WEBSTER'S NEW EXPLORER DICTIONARY AND THESAURUS

Created in Cooperation with the Editors of
MERRIAM-WEBSTER

FEDERAL STREET PRESS

A Division of Merriam-Webster, Incorporated
Springfield, Massachusetts

This edition published by
Federal Street Press,
A Division of Merriam-Webster, Incorporated
P.O. Box 281
Springfield, MA 01102

Federal Street Press books are available for bulk purchase for sales promotion and premium use. For details write the manager of special sales, Federal Street Press, P.O. Box 281, Springfield, MA 01102

Library of Congress Catalog Card Number 99-62651

ISBN 1-892859-06-8

Printed in the United States of America

7 9 10 8 6

Contents

A 48-page full-color world atlas follows page 688

Preface

Webster's New Explorer Dictionary and Thesaurus, created in cooperation with the editors of Merriam-Webster, is designed to serve the reference needs of the entire family. The up-to-date, easy-to-use dictionary and thesaurus sections provide authoritative guidance in matters of spelling, pronunciation, and use of words in context in speech and writing. Clearly written Explanatory Notes appear in both sections, identifying all of the features and conventions of this volume.

At the end of the dictionary section, a Handbook of Style describes the use of punctuation, capitalization, italicization, and more. In addition, several sections filled with useful general information are provided. They are listed on the Contents page.

A special feature of *Webster's New Explorer Dictionary and Thesaurus* is a 48-page full-color atlas of the world. The maps, created and updated for this edition by the editors of Encyclopaedia Britannica, are a useful resource for classwork, business projects, and a more complete understanding of world events.

DICTIONARY

Preface

This section of *Webster's New Explorer Dictionary and Thesaurus* is designed to meet the day-to-day needs of dictionary users in the home, office, and classroom. It emphasizes practicality and ease of use and offers a range of material.

The heart of this book is the A-Z vocabulary. This vocabulary is a compilation of the words most likely to be looked up by any person searching for a meaning, spelling, pronunciation, or end-of-line division point.

The A-Z vocabulary is preceded by a section of Explanatory Notes that should be read carefully by every user of the dictionary. Following these notes is a page that lists and explains the pronunciation symbols used in this dictionary.

This dictionary was created in cooperation with the editors of Merriam-Webster Inc., a company that has been publishing dictionaries for over 150 years.

Explanatory Notes

Entries

A boldface letter or a combination of such letters, including punctuation marks and diacritics where needed, that is set flush with the left-hand margin of each column of type is a main entry. The main entry may consist of letters set solid, of letters joined by a hyphen or a diagonal, or of letters separated by one or more spaces:

alone . . . *adj*
avant-garde . . . *n*
and/or . . . *conj*
assembly language *n*

The material in lightface type that follows each main entry on the same line and on succeeding indented lines presents information about the main entry.

The main entries follow one another in alphabetical order letter by letter: *bill of health* follows *billion; Day of Atonement* follows *daylight saving time*. Those containing an Arabic numeral are alphabetized as if the numeral were spelled out: *4-H* comes between *fourfold* and *Four Hundred; 3-D* comes between *three* and *three-dimensional*. Those that often begin with the abbreviation *St.* in common usage have the abbreviation spelled out: *Saint Valentine's Day*.

A pair of guide words is printed at the top of each page. These indicate that the entries falling alphabetically between the words at the top of the outer column of each page are found on that page.

The guide words are usually the alphabetically first and the alphabetically last entries on the page:

affinity • agate

Occasionally the last printed entry is not the alphabetically last entry. On page 52, for example, *bittern* is the last main entry, but *bitterness*, a run-on entry at *bitter*, is the alphabetically last entry and is therefore the second guide word. The alphabetically last entry is not used, however, if it follows alphabetically the first guide word on the succeeding page. Thus on page 94 *cinematic* is not a guide word because it follows alphabetically the entry *cinematheque* which is the first guide word on page 95.

Any boldface word—a main entry with definition, a variant, an inflected form, a defined or undefined run-on, or a run-in entry—may be used as a guide word.

When one main entry has exactly the same written form as another, the two are distinguished by superscript numerals preceding each word:

[1]**melt** . . . *vb*　　[1]**pine** . . . *n*
[2]**melt** *n*　　[2]**pine** *vb*

Full words come before parts of words made up of the same letters; solid compounds come before hyphenated compounds; hyphenated compounds come before open compounds; and lowercase entries come before those with an initial capital:

[2]**super** *adj*
super- . . . *prefix*
run•down . . . *n*
run-down . . . *adj*
run down *vb*
dutch . . . *adv*
Dutch . . . *n*

The centered dots within entry words indicate division points at which a hyphen may be put at the end of a line of print or writing. Thus the noun *cap•puc•ci•no* may be ended on one line and continued on the next in this manner:

cap-
puccino
cappuc-
cino
cappucci-
no

Centered dots are not shown after a single initial letter or before a single terminal letter because typesetters seldom cut off a single letter:

abyss . . . *n*
flighty . . . *adj*
idea . . . *n*

Nor are they usually shown at the second and succeeding homographs unless they differ among themselves:

[1]**sig•nal** . . . *n*
[2]**signal** *vb*
[3]**signal** *adj*
[1]**min•ute** . . . *n*
[2]**mi•nute** . . . *adj*

There are acceptable alternative end-of-line divisions just as there are acceptable variant spellings and pronunciations, but no more than one division is shown for any entry in this dictionary.

A double hyphen at the end of a line in this dictionary (as in the definition at **ant lion**) stands for a hyphen that is retained when the word is written as a unit on one line. This kind of fixed hyphen is always represented in boldface words in this dictionary with an en dash.

When a main entry is followed by the word *or* and another spelling, the two spellings are equal variants. Both are standard, and either one may be used according to personal inclination:

ocher *or* **ochre**

If two variants joined by *or* are out of alphabetical order, they remain equal variants. The one printed first is, however, slightly more common than the second:

[1]**plow** *or* **plough**

When another spelling is joined to the main entry by the word *also*, the spelling after *also* is a secondary variant and occurs less frequently than the first:

absinthe *also* **absinth**

Secondary variants belong to standard usage and may be used according to personal inclination. Once the word *also* is used to signal a secondary variant, all following variants are joined by *or:*

[2]**wool·ly** *also* **wool·ie** *or* **wooly**

Variants whose spelling puts them alphabetically more than a column away from the main entry are entered at their own alphabetical places and usually not at the main entry:

li·chee *var of* LITCHI

Variants having a usage label appear only at their own alphabetical places:

me·tre . . . *chiefly Brit var of* METER

To show all the stylings that are found for English compounds would require space that can be better used for other information. So this dictionary limits itself to a single styling for a compound:

peace·mak·er
pell–mell
boom box

When a compound is widely used and one styling predominates, that styling is shown. When a compound is uncommon or when the evidence indicates that two or three stylings are approximately equal in frequency, the styling shown is based on the comparison of other similar compounds.

A main entry may be followed by one or more derivatives or by a homograph with a different functional label. These are run-on entries. Each is introduced by a boldface dash and each has a functional label. They are not defined, however, since their meanings are readily understood from the meaning of the root word:

fear·less . . . *adj* . . . — **fear·less·ly** *adv*
— **fear·less·ness** *n*
hic·cup . . . *n* . . . — **hiccup** *vb*

A main entry may be followed by one or more phrases containing the entry word or an inflected form of it. These are also run-on entries. Each is introduced by a boldface dash but there is no functional label. They are, however, defined since their meanings are more than the sum of the meanings of their elements:

[1]**set** . . . *vb* . . . — **set sail :** . . .
[1]**hand** . . . *n* . . . — **at hand :** . . .

Defined phrases of this sort are run on at the entry defining the first major word in the phrase. When there are variants, however, the run-on appears at the entry defining the first major word which is invariable in the phrase:

[1]**seed** . . . *n* . . . — **go to seed** *or* **run to seed 1 :** . . .

Boldface words that appear within parentheses (as **co·ca** at **co·caine** and **jet engine** and **jet propulsion** at **jet–propelled**) are run-in entries.

Attention is called to the definition of *vocabulary entry* on page 587. The term *dictionary entry* includes all vocabulary entries as well as all boldface entries in the section headed "Foreign Words and Phrases."

Pronunciation

The matter between a pair of reversed virgules \ \ following the entry word indicates the pronunciation. The symbols used are explained in the chart on page 14a.

A hyphen is used in the pronunciation to show syllabic division. These hyphens sometimes coincide with the centered dots in the entry word that indicate end-of-line division:

ab·sen·tee \ˌab-sən-ˈtē\

Sometimes they do not:

met·ric \ˈme-trik\

A high-set mark ˈ indicates major (primary) stress or accent; a low-set mark ˌ indicates minor (secondary) stress or accent:

heart•beat \ˈhärt-ˌbēt\

The stress mark stands at the beginning of the syllable that receives the stress.

A syllable with neither a high-set mark nor a low-set mark is unstressed:

[1]**struc•ture** \ˈstrək-chər\

The presence of variant pronunciations indicates that not all educated speakers pronounce words the same way. A second-place variant is not to be regarded as less acceptable than the pronunciation that is given first. It may, in fact, be used by as many educated speakers as the first variant, but the requirements of the printed page are such that one must precede the other:

apri•cot \ˈa-prə-ˌkät, ˈā-\
pro•vost \ˈprō-ˌvōst, ˈprä-vəst\

Symbols enclosed by parentheses represent elements that are present in the pronunciation of some speakers but are absent from the pronunciation of other speakers, or elements that are present in some but absent from other utterances of the same speaker:

[1]**om•ni•bus** \ˈäm-ni-(ˌ)bəs\
ad•di•tion•al \ə-ˈdi-sh(ə-)nəl\

Thus, the above parentheses indicate that some people say \ˈäm-ni-ˌbəs\ and others say \ˈäm-ni-bəs\; some \ə-ˈdi-shə-nəl\, others \ə-ˈdi-shnəl\.

When a main entry has less than a full pronunciation, the missing part is to be supplied from a pronunciation in a preceding entry or within the same pair of reversed virgules:

cham•pi•on•ship \-ˌship\
pa•la•ver \pə-ˈla-vər, -ˈlä-\

The pronunciation of the first three syllables of *championship* is found at the main entry *champion*. The hyphens before and after \ˈlä\ in the pronunciation of *palaver* indicate that both the first and the last parts of the pronunciation are to be taken from the immediately preceding pronunciation.

In general, no pronunciation is indicated for open compounds consisting of two or more English words that have own-place entry:

witch doctor *n*

Only the first entry in a sequence of numbered homographs is given a pronunciation if their pronunciations are the same:

[1]**re•ward** \ri-ˈwȯrd\ *vb*
[2]**reward** *n*

The absent but implied pronunciation of derivatives and compounds run on after a main entry is a combination of the pronunciation at the main entry and the pronunciation of the other element as given at its alphabetical place in the vocabulary:

— **quick•ness** *n*
— **hold forth**

Thus, the pronunciation of *quickness* is the sum of the pronunciations given at *quick* and *-ness;* that of *hold forth*, the sum of the pronunciations of the two elements that make up the phrase.

Functional Labels

An italic label indicating a part of speech or another functional classification follows the pronunciation or, if no pronunciation is given, the main entry. The eight traditional parts of speech are indicated as follows:

bold . . . *adj*
forth•with . . . *adv*
[1]**but** . . . *conj*
ge•sund•heit . . . *interj*
bo•le•ro . . . *n*
[2]**un•der** . . . *prep*
[1]**it** . . . *pron*
slap . . . *vb*

Other italicized labels used to indicate functional classifications that are not traditional parts of speech include:

ATM *abbr*
self- *comb form*
un- . . . *prefix*
-ial *adj suffix*
[2]**-ly** *adv suffix*
[2]**-er** . . . *n suffix*
-ize . . . *vb suffix*
Fe *symbol*
may . . . *verbal auxiliary*

Functional labels are sometimes combined:

afloat . . . *adj or adv*

Inflected Forms

Nouns

The plurals of nouns are shown in this dictionary when suffixation brings about a change of final *-y* to *-i-*, when the noun ends in a consonant plus *-o* or in *-ey*, when the noun ends in *-oo*, when the noun has an irregular plural or a zero plural or a foreign plural, when the noun is a compound that pluralizes any element but the last, when a final consonant is doubled, when the noun has variant plurals, and when it is believed that the dictionary user might have reasonable doubts about the spelling of the plural or when the plural is spelled in a way contrary to what is expected:

[2]**spy** *n, pl* **spies**
si•lo . . . *n, pl* **silos**
val•ley . . . *n, pl* **valleys**
[2]**shampoo** *n, pl* **shampoos**
[1]**quiz** . . . *n, pl* **quiz•zes**
[1]**fish** . . . *n, pl* **fish** *or* **fish•es**
mouse . . . *n, pl* **mice**
moose . . . *n, pl* **moose**
cri•te•ri•on . . . *n, pl* **-ria**
son–in–law . . . *n, pl* **sons–in–law**
pi . . . *n, pl* **pis**
[3]**dry** *n, pl* **drys**

Cutback inflected forms are used when the noun has three or more syllables:

ame•ni•ty . . . *n, pl* **-ties**

The plurals of nouns are usually not shown when the base word is unchanged by suffixation, when the noun is a compound whose second element is readily recognizable as a regular free form entered at its own place, or when the noun is unlikely to occur in the plural:

night . . . *n*
fore•foot . . . *n*
mo•nog•a•my . . . *n*

Nouns that are plural in form and that regularly occur in plural construction are labeled *n pl*:

munch•ies . . . *n pl*

Nouns that are plural in form but that are not always construed as plurals are appropriately labeled:

lo•gis•tics . . . *n sing or pl*

Verbs

The principal parts of verbs are shown in this dictionary when suffixation brings about a doubling of a final consonant or an elision of a final *-e* or a change of final *-y* to *-i-*, when final *-c* changes to *-ck* in suffixation, when the verb ends in *-ey*, when the inflection is irregular, when there are variant inflected forms, and when it is believed that the dictionary user might have reasonable doubts about the spelling of an inflected form or when the inflected form is spelled in a way contrary to what is expected:

[2]**snag** *vb* **snagged; snag•ging**
[1]**move** . . . *vb* **moved; mov•ing**
[1]**cry** . . . *vb* **cried; cry•ing**
[1]**frol•ic** . . . *vb* **frol•icked; frol•ick•ing**
[1]**sur•vey** . . . *vb* **sur•veyed; sur•vey•ing**
[1]**drive** . . . *vb* **drove** . . .; **driv•en** . . .; **driv•ing**
[2]**bus** *vb* **bused** *or* **bussed; bus•ing** *or* **bus•sing**
[2]**visa** *vb* **vi•saed** . . .; **vi•sa•ing**
[2]**chagrin** *vb* **cha•grined** . . .; **cha•grin•ing**

The principal parts of a regularly inflected verb are shown when it is desirable to indicate the pronunciation of one of the inflected forms:

learn . . . *vb* **learned** \ˈlərnd, ˈlərnt\; **learn•ing**
[1]**al•ter** \ˈȯl-tər\ *vb* **al•tered; al•ter•ing** \-t(ə-)riŋ\

Cutback inflected forms are usually used when the verb has three or more syllables, when it is a two-syllable word that ends in *-l* and has variant spellings, and when it is a compound whose second element is readily recognized as an irregular verb:

elim•i•nate . . . *vb* **-nat•ed; -nat•ing**
[2]**quarrel** *vb* **-reled** *or* **-relled; -rel•ing** *or* **-rel•ling**
[1]**re•take** . . . *vb* **-took** . . .; **-tak•en** . . .; **-tak•ing**

The principal parts of verbs are usually not shown when the base word is unchanged by suffixation or when the verb is a compound whose second element is readily recognizable as a regular free form entered at its own place:

[1]**jump** . . . *vb*
pre•judge . . . *vb*

Another inflected form of English verbs is the third person singular of the present tense, which is regularly formed by the addition of *-s* or *-es* to the base form of the verb. This inflected form is not shown except at a handful of entries (as *have* and *do*) for which it is in some way anomalous.

Adjectives & Adverbs

The comparative and superlative forms of adjectives and adverbs are shown in this dictionary when suffixation brings about a doubling of a final consonant or an elision of a final *-e* or a change of final *-y* to *-i-*, when the word ends in *-ey*, when the inflection is irregular, and when there are variant inflected forms:

[1]**red** . . . *adj* **red•der; red•dest**

[1]tame . . . *adj* **tam•er; tam•est**

[1]kind•ly . . . *adj* **kind•li•er; -est**

hors•ey *or* **horsy** . . . *adj* **hors•i•er; -est**

[1]good . . . *adj* **bet•ter** . . .; **best**

[1]far . . . *adv* **far•ther** . . . *or* **fur•ther** . . .; **far•thest** *or* **fur•thest**

The superlative forms of adjectives and adverbs of two or more syllables are usually cut back:

[3]fancy *adj* **fan•ci•er; -est**

[1]ear•ly . . . *adv* **ear•li•er; -est**

The comparative and superlative forms of regularly inflected adjectives and adverbs are shown when it is desirable to indicate the pronunciation of the inflected forms:

[1]young \ˈyəŋ\ *adj* **youn•ger** \ˈyəŋ-gər\; **youn•gest** \ˈyəŋ-gəst\

The inclusion of inflected forms in *-er* and *-est* at adjective and adverb entries means nothing more about the use of *more* and *most* with these adjectives and adverbs than that their comparative and superlative degrees may be expressed in either way: *lazier* or *more lazy; laziest* or *most lazy.*

At a few adjective entries only the superlative form is shown:

[2]mere *adj, superlative* **mer•est**

The absence of the comparative form indicates that there is no evidence of its use.

The comparative and superlative forms of adjectives and adverbs are usually not shown when the base word is unchanged by suffixation, when the inflected forms of the word are identical with those of a preceding homograph, or when the word is a compound whose second element is readily recognizable as a regular free form entered at its own place:

[1]near . . . *adv*

[3]good *adv*

un•wor•thy . . . *adj*

Inflected forms are not shown at undefined run-ons.

Capitalization

Most entries in this dictionary begin with a lowercase letter. A few of these have an italicized label *often cap*, which indicates that the word is as likely to be capitalized as not and that it is as acceptable with an uppercase initial as it is with one in lowercase. Some entries begin with an uppercase letter, which indicates that the word is usually capitalized. The absence of an initial capital or of an *often cap* label indicates that the word is not ordinarily capitalized:

salm•on . . . *n*

gar•gan•tuan . . . *adj, often cap*

Mo•hawk . . . *n*

The capitalization of entries that are open or hyphenated compounds is similarly indicated by the form of the entry or by an italicized label:

dry goods . . . *n pl*

french fry *vb, often cap 1st F*

un–Amer•i•can . . . *adj*

Par•kin•son's disease . . . *n*

lazy Su•san . . . *n*

Jack Frost *n*

A word that is capitalized in some senses and lowercase in others shows variations from the form of the main entry by the use of italicized labels at the appropriate senses:

Trin•i•ty . . . *n* . . . **2** *not cap*

To•ry . . . *n* . . . **3** *often not cap*

ti•tan . . . *n* **1** *cap*

re•nais•sance . . . *n* . . . **1** *cap* . . . **2** *often cap*

Etymology

This dictionary gives the etymologies for a number of the vocabulary entries. These etymologies are in boldface square brackets preceding the definition. Meanings given in roman type within these brackets are not definitions of the entry, but are meanings of the Middle English, Old English, or non-English words within the brackets.

The etymology gives the language from which words borrowed into English have come. It also gives the form of the word in that language or a representation of the word in our alphabet if the form in that language differs from that in English:

philo•den•dron . . . [NL, fr. Gk, neut. of *philodendros* loving trees . . .]

[1]sav•age . . . [ME *sauvage,* fr. MF, fr. ML *salvaticus,* alter. of L *silvaticus* of the woods, wild . . .]

An etymology beginning with the name of a language (including ME or OE) and not giving the foreign (or Middle English or Old English) form indicates that this form is the same as the form of the entry word:

le•gume . . . [F]

[1]jour•ney . . . [ME, fr. OF . . .]

An etymology beginning with the name of a language (including ME or OE) and not giving the foreign (or Middle English or Old English) meaning indicates that this meaning is the same as the meaning expressed in the first definition in the entry:

ug·ly . . . *adj* . . . [ME, fr. ON *uggligr* . . .] **1** : FRIGHTFUL, DIRE

Usage

Three types of status labels are used in this dictionary—temporal, regional, and stylistic—to signal that a word or a sense of a word is not part of the standard vocabulary of English.

The temporal label *obs* for "obsolete" means that there is no evidence of use since 1755:

[3]post *n* **1** *obs*

The label *obs* is a comment on the word being defined. When a thing, as distinguished from the word used to designate it, is obsolete, appropriate orientation is usually given in the definition:

cat·a·pult . . . *n* **1** : an ancient military machine for hurling missiles

The temporal label *archaic* means that a word or sense once in common use is found today only sporadically or in special contexts:

[1]mete . . . *vb* . . . **1** *archaic*
[1]thou . . . *pron, archaic*

A word or sense limited in use to a specific region of the U.S. has an appropriate label. The adverb *chiefly* precedes a label when the word has some currency outside the specified region, and a double label is used to indicate considerable currency in each of two specific regions:

[2]wash *n* . . . **5** *West*
do·gie . . . *n, chiefly West*
crul·ler . . . *n* . . . **2** *Northern & Midland*

Words current in all regions of the U.S. have no label.

A word or sense limited in use to one of the other countries of the English-speaking world has an appropriate regional label:

chem·ist . . . *n* . . . **2** *Brit*
loch . . . *n, Scot*
[2]wireless *n* . . . **2** *chiefly Brit*

The label *dial* for "dialect" indicates that the pattern of use of a word or sense is too complex for summary labeling: it usually includes several regional varieties of American English or of American and British English:

[2]mind *vb* **1** *chiefly dial*

The stylistic label *slang* is used with words or senses that are especially appropriate in contexts of extreme informality:

[3]can . . . *vb* . . . **2** *slang*
[2]grand *n, slang*

There is no satisfactory objective test for slang, especially with reference to a word out of context. No word, in fact, is invariably slang, and many standard words can be given slang applications.

Definitions are sometimes followed by verbal illustrations that show a typical use of the word in context. These illustrations are enclosed in angle brackets, and the word being illustrated is usually replaced by a lightface swung dash. The swung dash stands for the boldface entry word, and it may be followed by an italicized suffix:

[1]jump . . . *vb* . . . **5** . . . ⟨~ the gun⟩
all–around . . . *adj* **1** . . . ⟨best ~ performance⟩
[1]can·on . . . *n* . . . **3** . . . ⟨the ~*s* of good taste⟩
en·joy . . . *vb* . . . **2** . . . ⟨~*ed* the concert⟩

The swung dash is not used when the form of the boldface entry word is changed in suffixation, and it is not used for open compounds:

[2]deal *vb* . . . **2** . . . ⟨*dealt* him a blow⟩
drum up *vb* **1** . . . ⟨*drum up* business⟩

Definitions are sometimes followed by usage notes that give supplementary information about such matters as idiom, syntax, and semantic relationship. A usage note is introduced by a lightface dash:

[2]cry *n* . . . **5** . . . — usu. used in the phrase *a far cry*
[2]drum *vb* . . . **4** . . . — usu. used with *out*
[1]jaw . . . *n* . . . **2** . . . — usu. used in pl.
[1]ada·gio . . . *adv or adj* . . . — used as a direction in music
hajji . . . *n* . . . — often used as a title

Sometimes a usage note is used in place of a definition. Some function words (as conjunctions and prepositions) have chiefly grammatical meaning and little or no lexical meaning; most interjections express feelings but are otherwise untranslatable into lexical meaning; and some other words (as honorific titles) are more amenable to comment than to definition:

or . . . *conj* — used as a function word to indicate an alternative

[1]at . . . *prep* **1** — used to indicate a point in time or space

auf Wie•der•seh•en . . . *interj* . . . — used to express farewell

sir . . . *n* . . . **2** — used as a usu. respectful form of address

Sense Division

A boldface colon is used in this dictionary to introduce a definition:

equine . . . *adj* . . . **:** of or relating to the horse

It is also used to separate two or more definitions of a single sense:

no•ti•fy . . . *vb* . . . **1 :** to give notice of **:** report the occurrence of

Boldface Arabic numerals separate the senses of a word that has more than one sense:

add . . . *vb* **1 :** to join to something else so as to increase in number or amount **2 :** to say further . . . **3 :** to combine (numbers) into one sum

A particular semantic relationship between senses is sometimes suggested by the use of one of the two italic sense dividers *esp* or *also.*

The sense divider *esp* (for *especially*) is used to introduce the most common meaning included in the more general preceding definition:

crys•tal . . . *n* . . . **2 :** something resembling crystal (as in transparency); *esp* **:** a clear glass used for table articles

The sense divider *also* is used to introduce a meaning related to the preceding sense by an easily understood extension of that sense:

chi•na . . . *n* **:** porcelain ware; *also* **:** domestic pottery in general

The order of senses is historical: the sense known to have been first used in English is entered first. This is not to be taken to mean, however, that each sense of a multisense word developed from the immediately preceding sense. It is altogether possible that sense 1 of a word has given rise to sense 2 and sense 2 to sense 3, but frequently sense 2 and sense 3 may have developed independently of one another from sense 1.

When an italicized label follows a boldface numeral, the label applies only to that specific numbered sense. It does not apply to any other boldface numbered senses:

craft . . . *n* . . . **3** *pl usu* **craft**

[1]fa•ther . . . *n* . . . **2** *cap* . . . **5** *often cap*

dul•ci•mer . . . *n* . . . **2** *or* **dul•ci•more** \-ˌmōr\

[2]lift *n* . . . **5** *chiefly Brit*

At *craft* the *pl* label applies to sense 3 but to none of the other numbered senses. At *father* the *cap* label applies only to sense 2 and the *often cap* label only to sense 5. At *dulcimer* the variant spelling and pronunciation apply only to sense 2, and the *chiefly Brit* label at *lift* applies only to sense 5.

Cross-Reference

Four different kinds of cross-references are used in this dictionary: directional, synonymous, cognate, and inflectional. In each instance the cross-reference is readily recognized by the lightface small capitals in which it is printed.

A cross-reference following a lightface dash and beginning with *see* is a directional cross-reference. It directs the dictionary user to look elsewhere for further information:

ri•al . . . *n* — see MONEY table

A cross-reference following a boldface colon is a synonymous cross-reference. It may stand alone as the only definition for an entry or for a sense of an entry; it may follow an analytical definition; it may be one of two or more synonymous cross-references separated by commas:

pa•pa . . . *n* **:** FATHER

[1]par•tic•u•lar . . . *adj* . . . **4 :** attentive to details **:** PRECISE

[2]main *adj* **1 :** CHIEF, PRINCIPAL

[1]fig•ure . . . *n* . . . **6 :** SHAPE, FORM, OUTLINE

A synonymous cross-reference indicates that an entry, a definition at the entry, or a specific sense at the entry cross-referred to can be substituted as a definition for the entry or the sense in which the cross-reference appears.

A cross-reference following an italic *var of* ("variant of") is a cognate cross-reference:

pick•a•back . . . *var of* PIGGYBACK

Occasionally a cognate cross-reference has a limiting label preceding *var of* as an indication that the variant is not standard English:

aero•plane . . . *chiefly Brit var of* AIRPLANE

A cross-reference following an italic label that identifies an entry as an inflected form (as of a noun or verb) is an inflectional cross-reference:

calves *pl of* CALF

woven *past part of* WEAVE

Inflectional cross-references appear only when the inflected form falls at least a column away from the entry cross-referred to.

Synonyms

A boldface **syn** near the end of an entry introduces words that are synonymous with the word being defined:

alone . . . *adj* . . . **syn** lonely, lonesome, lone, solitary

Synonyms are not definitions although they may often be substituted for each other in context.

Combining Forms, Prefixes, & Suffixes

An entry that begins or ends with a hyphen is a word element that forms part of an English compound:

-wise . . . *adv comb form* . . . ⟨slant*wise*⟩
ex- . . . *prefix* . . . ⟨*ex*-president⟩
-let . . . *n suffix* **1** . . . ⟨book*let*⟩

Combining forms, prefixes, and suffixes are entered in this dictionary for two reasons: to make understandable the meaning of many undefined run-ons and to make recognizable the meaningful elements of words that are not entered in the dictionary.

Lists of Undefined Words

Lists of undefined words occur after the entries *anti-*, *in-*, *non-*, *over-*, *re-*, *self-*, *semi-*, *sub-*, *super-*, and *un-*. These words are undefined because they are self-explanatory: their meanings are simply the sum of a meaning of the prefix or combining form and a meaning of the root word.

Abbreviations & Symbols

Abbreviations and symbols for chemical elements are included as main entries in the vocabulary:

RSVP *abbr* . . . please reply
Ca *symbol* calcium

Abbreviations have been normalized to one form. In practice, however, there is considerable variation in the use of periods and in capitalization (as *vhf*, *v.h.f.*, *VHF*, and *V.H.F.*), and stylings other than those given in this dictionary are often acceptable.

Symbols that are not capable of being alphabetized are included in a separate section of the back matter headed "Signs and Symbols."

Abbreviations Used in This Work

ab	about
abbr	abbreviation
abl	ablative
acc	accusative
A.D.	anno Domini
adj	adjective
adv	adverb
alter	alteration
Am	American
AmerF	American French
AmerInd	American Indian
AmerSp	American Spanish
Ar	Arabic
Aram	Aramaic
B.C.	before Christ
Brit	British
C	Celsius
Calif	California
CanF	Canadian French
cap	capital, capitalized
Celt	Celtic
cent	century
Chin	Chinese
comb	combining
compar	comparative
conj	conjunction

D	Dutch
Dan	Danish
dat	dative
deriv	derivative
dial	dialect
dim	diminutive
E	English
Egypt	Egyptian
Eng	English
esp	especially
F	Fahrenheit, French
fem	feminine
fr	from
G	German
Gk	Greek
Gmc	Germanic
Heb	Hebrew
Hung	Hungarian
Icel	Icelandic
imit	imitative
imper	imperative
interj	interjection
Ir	Irish
irreg	irregular
It, Ital	Italian
Jp	Japanese
K	Kelvin
L	Latin
LaF	Louisiana French
LG	Low German
LGk	Late Greek
LHeb	Late Hebrew
lit	literally
LL	Late Latin
masc	masculine
MD	Middle Dutch
ME	Middle English
MexSp	Mexican Spanish
MF	Middle French
MGk	Middle Greek
ML	Medieval Latin
modif	modification
MS	manuscript
n	noun
neut	neuter
NewEng	New England
NGk	New Greek
NHeb	New Hebrew
NL	New Latin
No	North
Norw	Norwegian
n pl	noun plural
obs	obsolete
OE	Old English
OF	Old French
OIt	Old Italian
ON	Old Norse
OPer	Old Persian
OProv	Old Provençal
orig	originally
part	participle
Per	Persian
perh	perhaps
Pg	Portuguese
pl	plural
Pol	Polish
pp	past participle
prep	preposition
pres	present
prob	probably
pron	pronoun, pronunciation
Prov	Provençal
prp	present participle
Russ	Russian
Sc	Scotch, Scots
Scand	Scandinavian
ScGael	Scottish Gaelic
Scot	Scottish
sing	singular
Skt	Sanskrit
Slav	Slavic
So	South
Sp	Spanish
St	Saint
superl	superlative
Sw	Swedish
syn	synonym, synonymy
trans	translation
Turk	Turkish
US	United States
USSR	Union of Soviet Socialist Republics
usu	usually
var	variant
vb	verb
vi	verb intransitive
VL	Vulgar Latin
vt	verb transitive
W	Welsh

Pronunciation Symbols

ə ..... **a**but, c**o**llect, supp**o**se

ˈə, ˌə humdrum

ə ..... (in əl, ən) batt**le**, cott**on**; (in lə, mə, rə) French tab**le**, pris**me**, tit**re**

ər .... op**er**ation, f**ur**th**er**

a ..... m**a**p, p**a**tch

ā ..... d**ay**, f**a**te

ä ..... b**o**ther, c**o**t, f**a**ther

å ..... a sound between \a\ and \ä\, as in an Eastern New England pronunciation of **au**nt, **a**sk

au̇ .... n**ow**, **ou**t

b ..... **b**a**b**y, ri**b**

ch .... **ch**in, ca**tch**

d ..... **d**i**d**, a**dd**er

e ..... s**e**t, r**e**d

ē ..... b**ea**t, **ea**sy

f ..... **f**i**f**ty, cu**ff**

g ..... **g**o, bi**g**

h ..... **h**at, a**h**ead

hw .... **wh**ale

i ..... t**i**p, ban**i**sh

ī ..... s**i**te, b**uy**

j ..... **j**ob, e**dge**

k ..... **k**in, **c**oo**k**

k̲ ..... German Ba**ch**, Scots lo**ch**

l ..... **l**i**l**y, coo**l**

m .... **m**ur**m**ur, di**m**

n ..... **n**i**n**e, ow**n**

ⁿ ..... indicates that a preceding vowel is pronounced through both nose and mouth, as in French bon \bōⁿ\

ŋ ..... si**ng**, si**ng**er, fi**ng**er, i**n**k

ō ..... b**o**ne, holl**ow**

ȯ ..... s**aw**

œ .... French b**œu**f, German H**ö**lle

œ̄ .... French f**eu**, German H**öh**le

ȯi .... t**oy**

p ..... **p**e**pp**er, li**p**

r ..... **r**arity

s ..... **s**our**c**e, le**ss**

sh .... **sh**y, mi**ss**ion

t ..... **t**ie, a**tt**ack

th .... **th**in, e**th**er

th̲ .... **th**en, ei**th**er

ü ..... b**oo**t, few \ˈfyü\

u̇ ..... p**u**t, pure \ˈpyu̇r\

ue .... German f**ü**llen

ue̅ .... French r**ue**, German f**üh**len

v ..... **v**i**v**id, gi**v**e

w .... **w**e, a**w**ay

y ..... **y**ard, cue \ˈkyü\

ʸ ..... indicates that a preceding \l\, \n\, or \w\ is modified by having the tongue approximate the position for \y\, as in French di**gne** \dēnʸ\

z ..... **z**one, rai**se**

zh .... vi**si**on, plea**s**ure

\ ..... slant line used in pairs to mark the beginning and end of a transcription: \ˈpen\

ˈ ..... mark at the beginning of a syllable that has primary (strongest) stress: \ˈshə-fəl-ˌbōrd\

ˌ ..... mark at the beginning of a syllable that has secondary (next-strongest) stress: \ˈshə-fəl-ˌbōrd\

- ..... mark of a syllable division in pronunciations (the mark of end-of-line division in boldface entries is a centered dot •)

( ) .... indicate that what is symbolized between sometimes occurs and sometimes does not occur in the pronunciation of the word: **bakery** \ˈbā-k(ə-)rē\ = \ˈbā-kə-rē, ˈbā-krē\

A

[1]a \ˈā\ *n, pl* **a's** *or* **as** \ˈāz\ *often cap* **1 :** the 1st letter of the English alphabet **2 :** a grade rating a student's work as superior

[2]a \ə, (ˈ)ā\ *indefinite article* **:** ONE, SOME — used to indicate an unspecified or unidentified individual ⟨there's ~ man outside⟩

[3]a *abbr, often cap* **1** absent **2** acre **3** alto **4** answer **5** are **6** area

AA *abbr* **1** Alcoholics Anonymous **2** antiaircraft **3** associate in arts

AAA *abbr* American Automobile Association

A and M *abbr* agricultural and mechanical

A and R *abbr* artists and repertory

aard•vark \ˈärd-ˌvärk\ *n* [obs. Afrikaans, fr. Afrikaans *aard* earth + *vark* pig] **:** a large burrowing African ungulate mammal that feeds on ants and termites with its sticky tongue

[1]ab \ˈab\ *n* **:** an abdominal muscle

[2]ab *abbr* about

AB *abbr* **1** able-bodied seaman **2** airman basic **3** [NL *artium baccalaureus*] bachelor of arts

ABA *abbr* American Bar Association

aback \ə-ˈbak\ *adv* **:** by surprise ⟨taken ~⟩

aba•cus \ˈa-bə-kəs\ *n, pl* **aba•ci** \-ˌsī, -ˌkē\ *or* **aba•cus•es :** an instrument for making calculations by sliding counters along rods or grooves

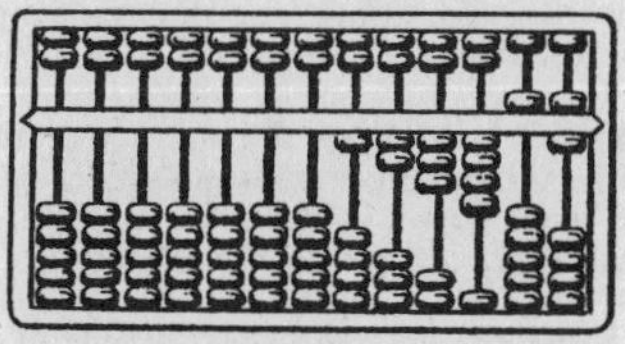

abacus

[1]abaft \ə-ˈbaft\ *prep* **:** to the rear of

[2]abaft *adv* **:** toward or at the stern **:** AFT

ab•a•lo•ne \ˌa-bə-ˈlō-nē, ˈa-bə-ˌ\ *n* **:** a large edible sea mollusk with a flattened slightly spiral shell with holes along the edge

[1]aban•don \ə-ˈban-dən\ *vb* [ME *abandounen,* fr. MF *abandoner,* fr. *abandon,* n., surrender, fr. *a bandon* in one's power] **:** to give up completely **:** FORSAKE, DESERT — **aban•don•ment** *n*

[2]abandon *n* **:** a thorough yielding to natural impulses; *esp* **:** EXUBERANCE

aban•doned \ə-ˈban-dənd\ *adj* **:** morally unrestrained **syn** profligate, dissolute, reprobate

abase \ə-ˈbās\ *vb* **abased; abas•ing :** HUMBLE, DEGRADE — **abase•ment** *n*

abash \ə-ˈbash\ *vb* **:** to destroy the composure of **:** EMBARRASS — **abash•ment** *n*

abate \ə-ˈbāt\ *vb* **abat•ed; abat•ing 1 :** to put an end to ⟨~ a nuisance⟩ **2 :** to decrease in amount, number, or degree

abate•ment \ə-ˈbāt-mənt\ *n* **1 :** DECREASE **2 :** an amount abated; *esp* **:** a deduction from a tax

ab•at•toir \ˈa-bə-ˌtwär\ *n* [F] **:** SLAUGHTERHOUSE

ab•ba•cy \ˈa-bə-sē\ *n, pl* **-cies :** the office or term of office of an abbot or abbess

ab•bé \a-ˈbā, ˈa-ˌ\ *n* **:** a member of the French secular clergy — used as a title

ab•bess \ˈa-bəs\ *n* **:** the superior of a convent for nuns

ab•bey \ˈa-bē\ *n, pl* **abbeys 1 :** MONASTERY **2 :** CONVENT **3 :** an abbey church

ab•bot \ˈa-bət\ *n* [ME *abbod,* fr. OE, fr. LL *abbat-, abbas,* fr. LGk *abbas,* fr. Aramaic *abbā* father] **:** the superior of a monastery for men

abbr *abbr* abbreviation

ab•bre•vi•ate \ə-ˈbrē-vē-ˌāt\ *vb* **-at•ed; -at•ing :** SHORTEN, CURTAIL; *esp* **:** to reduce to an abbreviation

ab•bre•vi•a•tion \ə-ˌbrē-vē-ˈā-shən\ *n* **1 :** the act or result of abbreviating **2 :** a shortened form of a word or phrase used for brevity esp. in writing

[1]ABC \ˌā-(ˌ)bē-ˈsē\ *n, pl* **ABC's** *or* **ABCs** \-ˈsēz\ **1 :** ALPHABET — usu. used in pl. **2 :** RUDIMENTS

[2]ABC *abbr* American Broadcasting Company

Ab•di•as \ab-ˈdī-əs\ *n* **:** OBADIAH

ab•di•cate \ˈab-di-ˌkāt\ *vb* **-cat•ed; -cat•ing :** to give up (as a throne) formally — **ab•di•ca•tion** \ˌab-di-ˈkā-shən\ *n*

ab•do•men \ˈab-də-mən, ab-ˈdō-\ *n* **1 :** the cavity in or area of the body between the chest and the pelvis **2 :** the part of the body posterior to the thorax in an arthropod — **ab•dom•i•nal** \ab-ˈdä-mən-ᵊl\ *adj* — **ab•dom•i•nal•ly** *adv*

ab•duct \ab-ˈdəkt\ *vb* **:** to take away (a person) by force **:** KIDNAP — **ab•duc•tion** \-ˈdək-shən\ *n* — **ab•duc•tor** \-tər\ *n*

abeam \ə-ˈbēm\ *adv or adj* **:** on a line at right angles to a ship's keel

abed \ə-ˈbed\ *adv or adj* **:** in bed

Abe•na•ki \ˌa-bə-ˈnä-kē\ *n, pl* **Abenaki** *or* **Abenakis :** a member of a group of American Indian peoples of northern New England and southern Quebec

ab•er•ra•tion \ˌa-bə-ˈrā-shən\ *n* **1 :** deviation esp. from a moral standard or normal state **2 :** failure of a mirror or lens to produce exact point-to-point correspondence between an object and its image **3 :** unsoundness of mind **:** DERANGEMENT — **ab•er•rant** \a-ˈber-ənt\ *adj*

abet \ə-ˈbet\ *vb* **abet•ted; abet•ting** [ME *abetten,* fr. MF *abeter,* fr. OF *beter* to bait] **1 :** INCITE, ENCOURAGE **2 :** to assist or support in the achievement of a purpose — **abet•tor** *or* **abet•ter** \-ˈbe-tər\ *n*

abey•ance \ə-ˈbā-əns\ *n* **:** a condition of suspended activity

ab•hor \əb-ˈhȯr, ab-\ *vb* **ab•horred; ab•hor•ring** [ME *abhorren,* fr. L *abhorrēre,* fr. *ab-* + *horrēre* to shudder] **:** LOATHE, DETEST — **ab•hor•rence** \-əns\ *n*

ab•hor•rent \-ənt\ *adj* **:** LOATHSOME, DETESTABLE

abide \ə-ˈbīd\ *vb* **abode** \-ˈbōd\ *or* **abid•ed; abid•ing 1 :** BEAR, ENDURE **2 :** DWELL, REMAIN, LAST

abil•i•ty \ə-ˈbi-lə-tē\ *n, pl* **-ties :** the quality of being able **:** POWER, SKILL

-ability *also* **-ibility** *n suffix* **:** capacity, fitness, or tendency to act or be acted on in a (specified) way ⟨flam*mability*⟩

ab•ject \ˈab-ˌjekt, ab-ˈjekt\ *adj* **:** low in spirit or hope **:** CRINGING — **ab•jec•tion** \ab-ˈjek-shən\ *n* — **ab•ject•ly** *adv* — **ab•ject•ness** *n*

ab•jure \ab-ˈju̇r\ *vb* **ab•jured; ab•jur•ing 1 :** to renounce solemnly **:** RECANT **2 :** to abstain from — **ab•ju•ra•tion** \ˌab-jə-ˈrā-shən\ *n*

abl *abbr* ablative

ab•late \a-ˈblāt\ *vb* **ab•lat•ed; ab•lat•ing :** to remove or become removed esp. by cutting, abrading, or vaporizing

ab•la•tion \a-ˈblā-shən\ *n* **1 :** surgical cutting and removal **2 :** loss of a part (as the outside of a nose cone) by melting or vaporization

ab•la•tive \ˈab-lə-tiv\ *adj* **:** of, relating to, or constituting a grammatical case (as in Latin) expressing typically the relation of separation and source — **ablative** *n*

ablaze \ə-ˈblāz\ *adj or adv* **:** being on fire **:** BLAZING

able \ˈā-bəl\ *adj* **abler** \-b(ə-)lər\; **ablest** \-b(ə-)ləst\ **1 :** having sufficient power, skill, or resources to accomplish an object **2 :** marked by skill or efficiency — **ably** \-blē\ *adv*

-able *also* **-ible** *adj suffix* **1 :** capable of, fit for, or wor-

thy of (being so acted upon or toward) ⟨break*able*⟩ ⟨collect*ible*⟩ **2** : tending, given, or liable to ⟨knowledge*able*⟩ ⟨perish*able*⟩
able–bod•ied \ˌā-bəl-ˈbä-dēd\ *adj* : having a sound strong body
abloom \ə-ˈblüm\ *adj* : BLOOMING
ab•lu•tion \ə-ˈblü-shən, a-\ *n* : the washing of one's body or part of it
ABM \ˌā-(ˌ)bē-ˈem\ *n, pl* **ABM's** *or* **ABMs** : ANTIBALLISTIC MISSILE
Ab•na•ki \ab-ˈnä-kē\ *var of* ABENAKI
ab•ne•gate \ˈab-ni-ˌgāt\ *vb* **-gat•ed; -gat•ing 1** : DENY, RENOUNCE **2** : SURRENDER, RELINQUISH — **ab•ne•ga•tion** \ˌab-ni-ˈgā-shən\ *n*
ab•nor•mal \ab-ˈnȯr-məl\ *adj* : deviating from the normal or average — **ab•nor•mal•i•ty** \ˌab-nȯr-ˈma-lə-tē\ *n* — **ab•nor•mal•ly** *adv*
¹aboard \ə-ˈbōrd\ *adv* **1** : ALONGSIDE **2** : on, onto, or within a car, ship, or aircraft **3** : in or into a group or association ⟨welcome new workers ∼⟩
²aboard *prep* : ON, ONTO, WITHIN
abode \ə-ˈbōd\ *n* **1** : STAY, SOJOURN **2** : HOME, RESIDENCE
abol•ish \ə-ˈbä-lish\ *vb* : to do away with : ANNUL — **ab•o•li•tion** \ˌa-bə-ˈli-shən\ *n*
ab•o•li•tion•ism \ˌa-bə-ˈli-shə-ˌni-zəm\ *n* : advocacy of the abolition of slavery — **ab•o•li•tion•ist** \-ˈli-sh(ə-)nist\ *n or adj*
A–bomb \ˈā-ˌbäm\ *n* : ATOMIC BOMB — **A–bomb** *vb*
abom•i•na•ble \ə-ˈbä-mə-nə-bəl\ *adj* : ODIOUS, LOATHSOME, DETESTABLE
abominable snow•man \-ˈsnō-mən, -ˌman\ *n, often cap A&S* : a mysterious creature with human or apelike characteristics reported to exist in the high Himalayas
abom•i•nate \ə-ˈbä-mə-ˌnāt\ *vb* **-nat•ed; -nat•ing** [L *abominari,* lit., to deprecate as an ill omen, fr. *ab-* away + *omen* omen] : LOATHE, DETEST
abom•i•na•tion \ə-ˌbä-mə-ˈnā-shən\ *n* **1** : something abominable **2** : DISGUST, LOATHING
ab•orig•i•nal \ˌa-bə-ˈri-jə-nəl\ *adj* : ORIGINAL, INDIGENOUS, PRIMITIVE
ab•orig•i•ne \ˌa-bə-ˈri-jə-nē\ *n* : a member of the original race of inhabitants of a region : NATIVE
aborn•ing \ə-ˈbȯr-niŋ\ *adv* : while being born or produced
¹abort \ə-ˈbȯrt\ *vb* **1** : to cause or undergo abortion **2** : to terminate prematurely ⟨∼ a spaceflight⟩ — **abor•tive** \-ˈbȯr-tiv\ *adj*
²abort *n* : the premature termination of a mission of or a procedure relating to an aircraft or spacecraft
abor•tion \ə-ˈbȯr-shən\ *n* : the spontaneous or induced termination of a pregnancy after, accompanied by, resulting in, or closely followed by the death of the embryo or fetus
abor•tion•ist \-sh(ə-)nist\ *n* : one who induces abortions
abound \ə-ˈbau̇nd\ *vb* **1** : to be plentiful : TEEM **2** : to be fully supplied
¹about \ə-ˈbau̇t\ *adv* **1** : reasonably close to; *also* : on the verge of ⟨∼ to join the army⟩ **2** : on all sides **3** : NEARBY
²about *prep* **1** : on every side of **2** : near to **3** : CONCERNING
about–face \-ˈfās\ *n* : a reversal of direction or attitude — **about–face** *vb*
¹above \ə-ˈbəv\ *adv* **1** : in the sky; *also* : in or to heaven **2** : in or to a higher place; *also* : higher on the same page or on a preceding page
²above *prep* **1** : in or to a higher place than : OVER ⟨storm clouds ∼ the bay⟩ **2** : superior to ⟨he thought her far ∼ him⟩ **3** : more than : EXCEEDING **4** : as distinct from ⟨∼ the noise⟩
above•board \-ˌbōrd\ *adv or adj* : without concealment or deception : OPENLY
abp *abbr* archbishop
abr *abbr* abridged; abridgment
ab•ra•ca•dab•ra \ˌa-brə-kə-ˈda-brə\ *n* **1** : a magical charm or incantation against calamity **2** : GIBBERISH
abrade \ə-ˈbrād\ *vb* **abrad•ed; abrad•ing 1** : to wear away by friction **2** : to wear down in spirit : IRRITATE — **abra•sion** \-ˈbrā-zhən\ *n*
¹abra•sive \ə-ˈbrā-siv\ *n* : a substance (as pumice) for abrading, smoothing, or polishing
²abrasive *adj* : tending to abrade : causing irritation ⟨∼ relationships⟩ — **abra•sive•ly** *adv* — **abra•sive•ness** *n*
abreast \ə-ˈbrest\ *adv or adj* **1** : side by side **2** : up to a standard or level esp. of knowledge
abridge \ə-ˈbrij\ *vb* **abridged; abridg•ing** [ME *abregen,* fr. MF *abregier,* fr. LL *abbreviare,* fr. L *ad* to + *brevis* short] : to lessen in length or extent : SHORTEN — **abridg•ment** *or* **abridge•ment** *n*
abroad \ə-ˈbrȯd\ *adv or adj* **1** : over a wide area **2** : away from one's home **3** : outside one's country
ab•ro•gate \ˈa-brə-ˌgāt\ *vb* **-gat•ed; -gat•ing** : ANNUL, REVOKE — **ab•ro•ga•tion** \ˌa-brə-ˈgā-shən\ *n*
abrupt \ə-ˈbrəpt\ *adj* **1** : broken or as if broken off **2** : SUDDEN, HASTY **3** : so quick as to seem rude **4** : DISCONNECTED **5** : STEEP — **abrupt•ly** *adv*
abs *abbr* absolute
ab•scess \ˈab-ˌses\ *n, pl* **ab•scess•es** [L *abscessus,* lit., act of going away, fr. *abscedere* to go away, fr. *abs-, ab-* away + *cedere* to go] : a localized collection of pus surrounded by inflamed tissue — **ab•scessed** \-ˌsest\ *adj*
ab•scis•sa \ab-ˈsi-sə\ *n, pl* **abscissas** *also* **ab•scis•sae** \-ˈsi-(ˌ)sē\ : the horizontal coordinate of a point in a plane coordinate system obtained by measuring parallel to the x-axis
ab•scis•sion \ab-ˈsi-zhən\ *n* **1** : the act or process of cutting off **2** : the natural separation of flowers, fruits, or leaves from plants — **ab•scise** \ab-ˈsīz\ *vb*
ab•scond \ab-ˈskänd\ *vb* : to depart secretly and hide oneself
ab•sence \ˈab-səns\ *n* **1** : the state or time of being absent **2** : WANT, LACK **3** : INATTENTION
¹ab•sent \ˈab-sənt\ *adj* **1** : not present **2** : LACKING **3** : INATTENTIVE
²ab•sent \ab-ˈsent\ *vb* : to keep (oneself) away
³ab•sent \ˈab-sənt\ *prep* : in the absence of : WITHOUT
ab•sen•tee \ˌab-sən-ˈtē\ *n* : one that is absent or keeps away
absentee ballot *n* : a ballot submitted (as by mail) in advance of an election by a voter who is unable to be present at the polls
ab•sen•tee•ism \ˌab-sən-ˈtē-ˌi-zəm\ *n* : chronic absence (as from work or school)
ab•sent•mind•ed \ˌab-sənt-ˈmīn-dəd\ *adj* : unaware of one's surroundings or actions : INATTENTIVE — **ab•sent•mind•ed•ly** *adv* — **ab•sent•mind•ed•ness** *n*
ab•sinthe *also* **ab•sinth** \ˈab-ˌsinth\ *n* [F] : a liqueur flavored esp. with wormwood and anise
ab•so•lute \ˈab-sə-ˌlüt, ˌab-sə-ˈlüt\ *adj* **1** : free from imperfection or mixture **2** : free from control, restriction, or qualification **3** : lacking grammatical connection with any other word in a sentence ⟨∼ construction⟩ **4** : POSITIVE ⟨∼ proof⟩ **5** : relating to the fundamental units of length, mass, and time **6** : FUNDAMENTAL, ULTIMATE — **ab•so•lute•ly** *adv*
absolute pitch *n* **1** : the position of a tone in a standard scale independently determined by its rate of vibration **2** : the ability to sing a note asked for or to name a note heard
absolute value *n* : the numerical value of a real number that for a positive number or zero is equal to the number itself and for a negative number is equal to the positive number which when added to it is equal to zero
absolute zero *n* : a theoretical temperature marked by a complete absence of heat and equivalent to exactly −273.15°C or −459.67°F

ab•so•lu•tion \ˌab-sə-ˈlü-shən\ *n* : the act of absolving; *esp* : a remission of sins pronounced by a priest in the sacrament of reconciliation

ab•so•lut•ism \ˈab-sə-ˌlü-ˌti-zəm\ *n* **1** : the theory that a ruler or government should have unlimited power **2** : government by an absolute ruler or authority

ab•solve \əb-ˈzälv, -ˈsälv\ *vb* **ab•solved; ab•solv•ing** : to set free from an obligation or the consequences of guilt

ab•sorb \əb-ˈsȯrb, -ˈzȯrb\ *vb* **1** : to take in and make part of an existent whole **2** : to suck up or take in in the manner of a sponge **3** : to engage (one's attention) : ENGROSS **4** : to receive without recoil or echo ⟨a ceiling that ~*s* sound⟩ **5** : ASSUME, BEAR ⟨~ all costs⟩ **6** : to transform (radiant energy) into a different form usu. with a resulting rise in temperature — **ab•sorb•ing** *adj* — **ab•sorb•ing•ly** *adv*

ab•sor•bent *also* **ab•sor•bant** \əb-ˈsȯr-bənt, ˈ-zȯr-\ *adj* : able to absorb ⟨~ cotton⟩ — **ab•sor•ben•cy** \-bən-sē\ *n* — **absorbent** *also* **absorbant** *n*

ab•sorp•tion \əb-ˈsȯrp-shən, -ˈzȯrp-\ *n* **1** : a process of absorbing or being absorbed **2** : concentration of attention — **ab•sorp•tive** \-tiv\ *adj*

ab•stain \əb-ˈstān\ *vb* : to refrain from an action or practice — **ab•stain•er** *n* — **ab•sten•tion** \-ˈsten-chən\ *n*

ab•ste•mi•ous \ab-ˈstē-mē-əs\ *adj* : sparing in use of food or drink : TEMPERATE — **ab•ste•mi•ous•ly** *adv* — **ab•ste•mi•ous•ness** *n*

ab•sti•nence \ˈab-stə-nəns\ *n* : voluntary refraining esp. from eating certain foods or drinking liquor — **ab•sti•nent** \-nənt\ *adj*

abstr *abbr* abstract

[1]**ab•stract** \ab-ˈstrakt, ˈab-ˌstrakt\ *adj* **1** : considered apart from a particular instance **2** : expressing a quality apart from an object ⟨*whiteness* is an ~ word⟩ **3** : having only intrinsic form with little or no pictorial representation ⟨~ painting⟩ — **ab•stract•ly** *adv* — **ab•stract•ness** *n*

[2]**ab•stract** \ˈab-ˌstrakt; *2 also* ab-ˈstrakt\ *n* **1** : SUMMARY, EPITOME **2** : an abstract thing or state

[3]**ab•stract** \ab-ˈstrakt, ˈab-ˌstrakt; *2 usu* ˈab-ˌstrakt\ *vb* **1** : REMOVE, SEPARATE **2** : to make an abstract of : SUMMARIZE **3** : to draw away the attention of **4** : STEAL — **ab•stract•ed•ly** \ab-ˈstrak-təd-lē, ˈab-ˌstrak-\ *adv*

abstract expressionism *n* : art that expresses the artist's attitudes and emotions through abstract forms — **abstract expressionist** *n*

ab•strac•tion \ab-ˈstrak-shən\ *n* **1** : the act of abstracting : the state of being abstracted **2** : an abstract idea **3** : an abstract work of art

ab•struse \ab-ˈstrüs\ *adj* : hard to understand : RECONDITE — **ab•struse•ly** *adv* — **ab•struse•ness** *n*

ab•surd \əb-ˈsərd, -ˈzərd\ *adj* [MF *absurde*, fr. L *absurdus*, fr. *ab-* from + *surdus* deaf, stupid] : RIDICULOUS, UNREASONABLE — **ab•sur•di•ty** \-ˈsər-də-tē, -ˈzər-\ *n* — **ab•surd•ly** *adv*

abun•dant \ə-ˈbən-dənt\ *adj* [ME, fr. MF, fr. L *abundant-*, *abundans*, prp. of *abundare* to abound, fr. *ab-* from + *unda* wave] : more than enough : amply sufficient **syn** copious, plentiful, ample, bountiful — **abun•dance** \-dəns\ *n* — **abun•dant•ly** *adv*

[1]**abuse** \ə-ˈbyüs\ *n* **1** : a corrupt practice **2** : MISUSE ⟨drug ~⟩ **3** : coarse and insulting speech **4** : MISTREATMENT ⟨child ~⟩

[2]**abuse** \ə-ˈbyüz\ *vb* **abused; abus•ing 1** : to put to a wrong use : MISUSE **2** : MISTREAT **3** : to attack in words : REVILE — **abus•er** *n* — **abu•sive** \-ˈbyü-siv\ *adj* — **abu•sive•ly** *adv* — **abu•sive•ness** *n*

abut \ə-ˈbət\ *vb* **abut•ted; abut•ting** : to touch along a border : border on

abut•ment \ə-ˈbət-mənt\ *n* : the part of a structure (as a bridge) that supports weight or withstands lateral pressure

abut•ter \ə-ˈbə-tər\ *n* : one that abuts; *esp* : the owner of a contiguous property

abys•mal \ə-ˈbiz-məl\ *adj* **1** : immeasurably deep : BOTTOMLESS **2** : absolutely wretched ⟨~ living conditions of the poor⟩ — **abys•mal•ly** *adv*

abyss \ə-ˈbis\ *n* **1** : the bottomless pit in old accounts of the universe **2** : an immeasurable depth

abys•sal \ə-ˈbi-səl\ *adj* : of or relating to the bottom waters of the ocean depths

ac *abbr* account

-ac *n suffix* : one affected with ⟨hypochondri*ac*⟩

Ac *symbol* actinium

AC *abbr* **1** air-conditioning **2** alternating current **3** [L *ante Christum*] before Christ **4** [L *ante cibum*] before meals **5** area code

aca•cia \ə-ˈkā-shə\ *n* : any of numerous leguminous trees or shrubs with round white or yellow flower clusters and often fernlike leaves

acad *abbr* academic; academy

ac•a•deme \ˈa-kə-ˌdēm, ˌa-kə-ˈ\ *n* : SCHOOL; *also* : academic environment

[1]**ac•a•dem•ic** \ˌa-kə-ˈde-mik\ *n* : a person who is academic in background, outlook, or methods

[2]**academic** *adj* **1** : of, relating to, or associated with schools or colleges **2** : literary or general rather than technical **3** : theoretical rather than practical — **ac•a•dem•i•cal•ly** \-mi-k(ə-)lē\ *adv*

ac•a•de•mi•cian \ˌa-kə-də-ˈmi-shən, ə-ˌka-də-\ *n* **1** : a member of a society of scholars or artists **2** : ACADEMIC

ac•a•dem•i•cism \ˌa-kə-ˈde-mə-ˌsi-zəm\ *also* **acad•e•mism** \ə-ˈka-də-ˌmi-zəm\ *n* **1** : a formal academic quality **2** : purely speculative thinking

acad•e•my \ə-ˈka-də-mē\ *n, pl* **-mies** [Gk *Akadēmeia*, school of philosophy founded by Plato, fr. *Akadēmeia*, gymnasium where Plato taught, fr. *Akadēmos* Greek mythological hero] **1** : a school above the elementary level; *esp* : a private high school **2** : a society of scholars or artists

acan•thus \ə-ˈkan-thəs\ *n, pl* **acanthus 1** : any of a genus of prickly herbs of the Mediterranean region **2** : an ornamentation (as on a column) representing the leaves of the acanthus

a cap•pel•la *also* **a ca•pel•la** \ˌä-kə-ˈpe-lə\ *adv or adj* [It *a cappella* in chapel style] : without instrumental accompaniment

acc *abbr* accusative

ac•cede \ak-ˈsēd\ *vb* **ac•ced•ed; ac•ced•ing 1** : to become a party to an agreement **2** : to express approval **3** : to enter upon an office **syn** agree, acquiesce, assent, consent, subscribe

ac•cel•er•ate \ik-ˈse-lə-ˌrāt, ak-\ *vb* **-at•ed; -at•ing 1** : to bring about earlier **2** : to speed up : QUICKEN — **ac•cel•er•a•tion** \-ˌse-lə-ˈrā-shən\ *n*

ac•cel•er•a•tor \ik-ˈse-lə-ˌrā-tər, ak-\ *n* **1** : one that accelerates **2** : a pedal for controlling the speed of a motor-vehicle engine **3** : an apparatus for imparting high velocities to charged particles

ac•cel•er•om•e•ter \ik-ˌse-lə-ˈrä-mə-tər, ak-\ *n* : an instrument for measuring acceleration or vibrations

[1]**ac•cent** \ˈak-ˌsent, ak-ˈsent\ *vb* : STRESS, EMPHASIZE

[2]**ac•cent** \ˈak-ˌsent\ *n* **1** : a distinctive manner of pronunciation ⟨a foreign ~⟩ **2** : prominence given to one syllable of a word esp. by stress **3** : a mark (as ´, `, ˆ) over a vowel used usu. to indicate a difference in pronunciation from a vowel not so marked — **ac•cen•tu•al** \ak-ˈsen-chə-wəl\ *adj*

ac•cen•tu•ate \ak-ˈsen-chə-ˌwāt\ *vb* **-at•ed; -at•ing** : ACCENT — **ac•cen•tu•a•tion** \-ˌsen-chə-ˈwā-shən\ *n*

ac•cept \ik-ˈsept, ak-\ *vb* **1** : to receive willingly **2** : to agree to **3** : to assume an obligation to pay

ac•cept•able \ik-ˈsep-tə-bəl, ak-\ *adj* : capable or worthy of being accepted — **ac•cept•abil•i•ty** \ik-ˌsep-tə-ˈbi-lə-tē, ak-\ *n*

ac•cep•tance \ik-ˈsep-təns, ak-\ *n* **1** : the act of accepting **2 :** the state of being accepted or acceptable **3 :** an accepted bill of exchange

ac·cep·ta·tion \ˌak-ˌsep-ˈtā-shən\ *n* **:** the generally understood meaning of a word

1**ac·cess** \ˈak-ˌses\ *n* **1 :** capacity to enter or approach **2 :** a way of approach **:** ENTRANCE

2**access** *vb* **:** to get at **:** gain access to

ac·ces·si·ble \ik-ˈse-sə-bəl, ak-, ek-\ *adj* **1 :** capable of being reached ⟨~ by train⟩ **2 :** capable of being used, seen, or known **:** OBTAINABLE ⟨~ information⟩ — **ac·ces·si·bil·i·ty** \-ˌse-sə-ˈbi-lə-tē\ *n*

ac·ces·sion \ik-ˈse-shən, ak-\ *n* **1 :** increase by something added **2 :** something added **3 :** the act of coming to a high office or position

ac·ces·so·ry *also* **ac·ces·sa·ry** \ik-ˈse-sə-rē, ak-\ *n, pl* **-ries 1 :** a person who though not present abets or assists in the commission of an offense **2 :** something helpful but not essential **syn** appurtenance, adjunct, appendage, appendix — **accessory** *adj*

ac·ci·dent \ˈak-sə-dənt\ *n* **1 :** an event occurring by chance or unintentionally **2 :** CHANCE ⟨met by ~⟩ **3 :** a nonessential property

1**ac·ci·den·tal** \ˌak-sə-ˈdent-ᵊl\ *adj* **1 :** happening unexpectedly or by chance **2 :** happening without intent or through carelessness **syn** casual, fortuitous, incidental, chance — **ac·ci·den·tal·ly** \-ˈden-tə-lē\ *also* **ac·ci·dent·ly** \-ˈdent-lē\ *adv*

2**accidental** *n* **:** a musical note foreign to a key indicated by a signature

ac·claim \ə-ˈklām\ *vb* **1 :** APPLAUD, PRAISE **2 :** to declare by acclamation **syn** extol, laud, commend, hail — **acclaim** *n*

ac·cla·ma·tion \ˌa-klə-ˈmā-shən\ *n* **1 :** loud eager applause **2 :** an overwhelming affirmative vote by shouting or applause rather than by ballot

ac·cli·mate \ˈa-klə-ˌmāt, ə-ˈklī-mət\ *vb* **-mat·ed; -mat·ing :** ACCLIMATIZE — **ac·cli·ma·tion** \ˌa-klə-ˈmā-shən, -ˌklī-\ *n*

ac·cli·ma·tise *Brit var of* ACCLIMATIZE

ac·cli·ma·tize \ə-ˈklī-mə-ˌtīz\ *vb* **-tized; -tiz·ing :** to accustom or become accustomed to a new climate or situation — **ac·cli·ma·ti·za·tion** \-ˌklī-mə-tə-ˈzā-shən\ *n*

ac·cliv·i·ty \ə-ˈkli-və-tē\ *n, pl* **-ties :** an ascending slope

ac·co·lade \ˈa-kə-ˌlād\ *n* [F, fr. *accoler* to embrace, fr. L *ad-* to + *collum* neck] **:** an expression of praise **:** AWARD

ac·com·mo·date \ə-ˈkä-mə-ˌdāt\ *vb* **-dat·ed; -dat·ing 1 :** to make fit or suitable **:** ADAPT, ADJUST **2 :** HARMONIZE, RECONCILE **3 :** to provide with something needed **4 :** to hold without crowding **5 :** to undergo visual accommodation

ac·com·mo·dat·ing *adj* **:** OBLIGING

ac·com·mo·da·tion \ə-ˌkä-mə-ˈdā-shən\ *n* **1 :** something supplied to satisfy a need; *esp* **:** LODGINGS — usu. used in pl. **2 :** the act of accommodating **:** ADJUSTMENT **3 :** the automatic adjustment of the eye for seeing at different distances

ac·com·pa·ni·ment \ə-ˈkəm-pə-nē-mənt, -ˈkəmp-nē-\ *n* **:** something that accompanies another; *esp* **:** subordinate music to support a principal voice or instrument

ac·com·pa·ny \-nē\ *vb* **-nied; -ny·ing 1 :** to go or occur with **:** ATTEND **2 :** to play an accompaniment for — **ac·com·pa·nist** \-nist\ *n*

ac·com·plice \ə-ˈkäm-pləs, -ˈkəm-\ *n* **:** an associate in crime

ac·com·plish \ə-ˈkäm-plish, -ˈkəm-\ *vb* **:** to bring to completion **syn** achieve, effect, execute, perform — **ac·com·plish·er** *n*

ac·com·plished *adj* **1 :** EXPERT, SKILLED **2 :** established beyond doubt

ac·com·plish·ment \ə-ˈkäm-plish-mənt, -ˈkəm-\ *n* **1 :** COMPLETION **2 :** something completed or effected **3 :** an acquired excellence or skill

1**ac·cord** \ə-ˈkȯrd\ *vb* [ME, fr. OF *acorder,* fr. L *ad-* to + *cord-, cor* heart] **1 :** GRANT, CONCEDE **2 :** AGREE, HARMONIZE — **ac·cor·dant** \-ˈkȯrd-ᵊnt\ *adj*

2**accord** *n* **1 :** AGREEMENT, HARMONY **2 :** willingness to act ⟨gave of their own ~⟩

ac·cor·dance \ə-ˈkȯrd-ᵊns\ *n* **1 :** ACCORD **2 :** the act of granting

ac·cord·ing·ly \ə-ˈkȯr-diŋ-lē\ *adv* **1 :** in accordance **2 :** CONSEQUENTLY, SO

according to *prep* **1 :** in conformity with ⟨paid *according to* ability⟩ **2 :** as stated or attested by ⟨*according to* you⟩

1**ac·cor·di·on** \ə-ˈkȯr-dē-ən\ *n* [G *Akkordion,* fr. *Akkord* chord] **:** a portable keyboard instrument with a bellows and reeds — **ac·cor·di·on·ist** \-ə-nist\ *n*

accordion

2**accordion** *adj* **:** folding like the bellows of an accordion ⟨~ pleats⟩

ac·cost \ə-ˈkȯst\ *vb* [MF *accoster,* ultim. fr. L *ad-* to + *costa* rib, side] **:** to approach and speak to esp. aggressively

1**ac·count** \ə-ˈkau̇nt\ *n* **1 :** a statement of business transactions **2 :** an arrangement with a vendor to supply credit **3 :** a statement of reasons, causes, or motives **4 :** VALUE, IMPORTANCE **5 :** a sum of money deposited in a bank and subject to withdrawal by the depositor — **on account of :** BECAUSE OF — **on no account :** under no circumstances — **on one's own account :** on one's own behalf

2**account** *vb* **1 :** CONSIDER ⟨I ~ him lucky⟩ **2 :** to give an explanation — used with *for*

ac·count·able \ə-ˈkau̇n-tə-bəl\ *adj* **1 :** ANSWERABLE, RESPONSIBLE **2 :** EXPLICABLE — **ac·count·abil·i·ty** \-ˌkau̇n-tə-ˈbi-lə-tē\ *n*

ac·coun·tant \ə-ˈkau̇nt-ᵊnt\ *n* **:** a person skilled in accounting — **ac·coun·tan·cy** \-ᵊn-sē\ *n*

account executive *n* **:** a business executive in charge of a client's account

ac·count·ing \ə-ˈkau̇n-tiŋ\ *n* **:** the art or system of keeping and analyzing financial records

ac·cou·tre *or* **ac·cou·ter** \ə-ˈkü-tər\ *vb* **-cou·tred** *or* **-cou·tered; -cou·tring** *or* **-cou·ter·ing** \-ˈkü-t(ə-)riŋ\ **:** EQUIP, OUTFIT

ac·cou·tre·ment *or* **ac·cou·ter·ment** \ə-ˈkü-trə-mənt, -ˈkü-tər-\ *n* [F] **1 :** an accessory item — usu. used in pl. **2 :** an identifying characteristic

ac·cred·it \ə-ˈkre-dət\ *vb* **1 :** to endorse or approve officially **2 :** CREDIT — **ac·cred·i·ta·tion** \-ˌkre-də-ˈtā-shən\ *n*

ac·cre·tion \ə-ˈkrē-shən\ *n* **1 :** growth or enlargement esp. by addition from without **2 :** a product of accretion

ac·crue \ə-ˈkrü\ *vb* **ac·crued; ac·cru·ing 1 :** to come by way of increase **2 :** to be added by periodic growth — **ac·cru·al** \-əl\ *n*

acct *abbr* account; accountant

ac·cul·tur·a·tion \ə-ˌkəl-chə-ˈrā-shən\ *n* **:** cultural modification of an individual or group by borrowing and adapting traits from another culture

ac•cu•mu•late \ə-ˈkyü-myə-ˌlāt\ *vb* **-lat•ed; -lat•ing** [L *accumulare,* fr. *ad-* to + *cumulare* to heap up] : to heap or pile up **syn** amass, gather, collect, stockpile — **ac•cu•mu•la•tion** \-ˌkyü-myə-ˈlā-shən\ *n* — **ac•cu•mu•la•tive** \-ˈkyü-myə-lə-tiv\ *adj* — **ac•cu•mu•la•tor** \-ˈkyü-myə-ˌlā-tər\ *n*

ac•cu•rate \ˈa-kyə-rət\ *adj* : free from error : EXACT, PRECISE — **ac•cu•ra•cy** \-rə-sē\ *n* — **ac•cu•rate•ly** *adv* — **ac•cu•rate•ness** *n*

ac•cursed \ə-ˈkərst, -ˈkər-səd\ *or* **ac•curst** \ə-ˈkərst\ *adj* **1** : being under a curse **2** : DAMNABLE, EXECRABLE

ac•cu•sal \ə-ˈkyü-zəl\ *n* : ACCUSATION

ac•cu•sa•tive \ə-ˈkyü-zə-tiv\ *adj* : of, relating to, or being a grammatical case marking the direct object of a verb or the object of a preposition — **accusative** *n*

ac•cuse \ə-ˈkyüz\ *vb* **ac•cused; ac•cus•ing** : to charge with an offense : BLAME — **ac•cu•sa•tion** \ˌa-kyə-ˈzā-shən\ *n* — **ac•cus•er** *n*

ac•cused \ə-ˈkyüzd\ *n, pl* **accused** : the defendant in a criminal case

ac•cus•tom \ə-ˈkəs-təm\ *vb* : to make familiar through use or experience

ac•cus•tomed \ə-ˈkəs-təmd\ *adj* : USUAL, CUSTOMARY

¹ace \ˈās\ *n* [ME *as* a die face marked with one spot, fr. OF, fr. L, unit, a copper coin] **1** : a playing card bearing a single large pip in its center **2** : a point (as in tennis) won on a serve that goes untouched **3** : a golf score of one stroke on a hole **4** : a combat pilot who has downed five or more enemy planes **5** : one that excels

²ace *vb* **aced; ac•ing 1** : to score an ace against (an opponent) or on (a golf hole) **2** : to defeat decisively

³ace *adj* : of first rank or quality

acer•bic \ə-ˈsər-bik, a-\ *adj* : acid in temper, mood, or tone

acer•bi•ty \ə-ˈsər-bə-tē\ *n, pl* **-ties** : SOURNESS, BITTERNESS

acet•amin•o•phen \ə-ˌsē-tə-ˈmi-nə-fən\ *n* : a crystalline compound used in chemical synthesis and in medicine to relieve pain and fever

ac•e•tate \ˈa-sə-ˌtāt\ *n* **1** : a salt or ester of acetic acid **2** : a textile fiber made from cellulose and acetic acid; *also* : a fabric or plastic made of this fiber

ace•tic acid \ə-ˈsē-tik-\ *n* : a colorless pungent liquid acid that is the chief acid of vinegar and is used esp. in making chemical compounds

ac•e•tone \ˈa-sə-ˌtōn\ *n* : a volatile flammable fragrant liquid compound used in making other chemical compounds and as a solvent

ace•tyl•cho•line \ə-ˌsēt-ᵊl-ˈkō-ˌlēn\ *n* : a compound that is released at nerve endings of the autonomic nervous system and is active in the transmission of nerve impulses

acet•y•lene \ə-ˈset-ᵊl-ən, -ᵊl-ˌēn\ *n* : a colorless flammable gas used as a fuel (as in welding and soldering)

ace•tyl•sal•i•cyl•ic acid \ə-ˈsēt-ᵊl-ˌsa-lə-ˌsi-lik-\ *n* : ASPIRIN 1

ache \ˈāk\ *vb* **ached; ach•ing 1** : to suffer a usu. dull persistent pain **2** : LONG, YEARN — **ache** *n*

achieve \ə-ˈchēv\ *vb* **achieved; achiev•ing** [ME *acheven,* fr. MF *achever* to finish, fr. *a-* to (fr. L *ad-*) + *chief* end, head, fr. L *caput*] : to gain by work or effort **syn** accomplish, attain, realize — **achiev•able** \-ˈchē-və-bəl\ *adj* — **achieve•ment** *n* — **achiev•er** *n*

Achil•les' heel \ə-ˌki-lēz-\ *n* [fr. the story that the Greek warrior Achilles was vulnerable only in the heel] : a vulnerable point

Achil•les tendon \ə-ˌki-lēz-\ *n* : the tendon joining the muscles in the calf of the leg to the bone of the heel

ach•ro•mat•ic \ˌa-krə-ˈma-tik\ *adj* : giving an image almost free from extraneous colors ⟨~ lens⟩

achy \ˈā-kē\ *adj* **ach•i•er; ach•i•est** : afflicted with aches — **ach•i•ness** *n*

¹ac•id \ˈa-səd\ *adj* **1** : sour or biting to the taste; *also* : sharp or sour in manner **2** : of or relating to an acid — **acid•i•ty** \ə-ˈsi-də-tē\ *n* — **acid•ly** *adv*

²acid *n* **1** : a sour substance **2** : a usu. water-soluble chemical compound that has a sour taste, reacts with a base to form a salt, and reddens litmus **3** : LSD — **acid•ic** \ə-ˈsi-dik\ *adj*

acid•i•fy \ə-ˈsi-də-ˌfī\ *vb* **-fied; -fy•ing 1** : to make or become acid **2** : to change into an acid — **acid•i•fi•ca•tion** \-ˌsi-də-fə-ˈkā-shən\ *n*

ac•i•do•sis \ˌa-sə-ˈdō-səs\ *n, pl* **-do•ses** \-ˌsēz\ : an abnormal state of reduced alkalinity of the blood and body tissues

acid precipitation *n* : precipitation with above normal acidity that is caused esp. by atmospheric pollutants

acid rain *n* : acid precipitation in the form of rain

acid test *n* : a severe or crucial test

acid•u•lous \ə-ˈsi-jə-ləs\ *adj* : somewhat acid or harsh in taste or manner

ack *abbr* acknowledge; acknowledgment

ac•knowl•edge \ik-ˈnä-lij, ak-\ *vb* **-edged; -edg•ing 1** : to recognize the rights or authority of **2** : to admit as true **3** : to express thanks for; *also* : to report receipt of **4** : to recognize as valid — **ac•knowl•edg•ment** *or* **ac•knowl•edge•ment** *n*

ACLU *abbr* American Civil Liberties Union

ac•me \ˈak-mē\ *n* [Gk *akmē*] : the highest point

ac•ne \ˈak-nē\ *n* [Gk *aknē,* MS var. of *akmē,* lit., point] : a skin disorder marked by inflammation of skin glands and hair follicles and by pimple formation esp. on the face

ac•o•lyte \ˈa-kə-ˌlīt\ *n* **1** : one who assists a member of the clergy in a liturgical service **2** : FOLLOWER

ac•o•nite \ˈa-kə-ˌnīt\ *n* **1** : MONKSHOOD **2** : a drug obtained from a common Old World monkshood

acorn \ˈā-ˌkȯrn, -kərn\ *n* : the nut of the oak

acorn squash *n* : an acorn-shaped dark green winter squash with a ridged surface

acous•tic \ə-ˈkü-stik\ *or* **acous•ti•cal** \-sti-kəl\ *adj* **1** : of or relating to the sense or organs of hearing, to sound, or to the science of sounds **2** : deadening sound ⟨~ tile⟩ **3** : operated by or utilizing sound waves — **acous•ti•cal•ly** \-k(ə-)lē\ *adv*

acous•tics \ə-ˈkü-stiks\ *n sing or pl* **1** : the science of sound **2** : the qualities in a room that make it easy or hard for a person in it to hear distinctly

ac•quaint \ə-ˈkwānt\ *vb* [ME, ultim. fr. L *ad-* + *cognoscere* to know] **1** : to cause to know personally **2** : INFORM

ac•quain•tance \ə-ˈkwānt-ᵊns\ *n* **1** : personal knowledge **2** : a person with whom one is acquainted — **ac•quain•tance•ship** *n*

ac•qui•esce \ˌa-kwē-ˈes\ *vb* **-esced; -esc•ing** : to accept, comply, or submit without open opposition **syn** consent, agree, assent, accede — **ac•qui•es•cence** \-ˈes-ᵊns\ *n* — **ac•qui•es•cent** \-ᵊnt\ *adj* — **ac•qui•es•cent•ly** *adv*

ac•quire \ə-ˈkwīr\ *vb* **ac•quired; ac•quir•ing** : to gain possession of : GET — **ac•quir•able** \-ˈkwī-rə-bəl\ *adj*

ac•quired \ə-ˈkwīrd\ *adj* **1** : gained by or as a result of effort or experience **2** : caused by environmental forces and not passed from parent to offspring in the genes ⟨~ characteristics⟩

acquired immune deficiency syndrome *n* : AIDS

acquired immunodeficiency syndrome *n* : AIDS

ac•quire•ment *n* **1** : ATTAINMENT, ACCOMPLISHMENT **2** : the act of acquiring

ac•qui•si•tion \ˌa-kwə-ˈzi-shən\ *n* **1** : ACQUIREMENT **2** : something acquired

ac•quis•i•tive \ə-ˈkwi-zə-tiv\ *adj* : eager to acquire : GREEDY — **ac•quis•i•tive•ly** *adv* — **ac•quis•i•tive•ness** *n*

ac•quit \ə-ˈkwit\ *vb* **ac•quit•ted; ac•quit•ting 1** : to pronounce not guilty **2** : to conduct (oneself) usu. satisfactorily — **ac•quit•tal** \-ᵊl\ *n*

acre \ˈā-kər\ *n* **1** *pl* : LANDS, ESTATE **2** — see WEIGHT table

acre•age \ˈā-k(ə-)rij\ *n* : area in acres

ac•rid \ˈa-krəd\ *adj* **1** : sharp and biting in taste or odor

2 : deeply bitter : CAUSTIC — **acrid•i•ty** \a-ˈkri-də-tē\ *n* — **ac•rid•ly** *adv* — **ac•rid•ness** *n*

ac•ri•mo•ny \ˈa-krə-ˌmō-nē\ *n, pl* **-nies** : harsh or biting sharpness of language or feeling — **ac•ri•mo•ni•ous** \ˌa-krə-ˈmō-nē-əs\ *adj* — **ac•ri•mo•ni•ous•ly** *adv* — **ac•ri•mo•ni•ous•ness** *n*

ac•ro•bat \ˈa-krə-ˌbat\ *n* [F *acrobate,* fr. Gk *akrobatēs,* fr. *akros* topmost + *bainein* to go] : a performer of gymnastic feats — **ac•ro•bat•ic** \ˌa-krə-ˈba-tik\ *adj* — **ac•ro•bat•i•cal•ly** \-ti-k(ə-)lē\ *adv*

ac•ro•bat•ics \ˌa-krə-ˈba-tiks\ *n sing or pl* : the performance of an acrobat

ac•ro•nym \ˈa-krə-ˌnim\ *n* : a word (as *radar*) formed from the initial letter or letters of each of the successive parts or major parts of a compound term

ac•ro•pho•bia \ˌa-krə-ˈfō-bē-ə\ *n* : abnormal dread of being at a great height

acrop•o•lis \ə-ˈkrä-pə-ləs\ *n* [Gk *akropolis,* fr. *akros* topmost + *polis* city] : the upper fortified part of an ancient Greek city

¹across \ə-ˈkrȯs\ *adv* **1** : to or on the opposite side **2** : so as to be understandable ⟨get the point ~⟩

²across *prep* **1** : to or on the opposite side of ⟨ran ~ the street⟩ **2** : on so as to cross or pass at an angle ⟨a log ~ the road⟩

across–the–board *adj* **1** : placed to win if a competitor wins, places, or shows ⟨an ~ bet⟩ **2** : including all classes or categories ⟨an ~ wage increase⟩

acros•tic \ə-ˈkrȯs-tik\ *n* : a composition usu. in verse in which the initial or final letters of the lines taken in order form a word or phrase — **acrostic** *adj*

acryl•ic \ə-ˈkri-lik\ *n* **1** : ACRYLIC RESIN **2** : a paint in which the vehicle is acrylic resin **3** : a quick-drying synthetic textile fiber

acrylic resin *n* : a glassy thermoplastic used for cast and molded parts or as coatings and adhesives

¹act \ˈakt\ *n* **1** : a thing done : DEED **2** : STATUTE, DECREE **3** : a main division of a play; *also* : an item on a variety program **4** : an instance of insincere behavior : PRETENSE

²act *vb* **1** : to perform by action esp. on the stage; *also* : FEIGN, SIMULATE, PRETEND **2** : to take action **3** : to conduct oneself : BEHAVE **4** : to perform a specified function **5** : to produce an effect

³act *abbr* **1** active **2** actual

ACT *abbr* Australian Capital Territory

actg *abbr* acting

ACTH \ˌā-(ˌ)sē-(ˌ)tē-ˈāch\ *n* : a protein hormone of the pituitary gland that stimulates the adrenal cortex

act•ing \ˈak-tiŋ\ *adj* : doing duty temporarily or for another ⟨~ president⟩

ac•tin•i•um \ak-ˈti-nē-əm\ *n* : a radioactive metallic chemical element — see ELEMENT table

ac•tion \ˈak-shən\ *n* **1** : a legal proceeding **2** : the manner or method of performing **3** : ACTIVITY **4** : ACT, DEED **5** : the accomplishment of a thing usu. over a period of time, in stages, or with the possibility of repetition **6** *pl* : CONDUCT **7** : COMBAT, BATTLE **8** : the events of a literary plot **9** : an operating mechanism ⟨the ~ of a gun⟩; *also* : the way it operates ⟨stiff ~⟩

ac•tion•able \ˈak-sh(ə-)nə-bəl\ *adj* : affording ground for an action or suit at law — **ac•tion•ably** \-blē\ *adv*

ac•ti•vate \ˈak-tə-ˌvāt\ *vb* **-vat•ed; -vat•ing 1** : to spur into action; *also* : to make active, reactive, or radioactive **2** : to treat (as carbon) so as to improve adsorptive properties **3** : to set up (a military unit) formally; *also* : to call to active duty — **ac•ti•va•tion** \ˌak-tə-ˈvā-shən\ *n* — **ac•ti•va•tor** \ˈak-tə-ˌvā-tər\ *n*

ac•tive \ˈak-tiv\ *adj* **1** : causing or involving action or change **2** : asserting that the grammatical subject performs the action represented by the verb ⟨~ voice⟩ **3** : BRISK, LIVELY **4** : erupting or likely to erupt ⟨~ volcano⟩ **5** : presently in operation or use **6** : tending to progress or to cause degeneration ⟨~ tuberculosis⟩ — **active** *n* — **ac•tive•ly** *adv* — **ac•tive•ness** *n*

ac•tiv•ism \ˈak-ti-ˌvi-zəm\ *n* : a doctrine or practice that emphasizes vigorous action for political ends — **ac•tiv•ist** \-vist\ *n or adj*

ac•tiv•i•ty \ak-ˈti-və-tē\ *n, pl* **-ties 1** : the quality or state of being active **2** : forceful or energetic action **3** : an occupation in which one is engaged

ac•tor \ˈak-tər\ *n* : a person who acts in a play or motion picture

ac•tress \ˈak-trəs\ *n* : a woman who is an actor

Acts \ˈakts\ *or* **Acts of the Apostles** *n* — see BIBLE table

ac•tu•al \ˈak-chə-wəl, -shə-\ *adj* : really existing : REAL — **ac•tu•al•i•ty** \ˌak-chə-ˈwa-lə-tē, -shə-\ *n* — **ac•tu•al•iza•tion** \ˌak-chə-wə-lə-ˈzā-shən, -shə-\ *n* — **ac•tu•al•ize** \ˈak-chə-wə-ˌlīz, -shə-\ *vb*

ac•tu•al•ly \ˈak-chə-wə-lē, -shə-\ *adv* : in fact or in truth : REALLY

ac•tu•ary \ˈak-chə-ˌwer-ē, -shə-\ *n, pl* **-ar•ies** : a person who calculates insurance risks and premiums — **ac•tu•ar•i•al** \ˌak-chə-ˈwer-ē-əl, -shə-\ *adj*

ac•tu•ate \ˈak-chə-ˌwāt\ *vb* **-at•ed; -at•ing 1** : to put into action **2** : to move to action — **ac•tu•a•tion** \ˌak-chə-ˈwā-shən, -shə-\ *n* — **ac•tu•a•tor** \ˈak-chə-ˌwā-tər, -shə-\ *n*

act up *vb* **1** : MISBEHAVE **2** : to function improperly

acu•ity \ə-ˈkyü-ə-tē\ *n, pl* **-ities** : keenness of perception

acu•men \ə-ˈkyü-mən\ *n* : mental keenness and penetration **syn** discernment, insight, percipience, perspicacity

acu•pres•sure \ˈa-kyů-ˌpre-shər\ *n* : SHIATSU

acu•punc•ture \-ˌpəŋk-chər\ *n* : an orig. Chinese practice of puncturing the body (as with needles) at specific points to cure disease or relieve pain — **acu•punc•tur•ist** \ˌa-kyů-ˈpəŋk-chə-rist\ *n*

acute \ə-ˈkyüt\ *adj* **acut•er; acut•est** [L *acutus,* pp. of *acuere* to sharpen, fr. *acus* needle] **1** : SHARP, POINTED **2** : containing less than 90 degrees ⟨an ~ angle⟩ **3** : sharply perceptive; *esp* : mentally keen **4** : SEVERE ⟨~ distress⟩; *also* : having a sudden onset, sharp rise, and short duration ⟨~ inflammation⟩ **5** : of, marked by, or being an accent mark having the form ´ — **acute•ly** *adv* — **acute•ness** *n*

acy•clo•vir \(ˌ)ā-ˈsī-klō-ˌvir\ *n* : a drug used esp. to treat the genital form of herpes simplex

ad \ˈad\ *n* : ADVERTISEMENT

AD *abbr* **1** after date **2** [L *anno Domini*] in the year of our Lord — often printed in small capitals and often punctuated **3** assistant director **4** athletic director

ad•age \ˈa-dij\ *n* : an old familiar saying : PROVERB, MAXIM

¹ada•gio \ə-ˈdä-j(ē-ˌ)ō, -zh(ē-ˌ)ō\ *adv or adj* [It] : at a slow tempo — used as a direction in music

²adagio *n, pl* **-gios 1** : an adagio movement **2** : a ballet duet or trio displaying feats of lifting and balancing

¹ad•a•mant \ˈa-də-mənt, -ˌmant\ *n* [ME, fr. OF, fr. L *adamant-, adamas* hardest metal, diamond, fr. Gk] : a stone believed to be impenetrably hard — **ad•a•man•tine** \ˌa-də-ˈman-ˌtēn, -ˌtīn\ *adj*

²adamant *adj* : INFLEXIBLE, UNYIELDING — **ad•a•mant•ly** *adv*

Ad•am's apple \ˈa-dəmz-\ *n* : the projection in front of the neck formed by the largest cartilage of the larynx

adapt \ə-ˈdapt\ *vb* : to make suitable or fit (as for a new use or for different conditions) **syn** adjust, accommodate, conform — **adapt•abil•i•ty** \ə-ˌdap-tə-ˈbi-lə-tē\ *n* — **adapt•able** *adj* — **ad•ap•ta•tion** \ˌa-ˌdap-ˈtā-shən\ *n* — **ad•ap•ta•tion•al** \-sh(ə-)nəl\ *adj* — **adap•tive** \ə-ˈdap-tiv\ *adj* — **ad•ap•tiv•i•ty** \ˌa-ˌdap-ˈti-və-tē\ *n*

adapt•er *also* **adap•tor** \ə-ˈdap-tər\ *n* **1** : one that adapts **2** : a device for connecting two dissimilar parts of an apparatus **3** : an attachment for adapting apparatus for uses not orig. intended

ADC *abbr* **1** aide-de-camp **2** Aid to Dependent Children

add \ˈad\ *vb* **1** : to join to something else so as to increase in number or amount **2** : to say further ⟨let me ~ this⟩ **3** : to combine (numbers) into one sum

ad•dend \ˈa-ˌdend\ *n* : a number to be added to another

ad•den•dum \ə-ˈden-dəm\ *n, pl* **-da** \-də\ [L] : something added; *esp* : a supplement to a book

[1]**ad•der** \ˈa-dər\ *n* **1** : a poisonous European viper or a related snake **2** : any of various harmless No. American snakes (as the hognose snake)

[2]**add•er** \ˈa-dər\ *n* : one that adds; *esp* : a device that performs addition

[1]**ad•dict** \ə-ˈdikt\ *vb* **1** : to devote or surrender (oneself) to something habitually or excessively **2** : to cause addiction to a substance in (as a person) — **ad•dic•tive** \-ˈdik-tiv\ *adj*

[2]**ad•dict** \ˈa-(ˌ)dikt\ *n* : one who is addicted to a substance

ad•dic•tion \ə-ˈdik-shən\ *n* **1** : the quality or state of being addicted **2** : compulsive need for and use of a habit-forming substance (as heroin, nicotine, or alcohol) characterized by well-defined physiological symptoms upon withdrawal; *also* : persistent compulsive use of a substance known by the user to be harmful

ad•di•tion \ə-ˈdi-shən\ *n* **1** : the act or process of adding; *also* : something added **2** : the operation of combining numbers to obtain their sum **syn** accretion, increment, accession, augmentation

ad•di•tion•al \ə-ˈdi-sh(ə-)nəl\ *adj* : coming by way of addition : ADDED, EXTRA

ad•di•tion•al•ly \ə-ˈdi-sh(ə-)nə-lē\ *adv* : in or by way of addition : FURTHERMORE

[1]**ad•di•tive** \ˈa-də-tiv\ *adj* **1** : of, relating to, or characterized by addition **2** : produced by addition — **ad•di•tiv•i•ty** \ˌa-də-ˈti-və-tē\ *n*

[2]**additive** *n* : a substance added to another in small quantities to effect a desired change in properties ⟨food ~*s*⟩

ad•dle \ˈad-ᵊl\ *vb* **ad•dled; ad•dling 1** : to throw into confusion : MUDDLE **2** : to become rotten ⟨*addled* eggs⟩

addn *abbr* addition

addnl *abbr* additional

add–on \ˈad-ˌȯn, -ˌän\ *n* : something (as a feature or accessory) added esp. as an enhancement

[1]**ad•dress** \ə-ˈdres\ *vb* **1** : to direct the attention of (oneself) **2** : to direct one's remarks to : deliver an address to **3** : to mark directions for delivery on **4** : to identify (as a memory location) by an address

[2]**ad•dress** \ə-ˈdres, ˈa-ˌdres\ *n* **1** : skillful management **2** : a formal speech : LECTURE **3** : the place where a person or organization may be communicated with **4** : the directions for delivery placed on mail **5** : a location (as in a computer's memory) where particular data is stored

ad•dress•ee \ˌa-ˌdre-ˈsē, ə-ˌdre-ˈsē\ *n* : one to whom something is addressed

ad•duce \ə-ˈdüs, -ˈdyüs\ *vb* **ad•duced; ad•duc•ing** : to offer as argument, reason, or proof **syn** advance, allege, cite, submit — **ad•duc•er** *n*

-ade *n suffix* **1** : act : action ⟨block*ade*⟩ **2** : product; *esp* : sweet drink ⟨lime*ade*⟩

ad•e•nine \ˈad-ᵊn-ˌēn\ *n* : one of the purine bases that make up the genetic code of DNA and RNA

ad•e•noid \ˈad-ˌnȯid, -ᵊn-ˌȯid\ *n* : an enlarged mass of tissue near the opening of the nose into the throat — usu. used in pl. — **adenoid** *or* **ad•e•noi•dal** \ˌad-ˈnȯi-dəl, -ᵊn-ˈȯi-\ *adj*

aden•o•sine tri•phos•phate \ə-ˈde-nə-ˌsēn-trī-ˈfäs-ˌfāt\ *n* : ATP

[1]**ad•ept** \ˈa-ˌdept\ *n* : EXPERT

[2]**adept** \ə-ˈdept\ *adj* : highly skilled : EXPERT — **adept•ly** *adv* — **adept•ness** *n*

ad•e•quate \ˈa-di-kwət\ *adj* : equal to or sufficient for a specific requirement — **ad•e•qua•cy** \-kwə-sē\ *n* — **ad•e•quate•ly** *adv* — **ad•e•quate•ness** *n*

ad•here \ad-ˈhir\ *vb* **ad•hered; ad•her•ing 1** : to give support : maintain loyalty **2** : to stick fast : CLING — **ad•her•ence** \-ˈhir-əns\ *n* — **ad•her•ent** \-ənt\ *adj or n*

ad•he•sion \ad-ˈhē-zhən\ *n* **1** : the act or state of adhering **2** : the union of bodily tissues abnormally grown together after inflammation; *also* : the newly formed uniting tissue **3** : the molecular attraction between the surfaces of bodies in contact

[1]**ad•he•sive** \-ˈhē-siv, -ziv\ *adj* **1** : tending to adhere : STICKY **2** : prepared for adhering

[2]**adhesive** *n* : an adhesive substance

adhesive tape *n* : tape coated on one side with an adhesive mixture; *esp* : one used for covering wounds

[1]**ad hoc** \ˈad-ˈhäk, -ˈhōk\ *adv* [L, for this] : for the case at hand apart from other applications

[2]**ad hoc** *adj* : concerned with or formed for a particular purpose ⟨an *ad hoc* committee⟩ ⟨*ad hoc* solutions⟩

adi•a•bat•ic \ˌa-dē-ə-ˈba-tik\ *adj* : occurring without loss or gain of heat — **adi•a•bat•i•cal•ly** \-ti-k(ə-)lē\ *adv*

adieu \ə-ˈdü, -ˈdyü\ *n, pl* **adieus** *or* **adieux** \ə-ˈdüz, -ˈdyüz\ : FAREWELL — often used interjectionally

ad in•fi•ni•tum \ˌad-ˌin-fə-ˈnī-təm\ *adv or adj* : without end or limit

ad in•ter•im \ad-ˈin-tə-rəm, -ˌrim\ *adv* : for the intervening time — **ad interim** *adj*

adi•os \ˌa-dē-ˈōs, ˌä-\ *interj* [Sp *adiós*, lit., to God] — used to express farewell

ad•i•pose \ˈa-də-ˌpōs\ *adj* : of or relating to animal fat : FATTY

adj *abbr* **1** adjective **2** adjutant

ad•ja•cent \ə-ˈjās-ᵊnt\ *adj* : situated near or next **syn** adjoining, contiguous, abutting, juxtaposed, conterminous — **ad•ja•cent•ly** *adv*

ad•jec•tive \ˈa-jik-tiv\ *n* : a word that typically serves as a modifier of a noun — **ad•jec•ti•val** \ˌa-jik-ˈtī-vəl\ *adj* — **ad•jec•ti•val•ly** *adv*

ad•join \ə-ˈjȯin\ *vb* : to be situated next to

ad•join•ing *adj* : touching or bounding at a point or line

ad•journ \ə-ˈjərn\ *vb* **1** : to suspend indefinitely or until a stated time **2** : to transfer to another place — **ad•journ•ment** *n*

ad•judge \ə-ˈjəj\ *vb* **ad•judged; ad•judg•ing 1** : JUDGE, ADJUDICATE **2** : to hold or pronounce to be : DEEM **3** : to award by judicial decision

ad•ju•di•cate \ə-ˈjü-di-ˌkāt\ *vb* **-cat•ed; -cat•ing** : to settle judicially — **ad•ju•di•ca•tion** \ə-ˌjü-di-ˈkā-shən\ *n*

ad•junct \ˈa-ˌjəŋkt\ *n* : something joined or added to another but not essentially a part of it **syn** appendage, appurtenance, accessory, appendix

ad•jure \ə-ˈjür\ *vb* **ad•jured; ad•jur•ing** : to command solemnly : urge earnestly **syn** beg, beseech, implore — **ad•ju•ra•tion** \ˌa-jə-ˈrā-shən\ *n*

ad•just \ə-ˈjəst\ *vb* **1** : to bring to agreement : SETTLE **2** : to cause to conform : ADAPT, FIT **3** : REGULATE ⟨~ a watch⟩ — **ad•just•able** *adj* — **ad•just•er** *also* **ad•jus•tor** \ə-ˈjəs-tər\ *n* — **ad•just•ment** \ə-ˈjəst-mənt\ *n*

ad•ju•tant \ˈa-jə-tənt\ *n* : one who assists; *esp* : an officer who assists a commanding officer by handling correspondence and keeping records

ad•ju•vant \ˈa-jə-vənt\ *n* : one that helps or facilitates; *esp* : something that enhances the effectiveness of medical treatment — **adjuvant** *adj*

[1]**ad–lib** \ˈad-ˈlib\ *vb* **ad–libbed; ad–lib•bing** : IMPROVISE — **ad–lib** *n*

[2]**ad–lib** *adj* : spoken, composed, or performed without preparation

ad lib \ˈad-ˈlib\ *adv* [NL *ad libitum*] **1** : at one's pleasure **2** : without limit

adm *abbr* administration; administrative

ADM *abbr* admiral

ad•man \ˈad-ˌman\ *n* : one who writes, solicits, or places advertisements

admin *abbr* administration; administrative

ad•min•is•ter \əd-ˈmi-nə-stər\ *vb* **1** : MANAGE, SUPERINTEND **2** : to mete out : DISPENSE **3** : to give ritually or remedially ⟨~ quinine for malaria⟩ **4** : to perform the office of administrator — **ad•min•is•tra•ble** \-strə-bəl\ *adj* — **ad•min•is•trant** \-strənt\ *n*

ad•min•is•tra•tion \ad-ˌmi-nə-ˈstrā- shən\ *n* **1** : the act or process of administering **2** : MANAGEMENT **3** : the officials directing the government of a country **4** : the term of office of an administrative officer or body — **ad•min•is•tra•tive** \ad-ˈmi-nə-ˌstrā-tiv\ *adj* — **ad•min•is•tra•tive•ly** *adv*

ad•min•is•tra•tor \ad-ˈmi-nə-ˌstrā-tər\ *n* : one that administers; *esp* : one who settles an intestate estate

ad•mi•ra•ble \ˈad-m(ə-)rə-bəl\ *adj* : worthy of admiration : EXCELLENT — **ad•mi•ra•bil•i•ty** \ˌad-m(ə-)rə-ˈbi-lə-tē\ *n* — **ad•mi•ra•ble•ness** *n* — **ad•mi•ra•bly** \-blē\ *adv*

ad•mi•ral \ˈad-m(ə-)rəl\ *n* [ME, ultim. fr. Ar *amīr-al-* commander of the (as in *amīr-al-baḥr* commander of the sea)] : a commissioned officer in the navy ranking next below a fleet admiral

ad•mi•ral•ty \ˈad-m(ə-)rəl-tē\ *n* **1** *cap* : a British government department formerly having authority over naval affairs **2** : the court having jurisdiction over questions of maritime law

ad•mire \əd-ˈmīr\ *vb* **ad•mired; ad•mir•ing** [MF *admirer*, fr. L *admirari*, fr. *ad-* to + *mirari* to wonder] : to regard with high esteem — **ad•mi•ra•tion** \ˌad-mə-ˈrā-shən\ *n* — **ad•mir•er** *n* — **ad•mir•ing•ly** \-ˈmī-riŋ-lē\ *adv*

ad•mis•si•ble \əd-ˈmi-sə-bəl\ *adj* : that can be or is worthy to be admitted or allowed : ALLOWABLE ⟨~ evidence⟩ — **ad•mis•si•bil•i•ty** \-ˌmi-sə-ˈbi-lə-tē\ *n*

ad•mis•sion \əd-ˈmi-shən\ *n* **1** : the act of admitting **2** : the privilege of being admitted **3** : a fee paid for admission **4** : the granting of an argument **5** : the acknowledgment of a fact

ad•mit \əd-ˈmit\ *vb* **ad•mit•ted; ad•mit•ting 1** : PERMIT, ALLOW **2** : to recognize as genuine or valid **3** : to allow to enter

ad•mit•tance \əd-ˈmit-ᵊns\ *n* : permission to enter

ad•mit•ted•ly \əd-ˈmi-təd-lē\ *adv* **1** : as has been or must be admitted **2** : it must be admitted

ad•mix \ad-ˈmiks\ *vb* : to mix in

ad•mix•ture \ad-ˈmiks-chər\ *n* **1** : something added in mixing **2** : MIXTURE

ad•mon•ish \ad-ˈmä-nish\ *vb* : to warn gently : reprove with a warning **syn** chide, reproach, rebuke, reprimand, reprove — **ad•mon•ish•er** *n* — **ad•mon•ish•ing•ly** *adv* — **ad•mon•ish•ment** *n* — **ad•mo•ni•tion** \ˌad-mə-ˈni-shən\ *n* — **ad•mon•i•to•ry** \ad-ˈmä-nə-ˌtōr-ē\ *adj*

ad nau•se•am \ad-ˈnȯ-zē-əm\ *adv* [L] : to a sickening or excessive degree

ado \ə-ˈdü\ *n* **1** : bustling excitement : FUSS **2** : TROUBLE

ado•be \ə-ˈdō-bē\ *n* **1** : sun-dried brick; *also* : clay for making such bricks **2** : a structure made of adobe bricks

ad•o•les•cence \ˌad-ᵊl-ˈes-ᵊns\ *n* : the process or period of growth between childhood and maturity — **ad•o•les•cent** \-ᵊnt\ *adj or n*

adopt \ə-ˈdäpt\ *vb* **1** : to take (a child of other parents) as one's own child **2** : to take up and practice as one's own **3** : to accept formally and put into effect — **adopt•able** \-ˈdäp-tə-bəl\ *adj* — **adopt•er** *n* — **adop•tion** \-ˈdäp-shən\ *n*

adop•tive \ə-ˈdäp-tiv\ *adj* : made or acquired by adoption ⟨~ father⟩ — **adop•tive•ly** *adv*

ador•able \ə-ˈdōr-ə-bəl\ *adj* **1** : worthy of adoration **2** : extremely charming — **ador•able•ness** *n* — **ador•ably** \-blē\ *adv*

adore \ə-ˈdōr\ *vb* **adored; ador•ing** [ME *adouren*, fr. MF *adorer*, fr. L *adorare*, fr. *ad-* to + *orare* to speak, pray] **1** : WORSHIP **2** : to regard with loving admiration **3** : to be extremely fond of — **ad•o•ra•tion** \ˌa-də-ˈrā-shən\ *n*

adorn \ə-ˈdȯrn\ *vb* : to enhance the appearance of esp. with ornaments — **adorn•ment** *n*

ad•re•nal \ə-ˈdrēn-ᵊl\ *adj* : of, relating to, or being a pair of endocrine organs (**adrenal glands**) that are located near the kidneys and produce several hormones and esp. epinephrine

adren•a•line \ə-ˈdren-ᵊl-ən\ *n* : EPINEPHRINE

adrift \ə-ˈdrift\ *adv or adj* **1** : afloat without motive power or moorings **2** : without guidance or purpose

adroit \ə-ˈdrȯit\ *adj* [F, fr. OF, fr. *a-* to + *droit* right] **1** : dexterous with one's hands **2** : SHREWD, RESOURCEFUL **syn** canny, clever, cunning, ingenious — **adroit•ly** *adv* — **adroit•ness** *n*

ad•sorb \ad-ˈsȯrb, -ˈzȯrb\ *vb* : to take up (as molecules of gases) and hold on the surface of a solid or liquid — **ad•sorp•tion** \-ˈsȯrp-shən, -ˈzȯrp-\ *n*

ad•u•late \ˈa-jə-ˌlāt\ *vb* **-lat•ed; -lat•ing** : to flatter or admire excessively — **ad•u•la•tion** \ˌa-jə-ˈlā-shən\ *n* — **ad•u•la•tor** \ˈa-jə-ˌlā-tər\ *n* — **ad•u•la•to•ry** \-lə-ˌtōr-ē\ *adj*

[1]**adult** \ə-ˈdəlt, ˈa-ˌ\ *adj* [L *adultus*, pp. of *adolescere* to grow up, fr. *ad-* to + *alescere* to grow] : fully developed and mature — **adult•hood** *n*

[2]**adult** *n* : one that is adult; *esp* : a human being after an age (as 18) specified by law

adul•ter•ant \ə-ˈdəl-tə-rənt\ *n* : something used to adulterate another

adul•ter•ate \ə-ˈdəl-tə-ˌrāt\ *vb* **-at•ed; -at•ing** [L *adulterare*, fr. *ad-* to + *alter* other] : to make impure by mixing in a foreign or inferior substance — **adul•ter•a•tion** \-ˌdəl-tə-ˈrā-shən\ *n*

adul•tery \ə-ˈdəl-t(ə-)rē\ *n, pl* **-ter•ies** : sexual unfaithfulness of a married person — **adul•ter•er** \-tər-ər\ *n* — **adul•ter•ess** \-t(ə-)rəs\ *n* — **adul•ter•ous** \-t(ə-)rəs\ *adj*

ad•um•brate \ˈa-dəm-ˌbrāt\ *vb* **-brat•ed; -brat•ing 1** : to foreshadow vaguely : INTIMATE **2** : to suggest or disclose partially **3** : SHADE, OBSCURE — **ad•um•bra•tion** \ˌa-dəm-ˈbrā-shən\ *n*

adv *abbr* **1** adverb **2** advertisement

ad va•lor•em \ˌad-və-ˈlōr-əm\ *adj* [L, according to the value] : imposed at a percentage of the value ⟨an *ad valorem* tax⟩

[1]**ad•vance** \əd-ˈvans\ *vb* **ad•vanced; ad•vanc•ing 1** : to assist the progress of **2** : to bring or move forward **3** : to promote in rank **4** : to make earlier in time **5** : PROPOSE **6** : LEND **7** : to raise in rate : INCREASE — **ad•vance•ment** *n*

[2]**advance** *n* **1** : a forward movement **2** : IMPROVEMENT **3** : a rise esp. in price or value **4** : OFFER — **in advance** : BEFOREHAND

[3]**advance** *adj* : made, sent, or furnished ahead of time

ad•van•tage \əd-ˈvan-tij\ *n* **1** : superiority of position **2** : BENEFIT, GAIN **3** : the 1st point won in tennis after deuce — **ad•van•ta•geous** \ˌad-van-ˈtā-jəs\ *adj* — **ad•van•ta•geous•ly** *adv*

ad•vent \ˈad-ˌvent\ *n* **1** *cap* : a penitential period beginning four Sundays before Christmas **2** *cap* : the coming of Christ **3** : a coming into being or use

ad•ven•ti•tious \ˌad-vən-ˈti-shəs\ *adj* **1** : ACCIDENTAL, INCIDENTAL **2** : arising or occurring sporadically or in other than the usual location ⟨~ buds⟩ — **ad•ven•ti•tious•ly** *adv*

[1]**ad•ven•ture** \əd-ˈven-chər\ *n* **1** : a risky undertaking **2** : a remarkable and exciting experience — **ad•ven•tur•ous** \-ch(ə-)rəs\ *adj*

[2]**adventure** *vb* **-ven•tured; -ven•tur•ing** \-ˈven-ch(ə-)riŋ\ : RISK, HAZARD

ad•ven•tur•er \əd-ˈven-ch(ə-)rər\ *n* **1** : a person who engages in new and risky undertakings **2** : a person who follows a military career for adventure or profit **3** : a person who tries to gain wealth by questionable means

ad•ven•ture•some \əd-ˈven-chər-səm\ *adj* : inclined to take risks

ad·ven·tur·ess \əd-ˈven-ch(ə-)rəs\ *n* : a female adventurer

ad·verb \ˈad-ˌvərb\ *n* : a word that typically serves as a modifier of a verb, an adjective, or another adverb — **ad·ver·bi·al** \ad-ˈvər-bē-əl\ *adj* — **ad·ver·bi·al·ly** *adv*

[1]**ad·ver·sary** \ˈad-vər-ˌser-ē\ *n, pl* **-sar·ies** : FOE

[2]**adversary** *adj* : involving antagonistic parties or interests

ad·verse \ad-ˈvərs, ˈad-ˌvərs\ *adj* **1** : acting against or in a contrary direction **2** : UNFAVORABLE — **ad·verse·ly** *adv*

ad·ver·si·ty \ad-ˈvər-sə-tē\ *n, pl* **-ties** : hard times : MISFORTUNE

ad·vert \ad-ˈvərt\ *vb* : REFER

ad·ver·tise \ˈad-vər-ˌtīz\ *vb* **-tised; -tis·ing 1** : INFORM, NOTIFY **2** : to call public attention to esp. in order to sell — **ad·ver·tis·er** *n*

ad·ver·tise·ment \ˌad-vər-ˈtīz-mənt; əd-ˈvər-təs-mənt\ *n* **1** : the act of advertising **2** : a public notice intended to advertise something

ad·ver·tis·ing \ˈad-vər-ˌtī-ziŋ\ *n* : the business of preparing advertisements

ad·vice \əd-ˈvīs\ *n* **1** : recommendation with regard to a course of action : COUNSEL **2** : INFORMATION, REPORT

ad·vis·able \əd-ˈvī-zə-bəl\ *adj* : proper to be done : EXPEDIENT — **ad·vis·abil·i·ty** \-ˌvī-zə-ˈbi-lə-tē\ *n*

ad·vise \əd-ˈvīz\ *vb* **ad·vised; ad·vis·ing 1** : to give advice to : COUNSEL **2** : INFORM, NOTIFY **3** : CONSULT, CONFER — **ad·vis·er** *or* **ad·vi·sor** \-ˈvī-zər\ *n*

ad·vised \əd-ˈvīzd\ *adj* : thought out : CONSIDERED ⟨well-*advised*⟩ — **ad·vis·ed·ly** \-ˈvī-zəd-lē\ *adv*

ad·vise·ment \əd-ˈvīz-mənt\ *n* **1** : careful consideration **2** : the act of advising

ad·vi·so·ry \əd-ˈvī-zə-rē\ *adj* **1** : having or exercising power to advise **2** : containing advice

[1]**ad·vo·cate** \ˈad-və-kət, -ˌkāt\ *n* [ultim. fr. L *advocare* to summon, fr. *ad-* to + *vocare* to call] **1** : one who pleads another's cause **2** : one who argues or pleads for a cause or proposal — **ad·vo·ca·cy** \-və-kə-sē\ *n*

[2]**ad·vo·cate** \-ˌkāt\ *vb* **-cat·ed; -cat·ing** : to plead in favor of — **ad·vo·ca·tion** \ˌad-və-ˈkā-shən\ *n*

advt *abbr* advertisement

adze *also* **adz** \ˈadz\ *n* : a tool with a curved blade set at right angles to the handle that is used in shaping wood

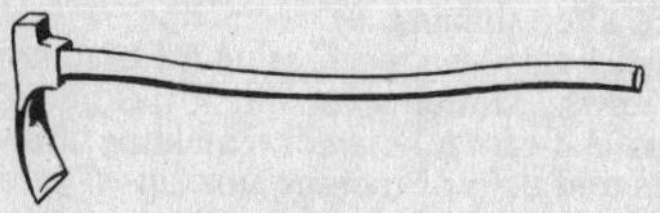

adze

AEC *abbr* Atomic Energy Commission

ae·gis \ˈē-jəs\ *n* **1** : SHIELD, PROTECTION **2** : PATRONAGE, SPONSORSHIP

ae·o·li·an harp \ē-ˈō-lē-ən-\ *n* : a box with strings that produce musical sounds when the wind blows on them

ae·on \ˈē-ən, -ˌän\ *n* : an indefinitely long time : AGE

aer·ate \ˈa(-ə)r-ˌāt\ *vb* **aer·at·ed; aer·at·ing 1** : to supply (blood) with oxygen by respiration **2** : to supply, impregnate, or combine with a gas and esp. air — **aer·a·tion** \ˌa(-ə)r-ˈā-shən\ *n* — **aer·a·tor** \ˈa(-ə)r-ˌā-tər\ *n*

[1]**ae·ri·al** \ˈar-ē-əl\ *adj* **1** : inhabiting, occurring in, or done in the air **2** : AIRY **3** : of or relating to aircraft

[2]**aer·i·al** \ˈar-ē-əl\ *n* : ANTENNA 2

ae·ri·al·ist \ˈar-ē-ə-list\ *n* : a performer of feats above the ground esp. on a trapeze

ae·rie \ˈar-ē, ˈir-ē\ *n* : a highly placed nest (as of an eagle)

aer·o·bat·ics \ˌar-ə-ˈba-tiks\ *n sing or pl* : spectacular flying feats and maneuvers

aer·o·bic \ˌa(-ə)r-ˈrō-bik\ *adj* **1** : living or active only in the presence of oxygen ⟨~ bacteria⟩ **2** : of or relating to aerobics — **aer·o·bi·cal·ly** \-bi-k(ə-)lē\ *adv*

aer·o·bics \-biks\ *n sing or pl* : strenuous exercises that produce a marked temporary increase in respiration and heart rate; *also* : a system of physical conditioning involving these

aero·drome \ˈar-ə-ˌdrōm\ *n, chiefly Brit* : AIRPORT

aero·dy·nam·ics \ˌar-ō-dī-ˈna-miks\ *n* : the science dealing with the forces acting on bodies in motion in a gas (as air) — **aero·dy·nam·ic** \-mik\ *also* **aero·dy·nam·i·cal** \-mi-kəl\ *adj* — **aero·dy·nam·i·cal·ly** \-mi-k(ə-)lē\ *adv*

aero·naut \ˈar-ə-ˌnȯt\ *n* : one who operates or travels in an airship or balloon

aero·nau·tics \ˌar-ə-ˈnȯ-tiks\ *n* : the science of aircraft operation — **aero·nau·ti·cal** \-ti-kəl\ *also* **aero·nau·tic** \-tik\ *adj*

aero·plane \ˈar-ə-ˌplān\ *chiefly Brit var of* AIRPLANE

aero·sol \ˈar-ə-ˌsäl, -ˌsȯl\ *n* **1** : a suspension of fine solid or liquid particles in a gas **2** : a substance (as an insecticide) dispensed from a pressurized container as an aerosol

aero·space \ˈar-ō-ˌspās\ *n* : the earth's atmosphere and the space beyond — **aerospace** *adj*

aery \ˈar-ē\ *adj* **aer·i·er; -est** : having an aerial quality : ETHEREAL

aes·thete \ˈes-ˌthēt\ *n* : a person having or affecting sensitivity to beauty esp. in art

aes·thet·ic \es-ˈthe-tik\ *adj* **1** : of or relating to aesthetics : ARTISTIC **2** : appreciative of the beautiful — **aes·thet·i·cal·ly** \-ti-k(ə-)lē\ *adv*

aes·thet·ics \-tiks\ *n* : a branch of philosophy dealing with the nature, creation, and appreciation of beauty

ae·ti·ol·o·gy *chiefly Brit var of* ETIOLOGY

AF *abbr* **1** air force **2** audio frequency

[1]**afar** \ə-ˈfär\ *adv* : from, at, or to a great distance

[2]**afar** *n* : a great distance

AFB *abbr* air force base

AFC *abbr* **1** American Football Conference **2** automatic frequency control

AFDC *abbr* Aid to Families with Dependent Children

af·fa·ble \ˈa-fə-bəl\ *adj* : courteous and agreeable in conversation — **af·fa·bil·i·ty** \ˌa-fə-ˈbi-lə-tē\ *n* — **af·fa·bly** \ˈa-fə-blē\ *adv*

af·fair \ə-ˈfar\ *n* [ME *affaire,* fr. MF, fr. *a faire* to do] **1** : something that relates to or involves one : CONCERN **2** : a romantic or sexual attachment of limited duration

[1]**af·fect** \ə-ˈfekt, a-\ *vb* **1** : to be fond of using or wearing **2** : SIMULATE, ASSUME, PRETEND

[2]**affect** *vb* : to produce an effect on : INFLUENCE

af·fec·ta·tion \ˌa-ˌfek-ˈtā-shən\ *n* : an attitude or behavior that is assumed by a person but not genuinely felt

af·fect·ed \a-ˈfek-təd\ *adj* **1** : given to affectation **2** : artificially assumed to impress others — **af·fect·ed·ly** *adv*

af·fect·ing \a-ˈfek-tiŋ\ *adj* : arousing pity, sympathy, or sorrow ⟨an ~ story⟩ — **af·fect·ing·ly** *adv*

af·fec·tion \ə-ˈfek-shən\ *n* : tender attachment — **af·fec·tion·ate** \-sh(ə-)nət\ *adj* — **af·fec·tion·ate·ly** *adv*

af·fer·ent \ˈa-fə-rənt, -ˌfer-ənt\ *adj* : bearing or conducting inward toward a more central part and esp. a nerve center (as the brain or spinal cord)

af·fi·ance \ə-ˈfī-əns\ *vb* **-anced; -anc·ing** : BETROTH, ENGAGE

af·fi·da·vit \ˌa-fə-ˈdā-vət\ *n* [ML, he has made an oath] : a sworn statement in writing

[1]**af·fil·i·ate** \ə-ˈfi-lē-ˌāt\ *vb* **-at·ed; -at·ing** : to associate as a member or branch — **af·fil·i·a·tion** \-ˌfi-lē-ˈā-shən\ *n*

[2]**af·fil·i·ate** \ə-ˈfi-lē-ət\ *n* : an affiliated person or organization

af•fin•i•ty \ə-ˈfi-nə-tē\ *n, pl* **-ties 1 :** KINSHIP, RELATIONSHIP **2 :** attractive force **:** ATTRACTION, SYMPATHY
af•firm \ə-ˈfərm\ *vb* **1 :** CONFIRM **2 :** to assert positively **3 :** to make a solemn and formal declaration or assertion in place of an oath **syn** aver, avow, avouch, declare, assert — **af•fir•ma•tion** \ˌa-fər-ˈmā-shən\ *n*
¹**af•fir•ma•tive** \ə-ˈfər-mə-tiv\ *adj* **:** asserting that the fact is so **:** POSITIVE
²**affirmative** *n* **1 :** an expression of affirmation or assent **2 :** the side that upholds the proposition stated in a debate
affirmative action *n* **:** an active effort to improve the employment or educational opportunities of members of minority groups and women
¹**af•fix** \ə-ˈfiks\ *vb* **:** ATTACH, ADD
²**af•fix** \ˈa-ˌfiks\ *n* **:** one or more sounds or letters attached to the beginning or end of a word that produce a derivative word or an inflectional form
af•fla•tus \ə-ˈflā-təs\ *n* **:** divine inspiration
af•flict \ə-ˈflikt\ *vb* **:** to cause pain and distress to **syn** rack, try, torment, torture — **af•flic•tion** \-ˈflik-shən\ *n*
af•flic•tive \ə-ˈflik-tiv\ *adj* **:** causing affliction **:** DISTRESSING — **af•flic•tive•ly** *adv*
af•flu•ence \ˈa-ˌflü-ən(t)s, a-ˈflü-\ *n* **:** abundant supply; *also* **:** WEALTH, RICHES — **af•flu•ent** \-ənt\ *adj*
af•ford \ə-ˈfōrd\ *vb* **1 :** to manage to bear or bear the cost of without serious harm or loss **2 :** PROVIDE, FURNISH
af•for•es•ta•tion \a-ˌfȯr-ə-ˈstā-shən\ *n* **:** the act or process of establishing a forest — **af•for•est** \a-ˈfȯr-əst, -ˈfär-\ *vb*
af•fray \ə-ˈfrā\ *n* **:** FIGHT, FRAY
af•fright \ə-ˈfrīt\ *vb* **:** FRIGHTEN, ALARM — **affright** *n*
af•front \ə-ˈfrənt\ *vb* **1 :** INSULT **2 :** CONFRONT — **affront** *n*
af•ghan \ˈaf-ˌgan\ *n* **1** *cap* **:** a native or inhabitant of Afghanistan **2 :** a blanket or shawl of colored wool knitted or crocheted in sections — **Afghan** *adj*
Afghan hound *n* **:** any of a breed of tall slim swift hunting dogs with a coat of silky thick hair and a long silky top knot
af•ghani \af-ˈga-nē\ *n* — see MONEY table
afi•cio•na•do \ə-ˌfi-sh(ē-)ə-ˈnä-dō, -sē-ə-\ *n, pl* **-dos** [Sp, fr. pp. of *aficionar* to inspire affection] **:** DEVOTEE, FAN
afield \ə-ˈfēld\ *adv or adj* **1 :** to, in, or on the field **2 :** away from home **3 :** out of the way **:** ASTRAY
afire \ə-ˈfīr\ *adj or adv* **:** being on fire **:** BURNING
AFL *abbr* American Football League
aflame \ə-ˈflām\ *adj or adv* **:** FLAMING
AFL–CIO *abbr* American Federation of Labor and Congress of Industrial Organizations
afloat \ə-ˈflōt\ *adj or adv* **1 :** borne on or as if on the water **2 :** CIRCULATING ⟨rumors were ~⟩ **3 :** ADRIFT
aflut•ter \ə-ˈflə-tər\ *adj* **1 :** FLUTTERING **2 :** nervously excited
afoot \ə-ˈfu̇t\ *adv or adj* **1 :** on foot **2 :** in action **:** in progress
afore•men•tioned \ə-ˈfōr-ˈmen-chənd\ *adj* **:** mentioned previously
afore•said \-ˌsed\ *adj* **:** said or named before
afore•thought \-ˌthȯt\ *adj* **:** PREMEDITATED ⟨with malice ~⟩
a for•ti•o•ri \ˌä-ˌfȯr-tē-ˈōr-ē\ *adv* [NL, lit., from the stronger (argument)] **:** with even greater reason
afoul of \ə-ˈfau̇l-əv\ *prep* **1 :** in or into conflict with **2 :** in or into collision or entanglement with
Afr *abbr* Africa; African
afraid \ə-ˈfrād\ *adj* **:** FRIGHTENED, FEARFUL
A–frame \ˈā-ˌfrām\ *n* **:** a building having triangular front and rear walls with the roof reaching to the ground
afresh \ə-ˈfresh\ *adv* **:** ANEW, AGAIN
Af•ri•can \ˈa-fri-kən\ *n* **1 :** a native or inhabitant of Africa **2 :** a person of African ancestry — **African** *adj*
Af•ri•can–Amer•i•can \-ə-ˈmer-ə-kən\ *n* **:** AFRO-AMERICAN — **African–American** *adj*
Af•ri•can•ized bee \ˈa-frə-kə-ˌnīzd-\ *n* **:** a highly aggressive hybrid honeybee accidentally produced from Brazilian and African stocks that has spread from So. America into Mexico and the southern U.S.
Africanized honeybee *n* **:** AFRICANIZED BEE
African violet *n* **:** a tropical African plant widely grown indoors for its velvety fleshy leaves and showy purple, pink, or white flowers
Af•ri•kaans \ˌa-fri-ˈkäns\ *n* **:** a language developed from 17th century Dutch that is one of the official languages of the Republic of So. Africa
¹**Af•ro** \ˈa-frō\ *adj* **:** having the hair shaped into a round bushy mass
²**Afro** *n, pl* **Afros :** an Afro hairstyle
Af•ro–Amer•i•can \ˌa-frō-ə-ˈmer-ə-kən\ *n* **:** an American of African and esp. of black African descent — **Afro–American** *adj*
aft \ˈaft\ *adv* **:** near, toward, or in the stern of a ship or the tail of an aircraft
AFT *abbr* American Federation of Teachers
¹**af•ter** \ˈaf-tər\ *adv* **:** AFTERWARD, SUBSEQUENTLY
²**after** *prep* **1 :** behind in place **2 :** later than **3 :** in pursuit or search of ⟨he's ~ your job⟩
³**after** *conj* **:** following the time when
⁴**after** *adj* **1 :** LATER **2 :** located toward the rear
af•ter•birth \ˈaf-tər-ˌbərth\ *n* **:** the placenta and membranes of the fetus that are expelled after childbirth
af•ter•burn•er \-ˌbər-nər\ *n* **:** a device incorporated in the tail pipe of a turbojet engine for injecting fuel into the hot exhaust gases and burning it to provide extra thrust
af•ter•care \-ˌker\ *n* **:** the care, nursing, or treatment of a convalescent patient
af•ter•deck \-ˌdek\ *n* **:** the rear half of the deck of a ship
af•ter•ef•fect \-ə-ˌfekt\ *n* **:** an effect that follows its cause after an interval
af•ter•glow \-ˌglō\ *n* **:** a glow remaining where a light has disappeared
af•ter•im•age \-ˌim-ij\ *n* **:** a usu. visual sensation continuing after the stimulus causing it has ended
af•ter•life \-ˌlīf\ *n* **:** an existence after death
af•ter•math \-ˌmath\ *n* **1 :** a second-growth crop esp. of hay **2 :** CONSEQUENCES, EFFECTS **syn** aftereffect, upshot, result, outcome
af•ter•noon \ˌaf-tər-ˈnün\ *n* **:** the time between noon and evening
af•ter•shave \ˈaf-tər-ˌshāv\ *n* **:** a usu. scented lotion for the face after shaving
af•ter•taste \-ˌtāst\ *n* **:** a sensation (as of flavor) continuing after the stimulus causing it has ended
af•ter–tax \ˈaf-tər-ˈtaks\ *adj* **:** remaining after payment of taxes and esp. of income tax ⟨an ~ profit⟩
af•ter•thought \-ˌthȯt\ *n* **:** a later thought; *also* **:** something thought of later
af•ter•ward \-wərd\ *or* **af•ter•wards** \-wərdz\ *adv* **:** at a later time
Ag *symbol* [L *argentum*] silver
AG *abbr* **1** adjutant general **2** attorney general
again \ə-ˈgen, -ˈgin\ *adv* **1 :** once more **:** ANEW **2 :** on the other hand **3 :** in addition **:** BESIDES
against \ə-ˈgenst\ *prep* **1 :** in opposition to **2 :** directly opposite to **:** FACING **3 :** as defense from **4 :** so as to touch or strike ⟨threw him ~ the wall⟩; *also* **:** TOUCHING
¹**aga•pe** \ä-ˈgä-pā, ˈä-gə-ˌpā\ *n* [Gk, lit., love] **:** unselfish unconditional love for another
²**agape** \ə-ˈgāp\ *adj or adv* **:** having the mouth open in wonder or surprise **:** GAPING
agar \ˈä-ˌgär\ *n* **1 :** a jellylike substance extracted from a red alga and used esp. as a gelling and stabilizing agent in foods **2 :** a culture medium containing agar
agar–agar \ˌä-ˌgär-ˈä-ˌgär\ *n* **:** AGAR
ag•ate \ˈa-gət\ *n* **1 :** a striped or clouded quartz **2 :** a playing marble of agate or of glass

aga•ve \ə-ˈgä-vē\ *n* : any of a genus of spiny-leaved plants (as a century plant) related to the amaryllis

agcy *abbr* agency

[1]**age** \ˈāj\ *n* **1** : the length of time during which a being or thing has lived or existed **2** : the time of life at which some particular qualification is achieved; *esp* : MAJORITY **3** : the latter part of life **4** : a long time **5** : a period in history

[2]**age** *vb* **aged; ag•ing** *or* **age•ing 1** : to grow old or cause to grow old **2** : to become or cause to become mature or mellow

-age *n suffix* **1** : aggregate : collection ⟨track*age*⟩ **2** : action : process ⟨haul*age*⟩ **3** : cumulative result of ⟨break*age*⟩ **4** : rate of ⟨dos*age*⟩ **5** : house or place of ⟨orphan*age*⟩ **6** : state : rank ⟨vassal*age*⟩ **7** : fee : charge ⟨post*age*⟩

aged \ˈā-jəd *for 1;* ˈājd *for 2*\ *adj* **1** : of advanced age **2** : having attained a specified age ⟨a man ~ 40 years⟩

age•less \ˈāj-ləs\ *adj* **1** : not growing old or showing the effects of age **2** : TIMELESS, ETERNAL ⟨~ truths⟩

agen•cy \ˈā-jən-sē\ *n, pl* **-cies 1** : one through which something is accomplished : INSTRUMENTALITY **2** : the office or function of an agent **3** : an establishment doing business for another **4** : an administrative division (as of a government) **syn** means, medium, vehicle

agen•da \ə-ˈjen-də\ *n* : a list of things to be done : PROGRAM

agent \ˈā-jənt\ *n* **1** : one that acts **2** : MEANS, INSTRUMENT **3** : a person acting or doing business for another **syn** attorney, deputy, proxy, delegate

Agent Orange *n* : an herbicide widely used in the Vietnam War that is composed of 2,4-D and 2,4,5-T and contains a toxic contaminant

agent pro•vo•ca•teur \ˈä-ˌzhä^{n}-prō-ˌvä-kə-ˈtər, ˈā-jənt-\ *n, pl* **agents provocateurs** \ˈä-ˌzhä^{n}-prō-ˌväk-ə-ˈtər, ˈā-jənts-prō-\ [F] : a person hired to infiltrate a group and incite its members to illegal action

age of consent : the age at which one is legally competent to give consent esp. to marriage or to sexual intercourse

age–old \ˈāj-ˈōld\ *adj* : having existed for ages : ANCIENT

ag•er•a•tum \ˌa-jə-ˈrā-təm\ *n, pl* **-tum** *also* **-tums** : any of a large genus of tropical American plants that are related to the daisies and have small showy heads of blue or white flowers

Ag•ge•us \a-ˈgē-əs\ *n* : HAGGAI

[1]**ag•glom•er•ate** \ə-ˈglä-mə-ˌrāt\ *vb* **-at•ed; -at•ing** [L *agglomerare* to heap up, join, fr. *ad-* to + *glomer-, glomus* ball] : to gather into a mass : CLUSTER — **ag•glom•er•a•tion** \-ˌglä-mə-ˈrā-shən\ *n*

[2]**ag•glom•er•ate** \-rət\ *n* : rock composed of volcanic fragments

ag•glu•ti•nate \ə-ˈglüt-^{ə}n-ˌāt\ *vb* **-nat•ed; -nat•ing 1** : to cause to adhere : gather into a group or mass **2** : to cause (as red blood cells or bacteria) to collect into clumps — **ag•glu•ti•na•tion** \-ˌglüt-^{ə}n-ˈā-shən\ *n*

ag•gran•dise *Brit var of* AGGRANDIZE

ag•gran•dize \ə-ˈgran-ˌdīz, ˈa-grən-\ *vb* **-dized; -diz•ing** : to make great or greater — **ag•gran•dize•ment** \ə-ˈgran-dəz-mənt, -ˌdīz-; ˌa-grən-ˈdīz-\ *n*

ag•gra•vate \ˈa-grə-ˌvāt\ *vb* **-vat•ed; -vat•ing 1** : to make more severe : INTENSIFY **2** : IRRITATE — **ag•gra•va•tion** \ˌa-grə-ˈvā-shən\ *n*

[1]**ag•gre•gate** \ˈa-gri-gət\ *adj* : formed by the gathering of units into one mass

[2]**ag•gre•gate** \-ˌgāt\ *vb* **-gat•ed; -gat•ing** : to collect into one mass

[3]**ag•gre•gate** \-gət\ *n* : a mass or body of units or parts somewhat loosely associated with one another; *also* : the whole amount

ag•gre•ga•tion \ˌa-gri-ˈgā-shən\ *n* **1** : a group, body, or mass composed of many distinct parts **2** : the collecting of units or parts into a mass or whole

ag•gres•sion \ə-ˈgre-shən\ *n* **1** : an unprovoked attack **2** : the practice of making attacks **3** : hostile, injurious, or destructive behavior or outlook esp. when caused by frustration — **ag•gres•sor** \-ˈgre-sər\ *n*

ag•gres•sive \ə-ˈgre-siv\ *adj* **1** : tending toward or exhibiting aggression; *esp* : marked by combative readiness **2** : marked by driving energy or initiative : ENTERPRISING **3** : more intensive or comprehensive esp. in dosage or extent — **ag•gres•sive•ly** *adv* — **ag•gres•sive•ness** *n*

ag•grieve \ə-ˈgrēv\ *vb* **ag•grieved; ag•griev•ing 1** : to cause grief to **2** : to inflict injury on : WRONG

aghast \ə-ˈgast\ *adj* : struck with amazement or horror

ag•ile \ˈa-jəl\ *adj* : able to move quickly and easily — **agil•i•ty** \ə-ˈji-lə-tē\ *n*

ag•i•tate \ˈa-jə-ˌtāt\ *vb* **-tat•ed; -tat•ing 1** : to move with an irregular rapid motion **2** : to stir up : EXCITE **3** : to discuss earnestly **4** : to attempt to arouse public feeling — **ag•i•ta•tion** \ˌa-jə-ˈtā-shən\ *n* — **ag•i•ta•tor** \ˈa-jə-ˌtā-tər\ *n*

ag•it•prop \ˈa-jət-ˌpräp\ *n* [Russ] : political propaganda promulgated esp. through the arts

agleam \ə-ˈglēm\ *adj* : GLEAMING

aglit•ter \ə-ˈgli-tər\ *adj* : GLITTERING

aglow \ə-ˈglō\ *adj* : GLOWING

ag•nos•tic \ag-ˈnäs-tik\ *adj* [Gk *agnōstos* unknown, unknowable, fr. *a-* un- + *gnōstos* known] : of or relating to the belief that the existence of any ultimate reality (as God) is unknown and prob. unknowable — **agnostic** *n* — **ag•nos•ti•cism** \-ˈnäs-tə-ˌsi-zəm\ *n*

ago \ə-ˈgō\ *adj or adv* : earlier than the present time

agog \ə-ˈgäg\ *adj* [MF *en gogues* in mirth] : full of excitement : EAGER

a–go–go \ä-ˈgō-ˌgō\ *adj* [*Whisky à Gogo*, café and disco in Paris, France, fr. F *à gogo* galore] : GO-GO

ag•o•nise *Brit var of* AGONIZE

ag•o•nize \ˈa-gə-ˌnīz\ *vb* **-nized; -niz•ing** : to suffer or cause to suffer agony — **ag•o•niz•ing•ly** *adv*

ag•o•ny \ˈa-gə-nē\ *n, pl* **-nies** [ME *agonie*, fr. L *agonia*, fr. Gk *agōnia* struggle, anguish, fr. *agōn* gathering, contest for a prize] : extreme pain of mind or body **syn** suffering, distress, misery

ago•ra \ˌä-gə-ˈrä\ *n, pl* **ago•rot** \-ˈrōt\ — see *shekel* at MONEY table

ag•o•ra•pho•bia \ˌa-gə-rə-ˈfō-bē-ə\ *n* : abnormal fear of being in a helpless, embarrassing, or inescapable situation characterized esp. by avoidance of open or public places — **ag•o•ra•pho•bic** \-ˈfō-bik, -ˈfä-\ *adj or n*

agr *abbr* agricultural; agriculture

agrar•i•an \ə-ˈgrer-ē-ən\ *adj* **1** : of or relating to land or its ownership ⟨~ reforms⟩ **2** : of or relating to farmers or farming interests — **agrarian** *n* — **agrar•i•an•ism** *n*

agree \ə-ˈgrē\ *vb* **agreed; agree•ing 1** : ADMIT, CONCEDE **2** : to be similar : CORRESPOND **3** : to express agreement or approval **4** : to be in harmony **5** : to settle by common consent **6** : to be fitting or healthful : SUIT

agree•able \ə-ˈgrē-ə-bəl\ *adj* **1** : PLEASING, PLEASANT **2** : ready to consent **3** : being in harmony : CONSONANT — **agree•able•ness** *n* — **agree•ably** \-blē\ *adv*

agree•ment \ə-ˈgrē-mənt\ *n* **1** : harmony of opinion or action **2** : mutual understanding or arrangement; *also* : a document containing such an arrangement

ag•ri•busi•ness \ˈa-grə-ˌbiz-nəs, -nəz\ *n* : an industry engaged in the manufacture and sale of farm equipment and supplies and in the production, processing, storage, and sale of farm commodities

agric *abbr* agricultural; agriculture

ag•ri•cul•ture \ˈa-gri-ˌkəl-chər\ *n* : FARMING, HUSBANDRY — **ag•ri•cul•tur•al** \ˌa-gri-ˈkəl-ch(ə-)rəl\ *adj* — **ag•ri•cul•tur•ist** \-ch(ə-)rist\ *or* **ag•ri•cul•tur•al•ist** \-ch(ə-)rə-list\ *n*

agron•o•my \ə-ˈgrä-nə-mē\ *n* : a branch of agriculture that deals with the raising of crops and the care of the

soil — **ag•ro•nom•ic** \ˌa-grə-ˈnä-mik\ *adj* — **agron•o•mist** \ə-ˈgrä-nə-mist\ *n*
aground \ə-ˈgraůnd\ *adv or adj* : on or onto the bottom or shore ⟨ran ~⟩
agt *abbr* agent
ague \ˈā-gyü\ *n* : a fever (as malaria) with recurrent chills and sweating
ahead \ə-ˈhed\ *adv or adj* **1** : in or toward the front **2** : into or for the future ⟨plan ~⟩ **3** : in or toward a more advantageous position
ahead of *prep* **1** : in front or advance of **2** : in excess of : ABOVE
AHL *abbr* American Hockey League
ahoy \ə-ˈhȯi\ *interj* — used in hailing ⟨ship ~⟩
AI *abbr* artificial intelligence
[1]**aid** \ˈād\ *vb* : to provide with what is useful in achieving an end : ASSIST
[2]**aid** *n* **1** : ASSISTANCE **2** : ASSISTANT
AID *abbr* Agency for International Development
aide \ˈād\ *n* : a person who acts as an assistant; *esp* : a military officer assisting a superior
aide–de–camp \ˌād-di-ˈkamp, -ˈkäⁿ\ *n, pl* **aides–de–camp** \ˌādz-di-\ [F] : AIDE
AIDS \ˈādz\ *n* [*a*cquired *i*mmuno*d*eficiency *s*yndrome] : a serious disease of the human immune system that is caused by infection with HIV, that is characterized by severe reduction in the numbers of helper T cells, that in modern industrialized nations occurs esp. in intravenous users of illicit drugs and in homosexual and bisexual men, and that is transmitted esp. in blood and bodily secretions (as semen)
AIDS–related complex *n* : a group of symptoms (as fever, weight loss, and lymphadenopathy) that is associated with the presence of antibodies to HIV and is followed by the development of AIDS in a certain proportion of cases
AIDS virus *n* : HIV
ai•grette \ā-ˈgret, ˈā-ˌ\ *n* [F, plume, egret] : a plume or decorative tuft for the head
ail \ˈāl\ *vb* **1** : to be the matter with : TROUBLE **2** : to be unwell
ai•lan•thus \ā-ˈlan-thəs\ *n* : any of a genus of Asian trees or shrubs with pinnate leaves and ill-scented greenish flowers
ai•le•ron \ˈā-lə-ˌrän\ *n* : a movable part of an airplane wing used in banking
ail•ment \ˈāl-mənt\ *n* : a bodily disorder
[1]**aim** \ˈām\ *vb* [ME, fr. MF *aesmer & esmer;* MF *aesmer,* fr. OF, fr. *a-* to (fr. L *ad-*) + *esmer* to estimate, fr. L *aestimare*] **1** : to point a weapon at an object **2** : to direct one's efforts : ASPIRE **3** : to direct to or toward a specified object or goal
[2]**aim** *n* **1** : the pointing of a weapon at an object **2** : the ability to hit a target **3** : OBJECT, PURPOSE — **aim•less** \-ləs\ *adj* — **aim•less•ly** *adv* — **aim•less•ness** *n*
AIM *abbr* American Indian Movement
ain't \ˈānt\ **1** : are not **2** : is not **3** : am not — though disapproved by many and more common in less educated speech, used orally in most parts of the U.S. by many educated speakers esp. in the phrase *ain't I*
Ai•nu \ˈī-nü\ *n, pl* **Ainu** *or* **Ainus** **1** : a member of an indigenous people of northern Japan **2** : the language of the Ainu people
[1]**air** \ˈar\ *n* **1** : the gaseous mixture surrounding the earth **2** : a light breeze **3** : MELODY, TUNE **4** : the outward appearance of a person or thing : MANNER **5** : an artificial manner **6** : COMPRESSED AIR ⟨~ sprayer⟩ **7** : AIRCRAFT ⟨~ patrol⟩ **8** : AVIATION ⟨~ safety⟩ **9** : the medium of transmission of radio waves; *also* : RADIO, TELEVISION
[2]**air** *vb* **1** : to expose to the air **2** : to expose to public view
air bag *n* : a bag designed to inflate automatically to protect automobile occupants in case of collision
air•boat \ˈar-ˌbōt\ *n* : a shallow-draft boat driven by an airplane propeller
air•borne \-ˌbōrn\ *adj* : done or being in the air
air brake *n* **1** : a brake operated by a piston driven by compressed air **2** : a surface projected into the airflow to lower an airplane's speed
air•brush \ˈar-ˌbrəsh\ *n* : a device for applying a fine spray (as of paint) by compressed air — **airbrush** *vb*
air–con•di•tion \ˌar-kən-ˈdi-shən\ *vb* : to equip with an apparatus for filtering air and controlling its humidity and temperature — **air con•di•tion•er** \-ˈdi-sh(ə-)nər\ *n*
air•craft \ˈar-ˌkraft\ *n, pl* **aircraft** : a vehicle for traveling through the air
aircraft carrier *n* : a warship with a deck on which airplanes can be launched and landed
air•drop \ˈar-ˌdräp\ *n* : delivery of cargo or personnel by parachute from an airplane in flight — **air–drop** *vb*
Aire•dale terrier \ˈar-ˌdāl-\ *n* : any of a breed of large terriers with a hard wiry coat
air•fare \ˈar-ˌfar\ *n* : fare for travel by airplane
air•field \-ˌfēld\ *n* : AIRPORT
air•flow \-ˌflō\ *n* : the motion of air relative to a body in it
air•foil \-ˌfȯil\ *n* : an airplane surface designed to produce reaction forces from the air through which it moves
air force *n* : the military organization of a nation for air warfare
air•frame \ˈar-ˌfrām\ *n* : the structure of an aircraft, rocket, or missile without the power plant
air•freight \-ˈfrāt\ *n* : freight transport by aircraft in volume; *also* : the charge for this service
air gun *n* **1** : a gun operated by compressed air **2** : a hand tool that works by compressed air; *esp* : AIRBRUSH
air•head \ˈar-ˌhed\ *n* : a mindless or stupid person
air lane *n* : AIRWAY 1
air•lift \ˈar-ˌlift\ *n* : transportation (as of supplies or passengers) by aircraft — **airlift** *vb*
air•line \-ˌlīn\ *n* : a transportation system using airplanes
air•lin•er \-ˌlī-nər\ *n* : a large passenger airplane operated by an airline
air lock *n* : an airtight chamber separating areas of different pressure
air•mail \ˈar-ˌmāl\ *n* : the system of transporting mail by aircraft; *also* : mail so transported — **airmail** *vb*
air•man \-mən\ *n* **1** : AVIATOR, PILOT **2** : an enlisted man in the air force in one of the three ranks below sergeant
airman basic *n* : an enlisted man of the lowest rank in the air force
airman first class *n* : an enlisted man in the air force with a rank just below that of sergeant
air mass *n* : a large horizontally homogeneous body of air
air•mo•bile \ˈar-ˌmō-bəl, -ˌbēl\ *adj* : of, relating to, or being a military unit whose members are transported to combat areas usu. by helicopter
air•plane \-ˌplān\ *n* : a powered heavier-than-air aircraft that has fixed wings from which it derives lift
air•play \-ˌplā\ *n* : the playing of a musical recording on the air by a radio station
air pocket *n* : a condition of the atmosphere that causes an airplane to drop suddenly
air police *n* : the military police of an air force
air•port \ˈar-ˌpōrt\ *n* : a place from which aircraft operate that usu. has paved runways and a terminal
air raid *n* : an attack by armed airplanes on a surface target
air•ship \ˈar-ˌship\ *n* : a lighter-than-air aircraft having propulsion and steering systems
air•sick \-ˌsik\ *adj* : affected with motion sickness associated with flying — **air•sick•ness** *n*

air•space \-ˌspās\ *n* : the space above a nation and under its jurisdiction
air•speed \-ˌspēd\ *n* : the speed of an object (as an airplane) with relation to the surrounding air
air•strip \-ˌstrip\ *n* : a runway without normal airport facilities
air•tight \ˈar-ˈtīt\ *adj* **1** : so tightly sealed that no air can enter or escape **2** : leaving no opening for attack
air–to–air *adj* : launched from one airplane in flight at another; *also* : involving aircraft in flight
air•waves \ˈar-ˌwāvz\ *n pl* : AIR 9
air•way \-ˌwā\ *n* **1** : a regular route for airplanes **2** : AIRLINE
air•wor•thy \-ˌwər-thē\ *adj* : fit for operation in the air ⟨an ~ plane⟩ — **air•wor•thi•ness** *n*
airy \ˈar-ē\ *adj* **air•i•er; -est 1** : LOFTY **2** : lacking in reality : EMPTY **3** : DELICATE **4** : BREEZY
aisle \ˈīl\ *n* [ME *ile*, fr. MF *ele* wing, fr. L *ala*] **1** : the side of a church nave separated by piers from the nave proper **2** : a passage between sections of seats
ajar \ə-ˈjär\ *adj or adv* : partly open
AK *abbr* Alaska
aka *abbr* also known as
AKC *abbr* American Kennel Club
akim•bo \ə-ˈkim-bō\ *adj or adv* : having the hand on the hip and the elbow turned outward
akin \ə-ˈkin\ *adj* **1** : related by blood **2** : similar in kind
Al *symbol* aluminum
AL *abbr* **1** Alabama **2** American League **3** American Legion
[1]**-al** *adj suffix* : of, relating to, or characterized by ⟨directional⟩
[2]**-al** *n suffix* : action : process ⟨rehearsal⟩
Ala *abbr* Alabama
al•a•bas•ter \ˈa-lə-ˌbas-tər\ *n* **1** : a compact fine-textured usu. white and translucent gypsum often carved into objects (as vases) **2** : a hard translucent calcite
à la carte \ˌa-lə-ˈkärt, ˌä-\ *adv or adj* [F] : with a separate price for each item on the menu
alac•ri•ty \ə-ˈla-krə-tē\ *n* : cheerful readiness : BRISKNESS
à la mode \ˌa-lə-ˈmōd, ˌä-\ *adj* [F, according to the fashion] **1** : FASHIONABLE, STYLISH **2** : topped with ice cream
[1]**alarm** \ə-ˈlärm\ *also* **ala•rum** \ə-ˈlär-əm, -ˈlar-\ *n* [ME *alarme*, fr. MF, fr. OIt *all'arme*, lit., to the weapon] **1** : a warning signal or device **2** : the terror caused by sudden danger
[2]**alarm** *also* **alarum** *vb* **1** : to warn of danger **2** : FRIGHTEN
alarm•ist \ə-ˈlär-mist\ *n* : a person who alarms others esp. needlessly
alas \ə-ˈlas\ *interj* — used to express unhappiness, pity, or concern
al•ba•core \ˈal-bə-ˌkōr\ *n, pl* **-core** *or* **-cores** : a large tuna that is a source of canned tuna
Al•ba•nian \al-ˈbā-nē-ən\ *n* : a native or inhabitant of Albania
al•ba•tross \ˈal-bə-ˌtrȯs, -ˌträs\ *n, pl* **-tross** *or* **-trosses** : any of a family of large web-footed seabirds
al•be•do \al-ˈbē-(ˌ)dō\ *n, pl* **-dos** : the fraction of incident radiation that is reflected by a body or surface
al•be•it \ȯl-ˈbē-ət, al-\ *conj* : even though : ALTHOUGH
al•bi•no \al-ˈbī-nō\ *n, pl* **-nos** : a person or nonhuman mammal lacking coloring matter in the skin, hair, and eyes — **al•bi•nism** \ˈal-bə-ˌni-zəm\ *n*
al•bum \ˈal-bəm\ *n* **1** : a book with blank pages used for making a collection (as of stamps) **2** : one or more recordings (as on tape or disk) produced as a single unit
al•bu•men \al-ˈbyü-mən\ *n* **1** : the white of an egg **2** : ALBUMIN
al•bu•min \al-ˈbyü-mən\ *n* : any of numerous water-soluble proteins of blood, milk, egg white, and plant and animal tissues
al•bu•min•ous \al-ˈbyü-mə-nəs\ *adj* : containing or resembling albumen or albumin
alc *abbr* alcohol
al•cal•de \al-ˈkäl-dē\ *n* : the chief administrative and judicial officer of a Spanish or Spanish-American town
al•ca•zar \al-ˈkä-zər, -ˈka-\ *n* [Sp *alcázar*, fr. Ar *al-qaṣr* the castle] : a Spanish fortress or palace
al•che•my \ˈal-kə-mē\ *n* : medieval chemistry chiefly concerned with efforts to turn base metals into gold — **al•che•mist** \ˈal-kə-mist\ *n*
al•co•hol \ˈal-kə-ˌhȯl\ *n* [NL, fr. ML, powdered antimony, fr. Sp, fr. Ar *al-kuḥul* the powdered antimony] **1** : a colorless flammable liquid that is the intoxicating agent in fermented and distilled liquors **2** : any of various carbon compounds similar to alcohol **3** : beverages containing alcohol
[1]**al•co•hol•ic** \ˌal-kə-ˈhȯ-lik, -ˈhä-\ *adj* **1** : of, relating to, caused by, or containing alcohol **2** : affected with alcoholism — **al•co•hol•i•cal•ly** \-li-k(ə-)lē\ *adv*
[2]**alcoholic** *n* : a person affected with alcoholism
al•co•hol•ism \ˈal-kə-ˌhȯ-ˌli-zəm\ *n* : continued excessive and usu. uncontrollable use of alcoholic drinks; *also* : a complex chronic psychological and nutritional disorder associated with such use
al•cove \ˈal-ˌkōv\ *n* **1** : a nook or small recess opening off a larger room **2** : a niche or arched opening (as in a wall)
ald *abbr* alderman
al•der \ˈȯl-dər\ *n* : a tree or shrub related to the birches and growing in wet areas
al•der•man \ˈȯl-dər-mən\ *n* : a member of a city legislative body
ale \ˈāl\ *n* : an alcoholic beverage brewed from malt and hops that is usu. more bitter than beer
ale•a•tor•ic \ˌā-lē-ə-ˈtȯr-ik\ *adj* : characterized by chance or random elements ⟨~ music⟩
ale•a•to•ry \ˈā-lē-ə-ˌtōr-ē\ *adj* : ALEATORIC
alee \ə-ˈlē\ *adv* : on or toward the lee
ale•house \ˈāl-ˌhau̇s\ *n* : a place where ale is sold to be drunk on the premises
[1]**alert** \ə-ˈlərt\ *adj* [It *all' erta*, lit., on the ascent] **1** : watchful against danger **2** : quick to perceive and act — **alert•ly** *adv* — **alert•ness** *n*
[2]**alert** *n* **1** : ALARM 1 **2** : the period during which an alert is in effect
[3]**alert** *vb* **1** : WARN **2** : to make aware of
Aleut \ˌa-lē-ˈüt, ə-ˈlüt\ *n* **1** : a member of a people of the Aleutian and Shumagin islands and the western part of Alaska Peninsula **2** : the language of the Aleuts
ale•wife \ˈāl-ˌwīf\ *n* : a food fish of the herring family abundant esp. on the Atlantic coast
Al•ex•an•dri•an \ˌa-lig-ˈzan-drē-ən\ *adj* **1** : of or relating to Alexander the Great **2** : HELLENISTIC
al•ex•an•drine \-ˈzan-drən\ *n, often cap* : a line of six iambic feet
al•fal•fa \al-ˈfal-fə\ *n* : a leguminous plant widely grown for hay and forage
al•fres•co \al-ˈfres-kō\ *adj or adv* [It] : taking place in the open air
alg *abbr* algebra
al•ga \ˈal-gə\ *n, pl* **al•gae** \ˈal-(ˌ)jē\ : any of a group of lower plants having chlorophyll but no vascular system and including seaweeds and related freshwater plants — **al•gal** \-gəl\ *adj*
al•ge•bra \ˈal-jə-brə\ *n* [ML, fr. Ar *al-jabr*] : a branch of mathematics using symbols (as letters) to explore the relationships between numbers and the operations used to work with them — **al•ge•bra•ic** \ˌal-jə-ˈbrā-ik\ *adj* — **al•ge•bra•i•cal•ly** \-ˈbrā-ə-k(ə-)lē\ *adv*
Al•ge•ri•an \al-ˈjir-ē-ən\ *n* : a native or inhabitant of Algeria — **Algerian** *adj*
Al•gon•quin \al-ˈgän-kwən, -ˈgäŋ-\ *n* : a member of an American Indian people of the Ottawa River valley
al•go•rithm \ˈal-gə-ˌri-thəm\ *n* : a procedure for solv-

ing a problem esp. in mathematics or computing — **al•go•rith•mic** \ˌal-gə-ˈrith-mik\ *adj* — **al•go•rith•mi•cal•ly** \-mi-k(ə-)lē\ *adv*

[1]alias \ˈā-lē-əs, ˈāl-yəs\ *adv* [L, otherwise, fr. *alius* other] : otherwise called

[2]alias *n* : an assumed name

[1]al•i•bi \ˈa-lə-ˌbī\ *n* [L, elsewhere, fr. *alius* other] **1** : a plea offered by an accused person of not having been at the scene of an offense **2** : an excuse (as for failure)

[2]alibi *vb* **-bied; -bi•ing 1** : to furnish an excuse for **2** : to offer an excuse

[1]alien \ˈā-lē-ən, ˈāl-yən\ *adj* : belonging to another : FOREIGN

[2]alien *n* **1** : a foreign-born resident who has not been naturalized **2** : EXTRATERRESTRIAL

alien•able \ˈāl-yə-nə-bəl, ˈā-lē-ə-nə-\ *adj* : transferable to the ownership of another ⟨~ property⟩

alien•ate \ˈā-lē-ə-ˌnāt, ˈāl-yə-\ *vb* **-at•ed; -at•ing 1** : to make hostile : ESTRANGE **2** : to transfer (property) to another — **alien•ation** \ˌā-lē-ə-ˈnā-shən, ˌāl-yə-\ *n*

alien•ist \ˈā-lē-ə-nist, ˈāl-yə-\ *n* : PSYCHIATRIST

[1]alight \ə-ˈlīt\ *vb* **alight•ed** *also* **alit** \ə-ˈlit\ **alight•ing 1** : to get down (as from a vehicle) **2** : to come to rest from the air **syn** settle, land, perch

[2]alight *adj* : lighted up

align *also* **aline** \ə-ˈlīn\ *vb* **1** : to bring into line **2** : to array on the side of or against a cause — **align•er** *n* — **align•ment** *also* **aline•ment** *n*

[1]alike \ə-ˈlīk\ *adv* : EQUALLY

[2]alike *adj* : LIKE **syn** akin, analogous, similar, comparable

al•i•ment \ˈa-lə-mənt\ *n* : NOURISHMENT 1 — **aliment** *vb*

al•i•men•ta•ry \ˌa-lə-ˈmen-t(ə-)rē\ *adj* : of, relating to, or functioning in nourishment or nutrition

alimentary canal *n* : the tube that extends from the mouth to the anus and functions in the digestion and absorption of food and the elimination of residues

al•i•mo•ny \ˈa-lə-ˌmō-nē\ *n, pl* **-nies** [L *alimonia* sustenance, fr. *alere* to nourish] : an allowance made to one spouse by the other for support pending or after legal separation or divorce

A–line \ˈā-ˌlīn\ *adj* : having a flared bottom and a close-fitting top ⟨an ~ skirt⟩

alive \ə-ˈlīv\ *adj* **1** : having life **2** : being in force or operation **3** : SENSITIVE ⟨~ to the danger⟩ **4** : ALERT, BRISK **5** : ANIMATED ⟨streets ~ with traffic⟩ — **alive•ness** *n*

alk *abbr* alkaline

al•ka•li \ˈal-kə-ˌlī\ *n, pl* **-lies** *or* **-lis 1** : a substance (as a hydroxide) that has a bitter taste and neutralizes acids **2** : a mixture of salts in the soil of some dry regions in such amount as to make ordinary farming impossible — **al•ka•line** \-kə-lən, -ˌlīn\ *adj* — **al•ka•lin•i•ty** \ˌal-kə-ˈli-nə-tē\ *n*

al•ka•loid \ˈal-kə-ˌlȯid\ *n* : any of various usu. basic and bitter organic compounds found esp. in seed plants

al•kane \ˈal-ˌkān\ *n* : a hydrocarbon in which each carbon atom is bonded to 4 other atoms

al•kyd \ˈal-kəd\ *n* : any of numerous synthetic resins used esp. for protective coatings and in paint

[1]all \ˈȯl\ *adj* **1** : the whole of **2** : every member of **3** : EVERY ⟨~ manner of problems⟩ **4** : any whatever ⟨beyond ~ doubt⟩ **5** : nothing but ⟨~ ears⟩ **6** : being more than one person or thing ⟨who ~ is coming⟩

[2]all *adv* **1** : WHOLLY **2** : selected as the best — used in combination ⟨*all*-state champs⟩ **3** : so much ⟨~ the better for it⟩ **4** : for each side ⟨the score is two ~⟩

[3]all *pron* **1** : the whole number, quantity, or amount ⟨~ of it is gone⟩ **2** : EVERYBODY, EVERYTHING ⟨that is ~⟩

[4]all *n* : the whole of one's resources ⟨gave his ~⟩

Al•lah \ˈä-lä, ˈa-; ä-ˈlä\ *n* [Ar] : GOD 1 — used in Islam

all along *adv* : all the time ⟨knew it *all along*⟩

all–Amer•i•can \ˌȯl-ə-ˈmer-ə-kən\ *adj* **1** : selected as the best in the U.S. **2** : composed wholly of American elements **3** : typical of the U.S. — **all–American** *n*

all–around \ˌȯl-ə-ˈrau̇nd\ *adj* **1** : considered in all aspects ⟨best ~ performance⟩ **2** : competent in many fields : VERSATILE ⟨an ~ athlete⟩

al•lay \ə-ˈlā\ *vb* **1** : ALLEVIATE **2** : CALM **syn** lighten, relieve, ease, assuage

all clear *n* : a signal that a danger has passed

al•lege \ə-ˈlej\ *vb* **al•leged; al•leg•ing 1** : to assert without proof **2** : to offer as a reason — **al•le•ga•tion** \ˌa-li-ˈgā-shən\ *n* — **al•leg•ed•ly** \ə-ˈle-jəd-lē\ *adv*

al•le•giance \ə-ˈlē-jəns\ *n* **1** : loyalty owed by a citizen to a government **2** : loyalty to a person or cause

al•le•go•ry \ˈa-lə-ˌgȯr-ē\ *n, pl* **-ries** : the expression through symbolism of truths or generalizations about human experience — **al•le•gor•i•cal** \ˌa-lə-ˈgȯr-i-kəl\ *adj* — **al•le•gor•i•cal•ly** \-k(ə-)lē\ *adv*

[1]al•le•gro \ə-ˈle-grō, -ˈlā-\ *n, pl* **-gros** : an allegro movement

[2]allegro *adv or adj* [It, merry] : at a brisk lively tempo — used as a direction in music

al•le•lu•ia \ˌa-lə-ˈlü-yə\ *interj* : HALLELUJAH

Al•len wrench \ˈa-lən-\ *n* [*Allen* Manufacturing Company, Hartford, Conn.] : an L-shaped hexagonal metal bar of which either end fits the socket of a screw or bolt

al•ler•gen \ˈa-lər-jən\ *n* : something that causes allergy — **al•ler•gen•ic** \ˌa-lər-ˈje-nik\ *adj*

al•ler•gist \ˈa-lər-jist\ *n* : a specialist in allergies

al•ler•gy \ˈa-lər-jē\ *n, pl* **-gies** [G *Allergie*, fr. Gk *allos* other + *ergon* work] : exaggerated or abnormal reaction (as by sneezing) to substances or situations harmless to most people — **al•ler•gic** \ə-ˈlər-jik\ *adj*

al•le•vi•ate \ə-ˈlē-vē-ˌāt\ *vb* **-at•ed; -at•ing** : RELIEVE, LESSEN **syn** lighten, mitigate, allay — **al•le•vi•a•tion** \ə-ˌlē-vē-ˈā-shən\ *n*

al•ley \ˈa-lē\ *n, pl* **alleys 1** : a garden or park walk **2** : a place for bowling **3** : a narrow passageway esp. between buildings

al•ley–oop \ˌa-lē-ˈyüp\ *n* : a basketball play in which a player catches a pass above the basket and immediately dunks the ball

al•ley•way \ˈa-lē-ˌwā\ *n* : ALLEY 3

All•hal•lows \ȯl-ˈha-lōz\ *n, pl* **Allhallows** : ALL SAINTS' DAY

al•li•ance \ə-ˈlī-əns\ *n* : a union to promote common interests **syn** league, coalition, confederacy, federation

al•li•ga•tor \ˈa-lə-ˌgā-tər\ *n* [Sp *el lagarto* the lizard] : either of two large short-legged reptiles resembling crocodiles but having a shorter and broader snout

alligator

alligator pear *n* : AVOCADO

al•lit•er•ate \ə-ˈli-tə-ˌrāt\ *vb* **-at•ed; -at•ing 1** : to form an alliteration **2** : to arrange so as to make alliteration

al•lit•er•a•tion \ə-ˌli-tə-ˈrā-shən\ *n* : the repetition of initial sounds in adjacent words or syllables — **al•lit•er•a•tive** \-ˈli-tə-ˌrā-tiv\ *adj*

al•lo•cate \ˈa-lə-ˌkāt\ *vb* **-cat•ed; -cat•ing** : ALLOT, ASSIGN — **al•lo•ca•tion** \ˌa-lə-ˈkā-shən\ *n*

al•lot \ə-ˈlät\ *vb* **al•lot•ted; al•lot•ting** : to distribute as a share **syn** assign, apportion, allocate — **al•lot•ment** *n*

all–out \ˈȯl-ˈau̇t\ *adj* : made with maximum effort

all over *adv* : EVERYWHERE

al•low \ə-ˈlau̇\ *vb* **1** : to assign as a share ⟨~ time for rest⟩ **2** : to count as a deduction **3** : to make allowance ⟨~ for expansion⟩ **4** : ADMIT, CONCEDE **5** : PERMIT ⟨~s the dog to roam⟩ — **al•low•able** *adj*

al•low•ance \-əns\ *n* **1** : an allotted share **2** : money given regularly for expenses **3** : a taking into account of extenuating circumstances

al•loy \ˈa-ˌlȯi, ə-ˈlȯi\ *n* **1** : a substance composed of metals melted together **2** : an admixture that lessens value — **al•loy** \ə-ˈlȯi, ˈa-ˌlȯi\ *vb*

all right *adv* **1** : very well ⟨*all right*, let's go⟩ **2** : beyond doubt **3** : SATISFACTORILY — **all right** *adj*

All Saints' Day *n* : a Christian feast on November 1 in honor of all the saints

All Souls' Day *n* : a day of prayer observed by some Christian churches on November 2 for the souls of the faithful departed

all•spice \ˈȯl-ˌspīs\ *n* : the berry of a West Indian tree related to the European myrtle; *also* : the mildly pungent and aromatic spice made from it

all–star \ˈȯl-ˌstär\ *n* : a member of a team of star performers — **all–star** *adj*

all told *adv* : with everything counted

al•lude \ə-ˈlüd\ *vb* **al•lud•ed; al•lud•ing** [L *alludere*, lit., to play with] : to refer indirectly — **al•lu•sion** \-ˈlü-zhən\ *n* — **al•lu•sive** \-ˈlü-siv\ *adj* — **al•lu•sive•ly** *adv* — **al•lu•sive•ness** *n*

al•lure \ə-ˈlu̇r\ *vb* **al•lured; al•lur•ing** : CHARM, ENTICE — **allure** *n* — **al•lur•ing•ly** *adv*

al•lu•vi•um \ə-ˈlü-vē-əm\ *n, pl* **-vi•ums** *or* **-via** \-vē-ə\ : soil material (as clay) deposited by running water — **al•lu•vi•al** \-vē-əl\ *adj or n*

al•ly \ə-ˈlī, ˈa-ˌlī\ *vb* **al•lied; al•ly•ing** : to enter into an alliance — **al•ly** \ˈa-ˌlī, ə-ˈlī\ *n*

-ally *adv suffix* : [2]-LY ⟨specific*ally*⟩

al•ma ma•ter \ˌal-mə-ˈmä-tər\ *n* [L, fostering mother] **1** : an educational institute that one has attended **2** : the song or hymn of an alma mater

al•ma•nac \ˈȯl-mə-ˌnak, ˈal-\ *n* **1** : a publication esp. of astronomical and meteorological data **2** : a usu. annual publication of miscellaneous information

al•man•dite \ˈal-mən-ˌdīt\ *n* : a deep red garnet

al•mighty \ȯl-ˈmī-tē\ *adj* **1** *often cap* : having absolute power over all ⟨*Almighty* God⟩ **2** : relatively unlimited in power — **al•might•i•ness** *n*

Almighty *n* : GOD 1

al•mond \ˈä-mənd, ˈa-; ˈal-\ *n* : a small tree related to the peach; *also* : the edible nutlike kernel of its fruit

al•mo•ner \ˈal-mə-nər, ˈä-mə-\ *n* : a person who distributes alms

al•most \ˈȯl-ˌmōst, ȯl-ˈmōst\ *adv* : very nearly but not exactly

alms \ˈämz, ˈälmz\ *n, pl* **alms** [ME *almesse, almes*, fr. OE *ælmesse, ælms*, fr. L *eleemosyna* alms, fr. Gk *eleēmosynē* pity, alms, fr. *eleēmōn* merciful] : something given freely to relieve the poor

alms•house \-ˌhau̇s\ *n* : POORHOUSE

al•oe \ˈa-lō\ *n* **1** : any of a large genus of succulent chiefly southern African plants related to the lilies **2** *pl* : the dried juice of the leaves of an aloe used esp. formerly as a laxative

aloft \ə-ˈlȯft\ *adv* **1** : high in the air **2** : in flight

alo•ha \ə-ˈlō-ə, ä-ˈlō-hä\ *interj* [Hawaiian] — used to greet or bid farewell

alone \ə-ˈlōn\ *adj* **1** : separated from others **2** : not including anyone or anything else : ONLY **syn** lonely, lonesome, lone, solitary — **alone** *adv*

[1]along \ə-ˈlȯŋ\ *prep* **1** : in line with the direction of ⟨sail ~ the coast⟩ **2** : at a point on or during ⟨stopped ~ the way⟩

[2]along *adv* **1** : FORWARD, ON **2** : as a companion ⟨bring her ~⟩ **3** : at an advanced point ⟨plans are far ~⟩

along•shore \ə-ˈlȯŋ-ˈshōr\ *adv or adj* : along the shore or coast

[1]along•side \-ˌsīd\ *adv* : along or by the side

[2]alongside *prep* **1** : along or by the side of **2** : in association with

alongside of *prep* : ALONGSIDE

aloof \ə-ˈlüf\ *adj* : removed or distant physically or emotionally — **aloof•ness** *n*

al•o•pe•cia \ˌa-lə-ˈpē-sh(ē-)ə\ *n* : BALDNESS

aloud \ə-ˈlau̇d\ *adv* : with a loud voice

alp \ˈalp\ *n* : a high rugged mountain

al•paca \al-ˈpa-kə\ *n* : a domesticated mammal esp. of Peru that is related to the llama; *also* : its woolly hair or cloth made from this

al•pha \ˈal-fə\ *n* **1** : the 1st letter of the Greek alphabet — Α or α **2** : something first : BEGINNING

al•pha•bet \ˈal-fə-ˌbet\ *n* : the set of letters or characters used in writing a language

al•pha•bet•i•cal \ˌal-fə-ˈbe-ti-kəl\ *or* **al•pha•bet•ic** \-ˈbe-tik\ *adj* **1** : arranged in the order of the letters of the alphabet **2** : of or employing an alphabet — **al•pha•bet•i•cal•ly** \-ti-k(ə-)lē\ *adv*

al•pha•bet•ize \ˈal-fə-bə-ˌtīz\ *vb* **-ized; -iz•ing** : to arrange in alphabetical order — **al•pha•bet•iz•er** *n*

al•pha•nu•mer•ic \ˌal-fə-nu̇-ˈmer-ik, -nyu̇-\ *adj* : consisting of letters and numbers and often other symbols ⟨an ~ code⟩; *also* : being a character in an alphanumeric system

alpha particle *n* : a positively charged particle identical with the nucleus of a helium atom that is ejected at high speed in certain radioactive transformations

alpha rhythm *n* : ALPHA WAVE

alpha wave *n* : an electrical rhythm of the brain often associated with a state of wakeful relaxation

Al•pine \ˈal-ˌpīn\ *adj* **1** : relating to, located in, or resembling the Alps mountains **2** *often not cap* : of, relating to, or growing on upland slopes above timberline **3** : of or relating to competitive ski events consisting of slalom and downhill racing

al•ready \ȯl-ˈre-dē\ *adv* : by this time : PREVIOUSLY

al•right \ȯl-ˈrīt\ *adv* : ALL RIGHT

al•so \ˈȯl-sō\ *adv* : in addition : TOO

al•so–ran \-ˌran\ *n* **1** : a horse or dog that finishes out of the money in a race **2** : a contestant that does not win

alt *abbr* **1** alternate **2** altitude

Alta *abbr* Alberta

al•tar \ˈȯl-tər\ *n* **1** : a structure on which sacrifices are offered or incense is burned **2** : a table used as a center of ritual or worship

altar boy *n* : a boy who assists the celebrant at a church service

[1]al•ter \ˈȯl-tər\ *vb* **al•tered; al•ter•ing** \-t(ə-)riŋ\ **1** : to make or become different **2** : CASTRATE, SPAY — **al•ter•a•tion** \ˌȯl-tə-ˈrā-shən\ *n*

[2]alter *abbr* alteration

al•ter•ca•tion \ˌȯl-tər-ˈkā-shən\ *n* : a noisy or angry dispute

al•ter ego \ˌȯl-tər-ˈē-gō\ *n* [L, lit., second I] : a second self; *esp* : a trusted friend

[1]al•ter•nate \ˈȯl-tər-nət, ˈal-\ *adj* **1** : arranged or succeeding by turns **2** : every other **3** : being an alternative ⟨an ~ route⟩ — **al•ter•nate•ly** *adv*

[2]al•ter•nate \-ˌnāt\ *vb* **-nat•ed; -nat•ing** : to occur or cause to occur by turns — **al•ter•na•tion** \ˌȯl-tər-ˈnā-shən, ˌal-\ *n*

[3]alternate *n* : SUBSTITUTE

alternating current *n* : an electric current that reverses its direction at regular intervals

al•ter•na•tive \ȯl-ˈtər-nə-tiv, al-\ *adj* : offering a choice — **alternative** *n*

al•ter•na•tor \ˈȯl-tər-ˌnā-tər, ˈal-\ *n* : an electric generator for producing alternating current

al•though *also* **al•tho** \ȯl-ˈt͟hō\ *conj* : in spite of the fact that : even though

al•tim•e•ter \al-ˈti-mə-tər, ˈal-tə-ˌmē-tər\ *n* : an instrument for measuring altitude

al•ti•tude \ˈal-tə-ˌtüd, -ˌtyüd\ *n* **1** : angular distance above the horizon **2** : vertical distance : HEIGHT **3** : the perpendicular distance in a geometric figure from the vertex to the base, from the vertex of an angle to the side opposite, or from the base to a parallel side or face

al•to \ˈal-tō\ *n, pl* **altos** [It, lit., high, fr. L *altus*] : the lower female voice part in a 4-part chorus; *also* : a singer having this voice or part

[1]**al·to·geth·er** \ˌȯl-tə-ˈge-t͟hər\ *adv* **1** : WHOLLY **2** : in all **3** : on the whole

[2]**altogether** *n* : NUDE ⟨posed in the ~⟩

al·tru·ism \ˈal-trü-ˌi-zəm\ *n* : unselfish interest in the welfare of others — **al·tru·ist** \-ist\ *n* — **al·tru·is·tic** \ˌal-trü-ˈis-tik\ *adj* — **al·tru·is·ti·cal·ly** \-ti-k(ə-)lē\ *adv*

al·um \ˈa-ləm\ *n* : either of two colorless crystalline aluminum-containing compounds used esp. as an emetic or as an astringent and styptic

alu·mi·na \ə-ˈlü-mə-nə\ *n* : the oxide of aluminum occurring in nature as corundum and in bauxite

al·u·min·i·um \ˌal-yə-ˈmi-nē-əm\ *n, chiefly Brit* : ALUMINUM

alu·mi·nize \ə-ˈlü-mə-ˌnīz\ *vb* **-nized; -niz·ing** : to treat with aluminum

alu·mi·num \ə-ˈlü-mə-nəm\ *n* : a silver-white malleable ductile light metallic element that is the most abundant metal in the earth's crust — see ELEMENT table

alum·na \ə-ˈləm-nə\ *n, pl* **-nae** \-(ˌ)nē\ : a woman graduate or former student of a college or school

alum·nus \ə-ˈləm-nəs\ *n, pl* **-ni** \-ˌnī\ [L, foster son, pupil, fr. *alere* to nourish] : a graduate or former student of a college or school

al·ways \ˈȯl-wēz, -wəz, -(ˌ)wāz\ *adv* **1** : at all times : INVARIABLY **2** : FOREVER

Alz·hei·mer's disease \ˈälts-ˌhī-mərz-, ˈalts-\ *n* : a degenerative disease of the central nervous system characterized esp. by premature senile mental deterioration

am *pres 1st sing of* BE

[1]**Am** *abbr* America; American

[2]**Am** *symbol* americium

[1]**AM** \ˈā-ˌem\ *n* : a broadcasting system using amplitude modulation; *also* : a radio receiver for broadcasts made by such a system

[2]**AM** *abbr* **1** ante meridiem — often not cap. and often punctuated **2** [NL *artium magister*] master of arts

AMA *abbr* American Medical Association

amah \ˈä-(ˌ)mä\ *n* : an Oriental female servant; *esp* : a Chinese nurse

amain \ə-ˈmān\ *adv, archaic* : with full force or speed

amal·gam \ə-ˈmal-gəm\ *n* **1** : an alloy of mercury with another metal used in making dental cements **2** : a mixture of different elements

amal·gam·ate \ə-ˈmal-gə-ˌmāt\ *vb* **-at·ed; -at·ing** : to unite or merge into one body — **amal·ga·ma·tion** \-ˌmal-gə-ˈmā-shən\ *n*

aman·u·en·sis \ə-ˌman-yə-ˈwen-səs\ *n, pl* **-en·ses** \-ˌsēz\ : one employed to write from dictation or to copy what another has written : SECRETARY

am·a·ranth \ˈa-mə-ˌranth\ *n* **1** : any of a large genus of coarse herbs sometimes grown for their showy flowers **2** : a flower that never fades

am·a·ran·thine \ˌa-mə-ˈran-thən, -ˌthīn\ *adj* **1** : relating to or resembling an amaranth **2** : UNDYING

am·a·ryl·lis \ˌa-mə-ˈri-ləs\ *n* : any of various plants related to the lilies; *esp* : any of several African herbs having bulbs and grown for their clusters of large showy flowers

amass \ə-ˈmas\ *vb* : ACCUMULATE

am·a·teur \ˈa-mə-(ˌ)tər, -ˌtu̇r, -ˌtyu̇r, -ˌchu̇r, -chər\ *n* [F, fr. L *amator* lover, fr. *amare* to love] **1** : a person who engages in a pursuit for pleasure and not as a profession **2** : a person who is not expert — **am·a·teur·ish** \ˌa-mə-ˈtər-ish, -ˈtu̇r-, -ˈtyu̇r-, -ˈchu̇r-, -ˈchər-\ *adj* — **am·a·teur·ism** \ˈa-mə-(ˌ)tər-i-zəm, -ˌtu̇r-, -ˌtyu̇r-, -ˌchu̇r-, -ˌchər-\ *n*

am·a·tive \ˈa-mə-tiv\ *adj* : indicative of love : AMOROUS — **am·a·tive·ly** *adv* — **am·a·tive·ness** *n*

am·a·to·ry \ˈa-mə-ˌtōr-ē\ *adj* : of or expressing sexual love

amaze \ə-ˈmāz\ *vb* **amazed; amaz·ing** : to fill with wonder : ASTOUND **syn** astonish, surprise, dumbfound — **amaze·ment** *n* — **amaz·ing·ly** *adv*

am·a·zon \ˈa-mə-ˌzän, -zən\ *n* **1** *cap* : a member of a race of female warriors of Greek mythology **2** : a tall strong often masculine woman — **am·a·zo·ni·an** \ˌa-mə-ˈzō-nē-ən\ *adj, often cap*

amb *abbr* ambassador

am·bas·sa·dor \am-ˈba-sə-dər\ *n* : a representative esp. of a government — **am·bas·sa·do·ri·al** \-ˌba-sə-ˈdōr-ē-əl\ *adj* — **am·bas·sa·dor·ship** *n*

am·ber \ˈam-bər\ *n* : a yellowish or brownish fossil resin used esp. for ornamental objects; *also* : the color of this resin

am·ber·gris \ˈam-bər-ˌgris, -ˌgrēs\ *n* : a waxy substance from the sperm whale used in making perfumes

am·bi·dex·trous \ˌam-bi-ˈdek-strəs\ *adj* : using both hands with equal ease — **am·bi·dex·trous·ly** *adv*

am·bi·ence *or* **am·bi·ance** \ˈam-bē-əns, äⁿ-ˈbyäⁿs\ *n* : a pervading atmosphere

am·bi·ent \ˈam-bē-ənt\ *adj* : existing on all sides

am·big·u·ous \am-ˈbi-gyə-wəs\ *adj* : capable of being understood in more than one way — **am·bi·gu·i·ty** \ˌam-bə-ˈgyü-ə-tē\ *n* — **am·big·u·ous·ly** *adv*

am·bi·tion \am-ˈbi-shən\ *n* [ME, fr. MF or L; MF, fr. L *ambition-, ambitio,* lit., act of soliciting for votes, fr. *ambire* to go around] : eager desire for success or power

am·bi·tious \-shəs\ *adj* : characterized by ambition — **am·bi·tious·ly** *adv*

am·biv·a·lence \am-ˈbi-və-ləns\ *n* : simultaneous attraction toward and repulsion from a person, object, or action — **am·biv·a·lent** \-lənt\ *adj*

[1]**am·ble** \ˈam-bəl\ *vb* **am·bled; am·bling** \-b(ə-)liŋ\ : to go at an amble

[2]**amble** *n* : an easy gait esp. of a horse

am·bro·sia \am-ˈbrō-zh(ē-)ə\ *n* : the food of the Greek and Roman gods — **am·bro·sial** \-zh(ē-)əl\ *adj*

am·bu·lance \ˈam-byə-ləns\ *n* : a vehicle equipped for carrying the injured or sick

am·bu·lant \ˈam-byə-lənt\ *adj* : AMBULATORY

[1]**am·bu·la·to·ry** \ˈam-byə-lə-ˌtōr-ē\ *adj* **1** : of, relating to, or adapted to walking **2** : able to walk or move about

[2]**ambulatory** *n, pl* **-ries** : a sheltered place (as in a cloister) for walking

am·bus·cade \ˈam-bə-ˌskād\ *n* : AMBUSH

am·bush \ˈam-ˌbu̇sh\ *n* : a trap in which concealed persons wait to attack by surprise — **ambush** *vb*

amdt *abbr* amendment

ame·ba, ame·boid *var of* AMOEBA, AMOEBOID

ame·lio·rate \ə-ˈmēl-yə-ˌrāt\ *vb* **-rat·ed; -rat·ing** : to make or grow better : IMPROVE — **ame·lio·ra·tion** \-ˌmēl-yə-ˈrā-shən\ *n*

amen \(ˌ)ā-ˈmen, (ˌ)ä-\ *interj* — used esp. at the end of prayers to affirm or express approval

ame·na·ble \ə-ˈmē-nə-bəl, -ˈme-\ *adj* **1** : ANSWERABLE **2** : COMPLIANT

amend \ə-ˈmend\ *vb* **1** : to change for the better : IMPROVE **2** : to alter formally in phraseology — **amend·able** \-ˈmen-də-bəl\ *adj*

amend·ment \ə-ˈmend-mənt\ *n* **1** : correction of faults **2** : the process of amending a parliamentary motion or a constitution; *also* : the alteration so proposed or made

amends \ə-ˈmendz\ *n sing or pl* : compensation for injury or loss

ame·ni·ty \ə-ˈme-nə-tē, -ˈmē-\ *n, pl* **-ties** **1** : AGREEABLENESS **2** : a gesture observed in social relationships **3** : something that serves as a comfort or convenience

Amer *abbr* America; American

amerce \ə-ˈmərs\ *vb* **amerced; amerc·ing** **1** : to penalize by a fine determined by the court **2** : PUNISH — **amerce·ment** *n*

Amer·i·can \ə-ˈmer-ə-kən\ *n* **1** : a native or inhabitant of No. or So. America **2** : a citizen of the U.S. — **American** *adj* — **Amer•i•can•ism** \-ə-kə-ˌni-zəm\ *n* — **Amer•i•can•iza•tion** \ə-ˌmer-ə-kə-nə-ˈzā-shən\ *n* — **Amer•i•can•ize** \ə-ˈmer-ə-kə-ˌnīz\ *vb* — **Amer•i•can•ness** *n*

Amer•i•ca•na \ə-ˌmer-ə-ˈka-nə, -ˈkä-\ *n pl* : materials concerning or characteristic of America, its civilization, or its culture

American Indian *n* : a member of any of the aboriginal peoples of No. and So. America except the Eskimos

American plan *n* : a hotel plan whereby the daily rates cover the cost of room and three meals

American Sign Language *n* : a sign language for the deaf in which meaning is conveyed by a system of hand gestures and placement

am•er•i•ci•um \ˌam-ə-ˈrish-ē-əm, -ˈris-\ *n* : a radioactive metallic chemical element produced artificially from plutonium — see ELEMENT table

AmerInd *abbr* American Indian

Am•er•in•di•an \ˌa-mə-ˈrin-dē-ən\ *n* : AMERICAN INDIAN — **Amerindian** *adj*

am•e•thyst \ˈa-mə-thəst\ *n* [ME *amatiste*, fr. OF & L; OF, fr. L *amethystus*, fr. Gk *amethystos*, lit., remedy against drunkenness, fr. *a-* not + *methyein* to be drunk, fr. *methy* wine] : a gemstone consisting of clear purple or bluish violet quartz

ami•a•ble \ˈā-mē-ə-bəl\ *adj* **1** : AGREEABLE **2** : having a friendly and sociable disposition — **ami•a•bil•i•ty** \ˌā-mē-ə-ˈbi-lə-tē\ *n* — **ami•a•ble•ness** *n* — **ami•a•bly** \ˈā-mē-ə-blē\ *adv*

am•i•ca•ble \ˈa-mi-kə-bəl\ *adj* : FRIENDLY, PEACEABLE — **am•i•ca•bil•i•ty** \ˌa-mi-kə-ˈbi-lə-tē\ *n* — **am•i•ca•bly** \ˈa-mi-kə-blē\ *adv*

amid \ə-ˈmid\ *or* **amidst** \-ˈmidst\ *prep* : in or into the middle of : AMONG

amid•ships \ə-ˈmid-ˌships\ *adv* : in or near the middle of a ship

ami•no acid \ə-ˈmē-nō-\ *n* : any of numerous nitrogen-containing acids that include some which are used by cells to build proteins

¹amiss \ə-ˈmis\ *adv* **1** : WRONGLY **2** : ASTRAY **3** : IMPERFECTLY

²amiss *adj* **1** : WRONG **2** : out of place

am•i•ty \ˈa-mə-tē\ *n, pl* **-ties** : FRIENDSHIP; *esp* : friendly relations between nations

am•me•ter \ˈa-ˌmē-tər\ *n* : an instrument for measuring electric current in amperes

am•mo \ˈa-mō\ *n* : AMMUNITION

am•mo•nia \ə-ˈmō-nyə\ *n* [NL, fr. L *sal ammoniacus* sal ammoniac (ammonium chloride), lit., salt of Ammon, fr. Gk *ammōniakos* of Ammon, fr. *Ammōn* Ammon, Amen, an Egyptian god near one of whose temples it was prepared] **1** : a colorless gaseous compound of nitrogen and hydrogen used in refrigeration and in the making of fertilizers and explosives **2** : a solution (**ammonia water**) of ammonia in water

am•mo•ni•um \ə-ˈmō-nē-əm\ *n* : an ion or chemical group derived from ammonia by combination with hydrogen

ammonium chloride *n* : a white crystalline volatile salt used in batteries and as an expectorant

am•mu•ni•tion \ˌam-yə-ˈni-shən\ *n* **1** : projectiles fired from guns **2** : explosive items used in war **3** : material for use in attack or defense

Amn *abbr* airman

am•ne•sia \am-ˈnē-zhə\ *n* **1** : abnormal loss of memory **2** : the selective overlooking of events or acts not favorable to one's purpose — **am•ne•si•ac** \-zhē-ˌak, -zē-\ *or* **am•ne•sic** \-zik, -sik\ *adj or n*

am•nes•ty \ˈam-nə-stē\ *n, pl* **-ties** : an act granting a pardon to a group of individuals — **amnesty** *vb*

am•nio•cen•te•sis \ˌam-nē-ō-ˌsen-ˈtē-səs\ *n, pl* **-te•ses** \-ˌsēz\ : the surgical insertion of a hollow needle through the abdominal wall and uterus of a pregnant female esp. to obtain fluid used to check the fetus for chromosomal abnormality and to determine sex

amoe•ba \ə-ˈmē-bə\ *n, pl* **-bas** *or* **-bae** \-(ˌ)bē\ : any of various tiny one-celled protozoans that lack permanent cell organs and occur esp. in water and soil — **amoe•bic** \-bik\ *adj*

amoe•boid \-ˌbȯid\ *adj* : resembling an amoeba esp. in moving or readily changing shape

amok \ə-ˈmək, -ˈmäk\ *or* **amuck** \-ˈmək\ *adv* : in a violent, frenzied, or uncontrolled manner ⟨run ~⟩

among \ə-ˈməŋ\ *also* **amongst** \-ˈməŋst\ *prep* **1** : in or through the midst of **2** : in the number, class, or company of **3** : in shares to each of **4** : by common action of

amon•til•la•do \ə-ˌmän-tə-ˈlä-dō\ *n, pl* **-dos** [Sp] : a medium dry sherry

amor•al \ā-ˈmȯr-əl\ *adj* **1** : neither moral nor immoral; *esp* : being outside the sphere to which moral judgments apply **2** : lacking moral sensibility — **amor•al•ly** *adv*

am•o•rous \ˈa-mə-rəs\ *adj* **1** : inclined to love **2** : being in love **3** : of or indicative of love — **am•o•rous•ly** *adv* — **am•o•rous•ness** *n*

amor•phous \ə-ˈmȯr-fəs\ *adj* **1** : SHAPELESS, FORMLESS **2** : not crystallized

am•or•tize \ˈa-mər-ˌtīz, ə-ˈmȯr-\ *vb* **-tized; -tiz•ing** : to extinguish (as a mortgage) usu. by payment on the principal at the time of each periodic interest payment — **amor•ti•za•tion** \ˌa-mər-tə-ˈzā-shən, ə-ˌmȯr-\ *n*

Amos \ˈā-məs\ — see BIBLE table

¹amount \ə-ˈmau̇nt\ *vb* **1** : to be equivalent **2** : to reach a total : add up

²amount *n* **1** : the total number or quantity **2** : a principal sum plus the interest on it

amour \ə-ˈmu̇r, ä-, a-\ *n* **1** : a love affair esp. when illicit **2** : LOVER

amour pro•pre \ˌa-ˌmu̇r-ˈprōprᵊ, ˌä-, -ˈprȯprᵊ\ *n* [F] : SELF-ESTEEM

¹amp \ˈamp\ *n* : AMPLIFIER; *also* : a unit consisting of an electronic amplifier and a loudspeaker

²amp *abbr* ampere

am•per•age \ˈam-p(ə-)rij\ *n* : the strength of a current of electricity expressed in amperes

am•pere \ˈam-ˌpir\ *n* : a unit of electric current equivalent to a steady current produced by one volt applied across a resistance of one ohm

am•per•sand \ˈam-pər-ˌsand\ *n* [alter. of *and per se and*, spoken form of the phrase *& per se and*, lit., (the character) & by itself (stands for the word) *and*] : a character & used for the word *and*

am•phet•amine \am-ˈfe-tə-ˌmēn, -mən\ *n* : a compound or one of its derivatives that stimulates the central nervous system and is used esp. to treat hyperactive children and to suppress appetite

am•phib•i•an \am-ˈfi-bē-ən\ *n* **1** : an amphibious organism; *esp* : any of a class of vertebrate animals (as frogs and salamanders) intermediate between fishes and reptiles **2** : an airplane that can land on and take off from either land or water

am•phib•i•ous \am-ˈfi-bē-əs\ *adj* [Gk *amphibios*, lit., living a double life, fr. *amphi-* on both sides + *bios* mode of life] **1** : able to live both on land and in water **2** : adapted for both land and water **3** : made by joint action of land, sea, and air forces invading from the sea; *also* : trained for such action

am•phi•bole \ˈam-fə-ˌbōl\ *n* : any of a group of rock-forming minerals of similar crystal structure

am•phi•the•ater \ˈam-fə-ˌthē-ə-tər\ *n* **1** : an oval or circular structure with rising tiers of seats around an arena **2** : a very large auditorium

am•pho•ra \ˈam-fə-rə\ *n, pl* **-rae** \-ˌrē\ *or* **-ras** : an ancient Greek jar or vase with two handles that rise almost to the level of the mouth

am•ple \ˈam-pəl\ *adj* **am•pler** \-plər\ **am•plest** \-pləst\ **1** : LARGE, CAPACIOUS **2** : enough to satisfy : ABUNDANT — **am•ply** \-plē\ *adv*

am•pli•fy \ˈam-plə-ˌfī\ *vb* **-fied; -fy•ing** **1** : to expand

by extended treatment **2 :** to increase in magnitude or strength; *esp* **:** to make louder — **am•pli•fi•ca•tion** \ˌam-plə-fə-ˈkā-shən\ *n* — **am•pli•fi•er** \ˈam-plə-ˌfī(-ə)r\ *n*
am•pli•tude \-ˌtüd, -ˌtyüd\ *n* **1 :** ample extent **:** FULLNESS **2 :** the extent of a vibratory movement (as of a pendulum) or of an oscillation (as of an alternating current or a radio wave)
amplitude modulation *n* **:** modulation of the amplitude of a radio carrier wave in accordance with the strength of the signal; *also* **:** a broadcasting system using such modulation
am•poule *or* **am•pule** *also* **am•pul** \ˈam-ˌpyül, -pül\ *n* **:** a small sealed bulbous glass vessel used to hold a solution for hypodermic injection
am•pu•tate \ˈam-pyə-ˌtāt\ *vb* **-tat•ed; -tat•ing :** to cut off ⟨~ a leg⟩ — **am•pu•ta•tion** \ˌam-pyə-ˈtā-shən\ *n*
am•pu•tee \ˌam-pyə-ˈtē\ *n* **:** one who has had a limb amputated
AMSLAN *abbr* American Sign Language
amt *abbr* amount
amuck \ə-ˈmək\ *var of* AMOK
am•u•let \ˈam-yə-lət\ *n* **:** an ornament worn as a charm against evil
amuse \ə-ˈmyüz\ *vb* **amused; amus•ing :** to entertain in a light or playful manner **:** DIVERT — **amuse•ment** *n*
AM•VETS \ˈam-ˌvets\ *abbr* American Veterans (of World War II)
am•y•lase \ˈa-mə-ˌlās, -ˌlāz\ *n* **:** any of several enzymes that accelerate the breakdown of starch and glycogen
an \ən, (ˈ)an\ *indefinite article* **:** A — used before words beginning with a vowel sound
[1]**-an** *or* **-ian** *also* **-ean** *n suffix* **1 :** one that belongs to ⟨Americ*an*⟩ ⟨crustac*ean*⟩ **2 :** one skilled in or specializing in ⟨phonetic*ian*⟩
[2]**-an** *or* **-ian** *also* **-ean** *adj suffix* **1 :** of or belonging to ⟨Americ*an*⟩ **2 :** characteristic of **:** resembling ⟨Mozart*ean*⟩
AN *abbr* airman (Navy)
an•a•bol•ic steroid \ˌa-nə-ˈbä-lik-\ *n* **:** any of a group of synthetic steroid hormones sometimes abused by athletes in training to increase temporarily the size of their muscles
anach•ro•nism \ə-ˈna-krə-ˌni-zəm\ *n* **1 :** the error of placing a person or thing in the wrong period **2 :** one that is chronologically out of place — **anach•ro•nis•tic** \ə-ˌna-krə-ˈnis-tik\ *adj* — **anach•ro•nous** \-ˈna-krə-nəs\ *adj*
an•a•con•da \ˌa-nə-ˈkän-də\ *n* **:** a large So. American snake that suffocates and kills its prey by constriction
anae•mia, anae•mic *chiefly Brit var of* ANEMIA, ANEMIC
an•aer•obe \ˈa-nə-ˌrōb\ *n* **:** an anaerobic organism
an•aer•o•bic \ˌa-nə-ˈrō-bik\ *adj* **:** living, active, occurring, or existing in the absence of free oxygen
an•aes•the•sia, an•aes•thet•ic *chiefly Brit var of* ANESTHESIA, ANESTHETIC
ana•gram \ˈa-nə-ˌgram\ *n* **:** a word or phrase made by transposing the letters of another word or phrase
[1]**anal** \ˈā-nᵊl\ *adj* **1 :** of, relating to, or situated near the anus **2 :** of, relating to, or characterized by the stage of psychosexual development in psychoanalytic theory during which one is concerned esp. with feces **3 :** of, relating to, or characterized by personality traits (as parsimony and ill humor) considered typical of fixation at the anal stage of development — **anal•ly** *adv*
[2]**anal** *abbr* **1** analogy **2** analysis; analytic
an•al•ge•sia \ˌa-nᵊl-ˈjē-zhə\ *n* **:** insensibility to pain — **an•al•ge•sic** \-ˈjē-zik, -sik\ *adj*
an•al•ge•sic \-ˈjē-zik, -sik\ *n* **:** an agent for producing analgesia
analog computer \ˈa-nᵊl-ˌòg-, -ˌäg-\ *n* **:** a computer that operates with numbers represented by directly measurable quantities (as voltages)
anal•o•gous \ə-ˈna-lə-gəs\ *adj* **:** similar in one or more respects
an•a•logue *or* **an•a•log** \ˈa-nᵊl-ˌòg, -ˌag\ *n* **1 :** something that is analogous to something else **2 :** an organ similar in function to one of another animal or plant but different in structure or origin
anal•o•gy \ə-ˈna-lə-jē\ *n, pl* **-gies 1 :** inference that if two or more things agree in some respects they will probably agree in others **2 :** a likeness in one or more ways between things otherwise unlike — **an•a•log•i•cal** \ˌa-nᵊl-ˈä-ji-kəl\ *adj* — **an•a•log•i•cal•ly** \-k(ə-)lē\ *adv*
an•a•lyse *chiefly Brit var of* ANALYZE
anal•y•sis \ə-ˈna-lə-səs\ *n, pl* **-y•ses** \-ˌsēz\ [NL, fr. Gk, fr. *analyein* to break up, fr. *ana-* up + *lyein* to loosen] **1 :** separation of a thing into the parts or elements of which it is composed **2 :** an examination of a thing to determine its parts or elements; *also* **:** a statement showing the results of such an examination **3 :** PSYCHOANALYSIS — **an•a•lyst** \ˈa-nᵊl-ist\ *n* — **an•a•lyt•ic** \ˌa-nᵊl-ˈi-tik\ *or* **an•a•lyt•i•cal** \-ti-kəl\ *adj* — **an•a•lyt•i•cal•ly** *adv*
an•a•lyze \ˈa-nᵊl-ˌīz\ *vb* **-lyzed; -lyz•ing :** to make an analysis of
an•a•pest \ˈa-nə-ˌpest\ *n* **:** a metrical foot of two unaccented syllables followed by one accented syllable — **an•a•pes•tic** \ˌa-nə-ˈpes-tik\ *adj or n*
an•ar•chism \ˈa-nər-ˌki-zəm\ *n* **:** the theory that all government is undesirable — **an•ar•chist** \-kist\ *n or adj* — **an•ar•chis•tic** \ˌa-nər-ˈkis-tik\ *adj*
an•ar•chy \ˈa-nər-kē\ *n* **1 :** a social structure without government or law and order **2 :** utter confusion — **an•ar•chic** \a-ˈnär-kik\ *adj* — **an•ar•chi•cal•ly** \-ki-k(ə-)lē\ *adv*
anas•to•mo•sis \ə-ˌnas-tə-ˈmō-səs\ *n, pl* **-mo•ses** \-ˌsēz\ **1 :** the union of parts or branches (as of blood vessels) **2 :** NETWORK
anat *abbr* anatomical; anatomy
anath•e•ma \ə-ˈna-thə-mə\ *n* **1 :** a solemn curse **2 :** a person or thing accursed; *also* **:** one intensely disliked
anath•e•ma•tize \-ˌtīz\ *vb* **-tized; -tiz•ing :** to pronounce an anathema against **:** CURSE
anat•o•mise *Brit var of* ANATOMIZE
anat•o•mize \ə-ˈna-tə-ˌmīz\ *vb* **-mized; -miz•ing :** to dissect so as to examine the structure and parts; *also* **:** ANALYZE
anat•o•my \ə-ˈna-tə-mē\ *n, pl* **-mies** [LL *anatomia* dissection, fr. Gk *anatomē*, fr. *anatemnein* to dissect, fr. *ana-* up + *temnein* to cut] **1 :** a branch of science dealing with the structure of organisms **2 :** structural makeup esp. of an organism or any of its parts **3 :** a separating into parts for detailed study **:** ANALYSIS — **an•a•tom•ic** \ˌa-nə-ˈtä-mik\ *or* **an•a•tom•i•cal** \-mi-kəl\ *adj* — **an•a•tom•i•cal•ly** \-mi-k(ə-)lē\ *adv* — **anat•o•mist** \ə-ˈna-tə-mist\ *n*
anc *abbr* ancient
-ance *n suffix* **1 :** action or process ⟨further*ance*⟩ **:** instance of an action or process ⟨perform*ance*⟩ **2 :** quality or state **:** instance of a quality or state ⟨protuber*ance*⟩ **3 :** amount or degree ⟨conduct*ance*⟩
an•ces•tor \ˈan-ˌses-tər\ *n* [ME *ancestre*, fr. OF, fr. L *antecessor* predecessor, fr. *antecedere* to go before, fr. *ante-* before + *cedere* to go] **:** one from whom an individual is descended
an•ces•tress \ˈan-ˌses-trəs\ *n* **:** a female ancestor
an•ces•try \ˈan-ˌses-trē\ *n* **1 :** line of descent **:** LINEAGE **2 :** ANCESTORS — **an•ces•tral** \an-ˈses-trəl\ *adj*
[1]**an•chor** \ˈaŋ-kər\ *n* **1 :** a heavy metal device attached to a ship that catches hold of the bottom and holds the ship in place **2 :** ANCHORPERSON
[2]**anchor** *vb* **:** to hold or become held in place by or as if by an anchor
an•chor•age \ˈaŋ-k(ə-)rij\ *n* **:** a place suitable for ships to anchor

an·cho·rite \ˈaŋ-kə-ˌrīt\ *n* : HERMIT

an·chor·man \ˈaŋ-kər-ˌman\ *n* **1** : the member of a team who competes last **2** : an anchorperson who is a man

an·chor·per·son \-ˌpər-sən\ *n* : a broadcaster who reads the news and introduces the reports of other broadcasters

an·chor·wom·an \-ˌwu̇-mən\ *n* **1** : a woman who competes last **2** : an anchorperson who is a woman

an·cho·vy \ˈan-ˌchō-vē, an-ˈchō-\ *n, pl* **-vies** *or* **-vy** : a small herringlike fish used esp. for sauces and relishes

an·cien ré·gime \ä^{n}s-ya^{n}-rā-ˈzhēm\ *n* **1** : the political and social system of France before the Revolution of 1789 **2** : a system no longer prevailing

1**an·cient** \ˈān-shənt\ *adj* **1** : having existed for many years **2** : belonging to times long past; *esp* : belonging to the period before the Middle Ages

2**ancient** *n* **1** : an aged person **2** *pl* : the peoples of ancient Greece and Rome; *esp* : the classical authors of Greece and Rome

an·cil·lary \ˈan-sə-ˌler-ē\ *adj* **1** : SUBORDINATE, SUBSIDIARY **2** : AUXILIARY, SUPPLEMENTARY — **ancillary** *n*

-ancy *n suffix* : quality or state ⟨flamboy*ancy*⟩

and \ənd, (ˈ)and\ *conj* **1** — used to indicate connection or addition esp. of items within the same class or type or to join words or phrases of the same grammatical rank or function **2** — used to join one finite verb to another so that together they are equivalent to an infinitive of purpose ⟨come ~ see me⟩

1**an·dan·te** \än-ˈdän-ˌtā, -tē\ *adv or adj* [It, lit., going, prp. of *andare* to go] : moderately slow — used as a direction in music

2**andante** *n* : an andante movement

and·iron \ˈan-ˌdī(-ə)rn\ *n* : one of a pair of metal supports for firewood in a fireplace

and/or \ˈand-ˈȯr\ *conj* — used to indicate that either *and* or *or* may apply ⟨men ~ women means men *and* women or men *or* women⟩

An·dor·ran \an-ˈdȯr-ən\ *n* : a native or inhabitant of Andorra

an·dro·gen \ˈan-drə-jən\ *n* : a male sex hormone

an·drog·y·nous \an-ˈdrä-jə-nəs\ *adj* **1** : having the characteristics of both male and female **2** : suitable for either sex ⟨~ clothing⟩

an·droid \ˈan-ˌdrȯid\ *n* : a mobile robot usu. with a human form

an·ec·dot·al \ˌa-nik-ˈdōt-^{ə}l\ *adj* **1** : relating to or consisting of anecdotes **2** : based on reports of an unscientific nature — **an·ec·dot·al·ly** *adv*

an·ec·dote \ˈan-ik-ˌdōt\ *n, pl* **-dotes** *also* **-dota** \ˌa-nik-ˈdō-tə\ [F, fr. Gk *anekdota* unpublished items, fr. *a-* not + *ekdidonai* to publish] : a brief story of an interesting, amusing, or biographical incident

ane·mia \ə-ˈnē-mē-ə\ *n* **1** : a condition in which blood is deficient in quantity, in red blood cells, or in hemoglobin and which is marked by pallor, weakness, and irregular heart action **2** : lack of vitality — **ane·mic** \ə-ˈnē-mik\ *adj*

an·e·mom·e·ter \ˌa-nə-ˈmä-mə-tər\ *n* : an instrument for measuring the force or speed of the wind

anem·o·ne \ə-ˈne-mə-nē\ *n* : any of a large genus of herbs related to the buttercups that have showy flowers without petals but with conspicuous often colored sepals

anent \ə-ˈnent\ *prep* : CONCERNING

an·es·the·sia \ˌa-nəs-ˈthē-zhə\ *n* : loss of bodily sensation

an·es·the·si·ol·o·gy \-ˌthē-zē-ˈä-lə-jē\ *n* : a branch of medical science dealing with anesthesia and anesthetics — **an·es·the·si·ol·o·gist** \-jist\ *n*

1**an·es·thet·ic** \ˌa-nəs-ˈthe-tik\ *adj* : of, relating to, or capable of producing anesthesia

2**anesthetic** *n* : an agent that produces anesthesia — **anes·the·tist** \ə-ˈnes-thə-tist\ *n* — **anes·the·tize** \-thə-ˌtīz\ *vb*

anew \ə-ˈnü, -ˈnyü\ *adv* **1** : over again **2** : in a new form

an·gel \ˈān-jəl\ *n* [ME, fr. OF *angele*, fr. L *angelus*, fr. Gk *angelos*, lit., messenger] **1** : a spiritual being superior to man **2** : an attendant spirit **3** : a winged figure of human form in art **4** : MESSENGER, HARBINGER **5** : a person held to resemble an angel **6** : a financial backer — **an·gel·ic** \an-ˈje-lik\ *or* **an·gel·i·cal** \-li-kəl\ *adj* — **an·gel·i·cal·ly** \-k(ə-)lē\ *adv*

an·gel·fish \ˈān-jəl-ˌfish\ *n* : any of several bright-colored tropical fishes that are flattened from side to side

an·gel·i·ca \an-ˈje-li-kə\ *n* : a biennial herb related to the carrot whose roots and fruit furnish a flavoring oil

1**an·ger** \ˈaŋ-gər\ *vb* : to make angry

2**anger** *n* [ME, affliction, anger, fr. ON *angr* grief] : a strong feeling of displeasure **syn** wrath, ire, rage, fury, indignation

an·gi·na \an-ˈjī-nə\ *n* : a disorder (as of the heart) marked by attacks of intense pain; *esp* : ANGINA PECTORIS — **an·gi·nal** \an-ˈjīn-^{ə}l\ *adj*

angina pec·to·ris \-ˈpek-t(ə-)rəs\ *n* : a heart disease marked by brief attacks of sharp chest pain caused by deficient oxygenation of heart muscles

an·gio·gram \ˈan-jē-ə-ˌgram\ *n* : an X-ray photograph made by angiography

an·gi·og·ra·phy \ˌan-jē-ˈä-grə-fē\ *n* : the use of X rays to make blood vessels visible (as by photography) after injection of a substance opaque to radiation

an·gio·plas·ty \ˈan-jē-ə-ˌplas-tē\ *n* : surgical repair of a blood vessel esp. by using an inflatable catheter to unblock arteries clogged by atherosclerotic deposits

an·gio·sperm \-ˌspərm\ *n* : FLOWERING PLANT

1**an·gle** \ˈaŋ-gəl\ *n* **1** : a sharp projecting corner **2** : the figure formed by the meeting of two lines in a point **3** : a point of view **4** : a special technique or plan : GIMMICK — **an·gled** *adj*

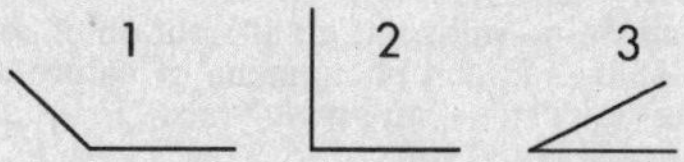

angle 2: *1* obtuse, *2* right, *3* acute

2**angle** *vb* **an·gled; an·gling** \-g(ə-)liŋ\ : to turn, move, or direct at an angle

3**angle** *vb* **an·gled; an·gling** \-g(ə-)liŋ\ : to fish with a hook and line — **an·gler** \-glər\ *n* — **an·gling** \-gliŋ\ *n*

an·gle·worm \ˈaŋ-gəl-ˌwərm\ *n* : EARTHWORM

An·gli·can \ˈaŋ-gli-kən\ *adj* **1** : of or relating to the established episcopal Church of England **2** : of or relating to England or the English nation — **Anglican** *n* — **An·gli·can·ism** \-kə-ˌni-zəm\ *n*

an·gli·cize \ˈaŋ-glə-ˌsīz\ *vb* **-cized; -ciz·ing** *often cap* **1** : to make English (as in habits, speech, character, or outlook) **2** : to borrow (a foreign word or phrase) into English without changing form or spelling and sometimes without changing pronunciation — **an·gli·ci·za·tion** \ˌaŋ-glə-sə-ˈzā-shən\ *n, often cap*

An·glo \ˈaŋ-glō\ *n, pl* **Anglos** : a non-Hispanic white inhabitant of the U.S.; *esp* : one of English origin and descent

An·glo–French \ˌaŋ-glō-ˈfrench\ *n* : the French language used in medieval England

An·glo·phile \ˈaŋ-glə-ˌfīl\ *also* **An·glo·phil** \-ˌfil\ *n* : one who greatly admires England and things English

An·glo·phobe \ˈaŋ-glə-ˌfōb\ *n* : one who is averse to England and things English

An·glo–Sax·on \ˌaŋ-glō-ˈsak-sən\ *n* **1** : a member of any of the Germanic peoples who invaded England in the 5th century A.D. **2** : a member of the English people **3** : Old English — **Anglo–Saxon** *adj*

an·go·ra \aŋ-ˈgōr-ə, an-\ *n* **1** : yarn or cloth made from the hair of an Angora goat or rabbit **2** *cap* : any of a breed of cats, goats, or rabbits with a long silky coat

an•gry \ˈaŋ-grē\ *adj* **an•gri•er; -est** : feeling or showing anger **syn** enraged, wrathful, irate, indignant, mad — **an•gri•ly** \-grə-lē\ *adv*

angst \ˈäŋst\ *n* [G] : a feeling of anxiety

ang•strom \ˈaŋ-strəm\ *n* : a unit of length equal to one ten-billionth of a meter

an•guish \ˈaŋ-gwish\ *n* : extreme pain or distress esp. of mind — **an•guished** \-gwisht\ *adj*

an•gu•lar \ˈaŋ-gyə-lər\ *adj* **1** : sharp-cornered **2** : having one or more angles **3** : being thin and bony — **an•gu•lar•i•ty** \ˌaŋ-gyə-ˈlar-ə-tē\ *n*

An•gus \ˈaŋ-gəs\ *n* : any of a breed of usu. black hornless beef cattle originating in Scotland

an•hy•drous \an-ˈhī-drəs\ *adj* : free from water

an•i•line \ˈan-ᵊl-ən\ *n* : an oily poisonous liquid used in making dyes, medicines, and explosives

an•i•mad•vert \ˌa-nə-ˌmad-ˈvərt\ *vb* : to remark critically : express censure — **an•i•mad•ver•sion** \-ˈvər-zhən\ *n*

[1]**an•i•mal** \ˈa-nə-məl\ *n* **1** : any of a kingdom of living things typically differing from plants in capacity for active movement, in rapid response to stimulation, and in lack of cellulose cell walls **2** : a lower animal as distinguished from human beings; *also* : MAMMAL

[2]**animal** *adj* **1** : of, relating to, or derived from animals **2** : of or relating to the physical as distinguished from the mental or spiritual **syn** carnal, fleshly, sensual

an•i•mal•cule \ˌa-nə-ˈmal-kyül\ *n* : a tiny animal usu. invisible to the naked eye

[1]**an•i•mate** \ˈa-nə-mət\ *adj* : having life

[2]**an•i•mate** \-ˌmāt\ *vb* **-mat•ed; -mat•ing 1** : to impart life to **2** : to give spirit and vigor to **3** : to make appear to move ⟨~ a cartoon for motion pictures⟩ — **an•i•mat•ed** *adj*

an•i•ma•tion \ˌa-nə-ˈmā-shən\ *n* **1** : VIVACITY, LIVELINESS **2** : a motion picture made from a series of drawings simulating motions by means of slight progressive changes

an•i•mism \ˈa-nə-ˌmi-zəm\ *n* : attribution of conscious life to objects in and phenomena of nature or to inanimate objects — **an•i•mist** \-mist\ *n* — **an•i•mis•tic** \ˌa-nə-ˈmis-tik\ *adj*

an•i•mos•i•ty \ˌa-nə-ˈmä-sə-tē\ *n, pl* **-ties** : ILL WILL, RESENTMENT

an•i•mus \ˈa-nə-məs\ *n* : deep-seated resentment and hostility

an•ion \ˈa-ˌnī-ən, -ˌnī-ˌän\ *n* : a negatively charged ion

an•ise \ˈa-nəs\ *n* : an herb related to the carrot with aromatic seeds (**aniseed** \-sēd\) used in flavoring

an•is•ette \ˌa-nə-ˈset, -ˈzet\ *n* [F] : a usu. colorless sweet liqueur flavored with aniseed

ankh \ˈäŋk\ *n* : a cross having a loop for its upper vertical arm and serving esp. in ancient Egypt as an emblem of life

an•kle \ˈaŋ-kəl\ *n* : the joint or region between the foot and the leg

an•kle•bone \ˈaŋ-kəl-ˌbōn\ *n* : the bone that in human beings bears the weight of the body and with the tibia and fibula forms the ankle joint

an•klet \ˈaŋ-klət\ *n* **1** : something (as an ornament) worn around the ankle **2** : a short sock reaching slightly above the ankle

ann *abbr* **1** annals **2** annual

an•nals \ˈan-ᵊlz\ *n pl* **1** : a record of events in chronological order **2** : historical records — **an•nal•ist** \-ᵊl-ist\ *n*

an•neal \ə-ˈnēl\ *vb* **1** : to make (as glass or steel) less brittle by heating and then cooling **2** : STRENGTHEN, TOUGHEN

[1]**an•nex** \ə-ˈneks, ˈa-ˌneks\ *vb* **1** : to attach as an addition **2** : to incorporate (as a territory) within a political domain — **an•nex•a•tion** \ˌa-ˌnek-ˈsā-shən\ *n*

[2]**an•nex** \ˈa-ˌneks, -niks\ *n* : a subsidiary or supplementary structure

an•nexe *chiefly Brit var of* ANNEX

an•ni•hi•late \ə-ˈnī-ə-ˌlāt\ *vb* **-lat•ed; -lat•ing** : to destroy completely — **an•ni•hi•la•tion** \-ˌnī-ə-ˈlā-shən\ *n*

an•ni•ver•sa•ry \ˌa-nə-ˈvər-sə-rē\ *n, pl* **-ries** : the annual return of the date of a notable event and esp. a wedding

an•no Do•mi•ni \ˌa-nō-ˈdä-mə-nē, -ˈdō-, -ˌnī\ *adv, often cap A* [ML, in the year of the Lord] — used to indicate that a time division falls within the Christian era

an•no•tate \ˈa-nə-ˌtāt\ *vb* **-tat•ed; -tat•ing** : to furnish with notes — **an•no•ta•tion** \ˌa-nə-ˈtā-shən\ *n* — **an•no•ta•tor** \ˈa-nə-ˌtā-tər\ *n*

an•nounce \ə-ˈnau̇ns\ *vb* **an•nounced; an•nounc•ing 1** : to make known publicly **2** : to give notice of the arrival or presence of — **an•nounce•ment** *n*

an•nounc•er \ə-ˈnau̇n-sər\ *n* : a person who introduces radio or television programs, makes commercial announcements, or gives station identification

an•noy \ə-ˈnȯi\ *vb* : to disturb or irritate esp. by repeated acts : VEX **syn** irk, bother, pester, tease, harass — **an•noy•ing•ly** *adv*

an•noy•ance \ə-ˈnȯi-əns\ *n* **1** : the act of annoying **2** : the state of being annoyed **3** : NUISANCE

[1]**an•nu•al** \ˈan-yə-wəl\ *adj* **1** : covering the period of a year **2** : occurring once a year : YEARLY **3** : completing the life cycle in one growing season ⟨~ plants⟩ — **an•nu•al•ly** *adv*

[2]**annual** *n* **1** : a publication appearing once a year **2** : an annual plant

annual ring *n* : the layer of wood produced by a single year's growth of a woody plant

an•nu•i•tant \ə-ˈnü-ə-tənt, -ˈnyü-\ *n* : a beneficiary of an annuity

an•nu•i•ty \ə-ˈnü-ə-tē, -ˈnyü-\ *n, pl* **-i•ties** : an amount payable annually; *also* : the right to receive such a payment

an•nul \ə-ˈnəl\ *vb* **an•nulled; an•nul•ling** : to make legally void — **an•nul•ment** *n*

an•nu•lar \ˈan-yə-lər\ *adj* : ring-shaped

an•nun•ci•ate \ə-ˈnən-sē-ˌāt\ *vb* **-at•ed; -at•ing** : ANNOUNCE

an•nun•ci•a•tion \ə-ˌnən-sē-ˈā-shən\ *n* **1** : ANNOUNCEMENT **2** *cap* : March 25 observed as a church festival commemorating the announcement of the Incarnation

an•nun•ci•a•tor \ə-ˈnən-sē-ˌā-tər\ *n* : one that annunciates; *specif* : a usu. electrically controlled signal board or indicator

an•ode \ˈa-ˌnōd\ *n* **1** : the positive electrode of an electrolytic cell **2** : the negative terminal of a battery **3** : the electron-collecting electrode of an electron tube — **an•od•ic** \a-ˈnä-dik\ *also* **an•od•al** \-ˈnōd-ᵊl\ *adj*

an•od•ize \ˈa-nə-ˌdīz\ *vb* **-ized; -iz•ing** : to subject (a metal) to electrolytic action as the anode of a cell in order to coat with a protective or decorative film

an•o•dyne \ˈa-nə-ˌdīn\ *n* : something that relieves pain : a soothing agent

anoint \ə-ˈnȯint\ *vb* **1** : to apply oil to esp. as a sacred rite **2** : CONSECRATE — **anoint•ment** *n*

anom•a•lous \ə-ˈnä-mə-ləs\ *adj* : deviating from a general rule : ABNORMAL

anom•a•ly \ə-ˈnä-mə-lē\ *n, pl* **-lies** : something anomalous : IRREGULARITY

[1]**anon** \ə-ˈnän\ *adv, archaic* : SOON

[2]**anon** *abbr* anonymous; anonymously

anon•y•mous \ə-ˈnä-nə-məs\ *adj* : of unknown or undeclared origin or authorship — **an•o•nym•i•ty** \ˌa-nə-ˈni-mə-tē\ *n* — **anon•y•mous•ly** *adv*

anoph•e•les \ə-ˈnä-fə-ˌlēz\ *n* [NL, genus name, fr. Gk *anōphelēs* useless, fr. *a-* not + *ophelos* advantage, help] : any of a genus of mosquitoes that includes all mosquitoes which transmit malaria to human beings

an•o•rec•tic \ˌa-nə-ˈrek-tik\ *adj* : ANOREXIC — **anorectic** *n*

an•o•rex•ia \ˌa-nə-ˈrek-sē-ə\ *n* **1** : loss of appetite esp. when prolonged **2** : ANOREXIA NERVOSA

anorexia ner•vo•sa \-nər-ˈvō-sə\ *n* : a serious disorder in eating behavior marked esp. by a pathological fear of weight gain leading to faulty eating patterns, malnutrition, and usu. excessive weight loss

an•orex•ic \ˌa-nə-ˈrek-sik\ *adj* **1** : lacking or causing loss of appetite **2** : affected with or as if with anorexia nervosa — **anorexic** *n*

[1]**an•oth•er** \ə-ˈnə-thər\ *adj* **1** : some other **2** : being one in addition : one more

[2]**another** *pron* **1** : an additional one : one more **2** : one that is different from the first or present one

ans *abbr* answer

[1]**an•swer** \ˈan-sər\ *n* **1** : something spoken or written in reply to a question **2** : a solution of a problem

[2]**answer** *vb* **1** : to speak or write in reply to **2** : to be responsible **3** : to be adequate — **an•swer•er** *n*

an•swer•able \ˈan-sə-rə-bəl\ *adj* **1** : subject to taking blame or responsibility **2** : capable of being refuted

answering machine *n* : a machine that receives telephone calls by playing a recorded message and usu. by recording messages from callers

answering service *n* : a commercial service that answers telephone calls for its clients

[1]**ant** \ˈant\ *n* : any of a family of small social insects related to the bees and living in communities usu. in earth or wood

[2]**ant** *abbr* antonym

Ant *abbr* Antarctica

ant- — see ANTI-

[1]**-ant** *n suffix* **1** : one that performs or promotes (a specified action) ⟨cool*ant*⟩ **2** : thing that is acted upon (in a specified manner) ⟨inhal*ant*⟩

[2]**-ant** *adj suffix* **1** : performing (a specified action) or being (in a specified condition) ⟨propell*ant*⟩ **2** : promoting (a specified action or process) ⟨expector*ant*⟩

ant•ac•id \ant-ˈa-səd\ *n* : an agent that counteracts acidity — **antacid** *adj*

an•tag•o•nism \an-ˈta-gə-ˌni-zəm\ *n* **1** : active opposition or hostility **2** : opposition in physiological action — **an•tag•o•nis•tic** \-ˌta-gə-ˈnis-tik\ *adj*

an•tag•o•nist \-nist\ *n* : ADVERSARY, OPPONENT

an•tag•o•nize \an-ˈta-gə-ˌnīz\ *vb* **-nized; -niz•ing** : to provoke the hostility of

ant•arc•tic \ant-ˈärk-tik, -ˈär-tik\ *adj, often cap* : of or relating to the south pole or the region near it

antarctic circle *n, often cap A&C* : the parallel of latitude that is approximately 66½ degrees south of the equator

[1]**an•te** \ˈan-tē\ *n* : a poker stake put up before the deal to build the pot; *also* : an amount paid : PRICE

[2]**ante** *vb* **an•ted; an•te•ing 1** : to put up (an ante) **2** : PAY

ant•eat•er \ˈant-ˌē-tər\ *n* : any of several mammals (as an aardvark) that feed mostly on ants or termites

an•te•bel•lum \ˌan-ti-ˈbe-ləm\ *adj* : existing before a war; *esp* : existing before the U.S. Civil War of 1861-65

an•te•ced•ent \ˌan-tə-ˈsēd-ᵊnt\ *n* **1** : a noun, pronoun, phrase, or clause referred to by a personal or relative pronoun **2** : a preceding event or cause **3** *pl* : the significant conditions of one's earlier life **4** *pl* : ANCESTORS — **antecedent** *adj*

an•te•cham•ber \ˈan-ti-ˌchām-bər\ *n* : ANTEROOM

an•te•date \ˈan-ti-ˌdāt\ *vb* **1** : to date (a paper) as of an earlier day than that on which the actual writing or signing is done **2** : to precede in time

an•te•di•lu•vi•an \ˌan-ti-də-ˈlü-vē-ən, -dī-\ *adj* **1** : of the period before the biblical flood **2** : ANTIQUATED

an•te•lope \ˈant-ᵊl-ˌōp\ *n, pl* **-lope** *or* **-lopes** [ME, fabulous heraldic beast, prob. fr. MF *antelop* savage animal with sawlike horns, fr. ML *anthalopus,* fr. LGk *antholops*] **1** : any of various Old World cud-chewing mammals related to the oxen but with smaller lighter bodies and horns that extend upward and backward **2** : PRONGHORN

an•te me•ri•di•em \ˈan-ti-mə-ˈri-dē-əm\ *adj* [L] : being before noon

an•ten•na \an-ˈte-nə\ *n, pl* **-nae** \-(ˌ)nē\ *or* **-nas** [ML, fr. L, sail yard] **1** : one of the long slender paired segmented sensory organs on the head of an arthropod (as an insect or crab) **2** *pl usu -nas* : a metallic device (as a rod or wire) for sending out or receiving radio waves

an•te•pe•nult \ˌan-ti-ˈpē-ˌnəlt\ *also* **an•te•pen•ul•ti•ma** \-pi-ˈnəl-tə-mə\ *n* : the 3d syllable of a word counting from the end — **an•te•pen•ul•ti•mate** \-pi-ˈnəl-tə-mət\ *adj or n*

an•te•ri•or \an-ˈtir-ē-ər\ *adj* **1** : situated before or toward the front **2** : situated near or nearer to the head **3** : coming before in time **syn** preceding, previous, prior, antecedent

an•te•room \ˈan-ti-ˌrüm, -ˌru̇m\ *n* : a room forming the entrance to another and often used as a waiting room

an•them \ˈan-thəm\ *n* **1** : a sacred vocal composition **2** : a song or hymn of praise or gladness

an•ther \ˈan-thər\ *n* : the part of a stamen of a seed plant that produces and contains pollen

ant•hill \ˈant-ˌhil\ *n* : a mound thrown up by ants or termites in digging their nest

an•thol•o•gy \an-ˈthä-lə-jē\ *n, pl* **-gies** [NL *anthologia* collection of epigrams, fr. MGk, fr. Gk, flower gathering, fr. *anthos* flower + *logia* collecting, fr. *legein* to gather] : a collection of literary selections — **an•thol•o•gist** \-jist\ *n* — **an•thol•o•gize** \-ˌjīz\ *vb*

an•thra•cite \ˈan-thrə-ˌsīt\ *n* : a hard glossy coal that burns without much smoke

an•thrax \ˈan-ˌthraks\ *n* : an infectious and usu. fatal bacterial disease of warm-blooded animals (as cattle and sheep) that is transmissible to humans; *also* : a bacterium causing anthrax

an•thro•po•cen•tric \ˌan-thrə-pə-ˈsen- trik\ *adj* : interpreting or regarding the world in terms of human values and experiences

an•thro•poid \ˈan-thrə-ˌpȯid\ *n* **1** : any of several large tailless apes (as a gorilla) **2** : a person resembling an ape — **anthropoid** *adj*

an•thro•pol•o•gy \ˌan-thrə-ˈpä-lə-jē\ *n* : the science of human beings and esp. of their physical characteristics, their origin and the distribution of races, their environment and social relations, and their culture — **an•thro•po•log•i•cal** \-pə-ˈlä-ji-kəl\ *adj* — **an•thro•pol•o•gist** \-ˈpä-lə-jist\ *n*

an•thro•po•mor•phism \ˌan-thrə-pə-ˈmȯr-ˌfi-zəm\ *n* : an interpretation of what is not human or personal in terms of human or personal characteristics : HUMANIZATION — **an•thro•po•mor•phic** \-fik\ *adj*

an•ti \ˈan-ˌtī, -tē\ *n, pl* **antis** : one who is opposed

anti- \ˌan-ti, -tē, -ˌtī\ *or* **ant-** *or* **anth-** *prefix* **1** : opposite in kind, position, or action **2** : opposing : hostile toward **3** : counteractive **4** : preventive of : curative of

antiaging
anti-AIDS
antiaircraft
antialcohol
anti-American
antiapartheid
antibacterial
anticapitalist
anti-Catholic
anticholesterol
anticlerical
anticolonial
anticommunism
anticommunist
antidemocratic
antiestablishment
antifascist
antigovernment
anti-imperialism
anti-imperialist
antiknock
antilabor
antimalarial
antimicrobial
antinausea
antipoverty
antislavery
antispasmodic
antistatic
antisubmarine
antitank
antitumor
antiviral

an•ti•abor•tion \ˌan-tē-ə-ˈbȯr-shən, ˌan-ˌtī-\ *adj* : opposed to abortion

an•ti•bal•lis•tic missile \ˌan-ti-bə-ˈlis-tik-, ˌan-ˌtī-\ *n* : a missile for intercepting and destroying ballistic missiles

an•ti•bi•ot•ic \-bī-ˈä-tik, -bē-\ *n* : a substance produced by or derived by chemical alteration of a substance produced by a microorganism (as a fungus or bacterium) that in dilute solution inhibits or kills another microorganism — **antibiotic** *adj*

an•ti•body \ˈan-ti-ˌbä-dē\ *n* : any of a large number of proteins of high molecular weight produced normally by specialized B cells after stimulation by an antigen and acting specifically against the antigen in an immune response

[1]**an•tic** \ˈan-tik\ *n* : an often wildly playful or funny act or action

[2]**antic** *adj* [It *antico* ancient, fr. L *antiquus*] **1** *archaic* : GROTESQUE **2** : PLAYFUL

an•ti•can•cer \ˌan-ti-ˈkan-sər, ˌan-ˌtī-\ *adj* : used against or tending to arrest cancer ⟨~ drugs⟩

An•ti•christ \ˈan-ti-ˌkrīst\ *n* **1** : one who denies or opposes Christ **2** : a false Christ

an•tic•i•pate \an-ˈti-sə-ˌpāt\ *vb* **-pat•ed; -pat•ing 1** : to foresee and provide for beforehand **2** : to look forward to — **an•tic•i•pa•tion** \-ˌti-sə-ˈpā-shən\ *n* — **an•tic•i•pa•to•ry** \-ˈti-sə-pə-ˌtōr-ē\ *adj*

an•ti•cli•max \ˌan-ti-ˈklī-ˌmaks\ *n* : something closing a series that is strikingly less important than what has preceded it — **an•ti•cli•mac•tic** \-klī-ˈmak-tik\ *adj*

an•ti•cline \ˈan-ti-ˌklīn\ *n* : an arch of layers of rock in the earth's crust

an•ti•co•ag•u•lant \ˌan-ti-kō-ˈa-gyə-lənt\ *n* : a substance that hinders the clotting of blood — **anticoagulant** *adj*

an•ti•cy•clone \ˌan-ti-ˈsī-ˌklōn\ *n* : a system of winds that rotates about a center of high atmospheric pressure — **an•ti•cy•clon•ic** \-sī-ˈklä-nik\ *adj*

[1]**an•ti•de•pres•sant** \ˌan-ti-di-ˈpres-ᵊnt, ˌan-ˌtī-\ *adj* : used or tending to relieve psychic depression ⟨~ drugs⟩

[2]**antidepressant** *n* : an antidepressant drug

an•ti•dote \ˈan-ti-ˌdōt\ *n* : a remedy to counteract the effects of poison

an•ti•drug \ˈan-ˌtī-ˌdrəg\ *adj* : acting against or opposing illicit drugs

an•ti•fer•til•i•ty \ˌan-ti-fər-ˈti-lə-tē\ *adj* : tending to control excess or unwanted fertility : CONTRACEPTIVE ⟨~ agents⟩

an•ti•freeze \ˈan-ti-ˌfrēz\ *n* : a substance added to a liquid to lower its freezing temperature

an•ti•gen \ˈan-ti-jən\ *n* : a usu. protein or carbohydrate substance (as a toxin or an enzyme) capable of stimulating an immune response — **an•ti•gen•ic** \ˌan-ti-ˈje-nik\ *adj* — **an•ti•ge•nic•i•ty** \-jə-ˈni-sə-tē\ *n*

an•ti•grav•i•ty \ˌan-ti-ˈgra-və-tē, ˌan-ˌtī-\ *adj* : reducing or canceling the effect of gravity

an•ti•he•ro \ˈan-ti-ˌhē-rō, ˈan-ˌtī-\ *n* : a protagonist who is notably lacking in heroic qualities (as courage)

an•ti•his•ta•mine \ˌan-ti-ˈhis-tə-ˌmēn, ˌan-ˌtī-, -mən\ *n* : any of various drugs used in treating allergies and colds

an•ti•hy•per•ten•sive \-ˌhī-pər-ˈten-siv\ *n* : a substance that is effective against high blood pressure — **antihypertensive** *adj*

an•ti–in•flam•ma•to•ry \-in-ˈfla-mə-ˌtōr-ē\ *adj* : counteracting inflammation — **anti–inflammatory** *n*

an•ti–in•tel•lec•tu•al \-ˌint-ᵊl-ˈek-chə- wəl\ *adj* : opposing or hostile to intellectuals or to an intellectual view or approach

an•ti•lock \ˈan-ti-ˌläk, ˈan-ˌtī-\ *adj* : being a braking system designed to prevent the wheels from locking

an•ti•log•a•rithm \ˌan-ti-ˈlȯ-gə-ˌri-t͟həm, ˌan-ˌtī-, -ˈlä-\ *n* : the number corresponding to a given logarithm

an•ti•ma•cas•sar \ˌan-ti-mə-ˈka-sər\ *n* : a cover to protect the back or arms of furniture

an•ti•mat•ter \ˈan-ti-ˌma-tər, ˈan-ˌtī-\ *n* : matter composed of antiparticles

an•ti•mo•ny \ˈan-tə-ˌmō-nē\ *n* : a brittle silvery white metallic chemical element used esp. in alloys — see ELEMENT table

an•ti•neu•tron \ˌan-ti-ˈnü-ˌträn, ˌan-ˌtī-, -ˈnyü-\ *n* : the antiparticle of the neutron

an•ti•no•mi•an \ˌan-ti-ˈnō-mē-ən\ *n* : one who denies the validity of moral laws

an•tin•o•my \an-ˈti-nə-mē\ *n, pl* **-mies** : a contradiction between two seemingly true statements

an•ti•nov•el \ˈan-ti-ˌnä-vəl, ˈan-ˌtī-\ *n* : a work of fiction that lacks all or most of the traditional features of the novel

an•ti•nu•cle•ar \ˌan-ti-ˈnü-klē-ər, -ˈnyü-\ *adj* : opposing the use or production of nuclear power plants

an•ti•ox•i•dant \ˌan-tē-ˈäk-sə-dənt, ˌan-ˌtī-\ *n* : a substance that inhibits oxidation — **antioxidant** *adj*

an•ti•par•ti•cle \ˈan-ti-ˌpär-ti-kəl, ˈan-ˌtī-\ *n* : a subatomic particle identical to another subatomic particle in mass but opposite to it in electric and magnetic properties

an•ti•pas•to \ˌan-ti-ˈpas-tō, ˌän-ti-ˈpäs-\ *n, pl* **-ti** \-(ˌ)tē\ : any of various typically Italian hors d'oeuvres

an•tip•a•thy \an-ˈti-pə-thē\ *n, pl* **-thies 1** : settled aversion or dislike **2** : an object of aversion — **an•ti•pa•thet•ic** \ˌan-ti-pə-ˈthe-tik\ *adj*

an•ti•per•son•nel \ˌan-ti-ˌpərs-ᵊn-ˈel, ˌan-ˌtī-\ *adj* : designed for use against military personnel ⟨~ mine⟩

an•ti•per•spi•rant \-ˈpər-spə-rənt\ *n* : a preparation used to check perspiration

an•tiph•o•nal \an-ˈti-fən-ᵊl\ *adj* : performed by two alternating groups — **an•tiph•o•nal•ly** *adv*

an•ti•pode \ˈan-tə-ˌpōd\ *n, pl* **an•tip•o•des** \an-ˈti-pə-ˌdēz\ [ME *antipodes,* pl., persons dwelling at opposite points on the globe, fr. L, fr. Gk, fr. pl. of *antipod-, antipous* with feet opposite, fr. *anti-* against + *pod-, pous* foot] : the parts of the earth diametrically opposite — usu. used in pl. — **an•tip•o•dal** \an-ˈti-pəd-ᵊl\ *adj* — **an•tip•o•de•an** \(ˌ)an-ˌti-pə-ˈdē-ən\ *adj*

an•ti•pol•lu•tion \ˌan-ti-pə-ˈlü-shən\ *adj* : designed to prevent, reduce, or eliminate pollution ⟨~ laws⟩

an•ti•pope \ˈan-ti-ˌpōp\ *n* : one elected or claiming to be pope in opposition to the pope canonically chosen

an•ti•pro•ton \ˌan-ti-ˈprō-ˌtän\ *n* : the antiparticle of the proton

an•ti•quar•i•an \ˌan-tə-ˈkwer-ē-ən\ *adj* **1** : of or relating to antiquities **2** : dealing in old books — **antiquarian** *n* — **an•ti•quar•i•an•ism** *n*

an•ti•quary \ˈan-tə-ˌkwer-ē\ *n, pl* **-quar•ies** : a person who collects or studies antiquities

an•ti•quat•ed \ˈan-tə-ˌkwā-təd\ *adj* : OUT-OF-DATE, OLD-FASHIONED

[1]**an•tique** \an-ˈtēk\ *n* : an object made in a bygone period

[2]**antique** *adj* **1** : belonging to antiquity **2** : OLD-FASHIONED **3** : of a bygone style or period

[3]**antique** *vb* **-tiqued; -tiqu•ing 1** : to finish or refinish in antique style : give an appearance of age to **2** : to shop around for antiques — **an•tiqu•er** *n*

an•tiq•ui•ty \an-ˈti-kwə-tē\ *n, pl* **-ties 1** : ancient times **2** : great age **3** *pl* : relics of ancient times **4** *pl* : matters relating to ancient culture

an•tis *pl of* ANTI

an•ti–Sem•i•tism \ˌan-ti-ˈse-mə-ˌti-zəm, ˌan-ˌtī-\ *n* : hostility toward Jews as a religious or social minority — **an•ti–Se•mit•ic** \-sə-ˈmi-tik\ *adj*

an•ti•sep•tic \ˌan-tə-ˈsep-tik\ *adj* **1** : killing or checking the growth of germs that cause decay or infection **2** : scrupulously clean : ASEPTIC — **antiseptic** *n* — **an•ti•sep•ti•cal•ly** *adv*

an•ti•se•rum \ˈan-ti-ˌsir-əm, ˈan-ˌtī-\ *n* : a serum containing antibodies

an•ti•so•cial \ˌan-ti-ˈsō-shəl\ *adj* **1** : disliking the society of others **2** : contrary or hostile to the well-being of society ⟨crime is ~⟩ — **an•ti•so•cial•ly** *adv*

an•tith•e•sis \an-ˈti-thə-səs\ *n, pl* **-e•ses** \-ˌsēz\ **1** : the opposition or contrast of ideas **2** : the direct opposite

an•ti•thet•i•cal \ˌan-tə-ˈthe-ti-kəl\ *also* **an•ti•thet•ic**

\-tik\ *adj* : constituting or marked by antithesis — **an·ti·thet·i·cal·ly** \-ti-k(ə-)lē\ *adv*
an·ti·tox·in \ˌan-ti-ˈtäk-sən\ *n* : an antibody that is able to neutralize a particular toxin or disease-causing agent; *also* : an antiserum containing an antitoxin
an·ti·trust \ˌan-ti-ˈtrəst\ *adj* : of or relating to legislation against trusts; *also* : consisting of laws to protect trade and commerce from unlawful restraints and monopolies or unfair business practices
an·ti·ven·in \-ˈve-nən\ *n* : an antitoxin to a venom; *also* : a serum containing such antitoxin
ant·ler \ˈant-lər\ *n* [ME *aunteler,* fr. MF *antoillier,* fr. (assumed) VL *anteocularis* located before the eye, fr. L *ante-* before + *oculus* eye] : one of the paired deciduous solid bone processes on the head of a deer; *also* : a branch of this — **ant·lered** \-lərd\ *adj*
ant lion *n* : any of various insects having a long-jawed larva that digs a conical pit in which it lies in wait for insects (as ants) on which it feeds
an·to·nym \ˈan-tə-ˌnim\ *n* : a word of opposite meaning
anus \ˈā-nəs\ *n* [L] : the lower or posterior opening of the alimentary canal
an·vil \ˈan-vəl\ *n* **1** : a heavy iron block on which metal is shaped **2** : INCUS
anx·i·ety \aŋ-ˈzī-ə-tē\ *n, pl* **-et·ies 1** : painful uneasiness of mind usu. over an anticipated ill **2** : abnormal apprehension and fear often accompanied by physiological signs (as sweating and increased pulse), by doubt about the nature and reality of the threat itself, and by self-doubt
anx·ious \ˈaŋk-shəs\ *adj* **1** : uneasy in mind : WORRIED **2** : earnestly wishing : EAGER — **anx·ious·ly** *adv*
¹any \ˈe-nē\ *adj* **1** : one chosen at random **2** : of whatever number or quantity
²any *pron* **1** : any one or ones ⟨take ~ of the books you like⟩ **2** : any amount ⟨~ of the money not used is to be returned⟩
³any *adv* : to any extent or degree : AT ALL ⟨could not walk ~ farther⟩
any·body \-ˌbä-dē, -bə-\ *pron* : ANYONE
any·how \-ˌhau̇\ *adv* **1** : in any way **2** : NEVERTHELESS; *also* : in any case
any·more \ˌe-nē-ˈmōr\ *adv* **1** : any longer **2** : at the present time
any·one \ˈe-nē-(ˌ)wən\ *pron* : any person
any·place \-ˌplās\ *adv* : ANYWHERE
any·thing \-ˌthiŋ\ *pron* : any thing whatever
any·time \ˈe-nē-ˌtīm\ *adv* : at any time whatever
any·way \-ˌwā\ *adv* : ANYHOW
any·where \-ˌhwer\ *adv* : in or to any place
any·wise \-ˌwīz\ *adv* : in any way whatever
A–OK \ˌā-ō-ˈkā\ *adv or adj* : very definitely OK
A1 \ˈā-ˈwən\ *adj* : of the finest quality
aor·ta \ā-ˈȯr-tə\ *n, pl* **-tas** *or* **-tae** \-tē\ : the main artery that carries blood from the heart — **aor·tic** \-tik\ *adj*
ap *abbr* **1** apostle **2** apothecaries'
AP *abbr* **1** American plan **2** Associated Press
apace \ə-ˈpās\ *adv* : SWIFTLY
Apache \ə-ˈpa-chē\ *n, pl* **Apache** *or* **Apach·es** \-ˈpa-chēz, -ˈpa-shəz\ : a member of an American Indian people of the southwestern U.S.; *also* : any of the languages of the Apache people — **Apach·e·an** \ə-ˈpa-chē-ən\ *adj or n*
ap·a·nage *var of* APPANAGE
apart \ə-ˈpärt\ *adv* **1** : separately in place or time **2** : ASIDE **3** : in two or more parts : to pieces
apart·heid \ə-ˈpär-ˌtāt, -ˌtīt\ *n* [Afrikaans] : a policy of racial segregation practiced in the Republic of So. Africa
apart·ment \ə-ˈpärt-mənt\ *n* : a room or set of rooms occupied as a dwelling; *also* : a building divided into individual dwelling units
ap·a·thy \ˈa-pə-thē\ *n* **1** : lack of emotion **2** : lack of interest : INDIFFERENCE — **ap·a·thet·ic** \ˌa-pə-ˈthe-tik\ *adj* — **ap·a·thet·i·cal·ly** \-ti-k(ə-)lē\ *adv*
ap·a·tite \ˈa-pə-ˌtīt\ *n* : any of a group of minerals that are phosphates of calcium and occur esp. in phosphate rock and in bones and teeth
APB *abbr* all points bulletin
¹ape \ˈāp\ *n* **1** : any of the larger tailless primates (as a baboon or gorilla); *also* : MONKEY **2** : MIMIC, IMITATOR; *also* : a large uncouth person
²ape *vb* **aped; ap·ing** : IMITATE, MIMIC
ape–man \ˈāp-ˌman\ *n* : a primate intermediate in character between Homo sapiens and the higher apes
aper·çu \ȧ-per-sǖ, ˌa-pər-ˈsü\ *n, pl* **aperçus** \-sǖ(z), -ˈsüz\ : an immediate impression; *esp* : INSIGHT
aper·i·tif \ˌä-ˌper-ə-ˈtēf\ *n* : an alcoholic drink taken as an appetizer
ap·er·ture \ˈa-pər-ˌchu̇r, -chər\ *n* : OPENING, HOLE
apex \ˈā-ˌpeks\ *n, pl* **apex·es** *or* **api·ces** \ˈā-pə-ˌsēz, ˈa-\ : the highest point : PEAK
apha·sia \ə-ˈfā-zh(ē-)ə\ *n* : loss or impairment of the power to use or comprehend words — **apha·sic** \-zik\ *adj or n*
aph·elion \a-ˈfēl-yən\ *n, pl* **-elia** \-yə\ [NL, fr. *apo-* away from + Gk *hēlios* sun] : the point in an object's orbit most distant from the sun
aphid \ˈā-fəd\ *n* : any of numerous small insects that suck the juices of plants
aphis \ˈā-fəs, ˈa-\ *n, pl* **aphi·des** \-fə-ˌdēz\ : APHID
aph·o·rism \ˈa-fə-ˌri-zəm\ *n* : a short saying stating a general truth : MAXIM — **aph·o·ris·tic** \ˌa-fə-ˈris-tik\ *adj*
aph·ro·di·si·ac \ˌa-frə-ˈdi-zē-ˌak, -ˈdē-zē-\ *n* : an agent that excites sexual desire — **aphrodisiac** *adj*
api·ary \ˈā-pē-ˌer-ē\ *n, pl* **-ar·ies** : a place where bees are kept — **api·a·rist** \-pē-ə-rist\ *n*
api·cal \ˈā-pi-kəl, ˈa-\ *adj* : of, relating to, or situated at an apex — **api·cal·ly** \-k(ə-)lē\ *adv*
apiece \ə-ˈpēs\ *adv* : for each one
aplen·ty \ə-ˈplen-tē\ *adj* : being in plenty or abundance
aplomb \ə-ˈpläm, -ˈpləm\ *n* [F, lit., perpendicularity, fr. MF, fr. *a plomb,* lit., according to the plummet] : complete composure or self-assurance
APO *abbr* army post office
Apoc *abbr* **1** Apocalypse **2** Apocrypha
apoc·a·lypse \ə-ˈpä-kə-ˌlips\ *n* **1** : a writing prophesying a cataclysm in which evil forces are destroyed **2** *cap* — see BIBLE table — **apoc·a·lyp·tic** \-ˌpä-kə-ˈlip-tik\ *also* **apoc·a·lyp·ti·cal** \-ti-kəl\ *adj*
Apoc·ry·pha \ə-ˈpä-krə-fə\ *n* **1** *not cap* : writings of dubious authenticity **2** : books included in the Septuagint and Vulgate but excluded from the Jewish and Protestant canons of the Old Testament — see BIBLE table **3** : early Christian writings not included in the New Testament
apoc·ry·phal \-fəl\ *adj* **1** : not canonical : SPURIOUS **2** *often cap* : of or resembling the Apocrypha — **apoc·ry·phal·ly** *adv* — **apoc·ry·phal·ness** *n*
apo·gee \ˈa-pə-(ˌ)jē\ *n* [F *apogée,* fr. NL *apogaeum,* fr. Gk *apogaion,* fr. *apo* away from + *gē* earth] : the point at which an orbiting object is farthest from the body being orbited
apo·lit·i·cal \ˌā-pə-ˈli-ti-kəl\ *adj* **1** : having an aversion for or no interest in political affairs **2** : having no political significance — **apo·lit·i·cal·ly** \-k(ə-)lē\ *adv*
apol·o·get·ic \ə-ˌpä-lə-ˈje-tik\ *adj* : expressing apology — **apol·o·get·i·cal·ly** \-ti-k(ə-)lē\ *adv*
ap·o·lo·gia \ˌa-pə-ˈlō-j(ē-)ə\ *n* : APOLOGY; *esp* : an argument in support or justification
apol·o·gise *Brit var of* APOLOGIZE
apol·o·gize \ə-ˈpä-lə-ˌjīz\ *vb* **-gized; -giz·ing** : to make an apology : express regret — **apol·o·gist** \-jist\ *n*
apol·o·gy \ə-ˈpä-lə-jē\ *n, pl* **-gies 1** : a formal justification : DEFENSE **2** : an expression of regret for a wrong
ap·o·plexy \ˈa-pə-ˌplek-sē\ *n* : STROKE 3 — **ap·o·plec·tic** \ˌa-pə-ˈplek-tik\ *adj*
aport \ə-ˈpōrt\ *adv* : on or toward the left side of a ship
apos·ta·sy \ə-ˈpäs-tə-sē\ *n, pl* **-sies** : a renunciation or

abandonment of a former loyalty (as to a religion) — **apos•tate** \ə-ˈpäs-ˌtāt, -tət\ *adj or n*

a pos•te•ri•o•ri \ˌä-pō-ˌstir-ē-ˈōr-ē\ *adj* [L, lit., from the latter] : relating to or derived by reasoning from observed facts — **a posteriori** *adv*

apos•tle \ə-ˈpä-səl\ *n* **1** : one of the group composed of Jesus' 12 original disciples and Paul **2** : the first prominent missionary to a region or group **3** : a person who initiates or first advocates a great reform — **apos•tle•ship** *n*

ap•os•tol•ic \ˌa-pə-ˈstä-lik\ *adj* **1** : of or relating to an apostle or to the New Testament apostles **2** : of or relating to a succession of spiritual authority from the apostles **3** : PAPAL

[1]**apos•tro•phe** \ə-ˈpäs-trə-(ˌ)fē\ *n* : the rhetorical addressing of a usu. absent person or a usu. personified thing (as in "O grave, where is thy victory?")

[2]**apostrophe** *n* : a punctuation mark ' used esp. to indicate the possessive case or the omission of a letter or figure

apos•tro•phise *Brit var of* APOSTROPHIZE

apos•tro•phize \ə-ˈpäs-trə-ˌfīz\ *vb* **-phized; -phiz•ing** : to address as if present or capable of understanding

apothecaries' weight *n* : a system of weights based on the troy pound and ounce and used chiefly by pharmacists — see WEIGHT table

apoth•e•cary \ə-ˈpä-thə-ˌker-ē\ *n, pl* **-car•ies** [ME *apothecarie*, fr. ML *apothecarius*, fr. LL, shopkeeper, fr. L *apotheca* storehouse, fr. Gk *apothēkē*, fr. *apotithenai* to put away] : DRUGGIST

ap•o•thegm \ˈa-pə-ˌthem\ *n* : APHORISM

apo•the•o•sis \ə-ˌpä-thē-ˈō-səs, ˌa-pə-ˈthē-ə-səs\ *n, pl* **-o•ses** \-ˌsēz\ **1** : DEIFICATION **2** : the perfect example

app *abbr* **1** apparatus **2** appendix

ap•pall *also* **ap•pal** \ə-ˈpȯl\ *vb* **ap•palled; ap•pall•ing** : to overcome with horror : DISMAY

Ap•pa•loo•sa \ˌa-pə-ˈlü-sə\ *n* : any of a breed of saddle horses developed in western No. America and usu. having a white or solid-colored coat with small spots

Appaloosa

ap•pa•nage \ˈa-pə-nij\ *n* **1** : provision (as a grant of land) made by a sovereign or legislative body for dependent members of the royal family **2** : a rightful adjunct

ap•pa•ra•tus \ˌa-pə-ˈra-təs, -ˈrā-\ *n, pl* **-tus•es** *or* **-tus** [L] **1** : a set of materials or equipment for a particular use **2** : a complex machine or device : MECHANISM **3** : the organization of a political party or underground movement

[1]**ap•par•el** \ə-ˈpar-əl\ *vb* **-eled** *or* **-elled; -el•ing** *or* **-el•ling** **1** : CLOTHE **2** : ADORN

[2]**apparel** *n* : CLOTHING, DRESS

ap•par•ent \ə-ˈpar-ənt\ *adj* **1** : open to view : VISIBLE **2** : EVIDENT, OBVIOUS **3** : appearing as real or true : SEEMING

ap•par•ent•ly \-lē\ *adv* : it seems apparent

ap•pa•ri•tion \ˌa-pə-ˈri-shən\ *n* : a supernatural appearance : GHOST

ap•peal \ə-ˈpēl\ *vb* **1** : to take steps to have (a case) reheard in a higher court **2** : to plead for help, corroboration, or decision **3** : to arouse a sympathetic response — **appeal** *n*

ap•pear \ə-ˈpir\ *vb* **1** : to become visible **2** : to come formally before an authority **3** : SEEM **4** : to become evident **5** : to come before the public

ap•pear•ance \ə-ˈpir-əns\ *n* **1** : outward aspect : LOOK **2** : the act of appearing **3** : PHENOMENON

ap•pease \ə-ˈpēz\ *vb* **ap•peased; ap•peas•ing** **1** : to cause to subside : ALLAY **2** : PACIFY, CONCILIATE; *esp* : to buy off by concessions — **ap•pease•ment** *n* — **ap•peas•able** \-ˈpē-zə-bəl\ *adj*

ap•pel•lant \ə-ˈpe-lənt\ *n* : one who appeals esp. from a judicial decision

ap•pel•late \ə-ˈpe-lət\ *adj* : having power to review decisions of a lower court

ap•pel•la•tion \ˌa-pə-ˈlā-shən\ *n* : NAME, DESIGNATION

ap•pel•lee \ˌa-pə-ˈlē\ *n* : one against whom an appeal is taken

ap•pend \ə-ˈpend\ *vb* : to attach esp. as something additional : AFFIX

ap•pend•age \ə-ˈpen-dij\ *n* **1** : something appended to a principal or greater thing **2** : a projecting part of the body (as an antenna) esp. when paired with one on each side **syn** accessory, adjunct, appendix, appurtenance

ap•pen•dec•to•my \ˌa-pən-ˈdek-tə-mē\ *n, pl* **-mies** : surgical removal of the intestinal appendix

ap•pen•di•ci•tis \ə-ˌpen-də-ˈsī-təs\ *n* : inflammation of the intestinal appendix

ap•pen•dix \ə-ˈpen-diks\ *n, pl* **-dix•es** *or* **-di•ces** \-də-ˌsēz\ [L] **1** : supplementary matter added at the end of a book **2** : a narrow blind tube usu. about three or four inches long that extends from the cecum in the lower right-hand part of the abdomen

ap•per•tain \ˌa-pər-ˈtān\ *vb* : to belong as a rightful part or privilege

ap•pe•tis•er, ap•pe•tis•ing *Brit var of* APPETIZER, APPETIZING

ap•pe•tite \ˈa-pə-ˌtīt\ *n* [ME *apetit*, fr. MF, fr. L *appetitus*, fr. *appetere* to strive after, fr. *ad-* to + *petere* to go to] **1** : natural desire for satisfying some want or need esp. for food **2** : TASTE, PREFERENCE

ap•pe•tiz•er \ˈa-pə-ˌtī-zər\ *n* : a food or drink taken just before a meal to stimulate the appetite

ap•pe•tiz•ing \-ziŋ\ *adj* : tempting to the appetite — **ap•pe•tiz•ing•ly** *adv*

appl *abbr* applied

ap•plaud \ə-ˈplȯd\ *vb* : to show approval esp. by clapping

ap•plause \ə-ˈplȯz\ *n* : approval publicly expressed (as by clapping)

ap•ple \ˈa-pəl\ *n* : a rounded fruit with firm white flesh and a seedy core; *also* : a tree that bears this fruit

ap•ple•jack \-ˌjak\ *n* : a liquor distilled from fermented cider

ap•pli•ance \ə-ˈplī-əns\ *n* **1** : INSTRUMENT, DEVICE **2** : a piece of household equipment (as a stove or toaster) operated by gas or electricity

ap•pli•ca•ble \ˈa-pli-kə-bəl, ə-ˈpli-kə-\ *adj* : capable of being applied : RELEVANT — **ap•pli•ca•bil•i•ty** \ˌa-pli-kə-ˈbi-lə-tē, ə-ˌpli-kə-\ *n*

ap•pli•cant \ˈa-pli-kənt\ *n* : one who applies

ap•pli•ca•tion \ˌa-plə-ˈkā-shən\ *n* **1** : the act of applying **2** : assiduous attention **3** : REQUEST; *also* : a form used in making a request **4** : something placed or spread on a surface **5** : capacity for use

ap•pli•ca•tor \ˈa-plə-ˌkā-tər\ *n* : a device for applying a substance (as medicine or polish)

ap•plied \ə-ˈplīd\ *adj* : put to practical use ⟨~ art⟩

ap•pli•qué \ˌa-plə-ˈkā\ *n* [F] : a fabric decoration cut out and fastened to a larger piece of material — **ap•pliqué** *vb*

ap•ply \ə-ˈplī\ *vb* **ap•plied; ap•ply•ing** **1** : to put to practical use **2** : to place in contact : put or spread on a surface **3** : to employ with close attention **4** : to have reference or connection **5** : to submit a request

ap•point \ə-ˈpȯint\ *vb* **1** : to fix or set officially ⟨~ a day for trial⟩ **2** : to name officially **3** : to fit out : EQUIP

ap·poin·tee \ə-ˌpȯin-ˈtē, ˌa-\ *n* : a person appointed

ap·point·ive \ə-ˈpȯin-tiv\ *adj* : subject to appointment

ap·point·ment \ə-ˈpȯint-mənt\ *n* **1** : the act of appointing **2** : an arrangement for a meeting **3** *pl* : FURNISHINGS, EQUIPMENT **4** : a nonelective office or position

ap·por·tion \ə-ˈpōr-shən\ *vb* : to distribute proportionately : ALLOT — **ap·por·tion·ment** *n*

ap·po·site \ˈa-pə-zət\ *adj* : APPROPRIATE, RELEVANT — **ap·po·site·ly** *adv* — **ap·po·site·ness** *n*

ap·po·si·tion \ˌa-pə-ˈzi-shən\ *n* : a grammatical construction in which a noun or pronoun is followed by another that has the same referent (as *the poet* and *Burns* in "a biography of the poet Burns")

ap·pos·i·tive \ə-ˈpä-zə-tiv, a-\ *adj* : of, relating to, or standing in grammatical apposition — **appositive** *n*

ap·praise \ə-ˈprāz\ *vb* **ap·praised; ap·prais·ing** : to set a value on — **ap·prais·al** \-ˈprā-zəl\ *n* — **ap·prais·er** *n*

ap·pre·cia·ble \ə-ˈprē-shə-bəl\ *adj* : large enough to be recognized and measured — **ap·pre·cia·bly** *adv*

ap·pre·ci·ate \ə-ˈprē-shē-ˌāt\ *vb* **-at·ed; -at·ing 1** : to value justly **2** : to be aware of **3** : to be grateful for **4** : to increase in value — **ap·pre·ci·a·tion** \-ˌprē-shē-ˈā-shən\ *n*

ap·pre·cia·tive \ə-ˈprē-shə-tiv, -shē-ˌāt-\ *adj* : having or showing appreciation — **ap·pre·cia·tive·ly** *adv*

ap·pre·hend \ˌa-pri-ˈhend\ *vb* **1** : ARREST **2** : to become aware of **3** : to look forward to with dread **4** : UNDERSTAND — **ap·pre·hen·sion** \-ˈhen-chən\ *n*

ap·pre·hen·sive \-ˈhen-siv\ *adj* : viewing the future with anxiety — **ap·pre·hen·sive·ly** *adv* — **ap·pre·hen·sive·ness** *n*

[1]ap·pren·tice \ə-ˈpren-təs\ *n* **1** : a person learning a craft under a skilled worker **2** : BEGINNER — **ap·pren·tice·ship** *n*

[2]apprentice *vb* **-ticed; -tic·ing** : to bind or set at work as an apprentice

ap·prise \ə-ˈprīz\ *vb* **ap·prised; ap·pris·ing** : INFORM

ap·proach \ə-ˈprōch\ *vb* **1** : to move nearer to **2** : to be almost the same as **3** : to make advances to esp. for the purpose of creating a desired result **4** : to take preliminary steps toward — **approach** *n* — **ap·proach·able** *adj*

ap·pro·ba·tion \ˌa-prə-ˈbā-shən\ *n* : APPROVAL

[1]ap·pro·pri·ate \ə-ˈprō-prē-ˌāt\ *vb* **-at·ed; -at·ing 1** : to take possession of **2** : to set apart for a particular use

[2]ap·pro·pri·ate \ə-ˈprō-prē-ət\ *adj* : fitted to a purpose or use : SUITABLE **syn** proper, fit, apt, befitting — **ap·pro·pri·ate·ly** *adv* — **ap·pro·pri·ate·ness** *n*

ap·pro·pri·a·tion \ə-ˌprō-prē-ˈā-shən\ *n* : something (as money) set aside by formal action for a specific use

ap·prov·al \ə-ˈprü-vəl\ *n* : an act of approving — **on approval** : subject to a prospective buyer's acceptance or refusal

ap·prove \ə-ˈprüv\ *vb* **ap·proved; ap·prov·ing 1** : to have or express a favorable opinion of **2** : to accept as satisfactory : RATIFY

approx *abbr* approximate; approximately

[1]ap·prox·i·mate \ə-ˈpräk-sə-mət\ *adj* : nearly correct or exact — **ap·prox·i·mate·ly** *adv*

[2]ap·prox·i·mate \-ˌmāt\ *vb* **-mat·ed; -mat·ing** : to come near : APPROACH — **ap·prox·i·ma·tion** \ə-ˌpräk-sə-ˈmā-shən\ *n*

appt *abbr* appoint; appointed; appointment

ap·pur·te·nance \ə-ˈpərt-nəns, -ᵊn-əns\ *n* : something that belongs to or goes with another thing **syn** accessory, adjunct, appendage, appendix — **ap·pur·te·nant** \ə-ˈpərt-nənt, -ᵊn-ənt\ *adj*

Apr *abbr* April

APR *abbr* annual percentage rate

apri·cot \ˈa-prə-ˌkät, ˈā-\ *n* [deriv. of Ar *al-birqūq*] : an oval orange-colored fruit resembling the related peach and plum in flavor; *also* : a tree bearing apricots

April \ˈā-prəl\ *n* [ME, fr. OF & L; OF *avrill*, fr. L *Aprilis*] : the 4th month of the year

a pri·o·ri \ˌä-prē-ˈōr-ē\ *adj* [L, from the former] **1** : characterized by or derived by reasoning from self-evident propositions **2** : independent of experience — **a priori** *adv*

apron \ˈā-prən\ *n* [ME, alter. (resulting fr. misdivision of *a napron*) of *napron*, fr. MF *naperon*, dim. of *nape* cloth, modif. of L *mappa* napkin] **1** : a garment tied over the front of the body to protect the clothes **2** : a paved area for parking or handling airplanes — **aproned** *adj*

[1]ap·ro·pos \ˌa-prə-ˈpō, ˈa-prə-ˌpō\ *adv* [F *à propos*, lit., to the purpose] **1** : OPPORTUNELY **2** : in passing : INCIDENTALLY

[2]apropos *adj* : being to the point

apropos of *prep* : with regard to

apse \ˈaps\ *n* : a projecting usu. semicircular and vaulted part of a building (as a church)

[1]apt \ˈapt\ *adj* **1** : well adapted : SUITABLE **2** : having an habitual tendency : LIKELY **3** : quick to learn — **apt·ly** *adv* — **apt·ness** \ˈapt-nəs\ *n*

[2]apt *abbr* **1** apartment **2** aptitude

ap·ti·tude \ˈap-tə-ˌtüd, -ˌtyüd\ *n* **1** : natural ability : TALENT **2** : capacity for learning **3** : APPROPRIATENESS

aqua \ˈa-kwə, ˈä-\ *n* : a light greenish blue color

aqua·cul·ture *also* **aqui·cul·ture** \ˈa-kwə-ˌkəl-chər, ˈä-\ *n* : the cultivation of aquatic plants or animals (as fish or shellfish) for human use

aqua·ma·rine \ˌa-kwə-mə-ˈrēn, ˌä-\ *n* **1** : a bluish green gem **2** : a pale blue to light greenish blue

aqua·naut \ˈa-kwə-ˌnȯt, ˈä-\ *n* : a person who lives in an underwater shelter for an extended period

aqua·plane \-ˌplān\ *n* : a board towed behind a motorboat and ridden by a person standing on it — **aquaplane** *vb*

aqua re·gia \ˌa-kwə-ˈrē-j(ē-)ə\ *n* [NL, lit., royal water] : a mixture of nitric and hydrochloric acids that dissolves gold or platinum

aquar·i·um \ə-ˈkwar-ē-əm\ *n, pl* **-i·ums** *or* **-ia** \-ē-ə\ **1** : a container (as a glass tank) in which living aquatic animals or plants are kept **2** : a place where aquatic animals and plants are kept and shown

Aquar·i·us \ə-ˈkwar-ē-əs\ *n* [L, lit., water carrier] **1** : a zodiacal constellation between Capricorn and Pisces usu. pictured as a man pouring water **2** : the 11th sign of the zodiac in astrology; *also* : one born under this sign

[1]aquat·ic \ə-ˈkwä-tik, -ˈkwa-\ *adj* **1** : growing or living in or frequenting water **2** : performed in or on water

[2]aquatic *n* : an aquatic animal or plant

aqua·vit \ˈä-kwə-ˌvēt\ *n* : a clear liquor flavored with caraway seeds

aqua vi·tae \ˌa-kwə-ˈvī-tē, ˌä-\ *n* [ME, fr. ML, lit., water of life] : a strong alcoholic liquor (as brandy)

aq·ue·duct \ˈa-kwə-ˌdəkt\ *n* **1** : a conduit for carrying running water **2** : a structure carrying a canal over a river or hollow **3** : a passage in a bodily part

aqueduct 1

aque·ous \ˈā-kwē-əs, ˈa-\ *adj* **1** : WATERY **2** : made of, by, or with water

aqueous humor *n* : a clear fluid occupying the space between the lens and the cornea of the eye

aqui·fer \ˈa-kwə-fər, ˈä-\ *n* : a water-bearing stratum of permeable rock, sand, or gravel

aq·ui·line \ˈa-kwə-ˌlīn, -lən\ *adj* **1** : of or resembling an eagle **2** : hooked like an eagle's beak ⟨an ~ nose⟩
ar *abbr* arrival; arrive
Ar *symbol* argon
AR *abbr* Arkansas
-ar *adj suffix* : of or relating to ⟨molecul*ar*⟩ : being ⟨spectacul*ar*⟩ : resembling ⟨oracul*ar*⟩
Ar·ab \ˈar-əb\ *n* **1** : a member of a Semitic people of the Arabian peninsula in southwestern Asia **2** : a member of an Arabic-speaking people — **Arab** *adj* — **Ara·bi·an** \ə-ˈrā-bē-ən\ *adj or n*
ar·a·besque \ˌar-ə-ˈbesk\ *n* : a design of interlacing lines forming figures of flowers, foliage, and sometimes animals — **arabesque** *adj*
[1]**Ar·a·bic** \ˈar-ə-bik\ *n* : a Semitic language of southwestern Asia and northern Africa
[2]**Arabic** *adj* **1** : of or relating to the Arabs, Arabic, or the Arabian peninsula in southwestern Asia **2** : expressed in or making use of Arabic numerals
Arabic numeral *n* : any of the number symbols 0, 1, 2, 3, 4, 5, 6, 7, 8, 9
ar·a·ble \ˈar-ə-bəl\ *adj* : fit for or used for the growing of crops
arach·nid \ə-ˈrak-nəd\ *n* : any of a class of usu. 8-legged arthropods comprising the spiders, scorpions, mites, and ticks — **arachnid** *adj*
Ar·a·ma·ic \ˌar-ə-ˈmā-ik\ *n* : an ancient Semitic language
ar·a·mid \ˈar-ə-məd, -ˌmid\ *n* : any of several light but very strong heat-resistant synthetic materials used esp. in textiles and plastics
Arap·a·ho *or* **Arap·a·hoe** \ə-ˈra-pə-ˌhō\ *n, pl* **-ho** *or* **-hos** *or* **-hoe** *or* **-hoes** : a member of an American Indian people of the western U.S.
ar·bi·ter \ˈär-bə-tər\ *n* : one having power to decide : JUDGE
ar·bi·trage \ˈär-bə-ˌträzh\ *n* [F, fr. MF, arbitration] : the purchase and sale of the same or equivalent securities in different markets in order to profit from price discrepancies
ar·bi·tra·geur \ˌär-bə-(ˌ)trä-ˈzhər\ *or* **ar·bi·trag·er** \ˈär-bə-ˌträ-zhər\ *n* : one who practices arbitrage
ar·bit·ra·ment \är-ˈbi-trə-mənt\ *n* **1** : the act of deciding a dispute **2** : the judgment given by an arbitrator
ar·bi·trary \ˈär-bə-ˌtrer-ē\ *adj* **1** : AUTOCRATIC, DESPOTIC **2** : determined by will or caprice : selected at random — **ar·bi·trari·ly** \ˌär-bə-ˈtrer-ə-lē\ *adv* — **ar·bi·trari·ness** \ˈär-bə-ˌtrer-ē-nəs\ *n*
ar·bi·trate \ˈär-bə-ˌtrāt\ *vb* **-trat·ed; -trat·ing** **1** : to act as arbitrator **2** : to act on as arbitrator **3** : to submit for decision to an arbitrator — **ar·bi·tra·tion** \ˌär-bə-ˈtrā-shən\ *n*
ar·bi·tra·tor \ˈär-bə-ˌtrā-tər\ *n* : one chosen to settle differences between two parties in a controversy
ar·bor \ˈär-bər\ *n* [ME *erber* plot of grass, arbor, fr. OF *herbier* plot of grass, fr. *herbe* herb, grass] : a shelter formed of or covered with vines or branches
ar·bo·re·al \är-ˈbōr-ē-əl\ *adj* **1** : of, relating to, or resembling a tree **2** : living in trees ⟨~ monkeys⟩
ar·bo·re·tum \ˌär-bə-ˈrē-təm\ *n, pl* **-retums** *or* **-re·ta** \-tə\ [L, plantation of trees, fr. *arbor* tree] : a place where trees and plants are grown for scientific and educational purposes
ar·bor·vi·tae \ˌär-bər-ˈvī-tē\ *n* : any of various evergreen trees and shrubs with scalelike leaves that are related to the cypresses
ar·bour *chiefly Brit var of* ARBOR
ar·bu·tus \är-ˈbyü-təs\ *n* : TRAILING ARBUTUS
[1]**arc** \ˈärk\ *n* **1** : a sustained luminous discharge of electricity (as between two electrodes) **2** : a continuous portion of a curved line (as part of the circumference of a circle)
[2]**arc** *vb* **arced** \ˈärkt\; **arc·ing** \ˈär-kiŋ\ : to form an electric arc
ARC *abbr* **1** AIDS-related complex **2** American Red Cross
ar·cade \är-ˈkād\ *n* **1** : an arched or covered passageway; *esp* : one lined with shops **2** : a row of arches with their supporting columns
ar·cane \är-ˈkān\ *adj* : SECRET, MYSTERIOUS
[1]**arch** \ˈärch\ *n* **1** : a curved structure spanning an opening (as a door) **2** : something resembling an arch **3** : ARCHWAY
[2]**arch** *vb* **1** : to cover with an arch **2** : to form or bend into an arch
[3]**arch** *adj* **1** : CHIEF, EMINENT **2** : ROGUISH, MISCHIEVOUS — **arch·ly** *adv* — **arch·ness** *n*
[4]**arch** *abbr* architect; architectural; architecture
ar·chae·ol·o·gy *or* **ar·che·ol·o·gy** \ˌär-kē-ˈä-lə-jē\ *n* : the study of past human life as revealed by relics left by ancient peoples — **ar·chae·o·log·i·cal** \-ə-ˈlä-ji-kəl\ *adj* — **ar·chae·ol·o·gist** \-ˈä-lə-jist\ *n*
ar·cha·ic \är-ˈkā-ik\ *adj* **1** : having the characteristics of the language of the past and surviving chiefly in specialized uses ⟨~ words⟩ **2** : belonging to an earlier time : ANTIQUATED — **ar·cha·i·cal·ly** \-i-k(ə-)lē\ *adv*
arch·an·gel \ˈär-ˌkān-jəl\ *n* : a chief angel
arch·bish·op \ärch-ˈbi-shəp\ *n* : a bishop of high rank
arch·bish·op·ric \-shə-(ˌ)prik\ *n* : the jurisdiction or office of an archbishop
arch·con·ser·va·tive \(ˌ)ärch-kən-ˈsər-və-tiv\ *n* : an extreme conservative — **archconservative** *adj*
arch·dea·con \-ˈdē-kən\ *n* : a church official who assists a diocesan bishop in ceremonial or administrative functions
arch·di·o·cese \-ˈdī-ə-səs, -ˌsēz\ *n* : the diocese of an archbishop
arch·duke \-ˈdük, -ˈdyük\ *n* **1** : a sovereign prince **2** : a prince of the imperial family of Austria
Ar·che·an \är-ˈkē-ən\ *adj* : of, relating to, or being the earliest eon of geologic history — **Archean** *n*
arch·en·e·my \ˌärch-ˈe-nə-mē\ *n, pl* **-mies** : a principal enemy
Ar·cheo·zo·ic \ˌär-kē-ə-ˈzō-ik\ *adj* : ARCHEAN — **Archeozoic** *n*
ar·chery \ˈär-chə-rē\ *n* : the art or practice of shooting with bow and arrows — **ar·cher** \ˈär-chər\ *n*
ar·che·type \ˈär-ki-ˌtīp\ *n* : the original pattern or model of all things of the same type
arch·fiend \ˌärch-ˈfēnd\ *n* : a chief fiend; *esp* : SATAN
ar·chi·epis·co·pal \ˌär-kē-ə-ˈpis-kə-pəl\ *adj* : of or relating to an archbishop
ar·chi·man·drite \ˌär-kə-ˈman-ˌdrīt\ *n* : a dignitary in an Eastern church ranking below a bishop
ar·chi·pel·a·go \ˌär-kə-ˈpe-lə-ˌgō, ˌär-chə-\ *n, pl* **-goes** *or* **-gos** : a group of islands
ar·chi·tect \ˈär-kə-ˌtekt\ *n* **1** : a person who plans buildings and oversees their construction **2** : a person who designs and guides a plan or undertaking
ar·chi·tec·ture \ˈär-kə-ˌtek-chər\ *n* **1** : the art or science of planning and building structures **2** : a method or style of building **3** : the manner in which the elements (as of a design) are arranged or organized — **ar·chi·tec·tur·al** \ˌar-kə-ˈtek-chə-rəl, -ˈtek-shrəl\ *adj* — **ar·chi·tec·tur·al·ly** *adv*
ar·chi·trave \ˈär-kə-ˌtrāv\ *n* : the supporting horizontal member just above the columns in a building in the classical style of architecture
ar·chive \ˈär-ˌkīv\ *n* : a place for keeping public records; *also* : public records — often used in pl.
ar·chi·vist \ˈär-kə-vist, -ˌkī-\ *n* : a person in charge of archives
ar·chon \ˈär-ˌkän, -kən\ *n* : a chief magistrate of ancient Athens
arch·way \ˈärch-ˌwā\ *n* : a passageway under an arch; *also* : an arch over a passage
arc lamp *n* : a gas-filled electric lamp that produces light when a current arcs between incandescent electrodes
[1]**arc·tic** \ˈärk-tik, ˈär-tik\ *adj* [ME *artik*, fr. L *arcticus*, fr. Gk *arktikos*, fr. *arktos* bear, Ursa Major, north] **1**

often cap : of or relating to the north pole or the region near it **2** : FRIGID

[2]**arc·tic** \ˈär-tik, ˈärk-tik\ *n* : a rubber overshoe that reaches to the ankle or above

arctic circle *n, often cap A&C* : the parallel of latitude that is approximately 66½ degrees north of the equator

-ard *also* **-art** *n suffix* : one that is characterized by performing some action, possessing some quality, or being associated with some thing esp. conspicuously or excessively ⟨bragg*art*⟩ ⟨dull*ard*⟩

ar·dent \ˈär-dᵊnt\ *adj* **1** : characterized by warmth of feeling : PASSIONATE **2** : FIERY, HOT **3** : GLOWING — **ar·dent·ly** *adv*

ar·dor \ˈär-dər\ *n* **1** : warmth of feeling : ZEAL **2** : sexual excitement

ar·dour *chiefly Brit var of* ARDOR

ar·du·ous \ˈär-jə-wəs, -dyu̇-wəs\ *adj* : DIFFICULT, LABORIOUS — **ar·du·ous·ly** *adv* — **ar·du·ous·ness** *n*

[1]**are** *pres 2d sing or pres pl of* BE

[2]**are** \ˈar\ *n* — see METRIC SYSTEM table

ar·ea \ˈar-ē-ə\ *n* **1** : a flat surface or space **2** : the amount of surface included (as within the lines of a geometric figure) **3** : range or extent of some thing or concept : FIELD **4** : REGION

area code *n* : a 3-digit number that identifies each telephone service area in a country (as the U.S. or Canada)

are·na \ə-ˈrē-nə\ *n* [L *harena, arena* sand, sandy place] **1** : an enclosed area used for public entertainment **2** : a sphere of activity or competition

Ar·gen·tine \ˈär-jən-ˌtēn, -ˌtīn\ *or* **Ar·gen·tin·ean** *or* **Ar·gen·tin·i·an** \ˌär-jən-ˈti-nē-ən\ *n* : a native or inhabitant of Argentina — **Argentine** *or* **Argentinean** *or* **Argentinian** *adj*

ar·gen·tite \ˈär-jən-ˌtīt\ *n* : a dark gray mineral that is an important ore of silver

ar·gon \ˈär-ˌgän\ *n* [Gk, neut. of *argos* idle, lazy, fr. *a-* not + *ergon* work; fr. its relative inertness] : a colorless odorless gaseous chemical element found in the air and used for filling electric lamps — see ELEMENT table

ar·go·sy \ˈär-gə-sē\ *n, pl* **-sies 1** : a large merchant ship **2** : FLEET

ar·got \ˈär-gət, -ˌgō\ *n* : the language of a particular group or class

argu·able \ˈär-gyü-ə-bəl\ *adj* : open to argument, dispute, or question

ar·gu·ably \ˈär-gyü-(ə-)blē\ *adv* : it can be argued

ar·gue \ˈär-gyü\ *vb* **ar·gued; ar·gu·ing 1** : to give reasons for or against something **2** : to contend in words : DISPUTE **3** : DEBATE **4** : to persuade by giving reasons

ar·gu·ment \ˈär-gyə-mənt\ *n* **1** : a reason offered in proof **2** : discourse intended to persuade **3** : QUARREL

ar·gu·men·ta·tion \ˌär-gyə-mən-ˈtā- shən\ *n* : the art of formal discussion

ar·gu·men·ta·tive \ˌär-gyə-ˈmen-tə-tiv\ *adj* : inclined to argue

ar·gyle *also* **ar·gyll** \ˈär-ˌgīl\ *n, often cap* : a geometric knitting pattern of varicolored diamonds on a single background color; *also* : a sock knit in this pattern

aria \ˈär-ē-ə\ *n* : an accompanied elaborate vocal solo forming part of a larger work

ar·id \ˈar-əd\ *adj* : very dry; *esp* : having insufficient rainfall to support agriculture — **arid·i·ty** \ə-ˈri-də-tē\ *n*

Ar·i·es \ˈar-ˌēz, -ē-ˌēz\ *n* [L, lit., ram] **1** : a zodiacal constellation between Pisces and Taurus pictured as a ram **2** : the 1st sign of the zodiac in astrology; *also* : one born under this sign

aright \ə-ˈrīt\ *adv* : RIGHT, CORRECTLY

arise \ə-ˈrīz\ *vb* **arose** \-ˈrōz\; **aris·en** \-ˈriz-ᵊn\; **aris·ing** \-ˈrī-ziŋ\ **1** : to get up **2** : ORIGINATE **3** : ASCEND **syn** rise, derive, spring, issue

ar·is·toc·ra·cy \ˌar-ə-ˈstä-krə-sē\ *n, pl* **-cies 1** : government by a noble or privileged class; *also* : a state so governed **2** : the governing class of an aristocracy **3** : UPPER CLASS — **aris·to·crat** \ə-ˈris-tə-ˌkrat\ *n* — **aris·to·crat·ic** \ə-ˌris-tə-ˈkra-tik\ *adj*

arith *abbr* arithmetic; arithmetical

arith·me·tic \ə-ˈrith-mə-ˌtik\ *n* **1** : a branch of mathematics that deals with computations usu. with nonnegative real numbers **2** : COMPUTATION, CALCULATION — **ar·ith·met·ic** \ˌar-ith-ˈme-tik\ *or* **ar·ith·met·i·cal** \-ti-kəl\ *adj* — **ar·ith·met·i·cal·ly** \-ti-k(ə-)lē\ *adv* — **arith·me·ti·cian** \ə-ˌrith-mə-ˈti-shən\ *n*

arithmetic mean *n* : the sum of a set of numbers divided by the number of numbers in the set

Ariz *abbr* Arizona

ark \ˈärk\ *n* **1** : a boat held to resemble that of Noah's at the time of the Flood **2** : the sacred chest in a synagogue representing to Hebrews the presence of God; *also* : the repository for the scrolls of the Torah

Ark *abbr* Arkansas

[1]**arm** \ˈärm\ *n* **1** : a human upper limb; *also* : a corresponding limb of a lower animal with a backbone **2** : something resembling an arm in shape or position ⟨an ~ of a chair⟩ **3** : POWER, MIGHT ⟨the ~ of the law⟩ — **armed** \ˈärmd\ *adj* — **arm·less** *adj*

[2]**arm** *vb* : to furnish with weapons

[3]**arm** *n* **1** : WEAPON **2** : a branch of the military forces **3** *pl* : the hereditary heraldic devices of a family

ar·ma·da \är-ˈmä-də, -ˈmā-\ *n* : a fleet of warships

ar·ma·dil·lo \ˌär-mə-ˈdi-lō\ *n, pl* **-los** : any of several small burrowing mammals with the head and body protected by an armor of bony plates

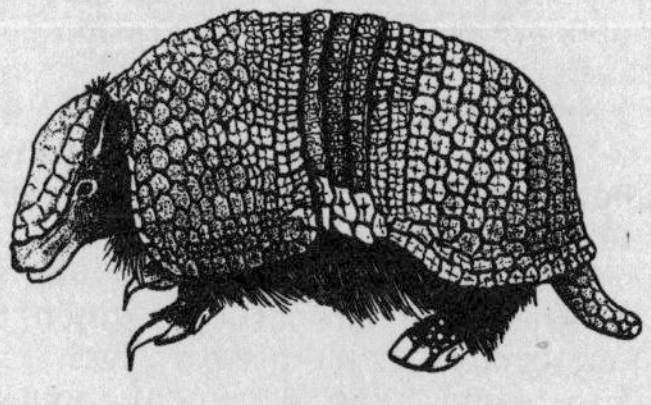

armadillo

Ar·ma·ged·don \ˌär-mə-ˈged-ᵊn\ *n* : a final conclusive battle between the forces of good and evil; *also* : the site or time of this

ar·ma·ment \ˈär-mə-mənt\ *n* **1** : military strength **2** : arms and equipment (as of a tank or combat unit) **3** : the process of preparing for war

ar·ma·ture \ˈär-mə-ˌchu̇r, -chər\ *n* **1** : a protective covering or structure (as the spines of a cactus) **2** : the rotating part of an electric generator or motor; *also* : the movable part in an electromagnetic device (as a loudspeaker)

arm·chair \ˈärm-ˌcher\ *n* : a chair with armrests

armed forces *n pl* : the combined military, naval, and air forces of a nation

Ar·me·nian \är-ˈmē-nē-ən\ *n* : a native or inhabitant of Armenia

arm·ful \ˈärm-ˌfu̇l\ *n, pl* **armfuls** *or* **arms·ful** \ˈärmz-ˌfu̇l\ : as much as the arm or arms can hold

arm·hole \ˈärm-ˌhōl\ *n* : an opening for the arm in a garment

ar·mi·stice \ˈär-mə-stəs\ *n* : temporary suspension of hostilities by mutual agreement : TRUCE

arm·let \ˈärm-lət\ *n* : a band worn around the upper arm

ar·mor \ˈär-mər\ *n* **1** : protective covering **2** : armored forces and vehicles — **ar·mored** \-mərd\ *adj*

ar·mor·er \ˈär-mər-ər\ *n* **1** : a person who makes arms and armor **2** : a person who services firearms

ar·mo·ri·al \är-ˈmōr-ē-əl\ *adj* : of or bearing heraldic arms

ar·mory \ˈär-mə-rē\ *n, pl* **ar·mor·ies 1** : a place where arms are stored **2** : a factory where arms are made

ar•mour, ar•moury *chiefly Brit var of* ARMOR, ARMORY
arm•pit \ˈärm-ˌpit\ *n* **:** the hollow under the junction of the arm and shoulder
arm•rest \-ˌrest\ *n* **:** a support for the arm
ar•my \ˈär-mē\ *n, pl* **armies 1 :** a body of men organized for war **2** *often cap* **:** the complete military organization of a country for land warfare **3 :** a great number **4 :** a body of persons organized to advance a cause
army ant *n* **:** any of various nomadic social ants
ar•my•worm \ˈär-mē-ˌwərm\ *n* **:** any of numerous moths whose larvae move about destroying crops
aro•ma \ə-ˈrō-mə\ *n* **:** a usu. pleasing odor **:** FRAGRANCE — **ar•o•mat•ic** \ˌar-ə-ˈma-tik\ *adj*
aro•ma•ther•a•py \ə-ˌrō-mə-ˈther-ə-pē\ *n* **:** massage with a preparation of fragrant oils extracted from herbs, flowers, and fruits
arose *past of* ARISE
[1]**around** \ə-ˈraund\ *adv* **1 :** in a circle or in circumference ⟨a tree five feet ~⟩ **2 :** in or along a circuit ⟨the road goes ~ by the lake⟩ **3 :** on all sides ⟨nothing for miles ~⟩ **4 :** NEARBY ⟨wait ~ awhile⟩ **5 :** from one place to another ⟨travels ~ on business⟩ **6 :** in an opposite direction ⟨turn ~⟩
[2]**around** *prep* **1 :** SURROUNDING ⟨trees ~ the house⟩ **2 :** to or on another side of ⟨~ the corner⟩ **3 :** NEAR ⟨stayed right ~ home⟩ **4 :** along the circuit of ⟨go ~ the world⟩
arouse \ə-ˈrauz\ *vb* **aroused; arous•ing 1 :** to awaken from sleep **2 :** to stir up — **arous•al** \-ˈrau̇-zəl\ *n*
ar•peg•gio \är-ˈpe-jē-ˌō, -ˈpe-jō\ *n, pl* **-gios** [It fr. *arpeggiare* to play on the harp, fr. *arpa* harp] **:** a chord whose notes are performed in succession and not simultaneously
arr *abbr* **1** arranged **2** arrival; arrive
ar•raign \ə-ˈrān\ *vb* **1 :** to call before a court to answer to an indictment **2 :** to accuse of wrong or imperfection — **ar•raign•ment** *n*
ar•range \ə-ˈrānj\ *vb* **ar•ranged; ar•rang•ing 1 :** to put in order **2 :** to adapt (a musical composition) to voices or instruments other than those for which it was orig. written **3 :** to come to an agreement about **:** SETTLE — **ar•range•ment** *n* — **ar•rang•er** *n*
ar•rant \ˈar-ənt\ *adj* **:** being notoriously without moderation **:** EXTREME
ar•ras \ˈar-əs\ *n, pl* **arras 1 :** TAPESTRY **2 :** a wall hanging or screen of tapestry
[1]**ar•ray** \ə-ˈrā\ *vb* **1 :** to dress esp. splendidly **2 :** to arrange in order
[2]**array** *n* **1 :** a regular arrangement **2 :** rich apparel **3 :** an imposing group
ar•rears \ə-ˈrirz\ *n pl* **1 :** a state of being behind in the discharge of obligations ⟨in ~ with the rent⟩ **2 :** overdue debts
[1]**ar•rest** \ə-ˈrest\ *vb* **1 :** STOP, CHECK **2 :** to take into legal custody
[2]**arrest** *n* **1 :** the act of stopping; *also* **:** the state of being stopped **2 :** the taking into custody by legal authority
ar•riv•al \ə-ˈrī-vəl\ *n* **1 :** the act of arriving **2 :** one that arrives
ar•rive \ə-ˈrīv\ *vb* **ar•rived; ar•riv•ing 1 :** to reach a destination **2 :** to make an appearance ⟨the guests have *arrived*⟩ **3 :** to attain success
ar•ro•gant \ˈar-ə-gənt\ *adj* **:** offensively exaggerating one's own importance — **ar•ro•gance** \-gəns\ *n* — **ar•ro•gant•ly** *adv*
ar•ro•gate \-ˌgāt\ *vb* **-gat•ed; -gat•ing :** to claim or seize without justification as one's right — **ar•ro•ga•tion** \ˌar-ə-ˈgā-shən\ *n*
ar•row \ˈar-ō\ *n* **1 :** a missile shot from a bow and usu. having a slender shaft, a pointed head, and feathers at the butt **2 :** a pointed mark used to indicate direction
ar•row•head \ˈar-ō-ˌhed\ *n* **:** the pointed end of an arrow
ar•row•root \-ˌrüt, -ˌru̇t\ *n* **:** an edible starch from the roots of any of several tropical American plants; *also* **:** a plant yielding arrowroot
ar•royo \ə-ˈrȯi-ə, -ō\ *n, pl* **-royos** [Sp] **1 :** a watercourse in a dry region **2 :** a water-carved gully or channel
ar•se•nal \ˈärs-nəl, ˈärs-ᵊn-əl\ *n* [ultim. fr. Ar *dārṣināʽah* house of manufacture] **1 :** a place for making and storing arms and military equipment **2 :** STORE, REPERTORY
ar•se•nic \ˈärs-nik, ˈärs-ᵊn-ik\ *n* **1 :** a solid brittle poisonous chemical element of grayish metallic luster — see ELEMENT table **2 :** a very poisonous oxygen compound of arsenic used in making insecticides
ar•son \ˈärs-ᵊn\ *n* **:** the willful or malicious burning of property — **ar•son•ist** \-ist\ *n*
[1]**art** \ˈärt\ *n* **1 :** skill acquired by experience or study **2 :** a branch of learning; *esp* **:** one of the humanities **3 :** an occupation requiring knowledge or skill **4 :** the use of skill and imagination in the production of things of beauty; *also* **:** works so produced **5 :** ARTFULNESS
[2]**art** *abbr* **1** article **2** artificial **3** artillery
-art — see -ARD
ar•te•fact *chiefly Brit var of* ARTIFACT
ar•te•ri•al \är-ˈtir-ē-əl\ *adj* **1 :** of or relating to an artery; *also* **:** relating to or being the oxygenated blood found in most arteries **2 :** of, relating to, or being a route for through traffic
ar•te•ri•ole \är-ˈtir-ē-ˌōl\ *n* **:** one of the small terminal branches of an artery that ends in capillaries — **ar•te•ri•o•lar** \-ˌtir-ē-ˈō-lər\ *adj*
ar•te•rio•scle•ro•sis \är-ˌtir-ē-ō-sklə-ˈrō-səs\ *n* **:** a chronic disease in which arterial walls are abnormally thickened and hardened — **ar•te•rio•scle•rot•ic** \-ˈrä-tik\ *adj or n*
ar•tery \ˈär-tə-rē\ *n, pl* **-ter•ies 1 :** one of the tubular vessels that carry blood from the heart **2 :** a main channel of transportation or communication
ar•te•sian well \är-ˈtē-zhən-\ *n* **:** a well from which the water flows to the surface by natural pressure; *also* **:** a deep well
art•ful \ˈärt-fəl\ *adj* **1 :** INGENIOUS **2 :** CRAFTY — **art•ful•ly** *adv* — **art•ful•ness** *n*
ar•thri•tis \är-ˈthrī-təs\ *n, pl* **-thri•ti•des** \-ˈthri-tə-ˌdēz\ **:** inflammation of the joints — **ar•thrit•ic** \-ˈthri-tik\ *adj or n*
ar•thro•pod \ˈär-thrə-ˌpäd\ *n* **:** any of a phylum of invertebrate animals comprising those (as insects, spiders, or crabs) with segmented bodies and jointed limbs — **arthropod** *adj*
ar•thros•co•py \är-ˈthräs-kə-pē\ *n, pl* **-pies :** visual examination of the interior of a joint (as the knee) with a special surgical instrument; *also* **:** joint surgery using arthroscopy — **ar•thro•scope** \ˈär-thrə-ˌskōp\ *n* — **ar•thro•scop•ic** \ˌär-thrə-ˈskä-pik\ *adj*
ar•ti•choke \ˈär-tə-ˌchōk\ *n* [It dial. *articiocco,* ultim. fr. Ar *al-khurshūf*] **:** a tall herb related to the daisies; *also* **:** its edible flower head

artichoke

ar•ti•cle \ˈär-ti-kəl\ *n* [ME, fr. OF, fr. L *articulus* joint, division, dim. of *artus* joint, limb] **1** : a distinct part of a written document **2** : a nonfictional prose composition forming an independent part of a publication **3** : a word (as *an, the*) used with a noun to limit or give definiteness to its application **4** : a member of a class of things; *esp* : COMMODITY

ar•tic•u•lar \är-ˈti-kyə-lər\ *adj* : of or relating to a joint

[1]ar•tic•u•late \är-ˈti-kyə-lət\ *adj* **1** : divided into meaningful parts : INTELLIGIBLE **2** : able to speak; *also* : expressing oneself readily and effectively **3** : JOINTED — **ar•tic•u•late•ly** *adv* — **ar•tic•u•late•ness** *n*

[2]ar•tic•u•late \-ˌlāt\ *vb* **-lat•ed; -lat•ing 1** : to utter distinctly **2** : to unite by or as if by joints — **ar•tic•u•la•tion** \-ˌti-kyə-ˈlā-shən\ *n*

ar•ti•fact \ˈär-tə-ˌfakt\ *n* : something made or modified by humans usu. for a purpose; *esp* : an object remaining from another time or culture ⟨prehistoric ~*s*⟩

ar•ti•fice \ˈär-tə-fəs\ *n* **1** : TRICK; *also* : TRICKERY **2** : an ingenious device; *also* : INGENUITY

ar•ti•fi•cer \är-ˈti-fə-sər, ˈär-tə-fə-sər\ *n* : a skilled worker

ar•ti•fi•cial \ˌär-tə-ˈfi-shəl\ *adj* **1** : produced by art rather than nature; *also* : made by humans to imitate nature **2** : not genuine : FEIGNED — **ar•ti•fi•ci•al•i•ty** \-ˌfi-shē-ˈa-lə-tē\ *n* — **ar•ti•fi•cial•ly** *adv* — **ar•ti•fi•cial•ness** *n*

artificial insemination *n* : introduction of semen into the uterus or oviduct by other than natural means

artificial intelligence *n* : the capability of a machine to imitate intelligent human behavior

artificial respiration *n* : the rhythmic forcing of air into and out of the lungs of a person whose breathing has stopped

ar•til•lery \är-ˈti-lə-rē\ *n, pl* **-ler•ies 1** : crew-served mounted firearms (as guns) **2** : a branch of the army armed with artillery — **ar•til•ler•ist** \-rist\ *n*

ar•ti•san \ˈär-tə-zən, -sən\ *n* : a skilled manual worker

art•ist \ˈär-tist\ *n* **1** : one who practices an art; *esp* : one who creates objects of beauty **2** : ARTISTE

ar•tiste \är-ˈtēst\ *n* : a skilled public performer

ar•tis•tic \är-ˈtis-tik\ *adj* : showing taste and skill — **ar•tis•ti•cal•ly** \-ti-k(ə-)lē\ *adv*

art•ist•ry \ˈär-tə-strē\ *n* : artistic quality or ability

art•less \ˈärt-ləs\ *adj* **1** : lacking art or skill **2** : free from artificiality : NATURAL **3** : free from guile : SINCERE — **art•less•ly** *adv* — **art•less•ness** *n*

art nou•veau \ˌär-nü-ˈvō, ˌärt-\ *n, often cap A&N* [F, lit., new art] : a late 19th century design style characterized by sinuous lines and leaf-shaped forms

arty \ˈär-tē\ *adj* **art•i•er; -est** : showily or pretentiously artistic — **art•i•ly** \ˈärt-ᵊl-ē\ *adv* — **art•i•ness** *n*

ar•um \ˈar-əm\ *n* : any of a family of plants (as the jack-in-the-pulpit or a skunk cabbage) with flowers in a fleshy enclosed spike

ARV *abbr* American Revised Version

[1]-ary *n suffix* : thing or person belonging to or connected with ⟨function*ary*⟩

[2]-ary *adj suffix* : of, relating to, or connected with ⟨budget*ary*⟩

Ary•an \ˈar-ē-ən, ˈer-; ˈär-yən\ *adj* **1** : INDO-EUROPEAN **2** : NORDIC — **Aryan** *n*

[1]as \əz, (ˌ)az\ *adv* **1** : to the same degree or amount : EQUALLY ⟨~ green as grass⟩ **2** : for instance ⟨various trees, ~ oak or pine⟩ **3** : when considered in a specified relation ⟨my opinion ~ distinguished from his⟩

[2]as *conj* **1** : in the same amount or degree in which ⟨green ~ grass⟩ **2** : in the same way that ⟨farmed ~ his father before him had farmed⟩ **3** : WHILE, WHEN ⟨spoke to me ~ I was leaving⟩ **4** : THOUGH ⟨improbable ~ it seems⟩ **5** : SINCE, BECAUSE ⟨~ I'm not wanted, I'll go⟩ **6** : that the result is ⟨so guilty ~ to leave no doubt⟩

[3]as *pron* **1** : THAT — used after *same* or *such* ⟨it's the same price ~ before⟩ **2** : a fact that ⟨he's rich, ~ you know⟩

[4]as *prep* : in the capacity or character of ⟨this will serve ~ a substitute⟩

As *symbol* arsenic

AS *abbr* **1** American Samoa **2** Anglo-Saxon **3** associate in science

asa•fet•i•da *or* **asa•foe•ti•da** \ˌa-sə-ˈfi-tə-dē, -ˈfe-tə-də\ *n* : an ill-smelling plant gum formerly used in medicine

ASAP *abbr* as soon as possible

as•bes•tos \as-ˈbes-təs, az-\ *n* : a noncombustible grayish mineral that occurs in fibrous form and has been used as a fireproof material

as•cend \ə-ˈsend\ *vb* **1** : to move upward : MOUNT, CLIMB **2** : to succeed to : OCCUPY ⟨he ~*ed* the throne⟩

as•cen•dan•cy *also* **as•cen•den•cy** \ə-ˈsen-dən-sē\ *n* : controlling influence : DOMINATION

[1]as•cen•dant *also* **as•cen•dent** \ə-ˈsen-dənt\ *n* : a dominant position

[2]ascendant *also* **ascendent** *adj* **1** : moving upward **2** : DOMINANT

as•cen•sion \ə-ˈsen-chən\ *n* : the act or process of ascending

Ascension Day *n* : the Thursday 40 days after Easter observed in commemoration of Christ's ascension into heaven

as•cent \ə-ˈsent\ *n* **1** : the act of mounting upward : CLIMB **2** : degree of upward slope

as•cer•tain \ˌas-ər-ˈtān\ *vb* : to learn with certainty — **as•cer•tain•able** *adj*

as•cet•ic \ə-ˈse-tik\ *adj* : practicing self-denial esp. for spiritual reasons : AUSTERE — **ascetic** *n* — **as•cet•i•cism** \-ˈse-tə-ˌsi-zəm\ *n*

ASCII \ˈas-kē\ *n* [*A*merican *S*tandard *C*ode for *I*nformation *I*nterchange] : a computer code for representing alphanumeric information

ascor•bic acid \ə-ˈskȯr-bik-\ *n* : VITAMIN C

as•cot \ˈas-kət, -ˌkät\ *n* [*Ascot* Heath, racetrack near Ascot, England] : a broad neck scarf that is looped under the chin

as•cribe \ə-ˈskrīb\ *vb* **as•cribed; as•crib•ing** : to refer to a supposed cause, source, or author : ATTRIBUTE — **as•crib•able** *adj* — **as•crip•tion** \-ˈskrip-shən\ *n*

asep•tic \ā-ˈsep-tik\ *adj* : free or freed from disease-causing germs

asex•u•al \ā-ˈsek-shə-wəl\ *adj* **1** : lacking sex or functional sex organs **2** : occurring or formed without the production and union of two kinds of germ cells ⟨~ reproduction⟩ — **asex•u•al•ly** *adv*

as for *prep* : with regard to : CONCERNING ⟨*as for* the others, they were late⟩

[1]ash \ˈash\ *n* **1** : any of a genus of trees related to the olive and having winged seeds and bark with grooves and ridges **2** : the tough elastic wood of an ash

[2]ash *n* **1** : the solid matter left when material is burned **2** : fine mineral particles from a volcano **3** *pl* : the remains of the dead human body after cremation or disintegration

ashamed \ə-ˈshāmd\ *adj* **1** : feeling shame **2** : restrained by anticipation of shame ⟨~ to say anything⟩ — **asham•ed•ly** \-ˈshā-məd-lē\ *adv*

ash•en \ˈa-shən\ *adj* : resembling ashes (as in color); *esp* : deadly pale

ash•lar \ˈash-lər\ *n* : hewn or squared stone; *also* : masonry of such stone

ashore \ə-ˈshōr\ *adv* : on or to the shore

as how *conj* : THAT ⟨allowed *as how* she was glad to be here⟩

ash•ram \ˈäsh-rəm\ *n* : a religious retreat esp. of a Hindu sage

ash•tray \ˈash-ˌtrā\ *n* : a receptacle for tobacco ashes

Ash Wednesday *n* : the 1st day of Lent

ashy \ˈa-shē\ *adj* **ash•i•er; -est** : ASHEN

Asian \ˈā-zhən\ *adj* : of, relating to, or characteristic of the continent of Asia or its people — **Asian** *n*

Asi•at•ic \ˌā-zhē-ˈa-tik\ *adj* : ASIAN — sometimes taken to be offensive — **Asiatic** *n*

[1]**aside** \ə-ˈsīd\ *adv* **1 :** to or toward the side **2 :** out of the way **:** AWAY

[2]**aside** *n* **:** an actor's words heard by the audience but supposedly not by other characters on stage

aside from *prep* **1 :** BESIDES ⟨*aside from* being pretty, she's intelligent⟩ **2 :** with the exception of ⟨*aside from* one D his grades are excellent⟩

as if *conj* **1 :** as it would be if ⟨it's *as if* nothing had changed⟩ **2 :** as one would if ⟨he acts *as if* he'd never been away⟩ **3 :** THAT ⟨it seems *as if* nothing ever happens around here⟩

as•i•nine \ˈas-ᵊn-ˌīn\ *adj* [L *asininus,* fr. *asinus* ass] **:** STUPID, FOOLISH — **as•i•nin•i•ty** \ˌa-sə-ˈni-nə-tē\ *n*

ask \ˈask\ *vb* **asked** \ˈaskt\; **ask•ing 1 :** to call on for an answer **2 :** UTTER ⟨~ a question⟩ **3 :** to make a request of ⟨~ him for help⟩ **4 :** to make a request for ⟨~ help of her⟩ **5 :** to set as a price ⟨~*ed* $800 for the car⟩ **6 :** INVITE

askance \ə-ˈskans\ *adv* **1 :** with a side glance **2 :** with distrust

askew \ə-ˈskyü\ *adv or adj* **:** out of line **:** AWRY

ASL *abbr* American Sign Language

[1]**aslant** \ə-ˈslant\ *adv or adj* **:** in a slanting direction

[2]**aslant** *prep* **:** over or across in a slanting direction

asleep \ə-ˈslēp\ *adv or adj* **1 :** in or into a state of sleep **2 :** DEAD **3 :** NUMB **4 :** INACTIVE

as long as *conj* **1 :** provided that ⟨do as you like *as long as* you get home on time⟩ **2 :** INASMUCH AS, SINCE ⟨*as long as* you're up, turn on the light⟩

aso•cial \(ˌ)ā-ˈsō-shəl\ *adj* **:** ANTISOCIAL

as of *prep* **:** AT, DURING, FROM, ON ⟨takes effect *as of* July 1⟩

asp \ˈasp\ *n* **:** a small poisonous African snake

as•par•a•gus \ə-ˈspar-ə-gəs\ *n* **:** a tall branching perennial herb related to the lilies; *also* **:** its edible young stalks

as•par•tame \as-ˈpär-ˌtām\ *n* **:** a crystalline low-calorie sweetener

ASPCA *abbr* American Society for the Prevention of Cruelty to Animals

as•pect \ˈas-ˌpekt\ *n* **1 :** a position facing a particular direction **2 :** APPEARANCE, LOOK **3 :** PHASE

as•pen \ˈas-pən\ *n* **:** any of several poplars with leaves that flutter in the slightest breeze

as per \ˈaz-ˌpər\ *prep* **:** in accordance with ⟨*as per* instructions⟩

as•per•i•ty \a-ˈsper-ə-tē\ *n, pl* **-ties 1 :** ROUGHNESS **2 :** harshness of temper

as•per•sion \ə-ˈspər-zhən\ *n* **:** a slanderous or defamatory remark

as•phalt \ˈas-ˌfölt\ *also* **as•phal•tum** \as-ˈföl-təm\ *n* **:** a dark substance found in natural beds or obtained as a residue in petroleum refining and used esp. in paving streets

asphalt jungle *n* **:** a big city or a specified part of a big city

as•pho•del \ˈas-fə-ˌdel\ *n* **:** any of several Old World herbs related to the lilies and bearing flowers in long erect spikes

as•phyx•ia \as-ˈfik-sē-ə\ *n* **:** a lack of oxygen or excess of carbon dioxide in the body usu. caused by interruption of breathing and causing unconsciousness

as•phyx•i•ate \-sē-ˌāt\ *vb* **-at•ed; -at•ing :** SUFFOCATE — **as•phyx•i•a•tion** \-ˌfik-sē-ˈā-shən\ *n*

as•pic \ˈas-pik\ *n* [F, lit., asp] **:** a savory meat jelly

as•pi•rant \ˈas-pə-rənt, ə-ˈspī-rənt\ *n* **:** one who aspires **syn** candidate, applicant, seeker

[1]**as•pi•rate** \ˈas-pə-rət\ *n* **1 :** an independent sound \h\ or a character (as the letter *h*) representing it **2 :** a consonant having aspiration as its final component

[2]**as•pi•rate** \ˈas-pə-ˌrāt\ *vb* **-rat•ed; -rat•ing :** to draw, remove, or take up or into by suction

as•pi•ra•tion \ˌas-pə-ˈrā-shən\ *n* **1 :** the pronunciation or addition of an aspirate; *also* **:** the aspirate or its symbol **2 :** a drawing of something in, out, up, or through by or as if by suction **3 :** a strong desire to achieve something noble; *also* **:** an object of this desire

as•pire \ə-ˈspīr\ *vb* **as•pired; as•pir•ing 1 :** to seek to attain or accomplish a particular goal **2 :** to rise aloft

as•pi•rin \ˈas-pə-rən\ *n, pl* **aspirin** *or* **aspirins 1 :** a white crystalline drug used to relieve pain and fever **2 :** a tablet of aspirin

as regards *also* **as respects** *prep* **:** in regard to **:** with respect to

ass \ˈas\ *n* **1 :** any of several long-eared mammals smaller than the related horses; *esp* **:** one of Africa ancestral to the donkey **2 :** a stupid person

as•sail \ə-ˈsāl\ *vb* **:** to attack violently — **as•sail•able** *adj* — **as•sail•ant** *n*

as•sas•sin \ə-ˈsas-ᵊn\ *n* [ML *assassinus,* fr. Ar *ḥashshāshīn,* pl. of *ḥashshāsh* hashish-user, fr. *hashīsh* hashish] **:** a murderer esp. for hire or fanatical reasons

as•sas•si•nate \ə-ˈsas-ᵊn-ˌāt\ *vb* **-nat•ed; -nat•ing :** to murder by sudden or secret attack — **as•sas•si•na•tion** \-ˌsas-ᵊn-ˈā-shən\ *n*

as•sault \ə-ˈsölt\ *n* **1 :** a violent attack **2 :** an unlawful attempt or threat to do harm to another — **assault** *vb*

assault rifle *n* **:** a military automatic rifle with a large-capacity magazine

[1]**as•say** \ˈa-ˌsā, a-ˈsā\ *n* **:** analysis to determine the quantity of one or more components present in a sample (as of an ore or drug)

[2]**as•say** \a-ˈsā, ˈa-ˌsā\ *vb* **1 :** TRY, ATTEMPT **2 :** to subject (as an ore or drug) to an assay **3 :** JUDGE 3

as•sem•blage \ə-ˈsem-blij, *3 & 4 also* ˌas-ˌäm-ˈbläzh\ *n* **1 :** a collection of persons or things **:** GATHERING **2 :** the act of assembling **3 :** an artistic composition made from scraps, junk, and odds and ends **4 :** the art of making assemblages

as•sem•ble \ə-ˈsem-bəl\ *vb* **-bled; -bling 1 :** to collect into one place **:** CONGREGATE **2 :** to fit together the parts of **3 :** to meet together **:** CONVENE

as•sem•bly \ə-ˈsem-blē\ *n, pl* **-blies 1 :** a gathering of persons **:** MEETING **2** *cap* **:** a legislative body; *esp* **:** the lower house of a legislature **3 :** a signal for troops to assemble **4 :** the fitting together of parts (as of a machine)

assembly language *n* **:** a computer language consisting of mnemonic codes corresponding to machine-language instructions

assembly line *n* **:** an arrangement of machines, equipment, and workers in which work passes from operation to operation in a direct line

as•sem•bly•man \ə-ˈsem-blē-mən\ *n* **:** a member of a legislative assembly

as•sem•bly•wom•an \-ˌwu̇-mən\ *n* **:** a woman who is a member of an assembly

as•sent \ə-ˈsent\ *vb* **:** AGREE, CONCUR — **assent** *n*

as•sert \ə-ˈsərt\ *vb* **1 :** to state positively **2 :** to demonstrate the existence of **syn** declare, affirm, protest, avow, claim — **as•ser•tive** \-ˈsər-tiv\ *adj* — **as•ser•tive•ness** *n*

as•ser•tion \ə-ˈsər-shən\ *n* **:** a positive statement

as•sess \ə-ˈses\ *vb* **1 :** to fix the rate or amount of **2 :** to impose (as a tax) at a specified rate **3 :** to evaluate for taxation — **as•sess•ment** *n* — **as•ses•sor** \-ˈse-sər\ *n*

as•set \ˈa-ˌset\ *n* **1** *pl* **:** the entire property of a person or company that may be used to pay debts **2 :** ADVANTAGE, RESOURCE

as•sev•er•ate \ə-ˈse-və-ˌrāt\ *vb* **-at•ed; -at•ing :** to assert earnestly — **as•sev•er•a•tion** \-ˌse-və-ˈrā-shən\ *n*

as•sid•u•ous \ə-ˈsi-jə-wəs\ *adj* **:** steadily attentive **:** DILIGENT — **as•si•du•i•ty** \ˌa-sə-ˈdü-ə-tē, -ˈdyü-\ *n* — **as•sid•u•ous•ly** *adv* — **as•sid•u•ous•ness** *n*

as•sign \ə-ˈsīn\ *vb* **1 :** to transfer (property) to another **2 :** to appoint to or as a duty ⟨~ a lesson⟩ **3 :** FIX, SPECIFY ⟨~ a limit⟩ **4 :** ASCRIBE ⟨~ a reason⟩ — **as•sign•able** *adj*

as•sig•na•tion \ˌa-sig-ˈnā-shən\ *n* **:** an appointment for a meeting; *esp* **:** TRYST

assigned risk *n* : a poor risk (as an accident-prone motorist) that an insurance company is forced to insure by state law

as•sign•ment \ə-ˈsīn-mənt\ *n* **1** : the act of assigning **2** : something assigned

as•sim•i•late \ə-ˈsi-mə-ˌlāt\ *vb* **-lat•ed; -lat•ing 1** : to take up and absorb as nourishment; *also* : to absorb into a cultural tradition **2** : COMPREHEND **3** : to make or become similar — **as•sim•i•la•tion** \-ˌsi-mə-ˈlā-shən\ *n*

¹as•sist \ə-ˈsist\ *vb* : HELP, AID — **as•sis•tance** \-ˈsis-təns\ *n*

²assist *n* **1** : an act of assistance **2** : the action of a player who enables a teammate to make a putout (as in baseball) or score a goal (as in hockey)

as•sis•tant \ə-ˈsis-tənt\ *n* : a person who assists : HELPER

as•size \ə-ˈsīz\ *n* **1** : a judicial inquest **2** *pl* : the former regular sessions of superior courts in English counties

assn *abbr* association

assoc *abbr* associate; associated; association

¹as•so•ci•ate \ə-ˈsō-shē-ˌāt, -sē-\ *vb* **-at•ed; -at•ing 1** : to join in companionship or partnership **2** : to connect in thought

²as•so•ciate \-shē-ət, -sē-; -shət\ *n* **1** : a fellow worker : PARTNER **2** : COMPANION **3** *often cap* : a degree conferred esp. by a junior college ⟨~ in arts⟩ — **associate** *adj*

as•so•ci•a•tion \ə-ˌsō-shē-ˈā-shən, -sē-\ *n* **1** : the act of associating **2** : an organization of persons : SOCIETY

as•so•cia•tive \ə-ˈsō-shē-ˌā-tiv, -sē-; -shə-tiv\ *adj* : of, relating to, or involved in association esp. of ideas or images

as•so•nance \ˈa-sə-nəns\ *n* : repetition of vowels esp. as an alternative to rhyme in verse — **as•so•nant** \-nənt\ *adj or n*

as soon as *conj* : immediately at or shortly after the time that ⟨we'll start *as soon as* they arrive⟩

as•sort \ə-ˈsȯrt\ *vb* **1** : to distribute into like groups : CLASSIFY **2** : HARMONIZE

as•sort•ed \-ˈsȯr-təd\ *adj* : consisting of various kinds

as•sort•ment \-ˈsȯrt-mənt\ *n* : a collection of assorted things or persons

asst *abbr* assistant

as•suage \ə-ˈswāj\ *vb* **as•suaged; as•suag•ing 1** : to make (as pain or grief) less : EASE **2** : SATISFY **syn** alleviate, relieve, lighten, mitigate

as•sume \ə-ˈsüm\ *vb* **as•sumed; as•sum•ing 1** : to take upon oneself **2** : to pretend to have or be **3** : to take as granted or true though not proved

as•sump•tion \ə-ˈsəmp-shən\ *n* **1** : the taking up of a person into heaven **2** *cap* : August 15 observed in commemoration of the Assumption of the Virgin Mary **3** : a taking upon oneself **4** : PRETENSION **5** : SUPPOSITION

as•sur•ance \ə-ˈshu̇r-əns\ *n* **1** : PLEDGE **2** *chiefly Brit* : INSURANCE **3** : SECURITY **4** : SELF-CONFIDENCE; *also* : AUDACITY

as•sure \ə-ˈshu̇r\ *vb* **as•sured; as•sur•ing 1** : INSURE **2** : to give confidence to **3** : to state confidently to **4** : to make certain the coming or attainment of

as•sured \ə-ˈshu̇rd\ *n, pl* **assured** *or* **assureds** : INSURED

as•ta•tine \ˈas-tə-ˌtēn\ *n* : an unstable radioactive chemical element — see ELEMENT table

as•ter \ˈas-tər\ *n* : any of various mostly fall-blooming leafy-stemmed composite herbs with daisylike purple, white, pink, or yellow flower heads

as•ter•isk \ˈas-tə-ˌrisk\ *n* [L *asteriscus,* fr. Gk *asteriskos,* lit., little star, dim. of *astēr*] : a character * used as a reference mark or as an indication of the omission of letters or words

astern \ə-ˈstərn\ *adv or adj* **1** : in, at, or toward the stern **2** : BACKWARD

as•ter•oid \ˈas-tə-ˌrȯid\ *n* : any of the numerous small celestial bodies found esp. between Mars and Jupiter

asth•ma \ˈaz-mə\ *n* : an often allergic disorder marked by difficulty in breathing and a cough — **asth•mat•ic** \az-ˈma-tik\ *adj or n*

as though *conj* : AS IF

astig•ma•tism \ə-ˈstig-mə-ˌti-zəm\ *n* : a defect in a lens or an eye causing improper focusing — **as•tig•mat•ic** \ˌas-tig-ˈma-tik\ *adj*

astir \ə-ˈstər\ *adj* **1** : being in action : MOVING **2** : being out of bed

as to *prep* **1** : ABOUT, CONCERNING ⟨uncertain *as to* what went on⟩ **2** : ACCORDING TO ⟨graded *as to* size⟩

as•ton•ish \ə-ˈstä-nish\ *vb* : to strike with sudden and usu. great wonder : AMAZE — **as•ton•ish•ing•ly** *adv* — **as•ton•ish•ment** *n*

as•tound \ə-ˈstau̇nd\ *vb* : to fill with bewilderment or wonder — **as•tound•ing•ly** *adv*

¹astrad•dle \ə-ˈstrad-ᵊl\ *adv* : on or above and extending onto both sides

²astraddle *prep* : ASTRIDE

as•tra•khan \ˈas-trə-kən, -ˌkan\ *n, often cap* **1** : karakul of Russian origin **2** : a cloth with a usu. wool, curled, and looped pile resembling karakul

as•tral \ˈas-trəl\ *adj* : of, relating to, or coming from the stars

astray \ə-ˈstrā\ *adv or adj* **1** : off the right path or route **2** : into error

¹astride \ə-ˈstrīd\ *adv* **1** : with one leg on each side **2** : with legs apart

²astride *prep* : with one leg on each side of

¹as•trin•gent \ə-ˈstrin-jənt\ *adj* : able or tending to shrink body tissues — **as•trin•gen•cy** \-jən-sē\ *n*

²astringent *n* : an astringent agent or substance

astrol *abbr* astrologer; astrology

as•tro•labe \ˈas-trə-ˌlāb\ *n* : an instrument formerly used for observing the positions of celestial bodies

as•trol•o•gy \ə-ˈsträ-lə-jē\ *n* : divination based on the supposed influence of the stars upon human events — **as•trol•o•ger** \-jər\ *n* — **as•tro•log•i•cal** \ˌas-trə-ˈlä-ji-kəl\ *adj*

astron *abbr* astronomer; astronomy

as•tro•naut \ˈas-trə-ˌnȯt\ *n* : a traveler in a spacecraft

as•tro•nau•tics \as-trə-ˈnȯ-tiks\ *n* : the science of the construction and operation of spacecraft — **as•tro•nau•tic** \-tik\ *or* **as•tro•nau•ti•cal** \-ti-kəl\ *adj*

as•tro•nom•i•cal \ˌas-trə-ˈnä-mi-kəl\ *also* **as•tro•nom•ic** \-mik\ *adj* **1** : of or relating to astronomy **2** : extremely large ⟨an ~ amount of money⟩

astronomical unit *n* : a unit of length used in astronomy equal to the mean distance of the earth from the sun or about 93 million miles (150 million kilometers)

as•tron•o•my \ə-ˈsträ-nə-mē\ *n, pl* **-mies** : the science of objects and matter beyond the earth's atmosphere — **as•tron•o•mer** \-mər\ *n*

as•tro•phys•ics \ˌas-trə-ˈfi-ziks\ *n* : astronomy dealing esp. with the physical properties and dynamic processes of celestial objects — **as•tro•phys•i•cal** \-zi-kəl\ *adj* — **as•tro•phys•i•cist** \-ˈfi-zə-sist\ *n*

as•tute \ə-ˈstüt, -ˈstyüt, a-\ *adj* [L *astutus,* fr. *astus* craft] : shrewdly discerning; *also* : WILY — **as•tute•ly** *adv* — **as•tute•ness** *n*

asun•der \ə-ˈsən-dər\ *adv or adj* **1** : into separate pieces ⟨torn ~⟩ **2** : separated in position from each other

ASV *abbr* American Standard Version

¹as well as *conj* : and in addition : and moreover ⟨brave *as well as* loyal⟩

²as well as *prep* : in addition to : BESIDES ⟨the coach, *as well as* the team, is ready⟩

asy•lum \ə-ˈsī-ləm\ *n* [ME, fr. L, fr. Gk *asylon,* neut. of *asylos* inviolable, fr. *a-* not + *sylon* right of seizure] **1** : a place of refuge **2** : protection given to esp. political fugitives **3** : an institution for the care of the needy or sick and esp. of the insane

asym•met•ri•cal \ˌā-sə-ˈme-tri-kəl\ *or* **asym•met•ric** \-trik\ *adj* : not symmetrical — **asym•me•try** \(ˌ)ā-ˈsi-mə-trē\ *n*

DICTIONARY

as•ymp•tote \ˈa-səmp-ˌtōt\ *n* : a straight line that is associated with a curve and tends to approximate it along an infinite branch — **as•ymp•tot•ic** \ˌa-səmp-ˈtä-tik\ *adj* — **as•ymp•tot•i•cal•ly** \-ti-k(ə-)lē\ *adv*

[1]**at** \ət, (ˈ)at\ *prep* **1** — used to indicate a point in time or space ⟨be here ~ 3 o'clock⟩ **2** — used to indicate a goal ⟨swung ~ the ball⟩ **3** — used to indicate position or condition ⟨~ rest⟩ **4** — used to indicate means, cause, or manner ⟨sold ~ auction⟩

[2]**at** \ˈät\ *n, pl* **at** — see *kip* at MONEY table

At *symbol* astatine

AT *abbr* automatic transmission

at all *adv* : in any way : in any circumstances ⟨not *at all* likely⟩

at•a•vism \ˈa-tə-ˌvi-zəm\ *n* : appearance in an individual of a character typical of an ancestral form; *also* : such an individual or character — **at•a•vis•tic** \ˌa-tə-ˈvis-tik\ *adj*

ate *past of* EAT

[1]**-ate** *n suffix* **1** : one acted upon (in a specified way) ⟨distill*ate*⟩ **2** : chemical compound or complex derived from a (specified) compound or element ⟨ace*tate*⟩

[2]**-ate** *n suffix* **1** : office : function : rank : group of persons holding a (specified) office or rank ⟨episcop*ate*⟩ **2** : state : dominion : jurisdiction ⟨emir*ate*⟩

[3]**-ate** *adj suffix* **1** : acted on (in a specified way) : being in a (specified) state ⟨temper*ate*⟩ ⟨degener*ate*⟩ **2** : marked by having ⟨vertebr*ate*⟩

[4]**-ate** *vb suffix* : cause to be modified or affected by ⟨pollin*ate*⟩ : cause to become ⟨activ*ate*⟩ : furnish with ⟨aer*ate*⟩

ate•lier \ˌat-əl-ˈyā\ *n* **1** : an artist's or designer's studio **2** : WORKSHOP

athe•ist \ˈā-thē-ist\ *n* : one who denies the existence of God — **athe•ism** \-ˌi-zəm\ *n* — **athe•is•tic** \ˌā-thē-ˈis-tik\ *adj*

ath•e•nae•um *or* **ath•e•ne•um** \ˌa-thə-ˈnē-əm\ *n* : LIBRARY 1

ath•ero•scle•ro•sis \ˌa-thə-rō-sklə-ˈrō-səs\ *n* : arteriosclerosis characterized by the deposition of fatty substances in and the hardening of the inner layer of the arteries — **ath•ero•scle•rot•ic** \-ˈrä-tik\ *adj*

athirst \ə-ˈthərst\ *adj* **1** *archaic* : THIRSTY **2** : EAGER, LONGING

ath•lete \ˈath-ˌlēt\ *n* [ME, fr. L *athleta,* fr. Gk *athlētēs,* fr. *athlein* to contend for a prize, fr. *athlon* prize, contest] : a person who is trained to compete in athletics

athlete's foot *n* : ringworm of the feet

ath•let•ic \ath-ˈle-tik\ *adj* **1** : of or relating to athletes or athletics **2** : VIGOROUS, ACTIVE **3** : STURDY, MUSCULAR

ath•let•ics \ath-ˈle-tiks\ *n sing or pl* : exercises and games requiring physical skill, strength, and endurance

athletic supporter *n* : an elastic pouch used to support the male genitals and worn esp. during athletic activity

[1]**athwart** \ə-ˈthwȯrt\ *prep* **1** : ACROSS **2** : in opposition to

[2]**athwart** *adv* : obliquely across

atilt \ə-ˈtilt\ *adv or adj* **1** : in a tilted position **2** : with lance in hand

-ation *n suffix* : action or process ⟨flirt*ation*⟩ : something connected with an action or process ⟨discolor*ation*⟩

Atl *abbr* Atlantic

at•las \ˈat-ləs\ *n* : a book of maps

atm *abbr* atmosphere; atmospheric

ATM *abbr* automated teller machine

at•mo•sphere \ˈat-mə-ˌsfir\ *n* **1** : the gaseous envelope of a celestial body; *esp* : the mass of air surrounding the earth **2** : a surrounding influence **3** : a unit of pressure equal to the pressure of air at sea level or about 14.7 pounds per square inch (10 newtons per square centimeter) **4** : a dominant effect — **at•mo•spher•ic** \ˌat-mə-ˈsfir-ik, -ˈsfer-\ *adj* — **at•mo•spher•i•cal•ly** \-i-k(ə-)lē\ *adv*

at•mo•sphe•rics \ˌat-mə-ˈsfir-iks, -ˈsfer-\ *n pl* : radio noise from atmospheric electrical phenomena

atoll \ˈa-ˌtȯl, -ˌtäl, ˈā-\ *n* : a coral island consisting of a reef surrounding a lagoon

atoll

at•om \ˈa-təm\ *n* [ME, fr. L *atomus,* fr. Gk *atomos,* fr. *atomos* indivisible, fr. *a-* not + *temnein* to cut] **1** : a tiny particle : BIT **2** : the smallest particle of a chemical element that can exist alone or in combination

atom•ic \ə-ˈtä-mik\ *adj* **1** : of or relating to atoms; *also* : NUCLEAR 2 ⟨~ energy⟩ **2** : extremely small

atomic bomb *n* : a very destructive bomb utilizing the energy released by splitting the atom

atomic clock *n* : a very precise clock regulated by the natural vibration of atoms or molecules (as of cesium)

atomic number *n* : the number of protons in the nucleus of an element

atomic weight *n* : the mass of one atom of an element

at•om•ise, at•om•is•er *Brit var of* ATOMIZE, ATOMIZER

at•om•ize \ˈa-tə-ˌmīz\ *vb* **-ized; -iz•ing** : to reduce to minute particles

at•om•iz•er \ˈa-tə-ˌmī-zər\ *n* : a device for dispensing a liquid (as perfume) as a mist

atom smasher *n* : ACCELERATOR 3

aton•al \ā-ˈtōn-əl\ *adj* : marked by avoidance of traditional musical tonality — **ato•nal•i•ty** \ˌā-tō-ˈna-lə-tē\ *n* — **aton•al•ly** \ā-ˈtōn-əl-ē\ *adv*

atone \ə-ˈtōn\ *vb* **atoned; aton•ing 1** : to make amends **2** : EXPIATE

atone•ment \ə-ˈtōn-mənt\ *n* **1** : the reconciliation of God and man through the death of Jesus Christ **2** : reparation for an offense : SATISFACTION

[1]**atop** \ə-ˈtäp\ *prep* : on top of

[2]**atop** *adv or adj* : on, to, or at the top

ATP \ˌā-ˌtē-ˈpē\ *n* [*a*denosine *t*ri*p*hosphate] : a compound that occurs widely in living tissue and supplies energy for many cellular processes by undergoing enzymatic hydrolysis

atri•um \ˈā-trē-əm\ *n, pl* **atria** \-trē-ə\ *also* **atri•ums 1** : the central room of a Roman house; *also* : an open patio or court in the center of a building (as a hotel) **2** : an anatomical cavity or passage; *esp* : one of the chambers of the heart that receives blood from the veins — **atri•al** \-əl\ *adj*

atro•cious \ə-ˈtrō-shəs\ *adj* **1** : savagely brutal, cruel, or wicked **2** : very bad : ABOMINABLE — **atro•cious•ly** *adv* — **atro•cious•ness** *n*

atroc•i•ty \ə-ˈträ-sə-tē\ *n, pl* **-ties 1** : ATROCIOUSNESS **2** : an atrocious act or object ⟨the *atrocities* of war⟩

at•ro•phy \ˈa-trə-fē\ *n, pl* **-phies** : decrease in size or wasting away of a bodily part or tissue — **atrophy** *vb*

at•ro•pine \ˈa-trə-ˌpēn\ *n* : a drug from belladonna and related plants used esp. to relieve spasms and to dilate the pupil of the eye

att *abbr* **1** attached **2** attention **3** attorney

at•tach \ə-ˈtach\ *vb* **1** : to seize legally in order to force payment of a debt **2** : to bind by personal ties **3** : FASTEN, CONNECT **4** : to be fastened or connected

at•ta•ché \ˌa-tə-ˈshā, ˌa-ˌta-, ə-ˌta-\ *n* [F] : a technical expert on the diplomatic staff of an ambassador

at•ta•ché case \ə-ˈta-shā-, ˌa-tə-ˈshā-\ *n* : a small thin suitcase used esp. for carrying business papers; *also* : BRIEFCASE

at•tach•ment \ə-ˈtach-mənt\ *n* **1** : legal seizure of property **2** : connection by ties of affection and regard **3** : a device attached to a machine or implement **4** : a connection by which one thing is attached to another

[1]at·tack \ə-ˈtak\ *vb* **1** : to set upon with force or words : ASSAIL, ASSAULT **2** : to set to work on

[2]attack *n* **1** : an offensive action **2** : a fit of sickness

at·tain \ə-ˈtān\ *vb* **1** : ACHIEVE, ACCOMPLISH **2** : to arrive at : REACH — **at·tain·abil·i·ty** \-ˌtā-nə-ˈbi-lə-tē\ *n* — **at·tain·able** *adj*

at·tain·der \ə-ˈtān-dər\ *n* : extinction of the civil rights of a person upon sentence of death or outlawry

at·tain·ment \ə-ˈtān-mənt\ *n* **1** : the act of attaining **2** : ACCOMPLISHMENT

at·taint \ə-ˈtānt\ *vb* : to condemn to loss of civil rights

at·tar \ˈa-tər\ *n* [Per *ʽaṭir* perfumed, fr. Ar, fr. *ʽiṭr* perfume] : a fragrant floral oil

at·tempt \ə-ˈtempt\ *vb* : to make an effort toward : TRY — **attempt** *n*

at·tend \ə-ˈtend\ *vb* **1** : to look after : TEND **2** : to be present with **3** : to be present at **4** : to apply oneself **5** : to pay attention **6** : to direct one's attention

at·ten·dance \ə-ˈten-dəns\ *n* **1** : the act or fact of attending **2** : the number of persons present; *also* : the number of times a person attends

[1]at·ten·dant \ə-ˈten-dənt\ *n* : one that attends another to render a service

[2]attendant *adj* : ACCOMPANYING ⟨~ circumstances⟩

at·ten·tion \ə-ˈten-chən\ *n* **1** : the act or state of applying the mind to an object **2** : CONSIDERATION **3** : an act of courtesy **4** : a position of readiness assumed on command by a soldier — **at·ten·tive** \-ˈten-tiv\ *adj* — **at·ten·tive·ly** *adv* — **at·ten·tive·ness** *n*

at·ten·u·ate \ə-ˈten-yə-ˌwāt\ *vb* **-at·ed; -at·ing 1** : to make or become thin **2** : WEAKEN — **attenuate** \-wət\ *adj* — **at·ten·u·a·tion** \-ˌten-yə-ˈwā-shən\ *n*

at·test \ə-ˈtest\ *vb* **1** : to certify as genuine by signing as a witness **2** : MANIFEST **3** : TESTIFY — **at·tes·ta·tion** \ˌa-ˌtes-ˈtā-shən\ *n*

at·tic \ˈa-tik\ *n* : the space or room in a building immediately below the roof

[1]at·tire \ə-ˈtīr\ *vb* **at·tired; at·tir·ing** : to put garments on : DRESS, ARRAY

[2]attire *n* : DRESS, CLOTHES

at·ti·tude \ˈa-tə-ˌtüd, -ˌtyüd\ *n* **1** : POSTURE **2** : a mental position or feeling with regard to a fact or state **3** : the position of something in relation to something else

at·ti·tu·di·nise *Brit var of* ATTITUDINIZE

at·ti·tu·di·nize \ˌa-tə-ˈtüd-ᵊn-ˌiz, -ˈtyüd-\ *vb* **-nized; -niz·ing** : to assume an affected mental attitude : POSE

attn *abbr* attention

at·tor·ney \ə-ˈtər-nē\ *n, pl* **-neys** : a legal agent qualified to act for persons in legal proceedings

attorney general *n, pl* **attorneys general** *or* **attorney generals** : the chief legal representative and adviser of a nation or state

at·tract \ə-ˈtrakt\ *vb* **1** : to draw to or toward oneself : cause to approach **2** : to draw by emotional or aesthetic appeal **syn** charm, fascinate, allure, captivate, enchant — **at·trac·tive** \-ˈtrak-tiv\ *adj* — **at·trac·tive·ly** *adv* — **at·trac·tive·ness** *n*

at·trac·tant \ə-ˈtrak-tənt\ *n* : a substance (as a pheromone) used to attract insects or other animals

at·trac·tion \ə-ˈtrak-shən\ *n* **1** : the act or power of attracting; *esp* : personal charm **2** : an attractive quality, object, or feature **3** : a force tending to draw particles together

attrib *abbr* attributive

[1]at·tri·bute \ˈa-trə-ˌbyüt\ *n* **1** : an inherent characteristic **2** : a word ascribing a quality; *esp* : ADJECTIVE

[2]at·trib·ute \ə-ˈtri-ˌbyüt, -byət\ *vb* **-ut·ed; -ut·ing 1** : to explain as to cause or origin ⟨~ the illness to fatigue⟩ **2** : to regard as a characteristic **syn** ascribe, credit, charge, impute — **at·trib·ut·able** *adj* — **at·tri·bu·tion** \ˌa-trə-ˈbyü-shən\ *n*

at·trib·u·tive \ə-ˈtrib-yə-tiv\ *adj* : joined directly to a modified noun without a linking verb ⟨*red* in *red hair* is an ~ adjective⟩ — **attributive** *n*

at·tri·tion \ə-ˈtri-shən\ *n* **1** : the act of wearing away by or as if by rubbing **2** : a reduction in numbers as a result of resignation, retirement, or death

at·tune \ə-ˈtün, -ˈtyün\ *vb* : to bring into harmony : TUNE — **at·tune·ment** *n*

atty *abbr* attorney

ATV *abbr* all-terrain vehicle

atyp·i·cal \ā-ˈti-pi-kəl\ *adj* : not typical : IRREGULAR — **atyp·i·cal·ly** \-k(ə-)lē\ *adv*

Au *symbol* [L *aurum*] gold

au·burn \ˈȯ-bərn\ *adj* : reddish brown — **auburn** *n*

au cou·rant \ˌō-ku̇-ˈräⁿ\ *adj* [F, lit., in the current] : UP-TO-DATE, STYLISH

[1]auc·tion \ˈȯk-shən\ *n* [L *auction-, auctio,* fr. *augēre* to increase] : public sale of property to the highest bidder

[2]auction *vb* **auc·tioned; auc·tion·ing** \-shə-niŋ\ : to sell at auction

auc·tion·eer \ˌȯk-shə-ˈnir\ *n* : an agent who conducts an auction

aud *abbr* audit; auditor

au·da·cious \ȯ-ˈdā-shəs\ *adj* **1** : DARING, BOLD **2** : INSOLENT — **au·da·cious·ly** *adv* — **au·da·cious·ness** *n* — **au·dac·i·ty** \-ˈda-sə-tē\ *n*

[1]au·di·ble \ˈȯ-də-bəl\ *adj* : capable of being heard — **au·di·bil·i·ty** \ˌȯ-də-ˈbi-lə-tē\ *n* — **au·di·bly** \ˈȯ-də-blē\ *adv*

[2]audible *n* : a play called at the line of scrimmage

au·di·ence \ˈȯ-dē-əns\ *n* **1** : a formal interview **2** : an opportunity of being heard **3** : an assembly of listeners or spectators

[1]au·dio \ˈȯ-dē-ˌō\ *adj* **1** : of or relating to frequencies (as of radio waves) corresponding to those of audible sound waves **2** : of or relating to sound or its reproduction and esp. high-fidelity reproduction **3** : relating to or used in the transmission or reception of sound

[2]audio *n* **1** : the transmission, reception, or reproduction of sound **2** : the section of television or motion-picture equipment that deals with sound

au·di·ol·o·gy \ˌȯ-dē-ˈä-lə-jē\ *n* : a branch of science dealing with hearing and esp. with the treatment of individuals having trouble with hearing — **au·di·o·log·i·cal** \-ə-ˈlä-ji-kəl\ *adj* — **au·di·ol·o·gist** \-ˈä-lə-jist\ *n*

au·dio·phile \ˈȯ-dē-ō-ˌfīl\ *n* : one who is enthusiastic about high-fidelity sound reproduction

au·dio·tape \ˈȯ-dē-ō-ˌtāp\ *n* : a tape recording of sound

au·dio·vi·su·al \ˌȯ-dē-ō-ˈvi-zhə-wəl\ *adj* : of, relating to, or making use of both hearing and sight

au·dio·vi·su·als \-wəlz\ *n pl* : audiovisual teaching materials (as videotapes)

[1]au·dit \ˈȯ-dət\ *n* : a formal examination and verification of financial accounts

[2]audit *vb* **1** : to perform an audit on or for **2** : to attend (a course) without expecting formal credit

[1]au·di·tion \ȯ-ˈdi-shən\ *n* : HEARING; *esp* : a trial performance to appraise an entertainer's merits

[2]audition *vb* **-tioned; -tion·ing** \-ˈdi-shə-niŋ\ : to give an audition to; *also* : to give a trial performance

au·di·tor \ˈȯ-də-tər\ *n* **1** : LISTENER **2** : a person who audits

au·di·to·ri·um \ˌȯ-də-ˈtōr-ē-əm\ *n, pl* **-riums** *or* **-ria** \-rē-ə\ **1** : the part of a public building where an audience sits **2** : a hall or building used for public gatherings

au·di·to·ry \ˈȯ-də-ˌtōr-ē\ *adj* : of or relating to hearing or to the sense or organs of hearing

auditory tube *n* : EUSTACHIAN TUBE

auf Wie·der·seh·en \au̇f-ˈvē-dər-ˌzān\ *interj* [G] — used to express farewell

Aug *abbr* August

au·ger \ˈȯ-gər\ *n* : a tool for boring

aught \ˈȯt, ˈät\ *n* : ZERO, CIPHER

aug·ment \ȯg-ˈment\ *vb* : ENLARGE, INCREASE — **aug·men·ta·tion** \ˌȯg-mən-ˈtā-shən\ *n*
au gra·tin \ō-ˈgrat-ᵊn, ȯ-, -ˈgrät-\ *adj* [F, lit., with the burnt scrapings from the pan] : covered with bread crumbs or grated cheese and browned
[1]au·gur \ˈȯ-gər\ *n* : DIVINER, SOOTHSAYER
[2]augur *vb* **1** : to foretell esp. from omens **2** : to give promise of : PRESAGE
au·gu·ry \ˈȯ-gyə-rē, -gə-\ *n, pl* **-ries 1** : divination from omens **2** : OMEN, PORTENT
au·gust \ȯ-ˈgəst\ *adj* : marked by majestic dignity or grandeur — **au·gust·ly** *adv* — **au·gust·ness** *n*
Au·gust \ˈȯ-gəst\ *n* [ME, fr. OE, fr. L *Augustus*, fr. *Augustus* Caesar] : the 8th month of the year
au jus \ō-ˈzhü, -ˈzhüs, -ˈjüs; ō-zhᵫ\ *adj* [F] : served in the juice obtained from roasting
auk \ˈȯk\ *n* : any of several stocky black-and-white diving seabirds that breed in colder parts of the northern hemisphere
auld \ˈȯl, ˈȯld, ˈäl, ˈäld\ *adj, chiefly Scot* : OLD
aunt \ˈant, ˈȧnt\ *n* **1** : the sister of one's father or mother **2** : the wife of one's uncle
au pair \ˈō-ˈpar\ *n* [F, on even terms] : a usu. young foreign person who does domestic work for a family in return for room and board and to learn the family's language
au·ra \ˈȯr-ə\ *n* **1** : a distinctive atmosphere surrounding a given source **2** : a luminous radiation
au·ral \ˈȯr-əl\ *adj* : of or relating to the ear or to the sense of hearing
aurar *pl of* EYRIR
au·re·ole \ˈȯr-ē-ˌōl\ *or* **au·re·o·la** \ȯ-ˈrē-ə-lə\ *n* : HALO, NIMBUS
au re·voir \ˌō-rə-ˈvwär\ *n* [F, lit., till seeing again] : GOOD-BYE
au·ri·cle \ˈȯr-i-kəl\ *n* : an atrium of the heart
au·ric·u·lar \ȯ-ˈri-kyə-lər\ *adj* **1** : told privately ⟨~ confession⟩ **2** : known or recognized by the sense of hearing
au·ro·ra \ə-ˈrōr-ə\ *n, pl* **auroras** *or* **au·ro·rae** \-(ˌ)ē\ : a luminous phenomenon of streamers or arches of light appearing in the upper atmosphere esp. of a planet's polar regions — **au·ro·ral** \-əl\ *adj*
aurora aus·tra·lis \-ȯ-ˈstrā-ləs\ *n* : an aurora that occurs in earth's southern hemisphere
aurora bo·re·al·is \-ˌbōr-ē-ˈa-ləs\ *n* : an aurora that occurs in earth's northern hemisphere
AUS *abbr* Army of the United States
aus·pice \ˈȯ-spəs\ *n, pl* **aus·pic·es** \-spə-səz, -ˌsēz\ [L *auspicium*, fr. *auspic-*, *auspex* diviner by birds, fr. *avis* bird + *specere* to look, look at] **1** : observation of birds by an augur **2** *pl* : kindly patronage and protection **3** : a prophetic sign or omen
aus·pi·cious \ȯ-ˈspi-shəs\ *adj* **1** : promising success : PROPITIOUS **2** : FORTUNATE, PROSPEROUS — **aus·pi·cious·ly** *adv* — **aus·pi·cious·ness** *n*
aus·tere \ȯ-ˈstir\ *adj* **1** : STERN, SEVERE, STRICT **2** : ABSTEMIOUS **3** : UNADORNED ⟨~ style⟩ — **aus·tere·ly** *adv* — **aus·ter·i·ty** \-ˈster-ə-tē\ *n*
aus·tral \ˈȯs-trəl\ *adj* : SOUTHERN
Aus·tra·lian \ȯ-ˈstrāl-yən\ *n* : a native or inhabitant of Australia — **Australian** *adj*
Aus·tri·an \ˈȯ-strē-ən\ *n* : a native or inhabitant of Austria — **Austrian** *adj*
Aus·tro·ne·sian \ˌȯs-trə-ˈnē-zhən\ *adj* : of, relating to, or constituting a family of languages spoken in the area extending from Madagascar eastward through the Malay Peninsula to Hawaii and Easter Island
auth *abbr* **1** authentic **2** author **3** authorized
au·then·tic \ə-ˈthen-tik, ȯ-\ *adj* : GENUINE, REAL — **au·then·ti·cal·ly** \-ti-k(ə-)lē\ *adv* — **au·then·tic·i·ty** \ˌȯ-ˌthen-ˈti-sə-tē\ *n*
au·then·ti·cate \ə-ˈthen-ti-ˌkāt, ȯ-\ *vb* **-cat·ed; -cat·ing** : to prove genuine — **au·then·ti·ca·tion** \-ˌthen-ti-ˈkā-shən\ *n*
au·thor \ˈȯ-thər\ *n* [ME *auctour*, ultim. fr. L *auctor* originator, author, fr. *augēre* to increase] **1** : one that originates or creates **2** : one that writes or composes a literary work
au·thor·ess \ˈȯ-thə-rəs\ *n* : a woman author
au·tho·rise *Brit var of* AUTHORIZE
au·thor·i·tar·i·an \ȯ-ˌthär-ə-ˈter-ē-ən, ə-, -ˌthȯr-\ *adj* **1** : characterized by or favoring the principle of blind obedience to authority **2** : characterized by or favoring concentration of political power in an authority not responsible to the people — **authoritarian** *n*
au·thor·i·ta·tive \ə-ˈthär-ə-ˌtā-tiv, ȯ-, -ˈthȯr-\ *adj* : supported by, proceeding from, or being an authority — **au·thor·i·ta·tive·ly** *adv* — **au·thor·i·ta·tive·ness** *n*
au·thor·i·ty \ə-ˈthär-ə-tē, ȯ-, -ˈthȯr-\ *n, pl* **-ties 1** : a citation used in support of a statement or in defense of an action; *also* : the source of such a citation **2** : one appealed to as an expert **3** : power to influence thought or behavior **4** : freedom granted : RIGHT **5** : persons in command; *esp* : GOVERNMENT **6** : convincing force
au·tho·rize \ˈȯ-thə-ˌrīz\ *vb* **-rized; -riz·ing 1** : SANCTION **2** : to give legal power to — **au·tho·ri·za·tion** \ˌȯ-thə-rə-ˈzā-shən\ *n*
au·thor·ship \ˈȯ-thər-ˌship\ *n* **1** : the state of being an author **2** : the source of a piece of writing, music, or art
au·tism \ˈȯ-ˌti-zəm\ *n* **1** : absorption in self-centered mental activity (as delusions and hallucinations) esp. when accompanied by withdrawal from reality **2** : a mental disorder orginating in infancy that is characterized esp. by inability to interact socially, repetitive behavior, and language disorder — **au·tis·tic** \ȯ-ˈtis-tik\ *adj*
[1]au·to \ˈȯ-tō\ *n, pl* **autos** : AUTOMOBILE
[2]auto *abbr* automatic
au·to·bahn \ˈȯ-tō-ˌbän, ˈau̇-\ *n* : a German, Swiss, or Austrian expressway
au·to·bi·og·ra·phy \ˌȯ-tə-bī-ˈä-grə-fē\ *n* : the biography of a person narrated by that person — **au·to·bi·og·ra·pher** \-fər\ *n* — **au·to·bi·o·graph·i·cal** \-ˌbī-ə-ˈgra-fi-kəl\ *adj* — **au·to·bi·o·graph·i·cal·ly** \-k(ə-)lē\ *adv*
au·toch·tho·nous \ȯ-ˈtäk-thə-nəs\ *adj* : INDIGENOUS, NATIVE
au·to·clave \ˈȯ-tō-ˌklāv\ *n* : an apparatus (as for sterilizing) using superheated high-pressure steam
au·toc·ra·cy \ȯ-ˈtä-krə-sē\ *n, pl* **-cies** : government by one person having unlimited power — **au·to·crat** \ˈȯ-tə-ˌkrat\ *n* — **au·to·crat·ic** \ˌȯ-tə-ˈkra-tik\ *adj* — **au·to·crat·i·cal·ly** \-ti-k(ə-)lē\ *adv*
[1]au·to·graph \ˈȯ-tə-ˌgraf\ *n* **1** : an original manuscript **2** : a person's signature written by hand
[2]autograph *vb* : to write one's signature on
au·to·im·mune \ˌȯ-tō-i-ˈmyün\ *adj* : of, relating to, or caused by antibodies or lymphocytes that attack molecules, cells, or tissues of the organism producing them ⟨~ diseases⟩ — **au·to·im·mu·ni·ty** \-i-ˈmyü-nə-tē\ *n*
au·to·mate \ˈȯ-tə-ˌmāt\ *vb* **-mat·ed; -mat·ing 1** : to operate automatically using mechanical or electronic devices **2** : to convert to automatic operation — **au·to·ma·tion** \ȯ-tə-ˈmā-shən\ *n*
automated teller machine *n* : a computer terminal allowing access to one's own bank accounts
[1]au·to·mat·ic \ˌȯ-tə-ˈma-tik\ *adj* **1** : INVOLUNTARY **2** : made so that certain parts act in a desired manner at the proper time : SELF-ACTING — **au·to·mat·i·cal·ly** \-ti-k(ə-)lē\ *adv*
[2]automatic *n* : an automatic device; *esp* : an automatic firearm
au·tom·a·ton \ȯ-ˈtä-mə-tən, -ˌtän\ *n, pl* **-atons** *or* **-a·ta** \-ə-tə, -ə-ˌtä\ **1** : an automatic machine; *esp* : ROBOT **2** : an individual who acts mechanically
au·to·mo·bile \ˈȯ-tə-mō-ˌbēl, ˌȯ-tə-mə-ˈbēl\ *n* : a usu. 4-wheeled automotive vehicle for passenger transportation

au•to•mo•tive \ˌȯ-tə-ˈmō-tiv\ *adj* **1 :** of or relating to automobiles, trucks, or buses **2 :** SELF-PROPELLED

au•to•nom•ic nervous system \ˌȯ-tə-ˈnä-mik-\ *n* **:** a part of the vertebrate nervous system that governs involuntary actions and that consists of the sympathetic nervous system and the parasympathetic nervous system

au•ton•o•mous \ȯ-ˈtä-nə-məs\ *adj* **:** having the right or power of self-government — **au•ton•o•mous•ly** *adv* — **au•ton•o•my** \-mē\ *n*

au•top•sy \ˈȯ-ˌtäp-sē, ˈȯ-təp-\ *n, pl* **-sies** [Gk *autopsia* act of seeing with one's own eyes, fr. *autos* self + *opsis* sight] **:** examination of a dead body usu. with dissection sufficient to determine the cause of death or extent of change produced by disease — **autopsy** *vb*

au•tumn \ˈȯ-təm\ *n* **:** the season between summer and winter — **au•tum•nal** \ȯ-ˈtəm-nəl\ *adj*

aux *abbr* auxiliary

[1]aux•il•ia•ry \ȯg-ˈzil-yə-rē, -ˈzi-lə-rē\ *adj* **1 :** providing help **2 :** functioning in a subsidiary capacity **3 :** accompanying a verb form to express person, number, mood, or tense ⟨~ verbs⟩

[2]auxiliary *n, pl* **-ries 1 :** an auxiliary person, group, or device **2 :** an auxiliary verb

aux•in \ˈȯk-sən\ *n* **:** a plant hormone that stimulates growth in length

av *abbr* **1** avenue **2** average **3** avoirdupois

AV *abbr* **1** ad valorem **2** audiovisual **3** Authorized Version

[1]avail \ə-ˈvāl\ *vb* **:** to be of use or advantage **:** HELP, BENEFIT

[2]avail *n* **:** USE ⟨effort was of no ~⟩

avail•able \ə-ˈvā-lə-bəl\ *adj* **1 :** USABLE **2 :** ACCESSIBLE — **avail•abil•i•ty** \-ˌvā-lə-ˈbi-lə-tē\ *n*

av•a•lanche \ˈa-və-ˌlanch\ *n* **:** a mass of snow, ice, earth, or rock sliding down a mountainside

avant–garde \ˌä-ˌvän-ˈgärd, -ˌvänt-\ *n* [F, vanguard] **:** those esp. in the arts who create or apply new or experimental ideas and techniques — **avant–garde** *adj*

av•a•rice \ˈa-və-rəs\ *n* **:** excessive desire for wealth **:** GREED — **av•a•ri•cious** \ˌa-və-ˈri-shəs\ *adj*

avast \ə-ˈvast\ *vb imper* — a nautical command to stop or cease

av•a•tar \ˈa-və-ˌtär\ *n* [Skt *avatāra* descent] **:** INCARNATION

avaunt \ə-ˈvȯnt\ *adv* **:** AWAY, HENCE

avdp *abbr* avoirdupois

ave *abbr* avenue

Ave Ma•ria \ˌä-ˌvā-mə-ˈrē-ə\ *n* **:** HAIL MARY

avenge \ə-ˈvenj\ *vb* **avenged; aveng•ing :** to take vengeance for — **aveng•er** *n*

av•e•nue \ˈa-və-ˌnü, -ˌnyü\ *n* **1 :** a way or route to a place or goal **:** PATH **2 :** a broad street

aver \ə-ˈvər\ *vb* **averred; aver•ring :** ALLEGE, ASSERT; *also* **:** DECLARE

[1]av•er•age \ˈa-və-rij, ˈa-vrij\ *n* [modif. of MF *avarie* damage to ship or cargo, fr. OIt *avaria,* fr. Ar *ʿawārīyah* damaged merchandise] **1 :** ARITHMETIC MEAN **2 :** a ratio of successful tries to total tries esp. in athletics ⟨batting ~ of .303⟩

[2]average *adj* **1 :** equaling or approximating an arithmetic mean **2 :** being about midway between extremes **3 :** not out of the ordinary **:** COMMON

[3]average *vb* **av•er•aged; av•er•ag•ing 1 :** to be at or come to an average **2 :** to be, do, or get usually **3 :** to find the average of

averse \ə-ˈvərs\ *adj* **:** having an active feeling of dislike or reluctance ⟨~ to exercise⟩

aver•sion \ə-ˈvər-zhən\ *n* **1 :** a feeling of repugnance for something with a desire to avoid it **2 :** something decidedly disliked

avert \ə-ˈvərt\ *vb* **1 :** to turn aside or away ⟨~ the eyes⟩ **2 :** to ward off

avg *abbr* average

avi•an \ˈā-vē-ən\ *adj* [L *avis* bird] **:** of, relating to, or derived from birds

avi•ary \ˈā-vē-ˌer-ē\ *n, pl* **-ar•ies :** a place for keeping birds confined

avi•a•tion \ˌā-vē-ˈā-shən, ˌa-\ *n* **1 :** the operation of heavier-than-air aircraft **2 :** aircraft manufacture, development, and design

avi•a•tor \ˈā-vē-ˌā-tər, ˈa-\ *n* **:** an airplane pilot

avi•a•trix \ˌā-vē-ˈā-triks, ˌa-\ *n, pl* **-trix•es** \-trik-səz\ *or* **-tri•ces** \-trə-ˌsēz\ **:** a woman airplane pilot

av•id \ˈa-vəd\ *adj* **1 :** craving eagerly **:** GREEDY **2 :** enthusiastic in pursuit of an interest — **avid•i•ty** \ə-ˈvi-də-tē, a-\ *n* — **av•id•ly** *adv* — **av•id•ness** *n*

avi•on•ics \ˌā-vē-ˈä-niks, ˌa-\ *n pl* **:** electronics designed for use in aerospace vehicles — **avi•on•ic** \-nik\ *adj*

avo \ˈa-(ˌ)vü\ *n, pl* **avos** — see *pataca* at MONEY table

av•o•ca•do \ˌa-və-ˈkä-dō, ˌä-\ *n, pl* **-dos** *also* **-does** [modif. of Sp *aguacate,* fr. Nahuatl *āhuacatl,* avocado, testicle] **:** a pulpy green to purple nutty-flavored edible fruit of a tropical American tree; *also* **:** this tree

av•o•ca•tion \ˌa-və-ˈkā-shən\ *n* **:** HOBBY

av•o•cet \ˈa-və-ˌset\ *n* **:** any of several long-legged shorebirds with webbed feet and slender upward-curving bills

avoid \ə-ˈvȯid\ *vb* **1 :** to keep away from **:** SHUN **2 :** to prevent the occurrence of **3 :** to refrain from — **avoid•able** *adj* — **avoid•ably** *adv* — **avoid•ance** \-ᵊns\ *n*

av•oir•du•pois \ˌa-vər-də-ˈpȯiz\ *n* [ME *avoir de pois* goods sold by weight, fr. OF, lit., goods of weight] **1 :** AVOIRDUPOIS WEIGHT **2 :** WEIGHT, HEAVINESS; *esp* **:** personal weight

avoirdupois weight *n* **:** a system of weights based on a pound of 16 ounces and an ounce of 16 drams (28 grams) — see WEIGHT table

avouch \ə-ˈvau̇ch\ *vb* **1 :** to declare positively **:** AVER **2 :** to vouch for

avow \ə-ˈvau̇\ *vb* **:** to declare openly — **avow•al** \-ˈvau̇(-ə)l\ *n*

avun•cu•lar \ə-ˈvəŋ-kyə-lər\ *adj* **:** of, relating to, or resembling an uncle

await \ə-ˈwāt\ *vb* **:** to wait for **:** EXPECT

[1]awake \ə-ˈwāk\ *vb* **awoke** \-ˈwōk\ *also* **awaked** \-ˈwākt\; **awo•ken** \-ˈwō-kən\ *or* **awaked** *also* **awoke; awak•ing :** to bring back to consciousness **:** wake up

[2]awake *adj* **:** not asleep; *also* **:** ALERT

awak•en \ə-ˈwā-kən\ *vb* **awak•ened; awak•en•ing** \-ˈwā-kə-niŋ\ **:** AWAKE

[1]award \ə-ˈwȯrd\ *vb* **1 :** to give by judicial decision ⟨~ damages⟩ **2 :** to give in recognition of merit or achievement

[2]award *n* **1 :** a final decision **:** JUDGMENT **2 :** something awarded **:** PRIZE

aware \ə-ˈwar\ *adj* **:** having perception or knowledge **:** CONSCIOUS, INFORMED — **aware•ness** *n*

awash \ə-ˈwȯsh, -ˈwäsh\ *adj* **1 :** washed by waves or tide **2 :** AFLOAT **3 :** FLOODED

[1]away \ə-ˈwā\ *adv* **1 :** from this or that place ⟨go ~⟩ **2 :** out of the way **3 :** in another direction ⟨turn ~⟩ **4 :** out of existence ⟨fade ~⟩ **5 :** from one's possession ⟨give ~⟩ **6 :** without interruption ⟨chatter ~⟩ **7 :** at a distance in space or time ⟨far ~⟩ ⟨~ back in 1910⟩

[2]away *adj* **1 :** ABSENT **2 :** distant in space or time ⟨a lake 10 miles ~⟩

[1]awe \ˈȯ\ *n* **1 :** profound and reverent dread of the supernatural **2 :** respectful fear inspired by authority

[2]awe *vb* **awed; aw•ing :** to inspire with awe

aweigh \ə-ˈwā\ *adj* **:** just clear of the bottom ⟨anchors ~⟩

awe•some \ˈȯ-səm\ *adj* **1 :** expressive of awe **2 :** inspiring awe

awe•struck \-ˌstrək\ *also* **awe•strick•en** \-ˌstri-kən\ *adj* **:** filled with awe

aw•ful \ˈȯ-fəl\ *adj* **1 :** inspiring awe **2 :** extremely disagreeable **3 :** very great ⟨an ~ lot of money⟩ — **aw·ful·ly** *adv*

awhile \ə-ˈhwīl\ *adv* **:** for a while

awhirl \ə-ˈhwərl\ *adj* **:** being in a whirl

awk·ward \ˈȯ-kwərd\ *adj* **1 :** CLUMSY **2 :** UNGRACEFUL **3 :** difficult to explain **:** EMBARRASSING **4 :** difficult to deal with — **awk·ward·ly** *adv* — **awk·ward·ness** *n*

awl \ˈȯl\ *n* **:** a pointed instrument for making small holes

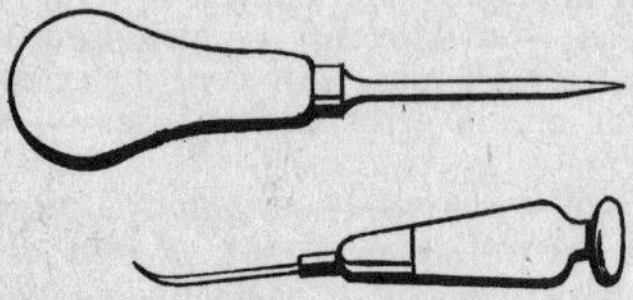

awls

aw·ning \ˈȯ-niŋ\ *n* **:** a rooflike cover (as of canvas) extended over or in front of a place as a shelter

AWOL \ˈā-ˌwȯl, ˌā-ˌdə-bəl-yü-ˌō-ˈel\ *n* **:** a person who is absent without leave — **AWOL** *adj or adv*

awry \ə-ˈrī\ *adv or adj* **1 :** ASKEW **2 :** AMISS

ax *or* **axe** \ˈaks\ *n* **:** a chopping or cutting tool with an edged head fitted parallel to a handle

ax·i·al \ˈak-sē-əl\ *adj* **1 :** of, relating to, or functioning as an axis **2 :** situated around, in the direction of, on, or along an axis — **ax·i·al·ly** *adv*

ax·i·om \ˈak-sē-əm\ *n* [L *axioma*, fr. Gk *axiōma*, lit., something worthy, fr. *axioun* to think worthy, fr. *axios* worth, worthy] **1 :** a statement generally accepted as true **:** MAXIM **2 :** a proposition regarded as a self-evident truth — **ax·i·om·at·ic** \ˌak-sē-ə-ˈma-tik\ *adj* — **ax·i·om·at·i·cal·ly** \-ti-k(ə-)lē\ *adv*

ax·is \ˈak-səs\ *n, pl* **ax·es** \-ˌsēz\ **1 :** a straight line around which a body rotates **2 :** a straight line or structure with respect to which a body or figure is symmetrical **3 :** one of the reference lines of a system of coordinates **4 :** an alliance between major powers

ax·le \ˈak-səl\ *n* **:** a shaft on which a wheel revolves

ayah \ˈī-ə\ *n* [Hindi *āyā*, fr. Pg *aia*, fr. L *avia* grandmother] **:** a nurse or maid native to India

aya·tol·lah \ˌī-ə-ˈtō-lə\ *n* [Per, lit., sign of God, fr. Ar *aya* sign, miracle + *allāh* God] **:** an Islamic religious leader — used as a title of respect

[1]**aye** *also* **ay** \ˈā\ *adv* **:** ALWAYS, EVER

[2]**aye** *also* **ay** \ˈī\ *adv* **:** YES

[3]**aye** *also* **ay** \ˈī\ *n, pl* **ayes :** an affirmative vote

AZ *abbr* Arizona

aza·lea \ə-ˈzāl-yə\ *n* **:** any of numerous rhododendrons with funnel-shaped blossoms and usu. deciduous leaves

az·i·do·thy·mi·dine \ə-ˌzi-dō-ˈthī-mə-ˌdēn\ *n* **:** AZT

az·i·muth \ˈa-zə-məth\ *n* **:** horizontal direction expressed as an angular distance from a fixed point

AZT \ˌā-(ˌ)zē-ˈtē\ *n* **:** an antiviral drug used to treat AIDS

Az·tec \ˈaz-ˌtek\ *n* **:** a member of a Nahuatl-speaking people that founded the Mexican empire and were conquered by Hernan Cortes in 1519 — **Az·tec·an** *adj*

azure \ˈa-zhər\ *n* **:** the blue of the clear sky — **azure** *adj*

B

[1]**b** \ˈbē\ *n, pl* **b's** *or* **bs** \ˈbēz\ *often cap* **1 :** the 2d letter of the English alphabet **2 :** a grade rating a student's work as good

[2]**b** *abbr, often cap* **1** bachelor **2** bass **3** bishop **4** book **5** born

B *symbol* boron

Ba *symbol* barium

BA *abbr* **1** bachelor of arts **2** batting average

bab·bitt \ˈba-bət\ *n* **:** an alloy used for lining bearings; *esp* **:** one containing tin, copper, and antimony

bab·ble \ˈba-bəl\ *vb* **bab·bled; bab·bling 1 :** to talk enthusiastically or excessively **2 :** to utter meaningless sounds — **babble** *n* — **bab·bler** \-b(ə-)lər\ *n*

babe \ˈbāb\ *n* **1 :** BABY **2** *slang* **:** GIRL, WOMAN

ba·bel \ˈbā-bəl, ˈba-\ *n, often cap* [fr. the Tower of *Babel*, Gen 11:4–9] **:** a place or scene of noise and confusion; *also* **:** a confused sound **syn** hubbub, racket, din, uproar, clamor

ba·boon \ba-ˈbün\ *n* [ME *babewin*, fr. MF *babouin*, fr. *baboue* grimace] **:** any of several large apes of Asia and Africa with doglike muzzles

ba·bush·ka \bə-ˈbüsh-kə, -ˈbu̇sh-\ *n* [Russ, grandmother, dim. of *baba* old woman] **:** a kerchief for the head

[1]**ba·by** \ˈbā-bē\ *n, pl* **babies 1 :** a very young child **:** INFANT **2 :** the youngest or smallest of a group **3 :** a childish person — **baby** *adj* — **ba·by·hood** *n* — **ba·by·ish** *adj*

[2]**baby** *vb* **ba·bied; ba·by·ing :** to tend or treat often with excessive care

baby boom *n* **:** a marked rise in birthrate — **baby boom·er** \-ˈbü-mər\ *n*

baby's breath *n* **:** any of a genus of herbs that are related to the pinks and have small delicate flowers

ba·by–sit \ˈbā-bē-ˌsit\ *vb* **-sat** \-ˌsat\; **-sit·ting :** to care for children usu. during a short absence of the parents — **ba·by–sit·ter** *n*

bac·ca·lau·re·ate \ˌba-kə-ˈlȯr-ē-ət\ *n* **1 :** the degree of bachelor conferred by colleges and universities **2 :** a sermon delivered to a graduating class

bac·ca·rat \ˌbä-kə-ˈrä, ˌba-\ *n* **:** a card game played esp. in European casinos

bac·cha·nal \ˈba-kən-ᵊl, ˌba-kə-ˈnal, ˌbä-kə-ˈnäl\ *n* **1 :** ORGY **2 :** REVELER

bac·cha·na·lia \ˌba-kə-ˈnāl-yə\ *n, pl* **bacchanalia :** a drunken orgy — **bac·cha·na·lian** \-ˈnāl-yən\ *adj or n*

bach·e·lor \ˈba-chə-lər\ *n* **1 :** a person who has received the usu. lowest degree conferred by a 4-year college **2 :** an unmarried man — **bach·e·lor·hood** *n*

bach·e·lor·ette \ˌba-chə-lə-ˈret\ *n* **:** a young unmarried woman

bachelor's button *n* **:** a European plant related to the daisies and having blue, pink, or white flower heads

ba·cil·lus \bə-ˈsi-ləs\ *n, pl* **-li** \-ˌlī\ [NL, fr. ML, small staff, dim. of L *baculus* staff] **:** any of numerous rod-shaped bacteria; *also* **:** a disease-producing bacterium — **bac·il·lary** \ˈba-sə-ˌler-ē\ *adj*

[1]**back** \ˈbak\ *n* **1 :** the rear or dorsal part of the human body; *also* **:** the corresponding part of a lower animal **2 :** the part or surface opposite the front **3 :** a player in the backfield in football — **back·less** \-ləs\ *adj*

[2]**back** *adv* **1 :** to, toward, or at the rear **2 :** AGO **3 :** so as to be restrained or retarded **4 :** to, toward, or in a former place or state **5 :** in return or reply

[3]**back** *adj* **1 :** located at or in the back; *also* **:** REMOTE **2 :** OVERDUE **3 :** moving or operating backward **4 :** not current

[4]**back** *vb* **1 :** SUPPORT, UPHOLD **2 :** to go or cause to go backward or in reverse **3 :** to furnish with a back **:** form the back of

back·ache \ˈba-ˌkāk\ *n* **:** a pain in the lower back

back–bench·er \-ˈben-chər\ *n* **:** a rank-and-file member of a British legislature

back•bite \-ˌbīt\ *vb* **-bit** \-ˌbit\; **-bit•ten** \-ˌbit-ᵊn\; **-bit•ing** \-ˌbī-tiŋ\ : to say mean or spiteful things about someone who is absent — **back•bit•er** *n*

back•board \-ˌbōrd\ *n* : a board placed at or serving as the back of something

back•bone \-ˌbōn\ *n* **1** : the bony column in the back of a vertebrate that is the chief support of the trunk and consists of a jointed series of vertebrae enclosing and protecting the spinal cord **2** : firm resolute character

back•drop \ˈbak-ˌdräp\ *n* : a painted cloth hung across the rear of a stage

back•er \ˈba-kər\ *n* : one that supports

back•field \-ˌfēld\ *n* : the football players whose positions are behind the line

[1]**back•fire** \-ˌfīr\ *n* : a loud noise caused by the improperly timed explosion of fuel in the cylinder of an internal combustion engine

[2]**backfire** *vb* **1** : to make or undergo a backfire **2** : to have a result opposite to what was intended

back•gam•mon \ˈbak-ˌga-mən\ *n* : a game played with pieces on a double board in which the moves are determined by throwing dice

back•ground \ˈbak-ˌgraùnd\ *n* **1** : the scenery behind something **2** : the setting within which something takes place; *also* : the sum of a person's experience, training, and understanding

back•hand \ˈbak-ˌhand\ *n* : a stroke (as in tennis) made with the back of the hand turned in the direction of movement; *also* : the side on which such a stroke is made — **back•hand** *vb*

backhand

back•hand•ed \ˈbak-ˈhan-dəd\ *adj* **1** : INDIRECT, DEVIOUS; *esp* : SARCASTIC **2** : using or made with a backhand

back•hoe \ˈbak-ˌhō\ *n* : an excavating machine having a bucket that is drawn toward the machine

back•ing \ˈba-kiŋ\ *n* **1** : something forming a back **2** : SUPPORT, AID; *also* : a body of supporters

back•lash \ˈbak-ˌlash\ *n* **1** : a sudden violent backward movement or reaction **2** : a strong adverse reaction

[1]**back•log** \-ˌlòg, -ˌläg\ *n* **1** : a large log at the back of a hearth fire **2** : an accumulation of tasks unperformed or materials not processed

[2]**backlog** *vb* : to accumulate in reserve

back of *prep* : BEHIND

back out *vb* : to withdraw esp. from a commitment or contest

[1]**back•pack** \ˈbak-ˌpak\ *n* : a camping pack supported by an aluminum frame and carried on the back

[2]**backpack** *vb* : to hike with a backpack — **back•pack•er** *n*

back•ped•al \ˈbak-ˌped-ᵊl\ *vb* : RETREAT

back•rest \-ˌrest\ *n* : a rest for the back

back•side \-ˌsīd\ *n* : BUTTOCKS

back•slap \-ˌslap\ *vb* : to display excessive cordiality — **back•slap•per** *n*

back•slide \-ˌslīd\ *vb* **-slid** \-ˌslid\; **-slid** *or* **-slid•den** \-ˌslid-ᵊn\; **-slid•ing** \-ˌslī-diŋ\ : to lapse morally or in religious practice — **back•slid•er** *n*

back•spin \-ˌspin\ *n* : a backward rotary motion of a ball

[1]**back•stage** \ˈbak-ˌstāj\ *adj* **1** : relating to or occurring in the area behind a stage **2** : of or relating to the private lives of theater people **3** : of or relating to the inner working or operation

[2]**back•stage** \ˈbak-ˈstāj\ *adv* **1** : in or to a backstage area **2** : SECRETLY

back•stairs \-ˌstarz\ *adj* : SECRET, FURTIVE; *also* : SORDID, SCANDALOUS

[1]**back•stop** \-ˌstäp\ *n* : something serving as a stop behind something else; *esp* : a screen or fence to keep a ball from leaving the field of play

[2]**backstop** *vb* **1** : SUPPORT **2** : to serve as a backstop to

back•stretch \ˈbak-ˈstrech\ *n* : the side opposite the homestretch on a racecourse

back•stroke \-ˌstrōk\ *n* : a swimming stroke executed on the back

back talk *n* : impudent, insolent, or argumentative replies

back•track \ˈbak-ˌtrak\ *vb* **1** : to retrace one's course **2** : to reverse a position or stand

back•up \-ˌəp\ *n* : one that serves as a substitute or alternative

[1]**back•ward** \ˈbak-wərd\ *or* **back•wards** \-wərdz\ *adv* **1** : toward the back **2** : with the back foremost **3** : in a reverse or contrary direction or way **4** : toward the past; *also* : toward a worse state

[2]**backward** *adj* **1** : directed, turned, or done backward **2** : DIFFIDENT, SHY **3** : retarded in development — **back•ward•ly** *adv* — **back•ward•ness** *n*

back•wash \ˈbak-ˌwȯsh, -ˌwäsh\ *n* : a backward flow or movement (as of water or air) produced by a propelling force (as the motion of oars)

back•wa•ter \-ˌwȯ-tər, -ˌwä-\ *n* **1** : water held or turned back in its course **2** : an isolated or backward place or condition

back•woods \-ˈwu̇dz\ *n pl* **1** : wooded or partly cleared areas far from cities **2** : a remote or isolated place

ba•con \ˈbā-kən\ *n* : salted and smoked meat from the sides or back of a pig

bacteria *pl of* BACTERIUM

bac•te•ri•cid•al \bak-ˌtir-ə-ˈsīd-ᵊl\ *adj* : destroying bacteria — **bac•te•ri•cide** \-ˈtir-ə-ˌsīd\ *n*

bac•te•ri•ol•o•gy \bak-ˌtir-ē-ˈä-lə-jē\ *n* **1** : a science dealing with bacteria **2** : bacterial life and phenomena — **bac•te•ri•o•log•ic** \-ə-ˈlä-jik\ *or* **bac•te•ri•o•log•i•cal** \-ə-ˈlä-ji-kəl\ *adj* — **bac•te•ri•ol•o•gist** \-ˈä-lə-jist\ *n*

bac•te•rio•phage \bak-ˈtir-ē-ə-ˌfāj\ *n* : any of various viruses that attack specific bacteria

bac•te•ri•um \bak-ˈtir-ē-əm\ *n, pl* **-ria** \-ē-ə\ [NL, fr. Gk *baktērion* staff] : any of a group of single-celled microorganisms including some that are disease producers and others that are valued esp. for their chemical effects (as fermentation) — **bac•te•ri•al** \-ē-əl\ *adj*

bad \ˈbad\ *adj* **worse** \ˈwərs\; **worst** \ˈwərst\ **1** : below standard : POOR; *also* : UNFAVORABLE ⟨a ~ report⟩ **2** : SPOILED, DECAYED **3** : WICKED; *also* : not well-behaved : NAUGHTY **4** : DISAGREEABLE ⟨a ~ taste⟩; *also* : HARMFUL **5** : DEFECTIVE, FAULTY ⟨~ wiring⟩; *also* : not valid ⟨a ~ check⟩ **6** : UNWELL, ILL **7** : SORRY, REGRETFUL **syn** evil, wrong, immoral, iniquitous — **bad•ly** *adv* — **bad•ness** *n*

bade *past and past part of* BID

badge \ˈbaj\ *n* : a device or token usu. worn as a sign of status

[1]**bad•ger** \ˈba-jər\ *n* : any of several sturdy burrowing mammals with long claws on their forefeet

☞ For illustration, see next page.

[2]**badger** *vb* : to harass or annoy persistently

ba•di•nage \ˌbad-ᵊn-ˈäzh\ *n* [F] : playful talk back and forth : BANTER

bad•land \ˈbad-ˌland\ *n* : a region marked by intricate

badger

erosional sculpturing and scanty vegetation — usu. used in pl.

bad·min·ton \ˈbad-ˌmint-ᵊn\ *n* : a court game played with light rackets and a shuttlecock volleyed over a net

bad–mouth \ˈbad-ˌmau̇th\ *vb* : to criticize severely

Bae·de·ker \ˈbā-di-kər, ˈbe-\ *n* : GUIDEBOOK

[1]**baf·fle** \ˈba-fəl\ *vb* **baf·fled; baf·fling** \-fə-liŋ\ : FRUSTRATE, THWART, FOIL; *also* : PERPLEX — **baf·fle·ment** *n*

[2]**baffle** *n* : a device (as a wall or screen) to deflect, check, or regulate flow (as of liquid or sound) — **baffled** \ˈba-fəld\ *adj*

[1]**bag** \ˈbag\ *n* : a flexible usu. closable container (as for storing or carrying)

[2]**bag** *vb* **bagged; bag·ging 1** : DISTEND, BULGE **2** : to put in a bag **3** : to get possession of; *esp* : to take in hunting **syn** trap, snare, catch, capture, collar

ba·gasse \bə-ˈgas\ *n* [F] : plant residue (as of sugarcane) left after a product (as juice) has been extracted

bag·a·telle \ˌba-gə-ˈtel\ *n* [F] : TRIFLE

ba·gel \ˈbā-gəl\ *n* [Yiddish *beygl*] : a hard glazed doughnut-shaped roll

bag·gage \ˈba-gij\ *n* **1** : the traveling bags and personal belongings of a traveler : LUGGAGE **2** : things that get in the way

bag·gy \ˈba-gē\ *adj* **bag·gi·er; -est** : puffed out or hanging like a bag — **bag·gi·ly** \-gə-lē\ *adv* — **bag·gi·ness** \-gē-nəs\ *n*

bag·man \ˈbag-mən\ *n* : a person who collects or distributes illicitly gained money on behalf of another

ba·gnio \ˈban-yō\ *n, pl* **bagnios** [It *bagno,* lit., public bath] : BROTHEL

bag of waters : a double-walled fluid-filled sac that encloses and protects the fetus in the womb and that breaks releasing its fluid during the process of birth

bag·pipe \ˈbag-ˌpīp\ *n* : a musical wind instrument consisting of a bag, a tube with valves, and sounding pipes — often used in pl.

ba·guette \ba-ˈget\ *n* [F, lit., rod] **1** : a gem having the shape of a narrow rectangle; *also* : the shape itself **2** : a long thin loaf of French bread

Ba·ha·mi·an \bə-ˈhā-mē-ən, -ˈhä-\ *n* : a native or inhabitant of the Bahama Islands

baht \ˈbät\ *n, pl* **baht** *also* **bahts** — see MONEY table

[1]**bail** \ˈbāl\ *n* : a container for ladling water out of a boat

[2]**bail** *vb* : to dip and throw out water from a boat — **bail·er** *n*

[3]**bail** *n* : security given to guarantee a prisoner's appearance when legally required; *also* : one giving such security or the release secured

[4]**bail** *vb* : to release under bail; *also* : to procure the release of by giving bail — **bail·able** \ˈbā-lə-bəl\ *adj*

[5]**bail** *n* : the arched handle (as of a pail or kettle)

bai·liff \ˈbā-ləf\ *n* **1** : an aide of a British sheriff who serves writs and makes arrests; *also* : a minor officer of a U.S. court **2** : an estate or farm manager esp. in Britain : STEWARD

bai·li·wick \ˈbā-li-ˌwik\ *n* : one's special province or domain **syn** territory, field, sphere

bail·out \ˈbā-ˌlau̇t\ *n* : a rescue from financial distress

bairn \ˈbarn\ *n, chiefly Scot* : CHILD

[1]**bait** \ˈbāt\ *vb* **1** : to persecute by continued attacks **2** : to harass with dogs usu. for sport ⟨~ a bear⟩ **3** : to furnish (as a hook) with bait **4** : ALLURE, ENTICE **5** : to give food and drink to (as an animal) **syn** badger, heckle, hound

[2]**bait** *n* **1** : a lure for catching animals (as fish) **2** : LURE, TEMPTATION **syn** snare, trap, decoy, come-on, enticement

bai·za \ˈbī-(ˌ)zä\ *n, pl* **baiza** *or* **baizas** — see *rial* at MONEY table

baize \ˈbāz\ *n* : a coarse feltlike fabric

[1]**bake** \ˈbāk\ *vb* **baked; bak·ing 1** : to cook or become cooked in dry heat esp. in an oven **2** : to dry and harden by heat ⟨~ bricks⟩ — **bak·er** *n*

[2]**bake** *n* : a social gathering featuring baked food

baker's dozen *n* : THIRTEEN

bak·ery \ˈbā-k(ə-)rē\ *n, pl* **-er·ies** : a place for baking or selling baked goods

bake·shop \ˈbāk-ˌshäp\ *n* : BAKERY

baking powder *n* : a powder that consists of a carbonate, an acid, and a starch and that makes the dough rise in baking cakes and biscuits

baking soda *n* : SODIUM BICARBONATE

bak·sheesh \ˈbak-ˌshēsh\ *n* : payment (as a tip or bribe) to expedite service

bal *abbr* balance

bal·a·lai·ka \ˌba-lə-ˈlī-kə\ *n* : a triangular 3-stringed instrument of Russian origin played by plucking or strumming

[1]**bal·ance** \ˈba-ləns\ *n* [ME, fr. OF, fr. LL *bilanc-, bilanx* having two scalepans, fr. L *bi* two + *lanc-, lanx* plate] **1** : a weighing device : SCALE **2** : a weight, force, or influence counteracting the effect of another **3** : an oscillating wheel used to regulate a timepiece **4** : a state of equilibrium **5** : REMAINDER, REST; *esp* : an amount in excess esp. on the credit side of an account — **bal·anced** \-lənst\ *adj*

[2]**balance** *vb* **bal·anced; bal·anc·ing 1** : to compute the balance of an account **2** : to arrange so that one set of elements equals another; *also* : to equal or equalize in weight, number, or proportions **3** : WEIGH **4** : to bring or come to a state or position of balance; *also* : to bring into harmony or proportion

bal·boa \bal-ˈbō-ə\ *n* — see MONEY table

bal·brig·gan \bal-ˈbri-gən\ *n* : a knitted cotton fabric used esp. for underwear

bal·co·ny \ˈbal-kə-nē\ *n, pl* **-nies 1** : a platform projecting from the side of a building and enclosed by a railing **2** : a gallery inside a building

bald \ˈbȯld\ *adj* **1** : lacking a natural or usual covering (as of hair) **2** : UNADORNED, PLAIN **syn** bare, barren, naked, nude — **bald·ly** *adv* — **bald·ness** *n*

bal·da·chin \ˈbȯl-də-kən, ˈbal-\ *or* **bal·da·chi·no** \ˌbal-də-ˈkē-nō\ *n, pl* **-chins** *or* **-chinos** : a canopylike structure over an altar

bald cypress *n* : either of two large swamp trees of the southern U.S. with hard red wood

bald eagle *n* : an eagle of No. America that when mature has white head and neck feathers and a white tail

bal·der·dash \ˈbȯl-dər-ˌdash\ *n* : NONSENSE

bald·ing \ˈbȯl-diŋ\ *adj* : getting bald

bal·dric \ˈbȯl-drik\ *n* : a belt worn over the shoulder to carry a sword or bugle

[1]**bale** \ˈbāl\ *n* : a large or closely packed bundle

[2]**bale** *vb* **baled; bal·ing** : to pack in a bale — **bal·er** *n*

ba·leen \bə-ˈlēn\ *n* : a horny substance attached in plates to the upper jaw of some large whales (**baleen whales**)

bale·ful \ˈbāl-fəl\ *adj* : DEADLY, HARMFUL; *also* : OMINOUS **syn** sinister, malefic, maleficent, malign

[1]**balk** \ˈbȯk\ *n* **1** : HINDRANCE, CHECK, SETBACK **2** : an illegal motion of the pitcher in baseball while in position

[2]**balk** *vb* **1** : BLOCK, THWART **2** : to stop short and refuse

to go on **3 :** to commit a balk in sports **syn** frustrate, baffle, foil, thwart — **balky** \ˈbȯ-kē\ *adj*

[1]**ball** \ˈbȯl\ *n* **1 :** a rounded body or mass (as at the base of the thumb or for use as a missile or in a game) **2 :** a game played with a ball **3 :** a pitched baseball that misses the strike zone and is not swung at by the batter **4 :** a hit or thrown ball in various games ⟨foul ~⟩ — **on the ball :** COMPETENT, KNOWLEDGEABLE, ALERT

[2]**ball** *vb* **:** to form into a ball

[3]**ball** *n* **:** a large formal dance

bal·lad \ˈba-ləd\ *n* **1 :** a narrative poem of strongly marked rhythm suitable for singing **2 :** a simple song **:** AIR **3 :** a slow romantic song

bal·lad·eer \ˌba-lə-ˈdir\ *n* **:** a singer of ballads

[1]**bal·last** \ˈba-ləst\ *n* **1 :** heavy material used to stabilize a ship or control a balloon's ascent **2 :** crushed stone laid in a railroad bed or used in making concrete

[2]**ballast** *vb* **:** to provide with ballast **syn** balance, stabilize, steady

ball bearing *n* **:** a bearing in which the revolving part turns upon steel balls that roll easily in a groove; *also* **:** one of the balls in such a bearing

ball·car·ri·er \ˈbȯl-ˌkar-ē-ər\ *n* **:** the football player carrying the ball in an offensive play

bal·le·ri·na \ˌba-lə-ˈrē-nə\ *n* **:** a female ballet dancer

bal·let \ˈba-ˌlā, ba-ˈlā\ *n* **1 :** dancing in which fixed poses and steps are combined with light flowing movements often to convey a story; *also* **:** a theatrical art form using ballet dancing **2 :** a company of ballet dancers

bal·let·o·mane \ba-ˈle-tə-ˌmān\ *n* **:** a devotee of ballet

bal·lis·tic missile \bə-ˈlis-tik-\ *n* **:** a missile that is guided during ascent and that falls freely during descent

bal·lis·tics \-tiks\ *n sing or pl* **1 :** the science of the motion of projectiles (as bullets) in flight **2 :** the flight characteristics of a projectile — **ballistic** *adj*

ball of fire : an unusually energetic person

[1]**bal·loon** \bə-ˈlün\ *n* **1 :** a bag filled with gas or heated air so as to rise and float in the atmosphere **2 :** a toy consisting of an inflatable bag — **bal·loon·ist** *n*

[2]**balloon** *vb* **1 :** to swell or puff out **2 :** to travel in a balloon **3 :** to increase rapidly

[1]**bal·lot** \ˈba-lət\ *n* [It *ballotta* small ball used in secret voting, fr. It dial., dim. of *balla* ball] **1 :** a piece of paper used to cast a vote **2 :** the action or a system of voting; *also* **:** the right to vote

[2]**ballot** *vb* **:** to decide by ballot **:** VOTE

[1]**ball·park** \ˈbȯl-ˌpärk\ *n* **:** a park in which ball games are played

[2]**ballpark** *adj* **:** approximately correct ⟨~ estimate⟩

ball·point \ˈbȯl-ˌpȯint\ *n* **:** a pen whose writing point is a small rotating metal ball that inks itself from an inner container

ball·room \ˈbȯl-ˌrüm, -ˌrům\ *n* **:** a large room for dances

bal·ly·hoo \ˈba-lē-ˌhü\ *n, pl* **-hoos :** extravagant statements and claims made for publicity — **ballyhoo** *vb*

balm \ˈbäm, ˈbälm\ *n* **1 :** a fragrant healing or soothing lotion or ointment **2 :** any of several spicy fragrant herbs of the mint family **3 :** something that comforts or soothes

balmy \ˈbä-mē, ˈbäl-\ *adj* **balm·i·er; -est 1 :** gently soothing **:** MILD **2 :** FOOLISH, ABSURD **syn** soft, bland, mild, gentle — **balm·i·ness** *n*

ba·lo·ney \bə-ˈlō-nē\ *n* **:** NONSENSE

bal·sa \ˈbȯl-sə\ *n* **:** the extremely light strong wood of a tropical American tree; *also* **:** the tree

bal·sam \ˈbȯl-səm\ *n* **1 :** a fragrant aromatic and usu. resinous substance oozing from various plants; *also* **:** a preparation containing or smelling like balsam **2 :** a balsam-yielding tree (as balsam fir) **3 :** a common garden ornamental plant — **bal·sam·ic** \bȯl-ˈsa-mik\ *adj*

balsam fir *n* **:** a resinous American evergreen tree that is widely used for pulpwood and as a Christmas tree

Bal·ti·more oriole \ˈbȯl-tə-ˌmōr-\ *n* **:** a common American oriole in which the male is brightly colored with orange, black, and white

bal·us·ter \ˈba-lə-stər\ *n* [F *balustre,* fr. It *balaustro,* fr. *balaustra* wild pomegranate flower, fr. L *balaustium;* fr. its shape] **:** an upright support for a rail (as of a staircase)

bal·us·trade \ˈba-lə-ˌstrād\ *n* **:** a row of balusters topped by a rail

bam·boo \bam-ˈbü\ *n, pl* **bamboos :** any of various woody mostly tall tropical grasses including some with strong hollow stems used for building, furniture, or utensils

bamboo curtain *n, often cap B&C* **:** a political, military, and ideological barrier in the Orient

bam·boo·zle \bam-ˈbü-zəl\ *vb* **-boo·zled; -boo·zling :** TRICK, HOODWINK

[1]**ban** \ˈban\ *vb* **banned; ban·ning :** PROHIBIT, FORBID

[2]**ban** *n* **1 :** CURSE **2 :** a legal or formal prohibiting

[3]**ban** \ˈbän\ *n, pl* **ba·ni** \ˈbä-nē\ — see *leu* at MONEY table

ba·nal \bə-ˈnäl, -ˈnal; ˈbān-ᵊl\ *adj* [F] **:** COMMONPLACE, TRITE — **ba·nal·i·ty** \bā-ˈna-lə-tē\ *n*

ba·nana \bə-ˈna-nə\ *n* **:** a treelike tropical plant bearing thick clusters of yellow or reddish finger-shaped fruit; *also* **:** this fruit

[1]**band** \ˈband\ *n* **1 :** something that binds, ties, or goes around **2 :** a strip or stripe that can be distinguished (as by color or texture) from nearby matter **3 :** a range of wavelengths (as in radio)

[2]**band** *vb* **1 :** to tie up, finish, or enclose with a band **2 :** to gather together or unite esp. for some common end — **band·er** *n*

[3]**band** *n* **:** a group of persons, animals, or things; *esp* **:** a group of musicians organized for playing together

[1]**ban·dage** \ˈban-dij\ *n* **:** a strip of material used esp. in dressing wounds

[2]**bandage** *vb* **ban·daged; ban·dag·ing :** to dress or cover with a bandage

ban·dan·na *or* **ban·dana** \ban-ˈda-nə\ *n* **:** a large colored figured handkerchief

B and B *abbr* bed-and-breakfast

band·box \ˈband-ˌbäks\ *n* **:** a usu. cylindrical box for carrying clothing

band·ed \ˈban-dəd\ *adj* **:** having or marked with bands

ban·de·role *or* **ban·de·rol** \ˈban-də-ˌrōl\ *n* **:** a long narrow forked flag or streamer

ban·dit \ˈban-dət\ *n* [It *bandito,* fr. *bandire* to banish] **1** *pl also* **ban·dit·ti** \ban-ˈdi-tē\ **:** an outlaw who lives by plunder; *esp* **:** a member of a band of marauders **2 :** ROBBER — **ban·dit·ry** \ˈban-də-trē\ *n*

ban·do·lier *or* **ban·do·leer** \ˌban-də-ˈlir\ *n* **:** a belt slung over the shoulder esp. to carry ammunition

band saw *n* **:** a saw in the form of an endless steel belt running over pulleys

band·stand \ˈband-ˌstand\ *n* **:** a usu. roofed platform on which a band or orchestra performs outdoors

b and w *abbr* black and white

band·wag·on \ˈband-ˌwa-gən\ *n* **1 :** a wagon carrying musicians in a parade **2 :** a movement that attracts growing support

[1]**ban·dy** \ˈban-dē\ *vb* **ban·died; ban·dy·ing 1 :** to exchange (as blows or quips) esp. in rapid succession **2 :** to use in a glib or offhand way

[2]**bandy** *adj* **:** curved outward ⟨~ legs⟩

bane \ˈbān\ *n* **1 :** POISON **2 :** WOE, HARM; *also* **:** a source of this — **bane·ful** *adj*

[1]**bang** \ˈbaŋ\ *vb* **1 :** BUMP ⟨fell and ~*ed* his knee⟩ **2 :** to strike, thrust, or move usu. with a loud noise

[2]**bang** *n* **1 :** a resounding blow **2 :** a sudden loud noise

[3]**bang** *adv* **:** DIRECTLY, RIGHT

[4]**bang** *n* **:** a fringe of hair cut short (as across the forehead) — usu. used in pl.

[5]**bang** *vb* **:** to cut a bang in

Ban·gla·deshi \ˌbäŋ-glə-ˈde-shē\ *n* **:** a native or inhabitant of Bangladesh — **Bangladeshi** *adj*

ban•gle \ˈbaŋ-gəl\ *n* : BRACELET; *also* : a loose-hanging ornament
bang–up \ˈbaŋ-ˌəp\ *adj* : FIRST-RATE, EXCELLENT ⟨a ~ job⟩
bani *pl of* ³BAN
ban•ish \ˈba-nish\ *vb* **1** : to require by authority to leave a country **2** : to drive out : EXPEL **syn** exile, ostracize, deport, relegate — **ban•ish•ment** *n*
ban•is•ter \ˈba-nə-stər\ *n* **1** : BALUSTER **2** : a handrail with its supporting posts **3** : HANDRAIL
ban•jo \ˈban-ˌjō\ *n, pl* **banjos** *also* **banjoes** : a musical instrument with a long neck, a drumlike body, and usu. five strings — **ban•jo•ist** \-ist\ *n*
¹**bank** \ˈbaŋk\ *n* **1** : a piled-up mass (as of cloud or earth) **2** : an undersea elevation **3** : rising ground bordering a lake, river, or sea **4** : the sideways slope of a surface along a curve or of a vehicle as it rounds a curve
²**bank** *vb* **1** : to form a bank about **2** : to cover (as a fire) with fuel to keep inactive **3** : to build (a curve) with the roadbed or track inclined laterally upward from the inside edge **4** : to pile or heap in a bank; *also* : to arrange in a tier **5** : to incline (an airplane) laterally
³**bank** *n* [ME, fr. MF or It; MF *banque,* fr. It *banca,* lit., bench] **1** : an establishment concerned esp. with the custody, loan, exchange, or issue of money, the extension of credit, and the transmission of funds **2** : a stock of or a place for holding something in reserve ⟨a blood ~⟩
⁴**bank** *vb* **1** : to conduct the business of a bank **2** : to deposit money or have an account in a bank — **bank•er** *n* — **bank•ing** *n*
⁵**bank** *n* : a group of objects arranged close together (as in a row or tier) ⟨a ~ of file drawers⟩
bank•book \ˈbaŋk-ˌbu̇k\ *n* : the depositor's book in which a bank records deposits and withdrawals
bank•card \-ˌkärd\ *n* : a credit card issued by a bank
bank•note \-ˌnōt\ *n* : a promissory note issued by a bank and circulating as money
bank•roll \-ˌrōl\ *n* : supply of money : FUNDS
¹**bank•rupt** \ˈbaŋ-(ˌ)krəpt\ *n* : an insolvent person; *esp* : one whose property is turned over by court action to a trustee to be handled for the benefit of his creditors — **bankrupt** *vb*
²**bankrupt** *adj* **1** : reduced to financial ruin; *esp* : legally declared a bankrupt **2** : wholly lacking in or deprived of some essential ⟨morally ~⟩ — **bank•rupt•cy** \ˈbaŋ-(ˌ)krəpt-sē\ *n*
¹**ban•ner** \ˈba-nər\ *n* **1** : a piece of cloth attached to a staff and used by a leader as his standard **2** : FLAG
²**banner** *adj* : distinguished from all others esp. in excellence ⟨a ~ year⟩
ban•nock \ˈba-nək\ *n* : a flat oatmeal or barley cake usu. cooked on a griddle
banns \ˈbanz\ *n pl* : public announcement esp. in church of a proposed marriage
ban•quet \ˈbaŋ-kwət\ *n* [MF, fr. It *banchetto,* fr. dim. of *banca* bench, bank] : a ceremonial dinner — **banquet** *vb*
ban•quette \baŋ-ˈket\ *n* : a long upholstered bench esp. along a wall
ban•shee \ˈban-shē\ *n* [Ir *bean sídhe* & ScGael *bean sìth,* lit., woman of fairyland] : a female spirit in Gaelic folklore whose wailing warns a family that one of them will soon die
ban•tam \ˈban-təm\ *n* **1** : any of numerous small domestic fowls that are often miniatures of standard breeds **2** : a small but pugnacious person
¹**ban•ter** \ˈban-tər\ *vb* : to speak to in a witty and teasing manner
²**banter** *n* : good-natured witty joking
Ban•tu \ˈban-ˌtü\ *n, pl* **Bantu** *or* **Bantus** **1** : a member of a group of African peoples of central and southern Africa **2** : a group of African languages spoken by the Bantu
Ban•tu•stan \ˌban-tu̇-ˈstan, ˌbän-tu̇-ˈstän\ *n* : an all-black enclave in the Republic of So. Africa with a limited degree of self-government
ban•yan \ˈban-yən\ *n* [earlier *banyan* Hindu merchant, fr. Hindi *baniyā;* fr. a merchant's pagoda erected under a tree of the species in Iran] : a large East Indian tree whose aerial roots grow downward to the ground and form new trunks

banyan

ban•zai \bän-ˈzī\ *n* : a Japanese cheer or cry of triumph
bao•bab \ˈbau̇-ˌbab, ˈbā-ə-\ *n* : an Old World tropical tree with short swollen trunk and sour edible gourd-like fruits
bap•tism \ˈbap-ˌti-zəm\ *n* **1** : a Christian sacrament signifying spiritual rebirth and symbolized by the ritual use of water **2** : an act of baptizing — **bap•tis•mal** \bap-ˈtiz-məl\ *adj*
baptismal name *n* : GIVEN NAME
Bap•tist \ˈbap-tist\ *n* : a member of any of several Protestant denominations emphasizing baptism by immersion of believers only
bap•tis•tery *or* **bap•tis•try** \ˈbap-tə-strē\ *n, pl* **-teries** *or* **-tries** : a place esp. in a church used for baptism
bap•tize \bap-ˈtīz, ˈbap-ˌtīz\ *vb* **bap•tized; bap•tiz•ing** [ME, fr. OF *baptiser,* fr. L *baptizare,* fr. Gk *baptizein* to dip, baptize, fr. *baptein* to dip] **1** : to administer baptism to; *also* : CHRISTEN **2** : to purify esp. by an ordeal
¹**bar** \ˈbär\ *n* **1** : a long narrow piece of material (as wood or metal) used esp. for a lever, fastening, or support **2** : BARRIER, OBSTACLE **3** : the railing in a law court at which prisoners are stationed; *also* : the legal profession or the whole body of lawyers **4** : a stripe, band, or line much longer than wide **5** : a counter at which food or esp. drink is served; *also* : BARROOM **6** : a vertical line across the musical staff
²**bar** *vb* **barred; bar•ring** **1** : to fasten, confine, or obstruct with or as if with a bar or bars **2** : to mark with bars : STRIPE **3** : to shut or keep out : EXCLUDE **4** : FORBID, PREVENT
³**bar** *prep* : EXCEPT
⁴**bar** *abbr* barometer; barometric
Bar *abbr* Baruch
barb \ˈbärb\ *n* **1** : a sharp projection extending backward (as from the point of an arrow) **2** : a biting critical remark — **barbed** \ˈbärbd\ *adj*
bar•bar•ian \bär-ˈber-ē-ən\ *adj* **1** : of, relating to, or being a land, culture, or people alien to and usu. believed to be inferior to another's **2** : lacking refinement, learning, or artistic or literary culture — **barbarian** *n*
bar•bar•ic \bär-ˈbar-ik\ *adj* **1** : BARBARIAN **2** : marked by a lack of restraint : WILD **3** : PRIMITIVE, UNSOPHISTICATED
bar•ba•rism \ˈbär-bə-ˌri-zəm\ *n* **1** : the social condition of barbarians; *also* : the use or display of barbarian or barbarous acts, attitudes, or ideas **2** : a word or expression that offends standards of correctness or purity
bar•ba•rous \ˈbär-bə-rəs\ *adj* **1** : lacking culture or refinement **2** : using linguistic barbarisms **3** : merciless-

ly harsh or cruel — **bar•bar•i•ty** \bär-ˈbar-ə-tē\ *n* — **bar•ba•rous•ly** *adv*

[1]**bar•be•cue** \ˈbär-bi-ˌkyü\ *n* : a social gathering at which barbecued food is served

[2]**barbecue** *vb* **-cued; -cu•ing 1** : to cook over hot coals or on a revolving spit **2** : to cook in a highly seasoned vinegar sauce

bar•bell \ˈbär-ˌbel\ *n* : a bar with adjustable weights attached to each end used for exercise and in weight-lifting competition

bar•ber \ˈbär-bər\ *n* [ME, fr. MF *barbeor,* fr. *barbe* beard, fr. L *barba*] : one whose business is cutting and dressing hair and shaving and trimming beards

bar•ber•ry \ˈbär-ˌber-ē\ *n* : any of a genus of spiny shrubs bearing yellow flowers and oblong red berries

bar•bi•tu•rate \bär-ˈbi-chə-rət\ *n* : any of various compounds (as a salt or ester) formed from an organic acid (**bar•bi•tu•ric acid** \ˌbär-bə-ˈtu̇r-ik-, -ˈtyu̇r-\); *esp* : one used as a sedative or hypnotic

bar•ca•role *or* **bar•ca•rolle** \ˈbär-kə-ˌrōl\ *n* : a Venetian boat song characterized by a beat suggesting a rowing rhythm; *also* : a piece of music imitating this

bar chart *n* : BAR GRAPH

bar code *n* : a set of printed and variously spaced bars and sometimes numerals that is designed to be scanned to identify the object it labels

bard \ˈbärd\ *n* : POET

[1]**bare** \ˈbar\ *adj* **bar•er; bar•est 1** : NAKED **2** : UNCONCEALED, EXPOSED **3** : EMPTY **4** : leaving nothing to spare : MERE **5** : PLAIN, UNADORNED **syn** nude, bald — **bare•ness** *n*

[2]**bare** *vb* **bared; bar•ing** : to make or lay bare : UNCOVER

bare•back \-ˌbak\ *or* **bare•backed** \-ˈbakt\ *adv or adj* : without a saddle

bare•faced \-ˈfāst\ *adj* **1** : having the face uncovered; *esp* : BEARDLESS **2** : not concealed : OPEN — **bare•faced•ly** \-ˈfā-səd-lē, -ˈfāst-lē\ *adv*

bare•foot \-ˌfu̇t\ *or* **bare•foot•ed** \-ˈfu̇-təd\ *adv or adj* : with bare feet

bare–hand•ed \-ˈhan-dəd\ *adv or adj* **1** : without gloves **2** : without tools or weapons

bare•head•ed \-ˈhe-dəd\ *adv or adj* : without a hat

bare•ly \ˈbar-lē\ *adv* **1** : PLAINLY, MEAGERLY **2** : by a narrow margin : only just ⟨~ enough money⟩

bar•fly \ˈbär-ˌflī\ *n* : a drinker who frequents bars

[1]**bar•gain** \ˈbär-gən\ *n* **1** : AGREEMENT **2** : an advantageous purchase **3** : a transaction, situation, or event regarded in the light of its results

[2]**bargain** *vb* **1** : to negotiate over the terms of an agreement; *also* : to come to terms **2** : BARTER

bar•gain–base•ment \ˈbär-gən-ˈbās-mənt\ *adj* : markedly inexpensive

[1]**barge** \ˈbärj\ *n* **1** : a broad flat-bottomed boat usu. moved by towing **2** : a motorboat supplied to a flagship (as for an admiral) **3** : a ceremonial boat elegantly furnished — **barge•man** \-mən\ *n*

[2]**barge** *vb* **barged; barg•ing 1** : to carry by barge **2** : to move or thrust oneself clumsily or rudely

bar graph *n* : a graphic technique for comparing amounts by rectangles whose lengths are proportional to the amounts they represent

bari•tone \ˈbar-ə-ˌtōn\ *n* [F *baryton* or It *baritono,* fr. Gk *barytonos* deep sounding, fr. *barys* heavy + *tonos* tone] : a male voice between bass and tenor; *also* : a man with such a voice

bar•i•um \ˈbar-ē-əm\ *n* : a silver-white metallic chemical element that occurs only in combination — see ELEMENT table

[1]**bark** \ˈbärk\ *vb* **1** : to make the short loud cry of a dog **2** : to speak or utter in a curt loud tone : SNAP

[2]**bark** *n* : the sound made by a barking dog

[3]**bark** *n* : the tough corky outer covering of a woody stem or root

[4]**bark** *vb* **1** : to strip the bark from **2** : to rub the skin from : ABRADE

[5]**bark** *n* : a ship of three or more masts with the aft mast fore-and-aft rigged and the others square-rigged

bar•keep \ˈbär-ˌkēp\ *also* **bar•keep•er** \-ˌkē-pər\ *n* : BARTENDER

bark•er \ˈbär-kər\ *n* : a person who stands at the entrance esp. to a show and tries to attract customers to it

bar•ley \ˈbär-lē\ *n* : a cereal grass with seeds used as food and in making malt liquors; *also* : its seed

bar mitz•vah \bär-ˈmits-və\ *n, often cap B&M* [Heb *bar miṣwāh,* lit., son of the (divine) law] **1** : a Jewish boy who at about 13 years of age assumes religious responsibilities **2** : the ceremony recognizing a boy as a bar mitzvah

barn \ˈbärn\ *n* [ME *bern,* fr. OE *bereærn,* fr. *bere* barley + *ærn* house, store] : a building used esp. for storing hay and grain and for housing livestock or farm equipment

bar•na•cle \ˈbär-ni-kəl\ *n* : any of numerous small marine crustaceans free-swimming when young but permanently fixed (as to rocks, whales, or ships) when adult

barn•storm \ˈbärn-ˌstȯrm\ *vb* : to travel through the country making brief stops to entertain (as with shows or flying stunts) or to campaign for political office

barn•yard \-ˌyärd\ *n* : a usu. fenced area adjoining a barn

baro•graph \ˈbar-ə-ˌgraf\ *n* : a recording barometer

ba•rom•e•ter \bə-ˈräm-ə-tər\ *n* : an instrument for measuring atmospheric pressure — **baro•met•ric** \ˌbar-ə-ˈme-trik\ *adj*

bar•on \ˈbar-ən\ *n* : a member of the lowest grade of the British peerage — **ba•ro•ni•al** \bə-ˈrō-nē-əl\ *adj* — **bar•ony** \ˈbar-ə-nē\ *n*

bar•on•age \ˈbar-ə-nij\ *n* : PEERAGE

bar•on•ess \ˈbar-ə-nəs\ *n* **1** : the wife or widow of a baron **2** : a woman holding a baronial title in her own right

bar•on•et \ˈbar-ə-nət\ *n* : a man holding a rank of honor below a baron but above a knight — **bar•on•et•cy** \-sē\ *n*

ba•roque \bə-ˈrōk, -ˈräk\ *adj* : marked by the use of complex forms, bold ornamentation, and the juxtapositioning of contrasting elements

ba•rouche \bə-ˈrüsh\ *n* [G *Barutsche,* fr. It *biroccio,* ultim. fr. LL *birotus* two-wheeled, fr. L *bi* two + *rota* wheel] : a 4-wheeled carriage with a high driver's seat in front and a folding top

bar•racks \ˈbar-əks\ *n sing or pl* : a building or group of buildings for lodging soldiers

bar•ra•cu•da \ˌbar-ə-ˈkü-də\ *n, pl* **-da** *or* **-das** : any of several large predaceous sea fishes including some used for food

bar•rage \bə-ˈräzh, -ˈräj\ *n* : a heavy concentration of fire (as of artillery)

barred \ˈbärd\ *adj* : STRIPED

[1]**bar•rel** \ˈbar-əl\ *n* **1** : a round bulging cask with flat ends of equal diameter **2** : the amount contained in a barrel **3** : a cylindrical or tubular part ⟨gun ~⟩ — **bar•reled** \-əld\ *adj*

[2]**barrel** *vb* **-reled** *or* **-relled; -rel•ing** *or* **-rel•ling 1** : to pack in a barrel **2** : to travel at high speed

bar•rel•head \-ˌhed\ *n* : the flat end of a barrel — **on the barrelhead** : asking for or granting no credit ⟨paid cash *on the barrelhead*⟩

barrel roll *n* : an airplane maneuver in which a complete revolution about the longitudinal axis is made

[1]**bar•ren** \ˈbar-ən\ *adj* **1** : STERILE, UNFRUITFUL **2** : unproductive of results ⟨a ~ scheme⟩ **3** : lacking interest or charm **4** : DULL, STUPID — **bar•ren•ness** \-nəs\ *n*

[2]**barren** *n* : a tract of barren land

bar•rette \bä-ˈret, bə-\ *n* : a clasp or bar for holding the hair in place

[1]**bar•ri•cade** \ˈbar-ə-ˌkād, ˌbar-ə-ˈkād\ *vb* **-cad•ed;**

-cad•ing : to block, obstruct, or fortify with a barricade

[2]barricade *n* [F, fr. MF, fr. *barriquer* to barricade, fr. *barrique* barrel] **1 :** a hastily thrown-up obstruction or fortification **2 :** BARRIER, OBSTACLE

bar•ri•er \ˈbar-ē-ər\ *n* : something that separates, demarcates, or serves as a barricade ⟨racial ∼*s*⟩

barrier island *n* : a long broad sandy island lying parallel to a shore

barrier reef *n* : a coral reef roughly parallel to a shore and separated from it by a lagoon

bar•ring \ˈbär-iŋ\ *prep* : excluding by exception : EXCEPTING

bar•rio \ˈbär-ē-ˌō, ˈbar-\ *n, pl* **-ri•os 1 :** a district of a city or town in a Spanish-speaking country **2 :** a Spanish-speaking quarter in a U.S. city

bar•ris•ter \ˈbar-ə-stər\ *n* : a British counselor admitted to plead in the higher courts

bar•room \ˈbär-ˌrüm, -ˌrům\ *n* : a room or establishment whose main feature is a bar for the sale of liquor

[1]bar•row \ˈbar-ō\ *n* : a large burial mound of earth and stones

[2]barrow *n* **1 :** WHEELBARROW **2 :** a cart with a boxlike body and two shafts for pushing it

Bart *abbr* baronet

bar•tend•er \ˈbär-ˌten-dər\ *n* : one that serves liquor at a bar

bar•ter \ˈbär-tər\ *vb* : to trade by exchange of goods — **barter** *n* — **bar•ter•er** *n*

Ba•ruch \ˈbär-ˌük, bə-ˈrük\ *n* — see BIBLE table

bas•al \ˈbā-səl\ *adj* **1 :** situated at or forming the base **2 :** BASIC

basal metabolism *n* : the turnover of energy in a fasting and resting organism using energy solely to maintain vital cellular activity, respiration, and circulation as measured by the rate at which heat is given off

ba•salt \bə-ˈsȯlt, ˈbā-ˌsȯlt\ *n* : a dark fine-grained igneous rock — **ba•sal•tic** \bə-ˈsȯl-tik\ *adj*

[1]base \ˈbās\ *n, pl* **bas•es** \ˈbā-səz\ **1 :** BOTTOM, FOUNDATION **2 :** a side or face on which a geometrical figure stands; *also* : the length of a base **3 :** a main ingredient or fundamental part **4 :** the point of beginning an act or operation **5 :** a place on which a force depends for supplies **6 :** a number (as 5 in 5^7) that is raised to a power; *esp* : a number that when raised to a power equal to the logarithm of a number yields the number itself ⟨the logarithm of 100 to ∼ 10 is 2 since $10^2 = 100$⟩ **7 :** the number of units in a given digit's place of a number system that is required to give the numeral 1 in the next higher place ⟨the decimal system uses a ∼ of 10⟩; *also* : such a system using an indicated base ⟨convert from ∼ 10 to ∼ 2⟩ **8 :** any of the four stations at the corners of a baseball diamond **9 :** a chemical compound (as lime or ammonia) that reacts with an acid to form a salt, has a bitter taste, and turns litmus blue **syn** basis, ground, groundwork, footing, foundation — **base•man** \ˈbās-mən\ *n*

[2]base *vb* **based; bas•ing 1 :** to form or serve as a base for **2 :** ESTABLISH

[3]base *adj* **1 :** of inferior quality : DEBASED, ALLOYED **2 :** CONTEMPTIBLE, IGNOBLE **3 :** MENIAL, DEGRADING **4 :** of little value **syn** low, vile, despicable, wretched — **base•ly** *adv* — **base•ness** *n*

base•ball \ˈbās-ˌbȯl\ *n* : a game played with a bat and ball by two teams on a field with four bases arranged in a diamond; *also* : the ball used in this game

base•board \-ˌbōrd\ *n* : a line of boards or molding covering the joint of a wall and the adjoining floor

base•born \-ˈbȯrn\ *adj* **1 :** MEAN, IGNOBLE **2 :** of humble birth **3 :** of illegitimate birth

base exchange *n* : a post exchange at a naval or air force base

base hit *n* : a hit in baseball that enables the batter to reach base safely with no error made and no base runner forced out

base•less \-ləs\ *adj* : having no base or basis : GROUNDLESS

base•line \ˈbās-ˌlīn\ *n* **1 :** a line serving as a basis esp. to calculate or locate something **2 :** the area within which a baseball player must keep when running between bases

base•ment \-mənt\ *n* **1 :** the part of a building that is wholly or partly below ground level **2 :** the lowest or fundamental part of something

base on balls : an advance to first base given to a baseball player who receives four balls

base runner *n* : a baseball player who is on base or is attempting to reach a base

[1]bash \ˈbash\ *vb* **1 :** to strike violently : HIT **2 :** to smash by a blow **3 :** to attack physically or verbally

[2]bash *n* **1 :** a heavy blow **2 :** a festive social gathering : PARTY

bash•ful \ˈbash-fəl\ *adj* : inclined to shrink from public attention — **bash•ful•ness** *n*

ba•sic \ˈbā-sik\ *adj* **1 :** of, relating to, or forming the base or essence : FUNDAMENTAL **2 :** of, relating to, or having the character of a chemical base **syn** underlying, basal, primary — **ba•sic•i•ty** \bā-ˈsi-sə-tē\ *n*

BA•SIC \ˈbā-sik\ *n* [*B*eginner's *A*ll-purpose *S*ymbolic *I*nstruction *C*ode] : a simplified language for programming a computer

ba•si•cal•ly \ˈbā-si-k(ə-)lē\ *adv* **1 :** at a basic level **2 :** for the most part **3 :** in a basic manner

ba•sil \ˈbā-zəl, ˈba-, -səl\ *n* : any of several mints with fragrant leaves used in cooking

ba•sil•i•ca \bə-ˈsi-li-kə, -ˈzi-\ *n* [L, fr. Gk *basilikē*, fr. fem. of *basilikos* royal, fr. *basileus* king] **1 :** an early Christian church building consisting of nave and aisles with clerestory and apse **2 :** a Roman Catholic church given ceremonial privileges

bas•i•lisk \ˈba-sə-ˌlisk, ˈba-zə-\ *n* [ME, fr. L *basiliscus*, fr. Gk *basiliskos*, fr. dim. of *basileus* king] : a legendary reptile with fatal breath and glance

ba•sin \ˈbās-ᵊn\ *n* **1 :** an open usu. circular vessel with sloping sides for holding liquid (as water) **2 :** a hollow or enclosed place containing water; *also* : the region drained by a river

ba•sis \ˈbā-səs\ *n, pl* **ba•ses** \-ˌsēz\ **1 :** FOUNDATION, BASE **2 :** a fundamental principle

bask \ˈbask\ *vb* **1 :** to expose oneself to comfortable heat **2 :** to enjoy something warmly comforting ⟨∼*ing* in his friends' admiration⟩

bas•ket \ˈbas-kət\ *n* : a container made of woven material (as twigs or grasses); *also* : any of various lightweight usu. wood containers — **bas•ket•ful** *n*

bas•ket•ball \-ˌbȯl\ *n* : a game played on a court by two teams who try to throw an inflated ball through a raised goal; *also* : the ball used in this game

basket case *n* **1 :** a person who has all four limbs amputated **2 :** one that is totally incapacitated or inoperative

basket weave *n* : a textile weave resembling the checkered pattern of a plaited basket

bas mitz•vah \bäs-ˈmits-və\ *n, often cap B&M* [Heb *bath miṣwāh*, lit., daughter of the (divine) law] **1 :** a Jewish girl who at about 13 years of age assumes religious responsibilities **2 :** the ceremony recognizing a girl as a bas mitzvah

Basque \ˈbask\ *n* **1 :** a member of a people inhabiting a region bordering on the Bay of Biscay in northern Spain and southwestern France **2 :** the language of the Basque people — **Basque** *adj*

bas–re•lief \ˌbä-ri-ˈlēf\ *n* [F] : a sculpture in relief with the design raised very slightly from the background

[1]bass \ˈbas\ *n, pl* **bass** *or* **bass•es :** any of numerous sport and food bony fishes (as a striped bass)

[2]bass \ˈbās\ *adj* : of low pitch

[3]bass \ˈbās\ *n* **1 :** a deep sound or tone **2 :** the lower half of the musical pitch range **3 :** the lowest part in a 4-part chorus; *also* : a singer having this voice or part

bas•set hound \ˈba-sət-\ *n* : any of an old breed of short=

legged hunting dogs of French origin having long ears and crooked front legs

bas•si•net \ˌba-sə-ˈnet\ *n* : a baby's bed that resembles a basket and often has a hood over one end

bas•so \ˈba-sō, ˈbä-\ *n, pl* **bassos** *or* **bas•si** \ˈbä-ˌsē\ [It] : a bass singer

bas•soon \bə-ˈsün\ *n* : a musical wind instrument lower in pitch than the oboe

bass•wood \ˈbas-ˌwu̇d\ *n* : any of several New World lindens or their wood

bast \ˈbast\ *n* : BAST FIBER

[1]**bas•tard** \ˈbas-tərd\ *n* **1** : an illegitimate child **2** : an offensive or disagreeable person

[2]**bastard** *adj* **1** : ILLEGITIMATE **2** : of an inferior or nontypical kind, size, or form; *also* : SPURIOUS — **bas•tardy** *n*

bas•tard•ise *Brit var of* BASTARDIZE

bas•tard•ize \ˈbas-tər-ˌdīz\ *vb* **-ized; -iz•ing** : to reduce from a higher to a lower state : DEBASE

[1]**baste** \ˈbāst\ *vb* **bast•ed; bast•ing** : to sew with long stitches so as to keep temporarily in place

[2]**baste** *vb* **bast•ed; bast•ing** : to moisten (as meat) at intervals with liquid while cooking

bast fiber *n* : a strong woody plant fiber obtained chiefly from phloem and used esp. in making ropes

bas•ti•na•do \ˌbas-tə-ˈnā-dō, -ˈnä-\ *or* **bas•ti•nade** \ˌbas-tə-ˈnād, -ˈnäd\ *n, pl* **-na•does** *or* **-nades 1** : a blow or beating esp. with a stick **2** : a punishment consisting of beating the soles of the feet

bas•tion \ˈbas-chən\ *n* : a projecting part of a fortification; *also* : a fortified position

[1]**bat** \ˈbat\ *n* **1** : a stout stick : CLUB **2** : a sharp blow **3** : an implement (as of wood) used to hit a ball (as in baseball) **4** : a turn at batting — usu. used with *at*

[2]**bat** *vb* **bat•ted; bat•ting** : to hit with or as if with a bat

[3]**bat** *n* : any of an order of night-flying mammals with forelimbs modified to form wings

[4]**bat** *vb* **bat•ted; bat•ting** : WINK, BLINK

batch \ˈbach\ *n* **1** : a quantity (as of bread) baked at one time **2** : a quantity of material for use at one time or produced at one operation

bate \ˈbāt\ *vb* **bat•ed; bat•ing** : MODERATE, REDUCE

bath \ˈbath, ˈbȧth\ *n, pl* **baths** \ˈbat͟hz, ˈbaths, ˈbȧt͟hz, ˈbȧths\ **1** : a washing of the body **2** : water for washing the body **3** : a liquid in which objects are immersed so that it can act on them **4** : BATHROOM **5** : a financial loss ⟨took a ~ in the market⟩

bathe \ˈbāt͟h\ *vb* **bathed; bath•ing 1** : to wash in liquid and esp. water; *also* : to apply water or a medicated liquid to ⟨*bathed* her eyes⟩ **2** : to take a bath; *also* : to take a swim **3** : to wash along, over, or against so as to wet **4** : to suffuse with or as if with light — **bath•er** *n*

bath•house \ˈbath-ˌhau̇s, ˈbȧth-\ *n* **1** : a building equipped for bathing **2** : a building containing dressing rooms for bathers

bathing suit *n* : SWIMSUIT

ba•thos \ˈbā-ˌthäs\ *n* [Gk, lit., depth] **1** : the sudden appearance of the commonplace in otherwise elevated matter or style **2** : insincere or overdone pathos — **ba•thet•ic** \bə-ˈthe-tik\ *adj*

bath•robe \ˈbath-ˌrōb, ˈbȧth-\ *n* : a loose often absorbent robe worn before and after bathing or as a dressing gown

bath•room \-ˌrüm, -ˌru̇m\ *n* : a room containing a bathtub or shower and usu. a sink and toilet

bath•tub \-ˌtəb\ *n* : a usu. fixed tub for bathing

ba•tik \bə-ˈtēk, ˈba-tik\ *n* [Javanese *batik*] **1** : an Indonesian method of hand-printing textiles by coating with wax the parts not to be dyed; *also* : a design so executed **2** : a fabric printed by batik

ba•tiste \bə-ˈtēst\ *n* : a fine sheer fabric of plain weave

bat•man \ˈbat-mən\ *n* : an orderly of a British military officer

ba•ton \bə-ˈtän\ *n* : STAFF, ROD; *esp* : a stick with which the leader directs an orchestra or band

bats•man \ˈbats-mən\ *n* : a batter esp. in cricket

bat•tal•ion \bə-ˈtal-yən\ *n* **1** : a large body of troops organized to act together : ARMY **2** : a military unit composed of a headquarters and two or more units (as companies)

[1]**bat•ten** \ˈbat-ᵊn\ *vb* **1** : to grow or make fat **2** : THRIVE

[2]**batten** *n* : a strip of wood used esp. to seal or strengthen a joint

[3]**batten** *vb* : to fasten with battens

[1]**bat•ter** \ˈba-tər\ *vb* : to beat or damage with repeated blows

[2]**batter** *n* : a soft mixture (as for cake) basically of flour and liquid

[3]**batter** *n* : one that bats; *esp* : the player whose turn it is to bat

battering ram *n* **1** : an ancient military machine for battering down walls **2** : a heavy metal bar with handles used to batter down doors

bat•tery \ˈba-tə-rē\ *n, pl* **-ter•ies 1** : BEATING; *esp* : unlawful beating or use of force on a person **2** : a grouping of artillery pieces for tactical purposes; *also* : the guns of a warship **3** : a group of electric cells for furnishing electric current; *also* : a single electric cell ⟨a flashlight ~⟩ **4** : a number of similar items grouped or used as a unit ⟨a ~ of tests⟩ **5** : the pitcher and catcher of a baseball team

bat•ting \ˈba-tiŋ\ *n* : layers or sheets of cotton or wool (as for lining quilts)

[1]**bat•tle** \ˈbat-ᵊl\ *n* [ME *batel*, fr. OF *bataille* battle, fortifying tower, battalion, fr. LL *battalia* combat, alter. of *battualia* fencing exercises, fr. L *battuere* to beat] : a general military engagement; *also* : an extended contest or controversy

[2]**battle** *vb* **bat•tled; bat•tling** : to engage in battle : CONTEND, FIGHT

bat•tle–ax \ˈbat-ᵊl-ˌaks\ *n* **1** : a long-handled ax formerly used as a weapon **2** : a quarrelsome domineering woman

battle fatigue *n* : COMBAT FATIGUE

bat•tle•field \ˈbat-ᵊl-ˌfēld\ *n* : a place where a battle is fought

bat•tle•ment \-mənt\ *n* : a decorative or defensive parapet on top of a wall

bat•tle•ship \-ˌship\ *n* : a warship of the most heavily armed and armored class

bat•tle•wag•on \-ˌwa-gən\ *n* : BATTLESHIP

bat•ty \ˈba-tē\ *adj* **bat•ti•er; -est** : CRAZY, FOOLISH

bau•ble \ˈbȯ-bəl\ *n* : TRINKET

baud \ˈbȯd, *Brit* ˈbōd\ *n, pl* **baud** *also* **bauds** : a unit of data transmission speed

baulk *chiefly Brit var of* BALK

baux•ite \ˈbȯk-ˌsīt\ *n* : a clayey mixture that is the chief ore of aluminum

bawd \ˈbȯd\ *n* **1** : MADAM 2 **2** : PROSTITUTE

bawdy \ˈbȯ-dē\ *adj* **bawd•i•er; -est** : OBSCENE, LEWD — **bawd•i•ly** \ˈbȯd-ᵊl-ē\ *adv* — **bawd•i•ness** \-dē-nəs\ *n*

[1]**bawl** \ˈbȯl\ *vb* : to cry or cry out loudly; *also* : to scold harshly

[2]**bawl** *n* : a long loud cry : BELLOW

[1]**bay** \ˈbā\ *adj* : reddish brown

[2]**bay** *n* **1** : a bay-colored animal **2** : a reddish brown color

[3]**bay** *n* **1** : a section or compartment of a building or vehicle **2** : a compartment projecting outward from the wall of a building and containing a window (**bay window**)

[4]**bay** *vb* : to bark with deep long tones

[5]**bay** *n* **1** : the position of one unable to escape and forced to face danger **2** : a baying of dogs

[6]**bay** *n* : an inlet of a body of water (as the sea) usu. smaller than a gulf

[7]**bay** *n* : the European laurel; *also* : a shrub or tree resembling this

bay•ber•ry \ˈbā-ˌber-ē\ *n* : a hardy deciduous shrub of coastal eastern No. America bearing small hard berries coated with a white wax used for candles; *also* : its fruit

bay leaf *n* : the dried leaf of the European laurel used in cooking

1**bay•o•net** \ˈbā-ə-nət, ˌbā-ə-ˈnet\ *n* : a daggerlike weapon made to fit on the muzzle end of a rifle

2**bayonet** *vb* **-net•ed** *also* **-net•ted; -net•ing** *also* **-net•ting** : to use or stab with a bayonet

bay•ou \ˈbī-yü, -ō\ *n* [Louisiana French, fr. Choctaw *bayuk*] : a marshy or sluggish body of water

bay rum *n* : a fragrant liquid used esp. as a cologne or after-shave lotion

ba•zaar \bə-ˈzär\ *n* **1** : a group of shops : MARKETPLACE **2** : a fair for the sale of articles usu. for charity

ba•zoo•ka \bə-ˈzü-kə\ *n* [*bazooka* (a crude musical instrument made of pipes and a funnel)] : a weapon consisting of a tube and launching an explosive rocket able to pierce armor

1**BB** \ˈbē-(ˌ)bē\ *n* : a small round shot pellet

2**BB** *abbr* base on balls

BBB *abbr* Better Business Bureau

BBC *abbr* British Broadcasting Corporation

bbl *abbr* barrel; barrels

BC *abbr* **1** before Christ — often printed in small capitals and often punctuated **2** British Columbia

B cell *n* [*b*one-marrow-derived *cell*] : any of the lymphocytes that secrete antibodies when mature

B complex *n* : VITAMIN B COMPLEX

bd *abbr* **1** board **2** bound

bdl *or* **bdle** *abbr* bundle

bdrm *abbr* bedroom

be \ˈbē\ *vb, past 1st & 3d sing* **was** \ˈwəz, ˈwäz\; *2d sing* **were** \ˈwər\; *pl* **were;** *past subjunctive* **were;** *past part* **been** \ˈbin\; *pres part* **be•ing** \ˈbē-iŋ\; *pres 1st sing* **am** \əm, ˈam\; *2d sing* **are** \ər, ˈär\; *3d sing* **is** \ˈiz, əz\; *pl* **are;** *pres subjunctive* **be** **1** : to equal in meaning or symbolically ⟨God *is* love⟩; *also* : to have a specified qualification or relationship ⟨leaves *are* green⟩ ⟨this fish *is* a trout⟩ **2** : to have objective existence ⟨I think, therefore I *am*⟩; *also* : to have or occupy a particular place ⟨here *is* your pen⟩ **3** : to take place : OCCUR ⟨the meeting *is* tonight⟩ **4** — used with the past participle of transitive verbs as a passive voice auxiliary ⟨the door *was* opened⟩ **5** — used as the auxiliary of the present participle in expressing continuous action ⟨he *is* sleeping⟩ **6** — used as an auxiliary with the past participle of some intransitive verbs to form archaic perfect tenses **7** — used as an auxiliary with *to* and the infinitive to express futurity, prearrangement, or obligation ⟨you *are* to come when called⟩

Be *symbol* beryllium

1**beach** \ˈbēch\ *n* : a sandy or gravelly part of the shore of an ocean or lake

2**beach** *vb* : to run or drive ashore

beach buggy *n* : DUNE BUGGY

beach•comb•er \ˈbēch-ˌkō-mər\ *n* : a person who searches along a shore for something of use or value

beach•head \ˈbēch-ˌhed\ *n* : a small area on an enemy-held shore occupied in the initial stages of an invasion

bea•con \ˈbē-kən\ *n* **1** : a signal fire **2** : a guiding or warning signal (as a lighthouse) **3** : a radio transmitter emitting signals for guidance of aircraft

1**bead** \ˈbēd\ *n* [ME *bede* prayer, prayer bead, fr. OE *bed, gebed* prayer] **1** *pl* : a series of prayers and meditations made with a rosary **2** : a small piece of material pierced for threading on a line (as in a rosary) **3** : a small globular body **4** : a narrow projecting rim or band — **bead•ing** *n* — **beady** *adj*

2**bead** *vb* : to form into a bead

bea•dle \ˈbēd-ᵊl\ *n* : a usu. English parish officer whose duties include keeping order in church

bea•gle \ˈbē-gəl\ *n* : a small short-legged smooth-coated hound

beak \ˈbēk\ *n* : the bill of a bird and esp. of a bird of

beagle

prey; *also* : a pointed projecting part — **beaked** \ˈbēkt\ *adj*

bea•ker \ˈbē-kər\ *n* **1** : a large widemouthed drinking cup **2** : a widemouthed thin-walled laboratory vessel

1**beam** \ˈbēm\ *n* **1** : a large long piece of timber or metal **2** : the bar of a balance from which the scales hang **3** : the breadth of a ship at its widest part **4** : a ray or shaft of light **5** : a collection of nearly parallel rays (as X rays) or particles (as electrons) **6** : a constant radio signal transmitted for the guidance of pilots; *also* : the course indicated by this signal

2**beam** *vb* **1** : to send out light **2** : to aim (a broadcast) by directional antennas **3** : to smile with joy

1**bean** \ˈbēn\ *n* : the edible seed borne in pods by some leguminous plants; *also* : a plant or a pod bearing these

2**bean** *vb* : to strike on the head with an object

bean•bag \ˈbēn-ˌbag\ *n* : a cloth bag partially filled typically with dried beans and used as a toy

bean•ball \ˈbēn-ˌbȯl\ *n* : a pitch thrown at a batter's head

bean curd *n* : TOFU

bean•ie \ˈbē-nē\ *n* : a small round tight-fitting skullcap

beano \ˈbē-nō\ *n, pl* **beanos** : BINGO

1**bear** \ˈbar\ *n, pl* **bears** **1** *or pl* **bear** : any of a family of large heavy mammals with shaggy hair and small tails **2** : a gruff or sullen person **3** : one who sells (as securities) in expectation of a price decline — **bear•ish** *adj*

2**bear** *vb* **bore** \ˈbōr\; **borne** \ˈbōrn\ *also* **born** \ˈbȯrn\; **bear•ing** **1** : CARRY **2** : to be equipped with **3** : to give as testimony ⟨~ witness to the facts of the case⟩ **4** : to give birth to; *also* : PRODUCE, YIELD ⟨a tree that ~*s* regularly⟩ **5** : ENDURE, SUSTAIN ⟨~ pain⟩ ⟨*bore* the weight on piles⟩; *also* : to exert pressure or influence **6** : to go in an indicated direction ⟨~ to the right⟩ — **bear•able** *adj* — **bear•er** *n*

1**beard** \ˈbird\ *n* **1** : the hair that grows on the face of a man **2** : a growth of bristly hairs (as on a goat's chin) — **beard•ed** \ˈbir-dəd\ *adj* — **beard•less** *adj*

2**beard** *vb* : to confront boldly

bear•ing \ˈbar-iŋ\ *n* **1** : manner of carrying oneself : COMPORTMENT **2** : a supporting object, purpose, or point **3** : a machine part in which another part (as an axle or pin) turns **4** : an emblem in a coat of arms **5** : the position or direction of one point with respect to another or to the compass; *also* : a determination of position **6** *pl* : comprehension of one's situation **7** : connection with or influence on something; *also* : SIGNIFICANCE

bear•skin \ˈbar-ˌskin\ *n* : an article made of the skin of a bear

beast \ˈbēst\ *n* **1** : ANIMAL 1; *esp* : a 4-footed mammal **2** : a contemptible person

1**beast•ly** \ˈbēst-lē\ *adj* **beast•li•er; -est** **1** : BESTIAL **2** : ABOMINABLE, DISAGREEABLE — **beast•li•ness** \-nəs\ *n*

2**beastly** *adv* : VERY

1**beat** \ˈbēt\ *vb* **beat; beat•en** \ˈbēt-ᵊn\ *or* **beat; beat•ing** **1** : to strike repeatedly **2** : TREAD **3** : to affect or alter by beating ⟨~ metal into sheets⟩ **4** : to sound (as an alarm) on a drum **5** : OVERCOME; *also* : SURPASS **6** : to act or arrive before ⟨~ his brother home⟩ **7** : THROB — **beat•er** *n*

²beat *n* **1** : a single stroke or blow esp. of a series; *also* : PULSATION **2** : a rhythmic stress in poetry or music or the rhythmic effect of these **3** : a regularly traversed course

³beat *adj* **1** : EXHAUSTED **2** : of or relating to beatniks

⁴beat *n* : BEATNIK

be•atif•ic \ˌbē-ə-ˈti-fik\ *adj* : giving or indicative of great joy or bliss

be•at•i•fy \bē-ˈa-tə-ˌfī\ *vb* **-fied; -fy•ing 1** : to make supremely happy **2** : to declare to have attained the blessedness of heaven and authorize the title "Blessed" for — **be•at•i•fi•ca•tion** \-ˌa-tə-fə-ˈkā-shən\ *n*

be•at•i•tude \bē-ˈa-tə-ˌtüd, -ˌtyüd\ *n* **1** : a state of utmost bliss **2** : any of the declarations made in the Sermon on the Mount (Mt 5:3–12) beginning "Blessed are"

beat•nik \ˈbēt-nik\ *n* : a person who rejects the mores of established society and indulges in exotic philosophizing and self-expression

beau \ˈbō\ *n, pl* **beaux** \ˈbōz\ *or* **beaus** [F, fr. *beau* beautiful, fr. L *bellus* pretty] **1** : a man of fashion : DANDY **2** : SUITOR, LOVER

beau geste \bō-ˈzhest\ *n, pl* **beaux gestes** *or* **beau gestes** \bō-ˈzhest\ : a graceful or magnanimous gesture

beau ide•al \ˌbō-ī-ˈdē(-ə)l\ *n, pl* **beau ideals** : the perfect type or model

Beau•jo•lais \ˌbō-zhō-ˈlā\ *n* : a French red table wine

beau monde \bō-ˈmänd, -ˈmōⁿd\ *n, pl* **beau mondes** \-ˈmänz, -ˈmändz\ *or* **beaux mondes** \bō-ˈmōⁿd\ : the world of high society and fashion

beau•te•ous \ˈbyü-tē-əs\ *adj* : BEAUTIFUL — **beau•te•ous•ly** *adv*

beau•ti•cian \byü-ˈti-shən\ *n* : COSMETOLOGIST

beau•ti•ful \ˈbyü-ti-fəl\ *adj* : characterized by beauty : LOVELY **syn** pretty, fair, comely — **beau•ti•ful•ly** \-f(ə-)lē\ *adv*

beautiful people *n pl, often cap B&P* : wealthy or famous people whose lifestyle is usu. expensive and well-publicized

beau•ti•fy \ˈbyü-tə-ˌfī\ *vb* **-fied; -fy•ing** : to make more beautiful — **beau•ti•fi•ca•tion** \ˌbyü-tə-fə-ˈkā-shən\ *n* — **beau•ti•fi•er** *n*

beau•ty \ˈbyü-tē\ *n, pl* **beauties** : qualities that give pleasure to the senses or exalt the mind : LOVELINESS; *also* : something having such qualities

beauty shop *n* : an establishment where hairdressing, facials, and manicures are done

beaux arts \bō-ˈzär\ *n pl* [F] : FINE ARTS

bea•ver \ˈbē-vər\ *n, pl* **beavers** : a large fur-bearing herbivorous rodent that builds dams and underwater houses of mud and sticks; *also* : its fur

be•calm \bi-ˈkäm, -ˈkälm\ *vb* : to keep (as a ship) motionless by lack of wind

be•cause \bi-ˈkȯz, -ˈkəz\ *conj* : for the reason that

because of *prep* : by reason of

beck \ˈbek\ *n* : a beckoning gesture; *also* : SUMMONS

beck•on \ˈbe-kən\ *vb* : to summon or signal esp. by a nod or gesture; *also* : ATTRACT

be•cloud \bi-ˈklau̇d\ *vb* : OBSCURE

be•come \bi-ˈkəm\ *vb* **-came** \-ˈkām\; **-come; -com•ing 1** : to come to be ⟨~ tired⟩ **2** : to suit or be suitable to ⟨her dress ~s her⟩

be•com•ing *adj* : SUITABLE, FIT; *also* : ATTRACTIVE — **be•com•ing•ly** *adv*

¹bed \ˈbed\ *n* **1** : an article of furniture to sleep on **2** : a plot of ground prepared for plants **3** : FOUNDATION, BOTTOM **4** : LAYER, STRATUM

²bed *vb* **bed•ded; bed•ding 1** : to put or go to bed **2** : to fix in a foundation : EMBED **3** : to plant in beds **4** : to lay or lie flat or in layers

bed–and–breakfast *n* : an establishment offering lodging and breakfast

be•daub \bi-ˈdȯb\ *vb* : SMEAR

be•daz•zle \bi-ˈda-zəl\ *vb* : to confuse by or as if by a strong light; *also* : FASCINATE — **be•daz•zle•ment** *n*

bed•bug \ˈbed-ˌbəg\ *n* : a wingless bloodsucking bug infesting houses and esp. beds

bed•clothes \ˈbed-ˌklōthz\ *n pl* : BEDDING 1

bed•ding \ˈbe-diŋ\ *n* **1** : materials for making up a bed **2** : FOUNDATION

be•deck \bi-ˈdek\ *vb* : ADORN

be•dev•il \bi-ˈde-vəl\ *vb* **1** : HARASS, TORMENT **2** : CONFUSE, MUDDLE

be•dew \bi-ˈdü, -ˈdyü\ *vb* : to wet with or as if with dew

bed•fast \ˈbed-ˌfast\ *adj* : BEDRIDDEN

bed•fel•low \-ˌfe-lō\ *n* **1** : one sharing the bed of another **2** : a close associate : ALLY

be•di•zen \bi-ˈdīz-ᵊn, -ˈdiz-\ *vb* : to dress or adorn with showy or vulgar finery

bed•lam \ˈbed-ləm\ *n* [*Bedlam,* popular name for the Hospital of St. Mary of Bethlehem, London, an insane asylum, fr. ME *Bedlem* Bethlehem] **1** : an insane asylum **2** : a scene of uproar and confusion

bed•ou•in *or* **bed•u•in** \ˈbe-də-wən\ *n, pl* **bedouin** *or* **bedouins** *or* **beduin** *or* **beduins** *often cap* [ME *Bedoyne,* fr. MF *bedoïn,* fr. Ar *badawī* desert dweller] : a nomadic Arab of the Arabian, Syrian, or No. African deserts

bed•pan \ˈbed-ˌpan\ *n* : a shallow vessel used by a bedridden person for urination or defecation

bed•post \-ˌpōst\ *n* : the post of a bed

be•drag•gled \bi-ˈdra-gəld\ *adj* : soiled and disordered as if by being drenched

bed•rid•den \ˈbed-ˌrid-ᵊn\ *adj* : kept in bed by illness or weakness

¹bed•rock \-ˈräk\ *n* : the solid rock underlying surface materials (as soil)

²bedrock *adj* : solidly fundamental, basic, or reliable ⟨traditional ~ values⟩

bed•roll \ˈbed-ˌrōl\ *n* : bedding rolled up for carrying

bed•room \-ˌrüm, -ˌru̇m\ *n* : a room containing a bed and used esp. for sleeping

bed•side \-ˌsīd\ *n* : the place beside a bed esp. of a sick or dying person

bed•sore \-ˌsōr\ *n* : an ulceration of tissue deprived of adequate blood supply by prolonged pressure

bed•spread \-ˌspred\ *n* : a usu. ornamental cloth cover for a bed

bed•stead \-ˌsted\ *n* : the framework of a bed

bed•time \-ˌtīm\ *n* : time for going to bed

bed–wet•ting \-ˌwe-tiŋ\ *n* : involuntary discharge of urine esp. in bed during sleep — **bed–wet•ter** *n*

¹bee \ˈbē\ *n* : HONEYBEE; *also* : any of various related insects

²bee *n* : a gathering of people for a specific purpose ⟨quilting ~⟩

beech \ˈbēch\ *n, pl* **beech•es** *or* **beech** : any of a genus of deciduous hardwood trees with smooth gray bark and small sweet triangular nuts; *also* : the wood of a beech — **beech•en** \ˈbē-chən\ *adj*

beech•nut \ˈbēch-ˌnət\ *n* : the nut of a beech

¹beef \ˈbēf\ *n, pl* **beefs** \ˈbēfs\ *or* **beeves** \ˈbēvz\ **1** : the flesh of a steer, cow, or bull; *also* : the dressed carcass of a beef animal **2** : a steer, cow, or bull esp. when fattened for food **3** : MUSCLE, BRAWN **4** *pl beefs* : COMPLAINT

²beef *vb* **1** : STRENGTHEN — usu. used with *up* **2** : COMPLAIN

beef•eat•er \ˈbē-ˌfē-tər\ *n* : a yeoman of the guard of an English monarch

beef•steak \-ˌstāk\ *n* : a slice of beef suitable for broiling or frying

beefy \ˈbē-fē\ *adj* **beef•i•er; -est** : THICKSET, BRAWNY

bee•hive \ˈbē-ˌhīv\ *n* : HIVE 1, 3

bee•keep•er \-ˌkē-pər\ *n* : a person who raises bees — **bee•keep•ing** *n*

bee•line \-ˌlīn\ *n* : a straight direct course

been *past part of* BE
beep·er \ˈbē-pər\ *n* : a small radio receiver that beeps when signaled to alert the person carrying it
beer \ˈbir\ *n* : an alcoholic beverage brewed from malt and hops — **beery** *adj*
bees·wax \ˈbēz-ˌwaks\ *n* : WAX 1
beet \ˈbēt\ *n* : a garden plant with edible leaves and a thick sweet root used as a vegetable, as a source of sugar, or as forage; *also* : its root
[1]**bee·tle** \ˈbēt-ᵊl\ *n* : any of an order of insects having four wings of which the stiff outer pair covers the membranous inner pair when not in flight
[2]**beetle** *vb* **bee·tled; bee·tling** : to jut out : PROJECT
be·fall \bi-ˈfȯl\ *vb* **-fell** \-ˈfel\; **-fall·en** \-ˈfȯ-lən\ : to happen to : OCCUR
be·fit \bi-ˈfit\ *vb* : to be suitable to
be·fog \bi-ˈfȯg, -ˈfäg\ *vb* : OBSCURE; *also* : CONFUSE
[1]**be·fore** \bi-ˈfōr\ *adv or adj* **1** : in front **2** : EARLIER
[2]**before** *prep* **1** : in front of ⟨stood ~ him⟩ **2** : earlier than ⟨got there ~ me⟩ **3** : in a more important category than ⟨put quality ~ quantity⟩
[3]**before** *conj* **1** : earlier than the time that ⟨he got here ~ I did⟩ **2** : more willingly than ⟨she'd starve ~ she'd steal⟩
be·fore·hand \bi-ˈfōr-ˌhand\ *adv or adj* : in advance
be·foul \bi-ˈfau̇l\ *vb* : SOIL
be·friend \bi-ˈfrend\ *vb* : to act as friend to
be·fud·dle \bi-ˈfəd-ᵊl\ *vb* : MUDDLE, CONFUSE
beg \ˈbeg\ *vb* **begged; beg·ging 1** : to ask as a charity; *also* : ENTREAT **2** : EVADE; *also* : assume as established, settled, or proved ⟨~ the question⟩
be·get \bi-ˈget\ *vb* **-got** \-ˈgät\; **-got·ten** \-ˈgät-ᵊn\ *or* **-got; -get·ting** : to become the father of : SIRE
[1]**beg·gar** \ˈbe-gər\ *n* : one that begs; *esp* : a person who begs as a way of life
[2]**beggar** *vb* : IMPOVERISH
beg·gar·ly \ˈbe-gər-lē\ *adj* **1** : contemptibly mean or inadequate **2** : marked by unrelieved poverty ⟨a ~ life⟩
beg·gary \ˈbe-gə-rē\ *n* : extreme poverty
be·gin \bi-ˈgin\ *vb* **be·gan** \-ˈgan\; **be·gun** \-ˈgən\; **be·gin·ning 1** : to do the first part of an action : COMMENCE **2** : to come into being : ARISE; *also* : FOUND **3** : ORIGINATE, INVENT — **be·gin·ner** *n*
beg off *vb* : to ask to be excused from something
be·gone \bi-ˈgȯn\ *vb* : to go away : DEPART — used esp. in the imperative
be·go·nia \bi-ˈgōn-yə\ *n* : any of a genus of tropical herbs widely grown for their showy leaves and waxy flowers
be·grime \bi-ˈgrīm\ *vb* **be·grimed; be·grim·ing** : to make dirty
be·grudge \bi-ˈgrəj\ *vb* **1** : to give or concede reluctantly **2** : to be reluctant to grant or allow
be·guile \-ˈgīl\ *vb* **be·guiled; be·guil·ing 1** : DECEIVE **2** : to while away **3** : to engage the interest of by guile
be·guine \bi-ˈgēn\ *n* [AmerF *béguine*, fr. F *béguin* flirtation] : a vigorous popular dance of the islands of Saint Lucia and Martinique
be·gum \ˈbā-gəm, ˈbē-\ *n* : a Muslim woman of high rank
be·half \bi-ˈhaf, -ˈhȧf\ *n* : BENEFIT, SUPPORT, DEFENSE
be·have \bi-ˈhāv\ *vb* **be·haved; be·hav·ing 1** : to bear, comport, or conduct oneself in a particular and esp. a proper way **2** : to act, function, or react in a particular way
be·hav·ior \bi-ˈhā-vyər\ *n* : way of behaving; *esp* : personal conduct — **be·hav·ior·al** \-vyə-rəl\ *adj*
be·hav·ior·ism \bi-ˈhā-vyə-ˌri-zəm\ *n* : a school of psychology concerned with the objective evidence of behavior without reference to conscious experience
be·hav·iour, be·hav·iour·ism *chiefly Brit var of* BEHAVIOR, BEHAVIORISM
be·head \bi-ˈhed\ *vb* : to cut off the head of
be·he·moth \bi-ˈhē-məth, ˈbē-ə-ˌmäth\ *n* : a huge powerful animal described in Job 40:15–24; *also* : something of monstrous size or power
be·hest \bi-ˈhest\ *n* **1** : COMMAND **2** : an urgent prompting
[1]**be·hind** \bi-ˈhīnd\ *adv or adj* **1** : BACK, BACKWARD ⟨look ~ ⟩ **2** : LATE, SLOW
[2]**behind** *prep* **1** : in or to a place or situation in back of or to the rear of ⟨look ~ you⟩ ⟨the staff stayed ~ the troops⟩ **2** : inferior to (as in rank) : BELOW ⟨three games ~ the first-place team⟩ **3** : in support of : SUPPORTING ⟨we're ~ you all the way⟩
be·hind·hand \bi-ˈhīnd-ˌhand\ *adj* : being in arrears **syn** tardy, late, overdue, belated
be·hold \bi-ˈhōld\ *vb* **-held** \-ˈheld\; **-hold·ing 1** : to have in sight : SEE **2** — used imperatively to direct the attention **syn** view, observe, notice, espy — **be·hold·er** *n*
be·hold·en \bi-ˈhōl-dən\ *adj* : OBLIGATED, INDEBTED
be·hoof \bi-ˈhüf\ *n* : ADVANTAGE, PROFIT
be·hoove \bi-ˈhüv\ *vb* **be·hooved; be·hoov·ing** : to be necessary, proper, or advantageous for
be·hove *chiefly Brit var of* BEHOOVE
beige \ˈbāzh\ *n* : a pale dull yellowish brown — **beige** *adj*
be·ing \ˈbē-iŋ\ *n* **1** : EXISTENCE; *also* : LIFE **2** : the qualities or constitution of an existent thing **3** : a living thing; *esp* : PERSON
be·la·bor \bi-ˈlā-bər\ *vb* : to assail (as with words) tiresomely or at length
be·la·bour *chiefly Brit var of* BELABOR
be·lat·ed \bi-ˈlā-təd\ *adj* : DELAYED, LATE
be·lay \bi-ˈlā\ *vb* **1** : to wind (a rope) around a pin or cleat in order to hold secure **2** : QUIT, STOP — used in the imperative
belch \ˈbelch\ *vb* **1** : to expel (gas) from the stomach through the mouth **2** : to gush forth ⟨a volcano ~*ing* lava⟩ — **belch** *n*
bel·dam *or* **bel·dame** \ˈbel-dəm\ *n* [ME *beldam* grandmother, fr. MF *bel* beautiful + ME *dam* lady, mother] : an old woman
be·lea·guer \bi-ˈlē-gər\ *vb* **1** : BESIEGE **2** : HARASS ⟨~*ed* parents⟩
bel·fry \ˈbel-frē\ *n, pl* **belfries** : a tower for a bell (as on a church); *also* : the part of the tower in which the bell hangs
Belg *abbr* Belgian; Belgium
Bel·gian \ˈbel-jən\ *n* : a native or inhabitant of Belgium — **Belgian** *adj*
be·lie \bi-ˈlī\ *vb* **-lied; -ly·ing 1** : MISREPRESENT **2** : to show (something) to be false **3** : to run counter to
be·lief \bə-ˈlēf\ *n* **1** : CONFIDENCE, TRUST **2** : something (as a tenet or creed) believed **syn** conviction, opinion, persuasion, sentiment
be·lieve \bə-ˈlēv\ *vb* **be·lieved; be·liev·ing 1** : to have religious convictions **2** : to have a firm conviction about something : accept as true **3** : to hold as an opinion : SUPPOSE — **be·liev·able** *adj* — **be·liev·er** *n*
be·like \bi-ˈlīk\ *adv, archaic* : PROBABLY
be·lit·tle \bi-ˈlit-ᵊl\ *vb* **-lit·tled; -lit·tling** : to make seem little or less; *also* : DISPARAGE
[1]**bell** \ˈbel\ *n* **1** : a hollow metallic device that makes a ringing sound when struck **2** : the sounding or stroke of a bell (as on shipboard to tell the time); *also* : time so indicated **3** : something with the flared form of a typical bell
[2]**bell** *vb* : to provide with a bell
bel·la·don·na \ˌbe-lə-ˈdä-nə\ *n* [It, lit., beautiful lady; fr. its cosmetic use] : a medicinal extract (as atropine) from a poisonous European herb related to the potato; *also* : this herb
bell–bot·toms \ˈbel-ˈbä-təmz\ *n pl* : pants with wide flaring bottoms — **bell–bottom** *adj*
bell·boy \ˈbel-ˌbȯi\ *n* : BELLHOP
belle \ˈbel\ *n* : an attractive and popular girl or woman
belles let·tres \bel-ˈletrᵊ\ *n pl* [F] : literature that is an end in itself and not practical or purely informative — **bel·le·tris·tic** \ˌbe-lə-ˈtris-tik\ *adj*
bell·hop \ˈbel-ˌhäp\ *n* : a hotel or club employee who

takes guests to rooms, carries luggage, and runs errands

bel·li·cose \ˈbe-li-ˌkōs\ *adj* : WARLIKE, PUGNACIOUS **syn** belligerent, quarrelsome, combative, contentious — **bel·li·cos·i·ty** \ˌbe-li-ˈkä-sə-tē\ *n*

bel·lig·er·en·cy \bə-ˈli-jə-rən-sē\ *n* **1** : the status of a nation engaged in war **2** : BELLIGERENCE, TRUCULENCE

bel·lig·er·ent \-rənt\ *adj* **1** : waging war **2** : TRUCULENT **syn** bellicose, pugnacious, combative, contentious, warlike — **bel·lig·er·ence** \-rəns\ *n* — **belligerent** *n*

bel·low \ˈbe-lō\ *vb* **1** : to make the deep hollow sound characteristic of a bull **2** : to shout in a deep voice — **bellow** *n*

bel·lows \-lōz, -ləz\ *n sing or pl* : a closed device with sides that can be spread apart and then pressed together to draw in air and expel it through a tube

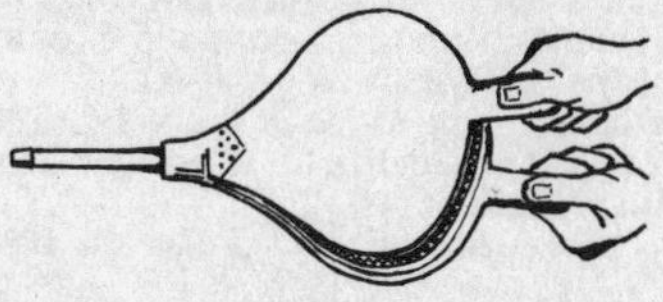

bellows

bell·weth·er \ˈbel-ˈwe-t͟hər, -ˌwe-\ *n* : one that takes the lead or initiative

[1]**bel·ly** \ˈbe-lē\ *n, pl* **bellies** [ME *bely* bellows, belly, fr. OE *belg* bag, skin] **1** : ABDOMEN; *also* : POTBELLY **2** : the underpart of an animal's body

[2]**belly** *vb* **bel·lied; bel·ly·ing** : BULGE

[1]**bel·ly·ache** \ˈbe-lē-ˌāk\ *n* : pain in the abdomen

[2]**bellyache** *vb* : COMPLAIN

belly button *n* : the human navel

belly dance *n* : a usu. solo dance emphasizing movement of the belly — **belly dance** *vb* — **belly dancer** *n*

belly laugh *n* : a deep hearty laugh

be·long \bi-ˈlȯŋ\ *vb* **1** : to be suitable or appropriate; *also* : to be properly situated ⟨shoes ~ in the closet⟩ **2** : to be the property ⟨this ~*s* to me⟩; *also* : to be attached (as through birth or membership) ⟨~ to a club⟩ **3** : to form an attribute or part ⟨this wheel ~*s* to the cart⟩ **4** : to be classified ⟨whales ~ among the mammals⟩

be·long·ings \-ˈlȯŋ-iŋz\ *n pl* : GOODS, EFFECTS, POSSESSIONS

be·loved \bi-ˈləvd, -ˈlə-vəd\ *adj* : dearly loved — **beloved** *n*

[1]**be·low** \bi-ˈlō\ *adv* **1** : in or to a lower place or rank **2** : on earth **3** : in hell

[2]**below** *prep* **1** : lower than **2** : inferior to (as in rank)

be·low·decks \bi-ˌlō-ˈdeks, -ˈlō-ˌdeks\ *adv* : inside the superstructure of a boat or down to a lower deck

[1]**belt** \ˈbelt\ *n* **1** : a strip (as of leather) worn about the waist **2** : a flexible continuous band to communicate motion or convey material **3** : a region marked by some distinctive feature; *esp* : one suited to a particular crop

[2]**belt** *vb* **1** : to encircle or secure with a belt **2** : to beat with or as if with a belt **3** : to mark with an encircling band **4** : to sing loudly

[3]**belt** *n* **1** : a jarring blow : WHACK **2** : DRINK ⟨a ~ of whiskey⟩

belt–tightening *n* : a reduction in spending

belt·way \ˈbelt-ˌwā\ *n* : a highway around a city

be·lu·ga \bə-ˈlü-gə\ *n* [Russ] : a white sturgeon of the Black Sea, Caspian Sea, and their tributaries that is a source of caviar; *also* : caviar from beluga roe

bel·ve·dere \ˈbel-və-ˌdir\ *n* [It, lit., beautiful view] : a structure (as a summerhouse) designed to command a view

be·mire \bi-ˈmīr\ *vb* : to cover or soil with or sink in mire

be·moan \bi-ˈmōn\ *vb* : LAMENT, DEPLORE **syn** bewail, grieve, moan, weep

be·muse \bi-ˈmyüz\ *vb* : BEWILDER, CONFUSE

[1]**bench** \ˈbench\ *n* **1** : a long seat for two or more persons **2** : the seat of a judge in court; *also* : the office or dignity of a judge **3** : COURT; *also* : JUDGES **4** : a table for holding work and tools ⟨a carpenter's ~⟩

[2]**bench** \ˈbench\ *vb* **1** : to furnish with benches **2** : to seat on a bench **3** : to remove from or keep out of a game

bench mark *n* **1** : a mark on a permanent object serving as an elevation reference in topographical surveys **2** *usu* **bench·mark** : a point of reference for measurement; *also* : STANDARD

bench press *n* : a press in weight lifting performed by a lifter lying on a bench — **bench–press** *vb*

bench warrant *n* : a warrant issued by a presiding judge or by a court against a person guilty of contempt or indicted for a crime

[1]**bend** \ˈbend\ *vb* **bent** \ˈbent\; **bend·ing** **1** : to draw (as a bow) taut **2** : to curve or cause a change of shape in ⟨~ a bar⟩ **3** : to make fast : SECURE **4** : DEFLECT **5** : to turn in a certain direction ⟨*bent* his steps toward town⟩ **6** : APPLY ⟨*bent* themselves to the task⟩ **7** : SUBDUE **8** : to curve downward **9** : YIELD, SUBMIT

[2]**bend** *n* **1** : an act or process of bending **2** : something bent; *esp* : CURVE **3** *pl* : a painful and sometimes fatal disorder caused by release of gas bubbles in the tissues upon too rapid decrease in air pressure after a stay in a compressed atmosphere

[3]**bend** *n* : a knot by which a rope is fastened (as to another rope)

bend·er \ˈben-dər\ *n* : SPREE

[1]**be·neath** \bi-ˈnēth\ *adv* : BELOW **syn** under, underneath

[2]**beneath** *prep* **1** : BELOW, UNDER ⟨stood ~ a tree⟩ **2** : unworthy of ⟨considered such behavior ~ her⟩ **3** : concealed by

bene·dic·tion \ˌbe-nə-ˈdik-shən\ *n* : the invocation of a blessing esp. at the close of a public worship service

ben·e·fac·tion \-ˈfak-shən\ *n* : a charitable donation **syn** contribution, alms, beneficence, offering

ben·e·fac·tor \ˈben-ə-ˌfak-tər\ *n* : one that confers a benefit and esp. a benefaction

ben·e·fac·tress \-ˌfak-trəs\ *n* : a woman who is a benefactor

ben·e·fice \ˈbe-nə-fəs\ *n* : an ecclesiastical office to which the revenue from an endowment is attached

be·nef·i·cence \bə-ˈne-fə-səns\ *n* **1** : beneficent quality **2** : BENEFACTION

be·nef·i·cent \-sənt\ *adj* : doing or producing good (as by acts of kindness or charity); *also* : BENEFICIAL

ben·e·fi·cial \ˌbe-nə-ˈfi-shəl\ *adj* : being of benefit or help : HELPFUL **syn** advantageous, profitable, favorable, propitious — **ben·e·fi·cial·ly** *adv*

ben·e·fi·cia·ry \ˌbe-nə-ˈfi-shē-ˌer-ē, -ˈfi-shə-rē\ *n, pl* **-ries** : one that receives a benefit (as the income of a trust or the proceeds of an insurance)

[1]**ben·e·fit** \ˈbe-nə-ˌfit\ *n* **1** : ADVANTAGE ⟨the ~*s* of exercise⟩ **2** : useful aid : HELP; *also* : material aid provided or due (as in sickness or unemployment) as a right **3** : a performance or event to raise funds

[2]**benefit** *vb* **-fit·ed** \-ˌfi-təd\ *also* **-fit·ted; -fit·ing** *also* **-fit·ting** **1** : to be useful or profitable to **2** : to receive benefit

be·nev·o·lence \bə-ˈne-və-ləns\ *n* **1** : charitable nature **2** : an act of kindness : CHARITY — **be·nev·o·lent** \-lənt\ *adj* — **be·nev·o·lent·ly** *adv*

be·night·ed \bi-ˈnī-təd\ *adj* **1** : overtaken by darkness or night **2** : living in ignorance

be·nign \bi-ˈnīn\ *adj* [ME *benigne,* fr. MF, fr. L *benignus*] **1** : of a gentle disposition; *also* : showing kindness **2** : of a mild kind; *esp* : not malignant ⟨~ tumors⟩ **syn** benignant, kind, kindly, good-hearted — **be·nig·ni·ty** \-ˈnig-nə-tē\ *n*

be•nig•nant \-ˈnig-nənt\ *adj* : BENIGN 1 **syn** kind, kindly, good-hearted
ben•i•son \ˈbe-nə-sən, -zən\ *n* : BLESSING, BENEDICTION
bent \ˈbent\ *n* **1** : strong inclination or interest; *also* : TALENT **2** : power of endurance **syn** talent, aptitude, gift, flair, knack, genius
ben•thic \ˈben-thik\ *adj* : of, relating to, or occurring at the bottom of a body of water
ben•ton•ite \ˈbent-ᵊn-ˌīt\ *n* : an absorptive clay used esp. as a filler (as in paper)
bent•wood \ˈbent-ˌwu̇d\ *adj* : made of wood bent into shape ⟨a ~ rocker⟩
be•numb \bi-ˈnəm\ *vb* **1** : DULL, DEADEN **2** : to make numb esp. by cold
ben•zene \ˈben-ˌzēn\ *n* : a colorless volatile flammable liquid hydrocarbon used in organic synthesis and as a solvent
ben•zine \ˈben-ˌzēn\ *n* : any of various flammable petroleum distillates used as solvents or as motor fuels
ben•zo•ate \ˈben-zə-ˌwāt\ *n* : a salt or ester of benzoic acid
ben•zo•ic acid \ben-ˈzō-ik-\ *n* : a white crystalline acid used as a preservative and antiseptic and in synthesizing chemicals
ben•zo•in \ˈben-zə-wən, -ˌzȯin\ *n* : a balsamlike resin from trees of southern Asia used esp. in medicine and perfumes
be•queath \bi-ˈkwēth, -ˈkwēth\ *vb* [ME *bequethen*, fr. OE *becwethan*, fr. *be-* + *cwethan* to say] **1** : to leave by will **2** : to hand down
be•quest \bi-ˈkwest\ *n* **1** : the action of bequeathing **2** : something bequeathed : LEGACY
be•rate \-ˈrāt\ *vb* : to scold harshly
Ber•ber \ˈbər-bər\ *n* : a member of any of various peoples living in northern Africa west of Tripoli
ber•ceuse \ber-ˈsœz, -ˈsüz\ *n, pl* **berceuses** *same or* -ˈsü-zəz\ [F, fr. *bercer* to rock] **1** : LULLABY **2** : a musical composition that resembles a lullaby
[1]**be•reaved** \bi-ˈrēvd\ *adj* : suffering the death of a loved one — **be•reave•ment** *n*
[2]**bereaved** *n, pl* **bereaved** : one who is bereaved
be•reft \-ˈreft\ *adj* **1** : deprived of or lacking something — usu. used with *of* **2** : BEREAVED
be•ret \bə-ˈrā\ *n* : a round soft cap with no visor
berg \ˈbərg\ *n* : ICEBERG
beri•beri \ˌber-ē-ˈber-ē\ *n* : a deficiency disease marked by weakness, wasting, and nerve damage and caused by lack of thiamine
berke•li•um \ˈbər-klē-əm\ *n* : an artificially prepared radioactive chemical element — see ELEMENT table
berm \ˈbərm\ *n* : a narrow shelf or path at the top or bottom of a slope; *also* : a mound or bank of earth
Ber•mu•das \bər-ˈmyü-dəz\ *n pl* : BERMUDA SHORTS
Bermuda shorts *n pl* : knee-length walking shorts
ber•ry \ˈber-ē\ *n, pl* **berries** **1** : a small pulpy fruit (as a strawberry) **2** : a simple fruit (as a grape, tomato, or banana) with the wall of the ripened ovary thick and pulpy **3** : the dry seed of some plants (as coffee)
ber•serk \bər-ˈsərk, -ˈzərk\ *adj* [ON *berserkr* warrior frenzied in battle, fr. *bjǫrn* bear + *serkr* shirt] : FRENZIED, CRAZED — **berserk** *adv*
[1]**berth** \ˈbərth\ *n* **1** : adequate distance esp. for a ship to maneuver **2** : the place where a ship is anchored or a vehicle rests **3** : ACCOMMODATIONS **4** : JOB, POSITION **syn** post, situation, office, appointment
[2]**berth** *vb* **1** : to bring or come into a berth **2** : to allot a berth to
ber•yl \ˈber-əl\ *n* : a hard silicate mineral occurring as green, yellow, pink, or white crystals
be•ryl•li•um \bə-ˈri-lē-əm\ *n* : a light strong metallic chemical element used as a hardener in alloys — see ELEMENT table
be•seech \bi-ˈsēch\ *vb* **-sought** \-ˈsȯt\ *or* **-seeched; -seech•ing** : to beg urgently : ENTREAT **syn** implore, plead, supplicate, importune
be•seem \bi-ˈsēm\ *vb, archaic* : BEFIT
be•set \-ˈset\ *vb* **1** : TROUBLE, HARASS **2** : ASSAIL; *also* : SURROUND
be•set•ting *adj* : persistently present
[1]**be•side** \bi-ˈsīd\ *prep* **1** : by the side of ⟨sit ~ me⟩ **2** : BESIDES **3** : not relevant to
[2]**beside** *adv, archaic* : BESIDES
[1]**be•sides** \bi-ˈsīdz\ *prep* **1** : other than **2** : together with
[2]**besides** *adv* **1** : as well : ALSO **2** : MOREOVER
be•siege \bi-ˈsēj\ *vb* : to lay siege to; *also* : to press with requests — **be•sieg•er** *n*
be•smear \-ˈsmir\ *vb* : SMEAR
be•smirch \-ˈsmərch\ *vb* : SMIRCH, SOIL
be•som \ˈbē-zəm\ *n* : BROOM
be•sot \bi-ˈsät\ *vb* **be•sot•ted; be•sot•ting** **1** : INFATUATE **2** : to make dull esp. by drinking
be•spat•ter \-ˈspa-tər\ *vb* : SPATTER
be•speak \bi-ˈspēk\ *vb* **-spoke** \-ˈspōk\; **-spo•ken** \-ˈspō-kən\; **-speak•ing** **1** : PREARRANGE **2** : ADDRESS **3** : REQUEST **4** : INDICATE, SIGNIFY **5** : FORETELL
be•sprin•kle \-ˈspriŋ-kəl\ *vb* : SPRINKLE
[1]**best** \ˈbest\ *adj, superlative of* GOOD **1** : excelling all others **2** : most productive (as of good or satisfaction) **3** : LARGEST, MOST
[2]**best** *adv, superlative of* WELL **1** : in the best way **2** : MOST
[3]**best** *n* : something that is best
[4]**best** *vb* : to get the better of : OUTDO
bes•tial \ˈbes-chəl\ *adj* **1** : of or relating to beasts **2** : resembling a beast esp. in brutality or lack of intelligence
bes•ti•al•i•ty \ˌbes-chē-ˈa-lə-tē, ˌbēs-\ *n, pl* **-ties** **1** : the condition or status of a lower animal **2** : display or gratification of bestial traits or impulses
bes•ti•ary \ˈbes-chē-ˌer-ē\ *n, pl* **-ar•ies** : a medieval allegorical or moralizing work on the appearance and habits of animals
be•stir \bi-ˈstər\ *vb* : to rouse to action
best man *n* : the principal groomsman at a wedding
be•stow \bi-ˈstō\ *vb* **1** : PUT, PLACE, STOW **2** : to present as a gift — **be•stow•al** *n*
be•stride \bi-ˈstrīd\ *vb* **-strode** \-ˈstrōd\; **-strid•den** \-ˈstrid-ᵊn\; **-strid•ing** : to ride, sit, or stand astride
[1]**bet** \ˈbet\ *n* **1** : something that is wagered, risked, or pledged usu. between two parties on the outcome of a contest; *also* : the making of such a bet **2** : OPTION ⟨the back road is your best ~⟩
[2]**bet** *vb* **bet** *also* **bet•ted; bet•ting** **1** : to stake on the outcome of an issue or a contest ⟨*bet* $2 on the race⟩ **2** : to make a bet with **3** : to lay a bet
[3]**bet** *abbr* between
be•ta \ˈbā-tə\ *n* : the 2d letter of the Greek alphabet — B or β
beta block•er \-ˌblä-kər\ *n* : any of a group of drugs that tend to decrease heart action and increase coronary blood flow
be•ta–car•o•tene \-ˈkar-ə-ˌtēn\ *n* : an isomer of carotene found in dark green and dark yellow vegetables and fruits
be•take \bi-ˈtāk\ *vb* **-took** \-ˈtu̇k\; **-tak•en** \-ˈtā-kən\; **-tak•ing** : to cause (oneself) to go
beta particle *n* : a high-speed electron; *esp* : one emitted by a radioactive nucleus
beta ray *n* **1** : BETA PARTICLE **2** : a stream of beta particles
be•tel \ˈbēt-ᵊl\ *n* : a climbing pepper whose leaves are chewed together with lime and betel nut as a stimulant esp. by southern Asians
betel nut *n* : the astringent seed of an Asian palm that is chewed with betel leaves
bête noire \ˌbet-ˈnwär, ˌbāt-\ *n, pl* **bêtes noires** *same or* -ˈnwärz\ [F, lit., black beast] : a person or thing strongly disliked or avoided
beth•el \ˈbe-thəl\ *n* [Heb *bēth'ēl* house of God] : a place of worship esp. for seamen
be•think \bi-ˈthiŋk\ *vb* **-thought** \-ˈthȯt\; **-think•ing** : REMEMBER; *also* : PONDER

be•tide \bi-ˈtīd\ *vb* : to happen to

be•times \bi-ˈtīmz\ *adv* : in good time : EARLY **syn** soon, seasonably, timely

be•to•ken \bi-ˈtō-kən\ *vb* **1** : PRESAGE **2** : to give evidence of **syn** indicate, attest, bespeak, testify

be•tray \bi-ˈtrā\ *vb* **1** : to lead astray; *esp* : SEDUCE **2** : to deliver to an enemy **3** : ABANDON **4** : to prove unfaithful to **5** : to reveal unintentionally; *also* : SHOW, INDICATE **syn** mislead, delude, deceive, beguile — **be•tray•al** *n* — **be•tray•er** *n*

be•troth \bi-ˈtrōth, -ˈtrȯth\ *vb* : to promise to marry — **be•troth•al** *n*

be•trothed *n* : the person to whom one is betrothed

1**bet•ter** \ˈbe-tər\ *adj, comparative of* GOOD **1** : greater than half **2** : improved in health **3** : more attractive, favorable, or commendable **4** : more advantageous or effective **5** : improved in accuracy or performance

2**better** *vb* **1** : to make or become better **2** : SURPASS, EXCEL

3**better** *adv, comparative of* WELL **1** : in a superior manner **2** : to a higher or greater degree; *also* : MORE

4**better** *n* **1** : something better; *also* : a superior esp. in merit or rank **2** : ADVANTAGE

5**better** *verbal auxiliary* : had better ⟨you ~ hurry⟩

bet•ter•ment \ˈbe-tər-mənt\ *n* : IMPROVEMENT

bet•tor *or* **bet•ter** \ˈbe-tər\ *n* : one that bets

1**be•tween** \bi-ˈtwēn\ *prep* **1** : by the common action of ⟨earned $10,000 ~ the two of them⟩ **2** : in the interval separating ⟨an alley ~ two buildings⟩; *also* : in intermediate relation to **3** : in point of comparison of ⟨choose ~ two cars⟩

2**between** *adv* : in an intervening space or interval

be•twixt \bi-ˈtwikst\ *adv or prep* : BETWEEN

1**bev•el** \ˈbe-vəl\ *n* **1** : a device for adjusting the slant of the surfaces of a piece of work **2** : the angle or slant that one surface or line makes with another when not at right angles

2**bevel** *vb* **-eled** *or* **-elled; -el•ing** *or* **-el•ling 1** : to cut or shape to a bevel **2** : INCLINE, SLANT

bev•er•age \ˈbev-rij\ *n* : a drinkable liquid

bevy \ˈbe-vē\ *n, pl* **bev•ies 1** : a large group or collection **2** : a group of animals and esp. quail together

be•wail \bi-ˈwāl\ *vb* : LAMENT **syn** deplore, bemoan, grieve, moan, weep

be•ware \-ˈwar\ *vb* : to be on one's guard : be wary of

be•wil•der \bi-ˈwil-dər\ *vb* : PERPLEX, CONFUSE **syn** mystify, distract, puzzle — **be•wil•der•ment** *n*

be•witch \-ˈwich\ *vb* **1** : to affect by witchcraft **2** : CHARM, FASCINATE **syn** enchant, attract, captivate — **be•witch•ment** *n*

bey \ˈbā\ *n* **1** : a former Turkish provincial governor **2** : the former native ruler of Tunis or Tunisia

1**be•yond** \bē-ˈänd\ *adv* **1** : FARTHER **2** : BESIDES

2**beyond** *prep* **1** : on or to the farther side of **2** : out of the reach or sphere of **3** : BESIDES

be•zel \ˈbē-zəl, ˈbe-\ *n* **1** : a rim that holds a transparent covering (as on a watch) **2** : the faceted part of a cut gem that rises above the setting

bf *abbr* boldface

BG *or* **B Gen** *abbr* brigadier general

bhang \ˈbaŋ\ *n* [Hindi *bhāṅg*] : a mildly intoxicating preparation of the leaves and flowering tops of uncultivated hemp

Bi *symbol* bismuth

BIA *abbr* Bureau of Indian Affairs

bi•an•nu•al \(ˌ)bī-ˈan-yə-wəl\ *adj* : occurring twice a year — **bi•an•nu•al•ly** *adv*

1**bi•as** \ˈbī-əs\ *n* **1** : a line diagonal to the grain of a fabric **2** : PREJUDICE, BENT

2**bias** *adv* : on the bias : DIAGONALLY

3**bias** *vb* **bi•ased** *or* **bi•assed; bi•as•ing** *or* **bi•as•sing** : PREJUDICE

bi•ath•lon \bī-ˈath-lən, -ˌlän\ *n* : a composite athletic contest consisting of cross-country skiing and target shooting with a rifle

1**bib** \ˈbib\ *n* : a cloth or plastic shield tied under the chin to protect the clothes while eating

2**bib** *abbr* Bible; biblical

bi•be•lot \ˈbē-bə-ˌlō\ *n, pl* **bibelots** *same or* -ˌlōz\ : a small household ornament or decorative object

bi•ble \ˈbī-bəl\ *n* [ME, fr. OF, fr. ML *biblia*, fr. Gk, pl. of *biblion* book, fr. *byblos* papyrus, book, fr. *Byblos*, ancient Phoenician city from which papyrus was exported] **1** *cap* : the sacred scriptures of Christians comprising the Old and New Testaments **2** *cap* : the sacred scriptures of Judaism; *also* : those of some other religion **3** : a publication that is considered authoritative for its subject — **bib•li•cal** \ˈbi-bli-kəl\ *adj*

☞ For table, see next page.

bib•li•og•ra•phy \ˌbi-blē-ˈä-grə-fē\ *n, pl* **-phies 1** : the history or description of writings or publications **2** : a list of writings (as on a subject or of an author) — **bib•li•og•ra•pher** \-fər\ *n* — **bib•li•o•graph•ic** \-ə-ˈgra-fik\ *also* **bib•li•o•graph•i•cal** \-fi-kəl\ *adj*

bib•lio•phile \ˈbi-blē-ə-ˌfīl\ *n* : a lover of books

bib•u•lous \ˈbi-byə-ləs\ *adj* **1** : highly absorbent **2** : fond of alcoholic beverages

bi•cam•er•al \ˈbī-ˈka-mə-rəl\ *adj* : having or consisting of two legislative branches

bicarb \(ˌ)bī-ˈkärb, ˈbī-ˌ\ *n* : SODIUM BICARBONATE

bi•car•bon•ate \(ˌ)bī-ˈkär-bə-ˌnāt, -nət\ *n* : an acid carbonate

bicarbonate of soda : SODIUM BICARBONATE

bi•cen•te•na•ry \ˌbī-sen-ˈte-nə-rē, bī-ˈsent-ᵊn-ˌer-ē\ *n* : BICENTENNIAL — **bicentenary** *adj*

bi•cen•ten•ni•al \ˌbī-sen-ˈte-nē-əl\ *n* : a 200th anniversary or its celebration — **bicentennial** *adj*

bi•ceps \ˈbī-ˌseps\ *n, pl* **biceps** *also* **bicepses** [NL, fr. L, two-headed, fr. *bi-* two + *caput* head] : a muscle (as in the front of the upper arm) having two points of origin

1**bick•er** \ˈbi-kər\ *n* : ALTERCATION

2**bicker** *vb* : to engage in a petty quarrel

bi•coast•al \bī-ˈkōst-ᵊl\ *adj* : living or working on both the East and West coasts of the U.S.

bi•con•cave \ˌbī-(ˌ)kän-ˈkāv, (ˌ)bī-ˈkän-ˌkāv\ *adj* : concave on both sides

bi•con•vex \ˌbī-(ˌ)kän-ˈveks, (ˌ)bī-ˈkän-ˌveks\ *adj* : convex on both sides

bi•cus•pid \bī-ˈkəs-pəd\ *n* : PREMOLAR

1**bi•cy•cle** \ˈbī-ˌsi-kəl\ *n* : a light 2-wheeled vehicle with a steering handle, saddle, and pedals

2**bicycle** *vb* **-cy•cled; -cy•cling** \-ˌsi-k(ə-)liŋ, -ˌsī-\ : to ride a bicycle — **bi•cy•cler** \-k(ə-)lər\ *n* — **bi•cy•clist** \-k(ə-)list\ *n*

1**bid** \ˈbid\ *vb* **bade** \ˈbad, ˈbād\ *or* **bid; bid•den** \ˈbid-ᵊn\ *or* **bid** *also* **bade; bid•ding 1** : COMMAND, ORDER **2** : INVITE **3** : to give expression to **4** : to make a bid : OFFER — **bid•der** *n*

2**bid** *n* **1** : the act of one who bids; *also* : an offer for something **2** : INVITATION **3** : an announcement in a card game of what a player proposes to accomplish **4** : an attempt to win or gain ⟨a ~ for mayor⟩

bid•da•ble \ˈbi-də-bəl\ *adj* **1** : OBEDIENT, DOCILE **2** : capable of being bid

bid•dy \ˈbi-dē\ *n, pl* **biddies** : HEN; *also* : a young chicken

bide \ˈbīd\ *vb* **bode** \ˈbōd\ *or* **bid•ed; bided; bid•ing 1** : to wait for **2** : WAIT, TARRY **3** : DWELL

bi•det \bi-ˈdā\ *n* : a bathroom fixture used esp. for bathing the external genitals and the posterior parts of the body

bi•di•rec•tion•al \ˌbī-də-ˈrek-sh(ə-)nəl\ *adj* : involving, moving, or taking place in two usu. opposite directions — **bi•di•rec•tion•al•ly** *adv*

bi•en•ni•al \bī-ˈe-nē-əl\ *adj* **1** : taking place once in two years **2** : lasting two years **3** : producing leaves the first year and fruiting and dying the second year — **biennial** *n* — **bi•en•ni•al•ly** *adv*

bi•en•ni•um \bī-ˈe-nē-əm\ *n, pl* **-niums** *or* **-nia** \-ə\ [L, fr. *bi-* two + *annus* year] : a period of two years

BOOKS OF THE OLD TESTAMENT

ROMAN CATHOLIC CANON	PROTESTANT CANON
Genesis	Genesis
Exodus	Exodus
Leviticus	Leviticus
Numbers	Numbers
Deuteronomy	Deuteronomy
Joshua	Joshua
Judges	Judges
Ruth	Ruth
1 & 2 Samuel	1 & 2 Samuel
1 & 2 Kings	1 & 2 Kings
1 & 2 Chronicles	1 & 2 Chronicles
Ezra	Ezra
Nehemiah	Nehemiah
Tobit	
Judith	
Esther	Esther
Job	Job
Psalms	Psalms
Proverbs	Proverbs
Ecclesiastes	Ecclesiastes
Song of Songs	Song of Solomon
Wisdom	
Sirach	
Isaiah	Isaiah
Jeremiah	Jeremiah
Lamentations	Lamentations
Baruch	
Ezekiel	Ezekiel
Daniel	Daniel
Hosea	Hosea
Joel	Joel
Amos	Amos
Obadiah	Obadiah
Jonah	Jonah
Micah	Micah
Nahum	Nahum
Habakkuk	Habakkuk
Zephaniah	Zephaniah
Haggai	Haggai
Zechariah	Zechariah
Malachi	Malachi
1 & 2 Macabees	

JEWISH SCRIPTURE

Law
Genesis
Exodus
Leviticus
Numbers
Deuteronomy
Prophets
Joshua
Judges
1 & 2 Samuel
1 & 2 Kings
Isaiah
Jeremiah
Ezekiel
Hosea
Joel
Amos
Obadiah
Jonah
Micah
Nahum
Habakkuk
Zephaniah
Haggai
Zechariah
Malachi
Hagiographa
Psalms
Proverbs
Job
Song of Songs
Ruth
Lamentations
Ecclesiastes
Esther
Daniel
Ezra
Nehemiah
1 & 2 Chronicles

PROTESTANT APOCRYPHA

1 & 2 Esdras
Tobit
Judith
Additions to Esther
Wisdom of Solomon
Ecclesiasticus *or* the Wisdom of Jesus Son of Sirach
Baruch
Prayer of Azariah and the Song of the Three Holy Children
Susanna
Bel and the Dragon
The Prayer of Manasses
1 & 2 Maccabees

BOOKS OF THE NEW TESTAMENT

Matthew
Mark
Luke
John
Acts of the Apostles
Romans
1 & 2 Corinthians
Galatians
Ephesians
Philippians
Colossians
1 & 2 Thessalonians
1 & 2 Timothy
Titus
Philemon
Hebrews
James
1 & 2 Peter
1, 2, 3 John
Jude
Revelation *or* Apocalypse

bier \ˈbir\ *n* **:** a stand bearing a coffin or corpse

bi•fo•cal \ˈbī-ˌfō-kəl\ *adj* **:** having two focal lengths

bifocals \-kəlz\ *n pl* **:** eyeglasses with lenses that have one part that corrects for near vision and one for distant vision

bi•fur•cate \ˈbī-fər-ˌkāt, bī-ˈfər-\ *vb* **-cat•ed; -cat•ing** **:** to divide into two branches or parts — **bi•fur•ca•tion** \ˌbī-fər-ˈkā-shən\ *n*

big \ˈbig\ *adj* **big•ger; big•gest 1 :** large in size, amount, or scope **2 :** PREGNANT; *also* **:** SWELLING **3 :** IMPORTANT, IMPOSING **4 :** POPULAR — **big•ness** *n*

big•a•my \ˈbi-gə-mē\ *n* **:** the act of marrying one person while still legally married to another — **big•a•mist** \-mist\ *n* — **big•a•mous** \-məs\ *adj*

big bang theory *n* **:** a theory in astronomy: the universe originated in an explosion (**big bang**) from a single point of nearly infinite energy density

big brother *n* **1 :** an older brother **2 :** a man who befriends a delinquent or friendless boy **3** *cap both Bs* **:** the leader of an authoritarian state or movement

Big Dipper *n* **:** the seven principal stars of Ursa Major in a form resembling a dipper

big•foot \ˈbig-ˌfu̇t\ *n* **:** SASQUATCH

big•horn \ˈbig-ˌhȯrn\ *n, pl* **bighorn** *or* **bighorns :** a wild sheep of mountainous western No. America

bighorn

bight \ˈbīt\ *n* **1 :** a curve in a coast; *also* **:** the bay formed by such a curve **2 :** a slack part in a rope

big–name \ˈbig-ˈnām\ *adj* **:** widely popular ⟨a ~ performer⟩ — **big name** *n*

big•ot \ˈbi-gət\ *n* **:** one intolerantly devoted to his or her own prejudices or opinions **syn** fanatic, enthusiast, zealot — **big•ot•ed** \-gə-təd\ *adj* — **big•ot•ry** \-trē\ *n*

big shot \ˈbig-ˌshät\ *n* **:** an important person

big time \-ˌtīm\ *n* **1 :** a high-paying vaudeville circuit requiring only two performances a day **2 :** the top rank of an activity or enterprise — **big–tim•er** *n*

big top *n* **1 :** the main tent of a circus **2 :** CIRCUS

big•wig \ˈbig-ˌwig\ *n* **:** BIG SHOT

bike \ˈbīk\ *n* **1 :** BICYCLE **2 :** MOTORCYCLE

bik•er *n* **:** MOTORCYCLIST; *esp* **:** one who is a member of an organized gang

bike•way \ˈbīk-ˌwā\ *n* **:** a thoroughfare for bicycles

bi•ki•ni \bə-ˈkē-nē\ *n* **:** a woman's brief 2-piece bathing suit

bi•lat•er•al \bī-ˈla-tə-rəl\ *adj* **1 :** having or involving two sides **2 :** affecting reciprocally two sides or parties — **bi•lat•er•al•ly** *adv*

bile \ˈbīl\ *n* **1 :** a bitter greenish fluid secreted by the liver that aids in the digestion of fats **2 :** an ill-humored mood

bilge \ˈbilj\ *n* **1 :** the part of a ship that lies between the bottom and the point where the sides go straight up **2 :** stale or worthless remarks or ideas

bi•lin•gual \bī-ˈliŋ-gwəl\ *adj* **:** expressed in, knowing, or using two languages

bil•ious \ˈbil-yəs\ *adj* **1 :** marked by or suffering from disordered liver function **2 :** IRRITABLE, ILL-TEMPERED — **bil•ious•ness** *n*
bilk \ˈbilk\ *vb* **:** CHEAT, SWINDLE
[1]**bill** \ˈbil\ *n* **:** the jaws of a bird together with their horny covering; *also* **:** a mouth structure (as of a turtle) resembling these — **billed** \ˈbild\ *adj*
[2]**bill** *vb* **:** to caress fondly
[3]**bill** *n* **1 :** an itemized statement of particulars; *also* **:** INVOICE **2 :** a written document or note **3 :** a printed advertisement (as a poster) announcing an event **4 :** a draft of a law presented to a legislature for enactment **5 :** a written statement of a legal wrong suffered or of some breach of law **6 :** a piece of paper money
[4]**bill** *vb* **1 :** to enter in or prepare a bill; *also* **:** to submit a bill or account to **2 :** to advertise by bills or posters
bill•board \-ˌbōrd\ *n* **:** a flat surface on which advertising bills are posted
[1]**bil•let** \ˈbi-lət\ *n* **1 :** an order requiring a person to provide lodging for a soldier; *also* **:** quarters assigned by or as if by such an order **2 :** POSITION, APPOINTMENT
[2]**billet** *vb* **:** to assign lodging to by billet
bil•let–doux \ˌbi-lā-ˈdü\ *n, pl* **billets–doux** *same or* -ˈdüz\ [F *billet doux,* lit., sweet letter] **:** a love letter
bill•fold \ˈbil-ˌfōld\ *n* **:** WALLET
bil•liards \ˈbil-yərdz\ *n* **:** any of several games played on an oblong table by driving balls against each other or into pockets with a cue
bil•lings•gate \ˈbi-liŋz-ˌgāt, *Brit usu* -git\ *n* [*Billingsgate,* old gate and fish market, London, England] **:** coarsely abusive language
bil•lion \ˈbil-yən\ *n* **1 :** a thousand millions **2** *Brit* **:** a million millions — **billion** *adj* — **bil•lionth** \-yənth\ *adj or n*
bill of health : a usu. favorable report following an examination
bill of sale : a legal document transferring ownership of goods
[1]**bil•low** \ˈbi-lō\ *n* **1 :** WAVE; *esp* **:** a great wave **2 :** a rolling mass (as of fog or flame) like a great wave — **billowy** \ˈbi-lə-wē\ *adj*
[2]**billow** *vb* **:** to rise and roll in waves; *also* **:** to swell out ⟨~*ing* sails⟩
bil•ly \ˈbi-lē\ *n, pl* **billies :** BILLY CLUB
billy club *n* **:** a heavy usu. wooden club; *esp* **:** a police officer's club
bil•ly goat \ˈbi-lē-\ *n* **:** a male goat
bi•met•al \ˈbī-ˌmet-ᵊl\ *adj* **:** BIMETALLIC — **bimetal** *n*
bi•me•tal•lic \ˌbī-mə-ˈta-lik\ *adj* **:** made of two different metals — often used of devices having a bonded expansive part — **bimetallic** *n*
bi•met•al•lism \bī-ˈmet-ᵊl-ˌi-zəm\ *n* **:** the use of two metals at fixed ratios to form a standard of value for a monetary system
[1]**bi•month•ly** \bī-ˈmənth-lē\ *adj* **1 :** occurring every two months **2 :** occurring twice a month **:** SEMIMONTHLY — **bimonthly** *adv*
[2]**bimonthly** *n* **:** a bimonthly publication
bin \ˈbin\ *n* **:** a box, crib, or enclosure used for storage
bi•na•ry \ˈbī-nə-rē, -ˌner-ē\ *adj* **1 :** consisting of two things or parts **2 :** relating to, being, or belonging to a system of numbers having 2 as its base ⟨the ~ digits 0 and 1⟩ **3 :** involving a choice between or condition of two alternatives only (as on-off, yes-no) — **binary** *n*
binary star *n* **:** a system of two stars revolving around each other
bin•au•ral \bī-ˈnȯr-əl\ *adj* **:** of or relating to sound reproduction involving the use of two separated microphones and two transmission channels to achieve a stereophonic effect
bind \ˈbīnd\ *vb* **bound** \ˈbau̇nd\; **bind•ing 1 :** TIE; *also* **:** to restrain as if by tying **2 :** to put under an obligation; *also* **:** to constrain with legal authority **3 :** BANDAGE **4 :** to unite into a mass **5 :** to compel as if by a pledge ⟨a handshake ~*s* the deal⟩ **6 :** to strengthen or decorate with a band **7 :** to fasten together and enclose in a cover ⟨~ books⟩ **8 :** to exert a tying, restraining, or compelling effect — **bind•er** *n*
bind•ing \ˈbīn-diŋ\ *n* **:** something (as a ski fastening, a cover, or an edging fabric) used to bind
[1]**binge** \ˈbinj\ *n* **:** SPREE
[2]**binge** *vb* **binged; binge•ing** *or* **bing•ing :** to go on a binge and esp. an eating binge — **bing•er** *n*
bin•go \ˈbiŋ-gō\ *n, pl* **bingos :** a game of chance played with cards having numbered squares corresponding to numbered balls drawn at random and won by covering five squares in a row
bin•na•cle \ˈbi-ni-kəl\ *n* [alter. of ME *bitakle,* fr. Pg or Sp; Pg *bitácola* & Sp *bitácula,* fr. L *habitaculum* dwelling place, fr. *habitare* to inhabit] **:** a container holding a ship's compass
[1]**bin•oc•u•lar** \bī-ˈnä-kyə-lər, bə-\ *adj* **:** of, relating to, or adapted to the use of both eyes — **bin•oc•u•lar•ly** *adv*
[2]**bin•oc•u•lar** \bə-ˈnä-kyə-lər, bī-\ *n* **1 :** a binocular optical instrument (as a microscope) **2 :** a hand-held optical instrument composed of two telescopes and a focusing device — usu. used in pl.
bi•no•mi•al \bī-ˈnō-mē-əl\ *n* **1 :** a mathematical expression consisting of two terms connected by the sign plus (+) or minus (−) **2 :** a biological species name consisting of two terms — **binomial** *adj*
bio•chem•is•try \ˌbī-ō-ˈke-mə-strē\ *n* **:** chemistry that deals with the chemical compounds and processes occurring in living things — **bio•chem•i•cal** \-mi-kəl\ *adj or n* — **bio•chem•ist** \-mist\ *n*
bio•de•grad•able \-di-ˈgrā-də-bəl\ *adj* **:** capable of being broken down esp. into innocuous products by the actions of living things (as microorganisms) ⟨a ~ detergent⟩ — **bio•de•grad•abil•i•ty** \-ˌgrā-də-ˈbi-lə-tē\ *n* — **bio•deg•ra•da•tion** \-ˌde-grə-ˈdā-shən\ *n* — **bio•de•grade** \-di-ˈgrād\ *vb*
bio•di•ver•si•ty \-də-ˈvər-sə-tē, -dī-\ *n* **:** biological diversity in an environment as indicated by numbers of different species of plants and animals
bio•eth•ics \-ˈe-thiks\ *n* **:** the ethics of biological research and its applications esp. in medicine — **bio•eth•i•cal** \-ˈe-thi-kəl\ *adj* — **bio•eth•i•cist** \-ˈe-thə-sist\ *n*
bio•feed•back \-ˈfēd-ˌbak\ *n* **:** the technique of making unconscious or involuntary bodily processes (as heartbeats or brain waves) objectively perceptible to the senses (as by use of an oscilloscope) in order to manipulate them by conscious mental control
biog *abbr* biographer; biographical; biography
bio•ge•og•ra•phy \ˌbī-ō-jē-ˈä-grə-fē\ *n* **:** a branch of biology that deals with the distribution of plants and animals — **bio•ge•og•ra•pher** *n*
bi•og•ra•phy \bī-ˈä-grə-fē, bē-\ *n, pl* **-phies :** a written history of a person's life; *also* **:** such writings in general — **bi•og•ra•pher** *n* — **bi•o•graph•i•cal** \ˌbī-ə-ˈgra-fi-kəl\ *also* **bi•o•graph•ic** \-fik\ *adj*
biol *abbr* biologic; biological; biologist; biology
bi•o•log•i•cal \ˌbī-ə-ˈlä-ji-kəl\ *also* **bi•o•log•ic** \-jik\ *adj* **1 :** of, relating to, or produced by biology or life and living processes **2 :** related by direct genetic relationship rather than by adoption or marriage ⟨~ parents⟩ — **bi•o•log•i•cal•ly** \-ji-k(ə-)lē\ *adv*
biological clock *n* **:** an inherent timing mechanism inferred to exist in some living systems (as a cell) in order to explain various cyclic physiological and behavioral responses
biological warfare *n* **:** warfare in which living organisms (as bacteria) are used as weapons
bi•ol•o•gy \bī-ˈä-lə-jē\ *n* [G *Biologie,* fr. Gk *bios* mode of life + *logos* word] **1 :** a science that deals with living beings and life processes **2 :** the life processes of an organism or group — **bi•ol•o•gist** \bī-ˈä-lə-jist\ *n*
bio•med•i•cal \ˌbī-ō-ˈme-di-kəl\ *adj* **:** of, relating to, or involving biological, medical, and physical science
bi•on•ic \bī-ˈä-nik\ *adj* **:** having normal biological ca-

pability or performance enhanced by or as if by electronic or mechanical devices

bio•phys•ics \ˌbī-ō-ˈfi-ziks\ *n* : a branch of science concerned with the application of physical principles and methods to biological problems — **bio•phys•i•cal** \-zi-kəl\ *adj* — **bio•phys•i•cist** \-ˈfi-zə-sist\ *n*

bi•op•sy \ˈbī-ˌäp-sē\ *n, pl* **-sies** : the removal of tissue, cells, or fluids from the living body for examination

bio•rhythm \ˈbī-ō-ˌri-thəm\ *n* : an inherent rhythm that appears to control or initiate various biological processes

bio•sphere \ˈbī-ə-ˌsfir\ *n* **1** : the part of the world in which life can exist **2** : living beings together with their environment

bio•tech \ˈbī-ō-ˌtek\ *n* : BIOTECHNOLOGY

bio•tech•nol•ogy \ˌbī-ō-tek-ˈnä-lə-jē\ *n* : biological science when applied esp. in genetic engineering and recombinant DNA technology

bi•ot•ic \bī-ˈä-tik\ *adj* : of or relating to life; *esp* : caused by living beings

bi•o•tin \ˈbī-ə-tən\ *n* : a vitamin of the vitamin B complex found esp. in yeast, liver, and egg yolk and active in growth promotion

bi•o•tite \ˈbī-ə-ˌtīt\ *n* : a dark mica containing iron, magnesium, potassium, and aluminum

bi•par•ti•san \bī-ˈpär-tə-zən\ *adj* : representing or composed of members of two parties

bi•par•tite \-ˈpär-ˌtīt\ *adj* **1** : being in two parts **2** : shared by two ⟨~ treaty⟩

bi•ped \ˈbī-ˌped\ *n* : a 2-footed animal — **bi•ped•al** \(ˌ)bī-ˈped-ᵊl\ *adj*

bi•plane \ˈbī-ˌplān\ *n* : an aircraft with two wings placed one above the other

bi•po•lar \bī-ˈpō-lər\ *adj* : having or involving the use of two poles — **bi•po•lar•i•ty** \ˌbī-pō-ˈlar-ə-tē\ *n*

bi•ra•cial \bī-ˈrā-shəl\ *adj* : of, relating to, or involving members of two races

¹birch \ˈbərch\ *n* **1** : any of a genus of mostly short-lived deciduous shrubs and trees with membranous outer bark and pale close-grained wood; *also* : this wood **2** : a birch rod or bundle of twigs for flogging — **birch** *or* **birch•en** \ˈbər-chən\ *adj*

²birch *vb* : WHIP, FLOG

¹bird \ˈbərd\ *n* : any of a class of warm-blooded egg-laying vertebrates having the body feathered and the forelimbs modified to form wings

²bird *vb* : to observe or identify wild birds in their native habitat — **bird•er** *n*

bird•bath \ˈbərd-ˌbath, -ˌbáth\ *n* : a usu. ornamental basin set up for birds to bathe in

bird•house \-ˌhaùs\ *n* : an artificial nesting place for birds; *also* : AVIARY

bird•ie \ˈbər-dē\ *n* : a score of one under par on a hole in golf

bird•lime \-ˌlīm\ *n* : a sticky substance smeared on twigs to snare small birds

bird of paradise : any of numerous brilliantly colored plumed birds of the New Guinea area

bird of prey : a carnivorous bird that feeds wholly or chiefly on carrion or on meat taken by hunting

bird•seed \ˈbərd-ˌsēd\ *n* : a mixture of small seeds (as of hemp or millet) used for feeding birds

bird's–eye \ˈbərdz-ˌī\ *adj* **1** : marked with spots resembling birds' eyes ⟨~ maple⟩ **2** : seen from above as if by a flying bird ⟨~ view⟩; *also* : CURSORY

bi•ret•ta \bə-ˈre-tə\ *n* : a square cap with three ridges on top worn esp. by Roman Catholic clergymen

birr \ˈbir, ˈbər\ *n, pl* **birr** — see MONEY table

birth \ˈbərth\ *n* **1** : the act or fact of being born or of bringing forth young **2** : LINEAGE, DESCENT **3** : ORIGIN, BEGINNING

birth canal *n* : the channel formed by the cervix, vagina, and vulva through which the fetus passes during birth

birth control *n* : control of the number of children born esp. by preventing or lessening the frequency of conception

birth•day \ˈbərth-ˌdā\ *n* : the day or anniversary of one's birth

birth defect *n* : a physical or biochemical defect present at birth and inherited or environmentally induced

birth•mark \ˈbərth-ˌmärk\ *n* : an unusual mark or blemish on the skin at birth

birth•place \-ˌplās\ *n* : place of birth or origin

birth•rate \-ˌrāt\ *n* : the number of births per number of individuals in a given area or group during a given time

birth•right \-ˌrīt\ *n* : a right, privilege, or possession to which one is entitled by birth **syn** legacy, patrimony, heritage, inheritance

birth•stone \-ˌstōn\ *n* : a gemstone associated symbolically with the month of one's birth

bis•cuit \ˈbis-kət\ *n* [ME *bisquite*, fr. MF *bescuit*, fr. (*pain*) *bescuit* twice-cooked bread] **1** : a crisp flat cake; *esp, Brit* : CRACKER 2 **2** : a small quick bread made from dough that has been rolled and cut or dropped from a spoon

bi•sect \ˈbī-ˌsekt\ *vb* : to divide into two usu. equal parts; *also* : CROSS, INTERSECT — **bi•sec•tion** \ˈbī-ˌsek-shən\ *n* — **bi•sec•tor** \-tər\ *n*

bi•sex•u•al \bī-ˈsek-shə-wəl\ *adj* **1** : possessing characters of or having sexual desire for both sexes **2** : of, relating to, or involving both sexes — **bisexual** *n* — **bi•sex•u•al•i•ty** \ˌbī-ˌsek-shə-ˈwal-ə-tē\ *n*

bish•op \ˈbi-shəp\ *n* [ME *bisshop*, fr. OE *bisceop*, fr. LL *episcopus*, fr. Gk *episkopos*, lit., overseer, fr. *epi-* on, over + *skeptesthai* to look] **1** : a member of the clergy ranking above a priest and typically governing a diocese **2** : any of various Protestant church officials who superintend other clergy **3** : a chess piece that can move diagonally across any number of adjoining unoccupied squares

bish•op•ric \ˈbi-shə-prik\ *n* **1** : DIOCESE **2** : the office of bishop

bis•muth \ˈbiz-məth\ *n* : a heavy brittle grayish white metallic chemical element used in alloys and medicine — see ELEMENT table

bi•son \ˈbīs-ᵊn, ˈbīz-\ *n, pl* **bison** : BUFFALO 2

bisque \ˈbisk\ *n* : a thick cream soup

bis•tro \ˈbēs-trō, ˈbis-\ *n, pl* **bistros** [F] **1** : a small or unpretentious restaurant **2** : BAR; *also* : NIGHTCLUB

¹bit \ˈbit\ *n* **1** : the biting or cutting edge or part of a tool **2** : the part of a bridle that is placed in a horse's mouth

²bit *n* **1** : a morsel of food; *also* : a small piece or quantity of something **2** : a small coin; *also* : a unit of value equal to 12½ cents **3** : something small or trivial **4** : an indefinite usu. small degree or extent ⟨a ~ tired⟩

³bit *n* [*b*inary dig*it*] : a unit of computer information equivalent to the result of a choice between two alternatives; *also* : its physical representation

¹bitch \ˈbich\ *n* **1** : a female canine; *esp* : a female dog **2** : a malicious, spiteful, and domineering woman

²bitch *vb* : COMPLAIN

¹bite \ˈbīt\ *vb* **bit** \ˈbit\; **bit•ten** \ˈbit-ᵊn\ *also* **bit; bit•ing** \ˈbī-tiŋ\ **1** : to grip with teeth or jaws; *also* : to wound or sting with or as if with fangs **2** : to cut or pierce with or as if with an edged instrument **3** : to cause to smart or sting **4** : CORRODE **5** : to take bait

²bite *n* **1** : the act or manner of biting **2** : FOOD **3** : a wound made by biting; *also* : a penetrating effect

bit•ing \ˈbī-tiŋ\ *adj* : SHARP, CUTTING

bit•ter \ˈbi-tər\ *adj* **1** : being or inducing the one of the basic taste sensations that is acrid, astringent, or disagreeable and is suggestive of hops **2** : marked by intensity or severity (as of distress or hatred) **3** : extremely harsh or cruel — **bit•ter•ly** *adv* — **bit•ter•ness** *n*

bit•tern \ˈbi-tərn\ *n* : any of various small or medium-sized herons

bit•ters \ˈbi-tərz\ *n sing or pl* : a usu. alcoholic solution of bitter and often aromatic plant products used in mixing drinks and as a mild tonic

¹bit•ter•sweet \ˈbi-tər-ˌswēt\ *n* **1** : a poisonous nightshade with purple flowers and orange-red berries **2** : a woody vine with yellow capsules that open when ripe and disclose scarlet seed coverings

²bittersweet *adj* : being at once both bitter and sweet

bi•tu•mi•nous coal \bə-ˈtü-mə-nəs-, bī-, -ˈtyü-\ *n* : a coal that when heated yields considerable volatile waste matter

bi•valve \ˈbī-ˌvalv\ *n* : an animal (as a clam) with a shell composed of two separate parts that open and shut — **bivalve** *adj*

¹biv•ouac \ˈbi-və-ˌwak\ *n* [F, fr. LG *biwacht*, fr. *bi* at + *wacht* guard] : a temporary encampment or shelter

²bivouac *vb* **-ouacked; -ouack•ing** : to form a bivouac : CAMP

¹bi•week•ly \ˌbī-ˈwē-klē\ *adj* **1** : occurring twice a week **2** : occurring every two weeks : FORTNIGHTLY — **biweekly** *adv*

²biweekly *n* : a biweekly publication

bi•year•ly \-ˈyir-lē\ *adj* **1** : BIANNUAL **2** : BIENNIAL

bi•zarre \bə-ˈzär\ *adj* : ODD, ECCENTRIC, FANTASTIC — **bi•zarre•ly** *adv*

bk *abbr* **1** bank **2** book

Bk *symbol* berkelium

bkg *abbr* banking

bkgd *abbr* background

bks *abbr* barracks

bkt *abbr* **1** basket **2** bracket

bl *abbr* **1** bale **2** barrel **3** blue

blab \ˈblab\ *vb* **blabbed; blab•bing** : TATTLE, GOSSIP

¹black \ˈblak\ *adj* **1** : of the color black; *also* : very dark **2** : SWARTHY **3** : of or relating to various groups of dark-skinned people **4** : of or relating to the Afro-American people or their culture **5** : SOILED, DIRTY **6** : lacking light ⟨a ~ night⟩ **7** : WICKED, EVIL ⟨~ magic⟩ **8** : DISMAL, GLOOMY ⟨a ~ outlook⟩ **9** : SULLEN ⟨a ~ mood⟩ — **black•ish** *adj* — **black•ly** *adv* — **black•ness** *n*

²black *n* **1** : a black pigment or dye; *also* : something (as clothing) that is black **2** : the characteristic color of soot or coal **3** : a person of a dark-skinned race **4** : AFRO-AMERICAN

³black *vb* : BLACKEN

black•a•moor \ˈbla-kə-ˌmu̇r\ *n* : a dark-skinned person

black–and–blue \ˌbla-kən-ˈblü\ *adj* : darkly discolored from blood effused by bruising

black•ball \ˈblak-ˌbȯl\ *vb* **1** : to vote against; *esp* : to exclude from membership by casting a negative vote **2** : OSTRACIZE — **black•ball** *n*

black bass *n* : any of several freshwater sunfishes native to eastern and central No. America

¹black belt \ˈblak-ˌbelt\ *n, often cap both Bs* : an area densely populated by blacks

²black belt \-ˈbelt\ *n* : one who holds the rating of expert (as in judo or karate); *also* : the rating itself

black•ber•ry \-ˌber-ē\ *n* : the usu. black or purple juicy but seedy edible fruit of various brambles; *also* : a plant bearing this fruit

black•bird \-ˌbərd\ *n* : any of various birds (as the red-winged blackbird) of which the male is largely or wholly black

black•board \-ˌbōrd\ *n* : a smooth usu. dark surface used for writing or drawing on with chalk

black•body \-ˈbä-dē\ *n* : a body or surface that completely absorbs incident radiation with no reflection

black box *n* **1** : a usu. complicated electronic device whose components and workings are unknown or mysterious to the user **2** : a device used in aircraft to record cockpit conversations and flight data

black death *n* : an epidemic of bacterial plague and esp. bubonic plague that spread rapidly in Europe and Asia in the 14th century

black•en \ˈbla-kən\ *vb* **black•ened; black•en•ing** **1** : to make or become black **2** : DEFAME, SULLY

black•ened *adj* : coated with spices and quickly seared in a very hot skillet ⟨~ swordfish⟩

black eye *n* : a discoloration of the skin around the eye from bruising

black–eyed Su•san \ˌblak-ˌīd-ˈsüz-ᵊn\ *n* : either of two No. American plants that are related to the daisies and have deep yellow to orange flower heads with dark conical centers

Black•foot \ˈblak-ˌfu̇t\ *n, pl* **Black•feet** *or* **Blackfoot** : a member of an American Indian people of Montana, Alberta, and Saskatchewan

black•guard \ˈbla-gərd, -ˌgärd\ *n* : SCOUNDREL, RASCAL

black•head \ˈblak-ˌhed\ *n* : a small usu. dark oily mass plugging the outlet of a skin gland

black hole *n* : a hypothetical celestial object with a gravitational field so strong that light cannot escape from it

black•ing \ˈbla-kiŋ\ *n* : a substance applied to something to make it black

¹black•jack \ˈblak-ˌjak\ *n* **1** : a leather-covered club with a flexible handle **2** : a card game in which the object is to be dealt cards having a higher count than the dealer but not exceeding 21

²blackjack *vb* : to hit with or as if with a blackjack

black light *n* : invisible ultraviolet light

black•list \ˈblak-ˌlist\ *n* : a list of persons who are disapproved of and are to be punished or boycotted — **blacklist** *vb*

black•mail \ˈblak-ˌmāl\ *n* : extortion by threats esp. of public exposure; *also* : something so extorted — **blackmail** *vb* — **black•mail•er** *n*

black market *n* : illicit trade in goods; *also* : a place where such trade is carried on

Black Mass *n* : a travesty of the Christian mass ascribed to worshipers of Satan

Black Muslim *n* : a member of a chiefly black group that professes Islamic religious belief

black nationalist *n, often cap B&N* : a member of a group of militant blacks who advocate separatism from whites and the formation of self-governing black communities — **black nationalism** *n, often cap B&N*

black•out \ˈbla-ˌkau̇t\ *n* **1** : a period of darkness due to electrical power failure **2** : a transitory loss or dulling of vision or consciousness **3** : the prohibition or restriction of the telecasting of a sports event — **black out** *vb*

black power *n* : the mobilization of the political and economic power of black Americans esp. to compel respect for their rights and improve their condition

black sheep *n* : a discreditable member of an otherwise respectable group

black•smith \ˈblak-ˌsmith\ *n* : a smith who forges iron — **black•smith•ing** *n*

black•thorn \-ˌthȯrn\ *n* : a European thorny plum

black•top \ˈblak-ˌtäp\ *n* : a dark tarry material (as asphalt) used esp. for surfacing roads — **blacktop** *vb*

black widow *n* : a venomous New World spider having the female black with an hourglass-shaped red mark on the underside of the abdomen

blad•der \ˈbla-dər\ *n* : a sac in which liquid or gas is stored; *esp* : one in a vertebrate into which urine passes from the kidneys

blade \ˈblād\ *n* **1** : a leaf of a plant and esp. of a grass; *also* : the flat part of a leaf as distinguished from its stalk **2** : something (as the flat part of an oar or an arm of a propeller) resembling the blade of a leaf **3** : the cutting part of an instrument or tool **4** : SWORD; *also* : SWORDSMAN **5** : a dashing fellow ⟨a gay ~⟩ **6** : the runner of an ice skate — **blad•ed** \ˈblā-dəd\ *adj*

blain \ˈblān\ *n* : an inflammatory swelling or sore

¹blame \ˈblām\ *vb* **blamed; blam•ing** [ME, fr. OF *blamer*, fr. L *blasphemare* to blaspheme, fr. Gk *blas-*

phēmein] **1 :** to find fault with **2 :** to hold responsible or responsible for **syn** censure, denounce, condemn, criticize — **blam•able** *adj*

[2]**blame** *n* **1 :** CENSURE, REPROOF **2 :** responsibility for fault or error **syn** guilt, fault, culpability, onus — **blame•less** *adj* — **blame•less•ly** *adv* — **blame•less•ness** *n*

blame•wor•thy \-ˌwər-t͟hē\ *adj* **:** deserving blame — **blame•wor•thi•ness** *n*

blanch \ˈblanch\ *vb* **:** to make or become white or pale **:** BLEACH

blanc•mange \blə-ˈmänj, -ˈmä^{n}zh\ *n* [ME *blancmanger,* fr. MF *blanc manger,* lit., white food] **:** a dessert made from gelatin or a starchy substance and milk usu. sweetened and flavored

bland \ˈbland\ *adj* **1 :** smooth in manner **:** SUAVE **2 :** gently soothing ⟨a ~ diet⟩; *also* **:** INSIPID **syn** gentle, mild, soft, balmy — **bland•ly** *adv* — **bland•ness** *n*

blan•dish•ment \ˈblan-dish-mənt\ *n* **:** flattering or coaxing speech or action **:** CAJOLERY

[1]**blank** \ˈblaŋk\ *adj* **1 :** showing or causing an appearance of dazed dismay; *also* **:** EXPRESSIONLESS **2 :** free from writing or marks; *also* **:** having spaces to be filled in **3 :** DULL, EMPTY ⟨~ moments⟩ **4 :** ABSOLUTE, DOWNRIGHT ⟨a ~ refusal⟩ **5 :** not shaped in final form — **blank•ly** *adv* — **blank•ness** *n*

[2]**blank** *n* **1 :** an empty space **2 :** a form with spaces for the entry of data **3 :** an unfinished form (as of a key) **4 :** a cartridge with propellant and a seal but no projectile

[3]**blank** *vb* **1 :** to cover or close up **:** OBSCURE **2 :** to keep from scoring

blank check *n* **1 :** a signed check with the amount unspecified **2 :** complete freedom of action

[1]**blan•ket** \ˈblaŋ-kət\ *n* **1 :** a heavy woven often woolen covering **2 :** a covering layer ⟨a ~ of snow⟩

[2]**blanket** *vb* **:** to cover with a blanket

[3]**blanket** *adj* **:** covering a group or class ⟨~ insurance⟩; *also* **:** applicable in all instances ⟨~ rules⟩

blank verse *n* **:** unrhymed iambic pentameter

blare \ˈblar\ *vb* **blared; blar•ing :** to sound loud and harsh; *also* **:** to proclaim loudly — **blare** *n*

blar•ney \ˈblär-nē\ *n* [*Blarney stone,* a stone in Blarney Castle, near Cork, Ireland, held to bestow skill in flattery on those who kiss it] **:** skillful flattery **:** BLANDISHMENT

bla•sé \blä-ˈzā\ *adj* [F] **:** apathetic to pleasure or excitement as a result of excessive indulgence; *also* **:** SOPHISTICATED

blas•pheme \blas-ˈfēm, ˈblas-ˌ\ *vb* **blas•phemed; blas•phem•ing 1 :** to speak of or address with irreverence **2 :** to utter blasphemy — **blas•phem•er** *n*

blas•phe•my \ˈblas-fə-mē\ *n, pl* **-mies 1 :** the act of expressing lack of reverence for God **2 :** irreverence toward something considered sacred — **blas•phe•mous** \-məs\ *adj*

[1]**blast** \ˈblast\ *n* **1 :** a violent gust of wind; *also* **:** its effect **2 :** sound made by a wind instrument **3 :** a current of air forced at high pressure through a hole in a furnace **(blast furnace) 4 :** a sudden withering esp. of plants **:** BLIGHT **5 :** EXPLOSION; *also* **:** the often destructive shock wave of an explosion

[2]**blast** *vb* **:** to shatter by or as if by an explosive

blast off *vb* **:** TAKE OFF 4 — used esp. of rocket-propelled vehicles — **blast•off** \ˈblast-ˌȯf\ *n*

bla•tant \ˈblāt-ᵊnt\ *adj* **:** offensively obtrusive **:** vulgarly showy **syn** vociferous, boisterous, clamorous, obstreperous — **bla•tan•cy** \-ᵊn-sē\ *n* — **bla•tant•ly** *adv*

blath•er \ˈbla-t͟hər\ *vb* **:** to talk foolishly at length — **blather** *n*

blath•er•skite \ˈbla-t͟hər-ˌskīt\ *n* **:** a person who blathers

[1]**blaze** \ˈblāz\ *n* **1 :** FIRE **2 :** intense direct light accompanied by heat **3 :** something (as a dazzling display or sudden outburst) suggesting fire ⟨a ~ of autumn leaves⟩ **syn** glare, glow, flame

[2]**blaze** *vb* **blazed; blaz•ing 1 :** to burn brightly; *also* **:** to flare up **2 :** to be conspicuously bright **:** GLITTER

[3]**blaze** *vb* **blazed; blaz•ing :** to make public or conspicuous

[4]**blaze** *n* **1 :** a usu. white stripe on the face of an animal **2 :** a trail marker; *esp* **:** one made on a tree

[5]**blaze** *vb* **blazed; blaz•ing :** to mark (as a tree or trail) with blazes

blaz•er \ˈblā-zər\ *n* **:** a sports jacket often with notched collar and pockets that are stitched on

[1]**bla•zon** \ˈblāz-ᵊn\ *n* **1 :** COAT OF ARMS **2 :** ostentatious display

[2]**blazon** *vb* **1 :** to publish widely **:** PROCLAIM **2 :** DECK, ADORN

bldg *abbr* building

bldr *abbr* builder

[1]**bleach** \ˈblēch\ *vb* **:** WHITEN, BLANCH

[2]**bleach** *n* **:** a preparation used in bleaching

bleach•ers \ˈblē-chərz\ *n sing or pl* **:** a usu. uncovered stand of tiered seats for spectators

bleak \ˈblēk\ *adj* **1 :** desolately barren and often windswept **2 :** lacking warm or cheering qualities — **bleak•ish** *adj* — **bleak•ly** *adv* — **bleak•ness** *n*

blear \ˈblir\ *adj* **:** dim with water or tears ⟨~ eyes⟩

bleary \ˈblir-ē\ *adj* **1 :** dull or dimmed esp. from fatigue or sleep **2 :** poorly outlined or defined

bleat \ˈblēt\ *n* **:** the cry of a sheep or goat or a sound like it — **bleat** *vb*

bleed \ˈblēd\ *vb* **bled** \ˈbled\; **bleed•ing 1 :** to lose or shed blood **2 :** to be wounded; *also* **:** to feel pain or distress **3 :** to flow or ooze from a wounded surface; *also* **:** to draw fluid from ⟨~ a tire⟩ **4 :** to extort money from

bleed•er \ˈblē-dər\ *n* **:** one that bleeds; *esp* **:** HEMOPHILIAC

bleeding heart *n* **1 :** a garden plant related to the poppies that has usu. deep pink drooping heart-shaped flowers **2 :** a person who shows extreme sympathy esp. for an object of alleged persecution

[1]**blem•ish** \ˈble-mish\ *vb* **:** to spoil by a flaw **:** MAR

[2]**blemish** *n* **:** a noticeable flaw

[1]**blench** \ˈblench\ *vb* [ME, to deceive, blench, fr. OE *blencan* to deceive] **:** FLINCH, QUAIL **syn** shrink, recoil, wince, start

[2]**blench** *vb* **:** to grow or make pale

[1]**blend** \ˈblend\ *vb* **blend•ed; blend•ing 1 :** to mix thoroughly **2 :** to prepare (as coffee) by mixing different varieties **3 :** to combine into an integrated whole **4 :** HARMONIZE **syn** fuse, merge, mingle, coalesce — **blend•er** *n*

[2]**blend** *n* **:** a product of blending **syn** compound, composite, alloy, mixture

bless \ˈbles\ *vb* **blessed** \ˈblest\ *also* **blest** \ˈblest\; **bless•ing** [ME, fr. OE *blētsian,* fr. *blōd* blood; fr. the use of blood in consecration] **1 :** to consecrate by religious rite or word **2 :** to sanctify with the sign of the cross **3 :** to invoke divine care for **4 :** PRAISE, GLORIFY **5 :** to confer happiness upon

bless•ed \ˈble-səd\ *also* **blest** \ˈblest\ *adj* **1 :** HOLY **2 :** BEATIFIED **3 :** DELIGHTFUL — **bless•ed•ly** *adv* — **bless•ed•ness** *n*

bless•ing \ˈble-siŋ\ *n* **1 :** the act or words of one who blesses; *also* **:** APPROVAL **2 :** a thing conducive to happiness **3 :** grace said at a meal

blew *past of* BLOW

[1]**blight** \ˈblīt\ *n* **1 :** a plant disease or injury marked by withering; *also* **:** an organism causing a blight **2 :** an impairing or frustrating influence; *also* **:** a deteriorated condition ⟨urban ~⟩

[2]**blight** *vb* **:** to affect with or suffer from blight

blimp \ˈblimp\ *n* **:** a nonrigid airship

[1]**blind** \ˈblīnd\ *adj* **1 :** lacking or grossly deficient in ability to see; *also* **:** intended for blind persons **2 :** not based on reason, evidence, or knowledge ⟨~ faith⟩ **3 :** not intelligently controlled or directed ⟨~ chance⟩ **4 :** performed solely by using aircraft instruments ⟨a ~

landing⟩ **5** : hard to discern or make out : HIDDEN ⟨a ~ seam⟩ **6** : lacking an opening or outlet ⟨a ~ alley⟩ — **blind•ly** *adv* — **blind•ness** \ˈblīnd-nəs\ *n*

²blind *vb* **1** : to make blind **2** : DAZZLE **3** : DARKEN; *also* : HIDE

³blind *n* **1** : something (as a shutter) to hinder vision or keep out light **2** : a place of concealment **3** : SUBTERFUGE

blind date *n* : a date between persons who have not previously met; *also* : either of these persons

blind•er \ˈblīn-dər\ *n* : either of two flaps on a horse's bridle to prevent it from seeing to the side

blind•fold \ˈblīnd-ˌfōld\ *vb* : to cover the eyes of with or as if with a bandage — **blindfold** *n*

¹blink \ˈbliŋk\ *vb* **1** : WINK **2** : TWINKLE **3** : EVADE, IGNORE

²blink *n* **1** : GLIMMER, SPARKLE **2** : a usu. involuntary shutting and opening of the eye

blink•er \ˈbliŋ-kər\ *n* : a blinking light used as a signal

blin•tze \ˈblint-sə\ *or* **blintz** \ˈblints\ *n* [Yiddish *blintse*] : a thin rolled pancake with a filling usu. of cream cheese

blip \ˈblip\ *n* **1** : a spot on a radar screen **2** : ABERRATION 1

bliss \ˈblis\ *n* : complete happiness : JOY **syn** beatitude, blessedness — **bliss•ful** \-fəl\ *adj* — **bliss•ful•ly** *adv*

¹blis•ter \ˈblis-tər\ *n* **1** : a raised area of skin containing watery fluid; *also* : an agent that causes blisters **2** : something (as a raised spot in paint) suggesting a blister **3** : a disease of plants marked by large swollen patches on the leaves

²blister *vb* : to develop a blister; *also* : to cause blisters

blithe \ˈblīth, ˈblīth\ *adj* **blith•er; blith•est** : happily lighthearted **syn** merry, jovial, jolly, jocund — **blithe•ly** *adv* — **blithe•some** \-səm\ *adj*

blitz \ˈblits\ *n* **1** : an intensive series of air raids **2** : a fast intensive campaign **3** : a rush of the passer by the defensive linebackers in football — **blitz** *vb*

blitz•krieg \-ˌkrēg\ *n* [G, lit., lightning war, fr. *Blitz* lightning + *Krieg* war] : a sudden violent enemy attack

bliz•zard \ˈbli-zərd\ *n* : a long severe snowstorm

blk *abbr* **1** black **2** block

bloat \ˈblōt\ *vb* : to swell by or as if by filling with water or air

blob \ˈbläb\ *n* : a small lump or drop of a thick consistency

bloc \ˈbläk\ *n* [F, lit., block] : a combination of individuals or groups (as nations) working for a common purpose

¹block \ˈbläk\ *n* **1** : a solid piece of substantial material (as wood or stone) **2** : HINDRANCE, OBSTRUCTION; *also* : interruption of normal function of body or mind ⟨heart ~⟩ **3** : a frame enclosing one or more pulleys and having a hook or strap by which it may be attached **4** : a piece of material with a hand-cut design on its surface from which copies are to be made **5** : a large building divided into separate units (as apartments or offices) **6** : a row of houses or shops **7** : a city square; *also* : the distance along one of the sides of such a square **8** : a quantity of things considered as a unit ⟨a ~ of seats⟩

²block *vb* **1** : OBSTRUCT, CHECK **2** : to outline roughly ⟨~ out a design⟩ **3** : to provide or support with a block ⟨~ up a wheel⟩ **syn** bar, impede, hinder, obstruct

block•ade \blä-ˈkād\ *n* : the isolation of a place usu. by troops or ships — **blockade** *vb* — **block•ad•er** *n*

block•age \ˈblä-kij\ *n* : an act or instance of obstructing : the state of being blocked

block•bust•er \ˈbläk-ˌbəs-tər\ *n* : one that is very large, successful, or violent ⟨a ~ of a movie⟩

block•head \ˈbläk-ˌhed\ *n* : DOLT, DUNCE

block•house \-ˌhau̇s\ *n* : a small strong building used as a shelter (as from enemy fire) or observation post

¹blond *or* **blonde** \ˈbländ\ *adj* : fair in complexion; *also* : of a light or bleached color ⟨~ mahogany⟩ — **blond•ish** \ˈblän-dish\ *adj*

²blond *or* **blonde** *n* : a person having blond hair

blood \ˈbləd\ *n* **1** : a usu. red liquid that circulates in the heart, arteries, and veins of animals **2** : LIFEBLOOD; *also* : LIFE **3** : LINEAGE, STOCK **4** : KINSHIP; *also* : KINDRED **5** : the taking of life **6** : TEMPER, PASSION **7** : DANDY 1 — **blood•less** *adj* — **bloody** *adj*

blood bank *n* : a place where blood or plasma is stored

blood•bath \ˈbləd-ˌbath, -ˌbȧth\ *n* : MASSACRE

blood count *n* : the determination of the number of blood cells in a specific volume of blood; *also* : the number of cells so determined

blood•cur•dling \ˈbləd-kərd-liŋ, -ˌkər-dᵊl-iŋ\ *adj* : arousing fright or horror

blood•ed \ˈblə-dəd\ *adj* **1** : having blood of a specified kind ⟨warm-*blooded* animals⟩ **2** : entirely or largely purebred ⟨~ horses⟩

blood group *n* : one of the classes into which human beings can be separated by the presence or absence in their blood of specific antigens

blood•hound \ˈbləd-ˌhau̇nd\ *n* : any of a breed of large powerful hounds with long drooping ears, a wrinkled face, and keen sense of smell

blood•let•ting \-ˌle-tiŋ\ *n* **1** : PHLEBOTOMY **2** : BLOODSHED

blood•line \-ˌlīn\ *n* : a sequence of direct ancestors esp. in a pedigree

blood•mo•bile \-mō-ˌbēl\ *n* : a motor vehicle equipped for collecting blood from donors

blood poisoning *n* : invasion of the bloodstream by virulent microorganisms from a focus of infection accompanied esp. by chills, fever, and prostration

blood pressure *n* : pressure of the blood on the walls of blood vessels and esp. arteries

blood•root \ˈbləd-ˌrüt, -ˌru̇t\ *n* : a plant related to the poppy that has a red root and sap, a solitary leaf, and a white flower in early spring

blood•shed \-ˌshed\ *n* : wounding or taking of life : CARNAGE, SLAUGHTER

blood•shot \-ˌshät\ *adj* : inflamed to redness ⟨~ eyes⟩

blood•stain \-ˌstān\ *n* : a discoloration caused by blood — **blood•stained** \-ˌstānd\ *adj*

blood•stone \-ˌstōn\ *n* : a green quartz sprinkled with red spots

blood•stream \-ˌstrēm\ *n* : the flowing blood in a circulatory system

blood•suck•er \-ˌsə-kər\ *n* : an animal that sucks blood; *esp* : LEECH — **blood•suck•ing** *adj*

blood test *n* : a test of the blood; *esp* : one for syphilis

blood•thirsty \ˈbləd-ˌthər-stē\ *adj* : eager to shed blood — **blood•thirst•i•ly** \-ˌthər-stə-lē\ *adv* — **blood•thirst•i•ness** \-stē-nəs\ *n*

blood type *n* : BLOOD GROUP — **blood–typ•ing** *n*

blood vessel *n* : a vessel (as a vein or artery) in which blood circulates in the body

Bloody Mary \-ˈmer-ē\ *n, pl* **Bloody Marys** : a drink made essentially of vodka and tomato juice

¹bloom \ˈblüm\ *n* **1** : FLOWER 1; *also* : flowers or amount of flowers (as of a plant) **2** : the period or state of flowering **3** : a state or time of beauty and vigor **4** : a powdery coating esp. on fruits and leaves **5** : rosy color; *also* : an appearance of freshness or health — **bloomy** *adj*

²bloom *vb* **1** : to produce or yield flowers **2** : MATURE **3** : to glow esp. with healthy color **syn** flower, blossom

bloo•mers \ˈblü-mərz\ *n pl* [Amelia *Bloomer* †1894 Am. reformer] : a woman's garment of short loose trousers gathered at the knee

bloop•er \ˈblü-pər\ *n* **1** : a fly ball hit barely beyond a baseball infield **2** : an embarrassing public blunder

¹blos•som \ˈblä-səm\ *n* **1** : the flower of a plant **2** : the period or state of flowering

²blossom *vb* : FLOWER, BLOOM

DICTIONARY

[1]blot \ˈblät\ *n* **1 :** SPOT, STAIN ⟨ink ~*s*⟩ **2 :** BLEMISH **syn** stigma, brand, slur

[2]blot *vb* **blot·ted; blot·ting 1 :** SPOT, STAIN **2 :** OBSCURE, ECLIPSE ⟨~ out the sun⟩ **3** *obs* **:** MAR; *esp* **:** DISGRACE **4 :** to dry or remove with or as if with an absorbing material **5 :** to make a blot

blotch \ˈbläch\ *n* **:** a usu. large and irregular spot or mark (as of ink or color) — **blotch** *vb* — **blotchy** *adj*

blot·ter \ˈblä-tər\ *n* **1 :** a piece of blotting paper **2 :** a book for preliminary records (as of sales or arrests)

blot·ting paper *n* **:** a spongy paper used to absorb ink

blouse \ˈblau̇s, ˈblau̇z\ *n* **1 :** a loose outer garment like a smock **2 :** a usu. loose garment reaching from the neck to about the waist

[1]blow \ˈblō\ *vb* **blew** \ˈblü\; **blown** \ˈblōn\; **blow·ing 1 :** to move forcibly ⟨the wind *blew*⟩ **2 :** to send forth a current of gas (as air) **3 :** to act on with a current of gas or vapor; *esp* **:** to drive with such a current **4 :** to sound or cause to sound ⟨~ a horn⟩ **5 :** PANT, GASP; *also* **:** to expel moist air in breathing ⟨the whale *blew*⟩ **6 :** BOAST; *also* **:** BLUSTER **7 :** MELT — used of an electrical fuse **8 :** to shape or form by blown or injected air ⟨~ glass⟩ **9 :** to shatter or destroy by or as if by explosion **10 :** to make breathless by exertion **11 :** to spend recklessly **12 :** to foul up hopelessly ⟨*blew* her lines⟩ — **blow·er** *n*

[2]blow *n* **1 :** a usu. strong blowing of air **:** GALE **2 :** BOASTING, BRAG **3 :** an act or instance of blowing

[3]blow *vb* **blew** \ˈblü\; **blown** \ˈblōn\; **blow·ing :** FLOWER, BLOOM

[4]blow *n* **1 :** a forcible stroke **2 :** COMBAT ⟨come to ~*s*⟩ **3 :** a severe and usu. unexpected calamity

blow–by–blow *adj* **:** minutely detailed ⟨~ account⟩

blow–dry \-ˌdrī\ *vb* **:** to dry and usu. style hair with a blow-dryer

blow–dryer \-ˌdrī(-ə)r\ *n* **:** a hand-held hair dryer

blow·fly \ˈblō-ˌflī\ *n* **:** any of a family of dipteran flies (as a bluebottle) that deposit their eggs or maggots on meat or in wounds

blow·gun \-ˌgən\ *n* **:** a tube from which an arrow or a dart may be shot by the force of the breath

blow·out \ˈblō-ˌau̇t\ *n* **:** a bursting of something (as a tire) because of pressure of the contents (as air)

blow·sy *also* **blow·zy** \ˈblau̇-zē\ *adj* **:** DISHEVELED, SLOVENLY

blow·torch \ˈblō-ˌtȯrch\ *n* **:** a small portable burner whose flame is made hotter by a blast of air or oxygen

blow·up \ˈblō-ˌəp\ *n* **1 :** EXPLOSION **2 :** an outburst of temper **3 :** a photographic enlargement

blowy \ˈblō-ē\ *adj* **:** WINDY

BLT \ˌbē-ˌel-ˈtē\ *n* **:** a bacon, lettuce, and tomato sandwich

[1]blub·ber \ˈblə-bər\ *vb* **:** to cry noisily

[2]blubber *n* **1 :** the fat of large sea mammals (as whales) **2 :** a noisy crying

[1]blud·geon \ˈblə-jən\ *n* **:** a short often loaded club

[2]bludgeon *vb* **:** to strike with or as if with a bludgeon

[1]blue \ˈblü\ *adj* **blu·er; blu·est 1 :** of the color blue; *also* **:** BLUISH **2 :** MELANCHOLY; *also* **:** DEPRESSING **3 :** PURITANICAL **4 :** INDECENT — **blue·ness** *n*

[2]blue *n* **1 :** a color between green and violet in the spectrum **:** the color of the clear daytime sky **2 :** something (as clothing or the sky) that is blue

blue baby *n* **:** a baby with bluish skin due to faulty circulation caused by a heart defect

blue·bell \-ˌbel\ *n* **:** any of various plants with blue bell-shaped flowers

blue·ber·ry \ˈblü-ˌber-ē, -bə-rē\ *n* **:** the edible blue or blackish berry of various shrubs of the heath family; *also* **:** one of these shrubs

blue·bird \-ˌbərd\ *n* **:** any of several small No. American thrushes that are blue above and reddish-brown or pale blue below

blue·bon·net \ˈblü-ˌbä-nət\ *n* **:** either of two low-growing annual lupines of Texas with silky foliage and blue flowers

blue·bot·tle \ˈblü-ˌbät-ᵊl\ *n* **:** any of several blowflies with iridescent blue bodies or abdomens

blue cheese *n* **:** cheese having veins of greenish blue mold

blue–col·lar \ˈblü-ˈkä-lər\ *adj* **:** of, relating to, or being the class of workers whose duties call for work clothes

blue·fish \-ˌfish\ *n* **:** a marine sport and food fish bluish above and silvery below

blue·grass \-ˌgras\ *n* **1 :** KENTUCKY BLUEGRASS **2 :** country music played on stringed instruments having free improvisation and close harmonies

blue jay \-ˌjā\ *n* **:** a crested bright blue No. American jay

blue jeans *n pl* **:** pants usu. made of blue denim

blue·nose \ˈblü-ˌnōz\ *n* **:** a person who advocates a rigorous moral code

blue·point \-ˌpȯint\ *n* **:** a small oyster typically from the south shore of Long Island, New York

blue·print \-ˌprint\ *n* **1 :** a photographic print in white on a blue ground used esp. for copying mechanical drawings and architects' plans **2 :** a detailed plan of action — **blueprint** *vb*

blues \ˈblüz\ *n pl* **1 :** MELANCHOLY **2 :** music in a style marked by recurrent minor intervals and melancholy lyrics

blue·stock·ing \ˈblü-ˌstä-kiŋ\ *n* **:** a woman having intellectual interests

blu·et \ˈblü-ət\ *n* **:** a low No. American herb with dainty bluish flowers

blue whale *n* **:** a very large baleen whale that may reach a weight of 150 tons (135 metric tons) and a length of 100 feet (30 meters)

[1]bluff \ˈbləf\ *adj* **1 :** having a broad flattened front **2 :** rising steeply with a broad flat front **3 :** OUTSPOKEN, FRANK **syn** abrupt, blunt, brusque, curt, gruff

[2]bluff *n* **:** a high steep bank **:** CLIFF

[3]bluff *vb* **:** to frighten or deceive by pretense or a mere show of strength

[4]bluff *n* **:** an act or instance of bluffing; *also* **:** one who bluffs

blu·ing *or* **blue·ing** \ˈblü-iŋ\ *n* **:** a preparation used in laundering to counteract yellowing of white fabrics

blu·ish \ˈblü-ish\ *adj* **:** somewhat blue

[1]blun·der \ˈblən-dər\ *vb* **1 :** to move clumsily or unsteadily **2 :** to make a stupid or needless mistake

[2]blunder *n* **:** an avoidable and usu. serious mistake

blun·der·buss \ˈblən-dər-ˌbəs\ *n* [obs. D *donderbus,* fr. D *donder* thunder + obs. D *bus* gun] **:** an obsolete short-barreled firearm with a flaring muzzle

blunderbuss

[1]blunt \ˈblənt\ *adj* **1 :** not sharp **:** DULL **2 :** lacking in tact **:** BLUFF **syn** brusque, curt, gruff, abrupt, crusty — **blunt·ly** *adv* — **blunt·ness** *n*

[2]blunt *vb* **:** to make or become dull

[1]blur \ˈblər\ *n* **1 :** a smear or stain that obscures **2 :** something vaguely perceived; *esp* **:** something moving too quickly to be clearly perceived — **blur·ry** \-ē\ *adj*

[2]blur *vb* **blurred; blur·ring :** DIM, CLOUD, OBSCURE

blurb \ˈblərb\ *n* **:** a short publicity notice (as on a book jacket)

blurt \ˈblərt\ *vb* **:** to utter suddenly and impulsively

blush \ˈbləsh\ *n* **:** a reddening of the face (as from modesty or confusion) **:** FLUSH — **blush** *vb* — **blush·ful** *adj*

blus·ter \ˈbləs-tər\ *vb* **1 :** to blow in stormy noisy gusts **2 :** to talk or act with noisy swaggering threats — **bluster** *n* — **blus·tery** \-tə-rē\ *adj*

blvd *abbr* boulevard
B lymphocyte *n* : B CELL
BM *abbr* bowel movement
B movie *n* : a cheaply produced motion picture
BO *abbr* **1** best offer **2** body odor **3** box office **4** branch office
boa \ˈbō-ə\ *n* **1** : a large snake (as the **boa con•stric•tor** \-kən-ˈstrik-tər\ or the related anaconda) that suffocates and kills its prey by constriction **2** : a fluffy scarf usu. of fur or feathers
boar \ˈbōr\ *n* : a male swine; *also* : WILD BOAR
[1]**board** \ˈbōrd\ *n* **1** : the side of a ship **2** : a thin flat length of sawed lumber; *also* : material (as cardboard) or a piece of material formed as a thin flat firm sheet **3** *pl* : STAGE 1 **4** : a table spread with a meal; *also* : daily meals esp. when furnished for pay **5** : a table at which a council or magistrates sit **6** : a group or association of persons organized for a special responsibility (as the management of a business or institution); *also* : an organized commercial exchange **7** : a sheet of insulating material carrying circuit elements and inserted in an electronic device
[2]**board** *vb* **1** : to go or put aboard ⟨~ a boat⟩ **2** : to cover with boards **3** : to provide or be provided with meals and often lodging — **board•er** *n*
board•ing•house \ˈbōr-diŋ-ˌhau̇s\ *n* : a house at which persons are boarded
board•walk \ˈbōrd-ˌwȯk\ *n* : a promenade (as of planking) along a beach
boast \ˈbōst\ *vb* **1** : to praise oneself **2** : to mention or assert with excessive pride **3** : to prize as a possession; *also* : HAVE ⟨the house ~*s* a fireplace⟩ — **boast** *n* — **boast•ful** \-fəl\ *adj* — **boast•ful•ly** *adv*
boat \ˈbōt\ *n* : a small vessel for travel on water; *also* : SHIP
boat•er \ˈbō-tər\ *n* **1** : one that travels in a boat **2** : a stiff straw hat
boat•man \ˈbōt-mən\ *n* : a man who operates, works on, or deals in boats
boat people *n pl* : refugees fleeing by boat
boat•swain \ˈbōs-ᵊn\ *n* : a subordinate officer of a ship in charge of the hull and related equipment
[1]**bob** \ˈbäb\ *vb* **bobbed; bob•bing 1** : to move up and down jerkily or repeatedly **2** : to emerge, arise, or appear suddenly or unexpectedly
[2]**bob** *n* : a bobbing movement
[3]**bob** *n* **1** : a knob, knot, twist, or curl esp. of ribbons, yarn, or hair **2** : a short haircut of a woman or child **3** : FLOAT 2 **4** : a weight hanging from a line
[4]**bob** *vb* **bobbed; bob•bing** : to cut hair in a bob
[5]**bob** *n, pl* **bob** *slang Brit* : SHILLING
bob•bin \ˈbä-bən\ *n* : a cylinder or spindle for holding or dispensing thread (as in a sewing machine)
bob•ble \ˈbä-bəl\ *vb* **bob•bled; bob•bling** : FUMBLE — **bobble** *n*
bob•by \ˈbä-bē\ *n, pl* **bobbies** [*Bobby,* nickname for Sir *Robert* Peel, who organized the London police force] *Brit* : a police officer
bobby pin *n* : a flat wire hairpin with prongs that press close together
bob•cat \ˈbäb-ˌkat\ *n* : a small usu. rusty-colored No. American lynx
bob•o•link \ˈbä-bə-ˌliŋk\ *n* : an American migratory songbird related to the meadowlarks
bob•sled \ˈbäb-ˌsled\ *n* **1** : a short sled usu. used as one of a joined pair **2** : a racing sled with two pairs of runners, a steering wheel, and a hand brake — **bobsled** *vb*
bob•white \(ˌ)bäb-ˈhwīt\ *n* : any of a genus of quail; *esp* : a popular game bird of the eastern and central U.S.
boc•cie *or* **boc•ci** *or* **boc•ce** \ˈbä-chē\ *n* : Italian lawn bowling played on a long narrow court
bock \ˈbäk\ *n* : a dark heavy beer usu. sold in early spring
bod \ˈbäd\ *n* : BODY
[1]**bode** \ˈbōd\ *vb* **bod•ed; bod•ing** : to indicate by signs : PRESAGE
[2]**bode** *past of* BIDE
bo•de•ga \bō-ˈdā-gə\ *n* [Sp, fr. L *apotheca* storehouse] : a store specializing in Hispanic groceries
bod•ice \ˈbä-dəs\ *n* [alter. of *bodies,* pl. of *body*] : the usu. close-fitting part of a dress above the waist
bodi•less \ˈbä-di-ləs\ *adj* : lacking a body or material form
[1]**bodi•ly** \ˈbäd-ᵊl-ē\ *adj* : of or relating to the body ⟨~ contact⟩
[2]**bodily** *adv* **1** : in the flesh **2** : as a whole ⟨lifted the crate up ~⟩
bod•kin \ˈbäd-kən\ *n* **1** : DAGGER **2** : a pointed implement for punching holes in cloth **3** : a blunt needle for drawing tape or ribbon through a loop or hem
body \ˈbä-dē\ *n, pl* **bod•ies 1** : the physical whole of a living or dead organism; *also* : the trunk or main mass of an organism as distinguished from its appendages **2** : a human being : PERSON **3** : the main part of something **4** : a mass of matter distinct from other masses **5** : GROUP **6** : VISCOSITY, FIRMNESS **7** : richness of flavor — used esp. of wines — **bod•ied** \ˈbä-dēd\ *adj*
body English *n* : bodily motions made in a usu. unconscious effort to influence the movement of a propelled object (as a ball)
body•guard \ˈbä-dē-ˌgärd\ *n* : a personal guard; *also* : RETINUE
body stocking *n* : a sheer close-fitting one-piece garment for the torso that often has sleeves and legs
body•work \ˈbä-dē-ˌwərk\ *n* : the making or repairing of vehicle bodies
Boer \ˈbōr, ˈbu̇r\ *n* [D, lit., farmer] : a South African of Dutch or Huguenot descent
[1]**bog** \ˈbäg, ˈbȯg\ *n* : wet, spongy, poorly drained, and usu. acid ground — **bog•gy** *adj*
[2]**bog** *vb* **bogged; bog•ging** : to sink into or as if into a bog
bo•gey *also* **bo•gie** *or* **bo•gy** \ˈbu̇-gē, ˈbō- *for 1*; ˈbō- *for 2*\ *n, pl* **bogeys** *also* **bogies 1** : SPECTER, HOBGOBLIN; *also* : a source of fear or annoyance **2** : a score of one over par on a hole in golf
bo•gey•man \ˈbu̇-gē-ˌman, ˈbō-, ˈbü-\ *n* : an imaginary monster used in threatening children
bog•gle \ˈbä-gəl\ *vb* **bog•gled; bog•gling** : to overwhelm or be overwhelmed with fright or amazement
bo•gus \ˈbō-gəs\ *adj* : SPURIOUS, SHAM
Bo•he•mi•an \bō-ˈhē-mē-ən\ *n* **1** : a native or inhabitant of Bohemia **2** *often not cap* : VAGABOND, WANDERER **3** *often not cap* : a person (as a writer or artist) living an unconventional life — **bohemian** *adj, often cap*
[1]**boil** \ˈbȯil\ *n* : an inflamed swelling on the skin containing pus
[2]**boil** *vb* **1** : to heat or become heated to a temperature (**boil•ing point**) at which vapor is formed and rises in bubbles ⟨water ~*s* and changes to steam⟩; *also* : to act on or be acted on by a boiling liquid ⟨~ eggs⟩ **2** : to be in a state of seething agitation
[3]**boil** *n* : the act or state of boiling
boil•er \ˈbȯi-lər\ *n* **1** : a container in which something is boiled **2** : a strong vessel used in making steam **3** : a tank holding hot water
boil•er•mak•er \ˈbȯi-lər-ˌmā-kər\ *n* : whiskey with a beer chaser
bois•ter•ous \ˈbȯi-st(ə-)rəs\ *adj* : noisily turbulent or exuberant — **bois•ter•ous•ly** *adv*
bok choy \ˈbäk-ˈchȯi\ *n* : a Chinese vegetable related to the mustards that forms a loose head of green leaves with long thick white stalks
bo•la \ˈbō-lə\ *or* **bo•las** \-ləs\ *n, pl* **bolas** \-ləz\ *also* **bo•las•es** [AmerSp *bolas,* fr. Sp *bola* ball] : a cord with weights attached to the ends for hurling at and entangling an animal
☞ For illustration, see next page.

bola

bold \ˈbōld\ *adj* **1** : COURAGEOUS, INTREPID **2** : IMPUDENT **3** : STEEP **4** : ADVENTUROUS, FREE ⟨a ~ thinker⟩ **syn** dauntless, brave, valiant — **bold•ly** *adv* — **bold•ness** \ˈbōld-nəs\ *n*

bold•face \ˈbōld-ˌfās\ *n* : a heavy-faced type; *also* : printing in boldface — **bold–faced** \-ˈfāst\ *adj*

bole \ˈbōl\ *n* : the trunk of a tree

bo•le•ro \bə-ˈler-ō\ *n, pl* **-ros 1** : a Spanish dance or its music **2** : a short loose jacket open at the front

bo•li•var \bə-ˈlē-ˌvär, ˈbä-lə-vər\ *n, pl* **-va•res** \ˌbä-lə-ˈvär-ˌās, ˌbō-\ *or* **-vars** — see MONEY table

Bo•liv•i•an \bə-ˈli-vē-ən\ *n* : a native or inhabitant of Bolivia — **Bolivian** *adj*

bo•li•vi•a•no \bə-ˈli-vē-ˈä-(ˌ)nō\ *n, pl* **-nos** — see MONEY table

boll \ˈbōl\ *n* : a seed pod (as of cotton)

boll weevil *n* : a small grayish weevil that infests the cotton plant both as a larva and as an adult

boll•worm \ˈbōl-ˌwərm\ *n* : any of several moths and esp. the corn earworm whose larvae feed on cotton bolls

bo•lo•gna \bə-ˈlō-nē\ *n* [short for *Bologna sausage,* fr. *Bologna,* Italy] : a large smoked sausage of beef, veal, and pork

Bol•she•vik \ˈbōl-shə-ˌvik\ *n, pl* **Bolsheviks** *also* **Bol•she•vi•ki** \ˌbōl-shə-ˈvi-kē\ [Russ *bol'shevik,* fr. *bol'shiĭ* larger] **1** : a member of the party that seized power in Russia in the revolution of November 1917 **2** : COMMUNIST — **Bolshevik** *adj*

bol•she•vism \ˈbōl-shə-ˌvi-zəm\ *n, often cap* : the doctrine or program of the Bolsheviks advocating violent overthrow of capitalism

¹bol•ster \ˈbōl-stər\ *n* : a long pillow or cushion

²bolster *vb* : to support with or as if with a bolster; *also* : REINFORCE

¹bolt \ˈbōlt\ *n* **1** : a missile (as an arrow) for a crossbow or catapult **2** : a flash of lightning : THUNDERBOLT **3** : a sliding bar used to fasten a door **4** : a roll of cloth or wallpaper of specified length **5** : a rod with a head at one end and a screw thread at the other used with a nut to fasten objects together **6** : a metal cylinder that drives the cartridge into the chamber of a firearm

²bolt *vb* **1** : to move suddenly (as in fright or hurry) : START, DASH **2** : to break away (as from association) ⟨~ from a political platform⟩ **3** : to produce seed prematurely **4** : to secure or fasten with a bolt **5** : to swallow hastily or without chewing

³bolt *n* : an act of bolting

bo•lus \ˈbō-ləs\ *n* **1** : a large pill **2** : a soft mass of chewed food

¹bomb \ˈbäm\ *n* **1** : a fused explosive device designed to detonate under specified conditions (as impact) **2** : an aerosol or foam dispenser (as of insecticide or hair spray) : SPRAY CAN **3** : a long pass in football

²bomb *vb* : to attack with bombs

bom•bard \bäm-ˈbärd\ *vb* **1** : to attack esp. with artillery or bombers **2** : to assail persistently **3** : to subject to the impact of rapidly moving particles (as electrons) — **bom•bard•ment** *n*

bom•bar•dier \ˌbäm-bər-ˈdir\ *n* : a bomber-crew member who releases the bombs

bom•bast \ˈbäm-ˌbast\ *n* [ME, cotton padding, fr. MF *bombace,* fr. ML *bombax* cotton, alter. of L *bombyx* silkworm, silk, fr. Gk] : pretentious wordy speech or writing — **bom•bas•tic** \bäm-ˈbas-tik\ *adj* — **bom•bas•ti•cal•ly** \-ti-k(ə-)lē\ *adv*

bom•ba•zine \ˌbäm-bə-ˈzēn\ *n* **1** : a twilled fabric with silk warp and worsted filling **2** : a silk fabric in twill weave dyed black

bomb•er \ˈbä-mər\ *n* : one that bombs; *esp* : an airplane for dropping bombs

bomb•proof \ˈbäm-ˌprüf\ *adj* : safe against the explosive force of bombs

bomb•shell \ˈbäm-ˌshel\ *n* **1** : BOMB 1 **2** : one that stuns, amazes, or completely upsets

bona fide \ˈbō-nə-ˌfīd, ˈbä-; ˌbō-nə-ˈfī-dē, -də\ *adj* [L, in good faith] **1** : made in good faith ⟨a *bona fide* agreement⟩ **2** : GENUINE, REAL ⟨a *bona fide* bargain⟩

bo•nan•za \bə-ˈnan-zə\ *n* [Sp, lit., calm sea, fr. ML *bonacia,* alter. of L *malacia,* fr. Gk *malakia,* lit., softness, fr. *malakos* soft] : something yielding a rich return

bon•bon \ˈbän-ˌbän\ *n* : a candy with a creamy center and a soft covering (as of chocolate)

¹bond \ˈbänd\ *n* **1** : FETTER **2** : a binding or uniting force or tie ⟨~*s* of friendship⟩ **3** : an agreement or obligation often made binding by a pledge of money or goods **4** : a person who acts as surety for another **5** : an interest-bearing certificate of public or private indebtedness **6** : the state of goods subject to supervision pending payment of taxes or duties due

²bond *vb* **1** : to assure payment of duties or taxes on (goods) by giving a bond **2** : to insure against losses caused by the acts of ⟨~ a bank teller⟩ **3** : to make or become firmly united as if by bonds ⟨~ iron to copper⟩

bond•age \ˈbän-dij\ *n* : SLAVERY, SERVITUDE

bond•hold•er \ˈbänd-ˌhōl-dər\ *n* : one that owns a government or corporation bond

bond•ing *n* **1** : the formation of a close personal relationship esp. through frequent or constant association **2** : the attaching of a material (as porcelain) to a tooth surface esp. for cosmetic purposes

bond•man \ˈbänd-mən\ *n* : SLAVE, SERF

¹bonds•man \ˈbändz-mən\ *n* : SURETY 3

²bondsman *n* : BONDMAN

bond•wom•an \ˈbänd-ˌwu̇-mən\ *n* : a female slave or serf

¹bone \ˈbōn\ *n* **1** : a hard largely calcareous tissue forming most of the skeleton of a vertebrate animal; *also* : one of the pieces of bone making up a vertebrate skeleton **2** : a hard animal substance (as ivory or baleen) similar to true bone **3** : something made of bone — **bone•less** *adj* — **bony** *also* **bon•ey** \ˈbō-nē\ *adj*

²bone *vb* **boned; bon•ing** : to free from bones ⟨~ a chicken⟩

bone black *n* : the black carbon residue from calcined bones used esp. as a pigment

bone meal *n* : crushed or ground bone used esp. as fertilizer or feed

bon•er \ˈbō-nər\ *n* : a stupid and ridiculous blunder

bone up *vb* **1** : CRAM 3 **2** : to refresh one's memory ⟨*boned up* on the speech before giving it⟩

bon•fire \ˈbän-ˌfīr\ *n* [ME *bonefire* a fire of bones, fr. *bon* bone + *fire*] : a large fire built in the open air

bon•go \ˈbäŋ-gō\ *n, pl* **bongos** *also* **bongoes** [AmerSp *bongó*] : one of a pair of small tuned drums played with the hands

bon•ho•mie \ˌbä-nə-ˈmē\ *n* [F *bonhomie,* fr. *bon-*

homme good-natured man, fr. *bon* good + *homme* man] : good-natured easy friendliness

bo•ni•to \bə-ˈnē-tō\ *n, pl* **-tos** *or* **-to** : any of several medium-sized tunas

bon mot \bō^{n}-ˈmō\ *n, pl* **bons mots** *same*\ *or* **bon mots** *same or* -ˈmō\ [F, lit., good word] : a clever remark

bon•net \ˈbä-nət\ *n* : a covering (as a cap) for the head; *esp* : a hat for a woman or infant tied under the chin

bon•ny \ˈbä-nē\ *adj* **bon•ni•er; -est** *chiefly Brit* : ATTRACTIVE, FAIR; *also* : FINE, EXCELLENT

bon•sai \bōn-ˈsī\ *n, pl* **bonsai** [Jp] : a potted plant (as a tree) dwarfed by special methods of culture; *also* : the art of growing such a plant

bo•nus \ˈbō-nəs\ *n* : something in addition to what is expected

bon vi•vant \ˌbän-vē-ˈvänt, ˌbō^{n}-vē-ˈvä^{n}\ *n, pl* **bons vivants** \ˌbän-vē-ˈvänts, ˌbō^{n}-vē-ˈvä^{n}\ *or* **bon vivants** *same*\ [F, lit., good liver] : a person having cultivated, refined, and sociable tastes esp. in food and drink

bon voy•age \ˌbō^{n}-ˌvȯi-ˈäzh, ˌbän-; ˌbō^{n}-ˌvwä-ˈyäzh\ *n* : FAREWELL — often used as an interjection

bony fish *n* : any of a very large group of fishes (as a salmon or marlin) with a bony rather than a cartilaginous skeleton

bonze \ˈbänz\ *n* : a Buddhist monk

boo \ˈbü\ *n, pl* **boos** : a shout of disapproval or contempt — **boo** *vb*

boo•by \ˈbü-bē\ *n, pl* **boobies** : an awkward foolish person : DOPE

booby hatch *n* : an insane asylum

booby prize *n* : an award for the poorest performance in a contest

booby trap *n* : a trap for the unwary; *esp* : a concealed explosive device set to go off when some harmless-looking object is touched — **booby–trap** *vb*

boo•dle \ˈbüd-^{ə}l\ *n* **1** : bribe money **2** : a large amount of money

[1]**book** \ˈbu̇k\ *n* **1** : a set of sheets bound into a volume **2** : a long written or printed narrative or record **3** : a major division of a long literary work **4** *cap* : BIBLE

[2]**book** *vb* **1** : to engage, reserve, or schedule by or as if by writing in a book ⟨~ seats on a plane⟩ **2** : to enter charges against in a police register

book•case \-ˌkās\ *n* : a piece of furniture consisting of shelves to hold books

book•end \-ˌend\ *n* : a support to hold up a row of books

book•ie \ˈbu̇-kē\ *n* : BOOKMAKER

book•ish \ˈbu̇-kish\ *adj* **1** : fond of books and reading **2** : inclined to rely unduly on book knowledge

book•keep•er \ˈbu̇k-ˌkē-pər\ *n* : one who records the accounts or transactions of a business — **book•keep•ing** *n*

book•let \ˈbu̇k-lət\ *n* : PAMPHLET

book•mak•er \ˈbu̇k-ˌmā-kər\ *n* : one who determines odds and receives and pays off bets — **book•mak•ing** *n*

book•mark \-ˌmärk\ *or* **book•mark•er** \-ˌmär-kər\ *n* : a marker for finding a place in a book

book•mo•bile \ˈbu̇k-mō-ˌbēl\ *n* : a truck that serves as a traveling library

book•plate \ˈbu̇k-ˌplāt\ *n* : a label pasted in a book to show who owns it

book•sell•er \ˈbu̇k-ˌse-lər\ *n* : one who sells books; *esp* : the proprietor of a bookstore

book•shelf \-ˌshelf\ *n* : a shelf for books

book•worm \ˈbu̇k-ˌwərm\ *n* : a person unusually devoted to reading and study

[1]**boom** \ˈbüm\ *vb* **1** : to make a deep hollow sound : RESOUND **2** : to grow or cause to grow rapidly esp. in value, esteem, or importance

[2]**boom** *n* **1** : a booming sound or cry **2** : a rapid expansion or increase esp. of economic activity

[3]**boom** *n* **1** : a long spar used to extend the bottom of a sail **2** : a line of floating timbers used to obstruct passage or catch floating objects **3** : a beam projecting from the upright pole of a derrick to support or guide the object lifted

boom box *n* : a large portable radio and often tape player

boo•mer•ang \ˈbü-mə-ˌraŋ\ *n* [Dharuk (an Australian aboriginal language *bumarin^{y}*] : a bent or angular club that can be so thrown as to return near the starting point

[1]**boon** \ˈbün\ *n* [ME, fr. ON *bōn* petition] : BENEFIT, BLESSING **syn** favor, gift, largess, present

[2]**boon** *adj* [ME *bon,* fr. MF, good] : CONVIVIAL ⟨a ~ companion⟩

boon•docks \ˈbün-ˌdäks\ *n pl* [Tagalog (language of the Philippines) *bundok* mountain] **1** : rough country filled with dense brush **2** : a rural area

boon•dog•gle \ˈbün-ˌdä-gəl, -ˌdȯ-\ *n* : a useless or wasteful project or activity

boor \ˈbu̇r\ *n* **1** : YOKEL **2** : a rude or insensitive person **syn** churl, lout, clown, clodhopper — **boor•ish** *adj*

boost \ˈbüst\ *vb* **1** : to push up from below **2** : INCREASE, RAISE ⟨~ prices⟩ **3** : AID, PROMOTE ⟨voted a bonus to ~ morale⟩ — **boost** *n* — **boost•er** *n*

[1]**boot** \ˈbüt\ *n, chiefly dial* : something to equalize a trade — **to boot** : BESIDES

[2]**boot** *vb, archaic* : AVAIL, PROFIT

[3]**boot** *n* **1** : a covering for the foot and leg **2** : a protective sheath (as of a flower) **3** *Brit* : an automobile trunk **4** : KICK; *also* : a discharge from employment **5** : a navy or marine corps trainee

[4]**boot** *vb* **1** : KICK **2** : to eject or discharge summarily

boot•black \ˈbüt-ˌblak\ *n* : a person who shines shoes

boo•tee *or* **boo•tie** \ˈbü-tē\ *n* : an infant's knitted or crocheted sock

booth \ˈbüth\ *n, pl* **booths** \ˈbüt͟hz, ˈbüths\ **1** : a small enclosed stall (as at a fair) **2** : a small enclosure giving privacy for a person ⟨voting ~⟩ ⟨telephone ~⟩ **3** : a restaurant accommodation having a table between backed benches

boot•leg \ˈbüt-ˌleg\ *vb* : to make, transport, or sell (as liquor) illegally — **boot•leg** *adj or n* — **boot•leg•ger** *n*

boot•less \ˈbüt-ləs\ *adj* : USELESS **syn** futile, vain, abortive, fruitless — **boot•less•ly** *adv* — **boot•less•ness** *n*

boo•ty \ˈbü-tē\ *n, pl* **booties** : PLUNDER, SPOIL

[1]**booze** \ˈbüz\ *vb* **boozed; booz•ing** : to drink liquor to excess — **booz•er** *n*

[2]**booze** *n* : intoxicating liquor — **boozy** *adj*

bop \ˈbäp\ *vb* **bopped; bop•ping** : HIT, SOCK — **bop** *n*

BOQ *abbr* bachelor officers' quarters

bor *abbr* borough

bo•rate \ˈbōr-ˌāt\ *n* : a salt or ester of boric acid

bo•rax \ˈbōr-ˌaks\ *n* : a crystalline borate of sodium that occurs as a mineral and is used as a flux and cleanser

bor•del•lo \bȯr-ˈde-lō\ *n, pl* **-los** [It] : BROTHEL

[1]**bor•der** \ˈbȯr-dər\ *n* **1** : EDGE, MARGIN **2** : BOUNDARY, FRONTIER **syn** rim, brim, brink, fringe, perimeter

[2]**border** *vb* **bor•dered; bor•der•ing 1** : to put a border on **2** : ADJOIN **3** : VERGE

bor•der•land \ˈbȯr-dər-ˌland\ *n* **1** : territory at or near a border **2** : an outlying or intermediate region often not clearly defined

bor•der•line \-ˌlīn\ *adj* : being in an intermediate position or state; *esp* : not quite up to what is standard or expected ⟨~ intelligence⟩

[1]**bore** \ˈbōr\ *vb* **bored; bor•ing 1** : to make a hole in with or as if with a drill **2** : to make (as a well) by boring or digging away material **syn** perforate, drill, prick, puncture — **bor•er** *n*

[2]**bore** *n* **1** : a hole made by or as if by boring **2** : a cylindrical cavity **3** : the diameter of a hole or tube; *esp* : the interior diameter of a gun barrel or engine cylinder

[3]**bore** *past of* BEAR

[4]**bore** *n* : a tidal flood with a high abrupt front

[5]**bore** *n* : one that causes boredom
[6]**bore** *vb* **bored; bor•ing** : to weary with tedious dullness
bo•re•al \ˈbōr-ē-əl\ *adj* : of, relating to, or located in northern regions
bore•dom \ˈbōr-dəm\ *n* : the condition of being bored
bo•ric acid \ˈbōr-ik-\ *n* : a white crystalline weak acid that contains boron and is used esp. as an antiseptic
born \ˈbȯrn\ *adj* **1** : brought into life by birth **2** : NATIVE ⟨American-*born*⟩ **3** : having special natural abilities or character from birth ⟨a ~ leader⟩
born–again *adj* : having experienced a revival of a personal faith or conviction ⟨~ believer⟩ ⟨~ liberal⟩
borne *past part of* BEAR
bo•ron \ˈbōr-ˌän\ *n* : a chemical element that occurs in nature only in combination (as in borax) — see ELEMENT table
bor•ough \ˈbər-ō\ *n* **1** : a British town that sends one or more members to Parliament; *also* : an incorporated British urban area **2** : an incorporated town or village in some U.S. states; *also* : any of the five political divisions of New York City **3** : a civil division of the state of Alaska corresponding to a county in most other states
bor•row \ˈbär-ō\ *vb* **1** : to take or receive (something) temporarily and with intent to return **2** : to take into possession or use from another source : DERIVE, APPROPRIATE ⟨~ a metaphor⟩
borscht \ˈbȯrsht\ *or* **borsch** \ˈbȯrsh\ *n* [Yiddish *borsht* & Ukrainian & Russ *borshch*] : a soup made mainly from beets
bosh \ˈbäsh\ *n* [Turk *boş* empty] : foolish talk or action : NONSENSE
bosky \ˈbäs-kē\ *adj* : covered with trees or shrubs
[1]**bos•om** \ˈbu̇-zəm, ˈbü-\ *n* **1** : the front of the human chest; *esp* : the female breasts **2** : the seat of secret thoughts and feelings **3** : the part of a garment covering the breast — **bos•omed** \-zəmd\ *adj*
[2]**bosom** *adj* : CLOSE, INTIMATE
[1]**boss** \ˈbäs, ˈbȯs\ *n* : a knoblike ornament : STUD
[2]**boss** *vb* : to ornament with bosses
[3]**boss** \ˈbȯs\ *n* **1** : one (as a foreman or manager) exercising control or supervision **2** : a politician who controls votes or dictates policies — **bossy** *adj*
[4]**boss** \ˈbȯs\ *vb* : to act as a boss : SUPERVISE
bo•sun \ˈbōs-ᵊn\ *var of* BOATSWAIN
bot *abbr* botanical; botanist; botany
bot•a•ny \ˈbät-ᵊn-ē, ˈbät-nē\ *n, pl* **-nies 1** : a branch of biology dealing with plants and plant life **2** : plant life (as of a given region); *also* : the biology of a plant or plant group — **bo•tan•i•cal** \bə-ˈta-ni-kəl\ *adj* — **bot•a•nist** \ˈbät-ᵊn-ist, ˈbät-nist\ *n* — **bot•a•nize** \-ᵊn-ˌīz\ *vb*
botch \ˈbäch\ *vb* : to foul up hopelessly : BUNGLE — **botch** *n*
[1]**both** \ˈbōth\ *pron* : both ones : the one as well as the other
[2]**both** *conj* — used as a function word to indicate and stress the inclusion of each of two or more things specified by coordinated words, phrases, or clauses ⟨~ New York and London⟩
[3]**both** *adj* : being the two : affecting the one and the other
both•er \ˈbä-t͟hər\ *vb* : WORRY, PESTER, TROUBLE **syn** vex, annoy, irk, provoke — **bother** *n* — **both•er•some** \-səm\ *adj*
[1]**bot•tle** \ˈbät-ᵊl\ *n* **1** : a container (as of glass) with a narrow neck and usu. no handles **2** : the quantity held by a bottle **3** : intoxicating liquor
[2]**bottle** *vb* **bot•tled; bot•tling 1** : to confine as if in a bottle : RESTRAIN **2** : to put into a bottle
bot•tle•neck \ˈbät-ᵊl-ˌnek\ *n* **1** : a narrow passage or point of congestion **2** : something that obstructs or impedes
[1]**bot•tom** \ˈbä-təm\ *n* **1** : an under or supporting surface; *also* : BUTTOCKS **2** : the surface on which a body of water lies **3** : the lowest part or place; *also* : an inferior position ⟨start at the ~⟩ **4** : BOTTOMLAND — **bottom** *adj* — **bot•tom•less** *adj*
[2]**bottom** *vb* **1** : to furnish with a bottom **2** : to reach the bottom **3** : to reach a low point before rebounding — usu. used with *out*
bot•tom•land \ˈbä-təm-ˌland\ *n* : low land along a river
bottom line *n* **1** : the essential point : CRUX **2** : the final result : OUTCOME
bot•u•lism \ˈbä-chə-ˌli-zəm\ *n* : an acute paralytic disease caused by a bacterial toxin esp. in food
bou•doir \ˈbü-ˌdwär, ˈbu̇-, ˌbü-ˈ, ˌbu̇-ˈ\ *n* [F, fr. *bouder* to pout] : a woman's dressing room or bedroom
bouf•fant \bü-ˈfänt, ˈbü-ˌfänt\ *adj* [F] : puffed out ⟨~ hairdos⟩
bough \ˈbau̇\ *n* : a usu. large or main branch of a tree
bought *past and past part of* BUY
bouil•la•baisse \ˌbü-yə-ˈbās\ *n* [F] : a highly seasoned fish stew made with at least two kinds of fish
bouil•lon \ˈbü-ˌyän; ˈbu̇l-ˌyän, -yən\ *n* : a clear soup made usu. from beef
boul•der \ˈbōl-dər\ *n* : a large detached rounded or worn mass of rock — **boul•dered** \-dərd\ *adj*
bou•le•vard \ˈbu̇-lə-ˌvärd, ˈbü-\ *n* [F, modif. of MD *bolwerc* bulwark] : a broad often landscaped thoroughfare
bounce \ˈbau̇ns\ *vb* **bounced; bounc•ing 1** : to cause to rebound ⟨~ a ball⟩ **2** : to rebound after striking — **bounce** *n* — **bouncy** \ˈbau̇n-sē\ *adj*
bounc•er \ˈbau̇n-sər\ *n* : a person employed in a public place to remove disorderly persons
[1]**bound** \ˈbau̇nd\ *adj* : intending to go
[2]**bound** *n* : LIMIT, BOUNDARY — **bound•less** *adj* — **bound•less•ness** *n*
[3]**bound** *vb* **1** : to set limits to **2** : to form the boundary of **3** : to name the boundaries of
[4]**bound** *past and past part of* BIND
[5]**bound** *adj* **1** : constrained by or as if by bonds : CONFINED, OBLIGED **2** : enclosed in a binding or cover **3** : RESOLVED, DETERMINED; *also* : SURE
[6]**bound** *n* **1** : LEAP, JUMP **2** : REBOUND, BOUNCE
[7]**bound** *vb* : SPRING, BOUNCE
bound•ary \ˈbau̇n-drē\ *n, pl* **-aries** : something that marks or fixes a limit (as of territory) **syn** border, frontier, march
bound•en \ˈbau̇n-dən\ *adj* : BINDING
boun•te•ous \ˈbau̇n-tē-əs\ *adj* **1** : GENEROUS **2** : ABUNDANT — **boun•te•ous•ly** *adv* — **boun•te•ous•ness** *n*
boun•ti•ful \ˈbau̇n-ti-fəl\ *adj* **1** : giving freely **2** : PLENTIFUL — **boun•ti•ful•ly** *adv* — **boun•ti•ful•ness** *n*
boun•ty \ˈbau̇n-tē\ *n, pl* **bounties** [ME *bounte* goodness, fr. OF *bonté*, fr. L *bonitas*, fr. *bonus* good] **1** : GENEROSITY **2** : something given liberally **3** : a reward, premium, or subsidy given usu. for doing something
bou•quet \bō-ˈkā, bü-\ *n* [F, fr. MF, thicket, fr. OF *bosc* forest] **1** : flowers picked and fastened together in a bunch **2** : a distinctive aroma (as of wine) **syn** scent, fragrance, perfume, redolence
bour•bon \ˈbər-bən\ *n* : a whiskey distilled from a corn mash
bour•geois \ˈbu̇rzh-ˌwä, bu̇rzh-ˈwä\ *n, pl* **bourgeois** *same or* -ˌwäz, -ˈwäz\ [MF, lit., citizen of a town, fr. *borc* town, borough, fr. L *burgus* fortified place, of Gmc origin] : a middle-class person — **bourgeois** *adj*
bour•geoi•sie \ˌbu̇rzh-ˌwä-ˈzē\ *n* : a social order dominated by bourgeois
bourne *also* **bourn** \ˈbōrn, ˈbu̇rn\ *n* : BOUNDARY; *also* : DESTINATION
bourse \ˈbu̇rs\ *n* : a European stock exchange
bout \ˈbau̇t\ *n* **1** : CONTEST, MATCH **2** : OUTBREAK, ATTACK ⟨a ~ of measles⟩ **3** : SESSION
bou•tique \bü-ˈtēk\ *n* : a small fashionable specialty shop
bou•ton•niere \ˌbüt-ᵊn-ˈiər\ *n* : a flower or bouquet worn in a buttonhole

[1]bo•vine \ˈbō-ˌvīn, -ˌvēn\ *adj* **1 :** of or relating to bovines **2 :** having qualities (as placidity or dullness) characteristic of oxen or cows
[2]bovine *n* **:** any of a group of mammals including oxen, buffalo, and their close relatives
[1]bow \ˈbau̇\ *vb* **1 :** SUBMIT, YIELD **2 :** to bend the head or body (as in submission, courtesy, or assent)
[2]bow *n* **:** an act or posture of bowing
[3]bow \ˈbō\ *n* **1 :** BEND, ARCH; *esp* **:** RAINBOW **2 :** a weapon for shooting arrows; *also* **:** ARCHER **3 :** a knot formed by doubling a line into two or more loops **4 :** a wooden rod strung with horsehairs for playing an instrument of the violin family
[4]bow \ˈbō\ *vb* **1 :** BEND, CURVE **2 :** to play (an instrument) with a bow
[5]bow \ˈbau̇\ *n* **:** the forward part of a ship — **bow** *adj*
bowd•ler•ise *Brit var of* BOWDLERIZE
bowd•ler•ize \ˈbōd-lə-ˌrīz, ˈbau̇d-\ *vb* **-ized; -iz•ing :** to expurgate by omitting parts considered vulgar
bow•el \ˈbau̇(-ə)l\ *n* **1 :** INTESTINE; *also* **:** one of the divisions of the intestine — usu. used in pl. **2** *pl* **:** the inmost parts ⟨the ∼*s* of the earth⟩
bow•er \ˈbau̇(-ə)r\ *n* **:** a shelter of boughs or vines **:** ARBOR
[1]bowl \ˈbōl\ *n* **1 :** a concave vessel used to hold liquids **2 :** a drinking vessel **3 :** a bowl-shaped part or structure — **bowl•ful** \-ˌfu̇l\ *n*
[2]bowl *n* **1 :** a ball for rolling on a level surface in bowling **2 :** a cast of the ball in bowling
[3]bowl *vb* **1 :** to play a game of bowling; *also* **:** to roll a ball in bowling **2 :** to travel (as in a vehicle) rapidly and smoothly **3 :** to strike or knock down with a moving object; *also* **:** to overwhelm with surprise
bowlder *var of* BOULDER
bow•legged \ˈbō-ˌle-gəd\ *adj* **:** having legs that bow outward at or below the knee — **bow•leg** \ˈbō-ˌleg\ *n*
[1]bowl•er \ˈbō-lər\ *n* **:** a person who bowls
[2]bow•ler \ˈbō-lər\ *n* **:** DERBY 3
bow•line \ˈbō-lən, -ˌlīn\ *n* **:** a knot used to form a loop that neither slips nor jams
bowl•ing \ˈbō-liŋ\ *n* **:** any of various games in which balls are rolled on a green or alley at an object or a group of objects; *esp* **:** TENPINS
bow•man \ˈbō-mən\ *n* **:** ARCHER
bow•sprit \ˈbau̇-ˌsprit\ *n* **:** a spar projecting forward from the prow of a ship
bow•string \ˈbō-ˌstriŋ\ *n* **:** the cord connecting the two ends of a shooting bow
[1]box \ˈbäks\ *n, pl* **box** *or* **box•es :** an evergreen shrub or small tree used esp. for hedges
[2]box *n* **1 :** a rigid typically rectangular receptacle often with a cover; *also* **:** the quantity held by a box **2 :** a small compartment (as for a group of theater patrons); *also* **:** a boxlike receptacle or division **3 :** any of six spaces on a baseball diamond where the batter, pitcher, coaches, and catcher stand **4 :** PREDICAMENT
[3]box *vb* **:** to enclose in or as if in a box
[4]box *n* **:** a punch or slap esp. on the ear
[5]box *vb* **1 :** to strike with the hand **2 :** to engage in boxing with
box•car \ˈbäks-ˌkär\ *n* **:** a roofed freight car usu. with sliding doors in the sides
[1]box•er \ˈbäk-sər\ *n* **:** a person who engages in boxing
[2]boxer *n* **:** a compact short-haired usu. fawn or brindled dog of a breed of German origin
box•ing \ˈbäk-siŋ\ *n* **:** the sport of fighting with the fists
box office *n* **:** an office (as in a theater) where admission tickets are sold
box•wood \ˈbäks-ˌwu̇d\ *n* **:** the tough hard wood of the box; *also* **:** a box tree or shrub
boy \ˈbȯi\ *n* **1 :** a male child **:** YOUTH **2 :** SON — **boy•hood** \-ˌhu̇d\ *n* — **boy•ish** *adj* — **boy•ish•ly** *adv* — **boy•ish•ness** *n*
boy•cott \ˈbȯi-ˌkät\ *vb* [Charles C. *Boycott* †1897 Eng. land agent in Ireland who was ostracized for refusing to reduce rents] **:** to refrain from having any dealings with — **boycott** *n*
boy•friend \ˈbȯi-ˌfrend\ *n* **1 :** a male friend **2 :** a frequent or regular male companion of a girl or woman
Boy Scout *n* **:** a member of any of various national scouting programs (as the Boy Scouts of America)
boy•sen•ber•ry \ˈbȯiz-ᵊn-ˌber-ē, ˈbȯis-\ *n* **:** a large bramble fruit with a raspberry flavor; *also* **:** the hybrid plant bearing it developed by crossing blackberries and raspberries
bo•zo \ˈbō-ˌzō\ *n, pl* **bozos :** a foolish or incompetent person
bp *abbr* **1** bishop **2** birthplace
BP *abbr* **1** batting practice **2** blood pressure **3** boiling point
bpl *abbr* birthplace
BPOE *abbr* Benevolent and Protective Order of Elks
br *abbr* **1** branch **2** brass **3** brown
[1]Br *abbr* Britain; British
[2]Br *symbol* bromine
BR *abbr* bedroom
bra \ˈbrä\ *n* **:** BRASSIERE
[1]brace \ˈbrās\ *vb* **braced; brac•ing 1** *archaic* **:** to make fast **:** BIND **2 :** to tighten preparatory to use; *also* **:** to get ready for **:** prepare oneself **3 :** INVIGORATE **4 :** to furnish or support with a brace; *also* **:** STRENGTHEN **5 :** to set firmly **6 :** to gain courage or confidence
[2]brace *n, pl* **brac•es 1** *or pl* **brace :** two of a kind ⟨a ∼ of dogs⟩ **2 :** a crank-shaped device for turning a bit **3 :** something (as a tie, prop, or clamp) that distributes, directs, or resists pressure or weight **4** *pl* **:** SUSPENDERS **5 :** an appliance for supporting a body part (as the shoulders) **6** *pl* **:** dental appliances used to exert pressure to straighten misaligned teeth **7 :** one of two marks { } used to connect words or items to be considered together
brace•let \ˈbrā-slət\ *n* [ME, fr. MF, dim. of *bras* arm, fr. L *bracchium,* fr. Gk *brachiōn*] **:** an ornamental band or chain worn around the wrist
bra•ce•ro \brä-ˈser-ō\ *n, pl* **-ros :** a Mexican laborer admitted to the U.S. esp. for seasonal farm work
brack•en \ˈbra-kən\ *n* **:** a large coarse fern; *also* **:** a growth of such ferns
[1]brack•et \ˈbra-kət\ *n* **1 :** a projecting framework or arm designed to support weight; *also* **:** a shelf on such framework **2 :** one of a pair of punctuation marks [ ] used esp. to enclose interpolated matter **3 :** a continuous section of a series; *esp* **:** one of a graded series of income groups
[2]bracket *vb* **1 :** to furnish or fasten with brackets **2 :** to place within brackets; *also* **:** to separate or group with or as if with brackets
brack•ish \ˈbra-kish\ *adj* **:** somewhat salty — **brack•ish•ness** *n*
bract \ˈbrakt\ *n* **:** an often modified leaf on or at the base of a flower stalk
brad \ˈbrad\ *n* **:** a slender nail with a small head
brae \ˈbrā\ *n, chiefly Scot* **:** a hillside esp. along a river
brag \ˈbrag\ *vb* **bragged; brag•ging :** to talk or assert boastfully — **brag** *n* — **brag•ger** *n*
brag•ga•do•cio \ˌbra-gə-ˈdō-shē-ˌō, -sē-, -chē-\ *n, pl* **-cios 1 :** BRAGGART, BOASTER **2 :** empty boasting **3 :** arrogant pretension **:** COCKINESS
brag•gart \ˈbra-gərt\ *n* **:** one who brags
Brah•man *or* **Brah•min** \ˈbrä-mən *for 1;* ˈbrā-, ˈbrä-, ˈbra- *for 2*\ *n* **1 :** a Hindu of the highest caste traditionally assigned to the priesthood **2 :** any of a breed of large vigorous humped cattle developed in the southern U.S. from Indian stock **3** *usu Brahmin* **:** a person of high social standing and cultivated intellect and taste
Brah•man•ism \ˈbrä-mə-ˌni-zəm\ *n* **:** orthodox Hinduism
[1]braid \ˈbrād\ *vb* **1 :** to form (strands) into a braid

: PLAIT; *also* : to make from braids **2** : to ornament with braid
[2]braid *n* **1** : a length of braided hair **2** : a cord or ribbon of three or more interwoven strands
braille \ˈbrāl\ *n, often cap* : a system of writing for the blind that uses characters made up of raised dots

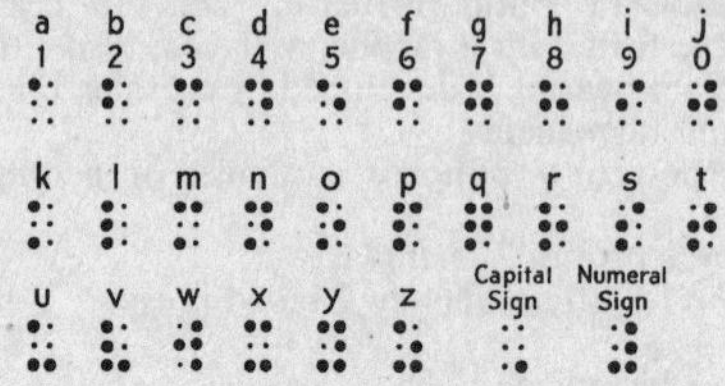

braille alphabet

[1]brain \ˈbrān\ *n* **1** : the part of the vertebrate nervous system that is the organ of thought and nervous coordination, is made up of nerve cells and their fibers, and is enclosed in the skull; *also* : a centralized mass of nerve tissue in an invertebrate **2** : INTELLECT, INTELLIGENCE — often used in pl. — **brained** \ˈbrānd\ *adj* — **brain•less** *adj* — **brainy** *adj*
[2]brain *vb* **1** : to kill by smashing the skull **2** : to hit on the head
brain•child \ˈbrān-ˌchīld\ *n* : a product of one's creative imagination
brain death *n* : final cessation of activity in the central nervous system esp. as indicated by a flat electroencephalogram — **brain–dead** \-ˌded\ *adj*
brain drain *n* : the departure of educated or professional people from one country, sector, or field to another usu. for better pay or living conditions
brain•storm \-ˌstȯrm\ *n* : a sudden inspiration or idea — **brainstorm** *vb*
brain•teas•er \-ˌtē-zər\ *n* : a challenging puzzle
brain•wash•ing \ˈbrān-ˌwȯ-shiŋ, -ˌwä-\ *n* **1** : a forcible indoctrination to induce someone to give up basic political, social, or religious beliefs and attitudes and to accept contrasting regimented ideas **2** : persuasion by propaganda or salesmanship — **brain•wash** *vb*
brain wave *n* **1** : BRAINSTORM **2** : rhythmic fluctuations of voltage between parts of the brain; *also* : a current produced by brain waves
braise \ˈbrāz\ *vb* **braised; brais•ing** : to cook (meat) slowly in fat and little moisture in a closed pot
[1]brake \ˈbrāk\ *n* : a common bracken fern
[2]brake *n* : rough or wet land heavily overgrown (as with thickets or reeds)
[3]brake *n* : a device for slowing or stopping motion esp. by friction — **brake•less** *adj*
[4]brake *vb* **braked; brak•ing 1** : to slow or stop by or as if by a brake **2** : to apply a brake
brake•man \ˈbrāk-mən\ *n* : a train crew member who inspects the train and assists the conductor
bram•ble \ˈbram-bəl\ *n* : any of a large genus of prickly shrubs (as a blackberry) related to the roses; *also* : any rough prickly shrub or vine — **bram•bly** \-b(ə-)lē\ *adj*
bran \ˈbran\ *n* : the edible broken husks of cereal grain sifted from flour or meal
[1]branch \ˈbranch\ *n* [ME, fr. OF *branche*, fr. LL *branca* paw] **1** : a natural subdivision (as a bough or twig) of a plant stem **2** : a division (as of an antler or a river) related to a whole like a plant branch to its stem **3** : a discrete element of a complex system ⟨the executive ~⟩; *esp* : a division of a family descended from one ancestor — **branched** \ˈbrancht\ *adj*
[2]branch *vb* **1** : to develop branches **2** : DIVERGE **3** : to extend activities ⟨the business is ~*ing* out⟩
[1]brand \ˈbrand\ *n* **1** : a piece of charred or burning wood **2** : a mark made (as by burning) usu. to identify; *also* : a mark of disgrace : STIGMA **3** : a class of goods identified as the product of a particular firm or producer **4** : a distinctive kind ⟨my own ~ of humor⟩
[2]brand *vb* **1** : to mark with a brand **2** : STIGMATIZE
bran•dish \ˈbran-dish\ *vb* : to shake or wave menacingly **syn** flourish, flash, flaunt
brand–new \ˈbran-ˈnü, -ˈnyü\ *adj* : conspicuously new and unused
bran•dy \ˈbran-dē\ *n, pl* **brandies** [short for *brandywine*, fr. D *brandewijn*, fr. MD *brantwijn*, fr. *brant* distilled + *wijn* wine] : a liquor distilled from wine or fermented fruit juice — **brandy** *vb*
brash \ˈbrash\ *adj* **1** : IMPETUOUS, AUDACIOUS **2** : aggressively self-assertive
brass \ˈbras\ *n* **1** : an alloy of copper and zinc; *also* : an object of brass **2** : brazen self-assurance **3** : persons of high rank (as in the military) — **brassy** *adj*
bras•siere \brə-ˈzir\ *n* : a woman's close-fitting undergarment designed to support the breasts
brat \ˈbrat\ *n* : an ill-behaved child — **brat•ti•ness** *n* — **brat•ty** *adj*
bra•va•do \brə-ˈvä-dō\ *n, pl* **-does** *or* **-dos 1** : blustering swaggering conduct **2** : a show of bravery
[1]brave \ˈbrāv\ *adj* **brav•er; brav•est** [MF, fr. It & Sp *bravo* courageous, wild, prob. fr. L *barbarus* barbarous] **1** : showing courage **2** : EXCELLENT, SPLENDID **syn** bold, intrepid, courageous, valiant — **brave•ly** *adv*
[2]brave *vb* **braved; brav•ing** : to face or endure bravely
[3]brave *n* : an American Indian warrior
brav•ery \ˈbrā-və-rē\ *n, pl* **-er•ies** : COURAGE
bra•vo \ˈbrä-vō\ *n, pl* **bravos** : a shout of approval — often used as an interjection in applauding
bra•vu•ra \brə-ˈvyu̇r-ə, -ˈvu̇r-\ *n* **1** : a florid brilliant musical style **2** : self-assured brilliant performance — **bravura** *adj*
brawl \ˈbrȯl\ *n* : a noisy quarrel **syn** fracas, row, rumpus, scrap, fray, melee — **brawl** *vb* — **brawl•er** *n*
brawn \ˈbrȯn\ *n* : strong muscles; *also* : muscular strength — **brawn•i•ness** *n* — **brawny** *adj*
bray \ˈbrā\ *n* : the characteristic harsh cry of a donkey — **bray** *vb*
braze \ˈbrāz\ *vb* **brazed; braz•ing** : to solder with an alloy (as brass) that melts at a lower temperature than the metals being joined — **braz•er** *n*
[1]bra•zen \ˈbrāz-ᵊn\ *adj* **1** : made of brass **2** : sounding harsh and loud **3** : of the color of brass **4** : marked by contemptuous boldness — **bra•zen•ly** *adv* — **bra•zen•ness** *n*
[2]brazen *vb* : to face boldly or defiantly
[1]bra•zier \ˈbrā-zhər\ *n* : a worker in brass
[2]brazier *n* **1** : a vessel holding burning coals (as for heating) **2** : a device on which food is grilled
Bra•zil•ian \brə-ˈzil-yən\ *n* : a native or inhabitant of Brazil — **Brazilian** *adj*
Bra•zil nut \brə-ˈzil-\ *n* : a triangular oily edible nut borne in large capsules by a tall So. American tree; *also* : the tree
[1]breach \ˈbrēch\ *n* **1** : a breaking of a law, obligation, tie (as of friendship), or standard (as of conduct) **2** : an interruption or opening made by or as if by breaking through **syn** violation, transgression, infringement, trespass
[2]breach *vb* **1** : to make a breach in **2** : to leap out of water ⟨whales ~*ing*⟩
[1]bread \ˈbred\ *n* **1** : baked food made basically of flour or meal **2** : FOOD
[2]bread *vb* : to cover with bread crumbs before cooking
bread•bas•ket \ˈbred-ˌbas-kət\ *n* : a major cereal-producing region
bread•fruit \-ˌfrüt\ *n* : a round usu. seedless fruit resembling bread in color and texture when baked; *also* : a tall tropical tree related to the mulberry and bearing breadfruit
bread•stuff \-ˌstəf\ *n* : GRAIN, FLOUR

breadth \ˈbredth, ˈbretth\ *n* **1** : WIDTH **2** : comprehensive quality : SCOPE ⟨~ of knowledge⟩
bread•win•ner \ˈbred-ˌwi-nər\ *n* : a member of a family whose wages supply its livelihood
[1]**break** \ˈbrāk\ *vb* **broke** \ˈbrōk\; **bro•ken** \ˈbrō-kən\; **break•ing** **1** : to separate into parts usu. suddenly or violently : come or force apart **2** : TRANSGRESS ⟨~ a law⟩ **3** : to force a way into, out of, or through **4** : to disrupt the order or unity of ⟨~ ranks⟩ ⟨~ up a gang⟩; *also* : to bring to submission or helplessness **5** : EXCEED, SURPASS ⟨~ a record⟩ **6** : RUIN **7** : to make known **8** : HALT, INTERRUPT; *also* : to act or change abruptly (as a course or activity) **9** : to come esp. suddenly into being or notice ⟨as day ~*s*⟩ **10** : to fail under stress **11** : HAPPEN, DEVELOP — **break•able** *adj or n*
[2]**break** *n* **1** : an act of breaking **2** : a result of breaking; *esp* : an interruption of continuity ⟨coffee ~⟩ ⟨a ~ for the commercial⟩ **3** : a stroke of good luck
break•age \ˈbrā-kij\ *n* **1** : the action of breaking **2** : articles or amount broken **3** : loss due to things broken
break•down \ˈbrāk-ˌdau̇n\ *n* **1** : functional failure; *esp* : a physical, mental, or nervous collapse **2** : DISINTEGRATION **3** : DECOMPOSITION **4** : ANALYSIS, CLASSIFICATION — **break down** *vb*
break•er \ˈbrā-kər\ *n* **1** : one that breaks **2** : a wave that breaks into foam (as against the shore)
break•fast \ˈbrek-fəst\ *n* : the first meal of the day — **breakfast** *vb*
break in *vb* **1** : to enter a building by force **2** : INTERRUPT; *also* : INTRUDE **3** : TRAIN — **break–in** \ˈbrāk-ˌin\ *n*
break•neck \ˈbrāk-ˈnek\ *adj* : very fast or dangerous ⟨~ speed⟩
break out *vb* **1** : to develop or erupt suddenly or with force **2** : to develop a skin rash
break•through \ˈbrāk-ˌthrü\ *n* **1** : an act or instance of breaking through an obstruction or defensive line **2** : a sudden advance in knowledge or technique
break•up \-ˌəp\ *n* **1** : DISSOLUTION **2** : a division into smaller units — **break up** *vb*
break•wa•ter \ˈbrāk-ˌwȯ-tər, -ˌwä-\ *n* : a structure protecting a harbor or beach from the force of waves
bream \ˈbrim, ˈbrēm\ *n, pl* **bream** *or* **breams** : any of various small freshwater sunfishes
breast \ˈbrest\ *n* **1** : either of the pair of mammary glands extending from the front of the chest esp. in pubescent and adult human females **2** : the front part of the body between the neck and the abdomen **3** : the seat of emotion and thought
breast•bone \ˈbrest-ˌbōn\ *n* : STERNUM
breast–feed \-ˌfēd\ *vb* : to feed (a baby) from a mother's breast rather than from a bottle
breast•plate \-ˌplāt\ *n* : a metal plate of armor for the breast
breast•stroke \-ˌstrōk\ *n* : a swimming stroke executed by extending both arms forward and then sweeping them back with palms out while kicking backward and outward with both legs
breast•work \-ˌwərk\ *n* : a temporary fortification
breath \ˈbreth\ *n* **1** : the act or power of breathing **2** : a slight breeze **3** : air inhaled or exhaled in breathing **4** : spoken sound **5** : SPIRIT — **breath•less** *adj* — **breath•less•ly** *adv* — **breath•less•ness** *n* — **breathy** \ˈbre-thē\ *adj*
breathe \ˈbrēth\ *vb* **breathed; breath•ing** **1** : to inhale and exhale **2** : LIVE **3** : to halt for rest **4** : to utter softly or secretly — **breath•able** *adj*
breath•er \ˈbrē-thər\ *n* **1** : one that breathes **2** : a short rest
breath•tak•ing \ˈbreth-ˌtā-kiŋ\ *adj* **1** : making one out of breath **2** : EXCITING, THRILLING ⟨~ beauty⟩ — **breath•tak•ing•ly** *adv*
brec•cia \ˈbre-chē-ə, -chə\ *n* : a rock consisting of sharp fragments held in fine-grained material
breech \ˈbrēch\ *n* **1** *pl* \ *usu* ˈbri-chəz\ : trousers ending near the knee; *also* : PANTS **2** : BUTTOCKS, RUMP **3** : the part of a firearm at the rear of the barrel
[1]**breed** \ˈbrēd\ *vb* **bred** \ˈbred\; **breed•ing** **1** : BEGET; *also* : ORIGINATE **2** : to propagate sexually; *also* : MATE **3** : BRING UP, NURTURE **4** : to produce (fissionable material) from material that is not fissionable **syn** generate, reproduce, procreate, propagate — **breed•er** *n*
[2]**breed** *n* **1** : a strain of similar and presumably related plants or animals usu. developed in domestication **2** : KIND, SORT, CLASS
breed•ing *n* **1** : ANCESTRY **2** : training in polite social interaction **3** : sexual propagation of plants or animals
[1]**breeze** \ˈbrēz\ *n* **1** : a light wind **2** : CINCH, SNAP — **breeze•less** *adj*
[2]**breeze** *vb* **breezed; breez•ing** : to progress quickly and easily
breeze•way \ˈbrēz-ˌwā\ *n* : a roofed open passage connecting two buildings (as a house and garage)
breezy \ˈbrē-zē\ *adj* **1** : swept by breezes **2** : briskly informal — **breez•i•ly** \ˈbrē-zə-lē\ *adv* — **breez•i•ness** \-zē-nəs\ *n*
breth•ren \ˈbreth-rən, ˈbre-thə-; ˈbre-thərn\ *pl of* BROTHER — used esp. in formal or solemn address
Brethren *n pl* : members of one of several Protestant denominations originating chiefly in a German religious movement and stressing personal religious experience
bre•via•ry \ˈbrē-vyə-rē, -vē-ˌer-ē\ *n, pl* **-ries** *often cap* : a book of prayers, hymns, psalms, and readings used by Roman Catholic priests
brev•i•ty \ˈbre-və-tē\ *n, pl* **-ties** **1** : shortness or conciseness of expression **2** : shortness of duration
brew \ˈbrü\ *vb* **1** : to prepare (as beer) by steeping, boiling, and fermenting **2** : to prepare (as tea) by steeping in hot water — **brew** *n* — **brew•er** *n* — **brew•ery** \ˈbrü-ə-rē, ˈbru̇(-ə)r-ē\ *n*
[1]**bri•ar** \ˈbrī-ər\ *var of* BRIER
[2]**briar** *n* : a tobacco pipe made from the root or stem of a brier
[1]**bribe** \ˈbrīb\ *n* [ME, something stolen, fr. MF, bread given to a beggar] : something (as money or a favor) given or promised to a person to influence conduct
[2]**bribe** *vb* **bribed; brib•ing** : to influence by offering a bribe — **brib•able** *adj* — **brib•er** *n* — **brib•ery** \ˈbrī-bə-rē\ *n*
bric–a–brac \ˈbri-kə-ˌbrak\ *n pl* [F] : small ornamental articles
[1]**brick** \ˈbrik\ *n* : a block molded from moist clay and hardened by heat used esp. for building
[2]**brick** *vb* : to close, cover, or pave with bricks
brick•bat \ˈbrik-ˌbat\ *n* **1** : a piece of a hard material (as a brick) esp. when thrown as a missile **2** : an uncomplimentary remark
brick•lay•er \ˈbrik-ˌlā-ər\ *n* : a person who builds or paves with bricks — **brick•lay•ing** *n*
[1]**brid•al** \ˈbrīd-ᵊl\ *n* [ME *bridale*, fr. OE *brȳdealu*, fr. *brȳd* bride + *ealu* ale] : MARRIAGE, WEDDING
[2]**bridal** *adj* : of or relating to a bride or a wedding
bride \ˈbrīd\ *n* : a woman just married or about to be married
bride•groom \ˈbrīd-ˌgrüm, -ˌgru̇m\ *n* : a man just married or about to be married
brides•maid \ˈbrīdz-ˌmād\ *n* : a woman who attends a bride at her wedding
[1]**bridge** \ˈbrij\ *n* **1** : a structure built over a depression or obstacle for use as a passageway **2** : something (as the upper part of the nose) resembling a bridge in form or function **3** : a curved piece raising the strings of a musical instrument **4** : the forward part of a ship's superstructure from which it is navigated **5** : an artificial replacement for missing teeth
[2]**bridge** *vb* **bridged; bridg•ing** : to build a bridge over — **bridge•able** *adj*
[3]**bridge** *n* : a card game for four players developed from whist

bridge·head \-ˌhed\ *n* : an advanced position seized in enemy territory
bridge·work \-ˌwərk\ *n* : dental bridges
[1]**bri·dle** \ˈbrīd-ᵊl\ *n* **1** : headgear with which a horse is controlled **2** : CURB, RESTRAINT
[2]**bridle** *vb* **bri·dled; bri·dling 1** : to put a bridle on; *also* : to restrain with or as if with a bridle **2** : to show hostility or scorn usu. by tossing the head
Brie \ˈbrē\ *n* : a soft cheese with a whitish rind and a pale yellow interior
[1]**brief** \ˈbrēf\ *adj* **1** : short in duration or extent **2** : CONCISE; *also* : CURT — **brief·ly** *adv* — **brief·ness** *n*
[2]**brief** *n* **1** : a concise statement or document; *esp* : one summarizing a law client's case or a legal argument **2** *pl* : short snug underpants
[3]**brief** *vb* : to give final instructions or essential information to
brief·case \ˈbrēf-ˌkās\ *n* : a flat flexible case for carrying papers
[1]**bri·er** \ˈbrī(-ə)r\ *n* : a plant (as a bramble or rose) with a thorny or prickly woody stem; *also* : a mass or twig of these — **bri·ery** \ˈbrī(-ə)r-ē\ *adj*
[2]**brier** *or* **briar** *n* : a heath of southern Europe whose roots and knotted stems are used for making tobacco pipes
[1]**brig** \ˈbrig\ *n* : a 2-masted square-rigged sailing ship
[2]**brig** *n* : the place of confinement for offenders on a naval ship
[3]**brig** *abbr* brigade
bri·gade \bri-ˈgād\ *n* **1** : a military unit composed of a headquarters, one or more units of infantry or armored forces, and supporting units **2** : a group organized for a particular purpose (as fire fighting)
brig·a·dier general \ˈbri-gə-ˌdir-\ *n* : a commissioned officer (as in the army) ranking next below a major general
brig·and \ˈbri-gənd\ *n* : BANDIT — **brig·and·age** \-gən-dij\ *n*
brig·an·tine \ˈbri-gən-ˌtēn\ *n* : a 2-masted square-rigged ship with a fore-and-aft mainsail
Brig Gen *abbr* brigadier general
bright \ˈbrīt\ *adj* **1** : SHINING, RADIANT **2** : ILLUSTRIOUS, GLORIOUS **3** : INTELLIGENT, CLEVER; *also* : LIVELY, CHEERFUL **syn** brilliant, lustrous, beaming — **bright** *adv* — **bright·ly** *adv* — **bright·ness** *n*
bright·en \ˈbrīt-ᵊn\ *vb* : to make or become bright or brighter — **bright·en·er** *n*
[1]**bril·liant** \ˈbril-yənt\ *adj* [F *brillant,* prp. of *briller* to shine, fr. It *brillare*] **1** : very bright **2** : STRIKING, DISTINCTIVE **3** : very intelligent **syn** radiant, lustrous, beaming, lucid, bright, lambent — **bril·liance** \-yəns\ *n* — **bril·lian·cy** \-yən-sē\ *n* — **bril·liant·ly** *adv*
[2]**brilliant** *n* : a gem cut in a particular form with many facets
[1]**brim** \ˈbrim\ *n* : EDGE, RIM **syn** brink, border, verge, fringe — **brim·less** *adj*
[2]**brim** *vb* **brimmed; brim·ming** : to be or become full often to overflowing
brim·ful \-ˈfu̇l\ *adj* : full to the brim
brim·stone \ˈbrim-ˌstōn\ *n* : SULFUR
brin·dled \ˈbrin-dᵊld\ *adj* : having dark streaks or flecks on a gray or tawny ground ⟨a ~ Great Dane⟩
brine \ˈbrīn\ *n* **1** : water saturated with salt **2** : OCEAN — **brin·i·ness** *n* — **briny** \ˈbrī-nē\ *adj*
bring \ˈbriŋ\ *vb* **brought** \ˈbrȯt\; **bring·ing** \ˈbriŋ-iŋ\ **1** : to cause to come with one **2** : INDUCE, PERSUADE, LEAD **3** : PRODUCE, EFFECT **4** : to sell for ⟨~ a good price⟩ — **bring·er** *n*
bring about *vb* : to cause to take place
bring up *vb* **1** : to give a parent's fostering care to **2** : to come or bring to a sudden halt **3** : to call to notice
brink \ˈbriŋk\ *n* **1** : an edge at the top of a steep place **2** : the point of onset
brio \ˈbrē-ō\ *n* : VIVACITY, SPIRIT
bri·quette *or* **bri·quet** \bri-ˈket\ *n* : a compacted often brick-shaped mass of fine material ⟨a charcoal ~⟩
brisk \ˈbrisk\ *adj* **1** : ALERT, LIVELY **2** : INVIGORATING **syn** agile, spry, nimble — **brisk·ly** *adv* — **brisk·ness** *n*
bris·ket \ˈbris-kət\ *n* : the breast or lower chest of a quadruped; *also* : a cut of beef from the brisket
bris·ling \ˈbriz-liŋ, ˈbris-\ *n* : SPRAT 1
[1]**bris·tle** \ˈbri-səl\ *n* : a short stiff coarse hair — **bris·tle·like** \ˈbri-səl-ˌlīk\ *adj* — **bris·tly** *adj*
[2]**bristle** *vb* **bris·tled; bris·tling 1** : to stand stiffly erect **2** : to show angry defiance **3** : to appear as if covered with bristles
Brit *abbr* Britain; British
Bri·tan·nic \bri-ˈta-nik\ *adj* : BRITISH
britch·es \ˈbri-chəz\ *n pl* : BREECHES, TROUSERS
Brit·ish \ˈbri-tish\ *n pl* : the people of Great Britain or the Commonwealth — **British** *adj* — **Brit·ish·ness** *n*
British thermal unit *n* : the quantity of heat needed to raise the temperature of one pound of water one degree Fahrenheit
Brit·on \ˈbrit-ᵊn\ *n* **1** : a member of a people inhabiting Britain before the Anglo-Saxon invasion **2** : a native or inhabitant of Great Britain
brit·tle \ˈbrit-ᵊl\ *adj* **brit·tler; brit·tlest** : easily broken : FRAGILE **syn** crisp, crumbly, friable — **brit·tle·ness** *n*
bro *abbr* brother
[1]**broach** \ˈbrōch\ *n* : a pointed tool
[2]**broach** *vb* **1** : to pierce (as a cask) in order to draw the contents **2** : to introduce as a topic of conversation
[1]**broad** \ˈbrȯd\ *adj* **1** : WIDE **2** : SPACIOUS **3** : CLEAR, OPEN **4** : OBVIOUS ⟨a ~ hint⟩ **5** : COARSE, CRUDE ⟨~ stories⟩ **6** : tolerant in outlook **7** : GENERAL **8** : dealing with essential points — **broad·ly** *adv* — **broad·ness** *n*
[2]**broad** *n, slang* : WOMAN
[1]**broad·cast** \ˈbrȯd-ˌkast\ *vb* **broadcast** *also* **broad·cast·ed; broad·cast·ing 1** : to scatter or sow broadcast **2** : to make widely known **3** : to transmit a broadcast — **broad·cast·er** *n*
[2]**broadcast** *adv* : to or over a wide area
[3]**broadcast** *n* **1** : the transmission of sound or images by radio or television **2** : a single radio or television program
broad·cloth \-ˌklȯth\ *n* **1** : a smooth dense woolen cloth **2** : a fine soft cloth of cotton, silk, or synthetic fiber
broad·en \ˈbrȯd-ᵊn\ *vb* : WIDEN
broad·loom \-ˌlüm\ *adj* : woven on a wide loom esp. in a solid color
broad–mind·ed \-ˈmīn-dəd\ *adj* : tolerant of varied opinions — **broad–mind·ed·ly** *adv* — **broad–mind·ed·ness** *n*
[1]**broad·side** \-ˌsīd\ *n* **1** : a sheet of paper printed usu. on one side (as an advertisement) **2** : all of the guns on one side of a ship; *also* : their simultaneous firing **3** : a volley of abuse or denunciation
[2]**broadside** *adv* **1** : with one side forward : SIDEWAYS **2** : from the side ⟨the car was hit ~⟩
broad–spectrum *adj* : effective against a wide range of organisms ⟨~ antibiotics⟩
broad·sword \ˈbrȯd-ˌsōrd\ *n* : a broad-bladed sword
broad·tail \-ˌtāl\ *n* : a karakul esp. with flat and wavy fur
bro·cade \brō-ˈkād\ *n* : a usu. silk fabric with a raised design
broc·co·li \ˈbrä-kə-lē\ *n* [It, pl. of *broccolo* flowering top of a cabbage, dim. of *brocco* small nail, sprout, fr. L *broccus* projecting] : the stems and immature usu. green or purple flower heads of either of two garden vegetable plants closely related to the cabbage; *also* : either of the plants
bro·chette \brō-ˈshet\ *n* : SKEWER
bro·chure \brō-ˈshu̇r\ *n* [F, fr. *brocher* to sew, fr. MF, to prick, fr. OF *brochier,* fr. *broche* pointed tool] : PAMPHLET, BOOKLET
bro·gan \ˈbrō-gən, brō-ˈgan\ *n* : a heavy shoe

brogue \ˈbrōg\ *n* : a dialect or regional pronunciation; *esp* : an Irish accent

broil \ˈbrȯil\ *vb* : to cook by exposure to radiant heat : GRILL — **broil** *n*

broil•er \ˈbrȯi-lər\ *n* **1** : a utensil for broiling **2** : a young chicken fit for broiling

[1]**broke** \ˈbrōk\ *past of* BREAK

[2]**broke** *adj* : PENNILESS

[1]**bro•ken** \ˈbrō-kən\ *past part of* BREAK

[2]**broken** *adj* **1** : SHATTERED **2** : having gaps or breaks : INTERRUPTED, DISRUPTED **3** : SUBDUED, CRUSHED **4** : BANKRUPT **5** : imperfectly spoken ⟨~ English⟩ — **bro•ken•ly** *adv*

bro•ken•heart•ed \ˌbrō-kən-ˈhär-təd\ *adj* : overcome by grief or despair

bro•ker \ˈbrō-kər\ *n* : an agent who negotiates contracts of purchase and sale — **broker** *vb*

bro•ker•age \ˈbrō-kə-rij\ *n* **1** : the business of a broker **2** : the fee or commission charged by a broker

bro•mide \ˈbrō-ˌmīd\ *n* : a compound of bromine and another element or chemical group including some (as potassium bromide) used as sedatives

bro•mid•ic \brō-ˈmi-dik\ *adj* : TRITE, UNORIGINAL

bro•mine \ˈbrō-ˌmēn\ *n* [F *brome* bromine, fr. Gk *brōmos* stink] : a deep red liquid corrosive chemical element that gives off an irritating vapor — see ELEMENT table

bronc \ˈbräŋk\ *n* : an unbroken or partly broken range horse of western No. America; *also* : MUSTANG

bron•chi•al \ˈbräŋ-kē-əl\ *adj* : of, relating to, or affecting the bronchi or their branches

bron•chi•tis \brän-ˈkī-təs, bräŋ-\ *n* : inflammation of the bronchi and their branches — **bron•chit•ic** \-ˈki-tik\ *adj*

bron•chus \ˈbräŋ-kəs\ *n, pl* **bron•chi** \ˈbräŋ-ˌkī, -ˌkē\ : either of the main divisions of the windpipe each leading to a lung

bron•co \ˈbräŋ-kō\ *n, pl* **broncos** [MexSp, fr. Sp, rough, wild] : BRONC

bron•to•sau•rus \ˌbrän-tə-ˈsȯr-əs\ *also* **bron•to•saur** \ˈbrän-tə-ˌsȯr\ *n* [NL, fr. Gk *brontē* thunder + *sauros* lizard] : any of a genus of large 4-footed and probably herbivorous sauropod dinosaurs of the Jurassic

Bronx cheer \ˈbräŋks-\ *n* : RASPBERRY 2

[1]**bronze** \ˈbränz\ *vb* **bronzed; bronz•ing** : to give the appearance of bronze to

[2]**bronze** *n* **1** : an alloy of copper and tin and sometimes other elements; *also* : something made of bronze **2** : a yellowish brown color — **bronzy** \ˈbrän-zē\ *adj*

brooch \ˈbrōch, ˈbrüch\ *n* : an ornamental clasp or pin

[1]**brood** \ˈbrüd\ *n* : a family of young animals or children and esp. of birds

[2]**brood** *adj* : kept for breeding ⟨a ~ mare⟩

[3]**brood** *vb* **1** : to sit on eggs to hatch them; *also* : to shelter (hatched young) with the wings **2** : to think anxiously or gloomily about something — **brood•ing•ly** *adv*

brood•er \ˈbrü-dər\ *n* **1** : one that broods **2** : a heated structure for raising young birds

[1]**brook** \ˈbru̇k\ *n* : a small natural stream

[2]**brook** *vb* : TOLERATE, BEAR

brook•let \ˈbru̇-klət\ *n* : a small brook

brook trout *n* : a common speckled cold-water char of No. America

broom \ˈbrüm, ˈbru̇m\ *n* **1** : any of several shrubs of the legume family with long slender branches and usu. yellow flowers **2** : an implement with a long handle (**broom•stick** \-ˌstik\) used for sweeping

bros *abbr* brothers

broth \ˈbrȯth\ *n, pl* **broths** \ˈbrȯths, ˈbrȯt͟hz\ **1** : liquid in which meat or sometimes vegetable food has been cooked **2** : a fluid culture medium

broth•el \ˈbrä-thəl, ˈbrȯ-\ *n* : a house of prostitution

broth•er \ˈbrə-t͟hər\ *n, pl* **brothers** *also* **breth•ren** \ˈbreth-rən, ˈbre-t͟hə-; ˈbre-t͟hərn\ **1** : a male having one or both parents in common with another individual **2** : a man who is a religious but not a priest **3** : KINSMAN; *also* : SOUL BROTHER — **broth•er•li•ness** \-lē-nəs\ *n* — **broth•er•ly** *adj*

broth•er•hood \ˈbrə-t͟hər-ˌhu̇d\ *n* **1** : the state of being brothers or a brother **2** : ASSOCIATION, FRATERNITY **3** : the whole body of persons in a business or profession

broth•er–in–law \ˈbrə-t͟hə-rən-ˌlȯ, ˈbrə-t͟hərn-ˌlȯ\ *n, pl* **brothers–in–law** \ˈbrə-t͟hər-zən-\ : the brother of one's spouse; *also* : the husband of one's sister or of one's spouse's sister

brougham \ˈbrü(-ə)m, ˈbrō(-ə)m\ *n* : a light closed horse-drawn carriage with the driver outside in front

brought *past and past part of* BRING

brou•ha•ha \ˈbrü-ˌhä-ˌhä\ *n* : HUBBUB, UPROAR

brow \ˈbrau̇\ *n* **1** : the eyebrow or the ridge on which it grows; *also* : FOREHEAD **2** : the projecting upper part of a steep place

brow•beat \ˈbrau̇-ˌbēt\ *vb* **-beat; -beat•en** \-ˈbēt-ᵊn\ *or* **-beat; -beat•ing** : to intimidate by sternness or arrogance

[1]**brown** \ˈbrau̇n\ *adj* : of the color brown; *also* : of dark or tanned complexion

[2]**brown** *n* : a color like that of coffee or chocolate that is a blend of red and yellow darkened by black — **brown•ish** *adj*

[3]**brown** *vb* : to make or become brown

brown bag•ging \-ˈba-giŋ\ *n* : the practice of carrying one's lunch usu. in a brown bag — **brown bag•ger** *n*

brown•ie \ˈbrau̇-nē\ *n* **1** : a legendary cheerful elf who performs good deeds at night **2** *cap* : a member of a program of the Girl Scouts for girls in the first through third grades

brown•out \ˈbrau̇-ˌnau̇t\ *n* : a period of reduced voltage of electricity caused esp. by high demand and resulting in reduced illumination

brown rice *n* : hulled but unpolished rice that retains most of the bran layers

brown•stone \ˈbrau̇n-ˌstōn\ *n* : a dwelling faced with reddish brown sandstone

[1]**browse** \ˈbrau̇z\ *vb* **browsed; brows•ing 1** : to feed on browse; *also* : GRAZE **2** : to read or look over something in a casual way

[2]**browse** *n* : tender shoots, twigs, and leaves fit for food for cattle

bru•in \ˈbrü-ən\ *n* : BEAR

[1]**bruise** \ˈbrüz\ *vb* **bruised; bruis•ing 1** : to inflict a bruise on; *also* : to become bruised **2** : to break down (as leaves or berries) by pounding

[2]**bruise** *n* : a surface injury to flesh : CONTUSION

bruis•er \ˈbrü-zər\ *n* : a big husky man

bruit \ˈbrüt\ *vb* : to make widely known by common report

brunch \ˈbrənch\ *n* : a meal that combines a late breakfast and an early lunch

bru•net *or* **bru•nette** \brü-ˈnet\ *adj* [F *brunet,* masc., *brunette,* fem., brownish, fr. OF, fr. *brun* brown] : having brown or black hair and usu. a relatively dark complexion — **brunet** *or* **brunette** *n*

brunt \ˈbrənt\ *n* : the main shock, force, or stress esp. of an attack; *also* : the greater burden

[1]**brush** \ˈbrəsh\ *n* **1** : BRUSHWOOD **2** : scrub vegetation or land covered with it

[2]**brush** *n* **1** : a device composed of bristles set in a handle and used esp. for cleaning or painting **2** : a bushy tail (as of a fox) **3** : an electrical conductor that makes contact between a stationary and a moving part (as of a motor) **4** : a quick light touch in passing

[3]**brush** *vb* **1** : to treat (as in cleaning or painting) with a brush **2** : to remove with or as if with a brush; *also* : to dismiss in an offhand manner **3** : to touch gently in passing

[4]**brush** *n* : SKIRMISH **syn** encounter, run-in

brush–off \ˈbrəsh-ˌȯf\ *n* : a curt offhand dismissal

brush up *vb* : to renew one's skill

brush•wood \ˈbrəsh-ˌwu̇d\ *n* **1** : small branches of

wood esp. when cut **2 :** a thicket of shrubs and small trees

brusque \ˈbrəsk\ *adj* [F *brusque,* fr. It *brusco,* fr. ML *bruscus* a plant with stiff twigs used for brooms] **:** CURT, BLUNT, ABRUPT **syn** gruff, bluff, crusty, short — **brusque•ly** *adv*

brus•sels sprout \ˈbrəs-əlz-\ *n, often cap B* **:** one of the edible small heads borne on the stalk of a plant closely related to the cabbage; *also, pl* **:** this plant

bru•tal \ˈbrüt-ᵊl\ *adj* **1 :** befitting a brute **:** UNFEELING, CRUEL **2 :** HARSH, SEVERE ⟨~ weather⟩ **3 :** unpleasantly accurate — **bru•tal•i•ty** \brü-ˈta-lə-tē\ *n* — **bru•tal•ly** *adv*

bru•tal•ise *Brit var of* BRUTALIZE

bru•tal•ize \ˈbrüt-ᵊl-ˌīz\ *vb* **-ized; -iz•ing 1 :** to make brutal **2 :** to treat brutally

[1]**brute** \ˈbrüt\ *adj* [ME, fr. MF *brut* rough, fr. L *brutus* brutish, lit., heavy] **1 :** of or relating to beasts **2 :** BRUTAL **3 :** UNREASONING; *also* **:** purely physical ⟨~ strength⟩

[2]**brute** *n* **1 :** BEAST 1 **2 :** a brutal person

brut•ish \ˈbrü-tish\ *adj* **1 :** BRUTE 1 **2 :** strongly sensual; *also* **:** showing little intelligence

BS *abbr* bachelor of science

BSA *abbr* Boy Scouts of America

bskt *abbr* basket

Bt *abbr* baronet

btry *abbr* battery

Btu *abbr* British thermal unit

bu *abbr* bushel

[1]**bub•ble** \ˈbə-bəl\ *n* **1 :** a globule of gas in a liquid **2 :** a thin film of liquid filled with gas **3 :** something lacking firmness or solidity — **bub•bly** *adj*

[2]**bubble** *vb* **bub•bled; bub•bling :** to form, rise in, or give off bubbles

bu•bo \ˈbü-bō, ˈbyü-\ *n, pl* **buboes :** an inflammatory swelling of a lymph gland

bu•bon•ic plague \bü-ˈbä-nik-, byü-\ *n* **:** plague caused by a bacterium transmitted to human beings by flea bites and marked esp. by chills and fever and by buboes usu. in the groin

buc•ca•neer \ˌbə-kə-ˈnir\ *n* **:** PIRATE

[1]**buck** \ˈbək\ *n, pl* **bucks 1** *or pl* **buck :** a male animal (as a deer or antelope) **2 :** DANDY **3 :** DOLLAR

[2]**buck** *vb* **1 :** to spring with an arching leap ⟨a ~*ing* horse⟩ **2 :** to charge against something; *also* **:** to strive for advancement sometimes without regard to ethical behavior

buck•board \-ˌbōrd\ *n* **:** a 4-wheeled horse-drawn wagon with a floor of long springy boards

buckboard

buck•et \ˈbə-kət\ *n* **1 :** PAIL **2 :** an object resembling a bucket in collecting, scooping, or carrying something — **buck•et•ful** *n*

bucket seat *n* **:** a low separate seat for one person (as in an automobile)

buck•eye \ˈbə-ˌkī\ *n* **:** a tree related to the horse chestnut that occurs chiefly in the central U.S.; *also* **:** its large nutlike seed

buck fever *n* **:** nervous excitement of an inexperienced hunter at the sight of game

[1]**buck•le** \ˈbə-kəl\ *n* **:** a clasp (as on a belt) for two loose ends

[2]**buckle** *vb* **buck•led; buck•ling 1 :** to fasten with a buckle **2 :** to apply oneself with vigor **3 :** to crumple up **:** BEND, COLLAPSE

[3]**buckle** *n* **:** BEND, FOLD, KINK

buck•ler \ˈbə-klər\ *n* **:** SHIELD

buck•ram \ˈbə-krəm\ *n* **:** a coarse stiff cloth used esp. for binding books

buck•saw \ˈbək-ˌsȯ\ *n* **:** a saw set in a usu. H-shaped frame for sawing wood

buck•shot \ˈbək-ˌshät\ *n* **:** lead shot that is from .24 to .33 inch (about 6.1 to 8.4 millimeters) in diameter

buck•skin \-ˌskin\ *n* **1 :** the skin of a buck **2 :** a soft usu. suede-finished leather — **buckskin** *adj*

buck•tooth \-ˈtüth\ *n* **:** a large projecting front tooth — **buck–toothed** \-ˈtütht\ *adj*

buck•wheat \-ˌhwēt\ *n* **:** either of two plants grown for their triangular seeds which are used as a cereal grain; *also* **:** these seeds

bu•col•ic \byü-ˈkä-lik\ *adj* [L *bucolicus,* fr. Gk *boukolikos,* fr. *boukolos* one who tends cattle, fr. *bous* head of cattle + *-kolos* (akin to L *colere* to cultivate)] **:** PASTORAL, RURAL

[1]**bud** \ˈbəd\ *n* **1 :** an undeveloped plant shoot (as of a leaf or a flower); *also* **:** a partly opened flower **2 :** an asexual reproductive structure that detaches from the parent and forms a new individual **3 :** something not yet fully developed ⟨nipped in the ~⟩

[2]**bud** *vb* **bud•ded; bud•ding 1 :** to form or put forth buds; *also* **:** to reproduce by asexual buds **2 :** to be or develop like a bud **3 :** to reproduce a desired variety (as of peach) by inserting a bud in a plant of a different variety

Bud•dhism \ˈbü-ˌdi-zəm, ˈbu̇-\ *n* **:** a religion of eastern and central Asia growing out of the teachings of Gautama Buddha — **Bud•dhist** \ˈbü-dist, ˈbu̇-\ *n or adj*

bud•dy \ˈbə-dē\ *n, pl* **buddies 1 :** COMPANION; *also* **:** FRIEND **2 :** FELLOW

budge \ˈbəj\ *vb* **budged; budg•ing :** MOVE, SHIFT; *also* **:** YIELD

bud•ger•i•gar \ˈbə-jə-rē-ˌgar\ *n* **:** a small brightly colored Australian parrot often kept as a pet

[1]**bud•get** \ˈbə-jət\ *n* [ME *bowgette,* fr. MF *bougette,* dim. of *bouge* leather bag, fr. L *bulga*] **1 :** STOCK, SUPPLY **2 :** a financial report containing estimates of income and expenses; *also* **:** a plan for coordinating income and expenses **3 :** the amount of money available for a particular use — **bud•get•ary** \ˈbə-jə-ˌter-ē\ *adj*

[2]**budget** *vb* **1 :** to allow for in a budget **2 :** to draw up a budget

[3]**budget** *adj* **:** INEXPENSIVE

bud•gie \ˈbə-jē\ *n* **:** BUDGERIGAR

[1]**buff** \ˈbəf\ *n* **1 :** a yellow to orange yellow color **2 :** FAN, ENTHUSIAST

[2]**buff** *adj* **:** of the color buff

[3]**buff** *vb* **:** POLISH, SHINE

buf•fa•lo \ˈbə-fə-ˌlō\ *n, pl* **-lo** *or* **-loes** *also* **-los 1 :** WATER BUFFALO **2 :** a large shaggy-maned No. American wild bovine mammal that has short horns and heavy forequarters with a large muscular hump

[1]**buf•fer** \ˈbə-fər\ *n* **:** something or someone that protects or shields (as from physical damage or a financial blow)

[2]**buffer** *n* **:** one that buffs

[1]**buf•fet** \ˈbə-fət\ *n* **:** BLOW, SLAP

[2]**buffet** *vb* **1 :** to strike with the hand; *also* **:** to pound repeatedly **2 :** to struggle against or on **syn** beat, batter, drub, pummel, thrash

[3]**buf•fet** \(ˌ)bə-ˈfā, bü-\ *n* **1 :** SIDEBOARD **2 :** a counter for refreshments; *also* **:** a meal at which people serve themselves informally

buff leather *n* **:** a strong supple oil-tanned leather

buf•foon \(ˌ)bə-ˈfün\ *n* [MF *bouffon,* fr. It *buffone*] **:** CLOWN 2 — **buf•foon•ery** \-ˈfü-nə-rē\ *n*

[1]**bug** \ˈbəg\ *n* **1 :** an insect or other creeping or crawling invertebrate animal; *esp* **:** an insect pest (as a bedbug)

2 : any of an order of insects with sucking mouthparts and incomplete metamorphosis that includes many plant pests **3** : an unexpected flaw or imperfection ⟨a ~ in a computer program⟩ **4** : a disease-producing germ; *also* : a disease caused by it **5** : a concealed listening device

²bug *vb* **bugged; bug•ging 1** : BOTHER, ANNOY **2** : to plant a concealed microphone in

³bug *vb* **bugged; bug•ging** *of the eyes* : PROTRUDE, BULGE

bug•a•boo \ˈbə-gə-ˌbü\ *n, pl* **-boos** : BOGEY 1

bug•bear \ˈbəg-ˌbar\ *n* : BOGEY 1; *also* : a source of dread

bug•gy \ˈbə-gē\ *n, pl* **buggies** : a light horse-drawn carriage; *also* : a carriage for a baby

bu•gle \ˈbyü-gəl\ *n* [ME, buffalo, instrument made of buffalo horn, bugle, fr. OF, fr. L *buculus,* dim. of *bos* head of cattle] : a valveless brass instrument resembling a trumpet and used esp. for military calls — **bugler** *n*

¹build \ˈbild\ *vb* **built** \ˈbilt\; **build•ing 1** : to form or have formed by ordering and uniting materials ⟨~ a house⟩; *also* : to bring into being or develop **2** : to produce or create gradually ⟨~ an argument on facts⟩ **3** : INCREASE, ENLARGE; *also* : ENHANCE **4** : to engage in building — **build•er** *n*

²build *n* : form or mode of structure; *esp* : PHYSIQUE

build•ing \ˈbil-diŋ\ *n* **1** : a usu. roofed and walled structure (as a house) for permanent use **2** : the art or business of constructing buildings

build•up \ˈbil-ˌdəp\ *n* : the act or process of building up; *also* : something produced by this

built–in \ˈbil-ˈtin\ *adj* **1** : forming an integral part of a structure **2** : INHERENT

bulb \ˈbəlb\ *n* **1** : an underground resting stage of a plant (as a lily or an onion) consisting of a short stem base bearing one or more buds enclosed in overlapping leaves; *also* : a fleshy plant structure (as a tuber) resembling a bulb **2** : a plant having or growing from a bulb **3** : a rounded more or less bulb-shaped object or part (as for an electric lamp) — **bul•bous** \ˈbəl-bəs\ *adj*

Bul•gar•i•an \ˌbəl-ˈgar-ē-ən, bu̇l-\ *n* : a native or inhabitant of Bulgaria — **Bulgarian** *adj*

¹bulge \ˈbəlj\ *vb* **bulged; bulg•ing** : to become or cause to become protuberant

²bulge *n* : a swelling projecting part

bu•li•mia \bü-ˈlē-mē-ə, byü-, -ˈli-\ *n* **1** : an abnormal and constant craving for food **2** : a serious eating disorder chiefly of females that is characterized by compulsive overeating usu. followed by self-induced vomiting or laxative or diuretic abuse — **bu•lim•ic** \-ˈlē-mik, -ˈli-\ *adj or n*

¹bulk \ˈbəlk\ *n* **1** : MAGNITUDE, VOLUME **2** : material that forms a mass in the intestine; *esp* : FIBER 2 **3** : a large mass **4** : the major portion

²bulk *vb* **1** : to cause to swell or bulge **2** : to appear as a factor : LOOM

bulk•head \ˈbəlk-ˌhed\ *n* **1** : a partition separating compartments **2** : a structure built to cover a shaft or a cellar stairway

bulky \ˈbəl-kē\ *adj* **bulk•i•er; -est** : having bulk; *esp* : being large and unwieldy

¹bull \ˈbu̇l\ *n* **1** : a male bovine animal; *also* : a usu. adult male of various large animals (as the moose, elephant, or whale) **2** : one who buys securities or commodities in expectation of a price increase — **bullish** *adj*

²bull *adj* **1** : of, relating to, or suggestive of a bull : MALE **2** : large of its kind

³bull *n* [ME *bulle,* fr. ML *bulla,* fr. L, bubble, amulet] **1** : a papal letter **2** : DECREE

⁴bull *n, slang* : NONSENSE

⁵bull *abbr* bulletin

¹bull•dog \ˈbu̇l-ˌdȯg\ *n* : any of a breed of compact muscular short-haired dogs of English origin

bulldog

²bulldog *vb* : to throw (a steer) by seizing the horns and twisting the neck

bull•doze \-ˌdōz\ *vb* **1** : to move, clear, or level with a tractor-driven machine (**bull•doz•er**) having a broad blade for pushing **2** : to force as if by using a bulldozer

bul•let \ˈbu̇-lət\ *n* [MF *boulette* small ball & *boulet* missile, dims. of *boule* ball] : a missile to be shot from a firearm — **bul•let•proof** \-ˌprüf\ *adj*

bul•le•tin \ˈbu̇-lət-ᵊn\ *n* **1** : a brief public report intended for immediate release on a matter of public interest **2** : a periodical publication (as of a college) — **bulletin** *vb*

bull•fight \ˈbu̇l-ˌfīt\ *n* : a spectacle in which people ceremonially fight with and usu. kill bulls in an arena — **bull•fight•er** *n*

bull•frog \-ˌfrȯg, -ˌfräg\ *n* : a large deep-voiced frog

bull•head \-ˌhed\ *n* : any of several common freshwater catfishes of the U.S.

bull•head•ed \-ˈhe-dəd\ *adj* : stupidly stubborn : HEADSTRONG

bul•lion \ˈbu̇l-yən\ *n* : gold or silver esp. in bars or ingots

bull•ock \ˈbu̇-lək\ *n* : a young bull; *also* : STEER

bull pen *n* : a place on a baseball field where pitchers warm up; *also* : the relief pitchers of a baseball team

bull session *n* : an informal discussion

bull's–eye \ˈbu̇l-ˌzī\ *n, pl* **bull's–eyes** : the center of a target; *also* : a shot that hits the bull's-eye

¹bul•ly \ˈbu̇-lē\ *n, pl* **bullies** : a person habitually cruel to others who are weaker

²bully *adj* : EXCELLENT, FIRST-RATE — often used interjectionally

³bully *vb* **bul•lied; bul•ly•ing** : to behave as a bully toward : DOMINEER **syn** browbeat, intimidate, hector

bul•rush \ˈbu̇l-ˌrəsh\ *n* : any of several large rushes or sedges of wetlands

bul•wark \ˈbu̇l-(ˌ)wərk, -ˌwȯrk; ˈbəl-(ˌ)wərk\ *n* **1** : a wall-like defensive structure **2** : a strong support or protection

¹bum \ˈbəm\ *adj* **1** : of poor quality ⟨~ advice⟩ **2** : DISABLED ⟨a ~ knee⟩

²bum *vb* **bummed; bum•ming 1** : to spend time unemployed and wandering; *also* : LOAF **2** : to obtain by begging

³bum *n* **1** : LOAFER **2** : a devotee of a recreational activity ⟨a ski ~⟩ **3** : TRAMP

bum•ble•bee \ˈbəm-bəl-ˌbē\ *n* : any of numerous large hairy social bees

bum•mer \ˈbə-mər\ *n* **1** : an unpleasant experience **2** : FAILURE

¹bump \ˈbəmp\ *n* **1** : a local bulge; *esp* : a swelling of tissue **2** : a sudden forceful blow or impact — **bumpy** *adj*

²bump *vb* **1** : to strike or knock forcibly; *also* : to move by or as if by bumping **2** : to collide with

¹bum•per \ˈbəm-pər\ *n* **1** : a cup or glass filled to the brim **2** : something unusually large — **bumper** *adj*

²bump•er \ˈbəm-pər\ *n* : a device for absorbing shock or preventing damage; *esp* : a usu. metal bar at either end of an automobile

DICTIONARY

bump•kin \ˈbəmp-kən\ *n* : an awkward and unsophisticated country person

bump•tious \ˈbəmp-shəs\ *adj* : obtusely and often noisily self-assertive

bun \ˈbən\ *n* : a sweet biscuit or roll

¹bunch \ˈbənch\ *n* **1** : SWELLING **2** : CLUSTER, GROUP — **bunchy** *adj*

²bunch *vb* : to form into a group or bunch

bun•co *or* **bun•ko** \ˈbəŋ-kō\ *n, pl* **buncos** *or* **bunkos** : a swindling scheme — **bunco** *vb*

¹bun•dle \ˈbən-dᵊl\ *n* **1** : several items bunched and fastened together; *also* : something wrapped for carrying **2** : a considerable amount : LOT **3** : a small band of mostly parallel nerve or muscle fibers

²bundle *vb* **bun•dled; bun•dling** : to gather or tie in a bundle

bun•dling \ˈbənd-(ᵊ-)liŋ\ *n* : a former custom of a courting couple's occupying the same bed without undressing

bung \ˈbəŋ\ *n* : the stopper in the bunghole of a cask

bun•ga•low \ˈbəŋ-gə-ˌlō\ *n* : a one-storied house with a low-pitched roof

bun•gee cord \ˈbən-jē-\ *n* : a long elastic cord used esp. in a sport (**bungee jump•ing**) in which it is fastened to a person to arrest a free fall from a high place (as a bridge)

bung•hole \ˈbəŋ-ˌhōl\ *n* : a hole for emptying or filling a cask

bun•gle \ˈbəŋ-gəl\ *vb* **bun•gled; bun•gling** : to do badly : BOTCH — **bungle** *n* — **bun•gler** *n*

bun•ion \ˈbən-yən\ *n* : an inflamed swelling of the first joint of the big toe

¹bunk \ˈbəŋk\ *n* : BED; *esp* : a built-in bed that is often one of a tier

²bunk *n* : BUNKUM, NONSENSE

bunk bed *n* : one of two single beds usu. placed one above the other

bun•ker \ˈbəŋ-kər\ *n* **1** : a bin or compartment for storage (as for coal on a ship) **2** : a protective embankment or dugout **3** : a sand trap or embankment constituting a hazard on a golf course

bun•kum *or* **bun•combe** \ˈbəŋ-kəm\ *n* [*Buncombe* County, N.C.; fr. a remark made by its congressman, who defended an irrelevant speech by claiming that he was speaking to Buncombe] : insincere or foolish talk

bun•ny \ˈbə-nē\ *n, pl* **-nies** : RABBIT

Bun•sen burner \ˈbən-sən-\ *n* : a gas burner usu. consisting of a straight tube with air holes at the bottom

¹bunt \ˈbənt\ *vb* **1** : ¹BUTT **2** : to push or tap a baseball lightly without swinging the bat

²bunt *n* : an act or instance of bunting; *also* : a bunted ball

¹bun•ting \ˈbən-tiŋ\ *n* : any of numerous small stout-billed finches

²bunting *n* : a thin fabric used esp. for flags; *also* : FLAGS

¹buoy \ˈbü-ē, ˈbȯi\ *n* **1** : a floating object anchored in water to mark something (as a channel) **2** : a float consisting of a ring of buoyant material to support a person who has fallen into the water

²buoy *vb* **1** : to mark by a buoy **2** : to keep afloat **3** : to raise the spirits of

buoy•an•cy \ˈbȯi-ən-sē, ˈbü-yən-\ *n* **1** : the tendency of a body to float or rise when submerged in a fluid **2** : the power of a fluid to exert an upward force on a body placed in it **3** : resilience of spirit — **buoy•ant** \-ənt, -yənt\ *adj*

¹bur \ˈbər\ *var of* BURR

²bur *abbr* bureau

¹bur•den \ˈbərd-ᵊn\ *n* **1** : LOAD; *also* : CARE, RESPONSIBILITY **2** : something oppressive : ENCUMBRANCE **3** : CARGO; *also* : capacity for cargo

²burden *vb* : LOAD, OPPRESS — **bur•den•some** \-səm\ *adj*

³burden *n* **1** : REFRAIN, CHORUS **2** : a main theme or idea : GIST

bur•dock \ˈbər-ˌdäk\ *n* : any of a genus of coarse composite herbs with globe-shaped flower heads surrounded by prickly bracts

bu•reau \ˈbyu̇r-ō\ *n, pl* **bureaus** *also* **bu•reaux** \-ōz\ [F, desk, cloth covering for desks, fr. OF *burel* woolen cloth, ultim. fr. L *burra* shaggy cloth] **1** : a chest of drawers **2** : an administrative unit (as of a government department) **3** : a branch of a publication or wire service in an important news center

bu•reau•cra•cy \byu̇-ˈrä-krə-sē\ *n, pl* **-cies 1** : a body of appointive government officials **2** : government marked by specialization of functions under fixed rules and a hierarchy of authority; *also* : an unwieldy administrative system burdened with excessive complexity and lack of flexibility — **bu•reau•crat** \ˈbyu̇r-ə-ˌkrat\ *n* — **bu•reau•crat•ic** \ˌbyu̇r-ə-ˈkra-tik\ *adj*

bur•geon \ˈbər-jən\ *vb* : to put forth fresh growth (as from buds) : grow vigorously : FLOURISH

burgh \ˈbər-ō\ *n* : a Scottish town

bur•gher \ˈbər-gər\ *n* **1** : TOWNSMAN **2** : a prosperous solid citizen

bur•glary \ˈbər-glə-rē\ *n, pl* **-glar•ies** : forcible entry into a building esp. at night with the intent to commit a crime (as theft) — **bur•glar** \-glər\ *n* — **bur•glar•ize** \ˈbər-glə-ˌrīz\ *vb*

bur•gle \ˈbər-gəl\ *vb* **bur•gled; bur•gling** : to commit burglary on

bur•go•mas•ter \ˈbər-gə-ˌmas-tər\ *n* : the chief magistrate of a town in some European countries

bur•gun•dy \ˈbər-gən-dē\ *n, pl* **-dies** *often cap* **1** : a red or white table wine from the Burgundy region of France **2** : an American red table wine

buri•al \ˈber-ē-əl\ *n* : the act or process of burying

burl \ˈbərl\ *n* : a hard woody often flattened hemispherical outgrowth on a tree

bur•lap \ˈbər-ˌlap\ *n* : a coarse fabric usu. of jute or hemp used esp. for bags

¹bur•lesque \(ˌ)bər-ˈlesk\ *n* [*burlesque*, adj., comic, droll, fr. F, fr. It *burlesco*, fr. *burla* joke, fr. Sp] **1** : a witty or derisive literary or dramatic imitative work **2** : broadly humorous theatrical entertainment consisting of several items (as songs, skits, or dances)

²burlesque *vb* **bur•lesqued; bur•lesqu•ing** : to make ludicrous by burlesque **syn** caricature, parody, travesty

bur•ly \ˈbər-lē\ *adj* **bur•li•er; -est** : strongly and heavily built : HUSKY **syn** muscular, brawny, beefy, hefty

Bur•mese \ˌbər-ˈmēz, -ˈmēs\ *n, pl* **Burmese** : a native or inhabitant of Burma (Myanmar) — **Burmese** *adj*

¹burn \ˈbərn\ *vb* **burned** \ˈbərnd, ˈbərnt\ *or* **burnt** \ˈbərnt\; **burn•ing 1** : to be on fire **2** : to feel or look as if on fire **3** : to alter or become altered by or as if by the action of fire or heat **4** : to use as fuel ⟨~ coal⟩; *also* : to destroy by fire ⟨~ trash⟩ **5** : to cause or make by fire ⟨~ a hole⟩; *also* : to affect as if by heat

²burn *n* : an injury or effect produced by or as if by burning

burn•er \ˈbər-nər\ *n* : the part of a fuel-burning or heat-producing device where the flame or heat is produced

bur•nish \ˈbər-nish\ *vb* : to make shiny esp. by rubbing : POLISH — **bur•nish•er** *n* — **bur•nish•ing** *adj or n*

bur•noose *or* **bur•nous** \(ˌ)bər-ˈnüs\ *n* : a hooded cloak worn esp. by Arabs

burn•out \ˈbər-ˌnau̇t\ *n* **1** : the cessation of operation of a jet or rocket engine **2** : exhaustion of one's physical or emotional strength; *also* : a person suffering from burnout

burp \ˈbərp\ *n* : an act of belching — **burp** *vb*

burp gun *n* : a small submachine gun

burr \ˈbər\ *n* **1** *usu* **bur** : a rough or prickly envelope of a fruit; *also* : a plant that bears burs **2** : roughness left in cutting or shaping metal **3** : WHIR — **bur•ry** *adj*

bur•ri•to \bə-ˈrē-tō\ *n* [AmerSp, fr. Sp, little donkey, dim. of *burro*] : a flour tortilla rolled around a filling and baked

bur•ro \ˈbər-ō, ˈbu̇r-\ *n, pl* **burros** [Sp] : a usu. small donkey
[1]**bur•row** \ˈbər-ō\ *n* : a hole in the ground made by an animal (as a rabbit)
[2]**burrow** *vb* **1** : to form by tunneling; *also* : to make a burrow **2** : to progress by or as if by digging — **bur•row•er** *n*
bur•sar \ˈbər-sər\ *n* : a treasurer esp. of a college
bur•si•tis \(ˌ)bər-ˈsī-təs\ *n* : inflammation of the serous sac (**bur•sa** \ˈbər-sə\) of a joint (as the elbow or shoulder)
[1]**burst** \ˈbərst\ *vb* **burst** *or* **burst•ed; burst•ing 1** : to fly apart or into pieces **2** : to show one's feelings suddenly; *also* : PLUNGE ⟨~ into song⟩ **3** : to enter or emerge suddenly : SPRING **4** : to be filled to the breaking point
[2]**burst** *n* **1** : a sudden outbreak : SPURT **2** : EXPLOSION **3** : result of bursting
Bu•run•di•an \bu̇-ˈrün-dē-ən\ *n* : a native or inhabitant of Burundi
bury \ˈber-ē\ *vb* **bur•ied; bury•ing 1** : to deposit in the earth; *also* : to inter with funeral ceremonies **2** : CONCEAL, HIDE **3** : SUBMERGE, ENGROSS — usu. used with *in*
[1]**bus** \ˈbəs\ *n, pl* **bus•es** *or* **bus•ses** [short for *omnibus*, fr. F, fr. L, for all, dat. pl. of *omnis* all] : a large motor vehicle for carrying passengers
[2]**bus** *vb* **bused** *or* **bussed; bus•ing** *or* **bus•sing 1** : to travel or transport by bus **2** : to work as a busboy
[3]**bus** *abbr* business
bus•boy \ˈbəs-ˌbȯi\ *n* : a waiter's helper
bus•by \ˈbəz-bē\ *n, pl* **busbies** : a military full-dress fur hat
bush \ˈbu̇sh\ *n* **1** : SHRUB **2** : rough uncleared country **3** : a thick tuft ⟨a ~ of hair⟩ — **bushy** *adj*
bushed \ˈbu̇sht\ *adj* : TIRED, EXHAUSTED
bush•el \ˈbu̇-shəl\ *n* — see WEIGHT table
bush•ing \ˈbu̇-shiŋ\ *n* : a usu. removable cylindrical lining for an opening of a mechanical part to limit the size of the opening, resist wear, or serve as a guide
bush•mas•ter \ˈbu̇sh-ˌmas-tər\ *n* : a large venomous tropical American pit viper
bush•whack \-ˌhwak\ *vb* **1** : AMBUSH **2** : to clear a path through esp. by chopping down bushes and branches — **bush•whack•er** *n*
busi•ly \ˈbi-zə-lē\ *adv* : in a busy manner
busi•ness \ˈbiz-nəs, -nəz\ *n* **1** : OCCUPATION; *also* : TASK, MISSION **2** : a commercial or industrial enterprise; *also* : TRADE ⟨~ is good⟩ **3** : AFFAIR, MATTER **4** : personal concern
busi•ness•man \-ˌman\ *n* : a man engaged in business esp. as an executive
busi•ness•per•son \-ˌpərs-ᵊn\ *n* : a businessman or businesswoman
busi•ness•wom•an \-ˌwu̇-mən\ *n* : a woman engaged in business esp. as an executive
bus•kin \ˈbəs-kən\ *n* **1** : a laced boot reaching halfway to the knee **2** : tragic drama
buss \ˈbəs\ *n* : KISS — **buss** *vb*
[1]**bust** \ˈbəst\ *n* [F *buste*, fr. It *busto*, fr. L *bustum* tomb] **1** : sculpture representing the upper part of the human figure **2** : the part of the human torso between the neck and the waist; *esp* : the breasts of a woman
[2]**bust** *vb* **bust•ed** *also* **bust; bust•ing 1** : BREAK, SMASH; *also* : BURST **2** : to ruin financially **3** : TAME **4** : DEMOTE **5** *slang* : ARREST; *also* : RAID
[3]**bust** *n* **1** : a drinking session **2** : a complete failure : FLOP **3** : a business depression **4** : PUNCH, SOCK **5** *slang* : a police raid; *also* : ARREST
[1]**bus•tle** \ˈbə-səl\ *vb* **bus•tled; bus•tling** : to move or work in a brisk busy manner
[2]**bustle** *n* : briskly energetic activity
[3]**bustle** *n* : a pad or frame worn to support the fullness at the back of a woman's skirt
[1]**busy** \ˈbi-zē\ *adj* **busi•er; -est 1** : engaged in action : not idle **2** : being in use ⟨~ telephones⟩ **3** : full of activity ⟨~ streets⟩ **4** : MEDDLING
[2]**busy** *vb* **bus•ied; busy•ing** : to make or keep busy : OCCUPY
busy•body \ˈbi-zē-ˌbä-dē\ *n* : MEDDLER
busy•work \-ˌwərk\ *n* : work that appears productive but only keeps one occupied
[1]**but** \ˈbət\ *conj* **1** : except for the fact ⟨would have protested ~ that he was afraid⟩ **2** : THAT ⟨there's no doubt ~ he won⟩ **3** : without the certainty that ⟨never rains ~ it pours⟩ **4** : on the contrary ⟨not one, ~ two job offers⟩ **5** : YET ⟨poor ~ proud⟩ **6** : with the exception of ⟨none ~ the strongest attempt it⟩
[2]**but** *prep* : other than : EXCEPT ⟨this letter is nothing ~ an insult⟩; *also* : with the exception of ⟨no one here ~ me⟩
bu•tane \ˈbyü-ˌtān\ *n* : either of two gaseous hydrocarbons used as a fuel
[1]**butch•er** \ˈbu̇-chər\ *n* [ME *bocher*, fr. OF *bouchier*, fr. *bouc* he-goat] **1** : one who slaughters animals or dresses their flesh; *also* : a dealer in meat **2** : one that kills brutally or needlessly **3** : one that botches — **butch•ery** \-chə-rē\ *n*
[2]**butcher** *vb* **1** : to slaughter and dress for meat ⟨~ hogs⟩ **2** : to kill barbarously **3** : BOTCH
but•ler \ˈbət-lər\ *n* [ME *buteler*, fr. OF *bouteillier* bottle bearer, fr. *bouteille* bottle] : the chief male servant of a household
[1]**butt** \ˈbət\ *vb* : to strike with the head or horns
[2]**butt** *n* : a blow or thrust with the head or horns
[3]**butt** *n* : a large cask
[4]**butt** *n* **1** : TARGET **2** : an object of abuse or ridicule
[5]**butt** *n* : a large, thicker, or bottom end of something
[6]**butt** *vb* **1** : ABUT **2** : to place or join edge to edge without overlapping
butte \ˈbyüt\ *n* : an isolated steep hill
[1]**but•ter** \ˈbə-tər\ *n* [ME, fr. OE *butere*, fr. L *butyrum* butter, fr. Gk *boutyron*, fr. *bous* cow + *tyros* cheese] **1** : a solid edible emulsion of fat obtained from cream by churning **2** : a substance resembling butter — **buttery** *adj*
[2]**butter** *vb* : to spread with or as if with butter
but•ter–and–eggs \ˌbə-tə-rə-ˈnegz\ *n sing or pl* : a common perennial herb related to the snapdragon that has showy yellow and orange flowers
but•ter•cup \ˈbə-tər-ˌkəp\ *n* : any of a genus of herbs having usu. yellow flowers with five petals and sepals
but•ter•fat \-ˌfat\ *n* : the natural fat of milk and chief constituent of butter
but•ter•fin•gered \-ˌfiŋ-gərd\ *adj* : likely to let things fall or slip through the fingers — **but•ter•fin•gers** \-gərz\ *n sing or pl*
but•ter•fly \-ˌflī\ *n* : any of a group of slender day-flying insects with four broad wings covered with bright-colored scales
but•ter•milk \-ˌmilk\ *n* : the liquid remaining after butter is churned
but•ter•nut \-ˌnət\ *n* : the sweet egg-shaped nut of an American tree related to the walnut; *also* : this tree
but•ter•scotch \-ˌskäch\ *n* : a candy made from brown sugar, corn syrup, and water; *also* : the flavor of such candy
but•tock \ˈbə-tək\ *n* **1** : the back of a hip that forms one of the fleshy parts on which a person sits **2** *pl* : the seat of the body : RUMP
[1]**but•ton** \ˈbət-ᵊn\ *n* **1** : a small knob secured to an article (as of clothing) and used as a fastener by passing it through a buttonhole or loop **2** : something that resembles a button **3** : PUSH BUTTON
[2]**button** *vb* : to close or fasten with or as if with buttons
[1]**but•ton•hole** \ˈbət-ᵊn-ˌhōl\ *n* : a slit or loop for a button to pass through
[2]**buttonhole** *vb* : to detain in conversation by or as if by holding on to the outer garments of
[1]**but•tress** \ˈbə-trəs\ *n* **1** : a projecting structure to support a wall **2** : PROP, SUPPORT
☞ For illustration, see next page.
[2]**buttress** *vb* : PROP, SUPPORT

buttress 1

bu•tut \bu̇-ˈtüt\ *n, pl* **bututs** *or* **butut** — see *dalasi* at MONEY table

bux•om \ˈbək-səm\ *adj* : healthily plump; *esp* : full-bosomed

¹buy \ˈbī\ *vb* **bought** \ˈbȯt\; **buy•ing 1** : to obtain for a price : PURCHASE; *also* : BRIBE **2** : to accept as true — **buy•er** *n*

²buy *n* **1** : PURCHASE 1, 2 **2** : an exceptional value : BARGAIN

¹buzz \ˈbəz\ *vb* **1** : to make a buzz **2** : to fly fast and close to

²buzz *n* **1** : a low humming sound **2** : RUMOR, GOSSIP

buz•zard \ˈbə-zərd\ *n* : any of various usu. large birds of prey and esp. the turkey vulture

buzz•er \ˈbə-zər\ *n* : a device that signals with a buzzing sound

buzz saw *n* : CIRCULAR SAW

buzz•word \ˈbəz-ˌwərd\ *n* : a voguish word or phrase often from technical jargon

BV *abbr* Blessed Virgin

BWI *abbr* British West Indies

bx *abbr* box

BX *abbr* base exchange

¹by \ˈbī, bə\ *prep* **1** : NEAR ⟨stood ~ the window⟩ **2** : through or through the medium of : VIA ⟨left ~ the door⟩ **3** : PAST ⟨drove ~ the house⟩ **4** : DURING, AT ⟨studied ~ night⟩ **5** : no later than ⟨get here ~ 3 p.m.⟩ **6** : through the means or direct agency of ⟨~ force⟩ **7** : in conformity with; *also* : ACCORDING TO ⟨did it ~ the book⟩ **8** : with respect to ⟨a vet ~ profession⟩ **9** : to the amount or extent of ⟨won ~ a nose⟩ **10** — used to express relationship in multiplication, in division, and in measurements ⟨divide *a* ~ *b*⟩ ⟨multiply ~ 6⟩ ⟨15 feet ~ 20 feet⟩

²by \ˈbī\ *adv* **1** : near at hand; *also* : IN ⟨stop ~⟩ **2** : PAST **3** : ASIDE, APART

bye \ˈbī\ *n* : a position of a participant in a tournament who advances to the next round without playing

by–elec•tion *also* **bye–election** \ˈbī-ə-ˌlek-shən\ *n* : a special election held between regular elections in order to fill a vacancy

by•gone \ˈbī-ˌgȯn\ *adj* : gone by : PAST — **bygone** *n*

by•law *or* **bye•law** \ˈbī-ˌlȯ\ *n* : a rule adopted by an organization for managing its internal affairs

by–line \ˈbī-ˌlīn\ *n* : a line at the beginning of a news story or magazine article giving the writer's name

BYO *abbr* bring your own

BYOB *abbr* bring your own beer; bring your own booze; bring your own bottle

¹by•pass \ˈbī-ˌpas\ *n* : a passage to one side or around a blocked or congested area; *also* : a surgical procedure establishing this ⟨a coronary ~⟩

²bypass *vb* : to avoid by means of a bypass

by•path \-ˌpath, -ˌpȧth\ *n* : BYWAY

by•play \ˈbī-ˌplā\ *n* : action engaged in on the side (as of a stage) while the main action proceeds

by–prod•uct \-ˌprä-(ˌ)dəkt\ *n* : a sometimes unexpected product or result produced in addition to the main product or result

by•stand•er \-ˌstan-dər\ *n* : one present but not participating **syn** onlooker, witness, spectator, eyewitness

byte \ˈbīt\ *n* : a group of 8 bits that a computer processes as a unit

by•way \ˈbī-ˌwā\ *n* **1** : a little-traveled side road **2** : a secondary aspect

by•word \-ˌwərd\ *n* **1** : PROVERB **2** : one that is noteworthy or notorious

Byz•an•tine \ˈbiz-ᵊn-ˌtēn, ˈbī-, -ˌtīn; bə-ˈzan-, bī-\ *adj* **1** : of, relating to, or characteristic of the ancient city of Byzantium or the Byzantine Empire **2** *often not cap* : intricately involved and often devious

C

¹c \ˈsē\ *n, pl* **c's** *or* **cs** \ˈsēz\ *often cap* **1** : the 3d letter of the English alphabet **2** *slang* : a sum of $100 **3** : a grade rating a student's work as fair

²c *abbr, often cap* **1** calorie **2** carat **3** Celsius **4** cent **5** centigrade **6** centimeter **7** century **8** chapter **9** circa **10** cocaine **11** copyright

C *symbol* carbon

ca *abbr* circa

Ca *symbol* calcium

CA *abbr* **1** California **2** chartered accountant **3** chief accountant **4** chronological age

cab \ˈkab\ *n* **1** : a light closed horse-drawn carriage **2** : TAXICAB **3** : the covered compartment for the engineer and controls of a locomotive; *also* : a similar compartment (as on a truck)

CAB *abbr* Civil Aeronautics Board

ca•bal \kə-ˈbäl, -ˈbal\ *n* [F *cabale,* fr. ML *cabbala* cabala, fr. Heb *qabbālāh,* lit., received (lore)] : a secret group of plotters or political conspirators

ca•ba•la \ˈka-bə-lə, kə-ˈbä-\ *n, often cap* **1** : a medieval Jewish mysticism marked by belief in creation through emanation and a cipher method of interpreting Scripture **2** : esoteric or mysterious doctrine

ca•bana \kə-ˈban-yə, -ˈba-nə\ *n* : a shelter at a beach or swimming pool

cab•a•ret \ˌka-bə-ˈrā\ *n* : NIGHTCLUB

cab•bage \ˈka-bij\ *n* [ME *caboche,* fr. OF, head] : a vegetable related to the mustard with a dense head of leaves

cab•bie *or* **cab•by** \ˈka-bē\ *n, pl* **cabbies** : a driver of a cab

cab•er•net sau•vi•gnon \ˌka-bər-ˈnā-sō-vē-ˈnyōⁿ\ *n* : a dry red wine made from a single variety of black grape

cab•in \ˈka-bən\ *n* **1** : a private room on a ship; *also* : a compartment below deck on a boat for passengers or crew **2** : an aircraft or spacecraft compartment for passengers, crew, or cargo **3** : a small simple one-story house

cabin boy *n* : a boy working as servant on a ship

cabin class *n* : a class of accommodations on a passenger ship superior to tourist class and inferior to first class

cabin cruiser *n* : CRUISER 3

cab•i•net \ˈkab-nit\ *n* **1** : a case or cupboard for holding or displaying articles **2** : the advisory council of a head of state (as a president or sovereign)

cab•i•net•mak•er \-ˌmā-kər\ *n* : a woodworker who makes fine furniture — **cab•i•net•mak•ing** *n*

cab•i•net•work \-ˌwərk\ *n* : the finished work of a cabinetmaker

¹ca•ble \ˈkā-bəl\ *n* **1** : a very strong rope, wire, or chain

2 : a bundle of insulated wires usu. twisted around a central core **3** : CABLEGRAM **4** : CABLE TELEVISION
[2]**cable** *vb* **ca•bled; ca•bling** : to telegraph by cable
cable car *n* : a vehicle moved by an endless cable
ca•ble•gram \ˈkā-bəl-ˌgram\ *n* : a message sent by a submarine telegraph cable
cable television *n* : a system of television reception in which signals from distant stations are sent by cable to the receivers of paying subscribers
cab•o•chon \ˈka-bə-ˌshän\ *n* : a gem or bead cut in convex form and highly polished but not given facets; *also* : this style of cutting — **cabochon** *adv*
ca•boose \kə-ˈbüs\ *n* : a car usu. at the rear of a freight train for the use of the train crew and railroad workers
cab•ri•o•let \ˌka-brē-ə-ˈlā\ *n* [F] **1** : a light 2-wheeled one-horse carriage **2** : a convertible coupe
cab•stand \ˈkab-ˌstand\ *n* : a place where cabs wait for passengers
ca•cao \kə-ˈkau̇, -ˈkā-ō\ *n, pl* **cacaos** [Sp] : a So. American tree whose seeds (**cacao beans**) are the source of cocoa and chocolate; *also* : its dried fatty seeds
cac•cia•to•re \ˌkä-chə-ˈtōr-ē\ *adj* [It] : cooked with tomatoes and herbs ⟨chicken ~⟩
cache \ˈkash\ *n* [F] : a hiding place esp. for preserving provisions; *also* : something hidden or stored in a cache — **cache** *vb*
ca•chet \ka-ˈshā\ *n* [F] **1** : a seal used esp. as a mark of official approval **2** : a feature or quality conferring prestige; *also* : PRESTIGE **3** : a design, inscription, or advertisement printed or stamped on mail
cack•le \ˈka-kəl\ *vb* **cack•led; cack•ling 1** : to make the sharp broken cry characteristic of a hen **2** : to laugh or chatter noisily — **cackle** *n* — **cack•ler** *n*
ca•coph•o•ny \ka-ˈkä-fə-nē\ *n, pl* **-nies** : harsh or discordant sound — **ca•coph•o•nous** \-nəs\ *adj*
cac•tus \ˈkak-təs\ *n, pl* **cac•ti** \-ˌtī\ *or* **cac•tus•es** *also* **cactus** : any of a large family of drought-resistant flowering plants with succulent stems and with leaves replaced by scales or prickles
cad \ˈkad\ *n* : a man who deliberately disregards another's feelings — **cad•dish** \ˈka-dish\ *adj* — **cad•dish•ly** *adv* — **cad•dish•ness** *n*
ca•dav•er \kə-ˈda-vər\ *n* : a dead body
ca•dav•er•ous \kə-ˈda-və-rəs\ *adj* : suggesting a corpse esp. in gauntness or pallor **syn** wasted, emaciated, gaunt — **ca•dav•er•ous•ly** *adv*
cad•die *or* **cad•dy** \ˈka-dē\ *n, pl* **caddies** [F *cadet* military cadet] : a person who assists a golfer esp. by carrying the clubs — **caddie** *or* **caddy** *vb*
cad•dy \ˈka-dē\ *n, pl* **caddies** [Malay *kati* a unit of weight] : a small box, can, or chest; *esp* : one to keep tea in
ca•dence \ˈkād-ᵊns\ *n* : the measure or beat of a rhythmical flow : RHYTHM — **ca•denced** \-ᵊnst\ *adj*
ca•den•za \kə-ˈden-zə\ *n* [It] : a brilliant sometimes improvised passage usu. toward the close of a musical composition
ca•det \kə-ˈdet\ *n* [F, fr. Prov (Gascony) *capdet* chief, fr. L *capitellum*, fr. L *caput* head] **1** : a younger son or brother **2** : a student in a service academy
Ca•dette \kə-ˈdet\ *n* : a member of a Girl Scout program for girls in sixth through ninth grades
cadge \ˈkaj\ *vb* **cadged; cadg•ing** : SPONGE, BEG — **cadg•er** *n*
cad•mi•um \ˈkad-mē-əm\ *n* : a bluish white metallic chemical element used esp. in protective platings — see ELEMENT table
cad•re \ˈka-ˌdrā, ˈkä-, -drē\ *n* [F] **1** : FRAMEWORK **2** : a central unit esp. of trained personnel able to assume control and train others **3** : a group of indoctrinated leaders active in promoting the interests of a revolutionary party
ca•du•ceus \kə-ˈdü-sē-əs, -ˈdyü-, -shəs\ *n, pl* **-cei** \-sē-ˌī\ [L] **1** : the staff of a herald; *esp* : a representation of a staff with two entwined snakes and two wings at the top **2** : an insignia bearing a caduceus and symbolizing a physician
cae•cum *var of* CECUM
Cae•sar \ˈsē-zər\ *n* **1** : any of the Roman emperors succeeding Augustus Caesar — used as a title **2** *often not cap* : a powerful ruler : AUTOCRAT, DICTATOR; *also* : the civil or temporal power
caesarean *also* **caesarian** *var of* CESAREAN
cae•si•um *chiefly Brit var of* CESIUM
cae•sura \si-ˈzhu̇r-ə\ *n, pl* **-suras** *or* **-su•rae** \-ˈzhu̇r-(ˌ)ē\ : a break in the flow of sound usu. in the middle of a line of verse
ca•fé \ka-ˈfā\ *n* [F, lit., coffee] **1** : RESTAURANT **2** : BARROOM **3** : NIGHTCLUB
ca•fé au lait \(ˌ)ka-ˌfā-ō-ˈlā\ *n* : coffee with hot milk in about equal parts
caf•e•te•ria \ˌka-fə-ˈtir-ē-ə\ *n* [AmerSp *cafetería* coffeehouse] : a restaurant in which the customers serve themselves or are served at a counter
caf•feine \ka-ˈfēn, ˈka-ˌfēn\ *n* : a stimulating alkaloid found esp. in coffee and tea
caf•fe lat•te \ˈkä-fā-ˈlä-tā\ *n* [It] : espresso mixed with hot or steamed milk
caf•tan \kaf-ˈtan, ˈkaf-ˌtan\ *n* [Russ *kaftan*, fr. Turk, fr. Per *qaftān*] : an ankle-length garment with long sleeves worn in countries of the eastern Mediterranean
[1]**cage** \ˈkāj\ *n* **1** : an openwork enclosure for confining an animal **2** : something resembling a cage
[2]**cage** *vb* **caged; cag•ing** : to put or keep in or as if in a cage
ca•gey *also* **ca•gy** \ˈkā-jē\ *adj* **ca•gi•er; -est** : wary of being trapped or deceived : SHREWD — **ca•gi•ly** \-jə-lē\ *adv* — **ca•gi•ness** \-jē-nəs\ *n*
CAGS *abbr* Certificate of Advanced Graduate Study
ca•hoot \kə-ˈhüt\ *n* : PARTNERSHIP, LEAGUE — usu. used in pl. ⟨officials in ~*s* with the underworld⟩
cai•man \ˈkā-mən; kā-ˈman, kī-\ *n* : any of several Central and So. American reptiles closely related to alligators and crocodiles
cairn \ˈkarn\ *n* : a heap of stones serving as a memorial or a landmark
cais•son \ˈkā-ˌsän, ˈkās-ᵊn\ *n* **1** : a usu. 2-wheeled vehicle for artillery ammunition **2** : a watertight chamber used in underwater construction work or as a foundation
caisson disease *n* : [2]BEND 3
cai•tiff \ˈkā-təf\ *adj* [ME *caitif*, fr. OF, captive, vile, fr. L *captivus* captive] : being base, cowardly, or despicable — **caitiff** *n*
ca•jole \kə-ˈjōl\ *vb* **ca•joled; ca•jol•ing** [F *cajoler*] : to persuade or coax esp. with flattery or false promises — **ca•jole•ment** *n* — **ca•jol•ery** \-ˈjō-lə-rē\ *n*
Ca•jun \ˈkā-jən\ *n* : a Louisianian descended from French-speaking immigrants from Acadia (Nova Scotia) — **Cajun** *adj*
[1]**cake** \ˈkāk\ *n* **1** : a baked or fried breadlike food usu. in a small flat shape **2** : a sweet baked food made from batter or dough usu. containing flour, sugar, or shortening, and a leaven (as baking powder) **3** : a hardened or compacted substance ⟨a ~ of soap⟩
[2]**cake** *vb* **caked; cak•ing 1** : ENCRUST **2** : to form or harden into a cake
cake•walk \ˈkāk-ˌwȯk\ *n* **1** : a stage dance typically involving a high prance with backward tilt **2** : a one-sided contest or an easy task
cal *abbr* **1** calendar **2** caliber
Cal *abbr* **1** California **2** calorie
cal•a•bash \ˈka-lə-ˌbash\ *n* : the fruit of a gourd; *also* : a utensil made from its hard shell
cal•a•boose \ˈka-lə-ˌbüs\ *n* [Sp *calabozo* dungeon] : JAIL
ca•la•di•um \kə-ˈlā-dē-əm\ *n* : any of a genus of tropical American ornamental plants related to the arums
cal•a•mari \ˌkä-lə-ˈmär-ē\ *n* [It] : squid used as food

DICTIONARY

cal•a•mine \ˈka-lə-ˌmīn\ *n* : a lotion of oxides of zinc and iron
ca•lam•i•ty \kə-ˈla-mə-tē\ *n, pl* **-ties** **1** : great distress or misfortune **2** : an event causing great harm or loss and affliction : DISASTER — **ca•lam•i•tous** \-təs\ *adj* — **ca•lam•i•tous•ly** *adv* — **ca•lam•i•tous•ness** *n*
calc *abbr* calculate; calculated
cal•car•e•ous \kal-ˈkar-ē-əs\ *adj* : resembling calcium carbonate in hardness; *also* : containing calcium or calcium carbonate
cal•cif•er•ous \kal-ˈsi-fə-rəs\ *adj* : producing or containing calcium carbonate
cal•ci•fy \ˈkal-sə-ˌfī\ *vb* **-fied; -fy•ing** : to make or become calcareous — **cal•ci•fi•ca•tion** \ˌkal-sə-fə-ˈkā-shən\ *n*
cal•ci•mine \ˈkal-sə-ˌmīn\ *n* : a thin water paint used esp. on plastered surfaces — **calcimine** *vb*
cal•cine \kal-ˈsīn\ *vb* **cal•cined; cal•cin•ing** : to heat to a high temperature but without fusing to drive off volatile matter and often to reduce to powder — **cal•ci•na•tion** \ˌkal-sə-ˈnā-shən\ *n*
cal•cite \ˈkal-ˌsīt\ *n* : a crystalline mineral consisting of calcium carbonate — **cal•cit•ic** \kal-ˈsi-tik\ *adj*
cal•ci•um \ˈkal-sē-əm\ *n* : a silver-white soft metallic chemical element occurring only in combination — see ELEMENT table
calcium carbonate *n* : a substance found in nature as limestone and marble and in plant ashes, bones, and shells
cal•cu•late \ˈkal-kyə-ˌlāt\ *vb* **-lat•ed; -lat•ing** [L *calculare,* fr. *calculus* small stone, pebble used in reckoning] **1** : to determine by mathematical processes : COMPUTE **2** : to reckon by exercise of practical judgment : ESTIMATE **3** : to design or adapt for a purpose **4** : COUNT, RELY — **cal•cu•la•ble** \-lə-bəl\ *adj* — **cal•cu•la•tor** \-ˌlā-tər\ *n*
cal•cu•lat•ed \-ˌlā-təd\ *adj* **1** : undertaken after estimating the probability of success or failure ⟨a ~ risk⟩ **2** : planned purposefully : DELIBERATE
cal•cu•lat•ing \-ˌlā-tiŋ\ *adj* : marked by shrewd consideration esp. of self-interest — **cal•cu•lat•ing•ly** *adv*
cal•cu•la•tion \ˌkal-kyə-ˈlā-shən\ *n* **1** : the process or an act of calculating **2** : the result of an act of calculating **3** : studied care; *also* : cold heartless planning to promote self-interest
cal•cu•lus \ˈkal-kyə-ləs\ *n, pl* **-li** \-ˌlī\ *also* **-lus•es** [L, pebble (used in reckoning)] **1** : a method of computation or calculation in a special notation (as of logic) **2** : a branch of higher mathematics comprising differential and integral calculus **3** : a concretion usu. of mineral salts esp. in hollow organs or ducts
cal•de•ra \kal-ˈder-ə, kȯl-, -ˈdir-\ *n* [Sp, lit., caldron] : a large crater usu. formed by the collapse of a volcanic cone
cal•dron *var of* CAULDRON
¹**cal•en•dar** \ˈka-lən-dər\ *n* **1** : an arrangement of time into days, weeks, months, and years; *also* : a sheet or folder containing such an arrangement for a period **2** : an orderly list
²**calendar** *vb* : to enter in a calendar
¹**cal•en•der** \ˈka-lən-dər\ *vb* : to press (as cloth or paper) between rollers or plates so as to make smooth or glossy or to thin into sheets
²**calender** *n* : a machine for calendering
ca•lends \ˈka-ləndz, ˈkā-\ *n sing or pl* : the first day of the ancient Roman month
ca•len•du•la \kə-ˈlen-jə-lə\ *n* : any of a genus of yellow-flowered herbs related to the daisies
¹**calf** \ˈkaf, ˈkȧf\ *n, pl* **calves** \ˈkavz, ˈkȧvz\ **1** : the young of the domestic cow; *also* : the young of various large mammals (as the elephant or whale) **2** : CALFSKIN
²**calf** *n, pl* **calves** \ˈkavz, ˈkȧvz\ : the fleshy back of the leg below the knee
calf•skin \ˈkaf-ˌskin, ˈkȧf-\ *n* : leather made of the skin of a calf
cal•i•ber *or* **cal•i•bre** \ˈka-lə-bər\ *n* [MF *calibre,* fr. It *calibro,* fr. Ar *qālib* shoemaker's last] **1** : degree of mental capacity, excellence, or importance **2** : the diameter of a projectile **3** : the diameter of the bore of a gun
cal•i•brate \ˈka-lə-ˌbrāt\ *vb* **-brat•ed; -brat•ing** : to adjust precisely
cal•i•bra•tion \ˌka-lə-ˈbrā-shən\ *n* : a set of graduated marks indicating values or positions — usu. used in pl.
¹**cal•i•co** \ˈka-li-ˌkō\ *n, pl* **-coes** *or* **-cos** : printed cotton fabric
²**calico** *adj* **1** : made of calico **2** : having blotched or spotted markings ⟨a ~ cat⟩
Calif *abbr* California
Cal•i•for•nia poppy \ˌka-lə-ˈfȯr-nyə-\ *n* : a widely cultivated herb with usu. yellow or orange flowers that is related to the poppies
cal•i•for•ni•um \ˌka-lə-ˈfȯr-nē-əm\ *n* : an artificially prepared radioactive chemical element — see ELEMENT table
cal•i•per \ˈka-lə-pər\ *n* **1** : any of various instruments having two arms, legs, or jaws used esp. to measure diameter or thickness — usu. used in pl. **2** : a device consisting of two plates lined with a frictional material that press against the sides of a rotating wheel or disk in certain brake systems
ca•liph \ˈkā-ləf, ˈka-\ *n* : a successor of Muhammad as head of Islam — used as a title — **ca•liph•ate** \-lə-ˌfāt, -fət\ *n*
cal•is•then•ics \ˌka-ləs-ˈthe-niks\ *n sing or pl* [Gk *kalos* beautiful + *sthenos* strength] : bodily exercises usu. done without apparatus — **cal•is•then•ic** *adj*
calk \ˈkȯk\ *var of* CAULK
¹**call** \ˈkȯl\ *vb* **1** : SHOUT, CRY; *also* : to utter a characteristic note or cry **2** : to utter in a loud clear voice **3** : to announce authoritatively **4** : SUMMON **5** : to make a request or demand ⟨~ for an investigation⟩ **6** : to halt (as a baseball game) because of unsuitable conditions **7** : to demand payment of (a loan); *also* : to demand surrender of (as a bond) for redemption **8** : to get or try to get in communication by telephone **9** : to make a brief visit **10** : to speak of or address by name : give a name to **11** : to estimate or consider for practical purposes ⟨~ it ten miles⟩ **12** : to temporarily transfer control of computer processing to (as a subroutine or procedure) — **call•er** *n*
²**call** *n* **1** : SHOUT **2** : the cry of an animal (as a bird) **3** : a request or a command to come or assemble : INVITATION, SUMMONS **4** : DEMAND, CLAIM; *also* : REQUEST **5** : a brief usu. formal visit **6** : an act of calling on the telephone **7** : DECISION ⟨a tough ~⟩ **8** : a temporary transfer of control of computer processing to a particular set of instructions
cal•la lily \ˈka-lə-\ *n* : a plant whose flowers form a fleshy yellow spike surrounded by a lilylike usu. white leaf
call•back \ˈkȯl-ˌbak\ *n* a calling back; *esp* : RECALL 5
call–board \-ˌbōrd\ *n* : a board for posting notices (as of rehearsal calls)
call down *vb* : REPRIMAND
call girl *n* : a prostitute with whom appointments are made by phone
cal•lig•ra•phy \kə-ˈli-grə-fē\ *n* : artistic or elegant handwriting; *also* : the art of producing such writing — **cal•lig•ra•pher** \-fər\ *n*
call–in \ˈkȯl-ˌin\ *adj* : allowing listeners to engage in broadcast telephone conversations ⟨a ~ show⟩
call in *vb* **1** : to order to return or be returned **2** : to summon to one's aid **3** : to report by telephone
call•ing \ˈkȯ-liŋ\ *n* **1** : a strong inner impulse toward a particular course of action **2** : the activity in which one customarily engages as an occupation
cal•li•ope \kə-ˈlī-ə-(ˌ)pē, ˈka-lē-ˌōp\ *n* [fr. *Calliope,* chief of the Muses, fr. L, fr. Gk *Kalliopē*] : a key-

board musical instrument similar to an organ and made up of a series of whistles

cal•li•per *chiefly Brit var of* CALIPER

call number *n* : a combination of characters assigned to a library book to indicate its place on a shelf

call off *vb* : CANCEL

cal•los•i•ty \ka-ˈlä-sə-tē\ *n, pl* **-ties 1** : the quality or state of being callous **2** : CALLUS 1

[1]**cal•lous** \ˈka-ləs\ *adj* **1** : being thickened and hardened ⟨~ skin⟩ **2** : feeling no emotion or sympathy — **cal•lous•ly** *adv* — **cal•lous•ness** *n*

[2]**callous** *vb* : to make callous

cal•low \ˈka-lō\ *adj* [ME *calu* bald, fr. OE] : lacking adult sophistication ⟨a ~ youth⟩ — **cal•low•ness** *n*

call–up \ˈkȯ-ˌləp\ *n* : an order to report for active military service

call up *vb* : to summon for active military duty

cal•lus \ˈka-ləs\ *n* **1** : a callous area on skin or bark **2** : tissue that is converted into bone in the healing of a bone fracture — **callus** *vb*

call–waiting *n* : a telephone service by which during a call in progress an incoming call is signaled (as by a click)

[1]**calm** \ˈkäm, ˈkälm\ *n* **1** : a period or a condition free from storms, high winds, or rough water **2** : complete or almost complete absence of wind **3** : a state of tranquillity

[2]**calm** *vb* : to make or become calm

[3]**calm** *adj* : marked by calm : STILL, UNRUFFLED — **calm•ly** *adv* — **calm•ness** *n*

cal•o•mel \ˈka-lə-məl, -ˌmel\ *n* : a chloride of mercury used esp. as a fungicide

ca•lor•ic \kə-ˈlȯ-rik\ *adj* **1** : of or relating to heat **2** : of or relating to calories

cal•o•rie *also* **cal•o•ry** \ˈka-lə-rē\ *n, pl* **-ries** : a unit for measuring heat; *esp* : one for measuring the value of foods for producing heat and energy in the human body equivalent to the amount of heat required to raise the temperature of one kilogram of water one degree Celsius

cal•o•rim•e•ter \ˌka-lə-ˈri-mə-tər\ *n* : an apparatus for measuring quantities of heat — **cal•o•rim•e•try** \-trē\ *n*

cal•u•met \ˈkal-yə-ˌmet, -mət\ *n* : an American Indian ceremonial pipe

ca•lum•ni•ate \kə-ˈləm-nē-ˌāt\ *vb* **-at•ed; -at•ing** : to make false and malicious statements about **syn** defame, malign, libel, slander, traduce — **ca•lum•ni•a•tion** \-ˌləm-nē-ˈā-shən\ *n* — **ca•lum•ni•a•tor** \-ˈləm-nē-ˌā-tər\ *n*

cal•um•ny \ˈka-ləm-nē\ *n, pl* **-nies** : false and malicious accusation — **ca•lum•ni•ous** \kə-ˈləm-nē-əs\ *adj*

calve \ˈkav, ˈkȧv\ *vb* **calved; calv•ing** : to give birth to a calf

calves *pl of* CALF

Cal•vin•ism \ˈkal-və-ˌni-zəm\ *n* : the theological system of John Calvin and his followers — **Cal•vin•ist** \-nist\ *n or adj* — **Cal•vin•is•tic** \ˌkal-və-ˈnis-tik\ *adj*

ca•lyp•so \kə-ˈlip-sō\ *n, pl* **-sos** : a style of music originating in the British West Indies and having lyrics that usu. satirize local personalities and events

ca•lyx \ˈkā-liks, ˈka-\ *n, pl* **ca•lyx•es** *or* **ca•ly•ces** \ˈkā-lə-ˌsēz, ˈka-\ : the usu. green or leaflike outer part of a flower consisting of sepals

cam \ˈkam\ *n* : a rotating or sliding piece in a mechanical linkage by which rotary motion is transformed into linear motion or vice versa

ca•ma•ra•de•rie \ˌkäm-ˈrä-də-rē, ˌkam-, -ˈra-\ *n* [F] : friendly feeling and goodwill among comrades

cam•bi•um \ˈkam-bē-əm\ *n, pl* **-bi•ums** *or* **-bia** \-bē-ə\ : a thin cellular layer between xylem and phloem of most higher plants from which new tissues develop — **cam•bi•al** \-əl\ *adj*

Cam•bo•di•an \kam-ˈbō-dē-ən\ *n* : a native or inhabitant of Cambodia — **Cambodian** *adj*

Cam•bri•an \ˈkam-brē-ən, ˈkām-\ *adj* : of, relating to, or being the earliest period of the Paleozoic era — **Cambrian** *n*

cam•bric \ˈkām-brik\ *n* : a fine thin white linen or cotton fabric

cam•cord•er \ˈkam-ˌkȯr-dər\ *n* : a small portable video camera and recorder

came *past of* COME

cam•el \ˈka-məl\ *n* : either of two large hoofed cud-chewing mammals used esp. in desert regions of Asia and Africa for carrying and riding

camel hair *also* **camel's hair** *n* **1** : the hair of a camel or a substitute for it **2** : cloth made of camel hair or of camel hair and wool

ca•mel•lia \kə-ˈmēl-yə\ *n* : any of a genus of shrubs and trees related to the tea plant and grown in warm regions and greenhouses for their showy roselike flowers

Cam•em•bert \ˈka-məm-ˌber\ *n* : a soft cheese with a grayish rind and yellow interior

cam•eo \ˈka-mē-ˌō\ *n, pl* **-eos 1** : a gem carved in relief; *also* : a small medallion with a profiled head in relief **2** : a brief appearance esp. by a well-known actor in a play or movie

cam•era \ˈkam-rə, ˈka-mər-ə\ *n* : a device with a lightproof chamber fitted with a lens through which the image of an object is projected onto a surface for recording (as on film) or for conversion into electrical signals (as for television broadcast) — **cam•era•man** \-ˌman, -mən\ *n* — **cam•era•wom•an** *n*

Cam•er•oo•ni•an \ˌka-mə-ˈrü-nē-ən\ *n* : a native or inhabitant of the Republic of Cameroon or the Cameroons region — **Cameroonian** *adj*

cam•i•sole \ˈka-mə-ˌsōl\ *n* : a short sleeveless garment for women

camomile *var of* CHAMOMILE

cam•ou•flage \ˈka-mə-ˌfläzh, -ˌfläj\ *n* [F] **1** : the disguising of military equipment with paint, nets, or foliage; *also* : the disguise itself **2** : deceptive behavior — **camouflage** *vb*

[1]**camp** \ˈkamp\ *n* **1** : a place where tents or buildings are erected for usu. temporary shelter **2** : a collection of tents or other shelters **3** : a body of persons encamped — **camp•ground** \-ˌgraund\ *n* — **camp•site** \-ˌsīt\ *n*

[2]**camp** *vb* **1** : to make or occupy a camp **2** : to live in a camp or outdoors

[3]**camp** *n* **1** : exaggerated effeminate mannerisms **2** : something so outrageous, inappropriate, or theatrical as to be considered amusing — **camp** *adj* — **camp•i•ly** \ˈkam-pə-lē\ *adv* — **camp•i•ness** \-pē-nəs\ *n* — **campy** \-pē\ *adj*

[4]**camp** *vb* : to engage in camp : exhibit the qualities of camp

cam•paign \kam-ˈpān\ *n* **1** : a series of military operations forming one distinct stage in a war **2** : a series of activities designed to bring about a particular result ⟨advertising ~⟩ — **campaign** *vb* — **cam•paign•er** *n*

cam•pa•ni•le \ˌkam-pə-ˈnē-lē\ *n, pl* **-ni•les** *or* **-ni•li** \-ˈnē-lē\ : a usu. freestanding bell tower

cam•pa•nol•o•gy \ˌkam-pə-ˈnä-lə-jē\ *n* : the art of bell ringing — **cam•pa•nol•o•gist** \-jist\ *n*

camp•er \ˈkam-pər\ *n* **1** : one that camps **2** : a portable dwelling (as a specially equipped vehicle) for use during casual travel and camping

Camp Fire Girl *n* : a member of a national organization of girls from ages 5 to 18

camp follower *n* **1** : a civilian (as a prostitute) who follows a military unit to attend or exploit its personnel **2** : a follower of a group who is not an adherent; *esp* : a politician who joins a movement solely for personal gain

cam•phor \ˈkam-fər\ *n* : a gummy volatile aromatic compound obtained from an evergreen Asian tree (**camphor tree**) and used esp. in medicine

camp meeting *n* : a series of evangelistic meetings usu. held outdoors

camp•o•ree \ˌkam-pə-ˈrē\ *n* : a gathering of Boy Scouts or Girl Scouts from a given geographic area

cam•pus \ˈkam-pəs\ *n* [L, plain] : the grounds and buildings of a college or school; *also* : grounds resembling a campus ⟨hospital ∼⟩

cam•shaft \ˈkam-ˌshaft\ *n* : a shaft to which a cam is fastened

[1]**can** \kən, ˈkan\ *vb, past* **could** \kəd, ˈku̇d\; *pres sing & pl* **can 1** : be able to **2** : may perhaps ⟨∼ he still be alive⟩ **3** : be permitted by conscience or feeling to ⟨you ∼ hardly blame her⟩ **4** : have permission to ⟨you ∼ go now⟩

[2]**can** \ˈkan\ *n* **1** : a usu. cylindrical container or receptacle ⟨garbage ∼⟩ ⟨coffee ∼⟩ **2** : JAIL **3** : TOILET

[3]**can** \ˈkan\ *vb* **canned; can•ning 1** : to put in a can : preserve by sealing in airtight cans or jars **2** *slang* : to discharge from employment **3** *slang* : to put a stop or an end to — **can•ner** *n*

Can *or* **Canad** *abbr* Canada; Canadian

Can•a•da goose \ˈka-nə-də-\ *n* : a common wild goose of No. America

Ca•na•di•an \kə-ˈnā-dē-ən\ *n* : a native or inhabitant of Canada — **Canadian** *adj*

ca•naille \kə-ˈnī, -ˈnāl\ *n* [F, fr. It *canaglia*, fr. *cane* dog] : RABBLE, RIFFRAFF

ca•nal \kə-ˈnal\ *n* **1** : a tubular passage in the body : DUCT **2** : an artificial waterway (as for boats or irrigation)

ca•na•lize \ˈkan-ᵊl-ˌīz\ *vb* **-lized; -liz•ing 1** : to provide with a canal or make into or like a channel **2** : to provide with an outlet; *esp* : to direct into preferred channels — **ca•nal•i•za•tion** \ˌkan-ᵊl-ə-ˈzā-shən\ *n*

can•a•pé \ˈka-nə-pē, -ˌpā\ *n* [F, lit., sofa, fr. ML *canopeum, canapeum* mosquito net] : a piece of bread or toast or a cracker topped with a savory food

ca•nard \kə-ˈnärd\ *n* : a false or unfounded report or story

ca•nary \kə-ˈner-ē\ *n, pl* **ca•nar•ies** [fr. the *Canary* islands] **1** : a usu. sweet wine similar to Madeira **2** : a usu. yellow or greenish finch often kept in a cage as a pet

ca•nas•ta \kə-ˈnas-tə\ *n* [Sp, lit., basket] : rummy played with two full decks of cards plus four jokers

canc *abbr* canceled

can•can \ˈkan-ˌkan\ *n* : a woman's dance of French origin characterized by high kicking

[1]**can•cel** \ˈkan-səl\ *vb* **-celed** *or* **-celled; -cel•ing** *or* **-cel•ling** [ME *cancellen*, fr. MF *canceller*, fr. LL *cancellare*, fr. L, to make like a lattice, fr. *cancelli* lattice] **1** : to destroy the force or validity of : ANNUL **2** : to match in force or effect : OFFSET **3** : to cross out : DELETE **4** : to remove (a common divisor) from a numerator and denominator; *also* : to remove (equivalents) on opposite sides of an equation or account **5** : to mark (a postage stamp or check) so that it cannot be reused **6** : to neutralize each other's strength or effect — **can•cel•la•tion** \ˌkan-sə-ˈlā-shən\ *n* — **can•cel•er** *or* **can•cel•ler** *n*

[2]**cancel** *n* **1** : CANCELLATION **2** : a deleted part

can•cer \ˈkan-sər\ *n* [L, lit., crab] **1** *cap* : a zodiacal constellation between Gemini and Leo usu. pictured as a crab **2** *cap* : the 4th sign of the zodiac in astrology; *also* : one born under this sign **3** : a malignant tumor that tends to spread in the body **4** : a malignant evil that spreads destructively — **can•cer•ous** \-sə-rəs\ *adj* — **can•cer•ous•ly** *adv*

can•de•la•bra \ˌkan-də-ˈlä-brə, -ˈla-\ *n* : an ornamental branched candlestick or lamp with several lights

can•de•la•brum \-brəm\ *n, pl* **-bra** *also* **-brums** : CANDELABRA

can•did \ˈkan-dəd\ *adj* **1** : FRANK, STRAIGHTFORWARD **2** : relating to photography of subjects acting naturally or spontaneously without being posed — **can•did•ly** *adv* — **can•did•ness** *n*

candelabra

can•di•da•cy \ˈkan-də-də-sē\ *n, pl* **-cies** : the state of being a candidate

can•di•date \ˈkan-də-ˌdāt, ˈka-nə-, -dət\ *n* [L *candidatus*, fr. *candidatus* clothed in white, fr. *candidus* white; fr. the white toga worn by office seekers in ancient Rome] : one who seeks or is proposed for an office, honor, or membership

can•di•da•ture \ˈkan-də-də-ˌchu̇r, ˈka-nə-\ *n, chiefly Brit* : CANDIDACY

can•died \ˈkan-dēd\ *adj* : preserved in or encrusted with sugar

[1]**can•dle** \ˈkan-dᵊl\ *n* : a usu. slender mass of tallow or wax molded around a wick that is burned to give light

[2]**candle** *vb* **can•dled; can•dling** : to examine (as eggs) by holding between the eye and a light — **can•dler** *n*

can•dle•light \ˈkan-dᵊl-ˌlīt\ *n* **1** : the light of a candle; *also* : any soft artificial light **2** : the time when candles are lit : TWILIGHT

can•dle•lit \-ˌlit\ *adj* : illuminated by candlelight ⟨a ∼ dinner⟩

Can•dle•mas \ˈkan-dᵊl-məs\ *n* : February 2 observed as a church festival in commemoration of the presentation of Christ in the temple

can•dle•stick \-ˌstik\ *n* : a holder with a socket for a candle

can•dle•wick \-ˌwik\ *n* : a soft cotton yarn; *also* : embroidery made with this yarn usu. in tufts

can•dor \ˈkan-dər\ *n* : FRANKNESS, OUTSPOKENNESS

can•dour *chiefly Brit var of* CANDOR

C and W *abbr* country and western

[1]**can•dy** \ˈkan-dē\ *n, pl* **candies** : a confection made from sugar often with flavoring and filling

[2]**candy** *vb* **can•died; can•dy•ing** : to encrust in sugar often by cooking in a syrup

candy strip•er \-ˈstrī-pər\ *n* : a teenage volunteer worker at a hospital

[1]**cane** \ˈkān\ *n* **1** : a slender hollow or pithy stem (as of a reed or bramble) **2** : a tall woody grass or reed (as sugarcane) **3** : a walking stick; *also* : a rod for flogging

[2]**cane** *vb* **caned; can•ing 1** : to beat with a cane **2** : to weave or make with cane — **can•er** *n*

cane•brake \ˈkān-ˌbrāk\ *n* : a thicket of cane

[1]**ca•nine** \ˈkā-ˌnīn\ *n* **1** : a pointed tooth between the outer incisor and the first premolar **2** : a canine mammal (as a domestic dog)

[2]**canine** *adj* [L *caninus*, fr. *canis* dog] : of or relating to dogs or to the family to which they belong

can•is•ter \ˈka-nə-stər\ *n* **1** : an often cylindrical container

can•ker \ˈkaŋ-kər\ *n* : a spreading sore that eats into tissue — **can•ker•ous** \-kə-rəs\ *adj*

can•ker•worm \-ˌwərm\ *n* : either of two moths and esp. their larvae that are pests of fruit and shade trees

can•na \ˈka-nə\ *n* : any of a genus of tropical herbs with large leaves and racemes of bright-colored flowers

can•na•bis \ˈka-nə-bəs\ *n* : any of the psychoactive preparations (as marijuana) or chemicals (as THC) derived from hemp; *also* : HEMP

canned \ˈkand\ *adj* : prepared in standardized form for general use or wide distribution

can•nery \ˈka-nə-rē\ *n, pl* **-ner•ies** : a factory for the canning of foods

can•ni•bal \ˈka-nə-bəl\ *n* [NL *Canibalis* a member of a Caribbean Indian people, fr. Sp *Caníbal*] : one that eats the flesh of its own kind — **can•ni•bal•ism** \-bə-ˌli-zəm\ *n* — **can•ni•bal•is•tic** \-bə-ˈlis-tik\ *adj*

can•ni•bal•ise *Brit var of* CANNIBALIZE

can•ni•bal•ize \ˈka-nə-bə-ˌlīz\ *vb* **-ized; -iz•ing 1** : to take usable parts from (as an inoperative machine) to construct or repair another machine **2** : to practice cannibalism

can•non \ˈka-nən\ *n, pl* **cannons** *or* **cannon** [MF *canon,* fr. It *cannone,* lit., large tube, fr. *canna* reed, tube, fr. L, cane, reed] : a large heavy gun; *esp* : one mounted on a carriage

can•non•ade \ˌka-nə-ˈnād\ *n* : a heavy fire of artillery — **cannonade** *vb*

can•non•ball \ˈka-nən-ˌbȯl\ *n* : a usu. round solid missile for a cannon

can•non•eer \ˌka-nə-ˈnir\ *n* : an artillery gunner

can•not \ˈka-ˌnät; kə-ˈnät\ : can not — **cannot but** : to be unable to do otherwise than

can•nu•la \ˈkan-yə-lə\ *n, pl* **-las** *or* **-lae** \-ˌlē\ : a small tube for insertion into a body cavity or into a duct or vessel

can•ny \ˈka-nē\ *adj* **can•ni•er; -est** : PRUDENT, SHREWD — **can•ni•ly** \ˈkan-ᵊl-ē\ *adv* — **can•ni•ness** \ˈka-nē-nəs\ *n*

ca•noe \kə-ˈnü\ *n* : a light narrow boat with sharp ends and curved sides that is usu. propelled by paddles — **canoe** *vb* — **ca•noe•ist** *n*

canoe

ca•no•la \kə-ˈnō-lə\ *n* : a rape plant producing seeds that are low in a toxic acid and yield an edible oil (**canola oil**) high in monounsaturated fatty acids; *also* : this oil

[1]**can•on** \ˈka-nən\ *n* **1** : a regulation decreed by a church council; *also* : a provision of canon law **2** : an official or authoritative list (as of the saints or the books of the Bible) **3** : an accepted principle ⟨the ∼s of good taste⟩

[2]**canon** *n* : a clergyman on the staff of a cathedral

ca•non•i•cal \kə-ˈnä-ni-kəl\ *adj* **1** : of, relating to, or forming a canon **2** : conforming to a general rule or acceptable procedure : ORTHODOX **3** : of or relating to a clergyman who is a canon — **ca•non•i•cal•ly** \-k(ə-)lē\ *adv*

can•on•ize \ˈka-nə-ˌnīz\ *vb* **can•on•ized** \-ˌnīzd\; **can•on•iz•ing 1** : to declare (a deceased person) an officially recognized saint **2** : GLORIFY, EXALT — **can•on•i•za•tion** \ˌka-nə-nə-ˈzā-shən\ *n*

canon law *n* : the law governing a church

can•o•py \ˈka-nə-pē\ *n, pl* **-pies** [ME *canope,* fr. ML *canopeum* mosquito net, fr. L *conopeum,* fr. Gk *kōnōpion,* fr. *kōnōps* mosquito] **1** : an overhanging cover, shelter, or shade **2** : a transparent cover for an airplane cockpit **3** : the fabric part of a parachute — **canopy** *vb*

[1]**cant** \ˈkant\ *vb* : to give a slant to

[2]**cant** *n* **1** : an oblique or slanting surface **2** : TILT, SLANT

[3]**cant** *vb* **1** : to beg in a whining manner **2** : to talk hypocritically

[4]**cant** *n* **1** : the special idiom of a profession or trade : JARGON **2** : insincere speech; *esp* : insincerely pious words or statements

Cant *abbr* Canticle of Canticles

can•ta•bi•le \kän-ˈtä-bə-ˌlā\ *adv or adj* [It] : in a singing manner — used as a direction in music

can•ta•loupe *also* **can•te•loupe** \ˈkant-ᵊl-ˌōp\ *n* : MUSKMELON; *esp* : one with orange flesh and rough skin

can•tan•ker•ous \kan-ˈtaŋ-kə-rəs\ *adj* : ILL-NATURED, QUARRELSOME — **can•tan•ker•ous•ly** *adv* — **can•tan•ker•ous•ness** *n*

can•ta•ta \kən-ˈtä-tə\ *n* [It] : a choral composition usu. sung to instrumental accompaniment

can•teen \kan-ˈtēn\ *n* [F *cantine* bottle case, canteen (store), fr. It *cantina* wine cellar] **1** : a flask for carrying liquids **2** : a place of recreation and entertainment for military personnel **3** : a small cafeteria or counter at which snacks are served

can•ter \ˈkan-tər\ *n* : a horse's 3-beat gait resembling but smoother and slower than a gallop — **canter** *vb*

Can•ter•bury bell \ˈkant-ər-ˌber-ē-\ *n* : any of several plants related to the bluebell that are cultivated for their showy flowers

can•ti•cle \ˈkan-ti-kəl\ *n* : SONG; *esp* : any of several liturgical songs taken from the Bible

Canticle of Canticles *n* : SONG OF SONGS

[1]**can•ti•le•ver** \ˈkant-ᵊl-ˌē-vər\ *n* : a projecting beam or structure supported only at one end; *also* : either of a pair of such structures projecting toward each other so that when joined they form a bridge

[2]**cantilever** *vb* **1** : to support by a cantilever ⟨a ∼*ed* shelf⟩ **2** : to build as a cantilever **3** : to project as a cantilever

can•tle \ˈkant-ᵊl\ *n* : the upwardly projecting rear part of a saddle

can•to \ˈkan-ˌtō\ *n, pl* **cantos** [It, fr. L *cantus* song] : one of the major divisions of a long poem

can•ton \ˈkant-ᵊn, ˈkan-ˌtän\ *n* : a small territorial division of a country; *esp* : one of the political divisions of Switzerland — **can•ton•al** \ˈkant-ᵊn-əl, kan-ˈtän-ᵊl\ *adj*

can•ton•ment \kan-ˈtōn-mənt, -ˈtän-\ *n* : usu. temporary quarters for troops

can•tor \ˈkan-tər\ *n* **1** : a choir leader **2** : a synagogue official who sings liturgical music and leads the congregation in prayer

can•vas *also* **can•vass** \ˈkan-vəs\ *n* **1** : a strong cloth formerly much used for making tents and sails **2** : a set of sails **3** : a group of tents **4** : a piece of cloth prepared as a surface to receive oil paint; *also* : an oil painting **5** : the canvas-covered floor of a boxing or wrestling ring

can•vas•back \ˈkan-vəs-ˌbak\ *n* : a No. American wild duck with red head and gray back

[1]**can•vass** *also* **can•vas** \ˈkan-vəs\ *vb* : to go through (a district) or to (persons) to solicit votes or orders for goods or to determine public opinion or sentiment — **can•vass•er** *n*

[2]**canvass** *n* : an act or instance of canvassing

can•yon \ˈkan-yən\ *n* : a deep narrow valley with high steep sides

[1]**cap** \ˈkap\ *n* **1** : a covering for the head esp. with a visor and no brim; *also* : something resembling such a covering **2** : a container holding an explosive charge **3** : an upper limit (as on expenditures)

[2]**cap** *vb* **capped; cap•ping 1** : to provide or protect with a cap **2** : to form a cap over : CROWN **3** : OUTDO, SURPASS **4** : CLIMAX

[3]**cap** *abbr* **1** capacity **2** capital **3** capitalize; capitalized

CAP *abbr* Civil Air Patrol

ca•pa•ble \ˈkā-pə-bəl\ *adj* : having ability, capacity, or power to do something : ABLE, COMPETENT — **ca•pa•bil•i•ty** \ˌkā-pə-ˈbi-lə-tē\ *n* — **ca•pa•bly** *adv*

ca•pa•cious \kə-ˈpā-shəs\ *adj* : able to contain much — **ca•pa•cious•ly** *adv* — **ca•pa•cious•ness** *n*

ca•pac•i•tance \kə-ˈpa-sə-təns\ *n* : the property of an electric nonconductor that permits the storage of energy

ca•pac•i•tor \kə-ˈpa-sə-tər\ *n* : an electronic circuit device for temporary storage of electrical energy

[1]**ca•pac•i•ty** \kə-ˈpa-sə-tē\ *n, pl* **-ties** **1** : legal qualification or fitness **2** : the ability to contain, receive, or accommodate **3** : the maximum amount or number that can be contained — see METRIC SYSTEM table, WEIGHT table **4** : ABILITY **5** : position or character assigned or assumed

[2]**capacity** *adj* : equaling maximum capacity ⟨a ~ crowd⟩

cap–a–pie *or* **cap–à–pie** \ˌka-pə-ˈpē\ *adv* [MF] : from head to foot : at all points

ca•par•i•son \kə-ˈpar-ə-sən\ *n* **1** : an ornamental covering for a horse **2** : TRAPPINGS, ADORNMENT — **caparison** *vb*

[1]**cape** \ˈkāp\ *n* **1** : a point of land jutting out into water **2** *often cap* : CAPE COD COTTAGE

[2]**cape** *n* : a sleeveless garment hanging from the neck over the shoulders

Cape Cod cottage \ˈkāp-ˈkäd-\ *n* : a compact rectangular dwelling of one or one-and-a-half stories usu. with a steep gable roof

[1]**ca•per** \ˈkā-pər\ *n* : the flower bud or young berry of a Mediterranean shrub pickled for use as a relish; *also* : this shrub

[2]**caper** *vb* **ca•pered; ca•per•ing** : to leap about in a playful manner

[3]**caper** *n* **1** : a frolicsome leap **2** : a capricious escapade **3** : an illegal or questionable act

cape•skin \ˈkāp-ˌskin\ *n* : a light flexible leather made from sheepskins

Cape Verd•ean \-ˈvər-dē-ən\ *n* : a native or inhabitant of the Republic of Cape Verde

cap•ful \ˈkap-ˌfu̇l\ *n, pl* **cap•fuls** *also* **caps•ful** \ˈkaps-\ : as much as a cap will hold

cap•il•lar•i•ty \ˌka-pə-ˈlar-ə-tē\ *n, pl* **-ties** : the action by which the surface of a liquid where it is in contact with a solid (as in a slender tube) is raised or lowered depending on the relative attraction of the molecules of the liquid for each other and for those of the solid

[1]**cap•il•lary** \ˈka-pə-ˌler-ē\ *adj* **1** : resembling a hair **2** : having a very small bore ⟨~ tube⟩ **3** : of or relating to capillaries or to capillarity

[2]**capillary** *n, pl* **-lar•ies** : any of the tiny thin-walled blood vessels that carry blood between the smallest arteries and their corresponding veins

[1]**cap•i•tal** \ˈka-pət-ᵊl\ *n* : the top part or piece of an architectural column

[2]**capital** *adj* **1** : conforming to the series A, B, C rather than a, b, c ⟨~ letters⟩ ⟨~ G⟩ **2** : punishable by death ⟨a ~ crime⟩ **3** : most serious ⟨a ~ error⟩ **4** : first in importance or position : CHIEF; *also* : being the seat of government ⟨the ~ city⟩ **5** : of or relating to capital ⟨~ expenditures⟩; *esp* : relating to or being assets that add to the long-term net worth of a corporation **6** : FIRST-RATE, EXCELLENT

[3]**capital** *n* **1** : accumulated wealth esp. as used to produce more wealth **2** : the total face value of shares of stock issued by a company **3** : persons holding capital **4** : ADVANTAGE, GAIN **5** : a letter larger than the ordinary small letter and often different in form **6** : the capital city of a state or country; *also* : a city preeminent in some activity ⟨the fashion ~⟩

capital gain *n* : the increase in value of an asset (as stock or real estate) between the time it is bought and the time it is sold

capital goods *n pl* : machinery, tools, factories, and commodities used in the production of goods

cap•i•tal•ise *Brit var of* CAPITALIZE

cap•i•tal•ism \ˈka-pət-ᵊl-ˌi-zəm\ *n* : an economic system characterized by private or corporate ownership of capital goods and by prices, production, and distribution of goods that are determined mainly by competition in a free market

[1]**cap•i•tal•ist** \-ist\ *n* **1** : a person who has capital esp. invested in business **2** : a person of great wealth : PLUTOCRAT **3** : a believer in capitalism

[2]**capitalist** *or* **cap•i•tal•is•tic** \ˌka-pət-ᵊl-ˈis-tik\ *adj* **1** : owning capital **2** : practicing or advocating capitalism **3** : marked by capitalism — **cap•i•tal•is•ti•cal•ly** \-ti-k(ə-)lē\ *adv*

cap•i•tal•iza•tion \ˌka-pət-ᵊl-ə-ˈzā-shən\ *n* **1** : the act or process of capitalizing **2** : the total amount of money used as capital in a business

cap•i•tal•ize \ˈka-pət-ᵊl-ˌīz\ *vb* **-ized; -iz•ing** **1** : to write or print with an initial capital or in capitals **2** : to convert into or use as capital **3** : to supply capital for **4** : to gain by turning something to advantage : PROFIT

cap•i•tal•ly \ˈka-pət-ᵊl-ē\ *adv* : ADMIRABLY, EXCELLENTLY

cap•i•ta•tion \ˌka-pə-ˈtā-shən\ *n* : a direct uniform tax levied on each person

cap•i•tol \ˈka-pət-ᵊl\ *n* : the building in which a legislature holds its sessions

ca•pit•u•late \kə-ˈpi-chə-ˌlāt\ *vb* **-lat•ed; -lat•ing** **1** : to surrender esp. on conditions agreed upon **2** : to cease resisting : ACQUIESCE **syn** submit, yield, succumb, cave, defer — **ca•pit•u•la•tion** \-ˌpi-chə-ˈlā-shən\ *n*

ca•pon \ˈkā-ˌpän, -pən\ *n* : a castrated male chicken

cap•puc•ci•no \ˌka-pə-ˈchē-nō, ˌkä-\ *n* [It, lit., Capuchin; fr. the likeness of its color to that of a Capuchin's habit] : espresso mixed with foamy hot milk or cream and often flavored with cinnamon

ca•pric•cio \kə-ˈprē-chē-ˌō, -chō\ *n, pl* **-cios** : an instrumental piece in free form usu. lively in tempo and brilliant in style

ca•price \kə-ˈprēs\ *n* [F, fr. It *capriccio*] **1** : a sudden whim or fancy **2** : an inclination to do things impulsively **3** : CAPRICCIO — **ca•pri•cious** \-ˈpri-shəs\ *adj* — **ca•pri•cious•ly** *adv* — **ca•pri•cious•ness** *n*

Cap•ri•corn \ˈka-pri-ˌkȯrn\ *n* **1** : a zodiacal constellation between Sagittarius and Aquarius usu. pictured as a goat **2** : the 10th sign of the zodiac in astrology; *also* : one born under this sign

cap•ri•ole \ˈka-prē-ˌōl\ *n* : [3]CAPER 1; *also* : an upward leap of a horse with a backward kick at the height of the leap — **capriole** *vb*

caps *abbr* **1** capitals **2** capsule

cap•si•cum \ˈkap-si-kəm\ *n* : PEPPER 2

cap•size \ˈkap-ˌsīz, kap-ˈsīz\ *vb* **cap•sized; cap•siz•ing** : UPSET, OVERTURN

cap•stan \ˈkap-stən, -ˌstan\ *n* **1** : a machine for moving or raising heavy weights that consists of a vertical drum which can be rotated and around which cable is turned **2** : a rotating shaft that drives recorder tape

cap•su•lar \ˈkap-sə-lər\ *adj* : of, relating to, or resembling a capsule

cap•su•lat•ed \-ˌlā-təd\ *adj* : enclosed in a capsule

[1]**cap•sule** \ˈkap-səl, -sül\ *n* **1** : a membrane or sac enclosing a body part (as of a joint) **2** : a case bearing spores or seeds **3** : a shell usu. of gelatin that is used for packaging something (as a drug); *also* : such a shell together with its contents **4** : a small pressurized compartment or vehicle (as for space flight)

[2]**capsule** *adj* **1** : very brief **2** : very compact

Capt *abbr* captain

[1]**cap•tain** \ˈkap-tən\ *n* **1** : a commander of a body of troops **2** : a commissioned officer in the army, air force, or marine corps ranking next below a major **3** : an officer in charge of a ship **4** : a commissioned officer in the navy ranking next below a rear admiral or a commodore **5** : a leader of a side or team **6** : a dominant figure — **cap•tain•cy** *n*

[2]**captain** *vb* : to be captain of : LEAD

cap•tion \ˈkap-shən\ *n* **1** : a heading esp. of an article or document : TITLE **2** : the explanatory matter accompanying an illustration **3** : a motion-picture subtitle — **cap•tion** *vb*

cap•tious \ˈkap-shəs\ *adj* : marked by an inclination to find fault — **cap•tious•ly** *adv* — **cap•tious•ness** *n*

cap•ti•vate \ˈkap-tə-ˌvāt\ *vb* **-vat•ed; -vat•ing** : to attract and hold irresistibly by some special charm or art — **cap•ti•va•tion** \ˌkap-tə-ˈvā-shən\ *n* — **cap•ti•va•tor** \ˈkap-tə-ˌvā-tər\ *n*

cap•tive \ˈkap-tiv\ *adj* **1** : made prisoner esp. in war **2** : kept within bounds : CONFINED **3** : held under control — **captive** *n* — **cap•tiv•i•ty** \kap-ˈti-və-tē\ *n*

cap•tor \ˈkap-tər\ *n* : one that captures

[1]**cap•ture** \ˈkap-chər\ *n* **1** : the act of capturing **2** : one that has been captured

[2]**capture** *vb* **cap•tured; cap•tur•ing 1** : to take captive : WIN, GAIN **2** : to preserve in a relatively permanent form

Ca•pu•chin \ˈka-pyə-shən\ *n* : a member of an austere branch of the order of St. Francis of Assisi engaged in missionary work and preaching

car \ˈkär\ *n* **1** : a vehicle moving on wheels **2** : the compartment of an elevator **3** : the part of a balloon or airship that carries passengers or equipment

car•a•cole \ˈkar-ə-ˌkōl\ *n* : a half turn to right or left executed by a mounted horse — **caracole** *vb*

car•a•cul \ˈkar-ə-ˌkəl\ *n* : the pelt of a karakul lamb after the curl begins to loosen

ca•rafe \kə-ˈraf, -ˈräf\ *n* : a bottle with a flaring lip used esp. to hold wine

car•am•bo•la \ˌkar-əm-ˈbō-lə\ *n* **1** : a five-angled green to yellow edible tropical fruit of star-shaped cross section **2** : a tropical tree widely cultivated for carambolas

car•a•mel \ˈkar-ə-məl, ˈkär-məl\ *n* **1** : an amorphous substance obtained by heating sugar and used for flavoring and coloring **2** : a firm chewy candy

car•a•pace \ˈkar-ə-ˌpās\ *n* : a protective case or shell on the back of some animals (as turtles or crabs)

[1]**carat** *var of* KARAT

[2]**car•at** \ˈkar-ət\ *n* : a unit of weight for precious stones equal to 200 milligrams

car•a•van \ˈkar-ə-ˌvan\ *n* **1** : a group of travelers journeying together through desert or hostile regions **2** : a group of vehicles traveling in a file

car•a•van•sa•ry \ˌkar-ə-ˈvan-sə-rē\ *or* **car•a•van•se•rai** \-sə-ˌrī\ *n, pl* **-ries** *or* **-rais** *or* **-rai** [Per *kārwānsarāī*, fr. *kārwān* caravan + *sarāī* palace, inn] **1** : an inn in eastern countries where caravans rest at night **2** : HOTEL, INN

car•a•vel \ˈkar-ə-ˌvel\ *n* : a small 15th and 16th century ship with a broad bow, high narrow poop, and usu. three masts

caravel

car•a•way \ˈkar-ə-ˌwā\ *n* : an aromatic herb related to the carrot with fruits (**caraway seed**) used in seasoning and medicine; *also* : its fruit

car•bide \ˈkär-ˌbīd\ *n* : a compound of carbon with another element

car•bine \ˈkär-ˌbēn, -ˌbīn\ *n* : a short-barreled lightweight rifle

car•bo•hy•drate \ˌkär-bō-ˈhī-ˌdrāt, -drət\ *n* : any of various compounds composed of carbon, hydrogen, and oxygen (as sugars and starches)

car•bol•ic acid \ˌkär-ˈbä-lik-\ *n* : PHENOL

car•bon \ˈkär-bən\ *n* **1** : a nonmetallic chemical element occurring in nature esp. as diamond and graphite and as a constituent of coal, petroleum, and limestone — see ELEMENT table **2** : a sheet of carbon paper; *also* : CARBON COPY 1 — **car•bon•less** \-ləs\ *adj*

car•bo•na•ceous \ˌkär-bə-ˈnā-shəs\ *adj* : relating to, containing, or composed of carbon

[1]**car•bon•ate** \ˈkär-bə-ˌnāt, -nət\ *n* : a salt or ester of carbonic acid

[2]**car•bon•ate** \-ˌnāt\ *vb* **-at•ed; -at•ing** : to combine or impregnate with carbon dioxide ⟨*carbonated* beverages⟩ — **car•bon•ation** \ˌkär-bə-ˈnā-shən\ *n*

carbon black *n* : any of various black substances consisting chiefly of carbon and used esp. as pigments

carbon copy *n* **1** : a copy made by carbon paper **2** : DUPLICATE

carbon dating *n* : the determination of the age of old material (as an archaeological specimen) by its content of carbon 14

carbon dioxide *n* : a heavy colorless gas that does not support combustion and is formed in animal respiration and in the combustion and decomposition of organic substances

carbon 14 *n* : a heavy radioactive form of carbon used esp. in dating archaeological materials

car•bon•ic acid \kär-ˈbä-nik-\ *n* : a weak acid that decomposes readily into water and carbon dioxide

car•bon•if•er•ous \ˌkär-bə-ˈni-fə-rəs\ *adj* **1** : producing or containing carbon or coal **2** *cap* : of, relating to, or being the period of the Paleozoic era between the Devonian and the Permian — **Carboniferous** *n*

carbon monoxide *n* : a colorless odorless very poisonous gas formed by the incomplete burning of carbon

carbon paper *n* : a thin paper coated with a pigment and used for making copies

carbon tet•ra•chlo•ride \-ˌte-trə-ˈklōr-ˌīd\ *n* : a colorless nonflammable toxic liquid used esp. as a solvent

carbon 12 *n* : the most abundant isotope of carbon having a nucleus of 6 protons and 6 neutrons and used as a standard for measurements of atomic weight

car•boy \ˈkär-ˌbȯi\ *n* [Per *qarāba*, fr. Ar *qarrābah* demijohn] : a large container for liquids

car•bun•cle \ˈkär-ˌbəŋ-kəl\ *n* : a painful inflammation of the skin and underlying tissue that discharges pus from several openings

car•bu•re•tor \ˈkär-bə-ˌrā-tər, -byə-\ *n* : an apparatus for supplying an internal combustion engine with an explosive mixture of vaporized fuel and air

car•bu•ret•tor *also* **car•bu•ret•ter** \ˌkär-byə-ˈre-tər, ˈkär-byə-ˌ\ *chiefly Brit var of* CARBURETOR

car•case *Brit var of* CARCASS

car•cass \ˈkär-kəs\ *n* : a dead body; *esp* : one of an animal dressed for food

car•cin•o•gen \kär-ˈsi-nə-jən\ *n* : an agent causing or inciting cancer — **car•ci•no•gen•ic** \ˌkärs-ᵊn-ō-ˈje-nik\ *adj* — **car•ci•no•ge•nic•i•ty** \-jə-ˈni-sə-tē\ *n*

car•ci•no•ma \ˌkärs-ᵊn-ˈō-mə\ *n, pl* **-mas** *or* **-ma•ta** \-tə\ : a malignant tumor of epithelial origin — **car•ci•no•ma•tous** \-təs\ *adj*

[1]**card** \ˈkärd\ *vb* : to comb with a card : cleanse and untangle before spinning — **card•er** *n*

[2]**card** *n* : an instrument for combing fibers (as wool or cotton)

[3]**card** *n* **1** : PLAYING CARD **2** *pl* : a game played with playing cards; *also* : card playing **3** : a usu. clownishly amusing person : WAG **4** : a flat stiff usu. small

piece of paper, cardboard, or plastic **5** : PROGRAM; *esp* : a sports program

[4]**card** *vb* **1** : to list or schedule on a card **2** : SCORE

[5]**card** *abbr* cardinal

car•da•mom \ˈkär-də-məm\ *n* : the aromatic capsular fruit of an East Indian herb related to the ginger whose seeds are used as a spice or condiment and in medicine; *also* : this plant

card•board \ˈkärd-ˌbōrd\ *n* : PAPERBOARD

card–car•ry•ing \ˈkärd-ˌkar-ē-iŋ\ *adj* : being a regularly enrolled member of an organized group and esp. of the Communist party

card catalog *n* : a catalog (as of books) in which the entries are arranged systematically on cards

car•di•ac \ˈkär-dē-ˌak\ *adj* **1** : of, relating to, or located near the heart **2** : of, relating to, or affected with heart disease

car•di•gan \ˈkär-di-gən\ *n* : a sweater or jacket usu. without a collar and with a full-length opening in the front

[1]**car•di•nal** \ˈkärd-nəl, ˈkär-dᵊn-əl\ *n* **1** : an ecclesiastical official of the Roman Catholic Church ranking next below the pope **2** : a crested No. American finch that is nearly completely red in the male

[2]**cardinal** *adj* [ME, fr. LL *cardinalis*, fr. L serving as a hinge, fr. *cardo* hinge] : of basic importance : CHIEF, MAIN, PRIMARY — **car•di•nal•ly** *adv*

car•di•nal•ate \ˈkärd-nə-lət, -ˈkär-dᵊn-ə-let, -ˌlāt\ *n* : the office, rank, or dignity of a cardinal

cardinal flower *n* : a No. American plant that bears a spike of brilliant red flowers

cardinal number *n* : a number (as 1, 5, 82, 357) that is used in simple counting and answers the question "how many?"

cardinal point *n* : one of the four principal compass points north, south, east, and west

car•di•ol•o•gy \ˌkär-dē-ˈä-lə-jē\ *n* : the study of the heart and its action and diseases — **car•di•ol•o•gist** \-jist\ *n*

car•dio•pul•mo•nary resuscitation \ˌkär-dē-ō-ˈpu̇l-mə-ˌner-ē-\ *n* : a procedure to restore normal breathing after cardiac arrest that includes the clearance of air passages to the lungs, mouth-to-mouth method of artificial respiration, and heart massage by the exertion of pressure on the chest

car•dio•vas•cu•lar \-ˈvas-kyə-lər\ *adj* : of or relating to the heart and blood vessels

card•sharp•er \ˈkärd-ˌshär-pər\ *or* **card•sharp** \-ˌshärp\ *n* : a cheater at cards

[1]**care** \ˈker\ *n* **1** : a disquieted state of uncertainty and responsibility : ANXIETY **2** : watchful attention : HEED **3** : CHARGE, SUPERVISION **4** : a person or thing that is an object of anxiety or solicitude

[2]**care** *vb* **cared; car•ing 1** : to feel anxiety **2** : to feel interest **3** : to give care **4** : to have a liking, fondness, taste, or inclination **5** : to be concerned about ⟨~ what happens⟩

CARE *abbr* Cooperative for American Relief to Everywhere

ca•reen \kə-ˈrēn\ *vb* **1** : to put (a ship or boat) on a beach esp. in order to clean or repair its hull **2** : to sway from side to side **3** : CAREER

[1]**ca•reer** \kə-ˈrir\ *n* [MF *carrière*, fr. OProv *carriera* street, fr. ML *carraria* road for vehicles, fr. L *carrus* car] **1** : COURSE, PASSAGE; *also* : speed in a course ⟨ran at full ~⟩ **2** : an occupation or profession followed as a life's work

[2]**career** *vb* : to go at top speed esp. in a headlong manner

care•free \ˈker-ˌfrē\ *adj* : free from care or worry

care•ful \-fəl\ *adj* **care•ful•ler; care•ful•lest 1** : using or taking care : VIGILANT **2** : marked by solicitude, caution, or prudence — **care•ful•ly** *adv* — **care•ful•ness** *n*

care•giv•er \-ˌgi-vər\ *n* : a person who provides direct care (as for children, the disabled, or the chronically ill)

care•less \-ləs\ *adj* **1** : free from care : UNTROUBLED **2** : UNCONCERNED, INDIFFERENT **3** : not taking care **4** : not showing or receiving care — **care•less•ly** *adv* — **care•less•ness** *n*

[1]**ca•ress** \kə-ˈres\ *n* : a tender or loving touch or embrace

[2]**caress** *vb* : to touch or stroke tenderly or lovingly — **ca•ress•er** *n*

car•et \ˈkar-ət\ *n* [L, there is lacking, fr. *carēre* to lack, be without] : a mark ʌ used to indicate the place where something is to be inserted

care•tak•er \ˈker-ˌtā-kər\ *n* **1** : one in charge usu. as occupant in place of an absent owner **2** : one temporarily fulfilling the functions of an office

care•worn \-ˌwōrn\ *adj* : showing the effects of grief or anxiety

car•fare \ˈkär-ˌfar\ *n* : passenger fare (as on a streetcar or bus)

car•go \ˈkär-gō\ *n, pl* **cargoes** *or* **cargos** : the goods carried in a ship, airplane, or vehicle : FREIGHT

Ca•rib•be•an \ˌkar-ə-ˈbē-ən, kə-ˈri-bē-ən\ *adj* : of or relating to the eastern and southern West Indies or the Caribbean Sea

car•i•bou \ˈkar-ə-ˌbü\ *n, pl* **caribou** *or* **caribous** : a large circumpolar gregarious deer of northern taiga and tundra that usu. has palmate antlers in both sexes — used esp. for one of the New World

car•i•ca•ture \ˈkar-i-kə-ˌchu̇r\ *n* **1** : distorted representation to produce a ridiculous effect **2** : a representation esp. in literature or art having the qualities of caricature — **caricature** *vb* — **car•i•ca•tur•ist** \-ist\ *n*

car•ies \ˈkar-ēz\ *n, pl* **caries** : tooth decay

car•il•lon \ˈkar-ə-ˌlän\ *n* : a set of tuned bells sounded by hammers controlled from a keyboard

car•i•ous \ˈkar-ē-əs\ *adj* : affected with caries

car•jack•ing \ˈkär-ˌja-kiŋ\ *n* : the theft of an automobile by force or intimidation — **car•jack•er** *n*

car•load \ˈkär-ˌlōd\ *n* : a load that fills a car

car•mi•na•tive \kär-ˈmi-nə-tiv\ *adj* : expelling gas from the alimentary canal — **carminative** *n*

car•mine \ˈkär-mən, -ˌmīn\ *n* : a vivid red

car•nage \ˈkär-nij\ *n* : great destruction of life : SLAUGHTER

car•nal \ˈkärn-ᵊl\ *adj* [ME, fr. LL *carnalis*, fr. L *carn-*, *caro* flesh] **1** : of or relating to the body **2** : relating to or given to sensual pleasures and appetites — **car•nal•i•ty** \kär-ˈna-lə-tē\ *n* — **car•nal•ly** *adv*

car•na•tion \kär-ˈnā-shən\ *n* : a cultivated pink of any of numerous usu. double-flowered varieties derived from an Old World species

car•nau•ba wax \kär-ˈnȯ-bə-, -ˈnau̇-; ˌkär-nə-ˈü-bə-\ *n* : a brittle yellowish wax from a Brazilian palm that is used esp. in polishes

car•ne•lian \kär-ˈnēl-yən\ *n* : a hard tough reddish quartz used as a gem

car•ni•val \ˈkär-nə-vəl\ *n* [It *carnevale*, alter. of *carnelevare*, lit., removal of meat] **1** : a season of merrymaking just before Lent **2** : a boisterous merrymaking **3** : a traveling enterprise offering amusements **4** : an organized program of entertainment

car•niv•o•ra \kär-ˈni-və-rə\ *n pl* : carnivorous mammals

car•ni•vore \ˈkär-nə-ˌvōr\ *n* : a flesh-eating animal; *esp* : any of an order of mammals (as dogs, cats, bears, minks, and seals) feeding mostly on animal flesh

car•niv•o•rous \kär-ˈni-və-rəs\ *adj* **1** : feeding on animal tissues **2** : of or relating to the carnivores — **car•niv•o•rous•ly** *adv* — **car•niv•o•rous•ness** *n*

car•ny *or* **car•ney** *or* **car•nie** \ˈkär-nē\ *n, pl* **carnies** *or* **carneys 1** : CARNIVAL 3 **2** : one who works with a carnival

car•ol \ˈkar-əl\ *n* : a song of joy or devotion — **carol** *vb* — **car•ol•er** *or* **car•ol•ler** *n*

car•om \ˈkar-əm\ *n* **1** : a shot in billiards in which the cue ball strikes two other balls **2 :** a rebounding esp. at an angle — **carom** *vb*

car•o•tene \ˈkar-ə-ˌtēn\ *n* **:** any of several orange to red pigments (as beta-carotene) formed esp. in plants and used as a source of vitamin A

ca•rot•id \kə-ˈrä-təd\ *adj* **:** of, relating to, or being the chief artery or pair of arteries that pass up the neck and supply the head — **carotid** *n*

ca•rous•al \kə-ˈraü-zəl\ *n* **:** CAROUSE

ca•rouse \kə-ˈraüz\ *n* [MF *carrousse,* fr. *carous,* adv., all out (in *boire carous* to empty the cup), fr. G *garaus*] **:** a drunken revel — **carouse** *vb* — **ca•rous•er** *n*

car•ou•sel \ˌkar-ə-ˈsel, ˈkar-ə-ˌsel\ *n* **1 :** MERRY-GO-ROUND **2 :** a circular conveyor

[1]**carp** \ˈkärp\ *vb* **:** to find fault **:** CAVIL, COMPLAIN — **carp** *n* — **carp•er** *n*

[2]**carp** *n, pl* **carp** *or* **carps :** a large variable Asian freshwater fish of sluggish waters often raised for food

[1]**car•pal** \ˈkär-pəl\ *adj* **:** relating to the wrist or the bones of the wrist

[2]**carpal** *n* **:** a carpal element or bone

carpal tunnel syndrome *n* **:** a condition characterized esp. by weakness, pain, and disturbances of sensation (as numbness) in the hand and caused by compression of a nerve in the wrist

car•pe di•em \ˈkär-pe-ˈdē-ˌem, -ˈdī-\ *n* [L, lit., pluck the day] **:** enjoyment of the present without concern for the future

car•pel \ˈkär-pəl\ *n* **:** one of the highly modified leaves that together form the ovary of a flower of a seed plant

car•pen•ter \ˈkär-pən-tər\ *n* **:** one who builds or repairs wooden structures — **carpenter** *vb* — **car•pen•try** \-trē\ *n*

car•pet \ˈkär-pət\ *n* **:** a heavy fabric used as a floor covering — **carpet** *vb*

car•pet•bag \-ˌbag\ *n* **:** a traveling bag common in the 19th century

car•pet•bag•ger \-ˌba-gər\ *n* **:** a Northerner in the South after the American Civil War usu. seeking private gain under the reconstruction governments

car•pet•ing \ˈkär-pə-tiŋ\ *n* **:** material for carpets; *also* **:** CARPETS

car pool *n* **:** an arrangement in which a group of people commute together by car; *also* **:** a group having this arrangement — **car•pool** \-ˌpül\ *vb*

car•port \ˈkär-ˌpōrt\ *n* **:** an open-sided automobile shelter

car•pus \ˈkär-pəs\ *n* **:** the wrist or its bones

car•ra•geen•an *or* **car•ra•geen•in** \ˌkar-ə-ˈgē-nən\ *n* **:** a colloid extracted esp. from a dark purple branching seaweed and used in foods esp. to stabilize and thicken them

car•rel \ˈkar-əl\ *n* **:** a table often partitioned or enclosed for individual study in a library

car•riage \ˈkar-ij\ *n* **1 :** the act of carrying **2 :** manner of holding the body **3 :** a wheeled vehicle **4** *Brit* **:** a railway passenger coach **5 :** a movable part of a machine for supporting some other moving part ⟨a typewriter ~⟩

carriage trade *n* **:** trade from well-to-do or upper-class people

car•ri•er \ˈkar-ē-ər\ *n* **1 :** one that carries **2 :** a person or organization in the transportation business **3 :** AIRCRAFT CARRIER **4 :** one whose system carries germs of a disease but who is immune to the disease **5 :** an individual having a gene for a trait or condition that is not expressed bodily **6 :** an electromagnetic wave whose amplitude or frequency is varied in order to convey a radio or television signal

carrier pigeon *n* **:** a pigeon used esp. to carry messages

car•ri•on \ˈkar-ē-ən\ *n* **:** dead and decaying flesh

car•rot \ˈkar-ət\ *n* **:** the elongated usu. orange root of a common garden plant that is eaten as a vegetable; *also* **:** this plant

car•rou•sel *var of* CAROUSEL

[1]**car•ry** \ˈkar-ē\ *vb* **car•ried; car•ry•ing 1 :** to move while supporting **:** TRANSPORT, CONVEY, TAKE **2 :** to influence by mental or emotional appeal **3 :** to get possession or control of **:** CAPTURE, WIN **4 :** to transfer from one place (as a column) to another ⟨~ a number in adding⟩ **5 :** to have or wear on one's person; *also* **:** to bear within one **6 :** INVOLVE, IMPLY **7 :** to hold or bear (oneself) in a specified way **8 :** to keep in stock for sale **9 :** to sustain the weight or burden of **:** SUPPORT **10 :** to prolong in space, time, or degree **11 :** to keep on one's books as a debtor **12 :** to succeed in (an election) **13 :** to win adoption (as in a legislature) **14 :** PUBLISH, PRINT **15 :** to reach or penetrate to a distance

[2]**carry** *n* **1 :** the range of a gun or projectile or of a struck or thrown ball **2 :** PORTAGE **3 :** an act or method of carrying ⟨fireman's ~⟩

car•ry•all \ˈkar-ē-ˌȯl\ *n* **:** a capacious bag or case

carry away *vb* **:** to arouse to a high and often excessive degree of emotion

carrying charge *n* **:** a charge added to the price of merchandise sold on the installment plan

car•ry–on *n* **:** a piece of luggage suitable for being carried aboard an airplane by a passenger — **carry–on** *adj*

carry on *vb* **1 :** CONDUCT, MANAGE **2 :** to behave in a foolish, excited, or improper manner **3 :** to continue in spite of hindrance or discouragement

carry out *vb* **1 :** to put into execution **2 :** to bring to a successful conclusion

car•sick \ˈkär-ˌsik\ *adj* **:** affected with motion sickness esp. in an automobile — **car sickness** *n*

[1]**cart** \ˈkärt\ *n* **1 :** a heavy 2-wheeled wagon **2 :** a small wheeled vehicle

[2]**cart** *vb* **:** to convey in or as if in a cart — **cart•er** *n*

cart•age \ˈkär-tij\ *n* **:** the act of or rate charged for carting

carte blanche \ˈkärt-ˈbläⁿsh\ *n, pl* **cartes blanches** *same or* -ˈbläⁿ-shəz\ [F, lit., blank document] **:** full discretionary power

car•tel \kär-ˈtel\ *n* **:** a combination of independent business enterprises designed to limit competition **syn** pool, syndicate, monopoly, trust

car•ti•lage \ˈkärt-ᵊl-ij\ *n* **:** a usu. translucent somewhat elastic tissue that composes most of the skeleton of young vertebrate embryos and later is mostly converted to bone in higher vertebrates — **car•ti•lag•i•nous** \ˌkärt-ᵊl-ˈa-jə-nəs\ *adj*

cartilaginous fish *n* **:** any of a class of fishes (as a shark or ray having the skeleton wholly or largely composed of cartilage

car•tog•ra•phy \kär-ˈtä-grə-fē\ *n* **:** the making of maps — **car•tog•ra•pher** *n*

car•ton \ˈkärt-ᵊn\ *n* **:** a paperboard box or container

car•toon \kär-ˈtün\ *n* **1 :** a preparatory sketch (as for a painting) **2 :** a drawing intended as humor, caricature, or satire **3 :** COMIC STRIP — **cartoon** *vb* — **car•toon•ist** *n*

car•tridge \ˈkär-trij\ *n* **1 :** a tube containing a complete charge for a firearm **2 :** a container of material for insertion into an apparatus **3 :** a small case containing a phonograph needle and transducer that is attached to a tonearm **4 :** a case containing a magnetic tape or disk **5 :** a case for holding integrated circuits containing a computer program

cart•wheel \ˈkärt-ˌhwēl\ *n* **1 :** a large coin (as a silver dollar) **2 :** a lateral handspring with arms and legs extended

carve \kärv\ *vb* **carved; carv•ing 1 :** to cut with care or precision **:** shape by cutting **2 :** to cut into pieces or slices **3 :** to slice and serve meat at table — **carv•er** *n*

cary•at•id \ˌkar-ē-ˈa-təd\ *n, pl* **-ids** *or* **-i•des** \-ˈa-tə-

ˌdēz\ : a sculptured draped female figure used as an architectural column

CAS *abbr* certificate of advanced study

ca•sa•ba \kə-ˈsä-bə\ *n* : any of several muskmelons with a yellow rind and sweet flesh

[1]**cas•cade** \ˌkas-ˈkād\ *n* **1** : a steep usu. small waterfall **2** : something arranged in a series or succession of stages so that each stage derives from or acts upon the product of the preceding

[2]**cascade** *vb* **cas•cad•ed; cas•cad•ing** : to fall, pass, or connect in or as if in a cascade

cas•cara \kas-ˈkar-ə\ *n* : the dried bark of a small Pacific coastal tree of the U.S. and southern Canada used as a laxative; *also* : this tree

[1]**case** \ˈkās\ *n* [ME *cas*, fr. OF, fr. L *casus* fall, chance, fr. *cadere* to fall] **1** : a particular instance or situation **2** : an inflectional form of a noun, pronoun, or adjective indicating its grammatical relation to other words; *also* : such a relation whether indicated by inflection or not **3** : what actually exists or happens : FACT **4** : a suit or action in law : CAUSE **5** : a convincing argument **6** : an instance of disease or injury; *also* : PATIENT **7** : INSTANCE, EXAMPLE — **in case** : as a precaution — **in case of** : in the event of

[2]**case** *n* [ME *cas*, fr. OF *casse*, fr. L *capsa*] **1** : a box or container for holding something; *also* : a box with its contents **2** : an outer covering **3** : a divided tray for holding printing type **4** : CASING 2

[3]**case** *vb* **cased; cas•ing 1** : to enclose in or cover with a case **2** : to inspect esp. with intent to rob

ca•sein \ˈkā-ˌsēn, kā-ˈ\ *n* : any of several phosphorus-containing proteins occurring in or produced from milk

case•ment \ˈkās-mənt\ *n* : a window that opens like a door

case•work \-ˌwərk\ *n* : social work that involves the individual person or family — **case•work•er** *n*

[1]**cash** \ˈkash\ *n* [MF or It; MF *casse* money box, fr. It *cassa*, fr. L *capsa* chest, case] **1** : ready money **2** : money or its equivalent paid at the time of purchase or delivery

[2]**cash** *vb* : to pay or obtain cash for

ca•shew \ˈka-shü, kə-ˈshü\ *n* : an edible kidney-shaped nut of a tropical American tree related to the sumacs; *also* : the tree

[1]**ca•shier** \ka-ˈshir\ *vb* : to dismiss from service; *esp* : to dismiss in disgrace

[2]**cash•ier** \ka-ˈshir\ *n* **1** : a bank official responsible for moneys received and paid out **2** : a person who receives and records payments

cashier's check *n* : a check drawn by a bank upon its own funds and signed by its cashier

cash in *vb* **1** : to convert into cash ⟨*cash in* bonds⟩ **2** : to settle accounts and withdraw from a gambling game or business deal **3** : to obtain financial profit or advantage

cash•mere \ˈkazh-ˌmir, ˈkash-\ *n* : fine wool from the undercoat of an Indian goat (**cashmere goat**) or a yarn spun of this; *also* : a soft twilled fabric orig. woven from this yarn

cash register *n* : a business machine that usu. has a money drawer, indicates each sale, and records the money received

cas•ing \ˈkā-siŋ\ *n* **1** : something that encases **2** : the frame of a door or window

ca•si•no \kə-ˈsē-nō\ *n, pl* **-nos** [It, fr. *casa* house] **1** : a building or room for social amusements; *esp* : one used for gambling **2** *also* **cas•si•no** : a card game in which players win cards by matching those on the table

cask \ˈkask\ *n* : a barrel-shaped container usu. for liquids; *also* : the quantity held by such a container

cas•ket \ˈkas-kət\ *n* **1** : a small box (as for jewels) **2** : COFFIN

casque \ˈkask\ *n* : HELMET

cas•sa•va \kə-ˈsä-və\ *n* : any of several tropical spurges with rootstocks yielding a nutritious starch from which tapioca is prepared; *also* : the rootstock or its starch

cas•se•role \ˈka-sə-ˌrōl\ *n* **1** : a dish in which food may be baked and served **2** : food cooked and served in a casserole

cas•sette *also* **ca•sette** \kə-ˈset\ *n* **1** : a lightproof container for photographic plates or film **2** : a plastic case containing magnetic tape

cas•sia \ˈka-shə\ *n* **1** : a coarse cinnamon bark **2** : any of a genus of leguminous herbs, shrubs, and trees of warm regions including several which yield senna

cas•sit•er•ite \kə-ˈsi-tə-ˌrīt\ *n* : a dark mineral that is the chief tin ore

cas•sock \ˈka-sək\ *n* : an ankle-length garment worn esp. by Roman Catholic and Anglican clergy

cas•so•wary \ˈka-sə-ˌwer-ē\ *n, pl* **-war•ies** : any of a genus of large birds closely related to the emu

[1]**cast** \ˈkast\ *vb* **cast; cast•ing 1** : THROW, FLING **2** : DIRECT ⟨~ a glance⟩ **3** : to deposit (a ballot) formally **4** : to throw off, out, or away : DISCARD, SHED **5** : COMPUTE; *esp* : to add up **6** : to assign the parts of (a play) to actors; *also* : to assign to a role or part **7** : to shape (a substance) by pouring in liquid or plastic form into a mold and letting harden without pressure **8** : to make (as a knot or stitch) by looping or catching up

[2]**cast** *n* **1** : THROW, FLING **2** : a throw of dice **3** : the set of actors in a dramatic production **4** : something formed in or as if in a mold; *also* : a rigid surgical dressing (as for protecting and supporting a fractured bone) **5** : TINGE, HUE **6** : APPEARANCE, LOOK **7** : something thrown out or off, shed, or expelled ⟨worm ~*s*⟩

cas•ta•net \ˌkas-tə-ˈnet\ *n* [Sp *castañeta*, fr. *castaña* chestnut, fr. L *castanea*] : a rhythm instrument consisting of two small wooden, ivory, or plastic shells held in the hand and clicked together

cast•away \ˈkas-tə-ˌwā\ *adj* **1** : thrown away : REJECTED **2** : cast adrift or ashore as a survivor of a shipwreck — **castaway** *n*

caste \ˈkast\ *n* [Port *casta*, lit., race, lineage, fr. fem. of *casto* pure, chaste, fr. L *castus*] **1** : one of the hereditary social classes in Hinduism **2** : a division of a society based on wealth, inherited rank, or occupation **3** : social position : PRESTIGE **4** : a system of rigid social stratification

cas•tel•lat•ed \ˈkas-tə-ˌlā-təd\ *adj* : having battlements like a castle

cast•er \ˈkas-tər\ *n* **1** *or* **cas•tor** : a small container to hold salt or pepper at the table **2** : a small wheel that turns freely and is used to support and move furniture, trucks, and equipment

cas•ti•gate \ˈkas-tə-ˌgāt\ *vb* **-gat•ed; -gat•ing** : to punish or criticize severely — **cas•ti•ga•tion** \ˌkas-tə-ˈgā-shən\ *n* — **cas•ti•ga•tor** \ˈkas-tə-ˌgā-tər\ *n*

cast•ing \ˈkas-tiŋ\ *n* **1** : CAST 7 **2** : something cast in a mold

casting vote *n* : a deciding vote cast by a presiding officer to break a tie

cast iron *n* : a hard brittle alloy of iron, carbon, and silicon cast in a mold

cas•tle \ˈka-səl\ *n* **1** : a large fortified building or set of buildings **2** : a large or imposing house **3** : [3]ROOK

castle in the air : an impracticable project

cast–off \ˈkas-ˌtȯf\ *adj* : thrown away or aside — **cast•off** *n*

cas•tor oil \ˈkas-tər-\ *n* : a thick yellowish oil extracted from the poisonous seeds of an herb (**castor–oil plant**) and used as a lubricant and purgative

cas•trate \ˈkas-ˌtrāt\ *vb* **cas•trat•ed; cas•trat•ing** : to deprive of sex glands and esp. testes — **cas•tra•tion** \kas-ˈtrā-shən\ *n* — **cas•tra•tor** \-ər\ *n*

ca•su•al \ˈka-zhə-wəl\ *adj* **1** : resulting from or occurring by chance **2** : OCCASIONAL, INCIDENTAL **3** : OFFHAND, NONCHALANT **4** : designed for informal use ⟨~ clothing⟩ — **ca•su•al•ly** *adv* — **ca•su•al•ness** *n*

ca•su•al•ty \ˈka-zhəl-tē, ˈka-zhə-wəl-\ *n, pl* **-ties 1** : serious or fatal accident **2 :** a military person lost through death, injury, sickness, or capture or through being missing in action **3 :** a person or thing injured, lost, or destroyed

ca•su•ist•ry \ˈka-zhə-wə-strē\ *n, pl* **-ries :** specious argument : RATIONALIZATION — **ca•su•ist** \-wist\ *n* — **ca•su•is•tic** \ˌka-zhə-ˈwis-tik\ *or* **ca•su•is•ti•cal** \-ti-kəl\ *adj*

ca•sus bel•li \ˌkä-səs-ˈbe-ˌlē, ˌkā-səs-ˈbe-ˌlī\ *n, pl* **casus belli** \ˌkä-ˌsüs-, ˌkā-\ [NL, occasion of war] **:** a cause or pretext for a declaration of war

[1]**cat** \ˈkat\ *n* **1 :** a carnivorous mammal long domesticated as a pet and for catching rats and mice **2 :** any of a family of animals (as the lion, lynx, or leopard) including the domestic cat **3 :** a spiteful woman **4 :** GUY

[2]**cat** *abbr* catalog

ca•tab•o•lism \kə-ˈta-bə-ˌli-zəm\ *n* **:** destructive metabolism involving the release of energy and resulting in the breakdown of complex materials — **cat•a•bol•ic** \ˌka-tə-ˈbä-lik\ *adj*

cat•a•clysm \ˈka-tə-ˌkli-zəm\ *n* **:** a violent change or upheaval — **cat•a•clys•mal** \ˌka-tə-ˈkliz-məl\ *or* **cat•a•clys•mic** \-ˈkliz-mik\ *adj*

cat•a•comb \ˈka-tə-ˌkōm\ *n* **:** an underground burial place with galleries and recesses for tombs

cat•a•falque \ˈka-tə-ˌfalk, -ˌfölk, -ˌfȯk\ *n* **:** an ornamental structure sometimes used in solemn funerals to hold the body

cat•a•lep•sy \ˈka-tə-ˌlep-sē\ *n, pl* **-sies :** a trancelike nervous condition characterized esp. by loss of voluntary motion — **cat•a•lep•tic** \ˌka-tə-ˈlep-tik\ *adj or n*

[1]**cat•a•log** *or* **cat•a•logue** \ˈkat-ᵊl-ˌȯg\ *n* **1 :** LIST, REGISTER **2 :** a systematic list of items with descriptive details; *also* **:** a book containing such a list

[2]**catalog** *or* **catalogue** *vb* **-loged** *or* **-logued; -log•ing** *or* **-logu•ing 1 :** to make a catalog of **2 :** to enter in a catalog — **cat•a•log•er** *or* **cat•a•logu•er** *n*

ca•tal•pa \kə-ˈtal-pə\ *n* **:** a broad-leaved tree with showy flowers and long slim pods

ca•tal•y•sis \kə-ˈta-lə-səs\ *n, pl* **-y•ses** \-ˌsēz\ **:** a change and esp. increase in the rate of a chemical reaction brought about by a substance (**cat•a•lyst** \ˈkat-ᵊl-ist\) that is itself unchanged at the end of the reaction — **cat•a•lyt•ic** \ˌkat-ᵊl-ˈi-tik\ *adj* — **cat•a•lyt•i•cal•ly** \-ti-k(ə-)lē\ *adv*

catalytic converter *n* **:** an automobile exhaust-system component in which a catalyst changes harmful gases into mostly harmless products

cat•a•lyze \ˈkat-ᵊl-ˌīz\ *vb* **-lyzed; -lyz•ing :** to bring about the catalysis of (a chemical reaction)

cat•a•ma•ran \ˌka-tə-mə-ˈran\ *n* [Tamil (a language of southern India) *kaṭṭumaram,* fr. *kaṭṭu* to tie + *maram* tree] **:** a boat with twin hulls

cat•a•mount \ˈka-tə-ˌmau̇nt\ *n* **:** COUGAR; *also* **:** LYNX

cat•a•pult \ˈka-tə-ˌpəlt, -ˌpu̇lt\ *n* **1 :** an ancient military machine for hurling missiles **2 :** a device for launching an airplane (as from an aircraft carrier) — **catapult** *vb*

cat•a•ract \ˈka-tə-ˌrakt\ *n* **1 :** a cloudiness of the lens of the eye obstructing vision **2 :** a large waterfall; *also* **:** steep rapids in a river

ca•tarrh \kə-ˈtär\ *n* **:** inflammation of a mucous membrane esp. of the nose and throat — **ca•tarrh•al** \-əl\ *adj*

ca•tas•tro•phe \kə-ˈtas-trə-(ˌ)fē\ *n* [Gk *katastrophē,* fr. *katastrephein* to overturn, fr. *kata-* down + *strephein* to turn] **1 :** a great disaster or misfortune **2 :** utter failure — **cat•a•stroph•ic** \ˌka-tə-ˈsträ-fik\ *adj* — **cat•a•stroph•i•cal•ly** \-fi-k(ə-)lē\ *adv*

cat•a•ton•ic \ˌka-tə-ˈtä-nik\ *adj* **:** of, relating to, or marked by schizophrenia characterized esp. by stupor, negativism, rigidity, purposeless excitement, and abnormal posturing — **catatonic** *n*

cat•bird \ˈkat-ˌbərd\ *n* **:** an American songbird with a catlike mewing call

cat•boat \ˈkat-ˌbōt\ *n* **:** a single-masted sailboat with a single large sail extended by a long boom

cat•call \-ˌkȯl\ *n* **:** a loud cry made esp. to express disapproval — **catcall** *vb*

[1]**catch** \ˈkach, ˈkech\ *vb* **caught** \ˈkȯt\; **catch•ing 1 :** to capture esp. after pursuit **2 :** TRAP **3 :** to discover unexpectedly ⟨*caught* in the act⟩ **4 :** to become suddenly aware of **5 :** to take hold of **:** SNATCH ⟨~ at a straw⟩ **6 :** INTERCEPT **7 :** to get entangled **8 :** to become affected with or by ⟨~ fire⟩ ⟨~ cold⟩ **9 :** to seize and hold firmly; *also* **:** FASTEN **10 :** OVERTAKE **11 :** to be in time for ⟨~ a train⟩ **12 :** to take in and retain **13 :** to look at or listen to

[2]**catch** *n* **1 :** something caught **2 :** the act of catching; *also* **:** a game consisting of throwing and catching a ball **3 :** something that catches or checks or holds immovable ⟨a door ~⟩ **4 :** one worth catching esp. as a mate **5 :** FRAGMENT, SNATCH **6 :** a concealed difficulty or complication

catch•all \ˈka-ˌchȯl, ˈke-\ *n* **:** something to hold a variety of odds and ends

catch–as–catch–can *adj* **:** using any means available

catch•er \ˈka-chər, ˈke-\ *n* **:** one that catches; *esp* **:** a player positioned behind home plate in baseball

catch•ing *adj* **1 :** INFECTIOUS, CONTAGIOUS **2 :** ALLURING, CATCHY

catch•ment \ˈkach-mənt, ˈkech-\ *n* **1 :** something that catches water **2 :** the action of catching water

catch on *vb* **1 :** UNDERSTAND **2 :** to become popular

catch•pen•ny \ˈkach-ˌpe-nē, ˈkech-\ *adj* **:** using sensationalism or cheapness for appeal ⟨a ~ newspaper⟩

catch–22 \-ˌtwen-tē-ˈtü\ *n, pl* **catch–22's** *or* **catch–22s** *often cap C* [fr. *Catch-22,* a paradoxical rule found in the novel *Catch-22* (1961) by Joseph Heller] **:** a problematic situation for which the only solution is denied by a circumstance inherent in the problem or by a rule; *also* **:** the circumstance or rule that denies a solution

catch•up \ˈke-chəp, ˈka-\ *var of* KETCHUP

catch up *vb* **:** to travel or work fast enough to overtake or complete

catch•word \ˈkach-ˌwərd, ˈkech-\ *n* **1 :** GUIDE WORD **2 :** a word or expression representative of a party, school, or point of view

catchy \ˈka-chē, ˈke-\ *adj* **catch•i•er; -est 1 :** likely to catch the interest or attention **2 :** TRICKY

cat•e•chism \ˈka-tə-ˌki-zəm\ *n* **:** a summary or test (as of religious doctrine) usu. in the form of questions and answers — **cat•e•chist** \-ˌkist\ *n* — **cat•e•chize** \-ˌkīz\ *vb*

cat•e•chu•men \ˌka-tə-ˈkyü-mən\ *n* **:** a religious convert receiving training before baptism

cat•e•gor•i•cal \ˌka-tə-ˈgȯr-i-kəl\ *adj* **1 :** ABSOLUTE, UNQUALIFIED **2 :** of, relating to, or constituting a category — **cat•e•gor•i•cal•ly** \-i-k(ə-)lē\ *adv*

cat•e•go•rise *Brit var of* CATEGORIZE

cat•e•go•rize \ˈka-ti-gə-ˌrīz\ *vb* **-rized; -riz•ing :** to put into a category **:** CLASSIFY — **cat•e•go•ri•za•tion** \ˌka-ti-gə-rə-ˈzā-shən\ *n*

cat•e•go•ry \ˈka-tə-ˌgōr-ē\ *n, pl* **-ries :** a division used in classification; *also* **:** CLASS, GROUP, KIND

ca•ter \ˈkā-tər\ *vb* **1 :** to provide a supply of food **2 :** to supply what is wanted — **ca•ter•er** *n*

cat•er•cor•ner \ˌka-tē-ˈkȯr-nər, ˌka-tə-, ˌki-tē-\ *or* **cat•er–cor•nered** *adv or adj* [obs. *cater* four + *corner*] **:** in a diagonal or oblique position

cat•er•pil•lar \ˈka-tər-ˌpi-lər\ *n* [ME *catyrpel,* fr. OF *catepelose,* lit., hairy cat] **:** a wormlike often hairy insect larva esp. of a butterfly or moth

cat•er•waul \ˈka-tər-ˌwȯl\ *vb* **:** to make a harsh cry — **caterwaul** *n*

cat•fish \ˈkat-ˌfish\ *n* **:** any of an order of chiefly freshwater stout-bodied fishes with slender tactile processes around the mouth

☞ For illustration, see next page.

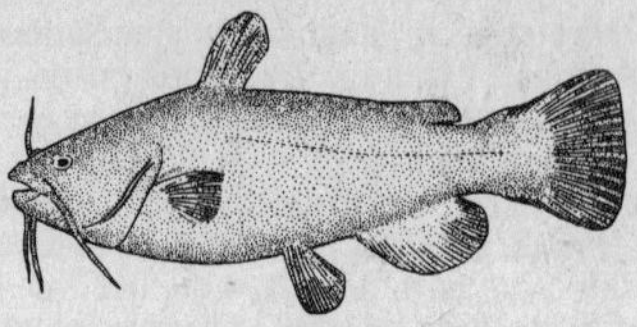
catfish

cat•gut \-ˌgət\ *n* : a tough cord made usu. from sheep intestines

ca•thar•sis \kə-ˈthär-səs\ *n, pl* **ca•thar•ses** \-ˌsēz\ **1** : an act of purging or purification **2** : elimination of a complex by bringing it to consciousness and affording it expression

¹ca•thar•tic \kə-ˈthär-tik\ *adj* : of, relating to, or producing catharsis

²cathartic *n* : PURGATIVE

ca•the•dral \kə-ˈthē-drəl\ *n* : the principal church of a diocese

cath•e•ter \ˈka-thə-tər\ *n* : a tube for insertion into a bodily passage or cavity usu. for injecting or drawing off material or for keeping a passage open

cath•ode \ˈka-ˌthōd\ *n* **1** : the negative electrode of an electrolytic cell **2** : the positive terminal of a battery **3** : the electron-emitting electrode of an electron tube — **cath•od•al** \ˈka-ˌthō-dᵊl\ *adj* — **ca•thod•ic** \ka-ˈthä-dik\ *adj*

cathode–ray tube *n* : a vacuum tube in which a beam of electrons is projected on a fluorescent screen to produce a luminous spot

cath•o•lic \ˈkath-lik, ˈka-thə-\ *adj* **1** *cap* : of or relating to Catholics and esp. Roman Catholics **2** : GENERAL, UNIVERSAL

Cath•o•lic \ˈkath-lik, ˈka-thə-\ *n* : a member of a church claiming historical continuity from the ancient undivided Christian church; *esp* : a member of the Roman Catholic Church — **Ca•thol•i•cism** \kə-ˈthä-lə-ˌsi-zəm\ *n*

cath•o•lic•i•ty \ˌka-thə-ˈli-sə-tē\ *n, pl* **-ties 1** *cap* : the character of being in conformity with a Catholic church **2** : liberality of sentiments or views **3** : comprehensive range

cat•ion \ˈkat-ˌī-ən\ *n* : the ion in an electrolyte that migrates to the cathode; *also* : a positively charged ion

cat•kin \ˈkat-kən\ *n* : a long flower cluster (as of a willow) bearing crowded flowers and prominent bracts

cat•like \-ˌlīk\ *adj* : resembling a cat or its behavior; *esp* : STEALTHY

cat•nap \-ˌnap\ *n* : a very short light nap — **catnap** *vb*

cat•nip \-ˌnip\ *n* : an aromatic mint that is esp. attractive to cats

cat–o'–nine–tails \ˌka-tə-ˈnīn-ˌtālz\ *n, pl* **cat–o'–nine–tails** : a whip made of usu. nine knotted cords fastened to a handle

CAT scan \ˈkat-\ *n* [computerized *a*xial *t*omography] : an image made by computed tomography

CAT scanner *n* : a medical instrument consisting of integrated X-ray and computing equipment that is used to make CAT scans

cat's cradle *n* : a game played with a string looped on the fingers in such a way as to resemble a small cradle

cat's–eye \ˈkats-ˌī\ *n, pl* **cat's–eyes** : any of various iridescent gems

cat's–paw \-ˌpȯ\ *n, pl* **cat's–paws** : a person used by another as a tool

cat•sup \ˈke-chəp, ˈka-; ˈkat-səp\ *var of* KETCHUP

cat•tail \ˈkat-ˌtāl\ *n* : a tall reedlike marsh plant with furry brown spikes of tiny flowers

cat•tle \ˈkat-ᵊl\ *n pl* : LIVESTOCK; *esp* : domestic bovines (as cows, bulls, or calves) — **cat•tle•man** \-mən, -ˌman\ *n*

cat•ty \ˈka-tē\ *adj* **cat•ti•er, -est** : slyly spiteful — **cat•ti•ly** \ˈka-tᵊl-ē\ *adv* — **cat•ti•ness** *n*

cat•ty–cor•ner *or* **cat•ty–cor•nered** *var of* CATERCORNER

CATV *abbr* community antenna television

cat•walk \ˈkat-ˌwȯk\ *n* : a narrow walk (as along a bridge)

Cau•ca•sian \kȯ-ˈkā-zhən\ *adj* : of or relating to the white race of mankind — **Caucasian** *n* — **Cau•ca•soid** \ˈkȯ-kə-ˌsȯid\ *adj or n*

cau•cus \ˈkȯ-kəs\ *n* : a meeting of a group of persons belonging to the same political party or faction usu. to decide upon policies and candidates — **caucus** *vb*

cau•dal \ˈkȯ-dᵊl\ *adj* : of, relating to, or located near the tail or the hind end of the body — **cau•dal•ly** *adv*

cau•di•llo \kau̇-ˈth̲ē-(ˌ)yō, -ˈth̲ēl-\ *n, pl* **-llos** : a Spanish or Latin-American military dictator

caught \ˈkȯt\ *past and past part of* CATCH

caul \ˈkȯl\ *n* : the inner fetal membrane of higher vertebrates esp. when covering the head at birth

caul•dron \ˈkȯl-drən\ *n* : a large kettle

cau•li•flow•er \ˈkȯ-li-ˌflau̇(-ə)r\ *n* [It *cavolfiore,* fr. *cavolo* cabbage + *fiore* flower] : a garden plant closely related to cabbage and grown for its compact edible head of undeveloped flowers; *also* : this head used as a vegetable

cauliflower ear *n* : an ear deformed from injury and excessive growth of scar tissue

¹caulk \ˈkȯk\ *vb* [ME, fr. OF *cauquer* to trample, fr. L *calcare,* fr. *calx* heel] : to stop up and make tight against leakage (as a boat or its seams) — **caulk•er** *n*

²caulk *also* **caulk•ing** *n* : material used to caulk

caus•al \ˈkȯ-zəl\ *adj* **1** : expressing or indicating cause **2** : relating to or acting as a cause — **cau•sal•i•ty** \kȯ-ˈza-lə-tē\ *n* — **caus•al•ly** *adv*

cau•sa•tion \kȯ-ˈzā-shən\ *n* **1** : the act or process of causing **2** : the means by which an effect is produced

¹cause \ˈkȯz\ *n* **1** : REASON, MOTIVE **2** : something that brings about a result; *esp* : a person or thing that is the agent of bringing something about **3** : a suit or action in court : CASE **4** : a question or matter to be decided **5** : a principle or movement earnestly supported — **cause•less** *adj*

²cause *vb* **caused; caus•ing** : to be the cause or occasion of — **caus•a•tive** \ˈkȯ-zə-tiv\ *adj* — **caus•er** *n*

cause cé•lè•bre \ˌkōz-sā-ˈlebrᵊ, ˌkȯz-\ *n, pl* **causes cé•lè•bres** *same*\ [F, lit., celebrated case] **1** : a legal case that excites widespread interest **2** : a notorious person, thing, incident, or episode

cau•se•rie \ˌkōz-ˈrē, ˌkō-zə-\ *n* [F] **1** : an informal conversation : CHAT **2** : a short informal essay

cause•way \ˈkȯz-ˌwā\ *n* : a raised way or road across wet ground or water

¹caus•tic \ˈkȯ-stik\ *adj* **1** : CORROSIVE **2** : SHARP, INCISIVE ⟨~ wit⟩

²caustic *n* **1** : a substance that burns or destroys organic tissue by chemical action **2** : SODIUM HYDROXIDE

cau•ter•ize \ˈkȯ-tə-ˌrīz\ *vb* **-ized; -iz•ing** : to burn or sear usu. to prevent infection or bleeding — **cau•ter•i•za•tion** \ˌkȯ-tə-rə-ˈzā-shən\ *n*

¹cau•tion \ˈkȯ-shən\ *n* **1** : ADMONITION, WARNING **2** : prudent forethought to minimize risk **3** : one that astonishes — **cau•tion•ary** \-shə-ˌner-ē\ *adj*

²caution *vb* : to advise caution to

cau•tious \ˈkȯ-shəs\ *adj* : marked by or given to caution : CAREFUL — **cau•tious•ly** *adv* — **cau•tious•ness** *n*

cav *abbr* **1** cavalry **2** cavity

cav•al•cade \ˌka-vəl-ˈkād\ *n* **1** : a procession of riders or carriages; *also* : a procession of vehicles **2** : a dramatic sequence or procession

¹cav•a•lier \ˌka-və-ˈlir\ *n* [MF, fr. It *cavaliere,* fr. OProv *cavalier,* fr. LL *caballarius* horseman, fr. L *caballus* horse] **1** : a mounted soldier : KNIGHT **2** *cap* : an adherent of Charles I of England **3** : GALLANT

[2]**cavalier** *adj* **1** : DEBONAIR **2** : DISDAINFUL, HAUGHTY — **cav•a•lier•ly** *adv*

cav•al•ry \ˈka-vəl-rē\ *n, pl* **-ries** : troops mounted on horseback or moving in motor vehicles — **cav•al•ry•man** \-mən, -ˌman\ *n*

[1]**cave** \ˈkāv\ *n* : a natural underground chamber open to the surface

[2]**cave** *vb* **caved; cav•ing 1** : to collapse or cause to collapse **2** : to cease to resist : SUBMIT — usu. used with *in*

ca•ve•at \ˈka-vē-ˌät, -ˌat; ˈkä-vē-ˌät\ *n* [L, let him beware] : WARNING

caveat emp•tor \-ˈemp-tər, -ˌtȯr\ *n* [NL, let the buyer beware] : a principle in commerce: without a warranty the buyer takes a risk

cave–in \ˈkā-ˌvin\ *n* **1** : the action of caving in **2** : a place where earth has caved in

cave•man \ˈkāv-ˌman\ *n* **1** : a cave dweller esp. of the Stone Age **2** : a man who acts in a rough or crude manner

cav•ern \ˈka-vərn\ *n* : CAVE; *esp* : one of large or unknown size — **cav•ern•ous** *adj* — **cav•ern•ous•ly** *adv*

cav•i•ar *or* **cav•i•are** \ˈka-vē-ˌär, ˈkä-\ *n* : the salted roe of a large fish (as sturgeon) used as an appetizer

cav•il \ˈka-vəl\ *vb* **-iled** *or* **-illed; -il•ing** *or* **-il•ling** : to make frivolous objections or raise trivial objections to — **cavil** *n* — **cav•il•er** *or* **cav•il•ler** *n*

cav•ing \ˈkā-viŋ\ *n* : the sport of exploring caves : SPELUNKING

cav•i•ta•tion \ˌka-və-ˈtā-shən\ *n* : the formation of partial vacuums in a liquid by a swiftly moving solid body (as a propeller) or by high-intensity sound waves

cav•i•ty \ˈka-və-tē\ *n, pl* **-ties 1** : an unfilled space within a mass : a hollow place **2** : an area of decay in a tooth

ca•vort \kə-ˈvȯrt\ *vb* : PRANCE, CAPER

ca•vy \ˈkā-vē\ *n, pl* **cavies** : GUINEA PIG 1

caw \ˈkȯ\ *vb* : to utter the harsh call of the crow or a similar cry — **caw** *n*

cay \ˈkē, ˈkā\ *n* : [4]KEY

cay•enne pepper \ˌkī-ˈen-, ˌkā-\ *n* : a condiment consisting of ground dried fruits or seeds of a hot pepper

cay•man *var of* CAIMAN

Ca•yu•ga \kā-ˈü-gə, kī-\ *n, pl* **Cayuga** *or* **Cayugas** : a member of an American Indian people of New York

Cay•use \ˈkī-ˌyüs, kī-ˈ\ *n* **1** *pl* **Cayuse** *or* **Cayuses** : a member of an American Indian people of Oregon and Washington **2** *pl cayuses, not cap, West* : a native range horse

Cb *symbol* columbium

CB \ˈsē-ˈbē\ *n* : CITIZENS BAND; *also* : the radio set used for citizens-band communications

CBC *abbr* Canadian Broadcasting Corporation

CBD *abbr* cash before delivery

CBS *abbr* Columbia Broadcasting System

CBW *abbr* chemical and biological warfare

cc *abbr* cubic centimeter

CC *abbr* **1** carbon copy **2** community college **3** country club

CCD \ˌsē-ˌsē-ˈdē\ *n* : CHARGE-COUPLED DEVICE

CCTV *abbr* closed-circuit television

CCU *abbr* **1** cardiac care unit **2** coronary care unit **3** critical care unit

ccw *abbr* counterclockwise

cd *abbr* cord

Cd *symbol* cadmium

[1]**CD** \ˌsē-ˈdē\ *n* : COMPACT DISC

[2]**CD** *abbr* **1** certificate of deposit **2** Civil Defense

CDR *abbr* commander

CD–ROM \ˌsē-ˌdē-ˈräm\ *n* : a compact disc containing data that can be read by a computer

CDT *abbr* central daylight (saving) time

Ce *symbol* cerium

CE *abbr* **1** chemical engineer **2** civil engineer **3** Corps of Engineers

cease \ˈsēs\ *vb* **ceased; ceas•ing** : to come or bring to an end : STOP

cease–fire \ˈsēs-ˈfīr\ *n* : a suspension of active hostilities

cease•less \ˈsēs-ləs\ *adj* : being without pause or stop : CONTINUOUS — **cease•less•ly** *adv* — **cease•less•ness** *n*

ce•cum \ˈsē-kəm\ *n, pl* **ce•ca** \-kə\ : the blind pouch at the beginning of the large intestine into which the small intestine opens — **ce•cal** \-kəl\ *adj*

ce•dar \ˈsē-dər\ *n* : any of numerous coniferous trees (as a juniper) noted for their fragrant durable wood; *also* : this wood

cede \ˈsēd\ *vb* **ced•ed; ced•ing 1** : to yield or give up esp. by treaty **2** : ASSIGN, TRANSFER — **ced•er** *n*

ce•di \ˈsā-dē\ *n* — see MONEY table

ce•dil•la \si-ˈdi-lə\ *n* : a mark placed under the letter *c* (as ç) to show that the *c* is to be pronounced like *s*

ceil•ing \ˈsē-liŋ\ *n* **1** : the overhead inside lining of a room **2** : the height above the ground of the base of the lowest layer of clouds when over half of the sky is obscured **3** : the greatest height at which an airplane can operate efficiently **4** : a prescribed upper limit ⟨price ~⟩

cel•an•dine \ˈse-lən-ˌdīn, -ˌdēn\ *n* : a yellow-flowered herb related to the poppies

cel•e•brate \ˈse-lə-ˌbrāt\ *vb* **-brat•ed; -brat•ing 1** : to perform (as a sacrament) with appropriate rites **2** : to honor (as a holiday) by solemn ceremonies or by refraining from ordinary business **3** : to observe a notable occasion with festivities **4** : EXTOL — **cel•e•brant** \-brənt\ *n* — **cel•e•bra•tion** \ˌse-lə-ˈbrā-shən\ *n* — **cel•e•bra•tor** \ˈse-lə-brā-tər\ *n* — **cel•e•bra•to•ry** \-brə-ˌtōr-ē, -ˌtȯr-; ˌse-lə-ˈbrā-tə-rē\ *adj*

cel•e•brat•ed *adj* : widely known and often referred to **syn** distinguished, renowned, noted, famous, illustrious, notorious

ce•leb•ri•ty \sə-ˈle-brə-tē\ *n, pl* **-ties 1** : the state of being celebrated : RENOWN **2** : a celebrated person

ce•ler•i•ty \sə-ˈler-ə-tē\ *n* : SPEED, RAPIDITY

cel•ery \ˈse-lə-rē\ *n, pl* **-er•ies** : a European herb related to the carrot and widely grown for the crisp edible stems of its leaves

celery cabbage *n* : CHINESE CABBAGE 2

ce•les•ta \sə-ˈles-tə\ *or* **ce•leste** \sə-ˈlest\ *n* : a keyboard instrument with hammers that strike steel plates

ce•les•tial \sə-ˈles-chəl\ *adj* **1** : HEAVENLY, DIVINE **2** : of or relating to the sky — **ce•les•tial•ly** *adv*

celestial navigation *n* : navigation by observation of the positions of stars

celestial sphere *n* : an imaginary sphere of infinite radius against which the celestial bodies appear to be projected

cel•i•ba•cy \ˈse-lə-bə-sē\ *n* **1** : the state of being unmarried; *esp* : abstention by vow from marriage **2** : abstention from sexual intercourse

cel•i•bate \ˈse-lə-bət\ *n* : one who lives in celibacy — **celibate** *adj*

cell \ˈsel\ *n* **1** : a small room (as in a convent or prison) usu. for one person; *also* : a small compartment, cavity, or bounded space **2** : a tiny mass of protoplasm that usu. contains a nucleus, is enclosed by a membrane, and forms the smallest structural unit of living matter capable of functioning independently **3** : a container holding an electrolyte either for generating electricity or for use in electrolysis **4** : a single unit in a device for converting radiant energy into electrical energy — **celled** \ˈseld\ *adj*

cel•lar \ˈse-lər\ *n* **1** : BASEMENT 1 **2** : the lowest position (as in an athletic league) **3** : a stock of wines

cel•lar•ette *or* **cel•lar•et** \ˌse-lə-ˈret\ *n* : a case or cabinet for a few bottles of wine or liquor

cel•lo \ˈche-lō\ *n, pl* **cellos** : a bass member of the violin family tuned an octave below the viola — **cel•list** \-list\ *n*

cel•lo•phane \ˈse-lə-ˌfān\ *n* : a thin transparent material made from cellulose and used as a wrapping

cel•lu•lar \ˈsel-yə-lər\ *adj* **1** : of, relating to, or consisting of cells **2** : of, relating to, or being a radiotelephone system in which a geographical area is divided into small sections each served by a transmitter of limited range

cel•lu•lite \ˈsel-yə-ˌlīt\ *n* : lumpy fat in the thighs, hips, and buttocks of some women

cel•lu•lose \ˈsel-yə-ˌlōs\ *n* : a complex carbohydrate of the cell walls of plants used esp. in making paper or rayon — **cel•lu•los•ic** \ˌsel-yə-ˈlō-sik\ *adj or n*

Cel•si•us \ˈsel-sē-əs\ *adj* : relating to or having a scale for measuring temperature on which the interval between the triple point and the boiling point of water is divided into 99.99 degrees with 0.01° being the triple point and 100.00° the boiling point

Celt \ˈkelt, ˈselt\ *n* : a member of any of a group of peoples (as the Irish or Welsh) of western Europe — **Celt•ic** *adj*

cem•ba•lo \ˈchem-bə-ˌlō\ *n, pl* **-ba•li** \-ˌlē\ *or* **-balos** [It] : HARPSICHORD

[1]**ce•ment** \si-ˈment\ *n* **1** : a powder that is produced from a burned mixture chiefly of clay and limestone and that is used in mortar and concrete; *also* : CONCRETE **2** : a binding element or agency **3** : CEMENTUM; *also* : a substance for filling cavities in teeth

[2]**cement** *vb* **1** : to unite by or as if by cement **2** : to cover with concrete — **ce•ment•er** *n*

ce•men•tum \si-ˈmen-təm\ *n* : a specialized external bony layer covering the dentin of the part of a tooth normally within the gum

cem•e•tery \ˈse-mə-ˌter-ē\ *n, pl* **-ter•ies** [ME *cimitery*, fr. MF *cimitere*, fr. LL *coemeterium*, fr. Gk *koimētērion* sleeping chamber, burial place, fr. *koiman* to put to sleep] : a burial ground : GRAVEYARD

cen•o•bite \ˈse-nə-ˌbīt\ *n* : a member of a religious group living together in a monastic community — **cen•o•bit•ic** \ˌse-nə-ˈbi-tik\ *adj*

ceno•taph \ˈse-nə-ˌtaf\ *n* [F *cénotaphe*, fr. L *cenotaphium*, fr. Gk *kenotaphion*, fr. *kenos* empty + *taphos* tomb] : a tomb or a monument erected in honor of a person whose body is elsewhere

Ce•no•zo•ic \ˌsē-nə-ˈzō-ik, ˌse-\ *adj* : of, relating to, or being the era of geologic history that extends from about 65 million years ago to the present — **Cenozoic** *n*

cen•ser \ˈsen-sər\ *n* : a vessel for burning incense (as in a religious ritual)

[1]**cen•sor** \ˈsen-sər\ *n* **1** : one of two early Roman magistrates whose duties included taking the census **2** : an official who inspects printed matter or sometimes motion pictures with power to suppress anything objectionable — **cen•so•ri•al** \sen-ˈsōr-ē-əl\ *adj*

[2]**censor** *vb* : to subject to censorship

cen•so•ri•ous \sen-ˈsōr-ē-əs\ *adj* : marked by or given to censure : CRITICAL — **cen•so•ri•ous•ly** *adv* — **cen•so•ri•ous•ness** *n*

cen•sor•ship \ˈsen-sər-ˌship\ *n* **1** : the action of a censor esp. in stopping the transmission or publication of matter considered objectionable **2** : the office of a Roman censor

[1]**cen•sure** \ˈsen-chər\ *n* **1** : the act of blaming or condemning sternly **2** : an official reprimand

[2]**censure** *vb* **cen•sured; cen•sur•ing** : to find fault with and criticize as blameworthy — **cen•sur•able** *adj* — **cen•sur•er** *n*

cen•sus \ˈsen-səs\ *n* **1** : a periodic governmental count of population **2** : COUNT, TALLY — **cen•sus** *vb*

[1]**cent** \ˈsent\ *n* [MF, hundred, fr. L *centum*] **1** : a monetary unit equal to 1/100 of a basic unit of value — see *birr, dollar, gulden, leone, lilangeni, lira, pound, rand, rupee, shilling* at MONEY table **2** : a coin, token, or note representing one cent

[2]**cent** *abbr* **1** centigrade **2** central **3** century

cen•taur \ˈsen-ˌtȯr\ *n* : any of a race of creatures in Greek mythology half man and half horse

[1]**cen•ta•vo** \sen-ˈtä-(ˌ)vō\ *n, pl* **-vos** — see *boliviano, colón, cordoba, lempira, peso, quetzal, sol, sucre* at MONEY table

[2]**cen•ta•vo** \-ˈtä-(ˌ)vü, -(ˌ)vō\ *n, pl* **-vos** — see *escudo, metical, real* at MONEY table

cen•te•nar•i•an \ˌsent-ᵊn-ˈer-ē-ən\ *n* : a person who is 100 or more years old

cen•te•na•ry \sen-ˈte-nə-rē, ˈsent-ᵊn-ˌer-ē\ *n, pl* **-ries** : CENTENNIAL — **centenary** *adj*

cen•ten•ni•al \sen-ˈte-nē-əl\ *n* : a 100th anniversary or its celebration — **centennial** *adj*

[1]**cen•ter** \ˈsen-tər\ *n* **1** : the point that is equally distant from all points on the circumference of a circle or surface of a sphere; *also* : MIDDLE 1 **2** : the point about which an activity concentrates or from which something originates **3** : a region of concentrated population **4** : a middle part **5** *often cap* : political figures holding moderate views esp. between those of conservatives and liberals **6** : a player occupying a middle position (as in football or basketball)

[2]**center** *vb* **1** : to place or fix at or around a center or central area **2** : to give a central focus or basis : CONCENTRATE **3** : to have a center : FOCUS

cen•ter•board \ˈsen-tər-ˌbōrd\ *n* : a retractable keel used esp. in sailboats

cen•ter•piece \-ˌpēs\ *n* **1** : an object in a central position; *esp* : an adornment in the center of a table **2** : one that is of central importance or interest in a larger whole

cen•tes•i•mal \sen-ˈte-sə-məl\ *adj* : marked by or relating to division into hundredths

[1]**cen•tes•i•mo** \chen-ˈte-zə-ˌmō\ *n, pl* **-mi** \-(ˌ)mē\ — see *lira* at MONEY table

[2]**cen•tes•i•mo** \sen-ˈte-sə-ˌmō\ *n, pl* **-mos** — see *balboa, peso* at MONEY table

cen•ti•grade \ˈsen-tə-ˌgrād, ˈsän-\ *adj* : relating to, conforming to, or having a thermometer scale on which the interval between the freezing and boiling points of water is divided into 100 degrees with 0° representing the freezing point and 100° the boiling point ⟨10° ~⟩

cen•ti•gram \-ˌgram\ *n* — see METRIC SYSTEM table

cen•ti•li•ter \ˈsen-ti-ˌlē-tər\ *n* — see METRIC SYSTEM table

cen•time \ˈsän-ˌtēm\ *n* — see *dinar, dirham, franc, gourde* at MONEY table

cen•ti•me•ter \ˈsen-tə-ˌmē-tər, ˈsän-\ *n* — see METRIC SYSTEM table

centimeter–gram–second *adj* : of, relating to, or being a system of units based on the centimeter as the unit of length, the gram as the unit of mass, and the second as the unit of time

cen•ti•mo \ˈsen-tə-ˌmō\ *n, pl* **-mos** — see *bolivar, colón, dobra, guarani, peseta* at MONEY table

cen•ti•pede \ˈsen-tə-ˌpēd\ *n* [L *centipeda*, fr. *centum* hundred + *pes* foot] : any of a class of long flattened segmented arthropods with one pair of legs on each segment except the first which has a pair of poison fangs

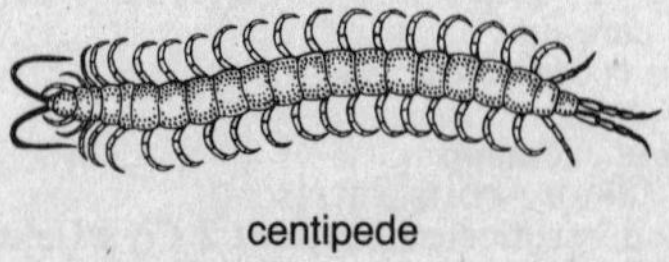

centipede

[1]**cen•tral** \ˈsen-trəl\ *adj* **1** : constituting a center **2** : ESSENTIAL, PRINCIPAL **3** : situated at, in, or near the center **4** : centrally placed and superseding separate units ⟨~ heating⟩ — **cen•tral•ly** *adv*

[2]**central** *n* : a central controlling office

cen•tral•ise *Brit var of* CENTRALIZE

cen•tral•ize \ˈsen-trə-ˌlīz\ *vb* **-ized; -iz•ing :** to bring to a central point or under central control — **cen•tral•i•za•tion** \ˌsen-trə-lə-ˈzā-shən\ *n* — **cen•tral•iz•er** \ˈsen-trə-ˌlī-zər\ *n*

central nervous system *n* **:** the part of the nervous system which integrates nervous function and activity and which in vertebrates consists of the brain and spinal cord

cen•tre *chiefly Brit var of* CENTER

cen•trif•u•gal \sen-ˈtri-fyə-gəl, -fi-\ *adj* [NL *centrifugus,* fr. *centr-* center + L *fugere* to flee] **1 :** proceeding or acting in a direction away from a center or axis **2 :** using or acting by centrifugal force

centrifugal force *n* **:** the force that tends to impel a thing or parts of a thing outward from a center of rotation

cen•tri•fuge \ˈsen-trə-ˌfyüj\ *n* **:** a machine using centrifugal force (as for separating substances of different densities or for removing moisture)

cen•trip•e•tal \sen-ˈtri-pət-ᵊl\ *adj* [NL *centripetus,* fr. *centr-* center + L *petere* seek] **:** proceeding or acting in a direction toward a center or axis

centripetal force *n* **:** the force needed to keep an object revolving about a point moving in a circular path

cen•trist \ˈsen-trist\ *n* **1** *often cap* **:** a member of a center party **2 :** one who holds moderate views

cen•tu•ri•on \sen-ˈtu̇r-ē-ən, -ˈtyu̇r-\ *n* **:** an officer commanding a Roman century

cen•tu•ry \ˈsen-chə-rē\ *n, pl* **-ries 1 :** a subdivision of a Roman legion **2 :** a group or sequence of 100 like things **3 :** a period of 100 years

century plant *n* **:** a Mexican agave maturing and flowering only once in many years and then dying

CEO \ˌsē-(ˌ)ē-ˈō\ *n* **:** the executive with the chief decision-making authority in an organization or business

ce•phal•ic \sə-ˈfa-lik\ *adj* **1 :** of or relating to the head **2 :** directed toward or situated on or in or near the head

ce•ram•ic \sə-ˈra-mik\ *n* **1** *pl* **:** the art or process of making articles from a nonmetallic mineral (as clay) by firing **2 :** a product produced by ceramics — **ceramic** *adj*

ce•ra•mist \sə-ˈra-mist\ *or* **ce•ram•i•cist** \sə-ˈra-mə-sist\ *n* **:** one who engages in ceramics

¹ce•re•al \ˈsir-ē-əl\ *adj* [L *cerealis,* fr. *Ceres,* the Roman goddess of agriculture] **:** relating to grain or to the plants that produce it; *also* **:** made of grain

²cereal *n* **1 :** a grass (as wheat) yielding grain suitable for food; *also* **:** its grain **2 :** a food and esp. a breakfast food prepared from the grain of a cereal

cer•e•bel•lum \ˌser-ə-ˈbe-ləm\ *n, pl* **-bellums** *or* **-bel•la** \-lə\ [ML, fr. L, dim. of *cerebrum*] **:** a part of the brain that projects over the medulla and is concerned esp. with coordination of muscular action and with bodily balance — **cer•e•bel•lar** \-lər\ *adj*

ce•re•bral \sə-ˈrē-brəl, ˈser-ə-\ *adj* **1 :** of or relating to the brain, intellect, or cerebrum **2 :** appealing to or involving the intellect — **ce•re•bral•ly** *adv*

cerebral cortex *n* **:** the surface layer of gray matter of the cerebrum that functions chiefly in coordination of sensory and motor information

cerebral palsy *n* **:** a disorder caused by brain damage usu. before, during, or shortly after birth and marked esp. by defective muscle control

cer•e•brate \ˈser-ə-ˌbrāt\ *vb* **-brat•ed; -brat•ing :** THINK — **cer•e•bra•tion** \ˌser-ə-ˈbrā-shən\ *n*

ce•re•brum \sə-ˈrē-brəm, ˈser-ə-\ *n, pl* **-brums** *or* **-bra** \-brə\ [L] **:** the enlarged front and upper part of the brain that contains the higher nervous centers

cere•ment \ˈser-ə-mənt, ˈsir-mənt\ *n* **:** a shroud for the dead

¹cer•e•mo•ni•al \ˌser-ə-ˈmō-nē-əl\ *adj* **:** of, relating to, or forming a ceremony; *also* **:** stressing careful attention to form and detail — **cer•e•mo•ni•al•ly** *adv*

²ceremonial *n* **:** a ceremonial act or system **:** RITUAL, FORM

cer•e•mo•ni•ous \ˌser-ə-ˈmō-nē-əs\ *adj* **1 :** devoted to forms and ceremony **2 :** CEREMONIAL **3 :** according to formal usage or procedure **4 :** marked by ceremony — **cer•e•mo•ni•ous•ly** *adv* — **cer•e•mo•ni•ous•ness** *n*

cer•e•mo•ny \ˈser-ə-ˌmō-nē\ *n, pl* **-nies 1 :** a formal act or series of acts prescribed by law, ritual, or convention **2 :** a conventional act of politeness **3 :** a mere outward form with no deeper significance **4 :** FORMALITY

ce•re•us \ˈsir-ē-əs\ *n* **:** any of various cacti of the western U.S. and tropical America

ce•rise \sə-ˈrēs\ *n* [F, lit., cherry] **:** a moderate red color

ce•ri•um \ˈsir-ē-əm\ *n* **:** a malleable metallic chemical element used esp. in alloys — see ELEMENT table

cer•met \ˈsər-ˌmet\ *n* **:** a strong alloy of a heat-resistant compound and a metal used esp. for turbine blades

cert *abbr* certificate; certification; certified; certify

¹cer•tain \ˈsərt-ᵊn\ *adj* **1 :** FIXED, SETTLED **2 :** of a specific but unspecified character ⟨~ people in authority⟩ **3 :** DEPENDABLE, RELIABLE **4 :** INDISPUTABLE, UNDENIABLE **5 :** assured in mind or action — **cer•tain•ly** *adv*

²certain *pron* **:** certain ones

cer•tain•ty \-tē\ *n, pl* **-ties 1 :** something that is certain **2 :** the quality or state of being certain

cer•tif•i•cate \sər-ˈti-fi-kət\ *n* **1 :** a document testifying to the truth of a fact **2 :** a document testifying that one has fulfilled certain requirements (as of a course or school) **3 :** a document giving evidence of ownership or debt ⟨~ of deposit⟩

cer•ti•fi•ca•tion \ˌsər-tə-fə-ˈkā-shən\ *n* **1 :** the act of certifying **:** the state of being certified **2 :** a certified statement

certified mail *n* **:** first class mail for which proof of delivery may be secured but no indemnity value is claimed

certified milk *n* **:** milk produced in dairies that operate under the rules and regulations of an authorized medical milk commission

certified public accountant *n* **:** an accountant who has met the requirements of a state law and has been granted a certificate

cer•ti•fy \ˈsər-tə-ˌfī\ *vb* **-fied; -fy•ing 1 :** VERIFY, CONFIRM **2 :** to endorse officially **3 :** to guarantee (a bank check) as good by a statement to that effect stamped on its face **4 :** to provide with a usu. professional certificate or license **syn** accredit, approve, sanction, endorse — **cer•ti•fi•able** \-ə-bəl\ *adj* — **cer•ti•fi•ably** \-blē\ *adv* — **cer•ti•fi•er** *n*

cer•ti•tude \ˈsər-tə-ˌtüd, -ˌtyüd\ *n* **:** the state of being or feeling certain

ce•ru•le•an \sə-ˈrü-lē-ən\ *adj* **:** AZURE

ce•ru•men \sə-ˈrü-mən\ *n* **:** EARWAX

cer•vi•cal \ˈsər-vi-kəl\ *adj* **:** of or relating to a neck or cervix

cervical cap *n* **:** a contraceptive device in the form of a thimble-shaped molded cap that fits over the uterine cervix and blocks sperm from entering the uterus

cer•vix \ˈsər-viks\ *n, pl* **cer•vi•ces** \-və-ˌsēz\ *or* **cer•vix•es 1 :** NECK; *esp* **:** the back part of the neck **2 :** a constricted portion of an organ or part; *esp* **:** the narrow outer end of the uterus

ce•sar•e•an *also* **ce•sar•i•an** \si-ˈzar-ē-ən, -ˈzer-\ *n* **:** CESAREAN SECTION — **cesarean** *also* **cesarian** *adj*

cesarean section *also* **cesarian section** *n* [fr. the belief that Julius Caesar was born this way] **:** surgical incision of the walls of the abdomen and uterus for delivery of offspring

ce•si•um \ˈsē-zē-əm\ *n* **:** a silver-white soft ductile chemical element — see ELEMENT table

ces•sa•tion \se-ˈsā-shən\ *n* **:** a temporary or final ceasing (as of action)

ces•sion \ˈse-shən\ *n* : a yielding (as of rights) to another
cess•pool \ˈses-ˌpül\ *n* : an underground pit or tank for receiving household sewage
ce•ta•cean \si-ˈtā-shən\ *n* : any of an order of aquatic mostly marine mammals that includes whales, porpoises, dolphins, and related forms — **cetacean** *adj*
cf *abbr* [L *confer*] compare
Cf *symbol* californium
CF *abbr* cystic fibrosis
CFC *abbr* chlorofluorocarbon
cg *abbr* centigram
CG *abbr* **1** coast guard **2** commanding general
cgs *abbr* centimeter-gram-second
ch *abbr* **1** chain **2** champion **3** chapter **4** church
CH *abbr* **1** clearinghouse **2** courthouse **3** customhouse
Cha•blis \sha-ˈblē, shə-, shä-; ˈsha-ˌblē\ *n, pl* **Cha•blis** \-ˈblēz, -(ˌ)blēz\ **1** : a dry sharp white Burgundy wine **2** : a white California wine
cha–cha \ˈchä-ˌchä\ *n* : a fast rhythmic ballroom dance of Latin American origin
Chad•ian \ˈcha-dē-ən\ *n* : a native or inhabitant of Chad — **Chadian** *adj*
chafe \ˈchāf\ *vb* **chafed; chaf•ing 1** : IRRITATE, VEX **2** : FRET **3** : to warm by rubbing **4** : to rub so as to wear away; *also* : to make sore by rubbing
cha•fer \ˈchā-fər\ *n* : any of various scarab beetles
[1]**chaff** \ˈchaf\ *n* **1** : debris (as husks) separated from grain in threshing **2** : something comparatively worthless — **chaffy** *adj*
[2]**chaff** *n* : light jesting talk : BANTER
[3]**chaff** *vb* : to tease good-naturedly
chaf•fer \ˈcha-fər\ *vb* : BARGAIN, HAGGLE — **chaf•fer•er** *n*
chaf•finch \ˈcha-ˌfinch\ *n* : a common European finch with a cheerful song
chaf•ing dish \ˈchā-fiŋ-\ *n* : a utensil for cooking food at the table
[1]**cha•grin** \shə-ˈgrin\ *n* : mental uneasiness or annoyance caused by failure, disappointment, or humiliation
[2]**chagrin** *vb* **cha•grined** \-ˈgrind\; **cha•grin•ing** : to cause to feel chagrin
[1]**chain** \ˈchān\ *n* [ME *cheyne,* fr. MF *chaeine,* fr. L *catena*] **1** : a flexible series of connected links **2** : a chainlike surveying instrument; *also* : a unit of length equal to 66 feet (about 20 meters) **3** *pl* : BONDS, FETTERS **4** : a series of things linked together **syn** train, string, sequence, succession, series
[2]**chain** *vb* : to fasten, bind, or connect with a chain; *also* : FETTER
chain gang *n* : a gang of convicts chained together
chain letter *n* : a letter sent to several persons with a request that each send copies to an equal number of persons
chain mail *n* : flexible armor of interlocking metal rings
chain reaction *n* **1** : a series of events in which each event initiates the succeeding one **2** : a chemical or nuclear reaction yielding products that cause further reactions of the same kind
chain saw *n* : a portable power saw that has teeth linked together to form an endless chain — **chain-saw** \ˈchān-ˌsȯ\ *vb*
chain–smoke \ˈchān-ˈsmōk\ *vb* : to smoke esp. cigarettes continuously
chain store *n* : any of numerous stores under the same ownership that sell the same lines of goods
[1]**chair** \ˈcher\ *n* **1** : a seat with a back for one person **2** : ELECTRIC CHAIR **3** : an official seat; *also* : an office or position of authority or dignity **4** : CHAIRMAN
[2]**chair** *vb* : to act as chairman of
chair•lift \ˈcher-ˌlift\ *n* : a motor-driven conveyor for skiers consisting of seats hung from a moving cable
chair•man \-mən\ *n* : the presiding officer of a meeting or of a committee — **chair•man•ship** *n*
chair•per•son \-ˌpər-sən\ *n* : CHAIRMAN
chair•wom•an \-ˌwu̇-mən\ *n* : a woman who acts as chairman
chaise \ˈshāz\ *n* : a 2-wheeled horse-drawn carriage with a folding top
chaise longue \ˈshāz-ˈlȯŋ\ *n, pl* **chaise longues** *same or* -ˈlȯŋz\ [F *chaise longue,* lit., long chair] : a long reclining chair
chaise lounge \-ˈlau̇nj\ *n* : CHAISE LONGUE
chal•ced•o•ny \kal-ˈsed-ᵊn-ē\ *n, pl* **-nies** : a translucent pale blue or gray quartz
chal•co•py•rite \ˌkal-kə-ˈpī-ˌrīt\ *n* : a yellow mineral constituting an important ore of copper
cha•let \sha-ˈlā\ *n* **1** : a herdsman's cabin in the Swiss mountains **2** : a building in the style of a Swiss cottage with a wide roof overhang

chalet 2

chal•ice \ˈcha-ləs\ *n* : a drinking cup; *esp* : the eucharistic cup
[1]**chalk** \ˈchȯk\ *n* **1** : a soft limestone **2** : chalk or chalky material esp. when used as a crayon — **chalky** *adj*
[2]**chalk** *vb* **1** : to rub or mark with chalk **2** : to record with or as if with chalk — usu. used with *up*
chalk•board \ˈchȯk-ˌbōrd\ *n* : BLACKBOARD
chalk up *vb* **1** : ASCRIBE, CREDIT **2** : ATTAIN, ACHIEVE
[1]**chal•lenge** \ˈcha-lənj\ *vb* **chal•lenged; chal•leng•ing** [ME *chalengen* to accuse, fr. OF *chalengier,* fr. L *calumniari* to accuse falsely, fr. *calumnia* calumny] **1** : to order to halt and prove identity **2** : to take exception to : DISPUTE **3** : to issue an invitation to compete against one esp. in single combat : DARE, DEFY — **chal•leng•er** *n*
[2]**challenge** *n* **1** : a summons to a duel **2** : an invitation to compete in a sport **3** : a calling into question **4** : an exception taken to a juror **5** : a sentry's command to halt and prove identity **6** : a stimulating or interesting task or problem
chal•lis \ˈsha-lē\ *n, pl* **chal•lises** \-lēz\ : a lightweight clothing fabric of wool, cotton, or synthetic yarns
cham•ber \ˈchām-bər\ *n* **1** : ROOM; *esp* : BEDROOM **2** : an enclosed space or cavity **3** : a hall for meetings of a legislative body **4** : a judge's consultation room — usu. used in pl. **5** : a legislative or judicial body; *also* : a council for a business purpose **6** : the part of a firearm that holds the cartridge or powder charge during firing — **cham•bered** \-bərd\ *adj*
cham•ber•lain \ˈchām-bər-lən\ *n* **1** : a chief officer in the household of a king or nobleman **2** : TREASURER
cham•ber•maid \-ˌmād\ *n* : a maid who takes care of bedrooms
chamber music *n* : music intended for performance by a few musicians before a small audience
chamber of commerce : an association of businesspeople for promoting commercial and industrial interests in the community
cham•bray \ˈsham-ˌbrā\ *n* : a lightweight clothing fabric of white and colored threads
cha•me•leon \kə-ˈmēl-yən\ *n* [ME *camelion,* fr. MF, fr. L *chamaeleon,* fr. Gk *chamaileōn,* fr. *chamai* on the ground + *leōn* lion] : a small lizard whose skin changes color esp. according to its surroundings

[1]cham•fer \ˈcham-fər\ *vb* **1** : to cut a furrow in (as a column) : GROOVE **2** : to make a chamfer on : BEVEL

[2]chamfer *n* : a beveled edge

cham•ois \ˈsha-mē\ *n, pl* **cham•ois** *same or* -mēz\ **1** : a small goatlike antelope of Europe and the Caucasus region of Russia **2** *also* **cham•my** \ˈsha-mē\ : a soft leather made esp. from the skin of the sheep or goat **3** : a cotton fabric made in imitation of chamois leather

cham•o•mile \ˈka-mə-ˌmīl, -ˌmēl\ *n* : any of a genus of strong-scented herbs related to the daisies and having flower heads that yield a bitter substance used esp. in tonics and teas

[1]champ \ˈchamp, ˈchämp\ *vb* **1** : to chew noisily **2** : to show impatience of delay or restraint

[2]champ \ˈchamp\ *n* : CHAMPION

cham•pagne \sham-ˈpān\ *n* : a white effervescent wine

[1]cham•pi•on \ˈcham-pē-ən\ *n* **1** : a militant advocate or defender **2** : one that wins first prize or place in a contest **3** : one that is acknowledged to be better than all others

[2]champion *vb* : to protect or fight for as a champion **syn** back, advocate, uphold, support

cham•pi•on•ship \-ˌship\ *n* **1** : the position or title of a champion **2** : the act of championing : DEFENSE **3** : a contest held to determine a champion

[1]chance \ˈchans\ *n* **1** : something that happens without apparent cause **2** : the unpredictable element in existence : LUCK, FORTUNE **3** : OPPORTUNITY **4** : the likelihood of a particular outcome in an uncertain situation : PROBABILITY **5** : RISK **6** : a raffle ticket — **chance** *adj* — **by chance** : in the haphazard course of events

[2]chance *vb* **chanced; chanc•ing** **1** : to take place by chance : HAPPEN **2** : to come casually and unexpectedly — used with *upon* **3** : to leave to chance **4** : to accept the risk of

chan•cel \ˈchan-səl\ *n* : the part of a church including the altar and choir

chan•cel•lery *or* **chan•cel•lory** \ˈchan-sə-lə-rē\ *n, pl* **-ler•ies** *or* **-lor•ies** **1** : the position or office of a chancellor **2** : the building or room where a chancellor works **3** : the office or staff of an embassy or consulate

chan•cel•lor \ˈchan-sə-lər\ *n* **1** : a high state official in various countries **2** : the head of a university **3** : a judge in the equity court in various states of the U.S. **4** : the chief minister of state in some European countries — **chan•cel•lor•ship** *n*

chan•cery \ˈchan-sə-rē\ *n, pl* **-cer•ies** **1** : any of various courts of equity in the U.S. and Britain **2** : a record office for public or diplomatic archives **3** : a chancellor's court or office **4** : the office of an embassy

chan•cre \ˈshaŋ-kər\ *n* [F, fr. L *cancer*] : a primary sore or ulcer at the site of entry of an infective agent (as of syphilis)

chan•croid \ˈchaŋ-ˌkrȯid\ *n* : a sexually transmitted disease caused by a bacterium and characterized by chancres that differ from those of syphilis in lacking hardened margins

chancy \ˈchan-sē\ *adj* **chanc•i•er; -est** **1** *Scot* : AUSPICIOUS **2** : RISKY

chan•de•lier \ˌshan-də-ˈlir\ *n* : a branched lighting fixture suspended from a ceiling

chan•dler \ˈchand-lər\ *n* [ME *chandeler* a maker or seller of candles, fr. MF *chandelier,* fr. OF, fr. *chandelle* candle, fr. L *candela*] : a dealer in provisions and supplies of a specified kind ⟨ship's ~⟩ — **chandlery** *n*

[1]change \ˈchānj\ *vb* **changed; chang•ing** **1** : to make or become different : ALTER **2** : to replace with another **3** : to give or receive an equivalent sum in notes or coins of usu. smaller denominations or of another currency **4** : to put fresh clothes or covering on ⟨~ a bed⟩ **5** : to put on different clothes **6** : EXCHANGE — **change•able** *adj* — **chang•er** *n*

[2]change *n* **1** : the act, process, or result of changing **2** : a fresh set of clothes **3** : money given in exchange for other money of higher denomination **4** : money returned when a payment exceeds the sum due **5** : coins esp. of small denominations — **change•ful** *adj*

change•ling \ˈchānj-liŋ\ *n* : a child secretly exchanged for another in infancy

change of life : MENOPAUSE

change•over \ˈchānj-ˌō-vər\ *n* : CONVERSION, TRANSITION

change ringing *n* : the art or practice of ringing a set of tuned bells in continually varying order

[1]chan•nel \ˈchan-ᵊl\ *n* **1** : the bed of a stream **2** : the deeper part of a waterway **3** : STRAIT **4** : a means of passage or transmission **5** : a range of frequencies of sufficient width for a single radio or television transmission **6** : a usu. tubular enclosed passage : CONDUIT **7** : a long gutter, groove, or furrow

[2]channel *vb* **-neled** *or* **-nelled; -nel•ing** *or* **-nel•ling** **1** : to make a channel in **2** : to direct into or through a channel

chan•nel•ize \ˈchan-ᵊl-ˌīz\ *vb* **-ized; -iz•ing** : CHANNEL — **chan•nel•iza•tion** \ˌchan-ᵊl-ə-ˈzā-shən\ *n*

chan•son \shäⁿ-ˈsōⁿ\ *n, pl* **chan•sons** *same or* -ˈsōⁿz\ : SONG; *esp* : a cabaret song

[1]chant \ˈchant\ *vb* **1** : SING; *esp* : to sing a chant **2** : to utter or recite in the manner of a chant **3** : to celebrate or praise in song — **chant•er** *n*

[2]chant *n* **1** : a repetitive melody in which several words are sung to one tone : SONG; *esp* : a liturgical melody **2** : a manner of singing or speaking in musical monotones

chan•teuse \shäⁿ-ˈtərz, shan-ˈtüz\ *n, pl* **chan•teuses** *same or* -ˈtər-zəz, -ˈtü-zəz\ [F] : a woman who is a concert or nightclub singer

chan•tey *or* **chan•ty** \ˈshan-tē, ˈchan-\ *n, pl* **chanteys** *or* **chanties** : a song sung by sailors in rhythm with their work

chan•ti•cleer \ˌchan-tə-ˈklir, ˌshan-\ *n* : ROOSTER

Cha•nu•kah \ˈkä-nə-kə, ˈhä-\ *var of* HANUKKAH

cha•os \ˈkā-ˌäs\ *n* **1** *often cap* : the confused unorganized state existing before the creation of distinct forms **2** : the inherent unpredictability in the behavior of a natural system (as the atmosphere or the beating heart) **3** : complete disorder **syn** confusion, jumble, snarl, muddle, disarray — **cha•ot•ic** \kā-ˈä-tik\ *adj* — **cha•ot•i•cal•ly** \-ti-k(ə-)lē\ *adv*

[1]chap \ˈchap\ *vb* **chapped; chap•ping** : to dry and crack open usu. from wind and cold ⟨*chapped* lips⟩

[2]chap *n* : a jaw with its fleshy covering — usu. used in pl.

[3]chap *n* : FELLOW

[4]chap *abbr* chapter

chap•ar•ral \ˌsha-pə-ˈral\ *n* **1** : a dense impenetrable thicket of shrubs or dwarf trees **2** : an ecological community esp. of southern California composed of shrubby plants

chap•book \ˈchap-ˌbu̇k\ *n* : a small book of ballads, tales, or tracts

cha•peau \sha-ˈpō\ *n, pl* **cha•peaus** \-ˈpōz\ *or* **cha•peaux** \-ˈpō, -ˈpōz\ [MF] : HAT

cha•pel \ˈcha-pəl\ *n* [ME, fr. OF *chapele,* fr. ML *cappella,* fr. LL *cappa* cloak; fr. the cloak of St. Martin of Tours preserved as a sacred relic in a chapel built for that purpose] **1** : a private or subordinate place of worship **2** : an assembly at an educational institution usu. including devotional exercises **3** : a place of worship used by a Christian group other than an established church

[1]chap•er•on *or* **chap•er•one** \ˈsha-pə-ˌrōn\ *n* [F *chaperon,* lit., hood, fr. MF, head covering, fr. *chape* cape, fr. LL *cappa*] **1** : a person (as a matron) who accompanies young unmarried women in public for propriety **2** : an older person who accompanies young people at a social gathering to ensure proper behavior

[2]chaperon *or* **chaperone** *vb* **-oned; -on•ing** **1** : ESCORT,

GUIDE **2** : to act as a chaperon to or for — **chap·er·on·age** \-ˌrō-nij\ *n*

chap·fall·en \ˈchap-ˌfȯ-lən, ˈchäp-\ *adj* **1** : having the lower jaw hanging loosely **2** : DEJECTED, DEPRESSED

chap·lain \ˈcha-plən\ *n* **1** : a member of the clergy officially attached to a special group (as the army) **2** : a person chosen to conduct religious exercises (as for a club) — **chap·lain·cy** \-sē\ *n*

chap·let \ˈcha-plət\ *n* **1** : a wreath for the head **2** : a string of beads : NECKLACE

chap·man \ˈchap-mən\ *n, Brit* : an itinerant dealer : PEDDLER

chaps \ˈshaps, ˈchaps\ *n pl* [MexSp *chaparreras*] : leather leggings resembling trousers without a seat that are worn esp. by western ranch hands

chap·ter \ˈchap-tər\ *n* **1** : a main division of a book **2** : a body of canons (as of a cathedral) **3** : a local branch of a society or fraternity

1**char** \ˈchär\ *n, pl* **char** *or* **chars** : any of a genus of trouts (as the common brook trout) with small scales

2**char** *vb* **charred; char·ring 1** : to burn or become burned to charcoal **2** : SCORCH

3**char** *vb* **charred; char·ring** : to work as a cleaning woman

char·ac·ter \ˈkar-ik-tər\ *n* [ME *caracter,* fr. MF *caractère,* fr. L *character* mark, distinctive quality, fr. Gk *charaktēr,* fr. *charassein* to scratch, engrave] **1** : a graphic symbol (as a letter) used in writing or printing **2** : a symbol that represents information; *also* : a representation of such a character that may be accepted by a computer **3** : a distinguishing feature : ATTRIBUTE **4** : the complex of mental and ethical traits marking a person or a group **5** : a person marked by conspicuous often peculiar traits **6** : one of the persons in a novel or play **7** : REPUTATION **8** : moral excellence

1**char·ac·ter·is·tic** \ˌkar-ik-tə-ˈris-tik\ *n* : a distinguishing trait, quality, or property

2**characteristic** *adj* : serving to mark individual character **syn** individual, peculiar, distinctive — **char·ac·ter·is·ti·cal·ly** \-ti-k(ə-)lē\ *adv*

char·ac·ter·ize \ˈkar-ik-tə-ˌrīz\ *vb* **-ized; -iz·ing 1** : to describe the character of **2** : to be a characteristic of — **char·ac·ter·iza·tion** \ˌkar-ik-tə-rə-ˈzā-shən\ *n*

cha·rades \shə-ˈrādz\ *n sing or pl* : a game in which some of the players try to guess a word or phrase from the actions of another player who may not speak

char·coal \ˈchär-ˌkōl\ *n* **1** : a porous carbon prepared from vegetable or animal substances **2** : a piece of fine charcoal used in drawing; *also* : a drawing made with charcoal

chard \ˈchärd\ *n* : SWISS CHARD

char·don·nay \ˌshard-ən-ˈā\ *n, often cap* [F] : a dry white wine made from a single variety of white grape

1**charge** \ˈchärj\ *n* **1** : a quantity (as of fuel or ammunition) required to fill something to capacity **2** : a store or accumulation of force **3** : an excess or deficiency of electrons in a body **4** : THRILL, KICK **5** : a task or duty imposed **6** : CARE, RESPONSIBILITY **7** : one given into another's care **8** : instructions from a judge to a jury **9** : COST, EXPENSE, PRICE; *also* : a debit to an account **10** : ACCUSATION, INDICTMENT **11** : ATTACK, ASSAULT

2**charge** *vb* **charged; charg·ing 1** : to load or fill to capacity **2** : to give an electric charge to; *also* : to restore the activity of (a storage battery) by means of an electric current **3** : to impose a task or responsibility on **4** : COMMAND, ORDER **5** : ACCUSE **6** : to rush against : rush forward in assault **7** : to make liable for payment; *also* : to record a debt or liability against **8** : to fix as a price — **charge·able** *adj*

charge–coupled device *n* : a semiconductor device used esp. as an optical sensor

char·gé d'af·faires \shär-ˌzhā-də-ˈfar\ *n, pl* **chargés d'affaires** \-ˌzhā-, -ˌzhāz-\ [F] : a diplomat who substitutes for an ambassador or minister

1**char·ger** \ˈchär-jər\ *n* : a large platter

2**charg·er** *n* **1** : a device or a workman that charges something **2** : WARHORSE

char·i·ot \ˈchar-ē-ət\ *n* : a 2-wheeled horse-drawn vehicle of ancient times used esp. in war and in races — **char·i·o·teer** \ˌchar-ē-ə-ˈtir\ *n*

cha·ris·ma \kə-ˈriz-mə\ *n* : a personal quality of leadership arousing popular loyalty or enthusiasm — **char·is·mat·ic** \ˌkar-əz-ˈma-tik\ *adj*

char·i·ta·ble \ˈchar-ə-tə-bəl\ *adj* **1** : liberal in giving to needy people **2** : merciful or lenient in judging others **syn** benevolent, philanthropic, altruistic, humanitarian — **char·i·ta·ble·ness** *n* — **char·i·ta·bly** \-blē\ *adv*

char·i·ty \ˈchar-ə-tē\ *n, pl* **-ties 1** : goodwill toward or love of humanity **2** : an act or feeling of generosity **3** : the giving of aid to the poor; *also* : ALMS **4** : an institution engaged in relief of the poor **5** : leniency in judging others **syn** mercy, clemency, lenity

char·la·tan \ˈshär-lə-tən\ *n* : a person making usu. showy pretenses to knowledge or ability : FRAUD, FAKER

Charles·ton \ˈchärl-stən\ *n* : a lively dance in which the knees are swung in and out and the heels are turned sharply outward on each step

char·ley horse \ˈchär-lē-ˌhȯrs\ *n* : a muscular pain, cramping, or stiffness from a strain or bruise

1**charm** \ˈchärm\ *n* [ME *charme,* fr. MF, fr. L *carmen* song, fr. *canere* to sing] **1** : a practice or expression believed to have magic power **2** : something worn about the person to ward off evil or bring good fortune : AMULET **3** : a trait that fascinates or allures **4** : physical grace or attraction **5** : a small ornament worn on a bracelet or chain

2**charm** *vb* **1** : to affect by or as if by a magic spell **2** : to protect by or as if by charms **3** : FASCINATE, ENCHANT **syn** allure, captivate, bewitch, attract — **charm·er** *n*

charm·ing \ˈchär-miŋ\ *adj* : PLEASING, DELIGHTFUL — **charm·ing·ly** *adv*

char·nel house \ˈchärn-əl-\ *n* : a building or chamber in which bodies or bones are deposited

1**chart** \ˈchärt\ *n* **1** : MAP **2** : a sheet giving information in the form of a table, list, or diagram; *also* : GRAPH

2**chart** *vb* **1** : to make a chart of **2** : PLAN

1**char·ter** \ˈchär-tər\ *n* **1** : an official document granting rights or privileges (as to a colony, town, or college) from a sovereign or a governing body **2** : CONSTITUTION **3** : a written instrument from a society creating a branch **4** : a mercantile lease of a ship

2**charter** *vb* **1** : to grant a charter to **2** *Brit* : CERTIFY ⟨~*ed* engineer⟩ **3** : to hire, rent, or lease for temporary use — **char·ter·er** *n*

charter member *n* : an original member of an organization

char·treuse \shär-ˈtrüz, -ˈtrüs\ *n* : a brilliant yellow green

char·wom·an \ˈchär-ˌwu̇-mən\ *n* : a cleaning woman esp. in large buildings

chary \ˈchar-ē\ *adj* **chari·er; -est** [ME, sorrowful, dear, fr. OE *cearig* sorrowful, fr. *caru* sorrow] **1** : CAUTIOUS, CIRCUMSPECT **2** : SPARING — **char·i·ly** \-ə-lē\ *adv*

1**chase** \ˈchās\ *n* **1** : PURSUIT; *also* : HUNTING **2** : QUARRY **3** : a tract of unenclosed land used as a game preserve

2**chase** *vb* **chased; chas·ing 1** : to follow rapidly : PURSUE **2** : HUNT **3** : to seek out ⟨*chasing* down clues⟩ **4** : to cause to depart or flee : drive away **5** : RUSH, HASTEN

3**chase** *vb* **chased; chas·ing** : to decorate (a metal surface) by embossing or engraving

4**chase** *n* : FURROW, GROOVE

chas·er \ˈchā-sər\ *n* **1** : one that chases **2** : a mild drink (as beer) taken after hard liquor

chasm \ˈka-zəm\ *n* : GORGE 2

chas·sis \ˈcha-sē, ˈsha-sē\ *n, pl* **chas·sis** \-sēz\ : the sup-

porting frame of a structure (as an automobile or television set)
chaste \ˈchāst\ *adj* **chast•er; chast•est 1 :** innocent of unlawful sexual intercourse : VIRTUOUS, PURE **2 :** CELIBATE **3 :** pure in thought : MODEST **4 :** severe or simple in design — **chaste•ly** *adv* — **chaste•ness** *n*
chas•ten \ˈchās-ᵊn\ *vb* : to correct through punishment or suffering : DISCIPLINE; *also* : PURIFY — **chas•ten•er** *n*
chas•tise \chas-ˈtīz\ *vb* **chas•tised; chas•tis•ing** [ME *chastisen*, alter. of *chasten*] **1 :** to punish esp. bodily **2 :** to censure severely : CASTIGATE — **chas•tise•ment** \-mənt, ˈchas-təz-\ *n*
chas•ti•ty \ˈchas-tə-tē\ *n* : the quality or state of being chaste; *esp* : sexual purity
cha•su•ble \ˈcha-zə-bəl, -sə-\ *n* : the outer vestment of the priest at mass
chat \ˈchat\ *n* : light familiar informal talk — **chat** *vb*
châ•teau \sha-ˈtō\ *n, pl* **châ•teaus** \-ˈtōz\ *or* **châ•teaux** \-ˈtō, -ˈtōz\ [F, fr. L *castellum* castle, dim. of *castra* camp] **1 :** a feudal castle in France **2 :** a large country house **3 :** a French vineyard estate
chat•e•laine \ˈshat-ᵊl-ˌān\ *n* **1 :** the mistress of a chateau **2 :** a clasp or hook for a watch, purse, or keys
chat•tel \ˈchat-ᵊl\ *n* **1 :** an item of tangible property other than real estate **2 :** SLAVE, BONDMAN
chat•ter \ˈcha-tər\ *vb* **1 :** to utter speechlike but meaningless sounds **2 :** to talk idly, incessantly, or fast **3 :** to click repeatedly or uncontrollably — **chatter** *n* — **chat•ter•er** *n*
chat•ter•box \ˈcha-tər-ˌbäks\ *n* : one who talks incessantly
chat•ty \ˈcha-tē\ *adj* **chat•ti•er; -est** : TALKATIVE — **chat•ti•ly** \-tə-lē\ *adv* — **chat•ti•ness** \-tē-nəs\ *n*
[1]**chauf•feur** \ˈshō-fər, shō-ˈfər\ *n* [F, lit., stoker, fr. *chauffer* to heat] : a person employed to drive an automobile
[2]**chauffeur** *vb* **chauf•feured; chauf•feur•ing 1 :** to do the work of a chauffeur **2 :** to transport in the manner of a chauffeur
chaunt \ˈchȯnt, ˈchänt\ *var of* CHANT
chau•vin•ism \ˈshō-və-ˌni-zəm\ *n* [F *chauvinisme*, fr. Nicolas *Chauvin*, fictional soldier of excessive patriotism and devotion to Napoleon] **1 :** excessive or blind patriotism **2 :** an attitude of superiority toward members of the opposite sex — **chau•vin•ist** \-nist\ *n or adj* — **chau•vin•is•tic** \ˌshō-və-ˈnis-tik\ *adj* — **chau•vin•is•ti•cal•ly** \-ti-k(ə-)lē\ *adv*
cheap \ˈchēp\ *adj* **1 :** INEXPENSIVE **2 :** costing little effort to obtain **3 :** worth little : SHODDY, TAWDRY **4 :** worthy of scorn **5 :** STINGY — **cheap** *adv* — **cheap•ly** *adv* — **cheap•ness** *n*
cheap•en \ˈchē-pən\ *vb* **1 :** to make or become cheap or cheaper in price or value **2 :** to make tawdry
cheap•skate \ˈchēp-ˌskāt\ *n* : a miserly or stingy person; *esp* : one who tries to avoid paying a fair share of costs
[1]**cheat** \ˈchēt\ *vb* **1 :** to deprive of something through fraud or deceit **2 :** to practice fraud or trickery **3 :** to violate rules (as of a game) dishonestly — **cheat•er** *n*
[2]**cheat** *n* **1 :** the act of deceiving : FRAUD, DECEPTION **2 :** one that cheats : a dishonest person
[1]**check** \ˈchek\ *n* **1 :** a sudden stoppage of progress **2 :** a sudden pause or break **3 :** something that stops or restrains **4 :** a standard for testing or evaluation **5 :** EXAMINATION, INVESTIGATION **6 :** the act of testing or verifying **7 :** a written order to a bank to pay money **8 :** a ticket or token showing ownership or identity **9 :** a slip indicating an amount due **10 :** a pattern in squares; *also* : a fabric in such a pattern **11 :** a mark typically ✓ placed beside an item to show that it has been noted **12 :** CRACK, SPLIT
[2]**check** *vb* **1 :** to slow down or stop : BRAKE **2 :** to restrain the action or force of : CURB **3 :** to compare with a source, original, or authority : VERIFY **4 :** to inspect or test for satisfactory condition **5 :** to mark with a check as examined **6 :** to consign for shipment for one holding a passenger ticket **7 :** to mark into squares **8 :** to leave or accept for safekeeping in a checkroom **9 :** to prove to be consistent or truthful **10 :** CRACK, SPLIT
check•book \ˈchek-ˌbu̇k\ *n* : a book containing blank checks
[1]**check•er** \ˈche-kər\ *n* : a piece in the game of checkers
[2]**checker** *vb* **1 :** to variegate with different colors or shades **2 :** to vary with contrasting elements ⟨a ~*ed* career⟩ **3 :** to mark into squares
[3]**checker** *n* : one that checks; *esp* : one who checks out purchases in a supermarket
check•er•ber•ry \ˈche-kər-ˌber-ē\ *n* : WINTERGREEN 1; *also* : the spicy red fruit of this plant
check•er•board \-ˌbōrd\ *n* : a board of 64 squares of alternate colors used in various games
check•ers \ˈche-kərz\ *n* : a game for two played on a checkerboard with each player having 12 pieces
check in *vb* : to report one's presence or arrival (as at a hotel)
check•list \ˈchek-ˌlist\ *n* : a list of things to be checked or done; *also* : a comprehensive list
check•mate \ˈchek-ˌmāt\ *vb* [ME *chekmaten*, fr. *chekmate*, interj. used to announce checkmate, fr. MF *eschec mat*, fr. Ar *shāh māt*, fr. Per, lit., the king is left unable to escape] **1 :** to thwart completely : DEFEAT, FRUSTRATE **2 :** to attack (an opponent's king) in chess so that escape is impossible — **checkmate** *n*
check•off \ˈche-ˌkȯf\ *n* : the deduction of union dues from a worker's paycheck by the employer
check•out \ˈche-ˌkau̇t\ *n* **1 :** the action or an instance of checking out **2 :** a counter at which checking out is done **3 :** the process of examining and testing something as to readiness for intended use
check out *vb* **1 :** to settle one's account (as at a hotel) and leave **2 :** to total or have totaled the cost of purchases in a store and to make or receive payment for them
check•point \ˈchek-ˌpȯint\ *n* : a point at which a check is performed
check•room \-ˌrüm, -ˌru̇m\ *n* : a room at which baggage, parcels, or clothing is checked
check•up \ˈche-ˌkəp\ *n* : EXAMINATION; *esp* : a general physical examination
ched•dar \ˈche-dər\ *n, often cap* : a hard mild to sharp white or yellow cheese of smooth texture
cheek \ˈchēk\ *n* **1 :** the fleshy side part of the face **2 :** IMPUDENCE, BOLDNESS, AUDACITY **3 :** BUTTOCK 1 — **cheeked** \ˈchēkt\ *adj*
cheek•bone \ˈchēk-ˌbōn\ *n* : the bone or bony ridge below the eye
cheeky \ˈchē-kē\ *adj* **cheek•i•er; -est** : IMPUDENT, SAUCY — **cheek•i•ly** \-kə-lē\ *adv* — **cheek•i•ness** \-kē-nəs\ *n*
cheep \ˈchēp\ *vb* : to utter faint shrill sounds : PEEP — **cheep** *n*
[1]**cheer** \ˈchir\ *n* [ME *chere* face, cheer, fr. OF, face, fr. ML *cara*, prob. fr. Gk *kara* head, face] **1 :** state of mind or heart : SPIRIT **2 :** ANIMATION, GAIETY **3 :** hospitable entertainment : WELCOME **4 :** food and drink for a feast **5 :** something that gladdens **6 :** a shout of applause or encouragement
[2]**cheer** *vb* **1 :** to give hope or courage to : COMFORT **2 :** to make glad **3 :** to urge on esp. by shouts **4 :** to applaud with shouts **5 :** to grow or be cheerful — usu. used with *up* — **cheer•er** *n*
cheer•ful \ˈchir-fəl\ *adj* **1 :** having or showing good spirits **2 :** conducive to good spirits : pleasant and bright — **cheer•ful•ly** *adv* — **cheer•ful•ness** *n*
cheer•lead•er \ˈchir-ˌlē-dər\ *n* : a person who directs organized cheering esp. at a sports event
cheer•less \ˈchir-ləs\ *adj* : BLEAK, DISPIRITING — **cheer•less•ly** *adv* — **cheer•less•ness** *n*

cheery \ˈchir-ē\ *adj* **cheer•i•er; -est** : CHEERFUL — **cheer•i•ly** \-ə-lē\ *adv* — **cheer•i•ness** \-ē-nəs\ *n*

cheese \ˈchēz\ *n* : the curd of milk usu. pressed into cakes and cured for use as food

cheese•burg•er \-ˌbər-gər\ *n* : a hamburger topped with cheese

cheese•cake \-ˌkāk\ *n* **1** : a dessert consisting of a creamy filling usu. containing cheese baked in a shell **2** : photographs of shapely scantily clad women

cheese•cloth \-ˌklȯth\ *n* : a lightweight coarse cotton gauze

cheese•par•ing \-ˌpar-iŋ\ *n* : miserly economizing — **cheeseparing** *adj*

cheesy \ˈchē-zē\ *adj* **chees•i•er; -est** **1** : resembling, suggesting, or containing cheese **2** *slang* : CHEAP 3

chee•tah \ˈchē-tə\ *n* [Hindu *cītā* leopard, fr. Skt *citraka*, fr. *citra* bright, variegated] : a large long-legged spotted swift-moving African and formerly Asian cat

cheetah

chef \ˈshef\ *n* **1** : a cook who manages the kitchen (as of a restaurant) **2** : COOK

chef d'oeu•vre \shā-ˈdœvrᵊ\ *n, pl* **chefs d'oeuvre** *same* \ : MASTERPIECE

chem *abbr* chemical; chemist; chemistry

[1]**chem•i•cal** \ˈke-mi-kəl\ *adj* **1** : of, relating to, used in, or produced by chemistry **2** : acting or operated or produced by chemicals — **chem•i•cal•ly** \-k(ə-)lē\ *adv*

[2]**chemical** *n* : a substance obtained by a chemical process or used for producing a chemical effect

chemical engineering *n* : engineering dealing with the industrial application of chemistry

chemical warfare *n* : warfare using incendiary mixtures, smokes, or irritant, burning, or asphyxiating gases

chemical weapon *n* : a weapon used in chemical warfare

che•mise \shə-ˈmēz\ *n* **1** : a woman's one-piece undergarment **2** : a loose straight-hanging dress

chem•ist \ˈke-mist\ *n* **1** : one trained in chemistry **2** *Brit* : PHARMACIST

chem•is•try \ˈke-mə-strē\ *n, pl* **-tries** **1** : the science that deals with the composition, structure, and properties of substances and of the changes they undergo **2** : chemical composition or properties ⟨the ~ of gasoline⟩ **3** : a strong mutual attraction

che•mo•ther•a•py \ˌkē-mō-ˈther-ə-pē\ *n* : the use of chemicals in the treatment or control of disease — **che•mo•ther•a•peu•tic** \-ˌther-ə-ˈpyü-tik\ *adj*

che•nille \shə-ˈnēl\ *n* [F, lit., caterpillar, fr. L *canicula*, dim. of *canis* dog] : a fabric with a deep fuzzy pile often used for bedspreads and rugs

cheque \ˈchek\ *chiefly Brit var of* [1]CHECK 7

che•quer *chiefly Brit var of* CHECKER

cher•ish \ˈcher-ish\ *vb* **1** : to hold dear : treat with care and affection **2** : to keep deeply in mind — **cher•ish•able** *adj* — **cher•ish•er** *n*

Cher•o•kee \ˈcher-ə-(ˌ)kē\ *n, pl* **Cherokee** *or* **Cherokees** : a member of an American Indian people orig. of Tennessee and No. Carolina; *also* : their language

che•root \shə-ˈrüt\ *n* : a cigar cut square at both ends

cher•ry \ˈcher-ē\ *n, pl* **cherries** [ME *chery*, fr. OF *cherise* (taken as a plural), fr. LL *ceresia*, fr. L *cerasus* cherry tree, fr. Gk *kerasos*] **1** : the small fleshy pale yellow to deep blackish red fruit of a tree related to the roses; *also* : the tree or its wood **2** : a moderate red

chert \ˈchərt, ˈchat\ *n* : a rock resembling flint and consisting essentially of fine crystalline quartz and fibrous chalcedony — **cherty** *adj*

cher•ub \ˈcher-əb\ *n* **1** *pl* **cher•u•bim** \ˈcher-ə-ˌbim\ : an angel of the 2d highest rank **2** *pl* **cherubs** : a chubby rosy person — **che•ru•bic** \chə-ˈrü-bik\ *adj*

chess \ˈches\ *n* : a game for two played on a chessboard with each player having 16 pieces — **chessman** \-ˌman, -mən\ *n*

chess•board \ˈches-ˌbōrd\ *n* : a checkerboard used in the game of chess

chest \ˈchest\ *n* **1** : a box, case, or boxlike receptacle for storage or shipping **2** : the part of the body enclosed by the ribs and sternum — **chest•ed** \ˈches-təd\ *adj* — **chest•ful** \ˈchest-ˌfu̇l\ *n*

ches•ter•field \ˈches-tər-ˌfēld\ *n* : an overcoat with a velvet collar

chest•nut \ˈches-(ˌ)nət\ *n* **1** : the edible nut of any of a genus of trees related to the beech and oaks; *also* : this tree **2** : a grayish to reddish brown **3** : an old joke or story

chet•rum \ˈche-trəm\ *n, pl* **chetrums** *or* **chetrum** — see *ngultrum* at MONEY table

che•val glass \shə-ˈval-\ *n* : a full-length mirror that may be tilted in a frame

che•va•lier \ˌshe-və-ˈlir, shə-ˈval-ˌyā\ *n* : a member of one of various orders of knighthood or of merit

chev•i•ot \ˈshe-vē-ət\ *n, often cap* **1** : a twilled fabric with a rough nap **2** : a sturdy soft-finished cotton fabric

chev•ron \ˈshe-vrən\ *n* : a sleeve badge of one or more V-shaped or inverted V-shaped stripes worn to indicate rank or service (as in the armed forces)

[1]**chew** \ˈchü\ *vb* : to crush or grind with the teeth — **chew•able** *adj* — **chew•er** *n*

[2]**chew** *n* **1** : an act of chewing **2** : something for chewing

chewy \ˈchü-ē\ *adj* : requiring much chewing ⟨~ candy⟩

Chey•enne \shī-ˈan, -ˈen\ *n, pl* **Cheyenne** *or* **Cheyennes** [CanF, fr. Dakota *šahíyena*] : a member of an American Indian people of the western plains of the U.S.; *also* : their language

chg *abbr* **1** change **2** charge

chi \ˈkī\ *n* : the 22d letter of the Greek alphabet — X or χ

Chi•an•ti \kē-ˈän-tē, -ˈan-\ *n* : a dry usu. red wine

chiar•oscu•ro \kē-ˌär-ə-ˈsku̇r-ō, -ˈskyu̇r-\ *n, pl* **-ros** [It, fr. *chiaro* clear, light + *oscuro* obscure, dark] **1** : pictorial representation in terms of light and shade without regard to color **2** : the arrangement or treatment of light and dark parts in a pictorial work of art

[1]**chic** \ˈshēk\ *n* : STYLISHNESS

[2]**chic** *adj* : cleverly stylish : SMART; *also* : currently fashionable

Chi•ca•na \chi-ˈkä-nə *also* shi-\ *n* : an American woman or girl of Mexican descent — **Chicana** *adj*

chi•cane \shi-ˈkān\ *n* : CHICANERY

chi•ca•nery \-ˈka-nə-rē\ *n, pl* **-ner•ies** : TRICKERY, DECEPTION

Chi•ca•no \chi-ˈkä-nō\ *n, pl* **-nos** : an American of Mexican descent — **Chicano** *adj*

chi•chi \ˈshē-(ˌ)shē, ˈchē-(ˌ)chē\ *adj* [F] **1** : SHOWY, FRILLY **2** : ARTY, PRECIOUS **3** : CHIC — **chichi** *n*

chick \ˈchik\ *n* **1** : a young chicken; *also* : a young bird **2** *slang* : a young woman

chick•a•dee \ˈchi-kə-(ˌ)dē\ *n* : any of several small grayish American birds with black or brown caps

Chick•a•saw \ˈchi-kə-ˌsȯ\ *n, pl* **Chickasaw** *or* **Chickasaws** : a member of an American Indian people of Mississippi and Alabama

[1]**chick•en** \ˈchi-kən\ *n* **1** : a common domestic fowl esp. when young; *also* : its flesh used as food **2** : COWARD

[2]**chicken** *adj* **1** : COWARDLY **2** *slang* : insistent on petty esp. military discipline

chicken feed *n, slang* : an insignificant sum of money

chick•en•heart•ed \ˌchi-kən-ˈhär-təd\ *adj* : TIMID, COWARDLY
chicken out *vb* : to lose one's courage
chicken pox *n* : an acute contagious virus disease esp. of children characterized by a low fever and vesicles
chicken wire *n* : a light wire netting of hexagonal mesh
chick–pea \ˈchik-ˌpē\ *n* : an Asian leguminous herb cultivated for its short pods with one or two edible seeds; *also* : its seed
chick•weed \ˈchik-ˌwēd\ *n* : any of several low-growing small-leaved weeds related to the pinks
chi•cle \ˈchi-kəl\ *n* : a gum from the latex of a tropical tree used as the chief ingredient of chewing gum
chic•o•ry \ˈchi-kə-rē\ *n, pl* **-ries** : a usu. blue-flowered herb related to the daisies and grown for its root and for use in salads; *also* : its dried ground root used to flavor or adulterate coffee
chide \ˈchīd\ *vb* **chid** \ˈchid\ *or* **chid•ed** \ˈchī-dəd\; **chid** *or* **chid•den** \ˈchid-ᵊn\ *or* **chided; chid•ing** : to speak disapprovingly to **syn** reproach, reprove, reprimand, admonish, scold, rebuke
¹chief \ˈchēf\ *adj* **1** : highest in rank **2** : most important **syn** principal, main, leading, major — **chief•ly** *adv*
²chief *n* **1** : the leader of a body or organization : HEAD **2** : the principal or most valuable part — **chief•dom** *n*
chief master sergeant *n* : a noncommissioned officer of the highest rank in the air force
chief of staff 1 : the ranking officer of a staff in the armed forces **2** : the ranking office of the army or air force
chief of state : the formal head of a national state as distinguished from the head of the government
chief petty officer *n* : an enlisted man in the navy ranking next below a senior chief petty officer
chief•tain \ˈchēf-tən\ *n* : a chief esp. of a band, tribe, or clan — **chief•tain•cy** \-sē\ *n* — **chief•tain•ship** *n*
chief warrant officer *n* : a warrant officer of senior rank
chif•fon \shi-ˈfän, ˈshi-ˌ\ *n* [F, lit., rag, fr. *chiffe* old rag] : a sheer fabric esp. of silk
chif•fo•nier \ˌshi-fə-ˈnir\ *n* : a high narrow chest of drawers
chig•ger \ˈchi-gər\ *n* : a bloodsucking larval mite that causes intense itching
chi•gnon \ˈshēn-ˌyän\ *n* [F, fr. MF *chignon* chain, collar, nape] : a knot of hair worn at the back of the head
Chi•hua•hua \chə-ˈwä-ˌwä\ *n* : any of a breed of very small large-eared dogs that originated in Mexico
chil•blain \ˈchil-ˌblān\ *n* : a sore or inflamed swelling (as on the feet or hands) caused by exposure to cold
child \ˈchīld\ *n, pl* **chil•dren** \ˈchil-drən\ **1** : an unborn or recently born person **2** : a young person between the periods of infancy and youth **3** : a male or female offspring : SON, DAUGHTER **4** : one strongly influenced by another or by a place or state of affairs — **child•ish** *adj* — **child•ish•ly** *adv* — **child•ish•ness** *n* — **child•less** *adj* — **child•less•ness** *n* — **child•like** *adj*
child•bear•ing \ˈchīld-ˌbar-iŋ\ *n* : CHILDBIRTH — **childbearing** *adj*
child•birth \-ˌbərth\ *n* : the act or process of giving birth to offspring
child•hood \-ˌhu̇d\ *n* : the state or time of being a child
child•proof \-ˌprüf\ *adj* : made to prevent tampering or opening by children
child's play *n* : a simple task or act
Chil•ean \ˈchi-lē-ən, chə-ˈlā-ən\ *n* : a native or inhabitant of Chile — **Chilean** *adj*
chili *or* **chile** *or* **chil•li** \ˈchi-lē\ *n, pl* **chil•ies** *or* **chil•es** *or* **chil•lies 1** : a pungent pepper related to the tomato **2** : a thick sauce of meat and chilies **3** : CHILI CON CARNE
chili con car•ne \ˌchi-lē-kän-ˈkär-nē\ *n* [Sp *chile con carne* chili with meat] : a spiced stew of ground beef and chilies or chili powder usu. with beans
chili powder *n* : a seasoning made of ground chilies and other spices
chili sauce *n* : a spiced tomato sauce usu. made with red and green peppers
¹chill \ˈchil\ *n* **1** : a feeling of coldness accompanied by shivering **2** : moderate coldness **3** : a check to enthusiasm or warmth of feeling
²chill *adj* **1** : moderately cold **2** : COLD, RAW **3** : DISTANT, FORMAL ⟨a ~ reception⟩ **4** : DEPRESSING, DISPIRITING
³chill *vb* **1** : to make or become cold or chilly **2** : to make cool esp. without freezing — **chill•er** *n*
chilly \ˈchi-lē\ *adj* **chill•i•er; -est 1** : noticeably cold **2** : unpleasantly affected by cold **3** : lacking warmth of feeling — **chill•i•ness** *n*
¹chime \ˈchīm\ *n* **1** : a set of bells musically tuned **2** : the sound of a set of bells — usu. used in pl. **3** : a musical sound suggesting bells
²chime *vb* **chimed; chim•ing 1** : to make bell-like sounds **2** : to indicate (as the time of day) by chiming **3** : to be or act in accord : be in harmony
chime in *vb* : to break into or join in a conversation
chi•me•ra *or* **chi•mae•ra** \kī-ˈmir-ə, kə-\ *n* [L *chimaera*, fr. Gk *chimaira* she-goat, chimera] **1** : an imaginary monster made up of incongruous parts **2** : an illusion or fabrication of the mind; *esp* : an impossible dream
chi•mer•i•cal \ki-ˈmer-i-kəl\ *also* **chi•mér•ic** \-ik\ *adj* **1** : FANTASTIC, IMAGINARY **2** : inclined to fantastic schemes
chim•ney \ˈchim-nē\ *n, pl* **chimneys 1** : a vertical structure extending above the roof of a building for carrying off smoke **2** : a glass tube around a lamp flame
chimp \ˈchimp\ *n* : CHIMPANZEE
chim•pan•zee \ˌchim-ˌpan-ˈzē, chim-ˈpan-zē\ *n* : an African ape related to the much larger gorilla
¹chin \ˈchin\ *n* : the part of the face below the lower lip including the prominence of the lower jaw — **chin•less** *adj*
²chin *vb* **chinned; chin•ning** : to raise (oneself) while hanging by the hands until the chin is level with the support
chi•na \ˈchī-nə\ *n* : porcelain ware; *also* : domestic pottery in general
Chi•na•town \-ˌtau̇n\ *n* : the Chinese quarter of a city
chinch bug \ˈchinch-\ *n* : a small black and white bug destructive to cereal grasses
chin•chil•la \chin-ˈchi-lə\ *n* **1** : either of two small So. American rodents with soft pearl-gray fur; *also* : this fur **2** : a heavy long-napped woolen cloth

chinchilla 1

chine \ˈchīn\ *n* : BACKBONE, SPINE; *also* : a cut of meat including all or part of the backbone
Chi•nese \chī-ˈnēz, -ˈnēs\ *n, pl* **Chinese 1** : a native or inhabitant of China **2** : any of a group of related languages of China — **Chinese** *adj*
Chinese cabbage *n* **1** : BOK CHOY **2** : an Asian garden plant related to the cabbage and widely grown in the U.S. for its tight elongate cylindrical heads of pale green to cream-colored leaves
Chinese checkers *n* : a game in which each player in

turn transfers a set of marbles from a home point to the opposite point of a pitted 6-pointed star

Chinese gooseberry *n* : a subtropical vine that bears kiwifruit; *also* : KIWIFRUIT

Chinese lantern *n* : a collapsible translucent cover for a light

¹**chink** \ˈchiŋk\ *n* : a small crack or fissure

²**chink** *vb* : to fill the chinks of : stop up

³**chink** *n* : a slight sharp metallic sound

⁴**chink** *vb* : to make a slight sharp metallic sound

chi•no \ˈchē-nō\ *n, pl* **chinos** **1** : a usu. khaki cotton twill **2** *pl* : an article of clothing made of chino

Chi•nook \shə-ˈnu̇k, chə-, -ˈnük\ *n, pl* **Chinook** *or* **Chinooks** : a member of an American Indian people of Oregon

chintz \ˈchints\ *n* : a usu. glazed printed cotton cloth

chintzy \ˈchint-sē\ *adj* **chintz•i•er; -est** **1** : decorated with or as if with chintz **2** : GAUDY, CHEAP **3** : STINGY

chin–up \ˈchi-ˌnəp\ *n* : the act of chinning oneself

¹**chip** \ˈchip\ *n* **1** : a small usu. thin and flat piece (as of wood) cut or broken off **2** : a thin crisp morsel of food **3** : a counter used in games (as poker) **4** *pl, slang* : MONEY **5** : a flaw left after a chip is removed **6** : INTEGRATED CIRCUIT **7** : a very small slice of silicon containing electronic circuits

²**chip** *vb* **chipped; chip•ping** **1** : to cut or break chips from **2** : to break off in small pieces at the edges **3** : to play a chip shot

chip in *vb* : CONTRIBUTE

chip•munk \ˈchip-ˌməŋk\ *n* : any of a genus of small striped No. American and Asian rodents closely related to the squirrels and marmots

chipped beef \ˈchipt-\ *n* : smoked dried beef sliced thin

¹**chip•per** \ˈchi-pər\ *n* : one that chips

²**chipper** *adj* : LIVELY, CHEERFUL

Chip•pe•wa \ˈchi-pə-ˌwȯ, -ˌwä, -ˌwā, -wə\ *n, pl* **Chippewa** *or* **Chippewas** : OJIBWA

chip shot *n* : a short usu. low shot to the green in golf

chi•rog•ra•phy \kī-ˈrä-grə-fē\ *n* : HANDWRITING, PENMANSHIP — **chi•ro•graph•ic** \ˌkī-rə-ˈgra-fik\ *adj*

chi•rop•o•dy \kə-ˈrä-pə-dē, shə-\ *n* : PODIATRY — **chi•rop•o•dist** \-dist\ *n*

chi•ro•prac•tic \ˈkī-rə-ˌprak-tik\ *n* : a system of therapy based esp. on manipulation of body structures — **chi•ro•prac•tor** \-tər\ *n*

chirp \ˈchərp\ *n* : a short sharp sound characteristic of a small bird or cricket — **chirp** *vb*

¹**chis•el** \ˈchi-zəl\ *n* : a metal tool with a sharpened edge at one end used to chip, carve, or cut into a solid material (as wood or stone)

²**chisel** *vb* **-eled** *or* **-elled; -el•ing** *or* **-el•ling** **1** : to work with or as if with a chisel **2** : to obtain by shrewd often unfair methods; *also* : CHEAT — **chis•el•er** *n*

¹**chit** \ˈchit\ *n* [ME *chitte* kitten, cub] **1** : CHILD **2** : a pert young woman

²**chit** *n* [Hindi *ciṭṭhī* letter, note] : a signed voucher for a small debt

chit•chat \ˈchit-ˌchat\ *n* : casual or trifling conversation — **chitchat** *vb*

chi•tin \ˈkīt-ᵊn\ *n* : a sugar polymer that forms part of the hard outer integument esp. of insects — **chi•tin•ous** *adj*

chit•ter•lings *or* **chit•lins** \ˈchit-lənz\ *n pl* : the intestines of hogs esp. when prepared as food

chi•val•ric \shə-ˈval-rik\ *adj* : relating to chivalry : CHIVALROUS

chiv•al•rous \ˈshi-vəl-rəs\ *adj* **1** : of or relating to chivalry **2** : marked by honor, courtesy, and generosity **3** : marked by especial courtesy to women — **chiv•al•rous•ly** *adv* — **chiv•al•rous•ness** *n*

chiv•al•ry \ˈshi-vəl-rē\ *n, pl* **-ries** **1** : mounted men-at-arms **2** : the system or practices of knighthood **3** : the spirit or character of the ideal knight

chive \ˈchīv\ *n* : an herb related to the onion that has leaves used for flavoring

chla•myd•ia \klə-ˈmi-dē-ə\ *n, pl* **-i•ae** \-dē-ˌē\ **1** : any of a genus of bacteria that cause various diseases of the eye and urogenital tract **2** : a disease or infection caused by chlamydiae

chlo•ral hydrate \ˈklōr-əl-\ *n* : a white crystalline compound used as a hypnotic and sedative

chlor•dane \ˈklȯr-ˌdān\ *n* : a highly chlorinated persistent insecticide

chlo•ride \ˈklōr-ˌīd\ *n* : a compound of chlorine with another element or group

chlo•ri•nate \ˈklōr-ə-ˌnāt\ *vb* **-nat•ed; -nat•ing** : to treat or combine with chlorine or a chlorine compound — **chlo•ri•na•tion** \ˌklōr-ə-ˈnā-shən\ *n* — **chlo•ri•na•tor** \ˈklōr-ə-ˌnā-tər\ *n*

chlo•rine \ˈklōr-ˌēn\ *n* : a nonmetallic chemical element that is found alone as a strong-smelling greenish yellow irritating gas and is used as a bleach, oxidizing agent, and disinfectant — see ELEMENT table

chlo•rite \ˈklōr-ˌīt\ *n* : a usu. green mineral found with and resembling mica

chlo•ro•flu•o•ro•car•bon \ˌklōr-ə-ˈflōr-ə-ˌkär-bən, -ˈflu̇r-\ *n* : any of several gaseous compounds that contain carbon, chlorine, fluorine, and sometimes hydrogen and are used esp. as solvents, refrigerants, and aerosol propellants

¹**chlo•ro•form** \ˈklōr-ə-ˌfȯrm\ *n* : a colorless heavy fluid with etherlike odor used as a solvent and anesthetic

²**chloroform** *vb* : to treat with chloroform to produce anesthesia or death

chlo•ro•phyll \-ˌfil\ *n* : the green coloring matter of plants that functions in photosynthesis

chm *abbr* chairman

chock \ˈchäk\ *n* : a wedge for steadying something or for blocking the movement of a wheel — **chock** *vb*

chock•a•block \ˈchä-kə-ˌbläk\ *adj* : very full : CROWDED

chock–full \ˈchək-ˈfu̇l, ˈchäk-\ *adj* : full to the limit : CRAMMED

choc•o•late \ˈchä-k(ə-)lət, ˈchȯ-\ *n* [Sp, fr. Nahuatl *chocolātl*] **1** : a food prepared from ground roasted cacao beans; *also* : a drink prepared from this **2** : a candy made of or with a coating of chocolate **3** : a dark brown color

Choc•taw \ˈchäk-ˌtȯ\ *n, pl* **Choctaw** *or* **Choctaws** : a member of an American Indian people of Mississippi, Alabama, and Louisiana; *also* : their language

¹**choice** \ˈchȯis\ *n* **1** : the act of choosing : SELECTION **2** : the power or opportunity of choosing : OPTION **3** : the best part **4** : a person or thing selected **5** : a variety offered for selection

²**choice** *adj* **choic•er; choic•est** **1** : worthy of being chosen **2** : selected with care **3** : of high quality

choir \ˈkwī(-ə)r\ *n* **1** : an organized company of singers (as in a church service) **2** : the part of a church occupied by the singers or by the clergy

choir•boy \ˈkwī(-ə)r-ˌbȯi\ *n* : a boy member of a church choir

choir•mas•ter \-ˌmas-tər\ *n* : the director of a choir (as in a church)

¹**choke** \ˈchōk\ *vb* **choked; chok•ing** **1** : to hinder breathing (as by obstructing the windpipe) : STRANGLE **2** : to check the growth or action of **3** : CLOG, OBSTRUCT **4** : to enrich the fuel mixture of (a motor) by restricting the carburetor air intake **5** : to perform badly in a critical situation

²**choke** *n* **1** : the act of choking **2** : a narrowing in size toward the muzzle in the bore of a gun **3** : a valve for choking a gasoline engine

chok•er \ˈchō-kər\ *n* : something (as a necklace) worn tightly around the neck

cho•ler \ˈkä-lər, ˈkō-\ *n* : a tendency toward anger : IRASCIBILITY

chol•era \ˈkä-lə-rə\ *n* : a disease marked by severe vomiting and dysentery; *esp* : an often fatal epidemic disease (**Asiatic cholera**) chiefly of southeastern Asia caused by a bacillus

cho•ler•ic \ˈkä-lə-rik, kə-ˈler-ik\ *adj* **1** : IRASCIBLE **2** : ANGRY, IRATE

cho•les•ter•ol \kə-ˈles-tə-ˌrȯl\ *n* : a physiologically important waxy steroid alcohol found in animal tissues and in high concentrations implicated as a cause of arteriosclerosis

chomp \ˈchämp, ˈchȯmp\ *vb* : to chew or bite on something heavily

chon \ˈchän\ *n, pl* **chon** — see *won* at MONEY table

choose \ˈchüz\ *vb* **chose** \chōz\; **cho•sen** \ˈchōz-ᵊn\; **choos•ing** \chü-ziŋ\ **1** : to select esp. after consideration **2** : DECIDE **3** : to have a preference for — **choos•er** *n*

choosy *or* **choos•ey** \ˈchü-zē\ *adj* **choos•i•er; -est** : very particular in making choices

[1]**chop** \ˈchäp\ *vb* **chopped; chop•ping** **1** : to cut by repeated blows **2** : to cut into small pieces : MINCE **3** : to strike (a ball) with a short quick downward stroke

[2]**chop** *n* **1** : a sharp downward blow or stroke **2** : a small cut of meat often including part of a rib **3** : a short abrupt motion (as of a wave)

[3]**chop** *n* **1** : an official seal or stamp **2** : a mark on goods to indicate quality or kind; *also* : QUALITY, GRADE

chop•house \ˈchäp-ˌhau̇s\ *n* : RESTAURANT

chop•per \ˈchä-pər\ *n* **1** : one that chops **2** *pl, slang* : TEETH **3** : HELICOPTER

chop•pi•ness \ˈchä-pē-nəs\ *n* : the quality or state of being choppy

[1]**chop•py** \ˈchä-pē\ *adj* **chop•pi•er; -est** **1** : rough with small waves **2** : JERKY, DISCONNECTED — **chop•pi•ly** \-pə-lē\ *adv*

[2]**choppy** *adj* **chop•pi•er; -est** : CHANGEABLE, VARIABLE ⟨a ~ wind⟩

chops \ˈchäps\ *n pl* : the fleshy covering of the jaws

chop•stick \ˈchäp-ˌstik\ *n* : one of a pair of sticks used chiefly in oriental countries for lifting food to the mouth

chop su•ey \chäp-ˈsü-ē\ *n, pl* **chop sueys** : a dish made of vegetables (as bean sprouts, bamboo shoots, water chestnuts, onions, mushrooms) and meat or fish and served with rice

cho•ral \ˈkōr-əl\ *adj* : of, relating to, or sung by a choir or chorus or in chorus — **cho•ral•ly** *adv*

cho•rale \kə-ˈral, -ˈräl\ *n* **1** : a hymn or psalm sung in church; *also* : a harmonization of a traditional melody **2** : CHORUS, CHOIR

[1]**chord** \ˈkȯrd\ *n* [alter. of ME *cord,* short for *accord*] : three or more musical tones sounded simultaneously

[2]**chord** *n* **1** : CORD 2 **2** : a straight line joining two points on a curve

chore \ˈchōr\ *n* **1** *pl* : the daily light work of a household or farm **2** : a routine task or job **3** : a difficult or disagreeable task

cho•rea \kə-ˈrē-ə\ *n* : a nervous disorder marked by spasmodic uncontrolled movements

cho•re•og•ra•phy \ˌkōr-ē-ˈä-grə-fē\ *n, pl* **-phies** : the art of composing and arranging dances and esp. ballets — **cho•reo•graph** \ˈkōr-ē-ə-ˌgraf\ *vb* — **cho•re•og•ra•pher** \ˌkōr-ē-ˈä-grə-fər\ *n* — **cho•reo•graph•ic** \ˌkōr-ē-ə-ˈgra-fik\ *adj* — **cho•reo•graph•i•cal•ly** \-fi-k(ə-)lē\ *adv*

cho•ris•ter \ˈkōr-ə-stər\ *n* : a singer in a choir

chor•tle \ˈchȯrt-ᵊl\ *vb* **chor•tled; chor•tling** : to laugh or chuckle esp. in satisfaction or exultation — **chortle** *n*

[1]**chorus** \ˈkōr-əs\ *n* **1** : an organized company of singers : CHOIR **2** : a group of dancers and singers (as in a musical comedy) **3** : a part of a song repeated at intervals **4** : a composition to be sung by a chorus; *also* : group singing **5** : sounds uttered by a number of persons or animals together ⟨a ~ of boos⟩

[2]**chorus** *vb* : to sing or utter in chorus

chose *past of* CHOOSE

cho•sen \ˈchōz-ᵊn\ *adj* : selected or marked for special favor or privilege

[1]**chow** \ˈchau̇\ *n* : FOOD

[2]**chow** *vb* : EAT — often used with *down*

[3]**chow** *n* : CHOW CHOW

chow•chow \ˈchau̇-ˌchau̇\ *n* : chopped mixed pickles in mustard sauce

chow chow \ˈchau̇-ˌchau̇\ *n* : any of a breed of thick-coated straight-legged muscular dogs of Chinese origin with a blue-black tongue and a short tail curled close to the back

chow•der \ˈchau̇-dər\ *n* : a soup or stew made from seafood or vegetables and containing milk or tomatoes

chow mein \ˈchau̇-ˈmān\ *n* : a seasoned stew of shredded or diced meat, mushrooms, and vegetables that is usu. served with fried noodles

chrism \ˈkri-zəm\ *n* : consecrated oil used esp. in baptism, confirmation, and ordination

Christ \ˈkrīst\ *n* [L *Christus,* fr. Gk *Christos,* lit., anointed] : Jesus esp. as the Messiah — **Christ•like** *adj* — **Christ•ly** *adj*

chris•ten \ˈkris-ᵊn\ *vb* **1** : BAPTIZE **2** : to name at baptism **3** : to name or dedicate (as a ship) by a ceremony suggestive of baptism — **chris•ten•ing** *n*

Chris•ten•dom \ˈkris-ᵊn-dəm\ *n* **1** : CHRISTIANITY **2** : the part of the world in which Christianity prevails

[1]**Chris•tian** \ˈkris-chən\ *n* : an adherent of Christianity

[2]**Christian** *adj* **1** : of or relating to Christianity **2** : based on or conforming with Christianity **3** : of or relating to a Christian **4** : professing Christianity

chris•ti•an•ia \ˌkris-chē-ˈa-nē-ə, ˌkris-tē-\ *n* : CHRISTIE

Chris•ti•an•i•ty \ˌkris-chē-ˈa-nə-tē\ *n* : the religion derived from Jesus Christ, based on the Bible as sacred scripture, and professed by Christians

Chris•tian•ize \ˈkris-chə-ˌnīz\ *vb* **-ized; -iz•ing** : to make Christian

Christian name *n* : GIVEN NAME

Christian Science *n* : a religion and system of healing founded by Mary Baker Eddy and taught by the Church of Christ, Scientist — **Christian Scientist** *n*

chris•tie *or* **chris•ty** \ˈkris-tē\ *n, pl* **christies** : a skiing turn made by shifting body weight forward and skidding into a turn with parallel skis

Christ•mas \ˈkris-məs\ *n* : December 25 celebrated as a church festival in commemoration of the birth of Christ and observed as a legal holiday

Christmas club *n* : a savings account in which regular deposits are made to provide money for Christmas shopping

Christ•mas•tide \ˈkris-məs-ˌtīd\ *n* : the season of Christmas

chro•mat•ic \krō-ˈma-tik\ *adj* **1** : of or relating to color **2** : proceeding by half steps of the musical scale — **chro•mat•i•cism** \-tə-ˌsi-zəm\ *n*

chro•mato•graph \krō-ˈma-tə-ˌgraf\ *n* : an instrument used in chromatography

chro•ma•tog•ra•phy \ˌkrō-mə-ˈtä-grə-fē\ *n* : the separation of a complex mixture into its component compounds as a result of the different rates at which the compounds travel through or over a stationary substance due to differing affinities for the substance — **chro•mato•graph•ic** \krō-ˌma-tə-ˈgra-fik\ *adj* — **chro•mato•graph•i•cal•ly** \-fi-k(ə-)lē\ *adv*

chrome \ˈkrōm\ *n* **1** : CHROMIUM **2** : a chromium pigment **3** : something plated with an alloy of chromium

chro•mi•um \ˈkrō-mē-əm\ *n* : a bluish white metallic element used esp. in alloys and chrome plating — see ELEMENT table

chro•mo•some \ˈkrō-mə-ˌsōm, -ˌzōm\ *n* : any of the linear or sometimes circular DNA-containing bodies of viruses, bacteria, and the nucleus of higher organisms that contain most or all of the individual's genes — **chro•mo•som•al** \ˌkrō-mə-ˈsō-məl, -ˈzō-\ *adj*

chro•mo•sphere \ˈkrō-mə-ˌsfir\ *n* : the lower part of a star's atmosphere

chron *abbr* **1** chronicle **2** chronological; chronology

Chron *abbr* Chronicles

chron•ic \ˈkrä-nik\ *adj* : marked by long duration or

frequent recurrence ⟨a ~ disease⟩; *also* : HABITUAL ⟨a ~ grumbler⟩ — **chron•i•cal•ly** \-ni-k(ə-)lē\ *adv*

[1]**chron•i•cle** \ˈkrä-ni-kəl\ *n* : HISTORY, NARRATIVE

[2]**chronicle** *vb* **-cled; -cling** : to record in or as if in a chronicle — **chron•i•cler** *n*

Chronicles *n* — see BIBLE table

chro•no•graph \ˈkrä-nə-ˌgraf\ *n* : an instrument for measuring and recording time intervals with accuracy — **chro•no•graph•ic** \ˌkrä-nə-ˈgra-fik\ *adj* — **chro•nog•ra•phy** \krə-ˈnä-grə-fē\ *n*

chro•nol•o•gy \krə-ˈnä-lə-jē\ *n, pl* **-gies** **1** : the science that deals with measuring time and dating events **2** : a chronological list or table **3** : arrangement of events in the order of their occurrence — **chron•o•log•i•cal** \ˌkrän-ᵊl-ˈä-ji-kəl\ *adj* — **chron•o•log•i•cal•ly** \-k(ə-)lē\ *adv* — **chro•nol•o•gist** \krə-ˈnä-lə-jist\ *n*

chro•nom•e•ter \krə-ˈnä-mə-tər\ *n* : a very accurate timepiece

chrys•a•lid \ˈkri-sə-ləd\ *n* : CHRYSALIS

chrys•a•lis \ˈkri-sə-ləs\ *n, pl* **chry•sal•i•des** \kri-ˈsa-lə-ˌdēz\ *or* **chrys•a•lis•es** : an insect pupa in a firm case without a cocoon

chry•san•the•mum \kri-ˈsan-thə-məm\ *n* [L, fr. Gk *chrysanthemon*, fr. *chrysos* gold + *anthemon* flower] : any of various plants related to the daisies including some grown for their showy flowers or for medicinal products or insecticides; *also* : a flower of a chrysanthemum

chub \ˈchəb\ *n, pl* **chub** *or* **chubs** : any of various small freshwater fishes related to the carp

chub•by \ˈchə-bē\ *adj* **chub•bi•er; -est** : PLUMP — **chub•bi•ness** *n*

[1]**chuck** \ˈchək\ *vb* **1** : to give a pat or tap **2** : TOSS **3** : DISCARD; *also* : EJECT **4** : to have done with

[2]**chuck** *n* **1** : a light pat under the chin **2** : TOSS

[3]**chuck** *n* **1** : a cut of beef including most of the neck and the parts around the shoulder blade and the first three ribs **2** : a device for holding work or a tool in a machine (as a lathe)

chuck•hole \ˈchək-ˌhōl\ *n* : POTHOLE

chuck•le \ˈchə-kəl\ *vb* **chuck•led; chuck•ling** : to laugh in a quiet hardly audible manner — **chuckle** *n*

chuck wagon *n* : a wagon equipped with a stove and food supplies

[1]**chug** \ˈchəg\ *n* : a dull explosive sound made by or as if by a laboring engine

[2]**chug** *vb* **chugged; chug•ging** : to move or go with chugs

chuk•ka \ˈchə-kə\ *n* : a usu. ankle-length leather boot

chuk•ker \ˈchə-kər\ *also* **chuk•ka** \ˈchə-kə\ *n* : a playing period of a polo game

[1]**chum** \ˈchəm\ *n* : a close friend

[2]**chum** *vb* **chummed; chum•ming** **1** : to room together **2** : to be a close friend

chum•my \ˈchə-mē\ *adj* **chum•mi•er; -est** : INTIMATE, SOCIABLE — **chum•mi•ly** \-mə-lē\ *adv* — **chum•mi•ness** \-mē-nəs\ *n*

chump \ˈchəmp\ *n* : FOOL, BLOCKHEAD

chunk \ˈchəŋk\ *n* **1** : a short thick piece **2** : a sizable amount

chunky \ˈchəŋ-kē\ *adj* **chunk•i•er; -est** **1** : STOCKY **2** : containing chunks

church \ˈchərch\ *n* [OE *cirice*, ultim. fr. LGk *kyriakon*, fr. Gk, neut. of *kyriakos* of the lord, fr. *kyrios* lord, master] **1** : a building esp. for Christian public worship **2** : the whole body of Christians **3** : DENOMINATION **4** : CONGREGATION **5** : public divine worship

church•go•er \ˈchərch-ˌgō(-ə)r\ *n* : one who habitually attends church — **church•go•ing** *adj or n*

church•less \ˈchərch-ləs\ *adj* : not affiliated with a church

church•man \ˈchərch-mən\ *n* **1** : CLERGYMAN **2** : a member of a church

church•war•den \ˈchərch-ˌwȯrd-ᵊn\ *n* : WARDEN 5

church•yard \-ˌyärd\ *n* : a yard that belongs to a church and is often used as a burial ground

churl \ˈchərl\ *n* **1** : a medieval peasant **2** : RUSTIC **3** : a rude ill-bred person — **churl•ish** *adj* — **churl•ish•ly** *adv* — **churl•ish•ness** *n*

[1]**churn** \ˈchərn\ *n* : a container in which milk or cream is violently stirred in making butter

[2]**churn** *vb* **1** : to stir in a churn; *also* : to make (butter) by such stirring **2** : to shake around violently

churn out *vb* : to produce mechanically or in large quantity

chute \ˈshüt\ *n* **1** : an inclined surface, trough, or passage down or through which something may pass ⟨a coal ~⟩ ⟨a mail ~⟩ **2** : PARACHUTE

chut•ney \ˈchət-nē\ *n, pl* **chutneys** : a thick sauce containing fruits, vinegar, sugar, and spices

chutz•pah \ˈhu̇t-spə, ˈk̲u̇t-, -(ˌ)spä\ *n* : supreme self-confidence

CIA *abbr* Central Intelligence Agency

cía *abbr* [Sp *compañía*] company

ciao \ˈchau̇\ *interj* — used to express greeting or farewell

ci•ca•da \sə-ˈkā-də\ *n* : any of a family of stout-bodied insects related to the aphids and having wide blunt heads and large transparent wings

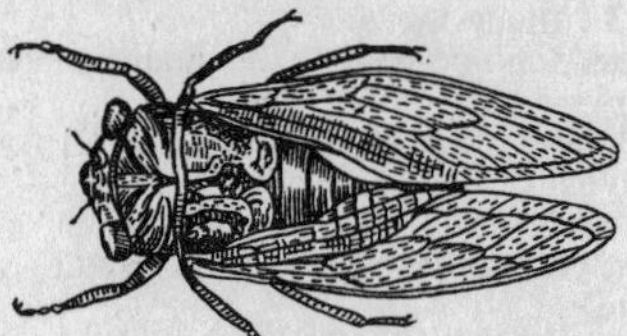

cicada

ci•ca•trix \ˈsi-kə-ˌtriks\ *n, pl* **ci•ca•tri•ces** \ˌsi-kə-ˈtrī-ˌsēz\ [L] : a scar resulting from formation and contraction of fibrous tissue in a wound

ci•ce•ro•ne \ˌsi-sə-ˈrō-nē, ˌchē-chə-\ *n, pl* **-ni** \-(ˌ)nē\ : a guide who conducts sightseers

CID *abbr* Criminal Investigation Department

ci•der \ˈsī-dər\ *n* : juice pressed from fruit (as apples) and used as a beverage, vinegar, or flavoring

cie *abbr* [F *compagnie*] company

ci•gar \si-ˈgär\ *n* : a roll of tobacco for smoking

cig•a•rette \ˌsi-gə-ˈret, ˈsi-gə-ˌret\ *n* [F, dim. of *cigare* cigar] : a slender roll of cut tobacco enclosed in paper for smoking

cig•a•ril•lo \ˌsi-gə-ˈri-lō, -ˈrē-ō\ *n, pl* **-los** [Sp] **1** : a very small cigar **2** : a cigarette wrapped in tobacco rather than paper

ci•lan•tro \si-ˈlän-trō, -ˈlan-\ *n* : leaves of coriander used as a flavoring or garnish; *also* : the coriander plant

cil•i•ate \ˈsi-lē-ˌāt\ *n* : any of a group of protozoans characterized by cilia

cil•i•um \ˈsi-lē-əm\ *n, pl* **-ia** \-lē-ə\ **1** : a minute short hairlike process; *esp* : one of a cell **2** : EYELASH

C in C *abbr* commander in chief

cinch \ˈsinch\ *n* **1** : a girth for a pack or saddle **2** : a sure or an easy thing — **cinch** *vb*

cin•cho•na \siŋ-ˈkō-nə\ *n* : any of a genus of So. American trees related to the madder; *also* : the bitter quinine-containing bark of a cinchona

cinc•ture \ˈsiŋk-chər\ *n* : BELT, SASH

cin•der \ˈsin-dər\ *n* **1** : SLAG **2** *pl* : ASHES **3** : a hot piece of partly burned wood or coal **4** : a fragment of lava from an erupting volcano — **cinder** *vb* — **cin•dery** *adj*

cinder block *n* : a building block made of cement and coal cinders

cin•e•ma \ˈsi-nə-mə\ *n* **1** : a motion-picture theater **2** : MOVIES — **cin•e•mat•ic** \ˌsi-nə-ˈma-tik\ *adj*

cin•e•ma•theque \ˌsi-nə-mə-ˈtek\ *n* : a small movie house specializing in avant-garde films

cin•e•ma•tog•ra•phy \ˌsi-nə-mə-ˈtä-grə-fē\ *n* : motion-picture photography — **cin•e•ma•tog•ra•pher** *n* — **cin•e•mat•o•graph•ic** \-ˌma-tə-ˈgra-fik\ *adj*

cin•e•plex \ˈsi-nə-ˌpleks\ *n* : a complex that houses several movie theaters

cin•er•ar•i•um \ˌsi-nə-ˈrer-ē-əm\ *n, pl* **-ia** \-ē-ə\ : a place to receive the ashes of the cremated dead — **cin•er•ary** \ˈsi-nə-ˌrer-ē\ *adj*

cin•na•bar \ˈsi-nə-ˌbär\ *n* : a red mineral that is the only important ore of mercury

cin•na•mon \ˈsi-nə-mən\ *n* : a spice prepared from the highly aromatic bark of any of several trees related to the true laurel; *also* : a tree that yields cinnamon

cinque•foil \ˈsiŋk-ˌfȯil, ˈsaŋk-\ *n* : any of a genus of plants related to the roses with leaves having five lobes

¹ci•pher \ˈsī-fər\ *n* [ME, fr. MF *cifre*, fr. ML *cifra*, fr. Ar *ṣifr* empty, zero] **1** : ZERO, NAUGHT **2** : a method of secret writing

²cipher *vb* : to compute arithmetically

cir *or* **circ** *abbr* circular

cir•ca \ˈsər-kə\ *prep* : ABOUT ⟨~ 1600⟩

cir•ca•di•an \ˌsər-ˈka-dē-ən, ˌsər-kə-ˈdī-ən\ *adj* : being, having, characterized by, or occurring in approximately 24-hour intervals (as of biological activity)

¹cir•cle \ˈsər-kəl\ *n* **1** : a closed curve every point of which is equally distant from a fixed point within it **2** : something circular **3** : an area of action or influence **4** : CYCLE **5** : a group bound by a common tie

²circle *vb* **cir•cled; cir•cling 1** : to enclose in a circle **2** : to move or revolve around; *also* : to move in a circle

cir•clet \ˈsər-klət\ *n* : a small circle; *esp* : a circular ornament

cir•cuit \ˈsər-kət\ *n* **1** : a boundary around an enclosed space **2** : a course around a periphery **3** : a regular tour (as by a judge) around an assigned territory **4** : the complete path of an electric current; *also* : an assemblage of electronic components **5** : LEAGUE; *also* : a chain of theaters — **cir•cuit•al** \-ᵊl\ *adj*

circuit breaker *n* : a switch that automatically interrupts an electric circuit under an abnormal condition

circuit court *n* : a court that sits at two or more places within one judicial district

cir•cu•i•tous \ˌsər-ˈkyü-ə-təs\ *adj* **1** : having a circular or winding course **2** : not being forthright or direct in language or action

cir•cuit•ry \ˈsər-kə-trē\ *n, pl* **-ries** : the plan or the components of an electric circuit

cir•cu•ity \ˌsər-ˈkyü-ə-tē\ *n, pl* **-ities** : INDIRECTION

¹cir•cu•lar \ˈsər-kyə-lər\ *adj* **1** : having the form of a circle : ROUND **2** : moving in or around a circle **3** : CIRCUITOUS **4** : intended for circulation ⟨a ~ letter⟩ — **cir•cu•lar•i•ty** \ˌsər-kyə-ˈlar-ə-tē\ *n*

²circular *n* : a paper (as a leaflet) intended for wide distribution

cir•cu•lar•ise *Brit var of* CIRCULARIZE

cir•cu•lar•ize \ˈsər-kyə-lə-ˌrīz\ *vb* **-ized; -iz•ing 1** : to send circulars to **2** : to poll by questionnaire

circular saw *n* : a power saw with a round cutting blade

cir•cu•late \ˈsər-kyə-ˌlāt\ *vb* **-lat•ed; -lat•ing 1** : to move or cause to move in a circle, circuit, or orbit **2** : to pass from place to place or from person to person — **cir•cu•la•tion** \ˌsər-kyə-ˈlā-shən\ *n*

cir•cu•la•to•ry \ˈsər-kyə-lə-ˌtōr-ē\ *adj* : of or relating to circulation or the circulatory system

circulatory system *n* : the system of blood, blood vessels, lymphatic vessels, and heart concerned with the circulation of the blood and lymph

cir•cum•am•bu•late \ˌsər-kəm-ˈam-byə-ˌlāt\ *vb* **-lat•ed; -lat•ing** : to circle on foot esp. as part of a ritual

cir•cum•cise \ˈsər-kəm-ˌsīz\ *vb* **-cised; -cis•ing** : to cut off the foreskin of — **cir•cum•ci•sion** \ˌsər-kəm-ˈsi-zhən\ *n*

cir•cum•fer•ence \sər-ˈkəm-f(ə-)rəns\ *n* **1** : the perimeter of a circle **2** : the external boundary or surface of a figure or object

cir•cum•flex \ˈsər-kəm-ˌfleks\ *n* : the mark ˆ over a vowel

cir•cum•lo•cu•tion \ˌsər-kəm-lō-ˈkyü-shən\ *n* : the use of unnecessary words in expressing an idea

cir•cum•lu•nar \-ˈlü-nər\ *adj* : revolving about or surrounding the moon

cir•cum•nav•i•gate \-ˈna-və-ˌgāt\ *vb* : to go completely around (as the earth) esp. by water — **cir•cum•nav•i•ga•tion** \-ˌna-və-ˈgā-shən\ *n*

cir•cum•po•lar \-ˈpō-lər\ *adj* **1** : continually visible above the horizon ⟨a ~ star⟩ **2** : surrounding or found near a pole of the earth

cir•cum•scribe \ˈsər-kəm-ˌskrīb\ *vb* **1** : to constrict the range or activity of **2** : to draw a line around — **cir•cum•scrip•tion** \ˌsər-kəm-ˈskrip-shən\ *n*

cir•cum•spect \ˈsər-kəm-ˌspekt\ *adj* : careful to consider all circumstances and consequences : PRUDENT — **cir•cum•spec•tion** \ˌsər-kəm-ˈspek-shən\ *n*

cir•cum•stance \ˈsər-kəm-ˌstans\ *n* **1** : a fact or event that must be considered along with another fact or event **2** : surrounding conditions **3** : CHANCE, FATE **4** *pl* : situation with regard to wealth **5** : CEREMONY

cir•cum•stan•tial \ˌsər-kəm-ˈstan-chəl\ *adj* **1** : consisting of or depending on circumstances **2** : INCIDENTAL **3** : containing full details — **cir•cum•stan•tial•ly** *adv*

cir•cum•vent \ˌsər-kəm-ˈvent\ *vb* : to check or defeat esp. by stratagem — **cir•cum•ven•tion** \ˈvent-shən\ *n*

cir•cus \ˈsər-kəs\ *n* **1** : a usu. traveling show that features feats of physical skill, wild animal acts, and performances by clowns **2** : a circus performance; *also* : the equipment, livestock, and personnel of a circus

cirque \ˈsərk\ *n* : a deep steep-walled mountain basin usu. forming the blunt end of a valley

cir•rho•sis \sə-ˈrō-səs\ *n, pl* **-rho•ses** \-ˌsēz\ [NL, fr. Gk *kirrhos* orange-colored] : fibrosis of the liver — **cir•rhot•ic** \-ˈrä-tik\ *adj or n*

cir•rus \ˈsir-əs\ *n, pl* **cir•ri** \ˈsir-ˌī\ : a wispy white cloud usu. of minute ice crystals at high altitudes

cis•lu•nar \(ˌ)sis-ˈlü-nər\ *adj* : lying between the earth and the moon or the moon's orbit

cis•sy *Brit var of* SISSY

cis•tern \ˈsis-tərn\ *n* : an often underground tank for storing water

cit *abbr* **1** citation; cited **2** citizen

cit•a•del \ˈsi-tə-dəl, -ˌdel\ *n* **1** : a fortress commanding a city **2** : STRONGHOLD

ci•ta•tion \sī-ˈtā-shən\ *n* **1** : an official summons to appear (as before a court) **2** : QUOTATION **3** : a formal statement of the achievements of a person; *also* : a specific reference in a military dispatch to meritorious performance of duty

cite \ˈsīt\ *vb* **cit•ed; cit•ing 1** : to summon to appear before a court **2** : QUOTE **3** : to refer to esp. in commendation or praise

cit•i•fied \ˈsi-ti-ˌfīd\ *adj* : of, relating to, or characterized by an urban style of living

cit•i•zen \ˈsi-tə-zən\ *n* **1** : an inhabitant of a city or town **2** : a person who owes allegiance to a government and is entitled to its protection — **cit•i•zen•ship** *n*

cit•i•zen•ry \-rē\ *n, pl* **-ries** : a whole body of citizens

citizens band *n* : a range of radio frequencies set aside for private radio communications

cit•ric acid \ˈsi-trik-\ *n* : a sour organic acid obtained from lemon and lime juices or by fermentation of sugars and used as a flavoring

cit•ron \ˈsi-trən\ *n* **1** : the oval lemonlike fruit of an Asian citrus tree; *also* : the tree **2** : a small hard-fleshed watermelon used esp. in pickles and preserves

cit•ro•nel•la \ˌsi-trə-ˈne-lə\ *n* : an oil obtained from a fragrant grass of southern Asia and used in perfumes and as an insect repellent

cit•rus \ˈsi-trəs\ *n, pl* **citrus** *or* **cit•rus•es** : any of a genus of often thorny evergreen trees or shrubs grown in warm regions for their fruits (as the orange, lemon, lime, and grapefruit); *also* : the fruit

city \ˈsi-tē\ *n, pl* **cit·ies** [ME *citie* large or small town, fr. OF *cité*, fr. ML *civitas*, fr. L, citizenship, state, city of Rome, fr. *civis* citizen] **1** : an inhabited place larger or more important than a town **2** : a municipality in the U.S. governed under a charter granted by the state; *also* : an incorporated municipal unit of the highest class in Canada

city manager *n* : an official employed by an elected council to direct the administration of a city government

city–state \ˈsi-tē-ˌstāt\ *n* : an autonomous state consisting of a city and surrounding territory

civ *abbr* **1** civil; civilian **2** civilization

civ·et \ˈsi-vət\ *n* : a yellowish strong-smelling substance obtained from a catlike mammal (**civet cat**) of Africa or Asia and used in making perfumes

civ·ic \ˈsi-vik\ *adj* : of or relating to a city, citizenship, or civil affairs

civ·ics \-viks\ *n* : a social science dealing with the rights and duties of citizens

civ·il \ˈsi-vəl\ *adj* **1** : of or relating to citizens or to the state as a political body **2** : COURTEOUS, POLITE **3** : of or relating to legal proceedings in connection with private rights and obligations ⟨the ~ code⟩ **4** : of or relating to the general population : not military or ecclesiastical

civil defense *n* : protective measures and emergency relief activities conducted by civilians in case of enemy attack or natural disaster

civil disobedience *n* : refusal to obey governmental commands esp. as a nonviolent means of protest

civil engineer *n* : an engineer whose training or occupation is in the design and construction esp. of public works (as roads or harbors) — **civil engineering** *n*

ci·vil·ian \sə-ˈvil-yən\ *n* : a person not on active duty in a military, police, or fire-fighting force

civ·i·li·sa·tion, civ·i·lise *chiefly Brit var of* CIVILIZATION, CIVILIZE

ci·vil·i·ty \sə-ˈvi-lə-tē\ *n, pl* **-ties 1** : POLITENESS, COURTESY **2** : a polite act or expression

civ·i·li·za·tion \ˌsi-və-lə-ˈzā-shən\ *n* **1** : a relatively high level of cultural and technological development **2** : the culture characteristic of a time or place

civ·i·lize \ˈsi-və-ˌlīz\ *vb* **-lized; -liz·ing 1** : to raise from a primitive state to an advanced and ordered stage of cultural development **2** : REFINE — **civ·i·lized** *adj*

civil liberty *n* : freedom from arbitrary governmental interference specifically by denial of governmental power — usu. used in pl.

civ·il·ly \ˈsi-vəl-lē\ *adv* **1** : in terms of civil rights, matters, or law ⟨~ dead⟩ **2** : in a civil manner : POLITELY

civil rights *n pl* : the nonpolitical rights of a citizen; *esp* : those guaranteed by the 13th and 14th amendments to the Constitution and by acts of Congress

civil servant *n* : a member of a civil service

civil service *n* : the administrative service of a government

civil war *n* : a war between opposing groups of citizens of the same country

civ·vies \ˈsi-vēz\ *n pl* : civilian clothes as distinguished from a military uniform

CJ *abbr* chief justice

ck *abbr* **1** cask **2** check

cl *abbr* **1** centiliter **2** class

Cl *symbol* chlorine

[1]**clack** \ˈklak\ *vb* **1** : CHATTER, PRATTLE **2** : to make or cause to make a clatter

[2]**clack** *n* **1** : rapid continuous talk : CHATTER **2** : a sound of clacking ⟨the ~ of a typewriter⟩

clad \ˈklad\ *adj* **1** : CLOTHED, COVERED **2** : being or consisting of coins made of outer layers of one metal bonded to a core of a different metal

[1]**claim** \ˈklām\ *vb* [ME, fr. MF *clamer*, fr. L *clamare* to cry out, shout] **1** : to ask for as one's own; *also* : to take as the rightful owner **2** : to call for : REQUIRE **3** : to state as a fact : MAINTAIN

[2]**claim** *n* **1** : a demand for something due **2** : a right to something usu. in another's possession **3** : an assertion open to challenge **4** : something claimed (as a tract of land)

claim·ant \ˈklā-mənt\ *n* : a person making a claim

clair·voy·ant \klar-ˈvȯi-ənt\ *adj* [F, fr. *clair* clear + *voyant* seeing] **1** : unusually perceptive **2** : having the power of discerning objects not present to the senses — **clair·voy·ance** \-əns\ *n* — **clairvoyant** *n*

clam \ˈklam\ *n* **1** : any of numerous bivalve mollusks including many that are edible **2** : DOLLAR

clam·bake \-ˌbāk\ *n* : a party or gathering (as at the seashore) at which food is cooked usu. on heated rocks covered by seaweed

clam·ber \ˈklam-bər\ *vb* : to climb awkwardly — **clam·ber·er** *n*

clam·my \ˈkla-mē\ *adj* **clam·mi·er; -est** : being damp, soft, sticky, and usu. cool — **clam·mi·ness** *n*

clam·or \ˈkla-mər\ *n* **1** : a noisy shouting **2** : a loud continuous noise **3** : insistent public expression (as of support or protest) — **clamor** *vb* — **clam·or·ous** *adj*

clam·our *chiefly Brit var of* CLAMOR

[1]**clamp** \ˈklamp\ *n* : a device that holds or presses parts together firmly

[2]**clamp** *vb* : to fasten with or as if with a clamp

clamp down *vb* : to impose restrictions : become repressive — **clamp·down** \ˈklamp-ˌdau̇n\ *n*

clam·shell \ˈklam-ˌshel\ *n* : a bucket or grapnel (as on a dredge) having two hinged jaws

clam up *vb* : to become silent

clan \ˈklan\ *n* [ME, fr. ScGael *clann* offspring, clan, fr. Old Irish *cland* plant, offspring, fr. L *planta* plant] : a group (as in the Scottish Highlands) made up of households whose heads claim descent from a common ancestor — **clan·nish** *adj* — **clan·nish·ness** *n*

clan·des·tine \klan-ˈdes-tən\ *adj* : held in or conducted with secrecy

clang \ˈklaŋ\ *n* : a loud metallic ringing sound — **clang** *vb*

clan·gor \ˈklaŋ-ər, -gər\ *n* : a resounding clang or medley of clangs

clan·gour *chiefly Brit var of* CLANGOR

clank \ˈklaŋk\ *n* : a sharp brief metallic ringing sound — **clank** *vb*

[1]**clap** \ˈklap\ *vb* **clapped; clap·ping 1** : to strike noisily **2** : APPLAUD

[2]**clap** *n* **1** : a loud noisy crash **2** : the noise made by clapping the hands

[3]**clap** *n* : GONORRHEA

clap·board \ˈkla-bərd, -ˌbōrd; ˈklap-ˌbōrd\ *n* : a narrow board thicker at one edge than the other used for siding — **clap·board** *vb*

clap·per \ˈkla-pər\ *n* : one that claps; *esp* : the tongue of a bell

clap·trap \ˈklap-ˌtrap\ *n* : pretentious nonsense

claque \ˈklak\ *n* [F, fr. *claquer* to clap] **1** : a group hired to applaud at a performance **2** : a group of sycophants

clar·et \ˈklar-ət\ *n* [ME, fr. MF (*vin*) *claret* clear wine] : a dry red wine

clar·i·fy \ˈklar-ə-ˌfī\ *vb* **-fied; -fy·ing** : to make or become clear — **clar·i·fi·ca·tion** \ˌklar-ə-fə-ˈkā-shən\ *n*

clar·i·net \ˌklar-ə-ˈnet\ *n* : a single-reed woodwind instrument in the form of a cylindrical tube with a moderately flaring end — **clar·i·net·ist** *or* **clar·i·net·tist** \-ˈne-tist\ *n*

clarinet

clar•i•on \ˈklar-ē-ən\ *adj* : brilliantly clear ⟨a ~ call⟩
clar•i•ty \ˈklar-ə-tē\ *n* : CLEARNESS
[1]**clash** \ˈklash\ *vb* **1** : to make or cause to make a clash **2** : CONFLICT, COLLIDE
[2]**clash** *n* **1** : a noisy usu. metallic sound of collision **2** : a hostile encounter; *also* : a conflict of opinion
clasp \ˈklasp\ *n* **1** : a device (as a hook) for holding objects or parts together **2** : EMBRACE, GRASP — **clasp** *vb*
[1]**class** \ˈklas\ *n* **1** : a group of students meeting regularly in a course; *also* : a group graduating together **2** : a course of instruction; *also* : the period when such a course is taught **3** : social rank; *also* : high quality **4** : a group of the same general status or nature; *esp* : a major category in biological classification that is above the order and below the phylum **5** : a division or rating based on grade or quality — **class•less** *adj*
[2]**class** *vb* : CLASSIFY
class action *n* : a legal action undertaken in behalf of the plaintiffs and all others having an identical interest in the alleged wrong
[1]**clas•sic** \ˈkla-sik\ *adj* **1** : serving as a standard of excellence; *also* : TRADITIONAL **2** : CLASSICAL 2 **3** : notable esp. as the best example **4** : AUTHENTIC
[2]**classic** *n* **1** : a work of enduring excellence and esp. of ancient Greece or Rome; *also* : its author **2** : a traditional event
clas•si•cal \ˈkla-si-kəl\ *adj* **1** : CLASSIC **2** : of or relating to the ancient Greek and Roman classics **3** : of or relating to a form or system of primary significance before modern times ⟨~ economics⟩ **4** : concerned with a general study of the arts and sciences — **clas•si•cal•ly** \-k(ə-)lē\ *adv*
clas•si•cism \ˈkla-sə-ˌsi-zəm\ *n* **1** : the principles or style of the literature or art of ancient Greece and Rome **2** : adherence to traditional standards believed to be universally valid — **clas•si•cist** \-sist\ *n*
clas•si•fied \ˈkla-sə-ˌfīd\ *adj* : withheld from general circulation for reasons of national security
clas•si•fy \ˈkla-sə-ˌfī\ *vb* **-fied; -fy•ing** : to arrange in or assign to classes — **clas•si•fi•able** *adj* — **clas•si•fi•ca•tion** \ˌkla-sə-fə-ˈkā-shən\ *n* — **clas•si•fi•er** *n*
class•mate \ˈklas-ˌmāt\ *n* : a member of the same class (as in a college)
class•room \-ˌrüm-, -ˌru̇m\ *n* : a place where classes meet
classy \ˈkla-sē\ *adj* **class•i•er; -est** : ELEGANT, STYLISH — **class•i•ness** *n*
clat•ter \ˈkla-tər\ *n* : a rattling sound ⟨the ~ of dishes⟩ — **clatter** *vb*
clause \ˈklȯz\ *n* **1** : a group of words having its own subject and predicate but forming only part of a compound or complex sentence **2** : a separate part of an article or document
claus•tro•pho•bia \ˌklȯ-strə-ˈfō-bē-ə\ *n* : abnormal dread of being in closed or narrow spaces — **claus•tro•pho•bic** \-bik\ *adj*
clav•i•chord \ˈkla-və-ˌkȯrd\ *n* : an early keyboard instrument in use before the piano
clav•i•cle \ˈkla-vi-kəl\ *n* [F *clavicule*, fr. NL *clavicula*, fr. L, dim. of L *clavis* key] : COLLARBONE
cla•vier \klə-ˈvir; ˈklā-vē-ər\ *n* **1** : the keyboard of a musical instrument **2** : an early keyboard instrument
[1]**claw** \ˈklȯ\ *n* **1** : a sharp usu. curved nail on the toe of an animal **2** : a sharp curved process (as on the foot of an insect); *also* : a pincerlike organ at the end of a limb of some arthropods (as a lobster) — **clawed** \ˈklȯd\ *adj*
[2]**claw** *vb* : to rake, seize, or dig with or as if with claws
clay \ˈklā\ *n* **1** : an earthy material that is plastic when moist but hard when fired and is used in making pottery; *also* : finely divided soil consisting largely of such clay **2** : EARTH, MUD **3** : a plastic substance used for modeling **4** : the mortal human body — **clay•ey** \ˈklā-ē\ *adj*
clay•more \ˈklā-ˌmōr\ *n* : a large 2-edged sword formerly used by Scottish Highlanders
clay pigeon *n* : a saucer-shaped target thrown from a trap in trapshooting
[1]**clean** \ˈklēn\ *adj* **1** : free from dirt or disease **2** : PURE; *also* : HONORABLE **3** : THOROUGH ⟨made a ~ sweep⟩ **4** : TRIM ⟨a ship with ~ lines⟩; *also* : EVEN **5** : habitually neat — **clean** *adv* — **clean•ly** \ˈklēn-lē\ *adv* — **clean•ness** \ˈklēn-nəs\ *n*
[2]**clean** *vb* : to make or become clean — **clean•er** *n*
clean–cut \ˈklēn-ˈkət\ *adj* **1** : cut so that the surface or edge is smooth and even **2** : sharply defined or outlined **3** : giving an effect of wholesomeness
clean•ly \ˈklen-lē\ *adj* **clean•li•er; -est** **1** : careful to keep clean **2** : habitually kept clean — **clean•li•ness** *n*
clean room \ˈklēn-ˌrüm, -ˌru̇m\ *n* : an uncontaminated room maintained for the manufacture or assembly of objects (as precision parts)
cleanse \ˈklenz\ *vb* **cleansed; cleans•ing** : to make clean — **cleans•er** *n*
[1]**clean•up** \ˈklē-ˌnəp\ *n* **1** : an act or instance of cleaning **2** : a very large profit
[2]**cleanup** *adj* : being 4th in the batting order of a baseball team
clean up *vb* : to make a spectacular business profit
[1]**clear** \ˈklir\ *adj* **1** : BRIGHT, LUMINOUS; *also* : UNTROUBLED, SERENE **2** : CLOUDLESS **3** : CLEAN, PURE; *also* : TRANSPARENT **4** : easily heard, seen, or understood **5** : capable of sharp discernment; *also* : free from doubt **6** : INNOCENT **7** : free from restriction, obstruction, or entanglement — **clear** *adv* — **clear•ness** *n*
[2]**clear** *vb* **1** : to make or become clear **2** : to go away : DISPERSE **3** : to free from accusation or blame; *also* : to certify as trustworthy **4** : EXPLAIN **5** : to get free from obstruction **6** : SETTLE **7** : NET **8** : to get rid of : REMOVE **9** : to jump or go by without touching; *also* : PASS
[3]**clear** *n* : a clear space or part
clear•ance \ˈklir-əns\ *n* **1** : an act or process of clearing **2** : the distance by which one object clears another **3** : AUTHORIZATION
clear–cut \ˈklir-ˈkət\ *adj* **1** : sharply outlined **2** : DEFINITE, UNEQUIVOCAL
clear•head•ed \-ˈhe-dəd\ *adj* : having a clear understanding : PERCEPTIVE
clear•ing \ˈklir-iŋ\ *n* **1** : a tract of land cleared of wood and brush **2** : the passage of checks and claims through a clearinghouse
clear•ing•house \-ˌhau̇s\ *n* : an institution maintained by banks for making an exchange of checks and claims held by each bank against other banks; *also* : an informal channel for information or assistance
clear•ly \ˈklir-lē\ *adv* **1** : in a clear manner **2** : it is clear
cleat \ˈklēt\ *n* : a piece of wood or metal fastened on or projecting from something to give strength, provide a grip, or prevent slipping
cleav•age \ˈklē-vij\ *n* **1** : a splitting apart : SPLIT **2** : the depression between a woman's breasts esp. when exposed by a low-cut dress
[1]**cleave** \ˈklēv\ *vb* **cleaved** \ˈklēvd\ *or* **clove** \ˈklōv\; **cleaved; cleav•ing** : ADHERE, CLING
[2]**cleave** *vb* **cleaved** \ˈklēvd\ *also* **cleft** \ˈkleft\ *or* **clove** \ˈklōv\; **cleaved** *also* **cleft** *or* **clo•ven** \ˈklō-vən\; **cleav•ing** **1** : to divide by force : split asunder **2** : DIVIDE
cleav•er \ˈklē-vər\ *n* : a heavy chopping knife for cutting meat
clef \ˈklef\ *n* : a sign placed on the staff in music to show what pitch is represented by each line and space
cleft \ˈkleft\ *n* : FISSURE, CRACK
cleft palate *n* : a split in the roof of the mouth that appears as a birth defect
clem•a•tis \ˈkle-mə-təs; kli-ˈma-təs\ *n* : any of a genus

of vines or herbs related to the buttercups that have showy usu. white or purple flowers

clem•en•cy \ˈkle-mən-sē\ *n, pl* **-cies 1 :** disposition to be merciful **2 :** mildness of weather

clem•ent \ˈkle-mənt\ *adj* **1 :** MERCIFUL, LENIENT **2 :** TEMPERATE, MILD

clench \ˈklench\ *vb* **1 :** CLINCH 1 **2 :** to hold fast **3 :** to set or close tightly

clere•sto•ry \ˈklir-ˌstōr-ē\ *n* **:** an outside wall of a room or building that rises above an adjoining roof and contains windows

cler•gy \ˈklər-jē\ *n* **:** a body of religious officials authorized to conduct services

cler•gy•man \-mən\ *n* **:** a member of the clergy

cler•ic \ˈkler-ik\ *n* **:** a member of the clergy

cler•i•cal \ˈkler-i-kəl\ *adj* **1 :** of or relating to the clergy **2 :** of or relating to a clerk

cler•i•cal•ism \ˈkler-i-kə-ˌli-zəm\ *n* **:** a policy of maintaining or increasing the power of a religious hierarchy

clerk \ˈklərk, *Brit* ˈklärk\ *n* **1 :** CLERIC **2 :** an official responsible for correspondence, records, and accounts; *also* **:** a person employed to perform general office work **3 :** a store salesperson — **clerk** *vb* — **clerk•ship** *n*

clev•er \ˈkle-vər\ *adj* **1 :** showing skill or resourcefulness **2 :** marked by wit or ingenuity — **clev•er•ly** *adv* — **clev•er•ness** *n*

clev•is \ˈkle-vəs\ *n* **:** a U-shaped shackle used for fastening

[1]clew \ˈklü\ *n* **1 :** CLUE **2 :** a metal loop on a lower corner of a sail

[2]clew *vb* **:** to haul (a sail) up or down by ropes through the clews

cli•ché \kli-ˈshā\ *n* [F] **:** a trite phrase or expression — **cli•chéd** \-ˈshād\ *adj*

[1]click \ˈklik\ *vb* **1 :** to make or cause to make a click **2 :** to fit or work together smoothly

[2]click *n* **:** a slight sharp noise

cli•ent \ˈklī-ənt\ *n* **1 :** DEPENDENT **2 :** a person who engages the professional services of another; *also* **:** PATRON, CUSTOMER

cli•en•tele \ˌklī-ən-ˈtel, ˌklē-\ *n* **:** a body of clients and esp. customers

cliff \ˈklif\ *n* **:** a high steep face of rock, earth, or ice

cliff–hang•er \-ˌhaŋ-ər\ *n* **1 :** an adventure serial or melodrama usu. presented in installments each of which ends in suspense **2 :** a contest whose outcome is in doubt up to the very end

cli•mac•ter•ic \klī-ˈmak-tə-rik\ *n* **1 :** a major turning point or critical stage **2 :** MENOPAUSE; *also* **:** a corresponding period in the male

cli•mate \ˈklī-mət\ *n* [ME *climat,* fr. MF, fr. LL *clima,* fr. Gk *klima* inclination, latitude, climate, fr. *klinein* to lean] **1 :** a region having specific climatic conditions **2 :** the average weather conditions at a place over a period of years **3 :** the prevailing set of conditions (as temperature and humidity) indoors **4 :** a prevailing atmosphere or environment ⟨the ~ of opinion⟩ — **cli•mat•ic** \klī-ˈma-tik\ *adj* — **cli•mat•i•cal•ly** \-ti-k(ə-)lē\ *adv*

cli•ma•tol•o•gy \ˌklī-mə-ˈtä-lə-jē\ *n* **:** the science that deals with climates — **cli•ma•to•log•i•cal** \-mət-ᵊl-ˈä-ji-kəl\ *adj* — **cli•ma•to•log•i•cal•ly** \-k(ə-)lē\ *adv* — **cli•ma•tol•o•gist** \-mə-ˈtä-lə-jist\ *n*

[1]cli•max \ˈklī-ˌmaks\ *n* [L, fr. Gk *klimax* ladder, fr. *klinein* to lean] **1 :** a series of ideas or statements so arranged that they increase in force and power from the first to the last; *also* **:** the last member of such a series **2 :** the highest point **3 :** ORGASM — **cli•mac•tic** \klī-ˈmak-tik\ *adj*

[2]climax *vb* **:** to come or bring to a climax

[1]climb \ˈklīm\ *vb* **1 :** to rise to a higher point **2 :** to go up or down esp. by use of hands and feet; *also* **:** to ascend in growing — **climb•er** *n*

[2]climb *n* **1 :** a place where climbing is necessary **2 :** the act of climbing **:** ascent by climbing

clime \ˈklīm\ *n* **:** CLIMATE

[1]clinch \ˈklinch\ *vb* **1 :** to turn over or flatten the end of something sticking out ⟨~ a nail⟩; *also* **:** to fasten by clinching **2 :** to make final **:** SETTLE **3 :** to hold fast or firmly

[2]clinch *n* **1 :** a fastening by means of a clinched nail, rivet, or bolt **2 :** an act or instance of clinching in boxing

clinch•er \ˈklin-chər\ *n* **:** one that clinches; *esp* **:** a decisive fact, argument, act, or remark

cling \ˈkliŋ\ *vb* **clung** \ˈkləŋ\; **cling•ing 1 :** to adhere as if glued; *also* **:** to hold or hold on tightly **2 :** to have a strong emotional attachment

cling•stone \ˈkliŋ-ˌstōn\ *n* **:** any of various fruits (as some peaches) whose flesh adheres strongly to the pit

clin•ic \ˈkli-nik\ *n* **1 :** a medical class in which patients are examined and discussed **2 :** a group meeting for teaching a certain skill and working on individual problems ⟨a reading ~⟩ **3 :** a facility (as of a hospital) for diagnosis and treatment of outpatients

clin•i•cal \ˈkli-ni-kəl\ *adj* **1 :** of, relating to, or typical of a clinic; *esp* **:** involving direct observation of the patient **2 :** scientifically dispassionate — **clin•i•cal•ly** \-k(ə-)lē\ *adv*

cli•ni•cian \kli-ˈni-shən\ *n* **:** a person qualified in the clinical practice of medicine, psychiatry, or psychology as distinguished from one specializing in laboratory or research techniques or in theory

[1]clink \ˈkliŋk\ *vb* **:** to make or cause to make a sharp short metallic sound

[2]clink *n* **:** a clinking sound

clin•ker \ˈkliŋ-kər\ *n* **:** stony matter fused together **:** SLAG

[1]clip \ˈklip\ *vb* **clipped; clip•ping :** to fasten with a clip

[2]clip *n* **1 :** a device that grips, clasps, or hooks **2 :** a cartridge holder for a rifle

[3]clip *vb* **clipped; clip•ping 1 :** to cut or cut off with shears **2 :** CURTAIL, DIMINISH **3 :** HIT, PUNCH **4 :** to illegally block (an opponent) in football

[4]clip *n* **1 :** a 2-bladed instrument for cutting esp. the nails **2 :** a sharp blow **3 :** a rapid pace

clip•board \ˈklip-ˌbōrd\ *n* **:** a small writing board with a spring clip at the top for holding papers

clip joint *n, slang* **:** an establishment (as a nightclub) that makes a practice of defrauding its customers

clip•per \ˈkli-pər\ *n* **1 :** an implement for clipping esp. the hair or nails — usu. used in pl. **2 :** a fast sailing ship

clip•ping \ˈkli-piŋ\ *n* **:** a piece clipped from something (as a newspaper)

clique \ˈklēk, ˈklik\ *n* [F] **:** a small exclusive group of people **:** COTERIE — **cliqu•ey** \ˈklē-kē, ˈkli-\ *adj* — **cliqu•ish** \-kish\ *adj*

cli•to•ris \ˈkli-tə-rəs\ *n, pl* **cli•to•ri•des** \kli-ˈtȯr-ə-ˌdēz\ **:** a small erectile organ at the anterior or ventral part of the vulva homologous to the penis — **cli•to•ral** \-rəl\ *adj*

clk *abbr* clerk

clo *abbr* clothing

[1]cloak \ˈklōk\ *n* **1 :** a loose outer garment **2 :** something that conceals

[2]cloak *vb* **:** to cover or hide with a cloak

cloak–and–dagger *adj* **:** involving or suggestive of espionage

clob•ber \ˈklä-bər\ *vb* **1 :** to pound mercilessly; *also* **:** to hit with force **:** SMASH **2 :** to defeat overwhelmingly

cloche \ˈklōsh\ *n* [F, lit., bell] **:** a woman's small close-fitting hat

[1]clock \ˈkläk\ *n* **:** a timepiece not intended to be carried on the person

[2]clock *vb* **1 :** to time (a person or a performance) by a timing device **2 :** to register (as speed) on a mechanical recording device — **clock•er** *n*

[3]clock *n* **:** an ornamental figure on a stocking or sock

clock•wise \ˈkläk-ˌwīz\ *adv* : in the direction in which the hands of a clock move — **clockwise** *adj*

clock•work \-ˌwərk\ *n* **1** : the machinery that runs a mechanical device (as a clock or toy) **2** : the precision or regularity associated with a clock

clod \ˈkläd\ *n* **1** : a lump esp. of earth or clay **2** : a dull or insensitive person

clod•hop•per \-ˌhä-pər\ *n* **1** : an uncouth rustic **2** : a large heavy shoe

[1]**clog** \ˈkläg\ *n* **1** : a weight so attached as to impede motion **2** : a thick-soled shoe

[2]**clog** *vb* **clogged; clog•ging 1** : to impede with a clog : HINDER **2** : to obstruct passage through **3** : to become filled with extraneous matter

cloi•son•né \ˌklȯiz-ᵊn-ˈā\ *adj* : a colored decoration made of enamels poured into the divided areas in a design outlined with wire or metal strips

[1]**clois•ter** \ˈklȯi-stər\ *n* [ME *cloistre*, fr. OF, fr. ML *claustrum*, fr. L, bar, bolt, fr. *claudere* to close] **1** : a monastic establishment **2** : a covered usu. colonnaded passage on the side of a court — **clois•tral** \-strəl\ *adj*

[2]**cloister** *vb* : to shut away from the world

clone \ˈklōn\ *n* [Gk *klōn* twig, slip] **1** : the offspring produced asexually from an individual (as a plant increased by grafting); *also* : a group of replicas of all or part of a large biological molecule (as DNA) **2** : an individual grown from a single body cell of its parent and genetically identical to the parent **3** : one that appears to be a copy of an original form — **clon•al** \ˈklōn-ᵊl\ *adj* — **clone** *vb*

clop \ˈkläp\ *n* : a sound made by or as if by a hoof or wooden shoe against pavement — **clop** *vb*

[1]**close** \ˈklōz\ *vb* **closed; clos•ing 1** : to bar passage through : SHUT **2** : to suspend the operations (as of a school) **3** : END, TERMINATE **4** : to bring together the parts or edges of; *also* : to fill up **5** : GRAPPLE ⟨∼ with the enemy⟩ **6** : to enter into an agreement — **clos•able** *or* **close•able** *adj*

[2]**close** \ˈklōz\ *n* : CONCLUSION, END

[3]**close** \ˈklōs\ *adj* **clos•er; clos•est 1** : having no openings **2** : narrowly restricting or restricted **3** : limited to a privileged class **4** : SECLUDED; *also* : SECRETIVE **5** : RIGOROUS **6** : SULTRY, STUFFY **7** : STINGY **8** : having little space between items or units **9** : fitting tightly; *also* : SHORT ⟨∼ haircut⟩ **10** : NEAR **11** : INTIMATE ⟨∼ friends⟩ **12** : ACCURATE **13** : decided by a narrow margin ⟨a ∼ game⟩ — **close** *adv* — **close•ly** *adv* — **close•ness** *n*

closed–circuit \ˈklōzd-ˈsər-kət\ *adj* : used in, shown on, or being a television installation in which the signal is transmitted by wire to a limited number of receivers

closed shop *n* : an establishment having only members of a labor union on the payroll

close•fist•ed \ˈklōz-ˈfis-təd, ˈklōs-\ *adj* : STINGY

close–knit \ˈklōs-ˈnit\ *adj* : closely bound together by social, cultural, economic, or political ties

close•mouthed \ˈklōz-ˈmau̇t͟hd, ˈklōs-ˈmau̇tht\ *adj* : cautious or reticent in speaking

close•out \ˈklō-ˌzau̇t\ *n* : a sale of a business's entire stock at low prices

close out *vb* **1** : to dispose of by a closeout **2** : to dispose of a business : SELL OUT

[1]**clos•et** \ˈklä-zət, ˈklō-\ *n* **1** : a small room for privacy **2** : a small compartment for household utensils or clothing **3** : a state or condition of secrecy ⟨came out of the ∼⟩

[2]**closet** *vb* : to take into a private room for an interview

close–up \ˈklō-ˌsəp\ *n* **1** : a photograph or movie shot taken at close range **2** : an intimate view or examination

clo•sure \ˈklō-zhər\ *n* **1** : an act of closing : the condition of being closed **2** : something that closes **3** : CLOTURE

clot \ˈklät\ *n* : a mass formed by a portion of liquid (as blood) thickening and sticking together — **clot** *vb*

cloth \ˈklȯth\ *n, pl* **cloths** \ˈklȯt͟hz, ˈklȯths\ **1** : a pliable fabric made usu. by weaving or knitting natural or synthetic fibers and filaments **2** : TABLECLOTH **3** : distinctive dress of the clergy; *also* : CLERGY

clothe \ˈklōt͟h\ *vb* **clothed** *or* **clad** \ˈklad\; **cloth•ing 1** : DRESS **2** : to express by suitably significant language

clothes \ˈklōt͟hz, ˈklōz\ *n pl* **1** : CLOTHING **2** : BEDDING 1

clothes•horse \-ˌhȯrs\ *n* **1** : a frame on which to hang clothes **2** : a conspicuously dressy person

clothes moth *n* : any of several small pale moths whose larvae eat wool, fur, and feathers

clothes•pin \ˈklōt͟hz-ˌpin, ˈklōz-\ *n* : a device for fastening clothes on a line

clothes•press \-ˌpres\ *n* : a receptacle for clothes

cloth•ier \ˈklōt͟h-yər, ˈklō-t͟hē-ər\ *n* : a maker or seller of clothing

cloth•ing \ˈklō-t͟hiŋ\ *n* : garments in general

clo•ture \ˈklō-chər\ *n* : the closing or limitation (as by calling for a vote) of debate in a legislative body

[1]**cloud** \ˈklau̇d\ *n* [ME, rock, cloud, fr. OE *clūd*] **1** : a visible mass of particles of condensed vapor (as water or ice) suspended in the atmosphere **2** : a usu. visible mass of minute airborne particles; *also* : a mass of obscuring matter in interstellar space **3** : CROWD, SWARM ⟨a ∼ of mosquitoes⟩ **4** : something having a dark or threatening aspect — **cloud•i•ness** \ˈklau̇-dē-nəs\ *n* — **cloud•less** *adj* — **cloudy** *adj*

[2]**cloud** *vb* **1** : to darken or hide with or as if with a cloud **2** : OBSCURE **3** : TAINT, SULLY

cloud•burst \-ˌbərst\ *n* : a sudden heavy rainfall

cloud•let \-lət\ *n* : a small cloud

cloud nine *n* : a feeling of extreme well-being or elation — usu. used with *on*

[1]**clout** \ˈklau̇t\ *n* **1** : a blow esp. with the hand **2** : PULL, INFLUENCE

[2]**clout** *vb* : to hit forcefully

[1]**clove** \ˈklōv\ *n* : one of the small bulbs that grows at the base of the scales of a large bulb ⟨a ∼ of garlic⟩

[2]**clove** *past of* CLEAVE

[3]**clove** *n* [ME *clowe*, fr. OF *clou* (*de girofle*), lit., nail of clove, fr. L *clavus* nail] : the dried flower bud of an East Indian tree used esp. as a spice

clo•ven \ˈklō-vən\ *past part of* CLEAVE

cloven foot *n* : CLOVEN HOOF — **cloven–foot•ed** \-ˈfu̇-təd\ *adj*

cloven hoof *n* : a foot (as of a sheep) with the front part divided into two parts — **cloven–hoofed** \-ˈhu̇ft, -ˈhu̇vd\ *adj*

clo•ver \ˈklō-vər\ *n* : any of a genus of leguminous herbs with usu. 3-parted leaves and dense flower heads

clo•ver•leaf \-ˌlēf\ *n, pl* **cloverleafs** \-ˌlēfs\ *or* **clo•ver•leaves** \-ˌlēvz\ : an interchange between two major highways that from above resembles a four-leaf clover

[1]**clown** \ˈklau̇n\ *n* **1** : BOOR **2** : a fool or comedian in an entertainment (as a circus) — **clown•ish** *adj* — **clown•ish•ly** *adv* — **clown•ish•ness** *n*

[2]**clown** *vb* : to act like a clown

cloy \ˈklȯi\ *vb* : to disgust or nauseate with excess of something orig. pleasing — **cloy•ing•ly** *adv*

clr *abbr* clear

[1]**club** \ˈkləb\ *n* **1** : a heavy wooden stick or staff used as a weapon; *also* : BAT **2** : any of a suit of playing cards marked with a black figure resembling a clover leaf **3** : a group of persons associated for a common purpose; *also* : the meeting place of such a group

[2]**club** *vb* **clubbed; club•bing 1** : to strike with a club **2** : to unite or combine for a common cause

club•foot \ˈkləb-ˈfu̇t\ *n* : a misshapen foot twisted out of position from birth; *also* : this deformed condition — **club•foot•ed** \-ˈfu̇-təd\ *adj*

club•house \ˈkləb-ˌhau̇s\ *n* **1** : a house occupied by a club **2** : locker rooms used by an athletic team

club sandwich *n* : a sandwich of three slices of bread with two layers of meat (as turkey) and lettuce, tomato, and mayonnaise
club soda *n* : SODA WATER
cluck \ˈklək\ *n* : the call of a hen esp. to her chicks — **cluck** *vb*
[1]**clue** \ˈklü\ *n* : something that guides through an intricate procedure or maze; *esp* : a piece of evidence leading to the solution of a problem
[2]**clue** *vb* **clued; clue•ing** *or* **clu•ing** : to provide with a clue; *also* : to give information to ⟨~ me in⟩
[1]**clump** \ˈkləmp\ *n* **1** : a group of things clustered together **2** : a heavy tramping sound
[2]**clump** *vb* : to tread clumsily and noisily
clum•sy \ˈkləm-zē\ *adj* **clum•si•er; -est 1** : lacking dexterity, nimbleness, or grace **2** : not tactful or subtle — **clum•si•ly** \-zə-lē\ *adv* — **clum•si•ness** \-zē-nəs\ *n*
clung *past and past part of* CLING
clunk•er \ˈkləŋ-kər\ *n* **1** : a dilapidated automobile **2** : a notable failure
[1]**clus•ter** \ˈkləs-tər\ *n* : GROUP, BUNCH
[2]**cluster** *vb* : to grow or gather in a cluster
[1]**clutch** \ˈkləch\ *vb* : to grasp with or as if with the hand
[2]**clutch** *n* **1** : the claws or a hand in the act of grasping; *also* : CONTROL, POWER **2** : a device for gripping an object **3** : a coupling used to connect and disconnect a driving and a driven part of a mechanism; *also* : a lever or pedal operating such a coupling **4** : a crucial situation
[3]**clutch** *adj* : made, done, or successful in a crucial situation
[4]**clutch** *n* **1** : a nest or batch of eggs; *also* : a brood of chicks **2** : GROUP, BUNCH
[1]**clut•ter** \ˈklə-tər\ *vb* : to fill or cover with a disorderly scattering of things
[2]**clutter** *n* : a crowded mass
cm *abbr* centimeter
Cm *symbol* curium
CM *abbr* [Commonwealth of the Northern Mariana Islands] Northern Mariana Islands
cmdr *abbr* commander
cml *abbr* commercial
CMSgt *abbr* chief master sergeant
CNO *abbr* chief of naval operations
CNS *abbr* central nervous system
co *abbr* **1** company **2** county
Co *symbol* cobalt
CO *abbr* **1** Colorado **2** commanding officer **3** conscientious objector
c/o *abbr* care of
[1]**coach** \ˈkōch\ *n* **1** : a large closed 4-wheeled carriage with an elevated outside front seat for the driver **2** : a railroad passenger car esp. for day travel **3** : BUS **4** : a private tutor; *also* : one who instructs or trains a team of performers

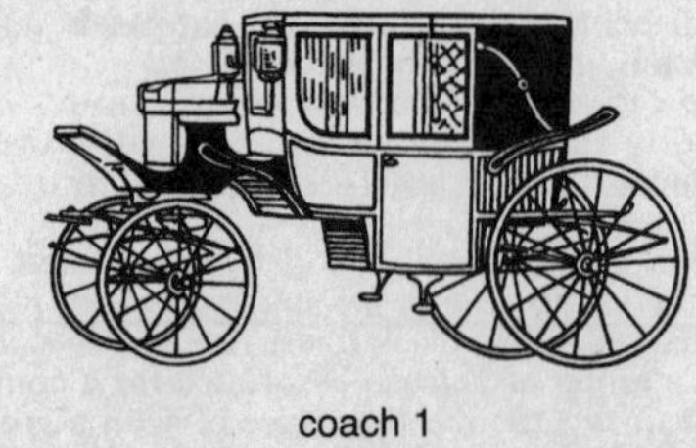

coach 1

[2]**coach** *vb* : to instruct, direct, or prompt as a coach
coach•man \-mən\ *n* : a man who drives a coach or carriage
co•ad•ju•tor \ˌkō-ə-ˈjü-tər, kō-ˈa-jə-tər\ *n* : ASSISTANT; *esp* : an assistant bishop having the right of succession
co•ag•u•lant \kō-ˈa-gyə-lənt\ *n* : something that produces coagulation
co•ag•u•late \-ˌlāt\ *vb* **-lat•ed; -lat•ing** : CLOT — **co•ag•u•la•tion** \kō-ˌa-gyə-ˈlā-shən\ *n*
[1]**coal** \ˈkōl\ *n* **1** : EMBER **2** : a black solid combustible mineral used as fuel
[2]**coal** *vb* **1** : to supply with coal **2** : to take in coal
co•a•lesce \ˌkō-ə-ˈles\ *vb* **co•a•lesced; co•a•lesc•ing** : to grow together; *also* : FUSE **syn** merge, blend, mingle, mix — **co•a•les•cence** \-ᵊns\ *n*
coal•field \ˈkōl-ˌfēld\ *n* : a region rich in coal deposits
coal gas *n* : gas from coal; *esp* : gas distilled from bituminous coal and used for heating
co•a•li•tion \ˌkō-ə-ˈli-shən\ *n* : UNION; *esp* : a temporary union for a common purpose — **co•a•li•tion•ist** *n*
coal oil *n* : KEROSENE
coal tar *n* : tar distilled from bituminous coal and used in dyes and drugs
co–an•chor \ˈkō-ˈaŋ-kər\ *n* : a newscaster who shares the duties of head broadcaster
coarse \ˈkōrs\ *adj* **coars•er; coars•est 1** : of ordinary or inferior quality **2** : composed of large parts or particles ⟨~ sand⟩ **3** : CRUDE ⟨~ manners⟩ **4** : ROUGH, HARSH — **coarse•ly** *adv* — **coarse•ness** *n*
coars•en \ˈkōrs-ᵊn\ *vb* : to make or become coarse
[1]**coast** \ˈkōst\ *n* [ME *cost*, fr. MF *coste*, fr. L *costa* rib, side] **1** : SEASHORE **2** : a slide down a slope **3** : the immediate area of view — used in the phrase *the coast is clear* — **coast•al** *adj*
[2]**coast** *vb* **1** : to sail along the shore **2** : to move (as downhill on a sled) without effort
coast•er *n* **1** : one that coasts **2** : a shallow container or a plate or mat to protect a surface
coaster brake *n* : a brake in the hub of the rear wheel of a bicycle
coast guard *n* : a military force employed in guarding or patrolling a coast — **coast•guards•man** \ˈkōst-ˌgärdz-mən\ *n*
coast•line \ˈkōst-ˌlīn\ *n* : the outline or shape of a coast
[1]**coat** \ˈkōt\ *n* **1** : an outer garment for the upper part of the body **2** : an external growth (as of fur or feathers) on an animal **3** : a covering layer — **coat•ed** \ˈkō-təd\ *adj*
[2]**coat** *vb* : to cover usu. with a finishing or protective coat
coat•ing \ˈkō-tiŋ\ *n* : COAT, COVERING
coat of arms : the heraldic bearings (as of a person) usu. depicted on an escutcheon
coat of mail : a garment of metal scales or rings worn as armor
co•au•thor \ˈkō-ˈȯ-thər\ *n* : a joint or associate author — **coauthor** *vb*
coax \ˈkōks\ *vb* : WHEEDLE; *also* : to gain by gentle urging or flattery
co•ax•i•al \ˈkō-ˈak-sē-əl\ *adj* : having coincident axes — **co•ax•i•al•ly** *adv*
coaxial cable *n* : a cable that consists of a tube of electrically conducting material surrounding a central conductor
cob \ˈkäb\ *n* **1** : a male swan **2** : CORN-COB **3** : a short-legged stocky horse
co•balt \ˈkō-ˌbȯlt\ *n* [G *Kobalt*, alter. of *Kobold*, lit., goblin; fr. its occurrence in silver ore, believed to be due to goblins] : a tough shiny silver-white magnetic metallic chemical element found with iron and nickel — see ELEMENT table
cob•ble \ˈkä-bəl\ *vb* **cob•bled; cob•bling** : to make or put together roughly or hastily
cob•bler \ˈkä-blər\ *n* **1** : a mender or maker of shoes **2** : a deep-dish fruit pie with a thick crust
cob•ble•stone \ˈkä-bəl-ˌstōn\ *n* : a naturally rounded stone larger than a pebble and smaller than a boulder
co•bra \ˈkō-brə\ *n* [Pg *cobra* (*de capello*), lit., hooded snake] : any of several venomous snakes of Asia and Africa that when excited expand the skin of the neck into a broad hood

cob•web \ˈkäb-ˌweb\ *n* [ME *coppeweb,* fr. *coppe* spider, fr. OE ātor*coppe*] **1 :** SPIDERWEB; *also* **:** a thread spun by a spider or insect larva **2 :** something flimsy or entangling

co•caine \kō-ˈkān, ˈkō-ˌkān\ *n* **:** a drug obtained from the leaves of a So. American shrub (**co•ca** \ˈkō-kə\) that can result in severe psychological dependence and is sometimes used in medicine as a local anesthetic and illegally to stimulate the central nervous system

coc•cus \ˈkä-kəs\ *n, pl* **coc•ci** \ˈkäk-ˌsī\ **:** a spherical bacterium

coc•cyx \ˈkäk-siks\ *n, pl* **coc•cy•ges** \ˈkäk-sə-ˌjēz\ *also* **coc•cyx•es** \ˈkäk-sik-səz\ **:** the end of the spinal column beyond the sacrum esp. in humans

co•chi•neal \ˈkä-chə-ˌnēl\ *n* **:** a red dye made from the dried bodies of females of a tropical American insect (**cochineal insect**)

co•chlea \ˈkō-klē-ə, ˈkä-\ *n, pl* **co•chle•as** *or* **co•chle•ae** \-klē-ˌē, -ˌī\ **:** the usu. spiral part of the inner ear containing nerve endings which carry information about sound to the brain — **co•chle•ar** \-klē-ər\ *adj*

[1]**cock** \ˈkäk\ *n* **1 :** the adult male of a bird and esp. of the common domestic chicken **2 :** VALVE, FAUCET **3 :** LEADER **4 :** the hammer of a firearm; *also* **:** the position of the hammer when ready for firing

[2]**cock** *vb* **1 :** to draw back the hammer of a firearm **2 :** to set or draw back in readiness for some action ⟨~ your arm to throw⟩ **3 :** to turn or tilt usu. to one side

[3]**cock** *n* **:** a small pile (as of hay)

cock•ade \kä-ˈkād\ *n* **:** an ornament worn on the hat as a badge

cock•a•tiel \ˌkä-kə-ˈtēl\ *n* **:** a small crested parrot often kept as a cage bird

cock•a•too \ˈkä-kə-ˌtü\ *n, pl* **-toos** [D *kaketoe,* fr. Malay *kakatua*] **:** any of various large noisy Australian crested parrots

cock•a•trice \ˈkä-kə-trəs, -ˌtrīs\ *n* **:** a legendary serpent with a deadly glance

cock•crow \ˈkäk-ˌkrō\ *n* **:** DAWN

cocked hat \ˈkäkt-\ *n* **:** a hat with the brim turned up on two or three sides

cock•er•el \ˈkä-kə-rəl\ *n* **:** a young male domestic chicken

cock•er spaniel \ˈkä-kər-\ *n* [*cocking* woodcock hunting] **:** any of a breed of small spaniels with long ears, square muzzle, and silky coat

cock•eyed \ˈkä-ˈkīd\ *adj* **1 :** turned or tilted to one side **2 :** slightly crazy **:** FOOLISH

cock•fight \ˈkäk-ˌfīt\ *n* **:** a contest of gamecocks usu. fitted with metal spurs

[1]**cock•le** \ˈkä-kəl\ *n* **:** any of several weedy plants related to the pinks

[2]**cockle** *n* **:** a bivalve mollusk with a heart-shaped shell

cock•le•shell \-ˌshel\ *n* **1 :** the shell of a cockle **2 :** a light flimsy boat

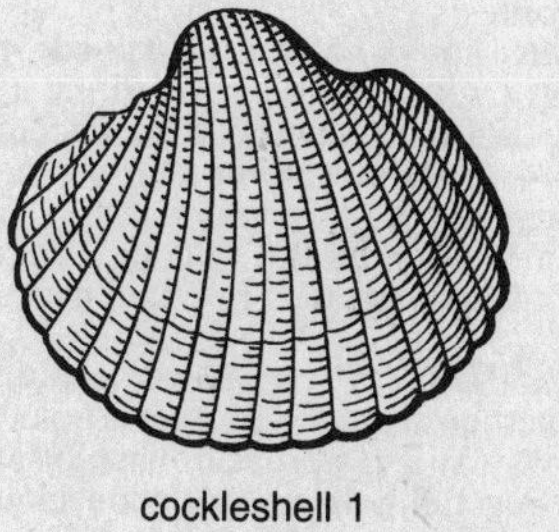

cockleshell 1

cock•ney \ˈkäk-nē\ *n, pl* **cockneys :** a native of London and esp. of the East End of London; *also* **:** the dialect of a cockney

cock•pit \ˈkäk-ˌpit\ *n* **1 :** a pit for cockfights **2 :** a space or compartment in a vehicle from which it is steered, piloted, or driven

cock•roach \ˈkäk-ˌrōch\ *n* [Sp *cucaracha*] **:** any of an order or suborder of active nocturnal insects including some which infest houses and ships

cock•sure \ˈkäk-ˈshu̇r\ *adj* **1 :** perfectly sure **:** CERTAIN **2 :** COCKY

cock•tail \ˈkäk-ˌtāl\ *n* **1 :** an iced drink made of liquor and flavoring ingredients **2 :** an appetizer (as tomato juice) served as a first course of a meal

cocky \ˈkä-kē\ *adj* **cock•i•er; -est :** marked by overconfidence **:** PERT, CONCEITED — **cock•i•ly** \-kə-lē\ *adv* — **cock•i•ness** \-kē-nəs\ *n*

co•coa \ˈkō-kō\ *n* **1 :** CACAO **2 :** chocolate deprived of some of its fat and powdered; *also* **:** a drink made of this heated with water or milk

co•co•nut \ˈkō-kə-(ˌ)nət\ *n* **:** a large edible nut produced by a tall tropical palm (**coconut palm**)

co•coon \kə-ˈkün\ *n* **:** a case usu. of silk formed by some insect larvae for protection during the pupal stage

cod \ˈkäd\ *n, pl* **cod** *also* **cods :** a bottom-dwelling bony fish of the No. Atlantic that is an important food fish; *also* **:** a related fish of the Pacific Ocean

COD *abbr* **1** cash on delivery **2** collect on delivery

co•da \ˈkō-də\ *n* **:** a closing section in a musical composition that is formally distinct from the main structure

cod•dle \ˈkäd-ᵊl\ *vb* **cod•dled; cod•dling 1 :** to cook slowly in water below the boiling point **2 :** PAMPER

[1]**code** \ˈkōd\ *n* **1 :** a systematic statement of a body of law **2 :** a system of principles or rules ⟨moral ~⟩ **3 :** a system of signals **4 :** a system of symbols (as in secret communication) with special meanings **5 :** GENETIC CODE

[2]**code** *vb* **cod•ed; cod•ing :** to put into the form or symbols of a code

co•deine \ˈkō-ˌdēn\ *n* **:** a narcotic drug obtained from opium and used esp. in cough remedies

co•dex \ˈkō-ˌdeks\ *n, pl* **co•di•ces** \ˈkō-də-ˌsēz, ˈkä-\ **:** a manuscript book (as of the Scriptures or classics)

cod•fish \ˈkäd-ˌfish\ *n* **:** COD

cod•ger \ˈkä-jər\ *n* **:** an odd or cranky and usu. elderly fellow

cod•i•cil \ˈkä-də-səl, -ˌsil\ *n* **:** a legal instrument modifying an earlier will

cod•i•fy \ˈkä-də-ˌfī, ˈkō-\ *vb* **-fied; -fy•ing :** to arrange in a systematic form — **cod•i•fi•ca•tion** \ˌkä-də-fə-ˈkā-shən, ˌkō-\ *n*

co•ed \ˈkō-ˌed\ *n* **:** a female student in a coeducational institution — **coed** *adj*

co•ed•u•ca•tion \ˌkō-ˌe-jə-ˈkā-shən\ *n* **:** the education of male and female students at the same institution — **co•ed•u•ca•tion•al** \-shə-nəl\ *adj* — **co•ed•u•ca•tion•al•ly** *adv*

co•ef•fi•cient \ˌkō-ə-ˈfi-shənt\ *n* **1 :** a constant factor as distinguished from a variable in a mathematical term **2 :** a number that serves as a measure of some property (as of a substance, device, or process)

coe•len•ter•ate \si-ˈlen-tə-ˌrāt, -rət\ *n* **:** any of a phylum of radially symmetrical invertebrate animals including the corals, sea anemones, and jellyfishes

co•equal \kō-ˈē-kwəl\ *adj* **:** equal with another — **coequal** *n* — **co•equal•i•ty** \ˌkō-ē-ˈkwä-lə-tē\ *n* — **coequal•ly** *adv*

co•erce \kō-ˈərs\ *vb* **co•erced; co•erc•ing 1 :** RESTRAIN, REPRESS **2 :** COMPEL **3 :** ENFORCE — **co•er•cion** \-ˈər-zhən, -shən\ *n* — **co•er•cive** \-ˈər-siv\ *adj*

co•e•val \kō-ˈē-vəl\ *adj* **:** of the same age — **coeval** *n*

co•ex•ist \ˌkō-ig-ˈzist\ *vb* **1 :** to exist together or at the same time **2 :** to live in peace with each other — **coex•is•tence** \-ˈzis-təns\ *n*

co•ex•ten•sive \ˌkō-ik-ˈsten-siv\ *adj* **:** having the same scope or extent in space or time

C of C *abbr* Chamber of Commerce

cof•fee \ˈkò-fē\ *n* [It & Turk; It *caffè,* fr. Turk *kahve,*

fr. Ar *qahwa*] : a drink made from the roasted and ground seeds of a fruit of a tropical shrub or tree; *also* : these seeds (**coffee beans**) or a plant producing them
cof•fee•house \-ˌhau̇s\ *n* : a place where refreshments (as coffee) are sold
coffee klatch \-ˌklach\ *n* : KAFFEE-KLATSCH
cof•fee•pot \-ˌpät\ *n* : a pot for brewing or serving coffee
coffee shop *n* : a small restaurant
coffee table *n* : a low table customarily placed in front of a sofa
cof•fer \ˈkȯ-fər\ *n* : a chest or box used esp. for valuables
cof•fer•dam \-ˌdam\ *n* : a watertight enclosure from which water is pumped to expose the bottom of a body of water and permit construction
cof•fin \ˈkȯ-fən\ *n* : a box or chest for a corpse to be buried in
C of S *abbr* chief of staff
[1]**cog** \ˈkäg\ *n* : a tooth on the rim of a wheel or gear — **cogged** \ˈkägd\ *adj*
[2]**cog** *abbr* cognate
co•gen•er•a•tion \ˌkō-ˌje-nə-ˈrā-shən\ *n* : the simultaneous generation of electricity and heat from the same fuel
co•gent \ˈkō-jənt\ *adj* : having power to compel or constrain : CONVINCING — **co•gen•cy** \-jən-sē\ *n*
cog•i•tate \ˈkä-jə-ˌtāt\ *vb* **-tat•ed; -tat•ing** : THINK, PONDER — **cog•i•ta•tion** \ˌkä-jə-ˈtā-shən\ *n* — **cog•i•ta•tive** \ˈkä-jə-ˌtā-tiv\ *adj*
co•gnac \ˈkōn-ˌyak\ *n* : a French brandy
cog•nate \ˈkäg-ˌnāt\ *adj* **1** : of the same or similar nature **2** : RELATED; *esp* : related by descent from the same ancestral language — **cognate** *n*
cog•ni•tive \ˈkäg-nə-tiv\ *adj* : of, relating to, or being conscious mental activity (as thinking, remembering, learning, or using language) — **cog•ni•tion** \käg-ˈni-shən\ *n*
cog•ni•zance \ˈkäg-nə-zəns\ *n* **1** : apprehension by the mind : AWARENESS **2** : NOTICE, HEED — **cog•ni•zant** \ˈkäg-nə-zənt\ *adj*
cog•no•men \käg-ˈnō-mən, ˈkäg-nə-\ *n, pl* **cognomens** *or* **cog•no•mi•na** \käg-ˈnä-mə-nə, -ˈnō-\ : NAME; *esp* : NICKNAME
co•gno•scen•te \ˌkän-yə-ˈshen-tē\ *n, pl* **-scen•ti** \-tē\ [obs. It] : CONNOISSEUR
cog•wheel \ˈkäg-ˌhwēl\ *n* : a wheel with cogs or teeth
co•hab•it \kō-ˈha-bət\ *vb* : to live together as husband and wife — **co•hab•i•ta•tion** \-ˌha-bə-ˈtā-shən\ *n*
co•here \kō-ˈhir\ *vb* **co•hered; co•her•ing** : to stick together
co•her•ent \kō-ˈhir-ənt\ *adj* **1** : having the quality of cohering **2** : logically consistent — **co•her•ence** \-əns\ *n* — **co•her•ent•ly** *adv*
co•he•sion \kō-ˈhē-zhən\ *n* **1** : a sticking together **2** : molecular attraction by which the particles of a body are united — **co•he•sive** \-siv\ *adj* — **co•he•sive•ly** *adv* — **co•he•sive•ness** *n*
co•ho \ˈkō-ˌhō\ *n, pl* **cohos** *or* **coho** : a rather small Pacific salmon with light-colored flesh
co•hort \ˈkō-ˌhȯrt\ *n* **1** : a group of warriors or followers **2** : COMPANION, ACCOMPLICE
coif \ˈkȯif; *2 usu* ˈkwäf\ *n* **1** : a close-fitting hat **2** : COIFFURE
coif•feur \kwä-ˈfər\ *n* [F] : HAIRDRESSER
coif•feuse \kwä-ˈfərz, -ˈfəz, -ˈfüz, -ˈfyüz\ *n* : a female hairdresser
coif•fure \kwä-ˈfyu̇r\ *n* : a manner of arranging the hair
[1]**coil** \ˈkȯil\ *vb* : to wind in a spiral shape
[2]**coil** *n* : a series of rings or loops (as of coiled rope, wire, or pipe) : RING, LOOP
[1]**coin** \ˈkȯin\ *n* [ME, fr. MF, wedge, corner, fr. L *cuneus* wedge] **1** : a piece of metal issued by government authority as money **2** : metal money
[2]**coin** *vb* **1** : to make (a coin) esp. by stamping : MINT **2** : CREATE, INVENT ⟨~ a phrase⟩ — **coin•er** *n*
coin•age \ˈkȯi-nij\ *n* **1** : the act or process of coining **2** : COINS
co•in•cide \ˌkō-ən-ˈsīd, ˈkō-ən-ˌsīd\ *vb* **-cid•ed; -cid•ing** **1** : to occupy the same place in space or time **2** : to correspond or agree exactly
co•in•ci•dence \kō-ˈin-sə-dəns\ *n* **1** : exact agreement **2** : occurrence together apparently without reason; *also* : an event that so occurs
co•in•ci•dent \-sə-dənt\ *adj* **1** : of similar nature **2** : occupying the same space or time — **co•in•ci•den•tal** \kō-ˌin-sə-ˈdent-ᵊl\ *adj*
co•i•tus \ˈkō-ə-təs\ *n* [L, fr. *coire* to come together] : SEXUAL INTERCOURSE — **co•i•tal** \-ᵊl\ *adj*
[1]**coke** \ˈkōk\ *n* : a hard gray porous fuel made by heating soft coal to drive off most of its volatile material
[2]**coke** *n* : COCAINE
[1]**col** *abbr* **1** colonial; colony **2** column
[2]**col** *or* **coll** *abbr* **1** collect, collected, collection **2** college, collegiate
Col *abbr* **1** colonel **2** Colorado **3** Colossians
COL *abbr* **1** colonel **2** cost of living
co•la \ˈkō-lə\ *n* : a carbonated soft drink usu. containing sugar, caffeine, caramel, and special flavoring
col•an•der \ˈkə-lən-dər, ˈkä-\ *n* : a perforated utensil for draining food
[1]**cold** \ˈkōld\ *adj* **1** : having a low or decidedly subnormal temperature **2** : lacking warmth of feeling **3** : suffering or uncomfortable from lack of warmth — **cold•ly** *adv* — **cold•ness** *n* — **in cold blood** : with premeditation : DELIBERATELY
[2]**cold** *n* **1** : a condition marked by low temperature; *also* : cold weather **2** : a chilly feeling **3** : a bodily disorder popularly associated with chilling; *esp* : COMMON COLD
[3]**cold** *adv* : TOTALLY, FINALLY
cold–blood•ed \ˈkōld-ˈblə-dəd\ *adj* **1** : lacking normal human feelings **2** : having a body temperature not internally regulated but close to that of the environment **3** : sensitive to cold
cold feet *n pl* : doubt or fear that prevents action
cold front *n* : an advancing edge of a cold air mass
cold shoulder *n* : cold or unsympathetic behavior — **cold–shoul•der** *vb*
cold sore *n* : a group of blisters appearing in or about the mouth in the oral form of herpes simplex
cold sweat *n* : concurrent perspiration and chill usu. associated with fear, pain, or shock
[1]**cold turkey** *n* : abrupt complete cessation of the use of an addictive drug
[2]**cold turkey** *adv* : without a period of adjustment : all at once
cold war *n* : a conflict characterized by the use of means short of sustained overt military action
cole•slaw \ˈkōl-ˌslȯ\ *n* [D *koolsla*, fr. *kool* cabbage + *sla* salad] : a salad made of raw cabbage
col•ic \ˈkä-lik\ *n* : sharp sudden abdominal pain — **col•icky** \ˈkä-li-kē\ *adj*
col•i•se•um \ˌkä-lə-ˈsē-əm\ *n* : a large structure esp. for athletic contests
col•lab•o•rate \kə-ˈla-bə-ˌrāt\ *vb* **-rat•ed; -rat•ing** **1** : to work jointly with others (as in writing a book) **2** : to cooperate with an enemy force occupying one's country — **col•lab•o•ra•tion** \-ˌla-bə-ˈrā-shən\ *n* — **col•lab•o•ra•tor** \-ˈla-bə-ˌrā-tər\ *n*
col•lage \kə-ˈläzh\ *n* [F, lit., gluing] : an artistic composition of fragments (as of printed matter) pasted on a surface
[1]**col•lapse** \kə-ˈlaps\ *vb* **col•lapsed; col•laps•ing** **1** : to shrink together abruptly **2** : DISINTEGRATE; *also* : to fall in : give way **3** : to break down physically or mentally; *esp* : to fall helpless or unconscious **4** : to fold down compactly — **col•laps•ible** *adj*
[2]**collapse** *n* : BREAKDOWN
[1]**col•lar** \ˈkä-lər\ *n* **1** : a band, strip, or chain worn around the neck or the neckline of a garment **2** : something resembling a collar — **col•lar•less** *adj*

²**collar** *vb* : to seize by the collar; *also* : ARREST, GRAB

col·lar·bone \-ˌbōn\ *n* : the bone of the shoulder that joins the breastbone and the shoulder blade

col·lard \ˈkä-lərd\ *n* : a stalked smooth-leaved kale — usu. used in pl.

col·late \kə-ˈlāt; ˈkä-ˌlāt, ˈkō-\ *vb* **col·lat·ed; col·lat·ing 1** : to compare (as two texts) carefully and critically **2** : to assemble in proper order

¹**col·lat·er·al** \kə-ˈla-tə-rəl\ *adj* **1** : associated but of secondary importance **2** : descended from the same ancestors but not in the same line **3** : PARALLEL **4** : of, relating to, or being collateral used as security; *also* : secured by collateral

²**collateral** *n* : property (as stocks) used as security for the repayment of a loan

col·la·tion \kä-ˈlā-shən, kō-\ *n* **1** : a light meal **2** : the act, process, or result of collating

col·league \ˈkä-ˌlēg\ *n* : an associate esp. in a profession

¹**col·lect** \ˈkä-likt, -ˌlekt\ *n* : a short prayer comprising an invocation, petition, and conclusion

²**col·lect** \kə-ˈlekt\ *vb* **1** : to bring or come together into one body or place : GATHER **2** : to gain control of ⟨~ his thoughts⟩ **3** : to receive payment of — **col·lect·ible** *or* **col·lect·able** *adj or n* — **col·lec·tor** \-ˈlek-tər\ *n*

³**col·lect** \kə-ˈlekt\ *adv or adj* : to be paid for by the receiver

col·lect·ed \kə-ˈlek-təd\ *adj* : SELF-POSSESSED, CALM

col·lec·tion \kə-ˈlek-shən\ *n* **1** : the act or process of collecting ⟨garbage ~⟩ **2** : something collected ⟨a stamp ~⟩ **3** : GROUP, AGGREGATE

¹**col·lec·tive** \kə-ˈlek-tiv\ *adj* **1** : of, relating to, or denoting a group of individuals considered as a whole **2** : involving all members of a group as distinct from its individuals **3** : shared or assumed by all members of the group — **col·lec·tive·ly** *adv*

²**collective** *n* **1** : GROUP **2** : a cooperative unit or organization

collective bargaining *n* : negotiation between an employer and a labor union

col·lec·tiv·ise *chiefly Brit var of* COLLECTIVIZE

col·lec·tiv·ism \kə-ˈlek-ti-ˌvi-zəm\ *n* : a political or economic theory advocating collective control esp. over production and distribution

col·lec·tiv·ize \-ˌvīz\ *vb* **-ized; -iz·ing** : to organize under collective control — **col·lec·tiv·i·za·tion** \-ˌlek-ti-və-ˈzā-shən\ *n*

col·leen \kä-ˈlēn, ˈkä-ˌlēn\ *n* : an Irish girl

col·lege \ˈkä-lij\ *n* [ME, fr. MF, fr. L *collegium* society, fr. *collega* colleague, fr. *com-* with + *legare* to appoint] **1** : a building used for an educational or religious purpose **2** : an institution of higher learning granting a bachelor's degree; *also* : an institution offering instruction esp. in a vocational or technical field ⟨barber ~⟩ **3** : an organized body of persons having common interests or duties ⟨~ of cardinals⟩ — **col·le·giate** \kə-ˈlē-jət\ *adj*

col·le·gi·al·i·ty \kə-ˌlē-jē-ˈa-lə-tē\ *n* : the relationship of colleagues

col·le·gian \kə-ˈlē-jən\ *n* : a college student or recent college graduate

col·le·gi·um \kə-ˈle-gē-əm, -ˈlā-\ *n, pl* **-gia** \-gē-ə\ *or* **-giums** : a group in which each member has approximately equal power

col·lide \kə-ˈlīd\ *vb* **col·lid·ed; col·lid·ing 1** : to come together with solid impact **2** : to come into conflict : CLASH

col·lid·er \kə-ˈlī-dər\ *n* : a particle accelerator in which two beams of particles are made to collide

col·lie \ˈkä-lē\ *n* : a large dog of a breed with rough-coated and smooth-coated varieties developed in Scotland for herding sheep

col·lier \ˈkäl-yər\ *n* **1** : a coal miner **2** : a ship for carrying coal

collie

col·liery \ˈkäl-yə-rē\ *n, pl* **-lier·ies** : a coal mine and its associated buildings

col·li·mate \ˈkä-lə-ˌmāt\ *vb* **-mat·ed; -mat·ing** : to make (as light rays) parallel

col·li·sion \kə-ˈli-zhən\ *n* : an act or instance of colliding

col·lo·ca·tion \ˌkä-lə-ˈkā-shən\ *n* : the act or result of placing or arranging together; *esp* : a noticeable arrangement or conjoining of linguistic elements (as words)

col·loid \ˈkä-ˌlȯid\ *n* : a substance in the form of submicroscopic particles that when in solution or suspension do not settle out; *also* : such a substance together with the medium in which it is dispersed — **col·loi·dal** \kə-ˈlȯid-ᵊl\ *adj*

colloq *abbr* colloquial

col·lo·qui·al \kə-ˈlō-kwē-əl\ *adj* : of, relating to, or characteristic of conversation and esp. of familiar and informal conversation

col·lo·qui·al·ism \-ˈlō-kwē-ə-ˌli-zəm\ *n* : a colloquial expression

col·lo·qui·um \kə-ˈlō-kwē-əm\ *n, pl* **-qui·ums** *or* **-quia** \-ə\ : CONFERENCE, SEMINAR

col·lo·quy \ˈkä-lə-kwē\ *n, pl* **-quies** : a usu. formal conversation or conference

col·lu·sion \kə-ˈlü-zhən\ *n* : secret agreement or cooperation for an illegal or deceitful purpose — **col·lu·sive** \-siv\ *adj*

Colo *abbr* Colorado

co·logne \kə-ˈlōn\ *n* [*Cologne*, Germany] : a perfumed liquid — **co·logned** \-ˈlōnd\ *adj*

Co·lom·bi·an \kə-ˈləm-bē-ən\ *n* : a native or inhabitant of Colombia — **Colombian** *adj*

¹**co·lon** \ˈkō-lən\ *n, pl* **colons** *or* **co·la** \-lə\ : the part of the large intestine extending from the cecum to the rectum — **co·lon·ic** \kō-ˈlä-nik\ *adj*

²**colon** *n, pl* **colons** : a punctuation mark : used esp. to direct attention to following matter (as a list)

co·lón *also* **co·lone** \kə-ˈlōn\ *n, pl* **co·lo·nes** \-ˈlō-ˌnās\ — see MONEY table

col·o·nel \ˈkərn-ᵊl\ *n* [alter. of *coronel*, fr. MF, fr. It *colonnello* column of soldiers, colonel, ultim. fr. L *columna*] : a commissioned officer (as in the army) ranking next below a brigadier general

¹**co·lo·nial** \kə-ˈlō-nē-əl\ *adj* **1** : of, relating to, or characteristic of a colony; *also* : possessing or composed of colonies **2** *often cap* : of or relating to the original 13 colonies forming the U.S.

²**colonial** *n* : a member or inhabitant of a colony

co·lo·nial·ism \-ə-ˌli-zəm\ *n* : control by one power over a dependent area or people; *also* : a policy advocating or based on such control — **co·lo·nial·ist** \-list\ *n or adj*

col·o·nise *Brit var of* COLONIZE

col·o·nist \ˈkä-lə-nist\ *n* **1** : COLONIAL **2** : one that colonizes or settles in a new country

col·o·nize \ˈkä-lə-ˌnīz\ *vb* **-nized; -niz·ing 1** : to establish a colony in or on **2 :** SETTLE — **col•o•ni•za•tion** \ˌkä-lə-nə-ˈzā-shən\ *n* — **col•o•niz•er** *n*

col•on•nade \ˌkä-lə-ˈnād\ *n* **:** an evenly spaced row of columns usu. supporting the base of a roof structure

col•o•ny \ˈkä-lə-nē\ *n, pl* **-nies 1 :** a body of people living in a new territory; *also* **:** the territory inhabited by these people **2 :** a localized population of organisms ⟨a ∼ of bees⟩ **3 :** a group with common interests situated in close association ⟨a writers' ∼⟩; *also* **:** the area occupied by such a group

col•o•phon \ˈkä-lə-fən, -ˌfän\ *n* **1 :** an inscription placed at the end of a book with facts relative to its production **2 :** a distinctive symbol used by a printer or publisher

[1]**col•or** \ˈkə-lər\ *n* **1 :** a phenomenon of light (as red or blue) or visual perception that enables one to differentiate otherwise identical objects; *also* **:** a hue as contrasted with black, white, or gray **2 :** APPEARANCE **3 :** complexion tint **4** *pl* **:** FLAG; *also* **:** military service ⟨a call to the ∼*s*⟩ **5 :** VIVIDNESS, INTEREST — **col•or•ful** *adj* — **col•or•less** *adj*

[2]**color** *vb* **1 :** to give color to; *also* **:** to change the color of **2 :** BLUSH

Col•o•ra•do potato beetle \ˌkä-lə-ˈra-dō-, -ˈrä-\ *n* **:** a black-and-yellow striped beetle that feeds on the leaves of the potato

col•or•ation \ˌkə-lə-ˈrā-shən\ *n* **:** use or arrangement of colors

col•or•a•tu•ra \ˌkə-lə-rə-ˈtu̇r-ə, -ˈtyu̇r-\ *n* **1 :** elaborate ornamentation in vocal music **2 :** a soprano specializing in coloratura

col•or–blind \ˈkə-lər-ˌblīnd\ *adj* **1 :** partially or totally unable to distinguish one or more chromatic colors **2 :** not recognizing differences of race — **color blindness** *n*

col•ored \ˈkə-lərd\ *adj* **1 :** having color **2 :** SLANTED, BIASED **3 :** of a race other than the white; *esp* **:** BLACK 4 — sometimes taken to be offensive

col•or•fast \ˈkə-lər-ˌfast\ *adj* **:** having color that does not fade or run — **col•or•fast•ness** *n*

col•or•ize \ˈkə-lə-ˌrīz\ *vb* **-ized; -iz•ing :** to add color to by means of a computer — **col•or•i•za•tion** \ˌkə-lə-rə-ˈzā-shən\ *n*

co•los•sal \kə-ˈlä-səl\ *adj* **:** of very great size or degree

Co•los•sians \kə-ˈlä-shənz\ *n* — see BIBLE table

co•los•sus \kə-ˈlä-səs\ *n, pl* **co•los•si** \-ˌsī\ [L] **:** a gigantic statue; *also* **:** something of great size or scope

col•our *chiefly Brit var of* COLOR

col•por•teur \ˈkäl-ˌpōr-tər\ *n* [F] **:** a peddler of religious books

colt \ˈkōlt\ *n* **:** FOAL; *also* **:** a young male horse, ass, or zebra — **colt•ish** *adj*

col•um•bine \ˈkä-ləm-ˌbīn\ *n* [ME, fr. ML *columbina*, fr. L, fem. of *columbinus* dovelike, fr. *columba* dove] **:** any of a genus of plants with showy spurred flowers that are related to the buttercups

co•lum•bi•um \kə-ˈləm-bē-əm\ *n* **:** NIOBIUM

Columbus Day \kə-ˈləm-bəs-\ *n* **:** the 2d Monday in October or formerly October 12 observed as a legal holiday in many states in commemoration of the landing of Columbus

col•umn \ˈkä-ləm\ *n* **1 :** one of two or more vertical sections of a printed page; *also* **:** one in a usu. regular series of articles (as in a newspaper) **2 :** a supporting pillar; *esp* **:** one consisting of a usu. round shaft, a capital, and a base **3 :** something resembling a column ⟨a ∼ of water⟩ **4 :** a long row (as of soldiers) — **co•lum•nar** \kə-ˈləm-nər\ *adj*

col•um•nist \ˈkä-ləm-nist\ *n* **:** a person who writes a newspaper or magazine column

com *abbr* **1** comedy; comic **2** comma

co•ma \ˈkō-mə\ *n* **:** a state of deep unconsciousness caused by disease, injury, or poison — **co•ma•tose** \ˈkō-mə-ˌtōs, ˈkä-\ *adj*

Co•man•che \kə-ˈman-chē\ *n, pl* **Comanche** *or* **Comanches :** a member of an American Indian people ranging from Wyoming and Nebraska south into New Mexico and Texas

[1]**comb** \ˈkōm\ *n* **1 :** a toothed instrument for arranging the hair or for separating and cleaning textile fibers **2 :** a fleshy crest on the head of a fowl **3 :** HONEYCOMB — **comb** *vb* — **combed** \ˈkōmd\ *adj*

[2]**comb** *abbr* combination; combining

com•bat \kəm-ˈbat, ˈkäm-ˌbat\ *vb* **-bat•ed** *or* **-bat•ted; -bat•ing** *or* **-bat•ting 1 :** FIGHT, CONTEND **2 :** to struggle against **:** OPPOSE — **com•bat** \ˈkäm-ˌbat\ *n* — **com•bat•ant** \kəm-ˈbat-ᵊnt, ˈkäm-bə-tənt\ *n* — **com•bat•ive** \kəm-ˈba-tiv\ *adj*

combat fatigue *n* **:** a traumatic neurotic or psychotic reaction occurring under conditions (as wartime combat) that cause intense stress

comb•er \ˈkō-mər\ *n* **1 :** one that combs **2 :** a long curling wave of the sea

com•bi•na•tion \ˌkäm-bə-ˈnā-shən\ *n* **1 :** a result or product of combining **2 :** a sequence of letters or numbers chosen in setting a lock **3 :** the act or process of combining; *also* **:** the quality or state of being combined

[1]**com•bine** \kəm-ˈbīn\ *vb* **com•bined; com•bin•ing :** to become one **:** UNITE

[2]**com•bine** \ˈkäm-ˌbīn\ *n* **1 :** a combination esp. of business or political interests **2 :** a machine that harvests and threshes grain while moving over a field

comb•ings \ˈkō-miŋz\ *n pl* **:** loose hairs or fibers removed by a comb

combining form *n* **:** a linguistic form that occurs only in compounds or derivatives

com•bo \ˈkäm-bō\ *n, pl* **combos :** a small jazz or dance band

com•bus•ti•ble \kəm-ˈbəs-tə-bəl\ *adj* **:** capable of being burned — **com•bus•ti•bil•i•ty** \-ˌbəs-tə-ˈbi-lə-tē\ *n* — **combustible** *n*

com•bus•tion \kəm-ˈbəs-chən\ *n* **1 :** an act or instance of burning **2 :** slow oxidation (as in the animal body)

comdg *abbr* commanding

comdr *abbr* commander

comdt *abbr* commandant

come \ˈkəm\ *vb* **came** \ˈkām\; **come; com•ing** \ˈkə-miŋ\ **1 :** APPROACH **2 :** ARRIVE **3 :** to reach the point of being or becoming ⟨∼ to a boil⟩ **4 :** AMOUNT ⟨the bill *came* to $10⟩ **5 :** to take place **6 :** ORIGINATE, ARISE **7 :** to be available **8 :** REACH, EXTEND — **come clean :** CONFESS — **come into :** ACQUIRE, ACHIEVE — **come to pass :** HAPPEN — **come to terms :** to reach an agreement

come•back \ˈkəm-ˌbak\ *n* **1 :** RETORT **2 :** a return to a former position or condition — **come back** *vb*

co•me•di•an \kə-ˈmē-dē-ən\ *n* **1 :** an actor in comedy **2 :** a comic person; *esp* **:** an entertainer specializing in comedy

co•me•di•enne \-ˌmē-dē-ˈen\ *n* **:** a woman who is a comedian

come•down \ˈkəm-ˌdau̇n\ *n* **:** a descent in rank or dignity

com•e•dy \ˈkä-mə-dē\ *n, pl* **-dies** [ME, fr. MF *comedie*, fr. L *comoedia*, fr. Gk *kōmōidia*, fr. *kōmos* revel + *aeidein* to sing] **1 :** a light amusing play with a happy ending **2 :** a literary work treating a comic theme or written in a comic style **3 :** humorous entertainment

come•ly \ˈkəm-lē\ *adj* **come•li•er; -est :** ATTRACTIVE, HANDSOME — **come•li•ness** *n*

come off *vb* **:** SUCCEED

come–on \ˈkə-ˌmȯn, -ˌmän\ *n* **:** INDUCEMENT, LURE

come out *vb* **1 :** to come into public view **2 :** to declare oneself **3 :** TURN OUT 5 ⟨everything *came out* all right⟩ — **come out with :** SAY 1

com•er \ˈkə-mər\ *n* **1 :** one that comes ⟨all ∼*s*⟩ **2 :** a promising beginner

[1]**co•mes•ti•ble** \kə-ˈmes-tə-bəl\ *adj* **:** EDIBLE

[2]**comestible** *n* **:** FOOD — usu. used in pl.

com•et \ˈkä-mət\ *n* [ME *comete*, fr. OE *cometa*, fr. L, fr. Gk *komētēs*, lit., long-haired, fr. *komē* hair] **:** a small bright celestial body that develops a long tail when near the sun

come to *vb* : to regain consciousness

come•up•pance \kə-ˈmə-pəns\ *n* : a deserved rebuke or penalty

com•fit \ˈkəm-fət\ *n* : a candied fruit or nut

1**com•fort** \ˈkəm-fərt\ *vb* **1** : to give strength and hope to **2** : CONSOLE

2**comfort** *n* **1** : CONSOLATION **2** : freedom from pain, trouble, or anxiety; *also* : something that gives such freedom

com•fort•able \ˈkəm-fər-tə-bəl, ˈkəmf-tər-\ *adj* **1** : providing comfort or security **2** : feeling at ease — **com•fort•ably** \-blē\ *adv*

com•fort•er \ˈkəm-fər-tər\ *n* **1** : one that comforts **2** : QUILT

com•fy \ˈkəm-fē\ *adj* : COMFORTABLE

1**com•ic** \ˈkä-mik\ *adj* **1** : relating to comedy or comic strips **2** : provoking laughter or amusement **syn** laughable, funny, farcical — **com•i•cal** *adj*

2**comic** *n* **1** : COMEDIAN **2** *pl* : the part of a newspaper devoted to comic strips

comic book *n* : a magazine containing sequences of comic strips

comic strip *n* : a group of cartoons in narrative sequence

coming \ˈkə-miŋ\ *adj* **1** : APPROACHING, NEXT **2** : gaining importance

co•mi•ty \ˈkä-mə-tē, ˈkō-\ *n, pl* **-ties** : friendly civility : COURTESY

coml *abbr* commercial

comm *abbr* **1** command; commander **2** commerce; commercial **3** commission; commissioner **4** committee **5** common **6** commonwealth

com•ma \ˈkä-mə\ *n* : a punctuation mark , used esp. as a mark of separation within the sentence

1**com•mand** \kə-ˈmand\ *vb* **1** : to direct authoritatively : ORDER **2** : DOMINATE, CONTROL, GOVERN **3** : to overlook from a strategic position

2**command** *n* **1** : an order given **2** : ability to control : MASTERY **3** : the act of commanding **4** : a signal that actuates a device (as a computer); *also* : the activation of a device by means of a signal **5** : a body of troops under a commander; *also* : an area or position that one commands **6** : a position of highest authority

com•man•dant \ˈkä-mən-ˌdant, -ˌdänt\ *n* : an officer in command

com•man•deer \ˌkä-mən-ˈdir\ *vb* : to take possession of by force

com•mand•er \kə-ˈman-dər\ *n* **1** : LEADER, CHIEF; *esp* : an officer commanding an army or subdivision of an army **2** : a commissioned officer in the navy ranking next below a captain

commander in chief : the supreme commander of the armed forces

com•mand•ment \kə-ˈmand-mənt\ *n* : COMMAND, ORDER; *esp* : any of the Ten Commandments

command module *n* : a space vehicle module designed to carry the crew and reentry equipment

com•man•do \kə-ˈman-dō\ *n, pl* **-dos** *or* **-does** [Afrikaans *kommando*, fr. Dutch *commando* command] : a member of a military unit trained for surprise raids

command sergeant major *n* : a noncommissioned officer in the army ranking above a first sergeant

com•mem•o•rate \kə-ˈme-mə-ˌrāt\ *vb* **-rat•ed; -rat•ing** **1** : to call or recall to mind **2** : to serve as a memorial of — **com•mem•o•ra•tion** \-ˌme-mə-ˈrā-shən\ *n*

com•mem•o•ra•tive \kə-ˈmem-rə-tiv, -ˈme-mə-ˌrā-tiv\ *adj* : intended to commemorate an event

com•mence \kə-ˈmens\ *vb* **com•menced; com•menc•ing** : BEGIN, START

com•mence•ment \-mənt\ *n* **1** : the act or time of a beginning **2** : the graduation exercises of a school or college

com•mend \kə-ˈmend\ *vb* **1** : to commit to one's care **2** : RECOMMEND **3** : PRAISE — **com•mend•able** \-ˈmen-də-bəl\ *adj* — **com•mend•ably** \-blē\ *adv* — **com•men•da•tion** \ˌkä-mən-ˈdā-shən, -ˌmen-\ *n* — **com•mend•er** *n*

com•men•su•ra•ble \kə-ˈmen-sə-rə-bəl\ *adj* : having a common measure or a common divisor

com•men•su•rate \kə-ˈmen-sə-rət, -ˈmen-chə-\ *adj* : equal in measure or extent; *also* : PROPORTIONAL, CORRESPONDING ⟨a job ~ with her abilities⟩

com•ment \ˈkä-ˌment\ *n* **1** : an expression of opinion **2** : an explanatory, illustrative, or critical note or observation : REMARK — **comment** *vb*

com•men•tary \ˈkä-mən-ˌter-ē\ *n, pl* **-tar•ies** : a systematic series of comments

com•men•ta•tor \-ˌtā-tər\ *n* : one who comments; *esp* : a person who discusses news events on radio or television

com•merce \ˈkä-(ˌ)mərs\ *n* : the buying and selling of commodities : TRADE

1**com•mer•cial** \kə-ˈmər-shəl\ *adj* : having to do with commerce; *also* : designed for profit or for mass appeal — **com•mer•cial•ly** *adv*

2**commercial** *n* : an advertisement broadcast on radio or television

com•mer•cial•ise *Brit var of* COMMERCIALIZE

com•mer•cial•ism \kə-ˈmər-shə-ˌli-zəm\ *n* **1** : a spirit, method, or practice characteristic of business **2** : excessive emphasis on profit

com•mer•cial•ize \-ˌlīz\ *vb* **-ized; -iz•ing** **1** : to manage on a business basis for profit **2** : to exploit for profit

com•mi•na•tion \ˌkä-mə-ˈnā-shən\ *n* : DENUNCIATION — **com•mi•na•to•ry** \ˈkä-mə-nə-ˌtōr-ē\ *adj*

com•min•gle \kə-ˈmiŋ-gəl\ *vb* : MINGLE, BLEND

com•mis•er•ate \kə-ˈmi-zə-ˌrāt\ *vb* **-at•ed; -at•ing** : to feel or express pity : SYMPATHIZE — **com•mis•er•a•tion** \-ˌmi-zə-ˈrā-shən\ *n*

com•mis•sar \ˈkä-mə-ˌsär\ *n* [Russ *komissar*] : a Communist party official

com•mis•sar•i•at \ˌkä-mə-ˈser-ē-ət\ *n* **1** : a system for supplying troops with food **2** : a department headed by a commissar

com•mis•sary \ˈkä-mə-ˌser-ē\ *n, pl* **-sar•ies** : a store for equipment and provisions esp. for military personnel

1**com•mis•sion** \kə-ˈmi-shən\ *n* **1** : a warrant granting certain powers and imposing certain duties **2** : a certificate conferring military rank and authority **3** : authority to act as agent for another; *also* : something to be done by an agent **4** : a body of persons charged with performing a duty **5** : the doing of some act; *also* : the thing done **6** : the allowance made to an agent for transacting business for another

2**commission** *vb* **1** : to give a commission to **2** : to order to be made **3** : to put (a ship) into a state of readiness for service

commissioned officer *n* : an officer of the armed forces holding rank by a commission from the president

com•mis•sion•er \kə-ˈmi-shə-nər\ *n* **1** : a member of a commission **2** : an official in charge of a department of public service **3** : the administrative head of a professional sport — **com•mis•sion•er•ship** *n*

com•mit \kə-ˈmit\ *vb* **com•mit•ted; com•mit•ting** **1** : to put into charge or trust : ENTRUST **2** : to put in a prison or mental institution **3** : TRANSFER, CONSIGN **4** : to carry into action : PERPETRATE ⟨~ a crime⟩ **5** : to pledge or assign to some particular course or use — **com•mit•ment** *n* — **com•mit•tal** *n*

com•mit•tee \kə-ˈmi-tē\ *n* : a body of persons selected to consider and act or report on some matter — **com•mit•tee•man** \-mən\ *n* — **com•mit•tee•wom•an** \-ˌwu̇-mən\ *n*

commo *abbr* commodore

com•mode \kə-ˈmōd\ *n* [F, fr. *commode*, adj., suitable, convenient, fr. L *commodus*, fr. *com-* with + *modus* measure] **1** : a movable washstand with cupboard below **2** : TOILET 3

com•mo•di•ous \kə-ˈmō-dē-əs\ *adj* : comfortably spacious : ROOMY

com•mod•i•ty \kə-ˈmä-də-tē\ *n, pl* **-ties** **1** : a product of agriculture or mining **2** : an article of commerce **3** : something useful or valued ⟨that valuable ~ patience⟩

com•mo•dore \ˈkä-mə-ˌdōr\ *n* **1** : a commissioned officer in the navy ranking next below a rear admiral **2** : an officer commanding a group of merchant ships **3** : the chief officer of a yacht club

[1]**com•mon** \ˈkä-mən\ *adj* **1** : belonging to or serving the community : PUBLIC **2** : shared by a number in a group **3** : widely or generally known, found, or observed : FAMILIAR ⟨~ knowledge⟩ **4** : VERNACULAR 3 ⟨~ names of plants⟩ **5** : not above the average esp. in social status **syn** universal, general, generic — **com•mon•ly** *adv*

[2]**common** *n* **1** *pl* : the common people **2** *pl* : a dining hall **3** *pl, cap* : the lower house of the British and Canadian parliaments **4** : a piece of land subject to common use — **in common** : shared together

com•mon•al•ty \ˈkä-mən-əl-tē\ *n, pl* **-ties** : the common people

common cold *n* : a contagious respiratory disease caused by a virus and characterized by a sore, swollen, and inflamed nose and throat, usu. by much mucus, and by coughing and sneezing

common denominator *n* **1** : a common multiple of the denominators of a number of fractions **2** : a common trait or theme

common divisor *n* : a number or expression that divides two or more numbers or expressions without remainder

com•mon•er \ˈkä-mə-nər\ *n* : one of the common people : a person having no rank of nobility

common fraction *n* : a fraction in which the numerator and denominator are both integers and are separated by a horizontal or slanted line

common law *n* : a group of legal practices and traditions based on judges' decisions and social customs and usu. having the same force as laws passed by legislative bodies

common logarithm *n* : a logarithm whose base is 10

common market *n* : an economic association formed to remove trade barriers among members

common multiple *n* : a multiple of each of two or more numbers or expressions

[1]**com•mon•place** \ˈkä-mən-ˌplās\ *n* : something that is ordinary or trite

[2]**commonplace** *adj* : ORDINARY

common sense *n* : ordinary good sense and judgment

com•mon•weal \ˈkä-mən-ˌwēl\ *n* **1** *archaic* : COMMONWEALTH **2** : the general welfare

com•mon•wealth \-ˌwelth\ *n* **1** : the body of people politically organized into a state **2** : STATE; *also* : an association or federation of autonomous states

com•mo•tion \kə-ˈmō-shən\ *n* **1** : DISTURBANCE, UPRISING **2** : AGITATION

com•mu•nal \kə-ˈmyün-əl, ˈkäm-yən-əl\ *adj* **1** : of or relating to a commune or community **2** : marked by collective ownership and use of property **3** : shared or used in common

[1]**com•mune** \kə-ˈmyün\ *vb* **com•muned; com•mun•ing** : to communicate intimately

[2]**com•mune** \ˈkäm-ˌyün; kə-ˈmyün\ *n* **1** : the smallest administrative district in some European countries **2** : a community organized on a communal basis

com•mu•ni•ca•ble \kə-ˈmyü-ni-kə-bəl\ *adj* : capable of being communicated ⟨~ diseases⟩ — **com•mu•ni•ca•bil•i•ty** \-ˌmyü-ni-kə-ˈbi-lə-tē\ *n*

com•mu•ni•cant \-ˈmyü-ni-kənt\ *n* **1** : a church member entitled to receive Communion **2** : one that communicates; *esp* : INFORMANT

com•mu•ni•cate \kə-ˈmyü-nə-ˌkāt\ *vb* **-cat•ed; -cat•ing** **1** : to make known **2** : to pass from one to another : TRANSMIT **3** : to receive Communion **4** : to be in communication **5** : JOIN, CONNECT

com•mu•ni•ca•tion \kə-ˌmyü-nə-ˈkā- shən\ *n* **1** : an act of transmitting **2** : MESSAGE **3** : exchange of information or opinions **4** : a means of communicating — **com•mu•ni•ca•tive** \-ˈmyü-nə-ˌkā-tiv, -ni-kə-tiv\ *adj*

com•mu•nion \kə-ˈmyü-nyən\ *n* **1** : a sharing of something with others **2** *cap* : a Christian sacrament in which bread and wine are consumed as the substance or symbols of Christ's body and blood in commemoration of the death of Christ **3** : intimate fellowship or rapport **4** : a body of Christians having a common faith and discipline

com•mu•ni•qué \kə-ˈmyü-nə-ˌkā, -ˌmyü-nə-ˈkā\ *n* : BULLETIN 1

com•mu•nism \ˈkäm-yə-ˌni-zəm\ *n* **1** : social organization in which goods are held in common **2** : a theory of social organization advocating common ownership of means of production and a distribution of products of industry based on need **3** *cap* : a political doctrine based on revolutionary Marxist socialism that was the official ideology of the U.S.S.R. and some other countries; *also* : a system of government in which one party controls state-owned means of production — **com•mu•nist** \-nist\ *n or adj, often cap* — **com•mu•nis•tic** \ˌkäm-yə-ˈnis-tik\ *adj, often cap*

com•mu•ni•ty \kə-ˈmyü-nə-tē\ *n, pl* **-ties** **1** : a body of people living in the same place under the same laws; *also* : a natural population of plants and animals that interact ecologically and live in one place (as a pond) **2** : society at large **3** : joint ownership **4** : SIMILARITY, LIKENESS

community college *n* : a 2-year government-supported college that offers an associate degree

community property *n* : property held jointly by husband and wife

com•mu•ta•tion \ˌkäm-yə-ˈtā-shən\ *n* : substitution of one form of payment or penalty for another

com•mu•ta•tive \ˈkäm-yə-ˌtā-tiv, kə-ˈmyü-tə-\ *adj* : of, relating to, having, or being the property that a given mathematical operation and set have when the result obtained using any two elements of the set with the operation does not differ with the order in which the numbers are used — **com•mu•ta•tiv•i•ty** \kə-ˌmyü-tə-ˈti-və-tē, ˌkäm-yə-tə-\ *n*

com•mu•ta•tor \ˈkäm-yə-ˌtā-tər\ *n* : a device (as on a generator or motor) for changing the direction of electric current

[1]**com•mute** \kə-ˈmyüt\ *vb* **com•mut•ed; com•mut•ing** **1** : EXCHANGE **2** : to revoke (a sentence) and impose a milder penalty **3** : to travel back and forth regularly — **com•mut•er** *n*

[2]**commute** *n* : a trip made in commuting

comp *abbr* **1** comparative; compare **2** compensation **3** compiled; compiler **4** composition; compositor **5** compound **6** comprehensive **7** comptroller

[1]**com•pact** \kəm-ˈpakt, ˈkäm-ˌpakt\ *adj* **1** : SOLID, DENSE **2** : BRIEF, SUCCINCT **3** : occupying a small volume by efficient use of space ⟨~ camera⟩ — **com•pact•ly** *adv* — **com•pact•ness** *n*

[2]**compact** *vb* : to pack together : COMPRESS — **com•pac•tor** \kəm-ˈpak-tər, ˈkäm-ˌpak-\ *n*

[3]**com•pact** \ˈkäm-ˌpakt\ *n* **1** : a small case for cosmetics **2** : a small automobile

[4]**com•pact** \ˈkäm-ˌpakt\ *n* : AGREEMENT, COVENANT

com•pact disc \ˈkäm-ˌpakt-\ *n* : a small plastic optical disc usu. containing recorded music

[1]**com•pan•ion** \kəm-ˈpan-yən\ *n* [OF *compagnon,* fr. LL *companion-, companio,* fr. L *com-* together + *panis* bread] **1** : an intimate friend or associate : COMRADE **2** : one that is closely connected with something similar — **com•pan•ion•able** *adj* — **com•pan•ion•ship** *n*

[2]**companion** *n* : COMPANIONWAY

com•pan•ion•way \-ˌwā\ *n* : a ship's stairway from one deck to another

com•pa•ny \ˈkəm-pə-nē\ *n, pl* **-nies 1** : association with others : FELLOWSHIP; *also* : COMPANIONS **2** : GUESTS **3** : a group of persons or things **4** : an infantry unit consisting of two or more platoons and normally commanded by a captain **5** : a group of musical or dramatic performers **6** : the officers and crew of a ship **7** : an association of persons for carrying on a business **syn** party, band, troop, troupe, corps, outfit

com•pa•ra•ble \ˈkäm-pə-rə-bəl, -prə-\ *adj* : capable of being compared **syn** parallel, similar, like, alike, corresponding — **com•pa•ra•bil•i•ty** \ˌkäm-pə-rə-ˈbi-lə-tē\ *n*

[1]**com•par•a•tive** \kəm-ˈpar-ə-tiv\ *adj* **1** : of, relating to, or constituting the degree of grammatical comparison that denotes increase in quality, quantity, or relation **2** : RELATIVE ⟨a ~ stranger⟩ — **com•par•a•tive•ly** *adv*

[2]**comparative** *n* : the comparative degree or form in a language

[1]**com•pare** \kəm-ˈpar\ *vb* **com•pared; com•par•ing 1** : to represent as similar : LIKEN **2** : to examine for likenesses and differences **3** : to inflect or modify (an adjective or adverb) according to the degrees of comparison

[2]**compare** *n* : the possibility of comparing ⟨beauty beyond ~⟩

com•par•i•son \kəm-ˈpar-ə-sən\ *n* **1** : the act of comparing **2** : change in the form of an adjective or adverb to show different levels of quality, quantity, or relation

com•part•ment \kəm-ˈpärt-mənt\ *n* **1** : a separate division **2** : a section of an enclosed space : ROOM

com•part•men•tal•ise *Brit var of* COMPARTMENTALIZE

com•part•men•tal•ize \kəm-ˌpärt-ˈment-ᵊl-ˌīz\ *vb* **-ized; -iz•ing** : to separate into compartments

[1]**com•pass** \ˈkəm-pəs, ˈkäm-\ *vb* [ME, fr. OF *compasser* to measure, fr. (assumed) VL *compassare* to pace off, fr. L *com-* + *passus* pace] **1** : CONTRIVE, PLOT **2** : ENCIRCLE, ENCOMPASS **3** : BRING ABOUT, ACHIEVE

[2]**compass** *n* **1** : BOUNDARY, CIRCUMFERENCE **2** : an enclosed space **3** : RANGE, SCOPE **4** : a device for determining direction by means of a magnetic needle swinging freely and pointing to the magnetic north; *also* : a nonmagnetic device that indicates direction **5** : an instrument for drawing circles or transferring measurements consisting of two legs joined by a pivot

com•pas•sion \kəm-ˈpa-shən\ *n* : sympathetic feeling : PITY, MERCY — **com•pas•sion•ate** \-shə-nət\ *adj* — **com•pas•sion•ate•ly** *adv*

com•pat•i•ble \kəm-ˈpa-tə-bəl\ *adj* : able to exist or act together harmoniously ⟨~ colors⟩ ⟨~ drugs⟩ **syn** consonant, congenial, sympathetic — **com•pat•i•bil•i•ty** \-ˌpa-tə-ˈbi-lə-tē\ *n*

com•pa•tri•ot \kəm-ˈpā-trē-ət, -ˌät\ *n* : a fellow countryman

com•peer \ˈkäm-ˌpir\ *n* : EQUAL, PEER

com•pel \kəm-ˈpel\ *vb* **com•pelled; com•pel•ling** : to drive or urge with force

com•pen•di•ous \kəm-ˈpen-dē-əs\ *adj* : concise and comprehensive; *also* : COMPREHENSIVE

com•pen•di•um \kəm-ˈpen-dē-əm\ *n, pl* **-di•ums** *or* **-dia** \-ə\ **1** : a brief summary of a larger work or of a field of knowledge **2** : COLLECTION

com•pen•sate \ˈkäm-pən-ˌsāt\ *vb* **-sat•ed; -sat•ing 1** : to be equivalent to : make up for **2** : PAY, REMUNERATE **syn** balance, offset, counterbalance, counterpoise — **com•pen•sa•tion** \ˌkäm-pən-ˈsā-shən\ *n* — **com•pen•sa•to•ry** \kəm-ˈpen-sə-ˌtōr-ē\ *adj*

com•pete \kəm-ˈpēt\ *vb* **com•pet•ed; com•pet•ing** : CONTEND, VIE

com•pe•tence \ˈkäm-pə-təns\ *n* **1** : adequate means for subsistence **2** : FITNESS, ABILITY

com•pe•ten•cy \-tən-sē\ *n, pl* **-cies** : COMPETENCE

com•pe•tent \-tənt\ *adj* : CAPABLE, FIT, QUALIFIED

com•pe•ti•tion \ˌkäm-pə-ˈti-shən\ *n* **1** : the act of competing : RIVALRY **2** : CONTEST, MATCH; *also* : one's competitors — **com•pet•i•tive** \kəm-ˈpe-tə-tiv\ *adj* — **com•pet•i•tive•ly** *adv* — **com•pet•i•tive•ness** *n*

com•pet•i•tor \kəm-ˈpe-tə-tər\ *n* : one that competes : RIVAL

com•pile \kəm-ˈpīl\ *vb* **com•piled; com•pil•ing** [ME, fr. MF *compiler,* fr. L *compilare* to plunder] **1** : to compose out of materials from other documents **2** : to collect and edit into a volume **3** : to translate (a computer program) with a compiler **4** : to build up gradually ⟨~ a record of four wins and two losses⟩ — **com•pi•la•tion** \ˌkäm-pə-ˈlā-shən\ *n*

com•pil•er \kəm-ˈpī-lər\ *n* **1** : one that compiles **2** : a computer program that translates any program correctly written in a specific programming language into machine language

com•pla•cence \kəm-ˈplās-ᵊns\ *n* : COMPLACENCY — **com•pla•cent** \-ᵊnt\ *adj* — **com•pla•cent•ly** *adv*

com•pla•cen•cy \-ᵊn-sē\ *n, pl* **-cies** : SATISFACTION; *esp* : SELF-SATISFACTION

com•plain \kəm-ˈplān\ *vb* **1** : to express grief, pain, or discontent **2** : to make a formal accusation — **com•plain•ant** *n* — **com•plain•er** *n*

com•plaint \kəm-ˈplānt\ *n* **1** : expression of grief, pain, or dissatisfaction **2** : a bodily ailment or disease **3** : a formal accusation against a person

com•plai•sance \kəm-ˈplās-ᵊns, ˌkäm-plā-ˈzans\ *n* [F] : disposition to please — **com•plai•sant** \-ᵊnt, -ˈzant\ *adj*

com•pleat \kəm-ˈplēt\ *adj* : PROFICIENT

com•plect•ed \kəm-ˈplek-təd\ *adj* : having a specified facial complexion ⟨dark-*complected*⟩

[1]**com•ple•ment** \ˈkäm-plə-mənt\ *n* **1** : something that fills up or completes; *also* : the full quantity, number, or amount that makes a thing complete **2** : an added word by which a predicate is made complete **3** : a group of proteins in blood that combines with antibodies to destroy antigens — **com•ple•men•ta•ry** \ˌkäm-plə-ˈmen-t(ə-)rē\ *adj*

[2]**com•ple•ment** \-ˌment\ *vb* : to be complementary to : fill out

[1]**com•plete** \kəm-ˈplēt\ *adj* **com•plet•er; -est 1** : having all parts or elements **2** : brought to an end **3** : fully carried out; *also* : ABSOLUTE 2 ⟨~ silence⟩ — **com•plete•ly** *adv* — **com•plete•ness** *n* — **com•ple•tion** \-ˈplē-shən\ *n*

[2]**complete** *vb* **com•plet•ed; com•plet•ing 1** : FINISH, CONCLUDE **2** : to make whole or perfect ⟨the hat ~*s* the outfit⟩

[1]**com•plex** \ˈkäm-ˌpleks\ *n* **1** : a whole made up of or involving intricately interrelated elements **2** : a group of repressed desires and memories that exert a dominating influence on one's personality and behavior ⟨a guilt ~⟩

[2]**com•plex** \käm-ˈpleks, ˈkäm-ˌpleks\ *adj* **1** : composed of two or more parts **2** : consisting of a main clause and one or more subordinate clauses ⟨~ sentence⟩ **3** : hard to separate, analyze, or solve — **com•plex•i•ty** \käm-ˈplek-sə-tē\ *n* — **com•plex•ly** *adv*

complex fraction *n* : a fraction with a fraction or mixed number in the numerator or denominator or both

com•plex•ion \kəm-ˈplek-shən\ *n* **1** : the hue or appearance of the skin esp. of the face **2** : overall appearance — **com•plex•ioned** \-shənd\ *adj*

complex number *n* : a number (as $3 + 4\sqrt{-1}$) formed by adding a real number to the product of a real number and the square root of minus one

com•pli•ance \kəm-ˈplī-əns\ *n* **1** : the act of complying to a demand or proposal **2** : a disposition to yield — **com•pli•ant** \-ənt\ *adj*

com•pli•cate \ˈkäm-plə-ˌkāt\ *vb* **-cat•ed; -cat•ing** : to make or become complex or intricate

com•pli•cat•ed \ˈkäm-plə-ˌkā-təd\ *adj* **1** : consisting of parts intricately combined **2** : difficult to analyze, understand, or explain — **com•pli•cat•ed•ly** *adv*

com·pli·ca·tion \ˌkäm-plə-ˈkā-shən\ *n* **1** : the quality or state of being complicated; *also* : a complex feature **2** : a disease or condition that develops during and affects the course of a primary disease or condition

com·plic·i·ty \kəm-ˈpli-sə-tē\ *n, pl* **-ties** : the state of being an accomplice

1**com·pli·ment** \ˈkäm-plə-mənt\ *n* **1** : an expression of approval or admiration; *esp* : a flattering remark **2** *pl* : best wishes : REGARDS

2**com·pli·ment** \-ˌment\ *vb* : to pay a compliment to

com·pli·men·ta·ry \ˌkäm-plə-ˈmen-t(ə-)rē\ *adj* **1** : containing or expressing a compliment **2** : given free as a courtesy ⟨~ ticket⟩

com·ply \kəm-ˈplī\ *vb* **com·plied; com·ply·ing** : CONFORM, YIELD

1**com·po·nent** \kəm-ˈpō-nənt, ˈkäm-ˌpō-\ *n* : a component part **syn** ingredient, element, factor, constituent

2**component** *adj* : serving to form a part of : CONSTITUENT

com·port \kəm-ˈpōrt\ *vb* **1** : AGREE, ACCORD **2** : CONDUCT **syn** behave, acquit, deport — **com·port·ment** *n*

com·pose \kəm-ˈpōz\ *vb* **com·posed; com·pos·ing 1** : to form by putting together : FASHION **2** : to produce (as pages of type) by composition **3** : ADJUST, ARRANGE **4** : CALM, QUIET **5** : to practice composition ⟨~ music⟩ — **com·pos·er** *n*

1**com·pos·ite** \käm-ˈpä-zət\ *adj* **1** : made up of distinct parts or elements **2** : of, relating to, or being a large family of flowering plants (as a daisy or aster) that bear many small flowers united into compact heads resembling single flowers

2**composite** *n* **1** : something composite **2** : a plant of the composite family **syn** blend, compound, mixture, amalgamation

com·po·si·tion \ˌkäm-pə-ˈzi-shən\ *n* **1** : the act or process of composing; *esp* : arrangement esp. in artistic form **2** : the arrangement or production of type for printing **3** : general makeup **4** : a product of mixing various elements or ingredients **5** : a literary, musical, or artistic product; *esp* : ESSAY

com·pos·i·tor \kəm-ˈpä-zə-tər\ *n* : one who sets type

com·post \ˈkäm-ˌpōst\ *n* : a fertilizing material consisting largely of decayed organic matter

com·po·sure \kəm-ˈpō-zhər\ *n* : CALMNESS, SELF-POSSESSION

com·pote \ˈkäm-ˌpōt\ *n* **1** : fruits cooked in syrup **2** : a bowl (as of glass) usu. with a base and stem for serving esp. fruit or compote

1**com·pound** \käm-ˈpaund, ˈkäm-ˌ\ *vb* [ME *compounen*, fr. MF *compondre*, fr. L *componere*, fr. *com-* together + *ponere* to put] **1** : COMBINE **2** : to form by combining parts ⟨~ a medicine⟩ **3** : SETTLE ⟨~ a dispute⟩; *also* : to refrain from prosecuting (an offense) in return for a consideration **4** : to increase (as interest) by an amount that can itself vary; *also* : to add to

2**com·pound** \ˈkäm-ˌpau̇nd\ *adj* **1** : made up of individual parts **2** : composed of united similar parts esp. of a kind usu. independent ⟨a ~ plant ovary⟩ **3** : formed by the combination of two or more otherwise independent elements ⟨~ sentence⟩

3**com·pound** \ˈkäm-ˌpau̇nd\ *n* **1** : a word consisting of parts that are words **2** : something formed from a union of elements or parts; *esp* : a distinct substance formed by the union of two or more chemical elements **syn** mixture, composite, blend, admixture, alloy

4**com·pound** \ˈkäm-ˌpau̇nd\ *n* [by folk etymology fr. Malay *kampung* group of buildings, village] : an enclosure containing buildings

compound interest *n* : interest computed on the sum of an original principal and accrued interest

com·pre·hend \ˌkäm-pri-ˈhend\ *vb* **1** : UNDERSTAND **2** : INCLUDE — **com·pre·hen·si·ble** \-ˈhen-sə-bəl\ *adj* — **com·pre·hen·sion** \-ˈhen-chən\ *n* — **com·pre·hen·sive** \-siv\ *adj*

1**com·press** \kəm-ˈpres\ *vb* : to squeeze together **syn** constrict, contract, shrink — **com·pres·sion** \-ˈpre-shən\ *n* — **com·pres·sor** \-ˈpre-sər\ *n*

2**com·press** \ˈkäm-ˌpres\ *n* : a folded pad or cloth used to press upon a body part

compressed air *n* : air under pressure greater than that of the atmosphere

com·prise \kəm-ˈprīz\ *vb* **com·prised; com·pris·ing 1** : INCLUDE, CONTAIN **2** : to be made up of **3** : COMPOSE, CONSTITUTE

1**com·pro·mise** \ˈkäm-prə-ˌmīz\ *n* : a settlement of differences reached by mutual concessions

2**compromise** *vb* **-mised; -mis·ing 1** : to settle by compromise **2** : to expose to suspicion or loss of reputation

comp·trol·ler \kən-ˈtrō-lər, ˈkämp-ˌtrō-\ *n* : an official who audits and supervises expenditures and accounts

com·pul·sion \kəm-ˈpəl-shən\ *n* **1** : an act of compelling **2** : a force that compels **3** : an irresistible impulse **syn** constraint, force, violence, duress — **com·pul·sive** \-siv\ *adj* — **com·pul·so·ry** \-sə-rē\ *adj*

com·punc·tion \kəm-ˈpəŋk-shən\ *n* : anxiety arising from guilt : REMORSE

com·pute \kəm-ˈpyüt\ *vb* **com·put·ed; com·put·ing** : CALCULATE, RECKON — **com·pu·ta·tion** \ˌkäm-pyu̇-ˈtā-shən\ *n* — **com·pu·ta·tion·al** *adj*

computed tomography *n* : radiography in which a three-dimensional image of a body structure is constructed by computer from a series of plane cross-sectional images made along an axis

com·put·er \kəm-ˈpyü-tər\ *n* : a programmable electronic device that can store, retrieve, and process data

com·put·er·ise *chiefly Brit var of* COMPUTERIZE

com·put·er·ize \kəm-ˈpyü-tə-ˌrīz\ *vb* **-ized; -iz·ing 1** : to carry out, control, or produce by means of a computer **2** : to provide with computers **3** : to store in a computer; *also* : put into a form that a computer can use — **com·put·er·iza·tion** \-ˌpyü-tə-rə-ˈzā-shən\ *n*

computerized axial tomography *n* : COMPUTED TOMOGRAPHY

com·rade \ˈkäm-ˌrad\ *n* [MF *comarade* group sleeping in one room, roommate, companion, fr. Sp *camarada*, fr. *cámara* room, fr. LL *camera*] : COMPANION, ASSOCIATE — **com·rade·ly** *adj* — **com·rade·ship** *n*

1**con** \ˈkän\ *vb* **conned; con·ning 1** : MEMORIZE **2** : STUDY

2**con** *adv* : in opposition : AGAINST

3**con** *n* : an opposing argument, person, or position ⟨pros and ~s⟩

4**con** *vb* **conned; con·ning 1** : SWINDLE **2** : PERSUADE, CAJOLE

5**con** *n* : CONVICT

conc *abbr* concentrated

con·cat·e·nate \kän-ˈka-tə-ˌnāt\ *vb* **-nat·ed; -nat·ing** : to link together in a series or chain — **con·cat·e·na·tion** \(ˌ)kän-ˌka-tə-ˈnā-shən\ *n*

con·cave \kän-ˈkāv, ˈkän-ˌ\ *adj* : curved or rounded inward like the inside of a bowl — **con·cav·i·ty** \kän-ˈka-və-tē\ *n*

con·ceal \kən-ˈsēl\ *vb* : to place out of sight : HIDE — **con·ceal·ment** *n*

con·cede \kən-ˈsēd\ *vb* **con·ced·ed; con·ced·ing 1** : to admit to be true **2** : GRANT, YIELD **syn** allow, acknowledge, avow, confess

con·ceit \kən-ˈsēt\ *n* **1** : excessively high opinion of one's self or ability : VANITY **2** : an elaborate or strained metaphor — **con·ceit·ed** *adj*

con·ceive \kən-ˈsēv\ *vb* **con·ceived; con·ceiv·ing 1** : to become pregnant or pregnant with ⟨~ a child⟩ **2** : to form an idea of : THINK, IMAGINE — **con·ceiv·able** \-ˈsē-və-bəl\ *adj* — **con·ceiv·ably** \-blē\ *adv*

con·cel·e·brant \kən-ˈse-lə-brənt\ *n* : one that jointly participates in celebrating the Eucharist

¹con•cen•trate \ˈkän-sən-ˌtrāt\ *vb* **-trat•ed; -trat•ing 1** : to gather into one body, mass, or force **2** : to make less dilute **3** : to fix one's powers, efforts, or attentions

²concentrate *n* : something concentrated

con•cen•tra•tion \ˌkän-sən-ˈtrā-shən\ *n* **1** : the act or process of concentrating : the state of being concentrated; *esp* : direction of attention on a single object **2** : the amount of a component in a given area or volume

concentration camp *n* : a camp where persons (as prisoners of war or political prisoners) are confined

con•cen•tric \kən-ˈsen-trik\ *adj* **1** : having a common center ⟨~ circles⟩ **2** : COAXIAL

con•cept \ˈkän-ˌsept\ *n* : THOUGHT, NOTION, IDEA — **con•cep•tu•al** \kən-ˈsep-chə-wəl\ *adj*

con•cep•tion \kən-ˈsep-shən\ *n* **1** : the process of conceiving or being conceived **2** : the power to form or understand ideas or concepts **3** : IDEA, CONCEPT **4** : the originating of something

con•cep•tu•al•ise *Brit var of* CONCEPTUALIZE

con•cep•tu•al•ize \-ˈsep-chə-wə-ˌlīz\ *vb* **-ized; -iz•ing** : to form a conception of

¹con•cern \kən-ˈsərn\ *vb* **1** : to relate to **2** : to be the business of : INVOLVE **3** : ENGAGE, OCCUPY

²concern *n* **1** : INTEREST, ANXIETY **2** : AFFAIR, MATTER **3** : a business organization **syn** care, worry, disquiet, unease

con•cerned *adj* **1** : ANXIOUS, UNEASY **2** : INVOLVED

con•cern•ing *prep* : relating to : REGARDING

con•cern•ment \kən-ˈsərn-mənt\ *n* **1** : something in which one is concerned **2** : IMPORTANCE, CONSEQUENCE

¹con•cert \ˈkän-(ˌ)sərt\ *n* **1** : agreement in a plan or design **2** : a concerted action **3** : a public performance (as of music)

²con•cert \kən-ˈsərt\ *vb* : to plan together

con•cert•ed \kən-ˈsər-təd\ *adj* : mutually agreed on; *also* : performed in unison

con•cer•ti•na \ˌkän-sər-ˈtē-nə\ *n* : an instrument of the accordion family

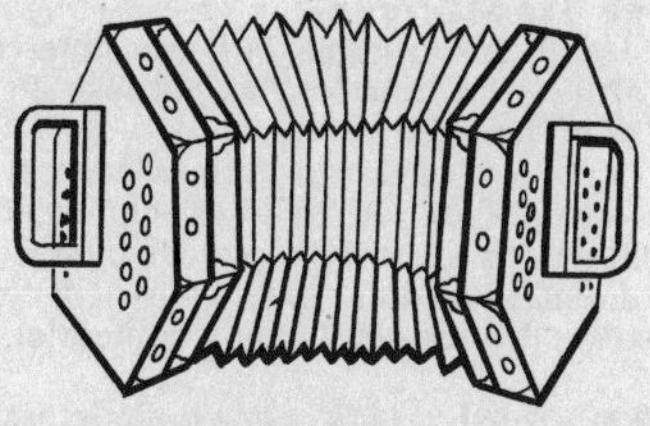

concertina

con•cert•mas•ter \ˈkän-sərt-ˌmas-tər\ *or* **con•cert•meis•ter** \-ˌmī-stər\ *n* : the leader of the first violins of an orchestra and assistant to the conductor

con•cer•to \kən-ˈcher-tō\ *n, pl* **-ti** \-(ˌ)tē\ *or* **-tos** [It] : a piece for one or more solo instruments and orchestra in three movements

con•ces•sion \kən-ˈse-shən\ *n* **1** : an act of conceding or yielding **2** : something yielded **3** : a grant by a government of land or of a right to use it **4** : a grant of a portion of premises for some specific purpose; *also* : the activities or enterprise carried on — **con•ces•sion•ary** \-ˈse-shə-ˌner-ē\ *adj*

con•ces•sion•aire \kən-ˌse-shə-ˈnar, -ˈner\ *n* : one that owns or operates a concession

conch \ˈkäŋk, ˈkänch\ *n, pl* **conchs** \ˈkäŋks\ *or* **conch•es** \ˈkän-chəz\ : a large spiral-shelled marine gastropod mollusk; *also* : its shell

con•cierge \kōⁿ-ˈsyerzh\ *n, pl* **con•cierges** *same or* -ˈsyer-zhəz\ [F] **1** : a resident in an apartment building who performs services for the tenants **2** : a usu. multilingual hotel staff member

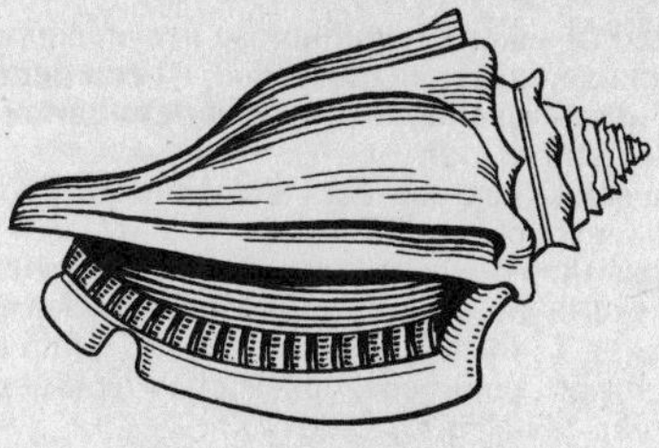

conch

con•cil•i•ate \kən-ˈsi-lē-ˌāt\ *vb* **-at•ed; -at•ing 1** : to bring into agreement : RECONCILE **2** : to gain the goodwill of — **con•cil•i•a•tion** \-ˌsi-lē-ˈā-shən\ *n* — **con•cil•ia•to•ry** \-ˈsi-lē-ə-ˌtōr-ē\ *adj*

con•cise \kən-ˈsīs\ *adj* : expressing much in few words : BRIEF — **con•cise•ly** *adv* — **con•cise•ness** *n*

con•clave \ˈkän-ˌklāv\ *n* [ML, fr. L, room that can be locked, fr. *com-* together + *clavis* key] : a private gathering; *also* : CONVENTION

con•clude \kən-ˈklüd\ *vb* **con•clud•ed; con•clud•ing 1** : to bring to a close : END **2** : DECIDE, JUDGE **3** : to bring about as a result **syn** close, finish, terminate, complete, halt

con•clu•sion \kən-ˈklü-zhən\ *n* **1** : the logical consequence of a reasoning process **2** : TERMINATION, END **3** : OUTCOME, RESULT — **con•clu•sive** \-siv\ *adj* — **con•clu•sive•ly** *adv*

con•coct \kən-ˈkäkt, kän-\ *vb* **1** : to prepare by combining raw materials **2** : DEVISE — **con•coc•tion** \-ˈkäk-shən\ *n*

con•com•i•tant \-ˈkä-mə-tənt\ *adj* : ACCOMPANYING, ATTENDING — **concomitant** *n*

con•cord \ˈkän-ˌkȯrd, ˈkäŋ-\ *n* : AGREEMENT, HARMONY

con•cor•dance \kən-ˈkȯr-dᵊns\ *n* **1** : an alphabetical index of words in a book or in an author's works with the passages in which they occur **2** : AGREEMENT, COVENANT

con•cor•dant \-dᵊnt\ *adj* : HARMONIOUS, AGREEING

con•cor•dat \kən-ˈkȯr-ˌdat\ *n* : CONCORDANCE 2

con•course \ˈkän-ˌkōrs\ *n* **1** : a spontaneous coming together : GATHERING **2** : an open space or hall (as in a bus terminal) where crowds gather

¹con•crete \kän-ˈkrēt, ˈkän-ˌkrēt\ *adj* **1** : naming a real thing or class of things : not abstract **2** : not theoretical : ACTUAL **3** : made of or relating to concrete

²con•crete \ˈkän-ˌkrēt, kän-ˈkrēt\ *vb* **con•cret•ed; con•cret•ing 1** : SOLIDIFY **2** : to cover with concrete

³con•crete \ˈkän-ˌkrēt, kän-ˈkrēt\ *n* : a hard building material made by mixing cement, sand, and gravel with water

con•cre•tion \kän-ˈkrē-shən\ *n* : a hard mass esp. when formed abnormally in the body

con•cu•bine \ˈkäŋ-kyu̇-ˌbīn\ *n* [ME, fr. MF, fr. L *concubina,* fr. *com-* with + *cubare* to lie] : a woman who is not legally a wife but lives with a man and sometimes has a recognized position in his household; *also* : MISTRESS — **con•cu•bi•nage** \kän-ˈkyü-bə-nij\ *n*

con•cu•pis•cence \kän-ˈkyü-pə-səns\ *n* : ardent sexual desire : LUST

con•cur \kən-ˈkər\ *vb* **con•curred; con•cur•ring 1** : to act together **2** : AGREE **3** : COINCIDE **syn** unite, combine, cooperate, band, join

con•cur•rence \-ˈkər-əns\ *n* **1** : agreement in action or opinion **2** : occurrence together : CONJUNCTION

con•cur•rent \-ˈkər-ənt\ *adj* **1** : happening or operating at the same time **2** : joint and equal in authority

con•cus•sion \kən-ˈkə-shən\ *n* **1** : a hard blow or collision; *also* : bodily injury (as to the brain) resulting from a sudden jar **2** : AGITATION, SHAKING

con•demn \kən-ˈdem\ *vb* **1** : to declare to be wrong **2** : to convict of guilt **3** : to sentence judicially **4** : to pronounce unfit for use ⟨~ a building⟩ **5** : to declare forfeited or taken for public use **syn** denounce, censure, blame, criticize, reprehend — **con•dem•na•tion** \ˌkän-ˌdem-ˈnā-shən\ *n* — **con•dem•na•to•ry** \kən-ˈdem-nə-ˌtōr-ē\ *adj*

con•den•sate \ˈkän-dən-ˌsāt, kən-ˈden-\ *n* : a product of condensation

con•dense \kən-ˈdens\ *vb* **con•densed; con•dens•ing 1** : to make or become more compact or dense : CONCENTRATE **2** : to change from vapor to liquid **syn** contract, shrink, compress, constrict — **con•den•sa•tion** \ˌkän-den-ˈsā-shən\ *n*

con•dens•er \kən-ˈden-sər\ *n* **1** : one that condenses **2** : CAPACITOR

con•de•scend \ˌkän-di-ˈsend\ *vb* : to assume an air of superiority — **con•de•scend•ing•ly** \-ˈsen-diŋ-lē\ *adv* — **con•de•scen•sion** \-ˈsen-chən\ *n*

con•dign \kən-ˈdīn, ˈkän-ˌdīn\ *adj* : DESERVED, APPROPRIATE ⟨~ punishment⟩

con•di•ment \ˈkän-də-mənt\ *n* : something used to make food savory; *esp* : a pungent seasoning (as pepper)

[1]**con•di•tion** \kən-ˈdi-shən\ *n* **1** : something essential to the occurrence of some other thing **2** : state of being **3** : social status **4** *pl* : state of affairs : CIRCUMSTANCES **5** : a bodily state in which something is wrong ⟨a heart ~⟩ **6** : a state of health, fitness, or working order ⟨in good ~⟩

[2]**condition** *vb* **1** : to put into proper condition for action or use **2** : to adapt, modify, or mold to respond in a particular way **3** : to modify so that an act or response previously associated with one stimulus becomes associated with another

con•di•tion•al \kən-ˈdi-shə-nəl\ *adj* : containing, implying, or depending on a condition — **con•di•tion•al•ly** *adv*

con•di•tioned *adj* : determined or established by conditioning

con•do \ˈkän-(ˌ)dō\ *n* : CONDOMINIUM 3

con•dole \kən-ˈdōl\ *vb* **con•doled; con•dol•ing** : to express sympathetic sorrow — **con•do•lence** \kən-ˈdō-ləns\ *n*

con•dom \ˈkän-dəm, ˈkən-\ *n* : a usu. rubber sheath worn over the penis (as to prevent pregnancy or venereal infection during sexual intercourse)

con•do•min•i•um \ˌkän-də-ˈmi-nē-əm\ *n, pl* **-ums 1** : joint sovereignty (as by two or more nations) **2** : a politically dependent territory under condominium **3** : individual ownership of a unit (as an apartment) in a multiunit structure; *also* : a unit so owned

con•done \kən-ˈdōn\ *vb* **con•doned; con•don•ing** : to overlook or forgive esp. by treating (an offense) as harmless or trivial **syn** excuse, pardon, forgive, remit — **con•do•na•tion** \ˌkän-də-ˈnā-shən\ *n*

con•dor \ˈkän-dər, -ˌdȯr\ *n* [Sp *cóndor,* fr. Quechua (a So. American Indian language) *kuntur*] : a very large American vulture of the high Andes; *also* : a related nearly extinct vulture of southern California now resident only in captivity

con•duce \kən-ˈdüs, -ˈdyüs\ *vb* **con•duced; con•duc•ing** : to lead or contribute to a particular result — **con•du•cive** *adj*

[1]**con•duct** \ˈkän-(ˌ)dəkt\ *n* **1** : MANAGEMENT, DIRECTION **2** : BEHAVIOR

[2]**con•duct** \kən-ˈdəkt\ *vb* **1** : GUIDE, ESCORT **2** : MANAGE, DIRECT **3** : to act as a medium for conveying or transmitting **4** : BEHAVE — **con•duc•tion** \-ˈdək-shən\ *n*

con•duc•tance \kən-ˈdək-təns\ *n* : the readiness with which a conductor transmits an electric current

con•duc•tive \kən-ˈdək-tiv\ *adj* : having the power to conduct (as heat or electricity) — **con•duc•tiv•i•ty** \ˌkän-ˌdək-ˈti-və-tē\ *n*

con•duc•tor \kən-ˈdək-tər\ *n* **1** : one that conducts; *esp* : a material that permits an electric current to flow easily **2** : a collector of fares in a public conveyance **3** : the leader of a musical ensemble

con•duit \ˈkän-ˌdü-ət, ˌdyü-, -dwət\ *n* **1** : a channel for conveying fluid **2** : a tube or trough for protecting electric wires or cables **3** : a means of transmitting or distributing

con•dyle \ˈkän-ˌdīl, -dᵊl\ *n* : an articular prominence of a bone — **con•dy•lar** \-də-lər\ *adj*

cone \ˈkōn\ *n* **1** : the scaly fruit of trees of the pine family **2** : a solid figure formed by rotating a right triangle about one of its legs **3** : a solid figure that slopes evenly to a point from a usu. circular base **4** : any of the conical light-sensitive receptor cells of the retina that function in color vision **5** : something shaped like a cone

Con•es•to•ga wagon \ˌkä-nə-ˈstō-gə-\ *n* : a broad-wheeled covered wagon used esp. for transporting freight across the prairies

co•ney \ˈkō-nē\ *n, pl* **coneys 1** : RABBIT; *also* : its fur **2** : PIKA

conf *abbr* **1** conference **2** confidential

con•fab \ˈkän-ˌfab, kən-ˈfab\ *n* : CONFABULATION 1

con•fab•u•la•tion \kən-ˌfab-yə-ˈlā-shən\ *n* **1** : CHAT; *also* : CONFERENCE **2** : a filling in of gaps in memory by fabrication

con•fec•tion \kən-ˈfek-shən\ *n* : a fancy dish or sweet; *also* : CANDY

con•fec•tion•er \-sh(ə-)nər\ *n* : a maker of or dealer in confections

con•fec•tion•ery \-shə-ˌner-ē\ *n, pl* **-er•ies 1** : sweet foods **2** : a confectioner's place of business

Confed *abbr* Confederate

con•fed•er•a•cy \kən-ˈfe-də-rə-sē\ *n, pl* **-cies 1** : LEAGUE, ALLIANCE **2** *cap* : the 11 southern states that seceded from the U.S. in 1860 and 1861

[1]**con•fed•er•ate** \kən-ˈfe-də-rət\ *adj* **1** : united in a league : ALLIED **2** *cap* : of or relating to the Confederacy

[2]**confederate** *n* **1** : ALLY, ACCOMPLICE **2** *cap* : an adherent of the Confederacy

[3]**con•fed•er•ate** \-ˈfe-də-ˌrāt\ *vb* **-at•ed; -at•ing** : to unite in a confederacy

con•fed•er•a•tion \kən-ˌfe-də-ˈrā-shən\ *n* **1** : an act of confederating : ALLIANCE **2** : LEAGUE

con•fer \kən-ˈfər\ *vb* **con•ferred; con•fer•ring 1** : GRANT, BESTOW **2** : to exchange views : CONSULT — **con•fer•ee** \ˌkän-fə-ˈrē\ *n*

con•fer•ence \ˈkän-f(ə-)rəns\ *n* **1** : an interchange of views; *also* : a meeting for this purpose **2** : an association of athletic teams

con•fess \kən-ˈfes\ *vb* **1** : to acknowledge or disclose one's misdeed, fault, or sin **2** : to acknowledge one's sins to God or to a priest **3** : to receive the confession of (a penitent) **syn** admit, own, avow, concede, grant

con•fessed•ly \-ˈfe-səd-lē\ *adv* : by confession : ADMITTEDLY

con•fes•sion \-ˈfe-shən\ *n* **1** : an act of confessing (as in the sacrament of penance) **2** : an acknowledgment of guilt **3** : a formal statement of religious beliefs **4** : a religious body having a common creed — **con•fes•sion•al** *adj*

con•fes•sion•al \-ˈfe-shə-nəl\ *n* : a place where a priest hears confessions

con•fes•sor \kən-ˈfe-sər\ *n* **1** : one that confesses **2** : a priest who hears confessions

con•fet•ti \kən-ˈfe-tē\ *n* [It, pl. of *confetto* sweetmeat, fr. ML *confectum,* fr. L, neut. of *confectus,* pp. of *conficere* to prepare] : bits of colored paper or ribbon for throwing (as at weddings)

con•fi•dant \ˈkän-fə-ˌdänt, -ˌdant\ *n* : one to whom secrets are confided

con•fi•dante \-ˌdänt, -ˌdant\ *n* : CONFIDANT; *esp* : one who is a woman

con•fide \kən-ˈfīd\ *vb* **con•fid•ed; con•fid•ing 1** : to have or show faith : TRUST ⟨~ in a friend⟩ **2** : to tell confidentially ⟨~ a secret⟩ **3** : ENTRUST

[1]**con•fi•dence** \ˈkän-fə-dəns\ *n* **1** : TRUST, RELIANCE **2** : SELF-ASSURANCE, BOLDNESS **3** : a state of trust or intimacy **4** : SECRET 2 — **con•fi•dent** \-dənt\ *adj* — **con•fi•dent•ly** *adv*

[2]**confidence** *adj* : of or relating to swindling by false promises ⟨a ~ game⟩
con•fi•den•tial \ˌkän-fə-ˈden-chəl\ *adj* **1** : SECRET, PRIVATE **2** : entrusted with confidences ⟨~ clerk⟩ — **con•fi•den•tial•ly** *adv*
con•fig•u•ra•tion \kən-ˌfi-gyə-ˈrā-shən\ *n* : structural arrangement of parts : SHAPE
con•fig•ure \kən-ˈfi-gyər\ *vb* **-ured; -ur•ing** : to set up for operation esp. in a particular way
con•fine \kən-ˈfīn\ *vb* **con•fined; con•fin•ing 1** : to hold within a location; *also* : IMPRISON **2** : to keep within limits ⟨will ~ my remarks to one subject⟩ — **con•fine•ment** *n* — **con•fin•er** *n*
con•fines \ˈkän-ˌfīnz\ *n pl* : BOUNDS, BORDERS
con•firm \kən-ˈfərm\ *vb* **1** : to give approval to : RATIFY **2** : to make firm or firmer **3** : to administer the rite of confirmation to **4** : VERIFY, CORROBORATE — **con•fir•ma•to•ry** \-ˈfər-mə-ˌtōr-ē\ *adj*
con•fir•ma•tion \ˌkän-fər-ˈmā-shən\ *n* **1** : a religious ceremony admitting a person to full membership in a church or synagogue **2** : an act of ratifying or corroborating; *also* : PROOF
con•fis•cate \ˈkän-fə-ˌskāt\ *vb* **-cat•ed; -cat•ing** [L *confiscare*, fr. *com-* with + *fiscus* treasury] : to take possession of by or as if by public authority — **con•fis•ca•tion** \ˌkän-fə-ˈskā-shən\ *n* — **con•fis•ca•to•ry** \kən-ˈfis-kə-ˌtōr-ē\ *adj*
con•fla•gra•tion \ˌkän-flə-ˈgrā-shən\ *n* : FIRE; *esp* : a large disastrous fire
[1]**con•flict** \ˈkän-ˌflikt\ *n* **1** : WAR **2** : a clash between hostile or opposing elements, ideas, or forces
[2]**con•flict** \kən-ˈflikt\ *vb* : to show opposition or irreconcilability : CLASH
con•flu•ence \ˈkän-ˌflü-əns, kən-ˈflü-\ *n* **1** : a coming together at one point **2** : the meeting or place of meeting of two or more streams — **con•flu•ent** \-ənt\ *adj*
con•flux \ˈkän-ˌfləks\ *n* : CONFLUENCE
con•form \kən-ˈfȯrm\ *vb* **1** : to be similar or identical; *also* : AGREE **2** : to obey customs or standards; *also* : COMPLY — **con•form•able** *adj*
con•for•mance \kən-ˈfȯr-məns\ *n* : CONFORMITY
con•for•ma•tion \ˌkän-fȯr-ˈmā-shən\ *n* : a forming into a whole by arranging parts
con•for•mi•ty \kən-ˈfȯr-mə-tē\ *n, pl* **-ties 1** : HARMONY, AGREEMENT **2** : COMPLIANCE, OBEDIENCE
con•found \kən-ˈfau̇nd, kän-\ *vb* **1** : to throw into disorder or confusion **2** : CONFUSE 2 **syn** bewilder, puzzle, perplex, befog
con•fra•ter•ni•ty \ˌkän-frə-ˈtər-nə-tē\ *n* : a society devoted esp. to a religious or charitable cause
con•frere \ˈkän-ˌfrer, ˈkōⁿ-\ *n* : COLLEAGUE, COMRADE
con•front \kən-ˈfrənt\ *vb* **1** : to face esp. in challenge : OPPOSE; *also* : to deal unflinchingly with ⟨~*ed* the issue⟩ **2** : to cause to face or meet — **con•fron•ta•tion** \ˌkän-frən-ˈtā-shən\ *n*
Con•fu•cian \kən-ˈfyü-shən\ *adj* : of or relating to the Chinese philosopher Confucius or his teachings — **Con•fu•cian•ism** \-shə-ˌni-zəm\ *n*
con•fuse \kən-ˈfyüz\ *vb* **con•fused; con•fus•ing 1** : to make mentally unclear or uncertain; *also* : to disturb the composure of **2** : to mix up : JUMBLE **syn** muddle, befuddle, addle, fluster — **con•fus•ed•ly** \-ˈfyü-zəd-lē\ *adv*
con•fu•sion \-ˈfyü-zhən\ *n* **1** : an act or instance of confusing **2** : the quality or state of being confused
con•fute \kən-ˈfyüt\ *vb* **con•fut•ed; con•fut•ing** : to overwhelm by argument : REFUTE — **con•fu•ta•tion** \ˌkän-fyu̇-ˈtā-shən\ *n*
cong *abbr* congress; congressional
con•ga \ˈkäŋ-gə\ *n* : a Cuban dance of African origin performed by a group usu. in single file
con•geal \kən-ˈjēl\ *vb* **1** : FREEZE **2** : to make or become hard or thick
con•ge•ner \ˈkän-jə-nər\ *n* : one related to another; *esp* : a plant or animal of the same taxonomic genus as another — **con•ge•ner•ic** \ˌkän-jə-ˈner-ik\ *adj*
con•ge•nial \kən-ˈjē-nyəl\ *adj* **1** : KINDRED, SYMPATHETIC **2** : suited to one's taste or nature : AGREEABLE — **con•ge•ni•al•i•ty** \-ˌjē-nē-ˈa-lə-tē\ *n* — **con•ge•nial•ly** *adv*
con•gen•i•tal \kən-ˈje-nə-tᵊl\ *adj* : existing at or dating from birth **syn** inborn, innate, natural
con•ger eel \ˈkän-gər-\ *n* : a large edible marine eel of the Atlantic
con•ge•ries \ˈkän-jə-(ˌ)rēz\ *n, pl* **congeries** : AGGREGATION, COLLECTION
con•gest \kən-ˈjest\ *vb* **1** : to cause excessive fullness of the blood vessels of (as a lung) **2** : to obstruct by overcrowding — **con•ges•tion** \-ˈjes-chən\ *n* — **con•ges•tive** \-ˈjes-tiv\ *adj*
congestive heart failure *n* : heart failure in which the heart is unable to keep enough blood circulating in the tissues or is unable to pump out the blood returned to it by the veins
[1]**con•glom•er•ate** \kən-ˈglä-mə-rət\ *adj* [L *conglomerare* to roll together, fr. *com-* together + *glomerare* to wind into a ball, fr. *glomer-, glomus* ball] : made up of parts from various sources
[2]**con•glom•er•ate** \-ˌrāt\ *vb* **-at•ed; -at•ing** : to form into a mass — **con•glom•er•a•tion** \-ˌglä-mə-ˈrā-shən\ *n*
[3]**con•glom•er•ate** \-rət\ *n* **1** : a mass formed of fragments from various sources; *esp* : a rock composed of fragments varying from pebbles to boulders held together by a cementing material **2** : a widely diversified corporation
Con•go•lese \ˌkäŋ-gə-ˈlēz, -ˈlēs\ *n* : a native or inhabitant of Congo — **Congolese** *adj*
con•grat•u•late \kən-ˈgra-chə-ˌlāt\ *vb* **-lat•ed; -lat•ing** : to express sympathetic pleasure to on account of success or good fortune : FELICITATE — **con•grat•u•la•tion** \-ˌgra-chə-ˈlā-shən\ *n* — **con•grat•u•la•to•ry** \-ˈgra-chə-lə-ˌtōr-ē\ *adj*
con•gre•gate \ˈkäŋ-gri-ˌgāt\ *vb* **-gat•ed; -gat•ing** [ME, fr. L *congregatus*, pp. of *congregare*, fr. *com-* together + *greg-, grex* flock] : ASSEMBLE
con•gre•ga•tion \ˌkäŋ-gri-ˈgā-shən\ *n* **1** : an assembly of persons met esp. for worship; *also* : a group that habitually so meets **2** : a religious community or order **3** : the act or an instance of congregating
con•gre•ga•tion•al \-shə-nəl\ *adj* **1** : of or relating to a congregation **2** *cap* : observing the faith and practice of certain Protestant churches which recognize the independence of each congregation in church matters — **con•gre•ga•tion•al•ism** \-nə-ˌli-zəm\ *n, often cap* — **con•gre•ga•tion•al•ist** \-list\ *n, often cap*
con•gress \ˈkäŋ-grəs\ *n* **1** : an assembly esp. of delegates for discussion and usu. action on some question **2** : the body of senators and representatives constituting a nation's legislature — **con•gres•sio•nal** \kən-ˈgre-shə-nəl\ *adj*
con•gress•man \ˈkäŋ-grəs-mən\ *n* : a member of a congress
con•gress•wom•an \-ˌwu̇-mən\ *n* : a female member of a congress
con•gru•ence \kən-ˈgrü-əns, ˈkäŋ-grü-\ *n* : the quality of agreeing or coinciding : CONGRUITY — **con•gru•ent** \kən-ˈgrü-ənt, ˈkäŋ-grü-\ *adj*
con•gru•en•cy \-sē\ *n, pl* **-cies** : CONGRUENCE
con•gru•ity \kän-ˈgrü-ə-tē\ *n, pl* **-ities** : correspondence between things — **con•gru•ous** \ˈkäŋ-grü-əs\ *adj*
con•ic \ˈkä-nik\ *adj* **1** : of or relating to a cone **2** : CONICAL
con•i•cal \ˈkä-ni-kəl\ *adj* : resembling a cone esp. in shape
co•ni•fer \ˈkä-nə-fər, ˈkō-\ *n* : any of an order of shrubs or trees (as the pines) that usu. are evergreen and bear cones — **co•nif•er•ous** \kō-ˈni-fə-rəs\ *adj*
conj *abbr* conjunction
con•jec•ture \kən-ˈjek-chər\ *n* : GUESS, SURMISE — **con•jec•tur•al** \-chə-rəl\ *adj* — **conjecture** *vb*

con•join \kən-ˈjȯin\ *vb* : to join together — **con•joint** \-ˈjȯint\ *adj*

con•ju•gal \ˈkän-ji-gəl\ *adj* : of or relating to marriage : MATRIMONIAL

[1]**con•ju•gate** \ˈkän-ji-gət, -jə-ˌgāt\ *adj* **1** : united esp. in pairs : COUPLED **2** : of kindred origin and meaning ⟨*sing* and *song* are ~⟩ — **con•ju•gate•ly** *adv*

[2]**con•ju•gate** \-jə-ˌgāt\ *vb* **-gat•ed; -gat•ing 1** : INFLECT ⟨~ a verb⟩ **2** : to join together : COUPLE

con•ju•ga•tion \ˌkän-jə-ˈgā-shən\ *n* **1** : an arrangement of the inflectional forms of a verb **2** : the act of conjugating : the state of being conjugated

con•junct \kän-ˈjəŋkt\ *adj* : JOINED, UNITED

con•junc•tion \kən-ˈjəŋk-shən\ *n* **1** : COMBINATION **2** : occurrence at the same time **3** : a word that joins together sentences, clauses, phrases, or words

con•junc•ti•va \ˌkän-ˌjəŋk-ˈtī-və\ *n, pl* **-vas** *or* **-vae** \-(ˌ)vē\ : the mucous membrane lining the inner surface of the eyelids and continuing over the forepart of the eyeball

con•junc•tive \kən-ˈjəŋk-tiv\ *adj* **1** : CONNECTIVE **2** : CONJUNCT **3** : being or functioning like a conjunction

con•junc•ti•vi•tis \kən-ˌjəŋk-ti-ˈvī-təs\ *n* : inflammation of the conjunctiva

con•junc•ture \kən-ˈjəŋk-chər\ *n* **1** : CONJUNCTION, UNION **2** : JUNCTURE 3

con•jure \ˈkän-jər, ˈkən- *for 1, 2;* kən-ˈju̇r *for 3*\ *vb* **con•jured; con•jur•ing 1** : to implore earnestly or solemnly **2** : to practice magic; *esp* : to summon (as a devil) by sorcery **3** : to practice sleight of hand — **con•ju•ra•tion** \ˌkän-ju̇-ˈrā-shən, ˌkən-\ *n* — **con•jur•er** *or* **con•ju•ror** \ˈkän-jər-ər, ˈkən-\ *n*

conk \ˈkäŋk\ *vb* : BREAK DOWN; *esp* : STALL ⟨the motor ~*ed* out⟩

Conn *abbr* Connecticut

con•nect \kə-ˈnekt\ *vb* **1** : JOIN, LINK **2** : to associate in one's mind — **con•nect•able** *adj* — **con•nec•tor** *n*

con•nec•tion \kə-ˈnek-shən\ *n* **1** : JUNCTION, UNION **2** : logical relationship : COHERENCE; *esp* : relation of a word to other words in a sentence **3** : family relationship **4** : BOND, LINK **5** : a person related by blood or marriage **6** : relationship in social affairs or in business **7** : an association of persons; *esp* : a religious denomination

[1]**con•nec•tive** \kə-ˈnek-tiv\ *adj* : serving to connect — **con•nec•tiv•i•ty** \ˌkä-ˌnek-ˈti-və-tē\ *n*

[2]**connective** *n* : a word (as a conjunction) that connects words or word groups

con•nex•ion *chiefly Brit var of* CONNECTION

con•ning tower \ˈkä-niŋ-\ *n* : a raised structure on the deck of a submarine

con•nip•tion \kə-ˈnip-shən\ *n* : a fit of rage, hysteria, or alarm

con•nive \kə-ˈnīv\ *vb* **con•nived; con•niv•ing** [F or L; F *conniver,* fr. L *conivēre* to close the eyes, connive] **1** : to pretend ignorance of something one ought to oppose as wrong **2** : to cooperate secretly : give secret aid — **con•niv•ance** *n* — **con•niv•er** *n*

con•nois•seur \ˌkä-nə-ˈsər\ *n* : a critical judge in matters of art or taste

con•no•ta•tion \ˌkä-nə-ˈtā-shən\ *n* : a meaning in addition to or apart from the thing explicitly named or described by a word

con•no•ta•tive \ˈkä-nə-ˌtā-tiv, kə-ˈnō-tə-\ *adj* **1** : connoting or tending to connote **2** : relating to connotation

con•note \kə-ˈnōt\ *vb* **con•not•ed; con•not•ing** : to suggest or mean as a connotation

con•nu•bi•al \kə-ˈnü-bē-əl, -ˈnyü-\ *adj* : of or relating to marriage : CONJUGAL

con•quer \ˈkäŋ-kər\ *vb* **1** : to gain by force of arms : WIN **2** : to get the better of : OVERCOME **syn** defeat, subjugate, subdue, overthrow, vanquish — **con•quer•or** \-ər\ *n*

con•quest \ˈkän-ˌkwest, ˈkäŋ-\ *n* **1** : an act of conquering : VICTORY **2** : something conquered

con•quis•ta•dor \kȯŋ-ˈkēs-tə-ˌdȯr, kän-ˈkwis-\ *n, pl* **-do•res** \-ˌkēs-tə-ˈdȯr-ēz, -ˌkwis-\ *or* **-dors** : CONQUEROR; *esp* : a leader in the Spanish conquest of the Americas in the 16th century

cons *abbr* consonant

con•san•guin•i•ty \ˌkän-ˌsan-ˈgwi-nə-tē, -ˌsaŋ-\ *n, pl* **-ties** : blood relationship — **con•san•guin•e•ous** \-nē-əs\ *adj*

con•science \ˈkän-chəns\ *n* : consciousness of the moral right and wrong of one's own acts or motives — **con•science•less** *adj*

con•sci•en•tious \ˌkän-chē-ˈen-chəs\ *adj* : guided by one's own sense of right and wrong **syn** scrupulous, honorable, honest, upright, just — **con•sci•en•tious•ly** *adv*

conscientious objector *n* : a person who refuses to serve in the armed forces or to bear arms on moral or religious grounds

con•scious \ˈkän-chəs\ *adj* **1** : AWARE **2** : known or felt by one's inner self **3** : mentally awake or alert : not asleep or unconscious **4** : INTENTIONAL — **con•scious•ly** *adv* — **con•scious•ness** *n*

con•script \kən-ˈskript\ *vb* : to enroll by compulsion for military or naval service — **conscript** \ˈkän-ˌskript\ *n* — **con•scrip•tion** \kən-ˈskrip-shən\ *n*

con•se•crate \ˈkän-sə-ˌkrāt\ *vb* **-crat•ed; -crat•ing 1** : to induct (as a bishop) into an office with a religious rite **2** : to make or declare sacred ⟨~ a church⟩ **3** : to devote solemnly to a purpose — **con•se•cra•tion** \ˌkän-sə-ˈkrā-shən\ *n*

con•sec•u•tive \kən-ˈse-kyə-tiv\ *adj* : following in regular order : SUCCESSIVE — **con•sec•u•tive•ly** *adv*

con•sen•su•al \kən-ˈsen-chə-wəl\ *adj* : involving or based on mutual consent

con•sen•sus \kən-ˈsen-səs\ *n* **1** : agreement in opinion, testimony, or belief **2** : collective opinion

[1]**con•sent** \kən-ˈsent\ *vb* : to give assent or approval

[2]**consent** *n* : approval or acceptance of something done or proposed by another

con•se•quence \ˈkän-sə-ˌkwens\ *n* **1** : RESULT **2** : IMPORTANCE **syn** effect, outcome, aftermath, upshot

con•se•quent \-kwənt, -ˌkwent\ *adj* : following as a result or effect

con•se•quen•tial \ˌkän-sə-ˈkwen-chəl\ *adj* **1** : having significant consequences **2** : showing self-importance

con•se•quent•ly \ˈkän-sə-ˌkwent-lē, -kwənt-\ *adv* : as a result : ACCORDINGLY

con•ser•van•cy \kən-ˈsər-vən-sē\ *n, pl* **-cies** : an organization or area designated to conserve natural resources

con•ser•va•tion \ˌkän-sər-ˈvā-shən\ *n* : PRESERVATION; *esp* : planned management of natural resources

con•ser•va•tion•ist \-shə-nist\ *n* : a person who advocates conservation esp. of natural resources

con•ser•va•tism \kən-ˈsər-və-ˌti-zəm\ *n* : disposition to keep to established ways : opposition to change

[1]**con•ser•va•tive** \kən-ˈsər-və-tiv\ *adj* **1** : PRESERVATIVE **2** : disposed to maintain existing views, conditions, or institutions **3** : MODERATE, CAUTIOUS — **con•ser•va•tive•ly** *adv*

[2]**conservative** *n* : a person who is conservative esp. in politics

con•ser•va•tor \kən-ˈsər-və-tər, ˈkän-sər-ˌvā-\ *n* **1** : PROTECTOR, GUARDIAN **2** : one named by a court to protect the interests of an incompetent (as a child)

con•ser•va•to•ry \kən-ˈsər-və-ˌtȯr-ē\ *n, pl* **-ries 1** : GREENHOUSE **2** : a place of instruction in one of the fine arts (as music)

[1]**con•serve** \kən-ˈsərv\ *vb* **con•served; con•serv•ing** : to keep from losing or wasting : PRESERVE

[2]**con•serve** \ˈkän-ˌsərv\ *n* **1** : CONFECTION; *esp* : a candied fruit **2** : PRESERVE; *esp* : one prepared from a mixture of fruits

con•sid•er \kən-ˈsi-dər\ *vb* [ME, fr. MF *considerer,* fr. L *considerare,* fr. *com-* together + *sider-, sidus* heavenly body] **1** : THINK, PONDER **2** : HEED, REGARD **3** : JUDGE, BELIEVE — **con·sid·ered** *adj*

con·sid·er·able \-ˈsi-dər-ə-bəl, -ˈsi-drə-bəl\ *adj* **1** : IMPORTANT **2** : large in extent, amount, or degree — **con·sid·er·ably** \-blē\ *adv*

con·sid·er·ate \kən-ˈsi-də-rət\ *adj* : observant of the rights and feelings of others **syn** thoughtful, attentive

con·sid·er·ation \kən-ˌsi-də-ˈrā-shən\ *n* **1** : careful thought : DELIBERATION **2** : a matter taken into account **3** : thoughtful attention **4** : JUDGMENT, OPINION **5** : RECOMPENSE

con·sid·er·ing *prep* : in view of : taking into account

con·sign \kən-ˈsīn\ *vb* **1** : ENTRUST, COMMIT **2** : to deliver formally **3** : to send (goods) to an agent for sale — **con·sign·ee** \ˌkän-sə-ˈnē, -ˌsī-; kən-ˌsī-\ *n* — **con·sign·or** \ˌkän-sə-ˈnȯr, -ˌsī-; kən-ˌsī-\ *n*

con·sign·ment \kən-ˈsīn-mənt\ *n* : something consigned esp. in a single shipment

con·sist \kən-ˈsist\ *vb* **1** : to be inherent : LIE — usu. used with *in* **2** : to be composed or made up — usu. used with *of*

con·sis·tence \kən-ˈsis-təns\ *n* : CONSISTENCY

con·sis·ten·cy \-tən-sē\ *n, pl* **-cies** **1** : COHESIVENESS, FIRMNESS **2** : agreement or harmony in parts or of different things **3** : UNIFORMITY ⟨∼ of behavior⟩ — **con·sis·tent** \-tənt\ *adj* — **con·sis·tent·ly** *adv*

con·sis·to·ry \kən-ˈsis-tə-rē\ *n, pl* **-ries** : a solemn assembly (as of Roman Catholic cardinals)

consol *abbr* consolidated

[1]**con·sole** \ˈkän-ˌsōl\ *n* **1** : the desklike part of an organ at which the organist sits **2** : the combination of displays and controls of a device or system **3** : a cabinet for a radio or television set resting directly on the floor **4** : a small storage cabinet between bucket seats in an automobile

[2]**con·sole** \kən-ˈsōl\ *vb* **con·soled; con·sol·ing** : to soothe the grief of : COMFORT, SOLACE — **con·so·la·tion** \ˌkän-sə-ˈlā-shən\ *n* — **con·so·la·to·ry** \kən-ˈsō-lə-ˌtōr-ē, -ˈsä-\ *adj*

con·sol·i·date \kən-ˈsä-lə-ˌdāt\ *vb* **-dat·ed; -dat·ing** **1** : to unite or become united into one whole : COMBINE **2** : to make firm or secure **3** : to form into a compact mass — **con·sol·i·da·tion** \-ˌsä-lə-ˈdā-shən\ *n*

con·som·mé \ˌkän-sə-ˈmā\ *n* [F] : a clear soup made from well-seasoned stock

con·so·nance \ˈkän-sə-nəns\ *n* **1** : AGREEMENT, HARMONY **2** : repetition of consonants esp. as an alternative to rhyme in verse

[1]**con·so·nant** \-nənt\ *adj* : having consonance, harmony, or agreement **syn** consistent, compatible, congruous, congenial, sympathetic — **con·so·nant·ly** *adv*

[2]**consonant** *n* **1** : a speech sound (as \p\, \g\, \n\, \l\, \s\, \r\) characterized by constriction or closure at one or more points in the breath channel **2** : a letter other than *a, e, i, o,* and *u* — **con·so·nan·tal** \ˌkän-sə-ˈnant-ᵊl\ *adj*

[1]**con·sort** \ˈkän-ˌsȯrt\ *n* **1** : a ship accompanying another **2** : SPOUSE, MATE

[2]**con·sort** \kən-ˈsȯrt\ *vb* **1** : to keep company **2** : ACCORD, HARMONIZE

con·sor·tium \kən-ˈsȯr-shəm; -shē-əm, -tē-\ *n, pl* **-sor·tia** \-shə-; -shē-ə, -tē-\ [L, fellowship] : an agreement or combination (as of companies) formed to undertake a large enterprise

con·spec·tus \kən-ˈspek-təs\ *n* **1** : a brief survey or summary **2** : SUMMARY

con·spic·u·ous \kən-ˈspi-kyə-wəs\ *adj* : attracting attention : PROMINENT, STRIKING **syn** noticeable, remarkable, outstanding — **con·spic·u·ous·ly** *adv*

con·spir·a·cy \kən-ˈspir-ə-sē\ *n, pl* **-cies** : an agreement among conspirators : PLOT

con·spir·a·tor \kən-ˈspir-ə-tər\ *n* : one that conspires — **con·spir·a·to·ri·al** \-ˌspir-ə-ˈtōr-ē-əl\ *adj*

con·spire \kən-ˈspīr\ *vb* **con·spired; con·spir·ing** [ME, fr. MF *conspirer,* fr. L *conspirare* to be in harmony, conspire, fr. *com-* with + *spirare* to breathe] : to plan secretly an unlawful act : PLOT

const *abbr* **1** constant **2** constitution; constitutional

con·sta·ble \ˈkän-stə-bəl, ˈkən-\ *n* [ME *conestable,* fr. OF, fr. LL *comes stabuli,* lit., officer of the stable] : a public officer responsible for keeping the peace

con·stab·u·lary \kən-ˈsta-byə-ˌler-ē\ *n, pl* **-lar·ies** **1** : the police of a particular district or country **2** : a police force organized like the military

con·stan·cy \ˈkän-stən-sē\ *n, pl* **-cies** **1** : firmness of mind **2** : STABILITY

[1]**con·stant** \-stənt\ *adj* **1** : STEADFAST, FAITHFUL **2** : FIXED, UNCHANGING **3** : continually recurring : REGULAR — **con·stant·ly** *adv*

[2]**constant** *n* : something unchanging

con·stel·la·tion \ˌkän-stə-ˈlā-shən\ *n* : any of 88 groups of stars forming patterns

con·ster·na·tion \ˌkän-stər-ˈnā-shən\ *n* : amazed dismay and confusion

con·sti·pa·tion \ˌkän-stə-ˈpā-shən\ *n* : abnormally difficult or infrequent bowel movements — **con·sti·pate** \ˈkän-stə-ˌpāt\ *vb*

con·stit·u·en·cy \kən-ˈsti-chə-wən-sē\ *n, pl* **-cies** : a body of constituents; *also* : an electoral district

[1]**con·stit·u·ent** \-wənt\ *n* **1** : a person entitled to vote for a representative for a district **2** : a component part

[2]**constituent** *adj* **1** : COMPONENT **2** : having power to create a government or frame or amend a constitution

con·sti·tute \ˈkän-stə-ˌtüt, -ˌtyüt\ *vb* **-tut·ed; -tut·ing** **1** : to appoint to an office or duty **2** : SET UP, ESTABLISH ⟨∼ a law⟩ **3** : MAKE UP, COMPOSE

con·sti·tu·tion \ˌkän-stə-ˈtü-shən, -ˈtyü-\ *n* **1** : an established law or custom **2** : the physical makeup of the individual **3** : the structure, composition, or makeup of something ⟨∼ of the sun⟩ **4** : the basic law in a politically organized body; *also* : a document containing such law

[1]**con·sti·tu·tion·al** \-shə-nəl\ *adj* **1** : of or relating to the constitution of body or mind **2** : being in accord with the constitution of a state or society; *also* : of or relating to such a constitution — **con·sti·tu·tion·al·ly** *adv*

[2]**constitutional** *n* : an exercise (as a walk) taken for one's health

con·sti·tu·tion·al·i·ty \-ˌtü-shə-ˈna-lə-tē, -ˌtyü-\ *n* : the quality or state of being constitutional

con·sti·tu·tive \ˈkän-stə-ˌtü-tiv, -tyü-, kən-ˈsti-chə-tiv\ *adj* **1** : CONSTRUCTIVE **2** : CONSTITUENT, ESSENTIAL

constr *abbr* construction

con·strain \kən-ˈstrān\ *vb* **1** : COMPEL, FORCE **2** : CONFINE **3** : RESTRAIN

con·straint \-ˈstrānt\ *n* **1** : COMPULSION; *also* : RESTRAINT **2** : repression of one's natural feelings

con·strict \kən-ˈstrikt\ *vb* : to draw together : SQUEEZE — **con·stric·tion** \-ˈstrik-shən\ *n* — **con·stric·tive** \-ˈstrik-tiv\ *adj*

con·stric·tor \kən-ˈstrik-tər\ *n* : a snake that kills its prey by crushing it in its coils

con·struct \kən-ˈstrəkt\ *vb* : BUILD, MAKE — **con·struc·tor** \-ˈstrək-tər\ *n*

con·struc·tion \kən-ˈstrək-shən\ *n* **1** : INTERPRETATION **2** : the art, process, or manner of building; *also* : something built, created, or established : STRUCTURE **3** : syntactical arrangement of words in a sentence — **con·struc·tive** \-tiv\ *adj*

con·struc·tion·ist \-shə-nist\ *n* : a person who construes a legal document (as the U.S. Constitution) in a specific way ⟨a strict ∼⟩

con·strue \kən-ˈstrü\ *vb* **con·strued; con·stru·ing** **1** : to analyze the mutual relations of words in a sentence; *also* : TRANSLATE **2** : EXPLAIN, INTERPRET — **con·stru·able** *adj*

con·sub·stan·ti·a·tion \ˌkän-səb-ˌstan-chē-ˈā-shən\ *n* : the actual substantial presence and combination of the body and blood of Christ with the eucharistic bread and wine

con•sul \ˈkän-səl\ *n* **1** : a chief magistrate of the Roman republic **2** : an official appointed by a government to reside in a foreign country to care for the commercial interests of the appointing government's citizens — **con•sul•ar** \-sə-lər\ *adj* — **con•sul•ate** \-lət\ *n* — **con•sul•ship** *n*

con•sult \kən-ˈsəlt\ *vb* **1** : to ask the advice or opinion of **2** : CONFER — **con•sul•tant** \-ᵊnt\ *n* — **con•sul•ta•tion** \ˌkän-səl-ˈtā-shən\ *n*

con•sume \kən-ˈsüm\ *vb* **con•sumed; con•sum•ing 1** : DESTROY ⟨*consumed* by fire⟩ **2** : to spend wastefully **3** : to eat up : DEVOUR **4** : to absorb the attention of : ENGROSS — **con•sum•able** *adj* — **con•sum•er** *n*

con•sum•er•ism \kən-ˈsü-mə-ˌri-zəm\ *n* : the promotion of consumers' interests (as against false advertising)

consumer price index *n* : an index measuring the change in the cost of widely purchased goods and services from the cost in some base period

[1]**con•sum•mate** \ˈkän-sə-mət, kən-ˈsə\ *adj* : PERFECT **syn** finished, accomplished

[2]**con•sum•mate** \ˈkän-sə-ˌmāt\ *vb* **-mat•ed; -mat•ing** : to make complete : FINISH, ACHIEVE — **con•sum•ma•tion** \ˌkän-sə-ˈmā-shən\ *n*

con•sump•tion \kən-ˈsəmp-shən\ *n* **1** : progressive bodily wasting away; *also* : TUBERCULOSIS **2** : the act of consuming or using up **3** : the use of economic goods

[1]**con•sump•tive** \-ˈsəmp-tiv\ *adj* **1** : tending to consume **2** : relating to or affected with consumption

[2]**consumptive** *n* : a person who has consumption

cont *abbr* **1** containing **2** contents **3** continent; continental **4** continued **5** control

[1]**con•tact** \ˈkän-ˌtakt\ *n* **1** : a touching or meeting of bodies **2** : ASSOCIATION, RELATIONSHIP; *also* : CONNECTION, COMMUNICATION **3** : a person serving as a go-between or source of information **4** : CONTACT LENS

[2]**contact** *vb* **1** : to come or bring into contact : TOUCH **2** : to get in communication with

contact lens *n* : a thin lens fitting over the cornea usu. to correct vision

con•ta•gion \kən-ˈtā-jən\ *n* **1** : a contagious disease; *also* : the transmission of such a disease **2** : a disease-producing agent (as a virus) **3** : transmission of an influence on the mind or emotions

con•ta•gious \-jəs\ *adj* **1** : transmitted by contact with an infected person, his or her bodily discharges, or something that has touched either **2** : communicated or transmitted like a contagious disease; *esp* : exciting similar emotion or conduct in others

con•tain \kən-ˈtān\ *vb* **1** : RESTRAIN **2** : to have within : HOLD **3** : COMPRISE, INCLUDE — **con•tain•ment** *n*

con•tain•er \kən-ˈtā-nər\ *n* : RECEPTACLE; *esp* : one for shipment of goods

con•tam•i•nant \kən-ˈta-mə-nənt\ *n* : something that contaminates

con•tam•i•nate \kən-ˈta-mə-ˌnāt\ *vb* **-nat•ed; -nat•ing** : to soil, stain, or infect by contact or association — **con•tam•i•na•tion** \-ˌta-mə-ˈnā-shən\ *n*

contd *abbr* continued

con•temn \kən-ˈtem\ *vb* : to view or treat with contempt : DESPISE

con•tem•plate \ˈkän-təm-ˌplāt\ *vb* **-plat•ed; -plat•ing** [L *contemplari*, fr. *com-* with + *templum* space marked out for observation of auguries] **1** : to view or consider with continued attention **2** : INTEND — **con•tem•pla•tion** \ˌkän-təm-ˈplā-shən\ *n* — **con•tem•pla•tive** \kən-ˈtem-plə-tiv, ˈkän-təm-ˌplā-\ *adj*

con•tem•po•ra•ne•ous \kən-ˌtem-pə-ˈrā-nē-əs\ *adj* : CONTEMPORARY 1

con•tem•po•rary \kən-ˈtem-pə-ˌrer-ē\ *adj* **1** : occurring or existing at the same time **2** : marked by characteristics of the present period — **contemporary** *n*

con•tempt \kən-ˈtempt\ *n* **1** : the act of despising : the state of mind of one who despises **2** : the state of being despised **3** : disobedience to or open disrespect of a court or legislature

con•tempt•ible \kən-ˈtemp-tə-bəl\ *adj* : deserving contempt : DESPICABLE — **con•tempt•ibly** \-blē\ *adv*

con•temp•tu•ous \-ˈtemp-chə-wəs\ *adj* : feeling or expressing contempt — **con•temp•tu•ous•ly** *adv*

con•tend \kən-ˈtend\ *vb* **1** : to strive against rivals or difficulties **2** : ARGUE **3** : MAINTAIN, ASSERT — **con•tend•er** *n*

[1]**con•tent** \kən-ˈtent\ *adj* : SATISFIED

[2]**content** *vb* : SATISFY; *esp* : to limit (oneself) in requirements or actions

[3]**content** *n* : CONTENTMENT

[4]**con•tent** \ˈkän-ˌtent\ *n* **1** : something contained ⟨~*s* of a room⟩ **2** : subject matter or topics treated (as in a book) **3** : MEANING, SIGNIFICANCE **4** : the amount of material contained

con•tent•ed \kən-ˈten-təd\ *adj* : SATISFIED — **con•tent•ed•ly** *adv* — **con•tent•ed•ness** *n*

con•ten•tion \kən-ˈten-chən\ *n* **1** : CONTEST, STRIFE **2** : an idea or point for which a person argues — **con•ten•tious** \-chəs\ *adj* — **con•ten•tious•ly** *adv*

con•tent•ment \kən-ˈtent-mənt\ *n* : ease of mind : SATISFACTION

con•ter•mi•nous \kän-ˈtər-mə-nəs\ *adj* : having the same or a common boundary — **con•ter•mi•nous•ly** *adv*

[1]**con•test** \kən-ˈtest\ *vb* **1** : to engage in strife : FIGHT **2** : CHALLENGE, DISPUTE — **con•tes•tant** \-ˈtes-tənt\ *n*

[2]**con•test** \ˈkän-ˌtest\ *n* : STRUGGLE, COMPETITION

con•text \ˈkän-ˌtekst\ *n* [L *contextus* connection of words, coherence, fr. *contexere* to weave together] : the parts of a discourse that surround a word or passage and help to explain its meaning; *also* : the circumstances surrounding an act or event — **con•tex•tu•al•ly** *adv*

con•tig•u•ous \kən-ˈti-gyə-wəs\ *adj* : being in contact : TOUCHING; *also* : NEXT, ADJOINING — **con•ti•gu•i•ty** \ˌkän-tə-ˈgyü-ə-tē\ *n*

con•ti•nence \ˈkänt-ᵊn-əns\ *n* **1** : SELF-RESTRAINT; *esp* : a refraining from sexual intercourse **2** : the ability to retain urine or feces voluntarily

[1]**con•ti•nent** \ˈkänt-ᵊn-ənt\ *adj* : exercising continence

[2]**continent** *n* **1** : any of the great divisions of land on the globe **2** *cap* : the continent of Europe

[1]**con•ti•nen•tal** \ˌkän-tə-ˈnent-ᵊl\ *adj* **1** : of or relating to a continent; *esp, often cap* : of or relating to the continent of Europe **2** *often cap* : of or relating to the colonies later forming the U.S. **3** : of or relating to cuisine based on classical European cooking

[2]**continental** *n* **1** *often cap* : a soldier in the Continental army **2** : EUROPEAN

continental drift *n* : a hypothetical slow movement of the continents over a fluid layer deep within the earth

continental shelf *n* : a shallow submarine plain forming a border to a continent

continental slope *n* : a usu. steep slope from a continental shelf to the ocean floor

con•tin•gen•cy \kən-ˈtin-jən-sē\ *n, pl* **-cies** : a chance or possible event

[1]**con•tin•gent** \-jənt\ *adj* **1** : liable but not certain to happen : POSSIBLE **2** : happening by chance : not planned **3** : dependent on something that may or may not occur **4** : CONDITIONAL **syn** accidental, casual, incidental, odd

[2]**contingent** *n* : a quota (as of troops) supplied from an area or group

con•tin•u•al \kən-ˈtin-yə-wəl\ *adj* **1** : CONTINUOUS, UNBROKEN **2** : steadily recurring — **con•tin•u•al•ly** *adv*

con•tin•u•ance \-yə-wəns\ *n* **1** : unbroken succession **2** : the extent of continuing : DURATION **3** : adjournment of legal proceedings

con•tin•u•a•tion \kən-ˌtin-yə-ˈwā-shən\ *n* **1** : extension or prolongation of a state or activity **2** : resumption after an interruption; *also* : something that carries on after a pause or break

con•tin•ue \kən-ˈtin-yü\ *vb* **-tin•ued; -tinu•ing 1 :** to maintain without interruption **2 :** ENDURE, LAST **3 :** to remain in a place or condition **4 :** to resume (as a story) after an intermission **5 :** EXTEND; *also* **:** to persist in **6 :** to allow to remain **7 :** to keep (a legal case) on the calendar or undecided

con•ti•nu•i•ty \ˌkän-tə-ˈnü-ə-tē, -ˈnyü-\ *n, pl* **-ties 1 :** the state of being continuous **2 :** something that has or provides continuity

con•tin•u•ous \kən-ˈtin-yə-wəs\ *adj* **:** continuing without interruption — **con•tin•u•ous•ly** *adv*

con•tin•u•um \-yə-wəm\ *n, pl* **-ua** \-yə-wə\ *also* **-u•ums :** something that is the same throughout or consists of a series of variations or of a sequence of things in regular order

con•tort \kən-ˈtȯrt\ *vb* **:** to twist out of shape — **con•tor•tion** \-ˈtȯr-shən\ *n*

con•tor•tion•ist \-ˈtȯr-shə-nist\ *n* **:** an acrobat able to twist the body into unusual postures

con•tour \ˈkän-ˌtu̇r\ *n* [F, fr. It *contorno* fr. *contornare* to round off, sketch in outline, fr. L *com-* together + *tornare* to turn in a lathe, fr. *tornus* lathe] **1 :** OUTLINE **2 :** SHAPE, FORM — often used in pl. ⟨the ∼*s* of a statue⟩

contr *abbr* contract; contraction

con•tra•band \ˈkän-trə-ˌband\ *n* **:** goods legally prohibited in trade; *also* **:** smuggled goods

con•tra•cep•tion \ˌkän-trə-ˈsep-shən\ *n* **:** intentional prevention of conception and pregnancy — **con•tra•cep•tive** \-ˈsep-tive\ *adj or n*

¹**con•tract** \ˈkän-ˌtrakt\ *n* **1 :** a binding agreement **2 :** an undertaking to win a specified number of tricks in bridge — **con•trac•tu•al** \kən-ˈtrak-chə-wəl\ *adj* — **con•trac•tu•al•ly** *adv*

²**con•tract** \kən-ˈtrakt, *2 usu* ˈkän-ˌtrakt\ *vb* **1 :** to become affected with ⟨∼ a disease⟩ **2 :** to establish or undertake by contract **3 :** SHRINK, LESSEN; *esp* **:** to draw together esp. so as to shorten ⟨∼ a muscle⟩ **4 :** to shorten (a word) by omitting letters or sounds in the middle — **con•tract•ible** \kən-ˈtrak-tə-bəl, ˈkän-ˌ\ *adj* — **con•trac•tion** \kən-ˈtrak-shən\ *n* — **con•trac•tor** \ˈkän-ˌtrak-tər, kən-ˈtrak-\ *n*

con•trac•tile \kən-ˈtrakt-^{ə}l\ *adj* **:** able to contract — **con•trac•til•i•ty** \ˌkän-ˌtrak-ˈti-lə-tē\ *n*

con•tra•dict \ˌkän-trə-ˈdikt\ *vb* **:** to assert the contrary of **:** deny the truth of — **con•tra•dic•tion** \-ˈdik-shən\ *n* — **con•tra•dic•to•ry** \-ˈdik-tə-rē\ *adj*

con•tra•dis•tinc•tion \ˌkän-trə-dis-ˈtiŋk-shən\ *n* **:** distinction by contrast

con•trail \ˈkän-ˌtrāl\ *n* **:** a streak of condensed water vapor created by an airplane or rocket at high altitudes

con•tra•in•di•ca•tion \ˌkän-trə-ˌin-də-ˈkā-shən\ *n* **:** something (as a symptom or condition) that makes a particular treatment or procedure inadvisable

con•tral•to \kən-ˈtral-tō\ *n, pl* **-tos :** the lowest female voice; *also* **:** a singer having such a voice

con•trap•tion \kən-ˈtrap-shən\ *n* **:** CONTRIVANCE, DEVICE

con•tra•pun•tal \ˌkän-trə-ˈpənt-^{ə}l\ *adj* **:** of or relating to counterpoint

con•tra•ri•ety \ˌkän-trə-ˈrī-ə-tē\ *n, pl* **-eties :** the state of being contrary **:** DISAGREEMENT, INCONSISTENCY

con•trari•wise \ˈkän-ˌtrer-ē-ˌwīz, kən-ˈtrer-\ *adv* **1 :** on the contrary **2 :** VICE VERSA

con•trary \ˈkän-ˌtrer-ē; *4 often* kən-ˈtrer-ē\ *adj* **1 :** opposite in nature or position **2 :** COUNTER, OPPOSED **3 :** UNFAVORABLE — used of wind or weather **4 :** unwilling to accept control or advice — **con•trari•ly** \-ˌtrer-ə-lē, -ˈtrer-\ *adv* — **con•trary** *n is* ˈkän-ˌtrer-ē, *adv is like adj*\ *n or adv*

¹**con•trast** \kən-ˈtrast\ *vb* [F *contraster,* fr. MF, to oppose, resist, fr. (assumed) VL *contrastare,* fr. L *contra-* against + *stare* to stand] **1 :** to show differences when compared **2 :** to compare in such a way as to show differences

²**con•trast** \ˈkän-ˌtrast\ *n* **1 :** diversity of adjacent parts in color, emotion, tone, or brightness ⟨the ∼ of a photograph⟩ **2 :** unlikeness as shown when things are compared **:** DIFFERENCE

con•tra•vene \ˌkän-trə-ˈvēn\ *vb* **-vened; -ven•ing 1 :** to go or act contrary to ⟨∼ a law⟩ **2 :** CONTRADICT

con•tre•temps \ˈkän-trə-ˌtä^n, kō^n-trə-ˈtä^n\ *n, pl* **con•tre•temps** \-ˌtä^n, -ˌtä^{n}z\ [F] **:** an inopportune or embarrassing occurrence

contrib *abbr* contribution; contributor

con•trib•ute \kən-ˈtri-byət\ *vb* **-ut•ed; -ut•ing :** to give along with others (as to a fund); *also* **:** HELP, ASSIST — **con•tri•bu•tion** \ˌkän-trə-ˈbyü-shən\ *n* — **con•trib•u•tor** \kən-ˈtri-byə-tər\ *n* — **con•trib•u•to•ry** \-byə-ˌtȯr-ē\ *adj*

con•trite \ˈkän-ˌtrīt, kən-ˈtrīt\ *adj* **:** PENITENT, REPENTANT — **con•trite•ly** *adv* — **con•tri•tion** \kən-ˈtri-shən\ *n*

con•triv•ance \kən-ˈtrī-vəns\ *n* **1 :** a mechanical device **2 :** SCHEME, PLAN

con•trive \kən-ˈtrīv\ *vb* **con•trived; con•triv•ing 1 :** PLAN, DEVISE **2 :** FRAME, MAKE **3 :** to bring about with difficulty — **con•triv•er** *n*

con•trived \-ˈtrīvd\ *adj* **:** lacking in natural or spontaneous quality

¹**con•trol** \kən-ˈtrōl\ *vb* **con•trolled; con•trol•ling 1 :** to exercise restraining or directing influence over **:** REGULATE **2 :** DOMINATE, RULE

²**control** *n* **1 :** power to direct or regulate **2 :** RESERVE, RESTRAINT **3 :** a device for regulating a mechanism

con•trol•ler \kən-ˈtrō-lər, ˈkän-ˌtrō-lər\ *n* **1 :** COMPTROLLER **2 :** one that controls

con•tro•ver•sy \ˈkän-trə-ˌvər-sē\ *n, pl* **-sies :** a clash of opposing views **:** DISPUTE — **con•tro•ver•sial** \ˌkän-trə-ˌvər-shəl, -sē-əl\ *adj*

con•tro•vert \ˈkän-trə-ˌvərt, ˌkän-trə-ˈvərt\ *vb* **:** DENY, CONTRADICT — **con•tro•vert•ible** *adj*

con•tu•ma•cious \ˌkän-tü-ˈmā-shəs, -tyü-\ *adj* **:** stubbornly disobedient **syn** rebellious, insubordinate, seditious — **con•tu•ma•cy** \kən-ˈtü-mə-sē, -ˈtyü-; ˈkän-tyə-\ *n* — **con•tu•ma•cious•ly** *adv*

con•tu•me•ly \kən-ˈtü-mə-lē, -ˈtyü-; ˈkän-tə-ˌmē-lē, -tyə-\ *n, pl* **-lies :** contemptuous treatment **:** INSULT

con•tu•sion \kən-ˈtü-zhən, -ˈtyü-\ *n* **:** BRUISE — **con•tuse** \-ˈtüz, -ˈtyüz\ *vb*

co•nun•drum \kə-ˈnən-drəm\ *n* **:** RIDDLE

conv *abbr* **1** convention **2** convertible

con•va•lesce \ˌkän-və-ˈles\ *vb* **-lesced; -lesc•ing :** to recover health gradually — **con•va•les•cence** \-^{ə}ns\ *n* — **con•va•les•cent** \-^{ə}nt\ *adj or n*

con•vec•tion \kən-ˈvek-shən\ *n* **:** circulatory motion in a fluid due to warmer portions rising and cooler denser portions sinking; *also* **:** the transfer of heat by such motion — **con•vec•tion•al** \-shə-nəl\ *adj* — **con•vec•tive** \-ˈvek-tiv\ *adj*

convection oven *n* **:** an oven with a fan that circulates hot air uniformly and continuously around the food

con•vene \kən-ˈvēn\ *vb* **con•vened; con•ven•ing :** ASSEMBLE, MEET

con•ve•nience \kən-ˈvē-nyəns\ *n* **1 :** SUITABLENESS **2 :** a laborsaving device **3 :** a suitable time ⟨at your ∼⟩ **4 :** personal comfort **:** EASE

con•ve•nient \-nyənt\ *adj* **1 :** suited to personal comfort or ease **2 :** placed near at hand — **con•ve•nient•ly** *adv*

con•vent \ˈkän-vənt, -ˌvent\ *n* [ME *covent,* fr. OF, fr. ML *conventus,* fr. L, assembly, fr. *convenire* to come together] **:** a local community or house of a religious order esp. of nuns — **con•ven•tu•al** \kän-ˈven-chə-wəl\ *adj*

con•ven•ti•cle \kən-ˈven-ti-kəl\ *n* **:** MEETING; *esp* **:** a secret meeting for worship

con•ven•tion \kən-ˈven-chən\ *n* **1 :** an agreement esp. between states on a matter of common concern **2 :** MEETING, ASSEMBLY **3 :** an assembly of delegates convened for some purpose **4 :** generally accepted custom, practice, or belief

con•ven•tion•al \-chə-nəl\ *adj* **1 :** sanctioned by general custom **2 :** COMMONPLACE, ORDINARY — **con•ven•tion•al•i•ty** \-ˌven-chə-ˈna-lə-tē\ *n* — **con•ven•tion•al•ize** \-ˈven-chə-nə-ˌlīz\ *vb* — **con•ven•tion•al•ly** *adv*

con•verge \kən-ˈvərj\ *vb* **con•verged; con•verg•ing :** to approach one common center or single point — **con•ver•gence** \kən-ˈvər-jəns\ *n* — **con•ver•gent** \-jənt\ *adj*

con•ver•sant \kən-ˈvərs-ᵊnt\ *adj* **:** having knowledge and experience — used with *with*

con•ver•sa•tion \ˌkän-vər-ˈsā-shən\ *n* **:** an informal talking together — **con•ver•sa•tion•al** \-shə-nəl\ *adj* — **con•ver•sa•tion•al•ly** *adv*

con•ver•sa•tion•al•ist \-shə-nᵊl-ist\ *n* **:** a person who converses a great deal or who excels in conversation

[1]**con•verse** \ˈkän-ˌvərs\ *n* **:** CONVERSATION

[2]**con•verse** \kən-ˈvərs\ *vb* **con•versed; con•vers•ing :** to engage in conversation

[3]**con•verse** \ˈkän-ˌvərs\ *n* **:** a statement related to another statement by having its hypothesis and conclusion or its subject and predicate reversed or interchanged

[4]**con•verse** \kən-ˈvərs, ˈkän-ˌvers\ *adj* **:** reversed in order or relation — **con•verse•ly** *adv*

con•ver•sion \kən-ˈvər-zhən\ *n* **1 :** a change in nature or form **2 :** an experience associated with a decisive adoption of religion

[1]**con•vert** \kən-ˈvərt\ *vb* **1 :** to turn from one belief or party to another **2 :** TRANSFORM, CHANGE **3 :** MISAPPROPRIATE **4 :** EXCHANGE — **con•vert•er** *or* **con•ver•tor** \-ˈvər-tər\ *n*

[2]**con•vert** \ˈkän-ˌvərt\ *n* **:** a person who has undergone religious conversion

[1]**con•vert•ible** \kən-ˈvər-tə-bəl\ *adj* **:** capable of being converted

[2]**convertible** *n* **:** an automobile with a top that may be lowered or removed

con•vex \kän-ˈveks, ˈkän-ˌveks\ *adj* **:** curved or rounded like the exterior of a sphere or circle — **con•vex•i•ty** \kän-ˈvek-sə-tē\ *n*

con•vey \kən-ˈvā\ *vb* **1 :** CARRY, TRANSPORT **2 :** TRANSMIT, TRANSFER — **con•vey•or** *also* **con•vey•er** \-ər\ *n*

con•vey•ance \-ˈvā-əns\ *n* **1 :** the act of conveying **2 :** a legal paper transferring ownership of property **3 :** VEHICLE

[1]**con•vict** \kən-ˈvikt\ *vb* **:** to prove or find guilty

[2]**con•vict** \ˈkän-ˌvikt\ *n* **:** a person serving a prison sentence

con•vic•tion \kən-ˈvik-shən\ *n* **1 :** the act of convicting esp. in a court **2 :** the state of being convinced **:** BELIEF

con•vince \kən-ˈvins\ *vb* **con•vinced; con•vinc•ing :** to bring (as by argument) to belief or action — **con•vinc•ing** *adj* — **con•vinc•ing•ly** *adv*

con•viv•ial \kən-ˈvi-vē-əl\ *adj* [LL *convivialis,* fr. L *convivium* banquet, fr. *com-* together + *vivere* to live] **:** enjoying companionship and the pleasures of feasting and drinking **:** JOVIAL, FESTIVE — **con•viv•i•al•i•ty** \-ˌvi-vē-ˈa-lə-tē\ *n* — **con•viv•ial•ly** *adv*

con•vo•ca•tion \ˌkän-və-ˈkā-shən\ *n* **1 :** a ceremonial assembly (as of the clergy) **2 :** the act of convoking

con•voke \kən-ˈvōk\ *vb* **con•voked; con•vok•ing :** to call together to a meeting

con•vo•lut•ed \ˈkän-və-ˌlü-təd\ *adj* **1 :** folded in curved or tortuous windings **2 :** INVOLVED, INTRICATE

con•vo•lu•tion \ˌkän-və-ˈlü-shən\ *n* **:** a tortuous or sinuous structure; *esp* **:** one of the ridges of the brain

[1]**con•voy** \ˈkän-ˌvȯi, kən-ˈvȯi\ *vb* **:** to accompany for protection

[2]**con•voy** \ˈkän-ˌvȯi\ *n* **1 :** one that convoys; *esp* **:** a protective escort (as for ships) **2 :** the act of convoying **3 :** a group of moving vehicles

con•vulse \kən-ˈvəls\ *vb* **con•vulsed; con•vuls•ing :** to agitate violently

con•vul•sion \kən-ˈvəl-shən\ *n* **1 :** an abnormal and violent involuntary contraction or series of contractions of muscle **2 :** a violent disturbance — **con•vul•sive** \-siv\ *adj* — **con•vul•sive•ly** *adv*

cony *var of* CONEY

coo \ˈkü\ *n* **:** a soft low sound made by doves or pigeons; *also* **:** a sound like this — **coo** *vb*

COO *abbr* chief operating officer

[1]**cook** \ˈku̇k\ *n* **:** a person who prepares food for eating

[2]**cook** *vb* **1 :** to prepare food for eating **2 :** to subject to heat or fire — **cook•er** *n* — **cook•ware** \-ˌwar\ *n*

cook•book \-ˌbu̇k\ *n* **:** a book of cooking directions and recipes

cook•ery \ˈku̇-kə-rē\ *n, pl* **-er•ies :** the art or practice of cooking

cook•ie *or* **cooky** \ˈku̇-kē\ *n, pl* **cook•ies :** a small sweet flat cake

cook•out \ˈku̇k-ˌau̇t\ *n* **:** an outing at which a meal is cooked and served in the open

[1]**cool** \ˈkül\ *adj* **1 :** moderately cold **2 :** not excited **:** CALM **3 :** not friendly **4 :** IMPUDENT **5 :** protecting from heat **6** *slang* **:** very good **syn** unflappable, composed, collected, unruffled, nonchalant — **cool•ly** *adv* — **cool•ness** *n*

[2]**cool** *vb* **:** to make or become cool

[3]**cool** *n* **1 :** a cool time or place **2 :** INDIFFERENCE; *also* **:** SELF-ASSURANCE, COMPOSURE ⟨kept his ~⟩

cool•ant \ˈkü-lənt\ *n* **:** a usu. fluid cooling agent

cool•er \ˈkü-lər\ *n* **1 :** a container for keeping food or drink cool **2 :** JAIL, PRISON **3 :** a tall iced drink

coo•lie \ˈkü-lē\ *n* [Hindi *kulī*] **:** an unskilled laborer usu. in or from the Far East

coon \ˈkün\ *n* **:** RACCOON

coon•hound \-ˌhau̇nd\ *n* **:** a sporting dog trained to hunt raccoons

coon•skin \-ˌskin\ *n* **:** the pelt of a raccoon; *also* **:** something (as a cap) made of this

[1]**coop** \ˈküp, ˈku̇p\ *n* **:** a small enclosure or building usu. for poultry

[2]**coop** *vb* **:** to confine in or as if in a coop — usu. used with *up*

co–op \ˈkō-ˌäp\ *n* **:** COOPERATIVE

coo•per \ˈkü-pər, ˈku̇-\ *n* **:** one who makes or repairs barrels or casks — **cooper** *vb* — **coo•per•age** \-pə-rij\ *n*

co•op•er•ate \kō-ˈä-pə-ˌrāt\ *vb* **:** to act jointly with another or others — **co•op•er•a•tion** \-ˌä-pə-ˈrā-shən\ *n* — **co•op•er•a•tor** \-ˈä-pə-ˌrā-tər\ *n*

[1]**co•op•er•a•tive** \kō-ˈä-prə-tiv, -ˈä-pə-ˌrā-\ *adj* **1 :** willing to work with others **2 :** of or relating to an association formed to enable its members to buy or sell to better advantage by eliminating middlemen's profits

[2]**cooperative** *n* **:** a cooperative association

co–opt \kō-ˈäpt\ *vb* **1 :** to choose or elect as a colleague **2 :** ABSORB, ASSIMILATE; *also* **:** TAKE OVER

[1]**co•or•di•nate** \kō-ˈȯrd-ᵊn-ət\ *adj* **1 :** equal in rank or order **2 :** of equal rank in a compound sentence ⟨~ clause⟩ **3 :** joining words or word groups of the same rank — **co•or•di•nate•ly** *adv*

[2]**co•or•di•nate** \-ˈȯrd-ᵊn-ˌāt\ *vb* **-nat•ed; -nat•ing 1 :** to make or become coordinate **2 :** to work or act together harmoniously — **co•or•di•na•tion** \-ˌȯrd-ᵊn-ˈā-shən\ *n* — **co•or•di•na•tor** \-ˈȯrd-ᵊn-ˌā-tər\ *n*

[3]**co•or•di•nate** \-ˈȯrd-ᵊn-ət\ *n* **1 :** one of a set of numbers used in specifying the location of a point on a surface or in space **2** *pl* **:** articles (as of clothing) designed to be used together and to attain their effect through pleasing contrast

coot \ˈküt\ *n* **1 :** a dark-colored ducklike bird related to the rails **2 :** any of several No. American sea ducks **3 :** a harmless simple person

coo•tie \ˈkü-tē\ *n* **:** a body louse

cop \ˈkäp\ *n* **:** POLICE OFFICER

co–pay•ment \ˈkō-ˌpā-mənt, ˌkō-ˈ\ *n* **:** a relatively small fixed fee required of a patient by a health insurer (as an HMO) at the time of each outpatient service or filling of a prescription

[1]**cope** \ˈkōp\ *n* **:** a long cloaklike ecclesiastical vestment

[2]**cope** *vb* **coped; cop•ing :** to struggle to overcome problems or difficulties

copi•er \ˈkä-pē-ər\ *n* **:** one that copies; *esp* **:** a machine for making copies

co•pi•lot \ˈkō-ˌpī-lət\ *n* **:** an assistant pilot of an aircraft or spacecraft

cop•ing \ˈkō-piŋ\ *n* **:** the top layer of a wall

co•pi•ous \ˈkō-pē-əs\ *adj* **:** LAVISH, ABUNDANT — **co•pi•ous•ly** *adv* — **co•pi•ous•ness** *n*

cop–out \ˈkäp-ˌau̇t\ *n* **:** an excuse for copping out; *also* **:** an act of copping out

cop out *vb* **:** to back out (as of an unwanted responsibility)

cop•per \ˈkä-pər\ *n* **1 :** a malleable reddish metallic chemical element that is one of the best conductors of heat and electricity — see ELEMENT table **2 :** a coin or token made of copper — **cop•pery** *adj*

cop•per•head \ˈkä-pər-ˌhed\ *n* **:** a largely coppery brown pit viper esp. of the eastern and central U.S.

cop•pice \ˈkä-pəs\ *n* **:** THICKET

co•pra \ˈkō-prə\ *n* **:** dried coconut meat yielding coconut oil

copse \ˈkäps\ *n* **:** THICKET

cop•ter \ˈkäp-tər\ *n* **:** HELICOPTER

cop•u•la \ˈkä-pyə-lə\ *n* **:** LINKING VERB — **cop•u•la•tive** \-lə-tiv, -ˌlā-\ *adj*

cop•u•late \ˈkä-pyə-ˌlāt\ *vb* **-lat•ed; -lat•ing :** to engage in sexual intercourse — **cop•u•la•tion** \ˌkä-pyə-ˈlā-shən\ *n* — **cop•u•la•to•ry** \ˈkä-pyə-lə-ˌtōr-ē\ *adj*

[1]**copy** \ˈkä-pē\ *n, pl* **cop•ies 1 :** an imitation or reproduction of an original work **2 :** material to be set in type **syn** duplicate, reproduction, facsimile, replica

[2]**copy** *vb* **cop•ied; copy•ing 1 :** to make a copy of **2 :** IMITATE — **copy•ist** *n*

copy•book \ˈkä-pē-ˌbu̇k\ *n* **:** a book formerly used to teach handwriting containing examples to be copied

copy•boy \-ˌbȯi\ *n* **:** a person who carries copy and runs errands (as in a newspaper office)

copy•cat \-ˌkat\ *n* **:** a slavish imitator

copy•desk \-ˌdesk\ *n* **:** the desk at which newspaper copy is edited

copy editor *n* **:** one who edits newspaper copy and writes headlines; *also* **:** one who reads and corrects manuscript copy in a publishing house

copy•read•er \-ˌrē-dər\ *n* **:** COPY EDITOR

[1]**copy•right** \-ˌrīt\ *n* **:** the sole right to reproduce, publish, and sell a literary or artistic work

[2]**copyright** *vb* **:** to secure a copyright on

copy•writ•er \ˈkä-pē-ˌrī-tər\ *n* **:** a writer of advertising copy

co•quet *or* **co•quette** \kō-ˈket\ *vb* **co•quet•ted; co•quet•ting :** FLIRT — **co•quet•ry** \ˈkō-kə-trē, kō-ˈke-trē\ *n*

co•quette \kō-ˈket\ *n* [F, fem. of *coquet,* flirtatious man, dim. of *coq* cock] **:** FLIRT — **co•quett•ish** *adj*

cor *abbr* corner

Cor *abbr* Corinthians

cor•a•cle \ˈkȯr-ə-kəl\ *n* [W *corwgl*] **:** a boat made of a frame covered usu. with hide or tarpaulin

cor•al \ˈkȯr-əl\ *n* **1 :** a stony or horny material that forms the skeleton of colonies of tiny sea polyps and includes a red form used in jewelry; *also* **:** a coral-forming polyp or polyp colony **2 :** a deep pink color — **coral** *adj*

coral snake *n* **:** any of several venomous chiefly tropical New World snakes brilliantly banded in red, black, and yellow or white

cor•bel \ˈkȯr-bəl\ *n* **:** a bracket-shaped architectural member that projects from a wall and supports a weight

[1]**cord** \ˈkȯrd\ *n* **1 :** a usu. heavy string consisting of several strands woven or twisted together **2 :** a long slender anatomical structure (as a tendon or nerve) **3 :** a small flexible insulated electrical cable used to connect an appliance with a receptacle **4 :** a cubic measure used esp. for firewood and equal to a stack 4×4×8 feet **5 :** a rib or ridge on cloth

[2]**cord** *vb* **1 :** to tie or furnish with a cord **2 :** to pile (wood) in cords

cord•age \ˈkȯr-dij\ *n* **:** ROPES, CORDS; *esp* **:** ropes in the rigging of a ship

[1]**cor•dial** \ˈkȯr-jəl\ *adj* [ME, fr. ML *cordialis,* fr. L *cord-, cor* heart] **:** warmly receptive or welcoming **:** HEARTFELT, HEARTY — **cor•di•al•i•ty** \ˌkȯr-jē-ˈa-lə-tē, kȯr-ˈja-\ *n* — **cor•dial•ly** *adv*

[2]**cordial** *n* **1 :** a stimulating medicine or drink **2 :** LIQUEUR

cor•dil•le•ra \ˌkȯr-dəl-ˈyer-ə, -də-ˈler-\ *n* [Sp] **:** a series of parallel mountain ranges

cord•less \ˈkȯrd-ləs\ *adj* **:** having no cord; *esp* **:** powered by a battery

cor•do•ba \ˈkȯr-də-bə, -və\ *n* — see MONEY table

cor•don \ˈkȯrd-ᵊn\ *n* **1 :** an ornamental cord or ribbon **2 :** an encircling line (as of troops or police) — **cordon** *vb*

cor•do•van \ˈkȯr-də-vən\ *n* **:** a soft fine-grained leather

cor•du•roy \ˈkȯr-də-ˌrȯi\ *n, pl* **-roys :** a heavy ribbed fabric; *also, pl* **:** trousers of this material

cord•wain•er \ˈkȯrd-ˌwā-nər\ *n* **:** SHOEMAKER

[1]**core** \ˈkōr\ *n* **1 :** the central usu. inedible part of some fruits (as the apple); *also* **:** an inmost part of something **2 :** GIST, ESSENCE

[2]**core** *vb* **cored; cor•ing :** to take out the core of — **cor•er** *n*

CORE \ˈkōr\ *abbr* Congress of Racial Equality

co•re•spon•dent \ˌkō-ri-ˈspän-dənt\ *n* **:** a person named as guilty of adultery with the defendant in a divorce suit

co•ri•an•der \ˈkōr-ē-ˌan-dər\ *n* **:** an herb related to the carrot; *also* **:** its aromatic dried fruit used as a flavoring

Cor•in•thi•ans \kə-ˈrin-thē-ənz\ *n* — see BIBLE table

[1]**cork** \ˈkȯrk\ *n* **1 :** the tough elastic bark of a European oak (**cork oak**) used esp. for stoppers and insulation; *also* **:** a stopper of this **2 :** a tissue of a woody plant making up most of the bark — **corky** *adj*

[2]**cork** *vb* **:** to furnish with or stop up with cork or a cork

cork•screw \ˈkȯrk-ˌskrü\ *n* **:** a device for drawing corks from bottles

corm \ˈkȯrm\ *n* **:** a solid bulblike underground part of a stem (as of the crocus or gladiolus)

cor•mo•rant \ˈkȯr-mə-rənt, -ˌrant\ *n* [ME *cormeraunt,* fr. MF *cormorant,* fr. OF *cormareng,* fr. *corp* raven + *marenc* of the sea, fr. L *marinus*] **:** any of a family of dark-colored water birds with a long neck, hooked bill, and distensible throat pouch

[1]**corn** \ˈkȯrn\ *n* **1 :** the seeds of a cereal grass and esp. of the chief cereal crop of a region (as wheat in Britain and Indian corn in the U.S.); *also* **:** a cereal grass **2 :** sweet corn served as a vegetable

[2]**corn** *vb* **:** to salt (as beef) in brine and preservatives

[3]**corn** *n* **:** a local hardening and thickening of skin (as on a toe)

[1]**corn•ball** \ˈkȯrn-ˌbȯl\ *n* **:** an unsophisticated person; *also* **:** something corny

[2]**cornball** *adj* **:** CORNY

corn bread *n* **:** bread made with cornmeal

corn•cob \-ˌkäb\ *n* **:** the woody core on which the kernels of Indian corn are arranged

corn•crib \-ˌkrib\ *n* **:** a crib for storing ears of Indian corn

cor•nea \ˈkȯr-nē-ə\ *n* **:** the transparent part of the coat of the eyeball covering the iris and the pupil — **cor•ne•al** *adj*

corn ear•worm \-ˈir-ˌwərm\ *n* **:** a moth whose larva is destructive esp. to Indian corn

[1]**cor•ner** \ˈkȯr-nər\ *n* [ME, fr. OF *cornere,* fr. *corne* horn, corner, fr. L *cornu* horn, point] **1 :** the point or angle formed by the meeting of lines, edges, or sides **2 :** the place where two streets come together **3 :** a quiet secluded place **4 :** a position from which retreat or escape is impossible **5 :** control of enough of the

available supply (as of a commodity) to permit manipulation of the price — **cor•nered** *adj*

[2]cor•ner *vb* **1** : to drive into a corner **2** : to get a corner on ⟨~ the wheat market⟩ **3** : to turn a corner

cor•ner•stone \ˈkȯr-nər-ˌstōn\ *n* **1** : a stone forming part of a corner in a wall; *esp* : such a stone laid at a formal ceremony **2** : something of basic importance

cor•net \kȯr-ˈnet\ *n* : a brass band instrument resembling the trumpet

corn flour *n, Brit* : CORNSTARCH

corn•flow•er \ˈkȯrn-ˌflau̇(-ə)r\ *n* : BACHELOR'S BUTTON

cor•nice \ˈkȯr-nəs\ *n* : the horizontal projecting part crowning the wall of a building

corn•meal \ˈkȯrn-ˌmēl\ *n* : meal ground from corn

corn•row \-ˌrō\ *n* : a section of hair braided flat to the scalp in rows — **cornrow** *vb*

corn•stalk \-ˌstȯk\ *n* : a stalk of Indian corn

corn•starch \-ˌstärch\ *n* : a starch made from corn and used in cookery as a thickening agent

corn syrup *n* : a sweet syrup obtained from cornstarch

cor•nu•co•pia \ˌkȯr-nə-ˈkō-pē-ə, -nyə-\ *n* [LL, fr. L *cornu copiae* horn of plenty] : a horn-shaped container filled with fruits and grain emblematic of abundance

cornucopia

corny \ˈkȯr-nē\ *adj* **corn•i•er; -est** : tiresomely simple or sentimental

co•rol•la \kə-ˈrä-lə, -ˈrō-\ *n* : the petals of a flower

cor•ol•lary \ˈkȯr-ə-ˌler-ē\ *n, pl* **-lar•ies 1** : a deduction from a proposition already proved true **2** : CONSEQUENCE, RESULT

co•ro•na \kə-ˈrō-nə\ *n* **1** : a colored circle often seen around and close to a luminous body (as the sun or moon) **2** : the outermost part of the atmosphere of a star (as the sun) — **co•ro•nal** \ˈkȯr-ən-ᵊl, kə-ˈrōn-ᵊl\ *adj*

cor•o•nal \ˈkȯr-ən-ᵊl\ *n* : a circlet for the head

[1]cor•o•nary \ˈkȯr-ə-ˌner-ē\ *adj* : of or relating to the heart or its blood vessels

[2]coronary *n, pl* **-nar•ies 1** : a coronary blood vessel **2** : CORONARY THROMBOSIS; *also* : HEART ATTACK

coronary thrombosis *n* : the blocking by a thrombus of one of the arteries supplying the heart tissues

cor•o•na•tion \ˌkȯr-ə-ˈnā-shən\ *n* : the act or ceremony of crowning a monarch

cor•o•ner \ˈkȯr-ə-nər\ *n* : a public official who investigates causes of deaths possibly not due to natural causes

cor•o•net \ˌkȯr-ə-ˈnet\ *n* **1** : a small crown **2** : an ornamental band worn around the temples

corp *abbr* **1** corporal **2** corporation

[1]cor•po•ral \ˈkȯr-p(ə-)rəl\ *adj* : of or relating to the body ⟨~ punishment⟩

[2]corporal *n* : a noncommissioned officer (as in the army) ranking next below a sergeant

cor•po•rate \ˈkȯr-p(ə-)rət\ *adj* **1** : INCORPORATED; *also* : belonging to an incorporated body **2** : combined into one body

cor•po•ra•tion \ˌkȯr-pə-ˈrā-shən\ *n* **1** : the municipal authorities of a town or city **2** : a legal creation authorized to act with the rights and liabilities of a person ⟨a business ~⟩

cor•po•re•al \kȯr-ˈpōr-ē-əl\ *adj* **1** : PHYSICAL, MATERIAL **2** *archaic* : BODILY — **cor•po•re•al•i•ty** \kȯr-ˌpōr-ē-ˈa-lə-tē\ *n* — **cor•po•re•al•ly** *adv*

corps \ˈkōr\ *n, pl* **corps** \ˈkōrz\ [F, fr. L *corpus* body] **1** : an organized subdivision of a country's military forces **2** : a group acting under common direction

corpse \ˈkȯrps\ *n* : a dead body

corps•man \ˈkōr-mən, ˈkōrz-\ *n* : an enlisted man trained to give first aid

cor•pu•lence \ˈkȯr-pyə-ləns\ *n* : excessive fatness : OBESITY

cor•pu•lent \-lənt\ *adj* : OBESE

cor•pus \ˈkȯr-pəs\ *n, pl* **cor•po•ra** \-pə-rə\ [ME, fr. L] **1** : BODY; *esp* : CORPSE **2** : a body of writings or works

cor•pus•cle \ˈkȯr-pə-səl, -ˌpə-\ *n* **1** : a minute particle **2** : a living cell (as in blood or cartilage) not aggregated into continuous tissues — **cor•pus•cu•lar** \kȯr-ˈpəs-kyə-lər\ *adj*

cor•pus de•lic•ti \ˌkȯr-pəs-di-ˈlik-ˌtī, -tē\ *n, pl* **corpora delicti** [NL, lit., body of the crime] **1** : the substantial fact proving that a crime has been committed **2** : the body of a victim of murder

corr *abbr* **1** correct; corrected; correction **2** correspondence; correspondent; corresponding

cor•ral \kə-ˈral\ *n* [Sp] : an enclosure for confining or capturing animals; *also* : an enclosure of wagons for defending a camp — **corral** *vb*

[1]cor•rect \kə-ˈrekt\ *vb* **1** : to make right **2** : REPROVE, CHASTISE — **cor•rect•able** \-ˈrek-tə-bəl\ *adj* — **cor•rec•tion** \-ˈrek-shən\ *n* — **cor•rec•tion•al** \-ˈrek-sh(ə-)nəl\ *adj* — **cor•rec•tive** \-ˈrek-tiv\ *adj*

[2]correct *adj* **1** : conforming to a conventional standard **2** : agreeing with fact or truth — **cor•rect•ly** *adv* — **cor•rect•ness** *n*

cor•re•late \ˈkȯr-ə-ˌlāt\ *vb* **-lat•ed; -lat•ing** : to connect in a systematic way : establish the mutual relations of — **cor•re•late** \-lət, -ˌlāt\ *n* — **cor•re•la•tion** \ˌkȯr-ə-ˈlā-shən\ *n*

cor•rel•a•tive \kə-ˈre-lə-tiv\ *adj* **1** : reciprocally related **2** : regularly used together (as *either* and *or*) — **correlative** *n* — **cor•rel•a•tive•ly** *adv*

cor•re•spond \ˌkȯr-ə-ˈspänd\ *vb* **1** : to be in agreement : SUIT, MATCH **2** : to communicate by letter — **cor•re•spond•ing•ly** *adv*

cor•re•spon•dence \-ˈspän-dəns\ *n* **1** : agreement between particular things **2** : communication by letters; *also* : the letters exchanged

[1]cor•re•spon•dent \-dənt\ *adj* **1** : SIMILAR **2** : FITTING, CONFORMING

[2]correspondent *n* **1** : something that corresponds **2** : a person with whom one communicates by letter **3** : a person employed to contribute news regularly from a place

cor•ri•dor \ˈkȯr-ə-dər, -ˌdȯr\ *n* **1** : a passageway into which compartments or rooms open (as in a hotel or school) **2** : a narrow strip of land esp. through foreign-held territory **3** : a densely populated strip of land including two or more major cities

cor•ri•gen•dum \ˌkȯr-ə-ˈjen-dəm\ *n, pl* **-da** \-də\ [L] : an error in a printed work discovered after printing and shown with its correction on a separate sheet

cor•ri•gi•ble \ˈkȯr-ə-jə-bəl\ *adj* : CORRECTABLE

cor•rob•o•rate \kə-ˈrä-bə-ˌrāt\ *vb* **-rat•ed; -rat•ing** [L *corroborare*, fr. *robur* strength] : to support with evidence : CONFIRM — **cor•rob•o•ra•tion** \-ˌrä-bə-ˈrā-shən\ *n* — **cor•rob•o•ra•tive** \-ˈrä-bə-ˌrā-tiv, -ˈrä-brə-\ *adj* — **cor•rob•o•ra•to•ry** \-ˈrä-bə-rə-ˌtōr-ē\ *adj*

cor•rode \kə-ˈrōd\ *vb* **cor•rod•ed; cor•rod•ing** : to wear or be worn away gradually (as by chemical action) — **cor•ro•sion** \-ˈrō-zhən\ *n* — **cor•ro•sive** \-ˈrō-siv\ *adj or n*

cor•ru•gate \ˈkȯr-ə-ˌgāt\ *vb* **-gat•ed; -gat•ing** : to form into wrinkles or ridges and grooves — **cor•ru•gat•ed** *adj* — **cor•ru•ga•tion** \ˌkȯr-ə-ˈgā-shən\ *n*

[1]**cor•rupt** \kə-ˈrəpt\ *vb* **1 :** to make evil : DEPRAVE; *esp* : BRIBE **2 :** ROT, SPOIL — **cor•rupt•ible** *adj* — **cor•rup•tion** \-ˈrəp-shən\ *n*
[2]**corrupt** *adj* **:** morally degenerate; *also* **:** characterized by improper conduct ⟨~ officials⟩
cor•sage \kȯr-ˈsäzh, -ˈsäj\ *n* [F, bust, bodice, fr. OF, bust, fr. *cors* body, fr. L *corpus*] **1 :** the waist or bodice of a dress **2 :** a bouquet to be worn or carried
cor•sair \ˈkȯr-ˌsar\ *n* **:** PIRATE
cor•set \ˈkȯr-sət\ *n* **:** a stiffened undergarment worn for support or to give shape to the waist and hips
cor•tege *also* **cor•tège** \kȯr-ˈtezh, ˈkȯr-ˌtezh\ *n* [F] **:** PROCESSION; *esp* **:** a funeral procession
cor•tex \ˈkȯr-ˌteks\ *n, pl* **cor•ti•ces** \ˈkȯr-tə-ˌsēz\ *or* **cor•tex•es :** an outer or covering layer of an organism or one of its parts ⟨the adrenal ~⟩ ⟨~ of a plant stem⟩; *esp* **:** the outer layer of gray matter of the brain — **cor•ti•cal** \ˈkȯr-ti-kəl\ *adj*
cor•ti•sone \ˈkȯr-tə-ˌsōn, -ˌzōn\ *n* **:** an adrenal hormone used in treating rheumatoid arthritis
co•run•dum \kə-ˈrən-dəm\ *n* **:** a very hard aluminum-containing mineral used as an abrasive or as a gem
cor•us•cate \ˈkȯr-ə-ˌskāt\ *vb* **-cat•ed; -cat•ing :** FLASH, SPARKLE — **cor•us•ca•tion** \ˌkȯr-ə-ˈskā-shən\ *n*
cor•vette \kȯr-ˈvet\ *n* **1 :** a naval sailing ship smaller than a frigate **2 :** an armed escort ship smaller than a destroyer
co•ry•za \kə-ˈrī-zə\ *n* **:** an inflammatory disorder of the upper respiratory tract; *esp* **:** COMMON COLD
COS *abbr* **1** cash on shipment **2** chief of staff
co•sig•na•to•ry \kō-ˈsig-nə-ˌtōr-ē\ *n* **:** a joint signer
co•sign•er \ˈkō-ˌsī-nər\ *n* **:** COSIGNATORY; *esp* **:** a joint signer of a promissory note
[1]**cos•met•ic** \käz-ˈme-tik\ *adj* [Gk *kosmētikos* skilled in adornment, fr. *kosmein* to arrange, adorn, fr. *kosmos* order, ornament, universe] **1 :** intended to beautify the hair or complexion **2 :** correcting physical defects esp. to improve appearance ⟨~ dentistry⟩ **3 :** SUPERFICIAL
[2]**cosmetic** *n* **:** a cosmetic preparation
cos•me•tol•o•gist \ˌkäz-mə-ˈtä-lə-jist\ *n* **:** one who gives beauty treatments — **cos•me•tol•o•gy** \-jē\ *n*
cos•mic \ˈkäz-mik\ *also* **cos•mi•cal** \-mi-kəl\ *adj* **1 :** of or relating to the cosmos **2 :** VAST, GRAND — **cos•mi•cal•ly** *adv*
cosmic ray *n* **:** a stream of very penetrating atomic nuclei that enter the earth's atmosphere from outer space
cos•mog•o•ny \käz-ˈmä-gə-nē\ *n, pl* **-nies :** the origin or creation of the world or universe
cos•mol•o•gy \-ˈmä-lə-jē\ *n, pl* **-gies :** a branch of astronomy dealing with the origin and structure of the universe — **cos•mo•log•i•cal** \ˌkäz-mə-ˈlä-ji-kəl\ *adj* — **cos•mol•o•gist** \käz-ˈmä-lə-jist\ *n*
cos•mo•naut \ˈkäz-mə-ˌnȯt\ *n* **:** a Soviet or Russian astronaut
cos•mo•pol•i•tan \ˌkäz-mə-ˈpä-lət-ᵊn\ *adj* **:** belonging to all the world **:** not local **syn** universal, global, catholic — **cosmopolitan** *n*
cos•mos \ˈkäz-məs, 1 *also* -ˌmōs, -ˌmäs\ *n* **1 :** UNIVERSE **2 :** a tall garden herb related to the daisies
co•spon•sor \ˈkō-ˌspän-sər, -ˈspän-\ *n* **:** a joint sponsor — **cosponsor** *vb*
cos•sack \ˈkä-ˌsak, -sək\ *n* [Pol & Ukrainian *kozak*, of Turkic origin] **:** a member of a group of frontiersmen of southern Russia organized as cavalry in the czarist army
[1]**cost** \ˈkȯst\ *n* **1 :** the amount paid or charged for something **:** PRICE **2 :** the loss or penalty incurred in gaining something **3** *pl* **:** expenses incurred in a law suit
[2]**cost** *vb* **cost; cost•ing 1 :** to require a specified amount in payment **2 :** to cause to pay, suffer, or lose
co–star \ˈkō-ˌstär\ *n* **:** one of two leading players in a motion picture or play — **co–star** *vb*
Cos•ta Ri•can \ˌkäs-tə-ˈrē-kən\ *n* **:** a native or inhabitant of Costa Rica — **Costa Rican** *adj*
cos•tive \ˈkäs-tiv\ *adj* **:** affected with or causing constipation
cost•ly \ˈkȯst-lē\ *adj* **cost•li•er; -est :** of great cost or value **:** not cheap **syn** dear, valuable, expensive — **cost•li•ness** *n*
cos•tume \ˈkäs-ˌtüm, -ˌtyüm\ *n* **1 :** the style of attire characteristic of a period or country **2 :** a special or fancy dress ⟨Halloween ~*s*⟩ — **cos•tum•er** \ˈkäs-ˌtü-mər, -ˌtyü-\ *n*
costume jewelry *n* **:** inexpensive jewelry
co•sy \ˈkō-zē\ *var of* COZY
[1]**cot** \ˈkät\ *n* **:** a small house **:** COTTAGE
[2]**cot** *n* **:** a small often collapsible bed
cote \ˈkōt, ˈkät\ *n* **:** a small shed or coop (as for sheep or doves)
co•te•rie \ˈkō-tə-ˌrē, ˌkō-tə-ˈrē\ *n* [F] **:** an intimate often exclusive group of persons with a common interest
co•ter•mi•nous \ˌkō-ˈtər-mə-nəs\ *adj* **:** having the same scope or duration
co•til•lion \kō-ˈtil-yən, kə-\ *n* **:** a formal ball
cot•tage \ˈkä-tij\ *n* **:** a small house — **cot•tag•er** *n*
cottage cheese *n* **:** a soft uncured cheese made from soured skim milk
cot•ter *or* **cot•tar** \ˈkä-tər\ *n* **:** a peasant or farm laborer occupying a cottage and often a small holding
cotter pin *n* **:** a metal strip bent into a pin whose ends can be spread apart after insertion through a hole or slot
cot•ton \ˈkät-ᵊn\ *n* [ME *coton*, fr. MF, fr. Ar *quṭun*] **1 :** a soft fibrous usu. white substance composed of hairs attached to the seeds of a plant related to the mallow; *also* **:** this plant **2 :** thread or cloth made of cotton — **cot•tony** *adj*
cotton candy *n* **:** a candy made of spun sugar
cot•ton•mouth \ˈkät-ᵊn-ˌmau̇th\ *n* **:** WATER MOCCASIN
cot•ton•seed \-ˌsēd\ *n* **:** the seed of the cotton plant yielding a protein-rich meal and a fatty oil (**cottonseed oil**) used esp. in cooking
cot•ton•tail \-ˌtāl\ *n* **:** an American rabbit with a white-tufted tail
cot•ton•wood \-ˌwu̇d\ *n* **:** a poplar having seeds with cottony hairs
cot•y•le•don \ˌkä-tə-ˈlēd-ᵊn\ *n* **:** the first leaf or one of the first pair or whorl of leaves developed by a seed plant
[1]**couch** \ˈkau̇ch\ *vb* **1 :** to lie or place on a couch **2 :** to phrase in a specified manner
[2]**couch** *n* **:** a piece of furniture (as a bed or sofa) that one can sit or lie on
couch•ant \ˈkau̇-chənt\ *adj* **:** lying down with the head raised ⟨coat of arms with lion ~⟩
couch potato *n* **:** one who spends a great deal of time watching television
cou•gar \ˈkü-gər\ *n, pl* **cougars** *also* **cougar** [F *couguar*, fr. NL *cuguacuarana*, modif. of Tupi (a Brazilian Indian language) *siwasuarána*, fr. *siwasú* deer + *-rana* resembling] **:** a large powerful tawny brown wild American cat
cough \ˈkȯf\ *vb* **:** to force air from the lungs with short sharp noises; *also* **:** to expel by coughing — **cough** *n*
could \kəd, ˈku̇d\ *past of* CAN — used as an auxiliary in the past or as a polite or less forceful alternative to *can* in the present
cou•lee \ˈkü-lē\ *n* **1 :** a small stream **2 :** a dry streambed **3 :** GULLY
cou•lomb \ˈkü-ˌläm, -ˌlōm\ *n* **:** a unit of electric charge equal to the electricity transferred by a current of one ampere in one second
coun•cil \ˈkau̇n-səl\ *n* **1 :** ASSEMBLY, MEETING **2 :** an official body of lawmakers ⟨city ~⟩ — **coun•cil•lor** *or* **coun•cil•or** \-sə-lər\ *n* — **coun•cil•man** \-səl-mən\ *n* — **coun•cil•wom•an** \-ˌwu̇-mən\ *n*
[1]**coun•sel** \ˈkau̇n-səl\ *n* **1 :** ADVICE **2 :** a plan of action **3 :** deliberation together **4** *pl* **counsel :** LAWYER
[2]**counsel** *vb* **-seled** *or* **-selled; -sel•ing** *or* **-sel•ling 1 :** ADVISE **2 :** CONSULT

coun•sel•or *or* **coun•sel•lor** \ˈkau̇n-sə-lər\ *n* **1** : ADVISER **2** : LAWYER **3** : one who has supervisory duties at a summer camp

¹count \ˈkau̇nt\ *vb* [ME *counten,* fr. MF *compter,* fr. L *computare,* fr. *com-* with + *putare* to consider] **1** : to name or indicate one by one in order to find the total number **2** : to recite numbers in order **3** : CONSIDER, ACCOUNT **4** : RELY ⟨you can ~ on me⟩ **5** : to be of value or account — **count•able** *adj*

²count *n* **1** : the act of counting; *also* : the total obtained by counting **2** : a particular charge in an indictment or legal declaration

³count *n* [MF *comte,* fr. LL *comes,* fr. L, companion, one of the imperial court, fr. *com-* with + *ire* to go] : a European nobleman whose rank corresponds to that of a British earl

count•down \ˈkau̇nt-ˌdau̇n\ *n* : a backward counting in fixed units (as seconds) to indicate the time remaining before an event (as the launching of a rocket) — **count down** *vb*

¹coun•te•nance \ˈkau̇nt-ᵊn-əns\ *n* **1** : the human face **2** : FAVOR, APPROVAL

²countenance *vb* **-nanced; -nanc•ing** : SANCTION, TOLERATE

¹count•er \ˈkau̇n-tər\ *n* **1** : a piece (as of metal or plastic) used in reckoning or in games **2** : a level surface over which business is transacted, food is served, or work is conducted

²count•er *n* : a device for recording a number or amount

³coun•ter *vb* : to act in opposition to

⁴coun•ter *adv* : in an opposite direction : CONTRARY

⁵coun•ter *n* **1** : OPPOSITE, CONTRARY **2** : an answering or offsetting force or blow

⁶coun•ter *adj* : CONTRARY, OPPOSITE

coun•ter•act \ˌkau̇n-tər-ˈakt\ *vb* : to lessen the force of : OFFSET — **coun•ter•ac•tive** \-ˈak-tiv\ *adj*

coun•ter•at•tack \ˈkau̇n-tər-ə-ˌtak\ *n* : an attack made to oppose an enemy's attack — **counterattack** *vb*

¹coun•ter•bal•ance \ˈkau̇n-tər-ˌba-ləns\ *n* : a weight or influence that balances another

²counterbalance \ˌkau̇n-tər-ˈba-ləns\ *vb* : to oppose with equal weight or influence

coun•ter•claim \ˈkau̇n-tər-ˌklām\ *n* : an opposing claim esp. in law

coun•ter•clock•wise \ˌkau̇n-tər-ˈkläk-ˌwīz\ *adv* : in a direction opposite to that in which the hands of a clock rotate — **counterclockwise** *adj*

coun•ter•cul•ture \ˈkau̇n-tər-ˌkəl-chər\ *n* : a culture esp. of the young with values and mores that run counter to those of established society

coun•ter•es•pi•o•nage \ˌkau̇n-tər-ˈes-pē-ə-ˌnäzh, -nij\ *n* : activities intended to discover and defeat enemy espionage

¹coun•ter•feit \ˈkau̇n-tər-ˌfit\ *adj* : SHAM, SPURIOUS; *also* : FORGED

²counterfeit *vb* **1** : to copy or imitate in order to deceive **2** : PRETEND, FEIGN — **coun•ter•feit•er** *n*

³counterfeit *n* : something counterfeit : FORGERY **syn** fraud, sham, fake, imposture, deceit, deception

coun•ter•in•sur•gen•cy \ˌkau̇n-tər-in-ˈsər-jən-sē\ *n* : military activity designed to deal with insurgents

coun•ter•in•tel•li•gence \-in-ˈte-lə-jəns\ *n* : organized activities of an intelligence service designed to counter the activities of an enemy's intelligence service

count•er•man \ˈkau̇n-tər-ˌman, -mən\ *n* : one who tends a counter

coun•ter•mand \ˈkau̇nt-ər-ˌmand\ *vb* : to withdraw (an order already given) by a contrary order

coun•ter•mea•sure \-ˌme-zhər\ *n* : an action or device designed to counter another

coun•ter•of•fen•sive \-ə-ˌfen-siv\ *n* : a large-scale counterattack

coun•ter•pane \-ˌpān\ *n* : BEDSPREAD

coun•ter•part \-ˌpärt\ *n* : a person or thing very closely like or corresponding to another person or thing

coun•ter•point \-ˌpȯint\ *n* : music in which one melody is accompanied by one or more other melodies all woven into a harmonious whole

coun•ter•poise \-ˌpȯiz\ *n* : COUNTERBALANCE

coun•ter•rev•o•lu•tion \ˌkau̇n-tər-ˌre-və-ˈlü-shən\ *n* : a revolution opposed to a current or earlier one — **coun•ter•rev•o•lu•tion•ary** \-shə-ˌner-ē\ *adj or n*

coun•ter•sign \ˈkau̇n-tər-ˌsīn\ *n* **1** : a confirmatory signature added to a writing already signed by another person **2** : a military secret signal that must be given by a person who wishes to pass a guard — **countersign** *vb*

coun•ter•sink \-ˌsiŋk\ *vb* **-sunk** \-ˌsəŋk\; **-sink•ing** **1** : to form a funnel-shaped enlargement at the outer end of a drilled hole **2** : to set the head of (as a screw) at or below the surface — **countersink** *n*

coun•ter•spy \-ˌspī\ *n* : a spy engaged in counterespionage

coun•ter•ten•or \-ˌte-nər\ *n* : a tenor with an unusually high range

coun•ter•vail \ˌkau̇n-tər-ˈvāl\ *vb* : COUNTERACT

coun•ter•weight \ˈkau̇n-tər-ˌwāt\ *n* : COUNTERBALANCE

count•ess \ˈkau̇n-təs\ *n* **1** : the wife or widow of a count or an earl **2** : a woman holding the rank of a count or an earl in her own right

count•ing•house \ˈkau̇n-tiŋ-ˌhau̇s\ *n* : a building or office for keeping books and conducting business

count•less \ˈkau̇nt-ləs\ *adj* : INNUMERABLE

coun•tri•fied *also* **coun•try•fied** \ˈkən-tri-ˌfīd\ *adj* **1** : RURAL, RUSTIC **2** : UNSOPHISTICATED **3** : played or sung in the manner of country music

¹coun•try \ˈkən-trē\ *n, pl* **countries** [ME *contree,* fr. OF *contrée,* fr. ML *contrata,* fr. L *contra* against, on the opposite side] **1** : REGION, DISTRICT **2** : FATHERLAND **3** : a nation or its territory **4** : rural regions as opposed to towns and cities **5** : COUNTRY MUSIC

²country *adj* **1** : RURAL **2** : of or relating to country music ⟨a ~ singer⟩

country and western *n* : COUNTRY MUSIC

country club *n* : a suburban club for social life and recreation; *esp* : one having a golf course

coun•try–dance \ˈkən-trē-ˌdans\ *n* : an English dance in which partners face each other esp. in rows

coun•try•man \ˈkən-trē-mən, *2 often* -ˌman\ *n* **1** : an inhabitant of a specified country **2** : COMPATRIOT **3** : one raised or living in the country : RUSTIC

country music *n* : music derived from or imitating the folk style of the southern U.S. or of the Western cowboy

coun•try•side \ˈkən-trē-ˌsīd\ *n* : a rural area or its people

coun•ty \ˈkau̇n-tē\ *n, pl* **counties** **1** : the domain of a count **2** : a territorial division of a country or state for purposes of local government

coup \ˈkü\ *n, pl* **coups** \ˈküz\ [F, blow, stroke] **1** : a brilliant sudden stroke or stratagem **2** : COUP D'ÉTAT

coup de grace \ˌkü-də-ˈgräs\ *n, pl* **coups de grace** *same*\ [F *coup de grâce,* lit., stroke of mercy] : DEATHBLOW; *also* : a final decisive stroke or event

coup d'état \ˌkü-də-ˈtä\ *n, pl* **coups d'état** *same or* -ˈtäz\ [F, lit., stroke of state] : a sudden violent overthrow of a government by a small group

cou•pé *or* **coupe** \kü-ˈpā, *2 often* ˈküp\ *n* [F *coupé,* fr. *couper* to cut] **1** : a closed horse-drawn carriage for two persons inside with an outside seat for the driver **2** *usu* *coupe* : a 2-door automobile with an enclosed body

¹cou•ple \ˈkə-pəl\ *n* **1** : two persons closely associated; *esp* : a man and a woman married or otherwise paired **2** : PAIR **3** : BOND, TIE **4** : an indefinite small number : FEW ⟨a ~ of days ago⟩

²couple *vb* **cou•pled; cou•pling** : to link together

cou•plet \ˈkə-plət\ *n* : two successive rhyming lines of verse

cou•pling \ˈkə-pliŋ (*usual for 2*), -pə-liŋ\ *n* **1** : CONNECTION **2** : a device for connecting two parts or things

cou•pon \ˈkü-ˌpän, ˈkyü-\ *n* **1** : a statement attached to a bond showing interest due and designed to be cut off and presented for payment **2** : a form surrendered in order to obtain an article, service, or accommodation **3** : a part of an advertisement to be cut off to use as an order blank or inquiry form or to obtain a discount on merchandise

cour•age \ˈkər-ij\ *n* : ability to conquer fear or despair : BRAVERY, VALOR — **cou•ra•geous** \kə-ˈrā-jəs\ *adj* — **cou•ra•geous•ly** *adv*

cou•ri•er \ˈku̇r-ē-ər, ˈkər-ē-\ *n* : one who bears messages or information esp. for the diplomatic or military services

[1]**course** \ˈkōrs\ *n* **1** : PROGRESS, PASSAGE; *also* : direction of progress **2** : the ground or path over which something moves **3** : method of procedure : CONDUCT, BEHAVIOR **4** : an ordered series of acts or proceedings : sequence of events **5** : a series of instruction periods dealing with a subject **6** : the series of studies leading to graduation from a school or college **7** : the part of a meal served at one time — **of course** : as might be expected

[2]**course** *vb* **coursed; cours•ing 1** : to hunt with dogs **2** : to run or go speedily

cours•er \ˈkōr-sər\ *n* : a swift or spirited horse

[1]**court** \ˈkōrt\ *n* **1** : the residence of a sovereign or similar dignitary **2** : a sovereign's formal assembly of officials and advisers as a governing power **3** : an assembly of the retinue of a sovereign **4** : an open space enclosed by a building or buildings **5** : a space walled or marked off for playing a game (as tennis or basketball) **6** : the place where justice is administered; *also* : a judicial body or a meeting of a judicial body **7** : attention intended to win favor

[2]**court** *vb* **1** : to try to gain the favor of **2** : WOO **3** : ATTRACT, TEMPT

cour•te•ous \ˈkər-tē-əs\ *adj* : marked by respect for others : CIVIL, POLITE — **cour•te•ous•ly** *adv*

cour•te•san \ˈkōr-tə-zən, -ˌzan\ *n* : PROSTITUTE

cour•te•sy \ˈkər-tə-sē\ *n, pl* **-sies 1** : courteous behavior : POLITENESS **2** : a favor courteously performed

court•house \ˈkōrt-ˌhau̇s\ *n* : a building in which courts of law are held or county offices are located

court•ier \ˈkōr-tē-ər\ *n* : a person in attendance at a royal court

court•ly \ˈkōrt-lē\ *adj* **court•li•er; -est** : REFINED, ELEGANT, POLITE **syn** gallant, gracious — **court•li•ness** *n*

court–mar•tial \ˈkōrt-ˌmär-shəl\ *n, pl* **courts–martial** : a military or naval court for trial of offenses against military or naval law; *also* : a trial by this court — **court–martial** *vb*

court•room \-ˌrüm, -ˌru̇m\ *n* : a room in which a court of law is held

court•ship \-ˌship\ *n* : the act of courting : WOOING

court•yard \-ˌyärd\ *n* : an enclosure next to a building

cous•in \ˈkə-zən\ *n* [ME *cosin,* fr. OF, fr. L *consobrinus,* fr. *com-* with + *sobrinus* second cousin, fr. *soror* sister] : a child of one's uncle or aunt

cou•ture \kü-ˈtu̇r, -ˈtu̅e̅r\ *n* [F] : the business of designing fashionable custom-made women's clothing; *also* : the designers and establishments engaged in this business

cou•tu•ri•er \kü-ˈtu̇r-ē-ər, -ē-ˌā\ *n* [F, dressmaker] : the owner of an establishment engaged in couture

cove \ˈkōv\ *n* : a small sheltered inlet or bay

co•ven \ˈkə-vən\ *n* : an assembly or band of witches

cov•e•nant \ˈkə-və-nənt\ *n* : a formal binding agreement : COMPACT — **cov•e•nant** \-nənt, -ˌnant\ *vb*

[1]**cov•er** \ˈkə-vər\ *vb* **1** : to bring or hold within range of a firearm **2** : PROTECT, SHIELD **3** : HIDE, CONCEAL **4** : to place something over or upon **5** : INCLUDE, COMPRISE **6** : to have as one's field of activity ⟨one salesman ∼*s* the state⟩ **7** : to buy (stocks) in order to have them for delivery on a previous short sale

[2]**cover** *n* **1** : something that protects or shelters **2** : LID, TOP **3** : CASE, BINDING **4** : TABLECLOTH **5** : a cloth used on a bed **6** : SCREEN, DISGUISE **7** : an envelope or wrapper for mail

cov•er•age \ˈkə-və-rij\ *n* **1** : the act or fact of covering **2** : the total group covered : SCOPE

cov•er•all \ˈkə-vər-ˌo̊l\ *n* : a one-piece outer garment worn to protect one's clothes — usu. used in pl.

cover charge *n* : a charge made by a restaurant or nightclub in addition to the charge for food and drink

cover crop *n* : a crop planted to prevent soil erosion and to provide humus

cov•er•let \ˈkə-vər-lət\ *n* : BEDSPREAD

[1]**co•vert** \ˈkō-ˌvərt, ˈkə-vərt\ *adj* **1** : HIDDEN, SECRET **2** : SHELTERED — **co•vert•ly** *adv*

[2]**co•vert** \ˈkə-vərt, ˈkō-\ *n* **1** : a secret or sheltered place; *esp* : a thicket sheltering game **2** : a feather covering the bases of the quills of the wings and tail of a bird

cov•er–up \ˈkə-vər-ˌəp\ *n* **1** : a device for masking or concealing **2** : a usu. concerted effort to keep an illegal or unethical act or situation from being made public

cov•et \ˈkə-vət\ *vb* : to desire enviously (what belongs to another) — **cov•et•ous** *adj* — **cov•et•ous•ness** *n*

cov•ey \ˈkə-vē\ *n, pl* **coveys** [ME, fr. MF *covee,* fr. OF, fr. *cover* to sit on, brood over, fr. L *cubare* to lie] **1** : a bird with her brood of young **2** : a small flock (as of quail)

[1]**cow** \ˈkau̇\ *n* **1** : the mature female of cattle or of an animal (as the moose, elephant, or whale) of which the male is called *bull* **2** : any domestic bovine animal irrespective of sex or age

[2]**cow** *vb* : INTIMIDATE, DAUNT, OVERAWE

cow•ard \ˈkau̇(-ə)rd\ *n* [ME, fr. OF *coart,* fr. *coe* tail, fr. L *cauda*] : one who lacks courage or shows shameful fear or timidity — **coward** *adj* — **cow•ard•ice** \ˈkau̇-ər-dəs\ *n* — **cow•ard•ly** *adv or adj*

cow•bird \ˈkau̇-ˌbərd\ *n* : a small No. American bird that lays its eggs in the nests of other birds

cow•boy \-ˌbo̊i\ *n* : one (as a mounted ranch hand) who tends cattle or horses

cow•er \ˈkau̇(-ə)r\ *vb* : to shrink or crouch down from fear or cold : QUAIL

cow•girl \ˈkau̇-ˌgərl\ *n* : a girl or woman who tends cattle or horses

cow•hand \ˈkau̇-ˌhand\ *n* : COWBOY

cow•hide \-ˌhīd\ *n* **1** : the hide of a cow; *also* : leather made from it **2** : a coarse whip of braided rawhide

cowl \ˈkau̇l\ *n* : a monk's hood

cow•lick \ˈkau̇-ˌlik\ *n* : a turned-up tuft of hair that resists control

cowl•ing \ˈkau̇-liŋ\ *n* : a usu. metal covering for the engine or another part of an airplane

cow•man \ˈkau̇-mən, -ˌman\ *n* : COWBOY; *also* : a cattle owner or rancher

co•work•er \ˈkō-ˌwər-kər\ *n* : a fellow worker

cow•poke \ˈkau̇-ˌpōk\ *n* : COWBOY

cow pony *n* : a strong and agile horse trained for herding cattle

cow•pox \ˈkau̇-ˌpäks\ *n* : a mild disease of the cow that when communicated to humans protects against smallpox

cow•punch•er \-ˌpən-chər\ *n* : COWBOY

cow•slip \ˈkau̇-ˌslip\ *n* **1** : a yellow-flowered European primrose **2** : MARSH MARIGOLD

cox•comb \ˈkäks-ˌkōm\ *n* : a conceited foolish person : FOP

cox•swain \ˈkäk-sən, -ˌswān\ *n* : the steersman of a ship's boat or a racing shell

coy \ˈko̊i\ *adj* [ME, quiet, shy, fr. MF *coi* calm, fr. L *quietus* quiet] **1** : BASHFUL, SHY **2** : marked by artful playfulness : COQUETTISH — **coy•ly** *adv* — **coy•ness** *n*

coy•ote \ˈkī-ˌōt, kī-ˈō-tē\ *n, pl* **coyotes** *or* **coyote** : a mammal of No. America smaller than the related wolves

☞ For illustration, see next page.

coyote

coy•pu \ˈkȯi-pü\ *n* : NUTRIA 2

coz•en \ˈkəz-ᵊn\ *vb* : CHEAT, DEFRAUD — **coz•en•age** \-ij\ *n* — **coz•en•er** *n*

[1]**co•zy** \ˈkō-zē\ *adj* **co•zi•er; -est** : SNUG, COMFORTABLE — **co•zi•ly** \-zə-lē\ *adv* — **co•zi•ness** \-zē-nəs\ *n*

[2]**cozy** *n, pl* **co•zies** : a padded covering for a vessel (as a teapot) to keep the contents hot

cp *abbr* **1** compare **2** coupon

CP *abbr* **1** cerebral palsy **2** chemically pure **3** command post **4** communist party

CPA *abbr* certified public accountant

CPB *abbr* Corporation for Public Broadcasting

cpd *abbr* compound

CPI *abbr* consumer price index

Cpl *abbr* corporal

CPO *abbr* chief petty officer

CPOM *abbr* master chief petty officer

CPOS *abbr* senior chief petty officer

CPR *abbr* cardiopulmonary resuscitation

CPT *abbr* captain

CQ *abbr* charge of quarters

cr *abbr* credit; creditor

Cr *symbol* chromium

[1]**crab** \ˈkrab\ *n* : any of various crustaceans with a short broad shell and small abdomen

[2]**crab** *n* : an ill-natured person

[3]**crab** *vb* **crabbed; crab•bing** : COMPLAIN, GROUSE

crab apple *n* : a small often highly colored sour apple; *also* : a tree that produces crab apples

crab•bed \ˈkra-bəd\ *adj* **1** : MOROSE, PEEVISH **2** : CRAMPED, IRREGULAR

crab•by \ˈkra-bē\ *adj* **crab•bi•er; -est** : CROSS, ILL-NATURED

crab•grass \ˈkrab-ˌgras\ *n* : a weedy grass with creeping or sprawling stems that root freely at the nodes

crab louse *n* : a louse infesting the pubic region in humans

[1]**crack** \ˈkrak\ *vb* **1** : to break with a sharp sudden sound **2** : to break with or without completely separating into parts **3** : to fail in tone or become harsh ⟨her voice *~ed*⟩ **4** : to subject (as a petroleum oil) to heat for breaking down into lighter products (as gasoline)

[2]**crack** *n* **1** : a sudden sharp noise **2** : a witty or sharp remark **3** : a narrow break or opening : FISSURE **4** : a sharp blow **5** : ATTEMPT, TRY **6** : highly purified cocaine in small chips used illicitly usu. for smoking

[3]**crack** *adj* : extremely proficient

crack•down \ˈkrak-ˌdau̇n\ *n* : an act or instance of taking positive disciplinary action ⟨a ~ on gambling⟩ — **crack down** *vb*

crack•er \ˈkra-kər\ *n* **1** : FIRECRACKER **2** : a dry thin crispy baked bread product made of flour and water

crack•er•jack \-ˌjak\ *n* : something very excellent — **crackerjack** *adj*

crack•le \ˈkra-kəl\ *vb* **crack•led; crack•ling 1** : to make small sharp snapping noises **2** : to develop fine cracks in a surface — **crackle** *n* — **crack•ly** \-k(ə-)lē\ *adj*

crack•pot \ˈkrak-ˌpät\ *n* : an eccentric person

crack–up \ˈkrak-ˌəp\ *n* : CRASH, WRECK; *also* : BREAKDOWN

crack up *vb* **1** : PRAISE ⟨isn't all it's *cracked up* to be⟩ **2** : to laugh or cause to laugh out loud **3** : to crash a vehicle

[1]**cra•dle** \ˈkrād-ᵊl\ *n* **1** : a baby's bed or cot **2** : a framework or support (as for a telephone receiver) **3** : INFANCY ⟨from ~ to the grave⟩ **4** : a place of origin

[2]**cradle** *vb* **cra•dled; cra•dling 1** : to place in or as if in a cradle **2** : SHELTER, REAR

craft \ˈkraft\ *n* **1** : ART, SKILL; *also* : an occupation requiring special skill **2** : CUNNING, GUILE **3** *pl usu* **craft** : a boat esp. of small size; *also* : AIRCRAFT, SPACECRAFT

crafts•man \ˈkrafts-mən\ *n* : a skilled artisan — **crafts•man•ship** *n*

crafty \ˈkraf-tē\ *adj* **craft•i•er; -est** : CUNNING, DECEITFUL, SUBTLE — **craft•i•ly** \-tə-lē\ *adv* — **craft•i•ness** \-tē-nəs\ *n*

crag \ˈkrag\ *n* : a steep rugged cliff or rock — **craggy** *adj*

cram \ˈkram\ *vb* **crammed; cram•ming 1** : to pack in tight : JAM **2** : to eat greedily **3** : to study rapidly under pressure for an examination

[1]**cramp** \ˈkramp\ *n* **1** : a sudden painful contraction of muscle **2** : sharp abdominal pain — usu. used in pl.

[2]**cramp** *vb* **1** : to affect with a cramp or cramps **2** : to restrain from free action : HAMPER

cran•ber•ry \ˈkran-ˌber-ē, -bə-rē\ *n* : the red acid berry of any of several trailing plants related to the heaths; *also* : one of these plants

[1]**crane** \ˈkrān\ *n* **1** : any of a family of tall wading birds related to the rails; *also* : any of several herons **2** : a machine for lifting and carrying heavy objects

[2]**crane** *vb* **craned; cran•ing** : to stretch one's neck to see better

crane fly *n* : any of numerous long-legged slender dipteran flies that resemble large mosquitoes but do not bite

cranial nerve *n* : any of the nerves that arise in pairs from the lower surface of the brain and pass through openings in the skull to the periphery of the body

cra•ni•um \ˈkrā-nē-əm\ *n, pl* **-ni•ums** *or* **-nia** \-ə\ : SKULL; *esp* : the part enclosing the brain — **cra•ni•al** \-əl\ *adj*

[1]**crank** \ˈkraŋk\ *n* **1** : a bent part of an axle or shaft or an arm at right angles to the end of a shaft by which circular motion is imparted to or received from it **2** : an eccentric person **3** : a bad-tempered person : GROUCH

[2]**crank** *vb* : to start or operate by or as if by turning a crank

crank•case \ˈkraŋk-ˌkās\ *n* : the housing of a crankshaft

crank out *vb* : to produce in a mechanical manner

crank•shaft \ˈkraŋk-ˌshaft\ *n* : a shaft turning or driven by a crank

cranky \ˈkraŋ-kē\ *adj* **crank•i•er; -est 1** : IRRITABLE **2** : operating uncertainly or imperfectly

cran•ny \ˈkra-nē\ *n, pl* **crannies** : CREVICE, CHINK

craps \ˈkraps\ *n* : a gambling game played with two dice

crap•shoot•er \ˈkrap-ˌshü-tər\ *n* : a person who plays craps

[1]**crash** \ˈkrash\ *vb* **1** : to break noisily : SMASH **2** : to damage an airplane in landing **3** : to enter or attend without invitation or without paying ⟨~ a party⟩

[2]**crash** *n* **1** : a loud sound (as of things smashing) **2** : an instance of crashing ⟨a plane ~⟩; *also* : COLLISION **3** : a sudden failure (as of a business)

[3]**crash** *adj* : marked by concerted effort over the shortest possible time

[4]**crash** *n* : coarse linen fabric used for towels and draperies

crash–land \ˈkrash-ˈland\ *vb* : to land an aircraft or

spacecraft under emergency conditions usu. with damage to the craft — **crash landing** *n*
crass \ˈkras\ *adj* : GROSS, INSENSITIVE — **crass·ly** *adv*
crate \ˈkrāt\ *n* : a container often of wooden slats — **crate** *vb*
cra·ter \ˈkrā-tər\ *n* [L, mixing bowl, crater, fr. Gk *kratēr*, fr. *kerannynai* to mix] **1** : the depression around the opening of a volcano **2** : a depression formed by the impact of a meteorite or by the explosion of a bomb or shell
cra·vat \krə-ˈvat\ *n* : NECKTIE
crave \ˈkrāv\ *vb* **craved; crav·ing 1** : to ask for earnestly : BEG **2** : to long for : DESIRE
cra·ven \ˈkrā-vən\ *adj* : COWARDLY — **craven** *n*
crav·ing \ˈkrā-viŋ\ *n* : an urgent or abnormal desire
craw·fish \ˈkrȯ-ˌfish\ *n* **1** : CRAYFISH 1 **2** : SPINY LOBSTER
[1]**crawl** \ˈkrȯl\ *vb* **1** : to move slowly by drawing the body along the ground **2** : to advance feebly, cautiously, or slowly **3** : to be swarming with or feel as if swarming with creeping things ⟨a place ~*ing* with ants⟩ ⟨her flesh ~*ed*⟩
[2]**crawl** *n* **1** : a very slow pace **2** : a prone speed swimming stroke
cray·fish \ˈkrā-ˌfish\ *n* **1** : any of numerous freshwater crustaceans usu. much smaller than the related lobsters **2** : SPINY LOBSTER

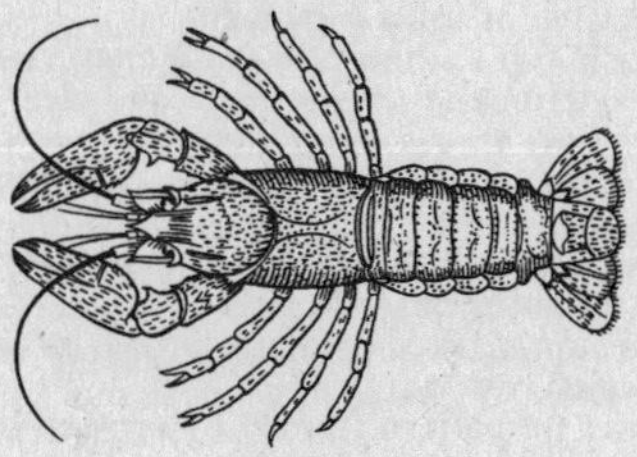

crayfish 1

cray·on \ˈkrā-ˌän, -ən\ *n* : a stick of chalk or wax used for writing, drawing, or coloring; *also* : a drawing made with such material — **crayon** *vb*
[1]**craze** \ˈkrāz\ *vb* **crazed; craz·ing** [ME *crasen* to crush, craze, of Scand origin] : to make or become insane
[2]**craze** *n* : FAD, MANIA
cra·zy \ˈkrā-zē\ *adj* **cra·zi·er; -est 1** : mentally disordered : INSANE **2** : wildly impractical; *also* : ERRATIC — **cra·zi·ly** \-zə-lē\ *adv* — **cra·zi·ness** \-zē-nəs\ *n*
CRC *abbr* Civil Rights Commission
creak \ˈkrēk\ *vb* : to make a prolonged squeaking or grating sound — **creak** *n* — **creaky** *adj*
[1]**cream** \ˈkrēm\ *n* **1** : the yellowish fat-rich part of milk **2** : a thick smooth sauce, confection, or cosmetic **3** : the choicest part **4** : a pale yellow color — **creamy** *adj*
[2]**cream** *vb* **1** : to prepare with a cream sauce **2** : to beat or blend into creamy consistency **3** : to defeat decisively
cream cheese *n* : a cheese made from whole milk enriched with cream
cream·ery \ˈkrē-mə-rē\ *n, pl* **-er·ies** : an establishment where butter and cheese are made or milk and cream are prepared for sale
crease \ˈkrēs\ *n* : a mark or line made by or as if by folding — **crease** *vb*
cre·ate \krē-ˈāt\ *vb* **cre·at·ed; cre·at·ing** : to bring into being : cause to exist : MAKE, PRODUCE — **cre·a·tive** \-ˈā-tiv\ *adj* — **cre·a·tiv·i·ty** \ˌkre-(ˌ)ā-ˈti-və-tē\ *n*
cre·a·tion \krē-ˈā-shən\ *n* **1** : the act of creating or producing ⟨~ of the world⟩ **2** : something that is created **3** : all created things : WORLD
cre·a·tion·ism \krē-ˈā-shə-ˌni-zəm\ *n* : a doctrine or theory holding that matter, the various forms of life, and the world were created by God out of nothing — **cre·a·tion·ist** \-nist\ *n or adj*
cre·a·tor \krē-ˈā-tər\ *n* **1** : one that creates : MAKER, AUTHOR **2** *cap* : GOD 1
crea·ture \ˈkrē-chər\ *n* : a lower animal; *also* : a human being
crèche \ˈkresh\ *n* [F, manger, crib] : a representation of the Nativity scene
cre·dence \ˈkrēd-ᵊns\ *n* : mental acceptance as true or real
cre·den·tial \kri-ˈden-chəl\ *n* : something that gives a basis for credit or confidence
cre·den·za \kri-ˈden-zə\ *n* [It, lit., belief, confidence] : a sideboard, buffet, or bookcase usu. without legs
cred·i·ble \ˈkre-də-bəl\ *adj* : TRUSTWORTHY, BELIEVABLE — **cred·i·bil·i·ty** \ˌkre-də-ˈbi-lə-tē\ *n*
[1]**cred·it** \ˈkre-dət\ *vb* **1** : BELIEVE **2** : to give credit to
[2]**credit** *n* [MF, fr. It *credito*, fr. L *creditum* something entrusted to another, loan, fr. *credere* to believe, entrust] **1** : the balance (as in a bank) in a person's favor **2** : time given for payment for goods sold on trust **3** : an accounting entry of payment received **4** : BELIEF, FAITH **5** : financial trustworthiness **6** : ESTEEM **7** : a source of honor or distinction **8** : a unit of academic work
cred·it·able \ˈkre-də-tə-bəl\ *adj* : worthy of esteem or praise — **cred·it·ably** \-blē\ *adv*
credit card *n* : a card authorizing purchases on credit
cred·i·tor \ˈkre-də-tər\ *n* : a person to whom money is owed
cre·do \ˈkrē-dō, ˈkrā-\ *n, pl* **credos** [ME, fr. L, I believe] : CREED
cred·u·lous \ˈkre-jə-ləs\ *adj* : inclined to believe esp. on slight evidence — **cre·du·li·ty** \kri-ˈdü-lə-tē, -ˈdyü-\ *n*
Cree \ˈkrē\ *n, pl* **Cree** *or* **Crees** : a member of an American Indian people of Canada
creed \ˈkrēd\ *n* [ME *crede*, fr. OE *crēda*, fr. L *credo* I believe, first word of the Apostles' and Nicene Creeds] : a statement of the essential beliefs of a religious faith
creek \ˈkrēk, ˈkrik\ *n* **1** *chiefly Brit* : a small inlet **2** : a stream smaller than a river and larger than a brook
Creek \ˈkrēk\ *n* : a member of an American Indian people of Alabama, Georgia, and Florida
creel \ˈkrēl\ *n* : a wicker basket esp. for carrying fish
creep \ˈkrēp\ *vb* **crept** \ˈkrept\; **creep·ing 1** : CRAWL **2** : to feel as though insects were crawling on the skin **3** : to grow over a surface like ivy — **creep** *n* — **creep·er** *n*
creep·ing \ˈkrē-piŋ\ *adj* : developing or advancing by imperceptible degrees
creepy \ˈkrē-pē\ *adj* **creep·i·er; -est** : having or producing a nervous shivery fear
cre·mate \ˈkrē-ˌmāt\ *vb* **cre·mat·ed; cre·mat·ing** : to reduce (a dead body) to ashes with fire — **cre·ma·tion** \kri-ˈmā-shən\ *n*
cre·ma·to·ry \ˈkrē-mə-ˌtōr-ē, ˈkre-\ *n, pl* **-ries** : a furnace for cremating; *also* : a structure containing such a furnace
crème \ˈkrem, ˈkrēm\ *n, pl* **crèmes** *same or* ˈkremz, ˈkrēmz\ [F, lit., cream] : a sweet liqueur
cren·el·lat·ed *or* **cren·el·at·ed** \ˈkren-ᵊl-ˌā-təd\ *adj* : having battlements — **cren·el·la·tion** \ˌkren-ᵊl-ˈā-shən\ *n*
Cre·ole \ˈkrē-ˌōl\ *n* **1** : a descendant of early French or Spanish settlers of the U.S. Gulf states preserving their speech and culture; *also* : a person of mixed French or Spanish and black descent speaking a dialect of French or Spanish **2** *not cap* : a language that has evolved from a pidgin but serves as the native language of a speech community
cre·o·sote \ˈkrē-ə-ˌsōt\ *n* : an oily liquid obtained by distillation of coal tar and used in preserving wood

crepe *or* **crêpe** \ˈkrāp\ *n* **:** a light crinkled fabric of any of various fibers
crêpe su•zette \ˌkrāp-sü-ˈzet\ *n, pl* **crêpes suzette** *same or* ˌkrāps-\ *or* **crêpe suzettes** \-sü-ˈzets\ *often cap S* **:** a thin folded or rolled pancake in a hot orange-butter sauce that is sprinkled with a liqueur and set ablaze for serving
cre•pus•cu•lar \kri-ˈpəs-kyə-lər\ *adj* **1 :** of, relating to, or resembling twilight **2 :** active in the twilight ⟨~ insects⟩
cre•scen•do \krə-ˈshen-dō\ *adv or adj* [It] **:** increasing in loudness — used as a direction in music — **crescendo** *n*
cres•cent \ˈkres-ᵊnt\ *n* [ME *cressant,* fr. MF *creissant,* fr. *creistre* to grow, increase, fr. L *crescere*] **:** the moon at any stage between new moon and first quarter and between last quarter and new moon; *also* **:** something shaped like the figure of the crescent moon with a convex and a concave edge — **cres•cen•tic** \kre-ˈsen-tik\ *adj*
cress \ˈkres\ *n* **:** any of several salad plants related to the mustards
¹**crest** \ˈkrest\ *n* **1 :** a tuft or process on the head of an animal (as a bird) **2 :** a heraldic device **3 :** an upper part, edge, or limit ⟨the ~ of a hill⟩ — **crest•ed** \ˈkres-təd\ *adj* — **crest•less** *adj*
²**crest** *vb* **1 :** CROWN **2 :** to reach the crest of **3 :** to rise to a crest
crest•fall•en \ˈkrest-ˌfȯ-lən\ *adj* **:** DISPIRITED, DEJECTED
Cre•ta•ceous \kri-ˈtā-shəs\ *adj* **:** of, relating to, or being the latest period of the Mesozoic era marked by great increase in flowering plants, diversification of mammals, and extinction of the dinosaurs — **Cretaceous** *n*
cre•tin \ˈkrēt-ᵊn\ *n* [F *crétin,* fr. F dial. *cretin,* lit., wretch, innocent victim, fr. L *christianus* Christian] **1 :** one affected with cretinism **2 :** a stupid person
cre•tin•ism \-ˌi-zəm\ *n* **:** a usu. congenital abnormal condition characterized by physical stunting and mental retardation
cre•tonne \ˈkrē-ˌtän\ *n* **:** a strong unglazed cotton cloth for curtains and upholstery
cre•vasse \kri-ˈvas\ *n* **:** a deep fissure esp. in a glacier
crev•ice \ˈkre-vəs\ *n* **:** a narrow fissure
¹**crew** \ˈkrü\ *chiefly Brit past of* CROW
²**crew** *n* [ME *crue,* lit., reinforcement, fr. MF *creue* increase, fr. *creistre* to grow, fr. L *crescere*] **1 :** a body of people trained to work together for certain purposes **2 :** a group of people who operate a ship, train, aircraft, or spacecraft **3 :** the rowers and coxswain of a racing shell; *also* **:** the sport of rowing engaged in by a crew — **crew•man** \-mən\ *n*
crew cut *n* **:** a very short bristly haircut
crew•el \ˈkrü-əl\ *n* **:** slackly twisted worsted yarn used for embroidery — **crew•el•work** \-ˌwərk\ *n*
¹**crib** \ˈkrib\ *n* **1 :** a manger for feeding animals **2 :** a child's bedstead with high sides **3 :** a building or bin for storage (as of grain) **4 :** something used for cheating in an exam
²**crib** *vb* **cribbed; crib•bing 1 :** to put in a crib **2 :** STEAL, PLAGIARIZE — **crib•ber** *n*
crib•bage \ˈkri-bij\ *n* **:** a card game usu. played by two players and scored on a board **(cribbage board)**
crib death *n* **:** SUDDEN INFANT DEATH SYNDROME
crick \ˈkrik\ *n* **:** a painful spasm of muscles (as of the neck)
¹**crick•et** \ˈkri-kət\ *n* **:** any of a family of leaping insects related to the grasshoppers and noted for the chirping noises of the male
²**cricket** *n* **:** a game played with a bat and ball by two teams on a field centering upon two wickets each defended by a batsman
cri•er \ˈkrī(-ə)r\ *n* **:** one who calls out proclamations and announcements
crime \ˈkrīm\ *n* **:** a serious offense against the public law
¹**crim•i•nal** \ˈkri-mən-ᵊl\ *adj* **1 :** involving or being a crime **2 :** relating to crime or its punishment — **crim•i•nal•i•ty** \ˌkri-mə-ˈna-lə-tē\ *n* — **crim•i•nal•ly** *adv*
²**criminal** *n* **:** one who has committed a crime
crim•i•nol•o•gy \ˌkri-mə-ˈnä-lə-jē\ *n* **:** the scientific study of crime and criminals — **crim•i•nol•o•gist** \ˌkri-mə-ˈnä-lə-jist\ *n*
¹**crimp** \ˈkrimp\ *vb* **:** to cause to become crinkled, wavy, or bent
²**crimp** *n* **:** something (as a curl in hair) produced by or as if by crimping
¹**crim•son** \ˈkrim-zən\ *n* **:** a deep purplish red color — **crimson** *adj*
²**crimson** *vb* **:** to make or become crimson
cringe \ˈkrinj\ *vb* **cringed; cring•ing :** to shrink in fear **:** WINCE, COWER
crin•kle \ˈkriŋ-kəl\ *vb* **crin•kled; crin•kling :** to form many short bends or curves; *also* **:** WRINKLE — **crinkle** *n* — **crin•kly** \-kə-lē\ *adj*
crin•o•line \ˈkrin-ᵊl-ən\ *n* **1 :** an open-weave cloth used for stiffening and lining **2 :** a full stiff skirt or underskirt made of crinoline
¹**crip•ple** \ˈkri-pəl\ *n* **:** a lame or disabled person — sometimes taken to be offensive
²**cripple** *vb* **crip•pled; crip•pling 1 :** to make lame **2 :** to make useless or imperfect
cri•sis \ˈkrī-səs\ *n, pl* **cri•ses** \-ˌsēz\ [L, fr. Gk *krisis,* lit., decision, fr. *krinein* to decide] **1 :** the turning point for better or worse in an acute disease or fever **2 :** a decisive or critical moment
crisp \ˈkrisp\ *adj* **1 :** CURLY, WAVY **2 :** BRITTLE **3 :** FIRM, FRESH ⟨~ lettuce⟩ **4 :** being sharp and clear **5 :** LIVELY, SPARKLING **6 :** FROSTY, SNAPPY; *also* **:** INVIGORATING — **crisp** *vb* — **crisp•ly** *adv* — **crisp•ness** *n* — **crispy** *adj*
¹**criss•cross** \ˈkris-ˌkrȯs\ *vb* **1 :** to mark with crossed lines **2 :** to go or pass back and forth
²**crisscross** *adj* **:** marked or characterized by crisscrossing — **crisscross** *adv*
³**crisscross** *n* **:** a pattern formed by crossed lines
crit *abbr* critical; criticism
cri•te•ri•on \krī-ˈtir-ē-ən\ *n, pl* **-ria** \-ē-ə\ **:** a standard on which a judgment may be based
crit•ic \ˈkri-tik\ *n* **1 :** a person who judges literary or artistic works **2 :** one inclined to find fault
crit•i•cal \ˈkri-ti-kəl\ *adj* **1 :** being or relating to a condition or disease involving danger of death **2 :** being a crisis **3 :** inclined to criticize **4 :** relating to criticism or critics **5 :** requiring careful judgment **6 :** UNCERTAIN — **crit•i•cal•ly** \-k(ə-)lē\ *adv*
crit•i•cise *Brit var of* CRITICIZE
crit•i•cism \ˈkri-tə-ˌsi-zəm\ *n* **1 :** the act of criticizing; *esp* **:** CENSURE **2 :** a judgment or review **3 :** the art of judging works of literature or art
crit•i•cize \ˈkri-tə-ˌsīz\ *vb* **-cized; -ciz•ing 1 :** to judge as a critic **:** EVALUATE **2 :** to find fault **:** express criticism **syn** blame, censure, condemn
cri•tique \krə-ˈtēk\ *n* **:** a critical estimate or discussion
crit•ter \ˈkri-tər\ *n* **:** CREATURE
croak \ˈkrōk\ *n* **:** a hoarse harsh cry (as of a frog) — **croak** *vb*
Croat \ˈkrō-ˌat\ *n* **:** CROATIAN
Cro•atian \krō-ˈā-shən\ *n* **:** a native or inhabitant of Croatia — **Croatian** *adj*
cro•chet \krō-ˈshā\ *n* [F, hook, crochet, fr. MF, dim. of *croche* hook] **:** needlework done with a single thread and hooked needle — **crochet** *vb*
crock \ˈkräk\ *n* **:** a thick earthenware pot or jar
crock•ery \ˈkrä-kə-rē\ *n* **:** EARTHENWARE
croc•o•dile \ˈkrä-kə-ˌdīl\ *n* [ME & L; ME *cocodrille,* fr. OF, fr. ML *cocodrillus,* alter. of L *crocodilus,* fr. Gk *krokodilos* lizard, crocodile, fr. *krokē* shingle, pebble + *drillos* worm] **:** any of several thick-skinned long-bodied carnivorous reptiles of tropical and subtropical waters
cro•cus \ˈkrō-kəs\ *n, pl* **cro•cus•es** *also* **crocus** *or* **cro-**

ci \-ˌkī\ : any of a large genus of low herbs related to the irises and having brightly colored flowers borne singly in early spring

crois•sant \krö-ˈsänt, krwä-ˈsä^{n}\ *n, pl* **croissants** *same or* -ˈsänts, -ˈsä^{n}z\ : a rich crescent-shaped roll

Cro–Ma•gnon \krō-ˈmag-nən, -ˈman-yən\ *n* : any of a tall erect human race known from skeletal remains found chiefly in southern France and usu. classified as the same species as present-day human beings — **Cro–Magnon** *adj*

crone \ˈkrōn\ *n* : HAG

cro•ny \ˈkrō-nē\ *n, pl* **cronies** : a close friend esp. of long standing

[1]**crook** \ˈkrůk\ *vb* : to curve or bend sharply

[2]**crook** *n* **1** : a bent or curved implement **2** : a bent or curved part; *also* : BEND, CURVE **3** : SWINDLER, THIEF

crook•ed \ˈkrů-kəd\ *adj* **1** : having a crook : BENT, CURVED **2** : DISHONEST — **crook•ed•ly** *adv* — **crook•ed•ness** *n*

croon \ˈkrün\ *vb* : to sing or hum in a gentle murmuring voice — **croon•er** *n*

[1]**crop** \ˈkräp\ *n* **1** : the handle of a whip; *also* : a short riding whip **2** : a pouch in the throat of many birds and insects where food is received **3** : something that can be harvested; *also* : the yield at harvest

[2]**crop** *vb* **cropped; crop•ping 1** : to remove the tips of : cut off short; *also* : TRIM **2** : to feed on by cropping **3** : to devote (land) to crops **4** : to appear unexpectedly

crop•land \-ˌland\ *n* : land devoted to the production of plant crops

crop•per \ˈkrä-pər\ *n* : a raiser of crops; *esp* : SHARECROPPER

cro•quet \krō-ˈkā\ *n* : a game in which mallets are used to drive wooden balls through a series of wickets set out on a lawn

cro•quette \krō-ˈket\ *n* [F] : a small often rounded mass of minced meat, fish, or vegetables fried in deep fat

cro•sier \ˈkrō-zhər\ *n* : a staff carried by bishops and abbots

[1]**cross** \ˈkrös\ *n* **1** : a structure consisting of an upright beam and a crossbar used esp. by the ancient Romans for execution **2** : a figure of the cross on which Christ was crucified used as a Christian symbol **3** : a hybridizing of unlike individuals or strains; *also* : a product of this **4** : a punch delivered with a circular motion over an opponent's lead

[2]**cross** *vb* **1** : to lie or place across; *also* : INTERSECT **2** : to cancel by marking a cross on or by lining through **3** : THWART, OBSTRUCT **4** : to go or extend across : TRAVERSE **5** : HYBRIDIZE **6** : to meet and pass on the way

[3]**cross** *adj* **1** : lying across **2** : CONTRARY, OPPOSED **3** : marked by bad temper **4** : HYBRID — **cross•ly** *adv*

cross•bar \ˈkrös-ˌbär\ *n* : a transverse bar or piece

cross•bow \-ˌbō\ *n* : a short bow mounted crosswise at the end of a wooden stock that shoots short arrows

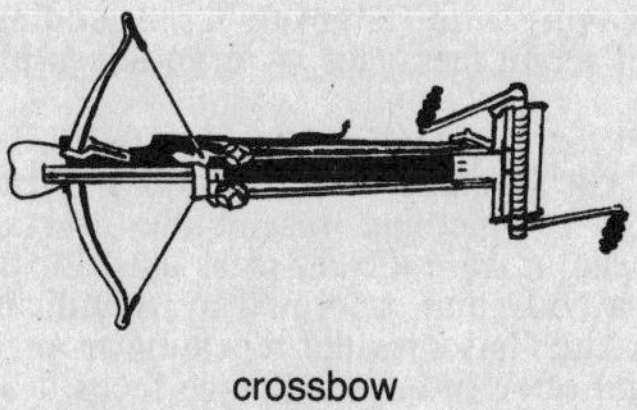

crossbow

cross•breed \ˈkrös-ˌbrēd, -ˈbrēd\ *vb* **-bred** \-ˈbred\; **-breed•ing** : HYBRIDIZE

cross–coun•try \-ˈkən-trē\ *adj* **1** : extending or moving across a country **2** : proceeding over the countryside (as fields and woods) and not by roads **3** : of or relating to racing or skiing over the countryside instead of over a track or run — **cross–country** *adv*

cross•cur•rent \-ˈkər-ənt\ *n* **1** : a current running counter to another **2** : a conflicting tendency — usu. used in pl.

[1]**cross•cut** \-ˌkət\ *vb* : to cut or saw crosswise esp. of the grain of wood

[2]**crosscut** *adj* **1** : made or used for crosscutting ⟨a ~ saw⟩ **2** : cut across the grain

[3]**crosscut** *n* : something that cuts through transversely

cross–ex•am•ine \ˌkrö-sig-ˈza-mən\ *vb* : to examine with questions to check the answers to previous questions — **cross–ex•am•i•na•tion** \-ˌza-mə-ˈnā-shən\ *n*

cross–eyed \ˈkrö-ˌsīd\ *adj* : having one or both eyes turned inward toward the nose

cross–fer•til•i•za•tion \-ˌfərt-^{ə}l-ə-ˈzā-shən\ *n* **1** : fertilization between sex cells produced by separate individuals or sometimes by individuals of different kinds; *also* : CROSS-POLLINATION **2** : a broadening or productive interchange (as between cultures) — **cross–fer•til•ize** \-ˈfərt-^{ə}l-ˌīz\ *vb*

cross fire *n* **1** : crossing lines of fire in combat **2** : rapid or angry interchange

cross•hair \ˈkrös-ˌhar\ *n* : a fine wire or thread in the eyepiece of an optical instrument used as a reference line

cross•hatch \ˈkrös-ˌhach\ *vb* : to mark with two series of parallel lines that intersect — **cross–hatch•ing** *n*

cross•ing \ˈkrö-siŋ\ *n* **1** : a place or structure for crossing something (as a river) **2** : a point of intersection (as of a street and a railroad track)

cross•over \ˈkrös-ˌō-vər\ *n* **1** : CROSSING **2** : a member of a political party who votes in the primary of the other party

cross•piece \ˈkrös-ˌpēs\ *n* : a horizontal member

cross–pol•li•na•tion \ˌkrös-ˌpä-lə-ˈnā- shən\ *n* : transfer of pollen from one flower to the stigma of another — **cross–pol•li•nate** \ˈkrös-ˈpä-lə-ˌnāt\ *vb*

cross–pur•pose \ˈkrös-ˈpər-pəs\ *n* : a purpose contrary to another purpose ⟨working at ~*s*⟩

cross–ques•tion \-ˈkwes-chən\ *vb* : CROSS-EXAMINE — **cross–question** *n*

cross–re•fer \ˌkrös-ri-ˈfər\ *vb* : to refer by a notation or direction from one place to another (as in a book or list) — **cross–ref•er•ence** \ˈkrös-ˈre-frəns\ *n*

cross•road \ˈkrös-ˌrōd\ *n* **1** : a road that crosses a main road or runs between main roads **2** : a place where roads meet — usu. used in pl. **3** : a crucial point where a decision must be made

cross section *n* **1** : a section cut across something; *also* : a representation made by or as if by such cutting **2** : a number of persons or things selected from a group that show the general nature of the whole group — **cross–sec•tion•al** *adj*

cross•walk \ˈkrös-ˌwök\ *n* : a marked path for pedestrians crossing a street

cross•ways \-ˌwāz\ *adv* : CROSSWISE

cross•wind \-ˌwind\ *n* : a wind not parallel to a course (as of an airplane)

cross•wise \-ˌwīz\ *adv* : so as to cross something : ACROSS — **crosswise** *adj*

cross•word \ˈkrös-ˌwərd\ *n* : a puzzle in which words are put into a pattern of numbered squares in answer to clues

crotch \ˈkräch\ *n* : an angle formed by the parting of two legs, branches, or members

crotch•et \ˈkrä-chət\ *n* : an odd notion : WHIM — **crotch•ety** *adj*

crouch \ˈkraůch\ *vb* **1** : to stoop or bend low **2** : CRINGE, COWER — **crouch** *n*

croup \ˈkrüp\ *n* : laryngitis esp. of infants marked by a hoarse ringing cough and difficult breathing — **croupy** *adj*

crou•pi•er \ˈkrü-pē-ər, -pē-ˌā\ *n* [F, lit., rider on the rump of a horse, fr. *croupe* rump] : an employee of a gambling casino who collects and pays bets at a gaming table

crou·ton \ˈkrü-ˌtän\ *n* [F *croûton,* dim. of *croûte* crust] : a small cube of bread toasted or fried crisp

¹crow \ˈkrō\ *n* **1** : any of various large glossy black birds related to the jays **2** *cap* : a member of an American Indian people of a region in Montana and Wyoming; *also* : the language of the Crow people

²crow *vb* **1** : to make the loud shrill sound characteristic of the cock **2** : to utter a sound expressive of pleasure **3** : EXULT, GLOAT; *also* : BRAG, BOAST

³crow *n* : the cry of the cock

crow·bar \ˈkrō-ˌbär\ *n* : a metal bar usu. wedge-shaped at the end for use as a pry or lever

¹crowd \ˈkrau̇d\ *vb* **1** : to press close **2** : to collect in numbers : THRONG **3** : CRAM, STUFF

²crowd *n* : a large number of people gathered together at random : THRONG

¹crown \ˈkrau̇n\ *n* **1** : a mark of victory or honor; *esp* : the title of a champion in a sport **2** : a royal headdress **3** : the top of the head **4** : the highest part (as of a tree or tooth) **5** *often cap* : sovereign power; *also* : MONARCH **6** : a formerly used British silver coin — **crowned** \ˈkrau̇nd\ *adj*

²crown *vb* **1** : to place a crown on **2** : HONOR **3** : TOP, SURMOUNT **4** : to fit (a tooth) with an artificial crown

crown vetch *n* : a European leguminous herb with umbels of pink-and-white flowers and sharp-angled pods

crow's–foot \ˈkrōz-ˌfu̇t\ *n, pl* **crow's–feet** \-ˌfēt\ : any of the wrinkles around the outer corners of the eyes — usu. used in pl.

crow's nest *n* : a partly enclosed platform high on a ship's mast for use as a lookout

¹CRT \ˌsē-(ˌ)är-ˈtē\ *n, pl* **CRTs** *or* **CRT's** : CATHODE-RAY TUBE; *also* : a display device incorporating a cathode-ray tube

²CRT *abbr* carrier route

cru·cial \ˈkrü-shəl\ *adj* : DECISIVE; *also* : IMPORTANT, SIGNIFICANT

cru·ci·ble \ˈkrü-sə-bəl\ *n* : a heat-resistant container in which material can be subjected to great heat

cru·ci·fix \ˈkrü-sə-ˌfiks\ *n* : a representation of Christ on the cross

cru·ci·fix·ion \ˌkrü-sə-ˈfik-shən\ *n* **1** *cap* : the crucifying of Christ **2** : the act of crucifying

cru·ci·form \ˈkrü-sə-ˌfȯrm\ *adj* : shaped like a cross

cru·ci·fy \ˈkrü-sə-ˌfī\ *vb* **-fied; -fy·ing 1** : to put to death by nailing or binding the hands and feet to a cross **2** : MORTIFY 1 **3** : TORTURE, PERSECUTE

¹crude \ˈkrüd\ *adj* **crud·er; crud·est 1** : not refined : RAW ⟨~ oil⟩ ⟨~ statistics⟩ **2** : lacking grace, taste, tact, or polish : RUDE — **crude·ly** *adv* — **cru·di·ty** \ˈkrü-də-tē\ *n*

²crude *n* : unrefined petroleum

cru·el \ˈkrü-əl\ *adj* **cru·el·er** *or* **cru·el·ler; cru·el·est** *or* **cru·el·lest** : causing pain and suffering to others : MERCILESS — **cru·el·ly** *adv* — **cru·el·ty** \-tē\ *n*

cru·et \ˈkrü-ət\ *n* : a small usu. glass bottle for vinegar, oil, or sauce

cruise \ˈkrüz\ *vb* **cruised; cruis·ing** [D *kruisen* to make a cross, cruise] **1** : to sail about touching at a series of ports **2** : to travel for enjoyment **3** : to travel about the streets at random **4** : to travel at the most efficient operating speed ⟨the *cruising* speed of an airplane⟩ — **cruise** *n*

cruis·er \ˈkrü-zər\ *n* **1** : SQUAD CAR **2** : a large fast moderately armored and gunned warship **3** : a motorboat equipped for living aboard

crul·ler \ˈkrə-lər\ *n* **1** : a small sweet cake in the form of a twisted strip fried in deep fat **2** *Northern & Midland* : an unraised doughnut

¹crumb \ˈkrəm\ *n* : a small fragment

²crumb *vb* **1** : to break into crumbs **2** : to cover with crumbs

crum·ble \ˈkrəm-bəl\ *vb* **crum·bled; crum·bling** : to break into small pieces : DISINTEGRATE — **crum·bly** *adj*

crum·my *also* **crumby** \ˈkrə-mē\ *adj* **crum·mi·er** *also* **crumb·i·er; -est 1** : MISERABLE, FILTHY **2** : CHEAP, WORTHLESS

crum·pet \ˈkrəm-pət\ *n* : a small round unsweetened bread cooked on a griddle

crum·ple \ˈkrəm-pəl\ *vb* **crum·pled; crum·pling 1** : to crush together : RUMPLE **2** : COLLAPSE

¹crunch \ˈkrənch\ *vb* : to chew with a grinding noise; *also* : to grind or press with a crushing noise

²crunch *n* **1** : an act of or a sound made by crunching **2** : a tight or critical situation — **crunchy** *adj*

cru·sade \krü-ˈsād\ *n* **1** *cap* : any of the expeditions in the 11th, 12th, and 13th centuries undertaken by Christian countries to take the Holy Land from the Muslims **2** : a reforming enterprise undertaken with zeal — **crusade** *vb* — **cru·sad·er** *n*

cruse \ˈkrüz, ˈkrüs\ *n* : a jar for water or oil

¹crush \ˈkrəsh\ *vb* **1** : to squeeze out of shape **2** : HUG, EMBRACE **3** : to grind or pound to small bits **4** : OVERWHELM, SUPPRESS

²crush *n* **1** : an act of crushing **2** : a violent crowding **3** : INFATUATION

crust \ˈkrəst\ *n* **1** : the outside part of bread; *also* : a piece of old dry bread **2** : the cover of a pie **3** : a hard surface layer — **crust·al** *adj*

crus·ta·cean \ˌkrəs-ˈtā-shən\ *n* : any of a large class of mostly aquatic arthropods (as lobsters or crabs) having a firm crustlike shell — **crustacean** *adj*

crusty *adj* **crust·i·er; -est 1** : having or being a crust **2** : CROSS, GRUMPY

crutch \ˈkrəch\ *n* : a supporting device; *esp* : a support fitting under the armpit for use by the disabled in walking

crux \ˈkrəks, ˈkru̇ks\ *n, pl* **crux·es 1** : a puzzling or difficult problem **2** : a crucial point

¹cry \ˈkrī\ *vb* **cried; cry·ing 1** : to call out : SHOUT **2** : to proclaim publicly : ADVERTISE **3** : WEEP

²cry *n, pl* **cries 1** : a loud outcry **2** : APPEAL, ENTREATY **3** : a fit of weeping **4** : the characteristic sound uttered by an animal **5** : DISTANCE — usu. used in the phrase *a far cry*

cry·ba·by \ˈkrī-ˌbā-bē\ *n* : one who cries easily or often

cryo·gen·ic \ˌkrī-ə-ˈje-nik\ *adj* : of or relating to the production of very low temperatures; *also* : involving the use of a very low temperature — **cryo·gen·i·cal·ly** \-ni-k(ə-)lē\ *adv*

cryo·gen·ics \-niks\ *n* : a branch of physics that relates to the production and effects of very low temperatures

cryo·lite \ˈkrī-ə-ˌlīt\ *n* : a usu. white mineral used in making aluminum

crypt \ˈkript\ *n* : a chamber wholly or partly underground

cryp·tic \ˈkrip-tik\ *adj* : meant to be puzzling or mysterious

cryp·to·gram \ˈkrip-tə-ˌgram\ *n* : a communication in cipher or code

cryp·tog·ra·phy \krip-ˈtä-grə-fē\ *n* : the coding and decoding of secret messages — **cryp·tog·ra·pher** \-fər\ *n*

crys·tal \ˈkrist-ᵊl\ *n* [ME *cristal,* fr. OF, fr. L *crystallum,* fr. Gk *krystallos* ice, crystal] **1** : transparent quartz **2** : something resembling crystal (as in transparency); *esp* : a clear glass used for table articles **3** : a body that is formed by solidification of a substance and has a regular repeating arrangement of atoms and often of external plane faces ⟨a salt ~⟩ **4** : the transparent cover of a watch dial

crys·tal·line \ˈkris-tə-lən\ *adj* **1** : made of or resembling crystal **2** : very clear or sparkling

crys·tal·lise *Brit var of* CRYSTALLIZE

crys·tal·lize \ˈkris-tə-ˌlīz\ *vb* **-lized; -liz·ing 1** : to assume or cause to assume a crystalline form **2** : to take or cause to take a definite form — **crys•tal•li•za•tion** \ˌkris-tə-lə-ˈzā-shən\ *n*

crys•tal•log•ra•phy \ˌkris-tə-ˈlä-grə-fē\ *n* : the science dealing with the forms and structures of crystals — **crys•tal•log•ra•pher** *n*

cs *abbr* case; cases

Cs *symbol* cesium

CS *abbr* **1** civil service **2** county seat

CSA *abbr* Confederate States of America

CSM *abbr* command sergeant major

CST *abbr* central standard time

ct *abbr* **1** carat **2** cent **3** count **4** county **5** court

CT *abbr* **1** central time **2** Connecticut

ctn *abbr* carton

ctr *abbr* **1** center **2** counter

CT scan \ˌsē-ˈtē-\ *n* : CAT SCAN

cu *abbr* cubic

Cu *symbol* [L *cuprum*] copper

cub \ˈkəb\ *n* : a young individual of some animals (as a fox, bear, or lion)

Cu•ban \ˈkyü-bən\ *n* : a native or inhabitant of Cuba — **Cuban** *adj*

cub•by•hole \ˈkə-bē-ˌhōl\ *n* : a snug place (as for storing things)

[1]**cube** \ˈkyüb\ *n* **1** : a solid having 6 equal square sides **2** : the product obtained by taking a number 3 times as a factor ⟨27 is the ~ of 3⟩

[2]**cube** *vb* **cubed; cub•ing 1** : to raise to the third power **2** : to form into a cube **3** : to cut into cubes

cube root *n* : a number whose cube is a given number

cu•bic \ˈkyü-bik\ *also* **cu•bi•cal** *adj* **1** : having the form of a cube **2** : being the volume of a cube whose edge is a specified unit **3** : having length, width, and height

cu•bi•cle \ˈkyü-bi-kəl\ *n* : a small separate space (as for sleeping or studying)

cubic measure *n* : a unit (as cubic inch) for measuring volume — see METRIC SYSTEM table, WEIGHT table

cub•ism \ˈkyü-ˌbi-zəm\ *n* : a style of art characterized by the abstraction of natural forms into fragmented geometric shapes — **cub•ist** \-bist\ *n or adj*

cu•bit \ˈkyü-bət\ *n* : an ancient unit of length equal to about 18 inches (46 centimeters)

Cub Scout *n* : a member of the program of the Boy Scouts for boys in the first through fifth grades in school

cuck•old \ˈkə-kəld, ˈku̇-\ *n* : a man whose wife is unfaithful — **cuckold** *vb*

[1]**cuck•oo** \ˈkü-kü, ˈku̇-\ *n, pl* **cuckoos** : a largely grayish brown European bird that lays its eggs in the nests of other birds for them to hatch

[2]**cuckoo** *adj* : SILLY, FOOLISH

cu•cum•ber \ˈkyü-(ˌ)kəm-bər\ *n* : the long fleshy many-seeded fruit of a vine of the gourd family that is grown as a garden vegetable; *also* : this vine

cud \ˈkəd\ *n* : food brought up into the mouth by some animals (as cows) from the rumen to be chewed again

cud•dle \ˈkəd-ᵊl\ *vb* **cud•dled; cud•dling** : to lie close : SNUGGLE

cud•gel \ˈkə-jəl\ *n* : a short heavy club — **cudgel** *vb*

[1]**cue** \ˈkyü\ *n* **1** : a word, phrase, or action in a play serving as a signal for the next actor to speak or act **2** : HINT — **cue** *vb*

[2]**cue** *n* : a tapered rod for striking the balls in billiards or pool

cue ball *n* : the ball a player strikes with a cue in billiards or pool

[1]**cuff** \ˈkəf\ *n* **1** : a part (as of a sleeve or glove) encircling the wrist **2** : the folded hem of a trouser leg

[2]**cuff** *vb* : to strike esp. with the open hand : SLAP

[3]**cuff** *n* : a blow with the hand esp. when open

cui•sine \kwi-ˈzēn\ *n* : style of cooking; *also* : the food prepared

cuke \ˈkyük\ *n* : CUCUMBER

cul–de–sac \ˌkəl-di-ˈsak, ˌku̇l-\ *n, pl* **culs–de–sac** *same or* ˌkəlz-, ˌku̇lz-\ *also* **cul–de–sacs** \ˌkəl-də-ˈsaks, ˌku̇l-\ [F, lit., bottom of the bag] : a street or passage closed at one end

cu•li•nary \ˈkə-lə-ˌner-ē, ˈkyü-\ *adj* : of or relating to the kitchen or cookery

[1]**cull** \ˈkəl\ *vb* : to pick out from a group

[2]**cull** *n* : something rejected from a group or lot as worthless or inferior

cul•mi•nate \ˈkəl-mə-ˌnāt\ *vb* **-nat•ed; -nat•ing** : to reach the highest point — **cul•mi•na•tion** \ˌkəl-mə-ˈnā-shən\ *n*

cu•lotte \ˈkü-ˌlät, ˌkyü-, ku̇-ˈlät, kyü-\ *n* [F, breeches, fr. dim. of *cul* backside] : a divided skirt; *also* : a garment having a divided skirt — often used in pl.

cul•pa•ble \ˈkəl-pə-bəl\ *adj* : deserving blame — **cul•pa•bil•i•ty** \ˌkəl-pə-ˈbi-lə-tē\ *n*

cul•prit \ˈkəl-prət\ *n* [Anglo-French (the French of medieval England) *cul.* (abbr. of *culpable* guilty) + *prest, prit* ready (i.e., to prove it), fr. L *praestus*] : one accused or guilty of a crime

cult \ˈkəlt\ *n* **1** : formal religious veneration **2** : a religious system; *also* : its adherents **3** : faddish devotion; *also* : a group of persons showing such devotion — **cult•ist** *n*

cul•ti•va•ble \ˈkəl-tə-və-bəl\ *adj* : capable of being cultivated

cul•ti•vate \ˈkəl-tə-ˌvāt\ *vb* **-vat•ed; -vat•ing 1** : to prepare for the raising of crops **2** : to foster the growth of by tilling or by labor and care ⟨~ vegetables⟩ **3** : REFINE, IMPROVE **4** : ENCOURAGE, FURTHER — **cul•ti•va•tion** \ˌkəl-tə-ˈvā-shən\ *n* — **cul•ti•va•tor** \ˈkəl-tə-ˌvā-tər\ *n*

cul•ture \ˈkəl-chər\ *n* **1** : TILLAGE, CULTIVATION **2** : the act of developing by education and training **3** : refinement of intellectual and artistic taste **4** : the customary beliefs, social forms, and material traits of a racial, religious, or social group — **cul•tur•al** \ˈkəl-chə-rəl\ *adj* — **cul•tur•al•ly** *adv* — **cul•tured** \-chərd\ *adj*

cul•vert \ˈkəl-vərt\ *n* : a drain crossing under a road or railroad

cum *abbr* cumulative

cum•ber \ˈkəm-bər\ *vb* : to weigh down : BURDEN, HINDER

cum•ber•some \ˈkəm-bər-səm\ *adj* : hard to handle or manage because of size or weight

cum•brous \ˈkəm-brəs\ *adj* : CUMBERSOME — **cum•brous•ly** *adv* — **cum•brous•ness** *n*

cum•in \ˈkə-mən, ˈkyü-\ *n* : a plant of the carrot family cultivated for its aromatic seeds; *also* : the fruit or seed of cumin used as a spice

cum•mer•bund \ˈkə-mər-ˌbənd, ˈkəm-bər-\ *n* [Hindi *kamarband,* fr. Per, fr. *kamar* waist + *band* band] : a broad sash worn as a waistband

cu•mu•la•tive \ˈkyü-myə-lə-tiv, -ˌlā-\ *adj* : increasing in force or value by successive additions

cu•mu•lo•nim•bus \ˌkyü-myə-lō-ˈnim-bəs\ *n* : an anvil-shaped cumulus cloud extending to great heights

cu•mu•lus \ˈkyü-myə-ləs\ *n, pl* **-li** \-ˌlī, -ˌlē\ : a massive cloud having a flat base and rounded outlines

cu•ne•i•form \kyu̇-ˈnē-ə-ˌfȯrm\ *adj* **1** : wedge-shaped **2** : composed of wedge-shaped characters

cun•ni•lin•gus \ˌkə-ni-ˈliŋ-gəs\ *also* **cun•ni•linc•tus** \-ˈliŋk-təs\ *n* : oral stimulation of the vulva or clitoris

[1]**cun•ning** \ˈkə-niŋ\ *adj* **1** : SKILLFUL, DEXTEROUS **2** : marked by wiliness and trickery **3** : CUTE — **cun•ning•ly** *adv*

[2]**cunning** *n* **1** : SKILL **2** : SLYNESS

[1]**cup** \ˈkəp\ *n* **1** : a small bowl-shaped drinking vessel **2** : the contents of a cup **3** : the consecrated wine of the Communion **4** : something resembling a cup : a small bowl or hollow **5** : a half pint — **cup•ful** *n*

[2]**cup** *vb* **cupped; cup•ping** : to curve into the shape of a cup

cup•board \ˈkə-bərd\ *n* : a small closet with shelves for food or dishes

cup•cake \ˈkəp-ˌkāk\ *n* : a small cake baked in a cup-like mold
cu•pid \ˈkyü-pəd\ *n* : a winged naked figure of an infant often with a bow and arrow that represents the god Cupid
cu•pid•i•ty \kyu̇-ˈpi-də-tē\ *n, pl* **-ties** : excessive desire for money
cu•po•la \ˈkyü-pə-lə, -ˌlō\ *n* : a small structure on top of a roof or building
[1]**cur** \ˈkər\ *n* : a mongrel dog
[2]**cur** *abbr* **1** currency **2** current
cu•rate \ˈkyu̇r-ət\ *n* **1** : a clergyman in charge of a parish **2** : a member of the clergy who assists a rector or vicar — **cu•ra•cy** \-ə-sē\ *n*
cu•ra•tive \-ə-tiv\ *adj* : relating to or used in the cure of diseases — **curative** *n*
cu•ra•tor \ˈkyu̇r-ˌā-tər, kyu̇-ˈrā-\ *n* : CUSTODIAN; *esp* : one in charge of a place of exhibit (as a museum or zoo)
[1]**curb** \ˈkərb\ *n* **1** : a bit that exerts pressure on a horse's jaws **2** : CHECK, RESTRAINT **3** : a raised edging (as of stone or concrete) along a paved street
[2]**curb** *vb* : to hold in or back : RESTRAIN
curb•ing \ˈkər-biŋ\ *n* **1** : the material for a curb **2** : CURB
curd \ˈkərd\ *n* : the thick protein-rich part of coagulated milk
cur•dle \ˈkərd-ᵊl\ *vb* **cur•dled; cur•dling** : to form curds; *also* : SPOIL, SOUR
[1]**cure** \ˈkyu̇r\ *n* **1** : spiritual care **2** : recovery or relief from disease **3** : a curative agent : REMEDY **4** : a course or period of treatment
[2]**cure** *vb* **cured; cur•ing** **1** : to restore to health : HEAL, REMEDY; *also* : to become cured **2** : to process for storage or use ⟨~ bacon⟩ — **cur•able** *adj*
cu•ré \kyu̇-ˈrā\ *n* [F] : a parish priest
cure–all \ˈkyu̇r-ˌo̊l\ *n* : a remedy for all ills : PANACEA
cu•ret•tage \ˌkyu̇r-ə-ˈtäzh\ *n* : a surgical scraping or cleaning of a body part (as the uterus)
cur•few \ˈkər-ˌfyü\ *n* [ME, fr. MF *covrefeu,* signal given to bank the hearth fire, curfew, fr. *covrir* to cover + *feu* fire, fr. L *focus* hearth] : a regulation that specified persons (as children) be off the streets at a set hour of the evening; *also* : the sounding of a signal (as a bell) at this hour
cu•ria \ˈkyu̇r-ē-ə, ˈku̇r-\ *n, pl* **cu•ri•ae** \ˈkyu̇r-ē-ˌē, ˈku̇r-ē-ˌī\ *often cap* : the body of congregations, tribunals, and offices through which the pope governs the Roman Catholic Church
cu•rie \ˈkyu̇r-ē\ *n* : a unit of radioactivity equal to 37 billion disintegrations per second
cu•rio \ˈkyu̇r-ē-ˌō\ *n, pl* **cu•ri•os** : an object or article valued because it is strange or rare
cu•ri•ous \ˈkyu̇r-ē-əs\ *adj* **1** : having a desire to investigate and learn **2** : STRANGE, UNUSUAL, ODD — **cu•ri•os•i•ty** \ˌkyu̇r-ē-ˈa-sə-tē\ *n* — **cu•ri•ous•ness**
cu•ri•ous•ly *adv* **1** : in a curious manner **2** : as is curious
cu•ri•um \ˈkyu̇r-ē-əm\ *n* : a metallic radioactive element produced artificially — see ELEMENT table
[1]**curl** \ˈkərl\ *vb* **1** : to form into ringlets **2** : CURVE, COIL — **curl•er** *n*
[2]**curl** *n* **1** : a lock of hair that coils : RINGLET **2** : something having a spiral or twisted form — **curly** *adj*
cur•lew \ˈkər-lü, ˈkərl-yü\ *n, pl* **curlews** *or* **curlew** : any of various long-legged brownish birds that have a down-curved bill and are related to the sandpipers and snipes
curli•cue \ˈkər-li-ˌkyü\ *n* : a fancifully curved or spiral figure
cur•rant \ˈkər-ənt\ *n* **1** : a small seedless raisin **2** : the acid berry of a shrub related to the gooseberry; *also* : this plant
cur•ren•cy \ˈkər-ən-sē\ *n, pl* **-cies** **1** : general use or acceptance **2** : something that is in circulation as a medium of exchange : MONEY
[1]**cur•rent** \ˈkər-ənt\ *adj* **1** : occurring in or belonging to the present **2** : used as a medium of exchange **3** : generally accepted or practiced
[2]**current** *n* **1** : the part of a body of fluid moving continuously in a certain direction; *also* : the swiftest part of a stream **2** : a flow of electric charge; *also* : the rate of such flow
cur•ric•u•lum \kə-ˈri-kyə-ləm\ *n, pl* **-la** \-lə\ *also* **-lums** [L, running, course, fr. *currere* to run] : the courses offered by an educational institution
[1]**cur•ry** \ˈkər-ē\ *vb* **cur•ried; cur•ry•ing** **1** : to clean the coat of (a horse) with a currycomb **2** : to treat (tanned leather) esp. by incorporating oil or grease — **curry favor** : to seek to gain favor by flattery or attention
[2]**cur•ry** *n, pl* **cur•ries** : a powder of pungent spices used in cooking; *also* : a food seasoned with curry
cur•ry•comb \-ˌkōm\ *n* : a comb used esp. to curry horses — **currycomb** *vb*
[1]**curse** \ˈkərs\ *n* **1** : a prayer for harm to come upon one **2** : something that is cursed **3** : evil or misfortune coming as if in response to a curse
[2]**curse** *vb* **cursed; curs•ing** **1** : to call on divine power to send injury upon **2** : BLASPHEME **3** : AFFLICT **syn** execrate, damn, anathematize, objurgate
cur•sive \ˈkər-siv\ *adj* : written with the strokes of the letters joined together and the angles rounded
cur•sor \ˈkər-sər\ *n* : a visual cue (as a pointer) on a computer screen that indicates position (as for data entry)
cur•so•ry \ˈkər-sə-rē\ *adj* : rapidly and often superficially done : HASTY — **cur•so•ri•ly** \-rə-lē\ *adj*
curt \ˈkərt\ *adj* : rudely short or abrupt — **curt•ly** *adv* — **curt•ness** *n*
cur•tail \(ˌ)kər-ˈtāl\ *vb* : to cut off the end of : SHORTEN — **cur•tail•ment** *n*
cur•tain \ˈkərt-ᵊn\ *n* **1** : a hanging screen that can be drawn back esp. at a window **2** : the screen between the stage and auditorium of a theater — **curtain** *vb*
curt•sy *or* **curt•sey** \ˈkərt-sē\ *n, pl* **curtsies** *or* **curtseys** : a courteous bow made by women chiefly by bending the knees — **curtsy** *or* **curtsey** *vb*
cur•va•ceous *also* **cur•va•cious** \ˌkər-ˈvā-shəs\ *adj* : having curves suggestive of a well-proportioned feminine figure
cur•va•ture \ˈkər-və-ˌchu̇r\ *n* : a measure or amount of curving : BEND
[1]**curve** \ˈkərv\ *vb* **curved; curv•ing** : to bend from a straight line or course
[2]**curve** *n* **1** : a line esp. when curved **2** : something that bends or curves without angles ⟨a ~ in the road⟩ **3** : a baseball pitch thrown so that it swerves esp. downward and to one side
cur•vet \(ˌ)kər-ˈvet\ *n* : a prancing leap of a horse — **curvet** *vb*
[1]**cush•ion** \ˈku̇-shən\ *n* **1** : a soft pillow or pad to rest on or against **2** : the springy pad inside the rim of a billiard table **3** : something soft that prevents discomfort or protects against injury
[2]**cushion** *vb* **1** : to provide (as a seat) with a cushion **2** : to soften or lessen the force or shock of
cusp \ˈkəsp\ *n* : a pointed end or part (as of a tooth)
cus•pid \ˈkəs-pəd\ *n* : a canine tooth
cus•pi•dor \ˈkəs-pə-ˌdo̊r\ *n* : SPITTOON
cus•tard \ˈkəs-tərd\ *n* : a sweetened cooked mixture of milk and eggs
cus•to•di•al \ˌkəs-ˈtō-dē-əl\ *adj* : marked by watching and protecting rather than seeking to cure ⟨~ care⟩
cus•to•di•an \ˌkəs-ˈtō-dē-ən\ *n* : one who has custody (as of a building)
cus•to•dy \ˈkəs-tə-dē\ *n, pl* **-dies** : immediate charge and control
[1]**cus•tom** \ˈkəs-təm\ *n* **1** : habitual course of action : recognized usage **2** *pl* : taxes levied on imports **3** : business patronage
[2]**custom** *adj* **1** : made to personal order **2** : doing work only on order
cus•tom•ary \ˈkəs-tə-ˌmer-ē\ *adj* **1** : based on or estab-

lished by custom **2** : commonly practiced or observed : HABITUAL — **cus•tom•ar•i•ly** *adv*

cus•tom–built \ˈkəs-təm-ˈbilt\ *adj* : built to individual order

cus•tom•er \ˈkəs-tə-mər\ *n* : BUYER, PURCHASER; *esp* : a regular or frequent buyer

cus•tom•house \ˈkəs-təm-ˌhau̇s\ *n* : the building where customs are paid

cus•tom•ise *Brit var of* CUSTOMIZE

cus•tom•ize \ˈkəs-tə-ˌmīz\ *vb* **-ized; -iz•ing** : to build, fit, or alter according to individual specifications

cus•tom–made \ˈkəs-təm-ˈmād\ *adj* : made to individual order

[1]**cut** \ˈkət\ *vb* **cut; cut•ting 1** : to penetrate or divide with a sharp edge : CLEAVE, GASH; *also* : to experience the growth of (a tooth) through the gum **2** : to hurt the feelings of **3** : to strike sharply **4** : SHORTEN, REDUCE **5** : to remove by severing or paring **6** : INTERSECT, CROSS **7** : to divide into parts **8** : to go quickly or change direction abruptly **9** : to cause to stop

[2]**cut** *n* **1** : something made by cutting : GASH, CLEFT **2** : SHARE **3** : a segment or section of a meat carcass **4** : an excavated channel or roadway **5** : BAND 4 **6** : a sharp stroke or blow **7** : REDUCTION ⟨∼ in wages⟩ **8** : the shape or manner in which a thing is cut

cut–and–dried \ˌkət-ᵊn-ˈdrīd\ *also* **cut–and–dry** \-ˈdrī\ *adj* : according to a plan, set procedure, or formula

cu•ta•ne•ous \kyu̇-ˈtā-nē-əs\ *adj* : of, relating to, or affecting the skin

cut•back \ˈkət-ˌbak\ *n* **1** : something cut back **2** : REDUCTION

cute \ˈkyüt\ *adj* **cut•er; cut•est** [short for *acute*] **1** : CLEVER, SHREWD **2** : daintily attractive : PRETTY

cu•ti•cle \ˈkyü-ti-kəl\ *n* **1** : an outer layer (as of skin or a leaf) **2** : dead or horny epidermis esp. around a fingernail — **cu•tic•u•lar** \kyu̇-ˈti-kyə-lər\ *adj*

cut in *vb* **1** : to thrust oneself between others **2** : to interrupt a dancing couple and take one as one's partner

cut•lass \ˈkət-ləs\ *n* : a short heavy curved sword

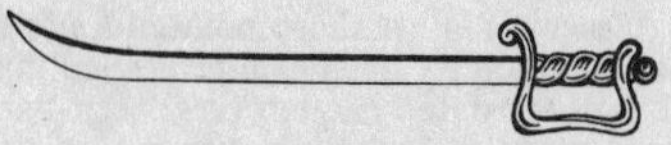

cutlass

cut•ler \ˈkət-lər\ *n* : one who makes, deals in, or repairs cutlery

cut•lery \ˈkət-lə-rē\ *n* : edged or cutting tools; *esp* : implements for cutting and eating food

cut•let \ˈkət-lət\ *n* : a slice of meat (as veal) for broiling or frying

cut•off \ˈkət-ˌȯf\ *n* **1** : the channel formed when a stream cuts through the neck of an oxbow; *also* : SHORTCUT **2** : a device for cutting off **3** *pl* : shorts orig. made from jeans with the legs cut off at the knees or higher

cut•out \ˈkət-ˌau̇t\ *n* : something cut out or prepared for cutting out from something else ⟨a page of animal ∼s⟩

cut out *vb* **1** : to be all that one can handle ⟨had her work *cut out* for her⟩ **2** : DISCONNECT **3** : to cease operating ⟨the engine *cut out*⟩ **4** : ELIMINATE ⟨*cut out* unnecessary expense⟩

cut–rate \ˈkət-ˈrāt\ *adj* : relating to or dealing in goods sold at reduced rates

cut•ter \ˈkə-tər\ *n* **1** : a tool or a machine for cutting **2** : a ship's boat for carrying stores and passengers **3** : a small armed vessel in government service **4** : a light sleigh

[1]**cut•throat** \ˈkət-ˌthrōt\ *n* : MURDERER

[2]**cutthroat** *adj* **1** : MURDEROUS, CRUEL **2** : RUTHLESS ⟨∼ competition⟩

cutthroat trout *n* : a large American trout with a red mark under the jaw

[1]**cut•ting** \ˈkə-tiŋ\ *n* : a piece of a plant able to grow into a new plant

[2]**cutting** *adj* **1** : SHARP, EDGED **2** : marked by piercing cold **3** : likely to hurt the feelings : SARCASTIC ⟨a ∼ remark⟩

cut•tle•fish \ˈkət-ᵊl-ˌfish\ *n* : a 10-armed mollusk related to the squid with an internal shell (**cut•tle•bone** \-ˌbōn\) composed of calcium compounds

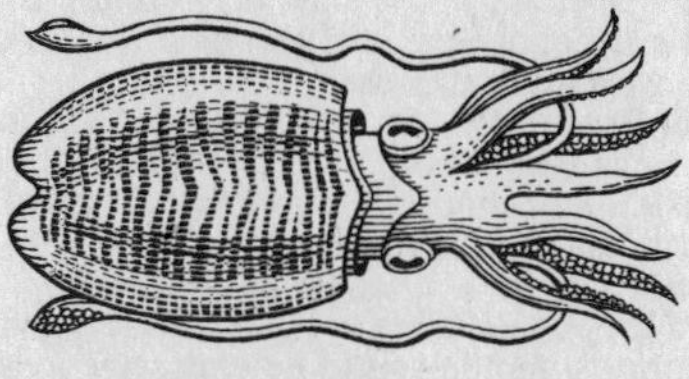

cuttlefish

cut•up \ˈkət-ˌəp\ *n* : a person who clowns or acts boisterously — **cut up** *vb*

cut•worm \-ˌwərm\ *n* : any of various smooth-bodied moth larvae that feed on plants at night

cw *abbr* clockwise

CWO *abbr* **1** cash with order **2** chief warrant officer

cwt *abbr* hundredweight

-cy \sē\ *n suffix* **1** : action : practice ⟨mendican*cy*⟩ **2** : rank : office ⟨chaplain*cy*⟩ **3** : body : class ⟨constituen*cy*⟩ **4** : state : quality ⟨accura*cy*⟩

cy•an \ˈsī-ˌan, -ən\ *n* : a greenish blue color

cy•a•nide \ˈsī-ə-ˌnīd, -nəd\ *n* : a poisonous compound of carbon and nitrogen with another element (as potassium)

cyber– *comb form* : computer : computer network

cy•ber•net•ics \ˌsī-bər-ˈne-tiks\ *n* : the science of communication and control theory that is concerned esp. with the comparative study of automatic control systems — **cy•ber•net•ic** *adj*

cy•ber•space \ˈsī-bər-ˌspās\ *n* : the on-line world of computer networks

cy•cla•men \ˈsī-klə-mən\ *n* : any of a genus of plants related to the primroses and grown for their showy nodding flowers

[1]**cy•cle** \ˈsī-kəl\ *n* **1** : a period of time occupied by a series of events that repeat themselves regularly and in the same order **2** : a recurring round of operations or events **3** : one complete occurrence of a periodic process (as a vibration or current alternation) **4** : a circular or spiral arrangement **5** : a long period of time : AGE **6** : BICYCLE **7** : MOTORCYCLE — **cy•clic** \ˈsī-klik, ˈsi-\ *or* **cy•cli•cal** \kli-kəl\ *adj* — **cy•cli•cal•ly** \-k(ə-)lē\ *also* **cy•clic•ly** *adv*

[2]**cy•cle** \ˈsī-kəl\ *vb* **cy•cled; cy•cling** : to ride a cycle — **cy•clist** \ˈsī-klist, -kə-list\ *n*

cy•clone \ˈsī-ˌklōn\ *n* **1** : a storm or system of winds that rotates about a center of low atmospheric pressure and advances at 20 to 30 miles (about 30 to 50 kilometers) an hour **2** : TORNADO — **cy•clon•ic** \sī-ˈklä-nik\ *adj*

cy•clo•pe•dia *or* **cy•clo•pae•dia** \ˌsī-klə-ˈpē-dē-ə\ *n* : ENCYCLOPEDIA

cy•clo•tron \ˈsī-klə-ˌträn\ *n* : a device for giving high speed to charged particles by magnetic and electric fields

cy•der *Brit var of* CIDER

cyg•net \ˈsig-nət\ *n* : a young swan

cyl *abbr* cylinder

cyl•in•der \ˈsi-lən-dər\ *n* : the solid figure formed by turning a rectangle about one side as an axis; *also* : a body or space of this form ⟨an engine ∼⟩ ⟨a bullet in the ∼ of a revolver⟩ — **cy•lin•dri•cal** \sə-ˈlin-dri-kəl\ *adj*

cym•bal \ˈsim-bəl\ *n* : a concave brass plate that produces a brilliant clashing sound

cyn•ic \ˈsi-nik\ *n* : one who attributes all actions to selfish motives — **cyn•i•cal** \-ni-kəl\ *adj* — **cyn•i•cal•ly** \-k(ə-)lē\ *adv* — **cyn•i•cism** \si-nə-ˌsi-zəm\ *n*

cy•no•sure \ˈsī-nə-ˌshu̇r, ˈsi-\ *n* [MF & L; MF, Ursa Minor, guide, fr. L *cynosura* Ursa Minor, fr. Gk *kynosoura*, fr. *kynos oura* dog's tail] : a center of attraction

CYO *abbr* Catholic Youth Organization

cy•pher *chiefly Brit var of* CIPHER

cy•press \ˈsī-prəs\ *n* **1** : any of a genus of scaly-leaved evergreen trees and shrubs **2** : BALD CYPRESS **3** : the wood of a cypress

Cyp•ri•ot \ˈsi-prē-ət, -ˌät\ *or* **Cyp•ri•ote** \-ˌōt, -ət\ *n* : a native or inhabitant of Cyprus — **Cypriot** *adj*

cyst \ˈsist\ *n* : an abnormal closed bodily sac usu. containing liquid — **cys•tic** \ˈsis-tik\ *adj*

cystic fibrosis *n* : a common hereditary disease marked esp. by deficiency of pancreatic enzymes, by respiratory symptoms, and by excessive loss of salt in the sweat

cy•tol•o•gy \sī-ˈtä-lə-jē\ *n* : a branch of biology dealing with cells — **cy•to•log•i•cal** \ˌsīt-ᵊl-ˈä-ji-kəl\ *or* **cy•to•log•ic** \-jik\ *adj* — **cy•tol•o•gist** \sī-ˈtä-lə-jist\ *n*

cy•to•plasm \ˈsī-tə-ˌpla-zəm\ *n* : the protoplasm of a cell that lies external to the nucleus — **cy•to•plas•mic** \ˌsī-tə-ˈplaz-mik\ *adj*

cy•to•sine \ˈsī-tə-ˌsēn\ *n* : a chemical base that is a pyrimidine coding genetic information in DNA and RNA

CZ *abbr* Canal Zone

czar \ˈzär, ˈtsär\ *n* [NL, fr. Russ *tsar'*, ultim. fr. L *Caesar* Caesar] : the ruler of Russia until 1917; *also* : one having great authority — **czar•ist** \-ist\ *n or adj*

cza•ri•na \zä-ˈrē-nə\ *n* : the wife of a czar

Czech \ˈchek\ *n* **1** : a native or inhabitant of Czechoslovakia or the Czech Republic **2** : the language of the Czechs — **Czech** *adj*

Czecho•slo•vak \ˌche-kə-ˈslō-ˌväk, -ˌvak\ *or* **Czecho•slo•va•ki•an** \-slō-ˈvä-kē-ən, -ˈva-\ *adj* : of, relating to, or characteristic of Czechoslovakia or its people — **Czechoslovak** *or* **Czechoslovakian** *n*

D

[1]**d** \ˈdē\ *n, pl* **d's** *or* **ds** \ˈdēz\ *often cap* **1** : the 4th letter of the English alphabet **2** : a grade rating a student's work as poor

[2]**d** *abbr, often cap* **1** date **2** daughter **3** day **4** dead **5** deceased **6** degree **7** Democrat **8** [L *denarius, denarii*] penny; pence **9** depart; departure **10** diameter

D *symbol* deuterium

DA *abbr* **1** deposit account **2** district attorney **3** don't answer

[1]**dab** \ˈdab\ *n* **1** : a sudden blow or thrust : POKE; *also* : PECK **2** : a gentle touch or stroke : PAT

[2]**dab** *vb* **dabbed; dab•bing 1** : to strike or touch gently : PAT **2** : to apply lightly or irregularly : DAUB — **dab•ber** *n*

[3]**dab** *n* **1** : DAUB **2** : a small amount

dab•ble \ˈda-bəl\ *vb* **dab•bled; dab•bling 1** : to wet by splashing : SPATTER **2** : to paddle or play in or as if in water **3** : to work or involve oneself without serious effort — **dab•bler** *n*

da ca•po \dä-ˈkä-(ˌ)pō\ *adv or adj* [It] : from the beginning — used as a direction in music to repeat

dace \ˈdās\ *n, pl* **dace** : any of various small No. American freshwater fishes related to the carp

da•cha \ˈdä-chə\ *n* [Russ] : a Russian country house

dachs•hund \ˈdäks-ˌhu̇nt\ *n, pl* **dachshunds** [G, fr. *Dachs* badger + *Hund* dog] : a small dog of a breed of German origin with a long body, short legs, and long drooping ears

dachshund

dac•tyl \ˈdakt-ᵊl\ *n* [ME *dactile*, fr. L *dactylus*, fr. Gk *daktylos*, lit., finger; fr. the fact that the three syllables have the first one longest like the joints of the finger] : a metrical foot of one accented syllable followed by two unaccented syllables — **dac•tyl•ic** \dak-ˈti-lik\ *adj or n*

dad \ˈdad\ *n* : FATHER 1

Da•da \ˈdä-(ˌ)dä\ *n* : a movement in art and literature based on deliberate irrationality and negation of traditional artistic values — **da•da•ism** \-ˌi-zəm\ *n, often cap* — **da•da•ist** \-ˌist\ *n or adj, often cap*

dad•dy \ˈda-dē\ *n, pl* **daddies** : FATHER 1

dad•dy long•legs \ˌda-dē-ˈlȯŋ-ˌlegz\ *n, pl* **daddy longlegs** : any of various arachnids resembling the true spiders but having small rounded bodies and long slender legs

dae•mon *var of* DEMON

daf•fo•dil \ˈda-fə-ˌdil\ *n* : any of a genus of bulbous herbs with usu. large flowers having a trumpetlike center

daf•fy \ˈda-fē\ *adj* **daf•fi•er; -est** : DAFT

daft \ˈdaft\ *adj* : FOOLISH; *also* : INSANE — **daft•ness** *n*

dag *abbr* dekagram

dag•ger \ˈda-gər\ *n* **1** : a sharp pointed knife for stabbing **2** : a character † used as a reference mark or to indicate a death date

da•guerre•o•type \də-ˈger-(ē-)ə-ˌtīp\ *n* : an early photograph produced on a silver or a silver-covered copper plate

dahl•ia \ˈdal-yə, ˈdäl-\ *n* : any of a genus of tuberous herbs related to the daisies and having showy flowers

[1]**dai•ly** \ˈdā-lē\ *adj* **1** : occurring, done, or used every day or every weekday **2** : of or relating to every day ⟨~ visitors⟩ **3** : computed in terms of one day ⟨~ wages⟩ **syn** diurnal, quotidian — **dai•li•ness** \-lē-nəs\ *n* — **daily** *adv*

[2]**daily** *n, pl* **dailies** : a newspaper published every weekday

daily double *n* : a system of betting on races in which the bettor must pick the winners of two stipulated races in order to win

[1]**dain•ty** \ˈdān-tē\ *n, pl* **dainties** [ME *deinte*, fr. OF *deintié*, fr. L *dignitas* dignity, worth] : something delicious or pleasing to the taste : DELICACY

[2]**dainty** *adj* **dain•ti•er; -est 1** : pleasing to the taste **2** : delicately pretty **3** : having or showing delicate taste; *also* : FASTIDIOUS **syn** choice, delicate, exquisite, rare, recherché — **dain•ti•ly** \-ti-lē\ *adv* — **dain•ti•ness** \-tē-nəs\ *n*

dai•qui•ri \ˈdī-kə-rē, ˈda-kə-rē\ *n* [*Daiquirí*, Cuba] : a cocktail made of rum, lime juice, and sugar

dairy \ˈder-ē\ *n, pl* **dair•ies** [ME *deyerie*, fr. *deye* dairymaid, fr. OE *dǣge* kneader of bread] **1** : CREAMERY **2** : a farm specializing in milk production

dairy•ing \ˈder-ē-iŋ\ *n* : the business of operating a dairy

dairy•maid \-ˌmād\ *n* : a woman employed in a dairy

dairy•man \-mən, -ˌman\ *n* : a person who operates a dairy farm or works in a dairy

da•is \ˈdā-əs\ *n* : a raised platform usu. above the floor of a hall or large room

dai•sy \ˈdā-zē\ *n, pl* **daisies** [ME *dayeseye,* fr. OE *dægesēage,* fr. *dæg* day + *ēage* eye] : any of numerous composite plants having flower heads in which the marginal flowers resemble petals

daisy wheel *n* : a disk with spokes bearing type that serves as the printing element of an electric typewriter or printer; *also* : a printer that uses such a disk

Da•ko•ta \də-ˈkō-tə\ *n, pl* **Dakotas** *also* **Dakota** : a member of an American Indian people of the northern Mississippi valley; *also* : their language

dal *abbr* dekaliter

da•la•si \dä-ˈlä-sē\ *n, pl* **dalasi** *or* **dalasis** — see MONEY table

dale \ˈdāl\ *n* : VALLEY

dal•ly \ˈda-lē\ *vb* **dal•lied; dal•ly•ing 1** : to act playfully; *esp* : to play amorously **2** : to waste time **3** : LINGER, DAWDLE **syn** flirt, coquet, toy, trifle — **dal•li•ance** \-lē-əns\ *n*

dal•ma•tian \dal-ˈmā-shən\ *n, often cap* : any of a breed of medium-sized dogs having a white short-haired coat with black or brown spots

dalmatian

[1]**dam** \ˈdam\ *n* : a female parent — used esp. of a domestic animal

[2]**dam** *n* : a barrier (as across a stream) to stop the flow of water — **dam** *vb*

[3]**dam** *abbr* dekameter

[1]**dam•age** \ˈda-mij\ *n* **1** : loss or harm due to injury to persons, property, or reputation **2** *pl* : compensation in money imposed by law for loss or injury ⟨bring a suit for ~*s*⟩

[2]**damage** *vb* **dam•aged; dam•ag•ing** : to cause damage to

dam•a•scene \ˈda-mə-ˌsēn\ *vb* **-scened; -scen•ing** : to ornament (as iron or steel) with wavy patterns or with inlaid work of precious metals

dam•ask \ˈda-məsk\ *n* **1** : a firm lustrous reversible figured fabric used for household linen **2** : a tough steel having decorative wavy lines

dame \ˈdām\ *n* **1** : a woman of rank, station, or authority **2** : an elderly woman **3** : WOMAN

damn \ˈdam\ *vb* [ME *dampnen,* fr. OF *dampner,* fr. L *damnare,* fr. *damnum* damage, loss, fine] **1** : to condemn esp. to hell **2** : CURSE — **damned** *adj*

dam•na•ble \ˈdam-nə-bəl\ *adj* **1** : liable to or deserving punishment **2** : DETESTABLE ⟨~ weather⟩ — **dam•na•bly** \-blē\ *adv*

dam•na•tion \dam-ˈnā-shən\ *n* **1** : the act of damning **2** : the state of being damned

[1]**damp** \ˈdamp\ *n* **1** : a noxious gas **2** : MOISTURE

[2]**damp** *vb* : DAMPEN

[3]**damp** *adj* : MOIST — **damp•ness** *n*

damp•en \ˈdam-pən\ *vb* **1** : to check or diminish in activity or vigor **2** : to make or become damp

damp•er \ˈdam-pər\ *n* : one that damps; *esp* : a valve or movable plate (as in the flue of a stove, furnace, or fireplace) to regulate the draft

dam•sel \ˈdam-zəl\ *n* : MAIDEN, GIRL

dam•sel•fly \-ˌflī\ *n* : any of a group of insects that are closely related to the dragonflies but fold their wings above the body when at rest

dam•son \ˈdam-zən\ *n* : a plum with acid purple fruit; *also* : its fruit

Dan *abbr* Daniel

[1]**dance** \ˈdans\ *vb* **danced; danc•ing 1** : to glide, step, or move through a set series of movements usu. to music **2** : to move quickly up and down or about **3** : to perform or take part in as a dancer — **danc•er** *n*

[2]**dance** *n* **1** : an act or instance of dancing **2** : a social gathering for dancing **3** : a piece of music (as a waltz) by which dancing may be guided **4** : the art of dancing

D & C *n* [*d*ilation *and c*urettage] : a surgical procedure used to test for cancer of the uterus or to perform an abortion that involves stretching the opening of the uterus and scraping the inside walls

dan•de•li•on \ˈdan-də-ˌlī-ən, -dē-\ *n* [MF *dent de lion,* lit., lion's tooth] : any of a genus of common yellow-flowered composite herbs

dan•der \ˈdan-dər\ *n* : ANGER, TEMPER

dan•di•fy \ˈdan-di-ˌfī\ *vb* **-fied; -fy•ing** : to cause to resemble a dandy

dan•dle \ˈdand-ᵊl\ *vb* **dan•dled; dan•dling** : to move up and down in one's arms or on one's knee in affectionate play **syn** caress, fondle, love, pet

dan•druff \ˈdan-drəf\ *n* : a whitish scurf on the scalp that comes off in small scales — **dan•druffy** \-drə-fē\ *adj*

[1]**dan•dy** \ˈdan-dē\ *n, pl* **dandies 1** : a man unduly attentive to personal appearance **2** : something excellent in its class **syn** fop, coxcomb, popinjay

[2]**dandy** *adj* **dan•di•er; -est** : very good : FIRST-RATE

Dane \ˈdān\ *n* **1** : a native or inhabitant of Denmark **2** : GREAT DANE

dan•ger \ˈdān-jər\ *n* **1** : exposure or liability to injury, harm, or evil **2** : something that may cause injury or harm **syn** peril, hazard, risk, jeopardy

dan•ger•ous \ˈdān-jə-rəs\ *adj* **1** : HAZARDOUS, PERILOUS **2** : able or likely to inflict injury — **dan•ger•ous•ly** *adv*

dan•gle \ˈdaŋ-gəl\ *vb* **dan•gled; dan•gling 1** : to hang loosely esp. with a swinging motion : SWING **2** : to be a hanger-on or dependent **3** : to be left without proper grammatical connection in a sentence **4** : to keep hanging uncertainly **5** : to offer as an inducement

Dan•iel \ˈdan-yəl\ *n* — see BIBLE table

Dan•ish \ˈdā-nish\ *n* : the language of the Danes — **Danish** *adj*

Danish pastry *n* : a pastry made of a rich yeast-raised dough

dank \ˈdaŋk\ *adj* : disagreeably wet or moist : DAMP — **dank•ness** *n*

dan•seuse \däⁿ-ˈsərz, -ˈsəz; dän-ˈsüz\ *n* [F] : a female ballet dancer

dap•per \ˈda-pər\ *adj* **1** : SPRUCE, TRIM **2** : being alert and lively in movement and manners : JAUNTY

dap•ple \ˈda-pəl\ *vb* **dap•pled; dap•pling** : to mark with different-colored spots

DAR *abbr* Daughters of the American Revolution

[1]**dare** \ˈdar\ *vb* **dared; dar•ing 1** : to have sufficient courage : be bold enough to **2** : CHALLENGE **3** : to confront boldly

[2]**dare** *n* : an act or instance of daring : CHALLENGE

dare•dev•il \-ˌde-vəl\ *n* : a recklessly bold person

dar•ing \ˈdar-iŋ\ *n* : venturesome boldness — **daring** *adj* — **dar•ing•ly** *adv*

[1]**dark** \ˈdärk\ *adj* **1** : being without light or without much light **2** : not light in color ⟨a ~ suit⟩ **3** : GLOOMY **4** *often cap* : being a period of stagnation or decline ⟨the *Dark* Ages⟩ **5** : SECRETIVE **syn** dim, dusky, murky, tenebrous — **dark•ly** *adv* — **dark•ness** *n*

[2]**dark** *n* **1** : absence of light : DARKNESS; *esp* : NIGHT **2** : a dark or deep color — **in the dark 1** : in secrecy **2** : in ignorance

dark•en \ˈdär-kən\ *vb* **1** : to make or grow dark or darker **2** : DIM **3** : BESMIRCH, TARNISH **4** : to make or become gloomy or forbidding

dark horse *n* : a contestant or a political figure whose abilities and chances as a contender are not known

dark•ling \ˈdär-kliŋ\ *adj* **1** : DARK ⟨a ~ plain⟩ **2** : MYSTERIOUS

dark•room \ˈdärk-ˌrüm, -ˌrům\ *n* : a lightproof room in which photographic materials are processed

[1]**dar•ling** \ˈdär-liŋ\ *n* **1** : a dearly loved person **2** : FAVORITE

[2]**darling** *adj* **1** : dearly loved : FAVORITE **2** : very pleasing : CHARMING

darn \ˈdärn\ *vb* : to mend with interlacing stitches — **darn•er** *n*

darning needle *n* **1** : a needle for darning **2** : DRAGONFLY

[1]**dart** \ˈdärt\ *n* **1** : a small missile with a point on one end and feathers on the other; *also, pl* : a game in which darts are thrown at a target **2** : something causing a sudden pain **3** : a stitched tapering fold in a garment **4** : a quick movement

[2]**dart** *vb* **1** : to throw with a sudden movement **2** : to thrust or move suddenly or rapidly **3** : to shoot with a dart containing a usu. tranquilizing drug

dart•er \ˈdär-tər\ *n* : any of numerous small American freshwater fishes related to the perches

Dar•win•ism \ˈdär-wə-ˌni-zəm\ *n* : a theory explaining the origin and continued existence of new species of plants and animals by means of natural selection acting on chance variations — **Dar•win•ist** \-nist\ *n or adj*

[1]**dash** \ˈdash\ *vb* **1** : SMASH **2** : to knock, hurl, or thrust violently **3** : SPLASH, SPATTER **4** : RUIN **5** : DEPRESS, SADDEN **6** : to perform or finish hastily **7** : to move with sudden speed

[2]**dash** *n* **1** : a sudden burst or splash **2** : a stroke of a pen **3** : a punctuation mark — that is used esp. to indicate a break in the thought or structure of a sentence **4** : a small addition ⟨a ~ of salt⟩ **5** : flashy showiness **6** : animation in style and action **7** : a sudden rush or attempt ⟨made a ~ for the door⟩ **8** : a short foot race **9** : DASHBOARD

dash•board \-ˌbōrd\ *n* : a panel in an automobile or aircraft below the windshield usu. containing dials and controls

dash•er \ˈda-shər\ *n* : a device (as in a churn) for agitating something

da•shi•ki \də-ˈshē-kē\ *or* **dai•shi•ki** \dī-\ *n* [modif. of Yoruba (an African language) *dàńṣíkí*] : a usu. brightly colored loose-fitting pullover garment

dash•ing \ˈda-shiŋ\ *adj* **1** : marked by vigorous action **2** : marked by smartness esp. in dress and manners **syn** stylish, chic, fashionable, modish, smart, swank

das•tard \ˈdas-tərd\ *n* **1** : COWARD **2** : a person who acts treacherously — **das•tard•ly** *adj*

dat *abbr* dative

da•ta \ˈdā-tə, ˈda-, ˈdä-\ *n sing or pl* [L, pl. of *datum*] : factual information (as measurements or statistics) used as a basis for reasoning, discussion, or calculation

da•ta•base \-ˌbās\ *n* : a usu. large collection of data organized esp. for rapid search and retrieval (as by a computer)

data processing *n* : the action or process of supplying a computer with information and having the computer use it to produce a desired result

[1]**date** \ˈdāt\ *n* [ME, fr. OF, ultim. fr. L *dactylus*, fr. Gk *daktylos*, lit., finger] : the edible fruit of a tall Old World palm; *also* : this palm

[2]**date** *n* [ME, fr. MF, fr. LL *data*, fr. *data* (as in *data Romae* given at Rome), fem. of L *datus*, pp. of *dare* to give] **1** : the day, month, or year of an event **2** : a statement giving the time of execution or making (as of a coin or check) **3** : the period to which something belongs **4** : APPOINTMENT; *esp* : a social engagement between two persons that often has a romantic character **5** : a person with whom one has a usu. romantic date — **to date** : up to the present moment

[3]**date** *vb* **dat•ed; dat•ing 1** : to record the date of or on **2** : to determine, mark, or reveal the date, age, or period of **3** : to make or have a date with **4** : ORIGINATE ⟨~*s* from ancient times⟩ **5** : EXTEND ⟨*dating* back to childhood⟩ **6** : to show qualities typical of a past period

dat•ed \ˈdā-təd\ *adj* **1** : provided with a date **2** : OLD-FASHIONED **syn** antiquated, archaic, old hat, outdated, outmoded, passé

date•less \ˈdāt-ləs\ *adj* **1** : ENDLESS **2** : having no date **3** : too ancient to be dated **4** : TIMELESS

date•line \ˈdāt-ˌlīn\ *n* : a line in a publication giving the date and place of composition or issue — **dateline** *vb*

da•tive \ˈdā-tiv\ *adj* : of, relating to, or constituting a grammatical case marking typically the indirect object of a verb — **dative** *n*

da•tum \ˈdā-təm, ˈda-, ˈdä-\ *n, pl* **da•ta** \-tə\ *or* **datums** : a single piece of data : FACT

dau *abbr* daughter

[1]**daub** \ˈdȯb\ *vb* **1** : to cover with soft adhesive matter **2** : SMEAR, SMUDGE **3** : to paint crudely — **daub•er** *n*

[2]**daub** *n* **1** : something daubed on : SMEAR **2** : a crude picture

daugh•ter \ˈdȯ-tər\ *n* **1** : a female offspring esp. of human beings **2** : a human female having a specified ancestor or belonging to a group of common ancestry — **daughter** *adj*

daugh•ter–in–law \ˈdȯ-tə-rən-ˌlȯ\ *n, pl* **daugh•ters–in–law** \-tər-zən-\ : the wife of one's son

daunt \ˈdȯnt\ *vb* [ME, fr. OF *danter*, alter. of *donter*, fr. L *domitare* to tame] : to lessen the courage of : INTIMIDATE, OVERWHELM

daunt•less \-ləs\ *adj* : FEARLESS, UNDAUNTED **syn** brave, bold, courageous, lionhearted — **daunt•less•ly** *adv*

dau•phin \ˈdȯ-fən\ *n, often cap* : the eldest son of a king of France

DAV *abbr* Disabled American Veterans

dav•en•port \ˈda-vən-ˌpōrt\ *n* : a large upholstered sofa

da•vit \ˈdā-vət, ˈda-\ *n* : a small crane on a ship used in pairs esp. to raise or lower boats

daw•dle \ˈdȯd-ᵊl\ *vb* **daw•dled; daw•dling 1** : to spend time wastefully or idly **2** : LOITER — **daw•dler** *n*

[1]**dawn** \ˈdȯn\ *vb* **1** : to begin to grow light as the sun rises **2** : to begin to appear or develop **3** : to begin to be understood ⟨the solution ~*ed* on him⟩

[2]**dawn** *n* **1** : the first appearance of light in the morning **2** : a first appearance : BEGINNING ⟨the ~ of a new era⟩

day \ˈdā\ *n* **1** : the period of light between one night and the next; *also* : DAYLIGHT **2** : the period of rotation of a planet (as earth) or a moon on its axis **3** : a period of 24 hours beginning at midnight **4** : a specified day or date ⟨wedding ~⟩ **5** : a specified time or period : AGE ⟨in olden ~*s*⟩ **6** : the conflict or contention of the day **7** : the time set apart by usage or law for work ⟨the 8-hour ~⟩

day•bed \ˈdā-ˌbed\ *n* : a couch that can be converted into a bed

day•book \-ˌbu̇k\ *n* : DIARY, JOURNAL

day•break \-ˌbrāk\ *n* : DAWN

day care *n* : supervision of and care for children or disabled adults provided during the day; *also* : a program offering day care

day•dream \ˈdā-ˌdrēm\ *n* : a pleasant reverie — **daydream** *vb*

day•light \ˈdā-ˌlīt\ *n* **1** : the light of day **2** : DAYTIME **3** : DAWN **4** : understanding of something that has been obscure **5** *pl* : CONSCIOUSNESS; *also* : WITS **6** : an opening or opportunity esp. for action

daylight saving time *n* : time usu. one hour ahead of standard time

Day of Atonement : YOM KIPPUR

day school *n* : a private school without boarding facilities

day student *n* : a student who attends regular classes at a college or preparatory school but does not live there

day•time \ˈdā-ˌtīm\ *n* : the period of daylight

daze \ˈdāz\ *vb* **dazed; daz•ing 1** : to stupefy esp. by a blow **2** : DAZZLE — **daze** *n* — **da•zed•ly** \ˈdā-zəd-lē\ *adv*

daz•zle \ˈda-zəl\ *vb* **daz•zled; daz•zling 1** : to overpower with light **2** : to impress greatly or confound with brilliance — **dazzle** *n*

dB *abbr* decibel

d/b/a *abbr* doing business as

dbl *or* **dble** *abbr* double

DC *abbr* **1** [It *da capo*] from the beginning **2** direct current **3** District of Columbia **4** doctor of chiropractic

DD *abbr* **1** days after date **2** demand draft **3** dishonorable discharge **4** doctor of divinity

D day *n* [*D*, abbr. for *day*] : a day set for launching an operation (as an invasion)

DDS *abbr* doctor of dental surgery

DDT \ˌdē-(ˌ)dē-ˈtē\ *n* : a persistent insecticide poisonous to many higher animals

DE *abbr* Delaware

dea•con \ˈdē-kən\ *n* [ME *dekene*, fr. OE *dēacon*, fr. LL *diaconus*, fr. Gk *diakonos*, lit., servant] : a subordinate officer in a Christian church

dea•con•ess \ˈdē-kə-nəs\ *n* : a woman chosen to assist in the church ministry

de•ac•ti•vate \dē-ˈak-tə-ˌvāt\ *vb* : to make inactive or ineffective

[1]**dead** \ˈded\ *adj* **1** : LIFELESS **2** : DEATHLIKE, DEADLY ⟨in a ~ faint⟩ **3** : NUMB **4** : very tired **5** : UNRESPONSIVE **6** : EXTINGUISHED ⟨~ coals⟩ **7** : INANIMATE, INERT **8** : no longer active or functioning ⟨a ~ battery⟩ **9** : lacking power, significance, or effect ⟨a ~ custom⟩ **10** : OBSOLETE ⟨a ~ language⟩ **11** : lacking in gaiety or animation ⟨a ~ party⟩ **12** : QUIET, IDLE, UNPRODUCTIVE ⟨~ capital⟩ **13** : lacking elasticity ⟨a ~ tennis ball⟩ **14** : not circulating : STAGNANT ⟨~ air⟩ **15** : lacking warmth, vigor, or taste ⟨~ wine⟩ **16** : absolutely uniform ⟨~ level⟩ **17** : UNERRING, EXACT ⟨a ~ shot⟩ **18** : ABRUPT ⟨a ~ stop⟩ **19** : COMPLETE ⟨a ~ loss⟩

[2]**dead** *n, pl* **dead 1** : one that is dead — usu. used collectively ⟨the living and the ~⟩ **2** : the time of greatest quiet ⟨the ~ of the night⟩

[3]**dead** *adv* **1** : UTTERLY ⟨~ right⟩ **2** : in a sudden and complete manner ⟨stopped ~⟩ **3** : DIRECTLY ⟨~ ahead⟩

dead•beat \-ˌbēt\ *n* : a person who persistently fails to pay personal debts or expenses

dead duck *n* : GONER

dead•en \ˈded-ᵊn\ *vb* **1** : to impair in vigor or sensation : BLUNT ⟨~ pain⟩ **2** : to lessen the luster or spirit of **3** : to make (as a wall) soundproof

dead end *n* **1** : an end (as of a street) without an exit **2** : a position, situation, or course of action that leads to nothing further — **dead–end** \ˌded-ˌend\ *adj*

dead heat *n* : a contest in which two or more contestants tie (as by crossing the finish line simultaneously)

dead letter *n* **1** : something that has lost its force or authority without being formally abolished **2** : a letter that cannot be delivered or returned

dead•line \ˈded-ˌlīn\ *n* : a date or time before which something must be done

dead•lock \ˈded-ˌläk\ *n* : a stoppage of action because neither faction in a struggle will give in — **deadlock** *vb*

[1]**dead•ly** \ˈded-lē\ *adj* **dead•li•er; -est 1** : likely to cause or capable of causing death **2** : HOSTILE, IMPLACABLE **3** : very accurate : UNERRING **4** : tending to deprive of force or vitality ⟨a ~ habit⟩ **5** : suggestive of death **6** : very great : EXTREME — **dead•li•ness** *n*

[2]**deadly** *adv* **1** : suggesting death ⟨~ pale⟩ **2** : EXTREMELY ⟨~ dull⟩

deadly sin *n* : one of seven sins of pride, covetousness, lust, anger, gluttony, envy, and sloth held to be fatal to spiritual progress

[1]**dead•pan** \ˈded-ˌpan\ *adj* : marked by an impassive manner or expression — **deadpan** *vb* — **deadpan** *adv*

[2]**deadpan** *n* : a completely expressionless face

dead reckoning *n* : the determination of the position of a ship or aircraft solely from the record of the direction and distance of its course

dead•weight \ˈded-ˈwāt\ *n* **1** : the unrelieved weight of an inert mass **2** : a ship's load including the weight of cargo, fuel, crew, and passengers

dead•wood \-ˌwu̇d\ *n* **1** : wood dead on the tree **2** : useless personnel or material

deaf \ˈdef\ *adj* **1** : unable to hear **2** : unwilling to hear or listen ⟨~ to all suggestions⟩ — **deaf•ness** *n*

deaf•en \ˈde-fən\ *vb* : to make deaf

deaf–mute \ˈdef-ˌmyüt\ *n* : a deaf person who has never learned to speak

[1]**deal** \ˈdēl\ *n* **1** : a usu. large or indefinite quantity or degree ⟨a great ~ of support⟩ **2** : the act or right of distributing cards to players in a card game; *also* : HAND

[2]**deal** *vb* **dealt** \ˈdelt\; **deal•ing 1** : DISTRIBUTE; *esp* : to distribute playing cards to players in a game **2** : ADMINISTER, DELIVER ⟨*dealt* him a blow⟩ **3** : to concern itself : TREAT ⟨the book ~*s* with crime⟩ **4** : to take action in regard to something ⟨~ with offenders⟩ **5** : TRADE; *also* : to sell or distribute something as a business ⟨~ in used cars⟩ **6** : to reach a state of acceptance ⟨~ with her child's death⟩ — **deal•er** *n*

[3]**deal** *n* **1** : BARGAINING, NEGOTIATION; *also* : TRANSACTION **2** : treatment received ⟨a raw ~⟩ **3** : an often secret agreement or arrangement for mutual advantage **4** : BARGAIN

[4]**deal** *n* : wood or a board of fir or pine

deal•er•ship \ˈdē-lər-ˌship\ *n* : an authorized sales agency

deal•ing \ˈdē-liŋ\ *n* **1** : a way of acting or of doing business **2** *pl* : friendly or business transactions

dean \ˈdēn\ *n* [ME *deen*, fr. MF *deien*, fr. LL *decanus*, lit., chief of ten, fr. Gk *dekanos*, fr. *deka* ten] **1** : a clergyman who is head of a group of canons or of joint pastors of a church **2** : the head of a division, faculty, college, or school of a university **3** : a college or secondary school administrator in charge of counseling and disciplining students **4** : DOYEN ⟨the ~ of a diplomatic corps⟩ — **dean•ship** *n*

dean•ery \ˈdē-nə-rē\ *n, pl* **-er•ies** : the office, jurisdiction, or official residence of a clerical dean

[1]**dear** \ˈdir\ *adj* **1** : highly valued : PRECIOUS **2** : AFFECTIONATE, FOND **3** : EXPENSIVE **4** : HEARTFELT — **dear•ly** *adv* — **dear•ness** *n*

[2]**dear** *n* : a loved one : DARLING

Dear John \-ˈjän\ *n* : a letter (as to a soldier) in which a woman breaks off a marital or romantic relationship

dearth \ˈdərth\ *n* : SCARCITY, FAMINE

death \ˈdeth\ *n* **1** : the end of life **2** : the cause of loss of life **3** : the state of being dead **4** : DESTRUCTION, EXTINCTION **5** : SLAUGHTER — **death•like** *adj*

death•bed \-ˌbed\ *n* **1** : the bed in which a person dies **2** : the last hours of life

death•blow \-ˌblō\ *n* : a destructive or killing stroke or event

death•less \-ləs\ *adj* : IMMORTAL, IMPERISHABLE ⟨~ fame⟩

death•ly \-lē\ *adj* **1** : FATAL **2** : of, relating to, or suggestive of death ⟨a ~ pallor⟩ — **deathly** *adv*

death rattle *n* : a sound produced by air passing

through mucus in the lungs and air passages of a dying person
death's–head \ˈdeths-ˌhed\ *n* : a human skull emblematic of death
death•watch \ˈdeth-ˌwäch\ *n* : a vigil kept over the dead or dying
deb \ˈdeb\ *n* : DEBUTANTE
de•ba•cle \di-ˈbä-kəl, -ˈba-\ *also* **dé•bâ•cle** \ *same or* dā-ˈbäk\ *n* [F *débâcle*] : DISASTER, FAILURE, ROUT ⟨stock market ~⟩
de•bar \di-ˈbär\ *vb* : to bar from having or doing something : PRECLUDE
de•bark \di-ˈbärk\ *vb* : DISEMBARK — **de•bar•ka•tion** \ˌdē-ˌbär-ˈkā-shən\ *n*
de•base \di-ˈbās\ *vb* : to lower in character, quality, or value **syn** degrade, corrupt, deprave — **de•base•ment** *n*
de•bate \di-ˈbāt\ *vb* **de•bat•ed; de•bat•ing 1** : to discuss a question by considering opposed arguments **2** : to take part in a debate — **de•bat•able** *adj* — **debate** *n* — **de•bat•er** *n*
de•bauch \di-ˈbȯch\ *vb* : SEDUCE, CORRUPT **syn** debase, demoralize, deprave, pervert — **de•bauch•ery** \-ˈbȯ-chə-rē\ *n*
de•ben•ture \di-ˈben-chər\ *n* : BOND; *esp* : one secured by the general credit of the issuer rather than a lien on particular assets
de•bil•i•tate \di-ˈbi-lə-ˌtāt\ *vb* **-tat•ed; -tat•ing** : to impair the health or strength of **syn** weaken, disable, enfeeble, undermine
de•bil•i•ty \di-ˈbi-lə-tē\ *n, pl* **-ties** : an infirm or weakened state
¹deb•it \ˈde-bət\ *vb* : to enter as a debit : charge with or as a debit
²debit *n* **1** : an entry in an account showing money paid out or owed **2** : DISADVANTAGE, SHORTCOMING
debit card *n* : a card by which money may be withdrawn or the cost of purchases paid directly from the holder's bank account
deb•o•nair \ˌde-bə-ˈnar\ *adj* [ME *debonere*, fr. OF *debonaire*, fr. *de bon aire* of good family or nature] : SUAVE, URBANE; *also* : LIGHTHEARTED
de•bouch \di-ˈbau̇ch, -ˈbüsh\ *vb* [F *déboucher*, fr. *dé-* out of + *bouche* mouth] : to come out into an open area : EMERGE
de•brief \di-ˈbrēf\ *vb* : to question (as a pilot back from a mission) in order to obtain useful information
de•bris \də-ˈbrē, dā-; ˈdā-ˌbrē\ *n, pl* **debris** \-ˈbrēz, -ˌbrēz\ **1** : the remains of something broken down or destroyed **2** : an accumulation of rock fragments **3** : RUBBISH
debt \ˈdet\ *n* **1** : SIN, TRESPASS **2** : something owed : OBLIGATION **3** : a condition of owing
debt•or \ˈde-tər\ *n* **1** : one guilty of neglect or violation of duty **2** : one that owes a debt
de•bug \(ˌ)dē-ˈbəg\ *vb* : to eliminate errors in
de•bunk \dē-ˈbəŋk\ *vb* : to expose the sham or falseness of ⟨~ a legend⟩
¹de•but \ˈdā-ˌbyü, dā-ˈbyü\ *n* **1** : a first appearance **2** : a formal entrance into society
²debut *vb* : to make a debut; *also* : INTRODUCE
deb•u•tante \ˈde-byu̇-ˌtänt\ *n* : a young woman making her formal entrance into society
dec *abbr* **1** deceased **2** decrease
Dec *abbr* December
de•cade \ˈde-ˌkād, de-ˈkād\ *n* : a period of 10 years
dec•a•dence \ˈde-kə-dəns, di-ˈkād-ᵊns\ *n* : DETERIORATION, DECLINE — **dec•a•dent** \ˈde-kə-dənt, di-ˈkād-ᵊnt\ *adj or n*
de•caf \ˈdē-ˌkaf\ *n* : decaffeinated coffee
de•caf•fein•at•ed \(ˌ)dē-ˈka-fə-nā-təd\ *adj* : having the caffeine removed ⟨~ coffee⟩
deca•gon \ˈde-kə-ˌgän\ *n* : a plane polygon of 10 angles and 10 sides
de•cal \ˈdē-ˌkal\ *n* : a picture, design, or label made to be transferred (as to glass) from specially prepared paper
de•cal•co•ma•nia \di-ˌkal-kə-ˈmā-nē-ə\ *n* [F *décalcomanie*, fr. *décalquer* to copy by tracing (fr. *calquer* to trace, fr. It *calcare*, lit., to tread, fr. L) + *manie* mania, fr. LL *mania*] : DECAL
Deca•logue \ˈde-kə-ˌlȯg\ *n* : TEN COMMANDMENTS
de•camp \di-ˈkamp\ *vb* **1** : to break up a camp **2** : to depart suddenly **syn** escape, abscond, flee
de•cant \di-ˈkant\ *vb* : to pour (as wine) gently from one vessel into another
de•cant•er \di-ˈkan-tər\ *n* : an ornamental glass bottle for serving wine
de•cap•i•tate \di-ˈka-pə-ˌtāt\ *vb* **-tat•ed; -tat•ing** : BEHEAD — **de•cap•i•ta•tion** \-ˌka-pə-ˈtā-shən\ *n* — **de•cap•i•ta•tor** \-ˈka-pə-ˌtā-tər\ *n*
deca•syl•lab•ic \ˌde-kə-sə-ˈla-bik\ *adj* : having or composed of verses having 10 syllables — **decasyllabic** *n*
de•cath•lon \di-ˈkath-lən, -ˌlän\ *n* : a 10-event athletic contest
de•cay \di-ˈkā\ *vb* **1** : to decline from a sound or prosperous condition **2** : to cause or undergo decomposition ⟨radium ~*s* slowly⟩; *esp* : to break down while spoiling : ROT — **decay** *n*
decd *abbr* deceased
de•cease \di-ˈsēs\ *n* : DEATH
¹de•ceased \-ˈsēst\ *adj* : no longer living; *esp* : recently dead
²deceased *n, pl* **deceased** : a dead person
de•ce•dent \di-ˈsēd-ᵊnt\ *n* : a deceased person
de•ceit \di-ˈsēt\ *n* **1** : DECEPTION **2** : TRICK **3** : DECEITFULNESS **syn** dissimulation, duplicity, guile
de•ceit•ful \-fəl\ *adj* **1** : practicing or tending to practice deceit **2** : MISLEADING, DECEPTIVE ⟨a ~ answer⟩ — **de•ceit•ful•ly** *adv* — **de•ceit•ful•ness** *n*
de•ceive \di-ˈsēv\ *vb* **de•ceived; de•ceiv•ing 1** : to cause to believe an untruth **2** : to use or practice deceit **syn** beguile, betray, delude, mislead — **de•ceiv•er** *n*
de•cel•er•ate \dē-ˈse-lə-ˌrāt\ *vb* **-at•ed; -at•ing** : to slow down
De•cem•ber \di-ˈsem-bər\ *n* [ME *Decembre*, fr. OF, fr. L *December* (tenth month), fr. *decem* ten] : the 12th month of the year
de•cen•cy \ˈdēs-ᵊn-sē\ *n, pl* **-cies 1** : PROPRIETY **2** : conformity to standards of taste, propriety, or quality **3** : standard of propriety — usu. used in pl.
de•cen•ni•al \di-ˈse-nē-əl\ *adj* **1** : consisting of 10 years **2** : happening every 10 years ⟨~ census⟩
de•cent \ˈdēs-ᵊnt\ *adj* **1** : conforming to standards of propriety, good taste, or morality **2** : modestly clothed **3** : free from immodesty or obscenity **4** : ADEQUATE ⟨~ housing⟩ — **de•cent•ly** *adv*
de•cen•tral•i•za•tion \dē-ˌsen-trə-lə-ˈzā-shən\ *n* **1** : the distribution of powers from a central authority to regional and local authorities **2** : the redistribution of population and industry from urban centers to outlying areas — **de•cen•tral•ize** \-ˈsen-trə-ˌlīz\ *vb*
de•cep•tion \di-ˈsep-shən\ *n* **1** : the act of deceiving **2** : the fact or condition of being deceived **3** : FRAUD, TRICK — **de•cep•tive** \-ˈsep-tiv\ *adj* — **de•cep•tive•ly** *adv* — **de•cep•tive•ness** *n*
deci•bel \ˈde-sə-ˌbel, -bəl\ *n* : a unit for measuring the relative loudness of sounds
de•cide \di-ˈsīd\ *vb* **de•cid•ed; de•cid•ing** [ME, fr. MF *decider*, fr. L *decidere*, lit., to cut off, fr. *de-* off + *caedere* to cut] **1** : to arrive at a solution that ends uncertainty or dispute about **2** : to bring to a definitive end ⟨one blow *decided* the fight⟩ **3** : to induce to come to a choice **4** : to make a choice or judgment
de•cid•ed \di-ˈsī-dəd\ *adj* **1** : UNQUESTIONABLE **2** : FIRM, DETERMINED — **de•cid•ed•ly** *adv*
de•cid•u•ous \di-ˈsi-jə-wəs\ *adj* **1** : falling off or out usu. at the end of a period of growth or function ⟨~ leaves⟩ ⟨a ~ tooth⟩ **2** : having deciduous parts ⟨~ trees⟩

deci•gram \ˈde-sə-ˌgram\ *n* — see METRIC SYSTEM table

deci•li•ter \-ˌlē-tər\ *n* — see METRIC SYSTEM table

¹dec•i•mal \ˈde-sə-məl\ *adj* **:** based on the number 10 **:** reckoning by tens

²decimal *n* **:** any number expressed in base 10; *esp* **:** DECIMAL FRACTION

decimal fraction *n* **:** a fraction (as .25 = 25/100 or .025 = 25/1000) or mixed number (as 3.025 = 3 25/1000) in which the denominator is a power of 10 usu. expressed by use of the decimal point

decimal point *n* **:** a period, centered dot, or in some countries a comma at the left of a decimal fraction (as .678) less than one or between a whole number and a decimal fraction in a mixed number (as 3.678)

dec•i•mate \ˈde-sə-ˌmāt\ *vb* **-mat•ed; -mat•ing 1 :** to take or destroy the 10th part of **2 :** to destroy a large part of

deci•me•ter \ˈde-sə-ˌmē-tər\ *n* — see METRIC SYSTEM table

de•ci•pher \di-ˈsī-fər\ *vb* **1 :** DECODE **2 :** to make out the meaning of despite indistinctness — **de•ci•pher•able** *adj*

de•ci•sion \di-ˈsi-zhən\ *n* **1 :** the act or result of deciding **2 :** promptness and firmness in deciding **:** DETERMINATION

de•ci•sive \-ˈsī-siv\ *adj* **1 :** having the power to decide ⟨the ~ vote⟩ **2 :** RESOLUTE, DETERMINED **3 :** CONCLUSIVE ⟨a ~ victory⟩ — **de•ci•sive•ly** *adv* — **de•ci•sive•ness** *n*

¹deck \ˈdek\ *n* **1 :** a floorlike platform of a ship; *also* **:** something resembling the deck of a ship **2 :** a pack of playing cards

²deck *vb* **1 :** ARRAY **2 :** DECORATE **3 :** to furnish with a deck **4 :** KNOCK DOWN, FLOOR

deck•hand \ˈdek-ˌhand\ *n* **:** a sailor who performs manual duties

deck•le edge \ˈdek-əl-\ *n* **:** the rough untrimmed edge of paper — **deck•le–edged** \-ˈejd\ *adj*

de•claim \di-ˈklām\ *vb* **:** to speak or deliver in the manner of a formal speech — **dec•la•ma•tion** \ˌde-klə-ˈmā-shən\ *n* — **de•clam•a•to•ry** \di-ˈkla-mə-ˌtōr-ē\ *adj*

de•clar•a•tive \di-ˈklar-ə-tiv\ *adj* **:** making a declaration ⟨~ sentence⟩

de•clare \di-ˈklar\ *vb* **de•clared; de•clar•ing 1 :** to make known formally, officially, or explicitly **:** ANNOUNCE ⟨~ war⟩ **2 :** to state emphatically **:** AFFIRM **3 :** to make a full statement of **syn** blazon, broadcast, proclaim, publish — **dec•la•ra•tion** \ˌde-klə-ˈrā-shən\ *n* — **de•clar•a•to•ry** \di-ˈklar-ə-ˌtōr-ē\ *adj* — **de•clar•er** *n*

de•clas•si•fy \dē-ˈkla-sə-ˌfī\ *vb* **:** to remove the security classification of — **de•clas•si•fi•ca•tion** \-ˌkla-sə-fə-ˈkā-shən\ *n*

de•clen•sion \di-ˈklen-chən\ *n* **1 :** the inflectional forms of a noun, pronoun, or adjective **2 :** DECLINE, DETERIORATION **3 :** DESCENT, SLOPE

¹de•cline \di-ˈklīn\ *vb* **de•clined; de•clin•ing 1 :** to slope downward **:** DESCEND **2 :** DROOP **3 :** RECEDE **4 :** WANE **5 :** to withhold consent; *also* **:** REFUSE, REJECT **6 :** INFLECT 2 ⟨~ a noun⟩ — **de•clin•able** *adj* — **dec•li•na•tion** \ˌde-klə-ˈnā-shən\ *n*

²decline *n* **1 :** a gradual sinking and wasting away **2 :** a change to a lower state or level **3 :** the time when something is approaching its end **4 :** a descending slope

de•cliv•i•ty \di-ˈkli-və-tē\ *n, pl* **-ties :** a steep downward slope

de•code \dē-ˈkōd\ *vb* **:** to convert (a coded message) into ordinary language — **de•cod•er** *n*

dé•col•le•té \dā-ˌkäl-ˈtā\ *adj* [F] **1 :** wearing a strapless or low-necked gown **2 :** having a low-cut neckline

de•com•mis•sion \ˌdē-kə-ˈmi-shən\ *vb* **:** to remove from service

de•com•pose \ˌdē-kəm-ˈpōz\ *vb* **1 :** to separate into constituent parts **2 :** to break down in decay **:** ROT — **de•com•po•si•tion** \dē-ˌkäm-pə-ˈzi-shən\ *n*

de•com•press \ˌdē-kəm-ˈpres\ *vb* **:** to release from pressure or compression — **de•com•pres•sion** \-ˈpre-shən\ *n*

de•con•ges•tant \ˌdē-kən-ˈjes-tənt\ *n* **:** an agent that relieves congestion (as of mucous membranes)

de•con•tam•i•nate \ˌdē-kən-ˈta-mə-ˌnāt\ *vb* **:** to rid of contamination (as radioactive material) — **de•con•tam•i•na•tion** \-ˌta-mə-ˈnā-shən\ *n*

de•con•trol \ˌdē-kən-ˈtrōl\ *vb* **:** to end control of ⟨~ prices⟩ — **decontrol** *n*

de•cor *or* **dé•cor** \dā-ˈkȯr, ˈdā-ˌkȯr\ *n* **:** DECORATION; *esp* **:** the style and layout of interior furnishings

dec•o•rate \ˈde-kə-ˌrāt\ *vb* **-rat•ed; -rat•ing 1 :** to furnish with something ornamental ⟨~ a room⟩ **2 :** to award a mark of honor (as a medal) to **syn** adorn, beautify, bedeck, garnish, ornament

dec•o•ra•tion \ˌde-kə-ˈrā-shən\ *n* **1 :** the act or process of decorating **2 :** ORNAMENT **3 :** a badge of honor

dec•o•ra•tive \ˈde-kə-rə-tiv\ *adj* **:** ORNAMENTAL

dec•o•ra•tor \ˈde-kə-ˌrā-tər\ *n* **:** one that decorates; *esp* **:** a person who designs or executes interiors and their furnishings

dec•o•rous \ˈde-kə-rəs, di-ˈkōr-əs\ *adj* **:** PROPER, SEEMLY, CORRECT

de•co•rum \di-ˈkōr-əm\ *n* [L] **1 :** conformity to accepted standards of conduct **2 :** ORDERLINESS, PROPRIETY

¹de•coy \ˈdē-ˌkȯi, di-ˈkȯi\ *n* **1 :** something that lures or entices; *esp* **:** an artificial bird used to attract live birds within shot **2 :** something used to draw attention away from another

²de•coy \di-ˈkȯi, ˈdē-ˌkȯi\ *vb* **:** to lure by or as if by a decoy **:** ENTICE

¹de•crease \di-ˈkrēs\ *vb* **de•creased; de•creas•ing :** to grow or cause to grow less **:** DIMINISH

²de•crease \ˈdē-ˌkrēs\ *n* **1 :** the process of decreasing **2 :** REDUCTION

¹de•cree \di-ˈkrē\ *n* **1 :** ORDER, EDICT **2 :** a judicial decision

²decree *vb* **de•creed; de•cree•ing 1 :** COMMAND **2 :** to determine or order judicially **syn** dictate, ordain, prescribe

dec•re•ment \ˈde-krə-mənt\ *n* **1 :** gradual decrease **2 :** the quantity lost by diminution or waste

de•crep•it \di-ˈkre-pət\ *adj* **:** broken down with age **:** WORN-OUT — **de•crep•i•tude** \-pə-ˌtüd, -ˌtyüd\ *n*

de•cre•scen•do \ˌdā-krə-ˈshen-dō\ *adv or adj* **:** with a decrease in volume — used as a direction in music

de•crim•i•nal•ize \dē-ˈkri-mən-ᵊl-ˌīz\ *vb* **:** to remove or reduce the criminal status of

de•cry \di-ˈkrī\ *vb* **:** to express strong disapproval of

ded•i•cate \ˈde-di-ˌkāt\ *vb* **-cat•ed; -cat•ing 1 :** to devote to the worship of a divine being esp. with sacred rites **2 :** to set apart for a definite purpose **3 :** to inscribe or address as a compliment — **ded•i•ca•tion** \ˌde-di-ˈkā-shən\ *n* — **ded•i•ca•tor** \ˈde-di-ˌkā-tər\ *n* — **ded•i•ca•to•ry** \-kə-ˌtōr-ē\ *adj*

de•duce \di-ˈdüs, -ˈdyüs\ *vb* **de•duced; de•duc•ing 1 :** to derive by reasoning **:** INFER **2 :** to trace the course of — **de•duc•ible** *adj*

de•duct \di-ˈdəkt\ *vb* **:** SUBTRACT — **de•duct•ible** *adj*

de•duc•tion \di-ˈdək-shən\ *n* **1 :** SUBTRACTION **2 :** something that is or may be subtracted **3 :** the deriving of a conclusion by reasoning **:** the conclusion so reached — **de•duc•tive** \-ˈdək-tiv\ *adj* — **de•duc•tive•ly** *adv*

¹deed \ˈdēd\ *n* **1 :** something done **2 :** FEAT, EXPLOIT **3 :** a document containing some legal transfer, bargain, or contract

²deed *vb* **:** to convey or transfer by deed

dee•jay \ˈdē-ˌjā\ *n* **:** DISC JOCKEY

deem \ˈdēm\ *vb* **:** THINK, JUDGE **syn** consider, account, reckon, regard, view

de–em•pha•size \dē-ˈem-fə-ˌsīz\ *vb* **:** to reduce in relative importance; *also* **:** to attach little importance to — **de–em•pha•sis** \-səs\ *n*

[1]**deep** \ˈdēp\ *adj* **1 :** extending far down, back, within, or outward **2 :** having a specified extension downward or backward **3 :** difficult to understand; *also* **:** MYSTERIOUS, OBSCURE ⟨a ~ dark secret⟩ **4 :** WISE **5 :** ENGROSSED, INVOLVED ⟨~ in thought⟩ **6 :** INTENSE, PROFOUND ⟨~ sleep⟩ **7 :** dark and rich in color ⟨a ~ red⟩ **8 :** having a low musical pitch or range ⟨a ~ voice⟩ **9 :** situated well within **10 :** covered, enclosed, or filled often to a specified degree — **deep•ly** *adv*

[2]**deep** *adv* **1 :** DEEPLY **2 :** far on **:** LATE ⟨~ in the night⟩

[3]**deep** *n* **1 :** an extremely deep place or part; *esp* **:** OCEAN **2 :** the middle or most intense part ⟨the ~ of winter⟩

deep•en \ˈdē-pən\ *vb* **:** to make or become deep or deeper

deep–freeze \ˈdēp-ˈfrēz\ *vb* **-froze** \-ˈfrōz\; **-fro•zen** \-ˈfrōz-ᵊn\ **:** QUICK-FREEZE

deep–fry *vb* **:** to cook in enough oil to cover the food being fried

deep pocket *n* **1 :** one having substantial financial resources **2** *pl* **:** substantial financial resources

deep–root•ed \ˈdēp-ˈrü-təd, -ˈrü-\ *adj* **:** deeply implanted or established

deep–sea \ˈdēp-ˈsē\ *adj* **:** of, relating to, or occurring in the deeper parts of the sea ⟨~ fishing⟩

deep–seat•ed \ˈdēp-ˈsē-təd\ *adj* **1 :** situated far below the surface **2 :** firmly established ⟨~ convictions⟩

deer \ˈdir\ *n, pl* **deer** [ME, deer, animal, fr. OE *dēor* beast] **:** any of numerous ruminant mammals with cloven hoofs and usu. antlers esp. in the males

deer•fly \-ˌflī\ *n* **:** any of numerous small horseflies

deer•skin \-ˌskin\ *n* **:** leather made from the skin of a deer; *also* **:** a garment of such leather

de–es•ca•late \dē-ˈes-kə-ˌlāt\ *vb* **:** to decrease in extent, volume, or scope **:** LIMIT — **de–es•ca•la•tion** \-ˌes-kə-ˈlā-shən\ *n*

def *abbr* **1** defendant **2** definite **3** definition

de•face \di-ˈfās\ *vb* **:** to destroy or mar the face or surface of — **de•face•ment** *n* — **de•fac•er** *n*

de fac•to \di-ˈfak-tō, dā-\ *adj or adv* **1 :** actually existing ⟨*de facto* segregation⟩ **2 :** actually exercising power ⟨*de facto* government⟩

de•fal•ca•tion \ˌdē-ˌfal-ˈkā-shən, -ˌfȯl-; ˌde-fəl-\ *n* **:** EMBEZZLEMENT

de•fame \di-ˈfām\ *vb* **de•famed; de•fam•ing :** to injure or destroy the reputation of by libel or slander **syn** calumniate, denigrate, libel, malign, slander, vilify — **def•a•ma•tion** \ˌde-fə-ˈmā-shən\ *n* — **de•fam•a•to•ry** \di-ˈfa-mə-ˌtōr-ē\ *adj*

de•fault \di-ˈfȯlt\ *n* **1 :** failure to do something required by duty or law; *also* **:** failure to appear for a legal proceeding **2 :** failure to compete in or to finish an appointed contest ⟨lose a race by ~⟩ — **default** *vb* — **de•fault•er** *n*

[1]**de•feat** \di-ˈfēt\ *vb* **1 :** FRUSTRATE, NULLIFY **2 :** to win victory over **:** BEAT

[2]**defeat** *n* **1 :** FRUSTRATION **2 :** an overthrow of an army in battle **3 :** loss of a contest

de•feat•ism \-ˈfē-ˌti-zəm\ *n* **:** acceptance of or resignation to defeat — **de•feat•ist** \-tist\ *n or adj*

def•e•cate \ˈde-fi-ˌkāt\ *vb* **-cat•ed; -cat•ing 1 :** to free from impurity or corruption **2 :** to discharge feces from the bowels — **def•e•ca•tion** \ˌde-fi-ˈkā-shən\ *n*

[1]**de•fect** \ˈdē-ˌfekt, di-ˈfekt\ *n* **:** BLEMISH, FAULT, IMPERFECTION

[2]**de•fect** \di-ˈfekt\ *vb* **:** to desert a cause or party esp. in order to espouse another — **de•fec•tion** \-ˈfek-shən\ *n* — **de•fec•tor** \-ˈfek-tər\ *n*

de•fec•tive \di-ˈfek-tiv\ *adj* **:** FAULTY, DEFICIENT — **defective** *n*

defence *chiefly Brit var of* DEFENSE

de•fend \di-ˈfend\ *vb* [ME, fr. OF *defendre,* fr. L *defendere,* fr. *de-* from + *-fendere* to strike] **1 :** to repel danger or attack from **2 :** to act as attorney for **3 :** to oppose the claim of another in a lawsuit **:** CONTEST **4 :** to maintain against opposition ⟨~ an idea⟩ — **de•fend•er** *n*

de•fen•dant \di-ˈfen-dənt\ *n* **:** a person required to make answer in a legal action or suit

de•fense \di-ˈfens\ *n* **1 :** the act of defending **:** resistance against attack **2 :** means, method, or capability of defending **3 :** an argument in support **4 :** the answer made by the defendant in a legal action **5 :** a defending party, group, or team — **de•fense•less** *adj* — **de•fen•si•ble** *adj*

defense mechanism *n* **:** an often unconscious mental process (as repression) that assists in reaching compromise solutions to personal problems

[1]**de•fen•sive** \di-ˈfen-siv\ *adj* **1 :** serving or intended to defend or protect **2 :** of or relating to the attempt to keep an opponent from scoring (as in a game) — **de•fen•sive•ly** *adv* — **de•fen•sive•ness** *n*

[2]**defensive** *n* **:** a defensive position

[1]**de•fer** \di-ˈfər\ *vb* **de•ferred; de•fer•ring** [ME *deferren, differren,* fr. MF *differer,* fr. L *differre* to postpone, be different] **:** POSTPONE, PUT OFF

[2]**defer** *vb* **deferred; deferring** [ME *deferren, differren,* fr. MF *deferer, defferer,* fr. LL *deferre,* fr. L, to bring down, bring, fr. *de-* down + *ferre* to carry] **:** to submit or yield to the opinion or wishes of another

def•er•ence \ˈde-fə-rəns\ *n* **:** courteous, respectful, or ingratiating regard for another's wishes **syn** honor, homage, obeisance, reverence — **def•er•en•tial** \ˌde-fə-ˈren-chəl\ *adj*

de•fer•ment \di-ˈfər-mənt\ *n* **:** the act of delaying; *esp* **:** official postponement of military service

de•fi•ance \di-ˈfī-əns\ *n* **1 :** CHALLENGE **2 :** disposition to resist or contend

de•fi•ant \-ənt\ *adj* **:** full of defiance **:** BOLD — **de•fi•ant•ly** *adv*

de•fi•bril•la•tor \dē-ˈfi-brə-ˌlā-tər\ *n* **:** an electronic device that applies an electric shock to restore the rhythm of a fibrillating heart — **de•fi•bril•late** \-ˌlāt\ *vb* — **de•fi•bril•la•tion** \-ˌfi-brə-ˈlā-shən\ *n*

deficiency disease *n* **:** a disease (as scurvy or beriberi) caused by a lack of essential dietary elements and esp. a vitamin or mineral

de•fi•cient \di-ˈfi-shənt\ *adj* **:** lacking in something necessary; *also* **:** not up to a normal standard — **de•fi•cien•cy** \-shən-sē\ *n*

def•i•cit \ˈde-fə-sət\ *n* **:** a deficiency in amount; *esp* **:** an excess of expenditures over revenue

[1]**de•file** \di-ˈfīl\ *vb* **de•filed; de•fil•ing 1 :** to make filthy **2 :** CORRUPT **3 :** to violate the chastity of **4 :** to violate the sanctity of **:** DESECRATE **5 :** DISHONOR **syn** contaminate, pollute, soil, taint — **de•file•ment** *n*

[2]**de•file** \di-ˈfīl, ˈdē-ˌfīl\ *n* **:** a narrow passage or gorge

de•fine \di-ˈfīn\ *vb* **de•fined; de•fin•ing 1 :** to set forth the meaning of ⟨~ a word⟩ **2 :** to fix or mark the limits of **3 :** to clarify in outline or character — **de•fin•able** *adj* — **de•fin•er** *n*

def•i•nite \ˈde-fə-nət\ *adj* **1 :** having distinct limits **:** FIXED **2 :** clear in meaning **3 :** typically designating an identified or immediately identifiable person or thing — **def•i•nite•ly** *adv* — **def•i•nite•ness** *n*

def•i•ni•tion \ˌde-fə-ˈni-shən\ *n* **1 :** an act of determining or settling **2 :** a statement of the meaning of a word or word group; *also* **:** the action or process of defining **3 :** the action or the power of making definite and clear **:** CLARITY, DISTINCTNESS

de•fin•i•tive \di-ˈfi-nə-tiv\ *adj* **1 :** DECISIVE, CONCLUSIVE **2 :** authoritative and apparently exhaustive **3 :** serving to define or specify precisely

de•flate \di-ˈflāt\ *vb* **de•flat•ed; de•flat•ing 1 :** to release air or gas from **2 :** to reduce in size, importance, or effectiveness; *also* **:** to reduce from a state of inflation **3 :** to become deflated

de•fla•tion \-ˈflā-shən\ *n* **1 :** an act or instance of deflating **:** the state of being deflated **2 :** reduction in the volume of available money or credit resulting in a decline of the general price level

de•flect \di-ˈflekt\ *vb* **:** to turn aside — **de•flec•tion** \-ˈflek-shən\ *n*

de•flo•ra•tion \ˌde-flə-ˈrā-shən\ *n* : rupture of the hymen

de•flow•er \dē-ˈflau̇(-ə)r\ *vb* : to deprive of virginity

de•fog \dē-ˈfȯg, -ˈfäg\ *vb* : to remove fog or condensed moisture from — **de•fog•ger** *n*

de•fo•li•ant \dē-ˈfō-lē-ənt\ *n* : a chemical spray or dust used to defoliate plants

de•fo•li•ate \-ˌāt\ *vb* : to deprive of leaves esp. prematurely — **de•fo•li•a•tion** \dē-ˌfō-lē-ˈā-shən\ *n* — **de•fo•li•a•tor** \dē-ˈfō-lē-ˌā-tər\ *n*

de•for•es•ta•tion \dē-ˌfȯr-ə-ˈstā-shən\ *n* : the action or process of clearing an area of forests; *also* : the state of having been cleared of forests — **de•for•est** \(ˌ)dē-ˈfȯr-əst, -ˈfär-\ *vb*

de•form \di-ˈfȯrm\ *vb* **1** : DISFIGURE, DEFACE **2** : to make or become misshapen or changed in shape — **de•for•ma•tion** \ˌdē-ˌfȯr-ˈmā-shən, ˌde-fər-\ *n*

de•for•mi•ty \di-ˈfȯr-mə-tē\ *n, pl* **-ties** **1** : the state of being deformed **2** : a physical blemish or distortion

de•fraud \di-ˈfrȯd\ *vb* : CHEAT

de•fray \di-ˈfrā\ *vb* : to provide for the payment of : PAY — **de•fray•al** *n*

de•frock \(ˌ)dē-ˈfräk\ *vb* : to deprive (as a priest) of the right to exercise the functions of office

de•frost \di-ˈfrȯst\ *vb* **1** : to thaw out **2** : to free from ice — **de•frost•er** *n*

deft \ˈdeft\ *adj* : quick and neat in action — **deft•ly** *adv* — **deft•ness** *n*

de•funct \di-ˈfəŋkt\ *adj* : DEAD, EXTINCT

de•fuse \dē-ˈfyüz\ *vb* **1** : to remove the fuse from (as a bomb) **2** : to make less harmful, potent, or tense

de•fy \di-ˈfī\ *vb* **de•fied; de•fy•ing** [ME, to renounce faith in, challenge, fr. OF *defier,* fr. *de-* from + *fier* to entrust, ultim. fr. L *fidere* to trust] **1** : CHALLENGE, DARE **2** : to refuse boldly to obey or to yield to : DISREGARD ⟨~ the law⟩ **3** : WITHSTAND, BAFFLE ⟨a scene that *defies* description⟩

deg *abbr* degree

de•gas \dē-ˈgas\ *vb* : to remove gas from

de•gen•er•a•cy \di-ˈje-nə-rə-sē\ *n, pl* **-cies** **1** : the state of being degenerate **2** : the process of becoming degenerate **3** : PERVERSION

[1]de•gen•er•ate \di-ˈje-nə-rət\ *adj* : fallen or deteriorated from a former, higher, or normal condition — **de•gen•er•a•tion** \-ˌje-nə-ˈrā-shən\ *n* — **de•gen•er•a•tive** \-ˈje-nə-ˌrā-tiv\ *adj*

[2]de•gen•er•ate \di-ˈje-nə-ˌrāt\ *vb* : to undergo deterioration (as in morality, intelligence, structure, or function)

[3]de•gen•er•ate \-rət\ *n* : a degenerate person; *esp* : a sexual pervert

de•grad•able \di-ˈgrā-də-bəl\ *adj* : capable of being chemically degraded

de•grade \di-ˈgrād\ *vb* **1** : to reduce from a higher to a lower rank or degree **2** : DEBASE, CORRUPT **3** : DECOMPOSE — **deg•ra•da•tion** \ˌde-grə-ˈdā-shən\ *n*

de•gree \di-ˈgrē\ *n* [ME, fr. OF *degré,* fr. (assumed) VL *degradus,* fr. L *de-* down + *gradus* step, grade] **1** : a step in a series **2** : a rank or grade of official, ecclesiastical, or social position; *also* : the civil condition of a person **3** : the extent, intensity, or scope of something esp. as measured by a graded series **4** : one of the forms or sets of forms used in the comparison of an adjective or adverb **5** : a title conferred upon students by a college, university, or professional school on completion of a program of study **6** : a line or space of the musical staff; *also* : a note or tone of a musical scale **7** : a unit of measure for angles that is equal to an angle with its vertex at the center of a circle and its sides cutting off 1/360 of the circumference; *also* : a unit of measure of the arc of a circle equal to the amount of arc cut off by an angle of one degree with its vertex at the center of the circle **8** : any of various units for measuring temperature

de•horn \dē-ˈhȯrn\ *vb* : to deprive of horns

de•hu•man•ize \dē-ˈhyü-mə-ˌnīz\ *vb* : to deprive of human qualities, personality, or spirit — **de•hu•man•i•za•tion** \ˌdē-ˌhyü-mə-nə-ˈzā-shən\ *n*

de•hu•mid•i•fy \ˌdē-hyü-ˈmi-də-ˌfī\ *vb* : to remove moisture from (as the air) — **de•hu•mid•i•fi•er** *n*

de•hy•drate \dē-ˈhī-ˌdrāt\ *vb* : to remove water from; *also* : to lose liquid — **de•hy•dra•tion** \ˌdē-hī-ˈdrā-shən\ *n*

de•hy•dro•ge•na•tion \ˌdē-(ˌ)hī-ˌdrä-jə-ˈnā-shən, -drə-\ *n* : the removal of hydrogen from a chemical compound — **de•hy•dro•ge•nate** \ˌdē-(ˌ)hī-ˈdrä-jə-ˌnāt, dē-ˈhī-drə-jə-\ *vb*

de•ice \dē-ˈīs\ *vb* : to keep free or rid of ice — **de•ic•er** *n*

de•i•fy \ˈdē-ə-ˌfī\ *vb* **-fied; -fy•ing** **1** : to make a god of **2** : WORSHIP, GLORIFY — **de•i•fi•ca•tion** \ˌdē-ə-fə-ˈkā-shən\ *n*

deign \ˈdān\ *vb* [ME, fr. OF *deignier,* fr. L *dignare, dignari,* fr. *dignus* worthy] : CONDESCEND

de•ion•ize \dē-ˈī-ə-ˌnīz\ *vb* : to remove ions from

de•ism \ˈdē-ˌi-zəm\ *n, often cap* : a system of thought advocating natural religion based on human morality and reason rather than divine revelation — **de•ist** \ˈdē-ist\ *n, often cap* — **de•is•tic** \dē-ˈis-tik\ *adj*

de•i•ty \ˈdē-ə-tē, ˈdā-\ *n, pl* **-ties** **1** : DIVINITY 2 **2** *cap* : GOD 1 **3** : a god or goddess

dé•jà vu \ˌdā-ˌzhä-ˈvü\ *n* [F, adj., already seen] : the feeling that one has seen or heard something before

de•ject•ed \di-ˈjek-təd\ *adj* : low in spirits : SAD — **de•ject•ed•ly** *adv*

de•jec•tion \di-ˈjek-shən\ *n* : lowness of spirits

de ju•re \dē-ˈju̇r-ē\ *adv or adj* [ML] : by legal right

deka•gram \ˈde-kə-ˌgram\ *n* — see METRIC SYSTEM table

deka•li•ter \-ˌlē-tər\ *n* — see METRIC SYSTEM table

deka•me•ter \-ˌmē-tər\ *n* — see METRIC SYSTEM table

del *abbr* delegate; delegation

Del *abbr* Delaware

Del•a•ware \ˈde-lə-ˌwar\ *n, pl* **Delaware** *or* **Delawares** : a member of an American Indian people orig. of the Delaware valley; *also* : their language

[1]de•lay \di-ˈlā\ *n* **1** : the act of delaying : the state of being delayed **2** : the time for which something is delayed

[2]delay *vb* **1** : POSTPONE, PUT OFF **2** : to stop, detain, or hinder for a time **3** : to move or act slowly

de•lec•ta•ble \di-ˈlek-tə-bəl\ *adj* **1** : highly pleasing : DELIGHTFUL **2** : DELICIOUS

de•lec•ta•tion \ˌdē-ˌlek-ˈtā-shən\ *n* : DELIGHT, PLEASURE, DIVERSION

[1]del•e•gate \ˈde-li-gət, -ˌgāt\ *n* **1** : DEPUTY, REPRESENTATIVE **2** : a member of the lower house of the legislature of Maryland, Virginia, or West Virginia

[2]del•e•gate \-ˌgāt\ *vb* **-gat•ed; -gat•ing** **1** : to entrust to another ⟨~ authority⟩ **2** : to appoint as one's delegate

del•e•ga•tion \ˌde-li-ˈgā-shən\ *n* **1** : the act of delegating **2** : one or more persons chosen to represent others

de•lete \di-ˈlēt\ *vb* **de•let•ed; de•let•ing** [L *delēre* to wipe out, destroy] : to eliminate esp. by blotting out, cutting out, or erasing — **de•le•tion** \-ˈlē-shən\ *n*

del•e•te•ri•ous \ˌde-lə-ˈtir-ē-əs\ *adj* : HARMFUL, NOXIOUS

delft \ˈdelft\ *n* **1** : a Dutch pottery with an opaque white glaze and predominantly blue decoration **2** : glazed pottery esp. when blue and white

delft•ware \-ˌwar\ *n* : DELFT

deli \ˈde-lē\ *n, pl* **del•is** : DELICATESSEN

[1]de•lib•er•ate \di-ˈli-bə-ˌrāt\ *vb* **-at•ed; -at•ing** : to consider carefully — **de•lib•er•a•tion** \-ˌli-bə-ˈrā-shən\ *n* — **de•lib•er•a•tive** \-ˈli-bə-ˌrā-tiv, -brə-tiv\ *adj* — **de•lib•er•a•tive•ly** *adv*

[2]de•lib•er•ate \di-ˈli-bə-rət, -ˈli-brət\ *adj* [L *deliberare* to consider carefully, fr. *libra* scale, pound] **1** : determined after careful thought **2** : done or said intentionally **3** : UNHURRIED, SLOW — **de•lib•er•ate•ly** *adv* — **de•lib•er•ate•ness** *n*

del•i•ca•cy \ˈde-li-kə-sē\ *n, pl* **-cies** **1** : something pleasing to eat and considered rare or luxurious **2** : FINENESS, DAINTINESS; *also* : FRAILTY **3** : nicety or expressiveness of touch **4** : precise perception and discrimination : SENSITIVITY **5** : sensibility in feeling or conduct; *also* : SQUEAMISHNESS **6** : the quality or state of requiring delicate handling

del•i•cate \ˈde-li-kət\ *adj* **1** : pleasing to the senses of taste or smell esp. in a mild or subtle way **2** : marked by daintiness or charm : EXQUISITE **3** : FASTIDIOUS, SQUEAMISH, SCRUPULOUS **4** : easily damaged : FRAGILE; *also* : SICKLY **5** : requiring skill or tact **6** : marked by care, skill, or tact **7** : marked by minute precision : very sensitive — **del•i•cate•ly** *adv*

del•i•ca•tes•sen \ˌde-li-kə-ˈtes-ᵊn\ *n pl* [G, pl. of *Delicatesse* delicacy, fr. F *délicatesse*] **1** : ready-to-eat food products (as cooked meats and prepared salads) **2** *sing, pl* **delicatessens** : a store where delicatessen are sold

de•li•cious \di-ˈli-shəs\ *adj* : affording great pleasure : DELIGHTFUL; *esp* : very pleasing to the taste or smell — **de•li•cious•ly** *adv* — **de•li•cious•ness** *n*

¹**de•light** \di-ˈlīt\ *n* **1** : great pleasure or satisfaction : JOY **2** : something that gives great pleasure — **delight•ful** \-fəl\ *adj* — **de•light•ful•ly** *adv*

²**delight** *vb* **1** : to take great pleasure **2** : to satisfy greatly : PLEASE

de•light•ed *adj* : highly pleased : GRATIFIED — **delight•ed•ly** *adv*

de•lim•it \di-ˈli-mət\ *vb* : to fix the limits of

de•lin•eate \di-ˈli-nē-ˌāt\ *vb* **-eat•ed; -eat•ing 1** : SKETCH, PORTRAY **2** : to picture in words : DESCRIBE — **de•lin•ea•tion** \-ˌli-nē-ˈā-shən\ *n*

de•lin•quen•cy \di-ˈliŋ-kwən-sē\ *n, pl* **-cies** : the quality or state of being delinquent

¹**de•lin•quent** \-kwənt\ *n* : a delinquent person

²**delinquent** *adj* **1** : offending by neglect or violation of duty or of law **2** : being overdue in payment

del•i•quesce \ˌde-li-ˈkwes\ *vb* **-quesced; -quesc•ing** : MELT, DISSOLVE — **del•i•ques•cent** \-ˈkwes-ᵊnt\ *adj*

de•lir•i•um \di-ˈlir-ē-əm\ *n* [L, fr. *delirare* to be crazy, lit., to leave the furrow (in plowing), fr. *de-* from + *lira* furrow] : mental disturbance marked by confusion, disordered speech, and hallucinations; *also* : frenzied excitement — **de•lir•i•ous** \-ē-əs\ *adj* — **de•lir•i•ous•ly** *adv*

delirium tre•mens \-ˈtrē-mənz, -ˈtre-\ *n* : a violent delirium with tremors that is induced by excessive and prolonged use of alcoholic liquors

de•liv•er \di-ˈli-vər\ *vb* **-ered; -er•ing 1** : to set free : SAVE **2** : CONVEY, TRANSFER ⟨~ a letter⟩ **3** : to assist in giving birth or at the birth of; *also* : to give birth to **4** : UTTER, COMMUNICATE **5** : to send to an intended target or destination — **de•liv•er•ance** *n* — **de•liv•er•er** *n*

de•liv•ery \di-ˈli-və-rē\ *n, pl* **-er•ies** : the act of delivering something; *also* : something delivered — **de•liv•ery•man** \-ˌman\ *n*

dell \ˈdel\ *n* : a small secluded valley

de•louse \dē-ˈlau̇s\ *vb* : to remove lice from

del•phin•i•um \del-ˈfi-nē-əm\ *n* : any of a genus of mostly perennial herbs related to the buttercups with tall branching spikes of irregular flowers

del•ta \ˈdel-tə\ *n* **1** : the 4th letter of the Greek alphabet — Δ or δ **2** : something shaped like a capital Δ; *esp* : the triangular silt-formed land at the mouth of a river — **del•ta•ic** \del-ˈtā-ik\ *adj*

de•lude \di-ˈlüd\ *vb* **de•lud•ed; de•lud•ing** : MISLEAD, DECEIVE, TRICK

¹**del•uge** \ˈdel-yüj\ *n* **1** : a flooding of land by water **2** : a drenching rain **3** : a great amount or number

²**deluge** *vb* **del•uged; del•ug•ing 1** : INUNDATE, FLOOD **2** : to overwhelm as if with a deluge

de•lu•sion \di-ˈlü-zhən\ *n* : a deluding or being deluded; *esp* : a persistent false psychotic belief — **de•lu•sion•al** \-ˈlü-zhə-nəl\ *adj* — **de•lu•sive** \-ˈlü-siv\ *adj*

de•luxe \di-ˈlu̇ks, -ˈləks, -ˈlüks\ *adj* : notably luxurious or elegant

delve \ˈdelv\ *vb* **delved; delv•ing 1** : DIG **2** : to seek laboriously for information

dely *abbr* delivery

Dem *abbr* Democrat; Democratic

de•mag•ne•tize \dē-ˈmag-nə-ˌtīz\ *vb* : to cause to lose magnetic properties — **de•mag•ne•ti•za•tion** \dē-ˌmag-nə-tə-ˈzā-shən\ *n*

dem•a•gogue *or* **dem•a•gog** \ˈde-mə-ˌgäg\ *n* [Gk *dēmagōgos*, fr. *dēmos* people + *agōgos* leading, fr. *agein* to lead] : a person who appeals to the emotions and prejudices of people esp. in order to gain political power — **dem•a•gogu•ery** \-ˌgä-gə-rē\ *n* — **dem•a•gogy** \-ˌgä-gē, -ˌgä-jē\ *n*

¹**de•mand** \di-ˈmand\ *n* **1** : an act of demanding; *also* : something claimed as due or just **2** : the ability and desire to buy goods or services; *also* : the quantity of goods wanted at a stated price **3** : a seeking or being sought after : urgent need **4** : a pressing need or requirement

²**demand** *vb* **1** : to ask for with authority : claim as due or just **2** : to ask earnestly or in the manner of a command **3** : REQUIRE, NEED

de•mar•cate \di-ˈmär-ˌkāt, ˈdē-ˌmär-\ *vb* **-cat•ed; -cat•ing 1** : DELIMIT **2** : SEPARATE — **de•mar•ca•tion** \ˌdē-ˌmär-ˈkā-shən\ *n*

dé•marche *or* **de•marche** \dā-ˈmärsh\ *n* : a course of action : MANEUVER

¹**de•mean** \di-ˈmēn\ *vb* **de•meaned; de•mean•ing** : to behave or conduct (oneself) usu. in a proper manner

²**demean** *vb* **de•meaned; de•mean•ing** : DEGRADE, DEBASE

de•mean•or \di-ˈmē-nər\ *n* : CONDUCT, BEARING

de•mean•our *Brit var of* DEMEANOR

de•ment•ed \di-ˈmen-təd\ *adj* : MAD, INSANE — **de•ment•ed•ly** *adv*

de•men•tia \di-ˈmen-chə\ *n* **1** : mental deterioration **2** : INSANITY

de•mer•it \di-ˈmer-ət\ *n* **1** : FAULT **2** : a mark placed against a person's record for some fault or offense

de•mesne \di-ˈmān, -ˈmēn\ *n* **1** : REALM **2** : manorial land actually possessed by the lord and not held by free tenants **3** : ESTATE **4** : REGION

demi•god \ˈde-mi-ˌgäd\ *n* : a mythological being with more power than a mortal but less than a god

demi•john \ˈde-mi-ˌjän\ *n* [F *dame-jeanne*, lit., Lady Jane] : a large narrow-necked bottle usu. enclosed in wickerwork

de•mil•i•ta•rize \dē-ˈmi-lə-tə-ˌrīz\ *vb* : to strip of military forces, weapons, or fortifications — **de•mil•i•tar•i•za•tion** \dē-ˌmi-lə-tə-rə-ˈzā-shən\ *n*

demi•mon•daine \ˌde-mi-ˌmän-ˈdān\ *n* : a woman of the demimonde

demi•monde \ˈde-mi-ˌmänd\ *n* [F *demi-monde*, fr. *demi-* half + *monde* world] **1** : a class of women on the fringes of respectable society supported by wealthy lovers **2** : a group engaged in activity of doubtful legality or propriety

de•min•er•al•ize \dē-ˈmi-nə-rə-ˌlīz\ *vb* : to remove the mineral matter from — **de•min•er•al•i•za•tion** \-ˌmi-nə-rə-lə-ˈzā-shən\ *n*

de•mise \di-ˈmīz\ *n* **1** : LEASE **2** : transfer of sovereignty to a successor ⟨~ of the crown⟩ **3** : DEATH **4** : loss of status

demi•tasse \ˈde-mi-ˌtas\ *n* : a small cup of black coffee; *also* : the cup used to serve it

de•mo•bi•lize \di-ˈmō-bə-ˌlīz, dē-\ *vb* **1** : DISBAND **2** : to discharge from military service — **de•mo•bi•li•za•tion** \di-ˌmō-bə-lə-ˈzā-shən, dē-\ *n*

de•moc•ra•cy \di-ˈmä-krə-sē\ *n, pl* **-cies** [MF *democratie*, fr. LL *democratia*, fr. Gk *dēmokratia*, fr. *dēmos* people + *kratos* strength, power] **1** : government by the people; *esp* : rule of the majority **2** : a government in which the supreme power is held by the people **3** : a political unit that has a democratic government 4 *cap* : the principles and policies of the Democratic party in the U.S. 5 : the common people esp. when constituting the source of political authority 6 : the absence of hereditary or arbitrary class distinctions or privileges

dem•o•crat \ˈde-mə-ˌkrat\ *n* 1 : one who believes in or practices democracy 2 *cap* : a member of the Democratic party of the U.S.

dem•o•crat•ic \ˌde-mə-ˈkra-tik\ *adj* 1 : of, relating to, or favoring democracy 2 *often cap* : of or relating to one of the two major political parties in the U.S. associated in modern times with policies of broad social reform and internationalism 3 : relating to or appealing to the common people ⟨~ art⟩ 4 : not snobbish — **dem•o•crat•i•cal•ly** \-ti-k(ə-)lē\ *adv*

de•moc•ra•tize \di-ˈmä-krə-ˌtīz\ *vb* **-tized; -tiz•ing** : to make democratic

dé•mo•dé \ˌdā-mō-ˈdā\ *adj* [F] : no longer fashionable : OUT-OF-DATE

de•mo•graph•ics \ˌde-mə-ˈgra-fiks, ˌdē-\ *n pl* : the statistical characteristics of human populations

de•mog•ra•phy \di-ˈmä-grə-fē\ *n* : the statistical study of human populations and esp. their size and distribution and the number of births and deaths — **de•mog•ra•pher** \-fər\ *n* — **de•mo•graph•ic** \ˌde-mə-ˈgra-fik, ˌdē-\ *adj* — **de•mo•graph•i•cal•ly** \-fi-k(ə-)lē\ *adv*

dem•oi•selle \ˌdem-wə-ˈzel\ *n* [F] : a young woman

de•mol•ish \di-ˈmä-lish\ *vb* 1 : to destroy by breaking apart : RAZE 2 : SMASH 3 : to put an end to

de•mo•li•tion \ˌde-mə-ˈli-shən, ˌdē-\ *n* : the act of demolishing; *esp* : destruction by means of explosives

de•mon *or* **dae•mon** \ˈdē-mən\ *n* 1 : an evil spirit : DEVIL 2 *usu daemon* : an attendant power or spirit 3 : one that has unusual drive or effectiveness

de•mon•e•tize \dē-ˈmä-nə-ˌtīz, -ˈmə-\ *vb* : to stop using as money or as a monetary standard ⟨~ silver⟩ — **de•mon•e•ti•za•tion** \dē-ˌmä-nə-tə-ˈzā-shən, -ˌmə-\ *n*

de•mo•ni•ac \di-ˈmō-nē-ˌak\ *also* **de•mo•ni•a•cal** \ˌdē-mə-ˈnī-ə-kəl\ *adj* 1 : possessed or influenced by a demon 2 : DEVILISH, FIENDISH

de•mon•ic \di-ˈmä-nik\ *also* **de•mon•i•cal** \-ni-kəl\ *adj* : DEMONIAC 2

de•mon•ol•o•gy \ˌdē-mə-ˈnä-lə-jē\ *n* 1 : the study of demons 2 : belief in demons

de•mon•stra•ble \di-ˈmän-strə-bəl\ *adj* 1 : capable of being demonstrated 2 : APPARENT, EVIDENT — **de•mon•stra•bly** \-blē\ *adv*

dem•on•strate \ˈde-mən-ˌstrāt\ *vb* **-strat•ed; -strat•ing** 1 : to show clearly 2 : to prove or make clear by reasoning or evidence 3 : to explain esp. with many examples 4 : to show publicly ⟨~ a new car⟩ 5 : to make a public display ⟨~ in protest⟩ — **dem•on•stra•tion** \ˌde-mən-ˈstrā-shən\ *n* — **dem•on•stra•tor** \ˈde-mən-ˌstrā-tər\ *n*

[1]**de•mon•stra•tive** \di-ˈmän-strə-tiv\ *adj* 1 : demonstrating as real or true 2 : characterized by demonstration 3 : pointing out the one referred to and distinguishing it from others of the same class ⟨~ pronoun⟩ 4 : marked by display of feeling : EFFUSIVE — **de•mon•stra•tive•ly** *adv* — **de•mon•stra•tive•ness** *n*

[2]**demonstrative** *n* : a demonstrative word and esp. a pronoun

de•mor•al•ize \di-ˈmȯr-ə-ˌlīz\ *vb* 1 : to corrupt in morals 2 : to weaken in discipline or spirit : DISORGANIZE — **de•mor•al•i•za•tion** \di-ˌmȯr-ə-lə-ˈzā-shən\ *n*

de•mote \di-ˈmōt\ *vb* **de•mot•ed; de•mot•ing** : to reduce to a lower grade or rank — **de•mo•tion** \-ˈmō-shən\ *n*

de•mot•ic \di-ˈmä-tik\ *adj* : COMMON, POPULAR

de•mur \di-ˈmər\ *vb* **de•murred; de•mur•ring** [ME *demeoren* to linger, fr. OF *demorer,* fr. L *demorari,* fr. *morari* to linger, fr. *mora* delay] : to take exception : OBJECT — **de•mur** *n*

de•mure \di-ˈmyu̇r\ *adj* 1 : quietly modest : DECOROUS 2 : affectedly modest, reserved, or serious : PRIM **syn** shy, bashful, coy, difficult, retiring, unassertive — **de•mure•ly** *adv*

de•mur•rer \di-ˈmər-ər\ *n* : a claim by the defendant in a legal action that the plaintiff does not have sufficient grounds to proceed

den \ˈden\ *n* 1 : LAIR 2 : HIDEOUT ⟨a robber's ~⟩; *also* : a place like a hideout or a center of secret activity ⟨opium ~⟩ ⟨a ~ of iniquity⟩ 3 : a cozy private little room

Den *abbr* Denmark

de•na•ture \dē-ˈnā-chər\ *vb* **de•na•tured; de•na•tur•ing** : to remove the natural qualities of; *esp* : to make (alcohol) unfit for drinking

den•drol•o•gy \den-ˈdrä-lə-jē\ *n* : the study of trees — **den•drol•o•gist** \-jist\ *n*

den•gue \ˈdeŋ-gē, -ˌgā\ *n* [Sp] : an acute infectious disease characterized by headache, severe joint pain, and rash

de•ni•al \di-ˈnī-əl\ *n* 1 : rejection of a request 2 : refusal to admit the truth of a statement or charge; *also* : assertion that something alleged is false 3 : DISAVOWAL 4 : restriction on one's own activity or desires

de•nier \ˈden-yər\ *n* : a unit of fineness for yarn

den•i•grate \ˈde-ni-ˌgrāt\ *vb* **-grat•ed; -grat•ing** [L *denigrare,* fr. *nigrare* to blacken, fr. *niger* black] : to cast aspersions on : DEFAME — **den•i•gra•tion** \ˌde-ni-ˈgrā-shən\ *n*

den•im \ˈde-nəm\ *n* [F *(serge) de Nîmes* serge of Nîmes, France] 1 : a firm durable twilled usu. cotton fabric woven with colored warp and white filling threads 2 *pl* : overalls or trousers of usu. blue denim

den•i•zen \ˈde-nə-zən\ *n* : INHABITANT

de•nom•i•nate \di-ˈnä-mə-ˌnāt\ *vb* : to give a name to : DESIGNATE

de•nom•i•na•tion \di-ˌnä-mə-ˈnā-shən\ *n* 1 : an act of denominating 2 : a value or size of a series of related values (as of money) 3 : NAME, DESIGNATION; *esp* : a general name for a category 4 : a religious organization uniting local congregations in a single body — **de•nom•i•na•tion•al** \-shə-nəl\ *adj*

de•nom•i•na•tor \di-ˈnä-mə-ˌnā-tər\ *n* : the part of a fraction that is below the line indicating division

de•no•ta•tive \ˈdē-nō-ˌtā-tiv, di-ˈnō-tə-tiv\ *adj* 1 : denoting or tending to denote 2 : relating to denotation

de•note \di-ˈnōt\ *vb* 1 : to mark out plainly : INDICATE 2 : to make known 3 : MEAN, NAME — **de•no•ta•tion** \ˌdē-nō-ˈtā-shən\ *n*

de•noue•ment \ˌdā-ˌnü-ˈmäⁿ\ *n* [F *dénouement,* lit., untying] : the final outcome of the dramatic complications in a literary work

de•nounce \di-ˈnau̇ns\ *vb* **de•nounced; de•nounc•ing** 1 : to pronounce esp. publicly to be blameworthy or evil 2 : to inform against : ACCUSE 3 : to announce formally the termination of (as a treaty) — **de•nounce•ment** *n*

de no•vo \di-ˈnō-vō\ *adv or adj* [L] : over again : ANEW

dense \ˈdens\ *adj* **dens•er; dens•est** 1 : marked by compactness or crowding together of parts : THICK ⟨~ forest⟩ ⟨a ~ fog⟩ 2 : DULL, STUPID — **dense•ly** *adv* — **dense•ness** *n*

den•si•ty \ˈden-sə-tē\ *n, pl* **-ties** 1 : the quality or state of being dense 2 : the quantity of something per unit volume, unit area, or unit length

dent \ˈdent\ *n* 1 : a small depressed place made by a blow or by pressure 2 : an impression or weakening effect made usu. against resistance 3 : initial progress — **dent** *vb*

den•tal \ˈdent-ᵊl\ *adj* : of or relating to teeth or dentistry — **den•tal•ly** *adv*

dental floss *n* : a thread used to clean between the teeth

dental hygienist *n* : a person licensed to clean and examine teeth

den•tate \ˈden-ˌtāt\ *adj* : having pointed projections : NOTCHED

den•ti•frice \ˈden-tə-frəs\ *n* [MF, fr. L *dentifricium,* fr.

dent-, dens tooth + *fricare* to rub] : a powder, paste, or liquid for cleaning the teeth
den•tin \ˈdent-ᵊn\ *or* **den•tine** \ˈden-ˌtēn, den-ˈtēn\ *n* : a calcareous material like bone but harder and denser that composes the principal mass of a tooth
den•tist \ˈden-tist\ *n* : a person licensed in the care, treatment, and replacement of teeth — **den•tist•ry** *n*
den•ti•tion \den-ˈti-shən\ *n* : the number, kind, and arrangement of teeth (as of a person or animal); *also* : TEETH
den•ture \ˈden-chər\ *n* : a set of teeth; *esp* : a partial or complete set of false teeth
de•nude \di-ˈnüd, -ˈnyüd\ *vb* **de•nud•ed; de•nud•ing** : to strip the covering from — **de•nu•da•tion** \ˌdē-nü-ˈdā-shən, -nyü-\ *n*
de•nun•ci•a•tion \di-ˌnən-sē-ˈā-shən\ *n* : the act of denouncing; *esp* : a public condemnation
de•ny \di-ˈnī\ *vb* **de•nied; de•ny•ing 1** : to declare untrue **2** : to refuse to recognize or acknowledge : DISAVOW **3** : to refuse to grant ⟨~ a request⟩ **4** : to reject as false ⟨~ a theory⟩
de•o•dar \ˈdē-ə-ˌdär\ *n* [Hindi *deodār,* fr. Skt *devadāru,* fr. *deva* god + *dāru* wood] : an East Indian cedar
de•odor•ant \dē-ˈō-də-rənt\ *n* : a preparation that gets rid of unpleasant odors
de•odor•ize \dē-ˈō-də-ˌrīz\ *vb* : to eliminate the offensive odor of
de•ox•i•dize \dē-ˈäk-sə-ˌdīz\ *vb* : to remove oxygen from
de•oxy•ri•bo•nu•cle•ic acid \dē-ˈäk-si-ˌrī-bō-nü-ˌklē-ik-, -nyü-\ *n* : DNA
de•oxy•ri•bose \dē-ˌäk-si-ˈrī-ˌbōs\ *n* : a sugar with five carbon and four oxygen atoms in each molecule that is part of DNA
dep *abbr* **1** depart; departure **2** deposit **3** deputy
de•part \di-ˈpärt\ *vb* **1** : to go away : go away from : LEAVE **2** : DIE **3** : to turn aside : DEVIATE
de•part•ment \di-ˈpärt-mənt\ *n* **1** : a distinct sphere or category esp. of an activity or attribute **2** : a functional or territorial division (as of a government, business, or college) — **de•part•men•tal** \di-ˌpärt-ˈment-ᵊl, ˌdē-\ *adj*
department store *n* : a store selling a wide variety of goods arranged in several departments
de•par•ture \di-ˈpär-chər\ *n* **1** : the act of going away **2** : a starting out (as on a journey) **3** : DIVERGENCE
de•pend \di-ˈpend\ *vb* **1** : to be determined, based, or contingent ⟨life ~*s* on food⟩ **2** : TRUST, RELY ⟨you can ~ on me⟩ **3** : to be dependent esp. for financial support **4** : to hang down ⟨a vine ~*ing* from a tree⟩
de•pend•able \di-ˈpen-də-bəl\ *adj* : TRUSTWORTHY, RELIABLE — **de•pend•abil•i•ty** \-ˌpen-də-ˈbi-lə-tē\ *n*
de•pen•dence *also* **de•pen•dance** \di-ˈpen-dəns\ *n* **1** : the quality or state of being dependent; *esp* : the quality or state of being influenced by or subject to another **2** : RELIANCE, TRUST **3** : something on which one relies **4** : drug addiction; *also* : HABITUATION 2
de•pen•den•cy \-dən-sē\ *n, pl* **-cies 1** : DEPENDENCE **2** : a territory under the jurisdiction of a nation but not formally annexed by it
[1]**de•pen•dent** \-dənt\ *adj* **1** : hanging down **2** : determined or conditioned by another; *also* : affected with drug dependence **3** : relying on another for support **4** : subject to another's jurisdiction **5** : SUBORDINATE 4
[2]**dependent** *also* **de•pen•dant** \-dənt\ *n* : one that is dependent; *esp* : a person who relies on another for support
de•pict \di-ˈpikt\ *vb* **1** : to represent by a picture **2** : to describe in words — **de•pic•tion** \-ˈpik-shən\ *n*
de•pil•a•to•ry \di-ˈpi-lə-ˌtōr-ē\ *n, pl* **-ries** : a preparation for removing hair, wool, or bristles
de•plane \dē-ˈplān\ *vb* : to get out of an airplane
de•plete \di-ˈplēt\ *vb* **de•plet•ed; de•plet•ing** : to exhaust esp. of strength or resources — **de•ple•tion** \-ˈplē-shən\ *n*
de•plor•able \di-ˈplōr-ə-bəl\ *adj* **1** : LAMENTABLE **2** : WRETCHED — **de•plor•ably** *adv*
de•plore \-ˈplōr\ *vb* **de•plored; de•plor•ing 1** : to feel or express grief for **2** : to regret strongly **3** : to consider unfortunate or deserving of disapproval
de•ploy \di-ˈplȯi\ *vb* : to spread out (as troops or ships) in order for battle — **de•ploy•ment** \-mənt\ *n*
de•po•nent \di-ˈpō-nənt\ *n* : one who gives evidence
de•pop•u•late \dē-ˈpä-pyə-ˌlāt\ *vb* : to reduce greatly the population of — **de•pop•u•la•tion** \-ˌpä-pyə-ˈlā-shən\ *n*
de•port \di-ˈpōrt\ *vb* **1** : CONDUCT, BEHAVE **2** : BANISH, EXILE — **de•por•ta•tion** \ˌdē-ˌpōr-ˈtā-shən\ *n*
de•port•ment \di-ˈpōrt-mənt\ *n* : BEHAVIOR, BEARING
de•pose \di-ˈpōz\ *vb* **de•posed; de•pos•ing 1** : to remove from high office (as of king) **2** : to testify under oath or by affidavit
[1]**de•pos•it** \di-ˈpä-zət\ *vb* **de•pos•it•ed** \-zə-təd\; **de•pos•it•ing 1** : to place for safekeeping or as a pledge; *esp* : to put money in a bank **2** : to lay down : PLACE **3** : to let fall or sink ⟨silt ~*ed* by a flood⟩ — **de•pos•i•tor** \-zə-tər\ *n*
[2]**deposit** *n* **1** : the state of being deposited ⟨money on ~⟩ **2** : something placed for safekeeping; *esp* : money deposited in a bank **3** : money given as a pledge **4** : an act of depositing **5** : something laid down ⟨a ~ of silt⟩ **6** : a natural accumulation (as of a mineral)
de•po•si•tion \ˌde-pə-ˈzi-shən, ˌdē-\ *n* **1** : an act of removing from a position of authority **2** : TESTIMONY **3** : the process of depositing **4** : DEPOSIT
de•pos•i•to•ry \di-ˈpä-zə-ˌtōr-ē\ *n, pl* **-ries** : a place where something is deposited esp. for safekeeping
de•pot *1, 2 usu* ˈde-pō, *3 usu* ˈdē-\ *n* **1** : STOREHOUSE **2** : a place where military supplies or replacements are kept or assembled **3** : a building for railroad or bus passengers
depr *abbr* depreciation
de•prave \di-ˈprāv\ *vb* **de•praved; de•prav•ing** [ME, fr. MF *depraver,* fr. L *depravare* to pervert, fr. *pravus* crooked, bad] : CORRUPT, PERVERT — **de•praved** *adj* — **de•prav•i•ty** \-ˈpra-və-tē\ *n*
dep•re•cate \ˈde-pri-ˌkāt\ *vb* **-cat•ed; -cat•ing** [L *deprecari* to avert by prayer, fr. *precari* to pray] **1** : to express disapproval of **2** : BELITTLE — **dep•re•ca•tion** \ˌde-pri-ˈkā-shən\ *n*
dep•re•ca•to•ry \ˈde-pri-kə-ˌtōr-ē\ *adj* **1** : APOLOGETIC **2** : serving to deprecate : DISAPPROVING
de•pre•ci•ate \di-ˈprē-shē-ˌāt\ *vb* **-at•ed; -at•ing** [LL *depretiare,* fr. L *pretium* price] **1** : BELITTLE, DISPARAGE **2** : to lessen in price or value — **de•pre•ci•a•tion** \-ˌprē-shē-ˈā-shən\ *n*
dep•re•da•tion \ˌde-prə-ˈdā-shən\ *n* : a laying waste or plundering — **dep•re•date** \ˈde-prə-ˌdāt\ *vb*
de•press \di-ˈpres\ *vb* **1** : to press down : cause to sink to a lower position **2** : to lessen the activity or force of **3** : SADDEN, DISCOURAGE **4** : to lessen in price or value — **de•pres•sor** \-ˈpre-sər\ *n*
de•pres•sant \di-ˈpres-ᵊnt\ *n* : one that depresses; *esp* : a chemical substance (as a drug) that reduces bodily functional activity — **depressant** *adj*
de•pressed *adj* **1** : low in spirits; *also* : affected with psychological depression **2** : suffering from economic depression
de•pres•sion \di-ˈpre-shən\ *n* **1** : an act of depressing : a state of being depressed **2** : a pressing down : LOWERING **3** : a state of feeling sad **4** : a psychological disorder marked esp. by sadness, inactivity, difficulty in thinking and concentration, and feelings of dejection **5** : a depressed area or part **6** : a period of low general economic activity with widespread unemployment
[1]**de•pres•sive** \di-ˈpre-siv\ *adj* **1** : tending to depress **2** : characterized or affected by psychological depression
[2]**depressive** *n* : a person affected with or prone to psychological depression

de•pres•sur•ize \(ˌ)dē-ˈpre-shə-ˌrīz\ *vb* : to release pressure from
dep•ri•va•tion \ˌde-prə-ˈvā-shən\ *n* **1** : an act or instance of depriving : LOSS **2** : PRIVATION 2
de•prive \di-ˈprīv\ *vb* **de•prived; de•priv•ing 1** : to take something away from **2** : to stop from having something
de•prived *adj* : marked by deprivation esp. of the necessities of life
de•pro•gram \(ˌ)dē-ˈprō-ˌgram, -grəm\ *vb* : to dissuade from convictions usu. of a religious nature often by coercive means
dept *abbr* department
depth \ˈdepth\ *n, pl* **depths** \ˈdepths\ **1** : something that is deep; *esp* : the deep part of a body of water **2** : a part that is far from the outside or surface; *also* : the middle or innermost part **3** : ABYSS **4** : a profound or intense state ⟨the ∼*s* of reflection⟩; *also* : the worst part ⟨during the ∼*s* of the depression⟩ **5** : a reprehensibly low condition **6** : the distance from top to bottom or from front to back **7** : the quality of being deep **8** : the degree of intensity
depth charge *n* : an explosive device for use underwater esp. against submarines
dep•u•ta•tion \ˌde-pyə-ˈtā-shən\ *n* **1** : the act of appointing a deputy **2** : DELEGATION
de•pute \di-ˈpyüt\ *vb* **de•put•ed; de•put•ing** : DELEGATE
dep•u•tize \ˈde-pyə-ˌtīz\ *vb* **-tized; -tiz•ing** : to appoint or act as deputy
dep•u•ty \ˈde-pyə-tē\ *n, pl* **-ties 1** : a person appointed to act for or in place of another **2** : an assistant empowered to act as a substitute in the absence of a superior **3** : a member of a lower house of a legislative assembly
der *or* **deriv** *abbr* derivation; derivative
de•rail \di-ˈrāl\ *vb* : to leave or cause to leave the rails — **de•rail•ment** *n*
de•rail•leur \di-ˈrā-lər\ *n* [F *dérailleur*] : a device for shifting gears on a bicycle by moving the chain from one set of exposed gears to another
de•range \di-ˈrānj\ *vb* **de•ranged; de•rang•ing 1** : DISARRANGE, UPSET **2** : to make insane — **de•range•ment** *n*
der•by \ˈdər-bē, *Brit* ˈdär-\ *n, pl* **derbies 1** : a horse race usu. for three-year-olds held annually **2** : a race or contest open to all **3** : a stiff felt hat with dome-shaped crown and narrow brim

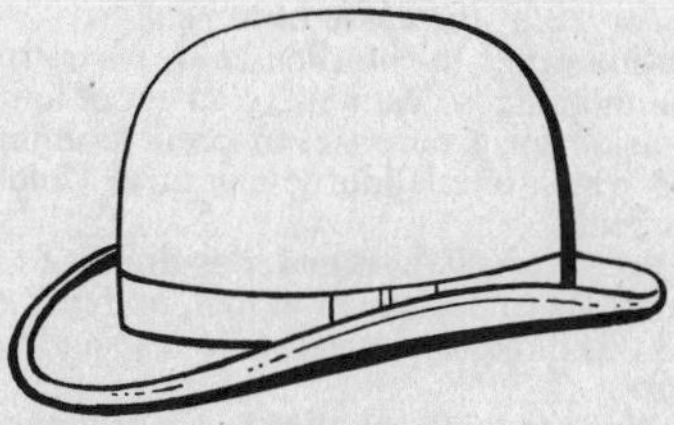
derby 3

de•reg•u•la•tion \(ˌ)dē-ˌre-gyü-ˈlā-shən\ *n* : the act of removing restrictions or regulations — **de•reg•u•late** \-ˈre-gyü-ˌlāt\ *vb*
[1]**der•e•lict** \ˈder-ə-ˌlikt\ *adj* **1** : abandoned by the owner or occupant **2** : NEGLIGENT ⟨∼ in his duty⟩
[2]**derelict** *n* **1** : something voluntarily abandoned; *esp* : a ship abandoned on the high seas **2** : a destitute homeless social misfit : VAGRANT, BUM
der•e•lic•tion \ˌder-ə-ˈlik-shən\ *n* **1** : the act of abandoning : the state of being abandoned **2** : a failure in duty
de•ride \di-ˈrīd\ *vb* **de•rid•ed; de•rid•ing** [L *deridēre*, fr. *ridēre* to laugh] : to laugh at scornfully : RIDICULE
de ri•gueur \də-rē-ˈgər\ *adj* [F] : prescribed or required by fashion, etiquette, or custom : PROPER
de•ri•sion \də-ˈri-zhən\ *n* : RIDICULE — **de•ri•sive** \-ˈrī-siv\ *adj* — **de•ri•sive•ly** *adv* — **de•ri•sive•ness** *n* — **de•ri•so•ry** \-ˈrī-sə-rē\ *adj*
der•i•va•tion \ˌder-ə-ˈvā-shən\ *n* **1** : the formation of a word from an earlier word or root; *also* : an act of ascertaining or stating the derivation of a word **2** : ETYMOLOGY **3** : SOURCE, ORIGIN; *also* : DESCENT **4** : an act or process of deriving
de•riv•a•tive \di-ˈri-və-tiv\ *n* **1** : a word formed by derivation **2** : something derived — **derivative** *adj*
de•rive \di-ˈrīv\ *vb* **de•rived; de•riv•ing** [ME, fr. MF *deriver*, fr. L *derivare*, lit., to draw off (water), fr. *de*- from + *rivus* stream] **1** : to receive or obtain from a source **2** : to obtain from a parent substance **3** : INFER, DEDUCE **4** : to trace the derivation of **5** : to come from a certain source
der•mal \ˈdər-məl\ *adj* : of or relating to the skin : CUTANEOUS
der•ma•ti•tis \ˌdər-mə-ˈtī-təs\ *n* : skin inflammation
der•ma•tol•o•gy \-ˈtä-lə-jē\ *n* : a branch of medical science dealing with the structure, functions, and diseases of the skin — **der•ma•tol•o•gist** \-jist\ *n*
der•mis \ˈdər-məs\ *n* : the sensitive vascular inner layer of the skin
der•o•gate \ˈder-ə-ˌgāt\ *vb* **-gat•ed; -gat•ing 1** : to cause to seem inferior : DISPARAGE **2** : DETRACT — **der•o•ga•tion** \ˌder-ə-ˈgā-shən\ *n* — **de•ro•ga•tive** \di-ˈrä-gə-tiv\ *adj*
de•rog•a•to•ry \di-ˈrä-gə-ˌtōr-ē\ *adj* : intended to lower the reputation of a person or thing : DISPARAGING — **de•rog•a•to•ri•ly** \-ˌrä-gə-ˈtōr-ə-lē\ *adv*
der•rick \ˈder-ik\ *n* [obs. *derrick* hangman, gallows, fr. *Derick*, name of 17th cent. Eng. hangman] **1** : a hoisting apparatus : CRANE **2** : a framework over a drill hole (as for oil) for supporting machinery
der•ri•ere *or* **der•ri•ère** \ˌder-ē-ˈer\ *n* : BUTTOCKS
der•ring–do \ˌder-iŋ-ˈdü\ *n* : DARING
der•rin•ger \ˈder-ən-jər\ *n* : a short-barreled pocket pistol
der•vish \ˈdər-vish\ *n* [Turk *derviş*, lit., beggar, fr. Per *darvīsh*] : a member of a Muslim religious order noted for devotional exercises (as bodily movements leading to a trance)
de•sal•i•nate \dē-ˈsa-lə-ˌnāt\ *vb* **-nat•ed; -nat•ing** : DESALT — **de•sal•i•na•tion** \-ˌsa-lə-ˈnā-shən\ *n*
de•sal•i•nize \dē-ˈsa-lə-ˌnīz\ *vb* **-nized; -niz•ing** : DESALT — **de•sal•i•ni•za•tion** \-ˌsa-lə-nə-ˈzā-shən\ *n*
de•salt \dē-ˈsȯlt\ *vb* : to remove salt from ⟨∼ seawater⟩ — **de•salt•er** *n*
des•cant \ˈdes-ˌkant\ *vb* **1** : to sing or play part music : SING **2** : to discourse or write at length
de•scend \di-ˈsend\ *vb* **1** : to pass from a higher to a lower place or level : pass, move, or climb down or down along **2** : DERIVE ⟨∼*ed* from royalty⟩ **3** : to pass by inheritance or transmission **4** : to incline, lead, or extend downward **5** : to swoop down or appear suddenly (as in an attack)
[1]**de•scen•dant** *or* **de•scen•dent** \di-ˈsen-dənt\ *adj* **1** : DESCENDING **2** : proceeding from an ancestor or source
[2]**descendant** *or* **descendent** *n* **1** : one descended from another or from a common stock **2** : one deriving directly from a precursor or prototype
de•scent \di-ˈsent\ *n* **1** : ANCESTRY, BIRTH, LINEAGE **2** : the act or process of descending **3** : SLOPE **4** : a descending way (as a downgrade) **5** : a sudden hostile raid or assault **6** : a downward step (as in station or value) : DECLINE
de•scribe \di-ˈskrīb\ *vb* **de•scribed; de•scrib•ing 1** : to represent or give an account of in words **2** : to trace the outline of — **de•scrib•able** *adj*
de•scrip•tion \di-ˈskrip-shən\ *n* **1** : an account of something; *esp* : an account that presents a picture to a person who reads or hears it **2** : KIND, SORT — **de•scrip•tive** \-ˈskrip-tiv\ *adj*
de•scry \di-ˈskrī\ *vb* **de•scried; de•scry•ing 1** : to catch

sight of 2 : to discover by observation or investigation
des•e•crate \ˈde-si-ˌkrāt\ *vb* **-crat•ed; -crat•ing** : PROFANE — **des•e•cra•tion** \ˌde-si-ˈkrā-shən\ *n*
de•seg•re•gate \dē-ˈse-gri-ˌgāt\ *vb* : to eliminate segregation in; *esp* : to free of any law or practice requiring isolation on the basis of race — **de•seg•re•ga•tion** \-ˌse-gri-ˈgā-shən\ *n*
de•sen•si•tize \dē-ˈsen-sə-ˌtīz\ *vb* : to make (a sensitized or hypersensitive individual) insensitive or nonreactive to a sensitizing agent — **de•sen•si•ti•za•tion** \-ˌsen-sə-tə-ˈzā-shən\ *n*
[1]**des•ert** \ˈde-zərt\ *n* : dry land with few plants and little rainfall
[2]**des•ert** \ˈde-zərt\ *adj* : of, relating to, or resembling a desert; *esp* : being barren and without life ⟨a ~ island⟩
[3]**de•sert** \di-ˈzərt\ *n* **1** : the quality or fact of deserving reward or punishment **2** : a just reward or punishment
[4]**de•sert** \di-ˈzərt\ *vb* **1** : to withdraw from **2** : ABANDON, FORSAKE — **de•sert•er** *n* — **de•ser•tion** \-ˈzər-shən\ *n*
de•serve \di-ˈzərv\ *vb* **de•served; de•serv•ing** : to be worthy of : MERIT — **de•serv•ing** *adj*
de•serv•ed•ly \-ˈzər-vəd-lē\ *adv* : according to merit : JUSTLY
des•ic•cate \ˈde-si-ˌkāt\ *vb* **-cat•ed; -cat•ing** : DRY, DEHYDRATE — **des•ic•ca•tion** \ˌde-si-ˈkā-shən\ *n* — **des•ic•ca•tor** \ˈde-si-ˌkā-tər\ *n*
de•sid•er•a•tum \di-ˌsi-də-ˈrä-təm, -ˌzi-, -ˈrā-\ *n, pl* **-ta** \-tə\ [L] : something desired as essential
[1]**de•sign** \di-ˈzīn\ *vb* **1** : to conceive and plan out in the mind **2** : INTEND **3** : to devise for a specific function or end **4** : to make a pattern or sketch of **5** : to conceive and draw the plans for
[2]**design** *n* **1** : a particular purpose : deliberate planning **2** : a mental project or scheme : PLAN **3** : a secret project or scheme : PLOT **4** *pl* : aggressive or evil intent — used with *on* or *against* **5** : a preliminary sketch or plan **6** : an underlying scheme that governs functioning, developing, or unfolding : MOTIF **7** : the arrangement of elements or details in a product or a work of art **8** : a decorative pattern **9** : the art of executing designs
[1]**des•ig•nate** \ˈde-zig-ˌnāt, -nət\ *adj* : chosen but not yet installed ⟨ambassador ~⟩
[2]**des•ig•nate** \-ˌnāt\ *vb* **-nat•ed; -nat•ing** **1** : to appoint and set apart for a special purpose **2** : to mark or point out : INDICATE; *also* : SPECIFY, STIPULATE **3** : to call by a name or title — **des•ig•na•tion** \ˌde-zig-ˈnā-shən\ *n*
designated hitter *n* : a baseball player designated at the start of the game to bat in place of the pitcher without causing the pitcher to be removed from the game
de•sign•er \di-ˈzī-nər\ *n* **1** : one who creates plans for a project or structure **2** : one who designs and manufactures high-fashion clothing — **designer** *adj*
de•sign•ing \di-ˈzī-niŋ\ *adj* : CRAFTY, SCHEMING
de•sir•able \di-ˈzī-rə-bəl\ *adj* **1** : PLEASING, ATTRACTIVE **2** : ADVISABLE ⟨~ legislation⟩ — **de•sir•abil•i•ty** \-ˌzī-rə-ˈbi-lə-tē\ *n* — **de•sir•able•ness** *n*
[1]**de•sire** \di-ˈzīr\ *vb* **de•sired; de•sir•ing** [ME, fr. OF *desirer*, fr. L *desiderare*, fr. *sider-*, *sidus* heavenly body] **1** : to long or hope for : exhibit or feel desire for **2** : REQUEST
[2]**desire** *n* **1** : a strong wish : LONGING, CRAVING **2** : sexual urge or appetite **3** : a usu. formal request for action **4** : something desired
de•sir•ous \di-ˈzīr-əs\ *adj* : eagerly wishing : DESIRING
de•sist \di-ˈzist, -ˈsist\ *vb* : to cease to proceed or act
desk \ˈdesk\ *n* [ME *deske*, fr. ML *desca*, fr. OIt *desco* table, fr. L *discus* dish, disc] **1** : a table, frame, or case esp. for writing and reading **2** : a counter, stand, or booth at which a person performs duties **3** : a specialized division of an organization (as a newspaper) ⟨city ~⟩
desk•top publishing \ˈdesk-ˌtäp-\ *n* : the production of printed matter by means of a microcomputer
[1]**des•o•late** \ˈde-sə-lət, -zə-\ *adj* **1** : DESERTED, ABANDONED **2** : FORSAKEN, LONELY **3** : DILAPIDATED **4** : BARREN, LIFELESS **5** : CHEERLESS, GLOOMY — **des•o•late•ly** *adv* — **des•o•late•ness** *n*
[2]**des•o•late** \-ˌlāt\ *vb* **-lat•ed; -lat•ing** : to make desolate : lay waste : make wretched
des•o•la•tion \ˌde-sə-ˈlā-shən, -zə-\ *n* **1** : the action of desolating **2** : GRIEF, SADNESS **3** : LONELINESS **4** : DEVASTATION, RUIN **5** : barren wasteland
des•oxy•ri•bo•nu•cle•ic acid \de-ˌzäk-sē-ˈrī-bō-nu̇-ˌklē-ik-, -nyu̇-\ *n* : DNA
[1]**de•spair** \di-ˈspar\ *vb* : to lose all hope or confidence — **de•spair•ing•ly** *adv*
[2]**despair** *n* **1** : utter loss of hope **2** : a cause of hopelessness
des•patch \dis-ˈpach\ *var of* DISPATCH
des•per•a•do \ˌdes-pə-ˈrä-dō, -ˈrā-\ *n, pl* **-does** *or* **-dos** : a bold or reckless criminal
des•per•ate \ˈdes-pə-rət, -prət\ *adj* **1** : being beyond or almost beyond hope : causing despair **2** : RASH **3** : extremely intense — **des•per•ate•ly** *adv* — **des•per•ate•ness** *n*
des•per•a•tion \ˌdes-pə-ˈrā-shən\ *n* **1** : a loss of hope and surrender to despair **2** : a state of hopelessness leading to rashness
de•spi•ca•ble \di-ˈspi-kə-bəl, ˈdes-pi-\ *adj* : deserving to be despised — **de•spi•ca•bly** \-blē\ *adv*
de•spise \di-ˈspīz\ *vb* **de•spised; de•spis•ing** **1** : to look down on with contempt or aversion : DISDAIN, DETEST **2** : to regard as negligible, worthless, or distasteful
de•spite \di-ˈspīt\ *prep* : in spite of
de•spoil \di-ˈspȯil\ *vb* : to strip of belongings, possessions, or value — **de•spoil•er** *n* — **de•spoil•ment** *n*
de•spo•li•a•tion \di-ˌspō-lē-ˈā-shən\ *n* : the act of plundering : the state of being despoiled
[1]**de•spond** \di-ˈspänd\ *vb* : to become discouraged or disheartened
[2]**despond** *n* : DESPONDENCY
de•spon•den•cy \-ˈspän-dən-sē\ *n* : DEJECTION, HOPELESSNESS — **de•spon•dent** \-dənt\ *adj* — **de•spon•dent•ly** *adv*
des•pot \ˈdes-pət, -ˌpät\ *n* [MF *despote*, fr. Gk *despotēs* master, lord, autocrat] **1** : a ruler with absolute power and authority **2** : a person exercising power tyrannically — **des•pot•ic** \des-ˈpä-tik\ *adj* — **des•po•tism** \ˈdes-pə-ˌti-zəm\ *n*
des•sert \di-ˈzərt\ *n* : a course of sweet food, fruit, or cheese served at the close of a meal
des•ti•na•tion \ˌdes-tə-ˈnā-shən\ *n* **1** : a purpose for which something is destined **2** : an act of appointing, setting aside for a purpose, or predetermining **3** : a place to which one is journeying or to which something is sent
des•tine \ˈdes-tən\ *vb* **des•tined; des•tin•ing** **1** : to settle in advance **2** : to designate, assign, or dedicate in advance **3** : to direct or set apart for a specific purpose or place
des•ti•ny \ˈdes-tə-nē\ *n, pl* **-nies** **1** : something to which a person or thing is destined : FATE, FORTUNE **2** : a predetermined course of events
des•ti•tute \ˈdes-tə-ˌtüt, -ˌtyüt\ *adj* **1** : lacking something needed or desirable **2** : suffering extreme poverty — **des•ti•tu•tion** \ˌdes-tə-ˈtü-shən, -ˈtyü-\ *n*
de•stroy \di-ˈstrȯi\ *vb* **1** : to put an end to : RUIN **2** : KILL
de•stroy•er \di-ˈstrȯi-ər\ *n* **1** : one that destroys **2** : a small speedy warship
de•struc•ti•ble \di-ˈstrək-tə-bəl\ *adj* : capable of being destroyed — **de•struc•ti•bil•i•ty** \-ˌstrək-tə-ˈbi-lə-tē\ *n*
de•struc•tion \di-ˈstrək-shən\ *n* **1** : RUIN **2** : the action or process of destroying something **3** : a destroying agency
de•struc•tive \di-ˈstrək-tiv\ *adj* **1** : causing destruction

: RUINOUS **2** : designed or tending to destroy — **de•struc•tive•ly** *adv* — **de•struc•tive•ness** *n*

de•sue•tude \ˈde-swi-ˌtüd, -ˌtyüd\ *n* : DISUSE

des•ul•to•ry \ˈde-səl-ˌtōr-ē\ *adj* : passing aimlessly from one thing or subject to another : DISCONNECTED

det *abbr* **1** detached; detachment **2** detail

de•tach \di-ˈtach\ *vb* **1** : to separate esp. from a larger mass **2** : DISENGAGE, WITHDRAW — **de•tach•able** *adj*

de•tached \di-ˈtacht\ *adj* **1** : not joined or connected : SEPARATE **2** : ALOOF, IMPARTIAL ⟨a ~ attitude⟩

de•tach•ment \di-ˈtach-mənt\ *n* **1** : SEPARATION **2** : the dispatching of a body of troops or part of a fleet from the main body for special service; *also* : the portion so dispatched **3** : a small permanent military unit of special composition **4** : indifference to worldly concerns : ALOOFNESS **5** : IMPARTIALITY

[1]**de•tail** \di-ˈtāl, ˈdē-ˌtāl\ *n* [F *détail*, fr. OF *detail* slice, piece, fr. *detaillier* to cut in pieces, fr. *taillier* to cut] **1** : a dealing with something item by item ⟨go into ~⟩; *also* : ITEM, PARTICULAR ⟨the ~s of a story⟩ **2** : selection (as of soldiers) for special duty; *also* : the persons thus selected

[2]**detail** *vb* **1** : to report in particulars : SPECIFY **2** : to assign to a special duty

de•tailed \di-ˈtāld, ˈdē-ˌtāld\ *adj* : marked by abundant detail

de•tain \di-ˈtān\ *vb* **1** : to hold in or as if in custody **2** : STOP, DELAY

de•tect \di-ˈtekt\ *vb* : to discover the nature, existence, presence, or fact of — **de•tect•able** *adj* — **de•tec•tion** \-ˈtek-shən\ *n* — **de•tec•tor** \-ˈtek-tər\ *n*

[1]**de•tec•tive** \di-ˈtek-tiv\ *adj* **1** : fitted or used for detection **2** : of or relating to detectives

[2]**detective** *n* : a person employed or engaged in detecting lawbreakers or getting information that is not readily accessible

dé•tente \dā-ˈtänt\ *n* [F] : a relaxation of strained relations or tensions (as between nations)

de•ten•tion \di-ˈten-chən\ *n* **1** : the act or fact of detaining : CONFINEMENT; *esp* : a period of temporary custody prior to disposition by a court **2** : a forced delay

de•ter \di-ˈtər\ *vb* **de•terred; de•ter•ring** [L *deterrēre*, fr. *terrēre* to frighten] **1** : to turn aside, discourage, or prevent from acting (as by fear) **2** : INHIBIT

de•ter•gent \di-ˈtər-jənt\ *n* : a cleansing agent; *esp* : a chemical product similar to soap in its cleaning ability

de•te•ri•o•rate \di-ˈtir-ē-ə-ˌrāt\ *vb* **-rat•ed; -rat•ing** : to make or become worse in quality or condition — **de•te•ri•o•ra•tion** \-ˌtir-ē-ə-ˈrā-shən\ *n*

de•ter•min•able \-ˈtər-mə-nə-bəl\ *adj* : capable of being determined; *esp* : ASCERTAINABLE

de•ter•mi•nant \-mə-nənt\ *n* **1** : something that determines or conditions **2** : GENE

de•ter•mi•nate \di-ˈtər-mə-nət\ *adj* **1** : having fixed limits : DEFINITE **2** : definitely settled — **de•ter•mi•nate•ness** *n*

de•ter•mi•na•tion \di-ˌtər-mə-ˈnā-shən\ *n* **1** : the act of coming to a decision; *also* : the decision or conclusion reached **2** : a fixing of the extent, position, or character of something **3** : accurate measurement (as of length or volume) **4** : firm or fixed purpose

de•ter•mine \di-ˈtər-mən\ *vb* **-mined; -min•ing 1** : to fix conclusively or authoritatively **2** : to come to a decision : SETTLE, RESOLVE **3** : to fix the form or character of beforehand : ORDAIN; *also* : REGULATE **4** : to find out the limits, nature, dimensions, or scope of ⟨~ a position at sea⟩ **5** : to bring about as a result

de•ter•mined \-ˈtər-mənd\ *adj* **1** : firmly resolved **2** : characterized by or showing determination — **de•ter•mined•ly** \-mənd-lē, -mə-nəd-lē\ *adv* — **de•ter•mined•ness** *n*

de•ter•min•ism \di-ˈtər-mə-ˌni-zəm\ *n* : a doctrine that acts of the will, natural events, or social changes are determined by preceding events or natural causes — **de•ter•min•ist** \-nist\ *n or adj*

de•ter•rence \di-ˈtər-əns\ *n* : the inhibition of criminal behavior by fear esp. of punishment

de•ter•rent \-ənt\ *adj* **1** : serving to deter **2** : relating to deterrence — **deterrent** *n*

de•test \di-ˈtest\ *vb* [L *detestari*, lit., to curse while calling a deity to witness, fr. *de-* from + *testari* to call to witness] : LOATHE, HATE — **de•test•able** *adj* — **de•tes•ta•tion** \ˌdē-ˌtes-ˈtā-shən\ *n*

de•throne \di-ˈthrōn\ *vb* : to remove from a throne : DEPOSE — **de•throne•ment** *n*

det•o•nate \ˈdet-ᵊn-ˌāt\ *vb* **-nat•ed; -nat•ing** : to explode or cause to explode with violence — **det•o•na•tion** \ˌdet-ᵊn-ˈā-shən\ *n*

det•o•na•tor \ˈdet-ᵊn-ˌā-tər\ *n* : a device for detonating an explosive

[1]**de•tour** \ˈdē-ˌtu̇r\ *n* : an indirect way replacing part of a route

[2]**detour** *vb* : to go by detour

de•tox \ˈdē-ˌtäks, di-ˈtäks\ *n* : detoxification from a substance (as alcohol) — **detox** *vb*

de•tox•i•fy \dē-ˈtäk-sə-ˌfī\ *vb* **-fied; -fy•ing 1** : to remove a poison or toxin or the effect of such from **2** : to free (as a drug user) from an intoxicating or addictive substance or from dependence on it — **de•tox•i•fi•ca•tion** \dē-ˌtäk-sə-fə-ˈkā-shən\ *n*

de•tract \di-ˈtrakt\ *vb* **1** : to take away or diminish the value or effect of something **2** : DIVERT — **de•trac•tion** \-ˈtrak-shən\ *n* — **de•trac•tor** \-ˈtrak-tər\ *n*

de•train \dē-ˈtrān\ *vb* : to leave or cause to leave a railroad train

det•ri•ment \ˈde-trə-mənt\ *n* : INJURY, DAMAGE; *also* : a cause of injury or damage — **det•ri•men•tal** \ˌde-trə-ˈment-ᵊl\ *adj* — **det•ri•men•tal•ly** *adv*

de•tri•tus \di-ˈtrī-təs\ *n, pl* **de•tri•tus** : fragments resulting from disintegration (as of rocks) : DEBRIS

deuce \ˈdüs, ˈdyüs\ *n* **1** : a two in cards or dice **2** : a tie in a tennis game with both sides at 40 **3** : DEVIL — used chiefly as a mild oath

Deut *abbr* Deuteronomy

deu•te•ri•um \dü-ˈtir-ē-əm, dyü-\ *n* : an isotope of hydrogen that has twice the mass of ordinary hydrogen

Deu•ter•on•o•my \ˌdü-tə-ˈrä-nə-mē, ˌdyü-\ *n* — see BIBLE table

deut•sche mark \ˈdȯi-chə-ˌmärk\ *n* — see MONEY table

dev *abbr* deviation

de•val•ue \dē-ˈval-yü\ *vb* : to reduce the international exchange value of ⟨~ a currency⟩ — **de•val•u•a•tion** \-ˌval-yə-ˈwā-shən\ *n*

dev•as•tate \ˈde-və-ˌstāt\ *vb* **-tat•ed; -tat•ing 1** : to bring to ruin **2** : to reduce to chaos or helplessness — **dev•as•ta•tion** \ˌde-və-ˈstā-shən\ *n*

de•vel•op \di-ˈve-ləp\ *vb* **1** : to unfold gradually or in detail **2** : to place (exposed photographic material) in chemicals to produce a visible image **3** : to bring out the possibilities of **4** : to make more available or usable ⟨~ land⟩ **5** : to acquire gradually ⟨~ a taste for olives⟩ **6** : to go through a natural process of growth, differentiation, or evolution **7** : to come into being gradually — **de•vel•op•er** *n* — **de•vel•op•ment** *n* — **de•vel•op•men•tal** \-ˌve-ləp-ˈment-ᵊl\ *adj*

de•vi•ant \ˈdē-vē-ənt\ *adj* : deviating esp. from some accepted norm ⟨~ behavior⟩ — **de•vi•ance** \-əns\ *n* — **de•vi•an•cy** \-ən-sē\ *n* — **deviant** *n*

de•vi•ate \ˈdē-vē-ˌāt\ *vb* **-at•ed; -at•ing** [LL *deviare*, fr. L *de-* from + *via* way] : to turn aside from a course, standard, principle, or topic — **de•vi•ate** \-vē-ət, -vē-ˌāt\ *n* — **de•vi•a•tion** \ˌdē-vē-ˈā-shən\ *n*

de•vice \di-ˈvīs\ *n* **1** : SCHEME, STRATAGEM **2** : a piece of equipment or a mechanism for a special purpose **3** : DESIRE, INCLINATION ⟨left to my own ~s⟩ **4** : an emblematic design

[1]**dev•il** \ˈde-vəl\ *n* [ME *devel*, fr. OE *dēofol*, fr. LL *diabolus*, fr. Gk *diabolos*, lit., slanderer, fr. *diaballein* to throw across, slander, fr. *dia-* across + *ballein* to throw] **1** *often cap* : the personal supreme spirit of

evil **2** : DEMON **3** : a wicked person **4** : an energetic, reckless, or dashing person **5** : FELLOW ⟨poor ~⟩ ⟨lucky ~⟩

²devil *vb* **-iled** *or* **-illed; -il•ing** *or* **-il•ling 1** : to season highly ⟨~*ed* eggs⟩ **2** : TEASE, ANNOY

dev•il•ish \ˈde-və-lish\ *adj* **1** : befitting a devil : EVIL; *also* : MISCHIEVOUS **2** : EXTREME — **dev•il•ish•ly** *adv* — **dev•il•ish•ness** *n*

dev•il•ment \ˈde-vəl-mənt, -ˌment\ *n* : MISCHIEF

dev•il•ry \-rē\ *or* **dev•il•try** \-trē\ *n, pl* **-il•ries** *or* **-il•tries 1** : action performed with the help of the devil **2** : MISCHIEF

de•vi•ous \ˈdē-vē-əs\ *adj* **1** : deviating from a straight line : ROUNDABOUT **2** : ERRANT 3 **3** : TRICKY, CUNNING

¹de•vise \di-ˈvīz\ *vb* **de•vised; de•vis•ing 1** : INVENT **2** : PLOT **3** : to give (real estate) by will

²devise *n* **1** : a disposing of real property by will **2** : a will or clause of a will disposing of real property **3** : property given by will

de•vi•tal•ize \dē-ˈvīt-ᵊl-ˌīz\ *vb* : to deprive of life or vitality

de•void \di-ˈvȯid\ *adj* : being without : VOID ⟨a book ~ of interest⟩

de•voir \də-ˈvwär\ *n* **1** : DUTY **2** : a formal act of civility or respect

de•volve \di-ˈvälv\ *vb* **de•volved; de•volv•ing** : to pass (as rights or responsibility) from one to another usu. by succession or transmission — **dev•o•lu•tion** \ˌde-və-ˈlü-shən, ˌdē-\ *n*

De•vo•ni•an \di-ˈvō-nē-ən\ *adj* : of, relating to, or being the period of the Paleozoic era between the Silurian and the Mississippian — **Devonian** *n*

de•vote \di-ˈvōt\ *vb* **de•vot•ed; de•vot•ing 1** : to commit to wholly or chiefly **2** : to set apart for a special purpose : DEDICATE

de•vot•ed \-ˈvō-təd\ *adj* : characterized by loyalty and devotion : FAITHFUL

dev•o•tee \ˌde-və-ˈtē, -ˈtā\ *n* : an ardent follower, supporter, or enthusiast

de•vo•tion \di-ˈvō-shən\ *n* **1** : religious fervor **2** : an act of prayer or private worship — usu. used in pl. **3** : a religious exercise for private use **4** : the fact or state of being dedicated and loyal ⟨~ to music⟩; *also* : the act of devoting — **de•vo•tion•al** \-shə-nəl\ *adj*

de•vour \di-ˈvau̇r\ *vb* **1** : to eat up greedily or ravenously **2** : WASTE, ANNIHILATE **3** : to enjoy avidly ⟨~ a book⟩ — **de•vour•er** *n*

de•vout \di-ˈvau̇t\ *adj* **1** : devoted to religion : PIOUS **2** : expressing devotion or piety **3** : EARNEST, SERIOUS — **de•vout•ly** *adv* — **de•vout•ness** *n*

dew \ˈdü, ˈdyü\ *n* : moisture that condenses on the surfaces of cool bodies at night — **dewy** *adj*

dew•ber•ry \ˈdü-ˌber-ē, ˈdyü-\ *n* : any of several sweet edible berries related to and resembling blackberries; *also* : a trailing bramble bearing these

dew•claw \-ˌklȯ\ *n* : a digit on the foot of a mammal that does not reach the ground; *also* : its claw or hoof

dew•lap \-ˌlap\ *n* : loose skin hanging under the neck of an animal

dew point *n* : the temperature at which the moisture in the air begins to condense

dex•ter•i•ty \dek-ˈster-ə-tē\ *n, pl* **-ties 1** : mental skill or quickness **2** : readiness and grace in physical activity; *esp* : skill and ease in using the hands

dex•ter•ous \ˈdek-strəs\ *adj* **1** : CLEVER **2** : done with skillfulness **3** : skillful and competent with the hands — **dex•ter•ous•ly** *adv*

dex•trose \ˈdek-ˌstrōs\ *n* : the naturally occurring form of glucose found in plants and blood

DFC *abbr* Distinguished Flying Cross

dg *abbr* decigram

DG *abbr* **1** [LL *Dei gratia*] by the grace of God **2** director general

DH \ˌdē-ˈāch\ *n* : DESIGNATED HITTER

dhow \ˈdau̇\ *n* : an Arab sailing ship usu. having a long overhang forward and a high poop

DI *abbr* drill instructor

dia *abbr* diameter

di•a•be•tes \ˌdī-ə-ˈbē-tēz, -təs\ *n* : an abnormal state marked by passage of excessive amounts of urine; *esp* : one (**diabetes mel•li•tus** \-ˈme-lə-təs\) characterized by deficient insulin, by excess sugar in the blood and urine, and by thrist, hunger, and loss of weight — **di•a•bet•ic** \-ˈbe-tik\ *adj or n*

di•a•bol•ic \ˌdī-ə-ˈbä-lik\ *or* **di•a•bol•i•cal** \-li-kəl\ *adj* : DEVILISH, FIENDISH — **di•a•bol•i•cal•ly** \-k(ə-)lē\ *adv*

di•a•crit•ic \ˌdī-ə-ˈkri-tik\ *n* : a mark accompanying a letter and indicating a sound value different from that of the same letter when unmarked — **di•a•crit•i•cal** \-ti-kəl\ *adj*

di•a•dem \ˈdī-ə-ˌdem\ *n* : CROWN; *esp* : a royal headband

di•aer•e•sis \dī-ˈer-ə-səs\ *n, pl* **-e•ses** \-ˌsēz\ : a mark ¨ placed over a vowel to show that it is pronounced in a separate syllable (as in *naïve*)

diag *abbr* **1** diagonal **2** diagram

di•ag•no•sis \ˌdī-ig-ˈnō-səs\ *n, pl* **-no•ses** \-ˌsēz\ : the art or act of identifying a disease from its signs and symptoms; *also* : the decision reached by diagnosis — **di•ag•nose** \ˈdī-ig-ˌnōs\ *vb* — **di•ag•nos•tic** \ˌdī-ig-ˈnäs-tik\ *adj* — **di•ag•nos•ti•cian** \-ˌnäs-ˈti-shən\ *n*

¹di•ag•o•nal \dī-ˈa-gə-nəl\ *adj* **1** : extending from one corner to the opposite corner in a 4-sided figure **2** : running in a slanting direction ⟨~ stripes⟩ **3** : having slanting markings or parts ⟨a ~ weave⟩ — **di•ag•o•nal•ly** *adv*

²diagonal *n* **1** : a diagonal line **2** : a diagonal row, pattern, or direction **3** : a mark / used esp. to mean "or," "and or," or "per"

¹di•a•gram \ˈdī-ə-ˌgram\ *n* : a design and esp. a drawing that makes something easier to understand — **di•a•gram•ma•ble** \-ˌgra-mə-bəl\ *adj* — **di•a•gram•mat•ic** \ˌdī-ə-grə-ˈma-tik\ *adj* — **di•a•gram•mat•i•cal•ly** \-ti-k(ə-)lē\ *adv*

²diagram *vb* **-grammed** *or* **-gramed** \-ˌgramd\; **-gram•ming** *or* **-gram•ing** : to represent by a diagram

¹di•al \ˈdī(-ə)l\ *n* [ME *dyal,* fr. ML *dialis* clock wheel revolving daily, fr. L *dies* day] **1** : the face of a sundial **2** : the face of a timepiece **3** : a face with a pointer and numbers that indicate something ⟨the ~ of a gauge⟩ **4** : a device used for making electrical connections or for regulating operation (as of a radio)

²dial *vb* **di•aled** *or* **di•alled; di•al•ing** *or* **di•al•ling 1** : to manipulate a dial so as to operate or select **2** : to make a telephone call or connection

³dial *abbr* dialect

di•a•lect \ˈdī-ə-ˌlekt\ *n* : a regional variety of a language

di•a•lec•tic \ˌdī-ə-ˈlek-tik\ *n* : the process or art of reasoning by discussion of conflicting ideas; *also* : the tension between opposing elements

di•a•logue \ˈdī-ə-ˌlȯg\ *n* **1** : a conversation between two or more parties **2** : the parts of a literary or dramatic work that represent conversation

di•al•y•sis \dī-ˈa-lə-səs\ *n, pl* **-y•ses** \-ˌsēz\ **1** : the separation of substances from solution by means of their unequal diffusion through semipermeable membranes **2** : the medical procedure of removing blood from an artery, purifying it by dialysis, and returning it to a vein

diam *abbr* diameter

di•am•e•ter \dī-ˈa-mə-tər\ *n* [ME *diametre,* fr. MF, fr. L *diametros,* fr. Gk, fr. *dia-* through + *metron* measure] **1** : a straight line passing through the center of a figure or body; *esp* : one that divides a circle in half **2** : the length of a diameter

di•a•met•ric \ˌdī-ə-ˈme-trik\ *or* **di•a•met•ri•cal** \-tri-kəl\ *adj* **1** : of, relating to, or constituting a diameter **2** : completely opposed or opposite — **di•a•met•ri•cal•ly** \-k(ə-)lē\ *adv*

di•a•mond \ˈdī-mənd, ˈdī-ə-\ *n* **1** : a hard brilliant mineral that consists of crystalline carbon and is used as a gem **2 :** a flat figure having four equal sides, two acute angles, and two obtuse angles **3 :** any of a suit of playing cards marked with a red diamond **4 :** INFIELD; *also* **:** the entire playing field in baseball

di·a·mond·back rattlesnake \-ˌbak-\ *n* **:** a large and deadly rattlesnake of the southern U.S.

di·an·thus \dī-ˈan-thəs\ *n* **:** [1]PINK 1

di·a·pa·son \ˌdī-ə-ˈpāz-ᵊn, -ˈpās-\ *n* **1 :** the organ stop governing the flue pipes that form the primary basis of organ tone **2 :** the entire range of musical tones

[1]**di·a·per** \ˈdī-pər, ˈdī-ə-\ *n* **1 :** a cotton or linen fabric woven in a simple geometric pattern **2 :** a garment for a baby drawn up between the legs and fastened about the waist

[2]**diaper** *vb* **1 :** to ornament with diaper designs **2 :** to put a diaper on

di·aph·a·nous \dī-ˈa-fə-nəs\ *adj* **:** of so fine a texture as to be transparent

di·a·pho·ret·ic \ˌdī-ə-fə-ˈre-tik\ *adj* **:** having the power to increase perspiration — **diaphoretic** *n*

di·a·phragm \ˈdī-ə-ˌfram\ *n* **1 :** a sheet of muscle between the chest and abdominal cavities of a mammal **2 :** a vibrating disk (as in a microphone) **3 :** a cup-shaped device usu. of thin rubber fitted over the uterine cervix to act as a mechanical contraceptive barrier — **di·a·phrag·mat·ic** \ˌdī-ə-frəg-ˈma-tik, -ˌfrag-\ *adj*

di·a·rist \ˈdī-ə-rist\ *n* **:** one who keeps a diary

di·ar·rhea \ˌdī-ə-ˈrē-ə\ *n* **:** abnormally frequent and watery bowel movements

di·ar·rhoea *chiefly Brit var of* DIARRHEA

di·a·ry \ˈdī-ə-rē\ *n, pl* **-ries :** a daily record esp. of personal experiences; *also* **:** a book used as a diary

di·as·to·le \dī-ˈas-tə-(ˌ)lē\ *n* **:** the stretching of the chambers of the heart during which they fill with blood — **di·a·stol·ic** \ˌdī-ə-ˈstä-lik\ *adj*

dia·ther·my \ˈdī-ə-ˌthər-mē\ *n* **:** the generation of heat in tissue by electric currents for medical or surgical purposes

di·a·tom \ˈdī-ə-ˌtäm\ *n* **:** any of a class of planktonic one-celled or colonial algae with skeletons of silica

di·atom·ic \ˌdī-ə-ˈtä-mik\ *adj* **:** having two atoms in the molecule

di·a·tribe \ˈdī-ə-ˌtrīb\ *n* **:** biting or abusive speech or writing

dib·ble \ˈdi-bəl\ *n* **:** a pointed hand tool for making holes (as for planting bulbs) in the ground — **dibble** *vb*

[1]**dice** \ˈdīs\ *n, pl* **dice :** DIE 1

[2]**dice** *vb* **diced; dic·ing 1 :** to cut into small cubes ⟨~ carrots⟩ **2 :** to play games with dice

di·chot·o·my \dī-ˈkä-tə-mē\ *n, pl* **-mies :** a division or the process of dividing into two esp. mutually exclusive or contradictory groups — **di·chot·o·mous** \-məs\ *adj*

dick·er \ˈdi-kər\ *vb* **:** BARGAIN, HAGGLE

dick·ey *or* **dicky** \ˈdi-kē\ *n, pl* **dickeys** *or* **dick·ies :** a small fabric insert worn to fill in the neckline

di·cot·y·le·don \ˌdī-ˌkät-ᵊl-ˈēd-ᵊn\ *n* **:** any of a group of seed plants having an embryo with two cotyledons — **di·cot·y·le·don·ous** *adj*

dict *abbr* dictionary

[1]**dic·tate** \ˈdik-ˌtāt\ *vb* **dic·tat·ed; dic·tat·ing 1 :** to speak or read for a person to transcribe or for a machine to record **2 :** COMMAND, ORDER — **dic·ta·tion** \dik-ˈtā-shən\ *n*

[2]**dic·tate** \ˈdik-ˌtāt\ *n* **:** an authoritative rule, prescription, or injunction **:** COMMAND ⟨the ~*s* of conscience⟩

dic·ta·tor \ˈdik-ˌtā-tər\ *n* **1 :** a person ruling absolutely and often brutally and oppressively **2 :** one that dictates

dic·ta·to·ri·al \ˌdik-tə-ˈtōr-ē-əl\ *adj* **:** of, relating to, or characteristic of a dictator or a dictatorship

dic·ta·tor·ship \dik-ˈtā-tər-ˌship, ˈdik-ˌtā-\ *n* **1 :** the office of a dictator **2 :** autocratic rule, control, or leadership **3 :** a government or country in which absolute power is held by a dictator or a small clique

dic·tion \ˈdik-shən\ *n* **1 :** choice of words esp. with regard to correctness, clearness, or effectiveness **:** WORDING **2 :** ENUNCIATION

dic·tio·nary \ˈdik-shə-ˌner-ē\ *n, pl* **-nar·ies :** a reference book containing words usu. alphabetically arranged along with information about their forms, pronunciations, functions, etymologies, meanings, and syntactical and idiomatic uses

dic·tum \ˈdik-təm\ *n, pl* **dic·ta** \-tə\ *also* **dictums :** a noteworthy, formal, or authoritative statement or observation

did *past of* DO

di·dac·tic \dī-ˈdak-tik\ *adj* **1 :** intended to instruct, inform, or teach a moral lesson **2 :** making moral observations

di·do \ˈdī-dō\ *n, pl* **didoes** *or* **didos :** a mischievous act **:** PRANK

[1]**die** \ˈdī\ *vb* **died; dy·ing** \ˈdī-iŋ\ **1 :** to stop living **:** EXPIRE **2 :** to pass out of existence ⟨a *dying* race⟩ **3 :** SUBSIDE 4 ⟨the wind *died* down⟩ **4 :** to long keenly ⟨*dying* to go⟩ **5 :** STOP ⟨the motor *died*⟩

[2]**die** \ˈdī\ *n* **1** *pl* **dice** \ˈdīs\ **:** a small cube marked on each face with one to six spots and used usu. in pairs in games and gambling **2** *pl* **dies** \ˈdīz\ **:** a device used to shape, finish, or impress an object

die·hard \ˈdī-ˌhärd\ *n* **:** one who is strongly devoted or determined

die·sel \ˈdē-zəl, -səl\ *n* **1 :** DIESEL ENGINE **2 :** a vehicle driven by a diesel engine

diesel engine *n* **:** an internal combustion engine in whose cylinders air is compressed to a temperature sufficiently high to ignite the fuel

die·sel·ing \ˈdē-zə-liŋ\ *n* **:** the continued operation of an internal combustion engine after the ignition has been turned off

[1]**di·et** \ˈdī-ət\ *n* [ME *diete,* fr. OF, fr. L *diaeta,* fr. Gk *diaita,* lit., manner of living, fr. *diaitasthai* to lead one's life] **1 :** food and drink regularly consumed **:** FARE **2 :** an allowance of food prescribed for a special reason (as to lose weight) — **di·e·tary** \-ə-ˌter-ē\ *adj or n*

[2]**diet** *vb* **:** to eat or cause to eat or drink less or according to a prescribed rule — **di·et·er** *n*

di·e·tet·ics \ˌdī-ə-ˈte-tiks\ *n sing or pl* **:** the science or art of applying the principles of nutrition to diet — **di·e·tet·ic** *adj*

di·e·ti·tian *or* **di·e·ti·cian** \ˌdī-ə-ˈti-shən\ *n* **:** a specialist in dietetics

dif *or* **diff** *abbr* difference

dif·fer \ˈdi-fər\ *vb* **dif·fered; dif·fer·ing 1 :** to be unlike **2 :** VARY **3 :** DISAGREE

dif·fer·ence \ˈdi-frəns, ˈdi-fə-\ *n* **1 :** UNLIKENESS ⟨~ in their looks⟩ **2 :** distinction or discrimination in preference **3 :** DISAGREEMENT; *also* **:** an instance or cause of disagreement ⟨unable to settle their ~*s*⟩ **4 :** the amount by which one number or quantity differs from another

dif·fer·ent \ˈdi-frənt, ˈdi-fə-\ *adj* **1 :** unlike in nature or quality **2 :** DISTINCT ⟨~ age groups⟩; *also* **:** VARIOUS ⟨~ members of the club⟩ **3 :** ANOTHER ⟨try a ~ channel⟩ **4 :** UNUSUAL, SPECIAL — **dif·fer·ent·ly** *adv*

[1]**dif·fer·en·tial** \ˌdi-fə-ˈren-chəl\ *adj* **:** showing, creating, or relating to a difference

[2]**differential** *n* **1 :** the amount or degree by which things differ **2 :** DIFFERENTIAL GEAR

differential calculus *n* **:** a branch of mathematics concerned with the study of the rate of change of functions with respect to their variables

differential gear *n* **:** an arrangement of gears in an automobile that allows one wheel to turn faster than another (as in rounding curves)

dif·fer·en·ti·ate \ˌdi-fə-ˈren-chē-ˌāt\ *vb* **-at·ed; -at·ing 1 :** to make or become different **2 :** to recognize or state the difference ⟨~ between them⟩ — **dif·fer·en·ti·a·tion** \-ˌren-chē-ˈā-shən\ *n*

dif·fi·cult \ˈdi-fi-(ˌ)kəlt\ *adj* **1** : hard to do or make **2** : hard to understand or deal with ⟨~ reading⟩ ⟨a ~ child⟩

dif·fi·cul·ty \-(ˌ)kəl-tē\ *n, pl* **-ties 1** : difficult nature ⟨the ~ of a task⟩ **2** : DISAGREEMENT ⟨settled their *difficulties*⟩ **3** : OBSTACLE ⟨overcome *difficulties*⟩ **4** : TROUBLE ⟨in financial *difficulties*⟩ **syn** hardship, rigor, vicissitude

dif·fi·dent \ˈdi-fə-dənt\ *adj* **1** : lacking confidence **2** : RESERVED 1 — **dif·fi·dence** \-dəns\ *n* — **dif·fi·dent·ly** *adv*

dif·frac·tion \di-ˈfrak-shən\ *n* : the bending or spreading of waves (as of light) esp. when passing through narrow slits

[1]**dif·fuse** \di-ˈfyüs\ *adj* **1** : VERBOSE, WORDY ⟨~ writing⟩ **2** : not concentrated or localized ⟨~ light⟩

[2]**dif·fuse** \di-ˈfyüz\ *vb* **dif·fused; dif·fus·ing 1** : to pour out or spread widely **2** : to undergo or cause to undergo diffusion **3** : to break up light by diffusion

dif·fu·sion \di-ˈfyü-zhən\ *n* **1** : a diffusing or a being diffused **2** : movement of particles (as of a gas) from a region of high to one of lower concentration **3** : the reflection of light from a rough surface or the passage of light through a translucent material

[1]**dig** \ˈdig\ *vb* **dug** \ˈdəg\; **dig·ging 1** : to turn up the soil (as with a spade) **2** : to hollow out or form by removing earth ⟨~ a hole⟩ **3** : to uncover or seek by turning up earth ⟨~ potatoes⟩ **4** : DISCOVER ⟨~ up information⟩ **5** : POKE, THRUST ⟨~ a person in the ribs⟩ **6** : to work hard **7** : UNDERSTAND, APPRECIATE; *also* : LIKE, ADMIRE

[2]**dig** *n* **1** : THRUST, POKE; *also* : a cutting remark : GIBE **2** *pl* : living accommodations

[3]**dig** *abbr* digest

[1]**di·gest** \ˈdī-ˌjest\ *n* : a summarized or shortened version esp. of a literary work

[2]**di·gest** \dī-ˈjest, də-\ *vb* **1** : to think over and arrange in the mind **2** : to convert (food) into simpler forms that can be absorbed by the body **3** : to compress into a short summary — **di·gest·ibil·i·ty** \-ˌjes-tə-ˈbi-lə-tē\ *n* — **di·gest·ible** *adj* — **di·ges·tion** \-ˈjes-chən\ *n* — **di·ges·tive** \-ˈjes-tiv\ *adj*

dig in *vb* **1** : to take a defensive stand esp. by digging trenches **2** : to firmly set to work **3** : to begin eating

dig·it \ˈdi-jət\ *n* [ME, fr. L *digitus* finger, toe] **1** : any of the Arabic numerals 1 to 9 and usu. the symbol 0 **2** : FINGER, TOE

dig·i·tal \ˈdi-jət-ᵊl\ *adj* **1** : of, relating to, or done with a finger or toe **2** : of, relating to, or using calculation directly with digits rather than through measurable physical quantities ⟨a ~ computer⟩ **3** : providing a readout in numerical digits ⟨a ~ watch⟩ — **dig·i·tal·ly** *adv*

dig·i·tal·is \ˌdi-jə-ˈta-ləs\ *n* : a drug from the common foxglove that is a powerful heart stimulant; *also* : FOXGLOVE

dig·ni·fied \ˈdig-nə-ˌfīd\ *adj* : showing or expressing dignity

dig·ni·fy \-ˌfī\ *vb* **-fied; -fy·ing** : to give dignity, distinction, or attention to

dig·ni·tary \ˈdig-nə-ˌter-ē\ *n, pl* **-tar·ies** : a person of high position or honor

dig·ni·ty \ˈdig-nə-tē\ *n, pl* **-ties 1** : the quality or state of being worthy, honored, or esteemed **2** : high rank, office, or position **3** : formal reserve of manner, language, or appearance

di·graph \ˈdī-ˌgraf\ *n* : a group of two successive letters whose phonetic value is a single sound (as *ea* in *bread*)

di·gress \dī-ˈgres, də-\ *vb* : to turn aside esp. from the main subject or argument — **di·gres·sion** \-ˈgre-shən\ *n* — **di·gres·sive** \-ˈgre-siv\ *adj*

dike \ˈdīk\ *n* : a bank of earth constructed to control water : LEVEE

dil *abbr* dilute

di·lap·i·dat·ed \də-ˈla-pə-ˌdā-təd\ *adj* : fallen into partial ruin or decay — **di·lap·i·da·tion** \-ˌla-pə-ˈdā-shən\ *n*

di·late \dī-ˈlāt, ˈdī-ˌlāt\ *vb* **di·lat·ed; di·lat·ing** : SWELL, DISTEND, EXPAND — **dil·a·ta·tion** \ˌdi-lə-ˈtā-shən\ *n* — **di·la·tion** \dī-ˈlā-shən\ *n*

dil·a·to·ry \ˈdi-lə-ˌtōr-ē\ *adj* **1** : DELAYING **2** : TARDY, SLOW

di·lem·ma \də-ˈle-mə\ *n* **1** : a usu. undesirable or unpleasant choice; *also* : a situation involving such a choice **2** : PREDICAMENT

dil·et·tante \ˌdi-lə-ˈtänt, -ˈtant\ *n, pl* **-tantes** *or* **-tan·ti** \-ˈtän-tē, -ˈtan-\ [It, fr. prp. of *dilettare* to delight, fr. L *dilectare*] : a person having a superficial interest in an art or a branch of knowledge

dil·i·gent \ˈdi-lə-jənt\ *adj* : characterized by steady, earnest, and energetic effort : PAINSTAKING — **dil·i·gence** \-jəns\ *n* — **dil·i·gent·ly** *adv*

dill \ˈdil\ *n* : an herb related to the carrot with aromatic leaves and seeds used in pickles

dil·ly \ˈdi-lē\ *n, pl* **dil·lies** : one that is remarkable or outstanding

dil·ly·dal·ly \ˈdi-lē-ˌda-lē\ *vb* : to waste time by loitering or delaying

[1]**di·lute** \dī-ˈlüt, də-\ *vb* **di·lut·ed; di·lut·ing** : to lessen the consistency or strength of by mixing with something else — **di·lu·tion** \-ˈlü-shən\ *n*

[2]**dilute** *adj* : DILUTED, WEAK

[1]**dim** \ˈdim\ *adj* **dim·mer; dim·mest 1** : LUSTERLESS, DULL **2** : not bright or distinct : OBSCURE, FAINT **3** : not seeing or understanding clearly — **dim·ly** *adv* — **dim·ness** *n*

[2]**dim** *vb* **dimmed; dim·ming 1** : to make or become dim or lusterless **2** : to reduce the light from

[3]**dim** *abbr* **1** dimension **2** diminished **3** diminutive

dime \ˈdīm\ *n* [ME, tenth part, tithe, fr. MF, fr. L *decima*, fr. fem. of *decimus* tenth, fr. *decem* ten] : a U.S. coin worth 1⁄10 dollar

di·men·sion \də-ˈmen-chən, dī-\ *n* **1** : the physical property of length, breadth, or thickness; *also* : a measure of this **2** : EXTENT, SCOPE, PROPORTIONS — usu. used in pl. — **di·men·sion·al** \-ˈmen-chə-nəl\ *adj* — **di·men·sion·al·i·ty** \-ˌmen-chə-ˈna-lə-tē\ *n*

di·min·ish \də-ˈmi-nish\ *vb* **1** : to make less or cause to appear less **2** : BELITTLE **3** : DWINDLE **4** : TAPER — **dim·i·nu·tion** \ˌdi-mə-ˈnü-shən, -ˈnyü-\ *n*

di·min·u·en·do \də-ˌmin-yə-ˈwen-dō\ *adv or adj* : DECRESCENDO

[1]**di·min·u·tive** \də-ˈmin-yə-tiv\ *n* **1** : a diminutive word or affix **2** : a diminutive individual

[2]**diminutive** *adj* **1** : indicating small size and sometimes the state or quality of being lovable, pitiable, or contemptible ⟨the ~ suffixes *-ette* and *-ling*⟩ **2** : extremely small : TINY

dim·i·ty \ˈdi-mə-tē\ *n, pl* **-ties** : a thin usu. corded cotton fabric

dim·mer \ˈdi-mər\ *n* : a device for controlling the amount of light from an electric lighting unit

di·mor·phic \(ˌ)dī-ˈmȯr-fik\ *adj* : occurring in two distinct forms — **di·mor·phism** \-ˌfi-zəm\ *n*

[1]**dim·ple** \ˈdim-pəl\ *n* : a small depression esp. in the cheek or chin

[2]**dimple** *vb* **dim·pled; dim·pling** : to form dimples (as in smiling)

din \ˈdin\ *n* : a loud confused mixture of noises

di·nar \di-ˈnär\ *n* **1** — see MONEY table **2** — see *rial* at MONEY table

dine \ˈdīn\ *vb* **dined; din·ing** [ME, fr. OF *diner*, fr. (assumed) VL *disjejunare* to break one's fast, ultim. fr. L *jejunus* fasting] **1** : to eat dinner **2** : to give a dinner to

din·er \ˈdī-nər\ *n* **1** : one that dines **2** : a railroad dining car **3** : a restaurant usu. resembling a dining car

di·nette \dī-ˈnet\ *n* : an alcove or small room used for dining

din•ghy \ˈdiŋ-ē\ *n, pl* **dinghies 1 :** a small boat **2 :** LIFE RAFT

din•gle \ˈdiŋ-gəl\ *n* **:** a small wooded valley

din•go \ˈdiŋ-gō\ *n, pl* **dingoes :** a reddish brown wild dog of Australia

dingo

din•gus \ˈdiŋ-gəs, -əs\ *n* **:** DOODAD

din•gy \ˈdin-jē\ *adj* **din•gi•er; -est :** DIRTY, DISCOLORED; *also* **:** SHABBY **— din•gi•ness** *n*

din•ky \ˈdiŋ-kē\ *adj* **din•ki•er; -est :** SMALL, INSIGNIFICANT

din•ner \ˈdi-nər\ *n* **:** the main meal of the day; *also* **:** a formal banquet

din•ner•ware \ˈdi-nər-ˌwar\ *n* **:** tableware other than flatware

di•no•fla•gel•late \ˌdī-nō-ˈfla-jə-lət, -ˌlāt\ *n* **:** any of an order of planktonic plantlike unicellular flagellates of which some cause red tide

di•no•saur \ˈdī-nə-ˌsȯr\ *n* [ultim. fr. Gk *deinos* terrifying + *sauros* lizard] **:** any of a group of extinct long-tailed Mesozoic reptiles often of huge size

dint \ˈdint\ *n* **1 :** FORCE ⟨by ~ of sheer grit⟩ **2 :** DENT

di•o•cese \ˈdī-ə-səs, -ˌsēz, -ˌsēs\ *n, pl* **-ces•es** \-sə-səz, -ˌsē-zəz, -ˌsē-səz\ **:** the territorial jurisdiction of a bishop **— di•oc•e•san** \dī-ˈä-sə-sən, ˌdī-ə-ˈsēz-ᵊn\ *adj or n*

di•ode \ˈdī-ˌōd\ *n* **1 :** an electronic device with two electrodes or terminals used esp. as a rectifier

di•ox•in \dī-ˈäk-sən\ *n* **:** a hydrocarbon that occurs esp. as a persistent toxic impurity in herbicides (as Agent Orange)

[1]dip \ˈdip\ *vb* **dipped; dip•ping 1 :** to plunge temporarily or partially under the surface (as of a liquid) **2 :** to thrust in a way to suggest immersion **3 :** to scoop up or out **:** LADLE **4 :** to lower and then raise quickly ⟨~ a flag in salute⟩ **5 :** to drop or slope down esp. suddenly ⟨the moon *dipped* below the crest⟩ **6 :** to decrease moderately and usu. temporarily ⟨prices *dipped*⟩ **7 :** to reach inside or as if inside or below a surface ⟨*dipped* into their savings⟩ **8 :** to delve casually into something; *esp* **:** to read superficially ⟨~ into a book⟩

[2]dip *n* **1 :** an act of dipping; *esp* **:** a short swim **2 :** inclination downward **:** DROP **3 :** something obtained by or used in dipping **4 :** a sauce or soft mixture into which food may be dipped **5 :** a liquid into which something may be dipped (as for cleansing or coloring)

diph•the•ria \dif-ˈthir-ē-ə\ *n* **:** an acute contagious bacterial disease marked by fever and by coating of the air passages with a membrane that interferes with breathing

diph•thong \ˈdif-ˌthȯŋ\ *n* **:** two vowel sounds joined in one syllable to form one speech sound (as *ou* in *out*)

dip•loid \ˈdi-ˌplȯid\ *adj* **:** having the basic chromosome number doubled **— diploid** *n*

di•plo•ma \də-ˈplō-mə\ *n, pl* **diplomas :** an official record of graduation from or of a degree conferred by a school

di•plo•ma•cy \də-ˈplō-mə-sē\ *n* **1 :** the art and practice of conducting negotiations between nations **2 :** TACT

dip•lo•mat \ˈdi-plə-ˌmat\ *n* **:** one employed or skilled in diplomacy **— dip•lo•mat•ic** \ˌdi-plə-ˈma-tik\ *adj*

di•plo•ma•tist \də-ˈplō-mə-tist\ *n* **:** DIPLOMAT

dip•per \ˈdi-pər\ *n* **1 :** any of a genus of birds that are related to the thrushes and are skilled in diving **2 :** something (as a ladle or scoop) that dips or is used for dipping **3** *cap* **:** BIG DIPPER **4** *cap* **:** LITTLE DIPPER

dip•so•ma•nia \ˌdip-sə-ˈmā-nē-ə\ *n* **:** an uncontrollable craving for alcoholic liquors **— dip•so•ma•ni•ac** \-nē-ˌak\ *n*

dip•stick \ˈdip-ˌstik\ *n* **:** a graduated rod for indicating depth

dip•ter•an \ˈdip-tə-rən\ *adj* **:** of, relating to, or being a fly (sense 2) **— dipteran** *n* **— dip•ter•ous** \-rəs\ *adj*

dir *abbr* **1** direction **2** director

dire \ˈdīr\ *adj* **dir•er; dir•est 1 :** very horrible **:** DREADFUL **2 :** warning of disaster **3 :** EXTREME

[1]di•rect \də-ˈrekt, dī-\ *vb* **1 :** ADDRESS ⟨~ a letter⟩; *also* **:** to impart orally **:** AIM ⟨~ a remark to the gallery⟩ **2 :** to regulate the activities or course of **:** guide the supervision, organizing, or performance of **3 :** to cause to turn, move, or point or to follow a certain course **4 :** to point, extend, or project in a specified line or course **5 :** to request or instruct with authority **6 :** to show or point out the way

[2]direct *adj* **1 :** stemming immediately from a source ⟨~ result⟩ **2 :** being or passing in a straight line of descent **:** LINEAL ⟨~ ancestor⟩ **3 :** leading from one point to another in time or space without turn or stop **:** STRAIGHT **4 :** NATURAL, STRAIGHTFORWARD ⟨a ~ manner⟩ **5 :** operating without an intervening agency or step ⟨~ action⟩ **6 :** effected by the action of the people or the electorate and not by representatives ⟨~ democracy⟩ **7 :** consisting of or reproducing the exact words of a speaker or writer **— direct** *adv* **— di•rect•ly** *adv* **— di•rect•ness** *n*

direct current *n* **:** an electric current flowing in one direction only

di•rec•tion \də-ˈrek-shən, dī-\ *n* **1 :** MANAGEMENT, GUIDANCE **2 :** COMMAND, ORDER, INSTRUCTION **3 :** the course or line along which something moves, lies, or points **4 :** TENDENCY, TREND **— di•rec•tion•al** \-shə-nəl\ *adj*

di•rec•tive \də-ˈrek-tiv, dī-\ *n* **:** something that directs and usu. impels toward an action or goal; *esp* **:** an order issued by a high-level body or official

direct mail *n* **:** printed matter used for soliciting business or contributions and mailed direct to individuals

di•rec•tor \də-ˈrek-tər, dī-\ *n* **1 :** one that directs **:** MANAGER, SUPERVISOR, CONDUCTOR **2 :** one of a group of persons who direct the affairs of an organized body **— di•rec•to•ri•al** \-ˌrek-ˈtōr-ē-əl\ *adj* **— di•rec•tor•ship** *n*

di•rec•tor•ate \-tə-rət\ *n* **1 :** the office or position of director **2 :** a board of directors; *also* **:** membership on such a board **3 :** an executive staff

di•rec•to•ry \-tə-rē\ *n, pl* **-ries :** an alphabetical or classified list esp. of names and addresses

dire•ful \ˈdīr-fəl\ *adj* **:** DREADFUL; *also* **:** OMINOUS

dirge \ˈdərj\ *n* **:** a song of lamentation; *also* **:** a slow mournful piece of music

dir•ham \ˈdir-həm\ *n* **1** — see MONEY table **2** — see *dinar, riyal* at MONEY table

di•ri•gi•ble \ˈdir-ə-jə-bəl, də-ˈri-jə-\ *n* **:** AIRSHIP

dirk \ˈdərk\ *n* **:** DAGGER 1

dirndl \ˈdərnd-ᵊl\ *n* [short for G *Dirndlkleid,* fr. G dial. *Dirndl* girl + G *Kleid* dress] **:** a full skirt with a tight waistband

dirt \ˈdərt\ *n* **1 :** a filthy or soiling substance (as mud, dust, or grime) **2 :** loose or packed earth **:** SOIL **3 :** moral uncleanness **4 :** scandalous gossip **5 :** embarrassing or incriminating information

[1]dirty \ˈdər-tē\ *adj* **dirt•i•er; -est 1 :** SOILED, FILTHY **2 :** INDECENT, SMUTTY ⟨~ jokes⟩ **3 :** BASE, UNFAIR ⟨a ~ trick⟩ **4 :** STORMY, FOGGY ⟨~ weather⟩ **5 :** not clear in color **:** DULL ⟨a ~ red⟩ **— dirt•i•ness** *n* **— dirty** *adv*

[2]dirty *vb* **dirt•ied; dirty•ing :** to make or become dirty

dis•able \di-ˈsā-bəl\ *vb* **dis•abled; dis•abling 1 :** to disqualify legally **2 :** to make unable to perform by or as if by illness, injury, or malfunction — **dis·abil·i·ty** \ˌdi-sə-ˈbi-lə-tē\ *n*

dis·abled *adj* **:** incapacitated by illness, injury, or wounds; *also* **:** physically or mentally impaired

dis·abuse \ˌdi-sə-ˈbyüz\ *vb* **:** to free from error, fallacy, or misconception

dis·ad·van·tage \ˌdi-səd-ˈvan-tij\ *n* **1 :** loss or damage esp. to reputation or finances **2 :** an unfavorable, inferior, or prejudicial condition; *also* **:** HANDICAP — **dis·ad·van·ta·geous** \di-ˌsad-ˌvan-ˈtā-jəs, -vən-\ *adj*

dis·ad·van·taged \-tijd\ *adj* **:** lacking in basic resources or conditions believed necessary for an equal position in society

dis·af·fect \ˌdi-sə-ˈfekt\ *vb* **:** to alienate the affection or loyalty of — **dis·af·fec·tion** \-ˈfek-shən\ *n*

dis·agree \ˌdi-sə-ˈgrē\ *vb* **1 :** to fail to agree **2 :** to differ in opinion **3 :** to cause discomfort or distress ⟨fried foods ~ with her⟩ — **dis·agree·ment** *n*

dis·agree·able \-ə-bəl\ *adj* **1 :** causing discomfort **:** UNPLEASANT, OFFENSIVE **2 :** ILL-TEMPERED, PEEVISH — **dis·agree·able·ness** *n* — **dis·agree·ably** \-blē\ *adv*

dis·al·low \ˌdi-sə-ˈlau̇\ *vb* **:** to refuse to admit or recognize **:** REJECT ⟨~ a claim⟩ — **dis·al·low·ance** *n*

dis·ap·pear \ˌdi-sə-ˈpir\ *vb* **1 :** to pass out of sight **2 :** to cease to be **:** become lost — **dis·ap·pear·ance** *n*

dis·ap·point \ˌdi-sə-ˈpȯint\ *vb* **:** to fail to fulfill the expectation or hope of — **dis·ap·point·ment** *n*

dis·ap·pro·ba·tion \di-ˌsa-prə-ˈbā-shən\ *n* **:** DISAPPROVAL

dis·ap·prov·al \ˌdi-sə-ˈprü-vəl\ *n* **:** adverse judgment **:** CENSURE

dis·ap·prove \-ˈprüv\ *vb* **1 :** CONDEMN **2 :** to feel or express disapproval ⟨~*s* of smoking⟩ **3 :** REJECT

dis·arm \di-ˈsärm\ *vb* **1 :** to take arms or weapons from **2 :** to reduce the size and strength of the armed forces of a country **3 :** to make harmless, peaceable, or friendly **:** win over ⟨a ~*ing* smile⟩ — **dis·ar·ma·ment** \-ˈsär-mə-mənt\ *n*

dis·ar·range \ˌdi-sə-ˈrānj\ *vb* **:** to disturb the arrangement or order of — **dis·ar·range·ment** *n*

dis·ar·ray \-ˈrā\ *n* **1 :** DISORDER, CONFUSION **2 :** disorderly or careless dress

dis·as·sem·ble \ˌdi-sə-ˈsem-bəl\ *vb* **:** to take apart

dis·as·so·ci·ate \-ˈsō-shē-ˌāt, -sē-\ *vb* **:** to detach from association

di·sas·ter \di-ˈzas-tər, -ˈsas-\ *n* [MF *desastre,* fr. It *disastro,* fr. *astro* star, fr. L *astrum*] **:** a sudden or great misfortune — **di·sas·trous** \-ˈzas-trəs\ *adj* — **di·sas·trous·ly** *adv*

dis·avow \ˌdi-sə-ˈvau̇\ *vb* **:** to deny responsibility for **:** REPUDIATE — **dis·avow·al** \-ˈvau̇-əl\ *n*

dis·band \dis-ˈband\ *vb* **:** to break up the organization of **:** DISPERSE

dis·bar \dis-ˈbär\ *vb* **:** to expel from the legal profession — **dis·bar·ment** *n*

dis·be·lieve \ˌdis-bə-ˈlēv\ *vb* **1 :** to hold not worthy of belief **:** not believe **2 :** to withhold or reject belief — **dis·be·lief** \-ˈlēf\ *n* — **dis·be·liev·er** *n*

dis·bur·den \dis-ˈbərd-ᵊn\ *vb* **:** to rid of a burden

dis·burse \dis-ˈbərs\ *vb* **dis·bursed; dis·burs·ing 1 :** to pay out **:** EXPEND **2 :** DISTRIBUTE — **dis·burse·ment** *n*

[1]disc *var of* DISK

[2]disc *abbr* discount

dis·card \dis-ˈkärd, ˈdis-ˌkärd\ *vb* **1 :** to let go a playing card from one's hand; *also* **:** to play (a card) from a suit other than a trump but different from the one led **2 :** to get rid of as unwanted — **dis·card** \ˈdis-ˌkärd\ *n*

disc brake *n* **:** a brake that operates by the friction of a pair of plates pressing against the sides of a rotating disc

dis·cern \di-ˈsərn, -ˈzərn\ *vb* **1 :** to detect with the eyes **:** DISTINGUISH **2 :** DISCRIMINATE **3 :** to come to know or recognize mentally — **dis·cern·ible** *adj* — **dis·cern·ment** *n*

dis·cern·ing *adj* **:** revealing insight and understanding

[1]dis·charge \dis-ˈchärj, ˈdis-ˌchärj\ *vb* **1 :** to relieve of a charge, load, or burden **:** UNLOAD; *esp* **:** to remove the electrical energy from ⟨~ a storage battery⟩ **2 :** to let or put off ⟨~ passengers⟩ **3 :** SHOOT ⟨~ an arrow⟩ **4 :** to set free ⟨~ a prisoner⟩ **5 :** to dismiss from service or employment ⟨~ a soldier⟩ **6 :** to get rid of by paying or doing ⟨~ a debt⟩ **7 :** to give forth fluid ⟨the river ~*s* into the ocean⟩

[2]dis·charge \ˈdis-ˌchärj, dis-ˈchärj\ *n* **1 :** the act of discharging, unloading, or releasing **2 :** something that discharges; *esp* **:** a certification of release or payment **3 :** a firing off (as of a gun) **4 :** a flowing out (as of blood from a wound); *also* **:** something that is emitted ⟨a purulent ~⟩ **5 :** release or dismissal esp. from an office or employment; *also* **:** complete separation from military service **6 :** a flow of electricity (as through a gas)

dis·ci·ple \di-ˈsī-pəl\ *n* **1 :** one who accepts and helps to spread the teachings of another; *also* **:** a convinced adherent **2** *cap* **:** a member of the Disciples of Christ

dis·ci·pli·nar·i·an \ˌdi-sə-plə-ˈner-ē-ən\ *n* **:** one who enforces order

dis·ci·plin·ary \ˈdi-sə-plə-ˌner-ē\ *adj* **:** of or relating to discipline; *also* **:** CORRECTIVE ⟨take ~ action⟩

[1]dis·ci·pline \ˈdi-sə-plən\ *n* **1 :** PUNISHMENT **2 :** a field of study **:** SUBJECT **3 :** training that corrects, molds, or perfects **4 :** control gained by obedience or training **:** orderly conduct **5 :** a system of rules governing conduct

[2]discipline *vb* **-plined; -plin·ing 1 :** PUNISH **2 :** to train or develop by instruction and exercise esp. in self-control **3 :** to bring under control ⟨~ troops⟩; *also* **:** to impose order upon

disc jockey *n* **:** an announcer of a radio show of popular recorded music

dis·claim \dis-ˈklām\ *vb* **:** DENY, DISAVOW — **dis·claim·er** *n*

dis·close \dis-ˈklōz\ *vb* **:** to expose to view — **dis·clo·sure** \-ˈklō-zhər\ *n*

dis·co \ˈdis-kō\ *n, pl* **discos 1 :** a nightclub for dancing to live or recorded music **2 :** popular dance music characterized by hypnotic rhythm, repetitive lyrics, and electronically produced sounds

dis·col·or \dis-ˈkə-lər\ *vb* **:** to alter or change in hue or color esp. for the worse — **dis·col·or·ation** \-ˌkə-lə-ˈrā-shən\ *n*

dis·com·bob·u·late \ˌdis-kəm-ˈbä-byu̇-ˌlāt\ *vb* **-lat·ed; -lat·ing :** UPSET, CONFUSE

dis·com·fit \dis-ˈkəm-fət, *esp Southern* ˌdis-kəm-ˈfit\ *vb* **:** UPSET, FRUSTRATE — **dis·com·fi·ture** \dis-ˈkəm-fə-ˌchu̇r\ *n*

[1]dis·com·fort \dis-ˈkəm-fərt\ *vb* **:** to make uncomfortable or uneasy

[2]discomfort *n* **:** mental or physical uneasiness

dis·com·mode \ˌdis-kə-ˈmōd\ *vb* **-mod·ed; -mod·ing :** INCONVENIENCE, TROUBLE

dis·com·pose \-kəm-ˈpōz\ *vb* **1 :** AGITATE **2 :** DISARRANGE — **dis·com·po·sure** \-ˈpō-zhər\ *n*

dis·con·cert \ˌdis-kən-ˈsərt\ *vb* **:** CONFUSE, UPSET

dis·con·nect \ˌdis-kə-ˈnekt\ *vb* **:** to undo the connection of — **dis·con·nec·tion** \-ˈnek-shən\ *n*

dis·con·nect·ed *adj* **:** not connected; *also* **:** INCOHERENT — **dis·con·nect·ed·ly** *adv*

dis·con·so·late \dis-ˈkän-sə-lət\ *adj* **1 :** CHEERLESS **2 :** hopelessly sad — **dis·con·so·late·ly** *adv*

dis·con·tent \ˌdis-kən-ˈtent\ *n* **:** uneasiness of mind **:** DISSATISFACTION — **dis·con·tent·ed** *adj*

dis·con·tin·ue \ˌdis-kən-ˈtin-yü\ *vb* **1 :** to break the continuity of **:** cease to operate, use, or take **2 :** END — **dis·con·tin·u·ance** \-yə-wəns\ *n* — **dis·con·ti·nu·i·ty** \dis-ˌkän-tə-ˈnü-ə-tē, -ˈnyü-\ *n* — **dis·con·tin·u·ous** \ˌdis-kən-ˈtin-yə-wəs\ *adj*

dis·cord \ˈdis-ˌkȯrd\ *n* **1 :** lack of agreement or harmony : DISSENSION, CONFLICT **2** : a harsh combination of musical sounds **3** : a harsh or unpleasant sound — **dis•cor•dant** \dis-ˈkȯrd-ᵊnt\ *adj* — **dis•cor•dant•ly** *adv*

dis•co•theque \ˈdis-kə-ˌtek\ *n* : DISCO 1

[1]**dis•count** \ˈdis-ˌkau̇nt\ *n* **1** : a reduction made from a regular or list price **2** : a deduction of interest in advance when lending money

[2]**dis•count** \ˈdis-ˌkau̇nt, dis-ˈkau̇nt\ *vb* **1** : to deduct from the amount of a bill, debt, or charge usu. for cash or prompt payment; *also* : to sell or offer for sale at a discount **2** : to lend money after deducting the discount ⟨~ a note⟩ **3** : DISREGARD; *also* : MINIMIZE **4** : to make allowance for bias or exaggeration **5** : to take into account (as a future event) in present calculations — **dis•count•able** *adj* — **dis•count•er** *n*

[3]**dis•count** \ˈdis-ˌkau̇nt\ *adj* : selling goods or services at a discount; *also* : sold at or reflecting a discount

dis•coun•te•nance \dis-ˈkau̇nt-ᵊn-əns\ *vb* **1** : EMBARRASS, DISCONCERT **2** : to look with disfavor on

dis•cour•age \dis-ˈkər-ij\ *vb* **-aged; -ag•ing 1** : to deprive of courage or confidence : DISHEARTEN **2** : to hinder by disfavoring **3** : to attempt to dissuade — **dis•cour•age•ment** *n* — **dis•cour•ag•ing•ly** *adv*

[1]**dis•course** \ˈdis-ˌkōrs\ *n* [ME *discours,* fr. ML & LL *discursus;* ML, argument, fr. LL, conversation, fr. L, act of running about, fr. *discurrere* to run about, fr. *currere* to run] **1** : CONVERSATION **2** : formal and usu. extended expression of thought on a subject

[2]**dis•course** \dis-ˈkōrs\ *vb* **dis•coursed; dis•cours•ing 1** : to express oneself in esp. oral discourse **2** : TALK, CONVERSE

dis•cour•te•ous \(ˌ)dis-ˈkər-tē-əs\ *adj* : lacking courtesy : UNCIVIL, RUDE — **dis•cour•te•ous•ly** *adv*

dis•cour•te•sy \-ˈkər-tə-sē\ *n* : RUDENESS; *also* : a rude act

dis•cov•er \dis-ˈkə-vər\ *vb* **1** : to make known or visible **2** : to obtain sight or knowledge of for the first time; *also* : FIND OUT — **dis•cov•er•er** *n*

dis•cov•ery \dis-ˈkə-və-rē\ *n, pl* **-er•ies 1** : the act or process of discovering **2** : something discovered **3** : the disclosure usu. before a civil trial of pertinent facts or documents

[1]**dis•cred•it** \(ˌ)dis-ˈkre-dət\ *vb* **1** : DISBELIEVE **2** : to cause disbelief in the accuracy or authority of **3** : DISGRACE — **dis•cred•it•able** *adj*

[2]**discredit** *n* **1** : loss of reputation **2** : lack or loss of belief or confidence

dis•creet \dis-ˈkrēt\ *adj* : showing good judgment; *esp* : capable of observing prudent silence — **dis•creet•ly** *adv*

dis•crep•an•cy \dis-ˈkre-pən-sē\ *n, pl* **-cies 1** : DIFFERENCE, DISAGREEMENT **2** : an instance of being discrepant

dis•crep•ant \-pənt\ *adj* [ME *discrepaunt,* fr. L *discrepans,* prp. of *discrepare* to sound discordantly, fr. *crepare* to rattle, creak] : being at variance : DISAGREEING

dis•crete \dis-ˈkrēt, ˈdis-ˌkrēt\ *adj* **1** : individually distinct **2** : NONCONTINUOUS

dis•cre•tion \dis-ˈkre-shən\ *n* **1** : the quality of being discreet : PRUDENCE **2** : individual choice or judgment **3** : power of free decision or latitude of choice — **dis•cre•tion•ary** *adj*

dis•crim•i•nate \dis-ˈkri-mə-ˌnāt\ *vb* **-nat•ed; -nat•ing 1** : DISTINGUISH, DIFFERENTIATE **2** : to make a difference in treatment on a basis other than individual merit — **dis•crim•i•na•tion** \-ˌkri-mə-ˈnā-shən\ *n*

dis•crim•i•nat•ing *adj* : marked by discrimination; *esp* : DISCERNING, JUDICIOUS

dis•crim•i•na•to•ry \dis-ˈkri-mə-nə-ˌtōr-ē\ *adj* : marked by esp. unjust discrimination ⟨~ treatment⟩

dis•cur•sive \dis-ˈkər-siv\ *adj* : passing from one topic to another : RAMBLING — **dis•cur•sive•ly** *adv* — **dis•cur•sive•ness** *n*

dis•cus \ˈdis-kəs\ *n, pl* **dis•cus•es** : a disk that is hurled for distance in a track-and-field contest

dis•cuss \di-ˈskəs\ *vb* [ME, fr. L *discussus,* pp. of *discutere* to disperse, fr. *dis-* apart + *quatere* to shake] **1** : to argue or consider carefully by presenting the various sides **2** : to talk about — **dis•cus•sion** \-ˈskə-shən\ *n*

dis•cus•sant \di-ˈskəs-ᵊnt\ *n* : one who takes part in a formal discussion

[1]**dis•dain** \dis-ˈdān\ *n* : CONTEMPT, SCORN — **dis•dain•ful** \-fəl\ *adj* — **dis•dain•ful•ly** *adv*

[2]**disdain** *vb* **1** : to look on with scorn **2** : to reject or refrain from because of disdain

dis•ease \di-ˈzēz\ *n* : an abnormal bodily condition that impairs functioning and can usu. be recognized by signs and symptoms : SICKNESS — **dis•eased** \-ˈzēzd\ *adj*

dis•em•bark \ˌdi-səm-ˈbärk\ *vb* : to go or put ashore from a ship — **dis•em•bar•ka•tion** \di-ˌsem-ˌbär-ˈkā-shən\ *n*

dis•em•body \ˌdi-səm-ˈbä-dē\ *vb* : to deprive of bodily existence

dis•em•bow•el \-ˈbau̇-əl\ *vb* : EVISCERATE 1 — **dis•em•bow•el•ment** *n*

dis•en•chant \ˌdis-ᵊn-ˈchant\ *vb* : DISILLUSION — **dis•en•chant•ment** *n*

dis•en•chant•ed \-ˈchan-təd\ *adj* : DISAPPOINTED, DISSATISFIED

dis•en•cum•ber \ˌdis-ᵊn-ˈkəm-bər\ *vb* : to free from something that burdens

dis•en•fran•chise \ˌdis-ᵊn-ˈfran-ˌchīz\ *vb* : DISFRANCHISE — **dis•en•fran•chise•ment** *n*

dis•en•gage \ˌdis-ᵊn-ˈgāj\ *vb* : RELEASE, EXTRICATE, DISENTANGLE — **dis•en•gage•ment** *n*

dis•en•tan•gle \ˌdis-ᵊn-ˈtaŋ-gəl\ *vb* : to free from entanglement : UNRAVEL

dis•equi•lib•ri•um \di-ˌsē-kwə-ˈli-brē-əm\ *n* : loss or lack of equilibrium

dis•es•tab•lish \ˌdi-sə-ˈsta-blish\ *vb* : to end the establishment of; *esp* : to deprive of the status of an established church — **dis•es•tab•lish•ment** *n*

dis•es•teem \ˌdi-sə-ˈstēm\ *n* : lack of esteem : DISFAVOR, DISREPUTE

dis•fa•vor \(ˌ)dis-ˈfā-vər\ *n* **1** : DISAPPROVAL, DISLIKE **2** : the state or fact of being no longer favored

dis•fig•ure \dis-ˈfi-gyər\ *vb* : to spoil the appearance of ⟨*disfigured* by a scar⟩ — **dis•fig•ure•ment** *n*

dis•fran•chise \dis-ˈfran-ˌchīz\ *vb* : to deprive of a franchise, a legal right, or a privilege; *esp* : to deprive of the right to vote — **dis•fran•chise•ment** *n*

dis•gorge \-ˈgȯrj\ *vb* : VOMIT; *also* : to discharge forcefully or confusedly

[1]**dis•grace** \di-ˈskrās, dis-ˈgrās\ *vb* : to bring reproach or shame to

[2]**disgrace** *n* **1** : SHAME, DISHONOR; *also* : a cause of shame **2** : the condition of being out of favor : loss of respect — **dis•grace•ful** \-fəl\ *adj* — **dis•grace•ful•ly** *adv*

dis•grun•tle \dis-ˈgrənt-ᵊl\ *vb* **dis•grun•tled; dis•grun•tling** : to put in bad humor

[1]**dis•guise** \dis-ˈgīz\ *vb* **dis•guised; dis•guis•ing 1** : to change the appearance of to conceal the identity or to resemble another **2** : HIDE, CONCEAL

[2]**disguise** *n* **1** : clothing put on to conceal one's identity or counterfeit another's **2** : an outward appearance that hides what something really is

[1]**dis•gust** \dis-ˈgəst\ *n* : AVERSION, REPUGNANCE — **dis•gust•ful** \-fəl\ *adj*

[2]**disgust** *vb* : to provoke to loathing, repugnance, or aversion : be offensive to — **dis•gust•ed•ly** *adv* — **dis•gust•ing•ly** *adv*

[1]**dish** \ˈdish\ *n* [ME, fr. OE *disc* plate, fr. L *discus* quoit, disk, dish, fr. Gk *diskos,* fr. *dikein* to throw] **1** : a vessel used for serving food **2** : the food served in a dish ⟨a ~ of berries⟩ **3** : food prepared in a partic-

ular way **4 :** something resembling a dish esp. in being shallow and concave

²dish *vb* **1 :** to put into a dish **2 :** to make concave like a dish

dis•ha•bille \ˌdi-sə-ˈbēl\ *n* [F *déshabillé*] **:** the state of being dressed in a casual or careless manner

dis•har•mo•ny \(ˌ)dis-ˈhär-mə-nē\ *n* **:** lack of harmony — **dis•har•mo•ni•ous** \ˌdis-(ˌ)här-ˈmō-nē-əs\ *adj*

dish•cloth \ˈdish-ˌklȯth\ *n* **:** a cloth for washing dishes

dis•heart•en \dis-ˈhärt-ᵊn\ *vb* **:** DISCOURAGE, DEJECT

dished \ˈdisht\ *adj* **:** CONCAVE

di•shev•el \di-ˈshe-vəl\ *vb* **-shev•eled** *or* **-shev•elled; -shev•el•ing** *or* **-shev•el•ling** [ME *discheveled* with disordered hair, fr. MF *deschevelé*, fr. pp. of *descheveler* to disarrange the hair, fr. *chevel* hair, fr. L *capillus*] **:** to throw into disorder or disarray — **di•shev•eled** *or* **di•shev•elled** *adj*

dis•hon•est \di-ˈsä-nəst\ *adj* **:** not honest **:** UNTRUSTWORTHY, DECEITFUL — **dis•hon•est•ly** *adv* — **dis•hon•es•ty** \-nə-stē\ *n*

¹dis•hon•or \di-ˈsä-nər\ *vb* **1 :** DISGRACE **2 :** to refuse to accept or pay ⟨~ a check⟩

²dishonor *n* **1 :** lack or loss of honor **2 :** SHAME, DISGRACE **3 :** a cause of disgrace **4 :** the act of dishonoring a negotiable instrument when presented for payment — **dis•hon•or•able** \di-ˈsä-nə-rə-bəl\ *adj* — **dis•hon•or•ably** \-blē\ *adv*

dish out *vb* **:** to give freely

dish•rag \ˈdish-ˌrag\ *n* **:** DISHCLOTH

dish•wash•er \-ˌwȯ-shər, -ˌwä-\ *n* **:** a person or machine that washes dishes

dish•wa•ter \-ˌwȯ-tər, -ˌwä-\ *n* **:** water used for washing dishes

dis•il•lu•sion \ˌdi-sə-ˈlü-zhən\ *vb* **:** to leave without illusion or naive faith and trust — **dis•il•lu•sion•ment** *n*

dis•il•lu•sioned *adj* **:** DISAPPOINTED, DISSATISFIED

dis•in•cli•na•tion \di-ˌsin-klə-ˈnā-shən\ *n* **:** a preference for avoiding something **:** slight aversion

dis•in•cline \ˌdis-ᵊn-ˈklīn\ *vb* **:** to make unwilling

dis•in•clined *adj* **:** unwilling because of dislike or disapproval

dis•in•fect \ˌdis-ᵊn-ˈfekt\ *vb* **:** to cleanse of infection-causing germs — **dis•in•fec•tant** \-ˈfek-tənt\ *n* — **dis•in•fec•tion** \-ˈfek-shən\ *n*

dis•in•for•ma•tion \-ˌin-fər-ˈmā-shən\ *n* **:** false information deliberately and often covertly spread

dis•in•gen•u•ous \ˌdis-ᵊn-ˈjen-yə-wəs\ *adj* **:** lacking in candor; *also* **:** giving a false appearance of simple frankness

dis•in•her•it \ˌdis-ᵊn-ˈher-ət\ *vb* **:** to deprive of the right to inherit

dis•in•te•grate \di-ˈsin-tə-ˌgrāt\ *vb* **1 :** to break or decompose into constituent parts or small particles **2 :** to destroy the unity or integrity of — **dis•in•te•gra•tion** \-ˌsin-tə-ˈgrā-shən\ *n*

dis•in•ter \ˌdis-ᵊn-ˈtər\ *vb* **1 :** to take from the grave or tomb **2 :** UNEARTH

dis•in•ter•est•ed \(ˌ)dis-ˈin-tə-rəs-təd, -ˌres-\ *adj* **1 :** not interested **2 :** free from selfish motive or interest **:** UNBIASED — **dis•in•ter•est•ed•ness** *n*

dis•join \(ˌ)dis-ˈjȯin\ *vb* **:** SEPARATE

dis•joint \(ˌ)dis-ˈjȯint\ *vb* **:** to disturb the orderly arrangement of; *also* **:** to separate at the joints

dis•joint•ed *adj* **1 :** DISCONNECTED; *esp* **:** INCOHERENT **2 :** separated at or as if at the joint

disk *or* **disc** \ˈdisk\ *n* **1 :** something round and flat; *esp* **:** a flat rounded anatomical structure (as the central part of the flower head of a composite plant or a pad of cartilage between vertebrae) **2** *usu disc* **:** a phonograph record **3 :** a round flat plate coated with a magnetic substance on which data for a computer is stored **4** *usu disc* **:** OPTICAL DISK

dis•kette \ˌdis-ˈket\ *n* **:** FLOPPY DISK

¹dis•like \(ˌ)dis-ˈlīk\ *n* **:** a feeling of aversion or disapproval

²dislike *vb* **:** to regard with dislike **:** DISAPPROVE

dis•lo•cate \ˈdis-lō-ˌkāt, dis-ˈlō-\ *vb* **1 :** to put out of place; *esp* **:** to displace (a bone or joint) from normal connections ⟨~ a shoulder⟩ **2 :** DISRUPT — **dis•lo•ca•tion** \ˌdis-(ˌ)lō-ˈkā-shən\ *n*

dis•lodge \(ˌ)dis-ˈläj\ *vb* **:** to force out of a place esp. of rest, hiding, or defense

dis•loy•al \(ˌ)dis-ˈlȯi-əl\ *adj* **:** lacking in loyalty — **dis•loy•al•ty** *n*

dis•mal \ˈdiz-məl\ *adj* [ME, fr. *dismal*, n., days marked as unlucky in medieval calendars, fr. AF, fr ML *dies mali*, lit., evil days] **1 :** showing or causing gloom or depression **2 :** lacking merit — **dis•mal•ly** *adv*

dis•man•tle \(ˌ)dis-ˈmant-ᵊl\ *vb* **-tled; -tling 1 :** to take apart **2 :** to strip of furniture and equipment — **dis•man•tle•ment** *n*

dis•may \dis-ˈmā\ *vb* **:** to cause to lose courage or resolution from alarm or fear **:** DAUNT — **dismay** *n* — **dis•may•ing•ly** *adv*

dis•mem•ber \dis-ˈmem-bər\ *vb* **1 :** to cut off or separate the limbs or parts of **2 :** to break up or tear into pieces — **dis•mem•ber•ment** *n*

dis•miss \dis-ˈmis\ *vb* **1 :** to send away **2 :** DISCHARGE 5 **3 :** to put aside or out of mind **4 :** to put out of judicial consideration ⟨~*ed* all charges⟩ — **dis•miss•al** *n*

dis•mount \dis-ˈmau̇nt\ *vb* **1 :** to get down from something (as a horse or bicycle) **2 :** UNHORSE **3 :** DISASSEMBLE

dis•obe•di•ence \ˌdi-sə-ˈbē-dē-əns\ *n* **:** neglect or refusal to obey — **dis•obe•di•ent** \-ənt\ *adj*

dis•obey \ˌdi-sə-ˈbā\ *vb* **:** to fail to obey **:** be disobedient

dis•oblige \ˌdi-sə-ˈblīj\ *vb* **1 :** to go counter to the wishes of **2 :** INCONVENIENCE

¹dis•or•der \di-ˈsȯr-dər\ *vb* **1 :** to disturb the order of **2 :** to disturb the regular or normal functions of ⟨a ~*ed* digestion⟩

²disorder *n* **1 :** lack of order **:** CONFUSION **2 :** breach of the peace or public order **:** TUMULT **3 :** an abnormal state of body or mind **:** AILMENT

dis•or•der•ly \-lē\ *adj* **1 :** offensive to public order **2 :** marked by disorder ⟨a ~ desk⟩ — **dis•or•der•li•ness** *n*

dis•or•ga•nize \di-ˈsȯr-gə-ˌnīz\ *vb* **:** to break up the regular system of **:** throw into disorder — **dis•or•ga•ni•za•tion** \di-ˌsȯr-gə-nə-ˈzā-shən\ *n*

dis•ori•ent \di-ˈsōr-ē-ˌent\ *vb* **:** to cause to be confused or lost — **dis•ori•en•ta•tion** \di-ˌsōr-ē-ən-ˈtā-shən\ *n*

dis•own \di-ˈsōn\ *vb* **:** REPUDIATE, RENOUNCE, DISCLAIM

dis•par•age \di-ˈspar-ij\ *vb* **-aged; -ag•ing** [ME to degrade by marriage below one's class, disparage, fr. MF *desparagier* to marry below one's class, fr. OF, fr. *parage* extraction, lineage, fr. *per* peer] **1 :** to lower in rank or reputation **:** DEGRADE **2 :** BELITTLE — **dis•par•age•ment** *n* — **dis•par•ag•ing•ly** *adv*

dis•pa•rate \ˈdis-pə-rət, dis-ˈpar-ət\ *adj* **:** distinct in quality or character — **dis•par•i•ty** \di-ˈspar-ə-tē\ *n*

dis•pas•sion•ate \(ˌ)dis-ˈpa-shə-nət\ *adj* **:** not influenced by strong feeling **:** CALM, IMPARTIAL — **dis•pas•sion** \-ˈpa-shən\ *n* — **dis•pas•sion•ate•ly** *adv*

¹dis•patch \di-ˈspach\ *vb* **1 :** to send off or away with promptness or speed esp. on official business **2 :** to put to death **3 :** to attend to rapidly or efficiently **4 :** DEFEAT — **dis•patch•er** *n*

²dis•patch \di-ˈspach, ˈdis-ˌpach\ *n* **1 :** MESSAGE **2 :** a news item sent in by a correspondent to a newspaper **3 :** the act of dispatching; *esp* **:** SHIPMENT **4 :** the act of putting to death **5 :** promptness and efficiency in performing a task

dis•pel \di-ˈspel\ *vb* **dis•pelled; dis•pel•ling :** to drive away by scattering **:** DISSIPATE

dis•pens•able \di-ˈspen-sə-bəl\ *adj* **:** capable of being dispensed with

dis·pen·sa·ry \di-ˈspen-sə-rē\ *n, pl* **-ries** : a place where medicine or medical or dental aid is dispensed

dis·pen·sa·tion \ˌdis-pən-ˈsā-shən\ *n* **1** : a system of rules for ordering affairs **2** : a particular arrangement or provision esp. of nature **3** : an exemption from a rule or from a vow or oath **4** : the act of dispensing **5** : something dispensed or distributed

dis·pense \di-ˈspens\ *vb* **dis·pensed; dis·pens·ing 1** : to portion out **2** : ADMINISTER ⟨~ justice⟩ **3** : EXEMPT **4** : to make up and give out (remedies) — **dis·pens·er** *n* — **dispense with 1** : SUSPEND **2** : to do without

dis·perse \di-ˈspərs\ *vb* **dis·persed; dis·pers·ing** : to break up and scatter about : SPREAD — **dis·per·sal** \-ˈspər-səl\ *n* — **dis·per·sion** \-ˈspər-zhən\ *n*

dis·pir·it \dis-ˈpir-ət\ *vb* : DEPRESS, DISCOURAGE, DISHEARTEN

dis·place \dis-ˈplās\ *vb* **1** : to remove from the usual or proper place; *esp* : to expel or force to flee from home or native land ⟨*displaced* persons⟩ **2** : to move out of position ⟨water *displaced* by a floating object⟩ **3** : to take the place of : REPLACE

dis·place·ment \-mənt\ *n* **1** : the act of displacing : the state of being displaced **2** : the volume or weight of a fluid (as water) displaced by a floating body (as a ship) **3** : the difference between the initial position of an object and a later position

[1]dis·play \di-ˈsplā\ *vb* : to present to view : make evident

[2]display *n* **1** : a displaying of something **2** : an electronic device (as a cathode-ray tube) that gives information in visual form; *also* : the visual information

dis·please \(ˌ)dis-ˈplēz\ *vb* **1** : to arouse the disapproval and dislike of **2** : to be offensive to : give displeasure

dis·plea·sure \-ˈple-zhər\ *n* : a feeling of dislike and irritation

dis·port \di-ˈspōrt\ *vb* **1** : DIVERT, AMUSE **2** : FROLIC **3** : DISPLAY

dis·pos·able \di-ˈspō-zə-bəl\ *adj* **1** : remaining after deduction of taxes ⟨~ income⟩ **2** : designed to be used once and then thrown away ⟨~ diapers⟩ — **disposable** *n*

dis·pos·al \di-ˈspō-zəl\ *n* **1** : CONTROL, COMMAND **2** : an orderly arrangement **3** : a getting rid of **4** : MANAGEMENT, ADMINISTRATION **5** : presenting or bestowing something ⟨~ of favors⟩ **6** : a device used to reduce waste matter (as by grinding)

dis·pose \di-ˈspōz\ *vb* **dis·posed; dis·pos·ing 1** : to give a tendency to : INCLINE ⟨*disposed* to accept⟩ **2** : to put in place : ARRANGE ⟨troops *disposed* for withdrawal⟩ **3** : SETTLE — **dis·pos·er** *n* — **dispose of 1** : to transfer to the control of another **2** : to get rid of **3** : to deal with conclusively

dis·po·si·tion \ˌdis-pə-ˈzi-shən\ *n* **1** : the act or power of disposing : DISPOSAL **2** : RELINQUISHMENT **3** : ARRANGEMENT **4** : TENDENCY, INCLINATION **5** : natural attitude toward things ⟨a cheerful ~⟩

dis·pos·sess \ˌdis-pə-ˈzes\ *vb* : to put out of possession or occupancy — **dis·pos·ses·sion** \-ˈze-shən\ *n*

dis·praise \(ˌ)dis-ˈprāz\ *vb* : DISPARAGE — **dispraise** *n* — **dis·prais·er** *n*

dis·pro·por·tion \ˌdis-prə-ˈpōr-shən\ *n* : lack of proportion, symmetry, or proper relation — **dis·pro·por·tion·ate** \-shə-nət\ *adj*

dis·prove \(ˌ)dis-ˈprüv\ *vb* : to prove to be false — **dis·proof** \-ˈprüf\ *n*

dis·pu·tant \di-ˈspyüt-ᵊnt, ˈdis-pyə-tənt\ *n* : one that is engaged in a dispute

dis·pu·ta·tion \ˌdis-pyu̇-ˈtā-shən\ *n* **1** : DEBATE **2** : an oral defense of an academic thesis

dis·pu·ta·tious \-shəs\ *adj* : inclined to dispute : ARGUMENTATIVE

[1]dis·pute \di-ˈspyüt\ *vb* **dis·put·ed; dis·put·ing 1** : ARGUE, DEBATE **2** : WRANGLE **3** : to deny the truth or rightness of **4** : to struggle against or over : OPPOSE — **dis·put·able** \di-ˈspyü-tə-bəl, ˈdis-pyə-tə-bəl\ *adj* — **dis·put·er** *n*

[2]dis·pute *n* **1** : DEBATE **2** : QUARREL

dis·qual·i·fy \(ˌ)dis-ˈkwä-lə-ˌfī\ *vb* : to make or declare unfit or not qualified — **dis·qual·i·fi·ca·tion** \-ˌkwä-lə-fə-ˈkā-shən\ *n*

[1]dis·qui·et \(ˌ)dis-ˈkwī-ət\ *vb* : to make uneasy or restless : DISTURB

[2]disquiet *n* : lack of peace or tranquillity : ANXIETY

dis·qui·etude \(ˌ)dis-ˈkwī-ə-ˌtüd, -ˌtyüd\ *n* : AGITATION, ANXIETY

dis·qui·si·tion \ˌdis-kwə-ˈzi-shən\ *n* : a formal inquiry or discussion

[1]dis·re·gard \ˌdis-ri-ˈgärd\ *vb* : to pay no attention to : treat as unworthy of notice or regard

[2]disregard *n* : the act of disregarding : the state of being disregarded : NEGLECT — **dis·re·gard·ful** *adj*

dis·re·pair \ˌdis-ri-ˈpar\ *n* : the state of being in need of repair

dis·rep·u·ta·ble \dis-ˈre-pyu̇-tə-bəl\ *adj* : having a bad reputation

dis·re·pute \ˌdis-ri-ˈpyüt\ *n* : lack or decline of reputation : low esteem

dis·re·spect \ˌdis-ri-ˈspekt\ *n* : DISCOURTESY — **dis·re·spect·ful** *adj*

dis·robe \dis-ˈrōb\ *vb* : UNDRESS

dis·rupt \dis-ˈrəpt\ *vb* **1** : to break apart **2** : to throw into disorder **3** : INTERRUPT — **dis·rup·tion** \-ˈrəp-shən\ *n* — **dis·rup·tive** \-ˈrəp-tiv\ *adj*

dis·sat·is·fac·tion \di-ˌsa-təs-ˈfak-shən\ *n* : DISCONTENT

dis·sat·is·fy \di-ˈsa-təs-ˌfī\ *vb* : to fail to satisfy : DISPLEASE

dis·sect \di-ˈsekt\ *vb* **1** : to divide into parts esp. for examination and study **2** : ANALYZE — **dis·sec·tion** \-ˈsek-shən\ *n* — **dis·sec·tor** \-ˈsek-tər\ *n*

dis·sect·ed *adj* : cut deeply into narrow lobes ⟨a ~ leaf⟩

dis·sem·ble \di-ˈsem-bəl\ *vb* **-bled; -bling 1** : to hide under or put on a false appearance : conceal facts, intentions, or feelings under some pretense **2** : SIMULATE — **dis·sem·bler** *n*

dis·sem·i·nate \di-ˈse-mə-ˌnāt\ *vb* **-nat·ed; -nat·ing** : to spread abroad as if sowing seed ⟨~ ideas⟩ — **dis·sem·i·na·tion** \-ˌse-mə-ˈnā-shən\ *n*

dis·sen·sion \di-ˈsen-chən\ *n* : disagreement in opinion : DISCORD

[1]dis·sent \di-ˈsent\ *vb* **1** : to withhold assent **2** : to differ in opinion

[2]dissent *n* **1** : difference of opinion; *esp* : religious nonconformity **2** : a written statement in which a justice disagrees with the opinion of the majority

dis·sent·er \di-ˈsen-tər\ *n* **1** : one that dissents **2** *cap* : an English Nonconformist

dis·ser·ta·tion \ˌdi-sər-ˈtā-shən\ *n* : an extended usu. written treatment of a subject; *esp* : one submitted for a doctorate

dis·ser·vice \di-ˈsər-vəs\ *n* : INJURY, HARM, MISCHIEF

dis·sev·er \di-ˈse-vər\ *vb* : SEPARATE, DISUNITE

dis·si·dent \ˈdi-sə-dənt\ *adj* [L *dissidens*, prp. of *dissidēre* to sit apart, disagree, fr. *dis-* apart + *sedēre* to sit] : disagreeing esp. with an established religious or political system, organization, or belief — **dis·si·dence** \-dəns\ *n* — **dissident** *n*

dis·sim·i·lar \di-ˈsi-mə-lər\ *adj* : UNLIKE — **dis·sim·i·lar·i·ty** \di-ˌsi-mə-ˈlar-ə-tē\ *n*

dis·sim·u·late \di-ˈsi-myə-ˌlāt\ *vb* : to hide under a false appearance : DISSEMBLE — **dis·sim·u·la·tion** \di-ˌsi-myə-ˈlā-shən\ *n*

dis·si·pate \ˈdi-sə-ˌpāt\ *vb* **-pat·ed; -pat·ing 1** : to break up and drive off : DISPERSE, SCATTER ⟨the breeze *dissipated* the fog⟩ **2** : SQUANDER **3** : to break up and vanish **4** : to be dissolute; *esp* : to drink alcoholic beverages to excess — **dis·si·pat·ed** *adj* — **dis·si·pa·tion** \ˌdi-sə-ˈpā-shən\ *n*

dis·so·ci·ate \di-ˈsō-shē-ˌāt\ *vb* **-at·ed; -at·ing** : DISCON-

NECT, DISUNITE — **dis•so•ci•a•tion** \di-ˌsō-shē-ˈā-shən\ *n*

dis•so•lute \ˈdi-sə-ˌlüt\ *adj* : loose in morals or conduct — **dis•so•lute•ly** *adv* — **dis•so•lute•ness** *n*

dis•so•lu•tion \ˌdi-sə-ˈlü-shən\ *n* **1** : the action or process of dissolving **2** : separation of a thing into its parts **3** : DECAY; *also* : DEATH **4** : the termination or breaking up of (as an assembly)

dis•solve \di-ˈzälv\ *vb* **1** : to separate into component parts **2** : to pass or cause to pass into solution ⟨sugar ~*s* in water⟩ **3** : TERMINATE, DISPERSE ⟨~ parliament⟩ **4** : to waste or fade away ⟨his courage *dissolved*⟩ **5** : to be overcome emotionally ⟨~ in tears⟩ **6** : to resolve itself as if by dissolution

dis•so•nance \ˈdi-sə-nəns\ *n* : DISCORD — **dis•so•nant** \-nənt\ *adj*

dis•suade \di-ˈswād\ *vb* **dis•suad•ed; dis•suad•ing** : to advise against a course of action : persuade or try to persuade not to do something — **dis•sua•sion** \-ˈswā-zhən\ *n* — **dis•sua•sive** \-ˈswā-siv\ *adj*

dist *abbr* **1** distance **2** district

[1]**dis•taff** \ˈdis-ˌtaf\ *n, pl* **distaffs** \-ˌtafs, -ˌtavz\ **1** : a staff for holding the flax, tow, or wool in spinning **2** : a woman's work or domain **3** : the female branch or side of a family

[2]**distaff** *adj* : MATERNAL, FEMALE

dis•tal \ˈdist-ᵊl\ *adj* **1** : away from the point of attachment or origin esp. on the body **2** : of, relating to, or being the surface of a tooth that is farthest from the middle of the front of the jaw — **dis•tal•ly** *adv*

[1]**dis•tance** \ˈdis-təns\ *n* **1** : measure of separation in space or time **2** : EXPANSE **3** : the full length ⟨go the ~⟩ **4** : spatial remoteness **5** : COLDNESS, RESERVE **6** : DIFFERENCE, DISPARITY **7** : a distant point

[2]**distance** *vb* **dis•tanced; dis•tanc•ing** : to leave far behind : OUTSTRIP

dis•tant \ˈdis-tənt\ *adj* **1** : separate in space : AWAY **2** : FAR-OFF **3** : far apart or behind **4** : not close in relationship ⟨a ~ cousin⟩ **5** : different in kind **6** : RESERVED, ALOOF, COLD ⟨~ politeness⟩ **7** : going a long distance — **dis•tant•ly** *adv* — **dis•tant•ness** *n*

dis•taste \(ˌ)dis-ˈtāst\ *n* : DISINCLINATION, DISLIKE — **dis•taste•ful** *adj*

dis•tem•per \(ˌ)dis-ˈtem-pər\ *n* : a bodily disorder usu. of a domestic animal; *esp* : a contagious often fatal virus disease of dogs

dis•tend \di-ˈstend\ *vb* : EXPAND, SWELL — **dis•ten•si•ble** \-ˈsten-sə-bəl\ *adj* — **dis•ten•sion** *or* **dis•ten•tion** \-chən\ *n*

dis•tich \ˈdis-(ˌ)tik\ *n* : a unit of two lines of poetry

dis•till *also* **dis•til** \di-ˈstil\ *vb* **dis•tilled; dis•till•ing** **1** : to fall or let fall in drops **2** : to obtain or purify by distillation — **dis•till•er** *n* — **dis•till•ery** \-ˈsti-lə-rē\ *n*

dis•til•late \ˈdis-tə-ˌlāt, -lət\ *n* : a liquid product condensed from vapor during distillation

dis•til•la•tion \ˌdis-tə-ˈlā-shən\ *n* : the process of purifying a liquid by successive evaporation and condensation

dis•tinct \di-ˈstiŋkt\ *adj* **1** : SEPARATE, INDIVIDUAL **2** : presenting a clear unmistakable impression — **dis•tinct•ly** *adv* — **dis•tinct•ness** *n*

dis•tinc•tion \di-ˈstiŋk-shən\ *n* **1** : the distinguishing of a difference; *also* : the difference distinguished **2** : something that distinguishes **3** : special honor or recognition

dis•tinc•tive \di-ˈstiŋk-tiv\ *adj* **1** : serving to distinguish **2** : having or giving style or distinction — **dis•tinc•tive•ly** *adv* — **dis•tinc•tive•ness** *n*

dis•tin•guish \di-ˈstiŋ-gwish\ *vb* [MF *distinguer,* fr. L *distinguere,* lit., to separate by pricking] **1** : to recognize by some mark or characteristic **2** : to hear or see clearly : DISCERN **3** : to make distinctions ⟨~ between right and wrong⟩ **4** : to give prominence or distinction to; *also* : to take special notice of — **dis•tin•guish•able** *adj*

dis•tin•guished \-gwisht\ *adj* **1** : marked by eminence or excellence **2** : befitting an eminent person

dis•tort \di-ˈstȯrt\ *vb* **1** : to twist out of the true meaning **2** : to twist out of a natural, normal, or original shape or condition **3** : to cause to be perceived unnaturally — **dis•tor•tion** \-ˈstȯr-shən\ *n*

distr *abbr* distribute; distribution

dis•tract \di-ˈstrakt\ *vb* **1** : to draw (the attention or mind) to a different object : DIVERT **2** : to stir up or confuse with conflicting emotions or motives — **dis•trac•tion** \-ˈstrak-shən\ *n*

dis•trait \di-ˈstrā\ *adj* : DISTRAUGHT 1

dis•traught \di-ˈstrȯt\ *adj* **1** : agitated with doubt or mental conflict **2** : INSANE

[1]**dis•tress** \di-ˈstres\ *n* **1** : suffering of body or mind : PAIN, ANGUISH **2** : TROUBLE, MISFORTUNE **3** : a condition of danger or desperate need — **dis•tress•ful** *adj*

[2]**distress** *vb* **1** : to subject to great strain or difficulties **2** : UPSET

dis•trib•ute \di-ˈstri-byüt\ *vb* **-ut•ed; -ut•ing** **1** : to divide among several or many **2** : to spread out : SCATTER; *also* : DELIVER **3** : CLASSIFY — **dis•tri•bu•tion** \ˌdis-trə-ˈbyü-shən\ *n*

dis•trib•u•tive \di-ˈstri-byu̇-tiv\ *adj* **1** : of or relating to distribution **2** : being or concerned with a mathematical operation (as multiplication in $a(b + c) = ab + ac$) that produces the same result when operating on a whole mathematical expression as when operating on each part and collecting the results — **dis•trib•u•tive•ly** *adv*

dis•trib•u•tor \di-ˈstri-byu̇-tər\ *n* **1** : one that distributes **2** : one that markets goods **3** : a device for directing current to the spark plugs of an engine

dis•trict \ˈdis-(ˌ)trikt\ *n* **1** : a fixed territorial division (as for administrative or electoral purposes) **2** : an area, region, or section with a distinguishing character

district attorney *n* : the prosecuting attorney of a judicial district

[1]**dis•trust** \dis-ˈtrəst\ *n* : a lack or absence of trust — **dis•trust•ful** \-fəl\ *adj* — **dis•trust•ful•ly** *adv*

[2]**distrust** *vb* : to have no trust or confidence in

dis•turb \di-ˈstərb\ *vb* **1** : to interfere with : INTERRUPT **2** : to alter the position or arrangement of; *also* : to upset the natural and esp. the ecological balance of **3** : to destroy the tranquillity or composure of : make uneasy **4** : to throw into disorder **5** : INCONVENIENCE — **dis•tur•bance** \-ˈstər-bəns\ *n* — **dis•turb•er** *n*

dis•turbed \-ˈstərbd\ *adj* : showing symptoms of emotional illness

dis•unite \ˌdis-yü-ˈnīt\ *vb* : DIVIDE, SEPARATE

dis•uni•ty \dis-ˈyü-nə-tē\ *n* : lack of unity; *esp* : DISSENSION

dis•use \-ˈyüs\ *n* : a cessation of use or practice

[1]**ditch** \ˈdich\ *n* : a long narrow channel or trench dug in the earth

[2]**ditch** *vb* **1** : to enclose with a ditch; *also* : to dig a ditch in **2** : to get rid of : DISCARD **3** : to make a forced landing of an airplane on water

dith•er \ˈdi-t͟hər\ *n* : a highly nervous, excited, or agitated state

dit•sy *or* **dit•zy** \ˈdit-sē\ *adj* **dits•i•er** *or* **ditz•i•er; -est** : eccentrically silly, giddy, or inane

dit•to \ˈdi-tō\ *n, pl* **dittos** [It *ditto, detto,* pp. of *dire* to say, fr. L *dicere*] **1** : a thing mentioned previously or above — used to avoid repeating a word **2** : a mark " or " used as a symbol for the word *ditto*

dit•ty \ˈdi-tē\ *n, pl* **ditties** : a short simple song

di•uret•ic \ˌdī-yə-ˈre-tik\ *adj* : tending to increase urine flow — **diuretic** *n*

di•ur•nal \dī-ˈərn-ᵊl\ *adj* **1** : DAILY **2** : of, relating to, occurring, or active in the daytime

div *abbr* **1** divided **2** dividend **3** division **4** divorced

di•va \ˈdē-və\ *n, pl* **divas** *or* **di•ve** \-ˌvā\ [It, lit., goddess, fr. L, fem. of *divus* divine, god] : PRIMA DONNA

di•va•gate \ˈdī-və-ˌgāt\ *vb* **-gat•ed; -gat•ing** : to wander or stray from a course or subject : DIVERGE — **di·va·ga·tion** \ˌdī-və-ˈgā-shən\ *n*

di·van \ˈdī-ˌvan, di-ˈvan\ *n* : COUCH, SOFA

[1]**dive** \ˈdīv\ *vb* **dived** \ˈdīvd\ *or* **dove** \ˈdōv\; **dived; div·ing 1** : to plunge into water headfirst **2** : SUBMERGE **3** : to come or drop down precipitously **4** : to descend in an airplane at a steep angle **5** : to plunge into some matter or activity **6** : DART, LUNGE — **div·er** *n*

[2]**dive** *n* **1** : the act or an instance of diving **2** : a sharp decline **3** : a disreputable bar or place of amusement

di·verge \də-ˈvərj, dī-\ *vb* **di·verged; di·verg·ing 1** : to move or extend in different directions from a common point : draw apart **2** : to differ in character, form, or opinion **3** : DEVIATE **4** : DEFLECT — **di·ver·gence** \-ˈvər-jəns\ *n* — **di·ver·gent** \-jənt\ *adj*

di·vers \ˈdī-vərz\ *adj* : VARIOUS

di·verse \dī-ˈvərs, də-, ˈdī-ˌvərs\ *adj* **1** : UNLIKE **2** : composed of distinct forms or qualities — **di·verse·ly** *adv*

di·ver·si·fy \də-ˈvər-sə-ˌfī, dī-\ *vb* **-fied; -fy·ing** : to make different or various in form or quality — **di·ver·si·fi·ca·tion** \-ˌvər-sə-fə-ˈkā-shən\ *n*

di·ver·sion \də-ˈvər-zhən, dī-\ *n* **1** : a turning aside from a course, activity, or use : DEVIATION **2** : something that diverts or amuses : PASTIME

di·ver·si·ty \də-ˈvər-sə-tē, dī-\ *n, pl* **-ties 1** : the condition of being diverse : VARIETY **2** : an instance of being diverse

di·vert \də-ˈvərt, dī-\ *vb* **1** : to turn from a course or purpose : DEFLECT **2** : DISTRACT **3** : ENTERTAIN, AMUSE

di·vest \dī-ˈvest, də-\ *vb* **1** : to deprive or dispossess esp. of property, authority, or rights **2** : to strip esp. of clothing, ornament, or equipment

[1]**di·vide** \də-ˈvīd\ *vb* **di·vid·ed; di·vid·ing 1** : SEPARATE; *also* : CLASSIFY **2** : CLEAVE, PART **3** : DISTRIBUTE, APPORTION **4** : to possess or make use of in common : share in **5** : to cause to be separate, distinct, or apart from one another **6** : to separate into opposing sides or parties **7** : to mark divisions on **8** : to subject to or use in mathematical division; *also* : to be used as a divisor with respect to **9** : to branch out

[2]**divide** *n* : WATERSHED 1

div·i·dend \ˈdi-və-ˌdend\ *n* **1** : an individual share of something distributed **2** : BONUS **3** : a number to be divided **4** : a sum or fund to be divided or distributed

di·vid·er \də-ˈvī-dər\ *n* **1** : one that divides (as a partition) ⟨room ~⟩ **2** *pl* : COMPASS 5

div·i·na·tion \ˌdi-və-ˈnā-shən\ *n* **1** : the art or practice of using omens or magic powers to foretell the future **2** : unusual insight or intuitive perception

[1]**di·vine** \də-ˈvīn\ *adj* **di·vin·er; -est 1** : of, relating to, or being God or a god **2** : supremely good : SUPERB; *also* : HEAVENLY — **di·vine·ly** *adv*

[2]**divine** *n* **1** : CLERGYMAN **2** : THEOLOGIAN

[3]**divine** *vb* **di·vined; di·vin·ing 1** : INFER, CONJECTURE **2** : PROPHESY **3** : DOWSE — **di·vin·er** *n*

divining rod *n* : a forked rod believed to reveal the presence of water or minerals by dipping downward when held over a vein

di·vin·i·ty \də-ˈvi-nə-tē\ *n, pl* **-ties 1** : THEOLOGY **2** : the quality or state of being divine **3** : a divine being; *esp* : GOD 1

di·vis·i·ble \də-ˈvi-zə-bəl\ *adj* : capable of being divided — **di·vis·i·bil·i·ty** \-ˌvi-zə-ˈbi-lə-tē\ *n*

di·vi·sion \də-ˈvi-zhən\ *n* **1** : DISTRIBUTION, SEPARATION **2** : one of the parts or groupings into which a whole is divided **3** : DISAGREEMENT, DISUNITY **4** : something that divides or separates **5** : the mathematical operation of finding how many times one number is contained in another **6** : a large self-contained military unit **7** : an administrative or operating unit of a governmental, business, or educational organization — **di·vi·sion·al** \-ˈvi-zhə-nəl\ *adj*

di·vi·sive \də-ˈvī-siv, -ˈvi-ziv\ *adj* : creating disunity or dissension — **di·vi·sive·ly** *adv* — **di·vi·sive·ness** *n*

di·vi·sor \də-ˈvī-zər\ *n* : the number by which a dividend is divided

di·vorce \də-ˈvōrs\ *n* **1** : an act or instance of legally dissolving a marriage **2** : SEPARATION, SEVERANCE — **divorce** *vb* — **di·vorce·ment** *n*

di·vor·cé \də-ˌvōr-ˈsā\ *n* [F] : a divorced man

di·vor·cée \də-ˌvōr-ˈsā, -ˈsē\ *n* : a divorced woman

div·ot \ˈdi-vət\ *n* : a piece of turf dug from a golf fairway in making a stroke

di·vulge \də-ˈvəlj, dī-\ *vb* **di·vulged; di·vulg·ing** : REVEAL, DISCLOSE

Dix·ie·land \ˈdik-sē-ˌland\ *n* : jazz music in duple time played in a style developed in New Orleans

diz·zy \ˈdi-zē\ *adj* **diz·zi·er; -est** [ME *disy,* fr. OE *dysig* stupid] **1** : FOOLISH, SILLY **2** : having a sensation of whirling : GIDDY **3** : causing or caused by giddiness — **diz·zi·ly** \-zə-lē\ *adv* — **diz·zi·ness** \-zē-nəs\ *n*

DJ *n, often not cap* : DISC JOCKEY

dk *abbr* **1** dark **2** deck **3** dock

dl *abbr* deciliter

DLitt *or* **DLit** *abbr* [NL *doctor litterarum*] doctor of letters; doctor of literature

DLO *abbr* dead letter office

dm *abbr* decimeter

DMD *abbr* [NL *dentariae medicinae doctor*] doctor of dental medicine

DMZ *abbr* demilitarized zone

dn *abbr* down

DNA \ˌdē-(ˌ)en-ˈā\ *n* : any of various nucleic acids that are usu. the molecular basis of heredity and are localized esp. in cell nuclei

[1]**do** \ˈdü\ *vb* **did** \ˈdid\; **done** \ˈdən\; **do·ing; does** \ˈdəz\ **1** : to bring to pass : ACCOMPLISH **2** : ACT, BEHAVE ⟨~ as I say⟩ **3** : to be active or busy ⟨up and ~*ing*⟩ **4** : HAPPEN ⟨what's ~*ing*?⟩ **5** : to be engaged in the study or practice of : work at ⟨he *does* tailoring⟩ **6** : COOK ⟨steak *done* rare⟩ **7** : to put in order (as by cleaning or arranging) ⟨~ the dishes⟩ **8** : DECORATE ⟨*did* the hall in blue⟩ **9** : GET ALONG ⟨~ well in school⟩ **10** : CARRY ON, MANAGE **11** : RENDER ⟨sleep will ~ you good⟩ **12** : FINISH ⟨when he had *done*⟩ **13** : EXERT ⟨*did* my best⟩ **14** : PRODUCE ⟨*did* a poem⟩ **15** : to play the part of **16** : CHEAT ⟨*did* him out of his share⟩ **17** : TRAVERSE, TOUR **18** : TRAVEL **19** : to spend or serve out a period of time ⟨*did* ten years in prison⟩ **20** : SUFFICE, SUIT **21** : to be fitting or proper **22** : USE ⟨doesn't ~ drugs⟩ **23** — used as an auxiliary verb (1) before the subject in an interrogative sentence ⟨*does* he work?⟩ and after some adverbs ⟨never *did* she say so⟩, (2) in a negative statement ⟨I *don't* know⟩, (3) for emphasis ⟨you ~ know⟩, and (4) as a substitute for a preceding predicate ⟨he works harder than I ~⟩ — **do·able** \ˈdü-ə-bəl\ *adj* — **do away with 1** : to put an end to **2** : DESTROY, KILL — **do by** : to deal with : TREAT ⟨*did* right *by* her⟩ — **do for** : to bring about the death or ruin of — **do the trick** : to produce a desired result

[2]**do** *n* **1** : AFFAIR, PARTY **2** : a command or entreaty to do something ⟨list of ~*s* and don'ts⟩ **3** : HAIRDO

[3]**do** *abbr* ditto

DOA *abbr* dead on arrival

DOB *abbr* date of birth

dob·bin \ˈdä-bən\ *n* [*Dobbin,* nickname for *Robert*] **1** : a farm horse **2** : a quiet plodding horse

Do·ber·man pin·scher \ˈdō-bər-mən-ˈpin-chər\ *n* : a short-haired medium-sized dog of a breed of German origin

do·bra \ˈdō-brə\ *n* — see MONEY table

[1]**doc** \ˈdäk\ *n* : DOCTOR

[2]**doc** *abbr* document

do·cent \ˈdō-sᵊnt, dōt-ˈsent\ *n* [obs. G (now *Dozent*), fr. L *docens,* prp. of *docēre* to teach] : TEACHER, LECTURER; *also* : a person who leads a guided tour

doc·ile \ˈdä-səl\ *adj* [L *docilis,* fr. *docēre* to teach] : easily taught, led, or managed : TRACTABLE — **do·cil·i·ty** \dä-ˈsi-lə-tē\ *n*

[1]**dock** \ˈdäk\ *n* **:** any of a genus of coarse weedy herbs related to buckwheat

[2]**dock** *vb* **1 :** to cut off the end of **:** cut short **2 :** to take away a part of **:** deduct from ⟨~ a worker's wages⟩

[3]**dock** *n* **1 :** an artificial basin to receive ships **2 :** [2]SLIP 2 **3 :** a wharf or platform for loading or unloading materials

[4]**dock** *vb* **1 :** to bring or come into dock **2 :** to join (as two spacecraft) mechanically in space

[5]**dock** *n* **:** the place in a court where a prisoner stands or sits during trial

dock•age \ˈdä-kij\ *n* **:** docking facilities

dock•et \ˈdä-kət\ *n* **1 :** a formal abridged record of the proceedings in a legal action; *also* **:** a register of such records **2 :** a list of legal causes to be tried **3 :** a calendar of matters to be acted on **:** AGENDA **4 :** a label attached to a document containing identification or directions — **docket** *vb*

dock•hand \ˈdäk-ˌhand\ *n* **:** LONGSHOREMAN

dock•work•er \-ˌwər-kər\ *n* **:** LONGSHOREMAN

dock•yard \-ˌyärd\ *n* **:** SHIPYARD

[1]**doc•tor** \ˈdäk-tər\ *n* [ME *doctour* teacher, doctor, fr. MF & ML; MF, fr. ML *doctor*, fr. L, teacher, fr. *docēre* to teach] **1 :** a person holding one of the highest academic degrees (as a PhD) conferred by a university **2 :** one skilled in healing arts; *esp* **:** an academically and legally qualified physician, surgeon, dentist, or veterinarian **3 :** a person who restores or repairs things — **doc•tor•al** \-tə-rəl\ *adj*

[2]**doctor** *vb* **1 :** to give medical treatment to **2 :** to practice medicine **3 :** REPAIR **4 :** to adapt or modify for a desired end **5 :** to alter deceptively

doc•tor•ate \ˈdäk-tə-rət\ *n* **:** the degree, title, or rank of a doctor

doc•tri•naire \ˌdäk-trə-ˈnar\ *n* [F] **:** one who attempts to put an abstract theory into effect without regard to practical difficulties — **doctrinaire** *adj*

doc•trine \ˈdäk-trən\ *n* **1 :** something that is taught **2 :** DOGMA, TENET — **doc•tri•nal** \-trən-ᵊl\ *adj*

docu•dra•ma \ˈdä-kyə-ˌdrä-mə, -ˌdra-\ *n* **:** a drama for television, motion pictures, or theater that deals freely with historical events

doc•u•ment \ˈdä-kyə-mənt\ *n* **:** a paper that furnishes information, proof, or support of something else — **doc•u•ment** \-ˌment\ *vb* — **doc•u•men•ta•tion** \ˌdä-kyə-mən-ˈtā-shən\ *n* — **doc•u•ment•er** *n*

doc•u•men•ta•ry \ˌdä-kyə-ˈmen-tə-rē\ *adj* **1 :** consisting of documents; *also* **:** being in writing ⟨~ proof⟩ **2 :** giving a factual presentation in artistic form ⟨a ~ movie⟩ — **documentary** *n*

DOD *abbr* Department of Defense

[1]**dod•der** \ˈdä-dər\ *n* **:** any of a genus of leafless elongated wiry parasitic herbs deficient in chlorophyll

[2]**dodder** *vb* **dod•dered; dod•der•ing 1 :** to tremble or shake usu. from age **2 :** to progress feebly and unsteadily

[1]**dodge** \ˈdäj\ *n* **1 :** an act of evading by sudden bodily movement **2 :** an artful device to evade, deceive, or trick **3 :** EXPEDIENT

[2]**dodge** *vb* **dodged; dodg•ing 1 :** to evade usu. by trickery **2 :** to move suddenly aside; *also* **:** to avoid or evade by so doing — **dodg•er** *n*

do•do \ˈdō-dō\ *n, pl* **dodoes** *or* **dodos** [Pg *doudo*, fr. *doudo* silly, stupid] **1 :** an extinct heavy flightless bird of the island of Mauritius related to the pigeons and larger than a turkey **2 :** one hopelessly behind the times; *also* **:** a stupid person

doe \ˈdō\ *n, pl* **does** *or* **doe :** an adult female of various mammals (as a deer, rabbit, or kangaroo) of which the male is called *buck*

DOE *abbr* Department of Energy

do•er \ˈdü-ər\ *n* **:** one that does

does *pres 3d sing of* DO, *pl of* DOE

doff \ˈdäf\ *vb* [ME, fr. *don* to do + *of* off] **1 :** to take off (the hat) in greeting or as a sign of respect **2 :** to rid oneself of

dodo 1

[1]**dog** \ˈdȯg\ *n* **1 :** a flesh-eating domestic mammal related to the wolves; *esp* **:** a male of this animal **2 :** a worthless person **3 :** FELLOW, CHAP ⟨you lucky ~⟩ **4 :** a mechanical device for holding something **5 :** uncharacteristic or affected stylishness or dignity ⟨put on the ~⟩ **6** *pl* **:** RUIN ⟨gone to the ~*s*⟩

[2]**dog** *vb* **dogged; dog•ging 1 :** to hunt or track like a hound **2 :** to worry as if by pursuit with dogs **:** PLAGUE

dog•bane \ˈdȯg-ˌbān\ *n* **:** any of a genus of mostly poisonous herbs with milky juice and often showy flowers

dog•cart \-ˌkärt\ *n* **:** a light one-horse carriage with two seats back to back

dog•catch•er \-ˌka-chər, -ˌke-\ *n* **:** a community official assigned to catch and dispose of stray dogs

dog–ear \ˈdȯ-gir\ *n* **:** the turned-down corner of a leaf of a book — **dog–ear** *vb* — **dog–eared** \-ˌgird\ *adj*

dog•fight \ˈdȯg-ˌfīt\ *n* **:** a fight between fighter planes at close range

dog•fish \-ˌfish\ *n* **:** any of various small sharks

dog•ged \ˈdȯ-gəd\ *adj* **:** stubbornly determined **:** TENACIOUS — **dog•ged•ly** *adv* — **dog•ged•ness** *n*

dog•ger•el \ˈdȯ-gə-rəl\ *n* **:** verse that is loosely styled and irregular in measure esp. for comic effect

dog•gie bag *or* **doggy bag** \ˈdȯ-gē-\ *n* **:** a container for carrying home leftover food from a restaurant meal

[1]**dog•gy** *or* **dog•gie** \ˈdȯ-gē\ *n, pl* **doggies :** a small dog

[2]**dog•gy** *adj* **dog•gi•er; -est :** of or resembling a dog ⟨a ~ odor⟩

dog•house \ˈdȯg-ˌhau̇s\ *n* **:** a shelter for a dog — **in the doghouse :** in a state of disfavor

do•gie \ˈdō-gē\ *n, chiefly West* **:** a motherless calf in a range herd

dog•leg \ˈdȯg-ˌleg\ *n* **:** a sharp bend or angle (as in a road) — **dogleg** *vb*

dog•ma \ˈdȯg-mə\ *n, pl* **dogmas** *also* **dog•ma•ta** \-mə-tə\ **1 :** a tenet or code of tenets **2 :** a doctrine or body of doctrines formally proclaimed by a church

dog•ma•tism \ˈdȯg-mə-ˌti-zəm\ *n* **:** positiveness in stating matters of opinion esp. when unwarranted or arrogant — **dog•mat•ic** \dȯg-ˈma-tik\ *adj* — **dog•mat•i•cal•ly** \-ti-k(ə-)lē\ *adv*

do–good•er \ˈdü-ˌgu̇-dər\ *n* **:** an earnest often naive humanitarian or reformer

dog•tooth violet \ˈdȯg-ˌtüth-\ *n* **:** any of a genus of wild spring-flowering bulbous herbs related to the lilies

dog•trot \ˈdȯg-ˌträt\ *n* **:** a gentle trot — **dogtrot** *vb*

dog•wood \ˈdȯg-ˌwu̇d\ *n* **:** any of a genus of trees and shrubs having heads of small flowers often with showy white, pink, or red bracts

doi•ly \ˈdȯi-lē\ *n, pl* **doilies :** a small often decorative mat

do in *vb* **1 :** RUIN **2 :** KILL **3 :** TIRE, EXHAUST **4 :** CHEAT

do•ings \ˈdü-iŋz\ *n pl* **:** GOINGS-ON

do–it–yourself *n* **:** the activity of doing or making something without professional training or help — **do–it–your•self•er** *n*

dol *abbr* dollar

dogwood

dol•drums \ˈdōl-drəmz, ˈdäl-\ *n pl* **1 :** a spell of listlessness or despondency **2** *often cap* **:** a part of the ocean near the equator known for calms **3 :** a state or period of inactivity, stagnation, or slump

[1]dole \ˈdōl\ *n* **1 :** a distribution esp. of food, money, or clothing to the needy; *also* **:** something so distributed **2 :** a grant of government funds to the unemployed

[2]dole *vb* **doled; dol•ing :** to give or distribute as a charity — usu. used with *out*

dole•ful \ˈdōl-fəl\ *adj* **:** full of grief **:** SAD — **dole•ful•ly** *adv*

dole out *vb* **1 :** to give or deliver in small portions **2 :** DISH OUT

doll \ˈdäl, ˈdȯl\ *n* **1 :** a small figure of a human being used esp. as a child's plaything **2 :** a pretty woman **3 :** an attractive person — **doll•ish** \ˈdä-lish, ˈdȯ-\ *adj*

dol•lar \ˈdä-lər\ *n* [Dutch or LG *daler,* fr. G *Taler,* short for *Joachimstaler,* fr. Sankt *Joachimsthal,* Bohemia, where talers were first made] **1 :** any of various basic monetary units (as in the U.S. and Canada) — see MONEY table **2 :** a coin, note, or token representing one dollar **3 :** RINGGIT

dol•lop \ˈdä-ləp\ *n* **1 :** LUMP, GLOB **2 :** PORTION 1 — **dollop** *vb*

doll up *vb* **1 :** to dress elegantly or extravagantly **2 :** to make more attractive **3 :** to get dolled up

dol•ly \ˈdä-lē\ *n, pl* **dollies :** a small cart or wheeled platform (as for a television or movie camera)

dol•men \ˈdōl-mən, ˈdäl-\ *n* **:** a prehistoric monument consisting of two or more upright stones supporting a horizontal stone slab

do•lo•mite \ˈdō-lə-ˌmīt, ˈdä-\ *n* **:** a mineral found in broad layers as a compact limestone

do•lor \ˈdō-lər, ˈdä-\ *n* **:** mental suffering or anguish **:** SORROW — **do•lor•ous** *adj* — **do•lor•ous•ly** *adv*

do•lour *chiefly Brit var of* DOLOR

dol•phin \ˈdäl-fən\ *n* **1 :** any of various small toothed whales with the snout more or less elongated into a beak **2 :** either of two active food fishes of tropical and temperate seas

dolt \ˈdōlt\ *n* **:** a stupid person — **dolt•ish** \ˈdōl-tish\ *adj* — **dolt•ish•ness** *n*

dom *abbr* **1** domestic **2** dominant **3** dominion

-dom *n suffix* **1 :** dignity **:** office ⟨duke*dom*⟩ **2 :** realm **:** jurisdiction ⟨king*dom*⟩ **3 :** state or fact of being ⟨free*dom*⟩ **4 :** those having a (specified) office, occupation, interest, or character ⟨official*dom*⟩

do•main \dō-ˈmān\ *n* **1 :** complete and absolute ownership of land **2 :** land completely owned **3 :** a territory over which dominion is exercised **4 :** a sphere of knowledge, influence, or activity ⟨the ~ of science⟩

dome \ˈdōm\ *n* **1 :** a large hemispherical roof or ceiling **2 :** a structure or natural formation that resembles the dome of a building **3 :** a roofed sports stadium — **dome** *vb*

[1]do•mes•tic \də-ˈmes-tik\ *adj* **1 :** living near or about human habitations **2 :** TAME, DOMESTICATED **3 :** relating and limited to one's own country or the country under consideration **4 :** of or relating to the household or the family **5 :** devoted to home duties and pleasures **6 :** INDIGENOUS — **do•mes•ti•cal•ly** \-ti-k(ə-)lē\ *adv*

[2]domestic *n* **:** a household servant

do•mes•ti•cate \də-ˈmes-ti-ˌkāt\ *vb* **-cat•ed; -cat•ing :** to adapt to life in association with and to the use of humans — **do•mes•ti•ca•tion** \-ˌmes-ti-ˈkā-shən\ *n*

do•mes•tic•i•ty \ˌdō-ˌmes-ˈti-sə-tē, ˌdə-\ *n, pl* **-ties 1 :** the quality or state of being domestic or domesticated **2 :** domestic activities or life

do•mi•cile \ˈdä-mə-ˌsīl, ˈdō-; ˈdä-mə-səl\ *n* **:** a dwelling place **:** HOME — **domicile** *vb* — **dom•i•cil•i•ary** \ˌdä-mə-ˈsi-lē-ˌer-ē, ˌdō-\ *adj*

dom•i•nance \ˈdä-mə-nəns\ *n* **1 :** AUTHORITY, CONTROL **2 :** the property of a genetic dominant that prevents expression of a genetic recessive

[1]dom•i•nant \-nənt\ *adj* **1 :** controlling or prevailing over all others **2 :** overlooking from a high position **3 :** producing or being a bodily characteristic that is expressed when a contrasting recessive gene or trait is present

[2]dominant *n* **:** a dominant gene or trait

dom•i•nate \ˈdä-mə-ˌnāt\ *vb* **-nat•ed; -nat•ing 1 :** RULE, CONTROL **2 :** to have a commanding position or controlling power over **3 :** to rise high above in a position suggesting power to dominate — **dom•i•na•tor** \-ˌnā-tər\ *n*

dom•i•na•tion \ˌdä-mə-ˈnā-shən\ *n* **1 :** supremacy or preeminence over another **2 :** exercise of mastery, ruling power, or preponderant influence

do•mi•na•trix \ˌdä-mə-ˈnā-triks\ *n, pl* **-trices** \-ˈnā-trə-ˌsēz, -nə-ˈtrī-sēz\ **:** a woman who dominates and abuses her sexual partner; *also* **:** a dominating woman

dom•i•neer \ˌdä-mə-ˈnir\ *vb* **1 :** to rule in an arrogant manner **2 :** to be overbearing

Do•min•i•can \də-ˈmi-ni-kən\ *n* **:** a native or inhabitant of the Dominican Republic — **Dominican** *adj*

do•mi•nie *1 usu* ˈdä-mə-nē, *2 usu* ˈdō-\ *n* **1** *chiefly Scot* **:** SCHOOLMASTER **2 :** CLERGYMAN

do•min•ion \də-ˈmin-yən\ *n* **1 :** DOMAIN **2 :** supreme authority **:** SOVEREIGNTY **3** *often cap* **:** a self-governing nation of the Commonwealth

dom•i•no \ˈdä-mə-ˌnō\ *n, pl* **-noes** *or* **-nos 1 :** a long loose hooded cloak usu. worn with a half mask as a masquerade costume **2 :** a flat rectangular block used as a piece in a game **(dominoes)**

[1]don \ˈdän\ *vb* **donned; don•ning** [ME, fr. *don* to do + *on*] **:** to put on (as clothes)

[2]don *n* [Sp, fr. L *dominus* lord, master] **1 :** a Spanish nobleman or gentleman — used as a title prefixed to the Christian name **2 :** a head, tutor, or fellow in an English university

do•ña \ˈdō-nyə\ *n* **:** a Spanish woman of rank — used as a title prefixed to the Christian name

do•nate \ˈdō-ˌnāt\ *vb* **do•nat•ed; do•nat•ing 1 :** to make a gift of **:** CONTRIBUTE **2 :** to make a donation

do•na•tion \dō-ˈnā-shən\ *n* **1 :** the making of a gift esp. to a charity **2 :** a free contribution **:** GIFT

[1]done \ˈdən\ *past part of* DO

[2]done *adj* **1 :** doomed to failure, defeat, or death **2 :** gone by **:** OVER ⟨when day is ~⟩ **3 :** cooked sufficiently **4 :** conformable to social convention

dong \ˈdȯŋ, ˈdäŋ\ *n* — see MONEY table

don•key \ˈdäŋ-kē, ˈdəŋ-\ *n, pl* **donkeys 1 :** a sturdy and patient domestic mammal classified with the asses **2 :** a stupid or obstinate person

don•ny•brook \ˈdä-nē-ˌbru̇k\ *n, often cap* [*Donnybrook* Fair, annual Irish event once known for its brawls] **:** an uproarious brawl

do•nor \ˈdō-nər\ *n* **:** one that gives, donates, or presents

donut *var of* DOUGHNUT

doo•dad \ˈdü-ˌdad\ *n* **:** an often small article whose common name is unknown or forgotten

doo•dle \ˈdüd-ᵊl\ *vb* **doo•dled; doo•dling :** to draw or scribble aimlessly while occupied with something else — **doodle** *n* — **doo•dler** *n*

doom \ˈdüm\ *n* **1 :** JUDGMENT; *esp* **:** a judicial condemnation or sentence **2 :** DESTINY **3 :** RUIN, DEATH — **doom** *vb*

dooms•day \ˈdümz-ˌdā\ *n* **:** JUDGMENT DAY

door \ˈdōr\ *n* **1 :** a barrier by which an entry is closed and opened; *also* **:** a similar part of a piece of furniture **2 :** DOORWAY **3 :** a means of access or participation **:** OPPORTUNITY
door•keep•er \-ˌkē-pər\ *n* **:** a person who tends a door
door•knob \-ˌnäb\ *n* **:** a knob that when turned releases a door latch
door•man \-ˌman, -mən\ *n* **:** a usu. uniformed attendant at the door of a building (as a hotel)
door•mat \-ˌmat\ *n* **:** a mat placed before or inside a door for wiping dirt from the shoes
door•plate \-ˌplāt\ *n* **:** a nameplate on a door
door•step \-ˌstep\ *n* **:** a step or series of steps before an outer door
door•way \-ˌwā\ *n* **1 :** the opening that a door closes **2 :** DOOR 3
do•pa \ˈdō-pə\ *n* **:** a form of an amino acid that is used esp. in the treatment of Parkinson's disease
[1]**dope** \ˈdōp\ *n* **1 :** a preparation for giving a desired quality **2 :** a drug esp. when narcotic or addictive and used illegally **3 :** a stupid person **4 :** INFORMATION
[2]**dope** *vb* **doped; dop•ing 1 :** to treat with dope; *esp* **:** to give a narcotic to **2 :** FIGURE OUT — usu. used with *out* **3 :** to take dope — **dop•er** *n*
dop•ey *also* **dopy** \ˈdō-pē\ *adj* **dop•i•er; -est 1 :** dulled by alcohol or a narcotic **2 :** SLUGGISH **3 :** STUPID — **dop•i•ness** *n*
Dopp•ler effect \ˈdä-plər-\ *n* **:** a change in the frequency at which waves (as of sound) reach an observer from a source in motion with respect to the observer
dork \ˈdȯrk\ *n, slang* **:** NERD; *also* **:** JERK 2
dorm \ˈdȯrm\ *n* **:** DORMITORY
dor•mant \ˈdȯr-mənt\ *adj* **:** INACTIVE; *esp* **:** not actively growing or functioning ⟨~ buds⟩ — **dor•man•cy** \-mən-sē\ *n*
dor•mer \ˈdȯr-mər\ *n* [MF *dormeor* dormitory, fr. L *dormitorium,* fr. *dormire* to sleep] **:** a window built upright in a sloping roof; *also* **:** the roofed structure containing such a window
dor•mi•to•ry \ˈdȯr-mə-ˌtōr-ē\ *n, pl* **-ries 1 :** a room for sleeping; *esp* **:** a large room containing a number of beds **2 :** a residence hall providing sleeping rooms
dor•mouse \ˈdȯr-ˌmau̇s\ *n* **:** any of numerous Old World squirrellike rodents
dor•sal \ˈdȯr-səl\ *adj* **:** of, relating to, or located near or on the surface of the body that in humans is the back but in most other animals is the upper surface — **dor•sal•ly** *adv*
do•ry \ˈdōr-ē\ *n, pl* **dories :** a flat-bottomed boat with high flaring sides and a sharp bow
DOS *abbr* disk operating system
[1]**dose** \ˈdōs\ *n* [ME, fr. MF, fr. LL *dosis,* fr. Gk, lit., act of giving, fr. *didonai* to give] **1 :** a measured quantity (as of medicine) to be taken or administered at one time **2 :** the quantity of radiation administered or absorbed — **dos•age** \ˈdō-sij\ *n*
[2]**dose** *vb* **dosed; dos•ing 1 :** to give in doses **2 :** to give medicine to
do•sim•e•ter \dō-ˈsi-mə-tər\ *n* **:** a device for measuring doses of X rays or of radioactivity — **do•sim•e•try** \-mə-trē\ *n*
dos•sier \ˈdȯs-ˌyā, ˈdȯ-sē-ˌā\ *n* [F, bundle of documents labeled on the back, dossier, fr. *dos* back, fr. L *dorsum*] **:** a file containing detailed records on a particular person or subject
[1]**dot** \ˈdät\ *n* **1 :** a small spot **:** SPECK **2 :** a small round mark **3 :** a precise point esp. in time ⟨be here on the ~⟩
[2]**dot** *vb* **dot•ted; dot•ting 1 :** to mark with a dot ⟨~ an *i*⟩ **2 :** to cover with or as if with dots — **dot•ter** *n*
DOT *abbr* Department of Transportation
dot•age \ˈdō-tij\ *n* **:** feebleness of mind esp. in old age **:** SENILITY
dot•ard \-tərd\ *n* **:** a person in dotage
dote \ˈdōt\ *vb* **dot•ed; dot•ing 1 :** to be feebleminded esp. from old age **2 :** to be lavish or excessive in one's attention, affection, or fondness ⟨*doted* on her niece⟩
dot matrix *n* **:** a rectangular arrangement of dots from which alphanumeric characters can be formed (as by a computer printer)
Dou•ay Version \dü-ˈā-\ *n* **:** an English translation of the Vulgate used by Roman Catholics
[1]**dou•ble** \ˈdə-bəl\ *adj* **1 :** TWOFOLD, DUAL **2 :** consisting of two members or parts **3 :** being twice as great or as many **4 :** folded in two **5 :** having more than one whorl of petals ⟨~ roses⟩
[2]**double** *vb* **dou•bled; dou•bling 1 :** to make, be, or become twice as great or as many **2 :** to make a call in bridge that increases the trick values and penalties of (an opponent's bid) **3 :** FOLD **4 :** CLENCH **5 :** to be or cause to be bent over **6 :** to take the place of another **7 :** to hit a double **8 :** to turn sharply and suddenly; *esp* **:** to turn back on one's course
[3]**double** *adv* **1 :** DOUBLY **2 :** two together
[4]**double** *n* **1 :** something twice another in size, strength, speed, quantity, or value **2 :** a base hit that enables the batter to reach second base **3 :** COUNTERPART, DUPLICATE; *esp* **:** a person who closely resembles another **4 :** UNDERSTUDY, SUBSTITUTE **5 :** a sharp turn **:** REVERSAL **6 :** FOLD **7 :** a combined bet placed on two different contests **8** *pl* **:** a game between two pairs of players **9 :** an act of doubling in a card game
double bond *n* **:** a chemical bond in which two atoms in a molecule share two pairs of electrons
double cross *n* **:** an act of betraying or cheating esp. an associate — **dou•ble–cross** \ˌdə-bəl-ˈkrȯs\ *vb* — **dou•ble–cross•er** *n*
dou•ble–deal•ing \ˌdə-bəl-ˈdē-liŋ\ *n* **:** DUPLICITY — **dou•ble–deal•er** \-ˈdē-lər\ *n* — **double–dealing** *adj*
dou•ble–deck•er \-ˈde-kər\ *n* **:** something having two decks, levels, or layers — **dou•ble–deck** \-ˌdek\ *or* **dou•ble–decked** \-ˌdekt\ *adj*
dou•ble–dig•it \ˌdə-bəl-ˈdi-jət\ *adj* **:** amounting to 10 percent or more
dou•ble en•ten•dre \ˌdüb-^{ə}l-ä^{n}-ˈtä^{n}d, ˌdə-bəl-, -ˈtändr^{ə}\ *n, pl* **double entendres** *same or* -ˈtän-drəz\ [obs. F, lit., double meaning] **:** a word or expression capable of two interpretations with one usu. risqué
dou•ble•head•er \ˌdə-bəl-ˈhe-dər\ *n* **:** two games played consecutively on the same day
double helix *n* **:** a helix or spiral consisting of two strands (as of DNA) in the surface of a cylinder which coil around its axis
dou•ble–hung \ˌdə-bəl-ˈhəŋ\ *adj, of a window* **:** having an upper and a lower sash that can slide past each other
dou•ble–joint•ed \-ˈjȯin-təd\ *adj* **:** having a joint that permits an exceptional degree of freedom of motion of the parts joined ⟨a ~ finger⟩
double play *n* **:** a play in baseball by which two players are put out
dou•blet \ˈdə-blət\ *n* **1 :** a man's close-fitting jacket worn in Europe esp. in the 16th century **2 :** one of two similar or identical things
dou•ble take \ˈdə-bəl-ˌtāk\ *n* **:** a delayed reaction to a surprising or significant situation after an initial failure to notice anything unusual
dou•ble–talk \-ˌtȯk\ *n* **:** language that appears to be meaningful but in fact is a mixture of sense and nonsense
double up *vb* **:** to share accommodations designed for one
double whammy *n* **:** a combination of two usu. adverse forces, circumstances, or effects
dou•bloon \ˌdə-ˈblün\ *n* **:** a former gold coin of Spain and Spanish America
dou•bly \ˈdə-blē\ *adv* **1 :** in a twofold manner **2 :** to twice the degree
[1]**doubt** \ˈdau̇t\ *vb* **1 :** to be uncertain about **2 :** to lack confidence in **:** DISTRUST **3 :** to consider unlikely — **doubt•able** *adj* — **doubt•er** *n*
[2]**doubt** *n* **1 :** uncertainty of belief or opinion **2 :** a con-

dition causing uncertainty, hesitation, or suspense ⟨the outcome was in ~⟩ **3** : DISTRUST **4** : an inclination not to believe or accept

doubt•ful \ˈdau̇t-fəl\ *adj* **1** : QUESTIONABLE **2** : UNDECIDED — **doubt•ful•ly** *adv* — **doubt•ful•ness** *n*

[1]**doubt•less** \ˈdau̇t-ləs\ *adv* **1** : without doubt **2** : PROBABLY

[2]**doubtless** *adj* : free from doubt : CERTAIN — **doubtless•ly** *adv*

douche \ˈdüsh\ *n* [F] **1** : a jet of fluid (as water) directed against a part or into a cavity of the body; *also* : a cleansing with a douche **2** : a device for giving douches — **douche** *vb*

dough \ˈdō\ *n* **1** : a mixture that consists of flour or meal and a liquid (as milk or water) and is stiff enough to knead or roll **2** : something resembling dough esp. in consistency **3** : MONEY — **doughy** \ˈdō-ē\ *adj*

dough•boy \-ˌbȯi\ *n* : an American infantryman esp. in World War I

dough•nut \-(ˌ)nət\ *n* : a small usu. ring-shaped cake fried in fat

dough•ty \ˈdau̇-tē\ *adj* **dough•ti•er; -est** : ABLE, STRONG, VALIANT

Doug•las fir \ˈdə-gləs-\ *n* : a tall evergreen timber tree of the western U.S.

do up *vb* **1** : to prepare (as by cleaning) for use **2** : to wrap up **3** : CLOTHE, DECORATE

dour \ˈdau̇r, ˈdu̇r\ *adj* [ME, fr. L *durus* hard] **1** : STERN, HARSH **2** : OBSTINATE **3** : SULLEN — **dour•ly** *adv*

douse \ˈdau̇s, ˈdau̇z\ *vb* **doused; dous•ing 1** : to plunge into water **2** : DRENCH **3** : EXTINGUISH

[1]**dove** \ˈdəv\ *n* **1** : any of numerous pigeons; *esp* : a small wild pigeon **2** : an advocate of peace or of a peaceful policy — **dov•ish** \ˈdə-vish\ *adj*

[2]**dove** \ˈdōv\ *past of* DIVE

[1]**dove•tail** \ˈdəv-ˌtāl\ *n* : something that resembles a dove's tail; *esp* : a flaring tenon and a mortise into which it fits tightly

[2]**dovetail** *vb* **1** : to join by means of dovetails **2** : to fit skillfully together to form a whole ⟨our plans ~ nicely⟩

dow•a•ger \ˈdau̇-i-jər\ *n* **1** : a widow owning property or a title from her deceased husband **2** : a dignified elderly woman

dowdy \ˈdau̇-dē\ *adj* **dowd•i•er; -est** : lacking neatness and charm : SHABBY, UNTIDY; *also* : lacking smartness

dow•el \ˈdau̇-əl\ *n* **1** : a pin used for fastening together two pieces of wood **2** : a round rod (as of wood) — **dowel** *vb*

[1]**dow•er** \ˈdau̇-ər\ *n* **1** : the part of a deceased husband's real estate which the law gives for life to his widow **2** : DOWRY

[2]**dower** *vb* : to supply with a dower or dowry : ENDOW

dow•itch•er \ˈdau̇-i-chər\ *n* : any of several long-billed wading birds related to the sandpipers

[1]**down** \ˈdau̇n\ *adv* **1** : toward or in a lower physical position **2** : to a lying or sitting position **3** : toward or to the ground, floor, or bottom **4** : as a down payment ⟨paid $5 ~⟩ **5** : on paper ⟨put ~ what he says⟩ **6** : in a direction that is the opposite of up **7** : SOUTH **8** : to or in a lower or worse condition or status **9** : from a past time **10** : to or in a state of less activity **11** : into defeat ⟨voted the motion ~⟩

[2]**down** *prep* : down in, on, along, or through : toward the bottom of

[3]**down** *vb* **1** : to go or cause to go or come down **2** : DEFEAT **3** : to cause (a football) to be out of play

[4]**down** *adj* **1** : occupying a low position; *esp* : lying on the ground **2** : directed or going downward **3** : being in a state of reduced or low activity **4** : DEPRESSED, DEJECTED **5** : SICK ⟨~ with a cold⟩ **6** : FINISHED, DONE

[5]**down** *n* **1** : a low or falling period (as in activity, emotional life, or fortunes) **2** : one of a series of attempts to advance a football

[6]**down** *n* : a rolling usu. treeless upland with sparse soil — usu. used in pl.

[7]**down** *n* **1** : a covering of soft fluffy feathers; *also* : such feathers **2** : a downlike covering or material

down•beat \ˈdau̇n-ˌbēt\ *n* : the downward stroke of a conductor indicating the principally accented note of a measure of music

down•burst \-ˌbərst\ *n* : a powerful downdraft usu. associated with a thunderstorm that is a hazard for low-flying aircraft; *also* : MICROBURST

down•cast \-ˌkast\ *adj* **1** : DEJECTED **2** : directed down ⟨a ~ glance⟩

down•draft \-ˌdraft\ *n* : a downward current of gas (as air)

down•er \ˈdau̇-nər\ *n* **1** : a depressant drug; *esp* : BARBITURATE **2** : someone or something depressing

down•fall \ˈdau̇n-ˌfȯl\ *n* **1** : a sudden fall (as from high rank) **2** : something that causes a downfall — **down•fall•en** \-ˌfȯ-lən\ *adj*

[1]**down•grade** \ˈdau̇n-ˌgrād\ *n* **1** : a downward slope (as of a road) **2** : a decline toward a worse condition

[2]**downgrade** *vb* : to lower in quality, value, extent, or status

down•heart•ed \-ˈhär-təd\ *adj* : DEJECTED

down•hill \ˈdau̇n-ˈhil\ *adv* : toward the bottom of a hill — **downhill** \-ˌhil\ *adj*

down•load \-ˌlōd\ *vb* : to transfer (data) from a computer to another device — **down•load•able** \-ˌlō-də-bəl\ *adj*

down payment *n* : a part of the full price paid at the time of purchase or delivery with the balance to be paid later

down•pour \ˈdau̇n-ˌpōr\ *n* : a heavy rain

down•range \-ˈrānj\ *adv* : away from a launching site

[1]**down•right** \-ˌrīt\ *adv* : THOROUGHLY

[2]**downright** *adj* **1** : ABSOLUTE, UTTER ⟨a ~ lie⟩ **2** : PLAIN, BLUNT ⟨a ~ man⟩

down•shift \-ˌshift\ *vb* : to shift an automotive vehicle into a lower gear

down•size \-ˌsīz\ *vb* : to reduce or undergo reduction in size or numbers

down•spout \-ˌspau̇t\ *n* : a vertical pipe used to drain rainwater from a roof

Down's syndrome \ˈdau̇nz-\ *or* **Down syndrome** \ˈdau̇n-\ *n* : a birth defect characterized by mental retardation, slanting eyes, a broad short skull, broad hands with short fingers, and the presence of an extra chromosome

down•stage \ˈdau̇n-ˈstāj\ *adv or adj* : toward or at the front of a theatrical stage

down•stairs \-ˈstarz\ *adv* : on or to a lower floor and esp. the main or ground floor — **down•stairs** \-ˌstarz\ *adj or n*

down•stream \-ˈstrēm\ *adv or adj* : in the direction of flow of a stream

down•stroke \-ˌstrōk\ *n* : a downward stroke

down•swing \-ˌswiŋ\ *n* **1** : a swing downward **2** : DOWNTURN

down–to–earth *adj* : PRACTICAL, REALISTIC

down•town \ˈdau̇n-ˌtau̇n\ *n* : the main business district of a town or city — **downtown** \ˈdau̇n-ˈtau̇n\ *adj or adv*

down•trod•den \ˈdau̇n-ˈträd-ᵊn\ *adj* : suffering oppression

down•turn \-ˌtərn\ *n* : a downward turn esp. in business activity

[1]**down•ward** \ˈdau̇n-wərd\ *or* **down•wards** \-wərdz\ *adv* **1** : from a higher to a lower place or condition **2** : from an earlier time **3** : from an ancestor or predecessor

[2]**downward** *adj* : directed toward or situated in a lower place or condition

down•wind \ˈdau̇n-ˈwind\ *adv or adj* : in the direction that the wind is blowing

downy \ˈdau̇-nē\ *adj* **down•i•er; -est** : resembling or covered with down

downy mildew *n* : any of various parasitic fungi producing whitish masses esp. on the underside of plant leaves; *also* : a plant disease caused by downy mildew

downy woodpecker *n* : a small black-and-white woodpecker of No. America

dow•ry \ˈdau̇r-ē\ *n, pl* **dowries** : the property that a woman brings to her husband in marriage

dowse \ˈdau̇z\ *vb* **dowsed; dows•ing** : to use a divining rod esp. to find water — **dows•er** *n*

dox•ol•o•gy \däk-ˈsä-lə-jē\ *n, pl* **-gies** : a usu. short hymn of praise to God

doy•en \ˈdȯi-ən, ˈdwä-ˌyaⁿ\ *n* : the senior or most experienced person in a group

doy•enne \dȯi-ˈyen, dwä-ˈyen\ *n* : a woman who is a doyen

doy•ley *chiefly Brit var of* DOILY

doz *abbr* dozen

doze \ˈdōz\ *vb* **dozed; doz•ing** : to sleep lightly — **doze** *n*

doz•en \ˈdəz-ᵊn\ *n, pl* **dozens** *or* **dozen** [ME *dozeine,* fr. OF *dozaine,* fr. *doze* twelve, fr. L *duodecim,* fr. *duo* two + *decem* ten] : a group of twelve — **doz•enth** \-ᵊnth\ *adj*

¹**DP** \ˌdē-ˈpē\ *n, pl* **DP's** *or* **DPs** : a displaced person

²**DP** *abbr* **1** data processing **2** double play

dpt *abbr* department

DPT *abbr* diphtheria-pertussis-tetanus (vaccines)

dr *abbr* **1** debtor **2** dram **3** drive **4** drum

Dr *abbr* doctor

DR *abbr* **1** dead reckoning **2** dining room

drab \ˈdrab\ *adj* **drab•ber; drab•best 1** : being of a light olive-brown color **2** : DULL, MONOTONOUS, CHEERLESS — **drab•ly** *adv* — **drab•ness** *n*

drach•ma \ˈdrak-mə\ *n, pl* **drach•mas** *or* **drach•mai** \-ˌmī\ *or* **drach•mae** \-(ˌ)mē\ — see MONEY table

dra•co•ni•an \drā-ˈkō-nē-ən, drə-\ *adj, often cap* : CRUEL; *also* : SEVERE

¹**draft** \ˈdraft, ˈdrȧft\ *n* **1** : the act of drawing or hauling **2** : the act or an instance of drinking or inhaling; *also* : the portion drunk or inhaled in one such act **3** : DOSE, POTION **4** : DELINEATION, PLAN, DESIGN; *also* : a preliminary sketch, outline, or version ⟨a rough ~ of a speech⟩ **5** : the act of drawing (as from a cask); *also* : a portion of liquid so drawn **6** : the depth of water a ship draws esp. when loaded **7** : a system for or act of selecting persons esp. for compulsory military service; *also* : the persons so selected **8** : an order for the payment of money drawn by one person or bank on another **9** : a heavy demand : STRAIN **10** : a current of air; *also* : a device to regulate air supply (as in a stove) — **on draft** : ready to be drawn from a receptacle ⟨beer *on draft*⟩

²**draft** *adj* **1** : used or adapted for drawing loads ⟨~ horses⟩ **2** : being or having been on draft ⟨~ beer⟩

³**draft** *vb* **1** : to select usu. on a compulsory basis; *esp* : to conscript for military service **2** : to draw the preliminary sketch, version, or plan of **3** : COMPOSE, PREPARE **4** : to draw off or away — **draft•ee** \draf-ˈtē, drȧf-\ *n*

drafts•man \ˈdraft-smən, ˈdrȧft-\ *n* : a person who draws plans (as for buildings or machinery)

drafty \ˈdraf-tē, ˈdrȧf-\ *adj* **draft•i•er; -est** : exposed to or abounding in drafts of air

¹**drag** \ˈdrag\ *n* **1** : a device pulled along under water for detecting or gathering **2** : something (as a harrow or sledge) that is dragged along over a surface **3** : the act or an instance of dragging **4** : something that hinders progress; *also* : something boring **5** : STREET ⟨the main ~⟩ **6** : clothing typical of one sex worn by a member of the opposite sex

²**drag** *vb* **dragged; drag•ging 1** : HAUL **2** : to move with painful or undue slowness or difficulty **3** : to force into or out of some situation, condition, or course of action **4** : PROTRACT ⟨~ a story out⟩ **5** : to hang or lag behind **6** : to explore, search, or fish with a drag **7** : to trail along on the ground **8** : DRAW, PUFF ⟨~ on a cigarette⟩ — **drag•ger** *n*

drag•net \-ˌnet\ *n* **1** : NET, TRAWL **2** : a network of planned actions for pursuing and catching ⟨a police ~⟩

drag•o•man \ˈdra-gə-mən\ *n, pl* **-mans** *or* **-men** \-mən\ : an interpreter employed esp. in the Near East

drag•on \ˈdra-gən\ *n* [ME, fr. OF, fr. L *dracon-, draco* serpent, dragon, fr. Gk *drakōn* serpent] : a fabulous animal usu. represented as a huge winged scaly serpent with a crested head and large claws

drag•on•fly \-ˌflī\ *n* : any of a group of large harmless 4-winged insects that hold the wings horizontal and unfolded in repose

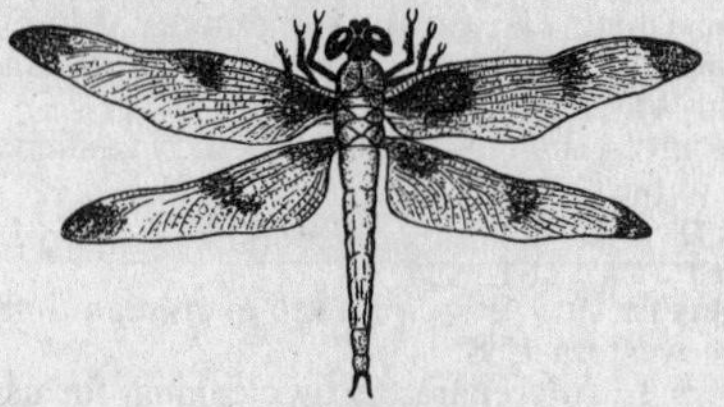

dragonfly

¹**dra•goon** \drə-ˈgün, dra-\ *n* [F *dragon* dragon, dragoon, fr. MF] : a heavily armed mounted soldier

²**dragoon** *vb* : to force or attempt to force into submission : COERCE

drag race *n* : an acceleration contest between vehicles

drag strip *n* : a site for drag races

¹**drain** \ˈdrān\ *vb* **1** : to draw off or flow off gradually or completely **2** : to exhaust physically or emotionally **3** : to make or become gradually dry or empty **4** : to carry away the surface water of : discharge surface or surplus water **5** : EMPTY, EXHAUST — **drain•er** *n*

²**drain** *n* **1** : a means (as a channel or sewer) of draining **2** : the act of draining **3** : a gradual outflow; *also* : something causing an outflow ⟨a ~ on our savings⟩

drain•age \ˈdrā-nij\ *n* **1** : the act or process of draining; *also* : something that is drained off **2** : a means for draining : DRAIN, SEWER **3** : an area drained

drain•pipe \ˈdrān-ˌpīp\ *n* : a pipe for drainage

drake \ˈdrāk\ *n* : a male duck

dram \ˈdram\ *n* **1** — see WEIGHT table **2** : FLUID DRAM **3** : a small drink

dra•ma \ˈdrä-mə, ˈdra-\ *n* [LL, fr. Gk, deed, drama, fr. *dran* to do, act] **1** : a literary composition designed for theatrical presentation **2** : dramatic art, literature, or affairs **3** : a series of events involving conflicting forces — **dra•mat•ic** \drə-ˈma-tik\ *adj* — **dra•mat•i•cal•ly** \-ti-k(ə-)lē\ *adv* — **dra•ma•tist** \ˈdra-mə-tist, ˈdrä-\ *n*

dramatise *Brit var of* DRAMATIZE

dra•ma•tize \ˈdra-mə-ˌtīz, ˈdrä-\ *vb* **-tized; -tiz•ing 1** : to adapt for or be suitable for theatrical presentation **2** : to present or represent in a dramatic manner — **dram•a•ti•za•tion** \ˌdra-mə-tə-ˈzā-shən, ˌdrä-\ *n*

dra•me•dy \ˈdrä-mə-dē, ˈdra-\ *n* : a situation comedy having dramatic scenes

drank *past and past part of* DRINK

¹**drape** \ˈdrāp\ *vb* **draped; drap•ing 1** : to cover or adorn with or as if with folds of cloth **2** : to cause to hang or stretch out loosely or carelessly **3** : to arrange or become arranged in flowing lines or folds

²**drape** *n* **1** : CURTAIN **2** : arrangement in or of folds **3** : the cut or hang of clothing

drap•er \ˈdrā-pər\ *n, chiefly Brit* : a dealer in cloth and sometimes in clothing and dry goods

drap•ery \ˈdrā-pə-rē\ *n, pl* **-er•ies 1** *Brit* : DRY GOODS **2** : a decorative fabric esp. when hung loosely and in folds; *also* : hangings of heavy fabric used as a curtain

dras•tic \ˈdras-tik\ *adj* : HARSH, RIGOROUS, SEVERE ⟨~ punishment⟩ — **dras•ti•cal•ly** \-ti-k(ə-)lē\ *adv*

draught \ˈdraft\, **draughty** \ˈdraf-tē\ *chiefly Brit var of* DRAFT, DRAFTY

draughts \ˈdrafts\ *n, Brit* : CHECKERS

draughts•man *chiefly Brit var of* DRAFTSMAN

[1]**draw** \ˈdrȯ\ *vb* **drew** \ˈdrü\; **drawn** \ˈdrȯn\; **draw•ing 1** : to cause to move toward a force exerted **2** : to cause to go in a certain direction ⟨*drew* him aside⟩ **3** : to move or go steadily or gradually ⟨night ~*s* near⟩ **4** : ATTRACT, ENTICE **5** : PROVOKE, ROUSE ⟨*drew* enemy fire⟩ **6** : INHALE ⟨~ a deep breath⟩ **7** : to bring or pull out ⟨*drew* a gun⟩ **8** : to cause to come out of a container ⟨~ water for a bath⟩ **9** : EVISCERATE **10** : to require (a specified depth) to float in **11** : ACCUMULATE, GAIN ⟨~*ing* interest⟩ **12** : to take money from a place of deposit : WITHDRAW **13** : to receive regularly ⟨~ a salary⟩ **14** : to take (cards) from a stack or the dealer **15** : to receive or take at random ⟨~ a winning number⟩ **16** : to bend (a bow) by pulling back the string **17** : WRINKLE, SHRINK **18** : to change shape by or as if by pulling or stretching ⟨a face *drawn* with sorrow⟩ **19** : to leave (a contest) undecided : TIE **20** : DELINEATE, SKETCH **21** : to write out in due form : DRAFT ⟨~ up a will⟩ **22** : FORMULATE ⟨~ comparisons⟩ **23** : INFER ⟨~ a conclusion⟩ **24** : to spread or elongate (metal) by hammering or by pulling through dies **25** : to produce or allow a draft or current of air ⟨the chimney ~*s* well⟩ **26** : to swell out in a wind ⟨all sails ~*ing*⟩

[2]**draw** *n* **1** : the act, process, or result of drawing **2** : a lot or chance drawn at random **3** : a contest left undecided or deadlocked : TIE **4** : one that draws attention or patronage

draw•back \ˈdrȯ-ˌbak\ *n* : DISADVANTAGE 2

draw•bridge \-ˌbrij\ *n* : a bridge made to be raised, lowered, or turned to permit or deny passage

draw•er \ˈdrȯr, ˈdrȯ-ər\ *n* **1** : one that draws **2** *pl* : an undergarment for the lower part of the body **3** : a sliding boxlike compartment (as in a table or desk)

draw•ing \ˈdrȯ-iŋ\ *n* **1** : an act or instance of drawing; *esp* : an occasion when something is decided by drawing lots ⟨tonight's lottery ~⟩ **2** : the act or art of making a figure, plan, or sketch by means of lines **3** : a representation made by drawing : SKETCH

drawing card *n* : DRAW 4

drawing room *n* : a formal reception room

drawl \ˈdrȯl\ *vb* : to speak or utter slowly with vowels greatly prolonged — **drawl** *n*

draw on *vb* : APPROACH ⟨night *draws on*⟩

draw out *vb* **1** : PROLONG **2** : to cause to speak freely

draw•string \ˈdrȯ-ˌstriŋ\ *n* : a string, cord, or tape for use in closing a bag or controlling fullness in garments or curtains

draw up *vb* **1** : to prepare a draft or version of **2** : to pull oneself erect **3** : to bring or come to a stop

dray \ˈdrā\ *n* : a strong low cart for carrying heavy loads

[1]**dread** \ˈdred\ *vb* **1** : to fear greatly **2** : to feel extreme reluctance to meet or face

[2]**dread** *n* : great fear esp. of some harm to come

[3]**dread** *adj* **1** : causing great fear or anxiety **2** : inspiring awe

dread•ful \ˈdred-fəl\ *adj* **1** : inspiring dread or awe : FRIGHTENING **2** : extremely distasteful, unpleasant, or shocking — **dread•ful•ly** *adv*

dread•locks \ˈdred-ˌläks\ *n pl* : long braids of hair over the entire head

dread•nought \ˈdred-ˌnȯt\ *n* : BATTLESHIP

[1]**dream** \ˈdrēm\ *n* [ME *dreem*, fr. OE *drēam* noise, joy, and ON *draumr* dream] **1** : a series of thoughts, images, or emotions occurring during sleep **2** : a dreamlike vision : DAYDREAM, REVERIE **3** : something notable for its beauty, excellence, or enjoyable quality **4** : IDEAL — **dreamy** *adj*

[2]**dream** \ˈdrēm\ *vb* **dreamed** \ˈdremt, ˈdrēmd\ *or* **dreamt** \ˈdremt\; **dream•ing 1** : to have a dream of **2** : to indulge in daydreams or fantasies : pass (time) in reverie or inaction **3** : IMAGINE — **dream•er** *n*

dream•land \ˈdrēm-ˌland\ *n* : an unreal delightful country that exists in imagination or in dreams

dream up *vb* : INVENT, CONCOCT

dream•world \-ˌwərld\ *n* : a world of illusion or fantasy

drear \ˈdrir\ *adj* : DREARY

drea•ry \ˈdrir-ē\ *adj* **drea•ri•er; -est** [ME *drery*, fr. OE *drēorig* sad, bloody, fr. *drēor* gore] **1** : DOLEFUL, SAD **2** : DISMAL, GLOOMY — **drea•ri•ly** \-ə-lē\ *adv*

[1]**dredge** \ˈdrej\ *vb* **dredged; dredg•ing** : to gather or search with or as if with a dredge — **dredg•er** *n*

[2]**dredge** *n* : a machine or barge for removing earth or silt

[3]**dredge** *vb* **dredged; dredg•ing** : to coat (food) by sprinkling (as with flour)

dregs \ˈdregz\ *n pl* **1** : SEDIMENT 1 **2** : the most undesirable part ⟨the ~ of humanity⟩

drench \ˈdrench\ *vb* : to wet thoroughly

[1]**dress** \ˈdres\ *vb* **1** : to make or set straight : ALIGN **2** : to prepare for use; *esp* : BUTCHER **3** : TRIM, EMBELLISH ⟨~ a store window⟩ **4** : to put clothes on : CLOTHE; *also* : to put on or wear formal or fancy clothes **5** : to apply dressings or medicine to **6** : to arrange (the hair) by combing, brushing, or curling **7** : to apply fertilizer to **8** : SMOOTH, FINISH ⟨~ leather⟩

[2]**dress** *n* **1** : APPAREL, CLOTHING **2** : a garment usu. consisting of a one-piece bodice and skirt — **dress•mak•er** \-ˌmā-kər\ *n* — **dress•mak•ing** \-ˌmā-kiŋ\ *n*

[3]**dress** *adj* : suitable for a formal occasion; *also* : requiring formal dress

dres•sage \drə-ˈsäzh\ *n* [F] : the execution by a trained horse of complex movements in response to barely perceptible signals from its rider

dress down *vb* : to scold severely

[1]**dress•er** \ˈdre-sər\ *n* : a chest of drawers or bureau with a mirror

[2]**dresser** *n* : one that dresses

dress•ing \ˈdre-siŋ\ *n* **1** : the act or process of one who dresses **2** : a sauce for adding to a dish (as a salad) **3** : a seasoned mixture usu. used as stuffing **4** : material used to cover an injury

dressing gown *n* : a loose robe worn esp. while dressing or resting

dressy \ˈdre-sē\ *adj* **dress•i•er; -est 1** : showy in dress **2** : STYLISH, SMART

drew *past of* DRAW

[1]**drib•ble** \ˈdri-bəl\ *vb* **drib•bled; drib•bling 1** : to fall or flow in drops : TRICKLE **2** : DROOL **3** : to propel by successive slight taps or bounces

[2]**dribble** *n* **1** : a small trickling stream or flow **2** : a drizzling shower **3** : the dribbling of a ball or puck

drib•let \ˈdri-blət\ *n* **1** : a trifling amount **2** : a drop of liquid

dri•er *or* **dry•er** \ˈdrī-ər\ *n* **1** : a substance that speeds drying (as of paint or ink) **2** *usu* *dryer* : a device for drying

[1]**drift** \ˈdrift\ *n* **1** : the motion or course of something drifting **2** : a mass of matter (as snow or sand) piled up esp. by wind **3** : earth, gravel, and rock deposited by a glacier **4** : a general underlying design or tendency : MEANING

[2]**drift** *vb* **1** : to float or be driven along by or as if by a current of water or air **2** : to become piled up by wind or water

drift•er \ˈdrif-tər\ *n* : a person without aim, ambition, or initiative

drift net *n* : a fishing net often miles in extent arranged to drift with the tide or current

drift•wood \ˈdrift-ˌwu̇d\ *n* : wood drifted or floated by water

[1]drill \ˈdril\ *n* **1 :** a tool for boring holes **2 :** the training of soldiers in marching and the handling of arms **3 :** a regularly practiced exercise

[2]drill *vb* **1 :** to instruct and exercise by repetition **2 :** to train in or practice military drill **3 :** to bore with a drill — **drill•er** *n*

[3]drill *n* **1 :** a shallow furrow or trench in which seed is sown **2 :** an agricultural implement for making furrows and dropping seed into them

[4]drill *n* **:** a firm cotton twilled fabric

drill•mas•ter \ˈdril-ˌmas-tər\ *n* **:** an instructor in military drill

drill press *n* **:** an upright drilling machine in which the drill is pressed to the work usu. by a hand lever

drily *var of* DRYLY

[1]drink \ˈdriŋk\ *vb* **drank** \ˈdraŋk\; **drunk** \ˈdrəŋk\ *or* **drank; drink•ing 1 :** to swallow liquid **:** IMBIBE **2 :** ABSORB **3 :** to take in through the senses ⟨~ in the beautiful scenery⟩ **4 :** to give or join in a toast **5 :** to drink alcoholic beverages esp. to excess — **drink•able** *adj* — **drink•er** *n*

[2]drink *n* **1 :** BEVERAGE; *also* **:** an alcoholic beverage **2 :** a draft or portion of liquid **3 :** excessive consumption of alcoholic beverages

[1]drip \ˈdrip\ *vb* **dripped; drip•ping 1 :** to fall or let fall in drops **2 :** to let fall drops of moisture or liquid ⟨a *dripping* faucet⟩ **3 :** to overflow with or as if with moisture

[2]drip *n* **1 :** a falling in drops **2 :** liquid that falls, overflows, or is extruded in drops **3 :** the sound made by or as if by falling drops

[1]drive \ˈdrīv\ *vb* **drove** \ˈdrōv\; **driv•en** \ˈdri-vən\; **driv•ing 1 :** to urge, push, or force onward **2 :** to carry through strongly ⟨~ a bargain⟩ **3 :** to set or keep in motion or operation **4 :** to direct the movement or course of **5 :** to convey in a vehicle **6 :** to bring into a specified condition ⟨the noise ~*s* me crazy⟩ **7 :** FORCE, COMPEL ⟨*driven* by hunger to steal⟩ **8 :** to project, inject, or impress forcefully ⟨*drove* the lesson home⟩ **9 :** to produce by opening a way ⟨~ a well⟩ **10 :** to progress with strong momentum ⟨a *driving* rain⟩ **11 :** to propel an object of play (as a golf ball) by a hard blow — **driv•er** *n*

[2]drive *n* **1 :** a trip in a carriage or automobile **2 :** a driving or collecting of animals ⟨a cattle ~⟩ **3 :** the guiding of logs downstream to a mill **4 :** the act of driving a ball; *also* **:** the flight of a ball **5 :** DRIVEWAY **6 :** a public road for driving (as in a park) **7 :** the state of being hurried and under pressure **8 :** an intensive campaign ⟨membership ~⟩ **9 :** the apparatus by which motion is imparted to a machine **10 :** an offensive or aggressive move **:** a military attack **11 :** NEED, LONGING **12 :** dynamic quality **13 :** a device for reading and writing on magnetic media (as magnetic tape or disks)

drive–in \ˈdrī-ˌvin\ *adj* **:** accommodating patrons while they remain in their automobiles — **drive–in** *n*

[1]driv•el \ˈdri-vəl\ *vb* **-eled** *or* **-elled; -el•ing** *or* **-el•ling 1 :** DROOL, SLAVER **2 :** to talk or utter stupidly, carelessly, or in an infantile way — **driv•el•er** *n*

[2]drivel *n* **:** NONSENSE

drive•shaft \ˈdrīv-ˌshaft\ *n* **:** a shaft that transmits mechanical power

drive•way \-ˌwā\ *n* **:** a short private road leading from the street to a house, garage, or parking lot

[1]driz•zle \ˈdri-zəl\ *n* **:** a fine misty rain

[2]drizzle *vb* **driz•zled; driz•zling :** to rain in very small drops

drogue \ˈdrōg\ *n* **:** a small parachute for slowing down or stabilizing something (as a space capsule)

droll \ˈdrōl\ *adj* [F *drôle,* fr. *drôle* scamp, fr. MF *drolle,* fr. MD, imp] **:** having a humorous, whimsical, or odd quality ⟨a ~ expression⟩ — **droll•ery** \ˈdrō-lə-rē\ *n* — **drol•ly** *adv*

drom•e•dary \ˈdrä-mə-ˌder-ē\ *n, pl* **-dar•ies** [ME *dromedarie,* fr. MF *dromedaire,* fr. LL *dromedarius,* fr. L *dromad-, dromas,* fr. Gk, running] **:** CAMEL; *esp* **:** a domesticated one-humped camel of western Asia and northern Africa

[1]drone \ˈdrōn\ *n* **1 :** a male honeybee **2 :** one that lives on the labors of others **:** PARASITE **3 :** an unmanned aircraft or ship guided by remote control

[2]drone *vb* **droned; dron•ing :** to sound with a low dull monotonous murmuring sound **:** speak monotonously

[3]drone *n* **:** a deep monotonous sound

drool \ˈdrül\ *vb* **1 :** to let liquid flow from the mouth **2 :** to talk foolishly

droop \ˈdrüp\ *vb* **1 :** to hang or incline downward **2 :** to sink gradually **3 :** LANGUISH — **droop** *n* — **droopy** *adj*

[1]drop \ˈdräp\ *n* **1 :** the quantity of fluid that falls in one spherical mass **2** *pl* **:** a dose of medicine measured by drops **3 :** a small quantity of drink **4 :** the smallest practical unit of liquid measure **5 :** something (as a pendant or a small round candy) that resembles a liquid drop **6 :** FALL **7 :** a decline in quantity or quality **8 :** a descent by parachute **9 :** the distance through which something drops **10 :** a slot into which something is to be dropped **11 :** something that drops or has dropped

[2]drop *vb* **dropped; drop•ping 1 :** to fall or let fall in drops **2 :** to let fall **:** LOWER ⟨~ a glove⟩ ⟨*dropped* his voice⟩ **3 :** SEND ⟨~ me a note⟩ **4 :** to let go **:** DISMISS ⟨~ the subject⟩ **5 :** to knock down **:** cause to fall **6 :** to go lower **:** become less ⟨prices *dropped*⟩ **7 :** to come or go unexpectedly or informally ⟨~ in to call⟩ **8 :** to pass from one state into a less active one ⟨~ off to sleep⟩ **9 :** to move downward or with a current **10 :** QUIT ⟨*dropped* out of the race⟩ — **drop back :** to move toward the rear — **drop behind :** to fail to keep up

drop•kick \-ˈkik\ *n* **:** a kick made by dropping a ball to the ground and kicking it at the moment it starts to rebound — **drop–kick** *vb*

drop•let \ˈdrä-plət\ *n* **:** a tiny drop

drop–off \ˈdräp-ˌȯf\ *n* **1 :** a steep or perpendicular descent **2 :** a marked decline ⟨a ~ in attendance⟩

drop off *vb* **:** to fall asleep

drop out *vb* **:** to withdraw from participation or membership; *esp* **:** to leave school before graduation — **drop•out** \ˈdräp-ˌau̇t\ *n*

drop•per \ˈdrä-pər\ *n* **1 :** one that drops **2 :** a short glass tube with a rubber bulb used to measure out liquids by drops

drop•pings *n pl* **:** MANURE, DUNG

drop•sy \ˈdräp-sē\ *n* [ME *dropesie,* short for *ydropesie,* fr. OF, fr. L *hydropisis,* fr. Gk *hydrōps,* fr. *hydōr* water] **:** EDEMA — **drop•si•cal** \-si-kəl\ *adj*

dross \ˈdräs\ *n* **1 :** the scum that forms on the surface of a molten metal **2 :** waste matter **:** REFUSE

drought \ˈdrau̇t\ *also* **drouth** \ˈdrau̇th\ *n* **:** a long spell of dry weather

[1]drove \ˈdrōv\ *n* **1 :** a group of animals driven or moving in a body **2 :** a large number **:** CROWD — usu. used in pl. ⟨tourists arriving in ~*s*⟩

[2]drove *past of* DRIVE

drov•er \ˈdrō-vər\ *n* **:** one that drives domestic animals usu. to market

drown \ˈdrau̇n\ *vb* **drowned** \ˈdrau̇nd\; **drown•ing 1 :** to suffocate by submersion esp. in water **2 :** to become drowned **3 :** to cover with water **4 :** to cause to be muted (as a sound) by a loud noise **5 :** OVERPOWER, OVERWHELM

drowse \ˈdrau̇z\ *vb* **drowsed; drows•ing :** DOZE — **drowse** *n*

drowsy \ˈdrau̇-zē\ *adj* **drows•i•er; -est 1 :** ready to fall asleep **2 :** making one sleepy — **drows•i•ly** \-zə-lē\ *adv* — **drows•i•ness** \-zē-nəs\ *n*

drub \ˈdrəb\ *vb* **drubbed; drub•bing 1 :** to beat severely **2 :** to defeat decisively

drudge \ˈdrəj\ *vb* **drudged; drudg•ing :** to do hard, menial, or monotonous work — **drudge** *n* — **drudg•ery** \ˈdrə-jə-rē\ *n*

[1]drug \ˈdrəg\ *n* **1 :** a substance used as or in medicine **2 :** a substance (as heroin or marijuana) that can cause addiction, a marked change in mental status, or psychological dependency

[2]drug *vb* **drugged; drug•ging :** to affect with or as if with drugs; *esp* **:** to stupefy with a narcotic

drug•gist \ˈdrə-gist\ *n* **:** a dealer in drugs and medicines; *also* **:** PHARMACIST

drug•store \ˈdrəg-ˌstōr\ *n* **:** a retail shop where medicines and miscellaneous articles are sold

dru•id \ˈdrü-əd\ *n, often cap* **:** one of an ancient Celtic priesthood appearing in Irish, Welsh, and Christian legends as magicians and wizards

[1]drum \ˈdrəm\ *n* **1 :** a percussion instrument usu. consisting of a hollow cylinder with a skin or plastic head stretched over one or both ends that is beaten with the hands or with a stick **2 :** the sound of a drum; *also* **:** a similar sound **3 :** a drum-shaped object

[2]drum *vb* **drummed; drum•ming 1 :** to beat a drum **2 :** to sound rhythmically **:** THROB, BEAT **3 :** to summon or enlist by or as if by beating a drum ⟨*drummed* into service⟩ **4 :** EXPEL — usu. used with *out* **5 :** to drive or force by steady effort ⟨∼ the facts into memory⟩ **6 :** to strike or tap repeatedly so as to produce rhythmic sounds

drum•beat \ˈdrəm-ˌbēt\ *n* **:** a stroke on a drum or its sound

drum major *n* **:** the leader of a marching band

drum ma•jor•ette \-ˌmā-jə-ˈret\ *n* **:** a girl or woman who leads a marching band; *also* **:** a baton twirler who accompanies a marching band

drum•mer \ˈdrə-mər\ *n* **1 :** one that plays a drum **2 :** a traveling salesman

drum•stick \ˈdrəm-ˌstik\ *n* **1 :** a stick for beating a drum **2 :** the lower segment of a fowl's leg

drum up *vb* **1 :** to bring about by persistent effort ⟨*drum up* business⟩ **2 :** INVENT, ORIGINATE

[1]drunk *past part of* DRINK

[2]drunk \ˈdrəŋk\ *adj* **1 :** having the faculties impaired by alcohol ⟨∼ drivers⟩ **2 :** dominated by an intense feeling ⟨∼ with power⟩ **3 :** of, relating to, or caused by intoxication

[3]drunk *n* **1 :** a period of excessive drinking **2 :** a drunken person

drunk•ard \ˈdrəŋ-kərd\ *n* **:** one who is habitually drunk

drunk•en \ˈdrəŋ-kən\ *adj* **1 :** DRUNK **2 :** given to habitual excessive use of alcohol **3 :** of, relating to, or resulting from intoxication **4 :** unsteady or lurching as if from intoxication — **drunk•en•ly** *adv* — **drunk•en•ness** *n*

drupe \ˈdrüp\ *n* **:** a partly fleshy one-seeded fruit (as a plum or cherry) that remains closed at maturity

[1]dry \ˈdrī\ *adj* **dri•er** \ˈdrī-ər\; **dri•est** \-əst\ **1 :** free or freed from water or liquid ⟨∼ fruits⟩; *also* **:** not being in or under water **2 :** characterized by lack of water or moisture ⟨∼ climate⟩ **3 :** lacking freshness **:** STALE **4 :** devoid of natural moisture; *also* **:** THIRSTY **5 :** no longer liquid or sticky ⟨the ink is ∼⟩ **6 :** not giving milk ⟨a ∼ cow⟩ **7 :** marked by the absence of alcoholic beverages **8 :** prohibiting the making or distributing of alcoholic beverages **9 :** not sweet ⟨∼ wine⟩ **10 :** solid as opposed to liquid ⟨∼ groceries⟩ **11 :** containing or employing no liquid **12 :** SEVERE; *also* **:** UNINTERESTING, WEARISOME **13 :** not productive **14 :** marked by a matter-of-fact, ironic, or terse manner of expression ⟨∼ humor⟩ — **dry•ly** *adv* — **dry•ness** *n*

[2]dry *vb* **dried; dry•ing :** to make or become dry

[3]dry *n, pl* **drys :** PROHIBITIONIST

dry•ad \ˈdrī-əd, -ˌad\ *n* **:** WOOD NYMPH

dry cell *n* **:** a battery whose contents are not spillable

dry–clean \ˈdrī-ˌklēn\ *vb* **:** to clean (fabrics) chiefly with solvents other than water — **dry cleaning** *n*

dry dock \ˈdrī-ˌdäk\ *n* **:** a dock that can be kept dry during ship construction or repair

dry•er *var of* DRIER

dry farm•ing *n* **:** farming without irrigation in areas of limited rainfall — **dry–farm** *vb* — **dry farm•er** *n*

dry goods \ˈdrī-ˌgu̇dz\ *n pl* **:** cloth goods (as fabrics, ribbon, and ready-to-wear clothing)

dry ice *n* **:** solid carbon dioxide

dry measure *n* **:** a series of units of capacity for dry commodities — see METRIC SYSTEM table, WEIGHT table

dry run *n* **:** REHEARSAL, TRIAL

dry•wall \ˈdrī-ˌwȯl\ *n* **:** PLASTERBOARD

DSC *abbr* **1** Distinguished Service Cross **2** doctor of surgical chiropody

DSM *abbr* Distinguished Service Medal

DST *abbr* daylight saving time

DTP *abbr* diphtheria, tetanus, pertussis (vaccines)

d.t.'s \ˌdē-ˈtēz\ *n pl, often cap D&T* **:** DELIRIUM TREMENS

du•al \ˈdü-əl, ˈdyü-\ *adj* **1 :** TWOFOLD, DOUBLE **2 :** having a double character or nature — **du•al•ism** \-ə-ˌli-zəm\ *n* — **du•al•i•ty** \dü-ˈa-lə-tē, dyü-\ *n*

[1]dub \ˈdəb\ *vb* **dubbed; dub•bing 1 :** to confer knighthood upon **2 :** NAME, NICKNAME

[2]dub *n* **:** a clumsy person **:** DUFFER

[3]dub *vb* **dubbed; dub•bing :** to add (sound effects) to a motion picture or to a radio or television production

du•bi•ety \dü-ˈbī-ə-tē, dyü-\ *n, pl* **-eties 1 :** UNCERTAINTY **2 :** a matter of doubt

du•bi•ous \ˈdü-bē-əs, ˈdyü-\ *adj* **1 :** UNCERTAIN **2 :** QUESTIONABLE **3 :** feeling doubt **:** UNDECIDED — **du•bi•ous•ly** *adv* — **du•bi•ous•ness** *n*

du•cal \ˈdü-kəl, ˈdyü-\ *adj* **:** of or relating to a duke or dukedom

duc•at \ˈdə-kət\ *n* **:** a gold coin formerly used in various European countries

duch•ess \ˈdə-chəs\ *n* **1 :** the wife or widow of a duke **2 :** a woman holding the rank of duke in her own right

duchy \ˈdə-chē\ *n, pl* **duch•ies :** the territory of a duke or duchess **:** DUKEDOM

[1]duck \ˈdək\ *n, pl* **ducks :** any of various swimming birds related to but smaller than geese and swans

[2]duck *vb* **1 :** to thrust or plunge under water **2 :** to lower the head or body suddenly **:** BOW; *also* **:** DODGE **3 :** to evade a duty, question, or responsibility ⟨∼ the issue⟩

[3]duck *n* **1 :** a durable closely woven usu. cotton fabric **2** *pl* **:** light clothes made of duck

duck•bill \ˈdək-ˌbil\ *n* **:** PLATYPUS

duck•ling \-liŋ\ *n* **:** a young duck

duck•pin \-ˌpin\ *n* **1 :** a small bowling pin shorter and wider in the middle than a tenpin **2** *pl but sing in constr* **:** a bowling game using duckpins

duct \ˈdəkt\ *n* **1 :** a tube or canal for conveying a bodily fluid **2 :** a pipe or tube through which a fluid (as air) flows — **duct•less** *adj*

duc•tile \ˈdəkt-ᵊl\ *adj* **1 :** capable of being drawn out (as into wire) or hammered thin **2 :** easily led **:** DOCILE — **duc•til•i•ty** \ˌdək-ˈti-lə-tē\ *n*

ductless gland *n* **:** an endocrine gland

dud \ˈdəd\ *n* **1** *pl* **:** CLOTHING **2 :** one that fails completely; *also* **:** a bomb or missile that fails to explode

dude \ˈdüd, ˈdyüd\ *n* **1 :** DANDY 1 **2 :** a city dweller; *esp* **:** an Easterner in the West **3 :** FELLOW, GUY

dude ranch *n* **:** a vacation resort offering activities (as horseback riding) typical of western ranches

dud•geon \ˈdə-jən\ *n* **:** a fit or state of indignation ⟨in high ∼⟩

[1]due \ˈdü, ˈdyü\ *adj* [ME, fr. MF *deu*, pp. of *devoir* to owe, fr. L *debēre*] **1 :** owed or owing as a debt **2 :** owed or owing as a right **3 :** APPROPRIATE, FITTING **4 :** SUFFICIENT, ADEQUATE **5 :** REGULAR, LAWFUL ⟨∼ process of law⟩ **6 :** ATTRIBUTABLE, ASCRIBABLE ⟨∼ to negligence⟩ **7 :** PAYABLE ⟨a bill ∼ today⟩ **8 :** SCHEDULED ⟨∼ to arrive soon⟩

[2]due *n* **1 :** something that rightfully belongs to one ⟨give everyone their ∼⟩ **2 :** DEBT **3** *pl* **:** FEES, CHARGES

DICTIONARY

[3]**due** *adv* : DIRECTLY, EXACTLY ⟨~ north⟩

du•el \ˈdü-əl, ˈdyü-\ *n* : a combat between two persons; *esp* : one fought with weapons in the presence of witnesses — **duel** *vb* — **du•el•ist** \-ə-list\ *n*

du•en•de \dü-ˈen-dā\ *n* [Sp dial., charm, fr. Sp, ghost, goblin, fr. *duen de casa,* prob. fr. *dueño de casa* owner of a house] : the power to attract through personal magnetism and charm

du•en•na \dü-ˈe-nə, dyü-\ *n* **1** : an elderly woman in charge of the younger ladies in a Spanish or Portuguese family **2** : CHAPERON

du•et \dü-ˈet, dyü-\ *n* : a musical composition for two performers

due to *prep* : BECAUSE OF

duf•fel bag \ˈdə-fəl-\ *n* : a large cylindrical bag for personal belongings

duf•fer \ˈdə-fər\ *n* : an incompetent or clumsy person

dug *past and past part of* DIG

dug•out \ˈdəg-ˌau̇t\ *n* **1** : a boat made by hollowing out a log **2** : a shelter dug in the ground **3** : a low shelter facing a baseball diamond that contains the players' bench

DUI *abbr* driving under the influence

duke \ˈdük, ˈdyük\ *n* **1** : a sovereign ruler of a continental European duchy **2** : a nobleman of the highest rank; *esp* : a member of the highest grade of the British peerage **3** *slang* : FIST 1 ⟨put up your ~*s*⟩ — **duke•dom** *n*

dul•cet \ˈdəl-sət\ *adj* **1** : pleasing to the ear **2** : AGREEABLE, SOOTHING

dul•ci•mer \ˈdəl-sə-mər\ *n* **1** : a stringed instrument of trapezoidal shape played with light hammers held in the hands **2** *or* **dul•ci•more** \-ˌmōr\ : an American folk instrument with three or four strings that is held on the lap and played by plucking or strumming

[1]**dull** \ˈdəl\ *adj* **1** : mentally slow : STUPID **2** : slow in perception or sensibility **3** : LISTLESS **4** : slow in action : SLUGGISH ⟨a ~ market⟩ **5** : lacking intensity; *also* : not resonant or ringing **6** : BLUNT **7** : lacking brilliance or luster **8** : low in saturation and lightness ⟨~ color⟩ **9** : CLOUDY, OVERCAST **10** : TEDIOUS, UNINTERESTING — **dull•ness** *or* **dul•ness** *n* — **dul•ly** *adv*

[2]**dull** *vb* : to make or become dull

dull•ard \ˈdə-lərd\ *n* : a stupid person

du•ly \ˈdü-lē, ˈdyü-\ *adv* : in a due manner or time

dumb \ˈdəm\ *adj* **1** : lacking the power of speech **2** : SILENT **3** : STUPID — **dumb•ly** *adv*

dumb•bell \ˈdəm-ˌbel\ *n* **1** : a bar with weights at the end used for exercise **2** : one who is stupid

dumb•found *or* **dum•found** \ˌdəm-ˈfau̇nd\ *vb* : ASTONISH, AMAZE

dumb•wait•er \ˈdəm-ˌwā-tər\ *n* : a small elevator for conveying food and dishes from one floor to another

dum•my \ˈdə-mē\ *n, pl* **dummies 1** : a person who cannot speak; *also* : a stupid person **2** : the exposed hand in bridge played by the declarer in addition to that player's own hand; *also* : a bridge player whose hand is a dummy **3** : an imitative substitute for something; *also* : MANNEQUIN **4** : one seeming to act alone but really acting for another **5** : a mock-up of matter to be reproduced esp. by printing

[1]**dump** \ˈdəmp\ *vb* : to let fall in a pile; *also* : to get rid of carelessly

[2]**dump** *n* **1** : a place for dumping something (as refuse) **2** : a reserve supply; *also* : a place where such supplies are kept ⟨an ammunition ~⟩ **3** : a messy or objectionable place

dump•ing \ˈdəm-piŋ\ *n* : the selling of goods in quantity at below market price

dump•ling \ˈdəm-pliŋ\ *n* **1** : a small mass of boiled or steamed dough **2** : a dessert of fruit baked in biscuit dough

dumps \ˈdəmps\ *n pl* : a gloomy state of mind : low spirits ⟨in the ~⟩

dump truck *n* : a truck for transporting and dumping bulk material

dumpy \ˈdəm-pē\ *adj* **dump•i•er; -est 1** : short and thick in build **2** : SHABBY

[1]**dun** \ˈdən\ *n* : a brownish dark gray

[2]**dun** *vb* **dunned; dun•ning 1** : to make persistent demands for payment **2** : PLAGUE, PESTER — **dun** *n*

dunce \ˈdəns\ *n* [John *Duns* Scotus, whose once accepted writings were ridiculed in the 16th cent.] : a slow stupid person

dun•der•head \ˈdən-dər-ˌhed\ *n* : DUNCE, BLOCKHEAD

dune \ˈdün, ˈdyün\ *n* : a hill or ridge of sand piled up by the wind

dune buggy *n* : a motor vehicle with oversize tires for use on sand

[1]**dung** \ˈdəŋ\ *n* : MANURE

[2]**dung** *vb* : to dress (land) with dung

dun•ga•ree \ˌdəŋ-gə-ˈrē\ *n* **1** : a heavy coarse cotton twill; *esp* : blue denim **2** *pl* : clothes made of blue denim

dun•geon \ˈdən-jən\ *n* [ME *donjon,* fr. MF, fr. (assumed) VL *domnion-, domnio* keep, mastery, fr. L *dominus* lord] : a dark prison commonly underground

dung•hill \ˈdəŋ-ˌhil\ *n* : a manure pile

dunk \ˈdəŋk\ *vb* **1** : to dip or submerge temporarily in liquid **2** : to submerge oneself in water **3** : to shoot a basketball into the basket from above the rim

duo \ˈdü-(ˌ)ō, ˈdyü-\ *n, pl* **du•os 1** : DUET **2** : PAIR 3

duo•dec•i•mal \ˌdü-ə-ˈde-sə-məl, ˌdyü-\ *adj* : of, relating to, or being a system of numbers with a base of 12

du•o•de•num \ˌdü-ə-ˈdē-nəm, ˌdyü-, du̇-ˈäd-ᵊn-əm, dyü-\ *n, pl* **-de•na** \-ˈdē-nə, -ᵊn-ə\ *or* **-denums** : the first part of the small intestine extending from the stomach to the jejunum — **du•o•de•nal** \-ˈdēn-ᵊl, -ᵊn-əl\ *adj*

dup *abbr* **1** duplex **2** duplicate

[1]**dupe** \ˈdüp, ˈdyüp\ *n* : one who is easily deceived or cheated : FOOL

[2]**dupe** *vb* **duped; dup•ing** : to make a dupe of : DECEIVE, FOOL

du•ple \ˈdü-pəl, ˈdyü-\ *adj* : having two beats or a multiple of two beats to the measure ⟨~ time⟩

[1]**du•plex** \ˈdü-ˌpleks, ˈdyü-\ *adj* : DOUBLE

[2]**duplex** *n* : something duplex; *esp* : a 2-family house

[1]**du•pli•cate** \ˈdü-pli-kət, ˈdyü-\ *adj* **1** : consisting of or existing in two corresponding or identical parts or examples **2** : being the same as another

[2]**du•pli•cate** \ˈdü-pli-ˌkāt, ˈdyü-\ *vb* **-cat•ed; -cat•ing 1** : to make double or twofold **2** : to make a copy of — **du•pli•ca•tion** \ˌdü-pli-ˈkā-shən, ˌdyü-\ *n*

[3]**du•pli•cate** \-kət\ *n* : a thing that exactly resembles another in appearance, pattern, or content : COPY

du•pli•ca•tor \ˈdü-pli-ˌkā-tər, ˈdyü-\ *n* : COPIER

du•plic•i•ty \du̇-ˈpli-sə-tē, dyu̇-\ *n, pl* **-ties** : the disguising of true intentions by deceptive words or action

du•ra•ble \ˈdu̇r-ə-bəl, ˈdyu̇r-\ *adj* : able to exist for a long time without significant deterioration ⟨~ goods⟩ — **du•ra•bil•i•ty** \ˌdu̇r-ə-ˈbi-lə-tē, ˌdyu̇r-\ *n*

du•rance \ˈdu̇r-əns, ˈdyu̇r-\ *n* : restraint by or as if by physical force ⟨held in ~ vile⟩

du•ra•tion \du̇-ˈrā-shən, dyu̇-\ *n* : the time during which something exists or lasts

du•ress \du̇-ˈres, dyu̇-\ *n* : compulsion by threat ⟨confession made under ~⟩

dur•ing \ˈdu̇r-iŋ, ˈdyu̇r-\ *prep* **1** : THROUGHOUT ⟨swims every day ~ the summer⟩ **2** : at some point in ⟨broke in ~ the night⟩

dusk \ˈdəsk\ *n* **1** : the darker part of twilight esp. at night **2** : partial darkness

dusky \ˈdəs-kē\ *adj* **dusk•i•er; -est 1** : somewhat dark in color **2** : SHADOWY — **dusk•i•ness** *n*

[1]**dust** \ˈdəst\ *n* **1** : fine particles of matter **2** : the particles into which something disintegrates **3** : something worthless **4** : the surface of the ground — **dustless** *adj* — **dusty** *adj*

[2]**dust** *vb* **1** : to make free of or remove dust **2** : to sprin-

kle with fine particles **3 :** to sprinkle in the form of dust
dust bowl *n* **:** a region suffering from long droughts and dust storms
dust devil *n* **:** a small whirlwind containing sand or dust
dust•er \ˈdəs-tər\ *n* **1 :** one that removes dust **2 :** a dress-length housecoat **3 :** one that scatters fine particles; *esp* **:** a device for applying insecticides to crops
dust•pan \ˈdəst-ˌpan\ *n* **:** a flat-ended pan for sweepings
dust storm *n* **:** a violent wind carrying dust across a dry region
dutch \ˈdəch\ *adv, often cap* **:** with each person paying his or her own way ⟨go ~⟩
Dutch \ˈdəch\ *n* **1 Dutch** *pl* **:** the people of the Netherlands **2 :** the language of the Netherlands — **Dutch** *adj* — **Dutch•man** \-mən\ *n*
Dutch elm disease *n* **:** a fungous disease of elms characterized by yellowing of the foliage, defoliation, and death
dutch treat *n, often cap D* **:** an entertainment (as a meal) for which each person pays his or her own way — **dutch treat** *adv, often cap D*
du•te•ous \ˈdü-tē-əs, ˈdyü-\ *adj* **:** DUTIFUL, OBEDIENT
du•ti•able \ˈdü-tē-ə-bəl, ˈdyü-\ *adj* **:** subject to a duty ⟨~ imports⟩
du•ti•ful \ˈdü-ti-fəl, ˈdyü-\ *adj* **1 :** motivated by a sense of duty ⟨a ~ son⟩ **2 :** coming from or showing a sense of duty ⟨~ affection⟩ — **du•ti•ful•ly** *adv* — **du•ti•ful•ness** *n*
du•ty \ˈdü-tē, ˈdyü-\ *n, pl* **duties 1 :** conduct or action required by one's occupation or position **2 :** assigned service or business; *esp* **:** active military service **3 :** a moral or legal obligation **4 :** TAX **5 :** the service required (as of a machine) **:** USE ⟨a heavy-*duty* tire⟩
DV *abbr* **1** [L *Deo volente*] God willing **2** Douay Version
DVM *abbr* doctor of veterinary medicine
[1]**dwarf** \ˈdwȯrf\ *n, pl* **dwarfs** \ˈdwȯrfs\ *or* **dwarves** \ˈdwȯrvz\ **:** one that is much below normal size — **dwarf•ish** *adj*
[2]**dwarf** *vb* **1 :** to restrict the growth or development of **:** STUNT **2 :** to cause to appear smaller ⟨*dwarfed* by comparison⟩
dwell \ˈdwel\ *vb* **dwelt** \ˈdwelt\ *or* **dwelled** \ˈdweld, ˈdwelt\; **dwell•ing** [ME, fr. OE *dwellan* to go astray, hinder] **1 :** ABIDE, REMAIN **2 :** RESIDE, EXIST **3 :** to keep the attention directed **4 :** to write or speak insistently — used with *on* or *upon* — **dwell•er** *n*
dwell•ing \ˈdwe-liŋ\ *n* **:** RESIDENCE
DWI *abbr* driving while intoxicated
dwin•dle \ˈdwind-ᵊl\ *vb* **dwin•dled; dwin•dling :** to make or become steadily less **:** DIMINISH
dwt *abbr* pennyweight
Dy *symbol* dysprosium
dyb•buk \ˈdi-bək\ *n, pl* **dyb•bu•kim** \ˌdi-bü-ˈkēm\ *also* **dybbuks :** a wandering soul believed in Jewish folklore to enter and possess a person
[1]**dye** \ˈdī\ *n* **1 :** color produced by dyeing **2 :** material used for coloring or staining
[2]**dye** *vb* **dyed; dye•ing 1 :** to impart a new color to esp. by impregnating with a dye **2 :** to take up or impart color in dyeing
dye•stuff \ˈdī-ˌstəf\ *n* **:** DYE 2
dying *pres part of* DIE
dyke *chiefly Brit var of* DIKE
dy•nam•ic \dī-ˈna-mik\ *also* **dy•nam•i•cal** \-mi-kəl\ *adj* **:** of or relating to physical force producing motion **:** ENERGETIC, FORCEFUL
[1]**dy•na•mite** \ˈdī-nə-ˌmīt\ *n* **:** an explosive made of nitroglycerin absorbed in a porous material; *also* **:** an explosive made without nitroglycerin
[2]**dynamite** *vb* **-mit•ed; -mit•ing :** to blow up with dynamite
dy•na•mo \ˈdī-nə-ˌmō\ *n, pl* **-mos :** an electrical generator
dy•na•mom•e•ter \ˌdī-nə-ˈmä-mə-tər\ *n* **:** an instrument for measuring mechanical power (as of an engine)
dy•nas•ty \ˈdī-nəs-tē, -ˌnas-\ *n, pl* **-ties 1 :** a succession of rulers of the same family **2 :** a powerful group or family that maintains its position for a long time — **dy•nas•tic** \dī-ˈnas-tik\ *adj*
dys•en•tery \ˈdis-ᵊn-ˌter-ē\ *n, pl* **-ter•ies :** a disease marked by diarrhea with blood and mucus in the feces; *also* **:** DIARRHEA
dys•lex•ia \dis-ˈlek-sē-ə\ *n* **:** a disturbance of the ability to read or use language — **dys•lex•ic** \-sik\ *adj or n*
dys•pep•sia \dis-ˈpep-shə, -sē-ə\ *n* **:** INDIGESTION — **dys•pep•tic** \-ˈpep-tik\ *adj or n*
dys•pro•si•um \dis-ˈprō-zē-əm\ *n* **:** a metallic chemical element that forms highly magnetic compounds — see ELEMENT table
dys•tro•phy \ˈdis-trə-fē\ *n, pl* **-phies :** a disorder involving atrophy of muscular tissue; *esp* **:** MUSCULAR DYSTROPHY
dz *abbr* dozen

E

[1]**e** \ˈē\ *n, pl* **e's** *or* **es** \ˈēz\ *often cap* **1 :** the 5th letter of the English alphabet **2 :** the base of the system of natural logarithms having the approximate value 2.71828 **3 :** a grade rating a student's work as poor or failing
[2]**e** *abbr, often cap* **1** east; eastern **2** error **3** excellent
ea *abbr* each
[1]**each** \ˈēch\ *adj* **:** being one of the class named ⟨~ man⟩
[2]**each** *pron* **:** every individual one
[3]**each** *adv* **:** APIECE ⟨cost five cents ~⟩
each other *pron* **:** each of two or more in reciprocal action or relation ⟨looked at *each other*⟩
ea•ger \ˈē-gər\ *adj* **:** marked by urgent or enthusiastic desire or interest ⟨~ to learn⟩ **syn** avid, anxious, ardent, keen — **ea•ger•ly** *adv* — **ea•ger•ness** *n*
ea•gle \ˈē-gəl\ *n* **1 :** a large bird of prey related to the hawks **2 :** a score of two under par on a hole in golf
ea•glet \ˈē-glət\ *n* **:** a young eagle
-ean — see -AN
E and OE *abbr* errors and omissions excepted
[1]**ear** \ˈir\ *n* **1 :** the organ of hearing; *also* **:** the outer part of this in a vertebrate **2 :** something resembling a mammal's ear in shape, position, or function **3 :** an ability to understand and appreciate something heard ⟨a good ~ for music⟩ **4 :** sympathetic attention
[2]**ear** *n* **:** the fruiting spike of a cereal (as wheat)
ear•ache \-ˌāk\ *n* **:** an ache or pain in the ear
ear•drum \-ˌdrəm\ *n* **:** a thin membrane that receives and transmits sound waves in the ear
eared \ˈird\ *adj* **:** having ears esp. of a specified kind or number ⟨a long-*eared* dog⟩
ear•ful \ˈir-ˌfu̇l\ *n* **:** a verbal outpouring (as of news, gossip, anger, or complaint)
earl \ˈərl\ *n* [ME *erl*, fr. OE *eorl* warrior, nobleman] **:** a member of the British peerage ranking below a marquess and above a viscount — **earl•dom** \-dəm\ *n*
ear•lobe \ˈir-ˌlōb\ *n* **:** the pendent part of the ear
[1]**ear•ly** \ˈər-lē\ *adv* **ear•li•er; -est :** at an early time (as in a period or series)
[2]**early** *adj* **ear•li•er; -est 1 :** of, relating to, or occurring near the beginning **2 :** ANCIENT, PRIMITIVE **3 :** occurring before the usual time ⟨an ~ breakfast⟩; *also* **:** occurring in the near future
[1]**ear•mark** \ˈir-ˌmärk\ *n* **:** an identification mark (as on

the ear of an animal); *also* : a distinguishing mark ⟨~*s* of poverty⟩

[2]earmark *vb* **1** : to mark with an earmark **2** : to designate for a specific purpose

ear•muff \-ˌməf\ *n* : one of a pair of ear coverings worn to protect against cold

earn \ˈərn\ *vb* **1** : to receive as a return for service **2** : DESERVE, MERIT **syn** gain, secure, get, obtain, acquire, win — **earn•er** *n*

[1]ear•nest \ˈər-nəst\ *n* : an intensely serious state of mind ⟨spoke in ~⟩

[2]earnest *adj* **1** : seriously intent and sober ⟨an ~ face⟩ ⟨an ~ attempt⟩ **2** : GRAVE, IMPORTANT **syn** solemn, sedate, staid — **ear•nest•ly** *adv* — **ear•nest•ness** *n*

[3]earnest *n* **1** : something of value given by a buyer to a seller to bind a bargain **2** : PLEDGE

earn•ings \ˈər-niŋz\ *n pl* **1** : something (as wages) earned **2** : the balance of revenue after deduction of costs and expenses

ear•phone \ˈir-ˌfōn\ *n* : a device that reproduces sound and is worn over or in the ear

ear•plug \-ˌpləg\ *n* : a protective device for insertion into the opening of the ear

ear•ring \-ˌriŋ\ *n* : an ornament for the earlobe

ear•shot \-ˌshät\ *n* : range of hearing

ear•split•ting \-ˌspli-tiŋ\ *adj* : intolerably loud or shrill

earth \ˈərth\ *n* **1** : SOIL, DIRT **2** : LAND, GROUND **3** *often cap* : the planet on which we live that is 3d in order from the sun — see PLANET table

earth•en \ˈər-thən\ *adj* : made of earth or baked clay

earth•en•ware \-ˌwar\ *n* : slightly porous opaque pottery fired at low heat

earth•ling \ˈərth-liŋ\ *n* : an inhabitant of the earth

earth•ly \ˈərth-lē\ *adj* : having to do with the earth esp. as distinguished from heaven — **earth•li•ness** *n*

earth•quake \-ˌkwāk\ *n* : a shaking or trembling of a portion of the earth

earth science *n* : any of the sciences (as geology or meteorology) that deal with the earth or one of its parts

earth•shak•ing \ˈərth-ˌshā-kiŋ\ *adj* : of great importance : MOMENTOUS

earth•ward \-wərd\ *also* **earth•wards** \-wərdz\ *adv* : toward the earth

earth•work \ˈərth-ˌwərk\ *n* : an embankment or fortification of earth

earth•worm \-ˌwərm\ *n* : a long segmented worm found in damp soil

earthy \ˈər-thē\ *adj* **earth•i•er; -est 1** : of, relating to, or consisting of earth; *also* : suggesting earth ⟨~ flavors⟩ **2** : PRACTICAL **3** : COARSE, GROSS — **earth•i•ness** *n*

ear•wax \ˈir-ˌwaks\ *n* : the yellow waxy secretion from the ear

ear•wig \-ˌwig\ *n* : any of numerous insects with slender many-jointed antennae and a pair of appendages resembling forceps at the end of the body

[1]ease \ˈēz\ *n* **1** : comfort of body or mind **2** : naturalness of manner **3** : freedom from difficulty or effort **syn** relaxation, rest, repose, leisure

[2]ease *vb* **eased; eas•ing 1** : to relieve from distress **2** : to lessen the pressure or tension of **3** : to make or become less difficult ⟨~ credit⟩

ea•sel \ˈē-zəl\ *n* [Dutch *ezel,* lit., ass] : a frame for supporting something (as an artist's canvas)

[1]east \ˈēst\ *adv* : to or toward the east

[2]east *adj* **1** : situated toward or at the east **2** : coming from the east

[3]east *n* **1** : the general direction of sunrise **2** : the compass point directly opposite to west **3** *cap* : regions or countries east of a specified or implied point — **east•er•ly** \ˈē-stər-lē\ *adv or adj* — **east•ward** *adv or adj* — **east•wards** *adv*

Eas•ter \ˈē-stər\ *n* : a church feast observed on a Sunday in March or April in commemoration of Christ's resurrection

east•ern \ˈē-stərn\ *adj* **1** *often cap* : of, relating to, or characteristic of a region designated East **2** *cap* : of, relating to, or being the Christian churches originating in the Church of the Eastern Roman Empire **3** : lying toward or coming from the east — **East•ern•er** *n*

easy \ˈē-zē\ *adj* **eas•i•er; -est 1** : marked by ease ⟨an ~ life⟩; *esp* : not causing distress or difficulty ⟨~ tasks⟩ **2** : MILD, LENIENT ⟨be ~ on him⟩ **3** : GRADUAL ⟨an ~ slope⟩ **4** : free from pain, trouble, or worry ⟨rest ~⟩ **5** : LEISURELY ⟨an ~ pace⟩ **6** : NATURAL ⟨an ~ manner⟩ **7** : COMFORTABLE ⟨an ~ chair⟩ — **eas•i•ly** \ˈē-zə-lē\ *adv* — **eas•i•ness** \-zē-nəs\ *n*

easy•go•ing \ˌē-zē-ˈgō-iŋ\ *adj* : relaxed and casual in style or manner

eat \ˈēt\ *vb* **ate** \ˈāt\; **eat•en** \ˈēt-ᵊn\; **eat•ing 1** : to take in as food : take food **2** : to use up : DEVOUR **3** : CORRODE — **eat•able** *adj or n* — **eat•er** *n*

eat•ery \ˈē-tə-rē\ *n, pl* **-er•ies** : LUNCHEONETTE, RESTAURANT

eaves \ˈēvz\ *n pl* : the overhanging lower edge of a roof

eaves•drop \ˈēvz-ˌdräp\ *vb* : to listen secretly — **eaves•drop•per** *n*

[1]ebb \ˈeb\ *n* **1** : the flowing back from shore of water brought in by the tide **2** : a point or state of decline

[2]ebb *vb* **1** : to recede from the flood **2** : DECLINE ⟨his fortunes ~*ed*⟩

EBCDIC \ˈeb-sə-ˌdik\ *n* [*ext*ended *b*inary *c*oded *d*ecimal *i*nterchange *c*ode] : a computer code for representing alphanumeric information

[1]eb•o•ny \ˈe-bə-nē\ *n, pl* **-nies** : a hard heavy wood of Old World tropical trees related to the persimmon

[2]ebony *adj* **1** : made of or resembling ebony **2** : BLACK, DARK

ebul•lient \i-ˈbu̇l-yənt, -ˈbəl-\ *adj* **1** : BOILING, AGITATED **2** : EXUBERANT — **ebul•lience** \-yəns\ *n*

EC *abbr* European Community

ec•cen•tric \ik-ˈsen-trik\ *adj* **1** : deviating from a usual or accepted pattern **2** : deviating from a circular path ⟨~ orbits⟩ **3** : set with axis or support off center ⟨an ~ cam⟩; *also* : being off center **syn** erratic, queer, singular, curious, odd — **eccentric** *n* — **ec•cen•tri•cal•ly** \-tri-k(ə-)lē\ *adv* — **ec•cen•tric•i•ty** \ˌek-ˌsen-ˈtri-sə-tē\ *n*

Eccles *abbr* Ecclesiastes

Ec•cle•si•as•tes \i-ˌklē-zē-ˈas-tēz\ *n* — see BIBLE table

ec•cle•si•as•tic \i-ˌklē-zē-ˈas-tik\ *n* : CLERGYMAN

ec•cle•si•as•ti•cal \-ti-kəl\ *or* **ec•cle•si•as•tic** \-tik\ *adj* : of or relating to a church esp. as an institution ⟨~ art⟩ — **ec•cle•si•as•ti•cal•ly** \-ti-k(ə-)lē\ *adv*

Ec•cle•si•as•ti•cus \i-ˌklē-zē-ˈas-ti-kəs\ *n* — see BIBLE table

Ecclus *abbr* Ecclesiasticus

ECG *abbr* electrocardiogram

ech•e•lon \ˈe-shə-ˌlän\ *n* [F *échelon,* lit., rung of a ladder] **1** : a steplike arrangement (as of troops or airplanes) **2** : a level (as of authority or responsibility) within an organization

echi•no•derm \i-ˈkī-nə-ˌdərm\ *n* : any of a phylum of marine animals (as starfishes and sea urchins) having similar body parts (as the arms of a starfish) arranged around a central axis and often having a calcium-containing outer skeleton

echo \ˈe-kō\ *n, pl* **ech•oes** *also* **ech•os** : repetition of a sound caused by a reflection of the sound waves; *also* : the reflection of a radar signal by an object — **echo** *vb* — **echo•ic** \e-ˈko-ik\ *adj*

echo•lo•ca•tion \ˌe-ko-lō-ˈkā-shən\ *n* : a process for locating distant or invisible objects by means of sound waves reflected back to the sender (as a bat) by the objects

éclair \ā-ˈklar\ *n* [F, lit., lightning] : an oblong shell of light pastry with whipped cream or custard filling

éclat \ā-ˈklä\ *n* [F] **1** : a dazzling effect or success **2** : ACCLAIM

eclec•tic \e-ˈklek-tik\ *adj* : selecting or made up of

what seems best of varied sources — **eclectic** *n*
[1]**eclipse** \i-ˈklips\ *n* **1 :** the total or partial obscuring of one heavenly body by another; *also* **:** a passing into the shadow of a heavenly body **2 :** a falling into obscurity or decline
[2]**eclipse** *vb* **eclipsed; eclips•ing :** to cause an eclipse of; *also* **:** SURPASS
eclip•tic \i-ˈklip-tik\ *n* **:** the great circle of the celestial sphere that is the apparent path of the sun
ec•logue \ˈek-ˌlȯg, -ˌläg\ *n* **:** a pastoral poem
ECM *abbr* European Common Market
ecol *abbr* ecological; ecology
ecol•o•gy \i-ˈkä-lə-jē, e-\ *n, pl* **-gies** [G *Ökologie,* fr. Gk *oikos* house + *logos* word] **1 :** a branch of science concerned with the relationships between organisms and their environment **2 :** the pattern of relations between one or more organisms and the environment — **eco•log•i•cal** \ˌē-kə-ˈlä-ji-kəl, ˌe-\ *also* **eco•log•ic** \-jik\ *adj* — **eco•log•i•cal•ly** \-ji-k(ə-)lē\ *adv* — **ecol•o•gist** \i-ˈkä-lə-jist, e-\ *n*
econ *abbr* economics; economist; economy
eco•nom•ic \ˌe-kə-ˈnä-mik, ˌē-\ *adj* **:** of or relating to the production, distribution, and consumption of goods and services
eco•nom•i•cal \-ˈnä-mi-kəl\ *adj* **1 :** THRIFTY **2 :** operating with little waste or at a saving **syn** frugal, sparing, provident — **ec•o•nom•i•cal•ly** \-k(ə-)lē\ *adv*
eco•nom•ics \ˌe-kə-ˈnä-miks, ˌē-\ *n sing or pl* **:** a social science dealing with the production, distribution, and consumption of goods and services — **econ•o•mist** \i-ˈkä-nə-mist\ *n*
econ•o•mise *Brit var of* ECONOMIZE
econ•o•mize \i-ˈkä-nə-ˌmīz\ *vb* **-mized; -miz•ing :** to practice economy **:** be frugal — **econ•o•miz•er** *n*
[1]**econ•o•my** \i-ˈkä-nə-mē\ *n, pl* **-mies** [MF *yconomie,* fr. ML *oeconomia,* fr. Gk *oikonomia,* fr. *oikonomos* household manager, fr. *oikos* house + *nemein* to manage] **1 :** thrifty and efficient use of resources; *also* **:** an instance of this **2 :** manner of arrangement or functioning **:** ORGANIZATION **3 :** an economic system ⟨a money ~⟩
[2]**economy** *adj* **:** ECONOMICAL ⟨~ cars⟩
eco•sys•tem \ˈē-kō-ˌsis-təm, ˈe-\ *n* **:** the complex of an ecological community and its environment functioning as a unit in nature
ecru \ˈe-krü, ˈā-\ *n* [F *écru,* lit., unbleached] **:** BEIGE — **ecru** *adj*
ec•sta•sy \ˈek-stə-sē\ *n, pl* **-sies :** extreme and usu. rapturous emotional excitement — **ec•stat•ic** \ek-ˈsta-tik, ik-\ *adj* — **ec•stat•i•cal•ly** \-ti-k(ə-)lē\ *adv*
Ecua *abbr* Ecuador
Ec•ua•dor•an \ˌe-kwə-ˈdȯr-ən\ *or* **Ec•ua•dor•ean** *or* **Ec•ua•dor•ian** \-ē-ən\ *n* **:** a native or inhabitant of Ecuador — **Ecuadorean** *or* **Ecuadorian** *adj*
ec•u•men•i•cal \ˌe-kyü-ˈme-ni-kəl\ *adj* **:** general in extent or influence; *esp* **:** promoting or tending toward worldwide Christian unity — **ec•u•men•i•cal•ly** \-k(ə-)lē\ *adv*
ec•ze•ma \ig-ˈzē-mə, ˈeg-zə-mə, ˈek-sə-\ *n* **:** an itching skin inflammation with oozing and then crusted lesions — **ec•zem•a•tous** \ig-ˈze-mə-təs\ *adj*
ed *abbr* **1** edited; edition; editor **2** education
[1]**-ed** \d *after a vowel or* b, g, j, l, m, n, ŋ, r, t͟h, v, z, zh; əd, id *after* d, t; t *after other sounds*\ *vb suffix or adj suffix* **1** — used to form the past participle of regular weak verbs ⟨end*ed*⟩ ⟨fad*ed*⟩ ⟨tri*ed*⟩ ⟨patt*ed*⟩ **2 :** having **:** characterized by ⟨cultur*ed*⟩ ⟨2-legg*ed*⟩; *also* **:** having the characteristics of ⟨bigot*ed*⟩
[2]**-ed** *vb suffix* — used to form the past tense of regular weak verbs ⟨judg*ed*⟩ ⟨deni*ed*⟩ ⟨dropp*ed*⟩
Edam \ˈē-dəm, -ˌdam\ *n* **:** a yellow Dutch pressed cheese made in balls
ed•dy \ˈe-dē\ *n, pl* **eddies :** WHIRLPOOL — **eddy** *vb*
edel•weiss \ˈād-ᵊl-ˌwīs, -ˌvīs\ *n* [G, fr. *edel* noble + *weiss* white] **:** a small perennial woolly composite herb that grows high in the Alps
ede•ma \i-ˈdē-mə\ *n* **:** abnormal accumulation of watery fluid in connective tissue or in a serous cavity — **edem•a•tous** \-ˈde-mə-təs\ *adj*
Eden \ˈēd-ᵊn\ *n* **:** PARADISE 2
[1]**edge** \ˈej\ *n* **1 :** the cutting side of a blade **2 :** SHARPNESS; *also* **:** FORCE, EFFECTIVENESS **3 :** the line where something begins or ends; *also* **:** the area adjoining such an edge **4 :** ADVANTAGE — **edged** \ˈejd\ *adj*
[2]**edge** *vb* **edged; edg•ing 1 :** to give or form an edge **2 :** to move or force gradually ⟨~ into a crowd⟩ **3 :** to defeat by a small margin ⟨*edged* out her opponent⟩ — **edg•er** *n*
edge•wise \ˈej-ˌwīz\ *adv* **:** SIDEWAYS
edg•ing \ˈe-jiŋ\ *n* **:** something that forms an edge or border ⟨a lace ~⟩
edgy \ˈe-jē\ *adj* **edg•i•er; -est 1 :** SHARP ⟨an ~ tone⟩ **2 :** TENSE, NERVOUS — **edg•i•ness** *n*
ed•i•ble \ˈe-də-bəl\ *adj* **:** fit or safe to be eaten — **ed•i•bil•i•ty** \ˌe-də-ˈbi-lə-tē\ *n* — **edible** *n*
edict \ˈē-ˌdikt\ *n* **:** ORDER, DECREE
ed•i•fi•ca•tion \ˌe-də-fə-ˈkā-shən\ *n* **:** instruction and improvement esp. in morality — **ed•i•fy** \ˈe-də-ˌfī\ *vb*
ed•i•fice \ˈe-də-fəs\ *n* **:** a usu. large building
ed•it \ˈe-dət\ *vb* **1 :** to revise, assemble, or prepare for publication or release (as a motion picture) **2 :** to direct the publication and policies of (as a newspaper) **3 :** DELETE — **ed•i•tor** \ˈe-də-tər\ *n* — **ed•i•tor•ship** *n* — **ed•i•tress** \-trəs\ *n*
edi•tion \i-ˈdi-shən\ *n* **1 :** the form in which a text is published **2 :** the total number of copies (as of a book) published at one time **3 :** VERSION
[1]**ed•i•to•ri•al** \ˌe-də-ˈtōr-ē-əl\ *adj* **1 :** of or relating to an editor or editing **2 :** being or resembling an editorial — **ed•i•to•ri•al•ly** *adv*
[2]**editorial** *n* **:** an article (as in a newspaper) giving the views of the editors or publishers; *also* **:** an expression of opinion resembling an editorial ⟨a television ~⟩
ed•i•to•ri•al•ize \ˌe-də-ˈtōr-ē-ə-ˌlīz\ *vb* **-ized; -iz•ing 1 :** to express an opinion in an editorial **2 :** to introduce opinions into factual reporting **3 :** to express an opinion — **ed•i•to•ri•al•i•za•tion** \-ˌtōr-ē-ə-lə-ˈzā-shən\ *n* — **ed•i•to•ri•al•iz•er** *n*
EDP *abbr* electronic data processing
EDT *abbr* Eastern daylight (saving) time
educ *abbr* education; educational
ed•u•ca•ble \ˈe-jə-kə-bəl\ *adj* **:** capable of being educated
ed•u•cate \ˈe-jə-ˌkāt\ *vb* **-cat•ed; -cat•ing 1 :** to provide with schooling **2 :** to develop mentally and morally; *also* **:** to provide with information **syn** train, discipline, school, instruct, teach — **ed•u•ca•tor** \-ˌkā-tər\ *n*
ed•u•ca•tion \ˌe-jə-ˈkā-shən\ *n* **1 :** the action or process of educating or being educated **2 :** a field of study dealing with methods of teaching and learning — **ed•u•ca•tion•al** \-shə-nəl\ *adj*
educational television *n* **:** PUBLIC TELEVISION
educe \i-ˈdüs, -ˈdyüs\ *vb* **educed; educ•ing 1 :** ELICIT, EVOKE **2 :** DEDUCE **syn** extract, evince, extort
ed•u•tain•ment \ˌe-jə-ˈtān-mənt\ *n* **:** a form of entertainment that is designed to be educational
[1]**-ee** \ˈē, (ˌ)ē\ *n suffix* **1 :** one that receives or benefits from (a specified action or thing) ⟨grant*ee*⟩ ⟨patent*ee*⟩ **2 :** a person who does (a specified action) ⟨escap*ee*⟩
[2]**-ee** *n suffix* **1 :** a particular esp. small kind of ⟨boot*ee*⟩ **2 :** one resembling or suggestive of ⟨goat*ee*⟩
EE *abbr* electrical engineer
EEC *abbr* European Economic Community
EEG *abbr* **1** electroencephalogram **2** electroencephalograph
eel \ˈēl\ *n* **:** any of numerous snakelike bony fishes with a smooth slimy skin
☞ For illustration, see next page.
EEO *abbr* equal employment opportunity

eel

ee•rie *also* **ee•ry** \ˈir-ē\ *adj* **ee•ri•er; -est** : WEIRD, UNCANNY — **ee•ri•ly** \ˈir-ə-lē\ *adv*

eff *abbr* efficiency

ef•face \i-ˈfās, e-\ *vb* **ef•faced; ef•fac•ing** : to obliterate or obscure by or as if by rubbing out **syn** erase, delete, annul, cancel, expunge — **ef•face•able** *adj* — **ef•face•ment** *n*

[1]**ef•fect** \i-ˈfekt\ *n* **1** : MEANING, INTENT **2** : RESULT **3** : APPEARANCE **4** : INFLUENCE **5** *pl* : GOODS, POSSESSIONS **6** : the quality or state of being operative : OPERATION **syn** consequence, outcome, upshot, aftermath, issue

[2]**effect** *vb* : to cause to happen ⟨~ repairs⟩ ⟨~ changes⟩

ef•fec•tive \i-ˈfek-tiv\ *adj* **1** : producing a decisive or desired effect **2** : IMPRESSIVE, STRIKING **3** : ready for service or action **4** : being in effect — **ef•fec•tive•ly** *adv* — **ef•fec•tive•ness** *n*

ef•fec•tu•al \i-ˈfek-chə-wəl\ *adj* : producing an intended effect : ADEQUATE — **ef•fec•tu•al•ly** *adv*

ef•fec•tu•ate \i-ˈfek-chə-ˌwāt\ *vb* **-at•ed; -at•ing** : BRING ABOUT, EFFECT

ef•fem•i•nate \ə-ˈfe-mə-nət\ *adj* : marked by qualities more typical of women than men — **ef•fem•i•na•cy** \-nə-sē\ *n*

ef•fen•di \e-ˈfen-dē\ *n* [Turk *efendi* master, fr. NGk *aphentēs*, alter. of Gk *authentēs*] : a man of property, authority, or education in an eastern Mediterranean country

ef•fer•ent \ˈe-fə-rənt\ *adj* : bearing or conducting outward from a more central part ⟨~ nerves⟩

ef•fer•vesce \ˌe-fər-ˈves\ *vb* **-vesced; -vesc•ing** : to bubble and hiss as gas escapes; *also* : to be exhilarated — **ef•fer•ves•cence** \-ˈves-ᵊns\ *n* — **ef•fer•ves•cent** \-ᵊnt\ *adj* — **ef•fer•ves•cent•ly** *adv*

ef•fete \e-ˈfēt\ *adj* **1** : having lost character, vitality, or strength; *also* : DECADENT **2** : EFFEMINATE

ef•fi•ca•cious \ˌe-fə-ˈkā-shəs\ *adj* : producing an intended effect ⟨~ remedies⟩ **syn** effectual, effective, efficient — **ef•fi•ca•cy** \ˈe-fi-kə-sē\ *n*

ef•fi•cient \i-ˈfi-shənt\ *adj* : productive of desired effects esp. without waste — **ef•fi•cien•cy** \-shən-sē\ *n* — **ef•fi•cient•ly** *adv*

ef•fi•gy \ˈe-fə-jē\ *n, pl* **-gies** : IMAGE; *esp* : a crude figure of a hated person

ef•flo•res•cence \ˌe-flə-ˈres-ᵊns\ *n* **1** : the period or state of flowering **2** : the action or process of developing **3** : fullness of development : FLOWERING

ef•flu•ence \ˈe-ˌflü-əns\ *n* : something that flows out

ef•flu•ent \ˈe-ˌflü-ənt\ *n* : something that flows out; *esp* : a fluid (as sewage) discharged as waste — **effluent** *adj*

ef•flu•vi•um \e-ˈflü-vē-əm\ *n, pl* **-via** \-vē-ə\ *or* **-vi•ums** [L, outflow] **1** : a usu. unpleasant emanation **2** : a by-product usu. in the form of waste

ef•fort \ˈe-fərt\ *n* **1** : EXERTION, ENDEAVOR; *also* : a product of effort **2** : active or applied force — **ef•fort•less** *adj* — **ef•fort•less•ly** *adv*

ef•fron•tery \i-ˈfrən-tə-rē\ *n, pl* **-ter•ies** : shameless boldness : IMPUDENCE **syn** temerity, audacity, brass, gall, nerve, chutzpah

ef•ful•gence \i-ˈfu̇l-jəns, -ˈfəl-\ *n* : radiant splendor : BRILLIANCE — **ef•ful•gent** \-jənt\ *adj*

ef•fu•sion \i-ˈfyü-zhən, e-\ *n* : a gushing forth; *also* : unrestrained utterance — **ef•fuse** \-ˈfyüz, e-\ *vb* — **ef•fu•sive** \i-ˈfyü-siv, e-\ *adj* — **ef•fu•sive•ly** *adv*

eft \ˈeft\ *n* : NEWT

EFT *or* **EFTS** *abbr* electronic funds transfer (system)

e.g. *abbr* [L *exempli gratia*] for example

Eg *abbr* Egypt; Egyptian

egal•i•tar•i•an•ism \i-ˌga-lə-ˈter-ē-ə-ˌni-zəm\ *n* : a belief in human equality esp. in social, political, and economic affairs — **egal•i•tar•i•an** *adj or n*

[1]**egg** \ˈeg\ *vb* [ME, fr. ON *eggja*; akin to OE *ecg* edge] : to urge to action — usu. used with *on*

[2]**egg** *n* [ME *egge*, fr. ON *egg*; akin to OE *ǣg* egg, L *ovum*] **1** : a rounded usu. hard-shelled reproductive body esp. of birds and reptiles from which the young hatches; *also* : the egg of the common domestic chicken as an article of food **2** : a germ cell produced by a female

egg•beat•er \ˈeg-ˌbē-tər\ *n* : a hand-operated kitchen utensil for beating, stirring, or whipping

egg cell *n* : EGG 2

egg•head \-ˌhed\ *n* : INTELLECTUAL, HIGHBROW

egg•nog \-ˌnäg\ *n* : a drink consisting of eggs beaten with sugar, milk or cream, and often alcoholic liquor

egg•plant \-ˌplant\ *n* : the edible usu. large and purplish fruit of a plant related to the potato; *also* : the plant

egg roll *n* : a thin egg-dough casing filled with minced vegetables and often bits of meat and usu. deep-fried

egg•shell \ˈeg-ˌshel\ *n* : the hard exterior covering of an egg

egis \ˈē-jəs\ *var of* AEGIS

eg•lan•tine \ˈe-glən-ˌtīn, -ˌtēn\ *n* : SWEETBRIER

ego \ˈē-gō\ *n, pl* **egos** [L, I] **1** : the self as distinguished from others **2** : the one of the three divisions of the psyche in psychoanalytic theory that is the organized conscious mediator between the person and reality

ego•cen•tric \ˌē-gō-ˈsen-trik\ *adj* : concerned or overly concerned with the self; *esp* : SELF-CENTERED

ego•ism \ˈē-gō-ˌi-zəm\ *n* **1** : a doctrine holding self-interest to be the motive or the valid end of action **2** : excessive concern for oneself with or without exaggerated feelings of self-importance — **ego•ist** \-ist\ *n* — **ego•is•tic** \ˌē-gō-ˈis-tik\ *adj* — **ego•is•ti•cal•ly** *adv*

ego•tism \ˈē-gə-ˌti-zəm\ *n* **1** : the practice of talking about oneself too much **2** : an exaggerated sense of self-importance : CONCEIT — **ego•tist** \-tist\ *n* — **ego•tis•tic** \ˌē-gə-ˈtis-tik\ *or* **ego•tis•ti•cal** \-ti-kəl\ *adj* — **ego•tis•ti•cal•ly** *adv*

ego trip *n* : an act that enhances and satisfies one's ego

egre•gious \i-ˈgrē-jəs\ *adj* [L *egregius* outstanding, fr. *ex, e* out of + *greg-, grex* flock, herd] : notably bad : FLAGRANT — **egre•gious•ly** *adv* — **egre•gious•ness** *n*

egress \ˈē-ˌgres\ *n* : a way out : EXIT

egret \ˈē-grət, i-ˈgret\ *n* : any of various herons that bear long plumes during the breeding season

Egyp•tian \i-ˈjip-shən\ *n* **1** : a native or inhabitant of Egypt **2** : the language of the ancient Egyptians from earliest times to about the 3d century A.D. — **Egyptian** *adj*

ei•der \ˈī-dər\ *n* : any of several northern sea ducks that yield a soft down

ei•der•down \-ˌdau̇n\ *n* **1** : the down of the eider **2** : a quilt filled with eiderdown

ei•do•lon \ī-ˈdō-lən\ *n, pl* **-lons** *or* **-la** \-lə\ **1** : PHANTOM **2** : IDEAL

eight \ˈāt\ *n* **1** : one more than seven **2** : the 8th in a set or series **3** : something having eight units — **eight** *adj or pron* — **eighth** \ˈātth\ *adj or adv or n*

eight ball *n* : a black pool ball numbered 8 — **behind the eight ball** : in a highly disadvantageous position

eigh•teen \ˈāt-ˈtēn\ *n* : one more than 17 — **eighteen** *adj or pron* — **eigh•teenth** \-ˈtēnth\ *adj or n*

eighty \ˈā-tē\ *n, pl* **eight•ies** : eight times 10 — **eight•i•eth** \ˈā-tē-əth\ *adj or n* — **eighty** *adj or pron*

ein•stei•ni•um \īn-ˈstī-nē-əm\ *n* : an artificially produced radioactive element — see ELEMENT table

ei•re•nic *chiefly Brit var of* IRENIC

[1]**ei•ther** \ˈē-t͟hər, ˈī-\ *adj* **1** : being the one and the other

of two : EACH ⟨trees on ~ side⟩ **2** : being the one or the other of two ⟨take ~ road⟩

[2]**either** *pron* : the one or the other

[3]**either** *conj* — used as a function word before the first of two or more words or word groups of which the last is preceded by *or* to indicate that they represent alternatives ⟨a statement is ~ true or false⟩

ejac•u•late \i-ˈja-kyə-ˌlāt\ *vb* **-lat•ed; -lat•ing 1** : to eject a fluid (as semen) **2** : to utter suddenly : EXCLAIM — **ejac•u•la•tion** \-ˌja-kyə-ˈlā-shən\ *n* — **ejac•u•la•to•ry** \-ˈja-kyə-lə-ˌtōr-ē\ *adj*

eject \i-ˈjekt\ *vb* : to drive or throw out or off **syn** expel, oust, evict, dismiss — **ejec•tion** \-ˈjek-shən\ *n*

eke \ˈēk\ *vb* **eked; ek•ing** : to gain, supplement, or extend usu. with effort — usu. used with *out* ⟨~ out a living⟩

EKG *abbr* [G *Elektrokardiogramm*] electrocardiogram; electrocardiograph

el *abbr* elevation

[1]**elab•o•rate** \i-ˈla-bə-rət, -ˈla-brət\ *adj* **1** : planned or carried out with great care **2** : being complex and usu. ornate — **elab•o•rate•ly** *adv* — **elab•o•rate•ness** *n*

[2]**elab•o•rate** \i-ˈla-bə-ˌrāt\ *vb* **-rat•ed; -rat•ing 1** : to build up from simpler ingredients **2** : to work out in detail : develop fully — **elab•o•ra•tion** \-ˌla-bə-ˈrā-shən\ *n*

élan \ā-ˈläⁿ\ *n* [F] : ARDOR, SPIRIT

eland \ˈē-lənd, -ˌland\ *n, pl* **eland** *also* **elands** [Afrikaans] : either of two large African antelopes with spirally twisted horns in both sexes

elapse \i-ˈlaps\ *vb* **elapsed; elaps•ing** : to slip by : PASS

[1]**elas•tic** \i-ˈlas-tik\ *adj* **1** : SPRINGY **2** : FLEXIBLE, PLIABLE **3** : ADAPTABLE **syn** resilient, supple, stretch — **elas•tic•i•ty** \-ˌlas-ˈti-sə-tē, ˌē-ˌlas-\ *n*

[2]**elastic** *n* **1** : elastic material **2** : a rubber band

elate \i-ˈlāt\ *vb* **elat•ed; elat•ing** : to fill with joy — **ela•tion** \-ˈlā-shən\ *n*

[1]**el•bow** \ˈel-ˌbō\ *n* **1** : the joint of the arm; *also* : the outer curve of the bent arm **2** : a bend or joint resembling an elbow in shape

[2]**elbow** *vb* : to push aside with the elbow; *also* : to make one's way by elbowing

el•bow•room \ˈel-ˌbō-ˌrüm, -ˌrům\ *n* : enough space for work or operation

[1]**el•der** \ˈel-dər\ *n* : ELDERBERRY 2

[2]**elder** *adj* **1** : OLDER **2** : EARLIER, FORMER **3** : of higher rank : SENIOR

[3]**elder** *n* **1** : an older individual : SENIOR **2** : one having authority by reason of age and experience **3** : a church officer

el•der•ber•ry \ˈel-dər-ˌber-ē\ *n* **1** : the edible black or red fruit of a shrub or tree related to the honeysuckle and bearing flat clusters of small white or pink flowers **2** : a tree or shrub bearing elderberries

el•der•ly \ˈel-dər-lē\ *adj* **1** : rather old; *esp* : past middle age **2** : of, relating to, or characteristic of later life

el•dest \ˈel-dəst\ *adj* : of the greatest age

El Do•ra•do \ˌel-də-ˈrä-dō, -ˈrā-\ *n* [Sp, lit., the gilded one] : a place of vast riches, abundance, or opportunity

elec *abbr* electric; electrical; electricity

[1]**elect** \i-ˈlekt\ *adj* **1** : CHOSEN, SELECT **2** : elected but not yet installed in office ⟨the president-*elect*⟩

[2]**elect** *n, pl* **elect 1** : a selected person **2** *pl* : a select or exclusive group

[3]**elect** *vb* **1** : to select by vote (as for office or membership) **2** : CHOOSE, PICK

elec•tion \i-ˈlek-shən\ *n* **1** : an act or process of electing **2** : the fact of being elected

elec•tion•eer \i-ˌlek-shə-ˈnir\ *vb* : to work for the election of a candidate or party

[1]**elec•tive** \i-ˈlek-tiv\ *adj* **1** : chosen or filled by election **2** : permitting a choice : OPTIONAL

[2]**elective** *n* : an elective course or subject of study

elec•tor \i-ˈlek-tər\ *n* **1** : one qualified to vote in an election **2** : one elected to an electoral college — **elec•tor•al** \i-ˈlek-tə-rəl\ *adj*

electoral college *n* : a body of electors who elect the president and vice president of the U.S.

elec•tor•ate \i-ˈlek-tə-rət\ *n* : a body of persons entitled to vote

elec•tric \i-ˈlek-trik\ *adj* [NL *electricus* produced from amber by friction, electric, fr. ML, of amber, fr. L *electrum* amber, fr. Gk *ēlektron*] **1** *or* **elec•tri•cal** \-tri-kəl\ : of, relating to, operated by, or produced by electricity **2** : ELECTRIFYING, THRILLING — **elec•tri•cal•ly** *adv*

electrical storm *n* : THUNDERSTORM

electric chair *n* : a chair used to carry out the death penalty by electrocution

electric eye *n* : PHOTOELECTRIC CELL

elec•tri•cian \i-ˌlek-ˈtri-shən\ *n* : a person who installs, operates, or repairs electrical equipment

elec•tric•i•ty \i-ˌlek-ˈtri-sə-tē\ *n, pl* **-ties 1** : a form of energy that occurs in nature and is observable in natural phenomena (as lightning) and that can be produced by friction, chemical reaction, or mechanical effort **2** : electric current

elec•tri•fy \i-ˈlek-trə-ˌfī\ *vb* **-fied; -fy•ing 1** : to charge with electricity **2** : to equip for use of electric power **3** : THRILL — **elec•tri•fi•ca•tion** \i-ˌlek-trə-fə-ˈkā-shən\ *n*

elec•tro•car•dio•gram \i-ˌlek-trō-ˈkär-dē-ə-ˌgram\ *n* : the tracing made by an electrocardiograph

elec•tro•car•dio•graph \-ˌgraf\ *n* : a device for recording the changes of electrical potential occurring during the heartbeat — **elec•tro•car•dio•graph•ic** \-ˌkär-dē-ə-ˈgra-fik\ *adj* — **elec•tro•car•di•og•ra•phy** \-dē-ˈä-grə-fē\ *n*

elec•tro•chem•is•try \-ˈke-mə-strē\ *n* : a branch of chemistry that deals with the relation of electricity to chemical changes — **elec•tro•chem•i•cal** \-ˈke-mi-kəl\ *adj*

elec•tro•cute \i-ˈlek-trə-ˌkyüt\ *vb* **-cut•ed; -cut•ing** : to kill by an electric shock; *esp* : to kill (a criminal) in this way — **elec•tro•cu•tion** \-ˌlek-trə-ˈkyü-shən\ *n*

elec•trode \i-ˈlek-ˌtrōd\ *n* : a conductor used to establish electrical contact with a nonmetallic part of a circuit

elec•tro•en•ceph•a•lo•gram \i-ˌlek-trō-in-ˈse-fə-lə-ˌgram\ *n* : the tracing made by an electroencephalograph

elec•tro•en•ceph•a•lo•graph \-ˌgraf\ *n* : an apparatus for detecting and recording brain waves — **elec•tro•en•ceph•a•lo•graph•ic** \-ˌse-fə-lə-ˈgra-fik\ *adj* — **elec•tro•en•ceph•a•log•ra•phy** \-ˈlä-grə-fē\ *n*

elec•trol•o•gist \i-ˌlek-ˈträ-lə-jist\ *n* : one that uses electrical means to remove hair, warts, moles, and birthmarks from the body

elec•trol•y•sis \i-ˌlek-ˈträ-lə-səs\ *n* **1** : the production of chemical changes by passage of an electric current through an electrolyte **2** : the destruction of hair roots with an electric current — **elec•tro•lyt•ic** \-trə-ˈli-tik\ *adj*

elec•tro•lyte \i-ˈlek-trə-ˌlīt\ *n* : a nonmetallic electric conductor in which current is carried by the movement of ions; *also* : a substance whose solution or molten form is such a conductor

elec•tro•mag•net \i-ˌlek-trō-ˈmag-nət\ *n* : a core of magnetic material surrounded by a coil of wire through which an electric current is passed to magnetize the core

elec•tro•mag•net•ic \-mag-ˈne-tik\ *adj* : of, relating to, or produced by electromagnetism — **elec•tro•mag•net•i•cal•ly** *adv*

electromagnetic radiation *n* : a series of electromagnetic waves

electromagnetic wave *n* : a wave (as a radio wave, an X ray, or a wave of visible light) that consists of associated electric and magnetic effects and that travels at the speed of light

elec•tro•mag•ne•tism \i-ˌlek-trō-ˈmag-nə-ˌti-zəm\ *n* **1** : magnetism developed by a current of electricity **2** : a natural force responsible for interactions between charged particles which result from their charge

elec•tro•mo•tive force \i-ˌlek-trə-ˈmō-tiv-\ *n* : the potential difference derived from an electrical source per unit quantity of electricity passing through the source

elec•tron \i-ˈlek-ˌträn\ *n* : a negatively charged elementary particle

elec•tron•ic \i-ˌlek-ˈträ-nik\ *adj* : of or relating to electrons or electronics — **elec•tron•i•cal•ly** \-ni-k(ə-)lē\ *adv*

electronic mail *n* : messages sent and received electronically

elec•tron•ics \i-ˌlek-ˈträ-niks\ *n* **1** : the physics of electrons and electronic devices **2** : electronic devices or equipment

electron microscope *n* : an instrument in which a focused beam of electrons is used to produce an enlarged image of a minute object

electron tube *n* : a device in which electrical conduction by electrons takes place within a sealed container and which is used for the controlled flow of electrons

elec•tro•pho•re•sis \i-ˌlek-trə-fə-ˈrē-səs\ *n* : the movement of suspended particles through a fluid by an electromotive force — **elec•tro•pho•ret•ic** \-ˈre-tik\ *adj*

elec•tro•plate \i-ˈlek-trə-ˌplāt\ *vb* : to coat (as with metal) by electrolysis

elec•tro•shock therapy \i-ˈlek-trō-ˌshäk-\ *n* : the treatment of mental disorder by the induction of coma with an electric current

elec•tro•stat•ics \i-ˌlek-trə-ˈsta-tiks\ *n* : physics dealing with the interactions of stationary electric charges

el•ee•mos•y•nary \ˌe-li-ˈmäs-ᵊn-ˌer-ē\ *adj* : CHARITABLE

el•e•gance \ˈe-li-gəns\ *n* **1** : refined gracefulness; *also* : tasteful richness (as of design) **2** : something marked by elegance — **el•e•gant** \-gənt\ *adj* — **el•e•gant•ly** *adv*

ele•giac \ˌe-lə-ˈjī-ək, -ˌak\ *adj* : of or relating to an elegy

el•e•gy \ˈe-lə-jē\ *n, pl* **-gies** : a song, poem, or speech expressing grief for one who is dead; *also* : a reflective poem usu. melancholy in tone

elem *abbr* elementary

el•e•ment \ˈe-lə-mənt\ *n* **1** *pl* : weather conditions; *esp* : severe weather ⟨boards exposed to the ~*s*⟩ **2** : natural environment ⟨in her ~⟩ **3** : a constituent part **4** *pl* : the simplest principles (as of an art or science) : RUDIMENTS **5** : a member of a mathematical set **6** : any of more than 100 fundamental substances that consist of atoms of only one kind **syn** component, ingredient, constituent — **el•e•men•tal** \ˌe-lə-ˈment-ᵊl\ *adj*

CHEMICAL ELEMENTS

ELEMENT	SYMBOL	ATOMIC NUMBER	ATOMIC WEIGHT (C = 12)
actinium	Ac	89	227.0278
aluminum	Al	13	26.98154
americium	Am	95	
antimony	Sb	51	121.75
argon	Ar	18	39.948
arsenic	As	33	74.9216
astatine	At	85	
barium	Ba	56	137.33
berkelium	Bk	97	
beryllium	Be	4	9.01218
bismuth	Bi	83	208.9804
boron	B	5	10.81
bromine	Br	35	79.904
cadmium	Cd	48	112.41
calcium	Ca	20	40.08
californium	Cf	98	
carbon	C	6	12.011
cerium	Ce	58	140.12
cesium	Cs	55	132.9054
chlorine	Cl	17	35.453
chromium	Cr	24	51.996
cobalt	Co	27	58.9332
copper	Cu	29	63.546
curium	Cm	96	
dysprosium	Dy	66	162.50
einsteinium	Es	99	
erbium	Er	68	167.26
europium	Eu	63	151.96
fermium	Fm	100	
fluorine	F	9	18.998403
francium	Fr	87	
gadolinium	Gd	64	157.25
gallium	Ga	31	69.72
germanium	Ge	32	72.59
gold	Au	79	196.9665
hafnium	Hf	72	178.49
helium	He	2	4.00260
holmium	Ho	67	164.9304
hydrogen	H	1	1.0079
indium	In	49	114.82
iodine	I	53	126.9045
iridium	Ir	77	192.22
iron	Fe	26	55.847
krypton	Kr	36	83.80
lanthanum	La	57	138.9055
lawrencium	Lr	103	
lead	Pb	82	207.2
lithium	Li	3	6.941
lutetium	Lu	71	174.967
magnesium	Mg	12	24.305
manganese	Mn	25	54.9380
mendelevium	Md	101	
mercury	Hg	80	200.59
molybdenum	Mo	42	95.94
neodymium	Nd	60	144.24
neon	Ne	10	20.179
neptunium	Np	93	237.0482
nickel	Ni	28	58.69
niobium	Nb	41	92.9064
nitrogen	N	7	14.0067
nobelium	No	102	
osmium	Os	76	190.2
oxygen	O	8	15.9994
palladium	Pd	46	106.42
phosphorus	P	15	30.97376
platinum	Pt	78	195.08
plutonium	Pu	94	
polonium	Po	84	
potassium	K	19	39.0983
praseodymium	Pr	59	140.9077
promethium	Pm	61	
protactinium	Pa	91	231.0359
radium	Ra	88	226.0254
radon	Rn	86	
rhenium	Re	75	186.207
rhodium	Rh	45	102.9055
rubidium	Rb	37	85.4678
ruthenium	Ru	44	101.07
samarium	Sm	62	150.36
scandium	Sc	21	44.9559
selenium	Se	34	78.96
silicon	Si	14	28.0855
silver	Ag	47	107.868

ELEMENT	SYMBOL	ATOMIC NUMBER	ATOMIC WEIGHT (C = 12)
sodium	Na	11	22.98977
strontium	Sr	38	87.62
sulfur	S	16	32.06
tantalum	Ta	73	180.9479
technetium	Tc	43	
tellurium	Te	52	127.60
terbium	Tb	65	158.9254
thallium	Tl	81	204.383
thorium	Th	90	232.0381
thulium	Tm	69	168.9342
tin	Sn	50	118.69
titanium	Ti	22	47.88
tungsten	W	74	183.85
unnilhexium	Unh	106	
unnilpentium	Unp	105	
unnilquadium	Unq	104	
uranium	U	92	238.0289
vanadium	V	23	50.9415
xenon	Xe	54	131.29
ytterbium	Yb	70	173.04
yttrium	Y	39	88.9059
zinc	Zn	30	65.38
zirconium	Zr	40	91.22

el•e•men•ta•ry \ˌe-lə-ˈmen-trē, -tə-rē\ *adj* **:** SIMPLE, RUDIMENTARY; *also* **:** of, relating to, or teaching the basic subjects of education

elementary particle *n* **:** a subatomic particle of matter and energy that does not appear to be made up of other smaller particles

elementary school *n* **:** a school usu. including the first six or the first eight grades

el•e•phant \ˈe-lə-fənt\ *n, pl* **elephants** *also* **elephant** **:** any of a family of huge thickset nearly hairless mammals that have the snout lengthened into a trunk and two long curving pointed ivory tusks

elephant

el•e•phan•ti•a•sis \ˌe-lə-fən-ˈtī-ə-səs\ *n, pl* **-a•ses** \-ˌsēz\ **:** enlargement and thickening of tissues in response esp. to infection by minute parasitic worms

el•e•phan•tine \ˌe-lə-ˈfan-ˌtēn, -ˌtīn, ˈe-lə-fən-\ *adj* **1 :** of great size or strength **2 :** CLUMSY, PONDEROUS

elev *abbr* elevation

el•e•vate \ˈe-lə-ˌvāt\ *vb* **-vat•ed; -vat•ing 1 :** to lift up **:** RAISE **2 :** EXALT, ENNOBLE **3 :** ELATE

el•e•va•tion \ˌe-lə-ˈvā-shən\ *n* **1 :** the height to which something is raised (as above sea level) **2 :** a lifting up **3 :** something (as a hill or swelling) that is elevated

el•e•va•tor \ˈe-lə-ˌvā-tər\ *n* **1 :** a cage or platform for conveying people or things from one level to another **2 :** a building for storing and discharging grain **3 :** a movable surface on an airplane to produce motion up or down

elev•en \i-ˈle-vən\ *n* **1 :** one more than 10 **2 :** the 11th in a set or series **3 :** something having 11 units; *esp* **:** a football team — **eleven** *adj or pron* — **elev•enth** \-vənth\ *adj or n*

elf \ˈelf\ *n, pl* **elves** \ˈelvz\ **:** a mischievous fairy — **elf•ish** \ˈel-fish\ *adj*

ELF *abbr* extremely low frequency

elf•in \ˈel-fən\ *adj* **:** of, relating to, or resembling an elf

elic•it \i-ˈli-sət\ *vb* **:** to draw out or forth **syn** evoke, educe, extract, extort

elide \i-ˈlīd\ *vb* **elid•ed; elid•ing :** to suppress or alter by elision

el•i•gi•ble \ˈe-lə-jə-bəl\ *adj* **:** qualified to participate or to be chosen — **el•i•gi•bil•i•ty** \ˌe-lə-jə-ˈbi-lə-tē\ *n* — **eligible** *n*

elim•i•nate \i-ˈli-mə-ˌnāt\ *vb* **-nat•ed; -nat•ing** [L *eliminatus,* pp. of *eliminare,* fr. *limen* threshold] **1 :** REMOVE, ERADICATE **2 :** to pass (wastes) from the body **3 :** to leave out **:** IGNORE — **elim•i•na•tion** \-ˌli-mə-ˈnā-shən\ *n*

eli•sion \i-ˈli-zhən\ *n* **:** the omission of a final or initial sound or a word; *esp* **:** the omission of an unstressed vowel or syllable in a verse to achieve a uniform rhythm

elite \ā-ˈlēt, ē-\ *n* [F *élite*] **1 :** the choice part; *also* **:** a superior group **2 :** a typewriter type providing 12 characters to the inch — **elite** *adj*

elit•ism \-ˈlē-ˌti-zəm\ *n* **:** leadership or rule by an elite; *also* **:** advocacy of such elitism

elix•ir \i-ˈlik-sər\ *n* [ME, fr. ML, fr. Ar *al-iksīr* the elixir, fr. *al* the + *iksīr* elixir] **1 :** a substance held capable of prolonging life indefinitely; *also* **:** PANACEA **2 :** a sweetened alcoholic medicinal solution

Eliz•a•be•than \i-ˌli-zə-ˈbē-thən\ *adj* **:** of, relating to, or characteristic of Elizabeth I of England or her times

elk \ˈelk\ *n, pl* **elk** *or* **elks 1 :** MOOSE — used for one of the Old World **2 :** a large gregarious deer of No. America, Europe, Asia, and northwestern Africa with curved antlers having many branches

[1]ell \ˈel\ *n* **:** a former English cloth measure of 45 inches

[2]ell *n* **:** an extension at right angles to a building

el•lipse \i-ˈlips, e-\ *n* **:** a closed curve of oval shape

el•lip•sis \i-ˈlip-səs, e-\ *n, pl* **el•lip•ses** \-ˌsēz\ **1 :** omission from an expression of a word clearly implied **2 :** marks (as . . .) to show omission

el•lip•soid \i-ˈlip-ˌsȯid, e-\ *n* **:** a surface all plane sections of which are circles or ellipses — **el•lip•soi•dal** \-ˌlip-ˈsȯid-ᵊl\ *also* **ellipsoid** *adj*

el•lip•ti•cal \i-ˈlip-ti-kəl, e-\ *or* **el•lip•tic** \-tik\ *adj* **1 :** of, relating to, or shaped like an ellipse **2 :** of, relating to, or marked by ellipsis — **el•lip•ti•cal•ly** \-ti-k(ə-)lē\ *adv*

elm \ˈelm\ *n* **:** any of a genus of large trees that have toothed leaves and nearly circular one-seeded winged fruits and are often grown as shade trees; *also* **:** the wood of an elm

el•o•cu•tion \ˌe-lə-ˈkyü-shən\ *n* **:** the art of effective public speaking — **el•o•cu•tion•ist** \-shə-nist\ *n*

elon•gate \i-ˈlȯŋ-ˌgāt\ *vb* **-gat•ed; -gat•ing :** to make or grow longer **syn** extend, lengthen, prolong, protract — **elon•ga•tion** \(ˌ)ē-ˌlȯŋ-ˈgā-shən\ *n*

elope \i-ˈlōp\ *vb* **eloped; elop•ing :** to run away esp. to be married — **elope•ment** *n* — **elop•er** *n*

el•o•quent \ˈe-lə-kwənt\ *adj* **1 :** having or showing clear and forceful expression **2 :** clearly showing some feeling or meaning — **el•o•quence** \-kwəns\ *n* — **el•o•quent•ly** *adv*

[1]else \ˈels\ *adv* **1 :** in a different or additional manner or place or at a different or additional time ⟨where ~ can we meet⟩ **2 :** OTHERWISE ⟨obey or ~ you'll be sorry⟩

[2]else *adj* **:** OTHER; *esp* **:** being in addition ⟨what ~ do you want⟩

else•where \-ˌhwer\ *adv* **:** in or to another place

elu•ci•date \i-ˈlü-sə-ˌdāt\ *vb* **-dat•ed; -dat•ing :** to make clear usu. by explanation **syn** clarify, explain, illuminate — **elu•ci•da•tion** \-ˌlü-sə-ˈdā-shən\ *n*

elude \ē-ˈlüd\ *vb* **elud•ed; elud•ing 1 :** EVADE **2 :** to escape the notice of

elu•sive \ē-ˈlü-siv\ *adj* **:** tending to elude **:** EVASIVE — **elu•sive•ly** *adv* — **elu•sive•ness** *n*

el•ver \ˈel-vər\ *n* [alter. of *eelfare* migration of eels] **:** a young eel

elves *pl of* ELF

Ely•si•um \i-ˈli-zhē-əm, -zē-\ *n, pl* **-si•ums** *or* **-sia** \-zhē-ə, -zē-\ : PARADISE 2 — **Ely•sian** \-ˈli-zhən\ *adj*

em \ˈem\ *n* : a length approximately the width of the letter *M*

EM *abbr* **1** electromagnetic **2** electron microscope **3** enlisted man

ema•ci•ate \i-ˈmā-shē-ˌāt\ *vb* **-at•ed; -at•ing** : to become or cause to become very thin — **ema•ci•a•tion** \-ˌmā-shē-ˈā-shən, -sē-\ *n*

E–mail \ˈē-ˌmāl\ *n* : ELECTRONIC MAIL

emalangeni *pl of* LILANGENI

em•a•nate \ˈe-mə-ˌnāt\ *vb* **-nat•ed; -nat•ing** : to come out from a source **syn** proceed, spring, rise, arise, originate — **em•a•na•tion** \ˌe-mə-ˈnā-shən\ *n*

eman•ci•pate \i-ˈman-sə-ˌpāt\ *vb* **-pat•ed; -pat•ing** : to set free **syn** liberate, release, deliver, discharge — **eman•ci•pa•tion** \-ˌman-sə-ˈpā-shən\ *n* — **eman•ci•pa•tor** \-ˈman-sə-ˌpā-tər\ *n*

emas•cu•late \i-ˈmas-kyù-ˌlāt\ *vb* **-lat•ed; -lat•ing** : CASTRATE, GELD; *also* : WEAKEN — **emas•cu•la•tion** \-ˌmas-kyù-ˈlā-shən\ *n*

em•balm \im-ˈbäm, -ˈbälm\ *vb* : to treat (a corpse) so as to protect from decay — **em•balm•er** *n*

em•bank•ment \im-ˈbaŋk-mənt\ *n* : a raised structure (as of earth) to hold back water or carry a roadway

em•bar•go \im-ˈbär-gō\ *n, pl* **-goes** [Sp, fr. *embargar* to bar] : a prohibition on commerce — **embargo** *vb*

em•bark \im-ˈbärk\ *vb* **1** : to put or go on board a ship or airplane **2** : to make a start — **em•bar•ka•tion** \ˌem-ˌbär-ˈkā-shən\ *n*

em•bar•rass \im-ˈbar-əs\ *vb* **1** : CONFUSE, DISCONCERT **2** : to involve in financial difficulties **3** : to cause to experience self-conscious distress **4** : HINDER, IMPEDE — **em•bar•rass•ing•ly** *adv* — **em•bar•rass•ment** *n*

em•bas•sy \ˈem-bə-sē\ *n, pl* **-sies 1** : a group of representatives headed by an ambassador **2** : the function, position, or mission of an ambassador **3** : the official residence and offices of an ambassador

em•bat•tle \im-ˈbat-ᵊl\ *vb* : to arrange in order for battle; *also* : FORTIFY

em•bat•tled *adj* **1** : engaged in battle, conflict, or controversy **2** : being a site of battle, conflict, or controversy **3** : characterized by conflict or controversy

em•bed \im-ˈbed\ *vb* **em•bed•ded; em•bed•ding 1** : to enclose closely in a surrounding mass **2** : to make something an integral part of

em•bel•lish \im-ˈbe-lish\ *vb* **1** : ADORN, DECORATE **2** : to add ornamental details to **syn** beautify, deck, bedeck, garnish, ornament, dress — **em•bel•lish•ment** *n*

em•ber \ˈem-bər\ *n* **1** : a glowing or smoldering fragment from a fire **2** *pl* : the smoldering remains of a fire

em•bez•zle \im-ˈbe-zəl\ *vb* **-zled; -zling** : to steal (as money) by falsifying records — **em•bez•zle•ment** *n* — **em•bez•zler** *n*

em•bit•ter \im-ˈbi-tər\ *vb* **1** : to arouse bitter feelings in **2** : to make bitter

em•bla•zon \-ˈblāz-ᵊn\ *vb* **1** : to adorn with heraldic devices **2** : to display conspicuously

em•blem \ˈem-bləm\ *n* : something (as an object or picture) suggesting another object or an idea : SYMBOL — **em•blem•at•ic** \ˌem-blə-ˈma-tik\ *also* **em•blem•at•i•cal** \-ti-kəl\ *adj*

em•body \im-ˈbä-dē\ *vb* **em•bod•ied; em•body•ing 1** : INCARNATE **2** : to express in definite form **3** : to incorporate into a system or body **4** : PERSONIFY **syn** combine, integrate — **em•bodi•ment** \-di-mənt\ *n*

em•bold•en \im-ˈbōl-dən\ *vb* : to inspire with courage

em•bo•lism \ˈem-bə-ˌli-zəm\ *n* : the obstruction of a blood vessel by a foreign or abnormal particle

em•bon•point \äⁿ-bōⁿ-ˈpwaⁿ\ *n* [F] : plumpness of person : STOUTNESS

em•boss \im-ˈbäs, -ˈbȯs\ *vb* : to ornament with raised work

em•bou•chure \ˈäm-bù-ˌshùr, ˌäm-bù-ˈshùr \ *n* [F, ultim. fr. *bouche* mouth] : the position and use of the lips, tongue, and teeth in playing a wind instrument

em•bow•er \im-ˈbaù-ər\ *vb* : to shelter or enclose in a bower

[1]**em•brace** \im-ˈbrās\ *vb* **em•braced; em•brac•ing 1** : to clasp in the arms; *also* : CHERISH, LOVE **2** : ENCIRCLE **3** : TAKE UP, ADOPT; *also* : WELCOME **4** : INCLUDE **5** : to participate in an embrace **syn** comprehend, involve, encompass, embody

[2]**embrace** *n* : an encircling with the arms

em•bra•sure \im-ˈbrā-zhər\ *n* **1** : an opening in a wall through which a cannon is fired **2** : a recess of a door or window

em•bro•ca•tion \ˌem-brə-ˈkā-shən\ *n* : LINIMENT

em•broi•der \im-ˈbrȯi-dər\ *vb* **1** : to ornament with or do needlework **2** : to elaborate with exaggerated detail

em•broi•dery \im-ˈbrȯi-də-rē\ *n, pl* **-der•ies 1** : the forming of decorative designs with needlework **2** : something embroidered

em•broil \im-ˈbrȯil\ *vb* **1** : to throw into confusion or disorder **2** : to involve in conflict or difficulties — **em•broil•ment** *n*

em•bryo \ˈem-brē-ˌō\ *n, pl* **embryos** : a living thing in its earliest stages of development — **em•bry•on•ic** \ˌem-brē-ˈä-nik\ *adj*

em•bry•ol•o•gy \ˌem-brē-ˈä-lə-jē\ *n* : a branch of biology dealing with embryos and their development — **em•bry•o•log•i•cal** \-brē-ə-ˈlä-ji-kəl\ *adj* — **em•bry•ol•o•gist** \-brē-ˈä-lə-jist\ *n*

em•cee \ˌem-ˈsē\ *n* : MASTER OF CEREMONIES — **emcee** *vb*

emend \ē-ˈmend\ *vb* : to correct usu. by altering the text of **syn** rectify, revise, amend — **emen•da•tion** \ˌē-ˌmen-ˈdā-shən\ *n*

emer *abbr* emeritus

[1]**em•er•ald** \ˈem-rəld, ˈe-mə-\ *n* : a green beryl prized as a gem

[2]**emerald** *adj* : brightly or richly green

emerge \i-ˈmərj\ *vb* **emerged; emerg•ing** : to rise, come forth, or come out into view — **emer•gence** \-ˈmər-jəns\ *n* — **emer•gent** \-jənt\ *adj*

emer•gen•cy \i-ˈmər-jən-sē\ *n, pl* **-cies** : an unforeseen event or condition requiring prompt action **syn** exigency, contingency, crisis, juncture

emergency room *n* : a hospital room for receiving and treating persons needing immediate medical care

emer•i•ta \i-ˈmer-ə-tə\ *adj* : EMERITUS — used of a woman

emer•i•tus \i-ˈmer-ə-təs\ *adj* [L] : retired from active duty ⟨professor ~⟩

em•ery \ˈe-mə-rē\ *n, pl* **em•er•ies** : a dark granular corundum used esp. for grinding and polishing

emet•ic \i-ˈme-tik\ *n* : an agent that induces vomiting — **emetic** *adj*

emf *n* [electro*m*otive *f*orce] : POTENTIAL DIFFERENCE

em•i•grate \ˈe-mə-ˌgrāt\ *vb* **-grat•ed; -grat•ing** : to leave a place (as a country) to settle elsewhere — **em•i•grant** \-mi-grənt\ *n* — **em•i•gra•tion** \ˌe-mə-ˈgrā-shən\ *n*

émi•gré *also* **emi•gré** \ˈe-mi-ˌgrā, ˌe-mi-ˈgrā\ *n* [F] : a person who emigrates esp. because of political conditions

em•i•nence \ˈe-mə-nəns\ *n* **1** : high rank or position; *also* : a person of high rank or attainments **2** : a lofty place

em•i•nent \ˈe-mə-nənt\ *adj* **1** : CONSPICUOUS, EVIDENT **2** : DISTINGUISHED, PROMINENT — **em•i•nent•ly** *adv*

eminent domain *n* : a right of a government to take private property for public use

emir \i-ˈmir, ā-\ *n* [Ar *amīr* commander] : a ruler, chief, or commander in Islamic countries — **emir•ate** \ˈe-mər-ət\ *n*

em•is•sary \ˈe-mə-ˌser-ē\ *n, pl* **-sar•ies** : AGENT; *esp* : a secret agent

emis•sion \ē-ˈmi-shən\ *n* : something emitted; *esp* : substances discharged into the air

emit \ē-ˈmit\ *vb* **emit•ted; emit•ting 1** : to give off or out ⟨~ light⟩; *also* : EJECT **2** : EXPRESS, UTTER — **emit•ter** *n*

emol•lient \i-ˈmäl-yənt\ *adj* : making soft or supple; *also* : soothing esp. to the skin or mucous membrane — **emol•lient** *n*

emol•u•ment \i-ˈmäl-yə-mənt\ *n* [ME, fr. L *emolumentum* advantage, fr. *emolere* to produce by grinding] : the product (as salary or fees) of an employment

emote \i-ˈmōt\ *vb* **emot•ed; emot•ing** : to give expression to emotion in or as if in a play

emo•tion \i-ˈmō-shən\ *n* : a usu. intense feeling (as of love, hate, or despair) — **emo•tion•al** \-shə-nəl\ *adj* — **emo•tion•al•ly** *adv*

emp *abbr* emperor; empress

em•pa•thy \ˈem-pə-thē\ *n* : the experiencing as one's own of the feelings of another; *also* : the capacity for this — **em•path•ic** \em-ˈpa-thik\ *adj*

em•pen•nage \ˌäm-pə-ˈnäzh, ˌem-\ *n* [F] : the tail assembly of an airplane

em•per•or \ˈem-pər-ər\ *n* : the sovereign male ruler of an empire

em•pha•sis \ˈem-fə-səs\ *n, pl* **-pha•ses** \-ˌsēz\ : particular prominence given (as to a syllable in speaking or to a phase of action)

em•pha•sise *Brit var of* EMPHASIZE

em•pha•size \-ˌsīz\ *vb* **-sized; -siz•ing** : to place emphasis on : STRESS

em•phat•ic \im-ˈfa-tik, em-\ *adj* : uttered with emphasis : STRESSED — **em•phat•i•cal•ly** \-ˈti-k(ə-)lē\ *adv*

em•phy•se•ma \ˌem-fə-ˈzē-mə, -ˈsē-\ *n* : a condition marked esp. by abnormal expansion of the air spaces of the lungs and often by impairment of heart action

em•pire \ˈem-ˌpīər\ *n* **1** : a large state or a group of states under a single sovereign who is usu. an emperor; *also* : something resembling a political empire **2** : imperial sovereignty or dominion

em•pir•i•cal \im-ˈpir-i-kəl\ *also* **em•pir•ic** \-ik\ *adj* : based on observation; *also* : subject to verification by observation or experiment ⟨~ laws⟩ — **em•pir•i•cal•ly** \-i-k(ə-)lē\ *adv*

em•pir•i•cism \im-ˈpir-ə-ˌsi-zəm, em-\ *n* : the practice of relying on observation and experiment esp. in the natural sciences — **em•pir•i•cist** \-sist\ *n*

em•place•ment \im-ˈplās-mənt\ *n* **1** : a prepared position for weapons or military equipment **2** : PLACEMENT

¹em•ploy \im-ˈplȯi\ *vb* **1** : to make use of **2** : to use the services of **3** : OCCUPY, DEVOTE — **em•ploy•er** *n*

²em•ploy \im-ˈplȯi; ˈim-ˌplȯi, ˈem-\ *n* : EMPLOYMENT

em•ploy•ee *or* **em•ploye** \im-ˌplȯi-ˈē, ˌem-; im-ˈplȯi-ˌē, em-\ *n* : a person who works for another

em•ploy•ment \im-ˈplȯi-mənt\ *n* **1** : OCCUPATION, ACTIVITY **2** : the act of employing : the condition of being employed

em•po•ri•um \im-ˈpōr-ē-əm, em-\ *n, pl* **-ri•ums** *also* **-ria** \-ē-ə\ [L, fr. Gk *emporion*, fr. *emporos* traveler, trader] : a commercial center; *esp* : a store carrying varied articles

em•pow•er \im-ˈpau̇-ər\ *vb* : to give authority or power to; *also* : ENABLE — **em•pow•er•ment** \-mənt\ *n*

em•press \ˈem-prəs\ *n* **1** : the wife or widow of an emperor **2** : a sovereign female ruler of an empire

¹emp•ty \ˈemp-tē\ *adj* **emp•ti•er; -est 1** : containing nothing **2** : UNOCCUPIED, UNINHABITED **3** : lacking value, force, sense, or purpose **syn** vacant, blank, void, stark, vacuous — **emp•ti•ness** *n*

²empty *vb* **emp•tied; emp•ty•ing 1** : to make or become empty **2** : to discharge contents; *also* : to remove from what holds or encloses

³empty *n, pl* **empties** : an empty container or vehicle

emp•ty–hand•ed \ˌemp-tē-ˈhan-dəd\ *adj* **1** : having or bringing nothing **2** : having acquired or gained nothing

em•py•re•an \ˌem-ˌpī-ˈrē-ən, -pə-\ *n* **1** : the highest heaven; *also* : FIRMAMENT **2** : an ideal place or state

EMT \ˌē-(ˌ)em-ˈtē\ *n* [*e*mergency *m*edical *t*echnician] : a specially trained medical technician licensed to provide basic medical services before and during transportation to a hospital

¹emu \ˈē-myü, -mü\ *n* : a swift-running flightless Australian bird smaller than the related ostrich

²emu *abbr* electromagnetic unit

em•u•late \ˈem-yu̇-ˌlāt\ *vb* **-lat•ed; -lat•ing** : to strive to equal or excel : IMITATE — **em•u•la•tion** \ˌem-yu̇-ˈlā-shən\ *n* — **em•u•lous** \ˈem-yu̇-ləs\ *adj*

emul•si•fi•er \i-ˈməl-sə-ˌfī-ər\ *n* : a substance (as a soap) that helps to form and stabilize an emulsion

emul•si•fy \-ˌfī\ *vb* **-fied; -fy•ing** : to disperse (as an oil) in an emulsion — **emul•si•fi•ca•tion** \i-ˌməl-sə-fə-ˈkā-shən\ *n*

emul•sion \i-ˈməl-shən\ *n* **1** : a mixture of mutually insoluble liquids in which one is dispersed in droplets throughout the other ⟨an ~ of oil in water⟩ **2** : a light-sensitive coating on photographic film or paper

en \ˈen\ *n* : a length approximately half the width of the letter *M*

¹-en *also* **-n** *adj suffix* : made of : consisting of ⟨earth*en*⟩

²-en *vb suffix* **1** : become or cause to be ⟨sharp*en*⟩ **2** : cause or come to have ⟨length*en*⟩

en•able \i-ˈnā-bəl\ *vb* **en•abled; en•abling 1** : to make able or feasible **2** : to give legal power, capacity, or sanction to

en•act \i-ˈnakt\ *vb* **1** : to make into law **2** : to act out — **en•act•ment** *n*

enam•el \i-ˈna-məl\ *n* **1** : a glasslike substance used to coat the surface of metal or pottery **2** : the hard outer layer of a tooth **3** : a usu. glossy paint that forms a hard coat — **enamel** *vb*

enam•el•ware \-ˌwar\ *n* : metal utensils coated with enamel

en•am•or \i-ˈna-mər\ *vb* : to inflame with love

en•am•our *chiefly Brit var of* ENAMOR

en bloc \äⁿ-ˈbläk\ *adv or adj* : as a whole : in a mass

enc *or* **encl** *abbr* enclosure

en•camp \in-ˈkamp\ *vb* : to make camp — **en•camp•ment** *n*

en•cap•su•late \in-ˈkap-sə-ˌlāt\ *vb* **-lat•ed; -lat•ing 1** : to encase or become encased in a capsule **2** : SUMMARIZE — **en•cap•su•la•tion** \-ˌkap-sə-ˈlā-shən\ *n*

en•case \in-ˈkās\ *vb* : to enclose in or as if in a case

-ence *n suffix* **1** : action or process ⟨emerg*ence*⟩ : instance of an action or process ⟨refer*ence*⟩ **2** : quality or state ⟨depend*ence*⟩

en•ceinte \äⁿn-ˈsant\ *adj* : PREGNANT

en•ceph•a•li•tis \in-ˌse-fə-ˈlī-təs\ *n, pl* **-lit•i•des** \-ˈli-tə-ˌdēz\ : inflammation of the brain — **en•ceph•a•lit•ic** \-ˈli-tik\ *adj*

en•chain \in-ˈchān\ *vb* : FETTER, CHAIN

en•chant \in-ˈchant\ *vb* **1** : BEWITCH **2** : ENRAPTURE, FASCINATE — **en•chant•er** *n* — **en•chant•ing•ly** *adv* — **en•chant•ment** *n* — **en•chant•ress** \-ˈchan-trəs\ *n*

en•chi•la•da \ˌen-chə-ˈlä-də\ *n* : a rolled filled tortilla covered with chili sauce and usu. baked

en•ci•pher \in-ˈsī-fər, en-\ *vb* : ENCODE

en•cir•cle \in-ˈsər-kəl\ *vb* : to pass completely around : SURROUND — **en•cir•cle•ment** *n*

en•clave \ˈen-ˌklāv; ˈän-ˌklāv\ *n* : a distinct territorial, cultural, or social unit enclosed within or as if within foreign territory

en•close \in-ˈklōz\ *vb* **1** : to shut up or in; *esp* : to surround with a fence **2** : to include along with something else in a parcel or envelope ⟨~ a check⟩ — **en•clo•sure** \-ˈklō-zhər\ *n*

en•code \in-ˈkōd, en-\ *vb* : to convert (a message) into code

en•co•mi•um \en-ˈkō-mē-əm\ *n, pl* **-mi•ums** *or* **-mia** \-mē-ə\ : high or glowing praise

en•com•pass \in-ˈkəm-pəs\ *vb* **1** : ENCIRCLE **2** : ENVELOP, INCLUDE

[1]**en·core** \ˈän-ˌkōr\ *n* : a demand for repetition or reappearance; *also* : a further performance (as of a singer) in response to such a demand

[2]**encore** *vb* **en·cored; en·cor·ing** : to request an encore from

[1]**en·coun·ter** \in-ˈkau̇n-tər\ *vb* **1** : to meet as an enemy : FIGHT **2** : to meet usu. unexpectedly

[2]**encounter** *n* **1** : a hostile meeting; *esp* : COMBAT **2** : a chance meeting

en·cour·age \in-ˈkər-ij\ *vb* **-aged; -ag·ing 1** : to inspire with courage and hope **2** : STIMULATE, INCITE **3** : FOSTER — **en·cour·age·ment** *n* — **en·cour·ag·ing·ly** *adv*

en·croach \in-ˈkrōch\ *vb* [ME *encrochen* to seize, fr. MF *encrochier*, fr. OF, fr. *croche* hook] : to enter gradually or stealthily upon another's property or rights — **en·croach·ment** *n*

en·crust \in-ˈkrəst\ *vb* : to provide with or form a crust

en·crus·ta·tion \(ˌ)in-ˌkrəs-ˈtā-shən, ˌen-\ *var of* INCRUSTATION

en·cum·ber \in-ˈkəm-bər\ *vb* **1** : to weigh down : BURDEN **2** : to hinder the function or activity of — **en·cum·brance** \-brəns\ *n*

ency *or* **encyc** *abbr* encyclopedia

-en·cy *n suffix* : quality or state ⟨despond*ency*⟩

[1]**en·cyc·li·cal** \in-ˈsi-kli-kəl, en-\ *adj* : addressed to all the individuals of a group

[2]**encyclical** *n* : an encyclical letter; *esp* : a papal letter to the bishops of the church

en·cy·clo·pe·dia *also* **en·cy·clo·pae·dia** \in-ˌsī-klə-ˈpē-dē-ə\ *n* [ML *encyclopaedia* course of general education, fr. Gk *enkyklios paideia* general education] : a work treating the various branches of learning — **en·cy·clo·pe·dic** \-ˈpē-dik\ *adj*

en·cyst \in-ˈsist, en-\ *vb* : to form or become enclosed in a cyst — **en·cyst·ment** *n*

[1]**end** \ˈend\ *n* **1** : the part of an area that lies at the boundary; *also* : a point which marks the extent or limit of something or at which something ceases to exist **2** : a ceasing of a course (as of action or activity); *also* : DEATH **3** : the ultimate state; *also* : RESULT, ISSUE **4** : REMNANT **5** : PURPOSE, OBJECTIVE **6** : a player stationed at the extremity of a line (as in football) **7** : a share, operation, or aspect of an undertaking

[2]**end** *vb* **1** : to bring or come to an end **2** : DESTROY; *also* : DIE **3** : to form or be at the end of **syn** close, conclude, terminate, finish, complete

en·dan·ger \in-ˈdān-jər\ *vb* : to bring into danger; *also* : to create danger

en·dan·gered *adj* : being or relating to an endangered species

endangered species *n* : a species threatened with extinction

en·dear \in-ˈdir\ *vb* : to cause to become beloved or admired

en·dear·ment \-mənt\ *n* : a sign of affection : CARESS

en·deav·or \in-ˈde-vər\ *vb* : TRY, ATTEMPT — **endeavor** *n*

en·deav·our *chiefly Brit var of* ENDEAVOR

en·dem·ic \en-ˈde-mik, in-\ *adj* : restricted to a particular place ⟨~ plants⟩ ⟨an ~ disease⟩ — **endemic** *n*

end·ing \ˈen-diŋ\ *n* : something that forms an end; *esp* : SUFFIX

en·dive \ˈen-ˌdīv\ *n* **1** : an herb related to chicory and grown as a salad plant **2** : the blanched shoot of chicory

end·less \ˈend-ləs\ *adj* **1** : having or seeming to have no end : ETERNAL **2** : united at the ends : CONTINUOUS ⟨an ~ belt⟩ **syn** interminable, everlasting, unceasing, ceaseless, unending — **end·less·ly** *adv*

end·most \-ˌmōst\ *adj* : situated at the very end

end·note \-ˌnōt\ *n* : a note placed at the end of a text

en·do·crine \ˈen-də-krən, -ˌkrīn, -ˌkrēn\ *adj* : producing secretions that are distributed by way of the bloodstream ⟨~ glands⟩ — **endocrine** *n* — **en·do·cri·nol·o·gist** \-kri-ˈnä-lə-jist\ *n* — **en·do·cri·nol·o·gy** \-jē\ *n*

en·dog·e·nous \en-ˈdä-jə-nəs\ *adj* : caused or produced by factors inside the organism or system ⟨~ psychic depression⟩ — **en·dog·e·nous·ly** *adv*

en·dorse \in-ˈdȯrs\ *vb* **en·dorsed; en·dors·ing 1** : to sign one's name on the back of (as a check) **2** : APPROVE, SANCTION — **en·dorse·ment** *n*

en·do·scope \ˈen-də-ˌskōp\ *n* : an instrument with which the interior of a hollow organ (as the rectum) may be visualized — **en·do·scop·ic** \ˌen-də-ˈskä-pik\ *adj* — **en·dos·co·py** \en-ˈdäs-kə-pē\ *n*

en·do·ther·mic \ˌen-də-ˈthər-mik\ *adj* : characterized by or formed with absorption of heat

en·dow \in-ˈdau̇\ *vb* **1** : to furnish with funds for support ⟨~ a school⟩ **2** : to furnish with something freely or naturally — **en·dow·ment** *n*

en·due \in-ˈdü, -ˈdyü\ *vb* **en·dued; en·du·ing** : PROVIDE, ENDOW

en·dur·ance \in-ˈdu̇r-əns, -ˈdyu̇r-\ *n* **1** : DURATION **2** : the ability to withstand hardship or stress : FORTITUDE

en·dure \in-ˈdu̇r, -ˈdyu̇r\ *vb* **en·dured; en·dur·ing 1** : LAST, PERSIST **2** : to suffer firmly or patiently : BEAR **3** : TOLERATE — **en·dur·able** *adj*

end·ways \ˈend-ˌwāz\ *adv or adj* **1** : LENGTHWISE **2** : with the end forward **3** : on end

end·wise \-ˌwīz\ *adv or adj* : ENDWAYS

ENE *abbr* east-northeast

en·e·ma \ˈe-nə-mə\ *n, pl* **enemas** *also* **ene·ma·ta** \ˌe-nə-ˈmä-tə, ˈe-nə-mə-tə\ : injection of liquid into the rectum; *also* : material so injected

en·e·my \ˈe-nə-mē\ *n, pl* **-mies** : one that attacks or tries to harm another : FOE; *esp* : a military opponent

en·er·get·ic \ˌe-nər-ˈje-tik\ *adj* : marked by energy : ACTIVE, VIGOROUS **syn** strenuous, lusty, dynamic, vital — **en·er·get·i·cal·ly** \-ti-k(ə-)lē\ *adv*

en·er·gise *Brit var of* ENERGIZE

en·er·gize \ˈe-nər-ˌjīz\ *vb* **-gized; -giz·ing** : to give energy to

en·er·gy \ˈe-nər-jē\ *n, pl* **-gies 1** : vigorous action : EFFORT **2** : capacity for action **3** : capacity for performing work **4** : usable power (as heat or electricity); *also* : the resources for producing such power

energy level *n* : one of the stable states of constant energy that may be assumed by a physical system (as the electrons in an atom)

en·er·vate \ˈe-nər-ˌvāt\ *vb* **-vat·ed; -vat·ing** : to lessen the strength or vigor of : weaken in mind or body — **en·er·va·tion** \ˌe-nər-ˈvā-shən\ *n*

en·fee·ble \in-ˈfē-bəl\ *vb* **-bled; -bling** : to make feeble **syn** weaken, debilitate, sap, undermine, cripple — **en·fee·ble·ment** *n*

en·fi·lade \ˈen-fə-ˌlād, -ˌläd\ *n* : gunfire directed along the length of an enemy battle line — **enfilade** *vb*

en·fold \in-ˈfōld\ *vb* **1** : ENVELOP **2** : EMBRACE

en·force \in-ˈfōrs\ *vb* **1** : COMPEL ⟨~ obedience by threats⟩ **2** : to execute effectively ⟨~ the law⟩ — **en·force·able** *adj* — **en·force·ment** *n*

en·forc·er \in-ˈfōr-sər\ *n* : one that enforces; *esp* : an aggressive player (as in ice hockey) known for rough play

en·fran·chise \in-ˈfran-ˌchīz\ *vb* **-chised; -chis·ing 1** : to set free (as from slavery) **2** : to admit to citizenship; *also* : to grant the vote to — **en·fran·chise·ment** \-ˌchīz-mənt, -chəz-\ *n*

eng *abbr* engine; engineer; engineering

Eng *abbr* England; English

en·gage \in-ˈgāj\ *vb* **en·gaged; en·gag·ing 1** : PLEDGE; *esp* : to bind by a pledge to marry **2** : EMPLOY, HIRE **3** : to attract and hold esp. by interesting; *also* : to cause to participate **4** : to commence or take part in a venture **5** : to bring or enter into conflict **6** : to connect or interlock with : MESH; *also* : to cause to mesh

en·gage·ment \in-ˈgāj-mənt\ *n* **1** : APPOINTMENT **2** : EMPLOYMENT **3** : a mutual promise to marry **4** : a hostile encounter

en·gag·ing *adj* : ATTRACTIVE — **en·gag·ing·ly** *adv*

en•gen•der \in-ˈjen-dər\ *vb* **1** : BEGET **2** : BRING ABOUT, CREATE **syn** generate, breed, occasion, produce

en•gine \ˈen-jən\ *n* [ME *engin,* fr. OF, fr. L *ingenium* natural disposition, talent] **1** : a mechanical device **2** : a machine for converting energy into mechanical motion **3** : LOCOMOTIVE

[1]**en•gi•neer** \ˌen-jə-ˈnir\ *n* **1** : a member of a military unit specializing in engineering work **2** : a designer or builder of engines **3** : one trained in engineering **4** : one that operates an engine

[2]**engineer** *vb* **1** : to lay out or manage as an engineer **2** : to guide the course of **syn** pilot, lead, steer

en•gi•neer•ing *n* : the practical applications of scientific and mathematical principles

En•glish \ˈiŋ-glish\ *n* **1** : the language of England, the U.S., and many areas now or formerly under British rule **2 English** *pl* : the people of England **3** : spin imparted to a ball that is driven or rolled — **English** *adj* — **En•glish•man** \-mən\ *n* — **En•glish•wom•an** \-ˌwu̇-mən\ *n*

English horn *n* : a woodwind instrument longer than and having a range lower than the oboe

English setter *n* : any of a breed of bird dogs with a flat silky coat of white or white with color

English sparrow *n* : HOUSE SPARROW

English system *n* : a system of weights and measures in which the foot is the principal unit of length and the pound is the principal unit of weight

engr *abbr* **1** engineer **2** engraved

en•gram \ˈen-ˌgram\ *n* : a hypothetical change in neural tissue postulated in order to account for persistence of memory

en•grave \in-ˈgrāv\ *vb* **en•graved; en•grav•ing 1** : to produce (as letters or lines) by incising a surface **2** : to cut figures, letters, or designs on for printing; *also* : to print from an engraved plate **3** : PHOTOENGRAVE — **en•grav•er** *n*

en•grav•ing \in-ˈgrā-viŋ\ *n* **1** : the art of one who engraves **2** : an engraved plate; *also* : a print made from it

en•gross \in-ˈgrōs\ *vb* : to take up the whole interest or attention of **syn** monopolize, absorb, consume

en•gulf \in-ˈgəlf\ *vb* : to flow over and enclose

en•hance \in-ˈhans\ *vb* **en•hanced; en•hanc•ing** : to increase or improve (as in value or desirability) **syn** heighten, intensify, magnify — **en•hance•ment** *n*

enig•ma \i-ˈnig-mə\ *n* [L *aenigma,* fr. Gk *ainigma,* fr. *ainissesthai* to speak in riddles, fr. *ainos* fable] : something obscure or hard to understand

enig•mat•ic \ˌen-ig-ˈma-tik\ *adj* : resembling an enigma **syn** obscure, cryptic, mystifying — **en•ig•mat•i•cal•ly** \-ti-k(ə-)lē\ *adv*

en•join \in-ˈjȯin\ *vb* **1** : COMMAND, ORDER **2** : FORBID **syn** direct, bid, charge, command, instruct

en•joy \in-ˈjȯi\ *vb* **1** : to have for one's benefit or use ⟨~ good health⟩ **2** : to take pleasure or satisfaction in ⟨~*ed* the concert⟩ — **en•joy•able** *adj* — **en•joy•ment** *n*

enl *abbr* **1** enlarged **2** enlisted

en•large \in-ˈlärj\ *vb* **en•larged; en•larg•ing 1** : to make or grow larger **2** : ELABORATE **syn** increase, augment, multiply, expand — **en•large•ment** *n*

en•light•en \in-ˈlīt-ᵊn\ *vb* **1** : INSTRUCT, INFORM **2** : to give spiritual insight to — **en•light•en•ment** *n*

en•list \in-ˈlist\ *vb* **1** : to secure the aid or support of **2** : to engage for service in the armed forces — **en•list•ee** \-ˌlis-ˈtē\ *n* — **en•list•ment** \-ˈlist-mənt\ *n*

en•list•ed \in-ˈlis-təd\ *adj* : of, relating to, or forming the part of a military force below commissioned or warrant officers

enlisted man *n* : a man or woman in the armed forces ranking below a commissioned or warrant officer

en•liv•en \in-ˈlī-vən\ *vb* : to give life, action, or spirit to : ANIMATE

en masse \äⁿ-ˈmas\ *adv* [F] : in a body : as a whole

en•mesh \in-ˈmesh\ *vb* : to catch or entangle in or as if in meshes

en•mi•ty \ˈen-mə-tē\ *n, pl* **-ties** : ILL WILL; *esp* : mutual hatred **syn** hostility, antipathy, animosity, rancor, antagonism

en•no•ble \i-ˈnō-bəl\ *vb* **-bled; -bling** : EXALT, ELEVATE; *esp* : to raise to noble rank — **en•no•ble•ment** *n*

en•nui \ˌän-ˈwē\ *n* [F] : BOREDOM

enor•mi•ty \i-ˈnȯr-mə-tē\ *n, pl* **-ties 1** : an outrageous, vicious, or immoral act **2** : great wickedness **3** : IMMENSITY

enor•mous \i-ˈnȯr-məs\ *adj* [L *enormis,* fr. *e, ex* out of + *norma* rule] **1** : exceedingly wicked **2** : great in size, number, or degree : HUGE **syn** immense, vast, gigantic, colossal, mammoth, elephantine

[1]**enough** \i-ˈnəf\ *adj* : SUFFICIENT

[2]**enough** *adv* **1** : SUFFICIENTLY **2** : FULLY, QUITE **3** : TOLERABLY

[3]**enough** *pron* : a sufficient number, quantity, or amount

en•quire \in-ˈkwīr\, **en•qui•ry** \ˈin-ˌkwīr-ē, in-ˈkwīr-; ˈin-kwə-rē, ˈiŋ-\ *var of* INQUIRE, INQUIRY

en•rage \in-ˈrāj\ *vb* : to fill with rage

en•rap•ture \in-ˈrap-chər\ *vb* **en•rap•tured; en•rap•tur•ing** : DELIGHT

en•rich \in-ˈrich\ *vb* **1** : to make rich or richer **2** : ORNAMENT, ADORN — **en•rich•ment** *n*

en•roll *or* **en•rol** \in-ˈrōl\ *vb* **en•rolled; en•roll•ing 1** : to enter or register on a roll or list **2** : to offer (oneself) for enrolling — **en•roll•ment** *n*

en route \än-ˈrüt, en-\ *adv or adj* : on or along the way

ENS *abbr* ensign

en•sconce \in-ˈskäns\ *vb* **en•sconced; en•sconc•ing 1** : SHELTER, CONCEAL **2** : to settle snugly or securely **syn** secrete, hide, cache, stash

en•sem•ble \än-ˈsäm-bəl\ *n* [F, fr. *ensemble* together, fr. L *insimul* at the same time] : a group (as of singers, dancers, or players) or a set (as of clothes) producing a single effect

en•sheathe \in-ˈshēth\ *vb* : to cover with or as if with a sheath

en•shrine \in-ˈshrīn\ *vb* **1** : to enclose in or as if in a shrine **2** : to cherish as sacred

en•shroud \in-ˈshrau̇d\ *vb* : SHROUD, OBSCURE

en•sign \ˈen-sən, *1 also* ˈen-ˌsīn\ *n* **1** : FLAG; *also* : BADGE, EMBLEM **2** : a commissioned officer in the navy ranking next below a lieutenant junior grade

en•slave \in-ˈslāv\ *vb* : to make a slave of — **en•slave•ment** *n*

en•snare \in-ˈsnar\ *vb* : SNARE, TRAP **syn** entrap, bag, catch, capture

en•sue \in-ˈsü\ *vb* **en•sued; en•su•ing** : to follow in time or as a result

en•sure \in-ˈshu̇r\ *vb* **en•sured; en•sur•ing** : INSURE, GUARANTEE

en•tail \in-ˈtāl\ *vb* **1** : to limit the inheritance of (property) to the owner's lineal descendants or to a class thereof **2** : to include or involve as a necessary step or result — **en•tail•ment** *n*

en•tan•gle \in-ˈtaŋ-gəl\ *vb* : TANGLE, CONFUSE — **en•tan•gle•ment** *n*

en•tente \än-ˈtänt\ *n* [F understanding, agreement] : an understanding providing for joint action; *also* : parties linked by such an entente

en•ter \ˈen-tər\ *vb* **1** : to go or come in or into **2** : to become a member of : JOIN ⟨~ the ministry⟩ **3** : BEGIN **4** : to take part in : CONTRIBUTE **5** : to go into or upon and take possession **6** : to set down (as in a list) : REGISTER **7** : to place (a complaint) before a court; *also* : to put on record ⟨~ a complaint⟩

en•ter•i•tis \ˌen-tə-ˈrī-təs\ *n* : intestinal inflammation; *also* : a disease marked by this

en•ter•prise \ˈen-tər-ˌprīz\ *n* **1** : UNDERTAKING, PROJECT **2** : readiness for daring action : INITIATIVE **3** : a business organization

DICTIONARY

en·ter·pris·ing \ˌprī-ziŋ\ *adj* : bold and vigorous in action : ENERGETIC

en·ter·tain \ˌen-tər-ˈtān\ *vb* **1** : to treat or receive as a guest **2** : AMUSE, DIVERT **3** : to hold in mind **syn** harbor, shelter, lodge, house, billet — **en·ter·tain·er** *n* — **en·ter·tain·ment** *n*

en·thrall *or* **en·thral** \in-ˈthrȯl\ *vb* **en·thralled; en·thrall·ing** **1** : ENSLAVE **2** : to hold spellbound

en·throne \in-ˈthrōn\ *vb* **1** : to seat on or as if on a throne **2** : EXALT

en·thuse \in-ˈthüz, -ˈthyüz\ *vb* **en·thused; en·thus·ing** **1** : to make enthusiastic **2** : to show enthusiasm

en·thu·si·asm \in-ˈthü-zē-ˌa-zəm, -ˈthyü-\ *n* [Gk *enthousiasmos,* fr. *enthousiazein* to be inspired, irreg. fr. *entheos* inspired, fr. *theos* god] **1** : strong warmth of feeling : keen interest : FERVOR **2** : a cause of fervor — **en·thu·si·ast** \-ˌast, -əst\ *n* — **en·thu·si·as·tic** \in-ˌthü-zē-ˈas-tik, -ˌthyü-\ *adj* — **en·thu·si·as·ti·cal·ly** \-ti-k(ə-)lē\ *adv*

en·tice \in-ˈtīs\ *vb* **en·ticed; en·tic·ing** : ALLURE, TEMPT — **en·tice·ment** *n*

en·tire \in-ˈtīr\ *adj* : COMPLETE, WHOLE **syn** sound, perfect, intact, undamaged — **en·tire·ly** *adv*

en·tire·ty \in-ˈtī-rə-tē, -ˈtīr-tē\ *n, pl* **-ties** **1** : COMPLETENESS **2** : WHOLE, TOTALITY

en·ti·tle \in-ˈtīt-ᵊl\ *vb* **en·ti·tled; en·ti·tling** **1** : NAME, DESIGNATE **2** : to give a right or claim to

en·ti·tle·ment \in-ˈtīt-ᵊl-mənt\ *n* : a government program providing benefits to members of a specified group

en·ti·ty \ˈen-tə-tē\ *n, pl* **-ties** **1** : EXISTENCE, BEING **2** : something with separate and real existence

en·tomb \in-ˈtüm\ *vb* : to place in a tomb : BURY — **en·tomb·ment** *n*

en·to·mol·o·gy \ˌen-tə-ˈmä-lə-jē\ *n* : a branch of zoology that deals with insects — **en·to·mo·log·i·cal** \-mə-ˈlä-ji-kəl\ *adj* — **en·to·mol·o·gist** \-jist\ *n*

en·tou·rage \ˌän-tu̇-ˈräzh\ *n* [F] : RETINUE

en·tr'acte \ˈäⁿ-ˌtrakt\ *n* [F] **1** : something (as a dance) performed between two acts of a play **2** : the interval between two acts of a play

en·trails \ˈen-ˌtrālz\ *n pl* : VISCERA; *esp* : INTESTINES

[1]**en·trance** \ˈen-trəns\ *n* **1** : permission or right to enter **2** : the act of entering **3** : a means or place of entry

[2]**en·trance** \in-ˈtrans\ *vb* **en·tranced; en·tranc·ing** : CHARM, DELIGHT

en·trant \ˈen-trənt\ *n* : one that enters esp. as a competitor

en·trap \in-ˈtrap\ *vb* : ENSNARE, TRAP — **en·trap·ment** *n*

en·treat \in-ˈtrēt\ *vb* : to ask urgently : BESEECH **syn** beg, implore, plead, supplicate — **en·treaty** \-ˈtrē-tē\ *n*

en·trée *or* **en·tree** \ˈän-ˌtrā\ *n* [F *entrée*] **1** : freedom of entry or access **2** : the main course of a meal in the U.S. **syn** admission, admittance, entrance

en·trench \in-ˈtrench\ *vb* **1** : to place within or surround with a trench esp. for defense; *also* : to establish solidly ⟨~*ed* customs⟩ **2** : ENCROACH, TRESPASS — **en·trench·ment** *n*

en·tre·pre·neur \ˌän-trə-prə-ˈnər, -ˈnu̇r, -ˈnyu̇r\ *n* [F, fr. OF, fr. *entreprendre* to undertake] : one who organizes and assumes the risk of a business or enterprise — **en·tre·pre·neur·ial** \-ˈnu̇r-ē-əl, -ˈnyu̇r-, -ˈnər-\ *adj*

en·tro·py \ˈen-trə-pē\ *n, pl* **-pies** **1** : the degree of disorder in a system **2** : an ultimate state of inert uniformity

en·trust \in-ˈtrəst\ *vb* **1** : to commit something to as a trust **2** : to commit to another with confidence **syn** confide, consign, relegate, commend

en·try \ˈen-trē\ *n, pl* **entries** **1** : ENTRANCE 2, 3; *also* : VESTIBULE 2 **2** : an entering in a record; *also* : an item so entered **3** : a headword with its definition or identification; *also* : VOCABULARY ENTRY **4** : one entered in a contest

en·twine \in-ˈtwīn\ *vb* : to twine together or around

enu·mer·ate \i-ˈnü-mə-ˌrāt, -ˈnyü-\ *vb* **-at·ed; -at·ing** **1** : to determine the number of : COUNT **2** : LIST — **enu·mer·a·tion** \-ˌnü-mə-ˈrā-shən, -ˌnyü-\ *n*

enun·ci·ate \ē-ˈnən-sē-ˌāt\ *vb* **-at·ed; -at·ing** **1** : to state definitely; *also* : ANNOUNCE, PROCLAIM **2** : PRONOUNCE, ARTICULATE — **enun·ci·a·tion** \-ˌnən-sē-ˈā-shən\ *n*

en·ure·sis \ˌen-yu̇-ˈrē-səs\ *n* : involuntary discharge of urine : BED-WETTING

env *abbr* envelope

en·vel·op \in-ˈve-ləp\ *vb* : to enclose completely with or as if with a covering — **en·vel·op·ment** *n*

en·ve·lope \ˈen-və-ˌlōp, ˈän-\ *n* **1** : a usu. paper container for a letter **2** : WRAPPER, COVERING

en·ven·om \in-ˈve-nəm\ *vb* **1** : to make poisonous **2** : EMBITTER

en·vi·able \ˈen-vē-ə-bəl\ *adj* : highly desirable — **en·vi·ably** \-blē\ *adv*

en·vi·ous \ˈen-vē-əs\ *adj* : feeling or showing envy — **en·vi·ous·ly** *adv* — **en·vi·ous·ness** *n*

en·vi·ron·ment \in-ˈvī-rən-mənt, -ˈvīrn-\ *n* **1** : SURROUNDINGS **2** : the whole complex of factors (as soil, climate, and living things) that influence the form and the ability to survive of a plant or animal or ecological community — **en·vi·ron·men·tal** \-ˌvī-rən-ˈment-ᵊl, -ˌvīrn-\ *adj*

en·vi·ron·men·tal·ist \-ˌvī-rən-ˈment-ᵊl-ist, -ˌvīrn-\ *n* : a person concerned about environmental quality esp. with respect to control of pollution

en·vi·rons \in-ˈvī-rənz\ *n pl* **1** : SUBURBS **2** : SURROUNDINGS; *also* : VICINITY

en·vis·age \in-ˈvi-zij\ *vb* **-aged; -ag·ing** : to have a mental picture of

en·vi·sion \in-ˈvi-zhən, en-\ *vb* : to picture to oneself ⟨~*s* world peace⟩

en·voy \ˈen-ˌvȯi, ˈän-\ *n* **1** : a diplomatic agent **2** : REPRESENTATIVE, MESSENGER

[1]**en·vy** \ˈen-vē\ *n, pl* **envies** [ME *envie,* fr. OF, fr. L *invidia,* fr. *invidus* envious, fr. *invidēre* to look askance at, envy, fr. *vidēre* to see] : painful or resentful awareness of another's advantages; *also* : an object of envy

[2]**envy** *vb* **en·vied; en·vy·ing** : to feel envy toward or on account of

en·zyme \ˈen-ˌzīm\ *n* : any of various complex proteins produced by living cells that catalyze specific biochemical reactions at body temperatures — **en·zy·mat·ic** \ˌen-zə-ˈma-tik\ *adj*

Eo·cene \ˈē-ə-ˌsēn\ *adj* : of, relating to, or being the epoch of the Tertiary between the Paleocene and the Oligocene — **Eocene** *n*

EOE *abbr* equal opportunity employer

eo·lian \ē-ˈō-lē-ən\ *adj* : borne, deposited, or produced by the wind

EOM *abbr* end of month

eon \ˈē-ən, ˈē-ˌän\ *var of* AEON

EP *abbr* European plan

EPA *abbr* Environmental Protection Agency

ep·au·let *also* **ep·au·lette** \ˌe-pə-ˈlet\ *n* [F *épaulette,* dim. of *épaule* shoulder] : a shoulder ornament esp. on a coat or military uniform

épée \ˈe-ˌpā, ā-ˈpā\ *n* [F] : a fencing or dueling sword

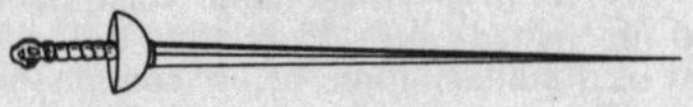

épée

Eph *or* **Ephes** *abbr* Ephesians

ephed·rine \i-ˈfe-drən\ *n* : a drug used in relieving hay fever, asthma, and nasal congestion

ephem•era \i-ˈfe-mər-ə\ *n pl* : collectibles (as posters or tickets) not intended to have lasting value
ephem•er•al \i-ˈfe-mə-rəl\ *adj* [Gk *ephēmeros* lasting a day, daily, fr. *epi*-on *hēmera* day] : SHORT-LIVED, TRANSITORY **syn** passing, fleeting, transient, evanescent
Ephe•sians \i-ˈfē-zhənz\ *n* — see BIBLE table
ep•ic \ˈe-pik\ *n* : a long poem in elevated style narrating the deeds of a hero — **epic** *adj*
epi•cen•ter \ˈe-pi-ˌsen-tər\ *n* : the point on the earth's surface directly above the point of origin of an earthquake
ep•i•cure \ˈe-pi-ˌkyu̇r\ *n* : a person with sensitive and discriminating tastes esp. in food and wine
ep•i•cu•re•an \ˌe-pi-kyu̇-ˈrē-ən, -ˈkyu̇r-ē-\ *n* : EPICURE — **epicurean** *adj*
[1]**ep•i•dem•ic** \ˌe-pə-ˈde-mik\ *adj* : affecting many persons at one time ⟨~ disease⟩; *also* : excessively prevalent
[2]**epidemic** *n* : an epidemic outbreak esp. of disease
epi•der•mis \ˌe-pə-ˈdər-məs\ *n* : an outer layer esp. of skin — **epi•der•mal** \-məl\ *adj*
epi•glot•tis \ˌe-pə-ˈglä-təs\ *n* : a thin plate of flexible tissue protecting the tracheal opening during swallowing
ep•i•gram \ˈe-pə-ˌgram\ *n* : a short witty poem or saying — **ep•i•gram•mat•ic** \ˌe-pə-grə-ˈma-tik\ *adj*
ep•i•lep•sy \ˈe-pə-ˌlep-sē\ *n, pl* **-sies** : a disorder typically marked by disturbed electrical rhythms of the central nervous system, by attacks of convulsions, and by loss of consciousness — **ep•i•lep•tic** \ˌe-pə-ˈlep-tik\ *adj or n*
ep•i•logue *also* **ep•i•log** \ˈe-pə-ˌlȯg, -ˌläg\ *n* : a speech addressed to the spectators by an actor at the end of a play
epi•neph•rine *also* **epi•neph•rin** \ˌe-pə-ˈne-frən\ *n* : an adrenal hormone used medicinally esp. as a heart stimulant, a muscle relaxant, and a vasoconstrictor
epiph•a•ny \i-ˈpi-fə-nē\ *n, pl* **-nies 1** *cap* : January 6 observed as a church festival in commemoration of the coming of the Magi to Jesus at Bethlehem **2** : a sudden striking understanding of something
epis•co•pa•cy \i-ˈpis-kə-pə-sē\ *n, pl* **-cies 1** : government of a church by bishops **2** : EPISCOPATE
epis•co•pal \i-ˈpis-kə-pəl\ *adj* **1** : of or relating to a bishop or episcopacy **2** *cap* : of or relating to the Protestant Episcopal Church
Epis•co•pa•lian \i-ˌpis-kə-ˈpāl-yən\ *n* : a member of the Protestant Episcopal Church
epis•co•pate \i-ˈpis-kə-pət, -ˌpāt\ *n* **1** : the rank, office, or term of a bishop **2** : a body of bishops
ep•i•sode \ˈe-pə-ˌsōd\ *n* [Gk *epeisodion*, fr. *epeisodios* coming in besides, fr. *eisodios* coming in, fr. *eis* into + *hodos* road, journey] **1** : a unit of action in a dramatic or literary work **2** : an incident in a course of events : OCCURRENCE ⟨a feverish ~⟩ — **ep•i•sod•ic** \ˌe-pə-ˈsä-dik\ *adj*
epis•tle \i-ˈpi-səl\ *n* **1** *cap* : one of the letters of the New Testament **2** : LETTER — **epis•to•lary** \i-ˈpis-tə-ˌler-ē\ *adj*
ep•i•taph \ˈe-pə-ˌtaf\ *n* : an inscription in memory of a dead person
ep•i•tha•la•mi•um \ˌe-pə-thə-ˈlā-mē-əm\ *or* **ep•i•tha•la•mi•on** \-mē-ən\ *n pl* **-mi•ums** *or* **-mia** \-mē-ə\ : a song or poem in honor of a bride and bridegroom
ep•i•the•li•um \ˌe-pə-ˈthē-lē-əm\ *n, pl* **-lia** \-lē-ə\ : a cellular membrane covering a bodily surface or lining a cavity — **ep•i•the•li•al** \-lē-əl\ *adj*
ep•i•thet \ˈe-pə-ˌthet, -thət\ *n* : a characterizing and often abusive word or phrase
epit•o•me \i-ˈpi-tə-mē\ *n* **1** : ABSTRACT, SUMMARY **2** : EMBODIMENT — **epit•o•mize** \-ˌmīz\ *vb*
ep•och \ˈe-pək, -ˌpäk\ *n* : a usu. extended period : ERA, AGE — **ep•och•al** \-pə-kəl, -ˌpä-\ *adj*
ep•oxy \i-ˈpäk-sē\ *vb* **ep•ox•ied** *or* **ep•oxyed; ep•oxy•ing** : to glue with epoxy resin
epoxy resin *n* : a synthetic resin used in coatings and adhesives
ep•si•lon \ˈep-sə-ˌlän, -lən\ *n* : the 5th letter of the Greek alphabet — Ε or ε
Ep•som salts \ˈep-səm-\ *n* : a bitter colorless or white magnesium salt with cathartic properties
eq *abbr* **1** equal **2** equation
equa•ble \ˈe-kwə-bəl, ˈē-\ *adj* : UNIFORM, EVEN; *esp* : free from unpleasant extremes — **eq•ua•bil•i•ty** \ˌe-kwə-ˈbi-lə-tē, ˌē-\ *n* — **eq•ua•bly** \ˈe-kwə-blē, ˈē-\ *adv*
[1]**equal** \ˈē-kwəl\ *adj* **1** : of the same measure, quantity, value, quality, number, degree, or status as another **2** : IMPARTIAL **3** : free from extremes **4** : able to cope with a situation or task — **equal•i•ty** \i-ˈkwä-lə-tē\ *n* — **equal•ly** *adv*
[2]**equal** *vb* **equaled** *or* **equalled; equal•ing** *or* **equal•ling** : to be or become equal to; *also* : to be identical in value to
[3]**equal** *n* : one that is equal
equal•ise *Brit var of* EQUALIZE
equal•ize \ˈē-kwə-ˌlīz\ *vb* **-ized; -iz•ing** : to make equal, uniform, or constant — **equal•i•za•tion** \ˌē-kwə-lə-ˈzā-shən\ *n* — **equal•iz•er** *n*
equals sign *or* **equal sign** *n* : a sign = indicating equivalence
equa•nim•i•ty \ˌē-kwə-ˈni-mə-tē, ˌe-\ *n, pl* **-ties** : COMPOSURE
equate \i-ˈkwāt\ *vb* **equat•ed; equat•ing** : to make, treat, or regard as equal or comparable
equa•tion \i-ˈkwā-zhən\ *n* **1** : an act of equating : the state of being equated **2** : a usu. formal statement of equivalence esp. of mathematical expressions
equa•tor \i-ˈkwā-tər, ˈē-ˌ\ *n* : an imaginary circle around the earth that is everywhere equally distant from the two poles — **equa•to•ri•al** \ˌē-kwə-ˈtōr-ē-əl, ˌe-\ *adj*
equer•ry \ˈe-kwə-rē, i-ˈkwer-ē\ *n, pl* **-ries 1** : an officer in charge of the horses of a prince or noble **2** : a personal attendant of a member of the British royal family
[1]**eques•tri•an** \i-ˈkwes-trē-ən\ *adj* : of or relating to horseback riding; *also* : representing a person on horseback ⟨an ~ statue⟩
[2]**equestrian** *n* : one who rides a horse
eques•tri•enne \i-ˌkwes-trē-ˈen\ *n* : a female rider on horseback
equi•dis•tant \ˌē-kwə-ˈdis-tənt\ *adj* : equally distant
equi•lat•er•al \ˌē-kwə-ˈla-tə-rəl\ *adj* : having all sides or faces equal ⟨~ triangles⟩
equi•lib•ri•um \ˌē-kwə-ˈli-brē-əm, ˌe-\ *n, pl* **-ri•ums** *or* **-ria** \-brē-ə\ : a state of intellectual or emotional balance; *also* : a state of balance between opposing forces or actions **syn** poise, balance, equipoise
equine \ˈē-ˌkwīn, ˈe-\ *adj* [L *equinus*, fr. *equus* horse] : of or relating to the horse — **equine** *n*
equi•noc•tial \ˌē-kwə-ˈnäk-shəl, ˌe-\ *adj* : relating to an equinox
equi•nox \ˈē-kwə-ˌnäks, ˈe-\ *n* : either of the two times each year when the sun appears directly overhead at the equator and day and night are everywhere of equal length
equip \i-ˈkwip\ *vb* **equipped; equip•ping** : to supply with needed resources
eq•ui•page \ˈe-kwə-pij\ *n* : a horse-drawn carriage usu. with its servants
equip•ment \i-ˈkwip-mənt\ *n* **1** : things used in equipping : SUPPLIES, OUTFIT **2** : the equipping of a person or thing : the state of being equipped
equi•poise \ˈe-kwə-ˌpȯiz, ˈē-\ *n* **1** : BALANCE, EQUILIBRIUM **2** : COUNTERBALANCE
eq•ui•ta•ble \ˈe-kwə-tə-bəl\ *adj* : JUST, FAIR — **eq•ui•ta•bly** \-blē\ *adv*
eq•ui•ta•tion \ˌe-kwə-ˈtā-shən\ *n* : the act or art of riding on horseback
eq•ui•ty \ˈe-kwə-tē\ *n, pl* **-ties 1** : JUSTNESS, IMPARTI-

ALITY **2 :** value of a property or of an interest in it in excess of claims against it

equiv *abbr* equivalent

equiv•a•lent \i-ˈkwi-və-lənt\ *adj* **:** EQUAL; *also* **:** virtually identical — **equiv•a•lence** \-ləns\ *n* — **equivalent** *n*

equiv•o•cal \i-ˈkwi-və-kəl\ *adj* **1 :** AMBIGUOUS **2 :** UNCERTAIN, UNDECIDED **3 :** SUSPICIOUS, DUBIOUS ⟨~ behavior⟩ **syn** obscure, dark, vague, enigmatic — **equiv•o•cal•ly** *adv*

equiv•o•cate \i-ˈkwi-və-ˌkāt\ *vb* **-cat•ed; -cat•ing 1 :** to use misleading language **2 :** to avoid giving a definite answer — **equiv•o•ca•tion** \-ˌkwi-və-ˈkā-shən\ *n*

[1]**-er** \ər\ *adj suffix or adv suffix* — used to form the comparative degree of adjectives and adverbs of one or two syllables ⟨hott*er*⟩ ⟨dri*er*⟩ ⟨silli*er*⟩ and sometimes of longer ones

[2]**-er** \ər\ *also* **-ier** \ē-ər, yər\ *or* **-yer** \yər\ *n suffix* **1 :** a person occupationally connected with ⟨hatt*er*⟩ ⟨law*yer*⟩ **2 :** a person or thing belonging to or associated with ⟨old-tim*er*⟩ **3 :** a native of **:** resident of ⟨New Zealand*er*⟩ **4 :** one that has ⟨double-deck*er*⟩ **5 :** one that produces or yields ⟨pork*er*⟩ **6 :** one that does or performs (a specified action) ⟨report*er*⟩ **7 :** one that is a suitable object of (a specified action) ⟨broil*er*⟩ **8 :** one that is ⟨foreign*er*⟩

Er *symbol* erbium

ER *abbr* emergency room

era \ˈir-ə, ˈer-ə, ˈē-rə\ *n* [LL *aera,* fr. L, counters, pl. of *aes* copper, money] **1 :** a chronological order or system of notation reckoned from a given date as basis **2 :** a period identified by some special feature **3 :** any of the four major divisions of geologic time **syn** age, epoch, period, time

ERA *abbr* Equal Rights Amendment

erad•i•cate \i-ˈra-də-ˌkāt\ *vb* **-cat•ed; -cat•ing** [L *eradicatus,* pp. of *eradicare,* fr. *e-* out + *radix* root] **:** UPROOT, ELIMINATE **syn** exterminate, annihilate, abolish, extinguish — **erad•i•ca•ble** \-di-kə-bəl\ *adj*

erase \i-ˈrās\ *vb* **erased; eras•ing :** to rub or scratch out (as written words); *also* **:** OBLITERATE **syn** cancel, efface, delete, expunge — **eras•er** *n* — **era•sure** \i-ˈrā-shər\ *n*

er•bi•um \ˈər-bē-əm\ *n* **:** a rare metallic element found with yttrium — see ELEMENT table

[1]**ere** \ˌer\ *prep* **:** BEFORE

[2]**ere** *conj* **:** BEFORE

[1]**erect** \i-ˈrekt\ *adj* **1 :** not leaning or lying down **:** UPRIGHT **2 :** being in a state of physiological erection

[2]**erect** *vb* **1 :** BUILD **2 :** to fix or set in an upright position **3 :** SET UP; *also* **:** ESTABLISH, DEVELOP

erec•tile \i-ˈrekt-ᵊl, -ˈrek-ˌtīl\ *adj* **:** capable of becoming erect ⟨~ tissue⟩ ⟨~ feathers of a bird⟩

erec•tion \i-ˈrek-shən\ *n* **1 :** the turgid state of a previously flaccid bodily part when it becomes dilated with blood **2 :** CONSTRUCTION

ere•long \er-ˈlȯŋ\ *adv* **:** before long

er•e•mite \ˈer-ə-ˌmīt\ *n* **:** HERMIT

er•go \ˈer-gō, ˈər-\ *adv* [L] **:** THEREFORE

er•got \ˈər-gət, -ˌgät\ *n* **1 :** a disease of rye and other cereals caused by a fungus; *also* **:** this fungus **2 :** a medicinal compound or preparation derived from an ergot fungus

Er•i•tre•an \ˌer-ə-ˈtrē-ən, -ˈtrā-\ *n* **:** a native or inhabitant of Eritrea — **Eritrean** *adj*

er•mine \ˈər-mən\ *n, pl* **ermines 1 :** any of several weasels with winter fur mostly white; *also* **:** the white fur of an ermine **2 :** a rank or office whose official robe is ornamented with ermine

erode \i-ˈrōd\ *vb* **erod•ed; erod•ing :** to diminish or destroy by degrees; *esp* **:** to gradually eat into or wear away ⟨soil *eroded* by wind and water⟩ — **erod•ible** \-ˈrō-də-bəl\ *adj*

erog•e•nous \i-ˈrä-jə-nəs\ *adj* **1 :** sexually sensitive ⟨~ zones⟩ **2 :** of, relating to, or arousing sexual feelings

ero•sion \i-ˈrō-zhən\ *n* **:** the process or state of being eroded — **ero•sion•al** \-ˈrō-zhə-nəl\ *adj* — **ero•sion•al•ly** *adv*

ero•sive \i-ˈrō-siv\ *adj* **:** tending to erode — **ero•sive•ness** *n*

erot•ic \i-ˈrä-tik\ *adj* **:** relating to or dealing with sexual love **:** AMATORY — **erot•i•cal•ly** \-ti-k(ə-)lē\ *adv* — **erot•i•cism** \-tə-ˌsi-zəm\ *n*

err \ˈər, ˈer\ *vb* **:** to be or do wrong

er•rand \ˈer-ənd\ *n* **:** a short trip taken to do something; *also* **:** the object or purpose of such a trip

er•rant \ˈer-ənt\ *adj* **1 :** WANDERING ⟨an ~ knight⟩ **2 :** straying outside proper bounds **3 :** deviating from an accepted pattern or standard

er•ra•ta \e-ˈrä-tə\ *n* **:** a list of corrigenda

er•rat•ic \i-ˈra-tik\ *adj* **1 :** having no fixed course **2 :** INCONSISTENT; *also* **:** ECCENTRIC — **er•rat•i•cal•ly** \-ti-k(ə-)lē\ *adv*

er•ra•tum \e-ˈrä-təm\ *n, pl* **-ta** \-tə\ **:** CORRIGENDUM

er•ro•ne•ous \i-ˈrō-nē-əs, e-ˈrō-\ *adj* **:** INCORRECT — **er•ro•ne•ous•ly** *adv*

er•ror \ˈer-ər\ *n* **1 :** a usu. ignorant or unintentional deviating from accuracy or truth ⟨made an ~ in adding⟩ **2 :** a defensive misplay in baseball **3 :** the state of one that errs ⟨to be in ~⟩ **4 :** a product of mistake ⟨a typographical ~⟩ — **er•ror•less** *adj*

er•satz \ˈer-ˌzäts\ *adj* [G *ersatz-,* fr. *Ersatz,* n., substitute] **:** being usu. an artificial and inferior substitute

erst \ˈərst\ *adv, archaic* **:** ERSTWHILE

[1]**erst•while** \-ˌhwīl\ *adv* **:** in the past **:** FORMERLY

[2]**erstwhile** *adj* **:** FORMER, PREVIOUS

er•u•di•tion \ˌer-ə-ˈdi-shən, ˌer-yə-\ *n* **:** SCHOLARSHIP, LEARNING — **er•u•dite** \ˈer-ə-ˌdīt, ˈer-yə-\ *adj*

erupt \i-ˈrəpt\ *vb* **1 :** to burst forth or cause to burst forth **:** EXPLODE **2 :** to break through a surface ⟨teeth *~ing* through the gum⟩ **3 :** to break out with or as if with a skin rash — **erup•tion** \-ˈrəp-shən\ *n* — **erup•tive** \-tiv\ *adj*

-ery *n suffix* **1 :** qualities collectively **:** character **:** -NESS ⟨snobb*ery*⟩ **2 :** art **:** practice ⟨cook*ery*⟩ **3 :** place of doing, keeping, producing, or selling (the thing specified) ⟨fish*ery*⟩ ⟨bak*ery*⟩ **4 :** collection **:** aggregate ⟨fin*ery*⟩ **5 :** state or condition ⟨slav*ery*⟩

ery•sip•e•las \ˌer-ə-ˈsi-pə-ləs, ˌir-\ *n* **:** an acute bacterial disease marked by fever and severe skin inflammation

er•y•the•ma \ˌer-ə-ˈthē-mə\ *n* **:** abnormal redness of the skin due to capillary congestion (as in inflammation)

eryth•ro•cyte \i-ˈri-thrə-ˌsīt\ *n* **:** RED BLOOD CELL

Es *symbol* einsteinium

[1]**-es** \əz, iz *after* s, z, sh, ch; z *after* v *or a vowel*\ *n pl suffix* — used to form the plural of most nouns that end in *s* ⟨glass*es*⟩, *z* ⟨fuzz*es*⟩, *sh* ⟨bush*es*⟩, *ch* ⟨peach*es*⟩, or a final *y* that changes to *i* ⟨lad*ies*⟩ and of some nouns ending in *f* that changes to *v* ⟨loav*es*⟩

[2]**-es** *vb suffix* — used to form the third person singular present of most verbs that end in *s* ⟨bless*es*⟩, *z* ⟨fizz*es*⟩, *sh* ⟨hush*es*⟩, *ch* ⟨catch*es*⟩, or a final *y* that changes to *i* ⟨def*ies*⟩

es•ca•late \ˈes-kə-ˌlāt\ *vb* **-lat•ed; -lat•ing :** to increase in extent, volume, number, intensity, or scope — **es•ca•la•tion** \ˌes-kə-ˈlā-shən\ *n*

es•ca•la•tor \ˈes-kə-ˌlā-tər\ *n* **:** a moving set of stairs

es•cal•lop \is-ˈkä-ləp, -ˈka-\ *var of* SCALLOP

es•ca•pade \ˈes-kə-ˌpād\ *n* [F, action of escaping] **:** a mischievous adventure

[1]**es•cape** \is-ˈkāp\ *vb* **es•caped; es•cap•ing** [ME, fr. OF *escaper,* fr. (assumed) VL *excappare,* fr. L *ex-* out + LL *cappa* head covering, cloak] **1 :** to get free or away **2 :** to avoid a threatening evil **3 :** AVOID 2 ⟨~ injury⟩ **4 :** ELUDE ⟨his name *~s* me⟩ **5 :** to be produced or uttered involuntarily by ⟨let a sob ~ him⟩

[2]**escape** *n* **1 :** flight from or avoidance of something unpleasant **2 :** LEAKAGE **3 :** a means of escape

[3]**escape** *adj* **:** providing a means or way of escape

es•cap•ee \is-ˌkā-ˈpē, ˌes-(ˌ)kā-\ *n* **:** one that has escaped esp. from prison

escape velocity *n* : the minimum velocity needed by a body (as a rocket) to escape from the gravitational field of a celestial body (as the earth)

es•cap•ism \is-ˈkā-ˌpi-zəm\ *n* : diversion of the mind to imaginative activity as an escape from routine — **es•cap•ist** \-pist\ *adj or n*

es•ca•role \ˈes-kə-ˌrōl\ *n* : ENDIVE 1

es•carp•ment \es-ˈkärp-mənt\ *n* **1** : a steep slope in front of a fortification **2** : a long cliff

es•chew \is-ˈchü\ *vb* : SHUN, AVOID

[1]**es•cort** \ˈes-ˌkȯrt\ *n* : one (as a person or warship) accompanying another esp. as a protection or courtesy

[2]**es•cort** \is-ˈkȯrt, es-\ *vb* : to accompany as an escort

es•crow \ˈes-ˌkrō\ *n* : something (as a deed or a sum of money) delivered by one person to another to be delivered to a third party only upon the fulfillment of a condition; *also* : a fund or deposit serving as an escrow

es•cu•do \is-ˈkü-dō\ *n, pl* **-dos 1** — see MONEY table **2** : the peso of Guinea-Bissau

es•cutch•eon \is-ˈkə-chən\ *n* : the usu. shield-shaped surface on which a coat of arms is shown

Esd *abbr* Esdras

Es•dras \ˈez-drəs\ *n* — see BIBLE table

ESE *abbr* east-southeast

Es•ki•mo \ˈes-kə-ˌmō\ *n* **1** : a member of a group of peoples of northern Canada, Greenland, Alaska, and eastern Siberia **2** : any of the languages of the Eskimo peoples

Eskimo dog *n* : a sled dog of American origin

ESL *abbr* English as a second language

esoph•a•gus \i-ˈsä-fə-gəs\ *n, pl* **-gi** \-ˌgī, -ˌjī\ : a muscular tube that leads from the cavity behind the mouth to the stomach — **esoph•a•geal** \-ˌsä-fə-ˈjē-əl\ *adj*

es•o•ter•ic \ˌe-sə-ˈter-ik\ *adj* **1** : designed for or understood only by the specially initiated **2** : PRIVATE, SECRET

esp *abbr* especially

ESP \ˌē-(ˌ)es-ˈpē\ *n* : EXTRASENSORY PERCEPTION

es•pa•drille \ˈes-pə-ˌdril\ *n* [F] : a flat sandal usu. having a fabric upper and a flexible sole

es•pal•ier \is-ˈpal-yər, -ˌyā\ *n* : a plant (as a fruit tree) trained to grow flat against a support — **espalier** *vb*

es•pe•cial \is-ˈpe-shəl\ *adj* : SPECIAL, PARTICULAR — **es•pe•cial•ly** *adv*

Es•pe•ran•to \ˌes-pə-ˈran-tō, -ˈrän-\ *n* : an artificial international language based esp. on words common to the chief European languages

es•pi•o•nage \ˈes-pē-ə-ˌnäzh, -nij\ *n* [F *espionnage*] : the practice of spying

es•pla•nade \ˈes-plə-ˌnäd\ *n* : a level open stretch or area; *esp* : one for walking or driving along a shore

es•pous•al \i-ˈspaụ-zəl\ *n* **1** : BETROTHAL; *also* : WEDDING **2** : a taking up (as of a cause) as a supporter — **es•pouse** \-ˈspaụz\ *vb*

espres•so \e-ˈspre-sō\ *n, pl* **-sos** [It (*caffè*) *espresso*, lit., pressed out coffee] : coffee brewed by forcing steam through finely ground darkly roasted coffee beans

es•prit \i-ˈsprē\ *n* : sprightly wit

es•prit de corps \i-ˌsprē-də-ˈkōr\ *n* [F] : the common spirit existing in the members of a group

es•py \i-ˈspī\ *vb* **es•pied; es•py•ing** : to catch sight of **syn** behold, see, view, descry

Esq *or* **Esqr** *abbr* esquire

es•quire \ˈes-ˌkwīr\ *n* [ME, fr. MF *esquier* squire, fr. LL *scutarius*, fr. L *scutum* shield] **1** : a man of the English gentry ranking next below a knight **2** : a candidate for knighthood serving as attendant to a knight **3** — used as a title of courtesy

-ess \əs, ˌes\ *n suffix* : female ⟨author*ess*⟩

[1]**es•say** \e-ˈsā, ˈe-ˌsā\ *vb* : ATTEMPT, TRY

[2]**es•say** *n* **1** \ˈe-ˌsā, e-ˈsā\ : ATTEMPT **2** \ˈe-ˌsā\ : a literary composition usu. dealing with a subject from a limited or personal point of view — **es•say•ist** \ˈe-ˌsā-ist\ *n*

es•sence \ˈes-ᵊns\ *n* **1** : fundamental nature or quality **2** : a substance distilled or extracted from another substance (as a plant or drug) and having the special qualities of the original substance **3** : PERFUME

[1]**es•sen•tial** \i-ˈsen-chəl\ *adj* **1** : of, relating to, or constituting an essence ⟨voting is an ~ right of citizenship⟩ ⟨~ oils⟩ **2** : of the utmost importance : INDISPENSABLE **syn** imperative, necessary, necessitous — **es•sen•tial•ly** *adv*

[2]**essential** *n* : something essential

est *abbr* **1** established **2** estimate; estimated

EST *abbr* eastern standard time

[1]**-est** \əst, ist\ *adj suffix or adv suffix* — used to form the superlative degree of adjectives and adverbs of one or two syllables ⟨fatt*est*⟩ ⟨lat*est*⟩ ⟨lucki*est*⟩ ⟨often*est*⟩ and less often of longer ones

[2]**-est** \əst, ist\ *or* **-st** \st\ *vb suffix* — used to form the archaic second person singular of English verbs (with *thou*) ⟨did*st*⟩

es•tab•lish \i-ˈsta-blish\ *vb* **1** : to institute permanently ⟨~ a law⟩ **2** : FOUND ⟨~ a settlement⟩; *also* : EFFECT **3** : to make firm or stable **4** : to put on a firm basis : SET UP ⟨~ a son in business⟩ **5** : to gain acceptance or recognition of ⟨the movie ~*ed* her as a star⟩; *also* : PROVE

es•tab•lish•ment \-mənt\ *n* **1** : something established **2** : a place of residence or business with its furnishings and staff **3** : an established ruling or controlling group ⟨the literary ~⟩ **4** : the act or state of establishing or being established

es•tate \i-ˈstāt\ *n* **1** : STATE, CONDITION; *also* : social standing : STATUS **2** : a social or political class ⟨the three ~*s* of nobility, clergy, and commons⟩ **3** : a person's possessions : FORTUNE **4** : a landed property

[1]**es•teem** \i-ˈstēm\ *n* : high regard

[2]**esteem** *vb* **1** : REGARD **2** : to set a high value on **syn** respect, admire, revere

es•ter \ˈes-tər\ *n* : an often fragrant organic compound formed by the reaction of an acid and an alcohol

Esth *abbr* Esther

Es•ther \ˈes-tər\ *n* — see BIBLE table

esthete, esthetic, esthetics *var of* AESTHETE, AESTHETIC, AESTHETICS

es•ti•ma•ble \ˈes-tə-mə-bəl\ *adj* : worthy of esteem

[1]**es•ti•mate** \ˈes-tə-ˌmāt\ *vb* **-mat•ed; -mat•ing 1** : to give or form an approximation (as of value, size, or cost) **2** : JUDGE, CONCLUDE **syn** evaluate, value, rate, appraise, assay, assess — **es•ti•ma•tor** \-ˌmā-tər\ *n*

[2]**es•ti•mate** \ˈes-tə-mət\ *n* **1** : OPINION, JUDGMENT **2** : a rough or approximate calculation **3** : a statement of the cost of work to be done

es•ti•ma•tion \ˌes-tə-ˈmā-shən\ *n* **1** : JUDGMENT, OPINION **2** : ESTIMATE **3** : ESTEEM, HONOR

es•ti•vate \ˈes-tə-ˌvāt\ *vb* **-vat•ed; -vat•ing** : to pass the summer in an inactive or resting state — **es•ti•va•tion** \ˌes-tə-ˈvā-shən\ *n*

Es•to•nian \e-ˈstō-nē-ən\ *n* : a native or inhabitant of Estonia — **Estonian** *adj*

es•trange \i-ˈstrānj\ *vb* **es•tranged; es•trang•ing** : to alienate the affections or confidence of — **es•trange•ment** *n*

es•tro•gen \ˈes-trə-jən\ *n* : a substance (as a sex hormone) that tends to cause estrus and the development of female secondary sex characteristics — **es•tro•gen•ic** \ˌes-trə-ˈje-nik\ *adj*

estrous cycle *n* : the cycle of changes in the endocrine and reproductive systems of a female mammal from the beginning of one period of estrus to the beginning of the next

es•trus \ˈes-trəs\ *n* : a periodic state of sexual excitability during which the female of most mammals is willing to mate with the male and is capable of becoming pregnant : HEAT — **es•trous** \-trəs\ *adj*

es•tu•ary \ˈes-chü-ˌwer-ē\ *n, pl* **-ar•ies :** an arm of the sea at the mouth of a river
ET *abbr* eastern time
eta \ˈā-tə\ *n* **:** the 7th letter of the Greek alphabet — H or η
ETA *abbr* estimated time of arrival
et al \et-ˈal\ *abbr* [L *et alii* (masc.), *et aliae* (fem.), or *et alia* (neut.)] and others
etc *abbr* et cetera
et cet•era \et-ˈse-tə-rə, -ˈse-trə\ [L] and others esp. of the same kind
etch \ˈech\ *vb* [D *etsen,* fr. G *ätzen* to etch, corrode, fr. OHG *azzen* to feed] **1 :** to produce (as a design) on a hard material by corroding its surface (as by acid) **2 :** to delineate clearly — **etch•er** *n*
etch•ing *n* **1 :** the action, process, or art of etching **2 :** a design produced on or print made from an etched plate
ETD *abbr* estimated time of departure
eter•nal \i-ˈtərn-ᵊl\ *adj* **:** EVERLASTING, PERPETUAL — **eter•nal•ly** *adv*
eter•ni•ty \i-ˈtər-nə-tē\ *n, pl* **-ties 1 :** infinite duration **2 :** IMMORTALITY
[1]**-eth** \əth, ith\ *or* **-th** \th\ *vb suffix* — used to form the archaic third person singular present of verbs ⟨do*th*⟩
[2]**-eth** — see [2]-TH
eth•ane \ˈe-ˌthān\ *n* **:** a colorless odorless gaseous hydrocarbon found in natural gas and used esp. as a fuel
eth•a•nol \ˈe-thə-ˌnȯl\ *n* **:** ALCOHOL 1
ether \ˈē-thər\ *n* **1 :** the upper regions of space; *also* **:** the gaseous element formerly held to fill these regions **2 :** a light flammable liquid used as an anesthetic and solvent
ethe•re•al \i-ˈthir-ē-əl\ *adj* **1 :** CELESTIAL, HEAVENLY **2 :** exceptionally delicate **:** AIRY, DAINTY — **ethe•re•al•ly** *adv* — **ethe•re•al•ness** *n*
eth•i•cal \ˈe-thi-kəl\ *adj* **1 :** of or relating to ethics **2 :** conforming to accepted and esp. professional standards of conduct **syn** virtuous, moral, principled — **eth•i•cal•ly** *adv*
eth•ics \ˈe-thiks\ *n sing or pl* **1 :** a discipline dealing with good and evil and with moral duty **2 :** moral principles or practice
Ethi•o•pi•an \ˌē-thē-ˈō-pē-ən\ *n* **:** a native or inhabitant of Ethiopia — **Ethiopian** *adj*
[1]**eth•nic** \ˈeth-nik\ *adj* [ME, heathen, fr. LL *ethnicus,* fr. Gk *ethnikos* national, gentile, fr. *ethnos* nation, people] **:** of or relating to races or large groups of people classed according to common traits and customs — **eth•ni•cal•ly** *adv*
[2]**ethnic** *n* **:** a member of a minority ethnic group who retains its customs, language, or social views
eth•nol•o•gy \eth-ˈnä-lə-jē\ *n* **:** a science dealing with the races of human beings, their origin, distribution, characteristics, and relations — **eth•no•log•i•cal** \ˌeth-nə-ˈlä-ji-kəl\ *adj* — **eth•nol•o•gist** \eth-ˈnä-lə-jist\ *n*
ethol•o•gy \ē-ˈthä-lə-jē\ *n* **:** the scientific and objective study of animal behavior — **etho•log•i•cal** \ˌē-thə-ˈlä-ji-kəl, ˌe-\ *adj* — **ethol•o•gist** \ē-ˈthä-lə-jist\ *n*
ethos \ˈē-ˌthäs\ *n* **:** the distinguishing character, sentiment, moral nature, or guiding beliefs of a person, group, or institution
ethyl alcohol *n* **:** ALCOHOL 1
eth•yl•ene \ˈe-thə-ˌlēn\ *n* **:** a colorless flammable gas found in coal gas or obtained from petroleum
eti•ol•o•gy \ˌē-tē-ˈä-lə-jē\ *n* **:** the causes of a disease or abnormal condition; *also* **:** a branch of medicine concerned with the causes and origins of diseases — **eti•o•log•ic** \ˌē-tē-ə-ˈlä-jik\ *or* **eti•o•log•i•cal** \-ji-kəl\ *adj*
et•i•quette \ˈe-ti-kət, -ˌket\ *n* [F *étiquette,* lit., ticket] **:** the forms prescribed by custom or authority to be observed in social, official, or professional life **syn** propriety, decorum, decency, dignity
Etrus•can \i-ˈtrəs-kən\ *n* **1 :** the language of the Etruscans **2 :** an inhabitant of ancient Etruria — **Etruscan** *adj*
et seq *abbr* [L *et sequens*] and the following one; [L *et sequentes* (masc. & fem. pl.) or *et sequentia* (neut. pl.)] and the following ones
-ette \ˈet, ˌet, ət, it\ *n suffix* **1 :** little one ⟨din*ette*⟩ **2 :** female ⟨usher*ette*⟩
étude \ˈā-ˌtüd, -ˌtyüd\ *n* [F, lit., study] **:** a musical composition for practice to develop technical skill
et•y•mol•o•gy \ˌe-tə-ˈmä-lə-jē\ *n, pl* **-gies 1 :** the history of a linguistic form (as a word) shown by tracing its development and relationships **2 :** a branch of linguistics dealing with etymologies — **et•y•mo•log•i•cal** \-mə-ˈlä-ji-kəl\ *adj* — **et•y•mol•o•gist** \-ˈmä-lə-jist\ *n*
Eu *symbol* europium
eu•ca•lyp•tus \ˌyü-kə-ˈlip-təs\ *n, pl* **-ti** \-ˌtī\ *or* **-tus•es :** any of a genus of mostly Australian evergreen trees widely grown for shade or their wood, oils, resins, and gums
Eu•cha•rist \ˈyü-kə-rəst\ *n* **:** COMMUNION 2 — **eu•cha•ris•tic** \ˌyü-kə-ˈris-tik\ *adj, often cap*
[1]**eu•chre** \ˈyü-kər\ *n* **:** a card game in which the side naming the trump must take three of five tricks to win
[2]**euchre** *vb* **eu•chred; eu•chring :** CHEAT, TRICK
eu•clid•e•an *also* **eu•clid•i•an** \yü-ˈkli-dē-ən\ *adj, often cap* **:** of or relating to the geometry of Euclid or a geometry based on similar axioms
eu•gen•ics \yü-ˈje-niks\ *n* **:** a science dealing with the improvement (as by selective breeding) of hereditary qualities esp. of human beings — **eu•gen•ic** \-nik\ *adj*
eu•lo•gy \ˈyü-lə-jē\ *n, pl* **-gies 1 :** a speech in praise of some person or thing **2 :** high praise — **eu•lo•gis•tic** \ˌyü-lə-ˈjis-tik\ *adj* — **eu•lo•gize** \ˈyü-lə-ˌjīz\ *vb*
eu•nuch \ˈyü-nək\ *n* **:** a castrated man
eu•phe•mism \ˈyü-fə-ˌmi-zəm\ *n* [Gk *euphēmismos,* fr. *euphēmos* auspicious, sounding good, fr. *eu-* good + *phēmē* speech] **:** the substitution of a mild or pleasant expression for one offensive or unpleasant; *also* **:** the expression substituted — **eu•phe•mis•tic** \ˌyü-fə-ˈmis-tik\ *adj*
eu•pho•ni•ous \yü-ˈfō-nē-əs\ *adj* **:** pleasing to the ear — **eu•pho•ni•ous•ly** *adv*
eu•pho•ny \ˈyü-fə-nē\ *n, pl* **-nies :** the effect produced by words so combined as to please the ear
eu•pho•ria \yü-ˈfȯr-ē-ə\ *n* **:** a marked feeling of well-being or elation — **eu•phor•ic** \-ˈfȯr-ik\ *adj*
Eur *abbr* Europe; European
Eur•asian \yü-ˈrā-zhən, -shən\ *adj* **1 :** of mixed European and Asian origin **2 :** of or relating to Europe and Asia — **Eurasian** *n*
eu•re•ka \yü-ˈrē-kə\ *interj* [Gk *heurēka* I have found, fr. *heuriskein* to find; fr. the exclamation attributed to Archimedes on discovering a method for determining the purity of gold] — used to express triumph on a discovery
Eu•ro•bond \ˈyür-ō-ˌbänd\ *n* **:** a bond of a U.S. corporation that is sold outside the U.S. but that is valued and paid for in dollars and yields interest in dollars
Eu•ro•cur•ren•cy \ˌyür-ō-ˈkər-ən-sē\ *n* **:** moneys (as of the U.S. and Japan) held outside their countries of origin and used in the money markets of Europe
Eu•ro•dol•lar \ˈyür-ō-ˌdä-lər\ *n* **:** a U.S. dollar held as Eurocurrency
Eu•ro•pe•an \ˌyür-ə-ˈpē-ən\ *n* **1 :** a native or inhabitant of Europe **2 :** a person of European descent — **European** *adj*
European plan *n* **:** a hotel plan whereby the daily rates cover only the cost of the room
eu•ro•pi•um \yü-ˈrō-pē-əm\ *n* **:** a rare metallic chemical element — see ELEMENT table
eu•sta•chian tube \yü-ˈstā-shən-\ *n, often cap E* **:** a tube connecting the inner cavity of the ear with the throat and equalizing air pressure on both sides of the eardrum

eu•tha•na•sia \ˌyü-thə-ˈnā-zhə\ *n* [Gk, easy death, fr. *eu-* good + *thanatos* death] : MERCY KILLING
EVA *abbr* extravehicular activity
evac•u•ate \i-ˈva-kyə-ˌwāt\ *vb* **-at•ed; -at•ing 1 :** EMPTY **2 :** to discharge wastes from the body **3 :** to remove or withdraw from : VACATE — **evac•u•a•tion** \-ˌva-kyə-ˈwā-shən\ *n*
evac•u•ee \i-ˌva-kyə-ˈwē\ *n* : a person removed from a dangerous place
evade \i-ˈvād\ *vb* **evad•ed; evad•ing :** to manage to avoid esp. by dexterity or slyness : ELUDE, ESCAPE
eval•u•ate \i-ˈval-yü-ˌwāt\ *vb* **-at•ed; -at•ing :** APPRAISE, VALUE — **eval•u•a•tion** \-ˌval-yü-ˈwā-shən\ *n*
ev•a•nes•cent \ˌe-və-ˈnes-ᵊnt\ *adj* : tending to vanish like vapor **syn** passing, transient, transitory, momentary — **ev•a•nes•cence** \-ᵊns\ *n*
evan•gel•i•cal \ˌē-ˌvan-ˈje-li-kəl, ˌe-vən-\ *adj* [LL *evangelium* gospel, fr. Gk *evangelion,* fr. *eu-* good + *angelos* messenger] **1 :** of or relating to the Christian gospel esp. as presented in the four Gospels **2 :** of or relating to certain Protestant churches emphasizing the authority of Scripture and the importance of preaching as contrasted with ritual **3 :** ZEALOUS ⟨~ fervor⟩ — **Evangelical** *n* — **Evan•gel•i•cal•ism** \-kə-ˌli-zəm\ *n* — **evan•gel•i•cal•ly** *adv*
evan•ge•lism \i-ˈvan-jə-ˌli-zəm\ *n* **1 :** the winning or revival of personal commitments to Christ **2 :** militant or crusading zeal — **evan•ge•lis•tic** \-ˌvan-jə-ˈlis-tik\ *adj* — **evan•ge•lis•ti•cal•ly** *adv*
evan•ge•list \i-ˈvan-jə-list\ *n* **1** *often cap* : the writer of any of the four Gospels **2 :** a person who evangelizes; *esp* : a Protestant minister or layman who preaches at special services
evan•ge•lize \i-ˈvan-jə-ˌlīz\ *vb* **-lized; -liz•ing 1 :** to preach the gospel **2 :** to convert to Christianity
evap *abbr* evaporate
evap•o•rate \i-ˈva-pə-ˌrāt\ *vb* **-rat•ed; -rat•ing 1 :** to pass off or cause to pass off in vapor **2 :** to disappear quickly **3 :** to drive out the moisture from (as by heat) — **evap•o•ra•tion** \-ˌva-pə-ˈrā-shən\ *n* — **evap•o•ra•tor** \-ˌrā-tər\ *n*
evap•o•rite \i-ˈva-pə-ˌrīt\ *n* : a sedimentary rock that originates by the evaporation of seawater in an enclosed basin
eva•sion \i-ˈvā-zhən\ *n* **1 :** a means of evading **2 :** an act or instance of evading — **eva•sive** \i-ˈvā-siv\ *adj* — **eva•sive•ness** *n*
eve \ˈēv\ *n* **1 :** EVENING **2 :** the period just before some important event
[1]**even** \ˈē-vən\ *adj* **1 :** LEVEL, FLAT **2 :** REGULAR, SMOOTH **3 :** EQUAL, FAIR **4 :** BALANCED; *also* : fully revenged **5 :** divisible by two **6 :** EXACT — **even•ly** *adv* — **even•ness** *n*
[2]**even** *adv* **1 :** EXACTLY, PRECISELY **2 :** FULLY, QUITE **3 :** at the very time **4** — used as an intensive to stress identity ⟨~ I know that⟩ **5** — used as an intensive to emphasize something extreme or highly unlikely ⟨so simple ~ a child can do it⟩ **6** — used as an intensive to stress the comparative degree ⟨did ~ better⟩ **7** — used as an intensive to indicate a small or minimum degree ⟨didn't ~ try⟩
[3]**even** *vb* : to make or become even
even•hand•ed \ˌē-vən-ˈhan-dəd\ *adj* : FAIR, IMPARTIAL — **even•hand•ed•ly** *adv*
eve•ning \ˈēv-niŋ\ *n* **1 :** the end of the day and early part of the night **2** *chiefly Southern & Midland* : AFTERNOON
evening primrose *n* : a coarse biennial herb with yellow flowers that open in the evening
evening star *n* : a bright planet (as Venus) seen esp. in the western sky at or after sunset
even•song \ˈē-vən-ˌsȯŋ\ *n, often cap* **1 :** VESPERS **2 :** evening prayer esp. when sung
event \i-ˈvent\ *n* [MF or L; MF, fr. L *eventus,* fr. *evenire* to happen, fr. *venire* to come] **1 :** OCCURRENCE **2 :** a noteworthy happening **3 :** CONTINGENCY ⟨in the ~ of rain⟩ **4 :** a contest in a program of sports — **event•ful** *adj*
even•tide \ˈē-vən-ˌtīd\ *n* : EVENING
even•tu•al \i-ˈven-chü-wəl\ *adj* : coming at some later time : ULTIMATE — **even•tu•al•ly** *adv*
even•tu•al•i•ty \i-ˌven-chü-ˈwa-lə-tē\ *n, pl* **-ties :** a possible event or outcome
even•tu•ate \i-ˈven-chü-ˌwāt\ *vb* **-at•ed; -at•ing :** to result finally
ev•er \ˈe-vər\ *adv* **1 :** ALWAYS **2 :** at any time **3 :** in any way : AT ALL
ev•er•glade \ˈe-vər-ˌglād\ *n* : a low-lying tract of swampy or marshy land
ev•er•green \-ˌgrēn\ *adj* : having foliage that remains green ⟨most coniferous trees are ~⟩ — **evergreen** *n*
[1]**ev•er•last•ing** \ˌe-vər-ˈlas-tiŋ\ *adj* **1 :** enduring forever : ETERNAL **2 :** having or being flowers or foliage that retain form or color for a long time when dried — **ev•er•last•ing•ly** *adv*
[2]**everlasting** *n* **1 :** ETERNITY ⟨from ~⟩ **2 :** a plant with everlasting flowers; *also* : its flower
ev•er•more \ˌe-vər-ˈmōr\ *adv* : FOREVER
ev•ery \ˈev-rē\ *adj* **1 :** being each one of a group **2 :** all possible ⟨given ~ chance⟩; *also* : COMPLETE ⟨have ~ confidence⟩
ev•ery•body \ˈev-ri-ˌbä-dē, -bə-\ *pron* : every person
ev•ery•day \ˈev-rē-ˌdā\ *adj* : encountered or used routinely : ORDINARY
ev•ery•one \-(ˌ)wən\ *pron* : EVERYBODY
ev•ery•thing \ˈev-rē-ˌthiŋ\ *pron* **1 :** all that exists **2 :** all that is relevant
ev•ery•where \ˈev-rē-ˌhwer\ *adv* : in every place or part
evg *abbr* evening
evict \i-ˈvikt\ *vb* **1 :** to put (a person) out from a property by legal process **2 :** EXPEL **syn** eject, oust, dismiss — **evic•tion** \-ˈvik-shən\ *n*
ev•i•dence \ˈe-və-dəns\ *n* **1 :** an outward sign **2 :** PROOF, TESTIMONY; *esp* : matter submitted in court to determine the truth of alleged facts
ev•i•dent \-dənt\ *adj* : clear to the vision and understanding **syn** manifest, distinct, obvious, apparent, plain
ev•i•dent•ly \ˈe-və-dənt-lē, ˌe-və-ˈdent-\ *adv* **1 :** in an evident manner **2 :** on the basis of available evidence
[1]**evil** \ˈē-vəl\ *adj* **evil•er** *or* **evil•ler; evil•est** *or* **evil•lest 1 :** WICKED **2 :** causing or threatening distress or harm : PERNICIOUS — **evil•ly** *adv*
[2]**evil** *n* **1 :** the fact of suffering, misfortune, and wrongdoing **2 :** a source of sorrow or distress
evil•do•er \ˌē-vəl-ˈdü-ər\ *n* : one who does evil
evil–mind•ed \-ˈmīn-dəd\ *adj* : having an evil disposition or evil thoughts — **evil–mind•ed•ly** *adv*
evince \i-ˈvins\ *vb* **evinced; evinc•ing :** SHOW, REVEAL
evis•cer•ate \i-ˈvi-sə-ˌrāt\ *vb* **-at•ed; -at•ing 1 :** to remove the entrails of **2 :** to deprive of vital content or force — **evis•cer•a•tion** \-ˌvi-sə-ˈrā-shən\ *n*
evoke \i-ˈvōk\ *vb* **evoked; evok•ing :** to call forth or up — **evo•ca•tion** \ˌē-vō-ˈkā-shən, ˌe-və-\ *n* — **evoc•a•tive** \i-ˈvä-kə-tiv\ *adj*
evo•lu•tion \ˌe-və-ˈlü-shən\ *n* **1 :** one of a set of prescribed movements (as in a dance) **2 :** a process of change in a particular direction **3 :** a theory that the various kinds of plants and animals are descended from other kinds that lived in earlier times and that the differences are due to inherited changes that occurred over many generations — **evo•lu•tion•ary** \-shə-ˌner-ē\ *adj* — **evo•lu•tion•ist** \-shə-nist\ *n*
evolve \i-ˈvälv\ *vb* **evolved; evolv•ing** [L *evolvere* to unroll] : to develop or change by or as if by evolution
EW *abbr* enlisted woman
ewe \ˈyü\ *n* : a female sheep
ew•er \ˈyü-ər\ *n* : a water pitcher
[1]**ex** \ˈeks\ *prep* [L] : out of : FROM
[2]**ex** *n* : a former spouse
[3]**ex** *abbr* **1** example **2** express **3** extra

DICTIONARY

Ex *abbr* Exodus

ex- \e *also occurs in this prefix where only* i *is shown below (as in "express") and* ks *sometimes occurs where only* gz *is shown (as in "exact")*\ *prefix* **1 :** out of : outside **2 :** former ⟨*ex*-president⟩

ex•ac•er•bate \ig-ˈza-sər-ˌbāt\ *vb* **-bat•ed; -bat•ing :** to make more violent, bitter, or severe — **ex•ac•er•ba•tion** \-ˌza-sər-ˈbā-shən\ *n*

[1]**ex•act** \ig-ˈzakt\ *vb* **1 :** to compel to furnish **2 :** to call for as suitable or necessary — **ex•ac•tion** \-ˈzak-shən\ *n*

[2]**exact** *adj* **:** precisely accurate or correct — **ex•act•ly** *adv* — **ex•act•ness** *n*

ex•act•ing \ig-ˈzak-tiŋ\ *adj* **1 :** greatly demanding ⟨an ~ taskmaster⟩ **2 :** requiring close attention and precision

ex•ac•ti•tude \ig-ˈzak-tə-ˌtüd, -ˌtyüd\ *n* **:** the quality or state of being exact

ex•ag•ger•ate \ig-ˈza-jə-ˌrāt\ *vb* **-at•ed; -at•ing** [L *exaggeratus,* pp. of *exaggerare,* lit., to heap up, fr. *agger* heap] **:** to enlarge (as a statement) beyond normal **:** OVERSTATE — **ex•ag•ger•at•ed•ly** *adv* — **ex•ag•ger•a•tion** \-ˌza-jə-ˈrā-shən\ *n* — **ex•ag•ger•a•tor** \-ˈza-jə-ˌrā-tər\ *n*

ex•alt \ig-ˈzȯlt\ *vb* **1 :** to raise up esp. in rank, power, or dignity **2 :** GLORIFY — **ex•al•ta•tion** \ˌeg-ˌzȯl-ˈtā-shən, ˌek-ˌsȯl-\ *n*

ex•am \ig-ˈzam\ *n* **:** EXAMINATION

ex•am•ine \ig-ˈza-mən\ *vb* **ex•am•ined; ex•am•in•ing 1 :** to inspect closely **2 :** QUESTION; *esp* **:** to test by questioning **syn** interrogate, query, quiz, catechize — **ex•am•i•na•tion** \-ˌza-mə-ˈnā-shən\ *n*

ex•am•ple \ig-ˈzam-pəl\ *n* **1 :** something forming a model to be followed or avoided **2 :** a representative sample **3 :** a problem to be solved in order to show the application of some rule

ex•as•per•ate \ig-ˈzas-pə-ˌrāt\ *vb* **-at•ed; -at•ing :** VEX, IRRITATE — **ex•as•per•a•tion** \ig-ˌzas-pə-ˈrā-shən\ *n*

exc *abbr* **1** excellent **2** except

ex•ca•vate \ˈek-skə-ˌvāt\ *vb* **-vat•ed; -vat•ing 1 :** to hollow out; *also* **:** to form by hollowing out **2 :** to dig out and remove (as earth) **3 :** to reveal to view by digging away a covering — **ex•ca•va•tion** \ˌek-skə-ˈvā-shən\ *n* — **ex•ca•va•tor** \ˈek-skə-ˌvā-tər\ *n*

ex•ceed \ik-ˈsēd\ *vb* **1 :** to go or be beyond the limit of **2 :** SURPASS

ex•ceed•ing•ly \-ˈsē-diŋ-lē\ *also* **ex•ceed•ing** *adv* **:** EXTREMELY, VERY

ex•cel \ik-ˈsel\ *vb* **ex•celled; ex•cel•ling :** SURPASS, OUTDO

ex•cel•lence \ˈek-sə-ləns\ *n* **1 :** the quality of being excellent **2 :** an excellent or valuable quality **:** VIRTUE **3 :** EXCELLENCY 2

ex•cel•len•cy \-lən-sē\ *n, pl* **-cies 1 :** EXCELLENCE **2** — used as a title of honor

ex•cel•lent \-lənt\ *adj* **:** very good of its kind **:** FIRST-CLASS — **ex•cel•lent•ly** *adv*

ex•cel•si•or \ik-ˈsel-sē-ər\ *n* **:** fine curled wood shavings used esp. for packing fragile items

[1]**ex•cept** \ik-ˈsept\ *also* **ex•cept•ing** *prep* **:** with the exclusion or exception of ⟨daily ~ Sundays⟩

[2]**except** *vb* **1 :** to take or leave out **2 :** OBJECT

[3]**except** *also* **excepting** *conj* **1 :** UNLESS ⟨~ you repent⟩ **2 :** ONLY ⟨I'd go, ~ it's too far⟩

ex•cep•tion \ik-ˈsep-shən\ *n* **1 :** the act of excepting **2 :** something excepted **3 :** OBJECTION

ex•cep•tion•able \ik-ˈsep-shə-nə-bəl\ *adj* **:** OBJECTIONABLE

ex•cep•tion•al \ik-ˈsep-shə-nəl\ *adj* **1 :** UNUSUAL **2 :** SUPERIOR — **ex•cep•tion•al•ly** *adv*

ex•cerpt \ˈek-ˌsərpt, ˈeg-ˌzərpt\ *n* **:** a passage selected or copied **:** EXTRACT — **excerpt** \ek-ˈsərpt, eg-ˈzərpt; ˈek-ˌsərpt, ˈeg-ˌzərpt\ *vb*

ex•cess \ik-ˈses, ˈek-ˌses\ *n* **1 :** SUPERFLUITY, SURPLUS **2 :** the amount by which one quantity exceeds another **3 :** INTEMPERANCE; *also* **:** an instance of intemperance — **excess** *adj* — **ex•ces•sive** \ik-ˈse-siv\ *adj* — **ex•ces•sive•ly** *adv*

exch *abbr* exchange; exchanged

[1]**ex•change** \iks-ˈchānj\ *n* **1 :** the giving or taking of one thing in return for another **:** TRADE **2 :** a substituting of one thing for another **3 :** interchange of valuables and esp. of bills of exchange or money of different countries **4 :** a place where things and services are exchanged; *esp* **:** a marketplace for securities **5 :** a central office in which telephone lines are connected for communication

[2]**exchange** *vb* **ex•changed; ex•chang•ing :** to transfer in return for some equivalent **:** BARTER, SWAP — **ex•change•able** \iks-ˈchān-jə-bəl\ *adj*

ex•che•quer \ˈeks-ˌche-kər\ *n* [ME *escheker,* fr. OF *eschequier* chessboard, counting table] **:** TREASURY; *esp* **:** a national treasury

ex•cise \ˈek-ˌsīz\ *n* **:** a tax on the manufacture, sale, or consumption of a commodity

ex•ci•sion \ik-ˈsi-zhən\ *n* **:** removal by or as if by cutting out esp. by surgical means — **ex•cise** \ik-ˈsīz\ *vb*

ex•cit•able \ik-ˈsī-tə-bəl\ *adj* **:** easily excited — **ex•cit•abil•i•ty** \-ˌsī-tə-ˈbi-lə-tē\ *n*

ex•cite \ik-ˈsīt\ *vb* **ex•cit•ed; ex•cit•ing 1 :** to stir up the emotions of **:** ROUSE **2 :** to increase the activity of **:** STIMULATE **syn** provoke, pique, quicken — **ex•ci•ta•tion** \ˌek-ˌsī-ˈtā-shən, ˌek-sə-\ *n* — **ex•cit•ed•ly** *adv* — **ex•cit•ing•ly** *adv*

ex•cite•ment \ik-ˈsīt-mənt\ *n* **:** AGITATION, STIR

ex•claim \iks-ˈklām\ *vb* **:** to cry out, speak, or utter sharply or vehemently — **ex•cla•ma•tion** \ˌeks-klə-ˈmā-shən\ *n* — **ex•clam•a•to•ry** \iks-ˈkla-mə-ˌtōr-ē\ *adj*

exclamation point *n* **:** a punctuation mark ! used esp. after an interjection or exclamation

ex•clude \iks-ˈklüd\ *vb* **ex•clud•ed; ex•clud•ing 1 :** to prevent from using or participating **:** BAR **2 :** to put out **:** EXPEL — **ex•clu•sion** \-ˈklü-zhən\ *n*

ex•clu•sive \iks-ˈklü-siv\ *adj* **1 :** reserved for particular persons **2 :** snobbishly aloof; *also* **:** STYLISH **3 :** SOLE ⟨~ rights⟩; *also* **:** UNDIVIDED **syn** chic, modish, smart, swank, fashionable — **exclusive** *n* — **ex•clu•sive•ly** *adv* — **ex•clu•sive•ness** *n* — **ex•clu•siv•i•ty** \ˌeks-ˌklü-si-və-tē, iks-, -zi-\ *n*

exclusive of *prep* **:** not taking into account

ex•cog•i•tate \ek-ˈskä-jə-ˌtāt\ *vb* **:** to think out **:** DEVISE

ex•com•mu•ni•cate \ˌek-skə-ˈmyü-nə-ˌkāt\ *vb* **:** to cut off officially from the rites of the church — **ex•com•mu•ni•ca•tion** \-ˌmyü-nə-ˈkā-shən\ *n*

ex•co•ri•ate \ek-ˈskōr-ē-ˌāt\ *vb* **-at•ed; -at•ing :** to criticize severely — **ex•co•ri•a•tion** \(ˌ)ek-ˌskōr-ē-ˈā-shən\ *n*

ex•cre•ment \ˈek-skrə-mənt\ *n* **:** waste discharged from the body and esp. from the alimentary canal — **ex•cre•men•tal** \ˌek-skrə-ˈment-ᵊl\ *adj*

ex•cres•cence \ik-ˈskres-ᵊns\ *n* **:** OUTGROWTH; *esp* **:** an abnormal outgrowth (as a wart)

ex•cre•ta \ik-ˈskrē-tə\ *n pl* **:** waste matter separated or eliminated from an organism

ex•crete \ik-ˈskrēt\ *vb* **ex•cret•ed; ex•cret•ing :** to separate and eliminate wastes from the body esp. in urine or sweat — **ex•cre•tion** \-ˈskrē-shən\ *n* — **ex•cre•to•ry** \ˈek-skrə-ˌtōr-ē\ *adj*

ex•cru•ci•at•ing \ik-ˈskrü-shē-ˌā-tiŋ\ *adj* [L *excruciare,* fr. *cruciare* to crucify, fr. *crux* cross] **:** intensely painful or distressing **syn** agonizing, harrowing, torturous — **ex•cru•ci•at•ing•ly** *adv*

ex•cul•pate \ˈek-(ˌ)skəl-ˌpāt\ *vb* **-pat•ed; -pat•ing :** to clear from alleged fault or guilt **syn** absolve, exonerate, acquit, vindicate, clear

ex•cur•sion \ik-ˈskər-zhən\ *n* **1 :** EXPEDITION; *esp* **:** a pleasure trip **2 :** DIGRESSION — **ex•cur•sion•ist** \-zhə-nist\ *n*

ex•cur•sive \-ˈskər-siv\ *adj* **:** constituting or characterized by digression

[1]**ex•cuse** \ik-ˈskyüz\ *vb* **ex•cused; ex•cus•ing** [ME, fr.

OF *excuser,* fr. L *excusare,* fr. *causa* cause, explanation] **1** : to make apology for **2** : PARDON **3** : to release from an obligation **4** : JUSTIFY — **ex•cus•able** *adj*

[2]**excuse** \ik-ˈskyüs\ *n* **1** : an act of excusing **2** : something that excuses or is a reason for excusing : JUSTIFICATION

exec *n* : EXECUTIVE

ex•e•cra•ble \ˈek-si-krə-bəl\ *adj* **1** : DETESTABLE **2** : very bad ⟨~ spelling⟩

ex•e•crate \ˈek-sə-ˌkrāt\ *vb* **-crat•ed; -crat•ing** [L *exsecratus,* pp. of *exsecrari* to put under a curse, fr. *ex*-out of + *sacer* sacred] : to denounce as evil or detestable; *also* : DETEST — **ex•e•cra•tion** \ˌek-sə-ˈkrā-shən\ *n*

ex•e•cute \ˈek-si-ˌkyüt\ *vb* **-cut•ed; -cut•ing 1** : to carry out fully : put completely into effect **2** : to do what is called for by (as a law) **3** : to put to death in accordance with a legal sentence **4** : to produce by carrying out a design **5** : to do what is needed to give validity to ⟨~ a deed⟩ — **ex•e•cu•tion** \ˌek-si-ˈkyü-shən\ *n* — **ex•e•cu•tion•er** *n*

[1]**ex•ec•u•tive** \ig-ˈze-kyə-tiv\ *adj* **1** : of or relating to the enforcement of laws and the conduct of affairs **2** : designed for or related to carrying out plans or purposes

[2]**executive** *n* **1** : the branch of government with executive duties **2** : one having administrative or managerial responsibility

ex•ec•u•tor \ig-ˈze-kyə-tər\ *n* : the person named in a will to execute it

ex•ec•u•trix \ig-ˈze-kyə-ˌtriks\ *n, pl* **ex•ec•u•tri•ces** \-ˌze-kyə-ˈtrī-ˌsēz\ *or* **ex•ec•u•trix•es** \-ˈze-kyə-ˌtrik-səz\ : a woman who is an executor

ex•e•ge•sis \ˌek-sə-ˈjē-səs\ *n, pl* **-ge•ses** \-ˈjē-ˌsēz\ : explanation or critical interpretation of a text

ex•e•gete \ˈek-sə-ˌjēt\ *n* : one who practices exegesis — **ex•e•get•i•cal** \ˌek-sə-ˈje-ti-kəl\ *adj*

ex•em•plar \ig-ˈzem-ˌplär, -plər\ *n* **1** : one that serves as a model or example; *esp* : an ideal model **2** : a typical instance or example

ex•em•pla•ry \ig-ˈzem-plə-rē\ *adj* : serving as a pattern; *also* : COMMENDABLE

ex•em•pli•fy \ig-ˈzem-plə-ˌfī\ *vb* **-fied; -fy•ing** : to illustrate by example : serve as an example of — **ex•em•pli•fi•ca•tion** \-ˌzem-plə-fə-ˈkā-shən\ *n*

[1]**ex•empt** \ig-ˈzempt\ *adj* : free from some liability to which others are subject

[2]**exempt** *vb* : to make exempt : EXCUSE — **ex•emp•tion** \ig-ˈzemp-shən\ *n*

[1]**ex•er•cise** \ˈek-sər-ˌsīz\ *n* **1** : EMPLOYMENT, USE ⟨~ of authority⟩ **2** : exertion made for the sake of training or physical fitness **3** : a task or problem done to develop skill **4** *pl* : a public exhibition or ceremony

[2]**exercise** *vb* **-cised; -cis•ing 1** : EXERT ⟨~ control⟩ **2** : to train by or engage in exercise **3** : WORRY, DISTRESS — **ex•er•cis•er** *n*

ex•ert \ig-ˈzərt\ *vb* : to bring or put into action ⟨~ influence⟩ ⟨~*ed* himself⟩ — **ex•er•tion** \-ˈzər-shən\ *n*

ex•hale \eks-ˈhāl\ *vb* **ex•haled; ex•hal•ing 1** : to breathe out **2** : to give or pass off in the form of vapor — **ex•ha•la•tion** \ˌeks-hə-ˈlā-shən\ *n*

[1]**ex•haust** \ig-ˈzȯst\ *vb* **1** : to use up wholly **2** : to tire or wear out **3** : to draw off or let out completely; *also* : EMPTY **4** : to develop (a subject) completely

[2]**exhaust** *n* **1** : the escape of used vapor or gas from an engine; *also* : the gas that escapes **2** : a system of pipes through which exhaust escapes

ex•haus•tion \ig-ˈzȯs-chən\ *n* : extreme weariness : FATIGUE

ex•haus•tive \ig-ˈzȯ-stiv\ *adj* : covering all possibilities : THOROUGH — **ex•haus•tive•ly** *adv*

[1]**ex•hib•it** \ig-ˈzi-bət\ *vb* **1** : to display esp. publicly **2** : to present to a court in legal form **syn** display, show, parade, flaunt — **ex•hi•bi•tion** \ˌek-sə-ˈbi-shən\ *n* — **ex•hib•i•tor** \ig-ˈzi-bə-tər\ *n*

[2]**exhibit** *n* **1** : an act or instance of exhibiting; *also* : something exhibited **2** : something produced and identified in court for use as evidence

ex•hi•bi•tion•ism \ˌek-sə-ˈbi-shə-ˌni-zəm\ *n* **1** : a perversion marked by a tendency to indecent exposure **2** : the act or practice of behaving so as to attract attention to oneself — **ex•hi•bi•tion•ist** \-nist\ *n or adj*

ex•hil•a•rate \ig-ˈzi-lə-ˌrāt\ *vb* **-rat•ed; -rat•ing** : ENLIVEN, STIMULATE — **ex•hil•a•ra•tion** \-ˌzi-lə-ˈrā-shən\ *n*

ex•hort \ig-ˈzȯrt\ *vb* : to urge, advise, or warn earnestly — **ex•hor•ta•tion** \ˌek-ˌsȯr-ˈtā-shən, ˌeg-ˌzȯr-, -zər-\ *n*

ex•hume \ig-ˈzüm, iks-ˈhyüm\ *vb* **ex•humed; ex•hum•ing** [F or ML; F *exhumer,* fr. ML *exhumare,* fr. L *ex* out of + *humus* earth] : DISINTER — **ex•hu•ma•tion** \ˌeks-hyü-ˈmā-shən, ˌeg-zü-\ *n*

ex•i•gen•cy \ˈek-sə-jən-sē, ig-ˈzi-jən-\ *n, pl* **-cies 1** *pl* : REQUIREMENTS **2** : urgent need — **ex•i•gent** \ˈek-sə-jənt\ *adj*

ex•ig•u•ous \ig-ˈzi-gyə-wəs\ *adj* : scanty in amount — **ex•i•gu•i•ty** \ˌeg-zi-ˈgyü-ə-tē\ *n*

[1]**ex•ile** \ˈeg-ˌzīl, ˈek-ˌsīl\ *n* **1** : BANISHMENT; *also* : voluntary absence from one's country or home **2** : a person driven from his or her native place

[2]**exile** *vb* **ex•iled; ex•il•ing** : BANISH, EXPEL **syn** expatriate, deport, ostracize

ex•ist \ig-ˈzist\ *vb* **1** : to have being **2** : to continue to be : LIVE

ex•is•tence \ig-ˈzis-təns\ *n* **1** : continuance in living **2** : actual occurrence **3** : something existing — **ex•is•tent** \-tənt\ *adj*

ex•is•ten•tial \ˌeg-zis-ˈten-chəl, ˌek-sis-\ *adj* **1** : of or relating to existence **2** : EMPIRICAL **3** : having being in time and space **4** : of or relating to existentialism or existentialists

ex•is•ten•tial•ism \ˌeg-zis-ˈten-chə-ˌli-zəm\ *n* : a philosophy centered on individual existence and personal responsibility for acts of free will in the absence of certain knowledge of what is right or wrong — **ex•is•ten•tial•ist** \-list\ *adj or n*

ex•it \ˈeg-zət, ˈek-sət\ *n* **1** : a departure from a stage **2** : a going out or away; *also* : DEATH **3** : a way out of an enclosed space **4** : a point of departure from an expressway — **exit** *vb*

exo•bi•ol•o•gy \ˌek-sō-bī-ˈä-lə-jē\ *n* : biology concerned with life originating or existing outside the earth or its atmosphere — **exo•bi•ol•o•gist** \-jist\ *n*

exo•crine gland \ˈek-sə-krən-, -ˌkrīn-, -ˌkrēn-\ *n* : a gland (as a salivary gland) that releases a secretion externally by means of a canal or duct

Exod *abbr* Exodus

ex•o•dus \ˈek-sə-dəs\ *n* **1** *cap* — see BIBLE table **2** : a mass departure : EMIGRATION

ex of•fi•cio \ˌek-sə-ˈfi-shē-ˌō\ *adv or adj* : by virtue of or because of an office ⟨*ex officio* chairman⟩

ex•og•e•nous \ek-ˈsä-jə-nəs\ *adj* : caused or produced by factors outside the organism or system — **ex•og•e•nous•ly** *adv*

ex•on•er•ate \ig-ˈzä-nə-ˌrāt\ *vb* **-at•ed; -at•ing** [ME, fr. L *exoneratus,* pp. of *exonerare* to unburden, fr. *ex*-out + *onus* load] : to free from blame **syn** acquit, absolve, exculpate, vindicate — **ex•on•er•a•tion** \-ˌzä-nə-ˈrā-shən\ *n*

ex•or•bi•tant \ig-ˈzȯr-bə-tənt\ *adj* : exceeding what is usual or proper

ex•or•cise \ˈek-ˌsȯr-ˌsīz, -sər-\ *vb* **-cised; -cis•ing 1** : to get rid of by or as if by solemn command **2** : to free of an evil spirit — **ex•or•cism** \-ˌsi-zəm\ *n* — **ex•or•cist** \-ˌsist\ *n*

exo•sphere \ˈek-sō-ˌsfir\ *n* : the outermost region of the atmosphere

exo•ther•mic \ˌek-sō-ˈthər-mik\ *adj* : characterized by or formed with evolution of heat

ex•ot•ic \ig-ˈzä-tik\ *adj* **1** : introduced from another country **2** : strikingly, excitingly, or mysteriously different or unusual — **exotic** *n* — **ex•ot•i•cal•ly** \-ti-k(ə-)lē\ *adv* — **ex•ot•i•cism** \-tə-ˌsi-zəm\ *n*

exp *abbr* **1** expense **2** experiment **3** export **4** express

ex•pand \ik-ˈspand\ *vb* **1** : to open up : UNFOLD **2** : ENLARGE **3** : to develop in detail **syn** amplify, swell, distend, inflate, dilate — **ex•pand•er** *n*

ex•panse \ik-ˈspans\ *n* : a broad extent (as of land or sea)

ex•pan•sion \ik-ˈspan-chən\ *n* **1** : the act or process of expanding **2** : the quality or state of being expanded **3** : an expanded part or thing

ex•pan•sive \ik-ˈspan-siv\ *adj* **1** : tending to expand or to cause expansion **2** : warmly benevolent, generous, or ready to talk **3** : of large extent or scope — **ex•pan•sive•ly** *adv* — **ex•pan•sive•ness** *n*

ex par•te \eks-ˈpär-tē\ *adv or adj* [ML] : from a one-sided point of view

ex•pa•ti•ate \ek-ˈspā-shē-ˌāt\ *vb* **-at•ed; -at•ing** : to talk or write at length — **ex•pa•ti•a•tion** \ek-ˌspā-shē-ˈā-shən\ *n*

1ex•pa•tri•ate \ek-ˈspā-trē-ˌāt\ *vb* **-at•ed; -at•ing** : EXILE — **ex•pa•tri•a•tion** \ek-ˌspā-trē-ˈā-shən\ *n*

2ex•pa•tri•ate \ek-ˈspā-trē-ˌāt, -trē-ət\ *adj* : living in a foreign country — **expatriate** *n*

ex•pect \ik-ˈspekt\ *vb* **1** : SUPPOSE, THINK **2** : to look forward to : ANTICIPATE **3** : to consider reasonable, due, or necessary **4** : to consider to be obliged

ex•pec•tan•cy \-ˈspek-tən-sē\ *n, pl* **-cies** **1** : EXPECTATION **2** : the expected amount (as of years of life)

ex•pec•tant \-tənt\ *adj* : marked by expectation; *esp* : expecting the birth of a child — **ex•pec•tant•ly** *adv*

ex•pec•ta•tion \ˌek-ˌspek-ˈtā-shən\ *n* **1** : the act or state of expecting **2** : prospect of good or bad fortune — usu. used in pl. **3** : something expected

ex•pec•to•rant \ik-ˈspek-tə-rənt\ *n* : an agent that promotes the discharge or expulsion of mucus from the respiratory tract — **expectorant** *adj*

ex•pec•to•rate \-ˌrāt\ *vb* **-rat•ed; -rat•ing** : SPIT — **ex•pec•to•ra•tion** \-ˌspek-tə-ˈrā-shən\ *n*

ex•pe•di•ence \ik-ˈspē-dē-əns\ *n* : EXPEDIENCY

ex•pe•di•en•cy \-ən-sē\ *n, pl* **-cies** **1** : fitness to some end **2** : use of expedient means and methods; *also* : something expedient

1ex•pe•di•ent \-ənt\ *adj* [ME, fr. MF or L; MF, fr. L *expediens*, prp. of *expedire* to extricate, prepare, be useful, fr. *ex-* out + *ped-*, *pes* foot] **1** : adapted for achieving a particular end **2** : marked by concern with what is advantageous; *esp* : governed by self-interest

2expedient *n* : something expedient; *esp* : a temporary means to an end

ex•pe•dite \ˈek-spə-ˌdīt\ *vb* **-dit•ed; -dit•ing** : to carry out promptly; *also* : to speed up

ex•pe•dit•er \-ˌdī-tər\ *n* : one that expedites; *esp* : one employed to ensure efficient movement of goods or supplies in a business

ex•pe•di•tion \ˌek-spə-ˈdi-shən\ *n* **1** : a journey for a particular purpose; *also* : the persons making it **2** : efficient promptness

ex•pe•di•tion•ary \-ˈdi-shə-ˌner-ē\ *adj* : of, relating to, or constituting an expedition; *also* : sent on military service abroad

ex•pe•di•tious \-ˈdi-shəs\ *adj* : marked by or acting with prompt efficiency **syn** swift, fast, rapid, speedy

ex•pel \ik-ˈspel\ *vb* **ex•pelled; ex•pel•ling** : to drive or force out : EJECT

ex•pend \ik-ˈspend\ *vb* **1** : to pay out : SPEND **2** : UTILIZE; *also* : USE UP — **ex•pend•able** *adj*

ex•pen•di•ture \ik-ˈspen-di-chər, -ˌchu̇r\ *n* **1** : the act or process of expending **2** : something expended

ex•pense \ik-ˈspens\ *n* **1** : EXPENDITURE **2** : COST **3** : a cause of expenditure **4** : SACRIFICE

ex•pen•sive \ik-ˈspen-siv\ *adj* : COSTLY, DEAR — **ex•pen•sive•ly** *adv*

1ex•pe•ri•ence \ik-ˈspir-ē-əns\ *n* **1** : observation of or participation in events resulting in or tending toward knowledge **2** : knowledge, practice, or skill derived from observation or participation in events; *also* : the length of such participation **3** : something encountered, undergone, or lived through (as by a person or community)

2experience *vb* **-enced; -enc•ing** **1** : FIND OUT, DISCOVER **2** : to have experience of : UNDERGO

ex•pe•ri•enced *adj* : made capable through experience

1ex•per•i•ment \ik-ˈsper-ə-mənt\ *n* : a controlled procedure carried out to discover, test, or demonstrate something; *also* : the process of testing — **ex•per•i•men•tal** \-ˌsper-ə-ˈment-ᵊl\ *adj*

2ex•per•i•ment \-ˌment\ *vb* : to make experiments — **ex•per•i•men•ta•tion** \ik-ˌsper-ə-mən-ˈtā-shən\ *n* — **ex•per•i•men•ter** *n*

1ex•pert \ˈek-ˌspərt\ *adj* : showing special skill or knowledge — **ex•pert•ly** *adv* — **ex•pert•ness** *n*

2ex•pert \ˈek-ˌspərt\ *n* : an expert person : SPECIALIST

ex•per•tise \ˌek-(ˌ)spər-ˈtēz\ *n* : the skill of an expert

expert system *n* : computer software that attempts to mimic the reasoning of a human specialist

ex•pi•ate \ˈek-spē-ˌāt\ *vb* **-at•ed; -at•ing** : to give satisfaction for : ATONE — **ex•pi•a•tion** \ˌek-spē-ˈā-shən\ *n*

ex•pi•a•to•ry \ˈek-spē-ə-ˌtōr-ē\ *adj* : serving to expiate

ex•pire \ik-ˈspīr, ek-\ *vb* **ex•pired; ex•pir•ing** **1** : to breathe one's last breath : DIE **2** : to come to an end **3** : to breathe out from or as if from the lungs — **ex•pi•ra•tion** \ˌek-spə-ˈrā-shən\ *n*

ex•plain \ik-ˈsplān\ *vb* [ME *explanen*, fr. L *explanare*, lit., to make level, fr. *planus* level, flat] **1** : to make clear **2** : to give the reason for — **ex•pla•na•tion** \ˌek-splə-ˈnā-shən\ *n* — **ex•plan•a•to•ry** \ik-ˈspla-nə-ˌtōr-ē\ *adj*

ex•ple•tive \ˈek-splə-tiv\ *n* : a usu. profane exclamation

ex•pli•ca•ble \ek-ˈspli-kə-bəl, ˈek-(ˌ)spli-\ *adj* : capable of being explained

ex•pli•cate \ˈek-splə-ˌkāt\ *vb* **-cat•ed; -cat•ing** : to give a detailed explanation of — **ex•pli•ca•tion** \ˌek-spli-ˈkā-shən\ *n*

ex•plic•it \ik-ˈspli-sət\ *adj* : clearly and precisely expressed — **ex•plic•it•ly** *adv* — **ex•plic•it•ness** *n*

ex•plode \ik-ˈsplōd\ *vb* **ex•plod•ed; ex•plod•ing** [L *explodere* to drive off the stage by clapping, fr. *ex-* out + *plaudere* to clap] **1** : DISCREDIT ⟨~ a belief⟩ **2** : to burst or cause to burst violently and noisily ⟨~ a bomb⟩ ⟨the boiler *exploded*⟩ **3** : to undergo a rapid chemical or nuclear reaction with production of heat and violent expansion of gas ⟨dynamite ~*s*⟩ **4** : to give forth a sudden strong and noisy outburst of emotion **5** : to increase rapidly

ex•plod•ed *adj* : showing the parts separated but in correct relationship to each other ⟨an ~ view of a carburetor⟩

1ex•ploit \ˈek-ˌsplȯit\ *n* : DEED; *esp* : a notable or heroic act

2ex•ploit \ik-ˈsplȯit\ *vb* **1** : to make productive use of : UTILIZE **2** : to use unfairly for one's own advantage — **ex•ploi•ta•tion** \ˌek-ˌsplȯi-ˈtā-shən\ *n*

ex•plore \ik-ˈsplōr\ *vb* **ex•plored; ex•plor•ing** **1** : to look into or travel over thoroughly **2** : to examine carefully ⟨~ a wound⟩ — **ex•plo•ra•tion** \ˌek-splə-ˈrā-shən\ *n* — **ex•plor•ato•ry** \ik-ˈsplōr-ə-ˌtōr-ē\ *adj* — **ex•plor•er** *n*

ex•plo•sion \ik-ˈsplō-zhən\ *n* : the act or an instance of exploding

ex•plo•sive \ik-ˈsplō-siv\ *adj* **1** : relating to or able to cause explosion **2** : tending to explode — **explosive** *n* — **ex•plo•sive•ly** *adv*

ex•po \ˈek-ˌspō\ *n, pl* **expos** : EXPOSITION 2

ex•po•nent \ik-ˈspō-nənt, ˈek-ˌspō-\ *n* **1** : a symbol written above and to the right of a mathematical expression (as ^{3} in a^3) to signify how many times it is to be used as a factor **2** : INTERPRETER, EXPOUNDER **3** : ADVOCATE, CHAMPION — **ex•po•nen•tial** \ˌek-spə-ˈnen-chəl\ *adj* — **ex•po•nen•tial•ly** *adv*

ex•po•nen•ti•a•tion \ˌek-spə-ˌnen-chē-ˈā-shen\ *n* : the mathematical operation of raising a quantity to a power
[1]**ex•port** \ek-ˈspōrt, ˈek-ˌspōrt\ *vb* : to send (as merchandise) to foreign countries — **ex•por•ta•tion** \ˌek-ˌspōr-ˈtā-shən, -spər-\ *n* — **ex•port•er** *n*
[2]**ex•port** \ˈek-ˌspōrt\ *n* **1** : something exported esp. for trade **2** : the act of exporting
ex•pose \ik-ˈspōz\ *vb* **ex•posed; ex•pos•ing 1** : to deprive of shelter or protection **2** : to submit or subject to an action or influence; *esp* : to subject (as photographic film) to radiant energy (as light) **3** : to bring to light : DISCLOSE **4** : to cause to be open to view
ex•po•sé *or* **ex•po•se** \ˌek-spō-ˈzā\ *n* : an exposure of something discreditable
ex•po•si•tion \ˌek-spə-ˈzi-shən\ *n* **1** : a setting forth of the meaning or purpose (as of a writing); *also* : discourse designed to convey information **2** : a public exhibition
ex•pos•i•tor \ik-ˈspä-zə-tər\ *n* : one who explains : COMMENTATOR
ex post fac•to \ˌeks-ˈpōst-ˌfak-tō\ *adv or adj* : after the fact
ex•pos•tu•late \ik-ˈspäs-chə-ˌlāt\ *vb* : to reason earnestly with a person esp. in dissuading : REMONSTRATE — **ex•pos•tu•la•tion** \-ˌspäs-chə-ˈlā-shən\ *n*
ex•po•sure \ik-ˈspō-zhər\ *n* **1** : the fact or condition of being exposed **2** : the act or an instance of exposing **3** : the length of time for which a film is exposed **4** : a section of a photographic film for one picture
ex•pound \ik-ˈspau̇nd\ *vb* **1** : STATE **2** : INTERPRET, EXPLAIN — **ex•pound•er** *n*
[1]**ex•press** \ik-ˈspres\ *adj* **1** : EXPLICIT; *also* : EXACT, PRECISE **2** : SPECIFIC ⟨this ~ purpose⟩ **3** : traveling at high speed and esp. with few stops ⟨an ~ train⟩; *also* : adapted to high speed use ⟨~ roads⟩ — **ex•press•ly** *adv*
[2]**express** *adv* : by express ⟨ship it ~⟩
[3]**express** *n* **1** : a system for the prompt transportation of goods; *also* : a company operating such a service or the shipments so transported **2** : an express vehicle
[4]**express** *vb* **1** : to make known : SHOW, STATE ⟨~ regret⟩; *also* : SYMBOLIZE **2** : to squeeze out : extract by pressing **3** : to send by express
ex•pres•sion \ik-ˈspre-shən\ *n* **1** : UTTERANCE **2** : something that represents or symbolizes : SIGN; *esp* : a mathematical symbol or combination of signs and symbols representing a quantity or operation **3** : a significant word or phrase; *also* : manner of expressing (as in writing or music) **4** : facial aspect or vocal intonation indicative of feeling — **ex•pres•sion•less** *adj*
ex•pres•sion•ism \ik-ˈspre-shə-ˌni-zəm\ *n* : a theory or practice in art of seeking to depict the artist's subjective responses to objects and events — **ex•pres•sion•ist** \-nist\ *n or adj* — **ex•pres•sion•is•tic** \-ˌspre-shə-ˈnis-tik\ *adj*
ex•pres•sive \ik-ˈspre-siv\ *adj* **1** : of or relating to expression **2** : serving to express — **ex•pres•sive•ly** *adv* — **ex•pres•sive•ness** *n*
ex•press•way \ik-ˈspres-ˌwā\ *n* : a divided superhighway with limited access
ex•pro•pri•ate \ek-ˈsprō-prē-ˌāt\ *vb* **-at•ed; -at•ing** : to deprive of possession or the right to own — **ex•pro•pri•a•tion** \(ˌ)ek-ˌsprō-prē-ˈā-shən\ *n*
expt *abbr* experiment
ex•pul•sion \ik-ˈspəl-shən\ *n* : an expelling or being expelled : EJECTION
ex•punge \ik-ˈspənj\ *vb* **ex•punged; ex•pung•ing** [L *expungere* to mark for deletion by dots, fr. *ex-* out + *pungere* to prick] : OBLITERATE, ERASE
ex•pur•gate \ˈek-spər-ˌgāt\ *vb* **-gat•ed; -gat•ing** : to clear (as a book) of objectionable passages — **ex•pur•ga•tion** \ˌek-spər-ˈgā-shən\ *n*
ex•qui•site \ek-ˈskwi-zət, ˈek-(ˌ)skwi-\ *adj* [ME *exquisit,* fr. L *exquisitus,* pp. of *exquirere* to search out, fr. *ex* out *quaerere* to seek] **1** : marked by flawless form or workmanship **2** : keenly appreciative or sensitive **3** : pleasingly beautiful or delicate **4** : INTENSE
ext *abbr* **1** extension **2** exterior **3** external **4** extra **5** extract
ex•tant \ˈek-stənt; ek-ˈstant\ *adj* : EXISTENT; *esp* : not lost or destroyed
ex•tem•po•ra•ne•ous \ek-ˌstem-pə-ˈrā-nē-əs\ *adj* : not planned beforehand : IMPROMPTU — **ex•tem•po•ra•ne•ous•ly** *adv*
ex•tem•po•rary \ik-ˈstem-pə-ˌrer-ē\ *adj* : EXTEMPORANEOUS
ex•tem•po•re \ik-ˈstem-pə-(ˌ)rē\ *adv* : EXTEMPORANEOUSLY
ex•tem•po•rise *Brit var of* EXTEMPORIZE
ex•tem•po•rize \ik-ˈstem-pə-ˌrīz\ *vb* **-rized; -riz•ing** : to do something extemporaneously
ex•tend \ik-ˈstend\ *vb* **1** : to spread or stretch forth or out (as in reaching) **2** : to exert or cause to exert to full capacity **3** : PROFFER ⟨~ credit⟩ **4** : PROLONG ⟨~ a note⟩ **5** : to make greater or broader ⟨~ knowledge⟩ ⟨~ a business⟩ **6** : to stretch out or reach across a distance, space, or time **syn** lengthen, elongate, protract — **ex•tend•able** *also* **ex•tend•ible** \-ˈsten-də-bəl\ *adj*
ex•ten•sion \ik-ˈsten-chən\ *n* **1** : an extending or being extended **2** : a program that geographically extends the educational resources of an institution **3** : an additional part; *also* : an extra telephone connected to a line
ex•ten•sive \ik-ˈsten-siv\ *adj* : of considerable extent : FAR-REACHING, BROAD — **ex•ten•sive•ly** *adv*
ex•tent \ik-ˈstent\ *n* **1** : the range or space over which something extends ⟨a property of large ~⟩ **2** : the point or degree to which something extends ⟨to the fullest ~ of the law⟩
ex•ten•u•ate \ik-ˈsten-yu̇-ˌwāt\ *vb* **-at•ed; -at•ing** : to lessen the seriousness of — **ex•ten•u•a•tion** \-ˌsten-yu̇-ˈwā-shən\ *n*
[1]**ex•te•ri•or** \ek-ˈstir-ē-ər\ *adj* **1** : EXTERNAL **2** : suitable for use on an outside surface ⟨~ paint⟩
[2]**exterior** *n* : an exterior part or surface
ex•ter•mi•nate \ik-ˈstər-mə-ˌnāt\ *vb* **-nat•ed; -nat•ing** : to get rid of completely usu. by killing off **syn** extirpate, eradicate, abolish, annihilate — **ex•ter•mi•na•tion** \-ˌstər-mə-ˈnā-shən\ *n* — **ex•ter•mi•na•tor** \-ˈstər-mə-ˌnā-tər\ *n*
[1]**ex•ter•nal** \ek-ˈstərn-ᵊl\ *adj* **1** : outwardly perceivable; *also* : SUPERFICIAL **2** : of, relating to, or located on the outside or an outer part **3** : arising or acting from without; *also* : FOREIGN ⟨~ affairs⟩ — **ex•ter•nal•ly** *adv*
[2]**external** *n* : an external feature
ex•tinct \ik-ˈstiŋkt\ *adj* **1** : EXTINGUISHED; *also* : no longer active ⟨an ~ volcano⟩ **2** : no longer existing or in use ⟨dinosaurs are ~⟩ ⟨~ languages⟩ — **ex•tinc•tion** \ik-ˈstiŋk-shən\ *n*
ex•tin•guish \ik-ˈstiŋ-gwish\ *vb* : to cause to stop burning; *also* : to bring to an end (as by destroying) — **ex•tin•guish•able** *adj* — **ex•tin•guish•er** *n*
ex•tir•pate \ˈek-stər-ˌpāt\ *vb* **-pat•ed; -pat•ing** [L *exstirpatus,* pp. of *exstirpare,* fr. *ex-* out + *stirps* trunk, root] **1** : to destroy completely **2** : UPROOT **syn** exterminate, eradicate, abolish, annihilate — **ex•tir•pa•tion** \ˌek-stər-ˈpā-shən\ *n*
ex•tol *also* **ex•toll** \ik-ˈstōl\ *vb* **ex•tolled; ex•tol•ling** : to praise highly : GLORIFY
ex•tort \ik-ˈstȯrt\ *vb* [L *extortus,* pp. of *extorquēre* to wrench out, extort, fr. *ex-* out + *torquēre* to twist] : to obtain by force or improper pressure ⟨~ a bribe⟩ — **ex•tor•tion** \-ˈstȯr-shən\ *n* — **ex•tor•tion•er** *n* — **ex•tor•tion•ist** *n*
ex•tor•tion•ate \ik-ˈstȯr-shə-nət\ *adj* : EXCESSIVE, EXORBITANT — **ex•tor•tion•ate•ly** *adv*
[1]**ex•tra** \ˈek-strə\ *adj* **1** : ADDITIONAL **2** : SUPERIOR
[2]**extra** *n* **1** : a special edition of a newspaper **2** : an added charge **3** : an additional worker or performer (as in a motion picture)

³extra *adv* : beyond what is usual

¹ex•tract \ik-ˈstrakt, *esp for 3* ˈek-ˌstrakt\ *vb* **1** : to draw out; *esp* : to pull out forcibly ⟨~ a tooth⟩ **2** : to withdraw (as a juice or a constituent) by a physical or chemical process **3** : to select for citation : QUOTE — **ex•tract•able** *adj* — **ex•trac•tion** \ik-ˈstrak-shən\ *n* — **ex•trac•tor** \-tər\ *n*

²ex•tract \ˈek-ˌstrakt\ *n* **1** : EXCERPT, CITATION **2** : a product (as a juice or concentrate) obtained by extracting

ex•tra•cur•ric•u•lar \ˌek-strə-kə-ˈri-kyə-lər\ *adj* : lying outside the regular curriculum; *esp* : of or relating to school-connected activities (as sports) usu. carrying no academic credit

ex•tra•dite \ˈek-strə-ˌdīt\ *vb* **-dit•ed; -dit•ing** : to obtain by or deliver up to extradition

ex•tra•di•tion \ˌek-strə-ˈdi-shən\ *n* : the surrender of an alleged criminal to a different jurisdiction for trial

ex•tra•mar•i•tal \ˌek-strə-ˈmar-ət-ᵊl\ *adj* : of or relating to sexual intercourse by a married person with someone other than his or her spouse

ex•tra•mu•ral \-ˈmyu̇r-əl\ *adj* : existing or functioning beyond the bounds of an organized unit

ex•tra•ne•ous \ek-ˈstrā-nē-əs\ *adj* **1** : coming from without **2** : not forming a vital part; *also* : IRRELEVANT — **ex•tra•ne•ous•ly** *adv*

ex•traor•di•nary \ik-ˈstrȯrd-ᵊn-ˌer-ē, ˌek-strə-ˈȯrd-\ *adj* **1** : notably unusual or exceptional **2** : employed on special service — **ex•traor•di•nari•ly** \-ˌstrȯrd-ᵊn-ˈer-ə-lē, ˌek-strə-ˌȯrd-\ *adv*

ex•trap•o•late \ik-ˈstra-pə-ˌlāt\ *vb* **-lat•ed; -lat•ing** : to infer (unknown data) from known data — **ex•trap•o•la•tion** \-ˌstra-pə-ˈlā-shən\ *n*

ex•tra•sen•so•ry \ˌek-strə-ˈsen-sə-rē\ *adj* : not acting or occurring through the known senses

extrasensory perception *n* : perception (as in telepathy) of events external to the self not gained through the senses and not deducible from previous experience

ex•tra•ter•res•tri•al \-tə-ˈres-trē-əl\ *adj* : originating or existing outside the earth or its atmosphere ⟨~ life⟩ — **extraterrestrial** *n*

ex•tra•ter•ri•to•ri•al \-ˌter-ə-ˈtōr-ē-əl\ *adj* : existing or taking place outside the territorial limits of a jurisdiction

ex•tra•ter•ri•to•ri•al•i•ty \-ˌtōr-ē-ˈa-lə-tē\ *n* : exemption from the application or jurisdiction of local law or tribunals ⟨diplomats enjoy ~⟩

ex•trav•a•gant \ik-ˈstra-vi-gənt\ *adj* **1** : EXCESSIVE ⟨~ claims⟩ **2** : unduly lavish : WASTEFUL **3** : too costly **syn** immoderate, exorbitant, extreme, inordinate, undue — **ex•trav•a•gance** \-gəns\ *n* — **ex•trav•a•gant•ly** *adv*

ex•trav•a•gan•za \ik-ˌstra-və-ˈgan-zə\ *n* **1** : a literary or musical work marked by extreme freedom of style and structure **2** : a spectacular show

ex•tra•ve•hic•u•lar \ˌek-strə-vē-ˈhi-kyə-lər\ *adj* : taking place outside a vehicle (as a spacecraft) ⟨~ activity⟩

¹ex•treme \ik-ˈstrēm\ *adj* **1** : very great or intense ⟨~ cold⟩ **2** : very severe or radical ⟨~ measures⟩ **3** : going to great lengths or beyond normal limits ⟨politically ~⟩ **4** : most remote ⟨the ~ end⟩ **5** : UTMOST; *also* : MAXIMUM — **ex•treme•ly** *adv*

²extreme *n* **1** : something located at one end or the other of a range or series **2** : EXTREMITY 4

extremely low frequency *n* : a radio frequency in the lowest range of the radio spectrum

ex•trem•ism \ik-ˈstrē-ˌmi-zəm\ *n* : the quality or state of being extreme; *esp* : advocacy of extreme political measures — **ex•trem•ist** \-mist\ *n or adj*

ex•trem•i•ty \ik-ˈstre-mə-tē\ *n, pl* **-ties 1** : the most remote part or point **2** : a limb of the body; *esp* : a human hand or foot **3** : the greatest need or danger **4** : the utmost degree; *also* : a drastic or desperate measure

ex•tri•cate \ˈek-strə-ˌkāt\ *vb* **-cat•ed; -cat•ing** [L *extricatus*, pp. of *extricare*, fr. *ex-* out + *tricae* trifles, perplexities] : to free from an entanglement or difficulty **syn** disentangle, untangle, disencumber — **ex•tri•ca•ble** \ik-ˈstri-kə-bəl, ek-; ˈek-(ˌ)stri-\ *adj* — **ex•tri•ca•tion** \ˌek-strə-ˈkā-shən\ *n*

ex•trin•sic \ek-ˈstrin-zik, -sik\ *adj* **1** : not forming part of or belonging to a thing **2** : EXTERNAL — **ex•trin•si•cal•ly** \-zi-k(ə-)lē, -si-\ *adv*

ex•tro•vert *also* **ex•tra•vert** \ˈek-strə-ˌvərt\ *n* : a gregarious and unreserved person — **ex•tro•ver•sion** *or* **ex•tra•ver•sion** \ˌek-strə-ˈvər-zhən\ *n* — **ex•tro•vert•ed** *also* **ex•tra•vert•ed** *adj*

ex•trude \ik-ˈstrüd\ *vb* **ex•trud•ed; ex•trud•ing 1** : to force, press, or push out **2** : to shape (as plastic) by forcing through a die — **ex•tru•sion** \-ˈstrü-zhən\ *n* — **ex•trud•er** *n*

ex•u•ber•ant \ig-ˈzü-bə-rənt\ *adj* **1** : unrestrained in enthusiasm or style **2** : PROFUSE — **ex•u•ber•ance** \-rəns\ *n* — **ex•u•ber•ant•ly** *adv*

ex•ude \ig-ˈzüd\ *vb* **ex•ud•ed; ex•ud•ing** [L *exsudare*, fr. *ex-* out + *sudare* to sweat] **1** : to discharge slowly through pores or cuts : OOZE **2** : to display conspicuously or abundantly ⟨~*s* charm⟩ — **ex•u•date** \ˈek-su̇-ˌdāt, -syu̇-\ *n* — **ex•u•da•tion** \ˌek-su̇-ˈdā-shən, -syu̇-\ *n*

ex•ult \ig-ˈzəlt\ *vb* : REJOICE, GLORY — **ex•ul•tant** \-ˈzəlt-ᵊnt\ *adj* — **ex•ul•tant•ly** *adv* — **ex•ul•ta•tion** \ˌek-(ˌ)səl-ˈtā-shən, ˌeg-(ˌ)zəl-\ *n*

ex•urb \ˈek-ˌsərb, ˈeg-ˌzərb\ *n* : a region outside a city and its suburbs inhabited chiefly by well-to-do families

ex•ur•ban•ite \ek-ˈsər-bə-ˌnīt; eg-ˈzər-\ *n* : one who lives in an exurb

ex•ur•bia \ek-ˈsər-bē-ə, eg-ˈzer-\ *n* : the generalized region of exurbs

-ey — see -Y

¹eye \ˈī\ *n* **1** : an organ of sight typically consisting in vertebrates of a globular structure that is located in a socket of the skull, is lined with a sensitive retina, and is normally paired **2** : VISION, PERCEPTION; *also* : faculty of discrimination ⟨an ~ for bargains⟩ **3** : POINT OF VIEW, JUDGMENT — often used in pl. ⟨in the ~*s* of the law⟩ **4** : something suggesting an eye ⟨the ~ of a needle⟩; *esp* : an undeveloped bud (as on a potato) **5** : the calm center of a cyclone — **eyed** \ˈīd\ *adj*

²eye *vb* **eyed; eye•ing** *or* **ey•ing** : to look at : WATCH

eye•ball \ˈī-ˌbȯl\ *n* : the globular capsule of the vertebrate eye

eye•brow \-ˌbrau̇\ *n* : the ridge over the eye or the hair growing on it

eye•drop•per \-ˌdrä-pər\ *n* : DROPPER 2

eye•glass \-ˌglas\ *n* : a lens worn to aid vision; *also, pl* : GLASSES

eye•lash \-ˌlash\ *n* **1** : the fringe of hair edging the eyelid — usu. used in pl. **2** : a single hair of the eyelashes

eye•let \-lət\ *n* **1** : a small hole intended for ornament or for passage of a cord or lace **2** : a typically metal ring for reinforcing an eyelet : GROMMET

eye•lid \-ˌlid\ *n* : either of the movable folds of skin and muscle that can be closed over the eyeball

eye•lin•er \-ˌlī-nər\ *n* : makeup used to emphasize the contour of the eyes

eye–open•er \-ˌō-pə-nər\ *n* : something startling or surprising — **eye–open•ing** *adj*

eye•piece \-ˌpēs\ *n* : the lens or combination of lenses at the eye end of an optical instrument

eye shadow *n* : a colored cosmetic applied to the eyelids to accent the eyes

eye•sight \-ˌsīt\ *n* : SIGHT, VISION

eye•sore \-ˌsōr\ *n* : something offensive to view

eye•strain \-ˌstrān\ *n* : weariness or a strained state of the eye

eye•tooth \-ˈtüth\ *n* : a canine tooth of the upper jaw

eye•wash \-ˌwȯsh, -ˌwäsh\ *n* **1** : an eye lotion **2** : misleading or deceptive statements, actions, or procedures

eye•wit•ness \-ˈwit-nəs\ *n* : a person who actually sees something happen

ey•rie \ˈīr-ē, *or like* AERIE\ *var of* AERIE

ey•rir \ˈā-ˌrir\ *n, pl* **au•rar** \ˈau̇-ˌrär\ — see *krona* at MONEY table

Ez *or* **Ezr** *abbr* Ezra

Ezech *abbr* Ezechiel

Eze•chiel \i-ˈzē-kyəl\ *n* — see BIBLE table

Ezek *abbr* Ezekiel

Eze•kiel \i-ˈzē-kyəl\ *n* — see BIBLE table

Ez•ra \ˈez-rə\ *n* — see BIBLE table

F

¹f \ˈef\ *n, pl* **f's** *or* **fs** \ˈefs\ *often cap* **1** : the 6th letter of the English alphabet **2** : a grade rating a student's work as failing

²f *abbr, often cap* **1** Fahrenheit **2** false **3** family **4** farad **5** female **6** feminine **7** forte **8** French **9** frequency **10** Friday

³f *symbol* focal length

F *symbol* fluorine

FAA *abbr* Federal Aviation Administration

Fa•bi•an \ˈfā-bē-ən\ *adj* : of, relating to, or being a society of socialists organized in England in 1884 to spread socialist principles gradually — **Fabian** *n* — **Fa•bi•an•ism** *n*

fa•ble \ˈfā-bəl\ *n* **1** : a legendary story of supernatural happenings **2** : a narration intended to teach a lesson; *esp* : one in which animals speak and act like people **3** : FALSEHOOD

fa•bled \ˈfā-bəld\ *adj* **1** : FICTITIOUS **2** : told or celebrated in fable

fab•ric \ˈfa-brik\ *n* [MF *fabrique,* fr. L *fabrica* workshop, structure] **1** : STRUCTURE, FRAMEWORK ⟨the ~ of society⟩ **2** : CLOTH; *also* : a material that resembles cloth

fab•ri•cate \ˈfa-bri-ˌkāt\ *vb* **-cat•ed; -cat•ing 1** : INVENT, CREATE **2** : to make up for the sake of deception **3** : CONSTRUCT, MANUFACTURE — **fab•ri•ca•tion** \ˌfa-bri-ˈkā-shən\ *n*

fab•u•lous \ˈfa-byə-ləs\ *adj* **1** : resembling a fable; *also* : INCREDIBLE, MARVELOUS **2** : told in or based on fable — **fab•u•lous•ly** *adv*

fac *abbr* **1** facsimile **2** faculty

fa•cade *also* **fa•çade** \fə-ˈsäd\ *n* [F *façade,* fr. It *facciata,* fr. *faccia* face] **1** : the principal face or front of a building **2** : a false, superficial, or artificial appearance ⟨a ~ of composure⟩ **syn** mask, disguise, front, guise, pretense, veneer

¹face \ˈfās\ *n* **1** : the front part of the head **2** : PRESENCE ⟨in the ~ of danger⟩ **3** : facial expression : LOOK ⟨put a sad ~ on⟩ **4** : GRIMACE ⟨made a ~⟩ **5** : outward appearance ⟨looks easy on the ~ of it⟩ **6** : CONFIDENCE; *also* : BOLDNESS **7** : DIGNITY, PRESTIGE ⟨afraid to lose ~⟩ **8** : SURFACE; *esp* : a front, principal, or bounding surface ⟨~ of a cliff⟩ ⟨the ~*s* of a cube⟩ — **faced** \ˈfāst, ˈfā-səd\ *adj*

²face *vb* **faced; fac•ing 1** : to confront brazenly **2** : to line near the edge esp. with a different material; *also* : to cover the front or surface of ⟨~ a building with marble⟩ **3** : to meet or bring in direct contact or confrontation ⟨*faced* the problem⟩ **4** : to stand or sit with the face toward ⟨~ the sun⟩ **5** : to have the front oriented toward ⟨a house *facing* the park⟩ **6** : to have as or be a prospect ⟨~ a grim future⟩ **7** : to turn the face or body in a specified direction — **face the music** : to meet the unpleasant consequences of one's actions

face•down \ˌfās-ˈdau̇n\ *adv* : with the face downward

face•less \-ləs\ *n* **1** : lacking a face **2** : lacking character or individuality

face–lift \ˈfās-ˌlift\ *n* **1** : a cosmetic surgical operation for removal of facial defects (as wrinkles) typical of aging **2** : MODERNIZATION — **face–lift** *vb*

face–off \ˈfās-ˌȯf\ *n* **1** : a method of beginning play by dropping a puck (as in ice hockey) between two opposing players each of whom attempts to control it **2** : CONFRONTATION

fac•et \ˈfa-sət\ *n* [F *facette,* dim. of *face*] **1** : a small plane surface of a cut gem **2** : ASPECT, PHASE

fa•ce•tious \fə-ˈsē-shəs\ *adj* **1** : joking often inappropriately **2** : JOCULAR, JOCOSE **syn** witty, humorous — **fa•ce•tious•ly** *adv* — **fa•ce•tious•ness** *n*

¹fa•cial \ˈfā-shəl\ *adj* **1** : of or relating to the face **2** : used to improve the appearance of the face

²facial *n* : a facial treatment

fac•ile \ˈfa-səl\ *adj* **1** : easily accomplished, handled, or attained **2** : SUPERFICIAL **3** : readily manifested and often insincere ⟨~ prose⟩ **4** : READY, FLUENT ⟨a ~ writer⟩

fa•cil•i•tate \fə-ˈsi-lə-ˌtāt\ *vb* **-tat•ed; -tat•ing** : to make easier

fa•cil•i•ty \fə-ˈsi-lə-tē\ *n, pl* **-ties 1** : the quality of being easily performed **2** : ease in performance : APTITUDE **3** : PLIANCY **4** : something that makes easier an action, operation, or course of conduct; *also* : REST ROOM — often used in pl. **5** : something (as a hospital) built or installed for a particular purpose

fac•ing \ˈfā-siŋ\ *n* **1** : a lining at the edge esp. of a garment **2** *pl* : the collar, cuffs, and trimmings of a uniform coat **3** : an ornamental or protective layer **4** : material for facing

fac•sim•i•le \fak-ˈsi-mə-lē\ *n* [L *fac simile* make similar] **1** : an exact copy **2** : a system of transmitting and reproducing printed matter or pictures by means of signals sent over telephone lines

fact \ˈfakt\ *n* **1** : DEED; *esp* : CRIME ⟨accessory after the ~⟩ **2** : the quality of being actual **3** : something that exists or occurs **4** : a piece of information

fac•tion \ˈfak-shən\ *n* : a group or combination (as in a government) acting together within and usu. against a larger body : CLIQUE — **fac•tion•al•ism** \-shə-nə-ˌli-zəm\ *n*

fac•tious \ˈfak-shəs\ *adj* **1** : of, relating to, or caused by faction **2** : inclined to faction or the formation of factions : causing dissension **syn** insubordinate, contumacious, insurgent, seditious, rebellious

fac•ti•tious \fak-ˈti-shəs\ *adj* : ARTIFICIAL, SHAM ⟨a ~ display of grief⟩

fac•toid \ˈfak-ˌtȯid\ *n* **1** : an invented fact believed to be true because of its appearance in print **2** : a brief and usu. trivial news item

¹fac•tor \ˈfak-tər\ *n* **1** : AGENT **2** : something that actively contributes to a result **3** : GENE **4** : any of the numbers or symbols in mathematics that when multiplied together form a product; *esp* : any of the integers that divide a given integer without a remainder

²factor *vb* **1** : to work as a factor **2** : to find the mathematical factors of and esp. the prime mathematical factors of

¹fac•to•ri•al \fak-ˈtōr-ē-əl\ *adj* : of, relating to, or being a factor

²factorial *n* : the product of all the positive integers from 1 to a given integer *n*

fac•to•ry \ˈfak-trē, -tə-rē\ *n, pl* **-ries 1** : a trading post where resident brokers trade **2** : a building or group of buildings used for manufacturing

fac•to•tum \fak-ˈtō-təm\ *n* [NL, lit., do everything, fr. L *fac* do + *totum* everything] : a person (as a servant) having numerous or varied duties

facts of life : the physiological processes and behavior involved in sex and reproduction

fac•tu•al \ˈfak-chə-wəl\ *adj* : of or relating to facts; *also* : based on fact — **fac•tu•al•ly** *adv*

fac•ul•ty \ˈfa-kəl-tē\ *n, pl* **-ties** **1** : ability to act or do : POWER; *also* : natural aptitude **2** : one of the powers of the mind or body ⟨the ∼ of hearing⟩ **3** : the teachers in a school or college or one of its divisions

fad \ˈfad\ *n* : a practice or interest followed for a time with exaggerated zeal : CRAZE — **fad•dish** *adj* — **fad•dist** *n*

fade \ˈfād\ *vb* **fad•ed; fad•ing** **1** : WITHER **2** : to lose or cause to lose freshness or brilliance of color **3** : VANISH **4** : to grow dim or faint

FADM *abbr* fleet admiral

fae•cal, fae•ces *var of* FECAL, FECES

fa•er•ie *also* **fa•ery** \ˈfā-rē, ˈfar-ē\ *n, pl* **fa•er•ies** **1** : FAIRYLAND **2** : FAIRY

[1]**fag** \ˈfag\ *vb* **fagged; fag•ging** **1** : DRUDGE **2** : to act as a fag **3** : TIRE, EXHAUST

[2]**fag** *n* **1** : an English public-school boy who acts as servant to another **2** : MENIAL, DRUDGE

[3]**fag** *n* : CIGARETTE

fag end *n* **1** : REMNANT **2** : the extreme end **3** : the last part or coarser end of a web of cloth **4** : the untwisted end of a rope

fag•ot *or* **fag•got** \ˈfa-gət\ *n* : a bundle of sticks or twigs

fag•ot•ing *or* **fag•got•ing** *n* : an embroidery produced by tying threads in hourglass-shaped clusters

Fah *or* **Fahr** *abbr* Fahrenheit

Fahr•en•heit \ˈfar-ən-ˌhīt\ *adj* : relating to, conforming to, or having a thermometer scale with the boiling point of water at 212 degrees and the freezing point at 32 degrees above zero

fa•ience *or* **fa•ïence** \fā-ˈäns\ *n* [F] : earthenware decorated with opaque colored glazes

[1]**fail** \ˈfāl\ *vb* **1** : to become feeble; *esp* : to decline in health **2** : to die away **3** : to stop functioning **4** : to fall short ⟨∼*ed* in his duty⟩ **5** : to be or become absent or inadequate **6** : to be unsuccessful **7** : to become bankrupt **8** : DISAPPOINT **9** : NEGLECT

[2]**fail** *n* : FAILURE ⟨without ∼⟩

[1]**fail•ing** \ˈfā-liŋ\ *n* : WEAKNESS, SHORTCOMING

[2]**failing** *prep* : in the absence or lack of

faille \ˈfīl\ *n* : a somewhat shiny closely woven ribbed fabric (as silk)

fail–safe \ˈfāl-ˌsāf\ *adj* **1** : incorporating a counteractive feature for a possible source of failure **2** : having no chance of failure

fail•ure \ˈfāl-yər\ *n* **1** : a failing to do or perform **2** : a state of inability to perform a normal function adequately ⟨heart ∼⟩ **3** : a fracturing or giving way under stress **4** : a lack of success **5** : BANKRUPTCY **6** : DEFICIENCY **7** : DETERIORATION, DECAY **8** : one that has failed

[1]**fain** \ˈfān\ *adj* **1** *archaic* : GLAD; *also* : INCLINED **2** : being obliged or compelled

[2]**fain** *adv* **1** : with pleasure **2** : by preference

[1]**faint** \ˈfānt\ *adj* [ME *faint, feint,* fr. OF, fr. *faindre, feindre* to feign, shirk] **1** : COWARDLY, SPIRITLESS **2** : weak, dizzy, and likely to faint **3** : lacking vigor or strength : FEEBLE ⟨∼ praise⟩ **4** : INDISTINCT, DIM — **faint•ly** *adv* — **faint•ness** *n*

[2]**faint** *vb* : to lose consciousness

[3]**faint** *n* : the action of fainting; *also* : the resulting condition

faint•heart•ed \ˌfānt-ˈhär-təd\ *adj* : lacking courage : TIMID

[1]**fair** \ˈfar\ *adj* **1** : pleasing in appearance : BEAUTIFUL **2** : superficially pleasing : SPECIOUS **3** : CLEAN, PURE **4** : CLEAR, LEGIBLE **5** : not stormy or cloudy **6** : JUST **7** : conforming with the rules : ALLOWED; *also* : being within the foul lines ⟨∼ ball⟩ **8** : open to legitimate pursuit or attack ⟨∼ game⟩ **9** : PROMISING, LIKELY ⟨a ∼ chance of winning⟩ **10** : favorable to a ship's course ⟨a ∼ wind⟩ **11** : light in complexion : BLOND **12** : ADEQUATE — **fair•ness** *n*

[2]**fair** *adv, chiefly Brit* : FAIRLY 4

[3]**fair** *n* **1** : a gathering of buyers and sellers at a stated time and place for trade **2** : a competitive exhibition (as of farm products) **3** : a sale of assorted articles usu. for a charitable purpose

fair•ground \-ˌgrau̇nd\ *n* : an area where outdoor fairs, circuses, or exhibitions are held

fair•ing \ˈfar-iŋ\ *n* : a structure for producing a smooth outline and reducing drag (as on an airplane)

fair•ly \ˈfar-lē\ *adv* **1** : HANDSOMELY **2** : in a manner of speaking ⟨∼ bursting with pride⟩ **3** : without bias **4** : to a full degree or extent : PLAINLY, DISTINCTLY **5** : SOMEWHAT, RATHER ⟨a ∼ easy job⟩

fair–spo•ken \ˈfar-ˈspō-kən\ *adj* : pleasant and courteous in speech

fair–trade \-ˈtrād\ *adj* : of, relating to, or being an agreement between a producer and a seller that branded merchandise will be sold at or above a specified price — **fair–trade** *vb*

fair•way \-ˌwā\ *n* : the mowed part of a golf course between tee and green

fairy \ˈfar-ē\ *n, pl* **fair•ies** [ME *fairie* fairyland, fairy people, fr. OF *faerie,* fr. *feie, fee* fairy, fr. L *Fata,* goddess of fate, fr. *fatum* fate] : an imaginary being of folklore and romance usu. having diminutive human form and magic powers — **fairy** *adj*

fairy•land \-ˌland\ *n* **1** : the land of fairies **2** : a beautiful or charming place

fairy tale *n* **1** : a children's story about fairies **2** : FIB

fait ac•com•pli \ˈfāt-ˌa-ˌkōⁿ-ˈplē\ *n, pl* **faits accomplis** *same or* -ˈplēz\ [F, accomplished fact] : a thing accomplished and presumably irreversible

faith \ˈfāth\ *n, pl* **faiths** \ˈfāths, ˈfāt͟hz\ [ME *feith,* fr. OF *feid, foi,* fr. L *fides*] **1** : allegiance to duty or a person : LOYALTY **2** : belief and trust in God **3** : complete trust **4** : a system of religious beliefs — **faith•ful** \-fəl\ *adj* — **faith•ful•ly** *adv* — **faith•ful•ness** *n*

faith•less \ˈfāth-ləs\ *adj* **1** : DISLOYAL **2** : not to be relied on **syn** false, traitorous, treacherous, unfaithful — **faith•less•ly** *adv* — **faith•less•ness** *n*

fa•ji•ta \fə-ˈhē-tə\ *n* : a marinated strip usu. of beef or chicken grilled or broiled and served usu. with a flour tortilla and savory fillings — usu. used in pl.

[1]**fake** \ˈfāk\ *adj* : COUNTERFEIT, SHAM

[2]**fake** *n* **1** : IMITATION, FRAUD; *also* : IMPOSTOR **2** : a simulated move in sports (as a pretended pass)

[3]**fake** *vb* **faked; fak•ing** **1** : to treat so as to falsify **2** : COUNTERFEIT **3** : to deceive (an opponent) in a sports contest by making a fake — **fak•er** *n*

fa•kir \fə-ˈkir\ *n* [Ar *faqīr,* lit., poor man] **1** : a Muslim mendicant : DERVISH **2** : a wandering Hindu ascetic

fal•con \ˈfal-kən, ˈfȯl-\ *n* **1** : a hawk trained for use in falconry **2** : any of various swift long-winged long-tailed hawks having a notched beak and usu. inhabiting open areas

fal•con•ry \ˈfal-kən-rē, ˈfȯl-\ *n* **1** : the art of training hawks to hunt in cooperation with a person **2** : the sport of hunting with hawks — **fal•con•er** *n*

[1]**fall** \ˈfȯl\ *vb* **fell** \ˈfel\; **fall•en** \ˈfȯ-lən\; **fall•ing** **1** : to descend freely by the force of gravity **2** : to hang freely **3** : to come or go as if by falling ⟨darkness *fell*⟩ **4** : to become uttered **5** : to lower or become lowered : DROP ⟨her eyes *fell*⟩ **6** : to leave an erect position suddenly and involuntarily **7** : STUMBLE, STRAY **8** : to drop down wounded or dead esp. in battle **9** : to become captured ⟨the city *fell* to the enemy⟩ **10** : to suffer ruin, defeat, or failure **11** : to commit an immoral act **12** : to move or extend in a downward direction **13** : SUBSIDE, ABATE **14** : to decline in quality, activity, quantity, or value **15** : to assume a look of shame or dejection ⟨her face *fell*⟩ **16** : to occur at a certain time **17** : to come by chance **18** : DEVOLVE ⟨the duties *fell* to him⟩ **19** : to have the proper place or station ⟨the accent ∼*s* on the first syllable⟩ **20** : to come within the scope of something **21** : to pass from one condition to another ⟨*fell* ill⟩ **22** : to set about heartily or actively ⟨∼ to work⟩ — **fall flat** : to produce no re-

sponse or result — **fall for 1** : to fall in love with **2** : to become a victim of — **fall foul** : to have a quarrel : CLASH — **fall from grace** : BACKSLIDE — **fall into line** : to comply with a certain course of action — **fall over oneself** *or* **fall over backward** : to display excessive eagerness — **fall short 1** : to be deficient **2** : to fail to attain

²fall *n* **1** : the act of falling **2** : a falling out, off, or away : DROPPING **3** : AUTUMN **4** : a thing or quantity that falls ⟨a light ~ of snow⟩ **5** : COLLAPSE, DOWNFALL **6** : the surrender or capture of a besieged place **7** : departure from virtue or goodness **8** : SLOPE **9** : WATERFALL — usu. used in pl. **10** : a decrease in size, quantity, degree, or value ⟨a ~ in price⟩ **11** : the distance which something falls **12** : an act of forcing a wrestler's shoulders to the mat; *also* : a bout of wrestling

fal·la·cious \fə-ˈlā-shəs\ *adj* **1** : embodying a fallacy ⟨a ~ argument⟩ **2** : MISLEADING, DECEPTIVE

fal·la·cy \ˈfa-lə-sē\ *n, pl* **-cies 1** : a false or mistaken idea **2** : an often plausible argument using false or illogical reasoning

fall back *vb* : RETREAT, RECEDE

fall guy *n* **1** : one that is easily duped **2** : SCAPEGOAT

fal·li·ble \ˈfa-lə-bəl\ *adj* **1** : liable to be erroneous **2** : capable of making a mistake — **fal·li·bly** \-blē\ *adv*

fall·ing–out \ˌfȯ-liŋ-ˈau̇t\ *n, pl* **fallings–out** *or* **falling–outs** : QUARREL

falling star *n* : METEOR

fal·lo·pi·an tube \fə-ˈlō-pē-ən-\ *n, often cap F* : either of the pair of anatomical tubes that carry the eggs from the ovary to the uterus

fall·out \ˈfȯ-ˌlau̇t\ *n* **1** : the often radioactive particles that result from a nuclear explosion and descend through the air **2** : a secondary and often lingering effect or result

fall out *vb* : QUARREL

¹fal·low \ˈfa-(ˌ)lō\ *n* : fallow land; *also* : the state or period of being fallow — **fallow** *vb*

²fallow *adj* **1** : left without tilling or sowing after plowing **2** : DORMANT, INACTIVE ⟨a writer's ~ period⟩

false \ˈfȯls\ *adj* **fals·er; fals·est 1** : not genuine : ARTIFICIAL **2** : intentionally untrue **3** : adjusted or made so as to deceive ⟨~ scales⟩ **4** : tending to mislead : DECEPTIVE ⟨~ promises⟩ **5** : not true ⟨~ concepts⟩ **6** : not faithful or loyal : TREACHEROUS **7** : not essential or permanent ⟨~ front⟩ **8** : inaccurate in pitch **9** : based on mistaken ideas — **false·ly** *adv* — **false·ness** *n* — **fal·si·ty** \ˈfȯl-sə-tē\ *n*

false·hood \ˈfȯls-ˌhu̇d\ *n* **1** : LIE **2** : absence of truth or accuracy **3** : the practice of lying

fal·set·to \fȯl-ˈse-tō\ *n, pl* **-tos** [It, fr. dim. of *falso* false] : an artificially high voice; *esp* : an artificial singing voice that overlaps and extends above the range of the full voice esp. of a tenor

fal·si·fy \ˈfȯl-sə-ˌfī\ *vb* **-fied; -fy·ing 1** : to prove to be false **2** : to alter so as to deceive **3** : LIE; *also* : MISREPRESENT — **fal·si·fi·ca·tion** \ˌfȯl-sə-fə-ˈkā-shən\ *n*

fal·ter \ˈfȯl-tər\ *vb* **1** : to move unsteadily : STUMBLE, TOTTER **2** : to hesitate in speech : STAMMER **3** : to hesitate in purpose or action : WAVER, FLINCH — **fal·ter·ing·ly** *adv*

fam *abbr* **1** familiar **2** family

fame \ˈfām\ *n* : public reputation : RENOWN — **famed** \ˈfāmd\ *adj*

fa·mil·ial \fə-ˈmil-yəl\ *adj* **1** : of, relating to, or suggestive of a family **2** : tending to occur in more members of a family than expected by chance alone ⟨a ~ disorder⟩

¹fa·mil·iar \fə-ˈmil-yər\ *n* **1** : COMPANION **2** : a spirit held to attend and serve or guard a person **3** : one who frequents a place

²familiar *adj* **1** : closely acquainted : INTIMATE **2** : of or relating to a family **3** : INFORMAL **4** : FORWARD, PRESUMPTUOUS **5** : frequently seen or experienced **6** : of everyday occurrence — **fa·mil·iar·ly** *adv*

fa·mil·iar·ise *Brit var of* FAMILIARIZE

fa·mil·iar·i·ty \fə-ˌmil-ˈyar-ə-tē, -ˌmi-lē-ˈar-\ *n, pl* **-ties 1** : close friendship : INTIMACY **2** : INFORMALITY **3** : an unduly bold or forward act or expression : IMPROPRIETY **4** : close acquaintance with something

fa·mil·iar·ize \fə-ˈmil-yə-ˌrīz\ *vb* **-ized; -iz·ing 1** : to make known or familiar **2** : to make thoroughly acquainted

fam·i·ly \ˈfam-lē, ˈfa-mə-\ *n, pl* **-lies** [ME *familie,* fr. L *familia* household, fr. *famulus* servant] **1** : a group of individuals living under one roof and under one head : HOUSEHOLD **2** : a group of persons of common ancestry : CLAN **3** : a group of things having common characteristics; *esp* : a group of related plants or animals ranking in biological classification above a genus and below an order **4** : a social unit usu. consisting of one or two parents and their children

family planning *n* : planning intended to determine the number and spacing of one's children by using birth control

family tree *n* : GENEALOGY; *also* : a genealogical diagram

fam·ine \ˈfa-mən\ *n* **1** : an extreme scarcity of food **2** : a great shortage

fam·ish \ˈfa-mish\ *vb* **1** : STARVE **2** : to suffer for lack of something necessary

fa·mous \ˈfā-məs\ *adj* **1** : widely known **2** : honored for achievement **3** : EXCELLENT, FIRST-RATE **syn** renowned, celebrated, noted, notorious, distinguished, eminent, illustrious

fa·mous·ly *adv* : SPLENDIDLY, EXCELLENTLY

¹fan \ˈfan\ *n* : a device (as a hand-waved triangular piece or a mechanism with blades) for producing a current of air

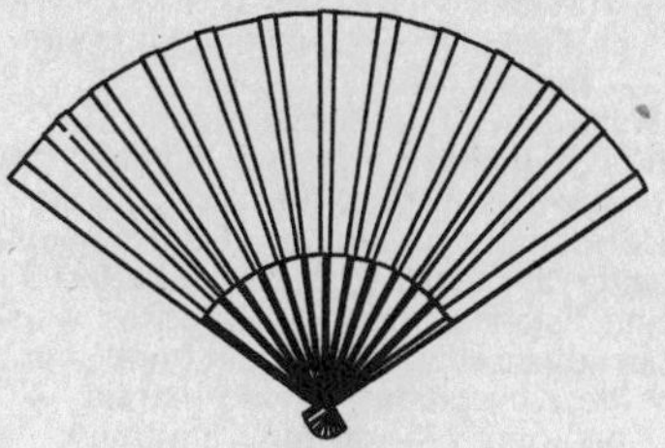

fan

²fan *vb* **fanned; fan·ning 1** : to drive away the chaff from grain by winnowing **2** : to move (air) with or as if with a fan **3** : to direct a current of air upon ⟨~ a fire⟩ **4** : to stir up to activity : STIMULATE **5** : to spread like a fan **6** : to strike out in baseball

³fan *n* : an enthusiastic follower or admirer

fa·nat·ic \fə-ˈna-tik\ *or* **fa·nat·i·cal** \-ti-kəl\ *adj* [L *fanaticus* inspired by a deity, frenzied, fr. *fanum* temple] : marked by excessive enthusiasm and often intense uncritical devotion — **fanatic** *n* — **fa·nat·i·cism** \-tə-ˌsi-zəm\ *n*

fan·ci·er \ˈfan-sē-ər\ *n* **1** : one that has a special liking or interest **2** : a person who breeds or grows some kind of animal or plant for points of excellence

fan·ci·ful \ˈfan-si-fəl\ *adj* **1** : marked by, existing in, or given to unrestrained imagination or whim rather than reason **2** : curiously made or shaped — **fan·ci·ful·ly** *adv*

¹fan·cy \ˈfan-sē\ *vb* **fan·cied; fan·cy·ing 1** : LIKE **2** : IMAGINE **3** : to believe without evidence or certainty **4** : to visualize or interpret as

²fancy *n, pl* **fancies** [ME *fantasie, fantsy* fantasy, fancy, fr. MF *fantasie,* fr. L *phantasia,* fr. Gk, appearance, imagination] **1** : LIKING, INCLINATION; *also* : LOVE **2** : WHIM, NOTION, IDEA ⟨a passing ~⟩ **3**

: IMAGINATION **4** : TASTE, JUDGMENT **syn** caprice, crotchet, vagary

3fancy *adj* **fan•ci•er; -est 1** : WHIMSICAL **2** : not plain : ORNAMENTAL, POSH **3** : of particular excellence **4** : bred esp. for a showy appearance **5** : EXCESSIVE **6** : executed with technical skill and style — **fan•ci•ly** \ˈfan-sə-lē\ *adv*

fancy dress *n* : a costume (as for a masquerade) chosen to suit a fancy

fan•cy–free \ˌfan-sē-ˈfrē\ *adj* : free from amorous attachment; *also* : free to imagine

fan•cy•work \ˈfan-sē-ˌwərk\ *n* : ornamental needlework (as embroidery)

fan•dan•go \fan-ˈdaŋ-gō\ *n, pl* **-gos 1** : a lively Spanish or Spanish-American dance **2** : TOMFOOLERY

fane \ˈfān\ *n* **1** : TEMPLE **2** : CHURCH

fan•fare \ˈfan-ˌfar\ *n* **1** : a flourish of trumpets **2** : a showy display

fang \ˈfaŋ\ *n* : a long sharp tooth; *esp* : a grooved or hollow tooth of a venomous snake — **fanged** \ˈfaŋd\ *adj*

fan•light \ˈfan-ˌlīt\ *n* : a semicircular window with radiating bars like a fan that is set over a door or window

fan•tail \ˈfan-ˌtāl\ *n* **1** : a fan-shaped tail or end **2** : an overhang at the stern of a ship

fan•ta•sia \fan-ˈtā-zhə, -zhē-ə, -zē-ə; ˌfan-tə-ˈzē-ə\ *n* : a musical composition free and fanciful in form

fan•ta•sise *Brit var of* FANTASIZE

fan•ta•size \ˈfan-tə-ˌsīz\ *vb* **-sized; -siz•ing** : IMAGINE, DAYDREAM

fan•tas•tic \fan-ˈtas-tik\ *also* **fan•tas•ti•cal** \-ti-kəl\ *adj* **1** : IMAGINARY, UNREAL **2** : conceived by unrestrained fancy **3** : exceedingly or unbelievably great **4** : ECCENTRIC **syn** chimerical, fanciful, imaginary — **fan•tas•ti•cal•ly** \-ti-k(ə-)lē\ *adv*

fan•ta•sy \ˈfan-tə-sē\ *n, pl* **-sies 1** : IMAGINATION, FANCY **2** : a product of the imagination : ILLUSION **3** : FANTASIA — **fantasy** *vb*

FAQ *abbr* frequently asked question

1far \ˈfär\ *adv* **far•ther** \-t͟hər\ *or* **fur•ther** \ˈfər-\; **far•thest** *or* **fur•thest** \-t͟həst\ **1** : at or to a considerable distance in space or time ⟨~ from home⟩ **2** : by a broad interval : WIDELY, MUCH ⟨~ better⟩ **3** : to or at a definite distance, point, or degree ⟨as ~ as I know⟩ **4** : to an advanced point or extent ⟨go ~ in his field⟩ — **by far** : by a considerable margin — **far and away** : DECIDEDLY — **so far** : until now

2far *adj* **farther** *or* **further; farthest** *or* **furthest 1** : remote in space or time **2** : DIFFERENT **3** : LONG ⟨a ~ journey⟩ **4** : being the more distant of two ⟨on the ~ side of the lake⟩

far•ad \ˈfar-ˌad, -əd\ *n* : a unit of capacitance equal to the capacitance of a capacitor having a potential difference of one volt between its plates when it is charged with one coulomb of electricity

far•away \ˈfär-ə-ˌwā\ *adj* **1** : DISTANT, REMOTE **2** : DREAMY

farce \ˈfärs\ *n* **1** : a broadly satirical comedy with an improbable plot **2** : the humor characteristic of farce or pretense **3** : a ridiculous or empty display — **far•ci•cal** \ˈfär-si-kəl\ *adj*

1fare \ˈfar\ *vb* **fared; far•ing 1** : GO, TRAVEL **2** : GET ALONG, SUCCEED **3** : EAT, DINE

2fare *n* **1** : range of food : DIET; *also* : material provided for use, consumption, or enjoyment **2** : the price charged to transport a person **3** : a person paying a fare : PASSENGER

1fare•well \far-ˈwel\ *vb imper* : get along well — used interjectionally to or by one departing

2farewell *n* **1** : a wish of well-being at parting : GOODBYE **2** : LEAVE-TAKING

3fare•well \ˈfar-ˌwel\ *adj* : PARTING, FINAL ⟨a ~ concert⟩

far–fetched \ˈfär-ˈfecht\ *adj* : not easily or naturally deduced or introduced : IMPROBABLE ⟨~ story⟩

far–flung \-ˈfləŋ\ *adj* : widely spread or distributed

fa•ri•na \fə-ˈrē-nə\ *n* [L, meal, flour] : a fine meal (as of wheat) used in puddings or as a breakfast cereal

far•i•na•ceous \ˌfar-ə-ˈnā-shəs\ *adj* **1** : having a mealy texture or surface **2** : containing or rich in starch

1farm \ˈfärm\ *n* [ME *ferme* rent, lease, fr. OF, lease, fr. *fermer* to fix, make a contract, fr. L *firmare* to make firm, fr. *firmus* firm] **1** : a tract of land used for raising crops or livestock **2** : a minor-league subsidiary of a major-league baseball team

2farm *vb* : to use (land) as a farm ⟨~*ed* 200 acres⟩; *also* : to raise crops or livestock — **farm•er** *n*

farm•hand \ˈfärm-ˌhand\ *n* : a farm laborer

farm•house \-ˌhau̇s\ *n* : a dwelling on a farm

farm•ing \ˈfär-miŋ\ *n* : the occupation or business of a person who farms

farm•land \ˈfärm-ˌland\ *n* : land used or suitable for farming

farm out *vb* : to turn over (as a task) to another

farm•stead \ˈfärm-ˌsted\ *n* : a farm with its buildings

farm•yard \-ˌyärd\ *n* : land around or enclosed by farm buildings

far–off \ˈfär-ˈȯf\ *adj* : remote in time or space : DISTANT

fa•rouche \fə-ˈrüsh\ *adj* [F] **1** : WILD **2** : marked by shyness and lack of polish

far–out \ˈfär-ˈau̇t\ *adj* : very unconventional ⟨~ clothes⟩

far•ra•go \fə-ˈrä-gō, -ˈrā-\ *n, pl* **-goes** [L, mixed fodder, mixture] : a confused collection : MIXTURE

far–reach•ing \ˈfär-ˈrē-chiŋ\ *adj* : having a wide range or effect

far•ri•er \ˈfar-ē-ər\ *n* : a person who shoes horses

1far•row \ˈfar-ō\ *vb* : to give birth to a litter of pigs

2farrow *n* : a litter of pigs

far•see•ing \ˈfär-ˌsē-iŋ\ *adj* : FARSIGHTED 1, 2

far•sight•ed \ˈfär-ˌsī-təd\ *adj* **1** : seeing or able to see to a great distance **2** : JUDICIOUS, WISE, SHREWD **3** : affected with an eye condition in which vision is better for distant than near objects — **far•sight•ed•ness** *n*

1far•ther \ˈfär-t͟hər\ *adv* **1** : at or to a greater distance or more advanced point **2** : to a greater degree or extent

2farther *adj* **1** : more distant **2** : ADDITIONAL

far•ther•most \-ˌmōst\ *adj* : FARTHEST

1far•thest \ˈfär-t͟həst\ *adj* : most distant

2farthest *adv* **1** : to or at the greatest distance : REMOTEST **2** : to the most advanced point **3** : by the greatest degree or extent : MOST

far•thing \ˈfär-t͟hiŋ\ *n* **1** : a former British monetary unit equal to ¼ of a penny; *also* : a coin representing this unit **2** : something of small value

fas•ci•cle \ˈfa-si-kəl\ *n* **1** : a small or slender bundle (as of pine needles or nerve fiber) **2** : one of the divisions of a book published in parts — **fas•ci•cled** \-kəld\ *adj*

fas•ci•nate \ˈfas-ᵊn-ˌāt\ *vb* **-nat•ed; -nat•ing** [L *fascinare*, fr. *fascinum* evil spell] **1** : to transfix and hold spellbound by an irresistible power **2** : ALLURE **3** : to be irresistibly attractive — **fas•ci•na•tion** \ˌfas-ᵊn-ˈā-shən\ *n*

fas•cism \ˈfa-ˌshi-zəm\ *n, often cap* : a political philosophy, movement, or regime that exalts nation and often race and stands for a centralized autocratic often militaristic government — **fas•cist** \-shist\ *n or adj, often cap* — **fas•cis•tic** \fa-ˈshis-tik\ *adj, often cap*

1fash•ion \ˈfa-shən\ *n* **1** : the make or form of something **2** : MANNER, WAY **3** : a prevailing custom, usage, or style **4** : the prevailing style (as in dress) **syn** mode, vogue, rage, trend

2fashion *vb* **1** : MOLD, CONSTRUCT **2** : FIT, ADAPT

fash•ion•able \ˈfa-shə-nə-bəl\ *adj* **1** : dressing or behaving according to fashion : STYLISH **2** : of or relating to the world of fashion ⟨~ resorts⟩ **syn** chic, modish, smart, swank — **fash•ion•ably** \-blē\ *adv*

1fast \ˈfast\ *adj* **1** : firmly fixed **2** : tightly shut **3** : adhering firmly **4** : STUCK **5** : STAUNCH ⟨~ friends⟩ **6**

: characterized by quick motion, operation, or effect ⟨a ~ trip⟩ ⟨a ~ track⟩ **7** : indicating ahead of the correct time ⟨the clock is ~⟩ **8** : not easily disturbed : SOUND ⟨a ~ sleep⟩ **9** : permanently dyed; *also* : being proof against fading ⟨colors ~ to sunlight⟩ **10** : DISSIPATED, WILD **11** : sexually promiscuous **syn** rapid, swift, fleet, quick, speedy, hasty

²fast *adv* **1** : in a firm or fixed manner ⟨stuck ~ in the mud⟩ **2** : SOUNDLY, DEEPLY ⟨~ asleep⟩ **3** : SWIFTLY **4** : RECKLESSLY

³fast *vb* **1** : to abstain from food **2** : to eat sparingly or abstain from some foods

⁴fast *n* **1** : the act or practice of fasting **2** : a time of fasting

fast•back \ˈfast-ˌbak\ *n* : an automobile having a roof with a long slope to the rear

fast•ball \-ˌbȯl\ *n* : a baseball pitch thrown at full speed

fas•ten \ˈfas-ᵊn\ *vb* **1** : to attach or join by or as if by pinning, tying, or nailing **2** : to make fast : fix securely **3** : to become fixed or joined **4** : to focus attention ⟨~*ed* onto the newest trends⟩ — **fas•ten•er** *n*

fas•ten•ing *n* : something that fastens : FASTENER

fast–food \ˌfast-ˈfüd\ *adj* : specializing in food that is prepared and served quickly ⟨a ~ restaurant⟩

fast–for•ward \-ˈfȯr-wərd\ *n* **1** : a function of a tape player that advances tape rapidly **2** : a state of rapid advancement — **fast–forward** *vb*

fas•tid•i•ous \fa-ˈsti-dē-əs\ *adj* **1** : overly difficult to please **2** : showing a meticulous or demanding attitude ⟨~ workmanship⟩ **syn** nice, finicky, fussy, particular, persnickety, squeamish — **fas•tid•i•ous•ly** *adv* — **fas•tid•i•ous•ness** *n*

fast•ness \ˈfast-nəs\ *n* **1** : the quality or state of being fast **2** : a fortified or secure place : STRONGHOLD

fast–talk \ˈfast-ˌtȯk\ *vb* : to influence by persuasive and usu. deceptive talk

fast–track \ˈfast-ˌtrak\ *vb* : to speed up the processing or production of

fast track *n* : a course leading to rapid advancement or success

¹fat \ˈfat\ *adj* **fat•ter; fat•test 1** : PLUMP, FLESHY **2** : OILY, GREASY **3** : well filled out : BIG **4** : well stocked : ABUNDANT **5** : richly rewarding — **fat•ness** *n*

²fat *n* **1** : animal tissue rich in greasy or oily matter **2** : any of numerous energy-rich esters that occur naturally in animal fats and in plants and are soluble in organic solvents (as ether) but not in water **3** : the best or richest portion ⟨lived on the ~ of the land⟩ **4** : OBESITY **5** : excess matter

fa•tal \ˈfāt-ᵊl\ *adj* **1** : FATEFUL ⟨that ~ day⟩ **2** : causing death or ruin ⟨a ~ mistake⟩ — **fa•tal•ly** *adv*

fa•tal•ism \-ˌi-zəm\ *n* : the belief that events are determined by fate — **fa•tal•ist** \-ist\ *n* — **fa•tal•is•tic** \ˌfāt-ᵊl-ˈis-tik\ *adj* — **fa•tal•is•ti•cal•ly** \-ti-k(ə-)lē\ *adv*

fa•tal•i•ty \fā-ˈta-lə-tē, fə-\ *n, pl* **-ties 1** : DEADLINESS **2** : FATE **3** : death resulting from a disaster or accident; *also* : one who suffers such a death

fat•back \ˈfat-ˌbak\ *n* : a fatty strip from the back of the hog usu. cured by salting and drying

fat cat *n* **1** : a wealthy contributor to a political campaign **2** : a wealthy privileged person

fate \ˈfāt\ *n* [ME, fr. MF or L; MF, fr. L *fatum,* lit., what has been spoken, fr. *fari* to speak] **1** : the cause or will that is held to determine events : DESTINY **2** : LOT, FORTUNE **3** : DISASTER; *esp* : DEATH **4** : END, OUTCOME **5** *cap, pl* : the three goddesses of classical mythology who determine the course of human life

fat•ed \ˈfā-təd\ *adj* : decreed, controlled, or marked by fate

fate•ful \ˈfāt-fəl\ *adj* **1** : OMINOUS, PROPHETIC **2** : IMPORTANT, DECISIVE **3** : DEADLY, DESTRUCTIVE **4** : determined by fate — **fate•ful•ly** *adv*

fath *abbr* fathom

fat•head \ˈfat-ˌhed\ *n* : a stupid person — **fat•head•ed** \-ˈhe-dəd\ *adj*

¹fa•ther \ˈfä-t͟hər\ *n* **1** : a male parent **2** *cap* : God esp. as the first person of the Trinity **3** : FOREFATHER **4** : one deserving the respect and love given to a father **5** *often cap* : an early Christian writer accepted by the church as an authoritative witness to its teaching and practice **6** : ORIGINATOR ⟨the ~ of modern radio⟩; *also* : SOURCE **7** : PRIEST — used esp. as a title **8** : one of the leading men ⟨city ~*s*⟩ — **fa•ther•hood** \-ˌhu̇d\ *n* — **fa•ther•less** *adj* — **fa•ther•ly** *adj*

²father *vb* **1** : BEGET **2** : to be the founder, producer, or author of **3** : to treat or care for as a father

father–in–law \ˈfä-t͟hə-rən-ˌlȯ\ *n, pl* **fa•thers–in–law** \-t͟hər-zən-\ : the father of one's husband or wife

fa•ther•land \ˈfä-t͟hər-ˌland\ *n* **1** : the native land of one's ancestors **2** : one's native land

¹fath•om \ˈfa-t͟həm\ *n* [ME *fadme,* fr. OE *fæthm* outstretched arms, fathom] : a unit of length equal to 6 feet (about 1.8 meters) used esp. for measuring the depth of water

²fathom *vb* **1** : to measure by a sounding line **2** : PROBE **3** : to penetrate and come to understand — **fath•om•able** \ˈfa-t͟hə-mə-bəl\ *adj*

fath•om•less \ˈfa-t͟həm-ləs\ *adj* : incapable of being fathomed

¹fa•tigue \fə-ˈtēg\ *n* [F] **1** : manual or menial work performed by military personnel **2** *pl* : the uniform or work clothing worn on fatigue and in the field **3** : weariness from labor or stress **4** : the tendency of a material to break under repeated stress

²fatigue *vb* **fa•tigued; fa•tigu•ing** : WEARY, TIRE

fat•ten \ˈfat-ᵊn\ *vb* : to make or grow fat

¹fat•ty \ˈfa-tē\ *adj* **fat•ti•er; -est 1** : containing fat esp. in unusual amounts **2** : GREASY

²fatty *n, pl* **fat•ties** : a fat person

fatty acid *n* : any of numerous acids that contain only carbon, hydrogen, and oxygen and that occur naturally in fats and various oils

fa•tu•ity \fə-ˈtü-ə-tē, -ˈtyü-\ *n, pl* **-ities** : FOOLISHNESS, STUPIDITY

fat•u•ous \ˈfa-chu̇-wəs\ *adj* : FOOLISH, INANE, SILLY — **fat•u•ous•ly** *adv*

fau•bourg \fō-ˈbu̇r\ *n* **1** : a suburb esp. of a French city **2** : a city quarter

fau•ces \ˈfȯ-ˌsēz\ *n pl* [L, throat] : the narrow passage located between the soft palate and the base of the tongue that joins the mouth to the pharynx

fau•cet \ˈfȯ-sət, ˈfä-\ *n* : a fixture for drawing off a liquid (as from a pipe)

¹fault \ˈfȯlt\ *n* **1** : a weakness in character : FAILING **2** : IMPERFECTION, IMPAIRMENT, DEFECT **3** : an error esp. in service in a net or racket game **4** : MISDEMEANOR; *also* : MISTAKE **5** : responsibility for something wrong **6** : a fracture in the earth's crust accompanied by a displacement of one side relative to the other — **fault•i•ly** \ˈfȯl-tə-lē\ *adv* — **fault•less** *adj* — **fault•less•ly** *adv* — **faulty** *adj*

²fault *vb* **1** : to commit a fault : ERR **2** : to fracture so as to produce a geologic fault **3** : to find a fault in

fault•find•er \ˈfȯlt-ˌfīn-dər\ *n* : a person who tends to find fault or complain **syn** critic, carper, caviler, complainer — **fault•find•ing** *n or adj*

faun \ˈfȯn\ *n* : a Roman god similar to but gentler than a satyr

fau•na \ˈfȯ-nə\ *n, pl* **faunas** *also* **fau•nae** \-ˌnē, -ˌnī\ [NL, fr. L *Fauna,* sister of Faunus (the Roman god of animals)] : animals or animal life esp. of a region, period, or environment — **fau•nal** \-nəl\ *adj*

fau•vism \ˈfō-ˌvi-zəm\ *n, often cap* : a movement in painting characterized by vivid colors, free treatment of form, and a vibrant and decorative effect — **fau•vist** \-vist\ *n, often cap*

faux pas \ˈfō-ˌpä, fō-ˈ\ *n, pl* **faux pas** *same or* -ˌpäz, -ˈpäz\ [F, lit., false step] : BLUNDER; *esp* : a social blunder

¹fa•vor \ˈfā-vər\ *n* **1** : friendly regard shown toward another esp. by a superior **2** : APPROVAL **3** : PARTIALITY **4** : POPULARITY **5** : gracious kindness; *also* : an act of

DICTIONARY

such kindness **6** *pl* : effort in one's behalf : ATTENTION **7** : a token of love (as a ribbon) usu. worn conspicuously **8** : a small gift or decorative item given out at a party **9** : a special privilege **10** : sexual privileges — usu. used in pl. **11** *archaic* : LETTER **12** : BEHALF, INTEREST

²**favor** *vb* **1** : to regard or treat with favor **2** : OBLIGE **3** : ENDOW ⟨~*ed* by nature⟩ **4** : to treat gently or carefully : SPARE ⟨~ a lame leg⟩ **5** : PREFER **6** : SUPPORT, SUSTAIN **7** : FACILITATE ⟨darkness ~*s* attack⟩ **8** : RESEMBLE ⟨he ~*s* his father⟩

fa•vor•able \ˈfā-və-rə-bəl\ *adj* **1** : APPROVING **2** : HELPFUL, PROMISING, ADVANTAGEOUS ⟨~ weather⟩ — **fa•vor•ably** \-blē\ *adv*

fa•vor•ite \ˈfā-və-rət, -vrət\ *n* **1** : a person or a thing that is favored above others **2** : a competitor regarded as most likely to win — **favorite** *adj*

favorite son *n* : a candidate supported by the delegates of his state at a presidential nominating convention

fa•vor•it•ism \ˈfā-və-rə-ˌti-zəm\ *n* : PARTIALITY, BIAS

fa•vour *chiefly Brit var of* FAVOR

¹**fawn** \ˈfȯn, ˈfän\ *vb* **1** : to show affection ⟨a dog ~*ing* on its master⟩ **2** : to court favor by a cringing or flattering manner **syn** grovel, kowtow, toady, truckle

²**fawn** *n* **1** : a young deer **2** : a light grayish brown

fax \ˈfaks\ *n* **1** : FACSIMILE 2 **2** : a device used to send or receive facsimile communications; *also* : such a communication — **fax** *vb*

fay \ˈfā\ *n* : FAIRY, ELF — **fay** *adj*

faze \ˈfāz\ *vb* **fazed; faz•ing** : to disturb the composure or courage of : DAUNT

FBI *abbr* Federal Bureau of Investigation

FCC *abbr* Federal Communications Commission

FD *abbr* fire department

FDA *abbr* Food and Drug Administration

FDIC *abbr* Federal Deposit Insurance Corporation

Fe *symbol* [L *ferrum*] iron

fe•al•ty \ˈfēl-tē\ *n, pl* **-ties** : LOYALTY, ALLEGIANCE **syn** fidelity, devotion, faithfulness, piety

¹**fear** \ˈfir\ *vb* **1** : to have a reverent awe of ⟨~ God⟩ **2** : to be afraid of : have fear **3** : to be apprehensive

²**fear** *n* **1** : an unpleasant often strong emotion caused by expectation or awareness of danger; *also* : an instance of or a state marked by this emotion **2** : anxious concern : SOLICITUDE **3** : profound reverence esp. toward God **syn** dread, fright, alarm, panic, terror, trepidation

fear•ful \-fəl\ *adj* **1** : causing fear **2** : filled with fear **3** : showing or caused by fear **4** : extremely bad, intense, or large — **fear•ful•ly** *adv*

fear•less \-ləs\ *adj* : free from fear : BRAVE — **fear•less•ly** *adv* — **fear•less•ness** *n*

fear•some \-səm\ *adj* **1** : causing fear **2** : TIMID

fea•si•ble \ˈfē-zə-bəl\ *adj* **1** : capable of being done or carried out ⟨a ~ plan⟩ **2** : SUITABLE **3** : REASONABLE, LIKELY **syn** possible, practicable, viable, workable — **fea•si•bil•i•ty** \ˌfē-zə-ˈbi-lə-tē\ *n* — **fea•si•bly** \ˈfē-zə-blē\ *adv*

¹**feast** \ˈfēst\ *n* **1** : an elaborate meal : BANQUET **2** : FESTIVAL 1

²**feast** *vb* **1** : to take part in a feast; *also* : to give a feast for **2** : to enjoy some unusual pleasure or delight **3** : DELIGHT, GRATIFY

feat \ˈfēt\ *n* : DEED, EXPLOIT, ACHIEVEMENT; *esp* : an act notable for courage, skill, endurance, or ingenuity

¹**feath•er** \ˈfe-t͟hər\ *n* **1** : any of the light horny outgrowths that form the external covering of the body of a bird **2** : PLUME **3** : PLUMAGE **4** : KIND, NATURE ⟨birds of a ~⟩ **5** : ATTIRE, DRESS ⟨in full ~⟩ **6** : CONDITION, MOOD ⟨in fine ~⟩ — **feath•ered** \-t͟hərd\ *adj* — **feath•er•less** *adj* — **feath•ery** *adj* — **a feather in one's cap** : a mark of distinction : HONOR

²**feather** *vb* **1** : to furnish with a feather ⟨~ an arrow⟩ **2** : to cover, clothe, line, or adorn with or as if with feathers — **feather one's nest** : to provide for oneself esp. while in a position of trust

feath•er•bed•ding \ˈfe-t͟hər-ˌbe-diŋ\ *n* : the requiring of an employer usu. under a union rule or safety statute to employ more workers than are needed

feath•er•edge \-ˌej\ *n* : a very thin sharp edge

feath•er•weight \-ˌwāt\ *n* : one that is very light in weight; *esp* : a boxer weighing more than 118 but not over 126 pounds

¹**fea•ture** \ˈfē-chər\ *n* **1** : the shape or appearance of the face or its parts **2** : a part of the face : LINEAMENT **3** : a prominent part or characteristic **4** : a special attraction (as in a newspaper) **5** : something offered to the public or advertised as particularly attractive — **fea•ture•less** *adj*

²**feature** *vb* **1** : to picture in the mind : IMAGINE **2** : to give special prominence to ⟨~ a story in a newspaper⟩ **3** : to play an important part

feaze \ˈfēz, ˈfāz\ *var of* FAZE

Feb *abbr* February

fe•brile \ˈfe-ˌbrīl\ *adj* : FEVERISH

Feb•ru•ary \ˈfe-b(y)ə-ˌwer-ē, ˈfe-brə-\ *n* [ME *Februarie*, fr. L *Februarius*, fr. *Februa*, pl., feast of purification] : the 2d month of the year

fe•ces \ˈfē-ˌsēz\ *n pl* : bodily waste discharged from the intestine — **fe•cal** \-kəl\ *adj*

feck•less \ˈfek-ləs\ *adj* **1** : WEAK, INEFFECTIVE **2** : WORTHLESS, IRRESPONSIBLE

fe•cund \ˈfe-kənd, ˈfē-\ *adj* : FRUITFUL, PROLIFIC — **fe•cun•di•ty** \fi-ˈkən-də-tē, fe-\ *n*

fe•cun•date \ˈfe-kən-ˌdāt, ˈfē-\ *vb* **-dat•ed; -dat•ing** **1** : to make fecund **2** : IMPREGNATE — **fe•cun•da•tion** \ˌfe-kən-ˈdā-shən, ˌfē-\ *n*

fed *abbr* federal; federation

fed•er•al \ˈfe-də-rəl, -drəl\ *adj* **1** : formed by a compact between political units that surrender individual sovereignty to a central authority but retain certain limited powers **2** : of or constituting a form of government in which power is distributed between a central authority and constituent territorial units **3** : of or relating to the central government of a federation **4** *cap* : FEDERALIST **5** *often cap* : of, relating to, or loyal to the federal government or the Union armies of the U.S. in the American Civil War — **fed•er•al•ly** *adv*

Federal *n* : a supporter of the U.S. government in the Civil War; *esp* : a soldier in the federal armies

federal district *n* : a district (as the District of Columbia) set apart as the seat of the central government of a federation

fed•er•al•ism \ˈfe-də-rə-li-zəm, -drə-\ *n* **1** *often cap* : the distribution of power in an organization (as a government) between a central authority and the constituent units **2** : support or advocacy of federalism **3** *cap* : the principles of the Federalists

fed•er•al•ist \-list\ *n* **1** : an advocate of federalism **2** *often cap* : an advocate of a federal union between the American colonies after the Revolution and of adoption of the U.S. Constitution **3** *cap* : a member of a major political party in the early years of the U.S. favoring a strong centralized national government — **federalist** *adj, often cap*

fed•er•al•ize \ˈfe-də-rə-ˌlīz, -drə-\ *vb* **-ized; -iz•ing** **1** : to unite in or under a federal system **2** : to bring under the jurisdiction of a federal government

fed•er•ate \ˈfe-də-ˌrāt\ *vb* **-at•ed; -at•ing** : to join in a federation

fed•er•a•tion \ˌfe-də-ˈrā-shən\ *n* **1** : the act of federating; *esp* : the forming of a federal union **2** : a federal government **3** : a union of organizations

fedn *abbr* federation

fe•do•ra \fi-ˈdōr-ə\ *n* : a low soft felt hat with the crown creased lengthwise

fed up *adj* : satiated, tired, or disgusted beyond endurance

fee \ˈfē\ *n* **1** : an estate in land held from a feudal lord **2** : an inherited or heritable estate in land **3** : a fixed charge; *also* : a charge for a service

fee•ble \ˈfē-bəl\ *adj* **fee•bler** \-bə-lər\; **fee•blest** \-bə-ləst\ [ME *feble,* fr. OF, fr. L *flebilis* lamentable, wretched, fr. *flēre* to weep] **1 :** DECREPIT, FRAIL **2 :** INEFFECTIVE, INADEQUATE ⟨a ~ protest⟩ — **fee•ble•ness** *n* — **fee•bly** \-blē\ *adv*

fee•ble•mind•ed \ˌfē-bəl-ˈmīn-dəd\ *adj* **:** lacking normal intelligence — **fee•ble•mind•ed•ness** *n*

[1]**feed** \ˈfēd\ *vb* **fed** \ˈfed\; **feed•ing 1 :** to give food to; *also* **:** to give as food **2 :** EAT 1; *also* **:** PREY **3 :** to furnish what is necessary to the growth or function of — **feed•er** *n*

[2]**feed** *n* **1 :** a usu. large meal **2 :** food for livestock **3 :** a mechanism for feeding material to a machine

feed•back \ˈfēd-ˌbak\ *n* **1 :** the return to the input of a part of the output of a machine, system, or process **2 :** response esp. to one in authority about an activity or policy

feed•lot \ˈfēd-ˌlät\ *n* **:** land on which cattle are fattened for market

feed•stuff \-ˌstəf\ *n* **:** FEED 2

[1]**feel** \ˈfēl\ *vb* **felt** \ˈfelt\; **feel•ing 1 :** to perceive or examine through physical contact **:** TOUCH, HANDLE **2 :** EXPERIENCE; *also* **:** to suffer from **3 :** to ascertain by cautious trial ⟨~ out public sentiment⟩ **4 :** to be aware of **5 :** to be conscious of an inward impression, state of mind, or physical condition **6 :** BELIEVE, THINK **7 :** to search for something with the fingers **:** GROPE **8 :** SEEM ⟨it ~*s* like spring⟩ **9 :** to have sympathy or pity

[2]**feel** *n* **1 :** the sense of touch **2 :** SENSATION, FEELING **3 :** the quality of a thing as imparted through touch

feel•er \ˈfē-lər\ *n* **1 :** one that feels; *esp* **:** a tactile organ (as on the head of an insect) **2 :** a proposal or remark made to find out the views of other people

[1]**feel•ing** \ˈfē-liŋ\ *n* **1 :** the sense of touch; *also* **:** a sensation perceived by this **2 :** a state of mind ⟨a ~ of loneliness⟩ **3** *pl* **:** general emotional condition **:** SENSIBILITIES ⟨hurt their ~*s*⟩ **4 :** OPINION, BELIEF **5 :** capacity to respond emotionally

[2]**feeling** *adj* **1 :** SENSITIVE; *esp* **:** easily moved emotionally **2 :** expressing emotion or sensitivity — **feel•ing•ly** *adv*

feet *pl of* FOOT

feign \ˈfān\ *vb* **1 :** to give a false appearance of **:** SHAM ⟨~ illness⟩ **2 :** to assert as if true **:** PRETEND

feint \ˈfānt\ *n* **:** something feigned; *esp* **:** a mock blow or attack intended to distract attention from the real point of attack — **feint** *vb*

feld•spar \ˈfeld-ˌspär\ *n* **:** any of a group of crystalline minerals consisting of silicates of aluminum with another element (as potassium or sodium)

fe•lic•i•tate \fi-ˈli-sə-ˌtāt\ *vb* **-tat•ed; -tat•ing :** CONGRATULATE — **fe•lic•i•ta•tion** \-ˌli-sə-ˈtā-shən\ *n*

fe•lic•i•tous \fi-ˈli-sə-təs\ *adj* **1 :** suitably expressed **:** APT **2 :** PLEASANT, DELIGHTFUL — **fe•lic•i•tous•ly** *adv*

fe•lic•i•ty \fi-ˈli-sə-tē\ *n, pl* **-ties 1 :** the quality or state of being happy; *esp* **:** great happiness **2 :** something that causes happiness **3 :** a pleasing manner or quality esp. in art or language **4 :** an apt expression

fe•line \ˈfē-ˌlīn\ *adj* [L *felinus,* fr. *felis* cat] **1 :** of or relating to cats or their kin **2 :** SLY, TREACHEROUS **3 :** STEALTHY — **feline** *n*

[1]**fell** \ˈfel\ *n* **:** SKIN, HIDE, PELT

[2]**fell** *vb* **1 :** to cut, beat, or knock down; *also* **:** KILL **2 :** to sew (a seam) by folding one raw edge under the other

[3]**fell** *past of* FALL

[4]**fell** *adj* **:** CRUEL, FIERCE; *also* **:** DEADLY

fel•lah \ˈfe-lə, fə-ˈlä\ *n, pl* **fel•la•hin** *or* **fel•la•heen** \ˌfe-lə-ˈhēn\ **:** a peasant or agricultural laborer in Arab countries (as Egypt or Syria)

fel•la•tio \fə-ˈlā-shē-ˌō\ *also* **fel•la•tion** \-shən\ *n* **:** oral stimulation of the penis

fel•low \ˈfe-lō\ *n* [ME *felawe,* fr. OE *fēolaga,* fr. ON *fēlagi,* fr. *fēlag* partnership, fr. *fē* cattle, money + *lag* act of laying] **1 :** COMRADE, ASSOCIATE **2 :** EQUAL, PEER **3 :** one of a pair **:** MATE **4 :** a member of an incorporated literary or scientific society **5 :** MAN, BOY **6 :** BOYFRIEND **7 :** a person granted a stipend for advanced study

fel•low•man \ˌfe-lō-ˈman\ *n* **:** a kindred human being

fel•low•ship \ˈfe-lō-ˌship\ *n* **1 :** the condition of friendly relationship existing among persons **:** COMRADESHIP **2 :** a community of interest or feeling **3 :** a group with similar interests **4 :** the position of a fellow (as of a university) **5 :** the stipend granted a fellow

fellow traveler *n* **:** a person who sympathizes with and often furthers the ideals and program of an organized group (as the Communist party) without joining it

fel•on \ˈfe-lən\ *n* **1 :** one who has committed a felony **2 :** WHITLOW

fel•o•ny \ˈfe-lə-nē\ *n, pl* **-nies :** a serious crime punishable by a heavy sentence — **fe•lo•ni•ous** \fə-ˈlō-nē-əs\ *adj*

fel•spar *chiefly Brit var of* FELDSPAR

[1]**felt** \ˈfelt\ *n* **1 :** a cloth made of wool and fur often mixed with natural or synthetic fibers **2 :** a material resembling felt

[2]**felt** *past and past part of* FEEL

fem *abbr* **1** female **2** feminine

fe•male \ˈfē-ˌmāl\ *adj* [ME, alter. of *femel,* fr. MF *femelle,* fr. ML *femella,* fr. L, girl, dim. of *femina* woman] **:** of, relating to, or being the sex that bears young; *also* **:** PISTILLATE **syn** feminine, womanly, womanlike, womanish, effeminate — **female** *n*

[1]**fem•i•nine** \ˈfe-mə-nən\ *adj* **1 :** of the female sex; *also* **:** characteristic of or appropriate or peculiar to women **2 :** of, relating to, or constituting the gender that includes most words or grammatical forms referring to females — **fem•i•nin•i•ty** \ˌfe-mə-ˈni-nə-tē\ *n*

[2]**feminine** *n* **:** a noun, pronoun, adjective, or inflectional form or class of the feminine gender; *also* **:** the feminine gender

fem•i•nism \ˈfe-mə-ˌni-zəm\ *n* **1 :** the theory of the political, economic, and social equality of the sexes **2 :** organized activity on behalf of women's rights and interests — **fem•i•nist** \-nist\ *n or adj*

femme fa•tale \ˌfem-fə-ˈtal\ *n, pl* **femmes fa•tales** *same or* -ˈtalz\ [F, lit., disastrous woman] **:** a seductive woman

fe•mur \ˈfē-mər\ *n, pl* **fe•murs** *or* **fem•o•ra** \ˈfe-mə-rə\ **:** the long leg bone extending from the hip to the knee — **fem•o•ral** \ˈfe-mə-rəl\ *adj*

[1]**fen** \ˈfen\ *n* **:** low swampy land

[2]**fen** \ˈfən\ *n, pl* **fen** — see *yuan* at MONEY table

[1]**fence** \ˈfens\ *n* [ME *fens,* short for *defens* defense] **1 :** a barrier (as of wood or wire) to prevent escape or entry or to mark a boundary **2 :** a person who receives stolen goods; *also* **:** a place where stolen goods are disposed of — **on the fence :** in a position of neutrality or indecision

[2]**fence** *vb* **fenced; fenc•ing 1 :** to enclose with a fence **2 :** to keep in or out with a fence **3 :** to practice fencing **4 :** to use tactics of attack and defense esp. in debate — **fenc•er** *n*

fenc•ing *n* **1 :** the art or practice of attack and defense with the foil, épée, or saber **2 :** the fences of a property or region **3 :** material used for building fences

fend \ˈfend\ *vb* **1 :** to keep or ward off **:** REPEL **2 :** SHIFT ⟨~ for yourself⟩

fend•er \ˈfen-dər\ *n* **:** a protective device (as a guard over the wheel of an automobile)

fen•es•tra•tion \ˌfe-nə-ˈstrā-shən\ *n* **:** the arrangement and design of windows and doors in a building

Fe•ni•an \ˈfē-nē-ən\ *n* **:** a member of a secret 19th century Irish and Irish-American organization dedicated to overthrowing British rule in Ireland

fen•nel \ˈfen-əl\ *n* **:** a garden plant related to the carrot and grown for its aromatic foliage and seeds

FEPC *abbr* Fair Employment Practices Commission

fe•ral \ˈfir-əl, ˈfer-\ *adj* **1 :** SAVAGE **2 :** WILD 1 **3 :** having escaped from domestication and become wild

fer–de–lance \ˈfer-də-ˈlans\ *n, pl* **fer–de–lance** [F, lit., lance iron, spearhead] : a large venomous pit viper of Central and So. America

[1]**fer•ment** \fər-ˈment\ *vb* **1** : to cause or undergo fermentation **2** : to be or cause to be in a state of agitation or intense activity

[2]**fer•ment** \ˈfər-ˌment\ *n* **1** : a living organism (as a yeast) causing fermentation by its enzymes; *also* : ENZYME **2** : AGITATION, TUMULT

fer•men•ta•tion \ˌfər-mən-ˈtā-shən, -ˌmen-\ *n* **1** : chemical decomposition of an organic substance (as in the souring of milk or the formation of alcohol from sugar) by enzymatic action in the absence of oxygen often with formation of gas **2** : FERMENT 2

fer•mi•um \ˈfer-mē-əm, ˈfər-\ *n* : an artificially produced radioactive metallic chemical element — see ELEMENT table

fern \ˈfərn\ *n* : any of an order of vascular plants resembling seed plants in having roots, stems, and leaflike fronds but reproducing by spores instead of by flowers and seeds

fern•ery \ˈfər-nə-rē\ *n, pl* **-er•ies 1** : a place for growing ferns **2** : a collection of growing ferns

fe•ro•cious \fə-ˈrō-shəs\ *adj* **1** : FIERCE, SAVAGE **2** : extremely intense — **fe•ro•cious•ly** *adv* — **fe•ro•cious•ness** *n*

fe•roc•i•ty \fə-ˈrä-sə-tē\ *n* : the quality or state of being ferocious

[1]**fer•ret** \ˈfer-ət\ *n* : a partially domesticated usu. white European mammal related to the weasels

[2]**ferret** *vb* **1** : to hunt game with ferrets **2** : to drive out of a hiding place **3** : to find and bring to light by searching ⟨~ out the truth⟩

fer•ric \ˈfer-ik\ *adj* : of, relating to, or containing iron

ferric oxide *n* : an oxide of iron found in nature as hematite and as rust and used as a pigment and for polishing

Fer•ris wheel \ˈfer-əs-\ *n* : an amusement device consisting of a large upright power-driven wheel with seats that remain horizontal around its rim

fer•ro•mag•net•ic \ˌfer-ō-mag-ˈne-tik\ *adj* : of or relating to substances that are easily magnetized

fer•rous \ˈfer-əs\ *adj* : of, relating to, or containing iron

fer•rule \ˈfer-əl\ *n* : a metal ring or cap around a slender wooden shaft to prevent splitting

[1]**fer•ry** \ˈfer-ē\ *vb* **fer•ried; fer•ry•ing** [ME *ferien,* fr. OE *ferian* to carry, convey] **1** : to carry by boat across a body of water **2** : to cross by a ferry **3** : to convey from one place to another

[2]**ferry** *n, pl* **ferries 1** : a place where persons or things are ferried **2** : FERRYBOAT

fer•ry•boat \ˈfer-ē-ˌbōt\ *n* : a boat used in ferrying

fer•tile \ˈfərt-ᵊl\ *adj* **1** : producing plentifully : PRODUCTIVE ⟨~ soils⟩ ⟨a ~ mind⟩ **2** : capable of developing or reproducing ⟨~ seed⟩ ⟨a ~ bull⟩ **syn** fruitful, prolific, fecund, productive — **fer•til•i•ty** \(ˌ)fər-ˈti-lə-tē\ *n*

fer•til•ize \ˈfərt-ᵊl-ˌīz\ *vb* **-ized; -iz•ing 1** : to unite with in the process of fertilization ⟨a sperm ~*s* an egg⟩ **2** : to apply fertilizer to — **fer•til•iza•tion** \ˌfərt-ᵊl-ə-ˈzā-shən\ *n*

fer•til•iz•er \-ˌī-zər\ *n* : material (as manure or a chemical mixture) for enriching land

fer•ule \ˈfer-əl\ *n* : a rod or ruler used to punish children

fer•ven•cy \ˈfər-vən-sē\ *n, pl* **-cies** : FERVOR

fer•vent \ˈfər-vənt\ *adj* **1** : very hot : GLOWING **2** : marked by great intensity of feeling **syn** impassioned, ardent, fervid, fiery, passionate — **fer•vent•ly** *adv*

fer•vid \-vəd\ *adj* **1** : very hot **2** : ARDENT, ZEALOUS — **fer•vid•ly** *adv*

fer•vor \ˈfər-vər\ *n* **1** : intense heat **2** : intensity of feeling or expression

fer•vour *chiefly Brit var of* FERVOR

fes•tal \ˈfest-ᵊl\ *adj* : FESTIVE

fester \ˈfes-tər\ *vb* **1** : to form pus **2** : PUTREFY, ROT **3** : RANKLE

fes•ti•val \ˈfes-tə-vəl\ *n* **1** : a time of celebration marked by special observances; *esp* : an occasion marked with religious ceremonies **2** : a periodic season or program of cultural events or entertainment ⟨a dance ~⟩

fes•tive \ˈfes-tiv\ *adj* **1** : of, relating to, or suitable for a feast or festival **2** : JOYFUL, GAY — **fes•tive•ly** *adv*

fes•tiv•i•ty \fes-ˈti-və-tē\ *n, pl* **-ties 1** : FESTIVAL 1 **2** : the quality or state of being festive **3** : festive activity

[1]**fes•toon** \fes-ˈtün\ *n* [F *feston,* fr. It *festone,* fr. *festa* festival] **1** : a decorative chain or strip hanging between two points **2** : a carved, molded, or painted ornament representing a decorative chain

[2]**festoon** *vb* **1** : to hang or form festoons on **2** : to shape into festoons

fe•tal \ˈfēt-ᵊl\ *adj* : of, relating to, or being a fetus

fetch \ˈfech\ *vb* **1** : to go or come after and bring or take back ⟨teach a dog to ~ a stick⟩ **2** : to bring in (as a price) **3** : to cause to come : bring out ⟨~*ed* tears from the eyes⟩ **4** : to give by striking ⟨~ him a blow⟩

fetch•ing *adj* : ATTRACTIVE, PLEASING — **fetch•ing•ly** *adv*

[1]**fete** *or* **fête** \ˈfāt, ˈfet\ *n* [F *fête,* fr. OF *feste*] **1** : FESTIVAL **2** : a large elaborate entertainment or party

[2]**fete** *or* **fête** *vb* **fet•ed** *or* **fêt•ed; fet•ing** *or* **fêt•ing 1** : to honor or commemorate with a fete **2** : to pay high honor to

fet•id \ˈfe-təd\ *adj* : having an offensive smell : STINKING

fe•tish *also* **fe•tich** \ˈfe-tish\ *n* [F & Pg; F *fétiche,* fr. Pg *feitiço,* fr. *feitiço* artificial, false, fr. L *facticius* factitious] **1** : an object (as an idol or image) believed to have magical powers (as in curing disease) **2** : an object of unreasoning devotion or concern **3** : an object whose real or fantasied presence is psychologically necessary for sexual gratification

fe•tish•ism \-ti-ˌshi-zəm\ *n* **1** : belief in or devotion to fetishes **2** : the pathological transfer of sexual interest and gratification to a fetish — **fe•tish•ist** \-shist\ *n* — **fe•tish•is•tic** \ˌfe-ti-ˈshis-tik\ *adj*

fet•lock \ˈfet-ˌläk\ *n* : a projection on the back of a horse's leg above the hoof; *also* : a tuft of hair on this

fet•ter \ˈfe-tər\ *n* **1** : a chain or shackle for the feet **2** : something that confines : RESTRAINT — **fetter** *vb*

fet•tle \ˈfet-ᵊl\ *n* : a state of fitness or order : CONDITION ⟨in fine ~⟩

fe•tus \ˈfē-təs\ *n* : an unborn or unhatched vertebrate esp. after its basic structure is laid down; *esp* : a developing human being in the uterus from usu. three months after pregnancy occurs to birth

feud \ˈfyüd\ *n* : a prolonged quarrel; *esp* : a lasting conflict between families or clans marked by violent attacks made for revenge — **feud** *vb*

feu•dal \ˈfyüd-ᵊl\ *adj* **1** : of, relating to, or having the characteristics of a medieval fee **2** : of, relating to, or characteristic of feudalism

feu•dal•ism \ˈfyüd-ᵊl-ˌi-zəm\ *n* : a system of political organization prevailing in medieval Europe in which a vassal renders service to a lord and receives protection and land in return; *also* : a similar political or social system — **feu•dal•is•tic** \ˌfyüd-ᵊl-ˈis-tik\ *adj*

[1]**feu•da•to•ry** \ˈfyü-də-ˌtōr-ē\ *adj* : owing feudal allegiance

[2]**feudatory** *n, pl* **-ries 1** : FIEF **2** : a person who holds lands by feudal law or usage

fe•ver \ˈfē-vər\ *n* **1** : a rise in body temperature above the normal; *also* : a disease of which this is a chief symptom **2** : a state of heightened emotion or activity **3** : CRAZE — **fe•ver•ish** *adj* — **fe•ver•ish•ly** *adv*

[1]**few** \ˈfyü\ *pron* : not many : a small number

[2]**few** *adj* **1** : consisting of or amounting to a small number **2** : not many but some ⟨caught a ~ fish⟩ — **few•ness** *n* — **few and far between** : RARE 3

[3]few *n* **1 :** a small number of units or individuals ⟨a ~ of them⟩ **2 :** a special limited number ⟨among the ~⟩
few•er \ˈfyü-ər\ *pron* **:** a smaller number of persons or things
fey \ˈfā\ *adj* **1** *chiefly Scot* **:** fated to die; *also* **:** marked by a foreboding of death or calamity **2 :** able to see into the future **:** VISIONARY **3 :** marked by an otherworldly air or attitude **4 :** CRAZY, TOUCHED
fez \ˈfez\ *n, pl* **fez•zes** *also* **fez•es :** a round red felt hat that has a flat top and a tassel but no brim

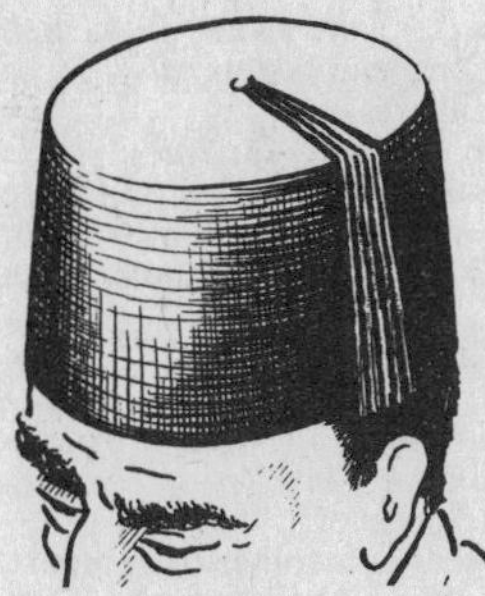

fez

ff *abbr* **1** folios **2** [*f*ollowing] and the following ones **3** fortissimo
FHA *abbr* Federal Housing Administration
fi•an•cé \ˌfē-ˌän-ˈsā\ *n* [F, fr. MF, fr. pp. of *fiancer* to promise, betroth, fr. OF *fiancier,* fr. *fiance* promise, trust, fr. *fier* to trust, ultim. fr. L *fidere*] **:** a man engaged to be married
fi•an•cée \ˌfē-ˌän-ˈsā\ *n* **:** a woman engaged to be married
fi•as•co \fē-ˈas-kō\ *n, pl* **-coes** [F] **:** a complete failure
fi•at \ˈfē-ət, -ˌat, -ˌät; ˈfī-ət, -ˌat\ *n* [L, let it be done] **:** an authoritative and often arbitrary order or decree
[1]fib \ˈfib\ *n* **:** a trivial or childish lie
[2]fib *vb* **fibbed; fib•bing :** to tell a fib **— fib•ber** *n*
fi•ber *or* **fi•bre** \ˈfī-bər\ *n* **1 :** a threadlike substance or structure (as a muscle cell or fine root); *esp* **:** a natural (as wool or flax) or artificial (as rayon) filament capable of being spun or woven **2 :** indigestible material in human food that stimulates the intestine to move its contents along **3 :** an element that gives texture or substance **4 :** basic toughness **:** STRENGTH **— fi•brous** \-brəs\ *adj*
fi•ber•board \ˈfī-bər-ˌbōrd\ *n* **:** a material made by compressing fibers (as of wood) into stiff sheets
fi•ber•fill \-ˌfil\ *n* **:** synthetic fibers used as a filling material (as for cushions)
fi•ber•glass \-ˌglas\ *n* **:** glass in fibrous form used in making various products (as insulation)
fiber optics *n* **1** *pl* **:** thin transparent fibers of glass or plastic that are enclosed by a less refractive material and that transmit light by internal reflection; *also* **:** a bundle of such fibers used in an instrument **2 :** the technique of the use of fiber optics **— fiber–optic** *adj*
fi•bril \ˈfī-brəl, ˈfi-\ *n* **:** a small fiber
fi•bril•la•tion \ˌfi-brə-ˈlā-shən, ˌfī-\ *n* **:** rapid irregular contractions of the heart muscle fibers resulting in a lack of synchronism between heartbeat and pulse **— fib•ril•late** \ˈfi-brə-ˌlāt, ˈfī-\ *vb*
fi•brin \ˈfī-brən\ *n* **:** a white insoluble fibrous protein formed in the clotting of blood
fi•broid \ˈfī-brȯid, ˈfi-\ *adj* **:** resembling, forming, or consisting of fibrous tissue ⟨~ tumors⟩
fi•bro•sis \fī-ˈbrō-səs\ *n* **:** a condition marked by abnormal increase of fiber-containing tissue
fib•u•la \ˈfi-byə-lə\ *n, pl* **-lae** \-lē, -lī\ *or* **-las :** the outer and usu. the smaller of the two bones between the knee and ankle **— fib•u•lar** \-lər\ *adj*

FICA *abbr* Federal Insurance Contributions Act
-fication *n comb form* **:** making **:** production ⟨simpli*fication*⟩
fiche \ˈfēsh\ *n, pl* **fiche :** MICROFICHE
fi•chu \ˈfi-shü\ *n* [F] **:** a woman's light triangular scarf draped over the shoulders and fastened in front
fick•le \ˈfi-kəl\ *adj* **:** not firm or steadfast in disposition or character **:** INCONSTANT **— fick•le•ness** *n*
fic•tion \ˈfik-shən\ *n* **1 :** something (as a story) invented by the imagination **2 :** fictitious literature (as novels) **— fic•tion•al** \-shə-nəl\ *adj* **— fic•tion•al•ly** *adv*
fic•ti•tious \fik-ˈti-shəs\ *adj* **1 :** of, relating to, or characteristic of fiction **:** IMAGINARY **2 :** FEIGNED **syn** chimerical, fanciful, fantastic, unreal
[1]fid•dle \ˈfid-ᵊl\ *n* **:** VIOLIN
[2]fiddle *vb* **fid•dled; fid•dling 1 :** to play on a fiddle **2 :** to move the hands or fingers restlessly **3 :** PUTTER **4 :** MEDDLE, TAMPER **— fid•dler** *n*
fiddler crab *n* **:** any of a genus of burrowing crabs with one claw much enlarged in the male
fid•dle•stick \ˈfid-ᵊl-ˌstik\ *n* **1** *archaic* **:** a violin bow **2** *pl* **:** NONSENSE — used as an interjection
fi•del•i•ty \fə-ˈde-lə-tē, fī-\ *n, pl* **-ties 1 :** the quality or state of being faithful **2 :** ACCURACY ⟨~ in sound reproduction⟩ **syn** allegiance, loyalty, devotion, fealty
[1]fidg•et \ˈfi-jət\ *n* **1** *pl* **:** uneasiness or restlessness as shown by nervous movements **2 :** one that fidgets **— fidg•ety** *adj*
[2]fidget *vb* **:** to move or cause to move or act restlessly or nervously
fi•du•cia•ry \fə-ˈdü-shē-ˌer-ē, -ˈdyü-, -shə-rē\ *adj* **1 :** involving a confidence or trust **2 :** held or holding in trust for another ⟨~ accounts⟩ **— fiduciary** *n*
fie \ˈfī\ *interj* — used to express disgust or disapproval
fief \ˈfēf\ *n* **:** a feudal estate **:** FEE
[1]field \ˈfēld\ *n* **1 :** open country **2 :** a piece of cleared land for cultivation or pasture **3 :** a piece of land yielding some special product **4 :** the place where a battle is fought; *also* **:** BATTLE **5 :** an area, division, or sphere of activity ⟨the ~ of science⟩ ⟨salesmen in the ~⟩ **6 :** an area for military exercises **7 :** an area for sports **8 :** a background on which something is drawn or projected ⟨a flag with white stars on a ~ of blue⟩ **9 :** a region or space in which a given effect (as magnetism) exists **— field** *adj*
[2]field *vb* **1 :** to handle a batted or thrown baseball while on defense **2 :** to put into the field **3 :** to answer satisfactorily ⟨~ a tough question⟩ **— field•er** *n*
field day *n* **1 :** a day devoted to outdoor sports and athletic competition **2 :** a time of extraordinary pleasure or opportunity
field event *n* **:** a track-and-field event (as weight-throwing) other than a race
field glass *n* **:** a hand-held binocular telescope — usu. used in pl.
field hockey *n* **:** a field game played between two teams of 11 players each whose object is to knock a ball into the opponent's goal with a curved stick
field marshal *n* **:** an officer (as in the British army) of the highest rank
field–test \-ˌtest\ *vb* **:** to test (as a new product) in a natural environment **— field test** *n*
fiend \ˈfēnd\ *n* **1 :** DEVIL 1 **2 :** DEMON **3 :** an extremely wicked or cruel person **4 :** a person excessively devoted to a pursuit **5 :** ADDICT ⟨dope ~⟩ **— fiend•ish** *adj* **— fiend•ish•ly** *adv*
fierce \ˈfirs\ *adj* **fierc•er; fierc•est 1 :** violently hostile or aggressive in temperament **2 :** PUGNACIOUS **3 :** INTENSE **4 :** furiously active or determined **5 :** wild or menacing in appearance **syn** ferocious, barbarous, savage, cruel **— fierce•ly** *adv* **— fierce•ness** *n*
fi•ery \ˈfī-ə-rē\ *adj* **fi•er•i•er; -est 1 :** consisting of fire **2 :** BURNING, BLAZING **3 :** FLAMMABLE **4 :** hot like a fire **:** INFLAMED, FEVERISH **5 :** RED **6 :** full of emotion or spirit **7 :** IRRITABLE **— fi•eri•ness** \-rē-nəs\ *n*

fi•es•ta \fē-ˈes-tə\ *n* [Sp] : FESTIVAL
fife \ˈfīf\ *n* [G *Pfeife* pipe, fife] : a small flute
FIFO *abbr* first in, first out
fif•teen \fif-ˈtēn\ *n* : one more than 14 — **fifteen** *adj or pron* — **fif•teenth** \-ˈtēnth\ *adj or n*
fifth \ˈfifth\ *n* **1** : one that is number five in a countable series **2** : one of five equal parts of something **3** : a unit of measure for liquor equal to ⅕ U.S. gallon (0.757 liter) — **fifth** *adj or adv*
fifth column *n* : a group of secret supporters of a nation's enemy that engage in espionage or sabotage within the country — **fifth columnist** *n*
fifth wheel *n* : one that is unnecessary and often burdensome
fif•ty \ˈfif-tē\ *n, pl* **fifties** : five times 10 — **fif•ti•eth** \-tē-əth\ *adj or n* — **fifty** *adj or pron*
fif•ty–fif•ty \ˌfif-tē-ˈfif-tē\ *adj* **1** : shared equally ⟨a ~ proposition⟩ **2** : half favorable and half unfavorable
[1]**fig** \ˈfig\ *n* : a usu. pear-shaped edible fruit of warm regions; *also* : a tree related to the mulberry that bears this fruit

fig: leaves and fruit

[2]**fig** *abbr* **1** figurative; figuratively **2** figure
[1]**fight** \ˈfīt\ *vb* **fought** \ˈfȯt\; **fight•ing** **1** : to contend against another in battle or physical combat **2** : BOX **3** : to put forth a determined effort **4** : STRUGGLE, CONTEND **5** : to attempt to prevent the success or effectiveness of **6** : WAGE **7** : to gain by struggle
[2]**fight** *n* **1** : a hostile encounter : BATTLE **2** : a boxing match **3** : a verbal disagreement **4** : a struggle for a goal or an objective **5** : strength or disposition for fighting ⟨full of ~⟩
fight•er \ˈfī-tər\ *n* **1** : one that fights; *esp* : WARRIOR **2** : BOXER **3** : a fast maneuverable warplane for destroying enemy aircraft
fig•ment \ˈfig-mənt\ *n* : something imagined or made up
fig•u•ra•tion \ˌfi-gyə-ˈrā-shən, -gə-\ *n* **1** : FORM, OUTLINE **2** : an act or instance of representation in figures and shapes
fig•u•ra•tive \ˈfi-gyə-rə-tiv, -gə-\ *adj* **1** : EMBLEMATIC **2** : SYMBOLIC, METAPHORICAL ⟨~ language⟩ — **fig•u•ra•tive•ly** *adv*
[1]**fig•ure** \ˈfi-gyər, -gər-\ *n* **1** : NUMERAL **2** *pl* : arithmetical calculations **3** : a written or printed character **4** : PRICE, SUM **5** : a combination of points, lines, or surfaces in geometry ⟨a circle is a closed plane ~⟩ **6** : SHAPE, FORM, OUTLINE **7** : the graphic representation of a form esp. of a person **8** : a diagram or pictorial illustration of textual matter **9** : PATTERN, DESIGN **10** : appearance made or impression produced ⟨they cut quite a ~⟩ **11** : a series of movements (as in a dance) **12** : PERSONAGE
[2]**figure** *vb* **fig•ured; fig•ur•ing** **1** : to represent by or as if by a figure or outline **2** : to decorate with a pattern **3** : to indicate or represent by numerals **4** : REGARD, CONSIDER **5** : to be or appear important or conspicuous **6** : COMPUTE, CALCULATE
fig•ure•head \ˈfi-gyər-ˌhed, -gər-\ *n* **1** : a figure on the bow of a ship **2** : a head or chief in name only
figure of speech : a form of expression (as a simile or metaphor) that often compares or identifies one thing with another to convey meaning or heighten effect
figure out *vb* **1** : FIND OUT, DISCOVER **2** : SOLVE
fig•u•rine \ˌfi-gyə-ˈrēn, -gə-\ *n* : a small carved or molded figure
Fi•ji•an \ˈfē-ˌjē-ən, fi-ˈjē-ən\ *n* : a native or inhabitant of the Pacific island country of Fiji — **Fijian** *adj*
fil•a•ment \ˈfi-lə-mənt\ *n* : a fine thread or threadlike object, part, or process — **fil•a•men•tous** \ˌfi-lə-ˈmen-təs\ *adj*
fil•bert \ˈfil-bərt\ *n* : the sweet thick-shelled nut of either of two European hazels; *also* : a shrub or small tree bearing filberts
filch \ˈfilch\ *vb* : to steal furtively
[1]**file** \ˈfīl\ *n* : a usu. steel tool with a ridged or toothed surface used esp. for smoothing a hard substance
[2]**file** *vb* **filed; fil•ing** : to rub, smooth, or cut away with a file
[3]**file** *vb* **filed; fil•ing** [ME, fr. MF *filer* to string documents on a string or wire, fr. *fil* thread, fr. L *filum*] **1** : to arrange in order **2** : to enter or record officially or as prescribed by law ⟨~ a lawsuit⟩ **3** : to send (copy) to a newspaper
[4]**file** *n* **1** : a device (as a folder or cabinet) by means of which papers may be kept in order **2** : a collection of papers or publications usu. arranged or classified **3** : a collection of data (as text) treated by a computer as a unit
[5]**file** *n* : a row of persons, animals, or things arranged one behind the other
[6]**file** *vb* **filed; fil•ing** : to march or proceed in file
fi•let mi•gnon \ˌfi-(ˌ)lā-mēn-ˈyō^{n}, fi-ˌlā-\ *n, pl* **filets mignons** \-(ˌ)lā-mēn-ˈyō^{n}z, -ˌlā-\ [F, lit., dainty fillet] : a thick slice of beef cut from the narrow end of a beef tenderloin
fil•ial \ˈfi-lē-əl, ˈfil-yəl\ *adj* : of, relating to, or befitting a son or daughter
fil•i•bus•ter \ˈfi-lə-ˌbəs-tər\ *n* [Sp *filibustero*, lit., freebooter] **1** : a military adventurer; *esp* : an American engaged in fomenting 19th century Latin American uprisings **2** : the use of delaying tactics (as extremely long speeches) esp. in a legislative assembly; *also* : an instance of this practice — **filibuster** *vb* — **fil•i•bus•ter•er** *n*
fil•i•gree \ˈfi-lə-ˌgrē\ *n* [F *filigrane*] : ornamental openwork (as of fine wire) — **fil•i•greed** \-ˌgrēd\ *adj*
fil•ing \ˈfī-liŋ\ *n* **1** : the act or instance of using a file **2** : a small piece scraped off by a file ⟨iron ~*s*⟩
Fil•i•pi•no \ˌfi-lə-ˈpē-nō\ *n, pl* **Filipinos** : a native or inhabitant of the Philippines — **Filipino** *adj*
[1]**fill** \ˈfil\ *vb* **1** : to make or become full **2** : to stop up : PLUG ⟨~ a cavity⟩ **3** : FEED, SATIATE **4** : SATISFY, FULFILL ⟨~ all requirements⟩ **5** : to occupy fully **6** : to spread through ⟨laughter ~*ed* the room⟩ **7** : OCCUPY ⟨~ the office of president⟩ **8** : to put a person in ⟨~ a vacancy⟩ **9** : to supply as directed ⟨~ a prescription⟩
[2]**fill** *n* **1** : a full supply; *esp* : a quantity that satisfies or satiates **2** : material used esp. for filling a low place
[1]**fill•er** \ˈfi-lər\ *n* **1** : one that fills **2** : a substance added to another substance (as to increase bulk or weight) **3** : a material used for filling cracks and pores in wood before painting
[2]**fil•ler** \ˈfi-ˌler\ *n, pl* **fillers** *or* **filler** — see *forint* at MONEY table
[1]**fil•let** \ˈfi-lət, *in sense 2* fi-ˈlā, ˈfi-(ˌ)lā\ *also* **fi•let** \fi-ˈlā, ˈfi-(ˌ)lā\ *n* [ME *filet*, fr. MF, dim. of *fil* thread] **1** : a narrow band, strip, or ribbon **2** : a piece or slice of boneless meat or fish; *esp* : the tenderloin of beef
[2]**fil•let** \ˈfi-lət, *in sense 2 also* fi-ˈlā, ˈfi-(ˌ)lā\ *vb* **1** : to bind or adorn with or as if with a fillet **2** : to cut into fillets
fill in *vb* **1** : to provide necessary or recent information **2** : to serve as a temporary substitute

DICTIONARY

fill·ing \ˈfi-liŋ\ *n* **1** : material used to fill something ⟨a ~ for a tooth⟩ **2** : the yarn interlacing the warp in a fabric **3** : a food mixture used to fill pastry or sandwiches

filling station *n* : SERVICE STATION

fil·lip \ˈfi-ləp\ *n* **1** : a blow or gesture made by a flick or snap of the finger across the thumb **2** : something that serves to arouse or excite — **fillip** *vb*

fill–up \ˈfil-ˌəp\ *n* : an act or instance of filling something

fil·ly \ˈfi-lē\ *n, pl* **fillies** : a young female horse usu. less than four years old

¹film \ˈfilm\ *n* **1** : a thin skin or membrane **2** : a thin coating or layer **3** : a flexible strip of chemically treated material used in taking pictures **4** : MOTION PICTURE — **filmy** *adj*

²film *vb* **1** : to cover with a film **2** : to make a motion picture of

film·dom \ˈfilm-dəm\ *n* : the motion-picture industry

film·og·ra·phy \fil-ˈmä-grə-fē\ *n, pl* **-phies** : a list of motion pictures featuring the work of a film figure or a particular topic

film·strip \ˈfilm-ˌstrip\ *n* : a strip of film bearing a sequence of images for projection as still pictures

fils \ˈfils\ *n, pl* **fils** — see *dinar, dirham, rial* at MONEY table

¹fil·ter \ˈfil-tər\ *n* **1** : a porous material through which a fluid is passed to separate out matter in suspension; *also* : a device containing such material **2** : a device for suppressing waves of certain frequencies; *esp* : one (as for a camera) that absorbs light of certain colors

²filter *vb* **1** : to remove by means of a filter **2** : to pass through a filter — **fil·ter·able** *also* **fil·tra·ble** \-tə-rə-bəl, -trə-\ *adj* — **fil·tra·tion** \fil-ˈtrā-shən\ *n*

filth \ˈfilth\ *n* [ME, fr. OE *fȳlth*, fr. *fūl* foul] **1** : foul matter; *esp* : loathsome dirt or refuse **2** : moral corruption **3** : OBSCENITY — **filth·i·ness** *n* — **filthy** \ˈfil-thē\ *adj*

fil·trate \ˈfil-ˌtrāt\ *n* : fluid that has passed through a filter

¹fin \ˈfin\ *n* **1** : one of the thin external processes by which an aquatic animal (as a fish) moves through water **2** : a fin-shaped part (as on an airplane) **3** : FLIPPER 2 — **finned** \ˈfind\ *adj*

²fin *abbr* **1** finance; financial **2** finish

fi·na·gle \fə-ˈnā-gəl\ *vb* **-gled; -gling 1** : to obtain by indirect or dishonest means : WANGLE **2** : to use devious dishonest methods to achieve one's ends — **fi·na·gler** *n*

¹fi·nal \ˈfī-ⁿl\ *adj* **1** : not to be altered or undone **2** : ULTIMATE **3** : relating to or occurring at the end or conclusion — **fi·nal·i·ty** \fī-ˈna-lə-tē, fə-\ *n* — **fi·nal·ly** *adv*

²final *n* **1** : a deciding match or game — usu. used in pl. **2** : the last examination in a course — often used in pl.

fi·na·le \fə-ˈna-lē, fi-ˈnä-\ *n* : the close or end of something; *esp* : the last section of a musical composition

fi·nal·ise *Brit var of* FINALIZE

fi·nal·ist \ˈfī-ⁿl-əst\ *n* : a contestant in the finals of a competition

fi·nal·ize \ˈfī-ⁿl-ˌīz\ *vb* **-ized; -iz·ing** : to put in final or finished form

¹fi·nance \fə-ˈnans, ˈfī-ˌnans\ *n* [ME, payment, ransom, fr. MF, fr. *finer* to end, pay, fr. *fin* end, fr. L *finis* boundary, end] **1** *pl* : money resources available esp. to a government or business **2** : management of money affairs

²finance *vb* **fi·nanced; fi·nanc·ing 1** : to raise or provide funds for **2** : to furnish with necessary funds **3** : to sell or supply on credit

finance company *n* : a company that makes usu. small short-term loans usu. to individuals

fi·nan·cial \fə-ˈnan-chəl, fī-\ *adj* : relating to finance or financiers — **fi·nan·cial·ly** *adv*

fi·nan·cier \ˌfi-nən-ˈsir, ˌfī-ˌnan-\ *n* **1** : a person skilled in managing public moneys **2** : a person who deals with large-scale finance and investment

finch \ˈfinch\ *n* : any of numerous songbirds with strong conical bills

¹find \ˈfīnd\ *vb* **found** \ˈfau̇nd\; **find·ing 1** : to meet with either by chance or by searching or study : ENCOUNTER, DISCOVER **2** : to obtain by effort or management ⟨~ time to read⟩ **3** : to arrive at : REACH ⟨the bullet *found* its mark⟩ **4** : EXPERIENCE, FEEL ⟨*found* happiness⟩ **5** : to gain or regain the use of ⟨*found* his voice again⟩ **6** : to determine and make a statement about ⟨~ a verdict⟩

²find *n* **1** : an act or instance of finding **2** : something found; *esp* : a valuable item of discovery

find·er \ˈfīn-dər\ *n* : one that finds; *esp* : VIEWFINDER

fin de siè·cle \ˌfaⁿ-də-sē-ˈeklᵊ\ *adj* [F, end of century] : of, relating to, or characteristic of the close of the 19th century

find·ing \ˈfīn-diŋ\ *n* **1** : the act of finding **2** : FIND 2 **3** : the result of a judicial proceeding or inquiry

find out *vb* : to learn by study, observation, or search : DISCOVER

¹fine \ˈfīn\ *n* : money exacted as a penalty for an offense

²fine *vb* **fined; fin·ing** : to impose a fine on : punish by a fine

³fine *adj* **fin·er; fin·est 1** : free from impurity **2** : very thin in gauge or texture **3** : not coarse **4** : SUBTLE, SENSITIVE ⟨a ~ distinction⟩ **5** : superior in quality or appearance **6** : ELEGANT, REFINED — **fine·ly** *adv* — **fine·ness** *n*

⁴fine *adv* : FINELY

fine art *n* : art (as painting, sculpture, or music) concerned primarily with the creation of beautiful objects — usu. used in pl.

fin·ery \ˈfī-nə-rē\ *n, pl* **-er·ies** : ORNAMENT, DECORATION; *esp* : showy clothing and jewels

fine·spun \ˈfīn-ˈspən\ *adj* : developed with extremely or excessively fine delicacy or detail

fi·nesse \fə-ˈnes\ *n* **1** : refinement or delicacy of workmanship, structure, or texture **2** : CUNNING, SUBTLETY — **finesse** *vb*

fine–tune \ˈfīn-ˈtün\ *vb* : to adjust so as to bring to the highest level of performance or effectiveness

fin·fish \ˈfin-ˌfish\ *n* : FISH 2

¹fin·ger \ˈfiŋ-gər\ *n* **1** : any of the five divisions at the end of the hand; *esp* : one other than the thumb **2** : something that resembles or does the work of a finger **3** : a part of a glove into which a finger is inserted

²finger *vb* **fin·gered; fin·ger·ing 1** : to touch or feel with the fingers : HANDLE **2** : to perform with the fingers or with a certain fingering **3** : to mark the notes of a piece of music as a guide in playing **4** : to point out

fin·ger·board \ˈfiŋ-gər-ˌbōrd\ *n* : the part of a stringed instrument against which the fingers press the strings to vary the pitch

finger bowl *n* : a small water bowl for rinsing the fingers at the table

fin·ger·ing \ˈfiŋ-gə-riŋ\ *n* **1** : handling or touching with the fingers **2** : the act or method of using the fingers in playing an instrument **3** : the marking of the method of fingering

fin·ger·ling \ˈfiŋ-gər-liŋ\ *n* : a small fish

fin·ger·nail \ˈfiŋ-gər-ˌnāl\ *n* : the nail of a finger

fin·ger·print \-ˌprint\ *n* : the pattern of marks made by pressing the tip of a finger or thumb on a surface; *esp* : an ink impression of such a pattern taken for the purpose of identification — **fingerprint** *vb*

fin·ger·tip \-ˌtip\ *n* : the tip of a finger

fin·i·al \ˈfi-nē-əl\ *n* : an ornamental projection or end (as on a spire)

fin·ick·ing \ˈfi-ni-kiŋ\ *adj* : FINICKY

fin·icky \ˈfi-ni-kē\ *adj* : excessively particular in taste or standards

fi·nis \ˈfi-nəs\ *n* : END, CONCLUSION

¹fin·ish \ˈfi-nish\ *vb* **1** : TERMINATE **2** : to use or dispose of entirely **3** : to bring to completion : ACCOMPLISH **4** : to put a final coat or surface on **5** : to come to the end of a course or undertaking — **fin•ish•er** *n*

²finish *n* **1** : END, CONCLUSION **2** : something that completes or perfects **3** : the final treatment or coating of a surface

fi•nite \ˈfī-ˌnīt\ *adj* **1** : having definite or definable limits; *also* : having a limited nature or existence **2** : being less than some positive integer in number or measure and greater than its negative **3** : showing distinction of grammatical person and number ⟨a ~ verb⟩

fink \ˈfiŋk\ *n* **1** : a contemptible person **2** : STRIKEBREAKER **3** : INFORMER

Finn \ˈfin\ *n* : a native or inhabitant of Finland

fin•nan had•die \ˌfi-nən-ˈha-dē\ *n* : smoked haddock

¹Finn•ish \ˈfi-nish\ *adj* : of or relating to Finland, the Finns, or Finnish

²Finnish *n* : the language of Finland

fin•ny \ˈfi-nē\ *adj* **1** : having or characterized by fins **2** : relating to or being fish

fiord *var of* FJORD

fir \ˈfər\ *n* : any of a genus of erect evergreen trees related to the pines; *also* : the light soft wood of a fir

¹fire \ˈfīr\ *n* **1** : the light or heat and esp. the flame of something burning **2** : ENTHUSIASM, ZEAL **3** : fuel that is burning (as in a stove or fireplace) **4** : destructive burning (as of a house) **5** : the firing of weapons — **fire•less** *adj*

²fire *vb* **fired; fir•ing 1** : KINDLE, IGNITE ⟨~ a house⟩ **2** : STIR, ENLIVEN ⟨~ the imagination⟩ **3** : to dismiss from employment **4** : SHOOT ⟨~ a gun⟩ ⟨~ an arrow⟩ **5** : BAKE ⟨*firing* pottery in a kiln⟩ **6** : to apply fire or fuel to something ⟨~ a furnace⟩

fire ant *n* : either of two small fiercely stinging South American ants that are pests in the southeastern U.S. esp. in fields used to grow crops

fire•arm \ˈfīr-ˌärm\ *n* : a weapon (as a pistol) from which a shot is discharged by gunpowder

fire•ball \-ˌbȯl\ *n* **1** : a ball of fire **2** : a very bright meteor **3** : the highly luminous cloud of vapor and dust created by a nuclear explosion **4** : a highly energetic person

fire•boat \-ˌbōt\ *n* : a boat equipped for fighting fires

fire•bomb \-ˌbäm\ *n* : an incendiary bomb — **firebomb** *vb*

fire•box \-ˌbäks\ *n* **1** : a chamber (as of a furnace) that contains a fire **2** : a box containing a fire alarm

fire•brand \-ˌbrand\ *n* **1** : a piece of burning wood **2** : a person who creates unrest or strife : AGITATOR

fire•break \-ˌbrāk\ *n* : a barrier of cleared or plowed land intended to check a forest or grass fire

fire•bug \-ˌbəg\ *n* : a person who deliberately sets destructive fires

fire•crack•er \-ˌkra-kər\ *n* : a paper tube containing an explosive and a fuse and set off to make a noise

fire department *n* : an organization for preventing or extinguishing fires; *also* : its members

fire engine *n* : a motor vehicle with equipment for extinguishing fires

fire escape *n* : a stairway or ladder for escape from a burning building

fire•fight•er \ˈfīr-ˌfī-tər\ *n* : a person who fights fires; *esp* : a member of a fire department

fire•fly \-ˌflī\ *n* : any of various small night-flying beetles that produce flashes of light for courtship purposes

fire•house \-ˌhau̇s\ *n* : FIRE STATION

fire irons *n pl* : tools for tending a fire esp. in a fireplace

fire•man \ˈfīr-mən\ *n* **1** : STOKER **2** : FIREFIGHTER

fire off *vb* : to write and send

fire•place \-ˌplās\ *n* **1** : a framed opening made in a chimney to hold an open fire **2** : an outdoor structure of brick or stone for an open fire

fire•plug \-ˌpləg\ *n* : HYDRANT

fire•pow•er \-ˌpau̇-ər\ *n* : the ability to deliver gunfire or warheads on a target

¹fire•proof \-ˈprüf\ *adj* : resistant to fire

²fireproof *vb* : to make fireproof

fire screen *n* : a protective screen before a fireplace

¹fire•side \ˈfīr-ˌsīd\ *n* **1** : a place near the fire or hearth **2** : HOME

²fireside *adj* : having an informal or intimate quality

fire station *n* : a building housing fire engines and usu. firefighters

fire•storm \ˈfīr-ˌstȯrm\ *n* **1** : a large destructive very hot fire **2** : a sudden or violent outburst ⟨~ of criticism⟩

fire tower *n* : a tower (as in a forest) from which a watch for fires is kept

fire•trap \ˈfīr-ˌtrap\ *n* : a building or place apt to catch on fire or difficult to escape from in case of fire

fire truck *n* : FIRE ENGINE

fire•wa•ter \ˈfīr-ˌwȯ-tər, -ˌwä-\ *n* : intoxicating liquor

fire•wood \-ˌwu̇d\ *n* : wood used for fuel

fire•work \-ˌwərk\ *n* : a device designed to produce a display of light, noise, and smoke by the burning of explosive or flammable materials

firing line *n* **1** : a line from which fire is delivered against a target **2** : the forefront of an activity

¹firm \ˈfərm\ *adj* **1** : securely fixed in place **2** : SOLID, VIGOROUS ⟨a ~ handshake⟩ **3** : having a solid or compact texture **4** : not subject to change or fluctuation : STEADY ⟨~ prices⟩ **5** : STEADFAST **6** : indicating firmness or resolution — **firm•ly** *adv* — **firm•ness** *n*

²firm *vb* : to make or become firm

³firm *n* [G *Firma,* fr. It, signature, ultim. fr. L *firmare* to make firm, confirm] **1** : the name under which a company transacts business **2** : a business partnership of two or more persons **3** : a business enterprise

fir•ma•ment \ˈfər-mə-mənt\ *n* : the arch of the sky : HEAVENS

firm•ware \ˈfirm-ˌwar\ *n* : computer programs contained permanently in a hardware device

¹first \ˈfərst\ *adj* : preceding all others as in time, order, or importance

²first *adv* **1** : before any other **2** : for the first time **3** : in preference to something else

³first *n* **1** : number one in a countable series **2** : something that is first **3** : the lowest forward gear in an automotive vehicle **4** : the winning or highest place in a competition or examination

first aid *n* : emergency care or treatment given an injured or ill person

first•born \ˈfərst-ˈbȯrn\ *adj* : ELDEST — **firstborn** *n*

first class *n* : the best or highest group in a classification — **first–class** *adj or adv*

first•hand \ˈfərst-ˈhand\ *adj* : coming from direct personal observation or experience — **firsthand** *adv*

first lady *n, often cap F&L* : the wife or hostess of the chief executive of a political unit (as a country)

first lieutenant *n* : a commissioned officer (as in the army) ranking next below a captain

first•ling \ˈfərst-liŋ\ *n* : one that comes or is produced first

first•ly \-lē\ *adv* : in the first place : FIRST

¹first–rate \-ˈrāt\ *adj* : of the first order of size, importance, or quality

²first–rate *adv* : very well

first sergeant *n* **1** : a noncommissioned officer serving as the chief assistant to the commander of a military unit **2** : a rank in the army below a command sergeant major and in the marine corps below a sergeant major

first strike *n* : a preemptive nuclear attack

first–string \ˈfərst-ˈstriŋ\ *adj* : being a regular as distinguished from a substitute

firth \ˈfərth\ *n* [ME, fr. ON *fjǫrthr*] : ESTUARY

fis•cal \ˈfis-kəl\ *adj* [L *fiscalis,* fr. *fiscus* basket, treasury] **1** : of or relating to taxation, public revenues, or public debt **2** : of or relating to financial matters — **fis•cal•ly** *adv*

[1]fish \ˈfish\ *n, pl* **fish** *or* **fish·es 1 :** a water-dwelling animal — usu. used in combination ⟨star*fish*⟩ ⟨shell*fish*⟩ **2 :** any of numerous cold-blooded water-breathing vertebrates with fins, gills, and usu. scales that include the bony fishes and usu. the cartilaginous and jawless fishes **3 :** the flesh of fish used as food
[2]fish *vb* **1 :** to attempt to catch fish **2 :** to seek something by roundabout means ⟨~ for praise⟩ **3 :** to search for something underwater **4 :** to engage in a search by groping **5 :** to draw forth
fish–and–chips *n pl* **:** fried fish and french fried potatoes
fish·bowl \ˈfish-ˌbōl\ *n* **1 :** a bowl for the keeping of live fish **2 :** a place or condition that affords no privacy
fish·er \ˈfi-shər\ *n* **1 :** one that fishes **2 :** a large dark brown No. American arboreal carnivorous mammal related to the weasels
fish·er·man \-mən\ *n* **:** a person engaged in fishing; *also* **:** a fishing boat
fish·ery \ˈfi-shə-rē\ *n, pl* **-er·ies :** the business of catching fish; *also* **:** a place for catching fish
fish·hook \ˈfish-ˌhu̇k\ *n* **:** a usu. barbed hook for catching fish
fish ladder *n* **:** an arrangement of pools in steps by which fish can pass over a dam
fish·net \ˈfish-ˌnet\ *n* **:** netting for catching fish **2 :** a coarse open-mesh fabric
fish·tail \-ˌtāl\ *vb* **:** to have the rear end slide from side to side out of control while moving forward
fish·wife \-ˌwīf\ *n* **1 :** a woman who sells fish **2 :** a vulgar abusive woman
fishy \ˈfi-shē\ *adj* **fish·i·er; -est 1 :** of or resembling fish **2 :** QUESTIONABLE
fis·sion \ˈfi-shən, -zhən\ *n* [L *fissio*, fr. *findere* to split] **1 :** a cleaving into parts **2 :** a method of reproduction in which a living cell or body divides into two or more parts each of which grows into a whole new individual **3 :** the splitting of an atomic nucleus resulting in the release of large amounts of energy — **fis·sion·able** \ˈfi-shə-nə-bəl, -zhə-\ *adj*
fis·sure \ˈfi-shər\ *n* **:** a narrow opening or crack
fist \ˈfist\ *n* **1 :** the hand with fingers folded into the palm **2 :** INDEX 6
fist·ful \ˈfist-ˌfu̇l\ *n* **:** HANDFUL
fist·i·cuffs \ˈfis-ti-ˌkəfs\ *n pl* **:** a fight with usu. bare fists
fis·tu·la \ˈfis-chə-lə\ *n, pl* **-las** *or* **-lae :** an abnormal passage leading from an abscess or hollow organ — **fis·tu·lous** \-ləs\ *adj*
[1]fit \ˈfit\ *adj* **fit·ter; fit·test 1 :** adapted to a purpose **:** APPROPRIATE **2 :** PROPER, RIGHT **3 :** PREPARED, READY **4 :** physically and mentally sound — **fit·ly** *adv* — **fit·ness** *n*
[2]fit *n* **1 :** a sudden violent attack (as of bodily disorder) **2 :** a sudden outburst
[3]fit *vb* **fit·ted** *also* **fit; fit·ting 1 :** to be suitable for or to **2 :** to be correctly adjusted to or shaped for **3 :** to insert or adjust until correctly in place **4 :** to make a place or room for **5 :** to be in agreement or accord with **6 :** PREPARE **7 :** ADJUST **8 :** SUPPLY, EQUIP ⟨*fitted* out with gear⟩ **9 :** BELONG — **fit·ter** *n*
[4]fit *n* **:** the fact, condition, or manner of fitting or being fitted
fit·ful \ˈfit-fəl\ *adj* **:** not regular **:** INTERMITTENT ⟨~ sleep⟩ — **fit·ful·ly** *adv*
[1]fit·ting \ˈfi-tiŋ\ *adj* **:** APPROPRIATE, SUITABLE — **fit·ting·ly** *adv*
[2]fitting *n* **1 :** the action or act of one that fits; *esp* **:** a trying on of clothes being made or altered **2 :** a small often standardized part ⟨a plumbing ~⟩
five \ˈfīv\ *n* **1 :** one more than four **2 :** the 5th in a set or series **3 :** something having five units; *esp* **:** a basketball team **4 :** a 5-dollar bill — **five** *adj or pron*
[1]fix \ˈfiks\ *vb* **1 :** to make firm, stable, or fast **2 :** to give a permanent or final form to **3 :** AFFIX, ATTACH **4 :** to hold or direct steadily ⟨~*es* his eyes on the horizon⟩ **5 :** ESTABLISH, SET **6 :** ASSIGN ⟨~ the blame⟩ **7 :** to set in order **:** ADJUST **8 :** PREPARE **9 :** to make whole or sound again **10 :** to get even with **11 :** to influence by improper or illegal methods ⟨~ a race⟩ — **fix·er** *n*
[2]fix *n* **1 :** PREDICAMENT **2 :** a determination of position (as of a ship) **3 :** an accurate determination or understanding **4 :** an act of improper influence **5 :** a supply or dose of something (as an addictive drug) strongly desired or craved **6 :** something that fixes or restores
fix·a·tion \fik-ˈsā-shən\ *n* **:** an obsessive or unhealthy preoccupation or attachment — **fix·ate** \ˈfik-ˌsāt\ *vb*
fix·a·tive \ˈfik-sə-tiv\ *n* **:** something that stabilizes or sets
fixed \ˈfikst\ *adj* **1 :** securely placed or fastened **:** STATIONARY **2 :** not volatile **3 :** SETTLED, FINAL **4 :** INTENT, CONCENTRATED ⟨a ~ stare⟩ **5 :** supplied with a definite amount of something needed (as money) — **fixed·ly** \ˈfik-səd-lē\ *adv* — **fixed·ness** \ˈfik-səd-nəs\ *n*
fix·i·ty \ˈfik-sə-tē\ *n, pl* **-ties :** the quality or state of being fixed or stable
fix·ture \ˈfiks-chər\ *n* **1 :** something firmly attached as a permanent part of some other thing **2 :** a familiar feature in a particular setting; *esp* **:** a person associated with a place or activity
[1]fizz \ˈfiz\ *vb* **:** to make a hissing or sputtering sound
[2]fizz *n* **:** an effervescent beverage
[1]fiz·zle \ˈfi-zəl\ *vb* **fiz·zled; fiz·zling 1 :** FIZZ **2 :** to fail after a good start — often used with *out*
[2]fizzle *n* **:** FAILURE
fjord \fē-ˈȯrd\ *n* [Norw] **:** a narrow inlet of the sea between cliffs or steep slopes

fjord

fl *abbr* **1** [L *floruit*] flourished **2** fluid
FL *or* **Fla** *abbr* Florida
flab \ˈflab\ *n* **:** soft flabby body tissue
flab·ber·gast \ˈfla-bər-ˌgast\ *vb* **:** ASTOUND
flab·by \ˈfla-bē\ *adj* **flab·bi·er; -est :** lacking firmness **:** FLACCID ⟨~ muscles⟩ — **flab·bi·ness** \-bē-nəs\ *n*
flac·cid \ˈflak-səd\ *adj* **:** deficient in firmness ⟨~ plant stems⟩
[1]flag \ˈflag\ *n* **:** any of various irises; *esp* **:** a wild iris
[2]flag *n* **1 :** a usu. rectangular piece of fabric of distinctive design that is used as a symbol (as of a nation) or as a signaling device **2 :** something used like a flag to signal or attract attention **3 :** one of the cross strokes of a musical note less than a quarter note in value
[3]flag *vb* **flagged; flag·ging 1 :** to signal with or as if with a flag; *esp* **:** to signal to stop ⟨~ a taxi⟩ **2 :** to put a flag on **3 :** to call a penalty on
[4]flag *vb* **flagged; flag·ging 1 :** to hang loose or limp **2 :** to become unsteady, feeble, or spiritless **3 :** to decline in interest or attraction ⟨the topic *flagged*⟩
[5]flag *n* **:** a hard flat stone suitable for paving
flag·el·late \ˈfla-jə-ˌlāt\ *vb* **-lat·ed; -lat·ing :** to punish by whipping — **flag·el·la·tion** \ˌfla-jə-ˈlā-shən\ *n*
fla·gel·lum \flə-ˈje-ləm\ *n, pl* **-la** \-lə\ *also* **-lums :** a

long whiplike process that is the primary organ of motion of many microorganisms — **fla•gel•lar** \-lər\ *adj*

fla•geo•let \ˌfla-jə-ˈlet, -ˈlā\ *n* [F] : a small woodwind instrument belonging to the flute class

fla•gi•tious \flə-ˈji-shəs\ *adj* : grossly wicked : VILLAINOUS

flag•on \ˈfla-gən\ *n* : a container for liquids usu. with a handle, spout, and lid

flag•pole \ˈflag-ˌpōl\ *n* : a pole on which to raise a flag

fla•grant \ˈflā-grənt\ *adj* [L *flagrans*, prp. of *flagrare* to burn] : conspicuously bad — **fla•grant•ly** *adv*

fla•gran•te de•lic•to \flə-ˌgran-tē-di-ˈlik-tō\ *adv or adj* [ML, lit., while the crime is blazing] : in the very act of committing a misdeed; *also* : in the midst of sexual activity

flag•ship \ˈflag-ˌship\ *n* **1** : the ship that carries the commander of a fleet or subdivision thereof and flies his flag **2** : the most important one of a group

flag•staff \-ˌstaf\ *n* : FLAGPOLE

flag•stone \-ˌstōn\ *n* : ⁵FLAG

¹**flail** \ˈflāl\ *n* : a tool for threshing grain by hand

²**flail** *vb* : to strike or swing with or as if with a flail

flair \ˈflar\ *n* [F, lit., sense of smell, fr. OF, odor, fr. *flairier* to give off an odor, fr. (assumed) VL *flagrare*, fr. L *fragrare*] **1** : ability to appreciate or make good use of something : BENT, TALENT **2** : a unique style

flak \ˈflak\ *n, pl* **flak** [G, fr. *Fliegerabwehrkanonen*, fr. *Flieger* flyer + *Abwehr* defense + *Kanonen* cannons] **1** : antiaircraft guns or bursting shells fired from them **2** : CRITICISM, OPPOSITION

¹**flake** \ˈflāk\ *n* **1** : a small loose mass or bit **2** : a thin flattened piece or layer : CHIP — **flaky** *adj*

²**flake** *vb* **flaked; flak•ing** : to form or separate into flakes

³**flake** *n* : a markedly eccentric person : ODDBALL — **flak•i•ness** \ˈflā-kē-nəs\ *n* — **flaky** *adj*

flam•beau \ˈflam-ˌbō\ *n, pl* **flambeaux** \-ˌbōz\ *or* **flambeaus** [F, fr. MF, fr. *flambe* flame] : a flaming torch

flam•boy•ant \flam-ˈbȯi-ənt\ *adj* : marked by or given to strikingly elaborate or colorful display or behavior — **flam•boy•ance** \-əns\ *n* — **flam•boy•an•cy** \-ən-sē\ *n* — **flam•boy•ant•ly** *adv*

flame \ˈflām\ *n* **1** : the glowing gaseous part of a fire **2** : a state of blazing combustion **3** : a flamelike condition **4** : burning zeal or passion **5** : BRILLIANCE **6** : SWEETHEART — **flame** *vb*

fla•men•co \flə-ˈmeŋ-kō\ *n, pl* **-cos** [Sp, fr. *flamenco* of the Gypsies, lit., Flemish, fr. MD *Vlaminc* Fleming] : a vigorous rhythmic dance style of the Spanish Gypsies

flame•throw•er \ˈflām-ˌthrō-ər\ *n* : a device that expels from a nozzle a burning stream of liquid or semiliquid fuel under pressure

fla•min•go \flə-ˈmiŋ-gō\ *n, pl* **-gos** *also* **-goes** : any of several long-legged long-necked tropical water birds with scarlet wings and a broad bill bent downward

flam•ma•ble \ˈfla-mə-bəl\ *adj* : easily ignited and quick-burning — **flam•ma•bil•i•ty** \ˌfla-mə-ˈbi-lə-tē\ *n* — **flammable** *n*

flange \ˈflanj\ *n* : a rim used for strengthening or guiding something or for attachment to another object

¹**flank** \ˈflaŋk\ *n* **1** : the fleshy part of the side between the ribs and the hip; *also* : the side of a quadruped **2** : SIDE **3** : the right or left of a formation

²**flank** *vb* **1** : to attack or threaten the flank of **2** : to be situated on the side of : BORDER

flank•er \ˈflaŋ-kər\ *n* : a football player stationed wide of the formation slightly behind the line of scrimmage as a pass receiver

flan•nel \ˈflan-ᵊl\ *n* **1** : a soft twilled wool or worsted fabric with a napped surface **2** : a stout cotton fabric napped on one side **3** *pl* : flannel underwear or trousers

¹**flap** \ˈflap\ *n* **1** : a stroke with something broad : SLAP **2** : something broad, limber, or flat and usu. thin that hangs loose **3** : the motion or sound of something broad and limber as it swings to and fro **4** : a state of excitement or confusion

²**flap** *vb* **flapped; flap•ping 1** : to beat with something broad and flat **2** : FLING **3** : to move (as wings) with a beating motion **4** : to sway loosely usu. with a noise of striking

flap•jack \ˈflap-ˌjak\ *n* : PANCAKE

flap•per \ˈfla-pər\ *n* **1** : one that flaps **2** : a young woman of the 1920s who showed freedom from conventions (as in conduct)

¹**flare** \ˈflar\ *vb* **flared; flar•ing 1** : to flame with a sudden unsteady light **2** : to become suddenly excited or angry ⟨~ up⟩ **3** : to spread outward

²**flare** *n* **1** : an unsteady glaring light **2** : a blaze of light used esp. to signal or illuminate; *also* : a device for producing such a blaze

flare–up \-ˌəp\ *n* : a sudden outburst or intensification

¹**flash** \ˈflash\ *vb* **1** : to break forth in or like a sudden flame **2** : to appear or pass suddenly or with great speed **3** : to send out in or as if in flashes ⟨~ a message⟩ **4** : to make a sudden display (as of brilliance or feeling) **5** : to gleam or glow intermittently **6** : to fill by a sudden rush of water **7** : to expose to view very briefly ⟨~ a badge⟩ **syn** glance, glint, sparkle, twinkle — **flash•er** *n*

²**flash** *n* **1** : a sudden burst of light **2** : a movement of a flag or light in signaling **3** : a sudden and brilliant burst (as of wit) **4** : a brief time **5** : SHOW, DISPLAY; *esp* : ostentatious display **6** : one that attracts notice; *esp* : an outstanding athlete **7** : GLIMPSE, LOOK **8** : a first brief news report **9** : FLASHLIGHT **10** : a device for producing a brief and very bright flash of light for taking photographs **11** : a quick-spreading flame or momentary intense outburst of radiant heat

³**flash** *adj* **1** : of sudden origin and short duration **2** : involving brief exposure to an intense agent (as heat or cold)

flash•back \ˈflash-ˌbak\ *n* **1** : interruption of the chronological sequence (as of a film or literary work) by an event of earlier occurrence **2** : a past event remembered vividly

flash back *vb* **1** : to vividly remember a past incident **2** : to employ a flashback

flash•bulb \-ˌbəlb\ *n* : an electric bulb that can be used only once to produce a brief and very bright flash of light for taking photographs

flash card *n* : a card bearing words, numbers, or pictures briefly displayed usu. as a learning aid

flash•cube \ˈflash-ˌkyüb\ *n* : a cubical device incorporating four flashbulbs

flash•gun \-ˌgən\ *n* : a device for producing a bright flash of light for photography

flash•ing \ˈfla-shiŋ\ *n* : sheet metal used in waterproofing (as at the angle between a chimney and a roof)

flash•light \ˈflash-ˌlīt\ *n* : a battery-operated portable electric light

flashy \ˈfla-shē\ *adj* **flash•i•er; -est 1** : momentarily dazzling **2** : superficially attractive or impressive : SHOWY — **flash•i•ly** \-shə-lē\ *adv* — **flash•i•ness** \-shē-nəs\ *n*

flask \ˈflask\ *n* : a flattened bottle-shaped container ⟨a whiskey ~⟩

¹**flat** \ˈflat\ *adj* **flat•ter; flat•test 1** : spread out along a surface; *also* : being or characterized by a horizontal line **2** : having a smooth, level, or even surface **3** : having a broad smooth surface and little thickness **4** : DOWNRIGHT, POSITIVE ⟨a ~ refusal⟩ **5** : FIXED, UNCHANGING ⟨charge a ~ rate⟩ **6** : EXACT, PRECISE ⟨in four minutes ~⟩ **7** : DULL, UNINTERESTING; *also* : INSIPID **8** : DEFLATED **9** : lower than the true pitch; *also* : lower by a half step **10** : free from gloss **11** : lacking depth of characterization — **flat•ly** *adv* — **flat•ness** *n*

²**flat** *n* **1** : a level surface of land : PLAIN **2** : a flat part or surface **3** : a character ♭ that indicates that a spec-

ified note is to be lowered by a half step; *also* : the resulting note **4** : something flat **5** : an apartment on one floor **6** : a deflated tire

[3]**flat** *adv* **1** : FLATLY **2** : COMPLETELY ⟨~ broke⟩ **3** : below the true musical pitch

[4]**flat** *vb* **flat•ted; flat•ting 1** : FLATTEN **2** : to lower in pitch esp. by a half step

flat•bed \ˈflat-ˌbed\ *n* : a truck or trailer with a body in the form of a platform or shallow box

flat•boat \-ˌbōt\ *n* : a flat-bottomed boat used esp. for carrying bulky freight

flat•car \-ˌkär\ *n* : a railroad freight car without sides or roof

flat•fish \-ˌfish\ *n* : any of an order of flattened marine bony fishes with both eyes on the upper side

flat•foot \-ˌfu̇t, -ˈfu̇t\ *n, pl* **flat•feet** \-ˌfēt, -ˈfēt\ : a condition in which the arch of the foot is flattened so that the entire sole rests upon the ground — **flat–foot•ed** \-ˈfu̇-təd\ *adj*

Flat•head \-ˌhed\ *n, pl* **Flatheads** *or* **Flathead** : a member of an American Indian people of Montana

flat•iron \-ˌīrn\ *n* : IRON 3

flat•land \-ˌland\ *n* : land lacking significant variation in elevation

flat–out \ˈflat-ˌau̇t\ *adj* **1** : being or going at maximum effort or speed **2** : OUT-AND-OUT, DOWNRIGHT ⟨it was a ~ lie⟩

flat out *adv* **1** : BLUNTLY, DIRECTLY **2** : at top speed **3** *usu* **flat–out** : to the greatest degree : COMPLETELY ⟨is just *flat-out* confusing⟩

flat•ten \ˈflat-ᵊn\ *vb* : to make or become flat

flat•ter \ˈfla-tər\ *vb* [ME *flateren*, fr. OF *flater* to lick, flatter] **1** : to praise too much or without sincerity **2** : to represent too favorably **3** : to display to advantage **4** : to judge (oneself) favorably or too favorably — **flat•ter•er** *n*

flat•tery \ˈfla-tə-rē\ *n, pl* **-ter•ies** : flattering speech or attentions : insincere or excessive praise

flat•top \ˈflat-ˌtäp\ *n* **1** : AIRCRAFT CARRIER **2** : CREW CUT

flat•u•lent \ˈfla-chə-lənt\ *adj* **1** : full of gas ⟨a ~ stomach⟩ **2** : INFLATED, POMPOUS — **flat•u•lence** \-ləns\ *n*

fla•tus \ˈflā-təs\ *n* : gas formed in the intestine or stomach

flat•ware \ˈflat-ˌwar\ *n* : eating and serving utensils

flat•worm \-ˌwərm\ *n* : any of a phylum of flattened mostly parasitic segmented worms (as trematodes and tapeworms)

flaunt \ˈflȯnt\ *vb* **1** : to display oneself to public notice **2** : to wave or flutter showily **3** : to display ostentatiously or impudently : PARADE — **flaunt** *n*

flau•tist \ˈflȯ-tist, ˈflau̇-\ *n* [It *flautista*] : FLUTIST

[1]**fla•vor** \ˈflā-vər\ *n* **1** : the quality of something that affects the sense of taste or of taste and smell **2** : a substance that adds flavor **3** : characteristic or predominant quality — **fla•vored** \-vərd\ *adj* — **fla•vor•ful** *adj* — **fla•vor•less** *adj* — **fla•vor•some** *adj*

[2]**flavor** *vb* : to give or add flavor to

fla•vor•ing *n* : FLAVOR 2

fla•vour *chiefly Brit var of* FLAVOR

flaw \ˈflȯ\ *n* : a small often hidden defect — **flaw•less** *adj* — **flaw•less•ly** *adv* — **flaw•less•ness** *n*

flax \ˈflaks\ *n* : a fiber that is the source of linen; *also* : a blue-flowered plant grown for this fiber and its oily seeds

flax•en \ˈflak-sən\ *adj* **1** : made of flax **2** : resembling flax esp. in pale soft straw color

flay \ˈflā\ *vb* **1** : to strip off the skin or surface of **2** : to criticize harshly

fl dr *abbr* fluid dram

flea \ˈflē\ *n* : any of an order of small wingless leaping bloodsucking insects

flea•bane \ˈflē-ˌbān\ *n* : any of various plants of the daisy family once believed to drive away fleas

flea–bit•ten \-ˌbit-ᵊn\ *adj* : bitten by or infested with fleas

flea market *n* : a usu. open-air market for secondhand articles and antiques

[1]**fleck** \ˈflek\ *vb* : STREAK, SPOT

[2]**fleck** *n* **1** : SPOT, MARK **2** : FLAKE, PARTICLE

fledge \ˈflej\ *vb* **fledged; fledg•ing** : to develop the feathers necessary for flying

fledg•ling \ˈflej-liŋ\ *n* **1** : a young bird with flight feathers newly developed **2** : an immature or inexperienced person

flee \ˈflē\ *vb* **fled** \ˈfled\; **flee•ing 1** : to run away often from danger or evil **2** : VANISH **3** : to run away from : SHUN

[1]**fleece** \ˈflēs\ *n* **1** : the woolly coat of an animal and esp. a sheep **2** : a soft or woolly covering — **fleecy** *adj*

[2]**fleece** *vb* **fleeced; fleec•ing 1** : to strip of money or property by fraud or extortion **2** : SHEAR

[1]**fleet** \ˈflēt\ *vb* : to pass rapidly

[2]**fleet** *n* [ME *flete*, fr. OE *flēot* ship, fr. *flēotan* to float] **1** : a group of warships under one command **2** : a group (as of ships, planes, or trucks) under one management

[3]**fleet** *adj* **1** : SWIFT, NIMBLE **2** : not enduring : FLEETING — **fleet•ness** *n*

fleet admiral *n* : an admiral of the highest rank in the navy

fleet•ing \ˈflē-tiŋ\ *adj* : passing swiftly

Flem•ing \ˈfle-miŋ\ *n* : a member of a Germanic people inhabiting chiefly northern Belgium

Flem•ish \ˈfle-mish\ *n* **1** : the Dutch language as spoken by the Flemings **2** **Flemish** *pl* : FLEMINGS — **Flemish** *adj*

flesh \ˈflesh\ *n* **1** : the soft parts of an animal's body; *esp* : muscular tissue **2** : MEAT **3** : the physical nature of humans as distinguished from the soul **4** : human beings; *also* : living beings **5** : STOCK, KINDRED **6** : fleshy plant tissue (as fruit pulp) — **fleshed** \ˈflesht\ *adj*

flesh fly *n* : a dipteran fly whose maggots feed on flesh

flesh•ly \ˈflesh-lē\ *adj* **1** : CORPOREAL, BODILY **2** : not spiritual : WORLDLY **3** : CARNAL, SENSUAL

flesh out *vb* : to make fuller or more nearly complete

flesh•pot \ˈflesh-ˌpät\ *n* **1** *pl* : bodily comfort : LUXURY **2** : a place of lascivious entertainment — usu. used in pl.

fleshy \ˈfle-shē\ *adj* **flesh•i•er; -est 1** : consisting of or resembling animal flesh **2** : PLUMP, FAT

flew *past of* [1]FLY

flex \ˈfleks\ *vb* : to bend esp. repeatedly — **flex** *n*

flex•i•ble \ˈflek-sə-bəl\ *adj* **1** : capable of being flexed : PLIANT **2** : yielding to influence : TRACTABLE **3** : readily changed or changing : ADAPTABLE **syn** elastic, supple, resilient, springy — **flex•i•bil•i•ty** \ˌflek-sə-ˈbi-lə-tē\ *n*

flex•ure \ˈflek-shər\ *n* : TURN, FOLD

flib•ber•ti•gib•bet \ˌfli-bər-tē-ˈji-bət\ *n* : a silly flighty person

[1]**flick** \ˈflik\ *n* **1** : a light sharp jerky stroke or movement **2** : a sound produced by a flick **3** : [2]FLICKER **4** : MOVIE — often used in pl.

[2]**flick** *vb* **1** : to strike lightly with a quick sharp motion **2** : FLUTTER, FLIT

[1]**flick•er** \ˈfli-kər\ *vb* **1** : to move irregularly or unsteadily : FLUTTER **2** : to burn fitfully or with a fluctuating light — **flick•er•ing•ly** *adv*

[2]**flicker** *n* **1** : an act of flickering **2** : a sudden brief movement ⟨a ~ of an eyelid⟩ **3** : a momentary stirring ⟨a ~ of interest⟩ **4** : a slight indication : HINT **5** : a wavering light

[3]**flicker** *n* : a large barred and spotted No. American woodpecker with a brown back that occurs as an eastern form with yellow on the underside of the wings and tail and a western form with red in these areas

flied *past and past part of* [3]FLY

fli•er \ˈflī-ər\ *n* **1** : one that flies; *esp* : PILOT **2** : a reckless or speculative undertaking **3** *usu* **fly•er :** an advertising circular

[1]**flight** \ˈflīt\ *n* **1 :** an act or instance of flying **2 :** the ability to fly **3 :** a passing through air or space **4 :** the distance covered in a flight **5 :** swift movement **6 :** a trip made by or in an airplane or spacecraft **7 :** a group of similar individuals (as birds or airplanes) flying as a unit **8 :** a passing (as of the imagination) beyond ordinary limits **9 :** a series of stairs from one landing to another — **flight•less** *adj*

[2]**flight** *n* **:** an act or instance of running away

flight bag *n* **1 :** a lightweight traveling bag with zippered outside pockets **2 :** a small canvas satchel

flight line *n* **:** a parking and servicing area for airplanes

flighty \ˈflī-tē\ *adj* **flight•i•er; -est 1 :** easily upset **:** VOLATILE **2 :** easily excited **:** SKITTISH **3 :** CAPRICIOUS, SILLY — **flight•i•ness** \-tē-nəs\ *n*

flim•flam \ˈflim-ˌflam\ *n* **:** DECEPTION, FRAUD — **flim-flam•mery** \-ˌfla-mə-re\ *n*

flim•sy \ˈflim-zē\ *adj* **flim•si•er; -est 1 :** lacking strength or substance **2 :** of inferior materials and workmanship **3 :** having little worth or plausibility ⟨a ~ excuse⟩ — **flim•si•ly** \-zə-lē\ *adv* — **flim•si•ness** \-zē-nəs\ *n*

flinch \ˈflinch\ *vb* [MF *flenchir* to bend] **:** to shrink from or as if from pain **:** WINCE — **flinch** *n*

[1]**fling** \ˈfliŋ\ *vb* **flung** \ˈfləŋ\; **fling•ing 1 :** to move hastily, brusquely, or violently ⟨*flung* out of the room⟩ **2 :** to kick or plunge vigorously **3 :** to throw with force or recklessness; *also* **:** to cast as if by throwing **4 :** to put suddenly into a state or condition

[2]**fling** *n* **1 :** an act or instance of flinging **2 :** a casual try **:** ATTEMPT **3 :** a period of self-indulgence

flint \ˈflint\ *n* **1 :** a hard quartz that produces a spark when struck by steel **2 :** an alloy used for producing a spark in lighters — **flinty** *adj*

flint glass *n* **:** heavy glass containing an oxide of lead and used in lenses and prisms

flint•lock \ˈflint-ˌläk\ *n* **1 :** a lock for a gun using a flint to ignite the charge **2 :** a firearm fitted with a flintlock

[1]**flip** \ˈflip\ *vb* **flipped; flip•ping 1 :** to turn by tossing ⟨~ a coin⟩ **2 :** to turn over; *also* **:** to leaf through **3 :** FLICK, JERK ⟨~ a light switch⟩ **4 :** to lose self-control — **flip** *n*

[2]**flip** *adj* **:** FLIPPANT, IMPERTINENT

flip•pant \ˈfli-pənt\ *adj* **:** lacking proper respect or seriousness — **flip•pan•cy** \ˈfli-pən-sē\ *n*

flip•per \ˈfli-pər\ *n* **1 :** a broad flat limb (as of a seal) adapted for swimming **2 :** a paddlelike shoe used in skin diving

flip side *n* **:** the reverse and usu. less popular side of a phonograph record

[1]**flirt** \ˈflərt\ *vb* **1 :** to move erratically **:** FLIT **2 :** to behave amorously without serious intent **3 :** to show casual interest ⟨~*ed* with the idea⟩; *also* **:** to come close to ⟨~ with danger⟩ — **flir•ta•tion** \ˌflər-ˈtā-shən\ *n* — **flir•ta•tious** \-shəs\ *adj*

[2]**flirt** *n* **1 :** an act or instance of flirting **2 :** a person who flirts

flit \ˈflit\ *vb* **flit•ted; flit•ting :** to pass or move quickly or abruptly from place to place **:** DART — **flit** *n*

flitch \ˈflich\ *n* **:** a side of cured meat; *esp* **:** a side of bacon

fliv•ver \ˈfli-vər\ *n* **:** a small cheap usu. old automobile

[1]**float** \ˈflōt\ *n* **1 :** something (as a raft) that floats **2 :** a cork buoying up the baited end of a fishing line **3 :** a hollow ball that floats at the end of a lever in a cistern or tank and regulates the liquid level **4 :** a vehicle with a platform to carry an exhibit **5 :** a soft drink with ice cream floating in it

[2]**float** *vb* **1 :** to rest on the surface of or be suspended in a fluid **2 :** to move gently on or through a fluid **3 :** to cause to float **4 :** WANDER **5 :** to offer (securities) in order to finance an enterprise **6 :** to finance by floating an issue of stocks or bonds **7 :** to arrange for ⟨~ a loan⟩ — **float•er** *n*

[1]**flock** \ˈfläk\ *n* **1 :** a group of birds or mammals assembled or herded together **2 :** a group of people under the guidance of a leader; *esp* **:** CONGREGATION **3 :** a large number

[2]**flock** *vb* **:** to gather or move in a flock

floe \ˈflō\ *n* **:** a flat mass of floating ice

flog \ˈfläg\ *vb* **flogged; flog•ging 1 :** to beat with or as if with a rod or whip **2 :** SELL ⟨~ encyclopedias⟩ — **flog•ger** *n*

[1]**flood** \ˈfləd\ *n* **1 :** a great flow of water over the land **2 :** the flowing in of the tide **3 :** an overwhelming volume

[2]**flood** *vb* **1 :** to cover or become filled with a flood **2 :** to fill abundantly or excessively; *esp* **:** to supply (a carburetor) with too much fuel **3 :** to pour forth in a flood — **flood•er** *n*

flood•gate \ˈfləd-ˌgāt\ *n* **:** a gate for controlling a body of water **:** SLUICE

flood•light \-ˌlīt\ *n* **:** a lamp that throws a broad beam of light; *also* **:** the beam itself — **floodlight** *vb*

flood•plain \-ˌplān\ *n* **:** a plain along a river or stream subject to periodic flooding

flood tide *n* **1 :** a rising tide **2 :** an overwhelming quantity **3 :** a high point

flood•wa•ter \ˈfləd-ˌwȯ-tər, -ˌwä-\ *n* **:** the water of a flood

[1]**floor** \ˈflōr\ *n* **1 :** the bottom of a room on which one stands **2 :** a ground surface **3 :** a story of a building **4 :** a main level space (as in a legislative chamber) distinguished from a platform or gallery **5 :** AUDIENCE **6 :** the right to address an assembly **7 :** a lower limit ⟨put a ~ under wheat prices⟩ — **floor•ing** *n*

[2]**floor** *vb* **1 :** to furnish with a floor **2 :** to knock down **3 :** AMAZE, DUMBFOUND **4 :** to press (a vehicle's accelerator) to the floorboard esp. rapidly

floor•board \-ˌbōrd\ *n* **1 :** a board in a floor **2 :** the floor of an automobile

floor leader *n* **:** a member of a legislative body who has charge of a party's organization and strategy on the floor

floor show *n* **:** a series of acts presented in a nightclub

floor•walk•er \ˈflōr-ˌwȯ-kər\ *n* **:** a person employed in a retail store to oversee the sales force and aid customers

floo•zy *or* **floo•zie** \ˈflü-zē\ *n, pl* **floozies :** a usu. young woman of loose morals

flop \ˈfläp\ *vb* **flopped; flop•ping 1 :** FLAP **2 :** to throw oneself down heavily, clumsily, or in a relaxed manner ⟨*flopped* into a chair⟩ **3 :** FAIL — **flop** *n* — **flop** *adv* — **flop•per** *n*

flop•house \ˈfläp-ˌhau̇s\ *n* **:** a cheap hotel

[1]**flop•py** \ˈflä-pē\ *adj* **flop•pi•er; -est :** tending to flop; *esp* **:** soft and flexible — **flop•pi•ly** \-pə-lē\ *adv*

[2]**floppy** *n, pl* **flop•pies :** FLOPPY DISK

floppy disk *n* **:** a small flexible disk with a magnetic coating on which computer data can be stored

flo•ra \ˈflōr-ə\ *n, pl* **floras** *also* **flo•rae** \-ˌē, -ˌī\ [L *Flora,* Roman goddess of flowers] **:** plants or plant life esp. of a region or period

flo•ral \ˈflōr-əl\ *adj* **:** of or relating to flowers or a flora

flo•res•cence \flȯ-ˈres-ᵊns, flə-\ *n* **:** a state or period of being in bloom or flourishing — **flo•res•cent** \-ᵊnt\ *adj*

flor•id \ˈflȯr-əd\ *adj* **1 :** very flowery in style **:** ORNATE ⟨~ prose⟩ **2 :** tinged with red **:** RUDDY **3 :** marked by emotional or sexual fervor

flo•rin \ˈflȯr-ən\ *n* **1 :** an old gold coin first struck at Florence, Italy, in 1252 **2 :** a gold coin of a European country patterned after the florin of Florence **3 :** any of several modern silver coins issued in Commonwealth countries **4 :** GULDEN

flo•rist \ˈflōr-ist\ *n* **:** a person who sells flowers or ornamental plants

[1]**floss** \ˈfläs\ *n* **1 :** soft thread of silk or mercerized cotton for embroidery **2 :** DENTAL FLOSS **3 :** fluffy fibrous material

[2]**floss** *vb* : to use dental floss on (one's teeth) : use dental floss

flossy \ˈflä-sē\ *adj* **floss·i·er; -est 1** : of, relating to, or having the characteristics of floss **2** : STYLISH, GLAMOROUS — **floss·i·ly** \-sə-lē\ *adv*

flo·ta·tion \flō-ˈtā-shən\ *n* : the process or an instance of floating

flo·til·la \flō-ˈti-lə\ *n* [Sp, dim. of *flota* fleet] : a fleet esp. of small ships

flot·sam \ˈflät-səm\ *n* : floating wreckage of a ship or its cargo

[1]**flounce** \ˈflau̇ns\ *vb* **flounced; flounc·ing 1** : to move with exaggerated jerky or bouncy motions **2** : to go with sudden determination

[2]**flounce** *n* : an act or instance of flouncing — **flouncy** \ˈflau̇n-sē\ *adj*

[3]**flounce** *n* : a strip of fabric attached by one edge; *also* : a wide ruffle

[1]**floun·der** \ˈflau̇n-dər\ *n, pl* **flounder** *or* **flounders** : FLATFISH; *esp* : any of various important marine food fishes

[2]**flounder** *vb* **1** : to struggle to move or obtain footing **2** : to proceed clumsily ⟨~*ed* through the speech⟩

[1]**flour** \ˈflau̇r\ *n* : finely ground and sifted meal of a grain (as wheat); *also* : a fine soft powder — **floury** *adj*

[2]**flour** *vb* : to coat with or as if with flour

[1]**flour·ish** \ˈflər-ish\ *vb* **1** : THRIVE, PROSPER **2** : to be in a state of activity or production ⟨~*ed* about 1850⟩ **3** : to reach a height of development or influence **4** : to make bold and sweeping gestures **5** : BRANDISH

[2]**flourish** *n* **1** : a florid bit of speech or writing; *also* : an ornamental touch or decorative detail **2** : FANFARE **3** : WAVE ⟨with a ~ of his cane⟩ **4** : showiness in doing something

[1]**flout** \ˈflau̇t\ *vb* : to treat with contemptuous disregard ⟨~ the law⟩ — **flout·er** *n*

[2]**flout** *n* : TAUNT

[1]**flow** \ˈflō\ *vb* **1** : to issue or move in a stream **2** : RISE ⟨the tide ebbs and ~*s*⟩ **3** : ABOUND **4** : to proceed smoothly and readily **5** : to have a smooth continuity **6** : to hang loose and billowing **7** : COME, ARISE **8** : MENSTRUATE

[2]**flow** *n* **1** : an act of flowing **2** : FLOOD 1, 2 **3** : a smooth uninterrupted movement **4** : STREAM; *also* : a mass of material that has flowed when molten **5** : the quantity that flows in a certain time **6** : MENSTRUATION **7** : a continuous transfer of energy — **flow·age** \ˈflō-ij\ *n*

flow·chart \ˈflō-ˌchärt\ *n* : a symbolic diagram showing step-by-step progression through a procedure

flow diagram *n* : FLOWCHART

[1]**flow·er** \ˈflau̇(-ə)r\ *n* **1** : a plant shoot modified for reproduction and bearing leaves specialized into floral organs; *esp* : one of a seed plant consisting of a calyx, corolla, stamens, and carpels **2** : a plant cultivated for its blossoms **3** : the best part or example **4** : the finest most vigorous period **5** : a state of blooming or flourishing — **flow·ered** \ˈflau̇(-ə)rd\ *adj* — **flow·er·less** *adj*

[2]**flower** *vb* **1** : DEVELOP; *also* : FLOURISH **2** : to produce flowers : BLOOM

flower girl *n* : a little girl who carries flowers at a wedding

flower head *n* : a compact cluster of small flowers without stems suggesting a single flower

flowering plant *n* : any of a major group of vascular plants (as magnolias, grasses, or roses) that produce flowers and fruit and have the seeds enclosed in an ovary

flow·er·pot \ˈflau̇(-ə)r-ˌpät\ *n* : a pot in which to grow plants

flow·ery \ˈflau̇(-ə)r-ē\ *adj* **1** : of, relating to, or resembling flowers **2** : full of fine words or phrases — **flow·er·i·ly** \-ə-lē\ *adv* — **flow·er·i·ness** \-ē-nəs\ *n*

flown \ˈflōn\ *past part of* [1]FLY

fl oz *abbr* fluid ounce

flu \ˈflü\ *n* **1** : INFLUENZA **2** : any of several virus diseases marked esp. by respiratory symptoms

flub \ˈfləb\ *vb* **flubbed; flub·bing** : BOTCH, BLUNDER — **flub** *n*

fluc·tu·ate \ˈflək-chə-ˌwāt\ *vb* **-at·ed; -at·ing 1** : WAVER **2** : to move up and down or back and forth — **fluc·tu·a·tion** \ˌflək-chə-ˈwā-shən\ *n*

flue \ˈflü\ *n* : a passage (as in a chimney) for directing a current (as of smoke or gases)

flu·ent \ˈflü-ənt\ *adj* **1** : capable of flowing : FLUID **2** : ready or facile in speech ⟨~ in French⟩ **3** : effortlessly smooth and rapid ⟨~ speech⟩ — **flu·en·cy** \-ən-sē\ *n* — **flu·ent·ly** *adv*

flue pipe *n* : an organ pipe whose tone is produced by an air current striking the beveled opening of the pipe

[1]**fluff** \ˈfləf\ *n* **1** : [7]DOWN 1 ⟨~ from a pillow⟩ **2** : something fluffy **3** : something inconsequential **4** : BLUNDER; *esp* : an actor's lapse of memory

[2]**fluff** *vb* **1** : to make or become fluffy ⟨~ up a pillow⟩ **2** : to make a mistake

fluffy \ˈflə-fē\ *adj* **fluff·i·er; -est 1** : covered with or resembling fluff **2** : being light and soft or airy ⟨a ~ omelet⟩ **3** : lacking in meaning or substance — **fluff·i·ly** \-fə-lē\ *adv*

[1]**flu·id** \ˈflü-əd\ *adj* **1** : capable of flowing **2** : subject to change or movement **3** : showing a smooth easy style ⟨~ movements⟩ **4** : available for a different use; *esp* : LIQUID 5 ⟨~ assets⟩ — **flu·id·i·ty** \flü-ˈi-də-tē\ *n* — **flu·id·ly** *adv*

[2]**fluid** *n* : a substance (as a liquid or gas) tending to flow or take the shape of its container

fluid dram *or* **flu·i·dram** \ˌflü-ə-ˈdram\ *n* — see WEIGHT table

fluid ounce *n* — see WEIGHT table

[1]**fluke** \ˈflük\ *n* : any of various trematode flatworms

[2]**fluke** *n* **1** : the part of an anchor that fastens in the ground **2** : a lobe of a whale's tail

[3]**fluke** *n* : a stroke of luck — **fluky** *also* **fluk·ey** \ˈflü-kē\ *adj*

flume \ˈflüm\ *n* **1** : an inclined channel for carrying water **2** : a ravine or gorge with a stream running through it

flung *past and past part of* FLING

flunk \ˈfləŋk\ *vb* : to fail esp. in an examination or course — **flunk** *n*

flun·ky *or* **flun·key** \ˈfləŋ-kē\ *n, pl* **flunkies** *or* **flunkeys 1** : a liveried servant; *also* : one performing menial or miscellaneous duties **2** : YES-MAN

fluo·res·cence \flȯ-ˈres-ᵊns\ *n* : luminescence caused by radiation absorption that ceases almost immediately after the incident radiation has stopped; *also* : the emitted radiation — **fluo·resce** \-ˈres\ *vb* — **fluo·res·cent** \-ˈres-ᵊnt\ *adj*

fluorescent lamp *n* : a tubular electric lamp in which light is produced by the action of ultraviolet light on a fluorescent material that coats the inner surface of the lamp

fluo·ri·date \ˈflȯr-ə-ˌdāt\ *vb* **-dat·ed; -dat·ing** : to add a fluoride to (as drinking water) to reduce tooth decay — **fluo·ri·da·tion** \ˌflȯr-ə-ˈdā-shən\ *n*

fluo·ride \ˈflȯr-ˌīd\ *n* : a compound of fluorine

fluo·ri·nate \ˈflȯr-ə-ˌnāt\ *vb* **-nat·ed; -nat·ing** : to treat or cause to combine with fluorine or a compound of fluorine — **fluo·ri·na·tion** \ˌflȯr-ə-ˈnā-shən\ *n*

fluo·rine \ˈflȯr-ˌēn, -ən\ *n* : a pale yellowish flammable irritating toxic gaseous chemical element — see ELEMENT table

fluo·rite \ˈflȯr-ˌīt\ *n* : a mineral that consists of the fluoride of calcium used as a flux and in making glass

fluo·ro·car·bon \ˌflȯr-ō-ˈkär-bən\ *n* : a compound containing fluorine and carbon used chiefly as a lubricant, refrigerant, or nonstick coating; *also* : CHLOROFLUOROCARBON

fluo·ro·scope \ˈflȯr-ə-ˌskōp\ *n* : an instrument for observing the internal structure of an opaque object (as the living body) by means of X rays — **fluo·ro·scop-**

ic \ˌflȯr-ə-ˈskä-pik\ *adj* — **fluo•ros•co•py** \-ˈä-skə-pē\ *n*

fluo•ro•sis \ˌflu̇-ˈrō-səs, ˌflȯ-\ *n* : an abnormal condition (as spotting of the teeth) caused by fluorine or its compounds

flur•ry \ˈflər-ē\ *n, pl* **flurries 1** : a gust of wind **2** : a brief light snowfall **3** : COMMOTION, BUSTLE **4** : a brief outburst of activity ⟨a ∼ of trading⟩ — **flurry** *vb*

[1]**flush** \ˈfləsh\ *vb* : to cause (a bird) to take wing suddenly

[2]**flush** *n* : a hand of cards all of the same suit

[3]**flush** *n* **1** : a sudden flow (as of water) **2** : a surge esp. of emotion ⟨a ∼ of triumph⟩ **3** : a tinge of red : BLUSH **4** : a fresh and vigorous state ⟨in the ∼ of youth⟩ **5** : a passing sensation of extreme heat

[4]**flush** *vb* **1** : to flow and spread suddenly and freely **2** : to glow brightly **3** : BLUSH **4** : to wash out with a rush of fluid **5** : INFLAME, EXCITE **6** : to cause to blush

[5]**flush** *adj* **1** : of a ruddy healthy color **2** : full of life and vigor **3** : filled to overflowing **4** : AFFLUENT **5** : readily available : ABUNDANT **6** : having an unbroken or even surface **7** : directly abutting : immediately adjacent **8** : set even with an edge of a type page or column — **flush•ness** *n*

[6]**flush** *adv* **1** : in a flush manner **2** : SQUARELY ⟨a blow ∼ on the chin⟩

[7]**flush** *vb* : to make flush

flus•ter \ˈfləs-tər\ *vb* : to put into a state of agitated confusion — **fluster** *n*

flute \ˈflüt\ *n* **1** : a hollow pipelike musical instrument **2** : a grooved pleat **3** : GROOVE — **flute** *vb* — **flut•ed** *adj*

flute 1

flut•ing *n* : fluted decoration

flut•ist \ˈflü-tist\ *n* : a flute player

[1]**flut•ter** \ˈflə-tər\ *vb* [ME *floteren* to float, flutter, fr. OE *floterian,* fr. *flotian* to float] **1** : to flap the wings rapidly **2** : to move with quick wavering or flapping motions **3** : to vibrate in irregular spasms **4** : to move about or behave in an agitated aimless manner — **flut•tery** \-tə-rē\ *adj*

[2]**flutter** *n* **1** : an act of fluttering **2** : a state of nervous confusion **3** : FLURRY

[1]**flux** \ˈfləks\ *n* **1** : an act of flowing **2** : a state of continuous change **3** : a substance used to aid in fusing metals

[2]**flux** *vb* : [1]FUSE

[1]**fly** \ˈflī\ *vb* **flew** \ˈflü\; **flown** \ˈflōn\; **fly•ing 1** : to move in or pass through the air with wings **2** : to move through the air or before the wind **3** : to float or cause to float, wave, or soar in the air **4** : FLEE **5** : to fade and disappear : VANISH **6** : to move or pass swiftly **7** : to become expended or dissipated rapidly **8** : to operate or travel in an aircraft or spacecraft **9** : to journey over by flying **10** : AVOID, SHUN **11** : to transport by flying

[2]**fly** *n, pl* **flies 1** : the action or process of flying : FLIGHT **2** *pl* : the space over a theater stage **3** : a garment closing concealed by a fold of cloth **4** : the length of an extended flag from its staff or support **5** : a baseball hit high into the air **6** : the outer canvas of a tent with a double top — **on the fly** : while still in the air

[3]**fly** *vb* **flied; fly•ing** : to hit a fly in baseball

[4]**fly** *n, pl* **flies 1** : a winged insect — usu. used in combination ⟨butter*fly*⟩ **2** : any of a large order of insects mostly with one pair of functional wings and another pair that if present are reduced to balancing organs and often with larvae without a head, eyes, or legs; *esp* : one (as a housefly) that is large and stout-bodied **3** : a fishhook dressed to suggest an insect

fly•able \ˈflī-ə-bəl\ *adj* : suitable for flying or being flown

fly ball *n* : [2]FLY 5

fly•blown \ˈflī-ˌblōn\ *adj* : not pure : TAINTED, CORRUPT

fly•by \-ˌbī\ *n, pl* **flybys 1** : a usu. low-altitude flight by an aircraft over a public gathering **2** : a flight of a spacecraft past a heavenly body (as Jupiter) close enough to obtain scientific data

fly–by–night \-bī-ˌnīt\ *adj* **1** : seeking a quick profit usu. by shady acts **2** : TRANSITORY, PASSING

fly casting *n* : the casting of artificial flies in fly-fishing or as a competitive sport

fly•catch•er \-ˌka-chər, -ˌke-\ *n* : any of various passerine birds that feed on insects caught in flight

fly•er *var of* FLIER

fly–fish•ing \ˈflī-ˌfi-shiŋ\ *n* : a method of fishing in which an artificial fly is used for bait

flying boat *n* : a seaplane with a hull designed for floating

flying buttress *n* : a projecting arched structure to support a wall or building

flying fish *n* : any of numerous sea fishes capable of long gliding flights out of water by spreading their large fins like wings

flying saucer *n* : an unidentified flying object reported to be saucer-shaped or disk-shaped

flying squirrel *n* : any of several No. American squirrels with folds of skin connecting the forelegs and hind legs that enable them to make long gliding leaps

fly•leaf \ˈflī-ˌlēf\ *n, pl* **fly•leaves** \-ˌlēvz\ : a blank leaf at the beginning or end of a book

fly•pa•per \-ˌpā-pər\ *n* : paper poisoned or coated with a sticky substance for killing or catching flies

fly•speck \-ˌspek\ *n* **1** : a speck of fly dung **2** : something small and insignificant — **flyspeck** *vb*

fly•way \-ˌwā\ *n* : an established air route of migratory birds

fly•wheel \-ˌhwēl\ *n* : a heavy wheel for regulating the speed of machinery

fm *abbr* fathom

Fm *symbol* fermium

FM \ˈef-ˌem\ *n* : a broadcasting system using frequency modulation; *also* : a radio receiver of such a system

fn *abbr* footnote

fo *or* **fol** *abbr* folio

FO *abbr* foreign office

foal \ˈfōl\ *n* : a young horse or related animal; *esp* : one under one year — **foal** *vb*

[1]**foam** \ˈfōm\ *n* **1** : a mass of bubbles formed on the surface of a liquid : FROTH, SPUME **2** : material (as rubber) in a lightweight cellular form — **foamy** *adj*

[2]**foam** *vb* : to form foam : FROTH

fob \ˈfäb\ *n* **1** : a short strap, ribbon, or chain attached esp. to a pocket watch **2** : a small ornament worn on a fob

FOB *abbr* free on board

fob off *vb* **1** : to put off with a trick, excuse, or inferior substitute **2** : to pass or offer as genuine **3** : to put aside

FOC *abbr* free of charge

focal length *n* : the distance of a focus from a lens or curved mirror

fo'•c'sle *var of* FORECASTLE

[1]**fo•cus** \ˈfō-kəs\ *n, pl* **fo•ci** \-ˌsī\ *also* **fo•cus•es** [NL, fr.

L, hearth] **1 :** a point at which rays (as of light, heat, or sound) meet or diverge or appear to diverge; *esp* **:** the point at which an image is formed by a mirror, lens, or optical system **2 :** FOCAL LENGTH **3 :** adjustment (as of eyes or eyeglasses) that gives clear vision **4 :** central point **:** CENTER — **fo•cal** \ˈfō-kəl\ *adj* — **fo•cal•ly** *adv*

2focus *vb* **-cused** *also* **-cussed; -cus•ing** *also* **-cus•sing 1 :** to bring or come to a focus ⟨∼ rays of light⟩ **2 :** CENTER ⟨∼ attention on a problem⟩ **3 :** to adjust the focus of

fod•der \ˈfä-dər\ *n* **:** coarse dry food (as cornstalks) for livestock

foe \ˈfō\ *n* [ME *fo,* fr. OE *fāh,* fr. *fāh* hostile] **:** ENEMY

FOE *abbr* Fraternal Order of Eagles

foehn *or* **föhn** \ˈfərn, ˈfœn, ˈfān\ *n* [G *Föhn*] **:** a warm dry wind blowing down a mountainside

foe•man \ˈfō-mən\ *n* **:** FOE

foe•tal, foe•tus *chiefly Brit var of* FETAL, FETUS

1fog \ˈfȯg, ˈfäg\ *n* **1 :** fine particles of water suspended in the lower atmosphere **2 :** mental confusion — **fog•gy** *adj*

2fog *vb* **fogged; fog•ging :** to obscure or be obscured with or as if with fog

fog•horn \ˈfȯg-ˌhȯrn, ˈfäg-\ *n* **:** a horn sounded in a fog to give warning

fo•gy *also* **fo•gey** \ˈfō-gē\ *n, pl* **fogies** *also* **fogeys :** a person with old-fashioned ideas ⟨an old ∼⟩

foi•ble \ˈfȯi-bəl\ *n* **:** a minor failing or weakness in character or behavior

1foil \ˈfȯil\ *vb* [ME, to trample, full cloth, fr. MF *fouler*] **1 :** to prevent from attaining an end **:** DEFEAT **2 :** to bring to naught **:** THWART

2foil *n* **:** a light fencing sword with a flexible blade tapering to a blunt point

3foil *n* [ME, leaf, fr. MF *foille, foil,* fr. L *folium*] **1 :** a very thin sheet of metal ⟨aluminum ∼⟩ **2 :** one that serves as a contrast to another

foist \ˈfȯist\ *vb* **:** to pass off (something false or worthless) as genuine

1fold \ˈfōld\ *n* **1 :** an enclosure for sheep **2 :** a group of people with a common faith, belief, or interest

2fold *vb* **:** to house (sheep) in a fold

3fold *vb* **1 :** to lay one part over or against another part **2 :** to clasp together **3 :** EMBRACE **4 :** to bend (as a layer of rock) into folds **5 :** to incorporate into a mixture by overturning repeatedly without stirring or beating **6 :** to become doubled or pleated **7 :** FAIL, COLLAPSE

4fold *n* **1 :** a doubling or folding over **2 :** a part doubled or laid over another part

fold•away \ˈfōl-də-ˌwā\ *adj* **:** designed to fold out of the way or out of sight

fold•er \ˈfōl-dər\ *n* **1 :** one that folds **2 :** a folded printed circular **3 :** a folded cover or large envelope for loose papers

fol•de•rol \ˈfäl-də-ˌräl\ *n* **1 :** a useless trifle **2 :** NONSENSE

fold•out \ˈfōl-ˌdau̇t\ *n* **:** a folded leaf (as in a magazine) larger in some dimension than the page

fo•liage \ˈfō-lē-ij\ *n* **:** a mass of leaves (as of a plant or forest)

fo•li•at•ed \ˈfō-lē-ˌā-təd\ *adj* **:** composed of or separable into layers

fo•lic acid \ˌfō-lik-\ *n* **:** a vitamin of the vitamin B complex used esp. to treat nutritional anemias

fo•lio \ˈfō-lē-ˌō\ *n, pl* **fo•li•os 1 :** a leaf of a book; *also* **:** a page number **2 :** the size of a piece of paper cut two from a sheet **3 :** a book printed on folio pages

1folk \ˈfōk\ *n, pl* **folk** *or* **folks 1 :** a group of people forming a tribe or nation; *also* **:** the largest number or most characteristic part of such a group **2** *pl* **:** PEOPLE, PERSONS ⟨country ∼⟩ ⟨old ∼*s*⟩ **3** *folks pl* **:** the persons of one's own family

2folk *adj* **:** of, relating to, or originating among the common people ⟨∼ music⟩

folk•lore \ˈfōk-ˌlōr\ *n* **:** customs, beliefs, stories, and sayings of a people handed down from generation to generation — **folk•lor•ist** \-ist\ *n*

folk mass *n* **:** a mass in which traditional liturgical music is replaced by folk music

folk•sing•er \ˈfōk-ˌsiŋ-ər\ *n* **:** a singer of folk songs — **folk•sing•ing** *n*

folksy \ˈfōk-sē\ *adj* **folks•i•er; -est 1 :** SOCIABLE, FRIENDLY **2 :** informal, casual, or familiar in manner or style

folk•way \ˈfōk-ˌwā\ *n* **:** a way of thinking, feeling, or acting common to a given group of people; *esp* **:** a traditional social custom

fol•li•cle \ˈfä-li-kəl\ *n* **1 :** a small anatomical cavity or gland ⟨a hair ∼⟩ **2 :** a small fluid-filled cavity in the ovary of a mammal enclosing a developing egg

fol•low \ˈfä-lō\ *vb* **1 :** to go or come after **2 :** to proceed along **3 :** to engage in as a way of life ⟨∼ the sea⟩ ⟨∼ a profession⟩ **4 :** OBEY **5 :** PURSUE **6 :** to come after in order or rank or natural sequence **7 :** to keep one's attention fixed on **8 :** to result from **syn** succeed, ensue, supervene — **fol•low•er** *n* — **follow suit 1 :** to play a card of the same suit as the card led **2 :** to follow an example set

1fol•low•ing \ˈfä-lə-wiŋ\ *adj* **1 :** next after **:** SUCCEEDING **2 :** that immediately follows

2following *n* **:** a group of followers, adherents, or partisans

3following *prep* **:** subsequent to **:** AFTER

follow–up \ˈfä-lə-ˌwəp\ *n* **:** a system or instance of pursuing an initial effort by supplementary action

fol•ly \ˈfä-lē\ *n, pl* **follies** [ME *folie,* fr. OF, fr. *fol* fool] **1 :** lack of good sense **2 :** a foolish act or idea **:** FOOLISHNESS **3 :** an excessively costly or unprofitable undertaking

fo•ment \fō-ˈment\ *vb* **:** INCITE

fo•men•ta•tion \ˌfō-mən-ˈtā-shən, -ˌmen-\ *n* **1 :** a hot moist material (as a damp cloth) applied to the body to ease pain **2 :** the act of fomenting **:** INSTIGATION

fond \ˈfänd\ *adj* [ME, fr. *fonne* fool] **1 :** FOOLISH, SILLY ⟨∼ pride⟩ **2 :** prizing highly **:** DESIROUS ⟨∼ of praise⟩ **3 :** strongly attracted or predisposed ⟨∼ of music⟩ **4 :** foolishly tender **:** INDULGENT; *also* **:** LOVING, AFFECTIONATE **5 :** CHERISHED, DEAR ⟨his ∼*est* hopes⟩ — **fond•ly** *adv* — **fond•ness** *n*

fon•dant \ˈfän-dənt\ *n* **:** a creamy preparation of sugar used as a basis for candies or icings

fon•dle \ˈfänd-ᵊl\ *vb* **fon•dled; fon•dling :** to touch or handle lovingly **:** CARESS

fon•due *also* **fon•du** \fän-ˈdü, -ˈdyü\ *n* [F] **:** a preparation of melted cheese often flavored with white wine

1font \ˈfänt\ *n* **1 :** a receptacle for baptismal or holy water **2 :** FOUNTAIN, SOURCE

2font *n* **:** an assortment of printing type of one size and style

food \ˈfüd\ *n* **1 :** material taken into an organism and used for growth, repair, and vital processes and as a source of energy; *also* **:** organic material produced by green plants and used by them as food **2 :** nourishment in solid form **3 :** something that nourishes, sustains, or supplies ⟨∼ for thought⟩

food chain *n* **:** a hierarchical arrangement of organisms in an ecological community such that each uses the next usu. lower member as a food source

food poisoning *n* **:** a digestive illness caused by bacteria or by chemicals in food

food•stuff \ˈfüd-ˌstəf\ *n* **:** a substance with food value; *esp* **:** a specific nutrient (as fat or protein)

1fool \ˈfül\ *n* [ME, fr. OF *fol,* fr. LL *follis,* fr. L, bellows, bag] **1 :** a person who lacks sense or judgment **2 :** JESTER **3 :** DUPE **4 :** IDIOT

2fool *vb* **1 :** to spend time idly or aimlessly **2 :** to meddle or tamper thoughtlessly or ignorantly **3 :** JOKE **4 :** DECEIVE **5 :** FRITTER ⟨∼*ed* away his time⟩

fool•ery \ˈfü-lə-rē\ *n, pl* **-er•ies 1 :** a foolish act, utterance, or belief **2 :** foolish behavior

fool•har•dy \ˈfül-ˌhär-dē\ *adj* : foolishly daring : RASH — **fool•har•di•ness** \-dē-nəs\ *n*

fool•ish \ˈfü-lish\ *adj* **1** : showing or arising from folly or lack of judgment **2** : ABSURD, RIDICULOUS **3** : ABASHED — **fool•ish•ly** *adv* — **fool•ish•ness** *n*

fool•proof \ˈfül-ˌprüf\ *adj* : so simple or reliable as to leave no opportunity for error, misuse, or failure ⟨a ~ plan⟩

fools•cap \ˈfül-ˌskap\ *n* [fr. the watermark of a fool's cap formerly applied to such paper] : a size of paper typically 16×13 inches

fool's gold *n* : PYRITE

¹foot \ˈfu̇t\ *n, pl* **feet** \ˈfēt\ *also* **foot 1** : the end part of a leg below the ankle of a vertebrate animal **2** — see WEIGHT table **3** : a group of syllables forming the basic unit of verse meter **4** : something resembling an animal's foot in position or use **5** : the lowest part : BOTTOM **6** : the part at the opposite end from the head **7** : the part (as of a stocking) that covers the foot

²foot *vb* **1** : DANCE **2** : to go on foot **3** : to add up **4** : to pay or provide for paying

foot•age \ˈfu̇-tij\ *n* : length expressed in feet

foot•ball \ˈfu̇t-ˌbȯl\ *n* **1** : any of several games played by two teams on a rectangular field with goalposts at each end in which the object is to get the ball over the goal line or between goalposts by running, passing, or kicking **2** : the ball used in football

foot•board \-ˌbōrd\ *n* **1** : a narrow platform on which to stand or brace the feet **2** : a board forming the foot of a bed

foot•bridge \-ˌbrij\ *n* : a bridge for pedestrians

foot•ed \ˈfu̇-təd\ *adj* : having a foot or feet of a specified kind or number ⟨flat-*footed*⟩ ⟨four-*footed*⟩

-foot•er \ˈfu̇-tər\ *comb form* : one that is a specified number of feet in height, length, or breadth ⟨a six=*footer*⟩

foot•fall \ˈfu̇t-ˌfȯl\ *n* : the sound of a footstep

foot•hill \-ˌhil\ *n* : a hill at the foot of higher hills or mountains

foot•hold \-ˌhōld\ *n* **1** : a hold for the feet : FOOTING **2** : a position usable as a base for further advance

foot•ing *n* **1** : the placing of one's feet in a stable position **2** : the act of moving on foot **3** : a place or space for standing : FOOTHOLD **4** : position with respect to one another : STATUS **5** : BASIS

foot•less \ˈfu̇t-ləs\ *adj* **1** : having no feet **2** : INEPT

foot•lights \-ˌlīts\ *n pl* **1** : a row of lights along the front of a stage floor **2** : the stage as a profession

foo•tling \ˈfüt-liŋ\ *adj* **1** : INEPT **2** : TRIVIAL

foot•lock•er \ˈfu̇t-ˌlä-kər\ *n* : a small trunk designed to be placed at the foot of a bed (as in a barracks)

foot•loose \-ˌlüs\ *adj* : having no ties : FREE, UNTRAMMELED

foot•man \-mən\ *n* : a male servant who attends a carriage, waits on table, admits visitors, and runs errands

foot•note \-ˌnōt\ *n* **1** : a note of reference, explanation, or comment placed usu. at the bottom of a page **2** : COMMENTARY

foot•pad \-ˌpad\ *n* : a round somewhat flat foot on the leg of a spacecraft for distributing weight to minimize sinking into a surface

foot•path \-ˌpath, -ˌpȧth\ *n* : a narrow path for pedestrians

foot•print \-ˌprint\ *n* **1** : an impression of the foot **2** : the area on a surface covered by something

foot•race \-ˌrās\ *n* : a race run on foot

foot•rest \-ˌrest\ *n* : a support for the feet

foot•sore \-ˌsōr\ *adj* : having sore or tender feet (as from much walking)

foot•step \-ˌstep\ *n* **1** : the mark of the foot : TRACK **2** : TREAD **3** : distance covered by a step : PACE **4** : a step on which to ascend or descend **5** : a way of life, conduct, or action

foot•stool \-ˌstül\ *n* : a low stool to support the feet

foot•wear \-ˌwar\ *n* : apparel (as shoes or boots) for the feet

foot•work \-ˌwərk\ *n* : the management of the feet (as in boxing)

fop \ˈfäp\ *n* : DANDY 1 — **fop•pery** \ˈfä-pə-rē\ *n* — **fop•pish** *adj*

¹for \fər, ˈfȯr\ *prep* **1** : as a preparation toward ⟨dress ~ dinner⟩ **2** : toward the purpose or goal of ⟨need time ~ study⟩ ⟨money ~ a trip⟩ **3** : so as to reach or attain ⟨run ~ cover⟩ **4** : as being ⟨took him ~ a fool⟩ **5** : because of ⟨cry ~ joy⟩ **6** — used to indicate a recipient ⟨a letter ~ you⟩ **7** : in support of ⟨fought ~ his country⟩ **8** : directed at : AFFECTING ⟨a cure ~ what ails you⟩ **9** — used with a noun or pronoun followed by an infinitive to form the equivalent of a noun clause ⟨~ you to go would be silly⟩ **10** : in exchange as equal to : so as to return the value of ⟨a lot of trouble ~ nothing⟩ ⟨pay $10 ~ a hat⟩ **11** : CONCERNING ⟨a stickler ~ detail⟩ **12** : CONSIDERING ⟨tall ~ her age⟩ **13** : through the period of ⟨served ~ three years⟩ **14** : in honor of

²for *conj* : BECAUSE

³for *abbr* **1** foreign **2** forestry

fora *pl of* FORUM

¹for•age \ˈfȯr-ij\ *n* **1** : food for animals esp. when taken by browsing or grazing **2** : a search for food or supplies

²forage *vb* **for•aged; for•ag•ing 1** : to collect forage from **2** : to search for food or supplies **3** : to get by foraging **4** : to make a search : RUMMAGE

for•ay \ˈfȯr-ˌā, fȯ-ˈrā\ *vb* : to raid esp. in search of plunder : PILLAGE — **foray** *n*

¹for•bear \fȯr-ˈbar\ *vb* **-bore** \-ˈbōr\; **-borne** \-ˈbōrn\; **-bear•ing 1** : to refrain from : ABSTAIN **2** : to be patient — **for•bear•ance** \-ˈbar-əns\ *n*

²forbear *var of* FOREBEAR

for•bid \fər-ˈbid\ *vb* **-bade** \-ˈbad, -ˈbād\ *or* **-bad** \-ˈbad\; **-bid•den** \-ˈbid-ᵊn\; **-bid•ding 1** : to command against : PROHIBIT **2** : HINDER, PREVENT **syn** enjoin, interdict, inhibit, ban

for•bid•ding *adj* : DISAGREEABLE, REPELLENT

for•bode *var of* FOREBODE

¹force \ˈfōrs\ *n* **1** : strength or energy esp. of an exceptional degree : active power **2** : capacity to persuade or convince **3** : military strength; *also, pl* : the whole military strength (as of a nation) **4** : a body (as of persons or ships) available for a particular purpose **5** : VIOLENCE, COMPULSION **6** : an influence (as a push or pull) that causes motion or a change of motion — **force•ful** \-fəl\ *adj* — **force•ful•ly** *adv* — **in force 1** : in great numbers **2** : VALID, OPERATIVE

²force *vb* **forced; forc•ing 1** : COMPEL, COERCE **2** : to cause through necessity ⟨*forced* to admit defeat⟩ **3** : to press, attain to, or effect against resistance or inertia ⟨~ your way through⟩ **4** : to raise or accelerate to the utmost ⟨~ the pace⟩ **5** : to produce with unnatural or unwilling effort ⟨*forced* a smile⟩ **6** : to hasten (as in growth) by artificial means

for•ceps \ˈfȯr-səps\ *n, pl* **forceps** [L] : a hand=held instrument for grasping, holding, or pulling objects esp. for delicate operations (as by a surgeon)

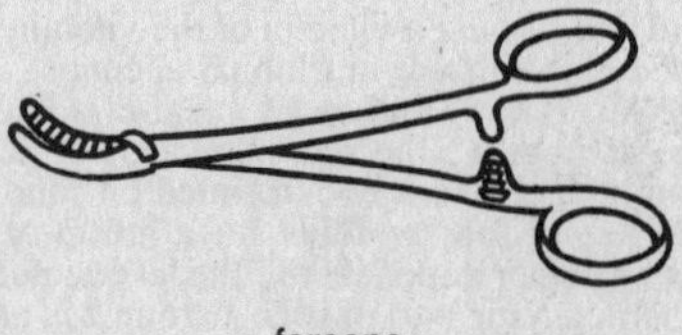

forceps

forc•ible \ˈfōr-sə-bəl\ *adj* **1** : obtained or done by force **2** : showing force or energy : POWERFUL — **forc•i•bly** \-blē\ *adv*

[1]ford \ˈfōrd\ *n* **:** a place where a stream may be crossed by wading
[2]ford *vb* **:** to cross (a body of water) by wading
[1]fore \ˈfōr\ *adv* **:** in, toward, or adjacent to the front **:** FORWARD
[2]fore *adj* **:** being or coming before in time, order, or space
[3]fore *n* **:** something that occupies a front position
[4]fore *interj* — used by a golfer to warn anyone within range of the probable line of flight of the ball
fore–and–aft \ˌfōr-ə-ˈnaft\ *adj* **:** lying, running, or acting along the length of a structure (as a ship)
[1]fore•arm \(ˌ)fōr-ˈärm\ *vb* **:** to arm in advance **:** PREPARE
[2]fore•arm \ˈfōr-ˌärm\ *n* **:** the part of the arm between the elbow and the wrist
fore•bear \-ˌbar\ *n* **:** ANCESTOR, FOREFATHER
fore•bode \fōr-ˈbōd\ *vb* **1 :** to have a premonition esp. of misfortune **2 :** FORETELL, PREDICT **syn** augur, bode, foreshadow, portend, promise — **fore•bod•ing** *n*
fore•cast \ˈfōr-ˌkast\ *vb* **-cast** *also* **-cast•ed; -cast•ing 1 :** PREDICT, CALCULATE ⟨~ weather conditions⟩ **2 :** to indicate as likely to occur — **forecast** *n* — **fore•cast•er** *n*
fore•cas•tle \ˈfōk-səl\ *n* **1 :** the forward part of the upper deck of a ship **2 :** the crew's quarters usu. in a ship's bow
fore•close \fōr-ˈklōz\ *vb* **1 :** to shut out **:** PRECLUDE **2 :** to take legal measures to terminate a mortgage and take possession of the mortgaged property
fore•clo•sure \-ˈklō-zhər\ *n* **:** the act of foreclosing; *esp* **:** the legal procedure of foreclosing a mortgage
fore•doom \fōr-ˈdüm\ *vb* **:** to doom beforehand
fore•fa•ther \ˈfōr-ˌfä-t͟hər\ *n* **1 :** ANCESTOR **2 :** a person of an earlier period and common heritage
fore•fend *var of* FORFEND
fore•fin•ger \-ˌfiŋ-gər\ *n* **:** the finger next to the thumb
fore•foot \-ˌfu̇t\ *n* **:** either of the front feet of a quadruped; *also* **:** the front part of the human foot
fore•front \-ˌfrənt\ *n* **:** the foremost part or place
fore•gath•er *var of* FORGATHER
[1]fore•go \fōr-ˈgō\ *vb* **-went** \-ˈwent\; **-gone** \-ˈgȯn\; **-go•ing :** PRECEDE
[2]forego *var of* FORGO
fore•go•ing *adj* **:** PRECEDING
fore•gone \ˈfōr-ˌgȯn\ *adj* **:** determined in advance ⟨a ~ conclusion⟩
fore•ground \-ˌgrau̇nd\ *n* **1 :** the part of a scene or representation that appears nearest to and in front of the spectator **2 :** a position of prominence
fore•hand \-ˌhand\ *n* **:** a stroke (as in tennis) made with the palm of the hand turned in the direction in which the hand is moving; *also* **:** the side on which such a stroke is made — **forehand** *adj*

forehand

fore•hand•ed \(ˌ)fōr-ˈhan-dəd\ *adj* **:** mindful of the future **:** PRUDENT
fore•head \ˈfȯr-əd, ˈfōr-ˌhed\ *n* **:** the part of the face above the eyes
for•eign \ˈfȯr-ən\ *adj* [ME *forein,* fr. OF, fr. LL *foranus* on the outside, fr. L *foris* outside] **1 :** situated outside a place or country and esp. one's own country **2 :** born in, belonging to, or characteristic of some place or country other than the one under consideration ⟨~ language⟩ **3 :** not connected, pertinent, or characteristically present **4 :** related to or dealing with other nations ⟨~ affairs⟩ **5 :** occurring in an abnormal situation in the living body ⟨a ~ body in the eye⟩
for•eign•er \ˈfȯr-ə-nər\ *n* **:** a person belonging to or owing allegiance to a foreign country
foreign minister *n* **:** a governmental minister for foreign affairs
fore•know \fōr-ˈnō\ *vb* **-knew** \-ˈnü, -ˈnyü\; **-known** \-ˈnōn\; **-know•ing :** to have previous knowledge of — **fore•knowl•edge** \ˈfōr-ˌnä-lij, fōr-ˈnä-\ *n*
fore•la•dy \ˈfōr-ˌlā-dē\ *n* **:** FOREWOMAN
fore•leg \-ˌleg\ *n* **:** a front leg
fore•limb \-ˌlim\ *n* **:** either of an anterior pair of limbs (as wings, arms, or fins)
fore•lock \-ˌläk\ *n* **:** a lock of hair growing from the front part of the head
fore•man \-mən\ *n* **1 :** a spokesperson of a jury **2 :** a person in charge of a group of workers
fore•mast \-ˌmast\ *n* **:** the mast nearest the bow of a ship
fore•most \-ˌmōst\ *adj* **:** first in time, place, or order **:** most important **:** PREEMINENT — **foremost** *adv*
fore•name \-ˌnām\ *n* **:** a first name
fore•named \-ˌnāmd\ *adj* **:** previously named **:** AFORESAID
fore•noon \-ˌnün\ *n* **:** MORNING
[1]fo•ren•sic \fə-ˈren-sik\ *adj* [L *forensis* public, forensic, fr. *forum* forum] **1 :** belonging to, used in, or suitable to courts of law or to public speaking or debate **2 :** relating to the application of scientific knowledge to legal problems ⟨~ medicine⟩
[2]forensic *n* **1 :** an argumentative exercise **2** *pl* **:** the art or study of argumentative discourse
fore•or•dain \ˌfōr-ȯr-ˈdān\ *vb* **:** to ordain or decree beforehand **:** PREDESTINE
fore•part \ˈfōr-ˌpärt\ *n* **1 :** the anterior part of something **2 :** the earlier part of a period of time
fore•quar•ter \-ˌkwȯr-tər\ *n* **:** the front half of a lateral half of the body or carcass of a quadruped ⟨a ~ of beef⟩
fore•run•ner \-ˌrə-nər\ *n* **1 :** one that goes before to give notice of the approach of others **:** HARBINGER **2 :** PREDECESSOR, ANCESTOR **syn** precursor, herald
fore•sail \-ˌsāl, -səl\ *n* **1 :** the lowest sail on the foremast of a square-rigged ship or schooner **2 :** the principal sail forward of the foremast (as of a sloop)
fore•see \fōr-ˈsē\ *vb* **-saw** \-ˈsȯ\; **-seen** \-ˈsēn\; **-see•ing :** to see or realize beforehand **:** EXPECT **syn** foreknow, divine, apprehend, anticipate — **fore•see•able** *adj*
fore•shad•ow \-ˈsha-dō\ *vb* **:** to give a hint or suggestion of beforehand
fore•short•en \fōr-ˈshȯrt-ᵊn\ *vb* **:** to shorten (a detail) in a drawing or painting so that it appears to have depth
fore•sight \ˈfōr-ˌsīt\ *n* **1 :** the act or power of foreseeing **2 :** care or provision for the future **:** PRUDENCE **3 :** an act of looking forward; *also* **:** a view forward — **fore•sight•ed** \-ˌsī-təd\ *adj* — **fore•sight•ed•ness** *n*
fore•skin \-ˌskin\ *n* **:** a fold of skin enclosing the end of the penis
for•est \ˈfȯr-əst\ *n* [ME, fr. OF, fr. LL *forestis* (*silva*) unenclosed (woodland), fr. L *foris* outside] **:** a large thick growth of trees and underbrush — **for•est•ed** \ˈfȯr-ə-stəd\ *adj* — **for•est•land** \ˈfȯr-əst-ˌland\ *n*
fore•stall \fōr-ˈstȯl, fȯr-\ *vb* **1 :** to keep out, hinder, or prevent by measures taken in advance **2 :** ANTICIPATE
forest ranger *n* **:** a person in charge of the management and protection of a portion of a forest

for·est·ry \ˈfȯr-ə-strē\ *n* **:** the science of growing and caring for forests — **for·est·er** \ˈfȯr-ə-stər\ *n*

fore·swear *var of* FORSWEAR

[1]**fore·taste** \ˈfōr-ˌtāst\ *n* **:** an advance indication, warning, or notion

[2]**fore·taste** \fōr-ˈtāst\ *vb* **:** to taste beforehand **:** ANTICIPATE

fore·tell \fōr-ˈtel\ *vb* **-told** \-ˈtōld\; **-tell·ing :** to tell of beforehand **:** PREDICT **syn** forecast, prophesy, prognosticate

fore·thought \ˈfōr-ˌthȯt\ *n* **1 :** PREMEDITATION **2 :** consideration for the future

fore·to·ken \fōr-ˈtō-kən\ *vb* **:** to indicate in advance

fore·top \ˈfōr-ˌtäp\ *n* **:** a platform near the top of a ship's foremast

for·ev·er \fȯr-ˈe-vər\ *adv* **1 :** for a limitless time **2 :** at all times **:** ALWAYS

for·ev·er·more \-ˌe-vər-ˈmōr\ *adv* **:** FOREVER

fore·warn \fōr-ˈwȯrn\ *vb* **:** to warn beforehand

forewent *past of* FOREGO

fore·wing \ˈfōr-ˌwiŋ\ *n* **:** either of the anterior wings of a 4-winged insect

fore·wom·an \ˈfōr-ˌwu̇-mən\ *n* **:** a woman having the responsibilities of a foreman

fore·word \-ˌwərd\ *n* **:** PREFACE

[1]**for·feit** \ˈfȯr-fət\ *n* **1 :** something forfeited **:** PENALTY, FINE **2 :** FORFEITURE **3 :** something deposited and then redeemed on payment of a fine **4** *pl* **:** a game in which forfeits are exacted

[2]**forfeit** *vb* **:** to lose or lose the right to by some error, offense, or crime

for·fei·ture \ˈfȯr-fə-ˌchu̇r\ *n* **1 :** the act of forfeiting **2 :** something forfeited **:** PENALTY

for·fend \fȯr-ˈfend\ *vb* **1 :** PREVENT **2 :** PROTECT, PRESERVE

for·gath·er \fōr-ˈga-t͟hər\ *vb* **1 :** to come together **:** ASSEMBLE **2 :** to meet someone usu. by chance

[1]**forge** \ˈfōrj\ *n* [ME, fr. OF, fr. L *fabrica*, fr. *faber* smith] **:** a furnace or shop with its furnace where metal is heated and worked

[2]**forge** *vb* **forged; forg·ing 1 :** to form (metal) by heating and hammering **2 :** FASHION, SHAPE ⟨~ an agreement⟩ **3 :** to make or imitate falsely esp. with intent to defraud ⟨~ a signature⟩ — **forg·er** *n* — **forg·ery** \ˈfōr-jə-rē\ *n*

[3]**forge** *vb* **forged; forg·ing :** to move ahead steadily but gradually

for·get \fər-ˈget\ *vb* **-got** \-ˈgät\; **-got·ten** \-ˈgät-ᵊn\ *or* **-got; -get·ting 1 :** to be unable to think of or recall **2 :** to fail to become mindful of at the proper time **3 :** NEGLECT, DISREGARD — **for·get·ful** \-ˈget-fəl\ *adj* — **for·get·ful·ly** *adv*

for·get–me–not \fər-ˈget-mē-ˌnät\ *n* **:** any of a genus of small herbs with bright blue or white flowers

forg·ing *n* **:** a piece of forged work

for·give \fər-ˈgiv\ *vb* **-gave** \-ˈgāv\; **-giv·en** \-ˈgi-vən\; **-giv·ing 1 :** to give up resentment of **2 :** PARDON, ABSOLVE **3 :** to grant relief from payment of — **for·giv·able** *adj* — **for·give·ness** *n*

for·giv·ing *adj* **1 :** willing or able to forgive **2 :** allowing room for error or weakness

for·go \fōr-ˈgō\ *vb* **-went** \-ˈwent\; **-gone** \-ˈgȯn\; **-go·ing :** to give up the enjoyment or advantage of **:** do without

fo·rint \ˈfȯr-int\ *n, pl* **forints** *also* **forint** — see MONEY table

[1]**fork** \ˈfȯrk\ *n* **1 :** an implement with two or more prongs for taking up (as in eating), pitching, or digging **2 :** a forked part, tool, or piece of equipment **3 :** a dividing into branches or a place where something branches; *also* **:** a branch of such a fork

[2]**fork** *vb* **1 :** to divide into two or more branches **2 :** to give the form of a fork to ⟨~*ing* her fingers⟩ **3 :** to raise or pitch with a fork ⟨~ hay⟩ **4 :** PAY, CONTRIBUTE — used with *over, out,* or *up*

forked \ˈfȯrkt, ˈfȯr-kəd\ *adj* **:** having a fork **:** shaped like a fork ⟨~ lightning⟩

fork·lift \ˈfōrk-ˌlift\ *n* **:** a machine for lifting heavy objects by means of steel fingers inserted under the load

for·lorn \fər-ˈlȯrn, fȯr-\ *adj* **1 :** sad and lonely because of isolation or desertion **2 :** WRETCHED **3 :** nearly hopeless — **for·lorn·ly** *adv* — **for·lorn·ness** *n*

[1]**form** \ˈfȯrm\ *n* **1 :** SHAPE, STRUCTURE **2 :** a body esp. of a person **:** FIGURE **3 :** the essential nature of a thing **4 :** established manner of doing or saying something **5 :** FORMULA **6 :** a document with blank spaces for insertion of information ⟨tax ~⟩ **7 :** CEREMONY **8 :** manner of performing according to recognized standards **9 :** a long seat **:** BENCH **10 :** a model of the human figure used for displaying clothes **11 :** MOLD ⟨a ~ for concrete⟩ **12 :** type or plates in a frame ready for printing **13 :** MODE, KIND, VARIETY ⟨coal is a ~ of carbon⟩ **14 :** orderly method of arrangement; *also* **:** a particular kind or instance of such arrangement ⟨the sonnet ~ in poetry⟩ **15 :** the structural element, plan, or design of a work of art **16 :** a bounded surface or volume **17 :** a grade in a British school or in some American private schools **18 :** RACING FORM **19 :** known ability to perform; *also* **:** condition (as of an athlete) suitable for performing **20 :** one of the ways in which a word is changed to show difference in use ⟨the plural ~ of a noun⟩ — **form·less** *adj*

[2]**form** *vb* **1 :** to give form or shape to **:** FASHION, MAKE **2 :** TRAIN, INSTRUCT **3 :** CONSTITUTE, COMPOSE **4 :** DEVELOP, ACQUIRE ⟨~ a habit⟩ **5 :** to arrange in order ⟨~ a battle line⟩ **6 :** to take form **:** ARISE ⟨clouds are ~*ing*⟩ **7 :** to take a definite form, shape, or arrangement

[1]**for·mal** \ˈfȯr-məl\ *adj* **1 :** according with conventional forms and rules ⟨a ~ dinner party⟩ **2 :** done in due or lawful form ⟨a ~ contract⟩ **3 :** CEREMONIOUS, PRIM ⟨a ~ manner⟩ **4 :** NOMINAL — **for·mal·ly** *adv*

[2]**formal** *n* **:** something (as a social event) formal in character

form·al·de·hyde \fȯr-ˈmal-də-ˌhīd\ *n* **:** a colorless pungent gas used in water solution as a preservative and disinfectant

for·mal·ise *Brit var of* FORMALIZE

for·mal·ism \ˈfȯr-mə-ˌli-zəm\ *n* **:** strict adherence to set forms

for·mal·i·ty \fȯr-ˈma-lə-tē\ *n, pl* **-ties 1 :** compliance with formal or conventional rules **2 :** the quality or state of being formal **3 :** an established form that is required or conventional

for·mal·ize \ˈfȯr-mə-ˌlīz\ *vb* **-ized; -iz·ing 1 :** to give a certain or definite form to **2 :** to make formal; *also* **:** to give formal status or approval to

[1]**for·mat** \ˈfȯr-ˌmat\ *n* **1 :** the general composition or style of a publication **2 :** the general plan or arrangement of something

[2]**format** *vb* **for·mat·ted; for·mat·ting :** to arrange (as material to be printed) in a particular format — **for·mat·ter** *n*

for·ma·tion \fȯr-ˈmā-shən\ *n* **1 :** an act of giving form to something **:** DEVELOPMENT **2 :** something that is formed **3 :** STRUCTURE, SHAPE **4 :** an arrangement of persons or things in a prescribed manner or for a certain purpose

for·ma·tive \ˈfȯr-mə-tiv\ *adj* **1 :** giving or capable of giving form **:** CONSTRUCTIVE **2 :** of, relating to, or characterized by important growth or formation ⟨a child's ~ years⟩

for·mer \ˈfȯr-mər\ *adj* **1 :** PREVIOUS, EARLIER **2 :** FOREGOING **3 :** being first mentioned or in order of two or more things

for·mer·ly \-lē\ *adv* **:** in time past **:** PREVIOUSLY

form·fit·ting \ˈfȯrm-ˌfi-tiŋ\ *adj* **:** conforming to the outline of the body

for·mi·da·ble \ˈfȯr-mə-də-bəl, fȯr-ˈmi-\ *adj* **1 :** exciting fear, dread, or awe **2 :** imposing serious difficulties — **for·mi·da·bly** \-blē\ *adv*

form letter *n* **1 :** a letter on a frequently recurring topic that can be sent to different people at different times **2** : a letter for mass circulation sent out in many printed copies

for•mu•la \ˈfȯr-myə-lə\ *n, pl* **-las** *or* **-lae** \-ˌlē, -ˌlī\ **1** : a set form of words for ceremonial use **2** : RECIPE, PRESCRIPTION **3** : a milk mixture or substitute for a baby **4** : a group of symbols or figures joined to express information concisely **5** : a customary or set form or method

for•mu•late \-ˌlāt\ *vb* **-lat•ed; -lat•ing 1** : to express in a formula **2** : DESIGN, DEVISE ⟨~ a policy⟩ **3** : to prepare according to a formula — **for•mu•la•tion** \ˌfȯr-myə-ˈlā-shən\ *n*

for•ni•ca•tion \ˌfȯr-nə-ˈkā-shən\ *n* : consensual sexual intercourse between two persons not married to each other — **for•ni•cate** \ˈfȯr-nə-ˌkāt\ *vb* — **for•ni•ca•tor** \-ˌkā-tər\ *n*

for•sake \fər-ˈsāk, fȯr-\ *vb* **for•sook** \-ˈsu̇k\; **for•sak•en** \-ˈsā-kən\; **for•sak•ing** [ME, fr. OE *forsacan*, fr. *sacan* to dispute] : to renounce or turn away from entirely

for•sooth \fər-ˈsüth\ *adv* : in truth : INDEED

for•swear \fȯr-ˈswar\ *vb* **for•swore** \-ˈswōr\; **for•sworn** \-ˈswōrn\; **for•swear•ing 1** : to swear falsely : commit perjury **2** : to renounce earnestly or under oath **3** : to deny under oath

for•syth•ia \fər-ˈsi-thē-ə\ *n* : any of a genus of shrubs related to the olive and having yellow bell-shaped flowers appearing before the leaves in early spring

fort \ˈfōrt\ *n* [ME *forte*, fr. MF *fort*, fr. *fort* strong, fr. L *fortis*] **1** : a fortified place **2** : a permanent army post

¹forte \ˈfōrt, ˈfȯr-ˌtā\ *n* [F *fort*, fr. *fort*, adj., strong] : one's strong point

²for•te \ˈfȯr-ˌtā\ *adv or adj* [It, fr. *forte* strong] : LOUD — used as a direction in music

forth \ˈfōrth\ *adv* **1** : FORWARD, ONWARD ⟨from that day ~⟩ **2** : out into view ⟨put ~ leaves⟩

forth•com•ing \fōrth-ˈkə-miŋ\ *adj* **1** : coming or available soon ⟨the ~ holidays⟩ **2** : marked by openness and candor : OUTGOING

forth•right \ˈfōrth-ˌrīt\ *adj* : free from ambiguity or evasiveness : going straight to the point ⟨a ~ answer⟩ — **forth•right•ly** *adv* — **forth•right•ness** *n*

forth•with \ˌfōrth-ˈwith\ *adv* : IMMEDIATELY

for•ti•fy \ˈfȯr-tə-ˌfī\ *vb* **-fied; -fy•ing 1** : to strengthen by military defenses **2** : to give physical strength or endurance to **3** : ENCOURAGE **4** : to strengthen or enrich with a material ⟨~ bread with vitamins⟩ — **for•ti•fi•ca•tion** \ˌfȯr-tə-fə-ˈkā-shən\ *n*

for•tis•si•mo \fȯr-ˈti-sə-ˌmō\ *adv or adj* : very loud — used as a direction in music

for•ti•tude \ˈfȯr-tə-ˌtüd, -ˌtyüd\ *n* : strength of mind that enables one to meet danger or bear pain or adversity with courage **syn** grit, backbone, pluck, guts

fort•night \ˈfōrt-ˌnīt\ *n* [ME *fourtenight*, alter. of *fourtene night* fourteen nights] : two weeks — **fort•night•ly** \-lē\ *adj or adv*

for•tress \ˈfȯr-trəs\ *n* : FORT 1

for•tu•itous \fȯr-ˈtü-ə-təs, -ˈtyü-\ *adj* **1** : happening by chance **2** : FORTUNATE

for•tu•ity \-ə-tē\ *n, pl* **-ities 1** : the quality or state of being fortuitous **2** : a chance event or occurrence

for•tu•nate \ˈfȯr-chə-nət\ *adj* **1** : bringing some good thing not foreseen **2** : LUCKY

for•tu•nate•ly \-lē\ *adv* **1** : in a fortunate manner **2** : it is fortunate that

for•tune \ˈfȯr-chən\ *n* **1** : prosperity attained partly through luck; *also* : CHANCE, LUCK **2** : what happens to a person : good or bad luck **3** : FATE, DESTINY **4** : RICHES, WEALTH

fortune hunter *n* : a person who seeks wealth esp. by marriage

for•tune–tell•er \-ˌte-lər\ *n* : a person who professes to tell future events — **for•tune–tell•ing** *n or adj*

for•ty \ˈfȯr-tē\ *n, pl* **forties** : four times 10 — **for•ti•eth** \ˈfȯr-tē-əth\ *adj or n* — **forty** *adj or pron*

for•ty–five \ˌfȯr-tē-ˈfīv\ *n* **1** : a .45 caliber handgun — usu. written .45 **2** : a phonograph record designed to be played at 45 revolutions per minute

for•ty–nin•er \-ˈnī-nər\ *n* : a person in the rush to California for gold in 1849

forty winks *n sing or pl* : a short sleep

fo•rum \ˈfōr-əm\ *n, pl* **forums** *also* **fo•ra** \-ə\ [L] **1** : the marketplace or central meeting place of an ancient Roman city **2** : a medium (as a publication) of open discussion **3** : COURT **4** : a public assembly, lecture, or program involving audience or panel discussion

¹for•ward \ˈfȯr-wərd\ *adj* **1** : being near or at or belonging to the front **2** : EAGER, READY **3** : BRASH, BOLD **4** : notably advanced or developed : PRECOCIOUS **5** : moving, tending, or leading toward a position in front **6** : EXTREME, RADICAL **7** : of, relating to, or getting ready for the future — **for•ward•ness** *n*

²forward *adv* : to or toward what is ahead or in front

³forward *vb* **1** : to help onward : ADVANCE **2** : to send forward : TRANSMIT **3** : to send or ship onward

⁴forward *n* : a player who plays at the front of a team's offensive formation near the opponent's goal

for•ward•er \-wər-dər\ *n* : one that forwards; *esp* : an agent who forwards goods — **for•ward•ing** *n*

for•wards \ˈfȯr-wərdz\ *adv* : FORWARD

¹fos•sil \ˈfä-səl\ *adj* [L *fossilis* obtained by digging, fr. *fodere* to dig] **1** : preserved from a past geologic age ⟨~ plants⟩ **2** : of or relating to fossil fuels

²fossil *n* **1** : a trace or impression or the remains of a plant or animal of a past geologic age preserved in the earth's crust **2** : a person whose ideas are out-of-date — **fos•sil•ize** \ˈfä-sə-ˌlīz\ *vb*

fossil fuel *n* : a fuel (as coal or oil) that is formed in the earth from plant or animal remains

¹fos•ter \ˈfȯs-tər\ *adj* [ME, fr. OE *fōstor-*, fr. *fōstor* food, feeding] : affording, receiving, or sharing nourishment or parental care though not related by blood or legal ties ⟨~ parent⟩ ⟨~ child⟩

²foster *vb* **1** : to give parental care to : NURTURE **2** : to promote the growth or development of : ENCOURAGE

foster home *n* : a household in which an orphaned, neglected, or delinquent child is placed for care

fos•ter•ling \-tər-liŋ\ *n* : a foster child

Fou•cault pendulum \ˌfü-ˈkō-\ *n* : a device that consists of a heavy weight hung by a long wire and that swings in a constant direction which appears to change showing that the earth rotates

fought *past and past part of* FIGHT

¹foul \ˈfau̇l\ *adj* **1** : offensive to the senses : LOATHSOME; *also* : clogged with dirt **2** : ODIOUS, DETESTABLE **3** : OBSCENE, ABUSIVE **4** : DISAGREEABLE, STORMY ⟨~ weather⟩ **5** : TREACHEROUS, DISHONORABLE, UNFAIR **6** : marking the bounds of a playing field ⟨~ lines⟩; *also* : being outside the foul line ⟨~ ball⟩ ⟨~ territory⟩ **7** : containing marked-up corrections **8** : ENTANGLED — **foul•ly** *adv* — **foul•ness** *n*

²foul *n* **1** : an entanglement or collision in fishing or sailing **2** : an infraction of the rules in a game or sport; *also* : a baseball hit outside the foul line

³foul *vb* **1** : to make or become foul or filthy **2** : to entangle or become entangled **3** : OBSTRUCT, BLOCK **4** : to collide with **5** : to make or hit a foul

⁴foul *adv* : in a foul manner

fou•lard \fü-ˈlärd\ *n* : a lightweight silk of plain or twill weave usu. decorated with a printed pattern

foul•mouthed \ˈfau̇l-ˈmau̇t͟hd, -ˈmau̇tht\ *adj* : given to the use of obscene, profane, or abusive language

foul play *n* : VIOLENCE; *esp* : MURDER

foul–up \ˈfau̇l-ˌəp\ *n* **1** : a state of being fouled up **2** : a mechanical difficulty

foul up *vb* **1** : to spoil by mistakes or poor judgment **2** : to cause a foul-up : BUNGLE

¹found \ˈfau̇nd\ *past and past part of* FIND

²found *vb* **1** : to take the first steps in building **2** : to set or ground on something solid : BASE **3** : to establish (as an institution) often with provision for future maintenance — **found•er** *n*

foun•da•tion \faůn-ˈdā-shən\ *n* **1** : the act of founding **2** : a basis upon which something stands or is supported ⟨suspicions without ~⟩ **3** : funds given for the permanent support of an institution : ENDOWMENT; *also* : an institution so endowed **4** : supporting structure : BASE **5** : CORSET — **foun•da•tion•al** \-shə-nəl\ *adj*

foun•der \ˈfaůn-dər\ *vb* **1** : to make or become lame ⟨the horse ~*ed*⟩ **2** : COLLAPSE **3** : SINK ⟨a ~*ing* ship⟩ **4** : FAIL

found•ling \ˈfaůnd-liŋ\ *n* : an infant found after its unknown parents have abandoned it

found•ry \ˈfaůn-drē\ *n, pl* **foundries** : a building or works where metal is cast

fount \ˈfaůnt\ *n* : SOURCE, FOUNTAIN

foun•tain \ˈfaůnt-ᵊn\ *n* **1** : a spring of water **2** : SOURCE **3** : an artificial jet of water **4** : a container for liquid that can be drawn off as needed

foun•tain•head \-ˌhed\ *n* : SOURCE

fountain pen *n* : a pen with a reservoir that feeds the writing point with ink

four \ˈfōr\ *n* **1** : one more than three **2** : the 4th in a set or series **3** : something having four units — **four** *adj or pron*

four–flush \-ˌfləsh\ *vb* : to make a false claim : BLUFF — **four–flush•er** *n*

four•fold \-ˌfōld, -ˈfōld\ *adj* **1** : being four times as great or as many **2** : having four units or members — **four•fold** \-ˈfōld\ *adv*

4–H \ˈfōr-ˈāch\ *adj* [fr. the fourfold aim of improving the head, heart, hands, and health] : of or relating to a program set up by the U.S. Department of Agriculture to help young people become productive citizens — **4–H'•er** *n*

Four Hundred *or* **400** *n* : the exclusive social set of a community — used with *the*

four–in–hand \ˈfōr-ən-ˌhand\ *n* **1** : a team of four horses driven by one person; *also* : a vehicle drawn by such a team **2** : a necktie tied in a slipknot with long ends overlapping vertically in front

four–o'clock \ˈfōr-ə-ˌkläk\ *n* : a garden plant with fragrant yellow, red, or white flowers without petals that open late in the afternoon

four–post•er \ˌfōr-ˈpō-stər\ *n* : a bed with tall corner posts orig. designed to support curtains or a canopy

four•score \ˈfōr-ˈskōr\ *adj* : being four times twenty : EIGHTY

four•some \ˈfōr-səm\ *n* **1** : a group of four persons or things **2** : a golf match between two pairs of partners

four•square \-ˈskwar\ *adj* **1** : SQUARE **2** : marked by boldness and conviction : FORTHRIGHT — **foursquare** *adv*

four•teen \fōr-ˈtēn\ *n* : one more than 13 — **fourteen** *adj or pron* — **four•teenth** \-ˈtēnth\ *adj or n*

fourth \ˈfōrth\ *n* **1** : one that is number four in a countable series **2** : one of four equal parts of something — **fourth** *adj or adv*

fourth estate *n, often cap F&E* : the public press

4WD *abbr* four-wheel drive

four–wheel \ˈfōr-ˌhwēl\ *or* **four–wheeled** \-ˌhwēld\ *adj* : acting on or by means of four wheels of a motor vehicle

[1]**fowl** \ˈfaůl\ *n, pl* **fowl** *or* **fowls** **1** : BIRD **2** : a cock or hen of the domestic chicken; *also* : the flesh of these used as food

[2]**fowl** *vb* : to hunt wildfowl

[1]**fox** \ˈfäks\ *n, pl* **fox•es** *also* **fox** **1** : any of various flesh-eating mammals related to the wolves but smaller and with shorter legs and a more pointed muzzle; *also* : the fur of a fox **2** : a clever crafty person **3** *cap* : a member of an American Indian people formerly living in what is now Wisconsin

[2]**fox** *vb* : TRICK, OUTWIT

fox•glove \ˈfäks-ˌgləv\ *n* : a common plant related to the snapdragons that is grown for its showy spikes of dotted white or purple tubular flowers and as a source of digitalis

fox•hole \-ˌhōl\ *n* : a pit dug for protection against enemy fire

fox•hound \-ˌhaůnd\ *n* : any of various large swift powerful hounds used in hunting foxes

fox terrier *n* : a small lively terrier that occurs in varieties with smooth dense coats or with harsh wiry coats

fox–trot \ˈfäks-ˌträt\ *n* **1** : a short broken slow trotting gait **2** : a ballroom dance in duple time

foxy \ˈfäk-sē\ *adj* **fox•i•er; -est** **1** : resembling or suggestive of a fox **2** : WILY **3** : physically attractive

foy•er \ˈfȯi-ər, ˈfȯi-ˌyā\ *n* [F, lit., fireplace, fr. (assumed) VL *focarium,* fr. L *focus* hearth] : LOBBY; *also* : an entrance hallway

fpm *abbr* feet per minute

FPO *abbr* fleet post office

fps *abbr* feet per second

fr *abbr* **1** father **2** franc **3** friar **4** from

[1]**Fr** *abbr* **1** France; French **2** Friday

[2]**Fr** *symbol* francium

fra•cas \ˈfrā-kəs, ˈfra-\ *n, pl* **fra•cas•es** \-kə-səz\ [F, din, row, fr. It *fracasso,* fr. *fracassare* to shatter] : BRAWL

frac•tal \ˈfrak-tᵊl\ *n* : an irregular curve or shape that repeats itself at any scale on which it is examined — **fractal** *adj*

frac•tion \ˈfrak-shən\ *n* **1** : a numerical representation (as ½, ¾, or 3.323) indicating the quotient of two numbers **2** : FRAGMENT **3** : PORTION — **frac•tion•al** \-shə-nəl\ *adj* — **frac•tion•al•ly** *adv*

frac•tious \ˈfrak-shəs\ *adj* **1** : tending to be troublesome : hard to handle or control **2** : QUARRELSOME, IRRITABLE

frac•ture \ˈfrak-chər\ *n* **1** : a breaking of something and esp. a bone **2** : CRACK, CLEFT — **fracture** *vb*

frag•ile \ˈfra-jəl, -ˌjīl\ *adj* : easily broken : DELICATE — **fra•gil•i•ty** \frə-ˈji-lə-tē\ *n*

[1]**frag•ment** \ˈfrag-mənt\ *n* : a part broken off, detached, or incomplete

[2]**frag•ment** \-ˌment\ *vb* : to break into fragments — **frag•men•ta•tion** \ˌfrag-mən-ˈtā-shən, -ˌmən-\ *n*

frag•men•tary \ˈfrag-mən-ˌter-ē\ *adj* : made up of fragments : INCOMPLETE

fra•grant \ˈfrā-grənt\ *adj* : sweet or agreeable in smell — **fra•grance** \-grəns\ *n* — **fra•grant•ly** *adv*

frail \ˈfrāl\ *adj* **1** : morally or physically weak **2** : FRAGILE, DELICATE

frail•ty \ˈfrāl-tē\ *n, pl* **frailties** **1** : the quality or state of being frail **2** : a fault due to weakness

[1]**frame** \ˈfrām\ *vb* **framed; fram•ing** **1** : PLAN, CONTRIVE **2** : SHAPE, CONSTRUCT **3** : FORMULATE **4** : DRAW UP ⟨~ a constitution⟩ **5** : to make appear guilty **6** : to fit or adjust for a purpose : ARRANGE **7** : to provide with or enclose in a frame — **fram•er** *n*

[2]**frame** *n* **1** : something made of parts fitted and joined together **2** : the physical makeup of the body **3** : an arrangement of structural parts that gives form or support **4** : a supporting or enclosing border or open case (as for a window or picture) **5** : one picture of a series (as on a length of film) **6** : FRAME-UP

[3]**frame** *adj* : having a wood frame

frame of mind *n* : mental attitude or outlook : MOOD

frame–up \ˈfrā-ˌməp\ *n* **1** : an act or series of actions in which someone is framed **2** : an action that is planned, contrived, or formulated

frame•work \ˈfrām-ˌwərk\ *n* : a basic supporting part or structure

franc \ˈfraŋk\ *n* — see MONEY table

fran•chise \ˈfran-ˌchīz\ *n* [ME, fr. MF, fr. *franchir* to free, fr. OF *franc* free] **1** : a special privilege granted to an individual or group ⟨a ~ to operate a ferry⟩ **2** : a constitutional or statutory right or privilege; *esp* : the right to vote

fran•chi•see \ˌfran-ˌchī-ˈzē, -chə-\ *n* : one granted a franchise

fran•chis•er \ˈfran-ˌchī-zər\ *n* **1** : FRANCHISEE **2** : FRANCHISOR

fran•chi•sor \ˌfran-ˌchī-ˈzȯr, -chə-\ *n* : one that grants a franchise

fran•ci•um \ˈfran-sē-əm\ *n* : a radioactive metallic chemical element — see ELEMENT table

Fran•co–Amer•i•can \ˌfraŋ-kō-ə-ˈmer-ə-kən\ *n* : an American of French or esp. French-Canadian descent — **Franco–American** *adj*

fran•gi•ble \ˈfran-jə-bəl\ *adj* : BREAKABLE — **fran•gi•bil•i•ty** \ˌfran-jə-ˈbi-lə-tē\ *n*

[1]**frank** \ˈfraŋk\ *adj* : marked by free, forthright, and sincere expression — **frank•ness** *n*

[2]**frank** *vb* : to mark (a piece of mail) with an official sign so that it can be mailed free; *also* : to mail free

[3]**frank** *n* **1** : the signature or mark on a piece of mail indicating free or paid postage **2** : the privilege of sending mail free

Fran•ken•stein \ˈfraŋ-kən-ˌstīn\ *n* **1** : a monstrous creation that usu. ruins its originator **2** : a monster in the shape of a man

frank•furt•er \ˈfraŋk-fər-tər, -ˌfər-\ *or* **frank•furt** \-fərt\ *n* : a seasoned sausage (as of beef or beef and pork)

frank•in•cense \ˈfraŋ-kən-ˌsens\ *n* : a fragrant resin burned as incense

frank•ly \ˈfraŋ-klē\ *adv* **1** : in a frank manner **2** : in truth : INDEED

fran•tic \ˈfran-tik\ *adj* : marked by uncontrolled emotion or disordered anxious activity — **fran•ti•cal•ly** \-ti-k(ə-)lē\ *adv*

frap•pé \fra-ˈpā\ *or* **frappe** *same or* ˈfrap\ [F *frappé*, fr. pp. of *frapper* to strike, chill] *n* **1** : an iced or frozen drink **2** : a thick milk shake — **frap•pé** \fra-ˈpā\ *adj*

fra•ter•nal \frə-ˈtərn-ᵊl\ *adj* **1** : of, relating to, or involving brothers **2** : of, relating to, or being a fraternity or society **3** : FRIENDLY, BROTHERLY — **fra•ter•nal•ly** *adv*

fra•ter•ni•ty \frə-ˈtər-nə-tē\ *n, pl* **-ties 1** : a social, honorary, or professional group; *esp* : a men's student organization **2** : BROTHERLINESS, BROTHERHOOD **3** : persons of the same class, profession, or tastes

frat•er•nize \ˈfra-tər-ˌnīz\ *vb* **-nized; -niz•ing 1** : to mingle as friends **2** : to associate on close terms with members of a hostile group — **frat•er•ni•za•tion** \ˌfra-tər-nə-ˈzā-shən\ *n*

frat•ri•cide \ˈfra-trə-ˌsīd\ *n* **1** : one that kills a sibling or countryman **2** : the act of a fratricide — **frat•ri•cid•al** \ˌfra-trə-ˈsīd-ᵊl\ *adj*

fraud \ˈfrȯd\ *n* **1** : DECEIT, TRICKERY **2** : TRICK **3** : IMPOSTOR, CHEAT

fraud•u•lent \ˈfrȯ-jə-lənt\ *adj* : characterized by, based on, or done by fraud : DECEITFUL — **fraud•u•lent•ly** *adv*

fraught \ˈfrȯt\ *adj* : full of or accompanied by something specified ⟨∼ with danger⟩

[1]**fray** \ˈfrā\ *n* : FIGHT, STRUGGLE; *also* : QUARREL, DISPUTE

[2]**fray** *vb* **1** : to wear (as an edge of cloth) by rubbing **2** : to separate the threads at the edge of **3** : STRAIN, IRRITATE ⟨∼*ed* nerves⟩

fraz•zle \ˈfra-zəl\ *vb* **fraz•zled; fraz•zling 1** : FRAY **2** : to put in a state of extreme physical or nervous fatigue — **frazzle** *n*

[1]**freak** \ˈfrēk\ *n* **1** : WHIM, CAPRICE **2** : a strange, abnormal, or unusual person or thing **3** *slang* : a person who uses an illicit drug **4** : an ardent enthusiast — **freak•ish** *adj*

[2]**freak** *vb* **1** : to experience the effects (as hallucinations) of taking illicit drugs — often used with *out* **2** : to distress or become distressed — often used with *out* — **freak–out** \ˈfrē-ˌkau̇t\ *n*

freck•le \ˈfre-kəl\ *n* : a brownish spot on the skin — **freckle** *vb*

[1]**free** \ˈfrē\ *adj* **fre•er; fre•est 1** : having liberty **2** : enjoying political or personal independence; *also* : not subject to or allowing slavery **3** : made or done voluntarily : SPONTANEOUS **4** : relieved from or lacking something unpleasant **5** : not subject to a duty, tax, or charge **6** : not obstructed : CLEAR **7** : not being used or occupied **8** : not fastened **9** : LAVISH **10** : OPEN, FRANK **11** : given without charge **12** : not literal or exact **13** : not restricted by conventional forms — **free•ly** *adv*

[2]**free** *vb* **freed; free•ing 1** : to set free **2** : RELIEVE, RID **3** : DISENTANGLE, CLEAR **syn** release, liberate, discharge, emancipate, loose

[3]**free** *adv* **1** : FREELY **2** : without charge

free•base \ˈfrē-ˌbās\ *n* : purified cocaine smoked as crack or heated to produce vapors for inhalation — **freebase** *vb*

free•bie *or* **free•bee** \ˈfrē-bē\ *n* : something given without charge

free•board \ˈfrē-ˌbōrd\ *n* : the vertical distance between the waterline and the upper edge of the side of a boat

free•boo•ter \-ˌbü-tər\ *n* [D *vrijbuiter,* fr. *vrijbuit* plunder, fr. *vrij* free + *buit* booty] : PLUNDERER, PIRATE

free•born \-ˈbȯrn\ *adj* **1** : not born in vassalage or slavery **2** : of, relating to, or befitting one that is freeborn

freed•man \ˈfrēd-mən, -ˌman\ *n* : a man freed from slavery

free•dom \ˈfrē-dəm\ *n* **1** : the quality or state of being free : INDEPENDENCE **2** : EXEMPTION, RELEASE **3** : EASE, FACILITY **4** : FRANKNESS **5** : unrestricted use **6** : a political right; *also* : FRANCHISE, PRIVILEGE

free enterprise *n* : freedom of private business to operate with little regulation by the government

free–for–all \ˈfrē-fə-ˌrȯl\ *n* : a competition or fight open to all comers and usu. with no rules : BRAWL — **free–for–all** *adj*

free•hand \-ˌhand\ *adj* : done without mechanical aids or devices

free•hold \ˈfrē-ˌhōld\ *n* : ownership of an estate for life usu. with the right to bequeath it to one's heirs; *also* : an estate thus owned — **free•hold•er** *n*

free•lance \-ˌlans\ *n* : one who pursues a profession (as writing) without a long-term commitment to any one employer — **free•lance** *adj or vb*

free–living \ˈfrē-ˈli-viŋ\ *adj* **1** : unrestricted in pursuing personal pleasures **2** : being neither parasitic nor symbiotic ⟨∼ organisms⟩

free•load \ˈfrē-ˌlōd\ *vb* : to impose upon another's hospitality — **free•load•er** *n*

free love *n* : the practice of living openly with one of the opposite sex without marriage

free•man \ˈfrē-mən, -ˌman\ *n* **1** : one who has civil or political liberty **2** : one having the full rights of a citizen

Free•ma•son \-ˌmās-ᵊn\ *n* : a member of a secret fraternal society called Free and Accepted Masons — **Free•ma•son•ry** \-rē\ *n*

free•stand•ing \ˈfrē-ˈstan-diŋ\ *adj* : standing alone or on its own foundation free of support

free•stone \ˈfrē-ˌstōn\ *n* **1** : a stone that may be cut freely without splitting **2** : a fruit stone to which the flesh does not cling; *also* : a fruit (as a peach or cherry) having such a stone

free•think•er \-ˈthiŋ-kər\ *n* : one who forms opinions on the basis of reason independently of authority; *esp* : one who doubts or denies religious dogma — **free•think•ing** *n or adj*

free trade *n* : trade between nations without restrictions (as high taxes on imports)

free verse *n* : verse whose meter is irregular or whose rhythm is not metrical

free•way \ˈfrē-ˌwā\ *n* : an expressway without tolls

free•wheel \-ˈhwēl\ *vb* : to move, live, or play freely or irresponsibly
free•will \ˈfrē-ˌwil\ *adj* : VOLUNTARY
free will *n* : voluntary choice or decision
[1]**freeze** \ˈfrēz\ *vb* **froze** \ˈfrōz\; **fro•zen** \ˈfrōz-ᵊn\; **freez•ing** **1** : to harden or cause to harden into a solid (as ice) by loss of heat **2** : to withstand freezing **3** : to chill or become chilled with cold **4** : to damage by frost **5** : to adhere solidly by or as if by freezing **6** : to become fixed, motionless, or incapable of speech **7** : to cause to grip tightly **8** : to become clogged with ice **9** : to fix at a certain stage or level
[2]**freeze** *n* **1** : an act or instance of freezing **2** : the state of being frozen **3** : a state of weather marked by low temperature
freeze–dry \ˈfrēz-ˈdrī\ *vb* : to dry in a frozen state under vacuum esp. for preservation — **freeze–dried** *adj*
freez•er \ˈfrē-zər\ *n* : a compartment, device, or room for freezing food or keeping it frozen
[1]**freight** \ˈfrāt\ *n* **1** : payment for carrying goods **2** : CARGO **3** : BURDEN **4** : the carrying of goods by a common carrier **5** : a train that carries freight
[2]**freight** *vb* **1** : to load with goods for transportation **2** : BURDEN, CHARGE **3** : to ship or transport by freight
freight•er \ˈfrā-tər\ *n* : a ship or airplane used chiefly to carry freight
French \ˈfrench\ *n* **1** : the language of France **2 French** *pl* : the people of France **3** : strong language — **French** *adj* — **French•man** \-mən\ *n* — **French•wom•an** \-ˌwu̇-mən\ *n*
French door *n* : a door with small panes of glass extending the full length
French dressing *n* **1** : a thin salad dressing usu. made of vinegar and oil with spices **2** : a creamy salad dressing flavored with tomatoes
french fry *vb, often cap 1st F* : to fry (as strips of potato) in deep fat until brown — **french fry** *n, often cap 1st F*
French horn *n* : a curved brass instrument with a funnel-shaped mouthpiece and a flaring bell
French toast *n* : bread dipped in a mixture of eggs and milk and fried at a low heat
fre•net•ic \fri-ˈne-tik\ *adj* : FRANTIC — **fre•net•i•cal•ly** \-ti-k(ə-)lē\ *adv*
fren•zy \ˈfren-zē\ *n, pl* **frenzies** **1** : temporary madness or a violently agitated state **2** : intense often disordered activity — **fren•zied** \-zēd\ *adj*
freq *abbr* frequency; frequent; frequently
fre•quen•cy \ˈfrē-kwən-sē\ *n, pl* **-cies** **1** : the fact or condition of occurring frequently **2** : rate of occurrence **3** : the number of cycles per second of an alternating current **4** : the number of waves (as of sound or electromagnetic energy) that pass a fixed point each second
frequency modulation *n* : variation of the frequency of a carrier wave according to another signal; *also* : FM
[1]**fre•quent** \frē-ˈkwent, ˈfrē-kwənt\ *vb* : to associate with, be in, or resort to habitually — **fre•quent•er** *n*
[2]**fre•quent** \ˈfrē-kwənt\ *adj* **1** : happening often or at short intervals **2** : HABITUAL — **fre•quent•ly** *adv*
fres•co \ˈfres-kō\ *n, pl* **frescoes** [It, fr. *fresco* fresh] : the art of painting on fresh plaster; *also* : a painting done by this method
fresh \ˈfresh\ *adj* **1** : VIGOROUS, REFRESHED **2** : not containing salt **3** : not altered by processing (as freezing or canning) **4** : free from taint : PURE **5** : fairly strong : BRISK ⟨~ breeze⟩ **6** : not stale, sour, or decayed ⟨~ bread⟩ **7** : not faded **8** : not worn or rumpled **9** : experienced, made, or received newly or anew **10** : ADDITIONAL, ANOTHER ⟨made a ~ start⟩ **11** : ORIGINAL, VIVID **12** : INEXPERIENCED **13** : newly come or arrived ⟨~ from school⟩ **14** : IMPUDENT — **fresh•ly** *adv* — **fresh•ness** *n*
fresh•en \ˈfre-shən\ *vb* : to make, grow, or become fresh
fresh•et \ˈfre-shət\ *n* : an overflowing of a stream (as by heavy rains)
fresh•man \ˈfresh-mən\ *n* **1** : a 1st-year student **2** : BEGINNER, NEWCOMER
fresh•wa•ter \-ˌwȯ-tər, -ˌwä-\ *n* : water that is not salty — **freshwater** *adj*
[1]**fret** \ˈfret\ *vb* **fret•ted; fret•ting** [ME, to devour, fret, fr. OE *fretan* to devour] **1** : WEAR, CORRODE; *also* : FRAY **2** : RUB, CHAFE **3** : to make by wearing away **4** : to become irritated : WORRY, VEX **5** : GRATE; *also* : AGITATE
[2]**fret** *n* : an irritated or worried state ⟨in a ~ about the interview⟩
[3]**fret** *n* : ornamental work esp. of straight lines in symmetrical patterns
[4]**fret** *n* : one of a series of ridges across the fingerboard of a stringed musical instrument — **fret•ted** *adj*
fret•ful \ˈfret-fəl\ *adj* : IRRITABLE — **fret•ful•ly** *adv* — **fret•ful•ness** *n*
fret•saw \-ˌsȯ\ *n* : a narrow-bladed saw used for cutting curved outlines
fret•work \-ˌwərk\ *n* **1** : decoration consisting of frets **2** : ornamental openwork or work in relief
Fri *abbr* Friday
fri•a•ble \ˈfrī-ə-bəl\ *adj* : easily crumbled or pulverized ⟨~ soil⟩
fri•ar \ˈfrī-ər\ *n* [ME *frere, fryer,* fr. OF *frere,* lit., brother, fr. L *frater*] : a member of a religious order that orig. lived by alms
fri•ary \ˈfrī-ər-ē\ *n, pl* **-ar•ies** : a monastery of friars
[1]**fric•as•see** \ˈfri-kə-ˌsē, ˌfri-kə-ˈsē\ *n* : a dish made of meat (as chicken) cut into pieces, stewed in stock, and served in sauce
[2]**fricassee** *vb* **-seed; -see•ing** : to cook as a fricassee
fric•tion \ˈfrik-shən\ *n* **1** : the rubbing of one body against another **2** : the force that resists motion between bodies in contact **3** : clash in opinions between persons or groups : DISAGREEMENT — **fric•tion•al** *adj*
friction tape *n* : a usu. cloth adhesive tape impregnated with insulating material and used esp. to protect and insulate electrical conductors
Fri•day \ˈfrī-dē, -(ˌ)dā\ *n* : the sixth day of the week
fridge \ˈfrij\ *n* : REFRIGERATOR
fried•cake \ˈfrīd-ˌkāk\ *n* : DOUGHNUT, CRULLER
friend \ˈfrend\ *n* **1** : one attached to another by respect or affection **2** : ACQUAINTANCE **3** : one who is not hostile **4** : one who supports or favors something ⟨a ~ of art⟩ **5** *cap* : a member of the Society of Friends : QUAKER — **friend•less** *adj* — **friend•li•ness** \-lē-nəs\ *n* — **friend•ly** *adj* — **friend•ship** \-ˌship\ *n*
frieze \ˈfrēz\ *n* : an ornamental often sculptured band extending around something (as a building or room)
frig•ate \ˈfri-gət\ *n* **1** : a square-rigged warship **2** : a warship smaller than a destroyer
fright \ˈfrīt\ *n* **1** : sudden terror : ALARM **2** : something that is ugly or shocking
fright•en \ˈfrīt-ᵊn\ *vb* **1** : to make afraid **2** : to drive away or out by frightening **3** : to become frightened — **fright•en•ing•ly** *adv*
fright•ful \ˈfrīt-fəl\ *adj* **1** : TERRIFYING **2** : STARTLING **3** : EXTREME ⟨~ thirst⟩ — **fright•ful•ly** *adv* — **fright•ful•ness** *n*
frig•id \ˈfri-jəd\ *adj* **1** : intensely cold **2** : lacking warmth or ardor : INDIFFERENT **3** : abnormally averse to or unable to achieve orgasm during sexual intercourse — used esp. of women — **fri•gid•i•ty** \fri-ˈji-də-tē\ *n*
frigid zone *n* : the area or region between the arctic circle and the north pole or between the antarctic circle and the south pole
frill \ˈfril\ *n* **1** : a gathered, pleated, or ruffled edging **2** : something unessential — **frilly** *adj*
fringe \ˈfrinj\ *n* **1** : an ornamental border consisting of short threads or strips hanging from an edge or band

2 : something that resembles a fringe : EDGE 3 : something that is additional or secondary to an activity, process, or subject — **fringe** *vb*

fringe benefit *n* **1** : an employment benefit paid for by an employer without affecting basic wage rates **2** : any additional benefit

frip•pery \ˈfri-pə-rē\ *n, pl* **-per•ies** [MF *friperie*] **1** : FINERY **2** : pretentious display

frisk \ˈfrisk\ *vb* **1** : to leap, skip, or dance in a lively or playful way : GAMBOL **2** : to search (a person) esp. for concealed weapons by running the hand rapidly over the clothing

frisky \ˈfris-kē\ *adj* **frisk•i•er; -est** : PLAYFUL — **frisk•i•ly** \-kə-lē\ *adv* — **frisk•i•ness** \-kē-nəs\ *n*

[1]**frit•ter** \ˈfri-tər\ *n* : a small lump of fried batter often containing fruit or meat

[2]**fritter** *vb* **1** : to reduce or waste piecemeal **2** : to break into small fragments

fritz \ˈfrits\ *n* : a state of disorder or disrepair ⟨the car is on the ~⟩

friv•o•lous \ˈfri-və-ləs\ *adj* **1** : of little importance : TRIVIAL **2** : lacking in seriousness — **fri•vol•i•ty** \fri-ˈvä-lə-tē\ *n* — **friv•o•lous•ly** *adv*

frizz \ˈfriz\ *vb* : to form into small tight curls — **frizz** *n* — **frizzy** *adj*

[1]**friz•zle** \ˈfri-zəl\ *vb* **friz•zled; friz•zling** : FRIZZ, CURL — **frizzle** *n*

[2]**frizzle** *vb* **friz•zled; friz•zling** **1** : to fry until crisp and curled **2** : to cook with a sizzling noise

fro \ˈfrō\ *adv* : BACK, AWAY — used in the phrase *to and fro*

frock \ˈfräk\ *n* **1** : an outer garment worn by monks and friars **2** : an outer garment worn esp. by men **3** : a woman's or girl's dress

frock coat *n* : a man's usu. double-breasted coat with knee-length skirts

frog \ˈfrȯg, ˈfräg\ *n* **1** : any of various largely aquatic smooth-skinned tailless leaping amphibians **2** : an ornamental braiding for fastening the front of a garment by a loop through which a button passes **3** : a condition in the throat causing hoarseness **4** : a small holder (as of metal, glass, or plastic) with perforations or spikes that is placed in a bowl or vase to keep cut flowers in position

frog•man \ˈfrȯg-ˌman, ˈfräg-, -mən\ *n* : a swimmer equipped to work underwater for long periods of time

[1]**frol•ic** \ˈfrä-lik\ *vb* **frol•icked; frol•ick•ing** **1** : to make merry **2** : to play about happily : ROMP

[2]**frolic** *n* **1** : a playful or mischievous action **2** : FUN, MERRIMENT — **frol•ic•some** \-səm\ *adj*

from \ˈfrəm, ˈfräm\ *prep* **1** — used to show a starting point ⟨a letter ~ home⟩ **2** — used to show removal or separation ⟨subtract 3 ~ 9⟩ **3** — used to show a material, source, or cause ⟨suffering ~ a cold⟩

frond \ˈfränd\ *n* : a usu. large divided leaf esp. of a fern or palm tree

[1]**front** \ˈfrənt\ *n* **1** : FOREHEAD; *also* : the whole face **2** : external and often feigned appearance **3** : a region of active fighting; *also* : a sphere of activity **4** : a political coalition **5** : the side of a building containing the main entrance **6** : the forward part or surface **7** : FRONTAGE **8** : a boundary between two dissimilar air masses **9** : a position directly before or ahead of something else **10** : a person, group, or thing used to mask the identity of the actual controlling agent

[2]**front** *vb* **1** : to have the principal side adjacent to something **2** : to serve as a front **3** : CONFRONT

front•age \ˈfrən-tij\ *n* **1** : a piece of land lying adjacent (as to a street or the ocean) **2** : the length of a frontage **3** : the front side of a building

front•al \ˈfrənt-ᵊl\ *adj* **1** : of, relating to, or next to the forehead **2** : of, relating to, or directed at the front ⟨a ~ attack⟩ — **fron•tal•ly** *adv*

fron•tier \ˌfrən-ˈtir\ *n* **1** : a border between two countries **2** : a region that forms the margin of settled territory **3** : the outer limits of knowledge or achievement ⟨the ~*s* of science⟩ — **fron•tiers•man** \-ˈtirz-mən\ *n*

fron•tis•piece \ˈfrən-tə-ˌspēs\ *n* : an illustration preceding and usu. facing the title page of a book

front man *n* : a person serving as a front or figurehead

front•ward \ˈfrənt-wərd\ *or* **front•wards** \-wərdz\ *adv or adj* : toward the front

[1]**frost** \ˈfrȯst\ *n* **1** : freezing temperature **2** : a covering of tiny ice crystals on a cold surface — **frosty** *adj*

[2]**frost** *vb* **1** : to cover with frost **2** : to put icing on (as a cake) **3** : to produce a slightly roughened surface on (as glass) **4** : to injure or kill by frost

[1]**frost•bite** \ˈfrȯst-ˌbīt\ *vb* **-bit** \-ˌbit\; **-bit•ten** \-ˌbit-ᵊn\; **-bit•ing** : to injure by frost or frostbite

[2]**frostbite** *n* : the freezing or the local effect of a partial freezing of some part of the body

frost heave *n* : an upthrust of pavement caused by freezing of moist soil

frost•ing \ˈfrȯ-stiŋ\ *n* **1** : ICING **2** : dull finish on metal or glass

froth \ˈfrȯth\ *n, pl* **froths** \ˈfrȯths, ˈfrȯt͟hz\ **1** : bubbles formed in or on a liquid **2** : something light or worthless — **frothy** *adj*

frou•frou \ˈfrü-ˌfrü\ *n* [F] **1** : a rustling esp. of a woman's skirts **2** : showy or frilly ornamentation

fro•ward \ˈfrō-wərd\ *adj* : DISOBEDIENT, WILLFUL

frown \ˈfrau̇n\ *vb* **1** : to wrinkle the forehead (as in displeasure or thought) **2** : to look with disapproval **3** : to express with a frown — **frown** *n*

frow•sy *or* **frow•zy** \ˈfrau̇-zē\ *adj* **frow•si•er** *or* **frow•zi•er; -est** : having a slovenly or uncared-for appearance

froze *past of* FREEZE

fro•zen \ˈfrōz-ᵊn\ *adj* **1** : treated, affected, or crusted over by freezing **2** : subject to long and severe cold **3** : incapable of being changed, moved, or undone : FIXED ⟨~ wages⟩ **4** : not available for present use ⟨~ capital⟩ **5** : expressing or characterized by cold unfriendliness

FRS *abbr* Federal Reserve System

frt *abbr* freight

fruc•ti•fy \ˈfrək-tə-ˌfī, ˈfru̇k-\ *vb* **-fied; -fy•ing** **1** : to bear fruit **2** : to make fruitful or productive

fru•gal \ˈfrü-gəl\ *adj* : ECONOMICAL, THRIFTY — **fru•gal•i•ty** \frü-ˈga-lə-tē\ *n* — **fru•gal•ly** *adv*

[1]**fruit** \ˈfrüt\ *n* [ME, fr. OF, fr. L *fructus* fruit, use, fr. *frui* to enjoy, have the use of] **1** : a product of plant growth; *esp* : a usu. edible and sweet reproductive body (as a strawberry or apple) of a seed plant **2** : a product of fertilization in a plant; *esp* : the ripe ovary of a seed plant with its contents and appendages **3** : CONSEQUENCE, RESULT — **fruit•ed** \ˈfrü-təd\ *adj*

[2]**fruit** *vb* : to bear or cause to bear fruit

fruit•cake \ˈfrüt-ˌkāk\ *n* : a rich cake containing nuts, dried or candied fruits, and spices

fruit fly *n* : any of various small dipteran flies whose larvae feed on fruit or decaying vegetable matter

fruit•ful \ˈfrüt-fəl\ *adj* **1** : yielding or producing fruit **2** : very productive ⟨a ~ soil⟩; *also* : bringing results ⟨a ~ idea⟩ — **fruit•ful•ly** *adv* — **fruit•ful•ness** *n*

fru•ition \frü-ˈi-shən\ *n* **1** : ENJOYMENT **2** : the state of bearing fruit **3** : REALIZATION, ACCOMPLISHMENT

fruit•less \ˈfrüt-ləs\ *adj* **1** : not bearing fruit **2** : UNSUCCESSFUL ⟨a ~ attempt⟩ — **fruit•less•ly** *adv*

fruity \ˈfrü-tē\ *adj* **fruit•i•er; -est** : resembling a fruit esp. in flavor

frumpy \ˈfrəm-pē\ *adj* **frump•i•er; -est** : DOWDY, DRAB

frus•trate \ˈfrəs-ˌtrāt\ *vb* **frus•trat•ed; frus•trat•ing** **1** : to balk or defeat in an endeavor **2** : to induce feelings of insecurity, discouragement, or dissatisfaction in **3** : to bring to nothing — **frus•trat•ing•ly** *adv* — **frus•tra•tion** \ˌfrəs-ˈtrā-shən\ *n*

frus•tum \ˈfrəs-təm\ *n, pl* **frustums** *or* **frus•ta** \-tə\ : the part of a cone or pyramid formed by cutting off the top by a plane parallel to the base

frwy *abbr* freeway

[1]**fry** \ˈfrī\ *vb* **fried; fry•ing 1 :** to cook in a pan or on a griddle over heat esp. with the use of fat **2 :** to undergo frying

[2]**fry** *n, pl* **fries 1 :** a social gathering where fried food is eaten **2 :** a dish of something fried; *esp, pl* **:** FRENCH FRIES

[3]**fry** *n, pl* **fry 1 :** recently hatched fishes; *also* **:** very small adult fishes **2 :** members of a group or class ⟨small ~⟩

fry•er \ˈfrī-ər\ *n* **1 :** something (as a young chicken) suitable for frying **2 :** a deep utensil for frying foods

FSLIC *abbr* Federal Savings and Loan Insurance Corporation

ft *abbr* **1** feet; foot **2** fort

FTC *abbr* Federal Trade Commission

fuch•sia \ˈfyü-shə\ *n* **1 :** any of a genus of shrubs related to the evening primrose and grown for their showy nodding often red or purple flowers **2 :** a vivid reddish purple color

fud•dle \ˈfəd-ᵊl\ *vb* **fud•dled; fud•dling :** MUDDLE, CONFUSE

fud•dy–dud•dy \ˈfə-dē-ˌdə-dē\ *n, pl* **-dies :** one that is old-fashioned, unimaginative, or conservative

[1]**fudge** \ˈfəj\ *vb* **fudged; fudg•ing 1 :** to exceed the proper bounds of something **2 :** CHEAT; *also* **:** FALSIFY **3 :** to fail to come to grips with

[2]**fudge** *n* **1 :** NONSENSE **2 :** a soft candy of milk, sugar, butter, and flavoring

[1]**fu•el** \ˈfyü-əl, ˈfyül\ *n* **:** a material used to produce heat or power by burning; *also* **:** a material from which nuclear energy can be liberated

[2]**fuel** *vb* **-eled** *or* **-elled; -el•ing** *or* **-el•ling :** to provide with or take in fuel

fuel cell *n* **:** a device that continuously changes the chemical energy of a fuel directly into electrical energy

[1]**fu•gi•tive** \ˈfyü-jə-tiv\ *n* **1 :** one who flees or tries to escape **2 :** something elusive or hard to find

[2]**fugitive** *adj* **1 :** running away or trying to escape **2 :** likely to vanish suddenly **:** not fixed or lasting

fugue \ˈfyüg\ *n* **1 :** a musical composition in which different parts successively repeat the theme **2 :** a disturbed state of consciousness characterized by acts that are not recalled upon recovery

füh•rer *or* **fueh•rer** \ˈfyu̇r-ər, ˈfir-\ *n* **:** LEADER; *esp* **:** TYRANT

[1]**-ful** \fəl\ *adj suffix, sometimes* **-ful•ler;** *sometimes* **-ful•lest 1 :** full of ⟨pride*ful*⟩ **2 :** characterized by ⟨peace*ful*⟩ **3 :** having the qualities of ⟨master*ful*⟩ **4 :** tending, given, or liable to ⟨help*ful*⟩

[2]**-ful** \ˌfu̇l\ *n suffix* **:** number or quantity that fills or would fill ⟨room*ful*⟩

ful•crum \ˈfu̇l-krəm, ˈfəl-\ *n, pl* **ful•crums** *or* **ful•cra** \-krə\ [LL, fr. L, bedpost] **:** the support on which a lever turns

F fulcrum

ful•fill *or* **ful•fil** \fu̇l-ˈfil\ *vb* **ful•filled; ful•fill•ing 1 :** to put into effect **2 :** to bring to an end **3 :** SATISFY **— ful•fill•ment** *n*

[1]**full** \ˈfu̇l\ *adj* **1 :** FILLED **2 :** complete esp. in detail, number, or duration **3 :** having all the distinguishing characteristics ⟨a ~ member⟩ **4 :** MAXIMUM **5 :** rounded in outline ⟨a ~ figure⟩ **6 :** possessing or containing an abundance ⟨~ of wrinkles⟩ **7 :** having an abundance of material ⟨a ~ skirt⟩ **8 :** satisfied esp. with food or drink **9 :** having volume or depth of sound **10 :** completely occupied with a thought or plan **— full•ness** *also* **ful•ness** *n*

[2]**full** *adv* **1 :** VERY, EXTREMELY **2 :** ENTIRELY **3 :** STRAIGHT, SQUARELY ⟨hit him ~ in the face⟩

[3]**full** *n* **1 :** the highest or fullest state or degree **2 :** the utmost extent **3 :** the requisite or complete amount

[4]**full** *vb* **:** to shrink and thicken (woolen cloth) by moistening, heating, and pressing **— full•er** *n*

full•back \ˈfu̇l-ˌbak\ *n* **:** a football back stationed between the halfbacks

full–blood•ed \ˈfu̇l-ˈblə-dəd\ *adj* **:** of unmixed ancestry **:** PUREBRED

full–blown \-ˈblōn\ *adj* **1 :** being at the height of bloom **2 :** fully mature or developed

full–bod•ied \-ˈbä-dēd\ *adj* **:** marked by richness and fullness

full dress *n* **:** the style of dress worn for ceremonial or formal occasions

full–fledged \ˈfu̇l-ˈflejd\ *adj* **1 :** fully developed **2 :** having attained complete status ⟨a ~ lawyer⟩

full house *n* **:** a poker hand containing three of a kind and a pair

full moon *n* **:** the moon with its whole disk illuminated

full–scale \ˈfu̇l-ˈskāl\ *adj* **1 :** identical to an original in proportion and size ⟨~ drawing⟩ **2 :** involving full use of available resources ⟨a ~ revolt⟩

full tilt *adv* **:** at high speed

full–time \ˈfu̇l-ˈtīm\ *adj or adv* **:** involving or working a normal or standard schedule

ful•ly \ˈfu̇-lē\ *adv* **1 :** in a full manner or degree **:** COMPLETELY **2 :** at least

ful•mi•nate \ˈfu̇l-mə-ˌnāt, ˈfəl-\ *vb* **-nat•ed; -nat•ing** [ME, fr. ML *fulminare,* fr. L, to strike (of lightning), fr. *fulmen* lightning] **:** to utter or send out censure or invective **:** condemn severely **— ful•mi•na•tion** \ˌfu̇l-mə-ˈnā-shən, ˌfəl-\ *n*

ful•some \ˈfu̇l-səm\ *adj* **1 :** COPIOUS, ABUNDANT ⟨~ detail⟩ **2 :** generous in amount or extent ⟨a ~ victory⟩ **3 :** excessively flattering ⟨~ praise⟩

fu•ma•role \ˈfyü-mə-ˌrōl\ *n* **:** a hole in a volcanic region from which hot gases issue

fum•ble \ˈfəm-bəl\ *vb* **fum•bled; fum•bling 1 :** to grope about clumsily **2 :** to fail to hold, catch, or handle properly **— fumble** *n*

[1]**fume** \ˈfyüm\ *n* **:** a usu. irritating smoke, vapor, or gas

[2]**fume** *vb* **fumed; fum•ing 1 :** to treat with fumes **2 :** to give off fumes **3 :** to express anger or annoyance

fu•mi•gant \ˈfyü-mi-gənt\ *n* **:** a substance used for fumigation

fu•mi•gate \ˈfyü-mə-ˌgāt\ *vb* **-gat•ed; -gat•ing :** to treat with fumes to disinfect or destroy pests **— fu•mi•ga•tion** \ˌfyü-mə-ˈgā-shən\ *n* **— fu•mi•ga•tor** \ˈfyü-mə-ˌgā-tər\ *n*

[1]**fun** \ˈfən\ *n* [E dial. *fun* to hoax] **1 :** something that provides amusement or enjoyment **2 :** ENJOYMENT

[2]**fun** *adj* **:** full of fun ⟨a ~ person⟩ ⟨had a ~ time⟩

[1]**func•tion** \ˈfəŋk-shən\ *n* **1 :** OCCUPATION **2 :** special purpose **3 :** the particular purpose for which a person or thing is specially fitted or used or for which a thing exists ⟨the ~ of a hammer⟩; *also* **:** the natural or proper action of a bodily part in a living thing ⟨the ~ of the heart⟩ **4 :** a formal ceremony or social affair **5 :** a mathematical relationship that assigns to each element of a set one and only one element of the same or another set **6 :** a variable (as a quality, trait, or measurement) that depends on and varies with another ⟨height is a ~ of age in children⟩ **— func•tion•al** \-shə-nəl\ *adj* **— func•tion•al•ly** *adv*

[2]**function** *vb* **:** to have or carry on a function

func•tion•ary \ˈfəŋk-shə-ˌner-ē\ *n, pl* **-ar•ies :** one who performs a certain function; *esp* **:** OFFICIAL

function word *n* **:** a word (as a preposition, auxiliary verb, or conjunction) expressing the grammatical relationship between other words

[1]**fund** \ˈfənd\ *n* [L *fundus* bottom, country estate] **1** : a sum of money or resources intended for a special purpose **2** : STORE, SUPPLY **3** *pl* : available money **4** : an organization administering a special fund

[2]**fund** *vb* **1** : to provide funds for **2** : to convert (a short-term obligation) into a long-term interest-bearing debt

fun•da•men•tal \ˌfən-də-ˈment-ᵊl\ *adj* **1** : serving as an origin : PRIMARY **2** : BASIC, ESSENTIAL **3** : RADICAL ⟨~ change⟩ **4** : of central importance : PRINCIPAL — **fundamental** *n* — **fun•da•men•tal•ly** *adv*

fun•da•men•tal•ism \-ˌi-zəm\ *n*, **1** *often cap* : a Protestant religious movement emphasizing the literal infallibility of the Bible **2** : a movement or attitude stressing strict adherence to a set of basic principles — **fun•da•men•tal•ist** \-ist\ *adj or n*

[1]**fu•ner•al** \ˈfyü-nə-rəl\ *adj* **1** : of, relating to, or constituting a funeral **2** : FUNEREAL 2

[2]**funeral** *n* : the ceremonies held for a dead person usu. before burial

fu•ner•ary \ˈfyü-nə-ˌrer-ē\ *adj* : of, used for, or associated with burial

fu•ne•re•al \fyu̇-ˈnir-ē-əl\ *adj* **1** : of or relating to a funeral **2** : suggesting a funeral

fun•gi•cide \ˈfən-jə-ˌsīd, ˈfəŋ-gə-\ *n* : an agent that kills or checks the growth of fungi — **fun•gi•cid•al** \ˌfən-jə-ˈsīd-ᵊl, ˌfən-gə-\ *adj*

fun•gus \ˈfəŋ-gəs\ *n, pl* **fun•gi** \ˈfən-ˌjī, ˈfəŋ-ˌgī\ *also* **fun•gus•es** \ˈfəŋ-gə-səz\ : any of a major group of organisms (as molds, mildews, and mushrooms) that lack chlorophyll and are usu. classified as plants — **fun•gal** \-gəl\ *adj* — **fun•gous** \-gəs\ *adj*

fu•nic•u•lar \fyu̇-ˈni-kyə-lər, fə-\ *n* : a cable railway ascending a mountain

funk \ˈfəŋk\ *n* : a depressed state of mind

funky \ˈfəŋ-kē\ *adj* **funk•i•er; -est 1** : having an earthy unsophisticated style and feeling; *esp* : having the style and feeling of older black American music **2** : odd or quaint in appearance or style

[1]**fun•nel** \ˈfən-ᵊl\ *n* **1** : a cone-shaped utensil with a tube used for catching and directing a downward flow (as of liquid) **2** : FLUE, SMOKESTACK

[2]**funnel** *vb* **-neled** *also* **-nelled; -nel•ing** *also* **-nel•ling 1** : to pass through or as if through a funnel **2** : to move to a central point or into a central channel

[1]**fun•ny** \ˈfə-nē\ *adj* **fun•ni•er; -est 1** : AMUSING **2** : FACETIOUS **3** : PECULIAR 3 **4** : UNDERHANDED — **funny** *adv*

[2]**funny** *n, pl* **funnies** : a comic strip or a comic section (as of a newspaper)

funny bone *n* : a place at the back of the elbow where a blow easily compresses a nerve and causes a painful tingling sensation

[1]**fur** \ˈfər\ *n* **1** : an article of clothing made of or with fur **2** : the hairy coat of a mammal esp. when fine, soft, and thick; *also* : this coat dressed for use — **fur** *adj* — **furred** \ˈfərd\ *adj*

[2]**fur** *abbr* furlong

fur•be•low \ˈfər-bə-ˌlō\ *n* **1** : FLOUNCE, RUFFLE **2** : showy trimming

fur•bish \ˈfər-bish\ *vb* **1** : to make lustrous : POLISH **2** : to give a new look to : RENOVATE

fu•ri•ous \ˈfyu̇r-ē-əs\ *adj* **1** : FIERCE, ANGRY, VIOLENT **2** : BOISTEROUS **3** : INTENSE — **fu•ri•ous•ly** *adv*

furl \ˈfərl\ *vb* **1** : to wrap or roll (as a sail or a flag) close to or around something **2** : to curl in furls — **furl** *n*

fur•long \ˈfər-ˌlȯŋ\ *n* [ME, fr. OE *furlang*, fr. *furh* furrow + *lang* long] : a unit of distance equal to 220 yards (about 201 meters)

fur•lough \ˈfər-lō\ *n* [D *verlof*, lit., permission] : a leave of absence from duty granted esp. to a soldier — **furlough** *vb*

fur•nace \ˈfər-nəs\ *n* : an enclosed structure in which heat is produced

fur•nish \ˈfər-nish\ *vb* **1** : to provide with what is needed : EQUIP **2** : SUPPLY, GIVE

fur•nish•ings \-ni-shiŋz\ *n pl* **1** : articles or accessories of dress **2** : FURNITURE

fur•ni•ture \ˈfər-ni-chər\ *n* : equipment that is necessary or desirable; *esp* : movable articles (as chairs or beds) for a room

fu•ror \ˈfyu̇r-ˌȯr\ *n* **1** : ANGER, RAGE **2** : a contagious excitement; *esp* : a fashionable craze **3** : UPROAR

fu•rore \-ˌōr\ *n* [It] : FUROR 2, 3

fur•ri•er \ˈfər-ē-ər\ *n* : one who prepares or deals in fur

fur•ring \ˈfər-iŋ\ *n* : wood or metal strips applied to a wall or ceiling to form a level surface or an air space

fur•row \ˈfər-ō\ *n* **1** : a trench in the earth made by a plow **2** : a narrow groove or wrinkle — **furrow** *vb*

fur•ry \ˈfər-ē\ *adj* **fur•ri•er; -est 1** : resembling or consisting of fur **2** : covered with fur

[1]**fur•ther** \ˈfər-t͟hər\ *adv* **1** : FARTHER 1 **2** : in addition : MOREOVER **3** : to a greater extent or degree

[2]**further** *vb* : to help forward — **fur•ther•ance** \ˈfər-thə-rəns\ *n*

[3]**further** *adj* **1** : FARTHER 1 **2** : ADDITIONAL

fur•ther•more \ˈfər-t͟hər-ˌmōr\ *adv* : in addition to what precedes : BESIDES

fur•ther•most \-ˌmōst\ *adj* : most distant : FARTHEST

fur•thest \ˈfər-t͟həst\ *adv or adj* : FARTHEST

fur•tive \ˈfər-tiv\ *adj* [F or L; F *furtif*, fr. L *furtivus*, fr. *furtum* theft, fr. *fur* thief] : done by stealth : SLY — **fur•tive•ly** *adv* — **fur•tive•ness** *n*

fu•ry \ˈfyu̇r-ē\ *n, pl* **furies 1** : intense and often destructive rage **2** : extreme fierceness or violence **3** : FRENZY

furze \ˈfərz\ *n* : GORSE

[1]**fuse** \ˈfyüz\ *vb* **fused; fus•ing 1** : MELT **2** : to unite by or as if by melting together — **fus•ible** *adj*

[2]**fuse** *n* : an electrical safety device having a metal wire or strip that melts and interrupts the circuit when the current becomes too strong

[3]**fuse** *n* **1** : a cord or cable that is set afire to ignite an explosive charge **2** *usu* **fuze** : a mechanical or electrical device for setting off the explosive charge of a projectile, bomb, or torpedo

[4]**fuse** *or* **fuze** \ˈfyüz\ *vb* **fused** *or* **fuzed; fus•ing** *or* **fuz•ing** : to equip with a fuse

fu•se•lage \ˈfyü-sə-ˌläzh, -zə-\ *n* : the central body portion of an aircraft

fu•sil•lade \ˈfyü-sə-ˌläd, -ˌlād\ *n* : a number of shots fired simultaneously or in rapid succession

fu•sion \ˈfyü-zhən\ *n* **1** : the act or process of melting or making plastic by heat **2** : union by or as if by melting **3** : the union of light atomic nuclei to form heavier nuclei with the release of huge quantities of energy

[1]**fuss** \ˈfəs\ *n* **1** : needless bustle or excitement : COMMOTION **2** : effusive praise **3** : a state of agitation **4** : OBJECTION, PROTEST **5** : DISPUTE

[2]**fuss** *vb* : to make a fuss

fuss•bud•get \ˈfəs-ˌbə-jət\ *n* : one who fusses or is fussy about trifles

fussy \ˈfə-sē\ *adj* **fuss•i•er; -est 1** : IRRITABLE **2** : overly decorated **3** : requiring or giving close attention or concern to details or niceties — **fuss•i•ly** \-sə-lē\ *adv* — **fuss•i•ness** \-sē-nəs\ *n*

fus•tian \ˈfəs-chən\ *n* **1** : a strong usu. cotton fabric **2** : pretentious writing or speech — **fustian** *adj*

fus•ty \ˈfəs-tē\ *adj* **fus•ti•er; -est** [ME, fr. *fust* wine cask, fr. MF, club, cask, fr. L *fustis*] **1** : MUSTY **2** : OLD-FASHIONED

fut *abbr* future

fu•tile \ˈfyüt-ᵊl, ˈfyü-ˌtīl\ *adj* **1** : USELESS, VAIN **2** : FRIVOLOUS, TRIVIAL — **fu•til•i•ty** \fyü-ˈti-lə-tē\ *n*

fu•ton \ˈfü-ˌtän\ *n* [Jp] : a usu. cotton-filled mattress used on the floor or in a frame

[1]**fu•ture** \ˈfyü-chər\ *adj* **1** : of, relating to, or constituting a verb tense that expresses time yet to come **2** : coming after the present

[2]future *n* **1** : time that is to come **2** : what is going to happen **3** : an expectation of advancement or progressive development **4** : the future tense; *also* : a verb form in it

fu•tur•ism \ˈfyü-chə-ˌri-zəm\ *n* : a modern movement in art, music, and literature that tries esp. to express the energy and activity of mechanical processes — **fu•tur•ist** \ˈfyü-chə-rist\ *n*

fu•tur•is•tic \ˌfyü-chə-ˈris-tik\ *adj* : of or relating to the future or to futurism; *also* : very modern

fu•tu•ri•ty \fyu̇-ˈtu̇r-ə-tē, -ˈtyu̇r-\ *n, pl* **-ties** **1** : FUTURE **2** : the quality or state of being future **3** *pl* : future events or prospects

fuze *var of* FUSE

fuzz \ˈfəz\ *n* : fine light particles or fibers (as of down or fluff)

fuzzy \ˈfə-zē\ *adj* **fuzz•i•er; -est** **1** : having or resembling fuzz **2** : INDISTINCT — **fuzz•i•ness** \-zē-nəs\ *n*

fwd *abbr* forward

FWD *abbr* front-wheel drive

FY *abbr* fiscal year

-fy *vb suffix* : make : form into ⟨dandi*fy*⟩

FYI *abbr* for your information

G

[1]g \ˈjē\ *n, pl* **g's** *or* **gs** \ˈjēz\ *often cap* **1** : the 7th letter of the English alphabet **2** : a unit of force equal to the force exerted by gravity on a body at rest and used to indicate the force to which a body is subjected when accelerated **3** *slang* : a sum of $1000

[2]g *abbr, often cap* **1** game **2** gauge **3** good **4** gram **5** gravity

ga *abbr* gauge

[1]Ga *abbr* Georgia

[2]Ga *symbol* gallium

GA *abbr* **1** general assembly **2** general average **3** general of the army **4** Georgia

gab \ˈgab\ *vb* **gabbed; gab•bing** : to talk in a rapid or thoughtless manner : CHATTER — **gab** *n*

gab•ar•dine \ˈga-bər-ˌdēn\ *n* **1** : GABERDINE 1 **2** : a firm durable twilled fabric having diagonal ribs and made of various fibers; *also* : a garment of gabardine

gab•ble \ˈga-bəl\ *vb* **gab•bled; gab•bling** : JABBER, BABBLE

gab•by \ˈga-bē\ *adj* **gab•bi•er; -est** : TALKATIVE, GARRULOUS

gab•er•dine \ˈga-bər-ˌdēn\ *n* **1** : a long loose outer garment worn in medieval times and associated esp. with Jews **2** : GABARDINE 2

gab•fest \ˈgab-ˌfest\ *n* **1** : an informal gathering for general talk **2** : an extended conversation

ga•ble \ˈgā-bəl\ *n* : the vertical triangular end of a building formed by the sides of the roof sloping from the ridge down to the eaves — **ga•bled** \-bəld\ *adj*

Gab•o•nese \ˌga-bə-ˈnēz, -ˈnēs\ *n* : a native or inhabitant of Gabon — **Gabonese** *adj*

gad \ˈgad\ *vb* **gad•ded; gad•ding** : to be constantly active without specific purpose — usu. used with *about* — **gad•der** *n*

gad•about \ˈga-də-ˌbau̇t\ *n* : a person who flits about in social activity

gad•fly \ˈgad-ˌflī\ *n* **1** : a fly that bites or harasses livestock **2** : a person who annoys esp. by persistent criticism

gad•get \ˈga-jət\ *n* : DEVICE, CONTRIVANCE — **gad•get•ry** \ˈga-jə-trē\ *n*

gad•o•lin•i•um \ˌgad-ᵊl-ˈi-nē-əm\ *n* : a magnetic metallic chemical element — see ELEMENT table

[1]Gael \ˈgāl\ *n* : a Celtic inhabitant of Ireland or Scotland

[2]Gael *abbr* Gaelic

Gael•ic \ˈgā-lik\ *adj* : of or relating to the Gaels or their languages — **Gaelic** *n*

gaff \ˈgaf\ *n* **1** : a spear used in taking fish or turtles; *also* : a metal hook for holding or lifting heavy fish **2** : the spar supporting the top of a fore-and-aft sail **3** : rough treatment : ABUSE — **gaff** *vb*

gaffe \ˈgaf\ *n* : a social blunder

gaf•fer \ˈga-fər\ *n* **1** : an old man **2** : a lighting electrician on a motion-picture or television set

[1]gag \ˈgag\ *vb* **gagged; gag•ging** **1** : to restrict use of the mouth with a gag **2** : to prevent from speaking freely **3** : to retch or cause to retch **4** : OBSTRUCT, CHOKE **5** : BALK **6** : to make quips — **gag•ger** *n*

[2]gag *n* **1** : something thrust into the mouth esp. to prevent speech or outcry **2** : an official check or restraint on free speech **3** : a laugh-provoking remark or act **4** : PRANK, TRICK

[1]gage \ˈgāj\ *n* **1** : a token of defiance; *esp* : a glove or cap cast on the ground as a pledge of combat **2** : SECURITY

[2]gage *var of* GAUGE

gag•gle \ˈga-gəl\ *n* [ME *gagyll,* fr. *gagelen* to cackle] **1** : a flock of geese **2** : GROUP, CLUSTER

gai•ety \ˈgā-ə-tē\ *n, pl* **-eties** **1** : festive activity : MERRYMAKING **2** : MERRIMENT **3** : FINERY **syn** mirth, festivity, glee, hilarity, jollity

gai•ly \ˈgā-lē\ *adv* : in a gay manner

[1]gain \ˈgān\ *n* **1** : PROFIT **2** : ACQUISITION, ACCUMULATION **3** : INCREASE

[2]gain *vb* **1** : to get possession of : EARN **2** : WIN ⟨~ a victory⟩ **3** : to increase in ⟨~ momentum⟩ **4** : PERSUADE **5** : to arrive at **6** : ACHIEVE ⟨~ strength⟩ **7** : to run fast ⟨the watch ~*s* a minute a day⟩ **8** : PROFIT **9** : INCREASE **10** : to improve in health **syn** accomplish, attain, realize — **gain•er** *n*

gain•ful \ˈgān-fəl\ *adj* : PROFITABLE — **gain•ful•ly** *adv*

gain•say \ˌgān-ˈsā\ *vb* **-said** \-ˈsād, -ˈsed\; **-say•ing; -says** \-ˈsāz, -ˈsez\ [ME *gainsayen,* fr. *gain-* against + *-sayen* to say] **1** : DENY, DISPUTE **2** : to speak against **syn** contradict, contravene, impugn, negate — **gain•say•er** *n*

gait \ˈgāt\ *n* : manner of moving on foot; *also* : a particular pattern or style of such moving — **gait•ed** *adj*

gai•ter \ˈgā-tər\ *n* **1** : a leg covering reaching from the instep to ankle, mid-calf, or knee **2** : an overshoe with a fabric upper **3** : an ankle-high shoe with elastic gores in the sides

[1]gal \ˈgal\ *n* : GIRL

[2]gal *abbr* gallon

Gal *abbr* Galatians

ga•la \ˈgā-lə, ˈga-, ˈgä-\ *n* : a gay celebration : FESTIVITY — **gala** *adj*

ga•lac•tic \gə-ˈlak-tik\ *adj* : of or relating to a galaxy

Ga•la•tians \gə-ˈlā-shənz\ *n* — see BIBLE table

gal•axy \ˈga-lək-sē\ *n, pl* **-ax•ies** [ME *galaxie, galaxias,* fr. LL *galaxias,* fr. Gk, fr. *galakt-, gala* milk] **1** *often cap* : MILKY WAY GALAXY — used with *the* **2** : a very large group of stars **3** : an assemblage of brilliant or famous persons or things

gale \ˈgāl\ *n* **1** : a strong wind **2** : an emotional outburst ⟨~*s* of laughter⟩

ga•le•na \gə-ˈlē-nə\ *n* : a lustrous bluish gray mineral that consists of the sulfide of lead and is the chief ore of lead

[1]gall \ˈgȯl\ *n* **1** : BILE **2** : something bitter to endure **3** : RANCOR **4** : IMPUDENCE **syn** effrontery, brass, cheek, chutzpah, audacity, presumption

[2]gall *n* : a skin sore caused by chafing

[3]gall *vb* **1** : CHAFE; *esp* : to become sore or worn by rubbing **2** : VEX, HARASS

[4]gall *n* : a swelling of plant tissue caused by parasites

[1]gal•lant \gə-ˈlant, -ˈlänt; ˈga-lənt\ *n* **1** : a young man of fashion **2** : a man who shows a marked fondness for the company of women and who is esp. attentive to them **3** : SUITOR

[2]**gal·lant** \ˈga-lənt *(usual for 2, 3, 4)*; gə-ˈlant, -ˈlänt *(usual for 5)*\ *adj* **1** : showy in dress or bearing : SMART **2** : SPLENDID, STATELY **3** : SPIRITED, BRAVE **4** : CHIVALROUS, NOBLE **5** : polite and attentive to women — **gal·lant·ly** *adv*

gal·lant·ry \ˈga-lən-trē\ *n, pl* **-ries 1** *archaic* : gallant appearance **2** : an act of marked courtesy **3** : courteous attention to a woman **4** : conspicuous bravery **syn** heroism, valor, prowess

gall·blad·der \ˈgȯl-ˌbla-dər\ *n* : a membranous muscular sac attached to the liver and serving to store bile

gal·le·on \ˈga-lē-ən\ *n* : a large square-rigged sailing ship formerly used esp. by the Spanish

galleon

gal·le·ria \ˌga-lə-ˈrē-ə\ *n* [It] : a roofed and usu. glass-enclosed promenade or court

gal·lery \ˈga-lə-rē\ *n, pl* **-ler·ies 1** : an outdoor balcony; *also* : PORCH, VERANDA **2** : a long narrow passage, apartment, or hall **3** : a narrow passage (as one made underground by a miner or through wood by an insect) **4** : a room where works of art are exhibited; *also* : an organization dealing in works of art **5** : a balcony in a theater, auditorium, or church; *esp* : the highest one in a theater **6** : the spectators at a tennis or golf match **7** : a photographer's studio — **gal·ler·ied** \-rēd\ *adj*

gal·ley \ˈga-lē\ *n, pl* **galleys 1** : a long low ship propelled esp. by oars and formerly used esp. in the Mediterranean Sea **2** : the kitchen esp. of a ship or airplane **3** : a proof of typeset matter esp. in a single column

Gal·lic \ˈga-lik\ *adj* : of or relating to Gaul or France

gal·li·mau·fry \ˌga-lə-ˈmȯ-frē\ *n, pl* **-fries** [MF *galimafree* stew] : HODGEPODGE

gal·li·nule \ˈga-lə-ˌnül, -ˌnyül\ *n* : any of several aquatic birds related to the rails

gal·li·um \ˈga-lē-əm\ *n* : a rare bluish white metallic chemical element — see ELEMENT table

gal·li·vant \ˈga-lə-ˌvant\ *vb* : to travel, roam, or move about for pleasure

gal·lon \ˈga-lən\ *n* — see WEIGHT table

[1]**gal·lop** \ˈga-ləp\ *vb* **1** : to go or cause to go at a gallop **2** : to run fast — **gal·lop·er** *n*

[2]**gallop** *n* **1** : a bounding gait of a quadruped; *esp* : a fast 3-beat gait of a horse **2** : a ride or run at a gallop

gal·lows \ˈga-lōz\ *n, pl* **gallows** *or* **gal·lows·es** : a frame usu. of two upright posts and a crosspiece from which criminals are hanged; *also* : the punishment of hanging

gall·stone \ˈgȯl-ˌstōn\ *n* : an abnormal concretion occurring in the gallbladder or bile passages

gal·lus·es \ˈga-lə-səz\ *n pl* : SUSPENDERS

ga·lore \gə-ˈlōr\ *adj* [Ir *go leor* enough] : ABUNDANT, PLENTIFUL

ga·losh \gə-ˈläsh\ *n* : a high overshoe

galv *abbr* galvanized

gal·va·nise *Brit var of* GALVANIZE

gal·va·nize \ˈgal-və-ˌnīz\ *vb* **-nized; -niz·ing 1** : to stimulate as if by an electric shock **2** : to coat (iron or steel) with zinc — **gal·va·ni·za·tion** \ˌgal-və-nə-ˈzā-shən\ *n* — **gal·va·niz·er** *n*

gal·va·nom·e·ter \ˌgal-və-ˈnä-mə-tər\ *n* : an instrument for detecting or measuring a small electric current

Gam·bi·an \ˈgam-bē-ən\ *n* : a native or inhabitant of Gambia — **Gambian** *adj*

gam·bit \ˈgam-bət\ *n* [It *gambetto*, lit., act of tripping someone, fr. *gamba* leg] **1** : a chess opening in which a player risks one or more minor pieces to gain an advantage in position **2** : a calculated move : STRATAGEM **syn** trick, artifice, gimmick, maneuver, play, ruse

[1]**gam·ble** \ˈgam-bəl\ *vb* **gam·bled; gam·bling 1** : to play a game for money or property **2** : BET, WAGER **3** : VENTURE, HAZARD — **gam·bler** *n*

[2]**gamble** *n* : a risky undertaking

gam·bol \ˈgam-bəl\ *vb* **-boled** *or* **-bolled; -bol·ing** *or* **-bol·ling** : to skip about in play : FRISK — **gambol** *n*

gam·brel roof \ˈgam-brəl-\ *n* : a roof with a lower steeper slope and an upper flatter one on each side

[1]**game** \ˈgām\ *n* **1** : AMUSEMENT, DIVERSION **2** : SPORT, FUN **3** : SCHEME, PROJECT **4** : a line of work : PROFESSION **5** : CONTEST **6** : animals hunted for sport or food; *also* : the flesh of a game animal

[2]**game** *vb* **gamed; gam·ing** : to play for a stake : GAMBLE

[3]**game** *adj* : PLUCKY — **game·ly** *adv* — **game·ness** *n*

[4]**game** *adj* : LAME ⟨a ~ leg⟩

game·cock \ˈgām-ˌkäk\ *n* : a rooster trained for fighting

game fish *n* : SPORT FISH

game·keep·er \ˈgām-ˌkē-pər\ *n* : a person in charge of the breeding and protection of game animals or birds in a private preserve

game·some \ˈgām-səm\ *adj* : MERRY **syn** playful, frolicsome, sportive, antic

game·ster \ˈgām-stər\ *n* : GAMBLER

gam·ete \ˈga-ˌmēt\ *n* : a mature germ cell — **ga·met·ic** \gə-ˈme-tik\ *adj*

game theory *n* : the analysis of a situation involving conflicting interests (as in business) in terms of gains and losses among opposing players

gam·in \ˈga-mən\ *n* [F] **1** : a boy who hangs around on the streets **2** : GAMINE 2

ga·mine \ga-ˈmēn\ *n* **1** : a girl who hangs around on the streets **2** : a small playfully mischievous girl

gam·ma \ˈga-mə\ *n* : the 3d letter of the Greek alphabet — Γ or γ

gamma globulin *n* : a blood protein fraction rich in antibodies; *also* : a solution of this from human blood donors that is given to provide immunity against some infectious diseases (as measles)

gamma ray *n* : a photon emitted by a radioactive substance; *also* : a high-energy photon — usu. used in pl.

gam·mer \ˈga-mər\ *n, archaic* : an old woman

gam·mon \ˈga-mən\ *n, chiefly Brit* : a cured ham or side of bacon

gam·ut \ˈga-mət\ *n* : an entire range or series **syn** scale, spectrum

gamy *or* **gam·ey** \ˈgā-mē\ *adj* **gam·i·er; -est 1** : GAME, PLUCKY **2** : having the flavor of game esp. when near tainting **3** : SCANDALOUS; *also* : DISREPUTABLE — **gam·i·ness** \-mē-nəs\ *n*

[1]**gan·der** \ˈgan-dər\ *n* : a male goose

[2]**gander** *n* : LOOK, GLANCE

[1]**gang** \ˈgaŋ\ *n* **1** : a set of implements or devices arranged to operate together **2** : a group of persons working or associated together; *esp* : a group of criminals or young delinquents

[2]**gang** *vb* **1** : to attack in a gang — usu. used with *up* **2** : to form into or move or act as a gang

gang·land \ˈgaŋ-ˌland\ *n* : the world of organized crime

gan•gling \ˈgaŋ-gliŋ\ *adj* : loosely and awkwardly built : LANKY

gan•gli•on \ˈgaŋ-glē-ən\ *n, pl* **-glia** \-ə\ *also* **-gli•ons** : a mass of nerve cells outside the central nervous system; *also* : NUCLEUS 3 — **gan•gli•on•ic** \ˌgaŋ-glē-ˈä-nik\ *adj*

gan•gly \ˈgaŋ-glē\ *adj* : GANGLING

gang•plank \ˈgaŋ-ˌplaŋk\ *n* : a movable bridge from a ship to the shore

gang•plow \-ˌplaů\ *n* : a plow that turns two or more furrows at one time

gan•grene \ˈgaŋ-ˌgrēn, gaŋ-ˈgrēn\ *n* : the death of soft tissues in a local area of the body due to loss of the blood supply — **gangrene** *vb* — **gan•gre•nous** \ˈgaŋ-grə-nəs\ *adj*

gang•ster \ˈgaŋ-stər\ *n* : a member of a gang of criminals : RACKETEER

gang•way \ˈgaŋ-ˌwā\ *n* **1** : PASSAGEWAY; *also* : GANGPLANK **2** : clear passage through a crowd

gan•net \ˈga-nət\ *n, pl* **gannets** *also* **gannet** : any of several large fish-eating usu. white and black marine birds that breed on offshore islands

gant•let \ˈgȯnt-lət\ *var of* GAUNTLET

gan•try \ˈgan-trē\ *n, pl* **gantries** : a frame structure on side supports over or around something

GAO *abbr* General Accounting Office

gaol \ˈjāl\, **gaol•er** \ˈjā-lər\ *chiefly Brit var of* JAIL, JAILER

gap \ˈgap\ *n* **1** : BREACH, CLEFT **2** : a mountain pass **3** : a blank space; *also* : an incomplete or deficient area **4** : a wide difference in character or attitude **5** : a problem caused by a disparity ⟨credibility ~⟩

gape \ˈgāp\ *vb* **gaped; gap•ing 1** : to open the mouth wide **2** : to open or part widely **3** : to stare with mouth open **4** : YAWN — **gape** *n*

[1]**gar** \ˈgär\ *n* : any of several fishes that have a long body resembling that of a pike and long narrow jaws

[2]**gar** *abbr* garage

GAR *abbr* Grand Army of the Republic

[1]**ga•rage** \gə-ˈräzh, -ˈräj\ *n* [F] : a shelter or repair shop for automobiles

[2]**garage** *vb* **ga•raged; ga•rag•ing** : to keep or put in a garage

garage sale *n* : a sale of used household or personal articles held on the seller's own premises

garb \ˈgärb\ *n* **1** : style of dress **2** : outward form : APPEARANCE — **garb** *vb*

gar•bage \ˈgär-bij\ *n* **1** : food waste **2** : unwanted or useless material — **gar•bage•man** \-ˌman\ *n*

gar•ble \ˈgär-bəl\ *vb* **gar•bled; gar•bling** [ME *garbelen,* fr. It *garbellare* to sift, fr. Ar *gharbala*] : to distort the meaning of ⟨~ a story⟩

gar•çon \gär-ˈsōⁿ\ *n, pl* **garçons** *same or* -ˈsoⁿz\ [F, boy, servant] : WAITER

[1]**gar•den** \ˈgärd-ᵊn\ *n* **1** : a plot for growing fruits, flowers, or vegetables **2** : a public recreation area; *esp* : one for displaying plants or animals

[2]**garden** *vb* : to lay out or work in a garden — **gar•den•er** *n*

gar•de•nia \gär-ˈdē-nyə\ *n* [NL, genus name, fr. Alexander *Garden* †1791 Scot. naturalist] : the fragrant white or yellow flower of any of a genus of trees or shrubs related to the madder; *also* : one of these trees

garden–variety *adj* : COMMONPLACE, ORDINARY

gar•fish \ˈgär-ˌfish\ *n* : GAR

gar•gan•tuan \gär-ˈgan-chə-wən\ *adj, often cap* : of tremendous size or volume **syn** huge, colossal, gigantic, mammoth, monstrous, titanic

gar•gle \ˈgär-gəl\ *vb* **gar•gled; gar•gling** : to rinse the throat with liquid agitated by air forced through it from the lungs — **gargle** *n*

gar•goyle \ˈgär-ˌgȯil\ *n* **1** : a waterspout in the form of a grotesque human or animal figure projecting from the roof or eaves of a building **2** : a grotesquely carved figure

gar•ish \ˈgar-ish\ *adj* : FLASHY, GLARING, SHOWY, GAUDY

[1]**gar•land** \ˈgär-lənd\ *n* : WREATH, CHAPLET

[2]**garland** *vb* : to form into or deck with a garland

gar•lic \ˈgär-lik\ *n* [ME *garlek,* fr. OE *gārlēac,* fr. *gār* spear + *lēac* leek] : an herb related to the lilies and grown for its pungent bulbs used in cooking; *also* : its bulb — **gar•licky** \-li-kē\ *adj*

gar•ment \ˈgär-mənt\ *n* : an article of clothing

gar•ner \ˈgär-nər\ *vb* **1** : to gather into storage **2** : to acquire by effort **3** : ACCUMULATE, COLLECT

gar•net \ˈgär-nət\ *n* [ME *grenat,* fr. MF, fr. *grenat,* adj., red like a pomegranate, fr. *(pomme) grenate* pomegranate] : a transparent deep red mineral sometimes used as a gem

gar•nish \ˈgär-nish\ *vb* **1** : DECORATE, EMBELLISH **2** : to add decorative or savory touches to (food) **3** : GARNISHEE — **garnish** *n*

gar•nish•ee \ˌgär-nə-ˈshē\ *vb* **-eed; -ee•ing 1** : to serve with a garnishment **2** : to take (as a debtor's wages) by legal authority

gar•nish•ment \ˈgär-nish-mənt\ *n* **1** : GARNISH **2** : a legal warning concerning the attachment of property to satisfy a debt; *also* : the attachment of such property

gar•ni•ture \-ni-chər, -ˌchůr\ *n* : EMBELLISHMENT, TRIMMING

gar•ret \ˈgar-ət\ *n* [ME *garette* watchtower, fr. MF *garite*] : the part of a house just under the roof : ATTIC

gar•ri•son \ˈgar-ə-sən\ *n* **1** : a military post; *esp* : a permanent military installation **2** : the troops stationed at a garrison — **garrison** *vb*

garrison state *n* : a state organized on a primarily military basis

gar•rote *or* **ga•rotte** \gə-ˈrät, -ˈrōt\ *n* [Sp *garrote*] **1** : a method of execution by strangulation; *also* : the apparatus used **2** : an implement (as a wire with handles) for strangulation — **garrote** *or* **garotte** *vb*

gar•ru•lous \ˈgar-ə-ləs\ *adj* : TALKATIVE, WORDY — **gar•ru•li•ty** \gə-ˈrü-lə-tē\ *n* — **gar•ru•lous•ly** *adv* — **gar•ru•lous•ness** *n*

gar•ter \ˈgär-tər\ *n* : a band or strap worn to hold up a stocking or sock

garter snake *n* : any of numerous harmless American snakes with longitudinal stripes on the back

[1]**gas** \ˈgas\ *n, pl* **gas•es** *also* **gas•ses** [NL, alter. of L *chaos* space, chaos] **1** : a fluid (as hydrogen or air) that tends to expand indefinitely **2** : a gas or mixture of gases used as a fuel or anesthetic **3** : a substance that can be used to produce a poisonous, asphyxiating, or irritant atmosphere **4** : GASOLINE — **gas•eous** \ˈga-sē-əs, -shəs\ *adj*

[2]**gas** *vb* **gassed; gas•sing 1** : to treat with gas; *also* : to poison with gas **2** : to fill with gasoline ⟨~ up the car⟩

gash \ˈgash\ *n* : a deep long cut — **gash** *vb*

gas•ket \ˈgas-kət\ *n* : material (as rubber) or a part used to seal a joint

gas•light \ˈgas-ˌlīt\ *n* **1** : light made by burning illuminating gas **2** : a gas flame; *also* : a gas lighting fixture

gas mask *n* : a mask with a chemical air filter used to protect the face and lungs against poison gas

gas•o•line \ˈga-sə-ˌlēn, ˌga-sə-ˈlēn\ *n* : a flammable liquid mixture made from petroleum and used esp. as a motor fuel

gasp \ˈgasp\ *vb* **1** : to catch the breath audibly (as with shock) **2** : to breathe laboriously : PANT **3** : to utter in a gasping manner — **gasp** *n*

gas•tric \ˈgas-trik\ *adj* : of or relating to the stomach

gastric juice *n* : the acid digestive secretion of the stomach

gas•tri•tis \gas-ˈtrī-təs\ *n* : inflammation of the lining of the stomach

gas•tro•en•ter•ol•o•gy \ˌgas-trō-ˌen-tə-ˈrä-lə-jē\ *n* : a branch of medicine concerned with the structure, functions, and diseases of the stomach and intestines — **gas•tro•en•ter•ol•o•gist** \-jist\ *n*

gas•tro•in•tes•ti•nal \ˌgas-trō-in-ˈtes-tən-ᵊl\ *adj* : of, relating to, affecting, or including both the stomach and intestine ⟨~ tract⟩ ⟨~ distress⟩

gas•tron•o•my \gas-ˈträ-nə-mē\ *n* [F *gastronomie,* fr. Gk *Gastronomia,* title of a 4th cent. B.C. poem, fr. *gastēr* belly + *-nomia* system of laws] : the art of good eating — **gas•tro•nom•ic** \ˌgas-trə-ˈnä-mik\ *also* **gas•tro•nom•i•cal** \-mi-kəl\ *adj*

gas•tro•pod \ˈgas-trə-ˌpäd\ *n* : any of a large class of mollusks (as snails and slugs) with a muscular foot and a spiral shell or none — **gastropod** *adj*

gas•works \ˈgas-ˌwərks\ *n sing or pl* : a plant for manufacturing gas

gate \ˈgāt\ *n* **1** : an opening for passage in a wall or fence **2** : a city or castle entrance often with defensive structures **3** : the frame or door that closes a gate **4** : a device (as a valve) for controlling the passage of a fluid or signal **5** : the total admission receipts or the number of people at an event

-gate \ˌgāt\ *n comb form* [Water*gate,* scandal that resulted in the resignation of President Richard Nixon in 1974] : usu. political scandal often involving the concealment of wrongdoing

gate–crash•er \ˈgāt-ˌkra-shər\ *n* : a person who enters without paying admission or attends without invitation

gate•keep•er \-ˌkē-pər\ *n* : a person who tends or guards a gate

gate•post \-ˌpōst\ *n* : the post to which a gate is hung or the one against which it closes

gate•way \-ˌwā\ *n* **1** : an opening for a gate **2** : a means of entrance or exit

[1]**gath•er** \ˈga-t͟hər\ *vb* **1** : to bring together : COLLECT **2** : PICK, HARVEST **3** : to pick up little by little **4** : to gain or win by gradual increase : ACCUMULATE ⟨~ speed⟩ **5** : to summon up ⟨~ courage to dive⟩ **6** : to draw about or close to something **7** : to pull (fabric) along a line of stitching into puckers **8** : GUESS, DEDUCE, INFER **9** : ASSEMBLE **10** : to swell out and fill with pus **11** : GROW, INCREASE **syn** congregate, forgather — **gath•er•er** *n*

[2]**gather** *n* : a puckering in cloth made by gathering

GATT \ˈgat\ *abbr* General Agreement on Tariffs and Trade

gauche \ˈgōsh\ *adj* [F, lit., left] **1** : lacking social experience or grace; *also* : not tactful **2** : crudely made or done **syn** clumsy, heavy-handed, inept, maladroit

gau•che•rie \ˌgō-shə-ˈrē\ *n* : a tactless or awkward action

gau•cho \ˈgau̇-chō\ *n, pl* **gauchos** : a cowboy of the So. American pampas

gaud \ˈgȯd\ *n* : ORNAMENT, TRINKET

gaudy \ˈgȯ-dē\ *adj* **gaud•i•er; -est 1** : ostentatiously or tastelessly ornamented **2** : marked by showiness or extravagance **syn** garish, flashy, glaring, tawdry — **gaud•i•ly** \-də-lē\ *adv* — **gaud•i•ness** \-dē-nəs\ *n*

[1]**gauge** *or* **gage** \ˈgāj\ *n* **1** : measurement according to some standard or system **2** : DIMENSIONS, SIZE **3** *usu gage* : an instrument for measuring, testing, or registering

[2]**gauge** *or* **gage** *vb* **gauged** *or* **gaged; gaug•ing** *or* **gag•ing 1** : MEASURE **2** : to determine the capacity or contents of **3** : ESTIMATE, JUDGE

gaunt \ˈgȯnt\ *adj* **1** : being thin and angular **2** : BARREN, DESOLATE **syn** bony, lank, lanky, lean, rawboned, skinny — **gaunt•ness** *n*

[1]**gaunt•let** \ˈgȯnt-lət\ *n* **1** : a protective glove **2** : an open challenge (as to combat) **3** : a dress glove extending above the wrist

[2]**gauntlet** *n* **1** : ORDEAL **2** : a double file of men armed with weapons (as clubs) with which to strike at an individual who is made to run between them

gauze \ˈgȯz\ *n* : a very thin often transparent fabric used esp. for draperies and surgical dressings — **gauzy** *adj*

gave *past of* GIVE

gav•el \ˈga-vəl\ *n* : the mallet of a presiding officer or auctioneer

ga•votte \gə-ˈvät\ *n* : a dance of French peasant origin marked by the raising rather than sliding of the feet

gawk \ˈgȯk\ *vb* : to gape or stare stupidly

gawky \ˈgȯ-kē\ *adj* **gawk•i•er; -est** : AWKWARD, CLUMSY — **gawk•i•ly** \-kə-lē\ *adv*

gay \ˈgā\ *adj* **1** : MERRY **2** : BRIGHT, LIVELY **3** : brilliant in color **4** : given to social pleasures; *also* : LICENTIOUS **5** : HOMOSEXUAL; *also* : of, relating to, or used by homosexuals

gay•ety, gay•ly *var of* GAIETY, GAILY

gaz *abbr* gazette

gaze \ˈgāz\ *vb* **gazed; gaz•ing** : to fix the eyes in a steady intent look **syn** gape, gawk, glare, goggle, peer, stare — **gaze** *n* — **gaz•er** *n*

ga•ze•bo \gə-ˈzē-bō\ *n, pl* **-bos 1** : BELVEDERE **2** : a freestanding roofed structure usu. open on the sides

ga•zelle \gə-ˈzel\ *n, pl* **gazelles** *also* **gazelle** : any of numerous small swift graceful antelopes

gazelle

ga•zette \gə-ˈzet\ *n* **1** : NEWSPAPER **2** : an official journal

gaz•et•teer \ˌga-zə-ˈtir\ *n* : a geographical dictionary

gaz•pa•cho \gəz-ˈpä-(ˌ)chō, gə-ˈspä-\ *n, pl* **-chos** [Sp] : a spicy soup usu. made from raw vegetables and served cold

GB *abbr* Great Britain

GCA *abbr* ground-controlled approach

gd *abbr* good

Gd *symbol* gadolinium

GDR *abbr* German Democratic Republic

Ge *symbol* germanium

gear \ˈgir\ *n* **1** : CLOTHING **2** : movable property : GOODS **3** : EQUIPMENT ⟨fishing ~⟩ **4** : a mechanism that performs a specific function ⟨steering ~⟩ **5** : a toothed wheel **6** : working adjustment of gears ⟨in ~⟩ **7** : an adjustment of transmission gears (as of an automobile or bicycle) that determines speed and direction of travel — **gear** *vb*

gear•box \ˈgir-ˌbäks\ *n* : TRANSMISSION 3

gear•shift \-ˌshift\ *n* : a mechanism by which transmission gears are shifted

gear•wheel \-ˌhwēl\ *n* : GEAR 5

GED *abbr* **1** General Educational Development (tests) **2** general equivalency diploma

geek \ˈgēk\ *n* : a person often of an intellectual bent who is disapproved of — **geeky** *adj*

geese *pl of* GOOSE

gee•zer \ˈgē-zər\ *n* : an odd or eccentric person

Gei•ger counter \ˈgī-gər-\ *n* : an electronic instrument for detecting the presence of cosmic rays or radioactive substances

gei•sha \ˈgā-shə, ˈgē-\ *n, pl* **geisha** *or* **geishas** [Jp, fr. *gei* art + *-sha* person] : a Japanese girl or woman who is trained to provide entertaining company for men

gel \ˈjel\ *n* **:** a solid jellylike colloid (as gelatin dessert) — **gel** *vb*

gel•a•tin *also* **gel•a•tine** \ˈje-lət-ᵊn\ *n* **:** glutinous material and esp. protein obtained from animal tissues by boiling and used as a food, in dyeing, and in photography; *also* **:** an edible jelly formed with gelatin — **ge•lat•i•nous** \jə-ˈlat-ᵊn-əs\ *adj*

geld \ˈgeld\ *vb* **:** CASTRATE

geld•ing *n* **:** a castrated male horse

gel•id \ˈje-ləd\ *adj* **:** extremely cold

gem \ˈjem\ *n* **1 :** JEWEL **2 :** a usu. valuable stone cut and polished for ornament **3 :** something valued for beauty or perfection

Gem•i•ni \ˈje-mə-(ˌ)nē, -ˌnī; ˈge-mə-ˌnē\ *n* **1 :** a zodiacal constellation between Taurus and Cancer usu. pictured as twins sitting together **2 :** the 3d sign of the zodiac in astrology; *also* **:** one born under this sign

gem•ol•o•gy *or* **gem•mol•o•gy** \je-ˈmä-lə-jē, jə-\ *n* **:** the science of gems — **gem•olog•i•cal** \ˌje-mə-ˈlä-ji-kəl\ *adj* — **gem•ol•o•gist** *or* **gem•mol•o•gist** \-jist\ *n*

gem•stone \ˈjem-ˌstōn\ *n* **:** a mineral or petrified material that when cut and polished can be used in jewelry

gen *abbr* **1** general **2** genitive

Gen *abbr* Genesis

Gen AF *abbr* general of the air force

gen•darme \ˈzhän-ˌdärm, ˈjän-\ *n* [F, intended as sing. of *gensdarmes,* pl. of *gent d'armes,* lit., armed people] **:** a member of a body of soldiers esp. in France serving as an armed police force

gen•der \ˈjen-dər\ *n* **1 :** any of two or more divisions within a grammatical class that determine agreement with and selection of other words or grammatical forms **2 :** SEX 1

gene \ˈjēn\ *n* **:** a part of DNA or RNA that contains chemical information needed to make a particular protein (as an enzyme) controlling or influencing an inherited bodily trait (as eye color) or activity or that influences or controls the activity of another gene or genes — **gen•ic** \ˈjē-nik, ˈje-\ *adj*

ge•ne•al•o•gy \ˌjē-nē-ˈä-lə-jē, ˌje-, -ˈa-\ *n, pl* **-gies :** PEDIGREE, LINEAGE; *also* **:** the study of family pedigrees — **ge•ne•a•log•i•cal** \ˌjē-nē-ə-ˈlä-ji-kəl, ˌje-\ *adj* — **ge•ne•a•log•i•cal•ly** \-k(ə-)lē\ *adv* — **ge•ne•al•o•gist** \ˌjē-nē-ˈä-lə-jist, ˌje-; -ˈa-\ *n*

genera *pl of* GENUS

[1]**gen•er•al** \ˈje-nə-rəl, ˈjen-rəl\ *adj* **1 :** of or relating to the whole **2 :** taken as a whole **3 :** relating to or covering all instances **4 :** not special or specialized **5 :** common to many ⟨a ~ custom⟩ **6 :** not limited in meaning **:** not specific **7 :** holding superior rank ⟨inspector ~⟩ **syn** generic, universal

[2]**general** *n* **1 :** something that involves or is applicable to the whole **2 :** a commissioned officer ranking next below a general of the army or a general of the air force **3 :** a commissioned officer of the highest rank in the marine corps — **in general :** for the most part

general assembly *n* **1 :** a legislative assembly; *esp* **:** a U.S. state legislature **2** *cap G&A* **:** the supreme deliberative body of the United Nations

gen•er•al•i•sa•tion, gen•er•al•ise *Brit var of* GENERALIZATION, GENERALIZE

gen•er•a•lis•si•mo \ˌje-nə-rə-ˈli-sə-ˌmō\ *n, pl* **-mos** [It, fr. *generale* general] **:** the chief commander of an army

gen•er•al•i•ty \ˌje-nə-ˈra-lə-tē\ *n, pl* **-ties 1 :** the quality or state of being general **2 :** GENERALIZATION 2 **3 :** a vague or inadequate statement **4 :** the greatest part **:** BULK

gen•er•al•i•za•tion \ˌje-nə-rə-lə-ˈzā-shən, ˌjen-rə-\ *n* **1 :** the act or process of generalizing **2 :** a general statement, law, principle, or proposition

gen•er•al•ize \ˈje-nə-rə-ˌlīz, ˈjen-rə-\ *vb* **-ized; -iz•ing 1 :** to make general **2 :** to draw general conclusions from **3 :** to reach a general conclusion esp. on the basis of particular instances **4 :** to extend throughout the body

gen•er•al•ly \ˈjen-rə-lē, ˈjē-nə-\ *adv* **1 :** in a general manner **2 :** as a rule

general of the air force : a commissioned officer of the highest rank in the air force

general of the army : a commissioned officer of the highest rank in the army

general practitioner *n* **:** a physician or veterinarian whose practice is not limited to a specialty

gen•er•al•ship \ˈje-nə-rəl-ˌship, ˈjen-rəl-\ *n* **1 :** office or tenure of office of a general **2 :** LEADERSHIP **3 :** military skill as a high commander

general store *n* **:** a retail store that carries a wide variety of goods but is not divided into departments

gen•er•ate \ˈje-nə-ˌrāt\ *vb* **-at•ed; -at•ing :** to bring into existence **:** PRODUCE **syn** create, originate, procreate, spawn

gen•er•a•tion \ˌje-nə-ˈrā-shən\ *n* **1 :** a body of living beings constituting a single step in the line of descent from an ancestor; *also* **:** the average period between generations **2 :** PRODUCTION

gen•er•a•tive \ˈje-nə-rə-tiv, -ˌrā-tiv\ *adj* **:** having the power or function of generating, originating, producing, or reproducing ⟨~ organs⟩

gen•er•a•tor \ˈje-nə-ˌrā-tər\ *n* **:** one that generates; *esp* **:** a machine by which mechanical energy is changed into electrical energy

ge•ner•ic \jə-ˈner-ik\ *adj* **1 :** not specific **:** GENERAL **2 :** not protected by a trademark ⟨a ~ drug⟩ **3 :** of or relating to a biological genus — **generic** *n* — **ge•ner•i•cal•ly** \-i-k(ə-)lē\ *adv*

gen•er•ous \ˈje-nə-rəs\ *adj* **1 :** free in giving or sharing **2 :** HIGH-MINDED, NOBLE **3 :** ABUNDANT, AMPLE, COPIOUS **syn** liberal, bountiful, munificent, openhanded — **gen•er•os•i•ty** \ˌje-nə-ˈrä-sə-tē\ *n* — **gen•er•ous•ly** \ˈje-nə-rəs-lē\ *adv* — **gen•er•ous•ness** *n*

gen•e•sis \ˈje-nə-səs\ *n, pl* **-e•ses** \-ˌsēz\ **:** the origin or coming into existence of something

Genesis *n* — see BIBLE table

gene–splic•ing \-ˌsplī-siŋ\ *n* **:** the technique by which recombinant DNA is produced and made to function in an organism

gene therapy *n* **:** the insertion of normal or altered genes into cells usu. to replace defective genes esp. in the treatment of genetic disorders

ge•net•ic \jə-ˈne-tik\ *adj* **:** of or relating to the origin, development, or causes of something; *also* **:** of or relating to genetics — **ge•net•i•cal•ly** \-ti-k(ə-)lē\ *adv*

genetic code *n* **:** the chemical code that is the basis of genetic inheritance and consists of triplets of three linked chemical groups in DNA and RNA which specify particular amino acids used to make proteins or which start or stop the process of making proteins

genetic engineering *n* **:** the directed alteration of genetic material by intervention in genetic processes; *esp* **:** GENE-SPLICING — **genetically engineered** *adj*

ge•net•ics \jə-ˈne-tiks\ *n* **:** a branch of biology dealing with heredity and variation — **ge•net•i•cist** \-tə-sist\ *n*

ge•nial \ˈjē-nyəl, ˈjē-nē-əl\ *adj* **1 :** favorable to growth or comfort ⟨~ sunshine⟩ **2 :** CHEERFUL, KINDLY ⟨a ~ host⟩ **syn** affable, congenial, cordial, gracious, sociable — **ge•nial•i•ty** \ˌjē-nē-ˈa-lə-tē, jēn-ˈya-\ *n* — **ge•nial•ly** *adv*

-gen•ic \ˈje-nik\ *adj comb form* **1 :** producing **:** forming **2 :** produced by **:** formed from **3 :** suitable for production or reproduction by (such) a medium

ge•nie \ˈjē-nē\ *n, pl* **ge•nies** *also* **ge•nii** \-nē-ˌī\ [F *génie,* fr. Ar *jinnīy*] **:** a supernatural spirit that often takes human form usu. serving the person who calls on it

gen•i•tal \ˈje-nət-ᵊl\ *adj* **1 :** concerned with reproduction ⟨~ organs⟩ **2 :** of, relating to, or characterized by the stage of psychosexual development in psychoanalytic theory in which oral and anal impulses are subordinated to adaptive interpersonal mechanisms — **gen•i•tal•ly** *adv*

gen•i•ta•lia \ˌje-nə-ˈtāl-yə\ *n pl* : reproductive organs; *esp* : the external genital organs — **gen•i•ta•lic** \-ˈta-lik, -ˈtā-\ *adj*

gen•i•tals \ˈje-nət-ᵊlz\ *n pl* : GENITALIA

gen•i•tive \ˈje-nə-tiv\ *adj* : of, relating to, or constituting a grammatical case marking typically a relationship of possessor or source — **genitive** *n*

gen•i•to•uri•nary \ˌje-nə-tō-ˈyu̇r-ə-ˌner-ē\ *adj* : of or relating to the genital and urinary organs or functions

ge•nius \ˈjē-nyəs\ *n, pl* **ge•nius•es** *or* **ge•nii** \-nē-ˌī\ [L, tutelary spirit, natural inclinations, fr. *gignere* to beget] **1** *pl genii* : an attendant spirit of a person or place; *also* : a person who influences another for good or evil **2** : a strong leaning or inclination **3** : a peculiar or distinctive character or spirit (as of a nation or a language) **4** *pl usu genii* : SPIRIT, GENIE **5** *pl usu geniuses* : a single strongly marked capacity or aptitude **6** : extraordinary intellectual power; *also* : a person having such power **syn** gift, faculty, flair, knack, talent

genl *abbr* general

geno•cide \ˈje-nə-ˌsīd\ *n* : the deliberate and systematic destruction of a racial, political, or cultural group

-genous \jə-nəs\ *adj comb form* **1** : producing : yielding ⟨ero*genous*⟩ **2** : having (such) an origin ⟨endo*genous*⟩

genre \ˈzhän-rə, ˈzhäⁿ-; ˈzhäⁿr; ˈjän-rə\ *n* **1** : a distinctive type or category esp. of literary composition **2** : a style of painting in which everyday subjects are treated realistically

gens \ˈjenz, ˈgens\ *n, pl* **gen•tes** \ˈjen-ˌtēz, ˈgen-ˌtās\ : a Roman clan embracing the families of the same stock in the male line

gent *n* : GENTLEMAN

gen•teel \jen-ˈtēl\ *adj* **1** : ARISTOCRATIC **2** : ELEGANT, STYLISH **3** : POLITE, REFINED **4** : maintaining the appearance of superior social status **5** : marked by false delicacy, prudery, or affectation — **gen•teel•ly** *adv* — **gen•teel•ness** *n*

gen•tian \ˈjen-chən\ *n* : any of numerous herbs with opposite leaves and showy usu. blue flowers in the fall

gen•tile \ˈjen-ˌtīl\ *n* [LL *gentilis* heathen, pagan, fr. L *gent-, gens* clan, nation] **1** *often cap* : a person who is not Jewish; *esp* : a Christian as distinguished from a Jew **2** : HEATHEN, PAGAN — **gentile** *adj, often cap*

gen•til•i•ty \jen-ˈti-lə-tē\ *n, pl* **-ties** **1** : good birth and family **2** : the qualities characteristic of a well-bred person **3** : good manners **4** : superior social status shown in manners or mode of life

[1]**gen•tle** \ˈjent-ᵊl\ *adj* **gen•tler** \ˈjent-lər, -ᵊl-ər\; **gen•tlest** \ˈjent-ləst, -ᵊl-əst\ **1** : belonging to a family of high social station **2** : of, relating to, or characteristic of a gentleman **3** : KIND, AMIABLE **4** : TRACTABLE, DOCILE **5** : not harsh, stern, or violent **6** : SOFT, DELICATE **7** : MODERATE — **gen•tle•ness** *n* — **gen•tly** *adv*

[2]**gentle** *vb* **gen•tled; gen•tling** **1** : to make or become mild, docile, soft, or moderate **2** : MOLLIFY, PLACATE

gen•tle•folk \ˈjent-ᵊl-ˌfōk\ *also* **gen•tle•folks** \-ˌfōks\ *n* : persons of good family and breeding

gen•tle•man \-mən\ *n* **1** : a man of good family **2** : a well-bred man **3** : MAN — used in pl. as a form of address — **gen•tle•man•ly** *adj*

gen•tle•wom•an \-ˌwu̇-mən\ *n* **1** : a woman of good family **2** : a woman attending a lady of rank **3** : a woman with very good manners : LADY

gen•tri•fi•ca•tion \ˌjen-trə-fə-ˈkā-shən\ *n* : the process of renewal accompanying the influx of middle-class people into deteriorating areas that often displaces earlier usu. poorer residents — **gen•tri•fy** \ˈjen-trə-fī\ *vb*

gen•try \ˈjen-trē\ *n, pl* **gentries** **1** : people of good birth, breeding, and education : ARISTOCRACY **2** : the class of English people between the nobility and the yeomanry **3** : persons of a designated class

gen•u•flect \ˈjen-yu̇-ˌflekt\ *vb* : to bend the knee esp. in worship — **gen•u•flec•tion** \ˌjen-yu̇-ˈflek-shən\ *n*

gen•u•ine \ˈjen-yə-wən\ *adj* **1** : AUTHENTIC, REAL **2** : SINCERE, HONEST **syn** bona fide, true, veritable — **gen•u•ine•ly** *adv* — **gen•u•ine•ness** *n*

ge•nus \ˈjē-nəs\ *n, pl* **gen•era** \ˈje-nə-rə\ [L, birth, race, kind] : a category of biological classification that ranks between the family and the species and contains related species

geo•cen•tric \ˌjē-ō-ˈsen-trik\ *adj* **1** : relating to or measured from the earth's center **2** : having or relating to the earth as a center

geo•chem•is•try \-ˈke-mə-strē\ *n* : a branch of geology that deals with the chemical composition of and chemical changes in the earth — **geo•chem•i•cal** \-mi-kəl\ *adj* — **geo•chem•ist** \-mist\ *n*

ge•ode \ˈjē-ˌōd\ *n* : a nodule of stone having a cavity lined with mineral matter

[1]**geo•de•sic** \ˌjē-ə-ˈde-sik\ *adj* : made of light straight structural elements ⟨a ~ dome⟩

[2]**geodesic** *n* : the shortest line between two points on a surface

geo•det•ic \ˌjē-ə-ˈde-tik\ *adj* : of, relating to, or being precise measurement of the earth and its features ⟨a ~ survey⟩

geog *abbr* geographic; geographical; geography

ge•og•ra•phy \jē-ˈä-grə-fē\ *n, pl* **-phies** **1** : a science that deals with the natural features of the earth and the climate, products, and inhabitants **2** : the natural features of a region — **ge•og•ra•pher** \-fər\ *n* — **geo•graph•ic** \ˌjē-ə-ˈgra-fik\ *or* **geo•graph•i•cal** \-fi-kəl\ *adj* — **geo•graph•i•cal•ly** \-fi-k(ə-)lē\ *adv*

geol *abbr* geologic; geological; geology

ge•ol•o•gy \jē-ˈä-lə-jē\ *n, pl* **-gies** **1** : a science that deals with the history of the earth and its life esp. as recorded in rocks; *also* : a study of the features of a celestial body (as the moon) **2** : the geologic features of an area — **ge•o•log•ic** \ˌjē-ə-ˈlä-jik\ *or* **ge•o•log•i•cal** \-ji-kəl\ *adj* — **geo•log•i•cal•ly** \-ji-k(ə-)lē\ *adv* — **ge•ol•o•gist** \jē-ˈä-lə-jist\ *n*

geom *abbr* geometric; geometrical; geometry

geo•mag•net•ic \ˌjē-ō-mag-ˈne-tik\ *adj* : of or relating to the magnetism of the earth — **geo•mag•ne•tism** \-ˈmag-nə-ˌti-zəm\ *n*

geometric mean *n* : the *n*th root of the product of *n* numbers; *esp* : a number that is the second term of three consecutive terms of a geometric progression ⟨the *geometric mean* of 9 and 4 is 6⟩

geometric progression *n* : a progression (as 1, ½, ¼) in which the ratio of a term to its predecessor is always the same

ge•om•e•try \jē-ˈä-mə-trē\ *n, pl* **-tries** [ultim. fr. Gk *geōmetria*, fr. *geōmetrein* to measure the earth, fr. *gē* earth + *metron* measure] : a branch of mathematics dealing with the relations, properties, and measurements of solids, surfaces, lines, points, and angles — **ge•om•e•ter** \-tər\ *n* — **ge•o•met•ric** \ˌjē-ə-ˈme-trik\ *or* **ge•o•met•ri•cal** \-tri-kəl\ *adj*

geo•phys•ics \ˌjē-ō-ˈfi-ziks\ *n* : the physics of the earth — **geo•phys•i•cal** \-zi-kəl\ *adj* — **geo•phys•i•cist** \-zə-sist\ *n*

geo•pol•i•tics \-ˈpä-lə-ˌtiks\ *n* : a combination of political and geographic factors relating to a state

Geor•gian \ˈjȯr-jən\ *n* : a native or inhabitant of the Republic of Georgia — **Georgian** *adj*

geo•ther•mal \ˌjē-ō-ˈthər-məl\ *adj* : of, relating to, or using the heat of the earth's interior

ger *abbr* gerund

Ger *abbr* German; Germany

ge•ra•ni•um \jə-ˈrā-nē-əm\ *n* [L, fr. Gk *geranion*, fr. *geranos* crane] **1** : any of a genus of herbs with usu. deeply cut leaves and pink, purple, or white flowers followed by long slender dry fruits **2** : any of a genus of herbs of the same family as the geraniums that

have clusters of scarlet, pink, or white flowers with the sepals joined at the base into a hollow tube closed at one end
ger•bil *also* **ger•bile** \ˈjər-bəl\ *n* : any of numerous Old World burrowing desert rodents with long hind legs
ge•ri•at•ric \ˌjer-ē-ˈa-trik\ *adj* **1** : of or relating to geriatrics or the process of aging **2** : of, relating to, or appropriate for elderly people **3** : OLD
ge•ri•at•rics \-triks\ *n* : a branch of medicine dealing with the problems and diseases of old age and aging
germ \ˈjərm\ *n* **1** : a bit of living matter capable of growth and development (as into an organism) **2** : SOURCE, RUDIMENTS **3** : MICROORGANISM; *esp* : one causing disease
Ger•man \ˈjər-mən\ *n* **1** : a native or inhabitant of Germany **2** : the language of Germany, Austria, and parts of Switzerland — **German** *adj* — **Ger•man•ic** \jər-ˈma-nik\ *adj*
ger•mane \jər-ˈmān\ *adj* [ME *germain*, lit., having the same parents, fr. MF, fr. L *germanus*, fr. *germen* sprout, bud] : RELEVANT, APPROPRIATE **syn** applicable, material, pertinent
ger•ma•ni•um \jər-ˈmā-nē-əm\ *n* : a grayish white hard chemical element used as a semiconductor — see ELEMENT table
German measles *n sing or pl* : an acute contagious virus disease milder than typical measles but damaging to the fetus when occurring early in pregnancy
German shepherd *n* : any of a breed of intelligent responsive working dogs of German origin often used in police work and as guide dogs for the blind
germ cell *n* : an egg or sperm or one of their antecedent cells
ger•mi•cide \ˈjər-mə-ˌsīd\ *n* : an agent that destroys germs — **ger•mi•cid•al** \ˌjər-mə-ˈsīd-ᵊl\ *adj*
ger•mi•nal \ˈjər-mə-nəl\ *adj* : of or relating to a germ or germ cell; *also* : EMBRYONIC
ger•mi•nate \ˈjər-mə-ˌnāt\ *vb* **-nat•ed; -nat•ing 1** : to cause to develop : begin to develop : SPROUT **2** : to come into being : EVOLVE — **ger•mi•na•tion** \ˌjər-mə-ˈnā-shən\ *n*
ger•on•tol•o•gy \ˌjer-ən-ˈtä-lə-jē\ *n* : a scientific study of aging and the problems of the aged — **ge•ron•to•log•i•cal** \jə-ˌränt-ᵊl-ˈä-ji-kəl\ *adj* — **ger•on•tol•o•gist** \ˌjer-ən-ˈtä-lə-jist\ *n*
ger•ry•man•der \ˈjer-ē-ˌman-dər\ *vb* : to divide into election districts so as to give one political party an advantage — **gerrymander** *n*
ger•und \ˈjer-ənd\ *n* : a word having the characteristics of both verb and noun
ge•sta•po \gə-ˈstä-pō\ *n, pl* **-pos** [G, fr. *Ge*heime *Sta*ats*po*lizei, lit., secret state police] : a usu. terrorist secret-police organization operating against persons suspected of disloyalty
ges•ta•tion \je-ˈstā-shən\ *n* : PREGNANCY, INCUBATION — **ges•tate** \ˈjes-ˌtāt\ *vb*
ges•tic•u•late \je-ˈsti-kyə-ˌlāt\ *vb* **-lat•ed; -lat•ing** : to make gestures esp. when speaking — **ges•tic•u•la•tion** \-ˌsti-kyə-ˈlā-shən\ *n*
ges•ture \ˈjes-chər\ *n* **1** : a movement usu. of the body or limbs that expresses or emphasizes an idea, sentiment, or attitude **2** : something said or done by way of formality or courtesy, as a symbol or token, or for its effect on the attitudes of others — **ges•tur•al** \-chə-rəl\ *adj* — **gesture** *vb*
ge•sund•heit \gə-ˈzünt-ˌhīt\ *interj* [G, lit., health] — used to wish good health esp. to one who has just sneezed
¹get \ˈget\ *vb* **got** \ˈgät\; **got** *or* **got•ten** \ˈgät-ᵊn\; **get•ting 1** : to gain possession of (as by receiving, acquiring, earning, buying, or winning) : PROCURE, OBTAIN, FETCH **2** : to succeed in coming or going ⟨*got* away to the lake⟩ **3** : to cause to come or go ⟨*got* the car to the station⟩ **4** : BEGET **5** : to cause to be in a certain condition or position ⟨don't ~ wet⟩ **6** : BECOME ⟨~ sick⟩ **7** : PREPARE **8** : SEIZE **9** : to move emotionally; *also* : IRRITATE **10** : BAFFLE, PUZZLE **11** : KILL **12** : HIT **13** : to be subjected to ⟨~ the measles⟩ **14** : to receive as punishment **15** : to find out by calculation **16** : HEAR; *also* : UNDERSTAND **17** : PERSUADE, INDUCE **18** : HAVE ⟨he's *got* no money⟩ **19** : to have as an obligation or necessity ⟨you have *got* to come⟩ **20** : to establish communication with **21** : to be able ⟨finally *got* to go to med school⟩ **22** : to come to be ⟨*got* talking about old times⟩ **23** : to leave at once
²get \ˈget\ *n* : OFFSPRING, PROGENY
get along *vb* **1** : GET BY **2** : to be on friendly terms
get•away \ˈge-tə-ˌwā\ *n* **1** : ESCAPE **2** : START
get by *vb* : to meet one's needs
get–to•geth•er \ˈget-tə-ˌge-t͟hər\ *n* : an informal social gathering
get•up \ˈget-ˌəp\ *n* **1** : OUTFIT, COSTUME **2** : general composition or structure
gew•gaw \ˈgü-ˌgȯ, ˈgyü-\ *n* : a showy trifle : BAUBLE, TRINKET
gey•ser \ˈgī-zər\ *n* [Icelandic *Geysir*, hot spring in Iceland] : a spring that intermittently shoots up hot water and steam
Gha•na•ian \gä-ˈnā-ən\ *n* : a native or inhabitant of Ghana — **Ghanaian** *adj*
ghast•ly \ˈgast-lē\ *adj* **ghast•li•er; -est 1** : HORRIBLE, SHOCKING **2** : resembling a ghost : DEATHLIKE, PALE **syn** gruesome, grim, lurid, grisly, macabre
ghat \ˈgȯt\ *n* [Hindi] : a broad flight of steps on an Indian riverbank that provides access to the water
gher•kin \ˈgər-kən\ *n* **1** : a small prickly fruit of a vine related to the cucumber used to make pickles **2** : an immature cucumber
ghet•to \ˈge-tō\ *n, pl* **ghettos** *or* **ghettoes** : a quarter of a city in which members of a minority group live because of social, legal, or economic pressure
¹ghost \ˈgōst\ *n* **1** : the seat of life : SOUL **2** : a disembodied soul; *esp* : the soul of a dead person believed to be an inhabitant of the unseen world or to appear in bodily form to living people **3** : SPIRIT, DEMON **4** : a faint trace ⟨a ~ of a smile⟩ **5** : a false image in a photographic negative or on a television screen — **ghost•ly** *adv*
²ghost *vb* : GHOSTWRITE
ghost•write \-ˌrīt\ *vb* **-wrote** \-ˌrōt\; **-writ•ten** \-ˌrit-ᵊn\ : to write for and in the name of another — **ghost•writ•er** *n*
ghoul \ˈgül\ *n* [Ar *ghūl*] : a legendary evil being that robs graves and feeds on corpses — **ghoul•ish** *adj*
GHQ *abbr* general headquarters
gi *abbr* gill
¹GI \ˌjē-ˈī\ *adj* [*g*alvanized *i*ron; fr. abbr. used in listing such articles as garbage cans, but taken as abbr. for *government issue*] **1** : provided by an official U.S. military supply department ⟨~ shoes⟩ **2** : of, relating to, or characteristic of U.S. military personnel **3** : conforming to military regulations or customs ⟨a ~ haircut⟩
²GI *n, pl* **GI's** *or* **GIs** \-ˈīz\ : a member or former member of the U.S. armed forces; *esp* : an enlisted man
³GI *abbr* **1** galvanized iron **2** gastrointestinal **3** general issue **4** government issue
gi•ant \ˈjī-ənt\ *n* **1** : a legendary humanlike being of great size and strength **2** : a living being or thing of extraordinary size or powers — **giant** *adj*
gi•ant•ess \ˈjī-ən-təs\ *n* : a female giant
gib•ber \ˈji-bər\ *vb* : to speak rapidly, inarticulately, and often foolishly
gib•ber•ish \ˈji-bə-rish\ *n* : unintelligible or confused speech or language
¹gib•bet \ˈji-bət\ *n* : GALLOWS
²gibbet *vb* **1** : to hang on a gibbet **2** : to expose to public scorn **3** : to execute by hanging
gib•bon \ˈgi-bən\ *n* : any of several tailless apes of southeastern Asia
gib•bous \ˈji-bəs, ˈgi-\ *adj* **1** : rounded like the exterior of a sphere or circle **2** : seen with more than half but

not all of the apparent disk illuminated ⟨∼ moon⟩ **3** : having a hump : HUMPBACKED

gibe \ˈjīb\ *vb* **gibed; gib•ing** : to utter taunting words : SNEER — **gibe** *n*

gib•lets \ˈjib-ləts\ *n pl* : the edible viscera of a fowl

Gib•son girl \ˈgib-sən-\ *adj* : of or relating to a style in women's clothing characterized by high necks, full sleeves, and slender waistlines

gid•dy \ˈgi-dē\ *adj* **gid•di•er; -est 1** : DIZZY **2** : causing dizziness **3** : not serious : FRIVOLOUS, SILLY — **gid•di•ness** \-dē-nəs\ *n*

gift \ˈgift\ *n* **1** : a special ability : TALENT **2** : something given : PRESENT **3** : the act or power of giving

gift•ed \ˈgif-təd\ *adj* : TALENTED

[1]**gig** \ˈgig\ *n* **1** : a long light ship's boat **2** : a light 2-wheeled one-horse carriage

[2]**gig** *n* : a pronged spear for catching fish — **gig** *vb*

[3]**gig** *n* : a job for a specified time; *esp* : an entertainer's engagement

[4]**gig** *n* : a military demerit — **gig** *vb*

giga•byte \ˈji-gə-ˌbīt, ˈgi-\ *n* : a unit of computer storage capacity approximately equal to one billion bytes

gi•gan•tic \jī-ˈgan-tik\ *adj* : exceeding the usual (as in size or force)

gig•gle \ˈgi-gəl\ *vb* **gig•gled; gig•gling** : to laugh with repeated short catches of the breath — **giggle** *n* — **gig•gly** \-gə-lē\ *adj*

GIGO *abbr* garbage in, garbage out

gig•o•lo \ˈji-gə-ˌlō\ *n, pl* **-los 1** : a man supported by a woman usu. in return for his attentions **2** : a professional dancing partner or male escort

Gi•la monster \ˈhē-lə-\ *n* : a large orange and black venomous lizard of the southwestern U.S.

[1]**gild** \ˈgild\ *vb* **gild•ed** *or* **gilt** \ˈgilt\; **gild•ing 1** : to overlay with or as if with a thin covering of gold **2** : to give an attractive but often deceptive appearance to

[2]**gild** *var of* GUILD

[1]**gill** \ˈjil\ *n* — see WEIGHT table

[2]**gill** \ˈgil\ *n* : an organ (as of a fish) for obtaining oxygen from water

[1]**gilt** \ˈgilt\ *adj* : of the color of gold

[2]**gilt** *n* : gold or a substance resembling gold laid on the surface of an object

[3]**gilt** *n* : a young female swine

gim•crack \ˈjim-ˌkrak\ *n* : a showy object of little use or value

gim•let \ˈgim-lət\ *n* : a small tool with screw point and cross handle for boring holes

gim•mick \ˈgi-mik\ *n* **1** : CONTRIVANCE, GADGET **2** : an important feature that is not immediately apparent : CATCH **3** : a new and ingenious scheme — **gim•micky** \-mi-kē\ *adj*

gim•mick•ry \ˈgi-mi-krē\ *n, pl* **-ries** : an array of or the use of gimmicks

gimpy \ˈgim-pē\ *adj* : CRIPPLED, LAME

[1]**gin** \ˈjin\ *n* [ME *gin*, modif. of OF *engin*] **1** : TRAP, SNARE **2** : a machine to separate seeds from cotton — **gin** *vb*

[2]**gin** *n* [by shortening & alter. fr. *geneva*, kind of gin] : a liquor distilled from a grain mash and flavored with juniper berries

gin•ger \ˈjin-jər\ *n* : the pungent aromatic rootstock of a tropical plant used esp. as a spice and in medicine; *also* : the spice or the plant

ginger ale *n* : a carbonated soft drink flavored with ginger

gin•ger•bread \ˈjin-jər-ˌbred\ *n* **1** : a cake made with molasses and flavored with ginger **2** : lavish or superfluous ornament

gin•ger•ly \ˈjin-jər-lē\ *adj* : very cautious or careful — **gingerly** *adv*

gin•ger•snap \-ˌsnap\ *n* : a thin brittle molasses cookie flavored with ginger

ging•ham \ˈgiŋ-əm\ *n* : a clothing fabric usu. of yarn-dyed cotton in plain weave

gin•gi•vi•tis \ˌjin-jə-ˈvī-təs\ *n* : inflammation of the gums

gink•go *also* **ging•ko** \ˈgiŋ-(ˌ)kō\ *n, pl* **ginkgoes** *or* **ginkgos** : a tree of eastern China with fan-shaped leaves often grown as a shade tree

gin•seng \ˈjin-ˌseŋ\ *n* : an aromatic root of a Chinese or No. American herb used esp. in Oriental medicine; *also* : one of these herbs

Gip•sy *chiefly Brit var of* GYPSY

gi•raffe \jə-ˈraf\ *n, pl* **giraffes** [It *giraffa*, fr. Ar *zirāfah*] : an African ruminant mammal with a very long neck and a short coat with dark blotches

gird \ˈgərd\ *vb* **gird•ed** *or* **girt** \ˈgərt\; **gird•ing 1** : to encircle or fasten with or as if with a belt ⟨∼ on a sword⟩ **2** : to invest esp. with power or authority **3** : PREPARE, BRACE

gird•er \ˈgər-dər\ *n* : a horizontal main supporting beam

gir•dle \ˈgərd-ᵊl\ *n* **1** : something (as a belt or sash) that encircles or confines **2** : a woman's supporting undergarment that extends from the waist to below the hips — **girdle** *vb*

girl \ˈgərl\ *n* **1** : a female child **2** : a young woman **3** : SWEETHEART — **girl•hood** \-ˌhu̇d\ *n* — **girl•ish** *adj*

girl Friday *n* : a female assistant (as in an office) entrusted with a wide variety of tasks

girl•friend \ˈgərl-ˌfrend\ *n* **1** : a female friend **2** : a frequent or regular female companion of a boy or man

Girl Scout *n* : a member of any of the scouting programs of the Girl Scouts of the United States of America

girth \ˈgərth\ *n* **1** : a band around an animal by which something (as a saddle) may be fastened on its back **2** : a measure around something

gist \ˈjist\ *n* [MF, it lies, fr. *gesir* to lie, ultim. fr. L *jacēre*] : the main point or part

[1]**give** \ˈgiv\ *vb* **gave** \ˈgāv\; **giv•en** \ˈgi-vən\; **giv•ing 1** : to make a present of **2** : to bestow by formal action **3** : to accord or yield to another **4** : to yield to force, strain, or pressure **5** : to put into the possession or keeping of another **6** : PROFFER **7** : DELIVER ⟨*gave* away the bride⟩ **8** : to present in public performance or to view **9** : PROVIDE ⟨∼ a party⟩ **10** : ATTRIBUTE **11** : to make, form, or yield as a product or result ⟨cows ∼ milk⟩ **12** : PAY **13** : to deliver by some bodily action ⟨*gave* me a push⟩ **14** : to offer as a pledge ⟨I ∼ you my word⟩ **15** : DEVOTE **16** : to cause to have or receive

[2]**give** *n* **1** : capacity or tendency to yield to force or strain **2** : the quality or state of being springy

give–and–take \ˌgiv-ən-ˈtāk\ *n* **1** : COMPROMISE **2** : a usu. good-natured exchange (as of remarks or ideas)

give•away \ˈgi-və-ˌwā\ *n* **1** : an unintentional revelation or betrayal **2** : something given away free; *esp* : PREMIUM

give in *vb* : SUBMIT, SURRENDER

[1]**giv•en** \ˈgi-vən\ *adj* **1** : DISPOSED, INCLINED ⟨∼ to swearing⟩ **2** : SPECIFIED, PARTICULAR ⟨at a ∼ time⟩

[2]**given** *prep* : CONSIDERING

given name *n* : a name that precedes one's surname

give out *vb* **1** : EMIT **2** : BREAK DOWN **3** : to become exhausted : COLLAPSE

give up *vb* **1** : SURRENDER **2** : to abandon (oneself) to a feeling, influence, or activity **3** : QUIT

giz•mo *also* **gis•mo** \ˈgiz-mō\ *n, pl* **gizmos** *also* **gismos** : GADGET

giz•zard \ˈgi-zərd\ *n* : the muscular usu. horny-lined enlargement of the alimentary canal of a bird used for churning and grinding up food

gla•cial \ˈglā-shəl\ *adj* **1** : extremely cold **2** : of or relating to glaciers **3** : being or relating to a past period of time when a large part of the earth was covered by glaciers **4** *cap* : PLEISTOCENE **5** : very slow ⟨a ∼ pace⟩ — **gla•cial•ly** *adv*

gla•ci•ate \ˈglā-shē-ˌāt\ *vb* **-at•ed; -at•ing 1** : to subject to glacial action **2** : to produce glacial effects in or on — **gla•ci•a•tion** \ˌglā-shē-ˈā-shən, -sē-\ *n*

gla•cier \ˈglā-shər\ *n* : a large body of ice moving slowly down a slope or spreading outward on a land surface

[1]**glad** \ˈglad\ *adj* **glad•der; glad•dest 1** : experiencing pleasure, joy, or delight **2** : PLEASED **3** : very willing **4** : PLEASANT, JOYFUL **5** : CHEERFUL — **glad•ly** *adv* — **glad•ness** *n*

[2]**glad** *n* : GLADIOLUS

glad•den \ˈglad-ᵊn\ *vb* : to make glad

glade \ˈglād\ *n* : a grassy open space surrounded by woods

glad•i•a•tor \ˈgla-dē-ˌā-tər\ *n* **1** : a person engaged in a fight to the death for public entertainment in ancient Rome **2** : a person engaging in a public fight or controversy; *also* : PRIZEFIGHTER — **glad•i•a•to•ri•al** \ˌgla-dē-ə-ˈtōr-ē-əl\ *adj*

glad•i•o•lus \ˌgla-dē-ˈō-ləs\ *n, pl* **-li** \-(ˌ)lē, -ˌlī\ [L, fr. dim. of *gladius* sword] : any of a genus of chiefly African plants related to the irises and having erect sword-shaped leaves and stalks of bright colored flowers

glad•some \ˈglad-səm\ *adj* : giving or showing joy : CHEERFUL

glad•stone \ˈglad-ˌstōn\ *n, often cap* : a suitcase with flexible sides on a rigid frame that opens flat into two compartments

glam•or•ise *Brit var of* GLAMORIZE

glam•or•ize *also* **glam•our•ize** \ˈgla-mə-ˌrīz\ *vb* **-ized; -iz•ing** : to make or look upon as glamorous

glam•our *or* **glam•or** \ˈgla-mər\ *n* [Sc *glamour* magic spell, alter. of E *grammar;* fr. the popular association of erudition with occult practices] : an exciting and often illusory and romantic attractiveness; *esp* : alluring personal attraction — **glam•or•ous** *also* **glam•our•ous** \-mə-rəs\ *adj*

[1]**glance** \ˈglans\ *vb* **glanced; glanc•ing 1** : to strike and fly off to one side **2** : GLEAM **3** : to give a quick look

[2]**glance** *n* **1** : a quick intermittent flash or gleam **2** : a deflected impact or blow **3** : a quick look

gland \ˈgland\ *n* : a cell or group of cells that prepares and secretes a substance (as saliva or sweat) for further use in or discharge from the body

glan•du•lar \ˈglan-jə-lər\ *adj* : of, relating to, or involving glands

glans \ˈglanz\ *n, pl* **glan•des** \ˈglan-ˌdēz\ [L, lit., acorn] : a conical vascular body forming the extremity of the penis or clitoris

[1]**glare** \ˈglar\ *vb* **glared; glar•ing 1** : to shine with a harsh dazzling light **2** : to stare fiercely or angrily

[2]**glare** *n* **1** : a harsh dazzling light **2** : an angry or fierce stare

glar•ing \ˈglar-iŋ\ *adj* : very conspicuous ⟨a ~ error⟩ — **glar•ing•ly** *adv*

glass \ˈglas\ *n* **1** : a hard brittle amorphous usu. transparent or translucent material consisting esp. of silica **2** : something made of glass; *esp* : TUMBLER 2 **3** *pl* : a pair of lenses used to correct defects of vision : SPECTACLES **4** : the quantity held by a glass container — **glass** *adj* — **glass•ful** \-ˌfu̇l\ *n* — **glassy** *adj*

glass•blow•ing \-ˌblō-iŋ\ *n* : the art of shaping a mass of glass that has been softened by heat by blowing air into it through a tube — **glass•blow•er** *n*

glass•ware \-ˌwar\ *n* : articles made of glass

glau•co•ma \glau̇-ˈkō-mə, glȯ-\ *n* : a disease of the eye marked by increased pressure within the eyeball resulting in damage to the retina and gradual loss of vision

[1]**glaze** \ˈglāz\ *vb* **glazed; glaz•ing 1** : to furnish (as a window frame) with glass **2** : to apply glaze to

[2]**glaze** *n* : a glassy coating or surface

gla•zier \ˈglā-zhər\ *n* : a person who sets glass in window frames

[1]**gleam** \ˈglēm\ *n* **1** : a transient subdued or partly obscured light **2** : GLINT **3** : a faint trace ⟨a ~ of hope⟩

[2]**gleam** *vb* **1** : to shine with subdued light or moderate brightness **2** : to appear briefly or faintly **syn** flash, glimmer, glisten, glitter, shimmer, sparkle

glean \ˈglēn\ *vb* **1** : to gather grain left by reapers **2** : to collect little by little or with patient effort — **glean•able** *adj* — **glean•er** *n*

glean•ings \ˈglē-niŋz\ *n pl* : things acquired by gleaning

glee \ˈglē\ *n* [ME, fr. OE *glēo* entertainment, music] **1** : JOY, HILARITY **2** : a part-song for three usu. male voices — **glee•ful** *adj*

glee club *n* : a chorus organized for singing usu. short choral pieces

glen \ˈglen\ *n* : a narrow hidden valley

glen•gar•ry \glen-ˈgar-ē\ *n, pl* **-ries** *often cap* : a woolen cap of Scottish origin

glib \ˈglib\ *adj* **glib•ber; glib•best** : speaking or spoken with careless ease — **glib•ly** *adv*

glide \ˈglīd\ *vb* **glid•ed; glid•ing 1** : to move smoothly and effortlessly **2** : to descend gradually without engine power ⟨~ in an airplane⟩ — **glide** *n*

glid•er \ˈglī-dər\ *n* **1** : one that glides **2** : an aircraft resembling an airplane but having no engine **3** : a porch seat suspended from an upright frame

[1]**glim•mer** \ˈgli-mər\ *vb* : to shine faintly or unsteadily

[2]**glimmer** *n* **1** : a faint unsteady light **2** : INKLING **3** : a small amount : HINT

[1]**glimpse** \ˈglimps\ *vb* **glimpsed; glimps•ing** : to take a brief look : see momentarily or incompletely

[2]**glimpse** *n* **1** : a faint idea : GLIMMER **2** : a short hurried look

glint \ˈglint\ *vb* **1** : to shine by reflection : SPARKLE, GLITTER, GLEAM **2** : to appear briefly or faintly — **glint** *n*

glis•san•do \gli-ˈsän-(ˌ)dō\ *n, pl* **-di** \-(ˌ)dē\ *or* **-dos** : a rapid sliding up or down the musical scale

[1]**glis•ten** \ˈglis-ᵊn\ *vb* : to shine by reflection with a soft luster or sparkle

[2]**glisten** *n* : GLITTER, SPARKLE

glis•ter \ˈglis-tər\ *vb* : GLITTER

glitch \ˈglich\ *n* : MALFUNCTION; *also* : SNAG 2

[1]**glit•ter** \ˈgli-tər\ *vb* **1** : to shine with brilliant or metallic luster : SPARKLE **2** : to shine with strong emotion : FLASH ⟨eyes ~*ing* in anger⟩ **3** : to be brilliantly attractive esp. in a superficial way

[2]**glitter** *n* **1** : sparkling brilliancy, showiness, or attractiveness **2** : small glittering objects used for ornamentation — **glit•tery** \ˈgli-tə-rē\ *adj*

glitz \ˈglits\ *n* : extravagant showiness — **glitzy** \ˈglit-sē\ *adj*

gloam•ing \ˈglō-miŋ\ *n* : TWILIGHT, DUSK

gloat \ˈglōt\ *vb* : to think about something with triumphant and often malicious delight

glob \ˈgläb\ *n* **1** : a small drop **2** : a large rounded mass

glob•al \ˈglō-bəl\ *adj* **1** : WORLDWIDE **2** : COMPREHENSIVE, GENERAL — **glob•al•ly** *adv*

globe \ˈglōb\ *n* **1** : BALL, SPHERE **2** : EARTH; *also* : a spherical representation of the earth

globe–trot•ter \ˈglōb-ˌträ-tər\ *n* : a person who travels widely — **globe–trot•ting** *n or adj*

glob•u•lar \ˈglä-byə-lər\ *adj* : having the shape of a globe or globule

glob•ule \ˈglä-(ˌ)byül\ *n* : a tiny globe or ball esp. of a liquid

glob•u•lin \ˈglä-byə-lən\ *n* : any of a class of simple proteins insoluble in pure water but soluble in dilute salt solutions that occur widely in plant and animal tissues

glock•en•spiel \ˈglä-kən-ˌshpēl, -ˌspēl\ *n* [G, fr. *Glocke* bell + *Spiel* play] : a percussion musical instrument consisting of a series of metal bars played with two hammers

gloom \ˈglüm\ *n* **1** : partial or total darkness **2** : lowness of spirits : DEJECTION **3** : an atmosphere of despondency — **gloom•i•ly** \ˈglü-mə-lē\ *adv* — **gloom•i•ness** \-mē-nəs\ *n* — **gloomy** \ˈglü-mē\ *adj*

glop \ˈgläp\ *n* : a messy mass or mixture

glo•ri•fy \ˈglōr-ə-ˌfī\ *vb* **-fied; -fy•ing 1** : to raise to heavenly glory **2** : to light up brilliantly **3** : EXTOL **4** : to give glory to (as in worship) — **glo•ri•fi•ca•tion** \ˌglōr-ə-fə-ˈkā-shən\ *n*

glo•ri•ous \ˈglōr-ē-əs\ *adj* **1** : possessing or deserving glory : PRAISEWORTHY **2** : conferring glory **3** : RESPLENDENT, MAGNIFICENT **4** : DELIGHTFUL, WONDERFUL — **glo•ri•ous•ly** *adv*

[1]**glo•ry** \ˈglōr-ē\ *n, pl* **glories** **1** : RENOWN **2** : honor and praise rendered in worship **3** : something that secures praise or renown **4** : a distinguishing quality or asset **5** : RESPLENDENCE, MAGNIFICENCE **6** : heavenly bliss **7** : a height of prosperity or achievement

[2]**glory** *vb* **glo•ried; glo•ry•ing** : to rejoice proudly : EXULT

[1]**gloss** \ˈgläs, ˈglȯs\ *n* **1** : LUSTER, SHEEN, BRIGHTNESS **2** : outward show

[2]**gloss** *vb* **1** : to give a false appearance of acceptableness to ⟨∼ over inadequacies⟩ **2** : to deal with too lightly or not at all

[3]**gloss** *n* [alter. of *gloze,* fr. ME *glose,* fr. MF, fr. ML *glosa, glossa,* fr. Gk *glōssa, glōtta* tongue, language, unusual word] **1** : an explanatory note (as in the margin of a text) **2** : GLOSSARY **3** : an interlinear translation **4** : a continuous commentary accompanying a text

[4]**gloss** *vb* : to furnish glosses for

glos•sa•ry \ˈglä-sə-rē, ˈglȯ-\ *n, pl* **-ries** : a collection of difficult or specialized terms with their meanings — **glos•sar•i•al** \glä-ˈsar-ē-əl, glȯ-\ *adj*

glos•so•la•lia \ˌglä-sə-ˈlā-lē-ə, ˌglȯ-\ *n* [Gk *glōssa* tongue, language + *lalia* chatter] : TONGUE 6

[1]**glossy** \ˈglä-sē, ˈglȯ-\ *adj* **gloss•i•er; -est** : having a surface luster or brightness — **gloss•i•ly** \-sə-lē\ *adv* — **gloss•i•ness** \-sē-nəs\ *n*

[2]**glossy** *n, pl* **gloss•ies** : a photograph printed on smooth shiny paper

glot•tis \ˈglä-təs\ *n, pl* **glot•tis•es** *or* **glot•ti•des** \-tə-ˌdēz\ : the slitlike opening between the vocal cords in the larynx — **glot•tal** \ˈglät-ᵊl\ *adj*

glove \ˈgləv\ *n* **1** : a covering for the hand having separate sections for each finger **2** : a padded leather covering for the hand for use in a sport

[1]**glow** \ˈglō\ *vb* **1** : to shine with or as if with intense heat **2** : to have a rich warm usu. ruddy color : FLUSH, BLUSH **3** : to feel hot **4** : to show exuberance or elation ⟨∼ with pride⟩

[2]**glow** *n* **1** : brightness or warmth of color; *esp* : REDNESS **2** : warmth of feeling or emotion **3** : a sensation of warmth **4** : light such as is emitted from a heated substance

glow•er \ˈglaů-ər\ *vb* : to stare angrily : SCOWL — **glower** *n*

glow•worm \ˈglō-ˌwərm\ *n* : any of various insect larvae or adults that give off light

glox•in•ia \gläk-ˈsi-nē-ə\ *n* : any of a genus of Brazilian herbs related to the African violets; *esp* : one with showy bell-shaped or slipper-shaped flowers

gloze \ˈglōz\ *vb* **glozed; gloz•ing** : to make appear right or acceptable : GLOSS

glu•cose \ˈglü-ˌkōs\ *n* **1** : a sugar known in two different forms; *esp* : DEXTROSE **2** : a sweet light-colored syrup made from cornstarch

glue \ˈglü\ *n* : a jellylike protein substance made from animal materials and used for sticking things together; *also* : any of various other strong adhesives — **glue** *vb* — **glu•ey** \ˈglü-ē\ *adj*

glum \ˈgləm\ *adj* **glum•mer; glum•mest** **1** : broodingly morose : SULLEN **2** : DREARY, GLOOMY **syn** crabbed, dour, saturnine, sulky

[1]**glut** \ˈglət\ *vb* **glut•ted; glut•ting** **1** : OVERSUPPLY **2** : to fill esp. with food to satiety : SATIATE

[2]**glut** *n* : an excessive supply

glu•ten \ˈglüt-ᵊn\ *n* : a gluey protein substance that causes dough to be sticky

glu•ti•nous \ˈglüt-ᵊn-əs\ *adj* : STICKY

glut•ton \ˈglət-ᵊn\ *n* : one that eats to excess — **glut•ton•ous** \ˈglət-ᵊn-əs\ *adj* — **glut•tony** \ˈglət-ᵊn-ē\ *n*

glyc•er•in *or* **glyc•er•ine** \ˈgli-sə-rən\ *n* : GLYCEROL

glyc•er•ol \ˈgli-sə-ˌrȯl, -ˌrōl\ *n* : a sweet syrupy alcohol usu. obtained from fats and used esp. as a solvent

gly•co•gen \ˈglī-kə-jən\ *n* : a white tasteless substance that is the chief storage carbohydrate of animals

gm *abbr* gram

GM *abbr* **1** general manager **2** guided missile

G–man \ˈjē-ˌman\ *n* : a special agent of the Federal Bureau of Investigation

GMT *abbr* Greenwich mean time

gnarled \ˈnärld\ *adj* **1** : KNOTTY **2** : GLOOMY, SULLEN

gnash \ˈnash\ *vb* : to grind (as teeth) together

gnat \ˈnat\ *n* : any of various small usu. biting dipteran flies

gnaw \ˈnȯ\ *vb* **1** : to consume, wear away, or make by persistent biting or nibbling **2** : to affect as if by gnawing — **gnaw•er** *n*

gneiss \ˈnīs\ *n* : a layered rock similar in composition to granite

gnome \ˈnōm\ *n* : a dwarf of folklore who lives inside the earth and guards precious ore or treasure — **gnom•ish** *adj*

GNP *abbr* gross national product

gnu \ˈnü\ *n, pl* **gnu** *or* **gnus** : either of two large African antelopes with an oxlike head and horns and a horselike mane and tail

gnu

[1]**go** \ˈgō\ *vb* **went** \ˈwent\; **gone** \ˈgȯn, ˈgän\; **go•ing; goes** \ˈgōz\ **1** : to move on a course : PROCEED ⟨∼ slow⟩ **2** : LEAVE, DEPART **3** : to take a certain course or follow a certain procedure ⟨reports ∼ through department channels⟩ **4** : EXTEND, RUN ⟨his land ∼*es* to the river⟩; *also* : LEAD ⟨that door ∼*es* to the cellar⟩ **5** : to be habitually in a certain state ⟨∼*es* armed after dark⟩ **6** : to become lost, consumed, or spent; *also* : DIE **7** : ELAPSE, PASS **8** : to pass by sale ⟨*went* for a good price⟩ **9** : to become impaired or weakened **10** : to give way under force or pressure : BREAK **11** : to move along in a specified manner ⟨it *went* well⟩ **12** : to be in general or on an average ⟨cheap, as yachts ∼⟩ **13** : to become esp. as the result of a contest ⟨the decision *went* against him⟩ **14** : to put or subject oneself ⟨∼ to great expense⟩ **15** : RESORT ⟨*went* to court to recover damages⟩ **16** : to begin or maintain an action or motion ⟨here ∼*es*⟩ **17** : to function properly ⟨the clock doesn't ∼⟩ **18** : to be known ⟨∼*es* by an alias⟩ **19** : to be or act in accordance ⟨a good rule to ∼ by⟩ **20** : to come to be applied **21** : to pass by award, assignment, or lot **22** : to contribute to a result ⟨qualities that ∼ to make a hero⟩ **23** : to be about, intending, or expecting something ⟨is ∼*ing* to leave town⟩ **24** : to arrive at a certain state or condition ⟨∼ to sleep⟩ **25** : to come to be ⟨the tire *went* flat⟩ **26** : to be capable of being sung or played ⟨the tune ∼*es* like this⟩ **27** : to be suitable or becoming : HARMONIZE **28** : to be capable of passing, extending, or being contained or inserted ⟨this coat will ∼ in the trunk⟩ **29** : to have a usual or proper place or position : BELONG ⟨these

books ~ on the top shelf⟩ **30** : to be capable of being divided ⟨3 ~*es* into 6 twice⟩ **31** : to have a tendency ⟨that ~*es* to show that he is honest⟩ **32** : to be acceptable, satisfactory, or adequate **33** : to empty the bladder or bowels **34** : to proceed along or according to : FOLLOW **35** : TRAVERSE **36** : BET, BID ⟨willing to ~ $50⟩ **37** : to assume the function or obligation of ⟨~ bail for a friend⟩ **38** : to participate to the extent of ⟨~ halves⟩ **39** : WEIGH **40** : ENDURE, TOLERATE **41** : AFFORD ⟨can't ~ the price⟩ **42** : SAY — used chiefly in oral narration of speech **43** : to engage in ⟨don't ~ telling everyone⟩ — **go at 1** : ATTACK, ATTEMPT **2** : UNDERTAKE — **go back on 1** : ABANDON **2** : BETRAY **3** : FAIL — **go by the board** : to be discarded — **go down the line** : to give wholehearted support — **go for 1** : to pass for or serve as **2** : to try to secure **3** : FAVOR — **go one better** : OUTDO, SURPASS — **go over 1** : EXAMINE **2** : REPEAT **3** : STUDY, REVIEW — **go places** : to be on the way to success — **go steady** : to date one person exclusively — **go to bat for** : DEFEND, CHAMPION — **go to town 1** : to work or act efficiently **2** : to be very successful

²go *n, pl* **goes 1** : the act or manner of going **2** : the height of fashion ⟨boots are all the ~⟩ **3** : a turn of affairs : OCCURRENCE **4** : ENERGY, VIGOR **5** : ATTEMPT, TRY **6** : a spell of activity — **no go** : USELESS, HOPELESS — **on the go** : constantly active

³go *adj* : functioning properly

goad \ˈgōd\ *n* [ME *gode,* fr. OE *gād* spear, goad] **1** : a pointed rod used to urge on an animal **2** : something that urges **syn** stimulus, impetus, incentive, spur, stimulant — **goad** *vb*

go–ahead \ˈgō-ə-ˌhed\ *n* : authority to proceed

goal \ˈgōl\ *n* **1** : the mark set as limit to a race; *also* : an area to be reached safely in children's games **2** : AIM, PURPOSE **3** : an area or object toward which play is directed to score; *also* : a successful attempt to score

goal•ie \ˈgō-lē\ *n* : GOALKEEPER

goal•keep•er \ˈgōl-ˌkē-pər\ *n* : a player who defends the goal in various games

goal•post \-ˌpōst\ *n* : one of the two vertical posts with a crossbar that constitute the goal in various games

goat \ˈgōt\ *n, pl* **goats** *or* **goat** : any of various hollow-horned ruminant mammals related to the sheep that have backward-curving horns, a short tail, and usu. straight hair

goa•tee \gō-ˈtē\ *n* : a small trim pointed or tufted beard on a man's chin

goat•herd \ˈgōt-ˌhərd\ *n* : a person who tends goats

goat•skin \-ˌskin\ *n* : the skin of a goat or a leather made from it

¹gob \ˈgäb\ *n* : LUMP, MASS

²gob *n* : SAILOR

gob•bet \ˈgä-bət\ *n* : LUMP, MASS

¹gob•ble \ˈgä-bəl\ *vb* **gob•bled; gob•bling 1** : to swallow or eat greedily **2** : to take eagerly : GRAB

²gobble *vb* **gob•bled; gob•bling** : to make the natural guttural noise of a male turkey

gob•ble•dy•gook *also* **gob•ble•de•gook** \ˈgä-bəl-dē-ˌgu̇k, -ˌgük\ *n* : generally unintelligible jargon

gob•bler \ˈgä-blər\ *n* : a male turkey

go–be•tween \ˈgō-bə-ˌtwēn\ *n* : an intermediate agent : BROKER

gob•let \ˈgä-blət\ *n* : a drinking glass with a foot and stem

gob•lin \ˈgä-blən\ *n* : an ugly or grotesque sprite that is mischievous and sometimes evil and malicious

god \ˈgäd, ˈgȯd\ *n* **1** *cap* : the supreme reality; *esp* : the Being worshiped as the creator and ruler of the universe **2** : a being or object believed to have supernatural attributes and powers and to require worship **3** : a person or thing of supreme value

god•child \ˈgäd-ˌchīld, ˈgȯd-\ *n* : a person for whom another person stands as sponsor at baptism

god•daugh•ter \-ˌdȯ-tər\ *n* : a female godchild

god•dess \ˈgä-dəs, ˈgȯ-\ *n* **1** : a female god **2** : a woman whose charm or beauty arouses adoration

god•fa•ther \ˈgäd-ˌfä-t͟hər, ˈgȯd-\ *n* **1** : a man who sponsors a person at baptism **2** : the leader of an organized crime syndicate

god•head \-ˌhed\ *n* **1** : divine nature or essence **2** *cap* : GOD 1; *also* : the nature of God esp. as existing in three persons

god•hood \-ˌhu̇d\ *n* : DIVINITY

god•less \-ləs\ *adj* : not acknowledging a deity or divine law — **god•less•ness** *n*

god•like \-ˌlīk\ *adj* : resembling or having the qualities of God or a god

god•ly \-lē\ *adj* **god•li•er; -est 1** : DIVINE **2** : PIOUS, DEVOUT — **god•li•ness** *n*

god•moth•er \-ˌmə-t͟hər\ *n* : a woman who sponsors a person at baptism

god•par•ent \-ˌpar-ənt\ *n* : a sponsor at baptism

god•send \-ˌsend\ *n* : a desirable or needed thing or event that comes unexpectedly

god•son \-ˌsən\ *n* : a male godchild

God•speed \-ˈspēd\ *n* : a prosperous journey : SUCCESS ⟨bade him ~⟩

go•fer \ˈgō-fər\ *n* [alter. of *go for*] : an employee whose duties include running errands

go–get•ter \ˈgō-ˌge-tər\ *n* : an aggressively enterprising person — **go–get•ting** *adj or n*

gog•gle \ˈgä-gəl\ *vb* **gog•gled; gog•gling** : to stare with wide or protuberant eyes

gog•gles \ˈgä-gəlz\ *n pl* : protective glasses set in a flexible frame that fits snugly against the face

go–go \ˈgō-ˌgō\ *adj* **1** : related to, being, or employed to entertain in a disco ⟨~ dancers⟩ **2** : aggressively enterprising and energetic

go•ings–on \ˌgō-iŋ-ˈzȯn, -ˈzän\ *n pl* : ACTIONS, EVENTS

goi•ter \ˈgȯi-tər\ *n* : an abnormally enlarged thyroid gland visible as a swelling at the base of the neck — **goi•trous** \-trəs, -tə-rəs\ *adj*

goi•tre *chiefly Brit var of* GOITER

gold \ˈgōld\ *n* **1** : a malleable yellow metallic chemical element used esp. for coins and jewelry — see ELEMENT table **2** : gold coins; *also* : MONEY **3** : a yellow color

gold•brick \ˈgōld-ˌbrik\ *n* : a person who shirks assigned work — **goldbrick** *vb*

gold coast *n, often cap G&C* : an exclusive residential district

gold digger *n* : a person who uses charm to extract money or gifts from others

gold•en \ˈgōl-dən\ *adj* **1** : made of or relating to gold **2** : having the color of gold; *also* : BLOND **3** : SHINING, LUSTROUS **4** : SUPERB **5** : FLOURISHING, PROSPEROUS **6** : radiantly youthful and vigorous **7** : FAVORABLE, ADVANTAGEOUS ⟨a ~ opportunity⟩ **8** : MELLOW, RESONANT

gold•en–ag•er \ˈgōl-dən-ˈā-jər\ *n* : an elderly and often retired person usu. engaging in club activities

golden hamster *n* : a small tawny hamster often kept as a pet

gold•en•rod \ˈgōl-dən-ˌräd\ *n* : any of numerous plants related to the daisies but having tall slender stalks with many tiny usu. yellow flower heads

gold•finch \-ˌfinch\ *n* **1** : a small largely red, black, and yellow Old World finch often kept in a cage **2** : any of three small American finches of which the males usu. become bright yellow and black in summer

gold•fish \-ˌfish\ *n* : a small usu. yellow or golden carp often kept as an aquarium or pond fish

gold•smith \-ˌsmith\ *n* : a person who makes or deals in articles of gold

golf \ˈgälf, ˈgȯlf\ *n* : a game played with a small ball and various clubs on a course having 9 or 18 holes — **golf** *vb* — **golf•er** *n*

-gon \ˌgän\ *n comb form* : figure having (so many) angles ⟨hexa*gon*⟩

go•nad \ˈgō-ˌnad\ *n* : a sperm- or egg-producing gland : OVARY, TESTIS — **go•nad•al** \gō-ˈnad-ᵊl\ *adj*

go•nad•o•trop•ic \gō-ˌna-də-ˈträ-pik\ *also* **go•nad•o•tro•phic** \-ˈtrō-fik,-ˈträ-\ *adj* : acting on or stimulating the gonads ⟨~ hormones⟩

go•nad•o•tro•pin \-ˈtrō-pən\ *also* **go•nad•o•tro•phin** \-fən\ *n* : a gonadotropic hormone

gon•do•la \ˈgän-də-lə (*usual for 1*), gän-ˈdō-\ *n* **1** : a long narrow boat used on the canals of Venice **2** : a railroad car used for hauling loose freight (as coal) **3** : an enclosure beneath an airship or balloon **4** : an enclosed car suspended from a cable and used esp. for transporting skiers

gondola 1

gon•do•lier \ˌgän-də-ˈlir\ *n* : a person who propels a gondola

[1]**gone** \ˈgȯn\ *past part of* GO

[2]**gone** *adj* **1** : DEAD **2** : LOST, RUINED **3** : SINKING, WEAK **4** : INVOLVED, ABSORBED **5** : INFATUATED **6** : PREGNANT **7** : PAST

gon•er \ˈgȯ-nər\ *n* : one whose case is hopeless

gong \ˈgäŋ, ˈgȯŋ\ *n* : a metallic disk that produces a resounding tone when struck

gono•coc•cus \ˌgä-nə-ˈkä-kəs\ *n, pl* **-coc•ci** \-ˈkäk-ˌsī, -(ˌ)sē, -ˈkä-ˌkī, -(ˌ)kē\ : a pus-producing bacterium causing gonorrhea — **gono•coc•cal** \-ˈkä-kəl\ *adj*

gon•or•rhea \ˌgä-nə-ˈrē-ə\ *n* : a contagious sexually transmitted inflammation of the genital tract caused by a bacterium — **gon•or•rhe•al** \-ˈrē-əl\ *adj*

goo \ˈgü\ *n* **1** : a viscid or sticky substance **2** : sentimental tripe — **goo•ey** \-ē\ *adj*

goo•ber \ˈgü-bər, ˈgu̇-\ *n, Southern & Midland* : PEANUT

[1]**good** \ˈgu̇d\ *adj* **bet•ter** \ˈbe-tər\; **best** \ˈbest\ **1** : of a favorable character or tendency **2** : BOUNTIFUL, FERTILE **3** : COMELY, ATTRACTIVE **4** : SUITABLE, FIT **5** : SOUND, WHOLE **6** : AGREEABLE, PLEASANT **7** : SALUTARY, WHOLESOME **8** : CONSIDERABLE, AMPLE **9** : FULL **10** : WELL-FOUNDED **11** : TRUE ⟨holds ~ for everybody⟩ **12** : legally valid or effectual **13** : ADEQUATE, SATISFACTORY **14** : conforming to a standard **15** : DISCRIMINATING **16** : COMMENDABLE, VIRTUOUS **17** : KIND **18** : UPPER-CLASS **19** : COMPETENT **20** : LOYAL, CLOSE — **good–heart•ed** \-ˈhär-təd\ *adj* — **good•ish** *adj* — **good–look•ing** \-ˈlu̇-kiŋ\ *adj* — **good–tem•pered** \-ˈtem-pərd\ *adj*

[2]**good** *n* **1** : something good **2** : GOODNESS **3** : BENEFIT, WELFARE ⟨for the ~ of mankind⟩ **4** : something that has economic utility **5** *pl* : personal property **6** *pl* : CLOTH **7** *pl* : WARES, MERCHANDISE **8** : good persons ⟨the ~ die young⟩ **9** *pl* : proof of wrongdoing — **for good** : FOREVER, PERMANENTLY — **to the good** : in a position of net gain or profit ⟨$10 *to the good*⟩

[3]**good** *adv* : WELL

good–bye *or* **good–by** \gu̇d-ˈbī, gə-\ *n* : a concluding remark at parting

good–for–noth•ing \ˈgu̇d-fər-ˌnə-thiŋ\ *n* : an idle worthless person

Good Friday *n* : the Friday before Easter observed as the anniversary of the crucifixion of Christ

good•ly \ˈgu̇d-lē\ *adj* **good•li•er; -est 1** : of pleasing appearance **2** : LARGE, CONSIDERABLE

good•man \ˈgu̇d-mən\ *n, archaic* : MR.

good–na•tured \ˈgu̇d-ˈnā-chərd\ *adj* : of a cheerful disposition — **good–na•tured•ly** \-chərd-lē\ *adv*

good•ness \-nəs\ *n* : EXCELLENCE, VIRTUE

good•wife \-ˌwīf\ *n, archaic* : MRS.

good•will \-ˈwil\ *n* **1** : BENEVOLENCE **2** : the value of the trade a business has built up over time **3** : cheerful consent **4** : willing effort

goody \ˈgu̇-dē\ *n, pl* **good•ies** : something that is good esp. to eat

goody–goody \ˌgu̇-dē-ˈgu̇-dē\ *adj* : affectedly good — **goody–goody** *n*

goof \ˈgüf\ *vb* **1** : to spend time idly or foolishly **2** : BLUNDER — often used with *off* — **goof** *n*

goof•ball \ˈgüf-ˌbȯl\ *n* **1** *slang* : a barbiturate sleeping pill **2** : a goofy person

go off *vb* **1** : EXPLODE **2** : to follow a course ⟨the party *went off* well⟩

goof–off \ˈgü-ˌfȯf\ *n* : one who evades work or responsibility

goofy \ˈgü-fē\ *adj* **goof•i•er; -est** : CRAZY, SILLY — **goof•i•ness** \-fē-nəs\ *n*

goon \ˈgün\ *n* : a man hired to terrorize or kill opponents

go on *vb* **1** : to continue in a course of action **2** : to take place : HAPPEN

goose \ˈgüs\ *n, pl* **geese** \ˈgēs\ **1** : any of numerous long-necked web-footed birds related to the swans and ducks; *esp* : a female goose as distinguished from a gander **2** : a foolish person **3** *pl* **goos•es** : a tailor's smoothing iron

goose•ber•ry \ˈgüs-ˌber-ē, ˈgüz-, -bə-rē\ *n* : the acid berry of any of several shrubs related to the currant and used esp. in jams and pies

goose bumps *n pl* : roughening of the skin caused usu. by cold, fear, or a sudden feeling of excitement

goose•flesh \-ˌflesh\ *n* : GOOSE BUMPS

goose pimples *n pl* : GOOSE BUMPS

go out *vb* **1** : to become extinguished **2** : to become a candidate ⟨*went out* for the football team⟩

go over *vb* : SUCCEED

GOP *abbr* Grand Old Party (Republican)

go•pher \ˈgō-fər\ *n* **1** : a burrowing American land tortoise **2** : any of a family of No. American burrowing rodents with large cheek pouches opening beside the mouth **3** : any of several small ground squirrels of the prairie region of No. America

[1]**gore** \ˈgōr\ *n* : BLOOD

[2]**gore** *n* : a tapering or triangular piece (as of cloth in a skirt)

[3]**gore** *vb* **gored; gor•ing** : to pierce or wound with something pointed

[1]**gorge** \ˈgȯrj\ *n* **1** : THROAT **2** : a narrow ravine **3** : a mass of matter that chokes up a passage

[2]**gorge** *vb* **gorged; gorg•ing** : to eat greedily : stuff to capacity : GLUT

gor•geous \ˈgȯr-jəs\ *adj* : resplendently beautiful

Gor•gon•zo•la \ˌgȯr-gən-ˈzō-lə\ *n* : a blue cheese of Italian origin

go•ril•la \gə-ˈri-lə\ *n* [NL, fr. Gk *Gorillai,* a tribe of hairy women in an account of a voyage around Africa] : an African anthropoid ape related to but much larger than the chimpanzee

gor•man•dise *chiefly Brit var of* GORMANDIZE

gor•man•dize \ˈgȯr-mən-ˌdīz\ *vb* **-dized; -diz•ing** : to eat ravenously — **gor•man•diz•er** *n*

gorp \ˈgȯrp\ *n* : a snack consisting of high-calorie food (as raisins and nuts)

gorse \ˈgȯrs\ *n* : a spiny yellow-flowered Old World evergreen shrub of the legume family

gory \ˈgōr-ē\ *adj* **gor•i•er; -est 1** : BLOODSTAINED **2** : HORRIBLE, SENSATIONAL

gos•hawk \ˈgäs-ˌhȯk\ *n* : any of several long-tailed hawks with short rounded wings

gos•ling \ˈgäz-liŋ, ˈgȯz-\ *n* : a young goose

[1]**gos•pel** \ˈgäs-pəl\ *n* [ME, fr. OE *gōdspel,* fr. *gōd* good + *spell* message, news] **1** : the teachings of Christ and the apostles **2** *cap* : any of the first four books of the

New Testament **3 :** something accepted as infallible truth

[2]gospel *adj* **1 :** of, relating to, or emphasizing the gospel **2 :** relating to or being American religious songs associated with evangelism

gos•sa•mer \ˈgä-sə-mər\ *n* [ME *gossomer,* fr. *gos* goose + *somer* summer] **1 :** a film of cobwebs floating in the air **2 :** something light, delicate, or tenuous

[1]gos•sip \ˈgä-səp\ *n* **1 :** a person who habitually reveals personal or sensational facts **2 :** rumor or report of an intimate nature **3 :** an informal conversation — **gos-sipy** *adj*

[2]gossip *vb* **:** to spread gossip

got *past and past part of* GET

Goth \ˈgäth\ *n* **:** a member of a Germanic people that early in the Christian era overran the Roman Empire

[1]Goth•ic \ˈgä-thik\ *adj* **1 :** of or relating to the Goths **2 :** of or relating to a style of architecture prevalent in western Europe from the middle 12th to the early 16th century

[2]Gothic *n* **1 :** the Germanic language of the Goths **2 :** the Gothic architectural style or decoration

gotten *past part of* GET

Gou•da \ˈgü-də\ *n* **:** a mild Dutch milk cheese shaped in balls

[1]gouge \ˈgau̇j\ *n* **1 :** a rounded troughlike chisel **2 :** a hole or groove made with or as if with a gouge

[2]gouge *vb* **gouged; goug•ing 1 :** to cut holes or grooves in with or as if with a gouge **2 :** DEFRAUD, CHEAT

gou•lash \ˈgü-ˌläsh, -ˌlash\ *n* [Hungarian *gulyás*] **:** a stew made with meat, assorted vegetables, and paprika

go under *vb* **:** to be overwhelmed, defeated, or destroyed **:** FAIL

gourd \ˈgōrd, ˈgu̇rd\ *n* **1 :** any of a family of tendril-bearing vines including the cucumber, squash, and melon **2 :** the fruit of a gourd; *esp* **:** any of various inedible hard-shelled fruits used esp. for ornament or implements

gourde \ˈgu̇rd\ *n* — see MONEY table

gour•mand \ˈgu̇r-ˌmänd\ *n* **1 :** one who is excessively fond of eating and drinking **2 :** GOURMET

gour•met \ˈgu̇r-ˌmā, gu̇r-ˈmā\ *n* [F, fr. MF, alter. of *gromet* boy servant, vintner's assistant] **:** a connoisseur of food and drink

gout \ˈgau̇t\ *n* **:** a metabolic disease marked by painful inflammation and swelling of the joints — **gouty** *adj*

gov *abbr* **1** government **2** governor

gov•ern \ˈgə-vərn\ *vb* **1 :** to control and direct the making and administration of policy in **:** RULE **2 :** CONTROL, DIRECT, INFLUENCE **3 :** DETERMINE, REGULATE **4 :** RESTRAIN — **gov•er•nance** \-vər-nəns\ *n*

gov•ern•ess \ˈgə-vər-nəs\ *n* **:** a woman who teaches and trains a child esp. in a private home

gov•ern•ment \ˈgə-vərn-mənt\ *n* **1 :** authoritative direction or control **:** RULE **2 :** the making of policy **3 :** the organization or agency through which a political unit exercises authority **4 :** the complex of institutions, laws, and customs through which a political unit is governed **5 :** the governing body — **gov•ern•men•tal** \ˌgə-vərn-ˈment-ᵊl\ *adj*

gov•er•nor \ˈgə-vər-nər\ *n* **1 :** one that governs; *esp* **:** a ruler, chief executive, or head of a political unit (as a state) **2 :** an attachment to a machine for automatic control of speed — **gov•er•nor•ship** *n*

govt *abbr* government

gown \ˈgau̇n\ *n* **1 :** a loose flowing outer garment **2 :** an official robe worn esp. by a judge, clergyman, or teacher **3 :** a woman's dress ⟨evening ~*s*⟩ **4 :** a loose robe — **gown** *vb*

gp *abbr* group

GP *abbr* general practitioner

GPO *abbr* **1** general post office **2** Government Printing Office

GQ *abbr* general quarters

gr *abbr* **1** grade **2** grain **3** gram **4** gravity **5** gross

grab \ˈgrab\ *vb* **grabbed; grab•bing :** to take hastily **:** SNATCH — **grab** *n*

[1]grace \ˈgrās\ *n* **1 :** unmerited help given to people by God (as in overcoming temptation) **2 :** freedom from sin through divine grace **3 :** a virtue coming from God **4** — used as a title for a duke, a duchess, or an archbishop **5 :** a short prayer at a meal **6 :** a temporary respite (as from the payment of a debt) **7 :** APPROVAL, ACCEPTANCE ⟨in his good ~*s*⟩ **8 :** CHARM **9 :** ATTRACTIVENESS, BEAUTY **10 :** fitness or proportion of line or expression **11 :** ease of movement **12 :** a musical trill or ornament — **grace•ful** \-fəl\ *adj* — **grace•ful•ly** *adv* — **grace•ful•ness** *n* — **grace•less** *adj*

[2]grace *vb* **graced; grac•ing 1 :** HONOR **2 :** ADORN, EMBELLISH

gra•cious \ˈgrā-shəs\ *adj* **1 :** marked by kindness and courtesy **2 :** GRACEFUL **3 :** characterized by charm and good taste **4 :** MERCIFUL — **gra•cious•ly** *adv* — **gra•cious•ness** *n*

grack•le \ˈgra-kəl\ *n* **:** any of several American blackbirds with glossy iridescent plumage

grad *abbr* graduate; graduated

gra•da•tion \grā-ˈdā-shən, grə-\ *n* **1 :** a series forming successive stages **2 :** a step, degree, or stage in a series **3 :** an advance by regular degrees **4 :** the act or process of grading

[1]grade \ˈgrād\ *vb* **grad•ed; grad•ing 1 :** to arrange in grades **:** SORT **2 :** to make level or evenly sloping ⟨~ a highway⟩ **3 :** to give a grade to ⟨~ a pupil in history⟩ **4 :** to assign to a grade

[2]grade *n* **1 :** a degree or stage in a series, order, or ranking **2 :** a position in a scale of rank, quality, or order **3 :** a class of persons or things of the same rank or quality **4 :** a division of the school course representing one year's work; *also* **:** the pupils in such a division **5** *pl* **:** the elementary school system **6 :** a mark or rating esp. of accomplishment in school **7 :** the degree of slope (as of a road); *also* **:** SLOPE

grad•er \ˈgrā-dər\ *n* **:** a machine for leveling earth

grade school *n* **:** ELEMENTARY SCHOOL

gra•di•ent \ˈgrā-dē-ənt\ *n* **:** SLOPE, GRADE

grad•u•al \ˈgra-jə-wəl\ *adj* **:** proceeding or changing by steps or degrees — **grad•u•al•ly** *adv*

grad•u•al•ism \-wə-ˌli-zəm\ *n* **:** the policy of approaching a desired end gradually

[1]grad•u•ate \ˈgra-jə-wət\ *n* **1 :** a holder of an academic degree or diploma **2 :** a graduated container for measuring contents

[2]graduate *adj* **1 :** holding an academic degree or diploma **2 :** of or relating to studies beyond the first or bachelor's degree ⟨~ school⟩

[3]grad•u•ate \ˈgra-jə-ˌwāt\ *vb* **-at•ed; -at•ing 1 :** to grant or receive an academic degree or diploma **2 :** to divide into grades, classes, or intervals **3 :** to admit to a particular standing or grade

grad•u•a•tion \ˌgra-jə-ˈwā-shən\ *n* **1 :** a mark that graduates something **2 :** an act or process of graduating **3 :** COMMENCEMENT 2

graf•fi•to \grə-ˈfē-tō, grə-\ *n, pl* **-ti** \-(ˌ)tē\ **:** an inscription or drawing made on a public surface (as a wall)

[1]graft \ˈgraft\ *n* **1 :** a grafted plant; *also* **:** the point of union in this **2 :** material (as skin) used in grafting **3 :** the getting of money or advantage dishonestly; *also* **:** the money or advantage so gained

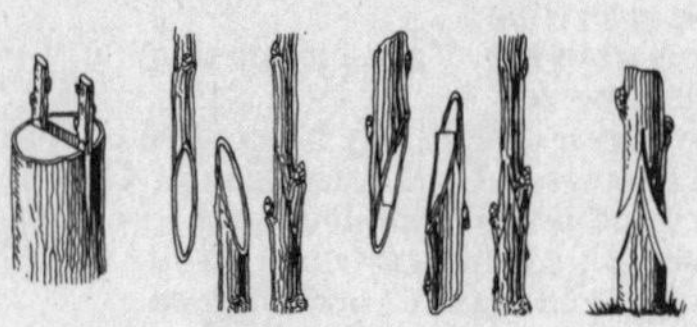

graft 1

[2]graft *vb* **1 :** to insert a shoot from one plant into another so that they join and grow; *also* **:** to join one thing to another as in plant grafting ⟨~ skin over a burn⟩ **2 :** to get (as money) dishonestly — **graft•er** *n*

gra•ham cracker \ˈgrā-əm-, ˈgram-\ *n* **:** a slightly sweet cracker made chiefly of whole wheat flour

Grail \ˈgrāl\ *n* **:** the cup or platter used according to medieval legend by Christ at the Last Supper and thereafter the object of knightly quests

grain \ˈgrān\ *n* **1 :** a seed or fruit of a cereal grass **2 :** seeds or fruits of various food plants and esp. cereal grasses; *also* **:** a plant (as wheat) producing grain **3 :** a small hard particle **4 :** a unit of weight based on the weight of a grain of wheat — see WEIGHT table **5 :** TEXTURE; *also* **:** the arrangement of fibers in wood **6 :** natural disposition — **grained** \ˈgrānd\ *adj*

grain alcohol *n* **:** ALCOHOL 1

grainy \ˈgrā-nē\ *adj* **grain•i•er; -est 1 :** resembling or having some characteristic of grain **:** not smooth or fine **2** *of a photograph* **:** appearing to be composed of grain-like particles

[1]gram \ˈgram\ *n* [F *gramme,* fr. LL *gramma,* a small weight, fr. Gk *gramma* letter, writing, a small weight, fr. *graphein* to write] **:** a metric unit of mass and weight equal to 1/1000 kilogram — see METRIC SYSTEM table

[2]gram *abbr* grammar; grammatical

-gram \ˌgram\ *n comb form* **:** drawing **:** writing **:** record ⟨tele*gram*⟩

gram•mar \ˈgra-mər\ *n* **1 :** the study of the classes of words, their inflections, and their functions and relations in the sentence **2 :** a study of what is to be preferred and what avoided in inflection and syntax **3 :** speech or writing evaluated according to its conformity to grammatical rules — **gram•mar•i•an** \grə-ˈmer-ē-ən, -ˈmar-\ *n* — **gram•mat•i•cal** \-ˈma-ti-kəl\ *adj* — **gram•mat•i•cal•ly** \-k(ə-)lē\ *adv*

grammar school *n* **1 :** a secondary school emphasizing Latin and Greek in preparation for college; *also* **:** a British college preparatory school **2 :** a school intermediate between the primary grades and high school **3 :** ELEMENTARY SCHOOL

gramme \ˈgram\ *chiefly Brit var of* GRAM

gram•o•phone \ˈgra-mə-ˌfōn\ *n* **:** PHONOGRAPH

gra•na•ry \ˈgrā-nə-rē, ˈgra-\ *n, pl* **-ries 1 :** a storehouse for grain **2 :** a region producing grain in abundance

[1]grand \ˈgrand\ *adj* **1 :** higher in rank or importance **:** FOREMOST, CHIEF **2 :** great in size **3 :** INCLUSIVE, COMPLETE ⟨a ~ total⟩ **4 :** MAGNIFICENT, SPLENDID **5 :** showing wealth or high social standing **6 :** IMPRESSIVE, STATELY **7 :** very good **:** FINE — **grand•ly** *adv* — **grand•ness** *n*

[2]grand *n, slang* **:** a thousand dollars

gran•dam \ˈgran-ˌdam, -dəm\ *or* **gran•dame** \-ˌdām, -dəm\ *n* **:** an old woman

grand•child \ˈgrand-ˌchīld\ *n* **:** a child of one's son or daughter

grand•daugh•ter \ˈgran-ˌdȯ-tər\ *n* **:** a daughter of one's son or daughter

grande dame \ˈgrän-ˈdäm\ *n, pl* **grandes dames :** a usu. elderly woman of great prestige or ability

gran•dee \gran-ˈdē\ *n* **:** a high-ranking Spanish or Portuguese nobleman

gran•deur \ˈgran-jər\ *n* **1 :** the quality or state of being grand **:** MAGNIFICENCE **2 :** something that is grand

grand•fa•ther \ˈgrand-ˌfä-t͟hər\ *n* **:** the father of one's father or mother; *also* **:** ANCESTOR

grandfather clock *n* **:** a tall clock that stands on the floor

gran•dil•o•quence \gran-ˈdi-lə-kwəns\ *n* **:** pompous eloquence — **gran•dil•o•quent** \-kwənt\ *adj*

gran•di•ose \ˈgran-dē-ˌōs, ˌgran-dē-ˈōs\ *adj* **:** IMPRESSIVE, IMPOSING; *also* **:** affectedly splendid — **gran•di•ose•ly** *adv* — **gran•di•os•i•ty** \ˌgran-dē-ˈä-sə-tē\ *n*

grand jury *n* **:** a jury that examines accusations of crime against persons and makes formal charges on which the persons are later tried

grand mal \ˈgrän-ˌmäl; ˈgrand-ˌmal\ *n* [F, lit., great illness] **:** severe epilepsy

grand•moth•er \ˈgrand-ˌmə-t͟hər\ *n* **:** the mother of one's father or mother; *also* **:** a female ancestor

grand•par•ent \-ˌpar-ənt\ *n* **:** a parent of one's father or mother

grand piano *n* **:** a piano with horizontal frame and strings

grand prix \ˈgrän-ˈprē\ *n, pl* **grand prix** *same or* -ˈprēz\ *often cap G&P* **:** a long-distance auto race over a road course

grand slam *n* **1 :** a total victory or success **2 :** a home run hit with three runners on base

grand•son \ˈgrand-ˌsən\ *n* **:** a son of one's son or daughter

grand•stand \-ˌstand\ *n* **:** a usu. roofed stand for spectators at a racecourse or stadium

grange \ˈgrānj\ *n* **1 :** a farm or farmhouse with its various buildings **2** *cap* **:** one of the lodges of a national association originally made up of farmers; *also* **:** the association itself — **grang•er** \ˈgrān-jər\ *n*

gran•ite \ˈgra-nət\ *n* **:** a hard granular igneous rock used esp. for building — **gra•nit•ic** \gra-ˈni-tik\ *adj*

gran•ite•ware \ˈgra-nət-ˌwar\ *n* **:** ironware with mottled enamel

gra•no•la \grə-ˈnō-lə\ *n* **:** a cereal made of rolled oats and usu. raisins and nuts

[1]grant \ˈgrant\ *vb* **1 :** to consent to **:** ALLOW, PERMIT **2 :** GIVE, BESTOW **3 :** to admit as true — **grant•er** *n* — **grant•or** \ˈgran-tər, -ˌtȯr\ *n*

[2]grant *n* **1 :** the act of granting **2 :** something granted; *esp* **:** a gift for a particular purpose ⟨a ~ for study abroad⟩ **3 :** a transfer of property by deed or writing; *also* **:** the instrument by which such a transfer is made **4 :** the property transferred by grant — **grant•ee** \gran-ˈtē\ *n*

gran•u•lar \ˈgra-nyə-lər\ *adj* **:** consisting of or appearing to consist of granules — **gran•u•lar•i•ty** \ˌgra-nyə-ˈlar-ə-tē\ *n*

gran•u•late \ˈgra-nyə-ˌlāt\ *vb* **-lat•ed; -lat•ing :** to form into grains or crystals — **gran•u•la•tion** \ˌgra-nyə-ˈlā-shən\ *n*

gran•ule \ˈgra-nyül\ *n* **:** a small grain or particle

grape \ˈgrāp\ *n* [ME, fr. OF *crape, grape* hook, grape stalk, bunch of grapes, grape] **1 :** a smooth-skinned juicy edible greenish white, deep red, or purple berry that is the chief source of wine **2 :** any of numerous woody vines widely grown for their bunches of grapes

grape•fruit \ˈgrāp-ˌfrüt\ *n* **1** *pl* **grapefruit** *or* **grapefruits :** a large edible yellow-skinned citrus fruit **2 :** a tree bearing grapefruit

grape hyacinth *n* **:** any of several small bulbous spring-flowering herbs with clusters of usu. blue flowers that are related to the lilies

grape•shot \ˈgrāp-ˌshät\ *n* **:** a cluster of small iron balls formerly fired at people from short range by a cannon

grape•vine \-ˌvīn\ *n* **1 :** GRAPE 2 **2 :** RUMOR; *also* **:** an informal means of circulating information or gossip

graph \ˈgraf\ *n* **:** a diagram that usu. by means of dots and lines shows change in one variable factor in comparison with one or more other factors — **graph** *vb*

-graph \ˌgraf\ *n comb form* **1 :** something written ⟨auto*graph*⟩ **2 :** instrument for making or transmitting records ⟨seismo*graph*⟩

[1]graph•ic \ˈgra-fik\ *also* **graph•i•cal** \-fi-kəl\ *adj* **1 :** being written, drawn, or engraved **2 :** vividly described **3 :** of or relating to the arts **(graphic arts)** of representation, decoration, and printing on flat surfaces — **graph•i•cal•ly** \-fi-k(ə-)lē\ *adv*

[2]graphic *n* **1 :** a picture, map, or graph used for illustration **2** *pl* **:** a display (as of pictures or graphs) generated by a computer on a screen, printer, or plotter

graph•ics tablet \-fiks-\ *n* **:** a computer input device for

entering pictorial information by drawing or tracing
graph•ite \ˈgra-ˌfīt\ *n* [G *Graphit,* fr. Gk *graphein* to write] : a soft black form of carbon used esp. for lead pencils and lubricants
grap•nel \ˈgrap-nəl\ *n* : a small anchor with usu. four claws used esp. in dragging or grappling operations
[1]**grap•ple** \ˈgra-pəl\ *n* [MF *grappelle,* dim. of *grape* hook] : the act of grappling
[2]**grapple** *vb* **grap•pled; grap•pling 1** : to seize or hold with or as if with a hooked implement **2** : to come to grips with : WRESTLE
[1]**grasp** \ˈgrasp\ *vb* **1** : to make the motion of seizing **2** : to take or seize firmly **3** : to enclose and hold with the fingers or arms **4** : COMPREHEND
[2]**grasp** *n* **1** : HANDLE **2** : EMBRACE **3** : HOLD, CONTROL **4** : the reach of the arms **5** : the power of seizing and holding **6** : COMPREHENSION
grasp•ing *adj* : GREEDY, AVARICIOUS
grass \ˈgras\ *n* **1** : herbage for grazing animals **2** : any of a large family of plants (as wheat, bamboo, or sugarcane) with jointed stems and narrow leaves **3** : grass-covered land **4** : MARIJUANA — **grassy** *adj*
grass•hop•per \-ˌhä-pər\ *n* : any of numerous leaping plant-eating insects
grass•land \-ˌland\ *n* : land covered naturally or under cultivation with grasses and low-growing herbs
grass roots *n pl* : society at the local level as distinguished from the centers of political leadership
[1]**grate** \ˈgrāt\ *vb* **grat•ed; grat•ing 1** : to pulverize by rubbing against something rough **2** : to grind or rub against with a rasping noise **3** : IRRITATE — **grat•er** *n* — **grat•ing•ly** *adv*
[2]**grate** *n* **1** : GRATING **2** : a frame of iron bars for holding fuel while it burns
grate•ful \ˈgrāt-fəl\ *adj* **1** : THANKFUL, APPRECIATIVE; *also* : expressing gratitude **2** : PLEASING — **grate•ful•ly** *adv* — **grate•ful•ness** *n*
grat•i•fy \ˈgra-tə-ˌfī\ *vb* **-fied; -fy•ing** : to afford pleasure to — **grat•i•fi•ca•tion** \ˌgra-tə-fə-ˈkā-shən\ *n*
grat•ing \ˈgrā-tiŋ\ *n* : a framework with parallel bars or crossbars
gra•tis \ˈgra-təs, ˈgrā-\ *adv or adj* : without charge or recompense : FREE
grat•i•tude \ˈgra-tə-ˌtüd, -ˌtyüd\ *n* : THANKFULNESS
gra•tu•itous \grə-ˈtü-ə-təs, -ˈtyü-\ *adj* **1** : done or provided without recompense : FREE **2** : UNWARRANTED
gra•tu•ity \-ə-tē\ *n, pl* **-ities** : [10]TIP
gra•va•men \grə-ˈvā-mən\ *n, pl* **-va•mens** *or* **-vam•i•na** \-ˈva-mə-nə\ [LL, burden] : the basic or significant part of a grievance or complaint
[1]**grave** \ˈgrāv\ *vb* **graved; grav•en** \ˈgrā-vən\ *or* **graved; grav•ing** : SCULPTURE, ENGRAVE
[2]**grave** *n* : an excavation in the earth as a place of burial; *also* : TOMB
[3]**grave** \ˈgrāv; *5 also* ˈgräv\ *adj* **1** : IMPORTANT **2** : threatening great harm or danger **3** : DIGNIFIED, SOLEMN **4** : drab in color : SOMBER **5** : of, marked by, or being an accent mark having the form ` — **grave•ly** *adv* — **grave•ness** *n*
grav•el \ˈgra-vəl\ *n* : pebbles and small pieces of rock larger than grains of sand — **grav•el•ly** *adj*
grave•stone \ˈgrāv-ˌstōn\ *n* : a burial monument
grave•yard \-ˌyärd\ *n* : CEMETERY
grav•id \ˈgra-vəd\ *adj* [L *gravidus,* fr. *gravis* heavy] : PREGNANT
gra•vi•me•ter \grə-ˈvi-mə-tər, ˈgra-və-ˌmē-\ *n* : a device for measuring variations in a gravitational field
grav•i•tate \ˈgra-və-ˌtāt\ *vb* **-tat•ed; -tat•ing** : to move or tend to move toward something
grav•i•ta•tion \ˌgra-və-ˈtā-shən\ *n* **1** : a natural force of attraction that tends to draw bodies together and that occurs because of the mass of the bodies **2** : the action or process of gravitating — **grav•i•ta•tion•al** \-shə-nəl\ *adj* — **grav•i•ta•tion•al•ly** *adv*
grav•i•ty \ˈgra-və-tē\ *n, pl* **-ties 1** : IMPORTANCE; *esp* : SERIOUSNESS **2** : [2]MASS 5 **3** : the gravitational attraction of the mass of a celestial object (as earth) for bodies close to it; *also* : GRAVITATION 1
gra•vure \grə-ˈvyůr\ *n* [F] : PHOTOGRAVURE
gra•vy \ˈgrā-vē\ *n, pl* **gravies 1** : a sauce made from the thickened and seasoned juices of cooked meat **2** : unearned or illicit gain : GRAFT
[1]**gray** \ˈgrā\ *adj* **1** : of the color gray; *also* : dull in color **2** : having gray hair **3** : CHEERLESS, DISMAL **4** : intermediate in position or character — **gray•ish** *adj* — **gray•ness** *n*
[2]**gray** *n* **1** : something of a gray color **2** : a neutral color ranging between black and white
[3]**gray** *vb* : to make or become gray
gray•beard \ˈgrā-ˌbird\ *n* : an old man
gray•ling \ˈgrā-liŋ\ *n, pl* **grayling** *also* **graylings** : any of several slender freshwater food and sport fishes related to the trouts
gray matter *n* **1** : the grayish part of nervous tissue consisting mostly of nerve cell bodies **2** : INTELLIGENCE
gray wolf *n* : a large wolf of northern No. America and Asia that is usu. gray
[1]**graze** \ˈgrāz\ *vb* **grazed; graz•ing 1** : to feed on herbage or pasture **2** : to feed (livestock) on grass or pasture — **graz•er** *n*
[2]**graze** *vb* **grazed; graz•ing 1** : to touch lightly in passing **2** : SCRATCH, ABRADE
[1]**grease** \ˈgrēs\ *n* **1** : rendered animal fat **2** : oily material **3** : a thick lubricant — **greasy** \ˈgrē-sē, -zē\ *adj*
[2]**grease** \ˈgrēs, ˈgrēz\ *vb* **greased; greas•ing** : to smear or lubricate with grease
grease•paint \ˈgrēs-ˌpānt\ *n* : theater makeup
great \ˈgrāt\ *adj* **1** : large in size : BIG **2** : ELABORATE, AMPLE **3** : large in number : NUMEROUS **4** : being beyond the average : MIGHTY, INTENSE ⟨a ~ weight⟩ ⟨in ~ pain⟩ **5** : EMINENT, GRAND **6** : long continued ⟨a ~ while⟩ **7** : MAIN, PRINCIPAL **8** : more distant in a family relationship by one generation ⟨a *great*-grandfather⟩ **9** : markedly superior in character, quality, or skill ⟨~ at bridge⟩ **10** : EXCELLENT, FINE ⟨had a ~ time⟩ — **great•ly** *adv* — **great•ness** *n*
great circle *n* : a circle on the surface of a sphere that has the same center as the sphere; *esp* : one on the surface of the earth an arc of which is the shortest travel distance between two points
great•coat \ˈgrāt-ˌkōt\ *n* : a heavy overcoat
Great Dane *n* : any of a breed of tall massive powerful smooth-coated dogs
great•heart•ed \ˈgrāt-ˈhär-təd\ *adj* **1** : COURAGEOUS **2** : MAGNANIMOUS
great power *n, often cap G&P* : one of the nations that figure most decisively in international affairs
great white shark *n* : a large and dangerous shark of warm seas that is light colored below and darker above becoming dirty white in older and larger specimens
grebe \ˈgrēb\ *n* : any of a family of lobe-toed diving birds related to the loons
Gre•cian \ˈgrē-shən\ *adj* : GREEK
greed \ˈgrēd\ *n* : acquisitive or selfish desire beyond reason — **greed•i•ly** \ˈgrē-də-lē\ *adv* — **greed•i•ness** \-dē-nəs\ *n* — **greedy** \ˈgrē-dē\ *adj*
[1]**Greek** \ˈgrēk\ *n* **1** : a native or inhabitant of Greece **2** : the ancient or modern language of Greece
[2]**Greek** *adj* **1** : of, relating to, or characteristic of Greece, the Greeks, or Greek **2** : ORTHODOX 3
[1]**green** \ˈgrēn\ *adj* **1** : of the color green **2** : covered with verdure; *also* : consisting of green plants or of the leafy parts of plants ⟨a ~ salad⟩ **3** : UNRIPE; *also* : IMMATURE **4** : having a sickly appearance **5** : not fully processed or treated ⟨~ liquor⟩ ⟨~ hides⟩ **6** : INEXPERIENCED; *also* : NAIVE **7** : concerned with or supporting environmentalism — **green•ish** *adj* — **green•ness** *n*
[2]**green** *vb* : to make or become green
[3]**green** *n* **1** : a color between blue and yellow in the

spectrum : the color of growing fresh grass or of the emerald **2** : something of a green color **3** : green vegetation; *esp, pl* : leafy herbs or leafy parts of a vegetable ⟨collard ~*s*⟩ ⟨beet ~*s*⟩ **4** : a grassy plot; *esp* : a smooth grassy area around the hole into which the ball must be played in golf

green•back \ˈgrēn-ˌbak\ *n* : a U.S. legal-tender note

green bean *n* : a kidney bean that is used as a snap bean when the pods are colored green

green•belt \ˈgrēn-ˌbelt\ *n* : a belt of parks or farmlands around a community

green•ery \ˈgrē-nə-rē\ *n, pl* **-er•ies** : green foliage or plants

green–eyed \ˈgrē-ˈnīd\ *adj* : JEALOUS

green•gro•cer \ˈgrēn-ˌgrō-sər\ *n* : a retailer of fresh vegetables and fruit

green•horn \-ˌhȯrn\ *n* : an inexperienced person; *also* : NEWCOMER

green•house \-ˌhau̇s\ *n* : a glass structure for the growing of tender plants

greenhouse effect *n* : warming of a planet's atmosphere that occurs when the sun's radiation passes through the atmosphere, is absorbed by the planet, and is reradiated as radiation of longer wavelength that can be absorbed by atmospheric gases

green manure *n* : an herbaceous crop (as clover) plowed under when green to enrich the soil

green onion *n* : a young onion pulled before the bulb has enlarged and used esp. in salads; *also* : SCALLION

green pepper *n* : a sweet pepper before it turns red at maturity

green•room \ˈgrēn-ˌrüm, -ˌru̇m\ *n* : a room in a theater or concert hall where actors or musicians relax before, between, or after appearances

green•sward \-ˌswȯrd\ *n* : turf that is green with growing grass

green thumb *n* : an unusual ability to make plants grow

Green•wich mean time \ˈgri-nij-, ˈgre-, -nich-\ *n* [*Greenwich,* England] : the time of the meridian of Greenwich used as the basis of worldwide standard time

Greenwich time *n* : GREENWICH MEAN TIME

green•wood \ˈgrēn-ˌwu̇d\ *n* : a forest green with foliage

greet \ˈgrēt\ *vb* **1** : to address with expressions of kind wishes **2** : to meet or react to in a specified manner **3** : to be perceived by — **greet•er** *n*

greet•ing *n* **1** : a salutation on meeting **2** *pl* : best wishes : REGARDS

greeting card *n* : a card that bears a message usu. sent on a special occasion

gre•gar•i•ous \gri-ˈgar-ē-əs\ *adj* [L *gregarius* of a flock or herd, fr. *greg-, grex* flock, herd] **1** : SOCIAL, COMPANIONABLE **2** : tending to flock together — **gre•gar•i•ous•ly** *adv* — **gre•gar•i•ous•ness** *n*

grem•lin \ˈgrem-lən\ *n* : a cause of error or equipment malfunction conceived of as a small gnome

gre•nade \grə-ˈnād\ *n* [MF, pomegranate, fr. LL *granata,* fr. L, fem. of *granatus* seedy, fr. *granum* grain] : a small bomb that is thrown by hand or launched (as by a rifle)

gren•a•dier \ˌgre-nə-ˈdir\ *n* : a member of a European regiment formerly armed with grenades

gren•a•dine \ˌgre-nə-ˈdēn, ˈgre-nə-ˌdēn\ *n* : a syrup flavored with pomegranates and used in mixed drinks

grew *past of* GROW

grey *var of* GRAY

grey•hound \ˈgrā-ˌhau̇nd\ *n* : any of a breed of tall slender dogs noted for speed and keen sight

grid \ˈgrid\ *n* **1** : GRATING **2** : a network of conductors for distributing electric power **3** : a network of horizontal and perpendicular lines (as for locating points on a map) **4** : GRIDIRON 2; *also* : FOOTBALL

grid•dle \ˈgrid-ᵊl\ *n* : a flat usu. metal surface for cooking food

greyhound

griddle cake *n* : PANCAKE

grid•iron \ˈgrid-ˌīrn, -ˌī-ərn\ *n* **1** : a grate for broiling food **2** : a football field

grid•lock \-ˌläk\ *n* : a traffic jam in which an intersection is so blocked that vehicles cannot move

grief \ˈgrēf\ *n* **1** : emotional distress caused by or as if by bereavement; *also* : a cause of such distress **2** : MISHAP **3** : DISASTER

griev•ance \ˈgrē-vəns\ *n* **1** : a cause of distress affording reason for complaint or resistance **2** : COMPLAINT

grieve \ˈgrēv\ *vb* **grieved; griev•ing** [ME *greven,* fr. OF *grever,* fr. L *gravare* to burden, fr. *gravis* heavy, grave] **1** : to cause grief or sorrow to : DISTRESS **2** : to feel grief : SORROW

griev•ous \ˈgrē-vəs\ *adj* **1** : causing suffering, grief, or sorrow : SEVERE ⟨a ~ wound⟩ **2** : OPPRESSIVE, ONEROUS **3** : SERIOUS, GRAVE — **griev•ous•ly** *adv*

¹grill \ˈgril\ *vb* **1** : to broil on a grill; *also* : to fry or toast on a griddle **2** : to question intensely

²grill *n* **1** : a cooking utensil of parallel bars on which food is grilled **2** : an informal restaurant

grille *or* **grill** \ˈgril\ *n* : a grating that forms a barrier or screen

grill•work \ˈgril-ˌwərk\ *n* : work constituting or resembling a grille

grim \ˈgrim\ *adj* **grim•mer; grim•mest** **1** : CRUEL, FIERCE **2** : harsh and forbidding in appearance **3** : ghastly or repellent in character **4** : RELENTLESS — **grim•ly** *adv* — **grim•ness** *n*

gri•mace \ˈgri-məs, gri-ˈmās\ *n* : a facial expression usu. of disgust or disapproval — **grimace** *vb*

grime \ˈgrīm\ *n* : soot, smut, or dirt adhering to or embedded in a surface; *also* : accumulated dirtiness and disorder — **grimy** *adj*

grin \ˈgrin\ *vb* **grinned; grin•ning** : to draw back the lips so as to show the teeth esp. in amusement — **grin** *n*

¹grind \ˈgrīnd\ *vb* **ground** \ˈgrau̇nd\; **grind•ing** **1** : to reduce to small particles **2** : to wear down, polish, or sharpen by friction **3** : OPPRESS **4** : to press with a grating noise : GRIT ⟨~ the teeth⟩ **5** : to operate or produce by turning a crank **6** : DRUDGE; *esp* : to study hard **7** : to move with difficulty or friction ⟨gears ~*ing*⟩

²grind *n* **1** : dreary monotonous labor, routine, or study **2** : one who works or studies excessively

grind•er \ˈgrīn-dər\ *n* **1** : MOLAR **2** *pl* : TEETH **3** : one that grinds **4** : SUBMARINE 2

grind•stone \ˈgrīnd-ˌstōn\ *n* : a flat circular stone of natural sandstone that revolves on an axle and is used for grinding, shaping, or smoothing

¹grip \ˈgrip\ *vb* **gripped; grip•ping** **1** : to seize or hold firmly **2** : to hold the interest of strongly

²grip *n* **1** : GRASP; *also* : strength in gripping **2** : a firm tenacious hold **3** : UNDERSTANDING **4** : a device for gripping **5** : TRAVELING BAG

gripe \ˈgrīp\ *vb* **griped; grip•ing** **1** : IRRITATE, VEX **2**

: to cause or experience spasmodic pains in the bowels **3** : COMPLAIN — **gripe** *n*

grippe \ˈgrip\ *n* : INFLUENZA

gris–gris \ˈgrē-ˌgrē\ *n, pl* **gris–gris** \-ˌgrēz\ [F] : an amulet or incantation used chiefly by people of black African ancestry

gris•ly \ˈgriz-lē\ *adj* **gris•li•er; -est** : HORRIBLE, GRUESOME

grist \ˈgrist\ *n* : grain to be ground or already ground

gris•tle \ˈgri-səl\ *n* : CARTILAGE — **gris•tly** \ˈgris-lē\ *adj*

grist•mill \ˈgrist-ˌmil\ *n* : a mill for grinding grain

¹grit \ˈgrit\ *n* **1** : a hard sharp granule (as of sand); *also* : material composed of such granules **2** : unyielding courage — **grit•ty** *adj*

²grit *vb* **grit•ted; grit•ting** : GRIND, GRATE

grits \ˈgrits\ *n pl* : coarsely ground hulled grain ⟨hominy ∼⟩

griz•zled \ˈgri-zəld\ *adj* : streaked or mixed with gray

griz•zly \ˈgriz-lē\ *adj* **griz•zli•er; -est** : GRIZZLED

grizzly bear *n* : a large pale-coated bear of western No. America

gro *abbr* gross

groan \ˈgrōn\ *vb* **1** : MOAN **2** : to make a harsh sound under sudden or prolonged strain ⟨the chair ∼*ed* under his weight⟩ — **groan** *n*

groat \ˈgrōt\ *n* : an old British coin worth four pennies

gro•cer \ˈgrō-sər\ *n* [ME, fr. MF *grossier* wholesaler, fr. *gros* coarse, wholesale, fr. L *grossus* coarse] : a dealer esp. in staple foodstuffs — **gro•cery** \ˈgrōs-rē, ˈgrōsh-, ˈgrō-sə-\ *n*

grog \ˈgräg\ *n* [*Old Grog*, nickname of Edward Vernon †1757 Eng. admiral responsible for diluting the sailors' rum] : alcoholic liquor; *esp* : liquor (as rum) mixed with water

grog•gy \ˈgrä-gē\ *adj* **grog•gi•er; -est** : weak and unsteady on the feet or in action — **grog•gi•ly** \-gə-lē\ *adv* — **grog•gi•ness** \-gē-nəs\ *n*

groin \ˈgrȯin\ *n* **1** : the juncture of the lower abdomen and inner part of the thigh; *also* : the region of this juncture **2** : the curved line or rib on a ceiling along which two vaults meet

grom•met \ˈgrä-mət, ˈgrə-\ *n* **1** : a ring of rope **2** : an eyelet of firm material to strengthen or protect an opening

¹groom \ˈgrüm, ˈgru̇m\ *n* **1** : a person responsible for the care of horses **2** : BRIDEGROOM

²groom *vb* **1** : to clean and care for (an animal) **2** : to make neat or attractive **3** : PREPARE

grooms•man \ˈgrümz-mən, ˈgru̇mz-\ *n* : a male friend who attends a bridegroom at his wedding

groove \ˈgrüv\ *n* **1** : a long narrow channel **2** : a fixed routine — **groove** *vb*

groovy \ˈgrü-vē\ *adj* **groov•i•er; -est 1** : EXCELLENT **2** : HIP

grope \ˈgrōp\ *vb* **groped; grop•ing 1** : to feel about or search for blindly or uncertainly ⟨∼ for the right word⟩ **2** : to feel one's way by groping

gros•beak \ˈgrōs-ˌbēk\ *n* : any of several finches of Europe or America with large stout conical bills

gro•schen \ˈgrō-shən\ *n, pl* **groschen** — see *schilling* at MONEY table

gros•grain \ˈgrō-ˌgrān\ *n* [F *gros grain* coarse texture] : a silk or rayon fabric with crosswise cotton ribs

¹gross \ˈgrōs\ *adj* **1** : glaringly noticeable **2** : OUT-AND-OUT, UTTER **3** : BIG, BULKY; *esp* : excessively fat **4** : GENERAL, BROAD **5** : consisting of an overall total exclusive of deductions ⟨∼ earnings⟩ **6** : CARNAL, EARTHY ⟨∼ pleasures⟩ **7** : UNREFINED; *also* : crudely vulgar **8** : lacking knowledge — **gross•ly** *adv* — **gross•ness** *n*

²gross *n* : an overall total exclusive of deductions — **gross** *vb*

³gross *n, pl* **gross** : a total of 12 dozen things ⟨a ∼ of pencils⟩

gross national product *n* : the total value of the goods and services produced in a nation during a year

gro•szy \ˈgrȯ-shē\ *n, pl* **groszy** — see *zloty* at MONEY table

grot \ˈgrät\ *n* : GROTTO

gro•tesque \grō-ˈtesk\ *adj* **1** : FANCIFUL, BIZARRE **2** : absurdly incongruous **3** : ECCENTRIC — **gro•tesque•ly** *adv*

grot•to \ˈgrä-tō\ *n, pl* **grottoes** *also* **grottos 1** : CAVE **2** : an artificial cavelike structure

grouch \ˈgrau̇ch\ *n* **1** : a fit of bad temper **2** : an habitually irritable or complaining person — **grouch** *vb* — **grouchy** *adj*

¹ground \ˈgrau̇nd\ *n* **1** : the bottom of a body of water **2** *pl* : sediment at the bottom of a liquid **3** : a basis for belief, action, or argument **4** : BACKGROUND **5** : the surface of the earth; *also* : SOIL **6** : an area with a particular use ⟨fishing ∼*s*⟩ **7** *pl* : the area about and belonging to a building **8** : a conductor that makes electrical connection with the earth — **ground•less** *adj*

²ground *vb* **1** : to bring to or place on the ground **2** : to run or cause to run aground **3** : to provide a reason or justification for **4** : to furnish with a foundation of knowledge **5** : to connect electrically with a ground **6** : to restrict to the ground; *also* : prohibit from some activity

³ground *past and past part of* GRIND

ground ball *n* : a batted baseball that rolls or bounces along the ground

ground cover *n* : low plants that grow over and cover the soil; *also* : a plant suitable for use as ground cover

ground•er \ˈgrau̇n-dər\ *n* : GROUND BALL

ground•hog \ˈgrau̇nd-ˌhȯg, -ˌhäg\ *n* : WOODCHUCK

ground•ling \ˈgrau̇nd-liŋ\ *n* : a spectator in the pit of an Elizabethan theater

ground rule *n* **1** : a sports rule adopted to modify play on a particular field, court, or course **2** : a rule of procedure

ground squirrel *n* : any of various burrowing rodents of No. America and Eurasia that are related to the squirrels and live in colonies in open areas

ground swell *n* **1** : a broad deep ocean swell caused by an often distant gale or earthquake **2** *usu* **ground-swell** : a rapid spontaneous growth (as of political opinion)

ground•wa•ter \ˈgrau̇nd-ˌwȯ-tər, -ˌwä-\ *n* : water within the earth that supplies wells and springs

ground•work \-ˌwərk\ *n* : FOUNDATION, BASIS

ground zero *n* : the point above, below, or at which a nuclear explosion occurs

¹group \ˈgrüp\ *n* **1** : a number of individuals related by a common factor (as physical association, community of interests, or blood) **2** : a combination of atoms commonly found together in a molecule ⟨a methyl ∼⟩

²group *vb* : to associate in groups : CLUSTER, AGGREGATE

grou•per \ˈgrü-pər\ *n, pl* **groupers** *also* **grouper** : any of numerous large solitary bottom fishes of warm seas

group•ie \ˈgrü-pē\ *n* : a fan of a rock group who usu. follows the group around on concert tours; *also* : ENTHUSIAST, FAN

group therapy *n* : therapy in the presence of a therapist in which several patients discuss their personal problems

¹grouse \ˈgrau̇s\ *n, pl* **grouse** *or* **grouses** : any of numerous ground-dwelling game birds that have feathered legs and are usu. of reddish brown or other protective color

²grouse *vb* **groused; grous•ing** : COMPLAIN, GRUMBLE

grout \ˈgrau̇t\ *n* : material (as mortar) used for filling spaces — **grout** *vb*

grove \ˈgrōv\ *n* : a small wood usu. without underbrush

grov•el \ˈgrä-vəl, ˈgrə-\ *vb* **-eled** *or* **-elled; -el•ing** *or* **-el•ling 1** : to creep or lie with the body prostrate in fear or humility **2** : to abase oneself

grow \ˈgrō\ *vb* **grew** \ˈgrü\; **grown** \ˈgrōn\; **grow·ing 1** : to spring up and develop to maturity **2** : to be able to grow : THRIVE **3** : to take on some relation through or as if through growth ⟨tree limbs *grown* together⟩ **4** : INCREASE, EXPAND **5** : to develop from a parent source **6** : BECOME **7** : to have an increasing influence **8** : to cause to grow — **grow·er** *n*

growl \ˈgrau̇l\ *vb* **1** : RUMBLE **2** : to utter a deep throaty sound **3** : GRUMBLE — **growl** *n*

grown–up \ˈgrō-ˌnəp\ *adj* : not childish : ADULT — **grown–up** *n*

growth \ˈgrōth\ *n* **1** : stage or condition attained in growing **2** : a process of growing esp. through progressive development or increase **3** : a result or product of growing ⟨a fine ~ of hair⟩; *also* : an abnormal mass of tissue (as a tumor)

[1]**grub** \ˈgrəb\ *vb* **grubbed; grub·bing 1** : to clear or root out by digging **2** : to dig in the ground usu. for a hidden object **3** : to search about

[2]**grub** *n* **1** : a soft thick wormlike insect larva ⟨beetle ~*s*⟩ **2** : DRUDGE; *also* : a slovenly person **3** : FOOD

grub·by \ˈgrə-bē\ *adj* **grub·bi·er; -est** : DIRTY, SLOVENLY — **grub·bi·ness** \-bē-nəs\ *n*

grub·stake \ˈgrəb-ˌstāk\ *n* : supplies or funds furnished a mining prospector in return for a share in his finds

[1]**grudge** \ˈgrəj\ *vb* **grudged; grudg·ing** : to be reluctant to give : BEGRUDGE

[2]**grudge** *n* : a feeling of deep-seated resentment or ill will

gru·el \ˈgrü-əl\ *n* : a thin porridge

gru·el·ing *or* **gru·el·ling** \ˈgrü-liŋ, ˈgrü-ə-\ *adj* : requiring extreme effort : EXHAUSTING

grue·some \ˈgrü-səm\ *adj* [fr. earlier *growsome,* fr. E dial. *grow, grue* to shiver] : inspiring horror or repulsion

gruff \ˈgrəf\ *adj* **1** : rough in speech or manner **2** : being deep and harsh : HOARSE — **gruff·ly** *adv*

grum·ble \ˈgrəm-bəl\ *vb* **grum·bled; grum·bling 1** : to mutter in discontent **2** : GROWL, RUMBLE — **grum·bler** *n*

grumpy \ˈgrəm-pē\ *adj* **grump·i·er; -est** : moodily cross : SURLY — **grump·i·ly** \-pə-lē\ *adv* — **grump·i·ness** \-pē-nəs\ *n*

grunge \ˈgrənj\ *n* **1**: one that is grungy **2** : heavy metal rock music expressing alienation and discontent **3** : untidy or tattered clothing typically worn by grunge fans

grun·gy \ˈgrən-jē\ *adj* **grun·gi·er; -est** : shabby or dirty in character or condition

grun·ion \ˈgrən-yən\ *n* : a fish of the California coast which comes inshore to spawn at nearly full moon

grunt \ˈgrənt\ *n* : a deep throaty sound (as that of a hog) — **grunt** *vb*

GSA *abbr* **1** General Services Administration **2** Girl Scouts of America

G suit *n* [gravity *suit*] : a suit for a pilot or astronaut designed to counteract the physiological effects of acceleration

GSUSA *abbr* Girl Scouts of the United States of America

gt *abbr* great

Gt Brit *abbr* Great Britain

gtd *abbr* guaranteed

GU *abbr* Guam

gua·ca·mo·le \ˌgwä-kə-ˈmō-lē\ *n* [MexSp] : mashed and seasoned avocado

gua·nine \ˈgwä-ˌnēn\ *n* : a purine base that codes genetic information in the molecular chain of DNA and RNA

gua·no \ˈgwä-nō\ *n* [Sp, fr. Quechua (a South American Indian language) *wanu* fertilizer, dung] : a substance composed chiefly of the excrement of seabirds and used as a fertilizer

gua·ra·ni \ˌgwär-ə-ˈnē\ *n, pl* **guaranies** *also* **guaranis** — see MONEY table

[1]**guar·an·tee** \ˌgar-ən-ˈtē\ *n* **1** : GUARANTOR **2** : GUARANTY 1 **3** : an agreement by which one person undertakes to secure another in the possession or enjoyment of something **4** : an assurance of the quality of or of the length of use to be expected from a product offered for sale **5** : GUARANTY 4

[2]**guarantee** *vb* **-teed; -tee·ing 1** : to undertake to answer for the debt, failure to perform, or faulty performance of (another) **2** : to undertake an obligation to establish, perform, or continue **3** : to give security to

guar·an·tor \ˌgar-ən-ˈtȯr\ *n* : one who gives a guarantee

[1]**guar·an·ty** \ˈgar-ən-tē\ *n, pl* **-ties 1** : an undertaking to answer for another's failure to pay a debt or perform a duty **2** : GUARANTEE 3 **3** : GUARANTOR **4** : PLEDGE, SECURITY

[2]**guaranty** *vb* **-tied; -ty·ing** : GUARANTEE

[1]**guard** \ˈgärd\ *n* **1** : a person or a body of persons on sentinel duty **2** *pl* : troops assigned to protect a sovereign **3** : a defensive position (as in boxing) **4** : the act or duty of protecting or defending **5** : PROTECTION **6** : a protective or safety device **7** : a football lineman playing between center and tackle; *also* : a basketball player stationed toward the rear — **on guard** : WATCHFUL, ALERT

[2]**guard** *vb* **1** : PROTECT, DEFEND **2** : to watch over **3** : to be on guard

guard·house \ˈgärd-ˌhau̇s\ *n* **1** : a building occupied by a guard or used as a headquarters by soldiers on guard duty **2** : a military jail

guard·ian \ˈgär-dē-ən\ *n* **1** : CUSTODIAN **2** : one who has the care of the person or property of another — **guard·ian·ship** *n*

guard·room \ˈgärd-ˌrüm\ *n* **1** : a room used by a military guard while on duty **2** : a room where military prisoners are confined

guards·man \ˈgärdz-mən\ *n* : a member of a military body called *guard* or *guards*

Gua·te·ma·lan \ˌgwä-tə-ˈmä-lən\ *n* : a native or inhabitant of Guatemala — **Guatemalan** *adj*

gua·va \ˈgwä-və\ *n* : the sweet yellow or pink acid fruit of a shrubby tropical American tree used esp. for making jam and jelly; *also* : the tree

gu·ber·na·to·ri·al \ˌgü-bər-nə-ˈtōr-ē-əl\ *adj* : of or relating to a governor

guer·don \ˈgərd-ᵊn\ *n* : REWARD, RECOMPENSE

Guern·sey \ˈgərn-zē\ *n, pl* **Guernseys** : any of a breed of fawn and white dairy cattle that produce rich yellowish milk

guer·ril·la *or* **gue·ril·la** \gə-ˈri-lə\ *n* [Sp *guerrilla,* fr. dim. of *guerra* war, of Gmc origin] : one who engages in irregular warfare esp. as a member of an independent unit

guess \ˈges\ *vb* **1** : to form an opinion from little or no evidence **2** : BELIEVE, SUPPOSE **3** : to conjecture correctly about : DISCOVER — **guess** *n*

guest \ˈgest\ *n* **1** : a person to whom hospitality (as of a house or a club) is extended **2** : a patron of a commercial establishment (as a hotel) **3** : a person not a regular member of a cast who appears on a program

guf·faw \(ˌ)gə-ˈfȯ\ *n* : a loud burst of laughter — **guffaw** *vb*

guid·ance \ˈgīd-ᵊns\ *n* **1** : the act or process of guiding **2** : ADVICE, DIRECTION

[1]**guide** \ˈgīd\ *n* **1** : one who leads or directs another's course **2** : one who shows and explains points of interest **3** : something that provides guiding information; *also* : SIGNPOST **4** : a device to direct the motion of something

[2]**guide** *vb* **guid·ed; guid·ing 1** : to act as a guide to **2** : MANAGE, DIRECT **3** : to superintend the training of — **guid·able** \ˈgī-də-bəl\ *adj*

guide·book \ˈgīd-ˌbu̇k\ *n* : a book of information for travelers

guided missile *n* : a missile whose course may be altered during flight

guide dog *n* : a dog trained to lead the blind
guide•line \ˈgīd-ˌlīn\ *n* : an indication or outline of policy or conduct
guide word *n* : a term at the head of a page of an alphabetical reference work that indicates the alphabetically first or last word on that page
gui•don \ˈgī-ˌdän, ˈgīd-ᵊn\ *n* : a small flag (as of a military unit)
guild \ˈgild\ *n* : an association of people with common aims and interests; *esp* : a medieval association of merchants or craftsmen — **guild•hall** \-ˌhȯl\ *n*
guil•der \ˈgil-dər\ *n* : GULDEN
guile \ˈgīl\ *n* : deceitful cunning : DUPLICITY — **guile•ful** *adj* — **guile•less•ness** *n*
guil•lo•tine \ˈgi-lə-ˌtēn, ˌgē-ə-ˈtēn\ *n* [F, fr. Joseph *Guillotin* †1814 Fr. physician] : a machine for beheading persons — **guillotine** *vb*
guilt \ˈgilt\ *n* **1** : the fact of having committed an offense esp. against the law **2** : BLAMEWORTHINESS **3** : a feeling of responsibility for wrongdoing — **guilt•less** *adj*
guilty \ˈgil-tē\ *adj* **guilt•i•er; -est 1** : having committed a breach of conduct or a crime **2** : suggesting or involving guilt **3** : aware of or suffering from guilt — **guilt•i•ly** \-tə-lē\ *adv* — **guilt•i•ness** \-tē-nəs\ *n*
guin•ea \ˈgi-nē\ *n* **1** : a British gold coin no longer issued worth 21 shillings **2** : a unit of value equal to 21 shillings
guinea fowl *n* : a gray and white spotted West African bird related to the pheasants and widely raised for food; *also* : any of several related birds
guinea hen *n* : a female guinea fowl; *also* : GUINEA FOWL
Guin•ean \ˈgi-nē-ən\ *n* : a native or inhabitant of Guinea — **Guinean** *adj*
guinea pig *n* **1** : a small stocky short-eared and nearly tailless So. American rodent often kept as a pet or used in lab research **2** : a subject of research or testing
guise \ˈgīz\ *n* **1** : a form or style of dress : COSTUME **2** : external appearance : SEMBLANCE
gui•tar \gi-ˈtär\ *n* : a musical instrument with usu. six strings plucked with a pick or with the fingers
gulch \ˈgəlch\ *n* : RAVINE
gul•den \ˈgül-dən, ˈgu̇l-\ *n, pl* **guldens** *or* **gulden** — see MONEY table
gulf \ˈgəlf\ *n* [ME *goulf,* fr. MF *golfe,* fr. It *golfo,* fr. LL *colpus,* fr. Gk *kolpos* bosom, gulf] **1** : a part of an ocean or sea partly or mostly surrounded by land **2** : ABYSS, CHASM **3** : a wide separation
¹gull \ˈgəl\ *n* : any of numerous mostly white or gray long-winged web-footed seabirds
²gull *vb* : to make a dupe of : DECEIVE — **gull•ible** \ˈgə-lə-bəl\ *adj*
³gull *n* : DUPE
gul•let \ˈgə-lət\ *n* : ESOPHAGUS; *also* : THROAT
gul•ly \ˈgə-lē\ *n, pl* **gullies** : a trench worn in the earth by and often filled with running water after rains
gulp \ˈgəlp\ *vb* **1** : to swallow hurriedly or greedily **2** : SUPPRESS ⟨~ down a sob⟩ **3** : to catch the breath as if in taking a long drink — **gulp** *n*
¹gum \ˈgəm\ *n* : the oral tissue that surrounds the necks of the teeth
²gum *n* **1** : a sticky plant exudate; *esp* : one that hardens on drying **2** : a sticky substance **3** : a preparation usu. of a plant gum sweetened and flavored and used for chewing — **gum•my** *adj*
gum arabic *n* : a water-soluble gum obtained from several acacias and used esp. in making inks, adhesives, confections, and pharmaceuticals
gum•bo \ˈgəm-bō\ *n* [AmerF *gombo,* of Bantu origin] : a rich thick soup usu. thickened with okra
gum•drop \ˈgəm-ˌdräp\ *n* : a candy made usu. from corn syrup with gelatin and coated with sugar crystals
gump•tion \ˈgəmp-shən\ *n* **1** : shrewd common sense **2** : ENTERPRISE, INITIATIVE
gum•shoe \ˈgəm-ˌshü\ *n* : DETECTIVE — **gumshoe** *vb*
¹gun \ˈgən\ *n* **1** : CANNON **2** : a portable firearm **3** : a discharge of a gun **4** : something suggesting a gun in shape or function **5** : THROTTLE — **gunned** \ˈgənd\ *adj*
²gun *vb* **gunned; gun•ning 1** : to hunt with a gun **2** : SHOOT **3** : to open up the throttle of so as to increase speed
gun•boat \ˈgən-ˌbōt\ *n* : a small lightly armed ship for use in shallow waters
gun•fight \-ˌfīt\ *n* : a duel with guns — **gun•fight•er** *n*
gun•fire \-ˌfīr\ *n* : the firing of guns
gung ho \ˈgəŋ-ˈhō\ *adj* [*Gung ho!,* motto (taken to mean "work together") adopted by certain U.S. marines in World War II, fr. Chin *gōnghé,* short for *Zhōngguó Gōngyè Hézuò Shè* Chinese Industrial Cooperatives Society] : extremely zealous or enthusiastic
gun•man \-mən\ *n* : a man armed with a gun; *esp* : a professional killer
gun•ner \ˈgə-nər\ *n* **1** : a soldier or airman who operates or aims a gun **2** : one who hunts with a gun
gun•nery \ˈgə-nə-rē\ *n* : the use of guns; *esp* : the science of the flight of projectiles and effective use of guns
gunnery sergeant *n* : a noncommissioned officer in the marine corps ranking next below a first sergeant
gun•ny•sack \ˈgə-nē-ˌsak\ *n* : a sack made of a coarse heavy fabric (as burlap)
gun•point \ˈgən-ˌpȯint\ *n* : the muzzle of a gun — **at gunpoint** : under a threat of death by being shot
gun•pow•der \-ˌpau̇-dər\ *n* : an explosive powder used in guns and blasting
gun•shot \-ˌshät\ *n* **1** : shot fired from a gun **2** : the range of a gun ⟨within ~⟩
gun–shy \-ˌshī\ *adj* **1** : afraid of a loud noise **2** : markedly distrustful
gun•sling•er \-ˌsliŋ-ər\ *n* : a skilled gunman esp. in the old West
gun•smith \-ˌsmith\ *n* : one who designs, makes, or repairs firearms
gun•wale *also* **gun•nel** \ˈgən-ᵊl\ *n* : the upper edge of a ship's or boat's side
gup•py \ˈgə-pē\ *n, pl* **guppies** [R.J.L. *Guppy* †1916 Trinidadian naturalist] : a small brightly colored tropical fish
gur•gle \ˈgər-gəl\ *vb* **gur•gled; gur•gling** : to make a sound like that of an irregularly flowing or gently splashing liquid — **gurgle** *n*
Gur•kha \ˈgu̇r-kə, ˈgər-\ *n* : a soldier from Nepal in the British or Indian army
gur•ney \ˈgər-nē\ *n, pl* **gurneys** : a wheeled cot or stretcher
gu•ru \ˈgu̇r-ü\ *n, pl* **gurus** [Hindi *gurū,* fr. Sanskrit *guru,* fr. *guru,* adj., heavy, venerable] **1** : a personal religious and spiritual teacher in Hinduism **2** : a teacher in matters of fundamental concern **3** : EXPERT ⟨a fitness ~⟩
gush \ˈgəsh\ *vb* **1** : to issue or pour forth copiously or violently : SPOUT **2** : to make an effusive display of affection or enthusiasm
gush•er \ˈgə-shər\ *n* : one that gushes; *esp* : an oil well with a large natural flow
gushy \ˈgə-shē\ *adj* **gush•i•er; -est** : marked by effusive sentimentality
gus•set \ˈgə-sət\ *n* : a triangular insert (as in a seam of a sleeve) to give width or strength — **gusset** *vb*
gus•sy up \ˈgə-sē-\ *vb* : to dress up
¹gust \ˈgəst\ *n* **1** : a sudden brief rush of wind **2** : a sudden outburst : SURGE — **gusty** *adj*
²gust *vb* : to blow in gusts
gus•ta•to•ry \ˈgəs-tə-ˌtōr-ē\ *adj* : relating to or associated with the sense of taste

gus•to \ˈgəs-tō\ *n, pl* **gustoes** : enthusiastic enjoyment; *also* : VITALITY 4

[1]**gut** \ˈgət\ *n* **1** *pl* : BOWELS, ENTRAILS **2** : the alimentary canal or a part of it (as the intestine); *also* : BELLY, ABDOMEN **3** *pl* : the inner essential parts **4** *pl* : COURAGE, PLUCK

[2]**gut** *vb* **gut•ted; gut•ting 1** : EVISCERATE **2** : to destroy the inside of

gutsy \ˈgət-sē\ *adj* **guts•i•er; -est** : marked by courage and determination

gut•ter \ˈgə-tər\ *n* : a groove or channel for carrying off esp. rainwater

gut•ter•snipe \-ˌsnīp\ *n* : a street urchin

gut•tur•al \ˈgə-tə-rəl\ *adj* **1** : sounded in the throat **2** : being or marked by an utterance that is strange, unpleasant, or disagreeable — **guttural** *n*

gut•ty \ˈgə-tē\ *adj* **gut•ti•er; -est 1** : GUTSY **2** : having a vigorous challenging quality

gut–wrench•ing \ˈgət-ˌren-chiŋ\ *adj* : causing emotional anguish

[1]**guy** \ˈgī\ *n* : a rope, chain, or rod attached to something as a brace or guide

[2]**guy** *vb* : to steady or reinforce with a guy

[3]**guy** *n* : MAN, FELLOW; *also, pl* : PERSONS ⟨all the ~s came⟩

[4]**guy** *vb* : to make fun of : RIDICULE

Guy•a•nese \ˌgī-ə-ˈnēz\ *n, pl* **Guyanese** : a native or inhabitant of Guyana — **Guyanese** *adj*

guz•zle \ˈgə-zəl\ *vb* **guz•zled; guz•zling** : to drink greedily

gym \ˈjim\ *n* : GYMNASIUM

gym•kha•na \jim-ˈkä-nə\ *n* : a meet featuring sports contests; *esp* : a contest of automobile-driving skill

gym•na•si•um *for 1* jim-ˈnā-zē-əm, -zhəm, *for 2* gim-ˈnä-zē-əm\ *n, pl* **-na•si•ums** *or* **-na•sia** \-ˈnā-zē-ə, -ˈnä-zhə; -ˈnä-zē-ə\ [L, exercise ground, school, fr. Gk *gymnasion,* fr. *gymnazein* to exercise naked, fr. *gymnos* naked] **1** : a room or building for indoor sports **2** : a European secondary school that prepares students for the university

gym•nas•tics \jim-ˈnas-tiks\ *n* : a competitive sport developed from physical exercises designed to demonstrate strength, balance, and body control — **gym•nast** \ˈjim-ˌnast\ *n* — **gym•nas•tic** *adj*

gym•no•sperm \ˈjim-nə-ˌspərm\ *n* : any of a class or subdivision of woody vascular seed plants (as conifers) that produce naked seeds not enclosed in an ovary

gyn *or* **gynecol** *abbr* gynecology

gy•nae•col•o•gy *chiefly Brit var of* GYNECOLOGY

gy•ne•col•o•gy \ˌgī-nə-ˈkä-lə-jē\ *n* : a branch of medicine dealing with the diseases and hygiene of women — **gy•ne•co•log•ic** \-ni-kə-ˈlä-jik\ *or* **gy•ne•co•log•i•cal** \-ji-kəl\ *adj* — **gy•ne•col•o•gist** \-nə-ˈkä-lə-jist\ *n*

gyp \ˈjip\ *n* **1** : CHEAT, SWINDLER **2** : FRAUD, SWINDLE — **gyp** *vb*

gyp•sum \ˈjip-səm\ *n* : a calcium-containing mineral used in making plaster of paris

Gyp•sy \ˈjip-sē\ *n, pl* **Gypsies** [by shortening & alter. fr. *Egyptian*] : a member of a traditionally traveling people coming orig. from India and living chiefly in Europe, Asia, and No. America; *also* : the language of the Gypsies

gypsy moth *n* : an Old World moth that was introduced into the U.S. where its caterpillar is a destructive defoliator of many trees

gy•rate \ˈjī-ˌrāt\ *vb* **gy•rat•ed; gy•rat•ing 1** : to revolve around a point or axis **2** : to oscillate with or as if with a circular or spiral motion — **gy•ra•tion** \jī-ˈrā-shən\ *n*

gyr•fal•con \ˈjər-ˌfal-kən, -ˌfȯl-\ *n* : an arctic falcon with several color forms that is the largest of all falcons

gy•ro \ˈjī-rō\ *n, pl* **gyros** : GYROSCOPE

gy•ro•scope \ˈjī-rō-ˌskōp\ *n* : a wheel or disk mounted to spin rapidly about an axis that is free to turn in various directions

Gy Sgt *abbr* gunnery sergeant

gyve \ˈjīv, ˈgīv\ *n* : FETTER — **gyve** *vb*

H

[1]**h** \ˈāch\ *n, pl* **h's** *or* **hs** \ˈā-chəz\ *often cap* : the 8th letter of the English alphabet

[2]**h** *abbr, often cap* **1** hard; hardness **2** heroin **3** hit **4** husband

H *symbol* hydrogen

[1]**ha** \ˈhä\ *interj* — used esp. to express surprise or joy

[2]**ha** *abbr* hectare

Hab *abbr* Habacuc; Habakkuk

Ha•ba•cuc \ˈha-bə-ˌkək, hə-ˈba-kək\ *n* : HABAKKUK

Ha•bak•kuk \ˈha-bə-ˌkək, hə-ˈba-kək\ *n* — see BIBLE table

ha•ba•ne•ra \ˌhä-bə-ˈner-ə\ *n* [Sp *(danza) habanera,* lit., dance of Havana] : a Cuban dance in slow time; *also* : the music for this dance

ha•be•as cor•pus \ˈhā-bē-əs-ˈkȯr-pəs\ *n* [ME, fr. ML, lit., you should have the body (the opening words of the writ)] : a writ issued to bring a party before a court

hab•er•dash•er \ˈha-bər-ˌda-shər\ *n* : a dealer in men's clothing and accessories

hab•er•dash•ery \-ˌda-shə-rē\ *n, pl* **-er•ies 1** : goods sold by a haberdasher **2** : a haberdasher's shop

ha•bil•i•ment \hə-ˈbi-lə-mənt\ *n* **1** *pl* : TRAPPINGS, EQUIPMENT **2** : DRESS; *esp* : the dress characteristic of an occupation or occasion — usu. used in pl.

hab•it \ˈha-bət\ *n* **1** : DRESS, GARB **2** : BEARING, CONDUCT **3** : PHYSIQUE **4** : mental makeup **5** : a usual manner of behavior : CUSTOM **6** : a behavior pattern acquired by frequent repetition **7** : ADDICTION **8** : mode of growth or occurrence ⟨trees with a spreading ~⟩

hab•it•able \ˈha-bə-tə-bəl\ *adj* : capable of being lived in — **hab•it•abil•i•ty** \ˌha-bə-tə-ˈbi-lə-tē\ *n*

hab•i•tat \ˈha-bə-ˌtat\ *n* [L, it inhabits] : the place or environment where a plant or animal naturally occurs

hab•i•ta•tion \ˌha-bə-ˈtā-shən\ *n* **1** : OCCUPANCY **2** : a dwelling place : RESIDENCE **3** : SETTLEMENT

hab•it–form•ing \ˈha-bət-ˌfȯr-miŋ\ *adj* : causing addiction : ADDICTIVE

ha•bit•u•al \hə-ˈbi-chə-wəl\ *adj* **1** : CUSTOMARY **2** : doing, practicing, or acting by force of habit **3** : inherent in an individual — **ha•bit•u•al•ly** *adv* — **ha•bit•u•al•ness** *n*

ha•bit•u•ate \hə-ˈbi-chə-ˌwāt\ *vb* **-at•ed; -at•ing 1** : ACCUSTOM **2** : to cause or undergo habituation

ha•bit•u•a•tion \hə-ˌbi-chə-ˈwā-shən\ *n* **1** : the process of making habitual **2** : psychological dependence on a drug after a period of use

ha•bi•tué *also* **ha•bi•tue** \hə-ˈbi-chə-ˌwā\ *n* [F] : one who may be regularly found in or at (as a place of entertainment)

ha•ci•en•da \ˌhä-sē-ˈen-də\ *n* **1** : a large estate in a Spanish-speaking country **2** : the main building of a farm or ranch

[1]**hack** \ˈhak\ *vb* **1** : to cut or sever with repeated irregular blows **2** : to cough in a short dry manner **3** : to manage successfully; *also* : TOLERATE

[2]**hack** *n* **1** : an implement for hacking **2** : a short dry cough **3** : a hacking blow

[3]**hack** *n* **1** : a horse hired or used for varied work **2** : a horse worn out in service **3** : a light easy often 3-gaited saddle horse **4** : HACKNEY, TAXICAB **5** : a per-

son who works solely for mercenary reasons; *esp* : a writer working solely for commercial success — **hack** *adj*

[4]**hack** *vb* : to operate a taxicab

hack•er \ˈha-kər\ *n* **1** : one that hacks; *also* : a person unskilled at something **2** : an expert at using a computer **3** : a person who illegally gains access to and sometimes tampers with information in a computer system

hack•ie \ˈha-kē\ *n* : a taxicab driver

hack•le \ˈha-kəl\ *n* **1** : one of the long feathers on the neck or back of a bird **2** *pl* : hairs (as on a dog's neck) that can be erected **3** *pl* : TEMPER, DANDER

hack•man \ˈhak-mən\ *n* : HACKIE

[1]**hack•ney** \ˈhak-nē\ *n, pl* **hackneys 1** : a horse for riding or driving **2** : a carriage or automobile kept for hire

[2]**hackney** *vb* : to make trite

hack•neyed \ˈhak-nēd\ *adj* : lacking in freshness or originality

hack•saw \ˈhak-ˌsȯ\ *n* : a fine-tooth saw in a frame for cutting metal

hack•work \-ˌwərk\ *n* : work done on order usu. according to a formula

had *past and past part of* HAVE

had•dock \ˈha-dək\ *n, pl* **haddock** *also* **haddocks** : an Atlantic food fish usu. smaller than the related cod

Ha•des \ˈhā-(ˌ)dēz\ *n* **1** : the abode of the dead in Greek mythology **2** *often not cap* : HELL

haem *chiefly Brit var of* HEME

hae•ma•tite *Brit var of* HEMATITE

haf•ni•um \ˈhaf-nē-əm\ *n* : a gray metallic chemical element — see ELEMENT table

haft \ˈhaft\ *n* : the handle of a weapon or tool

hag \ˈhag\ *n* **1** : an ugly or evil-looking old woman **2** : WITCH 1

Hag *abbr* Haggai

Hag•gai \ˈha-gē-ˌī, ˈha-ˌgī\ *n* — see BIBLE table

hag•gard \ˈha-gərd\ *adj* : having a worn or emaciated appearance **syn** careworn, wasted, drawn — **hag•gard•ly** *adv* — **hag•gard•ness** *n*

hag•gis \ˈha-gəs\ *n* : a traditionally Scottish dish made of the heart, liver, and lungs of a sheep or a calf minced with suet, onions, oatmeal, and seasonings

hag•gle \ˈha-gəl\ *vb* **hag•gled; hag•gling** : to argue in bargaining — **hag•gler** *n*

Ha•gi•og•ra•pha \ˌha-gē-ˈä-grə-fə, ˌhā-jē-\ *n pl* — see BIBLE table

ha•gi•og•ra•phy \ˌha-gē-ˈä-grə-fē, ˌhā-jē-\ *n* **1** : biography of saints or venerated persons **2** : idealizing or idolizing biography — **ha•gi•og•ra•pher** \-fər\ *n*

hai•ku \ˈhī-(ˌ)kü\ *n, pl* **haiku** : an unrhymed Japanese verse form of three lines containing usu. 5, 7, and 5 syllables respectively; *also* : a poem in this form

[1]**hail** \ˈhāl\ *n* **1** : precipitation in the form of small lumps of ice **2** : something that gives the effect of falling hail

[2]**hail** *vb* **1** : to precipitate hail **2** : to pour down and strike like hail

[3]**hail** *interj* [ME, fr. ON *heill*, fr. *heill* healthy] — used to express acclamation

[4]**hail** *vb* **1** : SALUTE, GREET **2** : SUMMON

[5]**hail** *n* **1** : an expression of greeting, approval, or praise **2** : hearing distance

Hail Mary *n* : a salutation and prayer to the Virgin Mary

hail•stone \ˈhāl-ˌstōn\ *n* : a pellet of hail

hail•storm \-ˌstȯrm\ *n* : a storm accompanied by hail

hair \ˈhar\ *n* : a threadlike outgrowth esp. from the skin of a mammal; *also* : a covering or growth of hairs of an animal or a body part — **haired** \ˈhard\ *adj* — **hair•less** *adj*

hair•breadth \ˈhar-ˌbredth\ *or* **hairs•breadth** \ˈharz-\ *n* : a very small distance or margin

hair•brush \-ˌbrəsh\ *n* : a brush for the hair

hair•cloth \-ˌklȯth\ *n* : a stiff wiry fabric used esp. for upholstery

hair•cut \-ˌkət\ *n* : the act, process, or style of cutting and shaping the hair

hair•do \-ˌdü\ *n, pl* **hairdos** : a way of wearing the hair

hair•dress•er \-ˌdre-sər\ *n* : one who dresses or cuts hair — **hair•dress•ing** *n*

hair•line \-ˌlīn\ *n* **1** : a very thin line **2** : the outline of the hair on the head

hair•piece \-ˌpēs\ *n* **1** : supplementary hair (as a switch) used in some women's hairdos **2** : TOUPEE

hair•pin \-ˌpin\ *n* **1** : a U-shaped pin to hold the hair in place **2** : a sharp U-shaped turn in a road — **hairpin** *adj*

hair–rais•ing \ˈhar-ˌrā-ziŋ\ *adj* : causing terror or astonishment

hair•split•ter \-ˌspli-tər\ *n* : a person who makes excessively fine distinctions in reasoning — **hair•split•ting** \-ˌspli-tiŋ\ *adj or n*

hair•style \-ˌstīl\ *n* : HAIRDO — **hair•styl•ing** *n*

hair•styl•ist \-ˌstī-list\ *n* : HAIRDRESSER

hair–trigger *adj* : immediately responsive to the slightest stimulus

hairy \ˈhar-ē\ *adj* **hair•i•er; -est 1** : covered with or as if with hair **2** : tending to cause nervous tension ⟨a few ~ moments⟩ — **hair•i•ness** \-ē-nəs\ *n*

hairy woodpecker *n* : a common No. American woodpecker with a white back that is larger than the similarly marked downy woodpecker

Hai•tian \ˈhā-shən\ *n* : a native or inhabitant of Haiti — **Haitian** *adj*

hajj \ˈhaj\ *n* : the Islamic religious pilgrimage to Mecca

hajji \ˈha-jē\ *n* : one who has made a pilgrimage to Mecca — often used as a title

hake \ˈhāk\ *n* : any of several marine food fishes related to the cod

ha•la•la \hə-ˈlä-lə\ *n, pl* **halala** *or* **halalas** — see *riyal* at MONEY table

hal•berd \ˈhal-bərd, ˈhȯl-\ *also* **hal•bert** \-bərt\ *n* : a weapon esp. of the 15th and 16th centuries consisting of a battle-ax and pike on a long handle

hal•cy•on \ˈhal-sē-ən\ *adj* [Gk *halkyōn*, a mythical bird believed to nest at sea and to calm the waves] : CALM, PEACEFUL

[1]**hale** \ˈhāl\ *adj* : free from defect, disease, or infirmity **syn** healthy, sound, robust, well

[2]**hale** *vb* **haled; hal•ing 1** : HAUL, PULL **2** : to compel to go

ha•ler \ˈhä-lər\ *n, pl* **ha•le•ru** \ˈhä-lə-ˌrü\ — see *koruna* at MONEY table

[1]**half** \ˈhaf, ˈhȧf\ *n, pl* **halves** \ˈhavz, ˈhȧvz\ **1** : either of two equal parts into which something is divisible **2** : one of a pair

[2]**half** *adj* **1** : being one of two equal parts **2** : amounting to nearly half **3** : PARTIAL, INCOMPLETE — **half** *adv*

half–and–half \ˌhaf-ᵊn-ˈhaf, ˌhȧf-ᵊn-ˈhȧf\ *n* : something that is half one thing and half another

half•back \ˈhaf-ˌbak, ˈhȧf-\ *n* **1** : a football back stationed on or near the flank **2** : a player stationed immediately behind the forward line

half–baked \-ˈbākt\ *adj* **1** : not thoroughly baked **2** : poorly planned; *also* : lacking common sense

half–breed \-ˌbrēd\ *n* : one of mixed racial descent — often used disparagingly — **half–breed** *adj*

half brother *n* : a brother related through one parent only

half–caste \ˈhaf-ˌkast, ˈhȧf-\ *n* : HALF-BREED — **half–caste** *adj*

half–dol•lar \-ˈdä-lər\ *n* **1** : a coin representing one half of a dollar **2** : the sum of fifty cents

half•heart•ed \-ˈhär-təd\ *adj* : lacking spirit or interest — **half•heart•ed•ly** *adv* — **half•heart•ed•ness** *n*

half–life \-ˌlīf\ *n* : the time required for half of something (as atoms or a drug) to undergo a process

half–mast \-ˈmast\ *n* : a point about halfway down from the top of a mast or staff

half note *n* : a musical note equal in time to one half of a whole note

half·pen·ny \ˈhāp-nē\ *n, pl* **half·pence** \ˈhā-pəns\ *or* **halfpennies** : a formerly used British coin representing one half of a penny

half–pint \ˈhaf-ˌpīnt, ˈhȧf-\ *adj* : of less than average size — **half–pint** *n*

half sister *n* : a sister related through one parent only

half sole *n* : a shoe sole extending from the shank forward — **half–sole** *vb*

half–staff \ˈhaf-ˈstaf, ˈhȧf-\ *n* : HALF-MAST

half step *n* : a musical interval equivalent to one twelfth of an octave

half·time \ˈhaf-ˌtīm, ˈhȧf-\ *n* : an intermission between halves of a game

half–track \-ˌtrak\ *n* : a motor vehicle propelled by an endless chain-track drive system; *esp* : such a vehicle lightly armored for military use

half–truth \-ˌtrüth\ *n* : a statement that is only partially true; *esp* : one that deliberately mixes truth and falsehood

half·way \-ˈwā\ *adj* **1** : midway between two points **2** : PARTIAL 1 — **halfway** *adv*

half–wit \-ˌwit\ *n* : a foolish or imbecilic person — **half–wit·ted** \-ˈwi-təd\ *adj* — **half–wit·ted·ness** *n*

hal·i·but \ˈha-lə-bət\ *n, pl* **halibut** *also* **halibuts** [ME *halybutte*, fr. *haly, holy* holy + *butte* flatfish; fr. its being eaten on holy days] : a large edible marine flatfish

ha·lite \ˈha-ˌlīt, ˈhā-\ *n* : ROCK SALT

hal·i·to·sis \ˌha-lə-ˈtō-səs\ *n* : the condition of having fetid breath

hall \ˈhȯl\ *n* **1** : the residence of a medieval king or noble; *also* : the house of a landed proprietor **2** : a large public building **3** : a college or university building; *also* : DORMITORY **4** : LOBBY; *also* : CORRIDOR **5** : AUDITORIUM

hal·le·lu·jah \ˌha-lə-ˈlü-yə\ *interj* [Heb *hallĕlūyāh* praise (ye) the Lord] — used to express praise, joy, or thanks

hall·mark \ˈhȯl-ˌmärk\ *n* **1** : a mark put on an article to indicate origin, purity, or genuineness **2** : a distinguishing characteristic

hal·low \ˈha-lō\ *vb* **1** : CONSECRATE **2** : REVERE — **hallowed** \-lōd, -lə-wəd\ *adj*

Hal·low·een *also* **Hal·low·e'en** \ˌha-lə-ˈwēn, ˌhä-\ *n* : the evening of October 31 observed esp. by children in merrymaking and masquerading

hal·lu·ci·nate \hə-ˈlüs-ᵊn-ˌāt\ *vb* **-nat·ed; -nat·ing** : to have hallucinations or experience as a hallucination

hal·lu·ci·na·tion \hə-ˌlüs-ᵊn-ˈā-shən\ *n* : perception of objects with no reality due usu. to use of drugs or to disorder of the nervous system; *also* : something so perceived **syn** delusion, illusion, mirage — **hal·lu·ci·na·to·ry** \-ᵊn-ə-ˌtōr-ē\ *adj*

hal·lu·ci·no·gen \hə-ˈlüs-ᵊn-ə-jən\ *n* : a substance that induces hallucinations — **hal·lu·ci·no·gen·ic** \-ˌlüs-ᵊn-ə-ˈje-nik\ *adj or n*

hall·way \ˈhȯl-ˌwā\ *n* **1** : an entrance hall **2** : CORRIDOR

ha·lo \ˈhā-lo\ *n, pl* **halos** *or* **haloes** [L *halos*, fr. Gk *halōs* threshing floor, disk, halo] **1** : a circle of light appearing to surround a shining body (as the sun) **2** : the aura of glory surrounding an idealized person or thing

hal·o·gen \ˈha-lə-jən\ *n* : any of the five elements fluorine, chlorine, bromine, iodine, and astatine

¹halt \ˈhȯlt\ *adj* : LAME

²halt *n* : STOP

³halt *vb* **1** : to stop marching or traveling **2** : DISCONTINUE, END

¹hal·ter \ˈhȯl-tər\ *n* **1** : a rope or strap for leading or tying an animal; *also* : HEADSTALL **2** : NOOSE **3** : a brief blouse held in place by straps around the neck and across the back

²halter *vb* **hal·tered; hal·ter·ing** **1** : to catch with or as if with a halter; *also* : to put a halter on (as a horse) **2** : HANG **3** : IMPEDE, RESTRAIN

halt·ing \ˈhȯl-tiŋ\ *adj* : UNCERTAIN, FALTERING — **halt·ing·ly** *adv*

halve \ˈhav, ˈhȧv\ *vb* **halved; halv·ing** **1** : to divide into two equal parts **2** : to reduce to one half

halv·ers \ˈha-vərz, ˈhȧ-\ *n pl* : half shares : HALVES

halves *pl of* HALF

hal·yard \ˈhal-yərd\ *n* : a rope or tackle for hoisting and lowering (as sails)

¹ham \ˈham\ *n* **1** : a buttock with its associated thigh — usu. used in pl. **2** : a cut of meat and esp. pork from the thigh **3** : a showy performer **4** : an operator of an amateur radio station — **ham** *adj*

²ham *vb* **hammed; ham·ming** : to overplay a part : OVERACT

ham·burg·er \ˈham-ˌbər-gər\ *or* **ham·burg** \-ˌbərg\ *n* [G *Hamburger* of Hamburg, Germany] **1** : ground beef **2** : a sandwich consisting of a ground-beef patty in a round roll

ham·let \ˈham-lət\ *n* : a small village

¹ham·mer \ˈha-mər\ *n* **1** : a hand tool used for pounding; *also* : something resembling a hammer in form or function **2** : the part of a gun whose striking action causes explosion of the charge **3** : a metal sphere hurled for distance in a track-and-field event **(hammer throw)** **4** : ACCELERATOR 2

²hammer *vb* **1** : to beat, drive, or shape with repeated blows of a hammer : POUND **2** : to produce or bring about as if by repeated blows — usu. used with *out*

ham·mer·head \ˈha-mər-ˌhed\ *n* **1** : the striking part of a hammer **2** : any of a family of medium-sized sharks with eyes at the ends of lateral extensions of the flattened head

hammerhead 2

ham·mer·lock \-ˌläk\ *n* : a wrestling hold in which an opponent's arm is held bent behind the back

ham·mer·toe \-ˌtō\ *n* : a toe deformed by having one or more joints permanently flexed

¹ham·mock \ˈha-mək\ *n* [Sp *hamaca*, of AmerInd origin] : a swinging couch hung by cords at each end

²hammock *n* : a fertile elevated area of the southern U.S. and esp. Florida with hardwood vegetation and soil rich in humus

¹ham·per \ˈham-pər\ *vb* : IMPEDE; *also* : RESTRAIN **syn** trammel, clog, fetter, shackle

²hamper *n* : a large basket

ham·ster \ˈham-stər\ *n* [G, fr. OHG *hamustro*, of Slavic origin] : any of a subfamily of small Old World rodents with large cheek pouches

¹ham·string \ˈham-ˌstriŋ\ *n* : any of several muscles at the back of the thigh or tendons at the back of the knee

²hamstring *vb* **-strung** \-ˌstrəŋ\; **-string·ing** **1** : to cripple by cutting the leg tendons **2** : to make ineffective or powerless

¹hand \ˈhand\ *n* **1** : the end of a front limb when modified (as in humans) for grasping **2** : an indicator or pointer on a dial **3** : personal possession — usu. used in pl.; *also* : CONTROL **4** : SIDE 5 **5** : a pledge esp. of betrothal **6** : HANDWRITING **7** : SKILL, ABILITY; *also* : a significant part **8** : ASSISTANCE; *also* : PARTICIPATION **9** : an outburst of applause **10** : a single round in a card game; *also* : the cards held by a player after a deal **11** : WORKER, EMPLOYEE; *also* : a member of a ship's crew — **hand·less** *adj* — **at hand** : near in time or place — **on hand** : in present possession or readily available

[2]hand *vb* **1** : to lead, guide, or assist with the hand **2** : to give, pass, or transmit with the hand

hand•bag \ˈhand-ˌbag\ *n* : a bag for carrying small personal articles and money

hand•ball \-ˌbȯl\ *n* : a game played by striking a small rubber ball against a wall with the hand

hand•bill \-ˌbil\ *n* : a small printed sheet for distribution by hand

hand•book \-ˌbu̇k\ *n* : a concise reference book : MANUAL

hand•car \-ˌkär\ *n* : a small 4-wheeled railroad car propelled by hand or by a small motor

hand•clasp \-ˌklasp\ *n* : HANDSHAKE

hand•craft \-ˌkraft\ *vb* : to fashion by manual skill

[1]hand•cuff \-ˌkəf\ *n* : a metal fastening that can be locked around a wrist and is usu. connected with another such fastening — usu. used in pl.

[2]handcuff *vb* : MANACLE

hand•ful \ˌhand-ˌfu̇l\ *n, pl* **hand•fuls** \-ˌfu̇lz\ *also* **hands•ful** \ˈhandz-ˌfu̇l\ **1** : as much or as many as the hand will grasp **2** : a small number **3** : as much as one can manage

hand•gun \-ˌgən\ *n* : a firearm held and fired with one hand

[1]hand•i•cap \ˈhan-di-ˌkap\ *n* [obs. E *handicap,* a game in which forfeits were held in a cap, fr. *hand in cap*] **1** : a contest in which an artificial advantage is given or disadvantage imposed on a contestant to equalize chances of winning; *also* : the advantage given or disadvantage imposed **2** : a disadvantage that makes achievement difficult

[2]handicap *vb* **-capped; -cap•ping 1** : to give a handicap to **2** : to put at a disadvantage

hand•i•capped *adj* : having a physical or mental disability that limits activity

hand•i•cap•per \-ˌka-pər\ *n* : a person who predicts the winners in a horse race usu. for a publication

hand•i•craft \ˈhan-di-ˌkraft\ *n* **1** : manual skill **2** : an occupation requiring manual skill **3** : the articles fashioned by those engaged in handicraft — **hand•i•craft•er** \-ˌkraf-tər\ *n* — **hand•i•crafts•man** \-ˌkrafts-mən\ *n*

hand in glove *or* **hand and glove** *adv* : in an extremely close relationship

hand•i•work \ˈhan-di-ˌwərk\ *n* : work done personally or by the hands

hand•ker•chief \ˈhaŋ-kər-chəf, -ˌchēf\ *n, pl* **-chiefs** \-chəfs, -ˌchēfs\ *also* **-chieves** \-ˌchēvz\ : a small piece of cloth used for various personal purposes (as the wiping of the face)

[1]han•dle \ˈhand-ᵊl\ *n* : a part (as of a tool) designed to be grasped by the hand — **han•dled** \-ᵊld\ *adj* — **off the handle** : into a state of sudden and violent anger — usu. used with *fly*

[2]handle *vb* **han•dled; han•dling 1** : to touch, hold, or manage with the hands **2** : to have responsibility for **3** : to deal or trade in **4** : to behave in a certain way when managed or directed ⟨a car that ∼*s* well⟩ — **han•dler** *n*

han•dle•bar \ˈhand-ᵊl-bär\ *n* : a usu. bent bar with a grip at each end (as for steering a bicycle) — usu. used in pl.

hand•made \ˈhand-ˈmād\ *adj* : made by hand or by a hand process

hand•maid•en \-ˌmād-ᵊn\ *also* **hand•maid** \-ˌmād\ *n* : a female attendant

hand–me–down \-me-ˌdau̇n\ *adj* : used by one person after having been used by another — **hand–me–down** *n*

hand•out \ˈhan-ˌdau̇t\ *n* **1** : a portion (as of food) given to a beggar **2** : a piece of printed information for free distribution; *also* : a prepared statement released to the press

hand•pick \ˈhand-ˈpik\ *vb* : to select personally ⟨a ∼*ed* candidate⟩

hand•rail \-ˌrāl\ *n* : a narrow rail for grasping as a support

hand•saw \-ˌsȯ\ *n* : a saw designed to be used with one hand

hands down *adv* **1** : with little effort **2** : without question

hand•sel \ˈhan-səl\ *n* **1** : a gift made as a token of good luck **2** : a first installment : earnest money

hand•set \ˈhand-ˌset\ *n* : a combined telephone transmitter and receiver mounted on a handle

hand•shake \-ˌshāk\ *n* : a clasping usu. of right hands by two people

hands–off \ˈhandz-ˈȯf\ *adj* : characterized by noninterference

hand•some \ˈhan-səm\ *adj* **hand•som•er; -est** [ME *handsom* easy to manipulate] **1** : SIZABLE, AMPLE **2** : GENEROUS, LIBERAL **3** : pleasing and usu. impressive in appearance **syn** beautiful, lovely, pretty, comely, fair — **hand•some•ly** *adv* — **hand•some•ness** *n*

hands–on \ˈhandz-ˈȯn, -ˈän\ *adj* **1** : being or providing direct practical experience in the operation of something **2** : characterized by active personal involvement ⟨∼ management⟩

hand•spring \ˈhand-ˌspriŋ\ *n* : an acrobatic feat in which the body turns in a full circle from a standing position and lands first on the hands and then on the feet

hand•stand \-ˌstand\ *n* : an act of supporting the body on the hands with the trunk and legs balanced in the air

hand–to–hand *adj* : involving physical contact or very close range ⟨∼ fighting⟩ — **hand to hand** *adv*

hand–to–mouth *adj* : having or providing nothing to spare

hand•wo•ven \ˈhand-ˌwō-vən\ *adj* : produced on a hand-operated loom

hand•writ•ing \-ˌrī-tiŋ\ *n* : writing done by hand; *also* : the form of writing peculiar to a person — **hand•writ•ten** \-ˌrit-ᵊn\ *adj*

handy \ˈhan-dē\ *adj* **hand•i•er; -est 1** : conveniently near **2** : easily used **3** : DEXTEROUS — **hand•i•ly** \-də-lē\ *adv* — **hand•i•ness** \-dē-nəs\ *n*

handy•man \-ˌman\ *n* **1** : one who does odd jobs **2** : one competent in a variety of small skills or repair work

[1]hang \ˈhaŋ\ *vb* **hung** \ˈhəŋ\ *also* **hanged; hang•ing 1** : to fasten or remain fastened to an elevated point without support from below; *also* : to fasten or be fastened so as to allow free motion on the point of suspension ⟨∼ a door⟩ **2** : to suspend by the neck until dead; *also* : to die by hanging **3** : DROOP ⟨*hung* his head in shame⟩ **4** : to fasten to a wall ⟨∼ wallpaper⟩ **5** : to prevent (a jury) from coming to a decision **6** : to display (pictures) in a gallery **7** : to remain stationary in the air **8** : to be imminent **9** : DEPEND **10** : to take hold for support **11** : to be burdensome **12** : to undergo delay **13** : to incline downward; *also* : to fit or fall from the figure in easy lines **14** : to be raptly attentive **15** : LINGER, LOITER — **hang•er** *n*

[2]hang *n* **1** : the manner in which a thing hangs **2** : an understanding of something

han•gar \ˈhaŋ-ər\ *n* [F] : a covered and usu. enclosed area for housing and repairing aircraft

hang•dog \ˈhaŋ-ˌdȯg\ *adj* **1** : ASHAMED, GUILTY **2** : ABJECT, COWED

hang•er–on \ˈhaŋ-ər-ˈȯn, -ˈän\ *n, pl* **hangers–on** : one who hangs around a person or place esp. for personal gain

hang in *vb* : to persist tenaciously

hang•ing *n* **1** : an execution by strangling or snapping the neck by a suspended noose **2** : something hung

hang•man \ˈhaŋ-mən\ *n* : a public executioner

hang•nail \-ˌnāl\ *n* : a bit of skin hanging loose at the edge of a fingernail

hang on *vb* **1** : HANG IN **2** : to keep a telephone connection open
hang•out \ˈhaŋ-ˌau̇t\ *n* : a favorite place for spending time
hang•over \-ˌō-vər\ *n* **1** : something that remains from what is past **2** : disagreeable physical effects following heavy drinking
hang–up \ˈhaŋ-ˌəp\ *n* : a source of mental or emotional difficulty
hang up *vb* **1** : to place on a hook or hanger **2** : to end a telephone conversation by replacing the receiver on the cradle **3** : to keep delayed or suspended
hank \ˈhaŋk\ *n* : COIL, LOOP
han•ker \ˈhaŋ-kər\ *vb* : to desire strongly or persistently — **han•ker•ing** *n*
han•kie *or* **han•ky** \ˈhaŋ-kē\ *n, pl* **hankies** : HANDKERCHIEF
han•ky–pan•ky \ˌhaŋ-kē-ˈpaŋ-kē\ *n* **1** : questionable or underhanded activity **2** : sexual dalliance
han•sel *var of* HANDSEL
han•som \ˈhan-səm\ *n* : a 2-wheeled covered carriage with the driver's seat elevated at the rear
Ha•nuk•kah \ˈk̲ä-nə-kə, ˈhä-\ *n* [Heb *ḥănukkāh* dedication] : an 8-day Jewish holiday commemorating the rededication of the Temple of Jerusalem after its defilement by Antiochus of Syria
hap \ˈhap\ *n* **1** : HAPPENING **2** : CHANCE, FORTUNE
[1]**hap•haz•ard** \hap-ˈha-zərd\ *n* : CHANCE
[2]**haphazard** *adj* : marked by lack of plan or order — **hap•haz•ard•ly** *adv* — **hap•haz•ard•ness** *n*
hap•less \ˈhap-ləs\ *adj* : UNFORTUNATE — **hap•less•ly** *adv* — **hap•less•ness** *n*
hap•loid \ˈhap-ˌlȯid\ *adj* : having the number of chromosomes characteristic of gametic cells — **haploid** *n*
hap•ly \ˈhap-lē\ *adv* : by chance
hap•pen \ˈha-pən\ *vb* **1** : to occur by chance **2** : to take place **3** : CHANCE 2
hap•pen•ing *n* **1** : OCCURRENCE **2** : an event that is especially interesting, entertaining, or important
hap•pi•ly \ˈha-pə-lē\ *adv* **1** : LUCKILY **2** : in a happy manner or state ⟨lived ~ ever after⟩ **3** : APTLY, SUCCESSFULLY
hap•pi•ness \ˈha-pē-nəs\ *n* **1** : a state of well-being and contentment; *also* : a pleasurable satisfaction **2** : APTNESS
hap•py \ˈha-pē\ *adj* **hap•pi•er; -est 1** : FORTUNATE **2** : APT, FELICITOUS **3** : enjoying well-being and contentment **4** : PLEASANT; *also* : PLEASED, GRATIFIED **syn** glad, cheerful, lighthearted, joyful, joyous
hap•py–go–lucky \ˌha-pē-gō-ˈlə-kē\ *adj* : CAREFREE
happy hour *n* : a period of time when the price of drinks at a bar is reduced
hara–kiri \ˌhar-i-ˈkir-ē, -ˈkar-ē\ *n* [Jp *harakiri,* fr. *hara* belly + *kiri* cutting] : ritual suicide by disembowelment
ha•rangue \hə-ˈraŋ\ *n* **1** : a ranting speech or writing **2** : LECTURE — **harangue** *vb* — **ha•rangu•er** *n*
ha•rass \hə-ˈras, ˈhar-əs\ *vb* [F *harasser,* fr. MF, fr. *harer* to set a dog on, fr. OF *hare,* interj. used to incite dogs, of Gmc origin] **1** : EXHAUST, FATIGUE **2** : to worry and impede by repeated raids **3** : to annoy continually **syn** harry, plague, pester, tease, bedevil — **ha•rass•ment** *n*
har•bin•ger \ˈhär-bən-jər\ *n* : one that announces or foreshadows what is coming : PRECURSOR; *also* : PORTENT
[1]**har•bor** \ˈhär-bər\ *n* **1** : a place of security and comfort **2** : a part of a body of water protected and deep enough to furnish anchorage : PORT
[2]**harbor** *vb* **1** : to give or take refuge : SHELTER **2** : to be the home or habitat of; *also* : LIVE **3** : to hold a thought or feeling ⟨~ a grudge⟩
har•bor•age \ˈhär-bə-rij\ *n* : HARBOR
har•bour *chiefly Brit var of* HARBOR
hard \ˈhärd\ *adj* **1** : not easily penetrated : not easily yielding to pressure **2** : high in alcoholic content **3** : containing salts that prevent lathering with soap ⟨~ water⟩ **4** : stable in value ⟨~ currency⟩ **5** : physically fit **6** : FIRM, DEFINITE ⟨~ agreement⟩; *also* : based on clear fact ⟨~ evidence⟩ **7** : CLOSE, SEARCHING ⟨~ look⟩ **8** : REALISTIC ⟨good ~ sense⟩ **9** : OBDURATE, UNFEELING ⟨~ heart⟩ **10** : difficult to bear ⟨~ times⟩; *also* : HARSH, SEVERE **11** : RESENTFUL ⟨~ feelings⟩ **12** : STRICT, UNRELENTING ⟨~ bargain⟩ **13** : INCLEMENT ⟨~ winter⟩ **14** : intense in force or manner ⟨~ blow⟩ **15** : ARDUOUS, STRENUOUS ⟨~ work⟩ **16** : sounding as in *arcing* and *geese* respectively — used of *c* and *g* **17** : TROUBLESOME ⟨~ problem⟩ **18** : having difficulty in doing something ⟨~ of hearing⟩ **19** : addictive and gravely detrimental to health ⟨~ drugs⟩ **20** : of or relating to the natural sciences and esp. the physical sciences — **hard** *adv* — **hard•ness** *n*
hard–and–fast *adj* : rigidly binding : STRICT ⟨a ~ rule⟩
hard•back \ˈhärd-ˌbak\ *n* : a hardcover book
hard•ball \-ˌbȯl\ *n* **1** : BASEBALL **2** : forceful uncompromising methods
hard–bit•ten \-ˈbit-ᵊn\ *adj* : SEASONED, TOUGH ⟨~ campaigners⟩
hard•board \-ˌbōrd\ *n* : a very dense fiberboard
hard–boiled \-ˈbȯild\ *adj* **1** *of an egg* : boiled until both white and yolk have solidified **2** : lacking sentiment : TOUGH; *also* : HARDHEADED 2
hard•bound \-ˌbau̇nd\ *adj* : HARDCOVER
hard copy *n* : copy of textual or graphic information (as from computer storage) produced on paper
hard–core \ˈhärd-ˈkōr\ *adj* **1** : extremely resistant to solution or improvement **2** : being the most determined or dedicated members of a specified group **3** : containing explicit depictions of sex acts — **hard core** *n*
hard•cov•er \-ˈkə-vər\ *adj* : having rigid boards on the sides covered in cloth or paper ⟨~ books⟩
hard disk *n* : a sealed rigid metal disk used as a computer storage device
hard•en \ˈhärd-ᵊn\ *vb* **1** : to make or become hard or harder **2** : to confirm or become confirmed in disposition or action — **hard•en•er** *n*
hard•hack \ˈhärd-ˌhak\ *n* : an American spirea with dense clusters of pink or white flowers and leaves having a hairy rusty yellow underside
hard hat *n* **1** : a protective hat worn esp. by construction workers **2** : a construction worker
hard•head•ed \ˈhärd-ˈhe-dəd\ *adj* **1** : STUBBORN, WILLFUL **2** : SOBER, REALISTIC — **hard•head•ed•ly** *adv* — **hard•head•ed•ness** *n*
hard–heart•ed \-ˈhär-təd\ *adj* : PITILESS, CRUEL — **hard–heart•ed•ly** *adv* — **hard–heart•ed•ness** *n*
har•di•hood \ˈhär-dē-ˌhu̇d\ *n* **1** : resolute courage and fortitude **2** : VIGOR, ROBUSTNESS
hard–line \ˈhärd-ˈlīn\ *adj* : advocating or involving a rigidly uncompromising course of action — **hard–lin•er** \-ˈlī-nər\ *n*
hard•ly \ˈhärd-lē\ *adv* **1** : with force **2** : SEVERELY **3** : with difficulty **4** : only just : BARELY **5** : certainly not
hard–nosed \ˈhärd-ˈnōzd\ *adj* : TOUGH, UNCOMPROMISING; *also* : HARDHEADED 2
hard palate *n* : the bony anterior part of the palate forming the roof of the mouth
hard•pan \ˈhärd-ˌpan\ *n* : a compact layer in soil that is impenetrable by roots
hard–pressed \-ˈprest\ *adj* : HARD PUT; *esp* : being under financial strain
hard put *adj* **1** : barely able **2** : faced with difficulty or perplexity
hard rock *n* : rock music marked by a heavy beat, high amplification, and usu. frenzied performances
hard–shell \ˈhärd-ˌshel\ *adj* : HIDEBOUND, UNCOMPROMISING ⟨a ~ conservative⟩
hard•ship \-ˌship\ *n* **1** : SUFFERING, PRIVATION **2** : something that causes suffering or privation
hard•tack \-ˌtak\ *n* : a saltless hard biscuit, bread, or cracker

hard•top \-ˌtäp\ *n* : an automobile having a permanent rigid top

hard•ware \-ˌwar\ *n* **1** : ware (as cutlery or tools) made of metal **2** : the physical components (as electronic devices) of a vehicle (as a spacecraft) or an apparatus (as a computer)

hard•wood \-ˌwu̇d\ *n* : the wood of a broad-leaved usu. deciduous tree as distinguished from that of a conifer; *also* : such a tree — **hardwood** *adj*

hard•work•ing \-ˈwər-kiŋ\ *adj* : INDUSTRIOUS

har•dy \ˈhär-dē\ *adj* **har•di•er; -est 1** : BOLD, BRAVE **2** : AUDACIOUS, BRAZEN **3** : ROBUST; *also* : able to withstand adverse conditions (as of weather) ⟨~ shrubs⟩ — **har•di•ly** \-də-lē\ *adv* — **har•di•ness** \-dē-nəs\ *n*

hare \ˈhar\ *n, pl* **hare** *or* **hares** : any of various swift timid long-eared mammals like the related rabbits but born with open eyes and fur

hare•bell \ˈhar-ˌbel\ *n* : a slender herb with bright blue bell-shaped flowers

hare•brained \-ˈbrānd\ *adj* : FOOLISH

hare•lip \-ˈlip\ *n* : a birth defect in which the upper lip is vertically split — **hare•lipped** \-ˈlipt\ *adj*

ha•rem \ˈhar-əm\ *n* [Ar *ḥarīm,* lit., something forbidden & *ḥaram,* lit., sanctuary] **1** : a house or part of a house allotted to women in a Muslim household **2** : the women and servants occupying a harem **3** : a group of females associated with one male

hark \ˈhärk\ *vb* : LISTEN

harken *var of* HEARKEN

har•le•quin \ˈhär-li-kən, -kwən\ *n* **1** *cap* : a character (as in comedy) with a shaved head, masked face, variegated tights, and wooden sword **2** : CLOWN 2

har•lot \ˈhär-lət\ *n* : PROSTITUTE

[1]**harm** \ˈhärm\ *n* **1** : physical or mental damage : INJURY **2** : MISCHIEF, HURT — **harm•ful** \-fəl\ *adj* — **harm•ful•ly** *adv* — **harm•ful•ness** *n* — **harm•less** *adj* — **harm•less•ly** *adv* — **harm•less•ness** *n*

[2]**harm** *vb* : to cause harm to : INJURE

[1]**har•mon•ic** \här-ˈmä-nik\ *adj* **1** : of or relating to musical harmony or harmonics **2** : pleasing to the ear — **har•mon•i•cal•ly** \-ni-k(ə-)lē\ *adv*

[2]**harmonic** *n* : a musical overtone

har•mon•i•ca \här-ˈmä-ni-kə\ *n* : a small wind instrument in which the sound is produced by metal reeds

har•mo•ni•ous \här-ˈmō-nē-əs\ *adj* **1** : musically concordant **2** : CONGRUOUS **3** : marked by accord in sentiment or action — **har•mo•ni•ous•ly** *adv* — **har•mo•ni•ous•ness** *n*

har•mo•nise *Brit var of* HARMONIZE

har•mo•ni•um \här-ˈmō-nē-əm\ *n* : a keyboard wind instrument in which the wind acts on a set of metal reeds

har•mo•nize \ˈhär-mə-ˌnīz\ *vb* **-nized; -niz•ing 1** : to play or sing in harmony **2** : to be in harmony **3** : to bring into consonance or accord — **har•mo•ni•za•tion** \ˌhär-mə-nə-ˈzā-shən\ *n*

har•mo•ny \ˈhär-mə-nē\ *n, pl* **-nies 1** : musical agreement of sounds; *esp* : the combination of tones into chords and progressions of chords **2** : a pleasing arrangement of parts; *also* : ACCORD **3** : internal calm

[1]**har•ness** \ˈhär-nəs\ *n* **1** : the gear other than a yoke of a draft animal **2** : something that resembles a harness

[2]**harness** *vb* **1** : to put a harness on; *also* : YOKE **2** : UTILIZE

[1]**harp** \ˈhärp\ *n* : a musical instrument consisting of a triangular frame set with strings plucked by the fingers — **harp•ist** \ˈhär-pist\ *n*

[2]**harp** *vb* **1** : to play on a harp **2** : to dwell on a subject tiresomely — **harp•er** *n*

har•poon \här-ˈpün\ *n* : a barbed spear used esp. in hunting whales — **harpoon** *vb* — **har•poon•er** *n*

harp•si•chord \ˈhärp-si-ˌkȯrd\ *n* : a keyboard instrument producing tones by the plucking of its strings with quills or with leather or plastic points

har•py \ˈhär-pē\ *n, pl* **harpies** [L *Harpyia,* a mythical predatory monster having a woman's head and a bird's body, fr. Gk] **1** : a predatory person : LEECH **2** : a shrewish woman

har•ri•dan \ˈhar-əd-ᵊn\ *n* : SHREW 2

[1]**har•ri•er** \ˈhar-ē-ər\ *n* **1** : any of a breed of medium-sized foxhounds **2** : a runner on a cross-country team

[2]**harrier** *n* : a slender long-legged hawk

[1]**har•row** \ˈhar-ō\ *n* : a cultivating tool that has spikes, spring teeth, or disks and is used esp. to pulverize and smooth the soil

[2]**harrow** *vb* **1** : to cultivate with a harrow **2** : TORMENT, VEX

har•ry \ˈhar-ē\ *vb* **har•ried; har•ry•ing 1** : RAID, PILLAGE **2** : to torment by or as if by constant attack **syn** worry, annoy, plague, pester

harsh \ˈhärsh\ *adj* **1** : disagreeably rough **2** : causing discomfort or pain **3** : unduly exacting : SEVERE — **harsh•ly** *adv* — **harsh•ness** *n*

hart \ˈhärt\ *n, chiefly Brit* : STAG

har•um–scar•um \ˌhar-əm-ˈskar-əm\ *adj* : RECKLESS, IRRESPONSIBLE

[1]**har•vest** \ˈhär-vəst\ *n* **1** : the season for gathering in crops; *also* : the act of gathering in a crop **2** : a mature crop **3** : the product or reward of effort

[2]**harvest** *vb* **1** : to gather in a crop : REAP **2** : to gather, hunt, or kill (as deer) for human use or population control — **har•vest•er** *n*

has *pres 3d sing of* HAVE

has–been \ˈhaz-ˌbin\ *n* : one that has passed the peak of ability, power, effectiveness, or popularity

[1]**hash** \ˈhash\ *vb* [F *hacher,* fr. OF *hachier,* fr. *hache* battle-ax, of Gmc origin] **1** : to chop into small pieces **2** : to talk about

[2]**hash** *n* **1** : chopped meat mixed with potatoes and browned **2** : HODGEPODGE, JUMBLE

[3]**hash** *n* : HASHISH

hash browns *n pl* : boiled potatoes that have been diced, mixed with chopped onions and shortening, and fried

hash•ish \ˈha-ˌshēsh, ha-ˈshēsh\ [Ar *ḥashīsh*] *n* : the concentrated resin from the flowering tops of the female hemp plant

hasp \ˈhasp\ *n* : a fastener (as for a door) consisting of a hinged metal strap that fits over a staple and is secured by a pin or padlock

hasp

has•sle \ˈha-səl\ *n* **1** : WRANGLE; *also* : FIGHT **2** : an annoying or troublesome concern — **hassle** *vb*

has•sock \ˈha-sək\ *n* : a cushion that serves as a seat or leg rest; *also* : a cushion to kneel on in prayer

haste \ˈhāst\ *n* **1** : rapidity of motion or action : SPEED **2** : rash or headlong action **3** : excessive eagerness — **hast•i•ly** \ˈhā-stə-lē\ *adv* — **hast•i•ness** \-stē-nəs\ *n* — **hasty** \ˈhā-stē\ *adj*

has•ten \ˈhās-ᵊn\ *vb* **1** : to urge on **2** : to move or act quickly : HURRY **syn** speed, accelerate, quicken

hat \ˈhat\ *n* : a covering for the head usu. having a shaped crown and brim

hat•box \ˈhat-ˌbäks\ *n* : a round piece of luggage esp. for carrying hats

[1]**hatch** \ˈhach\ *n* **1** : a small door or opening **2** : a door or cover for access down into a compartment of a ship

[2]**hatch** *vb* **1** : to produce by incubation; *also* : INCUBATE **2** : to emerge from an egg or pupa; *also* : to give forth young **3** : ORIGINATE — **hatch•ery** \ˈha-chə-rē\ *n*

hatch•back \ˈhach-ˌbak\ *n* : an automobile with a rear hatch that opens upward
hatch•et \ˈha-chət\ *n* **1** : a short-handled ax with a hammerlike part opposite the blade **2** : TOMAHAWK
hatchet man *n* : a person hired for murder, coercion, or unscrupulous attack
hatch•ing \ˈha-chiŋ\ *n* : the engraving or drawing of closely spaced fine lines chiefly to give an effect of shading; *also* : the pattern so created
hatch•way \ˈhach-ˌwā\ *n* : a hatch giving access usu. by a ladder or stairs
¹hate \ˈhāt\ *n* **1** : intense hostility and aversion **2** : an object of hatred — **hate•ful** \-fəl\ *adj* — **hate•ful•ly** *adv* — **hate•ful•ness** *n*
²hate *vb* **hat•ed; hat•ing 1** : to express or feel extreme enmity **2** : to find distasteful **syn** detest, abhor, abominate, loathe — **hat•er** *n*
ha•tred \ˈhā-trəd\ *n* : HATE; *also* : prejudiced hostility or animosity
hat•ter \ˈha-tər\ *n* : one that makes, sells, or cleans and repairs hats
hau•berk \ˈhȯ-bərk\ *n* : a coat of mail
haugh•ty \ˈhȯ-tē\ *adj* **haugh•ti•er; -est** [obs. *haught,* fr. ME *haute,* fr. MF *haut,* lit., high, fr. L *altus*] : disdainfully proud **syn** insolent, lordly, overbearing, arrogant — **haugh•ti•ly** \-tə-lē\ *adv* — **haugh•ti•ness** \-tē-nəs\ *n*
¹haul \ˈhȯl\ *vb* **1** : to exert traction on : DRAW, PULL **2** : to furnish transportation : CART — **haul•er** *n*
²haul *n* **1** : PULL, TUG **2** : the result of an effort to obtain, collect, or win **3** : the length or course of a transportation route; *also* : LOAD
haul•age \ˈhȯ-lij\ *n* **1** : the act or process of hauling **2** : a charge for hauling
haunch \ˈhȯnch\ *n* **1** : ²HIP 1 **2** : HINDQUARTER 2 — usu. used in pl. **3** : HINDQUARTER 1
¹haunt \ˈhȯnt\ *vb* **1** : to visit often : FREQUENT **2** : to recur constantly and spontaneously to; *also* : to reappear continually in **3** : to visit or inhabit as a ghost — **haunt•er** *n* — **haunt•ing•ly** *adv*
²haunt \ˈhȯnt, *2 is usu* ˈhant\ *n* **1** : a place habitually frequented **2** *chiefly dial* : GHOST
haute cou•ture \ˌōt-kü-ˈtu̇r\ *n* [F] : the establishments or designers that create exclusive and often trend-setting fashions for women; *also* : the fashions created
haute cui•sine \-kwi-ˈzēn\ *n* : artful or elaborate cuisine
hau•teur \hō-ˈtər, ō-, hō-\ *n* : ARROGANCE, HAUGHTINESS
¹have \ˈhav, həv, v; *in sense 2 before "to" usu* ˈhaf\ *vb* **had** \ˈhad, həd\; **hav•ing; has** \ˈhaz, həz, *in sense 2 before "to" usu* ˈhas\ **1** : to hold in possession; *also* : to hold in one's use, service, or regard **2** : to be compelled or forced ⟨~ to go now⟩ **3** : to stand in relationship to ⟨*has* many enemies⟩ **4** : OBTAIN; *also* : RECEIVE, ACCEPT **5** : to be marked by **6** : SHOW; *also* : USE, EXERCISE **7** : EXPERIENCE; *also* : TAKE ⟨~ a look⟩ **8** : to entertain in the mind ⟨~ an idea⟩ **9** : to cause to **10** : ALLOW **11** : to be competent in **12** : to hold in a disadvantageous position; *also* : TRICK **13** : BEGET **14** : to partake of **15** — used as an auxiliary with the past participle to form the present perfect, past perfect, or future perfect — **have at** : ATTACK — **have coming** : DESERVE — **have done with** : to be finished with — **have had it** : to have endured all one will permit or can stand — **have to do with** : to have in the way of relation with or effect on
²have \ˈhav\ *n* : one that has material wealth
ha•ven \ˈhā-vən\ *n* **1** : HARBOR, PORT **2** : a place of safety **3** : a place offering favorable conditions ⟨a tourist's ~⟩
have–not \ˈhav-ˌnät, -ˈnät\ *n* : one that is poor in material wealth
hav•er•sack \ˈha-vər-ˌsak\ *n* [F *havresac,* fr. G *Habersack* bag for oats] : a bag similar to a knapsack but worn over one shoulder
hav•oc \ˈha-vək\ *n* **1** : wide and general destruction **2** : great confusion and disorder
haw \ˈhȯ\ *n* : a hawthorn berry; *also* : HAWTHORN
Ha•wai•ian \hə-ˈwä-yən\ *n* : the Polynesian language of Hawaii
¹hawk \ˈhȯk\ *n* **1** : any of numerous mostly small or medium-sized day-flying birds of prey (as a falcon or kite) **2** : a supporter of a war or a warlike policy — **hawk•ish** *adj*
²hawk *vb* : to offer goods for sale by calling out in the street — **hawk•er** *n*
³hawk *vb* : to make a harsh coughing sound in or as if in clearing the throat; *also* : to raise by hawking
hawk•weed \ˈhȯk-ˌwēd\ *n* : any of several plants related to the daisies usu. having red or orange flower heads
haw•ser \ˈhȯ-zər\ *n* : a large rope for towing, mooring, or securing a ship
haw•thorn \ˈhȯ-ˌthȯrn\ *n* : any of a genus of spiny spring-flowering shrubs or trees related to the apple
¹hay \ˈhā\ *n* **1** : herbage (as grass) mowed and cured for fodder **2** : REWARD **3** *slang* : BED ⟨hit the ~⟩ **4** : a small amount of money
²hay *vb* : to cut, cure, and store for hay
hay•cock \ˈhā-ˌkäk\ *n* : a small conical pile of hay
hay fever *n* : an acute allergic reaction esp. to plant pollen that resembles a cold
hay•loft \ˈhā-ˌlȯft\ *n* : a loft for hay
hay•mow \-ˌmau̇\ *n* : a mow of or for hay
hay•rick \-ˌrik\ *n* : a large sometimes thatched outdoor stack of hay
hay•seed \-ˌsēd\ *n, pl* **hayseed** *or* **hayseeds 1** : clinging bits of straw or chaff from hay **2** : BUMPKIN, YOKEL
hay•stack \-ˌstak\ *n* : a stack of hay
hay•wire \-ˌwīr\ *adj* : being out of order or control : CRAZY
¹haz•ard \ˈha-zərd\ *n* [ME, a dice game, fr. MF *hasard,* fr. Ar *az-zahr* the die] **1** : a source of danger **2** : CHANCE; *also* : ACCIDENT **3** : an obstacle on a golf course — **haz•ard•ous** *adj*
²hazard *vb* : VENTURE, RISK
¹haze \ˈhāz\ *n* **1** : fine dust, smoke, or light vapor causing lack of transparency in the air **2** : vagueness of mind or perception
²haze *vb* **hazed; haz•ing** : to harass by abusive and humiliating tricks usu. by way of initiation
ha•zel \ˈhā-zəl\ *n* **1** : any of a genus of shrubs or small trees related to the birches and bearing edible nuts (**ha•zel•nuts** \-ˌnəts\) **2** : a light brown color
hazy \ˈhā-zē\ *adj* **haz•i•er; -est 1** : obscured or darkened by haze **2** : VAGUE, INDEFINITE — **haz•i•ly** \-zə-lē\ *adv* — **haz•i•ness** \-zē-nəs\ *n*
Hb *abbr* hemoglobin
HBM *abbr* Her Britannic Majesty; His Britannic Majesty
H–bomb \ˈāch-ˌbäm\ *n* : HYDROGEN BOMB
HC *abbr* **1** Holy Communion **2** House of Commons
hd *abbr* head
HD *abbr* heavy-duty
hdbk *abbr* handbook
hdkf *abbr* handkerchief
HDL \ˌāch-(ˌ)dē-ˈel\ *n* [*h*igh-*d*ensity *l*ipoprotein] : a cholesterol-poor protein-rich lipoprotein of blood plasma correlated with reduced risk of atherosclerosis
hdwe *abbr* hardware
he \ˈhē\ *pron* **1** : that male one **2** : a person : the person ⟨~ who hesitates is lost⟩
He *symbol* helium
HE *abbr* **1** Her Excellency **2** His Eminence **3** His Excellency
¹head \ˈhed\ *n* **1** : the front or upper part of the body containing the brain, the chief sense organs, and the mouth **2** : MIND; *also* : natural aptitude **3** : POISE **4**

DICTIONARY

: the obverse of a coin **5** : INDIVIDUAL; *also, pl* **head** : one of a number (as of cattle) **6** : the end that is upper or higher or opposite the foot; *also* : either end of something (as a drum) whose two ends need not be distinguished **7** : the source of a stream **8** : DIRECTOR, LEADER; *also* : a leading element (as of a procession) **9** : a projecting part; *also* : the striking part of a weapon **10** : the place of leadership or honor **11** : a separate part or topic **12** : the foam on a fermenting or effervescing liquid **13** : CRISIS — **head·ed** \ˈhe-dəd\ *adj* — **head·less** *adj*

[2]**head** *adj* : PRINCIPAL, CHIEF

[3]**head** *vb* **1** : to provide with or form a head; *also* : to form the head of **2** : LEAD, CONDUCT **3** : to get in front of esp. so as to stop; *also* : SURPASS **4** : to put or stand at the head **5** : to point or proceed in a certain direction

head·ache \ˈhe-ˌdāk\ *n* **1** : pain in the head **2** : a baffling situation or problem

head·band \ˈhed-ˌband\ *n* : a band worn on or around the head

head·board \-ˌbōrd\ *n* : a board forming the head (as of a bed)

head cold *n* : a common cold centered in the nasal passages and adjacent mucous tissues

head·dress \ˈhed-ˌdres\ *n* : an often elaborate covering for the head

head·first \-ˈfərst\ *adv* : HEADLONG 1 — **headfirst** *adj*

head·gear \-ˌgir\ *n* : a covering or protective device for the head

head–hunt·ing \-ˌhən-tiŋ\ *n* : the practice of seeking out and decapitating enemies and preserving their heads as trophies — **head·hunt·er** \-tər\ *n*

head·ing \ˈhe-diŋ\ *n* **1** : the compass direction in which the longitudinal axis of a ship or airplane points **2** : something that forms or serves as a head

head·land \ˈhed-lənd, -ˌland\ *n* : PROMONTORY

head·light \-ˌlīt\ *n* : a light mounted on the front of a vehicle to illuminate the road ahead

head·line \-ˌlīn\ *n* : a head of a newspaper story or article usu. printed in large type

head·lock \-ˌläk\ *n* : a wrestling hold in which one encircles the opponent's head with one arm

[1]**head·long** \-ˈlȯŋ\ *adv* **1** : with the head foremost **2** : RECKLESSLY **3** : without delay

[2]**head·long** \-ˌlȯŋ\ *adj* **1** : PRECIPITATE, RASH **2** : plunging with the head foremost

head·man \ˈhed-ˈman, -ˌman\ *n* : one who is a leader : CHIEF

head·mas·ter \-ˌmas-tər\ *n* : a man who is head of a private school

head·mis·tress \-ˌmis-trəs\ *n* : a woman who is head of a private school

head–on \ˈhed-ˈȯn, -ˈän\ *adj* : having the front facing in the direction of initial contact or line of sight ⟨~ collision⟩ — **head–on** *adv*

head·phone \-ˌfōn\ *n* : an earphone held on by a band over the head

head·piece \-ˌpēs\ *n* : a covering for the head

head·pin \-ˌpin\ *n* : a bowling pin that stands foremost in the arrangement of pins

head·quar·ters \-ˌkwȯr-tərz\ *n sing or pl* **1** : a place from which a commander exercises command **2** : the administrative center of an enterprise

head·rest \-ˌrest\ *n* **1** : a support for the head **2** : a pad at the top of the back of an automobile seat

head·room \-ˌrüm, -ˌru̇m\ *n* : vertical space in which to stand, sit, or move

head·set \-ˌset\ *n* : a pair of headphones

head·ship \-ˌship\ *n* : the position, office, or dignity of a head

heads·man \ˈhedz-mən\ *n* : EXECUTIONER

head·stall \ˈhed-ˌstȯl\ *n* : a part of a bridle or halter that encircles the head

head·stone \-ˌstōn\ *n* : a memorial stone at the head of a grave

head·strong \-ˌstrȯŋ\ *adj* **1** : not easily restrained **2** : directed by ungovernable will **syn** unruly, intractable, willful, pertinacious, refractory, stubborn

head·wait·er \-ˈwā-tər\ *n* : the head of the dining-room staff of a restaurant or hotel

head·wa·ter \-ˌwȯ-tər, -ˌwä-\ *n* : the source of a stream — usu. used in pl.

head·way \-ˌwā\ *n* : forward motion; *also* : PROGRESS

head wind *n* : a wind blowing in a direction opposite to a course esp. of a ship or aircraft

head·word \ˈhed-ˌwərd\ *n* **1** : a word or term placed at the beginning **2** : a word qualified by a modifier

head·work \-ˌwərk\ *n* : mental work or effort : THINKING

heady \ˈhe-dē\ *adj* **head·i·er; -est 1** : WILLFUL, RASH; *also* : IMPETUOUS **2** : INTOXICATING **3** : SHREWD

heal \ˈhēl\ *vb* **1** : to make or become healthy, sound, or whole **2** : CURE, REMEDY — **heal·er** *n*

health \ˈhelth\ *n* **1** : sound physical or mental condition; *also* : overall condition of the body ⟨in poor ~⟩ **2** : WELL-BEING **3** : a toast to someone's health or prosperity

health·ful \ˈhelth-fəl\ *adj* **1** : beneficial to health **2** : HEALTHY — **health·ful·ly** *adv* — **health·ful·ness** *n*

health maintenance organization *n* : HMO

healthy \ˈhel-thē\ *adj* **health·i·er; -est 1** : enjoying or typical of good health : WELL **2** : evincing or conducive to health **3** : PROSPEROUS; *also* : CONSIDERABLE — **health·i·ly** \-thə-lē\ *adv* — **health·i·ness** \-thē-nəs\ *n*

[1]**heap** \ˈhēp\ *n* : PILE; *also* : LOT

[2]**heap** *vb* **1** : to throw or lay in a heap **2** : to give in large quantities; *also* : to load heavily

hear \ˈhir\ *vb* **heard** \ˈhərd\; **hear·ing 1** : to perceive by the ear **2** : to gain knowledge of by hearing : LEARN **3** : HEED; *also* : ATTEND **4** : to give a legal hearing to or take testimony from — **hear·er** *n*

hear·ing *n* **1** : the process, function, or power of perceiving sound; *esp* : the special sense by which noises and tones are received as stimuli **2** : EARSHOT **3** : opportunity to be heard **4** : a listening to arguments (as in a court); *also* : a session of (as of a legislative committee) in which testimony is taken from witnesses

hear·ken \ˈhär-kən\ *vb* : to give attention : LISTEN **syn** hear, hark, heed

hear·say \ˈhir-ˌsā\ *n* : RUMOR

hearse \ˈhərs\ *n* : a vehicle for carrying the dead to the grave

heart \ˈhärt\ *n* **1** : a hollow muscular organ that by rhythmic contraction keeps up the circulation of the blood in the body; *also* : something resembling a heart in shape **2** : any of a suit of playing cards marked with a red figure of a heart; *also, pl* : a card game in which the object is to avoid taking tricks containing hearts **3** : the whole personality; *also* : the emotional or moral as distinguished from the intellectual nature **4** : COURAGE **5** : one's innermost being **6** : CENTER; *also* : the essential part **7** : the younger central part of a compact leafy cluster (as of lettuce) — **heart·ed** \ˈhär-təd\ *adj* — **by heart** : by rote or from memory

heart·ache \-ˌāk\ *n* : anguish of mind

heart attack *n* : an acute episode of heart disease due to insufficient blood supply to the heart muscle

heart·beat \ˈhärt-ˌbēt\ *n* : one complete pulsation of the heart

heart·break \-ˌbrāk\ *n* : crushing grief

heart·break·ing \-ˌbrā-kiŋ\ *adj* : causing extreme sorrow or distress — **heart·break·er** \-ˌbrā-kər\ *n*

heart·bro·ken \-ˌbrō-kən\ *adj* : overcome by sorrow

heart·burn \-ˌbərn\ *n* : a burning distress in the area of the heart usu. due to spasms of the esophagus or upper stomach

heart disease *n* : an abnormal organic condition of the heart or of the heart and circulation

heart•en \ˈhärt-ᵊn\ *vb* : ENCOURAGE, CHEER
heart•felt \ˈhärt-ˌfelt\ *adj* : deeply felt : SINCERE
hearth \ˈhärth\ *n* **1** : an area (as of brick) in front of a fireplace; *also* : the floor of a fireplace **2** : HOME
hearth•stone \ˈhärth-ˌstōn\ *n* **1** : stone forming a hearth **2** : HOME
heart•less \ˈhärt-ləs\ *adj* : CRUEL
heart•rend•ing \-ˌren-diŋ\ *adj* : HEARTBREAKING
heart•sick \-ˌsik\ *adj* : very despondent — **heart•sick•ness** *n*
heart•strings \-ˌstriŋz\ *n pl* : the deepest emotions or affections
heart•throb \-ˌthräb\ *n* **1** : the throb of a heart **2** : sentimental emotion **3** : SWEETHEART
heart–to–heart *adj* : SINCERE, FRANK
heart•warm•ing \ˈhärt-ˌwȯr-miŋ\ *adj* : inspiring sympathetic feeling
heart•wood \-ˌwu̇d\ *n* : the older harder nonliving and usu. darker wood of the central part of a tree trunk
¹hearty \ˈhär-tē\ *adj* **heart•i•er; -est 1** : giving full support; *also* : JOVIAL **2** : vigorously healthy **3** : ABUNDANT; *also* : NOURISHING **syn** sincere, wholehearted, unfeigned, heartfelt — **heart•i•ly** \-tə-lē\ *adv* — **heart•i•ness** \-tē-nəs\ *n*
²hearty *n, pl* **heart•ies** : an enthusiastic jovial fellow; *also* : SAILOR
¹heat \ˈhēt\ *vb* **1** : to make or become warm or hot **2** : EXCITE — **heat•ed•ly** *adv* — **heat•er** *n*
²heat *n* **1** : a condition of being hot : WARMTH **2** : a form of energy that when added to a body causes the body to rise in temperature, to fuse, to evaporate, or to expand **3** : high temperature **4** : intensity of feeling; *also* : sexual excitement esp. in a female mammal **5** : a preliminary race for narrowing the competition **6** : pungency of flavor **7** *slang* : POLICE **8** : PRESSURE, COERCION; *also* : ABUSE, CRITICISM
heat exchanger *n* : a device (as an automobile radiator) for transferring heat from one fluid to another without allowing them to mix
heat exhaustion *n* : a condition marked by weakness, nausea, dizziness, and profuse sweating resulting from physical exertion in a hot environment
heath \ˈhēth\ *n* **1** : any of a large family of often evergreen shrubby plants (as a blueberry or heather) of wet acid soils **2** : a tract of wasteland — **heathy** *adj*
hea•then \ˈhē-t͟hən\ *n, pl* **heathens** *or* **heathen 1** : an unconverted member of a people or nation that does not acknowledge the God of the Bible **2** : an uncivilized or irreligious person — **heathen** *adj* — **hea•then•dom** *n* — **hea•then•ish** *adj* — **hea•then•ism** *n*
heath•er \ˈhe-t͟hər\ *n* : a northern and alpine evergreen heath with usu. lavender flowers — **heath•ery** *adj*
heat lightning *n* : flashes of light without thunder ascribed to distant lightning reflected by high clouds
heat•stroke \ˈhēt-ˌstrōk\ *n* : a disorder marked esp. by high body temperature without sweating and by collapse that follows prolonged exposure to excessive heat
¹heave \ˈhēv\ *vb* **heaved** *or* **hove** \ˈhōv\; **heav•ing 1** : to rise or lift upward **2** : THROW **3** : to rise and fall rhythmically; *also* : PANT **4** : RETCH **5** : PULL, PUSH — **heav•er** *n*
²heave *n* **1** : an effort to lift or raise **2** : THROW, CAST **3** : an upward motion **4** *pl* : a chronic lung disease of horses marked by difficult breathing and persistent cough
heav•en \ˈhe-vən\ *n* **1** : FIRMAMENT — usu. used in pl. **2** *often cap* : the abode of the Deity and of the blessed dead; *also* : a spiritual state of everlasting communion with God **3** *cap* : GOD 1 **4** : a place of supreme happiness — **heav•en•ly** *adj* — **heav•en•ward** *adv or adj*
¹heavy \ˈhe-vē\ *adj* **heavi•er; -est 1** : having great weight **2** : hard to bear **3** : SERIOUS **4** : DEEP, PROFOUND **5** : burdened with something oppressive; *also* : PREGNANT **6** : SLUGGISH **7** : DRAB; *also* : DOLEFUL **8** : DROWSY **9** : greater than the average of its kind or class **10** : very rich and hard to digest; *also* : not properly raised or leavened **11** : producing goods (as steel) used in the production of other goods — **heavi•ly** \-və-lē\ *adv* — **heavi•ness** \-vē-nəs\ *n*
²heavy *n, pl* **heav•ies** : a theatrical role representing a dignified or imposing person; *also* : a villain esp. in a story
heavy–du•ty \ˌhe-vē-ˈdü-tē, -ˈdyü-\ *adj* : able to withstand unusual strain
heavy–hand•ed \-ˈhan-dəd\ *adj* **1** : CLUMSY **2** : OPPRESSIVE, HARSH
heavy•heart•ed \-ˈhär-təd\ *adj* : SADDENED, DESPONDENT
heavy metal *n* : energetic and highly amplified electronic rock music
heavy•set \ˌhe-vē-ˈset\ *adj* : stocky and compact in build
heavy water *n* : water enriched in deuterium
heavy•weight \ˈhe-vē-ˌwāt\ *n* : one above average in weight; *esp* : a boxer weighing over 175 pounds
Heb *abbr* Hebrews
He•bra•ism \ˈhē-brā-ˌi-zəm\ *n* : the thought, spirit, or practice characteristic of the Hebrews — **He•bra•ic** \hi-ˈbrā-ik\ *adj*
He•bra•ist \ˈhē-ˌbrā-ist\ *n* : a specialist in Hebrew and Hebraic studies
He•brew \ˈhē-brü\ *n* **1** : the language of the Hebrews **2** : a member of or descendant from a group of Semitic peoples; *esp* : ISRAELITE — **Hebrew** *adj*
He•brews \ˈhē-(ˌ)brüz\ *n* — see BIBLE table
hec•a•tomb \ˈhe-kə-ˌtōm\ *n* : an ancient Greek and Roman sacrifice of 100 oxen or cattle
heck•le \ˈhe-kəl\ *vb* **heck•led; heck•ling** : to harass with questions or gibes : BADGER — **heck•ler** *n*
hect•are \ˈhek-ˌtar\ *n* — see METRIC SYSTEM table
hec•tic \ˈhek-tik\ *adj* **1** : being hot and flushed **2** : filled with excitement, activity, or confusion — **hec•ti•cal•ly** \-ti-k(ə-)lē\ *adv*
hec•to•gram \ˈhek-tə-ˌgram\ *n* — see METRIC SYSTEM table
hec•to•li•ter \ˈhek-tə-ˌlē-tər\ *n* — see METRIC SYSTEM table
hec•to•me•ter \ˈhek-tə-ˌmē-tər, hek-ˈtä-mə-tər\ *n* — see METRIC SYSTEM table
hec•tor \ˈhek-tər\ *vb* [*hector* bully, fr. *Hector,* champion of Troy in Greek legend] **1** : SWAGGER **2** : to intimidate by bluster or personal pressure
¹hedge \ˈhej\ *n* **1** : a fence or boundary formed of shrubs or small trees **2** : BARRIER **3** : a means of protection (as against financial loss)
²hedge *vb* **hedged; hedg•ing 1** : ENCIRCLE **2** : HINDER **3** : to protect oneself financially by a counterbalancing action **4** : to evade the risk of commitment — **hedg•er** *n*
hedge•hog \ˈhej-ˌhȯg, -ˌhäg\ *n* : a small Old World insect-eating mammal covered with spines; *also* : PORCUPINE

hedgehog

hedge•hop \-ˌhäp\ *vb* : to fly an airplane very close to the ground

hedge•row \-ˌrō\ *n* : a row of shrubs or trees bounding or separating fields
he•do•nism \ˈhēd-ᵊn-ˌi-zəm\ *n* [Gk *hēdonē* pleasure] : the doctrine that pleasure is the chief good in life; *also* : a way of life based on this — **he•do•nist** \-ist\ *n* — **he•do•nis•tic** \ˌhēd-ᵊn-ˈi-stik\ *adj*
¹**heed** \ˈhēd\ *vb* : to pay attention
²**heed** *n* : ATTENTION, NOTICE — **heed•ful** \-fəl\ *adj* — **heed•ful•ly** *adv* — **heed•ful•ness** *n* — **heed•less** *adj* — **heed•less•ly** *adv* — **heed•less•ness** *n*
¹**heel** \ˈhēl\ *n* **1** : the hind part of the foot **2** : one of the crusty ends of a loaf of bread **3** : a solid attachment forming the back of the sole of a shoe **4** : a rear, low, or bottom part **5** : a contemptible person
²**heel** *vb* : to tilt to one side : LIST
¹**heft** \ˈheft\ *n* : WEIGHT, HEAVINESS
²**heft** *vb* : to test the weight of by lifting
hefty \ˈhef-tē\ *adj* **heft•i•er; -est 1** : marked by bigness, bulk, and usu. strength **2** : impressively large
he•ge•mo•ny \hi-ˈje-mə-nē\ *n* : preponderant influence or authority over others : DOMINATION
he•gi•ra \hi-ˈjī-rə\ *n* [the *Hegira*, flight of Muhammad from Mecca in A.D. 622, fr. ML, fr. Ar *hijrah*, lit., flight] : a journey esp. when undertaken to escape a dangerous or undesirable environment
heif•er \ˈhe-fər\ *n* : a young cow; *esp* : one that has not had a calf
height \ˈhīt\ *n* **1** : the highest part or point **2** : the distance from the bottom to the top of something standing upright **3** : ALTITUDE
height•en \ˈhīt-ᵊn\ *vb* **1** : to increase in amount or degree **2** : to make or become high or higher **syn** enhance, intensify, aggravate, magnify
Heim•lich maneuver \ˈhīm-lik-\ *n* [Henry J. *Heimlich* *b*1920 Am. surgeon] : the manual application of sudden upward pressure on the upper abdomen of a choking victim to force a foreign object from the windpipe
hei•nous \ˈhā-nəs\ *adj* [ME, fr. MF *haineus*, fr. *haine* hate, fr. *hair* to hate] : hatefully or shockingly evil — **hei•nous•ly** *adv* — **hei•nous•ness** *n*
heir \ˈar\ *n* : one who inherits or is entitled to inherit property, rank, title, or office — **heir•ship** *n*
heir apparent *n, pl* **heirs apparent** : an heir whose right to succeed (as to a title) cannot be taken away if he or she survives the present holder
heir•ess \ˈar-əs\ *n* : a female heir esp. to great wealth
heir•loom \ˈar-ˌlüm\ *n* **1** : a piece of personal property that descends by inheritance **2** : something handed on from one generation to another
heir presumptive *n, pl* **heirs presumptive** : an heir whose present right to inherit could be lost through the birth of a nearer relative
heist \ˈhīst\ *vb, slang* : to commit armed robbery on; *also* : STEAL — **heist** *n, slang*
held *past and past part of* HOLD
he•li•cal \ˈhe-li-kəl, ˈhē-\ *adj* : SPIRAL
he•li•cop•ter \ˈhe-lə-ˌkäp-tər, ˈhē-\ *n* [F *hélicoptère*, fr. Gk *helix* spiral + *pteron* wing] : an aircraft that is supported in the air by one or more rotors revolving on substantially vertical axes
he•lio•cen•tric \ˌhē-lē-ō-ˈsen-trik\ *adj* : having or relating to the sun as center
he•lio•trope \ˈhē-lē-ə-ˌtrōp\ *n* [L *heliotropium*, fr. Gk *hēliotropion*, fr. *hēlios* sun + *tropos* turn; fr. its flowers' turning toward the sun] : any of a genus of herbs or shrubs related to the forget-me-not that have small white or purple flowers
he•li•port \ˈhe-lə-ˌpōrt\ *n* : a landing and takeoff place for a helicopter
he•li•um \ˈhē-lē-əm\ *n* [NL, fr. Gk *hēlios* sun] : a very light nonflammable gaseous chemical element occurring in various natural gases — see ELEMENT table
he•lix \ˈhē-liks\ *n, pl* **he•li•ces** \ˈhe-lə-ˌsēz, ˈhē-\ *also* **he•lix•es** \ˈhē-lik-səz\ : something spiral in form
hell \ˈhel\ *n* **1** : a nether world in which the dead continue to exist **2** : the realm of the devil in which the damned suffer everlasting punishment **3** : a place or state of torment or destruction — **hell•ish** *adj*
hell–bent \ˈhel-ˌbent\ *adj* : stubbornly determined
hell•cat \-ˌkat\ *n* **1** : WITCH 2 **2** : a violently temperamental person; *esp* : an ill-tempered woman
hel•le•bore \ˈhe-lə-ˌbōr\ *n* **1** : any of a genus of poisonous herbs related to the buttercups; *also* : the dried root of a hellebore **2** : a poisonous plant related to the lilies; *also* : its dried roots used in medicine and insecticides
Hel•lene \ˈhe-ˌlēn\ *n* : GREEK
Hel•le•nism \ˈhe-lə-ˌni-zəm\ *n* : a body of humanistic and classical ideals associated with ancient Greece — **Hel•len•ic** \he-ˈle-nik\ *adj* — **Hel•le•nist** \ˈhe-lə-nist\ *n*
Hel•le•nis•tic \ˌhe-lə-ˈnis-tik\ *adj* : of or relating to Greek history, culture, or art after Alexander the Great
hell–for–leather *adv* : at full speed
hell•gram•mite \ˈhel-grə-ˌmīt\ *n* : an aquatic insect larva that is used as bait in fishing
hell•hole \ˈhel-ˌhōl\ *n* : a place of extreme misery or squalor
hel•lion \ˈhel-yən\ *n* : a troublesome or mischievous person
hel•lo \hə-ˈlō, he-\ *n, pl* **hellos** : an expression of greeting — used interjectionally
helm \ˈhelm\ *n* **1** : a lever or wheel for steering a ship **2** : a position of control
hel•met \ˈhel-mət\ *n* : a protective covering for the head
helms•man \ˈhelmz-mən\ *n* : the person at the helm : STEERSMAN
hel•ot \ˈhe-lət\ *n* : SLAVE, SERF
¹**help** \ˈhelp\ *vb* **1** : AID, ASSIST **2** : IMPROVE, RELIEVE **3** : to be of use; *also* : PROMOTE **4** : to change for the better **5** : to refrain from; *also* : PREVENT **6** : to serve with food or drink ⟨~ yourself⟩ — **help•er** *n*
²**help** *n* **1** : AID, ASSISTANCE; *also* : a source of aid **2** : REMEDY, RELIEF **3** : one who assists another **4** : EMPLOYEE — **help•ful** \-fəl\ *adj* — **help•ful•ly** *adv* — **help•ful•ness** *n* — **help•less** *adj* — **help•less•ly** *adv* — **help•less•ness** *n*
helper T cell *n* : a T cell of the immune system that has a protein on its surface to which HIV attaches and that is reduced to 20 percent or less of normal numbers in AIDS
help•ing *n* : a portion of food
help•mate \ˈhelp-ˌmāt\ *n* **1** : HELPER **2** : WIFE
help•meet \-ˌmēt\ *n* : HELPMATE
hel•ter–skel•ter \ˌhel-tər-ˈskel-tər\ *adv* **1** : in undue haste or disorder **2** : HAPHAZARDLY
helve \ˈhelv\ *n* : a handle of a tool or weapon
Hel•ve•tian \hel-ˈvē-shən\ *adj* : SWISS — **Helvetian** *n*
¹**hem** \ˈhem\ *n* **1** : a border of an article (as of cloth) doubled back and stitched down **2** : RIM, MARGIN
²**hem** *vb* **hemmed; hem•ming 1** : to make a hem in sewing; *also* : BORDER, EDGE **2** : to surround restrictively
he–man \ˈhē-ˌman\ *n* : a strong virile man
he•ma•tite \ˈhē-mə-ˌtīt\ *n* : a mineral that consists of an oxide of iron and that constitutes an important iron ore
he•ma•tol•o•gy \ˌhē-mə-ˈtä-lə-jē\ *n* : a branch of biology that deals with the blood and blood-forming organs — **he•ma•to•log•ic** \-tə-ˈlä-jik\ *also* **he•ma•to•log•i•cal** \-ji-kəl\ *adj* — **he•ma•tol•o•gist** \-ˈtä-lə-jist\ *n*
heme \ˈhēm\ *n* : the deep red iron-containing part of hemoglobin
hemi•sphere \ˈhe-mə-ˌsfir\ *n* **1** : one of the halves of the earth as divided by the equator into northern and southern parts (**northern hemisphere, southern hemisphere**) or by a meridian into two parts so that one half (**eastern hemisphere**) to the east of the Atlantic ocean includes Europe, Asia, and Africa and the half (**western hemisphere**) to the west includes

No. and So. America and surrounding waters **2** : either of two half spheres formed by a plane through the sphere's center — **hemi•spher•ic** \ˌhe-mə-ˈsfir-ik, -ˈsfer-\ *or* **hemi•spher•i•cal** \-ˈsfir-i-kəl, -ˈsfer-\ *adj*

hem•line \ˈhem-ˌlīn\ *n* : the line formed by the lower edge of a garment

hem•lock \ˈhem-ˌläk\ *n* **1** : any of several poisonous herbs related to the carrot **2** : an evergreen tree related to the pines; *also* : its soft light wood

he•mo•glo•bin \ˈhē-mə-ˌglō-bən\ *n* : an iron-containing compound found in red blood cells that carries oxygen from the lungs to the body tissues

he•mo•phil•ia \ˌhē-mə-ˈfi-lē-ə\ *n* : a hereditary blood defect usu. of males that slows blood clotting with resulting difficulty in stopping bleeding — **he•mo•phil•i•ac** \-lē-ˌak\ *adj or n*

hem•or•rhage \ˈhem-rij, ˈhe-mə-\ *n* : a large discharge of blood from the blood vessels — **hemorrhage** *vb* — **hem•or•rhag•ic** \ˌhe-mə-ˈra-jik\ *adj*

hem•or•rhoid \ˈhem-ˌrȯid, ˈhe-mə-\ *n* : a swollen mass of dilated veins at or just within the anus — usu. used in pl.

hemp \ˈhemp\ *n* : a tall widely grown Asian herb related to the mulberry that is the source of a tough fiber used in rope and of marijuana and hashish from its flowers and leaves; *also* : the fiber — **hemp•en** \ˈhem-pən\ *adj*

hem•stitch \ˈhem-ˌstich\ *vb* : to embroider (fabric) by drawing out parallel threads and stitching the exposed threads in groups to form designs

hen \ˈhen\ *n* : a female chicken esp. over a year old; *also* : a female bird

hence \ˈhens\ *adv* **1** : AWAY **2** : from this time **3** : CONSEQUENTLY **4** : from this source or origin

hence•forth \hens-ˌfōrth\ *adv* : from this point on

hence•for•ward \-ˈfȯr-wərd\ *adv* : HENCEFORTH

hench•man \ˈhench-mən\ *n* [ME *hengestman* groom, fr. *hengest* stallion] : a trusted follower or supporter

hen•na \ˈhe-nə\ *n* **1** : an Old World tropical shrub with fragrant white flowers; *also* : a reddish brown dye obtained from its leaves and used esp. on hair **2** : the color of henna dye

hen•peck \ˈhen-ˌpek\ *vb* : to nag and boss one's husband

hep \ˈhep\ *adj* : HIP

hep•a•rin \ˈhe-pə-rən\ *n* : a compound found esp. in liver that slows the clotting of blood and is used medically

he•pat•ic \hi-ˈpa-tik\ *adj* : of, relating to, or associated with the liver

he•pat•i•ca \hi-ˈpa-ti-kə\ *n* : any of a genus of herbs related to the buttercups that have lobed leaves and delicate white, pink, or bluish flowers

hep•a•ti•tis \ˌhe-pə-ˈtī-təs\ *n, pl* **-tit•i•des** \-ˈti-tə-ˌdēz\ : inflammation of the liver; *also* : a virus disease of which this is a feature

hep•tam•e•ter \hep-ˈta-mə-tər\ *n* : a line of verse containing seven metrical feet

[1]her \ˈhər\ *adj* : of or relating to her or herself

[2]her *pron, objective case of* SHE

[1]her•ald \ˈher-əld\ *n* **1** : an official crier or messenger **2** : HARBINGER **3** : ANNOUNCER **4** : ADVOCATE

[2]herald *vb* **1** : to give notice of **2** : HAIL, GREET; *also* : PUBLICIZE

he•ral•dic \he-ˈral-dik, hə-\ *adj* : of or relating to heralds or heraldry

her•ald•ry \ˈher-əl-drē\ *n, pl* **-ries 1** : the practice of devising and granting armorial insignia and of tracing genealogies **2** : INSIGNIA **3** : PAGEANTRY

herb \ˈərb, ˈhərb\ *n* **1** : a seed plant that lacks woody tissue and dies to the ground at the end of a growing season **2** : a plant or plant part valued for medicinal or savory qualities — **her•ba•ceous** \ˌər-ˈbā-shəs, ˌhər-\ *adj*

herb•age \ˈər-bij, ˈhər-\ *n* : green plants esp. when used or fit for grazing

herb•al•ist \ˈər-bə-list, ˈhər-\ *n* **1** : one who practices healing by the use of herbs **2** : one who collects or grows herbs

her•bar•i•um \ˌər-ˈbar-ē-əm, ˌhər-\ *n, pl* **-ia** \-ē-ə\ **1** : a collection of dried plant specimens **2** : a place that houses an herbarium

her•bi•cide \ˈər-bə-ˌsīd, ˈhər-\ *n* : an agent used to destroy or inhibit plant growth — **her•bi•cid•al** \ˌər-bə-ˈsīd-ᵊl, ˌhər-\ *adj*

her•biv•o•rous \ˌər-ˈbi-və-rəs, ˌhər-\ *adj* : feeding on plants — **her•bi•vore** \ˈər-bə-ˌvōr, ˈhər-\ *n*

her•cu•le•an \ˌhər-kyə-ˈlē-ən, ˌhər-ˈkyü-lē-\ *adj, often cap* [*Hercules*, hero of Greek myth renowned for his strength] : of extraordinary power, size, or difficulty

[1]herd \ˈhərd\ *n* **1** : a group of animals of one kind kept or living together **2** : a group of people with a common bond **3** : MOB

[2]herd *vb* : to assemble or move in a herd — **herd•er** *n*

herds•man \ˈhərdz-mən\ *n* : one who manages, breeds, or tends livestock

[1]here \ˈhir\ *adv* **1** : in or at this place; *also* : NOW **2** : at or in this point, particular, or case **3** : in the present life or state **4** : to this place

[2]here *n* : this place ⟨get away from ~⟩

here•abouts \ˈhir-ə-ˌbau̇ts\ *or* **here•about** \-ˌbau̇t\ *adv* : in this vicinity

[1]here•af•ter \hir-ˈaf-tər\ *adv* **1** : after this in sequence or in time **2** : in some future time or state

[2]hereafter *n, often cap* **1** : FUTURE **2** : an existence beyond earthly life

here•by \hir-ˈbī\ *adv* : by means of this

he•red•i•tary \hə-ˈre-də-ˌter-ē\ *adj* **1** : genetically passed or passable from parent to offspring **2** : passing by inheritance; *also* : having title or possession through inheritance **3** : of a kind established by tradition

he•red•i•ty \-də-tē\ *n* : the qualities and potentialities genetically derived from one's ancestors; *also* : the passing of these from ancestor to descendant

Here•ford \ˈhər-fərd\ *n* : any of a breed of red-coated beef cattle with white faces and markings

here•in \hir-ˈin\ *adv* : in this

here•of \-ˈəv, -ˈäv\ *adv* : of this

here•on \-ˈȯn, -ˈän\ *adv* : on this

her•e•sy \ˈher-ə-sē\ *n, pl* **-sies** [ME *heresie*, fr. OF, fr. LL *haeresis*, fr. LGk *hairesis*, fr. Gk, action of taking, choice, sect, fr. *hairein* to take] **1** : adherence to a religious opinion contrary to church dogma **2** : an opinion or doctrine contrary to church dogma **3** : dissent from a dominant theory, opinion, or practice — **her•e•tic** \-ˌtik\ *n* — **he•ret•i•cal** \hə-ˈre-ti-kəl\ *adj*

here•to \hir-ˈtü\ *adv* : to this document

here•to•fore \ˈhir-tə-ˌfōr\ *adv* : up to this time

here•un•der \hir-ˈən-dər\ *adv* : under this or according to this writing

here•un•to \hir-ˈən-tü\ *adv* : to this

here•upon \ˈhir-ə-ˌpȯn, -ˌpän\ *adv* : on this or immediately after this

here•with \ˈhir-ˈwith, -ˈwith\ *adv* **1** : with this **2** : HEREBY

her•i•ta•ble \ˈher-ə-tə-bəl\ *adj* : capable of being inherited

her•i•tage \ˈher-ə-tij\ *n* **1** : property that descends to an heir **2** : LEGACY **3** : BIRTHRIGHT

her•maph•ro•dite \(ˌ)hər-ˈma-frə-ˌdīt\ *n* : an animal or plant having both male and female reproductive organs — **hermaphrodite** *adj* — **her•maph•ro•dit•ic** \(ˌ)hər-ˌma-frə-ˈdi-tik\ *adj*

her•met•ic \hər-ˈme-tik\ *also* **her•met•i•cal** \-ti-kəl\ *adj* : AIRTIGHT — **her•met•i•cal•ly** \-ti-k(ə-)lē\ *adv*

her•mit \ˈhər-mət\ *n* [ME *eremite*, fr. OF, fr. LL *eremita*, fr. LGk *erēmitēs*, fr. Gk, adj., living in the desert, fr. *erēmia* desert, fr. *erēmos* desolate] : one who lives in solitude esp. for religious reasons

her•mit•age \-mə-tij\ *n* **1** : the dwelling of a hermit **2** : a secluded dwelling

her•nia \ˈhər-nē-ə\ *n, pl* **-ni•as** *or* **-ni•ae** \-nē-ˌē, -nē-ˌī\ : a protrusion of a bodily part (as a loop of intestine) into a pouch of the weakened wall of a cavity in which it is normally enclosed — **her•ni•ate** \-nē-ˌāt\ *vb* — **her•ni•a•tion** \ˌhər-nē-ˈā-shən\ *n*

he•ro \ˈhē-rō\ *n, pl* **heroes 1** : a mythological or legendary figure of great strength or ability **2** : a man admired for his achievements and qualities **3** : the chief male character in a literary or dramatic work **4** *pl usu* **heros** : SUBMARINE 2 — **he•ro•ic** \hi-ˈrō-ik\ *adj* — **he•ro•i•cal•ly** \-i-k(ə-)lē\ *adv*

heroic couplet *n* : a rhyming couplet in iambic pentameter

he•ro•ics \hi-ˈrō-iks\ *n pl* : heroic or showy behavior

her•o•in \ˈher-ə-wən\ *n* : an illicit addictive narcotic drug made from morphine

her•o•ine \ˈher-ə-wən\ *n* **1** : a woman admired for her achievements and qualities **2** : the chief female character in a literary or dramatic work

her•o•ism \ˈher-ə-ˌwi-zəm\ *n* **1** : heroic conduct **2** : the qualities of a hero **syn** valor, prowess, gallantry

her•on \ˈher-ən\ *n, pl* **herons** *also* **heron** : any of various long-legged long-billed wading birds with soft plumage

her•pes \ˈhər-pēz\ *n* : any of several virus diseases characterized by the formation of blisters on the skin or mucous membranes

herpes sim•plex \-ˈsim-ˌpleks\ *n* : either of two virus diseases marked in one by watery blisters above the waist (as on the mouth and lips) and in the other on the sex organs

herpes zos•ter \-ˈzäs-tər\ *n* : SHINGLES

her•pe•tol•o•gy \ˌhər-pə-ˈtä-lə-jē\ *n* : a branch of zoology dealing with reptiles and amphibians — **her•pe•tol•o•gist** \ˌhər-pə-ˈtä-lə-jist\ *n*

her•ring \ˈher-iŋ\ *n, pl* **herring** *or* **herrings** : a valuable narrow-bodied food fish of the north Atlantic; *also* : a related fish of the north Pacific harvested esp. for its roe

her•ring•bone \ˈher-iŋ-ˌbōn\ *n* : a pattern made up of rows of parallel lines with adjacent rows slanting in reverse directions; *also* : a twilled fabric with this pattern

hers \ˈhərz\ *pron* : one or the ones belonging to her

her•self \hər-ˈself\ *pron* : SHE, HER — used reflexively, for emphasis, or in absolute constructions

hertz \ˈhərts, ˈherts\ *n, pl* **hertz** : a unit of frequency equal to one cycle per second

hes•i•tant \ˈhe-zə-tənt\ *adj* : tending to hesitate — **hes•i•tance** \-təns\ *n* — **hes•i•tan•cy** \-tən-sē\ *n* — **hes•i•tant•ly** *adv*

hes•i•tate \ˈhe-zə-ˌtāt\ *vb* **-tat•ed; -tat•ing 1** : to hold back (as in doubt) **2** : PAUSE **syn** waver, vacillate, falter, shilly-shally — **hes•i•ta•tion** \ˌhe-zə-ˈtā-shən\ *n*

het•ero•dox \ˈhe-tə-rə-ˌdäks\ *adj* **1** : differing from an acknowledged standard **2** : holding unorthodox opinions — **het•er•o•doxy** \-ˌdäk-sē\ *n*

het•er•o•ge•neous \ˌhe-tə-rə-ˈjē-nē-əs, -nyəs\ *adj* : consisting of dissimilar ingredients or constituents : MIXED — **het•er•o•ge•ne•ity** \-jə-ˈnē-ə-tē\ *n* — **het•er•o•ge•neous•ly** *adv*

het•ero•sex•u•al \ˌhe-tə-rō-ˌsek-shə-wəl\ *adj* **1** : of, relating to, or marked by sexual interest in the opposite sex; *also* : of, relating to, or involving sexual intercourse between members of opposite sex **2** : of or relating to different sexes — **heterosexual** *n* — **het•ero•sex•u•al•i•ty** \-ˌsek-shə-ˈwa-lə-tē\ *n*

hew \ˈhyü\ *vb* **hewed; hewed** *or* **hewn** \ˈhyün\; **hew•ing 1** : to cut or fell with blows (as of an ax) **2** : to give shape to with or as if with an ax **3** : to conform strictly — **hew•er** *n*

HEW *abbr* Department of Health, Education, and Welfare

[1]**hex** \ˈheks\ *vb* **1** : to practice witchcraft **2** : JINX

[2]**hex** *n* : SPELL, JINX

[3]**hex** *adj* : HEXAGONAL

[4]**hex** *abbr* hexagon

hexa•gon \ˈhek-sə-ˌgän\ *n* : a polygon having six angles and six sides — **hex•ag•o•nal** \hek-ˈsa-gən-ᵊl\ *adj*

hex•am•e•ter \hek-ˈsa-mə-tər\ *n* : a line of verse containing six metrical feet

hey•day \ˈhā-ˌdā\ *n* : a period of greatest strength, vigor, or prosperity

hf *abbr* half

Hf *symbol* hafnium

HF *abbr* high frequency

hg *abbr* hectogram

Hg *symbol* [NL *hydrargyrum,* lit., water silver] mercury

hgt *abbr* height

hgwy *abbr* highway

HH *abbr* **1** Her Highness **2** His Highness **3** His Holiness

HHS *abbr* Department of Health and Human Services

HI *abbr* **1** Hawaii **2** humidity index

hi•a•tus \hī-ˈā-təs\ *n* [L, fr. *hiare* to yawn] **1** : a break in an object : GAP **2** : a lapse in continuity

hi•ba•chi \hi-ˈbä-chē\ *n* [Jp] : a charcoal brazier

hi•ber•nate \ˈhī-bər-ˌnāt\ *vb* **-nat•ed; -nat•ing** : to pass the winter in a torpid or resting state — **hi•ber•na•tion** \ˌhī-bər-ˈnā-shən\ *n* — **hi•ber•na•tor** \ˈhī-bər-ˌnā-tər\ *n*

hi•bis•cus \hī-ˈbis-kəs, hə-\ *n* : any of a genus of herbs, shrubs, and trees related to the mallows and noted for large showy flowers

hic•cup *also* **hic•cough** \ˈhi-(ˌ)kəp\ *n* : a spasmodic breathing movement checked by sudden closing of the glottis accompanied by a peculiar sound; *also, pl* : an attack of hiccuping — **hiccup** *vb*

hick \ˈhik\ *n* [*Hick,* nickname for *Richard*] : an awkward provincial person — **hick** *adj*

hick•o•ry \ˈhi-kə-rē\ *n, pl* **-ries** : any of a genus of No. American hardwood trees related to the walnuts; *also* : the wood of a hickory — **hickory** *adj*

hi•dal•go \hi-ˈdal-gō\ *n, pl* **-gos** *often cap* [Sp, fr. earlier *fijo dalgo,* lit., son of something] : a member of the lower nobility of Spain

hidden tax *n* **1** : a tax ultimately paid by someone other than the person on whom it is formally levied **2** : an economic injustice that reduces one's income or buying power

[1]**hide** \ˈhīd\ *vb* **hid** \ˈhid\; **hid•den** \ˈhid-ᵊn\ *or* **hid; hid•ing 1** : to put or remain out of sight **2** : to conceal for shelter or protection; *also* : to seek protection **3** : to keep secret **4** : to turn away in shame or anger — **hid•er** *n*

[2]**hide** *n* : the skin of an animal

hide–and–seek \ˌhīd-ᵊn-ˈsēk\ *n* : a children's game in which everyone hides from one player who tries to find them

hide•away \ˈhī-də-ˌwā\ *n* : HIDEOUT

hide•bound \ˈhīd-ˌbau̇nd\ *adj* : being inflexible or conservative

hid•eous \ˈhi-dē-əs\ *adj* [ME *hidous,* fr. OF, fr. *hisde, hide* terror] **1** : offensive to one of the senses : UGLY **2** : morally offensive : SHOCKING **syn** ghastly, grisly, gruesome, horrible, lurid, macabre — **hid•eous•ly** *adv* — **hid•eous•ness** *n*

hide•out \ˈhī-ˌdau̇t\ *n* : a place of refuge or concealment

hie \ˈhī\ *vb* **hied; hy•ing** *or* **hie•ing** : HASTEN

hi•er•ar•chy \ˈhī-ə-ˌrär-kē\ *n, pl* **-chies 1** : a ruling body of clergy organized into ranks **2** : persons or things arranged in a graded series — **hi•er•ar•chi•cal** \ˌhī-ə-ˈrär-ki-kəl\ *adj* — **hi•er•ar•chi•cal•ly** \-k(ə-)lē\ *adv*

hi•er•o•glyph•ic \ˌhī-ə-rə-ˈgli-fik\ *n* [MF *hieroglyphique,* adj., ultim. fr. Gk *hieroglyphikos,* fr. *hieros* sacred + *glyphein* to carve] **1** : a character in a system of picture writing (as of the ancient Egyptians) **2** : a symbol or sign difficult to decipher

hieroglyphic 1

hi–fi \ˈhī-ˈfī\ *n* **1** : HIGH FIDELITY **2** : equipment for reproduction of sound with high fidelity

hig•gle•dy–pig•gle•dy \ˌhi-gəl-dē-ˈpi-gəl-dē\ *adv* : in confusion

[1]high \ˈhī\ *adj* **1** : ELEVATED; *also* : TALL **2** : advanced toward fullness or culmination; *also* : slightly tainted **3** : advanced esp. in complexity ⟨∼*er* mathematics⟩ **4** : long past **5** : SHRILL, SHARP **6** : far from the equator ⟨∼ latitudes⟩ **7** : exalted in character **8** : of greater degree, size, or amount than average ⟨∼ in cholesterol⟩ **9** : of relatively great importance **10** : FORCIBLE, STRONG ⟨∼ winds⟩ **11** : showing elation or excitement **12** : INTOXICATED; *also* : excited or stupefied by or as if by a drug — **high•ly** *adv*

[2]high *adv* **1** : at or to a high place or degree **2** : LUXURIOUSLY ⟨living ∼⟩

[3]high *n* **1** : an elevated place **2** : a region of high barometric pressure **3** : a high point or level **4** : the gear of a vehicle giving the highest speed **5** : an excited or stupefied state produced by or as if by a drug

high•ball \ˈhī-ˌbȯl\ *n* : a usu. tall drink of liquor mixed with water or a carbonated beverage

high beam *n* : the long-range focus of a vehicle headlight

high•born \ˈhī-ˈbȯrn\ *adj* : of noble birth

high•boy \-ˌbȯi\ *n* : a high chest of drawers mounted on a base with legs

high•bred \-ˈbred\ *adj* : coming from superior stock

high•brow \-ˌbrau̇\ *n* : a person of superior learning or culture — **highbrow** *adj* — **high•brow•ism** \-ˌbrau̇-ˌi-zəm\ *n*

high–density li•po•pro•tein \-ˌlī-pō-ˈprō-tēn, -ˌli-\ *n* : HDL

high•er–up \ˌhī-ər-ˈəp\ *n* : a superior officer or official

high•fa•lu•tin \ˌhī-fə-ˈlüt-ᵊn\ *adj* : PRETENTIOUS, POMPOUS

high fashion *n* **1** : HIGH STYLE **2** : HAUTE COUTURE

high fidelity *n* : the reproduction of sound or image with a high degree of faithfulness to the original

high five *n* : a slapping of upraised right hands by two people (as in celebration) — **high–five** *vb*

high–flown \ˈhī-ˈflōn\ *adj* **1** : EXALTED **2** : BOMBASTIC

high frequency *n* : a radio frequency between 3 and 30 megahertz

high gear *n* **1** : HIGH 4 **2** : a state of intense or maximum activity

high–hand•ed \ˈhī-ˈhan-dəd\ *adj* : OVERBEARING — **high–hand•ed•ly** *adv* — **high–hand•ed•ness** *n*

high–hat \-ˈhat\ *adj* : SUPERCILIOUS, SNOBBISH — **high–hat** *vb*

high•land \ˈhī-lənd\ *n* : elevated or mountainous land

high•land•er \-lən-dər\ *n* **1** : an inhabitant of a highland **2** *cap* : an inhabitant of the Scottish Highlands

[1]high•light \-ˌlīt\ *n* : an event or detail of major importance

[2]highlight *vb* **1** : EMPHASIZE **2** : to constitute a highlight of

high–mind•ed \-ˈmīn-dəd\ *adj* : marked by elevated principles and feelings — **high–mind•ed•ness** *n*

high•ness \ˈhī-nəs\ *n* **1** : the quality or state of being high **2** — used as a title (as for kings)

high–pres•sure \-ˈpre-shər\ *adj* : using or involving aggressive and insistent sales techniques

high–rise \-ˈrīz\ *adj* : having several stories and being equipped with elevators ⟨∼ apartments⟩; *also* : of or relating to high-rise buildings

high road *n* : HIGHWAY

high school *n* : a school usu. including grades 9 to 12 or 10 to 12

high sea *n* : the open sea outside territorial waters — usu. used in pl.

high–sound•ing \ˈhī-ˈsau̇n-diŋ\ *adj* : POMPOUS, IMPOSING

high–spir•it•ed \-ˈspir-ə-təd\ *adj* : characterized by a bold or energetic spirit

high–strung \-ˈstrəŋ\ *adj* : having an extremely nervous or sensitive temperament

high style *n* : the newest in fashion or design

high•tail \ˈhī-ˌtāl\ *vb* : to retreat at full speed

high tech \-ˈtek\ *n* : HIGH TECHNOLOGY

high technology *n* : technology involving the use of advanced devices

high–ten•sion \ˈhī-ˈten-chən\ *adj* : having or using a high voltage

high–test \-ˈtest\ *adj* : having a high octane number

high–toned \-ˈtōnd\ *adj* **1** : high in social, moral, or intellectual quality **2** : PRETENTIOUS, POMPOUS

high•way \ˈhī-ˌwā\ *n* : a main direct road

high•way•man \ˈhī-ˌwā-mən\ *n* : a person who robs travelers on a road

hi•jack *also* **high•jack** \ˈhī-ˌjak\ *vb* : to steal esp. by stopping a vehicle on the highway; *also* : to commandeer a flying airplane — **hijack** *n* — **hi•jack•er** *n*

[1]hike \ˈhīk\ *vb* **hiked; hik•ing 1** : to move or raise with a sudden motion **2** : to take a long walk — **hik•er** *n*

[2]hike *n* **1** : a long walk **2** : RISE, INCREASE

hi•lar•i•ous \hi-ˈlar-ē-əs, hī-\ *adj* : marked by or providing boisterous merriment — **hi•lar•i•ous•ly** *adv* — **hi•lar•i•ty** \-ə-tē\ *n*

hill \ˈhil\ *n* **1** : a usu. rounded elevation of land **2** : a little heap or mound (as of earth) — **hilly** *adj*

hill•bil•ly \ˈhil-ˌbi-lē\ *n, pl* **-lies** : a person from a backwoods area

hill•ock \ˈhi-lək\ *n* : a small hill

hill•side \ˈhil-ˌsīd\ *n* : the part of a hill between the summit and the foot

hill•top \-ˌtäp\ *n* : the top of a hill

hilt \ˈhilt\ *n* : a handle esp. of a sword or dagger

him \ˈhim\ *pron, objective case of* HE

Hi•ma•la•yan \ˌhi-mə-ˈlā-ən, hi-ˈmäl-yən\ *adj* : of, relating to, or characteristic of the Himalaya mountains or the people living there

him•self \him-ˈself\ *pron* : HE, HIM — used reflexively, for emphasis, or in absolute constructions

[1]hind \ˈhīnd\ *n, pl* **hinds** *also* **hind** : a female of a common Eurasian deer

[2]hind *adj* : REAR

[1]hin•der \ˈhin-dər\ *vb* **1** : to impede the progress of **2** : to hold back **syn** obstruct, block, bar, impede

[2]hind•er \ˈhīn-dər\ *adj* : HIND

Hin•di \ˈhin-dē\ *n* : a literary and official language of northern India

hind•most \ˈhīnd-ˌmōst\ *adj* : farthest to the rear

hind•quar•ter \-ˌkwȯr-tər\ *n* **1** : one side of the back half of the carcass of a quadruped **2** *pl* : the part of the body of a quadruped behind the junction of hind limbs and trunk

hin•drance \ˈhin-drəns\ *n* **1** : the state of being hindered; *also* : the action of hindering **2** : IMPEDIMENT 1

hind•sight \ˈhīnd-ˌsīt\ *n* : understanding of an event after it has happened

Hindu–Arabic *adj* : relating to, being, or composed of Arabic numerals

Hin•du•ism \ˈhin-dü-ˌi-zəm\ *n* : a body of religious beliefs and practices native to India — **Hin•du** *n or adj*

hind wing *n* : either of the posterior wings of a 4-winged insect

[1]hinge \ˈhinj\ *n* : a jointed device on which a swinging part (as a door, gate, or lid) turns

[2]hinge *vb* **hinged; hing•ing 1** : to attach by or furnish with hinges **2** : to be contingent on a single consideration

hint \ˈhint\ *n* **1** : an indirect or summary suggestion **2**

: CLUE **3** : a very small amount **syn** dash, soupçon, suspicion, tincture, touch — **hint** *vb*

hin•ter•land \ˈhin-tər-ˌland\ *n* **1** : a region behind a coast **2** : a region remote from cities

[1]**hip** \ˈhip\ *n* : the fruit of a rose

[2]**hip** *n* **1** : the part of the body on either side below the waist consisting of the side of the pelvis and the upper thigh **2** : HIP JOINT

[3]**hip** *adj* **hip•per; hip•pest** : keenly aware of or interested in the newest developments or styles — **hip•ness** *n*

[4]**hip** *vb* **hipped; hip•ping** : TELL, INFORM

hip•bone \ˈhip-ˈbōn, -ˌbōn\ *n* : the large flaring bone that makes a lateral half of the pelvis in mammals

hip joint *n* : the articulation between the femur and the hipbone

hipped \ˈhipt\ *adj* : having hips esp. of a specified kind ⟨broad-*hipped*⟩

hip•pie *or* **hip•py** \ˈhi-pē\ *n, pl* **hippies** : a usu. young person who rejects established mores, advocates nonviolence, and often uses psychedelic drugs or marijuana; *also* : a long-haired unconventionally dressed young person

hip•po \ˈhi-pō\ *n, pl* **hippos** : HIPPOPOTAMUS

hip•po•drome \ˈhi-pə-ˌdrōm\ *n* : an arena for equestrian performances

hip•po•pot•a•mus \ˌhi-pə-ˈpä-tə-məs\ *n, pl* **-mus•es** *or* **-mi** \-ˌmī\ [L, fr. Gk *hippopotamos,* alter. of *hippos potamios,* lit., river horse] : a large thick-skinned river mammal of sub-Saharan Africa that is related to the swine

[1]**hire** \ˈhīr\ *n* **1** : payment for labor or personal services : WAGES **2** : EMPLOYMENT **3** : one who is hired

[2]**hire** *vb* **hired; hir•ing 1** : to employ for pay **2** : to engage the temporary use of for pay **3** : to take employment

hire•ling \ˈhīr-liŋ\ *n* : a hired person; *esp* : one with mercenary motives

hir•sute \ˈhər-ˌsüt, ˈhir-\ *adj* : HAIRY

[1]**his** \ˈhiz\ *adj* : of or relating to him or himself

[2]**his** *pron* : one or the ones belonging to him

His•pan•ic \hi-ˈspa-nik\ *adj* : of, relating to, or being a person of Latin-American descent living in the U.S. — **Hispanic** *n*

hiss \ˈhis\ *vb* : to make a sharp sibilant sound; *also* : to express disapproval of by hissing — **hiss** *n*

hist *abbr* historian; historical; history

his•ta•mine \ˈhis-tə-ˌmēn, -mən\ *n* : a compound widespread in animal tissues that plays a major role in allergic reactions (as hay fever)

his•to•gram \ˈhis-tə-ˌgram\ *n* : a representation of statistical data by rectangles whose widths represent class intervals and whose heights usu. represent corresponding frequencies

his•to•ri•an \hi-ˈstōr-ē-ən\ *n* : a student or writer of history

his•to•ric•i•ty \ˌhis-tə-ˈri-sə-tē\ *n* : historical actuality

his•to•ri•og•ra•pher \hi-ˌstōr-ē-ˈä-grə-fər\ *n* : HISTORIAN

his•to•ry \ˈhis-tə-rē\ *n, pl* **-ries** [L *historia,* fr. Gk, inquiry, history, fr. *histōr, istōr* knowing, learned] **1** : a chronological record of significant events often with an explanation of their causes **2** : a branch of knowledge that records and explains past events **3** : events that form the subject matter of history **4** : an established record ⟨a convict's ~ of violence⟩ — **his•tor•ic** \hi-ˈstȯr-ik\ *adj* — **his•tor•i•cal** \-i-kəl\ *adj* — **his•tor•i•cal•ly** \-k(ə-)lē\ *adv*

his•tri•on•ic \ˌhis-trē-ˈä-nik\ *adj* [LL *histrionicus,* fr. L *histrio* actor] **1** : deliberately affected **2** : of or relating to actors, acting, or the theater — **his•tri•on•i•cal•ly** \-ni-k(ə-)lē\ *adv*

his•tri•on•ics \-niks\ *n pl* **1** : theatrical performances **2** : deliberate display of emotion for effect

[1]**hit** \ˈhit\ *vb* **hit; hit•ting 1** : to reach with a blow : STRIKE; *also* : to arrive with a force like a blow ⟨the storm ~⟩ **2** : to make or bring into contact : COLLIDE **3** : to affect detrimentally ⟨was ~ by the flu⟩ **4** : to make a request of **5** : to come upon **6** : to accord with : SUIT **7** : REACH, ATTAIN **8** : to indulge in often to excess — **hit•ter** *n*

[2]**hit** *n* **1** : an act or instance of hitting or being hit **2** : a great success **3** : BASE HIT **4** : a dose of an illegal drug **5** : a murder committed by a gangster

[1]**hitch** \ˈhich\ *vb* **1** : to move by jerks **2** : to catch or fasten esp. by a hook or knot **3** : HITCHHIKE

[2]**hitch** *n* **1** : JERK, PULL **2** : a sudden halt **3** : a connection between something towed and its mover **4** : KNOT

hitch•hike \ˈhich-ˌhīk\ *vb* : to travel by securing free rides from passing vehicles — **hitch•hik•er** *n*

[1]**hith•er** \ˈhi-t͟hər\ *adv* : to this place

[2]**hither** *adj* : being on the near or adjacent side

hith•er•to \-ˌtü\ *adv* : up to this time

HIV \ˌāch-(ˌ)ī-ˈvē\ *n* [*h*uman *i*mmunodeficiency *v*irus] : any of several retroviruses that infect and destroy helper T cells causing the great reduction in their numbers diagnostic of AIDS

hive \ˈhīv\ *n* **1** : a container for housing honeybees **2** : a colony of bees **3** : a place swarming with busy occupants — **hive** *vb*

hives \ˈhīvz\ *n sing or pl* : an allergic disorder marked by raised itching patches on the skin or mucous membranes

hl *abbr* hectoliter

HL *abbr* House of Lords

hm *abbr* hectometer

HM *abbr* **1** Her Majesty; Her Majesty's **2** His Majesty; His Majesty's

HMO \ˌāch-(ˌ)em-ˈō\ *n* [*h*ealth *m*aintenance *o*rganization] : a comprehensive health-care organization financed by periodic fixed payments by voluntarily enrolled individuals and families

HMS *abbr* **1** Her Majesty's ship **2** His Majesty's ship

Ho *symbol* holmium

hoa•gie *also* **hoa•gy** \ˈhō-gē\ *n, pl* **hoagies** : SUBMARINE 2

hoard \ˈhōrd\ *n* : a hidden accumulation — **hoard** *vb* — **hoard•er** *n*

hoar•frost \ˈhōr-ˌfrȯst\ *n* : FROST 2

hoarse \ˈhōrs\ *adj* **hoars•er; hoars•est 1** : rough and harsh in sound **2** : having a grating voice — **hoarse•ly** *adv* — **hoarse•ness** *n*

hoary \ˈhōr-ē\ *adj* **hoar•i•er; -est 1** : gray or white with or as if with age **2** : ANCIENT — **hoar•i•ness** \ˈhōr-ē-nəs\ *n*

hoax \ˈhōks\ *n* : an act intended to trick or dupe; *also* : something accepted or established by fraud — **hoax** *vb* — **hoax•er** *n*

hob \ˈhäb\ *n* : MISCHIEF, TROUBLE

[1]**hob•ble** \ˈhä-bəl\ *vb* **hob•bled, hob•bling 1** : to limp along; *also* : to make lame **2** : FETTER

[2]**hobble** *n* **1** : a hobbling movement **2** : something used to hobble an animal

hob•by \ˈhä-bē\ *n, pl* **hobbies** : a pursuit or interest engaged in for relaxation — **hob•by•ist** \-ist\ *n*

hob•by•horse \ˈhä-bē-ˌhȯrs\ *n* **1** : a stick with a horse's head on which children pretend to ride **2** : a toy horse mounted on rockers **3** : a topic to which one constantly reverts

hob•gob•lin \ˈhäb-ˌgäb-lən\ *n* **1** : a mischievous goblin **2** : BOGEY 1

hob•nail \-ˌnāl\ *n* : a short large-headed nail for studding shoe soles — **hob•nailed** \-ˌnāld\ *adj*

hob•nob \-ˌnäb\ *vb* **hob•nobbed; hob•nob•bing** : to associate familiarly

ho•bo \ˈhō-bō\ *n, pl* **hoboes** *also* **hobos** : TRAMP 2

[1]**hock** \ˈhäk\ *n* : a joint or region in the hind limb of a quadruped just above the foot and corresponding to the human ankle

[2]**hock** *n* [D *hok* pen, prison] : PAWN; *also* : DEBT 3 — **hock** *vb*

hock•ey \ˈhä-kē\ *n* **1** : FIELD HOCKEY **2** : ICE HOCKEY

ho•cus–po•cus \ˌhō-kəs-ˈpō-kəs\ *n* **1** : SLEIGHT OF HAND **2** : nonsense or sham used to conceal deception

hod \ˈhäd\ *n* : a long-handled carrier for mortar or bricks

hodge•podge \ˈhäj-ˌpäj\ *n* : a heterogeneous mixture : JUMBLE

hoe \ˈhō\ *n* : a long-handled implement with a thin flat blade used esp. for cultivating, weeding, or loosening the earth around plants — **hoe** *vb*

hoe•cake \ˈhō-ˌkāk\ *n* : a small cornmeal cake

hoe•down \-ˌdau̇n\ *n* **1** : SQUARE DANCE **2** : a gathering featuring hoedowns

[1]**hog** \ˈhȯg, ˈhäg\ *n, pl* **hogs** *also* **hog** **1** : a domestic swine esp. when grown **2** : a selfish, gluttonous, or filthy person — **hog•gish** *adj*

[2]**hog** *vb* **hogged; hog•ging** : to take or hold selfishly

ho•gan \ˈhō-ˌgän\ *n* : a Navajo Indian dwelling usu. made of logs and mud

hogan

hog•back \ˈhȯg-ˌbak, ˈhäg-\ *n* : a ridge with a sharp summit and steep sides

hog•nose snake \ˈhȯg-ˌnōz-, ˈhäg-\ *or* **hog•nosed snake** \-ˌnōzd-\ *n* : any of a genus of rather small harmless stout-bodied No. American snakes that seldom bite but hiss wildly and often play dead when disturbed

hogs•head \ˈhȯgz-ˌhed, ˈhägz-\ *n* **1** : a large cask or barrel **2** : a liquid measure equal to 63 U.S. gallons

hog–tie \ˈhȯg-ˌtī, ˈhäg-\ *vb* **1** : to tie together the feet of ⟨~ a calf⟩ **2** : to make helpless

hog•wash \-ˌwȯsh, -ˌwäsh\ *n* **1** : SWILL, SLOP **2** : NONSENSE, BALONEY

hog–wild \-ˈwīld\ *adj* : lacking in restraint

hoi pol•loi \ˌhȯi-pə-ˈlȯi\ *n pl* [Gk, the many] : the general populace

[1]**hoist** \ˈhȯist\ *vb* : RAISE, LIFT

[2]**hoist** *n* **1** : LIFT **2** : an apparatus for hoisting

hoke \ˈhōk\ *vb* **hoked; hok•ing** : FAKE — usu. used with *up*

hok•ey \ˈhō-kē\ *adj* **hok•i•er; -est** : CORNY; *also* : PHONY

ho•kum \ˈhō-kəm\ *n* : NONSENSE

[1]**hold** \ˈhōld\ *vb* **held** \ˈheld\; **hold•ing** **1** : POSSESS; *also* : KEEP **2** : RESTRAIN **3** : to have a grasp on **4** : to support, remain, or keep in a particular situation or position **5** : SUSTAIN; *also* : RESERVE **6** : BEAR, COMPORT **7** : to maintain in being or action : PERSIST **8** : CONTAIN, ACCOMMODATE **9** : HARBOR, ENTERTAIN; *also* : CONSIDER, REGARD **10** : to carry on by concerted action; *also* : CONVOKE **11** : to occupy esp. by appointment or election **12** : to be valid **13** : HALT, PAUSE — **hold•er** *n* — **hold forth** : to speak at length — **hold to** : to adhere to : MAINTAIN — **hold with** : to agree with or approve of

[2]**hold** *n* **1** : STRONGHOLD **2** : CONFINEMENT; *also* : PRISON **3** : the act or manner of holding : GRIP **4** : a restraining, dominating, or controlling influence **5** : something that may be grasped as a support **6** : an order or indication that something is to be reserved or delayed — **on hold** : in a temporary state of waiting (as during a phone call); *also* : in a state of postponement ⟨plans *on hold*⟩

[3]**hold** *n* **1** : the interior of a ship below decks; *esp* : a ship's cargo deck **2** : an airplane's cargo compartment

hold•ing *n* **1** : land or other property owned **2** : a ruling of a court esp. on an issue of law

holding pattern *n* : a course flown by an aircraft waiting to land

hold out *vb* **1** : to continue to fight or work **2** : to refuse to come to an agreement — **hold•out** \ˈhōl-ˌdau̇t\ *n*

hold•over \ˈhōl-ˌdō-vər\ *n* : one that is held over

hold•up \ˈhōl-ˌdəp\ *n* **1** : DELAY **2** : robbery at the point of a gun

hole \ˈhōl\ *n* **1** : an opening into or through something **2** : a hollow place (as a pit or cave) **3** : DEN, BURROW **4** : a wretched or dingy place **5** : a unit of play from tee to cup in golf **6** : an awkward position — **hole** *vb*

hol•i•day \ˈhä-lə-ˌdā\ *n* [ME, fr. OE *hāligdæg,* fr. *hālig* holy + *dæg* day] **1** : a day set aside for special religious observance **2** : a day of freedom from work; *esp* : one in commemoration of an event **3** : VACATION — **holiday** *vb*

ho•li•ness \ˈhō-lē-nəs\ *n* : the quality or state of being holy — used as a title for various high religious officials

ho•lis•tic \hō-ˈlis-tik\ *adj* : relating to or concerned with integrated wholes or complete systems rather than with the analysis or treatment of separate parts ⟨~ medicine⟩ ⟨~ ecology⟩

hol•ler \ˈhä-lər\ *vb* : to cry out : SHOUT — **holler** *n*

[1]**hol•low** \ˈhä-lō\ *n* **1** : CAVITY, HOLE **2** : a surface depression

[2]**hollow** *adj* **hol•low•er** \ˈhä-lə-wər\; **hol•low•est** \-lə-wəst\ **1** : CONCAVE, SUNKEN **2** : having a cavity within **3** : lacking in real value, sincerity, or substance; *also* : FALSE **4** : MUFFLED ⟨a ~ sound⟩ — **hol•low•ness** *n*

[3]**hollow** *vb* : to make or become hollow

hol•low•ware *or* **hol•lo•ware** \ˈhä-lə-ˌwar\ *n* : vessels (as bowls or cups) with a significant depth and volume

hol•ly \ˈhä-lē\ *n, pl* **hollies** : either of two trees or shrubs with branches of usu. evergreen glossy spiny-margined leaves and red berries

hol•ly•hock \ˈhä-lē-ˌhäk, -ˌhȯk\ *n* [ME *holihoc,* fr. *holi* holy + *hoc* mallow] : a perennial Chinese herb related to the mallows that is widely grown for its tall stalks of showy flowers

hol•mi•um \ˈhōl-mē-əm\ *n* : a metallic chemical element — see ELEMENT table

ho•lo•caust \ˈhä-lə-ˌkȯst, ˈhō-\ *n* **1** : a thorough destruction esp. by fire **2** *often cap* : the killing of European Jews by the Nazis during World War II; *also* : GENOCIDE

Ho•lo•cene \ˈhō-lə-ˌsēn\ *adj* : of, relating to, or being the present geologic epoch — **Holocene** *n*

ho•lo•gram \ˈhō-lə-ˌgram, ˈhä-\ *n* : a three-dimensional image produced by an interference pattern of light (as laser light)

ho•lo•graph \ˈhō-lə-ˌgraf, ˈhä-\ *n* : a document wholly in the handwriting of its author

ho•log•ra•phy \hō-ˈlä-grə-fē\ *n* : the process of making a hologram — **ho•lo•graph•ic** \ˌhō-lə-ˈgra-fik, ˌhä-\ *adj*

Hol•stein \ˈhōl-ˌstēn, -ˌstīn\ *n* : any of a breed of large black-and-white dairy cattle that produce large quantities of comparatively low-fat milk

Hol•stein–Frie•sian \-ˈfrē-zhən\ *n* : HOLSTEIN

hol•ster \ˈhōl-stər\ *n* [D] : a usu. leather case for a firearm

ho•ly \ˈhō-lē\ *adj* **ho•li•er; -est** **1** : worthy of absolute devotion **2** : SACRED **3** : having a divine quality **syn** hallowed, blessed, sanctified, consecrated — **ho•li•ly** \-lə-lē\ *adv*

Holy Spirit *n* : the third person of the Christian Trinity

DICTIONARY

ho•ly•stone \ˈhō-lē-ˌstōn\ *n* : a soft sandstone used to scrub a ship's decks — **holystone** *vb*

hom•age \ˈä-mij, ˈhä-\ *n* [ME, fr. OF *hommage,* fr. *homme* man, vassal, fr. L *homo* human being] : expression of high regard; *also* : TRIBUTE 3

hom•bre \ˈäm-brē, ˈəm-, -ˌbrā\ *n* : GUY, FELLOW

hom•burg \ˈhäm-ˌbərg\ *n* [*Homburg,* Germany] : a man's felt hat with a stiff curled brim and a high crown creased lengthwise

[1]**home** \ˈhōm\ *n* **1** : one's residence; *also* : HOUSE **2** : the social unit formed by a family living together **3** : a congenial environment; *also* : HABITAT **4** : a place of origin **5** : the objective in various games

[2]**home** *vb* **homed; hom•ing 1** : to go or return home **2** : to proceed to or toward a source of radiated energy used as a guide

home•body \ˈhōm-ˌbä-dē\ *n* : one whose life centers in the home

home•boy \-ˌbȯi\ *n* **1** : a boy or man from one's neighborhood, hometown, or region **2** : a fellow member of a youth gang

home•bred \-ˈbred\ *adj* : produced at home : INDIGENOUS

home•com•ing \-ˌkə-miŋ\ *n* **1** : a return home **2** : the return of a group of people esp. on a special occasion to a place formerly frequented

home computer *n* : a small inexpensive microcomputer

home economics *n* : the theory and practice of homemaking

home•grown \ˈhōm-ˈgrōn\ *adj* **1** : grown domestically **2** : LOCAL, INDIGENOUS

home•land \-ˌland\ *n* **1** : native land **2** : an area set aside to be a state for a people of a particular national, cultural, or racial origin

[1]**home•less** \-ləs\ *adj* : having no home or permanent residence

[2]**homeless** *n pl* : persons esp. in urban areas that have no home

home•ly \ˈhōm-lē\ *adj* **home•li•er; -est 1** : FAMILIAR **2** : unaffectedly natural **3** : lacking beauty or proportion — **home•li•ness** \-lē-nəs\ *n*

home•made \ˈhōm-ˌmād\ *adj* : made in the home, on the premises, or by one's own efforts

home•mak•er \-ˌmā-kər\ *n* : one who manages a household esp. as a wife and mother — **home•mak•ing** \-kiŋ\ *n*

ho•me•op•a•thy \ˌhō-mē-ˈä-pə-thē\ *n* : a system of medical practice that treats disease esp. with minute doses of a remedy that would in healthy persons produce symptoms similar to those of the disease treated — **ho•meo•path** \ˈhō-mē-ə-ˌpath\ *n* — **ho•meo•path•ic** \ˌhō-mē-ə-ˈpa-thik\ *adj*

ho•meo•sta•sis \ˌhō-mē-ō-ˈstā-səs\ *n* : the maintence of a relatively stable state of equilibrium between interrelated physiological, psychological, or social factors characteristic of an individual or group — **ho•meo•stat•ic** \-ˈsta-tik\ *adj*

home plate *n* : a slab at the apex of a baseball diamond that a base runner must touch in order to score

hom•er \ˈhō-mər\ *n* : HOME RUN — **homer** *vb*

home•room \ˈhōm-ˌrüm, -ˌrу̇m\ *n* : a classroom where pupils report at the beginning of each school day

home run *n* : a hit in baseball that enables the batter to go around all the bases and score a run

home•school \ˈhōm-ˌskül\ *vb* : to teach school subjects to one's children at home — **home•school•er** \-ˌskü-lər\ *n*

home•sick \ˈhōm-ˌsik\ *adj* : longing for home and family while absent from them — **home•sick•ness** *n*

home•spun \-ˌspən\ *adj* **1** : spun or made at home; *also* : made of a loosely woven usu. woolen or linen fabric **2** : SIMPLE, HOMELY

[1]**home•stead** \-ˌsted\ *n* : the home and land occupied by a family

[2]**homestead** *vb* : to acquire or settle on public land — **home•stead•er** *n*

home•stretch \-ˈstrech\ *n* **1** : the part of a racecourse between the last curve and the winning post **2** : a final stage (as of a project)

[1]**home•ward** \-wərd\ *or* **home•wards** \-wərdz\ *adv* : toward home

[2]**homeward** *adj* : being or going toward home

home•work \-ˌwərk\ *n* **1** : an assignment given a student to be completed outside the classroom **2** : preparatory reading or research

hom•ey \ˈhō-mē\ *adj* **hom•i•er; -est** : characteristic of home

ho•mi•cide \ˈhä-mə-ˌsīd, ˈhō-\ *n* [L *homicida* murderer & *homicidium* manslaughter; both fr. *homo* human being + *caedere* to cut, kill] **1** : a person who kills another **2** : a killing of one human being by another — **hom•i•cid•al** \ˌhä-mə-ˈsīd-ᵊl\ *adj*

hom•i•ly \ˈhä-mə-lē\ *n, pl* **-lies** : SERMON — **hom•i•let•ic** \ˌhä-mə-ˈle-tik\ *adj*

homing pigeon *n* : a racing pigeon trained to return home

hom•i•nid \ˈhä-mə-nəd, -ˌnid\ *n* : any of a family of primate mammals that comprise all living humans and extinct ancestral and related forms — **hominid** *adj*

hom•i•ny \ˈhä-mə-nē\ *n* : hulled corn with the germ removed

ho•mo•ge•neous \ˌhō-mə-ˈjē-nē-əs, -nyəs\ *adj* : of the same or a similar kind; *also* : of uniform structure — **ho•mo•ge•ne•i•ty** \-jə-ˈnē-ə-tē\ *n* — **ho•mo•ge•neous•ly** *adv*

ho•mog•e•nise *Brit var of* HOMOGENIZE

ho•mog•e•nize \hō-ˈmä-jə-ˌnīz, hə-\ *vb* **-nized; -niz•ing 1** : to make homogeneous **2** : to reduce the particles in (as milk) to uniform size and distribute them evenly throughout the liquid — **ho•mog•e•ni•za•tion** \-ˌmä-jə-nə-ˈzā-shən\ *n* — **ho•mog•e•niz•er** *n*

ho•mo•graph \ˈhä-mə-ˌgraf, ˈhō-\ *n* : one of two or more words spelled alike but different in origin, meaning, or pronunciation (as the *bow* of a ship, a *bow* and arrow)

ho•mol•o•gy \hō-ˈmä-lə-jē, hə-\ *n, pl* **-gies 1** : structural likeness between corresponding parts of different plants or animals due to evolution from a common ancestor **2** : structural likeness between different parts of the same individual — **ho•mol•o•gous** \-ˈmä-lə-gəs\ *adj*

hom•onym \ˈhä-mə-ˌnim, ˈhō-\ *n* **1** : HOMOPHONE, HOMOGRAPH **2** : one of two or more words spelled and pronounced alike but different in meaning (as *pool* of water and *pool* the game)

ho•mo•pho•bia \ˈhō-mə-ˈfō-bē-ə\ *n* : irrational fear of, aversion to, or discrimination against homosexuality or homosexuals — **ho•mo•pho•bic** \-ˈfō-bik\ *adj*

ho•mo•phone \ˈhä-mə-ˌfōn, ˈhō-\ *n* : one of two or more words (as *to, too, two*) pronounced alike but different in meaning or derivation or spelling

Ho•mo sa•pi•ens \ˌhō-mō-ˈsā-pē-ənz, -ˈsa-\ *n* : HUMANKIND

ho•mo•sex•u•al \ˌhō-mō-ˈsek-shə-wəl\ *adj* : of, relating to, or marked by sexual interst in the same sex as oneself; *also* : of, relating to, or involving sexual intercourse between members of the same sex — **homosexual** *n* — **ho•mo•sex•u•al•i•ty** \-ˌsek-shə-ˈwa-lə-tē\ *n*

hon *abbr* honor; honorable; honorary

Hon•du•ran \hän-ˈdу̇r-ən\ *or* **Hon•du•ra•ne•an** *or* **Hon•du•ra•ni•an** \ˌhan-dü-ˈrā-nē-ən, -dyü-\ *n* : a native or inhabitant of Honduras — **Honduran** *or* **Honduranean** *or* **Honduranian** *adj*

hone \ˈhōn\ *n* : WHETSTONE — **hone** *vb* — **hon•er** *n*

hone in *vb* : to move toward or direct attention to an objective

[1]**hon•est** \ˈä-nəst\ *adj* **1** : free from deception : TRUTHFUL; *also* : GENUINE, REAL **2** : REPUTABLE **3** : CREDITABLE **4** : marked by integrity **5** : FRANK **syn** upright,

just, conscientious, honorable — **hon•est•ly** *adv* — **hon•es•ty** \-nə-stē\ *n*

²honest *adv* : HONESTLY; *also* : with all sincerity ⟨I didn't do it, ~⟩

hon•ey \ˈhə-nē\ *n, pl* **honeys** : a sweet sticky substance made by honeybees from the nectar of flowers

hon•ey•bee \ˈhə-nē-ˌbē\ *n* : a social and colonial 4-winged insect often kept in hives for the honey it produces

¹hon•ey•comb \-ˌkōm\ *n* : a mass of 6-sided wax cells built by honeybees; *also* : something of similar structure or appearance

²honeycomb *vb* : to make or become full of cavities like a honeycomb

hon•ey•dew \-ˌdü, -ˌdyü\ *n* : a sweetish deposit secreted on plants by aphids, scale insects, or fungi

honeydew melon *n* : a smooth-skinned muskmelon with sweet green flesh

honey locust *n* : a tall usu. spiny No. American leguminous tree with hard durable wood and long twisted pods

hon•ey•moon \ˈhə-nē-ˌmün\ *n* **1** : a period of harmony esp. just after marriage **2** : a holiday taken by a newly married couple — **honeymoon** *vb*

hon•ey•suck•le \ˈhə-nē-ˌsə-kəl\ *n* : any of a genus of shrubs or vines with tube-shaped flowers rich in nectar

honk \ˈhäŋk, ˈhȯŋk\ *n* : the cry of a goose; *also* : a similar sound (as of a horn) — **honk** *vb* — **honker** *n*

hon•ky–tonk \ˈhäŋ-kē-ˌtäŋk, ˈhȯŋ-kē-ˌtȯŋk\ *n* : a tawdry nightclub or dance hall — **honky–tonk** *adj*

¹hon•or \ˈä-nər\ *n* **1** : good name : REPUTATION; *also* : outward respect **2** : PRIVILEGE **3** : a person of superior standing — used esp. as a title **4** : one who brings respect or fame **5** : an evidence or symbol of distinction **6** : CHASTITY, PURITY **7** : INTEGRITY **syn** homage, reverence, deference, obeisance

²honor *vb* **1** : to regard or treat with honor **2** : to confer honor on **3** : to fulfill the terms of; *also* : to accept as payment — **hon•or•ee** \ˌä-nə-ˈrē\ *n* — **hon•or•er** *n*

hon•or•able \ˈä-nə-rə-bəl\ *adj* **1** : deserving of honor **2** : of great renown **3** : accompanied with marks of honor **4** : doing credit to the possessor **5** : characterized by integrity — **hon•or•able•ness** *n* — **hon•or•ably** \-blē\ *adv*

hon•o•rar•i•um \ˌä-nə-ˈrer-ē-əm\ *n, pl* **-ia** \-ē-ə\ *also* **-iums** : a reward usu. for services on which custom or propriety forbids a price to be set

hon•or•ary \ˈä-nə-ˌrer-ē\ *adj* **1** : having or conferring distinction **2** : conferred in recognition of achievement without the usual prerequisites ⟨~ degree⟩ **3** : UNPAID, VOLUNTARY — **hon•or•ari•ly** \ˌä-nə-ˈrer-ə-lē\ *adv*

hon•or•if•ic \ˌä-nə-ˈri-fik\ *adj* : conferring or conveying honor ⟨~ titles⟩

hon•our, hon•our•able *chiefly Brit var of* HONOR, HONORABLE

¹hood \ˈhu̇d\ *n* **1** : a covering for the head and neck and sometimes the face **2** : an ornamental fold (as at the back of an ecclesiastical vestment) **3** : a cover for parts of mechanisms; *esp* : the covering over an automobile engine — **hood•ed** \ˈhu̇-dəd\ *adj*

²hood \ˈhu̇d, ˈhüd\ *n* : HOODLUM

³hood \ˈhu̇d\ *n* : NEIGHBORHOOD 4

-hood \ˌhu̇d\ *n suffix* **1** : state : condition : quality : character ⟨boy*hood*⟩ ⟨hardi*hood*⟩ **2** : instance of a (specified) state or quality ⟨false*hood*⟩ **3** : individuals sharing a (specified) state or character ⟨brother*hood*⟩

hood•lum \ˈhüd-ləm, ˈhu̇d-\ *n* **1** : THUG **2** : a young ruffian

hoo•doo \ˈhü-dü\ *n, pl* **hoodoos** **1** : a body of magical practices traditional esp. among blacks in the southern U.S. **2** : something that brings bad luck — **hoodoo** *vb*

hood•wink \ˈhu̇d-ˌwiŋk\ *vb* : to deceive by false appearance

hoo•ey \ˈhü-ē\ *n* : NONSENSE

hoof \ˈhu̇f, ˈhüf\ *n, pl* **hooves** \ˈhu̇vz, ˈhüvz\ *or* **hoofs** : a horny covering that protects the ends of the toes of ungulate mammals (as horses or cattle); *also* : a hoofed foot — **hoofed** \ˈhu̇ft, ˈhüft\ *adj*

¹hook \ˈhu̇k\ *n* **1** : a curved or bent device for catching, holding, or pulling **2** : something curved or bent like a hook **3** : a flight of a ball (as in golf) that curves in a direction opposite to the dominant hand of the player propelling it **4** : a short punch delivered with a circular motion and with the elbow bent and rigid

²hook *vb* **1** : CURVE, CROOK **2** : to seize or make fast with a hook **3** : STEAL **4** : to work as a prostitute

hoo•kah \ˈhu̇-kə, ˈhü-\ *n* [Ar *ḥuqqah* bottle of a water pipe] : WATER PIPE

hook•er \ˈhu̇-kər\ *n* **1** : one that hooks **2** : PROSTITUTE

hook•up \ˈhu̇-ˌkəp\ *n* : an assemblage (as of apparatus or circuits) used for a specific purpose (as in radio)

hook•worm \ˈhu̇k-ˌwərm\ *n* : any of several parasitic intestinal nematode worms having hooks or plates around the mouth; *also* : infestation with or disease caused by hookworms

hoo•li•gan \ˈhü-li-gən\ *n* : RUFFIAN, HOODLUM

hoop \ˈhu̇p, ˈhüp\ *n* **1** : a circular strip used esp. for holding together the staves of a barrel **2** : a circular figure or object : RING **3** : a circle of flexible material for expanding a woman's skirt **4** : BASKETBALL — usu. used in pl.

hoop•la \ˈhüp-ˌlä, ˈhu̇p-\ *n* [F *houp-là*, interj.] : TO-DO; *also* : BALLYHOO

hoose•gow \ˈhüs-ˌgau̇\ *n* [Sp *juzgado* panel of judges, courtroom] : JAIL

¹hoot \ˈhüt\ *vb* **1** : to shout or laugh usu. in contempt **2** : to make the natural throat noise of an owl — **hooter** *n*

²hoot *n* **1** : a sound of hooting **2** : the least bit ⟨don't give a ~⟩ **3** : something or someone amusing ⟨the play is a real ~⟩

¹hop \ˈhäp\ *vb* **hopped; hop•ping** **1** : to move by quick springy leaps **2** : to make a quick trip **3** : to ride on esp. surreptitiously and without authorization

²hop *n* **1** : a short brisk leap esp. on one leg **2** : DANCE **3** : a short trip by air

³hop *n* : a vine related to the mulberry whose ripe dried pistillate catkins are used esp. in flavoring malt liquors; *also, pl* : its pistillate catkins

¹hope \ˈhōp\ *vb* **hoped; hop•ing** : to desire with expectation of fulfillment

²hope *n* **1** : TRUST, RELIANCE **2** : desire accompanied by expectation of fulfillment; *also* : something hoped for **3** : one that gives promise for the future — **hopeful** \-fəl\ *adj* — **hope•ful•ness** *n* — **hope•less** *adj* — **hope•less•ly** *adv* — **hope•less•ness** *n*

HOPE *abbr* Health Opportunity for People Everywhere

hope•ful•ly \ˈhōp-fə-lē\ *adv* **1** : in a hopeful manner **2** : it is hoped

Ho•pi \ˈhō-pē\ *n, pl* **Hopi** *also* **Hopis** : a member of an American Indian people of Arizona; *also* : the language of the Hopi people

hopped–up \ˈhäpt-ˈəp\ *adj* **1** : being under the influence of a narcotic; *also* : full of enthusiasm or excitement **2** : having more power than usual ⟨a ~ engine⟩

hop•per \ˈhä-pər\ *n* **1** : a usu. immature hopping insect (as a grasshopper) **2** : a usu. funnel-shaped container for delivering material (as grain) **3** : a freight car with hinged doors in a sloping bottom **4** : a box into which a bill to be considered by a legislative body is dropped **5** : a tank holding a liquid and having a device for releasing its contents through a pipe

hop•scotch \ˈhäp-ˌskäch\ *n* : a child's game in which a player tosses an object (as a stone) into areas of a figure drawn on the ground and hops through the figure to pick up the object

hor *abbr* horizontal
horde \ˈhōrd\ *n* : THRONG, SWARM
ho•ri•zon \hə-ˈrīz-ᵊn\ *n* [Gk *horizont-, horizōn,* fr. prp. of *horizein* to bound, fr. *horos* limit, boundary] **1** : the apparent junction of earth and sky **2** : range of outlook or experience
hor•i•zon•tal \ˌhȯr-ə-ˈzänt-ᵊl\ *adj* : parallel to the horizon : LEVEL — **horizontal** *n* — **hor•i•zon•tal•ly** *adv*
hor•mon•al \hȯr-ˈmōn-ᵊl\ *adj* : of, relating to, or effected by hormones
hor•mone \ˈhȯr-ˌmōn\ *n* [Gk *hormōn,* prp. of *horman* to stir up, fr. *hormē* impulse, assault] : a product of living cells that circulates in body fluids and has a specific effect on the activity of cells remote from its point of origin
horn \ˈhȯrn\ *n* **1** : one of the hard projections of bone or keratin on the head of many hoofed mammals **2** : something resembling or suggesting a horn **3** : a brass wind instrument **4** : a usu. electrical device that makes a noise ⟨automobile ~⟩ — **horned** \ˈhȯrnd\ *adj* — **horn•less** *adj*
horn•book \ˈhȯrn-ˌbu̇k\ *n* **1** : a child's primer consisting of a sheet of parchment or paper protected by a sheet of transparent horn **2** : a rudimentary treatise
horned toad *n* : any of several small harmless insect-eating lizards with spines on the head resembling horns and spiny scales on the body
hor•net \ˈhȯr-nət\ *n* : any of the larger social wasps
horn in *vb* : to participate without invitation : INTRUDE
horn•pipe \ˈhȯrn-ˌpīp\ *n* : a lively folk dance of the British Isles
horny \ˈhȯr-nē\ *adj* **horn•i•er; -est 1** : of or made of horn; *also* : HARD, CALLOUS **2** : having horns **3** : desiring sexual gratification; *also* : excited sexually
ho•rol•o•gy \hə-ˈrä-lə-jē\ *n* : the science of measuring time or constructing time-indicating instruments — **hor•o•log•ic** \ˌhȯr-ə-ˈlä-jik\ *adj* — **ho•rol•o•gist** \hə-ˈrä-lə-jist\ *n*
horo•scope \ˈhȯr-ə-ˌskōp\ *n* [ME *oruscope,* fr. MF *horoscope,* fr. L *horoscopus,* fr. Gk *hōroskopos,* fr. *hōra* hour + *skopos* watcher] **1** : a diagram of the relative positions of planets and signs of the zodiac at a particular time for use by astrologers to foretell events of a person's life **2** : an astrological forecast
hor•ren•dous \hȯ-ˈren-dəs\ *adj* : DREADFUL, HORRIBLE
hor•ri•ble \ˈhȯr-ə-bəl\ *adj* **1** : marked by or conducive to horror **2** : highly disagreeable — **hor•ri•ble•ness** *n* — **hor•ri•bly** \-blē\ *adv*
hor•rid \ˈhȯr-əd\ *adj* **1** : HIDEOUS **2** : REPULSIVE — **hor•rid•ly** *adv*
hor•ri•fy \ˈhȯr-ə-ˌfī\ *vb* **-fied; -fy•ing** : to cause to feel horror **syn** appall, daunt, dismay
hor•ror \ˈhȯr-ər\ *n* **1** : painful and intense fear, dread, or dismay **2** : intense repugnance **3** : something that horrifies
hors de com•bat \ˌȯr-də-kōⁿ-ˈbä\ *adv or adj* : in a disabled condition
hors d'oeuvre \ȯr-ˈdərv\ *n, pl* **hors d'oeuvres** *same or* -ˈdərvz\ *also* **hors d'oeuvre** [F *hors-d'oeuvre,* lit., outside of the work] : any of various savory foods usu. served as appetizers
horse \ˈhȯrs\ *n, pl* **hors•es** *also* **horse 1** : a large solid-hoofed herbivorous mammal domesticated as a draft and saddle animal **2** : a supporting framework usu. with legs — **horse•less** *adj*
[1]**horse•back** \ˈhȯrs-ˌbak\ *n* : the back of a horse
[2]**horseback** *adv* : on horseback
horse chestnut *n* : a large Asian tree with palmate leaves, erect conical clusters of showy flowers, and large glossy brown seeds enclosed in a prickly bur; *also* : its seed
horse•flesh \ˈhȯrs-ˌflesh\ *n* : horses for riding, driving, or racing
horse•fly \-ˌflī\ *n* : any of a family of large dipteran flies with bloodsucking females
horse•hair \-ˌhar\ *n* **1** : the hair of a horse esp. from the mane or tail **2** : cloth made from horsehair
horse•hide \-ˌhīd\ *n* **1** : the dressed or raw hide of a horse **2** : the ball used in baseball
horse latitudes *n pl* : either of two calm regions near 30°N and 30°S latitude
horse•laugh \ˈhȯrs-ˌlaf, -ˌlȧf\ *n* : a loud boisterous laugh
horse•man \-mən\ *n* **1** : one who rides horseback; *also* : one skilled in managing horses **2** : a breeder or raiser of horses — **horse•man•ship** *n*
horse•play \-ˌplā\ *n* : rough boisterous play
horse•play•er \-ər\ *n* : a bettor on horse races
horse•pow•er \ˈhȯrs-ˌpau̇-ər\ *n* : a unit of power equal in the U.S. to 746 watts
horse•rad•ish \-ˌra-dish\ *n* : a tall white-flowered herb related to the mustards whose pungent root is used as a condiment; *also* : the pungent condiment
horse•shoe \ˈhȯrs-ˌshü\ *n* **1** : a usu. U-shaped protective metal plate fitted to the rim of a horse's hoof **2** *pl* : a game in which horseshoes are pitched at a fixed object — **horse•shoe** *vb* — **horse•sho•er** *n*
horseshoe crab *n* : any of several marine arthropods with a broad crescent-shaped combined head and thorax
horse•tail \ˈhȯrs-ˌtāl\ *n* : any of a genus of primitive spore-producing plants with hollow jointed stems and leaves reduced to sheaths about the joints
horse•whip \-ˌhwip\ *vb* : to flog with a whip made to be used on a horse
horse•wom•an \-ˌwu̇-mən\ *n* : a woman skilled in riding horseback or in caring for or managing horses; *also* : a woman who breeds or raises horses
hors•ey *or* **horsy** \ˈhȯr-sē\ *adj* **hors•i•er; -est 1** : of, relating to, or suggesting a horse **2** : having to do with horses or horse racing
hort *abbr* horticultural; horticulture
hor•ta•tive \ˈhȯr-tə-tiv\ *adj* : giving exhortation
hor•ta•to•ry \ˈhȯr-tə-ˌtōr-ē\ *adj* : HORTATIVE
hor•ti•cul•ture \ˈhȯr-tə-ˌkəl-chər\ *n* : the science and art of growing fruits, vegetables, flowers, and ornamental plants — **hor•ti•cul•tur•al** \ˌhȯr-tə-ˈkəl-chə-rəl\ *adj* — **hor•ti•cul•tur•ist** \-rist\ *n*
Hos *abbr* Hosea
ho•san•na \hō-ˈza-nə, -ˈzä-\ *interj* [Gk *hōsanna,* fr. Heb *hōshīʿāh-nnā* pray, save (us)!] — used as a cry of acclamation and adoration — **hosanna** *n*
[1]**hose** \ˈhōz\ *n, pl* **hose** *or* **hos•es 1** *pl hose* : STOCKING, SOCK; *also* : a close-fitting garment covering the legs and waist **2** : a flexible tube for conveying fluids (as from a faucet)
[2]**hose** *vb* **hosed; hos•ing** : to spray, water, or wash with a hose
Ho•sea \hō-ˈzā-ə, -ˈzē-\ *n* — see BIBLE table
ho•siery \ˈhō-zhə-rē, -zə-\ *n* : STOCKINGS, SOCKS
hosp *abbr* hospital
hos•pice \ˈhäs-pəs\ *n* **1** : a lodging for travelers or for young persons or the underprivileged **2** : a facility or program for caring for dying persons
hos•pi•ta•ble \hä-ˈspi-tə-bəl, ˈhäs-(ˌ)pi-\ *adj* **1** : given to generous and cordial reception of guests **2** : readily receptive — **hos•pi•ta•bly** \-blē\ *adv*
hos•pi•tal \ˈhäs-ˌpit-ᵊl\ *n* [ME, fr. OF, fr. ML *hospitale* hospice, guest house, fr neut. of L *hospitalis* of a guest, fr. *hospit-, hospes* guest, host] : an institution where the sick or injured receive medical or surgical care
hos•pi•tal•ise *Brit var of* HOSPITALIZE
hos•pi•tal•i•ty \ˌhäs-pə-ˈta-lə-tē\ *n, pl* **-ties** : hospitable treatment, reception, or disposition
hos•pi•tal•ize \ˈhäs-ˌpit-ᵊl-ˌīz\ *vb* **-ized; -iz•ing** : to place in a hospital as a patient — **hos•pi•tal•i•za•tion** \ˌhäs-ˌpit-ᵊl-ə-ˈzā-shən\ *n*
[1]**host** \ˈhōst\ *n* [ME, fr. OF, fr. LL *hostis,* fr. L, stranger, enemy] **1** : ARMY **2** : MULTITUDE
[2]**host** *n* [ME *hoste* host, guest, fr. OF, fr. L *hospit-,*

hospes] **1** : one who receives or entertains guests **2** : an animal or plant on or in which a parasite lives — **host** *vb*

[3]host *n, often cap* [ultim. fr. L *hostia* sacrifice] : the eucharistic bread

hos•tage \ˈhäs-tij\ *n* **1** : a person kept as a pledge pending the fulfillment of an agreement **2** : a person taken by force to secure the taker's demands

hos•tel \ˈhäst-ᵊl\ *n* [ME, fr. OF, fr. ML *hospitale* hospice] **1** : INN **2** : a supervised lodging for youth — **hos•tel•er** *n*

hos•tel•ry \-rē\ *n, pl* **-ries** : INN, HOTEL

host•ess \ˈhō-stəs\ *n* : a woman who acts as host

hos•tile \ˈhäst-ᵊl, ˈhäs-ˌtīl\ *adj* : marked by usu. overt antagonism : UNFRIENDLY — **hostile** *n* — **hos•tile•ly** *adv*

hos•til•i•ty \hä-ˈsti-lə-tē\ *n, pl* **-ties** **1** : an unfriendly state or action **2** *pl* : overt acts of war

hos•tler \ˈhäs-lər, ˈäs-\ *n* : one who takes care of horses or mules

hot \ˈhät\ *adj* **hot•ter; hot•test** **1** : marked by a high temperature or an uncomfortable degree of body heat **2** : giving a sensation of heat or of burning **3** : ARDENT, FIERY **4** : sexually excited **5** : EAGER **6** : newly made or received **7** : PUNGENT **8** : unusually lucky or favorable ⟨~ dice⟩ **9** : recently and illegally obtained ⟨~ jewels⟩ — **hot** *adv* — **hot•ly** *adv* — **hot•ness** *n*

hot•bed \-ˌbed\ *n* **1** : a glass-covered bed of soil heated (as by fermenting manure) and used esp. for raising seedlings **2** : an environment that favors rapid growth or development

hot–blood•ed \-ˈblə-dəd\ *adj* : easily roused or excited

hot•box \-ˌbäks\ *n* : a bearing (as of a railroad car) overheated by friction

hot button *n* : an emotional issue or concern that triggers immediate intense reaction

hot•cake \-ˌkāk\ *n* : PANCAKE

hot dog *n* : a cooked frankfurter usu. served in a long split roll

ho•tel \hō-ˈtel\ *n* [F *hôtel*, fr. OF *hostel*, fr. ML *hospitale* hospice] : a building where lodging and usu. meals, entertainment, and various personal services are provided for the public

hot flash *n* : a sudden brief flushing and sensation of heat usu. associated with menopausal endocrine imbalance

hot•head•ed \ˈhät-ˈhe-dəd\ *adj* : FIERY, IMPETUOUS — **hot•head** \-ˌhed\ *n* — **hot•head•ed•ly** *adv* — **hot•head•ed•ness** *n*

hot•house \-ˌhau̇s\ *n* : a heated greenhouse esp. for raising tropical plants

hot line *n* : a telephone line for emergency use (as between governments or to a counseling service)

hot plate *n* : a simple portable appliance for heating or for cooking

hot potato *n* : an embarrassing or controversial issue

hot rod *n* : an automobile modified for high speed and fast acceleration — **hot–rod•der** \-ˈrä-dər\ *n*

hots \ˈhäts\ *n pl* : strong sexual desire — usu. used with *the*

hot seat *n* : a position of anxiety or embarrassment

hot•shot \ˈhät-ˌshät\ *n* : a showily skillful person

hot tub *n* : a large wooden tub of hot water in which bathers soak and usu. socialize

hot water *n* : TROUBLE, DIFFICULTY

hot–wire \ˈhät-ˌwīr\ *vb* : to start (an automobile) by short-circuiting the ignition system

[1]hound \ˈhau̇nd\ *n* **1** : : any of various long-eared hunting dogs that track prey by scent **2** : FAN, ADDICT

[2]hound *vb* : to pursue relentlessly

hour \ˈau̇r\ *n* **1** : the 24th part of a day : 60 minutes **2** : the time of day **3** : a particular or customary time **4** : a class session — **hour•ly** *adv or adj*

hour•glass \ˈau̇r-ˌglas\ *n* : a glass vessel for measuring time in which sand runs from an upper compartment to a lower compartment in an hour

hou•ri \ˈhu̇r-ē\ *n* [F, fr. Per *hūri*, fr. Ar *ḥūrīyah*] : one of the beautiful maidens of the Muslim paradise

[1]house \ˈhau̇s\ *n, pl* **hous•es** \ˈhau̇-zəz\ **1** : a building for human habitation **2** : an animal shelter (as a den or nest) **3** : a building in which something is stored **4** : HOUSEHOLD; *also* : FAMILY **5** : a residence for a religious community or for students; *also* : those in residence **6** : a legislative body **7** : a place of business or entertainment **8** : a business organization **9** : the audience in a theater or concert hall — **house•ful** *n*

[2]house \ˈhau̇z\ *vb* **housed; hous•ing** **1** : to provide with or take shelter : LODGE **2** : STORE

house•boat \ˈhau̇s-ˌbōt\ *n* : a pleasure boat fitted for use as a dwelling or for leisurely cruising

house•boy \-ˌbȯi\ *n* : a boy or man hired to act as a household servant

house•break \-ˌbrāk\ *vb* **house•broke; house•bro•ken; house•break•ing** : to train in excretory habits acceptable in indoor living

house•break•ing \-ˌbrā-kiŋ\ *n* : the act of breaking into a dwelling with the intent of committing a felony

house•clean \-ˌklēn\ *vb* : to clean a house and its furniture — **house•clean•ing** *n*

house•coat \-ˌkōt\ *n* : a woman's often long-skirted informal garment for wear around the house

house•fly \-ˌflī\ *n* : a dipteran fly that is common about human habitations

[1]house•hold \-ˌhōld\ *n* : those who dwell as a family under the same roof — **house•hold•er** *n*

[2]household *adj* **1** : DOMESTIC **2** : FAMILIAR, COMMON ⟨a ~ name⟩

house•keep•er \-ˌkē-pər\ *n* : a woman employed to take care of a house

house•keep•ing \-ˌkē-piŋ\ *n* : the care and management of a house or institutional property

house•lights \-ˌlīts\ *n pl* : the lights that illuminate the auditorium of a theater

house•maid \-ˌmād\ *n* : a female servant employed to do housework

house•moth•er \-ˌmə-t͟hər\ *n* : a woman acting as hostess, chaperon, and often housekeeper in a group residence

house•plant \-ˌplant\ *n* : a plant grown or kept indoors

house sparrow *n* : a Eurasian sparrow widely introduced in urban and agricultural areas

house•top \ˈhau̇s-ˌtäp\ *n* : ROOF

house•wares \-ˌwarz\ *n pl* : small articles of household equipment

house•warm•ing \-ˌwȯr-miŋ\ *n* : a party to celebrate the taking possession of a house or premises

house•wife \-ˌwīf\ *n* : a married woman in charge of a household — **house•wife•ly** *adj* — **house•wif•ery** \-ˌwī-fə-rē\ *n*

house•work \-ˌwərk\ *n* : the work of housekeeping

[1]hous•ing \ˈhau̇-ziŋ\ *n* **1** : SHELTER; *also* : dwellings provided for people **2** : something that covers or protects

[2]housing *n* : CAPARISON 1

HOV *abbr* high-occupancy vehicle

hove *past and past part of* HEAVE

hov•el \ˈhə-vəl, ˈhä-\ *n* : a small, wretched, and often dirty house : HUT

hov•er \ˈhə-vər, ˈhä-\ *vb* **hov•ered; hov•er•ing** **1** : FLUTTER; *also* : to move to and fro **2** : to be in an uncertain state

hov•er•craft \-ˌkraft\ *n* : a vehicle that rides on a cushion of air over a surface

[1]how \ˈhau̇\ *adv* **1** : in what way or manner ⟨~ was it done⟩ **2** : with what meaning ⟨~ do we interpret such behavior⟩ **3** : for what reason ⟨~ could you have done such a thing⟩ **4** : to what extent or degree ⟨~ deep is it⟩ **5** : in what state or condition ⟨~ are you⟩ — **how about** : what do you say to or think of ⟨*how about* coming with me⟩ — **how come** : why is it that

[2]how *conj* **1** : the way or manner in which ⟨remember ~ they fought⟩ **2** : HOWEVER ⟨do it ~ you like⟩

[1]how•be•it \hau̇-ˈbē-ət\ *conj* : ALTHOUGH

[2]**howbeit** *adv* : NEVERTHELESS

how•dah \ˈhau̇-də\ *n* [Hindi *haudā*] : a seat or covered pavilion on the back of an elephant or camel

[1]**how•ev•er** \hau̇-ˈe-vər\ *conj* : in whatever manner that

[2]**however** *adv* **1** : to whatever degree; *also* : in whatever manner **2** : in spite of that

how•it•zer \ˈhau̇-ət-sər\ *n* : a short cannon that shoots shells at a high angle

howl \ˈhau̇l\ *vb* **1** : to emit a loud long doleful sound characteristic of dogs **2** : to cry loudly — **howl** *n*

howl•er \ˈhau̇-lər\ *n* **1** : one that howls **2** : a humorous and ridiculous blunder

howl•ing *adj* **1** : DESOLATE, WILD **2** : very great ⟨a ~ success⟩

how•so•ev•er \ˌhau̇-sə-ˈwe-vər\ *adv* : HOWEVER 1

hoy•den \ˈhȯid-ᵊn\ *n* : a girl or woman of saucy, boisterous, or carefree behavior — **hoy•den•ish** *adj*

hp *abbr* horsepower

HP *abbr* high pressure

HPF *abbr* highest possible frequency

HQ *abbr* headquarters

hr *abbr* **1** here **2** hour

HR *abbr* House of Representatives

HRH *abbr* **1** Her Royal Highness **2** His Royal Highness

hrzn *abbr* horizon

HS *abbr* high school

HST *abbr* Hawaiian standard time

ht *abbr* height

HT *abbr* **1** Hawaii time **2** high-tension

http *abbr* hypertext transfer protocol

hua•ra•che \wə-ˈrä-chē\ *n* [MexSp] : a sandal with an upper made of interwoven leather strips

hub \ˈhəb\ *n* **1** : the central part of a circular object (as a wheel) **2** : a center of activity; *esp* : an airport or city with heavy air traffic

hub•bub \ˈhə-bəb\ *n* : UPROAR; *also* : TURMOIL

hub•cap \ˈhəb-ˌkap\ *n* : a removable metal cap over the end of an axle

hu•bris \ˈhyü-brəs\ *n* : exaggerated pride or self-confidence

huck•le•ber•ry \ˈhə-kəl-ˌber-ē\ *n* **1** : an American shrub related to the blueberry; *also* : its edible dark blue berry **2** : BLUEBERRY

huck•ster \ˈhək-stər\ *n* : PEDDLER, HAWKER — **huckster** *vb*

HUD *abbr* Department of Housing and Urban Development

[1]**hud•dle** \ˈhəd-ᵊl\ *vb* **hud•dled; hud•dling 1** : to crowd together **2** : CONFER

[2]**huddle** *n* **1** : a closely packed group **2** : MEETING, CONFERENCE

hue \ˈhyü\ *n* **1** : COLOR; *also* : gradation of color **2** : the attribute of colors that permits them to be classed as red, yellow, green, blue, or an intermediate color — **hued** \ˈhyüd\ *adj*

hue and cry *n* : a clamor of pursuit or protest

huff \ˈhəf\ *n* : a fit of anger or pique — **huff** *vb* — **huffy** *adj*

hug \ˈhəg\ *vb* **hugged; hug•ging 1** : EMBRACE **2** : to stay close to — **hug** *n*

huge \ˈhyüj\ *adj* **hug•er; hug•est** : very large or extensive — **huge•ly** *adv* — **huge•ness** *n*

hug•ger–mug•ger \ˈhə-gər-ˌmə-gər\ *n* **1** : SECRECY **2** : CONFUSION, MUDDLE

Hu•gue•not \ˈhyü-gə-ˌnät\ *n* : a French Protestant of the 16th and 17th centuries

hu•la \ˈhü-lə\ *n* : a sinuous Polynesian dance usu. accompanied by chants

hulk \ˈhəlk\ *n* **1** : a heavy clumsy ship **2** : an old ship unfit for service **3** : a bulky or unwieldy person or thing

hulk•ing \ˈhəl-kiŋ\ *adj* : BURLY, MASSIVE

[1]**hull** \ˈhəl\ *n* **1** : the outer covering of a fruit or seed **2** : the frame or body esp. of a ship or boat

[2]**hull** *vb* : to remove the hulls of — **hull•er** *n*

hul•la•ba•loo \ˈhə-lə-bə-ˌlü\ *n, pl* **-loos** : a confused noise : UPROAR

hul•lo \ˌhə-ˈlō\ *chiefly Brit var of* HELLO

hum \ˈhəm\ *vb* **hummed; hum•ming 1** : to utter a sound like that of the speech sound \m\ prolonged **2** : DRONE **3** : to be busily active **4** : to run smoothly **5** : to sing with closed lips — **hum** *n* — **hum•mer** *n*

[1]**hu•man** \ˈhyü-mən, ˈyü-\ *adj* **1** : of, relating to, being, or characteristic of humans **2** : having human form or attributes — **hu•man•ly** *adv* — **hu•man•ness** *n*

[2]**human** *n* : any of a species of primate mammals comprising all living persons and their recent ancestors; *also* : HOMINID

hu•mane \hyü-ˈmān, yü-\ *adj* **1** : marked by compassion, sympathy, or consideration for others **2** : HUMANISTIC — **hu•mane•ly** *adv* — **hu•mane•ness** *n*

human immunodeficiency virus *n* : HIV

hu•man•ism \ˈhyü-mə-ˌni-zəm, ˈyü-\ *n* **1** : devotion to the humanities; *also* : the revival of classical letters characteristic of the Renaissance **2** : a doctrine or way of life centered on human interests or values — **hu•man•ist** \-nist\ *n or adj* — **hu•man•is•tic** \ˌhyü-mə-ˈnis-tik, ˌyü-\ *adj*

hu•man•i•tar•i•an \hyü-ˌma-nə-ˈter-ē-ən, yü-\ *n* : one who practices philanthropy — **humanitarian** *adj* — **hu•man•i•tar•i•an•ism** *n*

hu•man•i•ty \hyü-ˈma-nə-tē, yü-\ *n, pl* **-ties 1** : the quality or state of being human or humane **2** *pl* : the branches of learning dealing with human concerns (as philosophy) as opposed to natural processes (as physics) **3** : the human race

hu•man•ize \ˈhyü-mə-ˌnīz, ˈyü-\ *vb* **-ized; -iz•ing** : to make human or humane — **hu•man•iza•tion** \ˌhyü-mə-nə-ˈzā-shən, ˌyü-\ *n* — **hu•man•iz•er** *n*

hu•man•kind \ˈhyü-mən-ˌkīnd, ˈyü-\ *n* : the human race

hu•man•oid \ˈhyü-mə-ˌnȯid, ˈyü-\ *adj* : having human form or characteristics — **humanoid** *n*

[1]**hum•ble** \ˈhəm-bəl\ *adj* **hum•bler** \-bə-lər\; **hum•blest** \-bə-ləst\ [ME, fr. OF, fr. L *humilis* low, humble, fr. *humus* earth] **1** : not proud or haughty **2** : not pretentious : UNASSUMING **3** : INSIGNIFICANT **syn** meek, modest, lowly — **hum•ble•ness** *n* — **hum•bly** *adv*

[2]**humble** *vb* **hum•bled; hum•bling 1** : to make humble **2** : to destroy the power or prestige of — **hum•bler** *n*

[1]**hum•bug** \ˈhəm-ˌbəg\ *n* **1** : HOAX, FRAUD **2** : NONSENSE

[2]**humbug** *vb* **hum•bugged; hum•bug•ging** : DECEIVE

hum•ding•er \ˈhəm-ˈdiŋ-ər\ *n* : a person or thing of striking excellence

hum•drum \ˈhəm-ˌdrəm\ *adj* : MONOTONOUS, DULL — **humdrum** *n*

hu•mer•us \ˈhyü-mə-rəs\ *n, pl* **hu•meri** \ˈhyü-mə-ˌrī, -ˌrē\ : the long bone extending from shoulder to elbow

hu•mid \ˈhyü-məd, ˈyü-\ *adj* : containing or characterized by perceptible moisture : DAMP — **hu•mid•ly** *adv*

hu•mid•i•fy \hyü-ˈmi-də-ˌfī\ *vb* **-fied; -fy•ing** : to make humid — **hu•mid•i•fi•ca•tion** \-ˌmi-də-fə-ˈkā-shən\ *n* — **hu•mid•i•fi•er** \-ˈmi-də-ˌfī-ər\ *n*

hu•mid•i•ty \hyü-ˈmi-də-tē, yü-\ *n, pl* **-ties** : the amount of atmospheric moisture

hu•mi•dor \ˈhyü-mə-ˌdȯr, ˈyü-\ *n* : a case (as for storing cigars) in which the air is kept properly humidified

hu•mil•i•ate \hyü-ˈmi-lē-ˌāt, yü-\ *vb* **-at•ed; -at•ing** : to injure the self-respect of : MORTIFY — **hu•mil•i•at•ing•ly** *adv* — **hu•mil•i•a•tion** \-ˌmi-lē-ˈā-shən\ *n*

hu•mil•i•ty \hyü-ˈmi-lə-tē, yü-\ *n* : the quality or state of being humble

hum•ming•bird \ˈhə-miŋ-ˌbərd\ *n* : any of a family of tiny American birds related to the swifts

hum•mock \ˈhə-mək\ *n* : a rounded mound : KNOLL — **hum•mocky** \-mə-kē\ *adj*

hu•mon•gous \hyü-ˈməŋ-gəs, -ˈmäŋ-\ *adj* [perh. alter. of *huge* + *monstrous*] : extremely large

[1]hu•mor \ˈhyü-mər, ˈyü-\ *n* **1** : TEMPERAMENT **2** : MOOD **3** : WHIM **4** : a quality that appeals to a sense of the ludicrous or incongruous; *also* : a keen perception of the ludicrous or incongruous **5** : comical or amusing entertainment — **hu•mor•ist** \ˈhyü-mə-rist, ˈyü-\ *n* — **hu•mor•less** \ˈhyü-mər-ləs, ˈyü-\ *adj* — **hu•mor•less•ly** *adv* — **hu•mor•less•ness** *n* — **hu•mor•ous** \ˈhyü-mə-rəs, ˈyü-\ *adj* — **hu•mor•ous•ly** *adv* — **hu•mor•ous•ness** *n*

[2]humor *vb* : to comply with the wishes or mood of

hu•mour *chiefly Brit var of* HUMOR

hump \ˈhəmp\ *n* **1** : a rounded protuberance (as on the back of a camel) **2** : a difficult phase or obstacle ⟨over the ~⟩ — **humped** *adj*

hump•back \ˈhəmp-ˌbak; *1 also* -ˈbak\ *n* **1** : HUNCHBACK **2** : HUMPBACK WHALE — **hump•backed** *adj*

humpback whale *n* : a large baleen whale having very long flippers

hu•mus \ˈhyü-məs, ˈyü-\ *n* : the dark organic part of soil formed from decaying matter

Hun \ˈhən\ *n* : a member of an Asian people that invaded Europe about A.D. 450

[1]hunch \ˈhənch\ *vb* **1** : to thrust oneself forward **2** : to assume or cause to assume a bent or crooked posture

[2]hunch *n* **1** : PUSH **2** : a strong intuitive feeling about what will happen

hunch•back \ˈhənch-ˌbak\ *n* : a person with a crooked back; *also* : a back with a hump — **hunch•backed** *adj*

hun•dred \ˈhən-drəd\ *n, pl* **hundreds** *or* **hundred** : 10 times 10 — **hundred** *adj* — **hun•dredth** \-drədth\ *adj or n*

hun•dred•weight \-ˌwāt\ *n, pl* **hundredweight** *or* **hundredweights** — see WEIGHT table

[1]hung *past and past part of* HANG

[2]hung *adj* : unable to reach a decision or verdict ⟨a ~ jury⟩

Hung *abbr* Hungarian; Hungary

Hun•gar•i•an \ˌhəŋ-ˈger-ē-ən\ *n* **1** : a native or inhabitant of Hungary **2** : the language of the Hungarians — **Hungarian** *adj*

hun•ger \ˈhəŋ-gər\ *n* **1** : a craving or urgent need for food **2** : a strong desire — **hunger** *vb* — **hun•gri•ly** *adv* — **hun•gry** *adj*

hung•over \ˈhəŋ-ˈō-vər\ *adj* : having a hangover

hung up *adj* **1** : DELAYED **2** : ENTHUSIASTIC; *also* : PREOCCUPIED

hunk \ˈhəŋk\ *n* **1** : a large piece **2** : an attractive well-built man — **hunky** *adj*

hun•ker \ˈhəŋ-kər\ *vb* **1** : CROUCH, SQUAT — usu. used with *down* **2** : to settle in for a sustained period — used with *down*

hun•ky–do•ry \ˌhəŋ-kē-ˈdōr-ē\ *adj* : quite satisfactory : FINE

[1]hunt \ˈhənt\ *vb* **1** : to pursue for food or in sport; *also* : to take part in a hunt **2** : to try to find : SEEK **3** : to drive or chase esp. by harrying **4** : to traverse in search of prey — **hunt•er** *n*

[2]hunt *n* : an act, practice, or instance of hunting

hunt•ress \ˈhən-trəs\ *n* : a woman who hunts game

hunts•man \ˈhənts-mən\ *n* **1** : HUNTER **2** : a person who manages a hunt and looks after the hounds

hur•dle \ˈhərd-ᵊl\ *n* **1** : a barrier to leap over in a race **2** : OBSTACLE — **hurdle** *vb* — **hur•dler** *n*

hur•dy–gur•dy \ˌhər-dē-ˈgər-dē, ˈhər-dē-ˌgər-dē\ *n, pl* **-gur•dies** : a musical instrument in which the sound is produced by turning a crank

hurl \ˈhərl\ *vb* **1** : to move or cause to move vigorously **2** : to throw down with violence **3** : FLING; *also* : PITCH — **hurl** *n* — **hurl•er** *n*

hur•ly–bur•ly \ˌhər-lē-ˈbər-lē\ *n* : UPROAR, TUMULT

Hu•ron \ˈhyu̇r-ən, ˈhyu̇r-ˌän\ *n, pl* **Hurons** *or* **Huron** : a member of a confederacy of American Indian peoples formerly living between Georgian Bay and Lake Ontario

hur•rah \hu̇-ˈrȯ, -ˈrä\ *also* **hur•ray** \hu̇-ˈrā\ *interj* — used to express joy, approval, or encouragement

hur•ri•cane \ˈhər-ə-ˌkān\ *n* [Sp *huracán*, of AmerInd origin] : a tropical cyclone with winds of 74 miles (118 kilometers) per hour or greater that is usu. accompanied by rain, thunder, and lightning

[1]hur•ry \ˈhər-ē\ *vb* **hur•ried; hur•ry•ing 1** : to carry or cause to go with haste **2** : to impel to a greater speed **3** : to move or act with haste — **hur•ried•ly** *adv* — **hur•ried•ness** *n*

[2]hurry *n* : extreme haste or eagerness

[1]hurt \ˈhərt\ *vb* **hurt; hurt•ing 1** : to feel or cause to feel physical or emotional pain **2** : to do harm to : DAMAGE **3** : OFFEND **4** : HAMPER **5** : to be in need — usu. used with *for* — **hurt** *adj*

[2]hurt *n* **1** : a bodily injury or wound **2** : SUFFERING **3** : HARM, WRONG — **hurt•ful** *adj* — **hurt•ful•ness** *n*

hur•tle \ˈhərt-ᵊl\ *vb* **hur•tled; hur•tling 1** : to move rapidly or forcefully **2** : HURL, FLING

[1]hus•band \ˈhəz-bənd\ *n* [ME *husbonde*, fr. OE *hūsbonda* master of a house, fr. ON *hūsbōndi*, fr. *hūs* house + *bōndi* householder] : a male partner in a marriage

[2]husband *vb* : to manage prudently

hus•band•man \ˈhəz-bənd-mən\ *n* : FARMER

hus•band•ry \ˈhəz-bən-drē\ *n* **1** : the control or judicious use of resources **2** : AGRICULTURE

[1]hush \ˈhəsh\ *vb* **1** : to make or become quiet or calm **2** : SUPPRESS

[2]hush *n* : SILENCE, QUIET

hush–hush \ˈhəsh-ˌhəsh\ *adj* : SECRET, CONFIDENTIAL

[1]husk \ˈhəsk\ *n* **1** : a usu. thin dry outer covering of a seed or fruit **2** : an outer layer : SHELL

[2]husk *vb* : to strip the husk from — **husk•er** *n*

[1]hus•ky \ˈhəs-kē\ *adj* **hus•ki•er; -est** : HOARSE — **hus•ki•ly** \-kə-lē\ *adv* — **hus•ki•ness** \-kē-nəs\ *n*

[2]husky *adj* **1** : BURLY, ROBUST **2** : LARGE

[3]husky *n, pl* **huskies** : a heavy-coated working dog of the New World arctic

hus•sar \(ˌ)hə-ˈzär\ *n* [Hung *huszár*] : a member of any of various European cavalry units

hus•sy \ˈhə-zē, -sē\ *n, pl* **hussies** [alter. of *housewife*] **1** : a lewd or brazen woman **2** : a pert or mischievous girl

hus•tings \ˈhəs-tiŋz\ *n pl* : a place where political campaign speeches are made; *also* : the proceedings in an election campaign

hus•tle \ˈhə-səl\ *vb* **hus•tled; hus•tling 1** : JOSTLE, SHOVE **2** : HASTEN, HURRY **3** : to work energetically — **hustle** *n* — **hus•tler** \ˈhəs-lər\ *n*

hut \ˈhət\ *n* : a small and often temporary dwelling : SHACK

hutch \ˈhəch\ *n* **1** : a chest or compartment for storage **2** : a cupboard usu. surmounted with open shelves **3** : a pen or coop for an animal **4** : HUT

huz•zah *or* **huz•za** \(ˌ)hə-ˈzä\ *n* : a shout of acclaim — often used interjectionally to express joy or approbation

HV *abbr* **1** high velocity **2** high voltage

HVAC *abbr* heating, ventilating and air-conditioning

hvy *abbr* heavy

HW *abbr* hot water

hwy *abbr* highway

hy•a•cinth \ˈhī-ə-(ˌ)sinth\ *n* : a bulbous Mediterranean herb related to the lilies that is widely grown for its spikes of fragrant bell-shaped flowers

hy•ae•na *var of* HYENA

hy•brid \ˈhī-brəd\ *n* **1** : an offspring of genetically differing parents (as members of different breeds or species) **2** : one of mixed origin or composition — **hybrid** *adj* — **hy•brid•i•za•tion** \ˌhī-brə-də-ˈzā-shən\ *n* — **hy•brid•ize** \ˈhī-brə-ˌdīz\ *vb* — **hy•brid•iz•er** *n*

hy•dra \ˈhī-drə\ *n* : any of numerous small tubular freshwater coelenterates that are polyps having at one end a mouth surrounded by tentacles

hy•dran•gea \hī-ˈdrān-jə\ *n* : any of a genus of shrubs related to the currants and grown for their showy clusters of white or tinted flowers

hy•drant \ˈhī-drənt\ *n* : a pipe with a valve and spout at which water may be drawn from a main pipe

hy•drate \ˈhī-ˌdrāt\ *n* : a compound formed by union of water with some other substance — **hydrate** *vb*

hy•drau•lic \hī-ˈdrȯ-lik\ *adj* **1** : operated, moved, or effected by means of water **2** : of or relating to hydraulics **3** : operated by the resistance offered or the pressure transmitted when a quantity of liquid is forced through a small orifice or through a tube **4** : hardening or setting under water

hy•drau•lics \-liks\ *n* : a science that deals with practical applications of liquid (as water) in motion

hydro \ˈhī-drō\ *n* : HYDROPOWER

hy•dro•car•bon \ˈhī-drō-ˌkär-bən\ *n* : an organic compound containing only carbon and hydrogen

hy•dro•ceph•a•lus \ˌhī-drō-ˈse-fə-ləs\ *n* : abnormal increase in the amount of fluid in the cranial cavity accompanied by enlargement of the skull and atrophy of the brain

hy•dro•chlo•ric acid \ˌhī-drə-ˈklōr-ik-\ *n* : a sharp-smelling corrosive acid used in the laboratory and in industry and present in dilute form in gastric juice

hy•dro•dy•nam•ics \ˌhī-drō-dī-ˈna-miks\ *n* : a science that deals with the motion of fluids and the forces acting on moving bodies immersed in fluids — **hy•dro•dy•nam•ic** *adj*

hy•dro•elec•tric \ˌhī-drō-i-ˈlek-trik\ *adj* : of or relating to production of electricity by waterpower — **hy•dro•elec•tric•i•ty** \-ˌlek-ˈtri-sə-tē\ *n*

hy•dro•foil \ˈhī-drə-ˌfȯil\ *n* : a boat that has fins attached to the bottom by struts for lifting the hull clear of the water to allow faster speeds

hy•dro•gen \ˈhī-drə-jən\ *n* [F *hydrogène*, fr. Gk *hydōr* water + *-genēs* born; fr. the fact that water is generated by its combustion] : a gaseous colorless odorless highly flammable chemical element that is the lightest of the elements — **hy•drog•e•nous** \hī-ˈdrä-jə-nəs\ *adj* — see ELEMENT table

hy•dro•ge•nate \hī-ˈdrä-jə-ˌnāt, ˈhī-drə-\ *vb* **-nat•ed; -nat•ing** : to combine or treat with hydrogen; *esp* : to add hydrogen to the molecule of — **hy•dro•ge•na•tion** \hī-ˌdrä-jə-ˈnā-shən, ˌhī-drə-\ *n*

hydrogen bomb *n* : a bomb whose violent explosive power is due to the sudden release of atomic energy resulting from the fusion of light nuclei (as of hydrogen atoms)

hydrogen peroxide *n* : an unstable compound of hydrogen and oxygen used esp. as an oxidizing and bleaching agent, an antiseptic, and a propellant

hy•dro•graph•ic \ˌhī-drə-ˈgra-fik\ *adj* : of or relating to the description and study of bodies of water — **hy•drog•ra•pher** *n* — **hy•drog•ra•phy** \hī-ˈdrä-grə-fē\ *n*

hy•drol•o•gy \hī-ˈdrä-lə-jē\ *n* : a science dealing with the properties, distribution, and circulation of water — **hy•dro•log•ic** \ˌhī-drə-ˈlä-jik\ *or* **hy•dro•log•i•cal** \-ji-kəl\ *adj* — **hy•drol•o•gist** \hī-ˈdrä-lə-jist\ *n*

hy•dro•ly•sis \hī-ˈdrä-lə-səs\ *n* : a chemical decomposition involving the addition of the elements of water

hy•drom•e•ter \hī-ˈdrä-mə-tər\ *n* : a floating instrument for determining specific gravities of liquids and hence the strength (as of alcoholic liquors)

hy•dro•pho•bia \ˌhī-drə-ˈfō-bē-ə\ *n* [LL, fr. Gk, fr. *hydōr* water + *phobos* fear] : RABIES

hy•dro•phone \ˈhī-drə-ˌfōn\ *n* : an underwater listening device

[1]**hy•dro•plane** \ˈhī-drə-ˌplān\ *n* **1** : a powerboat designed for racing that skims the surface of the water **2** : SEAPLANE

[2]**hydroplane** *vb* : to skid on a wet road due to loss of contact between the tires and road

hy•dro•pon•ics \ˌhī-drə-ˈpä-niks\ *n* : the growing of plants in nutrient solutions — **hy•dro•pon•ic** *adj*

hy•dro•pow•er \ˈhī-drə-ˌpau̇-ər\ *n* : hydroelectric power

hy•dro•sphere \ˈhī-drə-ˌsfir\ *n* : the water (as vapor or lakes) of the earth

hy•dro•stat•ic \ˌhī-drə-ˈsta-tik\ *adj* : of or relating to fluids at rest or to the pressures they exert or transmit

hy•dro•ther•a•py \ˌhī-drə-ˈther-ə-pē\ *n* : the use of water esp. externally in the treatment of disease or disability

hy•dro•ther•mal \ˌhī-drə-ˈthər-məl\ *adj* : of or relating to hot water

hy•drous \ˈhī-drəs\ *adj* : containing water

hy•drox•ide \hī-ˈdräk-ˌsīd\ *n* **1** : a negatively charged ion consisting of one atom of oxygen and one atom of hydrogen **2** : a compound of hydroxide with an element or group

hy•e•na \hī-ˈē-nə\ *n* [L *hyaena*, fr. Gk *hyaina*, fr. *hys* hog] : any of several large nocturnal carnivorous mammals of Asia and Africa

hy•giene \ˈhī-ˌjēn\ *n* **1** : a science concerned with establishing and maintaining good health **2** : conditions or practices conducive to health — **hy•gien•ic** \hī-ˈjenik, -ˈjē-\ *adj* — **hy•gien•i•cal•ly** \-ni-k(ə-)lē\ *adv* — **hy•gien•ist** \hī-ˈjē-nist, ˈhī-ˌjē-, hī-ˈje-\ *n*

hy•grom•e•ter \hī-ˈgrä-mə-tər\ *n* : any of several instruments for measuring the humidity of the atmosphere

hy•gro•scop•ic \ˌhī-grə-ˈskä-pik\ *adj* : readily taking up and retaining moisture

hying *pres part of* HIE

hy•men \ˈhī-mən\ *n* : a fold of mucous membrane partly closing the opening of the vagina

hy•me•ne•al \ˌhī-mə-ˈnē-əl\ *adj* : NUPTIAL

hymn \ˈhim\ *n* : a song of praise esp. to God — **hymn** *vb*

hym•nal \ˈhim-nəl\ *n* : a book of hymns

hyp *abbr* hypothesis; hypothetical

[1]**hype** \ˈhīp\ *vb* **hyped; hyp•ing 1** : STIMULATE — usu. used with *up* **2** : INCREASE — **hyped–up** *adj*

[2]**hype** *vb* **hyped; hyping 1** : DECEIVE **2** : PUBLICIZE

[3]**hype** *n* **1** : DECEPTION, PUT-ON **2** : PUBLICITY

hy•per \ˈhī-pər\ *adj* **1** : HIGH-STRUNG, EXCITABLE **2** : extremely active

hy•per•acid•i•ty \ˌhī-pər-ə-ˈsi-də-tē\ *n* : the condition of containing excessive acid esp. in the stomach — **hy•per•ac•id** \-ˈa-səd\ *adj*

hy•per•ac•tive \-ˈak-tiv\ *adj* : excessively or pathologically active — **hy•per•ac•tiv•i•ty** \-ˌak-ˈti-və-tē\ *n*

hy•per•bar•ic \ˌhī-pər-ˈbar-ik\ *adj* : of, relating to, or utilizing greater than normal pressure (as of oxygen)

hy•per•bo•la \hī-ˈpər-bə-lə\ *n, pl* **-las** *or* **-lae** \-(ˌ)lē\ : a curve formed by the intersection of a double right circular cone with a plane that cuts both halves of the cone — **hy•per•bol•ic** \ˌhī-pər-ˈbä-lik\ *adj*

hy•per•bo•le \hī-ˈpər-bə-(ˌ)lē\ *n* : extravagant exaggeration used as a figure of speech

hy•per•crit•i•cal \ˌhī-pər-ˈkri-ti-kəl\ *adj* : excessively critical — **hy•per•crit•i•cal•ly** \-k(ə-)lē\ *adv*

hy•per•opia \ˌhī-pə-ˈrō-pē-ə\ *n* : a condition in which visual images come to focus behind the retina resulting esp. in defective vision for near objects — **hy•per•opic** \-ˈrō-pik, -ˈrä-\ *adj*

hy•per•sen•si•tive \-ˈsen-sə-tiv\ *adj* **1** : excessively or abnormally sensitive **2** : abnormally susceptible physiologically to a specific agent (as a drug) — **hy•per•sen•si•tive•ness** *n* — **hy•per•sen•si•tiv•i•ty** \-ˌsen-sə-ˈti-və-tē\ *n*

hy•per•ten•sion \ˈhī-pər-ˌten-chən\ *n* : high blood pressure — **hy•per•ten•sive** \ˌhī-pər-ˈten-siv\ *adj or n*

hy•per•text \ˈhī-pər-ˌtekst\ *n* : a database format in which information related to that on display can be accessed directly from the display

hy•per•thy•roid•ism \ˌhī-pər-ˈthī-ˌrȯi-ˌdi-zəm\ *n* : excessive activity of the thyroid gland; *also* : the resulting bodily condition — **hy•per•thy•roid** \-ˈthī-ˌrȯid\ *adj*

hy•per•tro•phy \hī-ˈpər-trə-fē\ *n, pl* **-phies** : excessive development of a body part — **hy·per·tro·phic** \ˌhī-pər-ˈtrō-fik\ *adj* — **hypertrophy** *vb*

hy·per·ven·ti·late \ˌhī-pər-ˈven-tə-ˌlāt\ *vb* : to breathe rapidly and deeply esp. to the point of losing an abnormal amount of carbon dioxide from the blood — **hy·per·ven·ti·la·tion** \-ˌven-tə-ˈlā-shən\ *n*

hy·phen \ˈhī-fən\ *n* : a punctuation mark - used esp. to divide or to compound words or word parts — **hyphen** *vb*

hy·phen·ate \ˈhī-fə-ˌnāt\ *vb* **-at·ed; -at·ing** : to connect or divide with a hyphen — **hy·phen·ation** \ˌhī-fə-ˈnā-shən\ *n*

hyp·no·sis \hip-ˈnō-səs\ *n, pl* **-no·ses** \-ˌsēz\ : an induced state that resembles sleep and in which the subject is responsive to suggestions of the inducer (**hyp·no·tist** \ˈhip-nə-tist\) — **hyp·no·tism** \ˈhip-nə-ˌti-zəm\ *n* — **hyp·no·tiz·able** \ˈhip-nə-ˌtī-zə-bəl\ *adj* — **hyp·no·tize** \-ˌtīz\ *vb*

[1]**hyp·not·ic** \hip-ˈnä-tik\ *adj* **1** : inducing sleep : SOPORIFIC **2** : of or relating to hypnosis or hypnotism **3** : readily holding the attention — **hyp·not·i·cal·ly** \-ti-k(ə-)lē\ *adv*

[2]**hypnotic** *n* : a sleep-inducing drug

hy·po \ˈhī-pō\ *n, pl* **hypos** : SODIUM THIOSULFATE

hy·po·cen·ter \ˈhī-pə-ˌsen-tər\ *n* : the point of origin of an earthquake

hy·po·chon·dria \ˌhī-pə-ˈkän-drē-ə\ *n* [NL, fr. LL, pl., upper abdomen (formerly regarded as the seat of hypochondria), fr. Gk, lit., the parts under the cartilage (of the breastbone), fr. *hypo-* under + *chondros* cartilage] : depression of mind often centered on imaginary physical ailments — **hy·po·chon·dri·ac** \-drē-ˌak\ *adj or n*

hy·poc·ri·sy \hi-ˈpä-krə-sē\ *n, pl* **-sies** : a feigning to be what one is not or to believe what one does not; *esp* : the false assumption of an appearance of virtue or religion — **hyp·o·crite** \ˈhi-pə-ˌkrit\ *n* — **hyp·o·crit·i·cal** \ˌhi-pə-ˈkri-ti-kəl\ *adj* — **hyp·o·crit·i·cal·ly** \-k(ə-)lē\ *adv*

[1]**hy·po·der·mic** \ˌhī-pə-ˈdər-mik\ *adj* : administered by or used in making an injection beneath the skin

[2]**hypodermic** *n* : HYPODERMIC SYRINGE; *also* : an injection made with this

hypodermic needle *n* : NEEDLE 3; *also* : HYPODERMIC SYRINGE

hypodermic syringe *n* : a small syringe with a hollow needle for injecting material into or through the skin

hy·po·gly·ce·mia \ˌhī-pō-glī-ˈsē-mē-ə\ *n* : abnormal decrease of sugar in the blood — **hy·po·gly·ce·mic** \-mik\ *adj*

hy·pot·e·nuse \hī-ˈpät-ᵊn-ˌüs, -ˌyüs, -ˌüz, -ˌyüz\ *n* : the side of a triangle having a right angle that is opposite the right angle; *also* : its length

hy·poth·e·sis \hī-ˈpä-thə-səs\ *n, pl* **-e·ses** \-ˌsēz\ : an assumption made esp. in order to test its logical or empirical consequences — **hy·po·thet·i·cal** \ˌhī-pə-ˈthe-ti-kəl\ *adj* — **hy·po·thet·i·cal·ly** \-k(ə-)lē\ *adv*

hy·poth·e·size \-ˌsīz\ *vb* **-sized; -siz·ing** : to adopt as a hypothesis

hy·po·thy·roid·ism \ˌhī-pō-ˈthī-ˌrȯi-ˌdi-zəm\ *n* : deficient activity of the thyroid gland; *also* : a resultant lowered metabolic rate and general loss of vigor — **hy·po·thy·roid** *adj*

hys·sop \ˈhi-səp\ *n* : a European mint sometimes used as a potherb

hys·ter·ec·to·my \ˌhis-tə-ˈrek-tə-mē\ *n, pl* **-mies** : surgical removal of the uterus

hys·te·ria \hi-ˈster-ē-ə, -ˈstir-\ *n* [NL, fr. E *hysteric*, adj., fr. L *hystericus*, fr. Gk *hysterikos*, fr. *hystera* womb; fr. the Greek notion that hysteria was peculiar to women and caused by disturbances in the uterus] **1** : a nervous disorder marked esp. by defective emotional control **2** : unmanageable fear or outburst of emotion — **hys·ter·ic** \-ˈster-ik\ *n* — **hys·ter·i·cal** \-ˈster-i-kəl\ *also* **hysteric** *adj* — **hys·ter·i·cal·ly** \-k(ə-)lē\ *adv*

hys·ter·ics \-ˈster-iks\ *n pl* : a fit of uncontrollable laughter or crying

Hz *abbr* hertz

I

[1]**i** \ˈī\ *n, pl* **i's** *or* **is** \ˈīz\ *often cap* : the 9th letter of the English alphabet

[2]**i** *abbr, often cap* island; isle

[1]**I** \ˈī, ə\ *pron* : the one speaking or writing

[2]**I** *abbr* interstate

[3]**I** *symbol* iodine

Ia *or* **IA** *abbr* Iowa

-ial *adj suffix* : [1]-AL ⟨manor*ial*⟩

iamb \ˈī-ˌam\ *or* **iam·bus** \ī-ˈam-bəs\ *n, pl* **iambs** \ˈī-ˌamz\ *or* **iam·bus·es** : a metrical foot of one unaccented syllable followed by one accented syllable — **iam·bic** \ī-ˈam-bik\ *adj or n*

-ian — see -AN

-i·at·ric \ē-ˈa-trik\ *also* **-i·at·ri·cal** \-tri-kəl\ *adj comb form* : of or relating to (such) medical treatment or healing ⟨ped*iatric*⟩

-i·at·rics \ē-ˈa-triks\ *n pl comb form* : medical treatment ⟨ped*iatrics*⟩

ib *or* **ibid** *abbr* ibidem

ibex \ˈī-ˌbeks\ *n, pl* **ibex** *or* **ibex·es** [L] : any of several Old World wild goats with large curved horns

ibi·dem \ˈi-bə-ˌdem, i-ˈbī-dəm\ *adv* [L] : in the same place

-ibility — see -ABILITY

ibis \ˈī-bəs\ *n, pl* **ibis** *or* **ibis·es** [L, fr. Gk, fr. Egypt *hb*] : any of various wading birds related to the herons but having a downwardly curved bill

-ible — see -ABLE

ibu·pro·fen \ˌī-byü-ˈprō-fən\ *n* : a nonsteroidal anti-inflammatory drug used to relieve pain and fever

IC \ˌī-ˈsē\ *n* : INTEGRATED CIRCUIT

[1]**-ic** \ik\ *adj suffix* **1** : of, relating to, or having the form of : being ⟨panoram*ic*⟩ **2** : related to, derived from, or containing ⟨alcohol*ic*⟩ **3** : in the manner of : like that of : characteristic of **4** : associated or dealing with : utilizing ⟨electron*ic*⟩ **5** : characterized by : exhibiting ⟨nostalg*ic*⟩ : affected with ⟨allerg*ic*⟩ **6** : caused by **7** : tending to produce ⟨analges*ic*⟩

[2]**-ic** *n suffix* : one having the character or nature of : one belonging to or associated with : one exhibiting or affected by : one that produces

-i·cal \i-kəl\ *adj suffix* : -IC ⟨symmetr*ical*⟩ ⟨geolog*ical*⟩ — **-i·cal·ly** \i-kə-lē, -klē\ *adv suffix*

ICBM \ˌī-ˌsē-(ˌ)bē-ˈem\ *n, pl* **ICBM's** *or* **ICBMs** \-ˈemz\ : an intercontinental ballistic missile

ICC *abbr* Interstate Commerce Commission

[1]**ice** \ˈīs\ *n* **1** : frozen water **2** : a substance resembling ice **3** : a state of coldness (as from formality or reserve) **4** : a flavored frozen dessert; *esp* : one containing no milk or cream

[2]**ice** *vb* **iced; ic·ing 1** : FREEZE **2** : CHILL **3** : to cover with or as if with icing

ice age *n* : a time of widespread glaciation

ice bag *n* : a waterproof bag to hold ice for local application of cold to the body

ice·berg \ˈīs-ˌbərg\ *n* : a large floating mass of ice broken off from a glacier

iceberg lettuce *n* : any of various crisp light green lettuces that form a compact head like a cabbage

ice·boat \ˈīs-ˌbōt\ *n* : a boatlike frame on runners propelled on ice by sails

ice•bound \-ˌbau̇nd\ *adj* : surrounded, obstructed, or covered by ice
ice•box \-ˌbäks\ *n* : REFRIGERATOR
ice•break•er \-ˌbrā-kər\ *n* : a ship equipped to make a channel through ice
ice cap *n* : a glacier forming on relatively level land and flowing outward from its center
ice cream *n* : a frozen food containing sweetened or flavored cream or butterfat
ice hockey *n* : a game in which two teams of ice-skating players try to shoot a puck into the opponent's goal
ice•house \ˈīs-ˌhau̇s\ *n* : a building in which ice is made or stored
Ice•land•er \-ˌlan-dər, -lən-\ *n* : a native or inhabitant of Iceland
¹Ice•lan•dic \īs-ˈlan-dik\ *adj* : of, relating to, or characteristic of Iceland, the Icelanders, or their language
²Icelandic *n* : the language of Iceland
ice•man \ˈīs-ˌman\ *n* : one who sells or delivers ice
ice milk *n* : a sweetened frozen food made of skim milk
ice pick *n* : a hand tool ending in a spike for chipping ice
ice–skate \ˈīs-ˌskāt\ *vb* : to skate on ice — **ice–skater** *n*
ice storm *n* : a storm in which falling rain freezes on contact
ice water *n* : chilled or iced water esp. for drinking
ich•thy•ol•o•gy \ˌik-thē-ˈä-lə-jē\ *n* : a branch of zoology dealing with fishes — **ich•thy•ol•o•gist** \-jist\ *n*
ici•cle \ˈī-ˌsi-kəl\ *n* : a hanging mass of ice formed by the freezing of dripping water
ic•ing \ˈī-siŋ\ *n* : a sweet usu. creamy mixture used to coat baked goods
ICJ *abbr* International Court of Justice
icky \ˈi-kē\ *adj* **ick•i•er; -est** : OFFENSIVE, DISTASTEFUL — **ick•i•ness** *n*
icon \ˈī-ˌkän\ *n* **1** : IMAGE; *esp* : a religious image painted on a wood panel **2** : a small picture on a computer display that suggests the purpose of an available function
icon•o•clasm \ī-ˈkä-nə-ˌkla-zəm\ *n* : the doctrine, practice, or attitude of an iconoclast
icon•o•clast \-ˌklast\ *n* [ML *iconoclastes,* fr. MGk *eikonoklastēs,* lit., image destroyer, fr. Gk *eikōn* image + *klan* to break] **1** : one who destroys religious images or opposes their veneration **2** : one who attacks cherished beliefs or institutions
-ics \iks\ *n sing or pl suffix* **1** : study : knowledge : skill : practice ⟨linguist*ics*⟩ ⟨electron*ics*⟩ **2** : characteristic actions or activities ⟨acrobat*ics*⟩ **3** : characteristic qualities, operations, or phenomena ⟨mechan*ics*⟩
ic•tus \ˈik-təs\ *n* : the recurring stress or beat in a rhythmic or metrical series of sounds
ICU *abbr* intensive care unit
icy \ˈī-sē\ *adj* **ic•i•er; -est** **1** : covered with, abounding in, or consisting of ice **2** : intensely cold **3** : being cold and unfriendly — **ic•i•ly** \ˈī-sə-lē\ *adv* — **ic•i•ness** \-sē-nəs\ *n*
¹id \ˈid\ *n* [L, it] : the part of the psyche in psychoanalytic theory that is completely unconscious and concerned with instinctual needs and drives
²id *abbr* idem
ID *abbr* **1** Idaho **2** identification
idea \ī-ˈdē-ə\ *n* **1** : a plan for action : DESIGN **2** : something imagined or pictured in the mind **3** : a central meaning or purpose **syn** concept, conception, notion, impression
¹ide•al \ī-ˈdēl\ *adj* **1** : existing only in the mind : IMAGINARY; *also* : lacking practicality **2** : of or relating to an ideal or to perfection : PERFECT
²ideal *n* **1** : a standard of excellence **2** : one regarded as a model worthy of imitation **3** : GOAL **syn** archetype, example, exemplar, paradigm, pattern
ide•al•ise *Brit var of* IDEALIZE
ide•al•ism \ī-ˈdē-ə-ˌli-zəm\ *n* : the practice of forming ideals or living under their influence; *also* : an idealized representation — **ide•al•ist** \-list\ *n* — **ide•al•is•tic** \ī-ˌdē-ə-ˈlis-tik\ *adj* — **ide•al•is•ti•cal•ly** \-ti-k(ə-)lē\ *adv*
ide•al•ize \ī-ˈdē-ə-ˌlīz\ *vb* **-ized; -iz•ing** : to think of or represent as ideal — **ide•al•i•za•tion** \-ˌdē-ə-lə-ˈzā-shən\ *n*
ide•al•ly \ī-ˈdē-lē, -ˈdē-ə-lē\ *adv* **1** : in idea or imagination : MENTALLY **2** : in agreement with an ideal : PERFECTLY
ide•a•tion \ˌī-dē-ˈā-shən\ *n* : the forming of ideas — **ide•ate** \ˈī-dē-ˌāt\ *vb* — **ide•a•tion•al** \ˌī-dē-ˈā-shə-nəl\ *adj*
idem \ˈī-ˌdem, ˈē-, ˈi-\ *pron* [L, same] : something previously mentioned
iden•ti•cal \ī-ˈden-ti-kəl\ *adj* **1** : being the same **2** : essentially alike **syn** equivalent, equal, tantamount
iden•ti•fi•ca•tion \ī-ˌden-tə-fə-ˈkā-shən\ *n* **1** : an act of identifying : the state of being identified **2** : evidence of identity **3** : an unconscious psychological process by which an individual models thoughts, feelings, and actions after another person or an object
iden•ti•fy \ī-ˈden-tə-ˌfī\ *vb* **-fied; -fy•ing** **1** : to regard as identical **2** : ASSOCIATE **3** : to establish the identity of **4** : to practice psychological identification — **iden•ti•fi•able** \-ˌden-tə-ˈfī-ə-bəl\ *adj* — **iden•ti•fi•ably** \-blē\ *adv* — **iden•ti•fi•er** \-ˌfī(-ə)r\ *n*
iden•ti•ty \ī-ˈden-tə-tē\ *n, pl* **-ties** **1** : sameness of essential character **2** : INDIVIDUALITY **3** : the fact of being the same person or thing as claimed
identity crisis *n* : psychological conflict esp. in adolescence involving confusion about one's social role and one's personality
ideo•gram \ˈī-dē-ə-ˌgram, ˈi-\ *n* **1** : a picture or symbol used in a system of writing to represent a thing or an idea **2** : a character or symbol used in a system of writing to represent an entire word
ide•ol•o•gy \ˌī-dē-ˈä-lə-jē, ˌi-\ *also* **ide•al•o•gy** \-ˈä-lə-jē, -ˈa-\ *n, pl* **-gies** **1** : the body of ideas characteristic of a particular individual, group, or culture **2** : the assertions, theories, and aims that constitute a political, social, and economic program — **ide•o•log•i•cal** \ˌī-dē-ə-ˈlä-ji-kəl, ˌi-\ *adj* — **ide•ol•o•gist** \-dē-ˈä-lə-jist\ *n*
ides \ˈīdz\ *n sing or pl* : the 15th day of March, May, July, or October or the 13th day of any other month in the ancient Roman calendar
id•i•o•cy \ˈi-dē-ə-sē\ *n, pl* **-cies** **1** : extreme mental retardation **2** : something notably stupid or foolish
id•i•om \ˈi-dē-əm\ *n* **1** : the language peculiar to a person or group **2** : the characteristic form or structure of a language **3** : an expression that cannot be understood from the meanings of its separate words (as *give way*) — **id•i•o•mat•ic** \ˌi-dē-ə-ˈma-tik\ *adj* — **id•i•o•mat•i•cal•ly** \-ti-k(ə-)lē\ *adv*
id•i•o•path•ic \ˌi-dē-ə-ˈpa-thik\ *adj* : arising spontaneously or from an obscure or unknown cause ⟨an ~ disease⟩
id•i•o•syn•cra•sy \ˌi-dē-ə-ˈsiŋ-krə-sē\ *n, pl* **-sies** : personal peculiarity — **id•i•o•syn•crat•ic** \ˌi-dē-ō-sin-ˈkra-tik\ *adj* — **id•i•o•syn•crat•i•cal•ly** \-ˈkra-ti-k(ə-)lē\ *adv*
id•i•ot \ˈi-dē-ət\ *n* [ME, fr. L *idiota* ignorant person, fr. Gk *idiōtēs* one in a private station, ignorant person, fr. *idios* one's own, private] **1** : a mentally retarded person requiring complete custodial care **2** : a foolish or stupid person — **id•i•ot•ic** \ˌi-dē-ˈä-tik\ *adj* — **id•i•ot•i•cal•ly** \-ti-k(ə-)lē\ *adv*
¹idle \ˈīd-ᵊl\ *adj* **idler** \ˈī-də-lər\; **idlest** \ˈī-də-ləst\ **1** : GROUNDLESS, WORTHLESS, USELESS ⟨~ talk⟩ **2** : not occupied or employed : INACTIVE **3** : LAZY — **idle•ness** *n* — **idly** \ˈīd-lē\ *adv*
²idle *vb* **idled; idling** **1** : to spend time doing nothing **2** : to make idle **3** : to run without being connected so that power is not used for useful work — **idler** *n*
idol \ˈīd-ᵊl\ *n* **1** : an image worshiped as a god; *also* : a false god **2** : an object of passionate devotion

idol•a•ter *or* **idol•a•tor** \ī-ˈdä-lə-tər\ *n* : a worshiper of idols

idol•a•try \-trē\ *n, pl* **-tries 1** : the worship of a physical object as a god **2** : excessive devotion — **idol•a•trous** \-trəs\ *adj*

idol•ize \ˈīd-ᵊl-ˌīz\ *vb* **-ized; -iz•ing** : to make an idol of — **idol•i•za•tion** \ˌīd-ᵊl-ə-ˈzā-shən\ *n*

idyll \ˈīd-ᵊl\ *n* **1** : a simple work of writing or poetry that describes country life or suggests a peaceful setting **2** : a fit subject for an idyll — **idyl•lic** \ī-ˈdi-lik\ *adj*

i.e. \ˈī-ˈē\ *abbr* [L *id est*] that is

IE *abbr* industrial engineer

-ier — see -ER

if \ˈif \ *conj* **1** : in the event that ⟨~ he stays, I leave⟩ **2** : WHETHER ⟨ask ~ he left⟩ **3** — used as a function word to introduce an exclamation expressing a wish ⟨~ it would only rain⟩ **4** : even though ⟨an interesting ~ untenable argument⟩

IF *abbr* intermediate frequency

if•fy \ˈi-fē\ *adj* : full of contingencies or unknown conditions

-i•fy \ə-ˌfī\ *vb suffix* : -FY

IG *abbr* inspector general

ig•loo \ˈi-glü\ *n, pl* **igloos** [Inuit (an Eskimo language) *iglu* house] : an Eskimo house or hut often made of snow blocks and in the shape of a dome

ig•ne•ous \ˈig-nē-əs\ *adj* **1** : FIERY **2** : formed by solidification of molten rock

ig•nite \ig-ˈnīt\ *vb* **ig•nit•ed; ig•nit•ing** : to set afire or catch fire — **ig•nit•able** \-ˈnī-tə-bəl\ *adj*

ig•ni•tion \ig-ˈni-shən\ *n* **1** : a setting on fire **2** : the process or means (as an electric spark) of igniting the fuel mixture in an engine

ig•no•ble \ig-ˈnō-bəl\ *adj* **1** : of common birth **2** : not honorable : BASE, MEAN **syn** despicable, scurvy, sordid, vile, wretched — **ig•no•bly** *adv*

ig•no•min•i•ous \ˌig-nə-ˈmi-nē-əs\ *adj* **1** : DISHONORABLE **2** : DESPICABLE **3** : HUMILIATING, DEGRADING **syn** disreputable, discreditable, disgraceful, inglorious — **ig•no•min•i•ous•ly** *adv* — **ig•no•mi•ny** \ˈig-nə-ˌmi-nē, ig-ˈnä-mə-nē\ *n*

ig•no•ra•mus \ˌig-nə-ˈrā-məs\ *n* [*Ignoramus,* ignorant lawyer in *Ignoramus* (1615), play by George Ruggle] : an utterly ignorant person

ig•no•rance \ˈig-nə-rəns\ *n* : the state of being ignorant

ig•no•rant \ˈig-nə-rənt\ *adj* **1** : lacking knowledge **2** : resulting from or showing lack of knowledge or intelligence **3** : UNAWARE, UNINFORMED **syn** benighted, illiterate, uneducated, unlettered, untutored — **ig•no•rant•ly** *adv*

ig•nore \ig-ˈnōr\ *vb* **ig•nored; ig•nor•ing** : to refuse to take notice of **syn** overlook, slight, neglect

igua•na \i-ˈgwä-nə\ *n* : any of various large tropical American lizards

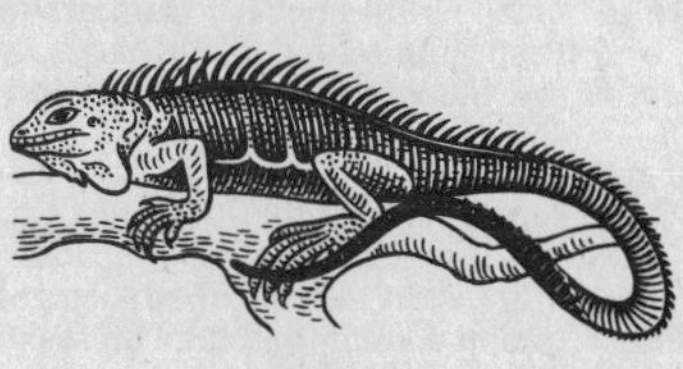

iguana

ihp *abbr* indicated horsepower

IHS \ˌī-ˌāch-ˈes\ [LL, part transliteration of Gk ΙΗΣ, abbreviation for ΙΗΣΟΥΣ *Iēsous* Jesus] — used as a Christian symbol and monogram for *Jesus*

ikon *var of* ICON

IL *abbr* Illinois

il•e•itis \ˌi-lē-ˈī-təs\ *n* : inflammation of the ileum

il•e•um \ˈi-lē-əm\ *n, pl* **il•ea** \-lē-ə\ : the part of the small intestine between the jejunum and the large intestine

il•i•ac \ˈi-lē-ˌak\ *adj* : of, relating to, or located near the ilium

il•i•um \ˈi-lē-əm\ *n* : the uppermost and largest of the three bones making up either side of the pelvis

ilk \ˈilk\ *n* : SORT, KIND

[1]**ill** \ˈil\ *adj* **worse** \ˈwərs\; **worst** \ˈwərst\ **1** : attended or caused by an evil intent ⟨~ deeds⟩ **2** : not normal or sound ⟨~ health⟩; *also* : not in good health : SICK **3** : BAD, UNLUCKY ⟨~ omen⟩ **4** : not right or proper ⟨~ manners⟩ **5** : UNFRIENDLY, HOSTILE ⟨~ feeling⟩

[2]**ill** *adv* **worse; worst 1** : with displeasure **2** : in a harsh manner **3** : HARDLY, SCARCELY ⟨can ~ afford it⟩ **4** : BADLY, UNLUCKILY **5** : in a faulty way

[3]**ill** *n* **1** : EVIL **2** : MISFORTUNE, DISTRESS **3** : AILMENT, SICKNESS; *also* : TROUBLE

[4]**ill** *abbr* illustrated; illustration; illustrator

Ill *abbr* Illinois

ill–ad•vised \ˌil-əd-ˈvīzd\ *adj* : not well counseled ⟨~ efforts⟩ — **ill–ad•vis•ed•ly** \-ˈvī-zəd-lē\ *adv*

ill–bred \-ˈbred\ *adj* : badly brought up : IMPOLITE

il•le•gal \il-ˈlē-gəl\ *adj* : not lawful; *also* : not sanctioned by official rules **syn** unlawful, criminal, illegitimate, illicit, wrongful — **il•le•gal•i•ty** \ˌi-li-ˈga-lə-tē\ *n* — **il•le•gal•ly** *adv*

il•leg•i•ble \il-ˈle-jə-bəl\ *adj* : not legible — **il•leg•i•bil•i•ty** \il-ˌle-jə-ˈbi-lə-tē\ *n* — **il•leg•i•bly** \il-ˈle-jə-blē\ *adv*

il•le•git•i•mate \ˌi-li-ˈji-tə-mət\ *adj* **1** : born of unmarried parents **2** : ILLOGICAL **3** : ILLEGAL — **il•le•git•i•ma•cy** \-ˈji-tə-mə-sē\ *n* — **il•le•git•i•mate•ly** *adv*

ill–fat•ed \ˈil-ˈfā-təd\ *adj* : UNFORTUNATE

ill–fa•vored \-ˈfā-vərd\ *adj* : UGLY, UNATTRACTIVE

ill–got•ten \-ˈgät-ᵊn\ *adj* : acquired by improper means ⟨~ gains⟩

ill–hu•mored \-ˈhyü-mərd, -ˈyü-\ *adj* : SURLY, IRRITABLE

il•lib•er•al \il-ˈli-bə-rəl\ *adj* : not liberal : NARROW, BIGOTED

il•lic•it \il-ˈli-sət\ *adj* : not permitted : UNLAWFUL — **il•lic•it•ly** *adv*

il•lim•it•able \il-ˈli-mə-tə-bəl\ *adj* : BOUNDLESS, MEASURELESS — **il•lim•it•ably** \-blē\ *adv*

Il•li•nois \ˌi-lə-ˈnȯi *also* -ˈnȯiz\ *n, pl* **Illinois** : a member of an American Indian people of Illinois, Iowa, and Wisconsin

il•lit•er•ate \il-ˈli-tə-rət\ *adj* **1** : having little or no education; *esp* : unable to read or write **2** : showing a lack of familiarity with the fundamentals of a particular field of knowledge — **il•lit•er•a•cy** \-ˈli-tə-rə-sē\ *n* — **illiterate** *n*

ill–man•nered \ˈil-ˈma-nərd\ *adj* : marked by bad manners : RUDE

ill–na•tured \-ˈnā-chərd\ *adj* : CROSS, SURLY — **ill–na•tured•ly** *adv*

ill•ness \ˈil-nəs\ *n* : SICKNESS

il•log•i•cal \il-ˈlä-ji-kəl\ *adj* : lacking sound reasoning; *also* : SENSELESS — **il•log•i•cal•ly** \-ji-k(ə-)lē\ *adv*

ill–starred \ˈil-ˈstärd\ *adj* : UNLUCKY 1

ill–tem•pered \-ˈtem-pərd\ *adj* : CROSS

ill–treat \-ˈtrēt\ *vb* : to treat cruelly or improperly : MALTREAT — **ill–treat•ment** *n*

il•lu•mi•nate \i-ˈlü-mə-ˌnāt\ *vb* **-nat•ed; -nat•ing 1** : to supply or brighten with light : light up **2** : to make clear : ELUCIDATE **3** : to decorate (as a manuscript) with designs or pictures in gold or colors — **il•lu•mi•nat•ing•ly** *adv* — **il•lu•mi•na•tion** \-ˌlü-mə-ˈnā-shən\ *n* — **il•lu•mi•na•tor** \-ˈlü-mə-ˌnā-tər\ *n*

il•lu•mine \i-ˈlü-mən\ *vb* **-mined; -min•ing** : ILLUMINATE

ill–us•age \ˈil-ˈyü-sij\ *n* : harsh, unkind, or abusive treatment

ill–use \-ˈyüz\ *vb* : MALTREAT, ABUSE

il•lu•sion \i-ˈlü-zhən\ *n* [ME, fr. MF, fr. LL *illusio,* fr. L, action of mocking, fr. *illudere* to mock at, fr. *ludere* to play, mock] **1** : a mistaken idea : MISCONCEP-

TION 2 : a misleading visual image; *also* : HALLUCINATION

il·lu·sion·ist \i-ˈlü-zhə-nist\ *n* : one that produces illusions; *esp* : a sleight-of-hand performer

il·lu·sive \i-ˈlü-siv\ *adj* : DECEPTIVE

il·lu·so·ry \i-ˈlü-sə-rē, -zə-\ *adj* : DECEPTIVE

illust *or* **illus** *abbr* illustrated; illustration

il·lus·trate \ˈi-ləs-ˌtrāt\ *vb* **-trat·ed; -trat·ing** [L *illustrare*, fr. *lustrare* to purify, make bright] **1** : to explain by use of examples : CLARIFY; *also* : DEMONSTRATE **2** : to provide with pictures or figures that explain or decorate **3** : to serve to explain or decorate — **il·lus·tra·tor** \ˈi-lə-ˌstrā-tər\ *n*

il·lus·tra·tion \ˌi-lə-ˈstrā-shən\ *n* **1** : the act of illustrating : the condition of being illustrated **2** : an example or instance that helps make something clear **3** : a picture or diagram that explains or decorates

il·lus·tra·tive \i-ˈləs-trə-tiv, ˈi-lə-ˌstrā-\ *adj* : serving, tending, or designed to illustrate — **il·lus·tra·tive·ly** *adv*

il·lus·tri·ous \i-ˈləs-trē-əs\ *adj* : notably outstanding because of rank or achievement **syn** distinguished, eminent, famous, great, notable, prominent — **il·lus·tri·ous·ness** *n*

ill will *n* : unfriendly feeling

ILS *abbr* instrument landing system

[1]**im·age** \ˈi-mij\ *n* **1** : a likeness or imitation of a person or thing; *esp* : STATUE **2** : a picture of an object formed by a device (as a mirror or lens) **3** : a person strikingly like another person ⟨he is the ~ of his father⟩ **4** : a mental picture or conception : IMPRESSION, IDEA, CONCEPT **5** : a vivid representation or description

[2]**image** *vb* **im·aged; im·ag·ing 1** : to call up a mental picture of **2** : to describe or portray in words **3** : to create a representation of **4** : REFLECT, MIRROR **5** : to make appear : PROJECT

im·ag·ery \ˈi-mij-rē\ *n* **1** : IMAGES; *also* : the art of making images **2** : figurative language **3** : mental images; *esp* : the products of imagination

imag·in·able \i-ˈma-jə-nə-bəl\ *adj* : capable of being imagined : CONCEIVABLE — **imag·in·ably** *adv*

imag·i·nary \i-ˈma-jə-ˌner-ē\ *adj* **1** : existing only in the imagination **2** : containing or relating to a quantity (**imaginary unit**) that is the positive square root of minus 1 ($\sqrt{-1}$)

imaginary number *n* : a complex number (as $2 + 3i$) with a nonzero term (**imaginary part**) containing the imaginary unit as a factor

imag·i·na·tion \i-ˌma-jə-ˈnā-shən\ *n* **1** : the act or power of forming a mental image of something not present to the senses or not previously known or experienced **2** : creative ability **3** : RESOURCEFULNESS **4** : a mental image : a creation of the mind — **imag·i·na·tive** \i-ˈma-jə-nə-tiv, -ˌnā-\ *adj* — **imag·i·na·tive·ly** *adv*

imag·ine \i-ˈma-jən\ *vb* **imag·ined; imag·in·ing 1** : to form a mental picture of something not present **2** : THINK, GUESS ⟨I ~ it will rain⟩

im·ag·ism \ˈi-mi-ˌji-zəm\ *n, often cap* : a movement in poetry advocating free verse and the expression of ideas and emotions through clear precise images — **im·ag·ist** \-jist\ *n*

ima·go \i-ˈmā-gō, -ˈmä-\ *n, pl* **imagoes** *or* **ima·gi·nes** \-ˈmā-gə-ˌnēz, -ˈmä-\ [NL, fr. L, image] : an insect in its final adult stage — **ima·gi·nal** \i-ˈmā-gən-ᵊl, -ˈmä-\ *adj*

im·bal·ance \ˈim-ˈba-ləns\ *n* : lack of balance : the state of being out of equilibrium or out of proportion

im·be·cile \ˈim-bə-səl, -ˌsil\ *n* **1** : a mentally retarded person who needs help in routine personal care **2** : FOOL, IDIOT — **imbecile** *or* **im·be·cil·ic** \ˌim-bə-ˈsi-lik\ *adj* — **im·be·cil·i·ty** \ˌim-bə-ˈsi-lə-tē\ *n*

imbed *var of* EMBED

im·bibe \im-ˈbīb\ *vb* **im·bibed; im·bib·ing 1** : to receive and retain in the mind **2** : DRINK **3** : to take in or up : ABSORB — **im·bib·er** *n*

im·bri·ca·tion \ˌim-brə-ˈkā-shən\ *n* **1** : an overlapping of edges (as of tiles) **2** : a pattern showing imbrication — **im·bri·cate** \ˈim-bri-kət\ *adj*

im·bro·glio \im-ˈbrōl-yō\ *n, pl* **-glios** [It, fr. *imbrogliare* to entangle] **1** : a confused mass **2** : a complicated situation; *also* : a serious or embarrassing misunderstanding

im·brue \im-ˈbrü\ *vb* **im·brued; im·bru·ing** : STAIN ⟨hands *imbrued* with blood⟩

im·bue \-ˈbyü\ *vb* **im·bued; im·bu·ing 1** : to permeate or influence as if by dyeing **2** : to tinge or dye deeply

IMF *abbr* International Monetary Fund

imit *abbr* imitative

im·i·ta·ble \ˈi-mə-tə-bəl\ *adj* : capable or worthy of being imitated or copied

im·i·tate \ˈi-mə-ˌtāt\ *vb* **-tat·ed; -tat·ing 1** : to follow as a model : COPY **2** : RESEMBLE **3** : REPRODUCE **4** : MIMIC, COUNTERFEIT — **im·i·ta·tor** \-ˌtā-tər\ *n*

im·i·ta·tion \ˌi-mə-ˈtā-shən\ *n* **1** : an act of imitating **2** : COPY, COUNTERFEIT **3** : a literary work that reproduces the style of another author — **imitation** *adj*

im·i·ta·tive \ˈi-mə-ˌtā-tiv\ *adj* **1** : marked by imitation **2** : inclined to imitate **3** : COUNTERFEIT

im·mac·u·late \i-ˈma-kyə-lət\ *adj* **1** : being without stain or blemish : PURE **2** : spotlessly clean ⟨~ linen⟩ — **im·mac·u·late·ly** *adv*

im·ma·nent \ˈi-mə-nənt\ *adj* : having existence only in the mind — **im·ma·nence** \-nəns\ *n* — **im·ma·nen·cy** \-nən-sē\ *n*

im·ma·te·ri·al \ˌi-mə-ˈtir-ē-əl\ *adj* **1** : not consisting of matter : SPIRITUAL **2** : UNIMPORTANT, TRIFLING **syn** bodiless, disembodied, incorporeal, insubstantial, nonphysical — **im·ma·te·ri·al·i·ty** \-ˌtir-ē-ˈa-lə-tē\ *n*

im·ma·ture \ˌi-mə-ˈtu̇r, -ˈtyu̇r\ *adj* : lacking complete development : not yet mature — **im·ma·tu·ri·ty** \-ˈtu̇r-ə-tē, -ˈtyu̇r-\ *n*

im·mea·sur·able \(ˌ)i-ˈme-zhə-rə-bəl\ *adj* : not capable of being measured : indefinitely extensive : ILLIMITABLE — **im·mea·sur·ably** \-blē\ *adv*

im·me·di·a·cy \i-ˈmē-dē-ə-sē\ *n, pl* **-cies 1** : the quality or state of being immediate **2** : something that is of immediate importance

im·me·di·ate \i-ˈmē-dē-ət\ *adj* **1** : acting directly and alone : DIRECT ⟨the ~ cause of death⟩ **2** : being next in line or relation ⟨members of the ~ family⟩ **3** : not distant : CLOSE **4** : made or done at once ⟨an ~ response⟩ **5** : near to or related to the present time ⟨the ~ future⟩ — **im·me·di·ate·ly** *adv*

im·me·mo·ri·al \ˌi-mə-ˈmōr-ē-əl\ *adj* : extending beyond the reach of memory, record, or tradition

im·mense \i-ˈmens\ *adj* [MF, fr. L *immensus* immeasurable, fr. *mensus*, pp. of *metiri* to measure] **1** : very great in size or degree : VAST, HUGE **2** : EXCELLENT — **im·mense·ly** *adv* — **im·men·si·ty** \-ˈmen-sə-tē\ *n*

im·merse \i-ˈmərs\ *vb* **im·mersed; im·mers·ing 1** : to plunge or dip esp. into a fluid **2** : ENGROSS, ABSORB **3** : to baptize by immersing — **im·mer·sion** \-ˈmər-zhən\ *n*

im·mi·grant \ˈi-mi-grənt\ *n* **1** : a person who immigrates **2** : a plant or animal that becomes established where it did not previously occur

im·mi·grate \ˈi-mə-ˌgrāt\ *vb* **-grat·ed; -grat·ing** : to come into a foreign country and take up residence — **im·mi·gra·tion** \ˌi-mə-ˈgrā-shən\ *n*

im·mi·nent \ˈi-mə-nənt\ *adj* : ready to take place; *esp* : hanging threateningly over one's head — **im·mi·nence** \-nəns\ *n* — **im·mi·nent·ly** *adv*

im·mis·ci·ble \(ˌ)i-ˈmi-sə-bəl\ *adj* : incapable of mixing — **im·mis·ci·bil·i·ty** \-ˌmi-sə-ˈbi-lə-tē\ *n*

im·mo·bile \(ˌ)i-ˈmō-bəl\ *adj* : incapable of being moved : IMMOVABLE, FIXED — **im·mo·bil·i·ty** \ˌi-mō-ˈbi-lə-tē\ *n*

im·mo·bi·lize \i-ˈmō-bə-ˌlīz\ *vb* : to make immobile — **im·mo·bi·li·za·tion** \i-ˌmō-bə-lə-ˈzā-shən\ *n*

im•mod•er•ate \(ˌ)i-ˈmä-də-rət\ *adj* : lacking in moderation : EXCESSIVE — **im•mod•er•a•cy** \-rə-sē\ *n* — **im•mod•er•ate•ly** *adv*

im•mod•est \(ˌ)i-ˈmä-dəst\ *adj* : not modest : BRAZEN, INDECENT ⟨an ~ dress⟩ ⟨~ conduct⟩ — **im•mod•est•ly** *adv* — **im•mod•es•ty** \-də-stē\ *n*

im•mo•late \ˈi-mə-ˌlāt\ *vb* **-lat•ed; -lat•ing** [L *immolare,* fr. *mola* grits; fr. the custom of sprinkling victims with sacrificial meal] : to offer in sacrifice; *esp* : to kill as a sacrificial victim — **im•mo•la•tion** \ˌi-mə-ˈlā-shən\ *n*

im•mor•al \(ˌ)i-ˈmȯr-əl\ *adj* : not moral — **im•mor•al•ly** *adv*

im•mo•ral•i•ty \ˌi-mȯ-ˈra-lə-tē, ˌi-mə-\ *n* **1** : WICKEDNESS; *esp* : UNCHASTITY **2** : an immoral act or practice

¹im•mor•tal \(ˌ)i-ˈmȯrt-ᵊl\ *adj* **1** : not mortal : exempt from death ⟨~ gods⟩ **2** : destined to be remembered forever ⟨those ~ words⟩ — **im•mor•tal•ly** *adv*

²immortal *n* **1** : one exempt from death **2** *pl, often cap* : the gods in Greek and Roman mythology **3** : a person whose fame is lasting ⟨an ~ of baseball⟩

im•mor•tal•ise *Brit var of* IMMORTALIZE

im•mor•tal•i•ty \ˌi-ˌmȯr-ˈta-lə-tē\ *n* : the quality or state of being immortal; *esp* : unending existence

im•mor•tal•ize \i-ˈmȯrt-ᵊl-ˌīz\ *vb* **-ized; -iz•ing** : to make immortal

im•mov•able \(ˌ)i-ˈmü-və-bəl\ *adj* **1** : firmly fixed, settled, or fastened : FAST, STATIONARY ⟨~ mountains⟩ **2** : STEADFAST, UNYIELDING **3** : IMPASSIVE — **im•mov•abil•ity** \-ˌmü-və-ˈbi-lə-tē\ *n* — **im•mov•ably** \-blē\ *adv*

im•mune \i-ˈmyün\ *adj* **1** : EXEMPT **2** : having a special capacity for resistance (as to a disease) **3** : containing or producing antibodies — **im•mu•ni•ty** \-ˈmyü-nə-tē\ *n*

immune response *n* : a response of the body to an antigen resulting in the formation of antibodies and cells designed to react with the antigen and render it harmless

immune system *n* : the bodily system that protects the body from foreign substances, cells, and tissues by producing the immune response and that includes esp. the thymus, spleen, lymph nodes, and lymphocytes

im•mu•nize \ˈi-myə-ˌnīz\ *vb* **-nized; -niz•ing** : to make immune — **im•mu•ni•za•tion** \ˌi-myə-nə-ˈzā-shən\ *n*

im•mu•no•de•fi•cien•cy \ˌi-myə-nō-di-ˈfi-shən-sē\ *n* : inability to produce the normal number of antibodies or immunologically sensitized cells esp. in response to specific antigens — **im•mu•no•de•fi•cient** \-ˈfi-shənt\ *adj*

im•mu•no•glob•u•lin \ˌi-myə-nō-ˈglä-byə-lən\ *n* : ANTIBODY

im•mu•nol•o•gy \ˌi-myə-ˈnä-lə-jē\ *n* : a science that deals with the immune system, immunity, and the immune response — **im•mu•no•log•ic** \-nə-ˈlä-jik\ *or* **im•mu•no•log•i•cal** \-ji-kəl\ *adj* — **im•mu•no•log•i•cal•ly** \-ji-k(ə-)lē\ *adv* — **im•mu•nol•o•gist** \-ˈnä-lə-jist\ *n*

im•mu•no•sup•pres•sion \ˌi-myə-nō-sə-ˈpre-shən\ *n* : suppression (as by drugs) of natural immune responses — **im•mu•no•sup•press** \-ˈpres\ *vb* — **im•mu•no•sup•pres•sive** \-ˈpre-siv\ *adj*

im•mu•no•ther•a•py \-ˈther-ə-pē\ *n* : treatment or prevention of disease by attempting to induce immunity

im•mure \i-ˈmyu̇r\ *vb* **im•mured; im•mur•ing** **1** : to enclose within or as if within walls **2** : to build into a wall; *esp* : to entomb in a wall

im•mu•ta•ble \(ˌ)i-ˈmyü-tə-bəl\ *adj* : UNCHANGEABLE, UNCHANGING — **im•mu•ta•bil•i•ty** \-ˌmyü-tə-ˈbi-lə-tē\ *n* — **im•mu•ta•bly** \-ˈmyü-tə-blē\ *adv*

¹imp \ˈimp\ *n* **1** : a small demon : FIEND **2** : a mischievous child

²imp *abbr* **1** imperative **2** imperfect **3** imperial **4** import; imported

¹im•pact \im-ˈpakt\ *vb* **1** : to press together **2** : to have an impact on

²im•pact \ˈim-ˌpakt\ *n* **1** : a forceful contact, collision, or onset; *also* : the impetus communicated in or as if in a collision **2** : EFFECT

im•pact•ed \im-ˈpak-təd\ *adj* **1** : packed or wedged in **2** : wedged between the jawbone and another tooth

im•pair \im-ˈpar\ *vb* : to diminish in quantity, value, excellence, or strength : DAMAGE, LESSEN — **im•pair•ment** *n*

im•paired \-ˈpard\ *adj* : being in a less than perfect or whole condition; *esp* : handicapped or functionally defective — often used in combination ⟨hearing-impaired⟩

im•pa•la \im-ˈpa-lə\ *n, pl* **impalas** *or* **impala** : a large brownish African antelope that in the male has slender curving horns

im•pale \im-ˈpāl\ *vb* **im•paled; im•pal•ing** : to pierce with or as if with something pointed — **im•pale•ment** *n*

im•pal•pa•ble \(ˌ)im-ˈpal-pə-bəl\ *adj* **1** : unable to be felt by touch : INTANGIBLE **2** : not easily seen or understood — **im•pal•pa•bly** \-blē\ *adv*

im•pan•el \im-ˈpan-ᵊl\ *vb* : to enter in or on a panel : ENROLL ⟨~ a jury⟩

im•part \im-ˈpärt\ *vb* **1** : to give from one's store or abundance ⟨the sun ~*s* warmth⟩ **2** : to make known

im•par•tial \(ˌ)im-ˈpär-shəl\ *adj* : not partial : UNBIASED, JUST — **im•par•tial•i•ty** \-ˌpär-shē-ˈa-lə-tē\ *n* — **im•par•tial•ly** *adv*

im•pass•able \(ˌ)im-ˈpa-sə-bəl\ *adj* : incapable of being passed, traversed, or crossed ⟨~ roads⟩ — **im•pass•ably** \-blē\ *adv*

im•passe \ˈim-ˌpas\ *n* **1** : an impassable road or way **2** : a predicament from which there is no obvious escape

im•pas•si•ble \(ˌ)im-ˈpa-sə-bəl\ *adj* : incapable of feeling : IMPASSIVE

im•pas•sioned \im-ˈpa-shənd\ *adj* : filled with passion or zeal : showing great warmth or intensity of feeling **syn** passionate, ardent, fervent, fervid

im•pas•sive \(ˌ)im-ˈpa-siv\ *adj* : showing no signs of feeling, emotion, or interest : EXPRESSIONLESS, INDIFFERENT **syn** stoic, phlegmatic, apathetic, stolid — **im•pas•sive•ly** *adv* — **im•pas•siv•i•ty** \ˌim-ˌpa-ˈsi-və-tē\ *n*

im•pas•to \im-ˈpas-tō, -ˈpäs-\ *n* : the thick application of a pigment to a canvas or panel in painting; *also* : the body of pigment so applied

im•pa•tiens \im-ˈpā-shənz, -shəns\ *n* : any of a genus of annual herbs with usu. spurred flowers and seed capsules that readily split open

im•pa•tient \(ˌ)im-ˈpā-shənt\ *adj* **1** : not patient : restless or short of temper esp. under irritation, delay, or opposition **2** : INTOLERANT ⟨~ of poverty⟩ **3** : prompted or marked by impatience **4** : ANXIOUS — **im•pa•tience** \-shəns\ *n* — **im•pa•tient•ly** *adv*

im•peach \im-ˈpēch\ *vb* [ME *empechen* to accuse, fr. MF *empeechier* to hinder, fr. LL *impedicare* to fetter, fr. L *pedica* fetter, fr. *ped-, pes* foot] **1** : to charge (a public official) before an authorized tribunal with misconduct in office **2** : to challenge the credibility or validity of **3** : to remove from public office for misconduct — **im•peach•ment** *n*

im•pec•ca•ble \(ˌ)im-ˈpe-kə-bəl\ *adj* **1** : not capable of sinning or wrongdoing **2** : FAULTLESS, IRREPROACHABLE ⟨a man of ~ character⟩ — **im•pec•ca•bil•i•ty** \-ˌpe-kə-ˈbi-lə-tē\ *n* — **im•pec•ca•bly** \-ˈpe-kə-blē\ *adv*

im•pe•cu•nious \ˌim-pi-ˈkyü-nyəs, -nē-əs\ *adj* : having little or no money — **im•pe•cu•nious•ness** *n*

im•ped•ance \im-ˈpēd-ᵊns\ *n* : the opposition in an electrical circuit to the flow of an alternating current

im•pede \im-ˈpēd\ *vb* **im•ped•ed; im•ped•ing** [L *impedire,* fr. *ped-, pes* foot] : to interfere with the progress of

im•ped•i•ment \im-ˈpe-də-mənt\ *n* **1** : something that impedes, hinders, or obstructs **2** : a speech defect

im•ped•i•men•ta \im-ˌpe-də-ˈmen-tə\ *n pl* : things that impede

im•pel \im-ˈpel\ *vb* **im•pelled; im•pel•ling** : to urge or drive forward or on : FORCE; *also* : PROPEL

im•pel•ler *also* **im•pel•lor** \im-ˈpe-lər\ *n* : a rotor esp. in a pump

im•pend \im-ˈpend\ *vb* **1** : to hover or hang over threateningly : MENACE **2** : to be about to occur

im•pen•e•tra•ble \(ˌ)im-ˈpe-nə-trə-bəl\ *adj* **1** : incapable of being penetrated or pierced ⟨an ~ jungle⟩ **2** : incapable of being comprehended : INSCRUTABLE ⟨an ~ mystery⟩ — **im•pen•e•tra•bil•i•ty** \-ˌpe-nə-trə-ˈbi-lə-tē\ *n* — **im•pen•e•tra•bly** \-ˈpe-nə-trə-blē\ *adv*

im•pen•i•tent \(ˌ)im-ˈpe-nə-tənt\ *adj* : not penitent : not repenting of sin — **im•pen•i•tence** \-təns\ *n*

im•per•a•tive \im-ˈper-ə-tiv\ *adj* **1** : expressing a command, request, or encouragement ⟨~ sentence⟩ **2** : having power to restrain, control, or direct **3** : NECESSARY — **imperative** *n* — **im•per•a•tive•ly** *adv*

im•per•cep•ti•ble \ˌim-pər-ˈsep-tə-bəl\ *adj* : not perceptible; *esp* : too slight to be perceived ⟨~ changes⟩ — **im•per•cep•ti•bly** \-blē\ *adv*

im•per•cep•tive \ˌim-pər-ˈsep-tiv\ *adj* : not perceptive

imperf *abbr* imperfect

[1]**im•per•fect** \(ˌ)im-ˈpər-fikt\ *adj* **1** : not perfect : DEFECTIVE, INCOMPLETE **2** : of, relating to, or being a verb tense used to designate a continuing state or an incomplete action esp. in the past — **im•per•fect•ly** *adv*

[2]**imperfect** *n* : the imperfect tense; *also* : a verb form in it

im•per•fec•tion \ˌim-pər-ˈfek-shən\ *n* : the quality or state of being imperfect; *also* : FAULT, BLEMISH

im•pe•ri•al \im-ˈpir-ē-əl\ *adj* **1** : of, relating to, or befitting an empire or an emperor; *also* : of or relating to the United Kingdom or to the Commonwealth or British Empire **2** : ROYAL, SOVEREIGN; *also* : REGAL, IMPERIOUS **3** : of unusual size or excellence

im•pe•ri•al•ism \im-ˈpir-ē-ə-ˌli-zəm\ *n* : the policy of seeking to extend the power, dominion, or territories of a nation — **im•pe•ri•al•ist** \-list\ *n or adj* — **im•pe•ri•al•is•tic** \-ˌpir-ē-ə-ˈlis-tik\ *adj* — **im•pe•ri•al•is•ti•cal•ly** \-ti-k(ə-)lē\ *adv*

im•per•il \im-ˈper-əl\ *vb* **-iled** *or* **-illed; -il•ing** *or* **-il•ling** : ENDANGER

im•pe•ri•ous \im-ˈpir-ē-əs\ *adj* **1** : COMMANDING, LORDLY **2** : ARROGANT, DOMINEERING **3** : IMPERATIVE, URGENT — **im•pe•ri•ous•ly** *adv*

im•per•ish•able \(ˌ)im-ˈper-i-shə-bəl\ *adj* : not perishable or subject to decay

im•per•ma•nent \(ˌ)im-ˈpər-mə-nənt\ *adj* : not permanent : TRANSIENT — **im•per•ma•nent•ly** *adv*

im•per•me•able \(ˌ)im-ˈpər-mē-ə-bəl\ *adj* : not permitting passage (as of a fluid) through its substance

im•per•mis•si•ble \ˌim-pər-ˈmi-sə-bəl\ *adj* : not permissible

im•per•son•al \(ˌ)im-ˈpər-sə-nəl\ *adj* **1** : not referring to any particular person or thing **2** : not involving human emotions — **im•per•son•al•i•ty** \-ˌpər-sə-ˈna-lə-tē\ *n* — **im•per•son•al•ly** *adv*

im•per•son•ate \im-ˈpər-sə-ˌnāt\ *vb* **-at•ed; -at•ing** : to assume or act the character of — **im•per•son•a•tion** \-ˌpər-sə-ˈnā-shən\ *n* — **im•per•son•a•tor** \-ˈpər-sə-ˌnā-tər\ *n*

im•per•ti•nent \(ˌ)im-ˈpərt-ᵊn-ənt\ *adj* **1** : IRRELEVANT **2** : not restrained within due or proper bounds : RUDE, INSOLENT, SAUCY — **im•per•ti•nence** \-əns\ *n* — **im•per•ti•nent•ly** *adv*

im•per•turb•able \ˌim-pər-ˈtər-bə-bəl\ *adj* : marked by extreme calm, impassivity, and steadiness : SERENE

im•per•vi•ous \(ˌ)im-ˈpər-vē-əs\ *adj* **1** : incapable of being penetrated (as by moisture) **2** : not capable of being affected or disturbed ⟨~ to criticism⟩

im•pe•ti•go \ˌim-pə-ˈtē-gō, -ˈtī-\ *n* : a contagious skin disease characterized by vesicles, pustules, and yellowish crusts

im•pet•u•ous \im-ˈpe-chə-wəs\ *adj* **1** : marked by impulsive vehemence ⟨~ temper⟩ **2** : marked by force and violence ⟨with ~ speed⟩ — **im•pet•u•os•i•ty** \(ˌ)im-ˌpe-chə-ˈwä-sə-tē\ *n* — **im•pet•u•ous•ly** *adv*

im•pe•tus \ˈim-pə-təs\ *n* [L, assault, impetus, fr. *impetere* to attack, fr. *petere* to go to, seek] **1** : a driving force : IMPULSE; *also* : INCENTIVE **2** : MOMENTUM

im•pi•e•ty \(ˌ)im-ˈpī-ə-tē\ *n, pl* **-ties 1** : the quality or state of being impious **2** : an impious act

im•pinge \im-ˈpinj\ *vb* **im•pinged; im•ping•ing 1** : to strike or dash esp. with a sharp collision **2** : ENCROACH, INFRINGE — **im•pinge•ment** *n*

im•pi•ous \ˈim-pē-əs, (ˌ)im-ˈpī-\ *adj* : not pious : IRREVERENT, PROFANE

imp•ish \ˈim-pish\ *adj* : of, relating to, or befitting an imp; *esp* : MISCHIEVOUS — **imp•ish•ly** *adv* — **imp•ish•ness** *n*

im•pla•ca•ble \(ˌ)im-ˈpla-kə-bəl, -ˈplā-\ *adj* : not capable of being appeased, pacified, mitigated, or changed ⟨an ~ enemy⟩ — **im•pla•ca•bil•i•ty** \-ˌpla-kə-ˈbi-lə-tē, -ˌplā-\ *n* — **im•pla•ca•bly** \-ˈpla-kə-blē\ *adv*

im•plant \im-ˈplant\ *vb* **1** : to set firmly or deeply **2** : to fix in the mind or spirit **3** : to insert in a living site for growth or absorption — **im•plant** \ˈim-ˌplant\ *n* — **im•plan•ta•tion** \ˌim-ˌplan-ˈtā-shən\ *n*

im•plau•si•ble \(ˌ)im-ˈplȯ-zə-bəl\ *adj* : not plausible — **im•plau•si•bil•i•ty** \-ˌplȯ-zə-ˈbi-lə-tē\ *n* — **im•plau•si•bly** \-ˈplȯ-zə-blē\ *adv*

[1]**im•ple•ment** \ˈim-plə-mənt\ *n* [ME, fr. LL *implementum* action of filling up, fr. L *implēre* to fill up] : TOOL, UTENSIL, INSTRUMENT

[2]**im•ple•ment** \-ˌment\ *vb* **1** : CARRY OUT; *esp* : to put into practice **2** : to provide implements for — **im•ple•men•ta•tion** \ˌim-plə-mən-ˈtā-shən\ *n*

im•pli•cate \ˈim-plə-ˌkāt\ *vb* **-cat•ed; -cat•ing 1** : IMPLY **2** : INVOLVE — **im•pli•ca•tion** \ˌim-plə-ˈkā-shən\ *n*

im•plic•it \im-ˈpli-sət\ *adj* **1** : understood though not directly stated or expressed : IMPLIED; *also* : POTENTIAL **2** : COMPLETE, UNQUESTIONING, ABSOLUTE ⟨~ faith⟩ — **im•plic•it•ly** *adv*

im•plode \im-ˈplōd\ *vb* **im•plod•ed; im•plod•ing** : to burst or collapse inward — **im•plo•sion** \-ˈplō-zhən\ *n* — **im•plo•sive** \-siv\ *adj*

im•plore \im-ˈplōr\ *vb* **im•plored; im•plor•ing** : BESEECH, ENTREAT **syn** supplicate, beg, importune, plead

im•ply \im-ˈplī\ *vb* **im•plied; im•ply•ing 1** : to involve or indicate by inference, association, or necessary consequence rather than by direct statement ⟨war *implies* fighting⟩ **2** : to express indirectly : hint at : SUGGEST

im•po•lite \ˌim-pə-ˈlīt\ *adj* : not polite : RUDE, DISCOURTEOUS

im•pol•i•tic \(ˌ)im-ˈpä-lə-ˌtik\ *adj* : not politic : RASH

im•pon•der•a•ble \(ˌ)im-ˈpän-də-rə-bəl\ *adj* : incapable of being weighed or evaluated with exactness — **imponderable** *n*

[1]**im•port** \im-ˈpōrt\ *vb* **1** : MEAN, SIGNIFY **2** : to bring (as merchandise) into a place or country from a foreign or external source — **im•port•er** *n*

[2]**im•port** \ˈim-ˌpōrt\ *n* **1** : IMPORTANCE, SIGNIFICANCE **2** : MEANING, SIGNIFICATION **3** : something (as merchandise) brought in from another country

im•por•tance \im-ˈpȯrt-ᵊns\ *n* : the quality or state of being important : MOMENT, SIGNIFICANCE **syn** consequence, import, weight

im•por•tant \im-ˈpȯrt-ᵊnt\ *adj* **1** : marked by importance : SIGNIFICANT **2** : giving an impression of importance — **im•por•tant•ly** *adv*

im•por•ta•tion \ˌim-ˌpōr-ˈtā-shən, -pər-\ *n* **1** : the act or practice of importing **2** : something imported

im•por•tu•nate \im-ˈpȯr-chə-nət\ *adj* **1** : troublesomely urgent or persistent **2** : BURDENSOME, TROUBLESOME

im•por•tune \ˌim-pər-ˈtün, -ˈtyün; im-ˈpȯr-chən\ *vb* **-tuned; -tun•ing** : to urge or beg with troublesome persistence — **im•por•tu•ni•ty** \-pər-ˈtü-nə-tē, -ˈtyü-\ *n*

im•pose \im-ˈpōz\ *vb* **im•posed; im•pos•ing 1** : to establish or apply by authority ⟨~ a tax⟩; *also* : to establish by force ⟨*imposed* a government⟩ **2** : OBTRUDE ⟨*imposed* herself on others⟩ **3** : to take unwarranted advantage of something ⟨~ on her good nature⟩ — **im•po•si•tion** \ˌim-pə-ˈzi-shən\ *n*

im•pos•ing *adj* : impressive because of size, bearing, dignity, or grandeur — **im•pos•ing•ly** *adv*

im•pos•si•ble \(ˌ)im-ˈpä-sə-bəl\ *adj* **1** : incapable of being or of occurring **2** : enormously difficult **3** : extremely undesirable : UNACCEPTABLE — **im•pos•si•bil•i•ty** \-ˌpä-sə-ˈbi-lə-tē\ *n* — **im•pos•si•bly** \-ˈpä-sə-blē\ *adv*

[1]**im•post** \ˈim-ˌpōst\ *n* : TAX, DUTY

[2]**impost** *n* : a block, capital, or molding from which an arch springs

im•pos•tor *or* **im•pos•ter** \im-ˈpäs-tər\ *n* : one that assumes an identity or title not one's own in order to deceive

im•pos•ture \im-ˈpäs-chər\ *n* : DECEPTION; *esp* : fraudulent impersonation

im•po•tent \ˈim-pə-tənt\ *adj* **1** : lacking in power or strength : HELPLESS **2** : unable to copulate; *also* : STERILE — **im•po•tence** \-təns\ *n* — **im•po•ten•cy** \-tən-sē\ *n* — **im•po•tent•ly** *adv*

im•pound \im-ˈpau̇nd\ *vb* **1** : CONFINE, ENCLOSE ⟨~ stray dogs⟩ **2** : to seize and hold in legal custody **3** : to collect in a reservoir ⟨~ water⟩ — **im•pound•ment** *n*

im•pov•er•ish \im-ˈpä-və-rish\ *vb* : to make poor; *also* : to deprive of strength, richness, or fertility — **im•pov•er•ish•ment** *n*

im•prac•ti•ca•ble \(ˌ)im-ˈprak-ti-kə-bəl\ *adj* : not practicable : incapable of being put into practice or use

im•prac•ti•cal \(ˌ)im-ˈprak-ti-kəl\ *adj* **1** : not practical **2** : IMPRACTICABLE

im•pre•cate \ˈim-pri-ˌkāt\ *vb* **-cat•ed; -cat•ing** : CURSE — **im•pre•ca•tion** \ˌim-pri-ˈkā-shən\ *n*

im•pre•cise \ˌim-pri-ˈsīs\ *adj* : not precise — **im•pre•cise•ly** *adv* — **im•pre•cise•ness** *n* — **im•pre•ci•sion** \-ˈsi-zhən\ *n*

im•preg•na•ble \im-ˈpreg-nə-bəl\ *adj* : incapable of being taken by assault : UNCONQUERABLE, UNASSAILABLE — **im•preg•na•bil•i•ty** \(ˌ)im-ˌpreg-nə-ˈbi-lə-tē\ *n*

im•preg•nate \im-ˈpreg-ˌnāt\ *vb* **-nat•ed; -nat•ing 1** : to fertilize or make pregnant **2** : to cause to be filled, permeated, or saturated — **im•preg•na•tion** \ˌim-ˌpreg-ˈnā-shən\ *n*

im•pre•sa•rio \ˌim-prə-ˈsär-ē-ˌō\ *n, pl* **-ri•os** [It, fr. *impresa* undertaking, fr. *imprendere* to undertake] **1** : the manager or conductor of an opera or concert company **2** : one who puts on an entertainment **3** : MANAGER, PRODUCER

[1]**im•press** \im-ˈpres\ *vb* **1** : to apply with or produce (as a mark) by pressure : IMPRINT **2** : to press, stamp, or print in or upon **3** : to produce a vivid impression of **4** : to affect esp. forcibly or deeply — **im•press•ible** *adj*

[2]**im•press** \ˈim-ˌpres\ *n* **1** : a characteristic or distinctive mark **2** : IMPRESSION, EFFECT **3** : IMPRESSION 2 **4** : an image of something formed by or as if by pressure; *esp* : SEAL **5** : a product of pressure or influence

[3]**im•press** \im-ˈpres\ *vb* **1** : to force into naval service **2** : to get the aid or services of by forcible argument or persuasion — **im•press•ment** *n*

im•pres•sion \im-ˈpre-shən\ *n* **1** : a characteristic trait or feature resulting from influence : IMPRESS **2** : a stamp, form, or figure made by impressing : IMPRINT **3** : an esp. marked influence or effect on feeling, sense, or mind **4** : a single print or copy (as from type or from an engraved plate or book) **5** : all the copies of a publication (as a book) printed for one issue : PRINTING **6** : a usu. vague notion or remembrance **7** : an imitation in caricature of a noted personality as a form of entertainment

im•pres•sion•able \im-ˈpre-shə-nə-bəl\ *adj* : capable of being easily impressed : easily molded or influenced

im•pres•sion•ism \im-ˈpre-shə-ˌni-zəm\ *n, often cap* : a theory or practice in modern art of depicting the natural appearances of objects by dabs or strokes of primary unmixed colors in order to simulate actual reflected light — **im•pres•sion•is•tic** \-ˌpre-shə-ˈnis-tik\ *adj*

im•pres•sion•ist \im-ˈpre-shə-nist\ *n* **1** *often cap* : a painter who practices impressionism **2** : an entertainer who does impressions

im•pres•sive \im-ˈpre-siv\ *adj* : making or tending to make a marked impression ⟨an ~ speech⟩ — **im•pres•sive•ly** *adv* — **im•pres•sive•ness** *n*

im•pri•ma•tur \ˌim-prə-ˈmä-ˌtu̇r\ *n* [NL, let it be printed] **1** : a license to print or publish; *also* : official approval of a publication by a censor **2** : SANCTION, APPROVAL

[1]**im•print** \im-ˈprint, ˈim-ˌprint\ *vb* **1** : to stamp or mark by or as if by pressure : IMPRESS **2** : to fix firmly (as on the memory)

[2]**im•print** \ˈim-ˌprint\ *n* **1** : something imprinted or printed **2** : a publisher's name printed at the foot of a title page **3** : an indelible distinguishing effect or influence

im•pris•on \im-ˈpriz-ᵊn\ *vb* : to put in or as if in prison : CONFINE — **im•pris•on•ment** *n*

im•prob•a•ble \(ˌ)im-ˈprä-bə-bəl\ *adj* : unlikely to be true or to occur — **im•prob•a•bil•i•ty** \-ˌprä-bə-ˈbi-lə-tē\ *n* — **im•prob•a•bly** \-ˈprä-bə-blē\ *adv*

im•promp•tu \im-ˈprämp-tü, -tyü\ *adj* [F, fr. *impromptu* extemporaneously, fr. L *in promptu* in readiness] **1** : made or done on or as if on the spur of the moment **2** : EXTEMPORANEOUS, UNREHEARSED — **impromptu** *adv or n*

im•prop•er \(ˌ)im-ˈprä-pər\ *adj* **1** : not proper, fit, or suitable **2** : INCORRECT, INACCURATE **3** : not in accord with propriety, modesty, or good manners — **im•prop•er•ly** *adv*

improper fraction *n* : a fraction whose numerator is equal to or larger than the denominator

im•pro•pri•e•ty \ˌim-prə-ˈprī-ə-tē\ *n, pl* **-ties 1** : an improper act or remark; *esp* : an unacceptable use of a word or of language **2** : the quality or state of being improper

im•prove \im-ˈprüv\ *vb* **im•proved; im•prov•ing 1** : to enhance or increase in value or quality **2** : to grow or become better ⟨your work is *improving*⟩ **3** : to make good use of ⟨~ the time by reading⟩ — **im•prov•able** \-ˈprü-və-bəl\ *adj*

im•prove•ment \im-ˈprüv-mənt\ *n* **1** : the act or process of improving **2** : increased value or excellence of something **3** : something that adds to the value or appearance of a thing

im•prov•i•dent \(ˌ)im-ˈprä-və-dənt\ *adj* : not providing for the future — **im•prov•i•dence** \-dəns\ *n*

im•pro•vise \ˈim-prə-ˌvīz\ *vb* **-vised; -vis•ing** [F *improviser*, fr. It *improvvisare*, fr. *improvviso* sudden, fr. L *improvisus*, lit., unforeseen] **1** : to compose, recite, play, or sing on the spur of the moment : EXTEMPORIZE ⟨~ on the piano⟩ **2** : to make, invent, or arrange offhand ⟨~ a sail out of shirts⟩ — **im•pro•vi•sa•tion** \im-ˌprä-və-ˈzā-shən, ˌim-prə-və-\ *n* — **im•pro•vis•er** *or* **im•pro•vi•sor** \ˌim-prə-ˈvī-zər, ˈim-prə-ˌvī-\ *n*

im•pru•dent \(ˌ)im-ˈprüd-ᵊnt\ *adj* : not prudent : lacking discretion — **im•pru•dence** \-ᵊns\ *n*

im•pu•dent \ˈim-pyu̇-dənt\ *adj* : marked by contemptuous boldness or disregard of others — **im•pu•dence** \-dəns\ *n* — **im•pu•dent•ly** *adv*

im•pugn \im-ˈpyün\ *vb* [ME, to assail, ultim. fr. L *inpugnare*, fr. *pugnare* to fight] : to attack by words or arguments : oppose or attack as false or as lacking integrity

im•puis•sance \im-ˈpwis-ᵊns, -ˈpyü-ə-səns\ *n* [ME, fr. MF] : the quality or state of being powerless : WEAKNESS

im•pulse \ˈim-ˌpəls\ *n* **1** : a force that starts a body into motion; *also* : the motion produced by such a force **2** : an arousing of the mind and spirit to some usu. unpremeditated action **3** : NERVE IMPULSE

im•pul•sion \im-ˈpəl-shən\ *n* **1** : the act of impelling : the state of being impelled **2** : a force that impels **3** : IMPULSE 2; *also* : COMPULSION 3

im•pul•sive \im-ˈpəl-siv\ *adj* **1** : having the power of or actually driving or impelling **2** : acting or prone to act on impulse ⟨~ buying⟩ — **im•pul•sive•ly** *adv* — **im•pul•sive•ness** *n*

im•pu•ni•ty \im-ˈpyü-nə-tē\ *n* [MF or L; MF *impunité*, fr. L *impunitas*, fr. *impune* without punishment, fr. *poena* penalty, punishment] : exemption from punishment, harm, or loss

im•pure \(ˌ)im-ˈpyu̇r\ *adj* **1** : not pure : UNCHASTE, OBSCENE **2** : DIRTY, FOUL **3** : ADULTERATED, MIXED — **im•pu•ri•ty** \-ˈpyu̇r-ə-tē\ *n*

im•pute \im-ˈpyüt\ *vb* **im•put•ed; im•put•ing 1** : to lay the responsibility or blame for often falsely or unjustly **2** : to credit to a person or a cause : ATTRIBUTE — **im•put•able** \-ˈpyü-tə-bəl\ *adj* — **im•pu•ta•tion** \ˌim-pyu̇-ˈtā-shən\ *n*

¹in \ˈin\ *prep* **1** — used to indicate physical surroundings ⟨swim ~ the lake⟩ **2** : INTO 1 ⟨ran ~ the house⟩ **3** : DURING ⟨~ the summer⟩ **4** : WITH ⟨written ~ pencil⟩ **5** — used to indicate one's situation or state of being ⟨~ luck⟩ ⟨~ love⟩ **6** — used to indicate manner or purpose ⟨~ a hurry⟩ ⟨said ~ reply⟩ **7** : INTO 2 ⟨broke ~ pieces⟩

²in *adv* **1** : to or toward the inside ⟨come ~⟩; *also* : to or toward some destination or place ⟨flew ~ from the South⟩ **2** : at close quarters : NEAR ⟨the enemy closed ~⟩ **3** : into the midst of something ⟨mix ~ the flour⟩ **4** : to or at its proper place ⟨fit a piece ~⟩ **5** : WITHIN ⟨locked ~⟩ **6** : in vogue or season **7** : in one's presence, possession, or control ⟨the results are ~⟩

³in *adj* **1** : located inside or within **2** : that is in position, operation, or power ⟨the ~ party⟩ **3** : directed inward : INCOMING ⟨the ~ train⟩ **4** : keenly aware of and responsive to what is new and smart ⟨the ~ crowd⟩; *also* : extremely fashionable ⟨the ~ thing to do⟩

⁴in *n* **1** : one who is in office or power or on the inside **2** : INFLUENCE, PULL ⟨he has an ~ with the owner⟩

⁵in *abbr* **1** inch **2** inlet

In *symbol* indium

IN *abbr* Indiana

in- \(ˌ)in\ *prefix* : not : absence of : NON-, UN-

inaccessibility
inaccessible
inaccuracy
inaccurate
inaction
inactive
inactivity
inadmissibility
inadmissible
inadvisability
inadvisable
inapparent
inapplicable
inapposite
inapproachable
inappropriate
inaptitude
inarguable
inartistic
inattentive
inaudible
inaudibly
inauspicious
inauthentic
incautious
incombustible
incomprehension
inconclusive
incongruent
inconsistency
inconsistent
incoordination
incurious
indecipherable
indemonstrable
indestructible
indeterminable
indiscernible
indistinguishable
inedible
ineducable
ineffaceable
inefficacious
inefficacy
inelastic
inelasticity
inequitable
inequity
ineradicable
inerrant
inexpedient
inexpensive
inexpressive
inextinguishable
infeasible
inharmonious
inhospitable
injudicious
inoffensive
insanitary
insensitive
insensitivity
insignificance
insignificant
insolvable
insusceptible

in•abil•i•ty \ˌi-nə-ˈbi-lə-tē\ *n* : the quality or state of being unable

in ab•sen•tia \ˌin-ab-ˈsen-chə, -chē-ə\ *adv* : in one's absence

in•ac•ti•vate \(ˌ)i-ˈnak-tə-ˌvāt\ *vb* : to make inactive — **in•ac•ti•va•tion** \(ˌ)i-ˌnak-tə-ˈvā-shən\ *n*

in•ad•e•quate \(ˌ)i-ˈna-di-kwət\ *adj* : not adequate : INSUFFICIENT — **in•ad•e•qua•cy** \-kwə-sē\ *n* — **in•ad•e•quate•ly** *adv* — **in•ad•e•quate•ness** *n*

in•ad•ver•tent \ˌi-nəd-ˈvərt-ᵊnt\ *adj* **1** : HEEDLESS, INATTENTIVE **2** : UNINTENTIONAL — **in•ad•ver•tence** \-ᵊns\ *n* — **in•ad•ver•ten•cy** \-ᵊn-sē\ *n* — **in•ad•ver•tent•ly** *adv*

in•alien•able \(ˌ)i-ˈnāl-yə-nə-bəl, -ˈnā-lē-ə-\ *adj* : incapable of being alienated, surrendered, or transferred ⟨~ rights⟩ — **in•alien•abil•i•ty** \(ˌ)i-ˌnāl-yə-nə-ˈbi-lə-tē, -ˌnā-lē-ə-\ *n* — **in•alien•ably** *adv*

in•amo•ra•ta \i-ˌnä-mə-ˈrä-tə\ *n* : a woman with whom one is in love

inane \i-ˈnān\ *adj* **inan•er; -est** : EMPTY, INSUBSTANTIAL; *also* : SHALLOW, SILLY — **inan•i•ty** \i-ˈna-nə-tē\ *n*

in•an•i•mate \(ˌ)i-ˈna-nə-mət\ *adj* : not animate or animated : lacking the qualities of living things — **in•an•i•mate•ly** *adv* — **in•an•i•mate•ness** *n*

in•ap•pre•cia•ble \ˌi-nə-ˈprē-shə-bəl\ *adj* : too small to be perceived — **in•ap•pre•cia•bly** \-blē\ *adv*

in•apt \(ˌ)i-ˈnapt\ *adj* **1** : not suitable **2** : INEPT — **in•apt•ly** *adv* — **in•apt•ness** *n*

in•ar•tic•u•late \ˌi-när-ˈti-kyə-lət\ *adj* **1** : not understandable as spoken words **2** : MUTE **3** : incapable of being expressed by speech; *also* : UNSPOKEN **4** : not having the power of distinct utterance or effective expression — **in•ar•tic•u•late•ly** *adv*

in•as•much as \ˌi-nəz-ˈməch-\ *conj* : seeing that : SINCE

in•at•ten•tion \ˌi-nə-ˈten-chən\ *n* : failure to pay attention : DISREGARD

¹in•au•gu•ral \i-ˈnȯ-gyə-rəl, -gə-\ *adj* **1** : of or relating to an inauguration **2** : marking a beginning

²inaugural *n* **1** : an inaugural address **2** : INAUGURATION

in•au•gu•rate \i-ˈnȯ-gyə-ˌrāt, -gə-\ *vb* **-rat•ed; -rat•ing 1** : to introduce into an office with suitable ceremonies : INSTALL **2** : to dedicate ceremoniously **3** : BEGIN, INITIATE — **in•au•gu•ra•tion** \-ˌnȯ-gyə-ˈrā-shən, -gə-\ *n*

in•board \ˈin-ˌbōrd\ *adv* **1** : inside the hull of a ship **2** : close or closest to the center line of a vehicle or craft — **inboard** *adj*

in•born \ˈin-ˈbȯrn\ *adj* **1** : present from or as if from birth **2** : HEREDITARY, INHERITED **syn** innate, congenital, native

in•bound \ˈin-ˌbau̇nd\ *adj* : inward bound ⟨~ traffic⟩

in•bred \ˈin-ˈbred\ *adj* **1** : ingrained in one's nature as deeply as if by heredity **2** : subjected to or produced by inbreeding

in•breed•ing \ˈin-ˌbrē-diŋ\ *n* **1** : the interbreeding of closely related individuals esp. to preserve and fix desirable characters of and to eliminate unfavorable characters from a stock **2** : confinement to a narrow range or a local or limited field of choice — **in•breed** \-ˈbrēd\ *vb*

inc *abbr* **1** incomplete **2** incorporated **3** increase

In•ca \ˈiŋ-kə\ *n* [Sp, fr. Quechua (a So. American Indian language) *inka* ruler of the Inca empire] **1** : a noble or a member of the ruling family of an Indian empire of Peru, Bolivia, and Ecuador until the Spanish conquest **2** : a member of any people under Inca influence

in•cal•cu•la•ble \(ˌ)in-ˈkal-kyə-lə-bəl\ *adj* : not capable of being calculated; *esp* : too large or numerous to be calculated — **in•cal•cu•la•bly** \-blē\ *adv*

in•can•des•cent \ˌin-kən-ˈdes-ᵊnt\ *adj* **1** : glowing with heat 2 : SHINING, BRILLIANT — **in•can•des•cence** \-ᵊns\ *n*

incandescent lamp *n* : a lamp in which an electrically heated filament emits light

in•can•ta•tion \ˌin-ˌkan-ˈtā-shən\ *n* : a use of spells or verbal charms spoken or sung as a part of a ritual of magic; *also* : a formula of words used in or as if in such a ritual

in•ca•pa•ble \(ˌ)in-ˈkā-pə-bəl\ *adj* : lacking ability or qualification for a particular purpose; *also* : UNQUALIFIED — **in•ca•pa•bil•i•ty** \-ˌkā-pə-ˈbi-lə-tē\ *n*

in•ca•pac•i•tate \ˌin-kə-ˈpa-sə-ˌtāt\ *vb* **-tat•ed; -tat•ing** : to make incapable or unfit : DISQUALIFY, DISABLE

in•ca•pac•i•ty \ˌin-kə-ˈpa-sə-tē\ *n, pl* **-ties** : the quality or state of being incapable

in•car•cer•ate \in-ˈkär-sə-ˌrāt\ *vb* **-at•ed; -at•ing** : IMPRISON, CONFINE — **in•car•cer•a•tion** \(ˌ)in-ˌkär-sə-ˈrā-shən\ *n*

in•car•na•dine \in-ˈkär-nə-ˌdīn, -ˌdēn\ *vb* **-dined; -din•ing** : REDDEN

in•car•nate \in-ˈkär-nət, -ˌnāt\ *adj* **1** : having bodily and esp. human form and substance **2** : PERSONIFIED — **in•car•nate** \-ˌnāt\ *vb*

in•car•na•tion \ˌin-ˌkär-ˈnā-shən\ *n* **1** : the embodiment of a deity or spirit in an earthly form **2** *cap* : the union of divine and human natures in Jesus Christ **3** : a person showing a trait or typical character to a marked degree **4** : the act of incarnating : the state of being incarnate

incase *var of* ENCASE

in•cen•di•ary \in-ˈsen-dē-ˌer-ē\ *adj* **1** : of or relating to a deliberate burning of property **2** : tending to excite or inflame **3** : designed to start fires ⟨an ~ bomb⟩ — **incendiary** *n*

¹**in•cense** \ˈin-ˌsens\ *n* **1** : material used to produce a fragrant odor when burned **2** : the perfume or smoke from some spices and gums when burned

²**in•cense** \in-ˈsens\ *vb* **in•censed; in•cens•ing** : to make extremely angry

in•cen•tive \in-ˈsen-tiv\ *n* [ME, fr. LL *incentivum*, fr. *incentivus* stimulating, fr. L, setting the tune, fr. *incinere* to set the tune, fr. *canere* to sing] : something that incites or is likely to incite to determination or action

in•cep•tion \in-ˈsep-shən\ *n* : BEGINNING, COMMENCEMENT

in•cer•ti•tude \(ˌ)in-ˈsər-tə-ˌtüd, -ˌtyüd\ *n* **1** : UNCERTAINTY, DOUBT, INDECISION **2** : INSECURITY, INSTABILITY

in•ces•sant \(ˌ)in-ˈses-ᵊnt\ *adj* : continuing or flowing without interruption ⟨~ rains⟩ — **in•ces•sant•ly** *adv*

in•cest \ˈin-ˌsest\ *n* [ME, fr. L *incestus* sexual impurity, fr. *incestus* impure, fr. *castus* pure] : sexual intercourse between persons so closely related that marriage is illegal — **in•ces•tu•ous** \in-ˈses-chü-wəs\ *adj*

¹**inch** \ˈinch\ *n* [ME, fr. OE *ynce*, fr. L *uncia* twelfth part, inch, ounce] — see WEIGHT table

²**inch** *vb* : to move by small degrees

in•cho•ate \in-ˈkō-ət, ˈin-kə-ˌwāt\ *adj* : being only partly in existence or operation : INCOMPLETE, INCIPIENT

inch•worm \ˈinch-ˌwərm\ *n* : LOOPER

in•ci•dence \ˈin-sə-dəns\ *n* : rate of occurrence or effect

¹**in•ci•dent** \-dənt\ *n* **1** : OCCURRENCE, HAPPENING **2** : an action likely to lead to grave consequences esp. in diplomatic matters

²**incident** *adj* **1** : occurring or likely to occur esp. in connection with some other happening **2** : falling or striking on something ⟨~ light rays⟩

¹**in•ci•den•tal** \ˌin-sə-ˈdent-ᵊl\ *adj* **1** : subordinate, nonessential, or attendant in position or significance ⟨~ expenses⟩ **2** : CASUAL, CHANCE

²**incidental** *n* **1** *pl* : minor items (as of expense) that are not individually accounted for **2** : something incidental

in•ci•den•tal•ly \ˌin-sə-ˈden-tə-lē, -ˈdent-lē\ *adv* **1** : in an incidental manner **2** : by the way

in•cin•er•ate \in-ˈsi-nə-ˌrāt\ *vb* **-at•ed; -at•ing** : to burn to ashes

in•cin•er•a•tor \in-ˈsi-nə-ˌrā-tər\ *n* : a furnace for burning waste

in•cip•i•ent \in-ˈsi-pē-ənt\ *adj* : beginning to be or become apparent

in•cise \in-ˈsīz\ *vb* **in•cised; in•cis•ing 1** : to cut into **2** : CARVE, ENGRAVE

in•ci•sion \in-ˈsi-zhən\ *n* : CUT, GASH; *esp* : a surgical cut

in•ci•sive \in-ˈsī-siv\ *adj* : impressively direct and decisive — **in•ci•sive•ly** *adv*

in•ci•sor \in-ˈsī-zər\ *n* : a front tooth typically adapted for cutting

in•cite \in-ˈsīt\ *vb* **in•cit•ed; in•cit•ing** : to arouse to action : stir up — **in•cite•ment** *n* — **in•cit•er** *n*

in•ci•vil•i•ty \ˌin-sə-ˈvi-lə-tē\ *n* **1** : RUDENESS, DISCOURTESY **2** : a rude or discourteous act

incl *abbr* include; included; including; inclusive

in•clem•ent \(ˌ)in-ˈkle-mənt\ *adj* : SEVERE, STORMY ⟨~ weather⟩ — **in•clem•en•cy** \-mən-sē\ *n*

in•cli•na•tion \ˌin-klə-ˈnā-shən\ *n* **1** : PROPENSITY, BENT; *esp* : LIKING **2** : BOW, NOD ⟨an ~ of the head⟩ **3** : a tilting of something **4** : SLANT, SLOPE

¹**in•cline** \in-ˈklīn\ *vb* **in•clined; in•clin•ing 1** : BOW, BEND **2** : to be drawn toward an opinion or course of action **3** : to deviate from the vertical or horizontal : SLOPE **4** : INFLUENCE, PERSUADE — **in•clin•er** *n*

²**in•cline** \ˈin-ˌklīn\ *n* : SLOPE

inclose, inclosure *var of* ENCLOSE, ENCLOSURE

in•clude \in-ˈklüd\ *vb* **in•clud•ed; in•clud•ing** : to take in or comprise as a part of a whole ⟨the price ~*s* tax⟩ — **in•clu•sion** \in-ˈklü-zhən\ *n* — **in•clu•sive** \-ˈklü-siv\ *adj*

incog *abbr* incognito

¹**in•cog•ni•to** \ˌin-ˌkäg-ˈnē-tō, in-ˈkäg-nə-ˌtō\ *n, pl* **-tos 1** : one appearing or living incognito **2** : the state or disguise of an incognito

²**incognito** *adv or adj* [It, fr. L *incognitus* unknown, fr. *cognoscere* to know] : with one's identity concealed

in•co•her•ent \ˌin-kō-ˈhir-ənt, -ˈher-\ *adj* **1** : not sticking closely or compactly together : LOOSE **2** : not clearly or logically connected : RAMBLING — **in•co•her•ence** \-əns\ *n* — **in•co•her•ent•ly** *adv*

in•come \ˈin-ˌkəm\ *n* : a gain usu. measured in money that derives from labor, business, or property

income tax *n* : a tax on the net income of an individual or business concern

in•com•ing \ˈin-ˌkə-miŋ\ *adj* : coming in ⟨the ~ tide⟩ ⟨~ freshmen⟩

in•com•men•su•rate \ˌin-kə-ˈmen-sə-rət, -ˈmen-chə-\ *adj* : not commensurate; *esp* : INADEQUATE

in•com•mode \ˌin-kə-ˈmōd\ *vb* **-mod•ed; -mod•ing** : INCONVENIENCE, DISTURB

in•com•mu•ni•ca•ble \ˌin-kə-ˈmyü-ni-kə-bəl\ *adj* : not communicable : not capable of being communicated or imparted; *also* : UNCOMMUNICATIVE

in•com•mu•ni•ca•do \ˌin-kə-ˌmyü-nə-ˈkä-dō\ *adv or adj* : without means of communication; *also* : in solitary confinement ⟨a prisoner held ~⟩

in•com•pa•ra•ble \(ˌ)in-ˈkäm-pə-rə-bəl, -prə-\ *adj* **1** : eminent beyond comparison : MATCHLESS **2** : not suitable for comparison — **in•com•pa•ra•bly** \-blē\ *adv*

in•com•pat•i•ble \ˌin-kəm-ˈpa-tə-bəl\ *adj* : incapable of or unsuitable for association or use together ⟨~ colors⟩ ⟨temperamentally ~⟩ — **in•com•pat•i•bil•i•ty** \ˌin-kəm-ˌpa-tə-ˈbi-lə-tē\ *n*

in•com•pe•tent \(ˌ)in-ˈkäm-pə-tənt\ *adj* **1** : not legally qualified **2** : not competent : lacking sufficient knowledge, skill, or ability — **in•com•pe•tence** \-təns\ *n* — **in•com•pe•ten•cy** \-tən-sē\ *n* — **incompetent** *n*

in·com·plete \ˌin-kəm-ˈplēt\ *adj* : lacking a part or parts : UNFINISHED, IMPERFECT — **in·com·plete·ly** *adv* — **in·com·plete·ness** *n*

in·com·pre·hen·si·ble \ˌin-ˌkäm-prē-ˈhen-sə-bəl\ *adj* : impossible to comprehend : UNINTELLIGIBLE

in·con·ceiv·able \ˌin-kən-ˈsē-və-bəl\ *adj* **1** : impossible to comprehend **2** : UNBELIEVABLE

in·con·gru·ous \(ˌ)in-ˈkäŋ-grü-wəs\ *adj* : not consistent with or suitable to the surroundings or associations — **in·con·gru·i·ty** \ˌin-kən-ˈgrü-ə-tē, -ˌkän-\ *n* — **in·con·gru·ous·ly** *adv*

in·con·se·quen·tial \ˌin-ˌkän-sə-ˈkwen-chəl\ *adj* **1** : ILLOGICAL; *also* : IRRELEVANT **2** : of no significance : UNIMPORTANT — **in·con·se·quence** \(ˌ)in-ˈkän-sə-ˌkwens\ *n* — **in·con·se·quen·tial·ly** *adv*

in·con·sid·er·able \ˌin-kən-ˈsi-də-rə-bəl\ *adj* : SLIGHT, TRIVIAL

in·con·sid·er·ate \ˌin-kən-ˈsi-də-rət\ *adj* : HEEDLESS, THOUGHTLESS; *esp* : not respecting the rights or feelings of others — **in·con·sid·er·ate·ly** *adv* — **in·con·sid·er·ate·ness** *n*

in·con·sol·able \ˌin-kən-ˈsō-lə-bəl\ *adj* : incapable of being consoled — **in·con·sol·ably** \-blē\ *adv*

in·con·spic·u·ous \ˌin-kən-ˈspi-kyə-wəs\ *adj* : not readily noticeable — **in·con·spic·u·ous·ly** *adv*

in·con·stant \(ˌ)in-ˈkän-stənt\ *adj* : not constant : CHANGEABLE **syn** fickle, capricious, mercurial, unstable, volatile — **in·con·stan·cy** \-stən-sē\ *n* — **in·con·stant·ly** *adv*

in·con·test·able \ˌin-kən-ˈtes-tə-bəl\ *adj* : not contestable : INDISPUTABLE — **in·con·test·ably** \-ˈtes-tə-blē\ *adv*

in·con·ti·nent \(ˌ)in-ˈkänt-ᵊn-ənt\ *adj* **1** : lacking self-restraint **2** : unable to retain a bodily discharge (as urine) voluntarily — **in·con·ti·nence** \-əns\ *n*

in·con·tro·vert·ible \ˌin-ˌkän-trə-ˈvər-tə-bəl\ *adj* : not open to question : INDISPUTABLE ⟨~ evidence⟩ — **in·con·tro·vert·ibly** \-blē\ *adv*

¹in·con·ve·nience \ˌin-kən-ˈvē-nyəns\ *n* **1** : something that is inconvenient **2** : the quality or state of being inconvenient

²inconvenience *vb* : to subject to inconvenience

in·con·ve·nient \ˌin-kən-ˈvē-nyənt\ *adj* : not convenient : causing trouble or annoyance : INOPPORTUNE — **in·con·ve·nient·ly** *adv*

in·cor·po·rate \in-ˈkȯr-pə-ˌrāt\ *vb* **-rat·ed; -rat·ing 1** : to unite closely or so as to form one body : BLEND **2** : to form, form into, or become a corporation **3** : to give material form to : EMBODY — **in·cor·po·ra·tion** \-ˌkȯr-pə-ˈrā-shən\ *n*

in·cor·po·re·al \ˌin-kȯr-ˈpōr-ē-əl\ *adj* : having no material body or form

in·cor·rect \ˌin-kə-ˈrekt\ *adj* **1** : INACCURATE, FAULTY **2** : not true : WRONG **3** : UNBECOMING, IMPROPER — **in·cor·rect·ly** *adv* — **in·cor·rect·ness** *n*

in·cor·ri·gi·ble \(ˌ)in-ˈkȯr-ə-jə-bəl\ *adj* : incapable of being corrected, amended, or reformed — **in·cor·ri·gi·bil·i·ty** \(ˌ)in-ˌkȯr-ə-jə-ˈbi-lə-tē\ *n* — **in·cor·ri·gi·bly** \-ˈkōr-ə-jə-blē\ *adv*

in·cor·rupt·ible \ˌin-kə-ˈrəp-tə-bəl\ *adj* **1** : not subject to decay or dissolution **2** : incapable of being bribed or morally corrupted — **in·cor·rupt·ibil·i·ty** \-ˌrəp-tə-ˈbi-lə-tē\ *n* — **in·cor·rupt·ibly** \-ˈrəp-tə-blē\ *adv*

incr *abbr* increase; increased

¹in·crease \in-ˈkrēs, ˈin-ˌkrēs\ *vb* **in·creased; in·creas·ing 1** : to become greater : GROW **2** : to multiply by the production of young ⟨rabbits ~ rapidly⟩ **3** : to make greater — **in·creas·ing·ly** \-ˈkrē-siŋ-lē\ *adv*

²in·crease \ˈin-ˌkrēs, in-ˈkrēs\ *n* **1** : addition or enlargement in size, extent, or quantity : GROWTH **2** : something that is added to an original stock or amount (as by growth)

in·cred·i·ble \(ˌ)in-ˈkre-də-bəl\ *adj* : too extraordinary and improbable to be believed; *also* : hard to believe — **in·cred·i·bil·i·ty** \(ˌ)in-ˌkre-də-ˈbi-lə-tē\ *n* — **in·cred·i·bly** \-ˈkre-də-blē\ *adv*

in·cred·u·lous \-ˈkre-jə-ləs\ *adj* **1** : SKEPTICAL **2** : expressing disbelief — **in·cre·du·li·ty** \ˌin-kri-ˈdü-lə-tē, -ˈdyü-\ *n* — **in·cred·u·lous·ly** *adv*

in·cre·ment \ˈiŋ-krə-mənt, ˈin-\ *n* **1** : the action or process of increasing esp. in quantity or value : ENLARGEMENT; *also* : QUANTITY **2** : something gained or added; *esp* : one of a series of regular consecutive additions — **in·cre·men·tal** \ˌiŋ-krə-ˈment-ᵊl, ˌin-\ *adj* — **in·cre·men·tal·ly** *adv*

in·crim·i·nate \in-ˈkri-mə-ˌnāt\ *vb* **-nat·ed; -nat·ing** : to charge with or prove involvement in a crime or fault : ACCUSE — **in·crim·i·na·tion** \-ˌkri-mə-ˈnā-shən\ *n* — **in·crim·i·na·to·ry** \-ˈkri-mə-nə-ˌtōr-ē\ *adj*

incrust *var of* ENCRUST

in·crus·ta·tion \ˌin-ˌkrəs-ˈtā-shən\ *n* **1** : CRUST; *also* : something resembling a crust ⟨~ of habits⟩ **2** : the act of encrusting : the state of being encrusted

in·cu·bate \ˈiŋ-kyü-ˌbāt, ˈin-\ *vb* **-bat·ed; -bat·ing** : to sit on (eggs) to hatch by the warmth of the body; *also* : to keep (as an embryo) under conditions favorable for development — **in·cu·ba·tion** \ˌiŋ-kyü-ˈbā-shən, ˌin-\ *n*

in·cu·ba·tor \ˈiŋ-kyü-ˌbāt-ər, ˈin-\ *n* : one that incubates; *esp* : an apparatus providing suitable conditions (as of warmth and moisture) for incubating something (as a premature baby)

in·cu·bus \ˈiŋ-kyə-bəs, ˈin-\ *n, pl* **-bi** \-ˌbī, -ˌbē\ *also* **-bus·es** [ME, fr. LL, fr. L *incubare* to lie on] **1** : a spirit supposed to work evil on persons in their sleep **2** : NIGHTMARE 1 **3** : one that oppresses like a nightmare

in·cul·cate \in-ˈkəl-ˌkāt, ˈin-(ˌ)kəl-\ *vb* **-cat·ed; -cat·ing** [L *inculcare*, lit., to tread on, fr. *calcare* to trample, fr. *calx* heel] : to teach and impress by frequent repetitions or admonitions — **in·cul·ca·tion** \ˌin-(ˌ)kəl-ˈkā-shən\ *n*

in·cul·pa·ble \(ˌ)in-ˈkəl-pə-bəl\ *adj* : free from guilt : INNOCENT

in·cul·pate \in-ˈkəl-ˌpāt, ˈin-(ˌ)kəl-\ *vb* **-pat·ed; -pat·ing** : INCRIMINATE

in·cum·ben·cy \in-ˈkəm-bən-sē\ *n, pl* **-cies 1** : something that is incumbent **2** : the quality or state of being incumbent **3** : the office or period of office of an incumbent

¹in·cum·bent \in-ˈkəm-bənt\ *n* : the holder of an office or position

²incumbent *adj* **1** : imposed as a duty **2** : occupying a specified office **3** : lying or resting on something else

in·cu·nab·u·lum \ˌin-kyə-ˈna-byə-ləm, iŋ-\ *n, pl* **-la** \-lə\ [NL, fr. L *incunabula*, pl., bands holding the baby in a cradle, fr. *cunae* cradle] : a book printed before 1501

in·cur \in-ˈkər\ *vb* **in·curred; in·cur·ring** : to become liable or subject to : bring down upon oneself

in·cur·able \(ˌ)in-ˈkyu̇r-ə-bəl\ *adj* **1** : not subject to cure **2** : not likely to be changed — **incurable** *n* — **in·cur·ably** \(ˌ)in-ˈkyu̇r-ə-blē\ *adv*

in·cur·sion \in-ˈkər-zhən\ *n* **1** : a sudden hostile invasion : RAID **2** : an entering in or into (as an activity)

in·cus \ˈiŋ-kəs\ *n, pl* **in·cu·des** \iŋ-ˈkyü-(ˌ)dēz\ [NL, fr. L, anvil] : the middle bone of a chain of three small bones in the ear of a mammal

ind *abbr* **1** independent **2** index **3** industrial; industry

Ind *abbr* **1** Indian **2** Indiana

in·debt·ed \in-ˈde-təd\ *adj* **1** : owing gratitude or recognition to another **2** : owing money — **in·debt·ed·ness** *n*

in·de·cent \(ˌ)in-ˈdēs-ᵊnt\ *adj* : not decent; *esp* : morally offensive — **in·de·cen·cy** \-ᵊn-sē\ *n* — **in·de·cent·ly** *adv*

in·de·ci·sion \ˌin-di-ˈsi-zhən\ *n* : a wavering between two or more possible courses of action : IRRESOLUTION

in·de·ci·sive \ˌin-di-ˈsī-siv\ *adj* **1** : INCONCLUSIVE **2** : marked by or prone to indecision **3** : INDEFINITE — **in·de·ci·sive·ly** *adv* — **in·de·ci·sive·ness** *n*

in•de•co•rous \(ˌ)in-ˈde-kə-rəs; ˌin-di-ˈkōr-əs\ *adj* : not decorous **syn** improper, unseemly, indecent, unbecoming, indelicate — **in•de•co•rous•ly** *adv* — **in•de•co•rous•ness** *n*

in•deed \in-ˈdēd\ *adv* **1** : without any question : TRULY — often used interjectionally to express irony, disbelief, or surprise **2** : in reality **3** : all things considered

indef *abbr* indefinite

in•de•fat•i•ga•ble \ˌin-di-ˈfa-ti-gə-bəl\ *adj* : UNTIRING — **in•de•fat•i•ga•bly** \-blē\ *adv*

in•de•fea•si•ble \-ˈfē-zə-bəl\ *adj* : not capable of being annulled or voided — **in•de•fea•si•bly** \-blē\ *adv*

in•de•fen•si•ble \-ˈfen-sə-bəl\ *adj* **1** : incapable of being maintained as right or valid **2** : INEXCUSABLE **3** : incapable of being protected against physical attack

in•de•fin•able \-ˈfī-nə-bəl\ *adj* : incapable of being precisely described or analyzed — **in•de•fin•ably** \-blē\ *adv*

in•def•i•nite \(ˌ)in-ˈde-fə-nət\ *adj* **1** : not defining or identifying ⟨*an* is an ~ article⟩ **2** : not precise : VAGUE **3** : having no fixed limit — **in•def•i•nite•ly** *adv* — **in•def•i•nite•ness** *n*

in•del•i•ble \in-ˈde-lə-bəl\ *adj* [ME, fr. ML *indelibilis,* alter. of L *indelebilis,* fr. *delēre* to delete, destroy] **1** : not capable of being removed or erased **2** : making marks that cannot be erased **3** : LASTING, UNFORGETTABLE — **in•del•i•bly** \in-ˈde-lə-blē\ *adv*

in•del•i•cate \(ˌ)in-ˈde-li-kət\ *adj* : not delicate; *esp* : IMPROPER, COARSE, TACTLESS **syn** indecent, unseemly, indecorous, unbecoming — **in•del•i•ca•cy** \in-ˈde-lə-kə-sē\ *n*

in•dem•ni•fy \in-ˈdem-nə-ˌfī\ *vb* **-fied; -fy•ing** [L *indemnis* unharmed, fr. *in-* not + *damnum* damage] **1** : to secure against hurt, loss, or damage **2** : to make compensation to for hurt, loss, or damage — **in•dem•ni•fi•ca•tion** \-ˌdem-nə-fə-ˈkā-shən\ *n*

in•dem•ni•ty \in-ˈdem-nə-tē\ *n, pl* **-ties** **1** : security against hurt, loss, or damage; *also* : exemption from incurred penalties or liabilities **2** : something that indemnifies

¹in•dent \in-ˈdent\ *vb* [ME, fr. MF *endenter,* fr. OF, fr. *dent* tooth, fr. L *dent-, dens*] **1** : to notch the edge of **2** : INDENTURE **3** : to set (as a line of a paragraph) in from the margin

²indent *vb* **1** : to force inward so as to form a depression **2** : to form a dent in

in•den•ta•tion \ˌin-ˌden-ˈtā-shən\ *n* **1** : NOTCH; also: a usu. deep recess (as in a coastline) **2** : the action of indenting : the condition of being indented **3** : DENT **4** : INDENTION 2

in•den•tion \in-ˈden-chən\ *n* **1** : INDENTATION 2 **2** : the blank space produced by indenting

¹in•den•ture \in-ˈden-chər\ *n* **1** : a written certificate or agreement; *esp* : a contract binding one person (as an apprentice) to work for another for a given period of time — usu. used in pl. **2** : INDENTATION 1 **3** : DENT

²indenture *vb* **in•den•tured; in•den•tur•ing** : to bind (as an apprentice) by indentures

in•de•pen•dence \ˌin-də-ˈpen-dəns\ *n* : the quality or state of being independent : FREEDOM

Independence Day *n* : July 4 observed as a legal holiday in commemoration of the adoption of the Declaration of Independence in 1776

in•de•pen•dent \ˌin-də-ˈpen-dənt\ *adj* **1** : SELF-GOVERNING; *also* : not affiliated with a larger controlling unit **2** : not requiring or relying on something else or somebody else ⟨an ~ conclusion⟩ ⟨~ of her parents⟩ **3** : not easily influenced : showing self-reliance and personal freedom ⟨an ~ mind⟩ **4** : not committed to a political party ⟨an ~ voter⟩ **5** : MAIN ⟨an ~ clause⟩ — **independent** *n* — **in•de•pen•dent•ly** *adv*

in•de•scrib•able \ˌin-di-ˈskrī-bə-bəl\ *adj* **1** : that cannot be described **2** : being too intense or great for description — **in•de•scrib•ably** \-blē\ *adv*

in•de•ter•mi•nate \ˌin-di-ˈtər-mə-nət\ *adj* **1** : VAGUE; *also* : not known in advance **2** : not limited in advance; *also* : not leading to a definite end or result — **in•de•ter•mi•na•cy** \-nə-sē\ *n* — **in•de•ter•mi•nate•ly** *adv*

¹in•dex \ˈin-ˌdeks\ *n, pl* **in•dex•es** *or* **in•di•ces** \-də-ˌsēz\ **1** : POINTER **2** : SIGN, INDICATION ⟨an ~ of character⟩ **3** : a guide for facilitating references; *esp* : an alphabetical list of items treated in a printed work with the page number where each item may be found **4** : a list of restricted or prohibited material **5** *pl usu* **indices** : a number or symbol or expression (as an exponent) associated with another to indicate a mathematical operation or use or position in an arrangement or expansion **6** : a character ☞ used to direct attention (as to a note) **7** : INDEX NUMBER

²index *vb* **1** : to provide with or put into an index **2** : to serve as an index of **3** : to regulate by indexation

in•dex•ation \ˌin-ˌdek-ˈsā-shən\ *n* : a system of economic control in which a body of variables (as wages and interest) rise or fall at the same rate as an index of the cost of living

index finger *n* : FOREFINGER

in•dex•ing *n* : INDEXATION

index number *n* : a number used to indicate change in magnitude (as of cost) as compared with the magnitude at some specified time usu. taken as 100

index of refraction : the ratio of the speed of radiation in one medium to that in another medium

in•dia ink \ˈin-dē-ə-\ *n, often cap 1st I* **1** : a solid black pigment used in drawing **2** : a fluid made from india ink

In•di•an \ˈin-dē-ən\ *n* **1** : a native or inhabitant of the subcontinent of India **2** : a person of Indian descent **3** : AMERICAN INDIAN — **Indian** *adj*

Indian corn *n* : a tall widely grown American cereal grass bearing seeds on long ears; *also* : its ears or seeds

Indian meal *n* : CORNMEAL

Indian paintbrush *n* : any of a genus of herbaceous plants related to the snapdragon that have brightly colored bracts

Indian pipe *n* : a waxy white leafless saprophytic herb of Asia and the U.S.

Indian summer *n* : a period of mild weather in late autumn or early winter

In•dia paper \ˈin-dē-ə-\ *n* **1** : a thin absorbent paper used esp. for taking impressions (as of steel engravings) **2** : a thin tough opaque printing paper

indic *abbr* indicative

in•di•cate \ˈin-də-ˌkāt\ *vb* **-cat•ed; -cat•ing** **1** : to point out or to **2** : to show indirectly **3** : to state briefly — **in•di•ca•tion** \ˌin-də-ˈkā-shən\ *n* — **in•di•ca•tor** \ˈin-də-ˌkā-tər\ *n*

¹in•dic•a•tive \in-ˈdi-kə-tiv\ *adj* **1** : of, relating to, or being a verb form that represents an act or state as a fact ⟨~ mood⟩ **2** : serving to indicate ⟨actions ~ of fear⟩

²indicative *n* **1** : the indicative mood of a language **2** : a form in the indicative mood

in•di•cia \in-ˈdi-shə, -shē-ə\ *n pl* **1** : distinctive marks **2** : postal markings often imprinted on mail or mailing labels

in•dict \in-ˈdīt\ *vb* [alter. of earlier *indite,* fr. ME, fr. OF *enditer,* lit., to write down] **1** : to charge with a fault or offense **2** : to charge with a crime by the finding of a jury — **in•dict•able** *adj* — **in•dict•ment** *n*

in•dif•fer•ent \in-ˈdi-frənt, -fə-rənt\ *adj* **1** : UNBIASED, UNPREJUDICED **2** : of no importance one way or the other **3** : marked by no special liking for or dislike of something **4** : being neither excessive nor inadequate **5** : PASSABLE, MEDIOCRE **6** : being neither right nor wrong — **in•dif•fer•ence** \-frəns, -fə-rəns\ *n* — **in•dif•fer•ent•ly** *adv*

in•dig•e•nous \in-ˈdi-jə-nəs\ *adj* : produced, growing, or living naturally in a particular region

in•di•gent \ˈin-di-jənt\ *adj* : IMPOVERISHED, NEEDY — **in•di•gence** \-jəns\ *n*

in•di•gest•ible \ˌin-dī-ˈjes-tə-bəl, -də-\ *adj* : not readily digested

in•di•ges•tion \-ˈjes-chən\ *n* : inadequate or difficult digestion : DYSPEPSIA

in•dig•nant \in-ˈdig-nənt\ *adj* : filled with or marked by indignation — **in•dig•nant•ly** *adv*

in•dig•na•tion \ˌin-dig-ˈnā-shən\ *n* : anger aroused by something unjust, unworthy, or mean

in•dig•ni•ty \in-ˈdig-nə-tē\ *n, pl* **-ties** : an offense against personal dignity or self-respect; *also* : humiliating treatment

in•di•go \ˈin-di-ˌgō\ *n, pl* **-gos** *or* **-goes** [It dial., fr. L *indicum,* fr. Gk *indikon,* fr. *indikos* Indic, fr. *Indos* India] **1** : a blue dye obtained from plants or synthesized **2** : a deep reddish blue color

in•di•rect \ˌin-də-ˈrekt, -dī-\ *adj* **1** : not straight ⟨an ~ route⟩ **2** : not straightforward and open ⟨~ methods⟩ **3** : not having a plainly seen connection ⟨an ~ cause⟩ **4** : not directly to the point ⟨an ~ answer⟩ — **in•di•rec•tion** \-ˈrek-shən\ *n* — **in•di•rect•ly** *adv* — **in•di•rect•ness** *n*

in•dis•creet \ˌin-di-ˈskrēt\ *adj* : not discreet : IMPRUDENT — **in•dis•creet•ly** *adv*

in•dis•cre•tion \ˌin-di-ˈskre-shən\ *n* **1** : IMPRUDENCE **2** : something marked by lack of discretion; *esp* : an act deviating from accepted morality

in•dis•crim•i•nate \ˌin-di-ˈskri-mə-nət\ *adj* **1** : not marked by discrimination or careful distinction **2** : HAPHAZARD, RANDOM **3** : UNRESTRAINED **4** : MOTLEY — **in•dis•crim•i•nate•ly** *adv*

in•dis•pens•able \ˌin-di-ˈspen-sə-bəl\ *adj* : absolutely essential : REQUISITE — **in•dis•pens•abil•i•ty** \-ˌspen-sə-ˈbi-lə-tē\ *n* — **indispensable** *n* — **in•dis•pens•ably** \-ˈspen-sə-blē\ *adv*

in•dis•posed \-ˈspōzd\ *adj* **1** : slightly ill **2** : AVERSE — **in•dis•po•si•tion** \(ˌ)in-ˌdis-pə-ˈzi-shən\ *n*

in•dis•put•able \ˌin-di-ˈspyü-tə-bəl, (ˌ)in-ˈdis-pyə-\ *adj* : not disputable : UNQUESTIONABLE ⟨~ proof⟩ — **in•dis•put•ably** \-blē\ *adv*

in•dis•sol•u•ble \ˌin-di-ˈsäl-yə-bəl\ *adj* : not capable of being dissolved, undone, or broken : PERMANENT

in•dis•tinct \ˌin-di-ˈstiŋkt\ *adj* **1** : not sharply outlined or separable : BLURRED, FAINT, DIM **2** : not readily distinguishable : UNCERTAIN — **in•dis•tinct•ly** *adv* — **in•dis•tinct•ness** *n*

in•dite \in-ˈdīt\ *vb* **in•dit•ed; in•dit•ing** : COMPOSE ⟨~ a poem⟩; *also* : to put in writing ⟨~ a letter⟩

in•di•um \ˈin-dē-əm\ *n* : a malleable silvery metallic chemical element — see ELEMENT table

indiv *abbr* individual

[1]**in•di•vid•u•al** \ˌin-də-ˈvi-jə-wəl\ *adj* **1** : of, relating to, or associated with an individual ⟨~ traits⟩ **2** : being an individual : existing as an indivisible whole **3** : intended for one person **4** : SEPARATE ⟨~ copies⟩ **5** : having marked individuality ⟨an ~ style⟩ — **in•di•vid•u•al•ly** *adv*

[2]**individual** *n* **1** : a single member of a category : a particular person, animal, or thing **2** : PERSON ⟨a disagreeable ~⟩

in•di•vid•u•al•ise *Brit var of* INDIVIDUALIZE

in•di•vid•u•al•ism \ˌin-də-ˈvi-jə-wə-ˌli-zəm\ *n* **1** : a doctrine that the interests of the individual are primary **2** : a doctrine holding that the individual has political or economic rights with which the state must not interfere **3** : INDIVIDUALITY

in•di•vid•u•al•ist \-list\ *n* **1** : one that pursues a markedly independent course in thought or action **2** : one that advocates or practices individualism — **individualist** *or* **in•di•vid•u•al•is•tic** \-ˌvi-jə-wə-ˈlis-tik\ *adj*

in•di•vid•u•al•i•ty \-ˌvi-jə-ˈwa-lə-tē\ *n, pl* **-ties** **1** : the sum of qualities that characterize and distinguish an individual from all others; *also* : PERSONALITY **2** : separate or distinct existence **3** : INDIVIDUAL, PERSON

in•di•vid•u•al•ize \-ˈvi-jə-wə-ˌlīz\ *vb* **-ized; -iz•ing** **1** : to make individual in character **2** : to treat or notice individually : PARTICULARIZE **3** : to adapt to the needs of an individual

individual retirement account *n* : IRA

in•di•vid•u•ate \ˌin-də-ˈvi-jə-ˌwāt\ *vb* **-at•ed; -at•ing** : to give individuality to : form into an individual — **in•di•vid•u•a•tion** \-ˌvi-jə-ˈwā-shən\ *n*

in•di•vis•i•ble \ˌin-də-ˈvi-zə-bəl\ *adj* : impossible to divide or separate — **in•di•vis•i•bil•i•ty** \-ˌvi-zə-ˈbi-lə-tē\ *n* — **in•di•vis•i•bly** *adv*

in•doc•tri•nate \in-ˈdäk-trə-ˌnāt\ *vb* **-nat•ed; -nat•ing** **1** : to instruct esp. in fundamentals or rudiments : TEACH **2** : to teach the beliefs and doctrines of a particular group — **in•doc•tri•na•tion** \(ˌ)in-ˌdäk-trə-ˈnā-shən\ *n* — **in•doc•tri•na•tor** *n*

In•do–Eu•ro•pe•an \ˌin-dō-ˌyu̇r-ə-ˈpē-ən\ *adj* : of, relating to, or constituting a family of languages comprising those spoken in most of Europe and in the parts of the world colonized by Europeans since 1500 and also in Persia, the subcontinent of India, and some other parts of Asia

in•do•lent \ˈin-də-lənt\ *adj* [LL *indolens* insensitive to pain, fr. L *dolēre* to feel pain] **1** : slow to develop or heal ⟨~ ulcers⟩ **2** : LAZY — **in•do•lence** \-ləns\ *n* — **in•do•lent•ly** *adv*

in•dom•i•ta•ble \in-ˈdä-mə-tə-bəl\ *adj* : UNCONQUERABLE ⟨~ courage⟩ — **in•dom•i•ta•bly** \-blē\ *adv*

In•do•ne•sian \ˌin-də-ˈnē-zhən\ *n* : a native or inhabitant of the Republic of Indonesia — **Indonesian** *adj*

in•door \ˈin-ˈdōr\ *adj* **1** : of or relating to the inside of a building **2** : living, located, or carried on within a building

in•doors \in-ˈdōrz\ *adv* : in or into a building

indorse *var of* ENDORSE

in•du•bi•ta•ble \(ˌ)in-ˈdü-bə-tə-bəl, -ˈdyü-\ *adj* : UNQUESTIONABLE — **in•du•bi•ta•bly** \-blē\ *adv*

in•duce \in-ˈdüs, -ˈdyüs\ *vb* **in•duced; in•duc•ing** **1** : PERSUADE, INFLUENCE **2** : BRING ABOUT **3** : to produce (as an electric current) by induction **4** : to determine by induction; *esp* : to infer from particulars — **in•duc•er** *n*

in•duce•ment \-mənt\ *n* **1** : something that induces : MOTIVE **2** : the act or process of inducing

in•duct \in-ˈdəkt\ *vb* **1** : to place in office **2** : to admit as a member **3** : to enroll for military training or service — **in•duct•ee** \-ˌdək-ˈtē\ *n*

in•duc•tance \in-ˈdək-təns\ *n* : a property of an electric circuit by which a varying current produces an electromotive force in that circuit or in a nearby circuit; *also* : the measure of this property

in•duc•tion \in-ˈdək-shən\ *n* **1** : the act or process of inducting; *also* : INITIATION **2** : the formality by which a civilian is inducted into military service **3** : inference of a generalized conclusion from particular instances; *also* : a conclusion so reached **4** : the act of causing or bringing on or about **5** : the process by which an electric current, an electric charge, or magnetism is produced in a body by the proximity of an electric or magnetic field

in•duc•tive \in-ˈdək-tiv\ *adj* : of, relating to, or employing induction

in•duc•tor \in-ˈdək-tər\ *n* : an electrical component that acts upon another or is itself acted upon by induction

in•dulge \in-ˈdəlj\ *vb* **in•dulged; in•dulg•ing** **1** : to give free rein to : GRATIFY **2** : HUMOR **3** : to gratify one's taste or desire for ⟨~ in alcohol⟩

in•dul•gence \in-ˈdəl-jəns\ *n* **1** : remission of temporal punishment due in Roman Catholic doctrine for sins whose eternal punishment has been remitted by reception of the sacrifice of penance **2** : the act of indulging : the state of being indulgent **3** : an indulgent act **4** : the thing indulged in **5** : SELF-INDULGENCE — **in•dul•gent** \-jənt\ *adj* — **in•dul•gent•ly** *adv*

in•du•rat•ed \ˈin-dyu̇-ˌrā-təd, -du̇-\ *adj* : physically or emotionally hardened — **in•du•ra•tion** \ˌin-dyu̇-ˈrā-shən, -du̇-\ *n*

in•dus•tri•al \in-ˈdəs-trē-əl\ *adj* **1** : of or relating to industry; *also* : HEAVY-DUTY **2** : characterized by highly developed industries — **in•dus•tri•al•ly** *adv*

in•dus•tri•al•ise *Brit var of* INDUSTRIALIZE

in•dus•tri•al•ist \-ə-list\ *n* : a person owning or engaged in the management of an industry

in•dus•tri•al•ize \in-ˈdəs-trē-ə-ˌlīz\ *vb* **-ized; -iz•ing** : to make or become industrial — **in•dus•tri•al•i•za•tion** \-ˌdəs-trē-ə-lə-ˈzā-shən\ *n*

in•dus•tri•ous \in-ˈdəs-trē-əs\ *adj* : DILIGENT, BUSY — **in•dus•tri•ous•ly** *adv* — **in•dus•tri•ous•ness** *n*

in•dus•try \ˈin-(ˌ)dəs-trē\ *n, pl* **-tries 1** : DILIGENCE **2** : a department or branch of a craft, art, business, or manufacture; *esp* : one that employs a large personnel and capital **3** : a distinct group of productive enterprises **4** : manufacturing activity as a whole

in•dwell \(ˌ)in-ˈdwel\ *vb* : to exist within as an activating spirit or force

[1]**in•ebri•ate** \i-ˈnē-brē-ˌāt\ *vb* **-at•ed; -at•ing** : to make drunk : INTOXICATE — **in•ebri•a•tion** \-ˌnē-brē-ˈā-shən\ *n*

[2]**in•ebri•ate** \-ət\ *n* : one that is drunk; *esp* : DRUNKARD

in•ef•fa•ble \(ˌ)in-ˈe-fə-bəl\ *adj* **1** : incapable of being expressed in words : INDESCRIBABLE ⟨~ joy⟩ **2** : UNSPEAKABLE ⟨~ disgust⟩ **3** : not to be uttered : TABOO — **in•ef•fa•bly** \-blē\ *adv*

in•ef•fec•tive \ˌi-nə-ˈfek-tiv\ *adj* **1** : INEFFECTUAL **2** : not able to perform efficiently or as expected : INCAPABLE — **in•ef•fec•tive•ly** *adv* — **in•ef•fec•tive•ness** *n*

in•ef•fec•tu•al \-ˈfek-chə-wəl\ *adj* **1** : not producing the proper or usual effect **2** : INEFFECTIVE 2 — **in•ef•fec•tu•al•ly** *adv*

in•ef•fi•cient \ˌi-nə-ˈfi-shənt\ *adj* **1** : not producing the desired effect **2** : wasteful of time or energy **3** : INCAPABLE, INCOMPETENT — **in•ef•fi•cien•cy** \-ˈfi-shən-sē\ *n* — **in•ef•fi•cient•ly** *adv*

in•el•e•gant \(ˌ)i-ˈne-li-gənt\ *adj* : lacking in refinement, grace, or good taste — **in•el•e•gance** \-gəns\ *n* — **in•el•e•gant•ly** *adv*

in•el•i•gi•ble \(ˌ)i-ˈne-lə-jə-bəl\ *adj* : not qualified for an office or position — **in•el•i•gi•bil•i•ty** \(ˌ)i-ˌne-lə-jə-ˈbi-lə-tē\ *n*

in•eluc•ta•ble \ˌi-ni-ˈlək-tə-bəl\ *adj* : not to be avoided, changed, or resisted — **in•eluc•ta•bly** \-blē\ *adv*

in•ept \i-ˈnept\ *adj* **1** : lacking in fitness or aptitude : UNFIT **2** : FOOLISH **3** : being out of place : INAPPROPRIATE **4** : generally incompetent : BUNGLING — **in•ept•ly** *adv* — **in•ept•ness** *n*

in•ep•ti•tude \(ˌ)i-ˈnep-ti-ˌtüd, -ˌtyüd\ *n* : the quality or state of being inept; *esp* : INCOMPETENCE

in•equal•i•ty \ˌi-ni-ˈkwä-lə-tē\ *n* **1** : the quality of being unequal or uneven; *esp* : UNEVENNESS, DISPARITY **2** : an instance of being unequal

in•ert \i-ˈnərt\ *adj* [L *inert-, iners* unskilled, idle, fr. *art-, ars* skill] **1** : powerless to move **2** : SLUGGISH **3** : lacking in active properties ⟨chemically ~⟩ — **in•ert•ly** *adv* — **in•ert•ness** *n*

in•er•tia \i-ˈnər-shə, -shē-ə\ *n* **1** : a property of matter whereby it remains at rest or continues in uniform motion unless acted upon by some outside force **2** : INERTNESS, SLUGGISHNESS — **in•er•tial** \-shəl\ *adj*

in•es•cap•able \ˌi-nə-ˈskā-pə-bəl\ *adj* : incapable of being escaped : INEVITABLE — **in•es•cap•ably** \-blē\ *adv*

in•es•ti•ma•ble \(ˌ)i-ˈnes-tə-mə-bəl\ *adj* **1** : incapable of being estimated or computed ⟨~ errors⟩ **2** : too valuable or excellent to be fully appreciated — **in•es•ti•ma•bly** \-blē\ *adv*

in•ev•i•ta•ble \i-ˈne-və-tə-bəl\ *adj* : incapable of being avoided or evaded : bound to happen — **in•ev•i•ta•bil•i•ty** \(ˌ)i-ˌne-və-tə-ˈbi-lə-tē\ *n*

in•ev•i•ta•bly \-blē\ *adv* **1** : in an inevitable way **2** : as is to be expected

in•ex•act \ˌi-nig-ˈzakt\ *adj* **1** : not precisely correct or true : INACCURATE **2** : not rigorous and careful — **in•ex•act•ly** *adv* — **in•ex•act•ness** *n*

in•ex•cus•able \ˌi-nik-ˈskyü-zə-bəl\ *adj* : being without excuse or justification — **in•ex•cus•ably** \-blē\ *adv*

in•ex•haust•ible \ˌi-nig-ˈzȯ-stə-bəl\ *adj* **1** : incapable of being used up ⟨an ~ supply⟩ **2** : UNTIRING — **in•ex•haust•ibly** \-blē\ *adv*

in•ex•o•ra•ble \(ˌ)i-ˈnek-sə-rə-bəl\ *adj* : not to be moved by entreaty : RELENTLESS — **in•ex•o•ra•bly** *adv*

in•ex•pe•ri•ence \ˌi-nik-ˈspir-ē-əns\ *n* : lack of experience or of knowledge gained by experience — **in•ex•pe•ri•enced** \-ənst\ *adj*

in•ex•pert \(ˌ)i-ˈnek-ˌspərt\ *adj* : not expert : UNSKILLED — **in•ex•pert•ly** *adv*

in•ex•pi•a•ble \(ˌ)i-ˈnek-spē-ə-bəl\ *adj* : not capable of being atoned for

in•ex•pli•ca•ble \ˌi-nik-ˈspli-kə-bəl, (ˌ)i-ˈnek-(ˌ)spli-\ *adj* : incapable of being explained or accounted for — **in•ex•pli•ca•bly** \-blē\ *adv*

in•ex•press•ible \-ˈspre-sə-bəl\ *adj* : not capable of being expressed — **in•ex•press•ibly** \-blē\ *adv*

in ex•tre•mis \ˌin-ik-ˈstrā-məs, -ˈstrē-\ *adv* : in extreme circumstances; *esp* : at the point of death

in•ex•tri•ca•ble \ˌi-nik-ˈstri-kə-bəl, (ˌ)i-ˈnek-(ˌ)stri-\ *adj* **1** : forming a maze or tangle from which it is impossible to get free **2** : incapable of being disentangled or untied — **in•ex•tri•ca•bly** \-blē\ *adv*

inf *abbr* **1** infantry **2** infinitive

in•fal•li•ble \(ˌ)in-ˈfa-lə-bəl\ *adj* **1** : incapable of error : UNERRING **2** : SURE, CERTAIN ⟨an ~ remedy⟩ — **in•fal•li•bil•i•ty** \(ˌ)in-ˌfa-lə-ˈbi-lə-tē\ *n* — **in•fal•li•bly** \(ˌ)in-ˈfa-lə-blē\ *adv*

in•fa•mous \ˈin-fə-məs\ *adj* **1** : having a reputation of the worst kind **2** : DISGRACEFUL — **in•fa•mous•ly** *adv*

in•fa•my \-mē\ *n, pl* **-mies 1** : evil reputation brought about by something grossly criminal, shocking, or brutal **2** : an extreme and publicly known criminal or evil act **3** : the state of being infamous

in•fan•cy \ˈin-fən-sē\ *n, pl* **-cies 1** : early childhood **2** : a beginning or early period of existence

in•fant \ˈin-fənt\ *n* [ME *enfaunt,* fr. MF *enfant,* fr. L *infant-, infans,* adj., incapable of speech, young, fr. *fant-, fans,* prp. of *fari* to speak] : BABY; *also* : a person who is a legal minor

in•fan•ti•cide \in-ˈfan-tə-ˌsīd\ *n* : the killing of an infant

in•fan•tile \ˈin-fən-ˌtīl, -tᵊl, -ˌtēl\ *adj* : of or relating to infants; *also* : CHILDISH

infantile paralysis *n* : POLIOMYELITIS

in•fan•try \ˈin-fən-trē\ *n, pl* **-tries** [MF & It; MF *infanterie,* fr. It *infanteria,* fr. *infante* boy, foot soldier] : soldiers trained, armed, and equipped to fight on foot — **in•fan•try•man** \-mən\ *n*

in•farct \ˈin-ˌfärkt\ *n* [L *infarctus,* pp. of *infarcire* to stuff] : an area of dead tissue (as of the heart wall) caused by blocking of local blood circulation — **in•farc•tion** \in-ˈfärk-shən\ *n*

in•fat•u•ate \in-ˈfa-chə-ˌwāt\ *vb* **-at•ed; -at•ing** : to inspire with a foolish or extravagant love or admiration — **in•fat•u•a•tion** \-ˌfa-chə-ˈwā-shən\ *n*

in•fect \in-ˈfekt\ *vb* **1** : to contaminate with disease-producing matter **2** : to communicate a germ or disease to **3** : to cause to share one's feelings

in•fec•tion \in-ˈfek-shən\ *n* **1** : a disease or condition caused by a germ or parasite; *also* : such a germ or parasite **2** : an act or process of infecting — **in•fec•tious** \-shəs\ *adj* — **in•fec•tive** \-ˈfek-tiv\ *adj*

infectious mononucleosis *n* : an acute infectious disease characterized by fever, swelling of lymph glands, and increased numbers of lymph cells in the blood

in•fe•lic•i•tous \ˌin-fi-ˈli-sə-təs\ *adj* : not appropriate in application or expression — **in•fe•lic•i•ty** \-sə-tē\ *n*

in•fer \in-ˈfər\ *vb* **in•ferred; in•fer•ring 1** : to derive as a conclusion from facts or premises **2** : GUESS, SURMISE **3** : to lead to as a conclusion or consequence **4** : HINT, SUGGEST **syn** deduce, conclude, judge, gather

— **in•fer•ence** \ˈin-frəns, -fə-rəns\ *n* — **in•fer•en•tial** \ˌin-fə-ˈren-chəl\ *adj*

in•fe•ri•or \in-ˈfir-ē-ər\ *adj* **1** : situated lower down **2** : of low or lower degree or rank **3** : of lesser quality **4** : of little or less importance, value, or merit — **inferior** *n* — **in•fe•ri•or•i•ty** \(ˌ)in-ˌfir-ē-ˈór-ə-tē\ *n*

in•fer•nal \in-ˈfərn-ᵊl\ *adj* **1** : of or relating to hell **2** : HELLISH, FIENDISH ⟨~ schemes⟩ **3** : DAMNABLE ⟨an ~ pest⟩ — **in•fer•nal•ly** *adv*

in•fer•no \in-ˈfər-nō\ *n, pl* **-nos** [It, hell, fr. LL *infernus* hell, fr. L, lower] : a place or a state that resembles or suggests hell; *also* : intense heat

in•fer•tile \(ˌ)in-ˈfərt-ᵊl\ *adj* : not fertile or productive : BARREN — **in•fer•til•i•ty** \ˌin-fər-ˈti-lə-tē\ *n*

in•fest \in-ˈfest\ *vb* : to trouble by spreading or swarming in or over; *also* : to live in or on as a parasite — **in•fes•ta•tion** \ˌin-ˌfes-ˈtā-shən\ *n*

in•fi•del \ˈin-fəd-ᵊl, -fə-ˌdel\ *n* **1** : one who is not a Christian or opposes Christianity **2** : an unbeliever esp. with respect to a particular religion

in•fi•del•i•ty \ˌin-fə-ˈde-lə-tē, -fī-\ *n, pl* **-ties 1** : lack of belief in a religion **2** : UNFAITHFULNESS, DISLOYALTY **3** : marital unfaithfulness or an instance of it

in•field \ˈin-ˌfēld\ *n* : the part of a baseball field inside the baselines — **in•field•er** *n*

in•fight•ing \ˈin-ˌfī-tiŋ\ *n* **1** : fighting at close quarters **2** : dissension or rivalry among members of a group

in•fil•trate \in-ˈfil-ˌtrāt, ˈin-(ˌ)fil-\ *vb* **-trat•ed; -trat•ing 1** : to enter or filter into or through something **2** : to pass into or through by or as if by filtering or permeating — **in•fil•tra•tion** \ˌin-(ˌ)fil-ˈtrā-shən\ *n* — **in•fil•tra•tor** *n*

in•fi•nite \ˈin-fə-nət\ *adj* **1** : LIMITLESS, BOUNDLESS, ENDLESS ⟨~ space⟩ ⟨~ patience⟩ **2** : VAST, IMMENSE; *also* : INEXHAUSTIBLE ⟨~ wealth⟩ **3** : greater than any preassigned finite value however large ⟨~ number of positive integers⟩; *also* : extending to infinity ⟨~ plane surface⟩ — **infinite** *n* — **in•fi•nite•ly** *adv*

in•fin•i•tes•i•mal \(ˌ)in-ˌfi-nə-ˈte-sə-məl\ *adj* : immeasurably or incalculably small — **in•fin•i•tes•i•mal•ly** *adv*

in•fin•i•tive \in-ˈfi-nə-tiv\ *n* : a verb form having the characteristics of both verb and noun and in English usu. being used with *to*

in•fin•i•tude \in-ˈfi-nə-ˌtüd, -ˌtyüd\ *n* **1** : the quality or state of being infinite **2** : something that is infinite esp. in extent

in•fin•i•ty \in-ˈfi-nə-tē\ *n, pl* **-ties 1** : the quality of being infinite **2** : unlimited extent of time, space, or quantity : BOUNDLESSNESS **3** : an indefinitely great number or amount

in•firm \in-ˈfərm\ *adj* **1** : deficient in vitality; *esp* : feeble from age **2** : weak of mind, will, or character : IRRESOLUTE **3** : not solid or stable : INSECURE

in•fir•ma•ry \in-ˈfər-mə-rē\ *n, pl* **-ries** : a place for the care of the infirm or sick

in•fir•mi•ty \in-ˈfər-mə-tē\ *n, pl* **-ties 1** : FEEBLENESS **2** : DISEASE, AILMENT **3** : a personal failing : FOIBLE

infl *abbr* influenced

in•flame \in-ˈflām\ *vb* **in•flamed; in•flam•ing 1** : KINDLE **2** : to excite to excessive or uncontrollable action or feeling; *also* : INTENSIFY **3** : to affect or become affected with inflammation

in•flam•ma•ble \in-ˈfla-mə-bəl\ *adj* **1** : FLAMMABLE **2** : easily inflamed, excited, or angered : IRASCIBLE

in•flam•ma•tion \ˌin-flə-ˈmā-shən\ *n* : a bodily response to injury in which an affected area becomes red, hot, and painful and congested with blood

in•flam•ma•to•ry \in-ˈfla-mə-ˌtōr-ē\ *adj* **1** : tending to excite the senses or to arouse anger, disorder, or tumult : SEDITIOUS **2** : causing or accompanied by inflammation ⟨an ~ disease⟩

in•flate \in-ˈflāt\ *vb* **in•flat•ed; in•flat•ing 1** : to swell with air or gas ⟨~ a balloon⟩ **2** : to puff up : ELATE **3** : to expand or increase abnormally ⟨~ prices⟩ — **in•flat•able** *adj*

in•fla•tion \in-ˈflā-shən\ *n* **1** : an act of inflating : the state of being inflated **2** : empty pretentiousness : POMPOSITY **3** : an increase in the volume of money and credit resulting in a continuing rise in the general price level

in•fla•tion•ary \-shə-ˌner-ē\ *adj* : of, characterized by, or productive of inflation

in•flect \in-ˈflekt\ *vb* **1** : to turn from a direct line or course : CURVE **2** : to vary a word by inflection **3** : to change or vary the pitch of the voice

in•flec•tion \in-ˈflek-shən\ *n* **1** : the act or result of curving or bending **2** : a change in pitch or loudness of the voice **3** : the change of form that words undergo to mark case, gender, number, tense, person, mood, or voice — **in•flec•tion•al** \-shə-nəl\ *adj*

in•flex•i•ble \(ˌ)in-ˈflek-sə-bəl\ *adj* **1** : UNYIELDING **2** : RIGID **3** : incapable of change — **in•flex•i•bil•i•ty** \-ˌflek-sə-ˈbi-lə-tē\ *n* — **in•flex•i•bly** \-ˈflek-sə-blē\ *adv*

in•flex•ion \in-ˈflek-shən\ *chiefly Brit var of* INFLECTION

in•flict \in-ˈflikt\ *vb* : AFFLICT; *also* : to give by or as if by striking — **in•flic•tion** \-ˈflik-shən\ *n*

in•flo•res•cence \ˌin-flə-ˈres-ᵊns\ *n* : the manner of development and arrangement of flowers on a stem; *also* : a flowering stem with its appendages : a flower cluster

in•flow \ˈin-ˌflō\ *n* : a flowing in

1**in•flu•ence** \ˈin-ˌflü-əns\ *n* **1** : the act or power of producing an effect without apparent force or direct authority **2** : the power or capacity of causing an effect in indirect or intangible ways ⟨under the ~ of liquor⟩ **3** : a person or thing that exerts influence — **in•flu•en•tial** \ˌin-flü-ˈen-chəl\ *adj*

2**influence** *vb* **-enced; -enc•ing 1** : to affect or alter by influence : SWAY **2** : to have an effect on the condition or development of : MODIFY

in•flu•en•za \ˌin-flü-ˈen-zə\ *n* [It, lit., influence, fr. ML *influentia;* fr. the belief that epidemics were due to the influence of the stars] : an acute and very contagious virus disease marked by fever, prostration, aches and pains, and respiratory inflammation; *also* : any of various feverish usu. virus diseases typically with respiratory symptoms

in•flux \ˈin-ˌfləks\ *n* : a coming in

in•fo \ˈin-(ˌ)fō\ *n* : INFORMATION

in•fold \in-ˈfōld\ *vb* **1** : ENFOLD **2** : to fold inward or toward one another

in•fo•mer•cial \ˈin-fō-ˌmər-shəl\ *n* : a television program that is an extended advertisement often including a discussion or demonstration

in•form \in-ˈfórm\ *vb* **1** : to communicate knowledge to : TELL **2** : to give information or knowledge **3** : to act as an informer **syn** acquaint, apprise, advise, notify

in•for•mal \(ˌ)in-ˈfór-məl\ *adj* **1** : conducted or carried out without formality or ceremony ⟨an ~ party⟩ **2** : characteristic of or appropriate to ordinary, casual, or familiar use ⟨~ clothes⟩ — **in•for•mal•i•ty** \ˌin-fór-ˈma-lə-tē, -fər-\ *n* — **in•for•mal•ly** \(ˌ)in-ˈfór-mə-lē\ *adv*

in•for•mant \in-ˈfór-mənt\ *n* : a person who gives information : INFORMER

in•for•ma•tion \ˌin-fər-ˈmā-shən\ *n* **1** : the communication or reception of knowledge or intelligence **2** : knowledge obtained from investigation, study, or instruction : FACTS, DATA — **in•for•ma•tion•al** \-shə-nəl\ *adj*

in•for•ma•tive \in-ˈfór-mə-tiv\ *adj* : imparting knowledge : INSTRUCTIVE

in•formed \in-ˈfórmd\ *adj* **1** : having or based on information **2** : EDUCATED, KNOWLEDGEABLE

informed consent *n* : consent to a medical procedure by someone who understands what is involved

in•form•er \-ˈfór-mər\ *n* : one that informs; *esp* : a person who informs against others for illegalities esp. for financial gain

in•fo•tain•ment \ˌin-fō-ˈtān-mənt\ *n* : a television program that presents information (as news) in a manner intended to be entertaining

in•frac•tion \in-ˈfrak-shən\ *n* [ME, fr. ML *infractio*, fr. L, subduing, fr. *infringere* to break, crush] : the act of infringing : VIOLATION

in•fra dig \ˌin-frə-ˈdig\ *adj* [short for L *infra dignitatem*] : being beneath one's dignity

in•fra•red \ˌin-frə-ˈred\ *adj* : being, relating to, or using radiation having wavelengths longer than those of red light — **infrared** *n*

in•fra•struc•ture \ˈin-frə-ˌstrək-chər\ *n* **1** : the underlying foundation or basic framework (as of a system or organization) **2** : the system of public works of a country, state, or region; *also* : the resources (as buildings or equipment) required for an activity

in•fre•quent \(ˌ)in-ˈfrē-kwənt\ *adj* **1** : seldom happening : RARE **2** : placed or occurring at wide intervals in space or time **syn** uncommon, scarce, sporadic — **in•fre•quent•ly** *adv*

in•fringe \in-ˈfrinj\ *vb* **in•fringed; in•fring•ing** **1** : VIOLATE, TRANSGRESS ⟨~ a patent⟩ **2** : ENCROACH, TRESPASS — **in•fringe•ment** *n*

in•fu•ri•ate \in-ˈfyu̇r-ē-ˌāt\ *vb* **-at•ed; -at•ing** : to make furious : ENRAGE — **in•fu•ri•at•ing•ly** *adv*

in•fuse \in-ˈfyüz\ *vb* **in•fused; in•fus•ing** **1** : to instill a principle or quality in : INTRODUCE **2** : INSPIRE, ANIMATE **3** : to steep (as tea) without boiling — **in•fu•sion** \-ˈfyü-zhən\ *n*

¹-ing \iŋ\ *n suffix* **1** : action or process ⟨sleep*ing*⟩ : instance of an action or process ⟨a meet*ing*⟩ **2** : product or result of an action or process ⟨an engrav*ing*⟩ ⟨earn*ings*⟩ **3** : something used in an action or process ⟨a bed cover*ing*⟩ **4** : something connected with, consisting of, or used in making (a specified thing) ⟨scaffold*ing*⟩ **5** : something related to (a specified concept) ⟨off*ing*⟩

²-ing *n suffix* : one of a (specified) kind

³-ing *vb suffix or adj suffix* — used to form the present participle ⟨sail*ing*⟩ and sometimes to form an adjective resembling a present participle but not derived from a verb ⟨swashbuckl*ing*⟩

in•ga•ther \ˈin-ˌga-t͟hər\ *vb* : to gather in : ASSEMBLE

in•ge•nious \in-ˈjēn-yəs\ *adj* **1** : marked by special aptitude at discovering, inventing, or contriving **2** : marked by originality, resourcefulness, and cleverness in conception or execution — **in•ge•nious•ly** *adv* — **in•ge•nious•ness** *n*

in•ge•nue *or* **in•gé•nue** \ˈan-jə-ˌnü, ˈän-; ˈaⁿ-zhə-, ˈäⁿ-\ *n* : a naive girl or young woman; *esp* : an actress portraying such a person

in•ge•nu•i•ty \ˌin-jə-ˈnü-ə-tē, -ˈnyü-\ *n, pl* **-ties** : skill or cleverness in planning or inventing : INVENTIVENESS

in•gen•u•ous \in-ˈjen-yə-wəs\ *adj* [L *ingenuus* native, freeborn, fr. *gignere* to beget] **1** : STRAIGHTFORWARD, FRANK **2** : NAIVE — **in•gen•u•ous•ly** *adv* — **in•gen•u•ous•ness** *n*

in•gest \in-ˈjest\ *vb* : to take in for or as if for digestion — **in•ges•tion** \-ˈjes-chən\ *n*

in•gle•nook \ˈiŋ-gəl-ˌnu̇k\ *n* : a nook by a large open fireplace; *also* : a bench occupying this nook

in•glo•ri•ous \(ˌ)in-ˈglōr-ē-əs\ *adj* **1** : SHAMEFUL **2** : not glorious : lacking fame or honor — **in•glo•ri•ous•ly** *adv*

in•got \ˈiŋ-gət\ *n* : a mass of metal cast in a form convenient for storage or transportation

¹in•grain \(ˌ)in-ˈgrān\ *vb* : to work indelibly into the natural texture or mental or moral constitution — **in•grained** *adj*

²in•grain \ˈin-ˌgrān\ *adj* **1** : made of fiber that is dyed before being spun into yarn **2** : made of yarn that is dyed before being woven or knitted **3** : INNATE — **in•grain** *n*

in•grate \ˈin-ˌgrāt\ *n* : an ungrateful person

in•gra•ti•ate \in-ˈgrā-shē-ˌāt\ *vb* **-at•ed; -at•ing** : to gain favor by deliberate effort

in•gra•ti•at•ing *adj* **1** : capable of winning favor : PLEASING ⟨an ~ smile⟩ **2** : FLATTERING ⟨an ~ manner⟩

in•grat•i•tude \(ˌ)in-ˈgra-tə-ˌtüd, -ˌtyüd\ *n* : lack of gratitude : UNGRATEFULNESS

in•gre•di•ent \in-ˈgrē-dē-ənt\ *n* : one of the substances that make up a mixture or compound : CONSTITUENT

in•gress \ˈin-ˌgres\ *n* : ENTRANCE, ACCESS — **in•gres•sion** \in-ˈgre-shən\ *n*

in•grow•ing \ˈin-ˌgrō-iŋ\ *adj* : growing or tending inward

in•grown \-ˌgrōn\ *adj* : grown in; *esp* : having the free tip or edge embedded in the flesh ⟨~ toenail⟩

in•gui•nal \ˈiŋ-gwən-ᵊl\ *adj* : of, relating to, or situated in or near the region of the groin

in•hab•it \in-ˈha-bət\ *vb* : to live or dwell in — **in•hab•it•able** *adj*

in•hab•i•tant \in-ˈha-bə-tənt\ *n* : a permanent resident in a place

in•hal•ant \in-ˈhā-lənt\ *n* : something (as a medicine) that is inhaled

in•ha•la•tor \ˈin-hə-ˌlā-tər\ *n* : a device that provides a mixture of carbon dioxide and oxygen for breathing

in•hale \in-ˈhāl\ *vb* **in•haled; in•hal•ing** : to breathe in — **in•ha•la•tion** \ˌin-hə-ˈlā-shən\ *n*

in•hal•er \in-ˈhā-lər\ *n* : a device by means of which medicinal material is inhaled

in•here \in-ˈhir\ *vb* **in•hered; in•her•ing** : to be inherent

in•her•ent \in-ˈhir-ənt, -ˈher-\ *adj* : established as an essential part of something : INTRINSIC — **in•her•ent•ly** *adv*

in•her•it \in-ˈher-ət\ *vb* : to receive esp. from one's ancestors — **in•her•it•able** \-ə-tə-bəl\ *adj* — **in•her•i•tance** \-ə-təns\ *n* — **in•her•i•tor** \-ə-tər\ *n*

in•hib•it \in-ˈhi-bət\ *vb* **1** : PROHIBIT, FORBID **2** : to hold in check : RESTRAIN

in•hi•bi•tion \ˌin-hə-ˈbi-shən\ *n* **1** : PROHIBITION, RESTRAINT **2** : a usu. inner check on free activity, expression, or functioning

in–house \ˈin-ˌhau̇s, -ˈhau̇s\ *adj* : existing, originating, or carried on within a group or organization

in•hu•man \(ˌ)in-ˈhyü-mən, -ˈyü-\ *adj* **1** : lacking pity, kindness, or mercy : SAVAGE **2** : COLD, IMPERSONAL **3** : not worthy of or conforming to the needs of human beings **4** : of or suggesting a nonhuman class of beings — **in•hu•man•ly** *adv* — **in•hu•man•ness** *n*

in•hu•mane \ˌin-hyü-ˈmān, -yü-\ *adj* : not humane : INHUMAN 1

in•hu•man•i•ty \-ˈma-nə-tē\ *n, pl* **-ties** **1** : the quality or state of being cruel or barbarous **2** : a cruel or barbarous act

in•im•i•cal \i-ˈni-mi-kəl\ *adj* **1** : being adverse often by reason of hostility **2** : HOSTILE, UNFRIENDLY — **in•im•i•cal•ly** *adv*

in•im•i•ta•ble \(ˌ)i-ˈni-mə-tə-bəl\ *adj* : not capable of being imitated

in•iq•ui•ty \i-ˈni-kwə-tē\ *n, pl* **-ties** [ME *iniquite*, fr. MF *iniquité*, fr. L *iniquitas*, fr. *iniquus* uneven, fr. *aequus* equal] **1** : WICKEDNESS **2** : a wicked act — **in•iq•ui•tous** \-təs\ *adj*

¹ini•tial \i-ˈni-shəl\ *adj* **1** : of or relating to the beginning : INCIPIENT **2** : FIRST — **ini•tial•ly** *adv*

²initial *n* : the first letter of a word or name

³initial *vb* **-tialed** *or* **-tialled; -tial•ing** *or* **-tial•ling** : to affix an initial to

¹ini•ti•ate \i-ˈni-shē-ˌāt\ *vb* **-at•ed; -at•ing** **1** : START, BEGIN **2** : to induct into membership by or as if by special ceremonies **3** : to instruct in the rudiments or principles of something — **ini•ti•a•tion** \-ˌni-shē-ˈā-shən\ *n*

²ini•tiate \i-ˈni-shē-ət\ *n* **1** : a person who is undergoing or has passed an initiation **2** : a person who is instructed or adept in some special field

ini·tia·tive \i-ˈni-shə-tiv\ *n* **1** : an introductory step **2** : self-reliant enterprise ⟨showed great ~⟩ **3** : a process by which laws may be introduced or enacted directly by vote of the people

ini·tia·to·ry \i-ˈni-shē-ə-ˌtōr-ē\ *adj* **1** : INTRODUCTORY **2** : tending or serving to initiate ⟨~ rites⟩

in·ject \in-ˈjekt\ *vb* **1** : to force into something ⟨~ serum with a needle⟩ **2** : to introduce as an element into some situation or subject ⟨~ a note of suspicion⟩ — **in·jec·tion** \-ˈjek-shən\ *n*

in·junc·tion \in-ˈjəŋk-shən\ *n* **1** : ORDER, ADMONITION **2** : a court writ whereby one is required to do or to refrain from doing a specified act

in·jure \ˈin-jər\ *vb* **in·jured; in·jur·ing** : WRONG, DAMAGE, HURT **syn** harm, impair, mar, spoil

in·ju·ry \ˈin-jə-rē\ *n, pl* **-ries 1** : an act that damages or hurts : WRONG **2** : hurt, damage, or loss sustained — **in·ju·ri·ous** \in-ˈju̇r-ē-əs\ *adj*

in·jus·tice \(ˌ)in-ˈjəs-təs\ *n* **1** : violation of a person's rights : UNFAIRNESS **2** : an unjust act or deed : WRONG

[1]**ink** \ˈiŋk\ *n* [ME *enke*, fr. OF, fr. LL *encaustum*, fr. L *encaustus* burned in, fr. Gk *enkaustos*, fr. *enkaiein* to burn in] : a usu. liquid and colored material for writing and printing — **inky** *adj*

[2]**ink** *vb* : to put ink on; *esp* : SIGN

ink·blot test \ˈiŋk-ˌblät-\ *n* : any of several psychological tests based on the interpretation of irregular figures

ink·horn \-ˌhȯrn\ *n* : a small bottle (as of horn) for holding ink

in–kind \ˈin-ˈkīnd\ *adj* : consisting of something (as goods) other than money

in·kling \ˈiŋ-kliŋ\ *n* **1** : HINT, INTIMATION **2** : a vague idea

ink·stand \ˈiŋk-ˌstand\ *n* : INKWELL; *also* : a pen and ink stand

ink·well \-ˌwel\ *n* : a container for ink

in·laid \ˈin-ˈlād\ *adj* : decorated with material set into a surface

[1]**in·land** \ˈin-ˌland, -lənd\ *adj* **1** *chiefly Brit* : not foreign : DOMESTIC ⟨~ revenue⟩ **2** : of or relating to the interior of a country

[2]**inland** *n* : the interior of a country

[3]**inland** *adv* : into or toward the interior

in–law \ˈin-ˌlȯ\ *n* : a relative by marriage

[1]**in·lay** \(ˌ)in-ˈlā, ˈin-ˌlā\ *vb* **in·laid** \-ˈlād\; **in·lay·ing** : to set (a material) into a surface or ground material esp. for decoration

[2]**in·lay** \ˈin-ˌlā\ *n* **1** : inlaid work **2** : a shaped filling cemented into a tooth

in·let \ˈin-ˌlet, -lət\ *n* **1** : a small or narrow bay **2** : an opening for intake esp. of a fluid

in–line skate *n* : a roller skate whose four wheels are set in a straight line

in·mate \ˈin-ˌmāt\ *n* : any of a group occupying a single place of residence; *esp* : a person confined (as in a hospital or prison)

in me·di·as res \in-ˌmā-dē-əs-ˈrās\ *adv* [L, lit., into the midst of things] : in or into the middle of a narrative or plot

in me·mo·ri·am \ˌin-mə-ˈmōr-ē-əm\ *prep* [L] : in memory of

in·most \ˈin-ˌmōst\ *adj* : deepest within : INNERMOST

inn \ˈin\ *n* : HOTEL, TAVERN

in·nards \ˈi-nərdz\ *n pl* **1** : the internal organs of a human being or animal; *esp* : VISCERA **2** : the internal parts of a structure or mechanism

in·nate \i-ˈnāt\ *adj* **1** : existing in, belonging to, or determined by factors present in an individual from birth : NATIVE **2** : INHERENT, INTRINSIC — **in·nate·ly** *adv*

in·ner \ˈi-nər\ *adj* **1** : situated farther in ⟨the ~ bark⟩ **2** : near a center esp. of influence ⟨the ~ circle⟩ **3** : of or relating to the mind or spirit

inner city *n* : the usu. older, poorer, and more densely populated section of a city — **inner–city** *adj*

in·ner–di·rect·ed \ˌi-nər-də-ˈrek-təd, -(ˌ)dī-\ *adj* : directed in thought and action by one's own scale of values as opposed to external norms

inner ear *n* : the part of the ear that is most important for hearing, is located in a cavity in the temporal bone, and contains sense organs of hearing and of awareness of position in space

in·ner·most \ˈi-nər-ˌmōst\ *adj* : farthest inward : INMOST

in·ner·sole \ˈi-nər-ˈsōl\ *n* : INSOLE

in·ner·spring \ˈi-nər-ˈspriŋ\ *adj* : having coil springs inside a padded casing

inner tube *n* : an airtight rubber tube inside a tire to hold air under pressure

in·ning \ˈi-niŋ\ *n* **1** *sing or pl* : a division of a cricket match **2** : a baseball team's turn at bat; *also* : a division of a baseball game consisting of a turn at bat for each team

inn·keep·er \ˈin-ˈkē-pər\ *n* **1** : a proprietor of an inn **2** : a hotel manager

in·no·cence \ˈi-nə-səns\ *n* **1** : BLAMELESSNESS; *also* : freedom from legal guilt **2** : GUILELESSNESS, SIMPLICITY; *also* : IGNORANCE

in·no·cent \-sənt\ *adj* [ME, fr. MF, fr. L *innocens*, fr. *nocens* wicked, fr. *nocēre* to harm] **1** : free from guilt or sin : BLAMELESS **2** : harmless in effect or intention; *also* : CANDID **3** : free from legal guilt or fault : LAWFUL **4** : INGENUOUS **5** : UNAWARE — **innocent** *n* — **in·no·cent·ly** *adv*

in·noc·u·ous \i-ˈnä-kyə-wəs\ *adj* **1** : HARMLESS **2** : not offensive; *also* : INSIPID

in·nom·i·nate \i-ˈnä-mə-nət\ *adj* : having no name; *also* : ANONYMOUS

in·no·vate \ˈi-nə-ˌvāt\ *vb* **-vat·ed; -vat·ing** : to introduce as or as if new : make changes — **in·no·va·tive** \-ˌvā-tiv\ *adj* — **in·no·va·tor** \-ˌvā-tər\ *n*

in·no·va·tion \ˌi-nə-ˈvā-shən\ *n* **1** : the introduction of something new **2** : a new idea, method, or device

in·nu·en·do \ˌin-yə-ˈwen-dō\ *n, pl* **-dos** *or* **-does** [L, by hinting, fr. *innuere* to hint, fr. *nuere* to nod] : HINT, INSINUATION; *esp* : a veiled reflection on character or reputation

in·nu·mer·a·ble \i-ˈnü-mə-rə-bəl, -ˈnyü-\ *adj* : too many to be numbered

in·oc·u·late \i-ˈnä-kyə-lāt\ *vb* **-lat·ed; -lat·ing** [ME, to insert a bud in a plant, fr. L *inoculare*, fr. *oculus* eye, bud] : to introduce something into; *esp* : to introduce a serum or antibody into (an organism) to treat or prevent a disease — **in·oc·u·la·tion** \-ˌnä-kyə-ˈlā-shən\ *n*

in·op·er·a·ble \(ˌ)i-ˈnä-pə-rə-bəl\ *adj* **1** : not suitable for surgery **2** : not operable

in·op·er·a·tive \-ˈnä-pə-rə-tiv, -ˈnä-pə-ˌrā-\ *adj* : not functioning

in·op·por·tune \(ˌ)i-ˌnä-pər-ˈtün, -ˈtyün\ *adj* : INCONVENIENT, INAPPROPRIATE — **in·op·por·tune·ly** *adv*

in·or·di·nate \i-ˈnȯrd-ᵊn-ət\ *adj* : exceeding reasonable limits : IMMODERATE ⟨an ~ curiosity⟩ — **in·or·di·nate·ly** *adv*

in·or·gan·ic \ˌi-ˌnȯr-ˈga-nik\ *adj* : being or composed of matter of other than plant or animal origin : MINERAL

in·pa·tient \ˈin-ˌpā-shənt\ *n* : a hospital patient who receives lodging and food as well as treatment

in·put \ˈin-ˌpu̇t\ *n* **1** : something put in **2** : power or energy put into a machine or system **3** : information fed into a computer or data processing system **4** : ADVICE, OPINION — **input** *vb*

in·quest \ˈin-ˌkwest\ *n* **1** : an official inquiry or examination esp. before a jury **2** : INQUIRY, INVESTIGATION

in·qui·etude \(ˌ)in-ˈkwī-ə-ˌtüd, -ˌtyüd\ *n* : UNEASINESS, RESTLESSNESS

in·quire \in-ˈkwīr\ *vb* **in·quired; in·quir·ing 1** : to ask about : ASK **2** : INVESTIGATE, EXAMINE — **in·quir·er** *n* — **in·quir·ing·ly** *adv*

in·qui·ry \ˈin-ˌkwīr-ē, in-ˈkwīr-ē; ˈin-kwə-rē, ˈiŋ-\ *n, pl* **-ries 1** : a request for information; *also* : RESEARCH

2 : a systematic investigation of a matter of public interest

in·qui·si·tion \ˌin-kwə-ˈzi-shən, ˌiŋ-\ *n* **1** : a judicial or official inquiry usu. before a jury **2** *cap* : a former Roman Catholic tribunal for the discovery and punishment of heresy **3** : a severe questioning — **in·quis·i·tor** \in-ˈkwi-zə-tər\ *n* — **in·quis·i·to·ri·al** \-ˌkwi-zə-ˈtōr-ē-əl\ *adj*

in·quis·i·tive \in-ˈkwi-zə-tiv\ *adj* **1** : given to examination or investigation ⟨an ~ mind⟩ **2** : unduly curious — **in·quis·i·tive·ly** *adv* — **in·quis·i·tive·ness** *n*

in re \in-ˈrā, -ˈrē\ *prep* : in the matter of

INRI *abbr* [L *Iesus Nazarenus Rex Iudaeorum*] Jesus of Nazareth, King of the Jews

in·road \ˈin-ˌrōd\ *n* **1** : INVASION, RAID **2** : ENCROACHMENT

in·rush \ˈin-ˌrəsh\ *n* : a crowding or flooding in

ins *abbr* **1** inches **2** insurance

INS *abbr* Immigration and Naturalization Service

in·sa·lu·bri·ous \ˌin-sə-ˈlü-brē-əs\ *adj* : UNWHOLESOME, NOXIOUS

ins and outs *n pl* **1** : characteristic peculiarities **2** : RAMIFICATIONS

in·sane \(ˌ)in-ˈsān\ *adj* **1** : exhibiting serious and debilitating mental disorder; *also* : used by or for the insane **2** : ABSURD — **in·sane·ly** *adv* — **in·san·i·ty** \in-ˈsa-nə-tē\ *n*

in·sa·tia·ble \(ˌ)in-ˈsā-shə-bəl\ *adj* : incapable of being satisfied — **in·sa·tia·bil·i·ty** \(ˌ)in-ˌsā-shə-ˈbi-lə-tē\ *n* — **in·sa·tia·bly** *adv*

in·sa·tiate \(ˌ)in-ˈsā-shē-ət, -shət\ *adj* : INSATIABLE — **in·sa·tiate·ly** *adv*

in·scribe \in-ˈskrīb\ *vb* **1** : to write, engrave, or print as a lasting record **2** : ENROLL **3** : to write, engrave, or print characters upon **4** : to dedicate to someone **5** : to draw within a figure so as to touch in as many places as possible — **in·scrip·tion** \-ˈskrip-shən\ *n*

in·scru·ta·ble \in-ˈskrü-tə-bəl\ *adj* : not readily comprehensible : MYSTERIOUS — **in·scru·ta·bly** \-blē\ *adv*

in·seam \ˈin-ˌsēm\ *n* : the seam on the inside of the leg of a pair of pants; *also* : the length of this seam

in·sect \ˈin-ˌsekt\ *n* [L *insectum*, fr. *insectus*, pp. of *insecare* to cut into, fr. *secare* to cut] : any of a class of small usu. winged arthropod animals (as flies, bees, beetles, and moths) with usu. three pairs of legs as adults

in·sec·ti·cide \in-ˈsek-tə-ˌsīd\ *n* : a preparation for destroying insects — **in·sec·ti·cid·al** \(ˌ)in-ˌsek-tə-ˈsīd-ᵊl\ *adj*

in·sec·tiv·o·rous \ˌin-ˌsek-ˈti-və-rəs\ *adj* : depending on insects as food

in·se·cure \ˌin-si-ˈkyu̇r\ *adj* **1** : UNCERTAIN **2** : not protected : UNSAFE **3** : LOOSE, SHAKY **4** : not highly stable; *also* : lacking assurance : ANXIOUS, FEARFUL — **in·se·cure·ly** *adv* — **in·se·cu·ri·ty** \-ˈkyu̇r-ə-tē\ *n*

in·sem·i·nate \in-ˈse-mə-ˌnāt\ *vb* **-nat·ed; -nat·ing** : to introduce semen into the genital tract of (a female) — **in·sem·i·na·tion** \-ˌse-mə-ˈnā-shən\ *n*

in·sen·sate \(ˌ)in-ˈsen-ˌsāt, -sət\ *adj* **1** : lacking sense or understanding; *also* : FOOLISH **2** : INANIMATE **3** : BRUTAL, INHUMAN ⟨~ rage⟩

in·sen·si·ble \(ˌ)in-ˈsen-sə-bəl\ *adj* **1** : IMPERCEPTIBLE; *also* : SLIGHT, GRADUAL **2** : INANIMATE **3** : UNCONSCIOUS **4** : lacking sensory perception or ability to react ⟨~ to pain⟩ **5** : APATHETIC, INDIFFERENT; *also* : UNAWARE ⟨~ of their danger⟩ **6** : MEANINGLESS **7** : lacking delicacy or refinement — **in·sen·si·bil·i·ty** \-ˌsen-sə-ˈbi-lə-tē\ *n* — **in·sen·si·bly** \-ˈsen-sə-blē\ *adv*

in·sen·tient \(ˌ)in-ˈsen-chē-ənt\ *adj* : lacking perception, consciousness, or animation — **in·sen·tience** \-chē-əns\ *n*

in·sep·a·ra·ble \(ˌ)in-ˈse-prə-bəl, -pə-rə-\ *adj* : incapable of being separated or disjoined — **in·sep·a·ra·bil·i·ty** \-ˌse-prə-ˈbi-lə-tē, -pə-rə-\ *n* — **inseparable** *n* — **in·sep·a·ra·bly** \-ˈse-prə-blē, -pə-rə-\ *adv*

¹in·sert \in-ˈsərt\ *vb* **1** : to put or thrust in ⟨~ a key in a lock⟩ ⟨~ a comma⟩ **2** : INTERPOLATE **3** : to set in (as a piece of fabric) and make fast

²in·sert \ˈin-ˌsərt\ *n* : something that is inserted or is for insertion; *esp* : written or printed material inserted (as between the leaves of a book)

in·ser·tion \in-ˈsər-shən\ *n* **1** : something that is inserted **2** : the act or process of inserting

in·set \ˈin-ˌset\ *vb* **inset** *or* **in·set·ted; in·set·ting** : to set in : INSERT — **inset** *n*

¹in·shore \ˈin-ˈshōr\ *adj* **1** : situated, living, or carried on near shore **2** : moving toward shore

²inshore *adv* : to or toward shore

¹in·side \in-ˈsīd, ˈin-ˌsīd\ *n* **1** : an inner side or surface : INTERIOR **2** : inward nature, thoughts, or feeling **3** *pl* : VISCERA, ENTRAILS **4** : a position of power, trust, or familiarity — **inside** *adj*

²inside *adv* **1** : on the inner side **2** : in or into the interior

³inside *prep* **1** : in or into the inside of **2** : WITHIN ⟨~ an hour⟩

inside of *prep* : INSIDE

in·sid·er \in-ˈsī-dər\ *n* : a person who is in a position of power or has access to confidential information

in·sid·i·ous \in-ˈsi-dē-əs\ *adj* [L *insidiosus*, fr. *insidiae* ambush, fr. *insidēre* to sit in, sit on, fr. *sedēre* to sit] **1** : SLY, TREACHEROUS **2** : SEDUCTIVE **3** : having a gradual and cumulative effect : SUBTLE — **in·sid·i·ous·ly** *adv* — **in·sid·i·ous·ness** *n*

in·sight \ˈin-ˌsīt\ *n* : the power, act, or result of seeing into a situation : UNDERSTANDING, PENETRATION — **in·sight·ful** \ˈin-ˌsīt-fəl, in-ˈsīt-\ *adj*

in·sig·nia \in-ˈsig-nē-ə\ *or* **in·sig·ne** \-(ˌ)nē\ *n, pl* **-nia** *or* **-ni·as** : a distinguishing mark esp. of authority or honor : BADGE

in·sin·cere \ˌin-sin-ˈsir\ *adj* : not sincere : HYPOCRITICAL — **in·sin·cere·ly** *adv* — **in·sin·cer·i·ty** \-ˈser-ə-tē\ *n*

in·sin·u·ate \in-ˈsin-yə-ˌwāt\ *vb* **-at·ed; -at·ing** [L *insinuare*, fr. *sinuare* to bend, curve, fr. *sinus* curve] **1** : to introduce gradually or in a subtle, indirect, or artful way **2** : to imply in a subtle or devious way — **in·sin·u·a·tion** \(ˌ)in-ˌsin-yə-ˈwā-shən\ *n*

in·sin·u·at·ing *adj* **1** : winning favor and confidence by imperceptible degrees **2** : tending gradually to cause doubt, distrust, or change of outlook

in·sip·id \in-ˈsi-pəd\ *adj* **1** : lacking taste or savor **2** : DULL, FLAT — **in·si·pid·i·ty** \ˌin-sə-ˈpi-də-tē\ *n*

in·sist \in-ˈsist\ *vb* [MF or L; MF *insister*, fr. L *insistere* to stand upon, persist, fr. *sistere* to take a stand] : to take a resolute stand

in·sis·tence \in-ˈsis-təns\ *n* : the act of insisting; *also* : an insistent attitude or quality : URGENCY

in·sis·tent \in-ˈsis-tənt\ *adj* : disposed to insist — **in·sis·tent·ly** *adv*

in si·tu \in-ˈsī-tü, -ˈsē-\ *adv or adj* [L, in position] : in the natural or original position

in·so·far as \ˌin-sə-ˈfär-\ *conj* : to the extent or degree that

insol *abbr* insoluble

in·so·la·tion \ˌin-(ˌ)sō-ˈlā-shən\ *n* : solar radiation that has been received

in·sole \ˈin-ˌsōl\ *n* **1** : an inside sole of a shoe **2** : a loose thin strip placed inside a shoe for warmth or comfort

in·so·lent \ˈin-sə-lənt\ *adj* : contemptuous, rude, disrespectful, or bold in behavior or language — **in·so·lence** \-ləns\ *n*

in·sol·u·ble \(ˌ)in-ˈsäl-yə-bəl\ *adj* **1** : having or admitting of no solution or explanation **2** : difficult or impossible to dissolve — **in·sol·u·bil·i·ty** \-ˌsäl-yə-ˈbi-lə-tē\ *n*

in·sol·vent \(ˌ)in-ˈsäl-vənt\ *adj* **1** : unable or insufficient to pay all debts ⟨an ~ estate⟩ **2** : IMPOVERISHED, DEFICIENT — **in·sol·ven·cy** \-vən-sē\ *n*

in·som·nia \in-ˈsäm-nē-ə\ *n* : prolonged and usu. abnormal sleeplessness

in·so·much as \ˌin-sə-ˈməch-\ *conj* : INASMUCH AS

insomuch that *conj* : to such a degree that : SO

in·sou·ci·ance \in-ˈsü-sē-əns, a^n-süs-ˈyä^{n}s\ *n* [F] : lighthearted unconcern — **in·sou·ci·ant** \in-ˈsü-sē-ənt, a^n-süs-ˈyä^n\ *adj*

insp *abbr* inspector

in·spect \in-ˈspekt\ *vb* : to view closely and critically : EXAMINE — **in·spec·tion** \-ˈspek-shən\ *n* — **in·spec·tor** \-tər\ *n*

inspector general *n* : the head of a system of inspection (as of an army)

in·spi·ra·tion \ˌin-spə-ˈrā-shən\ *n* **1** : the act or power of moving the intellect or emotions **2** : INHALATION **3** : the quality or state of being inspired; *also* : something that is inspired **4** : an inspiring agent or influence — **in·spi·ra·tion·al** \-shə-nəl\ *adj*

in·spire \in-ˈspīr\ *vb* **in·spired; in·spir·ing 1** : to influence, move, or guide by divine or supernatural inspiration **2** : exert an animating, enlivening, or exalting influence upon; *also* : AFFECT **3** : to communicate to an agent supernaturally; *also* : bring out or about **4** : INHALE **5** : INCITE **6** : to spread by indirect means — **in·spir·er** *n*

in·spir·it \in-ˈspir-ət\ *vb* : ENCOURAGE, HEARTEN

inst *abbr* **1** instant **2** institute; institution; institutional

in·sta·bil·i·ty \ˌin-stə-ˈbi-lə-tē\ *n* : lack of steadiness; *esp* : lack of emotional or mental stability

in·stall *or* **in·stal** \in-ˈstȯl\ *vb* **in·stalled; in·stall·ing 1** : to place formally in office : induct into an office, rank, or order **2** : to establish in an indicated place, condition, or status **3** : to set up for use or service — **in·stal·la·tion** \ˌin-stə-ˈlā-shən\ *n*

[1]**in·stall·ment** *also* **in·stal·ment** \in-ˈstȯl-mənt\ *n* : INSTALLATION

[2]**installment** *also* **instalment** *n* **1** : one of the parts into which a debt or sum is divided for payment **2** : one of several parts presented at intervals

[1]**in·stance** \ˈin-stəns\ *n* **1** : INSTIGATION, REQUEST **2** : EXAMPLE ⟨for ~⟩ **3** : an event or step that is part of a process or series **syn** case, illustration, sample, specimen

[2]**instance** *vb* **in·stanced; in·stanc·ing** : to mention as a case or example

[1]**in·stant** \ˈin-stənt\ *n* **1** : MOMENT ⟨the ~ we met⟩ **2** : the present or current month

[2]**instant** *adj* **1** : URGENT **2** : PRESENT, CURRENT **3** : IMMEDIATE ⟨~ relief⟩ **4** : premixed or precooked for easy final preparation ⟨~ cake mix⟩; *also* : immediately soluble in water ⟨~ coffee⟩

in·stan·ta·neous \ˌin-stən-ˈtā-nē-əs\ *adj* : done or occurring in an instant or without delay — **in·stan·ta·neous·ly** *adv*

in·stan·ter \in-ˈstan-tər\ *adv* : at once

in·stan·ti·ate \in-ˈstan-chē-ˌāt\ *vb* **-at·ed; -at·ing** : to represent (an abstraction) by a concrete example — **in·stan·ti·a·tion** \-ˌstan-chē-ˈā-shən\ *n*

in·stant·ly \ˈin-stənt-lē\ *adv* : at once : IMMEDIATELY

in·state \in-ˈstāt\ *vb* : to establish in a rank or office : INSTALL

in·stead \in-ˈsted\ *adv* **1** : as a substitute or equivalent **2** : as an alternative : RATHER

instead of *prep* : as a substitute for or alternative to

in·step \ˈin-ˌstep\ *n* : the arched part of the human foot in front of the ankle joint; *esp* : its upper surface

in·sti·gate \ˈin-stə-ˌgāt\ *vb* **-gat·ed; -gat·ing** : to goad or urge forward : PROVOKE, INCITE ⟨~ a revolt⟩ — **in·sti·ga·tion** \ˌin-stə-ˈgā-shən\ *n* — **in·sti·ga·tor** \ˈin-stə-ˌgā-tər\ *n*

in·still *also* **in·stil** \in-ˈstil\ *vb* **in·stilled; in·still·ing 1** : to cause to enter drop by drop **2** : to impart gradually

[1]**in·stinct** \ˈin-ˌstiŋkt\ *n* **1** : a natural aptitude **2** : a largely inheritable and unalterable tendency of an organism to make a complex and specific response to environmental stimuli without involving reason; *also* : behavior originating below the conscious level — **in·stinc·tive** \in-ˈstiŋk-tiv\ *adj* — **in·stinc·tive·ly** *adv*

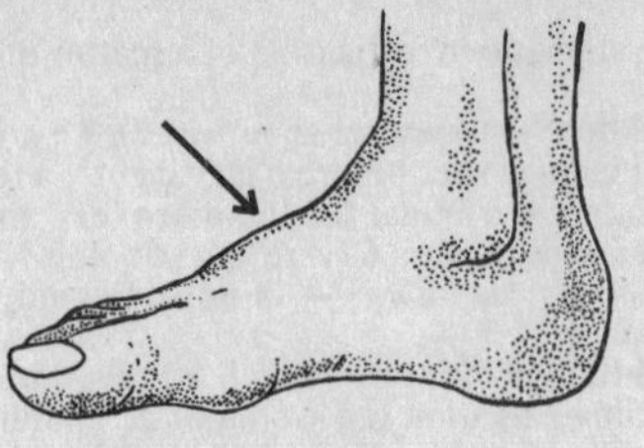

instep

[2]**in·stinct** \in-ˈstiŋkt, ˈin-ˌstiŋkt\ *adj* : IMBUED, INFUSED

in·stinc·tu·al \in-ˈstiŋk-chə-wəl\ *adj* : of, relating to, or based on instinct

[1]**in·sti·tute** \ˈin-stə-ˌtüt, -ˌtyüt\ *vb* **-tut·ed; -tut·ing 1** : to establish in a position or office **2** : ORGANIZE **3** : INAUGURATE, INITIATE

[2]**institute** *n* **1** : an elementary principle recognized as authoritative; *also, pl* : a collection of such principles and precepts **2** : an organization for the promotion of a cause : ASSOCIATION **3** : an educational institution **4** : a brief course of instruction on a particular field

in·sti·tu·tion \ˌin-stə-ˈtü-shən, -ˈtyü-\ *n* **1** : an act of originating, setting up, or founding **2** : an established practice, law, or custom **3** : a society or corporation esp. of a public character ⟨a charitable ~⟩; *also* : ASYLUM 3 — **in·sti·tu·tion·al** \-ˈtü-shə-nəl, -ˈtyü-\ *adj* — **in·sti·tu·tion·al·ize** \-nə-ˌlīz\ *vb* — **in·sti·tu·tion·al·ly** *adv*

instr *abbr* **1** instructor **2** instrument; instrumental

in·struct \in-ˈstrəkt\ *vb* [ME, fr. L *instructus*, pp. of *instruere*, fr. *struere* to build] **1** : TEACH **2** : INFORM **3** : to give an order or a command to

in·struc·tion \in-ˈstrək-shən\ *n* **1** : LESSON, PRECEPT **2** : COMMAND, ORDER **3** *pl* : DIRECTIONS **4** : the action, practice, or profession of a teacher — **in·struc·tion·al** \-shə-nəl\ *adj*

in·struc·tive \in-ˈstrək-tiv\ *adj* : carrying a lesson : ENLIGHTENING

in·struc·tor \in-ˈstrək-tər\ *n* : one that instructs; *esp* : a college teacher below professorial rank — **in·struc·tor·ship** *n*

in·stru·ment \ˈin-strə-mənt\ *n* **1** : a device used to produce music **2** : a means by which something is done **3** : a device for doing work and esp. precision work **4** : a legal document (as a deed) **5** : a device used in navigating an airplane — **in·stru·ment** \-ˌment\ *vb*

in·stru·men·tal \ˌin-strə-ˈment-ᵊl\ *adj* **1** : acting as an agent or means **2** : of, relating to, or done with an instrument **3** : relating to, composed for, or performed on a musical instrument

in·stru·men·tal·ist \-ˈmen-tə-list\ *n* : a player on a musical instrument

in·stru·men·tal·i·ty \ˌin-strə-mən-ˈta-lə-tē, -ˌmen-\ *n*, *pl* **-ties 1** : the quality or state of being instrumental **2** : MEANS, AGENCY

in·stru·men·ta·tion \ˌin-strə-mən-ˈtā-shən, -ˌmen-\ *n* **1** : ORCHESTRATION **2** : instruments for a particular purpose

instrument panel *n* : DASHBOARD

in·sub·or·di·nate \ˌin-sə-ˈbȯrd-ᵊn-ət\ *adj* : disobedient to authority — **in·sub·or·di·na·tion** \-ˌbȯrd-ᵊn-ˈā-shən\ *n*

in·sub·stan·tial \ˌin-səb-ˈstan-chəl\ *adj* **1** : lacking substance or reality **2** : lacking firmness or solidity

in·suf·fer·able \(ˌ)in-ˈsə-fə-rə-bəl\ *adj* : not to be endured : INTOLERABLE ⟨an ~ bore⟩ — **in·suf·fer·ably** \-blē\ *adv*

in·suf·fi·cient \ˌin-sə-ˈfi-shənt\ *adj* : not sufficient; *also* : INCOMPETENT — **in·suf·fi·cien·cy** \-shən-sē\ *n* — **in·suf·fi·cient·ly** *adv*

in·su·lar \ˈin-sə-lər, -syə-\ *adj* **1** : of, relating to, or forming an island **2** : dwelling or situated on an island

3 : NARROW-MINDED — **in•su•lar•i•ty** \ˌin-sə-ˈlar-ə-tē, -syə-\ *n*

in•su•late \ˈin-sə-ˌlāt\ *vb* **-lat•ed; -lat•ing** [L *insula* island] : ISOLATE; *esp* : to separate a conductor of electricity, heat, or sound from other conducting bodies by means of a nonconductor — **in•su•la•tion** \ˌin-sə-ˈlā-shən\ *n* — **in•su•la•tor** \ˈin-sə-ˌlā-tər\ *n*

in•su•lin \ˈin-sə-lən\ *n* : a pancreatic hormone essential esp. for the metabolism of carbohydrates and used in the control of diabetes mellitus

[1]**in•sult** \in-ˈsəlt\ *vb* [MF or L; MF *insulter,* fr. L *insultare,* lit., to spring upon, fr. *saltare* to leap] : to treat with insolence or contempt : AFFRONT — **in•sult•ing•ly** *adv*

[2]**in•sult** \ˈin-ˌsəlt\ *n* : a gross indignity

in•su•per•a•ble \(ˌ)in-ˈsü-pə-rə-bəl\ *adj* : incapable of being surmounted, overcome, passed over, or solved — **in•su•per•a•bly** \-blē\ *adv*

in•sup•port•able \ˌin-sə-ˈpōr-tə-bəl\ *adj* **1** : UNENDURABLE **2** : UNJUSTIFIABLE

in•sur•able \in-ˈshu̇-rə-bəl\ *adj* : capable of being or proper to be insured

in•sur•ance \in-ˈshu̇r-əns\ *n* **1** : the business of insuring persons or property **2** : coverage by contract whereby one party agrees to guarantee another against a specified loss **3** : the sum for which something is insured **4** : a means of guaranteeing protection or safety

in•sure \in-ˈshu̇r\ *vb* **in•sured; in•sur•ing 1** : to provide or obtain insurance on or for : UNDERWRITE **2** : to make certain : ENSURE

in•sured \in-ˈshu̇rd\ *n* : a person whose life or property is insured

in•sur•er \in-ˈshu̇r-ər\ *n* : one that insures; *esp* : an insurance company

in•sur•gent \in-ˈsər-jənt\ *n* **1** : a person who revolts against civil authority or an established government : REBEL **2** : a member of a political party who rebels against it — **in•sur•gence** \-jəns\ *n* — **in•sur•gen•cy** \-jən-sē\ *n* — **in•sur•gent** *adj*

in•sur•mount•able \ˌin-sər-ˈmau̇n-tə-bəl\ *adj* : INSUPERABLE — **in•sur•mount•ably** \-blē\ *adv*

in•sur•rec•tion \ˌin-sə-ˈrek-shən\ *n* : an act or instance of revolting against civil authority or an established government — **in•sur•rec•tion•ist** \-shə-nist\ *n*

int *abbr* **1** interest **2** interior **3** intermediate **4** internal **5** international **6** intransitive

in•tact \in-ˈtakt\ *adj* : untouched esp. by anything that harms or diminishes

in•ta•glio \in-ˈtal-yō\ *n, pl* **-glios** [It] : an engraving cut deeply into the surface of a hard material (as stone)

in•take \ˈin-ˌtāk\ *n* **1** : an opening through which fluid enters **2** : the act of taking in **3** : something taken in

in•tan•gi•ble \(ˌ)in-ˈtan-jə-bəl\ *adj* : incapable of being touched : IMPALPABLE — **intangible** *n* — **in•tan•gi•bly** \-blē\ *adv*

in•te•ger \ˈin-ti-jər\ *n* [L, adj., whole, entire] : a number (as 1, 2, 3, 12, 432) that is not a fraction and does not include a fraction, is the negative of such a number, or is 0

in•te•gral \ˈin-ti-grəl\ *adj* **1** : essential to completeness **2** : formed as a unit with another part **3** : composed of parts that make up a whole **4** : ENTIRE

integral calculus *n* : calculus concerned esp. with advanced methods of finding lengths, areas, and volumes

in•te•grate \ˈin-tə-ˌgrāt\ *vb* **-grat•ed; -grat•ing 1** : to form, coordinate, or blend into a functioning whole : UNITE **2** : to incorporate into a larger unit **3** : to end the segregation of and bring into equal membership in society or an organization; *also* : DESEGREGATE — **in•te•gra•tion** \ˌin-tə-ˈgrā-shən\ *n*

integrated circuit *n* : a group of tiny electronic components and their connections that is produced in or on a small slice of material (as silicon)

in•teg•ri•ty \in-ˈte-grə-tē\ *n* **1** : adherence to a code of values : INCORRUPTIBILITY **2** : SOUNDNESS **3** : COMPLETENESS

in•teg•u•ment \in-ˈte-gyə-mənt\ *n* : a covering layer (as a skin or cuticle) of an organism

in•tel•lect \ˈint-ᵊl-ˌekt\ *n* **1** : the power of knowing : the capacity for knowledge **2** : the capacity for rational or intelligent thought esp. when highly developed **3** : a person with great intellectual powers

in•tel•lec•tu•al \ˌint-ᵊl-ˈek-chə-wəl\ *adj* **1** : of, relating to, or performed by the intellect : RATIONAL **2** : given to study, reflection, and speculation **3** : engaged in activity requiring the creative use of the intellect — **intellectual** *n* — **in•tel•lec•tu•al•ly** *adv*

in•tel•lec•tu•al•ism \-chə-wə-ˌli-zəm\ *n* : devotion to the exercise of intellect or to intellectual pursuits

in•tel•li•gence \in-ˈte-lə-jəns\ *n* **1** : ability to learn and understand or to deal with new or trying situations **2** : mental acuteness **3** : INFORMATION, NEWS **4** : an agency engaged in obtaining information esp. concerning an enemy or possible enemy; *also* : the information so gained

intelligence quotient *n* : a number often used as a measure of a person's intelligence

in•tel•li•gent \in-ˈte-lə-jənt\ *adj* [L *intelligens,* fr. *intelligere* to understand, fr. *inter* between + *legere* to select] : having or showing intelligence or intellect — **in•tel•li•gent•ly** *adv*

in•tel•li•gen•tsia \in-ˌte-lə-ˈjent-sē-ə, -ˈgent-\ *n* [Russ *intelligentsiya,* fr. L *intelligentia* intelligence] : intellectuals forming a vanguard or elite

in•tel•li•gi•ble \in-ˈte-lə-jə-bəl\ *adj* : capable of being understood or comprehended — **in•tel•li•gi•bil•i•ty** \-ˌte-lə-jə-ˈbi-lə-tē\ *n* — **in•tel•li•gi•bly** \-ˈte-lə-jə-blē\ *adv*

in•tem•per•ance \(ˌ)in-ˈtem-pə-rəns\ *n* : lack of moderation; *esp* : habitual or excessive drinking of intoxicants — **in•tem•per•ate** \-pə-rət\ *adj* — **in•tem•per•ate•ness** *n*

in•tend \in-ˈtend\ *vb* [ME *entenden, intenden,* fr. MF *entendre* to purpose, fr. L *intendere* to stretch out, aim at, fr. *tendere* to stretch] **1** : to have in mind as a purpose or aim **2** : to design for a specified use or future

in•ten•dant \in-ˈten-dənt\ *n* : an official (as a governor) esp. under the French, Spanish, or Portuguese monarchies

[1]**in•tend•ed** *adj* **1** : expected to be such in the future; *esp* : BETROTHED **2** : INTENTIONAL

[2]**intended** *n* : an engaged person

in•tense \in-ˈtens\ *adj* **1** : existing in an extreme degree **2** : marked by great zeal, energy, or eagerness **3** : showing strong feeling; *also* : deeply felt — **in•tense•ly** *adv*

in•ten•si•fy \in-ˈten-sə-ˌfī\ *vb* **-fied; -fy•ing 1** : to make or become intense or more intensive **2** : to make more acute : SHARPEN **syn** aggravate, heighten, enhance, magnify — **in•ten•si•fi•ca•tion** \-ˌten-sə-fə-ˈkā-shən\ *n*

in•ten•si•ty \in-ˈten-sə-tē\ *n, pl* **-ties 1** : the quality or state of being intense; *esp* : degree of strength, energy, or force

[1]**in•ten•sive** \in-ˈten-siv\ *adj* **1** : highly concentrated **2** : serving to give emphasis — **in•ten•sive•ly** *adv*

[2]**intensive** *n* : an intensive word, particle, or prefix

intensive care *n* : special medical equipment and services for taking care of seriously ill patients ⟨an *intensive care* unit⟩

[1]**in•tent** \in-ˈtent\ *n* **1** : the state of mind with which an act is done : VOLITION **2** : PURPOSE, AIM **3** : MEANING, SIGNIFICANCE

[2]**intent** *adj* **1** : directed with keen attention ⟨an ~ gaze⟩ **2** : ENGROSSED; *also* : DETERMINED — **in•tent•ly** *adv* — **in•tent•ness** *n*

in•ten•tion \in-ˈten-chən\ *n* **1** : a determination to act in a certain way **2** : PURPOSE, AIM, END **syn** intent, design, object, objective, goal

in·ten·tion·al \in-ˈten-chə-nəl\ *adj* : done by intention or design : INTENDED — **in·ten·tion·al·ly** *adv*

in·ter \in-ˈtər\ *vb* **in·terred; in·ter·ring** : BURY

in·ter·ac·tion \ˌin-tər-ˈak-shən\ *n* : mutual or reciprocal action or influence — **in·ter·act** \-ˈakt\ *vb*

in·ter·ac·tive \-ˈak-tiv\ *adj* **1** : mutually or reciprocally active **2** : allowing two-way electronic communications (as between a person and a computer) — **in·ter·ac·tive·ly** *adv*

in·ter alia \ˌin-tər-ˈā-lē-ə, -ˈä-\ *adv* : among other things

in·ter·atom·ic \ˌin-tər-ə-ˈtä-mik\ *adj* : existing or acting between atoms

in·ter·breed \-ˈbrēd\ *vb* **-bred** \-ˈbred\; **-breed·ing** : to breed together

in·ter·ca·la·ry \in-ˈtər-kə-ˌler-ē\ *adj* **1** : INTERCALATED ⟨February 29 is an ~ day⟩ **2** : INTERPOLATED

in·ter·ca·late \-ˌlāt\ *vb* **-lat·ed; -lat·ing 1** : to insert (as a day) in a calendar **2** : to insert between or among existing elements or layers — **in·ter·ca·la·tion** \-ˌtər-kə-ˈlā-shən\ *n*

in·ter·cede \ˌin-tər-ˈsēd\ *vb* **-ced·ed; -ced·ing** : to act between parties with a view to reconciling differences

1in·ter·cept \ˌin-tər-ˈsept\ *vb* **1** : to stop or interrupt the progress or course of **2** : to include (as part of a curve or solid) between two points, curves, or surfaces **3** : to gain possession of (an opponent's pass in football) — **in·ter·cep·tion** \-ˈsep-shən\ *n*

2in·ter·cept \ˈin-tər-ˌsept\ *n* : INTERCEPTION; *esp* : the interception of a target by an interceptor or missile

in·ter·cep·tor \ˌin-tər-ˈsep-tər\ *n* : a fighter plane designed for defense against attacking bombers

in·ter·ces·sion \ˌin-tər-ˈse-shən\ *n* **1** : MEDIATION **2** : prayer or petition in favor of another — **in·ter·ces·sor** \-ˈse-sər\ *n* — **in·ter·ces·so·ry** \-ˈse-sə-rē\ *adj*

1in·ter·change \ˌin-tər-ˈchānj\ *vb* **1** : to put each in the place of the other **2** : EXCHANGE **3** : to change places mutually — **in·ter·change·able** \-ˈchān-jə-bəl\ *adj* — **in·ter·change·ably** \-blē\ *adv*

2in·ter·change \ˈin-tər-ˌchānj\ *n* **1** : EXCHANGE **2** : a highway junction that by separated levels permits passage between highways without crossing traffic streams

in·ter·col·le·giate \ˌin-tər-kə-ˈlē-jət\ *adj* : existing or carried on between colleges

in·ter·com \ˈin-tər-ˌkäm\ *n* : a two-way system for localized communication

in·ter·con·ti·nen·tal \-ˌkänt-ᵊn-ˈent-ᵊl\ *adj* **1** : extending among or carried on between continents ⟨~ trade⟩ **2** : capable of traveling between continents ⟨~ ballistic missiles⟩

in·ter·course \ˈin-tər-ˌkōrs\ *n* **1** : connection or dealings between persons or nations **2** : physical sexual contact between individuals that involves the genitalia of at least one person ⟨oral ~⟩; *esp* : SEXUAL INTERCOURSE

in·ter·de·nom·i·na·tion·al \ˌin-tər-di-ˌnä-mə-ˈnā-shə-nəl\ *adj* : involving different denominations

in·ter·de·part·men·tal \ˌin-tər-di-ˌpärt-ˈment-ᵊl, -ˌdē-\ *adj* : carried on between or involving different departments (as of a college)

in·ter·de·pen·dent \ˌin-tər-di-ˈpen-dənt\ *adj* : dependent upon one another — **in·ter·de·pen·dence** \-dəns\ *n*

in·ter·dict \ˌin-tər-ˈdikt\ *vb* **1** : to prohibit by decree **2** : to destroy, cut off, or damage (as an enemy line of supply) — **in·ter·dic·tion** \-ˈdik-shən\ *n*

in·ter·dis·ci·plin·ary \-ˈdi-sə-plə-ˌner-ē\ *adj* : involving two or more academic, scientific, or artistic disciplines

1in·ter·est \ˈin-trəst; ˈin-tə-rəst, -ˌrest\ *n* **1** : right, title, or legal share in something **2** : a charge for borrowed money that is generally a percentage of the amount borrowed; *also* : the return received by capital on its investment **3** : WELFARE, BENEFIT; *also* : SELF-INTEREST **4** : CURIOSITY, CONCERN **5** : readiness to be concerned with or moved by an object or class of objects **6** : a quality in a thing that arouses interest

2interest *vb* **1** : to persuade to participate or engage **2** : to engage the attention of

in·ter·est·ing *adj* : holding the attention — **in·ter·est·ing·ly** *adv*

1in·ter·face \ˈin-tər-ˌfās\ *n* **1** : a surface forming a common boundary of two bodies, spaces, or phases ⟨an oil-water ~⟩ **2** : the place at which two independent systems meet and act on or communicate with each other ⟨the man-machine ~⟩ **3** : the means by which interaction or communication is achieved at an interface — **in·ter·fa·cial** \ˌin-tər-ˈfā-shəl\ *adj*

2interface *vb* **-faced; -fac·ing 1** : to connect by means of an interface **2** : to serve as an interface

in·ter·faith \ˌin-tər-ˈfāth\ *adj* : involving persons of different religious faiths

in·ter·fere \ˌin-tər-ˈfir\ *vb* **-fered; -fer·ing** [MF *(s')entreferir* to strike one another, fr. OF, fr. *entre* between, among + *ferir* to strike, fr. L *ferire*] **1** : to come in collision or be in opposition : CLASH **2** : to enter into the affairs of others **3** : to affect one another

in·ter·fer·ence \-ˈfir-əns\ *n* **1** : the act or process of interfering **2** : something that interferes : OBSTRUCTION **3** : the mutual effect on meeting of two waves resulting in areas of increased and decreased amplitude **4** : the blocking of an opponent in football to make way for the ballcarrier **5** : the illegal hindering of an opponent in sports

in·ter·fer·om·e·ter \ˌin-tər-fə-ˈrä-mə-tər\ *n* : a device that uses the interference of waves (as of light) for making precise measurements — **in·ter·fer·om·e·try** \-fə-ˈrä-mə-trē\ *n*

in·ter·fer·on \ˌin-tər-ˈfir-ˌän\ *n* : any of a group of antiviral proteins of low molecular weight produced usu. by animal cells in response to a virus, a parasite in the cell, or a chemical

in·ter·ga·lac·tic \ˌin-tər-gə-ˈlak-tik\ *adj* : relating to or situated in the spaces between galaxies

in·ter·gla·cial \-ˈglā-shəl\ *n* : a warm period between successive glaciations

in·ter·gov·ern·men·tal \-ˌgə-vərn-ˈment-ᵊl\ *adj* : existing or occurring between two governments or levels of government

in·ter·im \ˈin-tə-rəm\ *n* [L, adv., meanwhile, fr. *inter* between] : a time intervening : INTERVAL — **interim** *adj*

1in·te·ri·or \in-ˈtir-ē-ər\ *adj* **1** : lying, occurring, or functioning within the limiting boundaries : INSIDE, INNER **2** : remote from the surface, border, or shore : INLAND

2interior *n* **1** : the inland part (as of a country) **2** : INSIDE **3** : the internal affairs of a state or nation **4** : a scene or view of the interior of a building

interior decoration *n* : INTERIOR DESIGN — **interior decorator** *n*

interior design *n* : the art or practice of planning and supervising the design and execution of architectural interiors and their furnishings — **interior designer** *n*

interj *abbr* interjection

in·ter·ject \ˌin-tər-ˈjekt\ *vb* : to throw in between or among other things

in·ter·jec·tion \ˌin-tər-ˈjek-shən\ *n* : an exclamatory word (as *ouch*) — **in·ter·jec·tion·al·ly** \-shə-nə-lē\ *adv*

in·ter·lace \ˌin-tər-ˈlās\ *vb* **1** : to unite by or as if by lacing together : INTERWEAVE **2** : INTERSPERSE

in·ter·lard \ˌin-tər-ˈlärd\ *vb* : to vary by inserting or interjecting something

in·ter·leave \ˌin-tər-ˈlēv\ *vb* **-leaved; -leav·ing** : to arrange in alternate layers

in·ter·leu·kin \ˌin-tər-ˈlü-kən\ *n* : any of several proteins of low molecular weight that are produced by cells of the body and regulate the immune system and immune responses

[1]**in·ter·line** \ˌin-tər-ˈlīn\ *vb* : to insert between lines already written or printed

[2]**interline** *vb* : to provide (as a coat) with an interlining

in·ter·lin·ear \ˌin-tər-ˈli-nē-ər\ *adj* : inserted between lines already written or printed ⟨an ~ translation of a text⟩

in·ter·lin·ing \ˈin-tər-ˌlī-niŋ\ *n* : a lining (as of a coat) between the ordinary lining and the outside fabric

in·ter·link \ˌin-tər-ˈliŋk\ *vb* : to link together

in·ter·lock \ˌin-tər-ˈläk\ *vb* **1** : to engage or interlace together : lock together : UNITE **2** : to connect so that action of one part affects action of another part — **in·ter·lock** \ˈin-tər-ˌläk\ *n*

in·ter·loc·u·tor \ˌin-tər-ˈlä-kyə-tər\ *n* : one who takes part in dialogue or conversation

in·ter·loc·u·to·ry \-ˌtōr-ē\ *adj* : pronounced during the progress of a legal action and having only provisional force ⟨an ~ decree⟩

in·ter·lope \ˌin-tər-ˈlōp\ *vb* **-loped; -lop·ing 1** : to encroach on the rights (as in trade) of others **2** : INTRUDE, INTERFERE — **in·ter·lop·er** *n*

in·ter·lude \ˈin-tər-ˌlüd\ *n* **1** : a usu. short simple play or dramatic entertainment **2** : an intervening period, space, or event **3** : a piece of music inserted between the parts of a longer composition or a religious service

in·ter·mar·riage \ˌin-tər-ˈmar-ij\ *n* **1** : marriage within one's own group as required by custom **2** : marriage between members of different groups

in·ter·mar·ry \-ˈmar-ē\ *vb* **1** : to marry each other **2** : to marry within a group **3** : to become connected by intermarriage

[1]**in·ter·me·di·ary** \ˌin-tər-ˈmē-dē-ˌer-ē\ *adj* **1** : INTERMEDIATE **2** : acting as a mediator

[2]**intermediary** *n, pl* **-ar·ies** : MEDIATOR, GO-BETWEEN

[1]**in·ter·me·di·ate** \ˌin-tər-ˈmē-dē-ət\ *adj* : being or occurring at the middle place or degree or between extremes

[2]**intermediate** *n* **1** : one that is intermediate **2** : INTERMEDIARY

intermediate school *n* **1** : JUNIOR HIGH SCHOOL **2** : a school usu. comprising grades 4–6

in·ter·ment \in-ˈtər-mənt\ *n* : BURIAL

in·ter·mez·zo \ˌin-tər-ˈmet-sō, -ˈmed-zō\ *n, pl* **-zi** \-sē, -zē\ *or* **-zos** [It, ultim. fr. L *intermedius* intermediate] : a short movement connecting major sections of an extended musical work (as a symphony); *also* : a short independent instrumental composition

in·ter·mi·na·ble \(ˌ)in-ˈtər-mə-nə-bəl\ *adj* : ENDLESS; *esp* : wearisomely protracted — **in·ter·mi·na·bly** \-blē\ *adv*

in·ter·min·gle \ˌin-tər-ˈmiŋ-gəl\ *vb* : to mingle or mix together

in·ter·mis·sion \ˌin-tər-ˈmi-shən\ *n* **1** : INTERRUPTION, BREAK **2** : a temporary halt esp. in a public performance

in·ter·mit \-ˈmit\ *vb* **-mit·ted; -mit·ting** : DISCONTINUE; *also* : to be intermittent

in·ter·mit·tent \-ˈmit-ᵊnt\ *adj* : coming and going at intervals **syn** recurrent, periodic, alternate — **in·ter·mit·tent·ly** *adv*

in·ter·mix \ˌin-tər-ˈmiks\ *vb* : to mix together : INTERMINGLE — **in·ter·mix·ture** \-ˈmiks-chər\ *n*

in·ter·mo·lec·u·lar \-mə-ˈle-kyə-lər\ *adj* : existing or acting between molecules

in·ter·mon·tane \ˌin-tər-ˈmän-ˌtān\ *adj* : situated between mountains

[1]**in·tern** \ˈin-ˌtərn, in-ˈtərn\ *vb* : to confine or impound esp. during a war — **in·tern·ee** \(ˌ)in-ˌtər-ˈnē\ *n* — **in·tern·ment** \in-ˈtərn-mənt\ *n*

[2]**in·tern** *also* **in·terne** \ˈin-ˌtərn\ *n* : an advanced student or recent graduate (as in medicine) gaining supervised practical experience — **in·tern·ship** *n*

[3]**in·tern** \ˈin-ˌtərn\ *vb* : to act as an intern

in·ter·nal \in-ˈtərn-ᵊl\ *adj* **1** : INWARD, INTERIOR **2** : relating to or located in the inside of the body ⟨~ pain⟩ **3** : of, relating to, or occurring within the confines of an organized structure ⟨~ affairs⟩ **4** : of, relating to, or existing within the mind **5** : INTRINSIC, INHERENT — **in·ter·nal·ly** *adv*

internal combustion engine *n* : an engine in which the fuel is ignited within the engine cylinder

internal medicine *n* : a branch of medicine that deals with the diagnosis and treatment of diseases not requiring surgery

[1]**in·ter·na·tion·al** \ˌin-tər-ˈna-shə-nəl\ *adj* **1** : common to or affecting two or more nations ⟨~ trade⟩ **2** : of, relating to, or constituting a group having members in two or more nations — **in·ter·na·tion·al·ly** *adv*

[2]**international** *n* : one that is international; *esp* : an organization of international scope

in·ter·na·tion·al·ise *Brit var of* INTERNATIONALIZE

in·ter·na·tion·al·ism \-ˈna-shə-nə-ˌli-zəm\ *n* : a policy of cooperation among nations; *also* : an attitude favoring such a policy

in·ter·na·tion·al·ize \-ˈna-shə-nə-ˌlīz\ *vb* : to make international; *esp* : to place under international control

in·ter·ne·cine \ˌin-tər-ˈne-ˌsēn, -ˈnē-ˌsīn\ *adj* [L *internecinus*, fr. *internecare* to destroy, kill, fr. *necare* to kill, fr. *nec-, nex* violent death] **1** : DEADLY; *esp* : mutually destructive **2** : of, relating to, or involving conflict within a group ⟨~ feuds⟩

In·ter·net \ˈin-tər-ˌnet\ *n* : an electronic communications network that connects computer networks worldwide

in·ter·nist \ˈin-ˌtər-nist\ *n* : a physician who specializes in internal medicine

in·ter·nun·cio \ˌin-tər-ˈnən-sē-ˌō, -ˈnün-\ *n* [It *internunzio*] : a papal legate of lower rank than a nuncio

in·ter·of·fice \-ˈȯ-fəs\ *adj* : functioning or communicating between the offices of an organization

in·ter·per·son·al \-ˈpərs-ᵊn-əl\ *adj* : being, relating to, or involving relations between persons — **in·ter·per·son·al·ly** *adv*

in·ter·plan·e·tary \ˌin-tər-ˈpla-nə-ˌter-ē\ *adj* : existing, carried on, or operating between planets ⟨~ space⟩

in·ter·play \ˈin-tər-ˌplā\ *n* : INTERACTION

in·ter·po·late \in-ˈtər-pə-ˌlāt\ *vb* **-lat·ed; -lat·ing 1** : to change (as a text) by inserting new or foreign matter **2** : to insert (as words) into a text or into a conversation **3** : to estimate values of (a function) between two known values — **in·ter·po·la·tion** \-ˌtər-pə-ˈlā-shən\ *n*

in·ter·pose \ˌin-tər-ˈpōz\ *vb* **-posed; -pos·ing 1** : to place between **2** : to thrust in : INTRUDE, INTERRUPT **3** : to inject between parts of a conversation or argument **4** : to come or be between **syn** interfere, intercede, intermediate, intervene — **in·ter·po·si·tion** \-pə-ˈzi-shən\ *n*

in·ter·pret \in-ˈtər-prət\ *vb* **1** : to explain the meaning of; *also* : to act as an interpreter : TRANSLATE **2** : to understand according to individual belief, judgment, or interest **3** : to represent artistically — **in·ter·pret·er** *n* — **in·ter·pre·tive** \-ˈtər-prə-tiv\ *adj*

in·ter·pre·ta·tion \in-ˌtər-prə-ˈtā-shən\ *n* **1** : EXPLANATION **2** : an instance of artistic interpretation in performance or adaptation — **in·ter·pre·ta·tive** \-ˈtər-prə-ˌtā-tiv\ *adj*

in·ter·ra·cial \-ˈrā-shəl\ *adj* : of, involving, or designed for members of different races

in·ter·reg·num \ˌin-tə-ˈreg-nəm\ *n, pl* **-nums** *or* **-na** \-nə\ **1** : the time during which a throne is vacant between two successive reigns or regimes **2** : a pause in a continuous series

in·ter·re·late \ˌin-tər-ri-ˈlāt\ *vb* : to bring into or have a mutual relationship — **in·ter·re·lat·ed·ness** \-lā-təd-nəs\ *n* — **in·ter·re·la·tion** \-ˈlā-shən\ *n* — **in·ter·re·la·tion·ship** *n*

interrog *abbr* interrogative

in·ter·ro·gate \in-ˈter-ə-ˌgāt\ *vb* **-gat·ed; -gat·ing** : to question esp. formally and systematically : ASK — **in·ter·ro·ga·tion** \-ˌter-ə-ˈgā-shən\ *n* — **in·ter·ro·ga·tor** \-ˈter-ə-ˌgā-tər\ *n*

in·ter·rog·a·tive \ˌin-tə-ˈrä-gə-tiv\ *adj* : asking a question ⟨~ sentence⟩ — **interrogative** *n* — **in·ter·rog·a·tive·ly** *adv*

in·ter·rog·a·to·ry \ˌin-tə-ˈrä-gə-ˌtōr-ē\ *adj* : INTERROGATIVE

in·ter·rupt \ˌin-tə-ˈrəpt\ *vb* **1** : to stop or hinder by breaking in **2** : to break the uniformity or continuity of **3** : to break in by speaking while another is speaking — **in·ter·rupt·er** *n* — **in·ter·rup·tion** \-ˈrəp-shən\ *n* — **in·ter·rup·tive** \-ˈrəp-tiv\ *adv*

in·ter·scho·las·tic \ˌin-tər-skə-ˈlas-tik\ *adj* : existing or carried on between schools

in·ter·sect \ˌin-tər-ˈsekt\ *vb* **1** : to divide by passing through or across **2** : to meet and cross (as at a point); *also* : OVERLAP — **in·ter·sec·tion** \-ˈsek-shən\ *n*

in·ter·sperse \ˌin-tər-ˈspərs\ *vb* **-spersed; -spers·ing 1** : to place something at intervals in or among **2** : to insert at intervals among other things — **in·ter·sper·sion** \-ˈspər-zhən\ *n*

¹in·ter·state \ˌin-tər-ˈstāt\ *adj* : relating to, including, or connecting two or more states esp. of the U.S.

²in·ter·state \ˈin-tər-ˌstāt\ *n* : an interstate highway

in·ter·stel·lar \ˌin-tər-ˈste-lər\ *adj* : located or taking place among the stars

in·ter·stice \in-ˈtər-stəs\ *n, pl* **-stic·es** \-stə-ˌsēz, -stə-səz\ : a space that intervenes between things : CHINK — **in·ter·sti·tial** \ˌin-tər-ˈsti-shəl\ *adj*

in·ter·tid·al \ˌin-tər-ˈtīd-ᵊl\ *adj* : of, relating to, or being the area that is above low-tide mark but exposed to tidal flooding ⟨life in the ~ mud⟩

in·ter·twine \-ˈtwīn\ *vb* : to twine or cause to twine about one another : INTERLACE — **in·ter·twine·ment** *n*

in·ter·twist \-ˈtwist\ *vb* : INTERTWINE

in·ter·ur·ban \-ˈər-bən\ *adj* : connecting cities or towns

in·ter·val \ˈin-tər-vəl\ *n* [ME *intervalle,* fr. MF, fr. L *intervallum* space between ramparts, interval, fr. *inter-* between + *vallum* rampart] **1** : a space of time between events or states : PAUSE **2** : a space between objects, units, or states **3** : the difference in pitch between two tones

in·ter·vene \ˌin-tər-ˈvēn\ *vb* **-vened; -ven·ing 1** : to occur, fall, or come between points of time or between events **2** : to enter or appear as an unrelated feature or circumstance ⟨rain *intervened* and we postponed the trip⟩ **3** : to come in or between in order to stop, settle, or modify ⟨~ in a quarrel⟩ **4** : to occur or lie between two things — **in·ter·ven·tion** \-ˈven-chən\ *n*

in·ter·ven·tion·ism \-ˈven-chə-ˌni-zəm\ *n* : interference by one country in the political affairs of another — **in·ter·ven·tion·ist** \-ˈven-chə-nist\ *n or adj*

in·ter·view \ˈin-tər-ˌvyü\ *n* **1** : a formal consultation usu. to evaluate qualifications **2** : a meeting at which a writer or reporter obtains information from a person; *also* : the recorded or written account of such a meeting — **interview** *vb* — **in·ter·view·ee** \ˌin-tər-(ˌ)vyü-ˈē\ *n* — **in·ter·view·er** *n*

in·ter·vo·cal·ic \ˌin-tər-vō-ˈka-lik\ *adj* : immediately preceded and immediately followed by a vowel

in·ter·weave \ˌin-tər-ˈwēv\ *vb* **-wove** \-ˈwōv\ *also* **-weaved; -wo·ven** \-ˈwō-vən\ *also* **-weaved; -weav·ing** : to weave or blend together : INTERTWINE, INTERMINGLE — **interwoven** *adj*

in·tes·tate \in-ˈtes-ˌtāt, -tət\ *adj* **1** : having made no valid will ⟨died ~⟩ **2** : not disposed of by will ⟨~ estate⟩

in·tes·tine \in-ˈtes-tən\ *n* : the tubular part of the alimentary canal that extends from stomach to anus and consists of a long narrow upper part (**small intestine**) followed by a broader shorter lower part (**large intestine**) — **in·tes·ti·nal** \-tən-ᵊl\ *adj*

¹in·ti·mate \ˈin-tə-ˌmāt\ *vb* **-mat·ed; -mat·ing 1** : ANNOUNCE, NOTIFY **2** : to communicate indirectly : HINT — **in·ti·ma·tion** \ˌin-tə-mā-shən\ *n*

²in·ti·mate \ˈin-tə-mət\ *adj* **1** : INTRINSIC; *also* : INNERMOST **2** : marked by very close association, contact, or familiarity **3** : marked by a warm friendship **4** : suggesting informal warmth or privacy **5** : of a very personal or private nature — **in·ti·ma·cy** \ˈin-tə-mə-sē\ *n* — **in·ti·mate·ly** *adv*

³in·ti·mate \ˈin-tə-mət\ *n* : an intimate friend, associate, or confidant

in·tim·i·date \in-ˈti-mə-ˌdāt\ *vb* **-dat·ed; -dat·ing** : to make timid or fearful : FRIGHTEN; *esp* : to compel or deter by or as if by threats **syn** cow, bulldoze, bully, browbeat — **in·tim·i·dat·ing·ly** *adv* — **in·tim·i·da·tion** \-ˌti-mə-ˈdā-shən\ *n*

intl *or* **intnl** *abbr* international

in·to \ˈin-tü\ *prep* **1** : to the inside of ⟨ran ~ the house⟩ **2** : to the state, condition, or form of ⟨got ~ trouble⟩ **3** : AGAINST ⟨ran ~ a wall⟩

in·tol·er·a·ble \(ˌ)in-ˈtä-lə-rə-bəl\ *adj* **1** : UNBEARABLE **2** : EXCESSIVE — **in·tol·er·a·bly** \-blē\ *adv*

in·tol·er·ant \(ˌ)in-ˈtä-lə-rənt\ *adj* **1** : unable or unwilling to endure **2** : unwilling to grant equality, freedom, or other social rights : BIGOTED — **in·tol·er·ance** \-rəns\ *n*

in·to·na·tion \ˌin-tō-ˈnā-shən\ *n* **1** : the act of intoning and esp. of chanting **2** : something that is intoned **3** : the manner of singing, playing, or uttering tones **4** : the rise and fall in pitch of the voice in speech

in·tone \in-ˈtōn\ *vb* **in·toned; in·ton·ing** : to utter in musical or prolonged tones : CHANT

in to·to \in-ˈtō-tō\ *adv* [L, on the whole] : TOTALLY, ENTIRELY

in·tox·i·cant \in-ˈtäk-si-kənt\ *n* : something that intoxicates; *esp* : an alcoholic drink — **intoxicant** *adj*

in·tox·i·cate \-sə-ˌkāt\ *vb* **-cat·ed; -cat·ing 1** : to affect by a drug (as alcohol or cocaine) esp. to the point of physical or mental impairment **2** : to excite to enthusiasm or frenzy — **in·tox·i·ca·tion** \-ˌtäk-sə-ˈkā-shən\ *n*

in·trac·ta·ble \(ˌ)in-ˈtrak-tə-bəl\ *adj* : not easily controlled : OBSTINATE

in·tra·mu·ral \-ˈmyu̇r-əl\ *adj* : being or occurring within the walls or limits (as of a city or college) ⟨~ sports⟩

in·tra·mus·cu·lar \-ˈməs-kyə-lər\ *adj* : situated within, occurring in, or administered by entering a muscle — **in·tra·mus·cu·lar·ly** *adv*

intrans *abbr* intransitive

in·tran·si·gent \-jənt\ *adj* : UNCOMPROMISING; *also* : IRRECONCILABLE — **in·tran·si·gence** \-jəns\ *n* — **intransigent** *n*

in·tran·si·tive \(ˌ)in-ˈtran-sə-tiv, -zə-\ *adj* : not transitive; *esp* : not having or containing an object ⟨an ~ verb⟩ — **in·tran·si·tive·ly** *adv* — **in·tran·si·tive·ness** *n*

in·tra·state \ˌin-trə-ˈstāt\ *adj* : existing or occurring within a state

in·tra·uter·ine device \-ˈyü-tə-rən-, -ˌrīn-\ *n* : a device (as a spiral of plastic) inserted and left in the uterus to prevent pregnancy

in·tra·ve·nous \ˌin-trə-ˈvē-nəs\ *adj* : being within or entering by way of the veins; *also* : used in or using intravenous procedures — **in·tra·ve·nous·ly** *adv*

intrench *var of* ENTRENCH

in·trep·id \in-ˈtre-pəd\ *adj* : characterized by resolute fearlessness, fortitude, and endurance — **in·tre·pid·i·ty** \ˌin-trə-ˈpi-də-tē\ *n*

in·tri·cate \ˈin-tri-kət\ *adj* [ME, fr. L *intricatus,* pp. of *intricare* to entangle, fr. *tricae* trifles, complications] **1** : having many complexly interrelated parts : COMPLICATED **2** : difficult to follow, understand, or solve — **in·tri·ca·cy** \-tri-kə-sē\ *n* — **in·tri·cate·ly** *adv*

¹in·trigue \in-ˈtrēg\ *vb* **in·trigued; in·trigu·ing 1** : to accomplish by intrigue **2** : to carry on an intrigue; *esp*

: PLOT, SCHEME **3** : to arouse the interest, desire, or curiosity of — **in·trigu·ing·ly** *adv*

[2]**in·trigue** \ˈin-ˌtrēg, in-ˈtrēg\ *n* **1** : a secret scheme : MACHINATION **2** : a clandestine love affair

in·trin·sic \in-ˈtrin-zik, -sik\ *adj* : belonging to the essential nature or constitution of a thing — **in·trin·si·cal·ly** \-zi-k(ə-)lē, -si-\ *adv*

introd *abbr* introduction

in·tro·duce \ˌin-trə-ˈdüs, -ˈdyüs\ *vb* **-duced; -duc·ing 1** : to lead or bring in esp. for the first time **2** : to bring into practice or use **3** : to cause to be acquainted **4** : to present for discussion **5** : PLACE, INSERT **syn** insinuate, interpolate, interpose, interject — **in·tro·duc·tion** \-ˈdək-shən\ *n* — **in·tro·duc·to·ry** \-ˈdək-tə-rē\ *adj*

in·troit \ˈin-ˌtrȯit, -ˌtrō-ət\ *n* **1** *often cap* : the first part of the traditional proper of the Mass **2** : a piece of music sung or played at the beginning of a worship service

in·tro·spec·tion \-ˈspek-shən\ *n* : a reflective looking inward : an examination of one's own thoughts or feelings — **in·tro·spect** \ˌin-trə-ˈspekt\ *vb* — **in·tro·spec·tive** \-ˈspek-tiv\ *adj* — **in·tro·spec·tive·ly** *adv*

in·tro·vert \ˈin-trə-ˌvərt\ *n* : a reserved or shy person — **in·tro·ver·sion** \ˌin-trə-ˈvər-zhən\ *n* — **introvert** *adj* — **in·tro·vert·ed** \ˈin-trə-ˌvər-təd\ *adj*

in·trude \in-ˈtrüd\ *vb* **in·trud·ed; in·trud·ing 1** : to thrust, enter, or force in or upon **2** : ENCROACH, TRESPASS — **in·trud·er** *n* — **in·tru·sion** \-ˈtrü-zhən\ *n* — **in·tru·sive** \-ˈtrü-siv\ *adj* — **in·tru·sive·ness** *n*

intrust *var of* ENTRUST

in·tu·it \in-ˈtü-ət, -ˈtyü-\ *vb* : to apprehend by intuition

in·tu·ition \ˌin-tu̇-ˈwi-shən, -tyu̇-\ *n* **1** : quick and ready insight **2** : the power or faculty of knowing things without conscious reasoning — **in·tu·i·tive** \in-ˈtü-ə-tiv, -ˈtyü-\ *adj* — **in·tu·i·tive·ly** *adv*

In·u·it \ˈi-nu̇-wət, ˈin-yu̇-\ *n* [Inuit *inuit,* pl. of *inuk* person] **1** : a member of the Eskimo people of No. America and Greenland **2** : the language of the Inuit people

in·un·date \ˈi-nən-ˌdāt\ *vb* **-dat·ed; -dat·ing** : to cover with or as if with a flood : OVERFLOW — **in·un·da·tion** \ˌi-nən-ˈdā-shən\ *n*

in·ure \i-ˈnu̇r, -ˈnyu̇r\ *vb* **in·ured; in·ur·ing** [ME *enuren,* fr. *en-* in + *ure,* n., use, custom, fr. MF *uevre* work, practice, fr. L *opera* work] **1** : to accustom to accept something undesirable **2** : to become of advantage

inv *abbr* **1** inventor **2** invoice

in vac·uo \in-ˈva-kyu̇-ˌwō\ *adv* [L] : in a vacuum

in·vade \in-ˈvād\ *vb* **in·vad·ed; in·vad·ing 1** : to enter for conquest or plunder **2** : to encroach upon **3** : to spread through and usu. harm ⟨germs ~ the tissues⟩ — **in·vad·er** *n*

[1]**in·val·id** \(ˌ)in-ˈva-ləd\ *adj* : being without foundation or force in fact, reason, or law — **in·va·lid·i·ty** \ˌin-və-ˈli-də-tē\ *n* — **in·val·id·ly** *adv*

[2]**in·va·lid** \ˈin-və-ləd\ *adj* : being in ill health : SICKLY

[3]**invalid** \ˈin-və-ləd\ *n* : a person in usu. chronic ill health — **in·va·lid·ism** \-lə-ˌdi-zəm\ *n*

[4]**in·va·lid** \ˈin-və-ləd, -ˌlid\ *vb* **1** : to remove from active duty by reason of sickness or disability **2** : to make sickly or disabled

in·val·i·date \(ˌ)in-ˈva-lə-ˌdāt\ *vb* : to make invalid; *esp* : to weaken or make valueless — **in·val·i·da·tion** \in-ˌva-lə-ˈdā-shən\ *n*

in·valu·able \-ˈval-yə-bəl, -yə-wə-bəl\ *adj* : valuable beyond estimation

in·vari·able \-ˈver-ē-ə-bəl\ *adj* : not changing or capable of change : CONSTANT — **in·vari·ably** \-blē\ *adv*

in·va·sion \in-ˈvā-zhən\ *n* : an act or instance of invading; *esp* : entry of an army into a country for conquest

in·va·sive \in-ˈvā-siv, -ziv\ *adj* **1** : tending to spread ⟨~ cancer cells⟩ **2** : involving entry into the living body (as by surgery) ⟨~ therapy⟩

in·vec·tive \in-ˈvek-tiv\ *n* **1** : an abusive expression or speech **2** : abusive language — **invective** *adj*

in·veigh \in-ˈvā\ *vb* : to protest or complain bitterly or vehemently : RAIL

in·vei·gle \in-ˈvā-gəl, -ˈvē-\ *vb* **in·vei·gled; in·vei·gling** [modif. of MF *aveugler* to blind, hoodwink] **1** : to win over by flattery : ENTICE **2** : to acquire by ingenuity or flattery

in·vent \in-ˈvent\ *vb* **1** : to think up **2** : to create or produce for the first time — **in·ven·tor** \-ˈven-tər\ *n*

in·ven·tion \in-ˈven-chən\ *n* **1** : INVENTIVENESS **2** : a creation of the imagination; *esp* : a false conception **3** : a device, contrivance, or process originated after study and experiment **4** : the act or process of inventing

in·ven·tive \in-ˈven-tiv\ *adj* **1** : CREATIVE, INGENIOUS ⟨an ~ composer⟩ **2** : characterized by invention ⟨an ~ turn of mind⟩ — **in·ven·tive·ness** *n*

in·ven·to·ry \ˈin-vən-ˌtōr-ē\ *n, pl* **-ries 1** : an itemized list of current goods or assets **2** : SURVEY, SUMMARY **3** : STOCK, SUPPLY **4** : the act or process of taking an inventory — **inventory** *vb*

[1]**in·verse** \(ˌ)in-ˈvərs, ˈin-ˌvərs\ *adj* : opposite in order, nature, or effect : REVERSED — **in·verse·ly** *adv*

[2]**inverse** *n* : something inverse or resulting in or from inversion : OPPOSITE

in·ver·sion \in-ˈvər-zhən\ *n* **1** : a reversal of position, order, or relationship; *esp* : an increase of temperature with altitude through a layer of air **2** : the act or process of inverting

in·vert \in-ˈvərt\ *vb* **1** : to reverse in position, order, or relationship **2** : to turn upside down or inside out **3** : to turn inward

[1]**in·ver·te·brate** \(ˌ)in-ˈvər-tə-brət, -ˌbrāt\ *adj* : lacking a backbone; *also* : of or relating to invertebrates

[2]**invertebrate** *n* : an invertebrate animal (as a jellyfish, insect, or worm)

[1]**in·vest** \in-ˈvest\ *vb* **1** : to install formally in an office or honor **2** : to furnish with power or authority : VEST **3** : to cover completely : ENVELOP **4** : CLOTHE, ADORN **5** : BESIEGE **6** : to endow with a quality or characteristic

[2]**invest** *vb* **1** : to commit (money) in order to earn a financial return **2** : to expend for future benefits or advantages **3** : to make an investment — **in·ves·tor** \-ˈves-tər\ *n*

in·ves·ti·gate \in-ˈves-tə-ˌgāt\ *vb* **-gat·ed; -gat·ing** [L *investigare* to track, investigate, fr. *vestigium* footprint, track] : to study by close examination and systematic inquiry — **in·ves·ti·ga·tion** \-ˌves-tə-ˈgā-shən\ *n* — **in·ves·ti·ga·tive** \-ˈves-tə-ˌgā-tiv\ *adj* — **in·ves·ti·ga·tor** \-ˌgā-tər\ *n*

in·ves·ti·ture \in-ˈves-tə-ˌchu̇r, -chər\ *n* **1** : the act of ratifying or establishing in office **2** : something that covers or adorns

[1]**in·vest·ment** \in-ˈvest-mənt\ *n* **1** : an outer layer : ENVELOPE **2** : INVESTITURE 1 **3** : BLOCKADE, SIEGE

[2]**investment** *n* : the outlay of money for income or profit; *also* : the sum invested or the property purchased

in·vet·er·ate \in-ˈve-tə-rət\ *adj* **1** : firmly established by age or long persistence **2** : confirmed in a habit

in·vi·a·ble \(ˌ)in-ˈvī-ə-bəl\ *adj* : incapable of surviving

in·vid·i·ous \in-ˈvi-dē-əs\ *adj* **1** : tending to cause discontent, animosity, or envy **2** : ENVIOUS **3** : OBNOXIOUS — **in·vid·i·ous·ly** *adv*

in·vig·o·rate \in-ˈvi-gə-ˌrāt\ *vb* **-rat·ed; -rat·ing** : to give life and energy to : ANIMATE — **in·vig·o·ra·tion** \-ˌvi-gə-ˈrā-shən\ *n*

in·vin·ci·ble \(ˌ)in-ˈvin-sə-bəl\ *adj* : incapable of being conquered, overcome, or subdued — **in·vin·ci·bil·i·ty** \-ˌvin-sə-ˈbi-lə-tē\ *n* — **in·vin·ci·bly** \-ˈvin-sə-blē\ *adv*

in·vi·o·la·ble \-ˈvī-ə-lə-bəl\ *adj* **1** : safe from violation or profanation **2** : UNASSAILABLE — **in·vi·o·la·bil·i·ty** \-ˌvī-ə-lə-ˈbi-lə-tē\ *n*

in·vi·o·late \-ˈvī-ə-lət\ *adj* : not violated or profaned : PURE

in·vis·i·ble \-ˈvi-zə-bəl\ *adj* **1** : incapable of being seen

⟨~ to the naked eye⟩ **2** : HIDDEN **3** : IMPERCEPTIBLE, INCONSPICUOUS — **in•vis•i•bil•i•ty** \-ˌvi-zə-ˈbi-lə-tē\ *n* — **in•vis•i•bly** \-ˈvi-zə-blē\ *adv*

in•vi•ta•tion•al \ˌin-və-ˈtā-shə-nəl\ *adj* : limited to invited participants ⟨an ~ tournament⟩ — **invitational** *n*

in•vite \in-ˈvīt\ *vb* **in•vit•ed; in•vit•ing 1** : ENTICE, TEMPT **2** : to increase the likelihood of **3** : to request the presence or participation of : ASK **4** : to request formally **5** : ENCOURAGE — **in•vi•ta•tion** \ˌin-və-ˈtā-shən\ *n*

in•vit•ing *adj* : ATTRACTIVE, TEMPTING

in vi•tro \in-ˈvē-trō, -ˈvī-, -ˈvi-\ *adv or adj* [NL, lit., in glass] : outside the living body and in an artificial environment ⟨*in vitro* fertilization⟩

in•vo•ca•tion \ˌin-və-ˈkā-shən\ *n* **1** : SUPPLICATION; *esp* : a prayer at the beginning of a service **2** : a formula for conjuring : INCANTATION

[1]**in•voice** \ˈin-ˌvȯis\ *n* [modif. of MF *envois*, pl. of *envoi* message] : an itemized list of goods shipped usu. specifying the price and the terms of sale : BILL

[2]**invoice** *vb* **in•voiced; in•voic•ing** : to send an invoice to or for : BILL

in•voke \in-ˈvōk\ *vb* **in•voked; in•vok•ing 1** : to petition for help or support **2** : to appeal to or cite as authority ⟨~ a law⟩ **3** : to call forth by incantation : CONJURE ⟨~ spirits⟩ **4** : to make an earnest request for : SOLICIT **5** : to put into effect or operation **6** : to bring about : CAUSE

in•vol•un•tary \(ˌ)in-ˈvä-lən-ˌter-ē\ *adj* **1** : done contrary to or without choice **2** : COMPULSORY **3** : not controlled by the will : REFLEX ⟨~ contractions⟩ — **in•vol•un•tari•ly** \-ˌvä-lən-ˈter-ə-lē\ *adv*

in•vo•lute \ˈin-və-ˌlüt\ *adj* : INVOLVED, INTRICATE

in•vo•lu•tion \ˌin-və-ˈlü-shən\ *n* **1** : the act or an instance of enfolding or entangling **2** : COMPLEXITY, INTRICACY

in•volve \in-ˈvälv\ *vb* **in•volved; in•volv•ing 1** : to draw in as a participant **2** : ENVELOP **3** : to occupy (as oneself) absorbingly; *esp* : to commit oneself emotionally **4** : to relate closely : CONNECT **5** : to have as part of itself : INCLUDE **6** : ENTAIL, IMPLY **7** : to have an effect on — **in•volve•ment** *n*

in•volved \-ˈvälvd\ *adj* : INTRICATE, COMPLEX ⟨an ~ plot⟩

in•vul•ner•a•ble \(ˌ)in-ˈvəl-nə-rə-bəl\ *adj* **1** : incapable of being wounded, injured, or damaged **2** : immune to or proof against attack — **in•vul•ner•a•bil•i•ty** \-ˌvəl-nə-rə-ˈbi-lə-tē\ *n* — **in•vul•ner•a•bly** \-ˈvəl-nə-rə-blē\ *adv*

[1]**in•ward** \ˈin-wərd\ *adj* **1** : situated on the inside **2** : MENTAL; *also* : SPIRITUAL **3** : directed toward the interior

[2]**inward** *or* **in•wards** \-wərdz\ *adv* **1** : toward the inside, center, or interior **2** : toward the inner being

in•ward•ly \ˈin-wərd-lē\ *adv* **1** : MENTALLY, SPIRITUALLY **2** : INTERNALLY ⟨bled ~⟩ **3** : to oneself ⟨cursed ~⟩

IOC *abbr* International Olympic Committee

io•dide \ˈī-ə-ˌdīd\ *n* : a compound of iodine with another element or group

io•dine \ˈī-ə-ˌdīn, -əd-ᵊn\ *n* **1** : a nonmetallic chemical element used esp. in medicine and photography — see ELEMENT table **2** : a solution of iodine used as a local antiseptic

io•dise *Brit var of* IODIZE

io•dize \ˈī-ə-ˌdīz\ *vb* **io•dized; io•diz•ing** : to treat with iodine or an iodide

ion \ˈī-ən, ˈī-ˌän\ *n* [Gk, neut. of *iōn*, prp. of *ienai* to go; so called because in electrolysis it goes to one of the two poles] : an electrically charged particle, atom, or group of atoms — **ion•ic** \ī-ˈä-nik\ *adj*

-ion *n suffix* : act, process, state, or condition ⟨valida*tion*⟩

ion•ise *Brit var of* IONIZE

ion•ize \ˈī-ə-ˌnīz\ *vb* **ion•ized; ion•iz•ing 1** : to convert wholly or partly into ions **2** : to become ionized — **ion•iz•able** \ˌī-ə-ˈnī-zə-bəl\ *adj* — **ion•iza•tion** \ˌī-ə-nə-ˈzā-shən\ *n* — **ion•iz•er** \ˈī-ə-ˌnī-zər\ *n*

ion•o•sphere \ī-ˈä-nə-ˌsfir\ *n* : the part of the earth's atmosphere extending from about 30 miles (50 kilometers) to the exosphere that contains ionized atmospheric gases — **ion•o•spher•ic** \ī-ˌä-nə-ˈsfir-ik, -ˈsfer-\ *adj*

IOOF *abbr* Independent Order of Odd Fellows

io•ta \ī-ˈō-tə\ *n* [L, fr. Gk *iōta*] **1** : the 9th letter of the Greek alphabet — Ι or ι **2** : a very small quantity : JOT

IOU \ˌī-(ˌ)ō-ˈyü\ *n* : an acknowledgement of a debt

IP *abbr* innings pitched

ip•e•cac \ˈi-pi-ˌkak\ *n* [Pg *ipecacuanha*] : an emetic and expectorant drug used esp. as a syrup in treating accidental poisoning; *also* : either of two So. American plants or their rhizomes and roots used to make ipecac

ip•so fac•to \ˌip-sō-ˈfak-tō\ *adv* [NL, lit., by the fact itself] : by the very nature of the case

iq *abbr* [L *idem quod*] the same as

IQ \ˈī-ˈkyü\ *n* : INTELLIGENCE QUOTIENT

[1]**Ir** *abbr* Irish

[2]**Ir** *symbol* iridium

IR *abbr* infrared

[1]**IRA** \ˌī-(ˌ)är-ˈā; ˈī-rə\ *n* [*i*ndividual *r*etirement *a*ccount] : a savings account in which a person may make tax deductible deposits up to a stipulated amount each year with deposits and interest taxable after the person's retirement

[2]**IRA** *abbr* Irish Republican Army

Ira•ni•an \i-ˈrā-nē-ən *also* -ˈrä-\ *n* : a native or inhabitant of Iran — **Iranian** *adj*

Iraqi \i-ˈrä-kē, -ˈra-\ *n* : a native or inhabitant of Iraq — **Iraqi** *adj*

iras•ci•ble \i-ˈra-sə-bəl\ *adj* : marked by hot temper and easily provoked anger **syn** choleric, testy, touchy, cranky, cross — **iras•ci•bil•i•ty** \-ˌra-sə-ˈbi-lə-tē\ *n*

irate \ī-ˈrāt\ *adj* **1** : roused to ire **2** : arising from anger — **irate•ly** *adv*

ire \ˈīr\ *n* : ANGER, WRATH — **ire•ful** *adj*

Ire *abbr* Ireland

ire•nic \ī-ˈre-nik\ *adj* : favoring, conducive to, or operating toward peace or conciliation

ir•i•des•cence \ˌir-ə-ˈdes-ᵊns\ *n* : a rainbowlike play of colors — **ir•i•des•cent** \-ᵊnt\ *adj*

irid•i•um \ir-ˈi-dē-əm\ *n* : a hard brittle heavy metallic chemical element — see ELEMENT table

iris \ˈī-rəs\ *n, pl* **iris•es** *or* **iri•des** \ˈī-rə-ˌdēz, ˈir-ə-\ [ME, fr. L *iris* rainbow, iris plant, fr. Gk, rainbow, iris plant, iris of the eye] **1** : the colored part around the pupil of the eye **2** : any of a large genus of plants with linear basal leaves and large showy flowers

Irish \ˈīr-ish\ *n* **1 Irish** *pl* : the people of Ireland **2** : the Celtic language of Ireland — **Irish** *adj* — **Irish•man** \-mən\ *n* — **Irish•wom•an** \-ˌwu̇-mən\ *n*

Irish bull *n* : an incongruous statement (as "it was hereditary in his family to have no children")

Irish coffee *n* : hot sugared coffee with Irish whiskey and whipped cream

Irish moss *n* : the dried and bleached plants of two red algae; *also* : either of these red algae

Irish setter *n* : any of a breed of bird dogs with a mahogany-red coat

irk \ˈərk\ *vb* : to make weary, irritated, or bored : ANNOY

irk•some \ˈərk-səm\ *adj* : tending to irk : ANNOYING — **irk•some•ly** *adv*

[1]**iron** \ˈīrn, ˈī-ərn\ *n* **1** : a heavy malleable magnetic metallic chemical element that rusts easily and is vital to biological processes — see ELEMENT table **2** : something made of metal and esp. iron; *also* : something (as handcuffs) used to bind or restrain ⟨put them in ~*s*⟩ **3** : a household device with a flat base that is

heated and used for pressing cloth **4** : STRENGTH, HARDNESS

²iron *vb* **1** : to press or smooth with or as if with a heated iron **2** : to remove (as wrinkles) by ironing — **iron•er** *n*

¹iron•clad \-ˈklad\ *adj* **1** : sheathed in iron armor **2** : so firm or secure as to be unbreakable

²iron•clad \-ˌklad\ *n* : an armored naval vessel esp. of the 19th century

iron curtain *n* : a political, military, and ideological barrier that isolates an area; *esp, often cap* : one isolating an area under Soviet control

iron•ic \ī-ˈrä-nik\ *or* **iron•i•cal** \-ni-kəl\ *adj* **1** : of, relating to, or marked by irony **2** : given to irony

iron•i•cal•ly \-ni-k(ə-)lē\ *adv* **1** : in an ironic manner **2** : it is ironic

iron•ing *n* : clothes ironed or to be ironed

iron lung *n* : a device for artificial respiration that encloses the chest in a chamber in which changes of pressure force air into and out of the lungs

iron out *vb* : to remove or lessen difficulties in or extremes of

iron oxide *n* : FERRIC OXIDE

iron•stone \ˈīrn-ˌstōn, ˈī-ərn-\ *n* **1** : a hard iron-rich sedimentary rock **2** : a hard heavy durable pottery developed in England in the 19th century

iron•ware \-ˌwar\ *n* : articles made of iron

iron•weed \-ˌwēd\ *n* : any of several mostly weedy American plants related to the asters that have terminal heads of red or purple flowers

iron•wood \-ˌwu̇d\ *n* : any of numerous trees or shrubs with exceptionally hard wood; *also* : the wood

iron•work \-ˌwərk\ *n* **1** : work in iron **2** *pl* : a mill or building where iron or steel is smelted or heavy iron or steel products are made — **iron•work•er** *n*

iro•ny \ˈī-rə-nē\ *n, pl* **-nies** [L *ironia,* fr. Gk *eirōnia,* fr. *eirōn* dissembler] **1** : the use of words to express the opposite of what one really means **2** : incongruity between the actual result of a sequence of events and the expected result

Ir•o•quois \ˈir-ə-ˌkwȯi\ *n, pl* **Iroquois** *same or* -ˌkwȯiz\ **1** *pl* : an American Indian confederacy of New York that consisted of the Cayuga, Mohawk, Oneida, Onondaga, and Seneca and later included the Tuscarora **2** : a member of any of the Iroquois peoples

ir•ra•di•ate \i-ˈrā-dē-ˌāt\ *vb* **-at•ed; -at•ing 1** : ILLUMINATE **2** : ENLIGHTEN **3** : to treat by exposure to radiation **4** : RADIATE — **ir•ra•di•a•tion** \-ˌrā-dē-ˈā-shən\ *n*

¹ir•ra•tio•nal \(ˌ)i-ˈra-shə-nəl\ *adj* **1** : incapable of reasoning ⟨~ beasts⟩; *also* : defective in mental power ⟨~ with fever⟩ **2** : not based on reason ⟨~ fears⟩ **3** : being or numerically equal to an irrational number — **ir•ra•tio•nal•i•ty** \(ˌ)i-ˌra-shə-ˈna-lə-tē\ *n* — **ir•ra•tio•nal•ly** *adv*

²irrational *n* : IRRATIONAL NUMBER

irrational number *n* : a real number that cannot be expressed as the quotient of two integers

ir•rec•on•cil•able \(ˌ)i-ˌre-kən-ˈsī-lə-bəl, -ˈre-kən-ˌsī-\ *adj* : impossible to reconcile, adjust, or harmonize — **ir•rec•on•cil•abil•i•ty** \(ˌ)i-ˌre-kən-ˌsī-lə-ˈbi-lə-tē\ *n*

ir•re•cov•er•able \ˌir-i-ˈkə-və-rə-bəl\ *adj* : not capable of being recovered or rectified : IRREPARABLE — **ir•re•cov•er•ably** \-blē\ *adv*

ir•re•deem•able \ˌir-i-ˈdē-mə-bəl\ *adj* **1** : not redeemable; *esp* : not terminable by payment of the principal ⟨an ~ bond⟩ **2** : not convertible into gold or silver at the will of the holder **3** : being beyond remedy : HOPELESS

ir•re•den•tism \-ˈden-ˌti-zəm\ *n* : a principle or policy directed toward the incorporation of a territory historically or ethnically part of another into that other — **ir•re•den•tist** \-tist\ *n or adj*

ir•re•duc•ible \ˌir-i-ˈdü-sə-bəl, -ˈdyü-\ *adj* : not reducible — **ir•re•duc•ibly** \-blē\ *adv*

ir•re•fut•able \ˌir-i-ˈfyü-tə-bəl, (ˌ)i-ˈre-fyət-\ *adj* : impossible to refute

irreg *abbr* irregular

ir•reg•u•lar \(ˌ)i-ˈre-gyə-lər\ *adj* **1** : not regular : not natural or uniform **2** : not conforming to the normal or usual manner of inflection ⟨~ verbs⟩ **3** : not belonging to a regular or organized army ⟨~ troops⟩ — **irregular** *n* — **ir•reg•u•lar•ly** *adv*

ir•reg•u•lar•i•ty \i-ˌre-gyə-ˈlar-ə-tē\ *n, pl* **-ties 1** : something that is irregular **2** : the quality or state of being irregular **3** : occasional constipation

ir•rel•e•vant \(ˌ)i-ˈre-lə-vənt\ *adj* : not relevant — **ir•rel•e•vance** \-vəns\ *n*

ir•re•li•gious \ˌir-i-ˈli-jəs\ *adj* : lacking religious emotions, doctrines, or practices

ir•re•me•di•a•ble \ˌir-i-ˈmē-dē-ə-bəl\ *adj* : impossible to remedy or correct

ir•re•mov•able \-ˈmü-və-bəl\ *adj* : not removable

ir•rep•a•ra•ble \(ˌ)i-ˈre-pə-rə-bəl\ *adj* : impossible to make good, undo, repair, or remedy ⟨~ damage⟩

ir•re•place•able \ˌir-i-ˈplā-sə-bəl\ *adj* : not replaceable

ir•re•press•ible \-ˈpre-sə-bəl\ *adj* : impossible to repress or control

ir•re•proach•able \-ˈprō-chə-bəl\ *adj* : not reproachable : BLAMELESS

ir•re•sist•ible \ˌir-i-ˈzis-tə-bəl\ *adj* : impossible to successfully resist — **ir•re•sist•ibly** \-blē\ *adv*

ir•res•o•lute \(ˌ)i-ˈre-zə-ˌlüt\ *adj* : uncertain how to act or proceed : VACILLATING — **ir•res•o•lute•ly** \-ˌlüt-lē; (ˌ)i-ˌre-zə-ˈlüt-\ *adv* — **ir•res•o•lu•tion** \(ˌ)i-ˌre-zə-ˈlü-shən\ *n*

ir•re•spec•tive of \ˌir-i-ˈspek-tiv-\ *prep* : without regard to

ir•re•spon•si•ble \-ˈspän-sə-bəl\ *adj* : not responsible — **ir•re•spon•si•bil•i•ty** \-ˌspän-sə-ˈbi-lə-tē\ *n* — **ir•re•spon•si•bly** \-ˈspän-sə-blē\ *adv*

ir•re•triev•able \ˌir-i-ˈtrē-və-bəl\ *adj* : not retrievable : IRRECOVERABLE

ir•rev•er•ence \(ˌ)i-ˈre-və-rəns\ *n* **1** : lack of reverence **2** : an irreverent act or utterance — **ir•rev•er•ent** \-rənt\ *adj*

ir•re•vers•ible \ˌir-i-ˈvər-sə-bəl\ *adj* : incapable of being reversed

ir•rev•o•ca•ble \(ˌ)i-ˈre-və-kə-bəl\ *adj* : incapable of being revoked or recalled — **ir•rev•o•ca•bly** \-blē\ *adv*

ir•ri•gate \ˈir-ə-ˌgāt\ *vb* **-gat•ed; -gat•ing** : to supply (as land) with water by artificial means; *also* : to flush with liquid — **ir•ri•ga•tion** \ˌir-ə-ˈgā-shən\ *n*

ir•ri•ta•bil•i•ty \ˌir-ə-tə-ˈbi-lə-tē\ *n* **1** : the property of living things and of protoplasm that enables reaction to stimuli **2** : the quality or state of being irritable; *esp* : readiness to become annoyed or angry

ir•ri•ta•ble \ˈir-ə-tə-bəl\ *adj* : capable of being irritated; *esp* : readily or easily irritated — **ir•ri•ta•bly** \-blē\ *adv*

ir•ri•tate \ˈir-ə-ˌtāt\ *vb* **-tat•ed; -tat•ing 1** : to excite to anger : EXASPERATE **2** : to make sore or inflamed — **ir•ri•tant** \ˈir-ə-tənt\ *adj or n* — **ir•ri•tat•ing•ly** *adv* — **ir•ri•ta•tion** \ˌir-ə-ˈtā-shən\ *n*

ir•rupt \(ˌ)i-ˈrəpt\ *vb* **1** : to rush in forcibly or violently **2** : to increase suddenly in numbers ⟨rabbits ~ in cycles⟩ — **ir•rup•tion** \-ˈrəp-shən\ *n*

IRS *abbr* Internal Revenue Service

is *pres 3d sing of* BE

Isa *or* **Is** *abbr* Isaiah

Isa•iah \ī-ˈzā-ə\ *n* — see BIBLE table

Isa•ias \ī-ˈzā-əs\ *n* : ISAIAH

ISBN *abbr* International Standard Book Number

-ish \ish\ *adj suffix* **1** : of, relating to, or being ⟨Finn*ish*⟩ **2** : characteristic of ⟨boy*ish*⟩ ⟨mul*ish*⟩ **3** : inclined or liable to ⟨book*ish*⟩ **4** : having a touch or trace of : somewhat ⟨purpl*ish*⟩ **5** : having the approximate age of ⟨forty*ish*⟩

isin•glass \ˈīz-ᵊn-ˌglas, ˈī-ziŋ-\ *n* **1** : a gelatin obtained from various fish **2** : mica esp. in thin sheets

isl *abbr* island

Is•lam \is-ˈläm, iz-, -ˈlam, ˈis-ˌ, ˈiz-ˌ\ *n* [Ar *islām* submission (to the will of God)] : the religious faith of Muslims; *also* : the civilization built on this faith — **Is•lam•ic** \is-ˈlä-mik, iz-, -ˈla-\ *adj*
is•land \ˈī-lənd\ *n* **1** : a body of land smaller than a continent surrounded by water **2** : something resembling an island in its isolation
is•land•er \ˈī-lən-dər\ *n* : a native or inhabitant of an island
isle \ˈīl\ *n* : ISLAND; *esp* : a small island
is•let \ˈī-lət\ *n* : a small island
ism \ˈi-ˌzəm\ *n* : a distinctive doctrine, cause, or theory
-ism \ˌi-zəm\ *n suffix* **1** : act : practice : process ⟨critic*ism*⟩ **2** : manner of action or behavior characteristic of a (specified) person or thing ⟨fanatic*ism*⟩ **3** : state : condition : property ⟨dual*ism*⟩ **4** : abnormal state or condition ⟨alcohol*ism*⟩ **5** : doctrine : theory : cult ⟨Buddh*ism*⟩ **6** : adherence to a set of principles ⟨stoic*ism*⟩ **7** : prejudice or discrimination on the basis of a (specified) attribute ⟨rac*ism*⟩ ⟨sex*ism*⟩ **8** : characteristic or peculiar feature or trait ⟨colloquial*ism*⟩
iso•bar \ˈī-sə-ˌbär\ *n* : a line on a map connecting places of equal barometric pressure — **iso•bar•ic** \ˌī-sə-ˈbär-ik, -ˈbar-\ *adj*
iso•late \ˈī-sə-ˌlāt\ *vb* **-lat•ed; -lat•ing** [fr. *isolated* set apart, fr. F *isolé*, fr. It *isolato*, fr. *isola* island, fr. L *insula*] : to place or keep by itself : separate from others — **iso•la•tion** \ˌī-sə-ˈlā-shən\ *n*
iso•lat•ed *adj* **1** : occurring alone or once : UNIQUE **2** : SPORADIC
iso•la•tion•ism \ˌī-sə-ˈlā-shə-ˌni-zəm\ *n* : a policy of national isolation by abstention from international political and economic relations — **iso•la•tion•ist** \-shə-nist\ *n or adj*
iso•mer \ˈī-sə-mər\ *n* : any of two or more chemical compounds that contain the same numbers of atoms of the same elements but differ in structural arrangement and properties — **iso•mer•ic** \ˌī-sə-ˈmer-ik\ *adj* — **isom•er•ism** \ī-ˈsä-mə-ˌri-zəm\ *n*
iso•met•rics \ˌī-sə-ˈme-triks\ *n sing or pl* : exercise involving a series of brief and intense contractions of muscles against each other or against an immovable resistance — **iso•met•ric** *adj*
iso•prene \ˈī-sə-ˌprēn\ *n* : a hydrocarbon used esp. in making synthetic rubber
isos•ce•les \ī-ˈsä-sə-ˌlēz\ *adj* : having two equal sides ⟨an ~ triangle⟩
iso•therm \ˈī-sə-ˌthərm\ *n* : a line on a map connecting points having the same temperature
iso•ther•mal \ˌī-sə-ˈthər-məl\ *adj* : of, relating to, or marked by equality of temperature
iso•tope \ˈī-sə-ˌtōp\ *n* [Gk *isos* equal + *topos* place] : any of the forms of a chemical element that differ chiefly in the number of neutrons in an atom — **iso•to•pic** \ˌī-sə-ˈtä-pik, -ˈtō-\ *adj* — **iso•to•pi•cal•ly** \-ˈtä-pi-k(ə-)lē, -ˈtō-\ *adv*
Isr *abbr* Israel; Israeli
Is•rae•li \iz-ˈrā-lē\ *n, pl* **Israelis** *also* **Israeli** : a native or inhabitant of Israel — **Israeli** *adj*
Is•ra•el•ite \ˈiz-rē-ə-ˌlīt\ *n* : a member of the Hebrew people descended from Jacob
is•su•ance \ˈi-shü-wəns\ *n* : the act of issuing or giving out esp. officially
[1]**is•sue** \ˈi-shü\ *n* **1** : the action of going, coming, or flowing out : EGRESS, EMERGENCE **2** : EXIT, OUTLET, VENT **3** : OFFSPRING, PROGENY **4** : OUTCOME, RESULT **5** : a point of debate or controversy; *also* : the point at which an unsettled matter is ready for a decision **6** : a discharge (as of blood) from the body **7** : something coming forth from a specified source **8** : the act of officially giving out or printing : PUBLICATION; *also* : the quantity of things given out at one time
[2]**issue** *vb* **is•sued; is•su•ing 1** : to go, come, or flow out **2** : to come forth or cause to come forth : EMERGE, DISCHARGE, EMIT **3** : ACCRUE **4** : to descend from a specified parent or ancestor **5** : to result in **6** : to put forth or distribute officially **7** : PUBLISH **8** : EMANATE, RESULT — **is•su•er** *n*
[1]**-ist** \ist\ *n suffix* **1** : one that performs a (specified) action ⟨cycl*ist*⟩ : one that makes or produces ⟨novel*ist*⟩ **2** : one that plays a (specified) musical instrument ⟨harp*ist*⟩ **3** : one that operates a (specified) mechanical instrument or contrivance ⟨machin*ist*⟩ **4** : one that specializes in a (specified) art or science or skill ⟨geolog*ist*⟩ **5** : one that adheres to or advocates a (specified) doctrine or system or code of behavior ⟨social*ist*⟩ or that of a (specified) individual ⟨Darwin*ist*⟩
[2]**-ist** *adj suffix* : -ISTIC
isth•mi•an \ˈis-mē-ən\ *adj* : of, relating to, or situated in or near an isthmus
isth•mus \ˈis-məs\ *n* : a narrow strip of land connecting two larger portions of land
-is•tic \ˈis-tik\ *or* **-is•ti•cal** \ˈis-ti-kəl\ *adj suffix* : of, relating to, or characteristic of ⟨altru*istic*⟩
[1]**it** \ˈit\ *pron* **1** : that one — used of a lifeless thing, a plant, a person or animal, or an abstract entity ⟨~'s a big building⟩ ⟨~'s a shade tree⟩ ⟨who is ~⟩ ⟨beauty is everywhere and ~ is a source of joy⟩ **2** — used as a subject of an impersonal verb that expresses a condition or action without reference to an agent ⟨~ is raining⟩ **3** — used as an anticipatory subject or object ⟨~'s good to see you⟩
[2]**it** \ˈit\ *n* : the player in a game who performs the principal action of the game (as trying to find others in hide-and-seek)
It *abbr* Italian; Italy
ital *abbr* italic; italicized
Ital *abbr* Italian
Ital•ian \i-ˈtal-yən\ *n* **1** : a native or inhabitant of Italy **2** : the language of Italy — **Italian** *adj*
ital•ic \i-ˈta-lik, ī-\ *adj* : relating to type in which the letters slope up toward the right (as in *"italic"*) — **italic** *n*
ital•i•cise *Brit var of* ITALICIZE
ital•i•cize \i-ˈta-lə-ˌsīz, ī-\ *vb* **-cized; -ciz•ing** : to print in italics
itch \ˈich\ *n* **1** : an uneasy irritating skin sensation prob. related to sensing pain **2** : a skin disorder accompanied by an itch **3** : a persistent desire — **itch** *vb* — **itchy** *adj*
-ite \ˌīt\ *n suffix* **1** : native : resident ⟨suburban*ite*⟩ **2** : adherent : follower ⟨Lenin*ite*⟩ **3** : product ⟨metabol*ite*⟩ **4** : mineral : rock ⟨quartz*ite*⟩
item \ˈī-təm\ *n* [L, likewise, also] **1** : a separate particular in a list, account, or series : ARTICLE **2** : a separate piece of news (as in a newspaper)
item•ise *Brit var of* ITEMIZE
item•ize \ˈī-tə-ˌmīz\ *vb* **-ized; -iz•ing** : to set down in detail : LIST — **item•i•za•tion** \ˌī-tə-mə-ˈzā-shən\ *n*
it•er•ate \ˈi-tə-ˌrāt\ *vb* **-at•ed; -at•ing** : REITERATE, REPEAT
it•er•a•tion \ˌi-tə-ˈrā-shən\ *n* **1** : REPETITION; *esp* : a computational process in which a series of operations is repeated until a condition is met **2** : one repetition of the series of operations in iteration
itin•er•ant \ī-ˈti-nə-rənt, ə-\ *adj* : traveling from place to place; *esp* : covering a circuit ⟨an ~ preacher⟩
itin•er•ary \ī-ˈti-nə-ˌrer-ē, ə-\ *n, pl* **-ar•ies 1** : the route of a journey or the proposed outline of one **2** : a travel diary **3** : GUIDEBOOK
its \ˈits\ *adj* : of or relating to it or itself
it•self \it-ˈself\ *pron* : that identical one — used reflexively, for emphasis, or in absolute constructions
-ity \ə-tē\ *n suffix* : quality : state : degree ⟨alkalin*ity*⟩
IUD \ˌī-(ˌ)yü-ˈdē\ *n* : INTRAUTERINE DEVICE
IV \ˌī-ˈvē\ *n* [*i*ntra*v*enous] : an apparatus used to give an intravenous injection or feeding; *also* : such an injection or feeding
-ive \iv\ *adj suffix* : that performs or tends toward an (indicated) action ⟨correct*ive*⟩
ivo•ry \ˈī-vrē, -və-rē\ *n, pl* **-ries** [ME *ivorie*, fr. OF

ivoire, fr. L *eboreus* of ivory, fr. *ebur* ivory] **1 :** the hard creamy-white material composing the tusks of an elephant or walrus **2 :** a pale yellow color **3 :** something made of ivory or of a similar substance

ivory tower *n* **1 :** an impractical lack of concern with urgent problems **2 :** a place of learning

ivy \ˈī-vē\ *n, pl* **ivies :** a trailing woody evergreen vine with small black berries that is related to ginseng

IWW *abbr* Industrial Workers of the World

-ize \ˌīz\ *vb suffix* **1 :** cause to be or conform to or resemble ⟨American*ize*⟩ **:** cause to be formed into ⟨union*ize*⟩ **2 :** subject to a (specified) action ⟨satir*ize*⟩ **3 :** saturate, treat, or combine with ⟨macadam*ize*⟩ **4 :** treat like ⟨idol*ize*⟩ **5 :** become **:** become like ⟨crystall*ize*⟩ **6 :** be productive in or of **:** engage in a (specified) activity ⟨philosoph*ize*⟩ **7 :** adopt or spread the manner of activity or the teaching of ⟨Christian*ize*⟩

J

[1]j \ˈjā\ *n, pl* **j's** *or* **js** \ˈjāz\ *often cap* **:** the 10th letter of the English alphabet

[2]j *abbr, often cap* **1** jack **2** journal **3** judge **4** justice

[1]jab \ˈjab\ *vb* **jabbed; jab•bing :** to thrust quickly or abruptly **:** POKE

[2]jab *n* **:** a usu. short straight punch

jab•ber \ˈja-bər\ *vb* **:** to talk rapidly, indistinctly, or unintelligibly **:** CHATTER — **jabber** *n* — **jab•ber•er** *n*

jab•ber•wocky \ˈja-bər-ˌwä-kē\ *n* **:** meaningless speech or writing

ja•bot \zha-ˈbō, ˈja-ˌbō\ *n* **:** a ruffle worn down the front of a dress or shirt

jac•a•ran•da \ˌja-kə-ˈran-də\ *n* **:** any of a genus of pinnate-leaved tropical American trees with clusters of showy blue flowers

[1]jack \ˈjak\ *n* **1 :** a mechanical device; *esp* **:** one used to raise a heavy body a short distance **2 :** a male donkey **3 :** a small target ball in lawn bowling **4 :** a small national flag flown by a ship **5 :** a small 6-pointed metal object used in a game **(jacks) 6 :** a playing card bearing the figure of a soldier or servant **7 :** a socket into which a plug is inserted for connecting electric circuits

[2]jack *vb* **1 :** to raise by means of a jack **2 :** INCREASE ⟨~ up prices⟩

jack•al \ˈja-kəl\ *n* [Turk *çakal,* fr. Per *shagāl*] **:** any of several mammals of Asia and Africa related to the wolves

jack•a•napes \ˈja-kə-ˌnāps\ *n* **1 :** MONKEY, APE **2 :** an impudent or conceited person

jack•ass \ˈjak-ˌas\ *n* **1 :** DONKEY; *esp* **:** a male donkey **2 :** a stupid person **:** FOOL

jack•boot \-ˌbüt\ *n* **1 :** a heavy military boot of glossy black leather extending above the knee **2 :** a laceless military boot reaching to the calf

jack•daw \ˈjak-ˌdò\ *n* **:** a black and gray Old World crowlike bird

jack•et \ˈja-kət\ *n* [ME *jaket,* fr. MF *jaquet,* dim. of *jaque* short jacket, fr. *jacque* peasant, fr. the name *Jacques* James] **1 :** a garment for the upper body usu. having a front opening, collar, and sleeves **2 :** an outer covering or casing ⟨a book ~⟩

Jack Frost *n* **:** frost or frosty weather personified

jack•ham•mer \ˈjak-ˌha-mər\ *n* **:** a pneumatic percussion tool for drilling rock or breaking pavement

jack–in–the–box *n, pl* **jack–in–the–boxes** *or* **jacks–in–the–box :** a toy consisting of a small box out of which a figure springs when the lid is raised

jack–in–the–pulpit *n, pl* **jack–in–the–pulpits** *or* **jacks–in–the–pulpit :** an American spring-flowering woodland herb having an upright club-shaped spadix arched over by a green and purple spathe

[1]jack•knife \ˈjak-ˌnīf\ *n* **1 :** a large pocketknife **2 :** a dive in which the diver bends from the waist and touches the ankles before straightening out

[2]jackknife *vb* **:** to fold like a jackknife ⟨the trailer truck *jackknifed*⟩

jack•leg \ˈjak-ˌleg\ *adj* **1 :** lacking skill or training **2 :** MAKESHIFT

jack–of–all–trades *n, pl* **jacks–of–all–trades :** one who is able to do passable work at various tasks

jack–o'–lan•tern \ˈja-kə-ˌlan-tərn\ *n* **:** a lantern made of a pumpkin cut to look like a human face

jack•pot \ˈjak-ˌpät\ *n* **1 :** a large sum of money formed by the accumulation of stakes from previous play (as in poker) **2 :** an impressive and often unexpected success or reward

jack•rab•bit \-ˌra-bət\ *n* **:** any of several large hares of western No. America with very long ears and hind legs

jack•straw \-ˌstrò\ *n* **1** *pl* **:** a game in which straws or thin sticks are let fall in a heap and each player in turn tries to remove them one at a time without disturbing the rest **2 :** one of the straws or sticks in jackstraws

jack–tar \-ˈtär\ *n, often cap* **:** SAILOR

Ja•cob's ladder \ˈjā-kəbz-\ *n* **:** any of several perennial herbs related to phlox that have pinnate leaves and blue or white bell-shaped flowers

jac•quard \ˈja-ˌkärd\ *n, often cap* **:** a fabric of intricate variegated weave or pattern

[1]jade \ˈjād\ *n* **1 :** a broken-down, vicious, or worthless horse **2 :** a disreputable woman

[2]jade *vb* **jad•ed; jad•ing 1 :** to wear out by overwork or abuse **2 :** to become weary **syn** exhaust, fatigue, tire

[3]jade *n* [F, fr. obs. Sp (*piedra de la*) *ijada,* lit., loin stone; fr. the belief that jade cures renal colic] **:** a usu. green gemstone that takes a high polish

jad•ed *adj* **:** dulled by a surfeit or excess

[1]jag \ˈjag\ *n* **:** a sharp projecting part

[2]jag *n* **:** SPREE

jag•ged \ˈja-gəd\ *adj* **:** sharply notched

jag•uar \ˈja-ˌgwär\ *n* **:** a black-spotted tropical American cat that is larger and stockier than the Old World leopard

jaguar

jai alai \ˈhī-ˌlī\ *n* [Sp, fr. Basque, fr. *jai* festival + *alai* merry] **:** a court game played by usu. two or four players with a ball and a curved wicker basket strapped to the wrist

jail \ˈjāl\ *n* [ME *jaiole,* fr. OF, fr. LL *caveola,* dim. of L *cavea* cage] **:** PRISON; *esp* **:** one for persons held in lawful custody — **jail** *vb*

jail•bird \-ˌbərd\ *n* **:** an habitual criminal

jail•break \-ˌbrāk\ *n* **:** a forcible escape from jail

jail•er *or* **jail•or** \ˈjā-lər\ *n* **:** a keeper of a jail

jal•ap \ˈja-ləp, ˈjä-\ *n* **:** a powdered purgative drug from the root of a Mexican plant related to the morning glory; *also* **:** this root or plant

ja•la•pe•ño \ˌhä-lə-ˈpān-(ˌ)yō\ *n* **:** a Mexican hot pepper

ja•lopy \jə-ˈlä-pē\ *n, pl* **ja•lop•ies** : a dilapidated vehicle (as an automobile)
jal•ou•sie \ˈja-lə-sē\ *n* [F, lit., jealousy] : a blind, window, or door with adjustable horizontal slats or louvers
¹jam \ˈjam\ *vb* **jammed; jam•ming 1** : to press into a close or tight position **2** : to cause to become wedged so as to be unworkable; *also* : to make or become unworkable through the jamming of a movable part **3** : to push forcibly ⟨~ on the brakes⟩ **4** : CRUSH, BRUISE **5** : to make unintelligible by sending out interfering signals or messages **6** : to take part in a jam session — **jam•mer** *n*
²jam *n* **1** : a crowded mass that impedes or blocks ⟨traffic ~⟩ **2** : a difficult state of affairs
³jam *n* : a food made by boiling fruit and sugar to a thick consistency
Jam *abbr* Jamaica
Ja•mai•can \jə-ˈmā-kən\ *n* : a native or inhabitant of Jamaica — **Jamaican** *adj*
jamb \ˈjam\ *n* [ME *jambe,* fr. MF, lit., leg] : an upright piece forming the side of an opening (as of a door)
jam•ba•laya \ˌjəm-bə-ˈlī-ə\ *n* [LaF] : rice cooked with ham, sausage, chicken, shrimp, or oysters and seasoned with herbs
jam•bo•ree \ˌjam-bə-ˈrē\ *n* : a large festive gathering
James \ˈjāmz\ *n* — see BIBLE table
jam–pack \ˈjam-ˈpak\ *vb* : to pack tightly or to excess
jam session *n* : an impromptu performance esp. by jazz musicians
Jan *abbr* January
jan•gle \ˈjaŋ-gəl\ *vb* **jan•gled; jan•gling** : to make a harsh or discordant sound — **jangle** *n*
jan•i•tor \ˈja-nə-tər\ *n* [L, fr. *janua* door] : a person who has the care of a building — **jan•i•to•ri•al** \ˌja-nə-ˈtōr-ē-əl\ *adj*
Jan•u•ary \ˈja-nyə-ˌwer-ē\ *n* [ME *Januarie,* fr. L *Januarius,* first month of the ancient Roman year, fr. *Janus,* two-faced god of gates and beginnings] : the 1st month of the year
¹ja•pan \jə-ˈpan\ *n* : a varnish giving a hard brilliant finish
²japan *vb* **ja•panned; ja•pan•ning** : to cover with a coat of japan
Jap•a•nese \ˌja-pə-ˈnēz, -ˈnēs\ *n, pl* **Japanese 1** : a native or inhabitant of Japan **2** : the language of Japan — **Japanese** *adj*
Japanese beetle *n* : a small metallic green and brown scarab beetle introduced from Japan that is a pest on the roots of grasses as a grub and on foliage and fruits as an adult
¹jape \ˈjāp\ *vb* **japed; jap•ing 1** : JOKE **2** : MOCK
²jape *n* : JEST, GIBE
¹jar \ˈjär\ *vb* **jarred; jar•ring 1** : to make a harsh or discordant sound **2** : to have a harsh or disagreeable effect **3** : VIBRATE, SHAKE
²jar *n* **1** : a state of conflict **2** : a harsh discordant sound **3** : JOLT **4** : a painful effect : SHOCK
³jar *n* : a widemouthed container usu. of glass or earthenware
jar•di•niere \ˌjärd-ᵊn-ˈir\ *n* : an ornamental stand for plants or flowers
jar•gon \ˈjär-gən\ *n* **1** : confused unintelligible language **2** : the special vocabulary of a particular group or activity **3** : obscure and often pretentious language
Jas *abbr* James
jas•mine \ˈjaz-mən\ *n* [F *jasmin,* fr. Ar *yāsamīn*] : any of various climbing shrubs with fragrant flowers
jas•per \ˈjas-pər\ *n* : a usu. red, yellow, or brown opaque quartz
jaun•dice \ˈjȯn-dəs\ *n* : yellowish discoloration of skin, tissues, and body fluids by bile pigments; *also* : an abnormal condition marked by jaundice
jaun•diced \-dəst\ *adj* **1** : affected with or as if with jaundice **2** : exhibiting envy, distaste, or hostility
jaunt \ˈjȯnt\ *n* : a short trip usu. for pleasure
jaun•ty \ˈjȯn-tē\ *adj* **jaun•ti•er; -est** : sprightly in manner or appearance : LIVELY — **jaun•ti•ly** \-tə-lē\ *adv* — **jaun•ti•ness** \-tē-nəs\ *n*
Ja•va•nese \ˌja-və-ˈnēz, ˌjä-, -ˈnēs\ *n* : a native or inhabitant of the Indonesian island of Java
jav•e•lin \ˈja-və-lən\ *n* **1** : a light spear **2** : a slender shaft thrown for distance in a track-and-field contest
¹jaw \ˈjȯ\ *n* **1** : either of the bony or cartilaginous structures that support the soft tissues enclosing the mouth and that usu. bear teeth **2** : the parts forming the walls of the mouth and serving to open and close it — usu. used in pl. **3** : one of a pair of movable parts for holding or crushing something — **jawed** \ˈjȯd\ *adj*
²jaw *vb* : to talk abusively, indignantly, or at length
jaw•bone \-ˌbōn\ *n* : JAW 1
jaw•break•er \-ˌbrā-kər\ *n* **1** : a word difficult to pronounce **2** : a round hard candy
jay \ˈjā\ *n* : any of various noisy brightly colored often largely blue birds smaller than the related crows
jay•bird \ˈjā-ˌbərd\ *n* : JAY
jay•vee \ˌjā-ˈvē\ *n* **1** : JUNIOR VARSITY **2** : a member of a junior varsity team
jay•walk \ˈjā-ˌwȯk\ *vb* : to cross a street carelessly without regard for traffic regulations — **jay•walk•er** *n*
¹jazz \ˈjaz\ *n* **1** : American music characterized by improvisation, syncopated rhythms, and contrapuntal ensemble playing **2** : empty talk **3** : similar but unspecified things : STUFF
²jazz *vb* : ENLIVEN ⟨~ things up⟩
jazzy \ˈja-zē\ *adj* **jazz•i•er; -est 1** : having the characteristics of jazz **2** : marked by unrestraint, animation, or flashiness
JCS *abbr* joint chiefs of staff
jct *abbr* junction
JD *abbr* **1** [L *juris doctor*] doctor of jurisprudence; doctor of law **2** [L *jurum doctor*] doctor of laws **3** justice department **4** juvenile delinquent
jeal•ous \ˈje-ləs\ *adj* **1** : demanding complete devotion **2** : suspicious of a rival or of one believed to enjoy an advantage **3** : VIGILANT — **jeal•ous•ly** *adv* — **jeal•ou•sy** \-lə-sē\ *n*
jeans \ˈjēnz\ *n pl* [pl. of *jean* twilled cloth, short for *jean fustian,* fr. ME *Gene* Genoa, Italy] : pants made of durable twilled cotton cloth
jeep \ˈjēp\ *n* [prob. fr. *g.p.* (abbr. of *general purpose*)] : a small four-wheel drive general-purpose motor vehicle used in World War II
¹jeer \ˈjir\ *vb* : to speak or cry out in derision : MOCK
²jeer *n* : TAUNT
Je•ho•vah \ji-ˈhō-və\ *n* : GOD 1
je•hu \ˈjē-hü, -hyü\ *n* : a driver of a coach or cab
je•june \ji-ˈjün\ *adj* [L *jejunus* empty of food, hungry, meager] : lacking interest or significance : DULL
je•ju•num \ji-ˈjü-nəm\ *n* [L] : the section of the small intestine between the duodenum and the ileum — **je•ju•nal** \-ˈjün-ᵊl\ *adj*
jell \ˈjel\ *vb* **1** : to come to the consistency of jelly **2** : to take shape
jel•ly \ˈje-lē\ *n, pl* **jellies 1** : a food with a soft elastic consistency due usu. to the presence of gelatin or pectin; *esp* : a fruit product made by boiling sugar and the juice of a fruit **2** : a substance resembling jelly — **jelly** *vb*
jelly bean *n* : a bean-shaped candy
jel•ly•fish \ˈje-lē-ˌfish\ *n* : a coelenterate with a saucer-shaped jellylike body
jen•net \ˈje-nət\ *n* **1** : a small Spanish horse **2** : a female donkey
jen•ny \ˈje-nē\ *n, pl* **jennies** : a female bird or donkey
jeop•ar•dy \ˈje-pər-dē\ *n* [ME *jeopardie,* fr. OF *jeu parti* alternative, lit., divided game] : exposure to death, loss, or injury **syn** peril, hazard, risk, danger — **jeop•ar•dize** \-ˌdīz\ *vb*
Jer *abbr* Jeremiah; Jeremias

jer•e•mi•ad \ˌjer-ə-ˈmī-əd, -ˌad\ *n* : a prolonged lamentation or complaint; *also* : a cautionary or angry harangue

Jer•e•mi•ah \ˌjer-ə-ˈmī-ə\ *n* — see BIBLE table

Jer•e•mi•as \ˌjer-ə-ˈmī-əs\ *n* : JEREMIAH

[1]**jerk** \ˈjərk\ *n* **1** : a short quick pull or twist : TWITCH **2** : an annoyingly stupid or foolish person — **jerk•i•ly** \ˈjər-kə-lē\ *adv* — **jerky** \ˈjər-kē\ *adj*

[2]**jerk** *vb* **1** : to give a sharp quick push, pull, or twist **2** : to move in short abrupt motions

jer•kin \ˈjər-kən\ *n* : a close-fitting usu. sleeveless jacket

jerk•wa•ter \ˈjərk-ˌwȯ-tər, -ˌwä-\ *adj* [fr. *jerkwater* rural train] : of minor importance : INSIGNIFICANT ⟨~ towns⟩

jer•ry–built \ˈjer-ē-ˌbilt\ *adj* : built cheaply and flimsily

jer•sey \ˈjər-zē\ *n, pl* **jerseys** [*Jersey,* one of the Channel islands] **1** : a plain weft-knitted fabric **2** : a close-fitting knitted shirt **3** *often cap* : any of a breed of small usu. fawn-colored dairy cattle

jess \ˈjes\ *n* : a leg strap by which a captive bird of prey may be controlled

jes•sa•mine \ˈje-sə-mən\ *var of* JASMINE

jest \ˈjest\ *n* **1** : an act intended to provoke laughter **2** : a witty remark **3** : a frivolous mood ⟨said in ~⟩ — **jest** *vb*

jest•er \ˈjes-tər\ *n* : a retainer formerly kept to provide casual entertainment

[1]**jet** \ˈjet\ *n* : a velvet-black coal that takes a good polish and is often used for jewelry

[2]**jet** *vb* **jet•ted; jet•ting** : to spout or emit in a stream

[3]**jet** *n* **1** : a forceful rush (as of liquid or gas) through a narrow opening; *also* : a nozzle for a jet of fluid **2** : a jet-propelled airplane

[4]**jet** *vb* **jet•ted; jet•ting** : to travel by jet

jet lag *n* : a condition that is marked esp. by fatigue and irritability and occurs following a long flight through several time zones — **jet–lagged** *adj*

jet•lin•er \ˈjet-ˌlī-nər\ *n* : a jet-propelled airliner

jet•port \-ˌpōrt\ *n* : an airport designed to handle jets

jet–pro•pelled \ˌjet-prə-ˈpeld\ *adj* : driven by an engine (**jet engine**) that produces propulsion (**jet propulsion**) by the rearward discharge of a jet of fluid (as heated air and exhaust gases)

jet•sam \ˈjet-səm\ *n* : jettisoned goods; *esp* : such goods washed ashore

jet set *n* : an international group of wealthy people who frequent fashionable resorts

jet stream *n* : a long narrow high-altitude current of high-speed winds blowing generally from the west

jet•ti•son \ˈje-tə-sən\ *vb* **1** : to throw (goods) overboard to lighten a ship or aircraft in distress **2** : DISCARD — **jettison** *n*

jet•ty \ˈje-tē\ *n, pl* **jetties 1** : a pier built to influence the current or to protect a harbor **2** : a landing wharf

jeu d'es•prit \zhœ-des-ˈprē\ *n, pl* **jeux d'esprit** *same*\ [F, lit., play of the mind] : a witty comment or composition

Jew \ˈjü\ *n* **1** : ISRAELITE **2** : one whose religion is Judaism — **Jew•ish** *adj*

[1]**jew•el** \ˈjü-əl\ *n* [ME *juel,* fr. OF, prob. dim. of *jeu* game, play, fr. L *jocus* game, joke] **1** : an ornament of precious metal **2** : GEMSTONE, GEM

[2]**jewel** *vb* **-eled** *or* **-elled; -el•ing** *or* **-el•ling** : to adorn or equip with jewels

jew•el•er *or* **jew•el•ler** \ˈjü-ə-lər\ *n* : a person who makes or deals in jewelry and related articles

jew•el•lery *chiefly Brit var of* JEWELRY

jew•el•ry \ˈjü-əl-rē\ *n* : JEWELS; *esp* : objects of precious metal set with gems and worn for personal adornment

Jew•ry \ˈju̇r-ē, ˈju̇-ər-ē, ˈjü-rē\ *n* : the Jewish people

jg *abbr* junior grade

[1]**jib** \ˈjib\ *n* : a triangular sail set on a line running from the bow to the mast

[2]**jib** *vb* **jibbed; jib•bing** : to refuse to proceed further

jibe \ˈjīb\ *vb* **jibed; jib•ing** : to be in accord : AGREE

jif•fy \ˈji-fē\ *n, pl* **jiffies** : MOMENT, INSTANT ⟨I'll be ready in a ~⟩

[1]**jig** \ˈjig\ *n* **1** : a lively dance in triple rhythm **2** : TRICK, GAME ⟨the ~ is up⟩ **3** : a device used to hold work during manufacture or assembly

[2]**jig** *vb* **jigged; jig•ging** : to dance a jig

jig•ger \ˈji-gər\ *n* : a measure usu. holding 1 to 2 ounces (30 to 60 milliliters) used in mixing drinks

jig•gle \ˈji-gəl\ *vb* **jig•gled; jig•gling** : to move with quick little jerks — **jiggle** *n*

jig•saw \ˈjig-ˌsȯ\ *n* : a machine saw with a narrow vertically reciprocating blade for cutting curved lines

jigsaw puzzle *n* : a puzzle consisting of small irregularly cut pieces to be fitted together to form a picture

ji•had \ji-ˈhäd, -ˈhad\ *n* **1** : a Muslim holy war **2** : CRUSADE 2

[1]**jilt** \ˈjilt\ *vb* : to drop (a lover) capriciously or unfeelingly

[2]**jilt** *n* : one who jilts a lover

jim crow \ˈjim-ˈkrō\ *n, often cap J&C* : discrimination against blacks esp. by legal enforcement or traditional sanctions — **jim crow** *adj, often cap J&C* — **jim crow•ism** \-ˈkrō-ˌi-zəm\ *n, often cap J&C*

jim–dan•dy \ˈjim-ˈdan-dē\ *n* : something excellent of its kind

jim•mies \ˈji-mēz\ *n pl* : tiny rod-shaped bits of usu. chocolate-flavored candy often sprinkled on ice cream

[1]**jim•my** \ˈji-mē\ *n, pl* **jimmies** : a small crowbar

[2]**jimmy** *vb* **jim•mied; jim•my•ing** : to force open with a jimmy

jim•son•weed \ˈjim-sən-ˌwēd\ *n, often cap* : a coarse poisonous weed related to the tomato that has large trumpet-shaped white or violet flowers

[1]**jin•gle** \ˈjiŋ-gəl\ *vb* **jin•gled; jin•gling** : to make a light clinking or tinkling sound

[2]**jingle** *n* **1** : a light clinking or tinkling sound **2** : a short verse or song with catchy repetition

jin•go•ism \ˈjiŋ-gō-ˌi-zəm\ *n* : extreme chauvinism or nationalism marked esp. by a belligerent foreign policy — **jin•go•ist** \-ist\ *n* — **jin•go•is•tic** \ˌjiŋ-gō-ˈis-tik\ *adj*

jin•rik•sha \jin-ˈrik-ˌshȯ\ *n* : RICKSHA

[1]**jinx** \ˈjiŋks\ *n* : one that brings bad luck

[2]**jinx** *vb* : to foredoom to failure or misfortune

jit•ney \ˈjit-nē\ *n, pl* **jitneys** : a small bus that serves a regular route on a flexible schedule

jit•ter•bug \ˈji-tər-ˌbəg\ *n* : a dance in which couples two-step, balance, and twirl vigorously in standardized patterns — **jitterbug** *vb*

jit•ters \ˈji-tərz\ *n pl* : extreme nervousness — **jit•tery** \-tə-rē\ *adj*

[1]**jive** \ˈjīv\ *n* **1** : swing music or dancing performed to it **2** : glib, deceptive, or foolish talk **3** : the jargon of jazz enthusiasts

[2]**jive** *vb* **jived; jiv•ing 1** : KID, TEASE **2** : to dance to or play jive

Jn *or* **Jno** *abbr* John

Jo *abbr* Joel

[1]**job** \ˈjäb\ *n* **1** : a piece of work **2** : something that has to be done : TASK **3** : a regular remunerative position — **job•less** *adj*

[2]**job** *vb* **jobbed; job•bing 1** : to do occasional pieces of work for hire **2** : to hire or let by the job

Job \ˈjōb\ *n* — see BIBLE table

job action *n* : a protest action by workers to force compliance with demands

job•ber \ˈjä-bər\ *n* **1** : a person who buys goods and then sells them to other dealers : MIDDLEMAN **2** : a person who does work by the job

job•hold•er \ˈjäb-ˌhōl-dər\ *n* : one having a regular job

jock \ˈjäk\ *n* [*jockstrap*] : ATHLETE; *esp* : a college athlete

[1]**jock•ey** \ˈjä-kē\ *n, pl* **jockeys** : one who rides a horse esp. as a professional in a race

[2]**jockey** *vb* **jock•eyed; jock•ey•ing** : to maneuver or manipulate by adroit or devious means

jock•strap \ˈjäk-ˌstrap\ *n* [E slang *jock* penis] : ATHLETIC SUPPORTER

jo•cose \jō-ˈkōs\ *adj* : MERRY, HUMOROUS **syn** jocular, facetious, witty

joc•u•lar \ˈjä-kyə-lər\ *adj* : marked by jesting : PLAYFUL — **joc•u•lar•i•ty** \ˌjäk-yə-ˈlar-ə-tē\ *n* — **joc•u•lar•ly** *adv*

jo•cund \ˈjä-kənd\ *adj* : marked by mirth or cheerfulness

jodh•pur \ˈjäd-pər\ *n* **1** *pl* : riding breeches loose above the knee and tight-fitting below **2** : an ankle-high boot fastened with a strap

Jo•el \ˈjō-əl\ *n* — see BIBLE table

[1]**jog** \ˈjäg\ *vb* **jogged; jog•ging 1** : to give a slight shake or push to **2** : to go at a slow monotonous pace **3** : to run or ride at a slow trot — **jog•ger** *n*

[2]**jog** *n* **1** : a slight shake **2** : a jogging movement or pace

[3]**jog** *n* **1** : a projecting or retreating part of a line or surface **2** : a brief abrupt change in direction

jog•gle \ˈjä-gəl\ *vb* **jog•gled; jog•gling** : to shake slightly — **joggle** *n*

john \ˈjän\ *n* **1** : TOILET **2** : a prostitute's client

John \ˈjän\ *n* — see BIBLE table

john•ny \ˈjä-nē\ *n, pl* **johnnies** : a short-sleeved gown opening in the back that is worn by hospital patients

John•ny–jump–up \ˌjä-nē-ˈjəmp-ˌəp\ *n* : any of various small-flowered cultivated pansies

joie de vi•vre \ˌzhwä-də-ˈvēvrᵊ\ *n* [F] : keen enjoyment of life

join \ˈjȯin\ *vb* **1** : to come or bring together so as to form a unit **2** : to come or bring into close association **3** : to become a member of **4** : ADJOIN **5** : to take part in a collective activity

join•er \ˈjȯi-nər\ *n* **1** : a worker who constructs articles by joining pieces of wood **2** : a gregarious person who joins many organizations

[1]**joint** \ˈjȯint\ *n* **1** : the point of contact between bones of an animal skeleton with the parts that surround and support it **2** : a cut of meat suitable for roasting **3** : a place where two things or parts are connected **4** : ESTABLISHMENT; *esp* : a shabby or disreputable establishment **5** : a marijuana cigarette — **joint•ed** *adj*

[2]**joint** *adj* **1** : UNITED **2** : common to two or more — **joint•ly** *adv*

[3]**joint** *vb* **1** : to unite by or provide with a joint **2** : to separate the joints of

joist \ˈjȯist\ *n* : any of the small beams ranged parallel from wall to wall in a building to support a floor or ceiling

[1]**joke** \ˈjōk\ *n* : something said or done to provoke laughter; *esp* : a brief narrative with a humorous climax

[2]**joke** *vb* **joked; jok•ing** : to make jokes — **jok•ing•ly** *adv*

jok•er \ˈjō-kər\ *n* **1** : a person who jokes **2** : an extra card used in some card games **3** : a misleading part of an agreement that works to one party's disadvantage

jol•li•fi•ca•tion \ˌjä-li-fə-ˈkā-shən\ *n* : a festive celebration

jol•li•ty \ˈjä-lə-tē\ *n, pl* **-ties** : GAIETY, MERRIMENT

jol•ly \ˈjä-lē\ *adj* **jol•li•er; -est** : full of high spirits : MERRY

[1]**jolt** \ˈjōlt\ *vb* **1** : to give a quick hard knock or blow to **2** : to move with a sudden jerky motion — **jolt•er** *n*

[2]**jolt** *n* **1** : an abrupt jerky blow or movement **2** : a sudden shock

Jon *abbr* Jonah; Jonas

Jo•nah \ˈjō-nə\ *n* — see BIBLE table

Jo•nas \ˈjō-nəs\ *n* : JONAH

jon•gleur \zhōⁿ-ˈglər\ *n* : an itinerant medieval minstrel

jon•quil \ˈjän-kwəl\ *n* [F *jonquille*, fr. Sp *junquillo*, dim. of *junco* reed, fr. L *juncus*] : a narcissus with fragrant clustered white or yellow flowers

Jor•da•ni•an \jȯr-ˈdā-nē-ən\ *n* : a native or inhabitant of Jordan — **Jordanian** *adj*

josh \ˈjäsh\ *vb* : TEASE, JOKE

Josh *abbr* Joshua

Josh•ua \ˈjä-shu̇-ə\ *n* — see BIBLE table

Joshua tree *n* : a tall branched yucca of the southwestern U.S.

jos•tle \ˈjä-səl\ *vb* **jos•tled; jos•tling 1** : to come in contact or into collision **2** : to make one's way by pushing and shoving

Jos•ue \ˈjä-shu̇-ē\ *n* : JOSHUA

[1]**jot** \ˈjät\ *n* : the least bit : IOTA

[2]**jot** *vb* **jot•ted; jot•ting** : to write briefly and hurriedly

jot•ting \ˈjä-tiŋ\ *n* : a brief note

joule \ˈjül\ *n* : a unit of work or energy equal to the work done by a force of one newton acting through a distance of one meter

jounce \ˈjau̇ns\ *vb* **jounced; jounc•ing** : JOLT — **jounce** *n*

jour *abbr* **1** journal **2** journeyman

jour•nal \ˈjərn-ᵊl\ *n* [ME, service book containing the day hours, fr. MF, fr. *journal* daily, fr. L *diurnalis*, fr. *dies* day] **1** : a brief account of daily events **2** : a record of proceedings (as of a legislative body) **3** : a periodical (as a newspaper) dealing esp. with current events **4** : the part of a rotating axle or spindle that turns in a bearing

jour•nal•ese \ˌjər-nə-ˈlēz, -ˈlēs\ *n* : a style of writing held to be characteristic of newspapers

jour•nal•ism \ˈjər-nə-ˌli-zəm\ *n* **1** : the business of writing for, editing, or publishing periodicals (as newspapers) **2** : writing designed for or characteristic of newspapers — **jour•nal•ist** \-list\ *n* — **jour•nal•is•tic** \ˌjər-nə-ˈlis-tik\ *adj*

[1]**jour•ney** \ˈjər-nē\ *n, pl* **journeys** [ME, fr. OF *journee* day's journey, fr. *jour* day] : a traveling from one place to another

[2]**journey** *vb* **jour•neyed; jour•ney•ing** : to go on a journey : TRAVEL

jour•ney•man \-mən\ *n* **1** : a worker who has learned a trade and works for another person **2** : an experienced reliable worker

[1]**joust** \ˈjau̇st\ *vb* : to engage in a joust

[2]**joust** *n* : a combat on horseback between two knights with lances esp. as part of a tournament

jo•vial \ˈjō-vē-əl\ *adj* : marked by good humor — **jo•vi•al•i•ty** \ˌjō-vē-ˈa-lə-tē\ *n* — **jo•vi•al•ly** *adv*

[1]**jowl** \ˈjau̇l\ *n* : loose flesh about the lower jaw or throat

[2]**jowl** *n* **1** : the lower jaw **2** : CHEEK

[1]**joy** \ˈjȯi\ *n* [ME, fr. OF *joie*, fr. L *gaudia*] **1** : a feeling of happiness that comes from success, good fortune, or a sense of well-being **2** : a source of happiness **syn** bliss, delight, enjoyment, pleasure — **joy•less** *adj*

[2]**joy** *vb* : REJOICE

joy•ful \-fəl\ *adj* : experiencing, causing, or showing joy — **joy•ful•ly** *adv*

joy•ous \ˈjȯi-əs\ *adj* : JOYFUL — **joy•ous•ly** *adv* — **joy•ous•ness** *n*

joy•ride \ˈjȯi-ˌrīd\ *n* : a ride for pleasure often marked by reckless driving — **joyride** *vb* — **joy•rid•er** *n* — **joy•rid•ing** *n*

joy•stick \-ˌstik\ *n* : a control device (as for a computer display) consisting of a lever capable of motion in two or more directions

JP *abbr* **1** jet propulsion **2** justice of the peace

Jr *abbr* junior

jt *or* **jnt** *abbr* joint

ju•bi•lant \ˈjü-bə-lənt\ *adj* [L *jubilans*, prp. of *jubilare* to rejoice] : EXULTANT — **ju•bi•lant•ly** *adv*

ju•bi•la•tion \ˌjü-bə-ˈlā-shən\ *n* : EXULTATION

ju•bi•lee \ˈjü-bə-ˌlē, ˌjü-bə-ˈlē\ *n* [ME, fr. MF & LL; MF *jubilé*, fr. LL *jubilaeus*, fr. LGk *iōbēlaios*, fr.

Heb *yōbhēl* ram's horn, trumpet, jubilee] **1** : a 50th anniversary **2** : a season or occasion of celebration

Jud *abbr* Judith

Ju•da•ic \jü-ˈdā-ik\ *also* **Ju•da•ical** \-ˈdā-ə-kəl\ *adj* : of, relating to, or characteristic of Jews or Judaism

Ju•da•ism \ˈjü-də-ˌi-zəm, -dā-, -dē-\ *n* : a religion developed among the ancient Hebrews and marked by belief in one God and by the moral and ceremonial laws of the Old Testament and the rabbinic tradition

Jude \ˈjüd\ *n* — see BIBLE table

Judg *abbr* Judges

[1]**judge** \ˈjəj\ *vb* **judged; judg•ing 1** : to form an authoritative opinion **2** : to decide as a judge : TRY **3** : to form an estimate or evaluation about something : THINK **syn** conclude, deduce, gather, infer

[2]**judge** *n* **1** : a public official authorized to decide questions brought before a court **2** : UMPIRE **3** : one who gives an authoritative opinion : CRITIC — **judge•ship** *n*

Judges *n* — see BIBLE table

judg•ment *or* **judge•ment** \ˈjəj-mənt\ *n* **1** : a decision or opinion given after judging; *esp* : a formal decision given by a court **2** *cap* : the final judging of mankind by God **3** : the process of forming an opinion by discerning and comparing **4** : the capacity for judging : DISCERNMENT

judg•men•tal \ˌjəj-ˈmen-təl\ *adj* **1** : of, relating to, or involving judgment **2** : characterized by a tendency to judge harshly — **judg•men•tal•ly** *adv*

Judgment Day *n* : the day of the final judging of all human beings by God

ju•di•ca•ture \ˈjü-di-kə-ˌchu̇r\ *n* **1** : the administration of justice **2** : JUDICIARY 1

ju•di•cial \jü-ˈdi-shəl\ *adj* **1** : of or relating to the administration of justice or the judiciary **2** : ordered or enforced by a court **3** : CRITICAL — **ju•di•cial•ly** *adv*

ju•di•cia•ry \jü-ˈdi-shē-ˌer-ē, -shə-rē\ *n* **1** : a system of courts of law; *also* : the judges of these courts **2** : a branch of government in which judicial power is vested — **judiciary** *adj*

ju•di•cious \jü-ˈdi-shəs\ *adj* : having, exercising, or characterized by sound judgment **syn** prudent, sage, sane, sensible, wise — **ju•di•cious•ly** *adv*

Ju•dith \ˈjü-dəth\ *n* — see BIBLE table

ju•do \ˈjü-dō\ *n* [Jp, fr. *jū* weakness + *dō* art] : a sport derived from jujitsu that emphasizes the use of quick movement and leverage to throw an opponent — **ju•do•ist** \-ist\ *n*

[1]**jug** \ˈjəg\ *n* **1** : a large deep container with a narrow mouth and a handle **2** : JAIL, PRISON

[2]**jug** *vb* **jugged; jug•ging** : JAIL, IMPRISON

jug•ger•naut \ˈjə-gər-ˌnȯt\ *n* [Hindi *Jagannāth,* title of Vishnu (a Hindu god), lit., lord of the world] : a massive inexorable force or object that crushes everything in its path

jug•gle \ˈjə-gəl\ *vb* **jug•gled; jug•gling 1** : to keep several objects in motion in the air at the same time **2** : to manipulate esp. in order to achieve a desired and often fraudulent end — **jug•gler** \ˈjə-glər\ *n*

jug•u•lar \ˈjə-gyə-lər\ *adj* : of, relating to, or situated in or on the throat or neck ⟨the ~ veins⟩

juice \ˈjüs\ *n* **1** : the extractable fluid contents of cells or tissues **2** *pl* : the natural fluids of an animal body **3** : something that supplies power; *esp* : ELECTRICITY 2

juic•er \ˈjü-sər\ *n* : an appliance for extracting juice (as from fruit)

juice up *vb* : to give life, energy, or spirit to

juicy \ˈjü-sē\ *adj* **juic•i•er; -est 1** : SUCCULENT **2** : rich in interest; *also* : RACY — **juic•i•ly** \-sə-lē\ *adv* — **juic•i•ness** \-sē-nəs\ *n*

ju•jit•su *or* **ju•jut•su** \jü-ˈjit-sü\ *n* [Jp *jūjutsu,* fr. *jū* weakness + *jutsu* art, skill] : an art of fighting employing holds, throws, and paralyzing blows

ju•jube \ˈjü-ˌjüb, ˈjü-jü-ˌbē\ *n* : a fruit-flavored gumdrop or lozenge

juke•box \ˈjük-ˌbäks\ *n* : a coin-operated machine that automatically plays selected recordings

Jul *abbr* July

ju•lep \ˈjü-ləp\ *n* [ME, sweetened water, fr. MF, fr. Ar *julāb,* fr. Per *gulāb,* fr. *gul* rose + *āb* water] : a drink made of bourbon, sugar, and mint served over crushed ice

Ju•ly \jü-ˈlī\ *n* [ME *Julie,* fr. OE *Julius,* fr. L, fr. Gaius *Julius* Caesar] : the 7th month of the year

[1]**jum•ble** \ˈjəm-bəl\ *vb* **jum•bled; jum•bling** : to mix in a confused mass

[2]**jumble** *n* : a disorderly mass or pile

jum•bo \ˈjəm-bō\ *n, pl* **jumbos** [*Jumbo,* a huge elephant exhibited by P.T. Barnum] : a very large specimen of its kind — **jumbo** *adj*

[1]**jump** \ˈjəmp\ *vb* **1** : to spring into the air : leap over **2** : to give a start **3** : to rise or increase suddenly or sharply **4** : to make a sudden attack **5** : ANTICIPATE ⟨~ the gun⟩ **6** : to leave hurriedly and often furtively ⟨~ town⟩ **7** : to act or move before (as a signal) — **jump bail** : to abscond after being released from custody on bail — **jump ship 1** : to leave the company of a ship without authority **2** : to desert a cause

[2]**jump** *n* **1** : a spring into the air; *esp* : one made for height or distance in a track meet **2** : a sharp sudden increase **3** : an initial advantage

[1]**jump•er** \ˈjəm-pər\ *n* : one that jumps

[2]**jumper** *n* **1** : a loose blouse **2** : a sleeveless one-piece dress worn usu. with a blouse **3** *pl* : a child's sleeveless coverall

jumping bean *n* : a seed of any of several Mexican shrubs that tumbles about because of the movements of a small moth larva inside it

jumping–off place *n* **1** : a remote or isolated place **2** : a place from which an enterprise is launched

jump–start \ˈjəmp-ˌstärt\ *vb* : to start (an engine or vehicle) by connection to an external power source

jump•suit \ˈjəmp-ˌsüt\ *n* **1** : a coverall worn by parachutists in jumping **2** : a one-piece garment consisting of a blouse or shirt with attached trousers or shorts

jumpy \ˈjəm-pē\ *adj* **jump•i•er; -est** : NERVOUS, JITTERY

jun *abbr* junior

Jun *abbr* June

junc *abbr* junction

jun•co \ˈjəŋ-kō\ *n, pl* **juncos** *or* **juncoes** : any of a genus of small common pink-billed American finches that are largely gray with conspicuous white feathers in the tail

junc•tion \ˈjəŋk-shən\ *n* **1** : an act of joining **2** : a place or point of meeting

junc•ture \ˈjeŋk-chər\ *n* **1** : JOINT, CONNECTION **2** : UNION **3** : a critical time or state of affairs

June \ˈjün\ *n* [ME, fr. L *Junius*] : the 6th month of the year

jun•gle \ˈjəŋ-gəl\ *n* **1** : a thick tangled mass of tropical vegetation; *also* : a tract overgrown with vegetation **2** : a place of ruthless struggle for survival

[1]**ju•nior** \ˈjü-nyər\ *adj* **1** : YOUNGER **2** : lower in rank **3** : of or relating to juniors

[2]**junior** *n* **1** : a person who is younger or of lower rank than another **2** : a student in the next-to-last year before graduating

junior college *n* : a school that offers studies corresponding to those of the 1st two years of college

junior high school *n* : a school usu. including grades 7–9

junior varsity *n* : a team whose members lack the experience or qualifications required for the varsity

ju•ni•per \ˈjü-nə-pər\ *n* : any of numerous coniferous shrubs or trees with leaves like needles or scales and female cones like berries

[1]**junk** \ˈjəŋk\ *n* **1** : old iron, glass, paper, or waste; *also* : discarded articles **2** : a shoddy product **3** *slang* : NARCOTICS; *esp* : HEROIN — **junky** *adj*

[2]**junk** *vb* : DISCARD, SCRAP

[3]junk *n* : a ship of eastern Asia with a high stern and 4-cornered sails

junk

junk•er \ˈjəŋ-kər\ *n* : something (as an old automobile) ready for scrapping

Jun•ker \ˈyu̇ŋ-kər\ *n* [G] : a member of the Prussian landed aristocracy

jun•ket \ˈjəŋ-kət\ *n* **1** : a pudding of sweetened flavored milk set by rennet **2** : a trip made by an official at public expense

junk food *n* : food that is high in calories but low in nutritional content

junk•ie *also* **junky** \ˈjəŋ-kē\ *n, pl* **junkies 1** *slang* : a narcotics peddler or addict **2** : one that derives inordinate pleasure from or is dependent on something ⟨sugar ~⟩

jun•ta \ˈhu̇n-tə, ˈjən-, ˈhən-\ *n* [Sp, fr. *junto* joined, fr. L *junctus,* pp. of *jungere* to join] : a group of persons controlling a government esp. after a revolutionary seizure of power

Ju•pi•ter \ˈjü-pə-tər\ *n* : the largest of the planets and the one 5th in order of distance from the sun — see PLANET table

Ju•ras•sic \ju̇-ˈra-sik\ *adj* : of, relating to, or being the period of the Mesozoic era between the Triassic and the Cretaceous that is marked esp. by the presence of dinosaurs — **Jurassic** *n*

ju•rid•i•cal \ju̇-ˈri-di-kəl\ *or* **ju•rid•ic** \-dik\ *adj* **1** : of or relating to the administration of justice **2** : LEGAL — **ju•rid•i•cal•ly** \-di-k(ə-)lē\ *adv*

ju•ris•dic•tion \ˌju̇r-əs-ˈdik-shən\ *n* **1** : the power, right, or authority to interpret and apply the law **2** : the authority of a sovereign power **3** : the limits or territory within which authority may be exercised — **ju•ris•dic•tion•al** \-shə-nəl\ *adj*

ju•ris•pru•dence \-ˈprüd-ᵊns\ *n* **1** : a system of laws **2** : the science or philosophy of law

ju•rist \ˈju̇r-ist\ *n* : one having a thorough knowledge of law; *esp* : JUDGE

ju•ris•tic \ju̇-ˈris-tik\ *adj* **1** : of or relating to a jurist or jurisprudence **2** : of, relating to, or recognized in law

ju•ror \ˈju̇r-ər, -ˌȯr\ *n* : a member of a jury

[1]ju•ry \ˈju̇r-ē\ *n, pl* **juries 1** : a body of persons sworn to inquire into a matter submitted to them and to give their verdict **2** : a committee for judging and awarding prizes

[2]jury *adj* : improvised for temporary use esp. in an emergency ⟨a ~ mast⟩

jury–rig \ˈju̇r-ē-ˌrig\ *vb* : to construct or arrange in a makeshift fashion

[1]just \ˈjəst\ *adj* **1** : having a basis in or conforming to fact or reason : REASONABLE ⟨~ comment⟩ **2** : CORRECT, PROPER ⟨~ proportions⟩ **3** : morally or legally right ⟨a ~ title⟩ **4** : DESERVED, MERITED ⟨~ punishment⟩ **syn** upright, honorable, conscientious, honest — **just•ly** *adv* — **just•ness** *n*

[2]just \ˈjəst, ˈjist\ *adv* **1** : EXACTLY ⟨~ right⟩ **2** : very recently ⟨has ~ left⟩ **3** : BARELY ⟨~ too late⟩ **4** : DIRECTLY ⟨~ west of here⟩ **5** : ONLY ⟨~ last year⟩ **6** : QUITE ⟨~ wonderful⟩ **7** : POSSIBLY ⟨it ~ might work⟩

jus•tice \ˈjəs-təs\ *n* **1** : the administration of what is just (as by assigning merited rewards or punishments) **2** : JUDGE **3** : the administration of law **4** : FAIRNESS; *also* : RIGHTEOUSNESS

justice of the peace : a local magistrate empowered chiefly to try minor cases, to administer oaths, and to perform marriages

jus•ti•fy \ˈjəs-tə-ˌfī\ *vb* **-fied; -fy•ing 1** : to prove to be just, right, or reasonable **2** : to pronounce free from guilt or blame **3** : to adjust spaces in a line of printed text so the margins are even — **jus•ti•fi•able** *adj* — **jus•ti•fi•ca•tion** \ˌjəs-tə-fə-ˈkā-shən\ *n*

jut \ˈjət\ *vb* **jut•ted; jut•ting** : PROJECT, PROTRUDE

jute \ˈjüt\ *n* : a strong glossy fiber from either of two tropical plants used esp. for making sacks and twine

juv *abbr* juvenile

[1]ju•ve•nile \ˈjü-və-ˌnīl, -nəl\ *adj* **1** : showing incomplete development **2** : of, relating to, or characteristic of children or young people

[2]juvenile *n* **1** : a young person; *esp* : one below the legally established age of adulthood **2** : a young animal (as a fish or a bird) or plant **3** : an actor or actress who plays youthful parts

juvenile delinquency *n* : violation of the law or antisocial behavior by a juvenile — **juvenile delinquent** *n*

jux•ta•pose \ˈjək-stə-ˌpōz\ *vb* **-posed; -pos•ing** : to place side by side — **jux•ta•po•si•tion** \ˌjək-stə-pə-ˈzi-shən\ *n*

JV *abbr* junior varsity

K

[1]k \ˈkā\ *n, pl* **k's** *or* **ks** \ˈkāz\ **1** *often cap* : the 11th letter of the English alphabet **2** *cap* : STRIKEOUT

[2]k *abbr* **1** karat **2** kitchen **3** knit **4** kosher — often enclosed in a circle

[1]K *abbr* Kelvin

[2]K *symbol* [NL *kalium*] potassium

ka•bob \kə-ˈbäb, ˈkā-ˌbäb\ *n* : cubes of meat cooked with vegetables usu. on a skewer

Ka•bu•ki \kə-ˈbü-kē\ *n* : traditional Japanese popular drama with highly stylized singing and dancing

kad•dish \ˈkä-dish\ *n, often cap* : a Jewish prayer recited in the daily synagogue ritual and by mourners at public services after the death of a close relative

kaf•fee•klatsch \ˈkȯ-fē-ˌklach, ˈkä-\ *n, often cap* [G] : an informal social gathering for coffee and conversation

kai•ser \ˈkī-zər\ *n* : EMPEROR; *esp* : the ruler of Germany from 1871 to 1918

kale \ˈkāl\ *n* : a hardy cabbage with curled leaves that do not form a head

ka•lei•do•scope \kə-ˈlī-də-ˌskōp\ *n* : a tube containing loose bits of colored material (as glass) and two mirrors at one end that shows many different patterns as it is turned — **ka•lei•do•scop•ic** \-ˌlī-də-ˈskä-pik\ *adj* — **ka•lei•do•scop•i•cal•ly** \-pi-k(ə-)lē\ *adv*

ka•ma•ai•na \ˌkä-mə-ˈī-nə\ *n* [Hawaiian *kama'āina,* fr. *kama* child + *'āina* land] : one who has lived in Hawaii for a long time

kame \ˈkām\ *n* [Sc, lit., comb] : a short ridge or mound of material deposited by water from a melting glacier

ka•mi•ka•ze \ˌkä-mi-ˈkä-zē\ *n* [Jp, lit., divine wind] : a member of a corps of Japanese pilots assigned to make a suicidal crash on a target; *also* : an airplane flown in such an attack

Kan *or* **Kans** *abbr* Kansas

kan•ga•roo \ˌkaŋ-gə-ˈrü\ *n, pl* **-roos** : any of various large leaping marsupial mammals of Australia and adjacent islands with powerful hind legs and a long thick tail

kangaroo court *n* : a court or an illegal self-appointed tribunal characterized by irresponsible, perverted, or irregular procedures

ka•o•lin \ˈkā-ə-lən\ *n* : a fine usu. white clay used in ceramics and refractories and for the treatment of diarrhea

ka•pok \ˈkā-ˌpäk\ *n* : silky fiber from the seeds of a tropical tree used esp. as a filling (as for life preservers)

Kap•o•si's sar•co•ma \ˈka-pə-sēz-sär-ˈkō-mə\ *n* : a neoplastic disease associated esp. with AIDS that affects esp. the skin and mucous membranes and is characterized usu. by the formation of pink to reddish-brown or bluish plaques

kap•pa \ˈka-pə\ *n* : the 10th letter of the Greek alphabet — Κ or κ

ka•put *also* **ka•putt** \kä-ˈpu̇t, kə-, -ˈpüt\ *adj* [G, fr. F *capot* not having made a trick at piquet] **1** : utterly defeated or destroyed **2** : unable to function : USELESS

kar•a•kul \ˈkar-ə-kəl\ *n* : the dark tightly curled pelt of the newborn lamb of a hardy Asian breed of sheep

kar•a•o•ke \ˌkar-ē-ˈō-kē\ *n* [Jp] : a device that plays instrumental accompaniments for songs to which the user sings along

kar•at \ˈkar-ət\ *n* : a unit for expressing proportion of gold in an alloy equal to 1/24 part of pure gold

ka•ra•te \kə-ˈrä-tē\ *n* [Jp, lit., empty hand] : an art of self-defense in which an attacker is disabled by crippling kicks and punches

kar•ma \ˈkär-mə\ *n, often cap* [Skt] : the force generated by a person's actions held in Hinduism and Buddhism to perpetuate reincarnation and to determine the nature of the person's next existence — **kar•mic** \-mik\ *adj*

karst \ˈkärst\ *n* [G] : an irregular limestone region with sinks, underground streams, and caverns

ka•ty•did \ˈkā-tē-ˌdid\ *n* : any of several large green tree-dwelling American grasshoppers with long antennae

kay•ak \ˈkī-ˌak\ *n* : an Eskimo canoe made of a skin-covered frame with a small opening and propelled by a double-bladed paddle; *also* : a similar portable boat

kayo \(ˌ)kā-ˈō, ˈkā-ō\ *n* : KNOCKOUT — **kayo** *vb*

ka•zoo \kə-ˈzü\ *n, pl* **kazoos** : a toy musical instrument consisting of a tube with a membrane sealing one end and a side hole to sing or hum into

KB *abbr* kilobyte

kc *abbr* kilocycle

KC *abbr* **1** Kansas City **2** King's Counsel **3** Knights of Columbus

kc/s *abbr* kilocycles per second

KD *abbr* knocked down

ke•bab *or* **ke•bob** \kə-ˈbäb\ *var of* KABOB

kedge \ˈkej\ *n* : a small anchor

[1]**keel** \ˈkēl\ *n* **1** : the chief structural member of a ship running lengthwise along the center of its bottom **2** : something (as a bird's breastbone) like a ship's keel in form or use — **keeled** \ˈkēld\ *adj*

[2]**keel** *vb* : FAINT, SWOON — usu. used with *over*

keel•boat \ˈkēl-ˌbōt\ *n* : a shallow covered keeled riverboat for freight that is usu. rowed, poled, or towed

keel•haul \-ˌhȯl\ *vb* : to haul under the keel of a ship as punishment

[1]**keen** \ˈkēn\ *adj* **1** : SHARP ⟨a ~ knife⟩ **2** : SEVERE ⟨a ~ wind⟩ **3** : ENTHUSIASTIC ⟨~ about swimming⟩ **4** : mentally alert ⟨a ~ mind⟩ **5** : STRONG, ACUTE ⟨~ eyesight⟩ **6** : WONDERFUL, EXCELLENT — **keen•ly** *adv* — **keen•ness** *n*

[2]**keen** *n* : a lamentation for the dead uttered in a loud wailing voice or in a wordless cry — **keen** *vb*

[1]**keep** \ˈkēp\ *vb* **kept** \ˈkept\; **keep•ing** **1** : FULFILL, OBSERVE ⟨~ a promise⟩ ⟨~ a holiday⟩ **2** : GUARD ⟨~ us from harm⟩; *also* : to take care of ⟨~ a neighbor's children⟩ **3** : MAINTAIN ⟨~ silence⟩ **4** : to have in one's service or at one's disposal ⟨~ a horse⟩ **5** : to preserve a record in ⟨~ a diary⟩ **6** : to have in stock for sale **7** : to retain in one's possession ⟨~ what you find⟩ **8** : to carry on (as a business) : CONDUCT **9** : HOLD, DETAIN ⟨~ him in jail⟩ **10** : to refrain from revealing ⟨~ a secret⟩ **11** : to continue in good condition ⟨meat will ~ in a freezer⟩ **12** : ABSTAIN, REFRAIN — **keep•er** *n*

[2]**keep** *n* **1** : FORTRESS **2** : the means or provisions by which one is kept — **for keeps 1** : with the provision that one keep what one has won ⟨play marbles *for keeps*⟩ **2** : PERMANENTLY

keep•ing *n* : CONFORMITY ⟨in ~ with good taste⟩

keep•sake \ˈkēp-ˌsāk\ *n* : MEMENTO

keep up *vb* **1** : to persevere in **2** : MAINTAIN, SUSTAIN **3** : to keep informed **4** : to continue without interruption

keg \ˈkeg\ *n* : a small cask or barrel

keg•ler \ˈke-glər\ *n* : [1]BOWLER

kelp \ˈkelp\ *n* : any of various coarse brown seaweeds; *also* : a mass of these or their ashes often used as fertilizer

Kelt \ˈkelt\ *var of* CELT

kel•vin \ˈkel-vən\ *n* : a unit of temperature equal to 1/273.16 of the Kelvin scale temperature of the triple point of water and equal to the Celsius degree

Kelvin *adj* : relating to, conforming to, or being a temperature scale according to which absolute zero is 0 K, the equivalent of −273.15°C

ken \ˈken\ *n* **1** : range of vision : SIGHT **2** : range of understanding

ken•nel \ˈken-ᵊl\ *n* : a shelter for a dog or cat; *also* : an establishment for the breeding or boarding of dogs or cats — **kennel** *vb*

ke•no \ˈkē-nō\ *n* : a game resembling bingo

Ken•tucky bluegrass \kən-ˈtə-kē-\ *n* : a valuable pasture and meadow grass of both Europe and America

Ke•nyan \ˈke-nyən, ˈkē-\ *n* : a native or inhabitant of Kenya — **Kenyan** *adj*

Ke•ogh plan \ˈkē-(ˌ)ō-\ *n* [Eugene James *Keogh* †1989 Am. politician] : an individual retirement account for the self-employed

ke•pi \ˈkā-pē, ˈke-\ *n* [F] : a military cap with a round flat top and a visor

ker•a•tin \ˈker-ət-ᵊn\ *n* : any of various sulfur-containing proteins that make up hair and horny tissues

kerb \ˈkərb\ *n, Brit* : CURB 3

ker•chief \ˈkər-chəf, -ˌchēf\ *n, pl* **kerchiefs** \-chəfs, -ˌchēfs\ *also* **kerchieves** \-ˌchēvz\ [ME *courchef*, fr. OF *cuevrechief*, fr. *covrir* to cover + *chief* head] **1** : a square of cloth worn by women esp. as a head covering **2** : HANDKERCHIEF

kerf \ˈkərf\ *n* : a slit or notch made by a saw or cutting torch

ker•nel \ˈkərn-ᵊl\ *n* **1** : the inner softer part of a seed, fruit stone, or nut **2** : a whole seed of a cereal ⟨a ~ of corn⟩ **3** : a central or essential part : CORE

ker•o•sene *or* **ker•o•sine** \ˈker-ə-ˌsēn, ˌker-ə-ˈsēn\ *n* : a flammable oil produced from petroleum and used for a fuel and as a solvent

ketch \ˈkech\ *n* : a large fore-and-aft rigged boat with two masts

ketch•up \ˈke-chəp, ˈka-\ *n* : a seasoned tomato puree

ket•tle \ˈket-ᵊl\ *n* : a metallic vessel for boiling liquids

ket•tle•drum \-ˌdrəm\ *n* : a brass, copper, or fiberglass drum with calfskin or plastic stretched across the top

[1]**key** \ˈkē\ *n* **1** : a usu. metal instrument by which the bolt of a lock is turned; *also* : a device having the form or function of a key **2** : a means of gaining or preventing entrance, possession, or control **3** : EXPLANATION, SOLUTION **4** : one of the levers pressed by a finger in operating or playing an instrument **5** : a leading individual or principle **6** : a system of seven

DICTIONARY

tones based on their relationship to a tonic; *also* **:** the tone or pitch of a voice **7 :** a small switch for opening or closing an electric circuit ⟨a telegraph ~⟩

[2]key *vb* **1 :** SECURE, FASTEN **2 :** to regulate the musical pitch of **3 :** to bring into harmony or conformity **4 :** to make nervous — usu. used with *up*

[3]key *adj* **:** BASIC, CENTRAL ⟨~ issues⟩

[4]key *n* **:** a low island or reef (as off the southern coast of Florida)

[5]key *n, slang* **:** a kilogram esp. of marijuana or heroin

key•board \-ˌbōrd\ *n* **1 :** a row of keys (as on a piano) **2 :** an assemblage of keys for operating a machine

key club *n* **:** a private club serving liquor and providing entertainment

key•hole \ˈkē-ˌhōl\ *n* **:** a hole for receiving a key

[1]key•note \-ˌnōt\ *n* **1 :** the first and harmonically fundamental tone of a scale **2 :** the central fact, idea, or mood

[2]keynote *vb* **1 :** to set the keynote of **2 :** to deliver the major address (as at a convention) — **key•not•er** *n*

key•punch \ˈkē-ˌpənch\ *n* **:** a machine with a keyboard used to cut holes or notches in punch cards — **keypunch** *vb* — **key•punch•er** *n*

key•stone \-ˌstōn\ *n* **:** the wedge-shaped piece at the crown of an arch that locks the other pieces in place

key•stroke \-ˌstrōk\ *n* **:** an act or instance of depressing a key on a keyboard

key word *n* **:** a word that is a key; *esp, usu* **key•word :** a significant word used as an indication of the content of or in searching (as a document or database)

kg *abbr* kilogram

KGB *abbr* [Russ *Komitet gosudarstvennoĭ bezopasnosti*] (Soviet) State Security Committee

kha•ki \ˈka-kē, ˈkä-\ *n* [Hindi *khaki* dust-colored, fr. *khāk* dust, fr. Per] **1 :** a light yellowish brown color **2 :** a khaki-colored cloth; *also* **:** a military uniform of this cloth

khan \ˈkän, ˈkan\ *n* **:** a Mongol leader; *esp* **:** a successor of Genghis Khan

khe•dive \kə-ˈdēv\ *n* **:** a ruler of Egypt from 1867 to 1914 governing as a viceroy of the sultan of Turkey

khoum \ˈküm\ *n* — see *ouguiya* at MONEY table

kHz *abbr* kilohertz

KIA *abbr* killed in action

kib•ble \ˈki-bəl\ *vb* **kib•bled; kib•bling :** to grind coarsely — **kibble** *n*

kib•butz \ki-ˈbu̇ts, -ˈbüts\ *n, pl* **kib•but•zim** \-ˌbu̇t-ˈsēm, -ˌbüt-\ [NHeb *qibbūṣ*] **:** a communal farm or settlement in Israel

ki•bitz•er \ˈki-bət-sər, kə-ˈbit-\ *n* **:** one who looks on and usu. offers unwanted advice esp. at a card game — **kib•itz** \ˈki-bəts\ *vb*

ki•bosh \ˈkī-ˌbäsh\ *n* **:** something that serves as a check or stop ⟨put the ~ on his plan⟩

[1]kick \ˈkik\ *vb* **1 :** to strike out or hit with the foot; *also* **:** to score by kicking a ball **2 :** to object strongly **3 :** to recoil when fired — **kick•er** *n*

[2]kick *n* **1 :** a blow or thrust with the foot; *esp* **:** a propelling of a ball with the foot **2 :** the recoil of a gun **3 :** a feeling or expression of objection **4 :** stimulating effect esp. of pleasure

kick•back \ˈkik-ˌbak\ *n* **1 :** a sharp violent reaction **2 :** a secret return of a part of a sum received

kick•box•ing \ˈkik-ˌbäk-siŋ\ *n* **:** boxing in which boxers are permitted to kick with bare feet

kick in *vb* **1 :** CONTRIBUTE **2** *slang* **:** DIE

kick•off \ˈkik-ˌȯf\ *n* **1 :** a kick that puts the ball in play (as in football) **2 :** COMMENCEMENT

kick off *vb* **1 :** to start or resume play with a placekick **2 :** to begin proceedings **3** *slang* **:** DIE

kick over *vb* **:** to begin or cause to begin to fire — used of an internal combustion engine

kick•shaw \ˈkik-ˌshȯ\ *n* [modif. of F *quelque chose* something] **1 :** DELICACY **2 :** TRINKET

kick•stand \ˈkik-ˌstand\ *n* **:** a swiveling metal bar attached to a 2-wheeled vehicle for holding it up when not in use

kicky \ˈki-kē\ *adj* **:** providing a kick or thrill **:** EXCITING

[1]kid \ˈkid\ *n* **1 :** a young goat **2 :** the flesh, fur, or skin of a young goat; *also* **:** something made of kid **3 :** CHILD, YOUNGSTER — **kid•dish** *adj*

[2]kid *vb* **kid•ded; kid•ding 1 :** FOOL **2 :** TEASE — **kid•der** *n* — **kid•ding•ly** *adv*

kid•nap \ˈkid-ˌnap\ *vb* **kid•napped** *or* **kid•naped** \-ˌnapt\; **kid•nap•ping** *or* **kid•nap•ing** \-ˌna-piŋ\ **:** to hold or carry a person away by unlawful force or by fraud and against one's will — **kid•nap•per** *or* **kid•nap•er** \-ˌna-pər\ *n*

kid•ney \ˈkid-nē\ *n, pl* **kidneys :** either of a pair of organs lying near the backbone that excrete waste products of the body in the form of urine

kidney bean *n* **1 :** an edible seed of the common cultivated bean; *esp* **:** one that is large and dark red **2 :** a plant bearing kidney beans

kid•skin \ˈkid-ˌskin\ *n* **:** the skin of a young goat used for leather

kiel•ba•sa \kēl-ˈbä-sə, kil-\ *n, pl* **-basas** *also* **-ba•sy** \-ˈbä-sē\ [Pol *kiełbasa*] **:** a smoked sausage of Polish origin

[1]kill \ˈkil\ *vb* **1 :** to deprive of life **2 :** to put an end to ⟨~ competition⟩; *also* **:** DEFEAT ⟨~ a proposed amendment⟩ **3 :** USE UP ⟨~ time⟩ **4 :** to mark for omission **syn** slay, murder, assassinate, execute — **kill•er** *n*

[2]kill *n* **1 :** an act of killing **2 :** an animal or animals killed (as in a hunt); *also* **:** an aircraft, ship, or vehicle destroyed by military action

kill•deer \ˈkil-ˌdir\ *n, pl* **killdeers** *or* **killdeer** [imit.] **:** an American plover with a plaintive penetrating cry

killdeer

killer bee *n* **:** AFRICANIZED BEE

killer whale *n* **:** a small gregarious black and white flesh-eating whale with a white oval patch behind each eye

kill•ing *n* **:** a sudden notable gain or profit

kill•joy \ˈkil-ˌjȯi\ *n* **:** one who spoils the pleasures of others

kiln \ˈkil, ˈkiln\ *n* **:** a heated enclosure (as an oven) for processing a substance by burning, firing, or drying — **kiln** *vb*

ki•lo \ˈkē-lō\ *n, pl* **kilos :** KILOGRAM

ki•lo•byte \ˈki-lə-ˌbīt, ˈkē-\ *n* **:** 1024 bytes

kilo•cy•cle \ˈki-lə-ˌsī-kəl\ *n* **:** KILOHERTZ

ki•lo•gram \ˈkē-lə-ˌgram, ˈki-\ *n* **1 :** the basic metric unit of mass that is nearly equal to the mass of 1000 cubic centimeters of water at its maximum density — see METRIC SYSTEM table **2 :** the weight of a kilogram mass under earth's gravity

ki•lo•hertz \ˈki-lə-ˌhərts, ˈkē-, -ˌherts\ *n* **:** 1000 hertz

kilo•li•ter \ˈki-lə-ˌlē-tər\ *n* — see METRIC SYSTEM table

ki•lo•me•ter \ki-ˈlä-mə-tər, ˈki-lə-ˌmē-\ *n* — see METRIC SYSTEM table

ki•lo•ton \ˈki-lə-ˌtən, ˈkē-lō-\ *n* **1 :** 1000 tons **2 :** an explosive force equivalent to that of 1000 tons of TNT

ki•lo•volt \-ˌvōlt\ *n* : 1000 volts
kilo•watt \ˈki-lə-ˌwät\ *n* : 1000 watts
kilowatt–hour *n* : a unit of energy equal to that expended by one kilowatt in one hour
kilt \ˈkilt\ *n* : a knee-length pleated skirt usu. of tartan worn by men in Scotland
kil•ter \ˈkil-tər\ *n* : proper condition ⟨out of ∼⟩
ki•mo•no \kə-ˈmō-nə\ *n, pl* **-nos 1** : a loose robe with wide sleeves traditionally worn with a wide sash as an outer garment by the Japanese **2** : a loose dressing gown or jacket
kin \ˈkin\ *n* **1** : an individual's relatives **2** : KINSMAN
ki•na \ˈkē-nə\ *n* — see MONEY table
[1]**kind** \ˈkīnd\ *n* **1** : essential quality or character **2** : a group united by common traits or interests : CATEGORY; *also* : VARIETY **3** : goods or commodities as distinguished from money
[2]**kind** *adj* **1** : of a sympathetic, forbearing, or pleasant nature **2** : arising from sympathy or forbearance ⟨∼ deeds⟩ **syn** benevolent, benign, benignant, kindly — **kind•ness** *n*
kin•der•gar•ten \ˈkin-dər-ˌgärt-ᵊn\ *n* [G, lit., children's garden] : a school or class for children usu. from four to six years old
kin•der•gart•ner \-ˌgärt-nər\ *n* **1** : a kindergarten pupil **2** : a kindergarten teacher
kind•heart•ed \ˌkīnd-ˈhär-təd\ *adj* : marked by a sympathetic nature
kin•dle \ˈkind-ᵊl\ *vb* **kin•dled; kin•dling 1** : to set on fire : start burning **2** : to stir up : AROUSE **3** : ILLUMINATE, GLOW
kin•dling \ˈkind-liŋ, ˈkin-lən\ *n* : easily combustible material for starting a fire
[1]**kind•ly** \ˈkīnd-lē\ *adj* **kind•li•er; -est 1** : of an agreeable or beneficial nature **2** : of a sympathetic or generous nature — **kind•li•ness** *n*
[2]**kindly** *adv* **1** : READILY ⟨does not take ∼ to criticism⟩ **2** : SYMPATHETICALLY **3** : COURTEOUSLY, OBLIGINGLY
kind of *adv* : to a moderate degree ⟨it's *kind of* late to begin⟩
[1]**kin•dred** \ˈkin-drəd\ *n* **1** : a group of related individuals **2** : one's relatives
[2]**kindred** *adj* : of a like nature or character
kine \ˈkīn\ *archaic pl of* COW
kin•e•ma \ˈki-nə-mə\ *Brit var of* CINEMA
ki•ne•mat•ics \ˌki-nə-ˈma-tiks\ *n* : a science that deals with motion apart from considerations of mass and force — **ki•ne•mat•ic** \-tik\ *or* **ki•ne•mat•i•cal** \-ti-kəl\ *adj*
kin•es•the•sia \ˌki-nəs-ˈthē-zhə, -zhē-ə\ *or* **kin•es•the•sis** \-ˈthē-səs\ *n, pl* **-the•sias** *or* **-the•ses** \-ˌsēz\ : a sense that perceives bodily movement, position, and weight and is mediated by nervous elements in tendons, muscles, and joints; *also* : sensory experience derived from this sense — **kin•es•thet•ic** \-ˈthe-tik\ *adj*
ki•net•ic \kə-ˈne-tik\ *adj* : of or relating to the motion of material bodies and the forces and energy (**kinetic energy**) associated with them
ki•net•ics \-tiks\ *n sing or pl* : a science that deals with the effects of forces upon the motions of material bodies or with changes in a physical or chemical system
kin•folk \ˈkin-ˌfōk\ *or* **kinfolks** *n pl* : RELATIVES
king \ˈkiŋ\ *n* **1** : a male sovereign **2** : a chief among competitors ⟨home-run ∼⟩ **3** : the principal piece in the game of chess **4** : a playing card bearing the figure of a king **5** : a checker that has been crowned — **king•less** *adj* — **king•ly** *adj* — **king•ship** *n*
king crab *n* **1** : HORSESHOE CRAB **2** : a large crab of the north Pacific caught commercially for food
king•dom \ˈkiŋ-dəm\ *n* **1** : a country whose head is a king or queen **2** : a realm or region in which something or someone is dominant ⟨a cattle ∼⟩ **3** : one of the three primary divisions of lifeless material, plants, and animals into which natural objects are grouped; *also* : a biological category that ranks above the phylum
king•fish•er \-ˌfi-shər\ *n* : any of numerous usu. bright-colored crested birds that feed chiefly on fish
king•pin \ˈkiŋ-ˌpin\ *n* **1** : HEADPIN **2** : the leader in a group or undertaking
Kings *n* — see BIBLE table
king–size \ˈkiŋ-ˌsīz\ *or* **king–sized** \-ˌsīzd\ *adj* **1** : longer than the regular or standard size **2** : unusually large **3** : having dimensions of about 76 by 80 inches (1.9 by 2.0 meters) ⟨a ∼ bed⟩; *also* : of a size that fits a king-size bed
kink \ˈkiŋk\ *n* **1** : a short tight twist or curl **2** : a mental peculiarity : QUIRK **3** : CRAMP ⟨a ∼ in the back⟩ **4** : an imperfection likely to cause difficulties in operation — **kinky** *adj*
kin•ship \ˈkin-ˌship\ *n* : RELATIONSHIP
kins•man \ˈkinz-mən\ *n* : RELATIVE; *esp* : a male relative
kins•wom•an \-ˌwu̇-mən\ *n* : a female relative
ki•osk \ˈkē-ˌäsk\ *n* : a small structure with one or more open sides
Ki•o•wa \ˈkī-ə-ˌwȯ, -ˌwä, -ˌwā\ *n, pl* **Kiowa** *or* **Kiowas** : a member of an American Indian people of Colorado, Kansas, New Mexico, Oklahoma, and Texas
kip \ˈkip, ˈgip\ *n, pl* **kip** *or* **kips** — see MONEY table
kip•per \ˈki-pər\ *n* : a fish (as a herring) preserved by salting and drying or smoking — **kipper** *vb*
kirk \ˈkərk, ˈkirk\ *n, chiefly Scot* : CHURCH
kir•tle \ˈkərt-ᵊl\ *n* : a long gown or dress worn by women
kis•met \ˈkiz-ˌmet, -mət\ *n, often cap* [Turk, fr. Ar *qismah* portion, lot] : FATE
[1]**kiss** \ˈkis\ *vb* **1** : to touch or caress with the lips as a mark of affection or greeting **2** : to touch gently or lightly
[2]**kiss** *n* **1** : a caress with the lips **2** : a gentle touch or contact **3** : a bite-size candy
kiss•er \ˈki-sər\ *n* **1** : one that kisses **2** *slang* : MOUTH **3** *slang* : FACE
kit \ˈkit\ *n* **1** : a set of articles for personal use; *also* : a set of tools or implements or of parts to be assembled **2** : a container (as a case) for a kit
kitch•en \ˈki-chən\ *n* **1** : a room with cooking facilities **2** : the personnel that prepares, cooks, and serves food
kitch•en•ette \ˌki-chə-ˈnet\ *n* : a small kitchen or an alcove containing cooking facilities
kitchen police *n* **1** : KP **2** : the work of KPs
kitch•en•ware \ˈki-chən-ˌwar\ *n* : utensils and appliances for kitchen use
kite \ˈkīt\ *n* **1** : any of various long-winged hawks often with deeply forked tails **2** : a light frame covered with paper or cloth and designed to be flown in the air at the end of a long string
kith \ˈkith\ *n* [ME, fr. OE *cȳthth*, fr. *cūth* known] : familiar friends, neighbors, or relatives ⟨∼ and kin⟩
kitsch \ˈkich\ *n* [G] : shoddy or cheap artistic or literary material — **kitschy** *adj*
kit•ten \ˈkit-ᵊn\ *n* : a young cat — **kit•ten•ish** *adj*
[1]**kit•ty** \ˈki-tē\ *n, pl* **kitties** : CAT; *esp* : KITTEN
[2]**kitty** *n, pl* **kitties** : a fund in a poker game made up of contributions from each pot; *also* : POOL
kit•ty–cor•ner *or* **kit•ty–cor•nered** *var of* CATER-CORNER
ki•wi \ˈkē-(ˌ)wē\ *n* : any of a small genus of flightless New Zealand birds
☞ For illustration, see next page.
ki•wi•fruit \-ˌfrüt\ *n* : a brownish hairy egg-shaped fruit of a subtropical vine that has sweet bright green flesh and small edible black seeds
KJV *abbr* King James Version
KKK *abbr* Ku Klux Klan
kl *abbr* kiloliter
klatch *or* **klatsch** \ˈklach\ *n* [G *Klatsch* gossip] : a gathering marked by informal conversation

kiwi

klep•to•ma•nia \ˌklep-tə-ˈmā-nē-ə\ *n* : a persistent neurotic impulse to steal esp. without economic motive — **klep•to•ma•ni•ac** \-nē-ˌak\ *n*
klieg light *or* **kleig light** \ˈklēg-\ *n* : a very bright lamp used in making motion pictures
klutz \ˈkləts\ *n* [Yiddish *klots,* lit., wooden beam] : a clumsy person — **klutzy** *adj*
km *abbr* kilometer
kn *abbr* knot
knack \ˈnak\ *n* **1** : a clever way of doing something **2** : natural aptitude
knap•sack \ˈnap-ˌsak\ *n* : a bag (as of canvas) strapped on the back and used esp. for carrying supplies
knave \ˈnāv\ *n* **1** : ROGUE **2** : JACK 6 — **knav•ery** \ˈnā-və-rē\ *n* — **knav•ish** \ˈnā-vish\ *adj*
knead \ˈnēd\ *vb* : to work and press into a mass with the hands; *also* : MASSAGE — **knead•er** *n*
knee \ˈnē\ *n* : the joint in the middle part of the leg — **kneed** \ˈnēd\ *adj*
knee•cap \ˈnē-ˌkap\ *n* : a thick flat movable bone forming the front of the knee
knee•hole \-ˌhōl\ *n* : a space (as under a desk) for the knees
kneel \ˈnēl\ *vb* **knelt** \ˈnelt\ *or* **kneeled; kneel•ing** : to bend the knee : fall or rest on the knees
[1]**knell** \ˈnel\ *vb* **1** : to ring esp. for a death or disaster **2** : to summon, announce, or proclaim by a knell
[2]**knell** *n* **1** : a stroke of a bell esp. when tolled (as for a funeral) **2** : an indication of the end or failure of something
knew *past of* KNOW
knick•ers \ˈni-kərz\ *n pl* : loose-fitting short pants gathered at the knee
knick•knack \ˈnik-ˌnak\ *n* : a small trivial article intended for ornament
[1]**knife** \ˈnīf\ *n, pl* **knives** \ˈnīvz\ **1** : a cutting instrument consisting of a sharp blade fastened to a handle **2** : a sharp cutting tool in a machine
[2]**knife** *vb* **knifed; knif•ing** : to stab, slash, or wound with a knife
[1]**knight** \ˈnīt\ *n* **1** : a mounted warrior of feudal times serving a king **2** : a man honored by a sovereign for merit and in Great Britain ranking below a baronet **3** : a man devoted to the service of a lady **4** : a member of an order or society **5** : a chess piece having an L-shaped move — **knight•ly** *adj*
[2]**knight** *vb* : to make a knight of
knight•hood \ˈnīt-ˌhu̇d\ *n* **1** : the rank, dignity, or profession of a knight **2** : CHIVALRY **3** : knights as a class or body
knish \kə-ˈnish\ *n* [Yiddish] : a small round or square of dough stuffed with a filling (as of meat or fruit) and baked or fried
[1]**knit** \ˈnit\ *vb* **knit** *or* **knit•ted; knit•ting 1** : to link firmly or closely **2** : WRINKLE ⟨~ her brows⟩ **3** : to form a fabric by interlacing yarn or thread in connected loops with needles **4** : to grow together — **knit•ter** *n*
[2]**knit** *n* **1** : a basic knitting stitch **2** : a knitted garment or fabric
knit•wear \-ˌwar\ *n* : knitted clothing
knob \ˈnäb\ *n* **1** : a rounded protuberance; *also* : a small rounded ornament or handle **2** : a rounded usu. isolated hill — **knobbed** \ˈnäbd\ *adj* — **knob•by** \ˈnä-bē\ *adj*
[1]**knock** \ˈnäk\ *vb* **1** : to strike with a sharp blow **2** : BUMP, COLLIDE **3** : to make a pounding noise; *esp* : to have engine knock **4** : to find fault with
[2]**knock** *n* **1** : a sharp blow **2** : a pounding noise; *esp* : one caused by abnormal ignition in an automobile engine
knock•down \ˈnäk-ˌdau̇n\ *n* **1** : the action of knocking down **2** : something (as a blow) that knocks down **3** : something that can be easily assembled or disassembled
knock down *vb* **1** : to strike to the ground with or as if with as sharp blow **2** : to take apart : DISASSEMBLE **3** : to receive as income or salary : EARN **4** : to make a reduction in
knock•er \ˈnä-kər\ *n* : one that knocks; *esp* : a device hinged to a door for use in knocking
knock–knee \ˈnäk-ˌnē\ *n* : a condition in which the legs curve inward at the knees — **knock–kneed** \-ˌnēd\ *adj*
knock•off \ˈnäk-ˌȯf\ *n* : a copy or imitation of someone or something popular
knock off *vb* **1** : to stop doing something **2** : to do quickly, carelessly, or routinely **3** : to deduct from a price **4** : KILL **5** : ROB **6** : COPY, IMITATE
knock•out \ˈnäk-ˌau̇t\ *n* **1** : a blow that fells and immobilizes an opponent (as in boxing) **2** : something sensationally striking or attractive
knock out *vb* **1** : to defeat by a knockout **2** : to make unconscious or inoperative **3** : to tire out : EXHAUST
knock•wurst *or* **knack•wurst** \ˈnäk-ˌwərst, -ˌvu̇rst\ *n* : a short thick heavily seasoned sausage
knoll \ˈnōl\ *n* : a small round hill
[1]**knot** \ˈnät\ *n* **1** : an interlacing (as of string) forming a lump or knob and often used for fastening or tying together **2** : PROBLEM **3** : a bond of union; *esp* : the marriage bond **4** : a protuberant lump or swelling in tissue **5** : a rounded cross-grained area in lumber that is a section through the junction of a tree branch with the trunk; *also* : the woody tissue forming this junction in a tree **6** : GROUP, CLUSTER **7** : an ornamental bow of ribbon **8** : one nautical mile per hour; *also* : one nautical mile — **knot•ty** *adj*
[2]**knot** *vb* **knot•ted; knot•ting 1** : to tie in or with a knot **2** : ENTANGLE
knot•hole \-ˌhōl\ *n* : a hole in a board or tree trunk where a knot has come out
knout \ˈnau̇t, ˈnüt\ *n* : a whip used for flogging
know \ˈnō\ *vb* **knew** \ˈnü, ˈnyü\; **known** \ˈnōn\; **know•ing 1** : to perceive directly : have understanding or direct cognition of; *also* : to recognize the nature of **2** : to be acquainted or familiar with **3** : to be aware of the truth of **4** : to have a practical understanding of — **know•able** *adj* — **know•er** *n* — **in the know** : possessing confidential information
know–how \ˈnō-ˌhau̇\ *n* : knowledge of how to do something smoothly and efficiently
know•ing *adj* **1** : having or reflecting knowledge, intelligence, or information **2** : shrewdly and keenly alert **3** : DELIBERATE, INTENTIONAL **syn** clever, bright, smart — **know•ing•ly** *adv*
knowl•edge \ˈnä-lij\ *n* **1** : understanding gained by actual experience ⟨a ~ of carpentry⟩ **2** : range of information ⟨to the best of my ~⟩ **3** : clear perception of truth **4** : something learned and kept in the mind
knowl•edge•able \ˈnä-li-jə-bəl\ *adj* : having or showing knowledge or intelligence
knuck•le \ˈnə-kəl\ *n* : the rounded knob at a joint and esp. at a finger joint
knuckle down *vb* : to apply oneself earnestly
knuckle under *vb* : SUBMIT, SURRENDER
knurl \ˈnərl\ *n* **1** : KNOB **2** : one of a series of small ridges on a metal surface to aid in gripping — **knurled** \ˈnərld\ *adj* — **knurly** *adj*
[1]**KO** \(ˌ)kā-ˈō, ˈkā-ō\ *n* : KNOCKOUT

[2]**KO** *vb* **KO'd; KO'•ing** : to knock out in boxing
ko•ala \kō-ˈä-lə\ *n* : a gray furry Australian marsupial with large hairy ears that feeds on eucalyptus leaves
ko•bo \ˈkō-(ˌ)bō\ *n, pl* **kobo** — see *naira* at MONEY table
K of C *abbr* Knights of Columbus
kohl•ra•bi \kōl-ˈrä-bē\ *n, pl* **-bies** [G, fr. It *cavolo rapa,* lit., cabbage turnip] : a cabbage that forms no head but has a swollen fleshy edible stem
ko•lin•sky \kə-ˈlin-skē\ *n, pl* **-skies** : the fur of various Asian minks
kook \ˈkük\ *n* : SCREWBALL 2
kooky *also* **kook•ie** \ˈkü-kē\ *adj* **kook•i•er; -est** : having the characteristics of a kook : CRAZY, ECCENTRIC — **kook•i•ness** *n*
ko•peck *or* **ko•pek** \ˈkō-ˌpek\ *n* [Russ *kopeĭka*] — see *ruble* at MONEY table
Ko•ran \kə-ˈran, -ˈrän\ *n* [Ar *qur'ān*] : a sacred book of Islam that contains revelations made to Muhammad by Allah
Ko•re•an \kə-ˈrē-ən\ *n* : a native or inhabitant of Korea — **Korean** *adj*
ko•ru•na \ˈkȯr-ə-ˌnä\ *n, pl* **ko•ru•ny** \-ə-nē\ *or* **korunas** *or* **ko•rum** \ˈkȯr-əm\ — see MONEY table
ko•sher \ˈkō-shər\ *adj* [Yiddish, fr. Heb *kāshēr* fit, proper] **1** : ritually fit for use according to Jewish law **2** : selling or serving kosher food
kow•tow \kau̇-ˈtau̇, ˈkau̇-ˌtau̇\ *vb* [Chin *kòutóu,* fr. *kòu* to knock + *tóu* head] **1** : to show obsequious deference **2** : to kneel and touch the forehead to the ground as a sign of homage or deep respect
KP \ˌkā-ˈpē\ *n* **1** : an enlisted man detailed to help the cooks in a military mess **2** : the work of KPs
kph *abbr* kilometers per hour
Kr *symbol* krypton
kraal \ˈkräl, ˈkrȯl\ *n* **1** : a native village in southern Africa **2** : an enclosure for domestic animals in southern Africa
kraut \ˈkrau̇t\ *n* : SAUERKRAUT
Krem•lin \ˈkrem-lən\ *n* : the Russian or Soviet government
Krem•lin•ol•o•gist \ˌkrem-lə-ˈnä-lə-jist\ *n* : a specialist in the policies and practices of the Soviet government
[1]**kro•na** \ˈkrō-nə\ *n, pl* **kro•nor** \-ˌnȯr\ [Sw] — see MONEY table
[2]**kro•na** \ˈkrō-nə\ *n, pl* **kro•nur** \-nər\ [Icel] — see MONEY table
kro•ne \ˈkrō-nə\ *n, pl* **kro•ner** \-nər\ — see MONEY table
Kru•ger•rand \ˈkrü-gər-ˌrand, -ˌränd\ *n* : a 1-ounce gold coin of the Republic of South Africa
kryp•ton \ˈkrip-ˌtän\ *n* : a gaseous chemical element used esp. in electric lamps — see ELEMENT table
KS *abbr* Kansas
kt *abbr* **1** karat **2** knight
ku•do \ˈkü-dō, ˈkyü-\ *n, pl* **kudos** [fr. *kudos* (taken as pl.)] **1** : AWARD, HONOR **2** : COMPLIMENT, PRAISE
ku•dos \ˈkü-ˌdäs, ˈkyü-\ *n* : fame and renown resulting from achievement
kud•zu \ˈku̇d-zü, ˈkəd-\ *n* [Jp *kuzu*] : a creeping leguminous vine used for hay, forage, and erosion control
ku•lak \kü-ˈlak, kyü-, -ˈläk\ *n* [Russ, lit., fist] **1** : a wealthy peasant farmer in 19th century Russia **2** : a farmer characterized by Communists as too wealthy
kum•quat \ˈkəm-ˌkwät\ *n* : any of several small citrus fruits with sweet spongy rind and acid pulp
kung fu \ˌkəŋ-ˈfü, ˌku̇ŋ-\ *n* : a Chinese art of self-defense resembling karate
ku•rus \kə-ˈrüsh\ *n, pl* **kurus** — see *lira* at MONEY table
Ku•waiti \ku̇-ˈwā-tē\ *n* : a native or inhabitant of Kuwait — **Kuwaiti** *adj*
kV *abbr* kilovolt
kvetch \ˈkvech, ˈkfech\ *vb* : to complain habitually — **kvetch** *n*
kW *abbr* kilowatt
kwa•cha \ˈkwä-chə\ *n, pl* **kwacha** — see MONEY table
kwan•za \ˈkwän-zə\ *n, pl* **kwanzas** *or* **kwanza** — see MONEY table
kwash•i•or•kor \ˌkwä-shē-ˈȯr-kȯr, -ȯr-ˈkȯr\ *n* : a disease of young children caused by deficient intake of protein
kWh *abbr* kilowatt-hour
Ky *or* **KY** *abbr* Kentucky
kyat \ˈchät\ *n* — see MONEY table
ky•bosh *chiefly Brit var of* KIBOSH

L

[1]**l** \ˈel\ *n, pl* **l's** *or* **ls** \ˈelz\ *often cap* : the 12th letter of the English alphabet
[2]**l** *abbr, often cap* **1** lake **2** large **3** left **4** [L *libra*] pound **5** line **6** liter
[1]**La** *abbr* Louisiana
[2]**La** *symbol* lanthanum
LA *abbr* **1** law agent **2** Los Angeles **3** Louisiana
lab \ˈlab\ *n* : LABORATORY
Lab *n* : LABRADOR RETRIEVER
[1]**la•bel** \ˈlā-bəl\ *n* **1** : a slip attached to something for identification or description **2** : a descriptive or identifying word or phrase **3** : BRAND 3
[2]**label** *vb* **-beled** *or* **-belled; -bel•ing** *or* **-bel•ling** **1** : to affix a label to **2** : to describe or name with a label
la•bi•al \ˈlā-bē-əl\ *adj* : of or relating to the lips or labia
la•bia ma•jo•ra \ˈlā-bē-ə-mə-ˈjōr-ə\ *n pl* : the outer fatty folds of the vulva
labia mi•no•ra \-mə-ˈnōr-ə\ *n pl* : the inner highly vascular folds of the vulva
la•bile \ˈlā-ˌbīl, -bəl\ *adj* **1** : UNSTABLE **2** : ADAPTABLE
la•bi•um \ˈlā-bē-əm\ *n, pl* **la•bia** \-ə\ [NL, fr. L, lip] : any of the folds at the margin of the vulva
[1]**la•bor** \ˈlā-bər\ *n* **1** : physical or mental effort; *also* : human activity that provides the goods or services in an economy **2** : the physical efforts of giving birth; *also* : the period of such labor **3** : TASK **4** : those who do manual labor or work for wages; *also* : labor unions or their officials
[2]**labor** *vb* **1** : WORK **2** : to move with great effort **3** : to be in the labor of giving birth **4** : to suffer from some disadvantage or distress ⟨~ under a delusion⟩ **5** : to treat or work out laboriously — **la•bor•er** *n*
lab•o•ra•to•ry \ˈla-brə-ˌtōr-ē, -bə-rə-\ *n, pl* **-ries** : a place equipped for making scientific experiments or tests
Labor Day *n* : the 1st Monday in September observed as a legal holiday in recognition of the working people
la•bored \ˈlā-bərd\ *adj* : not freely or easily done ⟨~ breathing⟩
la•bo•ri•ous \lə-ˈbōr-ē-əs\ *adj* **1** : INDUSTRIOUS **2** : requiring great effort — **la•bo•ri•ous•ly** *adv*
la•bor•sav•ing \ˈlā-bər-ˌsā-viŋ\ *adj* : designed to replace or decrease labor
labor union *n* : an organization of workers formed to advance its members' interest in respect to wages and working conditions
la•bour *chiefly Brit var of* LABOR
lab•ra•dor•ite \ˈla-brə-ˌdȯr-ˌīt\ *n* : an iridescent feldspar used in jewelry
Lab•ra•dor retriever \ˈla-brə-ˌdȯr-\ *n* : a strongly built retriever having a short dense black, yellow, or chocolate coat
la•bur•num \lə-ˈbər-nəm\ *n* : a leguminous shrub or tree with hanging clusters of yellow flowers
lab•y•rinth \ˈla-bə-ˌrinth\ *n* : a place constructed of or filled with confusing intricate passageways : MAZE

lab•y•rin•thine \ˌla-bə-ˈrin-thən, -ˌthīn, -ˌthēn\ *adj* : INTRICATE, INVOLVED

lac \ˈlak\ *n* : a resinous substance secreted by a scale insect and used chiefly in the form of shellac

[1]**lace** \ˈlās\ *vb* **laced; lac•ing 1** : TIE **2** : to adorn with lace **3** : INTERTWINE **4** : BEAT, LASH **5** : to add to something to impart zest or savor to

[2]**lace** *n* [ME, fr. OF *laz,* fr. L *laqueus* snare, noose] **1** : a cord or string used for drawing together two edges **2** : an ornamental braid **3** : a fine openwork usu. figured fabric made of thread — **lacy** \ˈlā-sē\ *adj*

lac•er•ate \ˈla-sə-ˌrāt\ *vb* **-at•ed; -at•ing** : to tear roughly — **lac•er•a•tion** \ˌla-sə-ˈrā-shən\ *n*

lace•wing \ˈlās-ˌwiŋ\ *n* : any of various insects with delicate wing veins, long antennae, and often brilliant eyes

lach•ry•mal *or* **lac•ri•mal** \ˈla-krə-məl\ *adj* **1** *usu lacrimal* : of, relating to, or being glands that produce tears **2** : of, relating to, or marked by tears

lach•ry•mose \ˈla-krə-ˌmōs\ *adj* **1** : TEARFUL **2** : MOURNFUL

[1]**lack** \ˈlak\ *vb* **1** : to be wanting or missing **2** : to be deficient in

[2]**lack** *n* : the fact or state of being wanting or deficient : NEED

lack•a•dai•si•cal \ˌla-kə-ˈdā-zi-kəl\ *adj* : lacking life, spirit, or zest — **lack•a•dai•si•cal•ly** \-k(ə-)lē\ *adv*

lack•ey \ˈla-kē\ *n, pl* **lackeys 1** : FOOTMAN, SERVANT **2** : TOADY

lack•lus•ter \ˈlak-ˌləs-tər\ *adj* : DULL

la•con•ic \lə-ˈkä-nik\ *adj* [L *laconicus* Spartan, fr. Gk *lakōnikos;* fr. the Spartan reputation for terseness of speech] : sparing of words : TERSE **syn** concise, curt, short, succinct, brusque — **la•con•i•cal•ly** \-ni-k(ə-)lē\ *adv*

lac•quer \ˈla-kər\ *n* : a clear or colored usu. glossy and quick-drying surface coating — **lacquer** *vb*

lac•ri•ma•tion \ˌla-krə-ˈmā-shən\ *n* : secretion of tears

la•crosse \lə-ˈkrȯs\ *n* [CanF *la crosse,* lit., the crosier] : a goal game in which players use a long-handled triangular-headed stick having a mesh pouch for catching, carrying, and throwing the ball

lac•tate \ˈlak-ˌtāt\ *vb* **lac•tat•ed; lac•tat•ing** : to secrete milk — **lac•ta•tion** \lak-ˈtā-shən\ *n*

lac•tic \ˈlak-tik\ *adj* **1** : of or relating to milk **2** : obtained from sour milk or whey

lactic acid *n* : a syrupy acid present in blood and muscle tissue and used in food and medicine

lac•tose \ˈlak-ˌtōs\ *n* : a sugar present in milk

la•cu•na \lə-ˈkü-nə, -ˈkyü-\ *n, pl* **la•cu•nae** \-nē\ *or* **la•cu•nas** [L, pool, pit, gap, fr. *lacus* lake] : a blank space or missing part : GAP

lad \ˈlad\ *n* : YOUTH; *also* : FELLOW

lad•der \ˈla-dər\ *n* : a structure for climbing that consists of two parallel sidepieces joined at intervals by crosspieces

lad•die \ˈla-dē\ *n* : a young lad

lad•en \ˈlād-ᵊn\ *adj* : LOADED, BURDENED

lad•ing \ˈlā-diŋ\ *n* : CARGO, FREIGHT

la•dle \ˈlād-ᵊl\ *n* : a deep-bowled long-handled spoon used in taking up and conveying liquids — **ladle** *vb*

la•dy \ˈlā-dē\ *n, pl* **ladies** [ME, fr. OE *hlǣfdīge,* fr. *hlāf* bread + *-dīge* (akin to *dǣge* kneader of bread)] **1** : a woman of property, rank, or authority; *also* : a woman of superior social position or of refinement **2** : WOMAN **3** : WIFE

lady beetle *n* : LADYBUG

la•dy•bird \ˈlā-dē-ˌbərd\ *n* : LADYBUG

la•dy•bug \-ˌbəg\ *n* : any of various small nearly hemispherical and usu. brightly colored beetles that feed mostly on other insects

la•dy•fin•ger \-ˌfiŋ-gər\ *n* : a small finger-shaped sponge cake

lady–in–waiting *n, pl* **ladies–in–waiting** : a lady appointed to attend or wait on a queen or princess

la•dy•like \ˈlā-dē-ˌlīk\ *adj* : WELL-BRED

la•dy•ship \-ˌship\ *n* : the condition of being a lady : rank of lady

lady's slipper *or* **lady slipper** *n* : any of several No. American orchids with slipper-shaped flowers

[1]**lag** \ˈlag\ *n* **1** : a slowing up or falling behind; *also* : the amount by which one lags **2** : INTERVAL

[2]**lag** *vb* **lagged; lag•ging 1** : to fail to keep up : stay behind **2** : to slacken gradually **syn** dawdle, dally, tarry, loiter

la•ger \ˈlä-gər\ *n* : a light-colored usu. dry beer

lag•gard \ˈla-gərd\ *adj* : tending to lag — **laggard** *n* — **lag•gard•ly** *adv or adj* — **lag•gard•ness** *n*

la•gniappe \ˈlan-ˌyap\ *n* : something given free esp. with a purchase

la•goon \lə-ˈgün\ *n* : a shallow sound, channel, or pond near or connected to a larger body of water

laid *past and past part of* LAY

laid–back \ˈlād-ˈbak\ *adj* : having a relaxed style or character ⟨~ music⟩

lain *past part of* [1]LIE

lair \ˈlar\ *n* : the resting or living place of a wild animal : DEN

laird \ˈlard\ *n, Scot* : a landed proprietor

lais•ser–faire *chiefly Brit var of* LAISSEZ-FAIRE

lais•sez–faire \ˌle-ˌsā-ˈfar, ˌlā-, -ˌzā-\ *n* [F *laissez faire* let do] : a doctrine opposing governmental control of economic affairs beyond that necessary to maintain peace and property rights

la•ity \ˈlā-ə-tē\ *n* **1** : the people of a religious faith as distinct from its clergy **2** : the mass of people as distinct from those of a particular field

lake \ˈlāk\ *n* : an inland body of standing water of considerable size; *also* : a pool of liquid (as lava or pitch)

[1]**lam** \ˈlam\ *vb* **lammed; lam•ming** : to flee hastily — **lam** *n*

[2]**lam** *abbr* laminated

Lam *abbr* Lamentations

la•ma \ˈlä-mə\ *n* : a Buddhist monk of Tibet or Mongolia

la•ma•sery \ˈlä-mə-ˌser-ē\ *n, pl* **-ser•ies** : a monastery for lamas

[1]**lamb** \ˈlam\ *n* **1** : a young sheep; *also* : its flesh used as food **2** : an innocent or gentle person

[2]**lamb** *vb* : to bring forth a lamb

lam•baste *or* **lam•bast** \lam-ˈbāst, -ˈbast\ *vb* **1** : BEAT **2** : EXCORIATE **syn** castigate, flay, lash

lamb•da \ˈlam-də\ *n* : the 11th letter of the Greek alphabet — Λ or λ

lam•bent \ˈlam-bənt\ *adj* [L *lambens,* prp. of *lambere* to lick] **1** : FLICKERING **2** : softly radiant ⟨~ eyes⟩ **3** : marked by lightness or brilliance ⟨~ humor⟩ **syn** effulgent, incandescent, lucent, luminous — **lam•ben•cy** \-bən-sē\ *n* — **lam•bent•ly** *adv*

lamb•skin \ˈlam-ˌskin\ *n* : a lamb's skin or a small fine-grade sheepskin or the leather made from either

[1]**lame** \ˈlām\ *adj* **lam•er; lam•est 1** : having a body part and esp. a limb so disabled as to impair freedom of movement; *also* : marked by stiffness and soreness **2** : lacking substance : WEAK — **lame•ly** *adv* — **lame•ness** *n*

[2]**lame** *vb* **lamed; lam•ing** : to make lame : CRIPPLE, DISABLE

la•mé \lä-ˈmā, la-\ *n* [F] : a brocaded clothing fabric with tinsel filling threads (as of gold or silver)

lame•brain \ˈlām-ˌbrān\ *n* : DOLT

lame duck *n* : an elected official continuing to hold office between an election and the inauguration of a successor — **lame–duck** *adj*

[1]**la•ment** \lə-ˈment\ *vb* **1** : to mourn aloud : WAIL **2** : to express sorrow or regret for : BEWAIL — **lam•en•ta•ble** \ˈla-mən-tə-bəl, lə-ˈmen-tə-\ *adj* — **lam•en•ta•bly** \-blē\ *adv* — **lam•en•ta•tion** \ˌla-mən-ˈtā-shən\ *n*

[2]**lament** *n* **1** : a crying out in grief : WAIL **2** : DIRGE, ELEGY **3** : COMPLAINT

Lamentations *n* — see BIBLE table

la•mia \ˈlā-mē-ə\ *n* : a female demon
lam•i•na \ˈla-mə-nə\ *n, pl* **-nae** \-ˌnē\ *or* **-nas** : a thin plate or scale
[1]**lam•i•nate** \ˈla-mə-ˌnāt\ *vb* **-nat•ed; -nat•ing** : to make by uniting layers of one or more materials — **lam•i•na•tion** \ˌla-mə-ˈnā-shən\ *n*
[2]**lam•i•nate** \-nət\ *n* : a product manufactured by laminating
lamp \ˈlamp\ *n* **1** : a vessel with a wick for burning a flammable liquid (as oil) to produce light **2** : a device for producing light or heat
lamp•black \-ˌblak\ *n* : black soot used esp. as a pigment
lamp•light•er \-ˌlī-tər\ *n* : one that lights a lamp
lam•poon \lam-ˈpün\ *n* : SATIRE; *esp* : a harsh satire directed against an individual — **lampoon** *vb*
lam•prey \ˈlam-prē\ *n, pl* **lampreys** : any of a family of eel-shaped jawless fishes that have well-developed eyes and a large disk-shaped sucking mouth armed with horny teeth
la•nai \lə-ˈnī\ *n* [Hawaiian *lānai*] : PORCH, VERANDA
[1]**lance** \ˈlans\ *n* **1** : a spear carried by mounted soldiers **2** : any of various sharp-pointed implements; *esp* : LANCET
[2]**lance** *vb* **lanced; lanc•ing** : to pierce or open with a lance ⟨~ a boil⟩
lance corporal *n* : an enlisted man in the marine corps ranking above a private first class and below a corporal
lanc•er \ˈlan-sər\ *n* : a cavalryman of a unit formerly armed with lances
lan•cet \ˈlan-sət\ *n* : a sharp-pointed and usu. 2-edged surgical instrument
[1]**land** \ˈland\ *n* **1** : the solid part of the surface of the earth; *also* : a part of the earth's surface ⟨fenced ~⟩ ⟨marshy ~⟩ **2** : NATION **3** : REALM, DOMAIN — **landless** *adj*
[2]**land** *vb* **1** : DISEMBARK; *also* : to touch at a place on shore **2** : to alight or cause to alight on a surface **3** : to bring to or arrive at a destination **4** : to catch and bring in ⟨~ a fish⟩; *also* : GAIN, SECURE ⟨~ a job⟩
lan•dau \ˈlan-ˌdau̇\ *n* : a 4-wheeled carriage with a top divided into two sections that can be lowered, thrown back, or removed
land•ed *adj* : having an estate in land ⟨~ gentry⟩
land•er \ˈlan-dər\ *n* : a space vehicle designed to land on a celestial body
land•fall \ˈland-ˌfȯl\ *n* : a sighting or making of land (as after a voyage); *also* : the land first sighted
land•fill \-ˌfil\ *n* : a low-lying area on which refuse is buried between layers of earth
land•form \-ˌfȯrm\ *n* : a natural feature of a land surface
land•hold•er \-ˌhōl-dər\ *n* : a holder or owner of land — **land•hold•ing** \-diŋ\ *adj or n*
land•ing \ˈlan-diŋ\ *n* **1** : the action of one that lands **2** : a place for discharging or taking on passengers and cargo **3** : a level part of a staircase
landing gear *n* : the part that supports the weight of an aircraft when it is on the ground
land•la•dy \ˈland-ˌlā-dē\ *n* : a woman who is a landlord
land•locked \-ˌläkt\ *adj* **1** : enclosed or nearly enclosed by land ⟨a ~ country⟩ **2** : confined to fresh water by some barrier ⟨~ salmon⟩
land•lord \-ˌlȯrd\ *n* **1** : the owner of property leased or rented to another **2** : a person who rents lodgings : INNKEEPER
land•lub•ber \-ˌlə-bər\ *n* : one who knows little of the sea or seamanship
land•mark \-ˌmärk\ *n* **1** : an object that marks a course or boundary or serves as a guide **2** : an event that marks a turning point **3** : a structure of unusual historical and usu. aesthetic interest
land•mass \-ˌmas\ *n* : a large area of land
land mine *n* **1** : a mine placed on or just below the surface of the ground and designed to be exploded by the weight of someone or something passing over it **2** : a trap for the unwary
land•own•er \-ˌō-nər\ *n* : an owner of land
[1]**land•scape** \-ˌskāp\ *n* **1** : a picture of natural inland scenery **2** : a portion of land that can be seen in one glance
[2]**landscape** *vb* **land•scaped; land•scap•ing** : to modify (a natural landscape) by grading, clearing, or decorative planting
land•slide \-ˌslīd\ *n* **1** : the slipping down of a mass of rocks or earth on a steep slope; *also* : the mass of material that slides **2** : an overwhelming victory esp. in a political contest
lands•man \ˈlandz-mən\ *n* : a person who lives on land; *esp* : LANDLUBBER
land•ward \ˈland-wərd\ *adv or adj* : to or toward the land
lane \ˈlān\ *n* **1** : a narrow passageway (as between fences) **2** : a relatively narrow way or track ⟨traffic ~⟩
lang *abbr* language
lan•guage \ˈlaŋ-gwij\ *n* [ME, fr. OF, fr. *langue* tongue, language, fr. L *lingua*] **1** : the words, their pronunciation, and the methods of combining them used and understood by a community **2** : form or style of verbal expression **3** : a system of signs and symbols and rules for using them that is used to carry information
lan•guid \ˈlaŋ-gwəd\ *adj* **1** : WEAK **2** : sluggish in character or disposition : LISTLESS **3** : SLOW — **lan•guid•ly** *adv* — **lan•guid•ness** *n*
lan•guish \ˈlaŋ-gwish\ *vb* **1** : to become languid **2** : to become dispirited : PINE **3** : to appeal for sympathy by assuming an expression of grief
lan•guor \ˈlaŋ-gər\ *n* **1** : a languid feeling **2** : listless indolence or inertia **syn** lethargy, lassitude, torpidity, torpor — **lan•guor•ous** *adj* — **lan•guor•ous•ly** *adv*
lank \ˈlaŋk\ *adj* **1** : not well filled out **2** : hanging straight and limp
lanky \ˈlaŋ-kē\ *adj* **lank•i•er; -est** : ungracefully tall and thin
lan•o•lin \ˈlan-ᵊl-ən\ *n* : the fatty coating of sheep's wool esp. when refined for use in ointments and cosmetics
lan•ta•na \lan-ˈtä-nə\ *n* : any of a genus of tropical shrubs related to the vervains with showy heads of small bright flowers
lan•tern \ˈlan-tərn\ *n* **1** : a usu. portable light with a protective covering **2** : the chamber in a lighthouse containing the light **3** : a projector for slides
lan•tha•num \ˈlan-thə-nəm\ *n* : a soft malleable metallic chemical element — see ELEMENT table
lan•yard \ˈlan-yərd\ *n* : a piece of rope for fastening something in ships; *also* : any of various cords
Lao•tian \lā-ˈō-shən, ˈlau̇-shən\ *n* : a native or inhabitant of Laos — **Laotian** *adj*
[1]**lap** \ˈlap\ *n* **1** : a loose panel of a garment **2** : the clothing that lies on the knees, thighs, and lower part of the trunk when one sits; *also* : the front part of the lower trunk and thighs of a seated person **3** : an environment of nurture ⟨the ~ of luxury⟩ **4** : CHARGE, CONTROL ⟨in the ~ of the gods⟩
[2]**lap** *vb* **lapped; lap•ping 1** : FOLD **2** : WRAP **3** : to lay over or near so as to partly cover
[3]**lap** *n* **1** : the amount by which an object overlaps another; *also* : the part of an object that overlaps another **2** : an act or instance of going over a course (as a track or swimming pool)
[4]**lap** *vb* **lapped; lap•ping 1** : to scoop up food or drink with the tip of the tongue; *also* : DEVOUR — usu. used with *up* **2** : to splash gently ⟨*lapping* waves⟩
[5]**lap** *n* **1** : an act or instance of lapping **2** : a gentle splashing sound
lap•dog \ˈlap-ˌdȯg\ *n* : a small dog that may be held in the lap
la•pel \lə-ˈpel\ *n* : the fold of the front of a coat that is usu. a continuation of the collar

[1]**lap·i·dary** \ˈla-pə-ˌder-ē\ *n, pl* **-dar·ies :** a person who cuts, polishes, or engraves precious stones

[2]**lapidary** *adj* **1 :** of, relating to, or suitable for engraved inscriptions **2 :** of or relating to precious stones or the art of cutting them

lap·in \ˈla-pən\ *n* **:** rabbit fur usu. sheared and dyed

la·pis la·zu·li \ˌla-pəs-ˈla-zə-lē, -zhə-\ *n* **:** a usu. blue semiprecious stone often having sparkling bits of pyrite

Lapp \ˈlap\ *n* **:** a member of a people of northern Scandinavia, Finland, and the Kola peninsula of Russia

lap·pet \ˈla-pət\ *n* **:** a fold or flap on a garment

[1]**lapse** \ˈlaps\ *n* [L *lapsus,* fr. *labi* to slip] **1 :** a slight error **2 :** a fall from a higher to a lower state **3 :** the termination of a right or privilege through failure to meet requirements **4 :** INTERRUPTION **5 :** APOSTASY **6 :** a passage of time; *also* **:** INTERVAL **syn** blooper, blunder, boner, goof, mistake, slip

[2]**lapse** *vb* **lapsed; laps·ing 1 :** to commit apostasy **2 :** to sink or slip gradually **:** SUBSIDE **3 :** CEASE

lap·top \ˈlap-ˌtäp\ *adj* **:** of a size that can be used conveniently on one's lap ⟨a ~ computer⟩ **— laptop** *n*

lap·wing \ˈlap-ˌwiŋ\ *n* **:** an Old World crested plover

lar·board \ˈlär-bərd\ *n* **:** [5]PORT

lar·ce·ny \ˈlär-sə-nē\ *n, pl* **-nies** [ME, fr. MF *larcin* theft, fr. L *latrocinium* robbery, fr. *latro* mercenary soldier] **:** THEFT **— lar·ce·nous** \-nəs\ *adj*

larch \ˈlärch\ *n* **:** any of a genus of trees related to the pines that shed their needles in the fall

[1]**lard** \ˈlärd\ *vb* **1 :** to insert strips of usu. pork fat into (meat) before cooking; *also* **:** GREASE **2** *obs* **:** ENRICH

[2]**lard** *n* **:** a soft white fat obtained by rendering fatty tissue of the hog

lar·der \ˈlär-dər\ *n* **:** a place where foods (as meat) are kept

lar·es and pe·na·tes \ˈlar-ēz . . . pə-ˈnā-tēz\ *n pl* **1 :** household gods **2 :** personal or household effects

large \ˈlärj\ *adj* **larg·er; larg·est 1 :** having more than usual power, capacity, or scope **2 :** exceeding most other things of like kind in quantity or size **syn** big, great, oversize **— large·ness** *n* **— at large 1 :** UNCONFINED **2 :** as a whole

large·ly \ˈlärj-lē\ *adv* **:** to a large extent

lar·gesse *or* **lar·gess** \lär-ˈzhes, -ˈjes\ *n* **1 :** liberal giving **2 :** a generous gift

[1]**lar·go** \ˈlär-gō\ *adv or adj* [It, slow, broad, fr. L *largus* abundant] **:** at a very slow tempo — used as a direction in music

[2]**largo** *n, pl* **largos :** a largo movement

lar·i·at \ˈlar-ē-ət\ *n* [AmerSp *la reata* the lasso, fr. Sp *la* the + AmerSp *reata* lasso, fr. Sp *reatar* to tie again] **:** a long rope used to catch or tether livestock **:** LASSO

[1]**lark** \ˈlärk\ *n* **:** any of a family of small songbirds; *esp* **:** SKYLARK

[2]**lark** *n* **:** something done solely for fun or adventure

[3]**lark** *vb* **:** to engage in harmless fun or mischief — often used with *about*

lark·spur \ˈlärk-ˌspər\ *n* **:** DELPHINIUM; *esp* **:** any of the cultivated annual delphiniums

lar·va \ˈlär-və\ *n, pl* **lar·vae** \-(ˌ)vē\ *also* **larvas** [L, specter, mask] **:** the wingless often wormlike form in which insects hatch from the egg; *also* **:** any young animal (as a tadpole) that is fundamentally unlike its parent **— lar·val** \-vəl\ *adj*

lar·yn·gi·tis \ˌlar-ən-ˈjī-təs\ *n* **:** inflammation of the larynx

lar·ynx \ˈlar-iŋks\ *n, pl* **la·ryn·ges** \lə-ˈrin-ˌjēz\ *or* **lar·ynx·es :** the upper part of the trachea containing the vocal cords **— la·ryn·ge·al** \lə-ˈrin-jəl\ *adj*

la·sa·gna \lə-ˈzän-yə\ *n* [It] **:** boiled broad flat noodles baked with a sauce usu. of tomatoes, cheese, and meat

las·car \ˈlas-kər\ *n* **:** an Indian sailor

las·civ·i·ous \lə-ˈsi-vē-əs\ *adj* **:** LUSTFUL, LEWD **syn** licentious, lecherous, libidinous, salacious **— las·civ·i·ous·ness** *n*

la·ser \ˈlā-zər\ *n* [*l*ight *a*mplification by *s*timulated *e*mission of *r*adiation] **:** a device that produces an intense monochromatic beam of light

laser disc *n* **:** an optical disk on which programs are recorded for playback on a television set

[1]**lash** \ˈlash\ *vb* **1 :** to move violently or suddenly **2 :** WHIP **3 :** to attack verbally

[2]**lash** *n* **1 :** a stroke esp. with a whip; *also* **:** WHIP **2 :** a stinging rebuke **3 :** EYELASH

[3]**lash** *vb* **:** to bind with or as if with a line

lass \ˈlas\ *n* **:** GIRL

lass·ie \ˈla-sē\ *n* **:** LASS

las·si·tude \ˈla-sə-ˌtüd, -ˌtyüd\ *n* **1 :** WEARINESS, FATIGUE **2 :** LANGUOR

las·so \ˈla-sō, la-ˈsü\ *n, pl* **lassos** *or* **lassoes** [Sp *lazo*] **:** a rope or long leather thong with a noose used for catching livestock **— lasso** *vb*

[1]**last** \ˈlast\ *vb* **1 :** to continue in existence or operation **2 :** to remain fresh or unimpaired **:** ENDURE **3 :** to manage to continue **4 :** to be enough for the needs of

[2]**last** *n* **:** a foot-shaped form on which a shoe is shaped or repaired

[3]**last** *vb* **:** to shape with a last

[4]**last** *adv* **1 :** at the end **2 :** most recently **3 :** in conclusion

[5]**last** *adj* **1 :** following all the rest **:** FINAL **2 :** next before the present **3 :** most up-to-date **4 :** farthest from a specified quality, attitude, or likelihood ⟨the ~ thing we want⟩ **4 :** CONCLUSIVE; *also* **:** SUPREME **— last·ly** *adv*

[6]**last** *n* **:** something that is last **— at last :** FINALLY

Last Supper *n* **:** the supper eaten by Jesus and his disciples on the night of his betrayal

lat *abbr* latitude

Lat *abbr* Latin

[1]**latch** \ˈlach\ *vb* **:** to catch or get hold

[2]**latch** *n* **:** a catch that holds a door or gate closed

[3]**latch** *vb* **:** to make fast with a latch

latch·et \ˈla-chət\ *n* **:** a strap, thong, or lace for fastening a shoe or sandal

latch·key \ˈlach-ˌkē\ *n* **:** a key for opening a door latch esp. from the outside

latch·string \-ˌstriŋ\ *n* **:** a string on a latch that may be left hanging outside the door for raising the latch

[1]**late** \ˈlāt\ *adj* **lat·er; lat·est 1 :** coming or remaining after the due, usual, or proper time **2 :** far advanced toward the close or end **3 :** recently deceased **4 :** made, appearing, or happening just previous to the present **:** RECENT **— late·ly** *adv* **— late·ness** *n*

[2]**late** *adv* **lat·er; lat·est 1 :** after the usual or proper time; *also* **:** at or to an advanced point in time **2 :** RECENTLY

late·com·er \ˈlāt-ˌkə-mər\ *n* **:** one who arrives late

la·teen \lə-ˈtēn\ *adj* **:** relating to or being a triangular sail extended by a long spar slung to a low mast

la·tent \ˈlāt-ᵊnt\ *adj* **:** present but not visible or active **syn** dormant, quiescent, potential **— la·ten·cy** \-ᵊn-sē\ *n*

[1]**lat·er·al** \ˈla-tə-rəl\ *adj* **:** situated on, directed toward, or coming from the side **— lat·er·al·ly** *adv*

[2]**lateral** *n* **1 :** a branch from the main part **2 :** a football pass thrown parallel to the line of scrimmage or away from the opponent's goal

la·tex \ˈlā-ˌteks\ *n, pl* **la·ti·ces** \ˈlā-tə-ˌsēz, ˈla-\ *or* **la·tex·es 1 :** a milky juice produced by various plant cells (as of milkweeds, poppies, and the rubber tree) **2 :** a water emulsion of a synthetic rubber or plastic used esp. in paint

lath \ˈlath, ˈlat͟h\ *n, pl* **laths** *or* **lath :** a thin narrow strip of wood used esp. as a base for plaster; *also* **:** a building material in sheets used for the same purpose **— lath** *vb*

lathe \ˈlāt͟h\ *n* **:** a machine in which a piece of material is held and turned while being shaped by a tool

[1]**lath·er** \ˈla-t͟hər\ *n* **1 :** a foam or froth formed when a

detergent is agitated in water; *also* : foam from profuse sweating (as by a horse) **2** : DITHER

[2]**lather** *vb* : to spread lather over; *also* : to form a lather

Lat•in \ˈlat-ᵊn\ *n* **1** : the language of ancient Rome **2** : a member of any of the peoples whose languages derive from Latin — **Latin** *adj*

Latin American *n* : a native or inhabitant of any of the countries of No., Central, or So. America whose official language is Spanish or Portuguese — **Latin–American** *adj*

La•ti•no \lə-ˈtē-nō\ *n, pl* **-nos** : a native or inhabitant of Latin America; *also* : a person of Latin-American origin living in the U.S. — **Latino** *adj*

lat•i•tude \ˈla-tə-ˌtüd, -ˌtyüd\ *n* **1** : angular distance north or south from the earth's equator measured in degrees **2** : a region marked by its latitude **3** : freedom of action or choice

lat•i•tu•di•nar•i•an \ˌla-tə-ˌtü-də-ˈner-ē-ən, -ˌtyü-\ *n* : a person who is liberal in religious belief and conduct

la•trine \lə-ˈtrēn\ *n* : TOILET

lat•ter \ˈla-tər\ *adj* **1** : more recent; *also* : FINAL **2** : of, relating to, or being the second of two things referred to

lat•ter–day *adj* **1** : of present or recent times **2** : of a later or subsequent time

Latter–day Saint *n* : a member of a religious body founded by Joseph Smith in 1830 and accepting the Book of Mormon as divine revelation : MORMON

lat•ter•ly \ˈla-tər-lē\ *adv* **1** : LATER **2** : of late : RECENTLY

lat•tice \ˈla-təs\ *n* **1** : a framework of crossed wood or metal strips; *also* : a window, door, or gate having a lattice **2** : a regular geometrical arrangement

lat•tice•work \-ˌwərk\ *n* : LATTICE; *also* : work made of lattices

Lat•vi•an \ˈlat-vē-ən\ *n* : a native or inhabitant of Latvia — **Latvian** *adj*

[1]**laud** \ˈlȯd\ *n* : PRAISE, ACCLAIM

[2]**laud** *vb* : PRAISE, EXTOL **syn** celebrate, eulogize, glorify, magnify — **laud•able** *adj* — **laud•ably** *adv*

lau•da•num \ˈlȯd-ᵊn-əm\ *n* : a tincture of opium

lau•da•to•ry \ˈlȯ-də-ˌtōr-ē\ *adj* : of, relating to, or expressive of praise

[1]**laugh** \ˈlaf, ˈlȧf\ *vb* : to show mirth, joy, or scorn with a smile and chuckle or explosive sound; *also* : to become amused or derisive — **laugh•able** *adj* — **laugh•ing•ly** *adv*

[2]**laugh** *n* **1** : the act of laughing **2** : JOKE; *also* : JEER **3** *pl* : SPORT 1

laugh•ing•stock \ˈla-fiŋ-ˌstäk, ˈlȧ-\ *n* : an object of ridicule

laugh•ter \ˈlaf-tər, ˈlȧf-\ *n* : the action or sound of laughing

[1]**launch** \ˈlȯnch\ *vb* [ME, fr. OF *lancher,* fr. LL *lanceare* to wield a lance] **1** : THROW, HURL; *also* : to send off ⟨~ a rocket⟩ **2** : to set afloat **3** : to set in operation : START — **launch•er** *n*

[2]**launch** *n* : an act or instance of launching

[3]**launch** *n* : a small open or half-decked motorboat

launch•pad \ˈlȯnch-ˌpad\ *n* : a platform from which a rocket is launched

laun•der \ˈlȯn-dər\ *vb* **1** : to wash or wash and iron clothing and household linens **2** : to transfer (as money of an illegal origin) through an outside party to conceal the true source — **laun•der•er** *n*

laun•dress \ˈlȯn-drəs\ *n* : a woman who is a laundry worker

laun•dry \ˈlȯn-drē\ *n, pl* **laundries** [fr. obs. *launder* launderer, fr. MF *lavandier,* fr. ML *lavandarius,* fr. L *lavandus* needing to be washed, fr. *lavare* to wash] **1** : a place where laundering is done **2** : clothes or linens that have been or are to be laundered — **laun•dry•man** \-mən\ *n*

lau•re•ate \ˈlȯr-ē-ət\ *n* : the recipient of honor for achievement in an art or science — **lau•re•ate•ship** *n*

lau•rel \ˈlȯ-rəl\ *n* **1** : any of a genus of evergreen trees related to the sassafras and cinnamon; *esp* : a small tree of southern Europe **2** : MOUNTAIN LAUREL **3** : a crown of laurel : HONOR — usu. used in pl.

lav *abbr* lavatory

la•va \ˈlä-və, ˈla-\ *n* [It] : melted rock coming from a volcano; *also* : such rock that has cooled and hardened

la•vage \lə-ˈväzh\ *n* [F] : WASHING; *esp* : the washing out (as of an organ) esp. for medicinal reasons

lav•a•to•ry \ˈla-və-ˌtōr-ē\ *n, pl* **-ries 1** : a fixed washbowl with running water and drainpipe **2** : BATHROOM

lave \ˈlāv\ *vb* **laved; lav•ing** : WASH

lav•en•der \ˈla-vən-dər\ *n* **1** : a Mediterranean mint or its dried leaves and flowers used to perfume clothing and bed linen **2** : a pale purple color

[1]**lav•ish** \ˈla-vish\ *adj* [ME *lavas* abundance, fr. MF *lavasse* downpour, fr. *laver* to wash] **1** : expending or bestowing profusely **2** : expended or produced in abundance **3** : marked by excess — **lav•ish•ly** *adv* — **lav•ish•ness** *n*

[2]**lavish** *vb* : to expend or give freely

law \ˈlȯ\ *n* **1** : a rule of conduct or action established by custom or laid down and enforced by a governing authority; *also* : the whole body of such rules **2** : the control brought about by enforcing rules **3** *cap* : the revelation of the divine will set forth in the Old Testament; *also* : the first part of the Jewish scriptures — see BIBLE table **4** : a rule or principle of construction or procedure **5** : the science that deals with laws and their interpretation and application **6** : the profession of a lawyer **7** : a rule or principle stating something that always works in the same way under the same conditions

law•break•er \ˈlȯ-ˌbrā-kər\ *n* : one who violates the law

law•ful \ˈlȯ-fəl\ *adj* **1** : permitted by law **2** : RIGHTFUL — **law•ful•ly** *adv*

law•giv•er \-ˌgi-vər\ *n* : LEGISLATOR

law•less \ˈlȯ-ləs\ *adj* **1** : having no laws **2** : UNRULY, DISORDERLY ⟨a ~ mob⟩ — **law•less•ly** *adv* — **law•less•ness** *n*

law•mak•er \-ˌmā-kər\ *n* : LEGISLATOR

law•man \ˈlȯ-mən\ *n* : a law enforcement official (as a sheriff or marshal)

[1]**lawn** \ˈlȯn\ *n* : ground (as around a house) covered with mowed grass

[2]**lawn** *n* : a fine sheer linen or cotton fabric

lawn bowling *n* : a bowling game played on a green with wooden balls which are rolled at a jack

law•ren•ci•um \lȯ-ˈren-sē-əm\ *n* : a short-lived radioactive element — see ELEMENT table

law•suit \ˈlȯ-ˌsüt\ *n* : a suit in law

law•yer \ˈlȯ-yər\ *n* : one who conducts lawsuits for clients or advises as to legal rights and obligations in other matters — **law•yer•ly** *adj*

lax \ˈlaks\ *adj* **1** : not strict ⟨~ discipline⟩ **2** : not tense or rigid **syn** remiss, negligent, neglectful, delinquent, derelict — **lax•i•ty** \ˈlak-sə-tē\ *n* — **lax•ly** *adv* — **lax•ness** *n*

[1]**lax•a•tive** \ˈlak-sə-tiv\ *adj* : relieving constipation

[2]**laxative** *n* : a usu. mild laxative drug

[1]**lay** \ˈlā\ *vb* **laid** \ˈlād\; **lay•ing 1** : to beat or strike down **2** : to put on or set down : PLACE **3** : to produce and deposit eggs **4** : SETTLE; *also* : ALLAY **5** : SPREAD **6** : PREPARE, CONTRIVE **7** : WAGER **8** : to impose esp. as a duty or burden **9** : to set in order or position **10** : to bring to a specified condition **11** : to put forward : SUBMIT

[2]**lay** *n* : the way in which something lies or is laid in relation to something else

[3]**lay** *past of* [1]LIE

[4]**lay** *n* **1** : a simple narrative poem **2** : SONG

[5]**lay** *adj* **1** : of or relating to the laity **2** : not of a particular profession; *also* : lacking extensive knowledge of a particular subject

lay•away \ˈlā-ə-ˌwā\ *n* : a purchasing agreement by

which a retailer agrees to hold merchandise secured by a deposit until the price is paid in full

lay•er \ˈlā-ər\ *n* **1 :** one that lays **2 :** one thickness, course, or fold laid or lying over or under another

lay•ette \lā-ˈet\ *n* [F, fr. MF, dim. of *laye* box] **:** an outfit of clothing and equipment for a newborn infant

lay•man \ˈlā-mən\ *n* **:** a person who is a member of the laity

lay•off \ˈlā-ˌȯf\ *n* **1 :** a period of inactivity **2 :** the act of dismissing an employee usu. temporarily

lay•out \ˈlā-ˌau̇t\ *n* **:** the final arrangement, plan, or design of something

lay•over \-ˌō-vər\ *n* **:** STOPOVER

lay•per•son \-ˌpər-sən\ *n* **:** a member of the laity

lay•wom•an \ˈlā-ˌwu̇-mən\ *n* **:** a woman who is a member of the laity

la•zar \ˈla-zər, ˈlā-\ *n* **:** LEPER

laze \ˈlāz\ *vb* **lazed; laz•ing :** to pass time in idleness or relaxation

la•zy \ˈlā-zē\ *adj* **la•zi•er; -est 1 :** disliking activity or exertion **2 :** encouraging idleness **3 :** SLUGGISH **4 :** DROOPY, LAX **5 :** not rigorous or strict — **la•zi•ly** \-zə-lē\ *adv* — **la•zi•ness** \-zē-nəs\ *n*

la•zy•bones \-ˌbōnz\ *n sing or pl* **:** a lazy person

lazy Su•san \ˌlā-zē-ˈsüz-ᵊn\ *n* **:** a revolving tray used for serving food

lb *abbr* [L *libra*] pound

lc *abbr* lowercase

LC *abbr* Library of Congress

1**LCD** \ˌel-(ˌ)sē-ˈdē\ *n* [*l*iquid *c*rystal *d*isplay] **:** a display (as of the time in a watch) that consists of segments of a liquid crystal whose reflectivity varies with the voltage applied to them

2**LCD** *abbr* least common denominator; lowest common denominator

LCDR *abbr* lieutenant commander

LCM *abbr* least common multiple; lowest common multiple

LCpl *abbr* lance corporal

LCS *abbr* League Championship Series

ld *abbr* **1** load **2** lord

LD *abbr* learning disabled; learning disability

LDC *abbr* less developed country

ldg *abbr* **1** landing **2** loading

LDL \ˌel-(ˌ)dē-ˈel\ *n* [*l*ow-*d*ensity *l*ipoprotein] **:** a cholesterol-rich protein-poor lipoprotein of blood plasma correlated with increased risk of atherosclerosis

L–do•pa \ˈel-ˈdō-pə\ *n* **:** an isomer of dopa used esp. in the treatment of Parkinson's disease

LDS *abbr* Latter-day Saints

lea \ˈlē, ˈlā\ *n* **:** PASTURE, MEADOW

leach \ˈlēch\ *vb* **:** to pass a liquid (as water) through to carry off the soluble components; *also* **:** to dissolve out by such means ⟨~ alkali from ashes⟩

1**lead** \ˈlēd\ *vb* **led** \ˈled\; **lead•ing 1 :** to guide on a way **2 :** LIVE ⟨~ a quiet life⟩ **3 :** to direct the operations, activity, or performance of ⟨~ an orchestra⟩ **4 :** to go at the head of **:** be first ⟨~ a parade⟩ **5 :** to begin play with; *also* **:** BEGIN, OPEN **6 :** to tend toward a definite result ⟨study *~ing* to a degree⟩ — **lead•er** *n* — **lead•er•less** *adj* — **lead•er•ship** *n*

2**lead** \ˈlēd\ *n* **1 :** a position at the front; *also* **:** a margin by which one leads **2 :** the privilege of leading in cards; *also* **:** the card or suit led **3 :** EXAMPLE **4 :** one that leads **5 :** a principal role (as in a play); *also* **:** one who plays such a role **6 :** INDICATION, CLUE **7 :** an insulated electrical conductor

3**lead** \ˈled\ *n* **1 :** a heavy malleable bluish white chemical element —see ELEMENT table **2 :** an article made of lead; *esp* **:** a weight for sounding at sea **3 :** a thin strip of metal used to separate lines of type in printing **4 :** a thin stick of marking substance in or for a pencil

4**lead** \ˈled\ *vb* **1 :** to cover, line, or weight with lead **2 :** to fix (glass) in position with lead **3 :** to treat or mix with lead or a lead compound

lead•en \ˈled-ᵊn\ *adj* **1 :** made of lead; *also* **:** of the color of lead **2 :** SLUGGISH, DULL

lead off *vb* **:** OPEN, BEGIN; *esp* **:** to bat first in an inning — **lead•off** \ˈlēd-ˌȯf\ *n or adj*

1**leaf** \ˈlēf\ *n, pl* **leaves** \ˈlēvz\ **1 :** a usu. flat and green outgrowth of a plant stem that is a unit of foliage and functions esp. in photosynthesis; *also* **:** FOLIAGE **2 :** something that is suggestive of a leaf — **leaf•less** *adj* — **leafy** *adj*

2**leaf** *vb* **1 :** to produce leaves **2 :** to turn the pages of a book

leaf•age \ˈlē-fij\ *n* **:** FOLIAGE

leafed \ˈlēft\ *adj* **:** LEAVED

leaf•hop•per \ˈlēf-ˌhä-pər\ *n* **:** any of a family of small leaping insects related to the cicadas that suck the juices of plants

leaf•let \ˈlē-flət\ *n* **1 :** a division of a compound leaf **2 :** PAMPHLET, FOLDER

leaf mold *n* **:** a compost or layer composed chiefly of decayed vegetable matter

leaf•stalk \ˈlēf-ˌstȯk\ *n* **:** PETIOLE

1**league** \ˈlēg\ *n* **:** a unit of distance equal to about three miles (five kilometers)

2**league** *n* **1 :** an association or alliance for a common purpose **2 :** CLASS, CATEGORY — **league** *vb* — **leagu•er** \ˈlē-gər\ *n*

1**leak** \ˈlēk\ *vb* **1 :** to enter or escape through a leak **2 :** to let a substance in or out through an opening **3 :** to become or make known

2**leak** *n* **1 :** a crack or hole that accidentally admits a fluid or light or lets it escape; *also* **:** something that secretly or accidentally permits the admission or escape of something else **2 :** LEAKAGE — **leaky** *adj*

leak•age \ˈlē-kij\ *n* **1 :** the act of leaking **2 :** the thing or amount that leaks

1**lean** \ˈlēn\ *vb* **1 :** to bend from a vertical position **:** INCLINE **2 :** to cast one's weight to one side for support **3 :** to rely on for support **4 :** to incline in opinion, taste, or desire — **lean** *n*

2**lean** *adj* **1 :** lacking or deficient in flesh and esp. in fat **2 :** lacking richness or productiveness **3 :** low in fuel content — **lean•ness** *n*

leant \ˈlent\ *chiefly Brit past of* LEAN

lean–to \ˈlēn-ˌtü\ *n, pl* **lean–tos** \-ˌtüz\ **:** a wing or extension of a building having a roof of only one slope; *also* **:** a rough shed or shelter with a similar roof

1**leap** \ˈlēp\ *vb* **leapt** \ˈlēpt, ˈlept\ *or* **leaped; leap•ing :** to spring free from a surface or over an obstacle **:** JUMP

2**leap** *n* **:** JUMP

leap•frog \ˈlēp-ˌfrȯg, -ˌfräg\ *n* **:** a game in which a player bends down and is vaulted over by another — **leapfrog** *vb*

leap year *n* **:** a year containing 366 days with February 29 as the extra day

learn \ˈlərn\ *vb* **learned** \ˈlərnd, ˈlərnt\; **learn•ing 1 :** to gain knowledge, understanding, or skill by study or experience; *also* **:** MEMORIZE **2 :** to find out **:** ASCERTAIN — **learn•er** *n*

learn•ed \ˈlər-nəd\ *adj* **:** SCHOLARLY, ERUDITE — **learn•ed•ly** *adv* — **learn•ed•ness** *n*

learn•ing \ˈlər-niŋ\ *n* **:** KNOWLEDGE, ERUDITION

learning disabled *adj* **:** having difficulty in learning a basic scholastic skill because of a disorder (as dyslexia) that interferes with the learning process — **learning disability** *n*

learnt \ˈlərnt\ *chiefly Brit past and past part of* LEARN

1**lease** \ˈlēs\ *n* **:** a contract transferring real estate for a term of years or at will usu. for a specified rent

2**lease** *vb* **leased; leas•ing 1 :** to grant by lease **2 :** to hold under a lease **syn** let, charter, hire, rent

lease•hold \ˈlēs-ˌhōld\ *n* **1 :** a tenure by lease **2 :** land held by lease — **lease•hold•er** *n*

leash \ˈlēsh\ *n* [ME *lees, leshe,* fr. OF *laisse,* fr. *laissier* to let go, fr. L *laxare* to loosen, fr. *laxus* slack]

: a line for leading or restraining an animal — **leash** *vb*

[1]**least** \ˈlēst\ *adj* **1** : lowest in importance or position **2** : smallest in size or degree **3** : SLIGHTEST

[2]**least** *n* : one that is least

[3]**least** *adv* : in the smallest or lowest degree

least common denominator *n* : the least common multiple of two or more denominators

least common multiple *n* : the smallest common multiple of two or more numbers

least•wise \ˈlēst-ˌwīz\ *adv* : at least

leath•er \ˈle-t͟hər\ *n* : animal skin dressed for use — **leath•ern** \-t͟hərn\ *adj* — **leath•ery** *adj*

leath•er•neck \-ˌnek\ *n* : MARINE

[1]**leave** \ˈlēv\ *vb* **left** \ˈleft\; **leav•ing 1** : to allow or cause to remain behind **2** : to have as a remainder **3** : BEQUEATH **4** : to let stay without interference **5** : to go away : depart from **6** : GIVE UP, ABANDON

[2]**leave** *n* **1** : PERMISSION; *also* : authorized absence from duty **2** : DEPARTURE

[3]**leave** *vb* **leaved; leav•ing** : LEAF

leaved \ˈlēvd\ *adj* : having leaves

[1]**leav•en** \ˈle-vən\ *n* **1** : a substance (as yeast) used to produce fermentation (as in dough) **2** : something that modifies or lightens

[2]**leaven** *vb* : to raise (dough) with a leaven; *also* : to permeate with a modifying or vivifying element

leav•en•ing *n* : LEAVEN

leaves *pl of* LEAF

leave–tak•ing \ˈlēv-ˌtā-kiŋ\ *n* : DEPARTURE, FAREWELL

leav•ings \ˈlē-viŋz\ *n pl* : REMNANT, RESIDUE

Leb•a•nese \ˌle-bə-ˈnēz, -ˈnēs\ *n* : a native or inhabitant of Lebanon — **Lebanese** *adj*

lech•ery \ˈle-chə-rē\ *n* : inordinate indulgence in sexual activity — **lech•er** \ˈle-chər\ *n* — **lech•er•ous** \ˈle-chə-rəs\ *adj* — **lech•er•ous•ly** *adv* — **lech•er•ous•ness** *n*

lec•i•thin \ˈle-sə-thən\ *n* : any of several waxy phosphorus-containing substances that are common in animals and plants, form colloidal solutions in water, and have emulsifying and wetting properties

lect *abbr* lecture; lecturer

lec•tern \ˈlek-tərn\ *n* : a stand to support a book for a standing reader

lec•tor \-tər\ *n* : one whose chief duty is to read the lessons in a church service

lec•ture \ˈlek-chər\ *n* **1** : a discourse given before an audience esp. for instruction **2** : REPRIMAND — **lecture** *vb* — **lec•tur•er** *n* — **lec•ture•ship** *n*

led *past and past part of* LEAD

LED \ˌel-(ˌ)ē-ˈdē\ *n* [*l*ight-*e*mitting *d*iode] : a semiconductor diode that emits light when a voltage is applied to it and is used esp. for electronic displays

le•der•ho•sen \ˈlā-dər-ˌhōz-ᵊn\ *n pl* : leather shorts often with suspenders worn esp. in Bavaria

ledge \ˈlej\ *n* [ME *legge* bar of a gate] **1** : a shelflike projection from a top or an edge **2** : REEF

led•ger \ˈle-jər\ *n* : a book containing accounts to which debits and credits are transferred in final form

lee \ˈlē\ *n* **1** : a protecting shelter **2** : the side (as of a ship) that is sheltered from the wind — **lee** *adj*

leech \ˈlēch\ *n* **1** : any of various segmented usu. freshwater worms that are related to the earthworms and have a sucker at each end **2** : a hanger-on who seeks gain

leek \ˈlēk\ *n* : an onionlike herb grown for its mildly pungent leaves and stalk

leer \ˈlir\ *n* : a suggestive, knowing, or malicious look — **leer** *vb*

leery \ˈlir-ē\ *adj* : SUSPICIOUS, WARY

lees \ˈlēz\ *n pl* : DREGS

[1]**lee•ward** \ˈlē-wərd, ˈlü-ərd\ *n* : the lee side

[2]**leeward** *adj* : situated away from the wind

lee•way \ˈlē-ˌwā\ *n* **1** : lateral movement of a ship when under way **2** : an allowable margin of freedom or variation

[1]**left** \ˈleft\ *adj* [ME, fr. OE, weak; fr. the left hand's being the weaker in most individuals] **1** : of, relating to, or being the side of the body in which the heart is mostly located; *also* : located nearer to this side than to the right **2** *often cap* : of, adhering to, or constituted by the political Left — **left** *adv*

[2]**left** *n* **1** : the left hand; *also* : the side or part that is on or toward the left side **2** *cap* : those professing political views marked by desire to reform the established order and usu. to give greater freedom to the common man

[3]**left** *past and past part of* LEAVE

left–hand *adj* **1** : situated on the left **2** : LEFT-HANDED

left–hand•ed \ˈleft-ˈhan-dəd\ *adj* **1** : using the left hand habitually or more easily than the right **2** : designed for or done with the left hand **3** : INSINCERE, BACK-HANDED ⟨a ~ compliment⟩ **4** : COUNTERCLOCKWISE — **left–handed** *adv*

left•ism \ˈlef-ˌti-zəm\ *n* **1** : the principles and views of the Left **2** : advocacy of the doctrines of the Left — **left•ist** \-tist\ *n or adj*

left•over \ˈleft-ˌō-vər\ *n* : something that remains unused or unconsumed

[1]**leg** \ˈleg\ *n* **1** : a limb of an animal used esp. for supporting the body and in walking; *also* : the part of the vertebrate leg between knee and foot **2** : something resembling or analogous to an animal leg ⟨table ~⟩ **3** : the part of an article of clothing that covers the leg **4** : a portion of a trip — **leg•ged** \ˈle-gəd\ *adj* — **leg•less** *adj*

[2]**leg** *vb* **legged; leg•ging** : to use the legs in walking or esp. in running

[3]**leg** *abbr* **1** legal **2** legislative; legislature

leg•a•cy \ˈle-gə-sē\ *n, pl* **-cies** : INHERITANCE; *also* : something that has come from a predecessor or the past

le•gal \ˈlē-gəl\ *adj* **1** : of or relating to law or lawyers **2** : LAWFUL; *also* : STATUTORY **3** : enforced in courts of law — **le•gal•i•ty** \li-ˈga-lə-tē\ *n* — **le•gal•ize** \ˈlē-gə-ˌlīz\ *vb* — **le•gal•ly** *adv*

le•gal•ism \ˈlē-gə-ˌli-zəm\ *n* **1** : strict, literal, or excessive conformity to the law or to a religious or moral code **2** : a legal term — **le•gal•is•tic** \ˌlē-gə-ˈlis-tik\ *adj*

leg•ate \ˈle-gət\ *n* : an official representative

leg•a•tee \ˌle-gə-ˈtē\ *n* : a person to whom a legacy is bequeathed

le•ga•tion \li-ˈgā-shən\ *n* **1** : a diplomatic mission headed by a minister **2** : the official residence and office of a minister in a foreign country

le•ga•to \li-ˈgä-tō\ *adv or adj* [It, lit., tied] : in a smooth and connected manner (as of music)

leg•end \ˈle-jənd\ *n* [ME *legende*, fr. MF & ML; MF *legende*, fr. ML *legenda*, fr. L *legere* to read] **1** : a story coming down from the past; *esp* : one popularly accepted as historical though not verifiable **2** : an inscription on an object; *also* : CAPTION **3** : an explanatory list of the symbols on a map or chart

leg•end•ary \ˈle-jən-ˌder-ē\ *adj* **1** : of, relating to, or characteristic of a legend **2** : FAMOUS — **leg•en•dari•ly** \-ˌder-ə-lē\ *adv*

leg•er•de•main \ˌle-jər-də-ˈmān\ *n* [ME, fr. MF *leger de main* light of hand] : SLEIGHT OF HAND

leg•ging *or* **leg•gin** \ˈle-gən, -giŋ\ *n* : a covering for the leg; *also* : TIGHTS

leg•gy \ˈle-gē\ *adj* **leg•gi•er; -est 1** : having unusually long legs **2** : having long and attractive legs **3** : SPINDLY — used of a plant

leg•horn \ˈleg-ˌhȯrn, ˈle-gərn\ *n* **1** : a fine plaited straw; *also* : a hat made of this straw **2** : any of a Mediterranean breed of small hardy fowls

leg•i•ble \ˈle-jə-bəl\ *adj* : capable of being read : CLEAR — **leg•i•bil•i•ty** \ˌle-jə-ˈbi-lə-tē\ *n* — **leg•i•bly** \ˈle-jə-blē\ *adv*

[1]**le•gion** \ˈlē-jən\ *n* **1** : a unit of the Roman army comprising 3000 to 6000 soldiers **2** : MULTITUDE **3** : an as-

sociation of ex-servicemen — **le•gion•ary** \-jə-ˌner-ē\ *n* — **le•gion•naire** \ˌlē-jə-ˈnar\ *n*

[2]**legion** *adj* : MANY, NUMEROUS

legis *abbr* legislation; legislative; legislature

leg•is•late \ˈle-jəs-ˌlāt\ *vb* **-lat•ed; -lat•ing** : to make or enact laws; *also* : to bring about by legislation — **leg•is•la•tor** \-ˌlā-tər\ *n*

leg•is•la•tion \ˌle-jəs-ˈlā-shən\ *n* **1** : the action of legislating **2** : laws made by a legislative body

leg•is•la•tive \ˈle-jəs-ˌlā-tiv\ *adj* **1** : having the power of legislating **2** : of or relating to a legislature or legislation

leg•is•la•ture \ˈle-jəs-ˌlā-chər\ *n* : an organized body of persons having the authority to make laws

le•git \li-ˈjit\ *adj, slang* : LEGITIMATE

[1]**le•git•i•mate** \li-ˈji-tə-mət\ *adj* **1** : lawfully begotten **2** : GENUINE **3** : LAWFUL **4** : conforming to recognized principles or accepted rules or standards — **le•git•i•ma•cy** \-mə-sē\ *n* — **le•git•i•mate•ly** *adv*

[2]**le•git•i•mate** \-ˌmāt\ *vb* : to make legitimate

le•git•i•mise *Brit var of* LEGITIMIZE

le•git•i•mize \li-ˈji-tə-ˌmīz\ *vb* **-mized; -miz•ing** : LEGITIMATE

leg•man \ˈleg-ˌman\ *n* **1** : a reporter assigned usu. to gather information **2** : an assistant who gathers information and runs errands

le•gume \ˈle-ˌgyüm, li-ˈgyüm\ *n* [F] **1** : any of a large family of plants having fruits that are dry pods and split when ripe and including important food and forage plants (as beans and clover); *also* : the part (as seeds or pods) of a legume used as food **2** : the pod of a legume — **le•gu•mi•nous** \li-ˈgyü-mə-nəs\ *adj*

[1]**lei** \ˈlā, ˈlā-ˌē\ *n* : a wreath or necklace usu. of flowers

[2]**lei** \ˈlā\ *pl of* LEU

lei•sure \ˈlē-zhər, ˈle-, ˈlā-\ *n* **1** : time free from work or duties **2** : EASE; *also* : CONVENIENCE **syn** relaxation, rest, repose — **lei•sure•ly** *adj or adv*

leit•mo•tiv *or* **leit•mo•tif** \ˈlīt-mō-ˌtēf\ *n* [G *Leitmotiv*, fr. *leiten* to lead + *Motiv* motive] : a dominant recurring theme

lek \ˈlek\ *n, pl* **leks** *or* **le•ke** *also* **lek** *or* **le•ku** — see MONEY table

lem•ming \ˈle-miŋ\ *n* [Norw] : any of various short-tailed northern rodents; *esp* : one of Europe noted for recurrent mass migrations

lem•on \ˈle-mən\ *n* **1** : an acid yellow usu. nearly oblong citrus fruit; *also* : a citrus tree that bears lemons **2** : something (as an automobile) unsatisfactory or defective — **lem•ony** *adj*

lem•on•ade \ˌle-mə-ˈnād\ *n* : a beverage of lemon juice, sugar, and water

lem•pi•ra \lem-ˈpir-ə\ *n* — see MONEY table

le•mur \ˈlē-mər\ *n* : any of various arboreal mammals largely of Madagascar that are related to the monkeys and have large eyes, very soft woolly fur, and a long furry tail

lemur

lend \ˈlend\ *vb* **lent** \ˈlent\; **lend•ing** **1** : to give for temporary use on condition that the same or its equivalent be returned **2** : AFFORD, FURNISH **3** : ACCOMMODATE — **lend•er** *n*

lend–lease \-ˈlēs\ *n* : the transfer of goods and services to an ally to aid in a common cause with payment made by a return of the items or their use in the cause or by a similar transfer of other goods and services

length \ˈleŋth\ *n* **1** : the longer or longest dimension of an object; *also* : a measured distance **2** : duration or extent in time or space **3** : the length of something taken as a unit of measure **4** : a single piece of a series of pieces that may be joined together ⟨a ~ of pipe⟩ — **at length 1** : in full **2** : FINALLY

length•en \ˈleŋ-thən\ *vb* : to make or become longer **syn** extend, elongate, prolong, protract

length•wise \ˈleŋth-ˌwīz\ *adv* : in the direction of the length — **lengthwise** *adj*

lengthy \ˈleŋ-thē\ *adj* **length•i•er; -est 1** : protracted excessively **2** : EXTENDED, LONG

le•nient \ˈlē-nē-ənt, -nyənt\ *adj* : of mild and tolerant disposition or effect **syn** indulgent, forbearing, merciful, tolerant — **le•ni•en•cy** \ˈlē-nē-ən-sē, -nyən-sē\ *n* — **le•ni•ent•ly** *adv*

len•i•tive \ˈle-nə-tiv\ *adj* : alleviating pain or harshness

len•i•ty \ˈle-nə-tē\ *n* : LENIENCY

lens \ˈlenz\ *n* [L *lent-, lens* lentil; so called fr. the shape of a convex lens] **1** : a curved piece of glass or plastic used singly or combined in an optical instrument for forming an image; *also* : a device for focusing radiation other than light **2** : a transparent body in the eye that focuses light rays on receptors at the back of the eye

Lent \ˈlent\ *n* : a 40-day period of penitence and fasting observed from Ash Wednesday to Easter by many churches — **Lent•en** \-ᵊn\ *adj*

len•til \ˈlent-ᵊl\ *n* : a Eurasian annual legume grown for its flat edible seeds and for fodder; *also* : its seed

Leo \ˈlē-ō\ *n* [L, lit., lion] **1** : a zodiacal constellation between Cancer and Virgo usu. pictured as a lion **2** : the 5th sign of the zodiac in astrology; *also* : one born under this sign

le•one \lē-ˈōn\ *n, pl* **leones** *or* **leone** — see MONEY table

le•o•nine \ˈlē-ə-ˌnīn\ *adj* : of, relating to, or resembling a lion

leop•ard \ˈle-pərd\ *n* : a large usu. tawny and black-spotted cat of southern Asia and Africa

le•o•tard \ˈlē-ə-ˌtärd\ *n* : a close-fitting garment worn esp. by dancers and for exercise

lep•er \ˈle-pər\ *n* **1** : a person affected with leprosy **2** : OUTCAST

lep•re•chaun \ˈle-prə-ˌkän\ *n* : a mischievous elf of Irish folklore

lep•ro•sy \ˈle-prə-sē\ *n* : a chronic bacterial disease marked esp. if not treated by slow-growing swellings with deformity and loss of sensation of affected parts — **lep•rous** \-prəs\ *adj*

lep•ton \lep-ˈtän\ *n, pl* **lep•ta** \-ˈtä\ — see *drachma* at MONEY table

les•bi•an \ˈlez-bē-ən\ *n, often cap* [fr. the reputed homosexual group associated with the poet Sappho of Lesbos] : a female homosexual — **lesbian** *adj, often cap* — **les•bi•an•ism** \-ə-ˌni-zəm\ *n*

lèse ma•jes•té *or* **lese maj•es•ty** \ˈlāz-ˈma-jə-stē, ˈlez-, ˈlēz-\ *n* [MF *lese majesté*, fr. L *laesa majestas*, lit., injured majesty] : an offense violating the dignity of a sovereign

le•sion \ˈlē-zhən\ *n* : an abnormal structural change in the body due to injury or disease; *esp* : one clearly marked off from healthy tissue around it

[1]**less** \ˈles\ *adj, comparative of* [1]LITTLE **1** : FEWER ⟨~ than six⟩ **2** : of lower rank, degree, or importance **3** : SMALLER; *also* : more limited in quantity

[2]**less** *adv, comparative of* [2]LITTLE : to a lesser extent or degree
[3]**less** *n, pl* **less 1** : a smaller portion **2** : something of less importance
[4]**less** *prep* : diminished by : MINUS
-less \ləs\ *adj suffix* **1** : destitute of : not having ⟨child*less*⟩ **2** : unable to be acted on or to act (in a specified way) ⟨daunt*less*⟩
les•see \le-ˈsē\ *n* : a tenant under a lease
less•en \ˈles-ᵊn\ *vb* : to make or become less **syn** decrease, diminish, dwindle, abate
less•er \ˈle-sər\ *adj, comparative of* [1]LITTLE : of less size, quality, or significance
les•son \ˈles-ᵊn\ *n* **1** : a passage from sacred writings read in a service of worship **2** : a reading or exercise to be studied by a pupil; *also* : something learned **3** : a period of instruction **4** : an instructive example
les•sor \ˈle-ˌsȯr, le-ˈsȯr\ *n* : one who conveys property by a lease
lest \ˌlest\ *conj* : for fear that
[1]**let** \ˈlet\ *n* [ME *lette,* fr. *letten* to delay, hinder, fr. OE *lettan*] **1** : HINDRANCE, OBSTACLE **2** : a shot or point in racket games that does not count
[2]**let** *vb* **let; let•ting** [ME *leten,* fr. OE *lǣtan*] **1** : to cause to : MAKE ⟨~ it be known⟩ **2** : RENT, LEASE; *also* : to assign esp. after bids **3** : ALLOW, PERMIT ⟨~ me go⟩
-let \lət\ *n suffix* **1** : small one ⟨book*let*⟩ **2** : article worn on ⟨wrist*let*⟩
let•down \ˈlet-ˌdau̇n\ *n* **1** : DISAPPOINTMENT **2** : a slackening of effort
le•thal \ˈlē-thəl\ *adj* : DEADLY, FATAL — **le•thal•ly** *adv*
leth•ar•gy \ˈle-thər-jē\ *n* **1** : abnormal drowsiness **2** : the quality or state of being lazy or indifferent **syn** languor, lassitude, torpor — **le•thar•gic** \li-ˈthär-jik\ *adj*
let on *vb* **1** : REVEAL 1 **2** : PRETEND
[1]**let•ter** \ˈle-tər\ *n* **1** : a symbol that stands for a speech sound and constitutes a unit of an alphabet **2** : a written or printed communication **3** *pl* : LITERATURE; *also* : LEARNING **4** : the literal meaning ⟨the ~ of the law⟩ **5** : a single piece of type
[2]**letter** *vb* : to mark with letters : INSCRIBE — **let•ter•er** *n*
let•ter•boxed \ˈle-tər-ˌbäkst\ *adj* : being a video recording formatted so as to display the full frame of a wide-screen motion picture
let•ter•head \ˈle-tər-ˌhed\ *n* : stationery with a printed or engraved heading; *also* : the heading itself
let•ter–per•fect \ˌle-tər-ˈpər-fikt\ *adj* : correct to the smallest detail
let•ter•press \ˈle-tər-ˌpres\ *n* : printing done directly by impressing the paper on an inked raised surface
letters of marque \-ˈmärk\ : a license granted to a private person by a government to fit out an armed ship to capture enemy shipping
letters patent *n pl* : a written grant from a government to a person in a form readily open for inspection by all
let•tuce \ˈle-təs\ *n* [ME *letuse,* fr. MF *laitues,* pl. of *laitue,* fr. L *lactuca,* fr. *lac* milk; fr. its milky juice] : a garden composite plant with crisp leaves used esp. in salads
let•up \ˈlet-ˌəp\ *n* : a lessening of effort
leu \ˈleu̇\ *n, pl* **lei** \ˈlā\ — see MONEY table
leu•kae•mia *chiefly Brit var of* LEUKEMIA
leu•ke•mia \lü-ˈkē-mē-ə\ *n* : a disease in which white blood cells increase greatly — **leu•ke•mic** \-mik\ *adj or n*
leu•ko•cyte \ˈlü-kə-ˌsīt\ *n* : any of the white or colorless cells with a nucleus found in bodily tissues and esp. blood
lev \ˈlef\ *n, pl* **le•va** \ˈle-və\ — see MONEY table
Lev *or* **Levit** *abbr* Leviticus
[1]**le•vee** \ˈle-vē; lə-ˈvē, -ˈvā\ *n* [F *lever* act of arising] : a reception held by or for a person of distinction
[2]**lev•ee** \ˈle-vē\ *n* : an embankment to prevent or confine flooding; *also* : a river landing place
[1]**lev•el** \ˈle-vəl\ *n* **1** : a device for establishing a horizontal line or plane **2** : horizontal condition **3** : a horizontal position, line, or surface often taken as an index of altitude; *also* : a flat area of ground **4** : height, position, rank, or size in a scale
[2]**level** *vb* **-eled** *or* **-elled; -el•ing** *or* **-el•ling 1** : to make flat or level; *also* : to come to a level **2** : AIM, DIRECT **3** : EQUALIZE **4** : RAZE — **lev•el•er** *n*
[3]**level** *adj* **1** : having a flat even surface **2** : HORIZONTAL **3** : of the same height or rank; *also* : UNIFORM **4** : steady and cool in judgment — **lev•el•ly** *adv* — **lev•el•ness** *n*
lev•el•head•ed \ˌle-vəl-ˈhe-dəd\ *adj* : having sound judgment : SENSIBLE
le•ver \ˈle-vər, ˈlē-\ *n* **1** : a bar used for prying or dislodging something; *also* : a means for achieving one's purpose **2** : a rigid piece turning about an axis and used for transmitting and changing force and motion
le•ver•age \ˈle-vrij, ˈlē-, -və-rij\ *n* : the action or mechanical effect of a lever
le•vi•a•than \li-ˈvī-ə-thən\ *n* **1** : a large sea animal **2** : something large or formidable
lev•i•tate \ˈle-və-ˌtāt\ *vb* **-tat•ed; -tat•ing** : to rise or cause to rise in the air in seeming defiance of gravitation — **lev•i•ta•tion** \ˌle-və-ˈtā-shən\ *n*
Le•vit•i•cus \li-ˈvi-tə-kəs\ *n* — see BIBLE table
lev•i•ty \ˈle-və-tē\ *n* : lack of seriousness **syn** lightness, flippancy, frivolity
[1]**levy** \ˈle-vē\ *n, pl* **lev•ies 1** : the imposition or collection of an assessment; *also* : an amount levied **2** : the enlistment or conscription of men for military service; *also* : troops raised by levy
[2]**levy** *vb* **lev•ied; levy•ing 1** : to impose or collect by legal authority **2** : to enlist for military service **3** : WAGE ⟨~ war⟩ **4** : to seize property
lewd \ˈlüd\ *adj* [ME *lewed* vulgar, fr. OE *lǣwede* lay, ignorant] **1** : sexually unchaste **2** : OBSCENE, VULGAR — **lewd•ly** *adv* — **lewd•ness** *n*
lex•i•cog•ra•phy \ˌlek-sə-ˈkä-grə-fē\ *n* **1** : the editing or making of a dictionary **2** : the principles and practices of dictionary making — **lex•i•cog•ra•pher** \-fər\ *n* — **lex•i•co•graph•i•cal** \-kō-ˈgra-fi-kəl\ *or* **lex•i•co•graph•ic** \-fik\ *adj*
lex•i•con \ˈlek-sə-ˌkän\ *n, pl* **lex•i•ca** \-si-kə\ *or* **lexicons 1** : DICTIONARY **2** : the vocabulary of a language, speaker, or subject
lg *abbr* **1** large **2** long
LH *abbr* **1** left hand **2** lower half
li *abbr* link
Li *symbol* lithium
LI *abbr* Long Island
li•a•bil•i•ty \ˌlī-ə-ˈbi-lə-tē\ *n, pl* **-ties 1** : the quality or state of being liable **2** *pl* : DEBTS **3** : DISADVANTAGE
li•a•ble \ˈlī-ə-bəl\ *adj* **1** : legally obligated : RESPONSIBLE **2** : LIKELY, APT ⟨~ to fall⟩ **3** : SUSCEPTIBLE
li•ai•son \ˈlē-ə-ˌzän, lē-ˈā-\ *n* [F] **1** : a close bond : INTERRELATIONSHIP **2** : an illicit sexual relationship **3** : communication for mutual understanding (as between parts of an armed force); *also* : one that carries on a liaison
li•ar \ˈlī-ər\ *n* : a person who lies
[1]**lib** \ˈlib\ *n* : LIBERATION
[2]**lib** *abbr* **1** liberal **2** librarian; library
li•ba•tion \lī-ˈbā-shən\ *n* **1** : an act of pouring a liquid as a sacrifice (as to a god); *also* : the liquid poured **2** : DRINK
[1]**li•bel** \ˈlī-bəl\ *n* [ME, written declaration, fr. MF, fr. L *libellus,* dim. of *liber* book] **1** : a spoken or written statement or a representation that gives an unjustly unfavorable impression of a person or thing **2** : the action or crime of publishing a libel — **li•bel•ous** *or* **li•bel•lous** \-bə-ləs\ *adj*
[2]**libel** *vb* **-beled** *or* **-belled; -bel•ing** *or* **-bel•ling** : to make or publish a libel — **li•bel•er** *n* — **li•bel•ist** *n*

[1]**lib•er•al** \ˈli-brəl, -bə-rəl\ *adj* [ME, fr. MF, fr. L *liberalis* suitable for a freeman, generous, fr. *liber* free] **1** : of, relating to, or based on the liberal arts **2** : GENEROUS, BOUNTIFUL **3** : not literal **4** : not narrow in opinion or judgment : TOLERANT; *also* : not orthodox **5** : not conservative — **lib•er•al•i•ty** \ˌli-bə-ˈra-lə-tē\ *n* — **lib•er•al•ize** \ˈli-brə-ˌlīz, -bə-rə-\ *vb* — **lib•er•al•ly** *adv*

[2]**liberal** *n* : a person who holds liberal views

liberal arts *n pl* : the studies (as language, philosophy, history, literature, or abstract science) in a college or university intended to provide chiefly general knowledge and to develop the general intellectual capacities

lib•er•al•ism \ˈli-brə-ˌli-zəm, -bə-rə-\ *n* : liberal principles and theories

lib•er•ate \ˈli-bə-ˌrāt\ *vb* **-at•ed; -at•ing 1** : to free from bondage or restraint; *also* : to raise to equal rights and status **2** : to free (as a gas) from combination — **lib•er•a•tion** \ˌli-bə-ˈrā-shən\ *n* — **lib•er•a•tor** \ˈli-bə-ˌrā-tər\ *n*

lib•er•at•ed *adj* : freed from or opposed to traditional social and sexual attitudes or roles ⟨a ∼ marriage⟩

Li•be•ri•an \lī-ˈbir-ē-ən\ *n* : a native or inhabitant of Liberia — **Liberian** *adj*

lib•er•tar•i•an \ˌli-bər-ˈter-ē-ən\ *n* **1** : an advocate of the doctrine of free will **2** : one who upholds the principles of unrestricted liberty

lib•er•tine \ˈli-bər-ˌtēn\ *n* : a person who leads a dissolute life

lib•er•ty \ˈli-bər-tē\ *n, pl* **-ties 1** : FREEDOM **2** : an action going beyond normal limits; *esp* : FAMILIARITY **3** : a short leave from naval duty

li•bid•i•nous \lə-ˈbid-ᵊn-əs\ *adj* **1** : LASCIVIOUS **2** : LIBIDINAL

li•bi•do \lə-ˈbē-dō, -ˈbī-\ *n, pl* **-dos** [NL, fr. L, desire, lust] **1** : psychic energy derived from basic biological urges **2** : sexual drive — **li•bid•i•nal** \lə-ˈbid-ᵊn-əl\ *adj*

Li•bra \ˈlē-brə\ *n* [L, lit., scales] **1** : a zodiacal constellation between Virgo and Scorpio usu. pictured as a balance scale **2** : the 7th sign of the zodiac in astrology; *also* : one born under this sign

li•brar•i•an \lī-ˈbrer-ē-ən\ *n* : a specialist in the management of a library

li•brary \ˈlī-ˌbrer-ē\ *n, pl* **-brar•ies 1** : a place in which books and related materials are kept for use but not for sale **2** : a collection of books

li•bret•to \lə-ˈbre-tō\ *n, pl* **-tos** *or* **-ti** \-tē\ [It, dim. of *libro* book, fr. L *liber*] : the text esp. of an opera — **li•bret•tist** \-tist\ *n*

Lib•y•an \ˈli-bē-ən\ *n* : a native or inhabitant of Libya — **Libyan** *adj*

lice *pl of* LOUSE

li•cense *or* **li•cence** \ˈlīs-ᵊns\ *n* **1** : permission to act **2** : a permission granted by authority to engage in an activity **3** : a document, plate, or tag providing proof of a license **4** : freedom used irresponsibly — **license** *vb*

licensed practical nurse *n* : a specially trained person who is licensed (as by a state) to provide routine care for the sick

licensed vocational nurse *n* : a licensed practical nurse licensed to practice in the states of California and Texas

li•cens•ee \ˌlīs-ᵊn-ˈsē\ *n* : a licensed person

licente *pl of* SENTE

li•cen•ti•ate \lī-ˈsen-chē-ət\ *n* : one licensed to practice a profession

li•cen•tious \lī-ˈsen-chəs\ *adj* : LEWD, LASCIVIOUS — **li•cen•tious•ly** *adv* — **li•cen•tious•ness** *n*

li•chee *var of* LITCHI

li•chen \ˈlī-kən\ *n* : any of various fungus complex lower plants made up of an alga and a fungus growing as a unit on a solid surface — **li•chen•ous** *adj*

lic•it \ˈli-sət\ *adj* : LAWFUL

[1]**lick** \ˈlik\ *vb* **1** : to draw the tongue over; *also* : to flicker over like a tongue **2** : THRASH; *also* : DEFEAT

[2]**lick** *n* **1** : a stroke of the tongue **2** : a small amount **3** : a hasty careless effort **4** : BLOW **5** : a natural deposit of salt that animals lick

lick•e•ty–split \ˌli-kə-tē-ˈsplit\ *adv* : at great speed

lick•spit•tle \ˈlik-ˌspit-ᵊl\ *n* : a fawning subordinate : TOADY

lic•o•rice \ˈli-kə-rish, -rəs\ *n* [ME *licorice,* fr. OF, fr. LL *liquiritia,* alter. of L *glycyrrhiza,* fr. Gk *glykyrrhiza,* fr. *glykys* sweet + *rhiza* root] **1** : the dried root of a European leguminous plant; *also* : an extract from it used esp. as a flavoring and in medicine **2** : a candy flavored with licorice **3** : a plant yielding licorice

lid \ˈlid\ *n* **1** : a movable cover **2** : EYELID **3** : something that confines or suppresses — **lid•ded** \ˈli-dəd\ *adj*

li•do \ˈlē-dō\ *n, pl* **lidos** : a fashionable beach resort

[1]**lie** \ˈlī\ *vb* **lay** \ˈlā\; **lain** \ˈlān\; **ly•ing** \ˈlī-iŋ\ **1** : to be in, stay at rest in, or assume a horizontal position; *also* : to be in a helpless or defenseless state **2** : EXTEND **3** : to occupy a certain relative position **4** : to have an effect esp. through mere presence

[2]**lie** *n* : the position in which something lies

[3]**lie** *vb* **lied; ly•ing** \ˈlī-iŋ\ : to tell a lie

[4]**lie** *n* : an untrue statement made with intent to deceive

lied \ˈlēt\ *n, pl* **lie•der** \ˈlē-dər\ [G] : a German song esp. of the 19th century

lie detector *n* : an instrument for detecting physiological evidence of the tension that accompanies lying

lief \ˈlēv, ˈlēf\ *adv* : GLADLY, WILLINGLY

[1]**liege** \ˈlēj\ *adj* : LOYAL, FAITHFUL

[2]**liege** *n* **1** : VASSAL **2** : a feudal superior

lien \ˈlēn, ˈlē-ən\ *n* : a legal claim on the property of another for the satisfaction of a debt or duty

lieu \ˈlü\ *n, archaic* : PLACE, STEAD — **in lieu of** : in the place of

lieut *abbr* lieutenant

lieu•ten•ant \lü-ˈte-nənt\ *n* [ME, fr. MF, fr. *lieu* place + *tenant* holding, fr. *tenir* to hold, fr. L *tenēre*] **1** : a representative of another in the performance of duty **2** : FIRST LIEUTENANT; *also* : SECOND LIEUTENANT **3** : a commissioned officer in the navy ranking next below a lieutenant commander — **lieu•ten•an•cy** \-nən-sē\ *n*

lieutenant colonel *n* : a commissioned officer (as in the army) ranking next below a colonel

lieutenant commander *n* : a commissioned officer in the navy ranking next below a commander

lieutenant general *n* : a commissioned officer (as in the army) ranking next below a general

lieutenant governor *n* : a deputy or subordinate governor

lieutenant junior grade *n, pl* **lieutenants junior grade** : a commissioned officer in the navy ranking next below a lieutenant

life \ˈlīf\ *n, pl* **lives** \ˈlīvz\ **1** : the quality that distinguishes a vital and functional being from a dead body or inanimate matter; *also* : a state of an organism characterized esp. by capacity for metabolism, growth, reaction to stimuli, and reproduction **2** : the physical and mental experiences of an individual **3** : BIOGRAPHY **4** : a specific phase or period ⟨adult ∼⟩ **5** : the period from birth to death; *also* : a sentence of imprisonment for the remainder of a person's life **6** : a way of living **7** : PERSON **8** : ANIMATION, SPIRIT; *also* : LIVELINESS **9** : living beings ⟨forest ∼⟩ **10** : animate activity ⟨signs of ∼⟩ **11** : one providing interest and vigor ⟨∼ of the party⟩ — **life•less** *adj* — **life•like** *adj*

life•blood \ˈlīf-ˌbləd\ *n* : a basic source of strength and vitality

life•boat \-ˌbōt\ *n* : a sturdy boat designed for use in saving lives at sea

life•guard \-ˌgärd\ *n* : a usu. expert swimmer employed to safeguard bathers

life•line \-ˌlīn\ *n* **1** : a line to which persons may cling

for safety **2 :** something considered vital for survival
life•long \-ˌlȯŋ\ *adj* **:** continuing through life
life preserver *n* **:** a buoyant device designed to save a person from drowning
lif•er \ˈlī-fər\ *n* **1 :** a person sentenced to life imprisonment **2 :** a person who makes a career in the armed forces
life raft *n* **:** a raft for use by people forced into the water
life•sav•ing \ˈlīf-ˌsā-viŋ\ *n* **:** the skill or practice of saving or protecting lives esp. of drowning persons — **life•sav•er** \-ˌsā-vər\ *n*
life science *n* **:** a branch of science (as biology, medicine, anthropology, or sociology) that deals with living organisms and life processes — usu. used in pl. — **life scientist** *n*
life•style \ˈlīf-stīl\ *n* **:** a way of living
life•time \-ˌtīm\ *n* **:** the duration of an individual's existence
life•work \-ˈwərk\ *n* **:** the entire or principal work of one's lifetime; *also* **:** a work extending over a lifetime
LIFO *abbr* last in, first out
[1]**lift** \ˈlift\ *vb* **1 :** RAISE, ELEVATE; *also* **:** RISE, ASCEND **2 :** to put an end to **:** STOP **3 :** to pay off ⟨~ a mortgage⟩ — **lift•er** *n*
[2]**lift** *n* **1 :** LOAD **2 :** the action or an instance of lifting **3 :** HELP; *also* **:** a ride along one's way **4 :** RISE, ADVANCE **5** *chiefly Brit* **:** ELEVATOR **6 :** an elevation of the spirits **7 :** the upward force that is developed by a moving airfoil and that opposes the pull of gravity
lift•off \ˈlif-ˌtȯf\ *n* **:** a vertical takeoff (as by a rocket)
lift truck *n* **:** a small truck for lifting and transporting loads
lig•a•ment \ˈli-gə-mənt\ *n* **:** a band of tough tissue that holds bones together or supports an organ in place
li•gate \ˈlī-ˌgāt\ *vb* **li•gat•ed; li•gat•ing :** to tie with a ligature — **li•ga•tion** \lī-ˈgā-shən\ *n*
lig•a•ture \ˈli-gə-ˌchu̇r, -chər\ *n* **1 :** something that binds or ties; *also* **:** a thread used in surgery esp. for tying blood vessels **2 :** a printed or written character consisting of two or more letters or characters (as æ) united
[1]**light** \ˈlīt\ *n* **1 :** something that makes vision possible **:** electromagnetic radiation visible to the human eye; *also* **:** the sensation aroused by stimulation of the visual sense organs **2 :** DAYLIGHT **3 :** a source of light (as a candle) **4 :** ENLIGHTENMENT; *also* **:** TRUTH **5 :** public knowledge ⟨facts brought to ~⟩ **6 :** a particular aspect presented to view ⟨saw the matter in a different ~⟩ **7 :** WINDOW **8** *pl* **:** STANDARDS ⟨according to his ~*s*⟩ **9 :** CELEBRITY **10 :** LIGHTHOUSE, BEACON; *also* **:** TRAFFIC LIGHT **11 :** a flame for lighting something
[2]**light** *adj* **1 :** having light **:** BRIGHT **2 :** PALE 2 ⟨~ blue⟩ — **light•ness** *n*
[3]**light** *vb* **lit** \ˈlit\ *or* **light•ed; light•ing 1 :** to make or become light **2 :** to cause to burn **:** BURN **3 :** to conduct with a light **4 :** ILLUMINATE
[4]**light** *adj* **1 :** not heavy **2 :** not serious ⟨~ reading⟩ **3 :** SCANTY ⟨~ rain⟩ **4 :** easily disturbed ⟨a ~ sleeper⟩ **5 :** GENTLE ⟨a ~ blow⟩ **6 :** easily endurable ⟨a ~ cold⟩; *also* **:** requiring little effort ⟨~ exercise⟩ **7 :** SWIFT, NIMBLE **8 :** FRIVOLOUS **9 :** DIZZY **10 :** made with lower calorie content or less of some ingredient than usual ⟨~ salad dressing⟩ **11 :** producing goods for direct consumption by the consumer ⟨~ industry⟩ — **lightly** *adv* — **light•ness** *n*
[5]**light** *adv* **1 :** LIGHTLY **2 :** with little baggage ⟨travel ~⟩
[6]**light** *vb* **lit** \ˈlit\ *or* **light•ed; light•ing 1 :** SETTLE, ALIGHT **2 :** to fall unexpectedly **3 :** HAPPEN
light–emitting diode *n* **:** LED
[1]**light•en** \ˈlīt-ᵊn\ *vb* **1 :** ILLUMINATE, BRIGHTEN **2 :** to give out flashes of lightning
[2]**lighten** *vb* **1 :** to relieve of a burden **2 :** GLADDEN **3 :** to become lighter
lighten up *vb* **:** to take things less seriously
[1]**ligh•ter** \ˈlī-tər\ *n* **:** a barge used esp. in loading or unloading ships
[2]**light•er** \ˈlī-tər\ *n* **:** one that lights; *esp* **:** a device for lighting
light•face \ˈlīt-ˌfās\ *n* **:** a type having light thin lines — **light•faced** \-ˌfāst\ *adj*
light–head•ed \ˈlīt-ˌhe-dəd\ *adj* **1 :** feeling confused or dizzy **2 :** lacking maturity or seriousness
light•heart•ed \-ˌhär-təd\ *adj* **:** free from worry — **light•heart•ed•ly** *adv* — **light•heart•ed•ness** *n*
light•house \-ˌhau̇s\ *n* **:** a structure with a powerful light for guiding sailors
light meter *n* **:** a usu. hand-held device for indicating correct photographic exposure
[1]**light•ning** \ˈlīt-niŋ\ *n* **:** the flashing of light produced by a discharge of atmospheric electricity; *also* **:** the discharge itself
[2]**lightning** *adj* **:** extremely fast
lightning bug *n* **:** FIREFLY
lightning rod *n* **:** a grounded metallic rod set up on a structure to protect it from lightning
light out *vb* **:** to leave in a hurry
light•proof \ˈlīt-ˌprüf\ *adj* **:** impenetrable by light
lights \ˈlīts\ *n pl* **:** the lungs esp. of a slaughtered animal
light•ship \ˈlīt-ˌship\ *n* **:** a ship with a powerful light moored at a place dangerous to navigation
light show *n* **:** a kaleidoscopic display (as of colored lights)
light•some \ˈlīt-səm\ *adj* **1 :** free from care **2 :** NIMBLE
[1]**light•weight** \ˈlīt-ˌwāt\ *n* **:** one of less than average weight; *esp* **:** a boxer weighing more than 126 but not over 135 pounds
[2]**lightweight** *adj* **1 :** INCONSEQUENTIAL **2 :** of less than average weight
light–year \ˈlīt-ˌyir\ *n* **1 :** an astronomical unit of distance equal to the distance that light travels in one year in a vacuum or about 5.88 trillion miles (9.46 trillion kilometers) **2 :** an extremely large measure of comparison ⟨saw it ~*s* ago⟩
lig•nin \ˈlig-nən\ *n* **:** a substance related to cellulose that occurs in the woody cell walls of plants and in the cementing material between them
lig•nite \ˈlig-ˌnīt\ *n* **:** brownish black soft coal
[1]**like** \ˈlīk\ *vb* **liked; lik•ing 1 :** ENJOY ⟨~*s* baseball⟩ **2 :** WANT **3 :** CHOOSE ⟨does as she ~*s*⟩ — **lik•able** *or* **like•able** \ˈlī-kə-bəl\ *adj*
[2]**like** *n* **:** PREFERENCE
[3]**like** *adj* **:** SIMILAR **syn** alike, analogous, comparable, parallel, uniform
[4]**like** *prep* **1 :** similar or similarly to ⟨it's ~ when we were kids⟩ **2 :** typical of **3 :** comparable to **4 :** as though there would be ⟨looks ~ rain⟩ **5 :** such as ⟨a subject ~ physics⟩
[5]**like** *n* **1 :** COUNTERPART **2 :** one that is similar to another — **and the like :** ET CETERA
[6]**like** *conj* **:** in the same way that
-like \ˌlīk\ *adj comb form* **:** resembling or characteristic of ⟨lady*like*⟩ ⟨life*like*⟩
like•li•hood \ˈlī-klē-ˌhu̇d\ *n* **:** PROBABILITY
[1]**like•ly** \ˈlī-klē\ *adj* **like•li•er; -est 1 :** very probable **2 :** BELIEVABLE **3 :** PROMISING ⟨a ~ place to fish⟩
[2]**likely** *adv* **:** in all probability
lik•en \ˈlī-kən\ *vb* **:** COMPARE
like•ness \ˈlīk-nəs\ *n* **1 :** COPY, PORTRAIT **2 :** SEMBLANCE **3 :** RESEMBLANCE
like•wise \-ˌwīz\ *adv* **1 :** in like manner **2 :** in addition **:** ALSO
lik•ing \ˈlī-kiŋ\ *n* **:** favorable regard; *also* **:** TASTE
li•ku•ta \li-ˈkü-tə\ *n, pl* **ma•ku•ta** \mä-\ — see *zaire* at MONEY table
li•lac \ˈlī-lək, -ˌlak, -ˌläk\ *n* [obs. F (now *lilas*), fr. Ar *līlak*, fr. Per *nīlak* bluish, fr. *nīl* blue, fr. Skt *nīla* dark blue] **1 :** a shrub related to the olive that produces large clusters of fragrant grayish pink, purple, or white flowers **2 :** a moderate purple color

lil•an•ge•ni \ˌli-lən-ˈge-nē\ *n, pl* **em•a•lan•ge•ni** \ˌe-mə-lən-ˈge-nē\ — see MONEY table

lil•li•pu•tian \ˌli-lə-ˈpyü-shən\ *adj, often cap* **1 :** SMALL, MINIATURE **2 :** PETTY

lilt \ˈlilt\ *n* **1 :** a cheerful lively song or tune **2 :** a rhythmical swing or flow

lily \ˈli-lē\ *n, pl* **lil•ies :** any of a genus of tall bulbous herbs with leafy stems and usu. funnel-shaped flowers; *also* **:** any of various related plants

lily of the valley : a low perennial herb related to the lilies that produces a raceme of fragrant nodding bell-shaped white flowers

li•ma bean \ˈlī-mə-\ *n* **:** a bushy or tall-growing bean widely cultivated for its flat edible usu. pale green or whitish seeds; *also* **:** the seed

limb \ˈlim\ *n* **1 :** one of the projecting paired appendages (as legs, arms, or wings) used by an animal esp. in moving or grasping **2 :** a large branch of a tree **:** BOUGH — **limb•less** *adj*

¹lim•ber \ˈlim-bər\ *adj* **1 :** FLEXIBLE, SUPPLE **2 :** LITHE, NIMBLE

²limber *vb* **:** to make or become limber

¹lim•bo \ˈlim-bō\ *n, pl* **limbos** [ME, fr. ML, abl. of *limbus* limbo, fr. L, border] **1** *often cap* **:** an abode of souls barred from heaven through no fault of their own **2 :** a place or state of confinement, oblivion, or uncertainty

²limbo *n, pl* **limbos :** a West Indian acrobatic dance orig. for men

Lim•burg•er \ˈlim-ˌbər-gər\ *n* **:** a pungent semisoft surface-ripened cheese

¹lime \ˈlīm\ *n* **:** a caustic powdery white solid that consists of calcium and oxygen, is obtained from limestone or shells, and is used in making cement and in fertilizer — **lime** *vb* — **limy** \ˈlī-mē\ *adj*

²lime *n* **:** a small yellowish green citrus fruit with juicy acid pulp

lime•ade \ˌlīm-ˈād, ˈlī-ˌmād\ *n* **:** a beverage of lime juice, sugar, and water

lime•light \ˈlīm-ˌlīt\ *n* **1 :** a device in which flame is directed against a cylinder of lime formerly used in the theater to cast a strong white light on the stage **2 :** the center of public attention

lim•er•ick \ˈli-mə-rik\ *n* **:** a light or humorous poem of 5 lines

lime•stone \ˈlīm-ˌstōn\ *n* **:** a rock that is formed by accumulation of organic remains (as shells), is used in building, and yields lime when burned

¹lim•it \ˈli-mət\ *n* **1 :** something that restrains or confines; *also* **:** the utmost extent **2 :** BOUNDARY; *also, pl* **:** BOUNDS **3 :** a prescribed maximum or minimum — **lim•it•less** *adj* — **lim•it•less•ness** *n*

²limit *vb* **1 :** to set limits to **2 :** to reduce in quantity or extent — **lim•i•ta•tion** \ˌli-mə-ˈtā-shən\ *n*

lim•it•ed *adj* **1 :** confined within limits **2 :** offering faster service esp. by making fewer stops

limn \ˈlim\ *vb* **limned; limn•ing** \ˈli-miŋ, ˈlim-niŋ\ **1 :** DRAW; *also* **:** PAINT **2 :** DELINEATE **3 :** DESCRIBE

limo \ˈli-(ˌ)mō\ *n, pl* **limos :** LIMOUSINE

li•mo•nite \ˈlī-mə-ˌnīt\ *n* **:** a ferric oxide that is a major ore of iron — **li•mo•nit•ic** \ˌlī-mə-ˈni-tik\ *adj*

lim•ou•sine \ˈli-mə-ˌzēn, ˌli-mə-ˈzēn\ *n* [F] **1 :** a large luxurious often chauffeur-driven sedan **2 :** a large vehicle for transporting passengers to and from an airport

¹limp \ˈlimp\ *vb* **:** to walk lamely; *also* **:** to proceed with difficulty

²limp *n* **:** a limping movement or gait

³limp *adj* **1 :** having no defined shape; *also* **:** not stiff or rigid **2 :** lacking in strength or firmness — **limp•ly** *adv* — **limp•ness** *n*

lim•pet \ˈlim-pət\ *n* **:** any of numerous gastropod sea mollusks with a conical shell that clings to rocks or timbers

lim•pid \ˈlim-pəd\ *adj* **:** CLEAR, TRANSPARENT

lin *abbr* **1** lineal **2** linear

lin•age \ˈlī-nij\ *n* **:** the number of lines of written or printed matter

linch•pin \ˈlinch-ˌpin\ *n* **:** a locking pin inserted crosswise (as through the end of an axle)

lin•den \ˈlin-dən\ *n* **:** any of a genus of trees with large heart-shaped leaves and clustered yellowish flowers rich in nectar

¹line \ˈlīn\ *n* **1 :** CORD, ROPE, WIRE; *also* **:** a length of material used in measuring and leveling **2 :** pipes for conveying a fluid ⟨a gas ∼⟩ **3 :** a horizontal row of written or printed characters; *also* **:** VERSE **4 :** NOTE **5 :** the words making up a part in a drama — usu. used in pl. **6 :** something distinct, long, and narrow; *also* **:** ROUTE **7 :** a state of agreement **8 :** a course of conduct, action, or thought; *also* **:** OCCUPATION **9 :** LIMIT **10 :** an arrangement of persons or objects of one kind in an orderly series ⟨waiting in ∼⟩ **11 :** a transportation system **12 :** the football players who are stationed on the line of scrimmage **13 :** a long narrow mark; *also* **:** EQUATOR **14 :** a geometric element that is the path of a moving point **15 :** CONTOUR **16 :** a general plan **17 :** an indication based on insight or investigation

²line *vb* **lined; lin•ing 1 :** to mark with a line **2 :** to place or form a line along **3 :** ALIGN

³line *vb* **lined; lin•ing :** to cover the inner surface of

lin•eage \ˈli-nē-ij\ *n* **:** lineal descent from a common progenitor; *also* **:** FAMILY

lin•eal \ˈli-nē-əl\ *adj* **1 :** LINEAR **2 :** consisting of or being in a direct line of ancestry; *also* **:** HEREDITARY

lin•ea•ment \ˈli-nē-ə-mənt\ *n* **:** an outline, feature, or contour of a body and esp. of a face — usu. used in pl.

lin•ear \ˈli-nē-ər\ *adj* **1 :** of, relating to, resembling, or having a graph that is a line and esp. a straight line **:** STRAIGHT **2 :** composed of simply drawn lines with little attempt at pictorial representation ⟨∼ script⟩ **3 :** being long and uniformly narrow

line•back•er \ˈlīn-ˌba-kər\ *n* **:** a defensive football player who lines up just behind the line of scrimmage

line drive *n* **:** a batted baseball hit in a flatter path than a fly ball

line•man \ˈlīn-mən\ *n* **1 :** a person who sets up or repairs communication or power lines **2 :** a player in the line in football

lin•en \ˈli-nən\ *n* **1 :** cloth made of flax; *also* **:** thread or yarn spun from flax **2 :** clothing or household articles made of linen cloth or similar fabric

line of scrimmage : an imaginary line in football parallel to the goal lines and tangent to the nose of the ball laid on the ground before a play

¹lin•er \ˈlī-nər\ *n* **:** a ship or airplane of a regular transportation line

²liner *n* **:** one that lines or is used as a lining — **lin•er•less** *adj*

line score *n* **:** a score of a baseball game giving the runs, hits, and errors made by each team

lines•man \ˈlīnz-mən\ *n* **1 :** LINEMAN 1 **2 :** an official who assists a referee

line•up \ˈlī-ˌnəp\ *n* **1 :** a list of players taking part in a game (as of baseball) **2 :** a line of persons arranged esp. for identification by police

ling \ˈliŋ\ *n* **:** any of various fishes related to the cod

-ling \liŋ\ *n suffix* **1 :** one associated with ⟨nest*ling*⟩ **2 :** young, small, or minor one ⟨duck*ling*⟩

lin•ger \ˈliŋ-gər\ *vb* **:** TARRY; *also* **:** PROCRASTINATE — **lin•ger•er** *n*

lin•ge•rie \ˌlän-jə-ˈrā, ˌlaⁿ-zhə-, -ˈrē\ *n* [F, fr. MF, fr. *linge* linen, fr. L *lineus* made of linen, fr. *linum* flax, linen] **:** women's intimate apparel

lin•go \ˈliŋ-gō\ *n, pl* **lingoes :** a usu. strange or incomprehensible language

lin•gua fran•ca \ˌliŋ-gwə-ˈfraŋ-kə\ *n, pl* **lingua francas** *or* **lin•guae fran•cae** \-gwē-ˈfraŋ-ˌkē\ [It] **1** *often cap* **:** a common language consisting of Italian mixed with French, Spanish, Greek, and Arabic that was former-

ly spoken in Mediterranean ports **2 :** a common or commercial tongue among speakers of different languages
lin•gual \ˈliŋ-gwəl\ *adj* **:** of, relating to, or produced by the tongue
lin•guist \ˈliŋ-gwist\ *n* **1 :** a person skilled in languages **2 :** a person who specializes in linguistics
lin•guis•tics \liŋ-ˈgwis-tiks\ *n* **:** the study of human speech including the units, nature, structure, and modification of language — **lin•guis•tic** \-tik\ *adj*
lin•i•ment \ˈli-nə-mənt\ *n* **:** a liquid preparation rubbed on the skin esp. to relieve pain
lin•ing \ˈlī-niŋ\ *n* **:** material used to line esp. an inner surface
link \ˈliŋk\ *n* **1 :** a connecting structure; *esp* **:** a single ring of a chain **2 :** BOND, TIE — **link** *vb* — **link•er** *n*
link•age \ˈliŋ-kij\ *n* **1 :** the manner or style of being united **2 :** the quality or state of being linked **3 :** a system of links
linking verb *n* **:** a word or expression (as a form of *be, become, feel,* or *seem*) that links a subject with its predicate
links \ˈliŋks\ *n pl* **:** a golf course
link•up \ˈliŋ-ˌkəp\ *n* **1 :** MEETING **2 :** something that serves as a linking device or factor
lin•net \ˈli-nət\ *n* **:** an Old World finch
li•no•leum \lə-ˈnō-lē-əm\ *n* [L *lin*um flax + *oleum* oil] **:** a floor covering with a canvas back and a surface of hardened linseed oil and a filler
lin•seed \ˈlin-ˌsēd\ *n* **:** the seeds of flax yielding a yellowish oil (**linseed oil**) used esp. in paints and linoleum
lin•sey–wool•sey \ˌlin-zē-ˈwu̇l-zē\ *n* **:** a coarse sturdy fabric of wool and linen or cotton
lint \ˈlint\ *n* **1 :** linen made into a soft fleecy substance **2 :** fine ravels and short fibers of yarn or fabric **3 :** the fibers that surround cotton seeds and form the cotton staple
lin•tel \ˈlint-ᵊl\ *n* **:** a horizontal piece across the top of an opening (as of a door) that carries the weight of the structure above it
li•on \ˈlī-ən\ *n, pl* **lions :** a large heavily-built cat of Africa and southern Asia with a shaggy mane in the male
li•on•ess \ˈlī-ə-nəs\ *n* **:** a female lion
li•on•heart•ed \ˌlī-ən-ˈhär-təd\ *adj* **:** COURAGEOUS, BRAVE
li•on•ise *Brit var of* LIONIZE
li•on•ize \ˈlī-ə-ˌnīz\ *vb* **-ized; -iz•ing :** to treat as an object of great interest or importance — **li•on•i•za•tion** \lī-ə-nə-ˈzā-shən\ *n*
lip \ˈlip\ *n* **1 :** either of the two fleshy folds that surround the mouth; *also* **:** the margin of the human lip **2 :** a part or projection suggesting a lip **3 :** the edge of a hollow vessel or cavity — **lipped** \ˈlipt\ *adj*
lip•id \ˈli-pəd\ *n* **:** any of various substances (as fats and waxes) that with proteins and carbohydrates make up the principal structural parts of living cells
li•po•pro•tein \ˌlī-pō-ˈprō-ˌtēn, ˌli-\ *n* **:** a protein that is a complex of protein and lipid
li•po•suc•tion \ˈli-pə-ˌsək-shən, ˈlī-\ *n* **:** surgical removal of local fat deposits (as in the thighs) esp. for cosmetic purposes
lip•read•ing \ˈlip-ˌrē-diŋ\ *n* **:** the interpreting of a speaker's words by watching lip and facial movements without hearing the voice
lip service *n* **:** an avowal of allegiance that is only verbal
lip•stick \ˈlip-ˌstik\ *n* **:** a waxy solid colored cosmetic in stick form for the lips — **lip•sticked** \-ˌstikt\ *adj*
liq *abbr* **1** liquid **2** liquor
liq•ue•fy *also* **liq•ui•fy** \ˈli-kwə-ˌfī\ *vb* **-fied; -fy•ing :** to make or become liquid — **liq•ue•fi•er** \-ˌfī-ər\ *n*
li•queur \li-ˈkər\ *n* [F] **:** a distilled alcoholic liquor flavored with aromatic substances and usu. sweetened
¹liq•uid \ˈli-kwəd\ *adj* **1 :** flowing freely like water **2 :** neither solid nor gaseous **3 :** shining and clear ⟨large ~ eyes⟩ **4 :** smooth and musical in tone; *also* **:** smooth and unconstrained in movement **5 :** consisting of or capable of ready conversion into cash ⟨~ assets⟩ — **li•quid•i•ty** \li-ˈkwi-də-tē\ *n*
²liquid *n* **:** a liquid substance
liq•ui•date \ˈli-kwə-ˌdāt\ *vb* **-dat•ed; -dat•ing 1 :** to settle the accounts and distribute the assets of (as a business) **2 :** to pay off ⟨~ a debt⟩ **3 :** to get rid of; *esp* **:** KILL — **liq•ui•da•tion** \ˌli-kwə-ˈdā-shən\ *n*
liquid crystal *n* **:** an organic liquid that resembles a crystal in having ordered molecular arrays
liquid crystal display *n* **:** LCD
liquid measure *n* **:** a unit or series of units for measuring liquid capacity — see METRIC SYSTEM table, WEIGHT table
li•quor \ˈli-kər\ *n* **:** a liquid substance; *esp* **:** a distilled alcoholic beverage
li•quo•rice *chiefly Brit var of* LICORICE
li•ra \ˈlir-ə, ˈlē-rə\ *n* — see MONEY table
lisente *pl of* SENTE
lisle \ˈlīl\ *n* **:** a smooth tightly twisted thread usu. made of long-staple cotton
lisp \ˈlisp\ *vb* **:** to pronounce \s\ and \z\ imperfectly esp. by turning them into \th\ and \th\; *also* **:** to speak childishly — **lisp** *n* — **lisp•er** *n*
lis•some *also* **lis•som** \ˈli-səm\ *adj* **1 :** easily flexed **2 :** LITHE 2 **3 :** NIMBLE — **lis•some•ly** *adv*
¹list \ˈlist\ *vb, archaic* **:** PLEASE; *also* **:** WISH
²list *vb, archaic* **:** LISTEN
³list *n* **1 :** a simple series of words or numerals; *also* **:** an official roster **2 :** CATALOG, CHECKLIST
⁴list *vb* **:** to make a list of; *also* **:** to include on a list — **list•ee** \li-ˈstē\ *n*
⁵list *vb* **:** TILT
⁶list *n* **:** a leaning to one side **:** TILT
lis•ten \ˈlis-ᵊn\ *vb* **1 :** to pay attention in order to hear **2 :** HEED — **lis•ten•er** *n*
lis•ten•er•ship \ˈlis-ᵊn-ər-ˌship\ *n* **:** the audience for a radio program or recording
list•ing \ˈlis-tiŋ\ *n* **1 :** an act or instance of making or including in a list **2 :** something that is listed
list•less \ˈlist-ləs\ *adj* **:** SPIRITLESS, LANGUID — **list•less•ly** *adv* — **list•less•ness** *n*
list price *n* **:** the price of an item as published in a catalog, price list, or advertisement before being discounted
lists \ˈlists\ *n pl* **:** an arena for combat (as jousting)
¹lit \ˈlit\ *past and past part of* LIGHT
²lit *abbr* **1** liter **2** literal; literally **3** literary **4** literature
lit•a•ny \ˈlit-ᵊn-ē\ *n, pl* **-nies** [ME *letanie,* fr. OF, fr. LL *litania,* fr. LGk *litaneia,* fr. Gk, entreaty, fr. *litanos* suppliant] **1 :** a prayer consisting of a series of supplications and responses said alternately by a leader and a group **2 :** a lengthy recitation ⟨a ~ of complaints⟩
li•tchi \ˈlē-chē, ˈlī-\ *n* [Chin (Beijing dialect) *lìzhī*] **1 :** an oval fruit with a hard scaly outer covering, a small hard seed, and edible flesh **2 :** an Asian tree bearing litchis
lite *var of* ³LIGHT 10
li•ter \ˈlē-tər\ *n* — see METRIC SYSTEM table
lit•er•al \ˈli-tə-rəl\ *adj* **1 :** adhering to fact or to the ordinary or usual meaning (as of a word) **2 :** UNADORNED; *also* **:** PROSAIC **3 :** VERBATIM
lit•er•al•ism \-rə-ˌli-zəm\ *n* **1 :** adherence to the explicit substance (as of an idea) **2 :** fidelity to observable fact — **lit•er•al•ist** \-list\ *n* — **lit•er•al•is•tic** \ˌli-tə-rə-ˈlis-tik\ *adj*
lit•er•al•ly \ˈli-tə-rə-lē, ˈli-trə-\ *adv* **1 :** ACTUALLY ⟨was ~ insane⟩ **2 :** VIRTUALLY ⟨~ poured out new ideas⟩
lit•er•ary \ˈli-tə-ˌrer-ē\ *adj* **1 :** of or relating to literature **2 :** WELL-READ
lit•er•ate \ˈli-trət, -tə-rət\ *adj* **1 :** EDUCATED; *also* **:** able to read and write **2 :** LITERARY; *also* **:** POLISHED, LUCID — **lit•er•a•cy** \ˈli-trə-sē, -tə-rə-\ *n* — **literate** *n*

li•te•ra•ti \ˌli-tə-ˈrä-tē\ *n pl* **1** : the educated class **2** : persons interested in literature or the arts

lit•er•a•ture \ˈli-trə-ˌchu̇r, -tə-rə-, -chər\ *n* **1** : the production of written works having excellence of form or expression and dealing with ideas of permanent interest **2** : the written works produced in a particular language, country, or age

lithe \ˈlīt͟h, ˈlīth\ *adj* **1** : SUPPLE **2** : characterized by effortless grace; *also* : athletically slim

lithe•some \ˈlīt͟h-səm, ˈlīth-\ *adj* : LISSOME

lith•i•um \ˈli-thē-əm\ *n* : a light silver-white metallic chemical element — see ELEMENT table

li•thog•ra•phy \li-ˈthä-grə-fē\ *n* : the process of printing from a plane surface (as a smooth stone or metal plate) on which the image to be printed is ink-receptive and the blank area ink-repellent — **lith•o•graph** \ˈli-thə-ˌgraf\ *vb* — **lithograph** *n* — **li•thog•ra•pher** \li-ˈthä-grə-fər, ˈli-thə-ˌgra-fər\ *n* — **lith•o•graph•ic** \ˌli-thə-ˈgra-fik\ *adj* — **lith•o•graph•i•cal•ly** \-fi-k(ə-)lē\ *adv*

li•thol•o•gy \li-ˈthä-lə-jē\ *n, pl* **-gies** : the study of rocks — **lith•o•log•ic** \ˌli-thə-ˈlä-jik\ *or* **lith•o•log•i•cal** \-ji-kəl\ *adj*

lith•o•sphere \ˈli-thə-ˌsfir\ *n* : the outer part of the solid earth

Lith•u•a•nian \ˌli-thü-ˈwā-nē-ən, -thyü-\ *n* **1** : a native or inhabitant of Lithuania **2** : the language of the Lithuanians — **Lithuanian** *adj*

lit•i•gant \ˈli-ti-gənt\ *n* : a party to a lawsuit — **litigant** *adj*

lit•i•gate \-ˌgāt\ *vb* **-gat•ed; -gat•ing** : to carry on a legal contest by judicial process; *also* : to contest at law — **lit•i•ga•tion** \ˌli-tə-ˈgā-shən\ *n*

li•ti•gious \lə-ˈti-jəs\ *adj* **1** : CONTENTIOUS **2** : prone to engage in lawsuits **3** : of or relating to litigation — **li•ti•gious•ly** *adv* — **li•ti•gious•ness** *n*

lit•mus \ˈlit-məs\ *n* : a coloring matter from lichens that turns red in acid solutions and blue in alkaline

litmus test *n* : a test in which a single factor (as an attitude) is decisive

Litt D *or* **Lit D** *abbr* [ML *litterarum doctor*] : doctor of letters; doctor of literature

[1]**lit•ter** \ˈli-tər\ *n* [ME, fr. OF *litiere*, fr. *lit* bed, fr. L *lectus*] **1** : a covered and curtained couch with shafts that is used to carry a single passenger; *also* : a device (as a stretcher) for carrying a sick or injured person **2** : material used as bedding for animals; *also* : material used to absorb the urine and feces of animals **3** : the offspring of an animal at one birth **4** : RUBBISH

litter 1

[2]**litter** *vb* **1** : to give birth to young **2** : to strew or mark with scattered objects

lit•ter•bug \ˈli-tər-ˌbəg\ *n* : one who litters a public area

[1]**lit•tle** \ˈlit-ᵊl\ *adj* **lit•tler** \ˈlit-ᵊl-ər\ *or* **less** \ˈles\ *or* **less•er** \ˈle-sər\; **lit•tlest** \ˈlit-ᵊl-əst\ *or* **least** \ˈlēst\ **1** : not big; *also* : YOUNG **2** : not important **3** : PETTY 3 **4** : not much — **lit•tle•ness** *n*

[2]**little** *adv* **less** \ˈles\; **least** \ˈlēst\ **1** : SLIGHTLY; *also* : not at all **2** : INFREQUENTLY

[3]**little** *n* **1** : a small amount or quantity **2** : a short time or distance

Little Dipper *n* : the seven bright stars of Ursa Minor arranged in a form resembling a dipper

little theater *n* : a small theater for low-cost dramatic productions designed for a limited audience

lit•to•ral \ˈli-tə-rəl; ˌli-tə-ˈral\ *adj* : of, relating to, or growing on or near a shore esp. of the sea — **littoral** *n*

lit•ur•gy \ˈli-tər-jē\ *n, pl* **-gies** : a rite or body of rites prescribed for public worship — **li•tur•gi•cal** \lə-ˈtər-ji-kəl\ *adj* — **li•tur•gi•cal•ly** \-k(ə-)lē\ *adv* — **lit•ur•gist** \ˈli-tər-jist\ *n*

liv•able *also* **live•able** \ˈli-və-bəl\ *adj* **1** : suitable for living in or with **2** : ENDURABLE — **liv•a•bil•i•ty** \ˌli-və-ˈbi-lə-tē\ *n*

[1]**live** \ˈliv\ *vb* **lived; liv•ing** **1** : to be or continue alive **2** : SUBSIST **3** : RESIDE **4** : to conduct one's life **5** : to remain in human memory or record

[2]**live** \ˈlīv\ *adj* **1** : having life **2** : BURNING, GLOWING ⟨a ~ cigar⟩ **3** : connected to electric power ⟨a ~ wire⟩ **4** : UNEXPLODED ⟨a ~ bomb⟩ **5** : of continuing interest ⟨a ~ issue⟩ **6** : of or involving the actual presence of real people ⟨~ audience⟩; *also* : broadcast directly at the time of production ⟨a ~ radio program⟩ **7** : being in play ⟨a ~ ball⟩

lived–in \ˈlivd-ˌin\ *adj* : of or suggesting long-term human habitation or use

live down *vb* : to live so as to wipe out the memory or effects of

live in *vb* : to live in one's place of employment — used of a servant — **live–in** \ˈliv-ˌin\ *adj*

live•li•hood \ˈlīv-lē-ˌhu̇d\ *n* : means of support or subsistence

live•long \ˈliv-ˌlȯŋ\ *adj* [ME *lef long*, fr. *lef* dear + *long* long] : WHOLE, ENTIRE ⟨the ~ day⟩

live•ly \ˈlīv-lē\ *adj* **live•li•er; -est** **1** : ANIMATED ⟨~ debate⟩ **2** : KEEN, VIVID ⟨~ interest⟩ **3** : showing activity or vigor ⟨a ~ manner⟩ **4** : quick to rebound ⟨a ~ ball⟩ **5** : full of life **syn** vivacious, sprightly, gay, spirited — **live•li•ness** *n* — **live•ly** *adv*

liv•en \ˈlī-vən\ *vb* : ENLIVEN

[1]**liv•er** \ˈli-vər\ *n* **1** : a large glandular organ of vertebrates that secretes bile and is a center of metabolic activity **2** : the liver of an animal (as a calf or chicken) eaten as food

[2]**liver** *n* : one that lives esp. in a specified way ⟨a fast ~⟩

liv•er•ish \ˈli-və-rish\ *adj* **1** : resembling liver esp. in color **2** : BILIOUS **3** : PEEVISH — **liv•er•ish•ness** *adj*

liv•er•wort \ˈli-vər-ˌwərt\ *n* : any of a class of flowerless plants resembling the related mosses

liv•er•wurst \-ˌwərst, -ˌwu̇rst\ *n* [part trans. of G *Leberwurst*, fr. *Leber* liver + *Wurst* sausage] : a sausage consisting chiefly of liver

liv•ery \ˈli-və-rē\ *n, pl* **-er•ies** **1** : a servant's uniform; *also* : distinctive dress **2** : the feeding, care, and stabling of horses for pay; *also* : an establishment (as a stable or business) keeping horses or vehicles for hire — **liv•er•ied** \-rēd\ *adj*

liv•ery•man \-mən\ *n* : the keeper of a livery

lives *pl of* LIFE

live•stock \ˈlīv-ˌstäk\ *n* : farm animals kept for use and profit

live wire *n* : an alert, active, or aggressive person

liv•id \ˈli-vəd\ *adj* [F *livide*, fr. L *lividus*, fr. *livēre* to be blue] **1** : discolored by bruising **2** : ASHEN, PALLID **3** : REDDISH **4** : ENRAGED — **li•vid•ity** \li-ˈvi-də-tē\ *n*

[1]**liv•ing** \ˈli-viŋ\ *adj* **1** : having life **2** : NATURAL **3** : full of life and vigor; *also* : VIVID

[2]**living** *n* **1** : the condition of being alive **2** : LIVELIHOOD **3** : manner of life

living room *n* : a room in a residence used for the common social activities of the occupants

living wage *n* : a wage sufficient to provide an acceptable standard of living

living will *n* : a document requesting that the signer not be kept alive by artificial means unless there is a reasonable expectation of recovery

livre \ˈlēvrᵊ\ *n* : the pound of Lebanon

liz•ard \ˈli-zərd\ *n* : any of a group of 4-legged reptiles with long tapering tails

Lk *abbr* Luke

ll *abbr* lines

lla•ma \ˈlä-mə\ *n* [Sp] : any of a genus of wild or domesticated So. American mammals related to the camels but smaller and without a hump

lla•no \ˈlä-nō\ *n, pl* **llanos** : an open grassy plain esp. of Latin America

LLD *abbr* [NL *legum doctor*] doctor of laws

LNG *abbr* liquefied natural gas

¹load \ˈlōd\ *n* **1** : PACK; *also* : CARGO **2** : a mass of weight supported by something **3** : something that burdens the mind or spirits **4** : a large quantity — usu. used in pl. **5** : a standard, expected, or authorized burden

²load *vb* **1** : to put a load in or on; *also* : to receive a load **2** : to encumber with an obligation or something heavy or disheartening **3** : to increase the weight of by adding something **4** : to supply abundantly **5** : to put a charge in (as a firearm)

load•ed *adj* **1** *slang* : HIGH 12 **2** : having a large amount of money

load•stone *var of* LODESTONE

¹loaf \ˈlōf\ *n, pl* **loaves** \ˈlōvz\ : a shaped or molded mass esp. of bread

²loaf *vb* : to spend time in idleness : LOUNGE — **loaf•er** *n*

loam \ˈlōm, ˈlüm\ *n* : SOIL; *esp* : a loose soil of mixed clay, sand, and silt — **loamy** *adj*

¹loan \ˈlōn\ *n* **1** : money lent at interest; *also* : something lent for the borrower's temporary use **2** : the grant of temporary use

²loan *vb* : LEND

loan shark *n* : a person who lends money at excessive rates of interest — **loan•shark•ing** \ˈlōn-ˌshär-kiŋ\ *n*

loan•word \ˈlōn-ˌwərd\ *n* : a word taken from another language and at least partly naturalized

loath \ˈlōth, ˈlōth\ *also* **loathe** \lōth, lōth\ *adj* : RELUCTANT

loathe \ˈlōth\ *vb* **loathed; loath•ing** : to dislike greatly **syn** abominate, abhor, detest, hate

loath•ing \ˈlō-thiŋ\ *n* : extreme disgust

loath•some \ˈlōth-səm, ˈlōth-\ *adj* : exciting loathing : REPULSIVE

lob \ˈläb\ *vb* **lobbed; lob•bing** : to throw, hit, or propel something in a high arc — **lob** *n*

¹lob•by \ˈlä-bē\ *n, pl* **lobbies** **1** : a corridor used esp. as a passageway or waiting room **2** : a group of persons engaged in lobbying

²lobby *vb* **lob•bied; lob•by•ing** : to try to influence public officials and esp. legislators — **lob•by•ist** *n*

lobe \ˈlōb\ *n* : a curved or rounded part esp. of a bodily organ — **lo•bar** \ˈlō-bər\ *adj* — **lobed** \ˈlōbd\ *adj*

lo•bot•o•my \lō-ˈbä-tə-mē\ *n, pl* **-mies** : surgical severance of certain nerve fibers in the brain for the relief of some mental disorders

lob•ster \ˈläb-stər\ *n* [ME, fr. OE *loppestre*, fr. *loppe* spider] : any of a family of edible marine crustaceans with two large pincerlike claws and four other pairs of legs; *also* : SPINY LOBSTER

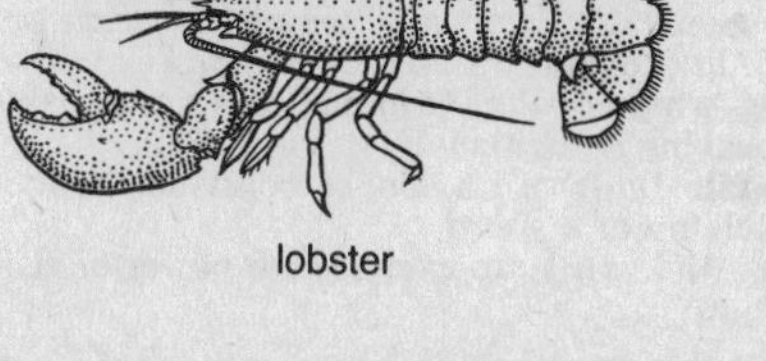

lobster

¹lo•cal \ˈlō-kəl\ *adj* **1** : of, relating to, or occupying a particular place **2** : serving a particular limited district; *also* : making all stops ⟨a ∼ train⟩ **3** : affecting a small part of the body ⟨∼ infection⟩ — **lo•cal•ly** *adv*

²local *n* : one that is local

lo•cale \lō-ˈkal\ *n* : a place that is the setting for a particular event

lo•cal•ise *Brit var of* LOCALIZE

lo•cal•i•ty \lō-ˈka-lə-tē\ *n, pl* **-ties** : a particular spot, situation, or location

lo•cal•ize \ˈlō-kə-ˌlīz\ *vb* **-ized; -iz•ing** : to fix in or confine to a definite place or locality — **lo•cal•i•za•tion** \ˌlō-kə-lə-ˈzā-shən\ *n*

lo•cate \ˈlō-ˌkāt, lō-ˈkāt\ *vb* **lo•cat•ed; lo•cat•ing** **1** : STATION, SETTLE **2** : to determine the site of **3** : to find or fix the place of in a sequence

lo•ca•tion \lō-ˈkā-shən\ *n* **1** : SITUATION, PLACE **2** : the process of locating **3** : a place outside a studio where a motion picture is filmed

loc cit *abbr* [L *loco citato*] in the place cited

loch \ˈläk, ˈläk\ *n, Scot* : LAKE; *also* : a bay or arm of the sea esp. when nearly landlocked

¹lock \ˈläk\ *n* : a tuft, strand, or ringlet of hair; *also* : a cohering bunch (as of wool or flax)

²lock *n* **1** : a fastening in which a bolt is operated **2** : the mechanism of a firearm by which the charge is exploded **3** : an enclosure (as in a canal) used in raising or lowering boats from level to level **4** : AIR LOCK **5** : a wrestling hold

³lock *vb* **1** : to fasten the lock of; *also* : to make fast with a lock **2** : to confine or exclude by means of a lock **3** : INTERLOCK **4** : to make or become motionless by the interlocking of parts

lock•er \ˈlä-kər\ *n* **1** : a drawer, cupboard, or compartment for individual storage use **2** : an insulated compartment for storing frozen food

lock•et \ˈlä-kət\ *n* : a small usu. metal case for a memento worn suspended from a chain or necklace

lock•jaw \ˈläk-ˌjȯ\ *n* : a symptom of tetanus marked by spasms of the jaw muscles and inability to open the jaws; *also* : TETANUS

lock•nut \-ˌnət\ *n* **1** : a nut screwed tight on another to prevent it from slacking back **2** : a nut designed to lock itself when screwed tight

lock•out \-ˌau̇t\ *n* : the suspension of work by an employer during a labor dispute in order to make employees accept the terms being offered

lock•smith \-ˌsmith\ *n* : one who makes or repairs locks

lock•step \-ˌstep\ *n* : a mode of marching in step by a body of men moving in a very close single file

lock•up \-ˌəp\ *n* : JAIL

lo•co \ˈlō-kō\ *adj* [Sp] *slang* : CRAZY, FRENZIED

lo•co•mo•tion \ˌlō-kə-ˈmō-shən\ *n* **1** : the act or power of moving from place to place **2** : TRAVEL

¹lo•co•mo•tive \ˌlō-kə-ˈmō-tiv\ *adj* : of or relating to locomotion or a locomotive

²locomotive *n* : a self-propelled vehicle used to move railroad cars

lo•co•mo•tor \ˌlō-kə-ˈmō-tər\ *adj* : of or relating to locomotion or organs used in locomotion

lo•co•weed \ˈlō-kō-ˌwēd\ *n* : any of several leguminous plants of western No. America that are poisonous to livestock

lo•cus \ˈlō-kəs\ *n, pl* **lo•ci** \ˈlō-ˌsī\ [L] **1** : PLACE, LOCALITY **2** : the set of all points whose location is determined by stated conditions

lo•cust \ˈlō-kəst\ *n* **1** : a usu. destructive migratory grasshopper **2** : CICADA **3** : any of various leguminous trees; *also* : the wood of a locust

lo•cu•tion \lō-ˈkyü-shən\ *n* : a particular form of expression; *also* : PHRASEOLOGY

lode \ˈlōd\ *n* : an ore deposit

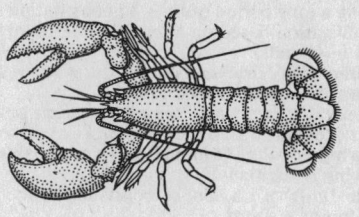

lode•stone \-ˌstōn\ *n* : an iron-containing rock with magnetic properties

[1]lodge \ˈläj\ *vb* **lodged; lodg•ing 1** : to provide quarters for; *also* : to settle in a place **2** : CONTAIN **3** : to come to a rest and remain **4** : to deposit for safekeeping **5** : to vest (as authority) in an agent **6** : FILE ⟨~ a complaint⟩

[2]lodge *n* **1** : a house set apart for residence in a special season or by an employee on an estate; *also* : INN **2** : a den or lair esp. of gregarious animals **3** : the meeting place of a branch of a fraternal organization; *also* : the members of such a branch

lodg•er \ˈlä-jər\ *n* : a person who occupies a rented room in another's house

lodg•ing \ˈlä-jiŋ\ *n* **1** : DWELLING **2** : a room or suite of rooms in another's house rented as a dwelling place — usu. used in pl.

lodg•ment *or* **lodge•ment** \ˈläj-mənt\ *n* **1** : a lodging place **2** : the act or manner of lodging **3** : DEPOSIT

loess \ˈles, ˈləs\ *n* : a usu. yellowish brown loamy deposit believed to be chiefly deposited by the wind

[1]loft \ˈlȯft\ *n* [ME, fr. OE, air, sky, fr. ON *lopt*] **1** : ATTIC **2** : GALLERY ⟨organ ~⟩ **3** : an upper floor (as in a warehouse or barn) esp. when not partitioned **4** : the thickness of a fabric or insulated material (as of a sleeping bag)

[2]loft *vb* : to strike or throw a ball so that it rises high in the air

lofty \ˈlȯf-tē\ *adj* **loft•i•er; -est 1** : NOBLE; *also* : SUPERIOR **2** : extremely proud **3** : HIGH, TALL — **loft•i•ly** \ˈlȯf-tə-lē\ *adv* — **loft•i•ness** \-tē-nəs\ *n*

[1]log \ˈlȯg, ˈläg\ *n* **1** : a bulky piece of unshaped timber **2** : an apparatus for measuring a ship's speed **3** : the daily record of a ship's progress; *also* : a regularly kept record of performance (as of an airplane)

[2]log *vb* **logged; log•ging 1** : to cut (trees) for lumber; *also* : to clear (land) of trees in lumbering **2** : to enter in a log **3** : to sail a ship or fly an airplane for (an indicated distance or period of time) **4** : to have (an indicated record) to one's credit : ACHIEVE — **log•ger** \ˈlȯ-gər, ˈlä-\ *n*

[3]log *n* : LOGARITHM

lo•gan•ber•ry \ˈlō-gən-ˌber-ē\ *n* : a red-fruited upright-growing dewberry; *also* : its fruit

log•a•rithm \ˈlȯ-gə-ˌri-t͟həm, ˈlä-\ *n* : the exponent that indicates the power to which a base is raised to produce a given number ⟨the ~ of 100 to base 10 is 2 since $10^2 = 100$⟩ — **log•a•rith•mic** \ˌlȯ-gə-ˈrit͟h-mik, ˌlä-\ *adj*

loge \ˈlōzh\ *n* **1** : a small compartment; *also* : a box in a theater **2** : a small partitioned area; *also* : the forward section of a theater mezzanine

log•ger•head \ˈlȯ-gər-ˌhed, ˈlä-\ *n* : a large sea turtle of subtropical and temperate waters — **at loggerheads** : in a state of quarrelsome disagreement

log•gia \ˈlō-jē-ə, ˈlȯ-jä\ *n, pl* **loggias** \ˈlō-jē-əz, ˈlȯ-jäz\ : a roofed open gallery

log•ic \ˈlä-jik\ *n* **1** : a science that deals with the rules and tests of sound thinking and proof by reasoning **2** : sound reasoning **3** : the arrangement of circuit elements for arithmetical computation in a computer — **log•i•cal** \-ji-kəl\ *adj* — **log•i•cal•ly** \-jik(ə-)lē\ *adv* — **lo•gi•cian** \lō-ˈji-shən\ *n*

lo•gis•tics \lō-ˈjis-tiks\ *n sing or pl* : the procurement, maintenance, and transportation of matériel, facilities, and personnel — **lo•gis•tic** \-tik\ *adj*

log•jam \ˈlȯg-ˌjam, ˈläg-\ *n* **1** : a deadlocked jumble of logs in a watercourse **2** : DEADLOCK

logo \ˈlō-gō\ *n, pl* **log•os** \-gōz\ : an identifying symbol (as for advertising)

logo•type \ˈlȯ-gə-ˌtīp, ˈlä-\ *n* : LOGO

log•roll•ing \-ˌrō-liŋ\ *n* : the trading of votes by legislators to secure favorable action on projects of individual interest

lo•gy \ˈlō-gē\ *also* **log•gy** \ˈlȯ-gē, ˈlä-\ *adj* **lo•gi•er; -est** : deficient in vitality : SLUGGISH

loin \ˈlȯin\ *n* **1** : the part of the body on each side of the spinal column and between the hip and the lower ribs; *also* : a cut of meat from this part of an animal **2** *pl* : the pubic region; *also* : the organs of reproduction

loin•cloth \-ˌklȯth\ *n* : a cloth worn about the loins often as the sole article of clothing in warm climates

loi•ter \ˈlȯi-tər\ *vb* **1** : LINGER **2** : to hang around idly **syn** dawdle, dally, procrastinate, lag, tarry — **loi•ter•er** *n*

loll \ˈläl\ *vb* **1** : DROOP, DANGLE **2** : LOUNGE

lol•li•pop *or* **lol•ly•pop** \ˈlä-li-ˌpäp\ *n* : a lump of hard candy on a stick

lol•ly•gag \ˈlä-lē-ˌgag\ *vb* **-gagged; -gag•ging** : DAWDLE

Lond *abbr* London

lone \ˈlōn\ *adj* **1** : SOLITARY ⟨a ~ sentinel⟩ **2** : SOLE, ONLY ⟨the ~ theater in town⟩ **3** : ISOLATED ⟨a ~ tree⟩

lone•ly \ˈlōn-lē\ *adj* **lone•li•er; -est 1** : being without company **2** : UNFREQUENTED ⟨a ~ spot⟩ **3** : LONESOME — **lone•li•ness** *n*

lon•er \ˈlō-nər\ *n* : one that avoids others

lone•some \ˈlōn-səm\ *adj* **1** : sad from lack of companionship **2** : REMOTE; *also* : SOLITARY — **lone•some•ly** *adv* — **lone•some•ness** *n*

[1]long \ˈlȯŋ\ *adj* **lon•ger** \ˈlȯŋ-gər\; **lon•gest** \ˈlȯŋ-gəst\ **1** : extending for a considerable distance; *also* : TALL, ELONGATED **2** : having a specified length **3** : extending over a considerable time; *also* : TEDIOUS **4** : containing many items in a series **5** : being a syllable or speech sound of relatively great duration **6** : extending far into the future **7** : well furnished with something — used with *on*

[2]long *adv* : for or during a long time

[3]long *n* : a long period of time

[4]long *vb* **longed; long•ing** \ˈlȯŋ-iŋ\ : to feel a strong desire or wish **syn** yearn, hanker, pine, hunger, thirst

[5]long *abbr* longitude

long•boat \ˈlȯŋ-ˌbōt\ *n* : a large boat usu. carried by a merchant sailing ship

long•bow \-ˌbō\ *n* : a wooden bow drawn by hand and used esp. by medieval English archers

lon•gev•i•ty \län-ˈje-və-tē\ *n* [LL *longaevitas*, fr. L *longaevus* long-lived, fr. *longus* long + *aevum* age] : a long duration of individual life; *also* : length of life

long•hair \ˈlȯŋ-ˌhar\ *n* **1** : a lover of classical music **2** : HIPPIE **3** : a domestic cat having long outer fur — **long•haired** \-ˌhard\ *or* **long•hair** *adj*

long•hand \-ˌhand\ *n* : HANDWRITING

long•horn \-ˌhȯrn\ *n* : any of the cattle with long horns formerly common in the southwestern U.S.

long hundredweight *n, Brit* — see WEIGHT table

long•ing \ˈlȯŋ-iŋ\ *n* : a strong desire esp. for something unattainable — **long•ing•ly** *adv*

lon•gi•tude \ˈlän-jə-ˌtüd, -ˌtyüd\ *n* : angular distance expressed usu. in degrees east or west from the prime meridian through Greenwich, England

lon•gi•tu•di•nal \ˌlän-jə-ˈtüd-ᵊn-əl, -ˈtyüd-\ *adj* **1** : extending lengthwise **2** : of or relating to length — **lon•gi•tu•di•nal•ly** *adv*

long•shore•man \ˈlȯŋ-ˌshōr-mən\ *n* : a laborer at a wharf who loads and unloads cargo

long–suf•fer•ing \-ˈsə-friŋ, -fə-riŋ\ *n* : long and patient endurance of offense

long–term \ˈlȯŋ-ˈtərm\ *adj* **1** : extending over or involving a long period of time **2** : constituting a financial obligation based on a term usu. of more than 10 years ⟨~ bonds⟩

long•time \ˈlȯŋ-ˈtīm\ *adj* : of long duration ⟨~ friends⟩

long ton *n* — see WEIGHT table

lon•gueur \lō^{n}-ˈgœr\ *n, pl* **longueurs** *same or* -ˈgœrz\ [F, lit., length] : a dull tedious passage or section

long–wind•ed \ˌlȯŋ-ˈwin-dəd\ *adj* : tediously long in speaking or writing

loo•fah \ˈlü-fə\ *n* : a sponge consisting of the fibrous skeleton of a gourd

[1]look \ˈlu̇k\ *vb* **1** : to exercise the power of vision : SEE

2 : EXPECT **3** : to have an appearance that befits ⟨~*s* the part⟩ **4** : SEEM ⟨~*s* thin⟩ **5** : to direct one's attention : HEED **6** : POINT, FACE **7** : to show a tendency — **look after** : to take care of — **look for** : EXPECT

²look *n* **1** : the action of looking : GLANCE **2** : EXPRESSION; *also* : physical appearance **3** : ASPECT

look down *vb* : to regard with contempt — used with *on* or *upon*

looking glass *n* : MIRROR

look•out \ˈlu̇k-ˌau̇t\ *n* **1** : a person assigned to watch (as on a ship) **2** : a careful watch **3** : VIEW **4** : a matter of concern

look up *vb* **1** : IMPROVE ⟨business is *looking up*⟩ **2** : to search for in or as if in a reference work **3** : to seek out esp. for a brief visit

¹loom \ˈlüm\ *n* : a frame or machine for weaving together threads or yarns into cloth

²loom *vb* **1** : to come into sight in an unnaturally large, indistinct, or distorted form **2** : to appear in an impressively exaggerated form

loon \ˈlün\ *n* : any of several web-footed black-and-white fish-eating diving birds

loo•ny *or* **loo•ney** \ˈlü-nē\ *adj* **loo•ni•er; -est** : CRAZY, FOOLISH

loony bin *n* : an insane asylum

loop \ˈlüp\ *n* **1** : a fold or doubling of a line through which another line or hook can be passed; *also* : a loop-shaped figure or course ⟨a ~ in a river⟩ **2** : a circular airplane maneuver executed in the vertical plane **3** : a piece of film or magnetic tape whose ends are spliced together to project or play continuously — **loop** *vb*

loop•er \ˈlü-pər\ *n* : any of numerous rather small hairless moth caterpillars that move with a looping movement

loop•hole \ˈlüp-ˌhōl\ *n* **1** : a small opening in a wall through which firearms may be discharged **2** : a means of escape; *esp* : an ambiguity or omission that allows one to evade the intent of a law or contract

¹loose \ˈlüs\ *adj* **loos•er; loos•est 1** : not rigidly fastened **2** : free from restraint or obligation **3** : not dense or compact in structure **4** : not chaste : LEWD **5** : SLACK **6** : not precise or exact — **loose•ly** *adv* — **loose•ness** *n*

²loose *vb* **loosed; loos•ing 1** : RELEASE **2** : UNTIE **3** : DETACH **4** : DISCHARGE **5** : RELAX, SLACKEN

³loose *adv* : LOOSELY

loos•en \ˈlüs-ᵊn\ *vb* **1** : FREE **2** : to make or become loose **3** : to relax the severity of

loot \ˈlüt\ *n* [Hindi *lūṭ;* akin to Skt *luṇṭati* he plunders] : goods taken in war or by robbery : PLUNDER — **loot** *vb* — **loot•er** *n*

¹lop \ˈläp\ *vb* **lopped; lop•ping** : to cut branches or twigs from : TRIM; *also* : to cut off

²lop *vb* **lopped; lop•ping** : to hang downward; *also* : to flop or sway loosely

lope \ˈlōp\ *n* : an easy bounding gait — **lope** *vb*

lop•sid•ed \ˈläp-ˈsī-dəd\ *adj* **1** : leaning to one side **2** : UNSYMMETRICAL — **lop•sid•ed•ly** *adv* — **lop•sid•ed•ness** *n*

lo•qua•cious \lō-ˈkwā-shəs\ *adj* : excessively talkative — **lo•quac•i•ty** \-ˈkwa-sə-tē\ *n*

¹lord \ˈlȯrd\ *n* [ME *loverd, lord,* fr. OE *hlāford,* fr. *hlāf* loaf + *weard* keeper] **1** : one having power and authority over others; *esp* : a person from whom a feudal fee or estate is held **2** : a man of rank or high position; *esp* : a British nobleman **3** *pl, cap* : the upper house of the British parliament **4** : a person of great power in some field

²lord *vb* : to act like a lord; *esp* : to put on airs — usu. used with *it*

lord chancellor *n, pl* **lords chancellor** : a British officer of state who presides over the House of Lords, serves as head of the British judiciary, and is usu. a leading member of the cabinet

lord•ly \-lē\ *adj* **lord•li•er; -est 1** : DIGNIFIED; *also* : NOBLE **2** : HAUGHTY

lord•ship \-ˌship\ *n* **1** : the rank or dignity of a lord — used as a title **2** : the authority or territory of a lord

Lord's Supper *n* : COMMUNION

lore \ˈlōr\ *n* : KNOWLEDGE; *esp* : traditional knowledge or belief

lor•gnette \lȯrn-ˈyet\ *n* [F, fr. *lorgner* to take a sidelong look at, fr. MF, fr. *lorgne* squinting] : a pair of eyeglasses or opera glasses with a handle

lorn \ˈlȯrn\ *adj* : FORSAKEN, DESOLATE

lor•ry \ˈlȯr-ē\ *n, pl* **lorries** *chiefly Brit* : MOTORTRUCK

lose \ˈlüz\ *vb* **lost** \ˈlȯst\; **los•ing** \ˈlü-ziŋ\ **1** : DESTROY **2** : to miss from a customary place : MISLAY **3** : to suffer deprivation of **4** : to fail to use : WASTE **5** : to fail to win or obtain ⟨~ the game⟩ **6** : to fail to keep or maintain ⟨~ his balance⟩ **7** : to wander from ⟨~ her way⟩ **8** : to get rid of — **los•er** *n*

loss \ˈlȯs\ *n* **1** : RUIN **2** : the harm resulting from losing **3** : something that is lost **4** *pl* : killed, wounded, or captured soldiers **5** : failure to win **6** : an amount by which the cost exceeds the selling price **7** : decrease in amount or degree

loss leader *n* : an article sold at a loss in order to draw customers

lost \ˈlȯst\ *adj* **1** : not used, won, or claimed **2** : no longer possessed or known **3** : ruined or destroyed physically or morally **4** : DENIED; *also* : HARDENED **5** : unable to find the way; *also* : HELPLESS **6** : ABSORBED, RAPT **7** : not appreciated or understood ⟨his jokes were ~ on me⟩

lot \ˈlät\ *n* **1** : an object used in deciding something by chance; *also* : the use of lots to decide something **2** : SHARE, PORTION; *also* : FORTUNE, FATE **3** : a plot of land **4** : a group of individuals : SET **5** : a considerable quantity

loth \ˈlōth, ˈlō*th*\ *var of* LOATH

lo•ti \ˈlō-tē\ *n, pl* **ma•lo•ti** \mə-ˈlō-tē\ — see MONEY table

lo•tion \ˈlō-shən\ *n* : a liquid preparation for cosmetic and external medicinal use

lot•tery \ˈlä-tə-rē\ *n, pl* **-ter•ies 1** : a drawing of lots in which prizes are given to the winning names or numbers **2** : a matter determined by chance

lo•tus \ˈlō-təs\ *n* **1** : a fruit held in Greek legend to cause dreamy contentment and forgetfulness **2** : any of various water lilies represented esp. in ancient Egyptian and Hindu art **3** : any of several leguminous forage plants

loud \ˈlau̇d\ *adj* **1** : marked by intensity or volume of sound **2** : CLAMOROUS, NOISY **3** : obtrusive or offensive in color or pattern ⟨a ~ suit⟩ — **loud** *adv* — **loud•ly** *adv* — **loud•ness** *n*

loud•mouthed \-ˌmau̇tht, -ˌmau̇*th*d\ *adj* : given to loud offensive talk

loud•speak•er \-ˌspē-kər\ *n* : a device that changes electrical signals into sound

¹lounge \ˈlau̇nj\ *vb* **lounged; loung•ing** : to act or move lazily or listlessly

²lounge *n* **1** : a room with comfortable furniture; *also* : a room (as in a theater) with lounging, smoking, and toilet facilities **2** : a long couch

lour \ˈlau̇r\, **loury** \ˈlau̇r-ē\ *var of* LOWER, LOWERY

louse \ˈlau̇s\ *n, pl* **lice** \ˈlīs\ **1** : any of various small wingless usu. flattened insects parasitic on warm-blooded animals **2** : a plant pest (as an aphid) **3** : a contemptible person

lousy \ˈlau̇-zē\ *adj* **lous•i•er; -est 1** : infested with lice **2** : POOR, INFERIOR **3** : amply supplied ⟨~ with money⟩ — **lous•i•ly** \-zə-lē\ *adv* — **lous•i•ness** \-zē-nəs\ *n*

lout \ˈlau̇t\ *n* : a stupid awkward fellow — **lout•ish** *adj* — **lout•ish•ly** *adv*

lou•ver *or* **lou•vre** \ˈlü-vər\ *n* **1** : an opening having parallel slanted slats to allow flow of air but to exclude rain or sun or to provide privacy; *also* : a slat in such an opening **2** : a device with movable slats for controlling the flow of air or light

[1]**love** \ˈləv\ *n* **1** : strong affection **2** : warm attachment ⟨~ of the sea⟩ **3** : attraction based on sexual desire **4** : a beloved person **5** : unselfish loyal and benevolent concern for others **6** : a score of zero in tennis — **love•less** *adj*

[2]**love** *vb* **loved; lov•ing 1** : CHERISH **2** : to feel a passion, devotion, or tenderness for **3** : CARESS **4** : to take pleasure in ⟨~*s* to play bridge⟩ — **lov•able** \ˈlə-və-bəl\ *adj* — **lov•er** *n*

love•bird \ˈləv-ˌbərd\ *n* : any of various small usu. gray or green parrots that seem to show caring behavior for their mates

love•lorn \-ˌlȯrn\ *adj* : deprived of love or of a lover

love•ly \ˈləv-lē\ *adj* **love•li•er; -est** : BEAUTIFUL — **love•li•ly** \ˈləv-lə-lē\ *adv* — **love•li•ness** *n* — **lovely** *adv*

love•mak•ing \-ˌmā-kiŋ\ *n* **1** : COURTSHIP **2** : sexual activity; *esp* : COPULATION

love•sick \-ˌsik\ *adj* **1** : YEARNING **2** : expressing a lover's longing — **love•sick•ness** *n*

lov•ing \ˈlə-viŋ\ *adj* **1** : AFFECTIONATE **2** : PAINSTAKING — **lov•ing•ly** *adv*

[1]**low** \ˈlō\ *vb* : MOO

[2]**low** *n* : MOO

[3]**low** *adj* **low•er** \ˈlō-ər\; **low•est** \ˈlō-əst\ **1** : not high or tall ⟨~ wall⟩; *also* : DÉCOLLETÉ **2** : situated or passing below the normal level or surface ⟨~ ground⟩; *also* : marking a nadir **3** : not loud ⟨~ voice⟩ **4** : being near the equator **5** : humble in status **6** : WEAK; *also* : DEPRESSED **7** : STRICKEN, PROSTRATE **8** : less than usual in number, amount, or value; *also* : of lesser degree than average **9** : falling short of a standard **10** : UNFAVORABLE — **low** *adv* — **low•ness** *n*

[4]**low** *n* **1** : something that is low **2** : a region of low barometric pressure **3** : the arrangement of gears in an automobile transmission that gives the slowest speed and greatest power

low beam *n* : the short-range focus of a vehicle headlight

low blow *n* : an unprincipled attack

low•brow \ˈlō-ˌbrau̇\ *n* : a person with little taste or intellectual interest

low–density lipoprotein *n* : LDL

low•down \-ˌdau̇n\ *n* : pertinent and esp. guarded information

low–down \-ˌdau̇n\ *adj* **1** : MEAN, CONTEMPTIBLE **2** : deeply emotional

low–end \-ˌend\ *adj* : of, relating to, or being the lowest-priced merchandise in a manufacturer's line

[1]**low•er** \ˈlau̇-ər\ *vb* **1** : FROWN **2** : to become dark, gloomy, and threatening

[2]**low•er** \ˈlō-ər\ *adj* **1** : relatively low (as in rank) **2** : situated beneath the earth's surface **3** : constituting the popular and more representative branch of a bicameral legislative body

[3]**low•er** \ˈlō-ər\ *vb* **1** : DROP; *also* : DIMINISH **2** : to let descend by its own weight; *also* : to reduce the height of **3** : to reduce in value, number, or amount **4** : DEGRADE; *also* : HUMBLE

low•er•case \ˌlō-ər-ˈkās\ *adj* : being a letter that belongs to or conforms to the series a, b, c, etc., rather than A, B, C, etc. — **lowercase** *n*

lower class *n* : a social class occupying a position below the middle class and having the lowest status in a society — **lower–class** \-ˈklas\ *adj*

low•er•most \ˈlō-ər-ˌmōst\ *adj* : LOWEST

low•ery \ˈlau̇-ə-rē\ *adj* : GLOOMY, LOWERING

lowest common denominator *n* **1** : LEAST COMMON DENOMINATOR **2** : something designed to appeal to a lowbrow audience; *also* : such an audience

lowest common multiple *n* : LEAST COMMON MULTIPLE

low–key \ˈlō-ˈkē\ *also* **low–keyed** \-ˈkēd\ *adj* : of low intensity : RESTRAINED

low•land \ˈlō-lənd, -ˌland\ *n* : low and usu. level country

low•life \ˈlō-ˌlīf\ *n, pl* **low•lifes** \-ˌlīfs\ *also* **low•lives** \-ˌlīvz\ : a person of low social status or moral character

low•ly \ˈlō-lē\ *adj* **low•li•er; -est 1** : HUMBLE, MEEK **2** : ranking low in some hierarchy — **low•li•ness** *n*

low–rise \ˈlō-ˈrīz\ *adj* **1** : having few stories and not equipped with elevators ⟨a ~ building⟩ **2** : of, relating to, or characterized by low-rise buildings

low–tech \ˈlō-ˈtek\ *adj* : technologically simple or unsophisticated

[1]**lox** \ˈläks\ *n* : liquid oxygen

[2]**lox** *n, pl* **lox** *or* **lox•es** : smoked salmon

loy•al \ˈlȯi-əl\ *adj* [MF, fr. OF *leial, leel,* fr. L *legalis* legal] **1** : faithful in allegiance to one's government **2** : faithful esp. to a cause or ideal : CONSTANT — **loy•al•ly** \ˈlȯi-ə-lē\ *adv* — **loy•al•ty** \ˈlȯi-əl-tē\ *n*

loy•al•ist \ˈlȯi-ə-list\ *n* : one who is or remains loyal to a political party, government, or sovereign

loz•enge \ˈlä-zənj\ *n* **1** : a diamond-shaped figure **2** : a small flat often medicated candy

LP *abbr* low pressure

LPG *abbr* liquefied petroleum gas

LPGA *abbr* Ladies Professional Golf Association

LPN \ˈel-ˈpē-ˈen\ *n* : LICENSED PRACTICAL NURSE

Lr *symbol* Lawrencium

LSD \ˌel-(ˌ)es-ˈdē\ *n* [G *Lysergsäure-Diäthylamid* lysergic acid diethylamide] : an illicit drug that causes psychotic symptoms similar to those of schizophrenia

lt *abbr* light

Lt *abbr* lieutenant

LT *abbr* long ton

LTC *or* **Lt Col** *abbr* lieutenant colonel

Lt Comdr *abbr* lieutenant commander

ltd *abbr* limited

LTG *or* **Lt Gen** *abbr* lieutenant general

LTJG *abbr* lieutenant, junior grade

ltr *abbr* letter

Lu *symbol* lutetium

lu•au \ˈlü-ˌau̇\ *n* : a Hawaiian feast

lub *abbr* lubricant; lubricating

lub•ber \ˈlə-bər\ *n* **1** : LOUT **2** : an unskilled seaman — **lub•ber•ly** *adj*

lube \ˈlüb\ *n* : LUBRICANT; *also* : an application of a lubricant

lu•bri•cant \ˈlü-bri-kənt\ *n* : a material capable of reducing friction when applied between moving parts

lu•bri•cate \ˈlü-brə-ˌkāt\ *vb* **-cat•ed; -cat•ing** : to apply a lubricant to — **lu•bri•ca•tion** \ˌlü-brə-ˈkā-shən\ *n* — **lu•bri•ca•tor** \ˈlü-brə-ˌkā-tər\ *n*

lu•bri•cious \lü-ˈbri-shəs\ *or* **lu•bri•cous** \ˈlü-bri-kəs\ *adj* **1** : SMOOTH, SLIPPERY **2** : LECHEROUS; *also* : SALACIOUS — **lu•bric•i•ty** \lü-ˈbri-sə-tē\ *n*

lu•cent \ˈlüs-ᵊnt\ *adj* **1** : LUMINOUS **2** : CLEAR, LUCID — **lu•cent•ly** *adv*

lu•cerne \lü-ˈsərn\ *n, chiefly Brit* : ALFALFA

lu•cid \ˈlü-səd\ *adj* **1** : SHINING **2** : mentally sound **3** : easily understood — **lu•cid•i•ty** \lü-ˈsi-də-tē\ *n* — **lu•cid•ly** *adv* — **lu•cid•ness** *n*

Lu•ci•fer \ˈlü-sə-fər\ *n* [ME, the morning star, a fallen rebel archangel, the Devil, fr. OE, fr. L, the morning star, fr. *lucifer* light-bearing] : DEVIL, SATAN

[1]**luck** \ˈlək\ *n* **1** : CHANCE, FORTUNE **2** : good fortune — **luck•less** *adj*

[2]**luck** *vb* **1** : to prosper or succeed esp. through chance or good fortune — usu. used with *out* **2** : to come upon something desirable by chance — usu. used with *out, on, onto,* or *into*

luck•i•ly \ˈlə-kə-lē\ *adv* **1** : in a lucky manner **2** : FORTUNATELY 2

lucky \ˈlə-kē\ *adj* **luck•i•er; -est 1** : favored by luck : FORTUNATE **2** : FORTUITOUS **3** : seeming to bring good luck — **luck•i•ness** *n*

lu•cra•tive \ˈlü-krə-tiv\ *adj* : PROFITABLE — **lu•cra•tive•ly** *adv* — **lu•cra•tive•ness** *n*

lu•cre \ˈlü-kər\ *n* [ME, fr. L *lucrum*] : PROFIT; *also* : MONEY

lu•cu•bra•tion \ˌlü-kyə-ˈbrā-shən, -kə-\ *n* : laborious study : MEDITATION

lu•di•crous \ˈlü-də-krəs\ *adj* : LAUGHABLE, RIDICULOUS — **lu•di•crous•ly** *adv* — **lu•di•crous•ness** *n*

luff \ˈləf\ *vb* : to turn the head of a ship toward the wind

¹lug \ˈləg\ *vb* **lugged; lug•ging 1** : DRAG, PULL **2** : to carry laboriously

²lug *n* **1** : a projecting piece (as for fastening, support, or traction) **2** : a nut securing a wheel on an automobile

lug•gage \ˈlə-gij\ *n* : containers (as suitcases) for carrying personal belongings : BAGGAGE

lu•gu•bri•ous \lu̇-ˈgü-brē-əs\ *adj* : mournful often to an exaggerated degree — **lu•gu•bri•ous•ly** *adv* — **lu•gu•bri•ous•ness** *n*

Luke \ˈlük\ *n* — see BIBLE table

luke•warm \ˈlük-ˈwȯrm\ *adj* **1** : moderately warm : TEPID **2** : not enthusiastic — **luke•warm•ly** *adv*

¹lull \ˈləl\ *vb* **1** : SOOTHE, CALM **2** : to cause to relax vigilance

²lull *n* **1** : a temporary calm (as during a storm) **2** : a temporary drop in activity

lul•la•by \ˈlə-lə-ˌbī\ *n, pl* **-bies** : a song to lull children to sleep

lum•ba•go \ˌləm-ˈbā-gō\ *n* : rheumatic pain in the lower back and loins

lum•bar \ˈləm-bər, -ˌbär\ *adj* : of, relating to, or constituting the loins or the vertebrae between the thoracic vertebrae and sacrum ⟨~ region⟩

¹lum•ber \ˈləm-bər\ *vb* : to move heavily or clumsily

²lumber *n* **1** : surplus or disused articles that are stored away **2** : timber or logs esp. when dressed for use

³lumber *vb* : to cut logs; *also* : to saw logs into lumber — **lum•ber•man** \-mən\ *n*

lum•ber•jack \-ˌjak\ *n* : LOGGER

lum•ber•yard \-ˌyärd\ *n* : a place where lumber is kept for sale

lu•mi•nary \ˈlü-mə-ˌner-ē\ *n, pl* **-nar•ies 1** : a very famous person **2** : a source of light; *esp* : a celestial body

lu•mi•nes•cence \ˌlü-mə-ˈnes-ᵊns\ *n* : the low-temperature emission of light (as by a chemical or physiological process); *also* : such light — **lu•mi•nes•cent** \-ᵊnt\ *adj*

lu•mi•nous \ˈlü-mə-nəs\ *adj* **1** : emitting light; *also* : LIGHTED **2** : CLEAR, INTELLIGIBLE — **lu•mi•nance** \-nəns\ *n* — **lu•mi•nos•i•ty** \ˌlü-mə-ˈnä-sə-tē\ *n* — **lu•mi•nous•ly** *adv*

lum•mox \ˈlə-məks\ *n* : a clumsy person

¹lump \ˈləmp\ *n* **1** : a piece or mass of indefinite size and shape **2** : AGGREGATE, TOTALITY **3** : a usu. abnormal swelling — **lump•ish** *adj* — **lumpy** *adj*

²lump *vb* **1** : to heap together in a lump **2** : to form into lumps

³lump *adj* : not divided into parts ⟨a ~ sum⟩

lu•na•cy \ˈlü-nə-sē\ *n, pl* **-cies 1** : INSANITY **2** : extreme folly

lu•nar \ˈlü-nər\ *adj* : of or relating to the moon

lu•na•tic \ˈlü-nə-ˌtik\ *adj* [ME *lunatik*, fr. LL *lunaticus*, fr. L *luna* moon; fr. the belief that lunacy fluctuated with the phases of the moon] **1** : INSANE; *also* : used for insane persons **2** : extremely foolish — **lunatic** *n*

¹lunch \ˈlənch\ *n* **1** : a light meal usu. eaten in the middle of the day **2** : the food prepared for a lunch

²lunch *vb* : to eat lunch

lun•cheon \ˈlən-chən\ *n* : a usu. formal lunch

lun•cheon•ette \ˌlən-chə-ˈnet\ *n* : a small restaurant serving light lunches

lunch•room \ˈlənch-ˌrüm, -ˌru̇m\ *n* **1** : LUNCHEONETTE **2** : a room (as in a school) where lunches are sold and eaten or lunches brought from home may be eaten

lu•nette \lü-ˈnet\ *n* : something shaped like a crescent

lung \ˈləŋ\ *n* **1** : one of the usu. paired baglike breathing organs in the chest of an air-breathing vertebrate **2** : a mechanical device to promote breathing and make it easier — **lunged** \ˈləŋd\ *adj*

lunge \ˈlənj\ *n* **1** : a sudden thrust or pass (as with a sword) **2** : a sudden forward stride or leap — **lunge** *vb*

lu•pine \ˈlü-pən\ *n* : any of a genus of leguminous plants with long upright clusters of pealike flowers

lu•pus \ˈlü-pəs\ *n* [ML, fr. L, wolf] : any of several diseases characterized by skin lesions; *esp* : SYSTEMIC LUPUS ERYTHEMATOSUS

lurch \ˈlərch\ *n* : a sudden swaying or tipping movement — **lurch** *vb*

¹lure \ˈlu̇r\ *n* **1** : ENTICEMENT; *also* : APPEAL **2** : an artificial bait for catching fish

²lure *vb* **lured; lur•ing** : to draw on with a promise of pleasure or gain

lu•rid \ˈlu̇r-əd\ *adj* **1** : wan and ghostly pale in appearance **2** : shining with the red glow of fire seen through smoke or cloud **3** : GRUESOME; *also* : SENSATIONAL **syn** ghastly, grisly, grim, horrible, macabre — **lu•rid•ly** *adv*

lurk \ˈlərk\ *vb* **1** : to move furtively : SNEAK **2** : to lie concealed

lus•cious \ˈlə-shəs\ *adj* **1** : having a pleasingly sweet taste or smell **2** : sensually appealing — **lus•cious•ly** *adv* — **lus•cious•ness** *n*

¹lush \ˈləsh\ *adj* : having or covered with abundant growth ⟨~ pastures⟩

²lush *n* : an habitual heavy drinker

lust \ˈləst\ *n* **1** : usu. intense or unbridled sexual desire : LASCIVIOUSNESS **2** : an intense longing — **lust** *vb* — **lust•ful** *adj*

lus•ter *or* **lus•tre** \ˈləs-tər\ *n* **1** : a shine or sheen esp. from reflected light **2** : BRIGHTNESS, GLITTER **3** : GLORY, SPLENDOR — **lus•ter•less** *adj* — **lus•trous** \-trəs\ *adj*

lus•tral \ˈləs-trəl\ *adj* : PURIFICATORY

lusty \ˈləs-tē\ *adj* **lust•i•er; -est** : full of vitality : ROBUST — **lust•i•ly** \ˈləs-tə-lē\ *adv* — **lust•i•ness** \-tē-nəs\ *n*

lute \ˈlüt\ *n* : a stringed musical instrument with a large pear-shaped body and a fretted fingerboard — **lu•te•nist** *or* **lu•ta•nist** \ˈlüt-ᵊn-ist\ *n*

lu•te•tium *also* **lu•te•cium** \lü-ˈtē-shē-əm, -shəm\ *n* : a metallic chemical element — see ELEMENT table

Lu•ther•an \ˈlü-thə-rən\ *n* : a member of a Protestant denomination adhering to the doctrines of Martin Luther — **Lu•ther•an•ism** \-rə-ˌni-zəm\ *n*

lux•u•ri•ant \ˌləg-ˈzhu̇r-ē-ənt, ˌlək-ˈshu̇r-\ *adj* **1** : yielding or growing abundantly : LUSH, PRODUCTIVE **2** : abundantly rich and varied; *also* : FLORID **syn** exuberant, lavish, opulent, prodigal, profuse, riotous — **lux•u•ri•ance** \-ē-əns\ *n* — **lux•u•ri•ant•ly** *adv*

lux•u•ri•ate \-ē-ˌāt\ *vb* **-at•ed; -at•ing 1** : to grow profusely **2** : REVEL

lux•u•ry \ˈlək-shə-rē, ˈləg-zhə-\ *n, pl* **-ries 1** : great ease and comfort **2** : something adding to pleasure or comfort but not absolutely necessary — **lux•u•ri•ous** \ˌləg-ˈzhu̇r-ē-əs, ˌlək-ˈshu̇r-\ *adj* — **lux•u•ri•ous•ly** *adv*

lv *abbr* leave

LVN *n* : LICENSED VOCATIONAL NURSE

lwei \lə-ˈwā\ *n, pl* **lwei** — see *kwanza* at MONEY table

LWV *abbr* League of Women Voters

¹-ly \lē\ *adj suffix* **1** : like in appearance, manner, or nature ⟨queen*ly*⟩ **2** : characterized by regular recurrence in (specified) units of time : every ⟨hour*ly*⟩

²-ly *adv suffix* **1** : in a (specified) manner ⟨slow*ly*⟩ **2** : from a (specified) point of view ⟨grammatical*ly*⟩

ly•ce•um \lī-ˈsē-əm, ˈlī-sē-\ *n* **1** : a hall for public lectures **2** : an association providing public lectures, concerts, and entertainments

lye \ˈlī\ *n* : a corrosive alkaline substance used esp. in making soap

ly·ing \ˈlī-iŋ\ *adj* : UNTRUTHFUL, FALSE

ly·ing–in \ˌlī-iŋ-ˈin\ *n, pl* **lyings–in** *or* **lying–ins** : the state during and consequent to childbirth : CONFINEMENT

Lyme disease \ˈlīm-\ *n* [*Lyme,* Connecticut, where it was first reported] : an acute inflammatory disease that is caused by a spirochete transmitted by ticks, is characterized esp. by chills and fever, and if left untreated may result in joint pain, arthritis, and cardiac and neurological disorders

lymph \ˈlimf\ *n* : a pale liquid consisting chiefly of blood plasma and white blood cells, circulating in thin-walled tubes (**lymphatic vessels**), and bathing the body tissues — **lym·phat·ic** \lim-ˈfa-tik\ *adj*

lymph·ade·nop·a·thy \ˌlim-ˌfad-ᵊn-ˈä-pə-thē\ *n, pl* **-thies** : abnormal enlargement of the lymph nodes

lymph node *n* : any of the rounded masses of lymphoid tissue surrounded by a capsule

lym·pho·cyte \ˈlim-fə-ˌsīt\ *n* : any of the weakly motile leukocytes produced in lymphoid tissue that are the typical cells in lymph and include the cellular mediators (as a B cell or a T cell) of immunity

lym·phoid \ˈlim-ˌfȯid\ *adj* **1** : of, relating to, or being tissue (as of the lymph nodes) containing lymphocytes **2** : of, relating to, or resembling lymph

lym·pho·ma \lim-ˈfō-mə\ *n, pl* **-mas** *or* **-ma·ta** \-mə-tə\ : a tumor of lymphoid tissue

lynch \ˈlinch\ *vb* : to put to death by mob action without legal sanction or due process of law — **lynch·er** *n*

lynx \ˈliŋks\ *n, pl* **lynx** *or* **lynx·es** : any of several wildcats with a short tail, long legs, and usu. tufted ears

lynx

lyre \ˈlīr\ *n* : a stringed musical instrument of the harp class used by the ancient Greeks

[1]**lyr·ic** \ˈlir-ik\ *n* **1** : a lyric poem **2** *pl* : the words of a popular song — **lyr·i·cal** \-i-kəl\ *adj*

[2]**lyric** *adj* **1** : suitable for singing : MELODIC **2** : expressing direct and usu. intense personal emotion

ly·ser·gic acid di·eth·yl·am·ide \lə-ˈsər-jik . . . ˌdī-ˌe-thə-ˈla-ˌmīd, lī-, -ˈla-məd\ *n* : LSD

LZ *abbr* landing zone

M

[1]**m** \ˈem\ *n, pl* **m's** *or* **ms** \ˈemz\ *often cap* : the 13th letter of the English alphabet

[2]**m** *abbr, often cap* **1** Mach **2** male **3** married **4** masculine **5** medium **6** [L *meridies*] noon **7** meter **8** mile **9** [L *mille*] thousand **10** minute **11** month **12** moon

ma \ˈmä, ˈmȯ\ *n* : MOTHER

MA *abbr* **1** [ML *magister artium*] master of arts **2** Massachusetts **3** mental age

ma'am \ˈmam, *after "yes" often* əm\ *n* : MADAM

Mac *abbr* Machabees

Mac *or* **Macc** *abbr* Maccabees

ma·ca·bre \mə-ˈkäb; ˈkä-brə, -bər\ *adj* [F] **1** : having death as a subject **2** : GRUESOME **3** : HORRIBLE

mac·ad·am \mə-ˈka-dəm\ *n* : a roadway or pavement of small closely packed broken stone — **mac·ad·am·ize** \-də-ˌmīz\ *vb*

ma·caque \mə-ˈkak, -ˈkäk\ *n* : any of a genus of short-tailed chiefly Asian monkeys

mac·a·ro·ni \ˌma-kə-ˈrō-nē\ *n* **1** : pasta made chiefly of wheat flour and shaped in the form of slender tubes **2** *pl* **-nis** *or* **-nies** : FOP, DANDY

mac·a·roon \ˌma-kə-ˈrün\ *n* : a small cookie made chiefly of egg whites, sugar, and ground almonds or coconut

ma·caw \mə-ˈkȯ\ *n* : any of numerous parrots of Central and So. America

Mac·ca·bees \ˈma-kə-ˌbēz\ *n* — see BIBLE table

[1]**mace** \ˈmās\ *n* : a spice made from the fibrous coating of the nutmeg

[2]**mace** *n* **1** : a heavy often spiked club used as a weapon esp. in the Middle Ages **2** : an ornamental staff carried as a symbol of authority

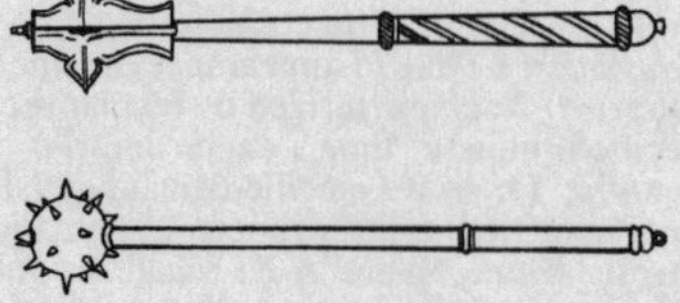

mace 1

Mac·e·do·nian \ˌma-sə-ˈdō-nyən, -nē-ən\ *n* : a native or inhabitant of Macedonia — **Macedonian** *adj*

mac·er·ate \ˈma-sə-ˌrāt\ *vb* **-at·ed; -at·ing 1** : to cause to waste away **2** : to soften by steeping or soaking so as to separate the parts — **mac·er·a·tion** \ˌma-sə-ˈrā-shən\ *n*

mach *abbr* machine; machinery; machinist

Mach \ˈmäk\ *n* : a speed expressed by a Mach number

Mach·a·bees \ˈma-kə-ˌbēz\ *n* : MACCABEES

ma·chete \mə-ˈshe-tē\ *n* : a large heavy knife used for cutting sugarcane and underbrush and as a weapon

Ma·chi·a·vel·lian \ˌma-kē-ə-ˈve-lē-ən\ *adj* [Niccolò *Machiavelli,* †1527 Ital. political philosopher] : characterized by cunning, duplicity, and bad faith — **Ma·chi·a·vel·lian·ism** *n*

mach·i·na·tion \ˌma-kə-ˈnā-shən, ˌma-shə-\ *n* : an act of planning esp. to do harm; *esp* : PLOT — **mach·i·nate** \ˈma-kə-ˌnāt, ˈma-shə-\ *vb*

[1]**ma·chine** \mə-ˈshēn\ *n* **1** : CONVEYANCE, VEHICLE; *esp* : AUTOMOBILE **2** : a combination of mechanical parts that transmit forces, motion, and energy one to another **3** : an instrument (as a lever) for transmitting or modifying force or motion **4** : an electrical, electronic, or mechanical device for performing a task ⟨a sewing ~⟩ **5** : a highly organized political group under the leadership of a boss or small clique

[2]**machine** *vb* **ma·chined; ma·chin·ing** : to shape or finish by machine-operated tools — **ma·chin·able** \-ˈshē-nə-bəl\ *adj*

machine gun *n* : an automatic gun capable of rapid continuous firing — **machine–gun** *vb* — **machine gunner** *n*

machine language *n* : the set of symbolic instruction codes used to represent operations and data in a machine (as a computer)

machine–readable *adj* : directly usable by a computer

ma·chin·ery \mə-ˈshē-nə-rē\ *n, pl* **-er·ies 1** : MACHINES; *also* : the working parts of a machine **2** : the means by which something is done

ma·chin·ist \mə-ˈshē-nist\ *n* : a person who makes or works on machines

ma·chis·mo \mä-ˈchēz-(ˌ)mō, -ˈchiz-\ *n* : a strong or exaggerated pride in one's masculinity

Mach number \ˈmäk-\ *n* : a number representing the ratio of the speed of a body to the speed of sound in the surrounding atmosphere
ma•cho \ˈmä-chō\ *adj* [Sp, lit., male, fr. L *masculus*] : characterized by machismo
mack•er•el \ˈma-kə-rəl\ *n, pl* **mackerel** *or* **mackerels** : a No. Atlantic food fish greenish above and silvery below
mack•i•naw \ˈma-kə-ˌnȯ\ *n* : a short heavy plaid coat
mack•in•tosh *also* **mac•in•tosh** \ˈma-kən-ˌtäsh\ *n* **1** *chiefly Brit* : RAINCOAT **2** : a lightweight waterproof fabric
mac•ra•mé *also* **mac•ra•me** \ˈma-krə-ˌmā\ *n* [ultim. fr. Ar *miqramah* coverlet] : a coarse lace or fringe made by knotting threads or cords in a geometrical pattern
mac•ro \ˈma-(ˌ)krō\ *adj* : very large; *also* : involving large quantities or being on a large scale
mac•ro•bi•ot•ic \ˌma-krō-bī-ˈä-tik, -bē-\ *adj* : relating to or being a very restricted diet (as one containing chiefly whole grains)
mac•ro•cosm \ˈma-krə-ˌkä-zəm\ *n* : the great world : UNIVERSE
ma•cron \ˈmā-ˌkrän, ˈma-\ *n* : a mark ¯ placed over a vowel (as in \māk\) to show that the vowel is long
mac•ro•scop•ic \ˌma-krə-ˈskä-pik\ *adj* : visible to the naked eye — **mac•ro•scop•i•cal•ly** \-pi-k(ə-)lē\ *adv*
mad \ˈmad\ *adj* **mad•der; mad•dest 1** : disordered in mind : INSANE **2** : being rash and foolish **3** : FURIOUS, ENRAGED **4** : carried away by enthusiasm **5** : RABID **6** : marked by wild gaiety and merriment **7** : FRANTIC — **mad•ly** *adv* — **mad•ness** *n*
Mad•a•gas•can \ˌma-də-ˈgas-kən\ *n* : a native or inhabitant of Madagascar
mad•am \ˈma-dəm\ *n* **1** *pl* **mes•dames** \mā-ˈdäm\ — used as a form of polite address to a woman **2** *pl* **mad•ams** : the female head of a house of prostitution
ma•dame \mə-ˈdam, *before a surname also* ˈma-dəm\ *n, pl* **mes•dames** \mā-ˈdäm\ : MISTRESS — used as a title equivalent to *Mrs.* for a married woman not of English-speaking nationality
mad•cap \ˈmad-ˌkap\ *adj* : WILD, RECKLESS — **mad•cap** *n*
mad•den \ˈmad-ᵊn\ *vb* : to make mad — **mad•den•ing•ly** *adv*
mad•der \ˈma-dər\ *n* : a Eurasian herb with yellow flowers and fleshy red roots; *also* : its root or a dye prepared from it
made *past and past part of* MAKE
Ma•dei•ra \mə-ˈdir-ə\ *n* : an amber-colored dessert wine
ma•de•moi•selle \ˌma-də-mə-ˈzel, -mwə-, mam-ˈzel\ *n, pl* **ma•de•moi•selles** \-ˈzelz\ *or* **mes•de•moi•selles** \ˌmā-də-me-ˈzel, -mwe-\ : an unmarried girl or woman — used as a title for an unmarried woman not of English-speaking nationality
made–up \ˈmā-ˈdəp\ *adj* **1** : fancifully conceived or falsely devised **2** : marked by the use of makeup
mad•house \ˈmad-ˌhau̇s\ *n* **1** : a place for the detention and care of the insane **2** : a place of great uproar
mad•man \ˈmad-ˌman, -mən\ *n* : LUNATIC
Ma•don•na \mə-ˈdä-nə\ *n* : a representation (as a picture or statue) of the Virgin Mary
ma•dras \ˈma-drəs; ˌmə-ˈdras, -ˈdräs\ *n* [*Madras*, India] : a fine usu. cotton fabric with various designs (as plaid)
mad•ri•gal \ˈma-dri-gəl\ *n* [It *madrigale*] **1** : a short lyrical poem in a strict poetic form **2** : an elaborate part-song esp. of the 16th and 17th centuries
mad•wom•an \ˈmad-ˌwu̇-mən\ *n* : a woman who is insane
mael•strom \ˈmāl-strəm\ *n* **1** : a violent whirlpool **2** : TUMULT
mae•stro \ˈmī-strō\ *n, pl* **maestros** *or* **mae•stri** \-ˌstrē\ [It] : a master in an art; *esp* : an eminent composer, conductor, or teacher of music
Ma•fia \ˈmä-fē-ə\ *n* [It] : a secret criminal society of Sicily or Italy; *also* : a similar organization elsewhere
ma•fi•o•so \ˌmä-fē-ˈō-(ˌ)sō\ *n, pl* **-si** \-(ˌ)sē\ : a member of the Mafia
[1]**mag** \ˈmag\ *n* : MAGAZINE
[2]**mag** *abbr* **1** magnetism **2** magneto **3** magnitude
mag•a•zine \ˈma-gə-ˌzēn\ *n* **1** : a storehouse esp. for military supplies **2** : a place for keeping gunpowder in a fort or ship **3** : a publication usu. containing stories, articles, or poems and issued periodically **4** : a container in a gun for holding cartridges; *also* : a chamber (as on a camera) for film
ma•gen•ta \mə-ˈjen-tə\ *n* : a deep purplish red color
mag•got \ˈma-gət\ *n* : the legless wormlike larva of a dipteran fly — **mag•goty** *adj*
ma•gi \ˈmā-jī\ *n pl, often cap* : the three wise men from the East who paid homage to the infant Jesus
mag•ic \ˈma-jik\ *n* **1** : the use of means (as charms or spells) believed to have supernatural power over natural forces **2** : an extraordinary power or influence seemingly from a supernatural force **3** : SLEIGHT OF HAND — **magic** *adj* — **mag•i•cal** \-ji-kəl\ *adj* — **mag•i•cal•ly** \-ji-k(ə-)lē\ *adv*
ma•gi•cian \mə-ˈji-shən\ *n* : one skilled in magic
mag•is•te•ri•al \ˌma-jə-ˈstir-ē-əl\ *adj* **1** : AUTHORITATIVE **2** : of or relating to a magistrate or a magistrate's office or duties
ma•gis•tral \ˈma-jə-strəl\ *adj* : AUTHORITATIVE
mag•is•trate \ˈma-jə-ˌstrāt\ *n* : an official entrusted with administration of the laws — **mag•is•tra•cy** \-strə-sē\ *n*
mag•ma \ˈmag-mə\ *n* : molten rock material within the earth — **mag•mat•ic** \mag-ˈma-tik\ *adj*
mag•nan•i•mous \mag-ˈna-nə-məs\ *adj* **1** : showing or suggesting a lofty and courageous spirit **2** : NOBLE, GENEROUS — **mag•na•nim•i•ty** \ˌmag-nə-ˈni-mə-tē\ *n* — **mag•nan•i•mous•ly** *adv* — **mag•nan•i•mous•ness** *n*
mag•nate \ˈmag-ˌnāt\ *n* : a person of rank, influence, or distinction
mag•ne•sia \mag-ˈnē-shə, -zhə\ *n* [NL, fr. *magnes carneus*, a white earth, lit., flesh magnet] : a light white oxide of magnesium used as a laxative
mag•ne•sium \mag-ˈnē-zē-əm, -zhəm\ *n* : a silver-white light malleable metallic chemical element — see ELEMENT table
mag•net \ˈmag-nət\ *n* **1** : LODESTONE **2** : a body that is able to attract iron **3** : something that attracts
mag•net•ic \mag-ˈne-tik\ *adj* **1** : having an unusual ability to attract ⟨a ~ leader⟩ **2** : of or relating to a magnet or magnetism **3** : magnetized or capable of being magnetized — **mag•net•i•cal•ly** \-ti-k(ə-)lē\ *adv*
magnetic disk *n* : DISK 3
magnetic north *n* : the northerly direction in the earth's magnetic field indicated by the north-seeking pole of a compass needle
magnetic resonance imaging *n* : a noninvasive diagnostic technique that produces computerized images of internal body tissues based on electromagnetically induced activity of atoms within the body
magnetic tape *n* : a ribbon coated with a magnetic material on which information (as sound) may be stored
mag•ne•tise *Brit var of* MAGNETIZE
mag•ne•tism \ˈmag-nə-ˌti-zəm\ *n* **1** : the power (as of a magnet) to attract iron **2** : the science that deals with magnetic phenomena **3** : an ability to attract
mag•ne•tite \ˈmag-nə-ˌtīt\ *n* : a black mineral that is an important iron ore
mag•ne•tize \ˈmag-nə-ˌtīz\ *vb* **-tized; -tiz•ing 1** : to induce magnetic properties in **2** : to attract like a magnet : CHARM — **mag•ne•tiz•able** *adj* — **mag•ne•ti•za•tion** \ˌmag-nə-tə-ˈzā-shən\ *n* — **mag•ne•tiz•er** *n*
mag•ne•to \mag-ˈnē-tō\ *n, pl* **-tos** : a generator used to produce sparks in an internal combustion engine
mag•ne•tom•e•ter \ˌmag-nə-ˈtä-mə-tər\ *n* : an instrument for measuring the strength of a magnetic field
mag•ne•to•sphere \mag-ˈnē-tə-ˌsfir, -ˈne-\ *n* : a region

around a celestial object (as the earth) in which charged particles are trapped by its magnetic field — **mag•ne•to•spher•ic** \-ˌnē-tə-ˈsfir-ik, -ˈsfer-\ *adj*

mag•ni•fi•ca•tion \ˌmag-nə-fə-ˈkā-shən\ *n* **1** : the act of magnifying **2** : the amount by which an optical lens or instrument magnifies

mag•nif•i•cent \mag-ˈni-fə-sənt\ *adj* **1** : characterized by grandeur or beauty : SPLENDID **2** : EXALTED, NOBLE **syn** imposing, stately, grand, majestic — **mag•nif•i•cence** \-səns\ *n* — **mag•nif•i•cent•ly** *adv*

mag•nif•i•co \mag-ˈni-fi-ˌkō\ *n, pl* **-coes** *or* **-cos 1** : a nobleman of Venice **2** : a person of high position

mag•ni•fy \ˈmag-nə-ˌfī\ *vb* **-fied; -fy•ing 1** : EXTOL, LAUD; *also* : to cause to be held in greater esteem **2** : INTENSIFY; *also* : EXAGGERATE **3** : to enlarge in fact or in appearance ⟨a microscope *magnifies* an object⟩ — **mag•ni•fi•er** \ˈmag-nə-ˌfī-ər\ *n*

mag•nil•o•quent \mag-ˈni-lə-kwənt\ *adj* : characterized by an exalted and often bombastic style or manner — **mag•nil•o•quence** \-kwəns\ *n*

mag•ni•tude \ˈmag-nə-ˌtüd, -tyüd\ *n* **1** : greatness of size or extent **2** : SIZE **3** : QUANTITY **4** : a number representing the brightness of a celestial body

mag•no•lia \mag-ˈnōl-yə\ *n* : any of a genus of usu. spring-flowering shrubs and trees with large often fragrant flowers

mag•num opus \ˈmag-nəm-ˈō-pəs\ *n* [L] : the greatest achievement of an artist or writer

mag•pie \ˈmag-ˌpī\ *n* : any of various long-tailed often black-and-white birds related to the jays

Mag•yar \ˈmag-ˌyär, ˈmäg-; ˈmä-ˌjär\ *n* : a member of the dominant people of Hungary — **Magyar** *adj*

ma•ha•ra•ja *or* **ma•ha•ra•jah** \ˌmä-hə-ˈrä-jə\ *n* : a Hindu prince ranking above a raja

ma•ha•ra•ni *or* **ma•ha•ra•nee** \-ˈrä-nē\ *n* **1** : the wife of a maharaja **2** : a Hindu princess ranking above a rani

ma•ha•ri•shi \ˌmä-hə-ˈrē-shē\ *n* : a Hindu teacher of mystical knowledge

ma•hat•ma \mə-ˈhät-mə, -ˈhat-\ *n* [Skt *mahātman,* fr. *mahātman* great-souled, fr. *mahat* great + *ātman* soul] : a person revered for high-mindedness, wisdom, and selflessness

Ma•hi•can \mə-ˈhē-kən\ *n, pl* **Mahican** *or* **Mahicans** : a member of an American Indian people of the upper Hudson River valley

ma•hog•a•ny \mə-ˈhä-gə-nē\ *n, pl* **-nies** : the reddish wood of any of various chiefly tropical trees that is used in furniture; *also* : a tree yielding this wood

ma•hout \mə-ˈhaůt\ *n* [Hindi *mahāut*] : a keeper and driver of an elephant

maid \ˈmād\ *n* **1** : an unmarried girl or young woman **2** : MAIDSERVANT

¹maid•en \ˈmād-ᵊn\ *n* : MAID 1 — **maid•en•ly** *adj*

²maiden *adj* **1** : UNMARRIED; *also* : VIRGIN **2** : of, relating to, or befitting a maiden **3** : FIRST ⟨~ voyage⟩

maid•en•hair fern \-ˌhar-\ *n* : any of a genus of ferns with delicate feathery fronds

maid•en•head \ˈmād-ᵊn-ˌhed\ *n* **1** : VIRGINITY **2** : HYMEN

maid•en•hood \-ˌhůd\ *n* : the condition or time of being a maiden

maid–in–waiting *n, pl* **maids–in–waiting** : a young woman appointed to attend a queen or princess

maid of honor : a bride's principal unmarried wedding attendant

maid•ser•vant \ˈmād-ˌsər-vənt\ *n* : a girl or woman who is a servant

¹mail \ˈmāl\ *n* [ME *male* bag, fr. OF] **1** : something sent or carried in the postal system **2** : a nation's postal system — often used in pl.

²mail *vb* : to send by mail

³mail *n* [ME *maille,* fr. MF, fr. L *macula* spot, mesh] : armor made of metal links or plates

mail•box \ˈmāl-ˌbäks\ *n* **1** : a public box for the collection of mail **2** : a private box for the delivery of mail

mail•man \-ˌman\ *n* : a man who delivers mail

maim \ˈmām\ *vb* : to mutilate, disfigure, or wound seriously : CRIPPLE

¹main \ˈmān\ *n* **1** : FORCE ⟨with might and ~⟩ **2** : MAINLAND; *also* : HIGH SEA **3** : the chief part **4** : a principal pipe, duct, or circuit of a utility system

²main *adj* **1** : CHIEF, PRINCIPAL **2** : fully exerted ⟨~ force⟩ **3** : expressing the chief predication in a complex sentence ⟨the ~ clause⟩ — **main•ly** *adv*

main•frame \ˈmān-ˌfrām\ *n* : a large fast computer

main•land \-ˌland, -lənd\ *n* : a continuous body of land constituting the chief part of a country or continent

main•line \-ˌlīn\ *vb, slang* : to inject a narcotic drug into a vein

main line *n* : a principal highway or railroad line

main•mast \ˈmān-ˌmast, -məst\ *n* : the principal mast on a sailing ship

main•sail \-ˌsāl, -səl\ *n* : the largest sail on the mainmast

main•spring \-ˌspriŋ\ *n* **1** : the chief spring in a mechanism (as of a watch) **2** : the chief motive, agent, or cause

main•stay \-ˌstā\ *n* **1** : a stay running from the head of the mainmast to the foot of the foremast **2** : a chief support

main•stream \-ˌstrēm\ *n* : a prevailing current or direction of activity or influence — **mainstream** *adj*

main•tain \mān-ˈtān\ *vb* [ME *mainteinen,* fr. OF *maintenir,* fr. ML *manutenēre,* fr. L *manu tenēre* to hold in the hand] **1** : to keep in an existing state (as of repair) **2** : to sustain against opposition or danger **3** : to continue in : CARRY ON **4** : to provide for : SUPPORT **5** : ASSERT — **main•tain•abil•i•ty** \-ˌtā-nə-ˈbi-lə-tē\ *n* — **main•tain•able** \-ˈtā-nə-bəl\ *adj* — **main•te•nance** \ˈmānt-ᵊn-əns\ *n*

main•top \ˈmān-ˌtäp\ *n* : a platform at the head of the mainmast of a square-rigged ship

mai•son•ette \ˌmāz-ᵊn-ˈet\ *n* **1** : a small house **2** : an apartment often on two floors

maî•tre d' *or* **mai•tre d'** \ˌmā-trə-ˈdē, ˌme-\ *n, pl* **maître d's** *or* **maitre d's** \-ˈdēz\ : MAÎTRE D'HÔTEL

maî•tre d'hô•tel \ˌmā-trə-dō-ˈtel, ˌme-\ *n, pl* **maîtres d'hôtel** *same*\ [F, lit., master of house] **1** : MAJORDOMO **2** : HEADWAITER

maize \ˈmāz\ *n* : INDIAN CORN

Maj *abbr* major

maj•es•ty \ˈma-jə-stē\ *n, pl* **-ties 1** : sovereign power, authority, or dignity; *also* : the person of a sovereign — used as a title **2** : GRANDEUR, SPLENDOR — **ma•jes•tic** \mə-ˈjes-tik\ *adj* — **ma•jes•ti•cal•ly** \-ti-k(ə-)lē\ *adv*

Maj Gen *abbr* Major General

ma•jol•i•ca \mə-ˈjä-li-kə\ *also* **ma•iol•i•ca** \-ˈyä-\ *n* : any of several faiences; *esp* : an Italian tin-glazed pottery

¹ma•jor \ˈmā-jər\ *adj* **1** : greater in number, extent, or importance ⟨a ~ poet⟩ **2** : notable or conspicuous in effect or scope ⟨a ~ improvement⟩ **3** : SERIOUS ⟨a ~ illness⟩ **4** : having half steps between the 3d and 4th and the 7th and 8th degrees ⟨~ scale⟩; *also* : based on a major scale ⟨~ key⟩ ⟨~ chord⟩

²major *n* **1** : a commissioned officer (as in the army) ranking next below a lieutenant colonel **2** : an academic subject chosen as a field of specialization; *also* : a student specializing in such a field

³major *vb* : to pursue an academic major

ma•jor•do•mo \ˌmā-jər-ˈdō-mō\ *n, pl* **-mos** [Sp *mayordomo* or obs. It *maiordomo,* fr. ML *major domus,* lit., chief of the house] **1** : a head steward **2** : BUTLER

ma•jor•ette \ˌmā-jə-ˈret\ *n* : DRUM MAJORETTE

major general *n* : a commissioned officer (as in the army) ranking next below a lieutenant general

ma•jor•i•ty \mə-ˈjȯr-ə-tē\ *n, pl* **-ties 1** : the age at which full civil rights are accorded; *also* : the status of one who has attained this age **2** : a number greater than half of a total; *also* : the excess of this greater number over the remainder **3** : the rank of a major

ma•jus•cule \ˈma-jəs-ˌkyül, mə-ˈjəs-\ *n* : a large letter (as a capital)

[1]**make** \ˈmāk\ *vb* **made** \ˈmād\; **mak•ing 1** : to cause to exist, occur, or appear; *also* : DESTINE ⟨was *made* to be an actor⟩ **2** : FASHION ⟨~ a dress⟩; *also* : COMPOSE **3** : to formulate in the mind ⟨~ plans⟩ **4** : CONSTITUTE ⟨house *made* of stone⟩ **5** : to compute to be **6** : to set in order : PREPARE ⟨~ a bed⟩ **7** : to cause to be or become; *also* : APPOINT **8** : ENACT; *also* : EXECUTE ⟨~ a will⟩ **9** : CONCLUDE ⟨didn't know what to ~ of it⟩ **10** : CARRY OUT, PERFORM ⟨~ a gesture⟩ **11** : COMPEL **12** : to assure the success of ⟨will ~ us or break us⟩ **13** : to amount to in significance ⟨~*s* no difference⟩ **14** : to be capable of developing or being fashioned into **15** : REACH, ATTAIN; *also* : GAIN **16** : to start out : GO **17** : to have weight or effect ⟨courtesy ~*s* for safer driving⟩ **syn** form, shape, fabricate, manufacture — **mak•er** *n* — **make believe** : PRETEND — **make do** : to manage with the means at hand — **make fun of** : RIDICULE, MOCK — **make good 1** : INDEMNIFY ⟨*make good* the loss⟩; *also* : to carry out successfully ⟨*make good* his promise⟩ **2** : SUCCEED — **make way 1** : to give room for passing, entering, or occupying **2** : to make progress

[2]**make** *n* **1** : the manner or style of construction; *also* : BRAND 3 **2** : MAKEUP **3** : the action of manufacturing — **on the make** : in search of wealth, social status, or sexual adventure

[1]**make–be•lieve** \ˈmāk-bə-ˌlēv\ *n* : a pretending to believe : PRETENSE

[2]**make–believe** *adj* : IMAGINED, PRETENDED

make–do \-ˌdü\ *adj* : MAKESHIFT

make out *vb* **1** : to draw up in writing ⟨*make out* a list⟩ **2** : to find or grasp the meaning of ⟨can you *make* that *out*⟩ **3** : to represent as being **4** : to pretend to be true **5** : DISCERN ⟨*make out* a ship in the fog⟩ **6** : GET ALONG, FARE ⟨*make out* well in life⟩ **7** : to engage in amorous kissing and caressing

make over *vb* : REMAKE, REMODEL — **make•over** \ˈmā-ˌkō-vər\ *n*

make•shift \ˈmāk-ˌshift\ *n* : a temporary expedient — **makeshift** *adj*

make•up \ˈmā-ˌkəp\ *n* **1** : the way in which something is put together; *also* : physical, mental, and moral constitution **2** : cosmetics esp. for the face; *also* : materials (as wigs and cosmetics) used in making up

make up *vb* **1** : FORM, COMPOSE **2** : to compensate for a deficiency **3** : SETTLE ⟨*made up* my mind⟩ **4** : INVENT, IMPROVISE **5** : to become reconciled **6** : to put on makeup (as for a play)

make–work \ˈmāk-ˌwərk\ *n* : BUSYWORK

mak•ings \ˈmā-kiŋz\ *n pl* : the material from which something is made

makuta *pl of* LIKUTA

Mal *abbr* Malachi

Mal•a•chi \ˈma-lə-ˌkī\ *n* — see BIBLE table

Mal•a•chi•as \ˌma-lə-ˈkī-əs\ *n* : MALACHI

mal•a•chite \ˈma-lə-ˌkīt\ *n* : a mineral that is a green carbonate of copper used for making ornamental objects

mal•adapt•ed \ˌma-lə-ˈdap-təd\ *adj* : poorly suited to a particular use, purpose, or situation

mal•ad•just•ed \ˌma-lə-ˈjəs-təd\ *adj* : poorly or inadequately adjusted (as to one's environment) — **mal•ad•just•ment** \-ˈjəst-mənt\ *n*

mal•adroit \ˌma-lə-ˈdrȯit\ *adj* : not adroit : INEPT

mal•a•dy \ˈma-lə-dē\ *n, pl* **-dies** : a disease or disorder of body or mind

mal•aise \mə-ˈlāz, ma-\ *n* [F] : a hazy feeling of not being well

mal•a•mute \ˈma-lə-ˌmyüt\ *n* : a dog often used to draw sleds esp. in northern No. America

mal•a•prop•ism \ˈma-lə-ˌprä-ˌpi-zəm\ *n* : a usu. humorous misuse of a word

mal•ap•ro•pos \ˌma-ˌla-prə-ˈpō, ma-ˈla-prə-ˌpō\ *adv* : in an inappropriate or inopportune way — **malapropos** *adj*

ma•lar•ia \mə-ˈler-ē-ə\ *n* [It, fr. *mala aria* bad air] : a disease marked by recurring chills and fever and caused by a protozoan parasite of the blood that is transmitted by anopheles mosquitoes — **ma•lar•i•al** \-əl\ *adj*

ma•lar•key \mə-ˈlär-kē\ *n* : insincere or foolish talk

mal•a•thi•on \ˌma-lə-ˈthī-ən, -ˌän\ *n* : an insecticide with a relatively low toxicity for mammals

Ma•la•wi•an \mə-ˈlä-wē-ən\ *n* : a native or inhabitant of Malawi — **Malawian** *adj*

Ma•lay \mə-ˈlā, ˈmā-ˌlā\ *n* **1** : a member of a people of the Malay Peninsula and Archipelago **2** : the language of the Malays — **Malay** *adj* — **Ma•lay•an** \mə-ˈlā-ən, ˈmā-ˌlā-\ *n or adj*

Ma•lay•sian \mə-ˈlā-zhən, -shən\ *n* : a native or inhabitant of Malaysia — **Malaysian** *adj*

mal•con•tent \ˌmal-kən-ˈtent\ *adj* : marked by a dissatisfaction with the existing state of affairs : DISCONTENTED — **malcontent** *n*

mal de mer \ˌmal-də-ˈmer\ *n* [F] : SEASICKNESS

[1]**male** \ˈmāl\ *adj* **1** : of, relating to, or being the sex that produces germ cells which fertilize the eggs of a female; *also* : STAMINATE **2** : MASCULINE — **male•ness** *n*

[2]**male** *n* : a male individual

male•dic•tion \ˌma-lə-ˈdik-shən\ *n* : CURSE, EXECRATION

male•fac•tor \ˈma-lə-ˌfak-tər\ *n* : EVILDOER; *esp* : one who commits an offense against the law — **mal•e•fac•tion** \ˌma-lə-ˈfak-shən\ *n*

ma•lef•ic \mə-ˈle-fik\ *adj* **1** : BALEFUL **2** : MALICIOUS

ma•lef•i•cent \-fə-sənt\ *adj* : working or productive of harm or evil

ma•lev•o•lent \mə-ˈle-və-lənt\ *adj* : having, showing, or arising from ill will, spite, or hatred **syn** malignant, malign, malicious, spiteful — **ma•lev•o•lence** \-ləns\ *n*

mal•fea•sance \mal-ˈfēz-ᵊns\ *n* : wrongful conduct esp. by a public official

mal•for•ma•tion \ˌmal-fȯr-ˈmā-shən\ *n* : irregular or faulty formation or structure; *also* : an instance of this — **mal•formed** \mal-ˈfȯrmd\ *adj*

mal•func•tion \mal-ˈfəŋk-shən\ *vb* : to fail to operate normally — **malfunction** *n*

Ma•li•an \ˈmä-lē-ən\ *n* : a native or inhabitant of Mali — **Malian** *adj*

mal•ice \ˈma-ləs\ *n* : desire to cause injury or distress to another — **ma•li•cious** \mə-ˈli-shəs\ *adj* — **ma•li•cious•ly** *adv*

[1]**ma•lign** \mə-ˈlīn\ *adj* **1** : evil in nature, influence, or effect; *also* : MALIGNANT 2 **2** : moved by ill will

[2]**malign** *vb* : to speak evil of : DEFAME

ma•lig•nant \mə-ˈlig-nənt\ *adj* **1** : INJURIOUS, MALIGN **2** : tending to produce death or deterioration ⟨a ~ tumor⟩ — **ma•lig•nan•cy** \-nən-sē\ *n* — **ma•lig•nant•ly** *adv* — **ma•lig•ni•ty** \-nə-tē\ *n*

ma•lin•ger \mə-ˈliŋ-gər\ *vb* [F *malingre* sickly] : to pretend illness so as to avoid duty — **ma•lin•ger•er** *n*

mal•i•son \ˈma-lə-sən, -zən\ *n* : CURSE

mall \ˈmȯl, ˈmal\ *n* **1** : a shaded walk : PROMENADE **2** : an urban shopping area featuring a variety of shops surrounding a concourse **3** : a usu. large enclosed suburban shopping area containing various shops

mal•lard \ˈma-lərd\ *n, pl* **mallard** *or* **mallards** : a common wild duck that is the source of domestic ducks

☞ For illustration, see next page.

mal•lea•ble \ˈma-lē-ə-bəl\ *adj* **1** : capable of being extended or shaped by beating with a hammer or by the pressure of rollers **2** : ADAPTABLE, PLIABLE **syn** plastic, pliant, ductile, supple — **mal•le•a•bil•i•ty** \ˌma-lē-ə-ˈbi-lə-tē\ *n*

mal•let \ˈma-lət\ *n* **1** : a tool with a large head for driving another tool or for striking a surface without mar-

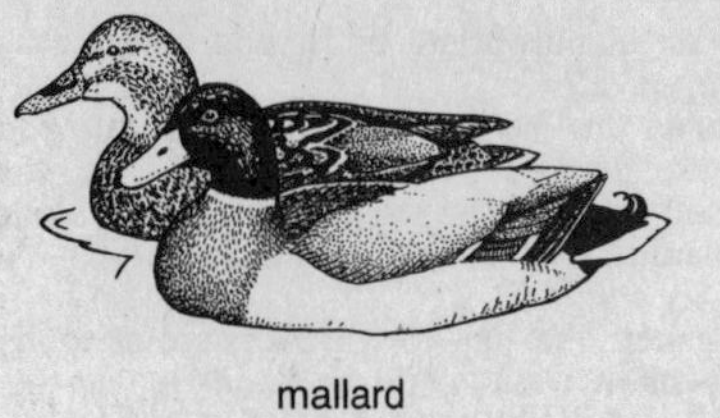
mallard

ring it **2 :** a long-handled hammerlike implement for striking a ball (as in croquet)

mal•le•us \ˈma-lē-əs\ *n, pl* **mal•lei** \-lē-ˌī, -lē-ˌē\ [NL, fr. L, hammer] **:** the outermost of the three small bones of the mammalian middle ear

mal•low \ˈma-lō\ *n* **:** any of a genus of herbs with lobed leaves, usu. showy flowers, and a disk-shaped fruit

malm•sey \ˈmälm-zē\ *n, often cap* **:** the sweetest variety of Madeira

mal•nour•ished \mal-ˈnər-isht\ *adj* **:** UNDERNOURISHED

mal•nu•tri•tion \ˌmal-nü-ˈtri-shən, -nyü-\ *n* **:** faulty and esp. inadequate nutrition

mal•oc•clu•sion \ˌma-lə-ˈklü-zhən\ *n* **:** faulty coming together of teeth in biting

mal•odor•ous \ma-ˈlō-də-rəs\ *adj* **:** ill-smelling — **mal•odor•ous•ly** *adv* — **mal•odor•ous•ness** *n*

ma•lo•ti \mə-ˈlō-tē\ *pl of* LOTI

mal•prac•tice \mal-ˈprak-təs\ *n* **:** a dereliction of professional duty or a failure of professional skill that results in injury, loss, or damage

malt \ˈmȯlt\ *n* **1 :** grain and esp. barley steeped in water until it has sprouted and used in brewing and distilling **2 :** liquor made with malt — **malty** *adj*

malted milk \ˈmȯl-təd-\ *n* **:** a powder prepared from dried milk and an extract from malt; *also* **:** a beverage of this powder in milk or other liquid

Mal•thu•sian \mal-ˈthü-zhən, -ˈthyü-\ *adj* **:** of or relating to a theory that population unless checked (as by war) tends to increase faster than its means of subsistence — **Malthusian** *n* — **Mal•thu•sian•ism** \-zhə-ˌni-zəm\ *n*

malt•ose \ˈmȯl-ˌtōs\ *n* **:** a sugar formed esp. from starch by the action of enzymes

mal•treat \mal-ˈtrēt\ *vb* **:** to treat cruelly or roughly **:** ABUSE — **mal•treat•ment** *n*

ma•ma *or* **mam•ma** \ˈmä-mə\ *n* **:** MOTHER

mam•bo \ˈmäm-bō\ *n, pl* **mambos :** a dance of Cuban origin related to the rumba — **mambo** *vb*

mam•mal \ˈma-məl\ *n* **:** any of a class of warm-blooded vertebrates that includes humans and all other animals which nourish their young with milk and have the skin more or less covered with hair — **mam•ma•li•an** \mə-ˈmā-lē-ən, ma-\ *adj or n*

mam•ma•ry \ˈma-mə-rē\ *adj* **:** of, relating to, or being the glands (**mammary glands**) that in female mammals secrete milk

mam•mo•gram \ˈma-mə-ˌgram\ *n* **:** an X-ray photograph of the breasts

mam•mog•ra•phy \ma-ˈmä-grə-fē\ *n* **:** X-ray examination of the breasts (as for early detection of cancer)

mam•mon \ˈma-mən\ *n, often cap* **:** material wealth having a debasing influence

¹mam•moth \ˈma-məth\ *n* **:** any of a genus of large hairy extinct elephants

²mammoth *adj* **:** of very great size **:** GIGANTIC **syn** colossal, enormous, immense, vast, elephantine

¹man \ˈman\ *n, pl* **men** \ˈmen\ **1 :** a human being; *esp* **:** an adult male **2 :** the human race **:** MANKIND **3 :** one possessing in high degree the qualities considered distinctive of manhood **4 :** an adult male servant or employee **5 :** the individual who can fulfill one's requirements ⟨he's your ~⟩ **6 :** one of the pieces with which various games (as chess) are played; *also* **:** one of the players on a team **7** *often cap* **:** white society or people

²man *vb* **manned; man•ning 1 :** to supply with men ⟨~ a fleet⟩ **2 :** FORTIFY, BRACE

³man *abbr* manual

Man *abbr* Manitoba

man–about–town *n, pl* **men–about–town :** a worldly and socially active man

man•a•cle \ˈma-ni-kəl\ *n* **1 :** a shackle for the hand or wrist **2 :** something used as a restraint

man•age \ˈma-nij\ *vb* **man•aged; man•ag•ing 1 :** HANDLE, CONTROL; *also* **:** to direct or carry on business or affairs **2 :** to make and keep compliant **3 :** to treat with care **:** HUSBAND **4 :** to achieve one's purpose **:** CONTRIVE — **man•age•abil•i•ty** \ˌma-ni-jə-ˈbi-lə-tē\ *n* — **man•age•able** \ˈma-ni-jə-bəl\ *adj* — **man•age•able•ness** *n* — **man•age•ably** \-blē\ *adv*

man•age•ment \ˈma-nij-mənt\ *n* **1 :** the act or art of managing **:** CONTROL **2 :** judicious use of means to accomplish an end **3 :** the group of those who manage or direct an enterprise

man•ag•er \ˈma-ni-jər\ *n* **:** one that manages — **man•a•ge•ri•al** \ˌma-nə-ˈjir-ē-əl\ *adj*

ma•ña•na \mən-ˈyä-nə\ [Sp, lit., tomorrow] *n* **:** an indefinite time in the future

man–at–arms *n, pl* **men–at–arms :** SOLDIER; *esp* **:** one who is heavily armed and mounted

man•a•tee \ˈma-nə-ˌtē\ *n* **:** any of a genus of chiefly tropical plant-eating aquatic mammals having a broad rounded tail

Man•chu•ri•an \man-ˈchu̇r-ē-ən\ *n* **:** a native or inhabitant of Manchuria, China — **Manchurian** *adj*

man•ci•ple \ˈman-sə-pəl\ *n* **:** a steward or purveyor esp. for a college or monastery

man•da•mus \man-ˈdā-məs\ *n* [L, we enjoin] **:** a writ issued by a superior court commanding that an official act or duty be performed

man•da•rin \ˈman-də-rən\ *n* **1 :** a public official of high rank under the Chinese Empire **2** *cap* **:** the chief dialect group of China **3 :** a yellow to reddish orange loose-skinned citrus fruit; *also* **:** a tree that bears mandarins

man•date \ˈman-ˌdāt\ *n* **1 :** an authoritative command **2 :** an authorization to act given to a representative **3 :** a commission granted by the League of Nations to a member nation for governing conquered territory; *also* **:** a territory so governed

man•da•to•ry \ˈman-də-ˌtōr-ē\ *adj* **1 :** containing or constituting a command **:** OBLIGATORY **2 :** of or relating to a League of Nations mandate

man•di•ble \ˈman-də-bəl\ *n* **1 :** JAW; *esp* **:** a lower jaw **2 :** either segment of a bird's bill — **man•dib•u•lar** \man-ˈdi-byə-lər\ *adj*

man•do•lin \ˌman-də-ˈlin, ˈmand-ᵊl-ən\ *n* **:** a stringed musical instrument with a pear-shaped body and a fretted neck

man•drake \ˈman-ˌdrāk\ *n* **1 :** an Old World herb of the nightshade family or its large forked root superstitiously credited with human and medicinal attributes **2 :** MAYAPPLE

man•drel *also* **man•dril** \ˈman-drəl\ *n* **1 :** an axle or spindle inserted into a hole in a piece of work to support it during machining **2 :** a metal bar used as a core around which material may be cast, shaped, or molded

man•drill \ˈman-drəl\ *n* **:** a large baboon of western central Africa

mane \ˈmān\ *n* **:** long heavy hair growing about the neck of some mammals (as a horse) — **maned** \ˈmānd\ *adj*

man–eat•er \ˈman-ˌē-tər\ *n* **:** one (as a shark or cannibal) that has or is thought to have an appetite for human flesh — **man–eat•ing** *adj*

ma•nège \ma-ˈnezh, mə-\ *n* **:** the art of horsemanship or of training horses

ma•nes \ˈmä-ˌnās, ˈmā-ˌnēz\ *n pl, often cap* **:** the spirits of the dead and gods of the lower world in ancient Roman belief

ma•neu•ver \mə-ˈnü-vər, -ˈnyü-\ *n* [F *manœuvre*, fr. OF *maneuvre* work done by hand, fr. ML *manuopera*, fr. L *manu operare* to work by hand] **1 :** a military or naval movement; *also* **:** an armed forces training exercise — often used in pl. **2 :** a procedure involving expert physical movement **3 :** an evasive movement or shift of tactics; *also* **:** an action taken to gain a tactical end — **maneuver** *vb* — **ma•neu•ver•abil•i•ty** \-ˌnü-və-rə-ˈbi-lə-tē, -ˌnyü-\ *n* — **ma•neu•ver•able** \-ˈnü-və-rə-bəl, -ˈnyü-\ *adj*

man Friday *n* **:** an efficient and devoted aide or employee

man•ful \ˈman-fəl\ *adj* **:** having or showing courage and resolution — **man•ful•ly** *adv*

man•ga•nese \ˈmaŋ-gə-ˌnēz, -ˌnēs\ *n* **:** a metallic chemical element resembling iron but not magnetic — see ELEMENT table

mange \ˈmānj\ *n* **:** any of several contagious itchy skin diseases esp. of domestic animals — **mangy** \ˈmān-jē\ *adj*

man•ger \ˈmān-jər\ *n* **:** a trough or open box for livestock feed or fodder

[1]**man•gle** \ˈmaŋ-gəl\ *vb* **man•gled; man•gling 1 :** to cut, bruise, or hack with repeated blows **2 :** to spoil or injure esp. through ineptitude — **man•gler** *n*

[2]**mangle** *n* **:** a machine with heated rollers for ironing laundry

man•go \ˈmaŋ-gō\ *n, pl* **mangoes** *also* **mangos** [Pg *manga*] **:** a usu. yellowish red slightly acid juicy tropical fruit borne by an evergreen tree related to the sumacs; *also* **:** this tree

man•grove \ˈman-ˌgrōv\ *n* **:** any of a genus of tropical maritime trees that send out many prop roots and form dense thickets important in coastal land building

man•han•dle \ˈman-ˌhand-ᵊl\ *vb* **:** to handle roughly

man•hat•tan \man-ˈhat-ᵊn\ *n, often cap* **:** a cocktail made of whiskey and vermouth

man•hole \ˈman-ˌhōl\ *n* **:** a hole through which a person may go esp. to gain access to an underground or enclosed structure

man•hood \-ˌhu̇d\ *n* **1 :** the condition of being an adult male **2 :** manly qualities **:** COURAGE **3 :** MEN ⟨the nation's ~⟩

man–hour \-ˈau̇r\ *n* **:** a unit of one hour's work by one person

man•hunt \-ˌhənt\ *n* **:** an organized hunt for a person and esp. for one charged with a crime

ma•nia \ˈmā-nē-ə, -nyə\ *n* **1 :** excitement of psychotic proportions accompanied by disorganized behavior and elevated mood **2 :** excessive enthusiasm

ma•ni•ac \ˈmā-nē-ˌak\ *n* **:** LUNATIC, MADMAN

ma•ni•a•cal \mə-ˈnī-ə-kəl\ *also* **ma•ni•ac** \ˈmā-nē-ak\ *adj* **1 :** affected with or suggestive of madness **2 :** FRANTIC

man•ic \ˈma-nik\ *adj* **:** affected with, relating to, or resembling mania — **manic** *n* — **man•i•cal•ly** \-ni-k(ə-)lē\ *adv*

man•ic–de•pres•sive \ˌma-nik-di-ˈpre-siv\ *adj* **:** characterized by mania or by psychotic depression or by alternating mania and depression — **manic–depressive** *n*

[1]**man•i•cure** \ˈma-nə-ˌkyu̇r\ *n* **1 :** MANICURIST **2 :** a treatment for the care of the hands and nails

[2]**manicure** *vb* **-cured; -cur•ing 1 :** to do manicure work on **2 :** to trim closely and evenly

man•i•cur•ist \-ˌkyu̇r-ist\ *n* **:** a person who gives manicure treatments

[1]**man•i•fest** \ˈma-nə-ˌfest\ *adj* [ME, fr. MF or L; MF *manifeste*, fr. L *manifestus*, caught in the act, flagrant, perh. fr. *manus* hand + *-festus* (akin to L *infestus* hostile)] **1 :** readily perceived by the senses and esp. by the sight **2 :** easily understood **:** OBVIOUS — **man•i•fest•ly** *adv*

[2]**manifest** *vb* **:** to make evident or certain by showing or displaying **syn** evince, demonstrate, exhibit

[3]**manifest** *n* **:** a list of passengers or an invoice of cargo for a ship or plane

man•i•fes•ta•tion \ˌma-nə-fə-ˈstā-shən\ *n* **:** DISPLAY, DEMONSTRATION

man•i•fes•to \ˌma-nə-ˈfes-tō\ *n, pl* **-tos** *or* **-toes :** a public declaration of intentions, motives, or views

[1]**man•i•fold** \ˈma-nə-ˌfōld\ *adj* **1 :** marked by diversity or variety **2 :** consisting of or operating many of one kind combined

[2]**manifold** *n* **:** a pipe fitting with several lateral outlets for connecting it with other pipes

[3]**manifold** *vb* **1 :** MULTIPLY **2 :** to make a number of copies of (as a letter)

man•i•kin *or* **man•ni•kin** \ˈma-ni-kən\ *n* **1 :** MANNEQUIN **2 :** a little man **:** DWARF

Ma•nila hemp \mə-ˈni-lə-\ *n* **:** a tough fiber from a Philippine plant related to the banana that is used for cordage

manila paper *n, often cap M* **:** a tough brownish paper made orig. from Manila hemp

man•i•oc \ˈma-nē-ˌäk\ *n* **:** CASSAVA

ma•nip•u•late \mə-ˈni-pyə-ˌlāt\ *vb* **-lat•ed; -lat•ing 1 :** to treat or operate manually or mechanically esp. with skill **2 :** to manage or use skillfully **3 :** to influence esp. with intent to deceive — **ma•nip•u•la•tion** \mə-ni-pyə-ˈlā-shən\ *n* — **ma•nip•u•la•tive** \-ˈni-pyə-ˌlā-tiv\ *adj* — **ma•nip•u•la•tor** \-ˌlā-tər\ *n*

man•kind *n* **1** \ˈman-ˈkīnd\ **:** the human race **2** \-ˌkīnd\ **:** men as distinguished from women

[1]**man•ly** \ˈman-lē\ *adj* **man•li•er; -est :** having qualities appropriate to or generally associated with a man **:** BOLD, RESOLUTE — **man•li•ness** *n*

[2]**manly** *adv* **:** in a manly manner

man–made \ˈman-ˈmād\ *adj* **:** made by humans rather than nature ⟨~ systems⟩; *esp* **:** SYNTHETIC ⟨~ fibers⟩

man•na \ˈma-nə\ *n* **1 :** food miraculously supplied to the Israelites in the wilderness **2 :** something of value that comes unexpectedly **:** WINDFALL

manned \ˈmand\ *adj* **:** carrying or performed by a person ⟨~ spaceflight⟩

man•ne•quin \ˈma-ni-kən\ *n* **1 :** a form representing the human figure used esp. for displaying clothes **2 :** a person employed to model clothing

man•ner \ˈma-nər\ *n* **1 :** KIND, SORT **2 :** a way of acting or proceeding ⟨worked in a brisk ~⟩; *also* **:** normal behavior ⟨spoke bluntly as was his ~⟩ **3 :** a method of artistic execution **4** *pl* **:** social conduct; *also* **:** BEARING **5** *pl* **:** BEHAVIOR ⟨taught the child good ~*s*⟩

man•nered \ˈma-nərd\ *adj* **1 :** having manners of a specified kind ⟨well-*mannered*⟩ **2 :** having an artificial character ⟨a highly ~ style⟩

man•ner•ism \ˈma-nə-ˌri-zəm\ *n* **1 :** ARTIFICIALITY, PRECIOSITY **2 :** a peculiarity of action, bearing, or treatment **syn** pose, air, affectation

man•ner•ly \ˈma-nər-lē\ *adj* **:** showing good manners **:** POLITE — **man•ner•li•ness** *n* — **mannerly** *adv*

man•nish \ˈma-nish\ *adj* **1 :** resembling or suggesting a man rather than a woman **2 :** generally associated with or characteristic of a man — **man•nish•ly** *adv* — **man•nish•ness** *n*

ma•noeu•vre \mə-ˈnü-vər, -ˈnyü-\ *chiefly Brit var of* MANEUVER

man–of–war \ˌman-əv-ˈwȯr\ *n, pl* **men–of–war** \ˌmen-\ **:** WARSHIP

ma•nom•e•ter \mə-ˈnä-mə-tər\ *n* **:** an instrument for measuring the pressure of gases and vapors — **mano•met•ric** \ˌma-nə-ˈme-trik\ *adj*

man•or \ˈma-nər\ *n* **1 :** the house or hall of an estate; *also* **:** a landed estate **2 :** an English estate of a feudal lord — **ma•no•ri•al** \mə-ˈnōr-ē-əl\ *adj* — **ma•no•ri•al•ism** \-ə-ˌli-zəm\ *n*

man power *n* **1 :** power available from or supplied by the physical effort of human beings **2** *usu* **man•power :** the total supply of persons available and fitted for service

man•qué \mäⁿ-ˈkā\ *adj* [F, fr. pp. of *manquer* to lack, fail] : short of or frustrated in the fulfillment of one's aspirations or talents ⟨a poet ~⟩

man•sard \ˈman-ˌsärd, -sərd\ *n* : a roof having two slopes on all sides with the lower slope steeper than the upper one

manse \ˈmans\ *n* : the residence esp. of a Presbyterian minister

man•ser•vant \ˈman-ˌsər-vənt\ *n, pl* **men•ser•vants** \ˈmen-ˌsər-vənts\ : a male servant

man•sion \ˈman-chən\ *n* : a large imposing residence; *also* : a separate apartment in a large structure

man–size \ˈman-ˌsīz\ *or* **man–sized** \-ˌsīzd\ *adj* : suitable for or requiring a man

man•slaugh•ter \-ˌslȯ-tər\ *n* : the unlawful killing of a human being without express or implied malice

man•ta \ˈman-tə\ *n* : a square piece of cloth or blanket used in southwestern U.S. and Latin America as a cloak or shawl

man•teau \man-ˈtō\ *n* : a loose cloak, coat, or robe

man•tel \ˈmant-ᵊl\ *n* : a beam, stone, or arch serving as a lintel to support the masonry above a fireplace; *also* : a shelf above a fireplace

man•tel•piece \ˈmant-ᵊl-ˌpēs\ *n* : the shelf of a mantel

man•til•la \man-ˈtē-yə, -ˈti-lə\ *n* : a light scarf worn over the head and shoulders esp. by Spanish and Latin-American women

man•tis \ˈman-təs\ *n, pl* **man•tis•es** *or* **man•tes** \-ˌtēz\ [NL, fr. Gk, lit., diviner, prophet] : any of a group of large usu. green insect-eating insects that hold their prey in forelimbs folded as if in prayer

man•tis•sa \man-ˈti-sə\ *n* : the part of a logarithm to the right of the decimal point

[1]**man•tle** \ˈmant-ᵊl\ *n* **1** : a loose sleeveless garment worn over other clothes **2** : something that covers, enfolds, or envelopes **3** : a lacy sheath that gives light by incandescence when placed over a flame **4** : the portion of the earth lying between the crust and the core **5** : MANTEL

[2]**mantle** *vb* **man•tled; man•tling 1** : to cover with a mantle **2** : BLUSH

man•tra \ˈman-trə\ *n* : a mystical formula of invocation or incantation (as in Hinduism)

[1]**man•u•al** \ˈman-yə-wəl\ *adj* **1** : of, relating to, or involving the hands; *also* : worked by hand ⟨a ~ pump⟩ **2** : requiring or using physical skill and energy — **man•u•al•ly** *adv*

[2]**manual** *n* **1** : a small book; *esp* : HANDBOOK **2** : the prescribed movements in the handling of a military item and esp. a weapon during a drill or ceremony ⟨the ~ of arms⟩ **3** : a keyboard esp. of an organ

man•u•fac•to•ry \ˌman-yə-ˈfak-tə-rē\ *n* : FACTORY

[1]**man•u•fac•ture** \ˌman-yə-ˈfak-chər\ *n* [MF, fr. ML *manufactura,* L *manu factus* made by hand] **1** : something made from raw materials **2** : the process of making wares by hand or by machinery; *also* : a productive industry using machinery

[2]**manufacture** *vb* **-tured; -tur•ing 1** : to make from raw materials by hand or by machinery; *also* : to engage in manufacture **2** : INVENT, FABRICATE; *also* : CREATE — **man•u•fac•tur•er** *n*

man•u•mit \ˌman-yə-ˈmit\ *vb* **-mit•ted; -mit•ting** : to free from slavery — **man•u•mis•sion** \-ˈmi-shən\ *n*

[1]**ma•nure** \mə-ˈnu̇r, -ˈnyu̇r\ *vb* **ma•nured; ma•nur•ing** : to fertilize land with manure

[2]**manure** *n* : FERTILIZER; *esp* : refuse from stables and barnyards — **ma•nu•ri•al** \-ˈnu̇r-ē-əl, -ˈnyu̇r-\ *adj*

man•u•script \ˈman-yə-ˌskript\ *n* [L *manu scriptus* written by hand] **1** : a written or typewritten composition or document; *also* : a document submitted for publication **2** : writing as opposed to print

Manx \ˈmaŋks\ *n pl* : the people of the Isle of Man — **Manx** *adj*

[1]**many** \ˈme-nē\ *adj* **more** \ˈmōr\; **most** \ˈmōst\ : consisting of or amounting to a large but indefinite number ⟨~ years ago⟩

[2]**many** *pron* : a large number ⟨~ are called⟩

[3]**many** *n* : a large but indefinite number ⟨a good ~ of them⟩

many•fold \ˌme-nē-ˈfōld\ *adv* : by many times

many–sid•ed \-ˈsī-dəd\ *adj* **1** : having many sides or aspects **2** : VERSATILE

Mao•ism \ˈmau̇-ˌi-zəm\ *n* : the theory and practice of Communism developed in China chiefly by Mao Tse-tung — **Mao•ist** \ˈmau̇-ist\ *n or adj*

Mao•ri \ˈmau̇r-ē\ *n, pl* **Maori** *or* **Maoris** : a member of a Polynesian people native to New Zealand

[1]**map** \ˈmap\ *n* [ML *mappa,* fr. L, napkin, towel] **1** : a representation usu. on a flat surface of the whole or part of an area **2** : a representation of the celestial sphere or part of it

[2]**map** *vb* **mapped; map•ping 1** : to make a map of **2** : to plan in detail ⟨~ out a program⟩ — **map•pa•ble** \ˈma-pə-bəl\ *adj* — **map•per** *n*

MAP *abbr* modified American plan

ma•ple \ˈmā-pəl\ *n* : any of a genus of trees or shrubs with 2-winged dry fruit and opposite leaves; *also* : the hard light-colored wood of a maple used esp. for floors and furniture

maple sugar *n* : sugar made by boiling maple syrup

maple syrup *n* : syrup made by concentrating the sap of maple trees and esp. the sugar maple

mar \ˈmär\ *vb* **marred; mar•ring** : to detract from the wholeness or perfection of : SPOIL **syn** injure, hurt, harm, damage, impair, blemish

Mar *abbr* March

ma•ra•ca \mə-ˈrä-kə, -ˈra-\ *n* [Pg *maracá*] : a rattle usu. made from a gourd and used as a percussion instrument

mar•a•schi•no cherry \ˌmar-ə-ˈskē-nō-, -ˈshē-\ *n, often cap M* : a cherry preserved in a sweet liqueur made from the juice of a bitter wild cherry

mar•a•thon \ˈmar-ə-ˌthän\ *n* [*Marathon,* Greece, site of a victory of Greeks over Persians in 490 B.C. the news of which was carried to Athens by a long-distance runner] **1** : a long-distance race esp. on foot **2** : an endurance contest

mar•a•thon•er \ˈmar-ə-ˌthä-nər\ *n* : a person who takes part in a marathon — **mar•a•thon•ing** *n*

ma•raud \mə-ˈrȯd\ *vb* : to roam about and raid in search of plunder : PILLAGE — **ma•raud•er** *n*

mar•ble \ˈmär-bəl\ *n* **1** : a limestone that can be polished and used in fine building work **2** : something resembling marble (as in coldness) **3** : a small ball (as of glass) used in various games; *also, pl* : a children's game played with these small balls — **marble** *adj*

mar•bling \-bə-liŋ, -bliŋ\ *n* : an intermixture of fat through the lean of a cut of meat

mar•cel \mär-ˈsel\ *n* : a deep soft wave made in the hair by the use of a heated curling iron — **marcel** *vb*

[1]**march** \ˈmärch\ *n* : a border region : FRONTIER

[2]**march** *vb* **1** : to move along in or as if in military formation **2** : to walk in a direct purposeful manner; *also* : PROGRESS, ADVANCE **3** : TRAVERSE ⟨~*ed* 10 miles⟩ — **march•er** *n*

[3]**march** *n* **1** : the action of marching; *also* : the distance covered (as by a military unit) in a march **2** : a regular measured stride or rhythmic step used in marching **3** : forward movement **4** : a piece of music with marked rhythm suitable for marching to

March *n* [ME, fr. OF, fr. L *martius,* fr. *martius* of Mars, fr. *Mart-, Mars,* Roman god of war] : the 3d month of the year

mar•chio•ness \ˈmär-shə-nəs\ *n* **1** : the wife or widow of a marquess **2** : a woman holding the rank of a marquess in her own right

Mar•di Gras \ˈmär-dē-ˌgrä\ *n* [F, lit., fat Tuesday] : the Tuesday before Ash Wednesday often observed with parades and merrymaking

[1]**mare** \ˈmar\ *n* : an adult female of the horse or a related mammal

[2]**ma•re** \ˈmär-(ˌ)ā\ *n, pl* **ma•ria** \ˈmär-ē-ə\ : any of sev-

eral large dark areas on the surface of the moon or Mars

mar·ga·rine \ˈmär-jə-rən\ *n* : a food product made usu. from vegetable oils churned with skimmed milk and used as a substitute for butter

mar·gin \ˈmär-jən\ *n* **1** : the part of a page outside the main body of printed or written matter **2** : EDGE **3** : a spare amount, measure, or degree allowed for use if needed **4** : measure or degree of difference ⟨a one-vote ~⟩

mar·gin·al \-jə-nəl\ *adj* **1** : written or printed in the margin **2** : of, relating to, or situated at a margin or border **3** : close to the lower limit of quality or acceptability **4** : excluded from or existing outside the mainstream of society or a group — **mar·gin·al·ly** *adv*

mar·gi·na·lia \ˌmär-jə-ˈnā-lē-ə\ *n pl* : marginal notes

mar·grave \ˈmär-ˌgrāv\ *n* : the military governor esp. of a medieval German border province

ma·ri·a·chi \ˌmär-ē-ˈä-chē, ˌmar-\ *n* : a Mexican street band; *also* : a member of or the music of such a band

mari·gold \ˈmar-ə-ˌgōld, ˈmer-\ *n* : any of a genus of tropical American herbs related to the daisies that are grown for their double yellow, orange, or reddish flower heads

mar·i·jua·na *also* **mar·i·hua·na** \ˌmar-ə-ˈwä-nə, -ˈhwä-\ *n* [MexSp *marihuana*] : the dried leaves and flowering tops of the female hemp plant smoked usu. illegally for their intoxicating effect; *also* : HEMP

ma·rim·ba \mə-ˈrim-bə\ *n* : a xylophone of southern Africa and Central America; *also* : a modern version of it

ma·ri·na \mə-ˈrē-nə\ *n* : a dock or basin providing secure moorings for pleasure boats

mar·i·na·ra \ˌmar-ə-ˈnar-ə\ *adj* [It *(alla) marinara,* lit., in sailor style] : made with tomatoes, onions, garlic, and spices; *also* : served with marinara sauce

mar·i·nate \ˈmar-ə-ˌnāt\ *vb* **-nat·ed; -nat·ing** : to steep (as meat or fish) in a brine or pickle

1**ma·rine** \mə-ˈrēn\ *adj* **1** : of or relating to the sea or its navigation or commerce **2** : of or relating to marines

2**marine** *n* **1** : the mercantile and naval shipping of a country **2** : any of a class of soldiers serving on shipboard or with a naval force

mar·i·ner \ˈmar-ə-nər\ *n* : SAILOR

mar·i·o·nette \ˌmar-ē-ə-ˈnet, ˌmer-\ *n* : a puppet moved by strings or by hand

mar·i·tal \ˈmar-ət-ᵊl\ *adj* : of or relating to marriage : CONJUGAL **syn** matrimonial, connubial, nuptial

mar·i·time \ˈmar-ə-ˌtīm\ *adj* **1** : of, relating to, or bordering on the sea **2** : of or relating to navigation or commerce of the sea

mar·jo·ram \ˈmär-jə-rəm\ *n* : any of various fragrant mints often used in cookery

1**mark** \ˈmärk\ *n* **1** : something (as a line or fixed object) designed to record position; *also* : the starting line or position in a track event **2** : TARGET; *also* : GOAL, OBJECT **3** : an object of abuse or ridicule **4** : the question under discussion **5** : NORM ⟨not up to the ~⟩ **6** : a visible sign : INDICATION; *also* : CHARACTERISTIC **7** : a written or printed symbol **8** : GRADE ⟨a ~ of B+⟩ **9** : IMPORTANCE, DISTINCTION **10** : a lasting impression ⟨made his ~ in the world⟩; *also* : a damaging impression left on a surface

2**mark** *vb* **1** : to set apart by a line or boundary **2** : to designate by a mark or make a mark on **3** : CHARACTERIZE ⟨the vehemence that ~*s* his speeches⟩; *also* : SIGNALIZE ⟨this year ~*s* our 50th anniversary⟩ **4** : to take notice of : OBSERVE — **mark·er** *n*

3**mark** *n* — see MONEY table

Mark \ˈmärk\ *n* — see BIBLE table

mark·down \ˈmärk-ˌdau̇n\ *n* **1** : a lowering of price **2** : the amount by which an original price is reduced

mark down *vb* : to put a lower price on

marked \ˈmärkt\ *adj* : NOTICEABLE — **mark·ed·ly** \ˈmär-kəd-lē\ *adv*

1**mar·ket** \ˈmär-kət\ *n* **1** : a meeting together of people for trade by purchase and sale; *also* : a public place where such a meeting is held **2** : the rate or price offered for a commodity or security **3** : a geographical area of demand for commodities; *also* : extent of demand **4** : a retail establishment usu. of a specific kind

2**market** *vb* : to go to a market to buy or sell; *also* : SELL — **mar·ket·able** *adj*

mar·ket·place \ˈmär-kət-ˌplās\ *n* **1** : an open square in a town where markets are held **2** : the world of trade or economic activity

mark·ka \ˈmär-ˌkä\ *n, pl* **mark·kaa** \ˈmär-ˌkä\ *or* **markkas** \-ˌkäz\ — see MONEY table

marks·man \ˈmärks-mən\ *n* : a person skillful at hitting a target — **marks·man·ship** *n*

mark·up \ˈmär-ˌkəp\ *n* **1** : a raising of price **2** : an amount added to the cost price of an article to determine the selling price

mark up *vb* : to put a higher price on

marl \ˈmärl\ *n* : an earthy deposit rich in lime used esp. as fertilizer — **marly** \ˈmär-lē\ *adj*

mar·lin \ˈmär-lən\ *n* : any of several large oceanic sport fishes related to sailfishes

mar·line·spike *also* **mar·lin·spike** \ˈmär-lən-ˌspīk\ *n* : a pointed iron tool used to separate strands of rope or wire (as in splicing)

mar·ma·lade \ˈmär-mə-ˌlād\ *n* : a clear jelly holding in suspension pieces of fruit and fruit rind

mar·mo·re·al \mär-ˈmōr-ē-əl\ *adj* : of, relating to, or suggestive of marble

mar·mo·set \ˈmär-mə-ˌset\ *n* : any of numerous small bushy-tailed tropical American monkeys

mar·mot \ˈmär-mət\ *n* : any of a genus of stout short-legged burrowing No. American rodents

marmot

1**ma·roon** \mə-ˈrün\ *vb* **1** : to put ashore (as on a desolate island) and leave to one's fate **2** : to leave in isolation and without hope of escape

2**maroon** *n* : a dark red color

mar·quee \mär-ˈkē\ *n* [modif. of F *marquise,* lit., marchioness] **1** : a large tent set up (as for an outdoor party) **2** : a usu. metal and glass canopy over an entrance (as of a theater)

mar·quess \ˈmär-kwəs\ *n* **1** : a nobleman of hereditary rank in Europe and Japan **2** : a member of the British peerage ranking below a duke and above an earl

mar·que·try \ˈmär-kə-trē\ *n* : inlaid work of wood, shell, or ivory (as on a table or cabinet)

mar·quis \ˈmär-kwəs, mär-ˈkē\ *n* : MARQUESS

mar·quise \mär-ˈkēz\ *n, pl* **mar·quises** *same or* -ˈkē-zəz\ : MARCHIONESS

mar·riage \ˈmar-ij\ *n* **1** : the state of being married **2** : a wedding ceremony and attendant festivities **3** : a close union — **mar·riage·able** *adj*

mar·row \ˈmar-ō\ *n* : a soft vascular tissue that fills the cavities of most bones

mar·row·bone \ˈmar-ə-ˌbōn, ˈmar-ō-\ *n* : a bone (as a shinbone) rich in marrow

mar·ry \ˈmar-ē\ *vb* **mar·ried; mar·ry·ing 1** : to join as

DICTIONARY

husband and wife according to law or custom **2 :** to take as husband or wife **:** WED **3 :** to enter into a close union — **mar•ried** *adj or n*

Mars \ˈmärz\ *n* **:** the planet 4th from the sun and conspicuous for its red color — see PLANET table

marsh \ˈmärsh\ *n* **:** a tract of soft wet land — **marshy** *adj*

1mar•shal \ˈmär-shəl\ *n* **1 :** a high official in a medieval household; *also* **:** a person in charge of the ceremonial aspects of a gathering **2 :** a general officer of the highest military rank **3 :** an administrative officer (as of a U.S. judicial district) having duties similar to a sheriff's **4 :** the administrative head of a city police or fire department

2marshal *vb* **mar•shaled** *or* **mar•shalled; mar•shal•ing** *or* **mar•shal•ling 1 :** to arrange in order, rank, or position **2 :** to bring together **3 :** to lead with ceremony **:** USHER

marsh gas *n* **:** METHANE

marsh•mal•low \ˈmärsh-ˌme-lō, -ˌma-\ *n* **:** a light creamy confection made from corn syrup, sugar, albumen, and gelatin

marsh marigold *n* **:** a swamp herb related to the buttercups that has bright yellow flowers

mar•su•pi•al \mär-ˈsü-pē-əl\ *n* **:** any of an order of primitive mammals (as opossums, kangaroos, or wombats) that bear very immature young which are nourished in a pouch on the abdomen of the female — **marsupial** *adj*

mart \ˈmärt\ *n* **:** MARKET

mar•ten \ˈmärt-ᵊn\ *n, pl* **marten** *or* **martens :** a slender weasellike mammal with fine gray or brown fur; *also* **:** this fur

mar•tial \ˈmär-shəl\ *adj* [L *martialis* of Mars, fr. *Mart-, Mars* Mars, Roman god of war] **1 :** of, relating to, or suited for war or a warrior ⟨~ music⟩ **2 :** of or relating to an army or military life **3 :** WARLIKE

martial law *n* **1 :** the law applied in occupied territory by the occupying military forces **2 :** the established law of a country administered by military forces in an emergency when civilian law enforcement agencies are unable to maintain public order and safety

mar•tian \ˈmär-shən\ *adj, often cap* **:** of or relating to the planet Mars or its hypothetical inhabitants — **martian** *n, often cap*

mar•tin \ˈmärt-ᵊn\ *n* **:** any of several small swallows and flycatchers

mar•ti•net \ˌmärt-ᵊn-ˈet\ *n* **:** a strict disciplinarian

mar•tin•gale \ˈmärt-ᵊn-ˌgāl\ *n* **:** a strap connecting a horse's girth to the bit or reins so as to hold down its head

mar•ti•ni \mär-ˈtē-nē\ *n* **:** a cocktail made of gin or vodka and dry vermouth

1mar•tyr \ˈmär-tər\ *n* [ME, fr. OE, fr. LL, fr. Gk *martyr-, martys,* lit., witness] **1 :** a person who dies rather than renounce a religion; *also* **:** a person who makes a great sacrifice for the sake of principle **2 :** a great or constant sufferer

2martyr *vb* **1 :** to put to death for adhering to a belief **2 :** TORTURE

mar•tyr•dom \ˈmär-tər-dəm\ *n* **1 :** the suffering and death of a martyr **2 :** TORTURE

1mar•vel \ˈmär-vəl\ *n* **1 :** something that causes wonder or astonishment **2 :** intense surprise or interest

2marvel *vb* **mar•veled** *or* **mar•velled; mar•vel•ing** *or* **mar•vel•ling :** to feel surprise, wonder, or amazed curiosity

mar•vel•ous *or* **mar•vel•lous** \ˈmär-və-ləs\ *adj* **1 :** causing wonder **2 :** of the highest kind or quality — **mar•vel•ous•ly** *adv* — **mar•vel•ous•ness** *n*

Marx•ism \ˈmärk-ˌsi-zəm\ *n* **:** the political, economic, and social principles and policies advocated by Karl Marx — **Marx•ist** \-sist\ *n or adj*

mar•zi•pan \ˈmärt-sə-ˌpän, -ˌpan; ˈmär-zə-ˌpan\ *n* [G] **:** a confection of almond paste, sugar, and egg whites

masc *abbr* masculine

mas•cara \mas-ˈkar-ə\ *n* **:** a cosmetic esp. for coloring the eyelashes

mas•car•po•ne \ˌmas-kär-ˈpō-nā\ *n* **:** an Italian cream cheese

mas•cot \ˈmas-ˌkät, -kət\ *n* [F *mascotte,* fr. Provençal *mascoto,* fr. *masco* witch, fr. ML *masca*] **:** a person, animal, or object believed to bring good luck

1mas•cu•line \ˈmas-kyə-lən\ *adj* **1 :** MALE; *also* **:** MANLY **2 :** of, relating to, or constituting the gender that includes most words or grammatical forms referring to males — **mas•cu•lin•i•ty** \ˌmas-kyə-ˈli-nə-tē\ *n*

2masculine *n* **:** a noun, pronoun, adjective, or inflectional form or class of the masculine gender; *also* **:** the masculine gender

1mash \ˈmash\ *n* **1 :** a mixture of ground feeds for livestock **2 :** crushed malt or grain steeped in hot water to make wort **3 :** a soft pulpy mass

2mash *vb* **1 :** to reduce to a soft pulpy state **2 :** CRUSH, SMASH ⟨~ a finger⟩ — **mash•er** *n*

MASH *abbr* mobile army surgical hospital

1mask \ˈmask\ *n* **1 :** a cover for the face usu. for disguise or protection **2 :** MASQUE **3 :** a figure of a head worn on the stage in antiquity **4 :** a copy of a face made by means of a mold ⟨death ~⟩ **5 :** something that conceals or disguises **6 :** the face of an animal

2mask *vb* **1 :** to conceal from view **:** DISGUISE **2 :** to cover for protection

mask•er \ˈmas-kər\ *n* **:** a participant in a masquerade

mas•och•ism \ˈma-sə-ˌki-zəm, ˈma-zə-\ *n* **1 :** a sexual perversion characterized by pleasure in being subjected to pain or humiliation **2 :** pleasure in being abused or dominated — **mas•och•ist** \-kist\ *n* — **mas•och•is•tic** \ˌma-sə-ˈkis-tik, ˌma-zə-\ *adj*

ma•son \ˈmās-ᵊn\ *n* **1 :** a skilled worker who builds with stone, brick, or concrete **2** *cap* **:** FREEMASON

Ma•son•ic \mə-ˈsä-nik\ *adj* **:** of or relating to Freemasons or Freemasonry

ma•son•ry \ˈmās-ᵊn-rē\ *n, pl* **-ries 1 :** something constructed of materials used by masons **2 :** the art, trade, or work of a mason **3** *cap* **:** FREEMASONRY

masque \ˈmask\ *n* **1 :** MASQUERADE **2 :** a short allegorical dramatic performance (as of the 17th century)

1mas•quer•ade \ˌmas-kə-ˈrād\ *n* **1 :** a social gathering of persons wearing masks; *also* **:** a costume for wear at such a gathering **2 :** DISGUISE

2masquerade *vb* **-ad•ed; -ad•ing 1 :** to disguise oneself **:** POSE **2 :** to take part in a masquerade — **mas•quer•ad•er** *n*

1mass \ˈmas\ *n* **1** *cap* **:** a sequence of prayers and ceremonies forming the eucharistic service of the Roman Catholic Church **2** *often cap* **:** a celebration of the Eucharist **3 :** a musical setting for parts of the Mass

2mass *n* **1 :** a quantity or aggregate of matter usu. of considerable size **2 :** EXPANSE, BULK; *also* **:** MASSIVENESS **3 :** the principal part **4 :** AGGREGATE, WHOLE **5 :** the quantity of matter that a body possesses as measured by its inertia **6 :** a large quantity, amount, or number **7 :** the great body of people — usu. used in pl. — **massy** *adj*

3mass *vb* **:** to form or collect into a mass

Mass *abbr* Massachusetts

mas•sa•cre \ˈma-si-kər\ *n* **1 :** the killing of many persons under cruel or atrocious circumstances **2 :** a wholesale slaughter — **massacre** *vb*

1mas•sage \mə-ˈsäzh, -ˈsäj\ *n* **:** manipulation of tissues (as by rubbing and kneading) esp. for therapeutic purposes

2massage *vb* **mas•saged; mas•sag•ing 1 :** to subject to massage **2 :** to treat flatteringly; *also* **:** MANIPULATE, DOCTOR ⟨~ data⟩

mas•seur \ma-ˈsər\ *n* **:** a man who practices massage

mas•seuse \-ˈsərz, -ˈsüz\ *n* **:** a woman who practices massage

mas•sif \ma-ˈsēf\ *n* **:** a principal mountain mass

mas•sive \ˈma-siv\ *adj* **1 :** forming or consisting of a large mass **2 :** large in structure, scope, or degree — **mas•sive•ly** *adv* — **mas•sive•ness** *n*

mass•less \ˈmas-ləs\ *adj* **:** having no mass ⟨~ particles⟩

mass medium *n, pl* **mass media :** a medium of communication (as the newspapers or television) that is designed to reach the mass of the people

mass–pro•duce \ˌmas-prə-ˈdüs, -ˈdyüs\ *vb* **:** to produce in quantity usu. by machinery — **mass production** *n*

[1]**mast** \ˈmast\ *n* **1 :** a long pole or spar rising from the keel or deck of a ship and supporting the yards, booms, and rigging **2 :** a slender vertical structure — **mast•ed** \ˈmas-təd\ *adj*

[2]**mast** *n* **:** nuts (as acorns) accumulated on the forest floor and often serving as food for animals (as hogs)

mas•tec•to•my \ma-ˈstek-tə-mē\ *n, pl* **-mies :** surgical removal of the breast

[1]**mas•ter** \ˈmas-tər\ *n* **1 :** a male teacher; *also* **:** a person holding an academic degree higher than a bachelor's but lower than a doctor's **2 :** one highly skilled (as in an art or profession) **3 :** one having authority or control **4 :** VICTOR, SUPERIOR **5 :** the commander of a merchant ship **6 :** a youth or boy too young to be called *mister* — used as a title **7 :** an original from which copies are made

[2]**master** *vb* **1 :** to become master of **:** OVERCOME **2 :** to become skilled or proficient in **3 :** to produce a master recording of (as a musical performance)

master chief petty officer *n* **:** a petty officer of the highest rank in the navy

mas•ter•ful \ˈmas-tər-fəl\ *adj* **1 :** inclined and usu. competent to act as a master **2 :** having or reflecting the skill of a master — **mas•ter•ful•ly** *adv* — **mas•ter•ful•ness** *n*

master gunnery sergeant *n* **:** a noncommissioned officer in the marine corps ranking above a master sergeant

master key *n* **:** a key designed to open several different locks

mas•ter•ly \ˈmas-tər-lē\ *adj* **:** indicating thorough knowledge or superior skill ⟨~ performance⟩ — **mas•ter•ly** *adv*

mas•ter•mind \-ˌmīnd\ *n* **:** a person who provides the directing or creative intelligence for a project — **mastermind** *vb*

master of ceremonies : a person who acts as host at a formal event or a program of entertainment

mas•ter•piece \ˈmas-tər-ˌpēs\ *n* **:** a work done with extraordinary skill

master plan *n* **:** an overall plan

mas•ter's \ˈmas-tərz\ *n* **:** a master's degree

master sergeant *n* **1 :** a noncommissioned officer in the army ranking next below a sergeant major **2 :** a noncommissioned officer in the air force ranking next below a senior master sergeant **3 :** a noncommissioned officer in the marine corps ranking next below a master gunnery sergeant

mas•ter•stroke \ˈmas-tər-ˌstrōk\ *n* **:** a masterly performance or move

mas•ter•work \-ˌwərk\ *n* **:** MASTERPIECE

mas•tery \ˈmas-tə-rē\ *n* **1 :** DOMINION; *also* **:** SUPERIORITY **2 :** possession or display of great skill or knowledge

mast•head \ˈmast-ˌhed\ *n* **1 :** the top of a mast **2 :** the printed matter in a newspaper or periodical giving the title and details of ownership and rates of subscription or advertising

mas•tic \ˈmas-tik\ *n* **:** a pasty material used as a coating or cement

mas•ti•cate \ˈmas-tə-ˌkāt\ *vb* **-cat•ed; -cat•ing :** CHEW — **mas•ti•ca•tion** \ˌmas-tə-ˈkā-shən\ *n*

mas•tiff \ˈmas-təf\ *n* **:** any of a breed of large smooth-coated dogs used esp. as guard dogs

mast•odon \ˈmas-tə-ˌdän\ *n* [NL, fr. Gk *mastos* breast + *odōn, odous* tooth] **:** any of numerous huge extinct mammals related to the mammoths

mas•toid \ˈmas-ˌtȯid\ *n* **:** a bony prominence behind the ear — **mastoid** *adj*

mas•tur•ba•tion \ˌmas-tər-ˈbā-shən\ *n* **:** stimulation of the genital organs apart from sexual intercourse, usu. to orgasm, and esp. by use of one's own hand — **mas•tur•bate** \ˈmas-tər-ˌbāt\ *vb* — **mas•tur•ba•to•ry** \ˈmas-tər-bə-ˌtōr-ē\ *adj*

[1]**mat** \ˈmat\ *n* **1 :** a piece of coarse woven or plaited fabric **2 :** something made up of many intertwined strands **3 :** a large thick pad used as a surface for wrestling and gymnastics

[2]**mat** *vb* **mat•ted; mat•ting 1 :** to provide with a mat **2 :** to form into a tangled mass

[3]**mat** *vb* **mat•ted; mat•ting 1 :** to make (as a color) matte **2 :** to provide (a picture) with a mat

[4]**mat** *var of* [2]MATTE

[5]**mat** *or* **matt** *or* **matte** *n* **:** a border going around a picture between picture and frame or serving as the frame

mat•a•dor \ˈma-tə-ˌdȯr\ *n* [Sp, fr. *matar* to kill] **:** a bullfighter whose role is to kill the bull in a bullfight

[1]**match** \ˈmach\ *n* **1 :** a person or thing equal or similar to another; *also* **:** one able to cope with another **:** RIVAL **2 :** a suitable pairing of persons or objects **3 :** a contest or game between two or more individuals **4 :** a marriage union; *also* **:** a prospective marriage partner — **match•less** *adj*

[2]**match** *vb* **1 :** to meet as an antagonist; *also* **:** PIT **2 :** to provide with a worthy competitor; *also* **:** to set in comparison with **3 :** MARRY **4 :** to combine suitably or congenially; *also* **:** ADAPT, SUIT **5 :** to provide with a counterpart

[3]**match** *n* **:** a short slender piece of flammable material (as wood) tipped with a combustible mixture that ignites through friction

match•book \ˈmach-ˌbu̇k\ *n* **:** a small folder containing rows of paper matches

match•lock \-ˌläk\ *n* **:** a musket with a slow-burning cord lowered over a hole in the breech to ignite the charge

match•mak•er \-ˌmā-kər\ *n* **:** one who arranges a match and esp. a marriage

match•wood \-ˌwu̇d\ *n* **:** small pieces of wood

[1]**mate** \ˈmāt\ *vb* **mat•ed; mat•ing :** CHECKMATE — **mate** *n*

[2]**mate** *n* **1 :** ASSOCIATE, COMPANION; *also* **:** HELPER **2 :** a deck officer on a merchant ship ranking below the captain **3 :** one of a pair; *esp* **:** either member of a married couple or a breeding pair of animals

[3]**mate** *vb* **mat•ed; mat•ing 1 :** to join or fit together **2 :** to come or bring together as mates **3 :** COPULATE

[1]**ma•te•ri•al** \mə-ˈtir-ē-əl\ *adj* **1 :** PHYSICAL ⟨~ world⟩; *also* **:** BODILY ⟨~ needs⟩ **2 :** of or relating to matter rather than form ⟨~ cause⟩; *also* **:** EMPIRICAL ⟨~ knowledge⟩ **3 :** highly important **:** SIGNIFICANT **4 :** of a physical or worldly nature ⟨~ progress⟩ — **ma•te•ri•al•ly** *adv*

[2]**material** *n* **1 :** the elements or substance of which something is composed or made **2 :** apparatus necessary for doing or making something

ma•te•ri•al•ise *Brit var of* MATERIALIZE

ma•te•ri•al•ism \mə-ˈtir-ē-ə-ˌli-zəm\ *n* **1 :** a theory that everything can be explained as being or coming from matter **2 :** a preoccupation with material rather than intellectual or spiritual things — **ma•te•ri•al•ist** \-list\ *n or adj* — **ma•te•ri•al•is•tic** \-ˌtir-ē-ə-ˈlis-tik\ *adj* — **ma•te•ri•al•is•ti•cal•ly** \-ti-k(ə-)lē\ *adv*

ma•te•ri•al•ize \mə-ˈtir-ē-ə-ˌlīz\ *vb* **-ized; -iz•ing 1 :** to give material form to; *also* **:** to assume bodily form **2 :** to make an often unexpected appearance — **ma•te•ri•al•i•za•tion** \mə-ˌtir-ē-ə-lə-ˈzā-shən\ *n*

ma•té•ri•el *or* **ma•te•ri•el** \mə-ˌtir-ē-ˈel\ *n* [F *matériel*] **:** equipment, apparatus, and supplies used by an organization

ma•ter•nal \mə-ˈtərn-ᵊl\ *adj* **1 :** MOTHERLY **2 :** related through or inherited or derived from a female parent — **ma•ter•nal•ly** *adv*

[1]ma•ter•ni•ty \mə-ˈtər-nə-tē\ *n, pl* **-ties 1 :** the quality or state of being a mother; *also* **:** MOTHERLINESS **2 :** a hospital facility for the care of women before and during childbirth and for newborn babies

[2]maternity *adj* **1 :** designed for wear during pregnancy ⟨a ~ dress⟩ **2 :** effective for the period close to and including childbirth ⟨~ leave⟩

[1]math \ˈmath\ *n* **:** MATHEMATICS

[2]math *abbr* mathematical; mathematician

math•e•mat•ics \ˌma-thə-ˈma-tiks\ *n* **:** the science of numbers and their properties, operations, and relations and with shapes in space and their structure and measurement — **math•e•mat•i•cal** \-ˈma-ti-kəl\ *adj* — **math•e•mat•i•cal•ly** \-ti-k(ə-)lē\ *adv* — **math•e•ma•ti•cian** \ˌma-thə-mə-ˈti-shən\ *n*

mat•i•nee *or* **mat•i•née** \ˌmat-ᵊn-ˈā\ *n* [F *matinée,* lit., morning, fr. OF, fr. *matin* morning, fr. L *matutinum,* fr. neut. of *matutinus* of the morning, fr. *Matuta,* goddess of morning] **:** a musical or dramatic performance in the daytime and esp. the afternoon

mat•ins \ˈmat-ᵊnz\ *n pl, often cap* **1 :** special prayers said between midnight and 4 a.m. **2 :** a morning service of liturgical prayer in Anglican churches

ma•tri•arch \ˈmā-trē-ˌärk\ *n* **:** a female who rules or dominates a family, group, or state — **ma•tri•ar•chal** \ˌmā-trē-ˈär-kəl\ *adj* — **ma•tri•ar•chy** \ˈmā-trē-ˌär-kē\ *n*

ma•tri•cide \ˈma-trə-ˌsīd, ˈmā-\ *n* **:** the murder of a mother by her child — **ma•tri•cid•al** \ˌma-trə-ˈsīd-ᵊl, ˌmā-\ *adj*

ma•tric•u•late \mə-ˈtri-kyə-ˌlāt\ *vb* **-lat•ed; -lat•ing :** to enroll as a member of a body and esp. of a college or university — **ma•tric•u•la•tion** \-ˌtri-kyə-ˈlā-shən\ *n*

mat•ri•mo•ny \ˈma-trə-ˌmō-nē\ *n* [ME, fr. MF *matremoine,* fr. L *matrimonium,* fr. *mater* mother, matron] **:** MARRIAGE — **mat•ri•mo•nial** \ˌma-trə-ˈmō-nē-əl\ *adj* — **mat•ri•mo•nial•ly** *adv*

ma•trix \ˈmā-triks\ *n, pl* **ma•tri•ces** \ˈmā-trə-ˌsēz, ˈma-\ *or* **ma•trix•es** \ˈmā-trik-səz\ **1 :** something within or from which something else originates, develops, or takes form **2 :** a mold from which a relief surface (as a piece of type) is made

ma•tron \ˈmā-trən\ *n* **1 :** a married woman usu. of dignified maturity or social distinction **2 :** a woman supervisor (as in a school or police station) — **ma•tron•ly** *adj*

Matt *abbr* Matthew

[1]matte *or* **matt** \ˈmat\ *var of* [3]MAT

[2]matte *also* **matt** \ˈmat\ *adj* **:** not shiny **:** DULL

[1]mat•ter \ˈma-tər\ *n* **1 :** a subject of interest or concern **2** *pl* **:** events or circumstances of a particular situation **3 :** the subject of a discourse or writing **4 :** TROUBLE, DIFFICULTY ⟨what's the ~⟩ **5 :** the substance of which a physical object is composed **6 :** PUS **7 :** an indefinite amount or quantity ⟨a ~ of a few days⟩ **8 :** something written or printed **9 :** MAIL

[2]matter *vb* **:** to be of importance

mat•ter–of–fact \ˌma-tə-rəv-ˈfakt\ *adj* **:** adhering to fact; *also* **:** being plain, straightforward, or unemotional — **mat•ter–of–fact•ly** *adv* — **mat•ter–of–fact•ness** *n*

Mat•thew \ˈma-thyü\ *n* — see BIBLE table

mat•tins *often cap, chiefly Brit var of* MATINS

mat•tock \ˈma-tək\ *n* **:** a digging and grubbing tool with features of an adze and an ax or pick

mat•tress \ˈma-trəs\ *n* **1 :** a fabric case filled with resilient material used as or for a bed **2 :** an inflatable airtight sack for use as a mattress

mat•u•rate \ˈma-chə-ˌrāt\ *vb* **-rat•ed; -rat•ing :** MATURE

mat•u•ra•tion \ˌma-chə-ˈrā-shən\ *n* **1 :** the process of becoming mature **2 :** the emergence of personal and behavioral characteristics through growth processes — **mat•u•ra•tion•al** \-shə-nəl\ *adj*

[1]ma•ture \mə-ˈtu̇r, -ˈtyu̇r\ *adj* **ma•tur•er; -est 1 :** based on slow careful consideration **2 :** having attained a final or desired state **3 :** of or relating to a condition of full development **4 :** due for payment — **ma•ture•ly** *adv*

[2]mature *vb* **ma•tured; ma•tur•ing :** to reach or bring to maturity or completion

ma•tu•ri•ty \mə-ˈtu̇r-ə-tē, -ˈtyu̇r-\ *n* **1 :** the quality or state of being mature; *esp* **:** full development **2 :** the date when a note becomes due for payment

ma•tu•ti•nal \ˌma-chu̇-ˈtīn-ᵊl; mə-ˈtüt-ᵊn-əl, -ˈtyüt-\ *adj* **:** of, relating to, or occurring in the morning **:** EARLY

mat•zo \ˈmät-sə\ *n, pl* **mat•zoth** \-ˌsōt, -ˌsōth, -sōs\ *or* **mat•zos** [Yiddish *matse,* fr. Heb *maṣṣāh*] **:** unleavened bread eaten esp. at the Passover

maud•lin \ˈmȯd-lən\ *adj* [alter. of Mary *Magdalene;* fr. her depiction as a weeping, penitent sinner] **1 :** drunk enough to be silly **2 :** weakly and effusively sentimental

[1]maul \ˈmȯl\ *n* **:** a heavy hammer often with a wooden head used esp. for driving wedges

[2]maul *vb* **1 :** BEAT, BRUISE; *also* **:** MANGLE **2 :** to handle roughly

maun•der \ˈmȯn-dər\ *vb* **1 :** to wander slowly and idly **2 :** to speak indistinctly or disconnectedly

mau•so•le•um \ˌmȯ-sə-ˈlē-əm, ˌmȯ-zə-\ *n, pl* **-leums** *or* **-lea** \-ˈlē-ə\ [L, fr. Gk *mausōleion,* fr. *Mausōlos* Mausolus † *ab* 353 B.C. ruler of Caria whose tomb was one of the seven wonders of the ancient world] **:** a large tomb; *esp* **:** a usu. stone building for entombment of the dead above ground

mauve \ˈmōv, ˈmȯv\ *n* **:** a moderate purple, violet, or lilac color

ma•ven *or* **ma•vin** \ˈmā-vən\ *n* [Yiddish *meyvn,* fr. LHeb *mēbhīn*] **:** EXPERT

mav•er•ick \ˈma-vrik, -və-rik\ *n* [perh. fr. Samuel A. *Maverick* † 1870 Am. pioneer who did not brand his calves] **1 :** an unbranded range animal **2 :** NONCONFORMIST

maw \ˈmȯ\ *n* **1 :** STOMACH; *also* **:** the crop of a bird **2 :** the throat, gullet, or jaws esp. of a voracious animal

mawk•ish \ˈmȯ-kish\ *adj* **:** sickly sentimental — **mawk•ish•ly** *adv* — **mawk•ish•ness** *n*

max *abbr* maximum

maxi \ˈmak-sē\ *n, pl* **max•is :** a long skirt, dress, or coat

maxi- *comb form* **1 :** extra long ⟨*maxi*-kilt⟩ **2 :** extra large ⟨*maxi*-problems⟩

max•il•la \mak-ˈsi-lə\ *n, pl* **max•il•lae** \-ˈsi-(ˌ)lē\ *or* **maxillas :** JAW 1; *esp* **:** an upper jaw — **max•il•lary** \ˈmak-sə-ˌler-ē\ *adj*

max•im \ˈmak-səm\ *n* **:** a proverbial saying

max•i•mal \ˈmak-sə-məl\ *adj* **:** MAXIMUM — **max•i•mal•ly** *adv*

max•i•mise *Brit var of* MAXIMIZE

max•i•mize \ˈmak-sə-ˌmīz\ *vb* **-mized; -miz•ing 1 :** to increase to a maximum **2 :** to make the most of — **max•i•mi•za•tion** \ˌmak-sə-mə-ˈzā-shən\ *n*

max•i•mum \ˈmak-sə-məm\ *n, pl* **-ma** \-mə\ *or* **-mums 1 :** the greatest quantity, value, or degree **2 :** an upper limit allowed by authority **3 :** the largest of a set of numbers — **maximum** *adj*

may \ˈmā\ *verbal auxiliary, past* **might** \ˈmīt\; *pres sing & pl* **may 1 :** have permission or liberty to ⟨you ~ go now⟩ **2 :** be in some degree likely to ⟨you ~ be right⟩ **3** — used as an auxiliary to express a wish, purpose, contingency, or concession

May \ˈmā\ *n* [ME, fr. OF *mai,* fr. L *Maius,* fr. *Maia,* Roman goddess] **:** the 5th month of the year

Ma•ya \ˈmī-ə\ *n, pl* **Maya** *or* **Mayas :** a member of a group of peoples of Yucatán, Guatemala, and adjacent areas — **Ma•yan** \ˈmī-ən\ *n or adj*

may•ap•ple \ˈmā-ˌa-pəl\ *n* **:** a No. American woodland herb related to the barberry that has a poisonous root, one or two large leaves, and an edible but insipid yellow fruit

may·be \ˈmā-bē, ˈme-\ *adv* : PERHAPS

May Day \ˈmā-ˌdā\ *n* : May 1 celebrated as a springtime festival and in some countries as Labor Day

may·flow·er \ˈmā-ˌflau̇-ər\ *n* : any of several spring blooming herbs (as the trailing arbutus or an anemone)

may·fly \ˈmā-flī\ *n* : any of an order of insects with an aquatic nymph and a short-lived fragile adult having membranous wings

may·hem \ˈmā-ˌhem, ˈmā-əm\ *n* **1** : willful and permanent crippling, mutilation, or disfigurement of a person **2** : needless or willful damage

may·on·naise \ˈmā-ə-ˌnāz\ *n* [F] : a dressing made of egg yolks, vegetable oil, and vinegar or lemon juice

may·or \ˈmā-ər\ *n* : an official elected to act as chief executive or nominal head of a city or borough — **may·or·al** \-əl\ *adj* — **may·or·al·ty** \-əl-tē\ *n*

may·pole \ˈmā-ˌpōl\ *n, often cap* : a tall flower-wreathed pole forming a center for May Day sports and dances

maze \ˈmāz\ *n* : a confusing intricate network of passages — **mazy** *adj*

ma·zur·ka \mə-ˈzər-kə\ *n* : a Polish dance in moderate triple measure

MB *abbr* Manitoba

MBA *abbr* master of business administration

mc *abbr* megacycle

[1]**MC** *n* : MASTER OF CEREMONIES

[2]**MC** *abbr* member of Congress

Mc·Coy \mə-ˈkȯi\ *n* : something that is neither imitation nor substitute ⟨the real ~⟩

MCPO *abbr* master chief petty officer

[1]**Md** *abbr* Maryland

[2]**Md** *symbol* mendelevium

MD *abbr* **1** [NL *medicinae doctor*] doctor of medicine **2** Maryland **3** muscular dystrophy

mdnt *abbr* midnight

mdse *abbr* merchandise

MDT *abbr* mountain daylight (saving) time

me \ˈmē\ *pron, objective case of* I

Me *abbr* Maine

ME *abbr* **1** Maine **2** mechanical engineer **3** medical examiner

[1]**mead** \ˈmēd\ *n* : an alcoholic beverage brewed from water and honey, malt, and yeast

[2]**mead** *n, archaic* : MEADOW

mead·ow \ˈme-dō\ *n* : land in or mainly in grass; *esp* : a tract of moist low-lying usu. level grassland — **mead·ow·land** \-ˌland\ *n* — **mead·owy** \ˈme-də-wē\ *adj*

mead·ow·lark \ˈme-dō-ˌlärk\ *n* : any of several No. American songbirds related to the orioles that are streaked brown above and in northernmost forms have a yellow breast marked with a black crescent

mead·ow·sweet \-ˌswēt\ *n* : a No. American native or naturalized spirea

mea·ger *or* **mea·gre** \ˈmē-gər\ *adj* **1** : THIN **2** : lacking richness, fertility, or strength; *also* : POOR **syn** scanty, scant, spare, sparse — **mea·ger·ly** *adv* — **mea·ger·ness** *n*

[1]**meal** \ˈmēl\ *n* **1** : an act or the time of eating a portion of food **2** : the portion of food eaten at a meal

[2]**meal** *n* **1** : usu. coarsely ground seeds of a cereal **2** : a product resembling seed meal — **mealy** *adj*

meal·time \ˈmēl-ˌtīm\ *n* : the usual time at which a meal is served

mealy·bug \ˈmē-lē-ˌbəg\ *n* : any of a family of scale insects with a white powdery covering that are destructive pests esp. of fruit trees

mealy·mouthed \ˈmē-lē-ˌmau̇t͟hd, -ˌmau̇tht\ *adj* : not plain and straightforward : DEVIOUS

[1]**mean** \ˈmēn\ *vb* **meant** \ˈment\; **mean·ing** **1** : to have in the mind as a purpose **2** : to serve to convey, show, or indicate : SIGNIFY **3** : to have importance to the degree of **4** : to direct to a particular individual

[2]**mean** *adj* **1** : HUMBLE **2** : lacking acumen : DULL **3** : SHABBY, CONTEMPTIBLE **4** : IGNOBLE, BASE **5** : STINGY **6** : pettily selfish or malicious **7** : VEXATIOUS **8** : EXCELLENT — **mean·ly** *adv* — **mean·ness** *n*

[3]**mean** *adj* **1** : occupying a middle position (as in space, order, or time) **2** : being a mean : AVERAGE ⟨a ~ value⟩

[4]**mean** *n* **1** : a middle point between extremes **2** *pl* : something helpful in achieving a desired end **3** *pl* : material resources affording a secure life **4** : ARITHMETIC MEAN

[1]**me·an·der** \mē-ˈan-dər\ *n* [L *maeander,* fr. Gk *maiandros,* fr. *Maiandros* (now *Menderes*), river in Asia Minor] **1** : a winding course **2** : a winding of a stream — **me·an·drous** \-drəs\ *adj*

[2]**meander** *vb* **1** : to follow a winding course **2** : to wander aimlessly or casually

mean·ing *n* **1** : the thing one intends to convey esp. by language; *also* : the thing that is thus conveyed **2** : AIM **3** : SIGNIFICANCE; *esp* : implication of a hidden significance **4** : CONNOTATION; *also* : DENOTATION — **mean·ing·ful** \-fəl\ *adj* — **mean·ing·ful·ly** *adv* — **mean·ing·less** *adj*

[1]**mean·time** \ˈmēn-ˌtīm\ *n* : the intervening time

[2]**meantime** *adv* : MEANWHILE

[1]**mean·while** \-ˌhwīl\ *n* : MEANTIME

[2]**meanwhile** *adv* **1** : during the intervening time **2** : at the same time

meas *abbr* measure

mea·sles \ˈmē-zəlz\ *n sing or pl* : an acute virus disease marked by fever and an eruption of distinct circular red spots

mea·sly \ˈmēz-lē, -zə-lē\ *adj* **mea·sli·er; -est** : contemptibly small or insignificant

[1]**mea·sure** \ˈme-zhər, ˈmā-\ *n* **1** : an adequate or moderate portion; *also* : a suitable limit **2** : the dimensions, capacity, or amount of something ascertained by measuring; *also* : an instrument for measuring **3** : a unit of measurement; *also* : a system of such units **4** : the act or process of measuring **5** : rhythmic structure or movement **6** : the part of a musical staff between two bars **7** : CRITERION **8** : a means to an end **9** : a legislative bill — **mea·sure·less** *adj*

[2]**measure** *vb* **mea·sured; mea·sur·ing** **1** : to mark or fix in multiples of a specific unit ⟨~ off five centimeters⟩ **2** : to find out the size, extent, or amount of **3** : to bring into comparison or competition **4** : to serve as a means of measuring **5** : to have a specified measurement — **mea·sur·able** \ˈme-zhə-rə-bəl, ˈmā-\ *adj* — **mea·sur·ably** \-blē\ *adv* — **mea·sur·er** *n*

mea·sure·ment \ˈme-zhər-mənt, ˈmā-\ *n* **1** : the act or process of measuring **2** : a figure, extent, or amount obtained by measuring

measure up *vb* **1** : to have necessary or fitting qualifications **2** : to equal esp. in ability

meat \ˈmēt\ *n* **1** : FOOD; *esp* : solid food as distinguished from drink **2** : animal and esp. mammal flesh considered as food **3** : the edible part inside a covering (as a shell or rind) — **meaty** *adj*

meat·ball \-ˌbȯl\ *n* : a small ball of chopped or ground meat

meat loaf *n* : a dish of ground meat seasoned and baked in the form of a loaf

mec·ca \ˈme-kə\ *n, often cap* [*Mecca,* Saudi Arabia, a destination of pilgrims in the Islamic world] : a center of activity sought as a goal by people sharing a common interest

mech *abbr* mechanical; mechanics

[1]**me·chan·ic** \mi-ˈka-nik\ *adj* : of or relating to manual work or skill

[2]**mechanic** *n* **1** : a manual worker **2** : MACHINIST; *esp* : one who repairs cars

me·chan·i·cal \mi-ˈka-ni-kəl\ *adj* **1** : of or relating to machinery, to manual operations, or to mechanics **2**

: done as if by a machine : AUTOMATIC **syn** instinctive, impulsive, spontaneous — **me·chan·i·cal·ly** \-k(ə-)lē\ *adv*

mechanical drawing *n* : drawing done with the aid of instruments

me·chan·ics \mi-ˈka-niks\ *n sing or pl* **1** : a branch of physics that deals with energy and forces and their effect on bodies **2** : the practical application of mechanics (as to the operation of machines) **3** : mechanical or functional details

mech·a·nism \ˈme-kə-ˌni-zəm\ *n* **1** : a piece of machinery; *also* : a process or technique for achieving a result **2** : mechanical operation or action **3** : the fundamental processes involved in or responsible for a natural phenomenon ⟨the visual ~⟩

mech·a·nis·tic \ˌme-kə-ˈnis-tik\ *adj* **1** : mechanically determined ⟨~ universe⟩ **2** : MECHANICAL — **mech·a·nis·ti·cal·ly** \-ti-k(ə-)lē\ *adv*

mech·a·nize \ˈme-kə-ˌnīz\ *vb* **-nized; -niz·ing 1** : to make mechanical **2** : to equip with machinery esp. in order to replace human or animal labor **3** : to equip with armed and armored motor vehicles — **mech·a·ni·za·tion** \ˌme-kə-nə-ˈzā-shən\ *n* — **mech·a·niz·er** *n*

med *abbr* **1** medical; medicine **2** medieval **3** medium

MEd *abbr* master of education

med·al \ˈmed-ᵊl\ *n* [MF *medaille,* fr. OIt *medaglia* coin worth half a denarius, medal, fr. (assumed) VL *medalis* half, alter. of LL *medialis* middle, fr. L *medius*] **1** : a small usu. metal object bearing a religious emblem or picture **2** : a piece of metal issued to commemorate a person or event or to award excellence or achievement

med·al·ist *or* **med·al·list** \ˈmed-ᵊl-ist\ *n* **1** : a designer or maker of medals **2** : a recipient of a medal as an award

me·dal·lion \mə-ˈdal-yən\ *n* **1** : a large medal **2** : a tablet or panel bearing a portrait or an ornament

med·dle \ˈmed-ᵊl\ *vb* **med·dled; med·dling** : to interfere without right or propriety — **med·dler** \ˈmed-ᵊl-ər\ *n*

med·dle·some \ˈmed-ᵊl-səm\ *adj* : inclined to meddle

me·dia \ˈmē-dē-ə\ *n, pl* **me·di·as** : MEDIUM 4

me·di·al \ˈmē-dē-əl\ *adj* : occurring in or extending toward the middle

[1]**me·di·an** \ˈmē-dē-ən\ *n* **1** : a value in an ordered set of values below and above which there are an equal number of values **2** : MEDIAN STRIP

[2]**median** *adj* **1** : being in the middle or in an intermediate position **2** : relating to or constituting a statistical median

median strip *n* : a strip dividing a highway into lanes according to the direction of travel

me·di·ate \ˈmē-dē-ˌāt\ *vb* **-at·ed; -at·ing 1** : to act as an intermediary; *esp* : to work with opposing sides in order to resolve (as a dispute) or bring about (as a settlement) **2** : to bring about, influence, or transmit (as a physical process or effect) by acting as an intermediate or controlling agent or mechanism **syn** intercede, intervene, interpose, interfere — **me·di·a·tion** \ˌmē-dē-ˈā-shən\ *n* — **me·di·a·tor** \ˈmē-dē-ˌā-tər\ *n*

med·ic \ˈme-dik\ *n* : one engaged in medical work; *esp* : CORPSMAN

med·i·ca·ble \ˈme-di-kə-bəl\ *adj* : CURABLE

med·ic·aid \ˈme-di-ˌkād\ *n, often cap* : a program of financial assistance for medical care designed for those unable to afford regular medical service and financed jointly by the state and federal governments

med·i·cal \ˈme-di-kəl\ *adj* : of or relating to the science or practice of medicine or the treatment of disease — **med·i·cal·ly** \-k(ə-)lē\ *adv*

medical examiner *n* : a public officer who performs autopsies on bodies to find the cause of death

me·di·ca·ment \mi-ˈdi-kə-mənt, ˈme-di-kə-\ *n* : a substance used in therapy

medi·care \ˈme-di-ˌker\ *n, often cap* : a government program of financial assistance for medical care esp. for the aged

med·i·cate \ˈme-də-ˌkāt\ *vb* **-cat·ed; -cat·ing** : to treat with medicine

med·i·ca·tion \ˌme-də-ˈkā-shən\ *n* **1** : the act or process of medicating **2** : MEDICINE 1

me·dic·i·nal \mə-ˈdis-ᵊn-əl\ *adj* : tending or used to cure disease or relieve pain — **me·dic·i·nal·ly** *adv*

med·i·cine \ˈme-də-sən\ *n* **1** : a substance or preparation used in treating disease **2** : a science and art dealing with the prevention and cure of disease

medicine ball *n* : a heavy stuffed leather ball used for conditioning exercises

medicine man *n* : a priestly healer or sorcerer esp. among the American Indians : SHAMAN

med·i·co \ˈme-di-ˌkō\ *n, pl* **-cos** : a medical practitioner or student

me·di·e·val *or* **me·di·ae·val** \ˌmē-dē-ˈē-vəl, ˌme-, mē-ˈdē-vəl\ *adj* **1** : of, relating to, or characteristic of the Middle Ages **2** : extremely outmoded or antiquated — **me·di·e·val·ism** \-və-ˌli-zəm\ *n* — **me·di·e·val·ist** \-list\ *n*

me·di·o·cre \ˌmē-dē-ˈō-kər\ *adj* [ME, fr. MF, fr. L *mediocris,* fr. *medius* middle + *ocris* stony mountain] : of moderate or low quality : ORDINARY — **me·di·oc·ri·ty** \-ˈä-krə-tē\ *n*

med·i·tate \ˈme-də-ˌtāt\ *vb* **-tat·ed; -tat·ing 1** : to muse over : CONTEMPLATE, PONDER **2** : INTEND, PLAN — **med·i·ta·tion** \ˌme-də-ˈtā-shən\ *n* — **med·i·ta·tive** \ˈme-də-ˌtā-tiv\ *adj* — **med·i·ta·tive·ly** *adv*

Med·i·ter·ra·nean \ˌme-də-tə-ˈrā-nē-ən, -ˈrā-nyən\ *adj* : of or relating to the Mediterranean Sea or to the lands or people around it

[1]**me·di·um** \ˈmē-dē-əm\ *n, pl* **mediums** *or* **me·dia** \-dē-ə\ [L] **1** : something in a middle position; *also* : a middle position or degree **2** : a means of effecting or conveying something **3** : a surrounding or enveloping substance **4** : a channel or system of communication, information, or entertainment **5** : a mode of artistic expression **6** : an individual held to be a channel of communication between the earthly world and a world of spirits **7** : a condition or environment in which something may function or flourish

[2]**medium** *adj* : intermediate in amount, quality, position, or degree

me·di·um·is·tic \ˌmē-dē-ə-ˈmis-tik\ *adj* : of, relating to, or being a spiritualistic medium

med·ley \ˈmed-lē\ *n, pl* **medleys 1** : HODGEPODGE **2** : a musical composition made up esp. of a series of songs

me·dul·la \mə-ˈdə-lə\ *n, pl* **-las** *or* **-lae** \-(ˌ)lē, -ˌlī\ : an inner or deep anatomical part; *also* : the posterior part (**medulla ob·lon·ga·ta** \-ˌä-ˌblȯŋ-ˈgä-tə\) of the vertebrate brain that is continuous with the spinal cord

meed \ˈmēd\ *n* : a fitting return

meek \ˈmēk\ *adj* **1** : characterized by patience and long-suffering **2** : deficient in spirit and courage **3** : MODERATE — **meek·ly** *adv* — **meek·ness** *n*

meer·schaum \ˈmir-shəm, -ˌshȯm\ *n* [G, fr. *Meer* sea + *Schaum* foam] : a tobacco pipe made of a light white clayey mineral

[1]**meet** \ˈmēt\ *vb* **met** \ˈmet\; **meet·ing 1** : to come upon : FIND **2** : JOIN, INTERSECT **3** : to appear to the perception of **4** : OPPOSE, FIGHT **5** : to join in conversation or discussion; *also* : ASSEMBLE **6** : to conform to **7** : to pay fully **8** : to cope with **9** : to provide for **10** : to be introduced to

[2]**meet** *n* : an assembling esp. for a hunt or for competitive sports

[3]**meet** *adj* : SUITABLE, PROPER

meet·ing \ˈmē-tiŋ\ *n* **1** : an act of coming together : ASSEMBLY **2** : JUNCTION, INTERSECTION

meet·ing·house \-ˌhau̇s\ *n* : a building for public assembly and esp. for Protestant worship

mega- *or* **meg-** *comb form* **1** : great : large ⟨*mega*hit⟩

2 : million : multiplied by one million ⟨*mega*hertz⟩

mega•byte \ˈme-gə-ˌbīt\ *n* : a unit of computer storage capacity equal to 1,048,576 bytes

mega•cy•cle \-ˌsī-kəl\ *n* : MEGAHERTZ

mega•death \-ˌdeth\ *n* : one million deaths — used as a unit in reference to nuclear warfare

mega•hertz \ˈme-gə-ˌhərts, -ˌherts\ *n* : a unit of frequency equal to one million hertz

mega•lith \ˈme-gə-ˌlith\ *n* : a large stone used in prehistoric monuments — **mega•lith•ic** \ˌme-gə-ˈli-thik\ *adj*

meg•a•lo•ma•nia \ˌme-gə-lō-ˈmā-nē-ə, -nyə\ *n* : a mental disorder marked by feelings of personal omnipotence and grandeur — **meg•a•lo•ma•ni•ac** \-ˈmā-nē-ˌak\ *adj or n*

meg•a•lop•o•lis \ˌme-gə-ˈlä-pə-ləs\ *n* : a very large urban unit

mega•phone \ˈme-gə-ˌfōn\ *n* : a cone-shaped device used to intensify or direct the voice — **megaphone** *vb*

mega•ton \-ˌtən\ *n* : an explosive force equivalent to that of one million tons of TNT

mega•vi•ta•min \-ˌvī-tə-mən\ *adj* : relating to or consisting of very large doses of vitamins — **mega•vi•ta•mins** *n pl*

mei•o•sis \mī-ˈō-səs\ *n* : a process of cell division in gamete-producing cells in which the number of chromosomes is reduced to one half — **mei•ot•ic** \mī-ˈä-tik\ *adj*

mel•an•cho•lia \ˌme-lən-ˈkō-lē-ə\ *n* : a mental disorder marked by extreme depression often with delusions

mel•an•chol•ic \ˌme-lən-ˈkä-lik\ *adj* **1** : DEPRESSED **2** : of or relating to melancholia

mel•an•choly \ˈme-lən-ˌkä-lē\ *n, pl* **-chol•ies** [ME *malencolie,* fr. MF *melancolie,* fr. LL *melancholia,* fr. Gk, fr. *melan-, melas* black + *cholē* bile; so called fr. the former belief that it was caused by an excess of black bile, a substance supposedly secreted by the kidneys or spleen] : depression of spirits : DEJECTION — **melancholy** *adj*

Mel•a•ne•sian \ˌme-lə-ˈnē-zhən\ *n* : a member of the dominant native group of the Pacific island grouping of Melanesia — **Melanesian** *adj*

mé•lange \mā-ˈlänzh, -ˈlänj\ *n* : a mixture esp. of incongruous elements

mel•a•nin \ˈme-lə-nən\ *n* : a dark brown or black animal or plant pigment

mel•a•nism \ˈme-lə-ˌni-zəm\ *n* : an increased amount of black or nearly black pigmentation

mel•a•no•ma \ˌme-lə-ˈnō-mə\ *n, pl* **-mas** *also* **-ma•ta** \-mə-tə\ : a usu. malignant tumor containing dark pigment

¹meld \ˈmeld\ *vb* : to show or announce for a score in a card game

²meld *n* : a card or combination of cards that is or can be melded

me•lee \ˈmā-ˌlā, mā-ˈlā\ *n* [F *mêlée*] : a confused struggle **syn** fracas, row, brawl, donnybrook

me•lio•rate \ˈmēl-yə-ˌrāt, ˈmē-lē-ə-\ *vb* **-rat•ed; -rat•ing** : AMELIORATE — **me•lio•ra•tion** \ˌmēl-yə-ˈrā-shən, ˌmē-lē-ə-\ *n* — **me•lio•ra•tive** \ˈmēl-yə-ˌrā-tiv, ˈmē-lē-ə-\ *adj*

mel•lif•lu•ous \me-ˈli-flə-wəs, mə-\ *adj* [LL *mellifluus,* fr. L *mel* honey + *fluere* to flow] : sweetly flowing — **mel•lif•lu•ous•ly** *adv* — **mel•lif•lu•ous•ness** *n*

¹mel•low \ˈme-lō\ *adj* **1** : soft and sweet because of ripeness; *also* : well aged and pleasingly mild ⟨~ wine⟩ **2** : made gentle by age or experience **3** : being rich and full but not garish or strident ⟨~ colors⟩ **4** : of soft loamy consistency ⟨~ soil⟩ — **mel•low•ness** *n*

²mellow *vb* : to make or become mellow

me•lo•di•ous \mə-ˈlō-dē-əs\ *adj* : pleasing to the ear — **me•lo•di•ous•ly** *adv* — **me•lo•di•ous•ness** *n*

melo•dra•ma \ˈme-lə-ˌdrä-mə, -ˌdra-\ *n* : an extravagantly theatrical play in which action and plot predominate over characterization — **melo•dra•mat•ic** \ˌme-lə-drə-ˈma-tik\ *adj* — **melo•dra•mat•i•cal•ly** \-ti-k(ə-)lē\ *adv* — **melo•dra•ma•tist** \ˌme-lə-ˈdra-mə-tist, -ˈdrä-\ *n*

mel•o•dy \ˈme-lə-dē\ *n, pl* **-dies 1** : sweet or agreeable sound **2** : a particular succession of notes : TUNE, AIR — **me•lod•ic** \mə-ˈlä-dik\ *adj* — **me•lod•i•cal•ly** \-di-k(ə-)lē\ *adv*

mel•on \ˈme-lən\ *n* : any of various fruits (as a muskmelon or watermelon) of the gourd family usu. eaten raw

¹melt \ˈmelt\ *vb* **1** : to change from a solid to a liquid state usu. by heat **2** : DISSOLVE, DISINTEGRATE; *also* : to cause to disperse or disappear **3** : to make or become tender or gentle

²melt *n* : a melted substance

melt•down \ˈmelt-ˌdau̇n\ *n* : the melting of the core of a nuclear reactor

melt•wa•ter \-ˌwȯ-tər, -ˌwä-\ *n* : water derived from the melting of ice and snow

mem *abbr* **1** member **2** memoir **3** memorial

mem•ber \ˈmem-bər\ *n* **1** : a part (as an arm, leg, leaf, or branch) of an animal or plant **2** : one of the individuals composing a group **3** : a constituent part of a whole

mem•ber•ship \-ˌship\ *n* **1** : the state or status of being a member **2** : the body of members

mem•brane \ˈmem-ˌbrān\ *n* : a thin pliable layer esp. of animal or plant origin — **mem•bra•nous** \-brə-nəs\ *adj*

me•men•to \mə-ˈmen-tō\ *n, pl* **-tos** *or* **-toes** [ME, fr. L, remember] : something that serves to warn or remind; *also* : SOUVENIR

memo \ˈme-mō\ *n, pl* **mem•os** : MEMORANDUM

mem•oir \ˈmem-ˌwär\ *n* **1** : MEMORANDUM **2** : AUTOBIOGRAPHY — usu. used in pl. **3** : an account of something noteworthy; *also, pl* : the record of the proceedings of a learned society

mem•o•ra•bil•ia \ˌme-mə-rə-ˈbi-lē-ə, -ˈbil-yə\ *n pl* [L] : things worthy of remembrance; *also* : MEMENTOS

mem•o•ra•ble \ˈme-mə-rə-bəl\ *adj* : worth remembering : NOTABLE — **mem•o•ra•bil•i•ty** \ˌme-mə-rə-ˈbi-lə-tē\ *n* — **mem•o•ra•ble•ness** *n* — **mem•o•ra•bly** \-blē\ *adv*

mem•o•ran•dum \ˌme-mə-ˈran-dəm\ *n, pl* **-dums** *or* **-da** \-də\ **1** : an informal record; *also* : a written reminder **2** : an informal written note

¹me•mo•ri•al \mə-ˈmōr-ē-əl\ *adj* : serving to preserve remembrance

²memorial *n* **1** : something designed to keep remembrance alive; *esp* : MONUMENT **2** : a statement of facts often accompanied with a petition — **me•mo•ri•al•ize** *vb*

Memorial Day *n* : the last Monday in May or formerly May 30 observed as a legal holiday in honor of those who died in war

mem•o•rise *Brit var of* MEMORIZE

mem•o•rize \ˈme-mə-ˌrīz\ *vb* **-rized; -riz•ing** : to learn by heart — **mem•o•ri•za•tion** \ˌme-mə-rə-ˈzā-shən\ *n* — **mem•o•riz•er** *n*

mem•o•ry \ˈme-mə-rē\ *n, pl* **-ries 1** : the power or process of remembering **2** : the store of things remembered **3** : COMMEMORATION **4** : something remembered **5** : the time within which past events are remembered **6** : a device (as in a computer) in which information can be stored **syn** remembrance, recollection, reminiscence

men *pl of* MAN

¹men•ace \ˈme-nəs\ *n* **1** : THREAT **2** : DANGER; *also* : NUISANCE

²menace *vb* **men•aced; men•ac•ing 1** : THREATEN **2** : ENDANGER — **men•ac•ing•ly** *adv*

mé•nage \mā-ˈnäzh\ *n* [F] : HOUSEHOLD

me•nag•er•ie \mə-ˈna-jə-rē\ *n* : a collection of wild animals esp. for exhibition

¹mend \ˈmend\ *vb* **1** : to improve in manners or morals

DICTIONARY

2 : to put into good shape : REPAIR 3 : to improve in or restore to health : HEAL — **mend·er** *n*

[2]**mend** *n* 1 : an act of mending 2 : a mended place

men·da·cious \men-ˈdā-shəs\ *adj* : given to deception or falsehood : UNTRUTHFUL **syn** dishonest, deceitful — **men·da·cious·ly** *adv* — **men·dac·i·ty** \-ˈda-sə-tē\ *n*

men·de·le·vi·um \ˌmen-də-ˈlē-vē-əm, -ˈlā-\ *n* : a radioactive chemical element artificially produced — see ELEMENT table

men·di·cant \ˈmen-di-kənt\ *n* 1 : BEGGAR 2 *often cap* : FRIAR — **men·di·can·cy** \-kən-sē\ *n* — **mendicant** *adj*

men·folk \ˈmen-ˌfōk\ *or* **men·folks** \-ˌfōks\ *n pl* 1 : men in general 2 : the men of a family or community

men·ha·den \men-ˈhād-ᵊn, mən-\ *n, pl* **-den** *also* **-dens** : a marine fish related to the herring that is abundant along the Atlantic coast of the U.S.

[1]**me·nial** \ˈmē-nē-əl, -nyəl\ *adj* 1 : of or relating to servants 2 : HUMBLE; *also* : SERVILE — **me·ni·al·ly** *adv*

[2]**menial** *n* : a domestic servant

men·in·gi·tis \ˌme-nən-ˈjī-təs\ *n, pl* **-git·i·des** \-ˈji-tə-ˌdēz\ : inflammation of the membranes enclosing the brain and spinal cord; *also* : a usu. bacterial disease marked by this

me·ninx \ˈmē-niŋks, ˈme-\ *n, pl* **me·nin·ges** \mə-ˈnin-(ˌ)jēz\ : any of the three membranes that envelop the brain and spinal cord — **men·in·ge·al** \ˌme-nən-ˈjē-əl\ *adj*

me·nis·cus \mə-ˈnis-kəs\ *n, pl* **me·nis·ci** \-ˈnis-ˌkī, -ˌkē\ *also* **me·nis·cus·es** 1 : CRESCENT 2 : the curved upper surface of a column of liquid

men·o·pause \ˈme-nə-ˌpȯz\ *n* : the period of life when menstruation stops naturally — **men·o·paus·al** \ˌme-nə-ˈpȯ-zəl\ *adj*

me·no·rah \mə-ˈnōr-ə\ *n* [Heb *mĕnōrāh* candlestick] : a candelabrum that is used in Jewish worship

men·ses \ˈmen-ˌsēz\ *n pl* : the menstrual flow

men·stru·a·tion \ˌmen-strə-ˈwā-shən, men-ˈstrā-\ *n* : a discharging of bloody matter at approximately monthly intervals from the uterus of breeding-age nonpregnant primate females; *also* : PERIOD 6 — **men·stru·al** \ˈmen-strə-wəl\ *adj* — **men·stru·ate** \ˈmen-strə-ˌwāt, -ˌstrāt\ *vb*

men·su·ra·ble \ˈmen-sə-rə-bəl, ˈ-chə-\ *adj* : MEASURABLE

men·su·ra·tion \ˌmen-sə-ˈrā-shən, ˌmen-chə-\ *n* : MEASUREMENT

-ment \mənt\ *n suffix* 1 : concrete result, object, or agent of a (specified) action ⟨embank*ment*⟩ ⟨entangle*ment*⟩ 2 : concrete means or instrument of a (specified) action ⟨entertain*ment*⟩ 3 : action : process ⟨encircle*ment*⟩ ⟨develop*ment*⟩ 4 : place of a (specified) action ⟨encamp*ment*⟩ 5 : state : condition ⟨amaze*ment*⟩

men·tal \ˈment-ᵊl\ *adj* 1 : of or relating to the mind 2 : of, relating to, or affected with a disorder of the mind ⟨~ illness⟩ — **men·tal·ly** *adv*

mental age *n* : a measure of a child's mental development in terms of the number of years it takes an average child to reach the same level

mental deficiency *n* : MENTAL RETARDATION

men·tal·i·ty \men-ˈta-lə-tē\ *n, pl* **-ties** 1 : mental power or capacity 2 : mode or way of thought

mental retardation *n* : subaverage intellectual ability present from infancy that is characterized by an IQ of 70 or less and problems in development, learning, and social adjustment

men·thol \ˈmen-ˌthȯl, -ˌthōl\ *n* : an alcohol occurring esp. in mint oils that has the odor and cooling properties of peppermint — **men·tho·lat·ed** \-thə-ˌlā-təd\ *adj*

[1]**men·tion** \ˈmen-chən\ *n* 1 : a brief or casual reference 2 : a formal citation for outstanding achievement

[2]**mention** *vb* 1 : to refer to : CITE 2 : to cite for superior achievement — **not to mention** : to say nothing of

men·tor \ˈmen-ˌtȯr, -tər\ *n* : a trusted counselor or guide; *also* : TUTOR, COACH

menu \ˈmen-yü, ˈmān-\ *n, pl* **menus** [F, fr. *menu* small, detailed, fr. L *minutus* minute (adj.)] 1 : a list of the dishes available (as in a restaurant) for a meal; *also* : the dishes served 2 : a list of offerings or options

me·ow \mē-ˈau̇\ *vb* : to make the characteristic cry of a cat — **meow** *n*

mer *abbr* meridian

mer·can·tile \ˈmər-kən-ˌtēl, -ˌtīl\ *adj* : of or relating to merchants or trading

[1]**mer·ce·nary** \ˈmərs-ᵊn-ˌer-ē\ *n, pl* **-nar·ies** : a person who serves merely for wages; *esp* : a soldier hired into foreign service

[2]**mercenary** *adj* 1 : serving merely for pay or gain 2 : hired for service in a foreign army

mer·cer \ˈmər-sər\ *n, Brit* : a dealer in usu. expensive fabrics

mer·cer·ise *Brit var of* MERCERIZE

mer·cer·ize \ˈmər-sə-ˌrīz\ *vb* **-ized; -iz·ing** : to treat cotton yarn or cloth with alkali so that it looks silky or takes a better dye

[1]**mer·chan·dise** \ˈmər-chən-ˌdīz, -ˌdīs\ *n* : the commodities or goods that are bought and sold in business

[2]**mer·chan·dise** \-ˌdīz\ *vb* **-dised; -dis·ing** : to buy and sell in business : TRADE — **mer·chan·dis·er** *n*

mer·chant \ˈmər-chənt\ *n* 1 : a buyer and seller of commodities for profit 2 : STOREKEEPER

mer·chant·able \ˈmər-chən-tə-bəl\ *adj* : acceptable to buyers : MARKETABLE

mer·chant·man \ˈmər-chənt-mən\ *n* : a ship used in commerce

merchant marine *n* : the commercial ships of a nation

merchant ship *n* : MERCHANTMAN

mer·ci·ful·ly \ˈmər-si-fə-lē\ *adv* 1 : in a merciful manner 2 : FORTUNATELY 2

mer·cu·ri·al \ˌmər-ˈkyu̇r-ē-əl\ *adj* 1 : unpredictably changeable 2 : MERCURIC — **mer·cu·ri·al·ly** *adv* — **mer·cu·ri·al·ness** *n*

mer·cu·ric \ˌmər-ˈkyu̇r-ik\ *adj* : of, relating to, or containing mercury

mercuric chloride *n* : a poisonous compound of mercury and chlorine used as an antiseptic and fungicide

mer·cu·ry \ˈmər-kyə-rē\ *n, pl* **-ries** 1 : a heavy silver-white liquid metallic chemical element used esp. in scientific instruments — see ELEMENT table 2 *cap* : the planet nearest the sun — see PLANET table

mer·cy \ˈmər-sē\ *n, pl* **mercies** [ME, fr. OF *merci*, fr. ML *merced-*, *merces*, fr. L, price paid, wages, fr. *merc-*, *merx* merchandise] 1 : compassion shown to an offender; *also* : imprisonment rather than death for first-degree murder 2 : a blessing resulting from divine favor or compassion; *also* : a fortunate circumstance 3 : compassion shown to victims of misfortune — **mer·ci·ful** \-si-fəl\ *adj* — **mer·ci·less** \-si-ləs\ *adj* — **mer·ci·less·ly** *adv* — **mercy** *adj*

mercy killing *n* : the act or practice of killing or permitting the death of hopelessly sick or injured persons or animals with as little pain as possible for reasons of mercy

[1]**mere** \ˈmir\ *n* : LAKE, POOL

[2]**mere** *adj, superlative* **mer·est** 1 : being nothing more than ⟨a ~ child⟩ 2 : not diluted : PURE — **mere·ly** *adv*

mer·e·tri·cious \ˌmer-ə-ˈtri-shəs\ *adj* [L *meretricius*, fr. *meretrix* prostitute, fr. *merēre* to earn] : tawdrily attractive; *also* : SPECIOUS — **mer·e·tri·cious·ly** *adv* — **mer·e·tri·cious·ness** *n*

mer·gan·ser \(ˌ)mər-ˈgan-sər\ *n* : any of various fish-eating wild ducks with a usu. crested head and a slender bill hooked at the end and serrated along the margins

merge \ˈmərj\ *vb* **merged; merg·ing** 1 : to blend gradually 2 : to combine, unite, or coalesce into one **syn** mingle, amalgamate, fuse, interfuse, intermingle

merg·er \ˈmər-jər\ *n* 1 : the act or process of merging

2 : absorption by a corporation of one or more others

me•rid•i•an \mə-ˈri-dē-ən\ *n* [ME, fr. MF *meridien*, fr. *meridien* of noon, fr. L *meridianus*, fr. *meridies* noon, south, irreg. fr. *medius* mid + *dies* day] **1** : the highest point : CULMINATION **2** : any of the imaginary circles on the earth's surface passing through the north and south poles — **meridian** *adj*

me•ringue \mə-ˈraŋ\ *n* [F] : a baked dessert topping of stiffly beaten egg whites and powdered sugar

me•ri•no \mə-ˈrē-nō\ *n, pl* **-nos** [Sp] **1** : any of a breed of sheep noted for fine soft wool **2** : a fine soft fabric or yarn of wool or wool and cotton

¹mer•it \ˈmer-ət\ *n* **1** : laudable or blameworthy traits or actions **2** : a praiseworthy quality; *also* : character or conduct deserving reward or honor **3** *pl* : the intrinsic nature of a legal case; *also* : legal significance

²merit *vb* : EARN, DESERVE

mer•i•toc•ra•cy \ˌmer-ə-ˈtä-krə-sē\ *n, pl* **-cies** : a system in which the talented are chosen and moved ahead based on their achievement; *also* : leadership by the talented

mer•i•to•ri•ous \ˌmer-ə-ˈtōr-ē-əs\ *adj* : deserving honor or esteem — **mer•i•to•ri•ous•ly** *adv* — **mer•i•to•ri•ous•ness** *n*

mer•maid \ˈmər-ˌmād\ *n* : a legendary sea creature with a woman's upper body and a fish's tail

mer•man \-ˌman, -mən\ *n* : a legendary sea creature with a man's upper body and a fish's tail

mer•ri•ment \ˈmer-i-mənt\ *n* **1** : HILARITY **2** : FESTIVITY

mer•ry \ˈmer-ē\ *adj* **mer•ri•er; -est** **1** : full of gaiety or high spirits **2** : marked by festivity **3** : BRISK ⟨a ~ pace⟩ **syn** blithe, jocund, jovial, jolly, mirthful — **mer•ri•ly** \ˈmer-ə-lē\ *adv*

merry–go–round \ˈmer-ē-gō-ˌraund\ *n* **1** : a circular revolving platform with benches and figures of animals on which people sit for a ride **2** : a busy round of activities

mer•ry•mak•ing \ˈmer-ē-ˌmā-kiŋ\ *n* **1** : jovial or festive activity **2** : a festive occasion — **mer•ry•mak•er** \-ˌmā-kər\ *n*

me•sa \ˈmā-sə\ *n* [Sp, lit., table, fr. L *mensa*] : a flat-topped hill with steep sides

mes•cal \me-ˈskal, mə-\ *n* **1** : a small cactus that is the source of a stimulant used esp. by Mexican Indians **2** : a usu. colorless liquor distilled from the leaves of an agave; *also* : this agave

mes•ca•line \ˈmes-kə-lən, -ˌlēn\ *n* : a hallucinatory alkaloid from the mescal cactus

mesdames *pl of* MADAM *or of* MADAME *or of* MRS.

mesdemoiselles *pl of* MADEMOISELLE

¹mesh \ˈmesh\ *n* **1** : one of the openings between the threads or cords of a net; *also* : one of the similar spaces in a network **2** : the fabric of a net **3** : NETWORK **4** : working contact (as of the teeth of gears) ⟨in ~⟩ — **meshed** \ˈmesht\ *adj*

²mesh *vb* **1** : to catch in or as if in a mesh **2** : to be in or come into mesh : ENGAGE **3** : to fit together properly

mesh•work \ˈmesh-ˌwərk\ *n* : NETWORK

me•si•al \ˈmē-zē-əl, -sē-\ *adj* : of, relating to, or being the surface of a tooth that is closest to the middle of the front of the jaw

mes•mer•ise *Brit var of* MESMERIZE

mes•mer•ize \ˈmez-mə-ˌrīz\ *vb* **-ized; -iz•ing** : HYPNOTIZE — **mes•mer•ic** \mez-ˈmer-ik\ *adj* — **mes•mer•ism** \ˈmez-mə-ˌri-zəm\ *n*

Me•so•lith•ic \ˌme-zə-ˈli-thik\ *adj* : of, relating to, or being a transitional period of the Stone Age between the Paleolithic and the Neolithic periods

me•so•sphere \ˈme-zə-ˌsfir\ *n* : a layer of the atmosphere between the stratosphere and the thermosphere

Me•so•zo•ic \ˌme-zə-ˈzō-ik, ˌmē-\ *adj* : of, relating to, or being the era of geologic history between the Paleozoic and the Cenozoic and extending from about 245 million years ago to about 65 million years ago — **Mesozoic** *n*

mes•quite \mə-ˈskēt, me-\ *n* : any of several spiny leguminous trees and shrubs chiefly of the southwestern U.S. with sugar-rich pods important as fodder; *also* : mesquite wood used esp. in grilling food

¹mess \ˈmes\ *n* **1** : a quantity of food; *also* : enough food of a specified kind for a dish or meal ⟨a ~ of beans⟩ **2** : a group of persons who regularly eat together; *also* : a meal eaten by such a group **3** : a place where meals are regularly served to a group **4** : a confused, dirty, or offensive state — **messy** *adj*

²mess *vb* **1** : to supply with meals; *also* : to take meals with a mess **2** : to make dirty or untidy; *also* : BUNGLE **3** : INTERFERE, MEDDLE **4** : PUTTER, TRIFLE

mes•sage \ˈme-sij\ *n* : a communication sent by one person to another

messeigneurs *pl of* MONSEIGNEUR

mes•sen•ger \ˈmes-ᵊn-jər\ *n* : one who carries a message or does an errand

messenger RNA *n* : an RNA that carries the code for a particular protein from DNA in the nucleus to a ribosome in the cytoplasm and acts as a template for the formation of that protein

Mes•si•ah \mə-ˈsī-ə\ *n* **1** : the expected king and deliverer of the Jews **2** : Jesus **3** *not cap* : a professed or accepted leader of a cause — **mes•si•an•ic** \ˌme-sē-ˈa-nik\ *adj*

messieurs *pl of* MONSIEUR

mess•mate \ˈmes-ˌmāt\ *n* : a member of a group who eat regularly together

Messrs. \ˈme-sərz\ *pl of* MR.

mes•ti•zo \me-ˈstē-zō\ *n, pl* **-zos** [Sp, fr. *mestizo* mixed, fr. LL *mixticius*, fr. L *mixtus*, pp. of *miscēre* to mix] : a person of mixed blood

¹met *past and past part of* MEET

²met *abbr* metropolitan

me•tab•o•lism \mə-ˈta-bə-ˌli-zəm\ *n* : the processes by which the substance of plants and animals incidental to life is built up and broken down; *also* : the processes by which a substance is handled in the body ⟨~ of sugar⟩ — **met•a•bol•ic** \ˌme-tə-ˈbä-lik\ *adj* — **me•tab•o•lize** \mə-ˈta-bə-ˌlīz\ *vb*

me•tab•o•lite \-ˌlīt\ *n* **1** : a product of metabolism **2** : a substance essential to the metabolism of a particular organism or to a metabolic process

meta•car•pal \ˌme-tə-ˈkär-pəl\ *n* : any of usu. five more or less elongated bones of the part of the hand or forefoot between the wrist and the bones of the digits — **metacarpal** *adj*

meta•car•pus \-ˈkär-pəs\ *n* : the part of the hand or forefoot that contains the metacarpals

met•al \ˈmet-ᵊl\ *n* **1** : any of various opaque, fusible, ductile, and typically lustrous substances that are good conductors of electricity and heat **2** : METTLE; *also* : the material out of which a person or thing is made — **me•tal•lic** \mə-ˈta-lik\ *adj*

met•al•lur•gy \ˈmet-ᵊl-ˌər-jē\ *n* : the science and technology of metals — **met•al•lur•gi•cal** \ˌmet-ᵊl-ˈər-ji-kəl\ *adj* — **met•al•lur•gist** \ˈmet-ᵊl-ˌər-jist\ *n*

met•al•ware \ˈmet-ᵊl-ˌwar\ *n* : metal utensils for household use

met•al•work \-ˌwərk\ *n* : work and esp. artistic work made of metal — **met•al•work•er** \-ˌwər-kər\ *n* — **met•al•work•ing** *n*

meta•mor•phism \ˌme-tə-ˈmȯr-ˌfi-zəm\ *n* : a change in the structure of rock; *esp* : a change to a more compact and more highly crystalline form produced by pressure, heat, and water — **meta•mor•phic** \-ˈmȯr-fik\ *adj*

meta•mor•pho•sis \ˌme-tə-ˈmȯr-fə-səs\ *n, pl* **-pho•ses** \-ˌsēz\ **1** : a change of physical form, structure, or substance esp. by supernatural means; *also* : a striking alteration (as in appearance or character) **2** : a fundamental change in form and often habits of an animal accompanying the transformation of a larva into an adult — **meta•mor•phose** \-ˌfōz, -ˌfōs\ *vb*

met•a•phor \ˈme-tə-ˌfȯr\ *n* : a figure of speech in which a word for one idea or thing is used in place of another to suggest a likeness between them (as in "the ship plows the sea") — **met•a•phor•i•cal** \ˌme-tə-ˈfȯr-i-kəl\ *adj*

meta•phys•ics \ˌme-tə-ˈfi-ziks\ *n* [ML *Metaphysica,* title of Aristotle's treatise on the subject, fr. Gk (*ta*) *meta* (*ta*) *physika,* lit., the (works) after the physical (works); fr. its position in his collected works] : the philosophical study of the ultimate causes and underlying nature of things — **meta•phys•i•cal** \-ˈfi-zi-kəl\ *adj* — **meta•phy•si•cian** \-fə-ˈzi-shən\ *n*

me•tas•ta•sis \mə-ˈtas-tə-səs\ *n, pl* **-ta•ses** \-ˌsēz\ : transfer of a health-impairing agency (as cancer cells) to a new site in the body; *also* : a secondary growth of a malignant tumor — **me•tas•ta•size** \-tə-ˌsīz\ *vb* — **met•a•stat•ic** \ˌme-tə-ˈsta-tik\ *adj*

meta•tar•sal \ˌme-tə-ˈtär-səl\ *n* : any of the bones of the foot between the tarsus and the bones of the digits that in humans include five more or less elongated bones — **metatarsal** *adj*

meta•tar•sus \-ˈtär-səs\ *n* : the part of the human foot or the hind foot in quadrupeds that contains the metatarsals

[1]**mete** \ˈmēt\ *vb* **met•ed; met•ing 1** *archaic* : MEASURE **2** : ALLOT

[2]**mete** *n* : BOUNDARY ⟨~*s* and bounds⟩

me•te•or \ˈmē-tē-ər, -ˌȯr\ *n* **1** : a small particle of matter in the solar system directly observable only by its glow from frictional heating on falling into the earth's atmosphere **2** : the streak of light produced by a meteor

me•te•or•ic \ˌmē-tē-ˈȯr-ik\ *adj* **1** : of, relating to, or resembling a meteor **2** : transiently brilliant ⟨a ~ career⟩ — **me•te•or•i•cal•ly** \-i-k(ə-)lē\ *adv*

me•te•or•ite \ˈmē-tē-ə-ˌrīt\ *n* : a meteor that reaches the surface of the earth

me•te•or•oid \ˈmē-tē-ə-ˌrȯid\ *n* : a small particle of matter in the solar system

me•te•o•rol•o•gy \ˌmē-tē-ə-ˈrä-lə-jē\ *n* : a science that deals with the atmosphere and its phenomena and esp. with weather forecasting — **me•te•o•ro•log•ic** \ˌmē-tē-ˌȯr-ə-ˈlä-jik\ *or* **me•te•o•ro•log•i•cal** \-ˈlä-ji-kəl\ *adj* — **me•te•o•rol•o•gist** \ˌmē-tē-ə-ˈrä-lə-jist\ *n*

[1]**me•ter** \ˈmē-tər\ *n* : rhythm in verse or music

[2]**meter** *n* : the basic metric unit of length — see METRIC SYSTEM table

[3]**meter** *n* : a measuring and sometimes recording instrument

[4]**meter** *vb* **1** : to measure by means of a meter **2** : to print postal indicia on by means of a postage meter ⟨~*ed* mail⟩

meter–kilogram–second *adj* : of, relating to, or being a system of units based on the meter, the kilogram, and the second

meter maid *n* : a policewoman assigned to write tickets for parking violations

meth•a•done \ˈme-thə-ˌdōn\ *also* **meth•a•don** \-ˌdän\ *n* : a synthetic addictive narcotic drug used esp. as a substitute narcotic in the treatment of heroin addiction

meth•am•phet•amine \ˌme-tham-ˈfe-tə-ˌmēn, -thəm-, -mən\ *n* : a drug used medically in the form of its hydrochloride in the treatment of obesity and often illicitly as a stimulant

meth•ane \ˈme-ˌthān\ *n* : a colorless odorless flammable gas produced by decomposition of organic matter or from coal and used esp. as a fuel

meth•a•nol \ˈme-thə-ˌnȯl, -ˌnōl\ *n* : a volatile flammable poisonous liquid alcohol used esp. as a solvent and as an antifreeze

meth•aqua•lone \me-ˈtha-kwə-ˌlōn\ *n* : a sedative and hypnotic habit-forming drug that is not a barbiturate

meth•od \ˈme-thəd\ *n* [MF *methode,* fr. L *methodus,* fr. Gk *methodos,* fr. *meta* with + *hodos* way] **1** : a procedure or process for achieving an end **2** : orderly arrangement : PLAN **syn** mode, manner, way, fashion, system — **me•thod•i•cal** \mə-ˈthä-di-kəl\ *adj* — **me•thod•i•cal•ly** \-k(ə-)lē\ *adv* — **me•thod•i•cal•ness** *n*

meth•od•ise *Brit var of* METHODIZE

Meth•od•ist \ˈme-thə-dist\ *n* : a member of a Protestant denomination adhering to the doctrines of John Wesley — **Meth•od•ism** \-ˌdi-zəm\ *n*

meth•od•ize \ˈme-thə-ˌdīz\ *vb* **-ized; -iz•ing** : SYSTEMATIZE

meth•od•ol•o•gy \ˌme-thə-ˈdä-lə-jē\ *n, pl* **-gies 1** : a body of methods and rules followed in a science or discipline **2** : the study of the principles or procedures of inquiry in a particular field

meth•yl \ˈme-thəl\ *n* : a chemical group consisting of carbon and hydrogen

methyl alcohol *n* : METHANOL

meth•yl•mer•cury \ˌme-thəl-ˈmər-kyə-rē\ *n* : any of various toxic compounds of mercury that often occur as pollutants which accumulate in animals esp. at the top of a food chain

met•i•cal \ˈme-ti-kəl\ *n* — see MONEY table

me•tic•u•lous \mə-ˈti-kyə-ləs\ *adj* [L *meticulosus* fearful, fr. *metus* fear] : extremely careful in attending to details — **me•tic•u•lous•ly** *adv* — **me•tic•u•lous•ness** *n*

mé•tier \ˈme-ˌtyā, me-ˈtyā\ *n* : an area of activity in which one is expert or successful

me•tre \ˈmē-tər\ *chiefly Brit var of* METER

met•ric \ˈme-trik\ *adj* **1** : of or relating to measurement; *esp* : of or relating to the metric system **2** : METRICAL 1

met•ri•cal \ˈme-tri-kəl\ *adj* **1** : of, relating to, or composed in meter **2** : METRIC 1 — **met•ri•cal•ly** \-k(ə-)lē\ *adv*

met•ri•ca•tion \ˌme-tri-ˈkā-shən\ *n* : the act or process of converting into or expressing in the metric system

met•ri•cize \ˈme-trə-ˌsīz\ *vb* **-cized; -ciz•ing** : to change into or express in the metric system

metric system *n* : a decimal system of weights and measures based on the meter and on the kilogram

metric ton *n* — see METRIC SYSTEM table

[1]**met•ro** \ˈme-trō\ *n, pl* **metros** : SUBWAY

[2]**metro** *adj* : of, relating to, or characteristic of a metropolis and sometimes including its suburbs

met•ro•nome \ˈme-trə-ˌnōm\ *n* : an instrument for marking exact time by a regularly repeated tick

me•trop•o•lis \mə-ˈträ-pə-ləs\ *n* [ME, fr. LL, fr. Gk *mētropolis,* fr. *mētēr* mother + *polis* city] : the chief or capital city of a country, state, or region — **met•ro•pol•i•tan** \ˌme-trə-ˈpä-lət-ᵊn\ *adj*

met•tle \ˈmet-ᵊl\ *n* **1** : SPIRIT, COURAGE **2** : quality of temperament

met•tle•some \ˈmet-ᵊl-səm\ *adj* : full of mettle : COURAGEOUS

MeV *abbr* million electron volts

[1]**mew** \ˈmyü\ *vb* : MEOW — **mew** *n*

[2]**mew** *vb* : CONFINE

mews \ˈmyüz\ *n pl, chiefly Brit* : stables usu. with living quarters built around a court; *also* : a narrow street with dwellings converted from stables

Mex *abbr* Mexican; Mexico

Mex•i•can \ˈmek-si-kən\ *n* : a native or inhabitant of Mexico — **Mexican** *adj*

mez•za•nine \ˈmez-ᵊn-ˌēn, ˌmez-ᵊn-ˈēn\ *n* **1** : a low-ceilinged story between two main stories of a building **2** : the lowest balcony in a theater; *also* : the first few rows of such a balcony

mez•zo for•te \ˌmet-(ˌ)sō-ˈfȯr-ˌtā, ˌmed-(ˌ)zō-, -tē\ *adj or adv* [It] : moderately loud — used as a direction in music

mez•zo pia•no \-pē-ˈä-(ˌ)nō\ *adj or adv* [It] : moderately soft — used as a direction in music

mez•zo–so•pra•no \-sə-ˈpra-nō, -ˈprä-\ *n* : a woman's

METRIC SYSTEM[1]

LENGTH

unit	abbreviation	number of meters	approximate U.S. equivalent
kilometer	km	1,000	0.62 mile
hectometer	hm	100	328.08 feet
dekameter	dam	10	32.81 feet
meter	m	1	39.37 inches
decimeter	dm	0.1	3.94 inches
centimeter	cm	0.01	0.39 inch
millimeter	mm	0.001	0.039 inch

AREA

unit	abbreviation	number of square meters	approximate U.S. equivalent
square kilometer	sq km *or* km^2	1,000,000	0.3861 square mile
hectare	ha	10,000	2.47 acres
are	a	100	119.60 square yards
square centimeter	sq cm *or* cm^2	0.0001	0.155 square inch

VOLUME

unit	abbreviation	number of cubic meters	approximate U.S. equivalent
cubic meter	m^3	1	1.307 cubic yards
cubic decimeter	dm^3	0.001	61.023 cubic inches
cubic centimeter	cu cm *or* cm^3 *also* cc	0.000001	0.061 cubic inch

CAPACITY

unit	abbreviation	number of liters	approximate U.S. equivalent *cubic*	*dry*	*liquid*
kiloliter	kl	1,000	1.31 cubic yards		
hectoliter	hl	100	3.53 cubic feet	2.84 bushels	
dekaliter	dal	10	0.35 cubic foot	1.14 pecks	2.64 gallons
liter	l	1	61.02 cubic inches	0.908 quart	1.057 quarts
deciliter	dl	0.1	6.1 cubic inches	0.18 pint	0.21 pint
centiliter	cl	0.01	0.61 cubic inch		0.338 fluid ounce
milliliter	ml	0.001	0.061 cubic inch		0.27 fluid dram

MASS AND WEIGHT

unit	abbreviation	number of grams	approximate U.S. equivalent
metric ton	t	1,000,000	1.102 short tons
kilogram	kg	1,000	2.2046 pounds
hectogram	hg	100	3.527 ounces
dekagram	dag	10	0.353 ounce
gram	g	1	0.035 ounce
decigram	dg	0.1	1.543 grains
centigram	cg	0.01	0.154 grain
milligram	mg	0.001	0.015 grain

[1]For metric equivalents of U.S. units see Weights and Measures table

voice having a range between that of the soprano and contralto; *also* : a singer having such a voice

MFA *abbr* master of fine arts

mfr *abbr* manufacture; manufacturer

mg *abbr* milligram

Mg *symbol* magnesium

MG *abbr* **1** machine gun **2** major general **3** military government

mgr *abbr* **1** manager **2** monseigneur **3** monsignor

mgt *or* **mgmt** *abbr* management

MGy Sgt *abbr* master gunnery sergeant

MHz *abbr* megahertz

mi *abbr* **1** mile; mileage **2** mill

MI *abbr* **1** Michigan **2** military intelligence

MIA \ˌem-(ˌ)ī-ˈā\ *n* [*m*issing *i*n *a*ction] : a member of the armed forces whose whereabouts following a combat mission are unknown

Mi•ami \mī-ˈa-mē, -mə\ *n, pl* **Mi•ami** *or* **Mi•am•is** : a member of an American Indian people orig. of Wisconsin and Indiana

mi•as•ma \mī-ˈaz-mə, mē-\ *n, pl* **-mas** *also* **-ma•ta** \-mə-tə\ **1** : a vapor from a swamp formerly believed to cause disease **2** : a harmful influence or atmosphere — **mi•as•mal** \-məl\ *adj* — **mi•as•mic** \-mik\ *adj*

Mic *abbr* Micah

mi•ca \ˈmī-kə\ *n* [NL, fr. L, grain, crumb] : any of various mineral silicates readily separable into thin transparent sheets

Mi•cah \ˈmī-kə\ *n* — see BIBLE table

mice *pl of* MOUSE

Mich *abbr* Michigan

Mi•che•as \ˈmī-kē-əs, mī-ˈkē-əs\ *n* : MICAH

Mic•mac \ˈmik-ˌmak\ *n, pl* **Micmac** *or* **Micmacs** : a member of an American Indian people of eastern Canada

micr- *or* **micro-** *comb form* **1** : small : minute ⟨*micro*capsule⟩ **2** : one millionth part of a specified unit ⟨*micro*second⟩

¹mi•cro \ˈmī-krō\ *adj* **1** : very small; *esp* : MICROSCOPIC **2** : involving minute quantities or variations

²micro *n* : MICROCOMPUTER

mi•crobe \ˈmī-ˌkrōb\ *n* : MICROORGANISM; *esp* : one causing disease — **mi•cro•bi•al** \mī-ˈkrō-bē-əl\ *adj*

mi•cro•bi•ol•o•gy \ˌmī-krō-bī-ˈä-lə-jē\ *n* : a branch of biology dealing esp. with microscopic forms of life — **mi•cro•bi•o•log•i•cal** \-ˌbī-ə-ˈlä-ji-kəl\ *adj* — **mi•cro•bi•ol•o•gist** \-bī-ˈä-lə-jist\ *n*

mi•cro•brew•ery \ˈmī-krō-ˌbrü-ə-rē\ *n* : a small brewery making specialty beer in limited quantities

mi•cro•burst \-ˌbərst\ *n* : a violent short-lived localized downdraft that creates extreme wind shears at low altitudes

mi•cro•cap•sule \ˈmī-krō-ˌkap-səl, -sül\ *n* : a tiny capsule containing material (as a medicine) released

when the capsule is broken, melted, or dissolved
mi•cro•chip \-ˌchip\ *n* : INTEGRATED CIRCUIT
mi•cro•cir•cuit \-ˌsər-kət\ *n* : a compact electronic circuit
mi•cro•com•put•er \-kəm-ˌpyü-tər\ *n* : a very small computer that uses a microprocessor
mi•cro•cosm \ˈmī-krə-ˌkä-zəm\ *n* : an individual or community thought of as a miniature world or universe
mi•cro•elec•tron•ics \ˈmī-krō-i-ˌlek-ˈträ-niks\ *n* : a branch of electronics that deals with the miniaturization of electronic circuits and components — **mi•cro•elec•tron•ic** \-nik\ *adj*
mi•cro•en•cap•su•late \ˌmī-krō-in-ˈkap-sə-ˌlāt\ *vb* : to enclose (as a drug) in a microcapsule — **mi•cro•en•cap•su•la•tion** \-in-ˌkap-sə-ˈlā-shən\ *n*
mi•cro•fiche \ˈmī-krō-ˌfēsh, -ˌfish\ *n, pl* **-fiche** *or* **-fiches** *same or* -ˌfē-shəz, -ˌfi-\ : a sheet of microfilm containing rows of images of pages of printed matter
mi•cro•film \-ˌfilm\ *n* : a film bearing a photographic record (as of print) on a reduced scale — **microfilm** *vb*
mi•cro•graph \ˈmī-krə-ˌgraf\ *n* : a graphic reproduction of the image of an object formed by a microscope
mi•cro•me•te•or•ite \ˌmī-krō-ˈmē-tē-ə-ˌrīt\ *n* : a very small particle in interplanetary space
mi•crom•e•ter \mī-ˈkrä-mə-tər\ *n* : an instrument used with a telescope or microscope for measuring minute distances
mi•cro•min•ia•tur•iza•tion \ˌmī-kro-ˌmi-nē-ə-ˌchu̇r-ə-ˈzā-shən, -ˌmi-ni-ˌchu̇r-, -chər-\ *n* : the process of producing things in a very small size and esp. in a size smaller than one considered miniature — **mi•cro•min•ia•tur•ized** \-ˈmi-nē-ə-chə-ˌrīzd, -ˈmi-ni-chə-\ *adj*
mi•cron \ˈmī-ˌkrän\ *n,* : one millionth of a meter
mi•cro•or•gan•ism \ˌmī-krō-ˈȯr-gə-ˌni-zəm\ *n* : an organism (as a bacterium) too tiny to be seen by the unaided eye
mi•cro•phone \ˈmī-krə-ˌfōn\ *n* : an instrument for converting sound waves into variations of an electric current for transmitting or recording sound
mi•cro•pho•to•graph \ˌmī-krə-ˈfō-tə-ˌgraf\ *n* : PHOTOMICROGRAPH
mi•cro•pro•ces•sor \ˌmī-krō-ˈprä-ˌse-sər\ *n* : a computer processor contained on a microchip
mi•cro•scope \ˈmī-krə-ˌskōp\ *n* : an instrument for making magnified images of minute objects usu. using light — **mi•cros•co•py** \mī-ˈkräs-kə-pē\ *n*
mi•cro•scop•ic \ˌmī-krə-ˈskä-pik\ *also* **mi•cro•scop•i•cal** \-pi-kəl\ *adj* **1** : of, relating to, or involving the use of the microscope **2** : too tiny to be seen without the use of a microscope : very small — **mi•cro•scop•i•cal•ly** \-pi-k(ə-)lē\ *adv*
mi•cro•sec•ond \ˈmī-krō-ˌse-kənd\ *n* : one millionth of a second
mi•cro•sur•gery \ˌmī-krō-ˈsər-jə-rē\ *n* : minute dissection or manipulation (as by a laser beam) of living structures or tissue — **mi•cro•sur•gi•cal** \-ˈsər-ji-kəl\ *adj*
¹mi•cro•wave \ˈmī-krə-ˌwāv\ *n* **1** : a radio wave between one millimeter and one meter in wavelength **2** : MICROWAVE OVEN
²microwave *vb* : to heat or cook in a microwave oven — **mi•cro•wav•able** *or* **mi•cro•wave•able** \ˌmī-krə-ˈwā-və-bəl\ *adj*
microwave oven *n* : an oven in which food is cooked by the absorption of microwave energy by water molecules in the food
¹mid \ˈmid\ *adj* : MIDDLE
²mid *abbr* middle
mid•air \ˈmid-ˈar\ *n* : a point or region in the air well above the ground
mid•day \ˈmid-ˌdā, -ˈdā\ *n* : NOON
mid•den \ˈmid-ᵊn\ *n* : a refuse heap
¹mid•dle \ˈmid-ᵊl\ *adj* **1** : equally distant from the extremes : MEDIAL, CENTRAL **2** : being at neither extreme : INTERMEDIATE **3** *cap* : constituting an intermediate period
²middle *n* **1** : a middle part, point, or position **2** : WAIST
middle age *n* : the period of life from about 40 to about 60 — **mid•dle–aged** \ˌmid-ᵊl-ˈājd\ *adj*
Middle Ages *n pl* : the period of European history from about A.D. 500 to about 1500
mid•dle•brow \ˈmid-ᵊl-ˌbrau̇\ *n* : a person who is moderately but not highly cultivated — **middlebrow** *adj*
middle class *n* : a social class holding a position between the upper class and the lower class — **middle–class** *adj*
middle ear *n* : a small membrane-lined cavity of the ear through which sound waves are transmitted by a chain of tiny bones
middle finger *n* : the midmost of the five digits of the hand
mid•dle•man \ˈmid-ᵊl-ˌman\ *n* : INTERMEDIARY; *esp* : one intermediate between the producer of goods and the retailer or consumer
middle–of–the–road *adj* : standing for or following a course of action midway between extremes; *esp* : being neither liberal nor conservative in politics — **mid•dle–of–the–road•er** \-ˈrō-dər\ *n* — **mid•dle–of–the–road•ism** \-ˈrō-ˌdi-zəm\ *n*
middle school *n* : a school usu. including grades 5 to 8 or 6 to 8
mid•dle•weight \ˈmid-ᵊl-ˌwāt\ *n* : one of average weight; *esp* : a boxer weighing more than 147 but not over 160 pounds
mid•dling \ˈmid-liŋ, -lən\ *adj* **1** : of middle, medium, or moderate size, degree, or quality **2** : MEDIOCRE
mid•dy \ˈmi-dē\ *n, pl* **middies** : MIDSHIPMAN
midge \ˈmij\ *n* : a very small fly : GNAT
midg•et \ˈmi-jət\ *n* **1** : a very small person **2** : something (as an animal) very small for its kind
midi \ˈmi-dē\ *n* : a calf-length dress, coat, or skirt
mid•land \ˈmid-lənd, -ˌland\ *n* : the interior or central region of a country
mid•life \ˈmid-ˈlīf\ *n* : MIDDLE AGE
midlife crisis *n* : a period of emotional turmoil in middle age characterized esp. by a strong desire for change
mid•most \-ˌmōst\ *adj* : being in or near the exact middle — **midmost** *adv*
mid•night \-ˌnīt\ *n* : 12 o'clock at night
mid•point \ˈmid-ˌpȯint, -ˈpȯint\ *n* : a point at or near the center or middle
mid•riff \ˈmi-ˌdrif\ *n* [ME *midrif,* fr. OE *midhrif,* fr. *midde* mid + *hrif* belly] **1** : DIAPHRAGM 1 **2** : the mid-region of the human torso
mid•sec•tion \-ˌsek-shən\ *n* : a section midway between the extremes; *esp* : MIDRIFF 2
mid•ship•man \ˈmid-ˌship-mən, (ˌ)mid-ˈship-\ *n* : a student in a naval academy
mid•ships \-ˌships\ *adv* : AMIDSHIPS
midst \ˈmidst\ *n* **1** : the interior or central part or point **2** : a position of proximity to the members of a group ⟨in our ~⟩ **3** : the condition of being surrounded or beset — **midst** *prep*
mid•stream \ˈmid-ˈstrēm, -ˌstrēm\ *n* : the middle of a stream
mid•sum•mer \-ˈsə-mər, -ˌsə-\ *n* **1** : the middle of summer **2** : the summer solstice
mid•town \ˈmid-ˌtau̇n, -ˈtau̇n\ *n* : a central section of a city; *esp* : one situated between sections called *downtown* and *uptown* — **midtown** *adj*
¹mid•way \ˈmid-ˌwā, -ˈwā\ *adv* : in the middle of the way or distance
²mid•way \-ˌwā\ *n* : an avenue (as at a carnival) for concessions and amusements
mid•week \-ˌwēk\ *n* : the middle of the week — **mid•week•ly** \-ˌwē-klē, -ˈwē-\ *adj or adv*
mid•wife \ˈmid-ˌwīf\ *n* : a person who helps women in childbirth — **mid•wife•ry** \-ˌwī-fə-rē\ *n*

mid•win•ter \ˈmid-ˈwin-tər, -ˌwin-\ *n* **1** : the winter solstice **2** : the middle of winter
mid•year \-ˌyir\ *n* **1** : the middle of a year **2** : a midyear examination — **midyear** *adj*
mien \ˈmēn\ *n* **1** : air or bearing esp. as expressive of mood or personality : DEMEANOR **2** : APPEARANCE, ASPECT
miff \ˈmif\ *vb* : to put into an ill humor
[1]**might** \ˈmīt\ *past of* MAY — used as an auxiliary to express permission or possibility in the past, a present condition contrary to fact, less probability or possibility than *may,* or as a polite alternative to *may, ought,* or *should*
[2]**might** *n* : the power, authority, or resources of an individual or a group
mighty \ˈmī-tē\ *adj* **might•i•er; -est 1** : very strong : POWERFUL **2** : GREAT, NOTABLE — **might•i•ly** \ˈmī-tə-lē\ *adv* — **might•i•ness** \-tē-nəs\ *n* — **mighty** *adv*
mi•gnon•ette \ˌmin-yə-ˈnet\ *n* : an annual garden herb with spikes of tiny fragrant flowers
mi•graine \ˈmī-ˌgrān\ *n* [F, fr. LL *hemicrania* pain in one side of the head, fr. Gk *hēmikrania,* fr. *hēmi-* half + *kranion* cranium] : a condition marked by recurrent severe headache and often nausea; *also* : an attack of migraine
mi•grant \ˈmī-grənt\ *n* : one that migrates; *esp* : a person who moves in order to find work (as picking crops) — **migrant** *adj*
mi•grate \ˈmī-ˌgrāt\ *vb* **mi•grat•ed; mi•grat•ing 1** : to move from one country or place to another **2** : to pass usu. periodically from one region or climate to another for feeding or breeding — **mi•gra•tion** \mī-ˈgrā-shən\ *n* — **mi•gra•to•ry** \ˈmī-grə-ˌtōr-ē\ *adj*
mi•ka•do \mə-ˈkä-dō\ *n, pl* **-dos** : an emperor of Japan
mike \ˈmīk\ *n* : MICROPHONE
[1]**mil** \ˈmil\ *n* : a unit of length equal to 1/1000 inch
[2]**mil** *abbr* military
milch \ˈmilk, ˈmilch\ *adj* : giving milk ⟨~ cow⟩
mild \ˈmīld\ *adj* **1** : gentle in nature or behavior **2** : moderate in action or effect **3** : TEMPERATE **syn** easy, complaisant, amiable, lenient — **mild•ly** *adv* — **mild•ness** *n*
mil•dew \ˈmil-ˌdü, -ˌdyü\ *n* : a superficial usu. whitish growth produced on organic matter and on plants by a fungus; *also* : a fungus producing this growth — **mildew** *vb*
mile \ˈmīl\ *n* [ME, fr. OE *mīl,* fr. L *milia* miles, fr. *milia passuum,* lit., thousands of paces] **1** — see WEIGHT table **2** : NAUTICAL MILE
mile•age \ˈmī-lij\ *n* **1** : an allowance for traveling expenses at a certain rate per mile **2** : distance in miles traveled (as in a day) **3** : the amount of service yielded (as by a tire) expressed in terms of miles of travel **4** : the average number of miles a car will travel on a gallon of gasoline
mile•post \ˈmīl-ˌpōst\ *n* : a post indicating the distance in miles from a given point
mile•stone \-ˌstōn\ *n* **1** : a stone serving as a milepost **2** : a significant point in development
mi•lieu \mēl-ˈyər, -ˈyü, -ˈyœ\ *n, pl* **mi•lieus** *or* **mi•lieux** *same or* -ˈyərz, -ˈyüz, -ˈyœz\ [F] : ENVIRONMENT, SETTING
mil•i•tant \ˈmi-lə-tənt\ *adj* **1** : engaged in warfare **2** : aggressively active esp. in a cause — **mil•i•tance** \-təns\ *n* — **mil•i•tan•cy** \-tən-sē\ *n* — **militant** *n* — **mil•i•tant•ly** *adv*
mil•i•ta•rise *Brit var of* MILITARIZE
mil•i•ta•rism \ˈmi-lə-tə-ˌri-zəm\ *n* **1** : predominance of the military class or its ideals **2** : a policy of aggressive military preparedness — **mil•i•ta•rist** \-rist\ *n* — **mil•i•ta•ris•tic** \ˌmi-lə-tə-ˈris-tik\ *adj*
mil•i•ta•rize \ˈmi-lə-tə-ˌrīz\ *vb* **-rized; -riz•ing 1** : to equip with military forces and defenses **2** : to give a military character to
[1]**mil•i•tary** \ˈmi-lə-ˌter-ē\ *adj* **1** : of or relating to soldiers, arms, or the army **2** : performed by armed forces; *also* : supported by armed force **syn** martial, warlike — **mil•i•tar•i•ly** \ˌmi-lə-ˈter-ə-lē\ *adv*
[2]**military** *n, pl* **military** *also* **mil•i•tar•ies 1** : the military, naval, and air forces of a nation **2** : military persons
mil•i•tate \ˈmi-lə-ˌtāt\ *vb* **-tat•ed; -tat•ing** : to have weight or effect
mi•li•tia \mə-ˈli-shə\ *n* : a part of the organized armed forces of a country liable to call only in emergency — **mi•li•tia•man** \-mən\ *n*
[1]**milk** \ˈmilk\ *n* **1** : a nutritive usu. whitish fluid secreted by female mammals for feeding their young **2** : a milklike liquid (as a plant juice) — **milk•i•ness** \ˈmil-kē-nəs\ *n* — **milky** *adj*
[2]**milk** *vb* **1** : to draw off the milk of ⟨~ a cow⟩ **2** : to draw something from as if by milking
milk•maid \ˈmilk-ˌmād\ *n* : DAIRYMAID
milk•man \-ˌman, -mən\ *n* : a person who sells or delivers milk
milk of magnesia : a milk-white mixture of hydroxide of magnesium and water used as an antacid and laxative
milk shake *n* : a thoroughly blended drink made of milk, a flavoring syrup, and often ice cream
milk•sop \ˈmilk-ˌsäp\ *n* : an unmanly man
milk•weed \-ˌwēd\ *n* : any of a genus of herbs with milky juice and clustered flowers
Milky Way *n* **1** : a broad irregular band of light that stretches across the sky and is caused by the light of a very great number of faint stars **2** : MILKY WAY GALAXY
Milky Way galaxy *n* : the galaxy of which the sun is a member and which includes the stars that comprise the Milky Way
[1]**mill** \ˈmil\ *n* **1** : a building with machinery for grinding grain into flour **2** : a machine used in processing (as by grinding, stamping, cutting, or finishing) raw material **3** : FACTORY
[2]**mill** *vb* **1** : to process in a mill **2** : to move in a circle or in an eddying mass
[3]**mill** *n* : one tenth of a cent
mill•age \ˈmi-lij\ *n* : a rate (as of taxation) expressed in mills
mil•len•ni•um \mə-ˈle-nē-əm\ *n, pl* **-nia** \-nē-ə\ *or* **-niums 1** : a period of 1000 years; *also* : a 1000th anniversary or its celebration **2** : the 1000 years mentioned in Revelation 20 when holiness is to prevail and Christ is to reign on earth **3** : a period of great happiness or perfect government
mill•er \ˈmi-lər\ *n* **1** : one that operates a mill and esp. a flour mill **2** : any of various moths having powdery wings
mil•let \ˈmi-lət\ *n* : any of several small-seeded cereal and forage grasses cultivated for grain or hay; *also* : the grain of a millet
mil•li•am•pere \ˌmi-lē-ˈam-ˌpir\ *n* : one thousandth of an ampere
mil•liard \ˈmil-ˌyärd, ˈmi-lē-ˌärd\ *n, Brit* : a thousand millions
mil•li•bar \ˈmi-lə-ˌbär\ *n* : a unit of atmospheric pressure
mil•li•gram \-ˌgram\ *n* — see METRIC SYSTEM table
mil•li•li•ter \-ˌlē-tər\ *n* — see METRIC SYSTEM table
mil•lime \mə-ˈlēm\ *n* — see *dinar* at MONEY table
mil•li•me•ter \ˈmi-lə-ˌmē-tər\ *n* — see METRIC SYSTEM table
mil•li•ner \ˈmi-lə-nər\ *n* [irreg. fr. *Milan,* Italy; fr. the importation of women's finery from Italy in the 16th century] : a person who designs, makes, trims, or sells women's hats
mil•li•nery \ˈmi-lə-ˌner-ē\ *n* **1** : women's apparel for the head **2** : the business or work of a milliner
mill•ing \ˈmi-liŋ\ *n* : a corrugated edge on a coin
mil•lion \ˈmil-yən\ *n, pl* **millions** *or* **million** : a thousand thousands — **million** *adj* — **mil•lionth** \-yənth\ *adj or n*

mil•lion•aire \ˌmil-yə-ˈner, ˈmil-yə-ˌner\ *n* : one whose wealth is estimated at a million or more (as of dollars or pounds)

mil•li•pede \ˈmi-lə-ˌpēd\ *n* : any of a class of arthropods related to the centipedes and having a long segmented body with a hard covering, two pairs of legs on most segments, and no poison fangs

mil•li•sec•ond \-ˌse-kənd\ *n* : one thousandth of a second

mil•li•volt \-ˌvōlt\ *n* : one thousandth of a volt

mill•pond \ˈmil-ˌpänd\ *n* : a pond made by damming a stream to produce a fall of water for operating a mill

mill•race \-ˌrās\ *n* : a canal in which water flows to and from a mill wheel

mill•stone \-ˌstōn\ *n* : either of two round flat stones used for grinding grain

mill•stream \-ˌstrēm\ *n* : a stream whose flow is used to run a mill; *also* : the stream in a millrace

mill wheel *n* : a waterwheel that drives a mill

mill•wright \ˈmil-ˌrīt\ *n* : a person who builds mills or sets up or maintains their machinery

milt \ˈmilt\ *n* : the sperm-containing fluid of a male fish

mime \ˈmīm\ *n* **1** : MIMIC **2** : PANTOMIME — **mime** *vb*

mim•eo•graph \ˈmi-mē-ə-ˌgraf\ *n* : a machine for making many copies by means of a stencil through which ink is pressed — **mimeograph** *vb*

mi•me•sis \mə-ˈmē-səs, mī-\ *n* : IMITATION, MIMICRY

mi•met•ic \-ˈme-tik\ *adj* **1** : IMITATIVE **2** : relating to, characterized by, or exhibiting mimicry

[1]**mim•ic** \ˈmi-mik\ *n* : one that mimics

[2]**mimic** *vb* **mim•icked** \-mikt\; **mim•ick•ing 1** : to imitate closely **2** : to ridicule by imitation **3** : to resemble by biological mimicry

mim•ic•ry \ˈmi-mi-krē\ *n, pl* **-ries 1** : an instance of mimicking **2** : a superficial resemblance of one organism to another or to natural objects among which it lives that gives it an advantage (as protection from predation)

mi•mo•sa \mə-ˈmō-sə, mī-, -zə\ *n* : any of a genus of leguminous trees, shrubs, and herbs of warm regions with ball-shaped heads of small white or pink flowers

min *abbr* **1** minim **2** minimum **3** mining **4** minister **5** minor **6** minute

min•a•ret \ˌmi-nə-ˈret\ *n* [F, fr. Turk *minare*, fr. Ar *manārah* lighthouse] : a tall slender tower of a mosque from which a muezzin calls the faithful to prayer

1 minaret

mi•na•to•ry \ˈmi-nə-ˌtōr-ē, ˈmī-\ *adj* : THREATENING, MENACING

mince \ˈmins\ *vb* **minced; minc•ing 1** : to cut into very small pieces **2** : to restrain (words) within the bounds of decorum **3** : to walk in a prim affected manner

mince•meat \ˈmins-ˌmēt\ *n* : a finely chopped mixture esp. of raisins, apples, spices, and often meat used as a filling for a pie

[1]**mind** \ˈmīnd\ *n* **1** : MEMORY **2** : the part of an individual that feels, perceives, thinks, wills, and esp. reasons **3** : INTENTION, DESIRE **4** : normal mental condition **5** : OPINION, VIEW **6** : MOOD **7** : mental qualities of a person or group **8** : intellectual ability

[2]**mind** *vb* **1** *chiefly dial* : REMEMBER **2** : to attend to closely **3** : HEED, OBEY **4** : to be concerned about; *also* : DISLIKE **5** : to be careful or cautious **6** : to take charge of **7** : to regard with attention

mind–bend•ing \ˈmīnd-ˌben-diŋ\ *adj* : MIND-BLOWING

mind–blow•ing \-ˌblō-iŋ\ *adj* : PSYCHEDELIC 1; *also* : MIND-BOGGLING

mind–bog•gling \-ˌbä-gə-liŋ\ *adj* : mentally or emotionally exciting or overwhelming

mind•ed \ˈmīn-dəd\ *adj* **1** : INCLINED, DISPOSED **2** : having a mind of a specified kind or concerned with a specific thing — usu. used in combination ⟨narrow-*minded*⟩

mind•ful \ˈmīnd-fəl\ *adj* : bearing in mind : AWARE — **mind•ful•ly** *adv* — **mind•ful•ness** *n*

mind•less \-ləs\ *adj* **1** : marked by a lack of mind or consciousness; *esp* : marked by no use of the intellect **2** : not mindful : HEEDLESS — **mind•less•ly** *adv* — **mind•less•ness** *n*

[1]**mine** \ˈmīn\ *pron* : that which belongs to me

[2]**mine** *n* **1** : an excavation in the earth from which minerals are taken; *also* : an ore deposit **2** : an underground passage beneath an enemy position **3** : an explosive device for destroying enemy personnel, vehicles, or ships **4** : a rich source of supply

[3]**mine** *vb* **mined; min•ing 1** : to dig a mine **2** : UNDERMINE **3** : to get ore from the earth **4** : to place military mines in — **min•er** *n*

mine•field \ˈmīn-ˌfēld\ *n* **1** : an area set with mines **2** : something resembling a minefield esp. in having many dangers

mine•lay•er \-ˌlā-ər\ *n* : a naval vessel for laying underwater mines

min•er•al \ˈmi-nə-rəl\ *n* **1** : a crystalline substance (as diamond or quartz) of inorganic origin **2** : a naturally occurring substance (as coal, salt, or water) obtained usu. from the ground — **mineral** *adj*

min•er•al•ise *Brit var of* MINERALIZE

min•er•al•ize \ˈmi-nə-rə-ˌlīz\ *vb* **-ized; -iz•ing 1** : to impregnate or supply with minerals **2** : to change into mineral form — **min•er•al•i•za•tion** \-rə-lə-ˈzā-shən\ *n*

min•er•al•o•gy \ˌmi-nə-ˈrä-lə-jē, -ˈra-\ *n* : a science dealing with minerals — **min•er•al•og•i•cal** \ˌmi-nə-rə-ˈlä-ji-kəl\ *adj* — **min•er•al•o•gist** \ˌmi-nə-ˈrä-lə-jist, -ˈra-\ *n*

mineral oil *n* : an oil of mineral origin; *esp* : a refined petroleum oil used as a laxative

mineral water *n* : water infused with mineral salts or gases

min•e•stro•ne \ˌmi-nə-ˈstrō-nē, -ˈstrōn\ *n* [It, fr. *minestra*, fr. *minestrare* to serve, dish up, fr. L *ministrare*, fr. *minister* servant] : a rich thick vegetable soup

mine•sweep•er \ˈmīn-ˌswē-pər\ *n* : a warship designed for removing or neutralizing underwater mines

min•gle \ˈmiŋ-gəl\ *vb* **min•gled; min•gling 1** : to bring or combine together : MIX **2** : ASSOCIATE; *also* : to move about (as in a group)

ming tree \ˈmiŋ-\ *n* : a dwarfed usu. evergreen tree grown as bonsai; *also* : an artificial plant resembling this

mini \ˈmi-nē\ *n, pl* **min•is** : something small of its kind — **mini** *adj*

mini- *comb form* : smaller or briefer than usual, normal, or standard

min•ia•ture \ˈmi-nē-ə-ˌchu̇r, ˈmi-ni-ˌchu̇r, -chər\ *n* [It *miniatura* art of illuminating a manuscript, fr. ML, fr. L *miniare* to color with red lead, fr. *minium* red lead] **1** : a copy on a much reduced scale; *also* : something small of its kind **2** : a small painting (as on ivory or metal) — **miniature** *adj* — **min•ia•tur•ist** \-ˌchu̇r-ist, -chər-\ *n*

min•ia•tur•ize \ˈmi-nē-ə-ˌchə-ˌrīz, ˈmi-ni-\ *vb* **-ized; -iz•ing** : to design or construct in small size — **min•ia•tur•i•za•tion** \ˌmi-nē-ə-ˌchu̇r-ə-ˈzā-shən, ˌmi-ni-, -chər-\ *n*

mini•bar \ˈmi-nē-ˌbär\ *n* : a small refrigerator in a hotel room that is stocked with beverages and snacks

mini•bike \ˈmi-nē-ˌbīk\ *n* : a small one-passenger motorcycle

mini•bus \-ˌbəs\ *n* : a small bus or van

mini•com•put•er \-kəm-ˌpyü-tər\ *n* : a computer between a mainframe and a microcomputer in size and speed

min•im \ˈmi-nəm\ *n* — see WEIGHT table

min•i•mal \ˈmi-nə-məl\ *adj* **1** : relating to or being a minimum : LEAST **2** : of or relating to minimalism or minimal art — **min•i•mal•ly** *adv*

minimal art *n* : abstract art consisting primarily of simple geometric forms executed in an impersonal style — **minimal artist** *n*

min•i•mal•ism \ˈmi-nə-mə-ˌli-zəm\ *n* : MINIMAL ART; *also* : a style (as in music or literature) marked by extreme spareness or simplicity — **min•i•mal•ist** \-list\ *n*

min•i•mise *Brit var of* MINIMIZE

min•i•mize \ˈmi-nə-ˌmīz\ *vb* **-mized; -miz•ing 1** : to reduce or keep to a minimum **2** : to underestimate intentionally; *also* : BELITTLE **syn** depreciate, decry, disparage

min•i•mum \ˈmi-nə-məm\ *n, pl* **-ma** \-mə\ *or* **-mums 1** : the least quantity assignable, admissible, or possible **2** : the least of a set of numbers **3** : the lowest degree or amount of variation (as of temperature) reached or recorded — **minimum** *adj*

min•ion \ˈmin-yən\ *n* [MF *mignon* darling] **1** : a servile dependent, follower, or underling **2** : one highly favored **3** : a subordinate official

min•is•cule \ˈmi-nəs-ˌkyül\ *var of* MINUSCULE

mini•se•ries \ˈmi-nē-ˌsir-ēz\ *n* : a television story presented in sequential episodes

mini•skirt \-ˌskərt\ *n* : a skirt with the hemline several inches above the knee

¹min•is•ter \ˈmi-nə-stər\ *n* **1** : AGENT **2** : a member of the clergy esp. of a Protestant communion **3** : a high officer of state who heads a division of governmental activities **4** : a diplomatic representative to a foreign state — **min•is•te•ri•al** \ˌmi-nə-ˈstir-ē-əl\ *adj*

²minister *vb* **1** : to perform the functions of a minister of religion **2** : to give aid or service — **min•is•tra•tion** \ˌmi-nə-ˈstrā-shən\ *n*

¹min•is•trant \ˈmi-nə-strənt\ *adj, archaic* : performing service as a minister

²ministrant *n* : one that ministers

min•is•try \ˈmi-nə-strē\ *n, pl* **-tries 1** : MINISTRATION **2** : the office, duties, or functions of a minister; *also* : the period of service or office **3** : CLERGY **4** : AGENCY **5** *often cap* : the body of ministers governing a nation or state; *also* : a government department headed by a minister

mini•van \ˈmi-nē-ˌvan\ *n* : a small van

mink \ˈmiŋk\ *n, pl* **mink** *or* **minks** : either of two slender mammals resembling the related weasels; *also* : the soft lustrous typically dark brown fur of a mink

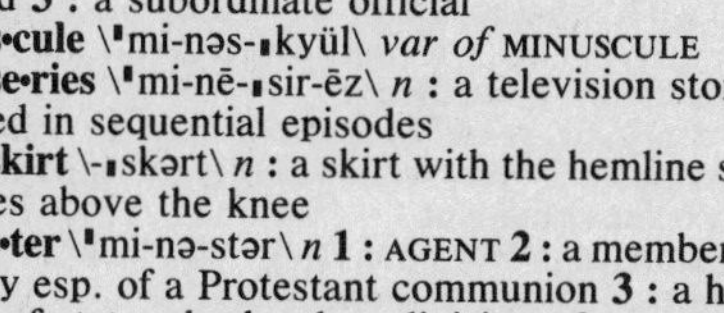

mink

Minn *abbr* Minnesota

min•ne•sing•er \ˈmi-ni-ˌsiŋ-ər, -ˌziŋ-\ *n* [G, fr. Middle High German, fr. *minne* love + *singer* singer] : any of a class of German lyric poets and musicians of the 12th to the 14th centuries

min•now \ˈmi-nō\ *n, pl* **minnows** *also* **minnow** : any of numerous small freshwater fishes

¹mi•nor \ˈmī-nər\ *adj* **1** : inferior in importance, size, or degree **2** : not having reached majority **3** : having the third, sixth, and sometimes the seventh degrees lowered by a half step ⟨~ scale⟩; *also* : based on a minor scale ⟨~ key⟩ **4** : not serious ⟨~ illness⟩

²minor *n* **1** : a person who has not attained majority **2** : a subject of academic study chosen as a secondary field of specialization

³minor *vb* : to pursue an academic minor

mi•nor•i•ty \mə-ˈnȯr-ə-tē, mī-\ *n, pl* **-ties 1** : the period or state of being a minor **2** : the smaller in number of two groups; *esp* : a group having less than the number of votes necessary for control **3** : a part of a population differing from others (as in race); *also* : a member of a minority

mi•nox•i•dil \mə-ˈnäk-sə-ˌdil\ *n* : a drug used orally to treat hypertension and topically in solution to promote hair regrowth in some forms of baldness

min•ster \ˈmin-stər\ *n* : a large or important church

min•strel \ˈmin-strəl\ *n* **1** : a medieval singer of verses; *also* : MUSICIAN, POET **2** : any of a group of performers usu. with blackened faces in a program of black American songs, jokes, and impersonations ⟨a ~ show⟩

min•strel•sy \-sē\ *n* : the singing and playing of a minstrel; *also* : a body of minstrels

¹mint \ˈmint\ *n* **1** : any of a large family of square-stemmed herbs and shrubs; *esp* : one (as spearmint) that is fragrant and is the source of a flavoring oil **2** : a mint-flavored piece of candy — **minty** *adj*

²mint *n* **1** : a place where coins are made **2** : a vast sum — **mint** *vb* — **mint•age** \-ij\ *n* — **mint•er** *n*

³mint *adj* : unmarred as if fresh from a mint ⟨in ~ condition⟩

min•u•end \ˈmin-yə-ˌwend\ *n* : a number from which another is to be subtracted

min•u•et \ˌmin-yə-ˈwet\ *n* : a slow graceful dance

¹mi•nus \ˈmī-nəs\ *prep* **1** : diminished by : LESS ⟨7 ~ 3 equals 4⟩ **2** : LACKING, WITHOUT ⟨~ his hat⟩

²minus *n* : a negative quantity or quality

³minus *adj* **1** : algebraically negative ⟨~ quantity⟩ **2** : having negative qualities

¹mi•nus•cule \ˈmi-nəs-ˌkyül\ *n* : a lowercase letter

²minuscule *adj* : very small

minus sign *n* : a sign – used in mathematics to indicate subtraction or a negative quantity

¹min•ute \ˈmi-nət\ *n* **1** : a 60th part of an hour or of a degree : 60 seconds **2** : a short space of time **3** *pl* : the official record of the proceedings of a meeting

²mi•nute \mī-ˈnüt, mə-, -ˈnyüt\ *adj* **mi•nut•er; -est 1** : very small **2** : of little importance : TRIFLING **3** : marked by close attention to details **syn** diminutive, tiny, miniature, wee — **mi•nute•ly** *adv* — **mi•nute•ness** *n*

min•ute•man \ˈmi-nət-ˌman\ *n* : a member of a group of armed men pledged to take the field at a minute's notice during and immediately before the American Revolution

mi•nu•tia \mə-ˈnü-shə, -ˈnyü-, -shē-ə\ *n, pl* **-ti•ae** \-shē-ˌē\ [L] : a minute or minor detail — usu. used in pl.

minx \ˈmiŋks\ *n* : a pert girl

Mio•cene \ˈmī-ə-ˌsēn\ *adj* : of, relating to, or being the epoch of the Tertiary between the Oligocene and the Pliocene — **Miocene** *n*

mir•a•cle \ˈmir-i-kəl\ *n* **1** : an extraordinary event manifesting divine intervention in human affairs **2** : an unusual event, thing, or accomplishment : WONDER, MARVEL — **mi•rac•u•lous** \mə-ˈra-kyə-ləs\ *adj* — **mi•rac•u•lous•ly** *adv*

miracle drug *n* : a usu. newly discovered drug that elicits a dramatic response in a patient's condition

mi•rage \mə-ˈräzh\ *n* **1** : an illusion that often appears as a pool of water or a mirror in which distant objects are seen inverted, is sometimes seen at sea, in the desert, or over a hot pavement, and results from atmospheric conditions **2** : something illusory and unattainable

[1]**mire** \ˈmīr\ *n* : heavy and often deep mud or slush — **miry** *adj*

[2]**mire** *vb* **mired; mir•ing** : to stick or sink in or as if in mire

[1]**mir•ror** \ˈmir-ər\ *n* **1** : a polished or smooth surface (as of glass) that forms images by reflection **2** : a true representation

[2]**mirror** *vb* : to reflect in or as if in a mirror

mirth \ˈmərth\ *n* : gladness or gaiety accompanied with laughter **syn** glee, jollity, hilarity, merriment — **mirth•ful** \-fəl\ *adj* — **mirth•ful•ly** *adv* — **mirth•ful•ness** *n* — **mirth•less** *adj*

MIRV \ˈmərv\ *n* [*m*ultiple *i*ndependently targeted *r*e-entry *v*ehicle] : an ICBM with multiple warheads that have different targets — **MIRV** *vb*

mis•ad•ven•ture \ˌmi-səd-ˈven-chər\ *n* : MISFORTUNE, MISHAP

mis•aligned \ˌmi-sə-ˈlīnd\ *adj* : not properly aligned — **mis•align•ment** \-ˈlīn-mənt\ *n*

mis•al•li•ance \ˌmi-sə-ˈlī-əns\ *n* : an improper or unsuitable marriage

mis•al•lo•ca•tion \ˌmi-ˌsa-lə-ˈkā-shən\ *n* : faulty or improper allocation

mis•an•thrope \ˈmis-^{ə}n-ˌthrōp\ *n* : one who hates mankind — **mis•an•throp•ic** \ˌmis-^{ə}n-ˈthrä-pik\ *adj* — **mis•an•throp•i•cal•ly** \-pi-k(ə-)lē\ *adv* — **mis•an•thro•py** \mi-ˈsan-thrə-pē\ *n*

mis•ap•ply \ˌmi-sə-ˈplī\ *vb* : to apply wrongly — **mis•ap•pli•ca•tion** \ˌmi-ˌsa-plə-ˈkā-shən\ *n*

mis•ap•pre•hend \ˌmi-ˌsa-pri-ˈhend\ *vb* : MISUNDERSTAND — **mis•ap•pre•hen•sion** \-ˈhen-chən\ *n*

mis•ap•pro•pri•ate \ˌmi-sə-ˈprō-prē-ˌāt\ *vb* : to appropriate wrongly (as by embezzlement) — **mis•ap•pro•pri•a•tion** \-ˌprō-prē-ˈā-shən\ *n*

mis•be•got•ten \-bi-ˈgät-^{ə}n\ *adj* : ILLEGITIMATE; *also* : ill-conceived

mis•be•have \ˌmis-bi-ˈhāv\ *vb* : to behave improperly — **mis•be•hav•er** *n* — **mis•be•hav•ior** \-ˈhā-vyər\ *n*

mis•be•liev•er \-bə-ˈlē-vər\ *n* : one who holds a false or unorthodox belief

mis•brand \mis-ˈbrand\ *vb* : to brand falsely or in a misleading manner

misc *abbr* miscellaneous

mis•cal•cu•late \mis-ˈkal-kyə-ˌlāt\ *vb* : to calculate wrongly — **mis•cal•cu•la•tion** \ˌmis-ˌkal-kyə-ˈlā-shən\ *n*

mis•call \mis-ˈkȯl\ *vb* : MISNAME

mis•car•riage \-ˈkar-ij\ *n* **1** : failure in the administration of justice **2** : spontaneous expulsion of a fetus before it is capable of independent life

mis•car•ry \-ˈkar-ē\ *vb* **1** : to have a miscarriage of a fetus **2** : to go wrong; *also* : to be unsuccessful

mis•ce•ge•na•tion \mi-se-jə-ˈnā-shən, ˌmi-si-jə-ˈnā-\ *n* [L *miscēre* to mix + *genus* race] : marriage or cohabitation between persons of different races

mis•cel•la•neous \ˌmi-sə-ˈlā-nē-əs\ *adj* **1** : consisting of diverse things or members **2** : having various traits; *also* : dealing with or interested in diverse subjects — **mis•cel•la•neous•ly** *adv* — **mis•cel•la•neous•ness** *n*

mis•cel•la•ny \ˈmi-sə-ˌlā-nē\ *n, pl* **-nies 1** : a collection of writings on various subjects **2** : HODGEPODGE

mis•chance \mis-ˈchans\ *n* : bad luck; *also* : MISHAP

mis•chief \ˈmis-chəf\ *n* **1** : injury caused by a particular agent **2** : a source of harm or irritation **3** : action that annoys; *also* : MISCHIEVOUSNESS

mis•chie•vous \ˈmis-chə-vəs\ *adj* **1** : HARMFUL, INJURIOUS **2** : causing annoyance or minor injury **3** : irresponsibly playful — **mis•chie•vous•ly** *adv* — **mis•chie•vous•ness** *n*

mis•ci•ble \ˈmi-sə-bəl\ *adj* : capable of being mixed

mis•com•mu•ni•ca•tion \ˌmis-kə-ˌmyü-nə-ˈkā-shən\ *n* : failure to communicate clearly

mis•con•ceive \ˌmis-kən-ˈsēv\ *vb* : to interpret incorrectly — **mis•con•cep•tion** \-ˈsep-shən\ *n*

mis•con•duct \mis-ˈkän-(ˌ)dəkt\ *n* **1** : MISMANAGEMENT **2** : intentional wrongdoing **3** : improper behavior

mis•con•strue \ˌmis-kən-ˈstrü\ *vb* : MISINTERPRET — **mis•con•struc•tion** \-ˈstrək-shən\ *n*

mis•count \mis-ˈkau̇nt\ *vb* : to count incorrectly : MISCALCULATE

mis•cre•ant \ˈmis-krē-ənt\ *n* : one who behaves criminally or viciously — **miscreant** *adj*

mis•cue \mis-ˈkyü\ *n* : MISTAKE, ERROR — **miscue** *vb*

mis•deed \mis-ˈdēd\ *n* : a wrong deed

mis•de•mean•or \ˌmis-di-ˈmē-nər\ *n* **1** : a crime less serious than a felony **2** : MISDEED

mis•di•rect \ˌmis-də-ˈrekt, -dī-\ *vb* : to give a wrong direction to — **mis•di•rec•tion** \-ˈrek-shən\ *n*

mis•do•ing \mis-ˈdü-iŋ\ *n* : WRONGDOING — **mis•do** \-ˈdü\ *vb* — **mis•do•er** \-ˈdü-ər\ *n*

mise–en–scène \ˌmē-ˌzä^{n}-ˈsen, -ˈsān\ *n, pl* **mise–en–scènes** *same or* -ˈsenz, -ˈsānz\ [F] **1** : the arrangement of the scenery, property, and actors on a stage **2** : SETTING; *also* : ENVIRONMENT

mi•ser \ˈmī-zər\ *n* [L *miser* miserable] : a person who hoards and is stingy with money — **mi•ser•li•ness** \-lē-nəs\ *n* — **mi•ser•ly** *adj*

mis•er•a•ble \ˈmi-zə-rə-bəl, ˈmiz-rə-\ *adj* **1** : wretchedly deficient; *also* : causing extreme discomfort **2** : being in a state of distress **3** : SHAMEFUL — **mis•er•a•ble•ness** *n* — **mis•er•a•bly** \-blē\ *adv*

mis•ery \ˈmi-zə-rē\ *n, pl* **-er•ies 1** : suffering and want caused by poverty or affliction **2** : a cause of suffering or discomfort **3** : emotional distress

mis•fea•sance \mis-ˈfēz-^{ə}ns\ *n* : the performance of a lawful action in an illegal or improper manner

mis•file \-ˈfīl\ *vb* : to file in the wrong place

mis•fire \-ˈfīr\ *vb* **1** : to fail to fire **2** : to miss an intended effect — **misfire** *n*

mis•fit \ˈmis-ˌfit, *sense 1 also* mis-ˈfit\ *n* **1** : something that fits badly **2** : one who is poorly adjusted to a situation or environment

mis•for•tune \mis-ˈfȯr-chən\ *n* **1** : bad luck **2** : an unfortunate condition or event

mis•giv•ing \-ˈgi-viŋ\ *n* : a feeling of doubt or suspicion esp. concerning a future event

mis•gov•ern \-ˈgə-vərn\ *vb* : to govern badly — **mis•gov•ern•ment** *n*

mis•guid•ance \mis-ˈgīd-^{ə}ns\ *n* : faulty guidance — **mis•guide** \-ˈgīd\ *vb*

mis•guid•ed \-ˈgī-dəd\ *adj* : led or prompted by wrong or inappropriate motives or ideals — **mis•guid•ed•ly** *adv*

mis•han•dle \-ˈhand-^{ə}l\ *vb* **1** : MALTREAT **2** : to manage wrongly

mis•hap \ˈmis-ˌhap\ *n* : an unfortunate accident

mish•mash \ˈmish-ˌmash, -ˌmäsh\ *n* : HODGEPODGE, JUMBLE

mis•in•form \ˌmis-^{ə}n-ˈfȯrm\ *vb* : to give false or misleading information to — **mis•in•for•ma•tion** \ˌmi-ˌsin-fər-ˈmā-shən\ *n*

mis•in•ter•pret \ˌmis-^{ə}n-ˈtər-prət\ *vb* : to understand or explain wrongly — **mis•in•ter•pre•ta•tion** \-ˌtər-prə-ˈtā- shən\ *n*

mis•judge \mis-ˈjəj\ *vb* **1** : to estimate wrongly **2** : to have an unjust opinion of — **mis•judg•ment** \mis-ˈjəj-mənt\ *n*

mis•la•bel \-ˈlā-bəl\ *vb* : to label incorrectly or falsely

mis•lay \mis-ˈlā\ *vb* **-laid** \-ˈlād\; **-lay•ing** : MISPLACE, LOSE

mis•lead \mis-ˈlēd\ *vb* **-led** \-ˈled\; **-lead•ing** : to lead in a wrong direction or into a mistaken action or belief — **mis•lead•ing•ly** *adv*

mis•like \-ˈlīk\ *vb* : DISLIKE — **mis•like** *n*

mis•man•age \-ˈma-nij\ *vb* : to manage badly — **mis•man•age•ment** *n*

mis·match \-ˈmach\ *vb* : to match unsuitably or badly — **mis·match** \mis-ˈmach, ˈmis-ˌmach\ *n*

mis·name \-ˈnām\ *vb* : to name incorrectly : MISCALL

mis·no·mer \mis-ˈnō-mər\ *n* : a wrong name or designation

mi·sog·y·ny \mə-ˈsä-jə-nē\ *n* [Gk *misogynia,* fr. *misein* to hate + *gynē* woman] : a hatred of women — **mi·sog·y·nist** \-nist\ *n or adj* — **mi·sog·y·nis·tic** \mə-ˌsä-jə-ˈnis-tik\ *adj*

mis·ori·ent \mi-ˈsōr-ē-ˌent\ *vb* : to orient improperly or incorrectly — **mis·ori·en·ta·tion** \mi-ˌsōr-ē-ən-ˈtā-shən\ *n*

mis·place \mis-ˈplās\ *vb* **1** : to put in a wrong or unremembered place **2** : to set on a wrong object ⟨~ trust⟩

mis·play \-ˈplā\ *n* : a wrong or unskillful play — **mis·play** \mis-ˈplā, ˈmis-ˌplā\ *vb*

mis·print \ˈmis-ˌprint\ *n* : a mistake in printed matter — **mis·print** \mis-ˈprint\ *vb*

mis·pro·nounce \ˌmis-prə-ˈnau̇ns\ *vb* : to pronounce incorrectly — **mis·pro·nun·ci·a·tion** \-prə-ˌnən-sē-ˈā-shən\ *n*

mis·quote \mis-ˈkwōt\ *vb* : to quote incorrectly — **mis·quo·ta·tion** \ˌmis-kwō-ˈtā-shən\ *n*

mis·read \-ˈrēd\ *vb* **-read** \-ˈred\; **-read·ing** \-ˈrē-diŋ\ : to read or interpret incorrectly

mis·rep·re·sent \ˌmis-ˌre-pri-ˈzent\ *vb* : to represent falsely or unfairly — **mis·rep·re·sen·ta·tion** \-ˌzen-ˈtā-shən\ *n*

1**mis·rule** \mis-ˈrül\ *vb* : MISGOVERN

2**misrule** *n* **1** : MISGOVERNMENT **2** : DISORDER

1**miss** \ˈmis\ *vb* **1** : to fail to hit, reach, or contact **2** : to feel the absence of **3** : to fail to obtain **4** : AVOID ⟨just ~*ed* hitting the other car⟩ **5** : OMIT **6** : to fail to understand **7** : to fail to perform or attend; *also* : MISFIRE

2**miss** *n* **1** : a failure to hit or to attain a result **2** : MISFIRE

3**miss** *n* **1** *cap* — used as a title prefixed to the name of an unmarried woman or girl **2** : a young unmarried woman or girl

Miss *abbr* Mississippi

mis·sal \ˈmi-səl\ *n* : a book containing all that is said or sung at mass during the entire year

mis·send \mis-ˈsend\ *vb* : to send incorrectly ⟨*missent* mail⟩

mis·shap·en \-ˈshā-pən\ *adj* : badly shaped : having an ugly shape

mis·sile \ˈmi-səl\ *n* [L, fr. neut. of *missilis* capable of being thrown, fr. *mittere* to let go, send] : an object (as a stone, bullet, or rocket) thrown or projected usu. so as to strike a target

miss·ing \ˈmi-siŋ\ *adj* : ABSENT; *also* : LOST ⟨~ in action⟩

mis·sion \ˈmi-shən\ *n* **1** : a group of missionaries; *also* : a place where missionaries work **2** : a group of envoys to a foreign country; *also* : a team of specialists or cultural leaders sent to a foreign country **3** : TASK

1**mis·sion·ary** \ˈmi-shə-ˌner-ē\ *adj* : of, relating to, or engaged in missions

2**missionary** *n, pl* **-ar·ies** : a person commissioned by a church to spread its faith or carry on humanitarian work

mis·sion·er \ˈmi-shə-nər\ *n* : MISSIONARY

Mis·sis·sip·pi·an \ˌmi-sə-ˈsi-pē-ən\ *adj* : of, relating to, or being the period of the Paleozoic era between the Devonian and the Pennsylvanian — **Mississippian** *n*

mis·sive \ˈmi-siv\ *n* : LETTER

mis·speak \mis-ˈspēk\ *vb* : to say imperfectly or incorrectly

mis·spell \-ˈspel\ *vb* : to spell incorrectly — **mis·spell·ing** *n*

mis·spend \-ˈspend\ *vb* **-spent** \-ˈspent\; **-spend·ing** : WASTE, SQUANDER ⟨my *misspent* youth⟩

mis·state \mis-ˈstāt\ *vb* : to state incorrectly — **mis·state·ment** *n*

mis·step \-ˈstep\ *n* **1** : a wrong step **2** : MISTAKE, BLUNDER

mist \ˈmist\ *n* **1** : water in the form of particles suspended or falling in the air **2** : something that obscures understanding — **mist** *vb*

mis·tak·able \mə-ˈstā-kə-bəl\ *adj* : capable of being misunderstood or mistaken

1**mis·take** \mi-ˈstāk\ *vb* **-took** \-ˈstu̇k\; **-tak·en** \-ˈstā-kən\; **-tak·ing** **1** : to blunder in the choice of **2** : MISINTERPRET **3** : to make a wrong judgment of the character or ability of **4** : to confuse with another — **mis·tak·en·ly** *adv* — **mis·tak·er** *n*

2**mistake** *n* **1** : a wrong judgment : MISUNDERSTANDING **2** : a wrong action or statement : ERROR

1**mis·ter** \ˈmis-tər\ *n* **1** *cap* — used sometimes instead of *Mr.* **2** : SIR — used without a name in addressing a man

2**mist·er** \ˈmis-tər\ *n* : a device for spraying mist

mis·tle·toe \ˈmi-səl-ˌtō\ *n* : a European parasitic green shrub with yellowish flowers and waxy white berries that grows on trees

mis·tral \ˈmis-trəl, mi-ˈsträl\ *n* [F, fr. Provençal, fr. *mistral* masterful, fr. LL *magistralis* of a teacher, fr. L *magister* master] : a strong cold dry northerly wind of southern France

mis·treat \mis-ˈtrēt\ *vb* : to treat badly : ABUSE — **mis·treat·ment** *n*

mis·tress \ˈmis-trəs\ *n* **1** : a woman who has power, authority, or ownership ⟨~ of the house⟩ **2** : something personified as female that rules or dominates ⟨when Rome was ~ of the world⟩ **3** : a woman other than his wife with whom a married man has sexual relations; *also, archaic* : SWEETHEART **4** — used archaically as a title prefixed to the name of a married or unmarried woman

mis·tri·al \ˈmis-ˌtrīl\ *n* : a trial that has no legal effect

1**mis·trust** \mis-ˈtrəst\ *n* : a lack of confidence : DISTRUST — **mis·trust·ful** \-fəl\ *adj* — **mis·trust·ful·ly** *adv* — **mis·trust·ful·ness** *n*

2**mistrust** *vb* : to have no trust or confidence in : SUSPECT

misty \ˈmis-tē\ *adj* **mist·i·er; -est** **1** : obscured by or as if by mist : INDISTINCT **2** : TEARFUL — **mist·i·ly** \-tə-lē\ *adv* — **mist·i·ness** \-tē-nəs\ *n*

mis·un·der·stand \ˌmi-ˌsən-dər-ˈstand\ *vb* **-stood** \-ˈstu̇d\; **-stand·ing** **1** : to fail to understand **2** : to interpret incorrectly

mis·un·der·stand·ing \-ˈstan-diŋ\ *n* **1** : MISINTERPRETATION **2** : DISAGREEMENT, QUARREL

mis·us·age \mis-ˈyü-sij\ *n* **1** : bad treatment : ABUSE **2** : wrong or improper use

mis·use \mis-ˈyüz\ *vb* **1** : to use incorrectly **2** : ABUSE, MISTREAT — **mis·use** \-ˈyüs\ *n*

mite \ˈmīt\ *n* **1** : any of numerous tiny arthropod animals related to the spiders that often live and feed on animals or plants **2** : a small coin or sum of money **3** : a small amount : BIT

1**mi·ter** *or* **mi·tre** \ˈmī-tər\ *n* [ME *mitre,* fr. MF, fr. L *mitra* headband, turban, fr. Gk] **1** : a headdress worn by bishops and abbots **2** : MITER JOINT

2**miter** *or* **mitre** *vb* **mi·tered** *or* **mi·tred; mi·ter·ing** *or* **mi·tring** \ˈmī-tə-riŋ\ **1** : to match or fit together in a miter joint **2** : to bevel the ends of for making a miter joint

miter joint *n* : a joint made by fitting together two parts with the ends cut at an angle

mit·i·gate \ˈmi-tə-ˌgāt\ *vb* **-gat·ed; -gat·ing** **1** : to make less harsh or hostile **2** : to make less severe or painful — **mit·i·ga·tion** \ˌmi-tə-ˈgā-shən\ *n* — **mit·i·ga·tive** \ˈmi-tə-ˌgā-tiv\ *adj*

mi·to·sis \mī-ˈtō-səs\ *n, pl* **-to·ses** \-ˌsēz\ : a process that takes place in the nucleus of a dividing cell and results in the formation of two new nuclei each of which has the same number of chromosomes as the parent nucleus; *also* : cell division in which mitosis occurs — **mi·tot·ic** \-ˈtä-tik\ *adj*

mitt \ˈmit\ *n* **1** : a baseball catcher's or first baseman's glove **2** *slang* : HAND

mit•ten \ˈmit-ᵊn\ *n* : a covering for the hand having a separate section for the thumb only

[1]**mix** \ˈmiks\ *vb* **1** : to combine into one mass **2** : ASSOCIATE **3** : to form by mingling components **4** : to produce (a recording) by electronically combining sounds from different sources **5** : HYBRIDIZE **6** : CONFUSE ⟨~*es* up the facts⟩ **7** : to become involved **syn** blend, merge, coalesce, amalgamate, fuse — **mix•able** *adj* — **mix•er** *n*

[2]**mix** *n* : a product of mixing; *esp* : a commercially prepared mixture of food ingredients

mixed number *n* : a number (as 5⅔) composed of an integer and a fraction

mixed–up \ˈmikst-ˈəp\ *adj* : CONFUSED

mixt *abbr* mixture

mix•ture \ˈmiks-chər\ *n* **1** : the act or process of mixing; *also* : the state of being mixed **2** : a product of mixing

mix–up \ˈmiks-ˌəp\ *n* **1** : an instance of confusion **2** : CONFLICT, FIGHT

miz•zen *also* **miz•en** \ˈmiz-ᵊn\ *n* **1** : a fore-and-aft sail set on the mizzenmast **2** : MIZZENMAST — **mizzen** *also* **mizen** *adj*

miz•zen•mast \-ˌmast, -məst\ *n* : the mast aft or next aft of the mainmast

mk *abbr* **1** mark **2** markka

Mk *abbr* Mark

mks *abbr* meter-kilogram-second

mkt *abbr* market

mktg *abbr* marketing

ml *abbr* milliliter

Mlle *abbr* [F] mademoiselle

Mlles *abbr* [F] mesdemoiselles

mm *abbr* millimeter

MM *abbr* [F] messieurs

Mme *abbr* [F] madame

Mmes *abbr* mesdames

Mn *symbol* manganese

MN *abbr* Minnesota

mne•mon•ic \nə-ˈmä-nik\ *adj* : assisting or designed to assist memory; *also* : of or relating to memory

mo *abbr* month

[1]**Mo** *abbr* **1** Missouri **2** Monday

[2]**Mo** *symbol* molybdenum

MO *abbr* **1** mail order **2** medical officer **3** Missouri **4** modus operandi **5** money order

moan \ˈmōn\ *n* : a low prolonged sound indicative of pain or grief — **moan** *vb*

moat \ˈmōt\ *n* : a deep wide usu. water-filled trench around a castle

[1]**mob** \ˈmäb\ *n* [L *mobile vulgus* vacillating crowd] **1** : MASSES, RABBLE **2** : a disorderly crowd **3** : a criminal gang

[2]**mob** *vb* **mobbed; mob•bing 1** : to crowd about and attack or annoy **2** : to crowd into or around ⟨shoppers *mobbed* the stores⟩

[1]**mo•bile** \ˈmō-bəl, -ˌbīl, -ˌbēl\ *adj* **1** : capable of moving or being moved **2** : changeable in appearance, mood, or purpose; *also* : ADAPTABLE **3** : having the opportunity for or undergoing a shift in social status **4** : using vehicles for transportation ⟨~ warfare⟩ — **mo•bil•i•ty** \mō-ˈbi-lə-tē\ *n*

[2]**mo•bile** \ˈmō-ˌbēl\ *n* : a construction or sculpture (as of wire and sheet metal) with parts that can be set in motion by air currents; *also* : a similar structure suspended so that it is moved by a current of air

mobile home *n* : a trailer used as a permanent dwelling

mo•bi•lise *chiefly Brit var of* MOBILIZE

mo•bi•lize \ˈmō-bə-ˌlīz\ *vb* **-lized; -liz•ing 1** : to put into movement or circulation **2** : to assemble and make ready for action ⟨~ army reserves⟩ — **mo•bi•li•za•tion** \ˌmō-bə-lə-ˈzā-shən\ *n* — **mo•bi•liz•er** \ˈmō-bə-ˌlī-zər\ *n*

mob•ster \ˈmäb-stər\ *n* : a member of a criminal gang

moc•ca•sin \ˈmä-kə-sən\ *n* **1** : a soft leather heelless shoe **2** : WATER MOCCASIN

mo•cha \ˈmō-kə\ *n* [*Mocha*, port in Yemen] **1** : choice coffee grown in Arabia **2** : a mixture of coffee and chocolate or cocoa **3** : a dark chocolate-brown color

[1]**mock** \ˈmäk, ˈmȯk\ *vb* **1** : to treat with contempt or ridicule **2** : DELUDE **3** : DEFY **4** : to mimic in sport or derision — **mock•er** *n* — **mock•ery** \ˈmä-kə-rē, ˈmȯ-\ *n* — **mock•ing•ly** *adv*

[2]**mock** *adj* : SHAM, PSEUDO

mock–he•ro•ic \ˌmäk-hi-ˈrō-ik, ˌmȯk-\ *adj* : ridiculing or burlesquing heroic style, character, or action ⟨a ~ poem⟩

mock•ing•bird \ˈmä-kiŋ-ˌbərd, ˈmȯ-\ *n* : a grayish No. American songbird related to the catbirds and thrashers that mimics the calls of other birds

mock–up \ˈmä-ˌkəp, ˈmȯ-\ *n* : a full-sized structural model built for study, testing, or display ⟨a ~ of a car⟩

[1]**mod** \ˈmäd\ *adj* **1** : of, relating to, or being the style of the 1960s British youth culture **2** : HIP, TRENDY

[2]**mod** *abbr* **1** moderate **2** modern **3** modification; modified

mode \ˈmōd\ *n* **1** : a particular form or variety of something; *also* : STYLE **2** : a manner of doing something **3** : the most frequent value of a set of data — **mod•al** \ˈmōd-ᵊl\ *adj*

[1]**mod•el** \ˈmäd-ᵊl\ *n* **1** : structural design **2** : a miniature representation; *also* : a pattern of something to be made **3** : an example for imitation or emulation **4** : one who poses for an artist; *also* : MANNEQUIN **5** : TYPE, DESIGN

[2]**model** *vb* **mod•eled** *or* **mod•elled; mod•el•ing** *or* **mod•el•ling 1** : SHAPE, FASHION, CONSTRUCT **2** : to work as a fashion model

[3]**model** *adj* **1** : serving as or worthy of being a pattern ⟨a ~ student⟩ **2** : being a miniature representation of something ⟨a ~ airplane⟩

mo•dem \ˈmō-dəm, -ˌdem\ *n* : a device that converts signals from one device (as a computer) to a form compatible with another (as a telephone)

[1]**mod•er•ate** \ˈmä-də-rət\ *adj* **1** : avoiding extremes; *also* : TEMPERATE **2** : AVERAGE; *also* : MEDIOCRE **3** : limited in scope or effect **4** : not expensive — **mod•erate** *n* — **mod•er•ate•ly** *adv* — **mod•er•ate•ness** *n*

[2]**mod•er•ate** \ˈmä-də-ˌrāt\ *vb* **-at•ed; -at•ing 1** : to lessen the intensity of : TEMPER **2** : to act as a moderator — **mod•er•a•tion** \ˌmä-də-ˈrā-shən\ *n*

mod•er•a•tor \ˈmä-də-ˌrā-tər\ *n* **1** : MEDIATOR **2** : one who presides over an assembly, meeting, or discussion

mod•ern \ˈmä-dərn\ *adj* [LL *modernus*, fr. L *modo* just now, fr. *modus* measure] : of, relating to, or characteristic of the present or the immediate past : CONTEMPORARY — **modern** *n* — **mo•der•ni•ty** \mə-ˈdər-nə-tē\ *n* — **mod•ern•ly** *adv* — **mod•ern•ness** *n*

mod•ern•ise *Brit var of* MODERNIZE

mod•ern•ism \ˈmä-dər-ˌni-zəm\ *n* : a practice, movement, or belief peculiar to modern times

mod•ern•ize \ˈmä-dər-ˌnīz\ *vb* **-ized; -iz•ing** : to make or become modern — **mod•ern•i•za•tion** \ˌmä-dər-nə-ˈzā-shən\ *n* — **mod•ern•iz•er** *n*

mod•est \ˈmä-dəst\ *adj* **1** : having a moderate estimate of oneself; *also* : DIFFIDENT **2** : observing the proprieties of dress and behavior **3** : limited in size, amount, or scope — **mod•est•ly** *adv* — **mod•es•ty** \-də-stē\ *n*

mod•i•cum \ˈmä-di-kəm\ *n* : a small amount

modif *abbr* modification

mod•i•fy \ˈmä-də-ˌfī\ *vb* **-fied; -fy•ing 1** : MODERATE **2** : to limit the meaning of esp. in a grammatical construction **3** : CHANGE, ALTER — **mod•i•fi•ca•tion** \ˌmä-də-fə-ˈkā-shən\ *n* — **mod•i•fi•er** \ˈmä-də-ˌfī-ər\ *n*

mod•ish \ˈmō-dish\ *adj* : FASHIONABLE, STYLISH — **mod•ish•ly** *adv* — **mod•ish•ness** *n*

mo•diste \mō-ˈdēst\ *n* : a maker of fashionable dresses and hats

mod•u•lar \ˈmä-jə-lər\ *adj* : constructed with standardized units

mod•u•lar•ized \ˈmä-jə-lə-ˌrīzd\ *adj* : containing or consisting of modules

mod•u•late \ˈmä-jə-ˌlāt\ *vb* **-lat•ed; -lat•ing 1** : to tune to a key or pitch **2** : to keep in proper measure or proportion : TEMPER **3** : to vary the amplitude or frequency of a carrier wave for the transmission of intelligence (as in radio or television) — **mod•u•la•tion** \ˌmä-jə-ˈlā-shən\ *n* — **mod•u•la•tor** \ˈmä-jə-ˌlā-tər\ *n* — **mod•u•la•to•ry** \-lə-ˌtōr-ē\ *adj*

mod•ule \ˈmä-jül\ *n* **1** : any in a series of standardized units for use together **2** : an assembly of wired electronic parts for use with other such assemblies **3** : an independent unit that constitutes a part of the total structure of a space vehicle ⟨a propulsion ~⟩

mo•dus ope•ran•di \ˌmō-dəs-ˌä-pə-ˈran-dē, -ˌdī\ *n, pl* **mo•di operandi** \ˈmō-ˌdē-ˌä-, ˈmō-ˌdī-\ [NL] : a method of procedure

[1]**mo•gul** \ˈmō-gəl, mō-ˈgəl\ *n* [fr. *Mogul,* member of a Muslim dynasty ruling northern India] : an important person : MAGNATE

[2]**mogul** \ˈmō-gəl\ *n* : a bump in a ski run

mo•hair \ˈmō-ˌhar\ *n* [modif. of obs. It *mocaiarro,* fr. Ar *mukhayyar,* lit., choice] : a fabric or yarn made wholly or in part from the long silky hair of the Angora goat; *also* : this goat hair

Mo•ham•med•an *var of* MUHAMMADAN

Mo•hawk \ˈmō-ˌhȯk\ *n, pl* **Mohawk** *or* **Mohawks** : a member of an American Indian people of the Mohawk River valley, New York; *also* : the language of the Mohawk people

Mo•he•gan \mō-ˈhē-gən, mə-\ *or* **Mo•hi•can** \-ˈhē-kən\ *n, pl* **Mohegan** *or* **Mohegans** *or* **Mohican** *or* **Mohicans** : a member of an American Indian people of southeastern Connecticut

Mo•hi•can \mō-ˈhē-kən, mə-\ *var of* MAHICAN

moi•e•ty \ˈmȯi-ə-tē\ *n, pl* **-ties** : one of two equal or approximately equal parts

moil \ˈmȯil\ *vb* : to work hard : DRUDGE — **moil** *n* — **moil•er** *n*

moi•ré \mȯ-ˈrā, mwä-\ *or* **moire** *same or* ˈmȯir, ˈmwär\ *n* : a fabric (as silk) having a watered appearance

moist \ˈmȯist\ *adj* : slightly or moderately wet — **moist•ly** *adv* — **moist•ness** *n*

moist•en \ˈmȯis-ᵊn\ *vb* : to make or become moist — **moist•en•er** *n*

mois•ture \ˈmȯis-chər\ *n* : the small amount of liquid that causes dampness

mois•tur•ise *Brit var of* MOISTURIZE

mois•tur•ize \ˈmȯis-chə-ˌrīz\ *vb* **-ized; -iz•ing** : to add moisture to — **mois•tur•iz•er** *n*

mol *abbr* molecular; molecule

mo•lar \ˈmō-lər\ *n* [ME *molares,* pl., fr. L *molaris,* fr. *molaris* of a mill, fr. *mola* millstone] : any of the broad teeth adapted to grinding food and located in the back of the jaw — **molar** *adj*

mo•las•ses \mə-ˈla-səz\ *n* : the thick brown syrup that is separated from raw sugar in sugar manufacture

[1]**mold** \ˈmōld\ *n* : crumbly soil rich in organic matter

[2]**mold** *n* **1** : distinctive nature or character **2** : the frame on or around which something is constructed **3** : a cavity in which something is shaped; *also* : an object so shaped **4** : MOLDING

[3]**mold** *vb* **1** : to shape in or as if in a mold **2** : to ornament with molding — **mold•er** *n*

[4]**mold** *n* : a surface growth of fungus esp. on damp or decaying matter; *also* : a fungus that forms molds — **mold•i•ness** \ˈmōl-dē-nəs\ *n* — **moldy** *adj*

[5]**mold** *vb* : to become moldy

mold•board \ˈmōld-ˌbōrd\ *n* : a curved iron plate attached above the plowshare to lift and turn the soil

mold•er \ˈmōl-dər\ *vb* : to crumble into small pieces

mold•ing \ˈmōl-diŋ\ *n* **1** : an act or process of shaping in a mold; *also* : an object so shaped **2** : a decorative surface, plane, or curved strip

[1]**mole** \ˈmōl\ *n* : a small often pigmented spot or protuberance on the skin

[2]**mole** *n* : any of numerous small burrowing insect-eating mammals related to the shrews and hedgehogs

[3]**mole** *n* : a massive breakwater or jetty

molecular biology *n* : a branch of biology dealing with the ultimate physical and chemical organization of living matter and esp. with the molecular basis of inheritance and protein synthesis — **molecular biologist** *n*

molecular weight *n* : the mass of a molecule that is equal to the sum of the masses of all atoms contained in the molecule's formula

mol•e•cule \ˈmä-li-ˌkyül\ *n* : the smallest particle of matter that is the same chemically as the whole mass — **mo•lec•u•lar** \mə-ˈle-kyə-lər\ *adj*

mole•hill \ˈmōl-ˌhil\ *n* : a little ridge of earth thrown up by a mole

mole•skin \-ˌskin\ *n* **1** : the skin of the mole used as fur **2** : a heavy durable cotton fabric

mo•lest \mə-ˈlest\ *vb* **1** : ANNOY, DISTURB **2** : to make annoying sexual advances to; *esp* : to force physical and usu. sexual contact on — **mo•les•ta•tion** \ˌmō-ˌles-ˈtā-shən\ *n* — **mo•lest•er** *n*

moll \ˈmäl\ *n* : a gangster's girlfriend

mol•li•fy \ˈmä-lə-ˌfī\ *vb* **-fied; -fy•ing 1** : to soothe in temper : APPEASE **2** : SOFTEN **3** : to reduce in intensity : ASSUAGE — **mol•li•fi•ca•tion** \ˌmä-lə-fə-ˈkā-shən\ *n*

mol•lusk *or* **mol•lusc** \ˈmä-ləsk\ *n* : any of a large phylum of usu. shelled and aquatic invertebrate animals (as snails, clams, and squids) — **mol•lus•can** *also* **mol•lus•kan** \mə-ˈləs-kən\ *adj*

[1]**mol•ly•cod•dle** \ˈmä-lē-ˌkäd-ᵊl\ *n* : a pampered man or boy

[2]**mollycoddle** *vb* **mol•ly•cod•dled; mol•ly•cod•dling** : PAMPER

Mo•lo•tov cocktail \ˈmä-lə-ˌtȯf-, ˈmȯ-\ *n* [Vyacheslav M. *Molotov* †1986 Soviet foreign minister] : a crude bomb made of a bottle filled usu. with gasoline and fitted with a wick (as a saturated rag) that is ignited just prior to hurling

[1]**molt** \ˈmōlt\ *vb* : to shed hair, feathers, outer skin, or horns periodically with the cast-off parts being replaced by new growth — **molt•er** *n*

[2]**molt** *n* : the act or process of molting

mol•ten \ˈmōlt-ᵊn\ *adj* **1** : fused or liquefied by heat **2** : GLOWING

mo•ly \ˈmō-lē\ *n* : a mythical herb with black root, white flowers, and magic powers

mo•lyb•de•num \mə-ˈlib-də-nəm\ *n* : a metallic chemical element used in strengthening and hardening steel — see ELEMENT table

mom \ˈmäm, ˈməm\ *n* : MOTHER

mom–and–pop *adj* : being a small owner-operated business

mo•ment \ˈmō-mənt\ *n* **1** : a minute portion of time : INSTANT **2** : a time of excellence ⟨he has his ~*s*⟩ **3** : IMPORTANCE **syn** consequence, significance, weight, import

mo•men•tari•ly \ˌmō-mən-ˈter-ə-lē\ *adv* **1** : for a moment **2** *archaic* : INSTANTLY **3** : at any moment : SOON

mo•men•tary \ˈmō-mən-ˌter-ē\ *adj* **1** : continuing only a moment; *also* : EPHEMERAL **2** : recurring at every moment — **mo•men•tar•i•ness** \-ˌter-ē-nəs\ *n*

mo•men•tous \mō-ˈmen-təs\ *adj* : very important — **mo•men•tous•ly** *adv* — **mo•men•tous•ness** *n*

mo•men•tum \mō-ˈmen-təm\ *n, pl* **mo•men•ta** \-ˈmen-tə\ *or* **momentums** : a property that a moving body has due to its mass and motion; *also* : IMPETUS

mom•my \ˈmä-mē, ˈmə-\ *n, pl* **mom•mies** : MOTHER

Mon *abbr* Monday

mon•arch \ˈmä-nərk, -ˌnärk\ *n* **1** : a person who reigns over a kingdom or an empire **2** : one holding preeminent position or power **3** : MONARCH BUTTERFLY —

mo•nar•chi•cal \mə-ˈnär-ki-kəl\ *also* **mo•nar•chic** \-ˈnär-kik\ *adj*

monarch butterfly *n* **:** a large orange and black migratory American butterfly whose larva feeds on milkweed

monarch butterfly

mon•ar•chist \ˈmä-nər-kist\ *n* **:** a believer in monarchical government — **mon•ar•chism** \-ˌki-zəm\ *n*

mon•ar•chy \ˈmä-nər-kē\ *n, pl* **-chies :** a nation or state governed by a monarch

mon•as•tery \ˈmä-nə-ˌster-ē\ *n, pl* **-ter•ies :** a house for persons under religious vows (as monks)

mo•nas•tic \mə-ˈnas-tik\ *adj* **:** of or relating to monasteries or to monks or nuns — **monastic** *n* — **mo•nas•ti•cal•ly** \-ti-k(ə-)lē\ *adv* — **mo•nas•ti•cism** \-tə-ˌsi-zəm\ *n*

mon•au•ral \mä-ˈnȯr-əl\ *adj* **:** MONOPHONIC — **mon•au•ral•ly** *adv*

Mon•day \ˈmən-dē, -ˌdā\ *n* **:** the second day of the week

mon•e•tary \ˈmä-nə-ˌter-ē, ˈmə-\ *adj* **:** of or relating to money or to the mechanisms by which it is supplied and circulated in the economy

mon•ey \ˈmə-nē\ *n, pl* **moneys** *or* **mon•ies** \ˈmə-nēz\ **1 :** something (as metal currency) accepted as a medium of exchange **2 :** wealth reckoned in monetary terms **3 :** the 1st, 2d, and 3d places in a horse or dog race

MONEY

NAME	SUBDIVISIONS	COUNTRY
afghani	100 puls	Afghanistan
baht *or* tical	100 satang	Thailand
balboa	100 centesimos	Panama
birr	100 cents	Ethiopia
bolivar	100 centimos	Venezuela
boliviano	100 centavos	Bolivia
cedi	100 pesewas	Ghana
colón	100 centimos	Costa Rica
colón	100 centavos	El Salvador
cordoba	100 centavos	Nicaragua
dalasi	100 bututs	Gambia
deutsche mark	100 pfennig	Germany
dinar	100 centimes	Algeria
dinar	1000 fils	Bahrain
dinar	1000 fils	Iraq
dinar	1000 fils	Jordan
dinar	1000 fils	Kuwait
dinar	1000 dirhams	Libya
dinar	1000 millimes	Tunisia
dinar	100 paras	Yugoslavia
dirham	100 centimes	Morocco
dirham	100 fils	United Arab Emirates
dobra	100 centimos	São Tomé and Príncipe
dollar[1]	100 cents	Antigua and Barbuda, Dominica, Grenada, St. Kitts-Nevis, St. Lucia, St. Vincent and the Grenadines
dollar	100 cents	Australia
dollar	100 cents	Bahamas
dollar	100 cents	Barbados
dollar	100 cents	Belize
dollar	100 cents	Bermuda
dollar	100 sen *or* cents	Brunei
dollar	100 cents	Canada
dollar *or* yuan	100 cents	China (Taiwan)
dollar	100 cents	Fiji
dollar	100 cents	Guyana
dollar	100 cents	Jamaica
dollar	100 cents	Liberia
dollar	100 cents	New Zealand
dollar	100 cents	Singapore
dollar	100 cents	Trinidad and Tobago
dollar	100 cents	United States
dollar	100 cents	Zimbabwe
dollar — see RINGGIT, below		
dong	100 xu	Vietnam
drachma	100 lepta	Greece
escudo	100 centavos	Cape Verde
escudo	100 centavos	Portugal
florin — see GULDEN, below		
forint	100 filler	Hungary
franc	100 centimes	Belgium
franc[2]	100 centimes	Benin, Burkina Faso, Cameroon, Central African Republic, Chad, Congo, Equatorial Guinea, Gabon, Ivory Coast, Mali, Niger, Senegal, Togo
franc	100 centimes	Burundi
franc	100 centimes	Djibouti
franc	100 centimes	France
franc	100 centimes	Guinea
franc	100 centimes	Luxembourg
franc	100 centimes	Madagascar
franc	100 centimes	Rwanda
franc	100 centimes *or* rappen	Switzerland
gourde	100 centimes	Haiti
guarani	100 centimos	Paraguay
gulden *or* guilder *or* florin	100 cents	Netherlands
gulden *or* guilder *or* florin	100 cents	Suriname
kina	100 toea	Papua New Guinea
kip	100 at	Laos
koruna	100 haleru	Czech Republic
krona	100 aurar (*sing* eyrir)	Iceland
krona	100 ore	Sweden
krone	100 ore	Denmark
krone	100 ore	Norway
kwacha	100 tambala	Malawi
kwacha	100 ngwee	Zambia
kwanza	100 lwei	Angola
kyat	100 pyas	Myanmar
lek	100 qindarka	Albania
lempira	100 centavos	Honduras
leone	100 cents	Sierra Leone
leu	100 bani	Romania
lev	100 stotinki	Bulgaria

NAME	SUBDIVISIONS	COUNTRY
lilangeni (*pl* emalangeni)	100 cents	Swaziland
lira	100 centesimi[3]	Italy
lira *or* pound	100 cents	Malta
lira	100 kurus	Turkey
livre — see POUND, below		
loti (*pl* maloti)	100 licente *or* lisente (*sing* sente)	Lesotho
mark — see DEUTSCHE MARK, above		
markka	100 pennia	Finland
metical	100 centavos	Mozambique
naira	100 kobo	Nigeria
ngultrum	100 chetrums	Bhutan
ouguiya	5 khoums	Mauritania
pa'anga	100 seniti	Tonga
pataca	100 avos	Macao
peseta	100 centimos	Spain
peso		Argentina
peso	100 centavos	Chile
peso	100 centavos	Colombia
peso	100 centavos	Cuba
peso	100 centavos	Dominican Republic
peso	100 centavos	Guinea-Bissau
peso	100 centavos	Mexico
peso *or* piso	100 sentimos *or* centavos	Philippines
peso	100 centesimos	Uruguay
pound	100 cents	Cyprus
pound	100 piastres	Egypt
pound	100 pence	Ireland
pound *or* livre	100 piastres	Lebanon
pound	100 piastres	Sudan
pound	100 piastres	Syria
pound	100 pence	United Kingdom
pound — see LIRA, above		
pula	100 thebe	Botswana
quetzal	100 centavos	Guatemala
rand	100 cents	South Africa
real	100 centavos	Brazil
rial	100 dinars	Iran
rial	1000 baiza	Oman
rial	100 fils	Yemen
riel	100 sen	Cambodia
ringgit *or* dollar	100 sen	Malaysia
riyal	100 dirhams	Qatar
riyal	100 halala	Saudi Arabia
ruble	100 kopecks	Russia
rupee	100 paise	India
rupee	100 cents	Mauritius
rupee	100 paisa	Nepal
rupee	100 paisa	Pakistan
rupee	100 cents	Seychelles
rupee	100 cents	Sri Lanka
rupiah	100 sen	Indonesia
schilling	100 groschen	Austria
shekel *or* sheqel	100 agorot	Israel
shilling	100 cents	Kenya
shilling	100 cents	Somalia
shilling	100 cents	Tanzania
shilling	100 cents	Uganda
sol	100 centavos	Peru
sucre	100 centavos	Ecuador
taka	100 paisa *or* poisha	Bangladesh
tala	100 sene	Western Samoa
tical — see BAHT, above		
tugrik	100 mongo	Mongolia
won	100 chon	North Korea
won	100 chon	South Korea
yen	100 sen[3]	Japan
yuan	100 fen	China (mainland)
yuan — see DOLLAR, above		
zaire	100 makuta (*sing* likuta)	Democratic Republic of Congo
zloty	100 groszy	Poland

[1] Dollars issued by the Eastern Caribbean Central Bank, established to promote economic cooperation among the member nations.
[2] Francs issued by the African Financial Community, established to promote economic cooperation among the member nations.
[3] No longer minted; a subdivision in name only.

mon•eyed \ˈmə-nēd\ *adj* **1** : having money : WEALTHY **2** : consisting in or derived from money

mon•ey•lend•er \ˈmə-nē-ˌlen-dər\ *n* : one (as a bank or pawnbroker) whose business is lending money

money market *n* : the trade in short-term negotiable financial instruments

money of account : a denominator of value or basis of exchange used in keeping accounts

money order *n* : an order purchased at a post office, bank, or telegraph office directing another office to pay a sum of money to a party named on it

mon•ger \ˈməŋ-gər, ˈmäŋ-\ *n* **1** : DEALER **2** : one who tries to stir up or spread something

mon•go \ˈmäŋ-(ˌ)gō\ *n, pl* **mongo** — see *tugrik* at MONEY table

Mon•gol \ˈmäŋ-gəl, ˈmän-ˌgōl\ *n* : a member of any of several traditionally pastoral peoples of Mongolia — **Mongol** *adj*

Mon•go•lian \män-ˈgōl-yən, mäŋ-, -ˈgō-lē-ən\ *n* **1** : a native or inhabitant of Mongolia **2** : a member of the Mongoloid racial stock — **Mongolian** *adj*

mon•gol•ism \ˈmäŋ-gə-ˌli-zəm\ *n* : DOWN'S SYNDROME

Mon•gol•oid \ˈmäŋ-gə-ˌlòid\ *adj* **1** : of or relating to a major racial stock native to Asia that includes peoples of northern and eastern Asia, Malaysians, Eskimos, and often American Indians **2** *often not cap* : of, relating to, or affected with Down's syndrome — **Mongoloid** *n*

mon•goose \ˈmän-ˌgüs, ˈmäŋ-\ *n, pl* **mon•goos•es** *also* **mon•geese** \-ˌgēs\ : any of a group of small agile Old World mammals that are related to the civet cats and feed on small animals and fruits

mon•grel \ˈmäŋ-grəl, ˈməŋ-\ *n* : an offspring of parents of different breeds; *esp* : one of uncertain ancestry

mo•nism \ˈmō-ˌni-zəm, ˈmä-\ *n* : a view that reality is basically one unitary organic whole — **mo•nist** \ˈmō-nist, ˈmä-\ *n*

mo•ni•tion \mō-ˈni-shən, mə-\ *n* : WARNING, CAUTION

[1]**mon•i•tor** \ˈmä-nə-tər\ *n* **1** : a student appointed to assist a teacher **2** : one that monitors; *esp* : a video display screen (as for a computer)

[2]**monitor** *vb* : to watch, check, or observe for a special purpose

mon•i•to•ry \ˈmä-nə-ˌtōr-ē\ *adj* : giving admonition : WARNING

[1]**monk** \ˈməŋk\ *n* [ME, fr. OE *munuc,* fr. LL *monachus,* fr. LGk *monachos,* fr. Gk, adj., single, fr. *monos* single, alone] : a man belonging to a religious order and living in a monastery — **monk•ish** *adj*

[2]**monk** *n* : MONKEY

[1]**mon•key** \ˈməŋ-kē\ *n, pl* **monkeys** : a nonhuman primate mammal; *esp* : one of the smaller, longer-tailed, and usu. more arboreal primates as contrasted with the apes

[2]**monkey** *vb* **mon•keyed; mon•key•ing 1** : FOOL, TRIFLE **2** : TAMPER

monkey bars *n pl* : a framework of bars on which children can play

mon•key•shine \ˈmən-kē-ˌshīn\ *n* : PRANK — usu. used in pl.

monkey wrench *n* : a wrench with one fixed and one adjustable jaw at right angles to a handle

monks•hood \ˈməŋks-ˌhu̇d\ *n* : any of a genus of poi-

DICTIONARY

sonous plants related to the buttercups; *esp* : a tall Old World plant with usu. purplish flowers

[1]mono \ˈmä-nō\ *adj* : MONOPHONIC

[2]mono *n* : INFECTIOUS MONONUCLEOSIS

mono•chro•mat•ic \ˌmä-nə-krō-ˈma-tik\ *adj* **1** : having or consisting of one color **2** : consisting of radiation (as light) of a single wavelength

mono•chrome \ˈmä-nə-ˌkrōm\ *adj* : involving or producing visual images in a single color or in varying tones of a single color ⟨~ television⟩

mon•o•cle \ˈmä-ni-kəl\ *n* : an eyeglass for one eye

mono•clo•nal \ˌmä-nə-ˈklō-nəl\ *adj* : produced by, being, or composed of cells derived from a single cell ⟨~ antibodies⟩

mono•cot•y•le•don \ˌmä-nə-ˌkät-ᵊl-ˈēd-ᵊn\ *n* : any of a class or subclass of chiefly herbaceous seed plants having an embryo with a single cotyledon and usu. parallel-veined leaves

mon•o•dy \ˈmä-nə-dē\ *n, pl* **-dies** : ELEGY, DIRGE — **mo•nod•ic** \mə-ˈnä-dik\ *or* **mo•nod•i•cal** \-di-kəl\ *adj* — **mon•o•dist** \ˈmä-nə-dist\ *n*

mo•nog•a•my \mə-ˈnä-gə-mē\ *n* **1** : marriage with but one person at a time **2** : the practice of having a single mate during a period of time — **mo•nog•a•mist** \-mist\ *n* — **mo•nog•a•mous** \-məs\ *adj*

mono•gram \ˈmä-nə-ˌgram\ *n* : a sign of identity composed of the combined initials of a name — **mono-gram** *vb*

mono•graph \ˈmä-nə-ˌgraf\ *n* : a learned treatise on a small area of learning

mono•lin•gual \ˌmä-nə-ˈliŋ-gwəl\ *adj* : knowing or using only one language

mono•lith \ˈmän-ᵊl-ˌith\ *n* **1** : a single great stone often in the form of a monument or column **2** : something large and powerful that acts as a single unified force — **mono•lith•ic** \ˌmän-ᵊl-ˈi-thik\ *adj*

mono•logue *also* **mono•log** \ˈmän-ᵊl-ˌȯg\ *n* **1** : a dramatic soliloquy; *also* : a long speech monopolizing conversation **2** : the routine of a stand-up comic — **mono•logu•ist** \-ˌȯg-ist\ *or* **mo•no•lo•gist** \mə-ˈnä-lə-jist; ˈmän-ᵊl-ˌȯ-gist\ *n*

mono•ma•nia \ˌmä-nə-ˈmā-nē-ə, -nyə\ *n* **1** : mental disorder limited in expression to one area of thought **2** : excessive concentration on a single object or idea — **mono•ma•ni•ac** \-nē-ˌak\ *n or adj*

mono•mer \ˈmä-nə-mər\ *n* : a simple chemical compound that can be polymerized

mono•nu•cle•o•sis \ˌmä-nō-ˌnü-klē-ˈō-səs, -ˌnyü-\ *n* : INFECTIOUS MONONUCLEOSIS

mono•phon•ic \ˌmä-nə-ˈfä-nik\ *adj* : of or relating to sound recording or reproduction involving a single transmission path

mono•plane \ˈmä-nə-ˌplān\ *n* : an airplane with only one set of wings

mo•nop•o•ly \mə-ˈnä-pə-lē\ *n, pl* **-lies** [L *monopolium*, fr. Gk *monopōlion*, fr. *monos* alone, single + *pōlein* to sell] **1** : exclusive ownership (as through command of supply) **2** : a commodity controlled by one party **3** : one that has a monopoly — **mo•nop•o•list** \-list\ *n* — **mo•nop•o•lis•tic** \mə-ˌnä-pə-ˈlis-tik\ *adj* — **mo•nop•o•li•za•tion** \-lə-ˈzā-shən\ *n* — **mo•nop•o•lize** \mə-ˈnä-pə-ˌlīz\ *vb*

mono•rail \ˈmä-nə-ˌrāl\ *n* : a single rail serving as a track for a vehicle; *also* : a vehicle traveling on such a track

mono•so•di•um glu•ta•mate \ˌmä-nə-ˌsō-dē-əm-ˈglü-tə-ˌmāt\ *n* : a crystalline salt used to enhance the flavor of food

mono•syl•la•ble \ˈmä-nə-ˌsi-lə-bəl\ *n* : a word of one syllable — **mono•syl•lab•ic** \ˌmä-nə-sə-ˈla-bik\ *adj* — **mono•syl•lab•i•cal•ly** \-bi-k(ə-)lē\ *adv*

mono•the•ism \ˈmä-nə-(ˌ)thē-ˌi-zəm\ *n* : a doctrine or belief that there is only one deity — **mono•the•ist** \-ˌthē-ist\ *n* — **mono•the•is•tic** \-thē-ˈis-tik\ *adj*

mono•tone \ˈmä-nə-ˌtōn\ *n* : a succession of syllables, words, or sentences in one unvaried key or pitch

mo•not•o•nous \mə-ˈnät-ᵊn-əs\ *adj* **1** : uttered or sounded in one unvarying tone **2** : tediously uniform — **mo•not•o•nous•ly** *adv* — **mo•not•o•nous•ness** *n*

mo•not•o•ny \mə-ˈnät-ᵊn-ē\ *n* : tedious sameness or uniformity

mono•un•sat•u•rat•ed \ˌmä-nō-ˌən-ˈsa-chə-ˌrā-təd\ *adj* : containing one double or triple bond per molecule — used esp. of an oil or fatty acid

mon•ox•ide \mə-ˈnäk-ˌsīd\ *n* : an oxide containing one atom of oxygen in a molecule

mon•sei•gneur \ˌmō^{n}-ˌsān-ˈyər\ *n, pl* **mes•sei•gneurs** \ˌmā-ˌsān-ˈyər, -ˈyərz\ : a French dignitary — used as a title

mon•sieur \məs-ˈyər, mə-ˈshər, *Fr* mə-ˈsyœ\ *n, pl* **mes•sieurs** *same or* -ˈyərz, -ˈshərz\ : a Frenchman of high rank or station — used as a title equivalent to *Mister*

mon•si•gnor \män-ˈsē-nyər\ *n, pl* **monsignors** *or* **mon-si•gno•ri** \ˌmän-ˌsēn-ˈyōr-ē\ [It *monsignore*] : a Roman Catholic prelate — used as a title

mon•soon \män-ˈsün\ *n* [obs. Dutch *monssoen*, fr. Pg *monção*, fr. Ar *mawsim* time, season] **1** : a periodic wind esp. in the Indian Ocean and southern Asia **2** : the season of the southwest monsoon esp. in India **3** : rainfall associated with the monsoon

[1]mon•ster \ˈmän-stər\ *n* **1** : an abnormally developed plant or animal **2** : an animal of strange or terrifying shape; *also* : one unusually large of its kind **3** : an extremely ugly, wicked, or cruel person — **mon•stros-i•ty** \män-ˈsträ-sə-tē\ *n* — **mon•strous** \ˈmän-strəs\ *adj* — **mon•strous•ly** *adv*

[2]monster *adj* : very large : ENORMOUS

mon•strance \ˈmän-strəns\ *n* : a vessel in which the consecrated Host is exposed for the adoration of the faithful

Mont *abbr* Montana

mon•tage \män-ˈtäzh\ *n* [F] **1** : a composite photograph made by combining several separate pictures **2** : an artistic composition made up of several different kinds of elements **3** : a varied mixture : JUMBLE

month \ˈmənth\ *n, pl* **months** \ˈməns, ˈmənths\ : one of the 12 parts into which the year is divided — **month•ly** *adv or adj or n*

month•long \ˈmənth-ˈlȯŋ\ *adj* : lasting a month

mon•u•ment \ˈmän-yə-mənt\ *n* **1** : a lasting reminder; *esp* : a structure erected in remembrance of a person or event **2** : NATIONAL MONUMENT

mon•u•men•tal \ˌmän-yə-ˈment-ᵊl\ *adj* **1** : of or relating to a monument **2** : MASSIVE; *also* : OUTSTANDING **3** : very great — **mon•u•men•tal•ly** *adv*

moo \ˈmü\ *vb* : to make the natural throat noise of a cow — **moo** *n*

[1]mood \ˈmüd\ *n* **1** : a conscious state of mind or predominant emotion : FEELING **2** : a prevailing attitude : DISPOSITION **3** : a distinctive atmosphere

[2]mood *n* : distinction of form of a verb to express whether its action or state is conceived as fact or in some other manner (as wish)

moody \ˈmü-dē\ *adj* **mood•i•er; -est** **1** : GLOOMY **2** : subject to moods : TEMPERAMENTAL — **mood•i•ly** \-də-lē\ *adv* — **mood•i•ness** \-dē-nəs\ *n*

[1]moon \ˈmün\ *n* **1** : the earth's natural satellite **2** : SATELLITE 2

[2]moon *vb* : to engage in idle reverie

moon•beam \ˈmün-ˌbēm\ *n* : a ray of light from the moon

[1]moon•light \-ˌlīt\ *n* : the light of the moon — **moon-lit** \-ˌlit\ *adj*

[2]moonlight *vb* **moon•light•ed; moon•light•ing** : to hold a second job in addition to a regular one — **moon-light•er** *n*

moon•scape \-ˌskāp\ *n* : the surface of the moon as seen or as pictured

moon•shine \-ˌshīn\ *n* **1** : MOONLIGHT **2** : empty talk **3** : intoxicating liquor usu. illegally distilled

moon•stone \-ˌstōn\ *n* : a transparent or translucent feldspar of pearly luster used as a gem

moon•struck \-ˌstrək\ *adj* **1** : mentally unbalanced **2** : romantically sentimental **3** : lost in fantasy

¹moor \ˈmu̇r\ *n* **1** *chiefly Brit* : an expanse of open rolling infertile land **2** : a boggy area; *esp* : one that is peaty and dominated by grasses and sedges

²moor *vb* : to make fast with or as if with cables, lines, or anchors

Moor \ˈmu̇r\ *n* : one of the Arab and Berber conquerors of Spain — **Moor•ish** *adj*

moor•ing \ˈmu̇r-iŋ\ *n* **1** : a place where or an object to which a craft can be made fast **2** : an established practice or stabilizing influence — usu. used in pl.

moor•land \-lənd, -ˌland\ *n* : land consisting of moors

moose \ˈmüs\ *n, pl* **moose** : a large heavy-antlered ruminant mammal of the deer family with humped shoulders and long legs that inhabits northern New and Old World forested areas

¹moot \ˈmüt\ *vb* : to bring up for discussion; *also* : DEBATE

²moot *adj* **1** : open to question; *also* : DISPUTED **2** : having no practical significance

¹mop \ˈmäp\ *n* : an implement made of absorbent material fastened to a handle and used esp. for cleaning floors

²mop *vb* **mopped; mop•ping** : to use a mop on : clean with a mop

mope \ˈmōp\ *vb* **moped; mop•ing 1** : to become dull, dejected, or listless **2** : DAWDLE

mo•ped \ˈmō-ˌped\ *n* : a light low-powered motorbike that can be pedaled

mop•pet \ˈmä-pət\ *n* [obs. E *mop* fool, child] : CHILD

mo•raine \mə-ˈrān\ *n* : an accumulation of earth and stones left by a glacier

¹mor•al \ˈmȯr-əl\ *adj* **1** : of or relating to principles of right and wrong **2** : conforming to a standard of right behavior; *also* : capable of right and wrong action **3** : probable but not proved ⟨a ~ certainty⟩ **4** : having the effects of such on the mind, confidence, or will ⟨a ~ victory⟩ **syn** virtuous, righteous, noble, ethical, principled — **mor•al•ly** *adv*

²moral *n* **1** : the practical meaning (as of a story) **2** *pl* : moral practices or teachings

mo•rale \mə-ˈral\ *n* **1** : MORALITY **2** : the mental and emotional attitudes of an individual to the tasks at hand; *also* : ESPRIT DE CORPS

mor•al•ise *Brit var of* MORALIZE

mor•al•ist \ˈmȯr-ə-list\ *n* **1** : one who leads a moral life **2** : a thinker or writer concerned with morals **3** : one concerned with regulating the morals of others — **mor•al•is•tic** \ˌmȯr-ə-ˈlis-tik\ *adj* — **mor•al•is•ti•cal•ly** \-ti-k(ə-)lē\ *adv*

mo•ral•i•ty \mə-ˈra-lə-tē\ *n, pl* **-ties** : moral conduct : VIRTUE

mor•al•ize \ˈmȯr-ə-ˌlīz\ *vb* **-ized; -iz•ing** : to make moral reflections — **mor•al•i•za•tion** \ˌmȯr-ə-lə-ˈzā-shən\ *n* — **mor•al•iz•er** \ˈmȯr-ə-ˌlī-zər\ *n*

mo•rass \mə-ˈras\ *n* : SWAMP; *also* : something that entangles, impedes, or confuses

mor•a•to•ri•um \ˌmȯr-ə-ˈtōr-ē-əm\ *n, pl* **-ri•ums** *or* **-ria** \-ē-ə\ [ultim. fr. L *mora* delay] : a suspension of activity

mo•ray \mə-ˈrā, ˈmȯr-ˌā\ *n* : any of numerous often brightly colored biting eels of warm seas

mor•bid \ˈmȯr-bəd\ *adj* **1** : of, relating to, or typical of disease; *also* : DISEASED, SICKLY **2** : characterized by gloomy or unwholesome ideas or feelings **3** : GRISLY, GRUESOME ⟨~ details⟩ — **mor•bid•i•ty** \mȯr-ˈbi-də-tē\ *n* — **mor•bid•ly** *adv* — **mor•bid•ness** *n*

mor•dant \ˈmȯrd-ᵊnt\ *adj* **1** : biting or caustic in manner or style **2** : BURNING, PUNGENT — **mor•dant•ly** *adv*

¹more \ˈmōr\ *adj* **1** : GREATER **2** : ADDITIONAL

²more *adv* **1** : in addition **2** : to a greater or higher degree

³more *n* **1** : a greater quantity, number, or amount ⟨the ~ the merrier⟩ **2** : an additional amount ⟨costs a little ~⟩

⁴more *pron* : additional persons or things or a greater amount

mo•rel \mə-ˈrel\ *n* : any of several pitted edible fungi

more•over \mōr-ˈō-vər\ *adv* : in addition : FURTHER

mo•res \ˈmȯr-ˌāz\ *n pl* [L, pl. of *mor-, mos* custom] **1** : the fixed morally binding customs of a group **2** : HABITS, MANNERS

Mor•gan \ˈmȯr-gən\ *n* : any of an American breed of lightly built horses

morgue \ˈmȯrg\ *n* : a place where the bodies of dead persons are kept until released for burial

mor•i•bund \ˈmȯr-ə-(ˌ)bənd\ *adj* : being in a dying condition

Mor•mon \ˈmȯr-mən\ *n* : a member of the Church of Jesus Christ of Latter-day Saints — **Mor•mon•ism** \-mə-ˌni-zəm\ *n*

morn \ˈmȯrn\ *n* : MORNING

morn•ing \ˈmȯr-niŋ\ *n* **1** : the early part of the day; *esp* : the time from the sunrise to noon **2** : BEGINNING

morning glory *n* : any of various twining plants related to the sweet potato that have often showy bell-shaped or funnel-shaped flowers

morning sickness *n* : nausea and vomiting that occur in the morning esp. during early pregnancy

morning star *n* : a bright planet (as Venus) seen in the eastern sky before or at sunrise

Mo•roc•can \mə-ˈrä-kən\ *n* : a native or inhabitant of Morocco

mo•roc•co \mə-ˈrä-kō\ *n* : a fine leather made of goatskins tanned with sumac

mo•ron \ˈmōr-ˌän\ *n* **1** : a mentally retarded person having a potential mental age of between 8 and 12 years and capable of doing routine work under supervision **2** : a very stupid person — **mo•ron•ic** \mə-ˈrä-nik\ *adj* — **mo•ron•i•cal•ly** \-ni-k(ə-)lē\ *adv*

mo•rose \mə-ˈrōs\ *adj* [L *morosus* hard to please, exacting, fr. *mor-, mos* custom, disposition] : having a sullen disposition; *also* : GLOOMY — **mo•rose•ly** *adv* — **mo•rose•ness** *n*

morph \ˈmȯrf\ *vb* : to change in form or character : TRANSFORM

mor•pheme \ˈmȯr-ˌfēm\ *n* : a meaningful linguistic unit that contains no smaller meaningful parts — **mor•phe•mic** \mȯr-ˈfē-mik\ *adj*

mor•phia \ˈmȯr-fē-ə\ *n* : MORPHINE

mor•phine \ˈmȯr-ˌfēn\ *n* [F, fr. Gk *Morpheus*, Greek god of dreams] : an addictive drug obtained from opium and used to ease pain or induce sleep

mor•phol•o•gy \mȯr-ˈfä-lə-jē\ *n* **1** : a branch of biology dealing with the form and structure of organisms **2** : a study and description of word formation in a language — **mor•pho•log•i•cal** \ˌmȯr-fə-ˈlä-ji-kəl\ *adj* — **mor•phol•o•gist** \mȯr-ˈfä-lə-jist\ *n*

mor•ris \ˈmȯr-əs\ *n* : a vigorous English dance traditionally performed by men wearing costumes and bells

mor•row \ˈmär-ō\ *n* : the next day

Morse code \ˈmȯrs-\ *n* : either of two codes consisting of dots and dashes or long and short sounds used for transmitting messages

mor•sel \ˈmȯr-səl\ *n* [ME, fr. OF, dim. of *mors* bite, fr. L *morsus*, fr. *mordēre* to bite] **1** : a small piece or quantity **2** : a tasty dish

mor•tal \ˈmȯrt-ᵊl\ *adj* **1** : causing death : FATAL; *also* : leading to eternal punishment ⟨~ sin⟩ **2** : subject to death ⟨~ man⟩ **3** : implacably hostile ⟨~ foe⟩ **4** : very great : EXTREME ⟨~ fear⟩ **5** : HUMAN ⟨~ limitations⟩ — **mortal** *n* — **mor•tal•i•ty** \mȯr-ˈta-lə-tē\ *n* — **mor•tal•ly** \ˈmȯrt-ᵊl-ē\ *adv*

¹mor•tar \ˈmȯr-tər\ *n* **1** : a strong bowl in which substances are pounded or crushed with a pestle **2** : a short-barreled cannon used to fire shells at high angles

[2]**mortar** *n* : a building material (as a mixture of lime and cement with sand and water) that is spread between bricks or stones to bind them together as it hardens — **mortar** *vb*

mor•tar•board \ˈmȯr-tər-ˌbōrd\ *n* **1** : a square board for holding mortar **2** : an academic cap with a flat square top

mort•gage \ˈmȯr-gij\ *n* [ME *morgage,* fr. MF, fr. OF, fr. *mort* dead + *gage* gage] : a transfer of rights to a piece of property usu. as security for the payment of a loan or debt that becomes void when the debt is paid — **mortgage** *vb* — **mort•gag•ee** \ˌmȯr-gi-ˈjē\ *n* — **mort•gag•or** \ˌmȯr-gi-ˈjȯr\ *n*

mor•ti•cian \mȯr-ˈti-shən\ *n* [L *mort-, mors* death + E *-ician* (as in *physician*)] : UNDERTAKER

mor•ti•fy \ˈmȯr-tə-ˌfī\ *vb* **-fied; -fy•ing 1** : to subdue (as the body) esp. by abstinence or self-inflicted pain **2** : HUMILIATE **3** : to become necrotic or gangrenous — **mor•ti•fi•ca•tion** \ˌmȯr-tə-fə-ˈkā-shən\ *n*

mor•tise *also* **mor•tice** \ˈmȯr-təs\ *n* : a hole cut in a piece of wood into which another piece fits to form a joint

mor•tu•ary \ˈmȯr-chə-ˌwer-ē\ *n, pl* **-ar•ies** : a place in which dead bodies are kept until burial

mos *abbr* months

mo•sa•ic \mō-ˈzā-ik\ *n* : a surface decoration made by inlaying small pieces (as of colored glass or stone) to form figures or patterns; *also* : a design made in mosaic — **mosaic** *adj*

mo•sey \ˈmō-zē\ *vb* **mo•seyed; mo•sey•ing** : SAUNTER

mosh \ˈmäsh\ *vb* : to engage in various uninhibited often frenzied activities with others near the stage at a rock concert

Mos•lem \ˈmäz-ləm\ *var of* MUSLIM

mosque \ˈmäsk\ *n* : a building used for public worship by Muslims

mos•qui•to \mə-ˈskē-tō\ *n, pl* **-toes** *also* **-tos** : any of a family of dipteran flies the female of which sucks the blood of animals

mosquito net *n* : a net or screen for keeping out mosquitoes

moss \ˈmȯs\ *n* : any of a class of green plants that lack flowers but have small leafy stems and often grow in clumps — **mossy** *adj*

moss•back \ˈmȯs-ˌbak\ *n* : an extremely conservative person : FOGY

[1]**most** \ˈmōst\ *adj* **1** : GREATEST ⟨the ∼ ability⟩ **2** : the majority of ⟨∼ people⟩

[2]**most** *adv* **1** : to the greatest or highest degree ⟨∼ beautiful⟩ **2** : to a very great degree ⟨a ∼ careful driver⟩

[3]**most** *n* : the greatest amount ⟨the ∼ I can do⟩

[4]**most** *pron* : the greatest number or part ⟨∼ became discouraged⟩

-most \ˌmōst\ *adj suffix* : most ⟨inner*most*⟩ : most toward ⟨end*most*⟩

most•ly \ˈmōst-lē\ *adv* : MAINLY

mot \ˈmō\ *n, pl* **mots** *same or* ˈmōz\ [F, word, saying, fr. LL *muttum* grunt] : a witty saying

mote \ˈmōt\ *n* : a small particle

mo•tel \mō-ˈtel\ *n* [blend of *motor* and *hotel*] : a hotel in which the rooms are accessible from the parking area

mo•tet \mō-ˈtet\ *n* : a choral work on a sacred text for several voices usu. without instrumental accompaniment

moth \ˈmȯth\ *n, pl* **moths** \ˈmȯt͟hz, ˈmȯths\ : any of various insects belonging to the same order as the butterflies but usu. night-flying and with a stouter body and smaller wings

moth•ball \ˈmȯth-ˌbȯl\ *n* **1** : a ball (as of naphthalene) used to keep moths out of clothing **2** *pl* : protective storage

[1]**moth•er** \ˈmə-t͟hər\ *n* **1** : a female parent **2** : the superior of a religious community of women **3** : SOURCE, ORIGIN — **moth•er•hood** \-ˌhu̇d\ *n* — **moth•er•less** *adj* — **moth•er•li•ness** \-lē-nəs\ *n* — **moth•er•ly** *adj*

[2]**mother** *vb* **1** : to give birth to; *also* : PRODUCE **2** : to care for or protect like a mother

moth•er•board \ˈmə-t͟hər-ˌbōrd\ *n* : the main circuit board esp. of a microcomputer

moth•er–in–law \ˈmə-t͟hər-ən-ˌlȯ\ *n, pl* **mothers–in–law** \ˈmə-t͟hərz-\ : the mother of one's spouse

moth•er•land \ˈmə-t͟hər-ˌland\ *n* **1** : the land of origin of something **2** : the native land of one's ancestors

moth•er–of–pearl \ˌmə-t͟hər-əv-ˈpərl\ *n* : the hard pearly matter forming the inner layer of a mollusk shell

mo•tif \mō-ˈtēf\ *n* [F, motive, motif] : a dominant idea or central theme (as in a work of art)

mo•tile \ˈmōt-ᵊl, ˈmō-ˌtīl\ *adj* : capable of spontaneous movement — **mo•til•i•ty** \mō-ˈti-lə-tē\ *n*

[1]**mo•tion** \ˈmō-shən\ *n* **1** : an act, process, or instance of moving **2** : a proposal for action (as by a deliberative body) **3** *pl* : ACTIVITIES, MOVEMENTS — **mo•tion•less** *adj* — **mo•tion•less•ly** *adv* — **mo•tion•less•ness** *n*

[2]**motion** *vb* : to direct or signal by a movement

motion picture *n* : a series of pictures projected on a screen so rapidly that they produce a continuous picture in which persons and objects seem to move

motion sickness *n* : sickness induced by motion and characterized by nausea

mo•ti•vate \ˈmō-tə-ˌvāt\ *vb* **-vat•ed; -vat•ing** : to provide with a motive : IMPEL — **mo•ti•va•tion** \ˌmō-tə-ˈvā-shən\ *n* — **mo•ti•va•tion•al** \-shə-nəl\ *adj* — **mo•ti•va•tor** \ˈmō-tə-ˌvā-tər\ *n*

[1]**mo•tive** \ˈmō-tiv, *2 also* mō-ˈtēv\ *n* **1** : something (as a need or desire) that causes a person to act **2** : a recurrent theme in a musical composition **3** : MOTIF — **mo•tive•less** *adj*

[2]**mo•tive** \ˈmō-tiv\ *adj* **1** : moving to action **2** : of or relating to motion

mot•ley \ˈmät-lē\ *adj* **1** : variegated in color **2** : made up of diverse often incongruous elements **syn** heterogeneous, miscellaneous, assorted, mixed, varied

[1]**mo•tor** \ˈmō-tər\ *n* **1** : one that imparts motion **2** : a machine that produces motion or power for doing work **3** : AUTOMOBILE

[2]**motor** *vb* : to travel or transport by automobile : DRIVE — **mo•tor•ist** *n*

mo•tor•bike \ˈmō-tər-ˌbīk\ *n* : a small lightweight motorcycle

mo•tor•boat \-ˌbōt\ *n* : a boat propelled by a motor

mo•tor•cade \-ˌkād\ *n* : a procession of motor vehicles

mo•tor•car \-ˌkär\ *n* : AUTOMOBILE

mo•tor•cy•cle \ˈmō-tər-ˌsī-kəl\ *n* : a 2-wheeled automotive vehicle — **mo•tor•cy•clist** \-k(ə-)list\ *n*

motor home *n* : a large motor vehicle equipped as living quarters

motor inn *n* : MOTEL

mo•tor•ise *Brit var of* MOTORIZE

mo•tor•ize \ˈmō-tə-ˌrīz\ *vb* **-ized; -iz•ing 1** : to equip with a motor **2** : to equip with automobiles

mo•tor•man \ˈmō-tər-mən\ *n* : an operator of a motor-driven vehicle (as a streetcar or subway train)

motor scooter *n* : a low 2- or 3-wheeled automotive vehicle resembling a child's scooter but having a seat

mo•tor•truck \ˈmō-tər-ˌtrək\ *n* : an automotive truck

motor vehicle *n* : an automotive vehicle (as an automobile) not operated on rails

mot•tle \ˈmät-ᵊl\ *vb* **mot•tled; mot•tling** : to mark with spots of different color : BLOTCH

mot•to \ˈmä-tō\ *n, pl* **mottoes** *also* **mottos** [It, fr. LL *muttum* grunt, fr. L *muttire* to mutter] **1** : a sentence, phrase, or word inscribed on something to indicate its character or use **2** : a short expression of a guiding rule of conduct

moue \ˈmü\ *n* : a little grimace

mould \ˈmōld\ *var of* MOLD

moult \ˈmōlt\ *var of* MOLT

mound \ˈmau̇nd\ *n* **1** : an artificial bank or hill of earth or stones **2** : KNOLL **3** : HEAP, PILE

[1]**mount** \ˈmau̇nt\ *n* : a high hill

²mount *vb* **1** : to increase in amount or extent; *also* : RISE, ASCEND **2** : to get up on something; *esp* : to seat oneself on (as a horse) for riding **3** : to put in position ⟨~ artillery⟩ **4** : to set on something that elevates **5** : to attach to a support **6** : to prepare esp. for examination or display — **mount•able** *adj* — **mount•er** *n*

³mount *n* **1** : FRAME, SUPPORT **2** : a means of conveyance; *esp* : SADDLE HORSE

moun•tain \ˈmau̇nt-ᵊn\ *n* : a landmass higher than a hill — **moun•tain•ous** \-ᵊn-əs\ *adj* — **moun•tainy** \-ᵊn-ē\ *adj*

mountain ash *n* : any of various trees related to the roses that have pinnate leaves and red or orange-red fruits

mountain bike *n* : a bicycle with wide knobby tires, straight handlebars, and 18 or 21 gears that is designed to operate esp. over unpaved terrain

moun•tain•eer \ˌmau̇nt-ᵊn-ˈir\ *n* **1** : a native or inhabitant of a mountainous region **2** : one who climbs mountains for sport

mountain goat *n* : a ruminant mammal of mountainous northwestern No. America that resembles a goat

mountain goat

mountain laurel *n* : a No. American evergreen shrub or small tree of the heath family with glossy leaves and clusters of rose-colored or white flowers

mountain lion *n* : COUGAR

moun•tain•side \ˈmau̇nt-ᵊn-ˌsīd\ *n* : the side of a mountain

moun•tain•top \-ˌtäp\ *n* : the summit of a mountain

moun•te•bank \ˈmau̇n-ti-ˌbaŋk\ *n* [It *montimbanco,* fr. *montare* to mount + *in* in, on + *banco, banca* bench] : QUACK, CHARLATAN

Mount•ie \ˈmau̇n-tē\ *n* : a member of the Royal Canadian Mounted Police

mount•ing \ˈmau̇n-tiŋ\ *n* : something that serves as a frame or support

mourn \ˈmōrn\ *vb* : to feel or express grief or sorrow — **mourn•er** *n*

mourn•ful \-fəl\ *adj* : expressing, feeling, or causing sorrow — **mourn•ful•ly** *adv* — **mourn•ful•ness** *n*

mourn•ing \ˈmōr-niŋ\ *n* **1** : an outward sign (as black clothes) of grief for a person's death **2** : a period of time during which signs of grief are shown

mouse \ˈmau̇s\ *n, pl* **mice** \ˈmīs\ **1** : any of numerous small rodents with pointed snout, long body, and slender tail **2** : a small manual device that controls cursor movement on a computer display

mous•er \ˈmau̇-sər\ *n* : a cat proficient at catching mice

mouse•trap \ˈmau̇s-ˌtrap\ *n* **1** : a trap for catching mice **2** : a stratagem that lures one to defeat or destruction — **mousetrap** *vb*

mousse \ˈmüs\ *n* [F, lit., froth] **1** : a molded chilled dessert made with sweetened and flavored whipped cream or egg whites and gelatin **2** : a foamy preparation used in styling hair — **mousse** *vb*

mous•tache \ˈməs-ˌtash, (ˌ)məs-ˈtash\ *var of* MUSTACHE

mousy *or* **mous•ey** \ˈmau̇-sē, -zē\ *adj* **mous•i•er; -est 1** : QUIET, STEALTHY **2** : TIMID **3** : grayish brown — **mous•i•ness** \ˈmau̇-sē-nəs, -zē-\ *n*

¹mouth \ˈmau̇th\ *n, pl* **mouths** \ˈmau̇t͟hz, ˈmau̇ths\ **1** : the opening through which an animal takes in food; *also* : the cavity that encloses the tongue, lips, and teeth in the typical vertebrate **2** : something resembling a mouth (as in affording entrance) — **mouthed** \ˈmau̇t͟hd, ˈmau̇tht\ *adj* — **mouth•ful** *n*

²mouth \ˈmau̇t͟h\ *vb* **1** : SPEAK; *also* : DECLAIM **2** : to repeat without comprehension or sincerity **3** : to form soundlessly with the lips

mouth•part \ˈmau̇th-ˌpärt\ *n* : a structure or appendage near the mouth (as of an insect) esp. when adapted for eating

mouth•piece \-ˌpēs\ *n* **1** : a part (as of a musical instrument) that goes in the mouth or to which the mouth is applied **2** : SPOKESMAN

mouth•wash \-ˌwȯsh, -ˌwäsh\ *n* : a usu. antiseptic liquid preparation for cleaning the mouth and teeth

mou•ton \ˈmü-ˌtän\ *n* : processed sheepskin that has been sheared or dyed to resemble beaver or seal

¹move \ˈmüv\ *vb* **moved; mov•ing 1** : to change or cause to change position or posture **2** : to go or cause to go from one point to another; *also* : DEPART **3** : to take or cause to take action **4** : to show marked activity **5** : to stir the emotions **6** : to make a formal request, application, or appeal **7** : to change one's residence **8** : EVACUATE 2 — **mov•able** *or* **move•able** \ˈmü-və-bəl\ *adj*

²move *n* **1** : an act of moving **2** : a calculated step taken to gain an objective **3** : a change of location **4** : an agile action esp. in sports

move•ment \ˈmüv-mənt\ *n* **1** : the act or process of moving : MOVE **2** : a series of organized activities working toward an objective **3** : the moving parts of a mechanism (as of a watch) **4** : RHYTHM **5** : a section of an extended musical composition **6** : an act of voiding the bowels; *also* : STOOL 4

mov•er \ˈmü-vər\ *n* : one that moves; *esp* : one that moves the belongings of others from one location to another

mov•ie \ˈmü-vē\ *n* **1** : MOTION PICTURE **2** *pl* : a showing of a motion picture **3** *pl* : the motion-picture industry

¹mow \ˈmau̇\ *n* : the part of a barn where hay or straw is stored

²mow \ˈmō\ *vb* **mowed; mowed** *or* **mown** \ˈmōn\; **mow•ing 1** : to cut (as grass) with a scythe or machine **2** : to cut the standing herbage of ⟨~ the lawn⟩ — **mow•er** *n*

Mo•zam•bi•can \ˌmō-zəm-ˈbē-kən\ *n* : a native or inhabitant of Mozambique

moz•za•rel•la \ˌmät-sə-ˈre-lə\ *n* [It] : a moist white unsalted unripened mild cheese of a smooth rubbery texture

MP *abbr* **1** melting point **2** member of parliament **3** metropolitan police **4** military police; military policeman

mpg *abbr* miles per gallon

mph *abbr* miles per hour

Mr. \ˈmis-tər\ *n, pl* **Messrs.** \ˈme-sərz\ — used as a conventional title of courtesy before a man's surname or his title of office

MRI *abbr* magnetic resonance imaging

Mrs. \ˈmi-səz, -səs, *esp Southern* ˈmi-zəz, -zəs\ *n, pl* **Mes•dames** \mā-ˈdäm, -ˈdam\ — used as a conventional title of courtesy before a married woman's surname

Ms. \ˈmiz\ *n, pl* **Mss.** *or* **Mses.** \ˈmi-zez\ — used instead of *Miss* or *Mrs.*

MS *abbr* **1** manuscript **2** master of science **3** military science **4** Mississippi **5** motor ship **6** multiple sclerosis

msec *abbr* millisecond

msg *abbr* message

MSG *abbr* **1** master sergeant **2** monosodium glutamate

msgr *abbr* **1** monseigneur **2** monsignor

MSgt *abbr* master sergeant

MSS *abbr* manuscripts

MST *abbr* mountain standard time

mt *abbr* mount; mountain

Mt *abbr* Matthew

MT *abbr* **1** metric ton **2** Montana **3** mountain time

mtg *abbr* **1** meeting **2** mortgage

mtge *abbr* mortgage

mu \ˈmyü, ˈmü\ *n* : the 12th letter of the Greek alphabet — M or μ

[1]**much** \ˈməch\ *adj* **more** \ˈmōr\; **most** \ˈmōst\ : great in quantity, amount, extent, or degree ⟨~ money⟩

[2]**much** *adv* **more; most 1** : to a great degree or extent ⟨~ happier⟩ **2** : ALMOST, NEARLY ⟨looks ~ as he did before⟩

[3]**much** *n* **1** : a great quantity, amount, extent, or degree **2** : something considerable or impressive

mu•ci•lage \ˈmyü-sə-lij\ *n* : a watery sticky solution (as of a gum) used esp. as an adhesive — **mu•ci•lag•i•nous** \ˌmyü-sə-ˈla-jə-nəs\ *adj*

muck \ˈmək\ *n* **1** : soft moist barnyard manure **2** : FILTH, DIRT **3** : a dark richly organic soil; *also* : MUD, MIRE — **mucky** *adj*

muck•rake \-ˌrāk\ *vb* : to expose publicly real or apparent misconduct of a prominent individual or business — **muck•rak•er** *n*

mu•cus \ˈmyü-kəs\ *n* : a slimy slippery protective secretion of membranes (**mucous membranes**) lining some body cavities — **mu•cous** \-kəs\ *adj*

mud \ˈməd\ *n* : soft wet earth : MIRE — **mud•di•ly** \ˈmə-də-lē\ *adv* — **mud•di•ness** \-dē-nəs\ *n* — **muddy** \ˈmə-dē\ *adj or vb*

mud•dle \ˈməd-ᵊl\ *vb* **mud•dled; mud•dling 1** : to make muddy **2** : to confuse esp. with liquor **3** : to mix up or make a mess of **4** : to think or act in a confused way

mud•dle•head•ed \ˌməd-ᵊl-ˈhe-dəd\ *adj* **1** : mentally confused **2** : INEPT

mud•flat \ˈməd-ˌflat\ *n* : a level tract alternately covered and left bare by the tide

mud•guard \ˈməd-ˌgärd\ *n* : a guard over or a flap behind a wheel of a vehicle to catch or deflect mud

mud•room \-ˌrüm, -ˌru̇m\ *n* : a room in a house for removing dirty or wet footwear and clothing

mud•sling•er \-ˌsliŋ-ər\ *n* : one who uses invective esp. against a political opponent — **mud•sling•ing** \-ˌsliŋ-iŋ\ *n*

Muen•ster \ˈmən-stər, ˈmün-, ˈmu̇n-\ *n* : a semisoft bland cheese

mu•ez•zin \mü-ˈez-ᵊn, myü-\ *n* : a Muslim crier who calls the hour of daily prayer

[1]**muff** \ˈməf\ *n* : a warm tubular covering for the hands

[2]**muff** *n* : a bungling performance; *esp* : a failure to hold a ball in attempting a catch — **muff** *vb*

muf•fin \ˈmə-fən\ *n* : a small soft cake baked in a cup-shaped container

muf•fle \ˈmə-fəl\ *vb* **muf•fled; muf•fling 1** : to wrap up so as to conceal or protect **2** : to wrap or pad with something to dull the sound of **3** : to keep down : SUPPRESS

muf•fler \ˈmə-flər\ *n* **1** : a scarf worn around the neck **2** : a device (as on a car's exhaust) to deaden noise

muf•ti \ˈməf-tē\ *n* : civilian clothes

[1]**mug** \ˈməg\ *n* : a usu. metal or earthenware cylindrical drinking cup

[2]**mug** *vb* **mugged; mug•ging 1** : to pose or make faces esp. to attract attention or for a camera **2** : PHOTOGRAPH

[3]**mug** *vb* **mugged; mug•ging** : to assault usu. with intent to rob — **mug•ger** *n*

mug•gy \ˈmə-gē\ *adj* **mug•gi•er; -est** : being warm and humid — **mug•gi•ness** \-gē-nəs\ *n*

mug•wump \ˈməg-ˌwəmp\ *n* [obs. slang *mugwump* kingpin, fr. Massachuset (a No. American Indian language) *mugquomp* war leader] : an independent in politics

Mu•ham•mad•an \mō-ˈha-mə-dən, -ˈhä-; mü-\ *n* : MUSLIM — **Mu•ham•mad•an•ism** \-də-ˌni-zəm\ *n*

mu•ja•hid•een *or* **mu•ja•hed•in** \mü-ˌja-hi-ˈdēn, -ˌjä-\ *n pl* [Ar *mujāhidīn*, pl. of *mujāhid*, lit., person who wages jihad] : Islamic guerrilla fighters esp. in the Middle East

muk•luk \ˈmək-ˌlək\ *n* **1** : an Eskimo boot of sealskin or reindeer skin **2** : a boot with a soft leather sole worn over several pairs of socks

mu•lat•to \mu̇-ˈla-tō, myu̇-, -ˈlä-\ *n, pl* **-toes** *or* **-tos** [Sp *mulato*, fr. *mulo* mule, fr. L *mulus*] : a first-generation offspring of a black person and a white person; *also* : a person of mixed white and black ancestry

mul•ber•ry \ˈməl-ˌber-ē\ *n* : any of a genus of trees with edible berrylike fruit and leaves used as food for silkworms; *also* : the fruit

mulch \ˈməlch\ *n* : a protective covering (as of straw or leaves) spread on the ground esp. to reduce evaporation or control weeds — **mulch** *vb*

[1]**mulct** \ˈməlkt\ *n* : FINE, PENALTY

[2]**mulct** *vb* **1** : FINE **2** : CHEAT, DEFRAUD

[1]**mule** \ˈmyül\ *n* **1** : a hybrid offspring of a male donkey and a female horse **2** : a very stubborn person — **mul•ish** \ˈmyü-lish\ *adj* — **mul•ish•ly** *adv* — **mul•ish•ness** *n*

[2]**mule** *n* : a slipper whose upper does not extend around the heel of the foot

mule deer *n* : a long-eared deer of western No. America

mu•le•teer \ˌmyü-lə-ˈtir\ *n* : one who drives mules

[1]**mull** \ˈməl\ *vb* : PONDER, MEDITATE

[2]**mull** *vb* : to heat, sweeten, and flavor (as wine) with spices

mul•lein \ˈmə-lən\ *n* : a tall herb related to the snapdragons that has coarse woolly leaves and flowers in spikes

mul•let \ˈmə-lət\ *n, pl* **mullet** *or* **mullets** : any of a family of largely gray chiefly marine bony fishes including valuable food fishes

mul•li•gan stew \ˈmə-li-gən-\ *n* : a stew made from whatever ingredients are available

mul•li•ga•taw•ny \ˌmə-li-gə-ˈtȯ-nē\ *n* : a soup usu. of chicken stock seasoned with curry

mul•lion \ˈməl-yən\ *n* : a vertical strip separating windowpanes

multi- *comb form* **1** : many : multiple ⟨*multi*unit⟩ **2** : many times over ⟨*multi*millionaire⟩

mul•ti•col•ored \ˌməl-ti-ˈkə-lərd\ *adj* : having many colors

mul•ti•cul•tur•al \ˌməl-tē-ˈkəl-chə-rəl, -ˌtī-\ *adj* : of, relating to, reflecting, or adapted to diverse cultures ⟨a ~ society⟩

mul•ti•di•men•sion•al \-ti-də-ˈmen-chə-nəl, -ˌtī-, -dī-\ *adj* : of, relating to, or having many facets or dimensions ⟨a ~ problem⟩ ⟨~ space⟩

mul•ti•fac•et•ed \-ˈfa-sə-təd\ *adj* : having several distinct facets

mul•ti•fam•i•ly \-ˈfam-lē, -ˈfa-mə-\ *adj* : designed for use by several families

mul•ti•far•i•ous \ˌməl-tə-ˈfar-ē-əs\ *adj* : having great variety : DIVERSE — **mul•ti•far•i•ous•ness** *n*

mul•ti•form \ˈməl-ti-ˌfȯrm\ *adj* : having many forms or appearances — **mul•ti•for•mi•ty** \ˌməl-ti-ˈfȯr-mə-tē\ *n*

mul•ti•lat•er•al \ˌməl-ti-ˈla-tə-rəl, -ˌtī-, -ˈla-trəl\ *adj* : having many sides or participants ⟨~ treaty⟩ — **mul•ti•lat•er•al•ism** \-ˈla-tə-rə-ˌli-zəm\ *n*

mul•ti•lev•el \-ˈle-vəl\ *adj* : having several levels

mul•ti•lin•gual \-ˈliŋ-gwəl\ *adj* : knowing or using several languages — **mul•ti•lin•gual•ism** \-gwə-ˌli-zəm\ *n*

mul•ti•me•dia \-ˈmē-dē-ə\ *adj* : using, involving, or encompassing several media ⟨a ~ advertising campaign⟩

mul·ti·mil·lion·aire \ˌməl-ti-ˌmil-yə-ˈnar, -ˌtī-, -ˈmil-yə-ˌnar\ *n* : a person worth several million dollars

mul·ti·na·tion·al \-ˈna-shə-nəl\ *adj* **1** : of or relating to several nationalities **2** : relating to or involving several nations **3** : having divisions in several countries ⟨a ~ corporation⟩ — **multinational** *n*

[1]**mul·ti·ple** \ˈməl-tə-pəl\ *adj* **1** : more than one; *also* : MANY **2** : VARIOUS

[2]**multiple** *n* : the product of a quantity by an integer ⟨35 is a ~ of 7⟩

multiple–choice *adj* : having several answers given from which the correct one is to be chosen ⟨a ~ question⟩

multiple personality *n* : a mental and emotional disorder which is a neurosis and in which the personality becomes separated into two or more parts each of which controls behavior part of the time

multiple sclerosis *n* : a disease marked by patches of hardened tissue in the brain or spinal cord and associated esp. with partial or complete paralysis and muscular tremor

mul·ti·plex \ˈməl-tə-ˌpleks\ *n* : CINEPLEX

mul·ti·pli·cand \ˌməl-tə-pli-ˈkand\ *n* : the number that is to be multiplied by another

mul·ti·pli·ca·tion \ˌməl-tə-plə-ˈkā-shən\ *n* **1** : INCREASE **2** : a short method of finding the result of adding a figure the number of times indicated by another figure

multiplication sign *n* **1** : TIMES SIGN **2** : a centered dot indicating multiplication

mul·ti·plic·i·ty \ˌməl-tə-ˈpli-sə-tē\ *n, pl* **-ties** : a great number or variety

mul·ti·pli·er \ˈməl-tə-ˌplī-ər\ *n* : one that multiplies; *esp* : a number by which another number is multiplied

mul·ti·ply \ˈməl-tə-ˌplī\ *vb* **-plied; -ply·ing 1** : to increase in number (as by breeding) **2** : to find the product of by multiplication; *also* : to perform multiplication

mul·ti·pur·pose \ˌməl-ti-ˈpər-pəs, -ˌtī-\ *adj* : having or serving several purposes

mul·ti·ra·cial \-ˈrā-shəl\ *adj* : composed of, involving, or representing various races

mul·ti·sense \-ˌsens\ *adj* : having several meanings ⟨~ words⟩

mul·ti·sto·ry \-ˌstōr-ē\ *adj* : having several stories ⟨~ buildings⟩

mul·ti·tude \ˈməl-tə-ˌtüd, -ˌtyüd\ *n* : a great number — **mul·ti·tu·di·nous** \ˌməl-tə-ˈtüd-ᵊn-əs, -ˈtyüd-\ *adj*

mul·ti·unit \ˌməl-ti-ˈyü-nət, -ˌtī-\ *adj* : having several units

mul·ti·vi·ta·min \-ˈvī-tə-mən\ *adj* : containing several vitamins and esp. all known to be essential to health

[1]**mum** \ˈməm\ *adj* : SILENT

[2]**mum** *n* : CHRYSANTHEMUM

[3]**mum** *chiefly Brit var of* MOM

mum·ble \ˈməm-bəl\ *vb* **mum·bled; mum·bling** : to speak in a low indistinct manner — **mumble** *n* — **mum·bler** *n* — **mum·bly** *adj*

mum·ble·ty–peg \ˈməm-bəl-tē-ˌpeg\ *also* **mum·ble–the–peg** \ˈməm-bəl-t͟hə-\ *n* : a game in which the players try to flip a knife from various positions so that the blade will stick into the ground

mum·bo jum·bo \ˌməm-bō-ˈjəm-bō\ *n* **1** : a complicated ritual with elaborate trappings **2** : GIBBERISH, NONSENSE

mum·mer \ˈmə-mər\ *n* **1** : an actor esp. in a pantomime **2** : a person who goes merrymaking in disguise during festivals — **mum·mery** *n*

mum·my \ˈmə-mē\ *n, pl* **mummies** [ME *mummie* powdered parts of a mummified body used as a drug, fr. MF *momie*, fr. ML *mumia*, fr. Ar *mūmiyah* bitumen, mummy, fr. Per *mūm* wax] : a body embalmed for burial in the manner of the ancient Egyptians — **mum·mi·fi·ca·tion** \ˌmə-mi-fə-ˈkā-shən\ *n* — **mum·mi·fy** \ˈmə-mi-ˌfī\ *vb*

mumps \ˈməmps\ *n sing or pl* [fr. pl. of obs. *mump* grimace] : a virus disease marked by fever and swelling esp. of the salivary glands

mun *or* **munic** *abbr* municipal

munch \ˈmənch\ *vb* : to eat with a chewing action; *also* : to snack on

munch·ies \ˈmən-chēz\ *n pl* **1** : hunger pangs **2** : light snack foods

mun·dane \ˌmən-ˈdān, ˈmən-ˌdān\ *adj* **1** : of or relating to the world **2** : concerned with the practical details of everyday life — **mun·dane·ly** *adv*

mu·nic·i·pal \myu̇-ˈni-sə-pəl\ *adj* **1** : of, relating to, or characteristic of a municipality **2** : restricted to one locality — **mu·nic·i·pal·ly** *adv*

mu·nic·i·pal·i·ty \myu̇-ˌni-sə-ˈpa-lə-tē\ *n, pl* **-ties** : an urban political unit with corporate status and usu. powers of self-government

mu·nif·i·cent \myu̇-ˈni-fə-sənt\ *adj* : liberal in giving : GENEROUS — **mu·nif·i·cence** \-səns\ *n*

mu·ni·tion \myu̇-ˈni-shən\ *n* : ARMAMENT, AMMUNITION

[1]**mu·ral** \ˈmyu̇r-əl\ *adj* **1** : of or relating to a wall **2** : applied to and made part of a wall or ceiling surface

[2]**mural** *n* : a mural painting — **mu·ral·ist** *n*

[1]**mur·der** \ˈmər-dər\ *n* **1** : the crime of unlawfully killing a person esp. with malice aforethought **2** : something unusually difficult or dangerous

[2]**murder** *vb* **1** : to commit a murder; *also* : to kill brutally **2** : to put an end to **3** : to spoil by performing poorly ⟨~ a song⟩ — **mur·der·er** *n*

mur·der·ess \ˈmər-də-rəs\ *n* : a woman who murders

mur·der·ous \ˈmər-də-rəs\ *adj* **1** : having or appearing to have the purpose of murder **2** : marked by or causing murder or bloodshed ⟨~ gunfire⟩ — **mur·der·ous·ly** *adv*

murk \ˈmərk\ *n* : DARKNESS, GLOOM — **murk·i·ly** \ˈmər-kə-lē\ *adv* — **murk·i·ness** \-kē-nəs\ *n* — **murky** *adj*

mur·mur \ˈmər-mər\ *n* **1** : a muttered complaint **2** : a low indistinct often continuous sound — **murmur** *vb* — **mur·mur·er** *n* — **mur·mur·ous** *adj*

mus *abbr* **1** museum **2** music; musical; musician

mus·ca·tel \ˌməs-kə-ˈtel\ *n* : a sweet fortified wine

[1]**mus·cle** \ˈmə-səl\ *n* [ME, fr. MF, fr. L *musculus*, fr. dim. of *mus* mouse] **1** : a body tissue consisting of long cells that contract when stimulated and produce motion; *also* : an organ consisting of this tissue and functioning in moving a body part **2** : STRENGTH, BRAWN — **mus·cled** \ˈmə-səld\ *adj* — **mus·cu·lar** \ˈməs-kyə-lər\ *adj* — **mus·cu·lar·i·ty** \ˌməs-kyə-ˈlar-ə-tē\ *n*

[2]**muscle** *vb* **mus·cled; mus·cling** : to force one's way

mus·cle–bound \ˈmə-səl-ˌbau̇nd\ *adj* : having some of the muscles abnormally enlarged and lacking in elasticity (as from excessive exercise)

muscular dystrophy *n* : any of a group of diseases characterized by progressive wasting of muscles

mus·cu·la·ture \ˈməs-kyə-lə-ˌchu̇r\ *n* : the muscles of the body or its parts

[1]**muse** \ˈmyüz\ *vb* **mused; mus·ing** [ME, fr. MF *muser* to gape, idle, muse, fr. *muse* mouth of an animal, fr. ML *musus*] : to become absorbed in thought — **mus·ing·ly** *adv*

[2]**muse** *n* [fr. *Muse* any of the nine sister goddesses of learning and the arts in Greek myth, fr. ME, fr. MF, fr. L *Musa*, fr. Gk *Mousa*] : a source of inspiration

mu·se·um \myu̇-ˈzē-əm\ *n* : an institution devoted to the procurement, care, and display of objects of lasting interest or value

[1]**mush** \ˈməsh\ *n* **1** : cornmeal boiled in water **2** : sentimental drivel

[2]**mush** *vb* : to travel esp. over snow with a sled drawn by dogs

[1]**mush·room** \ˈməsh-ˌrüm, -ˌru̇m\ *n* : the fleshy usu.

caplike spore-bearing organ of various fungi esp. when edible; *also* : such a fungus

[2]**mushroom** *vb* **1** : to collect wild mushrooms **2** : to spread out : EXPAND **3** : to grow rapidly

mushy \ˈmə-shē\ *adj* **mush·i·er; -est 1** : soft like mush **2** : excessively sentimental

mu·sic \ˈmyü-zik\ *n* **1** : the science or art of combining tones into a composition having structure and continuity; *also* : vocal or instrumental sounds having rhythm, melody, or harmony **2** : an agreeable sound

[1]**mu·si·cal** \ˈmyü-zi-kəl\ *adj* **1** : of or relating to music or musicians **2** : having the pleasing tonal qualities of music **3** : fond of or gifted in music — **mu·si·cal·ly** \-k(ə-)lē\ *adv*

[2]**musical** *n* : a film or theatrical production consisting of musical numbers and dialogue based on a unifying plot

mu·si·cale \ˌmyü-zi-ˈkal\ *n* : a usu. private social gathering featuring music

mu·si·cian \myü-ˈzi-shən\ *n* : a composer, conductor, or performer of music — **mu·si·cian·ly** *adj* — **mu·si·cian·ship** *n*

mu·si·col·o·gy \ˌmyü-zi-ˈkä-lə-jē\ *n* : the study of music as a field of knowledge or research — **mu·si·co·log·i·cal** \-kə-ˈlä-ji-kəl\ *adj* — **mu·si·col·o·gist** \-ˈkä-lə-jist\ *n*

musk \ˈməsk\ *n* : a substance obtained esp. from a small Asian deer **(musk deer)** and used as a perfume fixative — **musk·i·ness** \ˈməs-kē-nəs\ *n* — **musky** *adj*

mus·keg \ˈməs-ˌkeg\ *n* : BOG; *esp* : a mossy bog in northern No. America

mus·kel·lunge \ˈməs-kə-ˌlənj\ *n, pl* **muskellunge** : a large No. American pike that is a valuable sport fish

mus·ket \ˈməs-kət\ *n* [MF *mousquet,* fr. It *moschetto* arrow for a crossbow, musket, fr. dim. of *mosca* fly, fr. L *musca*] : a heavy large-caliber muzzle-loading shoulder firearm — **mus·ke·teer** \ˌməs-kə-ˈtir\ *n*

mus·ket·ry \ˈməs-kə-trē\ *n* **1** : MUSKETS **2** : MUSKETEERS **3** : musket fire

musk·mel·on \ˈməsk-ˌme-lən\ *n* : a small round to oval melon that has usu. a sweet edible green or orange flesh

musk ox *n* : a heavyset shaggy-coated wild ox of Greenland and the arctic tundra of northern No. America

musk·rat \ˈməs-ˌkrat\ *n, pl* **muskrat** *or* **muskrats** : a large No. American aquatic rodent with webbed feet and dark brown fur; *also* : its fur

Mus·lim \ˈməz-ləm\ *n* : an adherent of Islam — **Muslim** *adj*

mus·lin \ˈməz-lən\ *n* : a plain-woven sheer to coarse cotton fabric

[1]**muss** \ˈməs\ *n* : a state of disorder — **muss·i·ly** \ˈmə-sə-lē\ *adv* — **muss·i·ness** \-sē-nəs\ *n* — **mussy** *adj*

[2]**muss** *vb* : to make untidy : DISARRANGE

mus·sel \ˈmə-səl\ *n* **1** : a dark edible saltwater bivalve mollusk **2** : any of various freshwater bivalve mollusks of the central U.S. having shells with a pearly lining

[1]**must** \ˈməst\ *vb* — used as an auxiliary esp. to express a command, requirement, obligation, or necessity

[2]**must** *n* **1** : an imperative duty **2** : an indispensable item

mus·tache \ˈməs-ˌtash, (ˌ)məs-ˈtash\ *n* : the hair growing on the human upper lip — **mus·tached** \-ˌtasht, -ˈtasht\ *adj*

mus·tang \ˈməs-ˌtaŋ\ *n* [MexSp *mestengo,* fr. Sp, stray, fr. *mesteño* strayed, fr. *mesta* annual roundup of cattle that disposed of strays, fr. ML *(animalia) mixta* mixed animals] : a small hardy naturalized horse of the western plains of America; *also* : BRONC

mus·tard \ˈməs-tərd\ *n* **1** : a pungent yellow powder of the seeds of an herb related to the cabbage and used as a condiment or in medicine **2** : a plant that yields mustard; *also* : a closely related plant — **mustardy** *adj*

mustard gas *n* : a poison gas used in warfare that has violent irritating and blistering effects

[1]**mus·ter** \ˈməs-tər\ *n* **1** : an act of assembling (as for military inspection); *also* : critical examination **2** : an assembled group

[2]**muster** *vb* [ME *mustren* to show, muster, fr. OF *monstrer,* fr. L *monstrare* to show, fr. *monstrum* evil omen, monster] **1** : CONVENE, ASSEMBLE; *also* : to call the roll of **2** : ACCUMULATE **3** : to call forth : ROUSE **4** : to amount to : COMPRISE

muster out *vb* : to discharge from military service

musty \ˈməs-tē\ *adj* **mus·ti·er; -est** : MOLDY, STALE; *also* : tasting or smelling of damp or decay — **must·i·ly** \-tə-lē\ *adv* — **must·i·ness** \-tē-nəs\ *n*

mu·ta·ble \ˈmyü-tə-bəl\ *adj* **1** : prone to change : FICKLE **2** : capable of or liable to mutation : VARIABLE — **mu·ta·bil·i·ty** \ˌmyü-tə-ˈbi-lə-tē\ *n*

mu·tant \ˈmyüt-ᵊnt\ *adj* : of, relating to, or produced by mutation — **mu·tant** *n*

mu·tate \ˈmyü-ˌtāt\ *vb* **mu·tat·ed; mu·tat·ing** : to undergo or cause to undergo mutation — **mu·ta·tive** \ˈmyü-ˌtā-tiv, -tə-tiv\ *adj*

mu·ta·tion \myü-ˈtā-shən\ *n* **1** : CHANGE **2** : an inherited physical or biochemical change in genetic material; *also* : the process of producing a mutation **3** : an individual, strain, or trait resulting from mutation — **mu·ta·tion·al** *adj*

[1]**mute** \ˈmyüt\ *adj* **mut·er; mut·est 1** : unable to speak : DUMB **2** : SILENT — **mute·ly** *adv* — **mute·ness** *n*

[2]**mute** *n* **1** : a person who cannot or does not speak **2** : a device on a musical instrument that reduces, softens, or muffles the tone

[3]**mute** *vb* **mut·ed; mut·ing** : to muffle, reduce, or eliminate the sound of

mu·ti·late \ˈmyüt-ᵊl-ˌāt\ *vb* **-lat·ed; -lat·ing 1** : to cut up or alter radically so as to make imperfect **2** : MAIM, CRIPPLE — **mu·ti·la·tion** \ˌmyüt-ᵊl-ˈā-shən\ *n* — **mu·ti·la·tor** \ˈmyüt-ᵊl-ˌā-tər\ *n*

mu·ti·ny \ˈmyü-tə-nē\ *n, pl* **-nies** : willful refusal to obey constituted authority; *esp* : revolt against a superior officer — **mu·ti·neer** \ˌmyüt-ᵊn-ˈir\ *n* — **mu·ti·nous** \ˈmyüt-ᵊn-əs\ *adj* — **mu·ti·nous·ly** *adv* — **mutiny** *vb*

mutt \ˈmət\ *n* : MONGREL, CUR

mut·ter \ˈmə-tər\ *vb* **1** : to speak indistinctly or with a low voice and lips partly closed **2** : GRUMBLE — **mutter** *n*

mut·ton \ˈmət-ᵊn\ *n* [ME *motoun,* fr. OF *moton* ram] : the flesh of a mature sheep used for food — **muttony** *adj*

mut·ton·chops \ˈmət-ᵊn-ˌchäps\ *n pl* : whiskers on the side of the face that are narrow at the temple and broad and round by the lower jaws

mu·tu·al \ˈmyü-chə-wəl\ *adj* **1** : given and received in equal amount ⟨~ trust⟩ **2** : having the same feelings one for the other ⟨~ enemies⟩ **3** : COMMON, JOINT ⟨a ~ friend⟩ — **mu·tu·al·ly** *adv*

mutual fund *n* : an investment company that invests money of its shareholders in a usu. diversified group of securities of other corporations

muu·muu \ˈmü-ˌmü\ *n* : a loose dress of Hawaiian origin

[1]**muz·zle** \ˈmə-zəl\ *n* **1** : the nose and jaws of an animal; *also* : a covering for the muzzle to prevent biting or eating **2** : the mouth of a gun

[2]**muzzle** *vb* **muz·zled; muz·zling 1** : to put a muzzle on **2** : to restrain from expression : GAG

mV *abbr* millivolt

MV *abbr* motor vessel

MVP *abbr* most valuable player

MW *abbr* megawatt

my \ˈmī\ *adj* **1** : of or relating to me or myself **2** — used interjectionally esp. to express surprise

my·col·o·gy \mī-ˈkä-lə-jē\ *n* : a branch of biology deal-

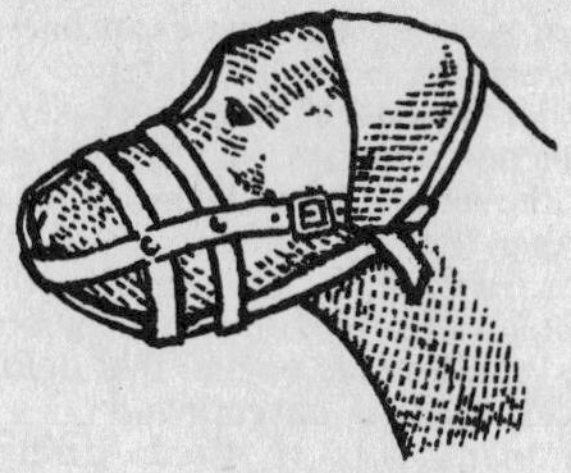

muzzle 1

ing with fungi — **my•co•log•i•cal** \ˌmī-kə-ˈlä-ji-kəl\ *adj* — **my•col•o•gist** \mī-ˈkä-lə-jist\ *n*

my•elo•ma \ˌmī-ə-ˈlō-mə\ *n, pl* **-mas** *or* **-ma•ta** \-mə-tə\ : a primary tumor of the bone marrow

my•nah *or* **my•na** \ˈmī-nə\ *n* : any of several Asian starlings; *esp* : a dark brown slightly crested bird sometimes taught to mimic speech

my•o•pia \mī-ˈō-pē-ə\ *n* : a condition in which visual images come to a focus in front of the retina resulting esp. in defective vision of distant objects — **my•o•pic** \-ˈō-pik, -ˈä-\ *adj* — **my•o•pi•cal•ly** \-pi-k(ə-)lē\ *adv*

¹myr•i•ad \ˈmir-ē-əd\ *n* [Gk *myriad-, myrias,* fr. *myrioi* countless, ten thousand] : an indefinitely large number

²myriad *adj* : consisting of a very great but indefinite number

myr•mi•don \ˈmər-mə-ˌdän\ *n* : a loyal follower; *esp* : one who executes orders without protest or pity

myrrh \ˈmər\ *n* : a fragrant aromatic plant gum used in perfumes and formerly for incense

myr•tle \ˈmərt-ᵊl\ *n* : an evergreen shrub of southern Europe with shiny leaves, fragrant flowers, and black berries; *also* : PERIWINKLE

my•self \mī-ˈself, mə-\ *pron* : I, ME — used reflexively, for emphasis, or in absolute constructions ⟨I hurt ~⟩ ⟨I ~ did it⟩ ⟨~ busy, I sent him instead⟩

mys•tery \ˈmis-tə-rē\ *n, pl* **-ter•ies 1** : a religious truth known by revelation alone **2** : something not understood or beyond understanding **3** : enigmatic quality or character **4** : a work of fiction dealing with the solution of a mysterious crime — **mys•te•ri•ous** \mis-ˈtir-ē-əs\ *adj* — **mys•te•ri•ous•ly** *adv* — **mys•te•ri•ous•ness** *n*

¹mys•tic \ˈmis-tik\ *adj* **1** : of or relating to mystics or mysticism **2** : MYSTERIOUS; *also* : MYSTIFYING

²mystic *n* : a person who follows, advocates, or experiences mysticism

mys•ti•cal \ˈmis-ti-kəl\ *adj* **1** : SPIRITUAL, SYMBOLIC **2** : of or relating to an intimate knowledge of or direct communion with God (as through contemplation or visions)

mys•ti•cism \ˈmis-tə-ˌsi-zəm\ *n* : the belief that direct knowledge of God or ultimate reality is attainable through immediate intuition or insight

mys•ti•fy \ˈmis-tə-ˌfī\ *vb* **-fied; -fy•ing 1** : to perplex the mind of **2** : to make mysterious — **mys•ti•fi•ca•tion** \ˌmis-tə-fə-ˈkā-shən\ *n*

mys•tique \mi-ˈstēk\ *n* [F] **1** : an air or attitude of mystery and reverence developing around something or someone **2** : the special esoteric skill essential in a calling or activity

myth \ˈmith\ *n* **1** : a usu. legendary narrative that presents part of the beliefs of a people or explains a practice or natural phenomenon **2** : an imaginary or unverifiable person or thing — **myth•i•cal** \ˈmi-thi-kəl\ *adj*

my•thol•o•gy \mi-ˈthä-lə-jē\ *n, pl* **-gies** : a body of myths and esp. of those dealing with the gods and heroes of a people — **myth•o•log•i•cal** \ˌmi-thə-ˈlä-ji-kəl\ *adj* — **my•thol•o•gist** \mi-ˈthä-lə-jist\ *n*

N

¹n \ˈen\ *n, pl* **n's** *or* **ns** \ˈenz\ *often cap* **1** : the 14th letter of the English alphabet **2** : an unspecified quantity

²n *abbr, often cap* **1** net **2** neuter **3** noon **4** normal **5** north; northern **6** note **7** noun **8** number

N *symbol* nitrogen

-n — see -EN

Na *symbol* [NL *natrium*] sodium

NA *abbr* **1** no account **2** North America **3** not applicable **4** not available

NAACP \ˌen-ˌdə-bəl-ˌā-ˌsē-ˈpē, ˌen-ˌā-ˌā-ˌsē-\ *abbr* National Association for the Advancement of Colored People

nab \ˈnab\ *vb* **nabbed; nab•bing** : SEIZE; *esp* : ARREST

NAB *abbr* New American Bible

na•bob \ˈnā-ˌbäb\ *n* [Urdu *nawwāb,* provincial governor (in the Mogul empire), fr. Ar *nuwwāb,* pl. of *nā'ib* governor] : a man of great wealth or prominence

na•celle \nə-ˈsel\ *n* : an enclosure (as for an engine) on an aircraft

na•cho \ˈnä-chō\ *n, pl* **nachos** [AmerSp] : a tortilla chip topped with melted cheese and often additional savory toppings

na•cre \ˈnā-kər\ *n* : MOTHER-OF-PEARL

na•dir \ˈnā-ˌdir, -dər\ *n* [ME, fr. MF, fr. Ar *naẓīr* opposite] **1** : the point of the celestial sphere that is directly opposite the zenith and directly beneath the observer **2** : the lowest point

¹nag \ˈnag\ *n* : HORSE; *esp* : an old or decrepit horse

²nag *vb* **nagged; nag•ging 1** : to find fault incessantly : COMPLAIN **2** : to irritate by constant scolding or urging **3** : to be a continuing source of annoyance ⟨a *nagging* backache⟩

³nag *n* : one who nags habitually

Nah *abbr* Nahum

Na•huatl \ˈnä-ˌwät-ᵊl\ *n* : a group of American Indian languages of central and southern Mexico

Na•hum \ˈnā-həm, -əm\ *n* — see BIBLE table

NAIA *abbr* National Association of Intercollegiate Athletes

na•iad \ˈnā-əd, ˈnī-, -ˌad\ *n, pl* **naiads** *or* **na•ia•des** \-ə-ˌdēz\ **1** : one of the nymphs in ancient mythology living in lakes, rivers, springs, and fountains **2** : an aquatic young of some insects (as a dragonfly)

¹na•ïf *or* **na•if** \nä-ˈēf\ *adj* : NAIVE

²naïf *or* **naif** *n* : a naive person

¹nail \ˈnāl\ *n* **1** : a horny sheath protecting the end of each finger and toe in humans and related primates **2** : a slender pointed fastener with a head designed to be pounded in

²nail *vb* : to fasten with or as if with a nail — **nail•er** *n*

nail down *vb* : to settle or establish clearly and unmistakably

nain•sook \ˈnān-ˌsu̇k\ *n* [Hindi *nainsukh,* fr. *nain* eye + *sukh* delight] : a soft lightweight muslin

nai•ra \ˈnī-rə\ *n* — see MONEY table

na•ive *or* **na•ïve** \nä-ˈēv\ *adj* **na•iv•er; -est** [F *naïve,* fem. of *naïf,* fr. OF, inborn, natural, fr. L *nativus* native] **1** : marked by unaffected simplicity : ARTLESS, INGENUOUS **2** : CREDULOUS **syn** natural, innocent, simple, unaffected, unsophisticated, unstudied — **na•ive•ly** *adv* — **na•ive•ness** *n*

na•ive•té *also* **na•ïve•té** *or* **na•ive•te** \ˌnä-ˌē-və-ˈtā, nä-ˈē-və-ˌtā\ *n* **1** : a naive remark or action **2** : the quality or state of being naive

na•ive•ty *also* **na•ïve•ty** \nä-ˈē-və-tē\ *n, pl* **-ties** : NAÏVETÉ

na•ked \ˈnā-kəd\ *adj* **1** : having no clothes on : NUDE **2** : UNSHEATHED ⟨a ~ sword⟩ **3** : lacking a usual or natural covering (as of foliage or feathers) **4** : PLAIN, UNADORNED ⟨the ~ truth⟩ **5** : not aided by artificial means ⟨seen by the ~ eye⟩ — **na•ked•ly** *adv* — **na•ked•ness** *n*

nam•by–pam•by \ˌnam-bē-ˈpam-bē\ *adj* **1** : INSIPID **2** : WEAK, INDECISIVE **syn** bland, flat, inane, jejune, vapid, wishy-washy

[1]**name** \ˈnām\ *n* **1** : a word or words by which a person or thing is known **2** : a disparaging epithet ⟨call him ~*s*⟩ **3** : REPUTATION; *esp* : distinguished reputation ⟨made a ~ for herself⟩ **4** : FAMILY, CLAN ⟨was a disgrace to their ~⟩ **5** : appearance as opposed to reality ⟨a friend in ~ only⟩

[2]**name** *vb* **named; nam•ing 1** : to give a name to : CALL **2** : to mention or identify by name **3** : NOMINATE, APPOINT **4** : to decide on : CHOOSE **5** : to mention explicitly : SPECIFY ⟨~ a price⟩ — **name•able** *adj*

[3]**name** *adj* **1** : of, relating to, or bearing a name ⟨~ tag⟩ **2** : having an established reputation ⟨~ brands⟩

name day *n* : the church feast day of the saint after whom one is named

name•less \ˈnām-ləs\ *adj* **1** : having no name **2** : not marked with a name ⟨a ~ grave⟩ **3** : not known by name ⟨a ~ hero⟩ **4** : too distressing to be described ⟨~ fears⟩ — **name•less•ly** *adv*

name•ly \-lē\ *adv* : that is to say : AS ⟨the cat family, ~, lions, tigers, and similar animals⟩

name•plate \-ˌplāt\ *n* : a plate or plaque bearing a name (as of a resident)

name•sake \-ˌsāk\ *n* : one that has the same name as another; *esp* : one named after another

Na•mib•i•an \nə-ˈmi-bē-ən, -byən\ *n* : a native or inhabitant of Namibia — **Namibian** *adj*

nan•keen \nan-ˈkēn\ *n* : a durable brownish yellow cotton fabric orig. woven by hand in China

nan•ny goat \ˈna-nē-\ *n* : a female domestic goat

nano•me•ter \ˈna-nə-ˌmē-tər\ *n* : one billionth of a meter

nano•sec•ond \-ˌse-kənd\ *n* : one billionth of a second

[1]**nap** \ˈnap\ *vb* **napped; nap•ping 1** : to sleep briefly esp. during the day : DOZE **2** : to be off guard ⟨was caught *napping*⟩

[2]**nap** *n* : a short sleep esp. during the day

[3]**nap** *n* : a soft downy fibrous surface (as on yarn and cloth) — **nap•less** *adj* — **napped** \ˈnapt\ *adj*

na•palm \ˈnā-ˌpälm, -ˌpäm\ *n* [*na*phthalene + *palm*itate, salt of a fatty acid] **1** : a thickener used in jelling gasoline (as for incendiary bombs) **2** : fuel jelled with napalm

nape \ˈnāp, ˈnap\ *n* : the back of the neck

na•pery \ˈnā-pə-rē\ *n* : household linen esp. for the table

naph•tha \ˈnaf-thə, ˈnap-\ *n* : any of various liquid hydrocarbon mixtures used chiefly as solvents

naph•tha•lene \-ˌlēn\ *n* : a crystalline substance used esp. in organic synthesis and as a moth repellent

nap•kin \ˈnap-kən\ *n* **1** : a piece of material (as cloth) used at table to wipe the lips or fingers and protect the clothes **2** : a small cloth or towel

na•po•leon \nə-ˈpōl-yən, -ˈpō-lē-ən\ *n* : an oblong pastry with a filling of cream, custard, or jelly

Na•po•le•on•ic \nə-ˌpō-lē-ˈä-nik\ *adj* : of, relating to, or characteristic of Napoleon I or his family

narc *also* **nark** \ˈnärk\ *n, slang* : a person (as a government agent) who investigates narcotics violations

nar•cis•sism \ˈnär-sə-ˌsi-zəm\ *n* [G *Narzissismus,* fr. *Narziss* Narcissus, beautiful youth of Greek mythology who fell in love with his own image] **1** : undue dwelling on one's own self or attainments **2** : love of or sexual desire for one's own body — **nar•cis•sist** \-sist\ *n or adj* — **nar•cis•sis•tic** \ˌnär-sə-ˈsis-tik\ *adj*

nar•cis•sus \när-ˈsi-səs\ *n, pl* **-cis•sus** *or* **-cis•sus•es** *or* **-cis•si** \-ˌsī, -ˌsē\ : DAFFODIL; *esp* : one with short-tubed flowers usu. borne separately

nar•co•sis \när-ˈkō-səs\ *n, pl* **-co•ses** \-ˌsēz\ : a state of stupor, unconsciousness, or arrested activity produced by the influence of chemicals (as narcotics)

nar•cot•ic \när-ˈkä-tik\ *n* [ME *narkotik,* fr. MF *narcotique,* fr. *narcotique,* adj., fr. ML *narcoticus,* fr. Gk *narkōtikos,* fr. *narkoun* to benumb, fr. *narkē* numbness] : a drug (as opium) that dulls the senses and induces sleep — **narcotic** *adj*

nar•co•tize \ˈnär-kə-ˌtīz\ *vb* **-tized; -tiz•ing 1** : to treat with or subject to a narcotic; *also* : to put into a state of narcosis **2** : to soothe to unconsciousness or unawareness

nard \ˈnärd\ *n* : a fragrant ointment of the ancients

na•res \ˈnar-(ˌ)ēz\ *n pl* [L] : the pair of openings of the nose

Nar•ra•gan•set \ˌnar-ə-ˈgan-sət\ *n, pl* **Narraganset** *or* **Narragansets** : a member of an American Indian people of Rhode Island

nar•rate \ˈnar-ˌāt\ *vb* **nar•rat•ed; nar•rat•ing** : to recite the details of (as a story) : RELATE, TELL — **nar•ra•tion** \na-ˈrā-shən\ *n* — **nar•ra•tor** \ˈnar-ˌā-tər\ *n*

nar•ra•tive \ˈnar-ə-tiv\ *n* **1** : something that is narrated : STORY **2** : the art or practice of narrating

[1]**nar•row** \ˈnar-ō\ *adj* **1** : of slender or less than standard width **2** : limited in size or scope : RESTRICTED **3** : not liberal in views : PREJUDICED **4** : interpreted or interpreting strictly **5** : CLOSE ⟨won by a ~ margin⟩; *also* : barely successful ⟨a ~ escape⟩ — **nar•row•ly** *adv* — **nar•row•ness** *n*

[2]**narrow** *n* : a narrow passage : STRAIT — usu. used in pl.

[3]**narrow** *vb* : to lessen in width or extent

nar•row–mind•ed \ˌnar-ō-ˈmīn-dəd\ *adj* : not liberal or broad-minded **syn** illiberal, bigoted, hidebound, intolerant

nar•whal \ˈnär-ˌhwäl, ˈnär-wəl\ *n* : an arctic sea mammal about 20 feet (6 meters) long that is related to the dolphins and in the male has a long twisted ivory tusk

narwhal

NAS *abbr* naval air station

NASA \ˈna-sə\ *abbr* National Aeronautics and Space Administration

[1]**na•sal** \ˈnā-zəl\ *n* **1** : a nasal part **2** : a nasal consonant or vowel

[2]**nasal** *adj* **1** : of or relating to the nose **2** : uttered through the nose — **na•sal•ly** *adv*

na•sal•ize \ˈnā-zə-ˌlīz\ *vb* **-ized; -iz•ing** : to make nasal or pronounce as a nasal sound — **na•sal•i•za•tion** \ˌnā-zə-lə-ˈzā-shən\ *n*

na•scent \ˈnas-ᵊnt, ˈnās-\ *adj* : coming into existence : beginning to grow or develop — **na•scence** \-ᵊns\ *n*

nas•tur•tium \nə-ˈstər-shəm, na-\ *n* : either of two widely cultivated watery-stemmed herbs with showy spurred flowers and pungent seeds

nas•ty \ˈnas-tē\ *adj* **nas•ti•er; -est 1** : FILTHY **2** : INDECENT, OBSCENE **3** : HARMFUL, DANGEROUS ⟨took a ~ fall⟩ **4** : DISAGREEABLE ⟨~ weather⟩ **5** : MEAN, ILL-NATURED ⟨a ~ temper⟩ **6** : DIFFICULT, VEXATIOUS ⟨a ~ problem⟩ **7** : UNFAIR, DIRTY ⟨a ~ trick⟩ — **nas•ti•ly** \ˈnas-tə-lē\ *adv* — **nas•ti•ness** \-tē-nəs\ *n*

nat *abbr* **1** national **2** native **3** natural

na•tal \ˈnāt-ᵊl\ *adj* **1** : NATIVE **2** : of, relating to, or present at birth

na•ta•to•ri•um \ˌnā-tə-ˈtōr-ē-əm, ˌna-\ *n* : a swimming pool esp. indoors

na•tion \ˈnā-shən\ *n* [ME *nacioun,* fr. MF *nation,* fr. L *nation-, natio* birth, race, nation, fr. *nasci* to be born] **1 :** NATIONALITY 5; *also* : a politically organized nationality **2 :** a community of people composed of one or more nationalities with its own territory and government **3 :** the territory of a nation **4 :** a federation of tribes (as of American Indians) — **na•tion•hood** *n*

[1]**na•tion•al** \ˈna-shə-nəl\ *adj* **1 :** of or relating to a nation **2 :** comprising or characteristic of a nationality **3 :** FEDERAL 3 — **na•tion•al•ly** *adv*

[2]**national** *n* **1 :** one who owes allegiance to a nation **2 :** a competition that is national in scope — usu. used in pl.

National Guard *n* **1 :** a militia force recruited by each state of the U.S., equipped by the federal government, and jointly maintained subject to the call of either **2** *often not cap* : a military force serving as a national constabulary and defense force

na•tion•al•ise *chiefly Brit var of* NATIONALIZE

na•tion•al•ism \ˈna-shə-nə-ˌli-zəm\ *n* : devotion to national interests, unity, and independence

na•tion•al•ist \-list\ *n* **1 :** an advocate of or believer in nationalism **2** *cap* : a member of a political party or group advocating national independence or strong national government — **nationalist** *adj, often cap* — **na•tion•al•is•tic** \ˌna-shə-nə-ˈlis-tik\ *adj*

na•tion•al•i•ty \ˌna-shə-ˈna-lə-tē\ *n, pl* **-ties 1 :** national character **2 :** a legal relationship involving allegiance of an individual and protection on the part of the state **3 :** membership in a particular nation **4 :** political independence or existence as a separate nation **5 :** a people having a common origin, tradition, and language and capable of forming a state **6 :** an ethnic group within a larger unit (as a nation)

na•tion•al•ize \ˈna-shə-nə-ˌlīz\ *vb* **-ized; -iz•ing 1 :** to make national : make a nation of **2 :** to remove from private ownership and place under government control — **na•tion•al•i•za•tion** \ˌna-shə-nə-lə-ˈzā-shən\ *n*

national monument *n* : a place of historic, scenic, or scientific interest set aside for preservation usu. by presidential proclamation

national park *n* : an area of special scenic, historical, or scientific importance set aside and maintained by a national government esp. for recreation or study

national seashore *n* : a recreational area adjacent to a seacoast and maintained by the federal government

na•tion•wide \ˌnā-shən-ˈwīd\ *adj* : extending throughout a nation

[1]**na•tive** \ˈnā-tiv\ *adj* **1 :** INBORN, NATURAL **2 :** born in a particular place or country **3 :** belonging to a person because of the place or circumstances of birth ⟨her ~ language⟩ **4 :** grown, produced, or originating in a particular place : INDIGENOUS **syn** aboriginal, autochthonous, endemic

[2]**native** *n* : one that is native; *esp* : a person who belongs to a particular country by birth

Native American *n* : AMERICAN INDIAN

na•tiv•ism \ˈnā-ti-ˌvi-zəm\ *n* **1 :** a policy of favoring native inhabitants over immigrants **2 :** the revival or perpetuation of a native culture esp. in opposition to acculturation

na•tiv•i•ty \nə-ˈti-və-tē, nā-\ *n, pl* **-ties 1 :** the process or circumstances of being born : BIRTH **2** *cap* : the birth of Christ

natl *abbr* national

NATO \ˈnā-(ˌ)tō\ *abbr* North Atlantic Treaty Organization

nat•ty \ˈna-tē\ *adj* **nat•ti•er; -est :** trimly neat and tidy : SMART — **nat•ti•ly** \-tə-lē\ *adv* — **nat•ti•ness** \-tē-nəs\ *n*

[1]**nat•u•ral** \ˈna-chə-rəl\ *adj* **1 :** determined by nature : INBORN, INNATE ⟨~ ability⟩ **2 :** BORN ⟨a ~ fool⟩ **3 :** ILLEGITIMATE **4 :** HUMAN **5 :** of or relating to nature **6 :** not artificial **7 :** being simple and sincere : not affected **8 :** LIFELIKE **9 :** being neither sharp nor flat **syn** ingenuous, naive, unsophisticated, artless, guileless — **nat•u•ral•ness** *n*

[2]**natural** *n* **1 :** IDIOT **2 :** a character placed on a line or space of the musical staff to nullify the effect of a preceding sharp or flat **3 :** one obviously suitable for a purpose **4 :** AFRO

natural childbirth *n* : a system of managing childbirth in which the mother prepares to remain conscious and assist in delivery with little or no use of drugs

natural gas *n* : a combustible gaseous mixture of hydrocarbons coming from the earth's crust and used chiefly as a fuel and raw material

natural history *n* **1 :** a treatise on some aspect of nature **2 :** the study of natural objects esp. from an amateur or popular point of view

nat•u•ral•ise *Brit var of* NATURALIZE

nat•u•ral•ism \ˈna-chə-rə-ˌli-zəm\ *n* **1 :** action or thought based only on natural desires and instincts **2 :** a doctrine that denies a supernatural explanation of the origin or development of the universe and holds that scientific laws account for all of nature **3 :** realism in art and literature — **nat•u•ral•is•tic** \ˌna-chə-rə-ˈlis-tik\ *adj*

nat•u•ral•ist \-list\ *n* **1 :** one that advocates or practices naturalism **2 :** a student of animals or plants esp. in the field

nat•u•ral•ize \-ˌlīz\ *vb* **-ized; -iz•ing 1 :** to become or cause to become established as if native ⟨~ new forage crops⟩ **2 :** to confer the rights of a citizen on — **nat•u•ral•iza•tion** \ˌna-chə-rə-lə-ˈzā-shən\ *n*

nat•u•ral•ly \ˈna-chə-rə-lē, ˈnach-rə-\ *adv* **1 :** by nature : by natural character or ability **2 :** as might be expected **3 :** without artificial aid; *also* : without affectation **4 :** REALISTICALLY

natural science *n* : a science (as physics, chemistry, or biology) that deals with matter, energy, and their interrelations and transformations or with objectively measurable phenomena — **natural scientist** *n*

natural selection *n* : the natural process that results in the survival of individuals or groups best adjusted to their environment

na•ture \ˈnā-chər\ *n* [ME, fr. MF, fr. L *natura,* fr. *natus,* pp. of *nasci* to be born] **1 :** the inherent quality or basic constitution of a person or thing **2 :** KIND, SORT **3 :** DISPOSITION, TEMPERAMENT **4 :** the physical universe **5 :** one's natural instincts or way of life ⟨quirks of human ~⟩; *also* : primitive state ⟨a return to ~⟩ **6 :** natural scenery or environment ⟨beauties of ~⟩

naught \ˈnȯt, ˈnät\ *n* **1 :** NOTHING **2 :** the arithmetical symbol 0 : ZERO

naugh•ty \ˈnȯ-tē, ˈnä-\ *adj* **naugh•ti•er; -est 1 :** guilty of disobedience or misbehavior **2 :** lacking in taste or propriety — **naugh•ti•ly** \-tə-lē\ *adv* — **naugh•ti•ness** \-tē-nəs\ *n*

nau•sea \ˈnȯ-zē-ə, -sē-; ˈnȯ-zhə, -shə\ *n* [L, seasickness, nausea, fr. Gk *nautia, nausia,* fr. *nautēs* sailor] **1 :** sickness of the stomach with a desire to vomit **2 :** extreme disgust

nau•se•ate \ˈnȯ-zē-ˌāt, -sē-, -zhē-, -shē-\ *vb* **-at•ed; -at•ing :** to affect or become affected with nausea — **nau•se•at•ing•ly** *adv*

nau•seous \ˈnȯ-shəs, -zē-əs\ *adj* **1 :** causing nausea or disgust **2 :** affected with nausea or disgust

naut *abbr* nautical

nau•ti•cal \ˈnȯ-ti-kəl\ *adj* : of or relating to sailors, navigation, or ships — **nau•ti•cal•ly** \-k(ə-)lē\ *adv*

nautical mile *n* : a unit of distance equal to about 6080 feet (1852 meters)

nau•ti•lus \ˈnȯt-ᵊl-əs\ *n, pl* **-lus•es** *or* **-li** \-ᵊl-ˌī, -ˌē\ : any of a genus of sea mollusks related to the octopuses but having a spiral chambered shell

nav *abbr* **1** naval **2** navigable; navigation

Na•va•jo *also* **Na•va•ho** \ˈna-və-ˌhō, ˈnä-\ *n, pl* **-jo** *or* **-jos** *also* **-ho** *or* **-hos :** a member of an American In-

dian people of northern New Mexico and Arizona; *also* : their language
na•val \ˈnā-vəl\ *adj* : of, relating to, or possessing a navy
naval stores *n pl* : products (as pitch, turpentine, or rosin) obtained from resinous conifers (as pines)
nave \ˈnāv\ *n* [ML *navis*, fr. L, ship] : the central part of a church running lengthwise
na•vel \ˈnā-vəl\ *n* : a depression in the middle of the abdomen that marks the point of attachment of fetus and mother
navel orange *n* : a seedless orange having a pit at the blossom end where the fruit encloses a small secondary fruit
nav•i•ga•ble \ˈna-vi-gə-bəl\ *adj* **1** : capable of being navigated ⟨a ~ river⟩ **2** : capable of being steered — **nav•i•ga•bil•i•ty** \ˌna-vi-gə-ˈbi-lə-tē\ *n*
nav•i•gate \ˈna-və-ˌgāt\ *vb* **-gat•ed; -gat•ing 1** : to sail on or through ⟨~ the Atlantic Ocean⟩ **2** : to steer or direct the course of a ship or aircraft **3** : MOVE; *esp* : WALK ⟨could hardly ~⟩ — **nav•i•ga•tion** \ˌna-və-ˈgā-shən\ *n* — **nav•i•ga•tor** \ˈna-və-ˌgā-tər\ *n*
na•vy \ˈnā-vē\ *n, pl* **navies 1** : FLEET; *also* : the warships belonging to a nation **2** *often cap* : a nation's organization for naval warfare
navy yard *n* : a yard where naval vessels are built or repaired
[1]**nay** \ˈnā\ *adv* **1** : NO
[2]**nay** *n* : a negative vote; *also* : a person casting such a vote
[3]**nay** *conj* : not merely this but also : not only so but ⟨he was happy, ~, ecstatic⟩
nay•say•er \ˈnā-ˌsā-ər\ *n* : one who denies, refuses, or opposes something
Na•zi \ˈnät-sē, ˈnat-\ *n* [G, fr. *Nationalsozialist*, lit., national socialist] : a member of a German fascist party controlling Germany from 1933 to 1945 under Adolf Hitler — **Nazi** *adj* — **Na•zism** \ˈnät-ˌsi-zəm, ˈnat-\ *or* **Na•zi•ism** \-sē-ˌi-zəm\ *n*
Nb *symbol* niobium
NB *abbr* **1** New Brunswick **2** nota bene
NBA *abbr* **1** National Basketball Association **2** National Boxing Association
NBC *abbr* National Broadcasting Company
NBS *abbr* National Bureau of Standards
NC *abbr* **1** no charge **2** North Carolina
NCAA *abbr* National Collegiate Athletic Association
NCE *abbr* New Catholic Edition
NCO \ˌen-ˌsē-ˈō\ *n* : NONCOMMISSIONED OFFICER
nd *abbr* no date
Nd *symbol* neodymium
ND *abbr* North Dakota
N Dak *abbr* North Dakota
Ne *symbol* neon
NE *abbr* **1** Nebraska **2** New England **3** northeast
Ne•an•der•thal \nē-ˈan-dər-ˌthȯl, nā-ˈän-dər-ˌtäl\ *adj* : of, relating to, or being an extinct Old World human; *also* : suggestive of a caveman — **Neanderthal** *n*
neap tide \ˈnēp-\ *n* : a tide of minimum range occurring at the first and third quarters of the moon
[1]**near** \ˈnir\ *adv* **1** : at, within, or to a short distance or time **2** : ALMOST
[2]**near** *prep* : close to
[3]**near** *adj* **1** : closely related or associated; *also* : INTIMATE **2** : not far away; *also* : being the closer or left-hand member of a pair **3** : barely avoided ⟨a ~ accident⟩ **4** : DIRECT, SHORT ⟨by the ~*est* route⟩ **5** : STINGY **6** : not real but very like ⟨~ silk⟩ — **near•ly** *adv* — **near•ness** *n*
[4]**near** *vb* : APPROACH
near beer *n* : any of various malt liquors low in alcohol
near•by \nir-ˈbī, ˈnir-ˌbī\ *adv or adj* : close at hand
near•sight•ed \ˈnir-ˈsī-təd\ *adj* : able to see near things more clearly than distant ones : MYOPIC — **near•sight•ed•ly** *adv* — **near•sight•ed•ness** *n*
neat \ˈnēt\ *adj* [MF *net*, fr. L *nitidus* bright, neat, fr. *nitēre* to shine] **1** : being orderly and clean **2** : not mixed or diluted ⟨~ brandy⟩ **3** : marked by tasteful simplicity **4** : PRECISE, SYSTEMATIC **5** : SKILLFUL, ADROIT **6** : FINE, ADMIRABLE **syn** shipshape, tidy, trig, trim — **neat** *adv* — **neat•ly** *adv* — **neat•ness** *n*
neath \ˈnēth\ *prep, dial* : BENEATH
neat's–foot oil \ˈnēts-ˌfu̇t-\ *n* [*neat* ox or cow] : a pale yellow fatty oil made esp. from the bones of cattle and used chiefly as a leather dressing
neb \ˈneb\ *n* **1** : the beak of a bird or tortoise; *also* : NOSE, SNOUT **2** : NIB
Neb *or* **Nebr** *abbr* Nebraska
NEB *abbr* New English Bible
neb•u•la \ˈne-byə-lə\ *n, pl* **-lae** \-ˌlē, -ˌlī\ *also* **-las** [NL, fr. L, mist, cloud] **1** : any of numerous clouds of gas or dust in interstellar space **2** : GALAXY — **neb•u•lar** \-lər\ *adj*
neb•u•liz•er \ˈne-byə-ˌlī-zər\ *n* : ATOMIZER
neb•u•lous \ˈne-byə-ləs\ *adj* **1** : of or relating to a nebula **2** : HAZY, INDISTINCT
[1]**nec•es•sary** \ˈne-sə-ˌser-ē\ *n, pl* **-saries** : an indispensable item
[2]**necessary** *adj* **1** : INEVITABLE, INESCAPABLE; *also* : CERTAIN **2** : PREDETERMINED **3** : COMPULSORY **4** : positively needed : INDISPENSABLE **syn** imperative, necessitous, essential — **nec•es•sar•i•ly** \ˌne-sə-ˈser-ə-lē\ *adv*
ne•ces•si•tate \ni-ˈse-sə-ˌtāt\ *vb* **-tat•ed; -tat•ing** : to make necessary
ne•ces•si•tous \ni-ˈse-sə-təs\ *adj* **1** : NEEDY, IMPOVERISHED **2** : URGENT **3** : NECESSARY
ne•ces•si•ty \ni-ˈse-sə-tē\ *n, pl* **-ties 1** : conditions that cannot be changed **2** : WANT, POVERTY **3** : something that is necessary **4** : very great need
[1]**neck** \ˈnek\ *n* **1** : the part of the body connecting the head and the trunk **2** : the part of a garment covering or near to the neck **3** : a relatively narrow part suggestive of a neck ⟨~ of a bottle⟩ ⟨~ of land⟩ **4** : a narrow margin esp. of victory ⟨won by a ~⟩ — **necked** \ˈnekt\ *adj*
[2]**neck** *vb* : to kiss and caress amorously
neck and neck *adv or adj* : very close (as in a race)
neck•er•chief \ˈne-kər-chəf, -ˌchēf\ *n, pl* **-chiefs** \-chəfs, -ˌchēfs\ *also* **-chieves** \-ˌchēvz\ : a square of cloth worn folded about the neck like a scarf
neck•lace \ˈne-kləs\ *n* : an ornament worn around the neck
neck•line \ˈnek-ˌlīn\ *n* : the outline of the neck opening of a garment
neck•tie \-ˌtī\ *n* : a strip of cloth worn around the neck and tied in front
ne•crol•o•gy \nə-ˈkrä-lə-jē\ *n, pl* **-gies 1** : OBITUARY **2** : a list of the recently dead
nec•ro•man•cy \ˈne-krə-ˌman-sē\ *n* **1** : the art or practice of conjuring up the spirits of the dead for purposes of magically revealing the future **2** : MAGIC, SORCERY — **nec•ro•man•cer** \-sər\ *n*
ne•crop•o•lis \nə-ˈkrä-pə-ləs, ne-\ *n, pl* **-lis•es** *or* **-les** \-ˌlēz\ *or* **-leis** \-ˌlās\ *or* **-li** \-ˌlī, -ˌlē\ : CEMETERY; *esp* : a large elaborate cemetery of an ancient city
ne•cro•sis \nə-ˈkrō-səs, ne-\ *n, pl* **ne•cro•ses** \-ˌsēz\ : usu. local death of body tissue — **ne•crot•ic** \-ˈkrä-tik\ *adj*
nec•tar \ˈnek-tər\ *n* **1** : the drink of the Greek and Roman gods; *also* : any delicious drink **2** : a sweet plant secretion that is the raw material of honey
nec•tar•ine \ˌnek-tə-ˈrēn\ *n* : a smooth-skinned peach
née *or* **nee** \ˈnā\ *adj* [F, lit., born] — used to identify a woman by her maiden family name
[1]**need** \ˈnēd\ *n* **1** : OBLIGATION ⟨no ~ to hurry⟩ **2** : a lack of something requisite, desirable, or useful **3** : a condition requiring supply or relief ⟨when the ~ arises⟩ **4** : POVERTY **syn** necessity, exigency
[2]**need** *vb* **1** : to be in want **2** : to have cause or occasion

for : REQUIRE ⟨he ~s advice⟩ **3** : to be under obligation or necessity ⟨we ~ to know the truth⟩

need•ful \ˈnēd-fəl\ *adj* : NECESSARY, REQUISITE

¹nee•dle \ˈnēd-əl\ *n* **1** : a slender pointed usu. steel implement used in sewing **2** : a slender rod (as for knitting, controlling a small opening, or transmitting vibrations to or from a recording) ⟨a phonograph ~⟩ **3** : a slender hollow instrument by which material is introduced into or withdrawn from the body **4** : a slender indicator on a dial **5** : a needle-shaped leaf (as of a pine)

²needle *vb* **nee•dled; nee•dling** : PROD, GOAD; *esp* : to incite to action by repeated gibes

nee•dle•point \ˈnēd-əl-ˌpȯint\ *n* **1** : lace worked with a needle over a paper pattern **2** : embroidery done on canvas across counted threads — **needlepoint** *adj*

need•less \ˈnēd-ləs\ *adj* : UNNECESSARY — **need•less•ly** *adv* — **need•less•ness** *n*

nee•dle•wom•an \ˈnēd-əl-ˌwu̇-mən\ *n* : a woman who does needlework; *esp* : SEAMSTRESS

nee•dle•work \-ˌwərk\ *n* : work done with a needle; *esp* : work (as embroidery) other than plain sewing

needs \ˈnēdz\ *adv* : of necessity : NECESSARILY ⟨must ~ be recognized⟩

needy \ˈnē-dē\ *adj* **need•i•er; -est** : being in want : POVERTY-STRICKEN

ne'er \ˈner\ *adv* : NEVER

ne'er–do–well \ˈner-du̇-ˌwel\ *n* : an idle worthless person — **ne'er–do–well** *adj*

ne•far•i•ous \ni-ˈfar-ē-əs\ *adj* [L *nefarius*, fr. *nefas* crime, fr. *ne-* not + *fas* right, divine law] : very wicked : EVIL **syn** bad, immoral, iniquitous, sinful, vicious — **ne•far•i•ous•ly** *adv*

neg *abbr* negative

ne•gate \ni-ˈgāt\ *vb* **ne•gat•ed; ne•gat•ing** **1** : to deny the existence or truth of **2** : to cause to be ineffective or invalid : NULLIFY

ne•ga•tion \ni-ˈgā-shən\ *n* **1** : the action or operation of negating or making negative **2** : a negative doctrine or statement

¹neg•a•tive \ˈne-gə-tiv\ *adj* **1** : marked by denial, prohibition, or refusal ⟨a ~ reply⟩ **2** : not positive or constructive; *esp* : not affirming the presence of what is sought or suspected to be present ⟨test results were ~⟩ **3** : less than zero ⟨a ~ number⟩ **4** : being, relating to, or charged with electricity of which the electron is the elementary unit **5** : having the light and dark parts opposite to what they were in the original photographic subject — **neg•a•tive•ly** *adv* — **neg•a•tive•ness** *n* — **neg•a•tiv•i•ty** \ˌne-gə-ˈti-və-tē\ *n*

²negative *n* **1** : a negative word or statement **2** : a negative vote or reply; *also* : REFUSAL **3** : something that is the opposite or negation of something else **4** : the side that votes or argues for the opposition (as in a debate) **5** : a negative number **6** : a negative photographic image on transparent material

³negative *vb* **-tived; -tiv•ing** **1** : to refuse to accept or approve **2** : to vote against **3** : DISPROVE

negative income tax *n* : a system of federal subsidy payments to families with incomes below a stipulated level

neg•a•tiv•ism \ˈne-gə-ti-ˌvi-zəm\ *n* : an attitude of skepticism and denial of nearly everything affirmed or suggested by others

¹ne•glect \ni-ˈglekt\ *vb* [L *neglegere*, *neclegere*, fr. *nec-* not + *legere* to gather] **1** : DISREGARD **2** : to leave undone or unattended to esp. through carelessness **syn** omit, ignore, over-look, slight, forget, miss

²neglect *n* **1** : an act or instance of neglecting something **2** : the condition of being neglected — **ne•glect•ful** *adj*

neg•li•gee *also* **neg•li•gé** \ˌne-glə-ˈzhā\ *n* : a woman's long flowing dressing gown

neg•li•gent \ˈne-gli-jənt\ *adj* : marked by neglect **syn** neglectful, remiss, delinquent, derelict — **neg•li•gence** \-jəns\ *n* — **neg•li•gent•ly** *adv*

neg•li•gi•ble \ˈne-gli-jə-bəl\ *adj* : so small as to be neglected or disregarded

ne•go•tiant \ni-ˈgō-shē-ənt\ *n* : NEGOTIATOR

ne•go•ti•ate \ni-ˈgō-shē-ˌāt\ *vb* **-at•ed; -at•ing** [L *negotiari* to carry on business, fr. *negotium* business, fr. *neg-* not + *otium* leisure] **1** : to confer with another so as to arrive at the settlement of some matter; *also* : to arrange for or bring about by such conferences ⟨~ a treaty⟩ **2** : to transfer to another by delivery or endorsement in return for equivalent value ⟨~ a check⟩ **3** : to get through, around, or over successfully ⟨~ a turn⟩ — **ne•go•tia•ble** \-shə-bəl, -shē-ə-\ *adj* — **ne•go•ti•a•tion** \ni-ˌgō-sē-ˈā-shən, -shē-\ *n* — **ne•go•ti•a•tor** \-ˈgō-shē-ˌā-tər\ *n*

ne•gri•tude \ˈne-grə-ˌtüd, -ˌtyüd, ˈnē-\ *n* : a consciousness of and pride in one's African heritage

Ne•gro \ˈnē-grō\ *n, pl* **Negroes** [Sp or Pg, fr. *negro* black] : a member of the black race — **Negro** *adj* — **Ne•groid** \ˈnē-ˌgrȯid\ *n or adj, often not cap*

Neh *abbr* Nehemiah

Ne•he•mi•ah \ˌnē-ə-ˈmī-ə\ *n* — see BIBLE table

neigh \ˈnā\ *n* : a loud prolonged cry of a horse — **neigh** *vb*

¹neigh•bor \ˈnā-bər\ *n* **1** : one living or located near another **2** : FELLOWMAN

²neighbor *vb* : to be next to or near to : border on

neigh•bor•hood \ˈnā-bər-ˌhu̇d\ *n* **1** : NEARNESS **2** : a place or region near : VICINITY; *also* : a number or amount near ⟨costs in the ~ of $10⟩ **3** : the people living near one another **4** : a section lived in by neighbors and usu. having distinguishing characteristics

neigh•bor•ly \-lē\ *adj* : befitting congenial neighbors; *esp* : FRIENDLY — **neigh•bor•li•ness** *n*

neigh•bour *chiefly Brit var of* NEIGHBOR

¹nei•ther \ˈnē-t͟hər, ˈnī-\ *pron* : neither one : not the one and not the other ⟨~ of the two⟩

²neither *conj* **1** : not either ⟨~ good nor bad⟩ **2** : NOR ⟨~ did I⟩

³neither *adj* : not either ⟨~ hand⟩

nel•son \ˈnel-sən\ *n* : a wrestling hold in which one applies leverage against an opponent's arm, neck, and head

nem•a•tode \ˈne-mə-ˌtōd\ *n* : any of a phylum of elongated cylindrical worms parasitic in animals or plants or free-living in soil or water

nem•e•sis \ˈne-mə-səs\ *n, pl* **-e•ses** \-ˌsēz\ [L *Nemesis*, goddess of divine retribution, fr. Gk] **1** : one that inflicts retribution or vengeance **2** : a formidable and usu. victorious rival **3** : an act or effect of retribution; *also* : CURSE

neo•clas•sic \ˌnē-ō-ˈkla-sik\ *or* **neo•clas•si•cal** \-si-kəl\ *adj* : of or relating to a revival or adaptation of the classical style esp. in literature, art, or music

neo•co•lo•nial•ism \ˌnē-ō-kə-ˈlō-nē-ə-ˌli-zəm\ *n* : the economic and political policies by which a nation indirectly maintains or extends its influence over other areas or peoples — **neo•co•lo•nial** *adj* — **neo•co•lo•nial•ist** \-list\ *n or adj*

neo•con•ser•va•tive \-kən-ˈsər-və-tiv\ *n* : a former liberal espousing political conservatism — **neo•con•ser•va•tism** \-və-ˌti-zəm\ *n* — **neoconservative** *adj*

neo•dym•i•um \ˌnē-ō-ˈdi-mē-əm\ *n* : a yellow metallic chemical element — see ELEMENT table

neo–im•pres•sion•ism \ˌnē-ō-im-ˈpre-shə-ˌni-zəm\ *n, often cap N&I* : a late 19th century French art movement that attempted to make impressionism more precise and to use a pointillist painting technique

Neo•lith•ic \ˌnē-ə-ˈli-thik\ *adj* : of or relating to the latest period of the Stone Age characterized by polished stone implements

ne•ol•o•gism \nē-ˈä-lə-ˌji-zəm\ *n* : a new word or expression

ne•on \ˈnē-ˌän\ *n* [Gk, neut. of *neos* new] **1** : a gaseous colorless chemical element used in electric lamps — see ELEMENT table **2** : a lamp in which a discharge through neon gives a reddish glow — **neon** *adj*

neo•na•tal \ˌnē-ō-ˈnāt-ᵊl\ *adj* : of, relating to, or affecting the newborn — **neo•na•tal•ly** *adv*
ne•o•nate \ˈnē-ə-ˌnāt\ *n* : a newborn child
neo•phyte \ˈnē-ə-ˌfīt\ *n* **1** : a new convert : PROSELYTE **2** : NOVICE **3** : BEGINNER **syn** apprentice, freshman, newcomer, rookie, tenderfoot, tyro
neo•plasm \ˈnē-ə-ˌpla-zəm\ *n* : a new growth of tissue serving no useful purpose in the body : TUMOR — **neo•plas•tic** \ˌnē-ə-ˈplas-tik\ *adj*
neo•prene \ˈnē-ə-ˌprēn\ *n* : a synthetic rubber used esp. for special-purpose clothing (as wet suits)
Ne•pali \nə-ˈpȯ-lē, -ˈpä-\ *n, pl* **Nepali** : a native or inhabitant of Nepal — **Nepali** *adj*
ne•pen•the \nə-ˈpen-thē\ *n* **1** : a potion used by the ancients to dull pain and sorrow **2** : something capable of making one forget grief or suffering
neph•ew \ˈne-fyü, *chiefly Brit* -vyü\ *n* : a son of one's brother, sister, brother-in-law, or sister-in-law
ne•phrit•ic \ni-ˈfri-tik\ *adj* **1** : RENAL **2** : of, relating to, or affected with nephritis
ne•phri•tis \ni-ˈfrī-təs\ *n, pl* **ne•phrit•i•des** \-ˈfri-tə-ˌdēz\ : kidney inflammation
ne plus ul•tra \ˌnē-ˌpləs-ˈəl-trə\ *n* [NL, (go) no more beyond] : the highest point capable of being attained
nep•o•tism \ˈne-pə-ˌti-zəm\ *n* [F *népotisme,* fr. It *nepotismo,* fr. *nepote* nephew, fr. L *nepot-, nepos* grandson, nephew] : favoritism shown to a relative (as in the granting of jobs)
Nep•tune \ˈnep-ˌtün, -ˌtyün\ *n* : the planet 8th in order from the sun — see PLANET table — **Nep•tu•ni•an** \nep-ˈtü-nē-ən, -ˈtyü-\ *adj*
nep•tu•ni•um \nep-ˈtü-nē-əm, -ˈtyü-\ *n* : a short-lived radioactive element — see ELEMENT table
nerd \ˈnərd\ *n* : an unstylish or socially inept person; *esp* : one slavishly devoted to intellectual pursuits — **nerdy** *adj*
Ne•re•id \ˈnir-ē-əd\ *n* : a sea nymph in Greek mythology
¹nerve \ˈnərv\ *n* **1** : SINEW, TENDON ⟨strain every ~⟩ **2** : any of the strands of nervous tissue that carry nerve impulses between the brain and spinal cord and every part of the body **3** : power of endurance or control : FORTITUDE; *also* : BOLDNESS, DARING **4** *pl* : NERVOUSNESS **5** : a vein of a leaf or insect wing — **nerved** \ˈnərvd\ *adj* — **nerve•less** *adj*
²nerve *vb* **nerved; nerv•ing** : to give strength or courage to
nerve cell *n* : NEURON; *also* : the nucleus-containing central part of a neuron exclusive of its processes
nerve gas *n* : a chemical weapon damaging esp. to the nervous and respiratory systems
nerve impulse *n* : a physical and chemical change that moves along a process of a neuron after stimulation and carries a record of sensation or an instruction to act
nerve–rack•ing *or* **nerve–wrack•ing** \ˈnərv-ˌra-kiŋ\ *adj* : extremely trying on the nerves
ner•vous \ˈnər-vəs\ *adj* **1** : FORCIBLE, SPIRITED **2** : of, relating to, or made up of nerve cells or nerves **3** : easily excited or annoyed : JUMPY **4** : TIMID, APPREHENSIVE ⟨a ~ smile⟩ **5** : UNEASY, UNSTEADY — **ner•vous•ly** *adv* — **ner•vous•ness** *n*
nervous breakdown *n* : an attack of mental or emotional disorder of sufficient severity to be incapacitating esp. when requiring hospitalization
nervous system *n* : a bodily system that in vertebrates is made up of the brain and spinal cord, nerves, ganglia, and parts of the sense organs and that receives and interprets stimuli and transmits nerve impulses
nervy \ˈnər-vē\ *adj* **nerv•i•er; -est** **1** : showing calm courage **2** : marked by impudence or presumption ⟨a ~ salesperson⟩ **3** : EXCITABLE, NERVOUS **syn** bold, cheeky, forward, fresh, impudent, saucy
-ness \nəs\ *n suffix* : state : condition : quality : degree ⟨good*ness*⟩
¹nest \ˈnest\ *n* **1** : the shelter prepared by a bird for its eggs and young **2** : a place where eggs (as of insects or fish) are laid and hatched **3** : a place of rest, retreat, or lodging **4** : DEN, HANGOUT ⟨a ~ of thieves⟩ **5** : the occupants of a nest **6** : a series of objects (as bowls or tables) fitting inside or under one another
²nest *vb* **1** : to build or occupy a nest **2** : to fit compactly together or within one another
nest egg *n* : a fund of money accumulated as a reserve
nes•tle \ˈne-səl\ *vb* **nes•tled; nes•tling** **1** : to settle snugly or comfortably **2** : to press closely and affectionately : CUDDLE **3** : to settle, shelter, or house as if in a nest
nest•ling \ˈnest-liŋ\ *n* : a bird too young to leave its nest
¹net \ˈnet\ *n* **1** : a meshed fabric twisted, knotted, or woven together at regular intervals **2** : a device made all or partly of net and used esp. to catch birds, fish, or insects **3** : something made of net used esp. for protecting, confining, carrying, or dividing ⟨a tennis ~⟩ **4** : SNARE, TRAP
²net *vb* **net•ted; net•ting** **1** : to cover or enclose with or as if with a net **2** : to catch in or as if in a net
³net *adj* : free from all charges or deductions ⟨~ profit⟩ ⟨~ weight⟩
⁴net *vb* **net•ted; net•ting** : to gain or produce as profit : CLEAR, YIELD ⟨his business *netted* $50,000 a year⟩
⁵net *n* : a net amount, profit, weight, or price
Neth *abbr* Netherlands
neth•er \ˈne-t͟hər\ *adj* : situated down or below ⟨the ~ regions of the earth⟩
Neth•er•land•er \ˈne-t͟hər-ˌlan-dər\ *n* : a native or inhabitant of the Netherlands
neth•er•most \-ˌmōst\ *adj* : LOWEST
neth•er•world \-ˌwərld\ *n* **1** : the world of the dead **2** : UNDERWORLD
nett *Brit var of* NET
net•ting *n* **1** : NETWORK **2** : the act or process of making a net or network
¹net•tle \ˈnet-ᵊl\ *n* : any of a genus of coarse herbs with stinging hairs
²nettle *vb* **net•tled; net•tling** : PROVOKE, VEX, IRRITATE
net•tle•some \ˈnet-ᵊl-səm\ *adj* : causing vexation : IRRITATING
net•work \ˈnet-ˌwərk\ *n* **1** : NET **2** : a system of elements (as lines or channels) that cross in the manner of the threads in a net **3** : a group or system of related or connected parts; *esp* : a chain of radio or television stations
net•work•ing \ˈnet-ˌwər-kiŋ\ *n* : the exchange of information or services among individuals, groups, or institutions
neu•ral \ˈnu̇r-əl, ˈnyu̇r-\ *adj* : of, relating to, or involving a nerve or the nervous system
neu•ral•gia \nu̇-ˈral-jə, nyu̇-\ *n* : acute pain that follows the course of a nerve — **neu•ral•gic** \-jik\ *adj*
neur•as•then•ic \ˌnu̇r-əs-ˈthe-nik, ˌnyu̇r-, -thē-\ *adj* : affected with or suggestive of mental disorder characterized esp. by fatiguing easily, lack of motivation, feelings of inadequacy, and psychosomatic symptoms — **neur•as•then•ia** \-ˈthē-nē-ə\ *n* — **neurasthenic** *n*
neu•ri•tis \-ˈrī-təs\ *n, pl* **-rit•i•des** \-ˈri-tə-ˌdēz\ *or* **-ri•tis•es** : inflammation of a nerve — **neu•rit•ic** \-ˈri-tik\ *adj or n*
neu•rol•o•gy \nu̇-ˈrä-lə-jē, nyu̇-\ *n* : the scientific study of the nervous system — **neu•ro•log•i•cal** \ˌnu̇r-ə-ˈlä-ji-kəl, ˌnyu̇r-\ *or* **neu•ro•log•ic** \-jik\ *adj* — **neu•ro•log•i•cal•ly** \-ji-k(ə-)lē\ *adv* — **neu•rol•o•gist** \nu̇-ˈrä-lə-jist, nyu̇-\ *n*
neu•ron \ˈnü-ˌrän, ˈnyü-\ *also* **neu•rone** \-ˌrōn\ *n* : a cell with specialized processes that is the fundamental functional unit of nervous tissue
neu•ro•sci•ence \ˌnu̇r-ō-ˈsī-əns, ˌnyu̇r-\ *n* : a branch of the life sciences that deals with the anatomy, physiology, biochemistry, or molecular biology of nerves and nervous tissue and with their relation to behavior and learning — **neu•ro•sci•en•tist** \-ən-tist\ *n*

neu•ro•sis \nu̇-ˈrō-səs, nyu̇-\ *n, pl* **-ro•ses** \-ˌsēz\ : a mental and emotional disorder that is less serious than a psychosis, is not characterized by disturbance of the use of language, and is accompanied by various bodily and mental disturbances (as visceral symptoms, anxieties, or phobias)

neu•ro•sur•gery \nu̇r-ō-ˈsər-jə-rē, ˌnyu̇r-\ *n* : surgery of nervous structures (as nerves, the brain, or the spinal cord) — **neu•ro•sur•geon** \-ˈsər-jən\ *n*

[1]**neu•rot•ic** \nu̇-ˈrä-tik, nyu̇-\ *adj* : of, relating to, being, or affected with a neurosis; *also* : NERVOUS — **neu•rot•i•cal•ly** \-ti-k(ə-)lē\ *adv*

[2]**neurotic** *n* : an emotionally unstable or neurotic person

neu•ro•trans•mit•ter \ˌnu̇r-ō-trans-ˈmi-tər, ˌnyu̇r-, -tranz-\ *n* : a substance (as acetylcholine) that transmits nerve impulses across the gap between neurons

neut *abbr* neuter

[1]**neu•ter** \ˈnü-tər, ˈnyü-\ *adj* [ME *neutre,* fr. MF & L; MF *neutre,* fr. L *neuter,* lit., neither, fr. *ne-* not + *uter* which of two] **1** : of, relating to, or constituting the gender that includes most words or grammatical forms referring to things classed as neither masculine nor feminine **2** : having imperfectly developed or no sex organs

[2]**neuter** *n* **1** : a noun, pronoun, adjective, or inflectional form or class of the neuter gender; *also* : the neuter gender **2** : WORKER 2; *also* : a spayed or castrated animal

[3]**neuter** *vb* : CASTRATE, SPAY

[1]**neu•tral** \ˈnü-trəl, ˈnyü-\ *n* **1** : one that is neutral **2** : a neutral color **3** : a position of disengagement (as of gears)

[2]**neutral** *adj* **1** : not favoring either side in a quarrel, contest, or war **2** : of or relating to a neutral state or power **3** : MIDDLING, INDIFFERENT **4** : having no hue : GRAY; *also* : not decided in color **5** : neither acid nor basic ⟨a ~ solution⟩ **6** : not electrically charged

neu•tral•ise *Brit var of* NEUTRALIZE

neu•tral•ism \ˈnü-trə-ˌli-zəm, ˈnyü-\ *n* : a policy or the advocacy of neutrality esp. in international affairs

neu•tral•i•ty \nü-ˈtra-lə-tē, nyü-\ *n* : the quality or state of being neutral; *esp* : refusal to take part in a war between other powers

neu•tral•ize \ˈnü-trə-ˌlīz, ˈnyü-\ *vb* **-ized; -iz•ing** : to make neutral; *esp* : COUNTERACT — **neu•tral•i•za•tion** \ˌnü-trə-lə-ˈzā-shən, ˌnyü-\ *n*

neu•tri•no \nü-ˈtrē-nō, nyü-\ *n, pl* **-nos** : an uncharged elementary particle held to be massless or very light

neu•tron \ˈnü-ˌträn, ˈnyü-\ *n* : an uncharged atomic particle that is nearly equal in mass to the proton

neutron bomb *n* : a nuclear bomb designed to produce lethal neutrons but less blast and fire damage than other nuclear bombs

neutron star *n* : a hypothetical dense celestial object that results from the collapse of a large star

Nev *abbr* Nevada

nev•er \ˈne-vər\ *adv* **1** : not ever **2** : not in any degree, way, or condition

nev•er•more \ˌne-vər-ˈmōr\ *adv* : never again

nev•er–nev•er land \ˌne-vər-ˈne-vər-\ *n* : an ideal or imaginary place

nev•er•the•less \ˌne-vər-t͟hə-ˈles\ *adv* : in spite of that : HOWEVER

ne•vus \ˈnē-vəs\ *n, pl* **ne•vi** \-ˌvī\ : a usu. pigmented birthmark

[1]**new** \ˈnü, ˈnyü\ *adj* **1** : not old : RECENT, MODERN **2** : recently discovered, recognized, or learned about ⟨~ drugs⟩ **3** : UNFAMILIAR **4** : different from the former **5** : not accustomed ⟨~ to the work⟩ **6** : beginning as a repetition of a previous act or thing ⟨a ~ year⟩ **7** : REFRESHED, REGENERATED ⟨rest made a ~ man of him⟩ **8** : being in a position or place for the first time ⟨a ~ member⟩ **9** *cap* : having been in use after medieval times : MODERN ⟨*New* Latin⟩ **syn** novel, newfangled, fresh — **new•ish** *adj* — **new•ness** *n*

[2]**new** *adv* : NEWLY ⟨*new*-mown hay⟩

New Age *adj* **1** : of, relating to, or being a late 20th century social movement incorporating various untraditional concepts and practices relating esp. to spiritual, emotional, and physical well-being **2** : of, relating to, or being a soft soothing form of instrumental music

[1]**new•born** \-ˌbȯrn\ *adj* **1** : recently born **2** : born anew ⟨~ hope⟩

[2]**newborn** *n, pl* **newborn** *or* **newborns** : a newborn individual

new•com•er \-ˌkə-mər\ *n* **1** : one recently arrived **2** : BEGINNER

New Deal *n* : the legislative and administrative program of President F. D. Roosevelt to promote economic recovery and social reform during the 1930s — **New Dealer** *n*

new•el \ˈnü-əl, ˈnyü-\ *n* : a post about which the steps of a circular staircase wind; *also* : a post at the foot of a stairway or one at a landing

new•fan•gled \ˈnü-ˈfaŋ-gəld, ˈnyü-\ *adj* **1** : attracted to novelty **2** : of the newest style : NOVEL

new–fash•ioned \-ˈfa-shənd\ *adj* **1** : made in a new fashion or form **2** : UP-TO-DATE

new•found \-ˈfau̇nd\ *adj* : newly found

New Left *n* : a radical political movement originating in the 1960s

new•ly \ˈnü-lē, ˈnyü-\ *adv* **1** : LATELY, RECENTLY **2** : ANEW, AFRESH

new•ly•wed \-ˌwed\ *n* : one recently married

new moon *n* : the phase of the moon with its dark side toward the earth; *also* : the thin crescent moon seen for a few days after the new moon phase

news \ˈnüz, ˈnyüz\ *n* **1** : a report of recent events : TIDINGS **2** : material reported in a newspaper or news periodical or on a newscast

news•boy \ˈnüz-ˌbȯi, ˈnyüz-\ *n* : one who delivers or sells newspapers

news•cast \-ˌkast\ *n* : a radio or television broadcast of news — **news•cast•er** \-ˌkas-tər\ *n*

news•let•ter \-ˌle-tər\ *n* : a small newspaper containing news or information of interest chiefly to a special group

news•mag•a•zine \-ˌma-gə-ˌzēn\ *n* : a usu. weekly magazine devoted chiefly to summarizing and analyzing news

news•man \-mən, -ˌman\ *n* : one who gathers, reports, or comments on the news : REPORTER

news•pa•per \-ˌpā-pər\ *n* : a paper that is published at regular intervals and contains news, articles of opinion, features, and advertising

news•pa•per•man \-ˌpā-pər-ˌman\ *n* : one who owns or is employed by a newspaper

news•print \-ˌprint\ *n* : paper made chiefly from wood pulp and used mostly for newspapers

news•reel \-ˌrēl\ *n* : a short motion picture portraying current events

news•stand \-ˌstand\ *n* : a place where newspapers and periodicals are sold

news•week•ly \-ˌwēk-lē\ *n* : a weekly newspaper or newsmagazine

news•wom•an \-ˌwu̇-mən\ *n* : a woman who gathers, reports, or comments on the news : REPORTER

news•wor•thy \-ˌwər-t͟hē\ *adj* : sufficiently interesting to the general public to warrant reporting (as in a newspaper)

newsy \ˈnü-zē, ˈnyü-\ *adj* **news•i•er; -est** : filled with news; *esp* : TALKATIVE

newt \ˈnüt, ˈnyüt\ *n* : any of various small chiefly aquatic salamanders

New Testament *n* : the second of the two chief divisions of the Bible — see BIBLE table

new•ton \ˈnüt-ᵊn, ˈnyüt-\ *n* : the unit of force in the metric system equal to the force required to impart an acceleration of one meter per second per second to a mass of one kilogram

new wave *n, often cap N&W* : the latest and esp. the most outrageous style — **new–wave** *adj*

New World *n* : the western hemisphere; *esp* : the continental landmass of No. and So. America

New Year *n* **1** : NEW YEAR'S DAY; *also* : the first days of the year **2** : ROSH HASHANAH

New Year's Day *n* : January 1 observed as a legal holiday

New Zea•land•er \nü-ˈzē-lən-dər, nyü-\ *n* : a native or inhabitant of New Zealand

[1]**next** \ˈnekst\ *adj* : immediately preceding or following : NEAREST

[2]**next** *prep* : nearest or adjacent to

[3]**next** *adv* **1** : in the time, place, or order nearest or immediately succeeding **2** : on the first occasion to come

nex•us \ˈnek-səs\ *n, pl* **nex•us•es** \-sə-səz\ *or* **nex•us** \-səs, -ˌsüs\ : CONNECTION, LINK

Nez Percé \ˈnez-ˈpərs, *F* nā-per-sā\ *n* : a member of an American Indian people of Idaho, Washington, and Oregon; *also* : the language of the Nez Percé

NF *abbr* Newfoundland

NFC *abbr* National Football Conference

NFL *abbr* National Football League

Nfld *abbr* Newfoundland

NG *abbr* **1** National Guard **2** no good

ngul•trum \eŋ-ˈgu̇l-trəm\ *n* — see MONEY table

ngwee \eŋ-ˈgwē\ *n, pl* **ngwee** — see *kwacha* at MONEY table

NH *abbr* New Hampshire

NHL *abbr* National Hockey League

Ni *symbol* nickel

ni•a•cin \ˈnī-ə-sən\ *n* : NICOTINIC ACID

nib \ˈnib\ *n* : POINT; *esp* : a pen point

[1]**nib•ble** \ˈni-bəl\ *vb* **nib•bled; nib•bling** : to bite gently or bit by bit

[2]**nibble** *n* : a small or cautious bite

ni•cad \ˈnī-ˌkad\ *n* : a rechargeable dry cell that has a nickel cathode and a cadmium anode

Nic•a•ra•guan \ˌni-kə-ˈrä-gwən\ *n* : a native or inhabitant of Nicaragua — **Nicaraguan** *adj*

nice \ˈnīs\ *adj* **nic•er; nic•est** [ME, foolish, wanton, fr. OF, fr. L *nescius* ignorant, fr. *nescire* to not know] **1** : FASTIDIOUS, DISCRIMINATING **2** : marked by delicate discrimination or treatment **3** : PLEASING, AGREEABLE; *also* : well-executed **4** : WELL-BRED ⟨~ people⟩ **5** : VIRTUOUS, RESPECTABLE **syn** choosy, finicky, particular, persnickety, picky — **nice•ly** *adv* — **nice•ness** *n*

nice–nel•ly \ˈnīs-ˈne-lē\ *adj, often cap 2d N* **1** : marked by euphemism **2** : PRUDISH — **nice nelly** *n, often cap 2d N* — **nice–nel•ly•ism** \-ˌi-zəm\ *n, often cap 2d N*

nice•ty \ˈnī-sə-tē\ *n, pl* **-ties** **1** : a dainty, delicate, or elegant thing ⟨enjoy the *niceties* of life⟩ **2** : a fine point or distinction ⟨*niceties* of workmanship⟩ **3** : EXACTNESS, PRECISION, ACCURACY

niche \ˈnich\ *n* [F] **1** : a recess in a wall esp. for a statue **2** : a place, employment, or activity for which a person or thing is best fitted **3** : the living space or role of an organism in an ecological community esp. with regard to food consumption

[1]**nick** \ˈnik\ *n* **1** : a small notch or groove **2** : the final critical moment ⟨in the ~ of time⟩

[2]**nick** *vb* : NOTCH, CHIP

nick•el \ˈni-kəl\ *n* **1** : a hard silver-white metallic chemical element capable of a high polish and used in alloys — see ELEMENT table **2** : the U.S. 5-cent piece made of copper and nickel; *also* : the Canadian 5-cent piece

nick•el•ode•on \ˌni-kə-ˈlō-dē-ən\ *n* **1** : an early movie theater to which admission cost five cents **2** : JUKEBOX

nick•er \ˈni-kər\ *vb* : NEIGH, WHINNY — **nicker** *n*

nick•name \ˈnik-ˌnām\ *n* [ME *nekename* additional name, alter. (from misdivision of *an ekename*) of *ekename*, fr. *eke* also + *name*] **1** : a usu. descriptive name given instead of or in addition to the one belonging to a person, place, or thing **2** : a familiar form of a proper name — **nickname** *vb*

nic•o•tine \ˈni-kə-ˌtēn\ *n* : a poisonous and addictive substance in tobacco that is used as an insecticide

nic•o•tin•ic acid \ˌni-kə-ˈtē-nik-, -ˈti-\ *n* : an organic acid of the vitamin B complex found in plants and animals and used against pellagra

niece \ˈnēs\ *n* : a daughter of one's brother, sister, brother-in-law, or sister-in-law

nif•ty \ˈnif-tē\ *adj* **nif•ti•er; -est** : very good : very attractive

Ni•ge•ri•an \nī-ˈjir-ē-ən\ *n* : a native or inhabitant of Nigeria — **Nigerian** *adj*

nig•gard \ˈni-gərd\ *n* : a stingy person : MISER — **nig•gard•li•ness** \-lē-nəs\ *n* — **nig•gard•ly** *adj or adv*

nig•gling \ˈni-gə-liŋ\ *adj* **1** : PETTY **2** : bothersome in a petty way **syn** inconsequential, measly, picayune, piddling, trifling, trivial

[1]**nigh** \ˈnī\ *adv* **1** : near in place, time, or relationship **2** : NEARLY, ALMOST

[2]**nigh** *adj* : CLOSE, NEAR

[3]**nigh** *prep* : NEAR

night \ˈnīt\ *n* **1** : the period between dusk and dawn **2** : the darkness of night **3** : a period of misery or unhappiness **4** : NIGHTFALL — **night** *adj*

night blindness *n* : reduced visual capacity in faint light (as at night)

night•cap \ˈnīt-ˌkap\ *n* **1** : a cloth cap worn with nightclothes **2** : a usu. alcoholic drink taken at bedtime

night•clothes \-ˌklōt͟hz, -ˌklōz\ *n pl* : garments worn in bed

night•club \-ˌkləb\ *n* : a place of entertainment open at night usu. serving food and liquor and providing music for dancing

night crawl•er \-ˌkrȯ-lər\ *n* : EARTHWORM; *esp* : a large earthworm found on the soil surface at night

night•dress \ˈnīt-ˌdres\ *n* : NIGHTGOWN

night•fall \-ˌfȯl\ *n* : the coming of night

night•gown \-ˌgau̇n\ *n* : a loose garment for wear in bed

night•hawk \-ˌhȯk\ *n* : any of a genus of American birds related to and resembling the whippoorwill

night•in•gale \ˈnīt-ᵊn-ˌgāl, ˈnī-tiŋ-\ *n* [ME, fr. OE *nihtegale*, fr. *niht* night + *galan* to sing] : any of several Old World thrushes noted for the sweet usu. nocturnal song of the male

night•life \ˈnīt-ˌlīf\ *n* : the activity of pleasure-seekers at night

night•ly \ˈnīt-lē\ *adj* **1** : happening, done, or produced by night or every night **2** : of or relating to the night or every night — **nightly** *adv*

night•mare \ˈnīt-ˌmar\ *n* **1** : a frightening dream **2** : a frightening or horrible experience — **nightmare** *adj* — **night•mar•ish** *adj*

night rider *n* : a member of a secret band who ride masked at night doing violence to punish or terrorize

night•shade \ˈnīt-ˌshād\ *n* : any of a large genus of herbs, shrubs, and trees that include poisonous forms (as belladonna) and important food plants (as the potato, tomato, and eggplant)

night•shirt \-ˌshərt\ *n* : a nightgown resembling a shirt

night soil *n* : human excrement used esp. for fertilizing the soil

night•stick \ˈnīt-ˌstik\ *n* : a police officer's club

night•time \-ˌtīm\ *n* : the time from dusk to dawn

night•walk•er \-ˌwȯ-kər\ *n* : a person who roves about at night esp. with criminal or immoral intent

ni•hil•ism \ˈnī-ə-ˌli-zəm, ˈnē-hə-\ *n* **1** : a viewpoint that traditional values and beliefs are unfounded and that existence is senseless and useless **2** : ANARCHISM **3** : TERRORISM — **ni•hil•ist** \-list\ *n or adj* — **ni•hil•is•tic** \ˌnī-ə-ˈlis-tik, ˌnē-hə-\ *adj*

nil \ˈnil\ *n* : ZERO, NOTHING

nim•ble \ˈnim-bəl\ *adj* **nim•bler; nim•blest** [ME *nimel*, fr. OE *numol* holding much, fr. *niman* to take] **1** : quick and light in motion : AGILE ⟨a ~ dancer⟩ **2**

: quick in understanding and learning : CLEVER ⟨a ~ mind⟩ **syn** active, brisk, sprightly, spry, zippy — **nim•ble•ness** *n* — **nim•bly** \-blē\ *adv*

nim•bus \ˈnim-bəs\ *n, pl* **nim•bi** \-ˌbī, -bē\ *or* **nim•bus•es** **1** : a figure (as a disk) in an art work suggesting radiant light about the head of a divinity, saint, or sovereign **2** : a rain cloud; *also* : THUNDERHEAD

NIMBY \ˈnim-bē\ *abbr* not in my backyard

nim•rod \ˈnim-ˌräd\ *n* : HUNTER

nin•com•poop \ˈnin-kəm-ˌpüp\ *n* : FOOL, SIMPLETON

nine \ˈnīn\ *n* **1** : one more than eight **2** : the 9th in a set or series **3** : something having nine units; *esp* : a baseball team — **nine** *adj or pron* — **ninth** \ˈnīnth\ *adj or adv or n*

nine days' wonder *n* : something that creates a short-lived sensation

nine•pins \ˈnīn-ˌpinz\ *n* : tenpins played without the headpin

nine•teen \ˈnīn-ˈtēn\ *n* : one more than 18 — **nineteen** *adj or pron* — **nine•teenth** \-ˈtēnth\ *adj or n*

nine•ty \ˈnīn-tē\ *n, pl* **nineties** : nine times 10 — **nine•ti•eth** \-tē-əth\ *adj or n* — **ninety** *adj or pron*

nin•ja \ˈnin-jə, -(ˌ)jä\ *n, pl* **ninja** *or* **ninjas** [Jp] : a person trained in ancient Japanese martial arts and employed esp. for espionage and assassinations

nin•ny \ˈni-nē\ *n, pl* **ninnies** : FOOL

ni•o•bi•um \nī-ˈō-bē-əm\ *n* : a gray metallic chemical element used in alloys — see ELEMENT table

[1]**nip** \ˈnip\ *vb* **nipped; nip•ping** **1** : to catch hold of and squeeze tightly between two surfaces, edges, or points **2** : [3]CLIP **3** : to destroy the growth, progress, or fulfillment of ⟨*nipped* in the bud⟩ **4** : to injure or make numb with cold : CHILL **5** : SNATCH, STEAL

[2]**nip** *n* **1** : a sharp stinging cold **2** : a biting or pungent flavor **3** : PINCH, BITE **4** : a small portion : BIT

[3]**nip** *n* : a small quantity of liquor : SIP

[4]**nip** *vb* **nipped; nip•ping** : to take liquor in nips : TIPPLE

nip and tuck *adj or adv* : so close that the lead shifts rapidly from one contestant to another

nip•per \ˈni-pər\ *n* **1** : one that nips **2** *pl* : PINCERS **3** : CHILD; *esp* : a small boy

nip•ple \ˈni-pəl\ *n* : the protuberance of a mammary gland through which milk is drawn off : TEAT; *also* : something resembling a nipple

nip•py \ˈni-pē\ *adj* **nip•pi•er; -est** **1** : PUNGENT, SHARP **2** : CHILLY

nir•va•na \nir-ˈvä-nə\ *n, often cap* [Skt *nirvāṇa*, lit., act of extinguishing, fr. *nis-* out + *vāti* it blows] **1** : the final freeing of a soul from all that enslaves it; *esp* : the supreme happiness that according to Buddhism comes when all passion, hatred, and delusion die out and the soul is released from the necessity of further purification **2** : OBLIVION; *also* : PARADISE

ni•sei \nē-ˈsā, ˈnē-ˌsā\ *n, pl* **nisei** *also* **niseis** : a son or daughter of immigrant Japanese parents who is born and educated in America

ni•si \ˈnī-ˌsī\ *adj* [L, unless, fr. *ne-* not + *si* if] : taking effect at a specified time unless previously modified or voided ⟨a divorce decree ~⟩

nit \ˈnit\ *n* : the egg of a parasitic insect (as a louse); *also* : the young insect

nite *var of* NIGHT

ni•ter \ˈnī-tər\ *n* : POTASSIUM NITRATE

nit–pick•ing \ˈnit-ˌpi-kiŋ\ *n* : minute and usu. unjustified criticism — **nit•pick•er** *n*

[1]**ni•trate** \ˈnī-ˌtrāt, -trət\ *n* **1** : a salt or ester of nitric acid **2** : sodium nitrate or potassium nitrate used as a fertilizer

[2]**ni•trate** \-ˌtrāt\ *vb* **ni•trat•ed; ni•trat•ing** : to treat or combine with nitric acid or a nitrate — **ni•tra•tion** \nī-ˈtrā-shən\ *n*

ni•tre *chiefly Brit var of* NITER

ni•tric acid \ˈnī-trik-\ *n* : a corrosive liquid acid used esp. in making dyes, explosives, and fertilizers

ni•tri•fi•ca•tion \ˌnī-trə-fə-ˈkā-shən\ *n* : the oxidation (as by bacteria) of ammonium salts to nitrites and then to nitrates — **ni•tri•fy•ing** \ˈnī-trə-fī-iŋ\ *adj*

ni•trite \ˈnī-ˌtrīt\ *n* : a salt of nitrous acid

ni•tro \ˈnī-trō\ *n, pl* **nitros** : any of various nitrated products; *esp* : NITROGLYCERIN

ni•tro•gen \ˈnī-trə-jən\ *n* : a tasteless odorless gaseous chemical element constituting 78 percent of the atmosphere by volume — see ELEMENT table — **ni•trog•e•nous** \nī-ˈträ-jə-nəs\ *adj*

nitrogen narcosis *n* : a state of euphoria and exhilaration caused by nitrogen forced into a diver's bloodstream from atmospheric air under pressure

ni•tro•glyc•er•in *or* **ni•tro•glyc•er•ine** \ˌnī-trə-ˈgli-sə-rən\ *n* : a heavy oily explosive liquid used to make dynamite and in medicine to dilate blood vessels

ni•trous acid \ˈnī-trəs-\ *n* : an unstable nitrogen-containing acid known only in solution or in the form of its salts

nitrous oxide *n* : a colorless gas used esp. as an anesthetic in dentistry

nit•ty–grit•ty \ˈni-tē-ˌgri-tē, ˌni-tē-ˈgri-tē\ *n* : what is essential and basic : specific practical details

nit•wit \ˈnit-ˌwit\ *n* : a scatterbrained or stupid person

[1]**nix** \ˈniks\ *n* : NOTHING

[2]**nix** *vb* : VETO, REJECT

[3]**nix** *adv* : NO

NJ *abbr* New Jersey

NL *abbr* National League

NLRB *abbr* National Labor Relations Board

NM *abbr* **1** nautical mile **2** New Mexico

N Mex *abbr* New Mexico

NMI *abbr* no middle initial

NNE *abbr* north-northeast

NNW *abbr* north-northwest

[1]**no** \ˈnō\ *adv* **1** — used to express the negative of an alternative ⟨shall we continue or ~⟩ **2** : in no respect or degree ⟨he is ~ better than the others⟩ **3** : not so ⟨~, I'm not ready⟩ **4** — used with an adjective to imply a meaning opposite to the positive statement ⟨in ~ uncertain terms⟩ **5** — used to introduce a more emphatic or explicit statement ⟨has the right, ~, the duty to continue⟩ **6** — used as an interjection to express surprise or doubt ⟨~—you don't say⟩ **7** — used in combination with a verb to form a compound adjective ⟨*no*-bake pie⟩

[2]**no** *adj* **1** : not any; *also* : hardly any **2** : not a ⟨she's ~ expert⟩

[3]**no** \ˈnō\ *n, pl* **noes** *or* **nos** \ˈnōz\ **1** : REFUSAL, DENIAL **2** : a negative vote or decision; *also, pl* : persons voting in the negative

[4]**no** *abbr* **1** north; northern **2** [L *numero*, abl. of *numerus*] number

[1]**No** *or* **Noh** \ˈnō\ *n, pl* **No** *or* **Noh** : classic Japanese dance-drama having a heroic theme, a chorus, and highly stylized action, costuming, and scenery

[2]**No** *symbol* nobelium

No•bel•ist \nō-ˈbe-list\ *n* : a winner of a Nobel prize

no•bel•i•um \nō-ˈbe-lē-əm\ *n* : a radioactive chemical element produced artificially — see ELEMENT table

No•bel prize \nō-ˈbel-, ˈnō-ˌbel-\ *n* : any of various annual prizes (as in peace, literature, or medicine) established by the will of Alfred Nobel for the encouragement of persons who work for the interests of humanity

no•bil•i•ty \nō-ˈbi-lə-tē\ *n* **1** : the quality or state of being noble **2** : nobles considered as forming a class

[1]**no•ble** \ˈnō-bəl\ *adj* **no•bler; no•blest** [ME, fr. OF, fr. L *nobilis* well known, noble, fr. *noscere* to come to know] **1** : ILLUSTRIOUS; *also* : FAMOUS, NOTABLE **2** : of high birth, rank, or station : ARISTOCRATIC **3** : EXCELLENT **4** : STATELY, IMPOSING ⟨a ~ edifice⟩ **5** : of a superior nature **syn** august, baronial, grand, grandiose, magnificent, majestic — **no•ble•ness** *n* — **no•bly** \-blē\ *adv*

[2]**no•ble** *n* : a person of noble rank or birth

no•ble•man \ˈnō-bəl-mən\ *n* : a member of the nobility : PEER

DICTIONARY

no•blesse oblige \nō-ˌbles-ə-ˈblēzh\ *n* [F, lit., nobility obligates] : the obligation of honorable, generous, and responsible behavior associated with high rank or birth

no•ble•wom•an \ˈnō-bəl-ˌwu̇-mən\ *n* : a woman of noble rank : PEERESS

[1]**no•body** \ˈnō-ˌbä-dē, -bə-\ *pron* : no person

[2]**nobody** *n, pl* **no•bod•ies** : a person of no influence or importance

no–brain•er \ˈnō-ˈbrā-nər\ *n* : something that requires a minimum of thought

noc•tur•nal \näk-ˈtərn-ᵊl\ *adj* **1** : of, relating to, or occurring in the night **2** : active at night ⟨a ~ bird⟩

noc•turne \ˈnäk-ˌtərn\ *n* : a work of art dealing with night; *esp* : a dreamy pensive composition for the piano

noc•u•ous \ˈnä-kyə-wəs\ *adj* : HARMFUL — **noc•u•ous•ly** *adv*

nod \ˈnäd\ *vb* **nod•ded; nod•ding 1** : to bend the head downward or forward (as in bowing, going to sleep, or giving assent) **2** : to move up and down ⟨tulips *nodding* in the breeze⟩ **3** : to show by a nod of the head ⟨~ agreement⟩ **4** : to make a slip or error in a moment of abstraction — **nod** *n*

nod•dle \ˈnäd-ᵊl\ *n* : HEAD

nod•dy \ˈnä-dē\ *n, pl* **noddies 1** : FOOL **2** : a stout-bodied tropical tern

node \ˈnōd\ *n* : a thickened, swollen, or differentiated area (as of tissue); *esp* : the part of a stem from which a leaf arises — **nod•al** \-ᵊl\ *adj*

nod•ule \ˈnä-jül\ *n* : a small lump or swelling — **nod•u•lar** \ˈnä-jə-lər\ *adj*

no•el \nō-ˈel\ *n* [F *noël* Christmas, carol, fr. L *natalis* birthday] **1** : a Christmas carol **2** *cap* : the Christmas season

noes *pl of* NO

no–fault \ˈnō-ˈfȯlt\ *adj* **1** : of, relating to, or being a motor vehicle insurance plan under which someone involved in an accident is compensated usu. up to a stipulated limit for actual losses by that person's own insurance company regardless of who is responsible **2** : of, relating to, or being a divorce law under which neither party is held responsible for the breakup of the marriage

nog•gin \ˈnä-gən\ *n* **1** : a small mug or cup; *also* : a small quantity of drink **2** : a person's head

no–good \ˈnō-ˈgu̇d\ *adj* : having no worth, virtue, use, or chance of success — **no–good** \ˈnō-ˌgu̇d\ *n*

Noh *var of* NO

no–hit•ter \(ˌ)nō-ˈhi-tər\ *n* : a baseball game or part of a game in which a pitcher allows no base hits

no•how \ˈnō-ˌhau̇\ *adv* : in no manner

[1]**noise** \ˈnȯiz\ *n* [ME, fr. OF, strife, quarrel, noise, fr. L *nausea* nausea] **1** : loud, confused, or senseless shouting or outcry **2** : SOUND; *esp* : one that lacks agreeable musical quality or is noticeably unpleasant **3** : unwanted electronic signal or disturbance — **noise•less** *adj* — **noise•less•ly** *adv*

[2]**noise** *vb* **noised; nois•ing** : to spread by rumor or report ⟨the story was *noised* abroad⟩

noise•mak•er \ˈnȯiz-ˌmā-kər\ *n* : one that makes noise; *esp* : a device used to make noise at parties

noise pollution *n* : annoying or harmful noise in an environment

noi•some \ˈnȯi-səm\ *adj* **1** : HARMFUL, UNWHOLESOME **2** : offensive to the senses (as smell) : DISGUSTING **syn** insalubrious, noxious, sickly, unhealthful, unhealthy

noisy \ˈnȯi-zē\ *adj* **nois•i•er; -est 1** : making loud noises **2** : full of noises : LOUD — **nois•i•ly** \-zə-lē\ *adv* — **nois•i•ness** \-zē-nəs\ *n*

nol•le pro•se•qui \ˌnä-lē-ˈprä-sə-ˌkwī\ *n* [L, to be unwilling to pursue] : an entry on the record of a legal action that the prosecutor or plaintiff will proceed no further in an action or suit or in some aspect of it

no•lo con•ten•de•re \ˌnō-lō-kən-ˈten-də-rē\ *n* [L, I do not wish to contend] : a plea in a criminal prosecution that subjects the defendant to conviction but does not admit guilt or preclude denying the charges in another proceeding

nol–pros \ˈnäl-ˈpräs\ *vb* **nol–prossed; nol–pros•sing** : to discontinue by entering a nolle prosequi

nom *abbr* nominative

no•mad \ˈnō-ˌmad\ *n* **1** : a member of a people who have no fixed residence but move from place to place **2** : an individual who roams about aimlessly — **nomad** *adj* — **no•mad•ic** \nō-ˈma-dik\ *adj*

no–man's–land \ˈnō-ˌmanz-ˌland\ *n* **1** : an area of unowned, unclaimed, or uninhabited land **2** : an unoccupied area between opposing troops

nom de guerre \ˌnäm-di-ˈger\ *n, pl* **noms de guerre** *same or* ˌnämz-\ [F, lit., war name] : PSEUDONYM

nom de plume \-ˈplüm\ *n, pl* **noms de plume** *same or* ˌnämz-\ [F, pen name; prob. coined in E] : PEN NAME

no•men•cla•ture \ˈnō-mən-ˌklā-chər\ *n* **1** : NAME, DESIGNATION **2** : a system of terms used in a science or art

nom•i•nal \ˈnä-mən-ᵊl\ *adj* **1** : being something in name or form only ⟨~ head of a party⟩ **2** : TRIFLING ⟨a ~ price⟩ — **nom•i•nal•ly** *adv*

nom•i•nate \ˈnä-mə-ˌnāt\ *vb* **-nat•ed; -nat•ing** : to choose as a candidate for election, appointment, or honor **syn** appoint, designate, name, tap — **nom•i•na•tion** \ˌnä-mə-ˈnā-shən\ *n*

nom•i•na•tive \ˈnä-mə-nə-tiv\ *adj* : of, relating to, or constituting a grammatical case marking typically the subject of a verb — **nominative** *n*

nom•i•nee \ˌnä-mə-ˈnē\ *n* : a person nominated for an office, duty, or position

non- \(ˈ)nän *or* ˌnän *before stressed syllables;* ˌnän *elsewhere*\ *prefix* **1** : not : reverse of : absence of **2** : having no importance

nonabrasive
nonabsorbent
nonacademic
nonacceptance
nonacid
nonactivated
nonadaptive
nonaddictive
nonadhesive
nonadjacent
nonadjustable
nonaggression
nonalcoholic
nonappearance
nonaromatic
nonathletic
nonattendance
nonbeliever
nonbelligerent
nonbreakable
noncancerous
noncandidate
noncellular
nonclerical
noncoital
noncombat
noncombustible
noncommercial
noncommunist
noncompeting
noncompetitive
noncompliance
noncomplying
nonconducting
nonconflicting
nonconformance
nonconforming
nonconstructive
noncontagious
noncontinuous
noncorroding
noncorrosive
noncritical
noncrystalline
nondeductible
nondelivery
nondemocratic
nondenominational
nondepartmental
nondestructive
nondevelopment
nondiscrimination
nondiscriminatory
nondistinctive
nondurable
noneconomic
noneducational
nonelastic
nonelection
nonelective
nonelectric
nonelectrical
nonemotional
nonenforcement
nonessential
nonethical
non-euclidean
nonexclusive
nonexempt
nonexistence
nonexistent
nonexplosive
nonfarm
nonfatal
nonfattening
nonfederated
nonferrous
nonfiction
nonfictional
nonfilamentous
nonfilterable
nonflammable

nonflowering
nonfood
nonfreezing
nonfulfillment
nonfunctional
nongraded
nonhereditary
nonhomogeneous
nonhomologous
nonhuman
nonidentical
nonimportation
nonindustrial
noninfectious
noninflammable
nonintellectual
nonintercourse
noninterference
nonintoxicant
nonintoxicating
noninvasive
nonionizing
nonirritating
nonlegal
nonlethal
nonlife
nonlinear
nonliterary
nonliving
nonlogical
nonmagnetic
nonmalignant
nonmaterial
nonmember
nonmembership
nonmigratory
nonmilitary
nonmoral
nonmotile
nonmoving
nonnegotiable
nonobservance
nonoccurrence
nonofficial
nonoily
nonorthodox
nonparallel
nonparasitic
nonparticipant
nonparticipating
nonpathogenic
nonpaying
nonpayment
nonperformance
nonperishable
nonphysical
nonpoisonous
nonpolar
nonpolitical
nonporous
nonpregnant
nonproductive
nonprofessional
nonprotein
nonradioactive
nonrandom
nonreactive
nonreciprocal
nonrecognition
nonrecurrent
nonrecurring
nonrefillable
nonreligious
nonrenewable
nonresidential
nonrestricted
nonreturnable
nonreversible
nonruminant
nonsalable
nonscientific
nonscientist
nonseasonal
nonsectarian
nonsegregated
nonselective
non-self-governing
nonsexist
nonsexual
nonshrinkable
nonsinkable
nonsmoker
nonsmoking
nonsocial
nonspeaking
nonspecialist
nonspecific
nonsteroidal
nonsuccess
nonsurgical
nontaxable
nonteaching
nontechnical
nontemporal
nontenured
nontheistic
nonthreatening
nontoxic
nontraditional
nontransferable
nontypical
nonuniform
nonvascular
nonvenomous
nonverbal
nonviable
nonvisual
nonvocal
nonvolatile
nonvoter
nonvoting
nonworker
nonworking
nonzero

non•age \ˈnä-nij, ˈnō-\ *n* **1 :** legal minority **2 :** a period of youth **3 :** IMMATURITY

no•na•ge•nar•i•an \ˌnō-nə-jə-ˈner-ē-ən, ˌnä-\ *n* **:** a person whose age is in the nineties

non•aligned \ˌnän-ə-ˈlīnd\ *adj* **:** not allied with other nations

non•book \ˈnän-ˌbu̇k\ *n* **:** a book of little literary merit that is often a compilation (as of pictures or speeches)

[1]**nonce** \ˈnäns\ *n* **:** the one, particular, or present occasion or purpose ⟨for the ~⟩

[2]**nonce** *adj* **:** occurring, used, or made only once or for a special occasion ⟨a ~ word⟩

non•cha•lant \ˌnän-shə-ˈlänt\ *adj* [F, fr. OF, fr. prp. of *nonchaloir* to disregard, fr. *non-* not + *chaloir* to concern, fr. L *calēre* to be warm] **:** giving an effect of unconcern or indifference **syn** collected, composed, cool, imperturbable, unflappable, unruffled — **non•cha•lance** \-ˈläns\ *n* — **non•cha•lant•ly** *adv*

non•com \ˈnän-ˌkäm\ *n* **:** NONCOMMISSIONED OFFICER

non•com•ba•tant \ˌnän-kəm-ˈbat-ᵊnt, nän-ˈkäm-bə-tənt\ *n* **:** a member (as a chaplain) of the armed forces whose duties do not include fighting; *also* **:** CIVILIAN — **noncombatant** *adj*

non•com•mis•sioned officer \ˌnän-kə-ˈmi-shənd-\ *n* **:** a subordinate officer in the armed forces appointed from enlisted personnel

non•com•mit•tal \ˌnän-kə-ˈmit-ᵊl\ *adj* **:** indicating neither consent nor dissent

non com•pos men•tis \ˌnän-ˌkäm-pəs-ˈmen-təs\ *adj* **:** not of sound mind

non•con•duc•tor \ˌnän-kən-ˈdək-tər\ *n* **:** a substance that is a very poor conductor of heat, electricity, or sound

non•con•form•ist \-kən-ˈfȯr-mist\ *n* **1** *often cap* **:** a person who does not conform to an established church and esp. the Church of England **2 :** a person who does not conform to a generally accepted pattern of thought or action **syn** dissenter, dissident, heretic, schismatic, sectary, separatist — **non•con•for•mi•ty** \-ˈfȯr-mə-tē\ *n*

non•co•op•er•a•tion \ˌnän-kō-ˌä-pə-ˈrā-shən\ *n* **:** failure or refusal to cooperate; *esp* **:** refusal through civil disobedience of a people to cooperate with the government of a country

non•cred•it \(ˌ)nän-ˈkre-dət\ *adj* **:** not offering credit toward a degree

non•cus•to•di•al \ˌnän-kə-ˈstō-dē-əl\ *adj* **:** of or being a parent who does not have legal custody of a child

non•dairy \ˈnän-ˈder-ē\ *adj* **:** containing no milk or milk products

non•de•script \ˌnän-di-ˈskript\ *adj* **1 :** not belonging to any particular class or kind **2 :** lacking distinctive qualities

non•drink•er \-ˈdriŋ-kər\ *n* **:** a person who abstains from alcohol

[1]**none** \ˈnən\ *pron* **1 :** not any ⟨~ of them went⟩ **2 :** not one ⟨~ of the family⟩ **3 :** not any such thing or person ⟨half a loaf is better than ~⟩

[2]**none** *adj, archaic* **:** not any **:** NO

[3]**none** *adv* **:** by no means **:** not at all ⟨he got there ~ too soon⟩

non•en•ti•ty \ˌnän-ˈen-tə-tē\ *n* **1 :** something that does not exist or exists only in the imagination **2 :** one of no consequence or significance **syn** nobody, nothing, whippersnapper

nones \ˈnōnz\ *n sing or pl* **:** the 7th day of March, May, July, or October or the 5th day of any other month in the ancient Roman calendar

none•such \ˈnən-ˌsəch\ *n* **:** one without an equal — **nonesuch** *adj*

none•the•less \ˌnən-t͟hə-ˈles\ *adv* **:** NEVERTHELESS

non•event \ˈnän-i-ˌvent\ *n* **1 :** an event that fails to take place or to satisfy expectations **2 :** a highly promoted event of little intrinsic interest

non•fat \-ˈfat\ *adj* **:** lacking fat solids **:** having fat solids removed ⟨~ milk⟩

non•gono•coc•cal \ˌnän-ˌgä-nə-ˈkä-kəl\ *adj* **:** not caused by a gonococcus

non•he•ro \ˈnän-ˈhē-rō\ *n* **:** ANTIHERO

non•in•ter•ven•tion \ˌnän-ˌin-tər-ˈven-chən\ *n* **:** refusal or failure to intervene (as in the affairs of other countries)

non•met•al \ˈnän-ˈmet-ᵊl\ *n* **:** a chemical element (as carbon) that lacks the characteristics of a metal — **non•me•tal•lic** \ˌnän-mə-ˈta-lik\ *adj*

non•neg•a•tive \-ˈne-gə-tiv\ *adj* **:** not negative **:** being either positive or zero

non•nu•cle•ar \ˈnän-ˈnü-klē-ər\ *adj* **1 :** not nuclear **2 :** not having, using, or involving nuclear weapons

non•ob•jec•tive \ˌnän-əb-ˈjek-tiv\ *adj* **1 :** not objective

2 : representing no natural or actual object, figure, or scene ⟨~ art⟩

[1]**non•pa•reil** \-pə-ˈrel\ *adj* : having no equal : PEERLESS

[2]**nonpareil** *n* **1** : an individual of unequaled excellence : PARAGON **2** : a small flat disk of chocolate covered with white sugar pellets

non•par•ti•san \ˈnän-ˈpär-tə-zən\ *adj* : not partisan; *esp* : not influenced by political party spirit or interests

non•per•son \-ˈpərs-ᵊn\ *n* **1** : UNPERSON **2** : a person having no social or legal status

non•plus \ˈnän-ˈpləs\ *vb* **-plussed** *also* **-plused** \-ˈpləst\; **-plus•sing** *also* **-plus•ing** : PUZZLE, PERPLEX

non•pre•scrip•tion \ˌnän-pri-ˈskrip-shən\ *adj* : available for sale legally without a doctor's prescription

non•prof•it \ˈnän-ˈprä-fət\ *adj* : not conducted or maintained for the purpose of making a profit ⟨a ~ organization⟩

non•pro•lif•er•a•tion \ˌnän-prə-ˌli-fə-ˈrā-shən\ *adj* : providing for the stoppage of proliferation (as of nuclear arms) ⟨a ~ treaty⟩

non•read•er \ˈnän-ˈrē-dər\ *n* : one who does not read

non•rep•re•sen•ta•tion•al \ˌnän-ˌre-pri-ˌzen-ˈtā-shə-nəl\ *adj* : NONOBJECTIVE 2

non•res•i•dent \ˈnän-ˈre-zə-dənt\ *adj* : not living in a particular place — **non•res•i•dence** \-dəns\ *n* — **nonresident** *n*

non•re•sis•tance \ˌnän-ri-ˈzis-təns\ *n* : the principles or practice of passive submission to authority even when unjust or oppressive

non•re•stric•tive \-ri-ˈstrik-tiv\ *adj* **1** : not serving or tending to restrict **2** : not limiting the reference of the word or phrase modified ⟨a ~ clause⟩

non•rig•id \nän-ˈri-jəd\ *adj* : maintaining form by pressure of contained gas ⟨a ~ airship⟩

non•sched•uled \ˈnän-ˈske-jüld\ *adj* : licensed to carry passengers or freight by air without a regular schedule

non•sense \ˈnän-ˌsens, -səns\ *n* **1** : foolish or meaningless words or actions **2** : things of no importance or value — **non•sen•si•cal** \nän-ˈsen-si-kəl\ *adj* — **non•sen•si•cal•ly** \-k(ə-)lē\ *adv*

non se•qui•tur \nän-ˈse-kwə-tər\ *n* [L, it does not follow] : an inference that does not follow from the premises

non•sked \ˈnän-ˈsked\ *n* : a nonscheduled transport plane or airline

non•skid \ˈnän-ˈskid\ *adj* : designed to prevent skidding

non•slip \-ˈslip\ *adj* : designed to prevent slipping

non•stan•dard \ˌnän-ˈstan-dərd\ *adj* **1** : not standard **2** : not conforming to the usage characteristic of educated native speakers of a language

non•start•er \ˈnän-ˈstär-tər\ *n* **1** : one that does not start **2** : one that is not productive or effective

non•stick \-ˈstik\ *adj* : allowing easy removal of cooked food particles

non•stop \-ˈstäp\ *adj* : done or made without a stop — **nonstop** *adv*

non•sup•port \ˌnän-sə-ˈpōrt\ *n* : failure to support; *esp* : failure on the part of one under obligation to provide maintenance

non–U \ˈnän-ˈyü\ *adj* : not characteristic of the upper classes

non•union \-ˈyü-nyən\ *adj* **1** : not belonging to a trade union ⟨~ carpenters⟩ **2** : not recognizing or favoring trade unions or their members ⟨~ employers⟩

non•us•er \-ˈyü-zər\ *n* : one who does not make use of something (as drugs)

non•vi•o•lence \ˈnän-ˈvī-ə-ləns\ *n* **1** : abstention from violence as a matter of principle **2** : avoidance of violence **3** : nonviolent political demonstrations — **non•vi•o•lent** \-lənt\ *adj*

non•white \ˌnän-ˈhwīt, -ˈwīt\ *n* : a person whose features and esp. skin color are different from those of peoples of northwestern Europe — **nonwhite** *adj*

non•wo•ven \ˈnän-ˈwō-vən\ *adj* : made of fibers held together by interlocking or bonding (as by chemical or thermal means) — **nonwoven** *n*

noo•dle \ˈnüd-ᵊl\ *n* [G *Nudel*] : a food paste made with egg and shaped typically in ribbon form

nook \ˈnu̇k\ *n* **1** : an interior angle or corner formed usu. by two walls ⟨a chimney ~⟩ **2** : a sheltered or hidden place ⟨searched every ~ and cranny⟩

noon \ˈnün\ *n* : the middle of the day : 12 o'clock in the daytime — **noon** *adj*

noon•day \ˈnün-ˌdā\ *n* : NOON, MIDDAY

no one *pron* : NOBODY

noon•tide \ˈnün-ˌtīd\ *n* : NOON

noon•time \-ˌtīm\ *n* : NOON

noose \ˈnüs\ *n* : a loop with a running knot (as in a lasso) that binds closer the more it is drawn

nope \ˈnōp\ *adv* : NO

nor \ˈnȯr\ *conj* : and not ⟨not for you ~ for me⟩ — used esp. to introduce and negate the second member and each later member of a series of items preceded by *neither* ⟨neither here ~ there⟩

Nor *abbr* Norway; Norwegian

Nor•dic \ˈnȯr-dik\ *adj* **1** : of or relating to the Germanic peoples of northern Europe and esp. of Scandinavia **2** : of or relating to competitive ski events involving cross-country racing, ski jumping, or biathlon — **Nordic** *n*

nor•epi•neph•rine \ˈnȯr-ˌe-pə-ˈne-frən\ *n* : a nitrogen-containing neurotransmitter in parts of the sympathetic and central nervous systems

norm \ˈnȯrm\ *n* [L *norma,* lit., carpenter's square] **1** : an authoritative standard or model; *esp* : a set standard of development or achievement usu. derived from the average or median achievement of a large group **2** : a typical or widespread practice, procedure, or custom **syn** average, mean, median, par

[1]**nor•mal** \ˈnȯr-məl\ *adj* **1** : REGULAR, STANDARD, NATURAL **2** : of average intelligence; *also* : sound in mind and body — **nor•mal•cy** \-sē\ *n* — **nor•mal•i•ty** \nȯr-ˈma-lə-tē\ *n* — **nor•mal•ly** *adv*

[2]**normal** *n* **1** : one that is normal **2** : the usual condition, level, or quantity

nor•mal•ise *Brit var of* NORMALIZE

nor•mal•ize \ˈnȯr-mə-ˌlīz\ *vb* **-ized; -iz•ing** : to make or restore to normal — **nor•mal•i•za•tion** \ˌnȯr-mə-lə-ˈzā-shən\ *n*

Nor•man \ˈnȯr-mən\ *n* **1** : a native or inhabitant of Normandy **2** : one of the 10th century Scandinavian conquerors of Normandy **3** : one of the Norman-French conquerors of England in 1066 — **Norman** *adj*

nor•ma•tive \ˈnȯr-mə-tiv\ *adj* : of, relating to, or determining norms — **nor•ma•tive•ly** *adv* — **nor•ma•tive•ness** *n*

Norse \ˈnȯrs\ *n, pl* **Norse 1** : NORWEGIAN; *also* : any of the western Scandinavian dialects or languages **2** *pl* : SCANDINAVIANS; *also* : NORWEGIANS

Norse•man \-mən\ *n* : any of the ancient Scandinavians

[1]**north** \ˈnȯrth\ *adv* : to, toward, or in the north

[2]**north** *adj* **1** : situated toward or at the north **2** : coming from the north

[3]**north** *n* **1** : the direction to the left of one facing east **2** : the compass point directly opposite to south **3** *cap* : regions or countries north of a specified or implied point — **north•er•ly** \ˈnȯr-t͟hər-lē\ *adv or adj* — **north•ern** \-t͟hərn\ *adj* — **North•ern•er** \-t͟hər-nər\ *n* — **north•ern•most** \-t͟hərn-ˌmōst\ *adj* — **north•ward** \ˈnȯrth-wərd\ *adv or adj* — **north•wards** \-wərdz\ *adv*

north•east \nȯr-ˈthēst\ *n* **1** : the general direction between north and east **2** : the compass point midway between north and east **3** *cap* : regions or countries northeast of a specified or implied point — **northeast** *adj or adv* — **north•east•er•ly** \-ˈthē-stər-lē\ *adv or adj* — **north•east•ern** \-stərn\ *adj*

north•east•er \-ˈthēs-tər\ *n* **1 :** a strong northeast wind **2 :** a storm with northeast winds
north•er \ˈnȯr-t͟hər\ *n* **1 :** a strong north wind **2 :** a storm with north winds
northern lights *n pl* **:** AURORA BOREALIS
north pole *n, often cap N&P* **:** the northernmost point of the earth
North Star *n* **:** the star toward which the northern end of the earth's axis points
north•west \nȯrth-ˈwest\ *n* **1 :** the general direction between north and west **2 :** the compass point midway between north and west **3** *cap* **:** regions or countries northwest of a specified or implied point — **northwest** *adj or adv* — **north•west•er•ly** \-ˈwe-stər-lē\ *adv or adj* — **north•west•ern** \-ˈwe-stərn\ *adj*
Norw *abbr* Norway; Norwegian
Nor•we•gian \nȯr-ˈwē-jən\ *n* **1 :** a native or inhabitant of Norway **2 :** the language of Norway — **Norwegian** *adj*
nos *abbr* numbers
¹nose \ˈnōz\ *n* **1 :** the part of the face or head containing the nostrils and covering the front of the nasal cavity **2 :** the sense of smell **3 :** something (as a point, edge, or projecting front part) that resembles a nose ⟨the ~ of a plane⟩ — **nosed** \ˈnōzd\ *adj*
²nose *vb* **nosed; nos•ing 1 :** to detect by or as if by smell **:** SCENT **2 :** to push or move with the nose **3 :** to touch or rub with the nose **:** NUZZLE **4 :** PRY **5 :** to move ahead slowly ⟨the ship *nosed* into her berth⟩
nose•bleed \ˈnōz-ˌblēd\ *n* **:** a bleeding from the nose
nose cone *n* **:** a protective cone constituting the forward end of an aerospace vehicle
nose dive *n* **1 :** a downward nose-first plunge (as of an airplane) **2 :** a sudden extreme drop (as in prices)
nose•gay \ˈnōz-ˌgā\ *n* **:** a small bunch of flowers **:** POSY
nose out *vb* **1 :** to discover often by prying **2 :** to defeat by a narrow margin
nose•piece \-ˌpēs\ *n* **1 :** a fitting at the lower end of a microscope tube to which the objectives are attached **2 :** the bridge of a pair of eyeglasses
no–show \ˈnō-ˈshō\ *n* **:** a person who reserves space (as on an airplane or at a concert) but neither uses nor cancels the reservation
nos•tal•gia \nä-ˈstal-jə\ *n* [NL, fr. Gk *nostos* return home + *algos* pain, grief] **1 :** HOMESICKNESS **2 :** a wistful yearning for something past or irrecoverable — **nos•tal•gic** \-jik\ *adj*
nos•tril \ˈnäs-trəl\ *n* [ME *nosethirl*, fr. OE *nosthyrl*, fr. *nosu* nose + *thyrel* hole] **1 :** either of the nares usu. with the adjoining nasal wall and passage **2 :** either fleshy lateral wall of the nose
nos•trum \ˈnäs-trəm\ *n* [L, neut. of *noster* our, ours, fr. *nos* we] **:** a questionable medicine or remedy
nosy *or* **nos•ey** \ˈnō-zē\ *adj* **nos•i•er; -est :** INQUISITIVE, PRYING
not \ˈnät\ *adv* **1** — used to make negative a group of words or a word ⟨the boys are ~ here⟩ **2** — used to stand for the negative of a preceding group of words ⟨sometimes hard to see and sometimes ~⟩
no•ta be•ne \ˌnō-tə-ˈbē-nē, -ˈbe-\ [L, mark well] — used to call attention to something important
no•ta•bil•i•ty \ˌnō-tə-ˈbi-lə-tē\ *n, pl* **-ties 1 :** the quality or state of being notable **2 :** NOTABLE
¹no•ta•ble \ˈnō-tə-bəl\ *adj* **1 :** NOTEWORTHY, REMARKABLE ⟨a ~ achievement⟩ **2 :** DISTINGUISHED, PROMINENT ⟨two ~ politicians made speeches⟩
²notable *n* **:** a person of note **syn** bigwig, eminence, nabob, personage, somebody, VIP
no•ta•bly \ˈnō-tə-blē\ *adv* **1 :** in a notable manner **2 :** ESPECIALLY, PARTICULARLY
no•tar•i•al \nō-ˈter-ē-əl\ *adj* **:** of, relating to, or done by a notary public
no•ta•rize \ˈnō-tə-ˌrīz\ *vb* **-rized; -riz•ing :** to acknowledge or make legally authentic as a notary public
no•ta•ry public \ˈnō-tə-rē-\ *n, pl* **notaries public** *or* **notary publics :** a public official who attests or certifies writings (as deeds) to make them legally authentic
no•ta•tion \nō-ˈtā-shən\ *n* **1 :** ANNOTATION, NOTE **2 :** the act, process, or method of representing data by marks, signs, figures, or characters; *also* **:** a system of symbols (as letters, numerals, or musical notes) used in such notation
¹notch \ˈnäch\ *n* **1 :** a V-shaped hollow in an edge or surface **2 :** a narrow pass between two mountains
²notch *vb* **1 :** to cut or make notches in **2 :** to score or record by or as if by cutting a series of notches ⟨~*ed* 20 points for the team⟩
notch•back \ˈnäch-ˌbak\ *n* **:** an automobile with a trunk whose lid forms a distinct deck
¹note \ˈnōt\ *vb* **not•ed; not•ing 1 :** to notice or observe with care; *also* **:** to record or preserve in writing **2 :** to make special mention of **:** REMARK
²note *n* **1 :** a musical sound **2 :** a cry, call, or sound esp. of a bird **3 :** a special tone in a person's words or voice ⟨a ~ of fear⟩ **4 :** a character in music used to indicate duration of a tone by its shape and pitch by its position on the staff **5 :** a characteristic feature **:** MOOD, QUALITY ⟨a ~ of optimism⟩ **6 :** MEMORANDUM **7 :** a brief and informal record; *also* **:** a written or printed comment or explanation **8 :** a written promise to pay a debt **9 :** a piece of paper money **10 :** a short informal letter **11 :** a formal diplomatic or official communication **12 :** DISTINCTION, REPUTATION ⟨an artist of ~⟩ **13 :** OBSERVATION, NOTICE, HEED ⟨take ~ of the time⟩
note•book \ˈnōt-ˌbu̇k\ *n* **:** a book for notes or memoranda
not•ed \ˈnō-təd\ *adj* **:** well known by reputation **:** EMINENT, CELEBRATED
note•wor•thy \ˈnōt-ˌwər-t͟hē\ *adj* **:** worthy of note **:** REMARKABLE
¹noth•ing \ˈnə-thiŋ\ *pron* **1 :** no thing ⟨leaves ~ to the imagination⟩ **2 :** no part **3 :** one of no interest, value, or importance ⟨she's ~ to me⟩
²nothing *adv* **:** not at all **:** in no degree
³nothing *n* **1 :** something that does not exist **2 :** ZERO **3 :** a person or thing of little or no value or importance
⁴nothing *adj* **:** of no account **:** worthless
noth•ing•ness \ˈnə-thiŋ-nəs\ *n* **1 :** the quality or state of being nothing **2 :** NONEXISTENCE; *also* **:** utter insignificance **3 :** something insignificant or valueless
¹no•tice \ˈnō-təs\ *n* **1 :** WARNING, ANNOUNCEMENT **2 :** notification of the termination of an agreement or contract at a specified time **3 :** ATTENTION, HEED ⟨bring the matter to my ~⟩ **4 :** a written or printed announcement **5 :** a short critical account or examination (as of a play) **:** REVIEW
²notice *vb* **no•ticed; no•tic•ing 1 :** to make mention of **:** remark on **:** NOTE **2 :** to take notice of **:** OBSERVE, MARK
no•tice•able \ˈnō-tə-sə-bəl\ *adj* **1 :** worthy of notice **2 :** capable of being or likely to be noticed — **no•tice•ably** \-blē\ *adv*
no•ti•fy \ˈnō-tə-ˌfī\ *vb* **-fied; -fy•ing 1 :** to give notice of **:** report the occurrence of **2 :** to give notice to — **no•ti•fi•ca•tion** \ˌnō-tə-fə-ˈkā-shən\ *n*
no•tion \ˈnō-shən\ *n* **1 :** IDEA, CONCEPTION ⟨have a ~ of what he means⟩ **2 :** a belief held **:** OPINION, VIEW **3 :** WHIM, FANCY ⟨a sudden ~ to go⟩ **4** *pl* **:** small useful articles (as pins, needles, or thread)
no•tion•al \ˈnō-shə-nəl\ *adj* **1 :** existing in the mind only **:** IMAGINARY, UNREAL **2 :** given to foolish or fanciful moods or ideas **:** WHIMSICAL
no•to•ri•ous \nō-ˈtōr-ē-əs\ *adj* **:** generally known and talked of; *esp* **:** widely and unfavorably known — **no•to•ri•ety** \ˌnō-tə-ˈrī-ə-tē\ *n* — **no•to•ri•ous•ly** \nō-ˈtōr-ē-əs-lē\ *adv*
¹not•with•stand•ing \ˌnät-with-ˈstan-diŋ, -wit͟h-\ *prep* **:** in spite of
²notwithstanding *adv* **:** NEVERTHELESS
³notwithstanding *conj* **:** ALTHOUGH
nou•gat \ˈnü-gət\ *n* [F, fr. Provençal, fr. Old Provençal

nogat, fr. *noga* nut, ultim. fr. L *nuc-, nux*] : a confection of nuts or fruit pieces in a sugar paste
nought \ˈnȯt, ˈnät\ *var of* NAUGHT
noun \ˈnau̇n\ *n* : a word that is the name of a subject of discourse (as a person or place)
nour•ish \ˈnər-ish\ *vb* : to promote the growth or development of
nour•ish•ing *adj* : giving nourishment
nour•ish•ment \ˈnər-ish-mənt\ *n* **1** : FOOD, NUTRIENT **2** : the action or process of nourishing
nou•veau riche \ˌnü-ˌvō-ˈrēsh\ *n, pl* **nou•veaux riches** *same* \ [F] : a person newly rich : PARVENU
Nov *abbr* November
no•va \ˈnō-və\ *n, pl* **novas** *or* **no•vae** \-(ˌ)vē, -ˌvī\ [NL, fem. of L *novus* new] : a star that suddenly increases greatly in brightness and then within a few months or years grows dim again
¹nov•el \ˈnä-vəl\ *adj* **1** : having no precedent : NEW **2** : STRANGE, UNUSUAL
²novel *n* : a long invented prose narrative dealing with human experience through a connected sequence of events — **nov•el•ist** \-və-list\ *n*
nov•el•ette \ˌnä-və-ˈlet\ *n* : a brief novel or long short story
nov•el•ize \ˈnä-və-ˌlīz\ *vb* **-ized; -iz•ing** : to convert into the form of a novel — **nov•el•i•za•tion** \ˌnä-və-lə-ˈzā-shən\ *n*
no•vel•la \nō-ˈve-lə\ *n, pl* **novellas** *or* **no•vel•le** \-ˈve-lē\ : NOVELETTE
nov•el•ty \ˈnä-vəl-tē\ *n, pl* **-ties** **1** : something new or unusual **2** : NEWNESS **3** : a small manufactured article intended mainly for personal or household adornment — usu. used in pl.
No•vem•ber \nō-ˈvem-bər\ *n* [ME *Novembre,* fr. OF, fr. L *November* (ninth month), fr. *novem* nine] : the 11th month of the year
no•ve•na \nō-ˈvē-nə\ *n* : a Roman Catholic nine-day period of prayer
nov•ice \ˈnä-vəs\ *n* **1** : a new member of a religious order who is preparing to take the vows of religion **2** : one who is inexperienced or untrained
no•vi•tiate \nō-ˈvi-shət\ *n* **1** : the period or state of being a novice **2** : a house where novices are trained **3** : NOVICE
¹now \ˈnau̇\ *adv* **1** : at the present time or moment **2** : in the time immediately before the present **3** : IMMEDIATELY, FORTHWITH **4** — used with the sense of present time weakened or lost (as to express command, introduce an important point, or indicate a transition) ⟨~ hear this⟩ **5** : SOMETIMES ⟨~ one and ~ another⟩ **6** : under the present circumstances **7** : at the time referred to
²now *conj* : in view of the fact ⟨~ that you're here, we'll start⟩
³now *n* : the present time or moment : PRESENT
⁴now *adj* **1** : of or relating to the present time ⟨the ~ president⟩ **2** : excitingly new ⟨~ clothes⟩; *also* : constantly aware of what is new ⟨~ people⟩
NOW *abbr* **1** National Organization for Women **2** negotiable order of withdrawal
now•a•days \ˈnau̇-ə-ˌdāz\ *adv* : at the present time
no•way \ˈnō-ˌwā\ *or* **no•ways** \-ˌwāz\ *adv* : NOWISE
no•where \-ˌhwer\ *adv* : not anywhere — **nowhere** *n*
nowhere near *adv* : not nearly
no•wise \ˈnō-ˌwīz\ *adv* : in no way
nox•ious \ˈnäk-shəs\ *adj* : harmful esp. to health or morals
noz•zle \ˈnä-zəl\ *n* : a short tube constricted in the middle or at one end and used (as on a hose) to speed up or direct a flow of fluid
np *abbr* **1** no pagination **2** no place (of publication)
Np *symbol* neptunium
NP *abbr* notary public
NR *abbr* not rated
NRA *abbr* National Rifle Association
NS *abbr* **1** not specified **2** Nova Scotia
NSA *abbr* National Security Agency
NSC *abbr* National Security Council
NSF *abbr* **1** National Science Foundation **2** not sufficient funds
NSW *abbr* New South Wales
NT *abbr* **1** New Testament **2** Northern Territory **3** Northwest Territories
nth \ˈenth\ *adj* **1** : numbered with an unspecified or indefinitely large ordinal number ⟨for the ~ time⟩ **2** : EXTREME, UTMOST ⟨to the ~ degree⟩
NTP *abbr* normal temperature and pressure
nt wt *or* **n wt** *abbr* net weight
nu \ˈnü, ˈnyü\ *n* : the 13th letter of the Greek alphabet— N or ν
NU *abbr* name unknown
nu•ance \ˈnü-ˌäns, ˈnyü-, nu̇-ˈäns, nyu̇-\ *n* [F] : a shade of difference : a delicate variation (as in tone or meaning)
nub \ˈnəb\ *n* **1** : KNOB, LUMP **2** : GIST, POINT ⟨the ~ of the story⟩
nub•bin \ˈnə-bən\ *n* **1** : something (as an ear of Indian corn) that is small for its kind, stunted, undeveloped, or imperfect **2** : a small projecting bit
nu•bile \ˈnü-ˌbīl, ˈnyü-, -bəl\ *adj* **1** : of marriageable condition or age **2** : sexually attractive ⟨~ young women⟩
nu•cle•ar \ˈnü-klē-ər, ˈnyü-\ *adj* **1** : of, relating to, or constituting a nucleus **2** : of, relating to, or using the atomic nucleus or energy derived from it **3** : of, relating to, or being a weapon whose destructive power results from an uncontrolled nuclear reaction
nu•cle•ate \ˈnü-klē-ˌāt, ˈnyü-\ *vb* **-at•ed; -at•ing** : to form, act as, or have a nucleus — **nu•cle•ation** \ˌnü-klē-ˈā-shən, ˌnyü-\ *n*
nu•cle•ic acid \nu̇-ˈklē-ik-, nyu̇-, -ˈklā-\ *n* : any of various complex organic acids (as DNA) found esp. in cell nuclei
nu•cle•us \ˈnü-klē-əs, ˈnyü-\ *n, pl* **nu•clei** \-klē-ˌī\ *also* **nu•cle•us•es** [NL, fr. L, kernel, dim. of *nuc-, nux* nut] **1** : a central mass or part about which matter gathers or is collected : CORE **2** : a cell part that is characteristic of all living things except viruses, bacteria, and certain algae, that is necessary for heredity and for making proteins, that contains the chromosomes with their genes, and that is enclosed in a membrane **3** : a mass of gray matter or group of nerve cells in the central nervous system **4** : the central part of an atom that comprises nearly all of the atomic mass
¹nude \ˈnüd, ˈnyüd\ *adj* **nud•er; nud•est** : BARE, NAKED, UNCLOTHED — **nu•di•ty** \ˈnü-də-tē, ˈnyü-\ *n*
²nude *n* **1** : a nude human figure esp. as depicted in art **2** : the condition of being nude ⟨in the ~⟩
nudge \ˈnəj\ *vb* **nudged; nudg•ing** : to touch or push gently (as with the elbow) usu. in order to seek attention — **nudge** *n*
nud•ism \ˈnü-ˌdi-zəm, ˈnyü-\ *n* : the practice of going nude esp. in mixed groups at specially secluded places — **nud•ist** \-dist\ *n*
nu•ga•to•ry \-gə-ˌtōr-ē\ *adj* **1** : INCONSEQUENTIAL, WORTHLESS **2** : having no force : INEFFECTUAL
nug•get \ˈnə-gət\ *n* : a lump of precious metal (as gold)
nui•sance \ˈnüs-ᵊns, ˈnyüs-\ *n* : an annoying or troublesome person or thing
nuisance tax *n* : an excise tax collected in small amounts directly from the consumer
¹nuke \ˈnük, ˈnyük\ *n* **1** : a nuclear weapon **2** : a nuclear power plant
²nuke *vb* **nuked; nuk•ing** **1** : to attack with nuclear weapons **2** : MICROWAVE
null \ˈnəl\ *adj* **1** : having no legal or binding force : INVALID, VOID **2** : amounting to nothing **2** : INSIGNIFICANT — **nul•li•ty** \ˈnə-lə-tē\ *n*
null and void *adj* : having no force, binding power, or validity
nul•li•fy \ˈnə-lə-ˌfī\ *vb* **-fied; -fy•ing** : to make null or

valueless; *also* : ANNUL — **nul·li·fi·ca·tion** \ˌnə-lə-fə-ˈkā-shən\ *n*
num *abbr* numeral
Num *or* **Numb** *abbr* Numbers
numb \ˈnəm\ *adj* : lacking sensation or emotion : BENUMBED — **numb** *vb* — **numb·ly** *adv* — **numbness** *n*
[1]**num·ber** \ˈnəm-bər\ *n* **1** : the total of individuals or units taken together **2** : an indefinite total ⟨a small ~ of tickets remain unsold⟩ **3** : an ascertainable total ⟨the sands of the desert are without ~⟩ **4** : a distinction of word form to denote reference to one or more than one **5** : a unit belonging to a mathematical system and subject to its laws; *also, pl* : ARITHMETIC **6** : a symbol used to represent a mathematical number; *also* : such a number used to identify or designate ⟨a phone ~⟩ **7** : one in a series ⟨the best ~ on the program⟩
☞ For table, see next page.
[2]**number** *vb* **1** : COUNT, ENUMERATE **2** : to include with or be one of a group **3** : to restrict to a small or definite number **4** : to assign a number to **5** : to comprise in number : TOTAL
num·ber·less \-ləs\ *adj* : INNUMERABLE, COUNTLESS
Numbers *n* — see BIBLE table
nu·mer·al \ˈnü-mə-rəl, ˈnyü-\ *n* : conventional symbol representing a number — **numeral** *adj*
nu·mer·ate \ˈnü-mə-ˌrāt, ˈnyü-\ *vb* **-at·ed; -at·ing** : ENUMERATE
nu·mer·a·tor \-ˌrā-tər\ *n* : the part of a fraction above the line
nu·mer·ic \nu̇-ˈmer-ik, nyu̇-\ *adj* : NUMERICAL; *esp* : denoting a number or a system of numbers
nu·mer·i·cal \-ˈmer-i-kəl\ *adj* **1** : of or relating to numbers **2** : expressed in or involving numbers — **numer·i·cal·ly** \-k(ə-)lē\ *adv*
nu·mer·ol·o·gy \ˌnü-mə-ˈrä-lə-jē, ˌnyü-\ *n* : the study of the occult significance of numbers — **nu·mer·ol·o·gist** \-jist\ *n*
nu·mer·ous \ˈnü-mə-rəs, ˈnyü-\ *adj* : consisting of, including, or relating to a great number : MANY
nu·mis·mat·ics \ˌnü-məz-ˈma-tiks, ˌnyü-\ *n* : the study or collection of monetary objects — **nu·mis·mat·ic** \-tik\ *adj* — **nu·mis·ma·tist** \nü-ˈmiz-mə-tist, nyü-\ *n*
num·skull \ˈnəm-ˌskəl\ *n* : a stupid person : DUNCE
nun \ˈnən\ *n* : a woman belonging to a religious order; *esp* : one under solemn vows of poverty, chastity, and obedience
nun·cio \ˈnən-sē-ˌō, ˈnu̇n-\ *n, pl* **-ci·os** [It, fr. L *nuntius* messenger] : a permanent high-ranking papal representative to a civil government
nun·nery \ˈnə-nə-rē\ *n, pl* **-ner·ies** : a convent of nuns
[1]**nup·tial** \ˈnəp-shəl\ *adj* : of or relating to marriage or a wedding
[2]**nuptial** *n* : MARRIAGE, WEDDING — usu. used in pl.
[1]**nurse** \ˈnərs\ *n* [ME, fr. OF *nurice,* fr. LL *nutricia,* fr. L, fem. of *nutricius* nourishing] **1** : a girl or woman employed to take care of children **2** : a person trained to care for sick people
[2]**nurse** *vb* **nursed; nurs·ing 1** : SUCKLE **2** : to take charge of and watch over **3** : TEND ⟨~ an invalid⟩ **4** : to treat with special care ⟨~ a headache⟩ **5** : to hold in one's mind or consideration ⟨~ a grudge⟩ **6** : to act or serve as a nurse
nurse·maid \ˈnərs-ˌmād\ *n* : NURSE 1
nurse–prac·ti·tion·er \-prak-ˈti-shə-nər\ *n* : a registered nurse who is qualified to assume some of the duties formerly assumed only by a physician
nurs·ery \ˈnər-sə-rē\ *n, pl* **-er·ies 1** : a room for children **2** : a place where children are temporarily cared for in their parents' absence **3** : a place where young plants are grown usu. for transplanting
nurs·ery·man \-mən\ *n* : a man who keeps or works in a plant nursery
nursery school *n* : a school for children under kindergarten age
nursing home *n* : a private establishment providing care for persons (as the aged or the chronically ill) who are unable to care for themselves
nurs·ling \ˈnərs-liŋ\ *n* **1** : one that is solicitously cared for **2** : a nursing child
[1]**nur·ture** \ˈnər-chər\ *n* **1** : TRAINING, UPBRINGING; *also* : the influences that modify the expression of an individual's heredity **2** : FOOD, NOURISHMENT
[2]**nurture** *vb* **nur·tured; nur·tur·ing 1** : to care for : FEED, NOURISH **2** : EDUCATE, TRAIN **3** : FOSTER
nut \ˈnət\ *n* **1** : a dry fruit or seed with a hard shell and a firm inner kernel; *also* : its kernel **2** : a metal block with a hole through it that is fastened to a bolt or screw by means of a screw thread within the hole **3** : the ridge on the upper end of the fingerboard in a stringed musical instrument over which the strings pass **4** : a foolish, eccentric, or crazy person **5** : ENTHUSIAST
nut·crack·er \ˈnət-ˌkra-kər\ *n* : an instrument for cracking nuts

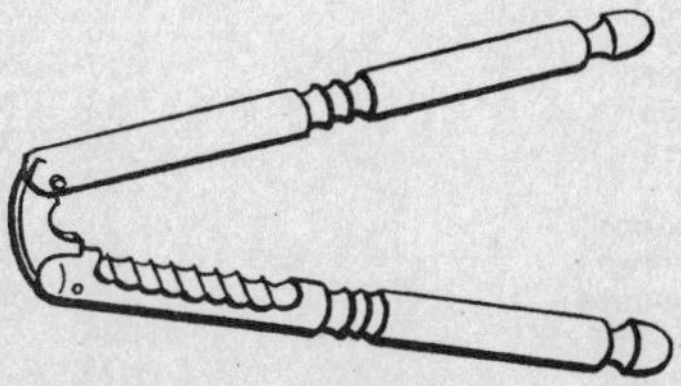
nutcracker

nut·hatch \-ˌhach\ *n* : any of various small tree-climbing chiefly insect-eating birds
nut·meg \-ˌmeg, -ˌmāg\ *n* [ME *notemuge,* ultim. fr. Old Provençal *noz muscada,* lit., musky nut] : a spice made by grinding the nutlike aromatic seed of a tropical tree; *also* : the seed or tree
nu·tria \ˈnü-trē-ə, ˈnyü-\ *n* [Sp] **1** : the durable usu. light brown fur of a nutria **2** : a So. American aquatic rodent with webbed hind feet
[1]**nu·tri·ent** \ˈnü-trē-ənt, ˈnyü-\ *adj* : NOURISHING
[2]**nutrient** *n* : a nutritive substance or ingredient
nu·tri·ment \-trə-mənt\ *n* : NUTRIENT
nu·tri·tion \nu̇-ˈtri-shən, nyu̇-\ *n* : the act or process of nourishing; *esp* : the processes by which an individual takes in and utilizes food material — **nu·tri·tion·al** \-shə-nəl\ *adj* — **nu·tri·tious** \-shəs\ *adj* — **nu·tri·tive** \ˈnü-trə-tiv, ˈnyü-\ *adj*
nuts \ˈnəts\ *adj* **1** : ENTHUSIASTIC, KEEN **2** : CRAZY, DEMENTED
nut·shell \ˈnət-ˌshel\ *n* : the shell of a nut — **in a nutshell** : in a few words ⟨that's the story *in a nutshell*⟩
nut·ty \ˈnə-tē\ *adj* **nut·ti·er; -est 1** : containing or suggesting nuts ⟨a ~ flavor⟩ **2** : mentally unbalanced
nuz·zle \ˈnə-zəl\ *vb* **nuz·zled; nuz·zling 1** : to root around, push, or touch with or as if with the nose **2** : NESTLE, SNUGGLE
NV *abbr* Nevada
NW *abbr* northwest
NWT *abbr* Northwest Territories
NY *abbr* New York
NYC *abbr* New York City
ny·lon \ˈnī-ˌlän\ *n* **1** : any of numerous strong tough elastic synthetic materials used esp. in textiles and plastics **2** *pl* : stockings made of nylon
nymph \ˈnimf\ *n* **1** : any of the lesser goddesses in ancient mythology represented as maidens living in the mountains, forests, meadows, and waters **2** : GIRL **3** : an immature insect resembling the adult but smaller, less differentiated, and usu. lacking wings
nym·pho·ma·nia \ˌnim-fə-ˈmā-nē-ə, -nyə\ *n* : excessive sexual desire by a female — **nym·pho·ma·ni·ac** \-nē-ˌak\ *n or adj*
NZ *abbr* New Zealand

TABLE OF NUMBERS

CARDINAL NUMBERS[1] NAME[2]	SYMBOL Hindu-Arabic	Roman[3]	ORDINAL NUMBERS[4] NAME[5]	SYMBOL
zero *or* naught *or* cipher	0		first	1st
one	1	I	second	2d *or* 2nd
two	2	II	third	3d *or* 3rd
three	3	III	fourth	4th
four	4	IV	fifth	5th
five	5	V	sixth	6th
six	6	VI	seventh	7th
seven	7	VII	eighth	8th
eight	8	VIII	ninth	9th
nine	9	IX	tenth	10th
ten	10	X	eleventh	11th
eleven	11	XI	twelfth	12th
twelve	12	XII	thirteenth	13th
thirteen	13	XIII	fourteenth	14th
fourteen	14	XIV	fifteenth	15th
fifteen	15	XV	sixteenth	16th
sixteen	16	XVI	seventeenth	17th
seventeen	17	XVII	eighteenth	18th
eighteen	18	XVIII	nineteenth	19th
nineteen	19	XIX	twentieth	20th
twenty	20	XX	twenty-first	21st
twenty-one	21	XXI	twenty-second	22d *or* 22nd
twenty-two	22	XXII	twenty-third	23d *or* 23rd
twenty-three	23	XXIII	twenty-fourth	24th
twenty-four	24	XXIV	twenty-fifth	25th
twenty-five	25	XXV	twenty-sixth	26th
twenty-six	26	XXVI	twenty-seventh	27th
twenty-seven	27	XXVII	twenty-eighth	28th
twenty-eight	28	XXVIII	twenty-ninth	29th
twenty-nine	29	XXIX	thirtieth	30th
thirty	30	XXX	thirty-first *etc*	31st
thirty-one *etc*	31	XXXI	fortieth	40th
forty	40	XL	fiftieth	50th
fifty	50	L	sixtieth	60th
sixty	60	LX	seventieth	70th
seventy	70	LXX	eightieth	80th
eighty	80	LXXX	ninetieth	90th
ninety	90	XC	hundredth *or*	100th
one hundred	100	C	one hundredth	
one hundred one *or*	101	CI	hundred and first *or*	101st
one hundred and one *etc*			one hundred and first *etc*	
two hundred	200	CC	two hundredth	200th
three hundred	300	CCC	three hundredth	300th
four hundred	400	CD	four hundredth	400th
five hundred	500	D	five hundredth	500th
six hundred	600	DC	six hundredth	600th
seven hundred	700	DCC	seven hundredth	700th
eight hundred	800	DCCC	eight hundredth	800th
nine hundred	900	CM	nine hundredth	900th
one thousand *or* ten	1,000	M	thousandth *or* one thousandth	1,000th
hundred *etc*			two thousandth *etc*	2,000th
two thousand *etc*	2,000	MM	five thousandth	5,000th
five thousand	5,000	$\overline{V}$	ten thousandth	10,000th
ten thousand	10,000	$\overline{X}$	hundred thousandth *or*	100,000th
one hundred thousand	100,000	$\overline{C}$	one hundred thousandth	
one million	1,000,000	$\overline{M}$	millionth *or* one millionth	1,000,000th

[1]The cardinal numbers are used in simple counting or in answer to "how many?" The words for these numbers may be used as nouns (I counted to *ten*), as pronouns (*ten* were found), or as adjectives (*ten* cows).

[2]In formal writing the numbers one to one hundred and in less formal writing the numbers one to nine are commonly written out, while larger numbers are given in numerals. A number occurring at the beginning of a sentence is usually written out. Except in very formal writing numerals are used for dates. Hindu-Arabic numerals from 1,000 to 9,999 are often written without commas (1000; 9999). Year numbers are always written without commas (1783).

[3]The Roman numerals are written either in capitals or in lowercase letters.

[4]The ordinal numbers are used to show the order in which such items as names, objects, and periods of time are considered (the *twelfth* month; the *fourth* row of seats; the *18th* century).

[5]Each of the names of the ordinal numbers except *first* and *second* is used for one of the equal parts into which a whole may be divided (a *fourth*; a *sixth*; a *tenth*) and also as the denominator in fractions (*one fourth; three fifths*). Fractions used as nouns are usually written as two words, but fractions used as adjectives are usually hyphenated (a *two-thirds* majority). When a two-word ordinal number is used as a noun to name a denominator, a hyphen is usually used to make sure that there is only one meaning (*six hundred ten-thousandths* means only 600/10,000 and not 610/1000). When fractions are written in numerals, the cardinal symbols are used (¼, ⅗, ⅘).

O

[1]**o** \ˈō\ *n, pl* **o's** *or* **os** \ˈōz\ *often cap* **1 :** the 15th letter of the English alphabet **2 :** ZERO

[2]**o** *abbr, often cap* **1** ocean **2** Ohio **3** ohm

[1]**O** \ˈō\ *var of* OH

[2]**O** *symbol* oxygen

o/a *abbr* on or about

oaf \ˈōf\ *n* **:** a stupid or awkward person — **oaf•ish** *adj*

oak \ˈōk\ *n, pl* **oaks** *or* **oak :** any of a genus of trees or shrubs related to the beech and chestnut and bearing a rounded thin-shelled nut surrounded at the base by a hardened cup; *also* **:** the usu. tough hard durable wood of an oak — **oak•en** \ˈō-kən\ *adj*

oa•kum \ˈō-kəm\ *n* **:** loosely twisted hemp or jute fiber impregnated with tar and used esp. in caulking ships

oar \ˈōr\ *n* **:** a long pole with a broad blade at one end used for propelling or steering a boat

oar•lock \ˈōr-ˌläk\ *n* **:** a U-shaped device for holding an oar in place

oars•man \ˈōrz-mən\ *n* **:** one who rows esp. in a racing crew

OAS *abbr* Organization of American States

oa•sis \ō-ˈā-səs\ *n, pl* **oa•ses** \-ˌsēz\ **:** a fertile or green area in an arid region

oat \ˈōt\ *n* **:** a cereal grass widely grown for its edible seed; *also* **:** this seed — **oat•en** \-ᵊn\ *adj*

oat•cake \ˈōt-ˌkāk\ *n* **:** a thin flat oatmeal cake

oath \ˈōth\ *n, pl* **oaths** \ˈōt͟hz, ˈōths\ **1 :** a solemn appeal to God to witness to the truth of a statement or the sacredness of a promise **2 :** an irreverent or careless use of a sacred name

oat•meal \ˈōt-ˌmēl\ *n* **1 :** ground or rolled oats **2 :** porridge made from ground or rolled oats

Ob *or* **Obad** *abbr* Obadiah

Oba•di•ah \ˌō-bə-ˈdī-ə\ *n* — see BIBLE table

ob•bli•ga•to \ˌä-blə-ˈgä-tō\ *n, pl* **-tos** *also* **-ti** \-ˈgä-tē\ [It] **:** an accompanying part usu. played by a solo instrument

ob•du•rate \ˈäb-də-rət, -dyə-\ *adj* **:** stubbornly resistant **:** UNYIELDING **syn** inflexible, adamant, rigid, uncompromising — **ob•du•ra•cy** \-rə-sē\ *n*

obe•di•ent \ō-ˈbē-dē-ənt\ *adj* **:** submissive to the restraint or command of authority **syn** docile, tractable, amenable, biddable — **obe•di•ence** \-əns\ *n* — **obe•di•ent•ly** *adv*

obei•sance \ō-ˈbē-səns, -ˈbā-\ *n* **:** a bow made to show respect or submission; *also* **:** DEFERENCE, HOMAGE

obe•lisk \ˈä-bə-ˌlisk\ *n* [MF *obelisque*, fr. L *obeliscus*, fr. Gk *obeliskos*, fr. dim. of *obelos* spit, pointed pillar] **:** a 4-sided pillar that tapers toward the top and ends in a pyramid

obese \ō-ˈbēs\ *adj* [L *obesus*, fr. *ob-* against + *esus*, pp. of *edere* to eat] **:** excessively fat **syn** corpulent, fleshy, gross, overweight, portly, stout — **obe•si•ty** \-ˈbē-sə-tē\ *n*

obey \ō-ˈbā\ *vb* **obeyed; obey•ing 1 :** to follow the commands or guidance of **:** behave obediently **2 :** to comply with ⟨~ orders⟩ **syn** conform, keep, mind, observe

ob•fus•cate \ˈäb-fə-ˌskāt\ *vb* **-cat•ed; -cat•ing 1 :** to make dark or obscure **2 :** CONFUSE — **ob•fus•ca•tion** \ˌäb-fəs-ˈkā-shən\ *n*

OB–GYN *abbr* obstetrician gynecologist; obstetrics gynecology

obi \ˈō-bē\ *n* [Jp] **:** a broad sash worn esp. with a Japanese kimono

obit \ō-ˈbit, ˈō-bət\ *n* **:** OBITUARY

obi•ter dic•tum \ˌō-bə-tər-ˈdik-təm\ *n, pl* **obiter dic•ta** \-tə\ [LL, lit., something said in passing] **:** an incidental remark or observation

obit•u•ary \ə-ˈbi-chə-ˌwer-ē\ *n, pl* **-ar•ies :** a notice of a person's death usu. with a short biographical account

obj *abbr* object; objective

[1]**ob•ject** \ˈäb-jikt\ *n* **1 :** something that may be seen or felt; *also* **:** something that may be perceived or examined mentally **2 :** something that arouses an emotional response (as of affection or pity) **3 :** AIM, PURPOSE **4 :** a word or word group denoting that on or toward which the action of a verb is directed; *also* **:** a noun or noun equivalent in a prepositional phrase

[2]**ob•ject** \əb-ˈjekt\ *vb* **1 :** to offer in opposition **2 :** to oppose something; *also* **:** DISAPPROVE **syn** protest, remonstrate, expostulate — **ob•jec•tor** \-ˈjek-tər\ *n*

ob•jec•ti•fy \əb-ˈjek-tə-ˌfī\ *vb* **-fied; -fy•ing :** to make objective

ob•jec•tion \əb-ˈjek-shən\ *n* **1 :** the act of objecting **2 :** a reason for or a feeling of disapproval

ob•jec•tion•able \əb-ˈjek-shə-nə-bəl\ *adj* **:** UNDESIRABLE, OFFENSIVE — **ob•jec•tion•ably** \-blē\ *adv*

[1]**ob•jec•tive** \əb-ˈjek-tiv\ *adj* **1 :** of or relating to an object or end **2 :** existing outside and independent of the mind **3 :** of, relating to, or constituting a grammatical case marking typically the object of a verb or preposition **4 :** treating or dealing with facts without distortion by personal feelings or prejudices — **ob•jec•tive•ly** *adv* — **ob•jec•tive•ness** *n* — **ob•jec•tiv•i•ty** \ˌäb-ˌjek-ˈti-və-tē\ *n*

[2]**objective** *n* **1 :** the lens (as in a microscope) nearest the object and forming an image of it **2 :** an aim, goal, or end of action

ob•jet d'art \ˌȯb-ˌzhā-ˈdär\ *n, pl* **ob•jets d'art** *same*\ [F] **:** an article of artistic worth; *also* **:** CURIO **syn** knickknack, bauble, bibelot, gewgaw, novelty, trinket

ob•jet trou•vé \ˈȯb-ˌzhā-trü-ˈvā\ *n, pl* **objets trouvés** *same*\ [F, lit., found object] **:** a found natural object (as a piece of driftwood) held to have aesthetic value; *also* **:** an artifact not orig. intended as art but displayed as a work of art

ob•jur•ga•tion \ˌäb-jər-ˈgā-shən\ *n* **:** a harsh rebuke — **ob•jur•gate** \ˈäb-jər-ˌgāt\ *vb*

obl *abbr* **1** oblique **2** oblong

ob•late \ä-ˈblāt\ *adj* **:** flattened or depressed at the poles ⟨an ~ spheroid⟩

ob•la•tion \ə-ˈblā-shən\ *n* **:** a religious offering

ob•li•gate \ˈä-blə-ˌgāt\ *vb* **-gat•ed; -gat•ing :** to bind legally or morally

ob•li•ga•tion \ˌä-blə-ˈgā-shən\ *n* **1 :** an act of obligating oneself to a course of action **2 :** something (as a promise or a contract) that binds one to a course of action **3 :** INDEBTEDNESS; *also* **:** LIABILITY **4 :** DUTY — **oblig•a•to•ry** \ə-ˈbli-gə-ˌtōr-ē\ *adj*

oblige \ə-ˈblīj\ *vb* **obliged; oblig•ing** [ME, fr. OF *obliger*, fr. L *obligare*, lit., to bind to, fr. *ob-* toward + *ligare* to bind] **1 :** FORCE, COMPEL **2 :** to bind by a favor; *also* **:** to do a favor for or do something as a favor

oblig•ing *adj* **:** willing to do favors — **oblig•ing•ly** *adv*

oblique \ō-ˈblēk\ *adj* **1 :** neither perpendicular nor parallel **:** SLANTING **2 :** not straightforward **:** INDIRECT — **oblique•ly** *adv* — **oblique•ness** *n* — **obliq•ui•ty** \-ˈbli-kwə-tē\ *n*

oblit•er•ate \ə-ˈbli-tə-ˌrāt\ *vb* **-at•ed; -at•ing** [L *oblitterare*, fr. *ob* in the way of + *littera* letter] **1 :** to make undecipherable by wiping out or covering over **2 :** to remove from recognition or memory **3 :** CANCEL — **oblit•er•a•tion** \-ˌbli-tə-ˈrā-shən\ *n*

obliv•i•on \ə-ˈbli-vē-ən\ *n* **1 :** the condition of being oblivious **2 :** the condition or state of being forgotten

obliv•i•ous \ə-ˈbli-ve-əs\ *adj* **1 :** lacking memory or mindful attention **2 :** UNAWARE — **obliv•i•ous•ly** *adv* — **obliv•i•ous•ness** *n*

ob•long \ˈä-ˌblȯŋ\ *adj* **:** deviating from a square, circular, or spherical form by elongation in one dimension — **oblong** *n*

ob•lo•quy \ˈä-blə-kwē\ *n, pl* **-quies 1 :** strongly condemnatory utterance or language **2 :** bad repute : DISGRACE **syn** dishonor, shame, infamy, disrepute, ignominy

ob•nox•ious \äb-ˈnäk-shəs\ *adj* : REPUGNANT, OFFENSIVE — **ob•nox•ious•ly** *adv* — **ob•nox•ious•ness** *n*

oboe \ˈō-bō\ *n* [It, fr. F *hautbois,* fr. *haut* high + *bois* wood] : a woodwind instrument with a slender conical tube and a double reed mouthpiece — **obo•ist** \ˈō-ˌbō-ist\ *n*

oboe

ob•scene \äb-ˈsēn\ *adj* **1 :** REPULSIVE **2 :** deeply offensive to morality or decency; *esp* : designed to incite to lust or depravity **syn** gross, vulgar, coarse, crude, indecent — **ob•scene•ly** *adv* — **ob•scen•i•ty** \-ˈse-nə-tē\ *n*

ob•scu•ran•tism \äb-ˈskyu̇r-ən-ˌti-zəm, ˌäb-skyu̇-ˈran-\ *n* **1 :** opposition to the spread of knowledge **2 :** deliberate vagueness or abstruseness — **ob•scu•ran•tist** \-tist\ *n or adj*

[1]**ob•scure** \äb-ˈskyu̇r\ *adj* **1 :** DIM, GLOOMY **2 :** not readily understood : VAGUE **3 :** REMOTE; *also* : HUMBLE **syn** dark, dusky, murky, tenebrous — **ob•scure•ly** *adv* — **ob•scu•ri•ty** \-ˈskyu̇r-ə-tē\ *n*

[2]**obscure** *vb* **ob•scured; ob•scur•ing 1 :** to make dark, dim, or indistinct **2 :** to conceal or hide by or as if by covering

ob•se•qui•ous \əb-ˈsē-kwē-əs\ *adj* : humbly or excessively attentive (as to a person in authority) : FAWNING, SYCOPHANTIC **syn** menial, servile, slavish, subservient — **ob•se•qui•ous•ly** *adv* — **ob•se•qui•ous•ness** *n*

ob•se•quy \ˈäb-sə-kwē\ *n, pl* **-quies :** a funeral or burial rite — usu. used in pl.

ob•serv•able \əb-ˈzər-və-bəl\ *adj* **1 :** NOTEWORTHY **2 :** capable of being observed — **ob•serv•abil•ity** \-ˈbi-lə-tē\ *n*

ob•ser•vance \əb-ˈzər-vəns\ *n* **1 :** a customary practice or ceremony **2 :** an act or instance of following a custom, rule, or law **3 :** OBSERVATION

ob•ser•vant \-vənt\ *adj* **1 :** WATCHFUL ⟨~ spectators⟩ **2 :** KEEN, PERCEPTIVE **3 :** MINDFUL ⟨~ of the amenities⟩

ob•ser•va•tion \ˌäb-sər-ˈvā-shən, -zər-\ *n* **1 :** an act or instance of observing **2 :** the gathering of information (as for scientific studies) by noting facts or occurrences **3 :** a conclusion drawn from observing; *also* : REMARK, STATEMENT **4 :** the fact of being observed

ob•ser•va•to•ry \əb-ˈzər-və-ˌtōr-ē\ *n, pl* **-ries :** a place or institution equipped for observation of natural phenomena (as in astronomy)

ob•serve \əb-ˈzərv\ *vb* **ob•served; ob•serv•ing 1 :** to conform one's action or practice to **2 :** CELEBRATE **3 :** to make a scientific observation of **4 :** to see or sense esp. through careful attention **5 :** to come to realize esp. through consideration of noted facts **6 :** REMARK — **ob•serv•er** *n*

ob•sess \əb-ˈses\ *vb* : to preoccupy intensely or abnormally

ob•ses•sion \äb-ˈse-shən\ *n* : a persistent disturbing preoccupation with an idea or feeling; *also* : an emotion or idea causing such a preoccupation — **ob•ses•sive** \-ˈse-siv\ *adj or n* — **ob•ses•sive•ly** *adv*

ob•sid•i•an \əb-ˈsi-dē-ən\ *n* : a dark natural glass formed by the cooling of molten lava

ob•so•les•cent \ˌäb-sə-ˈles-ᵊnt\ *adj* : going out of use : becoming obsolete — **ob•so•les•cence** \-ᵊns\ *n*

ob•so•lete \ˌäb-sə-ˈlēt, ˈäb-sə-ˌlēt\ *adj* : no longer in use; *also* : OLD-FASHIONED **syn** extinct, outworn, passé, superseded

ob•sta•cle \ˈäb-sti-kəl\ *n* : something that stands in the way or opposes

ob•stet•rics \əb-ˈste-triks\ *n sing or pl* : a branch of medicine that deals with birth and with its antecedents and sequels — **ob•stet•ric** \-trik\ *or* **ob•stet•ri•cal** \-tri-kəl\ *adj* — **ob•ste•tri•cian** \ˌäb-stə-ˈtri-shən\ *n*

ob•sti•nate \ˈäb-stə-nət\ *adj* : fixed and unyielding (as in an opinion or course) despite reason or persuasion : STUBBORN — **ob•sti•na•cy** \-nə-sē\ *n* — **ob•sti•nate•ly** *adv*

ob•strep•er•ous \əb-ˈstre-pə-rəs\ *adj* **1 :** uncontrollably noisy **2 :** stubbornly resistant to control : UNRULY — **ob•strep•er•ous•ness** *n*

ob•struct \əb-ˈstrəkt\ *vb* **1 :** to block by an obstacle **2 :** to impede the passage, action, or operation of **3 :** to cut off from sight — **ob•struc•tive** \-ˈstrək-tiv\ *adj* — **ob•struc•tor** \-tər\ *n*

ob•struc•tion \əb-ˈstrək-shən\ *n* **1 :** an act of obstructing : the state of being obstructed **2 :** something that obstructs : HINDRANCE

ob•struc•tion•ist \-shə-nist\ *n* : a person who hinders progress or business esp. in a legislative body — **ob•struc•tion•ism** \-shə-ˌni-zəm\ *n*

ob•tain \əb-ˈtān\ *vb* **1 :** to gain or attain usu. by planning or effort **2 :** to be generally recognized or established **syn** procure, secure, win, earn, acquire — **ob•tain•able** *adj*

ob•trude \əb-ˈtrüd\ *vb* **ob•trud•ed; ob•trud•ing 1 :** to thrust out **2 :** to thrust forward without warrant or request **3 :** INTRUDE — **ob•tru•sion** \-ˈtrü-zhən\ *n* — **ob•tru•sive** \-ˈtrü-siv\ *adj* — **ob•tru•sive•ly** *adv* — **ob•tru•sive•ness** *n*

ob•tuse \äb-ˈtüs, -ˈtyüs\ *adj* **ob•tus•er; -est 1 :** exceeding 90 degrees but less than 180 degrees ⟨~ angle⟩ **2 :** not pointed or acute : BLUNT **3 :** not sharp or quick of wit — **ob•tuse•ly** *adv* — **ob•tuse•ness** *n*

obv *abbr* obverse

[1]**ob•verse** \äb-ˈvərs, ˈäb-ˌvərs\ *adj* **1 :** facing the observer or opponent **2 :** being a counterpart or complement — **ob•verse•ly** *adv*

[2]**ob•verse** \ˈäb-ˌvərs, äb-ˈvərs\ *n* **1 :** the side (as of a coin) bearing the principal design and lettering **2 :** a front or principal surface **3 :** a counterpart having the opposite orientation or force

ob•vi•ate \ˈäb-vē-ˌāt\ *vb* **-at•ed; -at•ing :** to anticipate and prevent (as a situation) or make unnecessary (as an action) **syn** prevent, avert, forestall, forfend, preclude — **ob•vi•a•tion** \ˌäb-vē-ˈā-shən\ *n*

ob•vi•ous \ˈäb-vē-əs\ *adj* [L *obvius,* fr. *obviam* in the way, fr. *ob* in the way of + *viam,* acc. of *via* way] : easily found, seen, or understood : PLAIN **syn** evident, manifest, patent, clear — **ob•vi•ous•ly** *adv* — **ob•vi•ous•ness** *n*

OC *abbr* officer candidate

oc•a•ri•na \ˌä-kə-ˈrē-nə\ *n* [It] : a wind instrument typically having an oval body with finger holes and a projecting mouthpiece

occas *abbr* occasionally

[1]**oc•ca•sion** \ə-ˈkā-zhən\ *n* **1 :** a favorable opportunity **2 :** a direct or indirect cause **3 :** the time of an event **4 :** EXIGENCY **5** *pl* **:** AFFAIRS, BUSINESS **6 :** a special event : CELEBRATION

[2]**occasion** *vb* : BRING ABOUT, CAUSE

oc•ca•sion•al \ə-ˈkā-zhə-nəl\ *adj* **1 :** happening or met with now and then ⟨~ visits⟩ **2 :** used or designed for a special occasion ⟨~ verse⟩ **syn** infrequent, rare, sporadic — **oc•ca•sion•al•ly** *adv*

oc•ci•den•tal \ˌäk-sə-ˈdent-ᵊl\ *adj, often cap* [fr. *Occident* West, fr. ME, fr. L *occident-, occidens,* fr. prp.

of *occidere* to fall, set (of the sun)] : WESTERN — **Occidental** *n*

oc·clude \ə-ˈklüd\ *vb* **oc·clud·ed; oc·clud·ing 1** : OBSTRUCT ⟨an *occluded* artery⟩ **2** : to come together with opposing surfaces in contact — used of teeth — **oc·clu·sion** \-ˈklü-zhən\ *n* — **oc·clu·sive** \-ˈklü-siv\ *adj*

[1]**oc·cult** \ə-ˈkəlt\ *adj* **1** : not revealed : SECRET **2** : ABSTRUSE, MYSTERIOUS **3** : of or relating to supernatural agencies, their effects, or knowledge of them — **oc·cult·ism** \-ˈkəl-ˌti-zəm\ *n* — **oc·cult·ist** \-tist\ *n*

[2]**occult** *n* : occult matters — used with *the*

oc·cu·pan·cy \ˈä-kyə-pən-sē\ *n, pl* **-cies 1** : the act of occupying : the state of being occupied **2** : an occupied building or part of a building

oc·cu·pant \-pənt\ *n* : one who occupies something; *esp* : RESIDENT

oc·cu·pa·tion \ˌä-kyə-ˈpā-shən\ *n* **1** : an activity in which one engages; *esp* : VOCATION **2** : the taking possession of property; *also* : the taking possession of an area by a foreign military force — **oc·cu·pa·tion·al** \-shə-nəl\ *adj* — **oc·cu·pa·tion·al·ly** *adv*

occupational therapy *n* : therapy by means of activity; *esp* : creative activity prescribed for its effect in promoting recovery or rehabilitation — **occupational therapist** *n*

oc·cu·py \ˈä-kyə-ˌpī\ *vb* **-pied; -py·ing 1** : to engage the attention or energies of **2** : to fill up (an extent in space or time) **3** : to take or hold possession of **4** : to reside in as owner or tenant — **oc·cu·pi·er** *n*

oc·cur \ə-ˈkər\ *vb* **oc·curred; oc·cur·ring** [L *occurrere,* fr. *ob-* in the way + *currere* to run] **1** : to be found or met with : APPEAR **2** : HAPPEN **3** : to come to mind

oc·cur·rence \ə-ˈkər-əns\ *n* **1** : something that takes place **2** : the action or process of occurring

ocean \ˈō-shən\ *n* **1** : the whole body of salt water that covers nearly three fourths of the surface of the earth **2** : any of the large bodies of water into which the great ocean is divided — **oce·an·ic** \ˌō-shē-ˈa-nik\ *adj*

ocean·ar·i·um \ˌō-shə-ˈnar-ē-əm\ *n, pl* **-iums** *or* **-ia** \-ē-ə\ : a large marine aquarium

ocean·front \ˈō-shən-ˌfrənt\ *n* : a shore area on the ocean

ocean·go·ing \-ˌgō-iŋ\ *adj* : of, relating to, or suitable for travel on the ocean

ocean·og·ra·phy \ˌō-shə-ˈnä-grə-fē\ *n* : a science dealing with the ocean and its phenomena — **ocean·og·ra·pher** \-fər\ *n* — **ocean·o·graph·ic** \-nə-ˈgra-fik\ *adj*

oce·lot \ˈä-sə-ˌlät, ˈō-\ *n* : a medium-sized American wildcat ranging southward from Texas to northern Argentina and having a tawny yellow or gray coat with black markings

ocher *or* **ochre** \ˈō-kər\ *n* : an earthy usu. red or yellow iron ore used as a pigment; *also* : the color esp. of yellow ocher

o'·clock \ə-ˈkläk\ *adv* : according to the clock

OCR *abbr* optical character reader; optical character recognition

OCS *abbr* officer candidate school

oct *abbr* octavo

Oct *abbr* October

oc·ta·gon \ˈäk-tə-ˌgän\ *n* : a polygon of eight angles and eight sides — **oc·tag·o·nal** \äk-ˈta-gən-ᵊl\ *adj*

oc·tane \ˈäk-ˌtān\ *n* : OCTANE NUMBER

octane number *n* : a number used to measure the antiknock properties of gasoline that increases as the likelihood of knocking decreases

oc·tave \ˈäk-tiv\ *n* **1** : a musical interval embracing eight degrees; *also* : a tone or note at this interval or the whole series of notes, tones, or keys within this interval **2** : a group of eight

oc·ta·vo \äk-ˈtā-vō, -ˈtä-\ *n, pl* **-vos 1** : the size of a piece of paper cut eight from a sheet **2** : a book printed on octavo pages

oc·tet \äk-ˈtet\ *n* **1** : a musical composition for eight voices or eight instruments; *also* : the performers of such a composition **2** : a group or set of eight

Oc·to·ber \äk-ˈtō-bər\ *n* [ME *Octobre,* fr. OF, fr. L *October* (eighth month), fr. *octo* eight] : the 10th month of the year

oc·to·ge·nar·i·an \ˌäk-tə-jə-ˈner-ē-ən\ *n* : a person whose age is in the eighties

oc·to·pus \ˈäk-tə-pəs\ *n, pl* **-pus·es** *or* **-pi** \-ˌpī\ : any of various sea mollusks with eight long arms furnished with suckers

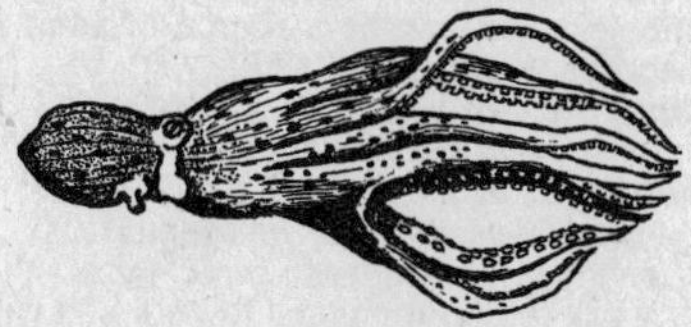

octopus

oc·to·syl·lab·ic \ˌäk-tə-sə-ˈla-bik\ *adj* : composed of verses having eight syllables — **octosyllabic** *n*

[1]**oc·u·lar** \ˈä-kyə-lər\ *adj* **1** : VISUAL **2** : of or relating to the eye or the eyesight

[2]**ocular** *n* : EYEPIECE

oc·u·list \ˈä-kyə-list\ *n* **1** : OPHTHALMOLOGIST **2** : OPTOMETRIST

[1]**OD** \ˌō-ˈdē\ *n* : an overdose of a drug and esp. a narcotic

[2]**OD** *vb* **OD'd** *or* **ODed; OD'ing** : to become ill or die from an OD

[3]**OD** *abbr* **1** doctor of optometry **2** [L *oculus dexter*] right eye **3** officer of the day **4** olive drab **5** overdraft **6** overdrawn

odd \ˈäd\ *adj* [ME *odde,* fr. ON *oddi* point of land, triangle, odd number] **1** : being only one of a pair or set ⟨an ~ shoe⟩ **2** : somewhat more than the number mentioned ⟨forty ~ years ago⟩ **3** : being an integer (as 1, 3, or 5) not divisible by two without leaving a remainder **4** : additional to what is usual ⟨~ jobs⟩ **5** : STRANGE ⟨an ~ way of behaving⟩ — **odd·ness** *n*

odd·ball \ˈäd-ˌbȯl\ *n* : one that is eccentric — **oddball** *adj*

odd·i·ty \ˈä-də-tē\ *n, pl* **-ties 1** : one that is odd **2** : the quality or state of being odd

odd·ly \ˈäd-lē\ *adv* **1** : in an odd manner **2** : it is odd that

odd·ment \ˈäd-mənt\ *n* : something left over : REMNANT

odds \ˈädz\ *n pl* **1** : a difference by which one thing is favored over another **2** : DISAGREEMENT — usu. used with *at* **3** : the ratio between the amount to be paid for a winning bet and the amount of the bet ⟨the horse went off at ~ of 6–1⟩

odds and ends *n pl* : miscellaneous things or matters

odds–on \ˈädz-ˈȯn, -ˈän\ *adj* : having a better than even chance to win

ode \ˈōd\ *n* : a lyric poem that expresses a noble feeling with dignity

odi·ous \ˈō-dē-əs\ *adj* : causing or deserving hatred or repugnance — **odi·ous·ly** *adv* — **odi·ous·ness** *n*

odi·um \ˈō-dē-əm\ *n* **1** : merited loathing : HATRED **2** : DISGRACE

odom·e·ter \ō-ˈdä-mə-tər\ *n* [F *odomètre,* fr. Gk *hodometron,* fr. *hodos* way, road + *metron* measure] : an instrument for measuring distance traveled (as by a vehicle)

odor \ˈō-dər\ *n* **1** : the quality of something that stimulates the sense of smell; *also* : a sensation resulting from such stimulation **2** : REPUTE, ESTIMATION — **odored** \ˈō-dərd\ *adj* — **odor·less** *adj* — **odor·ous** *adj*

odour *chiefly Brit var of* ODOR

od•ys•sey \ˈä-də-sē\ *n, pl* **-seys** [the *Odyssey,* epic poem attributed to Homer recounting the long wanderings of Odysseus] : a long wandering marked usu. by many changes of fortune
oe•cu•men•i•cal *esp Brit* ˌē-\ *var of* ECUMENICAL
OED *abbr* Oxford English Dictionary
oe•de•ma *chiefly Brit var of* EDEMA
oe•di•pal \ˈe-də-pəl, ˈē-\ *adj, often cap* : of, relating to, or resulting from the Oedipus complex
Oe•di•pus complex \-pəs-\ *n* : the positive sexual feelings of a child toward the parent of the opposite sex and hostile or jealous feelings toward the parent of the same sex that may be a source of adult personality disorder when unresolved
OEO *abbr* Office of Economic Opportunity
o'er \ˈōr\ *adv or prep* : OVER
OES *abbr* Order of the Eastern Star
oe•soph•a•gus *chiefly Brit var of* ESOPHAGUS
oeu•vre \œvrᵊ\ *n, pl* **oeuvres** *same* \ : a substantial body of work constituting the lifework of a writer, an artist, or a composer
of \ˈəv, ˈäv\ *prep* **1** : FROM ⟨a man ~ the West⟩ **2** : having as a significant background or character element ⟨a man ~ noble birth⟩ ⟨a woman ~ ability⟩ **3** : owing to ⟨died ~ flu⟩ **4** : BY ⟨the plays ~ Shakespeare⟩ **5** : having as component parts or material, contents, or members ⟨a house ~ brick⟩ ⟨a glass ~ water⟩ ⟨a pack ~ fools⟩ **6** : belonging to or included by ⟨the front ~ the house⟩ ⟨a time ~ life⟩ ⟨one ~ you⟩ ⟨the best ~ its kind⟩ ⟨the son ~ a doctor⟩ **7** : ABOUT ⟨tales ~ the West⟩ **8** : connected with : OVER ⟨the queen ~ England⟩ **9** : that is : signified as ⟨the city ~ Rome⟩ **10** — used to indicate apposition of the words it joins ⟨that fool ~ a husband⟩ **11** : as concerns : FOR ⟨love ~ nature⟩ **12** — used to indicate the application of an adjective ⟨fond ~ candy⟩ **13** : BEFORE ⟨quarter ~ ten⟩
OF *abbr* outfield
[1]**off** \ˈȯf\ *adv* **1** : from a place or position ⟨drove ~ in a new car⟩; *also* : ASIDE ⟨turned ~ into a side road⟩ **2** : at a distance in time or space ⟨stood ~ a few yards⟩ ⟨several years ~⟩ **3** : so as to be unattached or removed ⟨the lid blew ~⟩ **4** : to a state of discontinuance, exhaustion, or completion ⟨shut the radio ~⟩ **5** : away from regular work ⟨took time ~ for lunch⟩
[2]**off** *prep* **1** : away from ⟨just ~ the highway⟩ ⟨take it ~ the table⟩ **2** : to seaward of ⟨two miles ~ the coast⟩ **3** : FROM ⟨borrowed a dollar ~ me⟩ **4** : at the expense of ⟨lives ~ his parents⟩ **5** : not now engaged in ⟨~ duty⟩ **6** : abstaining from ⟨~ liquor⟩ **7** : below the usual level of ⟨~ his game⟩
[3]**off** *adj* **1** : more removed or distant **2** : started on the way **3** : not operating **4** : not correct **5** : REMOTE, SLIGHT **6** : INFERIOR **7** : provided for ⟨well ~⟩
[4]**off** *abbr* office; officer; official
of•fal \ˈȯ-fəl\ *n* : the waste or by-product of a process; *esp* : the viscera and trimmings of a butchered animal removed in dressing
off and on *adv* : INTERMITTENTLY
[1]**off•beat** \ˈȯf-ˌbēt\ *n* : the unaccented part of a musical measure
[2]**offbeat** *adj* : ECCENTRIC, UNCONVENTIONAL
off–col•or \ˈȯf-ˈkə-lər\ *or* **off–col•ored** \-lərd\ *adj* **1** : not having the right or standard color **2** : of doubtful propriety : verging on indecency ⟨~ stories⟩
of•fend \ə-ˈfend\ *vb* **1** : SIN, TRANSGRESS **2** : to cause discomfort or pain : HURT **3** : to cause dislike or vexation : ANNOY **syn** affront, insult, outrage — **of•fend•er** *n*
of•fense *or* **of•fence** \ə-ˈfens, *esp for 2 & 3* ˈä-ˌfens\ *n* **1** : something that outrages the senses **2** : ATTACK, ASSAULT **3** : the offensive team or members of a team playing offensive positions **4** : DISPLEASURE **5** : SIN, MISDEED **6** : an infraction of law : CRIME
[1]**of•fen•sive** \ə-ˈfen-siv *esp for 1 & 2* ˈä-ˌfen-\ *adj* **1** : AGGRESSIVE **2** : of or relating to an attempt to score in a game; *also* : of or relating to a team in possession of the ball or puck **3** : OBNOXIOUS **4** : INSULTING — **of•fen•sive•ly** *adv* — **of•fen•sive•ness** *n*
[2]**offensive** *n* : ATTACK
[1]**of•fer** \ˈȯ-fər\ *vb* **of•fered; of•fer•ing 1** : SACRIFICE **2** : to present for acceptance : TENDER; *also* : to propose as payment **3** : PROPOSE, SUGGEST; *also* : to declare one's readiness **4** : to try or begin to exert ⟨~ resistance⟩ **5** : to place on sale — **of•fer•ing** *n*
[2]**offer** *n* **1** : PROPOSAL **2** : BID **3** : TRY
of•fer•to•ry \ˈȯ-fər-ˌtōr-ē\ *n, pl* **-ries** : the presentation of offerings at a church service; *also* : the musical accompaniment during it
off•hand \ˈȯf-ˈhand\ *adv or adj* : without previous thought or preparation
off–hour \-ˌau̇(-ə)r\ *n* : a period of time other than a rush hour; *also* : a period of time other than business hours
of•fice \ˈȯ-fəs\ *n* **1** : a special duty or position; *esp* : a position of authority in government ⟨run for ~⟩ **2** : a prescribed form or service of worship; *also* : RITE **3** : an assigned or assumed duty or role **4** : a place where a business is transacted or a service is supplied
of•fice•hold•er \ˈȯ-fəs-ˌhōl-dər\ *n* : one holding a public office
of•fi•cer \ˈȯ-fə-sər\ *n* **1** : one charged with the enforcement of law **2** : one who holds an office of trust or authority **3** : a person who holds a position of authority or command in the armed forces; *esp* : COMMISSIONED OFFICER
[1]**of•fi•cial** \ə-ˈfi-shəl\ *n* : OFFICER 2
[2]**official** *adj* **1** : of or relating to an office or to officers **2** : AUTHORIZED, AUTHORITATIVE **3** : befitting or characteristic of a person in office — **of•fi•cial•ly** *adv*
of•fi•cial•dom \ə-ˈfi-shəl-dəm\ *n* : officials as a class
of•fi•cial•ism \ə-ˈfi-shə-ˌli-zəm\ *n* : lack of flexibility and initiative combined with excessive adherence to regulations
of•fi•ci•ant \ə-ˈfi-shē-ənt\ *n* : one (as a priest) who officiates at a religious rite
of•fi•ci•ate \ə-ˈfi-shē-ˌāt\ *vb* **-at•ed; -at•ing 1** : to perform a ceremony, function, or duty **2** : to act in an official capacity
of•fi•cious \ə-ˈfi-shəs\ *adj* : volunteering one's services where they are neither asked for nor needed — **of•fi•cious•ly** *adv* — **of•fi•cious•ness** *n*
off•ing \ˈȯ-fiŋ\ *n* : the near or foreseeable future
off–line \ˈȯf-ˈlīn\ *adj or adv* : not connected to or controlled directly by a computer
off of *prep* : OFF
off•print \ˈȯf-ˌprint\ *n* : a separately printed excerpt (as from a magazine)
off–road \-ˈrōd\ *adj* : of, relating to, or being a vehicle designed for use away from public roads
off–sea•son \-ˌsēz-ᵊn\ *n* : a time of suspended or reduced activity
[1]**off•set** \-ˌset\ *n* **1** : a sharp bend (as in a pipe) by which one part is turned aside out of line **2** : a printing process in which an inked impression is first made on a rubber-blanketed cylinder and then transferred to the paper
[2]**off•set** *vb* **off•set; off•set•ting 1** : to place over against : BALANCE **2** : to compensate for **3** : to form an offset in (as a wall)
off•shoot \ˈȯf-ˌshüt\ *n* **1** : a collateral or derived branch, descendant, or member **2** : a branch of a main stem (as of a plant)
[1]**off•shore** \ˈȯf-ˈshōr\ *adv* **1** : at a distance from the shore **2** : outside the country : ABROAD
[2]**off•shore** \ˈȯf-ˌshōr\ *adj* **1** : moving away from the shore **2** : situated off the shore but within waters under a country's control
off•side \-ˈsīd\ *adv or adj* : illegally in advance of the ball or puck
off•spring \-ˌspriŋ\ *n, pl* **offspring** *also* **offsprings** : PROGENY, YOUNG
off•stage \ˈȯf-ˈstāj, -ˌstāj\ *adv or adj* **1** : off or away

from the stage **2** : out of the public view ⟨deals made ~⟩
off–the–record *adj* : given or made in confidence and not for publication
off–the–shelf *adj* : available as a stock item : not specially designed or made
off–the–wall *adj* : highly unusual : BIZARRE
off•track \ˈȯf-ˈtrak\ *adv or adj* : away from a racetrack
off–white \ˈȯf-ˈhwīt\ *n* : a yellowish or grayish white color
off year *n* **1** : a year in which no major election is held **2** : a year of diminished activity or production
oft \ˈȯft\ *adv* : OFTEN
of•ten \ˈȯ-fən\ *adv* : many times : FREQUENTLY
of•ten•times \-ˌtīmz\ *or* **oft•times** \ˈȯf-ˌtīmz, ˈȯft-\ *adv* : OFTEN
ogle \ˈō-gəl\ *vb* **ogled; ogling** : to look at in a flirtatious way — **ogle** *n* — **ogler** *n*
ogre \ˈō-gər\ *n* **1** : a monster of fairy tales and folklore that eats people **2** : a dreaded person or object
ogress \ˈō-grəs\ *n* : a female ogre
oh \ˈō\ *interj* **1** — used to express an emotion or in response to physical stimuli **2** — used in direct address
OH *abbr* Ohio
ohm \ˈōm\ *n* : a unit of electrical resistance equal to the resistance of a circuit in which a potential difference of one volt produces a current of one ampere — **ohm•ic** \ˈō-mik\ *adj*
ohm•me•ter \ˈōm-ˌmē-tər\ *n* : an instrument for indicating resistance in ohms directly
[1]**oil** \ˈȯil\ *n* [ME *oile,* fr. OF, fr. L *oleum* olive oil, fr. Gk *elaion,* fr. *elaia* olive] **1** : any of numerous fatty or greasy liquid substances obtained from plants, animals, or minerals and used for fuel, food, medicines, and manufacturing **2** : PETROLEUM **3** : artists' colors made with oil; *also* : a painting in such colors — **oil•i•ness** \ˈȯi-lē-nəs\ *n* — **oily** \ˈȯi-lē\ *adj*
[2]**oil** *vb* : to put oil in or on — **oil•er** *n*
oil•cloth \ˈȯil-ˌklȯth\ *n* : cloth treated with oil or paint and used for table and shelf coverings
oil pan *n* : the lower section of a crankcase used as an oil reservoir
oil shale *n* : a rock (as shale) from which oil can be recovered
oil•skin \ˈȯil-ˌskin\ *n* **1** : an oiled waterproof cloth **2** : an oilskin raincoat **3** *pl* : an oilskin coat and trousers
oink \ˈȯiŋk\ *n* : the natural noise of a hog — **oink** *vb*
oint•ment \ˈȯint-mənt\ *n* : a salve for use on the skin
OJ *abbr* orange juice
Ojib•wa *or* **Ojib•way** \ō-ˈjib-ˌwā\ *n, pl* **Ojibwa** *or* **Ojibwas** *or* **Ojibway** *or* **Ojibways** : a member of an American Indian people of the region around Lake Superior and westward
OJT *abbr* on-the-job training
[1]**OK** *or* **okay** \ō-ˈkā\ *adv or adj* : all right
[2]**OK** *or* **okay** *vb* **OK'd** *or* **okayed; OK'•ing** *or* **okay•ing** : APPROVE, AUTHORIZE — **OK** *or* **okay** *n*
[3]**OK** *abbr* Oklahoma
Okla *abbr* Oklahoma
okra \ˈō-krə\ *n* : a tall annual plant related to the hollyhocks that has edible green pods; *also* : these pods
[1]**old** \ˈōld\ *adj* **1** : ANCIENT; *also* : of long standing **2** *cap* : belonging to an early period ⟨*Old* Irish⟩ **3** : having existed for a specified period of time **4** : of or relating to a past era **5** : advanced in years **6** : showing the effects of age or use **7** : no longer in use — **old•ish** \ˈōl-dish\ *adj*
[2]**old** *n* : old or earlier time ⟨days of ~⟩
old•en \ˈōl-dən\ *adj* : of or relating to a bygone era
[1]**old–fash•ioned** \ˈōld-ˈfa-shənd\ *adj* **1** : OUT-OF-DATE, ANTIQUATED **2** : CONSERVATIVE
[2]**old–fashioned** *n* : a cocktail usu. made with whiskey, bitters, sugar, a twist of lemon peel, and water or soda water
old guard *n, often cap O&G* : the conservative members of an organization
old hat *adj* **1** : OLD-FASHIONED **2** : STALE, TRITE
old•ie \ˈōl-dē\ *n* : something old; *esp* : a popular song from the past
old–line \ˈōld-ˈlīn\ *adj* **1** : ORIGINAL, ESTABLISHED ⟨an ~ business⟩ **2** : adhering to old policies or practices
old maid *n* **1** : SPINSTER **2** : a prim fussy person — **old–maid•ish** \ˈōld-ˈmā-dish\ *adj*
old man *n* **1** : HUSBAND **2** : FATHER
old•ster \ˈōld-stər\ *n* : an old or elderly person
Old Testament *n* : the first of the two chief divisions of the Bible — see BIBLE table
old–time \ˈōld-ˈtīm\ *adj* **1** : of, relating to, or characteristic of an earlier period **2** : of long standing
old–tim•er \-ˈtī-mər\ *n* VETERAN; *also* : OLDSTER
old–world \-ˈwərld\ *adj* : having old-fashioned charm
Old World *n* : the eastern hemisphere exclusive of Australia; *esp* : continental Europe
ole•ag•i•nous \ˌō-lē-ˈa-jə-nəs\ *adj* : OILY
ole•an•der \ˈō-lē-ˌan-dər\ *n* : a poisonous evergreen shrub often grown for its fragrant white to red flowers
oleo \ˈō-lē-ˌō\ *n, pl* **oleos** : MARGARINE
oleo•mar•ga•rine \ˌō-lē-ō-ˈmär-jə-rən\ *n* : MARGARINE
ol•fac•to•ry \äl-ˈfak-tə-rē, ōl-\ *adj* : of or relating to the sense of smell
oli•gar•chy \ˈä-lə-ˌgär-kē, ˈō-\ *n, pl* **-chies 1** : a government in which power is in the hands of a few **2** : a state having an oligarchy; *also* : the group holding power in such a state — **oli•garch** \-ˌgärk\ *n* — **oli•gar•chic** \ˌä-lə-ˈgär-kik, ˌō-\ *or* **oli•gar•chi•cal** \-ki-kəl\ *adj*
Oli•go•cene \ˈä-li-gō-ˌsēn, ə-ˈli-gə-ˌsēn\ *adj* : of, relating to, or being the epoch of the Tertiary between the Eocene and the Miocene — **Oligocene** *n*
olio \ˈō-lē-ˌō\ *n, pl* **oli•os** : HODGEPODGE, MEDLEY
ol•ive \ˈä-liv\ *n* **1** : an Old World evergreen tree grown in warm regions for its fruit that is a food and the source of an edible oil **(olive oil) 2** : a dull yellow to yellowish green color
olive drab *n* **1** : a grayish olive color **2** : an olive drab wool or cotton fabric; *also* : a uniform of this fabric
ol•iv•ine \ˈä-lə-ˌvēn\ *n* : a usu. greenish mineral that is a complex silicate of magnesium and iron
Olym•pic Games \ō-ˈlim-pik-\ *n pl* : a modified revival of an ancient Greek festival consisting of international athletic contests that are held at separate winter and summer gatherings at four-year intervals
om \ˈōm\ *n* : a mantra consisting of the sound "om" used in contemplating ultimate reality
Oma•ha \ˈō-mə-ˌhä, -ˌhȯ\ *n, pl* **Omaha** *or* **Omahas** : a member of an American Indian people of northeastern Nebraska
om•buds•man \ˈäm-ˌbu̇dz-mən, äm-ˈbu̇dz-\ *n, pl* **-men** \-mən\ **1** : a government official appointed to investigate complaints made by individuals against abuses or capricious acts of public officials **2** : one that investigates reported complaints (as from students or consumers)
ome•ga \ō-ˈmā-gə\ *n* : the 24th and last letter of the Greek alphabet — Ω or ω
om•elet *or* **om•elette** \ˈäm-lət, ˈä-mə-\ *n* [F *omelette,* alter. of MF *alumelle,* lit., knife blade, modif. of L *lamella,* dim. of *lamina* thin plate] : eggs beaten with milk or water, cooked without stirring until set, and folded over
omen \ˈō-mən\ *n* : an event or phenomenon believed to be a sign or warning of a future occurrence
om•i•cron \ˈä-mə-ˌkrän, ˈō-\ *n* : the 15th letter of the Greek alphabet — O or o
om•i•nous \ˈä-mə-nəs\ *adj* : foretelling evil : THREATENING — **om•i•nous•ly** *adv* — **om•i•nous•ness** *n*
omis•si•ble \ō-ˈmi-sə-bəl\ *adj* : that may be omitted
omis•sion \ō-ˈmi-shən\ *n* **1** : something neglected or left undone **2** : the act of omitting : the state of being omitted
omit \ō-ˈmit\ *vb* **omit•ted; omit•ting 1** : to leave out or leave unmentioned **2** : to fail to perform : NEGLECT

[1]**om•ni•bus** \ˈäm-ni-(ˌ)bəs\ *n* : BUS

[2]**omnibus** *adj* : of, relating to, or providing for many things at once ⟨an ~ bill⟩

om•nip•o•tent \äm-ˈni-pə-tənt\ *adj* : having unlimited authority or influence : ALMIGHTY — **om•nip•o•tence** \-əns\ *n* — **om•nip•o•tent•ly** *adv*

om•ni•pres•ent \ˌäm-ni-ˈprez-ᵊnt\ *adj* : present in all places at all times — **om•ni•pres•ence** \-ᵊns\ *n*

om•ni•scient \äm-ˈni-shənt\ *adj* : having infinite awareness, understanding, and insight — **om•ni•science** \-shəns\ *n* — **om•ni•scient•ly** *adv*

om•ni•um–gath•er•um \ˌäm-nē-əm-ˈga-thə-rəm\ *n, pl* **omnium–gatherums** : a miscellaneous collection

om•niv•o•rous \äm-ˈni-və-rəs\ *adj* : feeding on both animal and vegetable substances; *also* : AVID ⟨an ~ reader⟩ — **om•niv•o•rous•ly** *adv*

[1]**on** \ˈȯn, ˈän\ *prep* **1** : in or to a position over and in contact with ⟨jumped ~ his horse⟩ **2** : touching the surface of ⟨shadows ~ the wall⟩ **3** : AT, TO ⟨~ the right were the mountains⟩ **4** : IN, ABOARD ⟨went ~ the train⟩ **5** : during or at the time of ⟨came ~ Monday⟩ ⟨every hour ~ the hour⟩ **6** : through the agency of ⟨was cut ~ a tin can⟩ **7** : in a state or process of ⟨~ fire⟩ ⟨~ the wane⟩ **8** : connected with as a member or participant ⟨~ a committee⟩ ⟨~ tour⟩ **9** — used to indicate a basis, source, or standard of computation ⟨has it ~ good authority⟩ ⟨10 cents ~ the dollar⟩ **10** : with regard to ⟨a monopoly ~ wheat⟩ **11** : at or toward as an object ⟨crept up ~ her⟩ **12** : ABOUT, CONCERNING ⟨a book ~ minerals⟩

[2]**on** *adv* **1** : in or into a position of contact with or attachment to a surface **2** : FORWARD **3** : into operation

[3]**on** *adj* : being in operation or in progress

ON *abbr* Ontario

[1]**once** \ˈwəns\ *adv* **1** : one time only **2** : at any one time **3** : FORMERLY **4** : by one degree of relationship

[2]**once** *n* : one single time — **at once 1** : at the same time **2** : IMMEDIATELY

[3]**once** *adj* : FORMER

[4]**once** *conj* : AS SOON AS

once–over \ˈwəns-ˌō-vər\ *n* : a swift examination or survey

on•com•ing \ˈȯn-ˌkə-miŋ, ˈän-\ *adj* : APPROACHING ⟨~ traffic⟩

[1]**one** \ˈwən\ *adj* **1** : being a single unit or thing ⟨~ person went⟩ **2** : being one in particular ⟨early ~ morning⟩ **3** : being the same in kind or quality ⟨members of ~ race⟩; *also* : UNITED **4** : being not specified or fixed ⟨~ day soon⟩

[2]**one** *n* **1** : the number denoting unity **2** : the 1st in a set or series **3** : a single person or thing — **one•ness** \ˈwən-nəs\ *n*

[3]**one** *pron* **1** : a certain indefinitely indicated person or thing ⟨saw ~ of his friends⟩ **2** : a person in general ⟨~ never knows⟩ **3** — used in place of a first-person pronoun

Onei•da \ō-ˈnī-də\ *n, pl* **Oneida** *or* **Oneidas** : a member of an American Indian people orig. of New York

oner•ous \ˈä-nə-rəs, ˈō-\ *adj* : imposing or constituting a burden : TROUBLESOME **syn** oppressive, exacting, burdensome, weighty

one•self \(ˌ)wən-ˈself\ *also* **one's self** *pron* : one's own self — usu. used reflexively or for emphasis

one–sid•ed \ˈwən-ˈsī-dəd\ *adj* **1** : having or occurring on one side only; *also* : having one side prominent or more developed **2** : PARTIAL ⟨a ~ interpretation⟩

one•time \-ˌtīm\ *adj* : FORMER

one–to–one \ˌwən-tə-ˈwən\ *adj* : pairing each element of a set uniquely with an element of another set

one up *adj* : being in a position of advantage ⟨was *one up* on the others⟩

one–way *adj* : moving, allowing movement, or functioning in only one direction ⟨~ streets⟩

on•go•ing \ˈȯn-ˌgō-iŋ, ˈän-\ *adj* : continuously moving forward

on•ion \ˈən-yən\ *n* : the pungent edible bulb of a cultivated plant related to the lilies; *also* : this plant

on•ion•skin \-ˌskin\ *n* : a thin strong translucent paper of very light weight

on–line *adj or adv* : connected to or controlled directly by a computer

on•look•er \ˈȯn-ˌlu̇-kər, ˈän-\ *n* : SPECTATOR

[1]**on•ly** \ˈōn-lē\ *adj* **1** : unquestionably the best **2** : SOLE

[2]**only** *adv* **1** : MERELY, JUST ⟨~ $2⟩ **2** : SOLELY ⟨known ~ to me⟩ **3** : at the very least ⟨was ~ too true⟩ **4** : as a final result ⟨will ~ make you sick⟩

[3]**only** *conj* : except that

on•o•mato•poe•ia \ˌä-nə-ˌmä-tə-ˈpē-ə\ *n* **1** : formation of words in imitation of natural sounds (as *buzz* or *hiss*) **2** : the use of words whose sound suggests the sense — **on•o•mato•poe•ic** \-ˈpē-ik\ *or* **on•o•mato•po•et•ic** \-pō-ˈe-tik\ *adj* — **on•o•mato•poe•i•cal•ly** \-ˈpē-ə-k(ə-)lē\ *or* **on•o•mato•po•et•i•cal•ly** \-pō-ˈe-ti-k(ə-)lē\ *adv*

On•on•da•ga \ˌä-nən-ˈdȯ-gə, -ˈdā-, -ˈdä-\ *n, pl* **-ga** *or* **-gas** : a member of an American Indian people of New York and Canada

on•rush \ˈȯn-ˌrəsh, ˈän-\ *n* : a rushing onward — **on•rush•ing** *adj*

on•set \-ˌset\ *n* **1** : ATTACK **2** : BEGINNING

on•shore \-ˌshōr\ *adj* **1** : moving toward the shore **2** : situated on or near the shore — **on•shore** \-ˈshōr\ *adv*

on•slaught \ˈȯn-ˌslȯt, ˈän-\ *n* : a fierce attack; *also* : something resembling such an attack ⟨an ~ of questions⟩

Ont *abbr* Ontario

on•to \ˈȯn-tü, ˈän-\ *prep* : to a position or point on

onus \ˈō-nəs\ *n* **1** : BURDEN **2** : OBLIGATION **3** : BLAME

[1]**on•ward** \ˈȯn-wərd, ˈän-\ *also* **on•wards** \-wərdz\ *adv* : FORWARD

[2]**onward** *adj* : directed or moving onward : FORWARD

on•yx \ˈä-niks\ *n* [ME *onix*, fr. MF & L; MF, fr. L *onyx*, fr. Gk, lit., claw, nail] : a translucent chalcedony in parallel layers of different colors

oo•dles \ˈüd-ᵊlz\ *n pl* : a great quantity

oo•lite \ˈō-ə-ˌlīt\ *n* : a rock consisting of small round grains cemented together — **oo•lit•ic** \ˌō-ə-ˈli-tik\ *adj*

[1]**ooze** \ˈüz\ *n* **1** : a soft deposit (as of mud) on the bottom of a body of water **2** : soft wet ground : MUD — **oozy** \ˈü-zē\ *adj*

[2]**ooze** *vb* **oozed; ooz•ing 1** : to flow or leak out slowly or imperceptibly **2** : EXUDE

[3]**ooze** *n* : something that oozes

op *abbr* **1** operation; operative; operator **2** opportunity **3** opus

OP *abbr* **1** observation post **2** out of print

opac•i•ty \ō-ˈpa-sə-tē\ *n, pl* **-ties 1** : the quality or state of being opaque **2** : obscurity of meaning **3** : mental dullness **4** : an opaque spot in a normally transparent structure

opal \ˈō-pəl\ *n* : a mineral with iridescent colors that is used as a gem

opal•es•cent \ˌō-pə-ˈles-ᵊnt\ *adj* : IRIDESCENT — **opal•es•cence** \-ᵊns\ *n*

opaque \ō-ˈpāk\ *adj* **1** : blocking the passage of radiant energy and esp. light **2** : not easily understood **3** : OBTUSE — **opaque•ly** *adv* — **opaque•ness** *n*

op art \ˈäp-\ *n* : OPTICAL ART — **op artist** *n*

op cit *abbr* [L *opere citato*] in the work cited

ope \ˈōp\ *vb* **oped; op•ing** *archaic* : OPEN

OPEC *abbr* Organization of Petroleum Exporting Countries

[1]**open** \ˈō-pən\ *adj* **open•er; open•est 1** : not shut or shut up ⟨an ~ door⟩ **2** : not secret or hidden; *also* : FRANK **3** : not enclosed or covered ⟨an ~ fire⟩; *also* : not protected **4** : free to be entered or used ⟨an ~ tournament⟩ **5** : easy to get through or see ⟨~ country⟩ **6** : spread out : EXTENDED **7** : not decided ⟨an ~ question⟩ **8** : readily accessible and cooperative; *also* : GENEROUS **9** : having components separated by a space in writing and printing ⟨the name *Spanish moss*

is an ~ compound⟩ **10 :** having openings, interruptions, or spaces ⟨an ~ mesh⟩ **11 :** ready to operate ⟨stores are ~⟩ **12 :** free from restraints or controls ⟨~ season⟩ — **open·ly** *adv* — **open·ness** *n*

[2]**open** \ˈō-pən\ *vb* **opened; open·ing 1 :** to change or move from a shut position; *also* **:** to make open by clearing away obstacles **2 :** to make accessible **3 :** to make openings in **4 :** to make or become functional ⟨~ a store⟩ **5 :** REVEAL; *also* **:** ENLIGHTEN **6 :** BEGIN — **open·er** *n*

[3]**open** *n* **1 :** OUTDOORS **2 :** a contest or tournament open to all

open–air *adj* **:** OUTDOOR ⟨~ theaters⟩

open·hand·ed \ˌō-pən-ˈhan-dəd\ *adj* **:** GENEROUS — **open·hand·ed·ly** *adv*

open–heart *adj* **:** of, relating to, or performed on a heart temporarily relieved of circulatory function and laid open for inspection and treatment

open–hearth *adj* **:** of, relating to, or being a process of making steel in a furnace that reflects the heat from the roof onto the material

open·ing *n* **1 :** an act or instance of making or becoming open **2 :** BEGINNING **3 :** something that is open **4 :** OCCASION; *also* **:** an opportunity for employment

open–mind·ed \ˌō-pən-ˈmīn-dəd\ *adj* **:** free from rigidly fixed preconceptions

open sentence *n* **:** a statement (as in mathematics) containing at least one blank or unknown so that when the blank is filled or a quantity substituted for the unknown the statement becomes a complete statement that is either true or false

open shop *n* **:** an establishment having members and nonmembers of a labor union on the payroll

open·work \ˈō-pən-ˌwərk\ *n* **:** work so made as to show openings through its substance ⟨a railing of wrought-iron ~⟩ — **open–worked** \-ˌwərkt\ *adj*

[1]**opera** *pl of* OPUS

[2]**op·era** \ˈä-prə, -pə-rə\ *n* **:** a drama set to music — **op·er·at·ic** \ˌä-pə-ˈra-tik\ *adj*

op·er·a·ble \ˈä-pə-rə-bəl\ *adj* **1 :** fit, possible, or desirable to use **2 :** likely to result in a favorable outcome upon surgical treatment

opera glasses *n pl* **:** small binoculars for use in a theater

op·er·ate \ˈä-pə-ˌrāt\ *vb* **-at·ed; -at·ing 1 :** to perform work **:** FUNCTION **2 :** to produce an effect **3 :** to put or keep in operation **4 :** to perform or subject to an operation — **op·er·a·tor** \-ˌrā-tər\ *n*

operating system *n* **:** software that controls the operation of a computer

op·er·a·tion \ˌä-pə-ˈrā-shən\ *n* **1 :** a doing or performing of a practical work **2 :** an exertion of power or influence; *also* **:** method or manner of functioning **3 :** a surgical procedure **4 :** a process of deriving one mathematical expression from others according to a rule **5 :** a military action or mission — **op·er·a·tion·al** \-shə-nəl\ *adj*

[1]**op·er·a·tive** \ˈä-pə-rə-tiv, -ˌrā-\ *adj* **1 :** producing an appropriate effect **2 :** OPERATING ⟨an ~ force⟩ **3 :** having to do with physical operations; *also* **:** WORKING ⟨an ~ craftsman⟩ **4 :** based on or consisting of an operation ⟨~ dentistry⟩

[2]**operative** *n* **:** OPERATOR; *esp* **:** a secret agent

op·er·et·ta \ˌä-pə-ˈre-tə\ *n* [It, dim. of *opera* opera] **:** a light musical-dramatic work with a romantic plot, spoken dialogue, and dancing scenes

oph·thal·mic \äf-ˈthal-mik, äp-\ *adj* [Gk *ophthalmikos*, fr. *ophthalmos* eye] **:** of, relating to, or located near the eye

oph·thal·mol·o·gy \ˌäf-ˌthal-ˈmä-lə-jē, ˌäp-\ *n* **:** a branch of medicine dealing with the structure, functions, and diseases of the eye — **oph·thal·mol·o·gist** \-jist\ *n*

oph·thal·mo·scope \äf-ˈthal-mə-ˌskōp, äp-\ *n* **:** an instrument for use in viewing the interior of the eye and esp. the retina

opi·ate \ˈō-pē-ət, -pē-ˌāt\ *n* **:** a preparation or derivative of opium; *also* **:** a narcotic or a substance with similar activity — **opiate** *adj*

opine \ō-ˈpīn\ *vb* **opined; opin·ing :** to express an opinion **:** STATE

opin·ion \ə-ˈpin-yən\ *n* **1 :** a belief stronger than impression and less strong than positive knowledge **2 :** JUDGMENT **3 :** a formal statement by an expert after careful study

opin·ion·at·ed \ə-ˈpin-yə-ˌnā-təd\ *adj* **:** obstinately adhering to personal opinions

opi·um \ˈō-pē-əm\ *n* [ME, fr. L, fr. Gk *opion*, fr. dim. of *opos* sap] **:** an addictive narcotic drug that is the dried juice of a poppy

opos·sum \ə-ˈpä-səm\ *n, pl* **opossums** *also* **opossum :** a common omnivorous tree-dwelling marsupial mammal of the eastern U.S. that is active esp. at night

opp *abbr* opposite

op·po·nent \ə-ˈpō-nənt\ *n* **:** one that opposes **:** ADVERSARY

op·por·tune \ˌä-pər-ˈtün, -ˈtyün\ *adj* [ME, fr. MF *opportun*, fr. L *opportunus*, fr. *ob-* toward + *portus* port, harbor] **:** SUITABLE — **op·por·tune·ly** *adv*

op·por·tun·ism \ˌä-pər-ˈtü-ˌni-zəm, -ˈtyü-\ *n* **:** a taking advantage of opportunities or circumstances esp. with little regard for principles or ultimate consequences — **op·por·tun·ist** \-nist\ *n* — **op·por·tu·nis·tic** \-tü-ˈnis-tik, -tyü-\ *adj*

op·por·tu·ni·ty \ˌä-pər-ˈtü-nə-tē, -ˈtyü-\ *n, pl* **-ties 1 :** a favorable combination of circumstances, time, and place **2 :** a chance for advancement

op·pose \ə-ˈpōz\ *vb* **op·posed; op·pos·ing 1 :** to place opposite or against something (as to provide resistance or contrast) **2 :** to strive against **:** RESIST — **op·po·si·tion** \ˌä-pə-ˈzi-shən\ *n*

[1]**op·po·site** \ˈä-pə-zət\ *adj* **1 :** set over against something that is at the other end or side **2 :** OPPOSED, HOSTILE; *also* **:** CONTRARY **3 :** contrarily turned or moving — **op·po·site·ly** *adv* — **op·po·site·ness** *n*

[2]**opposite** *n* **:** one that is opposed or contrary

[3]**opposite** *adv* **:** on or to an opposite side

[4]**opposite** *prep* **:** across from and usu. facing ⟨the house ~ ours⟩

op·press \ə-ˈpres\ *vb* **1 :** to crush by abuse of power or authority **2 :** to weigh down **:** BURDEN **syn** aggrieve, wrong, persecute — **op·pres·sive** \-ˈpre-siv\ *adj* — **op·pres·sive·ly** *adv* — **op·pres·sor** \-ˈpre-sər\ *n*

op·pres·sion \ə-ˈpre-shən\ *n* **1 :** unjust or cruel exercise of power or authority **2 :** DEPRESSION

op·pro·bri·ous \ə-ˈprō-brē-əs\ *adj* **:** expressing or deserving opprobrium — **op·pro·bri·ous·ly** *adv*

op·pro·bri·um \-brē-əm\ *n* **1 :** something that brings disgrace **2 :** INFAMY

[1]**opt** \ˈäpt\ *vb* **:** to make a choice; *esp* **:** to decide in favor of something

[2]**opt** *abbr* **1** optical; optician; optics **2** option; optional

op·tic \ˈäp-tik\ *adj* **:** of or relating to vision or the eye

op·ti·cal \ˈäp-ti-kəl\ *adj* **1 :** relating to optics **2 :** OPTIC **3 :** of, relating to, or using light

optical art *n* **:** nonobjective art characterized by the use of geometric patterns often for an illusory effect

optical disk *n* **:** a disk on which information has been recorded digitally and which is read using a laser

optical fiber *n* **:** a single fiber-optic strand

op·ti·cian \äp-ˈti-shən\ *n* **1 :** a maker of or dealer in optical items and instruments **2 :** a person who makes or orders eyeglass and contact lenses to prescription and sells glasses

op·tics \ˈäp-tiks\ *n pl* **:** a science that deals with the nature and properties of light

op·ti·mal \ˈäp-tə-məl\ *adj* **:** most desirable or satisfactory — **op·ti·mal·ly** *adv*

op·ti·mism \ˈäp-tə-ˌmi-zəm\ *n* [F *optimisme*, fr. L *optimum*, n., best, fr. neut. of *optimus* best] **1 :** a doctrine that this world is the best possible world **2 :** an inclination to anticipate the best possible outcome of actions or events — **op•ti•mist** \-mist\ *n* — **op•ti•mis•tic** \ˌäp-tə-ˈmis-tik\ *adj* — **op•ti•mis•ti•cal•ly** \-ti-k(ə-)lē\ *adv*

op•ti•mum \ˈäp-tə-məm\ *n, pl* **-ma** \-mə\ *also* **-mums** [L] : the amount or degree of something most favorable to an end; *also* : greatest degree attained under implied or specified conditions

op•tion \ˈäp-shən\ *n* **1** : the power or right to choose **2** : a right to buy or sell something at a specified price during a specified period **3** : something offered for choice — **op•tion•al** \-shə-nəl\ *adj*

op•tom•e•try \äp-ˈtä-mə-trē\ *n* : the art or profession of examining the eyes for defects of vision and of prescribing corrective lenses or exercises — **op•tom•e•trist** \-trist\ *n*

opt out *vb* : to choose not to participate

op•u•lence \ˈä-pyə-ləns\ *n* **1** : WEALTH **2** : ABUNDANCE

op•u•lent \ˈä-pyə-lənt\ *adj* **1** : WEALTHY **2** : richly abundant — **op•u•lent•ly** *adv*

opus \ˈō-pəs\ *n, pl* **opera** \ˈō-pə-rə, ˈä-\ *also* **opus•es** \ˈō-pə-səz\ : WORK; *esp* : a musical composition

or \ˈȯr\ *conj* — used as a function word to indicate an alternative ⟨sink ~ swim⟩

OR *abbr* **1** operating room **2** Oregon

-or \ər\ *n suffix* : one that does a (specified) thing ⟨calculat*or*⟩

or•a•cle \ˈȯr-ə-kəl\ *n* **1** : one held to give divinely inspired answers or revelations **2** : an authoritative or wise utterance; *also* : a person of great authority or wisdom — **orac•u•lar** \ȯ-ˈra-kyə-lər\ *adj*

[1]**oral** \ˈōr-əl\ *adj* **1** : SPOKEN **2** : of or relating to the mouth **3** : of, relating to, or characterized by the first stage of psychosexual development in psychoanalytic theory in which libidinal gratification is derived from intake (as of food), by sucking, and later by biting **4** : relating to or characterized by personality traits of passive dependency and aggressiveness — **oral•ly** *adv*

[2]**oral** *n* : an oral examination — usu. used in pl.

orang \ə-ˈraŋ\ *n* : ORANGUTAN

or•ange \ˈȯr-inj\ *n* **1** : a juicy citrus fruit with reddish yellow rind; *also* : an evergreen tree with fragrant white flowers that bears this fruit **2** : a color between red and yellow

or•ange•ade \ˌȯr-in-ˈjād\ *n* : a beverage of orange juice, sugar, and water

orange hawkweed *n* : a weedy herb related to the daisies with bright orange-red flower heads

or•ange•ry \ˈȯr-inj-rē\ *n, pl* **-ries** : a protected place (as a greenhouse) for raising oranges in cool climates

orang•utan \ə-ˈraŋ-ə-ˌtaŋ, -ˌtan\ *n* [Bazaar Malay (Malay-based pidgin), fr. Malay *orang* man + *hutan* forest] : a large reddish brown tree-living anthropoid ape of Borneo and Sumatra

orate \ȯ-ˈrāt\ *vb* **orat•ed; orat•ing** : to speak in a declamatory manner

ora•tion \ə-ˈrā-shən\ *n* : an elaborate discourse delivered in a formal and dignified manner

or•a•tor \ˈȯr-ə-tər\ *n* : one noted for skill and power as a public speaker

or•a•tor•i•cal \ˌȯr-ə-ˈtȯr-i-kəl\ *adj* : of, relating to, or characteristic of an orator or oratory — **or•a•tor•i•cal•ly** \-ˈtȯr-i-k(ə-)lē\ *adv*

or•a•to•rio \ˌȯr-ə-ˈtōr-ē-ˌō\ *n, pl* **-rios** : a lengthy choral work usu. on a scriptural subject

[1]**or•a•to•ry** \ˈȯr-ə-ˌtōr-ē\ *n, pl* **-ries** : a private or institutional chapel

[2]**oratory** *n* : the art of speaking eloquently and effectively in public **syn** rhetoric, elocution

orb \ˈȯrb\ *n* : a spherical body; *also* : EYE

[1]**or•bit** \ˈȯr-bət\ *n* [L *orbita,* lit., path, rut] **1** : a path described by one body in its revolution about another **2** : range or sphere of activity — **or•bit•al** \-ᵊl\ *adj*

[2]**orbit** *vb* **1** : CIRCLE **2** : to send up and make revolve in an orbit ⟨~ a satellite⟩ — **or•bit•er** *n*

orch *abbr* orchestra

or•chard \ˈȯr-chərd\ *n* [ME, fr. OE *ortgeard,* fr. *ort-* (fr. L *hortus* garden) + *geard* yard] : a place where fruit trees, sugar maples, or nut trees are grown; *also* : the trees of such a place — **or•chard•ist** \-chər-dist\ *n*

or•ches•tra \ˈȯr-kə-strə\ *n* **1** : the front section of seats on the main floor of a theater **2** : a group of instrumentalists organized to perform ensemble music — **or•ches•tral** \ȯr-ˈkes-trəl\ *adj* — **or•ches•tral•ly** *adv*

or•ches•trate \ˈȯr-kə-ˌstrāt\ *vb* **-trat•ed; -trat•ing** **1** : to compose or arrange for an orchestra **2** : to arrange so as to achieve a desired effect — **or•ches•tra•tion** \ˌȯr-kə-ˈstrā-shən\ *n*

or•chid \ˈȯr-kəd\ *n* : any of a large family of plants having often showy flowers with three petals of which the middle one is enlarged into a lip; *also* : a flower of an orchid

ord *abbr* **1** order **2** ordnance

or•dain \ȯr-ˈdān\ *vb* **1** : to admit to the ministry or priesthood by the ritual of a church **2** : DECREE, ENACT; *also* : DESTINE — **or•dain•ment** *n*

or•deal \ȯr-ˈdēl, ˈȯr-ˌdēl\ *n* : a severe trial or experience

[1]**or•der** \ˈȯr-dər\ *vb* **1** : ARRANGE, REGULATE **2** : COMMAND **3** : to place an order

[2]**order** *n* **1** : a group of people formally united; *also* : a badge or medal of such a group **2** : any of the several grades of the Christian ministry; *also, pl* : ORDINATION **3** : a rank, class, or special group of persons or things **4** : a category of biological classification ranking above the family and below the class **5** : ARRANGEMENT, SEQUENCE; *also* : the prevailing state of things **6** : a customary mode of procedure; *also* : the rule of law or proper authority **7** : a specific rule, regulation, or authoritative direction **8** : a style of building; *also* : an architectural column forming the unit of a style **9** : condition esp. with regard to repair **10** : a written direction to pay money or to buy or sell goods; *also* : goods bought or sold

[1]**or•der•ly** \ˈȯr-dər-lē\ *adj* **1** : arranged according to some order; *also* : NEAT, TIDY **2** : well behaved ⟨an ~ crowd⟩ **syn** methodical, systematic, regular — **or•der•li•ness** *n*

[2]**orderly** *n, pl* **-lies** **1** : a soldier who attends a superior officer **2** : a hospital attendant who does general work

[1]**or•di•nal** \ˈȯrd-ᵊn-əl\ *n* : an ordinal number

[2]**ordinal** *adj* : indicating order or rank (as sixth) in a series

or•di•nance \ˈȯrd-ᵊn-əns\ *n* : an authoritative decree or law; *esp* : a municipal regulation

or•di•nary \ˈȯrd-ᵊn-ˌer-ē\ *adj* **1** : to be expected : USUAL **2** : of common quality, rank, or ability; *also* : POOR, INFERIOR **syn** customary, routine, normal, everyday — **or•di•nar•i•ly** \ˌȯrd-ᵊn-ˈer-ə-lē\ *adv* — **or•di•nar•i•ness** \ˈȯrd-ᵊn-ˌer-ē-nəs\ *n*

or•di•nate \ˈȯrd-ᵊn-ət, -ˌāt\ *n* : the coordinate of a point in a plane coordinate system that is the distance of the point from the horizontal axis found by measuring along a line parallel to the vertical axis

or•di•na•tion \ˌȯrd-ᵊn-ˈā-shən\ *n* : the act or ceremony by which a person is ordained

ord•nance \ˈȯrd-nəns\ *n* **1** : military supplies **2** : CANNON, ARTILLERY

Or•do•vi•cian \ˌȯr-də-ˈvi-shən\ *adj* : of, relating to, or being the period of the Paleozoic era between the Cambrian and the Silurian — **Ordovician** *n*

or•dure \ˈȯr-jər\ *n* : EXCREMENT

[1]**ore** \ˈōr\ *n* : a mineral mined to obtain a substance that it contains

[2]**ore** \ˈər-ə\ *n, pl* **ore** — see *krona, krone* at MONEY table

Ore *or* **Oreg** *abbr* Oregon

oreg•a•no \ə-ˈre-gə-ˌnō\ *n* : a bushy perennial mint used as a seasoning and a source of oil

org *abbr* organization; organized

or•gan \ˈȯr-gən\ *n* **1** : a musical instrument having sets of pipes sounded by compressed air and controlled by keyboards; *also* : an instrument in which the sounds of the pipe organ are approximated by electronic devices **2** : a differentiated animal or plant structure (as a heart or a leaf) made up of cells and tissues and performing some bodily function **3** : a group that performs a specialized function ⟨the various ~*s* of government⟩ **4** : PERIODICAL

or•gan•dy *also* **or•gan•die** \ˈȯr-gən-dē\ *n, pl* **-dies** [F *organdi*] : a fine transparent muslin with a stiff finish

or•gan•elle \ˌȯr-gə-ˈnəl\ *n* : a specialized cell part that resembles an organ in having a special function

or•gan•ic \ȯr-ˈga-nik\ *adj* **1** : of, relating to, or arising in a bodily organ **2** : of, relating to, or derived from living things **3** : of, relating to, or containing carbon compounds **4** : of or relating to a branch of chemistry dealing with carbon compounds **5** : involving, producing, or dealing in foods produced without the use of laboratory-made fertilizers, growth substances, antibiotics, or pesticides **6** : ORGANIZED ⟨an ~ whole⟩ — **or•gan•i•cal•ly** \-ni-k(ə-)lē\ *adv*

or•ga•nise *Brit var of* ORGANIZE

or•gan•ism \ˈȯr-gə-ˌni-zəm\ *n* : an individual living thing (as a person, animal, or plant) — **or•gan•is•mic** \ˌȯr-gə-ˈniz-mik\ *adj*

or•gan•ist \ˈȯr-gə-nist\ *n* : a person who plays an organ

or•ga•ni•za•tion \ˌȯr-gə-nə-ˈzā-shən\ *n* **1** : the act or process of organizing or of being organized; *also* : the condition or manner of being organized **2** : ASSOCIATION, SOCIETY **3** : an administrative structure (as a business or a political party) — **or•ga•ni•za•tion•al** \-shə-nəl\ *adj*

or•ga•nize \ˈȯr-gə-ˌnīz\ *vb* **-nized; -niz•ing 1** : to develop an organic structure **2** : to form into a complete and functioning whole **3** : to set up an administrative structure for **4** : to arrange by systematic planning and united effort **5** : to join in a union; *also* : UNIONIZE **syn** institute, found, establish, constitute — **or•ga•niz•er** *n*

or•gano•chlo•rine \ȯr-ˌga-nə-ˈklōr-ˌēn\ *adj* : of or relating to the chlorinated hydrocarbon pesticides (as DDT) — **organochlorine** *n*

or•gano•phos•phate \-ˈfäs-ˌfāt\ *n* : an organophosphorus pesticide — **organophosphate** *adj*

or•gano•phos•pho•rus \-ˈfäs-fə-rəs\ *also* **or•gano•phos•pho•rous** \-fäs-ˈfōr-əs\ *adj* : of, relating to, or being a phosphorus-containing organic pesticide (as malathion)

or•gan•za \ȯr-ˈgan-zə\ *n* : a sheer dress fabric resembling organdy and usu. made of silk, rayon, or nylon

or•gasm \ˈȯr-ˌga-zəm\ *n* : the climax of sexual excitement — **or•gas•mic** \ȯr-ˈgaz-mik\ *adj*

or•gi•as•tic \ˌȯr-jē-ˈas-tik\ *adj* : of, relating to, or marked by orgies

or•gu•lous \ˈȯr-gyə-ləs, -gə-\ *adj* : PROUD

or•gy \ˈȯr-jē\ *n, pl* **orgies** : a gathering marked by unrestrained indulgence (as in sexual activity, alcohol, or drugs)

ori•el \ˈōr-ē-əl\ *n* : a window built out from a wall and usu. supported by a bracket

ori•ent \ˈōr-ē-ˌent\ *vb* **1** : to set in a definite position esp. in relation to the points of the compass **2** : to acquaint with an existing situation or environment **3** : to direct toward the interests of a particular group — **ori•en•ta•tion** \ˌōr-ē-ən-ˈtā-shən\ *n*

Orient *n* : EAST 3; *esp* : the countries of eastern Asia

ori•en•tal \ˌōr-ē-ˈent-ᵊl\ *adj* [fr. *Orient* East, fr. ME, fr. MF, fr. L *orient-, oriens,* fr. prp. of *oriri* to rise] *often cap* : of or situated in the Orient — **Oriental** *n*

ori•en•tate \ˈōr-ē-ən-ˌtāt\ *vb* **-tat•ed; -tat•ing 1** : ORIENT **2** : to face east

or•i•fice \ˈȯr-ə-fəs\ *n* : OPENING, MOUTH

ori•flamme \ˈȯr-ə-ˌflam\ *n* : a brightly colored banner used as a standard or ensign in battle

orig *abbr* original; originally

ori•ga•mi \ˌȯr-ə-ˈgä-mē\ *n* : the art or process of Japanese paper folding

or•i•gin \ˈȯr-ə-jən\ *n* **1** : ANCESTRY **2** : rise, beginning, or derivation from a source; *also* : CAUSE **3** : the intersection of coordinate axes

¹**orig•i•nal** \ə-ˈri-jə-nəl\ *n* : something from which a copy, reproduction, or translation is made : PROTOTYPE

²**original** *adj* **1** : FIRST, INITIAL **2** : not copied from something else : FRESH **3** : INVENTIVE — **orig•i•nal•i•ty** \-ˌri-jə-ˈna-lə-tē\ *n* — **orig•i•nal•ly** \-ˈri-jən-ᵊl-ē\ *adv*

orig•i•nate \ə-ˈri-jə-ˌnāt\ *vb* **-nat•ed; -nat•ing 1** : to give rise to : INITIATE **2** : to come into existence : BEGIN — **orig•i•na•tor** \-ˌnā-tər\ *n*

ori•ole \ˈōr-ē-ˌōl\ *n* : any of various New World birds of which the males are usu. black and yellow or black and orange

or•i•son \ˈȯr-ə-sən\ *n* : PRAYER

or•mo•lu \ˈȯr-mə-ˌlü\ *n* : a golden or gilded brass used for decorative purposes

¹**or•na•ment** \ˈȯr-nə-mənt\ *n* : something that lends grace or beauty — **or•na•men•tal** \ˌȯr-nə-ˈment-ᵊl\ *adj*

²**or•na•ment** \-ˌment\ *vb* : to provide with ornament : ADORN — **or•na•men•ta•tion** \ˌȯr-nə-mən-ˈtā-shən\ *n*

or•nate \ȯr-ˈnāt\ *adj* : elaborately decorated — **or•nate•ly** *adv* — **or•nate•ness** *n*

or•nery \ˈȯr-nə-rē, ˈä-nə-\ *adj* : having an irritable disposition

or•ni•thol•o•gy \ˌȯr-nə-ˈthä-lə-jē\ *n, pl* **-gies** : a branch of zoology dealing with birds — **or•ni•tho•log•i•cal** \-thə-ˈlä-ji-kəl\ *adj* — **or•ni•thol•o•gist** \-ˈthä-lə-jist\ *n*

oro•tund \ˈȯr-ə-ˌtənd\ *adj* **1** : SONOROUS **2** : POMPOUS — **oro•tun•di•ty** \ȯr-ə-ˈtən-di-tē\ *n*

or•phan \ˈȯr-fən\ *n* : a child deprived by death of one or usu. both parents — **orphan** *vb*

or•phan•age \ˈȯr-fə-nij\ *n* : an institution for the care of orphans

or•tho•don•tia \ˌȯr-thə-ˈdän-chə, -chē-ə\ *n* : ORTHODONTICS

or•tho•don•tics \ˌȯr-thə-ˈdän-tiks\ *n* : a branch of dentistry concerned with the correction of faults in the arrangement and placing of the teeth — **or•tho•don•tist** \-ˈdän-tist\ *n*

or•tho•dox \ˈȯr-thə-ˌdäks\ *adj* [MF or LL; MF *orthodoxe,* fr. LL *orthodoxus,* fr. LGk *orthodoxos,* fr. Gk *orthos* right + *doxa* opinion] **1** : conforming to established doctrine esp. in religion **2** : CONVENTIONAL **3** *cap* : of or relating to a Christian church originating in the church of the Eastern Roman Empire — **or•tho•doxy** \-ˌdäk-sē\ *n*

or•thog•ra•phy \ȯr-ˈthä-grə-fē\ *n* : SPELLING — **or•tho•graph•ic** \ˌȯr-thə-ˈgra-fik\ *adj*

or•tho•pe•dics \ˌȯr-thə-ˈpē-diks\ *n sing or pl* : a branch of medicine concerned with the correction or prevention of skeletal deformities — **or•tho•pe•dic** \-dik\ *adj* — **or•tho•pe•dist** \-dist\ *n*

-ory \ˌōr-ē, ə-rē\ *adj suffix* **1** : of, relating to, or characterized by ⟨anticipat*ory*⟩ **2** : serving for, producing, or maintaining ⟨illus*ory*⟩

Os *symbol* osmium

OS *abbr* **1** [L *oculus sinister*] left eye **2** ordinary seaman **3** out of stock

Osage \ō-ˈsāj\ *n, pl* **Osag•es** *or* **Osage** : a member of an American Indian people orig. of Missouri

os•cil•late \ˈä-sə-ˌlāt\ *vb* **-lat•ed; -lat•ing 1** : to swing backward and forward like a pendulum **2** : to move or travel back and forth between two points **3** : VARY, FLUCTUATE — **os•cil•la•tion** \ˌä-sə-ˈlā-shən\ *n* — **os•cil•la•tor** \ˈä-sə-ˌlā-tər\ *n* — **os•cil•la•to•ry** \ˈä-sə-lə-ˌtōr-ē\ *adj*

os•cil•lo•scope \ä-ˈsi-lə-ˌskōp\ *n* : an instrument in which variations in current or voltage appear as a visible wave form on a fluorescent screen

os•cu•late \ˈäs-kyə-ˌlāt\ *vb* **-lat•ed; -lat•ing :** KISS — **os•cu•la•tion** \ˌäs-kyə-ˈlā-shən\ *n* — **os•cu•la•to•ry** \ˈäs-kyə-lə-ˌtōr-ē\ *adj*

Osee \ˈō-ˌzē, ō-ˈzā-ə\ *n* **:** HOSEA

OSHA \ˈō-shə\ *abbr* Occupational Safety and Health Administration

osier \ˈō-zhər\ *n* **:** any of various willows with pliable twigs used esp. in making baskets and furniture; *also* **:** a twig from an osier

os•mi•um \ˈäz-mē-əm\ *n* **:** a heavy hard brittle metallic chemical element used esp. as a catalyst and in alloys — see ELEMENT table

os•mo•sis \äz-ˈmō-səs, äs-\ *n* **:** movement of a solvent through a semipermeable membrane into a solution of higher concentration that tends to equalize the concentrations of the solutions on either side of the membrane — **os•mot•ic** \-ˈmä-tik\ *adj*

os•prey \ˈäs-prē, -ˌprā\ *n, pl* **ospreys :** a large brown and white fish-eating hawk

os•si•fy \ˈä-sə-ˌfī\ *vb* **-fied; -fy•ing :** to make or become hardened or set in one's ways — **os•si•fi•ca•tion** \ˌä-sə-fə-ˈkā-shən\ *n*

os•su•ary \ˈä-shə-ˌwer-ē, -syə-\ *n, pl* **-ar•ies :** a depository for the bones of the dead

os•ten•si•ble \ä-ˈsten-sə-bəl\ *adj* **:** shown outwardly **:** PROFESSED, APPARENT — **os•ten•si•bly** \-blē\ *adv*

os•ten•ta•tion \ˌäs-tən-ˈtā-shən\ *n* **:** pretentious or excessive display — **os•ten•ta•tious** \-shəs\ *adj* — **os•ten•ta•tious•ly** *adv*

os•teo•path \ˈäs-tē-ə-ˌpath\ *n* **:** a practitioner of osteopathy

os•te•op•a•thy \ˌäs-tē-ˈä-pə-thē\ *n* **:** a system of treating diseases emphasizing manipulation (as of joints) but not excluding other agencies (as the use of medicine and surgery) — **os•teo•path•ic** \ˌäs-tē-ə-ˈpa-thik\ *adj*

os•teo•po•ro•sis \ˌäs-tē-ō-pə-ˈrō-səs\ *n, pl* **-ro•ses** \-ˌsēz\ **:** a condition affecting esp. older women and characterized by fragile and porous bones

os•tra•cise *Brit var of* OSTRACIZE

os•tra•cize \ˈäs-trə-ˌsīz\ *vb* **-cized; -ciz•ing** [Gk *ostrakizein* to banish by voting with potsherds, fr. *ostrakon* shell, potsherd] **:** to exclude from a group by common consent — **os•tra•cism** \-ˌsi-zəm\ *n*

os•trich \ˈäs-trich, ˈȯs-\ *n* **:** a very large swift-footed flightless bird of Africa and Arabia

Os•we•go tea \ä-ˈswē-gō-\ *n* **:** a No. American mint with showy scarlet flowers

OT *abbr* **1** occupational therapy **2** Old Testament **3** overtime

¹oth•er \ˈə-t͟hər\ *adj* **1 :** being the one left; *also* **:** being the ones distinct from those first mentioned **2 :** ALTERNATE ⟨every ~ day⟩ **3 :** DIFFERENT **4 :** ADDITIONAL **5 :** recently past ⟨the ~ night⟩

²other *pron* **1 :** remaining one or ones **2 :** a different or additional one ⟨something or ~⟩

oth•er•wise \ˈə-t͟hər-ˌwīz\ *adv* **1 :** in a different way **2 :** in different circumstances **3 :** in other respects **4 :** if not **5 :** NOT — **otherwise** *adj*

oth•er•world \-ˌwərld\ *n* **:** a world beyond death or beyond present reality

oth•er•world•ly \ˌə-t͟hər-ˈwərld-lē\ *adj* **:** not worldly **:** concerned with spiritual, intellectual, or imaginative matters

oti•ose \ˈō-shē-ˌōs, ˈō-tē-\ *adj* **1 :** FUTILE **2 :** IDLE **3 :** USELESS

oto•lar•yn•gol•o•gy \ˌō-tō-ˌlar-ən-ˈgä-lə-jē\ *n* **:** a medical specialty concerned esp. with the ear, nose, and throat — **oto•lar•yn•gol•o•gist** \-jist\ *n*

oto•rhi•no•lar•yn•gol•o•gy \ˌō-tō-ˌrī-nō-ˌlar-ən-ˈgä-lə-jē\ *n* **:** OTOLARYNGOLOGY — **oto•rhi•no•lar•yn•gol•o•gist** \-jist\ *n*

OTS *abbr* officers' training school

Ot•ta•wa \ˈä-tə-wə, -ˌwä, -ˌwȯ\ *n, pl* **Ottawas** *or* **Ottawa :** a member of an American Indian people of Michigan and southern Ontario

ot•ter \ˈä-tər\ *n, pl* **otters** *also* **otter :** any of various web-footed fish-eating mammals with dark brown fur that are related to the weasels; *also* **:** the fur

otter

ot•to•man \ˈä-tə-mən\ *n* **:** an upholstered seat or couch usu. without a back; *also* **:** an overstuffed footstool

ou•bli•ette \ˌü-blē-ˈet\ *n* [F, fr. MF, fr. *oublier* to forget, ultim. fr. L *oblivisci*] **:** a dungeon with an opening at the top

ought \ˈȯt\ *verbal auxiliary* — used to express moral obligation, advisability, natural expectation, or logical consequence

ou•gui•ya \ü-ˈgwē-ə, -ˈgē\ *n, pl* **ouguiya** — see MONEY table

ounce \ˈau̇ns\ *n* [ME, fr. MF *unce,* fr. L *uncia* twelfth part, ounce, fr. *unus* one] **1 :** a unit of avoirdupois, troy, and apothecaries' weight — see WEIGHT table **2 :** FLUID OUNCE

our \är, ˈau̇r\ *adj* **:** of or relating to us or ourselves

ours \ˈau̇rz, ˈärz\ *pron* **:** that which belongs to us

our•selves \är-ˈselvz, au̇r-\ *pron* **:** our own selves — used reflexively, for emphasis, or in absolute constructions ⟨we pleased ~⟩ ⟨we'll do it ~⟩ ⟨we were tourists ~⟩

-ous \əs\ *adj suffix* **:** full of **:** abounding in **:** having **:** possessing the qualities of ⟨clamor*ous*⟩ ⟨poison*ous*⟩

oust \ˈau̇st\ *vb* **:** to eject from or deprive of property or position **:** EXPEL **syn** evict, dismiss, banish, deport

oust•er \ˈau̇s-tər\ *n* **:** EXPULSION

¹out \ˈau̇t\ *adv* **1 :** in a direction away from the inside or center **2 :** beyond control **3 :** to extinction, exhaustion, or completion **4 :** in or into the open **5 :** so as to retire a batter or base runner; *also* **:** so as to be retired

²out *vb* **:** to become known ⟨the truth will ~⟩

³out *prep* **1 :** out through ⟨looked ~ the window⟩ **2 :** outward on or along ⟨drive ~ the river road⟩

⁴out *adj* **1 :** situated outside or at a distance **2 :** not in **:** ABSENT; *also* **:** not being in power **3 :** not successful in reaching base **4 :** not being in vogue or fashion **:** not up-to-date

⁵out *n* **1 :** one who is out of office **2 :** the retiring of a batter or base runner

out•age \ˈau̇-tij\ *n* **:** a period or instance of interruption esp. of electricity

out–and–out *adj* **:** COMPLETE, THOROUGHGOING ⟨an ~ fraud⟩

out•bid \ˌau̇t-ˈbid\ *vb* **:** to make a higher bid than

¹out•board \ˈau̇t-ˌbōrd\ *adj* **1 :** situated outboard **2 :** having or using an outboard motor

²outboard *adv* **1 :** outside a ship's hull **:** away from the long axis of a ship **2 :** in a position closer to the wing tip of an airplane

outboard motor *n* **:** a small internal combustion engine with propeller attached for mounting at the stern of a small boat

out•bound \ˈau̇t-ˌbau̇nd\ *adj* **:** outward bound ⟨~ traffic⟩

out•break \-ˌbrāk\ *n* **1 :** a sudden increase in activity, incidence, or numbers **2 :** INSURRECTION, REVOLT

out•build•ing \-ˌbil-diŋ\ *n* **:** a building separate from but accessory to a main house

out•burst \-ˌbərst\ *n* **:** ERUPTION; *esp* **:** a violent expression of feeling

out·cast \-ˌkast\ *n* : one that is cast out by society
out·class \au̇t-ˈklas\ *vb* : SURPASS
out·come \ˈau̇t-ˌkəm\ *n* : a final consequence : RESULT
out·crop \-ˌkräp\ *n* : a coming out of bedrock to the surface of the ground; *also* : the part of a rock formation that thus appears — **outcrop** *vb*
out·cry \-ˌkrī\ *n* : a loud cry : CLAMOR
out·dat·ed \au̇t-ˈdā-təd\ *adj* : OUTMODED
out·dis·tance \-ˈdis-təns\ *vb* : to go far ahead of (as in a race) : OUTSTRIP
out·do \-ˈdü\ *vb* **-did** \-ˈdid\; **-done** \-ˈdən\; **-do·ing; -does** \-ˈdəz\ : to go beyond in action or performance
out·door \ˈau̇t-ˌdōr, -ˈdōr\ *also* **out·doors** \-ˌdōrz, -ˈdōrz\ *adj* **1** : of or relating to the outdoors **2** : performed outdoors **3** : not enclosed (as by a roof)
[1]**out·doors** \ˈau̇t-ˌdōrz, -ˈdōrz\ *adv* : in or into the open air
[2]**outdoors** *n* **1** : the open air **2** : the world away from human habitation
out·draw \au̇t-ˈdrȯ\ *vb* **-drew** \-ˈdrü\; **-drawn** \-ˈdrȯn\; **-draw·ing 1** : to attract a larger audience than **2** : to draw a handgun more quickly than
out·er \ˈau̇-tər\ *adj* **1** : EXTERNAL **2** : situated farther out; *also* : being away from a center
out·er·most \-ˌmōst\ *adj* : farthest out
outer space *n* : SPACE 5
out·face \au̇t-ˈfās\ *vb* **1** : to cause to waver or submit **2** : DEFY
out·field \ˈau̇t-ˌfēld\ *n* : the part of a baseball field beyond the infield and within the foul lines; *also* : players in the outfield — **out·field·er** \-ˌfēl-dər\ *n*
out·fight \au̇t-ˈfīt\ *vb* : to surpass in fighting : DEFEAT
[1]**out·fit** \ˈau̇t-ˌfit\ *n* **1** : the equipment or apparel for a special purpose or occasion **2** : GROUP
[2]**outfit** *vb* **out·fit·ted; out·fit·ting** : EQUIP — **out·fit·ter** *n*
out·flank \au̇t-ˈflaŋk\ *vb* : to get around the flank of (an opposing force)
out·flow \ˈau̇t-ˌflō\ *n* **1** : a flowing out **2** : something that flows out
out·fox \au̇t-ˈfäks\ *vb* : OUTWIT
out·go \ˈau̇t-ˌgō\ *n, pl* **outgoes** : EXPENDITURES, OUTLAY
out·go·ing \-ˌgō-iŋ\ *adj* **1** : going out ⟨~ tide⟩ **2** : retiring from a place or position **3** : FRIENDLY
out·grow \au̇t-ˈgrō\ *vb* **-grew** \-ˈgrü\; **-grown** \-ˈgrōn\; **-grow·ing 1** : to grow faster than **2** : to grow too large for
out·growth \ˈau̇t-ˌgrōth\ *n* : a product of growing out : OFFSHOOT; *also* : CONSEQUENCE, RESULT
out·guess \au̇t-ˈges\ *vb* : OUTWIT
out·gun \-ˈgən\ *vb* : to surpass in firepower
out·house \ˈau̇t-ˌhau̇s\ *n* : OUTBUILDING; *esp* : an outdoor toilet
out·ing \ˈau̇-tiŋ\ *n* : a brief stay or trip in the open
out·land·ish \au̇t-ˈlan-dish\ *adj* **1** : of foreign appearance or manner; *also* : BIZARRE **2** : remote from civilization — **out·land·ish·ly** *adv*
out·last \-ˈlast\ *vb* : to last longer than
[1]**out·law** \ˈau̇t-ˌlȯ\ *n* **1** : a person excluded from the protection of the law **2** : a lawless person
[2]**outlaw** *vb* **1** : to deprive of the protection of the law **2** : to make illegal — **out·law·ry** \ˈau̇t-ˌlȯr-ē\ *n*
out·lay \ˈau̇t-ˌlā\ *n* **1** : the act of spending **2** : EXPENDITURE
out·let \ˈau̇t-ˌlet, -lət\ *n* **1** : EXIT, VENT **2** : a means of release (as for an emotion) **3** : a market for a commodity **4** : a receptacle for the plug of an electrical device
[1]**out·line** \ˈau̇t-ˌlīn\ *n* **1** : a line marking the outer limits of an object or figure **2** : a drawing in which only contours are marked **3** : SUMMARY, SYNOPSIS **4** : PLAN
[2]**outline** *vb* **1** : to draw the outline of **2** : to indicate the chief features or parts of
out·live \au̇t-ˈliv\ *vb* : to live longer than **syn** outlast, survive
out·look \ˈau̇t-ˌlu̇k\ *n* **1** : a place offering a view; *also* : VIEW **2** : STANDPOINT **3** : the prospect for the future
out·ly·ing \-ˌlī-iŋ\ *adj* : distant from a center or main body
out·ma·neu·ver \ˌau̇t-mə-ˈnü-vər, -ˈnyü-\ *vb* : to defeat by more skillful maneuvering
out·mod·ed \au̇t-ˈmō-dəd\ *adj* **1** : no longer in style **2** : no longer acceptable or current
out·num·ber \-ˈnəm-bər\ *vb* : to exceed in number
out of *prep* **1** : out from within or behind ⟨walk *out of* the room⟩ ⟨look *out of* the window⟩ **2** : from a state of ⟨wake up *out of* a deep sleep⟩ **3** : beyond the limits of ⟨*out of* sight⟩ **4** : BECAUSE OF ⟨came *out of* curiosity⟩ **5** : FROM, WITH ⟨built it *out of* scrap⟩ **6** : in or into a state of loss or not having ⟨cheated him *out of* $5000⟩ ⟨we're *out of* matches⟩ **7** : from among ⟨one *out of* four⟩ — **out of it** : SQUARE, OLD-FASHIONED
out–of–bounds *adv or adj* : outside the prescribed boundaries or limits
out–of–date *adj* : no longer in fashion or in use : OUTMODED
out–of–door *or* **out–of–doors** *adj* : OUTDOOR
out–of–the–way *adj* **1** : UNUSUAL **2** : being off the beaten track
out·pa·tient \ˈau̇t-ˌpā-shənt\ *n* : a patient who visits a hospital or clinic for diagnosis or treatment without staying overnight
out·per·form \ˌau̇t-pər-ˈfȯrm\ *vb* : to perform better than
out·play \au̇t-ˈplā\ *vb* : to play more skillfully than
out·point \-ˈpȯint\ *vb* : to win more points than
out·post \ˈau̇t-ˌpōst\ *n* **1** : a security detachment dispatched by a main body of troops to protect it from enemy surprise; *also* : a military base established (as by treaty) in a foreign country **2** : an outlying or frontier settlement
out·pour·ing \-ˌpōr-iŋ\ *n* : something that pours out or is poured out
out·pull \au̇t-ˈpu̇l\ *vb* : OUTDRAW 1
[1]**out·put** \ˈau̇t-ˌpu̇t\ *n* **1** : the amount produced (as by a machine or factory) : PRODUCTION **2** : the information produced by a computer
[2]**output** *vb* **out·put·ted** *or* **output; out·put·ting** : to produce as output
[1]**out·rage** \ˈau̇t-ˌrāj\ *n* [ME, fr. MF, excess, outrage, fr. *outre* beyond, in excess, fr. L *ultra*] **1** : a violent or shameful act **2** : INJURY, INSULT **3** : the anger or resentment aroused by an outrage
[2]**outrage** *vb* **out·raged; out·rag·ing 1** : RAPE **2** : to subject to violent injury or gross insult **3** : to arouse to extreme resentment
out·ra·geous \au̇t-ˈrā-jəs\ *adj* : extremely offensive, insulting, or shameful : SHOCKING — **out·ra·geous·ly** *adv*
out·rank \-ˈraŋk\ *vb* : to rank higher than
ou·tré \ü-ˈtrā\ *adj* [F] : violating convention or propriety : BIZARRE
[1]**out·reach** \au̇t-ˈrēch\ *vb* **1** : to surpass in reach **2** : to get the better of by trickery
[2]**out·reach** \ˈau̇t-ˌrēch\ *n* **1** : the act of reaching out **2** : the extent of reach **3** : the extending of services beyond usual limits
out·rid·er \-ˌrī-dər\ *n* : a mounted attendant
out·rig·ger \-ˌri-gər\ *n* **1** : a frame that extends from the side of a canoe or boat to prevent upsetting **2** : a craft equipped with an outrigger
[1]**out·right** \au̇t-ˈrīt\ *adv* **1** : COMPLETELY **2** : INSTANTANEOUSLY
[2]**out·right** \ˈau̇t-ˌrīt\ *adj* **1** : being exactly what is stated ⟨an ~ lie⟩ **2** : given or made without reservation or encumbrance ⟨~ sale⟩
out·run \au̇t-ˈrən\ *vb* **-ran** \-ˈran\; **-run; -run·ning** : to run faster than; *also* : EXCEED
out·sell \-ˈsel\ *vb* **-sold** \-ˈsōld\; **-sell·ing** : to exceed in sales
out·set \ˈau̇t-ˌset\ *n* : BEGINNING, START

out•shine \au̇t-ˈshīn\ *vb* **-shone** \-ˈshōn\ *or* **-shined; -shin•ing 1 :** to shine brighter than **2 :** SURPASS

[1]**out•side** \au̇t-ˈsīd, ˈau̇t-ˌsīd\ *n* **1 :** a place or region beyond an enclosure or boundary **2 :** EXTERIOR **3 :** the utmost limit or extent

[2]**outside** *adj* **1 :** OUTER **2 :** coming from without ⟨~ influences⟩ **3 :** being apart from one's regular duties ⟨~ activities⟩ **4 :** REMOTE ⟨an ~ chance⟩

[3]**outside** *adv* **:** on or to the outside

[4]**outside** *prep* **1 :** on or to the outside of **2 :** beyond the limits of **3 :** EXCEPT

outside of *prep* **1 :** OUTSIDE **2 :** BESIDES

out•sid•er \au̇t-ˈsī-dər\ *n* **:** a person who does not belong to a group

out•size \ˈau̇t-ˌsīz\ *also* **out•sized** \-ˌsīzd\ *adj* **:** unusually large **:** extravagant in size or degree

out•skirts \-ˌskərts\ *n pl* **:** the outlying parts (as of a city) **:** BORDERS

out•smart \au̇t-ˈsmärt\ *vb* **:** OUTWIT

out•sourc•ing \ˈau̇t-ˌsōr-siŋ\ *n* **:** the subcontracting of manufacturing work to outside and esp. foreign and nonunion companies

out•spend \-ˈspend\ *vb* **1 :** to exceed the limits of in spending ⟨~*s* his income⟩ **2 :** to spend more than

out•spo•ken \au̇t-ˈspō-kən\ *adj* **:** direct and open in speech or expression **— out•spo•ken•ly** *adv* **— out•spo•ken•ness** *n*

out•spread \-ˈspred\ *vb* **-spread; -spread•ing :** to spread out

out•stand•ing \-ˈstan-diŋ\ *adj* **1 :** PROJECTING **2 :** UNPAID; *also* **:** UNRESOLVED **3 :** publicly issued and sold **4 :** CONSPICUOUS; *also* **:** DISTINGUISHED **— out•stand•ing•ly** *adv*

out•stay \-ˈstā\ *vb* **1 :** OVERSTAY **2 :** to surpass in endurance

out•stretched \-ˈstrecht\ *adj* **:** stretched out **:** EXTENDED

out•strip \-ˈstrip\ *vb* **1 :** to go faster than **2 :** EXCEL, SURPASS

out•take \ˈau̇t-ˌtāk\ *n* **:** something taken out; *esp* **:** a take that is not used in an edited version of a film or videotape

out•vote \-ˈvōt\ *vb* **:** to defeat by a majority of votes

[1]**out•ward** \ˈau̇t-wərd\ *adj* **1 :** moving or directed toward the outside **2 :** showing outwardly

[2]**outward** *or* **out•wards** \-wərdz\ *adv* **:** toward the outside

out•ward•ly \-wərd-lē\ *adv* **:** on the outside **:** EXTERNALLY

out•wear \au̇t-ˈwar\ *vb* **-wore** \-ˈwōr\; **-worn** \-ˈwōrn\; **-wear•ing :** to wear longer than **:** OUTLAST

out•weigh \-ˈwā\ *vb* **:** to exceed in weight, value, or importance

out•wit \-ˈwit\ *vb* **:** to get the better of by superior cleverness

[1]**out•work** \-ˈwərk\ *vb* **:** to outdo in working

[2]**out•work** \ˈau̇t-ˌwərk\ *n* **:** a minor defensive position outside a fortified area

out•worn \au̇t-ˈwōrn\ *adj* **:** OUTMODED

ou•zo \ˈü-(ˌ)zō\ *n* **:** a colorless anise-flavored unsweetened Greek liqueur

ova *pl of* OVUM

oval \ˈō-vəl\ *adj* [ML *ovalis*, fr. LL, of an egg, fr. L *ovum*] **:** egg-shaped; *also* **:** broadly elliptical **— oval** *n*

ova•ry \ˈō-və-rē\ *n, pl* **-ries 1 :** one of the usu. paired female reproductive organs producing eggs and in vertebrates sex hormones **2 :** the part of a flower in which seeds are produced **— ovar•i•an** \ō-ˈvar-ē-ən, -ˈver-\ *adj*

ovate \ˈō-ˌvāt\ *adj* **:** egg-shaped

ova•tion \ō-ˈvā-shən\ *n* [L *ovation-*, *ovatio*, fr. *ovare* to exult] **:** an enthusiastic popular tribute

ov•en \ˈə-vən\ *n* **:** a chamber (as in a stove) for baking, heating, or drying

oven•bird \-ˌbərd\ *n* **:** a large olive-green American warbler that builds its dome-shaped nest on the ground

[1]**over** \ˈō-vər\ *adv* **1 :** across a barrier or intervening space **2 :** across the brim ⟨boil ~⟩ **3 :** so as to bring the underside up **4 :** out of a vertical position **5 :** beyond some quantity, limit, or norm **6 :** ABOVE **7 :** at an end **8 :** THROUGH; *also* **:** THOROUGHLY **9 :** AGAIN ⟨do it ~⟩

[2]**over** *prep* **1 :** above in position, authority, or scope ⟨towered ~ her⟩ ⟨obeyed those ~ him⟩ **2 :** more than ⟨cost ~ $100⟩ **3 :** ON, UPON ⟨a cape ~ her shoulders⟩ **4 :** along the length of ⟨~ the road⟩ **5 :** through the medium of **:** ON ⟨spoke ~ TV⟩ **6 :** all through ⟨showed me ~ the house⟩ **7 :** on or to the other side or beyond ⟨jump ~ a ditch⟩ **8 :** DURING ⟨~ the past 25 years⟩ **9 :** on account of ⟨trouble ~ money⟩

[3]**over** *adj* **1 :** UPPER, HIGHER **2 :** REMAINING **3 :** ENDED

over- *prefix* **1 :** so as to exceed or surpass **2 :** excessive; excessively

overabundance
overabundant
overactive
overaggressive
overambitious
overanxious
overbid
overbold
overbuild
overburden
overbuy
overcapacity
overcapitalize
overcareful
overcautious
overcompensation
overconfidence
overconfident
overconscientious
overcook
overcritical
overcrowd
overdecorated
overdependence
overdetermined
overdevelop
overdress
overeager
overeat
overeducated
overemphasis
overemphasize
overenthusiastic
overestimate
overexcite
overexcited
overexert
overexertion
overextend
overfatigued
overfeed
overfill
overgeneralization
overgeneralize
overgenerous
overgraze
overhasty
overheat
overindulge
overindulgence
overindulgent
overlarge
overlearn
overload
overlong
overmodest
overnice
overoptimism
overoptimistic
overpay
overpraise
overproduce
overproduction
overprotect
overprotective
overrate
overreact
overreaction
overrefinement
overrepresented
overripe
oversensitive
oversensitiveness
oversimple
oversimplification
oversimplify
overspecialization
overspecialize
overspend
overstimulation
overstock
oversubtle
oversupply
overtax
overtired
overtrain
overuse
overvalue
overzealous

over•act \ˌō-vər-ˈakt\ *vb* **:** to exaggerate in acting

[1]**over•age** \ˌō-vər-ˈāj\ *adj* **1 :** too old to be useful **2 :** older than is normal for one's position, function, or grade

[2]**over•age** \ˈō-və-rij\ *n* **:** SURPLUS

over•all \ˌō-vər-ˈȯl\ *adj* **:** including everything ⟨~ expenses⟩

over•alls \ˈō-vər-ˌȯlz\ *n pl* **:** trousers of strong material usu. with a piece extending up to cover the chest

over•arm \-ˌärm\ *adj* **:** done with the arm raised above the shoulder

over•awe \ˌō-vər-ˈȯ\ *vb* **:** to restrain or subdue by awe

over•bal•ance \-ˈba-ləns\ *vb* **1** : OUTWEIGH **2** : to cause to lose balance
over•bear•ing \-ˈbar-iŋ\ *adj* : ARROGANT, DOMINEERING
over•blown \-ˈblōn\ *adj* **1** : PORTLY **2** : INFLATED, PRETENTIOUS
over•board \ˈō-vər-ˌbōrd\ *adv* **1** : over the side of a ship into the water **2** : to extremes of enthusiasm
¹over•cast \ˈō-vər-ˌkast\ *adj* : clouded over : GLOOMY
²overcast *n* : COVERING; *esp* : a covering of clouds
over•charge \ˌō-vər-ˈchärj\ *vb* **1** : to charge too much **2** : to fill or load too full — **over•charge** \ˈō-vər-ˌchärj\ *n*
over•coat \ˈō-vər-ˌkōt\ *n* : a warm coat worn over indoor clothing
over•come \ˌō-vər-ˈkəm\ *vb* **-came** \-ˈkām\; **-come; -com•ing** **1** : CONQUER **2** : to make helpless or exhausted
over•do \ˌō-vər-ˈdü\ *vb* **-did** \-ˈdid\; **-done** \-ˈdən\; **-do•ing; -does** \-ˈdəz\ **1** : to do too much; *also* : to tire oneself **2** : EXAGGERATE **3** : to cook too long
over•dose \ˈō-vər-ˌdōs\ *n* : too great a dose (as of medicine); *also* : a lethal or toxic amount (as of a drug) — **over•dose** \ˌō-vər-ˈdōs\ *vb*
over•draft \ˈō-vər-ˌdraft, -ˌdràft\ *n* : an overdrawing of a bank account; *also* : the sum overdrawn
over•draw \ˌō-vər-ˈdrȯ\ *vb* **-drew** \-ˈdrü\; **-drawn** \-ˈdrȯn\; **-draw•ing** **1** : to draw checks on a bank account for more than the balance **2** : EXAGGERATE
over•drive \ˈō-vər-ˌdrīv\ *n* : an automotive transmission gear that transmits to the driveshaft a speed greater than the engine speed
over•dub \ˌō-vər-ˈdəb\ *vb* : to transfer (recorded sound) onto an earlier recording for a combined effect — **over•dub** \ˈō-vər-ˌdəb\ *n*
over•due \-ˈdü, -ˈdyü\ *adj* **1** : unpaid when due; *also* : not appearing or presented on time **2** : more than ready
over•ex•pose \ˌō-vər-ik-ˈspōz\ *vb* : to expose (as film) for more time than is needed — **over•ex•po•sure** \-ˈspō-zhər\ *n*
¹over•flow \-ˈflō\ *vb* **1** : INUNDATE; *also* : to pour forth in a flood **2** : to flow over the brim or top of
²over•flow \ˈō-vər-ˌflō\ *n* **1** : FLOOD; *also* : SURPLUS **2** : an outlet for surplus liquid
over•fly \ˌō-vər-ˈflī\ *vb* **-flew** \-ˈflü\; **-flown** \-ˈflōn\; **-fly•ing** : to fly over in an airplane or spacecraft — **over•flight** \ˈō-vər-ˌflīt\ *n*
over•grow \ˌō-vər-ˈgrō\ *vb* **-grew** \-ˈgrü\; **-grown** \-ˈgrōn\; **-grow•ing** **1** : to grow over so as to cover **2** : OUTGROW **3** : to grow excessively
over•hand \ˈō-vər-ˌhand\ *adj* : made with the hand brought down from above — **overhand** *adv* — **over•hand•ed** \-ˌhan-dəd\ *adv or adj*
¹over•hang \ˈō-vər-ˌhaŋ, ˌō-vər-ˈhaŋ\ *vb* **-hung** \-ˌhəŋ, -ˈhəŋ\; **-hang•ing** **1** : to project over : jut out **2** : to hang over threateningly
²over•hang \ˈō-vər-ˌhaŋ\ *n* : a part (as of a roof) that overhangs
over•haul \ˌō-vər-ˈhȯl\ *vb* **1** : to examine thoroughly and make necessary repairs and adjustments **2** : OVERTAKE
¹over•head \ˌō-vər-ˈhed\ *adv* : ALOFT
²over•head \ˈō-vər-ˌhed\ *adj* : operating or lying above ⟨~ door⟩
³over•head \ˈō-vər-ˌhed\ *n* : business expenses not chargeable to a particular part of the work
over•hear \ˌō-vər-ˈhir\ *vb* **-heard** \-ˈhərd\; **-hear•ing** : to hear without the speaker's knowledge or intention
over•joyed \ˌō-vər-ˈjȯid\ *adj* : filled with great joy
over•kill \ˈō-vər-ˌkil\ *n* **1** : destructive capacity greatly exceeding that required for a target **2** : a large excess
over•land \ˈō-vər-ˌland, -lənd\ *adv or adj* : by, on, or across land
over•lap \ˌō-vər-ˈlap\ *vb* **1** : to lap over **2** : to have something in common — **over•lap** \ˈō-vər-ˌlap\ *n*
over•lay \ˌō-vər-ˈlā\ *vb* **-laid** \-ˈlād\; **-lay•ing** : to lay or spread over or across — **over•lay** \ˈō-vər-ˌlā\ *n*
over•leap \ˌō-vər-ˈlēp\ *vb* **-leaped** *or* **-leapt** \-ˈlēpt, -ˈlept\; **-leap•ing** **1** : to leap over or across **2** : to defeat (oneself) by going too far
over•lie \ˌō-vər-ˈlī\ *vb* **-lay** \-ˈlā\; **-lain** \-ˈlān\; **-ly•ing** : to lie over or upon
¹over•look \ˌō-vər-ˈlu̇k\ *vb* **1** : INSPECT **2** : to look down on from above **3** : to fail to see **4** : IGNORE; *also* : EXCUSE **5** : SUPERINTEND
²over•look \ˈō-vər-ˌlu̇k\ *n* : a place from which to look upon a scene below
over•lord \-ˌlȯrd\ *n* : a lord who has supremacy over other lords
over•ly \ˈō-vər-lē\ *adv* : EXCESSIVELY
over•match \ˌō-vər-ˈmach\ *vb* : to be more than a match for : DEFEAT
over•much \-ˈməch\ *adj or adv* : too much
¹over•night \-ˈnīt\ *adv* **1** : on or during the night **2** : SUDDENLY ⟨became famous ~⟩
²overnight *adj* : of, lasting, or staying the night ⟨~ guests⟩
over•pass \ˈō-vər-ˌpas\ *n* **1** : a crossing (as of two highways) at different levels by means of a bridge **2** : the upper level of an overpass
over•play \ˌō-vər-ˈplā\ *vb* **1** : EXAGGERATE; *also* : OVEREMPHASIZE **2** : to rely too much on the strength of
over•pop•u•la•tion \ˌō-vər-ˌpä-pyə-ˈlā-shən\ *n* : the condition of having a population so dense as to cause a decline in population or in living conditions — **over•pop•u•la•ted** \-ˈpä-pyə-ˌlā-təd\ *adj*
over•pow•er \-ˈpau̇-ər\ *vb* : to overcome by superior force
over•price \ˌō-vər-ˈprīs\ *vb* : to price too high
over•print \-ˈprint\ *vb* : to print over with something additional — **over•print** \ˈō-vər-ˌprint\ *n*
over•qual•i•fied \-ˈkwä-lə-ˌfīd\ *adj* : having more education, training, or experience than a job calls for
over•reach \ˌō-vər-ˈrēch\ *vb* : to defeat (oneself) by too great an effort
over•ride \-ˈrīd\ *vb* **-rode** \-ˈrōd\; **-rid•den** \-ˈrid-ᵊn\; **-rid•ing** **1** : to ride over or across **2** : to prevail over; *also* : to set aside ⟨~ a veto⟩
over•rule \-ˈrül\ *vb* **1** : to prevail over **2** : to rule against **3** : to set aside
¹over•run \-ˈrən\ *vb* **-ran** \-ˈran\; **-run•ning** **1** : to defeat and occupy the positions of **2** : OVERSPREAD; *also* : INFEST **3** : to go beyond **4** : to flow over
²over•run \ˈō-vər-ˌrən\ *n* **1** : an act or instance of overrunning; *esp* : an exceeding of estimated costs **2** : the amount by which something overruns
over•sea \ˌō-vər-ˈsē, ˈō-vər-ˌsē\ *adj or adv* : OVERSEAS
over•seas \ˌō-vər-ˈsēz, -ˌsēz\ *adv or adj* : beyond or across the sea : ABROAD
over•see \ˌō-vər-ˈsē\ *vb* **-saw** \-ˈsȯ\; **-seen** \-ˈsēn\; **-see•ing** **1** : OVERLOOK **2** : INSPECT; *also* : SUPERVISE — **over•seer** \ˈō-vər-ˌsir\ *n*
over•sell \ˌō-vər-ˈsel\ *vb* **-sold; -sel•ling** : to sell too much to or too much of
over•sexed \ˌō-vər-ˈsekst\ *adj* : exhibiting excessive sexual drive or interest
over•shad•ow \-ˈsha-dō\ *vb* **1** : to cast a shadow over **2** : to exceed in importance
over•shoe \ˈō-vər-ˌshü\ *n* : a protective outer shoe; *esp* : GALOSH
over•shoot \ˌō-vər-ˈshüt\ *vb* **-shot** \-ˈshät\; **-shoot•ing** **1** : to pass swiftly beyond **2** : to shoot over or beyond
over•sight \ˈō-vər-ˌsīt\ *n* **1** : SUPERVISION **2** : an inadvertent omission or error
over•size \ˌō-vər-ˈsīz\ *or* **over•sized** \-ˈsīzd\ *adj* : of more than ordinary size
over•sleep \ˌō-vər-ˈslēp\ *vb* **-slept** \-ˈslept\; **-sleep•ing** : to sleep beyond the time for waking

over•spread \-ˈspred\ *vb* **-spread; -spread•ing** : to spread over or above
over•state \-ˈstāt\ *vb* : EXAGGERATE — **over•state•ment** *n*
over•stay \-ˈstā\ *vb* : to stay beyond the time or limits of
over•step \-ˈstep\ *vb* : EXCEED
over•sub•scribe \-səb-ˈskrīb\ *vb* : to subscribe for more of than is available, asked for, or offered for sale
overt \ō-ˈvərt, ˈō-ˌvərt\ *adj* [ME, fr. MF *ouvert, overt,* fr. pp. of *ouvrir* to open] : not secret — **overt•ly** *adv*
over•take \ˌō-vər-ˈtāk\ *vb* **-took** \-ˈtu̇k\; **-tak•en** \-ˈtā-kən\; **-tak•ing** : to catch up with; *also* : to catch up with and pass by
over–the–counter *adj* : sold lawfully without a prescription ⟨~ drugs⟩
over•throw \ˌō-vər-ˈthrō\ *vb* **-threw** \-ˈthrü\; **-thrown** \-ˈthrōn\; **-throw•ing 1** : UPSET **2** : to bring down : DEFEAT ⟨~ a government⟩ **3** : to throw over or past — **over•throw** \ˈō-vər-ˌthrō\ *n*
over•time \ˈō-vər-ˌtīm\ *n* : time beyond a set limit; *esp* : working time in excess of a standard day or week — **overtime** *adv*
over•tone \-ˌtōn\ *n* **1** : one of the higher tones in a complex musical tone **2** : IMPLICATION, SUGGESTION
over•trick \ˈō-vər-ˌtrik\ *n* : a card trick won in excess of the number bid
over•ture \ˈō-vər-ˌchu̇r, -chər\ *n* [ME, lit., opening, fr. MF, fr. (assumed) VL *opertura,* alter. of L *apertura*] **1** : an opening offer **2** : an orchestral introduction to a musical dramatic work
over•turn \ˌō-vər-ˈtərn\ *vb* **1** : to turn over : UPSET **2** : INVALIDATE
over•view \ˈō-vər-ˌvyü\ *n* : a general survey : SUMMARY
over•ween•ing \ˌō-vər-ˈwē-niŋ\ *adj* **1** : ARROGANT **2** : IMMODERATE
over•weight \ˈō-vər-ˌwāt\ *n* **1** : weight above what is required or allowed **2** : bodily weight greater than normal — **overweight** *adj*
over•whelm \ˌō-vər-ˈhwelm\ *vb* **1** : OVERTHROW **2** : SUBMERGE **3** : to overcome completely
over•whelm•ing *adj* : EXTREME, GREAT ⟨~ joy⟩ — **over•whelm•ing•ly** *adv*
over•win•ter \-ˈwin-tər\ *vb* : to survive the winter
over•work \-ˈwərk\ *vb* **1** : to work or cause to work too hard or long **2** : to use too much — **overwork** *n*
over•wrought \ˌō-vər-ˈrȯt\ *adj* **1** : extremely excited **2** : elaborated to excess
ovi•duct \ˈō-və-ˌdəkt\ *n* : a tube that serves for the passage of eggs from an ovary
ovip•a•rous \ō-ˈvi-pə-rəs\ *adj* : reproducing by eggs that hatch outside the parent's body
ovoid \ˈō-ˌvȯid\ *or* **ovoi•dal** \ō-ˈvȯid-ᵊl\ *adj* : egg-shaped : OVAL
ovu•la•tion \ˌäv-yə-ˈlā-shən, ˌōv-\ *n* : the discharge of a mature egg from the ovary — **ovu•late** \ˈäv-yə-ˌlāt, ˈōv-\ *vb*
ovule \ˈäv-yül, ˈōv-\ *n* : any of the bodies in a plant ovary that after fertilization become seeds
ovum \ˈō-vəm\ *n, pl* **ova** \-və\ : EGG 2
ow \ˈau̇\ *interj* — used esp. to express sudden pain
owe \ˈō\ *vb* **owed; ow•ing 1** : to be under obligation to pay or render **2** : to be indebted to or for; *also* : to be in debt
owing to *prep* : BECAUSE OF
owl \ˈau̇l\ *n* : any of an order of chiefly nocturnal birds of prey with a large head and eyes and strong talons — **owl•ish** *adj* — **owl•ish•ly** *adv*
owl•et \ˈau̇-lət\ *n* : a young or small owl
[1]**own** \ˈōn\ *adj* : belonging to oneself — used as an intensive after a possessive adjective ⟨her ~ car⟩
[2]**own** *vb* **1** : to have or hold as property **2** : ACKNOWLEDGE; *also* : CONFESS — **own•er** *n* — **own•er•ship** *n*
[3]**own** *pron* : one or ones belonging to oneself
ox \ˈäks\ *n, pl* **ox•en** \ˈäk-sən\ *also* **ox** : any of the common large domestic cattle kept for milk, draft, and meat; *esp* : an adult castrated male ox
ox•blood \ˈäks-ˌbləd\ *n* : a moderate reddish brown
ox•bow \-ˌbō\ *n* **1** : a U-shaped collar worn by a draft ox **2** : a U-shaped bend in a river — **oxbow** *adj*
ox•ford \ˈäks-fərd\ *n* : a low shoe laced or tied over the instep
ox•i•dant \ˈäk-sə-dənt\ *n* : OXIDIZING AGENT — **oxi•dant** *adj*
ox•i•da•tion \ˌäk-sə-ˈdā-shən\ *n* : the act or process of oxidizing; *also* : the condition of being oxidized — **ox•i•da•tive** \ˈäk-sə-ˌdā-tiv\ *adj*
ox•ide \ˈäk-ˌsīd\ *n* : a compound of oxygen with another element or group
ox•i•dize \ˈäk-sə-ˌdīz\ *vb* **-dized; -diz•ing** : to combine with oxygen ⟨iron rusts because it is *oxidized* by exposure to the air⟩ — **ox•i•diz•er** *n*
oxidizing agent *n* : a substance (as oxygen or nitric acid) that oxidizes by taking up electrons
ox•y•gen \ˈäk-si-jən\ *n* [F *oxygène,* fr. Gk *oxys* acidic, lit., sharp + *-genēs* giving rise to; so called because it was once thought to be an essential element of all acids] : a colorless odorless gaseous chemical element that is found in the air, is essential to life, and is involved in combustion — see ELEMENT table
ox•y•gen•ate \ˈäk-si-jə-ˌnāt\ *vb* **-at•ed; -at•ing** : to impregnate, combine, or supply with oxygen — **ox•y•gen•a•tion** \ˌäk-si-jə-ˈnā-shən\ *n*
oxygen mask *n* : a device worn over the nose and mouth through which oxygen is supplied
oxygen tent *n* : a canopy which can be placed over a bedridden person and within which a flow of oxygen can be maintained
ox•y•mo•ron \ˌäk-sē-ˈmōr-ˌän\ *n* : a combination of contradictory words (as *cruel kindness*)
oys•ter \ˈoi-stər\ *n* : any of various marine mollusks with an irregular 2-valved shell that include commercially important edible shellfish and pearl producers — **oys•ter•ing** *n* — **oys•ter•man** \ˈoi-stər-mən\ *n*
oz *abbr* [obs. It *onza* (now *oncia*)] ounce; ounces
ozone \ˈō-ˌzōn\ *n* **1** : a bluish gaseous reactive form of oxygen that is formed naturally in the atmosphere and is used for disinfecting, deodorizing, and bleaching **2** : pure and refreshing air
ozone layer *n* : an atmospheric layer at heights of about 25 miles (40 kilometers) with high ozone content which blocks most solar ultraviolet radiation

P

[1]**p** \ˈpē\ *n, pl* **p's** *or* **ps** \ˈpēz\ *often cap* : the 16th letter of the English alphabet
[2]**p** *abbr, often cap* **1** page **2** participle **3** past **4** pawn **5** pence; penny **6** per **7** petite **8** pint **9** pressure **10** purl
P *symbol* phosphorus
pa \ˈpä, ˈpȯ\ *n* : FATHER
[1]**Pa** *abbr* **1** pascal **2** Pennsylvania
[2]**Pa** *symbol* protactinium
[1]**PA** \(ˌ)pē-ˈā\ *n* : PHYSICIAN'S ASSISTANT
[2]**PA** *abbr* **1** Pennsylvania **2** per annum **3** power of attorney **4** press agent **5** private account **6** professional association **7** public address **8** purchasing agent
pa•'an•ga \pä-ˈäŋ-gə\ *n* — see MONEY table
pab•u•lum \ˈpa-byə-ləm\ *n* [L, food, fodder] : usu. soft digestible food
Pac *abbr* Pacific
PAC *abbr* political action committee
[1]**pace** \ˈpās\ *n* **1** : rate of movement or progress (as in

walking or working) **2 :** a step in walking; *also* **:** a measure of length based on such a step **3 :** GAIT; *esp* **:** a horse's gait in which the legs on the same side move together

^{2}**pace** *vb* **paced; pac•ing 1 :** to go or cover at a pace or with slow steps **2 :** to measure off by paces **3 :** to set or regulate the pace of

^{3}**pace** \ˈpā-sē; ˈpä-ˌkā, -ˌchā\ *prep* **:** contrary to the opinion of

pace•mak•er \ˈpās-ˌmā-kər\ *n* **1 :** one that sets the pace for another **2 :** a body part (as of the heart) that serves to establish and maintain a rhythmic activity **3 :** an electrical device for stimulating or steadying the heartbeat

pac•er \ˈpā-sər\ *n* **1 :** a horse that paces **2 :** PACEMAKER

pachy•derm \ˈpa-ki-ˌdərm\ *n* [F *pachyderme,* fr. Gk *pachydermos* thick-skinned, fr. *pachys* thick + *derma* skin] **:** any of various thick-skinned hoofed mammals (as an elephant)

pach•ys•an•dra \ˌpa-ki-ˈsan-drə\ *n* **:** any of a genus of low shrubby evergreen plants used as a ground cover

pa•cif•ic \pə-ˈsi-fik\ *adj* **1 :** tending to lessen conflict **2 :** CALM, PEACEFUL

pac•i•fi•er \ˈpa-sə-ˌfī-ər\ *n* **:** one that pacifies; *esp* **:** a device for a baby to chew or suck on

pac•i•fism \ˈpa-sə-ˌfi-zəm\ *n* **:** opposition to war or violence as a means of settling disputes — **pac•i•fist** \-fist\ *n or adj* — **pac•i•fis•tic** \ˌpa-sə-ˈfis-tik\ *adj*

pac•i•fy \ˈpa-sə-ˌfī\ *vb* **-fied; -fy•ing 1 :** to allay anger or agitation in **:** SOOTHE **2 :** SETTLE; *also* **:** SUBDUE — **pac•i•fi•ca•tion** \ˌpa-sə-fə-ˈkā-shən\ *n*

^{1}**pack** \ˈpak\ *n* **1 :** a compact bundle; *also* **:** a flexible container for carrying a bundle esp. on the back **2 :** a large amount **:** HEAP **3 :** a set of playing cards **4 :** a group or band of people or animals **5 :** wet absorbent material for application to the body

^{2}**pack** *vb* **1 :** to stow goods in for transportation **2 :** to fill in or surround so as to prevent passage of air, steam, or water **3 :** to put into a protective container **4 :** to load with a pack ⟨~ a mule⟩ **5 :** to crowd in **6 :** to make into a pack **7 :** to cause to go without ceremony ⟨~ them off to school⟩ **8 :** WEAR, CARRY ⟨~ a gun⟩

^{3}**pack** *vb* **:** to make up fraudulently so as to secure a desired result ⟨~ a jury⟩

^{1}**pack•age** \ˈpa-kij\ *n* **1 :** BUNDLE, PARCEL **2 :** a group of related things offered as a whole

^{2}**package** *vb* **pack•aged; pack•ag•ing :** to make into or enclose in a package

package deal *n* **:** an offer containing several items all or none of which must be accepted

package store *n* **:** a store that sells alcoholic beverages in sealed containers for consumption off the premises

pack•er \ˈpa-kər\ *n* **:** one that packs; *esp* **:** a wholesale food dealer

pack•et \ˈpa-kət\ *n* **1 :** a small bundle or package **2 :** a passenger boat carrying mail and cargo on a regular schedule

pack•horse \ˈpak-ˌhȯrs\ *n* **:** a horse used to carry goods or supplies

pack•ing \ˈpa-kiŋ\ *n* **:** material used to pack something

pack•ing•house \-ˌhau̇s\ *n* **:** an establishment for processing and packing food and esp. meat and its by-products

pack rat *n* **:** a bushy-tailed rodent of the Rocky Mountain area that hoards food and miscellaneous objects

pack•sad•dle \ˈpak-ˌsad-ᵊl\ *n* **:** a saddle for supporting loads on the back of an animal

pack•thread \-ˌthred\ *n* **:** strong thread for tying

pact \ˈpakt\ *n* **:** AGREEMENT, TREATY

^{1}**pad** \ˈpad\ *n* **1 :** a cushioning part or thing **:** CUSHION **2 :** the cushioned underside of the foot or toes of some mammals **3 :** the floating leaf of a water plant **4 :** a writing tablet **5 :** LAUNCHPAD **6 :** living quarters; *also* **:** BED

^{2}**pad** *vb* **pad•ded; pad•ding 1 :** to furnish with a pad or padding **2 :** to expand with needless or fraudulent matter

pad•ding *n* **:** the material with which something is padded

^{1}**pad•dle** \ˈpad-ᵊl\ *vb* **pad•dled; pad•dling :** to move the hands and feet about in shallow water

^{2}**paddle** *n* **1 :** an implement with a flat blade used in propelling and steering a small craft (as a canoe) **2 :** an implement used for stirring, mixing, or beating **3 :** a broad board on the outer rim of a waterwheel or a paddle wheel

^{3}**paddle** *vb* **pad•dled; pad•dling 1 :** to move on or through water by or as if by using a paddle **2 :** to beat or stir with a paddle

paddle wheel *n* **:** a wheel with paddles around its outer edge used to move a boat

paddle wheeler *n* **:** a steam-driven vessel propelled by a paddle wheel

pad•dock \ˈpa-dək\ *n* **1 :** a usu. enclosed area for pasturing or exercising animals; *esp* **:** one where racehorses are saddled and paraded before a race **2 :** an area at a racecourse where racing cars are parked

pad•dy \ˈpa-dē\ *n, pl* **paddies :** wet land where rice is grown

paddy wagon *n* **:** an enclosed motortruck for carrying prisoners

pad•lock \ˈpad-ˌläk\ *n* **:** a removable lock with a curved piece that snaps into a catch — **padlock** *vb*

pa•dre \ˈpä-drā\ *n* [Sp or It or Pg, lit., father, fr. L *pater*] **1 :** PRIEST **2 :** a military chaplain

pae•an \ˈpē-ən\ *n* **:** an exultant song of praise or thanksgiving

pae•di•at•ric, pae•di•a•tri•cian, pae•di•at•rics *chiefly Brit var of* PEDIATRIC, PEDIATRICIAN, PEDIATRICS

pa•gan \ˈpā-gən\ *n* [ME, fr. LL *paganus,* fr. L, country dweller, fr. *pagus* country district] **:** HEATHEN — **pagan** *adj* — **pa•gan•ism** \-gə-ˌni-zəm\ *n*

^{1}**page** \ˈpāj\ *n* **:** ATTENDANT; *esp* **:** one employed to deliver messages

^{2}**page** *vb* **paged; pag•ing :** to summon by repeatedly calling out the name of

^{3}**page** *n* **:** a single leaf (as of a book); *also* **:** a single side of such a leaf

^{4}**page** *vb* **paged; pag•ing :** to mark or number the pages of

pag•eant \ˈpa-jənt\ *n* [ME *pagyn, padgeant,* lit., scene of a play, fr. ML *pagina,* perh. fr. L, page] **:** an elaborate spectacle, show, or procession esp. with tableaux or floats — **pag•eant•ry** \-jən-trē\ *n*

page•boy \ˈpāj-ˌbȯi\ *n* [^{1}*page*] **:** an often shoulder-length hairdo with the ends of the hair turned smoothly under

pag•er \ˈpā-jər\ *n* **:** one that pages; *esp* **:** BEEPER

pag•i•nate \ˈpa-jə-ˌnāt\ *vb* **-nat•ed; -nat•ing :** ^{4}PAGE

pag•i•na•tion \ˌpa-jə-ˈnā-shən\ *n* **1 :** the paging of written or printed matter **2 :** the number and arrangement of pages (as of a book)

pa•go•da \pə-ˈgō-də\ *n* **:** a tower with roofs curving upward at the division of each of several stories

paid *past and past part of* PAY

pail \ˈpāl\ *n* **:** a usu. cylindrical vessel with a handle — **pail•ful** \-ˌfu̇l\ *n*

^{1}**pain** \ˈpān\ *n* **1 :** PUNISHMENT, PENALTY **2 :** suffering or distress of body or mind; *also* **:** a basic bodily sensation marked by discomfort (as throbbing or aching) **3** *pl* **:** great care — **pain•ful** \-fəl\ *adj* — **pain•ful•ly** *adv* — **pain•less** *adj* — **pain•less•ly** *adv*

^{2}**pain** *vb* **:** to cause or experience pain

pain•kill•er \ˈpān-ˌki-lər\ *n* **:** something (as a drug) that relieves pain — **pain•kill•ing** *adj*

pains•tak•ing \-ˌstā-kiŋ\ *adj* **:** taking pains **:** showing care — **pains•taking** *n* — **pains•tak•ing•ly** *adv*

^{1}**paint** \ˈpānt\ *vb* **1 :** to apply color, pigment, or paint to **2 :** to produce or portray in lines or colors on a surface; *also* **:** to practice the art of painting **3 :** to decorate with colors **4 :** to use cosmetics **5 :** to describe vividly **6 :** SWAB — **paint•er** *n*

[2]**paint** *n* **1 :** something produced by painting **2 :** MAKEUP **3 :** a mixture of a pigment and a liquid that forms a thin adherent coating when spread on a surface; *also* **:** the dry pigment used in making this mixture **4 :** an applied coating of paint

paint•brush \ˈpānt-ˌbrəsh\ *n* **:** a brush for applying paint

painting *n* **1 :** a work (as a picture) produced by painting **2 :** the art or occupation of painting

[1]**pair** \ˈpar\ *n, pl* **pairs** *also* **pair** [ME *paire,* fr. OF, fr. L *paria* equal things, fr. neut. pl. of *par* equal] **1 :** two things of a kind designed for use together **2 :** something made up of two corresponding pieces ⟨a ~ of trousers⟩ **3 :** a set of two people or animals

[2]**pair** *vb* **1 :** to arrange in pairs **2 :** to form a pair **:** MATCH **3 :** to become associated with another

pai•sa \pī-ˈsä\ *n, pl* **paisa** *or* **pai•se** \-ˈsä\ — see *rupee, taka* at MONEY table

pais•ley \ˈpāz-lē\ *adj, often cap* **:** decorated with colorful curved abstract figures ⟨a ~ shawl⟩

Pai•ute \ˈpī-ˌüt, -ˌyüt\ *n* **:** a member of an American Indian people orig. of Utah, Arizona, Nevada, and California

pa•ja•mas \pə-ˈjä-məz, -ˈja-\ *n pl* **:** a loose suit for sleeping or lounging

Pak•i•stani \ˌpa-ki-ˈsta-nē, ˌpä-ki-ˈstä-nē\ *n* **:** a native or inhabitant of Pakistan — **Pak•i•stani** *adj*

pal \ˈpal\ *n* **:** a close friend

pal•ace \ˈpa-ləs\ *n* [ME *palais,* fr. OF, fr. L *palatium,* fr. *Palatium,* the Palatine Hill in Rome where the emperors' residences were built] **1 :** the official residence of a chief of state **2 :** MANSION

pal•a•din \ˈpa-lə-dən\ *n* **1 :** a trusted military leader (as for a medieval prince) **2 :** a leading champion of a cause

pa•laes•tra \pə-ˈles-trə\ *n, pl* **-trae** \-(ˌ)trē\ **:** a school in ancient Greece or Rome for sports (as wrestling)

pa•lan•quin \ˌpa-lən-ˈkēn\ *n* **:** an enclosed couch for one person borne on the shoulders of men by means of poles

pal•at•able \ˈpa-lə-tə-bəl\ *adj* **:** agreeable to the taste **syn** appetizing, savory, tasty, toothsome

pal•a•tal \ˈpa-lət-ᵊl\ *adj* **1 :** of or relating to the palate **2 :** pronounced with some part of the tongue near or touching the hard palate ⟨the \y\ in *yeast* and the \sh\ in *she* are ~ sounds⟩

pal•a•tal•ize \ˈpa-lət-ᵊl-ˌīz\ *vb* **-ized; -iz•ing :** to pronounce as or change into a palatal sound — **pal•a•tal•i•za•tion** \ˌpa-lət-ᵊl-ə-ˈzā-shən\ *n*

pal•ate \ˈpa-lət\ *n* **1 :** the roof of the mouth separating the mouth from the nasal cavity **2 :** TASTE

pa•la•tial \pə-ˈlā-shəl\ *adj* **1 :** of, relating to, or being a palace **2 :** MAGNIFICENT

pa•lat•i•nate \pə-ˈlat-ᵊn-ət\ *n* **:** the territory of a palatine

[1]**pal•a•tine** \ˈpa-lə-ˌtīn\ *adj* **1 :** possessing royal privileges; *also* **:** of or relating to a palatine or a palatinate **2 :** of or relating to a palace **:** PALATIAL

[2]**palatine** *n* **1 :** a feudal lord having sovereign power within his domains **2 :** a high officer of an imperial palace

pa•la•ver \pə-ˈla-vər, -ˈlä-\ *n* [Pg *palavra* word, speech, fr. LL *parabola* parable, speech] **1 :** a long parley **2 :** idle talk — **palaver** *vb*

[1]**pale** \ˈpāl\ *n* **1 :** a stake or picket of a fence **2 :** an enclosed place; *also* **:** a district or territory within certain bounds or under a particular jurisdiction **3 :** LIMITS, BOUNDS ⟨conduct beyond the ~⟩

[2]**pale** *vb* **paled; pal•ing :** to enclose with or as if with pales **:** FENCE

[3]**pale** *adj* **pal•er; pal•est 1 :** deficient in color or intensity **:** WAN ⟨~ face⟩ **2 :** lacking in brightness **:** DIM ⟨~ star⟩ **3 :** not dark or intense in hue ⟨~ blue⟩ — **pale•ness** *n*

[4]**pale** *vb* **paled; pal•ing :** to make or become pale

pale•face \ˈpāl-ˌfās\ *n* **:** a white person

Pa•leo•cene \ˈpā-lē-ə-ˌsēn\ *adj* **:** of, relating to, or being the earliest epoch of the Tertiary — **Paleocene** *n*

pa•le•og•ra•phy \ˌpā-lē-ˈä-grə-fē\ *n* [NL *palaeographia,* fr. Gk *palaios* ancient + *graphein* to write] **:** the study of ancient writings and inscriptions — **pa•le•og•ra•pher** *n*

Pa•leo•lith•ic \ˌpā-lē-ə-ˈli-thik\ *adj* **:** of or relating to the earliest period of the Stone Age characterized by rough or chipped stone implements

pa•le•on•tol•o•gy \ˌpā-lē-ˌän-ˈtä-lə-jē\ *n* **:** a science dealing with the life of past geologic periods as known from fossil remains — **pa•le•on•tol•o•gist** \-ˌän-ˈtä-lə-jist, -ən-\ *n*

Pa•leo•zo•ic \ˌpā-lē-ə-ˈzō-ik\ *adj* **:** of, relating to, or being the era of geologic history extending from about 570 million years ago to about 245 million years ago — **Paleozoic** *n*

pal•ette \ˈpa-lət\ *n* **:** a thin often oval board that a painter holds and mixes colors on; *also* **:** the colors on a palette

pal•frey \ˈpȯl-frē\ *n, pl* **palfreys** *archaic* **:** a saddle horse that is not a warhorse; *esp* **:** one suitable for a woman

pa•limp•sest \ˈpa-ləmp-ˌsest\ *n* [L *palimpsestus,* fr. Gk *palimpsēstos* scraped again] **:** writing material (as a parchment) used after the erasure of earlier writing

pal•in•drome \ˈpa-lən-ˌdrōm\ *n* **:** a word, verse, or sentence (as "Able was I ere I saw Elba") or a number (as 1881) that reads the same backward or forward

pal•ing \ˈpā-liŋ\ *n* **1 :** a fence of pales **2 :** material for pales **3 :** PALE, PICKET

pal•i•sade \ˌpa-lə-ˈsād\ *n* **1 :** a high fence of stakes esp. for defense **2 :** a line of steep cliffs

[1]**pall** \ˈpȯl\ *vb* **1 :** to lose in interest or attraction **2 :** SATIATE, CLOY

[2]**pall** *n* **1 :** a heavy cloth draped over a coffin **2 :** something that produces a gloomy atmosphere

pal•la•di•um \pə-ˈlā-dē-əm\ *n* **:** a silver-white metallic chemical element used esp. as a catalyst and in alloys — see ELEMENT table

pall•bear•er \ˈpȯl-ˌbar-ər\ *n* **:** a person who attends the coffin at a funeral

[1]**pal•let** \ˈpa-lət\ *n* **:** a small, hard, or makeshift bed

[2]**pallet** *n* **:** a portable platform for transporting and storing materials

pal•li•ate \ˈpa-lē-ˌāt\ *vb* **-at•ed; -at•ing 1 :** to ease (as a disease) without curing **2 :** to cover by excuses and apologies — **pal•li•a•tion** \ˌpa-lē-ˈā-shən\ *n* — **pal•li•a•tive** \ˈpa-lē-ˌā-tiv\ *adj or n*

pal•lid \ˈpa-ləd\ *adj* **:** PALE, WAN

pal•lor \ˈpa-lər\ *n* **:** PALENESS

[1]**palm** \ˈpäm, ˈpälm\ *n* [ME, fr. OE, fr. L *palma* palm of the hand, palm tree; fr. the resemblance of the tree's leaves to the outstretched hand] **1 :** any of a family of mostly tropical trees, shrubs, or vines usu. with a tall unbranched stem topped by a crown of large leaves **2 :** a symbol of victory; *also* **:** VICTORY

[2]**palm** *n* **:** the underpart of the hand between the fingers and the wrist

[3]**palm** *vb* **1 :** to conceal in or with the hand ⟨~ a card⟩ **2 :** to impose by fraud

pal•mate \ˈpal-ˌmāt, ˈpäl-\ *also* **pal•mat•ed** \-ˌmā-təd\ *adj* **:** resembling a hand with the fingers spread

pal•met•to \pal-ˈme-tō\ *n, pl* **-tos** *or* **-toes :** any of several usu. small palms with fan-shaped leaves

palm•ist•ry \ˈpä-mə-strē, ˈpäl-\ *n* **:** the practice of reading a person's character or future from the markings on the palms — **palm•ist** \ˈpä-mist, ˈpäl-\ *n*

Palm Sunday *n* **:** the Sunday preceding Easter and commemorating Christ's triumphal entry into Jerusalem

palmy \ˈpä-mē, ˈpäl-\ *adj* **palm•i•er; -est 1 :** abounding in or bearing palms **2 :** FLOURISHING, PROSPEROUS

pal•o•mi•no \ˌpa-lə-ˈmē-nō\ *n, pl* **-nos** [AmerSp, fr. Sp, like a dove, fr. L *palumbinus*, fr. *palumbes*, a species of dove] : a horse with a pale cream to golden coat and cream or white mane and tail

pal•pa•ble \ˈpal-pə-bəl\ *adj* **1** : capable of being touched or felt : TANGIBLE **2** : OBVIOUS, PLAIN **syn** perceptible, sensible, appreciable, tangible, detectable — **pal•pa•bly** \-blē\ *adv*

pal•pate \ˈpal-ˌpāt\ *vb* **pal•pat•ed; pal•pat•ing** : to examine by touch esp. medically — **pal•pa•tion** \pal-ˈpā-shən\ *n*

pal•pi•tate \ˈpal-pə-ˌtāt\ *vb* **-tat•ed; -tat•ing** : to beat rapidly and strongly : THROB — **pal•pi•ta•tion** \ˌpal-pə-ˈtā-shən\ *n*

pal•sy \ˈpȯl-zē\ *n, pl* **palsies 1** : PARALYSIS **2** : a condition marked by tremor — **pal•sied** \-zēd\ *adj*

pal•ter \ˈpȯl-tər\ *vb* **pal•tered; pal•ter•ing 1** : to act insincerely : EQUIVOCATE **2** : HAGGLE

pal•try \ˈpȯl-trē\ *adj* **pal•tri•er; -est 1** : TRASHY ⟨a ~ pamphlet⟩ **2** : MEAN, DESPICABLE ⟨a ~ trick⟩ **3** : TRIVIAL ⟨~ excuses⟩ **4** : MEAGER, MEASLY ⟨a ~ sum⟩

pam *abbr* pamphlet

pam•pas \ˈpam-pəz, ˈpäm-, -pəs\ *n pl* : wide grassy So. American plains

pam•per \ˈpam-pər\ *vb* : to treat with excessive attention : INDULGE **syn** coddle, humor, baby, spoil

pam•phlet \ˈpam-flət\ *n* [ME *pamflet* unbound booklet, fr. *Pamphilus seu De Amore* Pamphilus or On Love, popular Latin love poem of the 12th cent.] : an unbound printed publication

pam•phle•teer \ˌpam-flə-ˈtir\ *n* : a writer of pamphlets attacking something or urging a cause

[1]**pan** \ˈpan\ *n* **1** : a usu. broad, shallow, and open container for domestic use; *also* : something resembling such a container **2** : a basin or depression in land **3** : HARDPAN

[2]**pan** *vb* **panned; pan•ning 1** : to wash earth or gravel in a pan in searching for gold **2** : to criticize severely

Pan *abbr* Panama

pan•a•cea \ˌpa-nə-ˈsē-ə\ *n* : a remedy for all ills or difficulties : CURE-ALL

pa•nache \pə-ˈnash, -ˈnäsh\ *n* [MF *pennache*, ultim. fr. LL *pinnaculum* small wing] **1** : an ornamental tuft (as of feathers) esp. on a helmet **2** : dash or flamboyance in style and action

pan•a•ma \ˈpa-nə-ˌmä, -ˌmȯ\ *n, often cap* : a handmade hat braided from strips of the leaves from a tropical American tree

Pan•a•ma•ni•an \ˌpa-nə-ˈmā-nē-ən\ *n* : a native or inhabitant of Panama — **Panamanian** *adj*

pan•a•tela \ˌpa-nə-ˈte-lə\ *n* [Sp, fr. AmerSp, a long thin biscuit, ultim. fr. L *panis* bread] : a long slender cigar with straight sides

pan•cake \ˈpan-ˌkāk\ *n* : a flat cake made of thin batter and fried on both sides

pan•chro•mat•ic \ˌpan-krō-ˈma-tik\ *adj* : sensitive to all colors of visible light ⟨~ film⟩

pan•cre•as \ˈpaŋ-krē-əs, ˈpan-\ *n* : a large compound gland of vertebrates that produces insulin and discharges enzymes into the intestine — **pan•cre•at•ic** \ˌpaŋ-krē-ˈa-tik, ˌpan-\ *adj*

pan•da \ˈpan-də\ *n* **1** : a long-tailed Himalayan mammal related to and resembling the racoon **2** : a large black-and-white mammal of western China usu. classified with the bears

pan•dem•ic \pan-ˈde-mik\ *n* : a widespread outbreak of disease — **pandemic** *adj*

pan•de•mo•ni•um \ˌpan-də-ˈmō-nē-əm\ *n* : a wild uproar : TUMULT

[1]**pan•der** \ˈpan-dər\ *n* **1** : a go-between in love intrigues **2** : PIMP **3** : someone who caters to or exploits others' desires or weaknesses

[2]**pander** *vb* : to act as a pander

P & I *abbr* principal and interest

P & L *abbr* profit and loss

pan•dow•dy \pan-ˈdau̇-dē\ *n, pl* **-dies** : a deep-dish apple dessert spiced, sweetened, and covered with a crust

panda: *A* panda 1, *B* panda 2

pane \ˈpān\ *n* : a sheet of glass (as in a door or window)

pan•e•gy•ric \ˌpa-nə-ˈjir-ik\ *n* : a eulogistic oration or writing — **pan•e•gyr•ist** \-ˈjir-ist\ *n*

[1]**pan•el** \ˈpan-ᵊl\ *n* **1** : a list of persons appointed for special duty ⟨a jury ~⟩; *also* : a group of people taking part in a discussion or quiz program **2** : a section of something (as a wall or door) often sunk below the level of the frame; *also* : a flat piece of construction material **3** : a flat piece of wood on which a picture is painted **4** : a mount for controls or dials

[2]**panel** *vb* **-eled** *or* **-elled; -el•ing** *or* **-el•ling** : to decorate with panels

paneling *n* : decorative panels

pan•el•ist \ˈpan-ᵊl-ist\ *n* : a member of a discussion or quiz panel

panel truck *n* : a small motortruck with a fully enclosed body

pang \ˈpaŋ\ *n* : a sudden sharp spasm (as of pain) or attack (as of remorse)

[1]**pan•han•dle** \ˈpan-ˌhand-ᵊl\ *n* : a narrow projection of a larger territory (as a state) ⟨the Texas ~⟩

[2]**panhandle** *vb* **-dled; -dling** : to ask for money on the street — **pan•han•dler** *n*

[1]**pan•ic** \ˈpa-nik\ *n* : a sudden overpowering fright **syn** terror, consternation, dismay, alarm, dread, fear — **pan•icky** \-ni-kē\ *adj*

[2]**panic** *vb* **pan•icked** \-nikt\; **pan•ick•ing** : to affect or be affected with panic

pan•i•cle \ˈpa-ni-kəl\ *n* : a branched flower cluster (as of a lilac) in which each branch from the main stem has one or more flowers

pan•jan•drum \pan-ˈjan-drəm\ *n, pl* **-drums** *also* **-dra** \-drə\ : a powerful personage or pretentious official

pan•nier *also* **pan•ier** \ˈpan-yər\ *n* : a large basket esp. for bearing on the back

pan•o•ply \ˈpa-nə-plē\ *n, pl* **-plies 1** : a full suit of armor **2** : a protective covering **3** : an impressive array

pan•ora•ma \ˌpa-nə-ˈra-mə, -ˈrä-\ *n* **1** : a picture unrolled before one's eyes **2** : a complete view in every direction — **pan•oram•ic** \-ˈra-mik\ *adj*

pan out *vb* : TURN OUT; *esp* : SUCCEED

pan•sy \ˈpan-zē\ *n, pl* **pansies** [ME *pensee*, fr. MF *pensée*, fr. *pensée* thought, fr. *penser* to think, fr. L *pensare* to ponder] : a low-growing garden herb related to the violet; *also* : its showy flower

[1]**pant** \ˈpant\ *vb* [ME, fr. MF *pantaisier*, fr. (assumed) VL *phantasiare* to have hallucinations, fr. Gk *phantasioun*, fr. *phantasia* appearance, imagination] **1** : to breathe in a labored manner **2** : YEARN **3** : THROB

[2]**pant** *n* : a panting breath or sound

[3]**pant** *n* **1** : an outer garment covering each leg separately and usu. extending from the waist to the ankle — usu. used in pl. **2** *pl* : PANTIE

pan•ta•loons \ˌpan-tə-ˈlünz\ *n pl* **1 :** close-fitting trousers of the 19th century usu. having straps passing under the instep **2 :** loose-fitting usu. shorter than ankle-length trousers

pan•the•ism \ˈpan-thē-ˌi-zəm\ *n* **:** a doctrine that equates God with the forces and laws of the universe — **pan•the•ist** \-ist\ *n* — **pan•the•is•tic** \ˌpan-thē-ˈis-tik\ *adj*

pan•the•on \ˈpan-thē-ˌän, -ən\ *n* **1 :** a temple dedicated to all the gods; *also* **:** the gods of a people **2 :** a group of illustrious people

pan•ther \ˈpan-thər\ *n, pl* **panthers** *also* **panther 1 :** LEOPARD; *esp* **:** a black one **2 :** COUGAR **3 :** JAGUAR

pant•ie *or* **panty** \ˈpan-tē\ *n, pl* **pant•ies :** a woman's or child's short underpants — usu. used in pl.

pan•to•mime \ˈpan-tə-ˌmīm\ *n* **1 :** a play in which the actors use no words **2 :** expression of something by bodily or facial movements only — **pantomime** *vb* — **pan•to•mim•ic** \ˌpan-tə-ˈmi-mik\ *adj*

pan•try \ˈpan-trē\ *n, pl* **pantries :** a storage room for food or dishes

pant•suit \ˈpant-ˌsüt\ *n* **:** a woman's outfit consisting usu. of a long jacket and pants of the same material

panty hose *n pl* **:** a one-piece undergarment for women consisting of hosiery combined with a pantie

panty•waist \ˈpan-tē-ˌwāst\ *n* **:** SISSY

pap \ˈpap\ *n* **:** soft food for infants or invalids

pa•pa \ˈpä-pə\ *n* **:** FATHER

pa•pa•cy \ˈpā-pə-sē\ *n, pl* **-cies 1 :** the office of pope **2 :** a succession of popes **3 :** the term of a pope's reign **4** *cap* **:** the system of government of the Roman Catholic Church

pa•pa•in \pə-ˈpā-ən, -ˈpī-ən\ *n* **:** an enzyme in papaya juice used esp. as a meat tenderizer and in medicine

pa•pal \ˈpā-pəl\ *adj* **:** of or relating to the pope or to the Roman Catholic Church

pa•paw *n* **1** \pə-ˈpȯ\ **:** PAPAYA **2** \ˈpä-ˌpȯ\ **:** a No. American tree with yellow edible fruit; *also* **:** its fruit

pa•pa•ya \pə-ˈpī-ə\ *n* **:** a tropical American tree with large yellow black-seeded edible fruit; *also* **:** its fruit

pa•per \ˈpā-pər\ *n* [ME *papir,* fr. MF *papier,* fr. L *papyrus* papyrus, paper, fr. Gk *papyros* papyrus] **1 :** a pliable substance made usu. of vegetable matter and used to write or print on, to wrap things in, or to cover walls; *also* **:** a single sheet of this substance **2 :** a printed or written document **3 :** NEWSPAPER **4 :** WALLPAPER — **paper** *adj or vb* — **pa•pery** \ˈpā-pə-rē\ *adj*

pa•per•back \-ˌbak\ *n* **:** a paper-covered book

pa•per•board \-ˌbōrd\ *n* **:** a material made from cellulose fiber (as wood pulp) like paper but usu. thicker

pa•per•hang•er \ˈpā-pər-ˌhaŋ-ər\ *n* **:** one that applies wallpaper — **pa•per•hang•ing** *n*

pa•per•weight \-ˌwāt\ *n* **:** an object used to hold down loose papers by its weight

pa•pier–mâ•ché \ˌpā-pər-mə-ˈshā, ˌpa-ˌpyā-mə-, -ma-\ *n* [F, lit., chewed paper] **:** a molding material of wastepaper and additives (as glue) — **papier–mâché** *adj*

pa•pil•la \pə-ˈpi-lə\ *n, pl* **-lae** \-(ˌ)lē, -ˌlī\ [L, nipple] **:** a small projecting bodily part (as one of the nubs on the surface of the tongue) that resembles a tiny nipple in form — **pap•il•lary** \ˈpa-pə-ˌler-ē, pə-ˈpi-lə-rē\ *adj*

pa•poose \pa-ˈpüs, pə-\ *n* **:** a young child of No. American Indian parents

pa•pri•ka \pə-ˈprē-kə, pa-\ *n* [Hung] **:** a mild red spice made from the fruit of various cultivated sweet peppers

Pap smear \ˈpap-\ *n* **:** a method for the early detection of cancer esp. of the uterine cervix

Pap test *n* **:** PAP SMEAR

pap•ule \ˈpa-pyül\ *n* **:** a small solid usu. conical lesion of the skin — **pap•u•lar** \-pyə-lər\ *adj*

pa•py•rus \pə-ˈpī-rəs\ *n, pl* **-rus•es** *or* **-ri** \-(ˌ)rē, -ˌrī\ **1 :** a tall grassy sedge of the Nile valley **2 :** paper made from papyrus pith

[1]**par** \ˈpär\ *n* **1 :** a stated value (as of a security) **2 :** a common level **:** EQUALITY **3 :** an accepted standard or normal condition **4 :** the score standard set for each hole of a golf course — **par** *adj*

[2]**par** *abbr* **1** paragraph **2** parallel **3** parish

pa•ra \ˈpär-ə\ *n, pl* **paras** *or* **para** — see *dinar* at MONEY table

par•a•ble \ˈpar-ə-bəl\ *n* **:** a simple story told to illustrate a moral truth

pa•rab•o•la \pə-ˈra-bə-lə\ *n* **:** a plane curve formed by the intersection of a cone with a plane parallel to a straight line in its surface — **par•a•bol•ic** \ˌpar-ə-ˈbä-lik\ *adj*

para•chute \ˈpar-ə-ˌshüt\ *n* [F, fr. *para-* (as in *parasol*) + *chute* fall] **:** a device for slowing the descent of a person or object through the air that consists of a usu. hemispherical canopy beneath which the person or object is suspended — **parachute** *vb* — **para•chut•ist** \-ˈshü-tist\ *n*

[1]**pa•rade** \pə-ˈrād\ *n* **1 :** a pompous display **:** EXHIBITION **2 :** MARCH, PROCESSION; *esp* **:** a ceremonial formation and march **3 :** a place for strolling

[2]**parade** *vb* **pa•rad•ed; pa•rad•ing 1 :** to march in a parade **2 :** PROMENADE **3 :** SHOW OFF **4 :** MASQUERADE

par•a•digm \ˈpar-ə-ˌdīm, -ˌdim\ *n* **1 :** MODEL, PATTERN **2 :** a systematic inflection of a verb or noun showing a complete conjugation or declension — **par•a•dig•mat•ic** \ˌpar-ə-dig-ˈma-tik\ *adj*

par•a•dise \ˈpar-ə-ˌdīs, -ˌdīz\ *n* [ME *paradis,* fr. OF, fr. LL *paradisus,* fr. Gk *paradeisos,* lit., enclosed park, of Iranian origin] **1 :** HEAVEN **2 :** a place or state of bliss

par•a•di•si•a•cal \ˌpar-ə-də-ˈsī-ə-kəl\ *or* **par•a•dis•i•ac** \-ˈdi-zē-ˌak, -sē-\ *adj* **:** of, relating to, or resembling paradise

par•a•dox \ˈpar-ə-ˌdäks\ *n* **:** a statement that seems contrary to common sense and yet is perhaps true — **par•a•dox•i•cal** \ˌpar-ə-ˈdäk-si-kəl\ *adj* — **par•a•dox•i•cal•ly** \-k(ə-)lē\ *adv*

par•af•fin \ˈpar-ə-fən\ *n* **:** a waxy substance used esp. for making candles and sealing foods

par•a•gon \ˈpar-ə-ˌgän, -gən\ *n* **:** a model of perfection **:** PATTERN

[1]**para•graph** \ˈpar-ə-ˌgraf\ *n* **:** a subdivision of a written composition that deals with one point or gives the words of one speaker; *also* **:** a character (as ¶) marking the beginning of a paragraph

[2]**paragraph** *vb* **:** to divide into paragraphs

Par•a•guay•an \ˌpar-ə-ˈgwī-ən, -ˈgwā-\ *n* **:** a native or inhabitant of Paraguay — **Paraguayan** *adj*

par•a•keet \ˈpar-ə-ˌkēt\ *n* **:** any of numerous usu. small slender parrots with a long graduated tail

para•le•gal \ˌpar-ə-ˈlē-gəl\ *adj* **:** of, relating to, or being a paraprofessional who assists a lawyer — **paralegal** *n*

Par•a•li•pom•e•non \ˌpar-ə-lə-ˈpä-mə-ˌnän\ *n* **:** CHRONICLES

par•al•lax \ˈpar-ə-ˌlaks\ *n* **:** the difference in apparent direction of an object as seen from two different points

[1]**par•al•lel** \ˈpar-ə-ˌlel\ *adj* [L *parallelus,* fr. Gk *parallēlos,* fr. *para* beside + *allēlōn* of one another, fr. *allos . . . allos* one . . . another, fr. *allos* other] **1 :** lying or moving in the same direction but always the same distance apart **2 :** similar in essential parts — **par•al•lel•ism** \-ˌle-ˌli-zəm\ *n*

[2]**parallel** *n* **1 :** a parallel line, curve, or surface **2 :** one of the imaginary circles on the earth's surface that parallel the equator and mark the latitude **3 :** something essentially similar to another **4 :** SIMILARITY, LIKENESS

[3]**parallel** *vb* **1 :** COMPARE **2 :** to correspond to **3 :** to extend in a parallel direction with

par•al•lel•o•gram \ˌpar-ə-ˈle-lə-ˌgram\ *n* **:** a 4-sided geometric figure with opposite sides equal and parallel

par•a•lyse *Brit var of* PARALYZE

pa•ral•y•sis \pə-ˈra-lə-səs\ *n, pl* **-y•ses** \-ˌsēz\ **:** loss of function and esp. of feeling or the power of voluntary motion — **par•a•lyt•ic** \ˌpar-ə-ˈli-tik\ *adj or n*

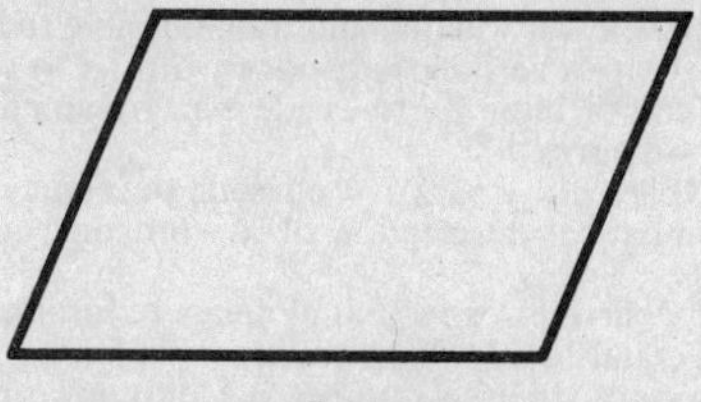

parallelogram

par•a•lyze \ˈpar-ə-ˌlīz\ *vb* **-lyzed; -lyz•ing 1 :** to affect with paralysis **2 :** to make powerless or inactive — **par•a•lyz•ing•ly** *adv*

par•a•me•cium \ˌpar-ə-ˈmē-shəm, -shē-əm, -sē-əm\ *n, pl* **-cia** \-shə, -shē-ə, -sē-ə\ *also* **-ciums :** any of a genus of slipper-shaped protozoans that move by cilia

para•med•ic \ˌpar-ə-ˈme-dik\ *also* **para•med•i•cal** \-di-kəl\ *n* **1 :** a person who assists a physician in a paramedical capacity **2 :** a specially trained medical technician licensed to provide a wide range of emergency services before or during transportation to a hospital

para•med•i•cal \ˌpar-ə-ˈme-di-kəl\ *also* **para•med•ic** \-ˈme-dik\ *adj* **:** concerned with supplementing the work of trained medical professionals

pa•ram•e•ter \pə-ˈra-mə-tər\ *n* **1 :** a quantity whose value characterizes a statistical population or a member of a system (as a family of curves) **2 :** a physical property whose value determines the characteristics or behavior of a system **3 :** a characteristic element **:** FACTOR — **para•met•ric** \ˌpar-ə-ˈme-trik\ *adj*

para•mil•i•tary \ˌpar-ə-ˈmi-lə-ˌter-ē\ *adj* **:** formed on a military pattern esp. as an auxiliary military force

par•a•mount \ˈpar-ə-ˌmau̇nt\ *adj* **:** superior to all others **:** SUPREME **syn** preponderant, predominant, dominant, chief, sovereign

par•amour \ˈpar-ə-ˌmu̇r\ *n* **:** an illicit lover

para•noia \ˌpar-ə-ˈnȯi-ə\ *n* **:** a psychosis marked by delusions and irrational suspicion usu. without hallucinations — **par•a•noid** \ˈpar-ə-ˌnȯid\ *adj or n*

par•a•pet \ˈpar-ə-pət, -ˌpet\ *n* **1 :** a protecting rampart **2 :** a low wall or railing (as at the edge of a bridge)

par•a•pher•na•lia \ˌpar-ə-fə-ˈnāl-yə, -fər-\ *n sing or pl* **1 :** personal belongings **2 :** EQUIPMENT, APPARATUS

para•phrase \ˈpar-ə-ˌfrāz\ *n* **:** a restatement of a text giving the meaning in different words — **paraphrase** *vb*

para•ple•gia \ˌpar-ə-ˈplē-jə, -jē-ə\ *n* **:** paralysis of the lower trunk and legs — **para•ple•gic** \-jik\ *adj or n*

para•pro•fes•sion•al \-prə-ˈfe-shə-nəl\ *n* **:** a trained aide who assists a professional — **paraprofessional** *adj*

para•psy•chol•o•gy \ˌpar-ə-sī-ˈkä-lə-jē\ *n* **:** a field of study concerned with investigating telepathy and related subjects — **para•psy•chol•o•gist** \-jist\ *n*

par•a•site \ˈpar-ə-ˌsīt\ *n* [MF, fr. L *parasitus,* fr. Gk *parasitos,* fr. *para-* beside + *sitos* grain, food] **1 :** a plant or animal living in, with, or on another organism usu. to its harm **2 :** one depending on another and not making adequate return — **par•a•sit•ic** \ˌpar-ə-ˈsi-tik\ *adj* — **par•a•sit•ism** \ˈpar-ə-sə-ˌti-zəm, -ˌsī-ˌti-\ *n* — **par•a•sit•ize** \-sə-ˌtīz\ *vb*

par•a•si•tol•o•gy \ˌpar-ə-sə-ˈtä-lə-jē\ *n* **:** a branch of biology dealing with parasites and parasitism esp. among animals — **par•a•si•tol•o•gist** \-jist\ *n*

para•sol \ˈpar-ə-ˌsȯl\ *n* [F, fr. It *parasole,* fr. *parare* to shield + *sole* sun, fr. L *sol*] **:** a lightweight umbrella used as a shield against the sun

para•sym•pa•thet•ic nervous system \ˌpar-ə-ˌsim-pə-ˈthe-tik-\ *n* **:** the part of the autonomic nervous system that tends to induce secretion, to increase the tone and contractility of smooth muscle, and to slow heart rate

para•thi•on \ˌpar-ə-ˈthī-ən, -ˌän\ *n* **:** an extremely toxic insecticide

para•thy•roid \-ˈthī-ˌrȯid\ *n* **:** PARATHYROID GLAND — **parathyroid** *adj*

parathyroid gland *n* **:** any of usu. four small endocrine glands adjacent to or embedded in the thyroid gland that produce a hormone (**parathyroid hormone**) concerned with calcium and phosphorus metabolism

para•troop•er \ˈpar-ə-ˌtrü-pər\ *n* **:** a member of the paratroops

para•troops \-ˌtrüps\ *n pl* **:** troops trained to parachute from an airplane

para•ty•phoid \ˌpar-ə-ˈtī-ˌfȯid\ *n* **:** a bacterial food poisoning resembling typhoid fever

par•boil \ˈpär-ˌbȯil\ *vb* **:** to boil briefly

[1]**par•cel** \ˈpär-səl\ *n* **1 :** a tract or plot of land **2 :** COLLECTION, LOT **3 :** a wrapped bundle **:** PACKAGE

[2]**parcel** *vb* **-celed** *or* **-celled; -cel•ing** *or* **-cel•ling :** to divide into portions

parcel post *n* **1 :** a mail service handling parcels **2 :** packages handled by parcel post

parch \ˈpärch\ *vb* **1 :** to toast under dry heat **2 :** to shrivel with heat

parch•ment \ˈpärch-mənt\ *n* **:** the skin of an animal prepared for writing on; *also* **:** a writing on such material

pard \ˈpärd\ *n* **:** LEOPARD

[1]**par•don** \ˈpärd-^{ə}n\ *n* **:** excuse of an offense without penalty; *esp* **:** an official release from legal punishment

[2]**pardon** *vb* **:** to free from penalty **:** EXCUSE, FORGIVE — **par•don•able** \ˈpärd-^{ə}n-ə-bəl\ *adj*

par•don•er \ˈpärd-^{ə}n-ər\ *n* **1 :** a medieval preacher delegated to raise money for religious works by soliciting offerings and granting indulgences **2 :** one that pardons

pare \ˈpar\ *vb* **pared; par•ing 1 :** to trim off an outside part (as the skin or rind) of **2 :** to reduce as if by paring ⟨~ expenses⟩ — **par•er** *n*

par•e•go•ric \ˌpar-ə-ˈgȯr-ik\ *n* **:** an alcoholic preparation of opium and camphor used esp. to relieve pain

par•ent \ˈpar-ənt\ *n* **1 :** one that begets or brings forth offspring **:** FATHER, MOTHER **2 :** one who brings up and cares for another **3 :** SOURCE, ORIGIN — **par•ent•age** \-ən-tij\ *n* — **pa•ren•tal** \pə-ˈrent-^{ə}l\ *adj* — **par•ent•hood** *n*

pa•ren•the•sis \pə-ˈren-thə-səs\ *n, pl* **-the•ses** \-ˌsēz\ **1 :** a word, phrase, or sentence inserted in a passage to explain or modify the thought **2 :** one of a pair of punctuation marks ( ) used esp. to enclose parenthetic matter — **par•en•thet•ic** \ˌpar-ən-ˈthe-tik\ *or* **par•en•thet•i•cal** \-ti-kəl\ *adj* — **par•en•thet•i•cal•ly** \-k(ə-)lē\ *adv*

pa•ren•the•size \pə-ˈren-thə-ˌsīz\ *vb* **-sized; -siz•ing :** to make a parenthesis of

par•ent•ing \ˈpar-ən-tiŋ, ˈper-\ *n* **:** the raising of a child by its parents

pa•re•sis \pə-ˈrē-səs, ˈpar-ə-\ *n, pl* **pa•re•ses** \-ˌsēz\ **:** a usu. incomplete paralysis; *also* **:** insanity caused by syphilitic alteration of the brain that leads to dementia and paralysis

par ex•cel•lence \ˌpär-ˌek-sə-ˈlä^{n}s\ *adj* [F, lit., by excellence] **:** being the best of a kind **:** PREEMINENT

par•fait \pär-ˈfā\ *n* [F, lit., something perfect] **:** a cold dessert made of layers of fruit, syrup, ice cream, and whipped cream

pa•ri•ah \pə-ˈrī-ə\ *n* **:** OUTCAST

pa•ri•etal \pə-ˈrī-ət-^{ə}l\ *adj* **1 :** of, relating to, or forming the walls of an anatomical structure **2 :** of or relating to college living or its regulation

pari–mu•tu•el \ˌpar-i-ˈmyü-chə-wəl\ *n* **:** a betting system in which winners share the total stakes minus a percentage for the management

par•ing \ˈpar-iŋ\ *n* **:** a pared-off piece

pa•ri pas•su \ˌpar-i-ˈpa-sü\ *adv or adj* [L, with equal step] **:** at an equal rate or pace

par•ish \ˈpar-ish\ *n* **1 :** a church district in the care of one pastor; *also* **:** the residents of such an area **2 :** a local church community **3 :** a civil division of the state of Louisiana : COUNTY

pa•rish•io•ner \pə-ˈri-shə-nər\ *n* **:** a member or resident of a parish

par•i•ty \ˈpar-ə-tē\ *n, pl* **-ties :** EQUALITY, EQUIVALENCE

[1]**park** \ˈpärk\ *n* **1 :** a tract of ground kept as a game preserve or recreation area **2 :** a place where vehicles (as automobiles) are parked **3 :** an enclosed stadium used esp. for ball games

[2]**park** *vb* **1 :** to leave a vehicle temporarily (as in a parking lot or garage) **2 :** to set and leave temporarily

par•ka \ˈpär-kə\ *n* **:** a very warm jacket with a hood

Par•kin•son's disease \ˈpär-kən-sənz-\ *n* **:** a chronic progressive nervous disease chiefly of later life marked by tremor and weakness of resting muscles and by a shuffling gait

Parkinson's law *n* **:** an observation in office organization: work expands so as to fill the time available for its completion

park•way \ˈpärk-ˌwā\ *n* **:** a broad landscaped thoroughfare

par•lance \ˈpär-ləns\ *n* **1 :** SPEECH **2 :** manner of speaking ⟨military ~⟩

[1]**par•lay** \ˈpär-ˌlā, -lē\ *vb* **:** to increase or change into something of much greater value

[2]**parlay** *n* **:** a series of bets in which the original stake plus its winnings are risked on successive wagers

par•ley \ˈpär-lē\ *n, pl* **parleys :** a conference usu. over matters in dispute : DISCUSSION — **parley** *vb*

par•lia•ment \ˈpär-lə-mənt\ *n* [ME, fr. OF *parlement,* fr. *parler* to speak, fr. ML *parabolare,* fr. LL *parabola* speech, parable] **1 :** a formal governmental conference **2** *cap* **:** an assembly that constitutes the supreme legislative body of a country (as the United Kingdom) — **par•lia•men•ta•ry** \ˌpär-lə-ˈmen-tə-rē\ *adj*

par•lia•men•tar•i•an \ˌpär-lə-ˌmen-ˈter-ē-ən\ *n* **1** *often cap* **:** an adherent of the parliament during the English Civil War **2 :** an expert in parliamentary procedure

par•lor \ˈpär-lər\ *n* **1 :** a room for conversation or the reception of guests **2 :** a place of business ⟨beauty ~⟩

par•lour \ˈpär-lər\ *chiefly Brit var of* PARLOR

par•lous \ˈpär-ləs\ *adj* **:** full of danger or risk : PRECARIOUS — **par•lous•ly** *adv*

Par•me•san \ˈpär-mə-ˌzän, -ˌzhän, -ˌzan\ *n* **:** a hard dry cheese with a sharp flavor

par•mi•gia•na \ˌpär-mi-ˈjä-nə, ˌpär-mi-ˈzhän\ *or* **par•mi•gia•no** \-ˈjä-(ˌ)nō\ *adj* **:** made or covered with Parmesan cheese ⟨veal ~⟩

pa•ro•chi•al \pə-ˈrō-kē-əl\ *adj* **1 :** of or relating to a church parish **2 :** limited in scope : NARROW, PROVINCIAL — **pa•ro•chi•al•ism** \-ə-ˌli-zəm\ *n*

parochial school *n* **:** a school maintained by a religious body

par•o•dy \ˈpar-ə-dē\ *n, pl* **-dies** [L *parodia,* fr. Gk *parōidia,* fr. *para-* beside + *aidein* to sing] **:** a humorous or satirical imitation — **parody** *vb*

pa•role \pə-ˈrōl\ *n* **:** a conditional release of a prisoner whose sentence has not expired — **parole** *vb* — **pa•rol•ee** \-ˌrō-ˈlē, -ˈrō-ˌlē\ *n*

par•ox•ysm \ˈpar-ək-ˌsi-zəm, pə-ˈräk-\ *n* **:** a sudden sharp attack (as of pain or coughing) : CONVULSION — **par•ox•ys•mal** \ˌpar-ək-ˈsiz-məl, pə-ˌräk-\ *adj*

par•quet \ˈpär-ˌkā, pär-ˈkā\ *n* [F] **1 :** a flooring of parquetry **2 :** the lower floor of a theater; *esp* **:** the forward part of the orchestra

par•que•try \ˈpär-kə-trē\ *n, pl* **-tries :** fine woodwork inlaid in patterns

par•ra•keet *var of* PARAKEET

par•ri•cide \ˈpar-ə-ˌsīd\ *n* **1 :** one that murders a parent or a close relative **2 :** the act of a parricide

par•rot \ˈpar-ət\ *n* **:** any of numerous bright-colored tropical birds that have a stout hooked bill

parrot fever *n* **:** an infectious disease of birds marked by diarrhea and wasting and transmissible to humans

par•ry \ˈpar-ē\ *vb* **par•ried; par•ry•ing 1 :** to ward off a weapon or blow **2 :** to evade esp. by an adroit answer — **parry** *n*

parse \ˈpärs *also* ˈpärz\ *vb* **parsed; pars•ing :** to give a grammatical description of a word or a group of words

par•sec \ˈpär-ˌsek\ *n* **:** a unit of measure for interstellar space equal to 3.26 light-years

par•si•mo•ny \ˈpär-sə-ˌmō-nē\ *n* **:** extreme or excessive frugality — **par•si•mo•ni•ous** \ˌpär-sə-ˈmō-nē-əs\ *adj* — **par•si•mo•ni•ous•ly** *adv*

pars•ley \ˈpär-slē\ *n* **:** a garden plant related to the carrot that has finely divided leaves used as a seasoning or garnish

pars•nip \ˈpär-snəp\ *n* **:** a garden plant related to the carrot that has a long edible usu. whitish root; *also* **:** this root

par•son \ˈpärs-ᵊn\ *n* [ME *persone,* fr. OF, fr. ML *persona,* lit., person, fr. L] **:** MINISTER 2, PASTOR

par•son•age \ˈpärs-ᵊn-ij\ *n* **:** a house provided by a church for its pastor

[1]**part** \ˈpärt\ *n* **1 :** a division or portion of a whole **2 :** the melody or score for a particular voice or instrument **3 :** a spare piece for a machine **4 :** DUTY, FUNCTION **5 :** one of the sides in a dispute **6 :** ROLE; *also* **:** an actor's lines in a play **7** *pl* **:** TALENTS, ABILITY **8 :** the line where one's hair divides (as in combing)

[2]**part** *vb* **1 :** to take leave of someone **2 :** to divide or break into parts : SEPARATE **3 :** to go away : DEPART; *also* **:** DIE **4 :** to give up possession ⟨~*ed* with her jewels⟩ **5 :** APPORTION, SHARE

[3]**part** *abbr* **1** participial; participle **2** particular

par•take \pär-ˈtāk\ *vb* **-took** \-ˈtu̇k\; **-tak•en** \-ˈtā-kən\; **-tak•ing 1 :** to have a share or part **2 :** to take a portion (as of food) — **par•tak•er** *n*

par•terre \pär-ˈter\ *n* [F, fr. MF, fr. *par terre* on the ground] **1 :** an ornamental garden with paths between the flower beds **2 :** the part of a theater floor behind the orchestra

par•the•no•gen•e•sis \ˌpär-thə-nō-ˈje-nə-səs\ *n* [NL, fr. Gk *parthenos* virgin + L *genesis* genesis] **:** development of a new individual from an unfertilized usu. female sex cell — **par•the•no•ge•net•ic** \-jə-ˈne-tik\ *adj*

par•tial \ˈpär-shəl\ *adj* **1 :** not total or general : affecting a part only **2 :** favoring one party over the other : BIASED **3 :** markedly fond — used with *to* — **par•tial•i•ty** \ˌpär-shē-ˈa-lə-tē\ *n* — **par•tial•ly** *adv*

par•tic•i•pate \pär-ˈti-sə-ˌpāt\ *vb* **-pat•ed; -pat•ing 1 :** to take part in something ⟨~ in a game⟩ **2 :** SHARE — **par•tic•i•pant** \-pənt\ *adj or n* — **par•tic•i•pa•tion** \-ˌti-sə-ˈpā-shən\ *n* — **par•tic•i•pa•tor** \-ˈti-sə-ˌpā-tər\ *n* — **par•tic•i•pa•to•ry** \-ˈti-sə-pə-ˌtōr-ē\ *adj*

par•ti•ci•ple \ˈpär-tə-ˌsi-pəl\ *n* **:** a word having the characteristics of both verb and adjective — **par•ti•cip•i•al** \ˌpär-tə-ˈsi-pē-əl\ *adj*

par•ti•cle \ˈpär-ti-kəl\ *n* **1 :** a very small bit of matter **2 :** a unit of speech (as an article, preposition, or conjunction) expressing some general aspect of meaning or some connective or limiting relation

par•ti•cle•board \-ˌbōrd\ *n* **:** a board made of very small pieces of wood bonded together

par•ti–col•or \ˌpär-tē-ˈkə-lər\ *or* **par•ti–col•ored** \-lərd\ *adj* **:** showing different colors or tints; *esp* **:** having one main color broken by patches of one or more other colors

[1]**par•tic•u•lar** \pər-ˈti-kyə-lər\ *adj* **1 :** of or relating to a specific person or thing ⟨the laws of a ~ state⟩ **2 :** DISTINCTIVE, SPECIAL ⟨the ~ point of his talk⟩ **3 :** SEPARATE, INDIVIDUAL ⟨each ~ hair⟩ **4 :** attentive to details : PRECISE **5 :** hard to please : EXACTING — **par•tic•u•lar•i•ty** \-ˌti-kyə-ˈlar-ə-tē\ *n* — **par•tic•u•lar•ly** *adv*

[2]**particular** *n* **:** an individual fact or detail

par•tic•u•lar•ise *Brit var of* PARTICULARIZE

par•tic•u•lar•ize \pər-ˈti-kyə-lə-ˌrīz\ *vb* **-ized; -iz•ing 1**

: to state in detail : SPECIFY **2** : to go into details
par•tic•u•late \pər-ˈti-kyə-lət, pär-, -ˌlāt\ *adj* : relating to or existing as minute separate particles — **particulate** *n*
[1]**part•ing** *n* : a place or point of separation or divergence
[2]**parting** *adj* : given, taken, or performed at parting ⟨a ~ kiss⟩
par•ti•san *also* **par•ti•zan** \ˈpär-tə-zən, -sən\ *n* **1** : one that takes the part of another : ADHERENT **2** : GUERRILLA — **partisan** *adj* — **par•ti•san•ship** *n*
par•tite \ˈpär-ˌtīt\ *adj* : divided into a usu. specified number of parts
par•ti•tion \pär-ˈti-shən\ *n* **1** : DIVISION **2** : something that divides or separates; *esp* : an interior dividing wall — **partition** *vb*
par•ti•tive \ˈpär-tə-tiv\ *adj* : of, relating to, or denoting a part
part•ly \ˈpärt-lē\ *adv* : in part : in some measure or degree
part•ner \ˈpärt-nər\ *n* **1** : ASSOCIATE, COLLEAGUE **2** : either of two persons who dance together **3** : one who plays on the same team with another **4** : SPOUSE **5** : one of two or more persons contractually associated as joint principals in a business — **part•ner•ship** *n*
part of speech : a class of words (as nouns or verbs) distinguished according to the kind of idea denoted and the function performed in a sentence
par•tridge \ˈpär-trij\ *n, pl* **partridge** *or* **par•tridg•es** : any of various stout-bodied game birds
part–song \ˈpärt-ˌsȯŋ\ *n* : a song with two or more voice parts
part–time \-ˈtīm\ *adj or adv* : involving or working less than a full or regular schedule — **part–tim•er** \-ˌtī-mər\ *n*
par•tu•ri•tion \ˌpär-tə-ˈri-shən, ˌpär-chə-, ˌpär-tyu̇-\ *n* : CHILDBIRTH
part•way \ˈpärt-ˈwā\ *adv* : to some extent : PARTLY
par•ty \ˈpär-tē\ *n, pl* **parties** **1** : a person or group taking one side of a question; *esp* : a group of persons organized for the purpose of directing the policies of a government **2** : a person or group concerned in an action or affair : PARTICIPANT **3** : a group of persons detailed for a common task **4** : a social gathering
par•ve•nu \ˈpär-və-ˌnü, -ˌnyü\ *n* [F, fr. pp. of *parvenir* to arrive, fr. L *pervenire*, fr. *per* through + *venire* to come] : one who has recently or suddenly risen to wealth or power but has not yet secured the social position associated with it
pas \ˈpä\ *n, pl* **pas** *same or* ˈpäz\ : a dance step or combination of steps
pas•cal \pas-ˈkal\ *n* : a unit of pressure in the metric system equal to one newton per square meter
pas•chal \ˈpas-kəl\ *adj* : of, relating to, appropriate for, or used during Passover or Easter ceremonies
pa•sha \ˈpä-shə, ˈpa-; pə-ˈshä\ *n* : a man (as formerly a governor in Turkey) of high rank
[1]**pass** \ˈpas\ *vb* **1** : MOVE, PROCEED **2** : to go away; *also* : DIE **3** : to move past, beyond, or over **4** : to allow to elapse : SPEND **5** : to go or make way through **6** : to go or allow to go unchallenged **7** : to undergo transfer **8** : to render a legal judgment **9** : OCCUR **10** : to secure the approval of (as a legislature) **11** : to go or cause to go through an inspection, test, or course of study successfully **12** : to be regarded **13** : CIRCULATE **14** : VOID 2 **15** : to transfer the ball or puck to another player **16** : to decline to bid or bet on one's hand in a card game **17** : to give a base on balls to — **passer** *n*
[2]**pass** *n* : a gap in a mountain range
[3]**pass** *n* **1** : the act or an instance of passing **2** : REALIZATION, ACCOMPLISHMENT **3** : a state of affairs **4** : a written authorization to leave, enter, or move about freely **5** : a transfer of a ball or puck from one player to another **6** : BASE ON BALLS **7** : EFFORT, TRY **8** : a sexually inviting gesture or approach
[4]**pass** *abbr* **1** passenger **2** passive
pass•able \ˈpa-sə-bəl\ *adj* **1** : capable of being passed or traveled on **2** : just good enough : TOLERABLE — **pass•ably** \-blē\ *adv*
pas•sage \ˈpa-sij\ *n* **1** : a means (as a road or corridor) of passing **2** : the action or process of passing **3** : a voyage esp. by sea or air **4** : a right or permission to pass **5** : ENACTMENT **6** : a usu. brief portion or section (as of a book)
pas•sage•way \-ˌwā\ *n* : a way that allows passage
pass•book \ˈpas-ˌbu̇k\ *n* : BANKBOOK
pas•sé \pa-ˈsā\ *adj* **1** : past one's prime **2** : not up-to-date : OUTMODED
pas•sel \ˈpa-səl\ *n* : a large number
pas•sen•ger \ˈpas-ᵊn-jər\ *n* : a traveler in a public or private conveyance
pass•er•by \ˈpa-sər-ˌbī\ *n, pl* **pass•ers•by** : one who passes by
pas•ser•ine \ˈpa-sə-ˌrīn\ *adj* : of or relating to the large order of birds comprising singing birds that perch
pas•sim \ˈpa-səm\ *adv* [L, fr. *passus* scattered, fr. pp. of *pandere* to spread] : here and there : THROUGHOUT
pass•ing *n* : the act of one that passes or causes to pass; *esp* : DEATH
pas•sion \ˈpa-shən\ *n* **1** *often cap* : the sufferings of Christ between the night of the Last Supper and his death **2** : strong feeling; *also, pl* : the emotions as distinguished from reason **3** : RAGE, ANGER **4** : LOVE; *also* : an object of affection or enthusiasm **5** : sexual desire — **pas•sion•ate** \ˈpa-shə-nət\ *adj* — **pas•sion•ate•ly** *adv* — **pas•sion•less** *adj*
pas•sion•flow•er \ˈpa-shən-ˌflau̇-ər\ *n* [fr. the fancied resemblance of parts of the flower to the instruments of Christ's crucifixion] : any of a genus of chiefly tropical woody climbing vines or erect herbs with showy flowers and pulpy often edible berries (**passion fruit**)
pas•sive \ˈpa-siv\ *adj* **1** : not active : acted upon **2** : asserting that the grammatical subject is subjected to or affected by the action represented by the verb ⟨~ voice⟩ **3** : making use of the sun's heat usu. without the aid of mechanical devices **4** : SUBMISSIVE, PATIENT — **passive** *n* — **pas•sive•ly** *adv* — **pas•siv•i•ty** \pa-ˈsi-və-tē\ *n*
pass•key \ˈpas-ˌkē\ *n* : a key for opening two or more locks
pass out *vb* : to lose consciousness
Pass•over \ˈpas-ˌō-vər\ *n* [fr. the exemption of the Israelites from the slaughter of the firstborn in Egypt (Exod 12:23–27)] : a Jewish holiday celebrated in March or April in commemoration of the Hebrews' liberation from slavery in Egypt
pass•port \ˈpas-ˌpōrt\ *n* : an official document issued by a country upon request to a citizen requesting protection during travel abroad
pass up *vb* : DECLINE, REJECT
pass•word \ˈpas-ˌwərd\ *n* **1** : a word or phrase that must be spoken by a person before being allowed to pass a guard **2** : a sequence of characters required for access to a computer system
[1]**past** \ˈpast\ *adj* **1** : AGO ⟨10 years ~⟩ **2** : just gone or elapsed ⟨the ~ month⟩ **3** : having existed or taken place in a period before the present : BYGONE **4** : of, relating to, or constituting a verb tense that expresses time gone by
[2]**past** *prep or adv* : BEYOND
[3]**past** *n* **1** : time gone by **2** : something that happened or was done in a former time **3** : the past tense; *also* : a verb form in it **4** : a secret past life
pas•ta \ˈpäs-tə\ *n* [It] **1** : a paste in processed form (as spaghetti) or in the form of fresh dough (as ravioli) **2** : a dish of cooked pasta
[1]**paste** \ˈpāst\ *n* **1** : DOUGH **2** : a smooth food product made by evaporation or grinding ⟨tomato ~⟩ **3** : a shaped dough (as spaghetti or ravioli) **4** : a prepara-

tion (as of flour and water) for sticking things together **5** : a brilliant glass used for artificial gems

²**paste** *vb* **past·ed; past·ing** : to cause to adhere by paste : STICK

paste·board \ˈpāst-ˌbōrd\ *n* : PAPERBOARD

¹**pas·tel** \pas-ˈtel\ *n* **1** : a paste made of powdered pigment; *also* : a crayon of such paste **2** : a drawing in pastel **3** : a pale or light color

²**pastel** *adj* **1** : of or relating to a pastel **2** : pale in color

pas·tern \ˈpas-tərn\ *n* : the part of a horse's foot extending from the fetlock to the top of the hoof

pas·teur·i·za·tion \ˌpas-chə-rə-ˈzā-shən, ˌpas-tə-\ *n* : partial sterilization of a substance (as milk) by heat or radiation — **pas·teur·ize** \ˈpas-chə-ˌrīz, ˈpas-tə-\ *vb* — **pas·teur·iz·er** *n*

pas·tiche \pas-ˈtēsh\ *n* : a composition (as in literature or music) made up of selections from different works

pas·tille \pas-ˈtēl\ *n* : an aromatic or medicated lozenge

pas·time \ˈpas-ˌtīm\ *n* : DIVERSION; *esp* : something that serves to make time pass agreeably

pas·tor \ˈpas-tər\ *n* [ME *pastour,* fr. OF, fr. L *pastor,* herdsman, fr. *pascere* to feed, pasture, nurture] : a minister or priest serving a local church or parish — **pas·tor·ate** \-tə-rət\ *n*

¹**pas·to·ral** \ˈpas-tə-rəl\ *adj* **1** : of or relating to shepherds or to rural life **2** : of or relating to spiritual guidance esp. of a congregation **3** : of or relating to the pastor of a church

²**pastoral** *n* : a literary work dealing with shepherds or rural life

pas·to·rale \ˌpas-tə-ˈräl, -ˈral\ *n* [It] : a musical composition having a pastoral theme

past participle *n* : a participle that typically expresses completed action, that is one of the principal parts of the verb, and that is used in the formation of perfect tenses in the active voice and of all tenses in the passive voice

pas·tra·mi \pə-ˈsträ-mē\ *n* [Yiddish *pastrame*] : a highly seasoned smoked beef prepared esp. from shoulder cuts

pas·try \ˈpā-strē\ *n, pl* **pastries** : sweet baked goods made of dough or with a crust made of enriched dough

pas·tur·age \ˈpas-chə-rij\ *n* : PASTURE

¹**pas·ture** \ˈpas-chər\ *n* **1** : plants (as grass) for the feeding esp. of grazing livestock **2** : land or a plot of land used for grazing

²**pasture** *vb* **pas·tured; pas·tur·ing** **1** : GRAZE **2** : to use as pasture

pasty \ˈpā-stē\ *adj* **past·i·er; -est** : resembling paste; *esp* : pallid and unhealthy in appearance

¹**pat** \ˈpat\ *n* **1** : a light tap esp. with the hand or a flat instrument; *also* : the sound made by it **2** : something (as butter) shaped into a small flat usu. square individual portion

²**pat** *adv* : in a pat manner : PERFECTLY

³**pat** *vb* **pat·ted; pat·ting** **1** : to strike lightly with a flat instrument **2** : to flatten, smooth, or put into place or shape with a pat **3** : to tap gently or lovingly with the hand

⁴**pat** *adj* **1** : exactly suited to the occasion : APT **2** : memorized exactly **3** : UNYIELDING

PAT *abbr* point after touchdown

pa·ta·ca \pə-ˈtä-kə\ *n* — see MONEY table

¹**patch** \ˈpach\ *n* **1** : a piece used to cover a torn or worn place; *also* : one worn on a garment as an ornament or insignia **2** : a small area distinct from that about it **3** : a shield worn over the socket of an injured or missing eye

²**patch** *vb* **1** : to mend or cover with a patch **2** : to make of fragments **3** : to repair usu. in hasty fashion

patch test *n* : a test for allergic sensitivity made by applying to the unbroken skin small pads soaked with the allergen to be tested

patch·work \ˈpach-ˌwərk\ *n* : something made of pieces of different materials, shapes, or colors

patchy \ˈpa-chē\ *adj* **patch·i·er; -est** : marked by or consisting of patches; *also* : irregular in appearance or quality — **patch·i·ness** \-chē-nəs\ *n*

pate \ˈpāt\ *n* : HEAD; *esp* : the crown of the head

pâ·té *also* **pate** \pä-ˈtā\ *n* [F] **1** : a meat or fish pie or patty **2** : a spread of finely chopped or pureed seasoned meat

pa·tel·la \pə-ˈte-lə\ *n, pl* **-lae** \-ˈte-(ˌ)lē, -ˌlī\ *or* **-las** [L] : KNEECAP

pat·en \ˈpat-ᵊn\ *n* **1** : PLATE; *esp* : one of precious metal for the eucharistic bread **2** : a thin disk

¹**pa·tent** *1 & 4 are* ˈpat-ᵊnt, *Brit also* ˈpāt-, *2 & 3 are* ˈpat-ᵊnt, ˈpāt-\ *adj* **1** : open to public inspection — used chiefly in the phrase *letters patent* **2** : free from obstruction **3** : EVIDENT, OBVIOUS **4** : protected by a patent **syn** manifest, distinct, apparent, palpable, plain, clear — **pat·ent·ly** *adv*

²**pat·ent** \ˈpat-ᵊnt, *Brit also* ˈpāt-\ *n* **1** : an official document conferring a right or privilege **2** : a document securing to an inventor for a term of years exclusive right to his or her invention **3** : something patented

³**pat·ent** *vb* : to secure by patent

pat·en·tee \ˌpat-ᵊn-ˈtē, *Brit also* ˌpāt-\ *n* : one to whom a grant is made or a privilege secured by patent

pat·ent medicine \ˈpat-ᵊnt-\ *n* : a packaged nonprescription drug protected by a trademark; *also* : any proprietary drug

pa·ter·fa·mil·i·as \ˌpā-tər-fə-ˈmi-lē-əs\ *n, pl* **pa·tres·fa·mil·i·as** \ˌpā-ˌtrēz-\ [L] : the father of a family : the male head of a household

pa·ter·nal \pə-ˈtərn-ᵊl\ *adj* **1** : FATHERLY **2** : related through or inherited or derived from a father — **pa·ter·nal·ly** *adv*

pa·ter·nal·ism \-ˌi-zəm\ *n* : a system under which an authority treats those under its control paternally (as by regulating their conduct and supplying their needs)

pa·ter·ni·ty \pə-ˈtər-nə-tē\ *n* **1** : FATHERHOOD **2** : descent from a father

¹**path** \ˈpath, ˈpȧth\ *n, pl* **paths** \ˈpat͟hz, ˈpaths, ˈpȧt͟hz, ˈpȧths\ **1** : a trodden way **2** : ROUTE, COURSE — **path·less** *adj*

²**path** *or* **pathol** *abbr* pathology

path·break·ing \ˈpath-ˌbrā-kiŋ\ *adj* : TRAILBLAZING

pa·thet·ic \pə-ˈthe-tik\ *adj* : evoking tenderness, pity, or sorrow **syn** pitiful, piteous, pitiable, poor — **pa·thet·i·cal·ly** \-ti-k(ə-)lē\ *adv*

path·find·er \ˈpath-ˌfīn-dər, ˈpȧth-\ *n* : one that discovers a way; *esp* : one that explores untraveled regions to mark out a new route

patho·gen \ˈpa-thə-jən\ *n* : a specific agent (as a bacterium) causing disease — **patho·gen·ic** \ˌpa-thə-ˈje-nik\ *adj* — **patho·ge·nic·i·ty** \-jə-ˈni-sə-tē\ *n*

pa·thol·o·gy \pə-ˈthä-lə-jē\ *n, pl* **-gies** **1** : the study of the essential nature of disease **2** : the abnormality of structure and function characteristic of a disease — **path·o·log·i·cal** \ˌpa-thə-ˈlä-ji-kəl\ *adj* — **pa·thol·o·gist** \pə-ˈthä-lə-jist\ *n*

pa·thos \ˈpā-ˌthäs, -ˌthōs\ *n* : an element in experience or artistic representation evoking pity or compassion

path·way \ˈpath-ˌwā, ˈpȧth-\ *n* : PATH

pa·tience \ˈpā-shəns\ *n* **1** : the capacity, habit, or fact of being patient **2** *chiefly Brit* : SOLITAIRE 2

¹**pa·tient** \ˈpā-shənt\ *adj* **1** : bearing pain or trials without complaint **2** : showing self-control : CALM **3** : STEADFAST, PERSEVERING — **pa·tient·ly** *adv*

²**patient** *n* : one under medical care

pa·ti·na \ˈpa-tə-nə, pə-ˈtē-\ *n, pl* **pa·ti·nas** \-nəz\ *or* **pa·ti·nae** \ˈpa-tə-ˌnē, -ˌnī\ **1** : a green film formed on copper and bronze by exposure to moist air **2** : a superficial covering or exterior

pa·tio \ˈpa-tē-ˌō, ˈpä-\ *n, pl* **pa·ti·os** **1** : COURTYARD **2** : an often paved area near a dwelling used esp. for outdoor dining

pa·tois \ˈpa-ˌtwä\ *n, pl* **pa·tois** \-ˌtwäz\ [F] **1** : a dialect other than the standard dialect; *esp* : uneducated or provincial speech **2** : JARGON 2

pa•tri•arch \ˈpā-trē-ˌärk\ *n* **1** : a man revered as father or founder (as of a tribe) **2** : a venerable old man **3** : an ecclesiastical dignitary (as the bishop of an Eastern Orthodox see) — **pa•tri•ar•chal** \ˌpā-trē-ˈär-kəl\ *adj* — **pa•tri•arch•ate** \ˈpā-trē-ˌär-kət, -ˌkāt\ *n* — **pa•tri•ar•chy** \-ˌär-kē\ *n*

pa•tri•cian \pə-ˈtri-shən\ *n* : a person of high birth : ARISTOCRAT — **patrician** *adj*

pat•ri•cide \ˈpa-tre-ˌsīd\ *n* **1** : one who murders his or her own father **2** : the murder of one's own father

pat•ri•mo•ny \ˈpa-trə-ˌmō-nē\ *n* : something (as an estate) inherited or derived esp. from one's father : HERITAGE — **pat•ri•mo•ni•al** \ˌpa-trə-ˈmō-nē-əl\ *adj*

pa•tri•ot \ˈpā-trē-ət, -ˌät\ *n* [MF *patriote* compatriot, fr. LL *patriota*, fr. Gk *patriōtēs*, fr. *patria* lineage, fr. *patr-*, *patēr* father] : one who loves his or her country — **pa•tri•ot•ic** \ˌpā-trē-ˈä-tik\ *adj* — **pa•tri•ot•i•cal•ly** \-ti-k(ə-)lē\ *adv* — **pa•tri•o•tism** \ˈpā-trē-ə-ˌti-zəm\ *n*

pa•tris•tic \pə-ˈtris-tik\ *adj* : of or relating to the church fathers or their writings

[1]**pa•trol** \pə-ˈtrōl\ *n* : the action of going the rounds (as of an area) for observation or the maintenance of security; *also* : a person or group performing such an action

[2]**patrol** *vb* **pa•trolled; pa•trol•ling** : to carry out a patrol

patrol car *n* : SQUAD CAR

pa•trol•man \pə-ˈtrōl-mən\ *n* : a police officer assigned to a beat

patrol wagon *n* : PADDY WAGON

pa•tron \ˈpā-trən\ *n* [ME, fr. MF, fr. ML & L; ML *patronus* patron saint, patron of a benefice, pattern, fr. L, defender, fr. *patr-*, *pater* father] **1** : a person chosen or named as special protector **2** : a wealthy or influential supporter ⟨~ of poets⟩; *also* : BENEFACTOR **3** : a regular client or customer

pa•tron•age \ˈpa-trə-nij, ˈpā-\ *n* **1** : the support or influence of a patron **2** : the trade of customers **3** : control of appointment to government jobs

pa•tron•ess \ˈpā-trə-nəs\ *n* : a woman who is a patron

pa•tron•ise *Brit var of* PATRONIZE

pa•tron•ize \ˈpā-trə-ˌnīz, ˈpa-\ *vb* **-ized; -iz•ing 1** : to be a customer of **2** : to treat condescendingly, haughtily, or coolly

pat•ro•nym•ic \ˌpa-trə-ˈni-mik\ *n* : a name derived from the name of one's father or a paternal ancestor usu. by the addition of an affix

pa•troon \pə-ˈtrün\ *n* : the proprietor of a manorial estate esp. in New York under Dutch rule

pat•sy \ˈpat-sē\ *n, pl* **pat•sies** : a person who is easily duped or victimized

[1]**pat•ter** \ˈpa-tər\ *vb* : to talk glibly or mechanically **syn** chatter, prate, chat, prattle, babble

[2]**patter** *n* **1** : a specialized lingo **2** : extremely rapid talk ⟨a comedian's ~⟩

[3]**patter** *vb* : to strike, pat, or tap rapidly

[4]**patter** *n* : a quick succession of taps or pats ⟨the ~ of rain⟩

[1]**pat•tern** \ˈpa-tərn\ *n* [ME *patron*, fr. MF, fr. ML *patronus*, fr. L, defender, fr. *patr-*, *pater* father] **1** : an ideal model **2** : something used as a model for making things ⟨a dressmaker's ~⟩ **3** : SAMPLE **4** : an artistic design **5** : CONFIGURATION

[2]**pattern** *vb* : to form according to a pattern

pat•ty *also* **pat•tie** \ˈpa-tē\ *n, pl* **patties 1** : a little pie **2** : a small flat cake esp. of chopped food

pau•ci•ty \ˈpò-sə-tē\ *n* : smallness of number or quantity

paunch \ˈpònch\ *n* : a usu. large belly : POTBELLY — **paunchy** *adj*

pau•per \ˈpò-pər\ *n* : a person without means of support except from charity — **pau•per•ism** \-pə-ˌri-zəm\ *n* — **pau•per•ize** \-pə-ˌrīz\ *vb*

[1]**pause** \ˈpòz\ *n* **1** : a temporary stop; *also* : a period of inaction **2** : a brief suspension of the voice **3** : a sign 𝄐 or 𝄑 above or below a musical note or rest to show it is to be prolonged **4** : a reason for pausing

[2]**pause** *vb* **paused; paus•ing** : to stop, rest, or linger for a time

pave \ˈpāv\ *vb* **paved; pav•ing** : to cover (as a road) with hard material in order to smooth or firm the surface

pave•ment \ˈpāv-mənt\ *n* **1** : a paved surface **2** : the material with which something is paved

pa•vil•ion \pə-ˈvil-yən\ *n* [ME *pavilon*, fr. OF *paveillon*, fr. L *papilion-*, *papilio* butterfly] **1** : a large tent **2** : a light structure (as in a park) used for entertainment or shelter

pav•ing \ˈpā-viŋ\ *n* : PAVEMENT

[1]**paw** \ˈpò\ *n* : the foot of a quadruped (as a dog or lion) having claws

[2]**paw** *vb* **1** : to touch or strike with a paw; *also* : to scrape with a hoof **2** : to feel or handle clumsily or rudely **3** : to flail about or grab for with the hands

pawl \ˈpòl\ *n* : a pivoted tongue or sliding bolt designed to fall into notches on another machine part to permit motion in one direction only

[1]**pawn** \ˈpòn\ *n* [ME *pown*, fr. MF *poon*, fr. ML *pedon-*, *pedo* foot soldier, fr. LL, one with broad feet, fr. L *ped-*, *pes* foot] : a chess piece of the least value

[2]**pawn** *n* **1** : something deposited as security for a loan; *also* : HOSTAGE **2** : the state of being pledged

[3]**pawn** *vb* : to deposit as a pledge

pawn•bro•ker \ˈpòn-ˌbrō-kər\ *n* : one who lends money on goods pledged

Paw•nee \pò-ˈnē\ *n, pl* **Pawnee** *or* **Pawnees** : a member of an American Indian people orig. of Kansas and Nebraska

pawn•shop \ˈpòn-ˌshäp\ *n* : a pawnbroker's place of business

paw•paw *var of* PAPAW

[1]**pay** \ˈpā\ *vb* **paid** \ˈpād\ *also in sense 7* **payed; pay•ing** [ME, fr. OF *paier*, fr. L *pacare* to pacify, fr. *pac-*, *pax* peace] **1** : to make due return to for goods or services **2** : to discharge indebtedness for : SETTLE ⟨~ a bill⟩ **3** : to give in forfeit ⟨~ the penalty⟩ **4** : REQUITE **5** : to give, offer, or make freely or as fitting ⟨~ attention⟩ **6** : to be profitable to : RETURN **7** : to make slack and allow to run out ⟨~ out a rope⟩ — **pay•able** *adj* — **pay•ee** \pā-ˈē\ *n* — **pay•er** *n*

[2]**pay** *n* **1** : something paid; *esp* : WAGES **2** : the status of being paid by an employer : EMPLOY

[3]**pay** *adj* **1** : containing something valuable (as gold) ⟨~ dirt⟩ **2** : equipped to receive a fee for use ⟨~ telephone⟩ **3** : requiring payment

pay•check \ˈpā-ˌchek\ *n* **1** : a check in payment of wages or salary **2** : WAGES, SALARY

pay•load \-ˌlōd\ *n* : the load carried by a vehicle in addition to what is necessary for its operation; *also* : the weight of such a load

pay•mas•ter \-ˌmas-tər\ *n* : one who distributes the payroll

pay•ment \ˈpā-mənt\ *n* **1** : the act of paying **2** : something paid

pay•off \-ˌȯf\ *n* **1** : PROFIT, REWARD; *also* : RETRIBUTION **2** : the climax of an incident or enterprise ⟨the ~ of a story⟩

pay–per–view *n* : a cable television service by which customers can order access to a single airing of a TV feature

pay•roll \-ˌrōl\ *n* : a list of persons entitled to receive pay; *also* : the money to pay those on such a list

payt *abbr* payment

pay up *vb* : to pay what is due; *also* : to pay in full

Pb *symbol* [L *plumbum*] lead

PBS *abbr* Public Broadcasting Service

PBX \ˌpē-(ˌ)bē-ˈeks\ *n* [*p*rivate *b*ranch e*x*change] : a private telephone switchboard

[1]**PC** \ˌpē-ˈsē\ *n, pl* **PCs** *or* **PC's** [*p*ersonal *c*omputer] : MICROCOMPUTER

[2]**PC** *abbr* **1** Peace Corps **2** percent; percentage **3** politically correct **4** postcard **5** [L *post cibum*] after meals **6** professional corporation

PCB \ˌpē-ˌsē-ˈbē\ *n* : POLYCHLORINATED BIPHENYL

PCP \ˌpē-ˌsē-ˈpē\ *n* : PHENCYCLIDINE

pct *abbr* percent; percentage

pd *abbr* paid

Pd *symbol* palladium

PD *abbr* **1** per diem **2** police department **3** potential difference

PDQ \ˌpē-ˌdē-ˈkyü\ *adv, often not cap* [abbr. of *pretty damned quick*] : IMMEDIATELY

PDT *abbr* Pacific daylight (saving) time

PE *abbr* **1** physical education **2** printer's error **3** professional engineer

pea \ˈpē\ *n, pl* **peas** *also* **pease** \ˈpēz\ **1** : the round edible protein-rich seed borne in the pod of a widely grown leguminous vine; *also* : this vine **2** : any of various plants resembling or related to the pea

peace \ˈpēs\ *n* **1** : a state of calm and quiet; *esp* : public security under law **2** : freedom from disturbing thoughts or emotions **3** : a state of concord (as between persons or governments); *also* : an agreement to end hostilities — **peace•able** \ˈpē-sə-bəl\ *adj* — **peace•ably** \-blē\ *adv* — **peace•ful** *adj* — **peace•ful•ly** *adv*

peace•keep•ing \ˈpēs-ˌkē-piŋ\ *n* : the preserving of peace; *esp* : international enforcement and supervision of a truce — **peace•keep•er** *n*

peace•mak•er \-ˌmā-kər\ *n* : one who settles an argument or stops a fight

peace•time \-ˌtīm\ *n* : a time when a nation is not at war

peach \ˈpēch\ *n* [ME *peche*, fr. MF, fr. LL *persica*, fr. L (*malum*) *Persicum*, lit., Persian fruit] : a sweet juicy fruit of a low tree with pink blossoms related to the cherry and plums; *also* : this tree

pea•cock \ˈpē-ˌkäk\ *n* [ME *pecok*, fr. *pe-* (fr. OE *pēa* peafowl, fr. L *pavo* peacock) + *cok* cock] : the male peafowl that can spread its long tail feathers to make a colorful display

pea•fowl \-ˌfau̇l\ *n* : either of two large domesticated Asian pheasants

peafowl: *A* female, *B* male

pea•hen \-ˌhen\ *n* : the female peafowl

[1]**peak** \ˈpēk\ *n* **1** : a pointed or projecting part **2** : the top of a hill or mountain; *also* : MOUNTAIN **3** : the front projecting part of a cap **4** : the narrow part of a ship's bow or stern **5** : the highest level or greatest degree — **peak** *adj*

[2]**peak** *vb* : to bring to or reach a maximum

peak•ed \ˈpē-kəd\ *adj* : THIN, SICKLY

[1]**peal** \ˈpēl\ *n* **1** : the loud ringing of bells **2** : a set of tuned bells **3** : a loud sound or succession of sounds

[2]**peal** *vb* : to give out peals : RESOUND

pea•nut \ˈpē-(ˌ)nət\ *n* **1** : an annual herb related to the pea but having pods that ripen underground; *also* : this pod or one of the edible seeds it bears **2** *pl* : a very small amount

pear \ˈpar\ *n* : the fleshy fruit of a tree related to the apple; *also* : this tree

pearl \ˈpərl\ *n* **1** : a small hard often lustrous body formed within the shell of some mollusks and used as a gem **2** : one that is choice or precious ⟨~*s* of wisdom⟩ **3** : a slightly bluish medium gray color — **pearly** \ˈpər-lē\ *adj*

peas•ant \ˈpez-ᵊnt\ *n* **1** : any of a class of small landowners or laborers tilling the soil **2** : a usu. uneducated person of low social status — **peas•ant•ry** \-ᵊn-trē\ *n*

pea•shoot•er \ˈpē-ˌshü-tər\ *n* : a toy blowgun for shooting peas

peat \ˈpēt\ *n* : a dark substance formed by partial decay of plants (as mosses) in water — **peaty** *adj*

peat moss *n* : SPHAGNUM

[1]**peb•ble** \ˈpe-bəl\ *n* : a small usu. round stone — **pebbly** \-b(ə-)lē\ *adj*

[2]**pebble** *vb* **peb•bled; peb•bling** : to produce a rough surface texture in ⟨~ leather⟩

pec \ˈpek\ *n* : PECTORAL MUSCLE

pe•can \pi-ˈkän, -ˈkan; ˈpē-ˌkan\ *n* : the smooth-shelled edible nut of a large American hickory; *also* : this tree

pec•ca•dil•lo \ˌpe-kə-ˈdi-lō\ *n, pl* **-loes** *or* **-los** : a slight offense

pec•ca•ry \ˈpe-kə-rē\ *n, pl* **-ries** : any of several American chiefly tropical mammals resembling but smaller than the related pigs

peccary

pec•ca•vi \pe-ˈkä-ˌvē\ *n* [L, I have sinned, fr. *peccare* to sin] : an acknowledgment of sin

[1]**peck** \ˈpek\ *n* — see WEIGHT table

[2]**peck** *vb* **1** : to strike or pierce with or as if with the bill **2** : to make (as a hole) by pecking **3** : to pick up with or as if with the bill

[3]**peck** *n* **1** : an impression made by pecking **2** : a quick sharp stroke

pecking order *also* **peck order** *n* : a basic pattern of social organization within a flock of poultry in which each bird pecks another lower in the scale without being pecked in return and submits to pecking by one of higher rank; *also* : a social hierarchy

pec•tin \ˈpek-tən\ *n* : any of various water-soluble plant substances that cause fruit jellies to set — **pec•tic** \-tik\ *adj*

pec•to•ral \ˈpek-tə-rəl\ *adj* : of or relating to the breast or chest

pectoral muscle *n* : either of two muscles on each side of the body which connect the front walls of the chest with the bones of the upper arm and shoulder

pe•cu•liar \pi-ˈkyül-yər\ *adj* [ME *peculier*, fr. L *peculiaris* of private property, special, fr. *peculium* private property, fr. *pecus* cattle] **1** : belonging exclusively to one person or group **2** : CHARACTERISTIC, DISTINCTIVE **3** : QUEER, ODD **syn** idiosyncratic, eccentric, singular, strange, weird — **pe•cu•liar•i-**

ty \-ˌkyül-ˈyar-ə-tē, -ˌkyü-lē-ˈar-\ *n* — **pe•cu•liar•ly** *adv*

pe•cu•ni•ary \pi-ˈkyü-nē-ˌer-ē\ *adj* : of or relating to money : MONETARY

ped•a•gogue *also* **ped•a•gog** \ˈpe-də-ˌgäg\ *n* : TEACHER, SCHOOLMASTER

ped•a•go•gy \ˈpe-də-ˌgō-jē, -ˌgä-\ *n* : the art or profession of teaching; *esp* : EDUCATION 2 — **ped•a•gog•ic** \ˌpe-də-ˈgä-jik, -ˈgō-\ *or* **ped•a•gog•i•cal** \-ji-kəl\ *adj*

[1]**ped•al** \ˈped-ᵊl\ *n* : a lever worked by the foot

[2]**pedal** *adj* : of or relating to the foot

[3]**ped•al** \ˈped-ᵊl\ *vb* **ped•aled** *also* **ped•alled; ped•al•ing** *also* **ped•al•ling 1** : to use or work a pedal (as of a piano or bicycle) **2** : to ride a bicycle

ped•ant \ˈped-ᵊnt\ *n* **1** : a person who makes a show of knowledge **2** : a formal uninspired teacher — **pe•dan•tic** \pi-ˈdan-tik\ *adj* — **ped•ant•ry** \ˈped-ᵊn-trē\ *n*

ped•dle \ˈped-ᵊl\ *vb* **ped•dled; ped•dling** : to sell or offer for sale from place to place — **ped•dler** *also* **ped•lar** \ˈped-lər\ *n*

ped•er•ast \ˈpe-də-ˌrast\ *n* [Gk *paiderastēs,* lit., lover of boys] : one that practices anal intercourse esp. with a boy — **ped•er•as•ty** \ˈpe-də-ˌras-tē\ *n*

ped•es•tal \ˈpe-dəst-ᵊl\ *n* **1** : the support or foot of something (as a column, statue, or vase) that is upright **2** : a position of high regard

[1]**pe•des•tri•an** \pə-ˈdes-trē-ən\ *adj* **1** : ORDINARY **2** : going on foot

[2]**pedestrian** *n* : WALKER

pe•di•at•rics \ˌpē-dē-ˈa-triks\ *n* : a branch of medicine dealing with the development, care, and diseases of children — **pe•di•at•ric** \-trik\ *adj* — **pe•di•a•tri•cian** \ˌpē-dē-ə-ˈtri-shən\ *n*

pedi•cab \ˈpe-di-ˌkab\ *n* : a pedal-driven tricycle with seats for a driver and two passengers

ped•i•cure \ˈpe-di-ˌkyu̇r\ *n* : care of the feet, toes, and nails; *also* : a single treatment of these parts — **ped•i•cur•ist** \-ˌkyu̇r-ist\ *n*

ped•i•gree \ˈpe-də-ˌgrē\ *n* [ME *pedegru,* fr. MF *pie de grue* crane's foot; fr. the shape made by the lines of a genealogical chart] **1** : a record of a line of ancestors **2** : an ancestral line — **ped•i•greed** \-grēd\ *adj*

ped•i•ment \ˈpe-də-mənt\ *n* : a low triangular gablelike decoration (as over a door or window) on a building

pe•dom•e•ter \pi-ˈdä-mə-tər\ *n* : an instrument that measures the distance one walks

pe•dun•cle \ˈpē-ˌdəŋ-kəl\ *n* : a narrow supporting stalk

peek \ˈpēk\ *vb* **1** : to look furtively **2** : to peer from a place of concealment **3** : GLANCE — **peek** *n*

[1]**peel** \ˈpēl\ *vb* [ME *pelen,* fr. MF *peler,* fr. L *pilare* to remove the hair from, fr. *pilus* hair] **1** : to strip the skin, bark, or rind from **2** : to strip off (as a coat); *also* : to come off **3** : to lose the skin, bark, or rind

[2]**peel** *n* : a skin or rind esp. of a fruit

peel•ing \ˈpē-liŋ\ *n* : a peeled-off piece or strip (as of skin or rind)

peen \ˈpēn\ *n* : the usu. hemispherical or wedge-shaped end of the head of a hammer opposite the face

[1]**peep** \ˈpēp\ *vb* : to utter a feeble shrill sound or the slightest sound

[2]**peep** *n* : a feeble shrill sound

[3]**peep** *vb* **1** : to look slyly esp. through an aperture : PEEK **2** : to begin to emerge — **peep•er** *n*

[4]**peep** *n* **1** : a first faint appearance **2** : a brief or furtive look

peep•hole \ˈpēp-ˌhōl\ *n* : a hole to peep through

[1]**peer** \ˈpir\ *n* **1** : one of equal standing with another : EQUAL **2** : NOBLE — **peer•age** \-ij\ *n*

[2]**peer** *vb* **1** : to look intently or curiously **2** : to come slightly into view

peer•ess \ˈpir-əs\ *n* : a woman who is a peer

peer•less \ˈpir-ləs\ *adj* : having no equal : MATCHLESS **syn** supreme, unequalled, unparalleled, incomparable

[1]**peeve** \ˈpēv\ *vb* **peeved; peev•ing** : to make resentful : ANNOY

[2]**peeve** *n* **1** : a feeling or mood of resentment **2** : a particular grievance

pee•vish \ˈpē-vish\ *adj* : querulous in temperament : FRETFUL **syn** irritable, petulant, huffy — **pee•vish•ly** *adv* — **pee•vish•ness** *n*

pee•wee \ˈpē-(ˌ)wē\ *n* : one that is diminutive or tiny

[1]**peg** \ˈpeg\ *n* **1** : a small pointed piece (as of wood) used to pin down or fasten things or to fit into holes **2** : a projecting piece used as a support or boundary marker **3** : SUPPORT, PRETEXT **4** : STEP, DEGREE **5** : THROW

[2]**peg** *vb* **pegged; peg•ging 1** : to put a peg into : fasten, pin down, or attach with or as if with pegs **2** : to work hard and steadily : PLUG **3** : HUSTLE **4** : to mark by pegs **5** : to hold (as prices) at a set level or rate **6** : IDENTIFY **7** : THROW

PEI *abbr* Prince Edward Island

pei•gnoir \pān-ˈwär, pen-\ *n* [F, lit., garment worn while combing the hair, fr. MF, fr. *peigner* to comb the hair, fr. L *pectinare,* fr. *pectin-, pecten* comb] : NEGLIGEE

[1]**pe•jo•ra•tive** \pi-ˈjȯr-ə-tiv\ *n* : a pejorative word or phrase

[2]**pejorative** *adj* : having negative connotations : DISPARAGING — **pe•jo•ra•tive•ly** *adv*

peke \ˈpēk\ *n, often cap* : PEKINGESE

Pe•king•ese *or* **Pe•kin•ese** \ˌpē-kə-ˈnēz, -ˈnēs; -kiŋ-ˈēz, -ˈēs\ *n, pl* **Pekingese** *or* **Pekinese** : any of a breed of Chinese origin of small short-legged long-haired dogs

pe•koe \ˈpē-(ˌ)kō\ *n* : a black tea made from young tea leaves

pel•age \ˈpe-lij\ *n* : the hairy covering of a mammal

pe•lag•ic \pə-ˈla-jik\ *adj* : OCEANIC

pelf \ˈpelf\ *n* : MONEY, RICHES

pel•i•can \ˈpe-li-kən\ *n* : any of a genus of large web-footed birds having a pouched lower bill used to scoop in fish

pel•la•gra \pə-ˈla-grə, -ˈlā-\ *n* : a disease caused by a diet with too little nicotinic acid and protein and marked by a skin rash, disease of the digestive system, and nervous symptoms

pel•let \ˈpe-lət\ *n* **1** : a little ball (as of medicine) **2** : BULLET — **pel•let•al** \-lə-təl\ *adj* — **pel•let•ize** \-ˌtīz\ *vb*

pell–mell \ˌpel-ˈmel\ *adv* **1** : in mingled confusion **2** : HEADLONG

pel•lu•cid \pə-ˈlü-səd\ *adj* : extremely clear : LIMPID, TRANSPARENT **syn** translucent, lucid, lucent

[1]**pelt** \ˈpelt\ *n* : a skin esp. of a fur-bearing animal

[2]**pelt** *vb* : to strike with a succession of blows or missiles

pel•vis \ˈpel-vəs\ *n, pl* **pel•vis•es** \-və-səz\ *or* **pel•ves** \-ˌvēz\ : a basin-shaped part of the vertebrate skeleton consisting of the large bone of each hip and the nearby bones of the spine — **pel•vic** \-vik\ *adj*

pem•mi•can *also* **pem•i•can** \ˈpe-mi-kən\ *n* : dried meat pounded fine and mixed with melted fat

[1]**pen** \ˈpen\ *vb* **penned; pen•ning** : to shut in or as if in a pen

[2]**pen** *n* **1** : a small enclosure for animals **2** : a small place of confinement or storage

[3]**pen** *n* **1** : an implement for writing or drawing with ink or a similar fluid **2** : a writing instrument regarded as a means of expression

[4]**pen** *vb* **penned; pen•ning** : WRITE

[5]**pen** *n* : PENITENTIARY

[6]**pen** *abbr* peninsula

PEN *abbr* International Association of Poets, Playwrights, Editors, Essayists and Novelists

pe•nal \ˈpēn-ᵊl\ *adj* : of or relating to punishment

pe•nal•ise *Brit var of* PENALIZE

pe•nal•ize \ˈpēn-ᵊl-ˌīz, ˈpen-\ *vb* **-ized; -iz•ing** : to put a penalty on

pen•al•ty \ˈpen-ᵊl-tē\ *n, pl* **-ties 1** : punishment for crime or offense **2** : something forfeited when a person fails to do something agreed to **3** : disadvantage, loss, or hardship due to some action

pen·ance \ˈpe-nəns\ *n* **1** : an act performed to show sorrow or repentance for sin **2** : a sacrament (as in the Roman Catholic Church) consisting of confession, absolution, and a penance directed by the confessor
pence \ˈpens\ *pl of* PENNY
pen·chant \ˈpen-chənt\ *n* [F, fr. prp. of *pencher* to incline, fr. (assumed) VL *pendicare,* fr. L *pendere* to weigh] : a strong inclination : LIKING **syn** leaning, propensity, predilection, predisposition
¹pen·cil \ˈpen-səl\ *n* : a writing or drawing tool consisting of or containing a slender cylinder of a solid marking substance
²pencil *vb* **-ciled** *or* **-cilled; -cil·ing** *or* **-cil·ling** : to draw or write with a pencil
pen·dant *also* **pen·dent** \ˈpen-dənt\ *n* : a hanging ornament (as an earring)
pen·dent *or* **pen·dant** \ˈpen-dənt\ *adj* : SUSPENDED, OVERHANGING
¹pend·ing \ˈpen-diŋ\ *prep* **1** : DURING **2** : while awaiting
²pending *adj* **1** : not yet decided **2** : IMMINENT
pen·du·lous \ˈpen-jə-ləs, -də-\ *adj* : hanging loosely : DROOPING
pen·du·lum \-ləm\ *n* : a body that swings freely from a fixed point
pe·ne·plain *also* **pe·ne·plane** \ˈpē-ni-ˌplān\ *n* : a large almost flat land surface shaped by erosion
pen·e·trate \ˈpe-nə-ˌtrāt\ *vb* **-trat·ed; -trat·ing 1** : to enter into : PIERCE **2** : PERMEATE **3** : to see into : UNDERSTAND **4** : to affect deeply — **pen·e·tra·ble** \-trə-bəl\ *adj* — **pen·e·tra·tion** \ˌpe-nə-ˈtrā-shən\ *n* — **pen·e·tra·tive** \ˈpe-nə-ˌtrā-tiv\ *adj*
pen·e·trat·ing *adj* **1** : having the power of entering, piercing, or pervading ⟨a ~ shriek⟩ ⟨a ~ odor⟩ **2** : ACUTE, DISCERNING ⟨a ~ look⟩
pen·guin \ˈpen-gwən, ˈpeŋ-\ *n* : any of various erect short-legged flightless seabirds of the southern hemisphere
pen·i·cil·lin \ˌpe-nə-ˈsi-lən\ *n* : any of several antibiotics produced by molds or synthetically and used against various bacteria
pen·in·su·la \pə-ˈnin-sə-lə\ *n* [L *paeninsula,* fr. *paene* almost + *insula* island] : a long narrow portion of land extending out into the water — **pen·in·su·lar** \-lər\ *adj*
pe·nis \ˈpē-nəs\ *n, pl* **pe·nes** \-ˌnēz\ *or* **pe·nis·es** : a male organ of copulation that in the human male also functions as the channel by which urine leaves the body
¹pen·i·tent \ˈpe-nə-tənt\ *adj* : feeling sorrow for sins or offenses : REPENTANT — **pen·i·tence** \-təns\ *n* — **pen·i·ten·tial** \ˌpe-nə-ˈten-chəl\ *adj*
²penitent *n* : a penitent person
¹pen·i·ten·tia·ry \ˌpe-nə-ˈten-chə-rē\ *n, pl* **-ries** : a state or federal prison
²penitentiary *adj* : of, relating to, or incurring confinement in a penitentiary
pen·knife \ˈpen-ˌnīf\ *n* : a small pocketknife
pen·light *or* **pen·lite** \-ˌlīt\ *n* : a small flashlight resembling a fountain pen in size or shape
pen·man \ˈpen-mən\ *n* **1** : COPYIST **2** : one skilled in penmanship **3** : AUTHOR
pen·man·ship \-ˌship\ *n* : the art or practice of writing with the pen
Penn *or* **Penna** *abbr* Pennsylvania
pen name *n* : an author's pseudonym
pen·nant \ˈpe-nənt\ *n* **1** : a tapering flag used esp. for signaling **2** : a flag symbolic of championship
pen·ni \ˈpe-nē\ *n, pl* **pen·nia** \-nē-ə\ *or* **pen·nis** \-nēz\ — see *markka* at MONEY table
pen·non \ˈpe-nən\ *n* **1** : a long narrow ribbonlike flag borne on a lance **2** : WING
Penn·syl·va·nian \ˌpen-səl-ˈvā-nyən\ *adj* : of, relating to, or being the period of the Paleozoic era between the Mississippian and the Permian — **Pennsylvanian** *n*
pen·ny \ˈpe-nē\ *n, pl* **pennies** \-nēz\ *or* **pence** \ˈpens\ **1** : a British monetary unit formerly equal to 1/12 shilling but now equal to 1/100 pound; *also* : a coin of this value — see *pound* at MONEY table **2** *pl* **pennies** : a cent of the U.S. or Canada — **pen·ni·less** \ˈpe-ni-ləs\ *adj*
pen·ny–pinch·ing \ˈpe-nē-ˌpin-chiŋ\ *n* : PARSIMONY — **pen·ny–pinch·er** *n* — **penny–pinching** *adj*
pen·ny·weight \-ˌwāt\ *n* — see WEIGHT table
pen·ny–wise \-ˌwīz\ *adj* : wise or prudent only in small matters
pe·nol·o·gy \pi-ˈnä-lə-jē\ *n* : a branch of criminology dealing with prisons and the treatment of offenders
¹pen·sion \ˈpen-chən\ *n* : a fixed sum paid regularly esp. to a person retired from service
²pension *vb* : to pay a pension to — **pen·sion·er** *n*
pen·sive \ˈpen-siv\ *adj* : musingly, dreamily, or sadly thoughtful **syn** reflective, speculative, contemplative, meditative — **pen·sive·ly** *adv*
pen·stock \ˈpen-ˌstäk\ *n* **1** : a sluice or gate for regulating a flow **2** : a pipe for carrying water
pent \ˈpent\ *adj* : shut up : CONFINED
pen·ta·gon \ˈpen-tə-ˌgän\ *n* : a polygon of five angles and five sides — **pen·tag·o·nal** \pen-ˈta-gən-əl\ *adj*
pen·tam·e·ter \pen-ˈta-mə-tər\ *n* : a line of verse containing five metrical feet
Pen·te·cost \ˈpen-ti-ˌkȯst\ *n* : the 7th Sunday after Easter observed as a church festival commemorating the descent of the Holy Spirit on the apostles — **Pen·te·cos·tal** \ˌpen-ti-ˈkäst-əl\ *adj*
Pentecostal *n* : a member of a Christian religious body that stresses expressive worship, evangelism, and spiritual gifts — **Pen·te·cos·tal·ism** \ˌpen-ti-ˈkäst-əl-ˌi-zəm\ *n*
pent·house \ˈpent-ˌhau̇s\ *n* [alter. of ME *pentis,* fr. MF *appentiz,* fr. *apent,* pp. of *apendre* to attach, hang against] **1** : a shed or sloping roof attached to a wall or building **2** : an apartment built on the roof of a building
pen·ul·ti·mate \pi-ˈnəl-tə-mət\ *adj* : next to the last ⟨~ syllable⟩
pen·um·bra \pə-ˈnəm-brə\ *n, pl* **-brae** \-(ˌ)brē\ *or* **-bras** : the partial shadow surrounding a complete shadow (as in an eclipse)
pe·nu·ri·ous \pə-ˈnu̇r-ē-əs, -ˈnyu̇r-\ *adj* **1** : marked by penury **2** : MISERLY **syn** stingy, close, tightfisted, parsimonious
pen·u·ry \ˈpe-nyə-rē\ *n* **1** : extreme poverty **2** : extreme frugality
pe·on \ˈpē-ˌän, -ən\ *n, pl* **peons** *or* **pe·o·nes** \pā-ˈō-nēz\ **1** : a member of the landless laboring class in Spanish America **2** : one bound to service for payment of a debt — **pe·on·age** \-ə-nij\ *n*
pe·o·ny \ˈpē-ə-nē\ *n, pl* **-nies** : any of a genus of chiefly Eurasian plants with large often double red, pink, or white flowers; *also* : the flower
¹peo·ple \ˈpē-pəl\ *n, pl* **people** [ME *peple,* fr. OF *peuple,* fr. L *populus*] **1** *pl* : human beings making up a group or linked by a common characteristic or interest **2** *pl* : human beings — often used in compounds instead of *persons* ⟨sales*people*⟩ **3** *pl* : the mass of persons in a community : POPULACE; *also* : ELECTORATE ⟨the ~'*s* choice⟩ **4** *pl* **peoples** : a body of persons (as a tribe, nation, or race) united by a common culture, sense of kinship, or political organization
²people *vb* **peo·pled; peo·pling** : to supply or fill with or as if with people
¹pep \ˈpep\ *n* : brisk energy or initiative — **pep·py** *adj*
²pep *vb* **pepped; pep·ping** : to put pep into : STIMULATE
¹pep·per \ˈpe-pər\ *n* **1** : either of two pungent condiments from the berry (**pep·per·corn** \-ˌkȯrn\) of an East Indian climbing plant; *also* : this plant **2** : a plant related to the tomato and widely grown for its hot or mild sweet fruit; *also* : this fruit
²pepper *vb* **pep·pered; pep·per·ing 1** : to sprinkle or season with or as if with pepper **2** : to shower with missiles or rapid blows
pep·per·mint \-ˌmint, -mənt\ *n* : a pungent aromatic mint; *also* : candy flavored with its oil

pep·per·o·ni \ˌpe-pə-ˈrō-nē\ *n* : a highly seasoned beef and pork sausage

pep·pery \ˈpe-pə-rē\ *adj* **1** : having the qualities of pepper : PUNGENT, HOT **2** : having a hot temper **3** : FIERY

pep·sin \ˈpep-sən\ *n* : an enzyme of the stomach that promotes digestion by breaking down proteins; *also* : a preparation of this used medicinally

pep·tic \ˈpep-tik\ *adj* **1** : relating to or promoting digestion **2** : caused by digestive juices ⟨a ~ ulcer⟩

Pe·quot \ˈpē-ˌkwät\ *n* : a member of an American Indian people of eastern Connecticut

[1]**per** \ˈpər\ *prep* **1** : by means of **2** : to or for each **3** : ACCORDING TO

[2]**per** *adv* : for each : APIECE

[3]**per** *abbr* **1** period **2** person

[1]**per·ad·ven·ture** \ˈpər-əd-ˌven-chər\ *adv, archaic* : PERHAPS

[2]**peradventure** *n* **1** : DOUBT **2** : CHANCE 4

per·am·bu·late \pə-ˈram-byə-ˌlāt\ *vb* **-lat·ed; -lat·ing** : to travel over esp. on foot — **per·am·bu·la·tion** \-ˌram-byə-ˈlā-shən\ *n*

per·am·bu·la·tor \pə-ˈram-byə-ˌlā-tər\ *n, chiefly Brit* : a baby carriage

per an·num \(ˌ)pər-ˈa-nəm\ *adv* [ML] : in or for each year : ANNUALLY

per·cale \(ˌ)pər-ˈkāl, ˈpər-ˌ; (ˌ)pər-ˈkal\ *n* : a fine woven cotton cloth

per cap·i·ta \(ˌ)pər-ˈka-pə-tə\ *adv or adj* [ML, by heads] : by or for each person

per·ceive \pər-ˈsēv\ *vb* **per·ceived; per·ceiv·ing** **1** : to attain awareness : REALIZE **2** : to become aware of through the senses — **per·ceiv·able** *adj*

[1]**per·cent** \pər-ˈsent\ *adv* [*per* + L *centum* hundred] : in each hundred

[2]**percent** *n, pl* **percent** *or* **percents** **1** : one part in a hundred : HUNDREDTH **2** : PERCENTAGE

per·cent·age \pər-ˈsen-tij\ *n* **1** : a part of a whole expressed in hundredths **2** : the result obtained by multiplying a number by a percent **3** : ADVANTAGE, PROFIT **4** : PROBABILITY; *also* : favorable odds

per·cen·tile \pər-ˈsen-ˌtīl\ *n* : a value on a scale of one hundred indicating the standing of a score or grade in terms of the percentage of scores or grades falling with or below it

per·cept \ˈpər-ˌsept\ *n* : an impression of an object obtained by use of the senses

per·cep·ti·ble \pər-ˈsep-tə-bəl\ *adj* : capable of being perceived — **per·cep·ti·bly** \-blē\ *adv*

per·cep·tion \pər-ˈsep-shən\ *n* **1** : an act or result of perceiving **2** : awareness of one's environment through physical sensation **3** : ability to understand : INSIGHT, COMPREHENSION **syn** penetration, discernment, discrimination

per·cep·tive \pər-ˈsep-tiv\ *adj* : capable of or exhibiting keen perception : OBSERVANT — **per·cep·tive·ly** *adv*

per·cep·tu·al \pər-ˈsep-chə-wəl\ *adj* : of, relating to, or involving sensory stimulus as opposed to abstract concept — **per·cep·tu·al·ly** *adv*

[1]**perch** \ˈpərch\ *n* **1** : a roost for a bird **2** : a high station or vantage point

[2]**perch** *vb* : ROOST

[3]**perch** *n, pl* **perch** *or* **perch·es** : either of two small freshwater bony fishes used for food; *also* : any of various fishes resembling or related to these

per·chance \pər-ˈchans\ *adv* : PERHAPS

per·cip·i·ent \pər-ˈsi-pē-ənt\ *adj* : capable of or characterized by perception — **per·cip·i·ence** \-əns\ *n*

per·co·late \ˈpər-kə-ˌlāt\ *vb* **-lat·ed; -lat·ing** **1** : to trickle or filter through a permeable substance **2** : to filter hot water through to extract the essence ⟨~ coffee⟩ — **per·co·la·tor** \-ˌlā-tər\ *n*

per con·tra \(ˌ)pər-ˈkän-trə\ *adv* [It, by the opposite side (of the ledger)] **1** : on the contrary **2** : by way of contrast

per·cus·sion \pər-ˈkə-shən\ *n* **1** : a sharp blow : IMPACT; *esp* : a blow upon a cap (**percussion cap**) designed to explode the charge in a firearm **2** : the beating or striking of a musical instrument; *also* : instruments sounded by striking, shaking, or scraping

per di·em \pər-ˈdē-əm, -ˈdī-\ *adv* [ML] : by the day — **per diem** *adj or n*

per·di·tion \pər-ˈdi-shən\ *n* **1** : eternal damnation **2** : HELL

per·du·ra·ble \(ˌ)pər-ˈdu̇r-ə-bəl, -ˈdyu̇r-\ *adj* : very durable — **per·du·ra·bil·i·ty** \-ˌdu̇r-ə-ˈbi-lə-tē, -ˌdyu̇r-\ *n*

per·e·gri·na·tion \ˌper-ə-grə-ˈnā-shən\ *n* : a traveling about esp. on foot

per·e·grine \ˈper-ə-grən, -grēn\ *n* : a swift nearly cosmopolitan falcon that often nests in cities and is used in falconry

pe·remp·to·ry \pə-ˈremp-tə-rē\ *adj* **1** : barring a right of action or delay **2** : expressive of urgency or command : IMPERATIVE **3** : marked by arrogant self-assurance **syn** imperious, masterful, domineering, magisterial — **pe·remp·to·ri·ly** \-tə-rə-lē\ *adv*

[1]**pe·ren·ni·al** \pə-ˈre-nē-əl\ *adj* **1** : present at all seasons of the year ⟨~ streams⟩ **2** : continuing to live from year to year ⟨~ plants⟩ **3** : recurring regularly : PERMANENT ⟨~ problems⟩ **syn** lasting, perpetual, enduring, everlasting — **pe·ren·ni·al·ly** *adv*

[2]**perennial** *n* : a perennial plant

perf *abbr* **1** perfect **2** perforated

[1]**per·fect** \ˈpər-fikt\ *adj* **1** : being without fault or defect **2** : EXACT, PRECISE **3** : COMPLETE **4** : relating to or being a verb tense that expresses an action or state completed at the time of speaking or at a time spoken of — **per·fect·ly** *adv* — **per·fect·ness** *n*

[2]**per·fect** \pər-ˈfekt\ *vb* : to make perfect

[3]**per·fect** \ˈpər-fikt\ *n* : the perfect tense; *also* : a verb form in it

per·fect·ible \pər-ˈfek-tə-bəl, ˈpər-fik-\ *adj* : capable of improvement or perfection — **per·fect·ibil·i·ty** \pər-ˌfek-tə-ˈbi-lə-tē, ˌpər-fik-\ *n*

per·fec·tion \pər-ˈfek-shən\ *n* **1** : the quality or state of being perfect **2** : the highest degree of excellence **3** : the act or process of perfecting

per·fec·tion·ist \-shə-nist\ *n* : a person who will not accept or be content with anything less than perfection

per·fec·to \pər-ˈfek-tō\ *n, pl* **-tos** : a cigar that is thick in the middle and tapers almost to a point at each end

per·fi·dy \ˈpər-fə-dē\ *n, pl* **-dies** [L *perfidia*, fr. *perfidus* faithless, fr. *per-* detrimental to + *fides* faith] : violation of faith or loyalty : TREACHERY — **per·fid·i·ous** \pər-ˈfi-dē-əs\ *adj* — **per·fid·i·ous·ly** *adv*

per·fo·rate \ˈpər-fə-ˌrāt\ *vb* **-rat·ed; -rat·ing** : to bore through : PIERCE; *esp* : to make a line of holes in to facilitate separation — **per·fo·ra·tion** \ˌpər-fə-ˈrā-shən\ *n*

per·force \pər-ˈfōrs\ *adv* : of necessity

per·form \pər-ˈfȯrm\ *vb* **1** : FULFILL **2** : CARRY OUT, DO **3** : FUNCTION **4** : to do in a set manner **5** : to give a performance — **per·form·er** *n*

per·for·mance \pər-ˈfȯr-ˌməns\ *n* **1** : the act or process of performing **2** : DEED, FEAT **3** : a public presentation

[1]**per·fume** \pər-ˈfyüm, ˈpər-ˌfyüm\ *n* **1** : a usu. pleasant odor : FRAGRANCE **2** : a preparation used for scenting

[2]**per·fume** \pər-ˈfyüm, ˈpər-ˌfyüm\ *vb* **per·fumed; per·fum·ing** : SCENT

per·fum·ery \ˌpər-ˈfyü-mə-rē\ *n* : PERFUMES

per·func·to·ry \pər-ˈfəŋk-tə-rē\ *adj* : done merely as a duty — **per·func·to·ri·ly** *adv*

per·go·la \ˈpər-gə-lə\ *n* [It] : a structure consisting of posts supporting an open roof in the form of a trellis

perh *abbr* perhaps

per·haps \pər-ˈhaps\ *adv* : possibly but not certainly

per·i·gee \ˈper-ə-ˌjē\ *n* [MF, fr. NL *perigeum*, fr. Gk *perigeion*, fr. *peri* around, near + *gē* earth] : the point at which an orbiting object is nearest the body (as the earth) being orbited

peri·he·lion \ˌper-ə-ˈhēl-yən\ *n, pl* **-he·lia** \-ˈhēl-yə\ : the point in the path of a celestial body (as a planet) that is nearest to the sun

per·il \ˈper-əl\ *n* : DANGER; *also* : a source of danger : RISK — **per·il·ous** *adj* — **per·il·ous·ly** *adv*

pe·rim·e·ter \pə-ˈri-mə-tər\ *n* **1** : the boundary of a closed plane figure; *also* : its length **2** : a line bounding or protecting an area

¹pe·ri·od \ˈpir-ē-əd\ *n* **1** : SENTENCE; *also* : the full pause closing the utterance of a sentence **2** : END, STOP **3** : a punctuation mark . used esp. to mark the end of a declarative sentence or an abbreviation **4** : an extent of time; *esp* : one regarded as a stage or division in a process or development **5** : a portion of time in which a recurring phenomenon completes one cycle and is ready to begin again **6** : a single cyclic occurrence of menstruation

²period *adj* : of or relating to a particular historical period ⟨~ furniture⟩

pe·ri·od·ic \ˌpir-ē-ˈä-dik\ *adj* **1** : occurring at regular intervals of time **2** : happening repeatedly **3** : of or relating to a sentence that has no trailing elements following full grammatical statement of the essential idea

¹pe·ri·od·i·cal \ˌpir-ē-ˈä-di-kəl\ *adj* **1** : PERIODIC **2** : published at regular intervals **3** : of or relating to a periodical — **pe·ri·od·i·cal·ly** \-k(ə-)lē\ *adv*

²periodical *n* : a periodical publication

periodic table *n* : an arrangement of chemical elements based on their atomic structure and on their properties

peri·odon·tal \ˌper-ē-ō-ˈdänt-ᵊl\ *adj* **1** : surrounding a tooth **2** : of or affecting periodontal tissues or regions ⟨~ disease⟩

per·i·pa·tet·ic \ˌper-ə-pə-ˈte-tik\ *adj* : performed or performing while moving about : ITINERANT

pe·riph·er·al \pə-ˈri-fər-əl\ *n* : a device connected to a computer to provide communication or auxiliary functions

peripheral nervous system *n* : the part of the nervous system that is outside the central nervous system and comprises the spinal nerves, the cranial nerves except the one supplying the retina, and the autonomic nervous system

pe·riph·ery \pə-ˈri-fə-rē\ *n, pl* **-er·ies** **1** : the boundary of a rounded figure **2** : outward bounds : border area — **pe·riph·er·al** \-fə-rəl\ *adj*

pe·riph·ra·sis \pə-ˈri-frə-səs\ *n, pl* **-ra·ses** \-ˌsēz\ : CIRCUMLOCUTION

peri·scope \ˈper-ə-ˌskōp\ *n* : a tubular optical instrument enabling an observer to see an otherwise blocked field of view

per·ish \ˈper-ish\ *vb* : to become destroyed or ruined : DIE

per·ish·able \ˈper-i-shə-bəl\ *adj* : easily spoiled ⟨~ foods⟩ — **perishable** *n*

peri·stal·sis \ˌper-ə-ˈstȯl-səs, -ˈstal-\ *n, pl* **-stal·ses** : waves of contraction passing along the walls of a hollow muscular organ and esp. the intestine and forcing its contents onward — **per·i·stal·tic** \-ˈstȯl-tik, -ˈstal-\ *adj*

peri·style \ˈper-ə-ˌstīl\ *n* : a row of columns surrounding a building or court

peri·to·ne·um \ˌper-ə-tə-ˈnē-əm\ *n, pl* **-ne·ums** *or* **-nea** : the smooth transparent serous membrane that lines the cavity of the abdomen — **peri·to·ne·al** \-ˈnē-əl\ *adj*

peri·to·ni·tis \ˌper-ə-tə-ˈnī-təs\ *n* : inflammation of the peritoneum

peri·wig \ˈper-i-ˌwig\ *n* : WIG

¹per·i·win·kle \ˈper-i-ˌwiŋ-kəl\ *n* : a usu. blue-flowered creeping plant cultivated as a ground cover

²periwinkle *n* : any of various small edible seashore snails

per·ju·ry \ˈpər-jə-rē\ *n* : the voluntary violation of an oath to tell the truth : lying under oath — **per·jure** \ˈpər-jər\ *vb* — **per·jur·er** *n*

¹perk \ˈpərk\ *vb* **1** : to thrust (as the head) up impudently or jauntily **2** : to regain vigor or spirit **3** : to make trim or brisk : FRESHEN — **perky** *adj*

²perk *vb* : PERCOLATE

³perk *n* : PERQUISITE — usu. used in pl.

per·lite \ˈpər-ˌlīt\ *n* : volcanic glass that when expanded by heat forms a lightweight material used esp. in concrete and plaster and for potting plants

¹perm \ˈpərm\ *n* : PERMANENT

²perm *vb* : to give (hair) a permanent

³perm *abbr* permanent

per·ma·frost \ˈpər-mə-ˌfrȯst\ *n* : a permanently frozen layer below the surface in frigid regions of a planet

¹per·ma·nent \ˈpər-mə-nənt\ *adj* : LASTING, STABLE — **per·ma·nence** \-nəns\ *n* — **per·ma·nen·cy** \-nən-sē\ *n* — **per·ma·nent·ly** *adv*

²permanent *n* : a long-lasting hair wave or straightening

permanent press *n* : the process of treating fabrics with chemicals (as resin) and heat for setting the shape and for aiding wrinkle resistance

per·me·able \ˈpər-mē-ə-bəl\ *adj* : having small openings that permit liquids or gases to seep through — **per·me·a·bil·i·ty** \ˌpər-mē-ə-ˈbi-lə-tē\ *n*

per·me·ate \ˈpər-mē-ˌāt\ *vb* **-at·ed; -at·ing** **1** : PERVADE **2** : to seep through the pores of : PENETRATE — **per·me·ation** \ˌpər-mē-ˈā-shən\ *n*

Perm·ian \ˈpər-mē-ən\ *adj* : of, relating to, or being the latest period of the Paleozoic era — **Permian** *n*

per·mis·si·ble \pər-ˈmi-sə-bəl\ *adj* : that may be permitted : ALLOWABLE

per·mis·sion \pər-ˈmi-shən\ *n* : formal consent : AUTHORIZATION

per·mis·sive \pər-ˈmi-siv\ *adj* : granting permission; *esp* : INDULGENT — **per·mis·sive·ly** *adv* — **per·mis·sive·ness** *n*

¹per·mit \pər-ˈmit\ *vb* **per·mit·ted; per·mit·ting** **1** : to consent to : ALLOW **2** : to make possible

²per·mit \ˈpər-ˌmit, pər-ˈmit\ *n* : a written permission : LICENSE

per·mu·ta·tion \ˌpər-myu̇-ˈtā-shən\ *n* **1** : a major or fundamental change **2** : the act or process of changing the order of an ordered set of objects **syn** innovation, mutation, vicissitude

per·ni·cious \pər-ˈni-shəs\ *adj* [ME, fr. MF *pernicieus*, fr. L *perniciosus*, fr. *pernicies* destruction, fr. *per-* through + *nec-, nex* violent death] : very destructive or injurious — **per·ni·cious·ly** *adv*

per·ora·tion \ˈper-ə-ˌrā-shən, ˈpər-\ *n* : the concluding part of a speech

¹per·ox·ide \pə-ˈräk-ˌsīd\ *n* : an oxide containing a large proportion of oxygen; *esp* : HYDROGEN PEROXIDE

²peroxide *vb* **-id·ed; -id·ing** : to bleach with hydrogen peroxide

perp *abbr* **1** perpendicular **2** perpetrator

per·pen·dic·u·lar \ˌpər-pən-ˈdi-kyə-lər\ *adj* **1** : standing at right angles to the plane of the horizon **2** : forming a right angle with each other or with a given line or plane — **perpendicular** *n* — **per·pen·dic·u·lar·i·ty** \-ˌdi-kyə-ˈlar-ə-tē\ *n* — **per·pen·dic·u·lar·ly** *adv*

per·pe·trate \ˈpər-pə-ˌtrāt\ *vb* **-trat·ed; -trat·ing** : to be guilty of : COMMIT — **per·pe·tra·tion** \ˌpər-pə-ˈtrā-shən\ *n* — **per·pe·tra·tor** \ˈpər-pə-ˌtrā-tər\ *n*

per·pet·u·al \pər-ˈpe-chə-wəl\ *adj* **1** : continuing forever : EVERLASTING **2** : occurring continually : CONSTANT ⟨~ annoyance⟩ **syn** ceaseless, unceasing, continual, continuous, incessant, unremitting — **per·pet·u·al·ly** *adv*

per·pet·u·ate \pər-ˈpe-chə-ˌwāt\ *vb* **-at·ed; -at·ing** : to make perpetual : cause to last indefinitely — **per·pet·u·a·tion** \-ˌpe-chə-ˈwā-shən\ *n*

per·pe·tu·i·ty \ˌpər-pə-ˈtü-ə-tē, -ˈtyü-\ *n, pl* **-ties** **1** : ETERNITY 1 **2** : the quality or state of being perpetual

per·plex \pər-ˈpleks\ *vb* : to disturb mentally; *esp* : CONFUSE — **per·plex·i·ty** \-ˈplek-sə-tē\ *n*

per·plexed \-ˈplekst\ *adj* **1** : filled with uncertainty : PUZZLED **2** : full of difficulty : COMPLICATED — **per·plexed·ly** \-ˈplek-səd-lē\ *adv*

per·qui·site \ˈpər-kwə-zət\ *n* : a privilege or profit beyond regular pay

pers *abbr* person; personal

per se \(ˌ)pər-ˈsā\ *adv* [L] : by, of, or in itself : as such

per·se·cute \ˈpər-si-ˌkyüt\ *vb* **-cut·ed; -cut·ing** : to pursue in such a way as to injure or afflict : HARASS; *esp* : to cause to suffer because of belief — **per·se·cu·tion** \ˌpər-si-ˈkyü-shən\ *n* — **per·se·cu·tor** \ˈpər-si-ˌkyü-tər\ *n*

per·se·vere \ˌpər-sə-ˈvir\ *vb* **-vered; -ver·ing** : to persist (as in an undertaking) in spite of difficulties — **per·se·ver·ance** \-ˈvir-əns\ *n*

Per·sian \ˈpər-zhən\ *n* **1** : a native or inhabitant of ancient Persia **2** : a member of one of the peoples of modern Iran **3** : the language of the Persians

Persian cat *n* : any of a breed of stocky round-headed domestic cats that have a long silky coat

Persian lamb *n* : a pelt that is obtained from lambs that are older than those yielding broadtail and that has very silky tightly curled fur

per·si·flage \ˈpər-si-ˌfläzh, ˈper-\ *n* [F, fr. *persifler* to banter, fr. *per-* thoroughly + *siffler* to whistle, hiss, boo, ultim. fr. L *sibilare*] : lightly jesting or mocking talk

per·sim·mon \pər-ˈsi-mən\ *n* : either of two trees related to the ebony; *also* : the edible orange-red plum-like fruit of a persimmon

per·sist \pər-ˈsist, -ˈzist\ *vb* **1** : to go on resolutely or stubbornly in spite of difficulties **2** : to continue to exist — **per·sis·tence** \-ˈsis-təns, -ˈzis-\ *n* — **per·sis·ten·cy** \-tən-sē\ *n* — **per·sis·tent** \-tənt\ *adj* — **per·sis·tent·ly** *adv*

per·snick·e·ty \pər-ˈsni-kə-tē\ *adj* : fussy about small details

per·son \ˈpər-sən\ *n* [ME, fr. OF *persone*, fr. L *persona* actor's mask, character in a play, person, prob. fr. Etruscan *phersu* mask, fr. Gk *prosōpa*, pl. of *prosōpon* face, mask] **1** : a human being : INDIVIDUAL — used in combination esp. by those who prefer to avoid *man* in compounds applicable to both sexes ⟨chair*person*⟩ **2** : one of the three modes of being in the Godhead as understood by Trinitarians **3** : the body of a human being **4** : the individual personality of a human being : SELF **5** : reference of a segment of discourse to the speaker, to one spoken to, or to one spoken of esp. as indicated by certain pronouns

per·son·able \ˈpər-sə-nə-bəl\ *adj* : pleasant in person : ATTRACTIVE

per·son·age \ˈpər-sə-nij\ *n* : a person of rank, note, or distinction

[1]**per·son·al** \ˈpər-sə-nəl\ *adj* **1** : of, relating to, or affecting a person : PRIVATE ⟨~ correspondence⟩ **2** : done in person ⟨a ~ inquiry⟩ **3** : relating to the person or body ⟨~ injuries⟩ **4** : relating to an individual esp. in an offensive way ⟨resented such ~ remarks⟩ **5** : of or relating to temporary or movable property as distinguished from real estate **6** : denoting grammatical person

[2]**personal** *n* **1** : a short newspaper paragraph relating to a person or group or to personal matters **2** : a short personal or private communication in the classified ads section of a newspaper

personal computer *n* : MICROCOMPUTER

per·son·al·ise *Brit var of* PERSONALIZE

per·son·al·i·ty \ˌpər-sə-ˈna-lə-tē\ *n, pl* **-ties 1** : an offensively personal remark ⟨indulges in *personalities*⟩ **2** : the collection of emotional and behavioral traits that characterize a person **3** : distinction of personal and social traits **4** : a well-known person ⟨a TV ~⟩ **syn** individuality, temperament, disposition, makeup

per·son·al·ize \ˈpər-sə-nə-ˌlīz\ *vb* **-ized; -iz·ing** : to make personal or individual; *esp* : to mark as belonging to a particular person

per·son·al·ly \-nə-lē\ *adv* **1** : in person **2** : as a person **3** : as far as oneself is concerned

per·son·al·ty \ˈpər-sə-nəl-tē\ *n, pl* **-ties** : personal property

per·so·na non gra·ta \pər-ˈsō-nə-ˌnän-ˈgra-tə, -ˈgrä-\ *adj* [L] : being personally unacceptable or unwelcome

per·son·ate \ˈpər-sə-ˌnāt\ *vb* **-at·ed; -at·ing** : IMPERSONATE, REPRESENT

per·son·i·fy \pər-ˈsä-nə-ˌfī\ *vb* **-fied; -fy·ing 1** : to think of or represent as a person **2** : to be the embodiment of : INCARNATE ⟨~ the law⟩ — **per·son·i·fi·ca·tion** \-ˌsä-nə-fə-ˈkā-shən\ *n*

per·son·nel \ˌpər-sə-ˈnel\ *n* : a body of persons employed

per·spec·tive \pər-ˈspek-tiv\ *n* **1** : the science of painting and drawing so that objects represented have apparent depth and distance **2** : the aspect in which a subject or its parts are mentally viewed; *esp* : a view of things (as objects or events) in their true relationship or relative importance

per·spi·ca·cious \ˌpər-spə-ˈkā-shəs\ *adj* : having or showing keen understanding or discernment — **per·spi·cac·i·ty** \-ˈka-sə-tē\ *n*

per·spic·u·ous \pər-ˈspi-kyə-wəs\ *adj* : plain to the understanding — **per·spi·cu·i·ty** \ˌpər-spə-ˈkyü-ə-tē\ *n*

per·spire \pər-ˈspīr\ *vb* **per·spired; per·spir·ing** : SWEAT — **per·spi·ra·tion** \ˌpər-spə-ˈrā-shən\ *n*

per·suade \pər-ˈswād\ *vb* **per·suad·ed; per·suad·ing** : to win over to a belief or course of action by argument or entreaty — **per·sua·sive** \-ˈswā-siv, -ziv\ *adj* — **per·sua·sive·ly** *adv* — **per·sua·sive·ness** *n*

per·sua·sion \pər-ˈswā-zhən\ *n* **1** : the act or process of persuading **2** : a system of religious beliefs; *also* : a group holding such beliefs

[1]**pert** \ˈpərt\ *adj* [ME, open, bold, pert, modif. of OF *apert*, fr. L *apertus* open, fr. pp. of *aperire* to open] **1** : saucily free and forward : IMPUDENT **2** : stylishly trim : JAUNTY **3** : LIVELY

[2]**pert** *abbr* pertaining

per·tain \pər-ˈtān\ *vb* **1** : to belong to as a part, quality, or function ⟨duties ~*ing* to the office⟩ **2** : to have reference : RELATE ⟨books ~*ing* to birds⟩

per·ti·na·cious \ˌpər-tə-ˈnā-shəs\ *adj* **1** : holding resolutely to an opinion or purpose **2** : obstinately persistent ⟨a ~ bill collector⟩ **syn** dogged, mulish, headstrong, perverse — **per·ti·nac·i·ty** \-ˈna-sə-tē\ *n*

per·ti·nent \ˈpərt-ᵊn-ənt\ *adj* : relating to the matter under consideration **syn** relevant, germane, applicable, apropos — **per·ti·nence** \-əns\ *n*

per·turb \pər-ˈtərb\ *vb* : to disturb greatly esp. in mind : UPSET — **per·tur·ba·tion** \ˌpər-tər-ˈbā-shən\ *n*

per·tus·sis \pər-ˈtə-səs\ *n* : WHOOPING COUGH

pe·ruke \pə-ˈrük\ *n* : WIG

pe·ruse \pə-ˈrüz\ *vb* **pe·rused; pe·rus·ing** : READ; *esp* : to read over attentively or leisurely — **pe·rus·al** \-ˈrü-zəl\ *n*

Pe·ru·vi·an \pə-ˈrü-vē-ən\ *n* : a native or inhabitant of Peru

per·vade \pər-ˈvād\ *vb* **per·vad·ed; per·vad·ing** : to spread through every part of : PERMEATE, PENETRATE — **per·va·sive** \-ˈvā-siv, -ziv\ *adj*

per·verse \pər-ˈvərs\ *adj* **1** : turned away from what is right or good : CORRUPT **2** : obstinate in opposing what is reasonable or accepted — **per·verse·ly** *adv* — **per·verse·ness** *n* — **per·ver·si·ty** \-ˈvər-sə-tē\ *n*

per·ver·sion \pər-ˈvər-zhən\ *n* **1** : the action of perverting : the condition of being perverted **2** : a perverted form of something; *esp* : aberrant sexual behavior

[1]**per·vert** \pər-ˈvərt\ *vb* **1** : to lead astray : CORRUPT ⟨~ the young⟩ **2** : to divert to a wrong purpose : MISAPPLY ⟨~ evidence⟩ **syn** deprave, debase, debauch, demoralize — **per·vert·er** *n*

[2]**per·vert** \ˈpər-ˌvərt\ *n* **:** one that is perverted; *esp* **:** one given to sexual perversion
pe·se·ta \pə-ˈsā-tə\ *n* — see MONEY table
pe·se·wa \pə-ˈsā-wə\ *n* — see *cedi* at MONEY table
pes·ky \ˈpes-kē\ *adj* **pes·ki·er; -est :** causing annoyance **:** TROUBLESOME
pe·so \ˈpā-sō\ *n, pl* **pesos** — see MONEY table
pes·si·mism \ˈpe-sə-ˌmi-zəm\ *n* [F *pessimisme*, fr. L *pessimus* worst] **:** an inclination to take the least favorable view (as of events) or to expect the worst — **pes·si·mist** \-mist\ *n* — **pes·si·mis·tic** \ˌpe-sə-ˈmis-tik\ *adj*
pest \ˈpest\ *n* **1 :** a destructive epidemic disease **:** PLAGUE **2 :** a plant or animal detrimental to humans **3 :** one that pesters **:** NUISANCE — **pesty** *adj*
pes·ter \ˈpes-tər\ *vb* **:** to harass with petty irritations **:** ANNOY
pes·ti·cide \ˈpes-tə-ˌsīd\ *n* **:** an agent used to destroy pests
pes·tif·er·ous \pes-ˈti-fə-rəs\ *adj* **1 :** PESTILENT **2 :** ANNOYING
pes·ti·lence \ˈpes-tə-ləns\ *n* **:** a destructive infectious swiftly spreading disease; *esp* **:** BUBONIC PLAGUE
pes·ti·lent \-lənt\ *adj* **1 :** dangerous to life **:** DEADLY **2 :** PERNICIOUS, HARMFUL **3 :** TROUBLESOME **4 :** INFECTIOUS, CONTAGIOUS
pes·ti·len·tial \ˌpes-tə-ˈlen-chəl\ *adj* **1 :** causing or tending to cause pestilence **:** DEADLY **2 :** morally harmful
pes·tle \ˈpes-əl, ˈpest-ᵊl\ *n* **:** an implement for grinding substances in a mortar — **pestle** *vb*
[1]**pet** \ˈpet\ *n* **1 :** FAVORITE, DARLING **2 :** a domesticated animal kept for pleasure rather than utility
[2]**pet** *adj* **1 :** kept or treated as a pet ⟨~ dog⟩ **2 :** expressing fondness ⟨~ name⟩ **3 :** particularly liked or favored
[3]**pet** *vb* **pet·ted; pet·ting 1 :** to stroke gently or lovingly **2 :** to make a pet of **:** PAMPER **3 :** to engage in amorous kissing and caressing
[4]**pet** *n* **:** a fit of peevishness, sulkiness, or anger — **pettish** *adj*
Pet *abbr* Peter
pet·al \ˈpet-ᵊl\ *n* **:** one of the modified leaves of a flower's corolla
pe·tard \pə-ˈtärd, -ˈtär\ *n* **:** a case containing an explosive to break down a door or gate or breach a wall
pe·ter \ˈpē-tər\ *vb* **:** to diminish gradually and come to an end ⟨his energy ~*ed* out⟩
Pe·ter \ˈpē-tər\ *n* — see BIBLE table
pet·i·ole \ˈpe-tē-ˌōl\ *n* **:** a slender stem that supports a leaf
pe·tite \pə-ˈtēt\ *adj* [F] **:** small and trim of figure ⟨a ~ woman⟩ — **petite** *n*
pe·tit four \ˌpe-tē-ˈfōr\ *n, pl* **petits fours** *or* **petit fours** \-ˈfōrz\ [F, lit., small oven] **:** a small cake cut from pound or sponge cake and frosted
[1]**pe·ti·tion** \pə-ˈti-shən\ *n* **:** an earnest request **:** ENTREATY; *esp* **:** a formal written request made to an authority
[2]**petition** *vb* **:** to make a request to or for — **pe·ti·tion·er** *n*
pe·trel \ˈpe-trəl\ *n* **:** any of numerous seabirds that fly far from land
pet·ri·fy \ˈpe-trə-ˌfī\ *vb* **-fied; -fy·ing 1 :** to convert (organic matter) into stone or stony material **2 :** to make rigid or inactive (as from fear or awe) — **pet·ri·fac·tion** \ˌpe-trə-ˈfak-shən\ *n*
pet·ro·chem·i·cal \ˌpe-trō-ˈke-mi-kəl\ *n* **:** a chemical isolated or derived from petroleum or natural gas — **pet·ro·chem·is·try** \-ˈke-mə-strē\ *n*
pet·rol \ˈpe-trəl\ *n, Brit* **:** GASOLINE
pet·ro·la·tum \ˌpe-trə-ˈlā-təm\ *n* **:** PETROLEUM JELLY
pe·tro·leum \pə-ˈtrō-lē-əm\ *n* [ML, fr. Gk *petra* rock + L *oleum* oil] **:** an oily flammable liquid obtained from wells drilled in the ground and refined into gasoline, fuel oils, and other products
petroleum jelly *n* **:** a tasteless, odorless, and oily or greasy substance from petroleum that is used esp. in ointments and dressings
[1]**pet·ti·coat** \ˈpe-tē-ˌkōt\ *n* **1 :** a skirt worn under a dress **2 :** an outer skirt
[2]**petticoat** *adj* **:** of, relating to, or exercised by women **:** FEMALE
pet·ti·fog \ˈpe-tē-ˌfòg, -ˌfäg\ *vb* **-fogged; -fog·ging 1 :** to engage in legal trickery **2 :** to quibble over insignificant details — **pet·ti·fog·ger** *n*
pet·ty \ˈpe-tē\ *adj* **pet·ti·er; -est** [ME *pety* small, minor, alter. of *petit*, fr. MF, small] **1 :** having secondary rank **:** MINOR ⟨~ prince⟩ **2 :** of little importance **:** TRIFLING ⟨~ faults⟩ **3 :** marked by narrowness or meanness — **pet·ti·ly** \ˈpe-tə-lē\ *adv* — **pet·ti·ness** \-tē-nəs\ *n*
petty officer *n* **:** a subordinate officer in the navy or coast guard appointed from among the enlisted men
petty officer first class *n* **:** a petty officer ranking below a chief petty officer
petty officer second class *n* **:** a petty officer ranking below a petty officer first class
petty officer third class *n* **:** a petty officer ranking below a petty officer second class
pet·u·lant \ˈpe-chə-lənt\ *adj* **:** marked by capricious ill humor **syn** irritable, peevish, fretful, fractious, querulous — **pet·u·lance** \-ləns\ *n* — **pet·u·lant·ly** *adv*
pe·tu·nia \pi-ˈtün-yə, -ˈtyün-\ *n* **:** any of a genus of tropical American herbs related to the potato and having bright funnel-shaped flowers
pew \ˈpyü\ *n* [ME *pewe*, fr. MF *puie* balustrade, fr. L *podia*, pl. of *podium* parapet, podium, fr. Gk *podion* base, dim. of *pod-, pous* foot] **:** any of the benches with backs fixed in rows in a church
pe·wee \ˈpē-(ˌ)wē\ *n* **:** any of various small flycatchers
pew·ter \ˈpyü-tər\ *n* **1 :** an alloy of tin used esp. for household utensils **2 :** a bluish gray color — **pewter** *adj* — **pew·ter·er** *n*
pey·o·te \pā-ˈō-tē\ *also* **pey·otl** \-ˈōt-ᵊl\ *n* **:** a stimulant drug derived from an American cactus; *also* **:** this cactus
pf *abbr* **1** pfennig **2** preferred
PFC *or* **Pfc** *abbr* private first class
pfd *abbr* preferred
pfen·nig \ˈfe-nig\ *n, pl* **pfennig** *also* **pfennigs** *or* **pfen·ni·ge** \ˈfe-ni-gə\ — see *deutsche mark* at MONEY table
pg *abbr* page
PG *abbr* postgraduate
PGA *abbr* Professional Golfers' Association
pH \(ˌ)pē-ˈāch\ *n* **:** a value used to express acidity and alkalinity; *also* **:** the condition represented by such a value
PH *abbr* **1** pinch hit **2** public health
pha·eton \ˈfā-ət-ᵊn\ *n* [F *phaéton*, fr. Gk *Phaethōn*, son of the sun god who persuaded his father to let him drive the chariot of the sun but who lost control of the horses with disastrous consequences] **1 :** a light 4-wheeled horse-drawn vehicle **2 :** an open automobile with two cross seats

phaeton 1

phage \ˈfāj\ *n* **:** BACTERIOPHAGE
pha·lanx \ˈfā-ˌlaŋks\ *n, pl* **pha·lanx·es** *or* **pha·lan·ges** \fə-ˈlan-ˌjēz\ **1 :** a group or body (as of troops) in

compact formation **2** *pl phalanges* : one of the digital bones of the hand or foot of a vertebrate

phal•a•rope \ˈfa-lə-ˌrōp\ *n, pl* **-ropes** *also* **-rope** : any of a genus of small shorebirds related to sandpipers

phal•lic \ˈfa-lik\ *adj* **1** : of, relating to, or resembling a phallus **2** : relating to or being the stage of psychosexual development in psychoanalytic theory during which children become interested in their own sexual organs

phal•lus \ˈfa-ləs\ *n, pl* **phal•li** \ˈfa-ˌlī\ *or* **phal•lus•es** : PENIS; *also* : a symbolic representation of the penis

Phan•er•o•zo•ic \ˌfa-nə-rə-ˈzō-ik\ *adj* : of, relating to, or being an eon of geologic history comprising the Paleozoic, Mesozoic, and Cenozoic

phan•tasm \ˈfan-ˌta-zəm\ *n* : a product of the imagination : ILLUSION — **phan•tas•mal** \ˌfan-ˈtaz-məl\ *adj*

phan•tas•ma•go•ria \fan-ˌtaz-mə-ˈgōr-ē-ə\ *n* : a constantly shifting complex succession of things seen or imagined; *also* : a scene that constantly changes or fluctuates

phantasy *var of* FANTASY

phan•tom \ˈfan-təm\ *n* **1** : something (as a specter) that is apparent to sense but has no substantial existence **2** : a mere show : SHADOW — **phantom** *adj*

pha•raoh \ˈfer-ō, ˈfā-rō\ *n, often cap* : a ruler of ancient Egypt

phar•i•sa•ical \ˌfar-ə-ˈsā-ə-kəl\ *adj* : hypocritically self-righteous

phar•i•see \ˈfar-ə-ˌsē\ *n* **1** *cap* : a member of an ancient Jewish sect noted for strict observance of rites and ceremonies of the traditional law **2** : a self-righteous or hypocritical person — **phar•i•sa•ic** \ˌfar-ə-ˈsā-ik\ *adj*

pharm *abbr* pharmaceutical; pharmacist; pharmacy

phar•ma•ceu•ti•cal \ˌfär-mə-ˈsü-ti-kəl\ *adj* : of, relating to, or engaged in pharmacy or the manufacture and sale of medicinal drugs — **pharmaceutical** *n*

phar•ma•col•o•gy \ˌfär-mə-ˈkä-lə-jē\ *n* **1** : the science of drugs esp. as related to medicinal uses **2** : the reactions and properties of one or more drugs — **phar•ma•co•log•i•cal** \-kə-ˈlä-ji-kəl\ *also* **phar•ma•co•log•ic** \-kə-ˈlä-jik\ *adj* — **phar•ma•col•o•gist** \-ˈkä-lə-jist\ *n*

phar•ma•co•poe•ia *also* **phar•ma•co•pe•ia** \-kə-ˈpē-ə\ *n* **1** : a book describing drugs and medicinal preparations **2** : a stock of drugs

phar•ma•cy \ˈfär-mə-sē\ *n, pl* **-cies** **1** : the art, practice, or profession of preparing and dispensing medical drugs **2** : DRUGSTORE — **phar•ma•cist** \-sist\ *n*

phar•ynx \ˈfar-iŋks\ *n, pl* **pha•ryn•ges** \fə-ˈrin-ˌjēz\ *also* **phar•ynx•es** : the space just back of the mouth into which the nostrils, esophagus, and trachea open — **pha•ryn•ge•al** \fə-ˈrin-jəl, ˌfar-ən-ˈjē-əl\ *adj*

phase \ˈfāz\ *n* **1** : a particular appearance in a recurring series of changes ⟨~s of the moon⟩ **2** : a stage or interval in a process or cycle ⟨first ~ of an experiment⟩ **3** : an aspect or part under consideration — **pha•sic** \ˈfā-zik\ *adj*

phase in *vb* : to introduce in stages

phase•out \ˈfā-ˌzau̇t\ *n* : a gradual stopping of operations or production

phase out *vb* : to stop production or use of in stages

PhD *abbr* [L *philosophiae doctor*] doctor of philosophy

pheas•ant \ˈfez-ᵊnt\ *n, pl* **pheasant** *or* **pheasants** : any of numerous long-tailed brilliantly colored game birds related to the domestic chicken

phen•cy•cli•dine \ˌfen-ˈsī-klə-ˌdēn\ *n* : a drug used esp. as a veterinary anesthetic and sometimes illicitly to induce vivid mental imagery

phe•no•bar•bi•tal \ˌfē-nō-ˈbär-bə-ˌtȯl\ *n* : a crystalline drug used as a hypnotic and sedative

phe•nol \ˈfē-ˌnȯl\ *n* : a corrosive poisonous acidic compound present in coal and wood tars and used in solution as a disinfectant

phe•nom•e•non \fi-ˈnä-mə-ˌnän, -nən\ *n, pl* **-na** \-nə\ *or* **-nons** [LL *phaenomenon*, fr. Gk *phainomenon*, fr. neut. of *phainomenos*, prp. of *phainesthai* to appear] **1** *pl -na* : an observable fact or event **2** : an outward sign of the working of a law of nature **3** *pl -nons* : an extraordinary person or thing : PRODIGY — **phe•nom•e•nal** \-ˈnä-mən-ᵊl\ *adj* — **phe•nom•e•non•al•ly** *adv*

pheasant

pher•o•mone \ˈfer-ə-ˌmōn\ *n* : a chemical substance that is produced by an animal and serves to stimulate a behavioral response in other individuals of the same species — **pher•o•mon•al** \ˌfer-ə-ˈmōn-ᵊl\ *adj*

phi \ˈfī\ *n* : the 21st letter of the Greek alphabet — Φ or φ

phi•al \ˈfī-əl\ *n* : VIAL

Phil *abbr* Philippians

phi•lan•der \fə-ˈlan-dər\ *vb* **1** : to make love without serious intent **2** : to have many love affairs — **phi•lan•der•er** *n*

phi•lan•thro•py \fə-ˈlan-thrə-pē\ *n, pl* **-pies** **1** : goodwill toward all people; *esp* : effort to promote human welfare **2** : a charitable act or gift; *also* : an organization that distributes or is supported by donated funds — **phil•an•throp•ic** \ˌfi-lən-ˈthrä-pik\ *adj* — **phil•an•throp•i•cal•ly** \-pi-k(ə-)lē\ *adv* — **phi•lan•thro•pist** \fə-ˈlan-thrə-pist\ *n*

phi•lat•e•ly \fə-ˈlat-ᵊl-ē\ *n* : the collection and study of postage and imprinted stamps — **phil•a•tel•ic** \ˌfi-lə-ˈte-lik\ *adj* — **phi•lat•e•list** \fə-ˈlat-ᵊl-ist\ *n*

Phi•le•mon \fə-ˈlē-mən, fī-\ *n* — see BIBLE table

Phi•lip•pi•ans \fə-ˈli-pē-ənz\ *n* — see BIBLE table

phi•lip•pic \fə-ˈli-pik\ *n* : TIRADE

phi•lis•tine \ˈfi-lə-ˌstēn; fə-ˈlis-tən\ *n, often cap* [*Philistine*, inhabitant of ancient Philistia (Palestine)] : a person who is smugly insensitive or indifferent to intellectual or artistic values — **philistine** *adj, often cap*

Phil•lips \ˈfi-ləps\ *adj* : of, relating to, or being a screw having a head with a cross slot or its corresponding screwdriver

philo•den•dron \ˌfi-lə-ˈden-drən\ *n, pl* **-drons** *or* **-dra** \-drə\ [NL, fr. Gk, neut. of *philodendros* loving trees, fr. *philos* dear, friendly + *dendron* tree] : any of various plants of the arum family grown for their showy foliage

phi•lol•o•gy \fə-ˈlä-lə-jē\ *n* **1** : the study of literature and relevant fields **2** : LINGUISTICS; *esp* : historical and comparative linguistics — **phil•o•log•i•cal** \ˌfi-lə-ˈlä-ji-kəl\ *adj* — **phi•lol•o•gist** \fə-ˈlä-lə-jist\ *n*

philos *abbr* philosopher; philosophy

phi•los•o•pher \fə-ˈlä-sə-fər\ *n* **1** : a reflective thinker : SCHOLAR **2** : a student of or specialist in philosophy **3** : a person whose philosophical perspective makes it possible to meet trouble calmly

phi•los•o•phise *Brit var of* PHILOSOPHIZE

phi•los•o•phize \fə-ˈlä-sə-ˌfīz\ *vb* **-phized; -phiz•ing** **1** : to reason like a philosopher : THEORIZE **2** : to expound a philosophy esp. superficially

phi•los•o•phy \fə-ˈlä-sə-fē\ *n, pl* **-phies** **1** : sciences and liberal arts exclusive of medicine, law, and theology ⟨doctor of ~⟩ **2** : a critical study of fundamental beliefs and the grounds for them **3** : a system of philosophical concepts ⟨Aristotelian ~⟩ **4** : a basic theory concerning a particular subject or sphere of activity **5 :** the sum of the ideas and convictions of an individual or group ⟨her ~ of life⟩ **6 :** calmness of temper and judgment — **phil·o·soph·ic** \ˌfi-lə-ˈsä-fik\ *or* **phil·o·soph·i·cal** \-fi-kəl\ *adj* — **phil·o·soph·i·cal·ly** \-k(ə-)lē\ *adv*

phil·ter *or* **phil·tre** \ˈfil-tər\ *n* **1 :** a potion, drug, or charm held to arouse sexual passion **2 :** a magic potion

phle·bi·tis \fli-ˈbī-təs\ *n* **:** inflammation of a vein

phle·bot·o·my \fli-ˈbä-tə-mē\ *n, pl* **-mies :** the opening of a vein esp. for removing or releasing blood

phlegm \ˈflem\ *n* **:** thick mucus secreted in abnormal quantity esp. in the nose and throat

phleg·mat·ic \fleg-ˈma-tik\ *adj* **:** having or showing a slow and stolid temperament **syn** impassive, apathetic, stoic

phlo·em \ˈflō-ˌem\ *n* **:** a vascular plant tissue external to the xylem that carries dissolved food material and functions in support and storage

phlox \ˈfläks\ *n, pl* **phlox** *or* **phlox·es :** any of a genus of American herbs that have tall stalks with showy spreading terminal clusters of flowers

pho·bia \ˈfō-bē-ə\ *n* **:** an irrational persistent fear or dread

phoe·be \ˈfē-(ˌ)bē\ *n* **:** a flycatcher of the eastern U.S. that has a slight crest and is grayish brown above and yellowish white below

phoe·nix \ˈfē-niks\ *n* **:** a legendary bird held to live for centuries and then to burn itself to death and rise fresh and young from its ashes

phon *abbr* phonetics

[1]**phone** \ˈfōn\ *n* **1 :** TELEPHONE **2 :** EARPHONE

[2]**phone** *vb* **phoned; phon·ing :** TELEPHONE

pho·neme \ˈfō-ˌnēm\ *n* **:** one of the elementary units of speech that distinguish one utterance from another — **pho·ne·mic** \fō-ˈnē-mik\ *adj*

pho·net·ics \fə-ˈne-tiks\ *n* **:** the study and systematic classification of the sounds made in spoken utterance — **pho·net·ic** \-tik\ *adj* — **pho·ne·ti·cian** \ˌfō-nə-ˈti-shən\ *n*

pho·nic \ˈfä-nik\ *adj* **1 :** of, relating to, or producing sound **2 :** of or relating to the sounds of speech or to phonics — **pho·ni·cal·ly** \-ni-k(ə-)lē\ *adv*

pho·nics \ˈfä-niks\ *n* **:** a method of teaching people to read and pronounce words by learning the phonetic value of letters, letter groups, and esp. syllables

pho·no·graph \ˈfō-nə-ˌgraf\ *n* **:** an instrument for reproducing sounds by means of the vibration of a needle following a spiral groove on a revolving disc

pho·nol·o·gy \fə-ˈnä-lə-jē\ *n* **:** a study and description of the sound changes in a language — **pho·no·log·i·cal** \ˌfō-nə-ˈlä-ji-kəl\ *adj* — **pho·nol·o·gist** \fə-ˈnä-lə-jist\ *n*

pho·ny *or* **pho·ney** \ˈfō-nē\ *adj* **pho·ni·er; -est :** marked by empty pretension **:** FAKE — **phony** *n*

phos·phate \ˈfäs-ˌfāt\ *n* **:** a salt of a phosphoric acid — **phos·phat·ic** \fäs-ˈfa-tik\ *adj*

phos·phor \ˈfäs-fər\ *n* **:** a phosphorescent substance

phos·pho·res·cence \ˌfäs-fə-ˈres-ᵊns\ *n* **1 :** luminescence caused by radiation absorption followed by emission that continues after the incident radiation stops **2 :** an enduring luminescence without sensible heat — **phos·pho·res·cent** \-ᵊnt\ *adj* — **phos·pho·res·cent·ly** *adv*

phosphoric acid \ˌfäs-ˈfȯr-ik-, -ˈfär-\ *n* **:** any of several oxygen-containing acids of phosphorus

phos·pho·rus \ˈfäs-fə-rəs\ *n* [NL, fr. Gk *phōsphoros* light-bearing, fr. *phōs* light + *pherein* to carry, bring] **:** a nonmetallic chemical element that has characteristics similar to nitrogen and occurs widely esp. as phosphates — see ELEMENT table — **phos·pho·ric** \fäs-ˈfȯr-ik, -ˈfär-\ *adj* — **phos·pho·rous** \ˈfäs-fə-rəs; fäs-ˈfȯr-əs, -ˈfȯr-\ *adj*

phot- *or* **photo-** *comb form* **1 :** light ⟨*photo*graphy⟩ **2 :** photograph **:** photographic ⟨*photo*engraving⟩ **3 :** photoelectric ⟨*photo*cell⟩

pho·to \ˈfō-tō\ *n, pl* **photos :** PHOTOGRAPH — **photo** *vb or adj*

pho·to·cell \ˈfō-tə-ˌsel\ *n* **:** PHOTOELECTRIC CELL

pho·to·chem·i·cal \ˌfō-tō-ˈke-mi-kəl\ *adj* **:** of, relating to, or resulting from the chemical action of radiant energy

pho·to·com·pose \-kəm-ˈpōz\ *vb* **:** to compose reading matter for reproduction by means of characters photographed on film — **pho·to·com·po·si·tion** \-ˌkäm-pə-ˈzi-shən\ *n*

pho·to·copy \ˈfō-tə-ˌkä-pē\ *n* **:** a photographic reproduction of graphic matter — **photocopy** *vb*

pho·to·elec·tric \ˌfō-tō-i-ˈlek-trik\ *adj* **:** relating to an electrical effect due to the interaction of light with matter — **pho·to·elec·tri·cal·ly** \-tri-k(ə-)lē\ *adv*

photoelectric cell *n* **:** a device whose electrical properties are modified by the action of light

pho·to·en·grave \ˌfō-tō-in-ˈgrāv\ *vb* **:** to make a photoengraving of

pho·to·en·grav·ing *n* **:** a process by which an etched printing plate is made from a photograph or drawing; *also* **:** a print made from such a plate

photo finish *n* **:** a race finish so close that a photograph of the finish is used to determine the winner

[1]**pho·tog** \fə-ˈtäg\ *n* **:** PHOTOGRAPHER

[2]**photog** *abbr* photographic; photography

pho·to·ge·nic \ˌfō-tə-ˈje-nik\ *adj* **:** eminently suitable esp. aesthetically for being photographed

pho·to·graph \ˈfō-tə-ˌgraf\ *n* **:** a picture taken by photography — **photograph** *vb* — **pho·tog·ra·pher** \fə-ˈtä-grə-fər\ *n*

pho·tog·ra·phy \fə-ˈtä-grə-fē\ *n* **:** the art or process of producing images on a sensitized surface (as film in a camera) by the action of light — **pho·to·graph·ic** \ˌfō-tə-ˈgra-fik\ *adj* — **pho·to·graph·i·cal·ly** \-fi-k(ə-)lē\ *adv*

pho·to·gra·vure \ˌfō-tə-grə-ˈvyu̇r\ *n* **:** a process for making prints from an intaglio plate prepared by photographic methods

pho·to·li·thog·ra·phy \ˌfō-tō-li-ˈthä-grə-fē\ *n* **:** the process of photographically transferring a pattern to a surface for etching (as in making an integrated circuit)

pho·tom·e·ter \fō-ˈtä-mə-tər\ *n* **:** an instrument for measuring the intensity of light — **pho·to·met·ric** \ˌfō-tə-ˈme-trik\ *adj* — **pho·tom·e·try** \fō-ˈtä-mə-trē\ *n*

pho·to·mi·cro·graph \ˌfō-tə-ˈmī-krə-ˌgraf\ *n* **:** a photograph of a microscope image — **pho·to·mi·crog·ra·phy** \-mī-ˈkrä-grə-fē\ *n*

pho·ton \ˈfō-ˌtän\ *n* **:** a quantum of electromagnetic radiation

pho·to·play \ˈfō-tō-ˌplā\ *n* **:** MOTION PICTURE

pho·to·sen·si·tive \ˌfō-tə-ˈsen-sə-tiv\ *adj* **:** sensitive or sensitized to the action of radiant energy

pho·to·sphere \ˈfō-tə-ˌsfir\ *n* **:** the luminous surface of a star — **pho·to·spher·ic** \ˌfō-tə-ˈsfir-ik, -ˈsfer-\ *adj*

pho·to·syn·the·sis \ˌfō-tō-ˈsin-thə-səs\ *n* **:** the process by which chlorophyll-containing plants make carbohydrates from water and from carbon dioxide in the air in the presence of light — **pho·to·syn·the·size** \-ˌsīz\ *vb* — **pho·to·syn·thet·ic** \-sin-ˈthe-tik\ *adj*

phr *abbr* phrase

[1]**phrase** \ˈfrāz\ *n* **1 :** a brief expression **2 :** a group of two or more grammatically related words that form a sense unit expressing a thought

[2]**phrase** *vb* **phrased; phras·ing :** to express in words

phrase·ol·o·gy \ˌfrā-zē-ˈä-lə-jē\ *n, pl* **-gies :** a manner of phrasing **:** STYLE

phras·ing *n* **:** style of expression

phre·net·ic \fri-ˈne-tik\ *adj* **:** FRENETIC

phren·ic \ˈfre-nik\ *adj* **:** of or relating to the diaphragm ⟨~ nerves⟩

phre·nol·o·gy \fri-ˈnä-lə-jē\ *n* **:** the study of the conformation of the skull based on the belief that it indicates mental faculties and character traits

phy•lac•tery \fə-ˈlak-tə-rē\ *n, pl* **-ter•ies** **1 :** one of two small square leather boxes containing slips inscribed with scripture passages and traditionally worn on the left arm and forehead by Jewish men during morning weekday prayers **2 :** AMULET

phy•lum \ˈfī-ləm\ *n, pl* **phy•la** \-lə\ [NL, fr. Gk *phylon* tribe, race] **:** a major division of the animal and in some classifications the plant kingdom; *also* **:** a group (as of people) apparently of common origin

phys *abbr* **1** physical **2** physics

[1]**phys•ic** \ˈfi-zik\ *n* **1 :** the profession of medicine **2 :** MEDICINE; *esp* **:** PURGATIVE

[2]**physic** *vb* **phys•icked; phys•ick•ing :** PURGE 2

[1]**phys•i•cal** \ˈfi-zi-kəl\ *adj* **1 :** of or relating to nature or the laws of nature **2 :** material as opposed to mental or spiritual **3 :** of, relating to, or produced by the forces and operations of physics **4 :** of or relating to the body — **phys•i•cal•ly** \-k(ə-)lē\ *adv*

[2]**physical** *n* **:** PHYSICAL EXAMINATION

physical education *n* **:** instruction in the development and care of the body ranging from simple calisthenics to training in hygiene, gymnastics, and the performance and management of athletic games

physical examination *n* **:** an examination of the bodily functions and condition of an individual

physical science *n* **:** any of the sciences (as physics and astronomy) that deal primarily with nonliving materials — **physical scientist** *n*

physical therapy *n* **:** the treatment of disease by physical and mechanical means (as massage, exercise, water, or heat) — **physical therapist** *n*

phy•si•cian \fə-ˈzi-shən\ *n* **:** a doctor of medicine

physician's assistant *n* **:** a person certified to provide basic medical care usu. under a licensed physician's supervision

phys•i•cist \ˈfi-zə-sist\ *n* **:** a scientist who specializes in physics

phys•ics \ˈfi-ziks\ *n* [L *physica,* pl., natural sciences, fr. Gk *physika,* fr. *physis* growth, nature, fr. *phyein* to bring forth] **1 :** the science of matter and energy and their interactions **2 :** the physical properties and composition of something

phys•i•og•no•my \ˌfi-zē-ˈäg-nə-mē\ *n, pl* **-mies :** facial appearance esp. as a reflection of inner character

phys•i•og•ra•phy \ˌfi-zē-ˈä-grə-fē\ *n* **:** geography dealing with physical features of the earth — **phys•io•graph•ic** \ˌfi-zē-ō-ˈgra-fik\ *adj*

phys•i•ol•o•gy \ˌfi-zē-ˈä-lə-jē\ *n* **1 :** a branch of biology dealing with the functions and functioning of living matter and organisms **2 :** functional processes in an organism or any of its parts — **phys•i•o•log•i•cal** \-zē-ə-ˈlä-ji-kəl\ *or* **phys•i•o•log•ic** \-jik\ *adj* — **phys•i•o•log•i•cal•ly** \-ji-k(ə-)lē\ *adv* — **phys•i•ol•o•gist** \-zē-ˈä-lə-jist\ *n*

phys•io•ther•a•py \ˌfi-zē-ō-ˈther-ə-pē\ *n* **:** PHYSICAL THERAPY — **phys•io•ther•a•pist** \-pist\ *n*

phy•sique \fə-ˈzēk\ *n* **:** the build of a person's body **:** bodily constitution

phy•to•plank•ton \ˈfī-tō-ˌplaŋk-tən\ *n* **:** plant life of the plankton

pi \ˈpī\ *n, pl* **pis** \ˈpīz\ **1 :** the 16th letter of the Greek alphabet — Π or π **2 :** the symbol π denoting the ratio of the circumference of a circle to its diameter; *also* **:** the ratio itself equal to approximately 3.1416

PI *abbr* private investigator

pi•a•nis•si•mo \ˌpē-ə-ˈni-sə-ˌmō\ *adv or adj* **:** very softly — used as a direction in music

pi•a•nist \pē-ˈa-nist, ˈpē-ə-\ *n* **:** one who plays the piano

[1]**pi•a•no** \pē-ˈä-nō\ *adv or adj* **:** SOFTLY — used as a direction in music

[2]**piano** \pē-ˈa-nō\ *n, pl* **pianos** [It, short for *pianoforte,* fr. *gravicembalo col piano e forte,* lit., harpsichord with soft and loud; fr. the fact that its tones could be varied in loudness] **:** a musical instrument having steel strings sounded by felt-covered hammers operated from a keyboard

pi•ano•forte \pē-ˌa-nō-ˈfȯr-ˌtā, -tē; pē-ˈa-nə-ˌfȯrt\ *n* **:** PIANO

pi•as•tre *also* **pi•as•ter** \pē-ˈas-tər\ *n* — see *pound* at MONEY table

pi•az•za \pē-ˈa-zə, *esp for 1* -ˈat-sə\ *n, pl* **piazzas** *or* **pi•az•ze** \-ˈat-(ˌ)sā, -ˈät-\ [It, fr. L *platea* broad street] **1 :** an open square esp. in an Italian town **2 :** a long hall with an arched roof **3** *dial* **:** VERANDA, PORCH

pi•broch \ˈpē-ˌbräk\ *n* **:** a set of variations for the bagpipe

pic \ˈpik\ *n, pl* **pics** *or* **pix** \ˈpiks\ **1 :** PHOTOGRAPH **2 :** MOTION PICTURE

pi•ca \ˈpī-kə\ *n* **:** a typewriter type with 10 characters to the inch

pi•ca•resque \ˌpi-kə-ˈresk, ˌpē-\ *adj* **:** of or relating to rogues ⟨~ fiction⟩

pic•a•yune \ˌpi-kē-ˈyün\ *adj* **:** of little value **:** TRIVIAL; *also* **:** PETTY

pic•ca•lil•li \ˌpi-kə-ˈli-lē\ *n* **:** a relish of chopped vegetables and spices

pic•co•lo \ˈpi-kə-ˌlō\ *n, pl* **-los** [It, short for *piccolo flauto* small flute] **:** a small shrill flute pitched an octave higher than the ordinary flute

pice \ˈpīs\ *n, pl* **pice :** PAISA

[1]**pick** \ˈpik\ *vb* **1 :** to pierce or break up with a pointed instrument **2 :** to remove bit by bit; *also* **:** to remove covering matter from **3 :** to gather by plucking ⟨~ apples⟩ **4 :** CULL, SELECT **5 :** ROB ⟨~ a pocket⟩ **6 :** PROVOKE ⟨~ a quarrel⟩ **7 :** to dig into or pull lightly at **8 :** to pluck with fingers or a pick **9 :** to loosen or pull apart with a sharp point ⟨~ wool⟩ **10 :** to unlock with a wire **11 :** to eat sparingly — **pick•er** *n*

[2]**pick** *n* **1 :** the act or privilege of choosing **2 :** the best or choicest one **3 :** the part of a crop gathered at one time

[3]**pick** *n* **1 :** a heavy wooden-handled tool pointed at one or both ends **2 :** a pointed implement used for picking **3 :** a small thin piece (as of plastic) used to pluck the strings of a stringed instrument

pick•a•back \ˈpi-gē-ˌbak, ˈpi-kə-\ *var of* PIGGYBACK

pick•ax \ˈpik-ˌaks\ *n* **:** [3]PICK 1

pick•er•el \ˈpi-kə-rəl\ *n, pl* **pickerel** *or* **pickerels :** either of two bony fishes related to the pikes; *also* **:** WALLEYE 2

pickerel

pick•er•el•weed \-ˌwēd\ *n* **:** an American shallow-water herb that bears spikes of blue flowers

[1]**pick•et** \ˈpi-kət\ *n* **1 :** a pointed stake (as for a fence) **2 :** a detached body of soldiers on outpost duty; *also* **:** SENTINEL **3 :** a person posted by a labor union where workers are on strike; *also* **:** a person posted for a protest

[2]**picket** *vb* **1 :** to guard with pickets **2 :** TETHER **3 :** to post pickets at ⟨~ a factory⟩ **4 :** to serve as a picket

pick•ings \ˈpi-kiŋz, -kənz\ *n pl* **1 :** gleanable or eatable fragments **:** SCRAPS **2 :** yield for effort expended **:** RETURN

pick•le \ˈpi-kəl\ *n* **1 :** a brine or vinegar solution for preserving foods; *also* **:** a food (as a cucumber) preserved in a pickle **2 :** a difficult situation **:** PLIGHT — **pickle** *vb*

pick•lock \ˈpik-ˌläk\ *n* **1 :** BURGLAR, THIEF **2 :** a tool for picking locks

pick•pock•et \ˈpik-ˌpä-kət\ *n* : one who steals from pockets
pick•up \ˈpik-ˌəp\ *n* **1** : a hitchhiker who is given a ride **2** : a temporary chance acquaintance **3** : a picking up **4** : revival of business activity **5** : ACCELERATION **6** : the conversion of mechanical movements into electrical impulses in the reproduction of sound; *also* : a device for making such conversion **7** : a light truck having an enclosed cab and an open body with low sides and a tailgate
pick up *vb* **1** : to take hold of and lift **2** : IMPROVE **3** : to put in order
picky \ˈpi-kē\ *adj* **pick•i•er; -est** : FUSSY, FINICKY
[1]**pic•nic** \ˈpik-ˌnik\ *n* : an outing with food usu. provided by members of the group and eaten in the open
[2]**picnic** *vb* **pic•nicked; pic•nick•ing** : to go on a picnic : eat in picnic fashion
pi•cot \ˈpē-ˌkō\ *n* : one of a series of small loops forming an edging on ribbon or lace
pic•to•ri•al \pik-ˈtōr-ē-əl\ *adj* : of, relating to, or consisting of pictures
[1]**pic•ture** \ˈpik-chər\ *n* **1** : a representation made by painting, drawing, or photography **2** : a vivid description in words **3** : IMAGE, COPY **4** : a transitory visual image (as on a TV screen) **5** : MOTION PICTURE **6** : SITUATION
[2]**picture** *vb* **pic•tured; pic•tur•ing 1** : to paint or draw a picture of **2** : to describe vividly in words **3** : to form a mental image of
pic•tur•esque \ˌpik-chə-ˈresk\ *adj* **1** : resembling a picture ⟨a ~ landscape⟩ **2** : CHARMING, QUAINT ⟨a ~ character⟩ **3** : GRAPHIC, VIVID ⟨a ~ account⟩ — **pic•tur•esque•ness** *n*
picture tube *n* : a cathode-ray tube on which the picture in a television set appears
pid•dle \ˈpid-ᵊl\ *vb* **pid•dled; pid•dling** : to act or work idly : DAWDLE
pid•dling \ˈpid-ᵊl-ən, -iŋ\ *adj* : TRIVIAL, PALTRY
pid•gin \ˈpi-jən\ *n* [fr. *pidgin English,* fr. Chinese Pidgin English *pidgin* business] : a simplified speech used for communication between people with different languages
pie \ˈpī\ *n* : a dish consisting of a pastry crust and a filling (as of fruit or meat)
[1]**pie•bald** \ˈpī-ˌbȯld\ *adj* : of different colors; *esp* : blotched with white and black ⟨a ~ horse⟩
[2]**piebald** *n* : a piebald animal
[1]**piece** \ˈpēs\ *n* **1** : a part of a whole : FRAGMENT **2** : one of a group, set, or mass ⟨chess ~⟩; *also* : a single item ⟨a ~ of news⟩ **3** : a length, weight, or size in which something is made or sold **4** : a product (as an essay) of creative work **5** : FIREARM **6** : COIN
[2]**piece** *vb* **pieced; piec•ing 1** : to repair or complete by adding pieces : PATCH **2** : to join into a whole
pièce de ré•sis•tance \pē-ˌes-də-rā-ˌzē-ˈstäns\ *n, pl* **pièces de ré•sis•tance** *same*\ [F] **1** : the chief dish of a meal **2** : an outstanding item
piece•meal \ˈpēs-ˌmēl\ *adv or adj* : one piece at a time : GRADUALLY
piece•work \-ˌwərk\ *n* : work done and paid for by the piece — **piece•work•er** *n*
pie chart *n* : a circular chart that shows quantities or frequencies by parts of a circle shaped like pieces of pie
pied \ˈpīd\ *adj* : of two or more colors in blotches : VARIEGATED
pied–à–terre \pē-ˌā-də-ˈter\ *n, pl* **pieds–à–terre** *same*\ [F, lit., foot to the ground] : a temporary or second lodging
pier \ˈpir\ *n* **1** : a support for a bridge span **2** : a structure built out into the water for use as a landing place or a promenade or to protect or form a harbor **3** : an upright supporting part (as a pillar) of a building or structure
pierce \ˈpirs\ *vb* **pierced; pierc•ing 1** : to enter or thrust into sharply or painfully : STAB **2** : to make a hole in or through : PERFORATE **3** : to force or make a way into or through : PENETRATE **4** : to see through : DISCERN
pies *pl of* PI *or of* PIE
pi•ety \ˈpī-ə-tē\ *n, pl* **pi•et•ies 1** : fidelity to natural obligations (as to parents) **2** : dutifulness in religion : DEVOUTNESS **3** : a pious act
pif•fle \ˈpi-fəl\ *n* : trifling talk or action
pig \ˈpig\ *n* **1** : SWINE; *esp* : a young swine **2** : PORK **3** : one that resembles a pig (as in dirtiness or greed) **4** : a crude casting of metal (as iron)
pi•geon \ˈpi-jən\ *n* : any of numerous stout-bodied short-legged birds with smooth thick plumage
[1]**pi•geon•hole** \ˈpi-jən-ˌhōl\ *n* : a small open compartment (as in a desk) for keeping letters or documents
[2]**pigeonhole** *vb* **1** : to place in or as if in a pigeonhole : FILE **2** : to lay aside **3** : CLASSIFY
pi•geon–toed \-ˌtōd\ *adj* : having the toes turned in
pig•gish \ˈpi-gish\ *adj* **1** : GREEDY **2** : STUBBORN
pig•gy•back \ˈpi-gē-ˌbak\ *adv or adj* **1** : up on the back and shoulders **2** : on a railroad flatcar
pig•head•ed \ˈpig-ˈhe-dəd\ *adj* : OBSTINATE, STUBBORN
pig latin *n, often cap L* : a jargon that is made by systematic alteration of English
pig•let \ˈpi-glət\ *n* : a small usu. young swine
pig•ment \ˈpig-mənt\ *n* **1** : coloring matter **2** : a powder mixed with a liquid to give color (as in paints)
pig•men•ta•tion \ˌpig-mən-ˈtā-shən\ *n* : coloration with or deposition of pigment; *esp* : an excessive deposition of bodily pigment
pig•my *var of* PYGMY
pig•nut \ˈpig-ˌnət\ *n* : the bitter nut of any of several hickory trees; *also* : any of these trees
pig•pen \-ˌpen\ *n* **1** : a pen for pigs **2** : a dirty place
pig•skin \-ˌskin\ *n* **1** : the skin of a swine or leather made of it **2** : FOOTBALL 2
pig•sty \-ˌstī\ *n* : PIGPEN
pig•tail \-ˌtāl\ *n* : a tight braid of hair
pi•ka \ˈpī-kə\ *n* : any of various small short-eared mammals related to the rabbits and occurring in rocky uplands of Asia and western No. America
[1]**pike** \ˈpīk\ *n* : a sharp point or spike
[2]**pike** *n, pl* **pike** *or* **pikes** : a large slender long-snouted freshwater bony fish valued for food; *also* : any of various related fishes
[3]**pike** *n* : a long wooden shaft with a pointed steel head formerly used as a foot soldier's weapon
[4]**pike** *n* : TURNPIKE
pik•er \ˈpī-kər\ *n* **1** : one who does things in a small way or on a small scale **2** : TIGHTWAD, CHEAPSKATE
pike•staff \ˈpīk-ˌstaf\ *n* : the staff of a foot soldier's pike
pi•laf *or* **pi•laff** \pi-ˈläf, ˈpē-ˌläf\ *or* **pi•lau** \pi-ˈlō, -ˈlȯ, ˈpē-lō, -lȯ\ *n* : a dish made of seasoned rice often with meat
pi•las•ter \pi-ˈlas-tər, ˈpī-ˌlas-tər\ *n* : an architectural support that looks like a rectangular column and projects slightly from a wall
pil•chard \ˈpil-chərd\ *n* : any of several fishes related to the herrings and often packed as sardines
[1]**pile** \ˈpīl\ *n* : a long slender column (as of wood or steel) driven into the ground to support a vertical load
[2]**pile** *n* **1** : a quantity of things heaped together **2** : PYRE **3** : a great number or quantity : LOT
[3]**pile** *vb* **piled; pil•ing 1** : to lay in a pile : STACK **2** : to heap up : ACCUMULATE **3** : to press forward in a mass : CROWD
[4]**pile** *n* : a velvety surface of fine short hairs or threads (as on cloth) — **piled** \ˈpīld\ *adj* — **pile•less** *adj*
piles \ˈpīlz\ *n pl* : HEMORRHOIDS
pil•fer \ˈpil-fər\ *vb* : to steal in small quantities
pil•grim \ˈpil-grəm\ *n* [ME, fr. OF *peligrin,* fr. LL *pelegrinus,* alter. of L *peregrinus* foreigner, fr. *peregrinus* foreign, fr. *peregri* abroad, fr. *per* through + *ager* land] **1** : one who journeys in foreign lands : WAYFARER **2** : one who travels to a shrine or holy

place as an act of devotion **3** *cap* : one of the English settlers founding Plymouth colony in 1620
pil•grim•age \-grə-mij\ *n* : a journey of a pilgrim esp. to a shrine or holy place
pil•ing \ˈpī-liŋ\ *n* : a structure of piles
pill \ˈpil\ *n* **1** : a medicine in a small rounded mass to be swallowed whole **2** : a disagreeable or tiresome person **3** *often cap* : an oral contraceptive — usu. used with *the*
pil•lage \ˈpi-lij\ *vb* **pil•laged; pil•lag•ing** : to take booty : LOOT, PLUNDER — **pillage** *n* — **pil•lag•er** *n*
pil•lar \ˈpi-lər\ *n* **1** : a strong upright support (as for a roof) **2** : a column or shaft standing alone esp. as a monument — **pil•lared** \-lərd\ *adj*
pill•box \ˈpil-ˌbäks\ *n* **1** : a shallow round box for pills **2** : a low concrete emplacement esp. for machine guns
pil•lion \ˈpil-yən\ *n* **1** : a pad or cushion placed behind a saddle for an extra rider **2** *chiefly Brit* : a motorcycle or bicycle saddle for a passenger
¹pil•lo•ry \ˈpi-lə-rē\ *n, pl* **-ries** : a wooden frame for public punishment having holes in which the head and hands can be locked
²pillory *vb* **-ried; -ry•ing** **1** : to set in a pillory **2** : to expose to public scorn
¹pil•low \ˈpi-lō\ *n* : a case filled with springy material (as feathers) and used to support the head of a resting person
²pillow *vb* : to rest or place on or as if on a pillow; *also* : to serve as a pillow for
pil•low•case \-ˌkās\ *n* : a removable covering for a pillow
¹pi•lot \ˈpī-lət\ *n* **1** : HELMSMAN, STEERSMAN **2** : a person qualified and licensed to take ships into and out of a port **3** : GUIDE, LEADER **4** : one that flies an aircraft or spacecraft **5** : a television show filmed or taped as a sample of a proposed series — **pi•lot•less** *adj*
²pilot *vb* : CONDUCT, GUIDE; *esp* : to act as pilot of
³pilot *adj* : serving as a guiding or activating device or as a testing or trial unit ⟨a ~ light⟩ ⟨a ~ factory⟩
pi•lot•house \ˈpī-lət-ˌhau̇s\ *n* : a shelter on the upper deck of a ship for the steering gear and the helmsman
pil•sner *also* **pil•sen•er** \ˈpilz-nər, ˈpil-zə-\ *n* [G, lit., of Pilsen (Plzeň), city in the Czech Republic] **1** : a light beer with a strong flavor of hops **2** : a tall slender footed glass for beer
pi•men•to \pə-ˈmen-tō\ *n, pl* **pimentos** *or* **pimento** [Sp *pimienta* allspice, pepper, fr. LL *pigmenta,* pl. of *pigmentum* plant juice, fr. L, pigment] **1** : ALLSPICE **2** : PIMIENTO
pi•mien•to \pə-ˈmen-tō\ *n, pl* **-tos** : any of various mild red sweet pepper fruits used esp. to stuff olives and to make paprika
pimp \ˈpimp\ *n* : a man who solicits clients for a prostitute — **pimp** *vb*
pim•per•nel \ˈpim-pər-ˌnel, -nəl\ *n* : any of a genus of herbs related to the primroses
pim•ple \ˈpim-pəl\ *n* : a small inflamed swelling on the skin often containing pus — **pim•ply** \-p(ə-)lē\ *adj*
¹pin \ˈpin\ *n* **1** : a piece of wood or metal used esp. for fastening articles together or as a support by which one article may be suspended from another; *esp* : a small pointed piece of wire with a head used for fastening clothes or attaching papers **2** : an ornament or emblem fastened to clothing with a pin **3** : one of the wooden pieces constituting the target (as in bowling); *also* : the staff of the flag marking a hole on a golf course **4** : LEG
²pin *vb* **pinned; pin•ning** **1** : to fasten, join, or secure with a pin **2** : to hold fast or immobile **3** : ATTACH, HANG ⟨*pinned* their hopes on one man⟩ **4** : to assign the blame for ⟨~ a crime on someone⟩ **5** : to define clearly : ESTABLISH ⟨~ down an idea⟩
PIN *abbr* personal identification number
pi•ña co•la•da \ˌpēn-yə-kō-ˈlä-də, ˌpē-nə-\ *n* [Sp, lit., strained pineapple] : a tall drink made of rum, cream of coconut, and pineapple juice mixed with ice
pin•afore \ˈpi-nə-ˌfōr\ *n* : a sleeveless dress or apron fastened at the back
pince–nez \paⁿs-ˈnā\ *n, pl* **pince–nez** *same or* -ˈnāz\ [F, lit., pinch-nose] : eyeglasses clipped to the nose by a spring
pin•cer \ˈpin-sər\ *n* **1** *pl* : a gripping instrument with two handles and two grasping jaws **2** : a claw (as of a lobster) resembling pincers
¹pinch \ˈpinch\ *vb* **1** : to squeeze between the finger and thumb or between the jaws of an instrument **2** : to compress painfully **3** : CONTRACT, SHRIVEL **4** : to be miserly; *also* : to subject to strict economy **5** : to confine or limit narrowly **6** : STEAL **7** : ARREST
²pinch *n* **1** : a critical point : EMERGENCY **2** : painful effect **3** : an act of pinching **4** : a very small quantity **5** : ARREST
³pinch *adj* : SUBSTITUTE ⟨a ~ runner⟩
pinch–hit \ˌpinch-ˈhit\ *vb* **1** : to bat in the place of another player esp. when a hit is particularly needed **2** : to act or serve in place of another — **pinch hit** *n* — **pinch hitter** *n*
pin curl *n* : a curl made usu. by dampening a strand of hair, coiling it, and securing it by a hairpin or clip
pin•cush•ion \ˈpin-ˌku̇-shən\ *n* : a cushion for pins not in use
¹pine \ˈpīn\ *n* : any of a genus of evergreen cone-bearing trees; *also* : the light durable resinous wood of a pine
²pine *vb* **pined; pin•ing** **1** : to lose vigor or health through distress **2** : to long for something intensely
pi•ne•al \ˈpī-nē-əl, pī-ˈnē-əl\ *n* : PINEAL GLAND — **pineal** *adj*
pineal gland *n* : a small usu. conical appendage of the brain of all vertebrates with a cranium that functions primarily as an endocrine organ
pine•ap•ple \ˈpīn-ˌa-pəl\ *n* : a tropical plant bearing an edible juicy fruit; *also* : its fruit
pin•feath•er \ˈpin-ˌfe-t͟hər\ *n* : a new feather just coming through the skin
ping \ˈpiŋ\ *n* **1** : a sharp sound like that of a bullet striking **2** : engine knock
pin•hole \ˈpin-ˌhōl\ *n* : a small hole made by, for, or as if by a pin
¹pin•ion \ˈpin-yən\ *n* : the end section of a bird's wing; *also* : WING
²pinion *vb* : to restrain by binding the arms; *also* : SHACKLE
³pinion *n* : a gear with a small number of teeth designed to mesh with a larger wheel or rack
¹pink \ˈpiŋk\ *n* **1** : any of a genus of plants with narrow leaves often grown for their showy flowers **2** : the highest degree : HEIGHT ⟨the ~ of condition⟩
²pink *n* : a light tint of red
³pink *adj* **1** : of the color pink **2** : holding socialistic views — **pink•ish** *adj*
⁴pink *vb* **1** : to perforate in an ornamental pattern **2** : PIERCE, STAB **3** : to cut a saw-toothed edge on
pink elephants *n pl* : hallucinations arising esp. from heavy drinking or use of narcotics
pink•eye \ˈpiŋk-ˌī\ *n* : an acute contagious eye inflammation
pin•kie *or* **pin•ky** \ˈpiŋ-kē\ *n, pl* **pinkies** : the smallest finger of the hand
pin•nace \ˈpi-nəs\ *n* **1** : a light sailing ship **2** : a ship's boat
pin•na•cle \ˈpi-ni-kəl\ *n* [ME *pinacle,* fr. MF, fr. LL *pinnaculum* small wing, gable, fr. L *pinna* wing, battlement] **1** : a turret ending in a small spire **2** : a lofty peak **3** : ACME
pin•nate \ˈpi-ˌnāt\ *adj* : resembling a feather esp. in having similar parts arranged on each side of an axis ⟨a ~ leaf⟩ — **pin•nate•ly** *adv*
pi•noch•le \ˈpē-ˌnə-kəl\ *n* : a card game played with a 48-card deck
pi•ñon *or* **pin•yon** \ˈpin-ˌyōn, -ˌyän\ *n, pl* **pi•ñons** *or*

DICTIONARY

pin•yons *or* **pi•ño•nes** \pin-ˈyō-nēz\ [AmerSp *piñón*] : any of various low-growing pines of western No. America with edible seeds; *also* : the edible seed of a piñon

pin•point \ˈpin-ˌpȯint\ *vb* : to locate, hit, or aim with great precision

pin•prick \-ˌprik\ *n* **1** : a small puncture made by or as if by a pin **2** : a petty irritation or annoyance

pins and needles *n pl* : a pricking tingling sensation in a limb growing numb or recovering from numbness — **on pins and needles** : in a nervous or jumpy state of anticipation

pin•stripe \ˈpin-ˌstrīp\ *n* : a narrow stripe on a fabric; *also* : a suit with such stripes — **pin–striped** \-ˌstrīpt\ *adj*

pint \ˈpīnt\ *n* — see WEIGHT table

pin•to \ˈpin-ˌtō\ *n, pl* **pintos** *also* **pintoes** : a spotted horse or pony

pinto bean *n* : a spotted seed produced by a kind of kidney bean and used for food

pin•up \ˈpin-ˌəp\ *adj* : suitable or designed for hanging on a wall; *also* : suited (as by beauty) to be the subject of a pinup photograph

pin•wheel \-ˌhwēl, -ˌwēl\ *n* **1** : a fireworks device in the form of a revolving wheel of colored fire **2** : a toy consisting of lightweight vanes that revolve at the end of a stick

pin•worm \-ˌwərm\ *n* : a nematode worm parasitic in the human intestine

pin•yin \ˈpin-ˈyin\ *n, often cap* : a system for writing Chinese ideograms by using Roman letters to represent the sounds

¹**pi•o•neer** \ˌpī-ə-ˈnir\ *n* **1** : one that originates or helps open up a new line of thought or activity **2** : an early settler in a territory

²**pioneer** *vb* **1** : to act as a pioneer **2** : to open or prepare for others to follow; *also* : SETTLE

pi•ous \ˈpī-əs\ *adj* **1** : marked by reverence for deity : DEVOUT **2** : excessively or affectedly religious **3** : SACRED, DEVOTIONAL **4** : showing loyal reverence for a person or thing : DUTIFUL **5** : marked by sham or hypocrisy — **pi•ous•ly** *adv*

¹**pip** \ˈpip\ *n* : one of the dots used on dice and dominoes to indicate numerical value

²**pip** *n* : a small fruit seed (as of an apple)

¹**pipe** \ˈpīp\ *n* **1** : a tubular musical instrument played by forcing air through it **2** : BAGPIPE **3** : a tube designed to conduct something (as water, steam, or oil) **4** : a device for smoking having a tube with a bowl at one end and a mouthpiece at the other

²**pipe** *vb* **piped; pip•ing 1** : to play on a pipe **2** : to speak in a high or shrill voice **3** : to convey by or as if by pipes — **pip•er** *n*

pipe down *vb* : to stop talking or making noise

pipe dream *n* : an illusory or fantastic hope

pipe•line \ˈpīp-ˌlīn\ *n* **1** : a line of pipe with pumps, valves, and control devices for conveying fluids **2** : a channel for information

pi•pette *or* **pi•pet** \pī-ˈpet\ *n* : a device for measuring and transferring small volumes of liquid

pipe up *vb* : to speak loudly and distinctly; *also* : to express an opinion freely

pip•ing \ˈpī-piŋ\ *n* **1** : the music of pipes **2** : a narrow fold of material used to decorate edges or seams

piping hot *adj* : very hot

pip•pin \ˈpi-pən\ *n* : any of several yellowish apples

pip–squeak \ˈpip-ˌskwēk\ *n* : one that is small or insignificant

pi•quant \ˈpē-kənt\ *adj* **1** : pleasantly savory : PUNGENT **2** : engagingly provocative; *also* : having a lively charm — **pi•quan•cy** \-kən-sē\ *n*

¹**pique** \ˈpēk\ *n* [F] : a passing feeling of wounded vanity : RESENTMENT

²**pique** *vb* **piqued; piqu•ing 1** : IRRITATE 1 **2** : to arouse by a provocation or challenge : GOAD

pi•qué *or* **pi•que** \pi-ˈkā\ *n* : a durable ribbed clothing fabric

pi•quet \pi-ˈkā\ *n* : a 2-handed card game played with 32 cards

pi•ra•cy \ˈpī-rə-sē\ *n, pl* **-cies 1** : robbery on the high seas; *also* : an act resembling such robbery **2** : the unauthorized use of another's production or invention

pi•ra•nha \pə-ˈrä-nə, -ˈrän-yə\ *n* [Pg, fr. Tupi (So. American Indian language) *pirãya,* fr. *pira* fish + *ãya* tooth] : any of various usu. small So. American fishes with sharp teeth that include some known to attack humans and large animals

pi•rate \ˈpī-rət\ *n* [ME, fr. MF or L; MF, fr. L *pirata,* fr. Gk *peiratēs,* fr. *peiran* to attempt, test] : one who commits piracy — **pirate** *vb* — **pi•rat•i•cal** \pə-ˈra-ti-kəl, pī-\ *adj*

pir•ou•ette \ˌpir-ə-ˈwet\ *n* [F] : a rapid whirling about of the body; *esp* : a full turn on the toe or ball of one foot in ballet — **pirouette** *vb*

pis *pl of* PI

pis•ca•to•ri•al \ˌpis-kə-ˈtōr-ē-əl\ *adj* : of or relating to fishing

Pi•sces \ˈpī-sēz\ *n* [ME, fr. L, lit., fishes] **1** : a zodiacal constellation between Aquarius and Aries usu. pictured as a fish **2** : the 12th sign of the zodiac in astrology; *also* : one born under this sign

pis•mire \ˈpis-ˌmīr\ *n* : ANT

pi•so \ˈpē-(ˌ)sō\ *n* : the peso of the Philippines

pis•ta•chio \pə-ˈsta-shē-ˌō, -ˈstä-\ *n, pl* **-chios** : the greenish edible seed of a small Asian tree related to the sumacs; *also* : the tree

pis•til \ˈpist-ᵊl\ *n* : the female reproductive organ in a flower — **pis•til•late** \ˈpis-tə-ˌlāt\ *adj*

pis•tol \ˈpist-ᵊl\ *n* : a handgun whose chamber is integral with the barrel

pis•tol–whip \-ˌhwip\ *vb* : to beat with a pistol

pis•ton \ˈpis-tən\ *n* : a sliding piece that receives and transmits motion and that usu. consists of a short cylinder inside a large cylinder

¹**pit** \ˈpit\ *n* **1** : a hole, shaft, or cavity in the ground **2** : an often sunken area designed for a particular use; *also* : an enclosed place (as for cockfights) **3** : HELL; *also, pl* : WORST ⟨it's the ~*s*⟩ **4** : a natural hollow or indentation in a surface **5** : a small indented mark or scar (as from disease or corrosion) **6** : an area beside a racecourse where cars are fueled and repaired during a race

²**pit** *vb* **pit•ted; pit•ting 1** : to form pits in or become marred with pits **2** : to match for fighting

³**pit** *n* : the stony seed of some fruits (as the cherry, peach, and date)

⁴**pit** *vb* **pit•ted; pit•ting** : to remove the pit from

pi•ta \ˈpē-tə\ *n* [NGk] : a thin flat bread

pit–a–pat \ˌpi-ti-ˈpat\ *n* : PITTER-PATTER — **pit–a–pat** *adv or adj*

pit bull *n* : a powerful compact short-haired dog developed for fighting

¹**pitch** \ˈpich\ *n* **1** : a dark sticky substance left over esp. from distilling tar or petroleum **2** : resin from various conifers — **pitchy** *adj*

²**pitch** *vb* **1** : to erect and fix firmly in place ⟨~ a tent⟩ **2** : THROW, FLING **3** : to deliver a baseball to a batter **4** : to toss (as coins) toward a mark **5** : to set at a particular level ⟨~ the voice low⟩ **6** : to fall headlong **7** : to have the front end (as of a ship) alternately plunge and rise **8** : to incline downward : SLOPE

³**pitch** *n* **1** : the action or a manner of pitching **2** : degree of slope ⟨~ of a roof⟩ **3** : the relative level of some quality or state ⟨a high ~ of excitement⟩ **4** : highness or lowness of sound; *also* : a standard frequency for tuning instruments **5** : an often high-pressure sales talk **6** : the delivery of a baseball to a batter; *also* : the baseball delivered

pitch•blende \ˈpich-ˌblend\ *n* : a dark mineral that is the chief source of uranium

¹pitch•er \ˈpi-chər\ *n* : a container for liquids that usu. has a lip and a handle
²pitcher *n* : one that pitches esp. in a baseball game
pitcher plant *n* : any of various plants with leaves modified to resemble pitchers in which insects are trapped and digested
pitch•fork \ˈpich-ˌfȯrk\ *n* : a long-handled fork used esp. in pitching hay
pitch in *vb* **1** : to begin to work **2** : to contribute to a common effort
pitch•man \ˈpich-mən\ *n* : SALESMAN; *esp* : one who sells merchandise on the streets or from a concession
pit•e•ous \ˈpi-tē-əs\ *adj* : arousing pity : PITIFUL — **pit•e•ous•ly** *adv*
pit•fall \ˈpit-ˌfȯl\ *n* **1** : TRAP, SNARE; *esp* : a covered pit used for capturing animals **2** : a hidden danger or difficulty
pith \ˈpith\ *n* **1** : loose spongy tissue esp. in the center of the stem of vascular plants **2** : the essential part : CORE
pithy \ˈpi-thē\ *adj* **pith•i•er; -est 1** : consisting of or filled with pith **2** : having substance and point : CONCISE
piti•able \ˈpi-tē-ə-bəl\ *adj* : PITIFUL
piti•ful \ˈpi-ti-fəl\ *adj* **1** : arousing or deserving pity ⟨a ∼ sight⟩ **2** : MEAN, MEAGER — **piti•ful•ly** *adv*
piti•less \ˈpi-ti-ləs\ *adj* : devoid of pity : MERCILESS — **pit•i•less•ly** *adv*
pi•ton \ˈpē-ˌtän\ *n* [F] : a spike, wedge, or peg that can be driven into a rock or ice surface as a support
pit•tance \ˈpit-ᵊns\ *n* : a small portion, amount, or allowance
pit•ted \ˈpi-təd\ *adj* : marked with pits
pit•ter–pat•ter \ˈpi-tər-ˌpa-tər, ˈpi-tē-\ *n* : a rapid succession of light taps or sounds — **pitter–patter** \ˌpi-tər-ˈpa-tər, ˌpi-tē-\ *adv or adj* — **pitter–patter** *same as adv*\ *vb*
pi•tu•i•tary \pə-ˈtü-ə-ˌter-ē, -ˈtyü-\ *n, pl* **-itar•ies** : PITUITARY GLAND — **pituitary** *adj*
pituitary gland *n* : a small oval endocrine gland attached to the brain which produces various hormones that affect most basic bodily functions
pit viper *n* : any of various mostly New World venomous snakes with a sensory pit on each side of the head and hollow perforated fangs
¹pity \ˈpi-tē\ *n, pl* **pit•ies** [ME *pite*, fr. OF *pité*, fr. L *pietas* piety, pity, fr. *pius* pious] **1** : sympathetic sorrow : COMPASSION **2** : something to be regretted
²pity *vb* **pit•ied; pity•ing** : to feel pity for
¹piv•ot \ˈpi-vət\ *n* : a fixed pin on which something turns — **pivot** *adj* — **piv•ot•al** \ˈpi-vət-ᵊl\ *adj*
²pivot *vb* : to turn on or as if on a pivot
pix *pl of* PIC
pix•el \ˈpik-səl, -ˌsel\ *n* : any of the small elements that together make up an image (as on a television screen)
pix•ie *or* **pixy** \ˈpik-sē\ *n, pl* **pix•ies** : FAIRY; *esp* : a mischievous sprite
piz•za \ˈpēt-sə\ *n* [It] : an open pie made of rolled bread dough spread with a spiced mixture (as of tomatoes, cheese, and ground meat) and baked
piz•zazz *or* **pi•zazz** \pə-ˈzaz\ *n* **1** : GLAMOUR **2** : VITALITY
piz•ze•ria \ˌpēt-sə-ˈrē-ə\ *n* : an establishment where pizzas are made and sold
piz•zi•ca•to \ˌpit-si-ˈkä-tō\ *adv or adj* [It] : by means of plucking instead of bowing — used as a direction in music
pj's \ˈpē-ˌjāz\ *n pl* : PAJAMAS
pk *abbr* **1** park **2** peak **3** peck **4** pike
pkg *abbr* package
pkt *abbr* **1** packet **2** pocket
pkwy *abbr* parkway
pl *abbr* **1** place **2** plate **3** plural
¹plac•ard \ˈpla-kərd, -ˌkärd\ *n* : a notice posted in a public place : POSTER
²plac•ard \-ˌkärd, -kərd\ *vb* **1** : to cover with or as if with placards **2** : to announce by or as if by posting
pla•cate \ˈplā-ˌkāt, ˈpla-\ *vb* **pla•cat•ed; pla•cat•ing** : to soothe esp. by concessions : APPEASE — **pla•ca•ble** \ˈpla-kə-bəl, ˈplā-\ *adj*
¹place \ˈplās\ *n* [ME, fr. OF, open space, fr. L *platea* broad street, fr. Gk *plateia (hodos)*, fr. fem. of *platys* broad, flat] **1** : SPACE, ROOM **2** : an indefinite region : AREA **3** : a building or locality used for a special purpose **4** : a center of population **5** : a particular part of a surface : SPOT **6** : relative position in a scale or sequence; *also* : position at the end of a competition ⟨last ∼⟩ **7** : ACCOMMODATION; *esp* : SEAT **8** : the position of a figure within a numeral ⟨12 is a two ∼ number⟩ **9** : JOB; *esp* : public office **10** : a public square **11** : 2d place at the finish (as of a horse race)
²place *vb* **placed; plac•ing 1** : to put in a particular place : SET **2** : to distribute in an orderly manner : ARRANGE **3** : IDENTIFY **4** : to give an order for ⟨∼ a bet⟩ **5** : to earn a given spot in a competition; *esp* : to come in 2d
pla•ce•bo \plə-ˈsē-bō\ *n, pl* **-bos** [L, I shall please] : an inert medication used for its psychological effect or for purposes of comparison in an experiment
place•hold•er \ˈplās-ˌhōl-dər\ *n* : a symbol in a mathematical or logical expression that may be replaced by the name of any element of a set
place•kick \-ˌkik\ *n* : the kicking of a ball placed or held on the ground — **placekick** *vb* — **place•kick•er** *n*
place•ment \ˈplās-mənt\ *n* : an act or instance of placing
place–name \-ˌnām\ *n* : the name of a geographical locality
pla•cen•ta \plə-ˈsen-tə\ *n, pl* **-tas** *or* **-tae** \-(ˌ)tē\ [NL, fr. L, flat cake] : the organ in most mammals by which the fetus is joined to the maternal uterus and is nourished — **pla•cen•tal** \-ˈsent-ᵊl\ *adj*
plac•er \ˈpla-sər\ *n* : a deposit of sand or gravel containing particles of valuable mineral (as gold)
plac•id \ˈpla-səd\ *adj* : UNDISTURBED, PEACEFUL **syn** tranquil, serene, calm — **pla•cid•i•ty** \pla-ˈsi-də-tē\ *n* — **plac•id•ly** *adv*
plack•et \ˈpla-kət\ *n* : a slit in a garment
pla•gia•rise *Brit var of* PLAGIARIZE
pla•gia•rize \ˈplā-jə-ˌrīz\ *vb* **-rized; -riz•ing** : to present the ideas or words of another as one's own — **pla•gia•rism** \-ˌri-zəm\ *n* — **pla•gia•rist** \-rist\ *n*
¹plague \ˈplāg\ *n* **1** : a disastrous evil or influx; *also* : NUISANCE **2** : PESTILENCE; *esp* : a destructive contagious bacterial disease (as bubonic plague)
²plague *vb* **plagued; plagu•ing 1** : to afflict with or as if with disease or disaster **2** : TEASE, TORMENT, HARASS
plaid \ˈplad\ *n* **1** : a rectangular length of tartan worn esp. over the left shoulder as part of the Scottish national costume **2** : a twilled woolen fabric with a tartan pattern **3** : a pattern of unevenly spaced repeated stripes crossing at right angles — **plaid** *adj*
¹plain \ˈplān\ *n* : an extensive area of level or rolling treeless country
²plain *adj* **1** : lacking ornament ⟨a ∼ dress⟩ **2** : free of extraneous matter **3** : OPEN, UNOBSTRUCTED ⟨∼ view⟩ **4** : EVIDENT, OBVIOUS **5** : easily understood : CLEAR **6** : CANDID, BLUNT **7** : SIMPLE, UNCOMPLICATED ⟨∼ cooking⟩ **8** : lacking beauty or ugliness — **plain•ly** *adv* — **plain•ness** *n*
plain•clothes•man \ˈplān-ˈklōt͟hz-mən, -ˈklōz-, -ˌman\ *n* : a police officer who wears civilian clothes instead of a uniform while on duty : DETECTIVE
plain•spo•ken \-ˈspō-kən\ *adj* : FRANK
plaint \ˈplānt\ *n* **1** : LAMENTATION, WAIL **2** : PROTEST, COMPLAINT
plain•tiff \ˈplān-təf\ *n* : the complaining party in a lawsuit

DICTIONARY

PLANETS

SYMBOL	NAME	MEAN DISTANCE FROM THE SUN astronomical units	MEAN DISTANCE FROM THE SUN million miles	PERIOD OF REVOLUTION IN DAYS OR YEARS	EQUATORIAL DIAMETER IN MILES
☿	Mercury	0.387	36.0	87.97 d.	3,032
♀	Venus	0.723	67.2	224.70 d.	7,523
⊕	Earth	1.000	92.9	365.26 d.	7,928
♂	Mars	1.524	141.5	686.98 d.	4,218
♃	Jupiter	5.203	483.4	11.86 y.	88,900
♄	Saturn	9.522	884.6	29.46 y.	74,900
♅	Uranus	19.201	1783.8	84.01 y.	31,800
♆	Neptune	30.074	2793.9	164.79 y.	30,800
♇	Pluto	39.725	3690.5	247.69 y.	1,400

plain•tive \ˈplān-tiv\ *adj* : expressive of suffering or woe : MELANCHOLY — **plain•tive•ly** *adv*

plait \ˈplāt, ˈplat\ *n* **1** : PLEAT **2** : a braid esp. of hair or straw — **plait** *vb*

[1]**plan** \ˈplan\ *n* **1** : a drawing or diagram showing the parts or details of something **2** : a method for accomplishing an objective; *also* : GOAL, AIM

[2]**plan** *vb* **planned; plan•ning 1** : to form a plan of ⟨~ a new city⟩ **2** : INTEND ⟨*planned* to go⟩ — **plan•ner** *n*

[1]**plane** \ˈplān\ *vb* **planed; plan•ing** : to smooth or level off with or as if with a plane — **plan•er** *n*

[2]**plane** *n* : PLANE TREE

[3]**plane** *n* : a tool for smoothing or shaping a wood surface

[4]**plane** *n* **1** : a level or flat surface **2** : a level of existence, consciousness, or development **3** : AIRPLANE

[5]**plane** *adj* **1** : FLAT, LEVEL **2** : dealing with flat surfaces or figures ⟨~ geometry⟩

plane•load \ˈplān-ˌlōd\ *n* : a load that fills an airplane

plan•et \ˈpla-nət\ *n* [ME *planete*, fr. OF, fr. LL *planeta*, modif. of Gk *planēt-*, *planēs*, lit., wanderer, fr. *planasthai* to wander] : any of the large bodies in the solar system that revolve around the sun — **plan•e•tary** \-nə-ˌter-ē\ *adj*

plan•e•tar•i•um \ˌpla-nə-ˈter-ē-əm\ *n, pl* **-i•ums** *or* **-ia** \-ē-ə\ : a building or room housing a device to project images of celestial bodies

plan•e•tes•i•mal \ˌpla-nə-ˈtes-ə-məl\ *n* : any of numerous small solid celestial bodies which may have existed during the formation of the solar system

plan•e•toid \ˈpla-nə-ˌtȯid\ *n* : a body resembling a planet; *esp* : ASTEROID

plane tree *n* : any of a genus of trees (as a sycamore) with large lobed leaves and globe-shaped fruit

plan•gent \ˈplan-jənt\ *adj* **1** : having a loud reverberating sound **2** : having an expressive esp. plaintive quality — **plan•gen•cy** \-jən-sē\ *n*

[1]**plank** \ˈplaŋk\ *n* **1** : a heavy thick board **2** : an article in the platform of a political party

[2]**plank** *vb* **1** : to cover with planks **2** : to set or lay down forcibly **3** : to cook and serve on a board

plank•ing \ˈplaŋ-kiŋ\ *n* : a quantity or covering of planks

plank•ton \ˈplaŋk-tən\ *n* [G, fr. Gk, neut. of *planktos* drifting] : the passively floating or weakly swimming animal and plant life of a body of water — **plank•ton•ic** \plaŋk-ˈtä-nik\ *adj*

[1]**plant** \ˈplant\ *vb* **1** : to set in the ground to grow **2** : ESTABLISH, SETTLE **3** : to stock or provide with something **4** : to place firmly or forcibly **5** : to hide or arrange with intent to deceive

[2]**plant** *n* **1** : any of a kingdom of living things that usu. have no locomotor ability or obvious sense organs and have cellulose cell walls and usu. capacity for indefinite growth **2** : the land, buildings, and machinery used in carrying on a trade or business

[1]**plan•tain** \ˈplant-ᵊn\ *n* [ME, fr. OF, fr. L *plantagin-*, *plantago*, fr. *planta* sole of the foot; fr. its broad leaves] : any of a genus of short-stemmed weedy herbs with spikes of tiny greenish flowers

[2]**plantain** *n* [Sp *plántano*, *plátano* plane tree, banana tree, fr. ML *plantanus* plane tree, alter. of L *platanus*] : a banana plant with starchy greenish fruit that are eaten cooked; *also* : its fruit

plan•tar \ˈplan-tər, -ˌtär\ *adj* : of or relating to the sole of the foot

plan•ta•tion \plan-ˈtā-shən\ *n* **1** : a large group of plants and esp. trees under cultivation **2** : an agricultural estate usu. worked by resident laborers

plant•er \ˈplan-tər\ *n* **1** : one that plants or sows; *esp* : an owner or operator of a plantation **2** : a container for plants

plant louse *n* : APHID

plaque \ˈplak\ *n* [F] **1** : an ornamental brooch **2** : a flat thin piece (as of metal) used for decoration; *also* : a commemorative tablet **3** : a bacteria-containing film on a tooth

plash \ˈplash\ *n* : SPLASH — **plash** *vb*

plas•ma \ˈplaz-mə\ *n* **1** : the fluid part of blood, lymph, or milk **2** : a gas composed of ionized particles — **plas•mat•ic** \plaz-ˈma-tik\ *adj*

[1]**plas•ter** \ˈplas-tər\ *n* **1** : a dressing consisting of a backing spread with an often medicated substance that clings to the skin ⟨adhesive ~⟩ **2** : a paste that hardens as it dries and is used for coating walls and ceilings

[2]**plaster** *vb* : to cover with or as if with plaster — **plas•ter•er** *n*

plas•ter•board \ˈplas-tər-ˌbōrd\ *n* : a wallboard consisting of fiberboard, paper, or felt over a plaster core

plaster of par•is \-ˈpar-əs\ *often cap 2d P* : a white powder made from gypsum and used as a quick-setting paste with water for casts and molds

[1]**plas•tic** \ˈplas-tik\ *adj* [L *plasticus* of molding, fr. Gk *plastikos*, fr. *plassein* to mold, form] **1** : capable of being molded ⟨~ clay⟩ **2** : characterized by or using modeling ⟨~ arts⟩ **3** : made or consisting of a plastic **syn** pliable, pliant, ductile, malleable, adaptable — **plas•tic•i•ty** \plas-ˈti-sə-tē\ *n*

[2]**plastic** *n* : a plastic substance; *esp* : a synthetic or processed material that can be formed into rigid objects or into films or filaments

plastic surgery *n* : surgery to repair, restore, or improve lost, injured, defective, or misshapen body parts — **plastic surgeon** *n*

[1]**plat** \ˈplat\ *n* **1** : a small plot of ground **2** : a plan of a piece of land with actual or proposed features (as lots)

[2]**plat** *vb* **plat•ted; plat•ting** : to make a plat of

[1]**plate** \ˈplāt\ *n* **1 :** a flat thin piece of material **2 :** domestic hollowware made of or plated with gold, silver, or base metals **3 :** DISH **4 :** HOME PLATE **5 :** the molded metal or plastic cast of a page of type to be printed from **6 :** a sheet of glass coated with a chemical sensitive to light and used in photography **7 :** the part of a denture that fits to the mouth; *also* **:** DENTURE **8 :** something printed from an engraving **9 :** a huge mobile segment of the earth's crust

[2]**plate** *vb* **plat•ed; plat•ing 1 :** to overlay with metal (as gold or silver) **2 :** to make a printing plate of

pla•teau \pla-ˈtō\ *n, pl* **plateaus** *or* **pla•teaux** \-ˈtōz\ [F] **:** a large level area of high land

plate glass *n* **:** rolled, ground, and polished sheet glass

plat•en \ˈplat-ᵊn\ *n* **1 :** a flat plate; *esp* **:** one that exerts or receives pressure (as in a printing press) **2 :** the roller of a typewriter or printer

plate tectonics *n* **:** a theory in geology that the lithosphere is divided into plates at the boundaries of which much of earth's seismic activity occurs

plat•form \ˈplat-ˌfȯrm\ *n* **1 :** a raised flooring or stage for speakers, performers, or workers **2 :** a declaration of the principles on which a group of persons (as a political party) stands

plat•ing \ˈplā-tiŋ\ *n* **:** a coating of metal plates or plate ⟨the ~ of a ship⟩

plat•i•num \ˈplat-ᵊn-əm\ *n* **:** a heavy grayish white metallic chemical element — see ELEMENT table

plat•i•tude \ˈpla-tə-ˌtüd, -ˌtyüd\ *n* **:** a flat or trite remark — **plat•i•tu•di•nous** \-ˈtüd-ᵊn-əs, -ˈtyüd-\ *adj*

pla•ton•ic love \plə-ˈtä-nik-, plā-\ *n, often cap P* **:** a close relationship between two persons without sexual desire

pla•toon \plə-ˈtün\ *n* [F *peloton* small detachment, lit., ball, fr. *pelote* little ball] **1 :** a subdivision of a company-size military unit usu. consisting of two or more squads or sections **2 :** a group of football players trained either for offense or for defense and sent into the game as a body

platoon sergeant *n* **:** a noncommissioned officer in the army ranking below a first sergeant

plat•ter \ˈpla-tər\ *n* **1 :** a large serving plate **2 :** a phonograph record

platy \ˈpla-tē\ *n, pl* **platy** *or* **plat•ys** *or* **plat•ies :** either of two small stocky often brilliantly colored bony fishes that are popular for tropical aquariums

platy•pus \ˈpla-ti-pəs\ *n, pl* **platy•pus•es** *also* **platy-pi** \-ˌpī\ [NL, fr. Gk *platypous* flat-footed, fr. *platys* broad, flat + *pous* foot] **:** a small aquatic egg-laying marsupial mammal of Australia with webbed feet and a fleshy bill like a duck's

platypus

plau•dit \ˈplȯ-dət\ *n* **:** an act of applause

plau•si•ble \ˈplȯ-zə-bəl\ *adj* [L *plausibilis* worthy of applause, fr. *plausus*, pp. of *plaudere* to applaud] **:** seemingly worthy of belief — **plau•si•bil•i•ty** \ˌplȯ-zə-ˈbi-lə-tē\ *n* — **plau•si•bly** \ˈplȯ-zə-blē\ *adv*

[1]**play** \ˈplā\ *n* **1 :** brisk handling of something (as a weapon) **2 :** the course of a game; *also* **:** a particular act or maneuver in a game **3 :** recreational activity; *esp* **:** the spontaneous activity of children **4 :** JEST ⟨said in ~⟩ **5 :** the act or an instance of punning **6 :** GAMBLING **7 :** OPERATION ⟨bring extra force into ~⟩ **8 :** a brisk or light movement **9 :** free motion (as of part of a machine) **10 :** scope for action **11 :** PUBLICITY **12 :** an effort to arouse liking ⟨made a ~ for her⟩ **13 :** a stage representation of a drama; *also* **:** a dramatic composition — **play•ful** \-fəl\ *adj* — **play•ful•ly** *adv* — **play•ful•ness** *n* — **in play :** in condition or position to be played

[2]**play** *vb* **1 :** to engage in recreation **:** FROLIC **2 :** to handle or behave lightly or absentmindedly **3 :** to make a pun ⟨~ on words⟩ **4 :** to take advantage ⟨~ on fears⟩ **5 :** to move or operate in a brisk or irregular manner ⟨a flashlight *~ed* over the wall⟩ **6 :** to perform music ⟨~ on a violin⟩; *also* **:** to perform (music) on an instrument ⟨~ a waltz⟩ **7 :** to perform music upon ⟨~ the piano⟩; *also* **:** to sound in performance ⟨the organ is *~ing*⟩ **8 :** to cause to emit sounds ⟨~ a radio⟩ **9 :** to act in a dramatic medium; *also* **:** to act in the character of ⟨~ the hero⟩ **10 :** GAMBLE **11 :** to behave in a specified way ⟨~ safe⟩; *also* **:** COOPERATE ⟨~ along with him⟩ **12 :** to deal with; *also* **:** EMPHASIZE ⟨~ up her good qualities⟩ **13 :** to perform for amusement ⟨~ a trick⟩ **14 :** WREAK **15 :** to contend with in a game; *also* **:** to fill (a certain position) on a team **16 :** to make wagers on ⟨~ the races⟩ **17 :** WIELD, PLY **18 :** to keep in action — **play•er** *n*

play•act•ing \ˈplā-ˌak-tiŋ\ *n* **1 :** performance in theatrical productions **2 :** insincere or artificial behavior

play•back \-ˌbak\ *n* **:** an act of reproducing recorded sound or pictures — **play back** *vb*

play•bill \-ˌbil\ *n* **:** a poster advertising the performance of a play

play•book \-ˌbu̇k\ *n* **:** a notebook containing diagrammed football plays

play•boy \-ˌbȯi\ *n* **:** a man whose chief interest is the pursuit of pleasure

play•go•er \-ˌgō-ər\ *n* **:** a person who frequently attends plays

play•ground \-ˌgrau̇nd\ *n* **:** an area used for games and play esp. by children

play•house \-ˌhau̇s\ *n* **1 :** THEATER **2 :** a small house for children to play in

playing card *n* **:** any of a set of 24 to 78 cards marked to show its rank and suit and used to play a game of cards

play•let \ˈplā-lət\ *n* **:** a short play

play•mate \-ˌmāt\ *n* **:** a companion in play

play–off \-ˌȯf\ *n* **:** a contest or series of contests to break a tie or determine a championship

play•pen \-ˌpen\ *n* **:** a portable enclosure in which a young child may play

play•suit \-ˌsüt\ *n* **:** a sports and play outfit for women and children

play•thing \-ˌthiŋ\ *n* **:** TOY

play•wright \-ˌrīt\ *n* **:** a writer of plays

pla•za \ˈpla-zə, ˈplä-\ *n* [Sp, fr. L *platea* broad street] **1 :** a public square in a city or town **2 :** a shopping center

PLC *abbr, Brit* public limited company

plea \ˈplē\ *n* **1 :** a defendant's answer in law to a charge or indictment **2 :** something alleged as an excuse **3 :** ENTREATY, APPEAL

plead \ˈplēd\ *vb* **plead•ed** *or* **pled** \ˈpled\; **plead•ing 1 :** to argue before a court or authority ⟨~ a case⟩ **2 :** to answer to a charge or indictment ⟨~ guilty⟩ **3 :** to argue for or against something ⟨~ for acquittal⟩ **4 :** to appeal earnestly ⟨*~s* for help⟩ **5 :** to offer as a plea (as in defense) ⟨*~ed* illness⟩ — **plead•er** *n*

pleas•ant \ˈplez-ᵊnt\ *adj* **1 :** giving pleasure **:** AGREEABLE ⟨a ~ experience⟩ **2 :** marked by pleasing behavior or appearance ⟨a ~ person⟩ — **pleas•ant•ly** *adv* — **pleas•ant•ness** *n*

pleas•ant•ry \-ᵊn-trē\ *n, pl* **-ries :** a pleasant and casual act or speech

[1]please \ˈplēz\ *vb* **pleased; pleas•ing 1 :** to give pleasure or satisfaction to **2 :** LIKE ⟨do as you ~⟩ **3 :** to be the will or pleasure of ⟨may it ~ his Majesty⟩

[2]please *adv* — used as a function word to express politeness or emphasis in a request ⟨~ come in⟩

pleas•ing *adj* **:** giving pleasure — **pleas•ing•ly** *adv*

plea•sur•able \ˈple-zhə-rə-bəl\ *adj* **:** PLEASANT, GRATIFYING — **plea•sur•ably** \-blē\ *adv*

plea•sure \ˈple-zhər\ *n* **1 :** DESIRE, INCLINATION ⟨await your ~⟩ **2 :** a state of gratification **:** ENJOYMENT **3 :** a source of delight or joy

[1]pleat \ˈplēt\ *vb* **1 :** FOLD; *esp* **:** to arrange in pleats **2 :** BRAID

[2]pleat *n* **:** a fold (as in cloth) made by doubling material over on itself

plebe \ˈplēb\ *n* **:** a freshman at a military or naval academy

[1]ple•be•ian \pli-ˈbē-ən\ *n* **1 :** a member of the Roman plebs **2 :** one of the common people

[2]plebeian *adj* **1 :** of or relating to plebeians **2 :** COMMON, VULGAR

pleb•i•scite \ˈple-bə-ˌsīt, -sət\ *n* **:** a vote of the people (as of a country) on a proposal submitted to them

plebs \ˈplebz\ *n, pl* **ple•bes** \ˈplē-bēz\ **1 :** the general populace **2 :** the common people of ancient Rome

plec•trum \ˈplek-trəm\ *n, pl* **plec•tra** \-trə\ *or* **plec•trums** [L] **:** [3]PICK 3

[1]pledge \ˈplej\ *n* **1 :** something given as security for the performance of an act **2 :** the state of being held as a security or guaranty **3 :** TOAST 3 **4 :** PROMISE, VOW

[2]pledge *vb* **pledged; pledg•ing 1 :** to deposit as a pledge **2 :** TOAST **3 :** to bind by a pledge **:** PLIGHT **4 :** PROMISE

Pleis•to•cene \ˈplī-stə-ˌsēn\ *adj* **:** of, relating to, or being the earlier epoch of the Quaternary — **Pleistocene** *n*

ple•na•ry \ˈplē-nə-rē, ˈple-\ *adj* **1 :** FULL ⟨~ power⟩ **2 :** including all entitled to attend ⟨~ session⟩

pleni•po•ten•tia•ry \ˌple-nə-pə-ˈten-chə-rē, -ˈten-chē-ˌer-ē\ *n, pl* **-ries :** a diplomatic agent having full authority — **plenipotentiary** *adj*

plen•i•tude \ˈple-nə-ˌtüd, -ˌtyüd\ *n* **1 :** COMPLETENESS **2 :** ABUNDANCE

plen•te•ous \ˈplen-tē-əs\ *adj* **1 :** FRUITFUL **2 :** existing in plenty

plen•ti•ful \ˈplen-ti-fəl\ *adj* **1 :** containing or yielding plenty **2 :** ABUNDANT — **plen•ti•ful•ly** *adv*

plen•ty \ˈplen-tē\ *n* **:** a more than adequate number or amount

ple•num \ˈple-nəm, ˈplē-\ *n, pl* **-nums** *or* **-na** \-nə\ **:** a general assembly of all members esp. of a legislative body

pleth•o•ra \ˈple-thə-rə\ *n* **:** an excessive quantity or fullness; *also* **:** PROFUSION

pleu•ri•sy \ˈplu̇r-ə-sē\ *n* **:** inflammation of the membrane that lines the chest and covers the lungs

plex•us \ˈplek-səs\ *n, pl* **plex•us•es** \-sə-səz\ **:** an interlacing network esp. of blood vessels or nerves

pli•able \ˈplī-ə-bəl\ *adj* **1 :** FLEXIBLE **2 :** yielding easily to others **syn** plastic, pliant, ductile, malleable, adaptable — **pli•abil•i•ty** \ˌplī-ə-ˈbi-lə-tē\ *n*

pli•ant \ˈplī-ənt\ *adj* **1 :** FLEXIBLE **2 :** easily influenced **:** PLIABLE — **pli•an•cy** \-ən-sē\ *n*

pli•ers \ˈplī-ərz\ *n pl* **:** small pincers for bending or cutting wire or handling small objects

[1]plight \ˈplīt\ *vb* **:** to put or give in pledge **:** ENGAGE

[2]plight *n* **:** an unfortunate, difficult, or precarious situation

plinth \ˈplinth\ *n* **:** the lowest part of the base of an architectural column

Plio•cene \ˈplī-ə-ˌsēn\ *adj* **:** of, relating to, or being the latest epoch of the Tertiary — **Pliocene** *n*

PLO *abbr* Palestine Liberation Organization

plod \ˈpläd\ *vb* **plod•ded; plod•ding 1 :** to walk heavily or slowly **:** TRUDGE **2 :** to work laboriously and monotonously **:** DRUDGE — **plod•der** *n* — **plod•ding•ly** *adv*

plop \ˈpläp\ *vb* **plopped; plop•ping 1 :** to fall or move with a sound like that of something dropping into water **2 :** to set, drop, or throw heavily — **plop** *n*

[1]plot \ˈplät\ *n* **1 :** a small area of ground **2 :** a ground plan (as of an area) **3 :** the main story (as of a book or movie) **4 :** a secret scheme **:** INTRIGUE

[2]plot *vb* **plot•ted; plot•ting 1 :** to make a plot or plan of **2 :** to mark on or as if on a chart **3 :** to plan or contrive esp. secretly — **plot•ter** *n*

plo•ver \ˈplə-vər, ˈplō-\ *n, pl* **plover** *or* **plovers :** any of a family of shore-inhabiting birds that differ from the sandpipers in having shorter stouter bills

[1]plow *or* **plough** \ˈplau̇\ *n* **1 :** an implement used to cut, lift, turn over, and partly break up soil **2 :** a device (as a snowplow) operating like a plow

[2]plow *or* **plough** *vb* **1 :** to open, break up, or work with a plow **2 :** to move through like a plow ⟨a ship *~ing* the waves⟩ **3 :** to proceed laboriously — **plow•able** *adj* — **plow•er** *n*

plow•boy \ˈplau̇-ˌbȯi\ *n* **:** a boy who leads the horse drawing a plow

plow•man \-mən, -ˌman\ *n* **1 :** a man who guides a plow **2 :** a farm laborer

plow•share \-ˌsher\ *n* **:** a part of a plow that cuts the earth

ploy \ˈplȯi\ *n* **:** a tactic intended to embarrass or frustrate an opponent

[1]pluck \ˈplək\ *vb* **1 :** to pull off or out **:** PICK; *also* **:** to pull something from **2 :** to play (an instrument) by pulling the strings **3 :** TUG, TWITCH

[2]pluck *n* **1 :** an act or instance of plucking **2 :** SPIRIT, COURAGE

plucky \ˈplə-kē\ *adj* **pluck•i•er; -est :** COURAGEOUS, SPIRITED

[1]plug \ˈpləg\ *n* **1 :** STOPPER; *also* **:** an obstructing mass **2 :** a cake of tobacco **3 :** a poor or worn-out horse **4 :** SPARK PLUG **5 :** a lure with several hooks used in fishing **6 :** a device on the end of a cord for making an electrical connection **7 :** a piece of favorable publicity

[2]plug *vb* **plugged; plug•ging 1 :** to stop, make tight, or secure by inserting a plug **2 :** HIT, SHOOT **3 :** to publicize insistently **4 :** PLOD, DRUDGE

plum \ˈpləm\ *n* [ME, fr. OE *plūme,* modif. of L *prunum* plum, fr. Gk *proumnon*] **1 :** a smooth-skinned juicy fruit borne by trees related to the peach and cherry; *also* **:** a tree bearing plums **2 :** a raisin when used in desserts (as puddings) **3 :** something excellent; *esp* **:** something desirable given in return for a favor

plum•age \ˈplü-mij\ *n* **:** the feathers of a bird — **plum•aged** \-mijd\ *adj*

[1]plumb \ˈpləm\ *n* **:** a weight on the end of a line (**plumb line**) used esp. by builders to show vertical direction

[2]plumb *adv* **1 :** VERTICALLY **2 :** COMPLETELY **3 :** EXACTLY; *also* **:** IMMEDIATELY

[3]plumb *vb* **:** to sound, adjust, or test with a plumb ⟨~ the depth of a well⟩

[4]plumb *adj* **1 :** VERTICAL **2 :** COMPLETE

plumb•er \ˈplə-mər\ *n* **:** a worker who fits or repairs pipes and fixtures

plumb•ing \ˈplə-miŋ\ *n* **:** a system of pipes in a building for supplying and carrying off water

[1]plume \ˈplüm\ *n* **:** FEATHER; *esp* **:** a large, conspicuous, or showy feather — **plumed** \ˈplümd\ *adj* — **plumy** \ˈplü-mē\ *adj*

[2]plume *vb* **plumed; plum•ing 1 :** to provide or deck with feathers **2 :** to indulge (oneself) in pride

[1]plum•met \ˈplə-mət\ *n* **:** PLUMB; *also* **:** PLUMB LINE

[2]plummet *vb* **:** to drop or plunge straight down

[1]plump \ˈpləmp\ *vb* **1 :** to drop or fall suddenly or heavily **2 :** to favor something strongly ⟨*~ing* for change⟩

[2]plump *n* **:** a sudden heavy fall or blow; *also* **:** the sound made by it

[3]plump *adv* **1 :** straight down; *also* **:** straight ahead **2 :** UNQUALIFIEDLY

[4]**plump** *adj* : having a full rounded usu. pleasing form **syn** fleshy, stout, roly-poly, rotund — **plump•ness** *n*

[1]**plun•der** \ˈplən-dər\ *vb* : to take the goods of by force or wrongfully : PILLAGE — **plun•der•er** *n*

[2]**plunder** *n* : something taken by force or theft : LOOT

[1]**plunge** \ˈplənj\ *vb* **plunged; plung•ing 1** : IMMERSE, SUBMERGE **2** : to enter or cause to enter a state or course of action suddenly or violently ⟨~ into war⟩ **3** : to cast oneself into or as if into water **4** : to gamble heavily and recklessly **5** : to descend suddenly

[2]**plunge** *n* : a sudden dive, leap, or rush

plung•er \ˈplən-jər\ *n* **1** : one that plunges **2** : a sliding piece driven by or against fluid pressure : PISTON **3** : a rubber cup on a handle pushed against an opening to free a waste outlet of an obstruction

plunk \ˈpləŋk\ *vb* **1** : to make or cause to make a hollow metallic sound **2** : to drop heavily or suddenly — **plunk** *n*

plu•per•fect \(ˌ)plü-ˈpər-fikt\ *adj* [ME *pluperfyth,* modif. of LL *plusquamperfectus,* lit., more than perfect] : of, relating to, or constituting a verb tense that denotes an action or state as completed at or before a past time spoken of — **pluperfect** *n*

plu•ral \ˈplu̇r-əl\ *adj* [ME, fr. MF & L; MF *plurel,* fr. L *pluralis,* fr. *plur-, plus* more] : of, relating to, or constituting a word form used to denote more than one — **plural** *n*

plu•ral•i•ty \plu̇-ˈra-lə-tē\ *n, pl* **-ties 1** : the state of being plural **2** : an excess of votes over those cast for an opposing candidate **3** : the greatest number of votes cast when not a majority

plu•ral•ize \ˈplu̇r-ə-ˌlīz\ *vb* **-ized; -iz•ing** : to make plural or express in the plural form — **plu•ral•i•za•tion** \ˌplu̇r-ə-lə-ˈzā-shən\ *n*

[1]**plus** \ˈpləs\ *adj* [L, more] **1** : mathematically positive **2** : having or being in addition to what is anticipated **3** : falling high in a specified range ⟨a grade of B ~⟩

[2]**plus** *n, pl* **plus•es** \ˈplə-səz\ *also* **plus•ses 1** : a sign + (**plus sign**) used in mathematics to indicate addition or a positive quantity **2** : an added quantity; *also* : a positive quality **3** : SURPLUS

[3]**plus** *prep* **1** : increased by : with the addition of ⟨3 ~ 4⟩ **2** : BESIDES

[4]**plus** *conj* : AND ⟨soup ~ salad and bread⟩

[1]**plush** \ˈpləsh\ *n* : a fabric with a pile longer and less dense than velvet pile — **plushy** *adj*

[2]**plush** *adj* : notably luxurious — **plush•ly** *adv* — **plush•ness** *n*

Plu•to \ˈplü-tō\ *n* : the planet farthest from the sun — see PLANET table

plu•toc•ra•cy \plü-ˈtä-krə-sē\ *n, pl* **-cies 1** : government by the wealthy **2** : a controlling class of the wealthy — **plu•to•crat** \ˈplü-tə-ˌkrat\ *n* — **plu•to•crat•ic** \ˌplü-tə-ˈkra-tik\ *adj*

plu•to•ni•um \plü-ˈtō-nē-əm\ *n* : a radioactive chemical element formed by the decay of neptunium — see ELEMENT table

plu•vi•al \ˈplü-vē-əl\ *adj* **1** : of or relating to rain **2** : characterized by abundant rain

[1]**ply** \ˈplī\ *vb* **plied; ply•ing 1** : to use, practice, or work diligently ⟨~ a trade⟩ **2** : to keep supplying something to ⟨*plied* them with liquor⟩ **3** : to go or travel regularly esp. by sea

[2]**ply** *n, pl* **plies** : one of the folds, thicknesses, or strands of which something (as plywood or yarn) is made

[3]**ply** *vb* **plied; ply•ing** : to twist together ⟨~ yarns⟩

Plym•outh Rock \ˈpli-məth-\ *n* : any of an American breed of medium-sized single-combed domestic fowls

ply•wood \ˈplī-ˌwu̇d\ *n* : material made of thin sheets of wood glued and pressed together

pm *abbr* premium

Pm *symbol* promethium

PM *abbr* **1** paymaster **2** police magistrate **3** postmaster **4** post meridiem — often not cap. and often punctuated **5** postmortem **6** prime minister **7** provost marshal

pmk *abbr* postmark

PMS *abbr* premenstrual syndrome

pmt *abbr* payment

pneu•mat•ic \nu̇-ˈma-tik, nyu̇-\ *adj* **1** : of, relating to, or using air or wind **2** : moved by air pressure **3** : filled with compressed air — **pneu•mat•i•cal•ly** \-ti-k(ə-)lē\ *adv*

pneu•mo•co•ni•o•sis \ˌnü-mō-ˌkō-nē-ˈō-səs, ˌnyü-\ *n* : a disease of the lungs caused by habitual inhalation of irritant mineral or metallic particles

pneu•mo•nia \nu̇-ˈmō-nyə, nyu̇-\ *n* : an inflammatory disease of the lungs

Po *symbol* polonium

PO *abbr* **1** petty officer **2** post office

[1]**poach** \ˈpōch\ *vb* [ME *pochen,* fr. MF *pocher,* fr. OF *pochier,* lit., to put into a bag, fr. *poche* bag, pocket, of Gmc origin] : to cook (as an egg or fish) in simmering liquid

[2]**poach** *vb* : to hunt or fish unlawfully — **poach•er** *n*

POB *abbr* post office box

pock \ˈpäk\ *n* : a small swelling on the skin (as in smallpox); *also* : a spot suggesting this

[1]**pock•et** \ˈpä-kət\ *n* **1** : a small bag open at the top or side inserted in a garment **2** : supply of money : MEANS **3** : RECEPTACLE, CONTAINER **4** : a small isolated area or group **5** : a small body of ore — **pock•et•ful** *n*

[2]**pocket** *vb* **1** : to put in or as if in a pocket **2** : STEAL

[3]**pocket** *adj* **1** : small enough to fit in a pocket; *also* : SMALL, MINIATURE **2** : carried in or paid from one's own pocket

[1]**pock•et•book** \-ˌbu̇k\ *n* **1** : PURSE; *also* : HANDBAG **2** : financial resources

[2]**pocketbook** *adj* : relating to money

pocket gopher *n* : GOPHER 2

pock•et•knife \ˈpä-kət-ˌnīf\ *n* : a knife with a folding blade to be carried in the pocket

pocket veto *n* : an indirect veto of a legislative bill by an executive through retention of the bill unsigned until after adjournment of the legislature

pock•mark \ˈpäk-ˌmärk\ *n* : a pit or scar caused by smallpox or acne — **pock•marked** \-ˌmärkt\ *adj*

po•co \ˈpō-kō, ˌpȯ-\ *adv* [It, little, fr. L *paucus*] : SOMEWHAT — used to qualify a direction in music ⟨~ allegro⟩

po•co a po•co \ˌpō-kō-ä-ˈpō-kō, ˌpȯ-kō-ä-ˈpȯ-\ *adv* : little by little : GRADUALLY — used as a direction in music

pod \ˈpäd\ *n* **1** : a dry fruit (as of a pea) that splits open when ripe **2** : an external streamlined compartment (as for a jet engine) on an airplane **3** : a compartment (as for personnel, a power unit, or an instrument) on a ship or craft

POD *abbr* pay on delivery

po•di•a•try \pə-ˈdī-ə-trē, pō-\ *n* : the medical care and treatment of the human foot — **po•di•a•trist** \pə-ˈdī-ə-trist, pō-\ *n*

po•di•um \ˈpō-dē-əm\ *n, pl* **podiums** *or* **po•dia** \-dē-ə\ **1** : a dais esp. for an orchestral conductor **2** : LECTERN

POE *abbr* port of entry

po•em \ˈpō-əm\ *n* : a composition in verse

po•esy \ˈpō-ə-zē\ *n* : POETRY

po•et \ˈpō-ət\ *n* [ME, fr. OF *poete,* fr. L *poeta,* fr. Gk *poiētēs* maker, poet, fr. *poiein* to make] : a writer of poetry; *also* : a creative artist of great sensitivity

po•et•as•ter \ˈpō-ə-ˌtas-tər\ *n* : an inferior poet

po•et•ess \ˈpō-ə-təs\ *n* : a girl or woman who is a poet

poetic justice *n* : an outcome in which vice is punished and virtue rewarded usu. in a manner peculiarly or ironically appropriate

po•et•ry \ˈpō-ə-trē\ *n* **1** : metrical writing **2** : POEMS — **po•et•ic** \pō-ˈe-tik\ *or* **po•et•i•cal** \-ti-kəl\ *adj*

po•grom \ˈpō-grəm, pō-ˈgräm\ *n* [Yiddish, fr. Russ, lit., devastation] : an organized massacre of helpless people and esp. of Jews

poi \ˈpȯi\ *n, pl* **poi** *or* **pois** : a Hawaiian food of taro root cooked, pounded, and kneaded to a paste and often allowed to ferment

poi•gnant \ˈpȯi-nyənt\ *adj* **1** : painfully affecting the feelings ⟨~ grief⟩ **2** : deeply moving ⟨~ scene⟩ — **poi•gnan•cy** \-nyən-sē\ *n*

poin•ci•ana \ˌpȯin-sē-ˈa-nə\ *n* : any of several ornamental tropical leguminous trees or shrubs with bright orange or red flowers

poin•set•tia \pȯin-ˈse-tē-ə\ *n* : any of several showy tropical American spurges with usu. scarlet bracts around their small greenish flowers

¹point \ˈpȯint\ *n* **1** : an individual detail; *also* : the most important essential **2** : PURPOSE **3** : a geometric element that has position but no size **4** : a particular place : LOCALITY **5** : a particular stage or degree **6** : a sharp end : TIP **7** : a projecting piece of land **8** : a punctuation mark; *esp* : PERIOD **9** : DECIMAL POINT **10** : one of the divisions of the compass **11** : a unit of counting (as in a game score) — **point•less** *adj* — **beside the point** : IRRELEVANT — **to the point** : RELEVANT, PERTINENT

²point *vb* **1** : to furnish with a point : SHARPEN **2** : PUNCTUATE **3** : to separate (a decimal fraction) from an integer by a decimal point — usu. used with *off* **4** : to indicate the position of esp. by extending a finger **5** : to direct attention to ⟨~ out an error⟩ **6** : AIM, DIRECT **7** : to lie extended, aimed, or turned in a particular direction : FACE, LOOK

point–blank \ˈpȯint-ˈblaŋk\ *adj* **1** : so close to the target that a missile fired will travel in a straight line to the mark **2** : DIRECT, BLUNT — **point–blank** *adv*

point•ed \ˈpȯin-təd\ *adj* **1** : having a point **2** : being to the point : DIRECT **3** : aimed at a particular person or group; *also* : CONSPICUOUS, MARKED — **point•ed•ly** *adv*

point•er \ˈpȯin-tər\ *n* **1** : one that points out : INDICATOR **2** : a large short-haired hunting dog **3** : HINT, TIP

poin•til•lism \ˈpwan-tē-ˌyi-zəm, ˈpȯint-ᵊl-ˌi-zəm\ *n* [F *pointillisme*, fr. *pointiller* to stipple, fr. *point* point] : the theory or practice in painting of applying small strokes or dots of color to a surface so that from a distance they blend together — **poin•til•list** *also* **poin•til•liste** \ˌpwan-tē-ˈyēst, ˈpȯint-ᵊl-ist\ *n or adj*

point of no return : a critical point at which turning back or reversal is not possible

point of view : a position from which something is considered or evaluated

¹poise \ˈpȯiz\ *n* **1** : BALANCE **2** : self-possessed calmness; *also* : a particular way of carrying oneself

²poise *vb* **poised; pois•ing** : BALANCE

poi•sha \ˈpȯi-shə\ *n, pl* **poisha** : the paisa of Bangladesh

¹poi•son \ˈpȯiz-ᵊn\ *n* [ME, fr. OF, drink, poisonous drink, poison, fr. L *potion-, potio* drink] : a substance that through its chemical action can injure or kill — **poi•son•ous** \-ᵊn-əs\ *adj*

²poison *vb* **1** : to injure or kill with poison **2** : to treat or taint with poison **3** : to affect destructively : CORRUPT ⟨~*ed* her mind⟩ — **poi•son•er** *n*

poison hemlock *n* : a large branching poisonous herb with finely divided leaves and white flowers that is related to the carrot

poison ivy *n* **1** : a usu. climbing plant related to the sumacs that has leaves composed of three shiny leaflets and produces an irritating oil causing a usu. intensely itching skin rash; *also* : any of several related plants **2** : a skin rash caused by poison ivy

poison oak *n* : any of several shrubby plants closely related to poison ivy and having similar properties

poison sumac *n* : a smooth American swamp shrub with pinnate leaves, greenish flowers, greenish white berries, and irritating properties like the related poison ivy

¹poke \ˈpōk\ *n* : BAG, SACK

²poke *vb* **poked; pok•ing** **1** : PROD; *also* : to stir up by prodding **2** : to make a prodding or jabbing movement esp. repeatedly **3** : HIT, PUNCH **4** : to thrust forward obtrusively **5** : RUMMAGE **6** : MEDDLE, PRY **7** : DAWDLE — **poke fun at** : RIDICULE, MOCK

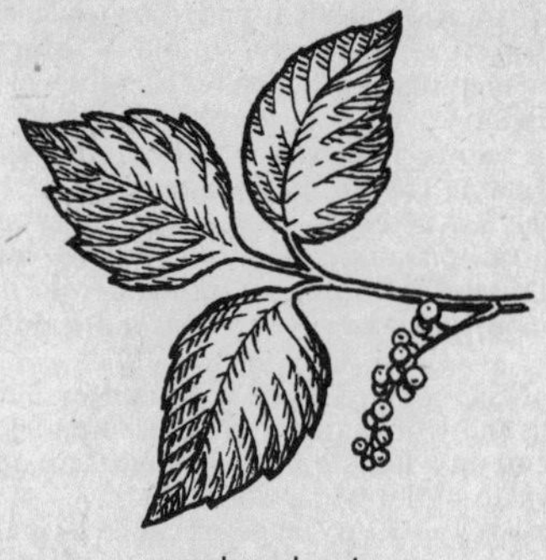

poison ivy 1

³poke *n* : a quick thrust; *also* : PUNCH

¹pok•er \ˈpō-kər\ *n* : a metal rod for stirring a fire

²po•ker \ˈpō-kər\ *n* : any of several card games in which the player with the highest hand at the end of the betting wins

poker: hands in descending value: *1* five of a kind, *2* royal flush, *3* straight flush, *4* four of a kind, *5* full house, *6* flush, *7* straight, *8* three of a kind, *9* two pairs, *10* one pair

poke•weed \ˈpōk-ˌwēd\ *n* : a coarse American perennial herb with clusters of white flowers and dark purple juicy berries

poky *or* **pok•ey** \ˈpō-kē\ *adj* **pok•i•er; -est** **1** : small and cramped **2** : SHABBY, DULL **3** : annoyingly slow

pol \ˈpäl\ *n* : POLITICIAN

po•lar \ˈpō-lər\ *adj* **1** : of or relating to a geographical pole **2** : of or relating to a pole (as of a magnet)

polar bear *n* : a large creamy-white bear that inhabits arctic regions

polar bear

Po•lar•is \pə-ˈlar-əs\ *n* : NORTH STAR

po•lar•ise *Brit var of* POLARIZE

po•lar•i•ty \pō-ˈlar-ə-tē\ *n, pl* **-ties** : the condition of having poles and esp. magnetic or electrical poles

po•lar•i•za•tion \ˌpō-lə-rə-ˈzā-shən\ *n* **1** : the action of polarizing : the state of being polarized **2** : concentration about opposing extremes

po•lar•ize \ˈpō-lə-ˌrīz\ *vb* **-ized; -iz•ing 1** : to cause (light waves) to vibrate in a definite way **2** : to give physical polarity to **3** : to break up into opposing groups

pol•der \ˈpōl-dər, ˈpäl-\ *n* [D] : a tract of low land reclaimed from the sea

¹pole \ˈpōl\ *n* : a long slender piece of wood or metal ⟨telephone ~⟩

²pole *vb* **poled; pol•ing** : to impel or push with a pole

³pole *n* **1** : either end of an axis esp. of the earth **2** : either of the terminals of an electric device (as a battery or generator) **3** : one of two or more regions in a magnetized body at which the magnetism is concentrated — **pole•ward** \ˈpōl-wərd\ *adj or adv*

Pole \ˈpōl\ *n* : a native or inhabitant of Poland

¹pole•ax \ˈpō-ˌlaks\ *n* : a battle-ax with a short handle

²poleax *vb* : to attack or fell with or as if with a poleax

pole•cat \ˈpōl-ˌkat\ *n, pl* **polecats** *or* **polecat 1** : a European carnivorous mammal of which the ferret is considered a domesticated variety **2** : SKUNK

po•lem•ic \pə-ˈle-mik\ *n* : the art or practice of disputation — usu. used in pl. — **po•lem•i•cal** \-mi-kəl\ *also* **po•lem•ic** \-mik\ *adj* — **po•lem•i•cist** \-sist\ *n*

pole•star \ˈpōl-ˌstär\ *n* **1** : NORTH STAR **2** : a directing principle : GUIDE

pole vault *n* : a field contest in which each contestant uses a pole to vault for height over a crossbar — **pole–vault** *vb* — **pole–vault•er** *n*

¹po•lice \pə-ˈlēs\ *vb* **po•liced; po•lic•ing 1** : to control, regulate, or keep in order esp. by use of police ⟨~ a highway⟩ **2** : to make clean and put in order

²police *n, pl* **police** [MF, government, fr. LL *politia,* fr. Gk *politeia,* fr. *politēs* citizen, fr. *polis* city, state] **1** : the department of government that keeps public order and safety and enforces the laws; *also* : the members of this department **2** : a private organization resembling a police force; *also* : its members **3** : military personnel detailed to clean and put in order

po•lice•man \-mən\ *n* : POLICE OFFICER

police officer *n* : a member of a police force

police state *n* : a state characterized by repressive, arbitrary, totalitarian rule by means of secret police

po•lice•wom•an \pə-ˈlēs-ˌwu̇-mən\ *n* : a woman who is a police officer

¹pol•i•cy \ˈpä-lə-sē\ *n, pl* **-cies** : a definite course or method of action selected to guide and determine present and future decisions

²policy *n, pl* **-cies** : a writing whereby a contract of insurance is made

pol•i•cy•hold•er \ˈpä-lə-sē-ˌhōl-dər\ *n* : one granted an insurance policy

po•lio \ˈpō-lē-ˌō\ *n* : POLIOMYELITIS — **polio** *adj*

po•lio•my•eli•tis \-ˌmī-ə-ˈlī-təs\ *n* : an acute virus disease marked by inflammation of the nerve cells of the spinal cord

¹pol•ish \ˈpä-lish\ *vb* **1** : to make smooth and glossy usu. by rubbing **2** : to refine or improve in manners, condition, or style

²polish *n* **1** : a smooth glossy surface : LUSTER **2** : REFINEMENT, CULTURE **3** : the action or process of polishing **4** : a preparation used to produce a gloss

Pol•ish \ˈpō-lish\ *n* : the Slavic language of the Poles — **Polish** *adj*

polit *abbr* political; politician

po•lit•bu•ro \ˈpä-lət-ˌbyu̇r-ō, ˈpō-, pə-ˈlit-\ *n* [Russ *politbyuro*] : the principal policy-making committee of a Communist party

po•lite \pə-ˈlīt\ *adj* **po•lit•er; -est 1** : REFINED, CULTIVATED ⟨~ society⟩ **2** : marked by correct social conduct : COURTEOUS; *also* : CONSIDERATE, TACTFUL — **po•lite•ly** *adv* — **po•lite•ness** *n*

po•li•tesse \ˌpä-li-ˈtes\ *n* [F] : formal politeness

pol•i•tic \ˈpä-lə-ˌtik\ *adj* **1** : wise in promoting a policy ⟨a ~ statesman⟩ **2** : shrewdly tactful ⟨a ~ move⟩

po•lit•i•cal \pə-ˈli-ti-kəl\ *adj* **1** : of or relating to government or politics **2** : involving or charged or concerned with acts against a government or a political system ⟨~ prisoners⟩ — **po•lit•i•cal•ly** \-k(ə-)lē\ *adv*

politically correct *adj* : conforming to a belief that language and practices which could offend sensibilities (as in matters of sex or race) should be eliminated

pol•i•ti•cian \ˌpä-lə-ˈti-shən\ *n* : a person actively engaged in government or politics

pol•i•tick \ˈpä-lə-ˌtik\ *vb* : to engage in political discussion or activity

po•lit•i•co \pə-ˈli-ti-ˌkō\ *n, pl* **-cos** *also* **-coes** : POLITICIAN

pol•i•tics \ˈpä-lə-ˌtiks\ *n sing or pl* **1** : the art or science of government, of guiding or influencing governmental policy, or of winning and holding control over a government **2** : political affairs or business; *esp* : competition between groups or individuals for power and leadership **3** : political opinions

pol•i•ty \ˈpä-lə-tē\ *n, pl* **-ties** : a politically organized unit; *also* : the form or constitution of such a unit

pol•ka \ˈpōl-kə, ˈpō-kə\ *n* [Czech, fr. *Polka* Polish woman, fem. of *Polák* Pole] : a lively couple dance of Bohemian origin; *also* : music for this dance — **polka** *vb*

pol•ka dot \ˈpō-kə-ˌdät\ *n* : a dot in a pattern of regularly distributed dots — **polka–dot** *or* **polka–dotted** \-ˌdä-təd\ *adj*

¹poll \ˈpōl\ *n* **1** : HEAD **2** : the casting and recording of votes; *also* : the total vote cast **3** : the place where votes are cast — usu. used in pl. **4** : a questioning of persons to obtain information or opinions to be analyzed

²poll *vb* **1** : to cut off or shorten a growth or part of : CLIP, SHEAR **2** : to receive and record the votes of **3** : to receive (as votes) in an election **4** : to question in a poll

pol•lack *or* **pol•lock** \ˈpä-lək\ *n, pl* **pollack** *or* **pollock** : an important Atlantic food fish that is related to the cods; *also* : a related food fish of the north Pacific

pol•len \ˈpä-lən\ *n* [NL, fr. L, fine flour] : a mass of male spores of a seed plant usu. appearing as a yellow dust

pol•li•na•tion \ˌpä-lə-ˈnā-shən\ *n* : the carrying of pollen to the female part of a plant to fertilize the seed — **pol•li•nate** \ˈpä-lə-ˌnāt\ *vb* — **pol•li•na•tor** \-ˌnā-tər\ *n*

poll•ster \ˈpōl-stər\ *n* : one that conducts a poll or compiles data obtained by a poll

poll tax *n* : a tax of a fixed amount per person levied on adults

pol•lute \pə-ˈlüt\ *vb* **pol•lut•ed; pol•lut•ing** : to make impure; *esp* : to contaminate (an environment) esp. with man-made waste — **pol•lut•ant** \-ˈlüt-ᵊnt\ *n* — **pol•lut•er** *n* — **pol•lu•tion** \-ˈlü-shən\ *n*

pol•ly•wog *or* **pol•li•wog** \ˈpä-lē-ˌwäg\ *n* : TADPOLE

po•lo \ˈpō-lō\ *n* : a game played by two teams on horseback using long-handled mallets to drive a wooden ball

po•lo•ni•um \pə-ˈlō-nē-əm\ *n* [NL, fr. ML *Polonia* Poland, birthplace of its discoverer, Mme. Curie] : a radioactive metallic chemical element — see ELEMENT table

pol•ter•geist \ˈpōl-tər-ˌgīst\ *n* [G, fr. *poltern* to knock + *Geist* spirit] : a noisy usu. mischievous ghost held to be responsible for unexplained noises

pol•troon \päl-ˈtrün\ *n* : COWARD

poly- *comb form* **1** : many : several ⟨*poly*syllabic⟩ **2** : polymeric ⟨*poly*ester⟩

poly•chlo•ri•nat•ed bi•phe•nyl \ˌpä-li-ˈklōr-ə-ˌnā-təd-ˌbī-ˈfen-ᵊl, -ˈfēn-\ *n* : any of several industrial compounds that are poisonous environmental pollutants

poly•clin•ic \ˌpä-li-ˈkli-nik\ *n* : a clinic or hospital treating diseases of many sorts

poly•es•ter \ˈpä-lē-ˌes-tər\ *n* : a polymer composed of ester groups used esp. in making fibers or plastics

poly•eth•yl•ene \ˌpä-lē-ˈe-thə-ˌlēn\ *n* : a lightweight

DICTIONARY

plastic resistant to chemicals and moisture and used chiefly in packaging

po·lyg·a·my \pə-ˈli-gə-mē\ *n* : the practice of having more than one wife or husband at one time — **po·lyg·a·mist** \-mist\ *n* — **po·lyg·a·mous** \-məs\ *adj*

poly·glot \ˈpä-li-ˌglät\ *adj* **1** : speaking or writing several languages **2** : containing or made up of several languages — **polyglot** *n*

poly·gon \ˈpä-li-ˌgän\ *n* : a closed plane figure bounded by straight lines — **po·lyg·o·nal** \pə-ˈli-gən-ᵊl\ *adj*

poly·graph \ˈpä-li-ˌgraf\ *n* : an instrument for recording variations of several bodily functions (as blood pressure) simultaneously — **po·lyg·ra·pher** \pə-ˈli-grə-fər, ˈpä-li-ˌgra-fər\ *n*

poly·he·dron \ˌpä-li-ˈhē-drən\ *n* : a solid formed by plane faces that are polygons — **poly·he·dral** \-drəl\ *adj*

poly·math \ˈpä-li-ˌmath\ *n* : a person of encyclopedic learning

poly·mer \ˈpä-lə-mər\ *n* : a chemical compound formed by union of small molecules and usu. consisting of repeating structural units — **poly·mer·ic** \ˌpä-lə-ˈmer-ik\ *adj*

po·lym·er·i·za·tion \pə-ˌli-mə-rə-ˈzā-shən\ *n* : a chemical reaction in which two or more small molecules combine to form polymers — **po·lym·er·ize** \pə-ˈli-mə-ˌrīz\ *vb*

Poly·ne·sian \ˌpä-lə-ˈnē-zhən\ *n* **1** : a member of any of the indigenous peoples of Polynesia **2** : a group of Austronesian languages spoken in Polynesia — **Polynesian** *adj*

poly·no·mi·al \ˌpä-lə-ˈnō-mē-əl\ *n* : an algebraic expression having one or more terms each of which consists of a constant multiplied by one or more variables raised to a nonnegative integral power — **polynomial** *adj*

pol·yp \ˈpä-ləp\ *n* **1** : an invertebrate animal (as a coral) that is a coelenterate having a hollow cylindrical body closed at one end **2** : a projecting mass of swollen and hypertrophied or tumorous membrane ⟨a rectal ∼⟩

po·lyph·o·ny \pə-ˈli-fə-nē\ *n* : music consisting of two or more melodically independent but harmonizing voice parts — **poly·phon·ic** \ˌpä-li-ˈfä-nik\ *adj*

poly·pro·pyl·ene \ˌpä-lē-ˈprō-pə-ˌlēn\ *n* : any of various polymer plastics or fibers

poly·sty·rene \ˌpä-li-ˈstīr-ˌēn\ *n* : a rigid transparent nonconducting thermoplastic used esp. in molded products and foams

poly·syl·lab·ic \-sə-ˈla-bik\ *adj* **1** : having more than three syllables **2** : characterized by polysyllabic words

poly·syl·la·ble \ˈpä-li-ˌsi-lə-bəl\ *n* : a polysyllabic word

poly·tech·nic \ˌpä-li-ˈtek-nik\ *adj* : of, relating to, or instructing in many technical arts or applied sciences

poly·the·ism \ˈpä-li-thē-ˌi-zəm\ *n* : belief in or worship of many gods — **poly·the·ist** \-ˌthē-ist\ *adj or n* — **poly·the·is·tic** \ˌpä-li-thē-ˈis-tik\ *adj*

poly·un·sat·u·rat·ed \ˌpä-lē-ˌən-ˈsa-chə-ˌrā-təd\ *adj* : having many double or triple bonds in a molecule — used esp. of an oil or fatty acid

poly·ure·thane \ˌpä-lē-ˈyůr-ə-ˌthān\ *n* : any of various polymers used esp. in foams and in resins (as for coatings)

poly·vi·nyl \ˌpä-li-ˈvīn-ᵊl\ *adj* : of, relating to, or being a polymerized vinyl compound, resin, or plastic — often used in combination

pome·gran·ate \ˈpä-mə-ˌgra-nət\ *n* [ME *poumgrenet*, fr. MF *pomme grenate*, lit., seedy apple] : a tropical reddish fruit with many seeds and an edible crimson pulp; *also* : the tree that bears it

[1]**pom·mel** \ˈpə-məl, ˈpä-\ *n* **1** : the knob on the hilt of a sword **2** : the knoblike bulge at the front and top of a saddlebow

[2]**pom·mel** \ˈpə-məl\ *vb* **-meled** *or* **-melled; -mel·ing** *or* **-mel·ling** : PUMMEL

pomp \ˈpämp\ *n* **1** : brilliant display : SPLENDOR **2** : OSTENTATION

pom·pa·dour \ˈpäm-pə-ˌdōr\ *n* : a style of dressing the hair high over the forehead

pom·pa·no \ˈpäm-pə-ˌnō, ˈpəm-\ *n, pl* **-no** *or* **-nos** : a New World fish esp. of warmer Atlantic coasts

pom–pom \ˈpäm-ˌpäm\ *n* **1** : an ornamental ball or tuft used on a cap or costume **2** : a fluffy ball flourished by cheerleaders

pom·pon \ˈpäm-ˌpän\ *n* **1** : POM-POM **2** : a chrysanthemum or dahlia with small rounded flower heads

pomp·ous \ˈpäm-pəs\ *adj* **1** : suggestive of pomp; *esp* : OSTENTATIOUS **2** : pretentiously dignified **3** : excessively elevated or ornate **syn** arrogant, magisterial, self-important — **pom·pos·i·ty** \päm-ˈpä-sə-tē\ *n* — **pomp·ous·ly** *adv*

pon·cho \ˈpän-chō\ *n, pl* **ponchos** [AmerSp, fr. Araucanian (American Indian language of Chile)] **1** : a blanket with a slit in the middle for the head so that it can be worn as a garment **2** : a waterproof garment resembling a poncho

pond \ˈpänd\ *n* : a small body of water

pon·der \ˈpän-dər\ *vb* **pon·dered; pon·der·ing** **1** : to weigh in the mind **2** : to consider carefully

pon·der·o·sa pine \ˈpän-də-ˌrō-sə-, -zə-\ *n* : a tall pine of western No. America with long needles; *also* : its strong reddish wood

pon·der·ous \ˈpän-də-rəs\ *adj* **1** : of very great weight **2** : UNWIELDY, CLUMSY ⟨a ∼ weapon⟩ **3** : oppressively dull ⟨a ∼ speech⟩ **syn** cumbrous, cumbersome, weighty

pone \ˈpōn\ *n, Southern & Midland* : an oval-shaped cornmeal cake; *also* : corn bread in the form of pones

pon·iard \ˈpän-yərd\ *n* : DAGGER

pon·tiff \ˈpän-təf\ *n* : POPE — **pon·tif·i·cal** \pän-ˈti-fi-kəl\ *adj*

[1]**pon·tif·i·cate** \pän-ˈti-fi-kət, -fə-ˌkāt\ *n* : the state, office, or term of office of a pontiff

[2]**pon·tif·i·cate** \pän-ˈti-fə-ˌkāt\ *vb* **-cat·ed; -cat·ing** : to deliver dogmatic opinions

pon·toon \pän-ˈtün\ *n* **1** : a flat-bottomed boat **2** : a boat or float used in building a floating temporary bridge **3** : a float of a seaplane

po·ny \ˈpō-nē\ *n, pl* **ponies** : a small horse

po·ny·tail \-ˌtāl\ *n* : a style of arranging hair to resemble the tail of a pony

pooch \ˈpüch\ *n* : DOG

poo·dle \ˈpüd-ᵊl\ *n* [G *Pudel*, short for *Pudelhund*, fr. *pudeln* to splash + *Hund* dog] : a dog of any of three breeds of active intelligent heavy-coated solid-colored dogs

pooh–pooh \ˈpü-ˈpü\ *also* **pooh** \ˈpü\ *vb* **1** : to express contempt or impatience **2** : DERIDE, SCORN

[1]**pool** \ˈpül\ *n* **1** : a small deep body of usu. fresh water **2** : a small body of standing liquid **3** : SWIMMING POOL

[2]**pool** *vb* : to form a pool

[3]**pool** *n* **1** : all the money bet on the result of a particular event **2** : any of several games of billiards played on a table having six pockets **3** : the amount contributed by the participants in a joint venture **4** : a combination between competing firms for mutual profit **5** : a readily available supply

[4]**pool** *vb* : to combine (as resources) in a common fund or effort

[1]**poop** \ˈpüp\ *n* : an enclosed superstructure at the stern of a ship

[2]**poop** *n, slang* : INFORMATION

poop deck *n* : a partial deck above a ship's main afterdeck

poor \ˈpůr\ *adj* **1** : lacking material possessions ⟨∼ people⟩ **2** : less than adequate : MEAGER ⟨∼ crop⟩ **3** : arousing pity ⟨you ∼ thing⟩ **4** : inferior in quality or value **5** : UNPRODUCTIVE, BARREN ⟨∼ soil⟩ **6** : fairly unsatisfactory ⟨∼ prospects⟩; *also* : UNFAVORABLE ⟨∼ opinion⟩ — **poor·ly** *adv*

poor boy \ˈpō-ˌbȯi, ˈpōr-\ *n* : SUBMARINE 2
poor•house \ˈpu̇r-ˌhau̇s\ *n* : a publicly supported home for needy or dependent persons
poor–mouth \-ˌmau̇th, -ˌmau̇th\ *vb* : to plead poverty as a defense or excuse
1**pop** \ˈpäp\ *vb* **popped; pop•ping 1** : to go, come, enter, or issue forth suddenly or quickly ⟨~ into bed⟩ **2** : to put or thrust suddenly ⟨~ questions⟩ **3** : to burst or cause to burst with a sharp sound; *also* : to make a sharp sound **4** : to protrude from the sockets **5** : SHOOT **6** : to hit a pop-up
2**pop** *n* **1** : a sharp explosive sound **2** : SHOT **3** : SODA POP
3**pop** *n* : FATHER
4**pop** *adj* **1** : POPULAR ⟨~ music⟩ **2** : of or relating to pop music ⟨~ singer⟩ **3** : of or relating to the popular culture disseminated through the mass media ⟨~ psychology⟩ **4** : of, relating to, or imitating pop art ⟨~ painter⟩
5**pop** *n* : pop music or culture; *also* : POP ART
6**pop** *abbr* population
pop art *n* : art in which commonplace objects (as comic strips or soup cans) are used as subject matter — **pop artist** *n*
pop•corn \ˈpäp-ˌkȯrn\ *n* : an Indian corn whose kernels burst open into a white starchy mass when heated; *also* : the burst kernels
pope \ˈpōp\ *n, often cap* : the head of the Roman Catholic Church
pop–eyed \ˈpäp-ˌīd\ *adj* : having eyes that bulge (as from disease)
pop fly *n* : POP-UP
pop•gun \ˈpäp-ˌgən\ *n* : a toy gun for shooting pellets with compressed air
pop•in•jay \ˈpä-pən-ˌjā\ *n* [ME *papejay* parrot, fr. MF *papegai, papejai,* fr. Ar *babghā'*] : a strutting supercilious person
pop•lar \ˈpä-plər\ *n* **1** : any of a genus of slender quick-growing trees (as a cottonwood) related to the willows **2** : the wood of a poplar
pop•lin \ˈpä-plən\ *n* : a strong plain-woven fabric with crosswise ribs
pop•over \ˈpäp-ˌō-vər\ *n* : a hollow muffin made from a thin batter rich in egg
pop•per \ˈpä-pər\ *n* : a utensil for popping corn
pop•py \ˈpä-pē\ *n, pl* **poppies** : any of a genus of herbs with showy flowers including one that yields opium
pop•py•cock \-ˌkäk\ *n* : empty talk or writing : NONSENSE
pop•u•lace \ˈpä-pyə-ləs\ *n* **1** : the common people **2** : POPULATION
pop•u•lar \ˈpä-pyə-lər\ *adj* **1** : of or relating to the general public ⟨~ government⟩ **2** : suited to the tastes of the general public ⟨~ style⟩ **3** : INEXPENSIVE ⟨~ rates⟩ **4** : frequently encountered or widely accepted ⟨~ notion⟩ **5** : commonly liked or approved ⟨~ teacher⟩ — **pop•u•lar•i•ty** \ˌpä-pyə-ˈlar-ə-tē\ *n* — **pop•u•lar•ize** \ˈpä-pyə-lə-ˌrīz\ *vb* — **pop•u•lar•ly** *adv*
pop•u•late \ˈpä-pyə-ˌlāt\ *vb* **-lat•ed; -lat•ing 1** : to have a place in : INHABIT **2** : PEOPLE
pop•u•la•tion \ˌpä-pyə-ˈlā-shən\ *n* **1** : the people or number of people in an area **2** : the organisms inhabiting a particular locality **3** : a group of individuals or items from which samples are taken for statistical measurement
population explosion *n* : a pyramiding of numbers of a biological population; *esp* : the recent great increase in human numbers resulting from increased survival and exponential population growth
pop•u•list \ˈpä-pyə-list\ *n* : a believer in or advocate of the rights, wisdom, or virtues of the common people — **pop•u•lism** \-ˌli-zəm\ *n*
pop•u•lous \ˈpä-pyə-ləs\ *adj* **1** : densely populated; *also* : having a large population **2** : CROWDED — **pop•u•lous•ness** *n*
pop–up \ˈpäp-ˌəp\ *n* : a short high fly in baseball
por•ce•lain \ˈpōr-sə-lən\ *n* : a fine-grained translucent ceramic ware
porch \ˈpōrch\ *n* : a covered entrance usu. with a separate roof
por•cine \ˈpȯr-ˌsīn\ *adj* : of, relating to, or suggesting swine
por•cu•pine \ˈpȯr-kyə-ˌpīn\ *n* [ME *porkepin,* fr. MF *porc espin,* fr. It *porcospino,* fr. L *porcus* pig + *spina* spine, prickle] : any of various mammals having stiff sharp spines mingled with their hair
1**pore** \ˈpōr\ *vb* **pored; por•ing 1** : to read studiously or attentively ⟨~ over a book⟩ **2** : PONDER, REFLECT
2**pore** *n* : a tiny hole or space (as in the skin or soil) — **pored** \ˈpōrd\ *adj*
pork \ˈpōrk\ *n* : the flesh of swine dressed for use as food
pork barrel *n* : government projects or appropriations yielding rich patronage benefits
pork•er \ˈpōr-kər\ *n* : HOG; *esp* : a young pig suitable for use as fresh pork
por•nog•ra•phy \pȯr-ˈnä-grə-fē\ *n* : the depiction of erotic behavior intended to cause sexual excitement — **por•no•graph•ic** \ˌpȯr-nə-ˈgra-fik\ *adj*
po•rous \ˈpōr-əs\ *adj* **1** : full of pores **2** : permeable to fluids : ABSORPTIVE — **po•ros•i•ty** \pə-ˈrä-sə-tē\ *n*
por•phy•ry \ˈpȯr-fə-rē\ *n, pl* **-ries** : a rock consisting of feldspar crystals embedded in a compact fine-grained base material — **por•phy•rit•ic** \ˌpȯr-fə-ˈri-tik\ *adj*
por•poise \ˈpȯr-pəs\ *n* [ME *porpoys,* fr. MF *porpois,* fr. ML *porcopiscis,* fr. L *porcus* pig + *piscis* fish] : any of a family of small gregarious toothed whales; *also* : DOLPHIN 1
por•ridge \ˈpȯr-ij\ *n* : a soft food made by boiling meal of grains or legumes in milk or water
por•rin•ger \ˈpȯr-ən-jər\ *n* : a low one-handled metal bowl or cup
1**port** \ˈpōrt\ *n* **1** : HARBOR **2** : a city with a harbor **3** : AIRPORT
2**port** *n* **1** : an inlet or outlet (as in an engine) for a fluid **2** : PORTHOLE
3**port** *vb* : to turn or put a helm to the left
4**port** *n* : the left side of a ship or airplane looking forward — **port** *adj*
5**port** *n* : a sweet fortified wine
por•ta•ble \ˈpōr-tə-bəl\ *adj* : capable of being carried — **portable** *n*
1**por•tage** \ˈpōr-tij, pȯr-ˈtäzh\ *n* [ME, fr. MF, fr. *porter* to carry] : the carrying of boats and goods overland between navigable bodies of water; *also* : a route for such carrying
2**portage** *vb* **por•taged; por•tag•ing** : to carry gear over a portage
por•tal \ˈpōrt-ᵊl\ *n* : DOOR, ENTRANCE; *esp* : a grand or imposing one
portal–to–portal *adj* : of or relating to the time spent by a worker in traveling from the entrance to an employer's property to the worker's actual job site (as in a mine)
port•cul•lis \pōrt-ˈkə-ləs\ *n* : a grating at the gateway of a castle or fortress that can be let down to stop entrance
porte co•chere \ˌpōrt-kō-ˈsher\ *n* [F *porte cochère,* lit., coach door] : a roofed structure extending from the entrance of a building over an adjacent driveway and sheltering those getting in or out of vehicles
por•tend \pȯr-ˈtend\ *vb* **1** : to give a sign or warning of beforehand **2** : INDICATE, SIGNIFY **syn** augur, prognosticate, foretell, predict, forecast, prophesy
por•tent \ˈpȯr-ˌtent\ *n* **1** : something that foreshadows a coming event : OMEN **2** : MARVEL, PRODIGY
por•ten•tous \pȯr-ˈten-təs\ *adj* **1** : of, relating to, or constituting a portent **2** : PRODIGIOUS **3** : self-consciously solemn : POMPOUS
1**por•ter** \ˈpōr-tər\ *n, chiefly Brit* : DOORKEEPER
2**porter** *n* **1** : a person who carries burdens; *esp* : one

employed (as at a terminal) to carry baggage **2 :** an attendant in a railroad car **3 :** a dark heavy ale

por·ter·house \ˈpōr-tər-ˌhau̇s\ *n* **:** a choice beefsteak with a large tenderloin

port·fo·lio \pōrt-ˈfō-lē-ˌō\ *n, pl* **-li·os 1 :** a portable case for papers or drawings **2 :** the office and functions of a minister of state **3 :** the securities held by an investor

port·hole \ˈpōrt-ˌhōl\ *n* **:** an opening (as a window) in the side of a ship or aircraft

por·ti·co \ˈpōr-ti-ˌkō\ *n, pl* **-coes** *or* **-cos** [It] **:** a row of columns supporting a roof around or at the entrance of a building

[1]**por·tion** \ˈpōr-shən\ *n* **1 :** one's part or share ⟨a ~ of food⟩ **2 :** DOWRY **3 :** an individual's lot **4 :** a part of a whole ⟨a ~ of the sky⟩

[2]**portion** *vb* **1 :** to divide into portions **2 :** to allot to as a portion

port·land cement \ˈpōrt-lənd-\ *n* **:** a cement made by calcining and grinding a mixture of clay and limestone

port·ly \ˈpōrt-lē\ *adj* **port·li·er; -est :** somewhat stout

port·man·teau \pōrt-ˈman-ˌtō\ *n, pl* **-teaus** *or* **-teaux** \-ˌtōz\ [MF *portemanteau,* fr. *porter* to carry + *manteau* mantle, fr. L *mantellum*] **:** a large traveling bag

port of call : an intermediate port where ships customarily stop for supplies, repairs, or transshipment of cargo

port of entry 1 : a place where foreign goods may be cleared through a customhouse **2 :** a place where an alien may enter a country

por·trait \ˈpōr-trət, -ˌtrāt\ *n* **:** a picture (as a painting or photograph) of a person usu. showing the face

por·trait·ist \-trə-tist\ *n* **:** a maker of portraits

por·trai·ture \ˈpōr-trə-ˌchu̇r\ *n* **:** the practice or art of making portraits

por·tray \pōr-ˈtrā\ *vb* **1 :** to make a picture of **:** DEPICT **2 :** to describe in words **3 :** to play the role of — **por·tray·al** *n*

Por·tu·guese \ˈpōr-chə-ˌgēz, -ˌgēs; ˌpōr-chə-ˈgēz, -ˈgēs\ *n, pl* **Portuguese 1 :** a native or inhabitant of Portugal **2 :** the language of Portugal and Brazil — **Portuguese** *adj*

Portuguese man–of–war *n* **:** any of several large colonial marine invertebrate animals related to the jellyfishes and having a large sac by which the colony floats at the surface

por·tu·laca \ˌpōr-chə-ˈla-kə\ *n* **:** a tropical succulent herb cultivated for its showy flowers

pos *abbr* **1** position **2** positive

[1]**pose** \ˈpōz\ *vb* **posed; pos·ing 1 :** to assume or cause to assume a posture usu. for artistic purposes **2 :** to set forth **:** PROPOSE ⟨~ a question⟩ **3 :** to affect an attitude or character

[2]**pose** *n* **1 :** a sustained posture; *esp* **:** one assumed by a model **2 :** an attitude assumed for effect **:** PRETENSE

[1]**pos·er** \ˈpō-zər\ *n* **:** a puzzling question

[2]**poser** *n* **:** a person who poses

po·seur \pō-ˈzər\ *n* [F, lit., poser] **:** an affected or insincere person

posh \ˈpäsh\ *adj* **:** FASHIONABLE

pos·it \ˈpä-zət\ *vb* **:** to assume the existence of **:** POSTULATE

po·si·tion \pə-ˈzi-shən\ *n* **1 :** an arranging in order **2 :** the stand taken on a question **3 :** the point or area occupied by something **:** SITUATION **4 :** a certain arrangement of bodily parts ⟨exercise in a sitting ~⟩ **5 :** RANK, STATUS **6 :** EMPLOYMENT, JOB — **position** *vb*

[1]**pos·i·tive** \ˈpä-zə-tiv\ *adj* **1 :** expressed definitely ⟨her answer was a ~ *no*⟩ **2 :** CONFIDENT, CERTAIN **3 :** of, relating to, or constituting the degree of grammatical comparison that denotes no increase in quality, quantity, or relation **4 :** not fictitious **:** REAL **5 :** active and effective in function ⟨~ leadership⟩ **6 :** having the light and shade as existing in the original subject ⟨a ~ photograph⟩ **7 :** numerically greater than zero ⟨a ~ number⟩ **8 :** being, relating to, or charged with electricity of which the proton is the elementary unit **9 :** AFFIRMATIVE ⟨a ~ response⟩ — **pos·i·tive·ly** *adv* — **pos·i·tive·ness** *n*

[2]**positive** *n* **1 :** the positive degree or a positive form in a language **2 :** a positive photograph

pos·i·tron \ˈpä-zə-ˌträn\ *n* **:** a positively charged particle having the same mass and magnitude of charge as the electron

poss *abbr* possessive

pos·se \ˈpä-sē\ *n* [ML *posse comitatus,* lit., power or authority of the county] **:** a body of persons organized to assist a sheriff in an emergency

pos·sess \pə-ˈzes\ *vb* **1 :** to have as property **:** OWN **2 :** to have as an attribute, knowledge, or skill **3 :** to enter into and control firmly ⟨~*ed* by a devil⟩ — **pos·ses·sor** \-ˈze-sər\ *n*

pos·ses·sion \-ˈze-shən\ *n* **1 :** control or occupancy of property **2 :** OWNERSHIP **3 :** something owned **:** PROPERTY **4 :** domination by something (as an evil spirit, a passion, or an idea) **5 :** SELF-CONTROL

pos·ses·sive \pə-ˈze-siv\ *adj* **1 :** of, relating to, or constituting a grammatical case denoting ownership **2 :** showing the desire to possess ⟨a ~ nature⟩ — **possessive** *n* — **pos·ses·sive·ness** *n*

pos·si·ble \ˈpä-sə-bəl\ *adj* **1 :** being within the limits of ability, capacity, or realization **2 :** being something that may or may not occur ⟨~ dangers⟩ **3 :** able or fitted to become ⟨a ~ site for a bridge⟩ — **pos·si·bil·i·ty** \ˌpä-sə-ˈbi-lə-tē\ *n* — **pos·si·bly** \ˈpä-sə-blē\ *adv*

pos·sum \ˈpä-səm\ *n* **:** OPOSSUM

[1]**post** \ˈpōst\ *n* **1 :** an upright piece of timber or metal serving esp. as a support **:** PILLAR **2 :** a pole or stake set up as a mark or indicator

[2]**post** *vb* **1 :** to affix to a usual place (as a wall) for public notices **2 :** to publish or announce by or as if by a public notice ⟨~ grades⟩ **3 :** to forbid (property) to trespassers by putting up a notice **4 :** SCORE 4

[3]**post** *n* **1** *obs* **:** COURIER **2** *chiefly Brit* **:** [1]MAIL; *also* **:** POST OFFICE

[4]**post** *vb* **1 :** to ride or travel with haste **:** HURRY **2 :** MAIL ⟨~ a letter⟩ **3 :** to enter in a ledger **4 :** INFORM ⟨kept him ~*ed* on new developments⟩

[5]**post** *n* **1 :** the place at which a soldier is stationed; *esp* **:** a sentry's beat or station **2 :** a station or task to which a person is assigned **3 :** the place at which a body of troops is stationed **:** CAMP **4 :** OFFICE, POSITION **5 :** a trading settlement or station

[6]**post** *vb* **1 :** to station in a given place **2 :** to put up (as bond)

post·age \ˈpōs-tij\ *n* **:** the fee for postal service; *also* **:** stamps representing this fee

post·al \ˈpōst-ᵊl\ *adj* **:** of or relating to the mails or the post office

postal card *n* **:** POSTCARD

postal service *n* **:** a government agency or department handling the transmission of mail

post·card \ˈpōst-ˌkärd\ *n* **:** a card on which a message may be written for mailing without an envelope

post chaise *n* **:** a 4-wheeled closed carriage for two to four persons

post·date \ˌpōst-ˈdāt\ *vb* **:** to date with a date later than that of execution ⟨~ a check⟩

post·doc·tor·al \-ˈdäk-tə-rəl\ *also* **post·doc·tor·ate** \-tə-rət\ *adj* **:** of, relating to, or engaged in advanced academic or professional work beyond a doctor's degree

post·er \ˈpō-stər\ *n* **:** a bill or placard for posting often in a public place

[1]**pos·te·ri·or** \pō-ˈstir-ē-ər, pä-\ *adj* **1 :** later in time **2 :** situated behind

[2]**pos·te·ri·or** \pä-ˈstir-ē-ər, pō-\ *n* **:** the hinder bodily parts; *esp* **:** BUTTOCKS

pos·ter·i·ty \pä-ˈster-ə-tē\ *n* **1 :** the descendants from one ancestor **2 :** all future generations

pos·tern \ˈpōs-tərn, ˈpäs-\ *n* **1** : a back door or gate **2** : a private or side entrance
post exchange *n* : a store at a military post that sells to military personnel and authorized civilians
post·grad·u·ate \(ˌ)pōst-ˈgra-jə-wət\ *adj* : of or relating to studies beyond the bachelor's degree — **post-graduate** *n*
post·haste \ˈpōst-ˈhāst\ *adv* : with all possible speed
post·hole \-ˌhōl\ *n* : a hole for a post and esp. a fence post
post·hu·mous \ˈpäs-chə-məs\ *adj* **1** : born after the death of the father **2** : published after the death of the author — **post·hu·mous·ly** *adv*
post·hyp·not·ic \ˌpōst-hip-ˈnä-tik\ *adj* : of, relating to, or characteristic of the period following a hypnotic trance
pos·til·ion *or* **pos·til·lion** \pō-ˈstil-yən\ *n* : a rider on the left-hand horse of a pair drawing a coach
Post·im·pres·sion·ism \ˌpōst-im-ˈpre-shə-ˌni-zəm\ *n* : a late 19th century French theory or practice of art that stresses variously volume, picture structure, or expressionism
post·lude \ˈpōst-ˌlüd\ *n* : an organ solo played at the end of a church service
post·man \-mən, -ˌman\ *n* : MAILMAN
post·mark \-ˌmärk\ *n* : an official postal marking on a piece of mail; *esp* : the mark canceling the postage stamp — **postmark** *vb*
post·mas·ter \-ˌmas-tər\ *n* : a person who has charge of a post office
postmaster general *n, pl* **postmasters general** : an official in charge of a national postal service
post me·ri·di·em \ˌpōst-mə-ˈri-dē-əm\ *adj* [L] : being after noon
post·mis·tress \ˈpōst-ˌmis-trəs\ *n* : a woman in charge of a post office
¹**post·mor·tem** \ˌpōst-ˈmȯr-təm\ *adj* [L *post mortem* after death] **1** : done, occurring, or collected after death **2** : following the event
²**postmortem** *n* **1** : an analysis or discussion of an event after it is over **2** : AUTOPSY
post·na·sal drip \ˈpōst-ˌnā-zəl-\ *n* : flow of mucous secretion from the posterior part of the nasal cavity onto the wall of the pharynx
post·na·tal \(ˌ)pōst-ˈnāt-ᵊl\ *adj* : occurring or being after birth; *esp* : of or relating to a newborn infant
post office *n* **1** : POSTAL SERVICE **2** : a local branch of a post office department
post·op·er·a·tive \(ˌ)pōst-ˈä-prə-tiv, -pə-ˌrā-\ *adj* : following or having undergone a surgical operation ⟨~ care⟩
post·paid \ˈpōst-ˈpād\ *adv* : with the postage paid by the sender and not chargeable to the receiver
post·par·tum \(ˌ)pōst-ˈpär-təm\ *adj* [NL *post partum* after birth] : following parturition — **postpartum** *adv*
post·pone \pōst-ˈpōn\ *vb* **post·poned; post·pon·ing** : to put off to a later time — **post·pone·ment** *n*
post road *n* : a road over which mail is carried
post·script \ˈpōst-ˌskript\ *n* : a note added esp. to a completed letter
post time *n* : the designated time for the start of a horse race
pos·tu·lant \ˈpäs-chə-lənt\ *n* : a probationary candidate for membership in a religious order
¹**pos·tu·late** \ˈpäs-chə-ˌlāt\ *vb* **-lat·ed; -lat·ing** : to assume as true
²**pos·tu·late** \ˈpäs-chə-lət, -ˌlāt\ *n* : a proposition taken for granted as true esp. as a basis for a chain of reasoning
¹**pos·ture** \ˈpäs-chər\ *n* **1** : the position or bearing of the body or one of its parts **2** : STATE, CONDITION **3** : ATTITUDE
²**posture** *vb* **pos·tured; pos·tur·ing** : to strike a pose esp. for effect
post·war \ˈpōst-ˈwȯr\ *adj* : of or relating to the period after a war
po·sy \ˈpō-zē\ *n, pl* **posies 1** : a brief sentiment : MOTTO **2** : a bunch of flowers; *also* : FLOWER
¹**pot** \ˈpät\ *n* **1** : a rounded container used chiefly for domestic purposes **2** : the total of the bets at stake at one time **3** : RUIN ⟨go to ~⟩ — **pot·ful** *n*
²**pot** *vb* **pot·ted; pot·ting 1** : to preserve or place in a pot **2** : SHOOT
³**pot** *n* : MARIJUANA
po·ta·ble \ˈpō-tə-bəl\ *adj* : suitable for drinking — **po·ta·bil·i·ty** \ˌpō-tə-ˈbi-lə-tē\ *n*
po·tage \pȯ-ˈtäzh\ *n* : a thick soup
pot·ash \ˈpät-ˌash\ *n* [sing. of *pot ashes*] : potassium or any of its various compounds esp. as used in agriculture
po·tas·si·um \pə-ˈta-sē-əm\ *n* : a silver-white soft metallic chemical element that occurs abundantly in nature — see ELEMENT table
potassium bromide *n* : a crystalline salt used as a sedative and in photography
potassium carbonate *n* : a white salt used in making glass and soap
potassium nitrate *n* : a soluble salt used in making gunpowder, as a fertilizer, and in medicine
po·ta·tion \pō-ˈtā-shən\ *n* : a usu. alcoholic drink; *also* : the act of drinking
po·ta·to \pə-ˈtā-tō\ *n, pl* **-toes** : the edible starchy tuber of a plant related to the tomato; *also* : this plant
potato beetle *n* : COLORADO POTATO BEETLE
potato bug *n* : COLORADO POTATO BEETLE
pot·bel·ly \ˈpät-ˌbe-lē\ *n* : a protruding abdomen — **pot·bel·lied** \-lēd\ *adj*
pot·boil·er \-ˌbȯi-lər\ *n* : a usu. inferior work of art or literature produced chiefly for profit
po·tent \ˈpōt-ᵊnt\ *adj* **1** : having authority or influence : POWERFUL **2** : chemically or medicinally effective **3** : able to copulate — used esp. of the male **syn** forceful, forcible, mighty, puissant — **po·ten·cy** \-ᵊn-sē\ *n*
po·ten·tate \ˈpōt-ᵊn-ˌtāt\ *n* : one who wields controlling power : RULER
¹**po·ten·tial** \pə-ˈten-chəl\ *adj* : existing in possibility : capable of becoming actual ⟨a ~ champion⟩ **syn** dormant, latent, quiescent — **po·ten·ti·al·i·ty** \pə-ˌten-chē-ˈa-lə-tē\ *n* — **po·ten·tial·ly** \-ˈten-chə-lē\ *adv*
²**potential** *n* **1** : something that can develop or become actual ⟨a ~ for violence⟩ **2** : the work required to move a unit positive charge from infinity to a point in question; *also* : POTENTIAL DIFFERENCE
potential difference *n* : the difference in potential between two points that represents the work involved in the transfer of a unit quantity of electricity from one point to the other
potential energy *n* : the energy an object has because of its position or the arrangement of its parts
po·ten·ti·ate \pə-ˈten-chē-ˌāt\ *vb* **-at·ed; -at·ing** : to make potent; *esp* : to augment the activity of (as a drug) synergistically — **po·ten·ti·a·tion** \-ˌten-chē-ˈā-shən\ *n*
pot·head \ˈpät-ˌhed\ *n* : a person who smokes marijuana
poth·er \ˈpä-t͟hər\ *n* : a noisy disturbance; *also* : FUSS
pot·herb \ˈpät-ˌərb, -ˌhərb\ *n* : an herb whose leaves or stems are boiled for greens or used to season food
pot·hole \ˈpät-ˌhōl\ *n* : a large pit or hole (as in a road surface)
pot·hook \-ˌhu̇k\ *n* : an S-shaped hook for hanging pots and kettles over an open fire
po·tion \ˈpō-shən\ *n* : a mixture of liquids (as liquor or medicine)
pot·luck \ˈpät-ˈlək\ *n* : the regular meal available to a guest for whom no special preparations have been made
pot·pie \-ˈpī\ *n* : pastry-covered meat and vegetables cooked in a deep dish
pot·pour·ri \ˌpō-pu̇-ˈrē\ *n* [F *pot pourri,* lit., rotten

pot] **1 :** a mixture of flowers, herbs, and spices used for scent **2 :** a miscellaneous collection

pot•sherd \ˈpät-ˌshərd\ *n* **:** a pottery fragment

pot•shot \-ˌshät\ *n* **1 :** a shot taken from ambush or at a random or easy target **2 :** a critical remark made in a random or sporadic manner

pot•tage \ˈpä-tij\ *n* **:** a thick soup of vegetables and often meat

[1]**pot•ter** \ˈpä-tər\ *n* **:** one that makes pottery

[2]**potter** *vb* **:** PUTTER

pot•tery \ˈpä-tə-rē\ *n, pl* **-ter•ies 1 :** a place where earthen pots and dishes are made **2 :** the art of the potter **3 :** dishes, pots, and vases made from clay

[1]**pouch** \ˈpau̇ch\ *n* **1 :** a small bag (as for tobacco) carried on the person **2 :** a bag for storing or transporting goods ⟨mail ~⟩ ⟨diplomatic ~⟩ **3 :** an anatomical sac; *esp* **:** one for carrying the young on the abdomen of a female marsupial (as a kangaroo)

[2]**pouch** *vb* **:** to put or form into or as if into a pouch

poult \ˈpōlt\ *n* **:** a young fowl; *esp* **:** a young turkey

poul•ter•er \ˈpōl-tər-ər\ *n* **:** one that deals in poultry

poul•tice \ˈpōl-təs\ *n* **:** a soft usu. heated and medicated mass spread on cloth and applied to a sore or injury — **poultice** *vb*

poul•try \ˈpōl-trē\ *n* **:** domesticated birds kept for eggs or meat — **poul•try•man** \-mən\ *n*

pounce \ˈpau̇ns\ *vb* **pounced; pounc•ing :** to spring or swoop upon and seize something

[1]**pound** \ˈpau̇nd\ *n, pl* **pounds** *also* **pound 1 :** a unit of avoirdupois, troy, and apothecaries' weight — see WEIGHT table **2** — see MONEY table

[2]**pound** *n* **:** a public enclosure where stray animals are kept

[3]**pound** *vb* **1 :** to crush to a powder or pulp by beating **2 :** to strike or beat heavily or repeatedly **3 :** DRILL 1 **4 :** to move or move along heavily

pound•age \ˈpau̇n-dij\ *n* **:** POUNDS; *also* **:** weight in pounds

pound cake *n* **:** a rich cake made with a large proportion of eggs and shortening

pound–fool•ish \ˈpau̇nd-ˈfü-lish\ *adj* **:** imprudent in dealing with large sums or large matters

pour \ˈpōr\ *vb* **1 :** to flow or cause to flow in a stream or flood **2 :** to rain hard **3 :** to supply freely and copiously

pour•boire \pu̇r-ˈbwär\ *n* [F, fr. *pour boire* for drinking] **:** TIP, GRATUITY

pout \ˈpau̇t\ *vb* **:** to show displeasure by thrusting out the lips; *also* **:** to look sullen — **pout** *n*

pov•er•ty \ˈpä-vər-tē\ *n* [ME *poverte*, fr. OF *poverté*, fr. L *paupertat-, paupertas*, fr. *pauper* poor] **1 :** lack of money or material possessions **:** WANT **2 :** poor quality (as of soil)

poverty line *n* **:** a level of personal or family income below which one is classified as poor according to government standards

pov•er•ty–strick•en \ˈpä-vər-tē-ˌstri-kən\ *adj* **:** very poor **:** DESTITUTE

POW \ˌpē-(ˌ)ō-ˈdə-bəl-(ˌ)yü\ *n* **:** PRISONER OF WAR

[1]**pow•der** \ˈpau̇-dər\ *n* [ME *poudre*, fr. OF, fr. L *pulver-, pulvis* dust] **1 :** dry material made up of fine particles; *also* **:** a usu. medicinal or cosmetic preparation in this form **2 :** a solid explosive (as gunpowder) — **pow•dery** *adj*

[2]**powder** *vb* **1 :** to sprinkle or cover with or as if with powder **2 :** to reduce to powder

powder room *n* **:** a rest room for women

[1]**pow•er** \ˈpau̇-ər\ *n* **1 :** the ability to act or produce an effect **2 :** a position of ascendancy over others **:** AUTHORITY **3 :** one that has control or authority; *esp* **:** a sovereign state **4 :** physical might; *also* **:** mental or moral vigor **5 :** the number of times as indicated by an exponent a number is to be multiplied by itself; *also* **:** the product itself **6 :** force or energy used to do work; *also* **:** the time rate at which work is done or energy transferred **7 :** MAGNIFICATION 2 — **pow•er•ful** \-fəl\ *adj* — **pow•er•ful•ly** *adv* — **pow•er•less** *adj*

[2]**power** *vb* **:** to supply with power and esp. motive power

pow•er•boat \-ˈbōt\ *n* **:** MOTORBOAT

pow•er•house \ˈpau̇-ər-ˌhau̇s\ *n* **1 :** POWER PLANT 1 **2 :** one having great drive, energy, or ability

power plant *n* **1 :** a building in which electric power is generated **2 :** an engine and related parts supplying the motive power of a self-propelled vehicle

pow•wow \ˈpau̇-ˌwau̇\ *n* **1 :** a No. American Indian ceremony (as for victory in war) **2 :** a meeting for discussion **:** CONFERENCE

pox \ˈpäks\ *n, pl* **pox** *or* **pox•es :** any of various diseases (as smallpox or syphilis) marked by a rash on the skin

pp *abbr* **1** pages **2** pianissimo

PP *abbr* **1** parcel post **2** past participle **3** postpaid **4** prepaid

ppd *abbr* **1** postpaid **2** prepaid

PPS *abbr* [L *post postscriptum*] an additional postscript

ppt *abbr* precipitate

PQ *abbr* Province of Quebec

pr *abbr* **1** pair **2** price

Pr *symbol* praseodymium

PR *abbr* **1** payroll **2** public relations **3** Puerto Rico

prac•ti•ca•ble \ˈprak-ti-kə-bəl\ *adj* **:** capable of being put into practice, done, or accomplished — **prac•ti•ca•bil•i•ty** \ˌprak-ti-kə-ˈbi-lə-tē\ *n*

prac•ti•cal \ˈprak-ti-kəl\ *adj* **1 :** of, relating to, or shown in practice ⟨~ questions⟩ **2 :** VIRTUAL ⟨~ control⟩ **3 :** capable of being put to use ⟨a ~ knowledge of French⟩ **4 :** inclined to action as opposed to speculation ⟨a ~ person⟩ **5 :** qualified by practice ⟨a good ~ mechanic⟩ — **prac•ti•cal•i•ty** \ˌprak-ti-ˈka-lə-tē\ *n* — **prac•ti•cal•ly** \-k(ə-)lē\ *adv*

practical joke *n* **:** a prank intended to trick or embarrass someone or cause physical discomfort

practical nurse *n* **:** a professional nurse without all of the qualifications of a registered nurse; *esp* **:** LICENSED PRACTICAL NURSE

[1]**prac•tice** *or* **prac•tise** \ˈprak-təs\ *vb* **prac•ticed** *or* **prac•tised; prac•tic•ing** *or* **prac•tis•ing 1 :** CARRY OUT, APPLY ⟨~ what you preach⟩ **2 :** to perform or work at repeatedly so as to become proficient ⟨~ tennis strokes⟩ **3 :** to do or perform customarily ⟨~ politeness⟩ **4 :** to be professionally engaged in ⟨~ law⟩

[2]**practice** *also* **practise** *n* **1 :** actual performance or application **2 :** customary action **:** HABIT **3 :** systematic exercise for proficiency **4 :** the exercise of a profession; *also* **:** a professional business

prac•ti•tion•er \prak-ˈti-shə-nər\ *n* **:** one who practices a profession

prae•tor \ˈprē-tər\ *n* **:** an ancient Roman magistrate ranking below a consul — **prae•to•ri•an** \prē-ˈtōr-ē-ən, -ˈtȯr-\ *adj*

prag•mat•ic \prag-ˈma-tik\ *also* **prag•mat•i•cal** \-ti-kəl\ *adj* **1 :** of or relating to practical affairs **2 :** concerned with the practical consequences of actions or beliefs — **pragmatic** *n* — **prag•mat•i•cal•ly** \-ti-k(ə-)lē\ *adv*

prag•ma•tism \ˈprag-mə-ˌti-zəm\ *n* **:** a practical approach to problems and affairs

prai•rie \ˈprer-ē\ *n* **:** a broad tract of level or rolling grassland

prairie dog *n* **:** an American burrowing black-tailed rodent related to the squirrels and living in colonies

prairie schooner *n* **:** a covered wagon used by pioneers in cross-country travel

praise \ˈprāz\ *vb* **praised; prais•ing 1 :** to express approval of **:** COMMEND **2 :** to glorify (a divinity or a saint) esp. in song — **praise** *n*

praise•wor•thy \-ˌwər-t͟hē\ *adj* **:** LAUDABLE

pra•line \ˈprä-ˌlēn, ˈprā-\ *n* [F] **:** a confection of nuts and sugar

pram \ˈpram\ *n, chiefly Brit* **:** PERAMBULATOR

prance \ˈprans\ *vb* **pranced; pranc•ing 1 :** to spring from the hind legs ⟨a *prancing* horse⟩ **2 :** SWAGGER; *also* **:** CAPER — **prance** *n* — **pranc•er** *n*
prank \ˈpraŋk\ *n* **:** a playful or mildly mischievous act **:** TRICK
prank•ster \ˈpraŋk-stər\ *n* **:** a person who plays pranks
pra•seo•dym•i•um \ˌprā-zē-ō-ˈdi-mē-əm\ *n* **:** a yellowish white metallic chemical element — see ELEMENT table
prate \ˈprāt\ *vb* **prat•ed; prat•ing :** to talk long and idly **:** chatter foolishly
prat•fall \ˈprat-ˌfȯl\ *n* **1 :** a fall on the buttocks **2 :** a humiliating blunder
[1]**prat•tle** \ˈprat-ᵊl\ *vb* **prat•tled; prat•tling :** PRATE, BABBLE
[2]**prattle** *n* **:** trifling or childish talk
prawn \ˈprȯn\ *n* **:** any of numerous edible shrimplike crustaceans; *also* **:** SHRIMP 1
pray \ˈprā\ *vb* **1 :** ENTREAT, IMPLORE **2 :** to ask earnestly for something **3 :** to address God or a god esp. with supplication
prayer \ˈprar\ *n* **1 :** a supplication or expression addressed to God or a god; *also* **:** a set order of words used in praying **2 :** an earnest request or wish **3 :** the act or practice of praying to God or a god **4 :** a religious service consisting chiefly of prayers — often used in pl. **5 :** something prayed for **6 :** a slight chance
prayer book *n* **:** a book containing prayers and often directions for worship
prayer•ful \ˈprar-fəl\ *adj* **1 :** DEVOUT **2 :** EARNEST — **prayer•ful•ly** *adv*
praying mantis *n* **:** MANTIS
PRC *abbr* People's Republic of China
preach \ˈprēch\ *vb* **1 :** to deliver a sermon **2 :** to set forth in a sermon **3 :** to advocate earnestly — **preach•er** *n* — **preach•ment** *n*
pre•ad•o•les•cence \ˈprē-ˌad-ᵊl-ˈes-ᵊns\ *n* **:** the period of human development just preceding adolescence — **pre•ad•o•les•cent** \-ᵊnt\ *adj or n*
pre•am•ble \ˈprē-ˌam-bəl\ *n* [ME, fr. MF *preambule*, fr. ML *preambulum*, fr. LL, neut. of *praeambulus* walking in front of, fr. L *prae* in front of + *ambulare* to walk] **:** an introductory part ⟨the ~ to a constitution⟩
pre•ar•range \ˌprē-ə-ˈrānj\ *vb* **:** to arrange beforehand — **pre•ar•range•ment** *n*
pre•as•signed \ˌprē-ə-ˈsīnd\ *adj* **:** assigned beforehand
prec *abbr* preceding
Pre•cam•bri•an \ˈprē-ˈkam-brē-ən, -ˈkām-\ *adj* **:** of, relating to, or being the era that is earliest in geologic history and is characterized esp. by the appearance of single-celled organisms — **Precambrian** *n*
pre•can•cel \(ˌ)prē-ˈkan-səl\ *vb* **:** to cancel (a postage stamp) in advance of use — **precancel** *n* — **pre•can•cel•la•tion** \ˌprē-ˌkan-sə-ˈlā-shən\ *n*
pre•can•cer•ous \(ˌ)prē-ˈkan-sə-rəs\ *adj* **:** likely to become cancerous
pre•car•i•ous \pri-ˈkar-ē-əs\ *adj* **:** dependent on uncertain conditions **:** dangerously insecure **:** UNSTABLE ⟨a ~ foothold⟩ ⟨~ prosperity⟩ **syn** delicate, sensitive, ticklish, touchy, tricky — **pre•car•i•ous•ly** *adv* — **pre•car•i•ous•ness** *n*
pre•cau•tion \pri-ˈkȯ-shən\ *n* **:** a measure taken beforehand to prevent harm or secure good — **pre•cau•tion•ary** \-shə-ˌner-ē\ *adj*
pre•cede \pri-ˈsēd\ *vb* **pre•ced•ed; pre•ced•ing :** to be, go, or come ahead or in front of (as in rank or time)
pre•ce•dence \ˈpre-sə-dəns, pri-ˈsēd-ᵊns\ *n* **1 :** the act or fact of preceding **2 :** consideration based on order of importance **:** PRIORITY
[1]**pre•ce•dent** \pri-ˈsēd-ᵊnt, ˈpre-sə-dənt\ *adj* **:** prior in time, order, or significance
[2]**prec•e•dent** \ˈpre-sə-dənt\ *n* **:** something said or done that may serve to authorize or justify further words or acts of the same or a similar kind
pre•ced•ing \pri-ˈsē-diŋ\ *adj* **:** that precedes **syn** antecedent, foregoing, prior, former, anterior
pre•cen•tor \pri-ˈsen-tər\ *n* **:** a leader of the singing of a choir or congregation
pre•cept \ˈprē-ˌsept\ *n* **:** a command or principle intended as a general rule of action or conduct
pre•cep•tor \pri-ˈsep-tər, ˈprē-ˌsep-\ *n* **:** TUTOR
pre•ces•sion \prē-ˈse-shən\ *n* **:** a slow gyration of the rotation axis of a spinning body (as the earth) — **pre•cess** \prē-ˈses\ *vb* — **pre•ces•sion•al** \-ˈsə-shə-nəl\ *adj*
pre•cinct \ˈprē-ˌsiŋkt\ *n* **1 :** an administrative subdivision (as of a city) **:** DISTRICT ⟨police ~⟩ ⟨electoral ~⟩ **2 :** an enclosure bounded by the limits of a building or place — often used in pl. **3** *pl* **:** ENVIRONS
pre•ci•os•i•ty \ˌpre-shē-ˈä-sə-tē\ *n, pl* **-ties :** fastidious refinement
pre•cious \ˈpre-shəs\ *adj* **1 :** of great value ⟨~ jewels⟩ **2 :** greatly cherished **:** DEAR ⟨~ memories⟩ **3 :** AFFECTED ⟨~ language⟩
prec•i•pice \ˈpre-sə-pəs\ *n* **:** a steep cliff
pre•cip•i•tan•cy \pri-ˈsi-pə-tən-sē\ *n* **:** undue hastiness or suddenness
[1]**pre•cip•i•tate** \pri-ˈsi-pə-ˌtāt\ *vb* **-tat•ed; -tat•ing** [L *praecipitare*, fr. *praecipit-*, *praeceps* headlong, fr. *prae* in front of + *caput* head] **1 :** to throw violently **2 :** to throw down **3 :** to cause to happen quickly or abruptly ⟨~ a quarrel⟩ **4 :** to cause to separate from solution or suspension **5 :** to fall as rain, snow, or hail **syn** speed, accelerate, quicken, hasten, hurry
[2]**pre•cip•i•tate** \pri-ˈsi-pə-tət, -ˌtāt\ *n* **:** the solid matter that separates from a solution or suspension
[3]**pre•cip•i•tate** \pri-ˈsi-pə-tət\ *adj* **1 :** showing extreme or unwise haste **:** RASH **2 :** falling with steep descent; *also* **:** PRECIPITOUS — **pre•cip•i•tate•ly** *adv* — **pre•cip•i•tate•ness** *n*
pre•cip•i•ta•tion \pri-ˌsi-pə-ˈtā-shən\ *n* **1 :** rash haste **2 :** the process of precipitating or forming a precipitate **3 :** water that falls to earth esp. as rain or snow; *also* **:** the quantity of this water
pre•cip•i•tous \pri-ˈsi-pə-təs\ *adj* **1 :** PRECIPITATE **2 :** having the character of a precipice **:** very steep ⟨a ~ slope⟩; *also* **:** containing precipices ⟨~ trails⟩ — **pre•cip•i•tous•ly** *adv*
pré•cis \prā-ˈsē\ *n, pl* **pré•cis** \-ˈsēz\ [F] **:** a concise summary of essentials
pre•cise \pri-ˈsīs\ *adj* **1 :** exactly defined or stated **:** DEFINITE **2 :** highly accurate **:** EXACT **3 :** conforming strictly to a standard **:** SCRUPULOUS — **pre•cise•ly** *adv* — **pre•cise•ness** *n*
pre•ci•sion \pri-ˈsi-zhən\ *n* **:** the quality or state of being precise
pre•clude \pri-ˈklüd\ *vb* **pre•clud•ed; pre•clud•ing :** to make impossible **:** BAR, PREVENT
pre•co•cious \pri-ˈkō-shəs\ *adj* [L *praecoc-*, *praecox*, lit., ripening early, fr. *prae-* ahead + *coquere* to cook] **:** early in development and esp. in mental development — **pre•co•cious•ly** *adv* — **pre•coc•i•ty** \pri-ˈkä-sə-tē\ *n*
pre•con•ceive \ˌprē-kən-ˈsēv\ *vb* **:** to form an opinion of beforehand — **pre•con•cep•tion** \-ˈsep-shən\ *n*
pre•con•cert•ed \-ˈsər-təd\ *adj* **:** arranged or agreed on in advance
pre•con•di•tion \-ˈdi-shən\ *vb* **:** to put in proper or desired condition or frame of mind in advance
pre•cook \ˌprē-ˈku̇k\ *vb* **:** to cook partially or entirely before final cooking or reheating
pre•cur•sor \pri-ˈkər-sər\ *n* **:** one that precedes and indicates the approach of another **:** FORERUNNER
pred *abbr* predicate
pre•da•ceous *or* **pre•da•cious** \pri-ˈdā-shəs\ *adj* **:** living by preying on others **:** PREDATORY
pre•date \ˈprē-ˈdāt\ *vb* **:** ANTEDATE
pre•da•tion \pri-ˈdā-shən\ *n* **1 :** the act of preying or plundering **2 :** a mode of life in which food is primarily obtained by killing and consuming animals

pred•a•tor \ˈpre-də-tər\ *n* : an animal that lives by predation

pred•a•to•ry \ˈpre-də-ˌtōr-ē\ *adj* **1** : of or relating to plunder ⟨~ warfare⟩ **2** : disposed to exploit others **3** : preying upon other animals

pre•de•cease \ˌprē-di-ˈsēs\ *vb* **-ceased; -ceas•ing** : to die before another person

pre•de•ces•sor \ˈpre-də-ˌse-sər, ˈprē-\ *n* : a previous holder of a position to which another has succeeded

pre•des•ig•nate \(ˌ)prē-ˈde-zig-ˌnāt\ *vb* : to designate beforehand

pre•des•ti•na•tion \ˌprē-ˌdes-tə-ˈnā-shən\ *n* : the act of foreordaining to an earthly lot or eternal destiny by divine decree; *also* : the state of being so foreordained — **pre•des•ti•nate** \prē-ˈdes-tə-ˌnāt\ *vb*

pre•des•tine \prē-ˈdes-tən\ *vb* : to settle beforehand : FOREORDAIN

pre•de•ter•mine \ˌprē-di-ˈtər-mən\ *vb* : to determine beforehand

pred•i•ca•ble \ˈpre-di-kə-bəl\ *adj* : capable of being predicated or affirmed

pre•dic•a•ment \pri-ˈdi-kə-mənt\ *n* : a difficult or trying situation **syn** dilemma, pickle, quagmire, jam

¹pred•i•cate \ˈpre-di-kət\ *n* : the part of a sentence or clause that expresses what is said of the subject

²pred•i•cate \ˈpre-də-ˌkāt\ *vb* **-cat•ed; -cat•ing 1** : AFFIRM **2** : to assert to be a quality or attribute **3** : FOUND, BASE — **pred•i•ca•tion** \ˌpre-də-ˈkā-shən\ *n*

pre•dict \pri-ˈdikt\ *vb* : to declare in advance — **pre•dict•abil•i•ty** \-ˌdik-tə-ˈbi-lə-tē\ *n* — **pre•dict•able** \-ˈdik-tə-bəl\ *adj* — **pre•dict•ably** \-blē\ *adv* — **pre•dic•tion** \-ˈdik-shən\ *n*

pre•di•gest \ˌprē-dī-ˈjest\ *vb* : to simplify for easy use; *also* : to subject to artificial or natural partial digestion

pre•di•lec•tion \ˌpre-də-ˈlek-shən, ˌprē-\ *n* : an established preference for something

pre•dis•pose \ˌprē-di-ˈspōz\ *vb* : to incline in advance : make susceptible — **pre•dis•po•si•tion** \ˌprē-ˌdis-pə-ˈzi-shən\ *n*

pre•dom•i•nant \pri-ˈdä-mə-nənt\ *adj* : greater in importance, strength, influence, or authority — **pre•dom•i•nance** \-nəns\ *n*

pre•dom•i•nant•ly \-nənt-lē\ *adv* : for the most part : MAINLY

pre•dom•i•nate \pri-ˈdä-mə-ˌnāt\ *vb* : to be superior esp. in power or numbers : PREVAIL

pree•mie \ˈprē-mē\ *n* : a premature baby

pre•em•i•nent \prē-ˈe-mə-nənt\ *adj* : having highest rank : OUTSTANDING — **pre•em•i•nence** \-nəns\ *n* — **pre•em•i•nent•ly** *adv*

pre•empt \prē-ˈempt\ *vb* **1** : to settle upon (public land) with the right to purchase before others; *also* : to take by such right **2** : to seize upon before someone else can **3** : to take the place of **syn** usurp, confiscate, appropriate, expropriate — **pre•emp•tion** \-ˈemp-shən\ *n*

pre•emp•tive \prē-ˈemp-tiv\ *adj* : marked by the seizing of the initiative : initiated by oneself ⟨~ attack⟩

preen \ˈprēn\ *vb* **1** : to dress or smooth up : PRIMP **2** : to trim or dress with the bill — used of a bird **3** : to pride (oneself) for achievement

pre•ex•ist \ˌprē-ig-ˈzist\ *vb* : to exist before — **pre•ex•is•tence** \-ˈzis-təns\ *n* — **pre•ex•is•tent** \-tənt\ *adj*

pref *abbr* **1** preface **2** preference **3** preferred **4** prefix

pre•fab \(ˌ)prē-ˈfab, ˈprē-ˌfab\ *n* : a prefabricated structure

pre•fab•ri•cate \(ˌ)prē-ˈfa-brə-ˌkāt\ *vb* : to manufacture the parts of (a structure) beforehand for later assembly — **pre•fab•ri•ca•tion** \ˌprē-ˌfa-bri-ˈkā-shən\ *n*

¹pref•ace \ˈpre-fəs\ *n* : the introductory remarks of a speaker or writer — **pref•a•to•ry** \ˈpre-fə-ˌtōr-ē\ *adj*

²preface *vb* **pref•aced; pref•ac•ing** : to introduce with a preface

pre•fect \ˈprē-ˌfekt\ *n* **1** : a high official; *esp* : a chief officer or magistrate **2** : a student monitor

pre•fec•ture \ˈprē-ˌfek-chər\ *n* : the office, term, or residence of a prefect

pre•fer \pri-ˈfər\ *vb* **pre•ferred; pre•fer•ring 1** : PROMOTE **2** : to like better **3** : to bring (as a charge) against a person — **pref•er•a•ble** \ˈpre-fə-rə-bəl\ *adj* — **pref•er•a•bly** \-blē\ *adv*

pref•er•ence \ˈpre-frəns, -fə-rəns\ *n* **1** : a special liking for one thing over another **2** : CHOICE, SELECTION — **pref•er•en•tial** \ˌpre-fə-ˈren-chəl\ *adj*

pre•fer•ment \pri-ˈfər-mənt\ *n* : PROMOTION, ADVANCEMENT

pre•fig•ure \prē-ˈfi-gyər\ *vb* **1** : FORESHADOW **2** : to imagine beforehand

¹pre•fix \ˈprē-ˌfiks, prē-ˈfiks\ *vb* : to place before ⟨~ a title to a name⟩

²pre•fix \ˈprē-ˌfiks\ *n* : an affix occurring at the beginning of a word

pre•flight \ˌprē-ˈflīt\ *adj* : preparing for or preliminary to flight

pre•form \(ˌ)prē-ˈfȯrm, ˈprē-ˌfȯrm\ *vb* : to form or shape beforehand

preg•na•ble \ˈpreg-nə-bəl\ *adj* : vulnerable to capture ⟨a ~ fort⟩

preg•nant \ˈpreg-nənt\ *adj* **1** : containing unborn young within the body **2** : rich in significance : MEANINGFUL — **preg•nan•cy** \-nən-sē\ *n*

pre•heat \ˌprē-ˈhēt\ *vb* : to heat beforehand; *esp* : to heat (an oven) to a designated temperature before using

pre•hen•sile \prē-ˈhen-səl, -ˌsīl\ *adj* : adapted for grasping esp. by wrapping around ⟨a monkey with a ~ tail⟩

pre•his•tor•ic \ˌprē-his-ˈtȯr-ik\ *or* **pre•his•tor•i•cal** \-i-kəl\ *adj* : of, relating to, or existing in the period before written history began

pre•judge \(ˌ)prē-ˈjəj\ *vb* : to judge before full hearing or examination

¹prej•u•dice \ˈpre-jə-dəs\ *n* **1** : DAMAGE; *esp* : detriment to one's rights or claims **2** : an opinion made without adequate basis — **prej•u•di•cial** \ˌpre-jə-ˈdi-shəl\ *adj*

²prejudice *vb* **-diced; -dic•ing 1** : to damage by a judgment or action esp. at law **2** : to cause to have prejudice

prel•ate \ˈpre-lət\ *n* : an ecclesiastic (as a bishop) of high rank — **prel•a•cy** \-lə-sē\ *n*

pre•launch \ˈprē-ˈlȯnch\ *adj* : preparing for or preliminary to launch

pre•lim \ˈprē-ˌlim, pri-ˈlim\ *n or adj* : PRELIMINARY

¹pre•lim•i•nary \pri-ˈli-mə-ˌner-ē\ *n, pl* **-nar•ies** : something that precedes or introduces the main business or event

²preliminary *adj* : preceding the main discourse or business

pre•lude \ˈprel-ˌyüd; ˈpre-ˌlüd, ˈprā-\ *n* **1** : an introductory performance or event **2** : a musical section or movement introducing the main theme; *also* : an organ solo played at the beginning of a church service

prem *abbr* premium

pre•mar•i•tal \(ˌ)prē-ˈmar-ət-ᵊl\ *adj* : existing or occurring before marriage

pre•ma•ture \ˌprē-mə-ˈtu̇r, -ˈtyu̇r, -ˈchu̇r\ *adj* : happening, coming, born, or done before the usual or proper time — **pre•ma•ture•ly** *adv*

¹pre•med \ˌprē-ˈmed\ *n* : a premedical student or course of study

²premed *adj* : PREMEDICAL

pre•med•i•cal \(ˌ)prē-ˈme-di-kəl\ *adj* : preceding and preparing for the professional study of medicine

pre•med•i•tate \pri-ˈme-də-ˌtāt\ *vb* : to consider and plan beforehand — **pre•med•i•ta•tion** \-ˌme-də-ˈtā-shən\ *n*

pre•men•stru•al \(ˌ)prē-ˈmen-strə-wəl\ *adj* : of, relating to, or occurring in the period just before menstruation

premenstrual syndrome *n* : a varying group of symptoms manifested by some women prior to menstruation

pre•mie *var of* PREEMIE

[1]**pre•mier** \pri-ˈmir, -ˈmyir, ˈprē-mē-ər\ *adj* [ME *primier,* fr. MF *premier* first, chief, fr. L *primarius* of the first rank] : first in rank or importance : CHIEF; *also* : first in time : EARLIEST

[2]**premier** *n* : PRIME MINISTER — **pre•mier•ship** *n*

[1]**pre•miere** \pri-ˈmyer, -ˈmir\ *n* : a first performance

[2]**premiere** *or* **pre•mier** *same as* [1]PREMIERE\ *vb* **premiered; pre•mier•ing** : to give or receive a first public performance

prem•ise \ˈpre-məs\ *n* **1** : a statement of fact or a supposition made or implied as a basis of argument **2** *pl* : a piece of land with the structures on it; *also* : the place of business of an enterprise

pre•mi•um \ˈprē-mē-əm\ *n* [L *praemium* booty, reward, fr. *prae* before + *emere* to take, buy] **1** : REWARD, PRIZE **2** : a sum over and above the stated value **3** : something paid over and above a fixed wage or price **4** : something given with a purchase **5** : the sum paid for a contract of insurance **6** : an unusually high value

pre•mix \ˌprē-ˈmiks\ *vb* : to mix before use

[1]**pre•mo•lar** \(ˌ)prē-ˈmō-lər\ *adj* : situated in front of or preceding the molar teeth

[2]**premolar** *n* : any of the double-pointed grinding teeth which are located between the canines and the true molars and of which there are two on each side of each human jaw

pre•mo•ni•tion \ˌprē-mə-ˈni-shən, ˌpre-\ *n* **1** : previous warning **2** : PRESENTIMENT — **pre•mon•i•to•ry** \pri-ˈmä-nə-ˌtōr-ē\ *adj*

pre•na•tal \ˈprē-ˈnāt-ᵊl\ *adj* : occurring, existing, or taking place before birth

pre•oc•cu•pa•tion \prē-ˌä-kyə-ˈpā-shən\ *n* : complete absorption of the mind or interests; *also* : something that causes such absorption

pre•oc•cu•pied \prē-ˈä-kyə-ˌpīd\ *adj* **1** : lost in thought; *also* : absorbed in some preoccupation **2** : already occupied **syn** abstracted, absent, absentminded

pre•oc•cu•py \-ˌpī\ *vb* **1** : to occupy the attention of beforehand **2** : to take possession of before another

pre•op•er•a•tive \(ˌ)prē-ˈä-prə-tiv, -pə-ˌrā-\ *adj* : occurring before a surgical operation

pre•or•dain \ˌprē-ȯr-ˈdān\ *vb* : FOREORDAIN

pre–owned \(ˌ)prē-ˈōnd\ *adj* : SECONDHAND

prep *abbr* **1** preparatory **2** preposition

pre•pack•age \(ˌ)prē-ˈpa-kij\ *vb* : to package (as food) before offering for sale to the customer

preparatory school *n* **1** : a usu. private school preparing students primarily for college **2** *Brit* : a private elementary school preparing students primarily for public schools

pre•pare \pri-ˈpar\ *vb* **pre•pared; pre•par•ing 1** : to make or get ready ⟨~ dinner⟩ ⟨~ a student for college⟩ **2** : to get ready beforehand **3** : to put together : COMPOUND ⟨~ a prescription⟩ — **prep•a•ra•tion** \ˌpre-pə-ˈrā-shən\ *n* — **pre•pa•ra•to•ry** \pri-ˈpar-ə-ˌtōr-ē\ *adj*

pre•pared•ness \pri-ˈpar-əd-nəs\ *n* : a state of adequate preparation

pre•pay \(ˌ)prē-ˈpā\ *vb* **-paid** \-ˈpād\; **-pay•ing** : to pay or pay the charge on in advance

pre•pon•der•ant \pri-ˈpän-də-rənt\ *adj* : having greater weight, force, influence, or frequency — **pre•pon•der•ance** \-rəns\ *n* — **pre•pon•der•ant•ly** *adv*

pre•pon•der•ate \pri-ˈpän-də-ˌrāt\ *vb* **-at•ed; -at•ing** [L *praeponderare,* fr. *prae-* ahead + *ponder-, pondus* weight] : to exceed in weight, force, influence, or frequency : PREDOMINATE

prep•o•si•tion \ˌpre-pə-ˈzi-shən\ *n* : a word that combines with a noun or pronoun to form a phrase — **prep•o•si•tion•al** \-ˈzi-shə-nəl\ *adj*

pre•pos•sess \ˌprē-pə-ˈzes\ *vb* **1** : to cause to be preoccupied **2** : to influence beforehand esp. favorably

pre•pos•sess•ing *adj* : tending to create a favorable impression ⟨a ~ manner⟩

pre•pos•ses•sion \-ˈze-shən\ *n* **1** : PREJUDICE **2** : an exclusive concern with one idea or object

pre•pos•ter•ous \pri-ˈpäs-tə-rəs\ *adj* : contrary to nature or reason : ABSURD

prep•py *or* **prep•pie** \ˈpre-pē\ *n, pl* **preppies 1** : a student at or a graduate of a preparatory school **2** : a person deemed to dress or behave like a preppy

pre•puce \ˈprē-ˌpyüs\ *n* : FORESKIN

pre•quel \ˈprē-kwəl\ *n* : a literary or dramatic work whose story precedes that of an earlier work

pre•re•cord•ed \(ˌ)prē-ri-ˈkȯr-dəd\ *adj* : recorded for later broadcast

pre•req•ui•site \prē-ˈre-kwə-zət\ *n* : something required beforehand or for the end in view — **prerequisite** *adj*

pre•rog•a•tive \pri-ˈrä-gə-tiv\ *n* : an exclusive or special right, power, or privilege

pres *abbr* **1** present **2** president

[1]**pres•age** \ˈpre-sij\ *n* **1** : something that foreshadows a future event : OMEN **2** : FOREBODING

[2]**pre•sage** \ˈpre-sij, pri-ˈsāj\ *vb* **pre•saged; pre•sag•ing 1** : to give an omen or warning of : FORESHADOW **2** : FORETELL, PREDICT

pres•by•o•pia \ˌprez-bē-ˈō-pē-ə\ *n* : a visual condition in which loss of elasticity of the lens of the eye causes defective accommodation and inability to focus sharply for near vision — **pres•by•o•pic** \-ˈō-pik, -ˈä-\ *adj or n*

pres•by•ter \ˈprez-bə-tər\ *n* **1** : PRIEST, MINISTER **2** : an elder in a Presbyterian church

[1]**Pres•by•te•ri•an** \ˌprez-bə-ˈtir-ē-ən\ *n* : a member of a Presbyterian church

[2]**Presbyterian** *adj* **1** *often not cap* : characterized by a graded system of representative ecclesiastical bodies (as presbyteries) exercising legislative and judicial powers **2** : of or relating to a group of Protestant Christian bodies that are presbyterian in government — **Pres•by•te•ri•an•ism** \-ə-ˌni-zəm\ *n*

pres•by•tery \ˈprez-bə-ˌter-ē\ *n, pl* **-ter•ies 1** : the part of a church reserved for the officiating clergy **2** : a ruling body in Presbyterian churches consisting of the ministers and representative elders of a district

[1]**pre•school** \ˈprē-ˌsküt\ *adj* : of or relating to the period in a child's life from infancy to the age of five or six — **pre•school•er** \-ˌskü-lər\ *n*

[2]**preschool** *n* : NURSERY SCHOOL

pre•science \ˈpre-shəns, ˈprē-\ *n* : foreknowledge of events; *also* : FORESIGHT — **pre•scient** \-shənt, -shē-ənt\ *adj*

pre•scribe \pri-ˈskrīb\ *vb* **pre•scribed; pre•scrib•ing 1** : to lay down as a guide or rule of action **2** : to direct the use of (as a medicine) as a remedy

pre•scrip•tion \pri-ˈskrip-shən\ *n* **1** : the action of prescribing rules or directions **2** : a written direction for the preparation and use of a medicine; *also* : a medicine prescribed

pres•ence \ˈprez-ᵊns\ *n* **1** : the fact or condition of being present **2** : the space immediately around a person **3** : one that is present **4** : the bearing of a person; *esp* : stately bearing

[1]**pres•ent** \ˈprez-ᵊnt\ *n* : something presented : GIFT

[2]**pre•sent** \pri-ˈzent\ *vb* **1** : to bring into the presence or acquaintance of : INTRODUCE **2** : to bring before the public ⟨~ a play⟩ **3** : to make a gift to **4** : to give formally **5** : to lay (as a charge) before a court for inquiry **6** : to aim or direct (as a weapon) so as to face in a particular direction — **pre•sent•able** *adj* — **pre•sen•ta•tion** \ˌprē-ˌzen-ˈtā-shən, ˌprez-ᵊn-\ *n* — **pre•sent•ment** \pri-ˈzent-mənt\ *n*

[3]**pres•ent** \ˈprez-ᵊnt\ *adj* **1** : now existing or in progress ⟨~ conditions⟩ **2** : being in view or at hand ⟨~ at the meeting⟩ **3** : under consideration ⟨the ~ problem⟩ **4**

: of, relating to, or constituting a verb tense that expresses present time or the time of speaking

[4]**pres•ent** \ˈprez-ᵊnt\ *n* **1** *pl* : the present legal document **2** : the present tense; *also* : a verb form in it **3** : the present time

pres•ent–day \ˈprez-ᵊnt-ˈdā\ *adj* : now existing or occurring : CURRENT

pre•sen•ti•ment \pri-ˈzen-tə-mənt\ *n* : a feeling that something is about to happen : PREMONITION

pres•ent•ly \ˈprez-ᵊnt-lē\ *adv* **1** : SOON **2** : NOW

present participle *n* : a participle that typically expresses present action and that in English is formed with the suffix *-ing* and is used in the formation of the progressive tenses

[1]**pre•serve** \pri-ˈzərv\ *vb* **pre•served; pre•serv•ing 1** : to keep safe : GUARD, PROTECT **2** : to keep from decaying; *esp* : to process food (as by canning or pickling) to prevent spoilage **3** : MAINTAIN ⟨~ silence⟩ — **pres•er•va•tion** \ˌpre-zər-ˈvā-shən\ *n* — **pre•ser•va•tive** \pri-ˈzər-və-tiv\ *adj or n* — **pre•serv•er** *n*

[2]**preserve** *n* **1** : preserved fruit — often used in pl. **2** : an area for the protection of natural resources (as animals)

pre•set \(ˌ)prē-ˈset\ *vb* **-set; -set•ting** : to set beforehand

pre•shrunk \-ˈshrəŋk\ *adj* : subjected to a shrinking process during manufacture usu. to reduce later shrinking

pre•side \pri-ˈzīd\ *vb* **pre•sid•ed; pre•sid•ing** [L *praesidēre* to guard, preside over, fr. *prae* in front of + *sedēre* to sit] **1** : to exercise guidance or control **2** : to occupy the place of authority; *esp* : to act as chairman

pres•i•dent \ˈpre-zə-dənt\ *n* **1** : one chosen to preside ⟨~ of the assembly⟩ **2** : the chief officer of an organization (as a corporation or society) **3** : an elected official serving as both chief of state and chief political executive; *also* : a chief of state often with only minimal political powers — **pres•i•den•cy** \-dən-sē\ *n* — **pres•i•den•tial** \ˌpre-zə-ˈden-chəl\ *adj*

pre•si•dio \pri-ˈsē-dē-ˌō, -ˈsi-\ *n, pl* **-di•os** [Sp] : a military post or fortified settlement in areas currently or orig. under Spanish control

pre•sid•i•um \pri-ˈsi-dē-əm\ *n, pl* **-ia** \-dē-ə\ *or* **-iums** [Russ *prezidium*, fr. L *praesidium* garrison] : a permanent executive committee that acts for a larger body in a Communist country

[1]**pre•soak** \(ˌ)prē-ˈsōk\ *vb* : to soak beforehand

[2]**pre•soak** \ˈprē-ˌsōk\ *n* **1** : an instance of presoaking **2** : a preparation used in presoaking clothes

pre•sort \(ˌ)prē-ˈsȯrt\ *vb* : to sort (mail) by zip code usu. before delivery to a post office

[1]**press** \ˈpres\ *n* **1** : a crowded condition : THRONG **2** : a machine for exerting pressure **3** : CLOSET, CUPBOARD **4** : PRESSURE **5** : the properly creased condition of a freshly pressed garment **6** : PRINTING PRESS; *also* : the act or the process of printing **7** : a printing or publishing establishment **8** : the media (as newspapers and magazines) of public news and comment; *also* : persons (as reporters) employed in these media **9** : comment in newspapers and periodicals

[2]**press** *vb* **1** : to bear down upon : push steadily against **2** : ASSAIL, COMPEL **3** : to squeeze out the juice or contents of ⟨~ grapes⟩ **4** : to squeeze to a desired density, shape, or smoothness; *esp* : IRON **5** : to try hard to persuade : URGE **6** : to follow through : PROSECUTE **7** : CROWD **8** : to force one's way **9** : to require haste or speed in action — **press•er** *n*

press agent *n* : an agent employed to establish and maintain good public relations through publicity

press•ing *adj* : URGENT

press•man \ˈpres-mən, -ˌman\ *n* : the operator of a press and esp. a printing press

press•room \-rüm, -ˌrům\ *n* **1** : a room in a printing plant containing the printing presses **2** : a room for the use of reporters

[1]**pres•sure** \ˈpre-shər\ *n* **1** : the burden of physical or mental distress **2** : the action of pressing; *esp* : the application of force to something by something else in direct contact with it **3** : the force exerted over a surface divided by its area **4** : the stress or urgency of matters demanding attention

[2]**pressure** *vb* **pres•sured; pres•sur•ing** : to apply pressure to

pressure group *n* : a group that seeks to influence governmental policy but not to elect candidates to office

pressure suit *n* : an inflatable suit for high-altitude flight or spaceflight to protect the body from low pressure

pres•sur•ise *Brit var of* PRESSURIZE

pres•sur•ize \ˈpre-shə-ˌrīz\ *vb* **-ized; -iz•ing 1** : to maintain higher pressure within than without; *esp* : to maintain normal atmospheric pressure within (as an airplane cabin) during high-altitude flight or spaceflight **2** : to apply pressure to **3** : to design to withstand pressure — **pres•sur•i•za•tion** \ˌpre-shə-rə-ˈzā-shən\ *n*

pres•ti•dig•i•ta•tion \ˌpres-tə-ˌdi-jə-ˈtā-shən\ *n* : SLEIGHT OF HAND

pres•tige \pres-ˈtēzh, -ˈtēj\ *n* [F, fr. MF, conjuror's trick, illusion, fr. LL *praestigium*, fr. L *praestigiae*, pl., conjuror's tricks, fr. *praestringere* to graze, blunt, constrict, fr. *prae-* in front of + *stringere* to bind tight] : standing or estimation in the eyes of people : REPUTATION **syn** influence, authority, weight, cachet — **pres•ti•gious** \-ˈti-jəs, -ˈtē-\ *adj*

pres•to \ˈpres-tō\ *adv or adj* [It] **1** : suddenly as if by magic : IMMEDIATELY **2** : at a rapid tempo — used as a direction in music

pre•stress \(ˌ)prē-ˈstres\ *vb* : to introduce internal stresses into (as a structural beam) to counteract later load stresses

pre•sum•ably \pri-ˈzü-mə-blē\ *adv* : by reasonable assumption

pre•sume \pri-ˈzüm\ *vb* **pre•sumed; pre•sum•ing 1** : to take upon oneself without leave or warrant : DARE **2** : to take for granted : ASSUME **3** : to act or behave with undue boldness — **pre•sum•able** \-ˈzü-mə-bəl\ *adj*

pre•sump•tion \pri-ˈzəmp-shən\ *n* **1** : presumptuous attitude or conduct : AUDACITY **2** : an attitude or belief dictated by probability; *also* : the grounds lending probability to a belief — **pre•sump•tive** \-tiv\ *adj*

pre•sump•tu•ous \pri-ˈzəmp-chə-wəs\ *adj* : overstepping due bounds : taking liberties — **pre•sump•tu•ous•ly** *adv*

pre•sup•pose \ˌprē-sə-ˈpōz\ *vb* **1** : to suppose beforehand **2** : to require beforehand as a necessary condition — **pre•sup•po•si•tion** \(ˌ)prē-ˌsə-pə-ˈzi-shən\ *n*

pre•teen \ˈprē-ˈtēn\ *n* : a boy or girl not yet 13 years old — **preteen** *adj*

pre•tend \pri-ˈtend\ *vb* **1** : PROFESS ⟨doesn't ~ to be scientific⟩ **2** : FEIGN ⟨~ to be angry⟩ **3** : to lay claim ⟨~ to a throne⟩ — **pre•tend•er** *n*

pre•tense *or* **pre•tence** \ˈprē-ˌtens, pri-ˈtens\ *n* **1** : CLAIM; *esp* : one not supported by fact **2** : mere display : SHOW **3** : an attempt to attain a certain condition ⟨made a ~ at discipline⟩ **4** : false show : PRETEXT — **pre•ten•sion** \pri-ˈten-chən\ *n*

pre•ten•tious \pri-ˈten-chəs\ *adj* **1** : making or possessing usu. unjustified claims (as to excellence) ⟨a ~ literary style⟩ **2** : making demands on one's ability or means : AMBITIOUS ⟨too ~ an undertaking⟩ — **pre•ten•tious•ly** *adv* — **pre•ten•tious•ness** *n*

pret•er•it *or* **pret•er•ite** \ˈpre-tə-rət\ *adj* : PAST 3 — **preterit** *n*

pre•ter•nat•u•ral \ˌprē-tər-ˈna-chə-rəl\ *adj* **1** : exceeding what is natural **2** : inexplicable by ordinary means — **pre•ter•nat•u•ral•ly** *adv*

pre•text \ˈprē-ˌtekst\ *n* : a purpose stated or assumed to cloak the real intention or state of affairs

pret•ti•fy \ˈpri-ti-ˌfī\ *vb* **-fied; -fy•ing** : to make pretty — **pret•ti•fi•ca•tion** \ˌpri-ti-fə-ˈkā-shən\ *n*

[1]**pret•ty** \ˈpri-tē\ *adj* **pret•ti•er; -est** [ME *praty, prety,* fr. OE *prættig* tricky, fr. *prætt* trick] **1** : pleasing by delicacy or grace : having conventionally accepted elements of beauty ⟨~ flowers⟩ **2** : MISERABLE, TERRIBLE ⟨a ~ state of affairs⟩ **3** : moderately large ⟨a ~ profit⟩ **syn** comely, fair, beautiful, attractive, lovely — **pret•ti•ly** \-tə-lē\ *adv* — **pret•ti•ness** \-tē-nəs\ *n*

[2]**pretty** *adv* : in some degree : MODERATELY

[3]**pretty** *vb* **pret•tied; pret•ty•ing** : to make pretty

pret•zel \ˈpret-səl\ *n* [G *Brezel,* ultim. fr. L *brachiatus* having branches like arms, fr. *brachium* arm] : a brittle or chewy glazed usu. salted slender bread often shaped like a loose knot

prev *abbr* previous; previously

pre•vail \pri-ˈvāl\ *vb* **1** : to win mastery : TRIUMPH **2** : to become or become effective : SUCCEED **3** : to urge successfully ⟨~*ed* upon her to sing⟩ **4** : to be frequent : PREDOMINATE — **pre•vail•ing•ly** *adv*

prev•a•lent \ˈpre-və-lənt\ *adj* : generally or widely existent : WIDESPREAD — **prev•a•lence** \-ləns\ *n*

pre•var•i•cate \pri-ˈvar-ə-ˌkāt\ *vb* **-cat•ed; -cat•ing** : to deviate from the truth : EQUIVOCATE — **pre•var•i•ca•tion** \-ˌvar-ə-ˈkā-shən\ *n* — **pre•var•i•ca•tor** \-ˈvar-ə-ˌkā-tər\ *n*

pre•vent \pri-ˈvent\ *vb* **1** : to keep from happening or existing ⟨steps to ~ war⟩ **2** : to hold back : HINDER, STOP ⟨~ us from going⟩ — **pre•vent•able** *also* **pre•vent•ible** \-ˈven-tə-bəl\ *adj* — **pre•ven•tion** \-ˈven-chən\ *n* — **pre•ven•tive** \-ˈven-tiv\ *adj or n* — **pre•ven•ta•tive** \-ˈven-tə-tiv\ *adj or n*

pre•ver•bal \ˌprē-ˈvər-bəl\ *adj* : having not yet acquired the faculty of speech

[1]**pre•view** \ˈprē-ˌvyü\ *vb* : to see or discuss beforehand; *esp* : to view or show in advance of public presentation

[2]**preview** *n* **1** : an advance showing or viewing **2** *also* **pre•vue** \-ˌvyü\ : a showing of snatches from a motion picture advertised for future appearance **3** : FORETASTE

pre•vi•ous \ˈprē-vē-əs\ *adj* : going before : EARLIER, FORMER **syn** foregoing, prior, preceding, antecedent — **pre•vi•ous•ly** *adv*

pre•vi•sion \prē-ˈvi-zhən\ *n* **1** : FORESIGHT, PRESCIENCE **2** : FORECAST, PREDICTION

pre•war \ˈprē-ˈwȯr\ *adj* : occurring or existing before a war

[1]**prey** \ˈprā\ *n, pl* **prey** *also* **preys** **1** : an animal taken for food by a predator; *also* : VICTIM **2** : the act or habit of preying

[2]**prey** *vb* **1** : to raid for booty **2** : to seize and devour prey **3** : to have a harmful or wearing effect

prf *abbr* proof

[1]**price** \ˈprīs\ *n* **1** *archaic* : VALUE **2** : the amount of money paid or asked for the sale of a specified thing; *also* : the cost at which something is obtained

[2]**price** *vb* **priced; pric•ing** **1** : to set a price on **2** : to ask the price of **3** : to drive by raising prices ⟨*priced* themselves out of the market⟩

price–fix•ing \ˈprīs-ˌfik-siŋ\ *n* : the setting of prices artificially (as by producers or government)

price•less \-ləs\ *adj* : having a value beyond any price : INVALUABLE **syn** precious, costly, expensive

price support *n* : artificial maintenance of prices of a commodity at a level usu. fixed through government action

price war *n* : a period of commercial competition in which prices are repeatedly cut by the competitors

pric•ey *also* **pricy** \ˈprī-sē\ *adj* **pric•i•er; -est** : EXPENSIVE

[1]**prick** \ˈprik\ *n* **1** : a mark or small wound made by a pointed instrument **2** : something sharp or pointed **3** : an instance of pricking; *also* : a sensation of being pricked

[2]**prick** *vb* **1** : to pierce slightly with a sharp point; *also* : to have or cause a pricking sensation **2** : to affect with anguish or remorse ⟨~*s* his conscience⟩ **3** : to outline with punctures ⟨~ out a pattern⟩ **4** : to stand or cause to stand erect ⟨the dog's ears ~*ed* up at the sound⟩ **syn** punch, puncture, perforate, bore, drill

prick•er \ˈpri-kər\ *n* : BRIAR; *also* : THORN

[1]**prick•le** \ˈpri-kəl\ *n* **1** : a small sharp process (as on a plant) **2** : a slight stinging pain — **prick•ly** \ˈpri-klē\ *adj*

[2]**prickle** *vb* **prick•led; prick•ling** **1** : to prick lightly **2** : TINGLE

prickly heat *n* : a red cutaneous eruption with intense itching and tingling caused by inflammation around the ducts of the sweat glands

prickly pear *n* : any of numerous cacti with usu. yellow flowers and prickly flat or rounded joints; *also* : the sweet pulpy pear-shaped edible fruit of various prickly pears

[1]**pride** \ˈprīd\ *n* **1** : CONCEIT **2** : justifiable self-respect **3** : elation over an act or possession **4** : haughty behavior : DISDAIN **5** : ostentatious display — **pride•ful** *adj*

[2]**pride** *vb* **prid•ed; prid•ing** : to indulge (as oneself) in pride

priest \ˈprēst\ *n* [ME *preist,* fr. OE *prēost,* ultim. fr. LL *presbyter* elder, priest, fr. Gk *presbyteros,* fr. compar. of *presbys* old man, elder] : a person having authority to perform the sacred rites of a religion; *esp* : a member of the Anglican, Eastern, or Roman Catholic clergy ranking below a bishop and above a deacon — **priest•hood** *n* — **priest•li•ness** *n* — **priest•ly** *adj*

priest•ess \ˈprēs-təs\ *n* : a woman authorized to perform the sacred rites of a religion

prig \ˈprig\ *n* : one who irritates by rigid or pointed observance of proprieties — **prig•gish** \ˈpri-gish\ *adj* — **prig•gish•ly** *adv*

[1]**prim** \ˈprim\ *adj* **prim•mer; prim•mest** : stiffly formal and precise — **prim•ly** *adv* — **prim•ness** *n*

[2]**prim** *abbr* **1** primary **2** primitive

pri•ma•cy \ˈprī-mə-sē\ *n* **1** : the state of being first (as in rank) **2** : the office, rank, or character of an ecclesiastical primate

pri•ma don•na \ˌpri-mə-ˈdä-nə\ *n, pl* **prima donnas** [It, lit., first lady] **1** : a principal female singer (as in an opera company) **2** : an extremely sensitive, vain, or undisciplined person

pri•ma fa•cie \ˈprī-mə-ˈfā-shə, -sē, -shē\ *adj or adv* [L, at first view] **1** : based on immediate impression : APPARENT **2** : SELF-EVIDENT

pri•mal \ˈprī-məl\ *adj* **1** : ORIGINAL, PRIMITIVE **2** : first in importance

pri•mar•i•ly \prī-ˈmer-ə-lē\ *adv* **1** : FUNDAMENTALLY **2** : ORIGINALLY

[1]**pri•ma•ry** \ˈprī-ˌmer-ē, -mə-rē\ *adj* **1** : first in order of time or development; *also* : PREPARATORY **2** : of first rank or importance; *also* : FUNDAMENTAL **3** : not derived from or dependent on something else ⟨~ sources⟩

[2]**primary** *n, pl* **-ries** : a preliminary election in which voters nominate or express a preference among candidates usu. of their own party

primary color *n* : any of a set of colors from which all other colors may be derived

primary school *n* **1** : a school usu. including grades 1-3 and sometimes kindergarten **2** : ELEMENTARY SCHOOL

pri•mate \ˈprī-ˌmāt *or esp for 1* -mət\ *n* **1** *often cap* : the highest-ranking bishop of a province or nation **2** : any of an order of mammals including humans, apes, and monkeys

[1]**prime** \ˈprīm\ *n* **1** : the earliest stage of something; *esp* : SPRINGTIME **2** : the most active, thriving, or successful stage or period (as of one's life) **3** : the best individual; *also* : the best part of something **4** : any integer other than 0, +1, or −1 that is not divisible without remainder by any integer except +1, −1, and plus or minus itself; *esp* : any such integer that is positive

²prime *adj* **1 :** standing first (as in time, rank, significance, or quality) ⟨~ requisite⟩ **2 :** of, relating to, or being a number that is prime

³prime *vb* **primed; prim•ing 1 :** FILL, LOAD **2 :** to lay a preparatory coating upon (as in painting) **3 :** to put in working condition **4 :** to instruct beforehand **:** COACH

prime meridian *n* **:** the meridian of 0° longitude which runs through Greenwich, England, and from which other longitudes are reckoned east and west

prime minister *n* **1 :** the chief minister of a ruler or state **2 :** the chief executive of a parliamentary government

¹prim•er \ˈpri-mər\ *n* **1 :** a small book for teaching children to read **2 :** a small introductory book on a subject

²prim•er \ˈprī-mər\ *n* **1 :** one that primes **2 :** a device for igniting an explosive **3 :** material for priming a surface

prime rate *n* **:** an interest rate announced by a bank to be the lowest available to its most credit-worthy customers

prime time *n* **1 :** the time period when the television or radio audience is largest; *also* **:** prime-time television **2 :** the choicest or busiest time

pri•me•val \prī-ˈmē-vəl\ *adj* **:** of or relating to the earliest ages **:** PRIMITIVE

¹prim•i•tive \ˈpri-mə-tiv\ *adj* **1 :** ORIGINAL, PRIMARY **2 :** of, relating to, or characteristic of an early stage of development **3 :** ELEMENTAL, NATURAL **4 :** of, relating to, or produced by a tribal people or culture **5 :** SELF-TAUGHT; *also* **:** produced by a self-taught artist — **prim•i•tive•ly** *adv* — **prim•i•tive•ness** *n* — **prim•i•tiv•i•ty** \ˌpri-mə-ˈti-və-tē\ *n*

²primitive *n* **1 :** something primitive **2 :** a primitive artist **3 :** a member of a primitive people

prim•i•tiv•ism \ˈpri-mə-ti-ˌvi-zəm\ *n* **1 :** belief in the superiority of a simple way of life close to nature **2 :** the style of art of primitive peoples or primitive artists

pri•mo•gen•i•tor \ˌprī-mō-ˈje-nə-tər\ *n* **:** ANCESTOR, FOREFATHER

pri•mo•gen•i•ture \-ˈje-nə-ˌchu̇r\ *n* **1 :** the state of being the firstborn of a family **2 :** an exclusive right of inheritance belonging to the eldest son

pri•mor•di•al \prī-ˈmȯr-dē-əl\ *adj* **:** first created or developed **:** existing in its original state **:** PRIMEVAL

primp \ˈprimp\ *vb* **:** to dress in a careful or finicky manner

prim•rose \ˈprim-ˌrōz\ *n* **:** any of a genus of perennial herbs with large leaves arranged at the base of the stem and clusters of showy flowers on leafless stalks

prin *abbr* **1** principal **2** principle

prince \ˈprins\ *n* [ME, fr. OF, fr. L *princeps* leader, initiator, fr. *primus* first + *capere* to take] **1 :** MONARCH, KING **2 :** a male member of a royal family; *esp* **:** a son of the monarch **3 :** a person of high standing (as in a class) — **prince•dom** \-dəm\ *n* — **prince•ly** *adj*

prince•ling \-liŋ\ *n* **:** a petty prince

prin•cess \ˈprin-səs, -ˌses\ *n* **1 :** a female member of a royal family **2 :** the consort of a prince

¹prin•ci•pal \ˈprin-sə-pəl\ *adj* **:** most important — **prin•ci•pal•ly** *adv*

²principal *n* **1 :** a leading person (as in a play) **2 :** the chief officer of an educational institution **3 :** the person from whom an agent's authority derives **4 :** a capital sum placed at interest or used as a fund

prin•ci•pal•i•ty \ˌprin-sə-ˈpa-lə-tē\ *n, pl* **-ties :** the position, territory, or jurisdiction of a prince

principal parts *n pl* **:** the inflected forms of a verb

prin•ci•ple \ˈprin-sə-pəl\ *n* **1 :** a general or fundamental law, doctrine, or assumption **2 :** a rule or code of conduct; *also* **:** devotion to such a code **3 :** the laws or facts of nature underlying the working of an artificial device **4 :** a primary source **:** ORIGIN; *also* **:** an underlying faculty or endowment **5 :** the active part (as of a drug)

prin•ci•pled \-pəld\ *adj* **:** exhibiting, based on, or characterized by principle ⟨high-*principled*⟩

prink \ˈpriŋk\ *vb* **:** PRIMP

¹print \ˈprint\ *n* **1 :** a mark made by pressure **2 :** something stamped with an impression **3 :** printed state or form **4 :** printed matter **5 :** a copy made by printing **6 :** cloth with a pattern applied by printing

²print *vb* **1 :** to stamp (as a mark) in or on something **2 :** to produce impressions of (as from type) **3 :** to write in letters like those of printer's type **4 :** to make (a positive picture) from a photographic negative

print•able \ˈprin-tə-bəl\ *adj* **1 :** capable of being printed or of being printed from **2 :** worthy or fit to be published

print•er \ˈprin-tər\ *n* **:** one that prints; *esp* **:** a device that produces printout

print•ing *n* **1 :** reproduction in printed form **2 :** the art, practice, or business of a printer **3 :** IMPRESSION 5

printing press *n* **:** a machine that produces printed copies

print•out \ˈprint-ˌau̇t\ *n* **:** a printed output produced by a computer — **print out** *vb*

¹pri•or \ˈprī-ər\ *n* **:** the superior ranking next to the abbot or abbess of a religious house

²prior *adj* **1 :** earlier in time or order **2 :** taking precedence logically or in importance — **pri•or•i•ty** \prī-ˈȯr-ə-tē\ *n*

pri•or•ess \ˈprī-ə-rəs\ *n* **:** a nun corresponding in rank to a prior

pri•or•i•tize \prī-ˈȯr-ə-ˌtīz, ˈprī-ə-rə-ˌtīz\ *vb* **-tized; -tiz•ing :** to list or rate in order of priority

prior to *prep* **:** in advance of **:** BEFORE

pri•o•ry \ˈprī-ə-rē\ *n, pl* **-ries :** a religious house under a prior or prioress

prise *chiefly Brit var of* ⁵PRIZE

prism \ˈpri-zəm\ *n* [LL *prisma,* fr. Gk, lit., anything sawed, fr. *priein* to saw] **1 :** a solid whose sides are parallelograms and whose ends are parallel and alike in shape and size **2 :** a usu. 3-sided transparent object that refracts light so that it breaks up into rainbow colors — **pris•mat•ic** \priz-ˈma-tik\ *adj*

pris•on \ˈpriz-ᵊn\ *n* **:** a place or state of confinement esp. for criminals

pris•on•er \ˈpriz-ᵊn-ər\ *n* **:** a person deprived of his liberty; *esp* **:** one on trial or in prison

prisoner of war : a person captured in war

pris•sy \ˈpri-sē\ *adj* **pris•si•er; -est :** being overly prim and precise **:** PRIGGISH — **pris•si•ness** \-sē-nəs\ *n*

pris•tine \ˈpris-ˌtēn, pri-ˈstēn\ *adj* **1 :** PRIMITIVE **2 :** having the purity of its original state **:** UNSPOILED

prith•ee \ˈpri-t͟hē\ *interj, archaic* — used to express a wish or request

pri•va•cy \ˈprī-və-sē\ *n, pl* **-cies 1 :** the quality or state of being apart from others **2 :** SECRECY

¹pri•vate \ˈprī-vət\ *adj* **1 :** belonging to or intended for a particular individual or group ⟨~ property⟩ **2 :** restricted to the individual **:** PERSONAL ⟨~ opinion⟩ **3 :** carried on by the individual independently ⟨~ study⟩ **4 :** not holding public office ⟨a ~ citizen⟩ **5 :** withdrawn from company or observation ⟨a ~ place⟩ **6 :** not known publicly — **pri•vate•ly** *adv*

²private *n* **:** an enlisted man of the lowest rank in the marine corps or of one of the two lowest ranks in the army — **in private :** not openly or in public

pri•va•teer \ˌprī-və-ˈtir\ *n* **:** an armed private ship licensed to attack enemy shipping; *also* **:** a sailor on such a ship

private first class *n* **:** an enlisted man ranking next below a corporal in the army and next below a lance corporal in the marine corps

pri•va•tion \prī-ˈvā-shən\ *n* **1 :** DEPRIVATION 1 **2 :** the state of being deprived; *esp* **:** lack of what is needed for existence

priv•et \ˈpri-vət\ *n* **:** a nearly evergreen shrub related to the olive and widely used for hedges

¹priv•i•lege \ˈpriv-lij, ˈpri-və-\ *n* [ME, fr. OF, fr. L *priv-*

ilegium law for or against a private person, fr. *privus* private + *leg-, lex* law] : a right or immunity granted as an advantage or favor esp. to some and not others
²**privilege** *vb* **-leged; -leg•ing** : to grant a privilege to
priv•i•leged *adj* **1** : having or enjoying one or more privileges ⟨~ classes⟩ **2** : not subject to disclosure in a court of law ⟨a ~ communication⟩
¹**privy** \ˈpri-vē\ *adj* **1** : PERSONAL, PRIVATE **2** : SECRET **3** : admitted as one sharing in a secret ⟨~ to the conspiracy⟩ — **priv•i•ly** \ˈpri-və-lē\ *adv*
²**privy** *n, pl* **priv•ies** : TOILET; *esp* : OUTHOUSE
¹**prize** \ˈprīz\ *n* **1** : something offered or striven for in competition or in contests of chance **2** : something exceptionally desirable
²**prize** *adj* **1** : awarded or worthy of a prize ⟨a ~ essay⟩; *also* : awarded as a prize ⟨a ~ medal⟩ **2** : OUTSTANDING
³**prize** *vb* **prized; priz•ing** : to value highly : ESTEEM
⁴**prize** *n* : property (as a ship) lawfully captured in time of war
⁵**prize** *vb* **prized; priz•ing** : PRY
prize•fight \ˈprīz-ˌfīt\ *n* : a professional boxing match — **prize•fight•er** *n* — **prize•fight•ing** *n*
prize•win•ner \-ˌwi-nər\ *n* : a winner of a prize — **prize•win•ning** *adj*
¹**pro** \ˈprō\ *n, pl* **pros** : a favorable argument, person, or position
²**pro** *adv* : in favor : FOR
³**pro** *n or adj* : PROFESSIONAL
PRO *abbr* public relations officer
prob *abbr* **1** probable; probably **2** problem
prob•a•bil•i•ty \ˌprä-bə-ˈbi-lə-tē\ *n, pl* **-ties 1** : the quality or state of being probable **2** : something probable **3** : a measure of how often a particular event will occur if something (as tossing a coin) is done repeatedly which results in any of a number of possible events
prob•a•ble \ˈprä-bə-bəl\ *adj* **1** : apparently or presumably true ⟨a ~ hypothesis⟩ **2** : likely to be or become true or real ⟨a ~ result⟩ — **prob•a•bly** \-bə-blē\ *adv*
¹**pro•bate** \ˈprō-ˌbāt\ *n* : the judicial determination of the validity of a will
²**pro•bate** *vb* **pro•bat•ed; pro•bat•ing** : to establish (a will) by probate as genuine and valid
pro•ba•tion \prō-ˈbā-shən\ *n* **1** : subjection of an individual to a period of testing and trial to ascertain fitness (as for a job) **2** : the action of giving a convicted offender freedom during good behavior under the supervision of a probation officer — **pro•ba•tion•ary** \-shə-ˌner-ē\ *adj*
pro•ba•tion•er \-shə-nər\ *n* **1** : a person (as a newly admitted student nurse) whose fitness is being tested during a trial period **2** : a convicted offender on probation
pro•ba•tive \ˈprō-bə-tiv\ *adj* **1** : serving to test or try **2** : serving to prove
¹**probe** \ˈprōb\ *n* **1** : a slender instrument for examining a cavity (as a wound) **2** : an information-gathering device sent into outer space **3** : a penetrating investigation **syn** inquiry, inquest, research, inquisition
²**probe** *vb* **probed; prob•ing 1** : to examine with a probe **2** : to investigate thoroughly
pro•bi•ty \ˈprō-bə-tē\ *n* : UPRIGHTNESS, HONESTY
prob•lem \ˈprä-bləm\ *n* **1** : a question raised for consideration or solution **2** : an intricate unsettled question **3** : a source of perplexity or vexation — **problem** *adj*
prob•lem•at•ic \ˌprä-blə-ˈma-tik\ *or* **prob•lem•at•i•cal** \-ti-kəl\ *adj* **1** : difficult to solve or decide : PUZZLING **2** : DUBIOUS, QUESTIONABLE
pro•bos•cis \prə-ˈbä-səs, -ˈbäs-kəs\ *n, pl* **-bos•cis•es** *also* **-bos•ci•des** \-ˈbä-sə-ˌdēz\ [L, fr. Gk *proboskis,* fr. *pro-* before + *boskein* to feed] : a long flexible snout (as the trunk of an elephant)
proc *abbr* proceedings
pro•caine \ˈprō-ˌkān\ *n* : a drug used esp. as a local anesthetic
pro•ce•dure \prə-ˈsē-jər\ *n* **1** : a particular way of doing something ⟨democratic ~⟩ **2** : a series of steps followed in a regular order ⟨surgical ~⟩ — **pro•ce•dur•al** \-ˈsē-jə-rəl\ *adj*
pro•ceed \prō-ˈsēd\ *vb* **1** : to come forth : ISSUE **2** : to go on in an orderly way; *also* : CONTINUE **3** : to begin and carry on an action **4** : to take legal action **5** : to go forward : ADVANCE
pro•ceed•ing *n* **1** : PROCEDURE **2** *pl* : DOINGS **3** *pl* : legal action **4** : TRANSACTION **5** *pl* : an official record of things said or done
pro•ceeds \ˈprō-ˌsēdz\ *n pl* : the total amount or the profit arising from a business deal : RETURN
¹**pro•cess** \ˈprä-ˌses, ˈprō-\ *n, pl* **pro•cess•es** \-ˌse-səz, -sə-səz, -sə-ˌsēz\ **1** : PROGRESS, ADVANCE **2** : something going on : PROCEEDING **3** : a natural phenomenon marked by gradual changes that lead toward a particular result ⟨the ~ of growth⟩ **4** : a series of actions or operations directed toward a particular result ⟨a manufacturing ~⟩ **5** : legal action **6** : a mandate issued by a court; *esp* : SUMMONS **7** : a projecting part of an organism or organic structure
²**process** *vb* : to subject to a special process
pro•ces•sion \prə-ˈse-shən\ *n* : a group of individuals moving along in an orderly often ceremonial way
pro•ces•sion•al \-ˈse-shə-nəl\ *n* **1** : music for a procession **2** : a ceremonial procession
pro•ces•sor \ˈprä-ˌse-sər, ˈprō-\ *n* **1** : one that processes **2** : the part of a computer that operates on data
pro–choice \(ˌ)prō-ˈchȯis\ *adj* : favoring the legalization of abortion
pro•claim \prō-ˈklām\ *vb* : to make known publicly : DECLARE
proc•la•ma•tion \ˌprä-klə-ˈmā-shən\ *n* : an official public announcement
pro•cliv•i•ty \prō-ˈkli-və-tē\ *n, pl* **-ties** : an inherent inclination esp. toward something objectionable
pro•con•sul \-ˈkän-səl\ *n* **1** : a governor or military commander of an ancient Roman province **2** : an administrator in a modern colony or occupied area — **pro•con•su•lar** \-sə-lər\ *adj*
pro•cras•ti•nate \prə-ˈkras-tə-ˌnāt, prō-\ *vb* **-nat•ed; -nat•ing** [L *procrastinare,* fr. *pro-* forward + *crastinus* of tomorrow, fr. *cras* tomorrow] : to put off usu. habitually doing something that should be done **syn** dawdle, delay — **pro•cras•ti•na•tion** \-ˌkras-tə-ˈnā-shən\ *n* — **pro•cras•ti•na•tor** \-ˈkras-tə-ˌnā-tər\ *n*
pro•cre•ate \ˈprō-krē-ˌāt\ *vb* **-at•ed; -at•ing** : to beget or bring forth offspring **syn** reproduce, breed, generate, propagate — **pro•cre•ation** \ˌprō-krē-ˈā-shən\ *n* — **pro•cre•ative** \ˈprō-krē-ˌā-tiv\ *adj* — **pro•cre•ator** \-ˌā-tər\ *n*
pro•crus•te•an \prə-ˈkrəs-tē-ən\ *adj, often cap* [fr. *Procrustes,* villain of Greek mythology who made victims fit his bed by stretching them or cutting off their legs] : marked by arbitrary often ruthless disregard of individual differences or special circumstances
proc•tor \ˈpräk-tər\ *n* : one appointed to supervise students (as at an examination) — **proctor** *vb* — **proc•to•ri•al** \präk-ˈtōr-ē-əl\ *adj*
proc•u•ra•tor \ˈprä-kyə-ˌrā-tər\ *n* : a Roman provincial administrator
pro•cure \prə-ˈkyu̇r\ *vb* **pro•cured; pro•cur•ing 1** : to get possession of : OBTAIN **2** : to make women available for promiscuous sexual intercourse **3** : ACHIEVE **syn** secure, acquire, gain, win, earn — **pro•cur•able** \-ˈkyu̇r-ə-bəl\ *adj* — **pro•cure•ment** *n* — **pro•cur•er** *n*
¹**prod** \ˈpräd\ *vb* **prod•ded; prod•ding 1** : to thrust a pointed instrument into : GOAD **2** : INCITE, STIR — **prod** *n*
²**prod** *abbr* product; production
prod•i•gal \ˈprä-di-gəl\ *adj* **1** : recklessly extravagant; *also* : LUXURIANT **2** : WASTEFUL, LAVISH **syn** profuse, lush, opulent — **prodigal** *n* — **prod•i•gal•i•ty** \ˌprä-də-ˈga-lə-tē\ *n*

pro•di•gious \prə-ˈdi-jəs\ *adj* **1** : exciting wonder **2** : extraordinary in size or degree : ENORMOUS **syn** monstrous, tremendous, stupendous, monumental — **pro•di•gious•ly** *adv*

prod•i•gy \ˈprä-də-jē\ *n, pl* **-gies 1** : something extraordinary : WONDER **2** : a highly talented child

[1]pro•duce \prə-ˈdüs, -ˈdyüs\ *vb* **pro•duced; pro•duc•ing 1** : to present to view : EXHIBIT **2** : to give birth or rise to : YIELD **3** : EXTEND, PROLONG **4** : to give being or form to : BRING ABOUT, MAKE; *esp* : MANUFACTURE **5** : to cause to accrue ⟨~ a profit⟩ — **pro•duc•er** *n*

[2]pro•duce \ˈprä-(ˌ)düs, ˈprō- *also* -(ˌ)dyüs\ *n* : PRODUCT 2; *also* : agricultural products and esp. fresh fruits and vegetables

prod•uct \ˈprä-(ˌ)dəkt\ *n* **1** : the number resulting from multiplication **2** : something produced

pro•duc•tion \prə-ˈdək-shən\ *n* **1** : something produced : PRODUCT **2** : the act or process of producing — **pro•duc•tive** \-ˈdək-tiv\ *adj* — **pro•duc•tive•ness** *n* — **pro•duc•tiv•i•ty** \(ˌ)prō-ˌdək-ˈti-və-tē, ˌprä-(ˌ)dək-\ *n*

pro•em \ˈprō-ˌem\ *n* **1** : preliminary comment : PREFACE **2** : PRELUDE

prof *abbr* **1** professional **2** professor

[1]pro•fane \prō-ˈfān\ *vb* **pro•faned; pro•fan•ing 1** : to treat (something sacred) with irreverence or contempt **2** : to debase by an unworthy use — **prof•a•na•tion** \ˌprä-fə-ˈnā-shən\ *n*

[2]profane *adj* [ME *prophane*, fr. MF, fr. L *profanus*, fr. *pro-* before + *fanum* temple] **1** : not concerned with religion : SECULAR **2** : not holy because unconsecrated, impure, or defiled **3** : serving to debase what is holy : IRREVERENT ⟨~ language⟩ — **pro•fane•ly** *adv* — **pro•fane•ness** *n*

pro•fan•i•ty \prō-ˈfa-nə-tē\ *n, pl* **-ties 1** : the quality or state of being profane **2** : the use of profane language **3** : profane language

pro•fess \prə-ˈfes\ *vb* **1** : to declare or admit openly : AFFIRM **2** : to declare in words only : PRETEND **3** : to confess one's faith in **4** : to practice or claim to be versed in (a calling or occupation) — **pro•fess•ed•ly** \-ˈfe-səd-lē\ *adv*

pro•fes•sion \prə-ˈfe-shən\ *n* **1** : an open declaration or avowal of a belief or opinion **2** : a calling requiring specialized knowledge and often long academic preparation **3** : the whole body of persons engaged in a calling

[1]pro•fes•sion•al \prə-ˈfe-shə-nəl\ *adj* **1** : of, relating to, or characteristic of a profession **2** : engaged in one of the professions **3** : participating for gain in an activity often engaged in by amateurs — **pro•fes•sion•al•ly** *adv*

[2]professional *n* : one that engages in an activity professionally

pro•fes•sion•al•ism \-nə-ˌli-zəm\ *n* **1** : the conduct, aims, or qualities that characterize or mark a profession or a professional person **2** : the following of a profession (as athletics) for gain or livelihood

pro•fes•sion•al•ize \-nə-ˌlīz\ *vb* **-ized; -iz•ing** : to give a professional nature to

pro•fes•sor \prə-ˈfe-sər\ *n* : a teacher at a university or college; *esp* : a faculty member of the highest academic rank — **pro•fes•so•ri•al** \ˌprō-fə-ˈsōr-ē-əl, ˌprä-\ *adj* — **pro•fes•sor•ship** *n*

prof•fer \ˈprä-fər\ *vb* **prof•fered; prof•fer•ing** : to present for acceptance : OFFER — **proffer** *n*

pro•fi•cient \prə-ˈfi-shənt\ *adj* : well advanced in an art, occupation, or branch of knowledge **syn** adept, skillful, expert, masterful, masterly — **pro•fi•cien•cy** \-shən-sē\ *n* — **proficient** *n* — **pro•fi•cient•ly** *adv*

[1]pro•file \ˈprō-ˌfīl\ *n* [It *profilo*, fr. *profilare* to draw in outline, fr. *pro-* forward (fr. L) + *filare* to spin, fr. LL, fr. L *filum* thread] **1** : a representation of something in outline; *esp* : a human head seen in side view **2** : a concise biographical sketch **3** : degree or level of public exposure ⟨keep a low ~⟩

[2]profile *vb* **pro•filed; pro•fil•ing** : to write or draw a profile of

[1]prof•it \ˈprä-fət\ *n* **1** : a valuable return : GAIN **2** : the excess of the selling price of goods over their cost — **prof•it•less** *adj*

[2]profit *vb* **1** : to be of use : BENEFIT **2** : to derive benefit : GAIN — **prof•it•able** \ˈprä-fə-tə-bəl\ *adj* — **prof•it•ably** \-blē\ *adv*

prof•i•teer \ˌprä-fə-ˈtir\ *n* : one who makes what is considered an unreasonable profit — **profiteer** *vb*

prof•li•gate \ˈprä-fli-gət, -flə-ˌgāt\ *adj* **1** : completely given up to dissipation and licentiousness **2** : wildly extravagant — **prof•li•ga•cy** \-gə-sē\ *n* — **profligate** *n* — **prof•li•gate•ly** *adv*

pro for•ma \(ˌ)prō-ˈfȯr-mə\ *adj* : done or existing as a matter of form

pro•found \prə-ˈfau̇nd, prō-\ *adj* **1** : marked by intellectual depth or insight ⟨a ~ thought⟩ **2** : coming from or reaching to a depth ⟨a ~ sigh⟩ **3** : deeply felt : INTENSE ⟨~ sympathy⟩ — **pro•found•ly** *adv* — **pro•fun•di•ty** \-ˈfən-də-tē\ *n*

pro•fuse \prə-ˈfyüs, prō-\ *adj* : pouring forth liberally : ABUNDANT **syn** lavish, prodigal, luxuriant, exuberant — **pro•fuse•ly** *adv* — **pro•fu•sion** \-ˈfyü-zhən\ *n*

prog *abbr* program

pro•gen•i•tor \prō-ˈje-nə-tər\ *n* **1** : a direct ancestor : FOREFATHER **2** : ORIGINATOR, PRECURSOR

prog•e•ny \ˈprä-jə-nē\ *n, pl* **-nies** : OFFSPRING, CHILDREN, DESCENDANTS

pro•ges•ter•one \prō-ˈjes-tə-ˌrōn\ *n* : a female hormone that causes the uterus to undergo changes so as to provide a suitable environment for a fertilized egg

prog•na•thous \ˈpräg-nə-thəs\ *adj* : having the jaws projecting beyond the upper part of the face

prog•no•sis \präg-ˈnō-səs\ *n, pl* **-no•ses** \-ˌsēz\ **1** : the prospect of recovery from disease **2** : FORECAST

[1]prog•nos•tic \präg-ˈnäs-tik\ *n* **1** : PORTENT **2** : PROPHECY

[2]prognostic *adj* : of, relating to, or serving as ground for prognostication or a prognosis

prog•nos•ti•cate \präg-ˈnäs-tə-ˌkāt\ *vb* **-cat•ed; -cat•ing** : to foretell from signs or symptoms — **prog•nos•ti•ca•tion** \-ˌnäs-tə-ˈkā-shən\ *n* — **prog•nos•ti•ca•tor** \-ˈnäs-tə-ˌkā-tər\ *n*

[1]pro•gram \ˈprō-ˌgram, -grəm\ *n* **1** : a brief outline of the order to be pursued or the subjects included (as in a public entertainment); *also* : PERFORMANCE **2** : a plan of procedure **3** : coded instructions for a computer — **pro•gram•mat•ic** \ˌprō-grə-ˈma-tik\ *adj*

[2]program *also* **programme** *vb* **-grammed** *or* **-gramed; -gram•ming** *or* **-gram•ing 1** : to arrange or furnish a program of or for **2** : to enter in a program **3** : to provide (as a computer) with a program — **pro•gram•ma•bil•i•ty** \(ˌ)prō-ˌgra-mə-ˈbi-lə-tē\ *n* — **pro•gram•ma•ble** \ˈprō-ˌgra-mə-bəl\ *adj* — **pro•gram•mer** *also* **pro•gram•er** \ˈprō-ˌgra-mər, -grə-\ *n*

programme *chiefly Brit var of* PROGRAM

programmed instruction *n* : instruction through information given in small steps with each requiring a correct response by the learner before going on to the next step

pro•gram•ming *or* **pro•gram•ing** *n* **1** : the planning, scheduling, or performing of a program **2** : the process of instructing or learning by means of an instruction program **3** : the process of preparing an instruction program

[1]prog•ress \ˈprä-grəs, -ˌgres\ *n* **1** : a forward movement : ADVANCE **2** : a gradual betterment

[2]pro•gress \prə-ˈgres\ *vb* **1** : to move forward : PROCEED **2** : to develop to a more advanced stage : IMPROVE

pro•gres•sion \prə-ˈgre-shən\ *n* **1** : an act of progressing : ADVANCE **2** : a continuous and connected series

[1]pro•gres•sive \prə-ˈgre-siv\ *adj* **1** : of, relating to, or characterized by progress ⟨a ~ city⟩ **2** : moving forward or onward : ADVANCING **3** : increasing in extent or severity ⟨a ~ disease⟩ **4** *often cap* : of or relating to political Progressives **5 :** of, relating to, or constituting a verb form that expresses action in progress at the time of speaking or a time spoken of — **pro·gres·sive·ly** *adv*

[2]**progressive** *n* **1 :** one that is progressive **2 :** a person believing in moderate political change and social improvement by government action; *esp, cap* **:** a member of a Progressive Party in the U.S.

pro·hib·it \prō-ˈhi-bət\ *vb* **1 :** to forbid by authority **2 :** to prevent from doing something

pro·hi·bi·tion \ˌprō-ə-ˈbi-shən\ *n* **1 :** the act of prohibiting **2 :** the forbidding by law of the sale or manufacture of alcoholic beverages — **pro·hi·bi·tion·ist** \-ˈbi-shə-nist\ *n* — **pro·hib·i·tive** \prō-ˈhi-bə-tiv\ *adj* — **pro·hib·i·tive·ly** *adv* — **pro·hib·i·to·ry** \-ˈhi-bə-ˌtōr-ē\ *adj*

[1]**proj·ect** \ˈprä-ˌjekt, -jikt\ *n* **1 :** a specific plan or design **:** SCHEME **2 :** a planned undertaking ⟨a research ~⟩

[2]**pro·ject** \prə-ˈjekt\ *vb* **1 :** to devise in the mind **:** DESIGN **2 :** to throw forward **3 :** PROTRUDE **4 :** to cause (light or shadow) to fall into space or (an image) to fall on a surface ⟨~ a beam of light⟩ **5 :** to attribute (a thought, feeling, or personal characteristic) to a person, group, or object — **pro·jec·tion** \-ˈjek-shən\ *n*

pro·jec·tile \prə-ˈjekt-əl, -ˈjek-tīl\ *n* **1 :** a body hurled or projected by external force; *esp* **:** a missile for a firearm **2 :** a self-propelling weapon

pro·jec·tion·ist \prə-ˈjek-shə-nist\ *n* **:** one that operates a motion-picture projector or television equipment

pro·jec·tor \-ˈjek-tər\ *n* **:** one that projects; *esp* **:** a device for projecting pictures on a screen

pro·le·gom·e·non \ˌprō-li-ˈgä-mə-ˌnän, -nən\ *n, pl* **-e·na** \-nə\ **:** prefatory remarks

pro·le·tar·i·an \ˌprō-lə-ˈter-ē-ən\ *n* **:** a member of the proletariat — **proletarian** *adj*

pro·le·tar·i·at \-ē-ət\ *n* **:** the laboring class; *esp* **:** industrial workers who sell their labor to live

pro–life \(ˌ)prō-ˈlīf\ *n* **:** ANTIABORTION

pro·lif·er·ate \prə-ˈli-fə-ˌrāt\ *vb* **-at·ed; -at·ing :** to grow or increase by rapid production of new units (as cells or offspring) — **pro·lif·er·a·tion** \-ˌli-fə-ˈrā-shən\ *n*

pro·lif·ic \prə-ˈli-fik\ *adj* **1 :** producing young or fruit abundantly **2 :** marked by abundant inventiveness or productivity ⟨a ~ writer⟩ — **pro·lif·i·cal·ly** \-fi-k(ə-)lē\ *adv*

pro·lix \prō-ˈliks, ˈprō-ˌliks\ *adj* **:** VERBOSE **syn** wordy, diffuse, redundant — **pro·lix·i·ty** \prō-ˈlik-sə-tē\ *n*

pro·logue *also* **pro·log** \ˈprō-ˌlȯg, -ˌläg\ *n* **:** PREFACE ⟨~ of a play⟩

pro·long \prə-ˈlȯŋ\ *vb* **1 :** to lengthen in time **:** CONTINUE ⟨~ a meeting⟩ **2 :** to lengthen in extent or range **syn** protract, extend, elongate, stretch — **pro·lon·ga·tion** \ˌprō-ˌlȯŋ-ˈgā-shən\ *n*

prom \ˈpräm\ *n* **:** a formal dance given by a high school or college class

[1]**prom·e·nade** \ˌprä-mə-ˈnād, -ˈnäd\ *vb* **-nad·ed; -nad·ing 1 :** to take a promenade **2 :** to walk about in or on

[2]**promenade** *n* [F, fr. *promener* to take for a walk, fr. L *prominare* to drive forward] **1 :** a place for strolling **2 :** a leisurely walk for pleasure or display **3 :** an opening grand march at a formal ball

pro·me·thi·um \prə-ˈmē-thē-əm\ *n* **:** a metallic chemical element obtained from uranium or neodymium — see ELEMENT table

prom·i·nence \ˈprä-mə-nəns\ *n* **1 :** something prominent **2 :** the quality, state, or fact of being prominent or conspicuous **3 :** a mass of cloudlike gas that arises from the sun's chromosphere

prom·i·nent \-nənt\ *adj* **1 :** jutting out **:** PROJECTING **2 :** readily noticeable **:** CONSPICUOUS **3 :** DISTINGUISHED, EMINENT **syn** remarkable, outstanding, striking, salient — **prom·i·nent·ly** *adv*

pro·mis·cu·ous \prə-ˈmis-kyə-wəs\ *adj* **1 :** consisting of various sorts and kinds **:** MIXED **2 :** not restricted to one class or person **3 :** having a number of sexual partners **syn** miscellaneous, assorted, heterogeneous, motley, varied — **pro·mis·cu·i·ty** \ˌprä-mis-ˈkyü-ə-tē, ˌprō-ˌmis-\ *n* — **pro·mis·cu·ous·ly** *adv* — **pro·mis·cu·ous·ness** *n*

[1]**prom·ise** \ˈprä-məs\ *n* **1 :** a pledge to do or not to do something specified **2 :** ground for expectation of success or improvement **3 :** something promised

[2]**promise** *vb* **prom·ised; prom·is·ing 1 :** to engage to do, bring about, or provide ⟨~ help⟩ **2 :** to suggest beforehand ⟨dark clouds ~ rain⟩ **3 :** to give ground for expectation ⟨it ~*s* to be a good game⟩

prom·is·ing *adj* **:** likely to succeed or yield good results — **prom·is·ing·ly** *adv*

prom·is·so·ry \ˈprä-mə-ˌsōr-ē\ *adj* **:** containing a promise

prom·on·to·ry \ˈprä-mən-ˌtōr-ē\ *n, pl* **-ries :** a point of land jutting into the sea **:** HEADLAND

pro·mote \prə-ˈmōt\ *vb* **pro·mot·ed; pro·mot·ing 1 :** to advance in station, rank, or honor **2 :** to contribute to the growth or prosperity of **:** FURTHER **3 :** LAUNCH — **pro·mo·tion** \-ˈmō-shən\ *n* — **pro·mo·tion·al** \-shə-nəl\ *adj*

pro·mot·er \-ˈmō-tər\ *n* **:** one that promotes; *esp* **:** one that assumes the financial responsibilities of a sports event

[1]**prompt** \ˈprämpt\ *vb* **1 :** INCITE **2 :** to assist (one acting or reciting) by suggesting the next words **3 :** INSPIRE, URGE — **prompt·er** *n*

[2]**prompt** *adj* **1 :** being ready and quick to act; *also* **:** PUNCTUAL **2 :** performed readily or immediately ⟨~ service⟩ — **prompt·ly** *adv* — **prompt·ness** *n*

prompt·book \-ˌbu̇k\ *n* **:** a copy of a play with directions for performance used by a theater prompter

promp·ti·tude \ˈprämp-tə-ˌtüd, -ˌtyüd\ *n* **:** the quality or habit of being prompt **:** PROMPTNESS

pro·mul·gate \ˈprä-məl-ˌgāt; prō-ˈməl-\ *vb* **-gat·ed; -gat·ing :** to make known or put into force by open declaration — **prom·ul·ga·tion** \ˌprä-məl-ˈgā-shən, ˌprō-(ˌ)məl-\ *n*

pron *abbr* **1** pronoun **2** pronounced **3** pronunciation

prone \ˈprōn\ *adj* **1 :** having a tendency or inclination **:** DISPOSED **2 :** lying face downward; *also* **:** lying flat or prostrate **syn** subject, exposed, open, liable, susceptible — **prone·ness** *n*

prong \ˈprȯŋ\ *n* **:** one of the sharp points of a fork **:** TINE; *also* **:** a slender projecting part (as of an antler) — **pronged** \ˈprȯŋd\ *adj*

prong·horn \ˈprȯŋ-ˌhȯrn\ *n, pl* **pronghorn** *also* **pronghorns :** a ruminant mammal of treeless parts of western No. America that resembles an antelope

pronghorn

pro·noun \ˈprō-ˌnau̇n\ *n* **:** a word used as a substitute for a noun

pro·nounce \prə-ˈnau̇ns\ *vb* **pro·nounced; pro·nounc·ing 1 :** to utter officially or as an opinion ⟨~ sentence⟩ **2 :** to employ the organs of speech in order to produce ⟨~ a word⟩; *esp* **:** to say or speak correctly ⟨she can't

~ his name⟩ — **pro•nounce•able** *adj* — **pro•nun•ci•a•tion** \-ˌnən-sē-ˈā-shən\ *n*

pro•nounced *adj* : strongly marked : DECIDED

pro•nounce•ment \prə-ˈnau̇ns-mənt\ *n* : a formal declaration of opinion; *also* : ANNOUNCEMENT

pron•to \ˈprän-ˌtō\ *adv* [Sp, fr. L *promptus* prompt] : QUICKLY

pro•nu•clear \ˈprō-ˈnü-klē-ər, -ˈnyü-\ *adj* : supporting the use of nuclear-powered electric generating stations

pro•nun•ci•a•men•to \prō-ˌnən-sē-ə-ˈmen-tō\ *n, pl* **-tos** *or* **-toes** : PROCLAMATION, MANIFESTO

[1]**proof** \ˈprüf\ *n* **1** : the evidence that compels acceptance by the mind of a truth or fact **2** : a process or operation that establishes validity or truth : TEST **3** : a trial impression (as from type) **4** : a trial print from a photographic negative **5** : alcoholic content (as of a beverage) indicated by a number that is twice the percent by volume of alcohol present ⟨whiskey of 90 ~ is 45% alcohol⟩

[2]**proof** *adj* **1** : successful in resisting or repelling ⟨~ against tampering⟩ ⟨water*proof*⟩ **2** : of standard strength or quality or alcoholic content

proof•read \-ˌrēd\ *vb* : to read and mark corrections in — **proof•read•er** *n*

[1]**prop** \ˈpräp\ *n* : something that props

[2]**prop** *vb* **propped; prop•ping 1** : to support by placing something under or against **2** : SUSTAIN, STRENGTHEN

[3]**prop** *n* : PROPERTY 4

[4]**prop** *n* : PROPELLER

[5]**prop** *abbr* **1** property **2** proposition **3** proprietor

pro•pa•gan•da \ˌprä-pə-ˈgan-də, ˌprō-\ *n* [NL, fr. *Congregatio de propaganda fide* Congregation for propagating the faith, organization established by Pope Gregory XV] : the spreading of ideas or information to further or damage a cause; *also* : ideas or allegations spread for such a purpose — **pro•pa•gan•dist** \-dist\ *n*

pro•pa•gan•dize \-ˌdīz\ *vb* **-dized; -diz•ing** : to subject to or carry on propaganda

prop•a•gate \ˈprä-pə-ˌgāt\ *vb* **-gat•ed; -gat•ing 1** : to reproduce or cause to reproduce biologically : MULTIPLY **2** : to cause to spread — **prop•a•ga•tion** \ˌprä-pə-ˈgā-shən\ *n*

pro•pane \ˈprō-ˌpān\ *n* : a heavy flammable gas found in petroleum and natural gas and used esp. as a fuel

pro•pel \prə-ˈpel\ *vb* **pro•pelled; pro•pel•ling** : to drive forward or onward **syn** push, shove, thrust

pro•pel•lant *also* **pro•pel•lent** \-ˈpe-lənt\ *n* : something (as a fuel) that propels — **propellant** *or* **propellent** *adj*

pro•pel•ler \prə-ˈpe-lər\ *n* : a device consisting of a hub fitted with blades that is used to propel a vehicle (as a motorboat or an airplane)

pro•pen•si•ty \prə-ˈpen-sə-tē\ *n, pl* **-ties** : an often intense natural inclination or preference

[1]**prop•er** \ˈprä-pər\ *adj* **1** : referring to one individual only ⟨~ noun⟩ **2** : belonging characteristically to a species or individual : PECULIAR **3** : very satisfactory : EXCELLENT **4** : strictly limited to a specified thing ⟨the city ~⟩ **5** : CORRECT ⟨the ~ way to proceed⟩ **6** : strictly decorous : GENTEEL **7** : marked by suitability or rightness ⟨~ punishment⟩ **syn** meet, appropriate, fitting, seemly — **prop•er•ly** *adv*

[2]**proper** *n* : the parts of the Mass that vary according to the liturgical calendar

prop•er•tied \ˈprä-pər-tēd\ *adj* : owning property and esp. much property

prop•er•ty \ˈprä-pər-tē\ *n, pl* **-ties 1** : a quality peculiar to an individual or thing **2** : something owned; *esp* : a piece of real estate **3** : OWNERSHIP **4** : an article or object used in a play or motion picture other than painted scenery and actor's costumes

proph•e•cy *also* **proph•e•sy** \ˈprä-fə-sē\ *n, pl* **-cies** *also* **-sies 1** : an inspired utterance of a prophet **2** : PREDICTION

proph•e•sy \-ˌsī\ *vb* **-sied; -sy•ing 1** : to speak or utter by divine inspiration **2** : PREDICT — **proph•e•si•er** *n*

proph•et \ˈprä-fət\ *n* [ME *prophete*, fr. OF, fr. L *propheta*, fr. Gk *prophētēs*, fr. *pro* for + *phanai* to speak] **1** : one who utters divinely inspired revelations **2** : one who foretells future events

proph•et•ess \ˈprä-fə-təs\ *n* : a woman who is a prophet

pro•phet•ic \prə-ˈfe-tik\ *or* **pro•phet•i•cal** \-ti-kəl\ *adj* : of, relating to, or characteristic of a prophet or prophecy — **pro•phet•i•cal•ly** \-ti-k(ə-)lē\ *adv*

Proph•ets \ˈprä-fəts\ *n pl* — see BIBLE table

[1]**pro•phy•lac•tic** \ˌprō-fə-ˈlak-tik, ˌprä-\ *adj* **1** : preventing or guarding from disease **2** : PREVENTIVE

[2]**prophylactic** *n* : something prophylactic; *esp* : a device (as a condom) for preventing venereal infection or conception

pro•phy•lax•is \-ˈlak-səs\ *n, pl* **-lax•es** \-ˈlak-ˌsēz\ : measures designed to preserve health and prevent the spread of disease

pro•pin•qui•ty \prə-ˈpiŋ-kwə-tē\ *n* **1** : KINSHIP **2** : nearness in place or time : PROXIMITY

pro•pi•ti•ate \prō-ˈpi-shē-ˌāt\ *vb* **-at•ed; -at•ing** : to gain or regain the favor of : APPEASE — **pro•pi•ti•a•tion** \-ˌpi-shē-ˈā-shən\ *n* — **pro•pi•tia•to•ry** \-ˈpi-shē-ə-ˌtōr-ē\ *adj*

pro•pi•tious \prə-ˈpi-shəs\ *adj* **1** : favorably disposed ⟨~ deities⟩ **2** : being of good omen ⟨~ circumstances⟩

prop•man \ˈpräp-ˌman\ *n* : one who is in charge of stage properties

pro•po•nent \prə-ˈpō-nənt\ *n* : one who argues in favor of something

[1]**pro•por•tion** \prə-ˈpōr-shən\ *n* **1** : BALANCE, SYMMETRY **2** : SHARE, QUOTA **3** : the relation of one part to another or to the whole with respect to magnitude, quantity, or degree : RATIO **4** : SIZE, DEGREE — **in proportion** : PROPORTIONAL

[2]**proportion** *vb* **-tioned; -tion•ing 1** : to adjust (a part or thing) in size relative to other parts or things **2** : to make the parts of harmonious

pro•por•tion•al \prə-ˈpōr-shə-nəl\ *adj* : corresponding in size, degree, or intensity; *also* : having the same or a constant ratio — **pro•por•tion•al•ly** *adv*

pro•por•tion•ate \prə-ˈpōr-shə-nət\ *adj* : PROPORTIONAL — **pro•por•tion•ate•ly** *adv*

pro•pose \prə-ˈpōz\ *vb* **pro•posed; pro•pos•ing 1** : PLAN, INTEND ⟨~*s* to buy a house⟩ **2** : to make an offer of marriage **3** : to offer for consideration : SUGGEST ⟨~ a policy⟩ — **pro•pos•al** \-ˈpō-zəl\ *n* — **pro•pos•er** *n*

[1]**prop•o•si•tion** \ˌprä-pə-ˈzi-shən\ *n* **1** : something proposed for consideration : PROPOSAL **2** : a request for sexual intercourse **3** : a statement of something to be discussed, proved, or explained **4** : SITUATION, AFFAIR ⟨a tough ~⟩ — **prop•o•si•tion•al** \-ˈzi-shə-nəl\ *adj*

[2]**proposition** *vb* **-tioned; -tion•ing** : to make a proposal to; *esp* : to suggest sexual intercourse to

pro•pound \prə-ˈpau̇nd\ *vb* : to set forth for consideration ⟨~ a doctrine⟩

pro•pri•e•tary \prə-ˈprī-ə-ˌter-ē\ *adj* **1** : of, relating to, or characteristic of a proprietor ⟨~ rights⟩ **2** : made and sold by one with the sole right to do so ⟨~ medicines⟩

pro•pri•e•tor \prə-ˈprī-ə-tər\ *n* : OWNER — **pro•pri•e•tor•ship** *n*

pro•pri•e•tress \-ˈprī-ə-trəs\ *n* : a woman who is a proprietor

pro•pri•e•ty \prə-ˈprī-ə-tē\ *n, pl* **-ties 1** : the standard of what is socially acceptable in conduct or speech **2** *pl* : the customs of polite society

pro•pul•sion \prə-ˈpəl-shən\ *n* **1** : the action or process of propelling **2** : something that propels — **pro•pul•sive** \-siv\ *adj*

pro ra•ta \(ˌ)prō-ˈrā-tə, -ˈrä-\ *adv* : in proportion to the share of each : PROPORTIONATELY

pro•rate \(ˌ)prō-ˈrāt\ *vb* **pro•rat•ed; pro•rat•ing :** to divide, distribute, or assess proportionately

pro•rogue \prə-ˈrōg\ *vb* **pro•rogued; pro•rogu•ing :** to suspend or end a session of (a legislative body) — **pro•ro•ga•tion** \ˌprō-rō-ˈgā-shən\ *n*

pros *pl of* PRO

pro•sa•ic \prō-ˈzā-ik\ *adj* **:** lacking imagination or excitement **:** DULL

pro•sce•ni•um \prō-ˈsē-nē-əm\ *n* **1 :** the part of a stage in front of the curtain **2 :** the wall containing the arch that frames the stage

pro•scribe \prō-ˈskrīb\ *vb* **pro•scribed; pro•scrib•ing 1 :** OUTLAW **2 :** to condemn or forbid as harmful — **pro•scrip•tion** \-ˈskrip-shən\ *n*

prose \ˈprōz\ *n* [ME, fr. MF, fr. L *prosa,* fr. fem. of *prorsus, prosus,* straightforward, being in prose, alter. of *proversus,* pp. of *provertere* to turn forward] **:** the ordinary language people use in speaking or writing

pros•e•cute \ˈprä-si-ˌkyüt\ *vb* **-cut•ed; -cut•ing 1 :** to follow to the end ⟨~ an investigation⟩ **2 :** to seek legal punishment of ⟨~ a forger⟩ — **pros•e•cu•tion** \ˌprä-si-ˈkyü-shən\ *n* — **pros•e•cu•tor** \ˈprä-si-ˌkyü-tər\ *n*

[1]**pros•e•lyte** \ˈprä-sə-ˌlīt\ *n* **:** a new convert to a religion, belief, or party — **pros•e•ly•tism** \-ˌlī-ˌti-zəm\ *n*

[2]**proselyte** *vb* **-lyt•ed; -lyt•ing :** PROSELYTIZE

pros•e•ly•tise *Brit var of* PROSELYTIZE

pros•e•ly•tize \ˈprä-sə-lə-ˌtīz\ *vb* **-tized; -tiz•ing 1 :** to induce someone to convert to one's faith **2 :** to recruit someone to join one's party, institution, or cause

pros•o•dy \ˈprä-sə-dē, -zə-\ *n, pl* **-dies :** the study of versification and esp. of metrical structure

[1]**pros•pect** \ˈprä-ˌspekt\ *n* **1 :** an extensive view; *also* **:** OUTLOOK **2 :** the act of looking forward **3 :** a mental vision of something to come **4 :** something that is awaited or expected **:** POSSIBILITY **5 :** a potential buyer or customer; *also* **:** a likely candidate — **pro•spec•tive** \prə-ˈspek-tiv, ˈprä-ˌspek-\ *adj* — **pro•spec•tive•ly** *adv*

[2]**prospect** \ˈprä-ˌspekt\ *vb* **:** to explore esp. for mineral deposits — **pros•pec•tor** \-ˌspek-tər, prä-ˈspek-\ *n*

pro•spec•tus \prə-ˈspek-təs\ *n* **:** a preliminary statement that describes an enterprise and is distributed to prospective buyers or participants

pros•per \ˈpräs-pər\ *vb* **pros•pered; pros•per•ing :** SUCCEED; *esp* **:** to achieve economic success

pros•per•i•ty \präs-ˈper-ə-tē\ *n* **:** thriving condition **:** SUCCESS; *esp* **:** economic well-being

pros•per•ous \ˈpräs-pə-rəs\ *adj* **1 :** FAVORABLE ⟨~ winds⟩ **2 :** marked by success or economic well-being ⟨a ~ business⟩

pros•tate \ˈpräs-ˌtāt\ *n* **:** PROSTATE GLAND — **pros•tat•ic** \prä-ˈsta-tik\ *adj*

prostate gland *n* **:** a glandular body about the base of the male urethra that produces a secretion which is a major part of the fluid ejaculated during an orgasm

pros•ta•ti•tis \ˌpräs-tə-ˈtī-təs\ *n* **:** inflammation of the prostate gland

pros•the•sis \präs-ˈthē-səs, ˈpräs-thə-\ *n, pl* **-the•ses** \-ˌsēz\ **:** an artificial replacement for a missing body part — **pros•thet•ic** \präs-ˈthe-tik\ *adj*

pros•thet•ics \-ˈthe-tiks\ *n pl* **:** the surgical or dental specialty concerned with the design, construction, and fitting of prostheses

[1]**pros•ti•tute** \ˈpräs-tə-ˌtüt, -ˌtyüt\ *vb* **-tut•ed; -tut•ing 1 :** to offer indiscriminately for sexual activity esp. for money **2 :** to devote to corrupt or unworthy purposes — **pros•ti•tu•tion** \ˌpräs-tə-ˈtü-shən, -ˈtyü-\ *n*

[2]**prostitute** *n* **:** one who engages in sexual activities for money

[1]**pros•trate** \ˈprä-ˌstrāt\ *adj* **1 :** stretched out with face on the ground in adoration or submission **2 :** lying flat **3 :** completely overcome ⟨~ with a cold⟩

[2]**prostrate** *vb* **pros•trat•ed; pros•trat•ing 1 :** to throw or put into a prostrate position **2 :** to reduce to a weak or powerless condition — **pros•tra•tion** \prä-ˈstrā-shən\ *n*

prosy \ˈprō-zē\ *adj* **pros•i•er; -est 1 :** PROSAIC **2 :** TEDIOUS

Prot *abbr* Protestant

prot•ac•tin•i•um \ˌprō-ˌtak-ˈti-nē-əm\ *n* **:** a metallic radioactive chemical element of relatively short life — see ELEMENT table

pro•tag•o•nist \prō-ˈta-gə-nist\ *n* **1 :** the principal character in a drama or story **2 :** a leader or supporter of a cause

pro•te•an \ˈprō-tē-ən\ *adj* **:** able to assume different shapes or roles

pro•tect \prə-ˈtekt\ *vb* **:** to shield from injury **:** GUARD

pro•tec•tion \prə-ˈtek-shən\ *n* **1 :** the act of protecting **:** the state of being protected **2 :** one that protects ⟨wear a helmet as a ~⟩ **3 :** the supervision or support of one that is smaller and weaker **4 :** the freeing of producers from foreign competition in their home market by high duties on foreign competitive goods — **pro•tec•tive** \-ˈtek-tiv\ *adj*

pro•tec•tion•ist \-shə-nist\ *n* **:** an advocate of government economic protection for domestic producers through restrictions on foreign competitors — **pro•tec•tion•ism** \-shə-ˌni-zəm\ *n*

pro•tec•tor \prə-ˈtek-tər\ *n* **1 :** one that protects **:** GUARDIAN **2 :** a device used to prevent injury **:** GUARD **3 :** REGENT 1

pro•tec•tor•ate \-tə-rət\ *n* **1 :** government by a protector **2 :** the relationship of superior authority assumed by one state over a dependent one; *also* **:** the dependent political unit in such a relationship

pro•té•gé \ˈprō-tə-ˌzhā\ *n* [F] **:** one who is protected, trained, or guided by an influential person

pro•tein \ˈprō-ˌtēn\ *n* [F *protéine,* fr. LGk *prōteios* primary, fr. Gk *prōtos* first] **:** any of numerous complex nitrogen-containing substances that consist of chains of amino acids, are present in all living cells, and are an essential part of the human diet

pro tem \prō-ˈtem\ *adv* **:** PRO TEMPORE

pro tem•po•re \prō-ˈtem-pə-rē\ *adv* [L] **:** for the time being

Pro•te•ro•zo•ic \ˌprä-tə-rə-ˈzō-ik, ˌprō-\ *adj* **:** of, relating to, or being the eon of geologic history between the Archean and the Phanerozoic — **Proterozoic** *n*

[1]**pro•test** \ˈprō-ˌtest\ *n* **1 :** the act of protesting; *esp* **:** an organized public demonstration of disapproval **2 :** a complaint or objection against an idea, an act, or a course of action

[2]**pro•test** \prō-ˈtest\ *vb* **1 :** to assert positively **:** make solemn declaration of ⟨~*s* his innocence⟩ **2 :** to object strongly **:** make a protest against ⟨~ a ruling⟩ — **pro•tes•ta•tion** \ˌprä-təs-ˈtā-shən\ *n* — **pro•test•er** *or* **pro•tes•tor** \-tər\ *n*

Prot•es•tant \ˈprä-təs-tənt, *3 also* prə-ˈtes-\ *n* **1 :** a member or adherent of one of the Christian churches deriving from the Reformation **2 :** a Christian not of a Catholic or Orthodox church **3** *not cap* **:** one who makes a protest — **Prot•es•tant•ism** \ˈprä-təs-tən-ˌti-zəm\ *n*

pro•tha•la•mi•on \ˌprō-thə-ˈlā-mē-ən\ *or* **pro•tha•la•mi•um** \-mē-əm\ *n, pl* **-mia** \-mē-ə\ **:** a song in celebration of a marriage

pro•to•col \ˈprō-tə-ˌkȯl\ *n* [MF *prothocole,* fr. ML *protocollum,* fr. LGk *prōtokollon* first sheet of a papyrus roll bearing data of manufacture, fr. Gk *prōtos* first + *kollan* to glue together, fr. *kolla* glue] **1 :** an original draft or record **2 :** a preliminary memorandum of diplomatic negotiation **3 :** a code of diplomatic or military etiquette **4 :** a set of conventions for formatting data in an electronic communications system

pro•ton \ˈprō-ˌtän\ *n* [Gk *prōton,* neut. of *prōtos* first] **:** a positively charged atomic particle present in all atomic nuclei — **pro•ton•ic** \-ˈtä-nik\ *adj*

pro•to•plasm \ˈprō-tə-ˌpla-zəm\ *n* **:** the complex colloidal largely protein substance of living plant and animal cells — **pro•to•plas•mic** \ˌprō-tə-ˈplaz-mik\ *adj*

pro•to•type \ˈprō-tə-ˌtīp\ *n* : an original model : ARCHETYPE

pro•to•zo•an \ˌprō-tə-ˈzō-ən\ *n* : any of a phylum or subkingdom of unicellular lower invertebrate animals that include some pathogenic parasites of humans and domestic animals — **protozoan** *adj*

pro•tract \prō-ˈtrakt\ *vb* : to prolong in time or space **syn** extend, lengthen, elongate, stretch

pro•trac•tor \-ˈtrak-tər\ *n* : an instrument for drawing and measuring angles

pro•trude \prō-ˈtrüd\ *vb* **pro•trud•ed; pro•trud•ing** : to stick out or cause to stick out : jut out — **pro•tru•sion** \-ˈtrü-zhən\ *n*

pro•tu•ber•ance \prō-ˈtü-bə-rəns, -ˈtyü-\ *n* : something that protrudes

pro•tu•ber•ant \-rənt\ *adj* : extending beyond the surrounding surface in a bulge

proud \ˈpraůd\ *adj* **1** : having or showing excessive self-esteem : HAUGHTY **2** : highly pleased : EXULTANT **3** : having proper self-respect ⟨too ~ to beg⟩ **4** : GLORIOUS ⟨a ~ occasion⟩ **5** : SPIRITED ⟨a ~ steed⟩ **syn** arrogant, insolent, overbearing, disdainful — **proud•ly** *adv*

prov *abbr* **1** province; provincial **2** provisional

Prov *abbr* Proverbs

prove \ˈprüv\ *vb* **proved; proved** *or* **prov•en** \ˈprü-vən\; **prov•ing 1** : to test by experiment or by a standard **2** : to establish the truth of by argument or evidence **3** : to show to be correct, valid, or genuine **4** : to turn out esp. after trial or test ⟨the car *proved* to be a good choice⟩ — **prov•able** \ˈprü-və-bəl\ *adj*

prov•e•nance \ˈprä-və-nəns\ *n* : ORIGIN, SOURCE

Pro•ven•çal \ˌprō-ˌvän-ˈsäl, ˌprä-vən-\ *n* **1** : a native or inhabitant of Provence **2** : a Romance language spoken in southern France — **Provençal** *adj*

prov•en•der \ˈprä-vən-dər\ *n* **1** : dry food for domestic animals : FEED **2** : FOOD, VICTUALS

pro•ve•nience \prə-ˈvē-nyəns\ *n* : ORIGIN, SOURCE

prov•erb \ˈprä-ˌvərb\ *n* : a pithy popular saying : ADAGE

pro•ver•bi•al \prə-ˈver-bē-əl\ *adj* **1** : of, relating to, or resembling a proverb **2** : commonly spoken of

Proverbs *n* — see BIBLE table

pro•vide \prə-ˈvīd\ *vb* **pro•vid•ed; pro•vid•ing** [ME, fr. L *providēre*, lit., to see ahead, fr. *pro-* forward + *vidēre* to see] **1** : to take measures beforehand ⟨~ against inflation⟩ **2** : to make a proviso or stipulation **3** : to supply what is needed ⟨~ for a family⟩ **4** : EQUIP **5** : to supply for use : YIELD — **pro•vid•er** *n*

pro•vid•ed *conj* : on condition that : IF

prov•i•dence \ˈprä-və-dəns\ *n* **1** *often cap* : divine guidance or care **2** *cap* : GOD 1 **3** : the quality or state of being provident

prov•i•dent \-dənt\ *adj* **1** : making provision for the future : PRUDENT **2** : FRUGAL — **prov•i•dent•ly** *adv*

prov•i•den•tial \ˌprä-və-ˈden-chəl\ *adj* **1** : of, relating to, or determined by Providence **2** : OPPORTUNE, LUCKY

pro•vid•ing *conj* : PROVIDED

prov•ince \ˈprä-vəns\ *n* **1** : an administrative district or division of a country **2** *pl* : all of a country except the metropolises **3** : proper business or scope : SPHERE

pro•vin•cial \prə-ˈvin-chəl\ *adj* **1** : of or relating to a province **2** : limited in outlook : NARROW ⟨~ ideas⟩ — **pro•vin•cial•ism** \-chə-ˌli-zəm\ *n*

proving ground *n* : a place for scientific experimentation or testing

[1]**pro•vi•sion** \prə-ˈvi-zhən\ *n* **1** : the act or process of providing; *also* : a measure taken beforehand **2** : a stock of needed supplies; *esp* : a stock of food — usu. used in pl. **3** : PROVISO

[2]**provision** *vb* : to supply with provisions

pro•vi•sion•al \-ˈvi-zhə-nəl\ *adj* : provided for a temporary need : CONDITIONAL — **pro•vi•sion•al•ly** *adv*

pro•vi•so \prə-ˈvī-zō\ *n, pl* **-sos** *or* **-soes** [ME, fr. ML *proviso quod* provided that] : an article or clause that introduces a condition : STIPULATION

prov•o•ca•tion \ˌprä-və-ˈkā-shən\ *n* **1** : the act of provoking **2** : something that provokes

pro•voc•a•tive \prə-ˈvä-kə-tiv\ *adj* : serving to provoke or excite

pro•voke \prə-ˈvōk\ *vb* **pro•voked; pro•vok•ing 1** : to incite to anger : INCENSE **2** : to call forth : EVOKE ⟨a remark that *provoked* laughter⟩ **3** : to stir up on purpose ⟨~ an argument⟩ **syn** irritate, exasperate, aggravate, inflame, rile, pique — **pro•vok•er** *n*

pro•vo•lo•ne \ˌprō-və-ˈlō-nē\ *n* : a usu. firm pliant often smoked Italian cheese

pro•vost \ˈprō-ˌvōst, ˈprä-vəst\ *n* : a high official : DIGNITARY; *esp* : a high-ranking university administrative officer

pro•vost mar•shal \ˈprō-ˌvō-ˈmär-shəl\ *n* : an officer who supervises the military police of a command

prow \ˈpraů\ *n* : the bow of a ship

prow•ess \ˈpraů-əs\ *n* **1** : military valor and skill **2** : extraordinary ability

prowl \ˈpraůl\ *vb* : to roam about stealthily — **prowl** *n* — **prowl•er** *n*

prox•i•mal \ˈpräk-sə-məl\ *adj* **1** : next to or nearest the point of attachment or origin; *esp* : located toward the center of the body **2** : of, relating to, or being the mesial and distal surfaces of a tooth — **prox•i•mal•ly** *adv*

prox•i•mate \ˈpräk-sə-mət\ *adj* **1** : DIRECT ⟨the ~ cause⟩ **2** : very near

prox•im•i•ty \präk-ˈsi-mə-tē\ *n* : NEARNESS

prox•i•mo \ˈpräk-sə-ˌmō\ *adj* [L *proximo mense* in the next month] : of or occurring in the next month after the present

proxy \ˈpräk-sē\ *n, pl* **prox•ies** : the authority or power to act for another; *also* : a document giving such authorization — **proxy** *adj*

prude \ˈprüd\ *n* : a person who shows or affects extreme modesty — **prud•ery** \ˈprü-də-rē\ *n* — **prud•ish** *adj* — **prud•ish•ly** *adv*

pru•dent \ˈprüd-ᵊnt\ *adj* **1** : shrewd in the management of practical affairs **2** : CAUTIOUS, DISCREET **3** : PROVIDENT, FRUGAL **syn** judicious, foresighted, sensible, sane — **pru•dence** \-ᵊns\ *n* — **pru•den•tial** \prü-ˈden-chəl\ *adj* — **pru•dent•ly** *adv*

[1]**prune** \ˈprün\ *n* : a dried plum

[2]**prune** *vb* **pruned; prun•ing** : to cut off unwanted parts (as of a tree)

pru•ri•ent \ˈprůr-ē-ənt\ *adj* : LASCIVIOUS; *also* : exciting to lasciviousness — **pru•ri•ence** \-ē-əns\ *n*

[1]**pry** \ˈprī\ *vb* **pried; pry•ing** : to look closely or inquisitively; *esp* : SNOOP

[2]**pry** *vb* **pried; pry•ing 1** : to raise, move, or pull apart with a pry or lever **2** : to detach or open with difficulty

[3]**pry** *n* : a tool for prying

Ps *or* **Psa** *abbr* Psalms

PS *abbr* **1** [L *postscriptum*] postscript **2** public school

PSA *abbr* public service announcement

psalm \ˈsäm, ˈsälm\ *n, often cap* [ME, fr. OE *psealm*, fr. LL *psalmus*, fr. Gk *psalmos*, lit., twanging of a harp, fr. *psallein* to pluck, play a stringed instrument] : a sacred song or poem; *esp* : one of the hymns collected in the Book of Psalms — **psalm•ist** *n*

psalm•o•dy \ˈsä-mə-dē, ˈsäl-\ *n* : the singing of psalms in worship

Psalms *n* — see BIBLE table

Psal•ter \ˈsȯl-tər\ *n* : the Book of Psalms; *also* : a collection of the Psalms arranged for devotional use

pseud *abbr* pseudonym; pseudonymous

pseu•do \ˈsü-dō\ *adj* : SPURIOUS, SHAM

pseu•do•nym \ˈsü-də-ˌnim\ *n* : a fictitious name — **pseu•don•y•mous** \sü-ˈdä-nə-məs\ *adj*

PSG *abbr* platoon sergeant

[1]**psi** \ˈsī, ˈpsī\ *n* : the 23d letter of the Greek alphabet — Ψ or ψ

[2]**psi** *abbr* pounds per square inch

pso•ri•a•sis \sə-ˈrī-ə-səs\ *n* : a chronic skin disease characterized by red patches covered with white scales

PST *abbr* Pacific standard time

[1]**psych** *also* **psyche** \ˈsīk\ *vb* **psyched; psych•ing 1** : OUTWIT, OUTGUESS; *also* : to analyze beforehand **2** : INTIMIDATE; *also* : to prepare oneself psychologically ⟨get *psyched* up for the game⟩

[2]**psych** *abbr* psychology

psy•che \ˈsī-kē\ *n* : SOUL, SELF; *also* : MIND

psy•che•del•ic \ˌsī-kə-ˈde-lik\ *adj* **1** : of, relating to, or causing abnormal psychic effects ⟨~ drugs⟩ **2** : relating to the taking of psychedelic drugs ⟨~ experience⟩ **3** : imitating, suggestive of, or reproducing the effects of psychedelic drugs ⟨~ art⟩ ⟨~ colors⟩ — **psychedelic** *n* — **psy•che•del•i•cal•ly** \-li-k(ə-)lē\ *adv*

psy•chi•a•try \sə-ˈkī-ə-trē, sī-\ *n* : a branch of medicine dealing with mental, emotional, and behavioral disorders — **psy•chi•at•ric** \ˌsī-kē-ˈa-trik\ *adj* — **psy•chi•a•trist** \sə-ˈkī-ə-trist, sī-\ *n*

[1]**psy•chic** \ˈsī-kik\ *also* **psy•chi•cal** \-ki-kəl\ *adj* **1** : of or relating to the psyche **2** : lying outside the sphere of physical science **3** : sensitive to nonphysical or supernatural forces — **psy•chi•cal•ly** \-k(ə-)lē\ *adv*

[2]**psychic** *n* : a person apparently sensitive to nonphysical forces; *also* : MEDIUM 6

psy•cho \ˈsī-kō\ *n, pl* **psychos** : a mentally disturbed person — **psycho** *adj*

psy•cho•ac•tive \ˌsī-kō-ˈak-tiv\ *adj* : affecting the mind or behavior

psy•cho•anal•y•sis \ˌsī-kō-ə-ˈna-lə-səs\ *n* : a method of dealing with psychic disorders by having the patient talk freely about personal experiences and esp. about early childhood and dreams — **psy•cho•an•a•lyst** \-ˈan-ᵊl-ist\ *n* — **psy•cho•an•a•lyt•ic** \-ˌan-ᵊl-ˈi-tik\ *adj* — **psy•cho•an•a•lyze** \-ˈan-ᵊl-ˌīz\ *vb*

psy•cho•dra•ma \ˌsī-kə-ˈdrä-mə, -ˈdra-\ *n* **1** : an extemporized dramatization designed to afford catharsis for one or more of the participants from whose life the plot is taken **2** : a dramatic event or story with psychological overtones

psy•cho•gen•ic \-ˈje-nik\ *adj* : originating in the mind or in mental or emotional conflict

psychol *abbr* psychologist; psychology

psy•chol•o•gy \sī-ˈkä-lə-jē\ *n, pl* **-gies 1** : the science of mind and behavior **2** : the mental and behavioral characteristics of an individual or group — **psy•cho•log•i•cal** \ˌsī-kə-ˈlä-ji-kəl\ *adj* — **psy•cho•log•i•cal•ly** \-ji-k(ə-)lē\ *adv* — **psy•chol•o•gist** \sī-ˈkä-lə-jist\ *n*

psy•cho•path \ˈsī-kō-ˌpath\ *n* : a mentally ill or unstable person; *esp* : one who has not lost contact with reality but who engages in abnormally aggressive and seriously irresponsible behavior with little or no feeling of guilt — **psy•cho•path•ic** \ˌsī-kə-ˈpa-thik\ *adj*

psy•cho•sex•u•al \ˌsī-kō-ˈsek-shə-wəl\ *adj* **1** : of or relating to the mental, emotional, and behavioral aspects of sexual development **2** : of or relating to the physiological psychology of sex

psy•cho•sis \sī-ˈkō-səs\ *n, pl* **-cho•ses** \-ˌsēz\ : a serious mental illness (as schizophrenia) marked by loss of or greatly lessened ability to test whether what one is thinking and feeling about the real world is really true

psy•cho•so•mat•ic \ˌsī-kō-sə-ˈma-tik\ *adj* : of, relating to, involving, or concerned with bodily symptoms caused by mental or emotional disturbance

psy•cho•ther•a•py \ˌsī-kō-ˈther-ə-pē\ *n* : treatment of mental or emotional disorder or of related bodily ills by psychological means — **psy•cho•ther•a•pist** \-pist\ *n*

psy•chot•ic \sī-ˈkä-tik\ *adj* : of or relating to psychosis ⟨~ behavior⟩ — **psychotic** *n*

psy•cho•tro•pic \ˌsī-kə-ˈtrō-pik\ *adj* : acting on the mind ⟨~ drugs⟩

pt *abbr* **1** part **2** payment **3** pint **4** point **5** port

Pt *symbol* platinum

PT *abbr* **1** Pacific time **2** part-time **3** physical therapy **4** physical training

PTA *abbr* Parent-Teacher Association

ptar•mi•gan \ˈtär-mi-gən\ *n, pl* **-gan** *or* **-gans** : any of various grouses of northern regions with completely feathered feet

PT boat \(ˌ)pē-ˈtē-\ *n* [*p*atrol *t*orpedo] : a small fast patrol craft usu. armed with torpedos

pte *abbr, Brit* private

ptg *abbr* printing

PTO *abbr* **1** Parent-Teacher Organization **2** please turn over

pto•maine \ˈtō-ˌmān\ *n* : any of various chemical substances formed by bacteria in decaying matter (as meat) and including a few poisonous ones

PTV *abbr* public television

Pu *symbol* plutonium

[1]**pub** \ˈpəb\ *n, chiefly Brit* **1** : PUBLIC HOUSE 2 **2** : TAVERN

[2]**pub** *abbr* **1** public **2** publication **3** published; publisher; publishing

pu•ber•ty \ˈpyü-bər-tē\ *n* : the condition of being or period of becoming first capable of reproducing sexually — **pu•ber•tal** \-bərt-ᵊl\ *adj*

pu•bes \ˈpyü-bēz\ *n, pl* **pubes 1** : the hair that appears upon the lower middle region of the abdomen at puberty **2** : the pubic region

pu•bes•cence \pyü-ˈbes-ᵊns\ *n* **1** : the quality or state of being pubescent **2** : a pubescent covering or surface

pu•bes•cent \-ᵊnt\ *adj* **1** : arriving at or having reached puberty **2** : covered with fine soft short hairs

pu•bic \ˈpyü-bik\ *adj* : of, relating to, or situated near the pubes or the pubis

pu•bis \ˈpyü-bəs\ *n, pl* **pu•bes** \-bēz\ : the ventral and anterior of the three principal bones composing either half of the pelvis

publ *abbr* **1** publication **2** published; publisher

[1]**pub•lic** \ˈpə-blik\ *adj* **1** : exposed to general view ⟨the story became ~⟩ **2** : of, relating to, or affecting the people as a whole ⟨~ opinion⟩ **3** : CIVIC, GOVERNMENTAL ⟨~ expenditures⟩ **4** : of, relating to, or serving the community ⟨~ officials⟩ **5** : not private : SOCIAL ⟨~ morality⟩ **6** : open to all ⟨~ library⟩ **7** : well known : PROMINENT ⟨~ figures⟩ — **pub•lic•ly** *adv*

[2]**public** *n* **1** : the people as a whole : POPULACE **2** : a group of people having common interests

pub•li•can \ˈpə-bli-kən\ *n* **1** : a Jewish tax collector for the ancient Romans **2** *chiefly Brit* : the licensee of a pub

pub•li•ca•tion \ˌpə-blə-ˈkā-shən\ *n* **1** : the act or process of publishing **2** : a published work

public house *n* **1** : INN **2** *chiefly Brit* : a licensed saloon or bar

pub•li•cise *Brit var of* PUBLICIZE

pub•li•cist \ˈpə-blə-sist\ *n* : one that publicizes; *esp* : PRESS AGENT

pub•lic•i•ty \(ˌ)pə-ˈbli-sə-tē\ *n* **1** : information with news value issued to gain public attention or support **2** : public attention or acclaim

pub•li•cize \ˈpə-blə-ˌsīz\ *vb* **-cized; -ciz•ing** : to bring to public attention : ADVERTISE

public relations *n sing or pl* : the business of fostering public goodwill toward a person, firm, or institution; *also* : the degree of goodwill and understanding achieved

public school *n* **1** : an endowed secondary boarding school in Great Britain offering a classical curriculum and preparation for the universities or public service **2** : a free tax-supported school controlled by a local governmental authority

public–spirited *adj* : motivated by devotion to the general or national welfare

public television *n* : television supported by public funds and private contributions rather than by commercials

public works *n pl* : works (as schools or highways) constructed with public funds for public use

pub•lish \ˈpə-blish\ *vb* **1** : to make generally known : announce publicly **2** : to produce or release literature, information, musical scores or sometimes recordings, or art for sale to the public — **pub•lish•er** *n*

[1]**puck** \ˈpək\ *n* : a mischievous sprite — **puck•ish** *adj* — **puck•ish•ly** *adv*

[2]**puck** *n* : a disk used in ice hockey

[1]**puck•er** \ˈpə-kər\ *vb* **puck•ered; puck•er•ing** : to contract into folds or wrinkles

[2]**pucker** *n* : FOLD, WRINKLE

pud•ding \ˈpu̇-diŋ\ *n* : a soft, spongy, or thick creamy dessert

pud•dle \ˈpəd-ᵊl\ *n* : a very small pool of usu. dirty or muddy water

pu•den•dum \pyu̇-ˈden-dəm\ *n, pl* **-da** \-də\ [NL, fr. L *pudēre* to be ashamed] : the human external genital organs esp. of a woman

pudgy \ˈpə-jē\ *adj* **pudg•i•er; -est** : being short and plump : CHUBBY

pueb•lo \ˈpwe-blō, pü-ˈe-\ *n, pl* **-los** [Sp, village, lit., people, fr. L *populus*] **1** : an American Indian village of Arizona or New Mexico that consists of flat-roofed stone or adobe houses joined in groups sometimes several stories high **2** *cap* : a member of a group of American Indian peoples of the southwestern U.S.

pu•er•ile \ˈpyu̇-ə-rəl\ *adj* : CHILDISH, SILLY — **pu•er•il•i•ty** \ˌpyü-ə-ˈri-lə-tē\ *n*

pu•er•per•al \pyü-ˈər-pə-rəl\ *adj* : of, relating to, or occurring during childbirth or the period immediately following ⟨~ infection⟩ ⟨~ depression⟩

puerperal fever *n* : an abnormal condition that results from infection of the placental site following childbirth or abortion

Puer•to Ri•can \ˌpōr-tə-ˈrē-kən, ˌpwer-\ *n* : a native or inhabitant of Puerto Rico — **Puerto Rican** *adj*

[1]**puff** \ˈpəf\ *vb* **1** : to blow in short gusts **2** : PANT **3** : to emit small whiffs or clouds **4** : BLUSTER, BRAG **5** : INFLATE, SWELL **6** : to make proud or conceited **7** : to praise extravagantly

[2]**puff** *n* **1** : a short discharge (as of air or smoke); *also* : a slight explosive sound accompanying it **2** : a light fluffy pastry **3** : a slight swelling **4** : a fluffy mass; *also* : a small pad for applying cosmetic powder **5** : a laudatory notice or review — **puffy** *adj*

puff•ball \ˈpəf-ˌbȯl\ *n* : any of various globe-shaped and often edible fungi

puf•fin \ˈpə-fən\ *n* : any of several seabirds having a short neck and a deep grooved parti-colored bill

[1]**pug** \ˈpəg\ *n* **1** : any of a breed of small stocky short-haired dogs with a wrinkled face **2** : a close coil of hair

pug

[2]**pug** *n* : [1]BOXER

pu•gi•lism \ˈpyü-jə-ˌli-zəm\ *n* : BOXING — **pu•gi•list** \-list\ *n* — **pu•gi•lis•tic** \ˌpyü-jə-ˈlis-tik\ *adj*

pug•na•cious \ˌpəg-ˈnā-shəs\ *adj* : having a quarrelsome or combative nature **syn** belligerent, bellicose, contentious, truculent — **pug•nac•i•ty** \-ˈna-sə-tē\ *n*

puis•sance \ˈpwi-səns, ˈpyü-ə-\ *n* : POWER, STRENGTH — **puis•sant** \-sənt\ *adj*

puke \ˈpyük\ *vb* **puked; puk•ing** : VOMIT — **puke** *n*

puk•ka \ˈpə-kə\ *adj* [Hindi *pakkā* cooked, ripe, solid, fr. Skt *pakva*] : GENUINE, AUTHENTIC; *also* : FIRST-CLASS, COMPLETE

pul \ˈpül\ *n, pl* **puls** \ˈpülz\ *or* **pul** — see *afghani* at MONEY table

pu•la \ˈpü-lə, ˈpyü-\ *n, pl* **pula** — see MONEY table

pul•chri•tude \ˈpəl-krə-ˌtüd, -ˌtyüd\ *n* : BEAUTY — **pul•chri•tu•di•nous** \ˌpəl-krə-ˈtüd-ᵊn-əs, -ˈtyüd-\ *adj*

pule \ˈpyül\ *vb* **puled; pul•ing** : WHINE, WHIMPER

[1]**pull** \ˈpu̇l\ *vb* **1** : to exert force so as to draw (something) toward the force; *also* : MOVE ⟨~ out of a driveway⟩ **2** : PLUCK; *also* : EXTRACT ⟨~ a tooth⟩ **3** : STRETCH, STRAIN ⟨~ a tendon⟩ **4** : to draw apart : TEAR **5** : to make (as a proof) by printing **6** : REMOVE **7** : DRAW ⟨~ a gun⟩ **8** : to carry out esp. with daring ⟨~ a robbery⟩ **9** : PERPETRATE, COMMIT **10** : ATTRACT **11** : to express strong sympathy — **pull•er** *n*

[2]**pull** *n* **1** : the act or an instance of pulling **2** : the effort expended in moving **3** : ADVANTAGE; *esp* : special influence **4** : a device for pulling something or for operating by pulling **5** : a force that attracts or compels **6** : an injury from abnormal straining or stretching ⟨a muscle ~⟩

pull•back \ˈpu̇l-ˌbak\ *n* : an orderly withdrawal of troops

pul•let \ˈpu̇-lət\ *n* : a young hen esp. of the domestic chicken when less than a year old

pul•ley \ˈpu̇-lē\ *n, pl* **pulleys** : a wheel used to transmit power by means of a belt, rope, or chain; *esp* : one with a grooved rim that forms part of a tackle for hoisting or for changing the direction of a force

Pull•man \ˈpu̇l-mən\ *n* : a railroad passenger car with comfortable furnishings esp. for night travel

pull off *vb* : to accomplish successfully

pull•out \ˈpu̇l-ˌau̇t\ *n* : PULLBACK

pull•over \ˈpu̇l-ˌō-vər\ *adj* : put on by being pulled over the head ⟨~ sweater⟩ — **pull•over** *n*

pull–up \ˈpu̇l-ˌəp\ *n* : CHIN-UP

pull up *vb* : to bring or come to an often abrupt halt : STOP

pul•mo•nary \ˈpu̇l-mə-ˌner-ē, ˈpəl-\ *adj* : of, relating to, or carried on by the lungs ⟨the ~ circulation⟩

pulp \ˈpəlp\ *n* **1** : the soft juicy or fleshy part of a fruit or vegetable **2** : a soft moist mass **3** : the soft sensitive tissue that fills the central cavity of a tooth **4** : a material (as from wood) used in making paper **5** : a magazine using cheap paper and often dealing with sensational material — **pulpy** *adj*

pul•pit \ˈpu̇l-ˌpit\ *n* : a raised platform or high reading desk used in preaching or conducting a worship service

pulp•wood \ˈpəlp-ˌwu̇d\ *n* : wood used in making pulp for paper

pul•sar \ˈpəl-ˌsär\ *n* : a celestial source of pulsating electromagnetic radiation (as radio waves)

pul•sate \ˈpəl-ˌsāt\ *vb* **pul•sat•ed; pul•sat•ing** : to expand and contract rhythmically : BEAT — **pul•sa•tion** \ˌpəl-ˈsā-shən\ *n*

pulse \ˈpəls\ *n* **1** : the regular throbbing in the arteries caused by the contractions of the heart **2** : rhythmical beating, vibrating, or sounding **3** : a brief change in electrical current or voltage — **pulse** *vb*

pul•ver•ise *Brit var of* PULVERIZE

pul•ver•ize \ˈpəl-və-ˌrīz\ *vb* **-ized; -iz•ing 1** : to reduce (as by crushing or grinding) or be reduced to very small particles **2** : DEMOLISH

pu•ma \ˈpü-mə, ˈpyü-\ *n, pl* **pumas** *also* **puma** : COUGAR

pum•ice \ˈpə-məs\ *n* : a light porous volcanic glass used esp. for smoothing and polishing

pum•mel \ˈpə-məl\ *vb* **-meled** *also* **-melled; -mel•ing** *also* **-mel•ling** : POUND, BEAT

[1]**pump** \ˈpəmp\ *n* : a device for raising, transferring, or compressing fluids esp. by suction or pressure

[2]**pump** *vb* **1** : to raise (as water) with a pump **2** : to draw fluid from with a pump; *also* : to fill by means of a pump ⟨~ up a tire⟩ **3** : to force or propel in the manner of a pump — **pump•er** *n*

[3]**pump** *n* : a low shoe that grips the foot chiefly at the toe and heel

pum•per•nick•el \ˈpəm-pər-ˌni-kəl\ *n* : a dark rye bread

pump•kin \ˈpəmp-kən, ˈpəŋ-kən\ *n* : the large usu. orange fruit of a vine of the gourd family that is widely used as food; *also* : this vine

pun \ˈpən\ *n* : the humorous use of a word in a way that suggests two or more interpretations — **pun** *vb*

[1]**punch** \ˈpənch\ *vb* **1** : PROD, POKE; *also* : DRIVE, HERD ⟨~*ing* cattle⟩ **2** : to strike with the fist **3** : to emboss, perforate, or make with a punch **4** : to operate, produce, or enter (as data) by or as if by punching — **punch•er** *n*

[2]**punch** *n* **1** : a quick blow with or as if with the fist **2** : effective energy or forcefulness

[3]**punch** *n* : a tool for piercing, stamping, cutting, or forming

[4]**punch** *n* [perh. fr. Hindi *pāc* five, fr. Skt *pañca;* fr. the number of ingredients] : a drink usu. composed of wine or alcoholic liquor and nonalcoholic beverages; *also* : a drink composed of nonalcoholic beverages

punched card \ˈpəncht-\ *n* : a card with holes punched in particular positions to represent data

pun•cheon \ˈpən-chən\ *n* : a large cask

punch line *n* : the sentence or phrase in a joke that makes the point

punchy \ˈpən-chē\ *adj* **punch•i•er; -est 1** : having punch : FORCEFUL **2** : DAZED, CONFUSED

punc•til•io \ˌpəŋk-ˈti-lē-ˌō\ *n, pl* **-i•os 1** : a nice detail of conduct in a ceremony or in observance of a code **2** : careful observance of forms (as in social conduct)

punc•til•i•ous \ˌpəŋk-ˈti-lē-əs\ *adj* : marked by precise accordance with codes or conventions **syn** meticulous, scrupulous, careful, punctual

punc•tu•al \ˈpəŋk-chə-wəl\ *adj* : being on time : PROMPT — **punc•tu•al•i•ty** \ˌpəŋk-chə-ˈwa-lə-tē\ *n* — **punc•tu•al•ly** *adv*

punc•tu•ate \ˈpəŋk-chə-ˌwāt\ *vb* **-at•ed; -at•ing 1** : to mark or divide (written matter) with punctuation marks **2** : to break into at intervals **3** : EMPHASIZE

punc•tu•a•tion \ˌpəŋk-chə-ˈwā-shən\ *n* : the act, practice, or system of inserting standardized marks in written matter to clarify the meaning and separate structural units

[1]**punc•ture** \ˈpəŋk-chər\ *n* **1** : an act of puncturing **2** : a small hole or wound made by puncturing

[2]**puncture** *vb* **punc•tured; punc•tur•ing 1** : to make a hole in : PIERCE **2** : to make useless as if by a puncture

pun•dit \ˈpən-dət\ *n* **1** : a learned person : TEACHER **2** : AUTHORITY, CRITIC

pun•gent \ˈpən-jənt\ *adj* **1** : having a sharp incisive quality : CAUSTIC ⟨a ~ editorial⟩ **2** : causing a sharp or irritating sensation; *esp* : ACRID ⟨~ smell of burning leaves⟩ — **pun•gen•cy** \-jən-sē\ *n* — **pun•gent•ly** *adv*

pun•ish \ˈpə-nish\ *vb* **1** : to impose a penalty on for a fault or crime ⟨~ an offender⟩ **2** : to inflict a penalty for ⟨~ treason with death⟩ **3** : to inflict injury on : HURT **syn** chastise, castigate, chasten, discipline, correct — **pun•ish•able** *adj*

pun•ish•ment *n* **1** : retributive suffering, pain, or loss : PENALTY **2** : rough treatment

pu•ni•tive \ˈpyü-nə-tiv\ *adj* : inflicting, involving, or aiming at punishment

[1]**punk** \ˈpəŋk\ *n* **1** : a young inexperienced person **2** : a petty hoodlum

[2]**punk** *adj* : very poor : INFERIOR

[3]**punk** *n* : dry crumbly wood useful for tinder; *also* : a substance made from fungi for use as tinder

pun•kin \ˈpəŋ-kən\ *var of* PUMPKIN

pun•ster \ˈpən-stər\ *n* : one who is given to punning

[1]**punt** \ˈpənt\ *n* : a long narrow flat-bottomed boat with square ends

[2]**punt** *vb* : to propel (as a punt) with a pole

[3]**punt** *vb* : to kick a football or soccer ball dropped from the hands before it touches the ground

[4]**punt** *n* : the act or an instance of punting a ball

pu•ny \ˈpyü-nē\ *adj* **pu•ni•er; -est** [MF *puisné* younger, lit., born afterward, fr. *puis* afterward (fr. L *post*) + *né* born, fr. L *natus*] : slight in power, size, or importance : WEAK

pup \ˈpəp\ *n* : a young dog; *also* : one of the young of some other animals

pu•pa \ˈpyü-pə\ *n, pl* **pu•pae** \-(ˌ)pē\ *or* **pupas** [NL, fr. L *pupa* doll] : a form of some insects (as a bee, moth, or beetle) between the larva and the adult that usu. has a protective covering (as a cocoon) — **pu•pal** \-pəl\ *adj*

[1]**pu•pil** \ˈpyü-pəl\ *n* **1** : a child or young person in school or in the charge of a tutor **2** : DISCIPLE

[2]**pupil** *n* : the dark central opening of the iris of the eye

pup•pet \ˈpə-pət\ *n* [ME *popet,* fr. MF *poupette,* ultim. fr. L *pupa* doll] **1** : a small figure of a person or animal moved by hand or by strings or wires **2** : DOLL **3** : one whose acts are controlled by an outside force or influence

pup•pe•teer \ˌpə-pə-ˈtir\ *n* : one who manipulates puppets

pup•py \ˈpə-pē\ *n, pl* **puppies** : a young domestic dog

pur•blind \ˈpər-ˌblīnd\ *adj* **1** : partly blind **2** : lacking in insight : OBTUSE

[1]**pur•chase** \ˈpər-chəs\ *vb* **pur•chased; pur•chas•ing** : to obtain by paying money or its equivalent : BUY — **pur•chas•able** \-chə-sə-bəl\ *adj* — **pur•chas•er** *n*

[2]**purchase** *n* **1** : an act or instance of purchasing **2** : something purchased **3** : a secure hold or grasp; *also* : advantageous leverage

pur•dah \ˈpər-də\ *n* : seclusion of women from public observation among Muslims and some Hindus esp. in India; *also* : a state of seclusion

pure \ˈpyu̇r\ *adj* **pur•er; pur•est 1** : unmixed with any other matter : free from taint ⟨~ gold⟩ ⟨~ water⟩ **2** : SHEER, ABSOLUTE ⟨~ nonsense⟩ **3** : ABSTRACT, THEORETICAL ⟨~ mathematics⟩ **4** : free from what vitiates, weakens, or pollutes ⟨speaks a ~ French⟩ **5** : free from moral fault : INNOCENT **6** : CHASTE, CONTINENT — **pure•ly** *adv*

pure–blood•ed \-ˌblə-dəd\ *or* **pure–blood** \-ˌbləd\ *adj* : FULL-BLOODED — **pure•blood** *n*

pure•bred \-ˈbred\ *adj* : bred from members of a recognized breed, strain, or kind without crossbreeding over many generations — **pure•bred** \-ˌbred\ *n*

[1]**pu•ree** \pyu̇-ˈrā, -ˈrē\ *n* [F *purée,* fr. MF, fr. fem. of *puré,* pp. of *purer* to purify, strain, fr. L *purare* to purify] : a paste or thick liquid suspension usu. made from finely ground cooked food; *also* : a thick soup made of pureed vegetables

[2]**puree** *vb* **pu•reed; pu•ree•ing** : to make a puree of

pur•ga•tion \ˌpər-ˈgā-shən\ *n* : the act or result of purging

[1]**pur•ga•tive** \ˈpər-gə-tiv\ *adj* : purging or tending to purge

[2]**purgative** *n* : a strong laxative : CATHARTIC

pur•ga•to•ry \ˈpər-gə-ˌtōr-ē\ *n, pl* **-ries 1** : an intermediate state after death for expiatory purification **2** : a place or state of temporary punishment — **pur•ga•tor•i•al** \ˌpər-gə-ˈtōr-ē-əl\ *adj*

[1]**purge** \ˈpərj\ *vb* **purged; purg•ing 1** : to cleanse or purify esp. from sin **2** : to have or cause strong and usu. repeated emptying of the bowels **3** : to get rid of ⟨the leaders had been *purged*⟩

[2]**purge** *n* **1** : something that purges; *esp* : PURGATIVE **2**

: an act or result of purging; *esp* : a ridding of persons regarded as treacherous or disloyal

pu•ri•fy \ˈpyu̇r-ə-ˌfī\ *vb* **-fied; -fy•ing** : to make or become pure — **pu•ri•fi•ca•tion** \ˌpyu̇r-ə-fə-ˈkā-shən\ *n* — **pu•ri•fi•ca•to•ry** \pyu̇-ˈri-fi-kə-ˌtōr-ē\ *adj* — **pu•ri•fi•er** *n*

Pu•rim \ˈpu̇r-(ˌ)im\ *n* : a Jewish holiday celebrated in February or March in commemoration of the deliverance of the Jews from the massacre plotted by Haman

pu•rine \ˈpyu̇r-ˌēn\ *n* : any of a group of bases including several (as adenine or guanine) that are constituents of DNA or RNA

pur•ism \ˈpyu̇r-ˌi-zəm\ *n* : rigid adherence to or insistence on purity or nicety esp. in use of words — **purist** \-ist\ *n* — **pu•ris•tic** \pyu̇-ˈris-tik\ *adj*

pu•ri•tan \ˈpyu̇r-ət-ᵊn\ *n* **1** *cap* : a member of a 16th and 17th century Protestant group in England and New England opposing the ceremonies and government of the Church of England **2** : one who practices or preaches a stricter or professedly purer moral code than that which prevails — **pu•ri•tan•i•cal** \ˌpyu̇r-ə-ˈta-ni-kəl\ *adj* — **pu•ri•tan•i•cal•ly** *adv*

pu•ri•ty \ˈpyu̇r-ə-tē\ *n* : the quality or state of being pure

¹purl \ˈpərl\ *vb* : to knit in purl stitch

²purl *n* : a stitch in knitting

³purl *n* : a gentle murmur or movement (as of purling water)

⁴purl *vb* **1** : EDDY, SWIRL **2** : to make a soft murmuring sound

pur•lieu \ˈpər-lü, ˈpərl-yü\ *n* **1** : an outlying district : SUBURB **2** *pl* : ENVIRONS

pur•loin \(ˌ)pər-ˈlȯin, ˈpər-ˌlȯin\ *vb* : STEAL, FILCH

¹pur•ple \ˈpər-pəl\ *adj* **pur•pler; pur•plest 1** : of the color purple **2** : highly rhetorical ⟨a ~ passage⟩ **3** : PROFANE ⟨~ language⟩ — **pur•plish** *adj*

²purple *n* **1** : a bluish red color **2** : a purple robe emblematic esp. of regal rank or authority

¹pur•port \ˈpər-ˌpōrt\ *n* : meaning conveyed or implied; *also* : GIST

²pur•port \(ˌ)pər-ˈpōrt\ *vb* : to convey or profess outwardly as the meaning or intention : CLAIM — **pur•port•ed•ly** \-ˈpōr-təd-lē\ *adv*

¹pur•pose \ˈpər-pəs\ *n* **1** : an object or result aimed at : INTENTION **2** : RESOLUTION, DETERMINATION — **pur•pose•ful** \-fəl\ *adj* — **pur•pose•ful•ly** *adv* — **pur•pose•less** *adj* — **pur•pose•ly** *adv*

²purpose *vb* **pur•posed; pur•pos•ing** : to propose as an aim to oneself

purr \ˈpər\ *n* : a low murmur typical of a contented cat — **purr** *vb*

¹purse \ˈpərs\ *n* **1** : a receptacle (as a pouch) to carry money and often other small objects in **2** : RESOURCES **3** : a sum of money offered as a prize or present

²purse *vb* **pursed; purs•ing** : PUCKER

purs•er \ˈpər-sər\ *n* : an official on a ship who keeps accounts and attends to the comfort of passengers

purs•lane \ˈpər-slən, -ˌslān\ *n* : a fleshy-leaved weedy trailing plant with tiny yellow flowers that is sometimes used in salads

pur•su•ance \pər-ˈsü-əns\ *n* : the act of carrying out or into effect

pur•su•ant to \-ˈsü-ənt-\ *prep* : in carrying out : ACCORDING TO

pur•sue \pər-ˈsü\ *vb* **pur•sued; pur•su•ing 1** : to follow in order to overtake or overcome : CHASE **2** : to seek to accomplish ⟨~ a goal⟩ **3** : to proceed along ⟨~ a course⟩ **4** : to engage in ⟨~ a career⟩ — **pur•su•er** *n*

pur•suit \pər-ˈsüt\ *n* **1** : the act of pursuing **2** : OCCUPATION, BUSINESS

pu•ru•lent \ˈpyu̇r-ə-lənt, -yə-\ *adj* : containing or accompanied by pus ⟨a ~ discharge⟩ — **pu•ru•lence** \-ləns\ *n*

pur•vey \(ˌ)pər-ˈvā\ *vb* **pur•veyed; pur•vey•ing** : to supply (as provisions) usu. as a business — **pur•vey•ance** \-əns\ *n* — **pur•vey•or** \-ər\ *n*

pur•view \ˈpər-ˌvyü\ *n* **1** : the range or limit esp. of authority, responsibility, or intention **2** : range of vision, understanding, or cognizance

pus \ˈpəs\ *n* : thick yellowish white fluid matter (as in a boil) formed at a place of inflammation and infection (as an abscess) and containing germs, blood cells, and tissue debris

¹push \ˈpu̇sh\ *vb* [ME *pusshen,* fr. OF *poulser* to beat, push, fr. L *pulsare,* fr. *pellere* to drive, strike] **1** : to press against with force in order to drive or impel **2** : to thrust forward, downward, or outward **3** : to urge on : press forward **4** : to cause to increase ⟨~ prices to record levels⟩ **5** : to urge or press the advancement, adoption, or practice of; *esp* : to make aggressive efforts to sell **6** : to engage in the illicit sale of narcotics

²push *n* **1** : a vigorous effort : DRIVE **2** : an act of pushing : SHOVE **3** : vigorous enterprise : ENERGY

push–button *adj* **1** : operated or done by means of push buttons **2** : using or dependent on complex and more or less automatic mechanisms ⟨~ warfare⟩

push button *n* : a small button or knob that when pushed operates something esp. by closing an electric circuit

push•cart \ˈpu̇sh-ˌkärt\ *n* : a cart or barrow pushed by hand

push•er \ˈpu̇-shər\ *n* : one that pushes; *esp* : one that pushes illegal drugs

push•over \-ˌō-vər\ *n* **1** : an opponent easy to defeat **2** : SUCKER **3** : something easily accomplished

push–up \-ˌəp\ *n* : a conditioning exercise performed in a prone position by raising and lowering the body with the straightening and bending of the arms while keeping the back straight and supporting the body on the hands and toes

pushy \ˈpu̇-shē\ *adj* **push•i•er; -est** : aggressive often to an objectionable degree

pu•sil•lan•i•mous \ˌpyü-sə-ˈla-nə-məs\ *adj* [LL *pusillanimis,* fr. L *pusillus* very small (dim. of *pusus* boy) + *animus* spirit] : contemptibly timid : COWARDLY — **pu•sil•la•nim•i•ty** \ˌpyü-sə-lə-ˈni-mə-tē\ *n*

¹puss \ˈpu̇s\ *n* : CAT

²puss *n* : FACE

¹pussy \ˈpu̇-sē\ *n, pl* **puss•ies** : CAT

²pus•sy \ˈpə-sē\ *adj* **pus•si•er; -est** : full of or resembling pus

pussy•cat \ˈpu̇-sē-ˌkat\ *n* : CAT

pussy•foot \-ˌfu̇t\ *vb* **1** : to tread or move warily or stealthily **2** : to refrain from committing oneself

pussy willow \ˈpu̇-sē-\ *n* : a willow having large silky catkins

pus•tule \ˈpəs-chül\ *n* : a pus-filled pimple

put \ˈpu̇t\ *vb* **put; put•ting 1** : to bring into a specified position : PLACE ⟨~ the book on the table⟩ **2** : SEND, THRUST **3** : to throw with an upward pushing motion ⟨~ the shot⟩ **4** : to bring into a specified state ⟨~ the plan into effect⟩ **5** : SUBJECT ⟨~ traitors to death⟩ **6** : IMPOSE **7** : to set before one for decision ⟨~ the question⟩ **8** : EXPRESS, STATE **9** : TRANSLATE, ADAPT **10** : APPLY, ASSIGN ⟨~ them to work⟩ **11** : ESTIMATE ⟨~ the number at 20⟩ **12** : ATTACH, ATTRIBUTE ⟨~ a high value on it⟩ **13** : to take a specified course ⟨the ship ~ out to sea⟩

pu•ta•tive \ˈpyü-tə-tiv\ *adj* **1** : commonly accepted **2** : assumed to exist or to have existed

put–down \ˈpu̇t-ˌdau̇n\ *n* : a belittling remark

put in *vb* **1** : to come in with : INTERPOSE ⟨*put in* a good word for me⟩ **2** : to spend time at some occupation or job ⟨*put in* eight hours at the office⟩

put off *vb* : POSTPONE, DELAY

¹put–on \ˈpu̇t-ˌȯn, -ˌän\ *adj* : PRETENDED, ASSUMED

²put–on *n* **1** : a deliberate act of misleading someone **2** : PARODY, SPOOF

put·out \ˈpu̇t-ˌau̇t\ *n* : the retiring of a base runner or batter in baseball

put out *vb* **1** : EXTINGUISH **2** : ANNOY; *also* : INCONVENIENCE **3** : to cause to be out (as in baseball)

pu·tre·fy \ˈpyü-trə-ˌfī\ *vb* **-fied; -fy·ing** : to make or become putrid : ROT — **pu·tre·fac·tion** \ˌpyü-trə-ˈfak-shən\ *n* — **pu·tre·fac·tive** \-tiv\ *adj*

pu·tres·cent \pyü-ˈtres-ᵊnt\ *adj* : becoming putrid : ROTTING — **pu·tres·cence** \-ᵊns\ *n*

pu·trid \ˈpyü-trəd\ *adj* **1** : ROTTEN, DECAYED **2** : VILE, CORRUPT — **pu·trid·i·ty** \pyü-ˈtri-də-tē\ *n*

putsch \ˈpu̇ch\ *n* [G] : a secretly plotted and suddenly executed attempt to overthrow a government

putt \ˈpət\ *n* : a golf stroke made on the green to cause the ball to roll into the hole — **putt** *vb*

put·tee \ˌpə-ˈtē, ˈpə-tē\ *n* [Hindi *paṭṭī* strip of cloth] **1** : a cloth strip wrapped around the lower leg **2** : a leather legging

[1]**put·ter** \ˈpu̇-tər\ *n* : one that puts

[2]**putt·er** \ˈpə-tər\ *n* **1** : a golf club used in putting **2** : one that putts

[3]**put·ter** \ˈpə-tər\ *vb* **1** : to move or act aimlessly or idly **2** : TINKER

put·ty \ˈpə-tē\ *n, pl* **putties** [F *potée* potter's glaze, lit., potful, fr. OF, fr. *pot* pot] **1** : a doughlike cement used esp. to fasten glass in sashes **2** : one who is easily manipulated — **putty** *vb*

put up *vb* **1** : SHEATHE **2** : to prepare so as to preserve for later use **3** : to offer for public sale ⟨*put* the house *up* for auction⟩ **4** : ACCOMMODATE, LODGE **5** : BUILD **6** : to engage in ⟨*put up* a struggle⟩ **7** : CONTRIBUTE, PAY — **put up with** : TOLERATE 2

[1]**puz·zle** \ˈpə-zəl\ *vb* **puz·zled; puz·zling** **1** : to bewilder mentally : PERPLEX **2** : to solve with difficulty or ingenuity ⟨~ out a riddle⟩ **3** : to be in a quandary ⟨~ over what to do⟩ **4** : to attempt a solution of a puzzle ⟨~ over a person's words⟩ **syn** mystify, bewilder, nonplus, confound — **puz·zle·ment** *n* — **puz·zler** *n*

[2]**puzzle** *n* **1** : something that puzzles **2** : a question, problem, or contrivance designed for testing ingenuity

PVC *abbr* polyvinyl chloride

pvt *abbr* private

PW *abbr* prisoner of war

pwt *abbr* pennyweight

PX *abbr* post exchange

pya \pē-ˈä\ *n* — see *kyat* at MONEY table

pyg·my \ˈpig-mē\ *n, pl* **pygmies** [ME *pigmei*, fr. L *pygmaeus* of a pygmy, dwarfish, fr. Gk *pygmaios*, fr. *pygmē* fist, measure of length] **1** *cap* : any of a small people of equatorial Africa **2** : DWARF — **pygmy** *adj*

py·ja·mas \pə-ˈjä-məz\ *chiefly Brit var of* PAJAMAS

py·lon \ˈpī-ˌlän, -lən\ *n* **1** : a usu. massive gateway; *esp* : an Egyptian one flanked by flat-topped pyramids **2** : a tower that supports wires over a long span **3** : a post or tower marking the course in an airplane race

py·or·rhea \ˌpī-ə-ˈrē-ə\ *n* : an inflammation with pus of the sockets of the teeth

[1]**pyr·a·mid** \ˈpir-ə-ˌmid\ *n* **1** : a massive structure with a square base and four triangular faces meeting at a point **2** : a geometrical solid having a polygon for its base and three or more triangles for its sides that meet at a point to form the top — **py·ra·mi·dal** \pə-ˈra-məd-ᵊl, ˌpir-ə-ˈmid-\ *adj*

[2]**pyramid** *vb* **1** : to build up in the form of a pyramid : heap up **2** : to increase rapidly on a broadening base

pyre \ˈpīr\ *n* : a combustible heap for burning a dead body as a funeral rite

py·re·thrum \pī-ˈrē-thrəm\ *n* : an insecticide made from the dried heads of any of several Old World chrysanthemums

py·rim·i·dine \pī-ˈri-mə-ˌdēn\ *n* : any of a group of bases including several (as cytosine, thymine, or uracil) that are constituents of DNA or RNA

py·rite \ˈpī-ˌrīt\ *n* : a mineral containing sulfur and iron that is brass-yellow in color

py·rol·y·sis \pī-ˈrä-lə-səs\ *n* : chemical change caused by the action of heat

py·ro·ma·nia \ˌpī-rō-ˈmā-nē-ə\ *n* : an irresistible impulse to start fires — **py·ro·ma·ni·ac** \-nē-ˌak\ *n*

py·ro·tech·nics \ˌpī-rə-ˈtek-niks\ *n pl* **1** : a display of fireworks **2** : a spectacular display (as of extreme virtuosity) — **py·ro·tech·nic** \-nik\ *also* **py·ro·tech·ni·cal** \-ni-kəl\ *adj*

Pyr·rhic \ˈpir-ik\ *adj* : achieved at excessive cost ⟨a ~ victory⟩; *also* : costly to the point of outweighing expected benefits

Py·thag·o·re·an theorem \pī-ˌtha-gə-ˈrē-ən-\ *n* : a theorem in geometry: the square of the length of the hypotenuse of a right triangle equals the sum of the squares of the lengths of the other two sides

py·thon \ˈpī-ˌthän, -thən\ *n* [L, monstrous serpent killed by the god Apollo, fr. Gk *Pythōn*] : a large snake (as a boa) that squeezes and suffocates its prey; *esp* : any of the large Old World snakes that include the largest snakes living at the present time

pyx \ˈpiks\ *n* : a small case used to carry the Eucharist to the sick

Q

[1]**q** \ˈkyü\ *n, pl* **q's** *or* **qs** \ˈkyüz\ *often cap* : the 17th letter of the English alphabet

[2]**q** *abbr, often cap* **1** quart **2** quarto **3** queen **4** query **5** question

QB *abbr* quarterback

QED *abbr* [L *quod erat demonstrandum*] which was to be demonstrated

qin·tar \kin-ˈtär\ *n, pl* **qin·dar·ka** \kin-ˈdär-kə\ *or* **qintar** — see *lek* at MONEY table

qi·vi·ut \ˈkē-vē-ˌüt\ *n* [Inuit] : the wool of the undercoat of the musk ox

Qld *abbr* Queensland

QM *abbr* quartermaster

QMC *abbr* quartermaster corps

QMG *abbr* quartermaster general

qq v *abbr* [L *quae vide*] which (*pl*) see

qr *abbr* quarter

qt *abbr* **1** quantity **2** quart

q.t. \ˌkyü-ˈtē\ *n, often cap Q&T* : QUIET — usu. used in the phrase *on the q.t.*

qto *abbr* quarto

qty *abbr* quantity

qu *or* **ques** *abbr* question

[1]**quack** \ˈkwak\ *vb* : to make the characteristic cry of a duck

[2]**quack** *n* : a sound made by quacking

[3]**quack** *n* **1** : CHARLATAN **2** : a pretender to medical skill **syn** faker, impostor, mountebank — **quack** *adj* — **quack·ery** \ˈkwa-kə-rē\ *n* — **quack·ish** *adj*

[1]**quad** \ˈkwäd\ *n* : QUADRANGLE

[2]**quad** *n* : QUADRUPLET

[3]**quad** *abbr* quadrant

quad·ran·gle \ˈkwä-ˌdraŋ-gəl\ *n* **1** : QUADRILATERAL **2** : a 4-sided courtyard or enclosure — **quad·ran·gu·lar** \kwä-ˈdraŋ-gyə-lər\ *adj*

quad·rant \ˈkwä-drənt\ *n* **1** : one quarter of a circle : an arc of 90° **2** : any of the four quarters into which something is divided by two lines intersecting each other at right angles

qua·drat·ic \kwä-ˈdra-tik\ *adj* : having or being a term in which the variable (as *x*) is squared but containing no term in which the variable is raised to a higher power than a square ⟨a ~ equation⟩ — **quadratic** *n*

qua·dren·ni·al \kwä-ˈdre-nē-əl\ *adj* **1** : consisting of or

lasting for four years **2 :** occurring every four years
qua•dren•ni•um \-nē-əm\ *n, pl* **-ni•ums** *or* **-nia** \-nē-ə\ : a period of four years
¹quad•ri•lat•er•al \ˌkwä-drə-ˈla-tə-rəl\ *n* : a polygon of four sides
²quadrilateral *adj* : having four sides
qua•drille \kwä-ˈdril, kə-\ *n* : a square dance made up of five or six figures in various rhythms
quad•ri•par•tite \ˌkwä-drə-ˈpär-ˌtīt\ *adj* **1 :** consisting of four parts **2 :** shared by four parties or persons
qua•driv•i•um \kwä-ˈdri-vē-əm\ *n* : the four liberal arts of arithmetic, music, geometry, and astronomy in a medieval university
quad•ru•ped \ˈkwä-drə-ˌped\ *n* : an animal having four feet — **qua•dru•pe•dal** \kwä-ˈdrü-pəd-ᵊl, ˌkwä-drə-ˈped-\ *adj*
¹qua•dru•ple \kwä-ˈdrü-pəl, -ˈdrə-; ˈkwä-drə-\ *vb* **qua•dru•pled; qua•dru•pling :** to make or become four times as great or as many
²quadruple *adj* : FOURFOLD
qua•dru•plet \kwä-ˈdrə-plət, -ˈdrü-; ˈkwä-drə-\ *n* **1 :** one of four offspring born at one birth **2 :** a group of four of a kind
¹qua•dru•pli•cate \kwä-ˈdrü-pli-kət\ *adj* **1 :** repeated four times **2 :** FOURTH
²qua•dru•pli•cate \-plə-ˌkāt\ *vb* **-cat•ed; -cat•ing 1 :** QUADRUPLE **2 :** to prepare in quadruplicate — **qua•dru•pli•ca•tion** \-ˌdrü-plə-ˈkā-shən\ *n*
³qua•dru•pli•cate \-ˈdrü-pli-kət\ *n* **1 :** four copies all alike ⟨typed in ~⟩ **2 :** one of four like things
quaff \ˈkwäf, ˈkwaf\ *vb* : to drink deeply or repeatedly — **quaff** *n*
quag•mire \ˈkwag-ˌmīr, ˈkwäg-\ *n* **1 :** soft miry land that yields under the foot **2 :** PREDICAMENT
qua•hog \ˈkō-ˌhȯg, ˈkwȯ-, ˈkwō-, -ˌhäg\ *n* : a round thick-shelled edible No. American clam
quai \ˈkā\ *n* : QUAY
¹quail \ˈkwāl\ *n, pl* **quail** *or* **quails** [ME *quaille,* fr. MF, fr. ML *quaccula,* of imit. origin] : any of numerous small short-winged plump game birds (as a bobwhite) related to the domestic chicken
²quail *vb* [ME, to grow feeble, fr. MD *quelen*] : to lose heart : COWER **syn** recoil, shrink, flinch, wince, blanch
quaint \ˈkwānt\ *adj* : unusual or different in character or appearance; *esp* : pleasingly old-fashioned or unfamiliar **syn** odd, queer, curious, strange — **quaint•ly** *adv* — **quaint•ness** *n*
¹quake \ˈkwāk\ *vb* **quaked; quak•ing 1 :** to shake usu. from shock or instability **2 :** to tremble usu. from cold or fear
²quake *n* : a shaking or trembling; *esp* : EARTHQUAKE
Quak•er \ˈkwā-kər\ *n* : FRIEND 5
qual *abbr* quality
qual•i•fi•ca•tion \ˌkwä-lə-fə-ˈkā-shən\ *n* **1 :** LIMITATION, MODIFICATION **2 :** a special skill that fits a person for some work or position **3 :** REQUIREMENT
qual•i•fied \ˈkwä-lə-ˌfīd\ *adj* **1 :** fitted for a given purpose or job **2 :** limited in some way
qual•i•fi•er \ˈkwä-lə-ˌfī-ər\ *n* **1 :** one that satisfies requirements **2 :** a word or word group that limits the meaning of another word or word group
qual•i•fy \ˈkwä-lə-ˌfī\ *vb* **-fied; -fy•ing 1 :** to reduce from a general to a particular form : MODIFY **2 :** to make less harsh **3 :** to limit the meaning of (as a noun) **4 :** to fit by skill or training for some purpose **5 :** to give or have a legal right to do something **6 :** to demonstrate the necessary ability ⟨~ for the finals⟩ **syn** moderate, temper
qual•i•ta•tive \ˈkwä-lə-ˌtā-tiv\ *adj* : of, relating to, or involving quality — **qual•i•ta•tive•ly** *adv*
¹qual•i•ty \ˈkwä-lə-tē\ *n, pl* **-ties 1 :** peculiar and essential character : NATURE **2 :** degree of excellence **3 :** high social status **4 :** a distinguishing attribute
²quality *adj* : being of high quality
qualm \ˈkwäm, ˈkwälm\ *n* **1 :** a sudden attack (as of nausea) **2 :** a sudden feeling of doubt, fear, or uneasiness esp. in not following one's conscience or better judgment
qualm•ish \ˈkwä-mish, ˈkwäl-\ *adj* **1 :** feeling qualms : NAUSEATED **2 :** overly scrupulous : SQUEAMISH **3 :** of, relating to, or producing qualms
quan•da•ry \ˈkwän-drē\ *n, pl* **-ries :** a state of perplexity or doubt
quan•ti•ta•tive \ˈkwän-tə-ˌtā-tiv\ *adj* : of, relating to, or involving quantity — **quan•ti•ta•tive•ly** *adv*
quan•ti•ty \ˈkwän-tə-tē\ *n, pl* **-ties 1 :** AMOUNT, NUMBER **2 :** a considerable amount
quan•tize \ˈkwän-ˌtīz\ *vb* **quan•tized; quan•tiz•ing :** to subdivide (as energy) into small units
quan•tum \ˈkwän-təm\ *n, pl* **quan•ta** \-tə\ [L, neut. of *quantus* how much] **1 :** QUANTITY, AMOUNT **2 :** an elemental unit of energy
quantum mechanics *n sing or pl* : a theory of matter based on the concept of possession of wave properties by elementary particles — **quantum mechanical** *adj* — **quantum mechanically** *adv*
quantum theory *n* : a theory in physics based on the idea that radiant energy (as light) is composed of small separate packets of energy
quar *abbr* quarterly
quar•an•tine \ˈkwȯr-ən-ˌtēn\ *n* [modif. of It *quarantena,* lit., period of forty days, fr. *quaranta* forty, fr. L *quadraginta*] **1 :** a period during which a ship suspected of carrying contagious disease is forbidden contact with the shore **2 :** a restraint on the movements of persons or goods to prevent the spread of pests or disease **3 :** a place or period of quarantine **4 :** a state of enforced isolation — **quarantine** *vb*
quark \ˈkwȯrk, ˈkwärk\ *n* : a hypothetical elementary particle that carries a fractional charge and is held to be a constituent of heavier particles (as protons and neutrons)
¹quar•rel \ˈkwȯr-əl\ *n* **1 :** a ground of dispute **2 :** a verbal clash : CONFLICT — **quar•rel•some** \-səm\ *adj*
²quarrel *vb* **-reled** *or* **-relled; -rel•ing** *or* **-rel•ling 1 :** to find fault **2 :** to dispute angrily : WRANGLE
¹quar•ry \ˈkwȯr-ē\ *n, pl* **quarries** [ME *querre* entrails of game given to the hounds, fr. MF *cuiree*] **1 :** game hunted with hawks **2 :** PREY
²quarry *n, pl* **quarries** [ME *quarey,* alter. of *quarrere,* fr. MF *quarriere,* fr. (assumed) OF *quarre* squared stone, fr. L *quadrum* square] : an open excavation usu. for obtaining building stone or limestone — **quarry** *vb*
quart \ˈkwȯrt\ *n* — see WEIGHT table
¹quar•ter \ˈkwȯr-tər\ *n* **1 :** one of four equal parts **2 :** a fourth of a dollar; *also* : a coin of this value **3 :** a district of a city **4** *pl* : LODGINGS ⟨moved into new ~*s*⟩ **5 :** MERCY, CLEMENCY ⟨gave no ~⟩ **6 :** a fourth part of the moon's period
²quarter *vb* **1 :** to divide into four equal parts **2 :** to provide with shelter
¹quar•ter•back \-ˌbak\ *n* : a football player who calls the signals and directs the offensive play for the team
²quarterback *vb* **1 :** to direct the offensive play of a football team **2 :** LEAD, BOSS
quar•ter•deck \-ˌdek\ *n* : the stern area of a ship's upper deck
quarter horse *n* : any of a breed of compact muscular saddle horses characterized by great endurance and by high speed for short distances
¹quar•ter•ly \ˈkwȯr-tər-lē\ *adv* : at 3-month intervals
²quarterly *adj* : occurring, issued, or payable at 3-month intervals
³quarterly *n, pl* **-lies :** a periodical published four times a year
quar•ter•mas•ter \-ˌmas-tər\ *n* **1 :** a petty officer who attends to a ship's helm, binnacle, and signals **2 :** an army officer who provides clothing and subsistence for troops

quarter horse

quar•ter•staff \-ˌstaf\ *n, pl* **-staves** \-ˌstavz, -ˌstāvz\ : a long stout staff formerly used as a weapon

quar•tet *also* **quar•tette** \kwȯr-ˈtet\ *n* **1** : a musical composition for four instruments or voices **2** : a group of four and esp. of four musicians

quar•to \ˈkwȯr-tō\ *n, pl* **quartos 1** : the size of a piece of paper cut four from a sheet **2** : a book printed on quarto pages

quartz \ˈkwȯrts\ *n* : a common often transparent crystalline mineral that is a form of silica

quartz•ite \ˈkwȯrt-ˌsīt\ *n* : a compact granular rock composed of quartz and derived from sandstone

qua•sar \ˈkwā-ˌzär, -ˌsär\ *n* : any of a class of extremely distant starlike celestial objects

[1]**quash** \ˈkwäsh, ˈkwȯsh\ *vb* : to suppress or extinguish summarily and completely : QUELL

[2]**quash** *vb* : to set aside by judicial action

qua•si \ˈkwā-ˌzī, -ˌsī; ˈkwä-zē, -sē\ *adj* : being in some sense or degree ⟨a ~ corporation⟩

quasi- *comb form* [L, as if, as it were, approximately, fr. *quam* as + *si* if] : in some sense or degree ⟨*quasi*-historical⟩

Qua•ter•na•ry \ˈkwä-tər-ˌner-ē, kwə-ˈtər-nə-rē\ *adj* : of, relating to, or being the geologic period from the end of the Tertiary to the present — **Quaternary** *n*

qua•train \ˈkwä-ˌtrān\ *n* : a unit of four lines of verse

qua•tre•foil \ˈka-tər-ˌfȯil, ˈka-trə-\ *n* : a stylized figure often of a flower with four petals

qua•ver \ˈkwā-vər\ *vb* **1** : TREMBLE, SHAKE **2** : TRILL **3** : to speak in tremulous tones **syn** shudder, quake, twitter, quiver, shiver — **quaver** *n*

quay \ˈkē, ˈkwā, ˈkā\ *n* : WHARF

Que *abbr* Quebec

quean \ˈkwēn\ *n* : PROSTITUTE

quea•sy \ˈkwē-zē\ *adj* **quea•si•er; -est** : NAUSEATED — **quea•si•ly** \-zə-lē\ *adv* — **quea•si•ness** \-zē-nəs\ *n*

queen \ˈkwēn\ *n* **1** : the wife or widow of a king **2** : a female monarch **3** : a woman notable for rank, power, or attractiveness **4** : the most powerful piece in the game of chess **5** : a playing card bearing the figure of a queen **6** : a fertile female of a social insect (as a bee or termite) — **queen•ly** *adj*

Queen Anne's lace \-ˈanz-\ *n* : a widely naturalized Eurasian herb from which the cultivated carrot originated

queen consort *n, pl* **queens consort** : the wife of a reigning king

queen mother *n* : a dowager queen who is mother of the reigning sovereign

queen–size *adj* : having dimensions of approximately 60 inches by 80 inches ⟨~ bed⟩; *also* : of a size that fits a queen-size bed

[1]**queer** \ˈkwir\ *adj* **1** : differing from the usual or normal : PECULIAR, STRANGE **2** : COUNTERFEIT **syn** weird, bizarre, eccentric, curious — **queer** *n* — **queer•ly** *adv* — **queer•ness** *n*

[2]**queer** *vb* : to spoil the effect of : DISRUPT ⟨~*ed* our plans⟩

quell \ˈkwel\ *vb* **1** : to put an end to by force ⟨~ a riot⟩ **2** : CALM, PACIFY

quench \ˈkwench\ *vb* **1** : PUT OUT, EXTINGUISH **2** : SUBDUE **3** : SLAKE, SATISFY ⟨~*ed* his thirst⟩ — **quench•able** *adj* — **quench•er** *n* — **quench•less** *adj*

quer•u•lous \ˈkwer-ə-ləs, -yə-\ *adj* **1** : constantly complaining **2** : FRETFUL, WHINING **syn** petulant, pettish, irritable, peevish, huffy — **quer•u•lous•ly** *adv* — **quer•u•lous•ness** *n*

que•ry \ˈkwir-ē, ˈkwer-\ *n, pl* **queries** : QUESTION — **query** *vb*

quest \ˈkwest\ *n* : SEARCH — **quest** *vb*

[1]**ques•tion** \ˈkwes-chən\ *n* **1** : an interrogative expression : QUERY **2** : a subject for debate; *also* : a proposition to be voted on **3** : INQUIRY **4** : DISPUTE

[2]**question** *vb* **1** : to ask questions **2** : DOUBT, DISPUTE **3** : to subject to analysis : EXAMINE **syn** interrogate, quiz, query — **ques•tion•er** *n*

ques•tion•able \ˈkwes-chə-nə-bəl\ *adj* **1** : not certain or exact : DOUBTFUL **2** : not believed to be true, sound, or moral **syn** dubious, problematical, moot, debatable — **ques•tion•ably** \-blē\ *adv*

question mark *n* : a punctuation mark ? used esp. at the end of a sentence to indicate a direct question

ques•tion•naire \ˌkwes-chə-ˈnar\ *n* : a set of questions for obtaining information

quet•zal \ket-ˈsäl, -ˈsal\ *n, pl* **quetzals** *or* **quet•za•les** \-ˈsä-lās, -ˈsa-\ **1** : a Central American bird with brilliant plumage **2** *pl quetzales* — see MONEY table

[1]**queue** \ˈkyü\ *n* [F, lit., tail, fr. L *cauda, coda*] **1** : a braid of hair usu. worn hanging at the back of the head **2** : a waiting line (as of persons)

[2]**queue** *vb* **queued; queu•ing** *or* **queue•ing** : to line up in a queue

quib•ble \ˈkwi-bəl\ *n* **1** : an evasion of or shifting from the point at issue **2** : a minor objection or criticism — **quibble** *vb* — **quib•bler** *n*

[1]**quick** \ˈkwik\ *adj* **1** : LIVING **2** : RAPID, SPEEDY ⟨~ steps⟩ **3** : prompt to understand, think, or perceive : ALERT **4** : easily aroused ⟨a ~ temper⟩ **5** : turning or bending sharply ⟨a ~ turn in the road⟩ **syn** fleet, fast, hasty, expeditious — **quick** *adv* — **quick•ly** *adv* — **quick•ness** *n*

[2]**quick** *n* **1** : a sensitive area of living flesh **2** : a vital part : HEART

quick bread *n* : a bread made with a leavening agent that permits immediate baking of the dough or batter

quick•en \ˈkwi-kən\ *vb* **1** : to come to life : REVIVE **2** : AROUSE, STIMULATE **3** : to increase in speed : HASTEN **4** : to show vitality (as by growing or moving) **syn** animate, enliven, liven, vivify

quick–freeze \ˈkwik-ˈfrēz\ *vb* **-froze** \-ˈfrōz\; **-fro•zen** \-ˈfrōz-ᵊn\; **-freez•ing** : to freeze (food) for preservation so rapidly that the natural juices and flavor are not lost

quick•ie \ˈkwi-kē\ *n* : something hurriedly done or made

quick•lime \ˈkwik-ˌlīm\ *n* : [1]LIME

quick•sand \-ˌsand\ *n* : a deep mass of loose sand mixed with water

quick•sil•ver \-ˌsil-vər\ *n* : MERCURY 1

quick•step \-ˌstep\ *n* : a spirited march tune or dance

quick–wit•ted \ˈkwik-ˈwi-təd\ *adj* : mentally alert **syn** clever, bright, smart, intelligent

quid \ˈkwid\ *n* : a lump of something chewable ⟨a ~ of tobacco⟩

quid pro quo \ˌkwid-ˌprō-ˈkwō\ *n* [NL, something for something] : something given or received for something else

qui•es•cent \kwī-ˈes-ᵊnt\ *adj* : being at rest : QUIET **syn** latent, dormant, potential — **qui•es•cence** \-ᵊns\ *n*

[1]**qui•et** \ˈkwī-ət\ *n* : REPOSE

[2]**quiet** *adj* **1** : marked by little motion or activity : CALM **2** : GENTLE, MILD ⟨a ~ disposition⟩ **3** : enjoyed in peace and relaxation ⟨a ~ cup of tea⟩ **4** : free from noise or uproar **5** : not showy : MODEST ⟨~ clothes⟩ **6** : SECLUDED ⟨a ~ nook⟩ — **quiet** *adv* — **qui•et•ly** *adv* — **qui•et•ness** *n*

³quiet *vb* **1** : CALM, PACIFY **2** : to become quiet ⟨~ down⟩

qui•etude \ˈkwī-ə-ˌtüd, -ˌtyüd\ *n* : QUIETNESS, REPOSE

qui•etus \kwī-ˈē-təs\ *n* [ME *quietus est*, fr. ML, he is quit, formula of discharge from obligation] **1** : final settlement (as of a debt) **2** : DEATH

quill \ˈkwil\ *n* **1** : a large stiff feather; *also* : the hollow tubular part of a feather **2** : one of the hollow sharp spines of a hedgehog or porcupine **3** : a pen made from a feather

¹quilt \ˈkwilt\ *n* : a padded bed coverlet

²quilt *vb* **1** : to fill, pad, or line like a quilt **2** : to stitch or sew in layers with padding in between **3** : to make quilts

quince \ˈkwins\ *n* : a hard yellow applelike fruit; *also* : a tree related to the roses that bears this fruit

qui•nine \ˈkwī-ˌnīn\ *n* : a bitter white drug obtained from cinchona bark and used esp. in treating malaria

quint \ˈkwint\ *n* : QUINTUPLET

quin•tal \ˈkwint-ᵊl, ˈkant-\ *n* : HUNDREDWEIGHT

quin•tes•sence \kwin-ˈtes-ᵊns\ *n* **1** : the purest essence of something **2** : the most typical example — **quint•es•sen•tial** \ˌkwin-tə-ˈsen-chəl\ *adj* — **quin•tes•sen•tial•ly** *adv*

quin•tet *also* **quin•tette** \kwin-ˈtet\ *n* **1** : a musical composition for five instruments or voices **2** : a group of five and esp. of five musicians

¹quin•tu•ple \kwin-ˈtü-pəl, -ˈtyü-, -ˈtə-\ *adj* **1** : having five units or members **2** : being five times as great or as many — **quintuple** *n*

²quintuple *vb* **quin•tu•pled; quin•tu•pling** : to make or become five times as great or as many

quin•tu•plet \kwin-ˈtə-plət, -ˈtü-, -ˈtyü-\ *n* **1** : a group of five of a kind **2** : one of five offspring born at one birth

¹quin•tu•pli•cate \kwin-ˈtü-pli-kət, -ˈtyü-\ *adj* **1** : repeated five times **2** : FIFTH

²quintuplicate *n* **1** : one of five like things **2** : five copies all alike ⟨typed in ~⟩

³quin•tu•pli•cate \-plə-ˌkāt\ *vb* **-cat•ed; -cat•ing 1** : QUINTUPLE **2** : to provide in quintuplicate

¹quip \ˈkwip\ *n* : a clever remark : GIBE

²quip *vb* **quipped; quip•ping 1** : to make quips : GIBE **2** : to jest or gibe at

quire \ˈkwīr\ *n* : a set of 24 or sometimes 25 sheets of paper of the same size and quality

quirk \ˈkwərk\ *n* : a peculiarity of action or behavior — **quirky** *adj*

quirt \ˈkwərt\ *n* : a riding whip with a short handle and a rawhide lash

quis•ling \ˈkwiz-liŋ\ *n* [Vidkun *Quisling* †1945 Norw. politician who collaborated with the Nazis] : one who helps the invaders of one's own country

quit \ˈkwit\ *vb* **quit** *also* **quit•ted; quit•ting 1** : CONDUCT, BEHAVE ⟨~ themselves well⟩ **2** : to depart from : LEAVE; *also* : to bring to an end **3** : to give up for good ⟨~ smoking⟩ ⟨~ my job⟩ **syn** acquit, comport, deport, demean — **quit•ter** *n*

quite \ˈkwīt\ *adv* **1** : COMPLETELY, WHOLLY **2** : to an extreme : POSITIVELY **3** : to a considerable extent : RATHER

quits \ˈkwits\ *adj* : even or equal with another ⟨call it ~⟩

quit•tance \ˈkwit-ᵊns\ *n* : REQUITAL

¹quiv•er \ˈkwi-vər\ *n* : a case for carrying arrows

²quiver *vb* **quiv•ered; quiv•er•ing** : to shake with a slight trembling motion **syn** shiver, shudder, quaver, quake, tremble — **quiv•er•ing•ly** *adv*

³quiver *n* : the act or action of quivering : TREMOR

qui vive \kē-ˈvēv\ *n* [F *qui-vive*, fr. *qui vive?* long live who?, challenge of a French sentry] : ALERT ⟨on the *qui vive* for prowlers⟩

quix•ot•ic \kwik-ˈsä-tik\ *adj* [fr. Don *Quixote*, hero of the novel *Don Quixote de la Mancha* by Cervantes] : foolishly impractical esp. in the pursuit of ideals — **quix•ot•i•cal•ly** \-ti-kə-lē\ *adv*

¹quiz \ˈkwiz\ *n, pl* **quiz•zes 1** : an eccentric person **2** : PRACTICAL JOKE **3** : a short oral or written test

²quiz *vb* **quizzed; quiz•zing 1** : MOCK **2** : to look at inquisitively **3** : to question closely **syn** ask, interrogate, query

quiz•zi•cal \ˈkwi-zi-kəl\ *adj* **1** : comically quaint **2** : mildly teasing or mocking **3** : expressive of puzzlement, curiosity, or disbelief

quoit \ˈkwāt, ˈkwȯit, ˈkȯit\ *n* **1** : a flattened ring of iron or circle of rope used in a throwing game **2** *pl* : a game in which quoits are thrown at an upright pin in an attempt to ring the pin

quon•dam \ˈkwän-dəm, -ˌdam\ *adj* [L, at one time, formerly, fr. *quom, cum* when] : FORMER

quo•rum \ˈkwōr-əm\ *n* : the number of members required to be present for business to be legally transacted

quot *abbr* quotation

quo•ta \ˈkwō-tə\ *n* : a proportional part esp. when assigned : SHARE

quot•able \ˈkwō-tə-bəl\ *adj* : fit for or worth quoting — **quot•abil•i•ty** \-ˈbi-lə-tē\ *n*

quo•ta•tion \kwō-ˈtā-shən\ *n* **1** : the act or process of quoting **2** : the price currently bid or offered for something **3** : something that is quoted

quotation mark *n* : one of a pair of punctuation marks " " or ' ' used esp. to indicate the beginning and end of a quotation in which exact phraseology is directly cited

quote \ˈkwōt\ *vb* **quot•ed; quot•ing** [ML *quotare* to mark the number of, number references, fr. L *quotus* of what number or quantity, fr. *quot* how many, (as) many as] **1** : to speak or write a passage from another usu. with acknowledgment; *also* : to repeat a passage in substantiation or illustration **2** : to state the market price of a commodity, stock, or bond **3** : to inform a hearer or reader that matter following is quoted — **quote** *n*

quoth \ˈkwōth\ *vb past* [ME, past of *quethen* to say, fr. OE *cwethan*] *archaic* : SAID — usu. used in the 1st and 3d persons with the subject following

quo•tid•i•an \kwō-ˈti-dē-ən\ *adj* **1** : DAILY **2** : COMMONPLACE, ORDINARY

quo•tient \ˈkwō-shənt\ *n* : the number obtained by dividing one number by another

qv *abbr* [L *quod vide*] which see

qy *abbr* query

R

¹r \ˈär\ *n, pl* **r's** *or* **rs** \ˈärz\ *often cap* : the 18th letter of the English alphabet

²r *abbr, often cap* **1** rabbi **2** radius **3** rare **4** Republican **5** rerun **6** resistance **7** right **8** river **9** roentgen **10** rook **11** run

Ra *symbol* radium

RA *abbr* **1** regular army **2** Royal Academy

¹rab•bet \ˈra-bət\ *n* : a groove in the edge or face of a surface (as a board) esp. to receive another piece

²rabbet *vb* : to cut a rabbet in; *also* : to join by means of a rabbet

rab•bi \ˈra-ˌbī\ *n* [LL, fr. Gk *rhabbi*, fr. Heb *rabbī* my master, fr. *rabh* master + *-ī* my] **1** : MASTER, TEACHER — used by Jews as a term of address **2** : a Jew trained and ordained for professional religious leadership — **rab•bin•ic** \rə-ˈbi-nik\ *or* **rab•bin•i•cal** \-ni-kəl\ *adj*

rab•bin•ate \ˈra-bə-nət, -ˌnāt\ *n* **1** : the office of a rabbi **2** : the whole body of rabbis

rab•bit \ˈra-bət\ *n, pl* **rabbit** *or* **rabbits :** any of various long-eared burrowing mammals distinguished from the related hares by being blind, naked, and helpless at birth; *also* : the pelt of a rabbit
rabbit ears *n* : an indoor V-shaped television antenna
rabble \ˈra-bəl\ *n* **1 :** MOB 2 **2 :** the lowest class of people
rab•ble–rous•er \ˈra-bəl-ˌrau̇-zər\ *n* : one that stirs up (as to hatred or violence) the masses of the people
ra•bid \ˈra-bəd\ *adj* **1 :** VIOLENT, FURIOUS **2 :** being fanatical or extreme **3 :** affected with rabies — **ra•bid•ly** *adv*
ra•bies \ˈrā-bēz\ *n, pl* **rabies** [NL, fr. L, madness] : an acute deadly virus disease of the nervous system transmitted by the bite of an affected animal
rac•coon \ra-ˈkün\ *n, pl* **raccoon** *or* **raccoons :** a gray No. American chiefly tree-dwelling mammal with a black mask, a bushy ringed tail, and nocturnal habits; *also* : its pelt
¹race \ˈrās\ *n* **1 :** a strong current of running water; *also* : its channel **2 :** an onward course (as of time or life) **3 :** a contest of speed **4 :** a contest for a desired end (as election to office)
²race *vb* **raced; rac•ing 1 :** to run in a race **2 :** to run swiftly : RUSH **3 :** to engage in a race with **4 :** to drive or ride at high speed — **rac•er** *n*
³race *n* **1 :** a family, tribe, people, or nation of the same stock; *also* : MANKIND **2 :** a group of individuals within a biological species able to breed together — **ra•cial** \ˈrā-shəl\ *adj* — **ra•cial•ly** *adv*
race•course \ˈrās-ˌkōrs\ *n* : a course for racing
race•horse \-ˌhȯrs\ *n* : a horse bred or kept for racing
ra•ceme \rā-ˈsēm\ *n* [L *racemus* bunch of grapes] : a flower cluster with flowers borne along a stem and blooming from the base toward the tip — **rac•e•mose** \ˈra-sə-ˌmōs\ *adj*
race•track \ˈrās-ˌtrak\ *n* : a usu. oval course on which races are run
race•way \-ˌwā\ *n* **1 :** a channel for a current of water **2 :** RACECOURSE
ra•cial•ism \ˈrā-shə-ˌli-zəm\ *n* : RACISM — **ra•cial•ist** \-list\ *n* — **ra•cial•is•tic** \ˌrā-shə-ˈlis-tik\ *adj*
racing form *n* : a paper giving data about racehorses for use by bettors
rac•ism \ˈrā-ˌsi-zəm\ *n* : a belief that some races are by nature superior to others; *also* : discrimination based on such belief — **rac•ist** \-sist\ *n*
¹rack \ˈrak\ *n* **1 :** an instrument of torture on which a body is stretched **2 :** a framework on or in which something may be placed (as for display or storage) **3 :** a bar with teeth on one side to mesh with a pinion or worm gear
²rack *vb* **1 :** to torture on or as if on a rack **2 :** to stretch or strain by force **3 :** TORMENT **4 :** to place on or in a rack
¹rack•et *also* **rac•quet** \ˈra-kət\ *n* [MF *raquette*, ultim. fr. Ar *rāḥah* palm of the hand] : a light bat made of netting stretched in an oval open frame having a handle and used for striking a ball or shuttlecock
²racket *n* **1 :** confused noise : DIN **2 :** a fraudulent or dishonest scheme or activity
³racket *vb* : to make a racket
rack•e•teer \ˌra-kə-ˈtir\ *n* : a person who obtains money by an illegal enterprise usu. involving intimidation — **rack•e•teer•ing** *n*
rack up *vb* : ACCUMULATE, GAIN
ra•con•teur \ˌra-ˌkän-ˈtər\ *n* : one good at telling anecdotes
racy \ˈrā-sē\ *adj* **rac•i•er; -est 1 :** full of zest **2 :** PUNGENT, SPICY **3 :** RISQUÉ, SUGGESTIVE — **rac•i•ly** \ˈrā-sə-lē\ *adv* — **rac•i•ness** \-sē-nəs\ *n*
rad *abbr* **1** radical **2** radio **3** radius
ra•dar \ˈrā-ˌdär\ *n* [*ra*dio *d*etecting *a*nd *r*anging] : a device that emits radio waves for detecting and locating an object by the reflection of the radio waves and that may use this reflection to determine the object's direction and speed
ra•dar•scope \ˈrā-ˌdär-ˌskōp\ *n* : a visual display for a radar receiver
¹ra•di•al \ˈrā-dē-əl\ *adj* : arranged or having parts arranged like rays around a common center ⟨the ~ form of a starfish⟩ — **ra•di•al•ly** *adv*
²radial *n* : a pneumatic tire with cords laid perpendicular to the center line
radial engine *n* : an internal combustion engine with cylinders arranged radially like the spokes of a wheel
ra•di•ant \ˈrā-dē-ənt\ *adj* **1 :** SHINING, GLOWING **2 :** beaming with happiness **3 :** transmitted by radiation **syn** brilliant, bright, luminous, lustrous — **ra•di•ance** \-əns\ *n* — **ra•di•ant•ly** *adv*
radiant energy *n* : energy traveling as electromagnetic waves
ra•di•ate \ˈrā-dē-ˌāt\ *vb* **-at•ed; -at•ing 1 :** to send out rays : SHINE, GLOW **2 :** to issue in or as if in rays ⟨light ~*s*⟩ **3 :** to spread around as from a center — **ra•di•a•tion** \ˌrā-dē-ˈā-shən\ *n*
radiation sickness *n* : sickness that results from exposure to radiation and is commonly marked by fatigue, nausea, vomiting, loss of teeth and hair, and in more severe cases by damage to blood-forming tissue
ra•di•a•tor \ˈrā-dē-ˌā-tər\ *n* : any of various devices (as a set of pipes or tubes) for transferring heat from a fluid within to an area or object outside
¹rad•i•cal \ˈra-di-kəl\ *adj* [ME, fr. LL *radicalis*, fr. L *radic-*, *radix* root] **1 :** FUNDAMENTAL, EXTREME, THOROUGHGOING **2 :** of or relating to radicals in politics — **rad•i•cal•ism** \-kə-ˌli-zəm\ *n* — **rad•i•cal•ly** *adv*
²radical *n* **1 :** a person who favors rapid and sweeping changes in laws and methods of government **2 :** a group of atoms considered as a unit that remains unchanged during reactions **3 :** a mathematical expression indicating a root by means of a radical sign; *also* : RADICAL SIGN
rad•i•cal•ise *Brit var of* RADICALIZE
rad•i•cal•ize \-kə-ˌlīz\ *vb* **-ized; -iz•ing :** to make radical esp. in politics — **rad•i•cal•i•za•tion** \ˌra-di-kə-lə-ˈzā-shən\ *n*
radical sign *n* : the sign $\sqrt{}$ placed before a mathematical expression to indicate that its root is to be taken
radii *pl of* RADIUS
¹ra•dio \ˈrā-dē-ˌō\ *n, pl* **ra•di•os 1 :** the wireless transmission or reception of signals using electromagnetic waves **2 :** a radio receiving set **3 :** the radio broadcasting industry — **radio** *adj*
²radio *vb* : to communicate or send a message to by radio
ra•dio•ac•tiv•i•ty \ˌrā-dē-ō-ˌak-ˈti-və-tē\ *n* : the property that some elements or isotopes have of spontaneously emitting energetic particles by the disintegration of their atomic nuclei — **ra•dio•ac•tive** \-ˈak-tiv\ *adj*
radio astronomy *n* : astronomy dealing with radio waves received from outside the earth's atmosphere
ra•dio•car•bon \ˌrā-dē-ō-ˈkär-bən\ *n* : CARBON 14
radio frequency *n* : an electromagnetic wave frequency intermediate between audio frequencies and infrared frequencies used esp. in radio and television transmission
ra•dio•gram \ˈrā-dē-ō-ˌgram\ *n* : a message transmitted by radio
ra•dio•graph \-ˌgraf\ *n* : a photograph made by some form of radiation other than light; *esp* : an X-ray photograph — **radiograph** *vb* — **ra•dio•graph•ic** \ˌrā-dē-ō-ˈgra-fik\ *adj* — **ra•dio•graph•i•cal•ly** \-fi-k(ə-)lē\ *adv* — **ra•di•og•ra•phy** \ˌrā-dē-ˈä-grə-fē\ *n*
ra•dio•iso•tope \ˌrā-dē-ō-ˈī-sə-ˌtōp\ *n* : a radioactive isotope
ra•di•ol•o•gy \ˌrā-dē-ˈä-lə-jē\ *n* : the use of radiant en-

DICTIONARY

ergy (as X rays and radium radiations) in medicine — **ra•di•ol•o•gist** \-jist\ *n*

ra•dio•man \ˈrā-dē-ō-ˌman\ *n* : a radio operator or technician

ra•di•om•e•ter \ˌrā-dē-ˈä-mə-tər\ *n* : an instrument for measuring the intensity of radiant energy — **ra•dio•met•ric** \ˌrā-dē-ō-ˈme-trik\ *adj* — **ra•di•om•e•try** \-mə-trē\ *n*

ra•dio•phone \ˈrā-dē-ə-ˌfōn\ *n* : RADIOTELEPHONE

ra•dio•sonde \ˈrā-dē-ō-ˌsänd\ *n* : a small radio transmitter carried aloft (as by balloon) and used to transmit meteorological data

ra•dio•tele•phone \ˌrā-dē-ō-ˈte-lə-ˌfōn\ *n* : a telephone that uses radio waves wholly or partly instead of connecting wires — **ra•dio•te•le•pho•ny** \-tə-ˈle-fə-nē, -ˈte-lə-ˌfō-nē\ *n*

radio telescope *n* : a radio receiver-antenna combination used for observation in radio astronomy

ra•dio•ther•a•py \ˌrā-dē-ō-ˈther-ə-pē\ *n* : the treatment of disease by means of radiation (as X rays) — **ra•dio•ther•a•pist** \-pist\ *n*

rad•ish \ˈra-dish\ *n* [ME, alter. of OE *rædic*, fr. L *radic-, radix* root, radish] : a pungent fleshy root usu. eaten raw; *also* : a plant related to the mustards that produces this root

ra•di•um \ˈrā-dē-əm\ *n* : a very radioactive metallic chemical element that is used in the treatment of cancer — see ELEMENT table

ra•di•us \ˈrā-dē-əs\ *n, pl* **ra•dii** \-ē-ˌī\ *also* **ra•di•us•es 1** : a straight line extending from the center of a circle or a sphere to the circumference or surface; *also* : the length of a radius **2** : the bone on the thumb side of the human forearm **3** : a circular area defined by the length of its radius **syn** range, reach, scope, compass

RADM *abbr* rear admiral

ra•don \ˈrā-ˌdän\ *n* : a heavy radioactive gaseous chemical element — see ELEMENT table

RAF *abbr* Royal Air Force

raf•fia \ˈra-fē-ə\ *n* : fiber used esp. for making baskets and hats that is obtained from the stalks of the leaves of a Madagascar palm **(raffia palm)**

raff•ish \ˈra-fish\ *adj* : jaunty or sporty esp. in a flashy or vulgar manner — **raff•ish•ly** *adv* — **raff•ish•ness** *n*

[1]**raf•fle** \ˈra-fəl\ *vb* **raf•fled; raf•fling** : to dispose of by a raffle

[2]**raffle** *n* : a lottery in which the prize is won by one of a number of persons buying chances

[1]**raft** \ˈraft\ *n* **1** : a number of logs or timbers fastened together to form a float **2** : a flat structure for support or transportation on water

[2]**raft** *vb* **1** : to travel or transport by raft **2** : to make into a raft

[3]**raft** *n* : a large amount or number

raf•ter \ˈraf-tər\ *n* : any of the parallel beams that support a roof

[1]**rag** \ˈrag\ *n* **1** : a waste piece of cloth **2** : NEWSPAPER

[2]**rag** *n* : a composition in ragtime

ra•ga \ˈrä-gə\ *n* **1** : a traditional melodic pattern or mode in Indian music **2** : an improvisation based on a raga

rag•a•muf•fin \ˈra-gə-ˌmə-fən\ *n* [ME *Ragamuffyn*, name for a ragged, oafish person] : a ragged dirty person

[1]**rage** \ˈrāj\ *n* **1** : violent and uncontrolled anger **2** : VOGUE, FASHION

[2]**rage** *vb* **raged; rag•ing 1** : to be furiously angry : RAVE **2** : to continue out of control ⟨the fire *raged*⟩

rag•ged \ˈra-gəd\ *adj* **1** : TORN, TATTERED; *also* : wearing tattered clothes **2** : done in an uneven way ⟨a ~ performance⟩ — **rag•ged•ly** *adv* — **rag•ged•ness** *n*

rag•lan \ˈra-glən\ *n* : an overcoat with sleeves **(raglan sleeves)** sewn in with seams slanting from neck to underarm

ra•gout \ra-ˈgü\ *n* [F *ragoût*, fr. *ragoûter* to revive the taste, fr. *re-* + *a-* to (fr. L *ad-*) + *goût* taste, fr. L *gustus*] : a highly seasoned meat stew with vegetables

rag•pick•er \ˈrag-ˌpi-kər\ *n* : one who collects rags and refuse for a living

rag•time \-ˌtīm\ *n* : music in which there is more or less continuous syncopation in the melody

rag•top \ˈrag-ˌtäp\ *n* : CONVERTIBLE

rag•weed \-ˌwēd\ *n* : any of several chiefly No. American weedy composite herbs with allergenic pollen

[1]**raid** \ˈrād\ *n* : a sudden usu. surprise attack or invasion : FORAY

[2]**raid** *vb* : to make a raid on — **raid•er** *n*

[1]**rail** \ˈrāl\ *n* [ME *raile*, fr. MF *reille* ruler, bar, fr. L *regula* ruler, fr. *regere* to keep straight, direct, rule] **1** : a bar extending from one support to another as a guard or barrier **2** : a bar of steel forming a track for wheeled vehicles **3** : RAILROAD

[2]**rail** *vb* : to provide with a railing

[3]**rail** *n, pl* **rail** *or* **rails** : any of numerous small wading birds often hunted as game birds

[4]**rail** *vb* [ME, fr. MF *railler* to mock, fr. OProv *ralhar* to babble, joke] : to complain angrily : SCOLD, REVILE — **rail•er** *n*

rail•ing \ˈrā-liŋ\ *n* : a barrier of rails

rail•lery \ˈrā-lə-rē\ *n, pl* **-ler•ies** : good-natured ridicule : BANTER

[1]**rail•road** \ˈrāl-ˌrōd\ *n* : a permanent road with rails fixed to ties providing a track for cars; *also* : such a road and its assets constituting a property

[2]**railroad** *vb* **1** : to put through (as a law) too hastily **2** : to convict hastily or with insufficient or improper evidence **3** : to send by rail **4** : to work on a railroad — **rail•road•er** *n* — **rail•road•ing** *n*

rail•way \-ˌwā\ *n* : RAILROAD

rai•ment \ˈrā-mənt\ *n* : CLOTHING

[1]**rain** \ˈrān\ *n* **1** : water falling in drops from the clouds **2** : a shower of objects ⟨a ~ of bullets⟩ — **rainy** *adj*

[2]**rain** *vb* **1** : to send down rain **2** : to fall as or like rain **3** : to pour down

rain•bow \-ˌbō\ *n* : an arc or circle of colors formed by the refraction and reflection of the sun's rays in rain, spray, or mist

rainbow trout *n* : a large stout-bodied fish of western No. America closely related to the salmons of the Pacific and usu. having red or pink stripes with black dots along its sides

rain check *n* **1** : a ticket stub good for a later performance when the scheduled one is rained out **2** : an assurance of a deferred extension of an offer

rain•coat \ˈrān-ˌkōt\ *n* : a waterproof or water-repellent coat

rain•drop \-ˌdräp\ *n* : a drop of rain

rain•fall \-ˌfȯl\ *n* **1** : amount of precipitation measured by depth **2** : a fall of rain

rain forest *n* : a tropical woodland having an annual rainfall of at least 100 inches (254 centimeters) and marked by lofty broad-leaved evergreen trees forming a continuous canopy

rain•mak•ing \ˈrān-ˌmā-kiŋ\ *n* : the action or process of producing or attempting to produce rain by artificial means — **rain•mak•er** *n*

rain out *vb* : to interrupt or prevent by rain

rain•storm \ˈrān-ˌstȯrm\ *n* : a storm of or with rain

rain•wa•ter \-ˌwȯ-tər, -ˌwä-\ *n* : water fallen as rain

[1]**raise** \ˈrāz\ *vb* **raised; rais•ing 1** : to cause or help to rise : LIFT ⟨~ a window⟩ **2** : AWAKEN, AROUSE ⟨enough to ~ the dead⟩ **3** : BUILD, ERECT ⟨~ a monument⟩ **4** : PROMOTE ⟨was *raised* to captain⟩ **5** : END ⟨~ a siege⟩ **6** : COLLECT ⟨~ money⟩ **7** : BREED, GROW ⟨~ cattle⟩ ⟨~ corn⟩; *also* : BRING UP ⟨~ a family⟩ **8** : PROVOKE ⟨~ a laugh⟩ **9** : to bring to notice ⟨~ an objection⟩ **10** : INCREASE ⟨~ prices⟩; *also* : to bet more than **11** : to make light and spongy ⟨~ dough⟩ **12** : to multiply a quantity by itself a specified number of times **13** : to cause to form ⟨~ a blister⟩ **syn** lift, hoist, boost, elevate — **rais•er** *n*

[2]**raise** *n* : an increase in amount (as of a bid or bet); *also* : an increase in pay

rai•sin \ˈrāz-ᵊn\ *n* [ME, fr. MF, grape, fr. L *racemus* cluster of grapes or berries] : a grape dried for food

rai•son d'être \ˌrā-ˌzōⁿ-ˈdetrᵊ\ *n* : reason or justification for existence

ra•ja *or* **ra•jah** \ˈrä-jə\ *n* [Hindi *rājā*, fr. Skt *rājan* king] : an Indian prince

[1]**rake** \ˈrāk\ *n* : a long-handled garden tool having a crossbar with prongs

[2]**rake** *vb* **raked; rak•ing 1** : to gather, loosen, or smooth with or as if with a rake **2** : to sweep the length of (as a trench or ship) with gunfire

[3]**rake** *n* : inclination from either perpendicular or horizontal : SLANT

[4]**rake** *n* : a dissolute man : LIBERTINE

rake–off \ˈrāk-ˌȯf\ *n* : a percentage or cut taken

[1]**rak•ish** \ˈrā-kish\ *adj* : DISSOLUTE — **rak•ish•ly** *adv* — **rak•ish•ness** *n*

[2]**rakish** *adj* **1** : having a trim appearance indicative of speed ⟨a ∼ sloop⟩ **2** : JAUNTY, SPORTY ⟨∼ clothes⟩ — **rak•ish•ly** *adv* — **rak•ish•ness** *n*

[1]**ral•ly** \ˈra-lē\ *vb* **ral•lied; ral•ly•ing 1** : to bring together for a common purpose; *also* : to bring back to order ⟨a leader ∼*ing* his forces⟩ **2** : to arouse to activity or from depression or weakness **3** : to make a comeback **syn** stir, rouse, awaken, waken, kindle

[2]**rally** *n, pl* **rallies 1** : an act of rallying **2** : a mass meeting to arouse enthusiasm **3** : a competitive automobile event run over public roads

[3]**rally** *vb* **ral•lied; ral•ly•ing** : BANTER

[1]**ram** \ˈram\ *n* **1** : a male sheep **2** : BATTERING RAM

[2]**ram** *vb* **rammed; ram•ming 1** : to force or drive in or through **2** : CRAM, CROWD **3** : to strike against violently

RAM \ˈram\ *n* : RANDOM-ACCESS MEMORY

[1]**ram•ble** \ˈram-bəl\ *vb* **ram•bled; ram•bling** : to go about aimlessly : ROAM, WANDER

[2]**ramble** *n* : a leisurely excursion; *esp* : an aimless walk

ram•bler \ˈram-blər\ *n* **1** : a person who rambles **2** : any of various climbing roses with large clusters of small often double flowers

ram•bunc•tious \ram-ˈbəŋk-shəs\ *adj* : UNRULY

ra•mie \ˈrā-mē, ˈra-\ *n* : a strong lustrous bast fiber from an Asian nettle

ram•i•fi•ca•tion \ˌra-mə-fə-ˈkā-shən\ *n* **1** : the act or process of branching **2** : CONSEQUENCE, OUTGROWTH

ram•i•fy \ˈra-mə-ˌfī\ *vb* **-fied; -fy•ing** : to branch out

ramp \ˈramp\ *n* : a sloping passage or roadway connecting different levels

[1]**ram•page** \ˈram-ˌpāj, (ˌ)ram-ˈpāj\ *vb* **ram•paged; ram•pag•ing** : to rush about wildly

[2]**ram•page** \ˈram-ˌpāj\ *n* : a course of violent or riotous action or behavior — **ram•pa•geous** \ram-ˈpā-jəs\ *adj*

ram•pant \ˈram-pənt\ *adj* : unchecked in growth or spread : RIFE ⟨fear was ∼ in the town⟩ — **ram•pan•cy** \-pən-sē\ *n* — **ram•pant•ly** *adv*

ram•part \ˈram-ˌpärt\ *n* **1** : a protective barrier **2** : a broad embankment raised as a fortification

[1]**ram•rod** \ˈram-ˌräd\ *n* **1** : a rod used to ram a charge into a muzzle-loading gun **2** : a cleaning rod for small arms **3** : BOSS, OVERSEER

[2]**ramrod** *adj* : marked by rigidity or severity

[3]**ramrod** *vb* : to direct, supervise, and control

ram•shack•le \ˈram-ˌsha-kəl\ *adj* : RICKETY, TUMBLEDOWN

ran *past of* RUN

[1]**ranch** \ˈranch\ *n* [MexSp *rancho* small ranch, fr. Sp, camp, hut & Sp dial., small farm, fr. Old Spanish *ranchear* (*se*) to take up quarters, fr. MF (*se*) *ranger* to take up a position, fr. *ranger* to set in a row] **1** : an establishment for the raising and grazing of livestock (as cattle, sheep, or horses) **2** : a large farm devoted to a specialty **3** : RANCH HOUSE 2

[2]**ranch** *vb* : to live or work on a ranch — **ranch•er** *n*

ranch house *n* **1** : the main house on a ranch **2** : a one-story house typically with a low-pitched roof

ran•cho \ˈran-chō, ˈrän-\ *n, pl* **ranchos** : RANCH 1

ran•cid \ˈran-səd\ *adj* **1** : having a rank smell or taste **2** : ROTTEN, SPOILED — **ran•cid•i•ty** \ran-ˈsi-də-tē\ *n*

ran•cor \ˈraŋ-kər\ *n* : bitter deep-seated ill will **syn** antagonism, animosity, antipathy, enmity, hostility — **ran•cor•ous** *adj*

ran•cour *Brit var of* RANCOR

rand \ˈrand, ˈränd, ˈränt\ *n, pl* **rand** — see MONEY table

R & B *abbr* rhythm and blues

R and D *n* : research and development

ran•dom \ˈran-dəm\ *adj* : CHANCE, HAPHAZARD — **ran•dom•ly** *adv* — **ran•dom•ness** *n*

random–access *adj* : allowing access to stored data in any order the user desires

random–access memory *n* : a computer memory that provides the main internal storage for programs and data

ran•dom•ize \ˈran-də-ˌmīz\ *vb* **-ized; -iz•ing** : to select, assign, or arrange in a random way — **ran•dom•i•za•tion** \ˌran-də-mə-ˈzā-shən\ *n*

R and R *abbr* rest and recreation; rest and recuperation

rang *past of* RING

[1]**range** \ˈrānj\ *n* **1** : a series of things in a row **2** : a cooking stove having an oven and a flat top with burners **3** : open land where animals (as livestock) may roam and graze **4** : the act of ranging about **5** : the distance a weapon will shoot or is to be shot **6** : a place where shooting is practiced **7** : the space or extent included, covered, or used : SCOPE **8** : a variation within limits **syn** reach, compass, radius, circle

[2]**range** *vb* **ranged; rang•ing 1** : to set in a row or in proper order **2** : to set in place among others of the same kind **3** : to roam over or through : EXPLORE **4** : to roam at large or freely **5** : to correspond in direction or line **6** : to vary within limits **7** : to find the range of an object by instrument (as radar)

rang•er \ˈrān-jər\ *n* **1** : FOREST RANGER **2** : a member of a body of troops who range over a region **3** : an expert in close-range fighting and raiding tactics

rangy \ˈrān-jē\ *adj* **rang•i•er; -est** : being long-limbed and slender — **rang•i•ness** \ˈrān-jē-nəs\ *n*

ra•ni *or* **ra•nee** \rä-ˈnē, ˈrä-ˌnē\ *n* : a raja's wife

[1]**rank** \ˈraŋk\ *adj* **1** : strong and vigorous and usu. coarse in growth ⟨∼ weeds⟩ **2** : unpleasantly strong-smelling — **rank•ly** *adv* — **rank•ness** *n*

[2]**rank** *n* **1** : ROW **2** : a line of soldiers ranged side by side **3** *pl* : the body of enlisted personnel ⟨rose from the ∼*s*⟩ **4** : an orderly arrangement **5** : CLASS, DIVISION **6** : a grade of official standing (as in an army) **7** : position in a group **8** : superior position

[3]**rank** *vb* **1** : to arrange in lines or in regular formation **2** : RATE **3** : to rate above (as in official standing) **4** : to take or have a relative position

rank and file *n* : the general membership of a body as contrasted with its leaders

rank•ing \ˈraŋ-kiŋ\ *adj* **1** : having a high position : FOREMOST **2** : being next to the chairman in seniority

ran•kle \ˈraŋ-kəl\ *vb* **ran•kled; ran•kling** [ME *ranclen* to fester, fr. MF *rancler*, fr. OF *draoncler, raoncler*, fr. *draoncle, raoncle* festering sore, fr. (assumed) VL *dracunculus*, fr. L, dim. of *draco* serpent] : to cause anger, irritation, or bitterness

ran•sack \ˈran-ˌsak\ *vb* : to search thoroughly; *esp* : to search through and rob

[1]**ran•som** \ˈran-səm\ *n* [ME *ransoun*, fr. OF *rançon*, fr. L *redemption-, redemptio* act of buying back, fr. *redimere* to buy back, redeem] **1** : something paid or demanded for the freedom of a captive **2** : the act of ransoming

[2]**ransom** *vb* : to free from captivity or punishment by paying a price — **ran•som•er** *n*

rant \ˈrant\ *vb* **1 :** to talk loudly and wildly **2 :** to scold violently — **rant•er** *n* — **rant•ing•ly** *adv*

[1]rap \ˈrap\ *n* **1 :** a sharp blow **2 :** a sharp rebuke **3 :** a negative often undeserved reputation ⟨a bum ~⟩ **4 :** responsibility for or consequences of an action ⟨take the ~⟩

[2]rap *vb* **rapped; rap•ping 1 :** to strike sharply **:** KNOCK **2 :** to utter sharply **3 :** to criticize sharply

[3]rap *vb* **rapped; rap•ping 1 :** to talk freely and frankly **2 :** to perform rap music

[4]rap *n* **1 :** TALK, CONVERSATION **2 :** a rhythmic chanting of usu. rhymed couplets to a musical accompaniment; *also* **:** a piece so performed

ra•pa•cious \rə-ˈpā-shəs\ *adj* **1 :** excessively greedy or covetous **2 :** living on prey **3 :** RAVENOUS 2 — **ra•pa•cious•ly** *adv* — **ra•pa•cious•ness** *n* — **ra•pac•i•ty** \-ˈpa-sə-tē\ *n*

[1]rape \ˈrāp\ *n* **:** a European herb related to the mustards that is grown as a forage crop and for its seeds (**rape•seed** \-ˌsēd\)

[2]rape *vb* **raped; rap•ing :** to commit rape on — **rap•er** *n* — **rap•ist** \ˈrā-pist\ *n*

[3]rape *n* **1 :** a carrying away by force **2 :** sexual intercourse by a man with a woman without her consent and chiefly by force or deception; *also* **:** unlawful sexual intercourse of any kind by force or threat

[1]rap•id \ˈra-pəd\ *adj* [L *rapidus* strong-flowing, rapid, fr. *rapere* to seize, carry away] **:** very fast **:** SWIFT **syn** fleet, quick, speedy — **ra•pid•i•ty** \rə-ˈpi-də-tē\ *n* — **rap•id•ly** *adv*

[2]rapid *n* **:** a place in a stream where the current flows very fast usu. over obstructions — usu. used in pl.

rapid eye movement *n* **:** rapid conjugate movement of the eyes associated with REM sleep

rapid transit *n* **:** fast passenger transportation (as by subway) in cities

ra•pi•er \ˈrā-pē-ər\ *n* **:** a straight 2-edged sword with a narrow pointed blade

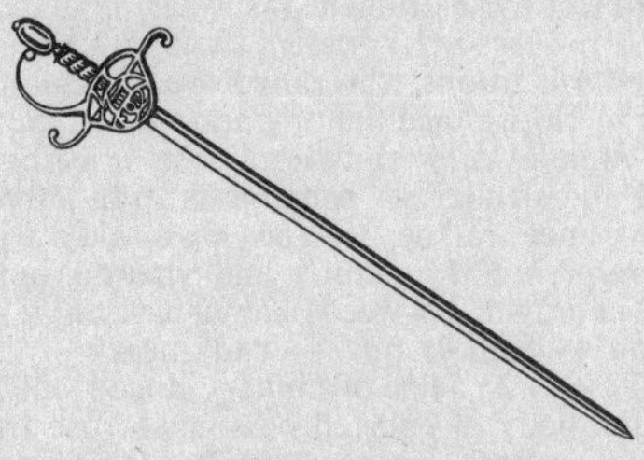

rapier

rap•ine \ˈra-pən, -pīn\ *n* **:** PILLAGE, PLUNDER

rap•pel \rə-ˈpel, ra-\ *vb* **-pelled; -pel•ling :** to descend (as from a cliff) by sliding down a rope

rap•pen \ˈrä-pən\ *n, pl* **rappen :** the centime of Switzerland

rap•port \ra-ˈpōr\ *n* **:** RELATION; *esp* **:** relation characterized by harmony

rap•proche•ment \ˌra-ˌprōsh-ˈmä^n, ra-ˈprōsh-ˌmä^n\ *n* **:** the establishment of or a state of having cordial relations

rap•scal•lion \rap-ˈskal-yən\ *n* **:** RASCAL, SCAMP

rapt \ˈrapt\ *adj* **1 :** carried away with emotion **2 :** ABSORBED, ENGROSSED — **rapt•ly** \ˈrapt-lē\ *adv* — **rapt•ness** *n*

rap•ture \ˈrap-chər\ *n* **:** spiritual or emotional ecstasy — **rap•tur•ous** \-chə-rəs\ *adj* — **rap•tur•ous•ly** *adv*

rapture of the deep : NITROGEN NARCOSIS

ra•ra avis \ˌrar-ə-ˈā-vəs\ *n* [L, rare bird] **:** a rare person or thing **:** RARITY

[1]rare \ˈrar\ *adj* **rar•er; rar•est 1 :** not thick or dense **:** THIN ⟨~ air⟩ **2 :** unusually fine **:** EXCELLENT, SPLENDID **3 :** seldom met with — **rare•ly** *adv* — **rare•ness** *n* — **rar•i•ty** \ˈrar-ə-tē\ *n*

[2]rare *adj* **rar•er; rar•est :** cooked so that the inside is still red ⟨~ beef⟩

rare•bit \ˈrar-bət\ *n* **:** WELSH RABBIT

rar•efac•tion \ˌrar-ə-ˈfak-shən\ *n* **1 :** the action or process of rarefying **2 :** the state of being rarefied

rar•e•fy *also* **rar•i•fy** \ˈrar-ə-ˌfī\ *vb* **-fied; -fy•ing :** to make or become rare, thin, or less dense

rar•ing \ˈrar-ən, -iŋ\ *adj* **:** full of enthusiasm or eagerness ⟨~ to go⟩

ras•cal \ˈras-kəl\ *n* **1 :** a mean or dishonest person **2 :** a mischievous person — **ras•cal•i•ty** \ras-ˈka-lə-tē\ *n* — **ras•cal•ly** \ˈras-kə-lē\ *adj*

[1]rash \ˈrash\ *adj* **:** having or showing little regard for consequences **:** too hasty in decision, action, or speech **:** RECKLESS **syn** daring, foolhardy, adventurous, venturesome — **rash•ly** *adv* — **rash•ness** *n*

[2]rash *n* **:** an eruption on the body

rash•er \ˈra-shər\ *n* **:** a thin slice of bacon or ham broiled or fried; *also* **:** a portion consisting of several such slices

[1]rasp \ˈrasp\ *vb* **1 :** to rub with or as if with a rough file **2 :** to grate harshly on (as one's nerves) **3 :** to speak in a grating tone

[2]rasp *n* **:** a coarse file with cutting points instead of ridges

rasp•ber•ry \ˈraz-ˌber-ē, -bə-rē\ *n* **1 :** any of various edible usu. black or red berries produced by some brambles; *also* **:** such a bramble **2 :** a sound of contempt made by protruding the tongue through the lips and expelling air forcibly

[1]rat \ˈrat\ *n* **1 :** any of numerous rodents larger than the related mice **2 :** a contemptible person; *esp* **:** one that betrays friends or associates

[2]rat *vb* **rat•ted; rat•ting 1 :** to betray or inform on one's associates **2 :** to hunt or catch rats

rat cheese *n* **:** CHEDDAR

ratch•et \ˈra-chət\ *n* **:** a device that consists of a bar or wheel having slanted teeth into which a pawl drops so as to allow motion in only one direction

ratchet wheel *n* **:** a toothed wheel held in position or turned by a pawl

[1]rate \ˈrāt\ *vb* **rat•ed; rat•ing :** to scold violently

[2]rate *n* **1 :** quantity, amount, or degree measured by some standard **2 :** an amount (as of payment) measured by its relation to some other amount (as of time) **3 :** a charge, payment, or price fixed according to a ratio, scale, or standard ⟨tax ~⟩ **4 :** RANK, CLASS

[3]rate *vb* **rat•ed; rat•ing 1 :** ESTIMATE **2 :** CONSIDER, REGARD **3 :** to settle the relative rank or class of **4 :** to be classed **:** RANK **5 :** to have a right to **:** DESERVE **6 :** to be of consequence — **rat•er** *n*

rath•er \ˈra-t͟hər, ˈrä-, ˈrə-\ *adv* [ME, fr. OE *hrathor,* compar. of *hrathe* quickly] **1 :** more properly **2 :** PREFERABLY **3 :** more correctly speaking **4 :** to the contrary **:** INSTEAD **5 :** SOMEWHAT

raths•kel•ler \ˈrät-ˌske-lər, ˈrat-\ *n* [obs. G (now *Ratskeller*), city-hall basement restaurant, fr. *Rat* council + *Keller* cellar] **:** a usu. basement tavern or restaurant

rat•i•fy \ˈra-tə-ˌfī\ *vb* **-fied; -fy•ing :** to approve and accept formally — **rat•i•fi•ca•tion** \ˌra-tə-fə-ˈkā-shən\ *n*

rat•ing \ˈrā-tiŋ\ *n* **1 :** a classification according to grade **:** RANK **2** *Brit* **:** a naval enlisted man **3 :** an estimate of the credit standing and business responsibility of a person or firm

ra•tio \ˈrā-shō, -shē-ō\ *n, pl* **ra•tios 1 :** the indicated quotient of two numbers or mathematical expressions **2 :** the relationship in number, quantity, or degree between two or more things

ra•ti•o•ci•na•tion \ˌra-tē-ˌōs-ᵊn-ˈā-shən, -shē-, -ˌäs-\ *n* **:** exact thinking **:** REASONING — **ra•ti•o•ci•nate** \-ˈōs-ᵊn-ˌāt, -ˈäs-\ *vb* — **ra•ti•o•ci•na•tive** \-ˈōs-ᵊn-ˌā-tiv, -ˈäs-\ *adj* — **ra•ti•o•ci•na•tor** \-ˈōs-ᵊn-ˌā-tər, -ˈäs-\ *n*

[1]ra•tion \ˈra-shən, ˈrā-\ *n* **1 :** a food allowance for one day **2** : FOOD, PROVISIONS, DIET — usu. used in pl. **3** : SHARE, ALLOTMENT

[2]**ration** *vb* **1** : to supply with or allot as rations **2** : to use or allot sparingly **syn** apportion, portion, prorate, parcel

[1]**ra•tio•nal** \ˈra-shə-nəl\ *adj* **1** : having reason or understanding **2** : of or relating to reason **3** : relating to, consisting of, or being one or more rational numbers — **ra•tio•nal•ly** *adv*

[2]**rational** *n* : RATIONAL NUMBER

ra•tio•nale \ˌra-shə-ˈnal\ *n* **1** : an explanation of principles controlling belief or practice **2** : an underlying reason

ra•tio•nal•ise *Brit var of* RATIONALIZE

ra•tio•nal•ism \ˈra-shə-nə-ˌli-zəm\ *n* : the practice of guiding one's actions and opinions solely by what seems reasonable — **ra•tio•nal•ist** \-list\ *n* — **rationalist** *or* **ra•tio•nal•is•tic** \ˌra-shə-nə-ˈlis-tik\ *adj*

ra•tio•nal•i•ty \ˌra-shə-ˈna-lə-tē\ *n, pl* **-ties** : the quality or state of being rational

ra•tio•nal•ize \ˈra-shə-nə-ˌlīz\ *vb* **-ized; -iz•ing 1** : to make (something irrational) appear rational or reasonable **2** : to provide a natural explanation of (as a myth) **3** : to justify (as one's behavior or weaknesses) esp. to oneself **4** : to find plausible but untrue reasons for conduct — **ra•tio•nal•i•za•tion** \ˌra-shə-nə-lə-ˈzā-shən\ *n*

rational number *n* : an integer or the quotient of an integer divided by a nonzero integer

rat race *n* : strenuous, tiresome, and usu. competitive activity or rush

rat•tan \ra-ˈtan, rə-\ *n* : a cane or switch made from one of the long stems of an Asian climbing palm; *also* : this palm

rat•ter \ˈra-tər\ *n* : a rat-catching dog or cat

[1]**rat•tle** \ˈrat-ᵊl\ *vb* **rat•tled; rat•tling 1** : to make or cause to make a series of clattering sounds **2** : to move with a clattering sound **3** : to say or do in a brisk lively fashion ⟨~ off the answers⟩ **4** : CONFUSE, UPSET ⟨~ a witness⟩

[2]**rattle** *n* **1** : a toy that produces a rattle when shaken **2** : a series of clattering and knocking sounds **3** : a rattling organ at the end of a rattlesnake's tail

rat•tler \ˈrat-lər\ *n* : RATTLESNAKE

rat•tle•snake \ˈrat-ᵊl-ˌsnāk\ *n* : any of various American pit vipers with a rattle at the end of the tail

rattlesnake

rat•tle•trap \ˈrat-ᵊl-ˌtrap\ *n* : something (as an old car) rickety and full of rattles

rat•tling \ˈrat-liŋ\ *adj* **1** : LIVELY, BRISK **2** : FIRST-RATE, SPLENDID

rat•trap \ˈrat-ˌtrap\ *n* **1** : a trap for rats **2** : a dilapidated building

rat•ty \ˈra-tē\ *adj* **rat•ti•er; -est 1** : infested with rats **2** : of, relating to, or suggestive of rats **3** : SHABBY

rau•cous \ˈrò-kəs\ *adj* **1** : HARSH, HOARSE, STRIDENT **2** : boisterously disorderly — **rau•cous•ly** *adv* — **rau•cous•ness** *n*

raun•chy \ˈròn-chē, ˈrän-\ *adj* **raun•chi•er; -est 1** : SLOVENLY, DIRTY **2** : OBSCENE, SMUTTY — **raun•chi•ness** \-chē-nəs\ *n*

[1]**rav•age** \ˈra-vij\ *n* [F] : an act or result of ravaging : DEVASTATION

[2]**ravage** *vb* **rav•aged; rav•ag•ing** : to lay waste : DEVASTATE — **rav•ag•er** *n*

[1]**rave** \ˈrāv\ *vb* **raved; rav•ing** [ME *raven*] **1** : to talk wildly in or as if in delirium : STORM, RAGE **2** : to talk with extreme enthusiasm

[2]**rave** *n* **1** : an act or instance of raving **2** : an extravagantly favorable criticism

[1]**rav•el** \ˈra-vəl\ *vb* **-eled** *or* **-elled; -el•ing** *or* **-el•ling 1** : UNRAVEL, UNTWIST **2** : TANGLE, CONFUSE

[2]**ravel** *n* **1** : something tangled **2** : something raveled out; *esp* : a loose thread

[1]**ra•ven** \ˈrā-vən\ *n* : a large black bird related to the crow

[2]**raven** *adj* : black and glossy like a raven's feathers

[3]**rav•en** \ˈra-vən\ *vb* **rav•ened; rav•en•ing 1** : to devour greedily **2** : DESPOIL, PLUNDER **3** : PREY

rav•en•ous \ˈra-və-nəs\ *adj* **1** : RAPACIOUS, VORACIOUS **2** : eager for food : very hungry — **rav•en•ous•ly** *adv* — **rav•en•ous•ness** *n*

ra•vine \rə-ˈvēn\ *n* : a small narrow steep-sided valley larger than a gully

rav•i•o•li \ˌra-vē-ˈō-lē\ *n* [It, fr. It dial., pl. of *raviolo*, lit., little turnip, dim. of *rava* turnip, fr. L *rapa*] : small cases of dough with a savory filling (as of meat or cheese)

rav•ish \ˈra-vish\ *vb* **1** : to seize and take away by violence **2** : to overcome with emotion and esp. with joy or delight **3** : RAPE — **rav•ish•er** *n* — **rav•ish•ment** *n*

[1]**raw** \ˈrò\ *adj* **raw•er** \ˈrò-ər\; **raw•est** \ˈrò-əst\ **1** : not cooked **2** : changed little from the original form : not processed ⟨~ materials⟩ **3** : having the surface abraded or irritated ⟨a ~ sore⟩ **4** : not trained or experienced ⟨~ recruits⟩ **5** : VULGAR, COARSE **6** : disagreeably cold and damp ⟨a ~ day⟩ **7** : UNFAIR ⟨~ deal⟩ — **raw•ness** *n*

[2]**raw** *n* : a raw place or state; *esp* : NUDITY

raw•boned \ˈrò-ˌbōnd\ *adj* **1** : LEAN, GAUNT **2** : having a heavy frame that seems to have little flesh

raw•hide \ˈrò-ˌhīd\ *n* : the untanned skin of cattle; *also* : a whip made of this

[1]**ray** \ˈrā\ *n* : any of an order of large flat cartilaginous fishes that have the eyes on the upper surface and the hind end of the body slender and taillike

[2]**ray** *n* [ME, fr. MF *rai*, fr. L *radius* rod, ray] **1** : any of the lines of light that appear to radiate from a bright object **2** : a thin beam of radiant energy (as light) **3** : light from a beam **4** : a thin line like a beam of light **5** : an animal or plant structure resembling a ray **6** : a tiny bit : PARTICLE ⟨a ~ of hope⟩

ray•on \ˈrā-ˌän\ *n* : a fiber made from cellulose; *also* : a yarn, thread, or fabric made from such fibers

raze \ˈrāz\ *vb* **razed; raz•ing 1** : to scrape, cut, or shave off **2** : to destroy to the ground : DEMOLISH

ra•zor \ˈrā-zər\ *n* : a sharp cutting instrument used to shave off hair

ra•zor–backed \ˈrā-zər-ˌbakt\ *or* **ra•zor•back** \-ˌbak\ *adj* : having a sharp narrow back ⟨~ horse⟩

razor clam *n* : any of a family of marine bivalve mollusks having a long narrow curved thin shell

[1]**razz** \ˈraz\ *n* : RASPBERRY 2

[2]**razz** *vb* : RIDICULE, TEASE

Rb *symbol* rubidium

RBC *abbr* red blood cells; red blood count

RBI \ˌär-(ˌ)bē-ˈī, ˈri-bē\ *n, pl* **RBIs** *or* **RBI** [*r*un *b*atted *i*n] : a run in baseball that is driven in by a batter

RC *abbr* **1** Red Cross **2** Roman Catholic

RCAF *abbr* Royal Canadian Air Force

RCMP *abbr* Royal Canadian Mounted Police

RCN *abbr* Royal Canadian Navy

rct *abbr* recruit

rd *abbr* **1** road **2** rod **3** round

RD *abbr* rural delivery

RDA *abbr* recommended daily allowance; recommended dietary allowance

re \ˈrā, ˈrē\ *prep* : with regard to

Re *symbol* rhenium

re- \rē, ˌrē, ˈrē\ *prefix* **1** : again : for a second time **2** : anew : in a new or different form **3** : back : backward

reabsorb
reacquire
reactivate
reactivation
readdress
readjust
readjustment
readmission
readmit
reaffirm
reaffirmation
realign
realignment
reallocate
reallocation
reanalysis
reanalyze
reanimate
reanimation
reannex
reannexation
reappear
reappearance
reapplication
reapply
reappoint
reappointment
reapportion
reapportionment
reappraisal
reappraise
rearm
rearmament
rearouse
rearrange
rearrangement
rearrest
reascend
reassemble
reassembly
reassert
reassess
reassessment
reassign
reassignment
reassume
reattach
reattachment
reattain
reattempt
reauthorization
reauthorize
reawaken
rebaptism
rebaptize
rebid
rebind
reboil
rebroadcast
reburial
rebury
recalculate
recalculation
rechannel
recharge
rechargeable
recharter
recheck
rechristen
reclassification
reclassify
recoin
recolonization
recolonize
recolor
recombine
recommence
recommission
recommit
recompile
recompose
recomputation
recompute
reconceive
reconcentrate
reconception
recondensation
recondense
reconfirm
reconfirmation
reconnect
reconquer
reconquest
reconsecrate
reconsecration
recontact
recontaminate
recontamination
reconvene
reconvert
recook
recopy
recross
recrystallize
recut
redecorate
redecoration
rededicate
rededication
redefine
redefinition
redeposit
redesign
redetermination
redetermine
redevelop
redevelopment
redirect
rediscount
rediscover
rediscovery
redissolve
redistill
redistillation
redraft
redraw
reecho
reedit
reelect
reelection
reemerge
reemergence
reemphasis
reemphasize
reemploy
reemployment
reenact
reenactment
reenergize
reenlist
reenlistment
reenter
reequip
reestablish
reestablishment
reevaluate
reevaluation
reexamination
reexamine
reexport
refashion
refight
refigure
refinish
refit
refix
refloat
refold
reforge
reformulate
reformulation
refortify
refound
refreeze
refuel
refurnish
regain
regather
regild
regive
regrade
regrind
regrow
regrowth
rehandle
rehear
reheat
rehouse
reimpose
reimposition
reincorporate
reinsert
reinsertion
reintegrate
reinterpret
reinterpretation
reintroduce
reintroduction
reinvention
reinvest
reinvestment
reinvigorate
reinvigoration
reissue
rejudge
rekindle
reknit
relaunch
relearn
relight
reline
reload
remanufacture
remap
remarriage
remarry
rematch
remelt
remigration
remix
remold
rename
renegotiate
renegotiation
renominate
renomination
renumber
reoccupy
reoccur
reopen
reorder
reorganization
reorganize
reorient
reorientation
repack
repaint
repass
repeople
rephotograph
rephrase
replant
repopulate
reprice
reprocess
reprogram
republication
republish
repurchase
reradiate
reread
rereading
rerecord
reroute
reschedule
rescore
rescreen
reseal
reseed
resell
reset
resettle
resettlement
resew
reshow
resocialization
resow
respell
restaff
restart
restate
restatement
restock
restrengthen
restructure
restudy
restuff
restyle
resubmit
resummon
resupply
resurface
resurvey
resynthesis
resynthesize
retaste
retell
retest
retool
retrain
retransmission
retransmit
retrial
reunification
reunify
reunite
reusable
reuse
revaluate
revaluation
revalue
revisit
rewarm
rewash
reweave

rewed **rewire**
reweigh **rezone**

[1]reach \ˈrēch\ *vb* **1** : to stretch out **2** : to touch or attempt to touch or seize **3** : to extend to **4** : to communicate with **5** : to arrive at **syn** gain, realize, achieve, attain — **reach•able** *adj* — **reach•er** *n*

[2]reach *n* **1** : an unbroken stretch of a river **2** : the act of reaching **3** : a reachable distance; *also* : ability to reach **4** : a range of knowledge or comprehension

re•act \rē-ˈakt\ *vb* **1** : to exert a return or counteracting influence **2** : to have or show a reaction **3** : to act in opposition to a force or influence **4** : to move or tend in a reverse direction **5** : to undergo chemical reaction

re•ac•tant \rē-ˈak-tənt\ *n* : a chemically reacting substance

re•ac•tion \rē-ˈak-shən\ *n* **1** : the act or process of reacting **2** : a counter tendency; *esp* : a tendency toward a former esp. outmoded political or social order or policy **3** : bodily, mental, or emotional response to a stimulus **4** : chemical change **5** : a process involving change in atomic nuclei

re•ac•tion•ary \rē-ˈak-shə-ˌner-ē\ *adj* : relating to, marked by, or favoring esp. political reaction — **reactionary** *n*

re•ac•tive \rē-ˈak-tiv\ *adj* : reacting or tending to react

re•ac•tor \rē-ˈak-tər\ *n* **1** : one that reacts **2** : a device for the controlled release of nuclear energy

[1]read \ˈrēd\ *vb* **read** \ˈred\; **read•ing** **1** : to understand language by interpreting written symbols for speech sounds **2** : to utter aloud written or printed words **3** : to learn by observing ⟨~ nature's signs⟩ **4** : to study by a course of reading ⟨~*s* law⟩ **5** : to discover the meaning of ⟨~ the clues⟩ **6** : to recognize or interpret as if by reading **7** : to attribute (a meaning) to something ⟨~ guilt in his manner⟩ **8** : INDICATE ⟨thermometer ~*s* 10°⟩ **9** : to consist in phrasing or meaning ⟨the two versions ~ differently⟩ — **read•abil•i•ty** \ˌrē-də-ˈbi-lə-tē\ *n* — **read•able** \ˈrē-də-bəl\ *adj* — **read•ably** \-blē\ *adv* — **read•er** *n*

[2]read \ˈred\ *adj* : informed by reading ⟨widely ~⟩

read•er•ship \ˈrē-dər-ˌship\ *n* : the mass or a particular group of readers

read•ing *n* **1** : something read or for reading **2** : a particular version **3** : data indicated by an instrument ⟨thermometer ~⟩ **4** : a particular interpretation (as of a law) **5** : a particular performance (as of a musical work) **6** : an indication of a certain state of affairs

read–only memory *n* : a computer memory that contains special-purpose information (as a program) which cannot be altered

read•out \ˈrēd-ˌau̇t\ *n* : the process of removing information from an automatic device (as a computer) and displaying it in an understandable form; *also* : the information removed from such a device

read out *vb* **1** : to read aloud **2** : to expel from an organization

[1]ready \ˈre-dē\ *adj* **read•i•er; -est** **1** : prepared for use or action **2** : likely to do something indicated; *also* : willingly disposed : INCLINED **3** : spontaneously prompt ⟨her ~ wit⟩ **4** : immediately available ⟨~ cash⟩ — **read•i•ly** \ˈre-də-lē\ *adv* — **read•i•ness** \-dē-nəs\ *n* — **at the ready** : ready for immediate use

[2]ready *vb* **read•ied; ready•ing** : to make ready : PREPARE

ready–made \ˌre-dē-ˈmād\ *adj* : already made up for general sale : not specially made — **ready–made** *n*

ready room *n* : a room in which pilots are briefed and await orders

re•agent \rē-ˈā-jənt\ *n* : a substance that takes part in or brings about a particular chemical reaction

[1]re•al \ˈrēl\ *adj* [ME, real, relating to things (in law), fr. MF, fr. ML & LL; ML *realis* relating to things (in law), fr. LL, real, fr. L *res* thing, fact] **1** : of or relating to fixed or immovable things (as land) ⟨~ property⟩ **2** : not artificial : GENUINE; *also* : not imaginary — **re•al•ness** *n* — **for real 1** : in earnest **2** : GENUINE

[2]real *adv* : VERY

[3]re•al \rā-ˈäl\ *n* — see MONEY table

real estate *n* : property in buildings and land

re•al•ism \ˈrē-ə-ˌli-zəm\ *n* **1** : the disposition to face facts and to deal with them practically **2** : true and faithful portrayal of nature and of people in art or literature — **re•al•ist** \-list\ *adj or n* — **re•al•is•tic** \ˌrē-ə-ˈlis-tik\ *adj* — **re•al•is•ti•cal•ly** \-ti-k(ə-)lē\ *adv*

re•al•i•ty \rē-ˈa-lə-tē\ *n, pl* **-ties** **1** : the quality or state of being real **2** : something real **3** : the totality of real things and events

re•al•ize \ˈrē-ə-ˌlīz\ *vb* **-ized; -iz•ing** **1** : to make actual : ACCOMPLISH **2** : to convert into money ⟨~ assets⟩ **3** : OBTAIN, GAIN ⟨~ a profit⟩ **4** : to be aware of : UNDERSTAND — **re•al•iz•able** *adj* — **re•al•i•za•tion** \ˌrē-ə-lə-ˈzā-shən\ *n*

re•al•ly \ˈrē-lē, ˈri-\ *adv* : in truth : in fact : ACTUALLY

realm \ˈrelm\ *n* **1** : KINGDOM **2** : SPHERE, DOMAIN

real number *n* : any of the numbers (as −2, 3, ⅞, .25, π) that are rational or irrational

re•al•po•li•tik \rā-ˈäl-ˌpō-li-ˌtēk\ *n* [G] : politics based on practical and material factors rather than on theoretical or ethical objectives

real time *n* : the actual time during which something takes place — **real–time** *adj*

re•al•ty \ˈrēl-tē\ *n* : REAL ESTATE

[1]ream \ˈrēm\ *n* [ME *reme*, fr. MF *raime*, fr. Ar *rizmah*, lit., bundle] : a quantity of paper that is variously 480, 500, or 516 sheets

[2]ream *vb* : to enlarge, shape, or clear with a reamer

ream•er \ˈrē-mər\ *n* : a tool with cutting edges that is used to enlarge or shape a hole

reap \ˈrēp\ *vb* **1** : to cut or clear with a scythe, sickle, or machine **2** : to gather by or as if by cutting : HARVEST ⟨~ a reward⟩ — **reap•er** *n*

[1]rear \ˈrir\ *vb* **1** : to erect by building **2** : to set or raise upright **3** : to breed and raise for use or market ⟨~ livestock⟩ **4** : BRING UP, FOSTER **5** : to lift or rise up; *esp* : to rise on the hind legs

[2]rear *n* **1** : the unit (as of an army) or area farthest from the enemy **2** : BACK; *also* : the position at the back of something

[3]rear *adj* : being at the back

rear admiral *n* : a commissioned officer in the navy or coast guard ranking next below a vice admiral

[1]rear•ward \ˈrir-wərd\ *adj* **1** : being at or toward the rear **2** : directed toward the rear

[2]rear•ward *also* **rear•wards** \-wərdz\ *adv* : at or toward the rear

reas *abbr* reasonable

[1]rea•son \ˈrēz-ᵊn\ *n* [ME *resoun*, fr. OF *raison*, fr. L *ration-, ratio* reason, computation] **1** : a statement offered in explanation or justification **2** : GROUND, CAUSE **3** : the power to think : INTELLECT **4** : a sane or sound mind **5** : due exercise of the faculty of logical thought

[2]reason *vb* **1** : to talk with another to cause a change of mind **2** : to use the faculty of reason : THINK **3** : to discover or formulate by the use of reason — **rea•son•er** *n* — **rea•son•ing** *n*

rea•son•able \ˈrēz-ᵊn-ə-bəl\ *adj* **1** : being within the bounds of reason : not extreme **2** : INEXPENSIVE **3** : able to reason : RATIONAL — **rea•son•able•ness** *n* — **rea•son•ably** \-blē\ *adv*

re•as•sure \ˌrē-ə-ˈshu̇r\ *vb* **1** : to assure again **2** : to restore confidence to : free from fear — **re•as•sur•ance** \-ˈshu̇r-əns\ *n* — **re•as•sur•ing•ly** *adv*

[1]re•bate \ˈrē-ˌbāt\ *vb* **re•bat•ed; re•bat•ing** : to make or give a rebate

[2]rebate *n* : a return of part of a payment **syn** deduction, abatement, discount

[3]re•bate \ˈra-bət, ˈrē-ˌbāt\ *chiefly Brit var of* RABBET

[1]reb•el \ˈre-bəl\ *adj* [ME, fr. OF *rebelle*, fr. L *rebellis*, fr. *re-* + *bellum* war] : of or relating to rebels

[2]rebel *n* : one that rebels against authority

[3]**re•bel** \ri-ˈbel\ *vb* **re•belled; re•bel•ling 1 :** to resist the authority of one's government **2 :** to act in or show disobedience **3 :** to feel or exhibit anger or revulsion

re•bel•lion \ri-ˈbel-yən\ *n* **:** resistance to authority; *esp* **:** defiance against a government through uprising or revolt

re•bel•lious \-yəs\ *adj* **1 :** given to or engaged in rebellion **2 :** inclined to resist authority — **re•bel•lious•ly** *adv* — **re•bel•lious•ness** *n*

re•birth \ˌrē-ˈbərth\ *n* **1 :** a new or 2d birth **2 :** RENAISSANCE, REVIVAL

re•born \-ˈbȯrn\ *adj* **:** born again **:** REGENERATED, REVIVED

[1]**re•bound** \ˌrē-ˈbau̇nd, ˈrē-ˌbau̇nd\ *vb* **1 :** to spring back on or as if on striking another body **2 :** to recover from a setback or frustration

[2]**re•bound** \ˈrē-ˌbau̇nd\ *n* **1 :** the action of rebounding **2 :** a rebounding ball **3 :** a reaction to setback or frustration

re•buff \ri-ˈbəf\ *vb* **:** to reject or criticize sharply **:** SNUB — **rebuff** *n*

re•build \(ˌ)rē-ˈbild\ *vb* **-built** \-ˈbilt\; **-build•ing 1 :** REPAIR, RECONSTRUCT; *also* **:** REMODEL **2 :** to build again

[1]**re•buke** \ri-ˈbyük\ *vb* **re•buked; re•buk•ing :** to reprimand sharply **:** REPROVE

[2]**rebuke** *n* **:** a sharp reprimand

re•bus \ˈrē-bəs\ *n* [L, by things, abl. pl. of *res* thing] **:** a representation of syllables or words by means of pictures; *also* **:** a riddle composed of such pictures

re•but \ri-ˈbət\ *vb* **re•but•ted; re•but•ting :** to refute esp. formally (as in debate) by evidence and arguments **syn** disprove, controvert, confute — **re•but•ter** *n*

re•but•tal \ri-ˈbət-ᵊl\ *n* **:** the act of rebutting

rec *abbr* **1** receipt **2** record; recording **3** recreation

re•cal•ci•trant \ri-ˈkal-sə-trənt\ *adj* [LL *recalcitrant-, recalcitrans,* prp. of *recalcitrare* to be stubbornly disobedient, fr. L, to kick back, fr. *re-* back, again + *calcitrare* to kick, fr. *calc-, calx* heel] **1 :** stubbornly resisting authority **2 :** resistant to handling or treatment **syn** refractory, headstrong, willful, unruly, ungovernable — **re•cal•ci•trance** \-trəns\ *n*

[1]**re•call** \ri-ˈkȯl\ *vb* **1 :** to call back **2 :** REMEMBER, RECOLLECT **3 :** REVOKE, CANCEL

[2]**re•call** \ri-ˈkȯl, ˈrē-ˌkȯl\ *n* **1 :** a summons to return **2 :** the procedure of removing an official by popular vote **3 :** remembrance of things learned or experienced **4 :** the act of revoking **5 :** a call by a manufacturer for the return of a product that may be defective or contaminated

re•cant \ri-ˈkant\ *vb* **:** to take back (something one has said) publicly **:** make an open confession of error — **re•can•ta•tion** \ˌrē-ˌkan-ˈtā-shən\ *n*

[1]**re•cap** \ˈrē-ˌkap, rē-ˈkap\ *vb* **re•capped; re•cap•ping :** RECAPITULATE — **re•cap** \ˈrē-ˌkap\ *n*

[2]**recap** *vb* **re•capped; re•cap•ping :** RETREAD — **re•cap** \ˈrē-ˌkap\ *n*

re•ca•pit•u•late \ˌrē-kə-ˈpi-chə-ˌlāt\ *vb* **-lat•ed; -lat•ing :** to restate briefly **:** SUMMARIZE — **re•ca•pit•u•la•tion** \-ˌpi-chə-ˈlā-shən\ *n*

re•cap•ture \(ˌ)rē-ˈkap-chər\ *vb* **1 :** to capture again **2 :** to experience again ⟨~ happy times⟩

re•cast \(ˌ)rē-ˈkast\ *vb* **1 :** to cast again **2 :** REVISE, REMODEL ⟨~ a sentence⟩

recd *abbr* received

re•cede \ri-ˈsēd\ *vb* **re•ced•ed; re•ced•ing 1 :** to move back or away **2 :** to slant backward **3 :** DIMINISH, CONTRACT

[1]**re•ceipt** \ri-ˈsēt\ *n* **1 :** RECIPE **2 :** the act of receiving **3 :** something received — usu. used in pl. **4 :** a written acknowledgment of something received

[2]**receipt** *vb* **1 :** to give a receipt for **2 :** to mark as paid

re•ceiv•able \ri-ˈsē-və-bəl\ *adj* **1 :** capable of being received; *esp* **:** acceptable as legal ⟨~ certificates⟩ **2 :** subject to call for payment ⟨notes ~⟩

re•ceive \ri-ˈsēv\ *vb* **re•ceived; re•ceiv•ing 1 :** to take in or accept (as something sent or paid) **:** come into possession of **:** GET **2 :** CONTAIN, HOLD **3 :** to permit to enter **:** GREET, WELCOME **4 :** to be at home to visitors **5 :** to accept as true or authoritative **6 :** to be the subject of **:** UNDERGO, EXPERIENCE ⟨~ a shock⟩ **7 :** to change incoming radio waves into sounds or pictures

re•ceiv•er \ri-ˈsē-vər\ *n* **1 :** one that receives **2 :** a person legally appointed to receive and have charge of property or money involved in a lawsuit **3 :** a device for converting electromagnetic waves or signals into audio or visual form ⟨telephone ~⟩

re•ceiv•er•ship \-ˌship\ *n* **1 :** the office or function of a receiver **2 :** the condition of being in the hands of a receiver

re•cen•cy \ˈrēs-ᵊn-sē\ *n* **:** RECENTNESS

re•cent \ˈrēs-ᵊnt\ *adj* **1 :** of the present time or time just past ⟨~ history⟩ **2 :** having lately come into existence **:** NEW, FRESH **3** *cap* **:** HOLOCENE — **re•cent•ly** *adv* — **re•cent•ness** *n*

re•cep•ta•cle \ri-ˈsep-ti-kəl\ *n* **1 :** something used to receive and hold something else **:** CONTAINER **2 :** the enlarged end of a flower stalk upon which the parts of the flower grow **3 :** an electrical fitting containing the live parts of a circuit

re•cep•tion \ri-ˈsep-shən\ *n* **1 :** the act of receiving **2 :** a social gathering at which guests are formally welcomed

re•cep•tion•ist \ri-ˈsep-shə-nist\ *n* **:** a person employed to greet callers

re•cep•tive \ri-ˈsep-tiv\ *adj* **:** able or inclined to receive; *esp* **:** open and responsive to ideas, impressions, or suggestions — **re•cep•tive•ly** *adv* — **re•cep•tive•ness** *n* — **re•cep•tiv•i•ty** \ˌrē-ˌsep-ˈti-və-tē\ *n*

re•cep•tor \ri-ˈsep-tər\ *n* **1 :** one that receives; *esp* **:** SENSE ORGAN **2 :** a chemical group or molecule in the outer cell membrane or in the cell interior that has an affinity for a specific chemical group, molecule, or virus

[1]**re•cess** \ˈrē-ˌses, ri-ˈses\ *n* **1 :** a secret or secluded place **2 :** an indentation in a line or surface (as an alcove in a room) **3 :** a suspension of business or procedure for rest or relaxation

[2]**recess** *vb* **1 :** to put into a recess **2 :** to make a recess in **3 :** to interrupt for a recess **4 :** to take a recess

re•ces•sion \ri-ˈse-shən\ *n* **1 :** the act of receding **:** WITHDRAWAL **2 :** a departing procession (as at the end of a church service) **3 :** a period of reduced economic activity

re•ces•sion•al \ri-ˈse-shə-nəl\ *n* **1 :** a hymn or musical piece at the conclusion of a service or program **2 :** RECESSION 2

[1]**re•ces•sive** \ri-ˈse-siv\ *adj* **1 :** tending to recede **2 :** producing or being a bodily characteristic that is masked or not expressed when a contrasting dominant gene or trait is present ⟨~ genes⟩ ⟨~ traits⟩

[2]**recessive** *n* **:** a recessive characteristic or gene; *also* **:** an individual that has one or more recessive characteristics

re•cher•ché \rə-ˌsher-ˈshā, -ˈsheər-ˌshā\ *adj* [F] **1 :** CHOICE, RARE **2 :** excessively refined

re•cid•i•vism \ri-ˈsi-də-ˌvi-zəm\ *n* **:** a tendency to relapse into a previous condition; *esp* **:** relapse into criminal behavior — **re•cid•i•vist** \-vist\ *n*

recip *abbr* reciprocal; reciprocity

rec•i•pe \ˈre-sə-(ˌ)pē\ *n* [L, take, imperative of *recipere* to take, receive, fr. *re-* back + *capere* to take] **1 :** a set of instructions for making something from various ingredients **2 :** a method of procedure **:** FORMULA

re•cip•i•ent \ri-ˈsi-pē-ənt\ *n* **:** one that receives

[1]**re•cip•ro•cal** \ri-ˈsi-prə-kəl\ *adj* **1 :** inversely related **2 :** MUTUAL, SHARED **3 :** serving to reciprocate **4 :** mutually corresponding — **re•cip•ro•cal•ly** *adv*

[2]**reciprocal** *n* **1 :** something in a reciprocal relationship to another **2 :** one of a pair of numbers (as ⅔, 3/2) whose product is one

re•cip•ro•cate \-ˌkāt\ *vb* **-cat•ed; -cat•ing 1 :** to move backward and forward alternately **2 :** to give and take mutually **3 :** to make a return for something done or given — **re•cip•ro•ca•tion** \-ˌsi-prə-ˈkā-shən\ *n*

rec•i•proc•i•ty \ˌre-sə-ˈprä-sə-tē\ *n, pl* **-ties 1 :** the quality or state of being reciprocal **2 :** mutual exchange of privileges (as trade advantages between countries)

re•cit•al \ri-ˈsīt-ᵊl\ *n* **1 :** an act or instance of reciting : ACCOUNT **2 :** a public reading or recitation ⟨a poetry ~⟩ **3 :** a concert given by a musician, dancer, or dance troupe **4 :** a public exhibition of skill given by music or dance pupils — **re•cit•al•ist** \-ᵊl-ist\ *n*

rec•i•ta•tion \ˌre-sə-ˈtā-shən\ *n* **1 :** RECITING, RECITAL **2 :** delivery before an audience usu. of something memorized **3 :** a classroom exercise in which pupils answer questions on a lesson they have studied

re•cite \ri-ˈsīt\ *vb* **re•cit•ed; re•cit•ing 1 :** to repeat verbatim (as something memorized) **2 :** to recount in some detail : RELATE **3 :** to reply to a teacher's questions on a lesson — **re•cit•er** *n*

reck•less \ˈre-kləs\ *adj* : lacking caution : RASH **syn** hasty, brash, hotheaded, thoughtless — **reck•less•ly** *adv* — **reck•less•ness** *n*

reck•on \ˈre-kən\ *vb* **1 :** COUNT, CALCULATE, COMPUTE **2 :** CONSIDER, REGARD **3** *chiefly dial* **:** THINK, SUPPOSE, GUESS

reck•on•ing *n* **1 :** an act or instance of reckoning **2 :** a settling of accounts ⟨day of ~⟩

re•claim \ri-ˈklām\ *vb* **1 :** to recall from wrong conduct : REFORM **2 :** to change from an undesirable to a desired condition ⟨~ marshy land⟩ **3 :** to obtain from a waste product or by-product **4 :** to demand or obtain the return of — **re•claim•able** *adj* — **rec•la•ma•tion** \ˌre-klə-ˈmā-shən\ *n*

re•cline \ri-ˈklīn\ *vb* **re•clined; re•clin•ing 1 :** to lean or incline backward **2 :** to lie down : REST

re•clin•er \ri-ˈklī-nər\ *n* : a chair with an adjustable back and footrest

re•cluse \ˈre-ˌklüs, ri-ˈklüs\ *n* : a person who leads a secluded or solitary life : HERMIT

rec•og•nise *chiefly Brit var of* RECOGNIZE

rec•og•ni•tion \ˌre-kəg-ˈni-shən\ *n* **1 :** the act of recognizing : the state of being recognized : ACKNOWLEDGMENT **2 :** special notice or attention

re•cog•ni•zance \ri-ˈkäg-nə-zəns\ *n* : a promise recorded before a court or magistrate to do something (as to appear in court or to keep the peace) usu. under penalty of a money forfeiture

rec•og•nize \ˈre-kəg-ˌnīz\ *vb* **-nized; -niz•ing 1 :** to acknowledge (as a speaker in a meeting) as one entitled to be heard at the time **2 :** to acknowledge the existence or the independence of (a country or government) **3 :** to take notice of **4 :** to acknowledge with appreciation **5 :** to acknowledge acquaintance with **6 :** to identify as previously known **7 :** to perceive clearly : REALIZE — **rec•og•niz•able** \ˈre-kəg-ˌnī-zə-bəl\ *adj* — **rec•og•niz•ably** \-blē\ *adv*

[1]**re•coil** \ri-ˈkȯil\ *vb* **1 :** to draw back : RETREAT **2 :** to spring back to or as if to a starting point **syn** shrink, flinch, wince, quail, blanch

[2]**re•coil** \ˈrē-ˌkȯil, ri-ˈkȯil\ *n* : the action of recoiling (as by a gun or spring)

re•coil•less \-ˌkȯil-ləs, -ˈkȯil-\ *adj* : venting expanding propellant gas before recoil is produced ⟨~ gun⟩

rec•ol•lect \ˌre-kə-ˈlekt\ *vb* : to recall to mind : REMEMBER **syn** recall, remind, reminisce, bethink

rec•ol•lec•tion \ˌre-kə-ˈlek-shən\ *n* **1 :** the act or power of recollecting **2 :** something recollected

re•com•bi•nant DNA \(ˌ)rē-ˈkäm-bə-nənt-\ *n* : genetically engineered DNA prepared in vitro by joining together DNA fragments usu. from more than one species of organism

rec•om•mend \ˌre-kə-ˈmend\ *vb* **1 :** to present as deserving of acceptance or trial **2 :** to give in charge : COMMIT **3 :** to make acceptable **4 :** ADVISE, COUNSEL — **rec•om•mend•able** \-ˈmen-də-bəl\ *adj*

rec•om•men•da•tion \ˌre-kə-mən-ˈdā-shən\ *n* **1 :** the act of recommending **2 :** something recommended **3 :** something that recommends

[1]**rec•om•pense** \ˈre-kəm-ˌpens\ *vb* **-pensed; -pens•ing 1 :** to give compensation to : pay for **2 :** to return in kind : REQUITE **syn** reimburse, indemnify, repay, compensate

[2]**recompense** *n* : COMPENSATION

rec•on•cile \ˈre-kən-ˌsīl\ *vb* **-ciled; -cil•ing 1 :** to cause to be friendly or harmonious again **2 :** ADJUST, SETTLE ⟨~ differences⟩ **3 :** to bring to submission or acceptance **syn** conform, accommodate, harmonize, coordinate — **rec•on•cil•able** *adj* — **rec•on•cile•ment** *n* — **rec•on•cil•er** *n*

rec•on•cil•i•a•tion \ˌre-kən-ˌsi-lē-ˈā-shən\ *n* **1 :** the action of reconciling **2 :** the Roman Catholic sacrament of penance

re•con•dite \ˈre-kən-ˌdīt\ *adj* **1 :** hard to understand : PROFOUND, ABSTRUSE **2 :** little known : OBSCURE

re•con•di•tion \ˌrē-kən-ˈdi-shən\ *vb* **1 :** to restore to good condition (as by replacing parts) **2 :** to condition anew

re•con•nais•sance \ri-ˈkä-nə-zəns, -səns\ *n* [F, lit., recognition] : a preliminary survey of an area; *esp* : an exploratory military survey of enemy territory

re•con•noi•ter *or* **re•con•noi•tre** \ˌrē-kə-ˈnȯi-tər, ˌre-\ *vb* **-noi•tered** *or* **-noi•tred; -noi•ter•ing** *or* **-noi•tring** : to make a reconnaissance of : engage in reconnaissance

re•con•sid•er \ˌrē-kən-ˈsi-dər\ *vb* : to consider again with a view to changing or reversing — **re•con•sid•er•a•tion** \-ˌsi-də-ˈrā-shən\ *n*

re•con•sti•tute \ˌrē-ˈkän-stə-ˌtüt, -ˌtyüt\ *vb* : to restore to a former condition by adding water ⟨~ powdered milk⟩

re•con•struct \ˌrē-kən-ˈstrəkt\ *vb* : to construct again : REBUILD

re•con•struc•tion \ˌrē-kən-ˈstrək-shən\ *n* **1 :** the action of reconstructing : the state of being reconstructed **2** *often cap* : the reorganization and reestablishment of the seceded states in the Union after the American Civil War **3 :** something reconstructed

[1]**re•cord** \ri-ˈkȯrd\ *vb* **1 :** to set down in writing **2 :** to register permanently **3 :** INDICATE, READ **4 :** to give evidence of **5 :** to cause (as sound or visual images) to be registered (as on magnetic tape) in a form that permits reproduction

[2]**rec•ord** \ˈre-kərd\ *n* **1 :** the act of being recorded **2 :** a written account of proceedings **3 :** known facts about a person; *also* : a collection of items of information (as in a database) treated as a unit **4 :** an attested top performance **5 :** something on which sound or visual images have been recorded

re•cord•er \ri-ˈkȯr-dər\ *n* **1 :** a judge in some city courts **2 :** one who records transactions officially **3 :** a recording device **4 :** a wind instrument with a whistle mouthpiece and eight fingerholes

re•cord•ing *n* : RECORD 5

re•cord•ist \ri-ˈkȯr-dist\ *n* : one who records sound esp. on film

[1]**re•count** \ri-ˈkau̇nt\ *vb* : to relate in detail : TELL **syn** recite, rehearse, narrate, describe, state, report

[2]**re•count** \ˈrē-ˌkau̇nt, (ˌ)rē-ˈkau̇nt\ *vb* : to count again

[3]**re•count** \ˈrē-ˌkau̇nt, (ˌ)rē-ˈkau̇nt\ *n* : a second or fresh count

re•coup \ri-ˈküp\ *vb* : to get an equivalent or compensation for : make up for something lost

re•course \ˈrē-ˌkōrs, ri-ˈkōrs\ *n* **1 :** a turning to someone or something for assistance or protection **2 :** a source of aid : RESORT

re•cov•er \ri-ˈkə-vər\ *vb* **-ered; -er•ing 1 :** to get back again : REGAIN, RETRIEVE **2 :** to regain normal health, poise, or status **3 :** to make up for : RECOUP ⟨~*ed* all his losses⟩ **4 :** RECLAIM ⟨~ land from the sea⟩ **5 :** to obtain a legal judgment in one's favor — **re•cov•er•able** *adj* — **re•cov•ery** \-ˈkə-və-rē\ *n*

re–cov•er \ˌrē-ˈkə-vər\ *vb* : to cover again

¹rec•re•ant \ˈre-krē-ənt\ *adj* [ME, fr. MF, fr. prp. of *recroire* to renounce one's cause in a trial by battle, fr. *re-* back + *croire* to believe, fr. L *credere*] **1 :** COWARDLY **2 :** UNFAITHFUL
²recreant *n* **1 :** COWARD **2 :** DESERTER
rec•re•ate \ˈre-krē-ˌāt\ *vb* **-at•ed; -at•ing 1 :** to give new life or freshness to **2 :** to take recreation — **rec•re•ative** \-ˌā-tiv\ *adj*
re–cre•ate \ˌrē-krē-ˈāt\ *vb* **:** to create again — **re–cre•ation** \-ˈā-shən\ *n* — **re–cre•ative** \-ˈā-tiv\ *adj*
rec•re•ation \ˌre-krē-ˈā-shən\ *n* **:** a refreshing of strength or spirits after work; *also* **:** a means of refreshment **syn** diversion, entertainment, amusement — **rec•re•ation•al** \-shə-nəl\ *adj*
recreational vehicle *n* **:** a vehicle designed for recreational use (as camping)
re•crim•i•na•tion \ri-ˌkri-mə-ˈnā-shən\ *n* **:** a retaliatory accusation — **re•crim•i•nate** \-ˈkri-mə-nāt\ *vb* — **re•crim•i•na•tory** \-ˈkri-mə-nə-ˌtōr-ē\ *adj*
re•cru•des•cence \ˌrē-krü-ˈdes-ᵊns\ *n* **:** a renewal or breaking out again esp. of something unhealthful or dangerous
¹re•cruit \ri-ˈkrüt\ *vb* **1 :** to form or strengthen with new members ⟨~ an army⟩ **2 :** to enlist as a member of an armed service **3 :** to secure the services of **4 :** to seek to enroll **5 :** to restore or increase in health or vigor ⟨resting to ~ his strength⟩ — **re•cruit•er** *n* — **re•cruit•ment** *n*
²recruit *n* [F *recrute, recrue* fresh growth, new levy of soldiers, fr. MF, fr. *recroistre* to grow up again, fr. L *recrescere*] **:** a newcomer to an activity or field; *esp* **:** a newly enlisted member of the armed forces
rec sec *abbr* recording secretary
rect *abbr* **1** receipt **2** rectangle; rectangular **3** rectified
rec•tal \ˈrekt-ᵊl\ *adj* **:** of or relating to the rectum — **rec•tal•ly** *adv*
rect•an•gle \ˈrek-ˌtaŋ-gəl\ *n* **:** a 4-sided figure with four right angles; *esp* **:** one with adjacent sides of unequal length — **rect•an•gu•lar** \rek-ˈtaŋ-gyə-lər\ *adj*
rec•ti•fi•er \ˈrek-tə-ˌfī-ər\ *n* **:** one that rectifies; *esp* **:** a device for converting alternating current into direct current
rec•ti•fy \ˈrek-tə-ˌfī\ *vb* **-fied; -fy•ing :** to make or set right **:** CORRECT **syn** emend, amend, mend, right — **rec•ti•fi•ca•tion** \ˌrek-tə-fə-ˈkā-shən\ *n*
rec•ti•lin•ear \ˌrek-tə-ˈli-nē-ər\ *adj* **1 :** moving in a straight line ⟨~ motion⟩ **2 :** characterized by straight lines
rec•ti•tude \ˈrek-tə-ˌtüd, -ˌtyüd\ *n* **1 :** moral integrity **2 :** correctness of procedure **syn** virtue, goodness, morality, probity
rec•to \ˈrek-tō\ *n, pl* **rectos :** a right-hand page
rec•tor \ˈrek-tər\ *n* **1 :** a priest or minister in charge of a parish **2 :** the head of a university or school — **rec•to•ri•al** \rek-ˈtōr-ē-əl\ *adj*
rec•to•ry \ˈrek-tə-rē\ *n, pl* **-ries :** the residence of a rector or a parish priest
rec•tum \ˈrek-təm\ *n, pl* **rectums** *or* **rec•ta** \-tə\ [ME, fr. ML, fr. *rectum intestinum,* lit., straight intestine] **:** the last part of the intestine joining the colon and anus
re•cum•bent \ri-ˈkəm-bənt\ *adj* **:** lying down **:** RECLINING
re•cu•per•ate \ri-ˈkü-pə-ˌrāt-, -ˈkyü-\ *vb* **-at•ed; -at•ing :** to get back (as health or strength) **:** RECOVER — **re•cu•per•a•tion** \-ˌkü-pə-ˈrā-shən, -ˌkyü-\ *n* — **re•cu•per•a•tive** \-ˈkü-pə-ˌrā-tiv, -ˈkyü-\ *adj*
re•cur \ri-ˈkər\ *vb* **re•curred; re•cur•ring 1 :** to go or come back in thought or discussion **2 :** to occur or appear again esp. after an interval **:** occur time after time — **re•cur•rence** \-ˈkər-əns\ *n* — **re•cur•rent** \-ənt\ *adj*
re•cy•cle \rē-ˈsī-kəl\ *vb* **1 :** to pass again through a cycle of changes or treatment **2 :** to process (as liquid body waste, glass, or cans) in order to regain materials for human use — **re•cy•cla•ble** \-k(ə)lə-bəl\ *adj* — **recycle** *n*
¹red \ˈred\ *adj* **red•der; red•dest 1 :** of the color red **2 :** endorsing radical social or political change esp. by force **3** *often cap* **:** of or relating to the former U.S.S.R. or its allies — **red•ly** *adv* — **red•ness** *n*
²red *n* **1 :** the color of blood or of the ruby **2 :** a revolutionary in politics **3** *cap* **:** COMMUNIST **4 :** the condition of showing a loss ⟨in the ~⟩
re•dact \ri-ˈdakt\ *vb* **1 :** to put in writing **:** FRAME **2 :** EDIT — **re•dac•tor** \-ˈdak-tər\ *n*
re•dac•tion \-ˈdak-shən\ *n* **1 :** an act or instance of redacting **2 :** EDITION
red alga *n* **:** any of a group of reddish usu. marine algae
red blood cell *n* **:** any of the hemoglobin-containing cells that carry oxygen from the lungs to the tissues and are responsible for the red color of vertebrate blood
red•breast \ˈred-ˌbrest\ *n* **:** ROBIN
red–carpet *adj* **:** marked by ceremonial courtesy
red cedar *n* **:** an American juniper with fragrant close-grained red wood; *also* **:** its wood
red clover *n* **:** a Eurasian clover with globe-shaped heads of reddish flowers widely cultivated for hay and forage
red•coat \ˈred-ˌkōt\ *n* **:** a British soldier esp. during the Revolutionary War
red•den \ˈred-ᵊn\ *vb* **:** to make or become red or reddish **:** FLUSH, BLUSH
red•dish \ˈre-dish\ *adj* **:** tinged with red — **red•dish•ness** *n*
re•deem \ri-ˈdēm\ *vb* [ME *redemen,* modif. of MF *redimer,* fr. L *redimere,* fr. *re-, red-* re- + *emere* to take, buy] **1 :** to recover (property) by discharging an obligation **2 :** to ransom, free, or rescue by paying a price **3 :** to free from the consequences of sin **4 :** to remove the obligation of by payment ⟨the government ~*s* savings bonds⟩; *also* **:** to convert into something of value **5 :** to make good (a promise) by performing **:** FULFILL **6 :** to atone for — **re•deem•able** *adj* — **re•deem•er** *n*
re•demp•tion \ri-ˈdemp-shən\ *n* **:** the act of redeeming **:** the state of being redeemed — **re•demp•tive** \-tiv\ *adj* — **re•demp•to•ry** \-tə-rē\ *adj*
re•de•ploy \ˌrē-di-ˈplȯi\ *vb* **1 :** to transfer from one area or activity to another **2 :** to relocate men or equipment — **re•de•ploy•ment** *n*
red–eye \ˈred-ˌī\ *n* **1 :** cheap whiskey **2 :** a late night or overnight flight
red fox *n* **:** a fox with orange-red to reddish brown fur

red fox

red giant *n* **:** a very large star with a relatively low surface temperature
red–hand•ed \ˈred-ˈhan-dəd\ *adv or adj* **:** in the act of committing a misdeed
red•head \-ˌhed\ *n* **:** a person having red hair — **red•head•ed** \-ˌhe-dəd\ *adj*
red herring *n* **:** a diversion intended to distract attention from the real issue
red–hot \ˈred-ˈhät\ *adj* **1 :** extremely hot; *esp* **:** glowing with heat **2 :** EXCITED, FURIOUS **3 :** very new ⟨~ news⟩
re•dial \ˈrē-ˌdīl\ *n* **:** a telephone function that automat-

ically repeats the dialing of the last number called — **redial** *vb*

re•dis•trib•ute \ˌrē-də-ˈstri-byüt\ *vb* **1** : to alter the distribution of **2** : to spread to other areas — **re•dis•tri•bu•tion** \(ˌ)rē-ˌdis-trə-ˈbyü-shən\ *n*

re•dis•trict \ˌrē-ˈdis-(ˌ)trikt\ *vb* : to organize into new territorial and esp. political divisions

red–let•ter \ˈred-ˌle-tər\ *adj* : of special significance : MEMORABLE

red–light district *n* : a district with many houses of prostitution

re•do \(ˌ)rē-ˈdü\ *vb* : to do over or again; *esp* : REDECORATE

red oak *n* : any of numerous American oaks with leaves usu. having spiny-tipped lobes and acorns that take two years to mature; *also* : the wood of a red oak

red•o•lent \ˈred-ᵊl-ənt\ *adj* **1** : FRAGRANT, AROMATIC **2** : having a specified fragrance ⟨a room ~ of cooked cabbage⟩ **3** : REMINISCENT, SUGGESTIVE — **red•o•lence** \-əns\ *n* — **red•o•lent•ly** *adv*

re•dou•ble \(ˌ)rē-ˈdə-bəl\ *vb* : to make twice as great in size or amount; *also* : INTENSIFY

re•doubt \ri-ˈdau̇t\ *n* [F *redoute*, fr. It *ridotto*, fr. ML *reductus* secret place, fr. L, withdrawn, fr. *reducere* to lead back, fr. *re-* back + *ducere* to lead] : a small usu. temporary fortification

re•doubt•able \ri-ˈdau̇-tə-bəl\ *adj* [ME *redoutable*, fr. MF, fr. *redouter* to dread, fr. *re-* re- + *douter* to doubt] : arousing dread or fear : FORMIDABLE

re•dound \ri-ˈdau̇nd\ *vb* **1** : to have an effect **2** : to become added or transferred : ACCRUE

red pepper *n* : CAYENNE PEPPER

[1]**re•dress** \ri-ˈdres\ *vb* **1** : to set right : REMEDY **2** : COMPENSATE **3** : to remove the cause of (a grievance) **4** : AVENGE

[2]**re•dress** *n* **1** : relief from distress **2** : means or possibility of seeking a remedy **3** : compensation for loss or injury **4** : an act or instance of redressing

red•shift \ˈred-ˈshift\ *n* : displacement of the spectrum of a heavenly body toward longer wavelength

red snapper *n* : any of various reddish fishes including several food fishes

red spider *n* : SPIDER MITE

red squirrel *n* : a common American squirrel with the upper parts chiefly red

red–tailed hawk \ˈred-ˌtāld-\ *n* : a common rodent-eating hawk of eastern No. America with a rather short typically reddish tail

red tape *n* [fr. the red tape formerly used to bind legal documents in England] : official routine or procedure marked by excessive complexity which results in delay or inaction

red tide *n* : seawater discolored by the presence of large numbers of dinoflagellates which produce a toxin that renders infected shellfish poisonous

re•duce \ri-ˈdüs, -ˈdyüs\ *vb* **re•duced; re•duc•ing 1** : LESSEN **2** : to bring to a specified state or condition ⟨*reduced* them to tears⟩ **3** : to put in a lower rank or grade **4** : CONQUER ⟨~ a fort⟩ **5** : to bring into a certain order or classification **6** : to correct (as a fracture) by restoration of displaced parts **7** : to lessen one's weight **syn** decrease, diminish, abate, dwindle, recede — **re•duc•er** *n* — **re•duc•ible** \-ˈdü-sə-bəl, -ˈdyü-\ *adj*

re•duc•tion \ri-ˈdək-shən\ *n* **1** : the act of reducing : the state of being reduced **2** : something made by reducing **3** : the amount taken off in reducing something

re•dun•dan•cy \ri-ˈdən-dən-sē\ *n, pl* **-cies 1** : the quality or state of being redundant : SUPERFLUITY **2** : something redundant or in excess **3** : the use of surplus words

re•dun•dant \-dənt\ *adj* : exceeding what is needed or normal : SUPERFLUOUS; *esp* : using more words than necessary — **re•dun•dant•ly** *adv*

red–winged blackbird \ˈred-ˌwiŋd-\ *n* : a No. American blackbird of which the adult male is black with a patch of bright scarlet on the wings

red•wood \ˈred-ˌwu̇d\ *n* : a tall coniferous timber tree esp. of coastal California; *also* : its durable wood

reed \ˈrēd\ *n* **1** : any of various tall slender grasses of wet areas; *also* : a stem or growth of reed **2** : a musical instrument made from the hollow stem of a reed **3** : an elastic tongue of cane, wood, or metal by which tones are produced in organ pipes and certain other wind instruments — **reedy** *adj*

re•ed•u•cate \(ˌ)rē-ˈe-jə-ˌkāt\ *vb* : to train again; *esp* : to rehabilitate through education — **re•ed•u•ca•tion** *n*

[1]**reef** \ˈrēf\ *n* **1** : a part of a sail taken in or let out in regulating the sail's size **2** : reduction in sail area by reefing

[2]**reef** *vb* : to reduce the area of a sail by rolling or folding part of it

[3]**reef** *n* : a ridge of rocks, sand or coral at or near the surface of the water

reef•er \ˈrē-fər\ *n* : a marijuana cigarette

[1]**reek** \ˈrēk\ *n* : a strong or disagreeable fume or odor

[2]**reek** *vb* **1** : to give off or become permeated with a strong or offensive odor **2** : to give a strong impression of some constituent quality ⟨an excuse that ~*ed* of falsehood⟩ — **reek•er** *n* — **reeky** \ˈrē-kē\ *adj*

[1]**reel** \ˈrēl\ *n* : a revolvable device on which something flexible (as film or tape) is wound; *also* : a quantity of something wound on such a device

[2]**reel** *vb* **1** : to wind on or as if on a reel **2** : to pull or draw (as a fish) by reeling a line — **reel•able** *adj* — **reel•er** *n*

[3]**reel** *vb* **1** : WHIRL; *also* : to be giddy **2** : to waver or fall back (as from a blow) **3** : to walk or move unsteadily

[4]**reel** *n* : a reeling motion

[5]**reel** *n* : a lively Scottish dance or its music

reel off *vb* : to tell or recite rapidly and easily ⟨*reeled off* the right answers⟩

re•en•try \rē-ˈen-trē\ *n* **1** : a second or new entry **2** : the action of reentering the earth's atmosphere from space

reeve \ˈrēv\ *vb* **rove** \ˈrōv\ *or* **reeved; reev•ing** : to pass (as a rope) through a hole in a block or cleat

[1]**ref** \ˈref\ *n* : REFEREE 2

[2]**ref** *abbr* **1** reference **2** referred **3** reformed **4** refunding

re•fec•tion \ri-ˈfek-shən\ *n* **1** : refreshment esp. after hunger or fatigue **2** : food and drink together : REPAST

re•fec•to•ry \ri-ˈfek-tə-rē\ *n, pl* **-ries** : a dining hall (as in a monastery or college)

re•fer \ri-ˈfər\ *vb* **re•ferred; re•fer•ring 1** : to assign to a certain source, cause, or relationship **2** : to direct or send to some person or place (as for information or help) **3** : to submit to someone else for consideration or action **4** : to have recourse (as for information or aid) **5** : to have connection : RELATE **6** : to direct attention : speak of : MENTION, ALLUDE **syn** recur, repair, resort, apply, go, turn — **re•fer•able** \ˈre-fə-rə-bəl, ri-ˈfər-ə-\ *adj*

[1]**ref•er•ee** \ˌre-fə-ˈrē\ *n* **1** : a person to whom an issue esp. in law is referred for investigation or settlement **2** : an umpire in certain games

[2]**referee** *vb* **-eed; -ee•ing** : to act as referee

ref•er•ence \ˈre-frəns, -fə-rəns\ *n* **1** : the act of referring **2** : RELATION, RESPECT **3** : ALLUSION, MENTION **4** : something that refers a reader to another passage or book **5** : consultation esp. for obtaining information ⟨books for ~⟩ **6** : a person of whom inquiries as to character or ability can be made **7** : a written recommendation of a person for employment

ref•er•en•dum \ˌre-fə-ˈren-dəm\ *n, pl* **-da** \-də\ *or* **-dums** : the submitting of legislative measures to the voters for approval or rejection; *also* : a vote on a measure so submitted

ref•er•ent \ˈre-frənt, -fə-rənt\ *n* : one that refers or is referred to; *esp* : the thing a word stands for — **referent** *adj*

re•fer•ral \ri-ˈfər-əl\ *n* **1** : the act or an instance of referring **2** : one that is referred

[1]**re•fill** \ˌrē-ˈfil\ *vb* : to fill again : REPLENISH — **re•fill•able** *adj*

[2]**re•fill** \ˈrē-ˌfil\ *n* : a new or fresh supply of something

re•fi•nance \ˌrē-fə-ˈnans, (ˌ)rē-ˈfī-nans\ *vb* : to renew or reorganize the financing of

re•fine \ri-ˈfīn\ *vb* **re•fined; re•fin•ing 1** : to free from impurities or waste matter **2** : IMPROVE, PERFECT **3** : to free or become free of what is coarse or uncouth **4** : to make improvements by introducing subtle changes — **re•fin•er** *n*

re•fined \ri-ˈfīnd\ *adj* **1** : freed from impurities **2** : CULTURED, CULTIVATED **3** : SUBTLE

re•fine•ment \ri-ˈfīn-mənt\ *n* **1** : the action of refining **2** : the quality or state of being refined **3** : a refined feature or method; *also* : something intended to improve or perfect

re•fin•ery \ri-ˈfī-nə-rē\ *n, pl* **-er•ies** : a building and equipment for refining metals, oil, or sugar

refl *abbr* reflex; reflexive

re•flect \ri-ˈflekt\ *vb* [ME, fr. L *reflectere* to bend back, fr. *re-* back + *flectere* to bend] **1** : to bend or cast back (as light, heat, or sound) **2** : to give back a likeness or image of as a mirror does **3** : to bring as a result ⟨~*ed* credit on him⟩ **4** : to cast reproach or blame ⟨their bad conduct ~*ed* on their training⟩ **5** : PONDER, MEDITATE — **re•flec•tion** \-ˈflek-shən\ *n* — **re•flec•tive** \-tiv\ *adj* — **re•flec•tiv•ity** \(ˌ)rē-ˌflek-ˈti-və-tē\ *n*

re•flec•tor \ri-ˈflek-tər\ *n* : one that reflects; *esp* : a polished surface for reflecting radiation (as light)

[1]**re•flex** \ˈrē-ˌfleks\ *n* **1** : an automatic and usu. inborn response to a stimulus not involving higher mental centers **2** *pl* : the power of acting or responding with enough speed ⟨an athlete with great ~*es*⟩

[2]**reflex** *adj* **1** : bent or directed back **2** : of, relating to, or produced by a reflex — **re•flex•ly** *adv*

re•flex•ion *chiefly Brit var of* REFLECTION

[1]**re•flex•ive** \ri-ˈflek-siv\ *adj* : of or relating to an action directed back upon the doer or the grammatical subject ⟨a ~ verb⟩ ⟨the ~ pronoun *himself*⟩ — **re•flex•ive•ly** *adv* — **re•flex•ive•ness** *n*

[2]**reflexive** *n* : a reflexive verb or pronoun

re•fo•cus \(ˌ)rē-ˈfō-kəs\ *vb* **1** : to focus again **2** : to change the emphasis or direction of ⟨~*ed* her life⟩

re•for•es•ta•tion \ˌrē-ˌfȯr-ə-ˈstā-shən\ *n* : the action of renewing forest cover by planting seeds or young trees — **re•for•est** \rē-ˈfȯr-əst\ *vb*

[1]**re•form** \ri-ˈfȯrm\ *vb* **1** : to make better or improve by removal of faults **2** : to correct or improve one's own character or habits **syn** correct, rectify, emend, remedy, redress, revise — **re•form•able** *adj* — **re•for•ma•tive** \-ˈfȯr-mə-tiv\ *adj*

[2]**reform** *n* : improvement or correction of what is corrupt or defective

re–form \ˌrē-ˈfȯrm\ *vb* : to form again

ref•or•ma•tion \ˌre-fər-ˈmā-shən\ *n* **1** : the act of reforming : the state of being reformed **2** *cap* : a 16th century religious movement marked by the establishment of the Protestant churches

[1]**re•for•ma•to•ry** \ri-ˈfȯr-mə-ˌtȯr-ē\ *adj* : aiming at or tending toward reformation : REFORMATIVE

[2]**reformatory** *n, pl* **-ries** : a penal institution for reforming esp. young or first offenders

re•form•er \ri-ˈfȯr-mər\ *n* **1** : one that works for or urges reform **2** *cap* : a leader of the Protestant Reformation

refr *abbr* refraction

re•fract \ri-ˈfrakt\ *vb* [L *refractus,* pp. of *refringere* to break open, break up, fr. *re-* back + *frangere* to break] : to subject to refraction

re•frac•tion \ri-ˈfrak-shən\ *n* : the bending of a ray (as of light) when it passes obliquely from one medium into another in which its speed is different — **re•frac•tive** \-tiv\ *adj*

re•frac•to•ry \ri-ˈfrak-tə-rē\ *adj* **1** : OBSTINATE, STUBBORN, UNMANAGEABLE **2** : capable of enduring high temperature ⟨~ bricks⟩ **syn** recalcitrant, intractable, ungovernable, unruly, headstrong, willful — **re•frac•to•ri•ness** \ri-ˈfrak-tə-rē-nəs\ *n* — **refractory** *n*

[1]**re•frain** \ri-ˈfrān\ *vb* : to hold oneself back : FORBEAR — **re•frain•ment** *n*

[2]**refrain** *n* : a phrase or verse recurring regularly in a poem or song

re•fresh \ri-ˈfresh\ *vb* **1** : to make or become fresh or fresher **2** : to revive by or as if by renewal of supplies ⟨~ one's memory⟩ **3** : to freshen up **4** : to supply or take refreshment **syn** restore, rejuvenate, renovate, refurbish — **re•fresh•er** *n* — **re•fresh•ing•ly** *adv*

re•fresh•ment \-mənt\ *n* **1** : the act of refreshing : the state of being refreshed **2** : something that refreshes **3** *pl* : a light meal; *also* : assorted light foods

re•fried beans \ˈrē-ˌfrīd-\ *n pl* : beans cooked with seasonings, fried, then mashed and fried again

refrig *abbr* refrigerating; refrigeration

re•frig•er•ate \ri-ˈfri-jə-ˌrāt\ *vb* **-at•ed; -at•ing** : to make cool; *esp* : to chill or freeze (food) for preservation — **re•frig•er•ant** \-jə-rənt\ *adj or n* — **re•frig•er•a•tion** \-ˌfri-jə-ˈrā-shən\ *n* — **re•frig•er•a•tor** \-ˈfri-jə-ˌrā-tər\ *n*

ref•uge \ˈre-ˌfyüj\ *n* **1** : shelter or protection from danger or distress **2** : a place that provides protection

ref•u•gee \ˌre-fyu̇-ˈjē\ *n* : one who flees for safety esp. to a foreign country

re•ful•gence \ri-ˈfu̇l-jəns, -ˈfəl-\ *n* : a radiant or resplendent quality or state — **re•ful•gent** \-jənt\ *adj*

[1]**re•fund** \ri-ˈfənd, ˈrē-ˌfənd\ *vb* : to give or put back (money) : REPAY — **re•fund•able** *adj*

[2]**re•fund** \ˈrē-ˌfənd\ *n* **1** : the act of refunding **2** : a sum refunded

re•fur•bish \ri-ˈfər-bish\ *vb* : to brighten or freshen up : RENOVATE

[1]**re•fuse** \ri-ˈfyüz\ *vb* **re•fused; re•fus•ing 1** : to decline to accept : REJECT **2** : to decline to do, give, or grant : DENY — **re•fus•al** \-ˈfyü-zəl\ *n*

[2]**ref•use** \ˈre-ˌfyüs, -ˌfyüz\ *n* : rejected or worthless matter : RUBBISH, TRASH

re•fute \ri-ˈfyüt\ *vb* **re•fut•ed; re•fut•ing** [L *refutare* to check, suppress, refute] : to prove to be false by argument or evidence — **ref•u•ta•tion** \ˌre-fyu̇-ˈtā-shən\ *n* — **re•fut•er** *n*

[1]**reg** \ˈreg\ *n* : REGULATION

[2]**reg** *abbr* **1** region **2** register; registered; registration **3** regular

re•gal \ˈrē-gəl\ *adj* **1** : of, relating to, or befitting a king : ROYAL **2** : STATELY, SPLENDID — **re•gal•ly** *adv*

re•gale \ri-ˈgāl\ *vb* **re•galed; re•gal•ing 1** : to entertain richly or agreeably **2** : to give pleasure or amusement to **syn** gratify, delight, please, rejoice, gladden

re•ga•lia \ri-ˈgāl-yə\ *n pl* **1** : the emblems, symbols, or paraphernalia of royalty (as the crown and scepter) **2** : the insignia of an office or order **3** : special costume : FINERY

[1]**re•gard** \ri-ˈgärd\ *n* **1** : CONSIDERATION, HEED; *also* : CARE, CONCERN **2** : GAZE, GLANCE, LOOK **3** : RESPECT, ESTEEM **4** *pl* : friendly greetings implying respect and esteem **5** : an aspect to be considered : PARTICULAR — **re•gard•ful** *adj* — **re•gard•less** *adj*

[2]**regard** *vb* **1** : to think of : CONSIDER **2** : to pay attention to **3** : to show respect for : HEED **4** : to hold in high esteem : care for **5** : to look at : gaze upon **6** *archaic* : to relate to

re•gard•ing *prep* : CONCERNING

regardless of \ri-ˈgärd-ləs-\ *prep* : in spite of

re•gat•ta \ri-ˈgä-tə, -ˈga-\ *n* : a boat race or a series of boat races

regd *abbr* registered

re•gen•cy \ˈrē-jən-sē\ *n, pl* **-cies 1** : the office or government of a regent or body of regents **2** : a body of regents **3** : the period during which a regent governs

re•gen•er•a•cy \ri-ˈje-nə-rə-sē\ *n* **:** the state of being regenerated

[1]**re•gen•er•ate** \ri-ˈje-nə-rət\ *adj* **1 :** formed or created again **2 :** spiritually reborn or converted

[2]**re•gen•er•ate** \ri-ˈje-nə-ˌrāt\ *vb* **1 :** to subject to spiritual renewal **2 :** to reform completely **3 :** to replace (a body part) by a new growth of tissue **4 :** to give new life to **:** REVIVE — **re•gen•er•a•tion** \-ˌje-nə-ˈrā-shən\ *n* — **re•gen•er•a•tive** \-ˈje-nə-ˌrā-tiv\ *adj* — **re•gen•er•a•tor** \-ˌrā-tər\ *n*

re•gent \ˈrē-jənt\ *n* **1 :** a person who rules during the childhood, absence, or incapacity of the sovereign **2 :** a member of a governing board (as of a state university) — **regent** *adj*

reg•gae \ˈre-ˌgā\ *n* **:** popular music of Jamaican origin that combines native styles with elements of rock and soul music

reg•i•cide \ˈre-jə-ˌsīd\ *n* **1 :** one who murders a king **2 :** murder of a king

re•gime *also* **ré•gime** \rā-ˈzhēm, ri-\ *n* **1 :** REGIMEN **2 :** a form or system of government **3 :** a government in power; *also* **:** a period of rule

reg•i•men \ˈre-jə-mən\ *n* **1 :** a systematic course of treatment or training ⟨a strict dietary ~⟩ **2 :** GOVERNMENT

[1]**reg•i•ment** \ˈre-jə-mənt\ *n* **:** a military unit consisting usu. of a number of battalions — **reg•i•men•tal** \ˌre-jə-ˈment-təl\ *adj*

[2]**reg•i•ment** \ˈre-jə-ˌment\ *vb* **:** to organize rigidly esp. for regulation or central control; *also* **:** to subject to order or uniformity — **reg•i•men•ta•tion** \ˌre-jə-mən-ˈtā-shən\ *n*

reg•i•men•tals \ˌre-jə-ˈmen-təlz\ *n pl* **1 :** a regimental uniform **2 :** military dress

re•gion \ˈrē-jən\ *n* [ME, fr. MF, fr. L *region-*, *regio*, fr. *regere* to rule] **:** an often indefinitely defined part or area

re•gion•al \ˈrē-jə-nəl\ *adj* **1 :** affecting a particular region **:** LOCALIZED **2 :** of, relating to, characteristic of, or serving a region — **re•gion•al•ly** *adv*

[1]**reg•is•ter** \ˈre-jə-stər\ *n* **1 :** a record of items or details; *also* **:** a book or system for keeping such a record **2 :** the range of a voice or instrument **3 :** a device to regulate ventilation or heating **4 :** an automatic device recording a number or quantity

[2]**register** *vb* **-tered; -ter•ing 1 :** to enter in a register (as in a list of guests) **2 :** to record automatically **3 :** to secure special care for (mail matter) by paying additional postage **4 :** to convey an impression of **:** EXPRESS **5 :** to make or adjust so as to correspond exactly

registered nurse *n* **:** a graduate trained nurse who has been licensed to practice by a state authority after passing qualifying examinations

reg•is•trant \ˈre-jə-strənt\ *n* **:** one that registers or is registered

reg•is•trar \-ˌsträr\ *n* **:** an official recorder or keeper of records (as at an educational institution)

reg•is•tra•tion \ˌre-jə-ˈstrā-shən\ *n* **1 :** the act of registering **2 :** an entry in a register **3 :** the number of persons registered **:** ENROLLMENT **4 :** a document certifying an act of registering

reg•is•try \ˈre-jə-strē\ *n, pl* **-tries 1 :** ENROLLMENT, REGISTRATION **2 :** a place of registration **3 :** an official record book or an entry in one

reg•nant \ˈreg-nənt\ *adj* **1 :** REIGNING **2 :** DOMINANT **3 :** of common or widespread occurrence

[1]**re•gress** \ˈrē-ˌgres\ *n* **1 :** an act or the privilege of going or coming back **2 :** RETROGRESSION

[2]**re•gress** \ri-ˈgres\ *vb* **:** to go or cause to go back or to a lower level — **re•gres•sive** *adj* — **re•gres•sor** \-ˈgre-sər\ *n*

re•gres•sion \ri-ˈgre-shən\ *n* **:** the act or an instance of regressing; *esp* **:** reversion to an earlier mental or behavioral level

[1]**re•gret** \ri-ˈgret\ *vb* **re•gret•ted; re•gret•ting 1 :** to mourn the loss or death of **2 :** to be very sorry for **3 :** to experience regret — **re•gret•ta•ble** \-ˈgre-tə-bəl\ *adj* — **re•gret•ter** *n*

[2]**regret** *n* **1 :** sorrow caused by something beyond one's power to remedy **2 :** an expression of sorrow **3** *pl* **:** a note politely declining an invitation — **re•gret•ful** \-fəl\ *adj* — **re•gret•ful•ly** *adv*

re•gret•ta•bly \-ˈgre-tə-blē\ *adv* **1 :** to a regrettable extent **2 :** it is to be regretted

re•group \(ˌ)rē-ˈgrüp\ *vb* **:** to form into a new grouping

regt *abbr* regiment

[1]**reg•u•lar** \ˈre-gyə-lər\ *adj* [ME *reguler*, fr. MF, fr. LL *regularis* regular, fr L, of a bar, fr. *regula* rule, straightedge, fr. *regere* to keep straight, rule] **1 :** belonging to a religious order **2 :** made, built, or arranged according to a rule, standard, or type; *also* **:** even or symmetrical in form or structure **3 :** ORDERLY, METHODICAL ⟨~ habits⟩; *also* **:** not varying **:** STEADY ⟨a ~ pace⟩ **4 :** made, selected, or conducted according to rule or custom **5 :** properly qualified ⟨not a ~ lawyer⟩ **6 :** conforming to the normal or usual manner or inflection **7 :** of, relating to, or constituting the permanent standing military force of a state — **reg•u•lar•i•ty** \ˌre-gyə-ˈlar-ə-tē\ *n* — **reg•u•lar•ize** \ˈre-gyə-lə-ˌrīz\ *vb* — **reg•u•lar•ly** *adv*

[2]**regular** *n* **1 :** one that is regular (as in attendance) **2 :** a member of the regular clergy **3 :** a soldier in a regular army **4 :** a player on an athletic team who is usu. in the starting lineup

reg•u•late \ˈre-gyə-ˌlāt\ *vb* **-lat•ed; -lat•ing 1 :** to govern or direct according to rule **:** CONTROL **2 :** to bring under the control of law or authority **3 :** to put in good order **4 :** to fix or adjust the time, amount, degree, or rate of — **reg•u•la•tive** \-ˌlā-tiv\ *adj* — **reg•u•la•tor** \-ˌlā-tər\ *n* — **reg•u•la•to•ry** \-lə-ˌtōr-ē\ *adj*

reg•u•la•tion \ˌre-gyə-ˈlā-shən\ *n* **1 :** the act of regulating **:** the state of being regulated **2 :** a rule dealing with details of procedure **3 :** an order issued by an executive authority of a government and having the force of law

re•gur•gi•tate \rē-ˈgər-jə-ˌtāt\ *vb* **-tat•ed; -tat•ing** [ML *regurgitare*, fr. L *re-* re- + LL *gurgitare* to engulf, fr. L *gurgit-*, *gurges* whirlpool] **:** to throw or be thrown back, up, or out ⟨~ food⟩ — **re•gur•gi•ta•tion** \-ˌgər-jə-ˈtā-shən\ *n*

re•hab \ˈrē-ˌhab\ *n* **1 :** REHABILITATION **2 :** a rehabilitated building — **rehab** *vb*

re•ha•bil•i•tate \ˌrē-hə-ˈbi-lə-ˌtāt, ˌrē-ə-\ *vb* **-tat•ed; -tat•ing 1 :** to restore to a former capacity, rank, or right **:** REINSTATE **2 :** to restore to good condition or health — **re•ha•bil•i•ta•tion** \-ˌbi-lə-ˈtā-shən\ *n* — **re•ha•bil•i•ta•tive** \-ˌtā-tiv\ *adj*

re•hash \ˌrē-ˈhash\ *vb* **:** to present again in another form without real change or improvement — **rehash** *n*

re•hear•ing \ˌrē-ˈhir-iŋ\ *n* **:** a second or new hearing by the same tribunal

re•hears•al \ri-ˈhər-səl\ *n* **1 :** something told again **:** RECITAL **2 :** a private performance or practice session preparatory to a public appearance

re•hearse \ri-ˈhərs\ *vb* **re•hearsed; re•hears•ing 1 :** to say again **:** REPEAT **2 :** to recount in order **:** ENUMERATE; *also* **:** RELATE 1 **3 :** to give a rehearsal of **4 :** to train by rehearsal **5 :** to engage in a rehearsal — **re•hears•er** *n*

[1]**reign** \ˈrān\ *n* **1 :** the authority or rule of a sovereign **2 :** the time during which a sovereign rules

[2]**reign** *vb* **1 :** to rule as a sovereign **2 :** to be predominant or prevalent

re•im•burse \ˌrē-əm-ˈbərs\ *vb* **-bursed; -burs•ing** [*re-* re- + obs. E *imburse* to put in the pocket, pay, fr. ML *imbursare* to put into a purse, fr. L *in-* in + ML *bursa* purse, fr. LL, hide of an ox, fr. Gk *byrsa*] **:** to pay back **:** make restitution **:** REPAY **syn** indemnify, recompense, requite, compensate — **re•im•burs•able** *adj* — **re•im•burse•ment** *n*

[1]**rein** \ˈrān\ *n* **1 :** a strap fastened to a bit by which a rider or driver controls an animal **2 :** a restraining influence **:** CHECK **3 :** controlling or guiding power **4 :** complete freedom — usu. used in the phrase *give rein to*

[2]**rein** *vb* **:** to check or direct by reins

re•in•car•na•tion \ˌrē-(ˌ)in-(ˌ)kär-ˈnā-shən\ *n* **:** rebirth of the soul in a new body — **re•in•car•nate** \ˌrē-in-ˈkär-ˌnāt\ *vb*

rein•deer \ˈrān-ˌdir\ *n* [ME *reindere,* fr. ON *hreinn* reindeer + ME *deer*] **:** CARIBOU — used esp. for the Old World caribou

reindeer moss *n* **:** a gray, erect, tufted, and much-branched edible lichen of northern regions that is an important food of reindeer

re•in•fec•tion \ˌrē-in-ˈfek-shən\ *n* **:** infection following another infection of the same type

re•in•force \ˌrē-ən-ˈfōrs\ *vb* **1 :** to strengthen with additional forces ⟨~ our troops⟩ **2 :** to strengthen with new force, aid, material, or support — **re•in•force•ment** *n* — **re•in•forc•er** *n*

re•in•state \ˌrē-in-ˈstāt\ *vb* **-stat•ed; -stat•ing :** to restore to a former position, condition, or capacity — **re•in•state•ment** *n*

re•in•vent \ˌrē-in-ˈvent\ *vb* **1 :** to make as if for the first time something already invented ⟨~ the wheel⟩ **2 :** to remake completely

re•it•er•ate \rē-ˈi-tə-ˌrāt\ *vb* **-at•ed; -at•ing :** to state or do over again or repeatedly — **re•it•er•a•tion** \-ˌi-tə-ˈrā-shən\ *n*

[1]**re•ject** \ri-ˈjekt\ *vb* **1 :** to refuse to accept, consider, use, or submit to **2 :** to refuse to hear, receive, or admit **:** REPEL **3 :** to rebuff or withhold love from **4 :** to throw out esp. as useless or unsatisfactory **5 :** to subject to the immunological process of sloughing off (foreign tissue) — **re•jec•tion** \-ˈjek-shən\ *n*

[2]**re•ject** \ˈrē-ˌjekt\ *n* **:** a rejected person or thing

re•joice \ri-ˈjȯis\ *vb* **re•joiced; re•joic•ing 1 :** to give joy to **:** GLADDEN **2 :** to feel joy or great delight — **re•joic•er** *n*

re•join \(ˌ)rē-ˈjȯin *for 1,* ri- *for 2*\ *vb* **1 :** to join again **2 :** to say in answer (as to a plaintiff's plea in court) **:** REPLY

re•join•der \ri-ˈjoin-dər\ *n* **:** REPLY; *esp* **:** an answer to a reply

re•ju•ve•nate \ri-ˈjü-və-ˌnāt\ *vb* **-nat•ed; -nat•ing :** to make young or youthful again **:** give new vigor to **syn** renew, refresh, renovate, restore — **re•ju•ve•na•tion** \-ˌjü-və-ˈnā-shən\ *n*

rel *abbr* **1** relating; relative **2** religion; religious

[1]**re•lapse** \ri-ˈlaps, ˈrē-ˌlaps\ *n* **1 :** the act or process of backsliding or worsening **2 :** a recurrence of illness after a period of improvement

[2]**re•lapse** \ri-ˈlaps\ *vb* **re•lapsed; re•laps•ing :** to slip or fall back into a former worse state (as of illness)

re•late \ri-ˈlāt\ *vb* **re•lat•ed; re•lat•ing 1 :** to give an account of **:** TELL, NARRATE **2 :** to show or establish logical or causal connection between **3 :** to have relationship or connection **4 :** to have or establish relationship ⟨the way a child ~*s* to a teacher⟩ **5 :** to respond favorably — **re•lat•able** *adj* — **re•lat•er** *or* **re•la•tor** \-ˈlā-tər\ *n*

re•lat•ed *adj* **1 :** connected by some understood relationship **2 :** connected through membership in the same family — **re•lat•ed•ness** *n*

re•la•tion \ri-ˈlā-shən\ *n* **1 :** NARRATION, ACCOUNT **2 :** CONNECTION, RELATIONSHIP **3 :** connection by blood or marriage **:** KINSHIP; *also* **:** RELATIVE **4 :** REFERENCE, RESPECT ⟨in ~ to⟩ **5 :** the state of being mutually interested or involved (as in social or commercial matters) **6** *pl* **:** DEALINGS, AFFAIRS **7** *pl* **:** SEXUAL INTERCOURSE — **re•la•tion•al** \-shə-nəl\ *adj*

re•la•tion•ship \-ˌship\ *n* **:** the state of being related or interrelated

[1]**rel•a•tive** \ˈre-lə-tiv\ *n* **1 :** a word referring grammatically to an antecedent **2 :** a thing having a relation to or a dependence upon another thing **3 :** a person connected with another by blood or marriage

[2]**relative** *adj* **1 :** introducing a subordinate clause qualifying an expressed or implied antecedent ⟨~ pronoun⟩; *also* **:** introduced by such a connective ⟨~ clause⟩ **2 :** PERTINENT, RELEVANT **3 :** not absolute or independent **:** COMPARATIVE **4 :** expressed as the ratio of the specified quantity to the total magnitude or to the mean of all quantities involved **syn** dependent, contingent, conditional — **rel•a•tive•ly** *adv* — **rel•a•tive•ness** *n*

relative humidity *n* **:** the ratio of the amount of water vapor actually present in the air to the greatest amount possible at the same temperature

rel•a•tiv•is•tic \ˌre-lə-ti-ˈvis-tik\ *adj* **1 :** of, relating to, or characterized by relativity **2 :** moving at a velocity that is a significant fraction of the speed of light so that effects predicted by the theory of relativity become evident ⟨a ~ electron⟩ — **rel•a•tiv•is•ti•cal•ly** \-ti-k(ə-)lē\ *adv*

rel•a•tiv•i•ty \ˌre-lə-ˈti-və-tē\ *n, pl* **-ties 1 :** the quality or state of being relative **2 :** a theory in physics that considers mass and energy to be equivalent and that predicts changes in mass, dimension, and time which are related to speed but are noticeable esp. at speeds approaching that of light

re•lax \ri-ˈlaks\ *vb* **1 :** to make or become less firm, tense, or rigid **2 :** to make less severe or strict **3 :** to seek rest or recreation — **re•lax•er** *n*

[1]**re•lax•ant** \ri-ˈlak-sənt\ *adj* **:** of, relating to, or producing relaxation

[2]**relaxant** *n* **:** a relaxing agent; *esp* **:** a drug that induces muscular relaxation

re•lax•ation \ˌrē-ˌlak-ˈsā-shən\ *n* **1 :** the act of relaxing or state of being relaxed **:** a lessening of tension **2 :** DIVERSION, RECREATION

[1]**re•lay** \ˈrē-ˌlā\ *n* **1 :** a fresh supply (as of horses or men) arranged beforehand to relieve others **2 :** a race between teams in which each team member covers a specified part of a course **3 :** an electromagnetic device in which the opening or closing of one circuit activates another device (as a switch in another circuit) **4 :** the act of passing along by stages

[2]**re•lay** \ˈrē-ˌlā, ri-ˈlā\ *vb* **re•layed; re•lay•ing 1 :** to place in or provide with relays **2 :** to pass along by relays **3 :** to control or operate by a relay

[3]**re•lay** \(ˌ)rē-ˈlā\ *vb* **-laid** \-ˈlād\; **-lay•ing :** to lay again

[1]**re•lease** \ri-ˈlēs\ *vb* **re•leased; re•leas•ing 1 :** to set free from confinement or restraint; *also* **:** DISMISS **2 :** to relieve from something that oppresses, confines, or burdens **3 :** RELINQUISH ⟨~ a claim⟩ **4 :** to permit publication, performance, exhibition, or sale of; *also* **:** to make available to the public **syn** emancipate, discharge, free, liberate

[2]**release** *n* **1 :** relief or deliverance from sorrow, suffering, or trouble **2 :** discharge from an obligation or responsibility **3 :** an act of setting free **:** the state of being freed **4 :** a document effecting a legal release **5 :** a releasing for performance or publication; *also* **:** the matter released (as to the press) **6 :** a device for holding or releasing a mechanism as required

rel•e•gate \ˈre-lə-ˌgāt\ *vb* **-gat•ed; -gat•ing 1 :** to send into exile **:** BANISH **2 :** to remove or dismiss to some less prominent position **3 :** to assign to a particular class or sphere **4 :** to submit to someone or something for appropriate action **:** DELEGATE **syn** commit, entrust, consign, commend — **rel•e•ga•tion** \ˌre-lə-ˈgā-shən\ *n*

re•lent \ri-ˈlent\ *vb* **1 :** to become less stern, severe, or harsh **2 :** SLACKEN

re•lent•less \-ləs\ *adj* **:** showing or promising no abatement of severity, intensity, or pace ⟨~ pressure⟩ — **re•lent•less•ly** *adv* — **re•lent•less•ness** *n*

rel•e•vance \ˈre-lə-vəns\ *n* **:** relation to the matter at hand; *also* **:** practical and esp. social applicability

rel•e•van•cy \-vən-sē\ *n* **:** RELEVANCE

DICTIONARY

rel•e•vant \ˈre-lə-vənt\ *adj* : bearing on the matter at hand : PERTINENT **syn** germane, material, applicable, apropos — **rel•e•vant•ly** *adv*

re•li•able \ri-ˈlī-ə-bəl\ *adj* : fit to be trusted or relied on : DEPENDABLE, TRUSTWORTHY — **re•li•abil•i•ty** \-ˌlī-ə-ˈbi-lə-tē\ *n* — **re•li•able•ness** *n* — **re•li•ably** \-ˈlī-ə-blē\ *adv*

re•li•ance \ri-ˈlī-əns\ *n* **1** : the act of relying **2** : the state of being reliant **3** : one relied on

re•li•ant \ri-ˈlī-ənt\ *adj* : having reliance on someone or something : DEPENDENT

rel•ic \ˈre-lik\ *n* **1** : an object venerated because of its association with a saint or martyr **2** : SOUVENIR, MEMENTO **3** *pl* : REMAINS, RUINS **4** : a remaining trace : VESTIGE

rel•ict \ˈre-likt\ *n* : WIDOW

re•lief \ri-ˈlēf\ *n* **1** : removal or lightening of something oppressive, painful, or distressing **2** : WELFARE 2 **3** : military assistance to an endangered post or force **4** : release from a post or from performance of a duty; *also* : one that takes the place of another on duty **5** : legal remedy or redress **6** : projection of figures or ornaments from the background (as in sculpture) **7** : the elevations of a land surface

relief pitcher *n* : a baseball pitcher who takes over for another during a game

re•lieve \ri-ˈlēv\ *vb* **re•lieved; re•liev•ing 1** : to free partly or wholly from a burden or from distress **2** : to bring about the removal or alleviation of : MITIGATE **3** : to release from a post or duty; *also* : to take the place of **4** : to break the monotony of **5** : to discharge the bladder or bowels of (oneself) **syn** alleviate, lighten, assuage, allay — **re•liev•er** *n*

relig *abbr* religion

re•li•gion \ri-ˈli-jən\ *n* **1** : the service and worship of God or the supernatural **2** : devotion to a religious faith **3** : a personal set or institutionalized system of religious beliefs, attitudes, and practices **4** : a cause, principle, or belief held to with faith and ardor — **re•li•gion•ist** *n*

¹re•li•gious \ri-ˈli-jəs\ *adj* **1** : relating or devoted to an acknowledged ultimate reality or deity **2** : of or relating to religious beliefs or observances **3** : scrupulously and conscientiously faithful **4** : FERVENT, ZEALOUS — **re•li•gious•ly** *adv*

²religious *n, pl* **religious** : a member of a religious order under monastic vows

re•lin•quish \ri-ˈliŋ-kwish, -ˈlin-\ *vb* **1** : to withdraw or retreat from : ABANDON, QUIT **2** : GIVE UP ⟨~ a title⟩ **3** : to let go of : RELEASE **syn** yield, leave, resign, surrender, cede, waive — **re•lin•quish•ment** *n*

rel•i•quary \ˈre-lə-ˌkwer-ē\ *n, pl* **-quar•ies** : a container for religious relics

¹rel•ish \ˈre-lish\ *n* [ME *reles* taste, fr. OF, something left behind, release, fr. *relessier* to relax, release, fr. L *relaxare*] **1** : characteristic flavor : SAVOR **2** : keen enjoyment or delight in something : GUSTO **3** : APPETITE, INCLINATION **4** : a highly seasoned sauce (as of pickles) eaten with other food to add flavor

²relish *vb* **1** : to add relish to **2** : to take pleasure in : ENJOY **3** : to eat with pleasure — **rel•ish•able** *adj*

re•live \(ˌ)rē-ˈliv\ *vb* : to live again or over again; *esp* : to experience again in the imagination

re•lo•cate \(ˌ)rē-ˈlō-ˌkāt, ˌrē-lō-ˈkāt\ *vb* **1** : to locate again **2** : to move to a new location — **re•lo•ca•tion** \ˌrē-lō-ˈkā-shən\ *n*

re•luc•tant \ri-ˈlək-tənt\ *adj* : feeling or showing aversion, hesitation or unwillingness ⟨~ to get involved⟩ **syn** disinclined, indisposed, hesitant, loath, averse — **re•luc•tance** \-təns\ — **re•luc•tant•ly** *adv*

re•ly \ri-ˈlī\ *vb* **re•lied; re•ly•ing** [ME *relien* to rally, fr. MF *relier* to connect, rally, fr. L *religare* to tie back, fr. *re-* back + *ligare* to tie] : to place faith or confidence : DEPEND

REM \ˈrem\ *n* : RAPID EYE MOVEMENT

re•main \ri-ˈmān\ *vb* **1** : to be left after others have been removed, subtracted, or destroyed **2** : to be something yet to be shown, done, or treated ⟨it ~*s* to be seen⟩ **3** : to stay after others have gone **4** : to continue unchanged

re•main•der \ri-ˈmān-dər\ *n* **1** : that which is left over : a remaining group, part, or trace **2** : the number left after a subtraction **3** : the number that is left over from the dividend after division and that is less than the divisor **4** : a book sold at a reduced price by the publisher after sales have slowed **syn** leavings, rest, balance, remnant, residue

re•mains \-ˈmānz\ *n pl* **1** : a remaining part or trace ⟨the ~ of a meal⟩ **2** : a dead body

¹re•make \(ˌ)rē-ˈmāk\ *vb* **-made** \-ˈmād\; **-mak•ing** : to make anew or in a different form

²re•make \ˈrē-ˌmāk\ *n* : one that is remade; *esp* : a new version of a motion picture

re•mand \ri-ˈmand\ *vb* : to order back; *esp* : to return to custody pending trial or for further detention

¹re•mark \ri-ˈmärk\ *n* **1** : the act of remarking : OBSERVATION, NOTICE **2** : a passing observation or comment

²remark *vb* **1** : to take notice of : OBSERVE **2** : to express as an observation or comment : SAY

re•mark•able \ri-ˈmär-kə-bəl\ *adj* : worthy of being or likely to be noticed : UNUSUAL, EXTRAORDINARY, NOTEWORTHY — **re•mark•able•ness** *n*

re•mark•ably \ri-ˈmär-kə-blē\ *adv* **1** : in a remarkable manner **2** : as is remarkable

re•me•di•a•ble \ri-ˈmē-dē-ə-bəl\ *adj* : capable of being remedied

re•me•di•al \ri-ˈmē-dē-əl\ *adj* : intended to remedy or improve

¹rem•e•dy \ˈre-mə-dē\ *n, pl* **-dies 1** : a medicine or treatment that cures or relieves a disease or condition **2** : something that corrects or counteracts an evil or compensates for a loss

²remedy *vb* **-died; -dy•ing** : to provide or serve as a remedy for

re•mem•ber \ri-ˈmem-bər\ *vb* **-bered; -ber•ing 1** : to bring to mind or think of again : RECOLLECT **2** : to keep from forgetting : keep in mind **3** : to convey greetings from **4** : COMMEMORATE

re•mem•brance \-brəns\ *n* **1** : an act of remembering : RECOLLECTION **2** : the ability to remember : MEMORY **3** : the period over which one's memory extends **4** : a memory of a person, thing, or event **5** : something that serves to bring to mind : REMINDER **6** : a greeting or gift recalling or expressing friendship or affection

re•mind \ri-ˈmīnd\ *vb* : to put in mind of something : cause to remember — **re•mind•er** *n*

rem•i•nisce \ˌre-mə-ˈnis\ *vb* **-nisced; -nisc•ing** : to indulge in reminiscence

rem•i•nis•cence \-ˈnis-ᵊns\ *n* **1** : a recalling or telling of a past experience **2** : an account of a memorable experience

rem•i•nis•cent \-ᵊnt\ *adj* **1** : of or relating to reminiscence **2** : marked by or given to reminiscence **3** : serving to remind : SUGGESTIVE — **rem•i•nis•cent•ly** *adv*

re•miss \ri-ˈmis\ *adj* **1** : negligent or careless in the performance of work or duty **2** : showing neglect or inattention **syn** lax, neglectful, delinquent, derelict — **re•miss•ly** *adv* — **re•miss•ness** *n*

re•mis•sion \ri-ˈmi-shən\ *n* **1** : the act or process of remitting **2** : a state or period during which something is remitted

re•mit \ri-ˈmit\ *vb* **re•mit•ted; re•mit•ting 1** : FORGIVE, PARDON **2** : to give or gain relief from (as pain) **3** : to refer for consideration, report, or decision **4** : to refrain from exacting or enforcing (as a penalty) **5** : to send (money) in payment of a bill

re•mit•tal \ri-ˈmit-ᵊl\ *n* : REMISSION

re•mit•tance \ri-ˈmit-ᵊns\ *n* **1** : a sum of money remitted **2** : transmittal of money (as to a distant place)

rem•nant \ˈrem-nənt\ *n* **1** : a usu. small part or trace remaining **2 :** an unsold or unused end of fabrics that are sold by the yard

re•mod•el \ˌrē-ˈmäd-ᵊl\ *vb* **:** to alter the structure of **:** MAKE OVER

re•mon•strance \ri-ˈmän-strəns\ *n* **:** an act or instance of remonstrating

re•mon•strant \-strənt\ *adj* **:** vigorously objecting or opposing — **remonstrant** *n* — **re•mon•strant•ly** *adv*

re•mon•strate \ri-ˈmän-ˌstrāt\ *vb* **-strat•ed; -strat•ing :** to plead in opposition to something **:** speak in protest or reproof **syn** expostulate, object, protest — **re•mon•stra•tion** \ri-ˌmän-ˈstrā-shən, ˌre-mən-\ *n* — **re•mon•stra•tor** \ri-ˈmän-ˌstrā-tər\ *n*

rem•o•ra \ˈre-mə-rə\ *n* **:** any of a family of marine bony fishes with sucking organs on the head by which they cling esp. to other fishes

re•morse \ri-ˈmȯrs\ *n* [ME, fr. MF *remors,* fr. ML *remorsus,* fr. LL, act of biting again, fr. L *remordēre* to bite again, fr. *re-* again + *mordēre* to bite] **:** a gnawing distress arising from a sense of guilt for past wrongs **syn** penitence, repentance, contrition — **re•morse•ful** *adj*

re•morse•less \-ləs\ *adj* **1 :** MERCILESS **2 :** PERSISTENT, RELENTLESS

[1]**re•mote** \ri-ˈmōt\ *adj* **re•mot•er; -est 1 :** far off in place or time **:** not near **2 :** not closely related **:** DISTANT **3 :** located out of the way **:** SECLUDED **4 :** acting, acted on, or controlled indirectly or from a distance **5 :** small in degree **:** SLIGHT ⟨a ~ chance⟩ **6 :** distant in manner — **re•mote•ly** *adv* — **re•mote•ness** *n*

[2]**remote** *n* **1 :** a radio or television program or a portion of a program originating outside the studio **2 :** REMOTE CONTROL 2

remote control *n* **1 :** control (as by radio signal) of operation from a point at some distance removed **2 :** a device or mechanism for controlling something from a distance

[1]**re•mount** \(ˌ)rē-ˈmau̇nt\ *vb* **1 :** to mount again **2 :** to furnish remounts to

[2]**re•mount** \ˈrē-ˌmau̇nt\ *n* **:** a fresh horse to replace one disabled or exhausted

[1]**re•move** \ri-ˈmüv\ *vb* **re•moved; re•mov•ing 1 :** to move from one place to another **:** TRANSFER **2 :** to move by lifting or taking off or away **3 :** DISMISS, DISCHARGE **4 :** to get rid of **:** ELIMINATE ⟨~ a fire hazard⟩ **5 :** to change one's residence or location **6 :** to go away **:** DEPART **7 :** to be capable of being removed — **re•mov•able** *adj* — **re•mov•al** \-ˈmü-vəl\ *n* — **re•mov•er** *n*

[2]**remove** *n* **1 :** a transfer from one location to another **:** MOVE **2 :** a degree or stage of separation

REM sleep *n* **:** a state of sleep associated esp. with rapid eye movements and dreaming and occurring approximately at 90-minute intervals

re•mu•ner•ate \ri-ˈmyü-nə-ˌrāt\ *vb* **-at•ed; -at•ing :** to pay an equivalent for or to **:** RECOMPENSE — **re•mu•ner•a•tor** \-ˌrā-tər\ *n*

re•mu•ner•a•tion \ri-ˌmyü-nə-ˈrā-shən\ *n* **:** COMPENSATION, PAYMENT

re•mu•ner•a•tive \ri-ˈmyü-nə-rə-tiv, -ˌrā-\ *adj* **:** serving to remunerate **:** GAINFUL

re•nais•sance \ˌre-nə-ˈsäns, -ˈzäns\ *n* **1** *cap* **:** the cultural revival and beginnings of modern science in Europe in the 14th-17th centuries; *also* **:** the period of the Renaissance **2** *often cap* **:** a movement or period of vigorous artistic and intellectual activity **3 :** REBIRTH, REVIVAL

re•nal \ˈrēn-ᵊl\ *adj* **:** of, relating to, or located in or near the kidneys

re•na•scence \ri-ˈnas-ᵊns, -ˈnās-\ *n, often cap* **:** RENAISSANCE

rend \ˈrend\ *vb* **rent** \ˈrent\; **rend•ing 1 :** to remove by violence **:** WREST **2 :** to tear forcibly apart **:** SPLIT

ren•der \ˈren-dər\ *vb* **1 :** to extract (as lard) by heating **2 :** to give to another; *also* **:** YIELD **3 :** to give in return **4 :** to do (a service) for another ⟨~ aid⟩ **5 :** to cause to be or become **:** MAKE **6 :** to reproduce or represent by artistic or verbal means **7 :** TRANSLATE ⟨~ into English⟩

[1]**ren•dez•vous** \ˈrän-di-ˌvü, -dā-\ *n, pl* **ren•dez•vous** \-ˌvüz\ [MF, fr. *rendez vous* present yourselves] **1 :** a place appointed for a meeting; *also* **:** a meeting at an appointed place **2 :** a place of popular resort **3 :** the process of bringing two spacecraft together

[2]**rendezvous** *vb* **-voused** \-ˌvüd\; **-vous•ing** \-ˌvü-iŋ\; **-vouses** \-ˌvüz\ **:** to come or bring together at a rendezvous

ren•di•tion \ren-ˈdi-shən\ *n* **:** an act or a result of rendering ⟨first ~ of the work into English⟩

ren•e•gade \ˈre-ni-ˌgād\ *n* [Sp *renegado,* fr. ML *renegatus,* fr. pp. of *renegare* to deny, fr. L *re-* re- + *negare* to deny] **:** a deserter from one faith, cause, principle, or party for another

re•nege \ri-ˈnig, -ˈneg, -ˈnēg, -ˈnāg\ *vb* **re•neged; re•neg•ing 1 :** to go back on a promise or commitment **2 :** to fail to follow suit when able in a card game in violation of the rules — **re•neg•er** *n*

re•new \ri-ˈnü, -ˈnyü\ *vb* **1 :** to make or become new, fresh, or strong again **2 :** to restore to existence **:** RECREATE, REVIVE **3 :** to make or do again **:** REPEAT ⟨~ a complaint⟩ **4 :** to begin again **:** RESUME ⟨~*ed* his efforts⟩ **5 :** REPLACE ⟨~ the lining of a coat⟩ **6 :** to grant or obtain an extension of or on ⟨~ a lease⟩ ⟨~ a subscription⟩ — **re•new•er** *n*

re•new•able \ri-ˈnü-ə-bəl, -ˈnyü-\ *adj* **1 :** capable of being renewed **2 :** capable of being replaced by natural ecological cycles or sound management procedures ⟨~ resources⟩

re•new•al \ri-ˈnü-əl, -ˈnyü-\ *n* **1 :** the act of renewing **:** the state of being renewed **2 :** something renewed

ren•net \ˈre-nət\ *n* **1 :** the contents of the stomach of an unweaned animal (as a calf) or the lining membrane of the stomach used for curdling milk **2 :** rennin or a substitute used to curdle milk

ren•nin \ˈre-nən\ *n* **:** a stomach enzyme that coagulates casein and is used commercially to curdle milk in the making of cheese

re•nounce \ri-ˈnau̇ns\ *vb* **re•nounced; re•nounc•ing 1 :** to give up, refuse, or resign usu. by formal declaration **2 :** to refuse further to follow, obey, or recognize **:** REPUDIATE — **re•nounce•ment** *n*

ren•o•vate \ˈre-nə-ˌvāt\ *vb* **-vat•ed; -vat•ing 1 :** to make like new again **:** put in good condition **:** REPAIR **2 :** to restore to vigor or activity — **ren•o•va•tion** \ˌre-nə-ˈvā-shən\ *n* — **ren•o•va•tor** \ˈre-nə-ˌvā-tər\ *n*

re•nown \ri-ˈnau̇n\ *n* **:** a state of being widely acclaimed and honored **:** FAME, CELEBRITY **syn** honor, glory, reputation, repute — **re•nowned** \-ˈnau̇nd\ *adj*

[1]**rent** \ˈrent\ *n* **1 :** money or the amount of money paid or due at intervals for the use of another's property **2 :** property rented or for rent

[2]**rent** *vb* **1 :** to give possession and use of in return for rent **2 :** to take and hold under an agreement to pay rent **3 :** to be for rent ⟨~*s* for $100 a month⟩ — **rent•er** *n*

[3]**rent** *n* **1 :** a tear in cloth **2 :** a split in a party or organized group **:** SCHISM

[1]**rent•al** \ˈren-təl\ *n* **1 :** an amount paid or collected as rent **2 :** something that is rented **3 :** an act of renting

[2]**rental** *adj* **:** of or relating to rent

re•nun•ci•a•tion \ri-ˌnən-sē-ˈā-shən\ *n* **:** the act of renouncing **:** REPUDIATION

rep *abbr* **1** repair **2** repeat **3** report; reporter **4** representative **5** republic

Rep *abbr* Republican

re•pack•age \(ˌ)rē-ˈpa-kij\ *vb* **:** to package again or anew; *esp* **:** to put into a more attractive form

[1]**re•pair** \ri-ˈpar\ *vb* [ME, fr. MF *repairier* to go back to one's country, fr. LL *repatriare,* fr. L *re-* re- + *patria* native country] **:** to make one's way **:** GO ⟨~*ed* to the drawing room⟩

[2]**repair** *vb* [ME, fr. MF *reparer,* fr. L *reparare,* fr. *re-*

re- + *parare* to prepare] **1** : to restore to good condition : FIX **2** : to restore to a healthy state **3** : REMEDY ⟨~ a wrong⟩ — **re·pair·er** *n* — **re·pair·man** \-ˌman\ *n*

³**repair** *n* **1** : a result of repairing **2** : an act of repairing **3** : condition with respect to need of repairing ⟨in bad ~⟩

rep·a·ra·tion \ˌre-pə-ˈrā-shən\ *n* **1** : the act of making amends for a wrong **2** : amends made for a wrong; *esp* : money paid by a defeated nation in compensation for damages caused during hostilities — usu. used in pl. **syn** redress, restitution, indemnity

re·par·a·tive \ri-ˈpar-ə-tiv\ *adj* **1** : of, relating to, or effecting repairs **2** : serving to make amends

rep·ar·tee \ˌre-pər-ˈtē\ *n* **1** : a witty reply **2** : a succession of clever replies; *also* : skill in making such replies

re·past \ri-ˈpast, ˈrē-ˌpast\ *n* : a supply of food and drink served as a meal

re·pa·tri·ate \rē-ˈpā-trē-ˌāt\ *vb* **-at·ed; -at·ing** : to send or bring back to the country of origin or citizenship ⟨~ prisoners of war⟩ — **re·pa·tri·ate** \-trē-ət, -trē-ˌāt\ *n* — **re·pa·tri·a·tion** \-ˌpā-trē-ˈā-shən\ *n*

re·pay \rē-ˈpā\ *vb* **-paid** \-ˈpād\; **-pay·ing** **1** : to pay back : REFUND **2** : to give or do in return or requital **3** : to make a return payment to : RECOMPENSE, REQUITE **syn** remunerate, compensate, reimburse, indemnify — **re·pay·able** *adj* — **re·pay·ment** *n*

re·peal \ri-ˈpēl\ *vb* : to annul by authoritative and esp. legislative action — **repeal** *n* — **re·peal·er** *n*

¹**re·peat** \ri-ˈpēt\ *vb* **1** : to say again **2** : to do again **3** : to say over from memory — **re·peat·able** *adj* — **re·peat·er** *n*

²**re·peat** \ri-ˈpēt, ˈrē-ˌpēt\ *n* **1** : the act of repeating **2** : something repeated or to be repeated (as a radio or television program)

re·peat·ed \ri-ˈpē-təd\ *adj* : done or recurring again and again : FREQUENT — **re·peat·ed·ly** *adv*

re·pel \ri-ˈpel\ *vb* **re·pelled; re·pel·ling** **1** : to drive away : REPULSE **2** : to fight against : RESIST **3** : to turn away : REJECT **4** : to cause aversion in : DISGUST

¹**re·pel·lent** *also* **re·pel·lant** \ri-ˈpe-lənt\ *adj* **1** : tending to drive away ⟨a mosquito-*repellent* spray⟩ **2** : causing disgust

²**repellent** *also* **repellant** *n* : something that repels; *esp* : a substance that repels insects

re·pent \ri-ˈpent\ *vb* **1** : to turn from sin and resolve to reform one's life **2** : to feel sorry for (something done) : REGRET — **re·pen·tance** \ri-ˈpent-ᵊns\ *n* — **re·pen·tant** \-ᵊnt\ *adj*

re·per·cus·sion \ˌrē-pər-ˈkə-shən, ˌre-\ *n* **1** : REVERBERATION **2** : a reciprocal action or effect **3** : a widespread, indirect, or unforeseen effect of something done or said

rep·er·toire \ˈre-pər-ˌtwär\ *n* [F] **1** : a list of plays, operas, pieces, or parts which a company or performer is prepared to present **2** : a list of the skills or devices possessed by a person or needed in his occupation

rep·er·to·ry \ˈre-pər-ˌtōr-ē\ *n, pl* **-ries** **1** : REPOSITORY **2** : REPERTOIRE **3** : a company that presents its repertoire in the course of one season at one theater

rep·e·ti·tion \ˌre-pə-ˈti-shən\ *n* **1** : the act or an instance of repeating **2** : the fact of being repeated

rep·e·ti·tious \-ˈti-shəs\ *adj* : marked by repetition; *esp* : tediously repeating — **rep·e·ti·tious·ly** *adv* — **rep·e·ti·tious·ness** *n*

re·pet·i·tive \ri-ˈpe-ti-tiv\ *adj* : REPETITIOUS — **re·pet·i·tive·ly** *adv* — **re·pet·i·tive·ness** *n*

re·pine \ri-ˈpīn\ *vb* **re·pined; re·pin·ing** **1** : to feel or express discontent or dejection **2** : to long for something

repl *abbr* replace; replacement

re·place \ri-ˈplās\ *vb* **1** : to restore to a former place or position **2** : to take the place of : SUPPLANT **3** : to put something new in the place of — **re·place·able** *adj* — **re·plac·er** *n*

re·place·ment \ri-ˈplās-mənt\ *n* **1** : the act of replacing : the state of being replaced **2** : one that replaces another esp. in a job or function

¹**re·play** \(ˌ)rē-ˈplā\ *vb* : to play again or over

²**re·play** \ˈrē-ˌplā\ *n* **1** : an act or instance of replaying **2** : the playing of a tape (as a videotape)

re·plen·ish \ri-ˈple-nish\ *vb* : to fill or build up again : stock or supply anew — **re·plen·ish·ment** *n*

re·plete \ri-ˈplēt\ *adj* **1** : fully provided **2** : FULL; *esp* : full of food — **re·plete·ness** *n*

re·ple·tion \ri-ˈplē-shən\ *n* : the state of being replete

rep·li·ca \ˈre-pli-kə\ *n* [It, repetition, fr. *replicare* to repeat, fr. LL, fr. L, to fold back, fr. *re-* back + *plicare* to fold] **1** : an exact reproduction (as of a painting) executed by the original artist **2** : a copy exact in all details : DUPLICATE

¹**rep·li·cate** \ˈre-plə-ˌkāt\ *vb* **-cat·ed; -cat·ing** : DUPLICATE, REPEAT

²**rep·li·cate** \-pli-kət\ *n* : one of several identical experiments or procedures

rep·li·ca·tion \ˌre-plə-ˈkā-shən\ *n* **1** : ANSWER, REPLY **2** : precise copying or reproduction; *also* : an act or process of this

¹**re·ply** \ri-ˈplī\ *vb* **re·plied; re·ply·ing** : to say or do in answer : RESPOND

²**reply** *n, pl* **replies** : ANSWER, RESPONSE

¹**re·port** \ri-ˈpōrt\ *n* [ME, fr. MF, fr. OF, fr. *reporter* to report, fr. L *reportare*, fr. *re-* back + *portare* to carry] **1** : common talk : RUMOR **2** : FAME, REPUTATION **3** : a usu. detailed account or statement **4** : an explosive noise

²**report** *vb* **1** : to give an account of : RELATE, TELL **2** : to serve as carrier of (a message) **3** : to prepare or present (as an account of an event) for a newspaper or a broadcast **4** : to make a charge of misconduct against **5** : to present oneself (as for work) **6** : to make known to the authorities ⟨~ a fire⟩ **7** : to return or present (as a matter referred to a committee) with conclusions and recommendations — **re·port·able** *adj*

re·port·age \ri-ˈpōr-tij, *esp for 2* ˌre-pər-ˈtäzh, ˌre-ˌpȯr-ˈ\ *n* [F] **1** : the act or process of reporting news **2** : writing intended to give an account of observed or documented events

report card *n* : a periodic report on a student's grades

re·port·ed·ly \ri-ˈpōr-təd-lē\ *adv* : according to report

re·port·er \ri-ˈpōr-tər\ *n* : one that reports; *esp* : a person who gathers and reports news for a news medium — **re·por·to·ri·al** \ˌre-pər-ˈtōr-ē-əl\ *adj*

¹**re·pose** \ri-ˈpōz\ *vb* **re·posed; re·pos·ing** **1** : to lay at rest **2** : to lie at rest **3** : to lie dead **4** : to take a rest **5** : to rest for support : LIE

²**repose** *n* **1** : a state of resting (as after exertion); *esp* : SLEEP **2** : eternal or heavenly rest **3** : CALM, PEACE **4** : cessation or absence of activity, movement, or animation **5** : composure of manner : POISE — **re·pose·ful** *adj*

³**repose** *vb* **re·posed; re·pos·ing** **1** : to place (as trust) in someone or something **2** : to place for control, management, or use

re·pos·i·to·ry \ri-ˈpä-zə-ˌtōr-ē\ *n, pl* **-ries** **1** : a place where something is deposited or stored **2** : a person to whom something is entrusted

re·pos·sess \ˌrē-pə-ˈzes\ *vb* **1** : to regain possession of **2** : to take possession of in default of the payment of installments due — **re·pos·ses·sion** \-ˈze-shən\ *n*

rep·re·hend \ˌre-pri-ˈhend\ *vb* : to express disapproval of : CENSURE **syn** criticize, condemn, denounce, blame, pan — **rep·re·hen·sion** \-ˈhen-chən\ *n*

rep·re·hen·si·ble \-ˈhen-sə-bəl\ *adj* : deserving blame or censure : CULPABLE — **rep·re·hen·si·bly** \-blē\ *adv*

rep·re·sent \ˌre-pri-ˈzent\ *vb* **1** : to present a picture or a likeness of : PORTRAY, DEPICT **2** : to serve as a sign or symbol of **3** : to act the role of **4** : to stand in the place of : act or speak for **5** : to be a member or example of : TYPIFY **6** : to serve as an elected represen-

DICTIONARY

tative of **7** : to describe as having a specified quality or character **8** : to state with the purpose of affecting judgment or action

rep•re•sen•ta•tion \ˌre-pri-ˌzen-ˈtā-shən\ *n* **1** : the act of representing **2** : one (as a picture or image) that represents something else **3** : the state of being represented in a legislative body; *also* : the body of persons representing a constituency **4** : a usu. formal statement made to effect a change

[1]**rep•re•sen•ta•tive** \ˌre-pri-ˈzen-tə-tiv\ *adj* **1** : serving to represent **2** : standing or acting for another **3** : founded on the principle of representation : carried on by elected representatives ⟨~ government⟩ — **rep•re•sen•ta•tive•ly** *adv* — **rep•re•sen•ta•tive•ness** *n*

[2]**representative** *n* **1** : a typical example of a group, class, or quality **2** : one that represents another; *esp* : one representing a district in a legislative body usu. as a member of a lower house

re•press \ri-ˈpres\ *vb* **1** : CURB, SUBDUE **2** : RESTRAIN, SUPPRESS **3** : to exclude from consciousness — **re•pres•sion** \-ˈpre-shən\ *n* — **re•pres•sive** \-ˈpre-siv\ *adj*

[1]**re•prieve** \ri-ˈprēv\ *vb* **re•prieved; re•priev•ing 1** : to delay the punishment or execution of **2** : to give temporary relief to

[2]**reprieve** *n* **1** : the act of reprieving : the state of being reprieved **2** : a formal temporary suspension of a sentence esp. of death **3** : a temporary respite

[1]**rep•ri•mand** \ˈre-prə-ˌmand\ *n* : a severe or formal reproof

[2]**reprimand** *vb* : to reprove severely or formally

[1]**re•print** \(ˌ)rē-ˈprint\ *vb* : to print again

[2]**re•print** \ˈrē-ˌprint\ *n* : a reproduction of printed matter

re•pri•sal \ri-ˈprī-zəl\ *n* : an act in retaliation for something done by another

re•prise \ri-ˈprēz\ *n* : a recurrence, renewal, or resumption of an action; *also* : a musical repetition

[1]**re•proach** \ri-ˈprōch\ *n* **1** : an expression of disapproval **2** : DISGRACE, DISCREDIT **3** : the act of reproaching : REBUKE **4** : a cause or occasion of blame or disgrace — **re•proach•ful** \-fəl\ *adj* — **re•proach•ful•ly** *adv* — **re•proach•ful•ness** *n*

[2]**reproach** *vb* **1** : CENSURE, REBUKE **2** : to cast discredit on **syn** chide, admonish, reprove, reprimand — **re•proach•able** *adj*

rep•ro•bate \ˈre-prə-ˌbāt\ *n* **1** : a person foreordained to damnation **2** : a thoroughly bad person : SCOUNDREL — **reprobate** *adj*

rep•ro•ba•tion \ˌre-prə-ˈbā-shən\ *n* : strong disapproval : CONDEMNATION

re•pro•duce \ˌrē-prə-ˈdüs, -ˈdyüs\ *vb* **1** : to produce again or anew **2** : to produce offspring — **re•pro•duc•ible** \-ˈdü-sə-bəl, -ˈdyü-\ *adj* — **re•pro•duc•tion** \-ˈdək-shən\ *n* — **re•pro•duc•tive** \-ˈdək-tiv\ *adj*

re•proof \ri-ˈprüf\ *n* : blame or censure for a fault

re•prove \ri-ˈprüv\ *vb* **re•proved; re•prov•ing 1** : to administer a rebuke to **2** : to express disapproval of **syn** reprimand, admonish, reproach, chide — **re•prov•er** *n*

rept *abbr* report

rep•tile \ˈrep-təl, -ˌtīl\ *n* [ME *reptil,* fr. MF or LL; MF *reptile,* fr. LL *reptile,* fr. L *repere* to crawl] : any of a large class of air-breathing scaly vertebrates including snakes, lizards, alligators, turtles, and extinct related forms (as dinosaurs) — **rep•til•i•an** \rep-ˈti-lē-ən\ *adj or n*

re•pub•lic \ri-ˈpə-blik\ *n* [F *république,* fr. MF *republique,* fr. L *respublica,* fr. *res* thing, wealth + *publica,* fem. of *publicus* public] **1** : a government having a chief of state who is not a monarch and is usu. a president; *also* : a nation or other political unit having such a government **2** : a government in which supreme power is held by the citizens entitled to vote and is exercised by elected officers and representatives governing according to law; *also* : a nation or other political unit having such a form of government **3** : a constituent political and territorial unit of the former nations of Czechoslovakia, the U.S.S.R., or Yugoslavia

[1]**re•pub•li•can** \-bli-kən\ *adj* **1** : of, relating to, or resembling a republic **2** : favoring or supporting a republic **3** *cap* : of, relating to, or constituting one of the two major political parties in the U.S. evolving in the mid-19th century — **re•pub•li•can•ism** *n, often cap*

[2]**republican** *n* **1** : one that favors or supports a republican form of government **2** *cap* : a member of a republican party and esp. of the Republican party of the U.S.

re•pu•di•ate \ri-ˈpyü-dē-ˌāt\ *vb* **-at•ed; -at•ing** [L *repudiare* to cast off, divorce, fr. *repudium* divorce] **1** : to cast off : DISOWN **2** : to refuse to have anything to do with : refuse to acknowledge, accept, or pay ⟨~ a charge⟩ ⟨~ a debt⟩ **syn** spurn, reject, decline — **re•pu•di•a•tion** \-ˌpyü-dē-ˈā-shən\ *n* — **re•pu•di•a•tor** \-ˈpyü-dē-ˌā-tər\ *n*

re•pug•nance \ri-ˈpəg-nəns\ *n* **1** : the quality or fact of being contradictory or inconsistent **2** : strong dislike, distaste, or antagonism

re•pug•nant \-nənt\ *adj* **1** : marked by repugnance **2** : contrary to a person's tastes or principles : exciting distaste or aversion **syn** repellent, abhorrent, distasteful, obnoxious, revolting, loathsome — **re•pug•nant•ly** *adv*

[1]**re•pulse** \ri-ˈpəls\ *vb* **re•pulsed; re•puls•ing 1** : to drive or beat back : REPEL **2** : to repel by discourtesy or denial : REBUFF **3** : to cause a feeling of repulsion in : DISGUST

[2]**repulse** *n* **1** : REBUFF, REJECTION **2** : the action of repelling an attacker : the fact of being repelled

re•pul•sion \ri-ˈpəl-shən\ *n* **1** : the action of repulsing : the state of being repulsed **2** : the force with which bodies, particles, or like forces repel one another **3** : a feeling of aversion

re•pul•sive \-siv\ *adj* **1** : serving or tending to repel or reject **2** : arousing aversion or disgust **syn** repugnant, revolting, loathsome, noisome — **re•pul•sive•ly** *adv* — **re•pul•sive•ness** *n*

rep•u•ta•ble \ˈre-pyə-tə-bəl\ *adj* : having a good reputation : ESTIMABLE — **rep•u•ta•bly** \-blē\ *adv*

rep•u•ta•tion \ˌre-pyù-ˈtā-shən\ *n* **1** : overall quality or character as seen or judged by people in general **2** : place in public esteem or regard

[1]**re•pute** \ri-ˈpyüt\ *vb* **re•put•ed; re•put•ing** : BELIEVE, CONSIDER

[2]**repute** *n* **1** : REPUTATION **2** : the state of being favorably known or spoken of

re•put•ed \ri-ˈpyü-təd\ *adj* **1** : REPUTABLE **2** : according to reputation : SUPPOSED — **re•put•ed•ly** *adv*

req *abbr* **1** request **2** require; required **3** requisition

[1]**re•quest** \ri-ˈkwest\ *n* **1** : an act or instance of asking for something **2** : a thing asked for **3** : the condition of being asked for ⟨available on ~⟩

[2]**request** *vb* **1** : to make a request to or of **2** : to ask for — **re•quest•er** *n*

re•qui•em \ˈre-kwē-əm, ˈrā-\ *n* [ME, fr. L (first word of the requiem mass), acc. of *requies* rest, fr. *quies* quiet, rest] **1** : a mass for a dead person; *also* : a musical setting for this **2** : a musical service or hymn in honor of the dead

re•quire \ri-ˈkwīr\ *vb* **re•quired; re•quir•ing 1** : to demand as necessary or essential **2** : COMMAND, ORDER

re•quire•ment \-mənt\ *n* **1** : something (as a condition or quality) required ⟨entrance ~s⟩ **2** : NECESSITY

req•ui•site \ˈre-kwə-zət\ *adj* : REQUIRED, NECESSARY — **requisite** *n*

req•ui•si•tion \ˌre-kwə-ˈzi-shən\ *n* **1** : formal application or demand (as for supplies) **2** : the state of being in demand or use — **requisition** *vb*

re•quite \ri-ˈkwīt\ *vb* **re•quit•ed; re•quit•ing 1** : to make return for : REPAY **2** : to make retaliation for

: AVENGE **3** : to make return to — **re•quit•al** \-ˈkwīt-ᵊl\ *n*

rere•dos \ˈrer-ə-ˌdäs\ *n* : a usu. ornamental wood or stone screen or partition wall behind an altar

re•run \ˈrē-ˌrən, (ˌ)rē-ˈrən\ *n* : the act or an instance of running again or anew; *esp* : a showing of a motion picture or television program after its first run — **re-run** \(ˌ)rē-ˈrən\ *vb*

res *abbr* **1** research **2** reservation; reserve **3** reservoir **4** residence; resident **5** resolution

re•sale \ˈrē-ˌsāl, (ˌ)rē-ˈsāl\ *n* : the act of selling again usu. to a new party — **re•sal•able** \(ˌ)rē-ˈsā-lə-bəl\ *adj*

re•scind \ri-ˈsind\ *vb* : REPEAL, CANCEL, ANNUL — **re-scis•sion** \-ˈsi-zhən\ *n*

re•script \ˈrē-ˌskript\ *n* : an official or authoritative order or decree

res•cue \ˈres-kyü\ *vb* **res•cued; res•cu•ing** [ME, fr. MF *rescourre,* fr. OF, fr. *re-* re- + *escourre* to shake out, fr. L *excutere*] : to free from danger, harm, or confinement — **rescue** *n* — **res•cu•er** *n*

re•search \ri-ˈsərch, ˈrē-ˌsərch\ *n* **1** : careful or diligent search **2** : studious inquiry or examination aimed at the discovery and interpretation of new knowledge **3** : the collecting of information about a particular subject — **research** *vb* — **re•search•er** *n*

re•sec•tion \ri-ˈsek-shən\ *n* : the surgical removal of part of an organ or structure

re•sem•blance \ri-ˈzem-bləns\ *n* : the quality or state of resembling

re•sem•ble \ri-ˈzem-bəl\ *vb* **-bled; -bling** : to be like or similar to

re•sent \ri-ˈzent\ *vb* : to feel or exhibit annoyance or indignation at — **re•sent•ful** \-fəl\ *adj* — **re•sent•ful-ly** *adv* — **re•sent•ment** *n*

re•ser•pine \ri-ˈsər-ˌpēn, -pən\ *n* : a drug used in treating high blood pressure and nervous tension

res•er•va•tion \ˌre-zər-ˈvā-shən\ *n* **1** : an act of reserving **2** : something (as a room in a hotel) arranged for in advance **3** : something reserved; *esp* : a tract of public land set aside for special use **4** : a limiting condition

¹re•serve \ri-ˈzərv\ *vb* **re•served; re•serv•ing 1** : to store for future or special use **2** : to hold back for oneself **3** : to set aside or arrange to have set aside or held for special use

²reserve *n* **1** : something reserved : STOCK, STORE **2** : a military force withheld from action for later use — usu. used in pl. **3** : the military forces of a country not part of the regular services; *also* : RESERVIST **4** : a tract set apart : RESERVATION **5** : an act of reserving **6** : restraint or caution in one's words or bearing **7** : money or its equivalent kept in hand or set apart to meet liabilities

re•served \ri-ˈzərvd\ *adj* **1** : restrained in words and actions **2** : set aside for future or special use — **re-serv•ed•ly** \-ˈzər-vəd-lē\ *adv* — **re•serv•ed•ness** \-vəd-nəs\ *n*

re•serv•ist \ri-ˈzər-vist\ *n* : a member of a military reserve

res•er•voir \ˈre-zə-ˌvwär, -zər-, -ˌvwȯr\ *n* [F] : a place where something is kept in store; *esp* : an artificial lake where water is collected as a water supply

re•shuf•fle \rē-ˈshə-fəl\ *vb* **1** : to shuffle again **2** : to reorganize usu. by redistribution of existing elements — **reshuffle** *n*

re•side \ri-ˈzīd\ *vb* **re•sid•ed; re•sid•ing 1** : to make one's home : DWELL **2** : to be present as a quality or vested as a right

res•i•dence \ˈre-zə-dəns\ *n* **1** : the act or fact of residing in a place as a dweller or in discharge of a duty or an obligation **2** : the place where one actually lives **3** : a building used as a home : DWELLING **4** : the period of living in a place

res•i•den•cy \ˈre-zə-dən-sē\ *n, pl* **-cies 1** : the residence of or the territory under a diplomatic resident **2** : a period of advanced training in a medical specialty

¹res•i•dent \-dənt\ *adj* **1** : RESIDING **2** : being in residence **3** : not migratory

²resident *n* **1** : one who resides in a place **2** : a diplomatic representative with governing powers (as in a protectorate) **3** : a physician serving a residency

res•i•den•tial \ˌre-zə-ˈden-chəl\ *adj* **1** : used as a residence or by residents **2** : occupied by or restricted to residences — **res•i•den•tial•ly** *adv*

¹re•sid•u•al \ri-ˈzi-jə-wəl\ *adj* : being a residue or remainder

²residual *n* **1** : a residual product or substance **2** : a payment (as to an actor or writer) for each rerun after an initial showing (as of a taped TV show)

re•sid•u•ary \ri-ˈzi-jə-ˌwer-ē\ *adj* : of, relating to, or constituting a residue esp. of an estate

res•i•due \ˈre-zə-ˌdü, -ˌdyü\ *n* : a part remaining after another part has been taken away : REMAINDER

re•sid•u•um \ri-ˈzi-jə-wəm\ *n, pl* **re•sid•ua** \-jə-wə\ [L] **1** : something remaining or residual after certain deductions are made **2** : a residual product

re•sign \ri-ˈzīn\ *vb* [ME, fr. MF *resigner,* fr. L *resignare,* lit., to unseal, cancel, fr. *signare* to sign, seal] **1** : to give up deliberately (as one's position) esp. by a formal act **2** : to give (oneself) over (as to grief or despair) without resistance — **re•sign•ed•ly** \-ˈzī-nəd-lē\ *adv*

re–sign \(ˌ)rē-ˈsīn\ *vb* : to sign again

res•ig•na•tion \ˌre-zig-ˈnā-shən\ *n* **1** : an act or instance of resigning; *also* : a formal notification of such an act **2** : the quality or state of being resigned

re•sil•ience \ri-ˈzil-yəns\ *n* **1** : the ability of a body to regain its original size and shape after being compressed, bent, or stretched **2** : an ability to recover from or adjust easily to change or misfortune

re•sil•ien•cy \-yən-sē\ *n* : RESILIENCE

re•sil•ient \-yənt\ *adj* : marked by resilience

res•in \ˈrez-ᵊn\ *n* : any of various substances obtained from the gum or sap of some trees and used esp. in varnishes, plastics, and medicine; *also* : a comparable synthetic product — **res•in•ous** *adj*

¹re•sist \ri-ˈzist\ *vb* **1** : to fight against : OPPOSE ⟨~ aggression⟩ **2** : to withstand the force or effect of ⟨~ disease⟩ **syn** combat, repel — **re•sist•ible** \-ˈzis-tə-bəl\ *adj* — **re•sist•less** *adj*

²resist *n* : something (as a coating) that resists or prevents a particular action

re•sis•tance \ri-ˈzis-təns\ *n* **1** : the act or an instance of resisting : OPPOSITION **2** : the power or capacity to resist; *esp* : the inherent ability of an organism to resist harmful influences (as disease or infection) **3** : the opposition offered by a body to the passage through it of a steady electric current

re•sis•tant \-tənt\ *adj* : giving or capable of resistance

re•sis•tor \ri-ˈzis-tər\ *n* : a device used to provide resistance to the flow of an electric current in a circuit

res•o•lute \ˈre-zə-ˌlüt\ *adj* : firmly determined in purpose : RESOLVED **syn** steadfast, staunch, faithful, true, loyal — **res•o•lute•ly** *adv* — **res•o•lute•ness** *n*

res•o•lu•tion \ˌre-zə-ˈlü-shən\ *n* **1** : the act or process of resolving **2** : the action of solving; *also* : SOLUTION **3** : the quality of being resolute : FIRMNESS, DETERMINATION **4** : a formal statement expressing the opinion, will, or intent of a body of persons

¹re•solve \ri-ˈzälv\ *vb* **re•solved; re•solv•ing 1** : to break up into constituent parts : ANALYZE **2** : to distinguish between or make visible adjacent parts of **3** : to find an answer to : SOLVE **4** : DETERMINE, DECIDE **5** : to make or pass a formal resolution — **re•solv•able** *adj*

²resolve *n* **1** : fixity of purpose **2** : something resolved

res•o•nance \ˈre-zə-nəns\ *n* **1** : the quality or state of being resonant **2** : a reinforcement of sound in a vibrating body caused by waves from another body vibrating at nearly the same rate

res•o•nant \-nənt\ *adj* **1** : continuing to sound : RE-

SOUNDING **2** : relating to or exhibiting resonance **3** : intensified and enriched by or as if by resonance — **res•o•nant•ly** *adv*

res•o•nate \-ˌnāt\ *vb* **-nat•ed; -nat•ing 1** : to produce or exhibit resonance **2** : REVERBERATE, RESOUND

res•o•na•tor \-ˌnā-tər\ *n* : something that resounds or exhibits resonance

re•sorp•tion \rē-ˈsȯrp-shən, -ˈzȯrp-\ *n* : the action or process of breaking down and assimilating something (as a tooth or an embryo)

[1]**re•sort** \ri-ˈzȯrt\ *n* [ME, fr. MF, resource, recourse, fr. *resortir* to rebound, resort, fr. OF, fr. *sortir* to escape, sally] **1** : one looked to for help : REFUGE **2** : RECOURSE **3** : frequent or general visiting ⟨place of ~⟩ **4** : a frequently visited place : HAUNT **5** : a place providing recreation esp. to vacationers

[2]**resort** *vb* **1** : to go often or habitually **2** : to have recourse ⟨~*ed* to violence⟩

re•sound \ri-ˈzau̇nd\ *vb* **1** : to become filled with sound : REVERBERATE, RING **2** : to sound loudly

re•sound•ing *adj* **1** : RESONATING, RESONANT **2** : impressively sonorous ⟨~ name⟩ **3** : EMPHATIC, UNEQUIVOCAL ⟨a ~ success⟩ — **re•sound•ing•ly** *adv*

re•source \ˈrē-ˌsōrs, ri-ˈsōrs\ *n* [F *ressource,* fr. OF *ressourse* relief, resource, fr. *resourdre* to relieve, lit., to rise again, fr. L *resurgere,* fr. *re-* again + *surgere* to rise] **1** : a source of supply or support — usu. used in pl. **2** *pl* : available funds **3** : a possibility of relief or recovery **4** : a means of spending leisure time **5** : ability to meet and handle situations — **re•source•ful** \ri-ˈsōrs-fəl\ *adj* — **re•source•ful•ness** *n*

resp *abbr* respective; respectively

[1]**re•spect** \ri-ˈspekt\ *n* **1** : relation to something usu. specified : REGARD ⟨in ~ to⟩ **2** : high or special regard : ESTEEM **3** *pl* : an expression of respect or deference **4** : DETAIL, PARTICULAR — **re•spect•ful** \-fəl\ *adj* — **re•spect•ful•ly** *adv* — **re•spect•ful•ness** *n*

[2]**respect** *vb* **1** : to consider deserving of high regard : ESTEEM **2** : to refrain from interfering with ⟨~ another's privacy⟩ **3** : to have reference to : CONCERN — **re•spect•er** *n*

re•spect•able \ri-ˈspek-tə-bəl\ *adj* **1** : worthy of respect : ESTIMABLE **2** : decent or correct in conduct : PROPER **3** : fair in size, quantity, or quality : MODERATE, TOLERABLE **4** : fit to be seen : PRESENTABLE — **re•spect•a•bil•i•ty** \-ˌspek-tə-ˈbi-lə-tē\ *n* — **re•spect•ably** \-ˈspek-tə-blē\ *adv*

re•spect•ing *prep* : with regard to

re•spec•tive \-tiv\ *adj* : PARTICULAR, SEPARATE ⟨returned to their ~ homes⟩

re•spec•tive•ly \-lē\ *adv* **1** : as relating to each **2** : each in the order given

res•pi•ra•tion \ˌres-pə-ˈrā-shən\ *n* **1** : an act or the process of breathing **2** : the physical and chemical processes (as breathing and oxidation) by which a living thing obtains oxygen and eliminates waste gases (as carbon dioxide) — **re•spi•ra•to•ry** \ˈres-pə-rə-ˌtōr-ē, ri-ˈspī-rə-\ *adj* — **re•spire** \ri-ˈspīr\ *vb*

res•pi•ra•tor \ˈres-pə-ˌrā-tər\ *n* **1** : a device covering the mouth or nose esp. to prevent inhaling harmful vapors **2** : a device for artificial respiration

re•spite \ˈres-pət\ *n* **1** : a temporary delay **2** : an interval of rest or relief

re•splen•dent \ri-ˈsplen-dənt\ *adj* : shining brilliantly : gloriously bright : SPLENDID — **re•splen•dence** \-dəns\ *n* — **re•splen•dent•ly** *adv*

re•spond \ri-ˈspänd\ *vb* **1** : ANSWER, REPLY **2** : REACT ⟨~*ed* to a call for help⟩ **3** : to show favorable reaction ⟨~ to medication⟩ — **re•spond•er** *n*

re•spon•dent \ri-ˈspän-dənt\ *n* : one who responds; *esp* : one who answers in various legal proceedings — **respondent** *adj*

re•sponse \ri-ˈspäns\ *n* **1** : an act of responding **2** : something constituting a reply or a reaction

re•spon•si•bil•i•ty \ri-ˌspän-sə-ˈbi-lə-tē\ *n, pl* **-ties 1** : the quality or state of being responsible **2** : something for which one is responsible

re•spon•si•ble \ri-ˈspän-sə-bəl\ *adj* **1** : liable to be called upon to answer for one's acts or decisions : ANSWERABLE **2** : able to fulfill one's obligations : RELIABLE, TRUSTWORTHY **3** : able to choose for oneself between right and wrong **4** : involving accountability or important duties ⟨~ position⟩ — **re•spon•si•ble•ness** *n* — **re•spon•si•bly** \-blē\ *adv*

re•spon•sive \-siv\ *adj* **1** : RESPONDING **2** : quick to respond : SENSITIVE **3** : using responses ⟨~ readings⟩ — **re•spon•sive•ly** *adv* — **re•spon•sive•ness** *n*

[1]**rest** \ˈrest\ *n* **1** : REPOSE, SLEEP **2** : freedom from work or activity **3** : a state of motionlessness or inactivity **4** : a place of shelter or lodging **5** : a silence in music equivalent in duration to a note of the same value; *also* : a character indicating this **6** : something used as a support — **rest•ful** \-fəl\ *adj* — **rest•ful•ly** *adv*

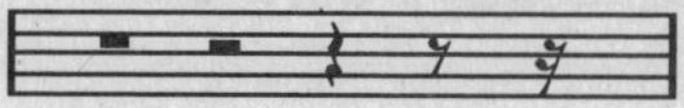

rest 5

[2]**rest** *vb* **1** : to get rest by lying down; *esp* : SLEEP **2** : to cease from action or motion **3** : to give rest to : set at rest **4** : to sit or lie fixed or supported **5** : to place on or against a support **6** : to remain based or founded **7** : to cause to be firmly fixed : GROUND **8** : to remain for action : DEPEND

[3]**rest** *n* : something left over

res•tau•rant \ˈres-trənt, -tə-ˌränt\ *n* [F, fr. prp. of *restaurer* to restore, fr. L *restaurare*] : a public eating place

res•tau•ra•teur \ˌres-tə-rə-ˈtər\ *also* **res•tau•ran•teur** \-ˌrän-\ *n* : the operator or proprietor of a restaurant

rest home *n* : an establishment that gives care for the aged or convalescent

res•ti•tu•tion \ˌres-tə-ˈtü-shən, -ˈtyü-\ *n* : the act of restoring : the state of being restored; *esp* : restoration of something to its rightful owner **syn** amends, redress, reparation, indemnity, compensation

res•tive \ˈres-tiv\ *adj* [ME, fr. MF *restif,* fr. *rester* to stop behind, remain, fr. L *restare,* fr. *re-* back + *stare* to stand] **1** : BALKY **2** : UNEASY, FIDGETY **syn** restless, impatient, nervous — **res•tive•ly** *adv* — **res•tive•ness** *n*

rest•less \ˈrest-ləs\ *adj* **1** : lacking or denying rest ⟨a ~ night⟩ **2** : never resting or settled : always moving ⟨the ~ sea⟩ **3** : marked by or showing unrest esp. of mind ⟨~ pacing back and forth⟩ **syn** restive, impatient, nervous, fidgety — **rest•less•ly** *adv* — **rest•less•ness** *n*

re•stor•able \ri-ˈstōr-ə-bəl\ *adj* : fit for restoring or reclaiming

res•to•ra•tion \ˌres-tə-ˈrā-shən\ *n* **1** : an act of restoring : the state of being restored **2** : something (as a building) that has been restored

re•stor•ative \ri-ˈstōr-ə-tiv\ *n* : something that restores esp. to consciousness or health — **restorative** *adj*

re•store \ri-ˈstōr\ *vb* **re•stored; re•stor•ing 1** : to give back : RETURN **2** : to put back into use or service **3** : to put or bring back into a former or original state **4** : to put again in possession of something — **re•stor•er** *n*

re•strain \ri-ˈstrān\ *vb* **1** : to prevent from doing something **2** : to limit, restrict, or keep under control : CURB **3** : to place under restraint or arrest — **re•strain•able** *adj* — **re•strain•er** *n*

re•strained \ri-ˈstrānd\ *adj* : marked by restraint : DISCIPLINED — **re•strain•ed•ly** \-ˈstrā-nəd-lē\ *adv*

restraining order *n* : a legal order directing one person to stay away from another

re•straint \ri-ˈstrānt\ *n* **1** : an act of restraining : the state of being restrained **2** : a restraining force, agency, or device **3** : deprivation or limitation of liberty : CONFINEMENT **4** : control over one's feelings : RESERVE

re•strict \ri-ˈstrikt\ *vb* **1** : to confine within bounds : LIMIT **2** : to place under restriction as to use — **re•stric•tive** *adj* — **re•stric•tive•ly** *adv*

re•stric•tion \ri-ˈstrik-shən\ *n* **1** : something (as a law or rule) that restricts **2** : an act of restricting : the state of being restricted

rest room *n* : a room or suite of rooms that includes sinks and toilets

¹re•sult \ri-ˈzəlt\ *vb* [ME, fr. ML *resultare*, fr. L, to rebound, fr. *re-* re- + *saltare* to leap] : to come about as an effect or consequence — **re•sul•tant** \-ˈzəlt-ᵊnt\ *adj or n*

²result *n* **1** : something that results : EFFECT, CONSEQUENCE **2** : beneficial or discernible effect **3** : something obtained by calculation or investigation

re•sume \ri-ˈzüm\ *vb* **re•sumed; re•sum•ing 1** : to take or assume again **2** : to return to or begin again after interruption **3** : to take back to oneself — **re•sump•tion** \-ˈzəmp-shən\ *n*

ré•su•mé *or* **re•su•me** *or* **re•su•mé** \ˈre-zə-ˌmā, ˌre-zə-ˈmā\ *n* [F *résumé*] : SUMMARY; *esp* : a short account of one's career and qualifications usu. prepared by a job applicant

re•sur•gence \ri-ˈsər-jəns\ *n* : a rising again into life, activity, or prominence — **re•sur•gent** \-jənt\ *adj*

res•ur•rect \ˌre-zə-ˈrekt\ *vb* **1** : to raise from the dead **2** : to bring to attention or use again

res•ur•rec•tion \ˌre-zə-ˈrek-shən\ *n* **1** *cap* : the rising of Christ from the dead **2** *often cap* : the rising to life of all human dead before the final judgment **3** : REVIVAL

re•sus•ci•tate \ri-ˈsə-sə-ˌtāt\ *vb* **-tat•ed; -tat•ing** : to revive from apparent death or unconsciousness; *also* : REVITALIZE — **re•sus•ci•ta•tion** \ri-ˌsə-sə-ˈtā-shən, ˌrē-\ *n* — **re•sus•ci•ta•tor** \-ˌtā-tər\ *n*

ret *abbr* **1** retain **2** retired **3** return

¹re•tail \ˈrē-ˌtāl, *esp for 2 also* ri-ˈtāl\ *vb* **1** : to sell in small quantities directly to the ultimate consumer **2** : to tell in detail or to one person after another — **re•tail•er** *n*

²re•tail \ˈrē-ˌtāl\ *n* : the sale of goods in small amounts to ultimate consumers — **retail** *adj or adv*

re•tain \ri-ˈtān\ *vb* **1** : to hold in possession or use **2** : to engage (as a lawyer) by paying a fee in advance **3** : to keep in a fixed place or position **syn** detain, withhold, reserve

¹re•tain•er \ri-ˈtā-nər\ *n* **1** : one that retains **2** : a servant in a wealthy household; *also* : EMPLOYEE

²retainer *n* : a fee paid to secure services (as of a lawyer)

¹re•take \(ˌ)rē-ˈtāk\ *vb* **-took** \-ˈtu̇k\; **-tak•en** \-ˈtā-kən\; **-tak•ing 1** : to take or seize again **2** : to photograph again

²re•take \ˈrē-ˌtāk\ *n* : a second photographing of a motion-picture scene

re•tal•i•ate \ri-ˈta-lē-ˌāt\ *vb* **-at•ed; -at•ing** : to return like for like; *esp* : to get revenge — **re•tal•i•a•tion** \-ˌta-lē-ˈā-shən\ *n* — **re•tal•ia•to•ry** \-ˈtal-yə-ˌtōr-ē\ *adj*

re•tard \ri-ˈtärd\ *vb* : to hold back : delay the progress of **syn** slow, slacken, detain — **re•tar•da•tion** \ˌrē-ˌtär-ˈdā-shən, ri-\ *n* — **re•tard•er** *n*

re•tard•ed *adj* : slow or limited in intellectual, emotional, or academic progress ⟨a ~ child⟩

retch \ˈrech\ *vb* : to try to vomit; *also* : VOMIT

re•ten•tion \ri-ˈten-chən\ *n* **1** : the act of retaining : the state of being retained **2** : the power of retaining esp. in the mind : RETENTIVENESS

re•ten•tive \-ˈten-tiv\ *adj* : having the power of retaining; *esp* : retaining knowledge easily — **re•ten•tive•ness** *n*

re•think \(ˌ)rē-ˈthiŋk\ *vb* **-thought** \-ˈtho̊t\; **-think•ing** : to think about again : RECONSIDER

ret•i•cent \ˈre-tə-sənt\ *adj* **1** : tending not to talk or give out information **2** : RELUCTANT **syn** reserved, taciturn, closemouthed — **ret•i•cence** \-səns\ *n* — **ret•i•cent•ly** *adv*

ret•i•na \ˈret-ᵊn-ə\ *n, pl* **retinas** *or* **ret•i•nae** \-ᵊn-ˌē\ : the sensory membrane lining the eye that receives the image formed by the lens — **ret•i•nal** \ˈret-ᵊn-əl\ *adj*

ret•i•nue \ˈret-ᵊn-ˌü, -ˌyü\ *n* : the body of attendants or followers of a distinguished person

re•tire \ri-ˈtīr\ *vb* **re•tired; re•tir•ing 1** : RETREAT **2** : to withdraw esp. for privacy **3** : to withdraw from one's occupation or position : conclude one's career **4** : to go to bed **5** : to cause to be out in baseball — **re•tire•ment** *n*

re•tired \ri-ˈtīrd\ *adj* **1** : SECLUDED, QUIET **2** : withdrawn from active duty or from one's career

re•tir•ee \ri-ˌtī-ˈrē\ *n* : a person who has retired from a career

re•tir•ing *adj* : SHY, RESERVED

¹re•tort \ri-ˈto̊rt\ *vb* [L *retortus*, pp. of *retorquēre*, lit., to twist back, hurl back, fr. *re-* back + *torquēre* to twist] **1** : to say in reply : answer back usu. sharply **2** : to answer (an argument) by a counter argument **3** : RETALIATE

²retort *n* : a quick, witty, or cutting reply

³re•tort \ri-ˈto̊rt, ˈrē-ˌto̊rt\ *n* [MF *retorte*, fr. ML *retorta*, fr. L, fem. of *retortus*, pp. of *retorquēre* to twist back; fr. its shape] : a vessel in which substances are distilled or broken up by heat

re•touch \(ˌ)rē-ˈtəch\ *vb* : TOUCH UP; *esp* : to change (as a photographic negative) in order to produce a more desirable appearance

re•trace \(ˌ)rē-ˈtrās\ *vb* : to go over again or in a reverse direction ⟨*retraced* his steps⟩

re•tract \ri-ˈtrakt\ *vb* **1** : to draw back or in **2** : to withdraw (as a charge or promise) : DISAVOW — **re•tract•able** *adj* — **re•trac•tion** \-ˈtrak-shən\ *n*

re•trac•tile \ri-ˈtrakt-ᵊl, -ˈtrak-ˌtīl\ *adj* : capable of being drawn back or in ⟨~ claws⟩

¹re•tread \(ˌ)rē-ˈtred\ *vb* **re•tread•ed; re•tread•ing** : to put a new tread on (a worn tire)

²re•tread \ˈrē-ˌtred\ *n* **1** : a retreaded tire **2** : one pressed into service again; *also* : REMAKE

¹re•treat \ri-ˈtrēt\ *n* **1** : an act of withdrawing esp. from something dangerous, difficult, or disagreeable **2** : a military signal for withdrawal; *also* : a military flag-lowering ceremony **3** : a place of privacy or safety : REFUGE **4** : a period of group withdrawal for prayer, meditation, and study

²retreat *vb* **1** : to make a retreat : WITHDRAW **2** : to slope backward

re•trench \ri-ˈtrench\ *vb* [obs. F *retrencher* (now *retrancher*), fr. MF *retrenchier*, fr. *re-* + *trenchier* to cut] **1** : to cut down or pare away : REDUCE, CURTAIL **2** : to cut down expenses : ECONOMIZE — **re•trench•ment** *n*

ret•ri•bu•tion \ˌre-trə-ˈbyü-shən\ *n* : something administered or exacted in recompense; *esp* : PUNISHMENT **syn** reprisal, vengeance, revenge, retaliation — **re•trib•u•tive** \ri-ˈtri-byə-tiv\ *adj* — **re•trib•u•to•ry** \-byə-ˌtōr-ē\ *adj*

re•trieve \ri-ˈtrēv\ *vb* **re•trieved; re•triev•ing 1** : to search about for and bring in (killed or wounded game) **2** : RECOVER, RESTORE — **re•triev•able** *adj* — **re•triev•al** \-ˈtrē-vəl\ *n*

re•triev•er \ri-ˈtrē-vər\ *n* : one that retrieves; *esp* : a dog of any of several breeds used esp. for retrieving game

ret•ro•ac•tive \ˌre-trō-ˈak-tiv\ *adj* : made effective as of a date prior to enactment ⟨a ~ pay raise⟩ — **ret•ro•ac•tive•ly** *adv*

ret•ro•fit \ˈre-tro-ˌfit, ˌre-trō-ˈfit\ *vb* : to furnish (as an

DICTIONARY

aircraft) with newly available equipment — **ret•ro•fit** \ˈre-trō-ˌfit\ *n*

[1]**ret•ro•grade** \ˈre-trə-ˌgrād\ *adj* **1** : moving or tending backward **2** : tending toward or resulting in a worse condition

[2]**retrograde** *vb* **1** : RETREAT **2** : DETERIORATE, DEGENERATE

ret•ro•gres•sion \ˌre-trə-ˈgre-shən\ *n* : return to a former and less complex level of development or organization — **ret•ro•gress** \ˌre-trə-ˈgres\ *vb* — **ret•ro•gres•sive** \ˌre-trə-ˈgre-siv\ *adj*

ret•ro–rock•et \ˈre-trō-ˌrä-kət\ *n* : an auxiliary rocket engine (as on a spacecraft) used to slow forward motion

ret•ro•spect \ˈre-trə-ˌspekt\ *n* : a review of past events — **ret•ro•spec•tion** \ˌre-trə-ˈspek-shən\ *n* — **ret•ro•spec•tive** \-ˈspek-tiv\ *adj* — **ret•ro•spec•tive•ly** *adv*

ret•ro•vi•rus \ˈre-trō-ˌvī-rəs\ *n* : any of a group of RNA-containing viruses (as HIV) that make DNA using RNA instead of the reverse

[1]**re•turn** \ri-ˈtərn\ *vb* **1** : to go or come back **2** : to pass, give, or send back to an earlier possessor **3** : to put back to or in a former place or state **4** : REPLY, ANSWER **5** : to report esp. officially **6** : to elect to office **7** : to bring in (as profit) : YIELD **8** : to give or perform in return — **re•turn•er** *n*

[2]**return** *n* **1** : an act of coming or going back to or from a former place or state **2** : RECURRENCE **3** : a report of the results of balloting **4** : a formal statement of taxable income **5** : the profit from labor, investment, or business : YIELD **6** : the act of returning something **7** : something that returns or is returned; *also* : a means for conveying something (as water) back to its starting point **8** : something given in repayment or reciprocation; *also* : ANSWER, RETORT **9** : an answering play — **return** *adj*

[1]**re•turn•able** \ri-ˈtər-nə-bəl\ *adj* : capable of being returned (as for reuse or recycling); *also* : permitted to be returned

[2]**returnable** *n* : a returnable beverage container

re•turn•ee \ri-ˌtər-ˈnē\ *n* : one who returns

re•union \rē-ˈyü-nyən\ *n* **1** : an act of reuniting : the state of being reunited **2** : a meeting of persons after separation

[1]**rev** \ˈrev\ *n* : a revolution of a motor

[2]**rev** *vb* **revved; rev•ving** : to increase the revolutions per minute of (a motor)

[3]**rev** *abbr* **1** revenue **2** reverse **3** review; reviewed **4** revised; revision **5** revolution

Rev *abbr* **1** Revelation **2** Reverend

re•vamp \(ˌ)rē-ˈvamp\ *vb* : RECONSTRUCT, REVISE; *also* : RENOVATE

re•vanche \rə-ˈväⁿsh\ *n* [F] : REVENGE; *esp* : a usu. political policy designed to recover lost territory or status

re•veal \ri-ˈvēl\ *vb* **1** : to make known **2** : to show plainly : open up to view

rev•eil•le \ˈre-və-lē\ *n* [modif. of F *réveillez,* imper. pl. of *réveiller* to awaken, fr. *eveiller* to awaken, fr. (assumed) VL *exvigilare,* fr. L *vigilare* to keep watch, stay awake] : a military signal sounded at about sunrise

[1]**rev•el** \ˈre-vəl\ *vb* **-eled** *or* **-elled; -el•ing** *or* **-el•ling 1** : to take part in a revel **2** : to take great pleasure or satisfaction — **rev•el•er** *or* **rev•el•ler** *n* — **rev•el•ry** \-vəl-rē\ *n*

[2]**revel** *n* : a usu. wild party or celebration

rev•e•la•tion \ˌre-və-ˈlā-shən\ *n* **1** : an act of revealing **2** : something revealed; *esp* : an enlightening or astonishing disclosure

Revelation *n* — see BIBLE table

[1]**re•venge** \ri-ˈvenj\ *vb* **re•venged; re•veng•ing** : to inflict harm or injury in return for (a wrong) : AVENGE — **re•veng•er** *n*

[2]**revenge** *n* **1** : a desire for revenge **2** : an act or instance of retaliation to get even **3** : an opportunity for getting satisfaction **syn** vengeance, retribution, reprisal — **re•venge•ful** *adj*

rev•e•nue \ˈre-və-ˌnü, -ˌnyü\ *n* [ME, fr. MF, fr. *revenir* to return, fr. L *revenire,* fr. *re-* back + *venire* to come] **1** : investment income **2** : money collected by a government (as through taxes)

rev•e•nu•er \ˈre-və-ˌnü-ər, -ˌnyü-\ *n* : a revenue officer or boat

re•verb \ri-ˈvərb, ˈrē-ˌvərb\ *n* : an electronically produced echo effect in recorded music; *also* : a device for producing reverb

re•ver•ber•ate \ri-ˈvər-bə-ˌrāt\ *vb* **-at•ed; -at•ing 1** : REFLECT ⟨~ light or heat⟩ **2** : to resound in or as if in a series of echoes — **re•ver•ber•a•tion** \-ˌvər-bə-ˈrā-shən\ *n*

re•vere \ri-ˈvir\ *vb* **re•vered; re•ver•ing** : to show honor and devotion to : VENERATE **syn** reverence, worship, adore

[1]**rev•er•ence** \ˈre-vrəns, -və-rəns\ *n* **1** : honor or respect felt or shown **2** : a gesture (as a bow or curtsy) of respect

[2]**reverence** *vb* **-enced; -enc•ing** : to regard or treat with reverence

[1]**rev•er•end** \ˈre-vrənd, -və-rənd\ *adj* **1** : worthy of reverence : REVERED **2** : being a member of the clergy — used as a title

[2]**reverend** *n* : a member of the clergy

rev•er•ent \ˈre-vrənt, -və-rənt\ *adj* : expressing reverence — **rev•er•ent•ly** *adv*

rev•er•en•tial \ˌre-və-ˈren-chəl\ *adj* : REVERENT

rev•er•ie *also* **rev•ery** \ˈre-və-rē\ *n, pl* **-er•ies 1** : DAYDREAM **2** : the state of being lost in thought

re•ver•sal \ri-ˈvər-səl\ *n* : an act or process of reversing

[1]**re•verse** \ri-ˈvərs\ *adj* **1** : opposite to a previous or normal condition ⟨in ~ order⟩ **2** : acting or working in a manner opposite the usual **3** : bringing about reverse movement ⟨~ gear⟩ — **re•verse•ly** *adv*

[2]**reverse** *vb* **re•versed; re•vers•ing 1** : to turn upside down or completely about in position or direction **2** : to set aside or change (as a legal decision) **3** : to change to the contrary ⟨~ a policy⟩ **4** : to go or cause to go in the opposite direction **5** : to put (as a car) in reverse — **re•vers•ible** \-ˈvər-sə-bəl\ *adj*

[3]**reverse** *n* **1** : something contrary to something else : OPPOSITE **2** : an act or instance of reversing; *esp* : a change for the worse **3** : the back of something **4** : a gear that reverses something

re•ver•sion \ri-ˈvər-zhən\ *n* **1** : the right of succession or future possession (as to a title or property) **2** : return toward some former or ancestral condition; *also* : a product of this — **re•ver•sion•ary** \-zhə-ˌner-ē\ *adj*

re•vert \ri-ˈvərt\ *vb* **1** : to come or go back ⟨~*ed* to savagery⟩ **2** : to return to a proprietor or his or her heirs **3** : to return to an ancestral type

[1]**re•view** \ri-ˈvyü\ *n* **1** : an act of revising **2** : a formal military inspection **3** : a general survey **4** : INSPECTION, EXAMINATION; *esp* : REEXAMINATION **5** : a critical evaluation (as of a book) **6** : a magazine devoted to reviews and essays **7** : a renewed study of previously studied material **8** : REVUE

[2]**re•view** \ri-ˈvyü, *1 also* ˈrē-\ *vb* **1** : to examine or study again; *esp* : to reexamine judicially **2** : to hold a review of ⟨~ troops⟩ **3** : to write a critical examination of ⟨~ a novel⟩ **4** : to look back over ⟨~*ed* her accomplishments⟩ **5** : to study material again

re•view•er \ri-ˈvyü-ər\ *n* : one that reviews; *esp* : a writer of critical reviews

re•vile \ri-ˈvīl\ *vb* **re•viled; re•vil•ing** : to abuse verbally : rail at **syn** vituperate, berate, rate, upbraid, scold — **re•vile•ment** *n* — **re•vil•er** *n*

re•vise \ri-ˈvīz\ *vb* **re•vised; re•vis•ing 1** : to look over something written in order to correct or improve **2** : to make a new version of — **re•vis•able** *adj* — **re•vise** *n* — **re•vis•er** *or* **re•vi•sor** \-ˈvī-zər\ *n* — **re•vi•sion** \-ˈvi-zhən\ *n*

re•vi•tal•ise *Brit var of* REVITALIZE

re•vi•tal•ize \ˌrē-ˈvīt-ᵊl-ˌīz\ *vb* **-ized; -iz•ing** : to give new life or vigor to — **re•vi•tal•i•za•tion** \(ˌ)rē-ˌvīt-ᵊl-ə-ˈzā-shən\ *n*

re•viv•al \ri-ˈvī-vəl\ *n* **1** : an act of reviving : the state of being revived **2** : a new publication or presentation (as of a book or play) **3** : an evangelistic meeting or series of meetings

re•vive \ri-ˈvīv\ *vb* **re•vived; re•viv•ing 1** : to bring back to life consciousness, or activity : make or become fresh or strong again **2** : to bring back into use — **re•viv•er** *n*

re•viv•i•fy \rē-ˈvi-və-ˌfī\ *vb* : REVIVE — **re•viv•i•fi•ca•tion** \-ˌvi-və-fə-ˈkā-shən\ *n*

re•vo•ca•ble \ˈre-və-kə-bəl *also* ri-ˈvō-kə-bəl\ *adj* : capable of being revoked

re•vo•ca•tion \ˌre-və-ˈkā-shən\ *n* : an act or instance of revoking

re•voke \ri-ˈvōk\ *vb* **re•voked; re•vok•ing 1** : to annul by recalling or taking back : REPEAL, RESCIND **2** : RENEGE 2 — **re•vok•er** *n*

[1]**re•volt** \ri-ˈvōlt\ *vb* **1** : to throw off allegiance to a ruler or government : REBEL **2** : to experience disgust or shock **3** : to turn or cause to turn away with disgust or abhorrence — **re•volt•er** *n*

[2]**revolt** *n* : REBELLION, INSURRECTION

re•volt•ing *adj* : extremely offensive — **re•volt•ing•ly** *adv*

rev•o•lu•tion \ˌre-və-ˈlü-shən\ *n* **1** : the action by a heavenly body of going round in an orbit **2** : ROTATION **3** : a sudden, radical, or complete change; *esp* : the overthrow or renunciation of one ruler or government and substitution of another by the governed

[1]**rev•o•lu•tion•ary** \-shə-ˌner-ē\ *adj* **1** : of or relating to revolution **2** : tending to or promoting revolution **3** : constituting or bringing about a major change

[2]**revolutionary** *n, pl* **-ar•ies** : one who takes part in a revolution or who advocates revolutionary doctrines

rev•o•lu•tion•ise *Brit var of* REVOLUTIONIZE

rev•o•lu•tion•ist \ˌre-və-ˈlü-shə-nist\ *n* : REVOLUTIONARY — **revolutionist** *adj*

rev•o•lu•tion•ize \-ˌnīz\ *vb* **-ized; -iz•ing** : to change fundamentally or completely : make revolutionary — **rev•o•lu•tion•iz•er** *n*

re•volve \ri-ˈvälv\ *vb* **re•volved; re•volv•ing 1** : to turn over in the mind : reflect upon : PONDER **2** : to move in an orbit; *also* : ROTATE — **re•volv•able** *adj*

re•volv•er \ri-ˈväl-vər\ *n* : a pistol with a revolving cylinder of several chambers

re•vue \ri-ˈvyü\ *n* : a theatrical production consisting typically of brief often satirical sketches and songs

re•vul•sion \ri-ˈvəl-shən\ *n* **1** : a strong sudden reaction or change of feeling **2** : a feeling of complete distaste or repugnance

revved *past and past part of* REV

revving *pres part of* REV

[1]**re•ward** \ri-ˈwȯrd\ *vb* **1** : to give a reward to or for **2** : RECOMPENSE

[2]**reward** *n* **1** : something given in return for good or evil done or received; *esp* : something given or offered for some service or attainment **2** : a stimulus that is administered to an organism after a response and that increases the probability of occurrence of the response **syn** premium, prize, award

[1]**re•wind** \(ˌ)rē-ˈwīnd\ *vb* **-wound; -wind•ing 1** : to wind again **2** : to reverse the winding of (as film)

[2]**re•wind** \ˈrē-ˌwīnd\ *n* **1** : something that rewinds **2** : an act of rewinding

re•work \(ˌ)rē-ˈwərk\ *vb* **1** : REVISE **2** : to reprocess for further use

[1]**re•write** \(ˌ)rē-ˈrīt\ *vb* **-wrote; -writ•ten; -writ•ing** : to make a revision of : REVISE

[2]**re•write** \ˈrē-ˌrīt\ *n* : an instance or a piece of rewriting

RF *abbr* radio frequency

RFD *abbr* rural free delivery

Rh *symbol* rhodium

RH *abbr* right hand

rhap•so•dy \ˈrap-sə-dē\ *n, pl* **-dies** [L *rhapsodia* portion of an epic poem adapted for recitation, fr. Gk *rhapsōidia* recitation of selections from epic poetry, fr. *rhaptein* to sew, stitch together + *aidein* to sing] **1** : an expression of extravagant praise or ecstasy **2** : an instrumental composition of irregular form — **rhap•sod•ic** \rap-ˈsä-dik\ *adj* — **rhap•sod•i•cal•ly** \-di-k(ə-)lē\ *adv* — **rhap•so•dize** \ˈrap-sə-ˌdīz\ *vb*

rhea \ˈrē-ə\ *n* : either of two large flightless 3-toed So. American birds that resemble but are smaller than the African ostrich

rhe•ni•um \ˈrē-nē-əm\ *n* : a rare heavy hard metallic chemical element — see ELEMENT table

rheo•stat \ˈrē-ə-ˌstat\ *n* : a resistor for regulating an electric current by means of variable resistances — **rheo•stat•ic** \ˌrē-ə-ˈsta-tik\ *adj*

rhe•sus monkey \ˈrē-səs-\ *n* : a pale brown Indian monkey often used in medical research

rhet•o•ric \ˈre-tə-rik\ *n* [ME *rethorik*, fr. MF *rethorique*, fr. L *rhetorica*, fr. Gk *rhētorikē*, lit., art of oratory, fr. *rhētōr* public speaker, fr. *eirein* to speak] : the art of speaking or writing effectively — **rhe•tor•i•cal** \ri-ˈtȯr-i-kəl\ *adj* — **rhet•o•ri•cian** \ˌre-tə-ˈri-shən\ *n*

rheum \ˈrüm\ *n* : a watery discharge from the mucous membranes esp. of the eyes or nose — **rheumy** *adj*

rheu•mat•ic fever \ru̇-ˈma-tik-\ *n* : an acute disease chiefly of children and young adults that is characterized by fever, by inflammation and pain in and around the joints, and by inflammation of the membranes surrounding the heart and the heart valves

rheu•ma•tism \ˈrü-mə-ˌti-zəm, ˈru̇-\ *n* : any of various conditions marked by stiffness, pain, or swelling in muscles or joints — **rheu•mat•ic** \ru̇-ˈma-tik\ *adj*

rheu•ma•toid arthritis \-ˌtȯid-\ *n* : a progressive constitutional disease characterized by inflammation and swelling of joint structures

Rh factor \ˌär-ˈāch-\ *n* [*rh*esus monkey (in which it was first detected)] : any of one or more inherited substances in red blood cells that may cause dangerous reactions in some infants or in transfusions

rhine•stone \ˈrīn-ˌstōn\ *n* : a colorless imitation stone of high luster made of glass, paste, or gem quartz

rhi•no \ˈrī-nō\ *n, pl* **rhino** *or* **rhinos** : RHINOCEROS

rhi•noc•er•os \rī-ˈnä-sə-rəs\ *n, pl* **-noc•er•os•es** *or* **-noc•er•os** *or* **-noc•eri** \-ˈnä-sə-ˌrī\ [ME *rinoceros*, fr. L *rhinoceros*, fr. Gk *rhinokerōs*, fr. *rhin-*, *rhis* nose + *keras* horn] : any of a family of large thick-skinned mammals of Africa and Asia with one or two upright horns of keratin on the snout and three toes on each foot

rhi•zome \ˈrī-ˌzōm\ *n* : a fleshy, rootlike, and usu. horizontal underground plant stem that forms shoots above and roots below — **rhi•zom•a•tous** \rī-ˈzä-mə-təs\ *adj*

Rh–neg•a•tive \ˌär-ˌāch-ˈne-gə-tiv\ *adj* : lacking Rh factors in the red blood cells

rho \ˈrō\ *n* : the 17th letter of the Greek alphabet — Ρ or ρ

rho•di•um \ˈrō-dē-əm\ *n* : a hard ductile metallic chemical element — see ELEMENT table

rho•do•den•dron \ˌrō-də-ˈden-drən\ *n* : any of a genus of shrubs or trees of the heath family with clusters of large bright flowers

rhom•boid \ˈräm-ˌbȯid\ *n* : a parallelogram with unequal adjacent sides and angles that are not right angles — **rhomboid** *or* **rhom•boi•dal** \räm-ˈbȯid-ᵊl\ *adj*

rhom•bus \ˈräm-bəs\ *n, pl* **rhom•bus•es** *or* **rhom•bi** \-ˌbī\ : a parallelogram having all four sides equal

☞ For illustration, see next page.

Rh–pos•i•tive \ˌär-ˌāch-ˈpä-zə-tiv\ *adj* : containing one or more Rh factors in the red blood cells

rhu•barb \ˈrü-ˌbärb\ *n* [ME *rubarbe*, fr. MF *reubarbe*,

DICTIONARY

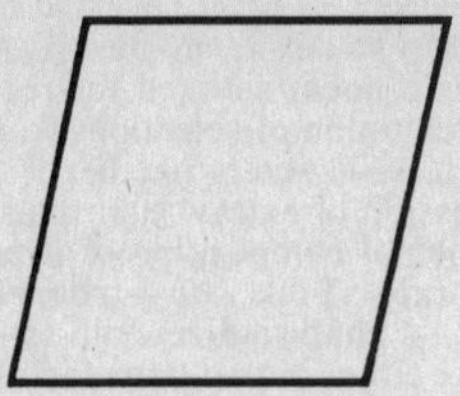
rhombus

fr. ML *reubarbarum,* alter. of *rha barbarum,* lit., barbarian rhubarb] : a garden plant related to the buckwheat having leaves with thick juicy edible pink and red stems

¹rhyme \ˈrīm\ *n* **1** : a composition in verse that rhymes; *also* : POETRY **2** : correspondence in terminal sounds (as of two lines of verse)

²rhyme *vb* **rhymed; rhym•ing 1** : to make rhymes; *also* : to write poetry **2** : to have rhymes : be in rhyme

rhythm \ˈri-thəm\ *n* **1** : regular rise and fall in the flow of sound in speech **2** : a movement or activity in which some action or element recurs regularly — **rhyth•mic** \ˈrith-mik\ *or* **rhyth•mi•cal** \-mi-kəl\ *adj* — **rhyth•mi•cal•ly** \-k(ə-)lē\ *adv*

rhythm and blues *n* : popular music based on blues and black folk music

rhythm method *n* : birth control by refraining from sexual intercourse during the time when ovulation is most likely to occur

RI *abbr* Rhode Island

ri•al \rē-ˈȯl, -ˈäl\ *n* — see MONEY table

¹rib \ˈrib\ *n* **1** : any of the series of curved bones of the chest of most vertebrates that are joined to the backbone in pairs and help to support the body wall and protect the organs inside **2** : something resembling a rib in shape or function **3** : any of the parallel ridges in a knitted or woven fabric

²rib *vb* **ribbed; rib•bing 1** : to furnish or strengthen with ribs **2** : to form ridges in knitting or weaving

³rib *vb* **ribbed; rib•bing** : to poke fun at : TEASE — **rib•ber** *n*

rib•ald \ˈri-bəld\ *adj* : coarse or indecent esp. in language ⟨~ jokes⟩ — **rib•ald•ry** \-bəl-drē\ *n*

rib•and \ˈri-bənd\ *n* : RIBBON

rib•bon \ˈri-bən\ *n* **1** : a narrow fabric typically of silk or velvet used for trimming and for badges **2** : a strip of inked cloth (as in a typewriter) **3** : TATTER, SHRED ⟨torn to ~*s*⟩

ri•bo•fla•vin \ˌrī-bə-ˈflā-vən, ˈrī-bə-ˌflā-vən\ *n* : a growth-promoting vitamin of the vitamin B complex occurring in milk and liver

ri•bo•nu•cle•ic acid \ˌrī-bō-nu̇-ˌklē-ik-, -nyu̇-, -ˌklā-\ *n* : RNA

ri•bose \ˈrī-ˌbōs\ *n* : a sugar with five carbon atoms and five oxygen atoms in each molecule that is part of RNA

ri•bo•some \ˈrī-bə-ˌsōm\ *n* : any of the RNA-rich cytoplasmic granules in a cell that are sites of protein synthesis — **ri•bo•som•al** \ˌrī-bə-ˈsō-məl\ *adj*

rice \ˈrīs\ *n* : the starchy seeds of an annual grass that are cooked and used for food; *also* : this widely cultivated grass of warm wet areas

rich \ˈrich\ *adj* **1** : possessing or controlling great wealth : WEALTHY **2** : COSTLY, VALUABLE **3** : deep and pleasing in color or tone **4** : ABUNDANT **5** : containing much sugar, fat, or seasoning; *also* : high in combustible content **6** : FRUITFUL, FERTILE — **rich•ly** *adv* — **rich•ness** *n*

rich•es \ˈri-chəz\ *n pl* [ME, sing. or pl., fr. *richesse,* lit., richness, fr. OF, fr. *riche* rich] : things that make one rich : WEALTH

Rich•ter scale \ˈrik-tər-\ *n* : a scale for expressing the magnitude of a seismic disturbance (as an earthquake) in terms of the energy dissipated in it

rick \ˈrik\ *n* : a large stack (as of hay) in the open air

rick•ets \ˈri-kəts\ *n* : a childhood deficiency disease marked esp. by soft deformed bones and caused by inadequate sunlight or inadequate vitamin D

rick•ett•sia \ri-ˈket-sē-ə\ *n, pl* **-si•as** *or* **-si•ae** \-sē-ˌē\ : any of a group of rod-shaped bacteria that cause various diseases (as typhus)

rick•ety \ˈri-kə-tē\ *adj* **1** : affected with rickets **2** : SHAKY; *also* : in unsound physical condition

rick•sha *or* **rick•shaw** \ˈrik-ˌshȯ\ *n* : a small covered 2-wheeled carriage pulled by one person and used orig. in Japan

¹ric•o•chet \ˈri-kə-ˌshā, *Brit also* -ˌshet\ *n* : a bouncing off at an angle (as of a bullet off a wall); *also* : an object that ricochets

²ricochet *vb* **-cheted** \-ˌshād\ *or* **-chet•ted** \-ˌshe-təd\; **-chet•ing** \-ˌshā-iŋ\ *or* **-chet•ting** \-ˌshe-tiŋ\ : to skip with or as if with glancing rebounds

rid \ˈrid\ *vb* **rid** *also* **rid•ded; rid•ding** : to make free : CLEAR, RELIEVE — **rid•dance** \ˈrid-ᵊns\ *n*

rid•den \ˈrid-ᵊn\ *adj* **1** : harassed, oppressed, or obsessed by ⟨debt-*ridden*⟩ **2** : excessively full of or supplied with ⟨slum-*ridden*⟩

¹rid•dle \ˈrid-ᵊl\ *n* : a puzzling question to be solved or answered by guessing

²riddle *vb* **rid•dled; rid•dling 1** : EXPLAIN, SOLVE **2** : to speak in riddles

³riddle *n* : a coarse sieve

⁴riddle *vb* **rid•dled; rid•dling 1** : to sift with a riddle **2** : to pierce with many holes **3** : PERMEATE

¹ride \ˈrīd\ *vb* **rode** \ˈrōd\; **rid•den** \ˈrid-ᵊn\; **rid•ing 1** : to go on an animal's back or in a conveyance (as a boat, car, or airplane); *also* : to sit on and control so as to be carried along ⟨~ a bicycle⟩ **2** : to float or move on water ⟨~ at anchor⟩; *also* : to move like a floating object **3** : to bear along : CARRY ⟨*rode* her on their shoulders⟩ **4** : to travel over a surface ⟨car ~*s* well⟩ **5** : to proceed over on horseback **6** : to torment by nagging or teasing

²ride *n* **1** : an act of riding; *esp* : a trip on horseback or by vehicle **2** : a way (as a road or path) suitable for riding **3** : a mechanical device (as a merry-go-round) for riding on **4** : a means of transportation

rid•er \ˈrī-dər\ *n* **1** : one that rides **2** : an addition to a document often attached on a separate piece of paper **3** : a clause dealing with an unrelated matter attached to a legislative bill during passage — **rid•er•less** *adj*

¹ridge \ˈrij\ *n* **1** : a range of hills **2** : a raised line or strip **3** : the line made where two sloping surfaces (as of a roof) meet — **ridgy** *adj*

²ridge *vb* **ridged; ridg•ing 1** : to form into a ridge **2** : to extend in ridges

¹rid•i•cule \ˈri-də-ˌkyül\ *n* : the act of exposing to laughter : DERISION

²ridicule *vb* **-culed; -cul•ing** : to laugh at or make fun of mockingly or contemptuously **syn** deride, taunt, twit, mock

ri•dic•u•lous \rə-ˈdi-kyə-ləs\ *adj* : arousing or deserving ridicule : ABSURD, PREPOSTEROUS **syn** laughable, ludicrous, farcical, risible — **ri•dic•u•lous•ly** *adv* — **ri•dic•u•lous•ness** *n*

ri•el \rē-ˈel\ *n* — see MONEY table

RIF *abbr* reduction in force

rife \ˈrīf\ *adj* : WIDESPREAD, PREVALENT, ABOUNDING — **rife** *adv* — **rife•ly** *adv*

riff \ˈrif\ *n* : a repeated phrase in jazz typically supporting a solo improvisation; *also* : a piece based on such a phrase — **riff** *vb*

riff•raff \rif-ˌraf\ *n* [ME *riffe raffe,* fr. *rif and raf* every single one, fr. MF *rif et raf* completely] **1** : RABBLE **2** : REFUSE, RUBBISH

¹ri•fle \ˈrī-fəl\ *vb* **ri•fled; ri•fling** : to ransack esp. with the intent to steal — **ri•fler** *n*

[2]**rifle** *vb* **ri•fled; ri•fling :** to cut spiral grooves into the bore of ⟨*rifled* pipe⟩ — **rifling** *n*

[3]**rifle** *n* **1 :** a shoulder weapon with a rifled bore **2** *pl* **:** soldiers armed with rifles — **ri•fle•man** \-fəl-mən\ *n*

rift \ˈrift\ *n* **1 :** CLEFT, FISSURE **2 :** FAULT 6 **3 :** ESTRANGEMENT, SEPARATION — **rift** *vb*

[1]**rig** \ˈrig\ *vb* **rigged; rig•ging 1 :** to fit out (as a ship) with rigging **2 :** CLOTHE, DRESS **3 :** EQUIP **4 :** to set up esp. as a makeshift ⟨~ up a shelter⟩

[2]**rig** *n* **1 :** the distinctive shape, number, and arrangement of sails and masts of a ship **2 :** a carriage with its horse **3 :** CLOTHING, DRESS **4 :** EQUIPMENT

[3]**rig** *vb* **rigged; rig•ging 1 :** to manipulate or control esp. by deceptive or dishonest means **2 :** to fix in advance for a desired result — **rig•ger** *n*

rig•ging \ˈri-giŋ, -gən\ *n* **1 :** the ropes and chains that hold and move masts, sails, and spars of a ship **2 :** a network (as in theater scenery) used for support and manipulation

[1]**right** \ˈrīt\ *adj* **1 :** RIGHTEOUS, UPRIGHT **2 :** JUST, PROPER **3 :** conforming to truth or fact **:** CORRECT **4 :** APPROPRIATE, SUITABLE **5 :** STRAIGHT ⟨a ~ line⟩ **6 :** GENUINE, REAL **7 :** of, relating to, or being the side of the body which is away from the heart and on which the hand is stronger and more skilled in most persons **8 :** located nearer to the right hand; *esp* **:** being on the right when facing in the same direction as the observer **9 :** made to be placed or worn outward ⟨~ side of a rug⟩ **10 :** NORMAL, SOUND ⟨not in her ~ mind⟩ **syn** correct, accurate, exact, precise, nice — **right•ness** *n*

[2]**right** *n* **1 :** qualities that constitute what is correct, just, proper, or honorable **2 :** something (as a power or privilege) to which one has a just or lawful claim **3 :** just action or decision **:** the cause of justice **4 :** the side or part that is on or toward the right side **5** *cap* **:** political conservatives **6** *often cap* **:** a conservative position — **right•ward** \-wərd\ *adj*

[3]**right** *adv* **1 :** according to what is right ⟨live ~⟩ **2 :** EXACTLY, PRECISELY ⟨~ here and now⟩ **3 :** DIRECTLY ⟨went ~ home⟩ **4 :** according to fact or truth ⟨guess ~⟩ **5 :** all the way **:** COMPLETELY ⟨~ to the end⟩ **6 :** IMMEDIATELY ⟨~ after lunch⟩ **7 :** QUITE, VERY ⟨~ nice weather⟩ **8 :** on or to the right ⟨looked ~ and left⟩

[4]**right** *vb* **1 :** to relieve from wrong **2 :** to adjust or restore to a proper state or position **3 :** to bring or restore to an upright position **4 :** to become upright — **right•er** *n*

right angle *n* **:** an angle whose measure is 90° **:** an angle whose sides are perpendicular to each other — **right–an•gled** \ˈrīt-ˈaŋ-gəld\ *or* **right–an•gle** \-gəl\ *adj*

right circular cone *n* **:** CONE 2

righ•teous \ˈrī-chəs\ *adj* **:** acting or being in accordance with what is just, honorable, and free from guilt or wrong **:** UPRIGHT **syn** virtuous, noble, moral, ethical — **righ•teous•ly** *adv* — **righ•teous•ness** *n*

right•ful \ˈrīt-fəl\ *adj* **1 :** JUST; *also* **:** FITTING **2 :** having or held by a legally just claim — **right•ful•ly** *adv* — **right•ful•ness** *n*

right–hand \ˈrīt-ˌhand\ *adj* **1 :** situated on the right **2 :** RIGHT-HANDED **3 :** chiefly relied on ⟨his ~ man⟩

right–hand•ed \-ˈhan-dəd\ *adj* **1 :** using the right hand habitually or better than the left **2 :** designed for or done with the right hand **3 :** CLOCKWISE ⟨a ~ twist⟩ — **right–handed** *adv* — **right–hand•ed•ly** *adv* — **right–hand•ed•ness** *n*

right•ly \ˈrīt-lē\ *adv* **1 :** FAIRLY, JUSTLY **2 :** PROPERLY **3 :** CORRECTLY, EXACTLY

right–of–way *n, pl* **rights–of–way 1 :** a legal right of passage over another person's ground **2 :** the area over which a right-of-way exists **3 :** the land on which a public road is built **4 :** the land occupied by a railroad **5 :** the land used by a public utility **6 :** the right of traffic to take precedence over other traffic

right on *interj* — used to express agreement or give encouragement

right–to–life *adj* **:** ANTIABORTION — **right–to–lifer** *n*

right triangle *n* **:** a triangle having one right angle

rig•id \ˈri-jəd\ *adj* **1 :** lacking flexibility **2 :** strictly observed **syn** severe, stern, rigorous, stringent — **ri•gid•i•ty** \rə-ˈji-də-tē\ *n* — **rig•id•ly** *adv*

rig•ma•role \ˈri-gə-mə-ˌrōl\ *n* [alter. of obs. *ragman roll* long list, catalog] **1 :** confused or senseless talk **2 :** a complex and ritualistic procedure

rig•or \ˈri-gər\ *n* **1 :** the quality of being inflexible or unyielding **:** STRICTNESS **2 :** HARSHNESS, SEVERITY **3 :** a tremor caused by a chill **4 :** strict precision **:** EXACTNESS — **rig•or•ous** *adj* — **rig•or•ous•ly** *adv*

rig•or mor•tis \ˌri-gər-ˈmȯr-təs\ *n* [NL, stiffness of death] **:** temporary rigidity of muscles occurring after death

rig•our *chiefly Brit var of* RIGOR

rile \ˈrīl\ *vb* **riled; ril•ing 1 :** to make angry **2 :** ROIL 1

rill \ˈril\ *n* **:** a very small brook

[1]**rim** \ˈrim\ *n* **1 :** the outer part of a wheel **2 :** an outer edge esp. of something curved **:** BORDER, MARGIN

[2]**rim** *vb* **rimmed; rim•ming 1 :** to serve as a rim for **:** BORDER **2 :** to run around the rim of

[1]**rime** \ˈrīm\ *n* **:** FROST 2 — **rimy** \ˈrī-mē\ *adj*

[2]**rime** *var of* RHYME

rind \ˈrīnd\ *n* **:** a usu. hard or tough outer layer ⟨lemon ~⟩

[1]**ring** \ˈriŋ\ *n* **1 :** a circular band worn as an ornament or token or used for holding or fastening ⟨wedding ~⟩ ⟨key ~⟩ **2 :** something circular in shape ⟨smoke ~⟩ **3 :** a place for contest or display ⟨boxing ~⟩; *also* **:** PRIZEFIGHTING **4 :** ANNUAL RING **5 :** a group of people who work together for selfish or dishonest purposes — **ringed** *adj* — **ring•like** \ˈriŋ-ˌlīk\ *adj*

[2]**ring** *vb* **ringed; ring•ing** \ˈriŋ-iŋ\ **1 :** ENCIRCLE **2 :** to throw a ring over (a mark) in a game (as quoits) **3 :** to move in a ring or spirally

[3]**ring** *vb* **rang** \ˈraŋ\; **rung** \ˈrəŋ\; **ring•ing** \ˈriŋ-iŋ\ **1 :** to sound resonantly when struck; *also* **:** to feel as if filled with such sound **2 :** to cause to make a clear metallic sound by striking **3 :** to announce or call by or as if by striking a bell ⟨~ an alarm⟩ **4 :** to repeat loudly and persistently **5 :** to summon esp. by a bell ⟨~ for the butler⟩

[4]**ring** *n* **1 :** a set of bells **2 :** the clear resonant sound of vibrating metal **3 :** resonant tone **:** SONORITY **4 :** a sound or character expressive of a particular quality **5 :** an act or instance of ringing; *esp* **:** a telephone call

[1]**ring•er** \ˈriŋ-ər\ *n* **1 :** one that sounds by ringing **2 :** one that enters a competition under false representations **3 :** one that closely resembles another

[2]**ringer** *n* **:** one that encircles or puts a ring around

ring finger *n* **:** the third finger of the left hand counting the forefinger as one

ring•git \ˈriŋ-git\ *n* — see MONEY table

ring•lead•er \ˈriŋ-ˌlē-dər\ *n* **:** a leader esp. of a group of troublemakers

ring•let \-lət\ *n* **:** a long curl

ring•mas•ter \-ˌmas-tər\ *n* **:** one in charge of performances in a circus ring

ring up *vb* **1 :** to total and record esp. by means of a cash register **2 :** ACHIEVE ⟨*rang up* many triumphs⟩

ring•worm \ˈriŋ-ˌwərm\ *n* **:** any of several contagious skin diseases caused by fungi and marked by ring-shaped discolored patches

rink \ˈriŋk\ *n* **:** a level extent of ice marked off for skating or various games; *also* **:** a similar surface (as of wood) marked off or enclosed for a sport or game ⟨roller-skating ~⟩

[1]**rinse** \ˈrins\ *vb* **rinsed; rins•ing** [ME *rincen,* fr. MF *rincer,* fr. (assumed) VL *recentiare,* fr. L *recent-, recens* fresh, recent] **1 :** to wash lightly or in water only **2 :** to cleanse (as of soap) with clear water **3 :** to treat (hair) with a rinse — **rins•er** *n*

[2]rinse *n* **1 :** an act of rinsing **2 :** a liquid used for rinsing **3 :** a solution that temporarily tints hair

ri•ot \ˈrī-ət\ *n* **1** *archaic* **:** disorderly behavior **2 :** disturbance of the public peace; *esp* **:** a violent public disorder **3 :** random or disorderly profusion ⟨a ~ of color⟩ **4 :** one that is wildly amusing ⟨the comedy is a ~⟩ — **riot** *vb* — **ri•ot•er** *n* — **ri•ot•ous** *adj*

[1]rip \ˈrip\ *vb* **ripped; rip•ping 1 :** to cut or tear open **2 :** to saw or split (wood) with the grain — **rip•per** *n*

[2]rip *n* **:** a rent made by ripping

RIP *abbr* [L *requiescat in pace*] may he rest in peace, may she rest in peace; [L *requiescant in pace*] may they rest in peace

ri•par•i•an \rə-ˈper-ē-ən\ *adj* **:** of or relating to the bank of a stream, river, or lake

rip cord *n* **:** a cord that is pulled to release the pilot parachute which lifts a main parachute out of its container

ripe \ˈrīp\ *adj* **rip•er; rip•est 1 :** fully grown and developed **:** MATURE ⟨~ fruit⟩ **2 :** fully prepared for some use or object **:** READY — **ripe•ly** *adv* — **ripe•ness** *n*

rip•en \ˈrī-pən\ *vb* **rip•ened; rip•en•ing 1 :** to grow or make ripe **2 :** to bring to completeness or perfection; *also* **:** to age or cure (cheese) to develop characteristic flavor, odor, body, texture, and color

rip–off \ˈrip-ˌȯf\ *n* **1 :** an act of stealing **:** THEFT **2 :** a cheap imitation — **rip off** *vb*

ri•poste \ri-ˈpōst\ *n* [F, modif. of It *risposta,* lit., answer] **1 :** a fencer's return thrust after a parry **2 :** a retaliatory maneuver or response; *esp* **:** a quick retort — **riposte** *vb*

rip•ple \ˈri-pəl\ *vb* **rip•pled; rip•pling 1 :** to become lightly ruffled on the surface **2 :** to make a sound like that of rippling water — **ripple** *n*

rip•saw \ˈrip-ˌsȯ\ *n* **:** a coarse-toothed saw used to cut wood in the direction of the grain

rip•stop \-ˌstäp\ *adj* **:** being a fabric woven in such a way that small tears do not spread ⟨~ nylon⟩ — **ripstop** *n*

[1]rise \ˈrīz\ *vb* **rose** \ˈrōz\; **ris•en** \ˈriz-ᵊn\; **ris•ing 1 :** to get up from sitting, kneeling, or lying **2 :** to get up from sleep or from one's bed **3 :** to return from death **4 :** to take up arms **5 :** to end a session **:** ADJOURN **6 :** to appear above the horizon **7 :** to move upward **:** ASCEND **8 :** to extend above other objects **9 :** to attain a higher level or rank **10 :** to increase in quantity or in intensity **11 :** to come into being **:** HAPPEN, BEGIN, ORIGINATE

[2]rise *n* **1 :** a spot higher than surrounding ground **2 :** an upward slope **3 :** an act of rising **:** a state of being risen **4 :** BEGINNING, ORIGIN **5 :** the elevation of one point above another **6 :** an increase in amount, number, or volume **7 :** an angry reaction

ris•er \ˈrī-zər\ *n* **1 :** one that rises **2 :** the upright part between stair treads

ris•i•bil•i•ty \ˌri-zə-ˈbi-lə-tē\ *n, pl* **-ties :** the ability or inclination to laugh — often used in pl.

ris•i•ble \ˈri-zə-bəl\ *adj* **1 :** able or inclined to laugh **2 :** arousing laughter; *esp* **:** amusingly ridiculous

[1]risk \ˈrisk\ *n* **:** exposure to possible loss or injury **:** DANGER, PERIL — **risk•i•ness** \ˈris-kē-nəs\ *n* — **risky** *adj*

[2]risk *vb* **1 :** to expose to danger ⟨~*ed* his life⟩ **2 :** to incur the danger of

ris•qué \ris-ˈkā\ *adj* [F] **:** verging on impropriety or indecency

ri•tard \ri-ˈtärd\ *adv or adj* **:** with a gradual slackening in tempo — used as a direction in music

rite \ˈrīt\ *n* **1 :** a set form for conducting a ceremony **2 :** the liturgy of a church **3 :** a ceremonial act or action

rit•u•al \ˈri-chə-wəl\ *n* **1 :** the established form esp. for a religious ceremony **2 :** a system of rites **3 :** a ceremonial act or action **4 :** a customarily repeated act or series of acts — **ritual** *adj* — **rit•u•al•ism** \-wə-ˌli-zəm\ *n* — **rit•u•al•is•tic** \ˌri-chə-wə-ˈlis-tik\ *adj* — **rit•u•al•is•ti•cal•ly** \-ti-k(ə-)lē\ *adv* — **rit•u•al•ly** *adv*

riv *abbr* river

[1]ri•val \ˈrī-vəl\ *n* [MF or L; MF, fr. L *rivalis* one using the same stream as another, rival in love, fr. *rivalis* of a stream, fr. *rivus* stream] **1 :** one of two or more trying to get what only one can have **2 :** one striving for competitive advantage **3 :** one that equals another esp. in desired qualities **:** MATCH, PEER

[2]rival *adj* **:** COMPETING

[3]rival *vb* **-valed** *or* **-valled; -val•ing** *or* **-val•ling 1 :** to be in competition with **2 :** to try to equal or excel **3 :** to have qualities that approach or equal another's

ri•val•ry \ˈrī-vəl-rē\ *n, pl* **-ries :** COMPETITION

rive \ˈrīv\ *vb* **rived** \ˈrīvd\; **riv•en** \ˈri-vən\ *also* **rived; riv•ing 1 :** SPLIT, REND **2 :** SHATTER

riv•er \ˈri-vər\ *n* **1 :** a natural stream larger than a brook **2 :** a large stream or flow

riv•er•bank \-ˌbaŋk\ *n* **:** the bank of a river

riv•er•bed \-ˌbed\ *n* **:** the channel occupied by a river

riv•er•boat \-ˌbōt\ *n* **:** a boat for use on a river

riv•er•front \-ˌfrənt\ *n* **:** the land or area along a river

riv•er•side \-ˌsīd\ *n* **:** the side or bank of a river

[1]riv•et \ˈri-vət\ *n* **:** a metal bolt with a head at one end used to join parts by being put through holes in them and then being flattened on the plain end to make another head

[2]rivet *vb* **:** to fasten with or as if with a rivet — **riv•et•er** *n*

riv•u•let \ˈri-vyə-lət, -və-\ *n* **:** a small stream

ri•yal \rē-ˈäl, -ˈal\ *n* — see MONEY table

rm *abbr* **1** ream **2** room

Rn *symbol* radon

[1]RN \ˌär-ˈen\ *n* **:** REGISTERED NURSE

[2]RN *abbr* Royal Navy

RNA \ˌär-(ˌ)en-ˈā\ *n* **:** any of various nucleic acids (as messenger RNA) that are found esp. in the cytoplasm of cells, have ribose as the 5-carbon sugar, and are associated with the control of cellular chemical activities

rnd *abbr* round

[1]roach \ˈrōch\ *n, pl* **roach** *also* **roach•es :** any of various bony fishes related to the carp; *also* **:** any of several sunfishes

[2]roach *n* **1 :** COCKROACH **2 :** the butt of a marijuana cigarette

road \ˈrōd\ *n* **1 :** ROADSTEAD — often used in pl. **2 :** an open way for vehicles, persons, and animals **:** HIGHWAY **3 :** ROUTE, PATH **4 :** a series of scheduled visits (as games or performances) in several locations or the travel necessary to make these visits ⟨the team is on the ~⟩

road•bed \ˈrōd-ˌbed\ *n* **1 :** the foundation of a road or railroad **2 :** the part of the surface of a road on which vehicles travel

road•block \-ˌbläk\ *n* **1 :** a barricade on the road ⟨a police ~⟩ **2 :** an obstruction to progress

road•ie \ˈrō-dē\ *n* **:** one who works for traveling entertainers

road•kill \ˈrōd-ˌkil\ *n* **:** an animal that has been killed on a road by a motor vehicle

road•run•ner \-ˌrə-nər\ *n* **:** a largely terrestrial bird of the southwestern U.S. and Mexico that is a speedy runner

road•side \ˈrōd-ˌsīd\ *n* **:** the strip of land along a road — **roadside** *adj*

road•stead \-ˌsted\ *n* **:** an anchorage for ships usu. less sheltered than a harbor

road•ster \ˈrōd-stər\ *n* **1 :** a driving horse **2 :** an open automobile that seats two

road•way \-ˌwā\ *n* **:** ROAD; *esp* **:** ROADBED

road•work \-ˌwərk\ *n* **1 :** work done in constructing or repairing roads **2 :** conditioning for an athletic contest (as a boxing match) consisting mainly of long runs

roam \ˈrōm\ *vb* **1 :** WANDER, ROVE **2 :** to range or wander over or about

[1]**roan** \ˈrōn\ *adj* : of dark color (as black, red, or brown) sprinkled with white ⟨a ~ horse⟩
[2]**roan** *n* : an animal (as a horse) with a roan coat; *also* : its color
[1]**roar** \ˈrōr\ *vb* **1 :** to utter a full loud prolonged sound **2 :** to make a loud confused sound (as of wind or waves) — **roar•er** *n*
[2]**roar** *n* : a sound of roaring
[1]**roast** \ˈrōst\ *vb* **1 :** to cook by dry heat (as before a fire or in an oven) **2 :** to criticize severely or kiddingly
[2]**roast** *n* **1 :** a piece of meat suitable for roasting **2 :** an outing at which food is roasted ⟨corn ~⟩ **3 :** severe criticism or kidding
[3]**roast** *adj* : ROASTED
roast•er \ˈrō-stər\ *n* **1 :** one that roasts **2 :** a device for roasting **3 :** something suitable for roasting
rob \ˈräb\ *vb* **robbed; rob•bing 1 :** to steal from **2 :** to deprive of something due or expected **3 :** to commit robbery — **rob•ber** *n*
robber fly *n* : any of a family of predaceous flies
rob•bery \ˈrä-bə-rē\ *n, pl* **-ber•ies :** the act or practice of robbing; *esp* : theft of something from a person by use of violence or threat
[1]**robe** \ˈrōb\ *n* **1 :** a long flowing outer garment; *esp* : one used for ceremonial occasions **2 :** a wrap or covering for the lower body (as for sitting outdoors)
[2]**robe** *vb* **robed; rob•ing 1 :** to clothe with or as if with a robe **2 :** DRESS
rob•in \ˈrä-bən\ *n* **1 :** a small chiefly European thrush with a somewhat orange face and breast **2 :** a large No. American thrush with a grayish back, a streaked throat, and a chiefly dull reddish breast
ro•bot \ˈrō-ˌbät, -bət\ *n* [Czech, fr. *robota* compulsory labor] **1 :** a machine that looks and acts like a human being **2 :** an efficient but insensitive person **3 :** a device that automatically performs esp. repetitive tasks **4 :** something guided by automatic controls — **ro•bot•ic** \rō-ˈbä-tik\ *adj*
ro•bot•ics \rō-ˈbä-tiks\ *n* : technology dealing with the design, construction, and operation of robots
ro•bust \rō-ˈbəst, ˈrō-(ˌ)bəst\ *adj* [L *robustus* oaken, strong, fr. *robur* oak, strength] : strong and vigorously healthy — **ro•bust•ly** *adv* — **ro•bust•ness** *n*
ROC *abbr* Republic of China (Taiwan)
[1]**rock** \ˈräk\ *vb* **1 :** to move back and forth in or as if in a cradle **2 :** to sway or cause to sway back and forth
[2]**rock** *n* **1 :** a rocking movement **2 :** popular music usu. played on electric instruments and characterized by a strong beat and much repetition
[3]**rock** *n* **1 :** a mass of stony material; *also* : broken pieces of stone **2 :** solid mineral deposits **3 :** something like a rock in firmness **4 :** GEM; *esp* : DIAMOND — **rock** *adj* — **rock•like** *adj* — **rocky** *adj*
rock and roll *n* : [2]ROCK 2
rock•bound \ˈräk-ˌbau̇nd\ *adj* : fringed or covered with rocks
rock•er \ˈrä-kər\ *n* **1 :** one of the curved pieces on which something (as a chair or cradle) rocks **2 :** a chair that rocks on rockers **3 :** a device that works with a rocking motion **4 :** a rock performer, song, or enthusiast
[1]**rock•et** \ˈrä-kət\ *n* [It *rocchetta*, lit., small distaff] **1 :** a firework that is propelled through the air by the discharge of gases produced by a burning substance **2 :** a jet engine that operates on the same principle as a firework rocket but carries the oxygen needed for burning its fuel **3 :** a rocket-propelled bomb or missile
[2]**rocket** *vb* **1 :** to convey by means of a rocket **2 :** to rise abruptly and rapidly
rock•et•ry \ˈrä-kə-trē\ *n* : the study or use of rockets
rocket ship *n* : a rocket-propelled spacecraft
rock•fall \ˈräk-ˌfȯl\ *n* : a mass of falling or fallen rocks
rock•fish \-ˌfish\ *n* : any of various market bony fishes that live among rocks or on rocky bottoms
rock salt *n* : common salt in rocklike masses or large crystals
Rocky Mountain sheep *n* : BIGHORN
ro•co•co \rə-ˈkō-kō\ *adj* [F, irreg. fr. *rocaille* style of ornament, lit., stone debris] : of or relating to an artistic style esp. of the 18th century marked by fanciful curved forms and elaborate ornamentation — **rococo** *n*
rod \ˈräd\ *n* **1 :** a straight slender stick **2 :** a stick or bundle of twigs used in punishing a person; *also* : PUNISHMENT **3 :** a staff borne to show rank **4** — see WEIGHT table **5 :** any of the rod-shaped receptor cells of the retina that are sensitive to faint light **6** *slang* : HANDGUN
rode *past of* RIDE
ro•dent \ˈrōd-ᵊnt\ *n* [ultim. fr. L *rodent-, rodens,* prp. of *rodere* to gnaw] : any of an order of relatively small mammals (as mice, squirrels, and beavers) with sharp front teeth used for gnawing
ro•deo \ˈrō-dē-ˌō, rə-ˈdā-ō\ *n, pl* **ro•de•os** [Sp, fr. *rodear* to surround, fr. *rueda* wheel, fr. L *rota*] **1** : ROUNDUP 1 **2 :** a public performance featuring cowboy skills (as riding and roping)
[1]**roe** \ˈrō\ *n, pl* **roe** *or* **roes :** DOE
[2]**roe** *n* : the eggs of a fish esp. while bound together in a mass
roe•buck \ˈrō-ˌbək\ *n, pl* **roebuck** *or* **roebucks :** a male roe deer
roe deer *n* : either of two small nimble European or Asian deers

roe deer

roent•gen \ˈrent-gən, ˈrənt-, -jən\ *n* : the international unit of measurement for X rays and gamma rays
rog•er \ˈrä-jər\ *interj* — used esp. in radio and signaling to indicate that a message has been received and understood
rogue \ˈrōg\ *n* **1 :** a dishonest person : SCOUNDREL **2 :** a mischievous person : SCAMP — **rogu•ery** \ˈrō-gə-rē\ *n* — **rogu•ish** *adj* — **rogu•ish•ly** *adv* — **rogu•ish•ness** *n*
roil \ˈrȯil, *for 2 also* ˈrīl\ *vb* **1 :** to make cloudy or muddy by stirring up **2 :** RILE 1 — **roily** \ˈrȯi-lē\ *adj*
rois•ter \ˈrȯi-stər\ *vb* **rois•tered; rois•ter•ing :** to engage in noisy revelry : CAROUSE — **rois•ter•er** *n* — **rois•ter•ous** \-stə-rəs\ *adj*
ROK *abbr* Republic of Korea (South Korea)
role *also* **rôle** \ˈrōl\ *n* **1 :** an assigned or assumed character; *also* : a part played (as by an actor) **2 :** FUNCTION
role model *n* : a person whose behavior in a particular role is imitated by others
[1]**roll** \ˈrōl\ *n* **1 :** a document containing an official record **2 :** an official list of names **3 :** something (as a bun) that is rolled up or rounded as if rolled **4 :** something that rolls : ROLLER
[2]**roll** *vb* **1 :** to move by turning over and over **2 :** to press with a roller **3 :** to move on wheels **4 :** to sound with a full reverberating tone **5 :** to make a continuous

DICTIONARY

beating sound (as on a drum) **6 :** to utter with a trill **7 :** to move onward as if by completing a revolution ⟨years ~*ed* by⟩ **8 :** to flow or seem to flow in a continuous stream or with a rising and falling motion ⟨the river ~*ed* on⟩ **9 :** to swing or sway from side to side **10 :** to shape or become shaped in rounded form

[3]roll *n* **1 :** a sound produced by rapid strokes on a drum **2 :** a heavy reverberating sound **3 :** a rolling movement or action **4 :** a swaying movement (as of a ship) **5 :** SOMERSAULT

roll•back \ˈrōl-ˌbak\ *n* **:** the act or an instance of rolling back

roll back *vb* **1 :** to reduce (as a commodity price) on a national scale **2 :** to cause to withdraw **:** push back

roll bar *n* **:** an overhead metal bar on an automobile designed to protect riders in case the automobile overturns

roll call *n* **:** the act or an instance of calling off a list of names (as of soldiers); *also* **:** a time for a roll call

roll•er \ˈrō-lər\ *n* **1 :** a revolving cylinder used for moving, pressing, shaping, applying, or smoothing something **2 :** a rod on which something is rolled up **3 :** a long heavy ocean wave

roll•er coast•er \ˈrō-lər-ˌkō-stər\ *n* **:** an amusement ride consisting of an elevated railway having sharp curves and steep slopes

roller skate *n* **:** a skate with wheels instead of a runner — **roller–skate** *vb* — **roller skater** *n*

rol•lick \ˈrä-lik\ *vb* **:** ROMP, FROLIC

rol•lick•ing *adj* **:** full of fun and good spirits

roly–poly \ˌrō-lē-ˈpō-lē\ *adj* **:** ROTUND

Rom *abbr* **1** Roman **2** Romance **3** Romania; Romanian **4** Romans

ROM \ˈräm\ *n* **:** READ-ONLY MEMORY

ro•maine \rō-ˈmān\ *n* [F, lit., Roman] **:** a garden lettuce with a tall loose head of long crisp leaves

[1]Ro•man \ˈrō-mən\ *n* **1 :** a native or resident of Rome **2** *not cap* **:** roman letters or type

[2]Roman *adj* **1 :** of or relating to Rome or the Romans and esp. the ancient Romans **2** *not cap* **:** relating to type in which the letters are upright (as in this definition) **3 :** of or relating to the Roman Catholic Church

Roman candle *n* **:** a cylindrical firework that discharges balls of fire

Roman Catholic *adj* **:** of, relating to, or being a Christian church led by the pope and having a liturgy centered in the Mass — **Roman Catholicism** *n*

[1]ro•mance \rō-ˈmans, ˈrō-ˌmans\ *n* [ME *romauns*, fr. OF *romans* French, something written in French, tale in verse, fr. ML *Romanice* in a vernacular language, ultim. fr. L *Romanus* Roman] **1 :** a medieval tale of knightly adventure **2 :** a prose narrative dealing with heroic or mysterious events set in a remote time or place **3 :** a love story **4 :** a romantic attachment or episode between lovers — **ro•manc•er** *n*

[2]romance *vb* **ro•manced; ro•manc•ing 1 :** to exaggerate or invent detail or incident **2 :** to have romantic fancies **3 :** to carry on a romantic episode with

Ro•mance \rō-ˈmans, ˈrō-ˌmans\ *adj* **:** of or relating to any of several languages developed from Latin

Ro•ma•nian \rù-ˈmā-nē-ən, rō-, -nyən\ *n* **1 :** a native or inhabitant of Romania **2 :** the language of the Romanians

Roman numeral *n* **:** a numeral in a system of notation that is based on the ancient Roman system

Ro•ma•no \rō-ˈmä-nō\ *n* **:** a hard Italian cheese that is sharper than Parmesan

Ro•mans \ˈrō-mənz\ *n* — see BIBLE table

[1]ro•man•tic \rō-ˈman-tik\ *n* **:** a romantic person; *esp* **:** a romantic writer, composer, or artist

[2]romantic *adj* **1 :** IMAGINARY **2 :** VISIONARY **3 :** having an imaginative or emotional appeal **4 :** of, relating to, or having the characteristics of romanticism — **ro•man•ti•cal•ly** \-ti-k(ə-)lē\ *adv*

ro•man•ti•cism \rō-ˈman-tə-ˌsi-zəm\ *n, often cap* **:** a literary movement (as in early 19th century England) marked esp. by emphasis on the imagination and the emotions and by the use of autobiographical material — **ro•man•ti•cist** \-sist\ *n, often cap*

romp \ˈrämp\ *vb* **1 :** to play actively and noisily **2 :** to win a contest easily — **romp** *n*

romp•er \ˈräm-pər\ *n* **1 :** one that romps **2 :** a child's one-piece garment with the lower part shaped like bloomers — usu. used in pl.

rood \ˈrüd\ *n* **:** CROSS, CRUCIFIX

[1]roof \ˈrüf, ˈrùf\ *n, pl* **roofs** \ˈrüfs, ˈrùfs; ˈrüvz, ˈrùvz\ **1 :** the upper covering part of a building **2 :** something suggesting a roof of a building — **roofed** \ˈrüft, ˈrùft\ *adj* — **roof•ing** *n* — **roof•less** *adj*

[2]roof *vb* **:** to cover with a roof

roof•top \-ˌtäp\ *n* **:** a roof esp. of a house

[1]rook \ˈrùk\ *n* **:** a common Old World bird resembling the related crow

[2]rook *vb* **:** CHEAT, SWINDLE

[3]rook *n* **:** a chess piece that can move parallel to the sides of the board across any number of unoccupied squares

rook•ery \ˈrù-kə-rē\ *n, pl* **-er•ies :** a breeding ground or haunt of gregarious birds or mammals; *also* **:** a colony of such birds or mammals

rook•ie \ˈrù-kē\ *n* **:** BEGINNER, RECRUIT; *esp* **:** a first-year player in a professional sport

[1]room \ˈrüm, ˈrùm\ *n* **1 :** an extent of space occupied by or sufficient or available for something **2 :** a partitioned part of a building **:** CHAMBER; *also* **:** the people in a room **3 :** OPPORTUNITY, CHANCE ⟨~ to develop his talents⟩ — **room•ful** *n* — **roomy** *adj*

[2]room *vb* **:** to occupy lodgings **:** LODGE — **room•er** *n*

room•ette \rü-ˈmet, rù-\ *n* **:** a small private room on a railroad sleeping car

room•mate \ˈrüm-ˌmāt, ˈrùm-\ *n* **:** one of two or more persons sharing the same room or dwelling

[1]roost \ˈrüst\ *n* **:** a support on which or a place where birds perch

[2]roost *vb* **:** to settle on or as if on a roost

roost•er \ˈrüs-tər, ˈrùs-\ *n* **:** an adult male domestic chicken **:** COCK

[1]root \ˈrüt, ˈrùt\ *n* **1 :** the leafless usu. underground part of a seed plant that functions in absorption, aeration, and storage or as a means of anchorage; *also* **:** an underground plant part esp. when fleshy and edible **2 :** something (as the basal part of a tooth or hair) resembling a root **3 :** SOURCE, ORIGIN **4 :** the essential core **:** HEART ⟨get to the ~ of the matter⟩ **5 :** a number that when taken as a factor an indicated number of times gives a specified number **6 :** the lower part — **root•less** *adj* — **root•like** *adj*

[2]root *vb* **1 :** to form roots **2 :** to fix or become fixed by or as if by roots **:** ESTABLISH **3 :** UPROOT

[3]root *vb* **1 :** to turn up or dig with the snout ⟨pigs ~*ing*⟩ **2 :** to poke or dig around (as in search of something)

[4]root \ˈrüt\ *vb* **1 :** to applaud or encourage noisily **:** CHEER **2 :** to wish success or lend support to — **root•er** *n*

root beer *n* **:** a sweetened carbonated beverage flavored with extracts of roots and herbs

root•let \ˈrüt-lət, ˈrùt-\ *n* **:** a small root

root•stock \-ˌstäk\ *n* **:** an underground part of a plant that resembles a rhizome

[1]rope \ˈrōp\ *n* **1 :** a large strong cord made of strands of fiber **2 :** a hangman's noose **3 :** a thick string (as of pearls) made by twisting or braiding

[2]rope *vb* **roped; rop•ing 1 :** to bind, tie, or fasten together with a rope **2 :** to separate or divide by means of a rope **3 :** LASSO

Ror•schach test \ˈròr-ˌshäk-\ *n* **:** a psychological test in which a subject interprets ink-blot designs in terms that reveal intellectual and emotional factors

ro•sa•ry \ˈrō-zə-rē\ *n, pl* **-ries 1** *often cap* **:** a Roman Catholic devotion consisting of meditation on sacred mysteries during recitation of Hail Marys **2** : a string of beads used in praying

[1]rose *past of* RISE

[2]rose \ˈrōz\ *n* **1** : any of a genus of usu. prickly often climbing shrubs with divided leaves and bright often fragrant flowers; *also* : one of these flowers **2** : something resembling a rose in form **3** : a moderate purplish red color — **rose** *adj*

ro•sé \rō-ˈzā\ *n* [F] : a light pink wine

ro•se•ate \ˈrō-zē-ət, -zē-ˌāt\ *adj* **1** : resembling a rose esp. in color **2** : OPTIMISTIC ⟨a ~ view of the future⟩

rose•bud \ˈrōz-ˌbəd\ *n* : the flower of a rose when it is at most partly open

rose•bush \-ˌbu̇sh\ *n* : a shrubby rose

rose•mary \ˈrōz-ˌmer-ē\ *n, pl* **-mar•ies** [ME *rosmarine*, fr. L *rosmarinus*, fr. *ros* dew + *marinus* of the sea, fr. *mare* sea] : a fragrant shrubby Old World mint; *also* : its leaves used as a seasoning

ro•sette \rō-ˈzet\ *n* [F] **1** : a usu. small badge or ornament of ribbon gathered in the shape of a rose **2** : a circular ornament filled with representations of leaves

rose•wa•ter \ˈrōz-ˌwȯ-tər, -ˌwä-\ *n* : a watery solution of the fragrant constituents of the rose used as a perfume

rose•wood \-ˌwu̇d\ *n* : any of various tropical trees with dark red wood streaked with black; *also* : this wood

Rosh Ha•sha•nah \ˌräsh-hə-ˈshä-nə, ˌrōsh-, -ˈshō-\ *n* [Heb *rōsh hashshānāh*, lit., beginning of the year] : the Jewish New Year observed as a religious holiday in September or October

ros•in \ˈräz-ᵊn\ *n* : a brittle resin obtained esp. from pine trees and used esp. in varnishes and on violin bows

ros•ter \ˈräs-tər\ *n* **1** : a list of personnel; *also* : the persons listed on a roster **2** : an itemized list

ros•trum \ˈräs-trəm\ *n, pl* **rostrums** *or* **ros•tra** \-trə\ [L *Rostra*, pl., a platform for speakers in the Roman Forum decorated with the beaks of captured ships, fr. pl. of *rostrum* beak, ship's beak, fr. *rodere* to gnaw] : a stage or platform for public speaking

rosy \ˈrō-zē\ *adj* **ros•i•er; -est 1** : of the color rose **2** : HOPEFUL, PROMISING — **ros•i•ly** \ˈrō-zə-lē\ *adv* — **ros•i•ness** \-zē-nəs\ *n*

[1]rot \ˈrät\ *vb* **rot•ted; rot•ting** : to undergo decomposition : DECAY

[2]rot *n* **1** : DECAY **2** : any of various diseases of plants or animals in which tissue breaks down **3** : NONSENSE

[1]ro•ta•ry \ˈrō-tə-rē\ *adj* **1** : turning on an axis like a wheel **2** : having a rotating part

[2]rotary *n, pl* **-ries 1** : a rotary machine **2** : a one-way circular road junction

ro•tate \ˈrō-ˌtāt\ *vb* **ro•tat•ed; ro•tat•ing 1** : to turn or cause to turn about an axis or a center : REVOLVE **2** : to alternate in a series **syn** turn, circle, spin, whirl, twirl — **ro•ta•tion** \rō-ˈtā-shən\ *n* — **ro•ta•tor** \ˈrō-ˌtā-tər\ *n* — **ro•ta•to•ry** \ˈrō-tə-ˌtōr-ē\ *adj*

ROTC *abbr* Reserve Officers' Training Corps

rote \ˈrōt\ *n* **1** : repetition from memory often without attention to meaning **2** : fixed routine or repetition — **rote** *adj*

ro•tis•ser•ie \rō-ˈti-sə-rē\ *n* [F] **1** : a restaurant specializing in broiled and barbecued meats **2** : an appliance fitted with a spit on which food is rotated before or over a source of heat

ro•to•gra•vure \ˌrō-tə-grə-ˈvyu̇r\ *n* : PHOTOGRAVURE

ro•tor \ˈrō-tər\ *n* **1** : a part that rotates; *esp* : the rotating part of an electrical machine **2** : a system of rotating horizontal blades for supporting a helicopter

ro•to•till•er \ˈrō-tō-ˌti-lər\ *n* : an engine-powered machine with rotating blades used to lift and turn over soil

rot•ten \ˈrät-ᵊn\ *adj* **1** : having rotted **2** : CORRUPT **3** : extremely unpleasant or inferior — **rot•ten•ness** *n*

rot•ten•stone \ˈrät-ᵊn-ˌstōn\ *n* : a decomposed siliceous limestone used for polishing

ro•tund \rō-ˈtənd\ *adj* : rounded out **syn** plump, chubby, portly, stout — **ro•tun•di•ty** \-ˈtən-də-tē\ *n*

ro•tun•da \rō-ˈtən-də\ *n* **1** : a round building; *esp* : one covered by a dome **2** : a large round room

rou•ble \ˈrü-bəl\ *var of* RUBLE

roué \ru̇-ˈā\ *n* [F, lit., broken on the wheel, fr. pp. of *rouer* to break on the wheel, fr. ML *rotare*, fr. L, to rotate; fr. the feeling that such a person deserves this punishment] : a man devoted to a life of sensual pleasure : RAKE

rouge \ˈrüzh, ˈrüj\ *n* [F, lit., red] : a cosmetic used to give a red color to cheeks and lips — **rouge** *vb*

[1]rough \ˈrəf\ *adj* **rough•er; rough•est 1** : uneven in surface : not smooth **2** : SHAGGY **3** : not calm : TURBULENT, TEMPESTUOUS **4** : marked by harshness or violence **5** : DIFFICULT, TRYING **6** : coarse or rugged in character or appearance **7** : marked by lack of refinement **8** : CRUDE, UNFINISHED **9** : done or made hastily or tentatively — **rough•ly** *adv* — **rough•ness** *n*

[2]rough *n* **1** : uneven ground covered with high grass esp. along a golf fairway **2** : a crude, unfinished, or preliminary state; *also* : something in such a state **3** : ROWDY, TOUGH

[3]rough *vb* **1** : ROUGHEN **2** : MANHANDLE **3** : to make or shape roughly esp. in a preliminary way — **rough•er** *n*

rough•age \ˈrə-fij\ *n* : FIBER 2; *also* : food containing much indigestible material acting as fiber

rough–and–ready \ˌrə-fən-ˈre-dē\ *adj* : rude or unpolished in nature, method, or manner but effective in action or use

rough–and–tum•ble \-ˈtəm-bəl\ *n* : rough unrestrained fighting or struggling — **rough–and–tumble** *adj*

rough•en \ˈrə-fən\ *vb* **rough•ened; rough•en•ing** : to make or become rough

rough–hewn \ˈrəf-ˈhyün\ *adj* **1** : being rough and unfinished ⟨~ beams⟩ **2** : lacking smooth manners or social grace — **rough–hew** \-ˈhyü\ *vb*

rough•house \ˈrəf-ˌhau̇s\ *vb* **rough•housed; rough•hous•ing** : to participate in rough noisy behavior — **roughhouse** *n*

rough•neck \ˈrəf-ˌnek\ *n* **1** : ROWDY, TOUGH **2** : a worker on a crew drilling oil wells

rough•shod \ˈrəf-ˌshäd\ *adv* : with no consideration for the wishes or feelings of others ⟨rode ~ over the opposition⟩

rou•lette \rü-ˈlet\ *n* [F, lit., small wheel] **1** : a gambling game in which a whirling wheel is used **2** : a wheel or disk with teeth around the outside

[1]round \ˈrau̇nd\ *adj* **1** : having every part of the surface or circumference the same distance from the center **2** : CYLINDRICAL **3** : COMPLETE, FULL **4** : approximately correct; *esp* : exact only to a specific decimal or place ⟨~ numbers⟩ **5** : liberal or ample in size or amount **6** : BLUNT, OUTSPOKEN **7** : moving in or forming a circle **8** : having curves rather than angles — **round•ish** *adj* — **round•ness** *n*

[2]round *prep or adv* : AROUND

[3]round *n* **1** : something round (as a circle, globe, or ring) **2** : a curved or rounded part (as a rung of a ladder) **3** : an indirect path or course; *also* : a regularly covered route (as of a security guard) **4** : a series or cycle of recurring actions or events **5** : one shot fired by a soldier or a gun; *also* : ammunition for one shot **6** : a period of time or a unit of play in a game or contest **7** : a cut of meat (as beef) esp. between the rump and the lower leg — **in the round 1** : FREESTANDING **2** : with a center stage surrounded by an audience ⟨theater *in the round*⟩

[4]round *vb* **1** : to make or become round **2** : to go or pass around or part way around **3** : COMPLETE, FINISH **4** : to become plump or shapely **5** : to express as a

DICTIONARY

round number — often used with *off* **6** : to follow a winding course : BEND

[1]**round•about** \ˈrau̇n-də-ˌbau̇t\ *adj* : INDIRECT, CIRCUITOUS

[2]**roundabout** *n, Brit* : MERRY-GO-ROUND

roun•de•lay \ˈrau̇n-də-ˌlā\ *n* **1** : a simple song with a refrain **2** : a poem with a recurring refrain

round•house \ˈrau̇nd-ˌhau̇s\ *n* **1** : a circular building for housing and repairing locomotives **2** : a blow with the hand made with a wide swing

round•ly \ˈrau̇nd-lē\ *adv* **1** : in a complete manner; *also* : WIDELY **2** : in a blunt way **3** : with vigor

round–shoul•dered \-ˌshōl-dərd\ *adj* : having the shoulders stooping or rounded

round–trip *n* : a trip to a place and back

round•up \ˈrau̇n-ˌdəp\ *n* **1** : the gathering together of cattle on the range by riding around them and driving them in; *also* : the ranch hands and horses engaged in a roundup **2** : a gathering in of scattered persons or things **3** : SUMMARY ⟨news ~⟩ — **round up** *vb*

round•worm \-ˌwərm\ *n* : NEMATODE

rouse \ˈrau̇z\ *vb* **roused; rous•ing 1** : to excite to activity : stir up **2** : to wake from sleep — **rous•er** *n*

roust•about \ˈrau̇s-tə-ˌbau̇t\ *n* : one who does heavy unskilled labor (as on a dock or in an oil field)

[1]**rout** \ˈrau̇t\ *n* **1** : MOB 1, 2 **2** : DISTURBANCE **3** : a fashionable gathering

[2]**rout** *vb* **1** : RUMMAGE **2** : to gouge out **3** : to expel by force

[3]**rout** *n* **1** : a state of wild confusion or disorderly retreat **2** : a disastrous defeat

[4]**rout** *vb* **1** : to put to flight **2** : to defeat decisively

[1]**route** \ˈrüt, ˈrau̇t\ *n* **1** : a traveled way **2** : CHANNEL **3** : a line of travel

[2]**route** *vb* **rout•ed; rout•ing** : to send by a selected route : DIRECT

route•man \-mən, -ˌman\ *n* : one who sells and makes deliveries on an assigned route

rout•er \ˈrau̇-tər\ *n* : a machine with a revolving spindle and cutter for shaping a surface (as of wood)

rou•tine \rü-ˈtēn\ *n* [F, fr. MF, fr. *route* traveled way] **1** : a regular course of procedure **2** : an often repeated speech or formula **3** : a part fully worked out ⟨a comedy ~⟩ **4** : a set of computer instructions that will perform a certain task — **routine** *adj* — **rou•tine•ly** *adv* — **rou•tin•ize** \-ˈtē-ˌnīz\ *vb*

[1]**rove** \ˈrōv\ *vb* **roved; rov•ing** : to wander over or through — **rov•er** *n*

[2]**rove** *past and past part of* REEVE

[1]**row** \ˈrō\ *vb* **1** : to propel a boat with oars **2** : to transport in a rowboat **3** : to pull an oar in a crew — **row•er** \ˈrō-ər\ *n*

[2]**row** *n* : an act or instance of rowing

[3]**row** *n* **1** : a number of objects in an orderly sequence **2** : WAY, STREET

[4]**row** \ˈrau̇\ *n* : a noisy quarrel

[5]**row** \ˈrau̇\ *vb* : to engage in a row

row•boat \ˈrō-ˌbōt\ *n* : a small boat designed to be rowed

row•dy \ˈrau̇-dē\ *adj* **row•di•er; -est** : coarse or boisterous in behavior : ROUGH — **row•di•ness** \ˈrau̇-dē-nəs\ *n* — **rowdy** *n* — **row•dy•ish** *adj* — **row•dy•ism** *n*

row•el \ˈrau̇-əl\ *n* : a small pointed wheel on a rider's spur — **rowel** *vb*

[1]**roy•al** \ˈrȯi-əl\ *adj* **1** : of or relating to a sovereign : REGAL **2** : fit for a king or queen ⟨a ~ welcome⟩ — **roy•al•ly** *adv*

[2]**royal** *n* : a person of royal blood

royal flush *n* : a straight flush having an ace as the highest card

roy•al•ist \ˈrȯi-ə-list\ *n* : an adherent of a king or of monarchical government

roy•al•ty \ˈrȯi-əl-tē\ *n, pl* **-ties 1** : the state of being royal **2** : royal persons **3** : a share of a product or profit (as of a mine or oil well) claimed by the owner for allowing another person to use the property **4** : a payment made to an author or composer for each copy of a work sold or to an inventor for each article sold under a patent

RP *abbr* **1** relief pitcher **2** Republic of the Philippines

rpm *abbr* revolutions per minute

rps *abbr* revolutions per second

rpt *abbr* **1** repeat **2** report

RR *abbr* **1** railroad **2** rural route

RS *abbr* **1** recording secretary **2** revised statutes **3** right side **4** Royal Society

RSV *abbr* Revised Standard Version

RSVP *abbr* [F *répondez s'il vous plaît*] please reply

rt *abbr* **1** right **2** route

RT *abbr* **1** radiotelephone **2** round-trip

rte *abbr* route

Ru *symbol* ruthenium

[1]**rub** \ˈrəb\ *vb* **rubbed; rub•bing 1** : to use pressure and friction on a body or object **2** : to fret or chafe with friction **3** : to scour, polish, erase, or smear by pressure and friction

[2]**rub** *n* **1** : DIFFICULTY, OBSTRUCTION **2** : something grating to the feelings

[1]**rub•ber** \ˈrə-bər\ *n* **1** : one that rubs **2** : ERASER **3** : a flexible waterproof elastic substance made from the milky juice esp. of a So. American tropical tree or made synthetically; *also* : something made of this material — **rubber** *adj* — **rub•ber•ize** \ˈrə-bə-ˌrīz\ *vb* — **rub•bery** *adj*

[2]**rubber** *n* **1** : a contest that consists of an odd number of games and is won by the side that takes a majority **2** : an extra game played to decide a tie

[1]**rub•ber•neck** \-ˌnek\ *n* **1** : an idly or overly inquisitive person **2** : a person on a guided tour

[2]**rubberneck** *vb* : to look about, stare, or listen with excessive curiosity — **rub•ber•neck•er** *n*

rub•bish \ˈrə-bish\ *n* **1** : useless waste or rejected matter : TRASH **2** : something worthless or nonsensical

rub•ble \ˈrə-bəl\ *n* : broken fragments esp. of a destroyed building

ru•bel•la \rü-ˈbe-lə\ *n* : GERMAN MEASLES

ru•bi•cund \ˈrü-bi-(ˌ)kənd\ *adj* : RED, RUDDY

ru•bid•i•um \rü-ˈbi-dē-əm\ *n* : a soft silvery metallic chemical element — see ELEMENT table

ru•ble \ˈrü-bəl\ *n* — see MONEY table

ru•bric \ˈrü-brik\ *n* [ME *rubrike* red ocher, heading in red letters of part of a book, fr. MF *rubrique*, fr. L *rubrica*, fr. *ruber* red] **1** : HEADING, TITLE; *also* : CLASS, CATEGORY **2** : a rule esp. for the conduct of a religious service

ru•by \ˈrü-bē\ *n, pl* **rubies** : a clear red precious stone — **ruby** *adj*

ru•by–throat•ed hummingbird \ˈrü-bē-ˌthrō-təd-\ *n* : a bright green and whitish hummingbird of eastern No. America with a red throat in the male

ruck•us \ˈrə-kəs\ *n* : ROW, DISTURBANCE

rud•der \ˈrə-dər\ *n* : a movable flat piece attached vertically at the rear of a ship or aircraft for steering

rud•dy \ˈrə-dē\ *adj* **rud•di•er; -est** : REDDISH; *esp* : of a healthy reddish complexion — **rud•di•ness** \ˈrə-dē-nəs\ *n*

rude \ˈrüd\ *adj* **rud•er; rud•est 1** : roughly made : CRUDE **2** : UNDEVELOPED, PRIMITIVE **3** : IMPOLITE **4** : UNSKILLED — **rude•ly** *adv* — **rude•ness** *n*

ru•di•ment \ˈrü-də-mənt\ *n* **1** : an elementary principle or basic skill — usu. used in pl. **2** : something not fully developed — usu. used in pl. — **ru•di•men•ta•ry** \ˌrü-də-ˈmen-tə-rē\ *adj*

[1]**rue** \ˈrü\ *n* : REGRET, SORROW — **rue•ful** \-fəl\ *adj* — **rue•ful•ly** *adv* — **rue•ful•ness** *n*

[2]**rue** *vb* **rued; ru•ing** : to feel regret, remorse, or penitence for

[3]**rue** *n* : a European strong-scented woody herb with bitter-tasting leaves

ruff \ˈrəf\ *n* **1** : a large round pleated collar worn about

1600 **2** : a fringe of long hair or feathers around the neck of an animal — **ruffed** \ˈrəft\ *adj*

ruf•fi•an \ˈrə-fē-ən\ *n* : a brutal person — **ruf•fi•an•ly** *adj*

[1]**ruf•fle** \ˈrə-fəl\ *vb* **ruf•fled; ruf•fling 1** : to roughen the surface of **2** : IRRITATE, VEX **3** : to erect (as hair or feathers) in or like a ruff **4** : to flip through (as pages) **5** : to draw into or provide with plaits or folds

[2]**ruffle** *n* **1** : a strip of fabric gathered or pleated on one edge **2** : RUFF 2 **3** : RIPPLE — **ruf•fly** \ˈrə-fə-lē, -flē\ *adj*

RU 486 \ˈär-ˌyü-ˌfōr-ˌā-tē-ˈsiks\ *n* : a drug taken orally to induce abortion esp. early in pregnancy

rug \ˈrəg\ *n* **1** : a covering for the legs, lap, and feet **2** : a piece of heavy fabric usu. with a nap or pile used as a floor covering

rug•by \ˈrəg-bē\ *n, often cap* [*Rugby* School, Rugby, England, where it was first played] : a football game in which play is continuous and interference and forward passing are not permitted

rug•ged \ˈrə-gəd\ *adj* **1** : having a rough uneven surface **2** : TURBULENT, STORMY **3** : HARSH, STERN **4** : ROBUST, STURDY — **rug•ged•ize** \ˈrə-gə-ˌdīz\ *vb* — **rug•ged•ly** *adv* — **rug•ged•ness** *n*

[1]**ru•in** \ˈrü-ən\ *n* **1** : complete collapse or destruction **2** : the remains of something destroyed — usu. used in pl. **3** : a cause of destruction **4** : the action of destroying

[2]**ruin** *vb* **1** : DESTROY **2** : to damage beyond repair **3** : BANKRUPT

ru•in•ation \ˌrü-ə-ˈnā-shən\ *n* : RUIN, DESTRUCTION

ru•in•ous \ˈrü-ə-nəs\ *adj* **1** : RUINED, DILAPIDATED **2** : causing ruin — **ru•in•ous•ly** *adv*

[1]**rule** \ˈrül\ *n* **1** : a guide or principle for governing action : REGULATION **2** : the usual way of doing something **3** : the exercise of authority or control : GOVERNMENT **4** : RULER 2

[2]**rule** *vb* **ruled; rul•ing 1** : CONTROL; *also* : GOVERN **2** : to be supreme or outstanding in **3** : to give or state as a considered decision **4** : to mark on paper with or as if with a ruler

rul•er \ˈrü-lər\ *n* **1** : SOVEREIGN **2** : a straight strip of material (as wood or metal) marked off in units and used for measuring or as a straightedge

rum \ˈrəm\ *n* **1** : an alcoholic liquor made from molasses or sugarcane **2** : alcoholic liquor

Ru•ma•nian \rü-ˈmā-nē-ən, -nyən\ *n* : ROMANIAN — **Rumanian** *adj*

rum•ba \ˈrəm-bə, ˈrüm-\ *n* : a dance of Cuban origin marked by strong rhythmic movements

[1]**rum•ble** \ˈrəm-bəl\ *vb* **rum•bled; rum•bling** : to make a low heavy rolling sound; *also* : to move along with such a sound — **rum•bler** *n*

[2]**rumble** *n* **1** : a low heavy rolling sound **2** : a street fight esp. among gangs

rumble seat *n* : a folding seat in the back of an automobile that is not covered by the top

rum•bling \ˈrəm-bliŋ\ *n* **1** : RUMBLE **2** : widespread talk or complaints — usu. used in pl.

ru•men \ˈrü-mən\ *n, pl* **ru•mi•na** \-mə-nə\ *or* **rumens** : the large first compartment of the stomach of a ruminant (as a cow)

[1]**ru•mi•nant** \ˈrü-mə-nənt\ *n* : a ruminant mammal

[2]**ruminant** *adj* **1** : chewing the cud; *also* : of or relating to a group of hoofed mammals (as cattle, deer, and camels) that chew the cud and have a complex usu. 4-chambered stomach **2** : MEDITATIVE

ru•mi•nate \ˈrü-mə-ˌnāt\ *vb* **-nat•ed; -nat•ing** [L *ruminari* to chew the cud, muse upon, fr. *rumin-, rumen* first stomach chamber of a ruminant] **1** : MEDITATE, MUSE **2** : to chew the cud — **ru•mi•na•tion** \ˌrü-mə-ˈnā-shən\ *n*

[1]**rum•mage** \ˈrə-mij\ *vb* **rum•maged; rum•mag•ing** : to search thoroughly — **rum•mag•er** *n*

[2]**rummage** *n* **1** : a miscellaneous collection **2** : an act of rummaging

rum•my \ˈrə-mē\ *n* : any of several card games for two or more players

ru•mor \ˈrü-mər\ *n* **1** : common talk **2** : a statement or report current but not authenticated — **rumor** *vb*

ru•mour *chiefly Brit var of* RUMOR

rump \ˈrəmp\ *n* **1** : the rear part of an animal; *also* : a cut of meat (as beef) behind the upper sirloin **2** : a small or inferior remnant (as of a group)

rum•ple \ˈrəm-pəl\ *vb* **rum•pled; rum•pling** : TOUSLE, MUSS, WRINKLE — **rumple** *n* — **rum•ply** \ˈrəm-pə-lē\ *adj*

rum•pus \ˈrəm-pəs\ *n* : DISTURBANCE, RUCKUS

rumpus room *n* : a room usu. in the basement of a home that is used for games, parties, and recreation

[1]**run** \ˈrən\ *vb* **ran** \ˈran\; **run; run•ning 1** : to go faster than a walk **2** : to take to flight : FLEE **3** : to go without restraint ⟨let chickens ~ loose⟩ **4** : to go rapidly or hurriedly : HASTEN, RUSH **5** : to make a quick or casual trip or visit **6** : to contend in a race; *esp* : to enter an election **7** : to put forward as a candidate for office **8** : to move on or as if on wheels : pass or slide freely **9** : to go back and forth : PLY **10** : to move in large numbers esp. to a spawning ground ⟨shad are *running*⟩ **11** : FUNCTION, OPERATE ⟨left the motor *running*⟩ **12** : to continue in force ⟨two years to ~⟩ **13** : to flow rapidly or under pressure : MELT, FUSE, DISSOLVE; *also* : DISCHARGE 7 ⟨my nose is *running*⟩ **14** : to tend to produce or to recur ⟨family ~*s* to blonds⟩ **15** : to take a certain direction **16** : to be worded or written **17** : to be current ⟨rumors *running* wild⟩ **18** : to cause to run **19** : TRACE ⟨~ down a rumor⟩ **20** : to perform or bring about by running **21** : to cause to pass ⟨~ a wire from the antenna⟩ **22** : to cause to collide **23** : SMUGGLE **24** : MANAGE, CONDUCT, OPERATE ⟨~ a business⟩ **25** : INCUR ⟨~ a risk⟩ **26** : to permit to accumulate before settling ⟨~ up a bill⟩

[2]**run** *n* **1** : an act or the action of running **2** : a migration of fish; *also* : the migrating fish **3** : a score in baseball **4** : BROOK, CREEK **5** : a continuous series esp. of similar things **6** : persistent heavy demands from depositors, creditors, or customers **7** : the quantity of work turned out in a continuous operation; *also* : a period of operation (as of a machine or plant) **8** : the usual or normal kind ⟨the ordinary ~ of students⟩ **9** : the distance covered in continuous travel or sailing **10** : a regular course or trip **11** : freedom of movement in a place or area ⟨has the ~ of the house⟩ **12** : an enclosure for animals **13** : an inclined course (as for skiing) **14** : a lengthwise ravel (as in a stocking) — **run•less** *adj*

run•about \ˈrə-nə-ˌbau̇t\ *n* : a light wagon, automobile, or motorboat

run•a•gate \ˈrə-nə-ˌgāt\ *n* **1** : VAGABOND **2** : FUGITIVE

run•around \ˈrə-nə-ˌrau̇nd\ *n* : evasive or delaying action esp. in response to a request

[1]**run•away** \ˈrə-nə-ˌwā\ *n* **1** : one that runs away : FUGITIVE **2** : the act of running away out of control; *also* : something (as a horse) that is running out of control

[2]**runaway** *adj* **1** : FUGITIVE **2** : won by a long lead; *also* : extremely successful **3** : subject to uncontrolled changes ⟨~ inflation⟩ **4** : operating out of control ⟨a ~ locomotive⟩

run•down \ˈrən-ˌdau̇n\ *n* : an item-by-item report or review : SUMMARY

run–down \ˈrən-ˈdau̇n\ *adj* **1** : EXHAUSTED, WORN-OUT ⟨that ~ feeling⟩ **2** : being in poor repair ⟨a ~ farm⟩

run down *vb* **1** : to collide with and knock down **2** : to chase until exhausted or captured **3** : to find by search **4** : DISPARAGE **5** : to cease to operate for lack of motive power **6** : to decline in physical condition

rune \ˈrün\ *n* **1** : any of the characters of any of several alphabets formerly used by the Germanic peoples **2** : MYSTERY, MAGIC **3** : a poem esp. in Finnish or Old Norse — **ru•nic** \ˈrü-nik\ *adj*

[1]**rung** *past part of* RING

[2]**rung** \ˈrəŋ\ *n* **1** : a rounded crosspiece between the legs

of a chair **2 :** one of the crosspieces of a ladder
run–in \ˈrən-ˌin\ *n* **1 :** ALTERCATION, QUARREL **2 :** something run in
run in *vb* **1 :** to insert as additional matter **2 :** to arrest esp. for a minor offense **3 :** to pay a casual visit
run•nel \ˈrən-ᵊl\ *n* **:** BROOK, STREAMLET
run•ner \ˈrə-nər\ *n* **1 :** one that runs **2 :** BASE RUNNER **3 :** BALLCARRIER **4 :** a thin piece or part on which something (as a sled or an ice skate) slides **5 :** the support of a drawer or a sliding door **6 :** a horizontal branch from the base of a plant that produces new plants **7 :** a plant producing runners **8 :** a long narrow carpet **9 :** a narrow decorative cloth cover for a table or dresser top
run•ner–up \ˈrə-nər-ˌəp\ *n, pl* **runners–up** *also* **runner–ups :** the competitor in a contest who finishes second
¹run•ning *adj* **1 :** FLOWING **2 :** FLUID, RUNNY **3 :** CONTINUOUS, INCESSANT **4 :** measured in a straight line ⟨cost per ~ foot⟩ **5 :** of or relating to an act of running **6 :** made or trained for running ⟨~ horse⟩ ⟨~ shoes⟩
²running *adv* **:** in succession
running light *n* **:** any of the lights carried by a vehicle (as a ship) at night
run•ny \ˈrə-nē\ *adj* **:** having a tendency to run ⟨a ~ dough⟩ ⟨a ~ nose⟩
run•off \ˈrən-ˌȯf\ *n* **:** a final contest (as an election) to a previous indecisive contest
run–of–the–mill *adj* **:** not outstanding **:** AVERAGE
run on *vb* **1 :** to talk at length **2 :** to continue (matter in type) without a break or a new paragraph **3 :** to place or add (as an entry in a dictionary) at the end of a paragraphed item — **run–on** \ˈrən-ˌȯn, -ˌän\ *n*
runt \ˈrənt\ *n* **:** an unusually small person or animal **:** DWARF — **runty** *adj*
run•way \ˈrən-ˌwā\ *n* **1 :** a beaten path made by animals; *also* **:** a passage for animals **2 :** a paved strip of ground for the landing and takeoff of aircraft **3 :** a narrow platform from a stage into an auditorium **4 :** a support (as a track) on which something runs
ru•pee \rü-ˈpē, ˈrü-ˌpē\ *n* — see MONEY table
ru•pi•ah \rü-ˈpē-ə\ *n, pl* **rupiah** *or* **rupiahs** — see MONEY table
¹rup•ture \ˈrəp-chər\ *n* **:** a breaking or tearing apart; *also* **:** HERNIA
²rupture *vb* **rup•tured; rup•tur•ing :** to cause or undergo rupture
ru•ral \ˈrůr-əl\ *adj* **:** of or relating to the country, country people, or agriculture
ruse \ˈrüs, ˈrüz\ *n* **:** a wily subterfuge **:** TRICK, ARTIFICE
¹rush \ˈrəsh\ *n* **:** any of various often tufted and hollow-stemmed grasslike marsh plants — **rushy** *adj*
²rush *vb* [ME *russhen,* fr. MF *ruser* to put to flight, deceive, fr. L *recusare* to refuse] **1 :** to move forward or act with too great haste or eagerness or without preparation **2 :** to perform in a short time or at high speed **3 :** ATTACK, CHARGE — **rush•er** *n*
³rush *n* **1 :** a violent forward motion **2 :** unusual demand or activity **3 :** a crowding of people to one place **4 :** a running play in football **5 :** a sudden feeling of pleasure
⁴rush *adj* **:** requiring or marked by special speed or urgency ⟨~ orders⟩
rush hour *n* **:** a time when the amount of traffic or business is at a peak
rusk \ˈrəsk\ *n* **:** a sweet or plain bread baked, sliced, and baked again until dry and crisp
Russ *abbr* Russia; Russian
rus•set \ˈrə-sət\ *n* **1 :** a coarse reddish brown cloth **2 :** a reddish brown or yellowish brown color **3 :** a baking potato — **russet** *adj*
Rus•sian \ˈrə-shən\ *n* **1 :** a native or inhabitant of Russia **2 :** a Slavic language of the Russian people — **Russian** *adj*
rust \ˈrəst\ *n* **1 :** a reddish coating formed on iron when it is exposed to esp. moist air **2 :** any of numerous plant diseases characterized by usu. reddish spots; *also* **:** a fungus causing rust **3 :** a reddish brown color — **rust** *vb* — **rusty** *adj*
¹rus•tic \ˈrəs-tik\ *adj* **:** of, relating to, or suitable for the country or country people — **rus•ti•cal•ly** \-ti-k(ə-)lē\ *adv* — **rus•tic•i•ty** \ˌrəs-ˈti-sə-tē\ *n*
²rustic *n* **:** a rustic person
rus•ti•cate \ˈrəs-ti-ˌkāt\ *vb* **-cat•ed; -cat•ing :** to go into or reside in the country — **rus•ti•ca•tion** \ˌrəs-ti-ˈkā-shən\ *n*
¹rus•tle \ˈrə-səl\ *vb* **rus•tled; rus•tling 1 :** to make or cause a rustle **2 :** to cause to rustle ⟨~ a newspaper⟩ **3 :** to act or move with energy or speed; *also* **:** to procure in this way **4 :** to forage food **5 :** to steal cattle from the range — **rus•tler** *n*
²rustle *n* **:** a quick series of small sounds ⟨~ of leaves⟩
¹rut \ˈrət\ *n* **:** state or period of sexual excitement esp. in male deer — **rut** *vb*
²rut *n* **1 :** a track worn by wheels or by habitual passage of something **2 :** a usual or fixed routine
ru•ta•ba•ga \ˌrü-tə-ˈbā-gə, ˌrů-\ *n* **:** a turnip with a large yellowish root
Ruth \ˈrüth\ *n* — see BIBLE table
ru•the•ni•um \rü-ˈthē-nē-əm\ *n* **:** a hard brittle metallic chemical element — see ELEMENT table
ruth•less \ˈrüth-ləs\ *adj* [fr. *ruth* compassion, pity, fr. ME *ruthe,* fr. *ruen* to rue, fr. OE *hrēowan*] **:** having no pity **:** MERCILESS, CRUEL — **ruth•less•ly** *adv* — **ruth•less•ness** *n*
¹RV \ˌär-ˈvē\ *n* **:** RECREATIONAL VEHICLE
²RV *abbr* Revised Version
R–value \ˈär-ˌval-yü\ *n* **:** a measure of resistance to the flow of heat through a substance (as insulation)
RW *abbr* **1** right worshipful **2** right worthy
rwy *or* **ry** *abbr* railway
-ry \rē\ *n suffix* **:** -ERY ⟨bigot*ry*⟩
rye \ˈrī\ *n* **1 :** a hardy annual grass grown for grain or as a cover crop; *also* **:** its seed **2 :** a whiskey distilled from a rye mash

S

¹s \ˈes\ *n, pl* **s's** *or* **ss** \ˈe-səz\ *often cap* **:** the 19th letter of the English alphabet
²s *abbr, often cap* **1** saint **2** second **3** senate **4** series **5** shilling **6** singular **7** small **8** son **9** south; southern
¹-s \s *after sounds* f, k, k̲, p, t, th; əz *after sounds* ch, j, s, sh, z, zh; z *after other sounds*\ *n pl suffix* — used to form the plural of most nouns that do not end in *s, z, sh,* or *ch* or in *y* following a consonant ⟨head*s*⟩ ⟨book*s*⟩ ⟨boy*s*⟩ ⟨belief*s*⟩, to form the plural of proper nouns that end in *y* following a consonant ⟨Mary*s*⟩, and with or without a preceding apostrophe to form the plural of abbreviations, numbers, letters, and symbols used as nouns ⟨MC*s*⟩ ⟨4*s*⟩ ⟨+ #*s*⟩ ⟨B'*s*⟩
²-s *adv suffix* — used to form adverbs denoting usual or repeated action or state ⟨works night*s*⟩
³-s *vb suffix* — used to form the third person singular present of most verbs that do not end in *s, z, sh,* or *ch* or in *y* followng a consonant ⟨fall*s*⟩ ⟨take*s*⟩ ⟨play*s*⟩
S *symbol* sulfur
SA *abbr* **1** Salvation Army **2** seaman apprentice **3** sex appeal **4** [L *sine anno* without year] without date **5** South Africa **6** South America **7** subject to approval
Sab•bath \ˈsa-bəth\ *n* [ME *sabat,* fr. OF & OE, fr. L *sabbatum,* fr. Gk *sabbaton,* fr. Heb *shabbāth,* lit., rest] **1 :** the 7th day of the week observed as a day of

worship by Jews and some Christians **2 :** Sunday observed among Christians as a day of worship

sab•bat•i•cal \sə-ˈba-ti-kəl\ *n* **:** a leave often with pay granted (as to a college professor) usu. every 7th year for rest, travel, or research

sa•ber *or* **sa•bre** \ˈsā-bər\ *n* [F *sabre*] **:** a cavalry sword with a curved blade and thick back

saber saw *n* **:** a portable electric saw with a pointed reciprocating blade

sa•ble \ˈsā-bəl\ *n, pl* **sables 1 :** the color black **2** *pl* **:** mourning garments **3 :** a dark brown mammal chiefly of northern Asia related to the weasels; *also* **:** its fur or pelt

[1]sab•o•tage \ˈsa-bə-ˌtäzh\ *n* [F] **1 :** deliberate destruction of an employer's property or hindering of production by workers **2 :** destructive or hampering action by enemy agents or sympathizers in time of war

[2]sabotage *vb* **-taged; -tag•ing :** to practice sabotage on **:** WRECK

sab•o•teur \ˌsa-bə-ˈtər\ *n* **:** a person who practices sabotage

sac \ˈsak\ *n* **:** a pouch in an animal or plant often containing a fluid

SAC *abbr* Strategic Air Command

sac•cha•rin \ˈsa-kə-rən\ *n* **:** a white crystalline compound used as an artificial calorie-free sweetener

sac•cha•rine \ˈsa-kə-rən\ *adj* **:** nauseatingly sweet ⟨~ poetry⟩

sac•er•do•tal \ˌsa-sər-ˈdōt-ᵊl, -kər-\ *adj* **:** PRIESTLY

sac•er•do•tal•ism \-ᵊl-ˌi-zəm\ *n* **:** a religious belief emphasizing the powers of priests as essential mediators between God and man

sa•chem \ˈsā-chəm\ *n* **:** a No. American Indian chief

sa•chet \sa-ˈshā\ *n* [F, fr. OF, dim. of *sac* bag] **:** a small bag filled with perfumed powder for scenting clothes

[1]sack \ˈsak\ *n* **1 :** a usu. rectangular-shaped bag (as of paper or burlap) **2 :** a loose jacket or short coat

[2]sack *vb* **:** DISMISS, FIRE

[3]sack *n* [modif. of MF *sec* dry, fr. L *siccus*] **:** a white wine popular in England in the 16th and 17th centuries

[4]sack *vb* **:** to plunder a captured town

sack•cloth \-ˌklȯth\ *n* **:** a rough garment worn as a sign of penitence

sac•ra•ment \ˈsa-krə-mənt\ *n* **1 :** a formal religious act or rite; *esp* **:** one (as baptism or the Eucharist) held to have been instituted by Christ **2 :** the elements of the Eucharist — **sac•ra•men•tal** \ˌsa-krə-ˈment-ᵊl\ *adj*

sa•cred \ˈsā-krəd\ *adj* **1 :** set apart for the service or worship of deity **2 :** devoted exclusively to one service or use **3 :** worthy of veneration or reverence **4 :** of or relating to religion **:** RELIGIOUS **syn** blessed, divine, hallowed, holy, sanctified — **sa•cred•ly** *adv* — **sa•cred•ness** *n*

sacred cow *n* **:** one that is often unreasonably immune from criticism

[1]sac•ri•fice \ˈsa-krə-ˌfīs\ *n* **1 :** the offering of something precious to deity **2 :** something offered in sacrifice **3 :** LOSS, DEPRIVATION **4 :** a bunt allowing a base runner to advance while the batter is put out; *also* **:** a fly ball allowing a runner to score after the catch — **sac•ri•fi•cial** \ˌsa-krə-ˈfi-shəl\ *adj* — **sac•ri•fi•cial•ly** *adv*

[2]sac•ri•fice *vb* **-ficed; -fic•ing 1 :** to offer up or kill as a sacrifice **2 :** to accept the loss or destruction of for an end, cause, or ideal **3 :** to make a sacrifice in baseball

sac•ri•lege \ˈsa-krə-lij\ *n* [ME, fr. OF, fr. L *sacrilegium,* fr. *sacrilegus* one who steals sacred things, fr. *sacr-, sacer* sacred + *legere* to gather, steal] **1 :** violation of something consecrated to God **2 :** gross irreverence toward a hallowed person, place, or thing — **sac•ri•le•gious** \ˌsa-krə-ˈli-jəs, -ˈlē-\ *adj* — **sac•ri•le•gious•ly** *adv*

sac•ris•tan \ˈsa-krə-stən\ *n* **1 :** a church officer in charge of the sacristy **2 :** SEXTON

sac•ris•ty \ˈsa-krə-stē\ *n, pl* **-ties :** VESTRY

sac•ro•il•i•ac \ˌsa-krō-ˈi-lē-ˌak\ *n* **:** the joint between the upper part of the hipbone and the sacrum

sac•ro•sanct \ˈsa-krō-ˌsaŋkt\ *adj* **:** SACRED, INVIOLABLE

sa•crum \ˈsa-krəm, ˈsā-\ *n, pl* **sa•cra** \ˈsa-krə, ˈsā-\ **:** the part of the vertebral column that is directly connected with or forms a part of the pelvis and in humans consists of five fused vertebrae

sad \ˈsad\ *adj* **sad•der; sad•dest 1 :** GRIEVING, MOURNFUL, DOWNCAST **2 :** causing sorrow **3 :** DULL, SOMBER — **sad•ly** *adv* — **sad•ness** *n*

sad•den \ˈsad-ᵊn\ *vb* **:** to make sad

[1]sad•dle \ˈsad-ᵊl\ *n* **1 :** a usu. padded leather-covered seat (as for a rider on horseback) **2 :** the upper back portion of a carcass (as of mutton)

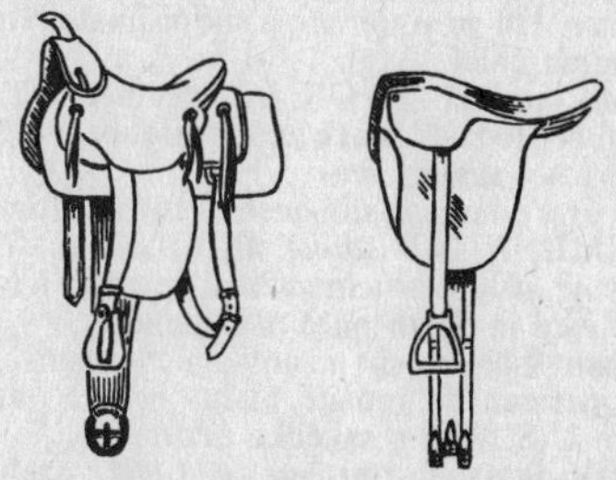

saddle 1

[2]saddle *vb* **sad•dled; sad•dling 1 :** to put a saddle on **2 :** OPPRESS, BURDEN

sad•dle•bow \ˈsad-ᵊl-ˌbō\ *n* **:** the arch in the front of a saddle

saddle horse *n* **:** a horse suited for or trained for riding

Sad•du•cee \ˈsa-jə-ˌsē, ˈsa-dyə-\ *n* **:** a member of an ancient Jewish sect consisting of a ruling class of priests and rejecting certain doctrines — **Sad•du•ce•an** \ˌsa-jə-ˈsē-ən, ˌsa-dyə-\ *adj*

sad•iron \ˈsa-ˌdi-ərn\ *n* **:** a flatiron with a removable handle

sa•dism \ˈsā-ˌdi-zəm, ˈsa-\ *n* **:** a sexual perversion in which gratification is obtained by inflicting physical or mental pain on others — **sa•dist** \ˈsā-dist, ˈsa-\ *n* — **sa•dis•tic** \sə-ˈdis-tik\ *adj* — **sa•dis•ti•cal•ly** \-ti-k(ə-)lē\ *adv*

SAE *abbr* **1** self-addressed envelope **2** Society of Automotive Engineers **3** stamped addressed envelope

sa•fa•ri \sə-ˈfär-ē, -ˈfar-\ *n* [Ar *safarīy* of a trip] **1 :** a hunting expedition esp. in eastern Africa **2 :** JOURNEY, TRIP

[1]safe \ˈsāf\ *adj* **saf•er; saf•est 1 :** free from harm or risk **2 :** affording safety; *also* **:** secure from danger or loss **3 :** RELIABLE — **safe•ly** *adv*

[2]safe *n* **:** a container for keeping articles (as valuables) safe

safe–con•duct \-ˈkän-(ˌ)dəkt\ *n* **:** a pass permitting a person to go through enemy lines

[1]safe•guard \-ˌgärd\ *n* **:** a measure or device for preventing accident

[2]safeguard *vb* **:** to provide a safeguard for **:** PROTECT

safe•keep•ing \ˈsāf-ˈkē-piŋ\ *n* **:** a keeping or being kept in safety

safe sex *n* **:** sexual activity and esp. sexual intercourse in which various measures (as the use of latex condoms) are taken to avoid disease (as AIDS) transmitted by sexual contact

safe•ty \ˈsāf-tē\ *n, pl* **safeties 1 :** freedom from danger **:** SECURITY **2 :** a protective device **3 :** a football play in which the ball is downed by the offensive team behind its own goal line **4 :** a defensive football back in the deepest position — **safety** *adj*

safety glass *n* **:** shatter-resistant material formed of two sheets of glass with a sheet of clear plastic between them

safety match *n* : a match that ignites only when struck on a special surface

saf•flow•er \ˈsa-ˌflau̇-ər\ *n* : a widely grown Old World herb related to the daisies that has large orange or red flower heads yielding a dyestuff and seeds rich in edible oil

saf•fron \ˈsa-frən\ *n* : a deep orange powder from the flower of a crocus used to color and flavor foods

sag \ˈsag\ *vb* **sagged; sag•ging 1** : to droop or settle from or as if from pressure **2** : to lose firmness or vigor — **sag** *n*

sa•ga \ˈsä-gə\ *n* [ON] : a narrative of heroic deeds; *esp* : one recorded in Iceland in the 12th and 13th centuries

sa•ga•cious \sə-ˈgā-shəs\ *adj* : of keen mind : SHREWD — **sa•gac•i•ty** \-ˈga-sə-tē\ *n*

sag•a•more \ˈsa-gə-ˌmōr\ *n* : a subordinate No. American Indian chief

[1]**sage** \ˈsāj\ *adj* [ME, fr. OF, fr. (assumed) VL *sapius*, fr. L *sapere* to taste, have good taste, be wise] : WISE, PRUDENT — **sage•ly** *adv*

[2]**sage** *n* : one who is distinguished for wisdom

[3]**sage** *n* [ME, fr. MF *sauge*, fr. L *salvia*, fr. *salvus* healthy; fr. its use as a medicinal herb] **1** : a mint with leaves used in flavoring **2** : SAGEBRUSH

sage•brush \ˈsāj-ˌbrəsh\ *n* : any of several low shrubby No. American composite plants; *esp* : one of the western U.S. with a sagelike odor

Sag•it•tar•i•us \ˌsa-jə-ˈter-ē-əs\ *n* [L, lit., archer] **1** : a zodiacal constellation between Scorpio and Capricorn usu. pictured as a centaur archer **2** : the 9th sign of the zodiac in astrology; *also* : one born under this sign

sa•go \ˈsā-gō\ *n, pl* **sagos** : a dry granulated starch esp. from the pith of various tropical palms (**sago palm**)

sa•gua•ro \sə-ˈwär-ə, -ˈgwär-, -ō\ *n, pl* **-ros** [MexSp] : a desert cactus of the southwestern U.S. and Mexico with a tall columnar simple or sparsely branched trunk of up to 60 feet (18 meters)

said *past and past part of* SAY

[1]**sail** \ˈsāl\ *n* **1** : a piece of fabric by means of which the wind is used to propel a ship **2** : a sailing ship **3** : something resembling a sail **4** : a trip on a sailboat

[2]**sail** *vb* **1** : to travel on a sailing ship **2** : to pass over in a ship **3** : to manage or direct the course of a ship **4** : to move with ease, grace, or nonchalance

sail•board \ˈsāl-ˌbōrd\ *n* : a modified surfboard having a mast and sailed by a standing person

sail•boat \-ˌbōt\ *n* : a boat propelled primarily by sail

sail•cloth \-ˌklȯth\ *n* : a heavy canvas used for sails, tents, or upholstery

sail•fish \-ˌfish\ *n* : any of a genus of large marine bony fishes with a large dorsal fin that are related to marlins

sail•ing *n* : the sport of handling or riding in a sailboat

sail•or \ˈsā-lər\ *n* : one that sails; *esp* : a member of a ship's crew

sail•plane \ˈsāl-ˌplān\ *n* : a glider designed to rise in an upward air current

saint \ˈsānt, *before a name* (ˌ)sānt *or* sənt\ *n* **1** : one officially recognized as preeminent for holiness **2** : one of the spirits of the departed in heaven **3** : a holy or godly person — **saint•ed** \-ˈsān-təd\ *adj* — **saint•hood** \-ˌhu̇d\ *n*

Saint Ber•nard \-bər-ˈnärd\ *n* : any of a Swiss alpine breed of tall powerful working dogs used esp. formerly in aiding lost travelers

saint•ly \ˈsānt-lē\ *adj* : relating to, resembling, or befitting a saint — **saint•li•ness** \-lē-nəs\ *n*

Saint Val•en•tine's Day \-ˈva-lən-ˌtīnz-\ *n* : February 14 observed in honor of St. Valentine and as a time for exchanging valentines

[1]**sake** \ˈsāk\ *n* **1** : END, PURPOSE **2** : personal or social welfare, safety, or well-being

[2]**sa•ke** *or* **sa•ki** \ˈsä-kē\ *n* : a Japanese alcoholic beverage of fermented rice

Saint Bernard

sa•laam \sə-ˈläm\ *n* [Ar *salām*, lit., peace] **1** : a salutation or ceremonial greeting in the East **2** : an obeisance performed by bowing very low and placing the right palm on the forehead — **salaam** *vb*

sa•la•cious \sə-ˈlā-shəs\ *adj* **1** : arousing sexual desire or imagination **2** : LUSTFUL — **sa•la•cious•ly** *adv* — **sa•la•cious•ness** *n*

sal•ad \ˈsa-ləd\ *n* : a cold dish (as of lettuce, vegetables, fish, eggs, or fruit) served with dressing

sal•a•man•der \ˈsa-lə-ˌman-dər\ *n* : any of numerous amphibians that look like lizards but have scaleless usu. smooth moist skin

sa•la•mi \sə-ˈlä-mē\ *n* [It] : a highly seasoned sausage of pork and beef

sal•a•ry \ˈsa-lə-rē\ *n, pl* **-ries** [ME *salarie*, fr. L *salarium* pension, salary, fr. neut. of *salarius* of salt, fr. *sal* salt] : payment made at regular intervals for services

sale \ˈsāl\ *n* **1** : transfer of ownership of property from one person to another in return for money **2** : ready market : DEMAND **3** : AUCTION **4** : a selling of goods at bargain prices — **sal•able** *or* **sale•able** \ˈsā-lə-bəl\ *adj*

sales•girl \ˈsālz-ˌgərl\ *n* : SALESWOMAN

sales•man \-mən\ *n* : a person who sells in a store or to outside customers — **sales•man•ship** *n*

sales•per•son \-ˌpər-sən\ *n* : a salesman or saleswoman

sales•wom•an \-ˌwu̇-mən\ *n* : a woman who sells merchandise

sal•i•cyl•ic acid \ˌsa-lə-ˈsi-lik-\ *n* : a crystalline organic acid used in the form of its salts and other derivatives to relieve pain and fever

[1]**sa•lient** \ˈsāl-yənt, ˈsā-lē-ənt\ *adj* : jutting forward beyond a line; *also* : PROMINENT **syn** conspicuous, striking, noticeable

[2]**salient** *n* : a projecting part in a line of defense

[1]**sa•line** \ˈsā-ˌlēn, -ˌlīn\ *adj* : consisting of or containing salt : SALTY — **sa•lin•i•ty** \sā-ˈli-nə-tē, sə-\ *n*

[2]**saline** *n* **1** : a metallic salt esp. with a purgative action **2** : a saline solution

sa•li•va \sə-ˈlī-və\ *n* : a liquid secreted into the mouth that helps digestion — **sal•i•vary** \ˈsa-lə-ˌver-ē\ *adj*

sal•i•vate \ˈsa-lə-ˌvāt\ *vb* **-vat•ed; -vat•ing** : to produce saliva esp. in excess — **sal•i•va•tion** \ˌsa-lə-ˈvā-shən\ *n*

sal•low \ˈsa-lō\ *adj* : of a yellowish sickly color ⟨a ~ face⟩

sal•ly \ˈsa-lē\ *n, pl* **sallies 1** : a rushing attack on besiegers by troops of a besieged place **2** : a witty remark or retort **3** : a brief excursion — **sally** *vb*

salm•on \ˈsa-mən\ *n, pl* **salmon** *also* **salmons 1** : any of several bony fishes with pinkish flesh used for food that are related to the trouts **2** : a strong yellowish pink color

sal•mo•nel•la \ˌsal-mə-ˈne-lə\ *n, pl* **-nel•lae** \-ˈne-(ˌ)lē, -ˌlī\ *or* **-nellas** *or* **-nella** : any of a genus of rod-shaped bacteria that cause various illnesses (as food poisoning)

sa•lon \sə-ˈlän, ˈsa-ˌlän, sa-ˈlōⁿ\ *n* [F] : an elegant

drawing room; *also* : a fashionable shop ⟨beauty ~⟩
sa•loon \sə-ˈlün\ *n* **1** : a large public cabin on a ship **2** : a place where liquors are sold and drunk : BARROOM **3** *Brit* : SEDAN 2
sal•sa \ˈsȯl-sə, ˈsäl-\ *n* : a spicy sauce of tomatoes, onions, and hot peppers
sal soda \ˈsal-ˈsō-də\ *n* : SODIUM CARBONATE
[1]**salt** \ˈsȯlt\ *n* **1** : a white crystalline substance that consists of sodium and chlorine and is used in seasoning foods **2** : a saltlike cathartic substance (as Epsom salts) **3** : a compound formed usu. by action of an acid on metal **4** : SAILOR — **salt•i•ness** \ˈsȯl-tē-nəs\ *n* — **salty** \ˈsȯl-tē\ *adj*
[2]**salt** *vb* : to preserve, season, or feed with salt
[3]**salt** *adj* : preserved or treated with salt; *also* : SALTY
SALT *abbr* Strategic Arms Limitation Talks
salt away *vb* : to lay away safely : SAVE
salt•box \ˈsȯlt-ˌbäks\ *n* : a frame dwelling with two stories in front and one behind and a long sloping roof
salt•cel•lar \-ˌse-lər\ *n* : a small container for holding salt at the table
sal•tine \sȯl-ˈtēn\ *n* : a thin crisp cracker sprinkled with salt
salt lick *n* : LICK 5
salt•pe•ter \ˈsȯlt-ˈpē-tər\ *n* [ME *salt petre,* alter. of *salpetre,* fr. MF, fr. ML *sal petrae,* lit., salt of the rock] **1** : POTASSIUM NITRATE **2** : SODIUM NITRATE
salt•wa•ter \-ˌwȯ-tər, -ˌwä-\ *adj* : of, relating to, or living in salt water
sa•lu•bri•ous \sə-ˈlü-brē-əs\ *adj* : favorable to health
sal•u•tary \ˈsal-yə-ˌter-ē\ *adj* : health-giving; *also* : BENEFICIAL
sal•u•ta•tion \ˌsal-yə-ˈtā-shən\ *n* : an expression of greeting, goodwill, or courtesy usu. by word or gesture
sa•lu•ta•to•ri•an \sə-ˌlü-tə-ˈtōr-ē-ən\ *n* : the student having the 2nd highest rank in a graduating class who delivers the salutatory address
sa•lu•ta•to•ry \sə-ˈlü-tə-ˌtōr-ē\ *adj* : relating to or being the welcoming oration delivered at an academic commencement
[1]**sa•lute** \sə-ˈlüt\ *vb* **sa•lut•ed; sa•lut•ing 1** : GREET **2** : to honor by special ceremonies **3** : to show respect to (a superior officer) by a formal position of hand, rifle, or sword
[2]**salute** *n* **1** : GREETING **2** : the formal position assumed in saluting a superior
[1]**sal•vage** \ˈsal-vij\ *n* **1** : money paid for saving a ship, its cargo, or passengers when the ship is wrecked or in danger **2** : the saving of a ship **3** : the saving of possessions in danger of being lost **4** : things saved from loss or destruction (as by a wreck or fire)
[2]**salvage** *vb* **sal•vaged; sal•vag•ing** : to rescue from destruction
sal•va•tion \sal-ˈvā-shən\ *n* **1** : the saving of a person from sin or its consequences esp. in the life after death **2** : the saving from danger, difficulty, or evil **3** : something that saves
[1]**salve** \ˈsav, ˈsȧv\ *n* **1** : a medicinal substance applied to the skin **2** : a soothing influence
[2]**salve** *vb* **salved; salv•ing** : EASE, SOOTHE
sal•ver \ˈsal-vər\ *n* [F *salve,* fr. Sp *salva* sampling of food to detect poison, tray, fr. *salvar* to save, sample food to detect poison, fr. LL *salvare* to save, fr. L *salvus* safe] : a small serving tray
sal•vo \ˈsal-vō\ *n, pl* **salvos** *or* **salvoes** : a simultaneous discharge of guns
Sam *or* **Saml** *abbr* Samuel
SAM \ˈsam, ˌes-ˌā-ˈem\ *n* [*s*urface-to-*a*ir *m*issile] : a guided missile for use against aircraft by ground units
sa•mar•i•um \sə-ˈmer-ē-əm\ *n* : a gray lustrous metallic chemical element — see ELEMENT table
[1]**same** \ˈsām\ *adj* **1** : being the one referred to : not different **2** : SIMILAR — **same•ness** *n*
[2]**same** *pron* : the same one or ones
[3]**same** *adv* : in the same manner
Sa•mo•an \sə-ˈmō-ən\ *n* : a native or inhabitant of Samoa — **Samoan** *adj*
sam•o•var \ˈsa-mə-ˌvär\ *n* [Russ, fr. *samo-* self + *varit'* to boil] : an urn with a spigot at the base used esp. in Russia to boil water for tea
sam•pan \ˈsam-ˌpan\ *n* : a flat-bottomed skiff of the Far East usu. propelled by two short oars
[1]**sam•ple** \ˈsam-pəl\ *n* : a representative piece, item, or set of individuals that shows the quality or nature of the whole from which it was taken : EXAMPLE, SPECIMEN
[2]**sample** *vb* **sam•pled; sam•pling** : to judge the quality of by a sample
sam•pler \ˈsam-plər\ *n* : a piece of needlework; *esp* : one testing skill in embroidering
Sam•u•el \ˈsam-yə-wəl\ *n* — see BIBLE table
sam•u•rai \ˈsa-mə-ˌrī, ˈsam-yə-\ *n, pl* **samurai** : a member of a Japanese feudal warrior class practicing a chivalric code
san•a•to•ri•um \ˌsa-nə-ˈtōr-ē-əm\ *n, pl* **-riums** *or* **-ria** \-ē-ə\ **1** : a health resort **2** : an establishment for the care esp. of convalescents or the chronically ill
sanc•ti•fy \ˈsaŋk-tə-ˌfī\ *vb* **-fied; -fy•ing 1** : to make holy : CONSECRATE **2** : to free from sin — **sanc•ti•fi•ca•tion** \ˌsaŋk-tə-fə-ˈkā-shən\ *n*
sanc•ti•mo•nious \ˌsaŋk-tə-ˈmō-nē-əs\ *adj* : hypocritically pious — **sanc•ti•mo•nious•ly** *adv*
[1]**sanc•tion** \ˈsaŋk-shən\ *n* **1** : authoritative approval **2** : a measure (as a threat or fine) designed to enforce a law or standard ⟨economic ~*s*⟩
[2]**sanction** *vb* : to give approval to : RATIFY **syn** endorse, accredit, certify, approve
sanc•ti•ty \ˈsaŋk-tə-tē\ *n, pl* **-ties 1** : GODLINESS **2** : SACREDNESS
sanc•tu•ary \ˈsaŋk-chə-ˌwer-ē\ *n, pl* **-ar•ies 1** : a consecrated place (as the part of a church in which the altar is placed) **2** : a place of refuge ⟨bird ~⟩
sanc•tum \ˈsaŋk-təm\ *n, pl* **sanctums** *also* **sanc•ta** \-tə\ : a private office or study : DEN ⟨an editor's ~⟩
[1]**sand** \ˈsand\ *n* : loose particles of hard broken rock — **sandy** *adj*
[2]**sand** *vb* **1** : to cover or fill with sand **2** : to scour, smooth, or polish with an abrasive (as sandpaper) — **sand•er** *n*
san•dal \ˈsand-ᵊl\ *n* : a shoe consisting of a sole strapped to the foot; *also* : a low or open slipper or rubber overshoe
san•dal•wood \-ˌwu̇d\ *n* : the fragrant yellowish heartwood of a parasitic tree of southern Asia that is much used in ornamental carving and cabinetwork; *also* : the tree
sand•bag \ˈsand-ˌbag\ *n* : a bag filled with sand and used in fortifications, as ballast, or as a weapon
sand•bank \-ˌbaŋk\ *n* : a deposit of sand (as in a bar or shoal)
sand•bar \-ˌbär\ *n* : a ridge of sand formed in water by tides or currents
sand•blast \-ˌblast\ *vb* : to treat with a stream of sand blown (as for cleaning stone) by compressed air — **sand•blast•er** *n*
sand dollar *n* : any of numerous flat circular sea urchins chiefly of sandy bottoms in shallow water
S & H *abbr* shipping and handling
sand•hog \ˈsand-ˌhȯg, -ˌhäg\ *n* : a laborer who builds underwater tunnels
sand•lot \-ˌlät\ *n* : a vacant lot esp. when used for the unorganized sports of children — **sand•lot** *adj* — **sand•lot•ter** *n*
sand•man \-ˌman\ *n* : the genie of folklore who makes children sleepy
sand•pa•per \-ˌpā-pər\ *n* : paper with abrasive (as sand) glued on one side used in smoothing and polishing surfaces — **sandpaper** *vb*
sand•pip•er \-ˌpī-pər\ *n* : any of numerous shorebirds with a soft-tipped bill longer than that of the related plovers

sand•stone \-ˌstōn\ *n* : rock made of sand united by a natural cement
sand•storm \-ˌstȯrm\ *n* : a windstorm that drives clouds of sand
sand trap *n* : a hazard on a golf course consisting of a hollow containing sand
[1]**sand•wich** \ˈsand-(ˌ)wich\ *n* [after John Montagu, 4th Earl of *Sandwich* †1792 Eng. diplomat] **1** : two or more slices of bread with a layer (as of meat or cheese) spread between them **2** : something resembling a sandwich
[2]**sandwich** *vb* : to squeeze or crowd in
sane \ˈsān\ *adj* **san•er; san•est** : mentally sound and healthy; *also* : SENSIBLE, RATIONAL — **sane•ly** *adv*
sang *past of* SING
sang•froid \ˈsäⁿ-ˈfrwä\ *n* [F *sang-froid,* lit., cold blood] : self-possession or an imperturbable state esp. under strain
san•gui•nary \ˈsaŋ-gwə-ˌner-ē\ *adj* : BLOODY ⟨~ battle⟩
san•guine \ˈsaŋ-gwən\ *adj* **1** : RUDDY **2** : CHEERFUL, HOPEFUL
sanit *abbr* sanitary; sanitation
san•i•tar•i•an \ˌsa-nə-ˈter-ē-ən\ *n* : a specialist in sanitation and public health
san•i•tar•i•um \ˌsa-nə-ˈter-ē-əm\ *n, pl* **-i•ums** *or* **-ia** \-ē-ə\ : SANATORIUM
san•i•tary \ˈsa-nə-ˌter-ē\ *adj* **1** : of or relating to health : HYGIENIC **2** : free from filth or infective matter
sanitary napkin *n* : a disposable absorbent pad used to absorb uterine flow (as during menstruation)
san•i•ta•tion \ˌsa-nə-ˈtā-shən\ *n* : the act or process of making sanitary; *also* : protection of health by maintenance of sanitary conditions
san•i•tize \ˈsa-nə-ˌtīz\ *vb* **-tized; -tiz•ing 1** : to make sanitary **2** : to make more acceptable by removing unpleasant features
san•i•ty \ˈsa-nə-tē\ *n* : soundness of mind
sank *past of* SINK
sans \ˈsanz\ *prep* : WITHOUT
San•skrit \ˈsan-ˌskrit\ *n* : an ancient language that is the classical language of India and of Hinduism — **Sanskrit** *adj*
San•ta Ana \ˌsan-tə-ˈa-nə\ *n* [*Santa Ana* Mountains in southern Calif.] : a hot dry wind from the north, northeast, or east in southern California
[1]**sap** \ˈsap\ *n* **1** : a vital fluid; *esp* : a watery fluid that circulates through a vascular plant **2** : a foolish gullible person — **sap•less** *adj*
[2]**sap** *vb* **sapped; sap•ping 1** : UNDERMINE **2** : to weaken gradually
sap•id \ˈsa-pəd\ *adj* : FLAVORFUL
sa•pi•ent \ˈsā-pē-ənt, ˈsa-\ *adj* : WISE, DISCERNING — **sa•pi•ence** \-əns\ *n*
sap•ling \ˈsa-pliŋ\ *n* : a young tree
sap•phire \ˈsa-ˌfīr\ *n* : a hard transparent usu. rich blue gem
sap•py \ˈsa-pē\ *adj* **sap•pi•er; -est 1** : full of sap **2** : overly sentimental **3** : SILLY, FOOLISH
sap•ro•phyte \ˈsa-prə-ˌfīt\ *n* : a living thing and esp. a plant living on dead or decaying organic matter — **sap•ro•phyt•ic** \ˌsa-prə-ˈfi-tik\ *adj*
sap•suck•er \ˈsap-ˌse-kər\ *n* : any of a genus of small No. American woodpeckers
sap•wood \-ˌwu̇d\ *n* : the younger active and usu. lighter and softer outer layer of wood (as of a tree trunk)
sar•casm \ˈsär-ˌka-zəm\ *n* **1** : a cutting or contemptuous remark **2** : ironic criticism or reproach — **sar•cas•tic** \sär-ˈkas-tik\ *adj* — **sar•cas•ti•cal•ly** \-ti-k(ə-)lē\ *adv*
sar•co•ma \sär-ˈkō-mə\ *n, pl* **-mas** *also* **-ma•ta** \-mə-tə\ : a malignant tumor esp. of connective tissue, bone, cartilage, or striated muscle
sar•coph•a•gus \sär-ˈkä-fə-gəs\ *n, pl* **-gi** \-ˌgī, -ˌjī\ *also* **-gus•es** [L *sarcophagus* (*lapis*) limestone used for coffins, fr. Gk (*lithos*) *sarkophagos,* lit., flesh-eating stone, fr. *sark-, sarx* flesh + *phagein* to eat] : a large stone coffin
sar•dine \sär-ˈdēn\ *n, pl* **sardines** *also* **sardine** : a young or small fish preserved for use as food
sar•don•ic \sär-ˈdä-nik\ *adj* : disdainfully or skeptically humorous : derisively mocking **syn** ironic, satiric, sarcastic — **sar•don•i•cal•ly** \-ni-k(ə-)lē\ *adv*
sa•ri *also* **sa•ree** \ˈsär-ē\ *n* [Hindi *sāṛī*] : a garment worn by women in southern Asia that consists of a long cloth draped around the body and head or shoulder
sa•rong \sə-ˈrȯŋ, -ˈräŋ\ *n* : a loose garment wrapped around the body and worn by men and women of the Malay Archipelago and the Pacific islands
sar•sa•pa•ril•la \ˌsas-ə-pə-ˈri-lə, ˌsärs-\ *n* **1** : the dried roots of a tropical American smilax used esp. for flavoring; *also* : the plant **2** : a sweetened carbonated beverage flavored with sassafras and an oil from a birch
sar•to•ri•al \sär-ˈtōr-ē-əl\ *adj* : of or relating to a tailor or tailored clothes — **sar•to•ri•al•ly** *adv*
SASE *abbr* self-addressed stamped envelope
[1]**sash** \ˈsash\ *n* : a broad band worn around the waist or over the shoulder
[2]**sash** *n, pl* **sash** *also* **sash•es** : a frame for panes of glass in a door or window; *also* : the movable part of a window
sa•shay \sa-ˈshā\ *vb* **1** : WALK, GLIDE, GO **2** : to strut or move about in an ostentatious manner **3** : to proceed in a diagonal or sideways manner
Sask *abbr* Saskatchewan
Sas•quatch \ˈsas-ˌkwach, -ˌkwäch\ *n* [Halkomelem (American Indian language of British Columbia) *sésq̓əc*] : a large hairy humanlike creature reported to exist in the northwestern U.S. and western Canada
sas•sa•fras \ˈsa-sə-ˌfras\ *n* [Sp *sasafrás*] : a No. American tree related to the laurel; *also* : its carcinogenic dried root bark
sassy \ˈsa-sē\ *adj* **sass•i•er; -est** : SAUCY
[1]**sat** *past and past part of* SIT
[2]**sat** *abbr* saturate; saturated; saturation
Sat *abbr* Saturday
Sa•tan \ˈsāt-ᵊn\ *n* : DEVIL
sa•tang \sə-ˈtäŋ\ *n, pl* **satang** *or* **satangs** — see *baht* at MONEY table
sa•tan•ic \sə-ˈta-nik, sā-\ *adj* **1** : of or characteristic of Satan **2** : extremely malicious or wicked — **sa•tan•i•cal•ly** \-ni-k(ə-)lē\ *adv*
satch•el \ˈsa-chəl\ *n* : SUITCASE
sate \ˈsāt\ *vb* **sat•ed; sat•ing** : to satisfy to the full; *also* : SURFEIT, GLUT
sa•teen \sa-ˈtēn, sə-\ *n* : a cotton cloth finished to resemble satin
sat•el•lite \ˈsat-ᵊl-ˌīt\ *n* [F, fr. L *satelles* attendant] **1** : an obsequious follower of a distinguished person : TOADY **2** : a celestial body that orbits a larger body **3** : a manufactured object that orbits a celestial body
sa•ti•ate \ˈsā-shē-ˌāt\ *vb* **-at•ed; -at•ing** : to satisfy fully or to excess
sa•ti•ety \sə-ˈtī-ə-tē\ *n* : fullness to the point of excess
sat•in \ˈsat-ᵊn\ *n* : a fabric (as of silk) with a glossy surface — **sat•iny** *adj*
sat•in•wood \ˈsat-ᵊn-ˌwu̇d\ *n* : a hard yellowish brown wood of satiny luster; *also* : a tree yielding this wood
sat•ire \ˈsa-ˌtīr\ *n* : biting wit, irony, or sarcasm used to expose vice or folly; *also* : a literary work having these qualities — **sa•tir•ic** \sə-ˈtir-ik\ *or* **sa•tir•i•cal** \-i-kəl\ *adj* — **sa•tir•i•cal•ly** *adv* — **sat•i•rist** \ˈsa-tə-rist\ *n* — **sat•i•rize** \-tə-ˌrīz\ *vb*
sat•is•fac•tion \ˌsa-təs-ˈfak-shən\ *n* **1** : payment through penance of punishment incurred by sin **2** : CONTENTMENT, GRATIFICATION **3** : reparation for an insult **4** : settlement of a claim
sat•is•fac•to•ry \-ˈfak-tə-rē\ *adj* : giving satisfaction : ADEQUATE — **sat•is•fac•to•ri•ly** \-ˈfak-tə-rə-lē\ *adv*
sat•is•fy \ˈsa-təs-ˌfī\ *vb* **-fied; -fy•ing 1** : to answer or discharge (a claim) in full **2** : to make happy : GRATIFY

3 : to pay what is due to 4 : CONVINCE 5 : to meet the requirements of — **sat•is•fy•ing•ly** *adv*

sa•trap \ˈsā-ˌtrap, ˈsa-\ *n* [ME, fr. L *satrapes,* fr. Gk *satrapēs,* fr. OPer *khshathrapāvan,* lit., protector of the dominion] : a petty prince : a subordinate ruler

sat•u•rate \ˈsa-chə-ˌrāt\ *vb* **-rat•ed; -rat•ing 1** : to soak thoroughly **2** : to treat or charge with something to the point where no more can be absorbed, dissolved, or retained — **sat•u•ra•ble** \ˈsa-chə-rə-bəl\ *adj* — **sat•u•ra•tion** \ˌsa-chə-ˈrā-shən\ *n*

Sat•ur•day \ˈsa-tər-dē, -ˌdā\ *n* : the 7th day of the week

Saturday night special *n* : a cheap easily concealed handgun

Sat•urn \ˈsa-tərn\ *n* : the planet 6th in order from the sun — see PLANET table

sat•ur•nine \ˈsa-tər-ˌnīn\ *adj* : SULLEN, SARDONIC

sa•tyr \ˈsā-tər\ *n* **1** *often cap* : a woodland deity in Greek mythology having certain characteristics of a horse or goat **2** : a lecherous man

¹sauce \ˈsȯs, *3 usu* ˈsas\ *n* **1** : a fluid dressing or topping for food **2** : stewed fruit **3** : IMPUDENCE

²sauce \ˈsȯs, *2 usu* ˈsas\ *vb* **sauced; sauc•ing 1** : to put sauce on; *also* : to add zest to **2** : to be impudent to

sauce•pan \ˈsȯs-ˌpan\ *n* : a small deep cooking pan with a handle

sau•cer \ˈsȯ-sər\ *n* : a rounded shallow dish for use under a cup

saucy \ˈsa-sē, ˈsȯ-\ *adj* **sauc•i•er; -est** : IMPUDENT, PERT — **sauc•i•ly** \-sə-lē\ *adv* — **sauc•i•ness** \-sē-nəs\ *n*

Sau•di \ˈsaù-dē, ˈsȯ-; sä-ˈü-dē\ *n* : SAUDI ARABIAN — **Saudi** *adj*

Saudi Arabian *n* : a native or inhabitant of Saudi Arabia — **Saudi Arabian** *adj*

sau•er•kraut \ˈsaù-ər-ˌkraùt\ *n* [G, fr. *sauer* sour + *Kraut* greens] : finely cut cabbage fermented in brine

sau•na \ˈsaù-nə\ *n* **1** : a Finnish steam bath in which the steam is provided by water thrown on hot stones **2** : a dry heat bath; *also* : a room or cabinet used for such a bath

saun•ter \ˈsȯn-tər, ˈsän-\ *vb* : STROLL

sau•ro•pod \ˈsȯr-ə-ˌpäd\ *n* : any of a suborder of plant-eating dinosaurs (as a brontosaurus) with a long neck and tail and a small head — **sauropod** *adj*

sau•sage \ˈsȯ-sij\ *n* [ultim. fr. LL *salsicia,* fr. L *salsus* salted] : minced and highly seasoned meat (as pork) usu. enclosed in a tubular casing

S Aust *abbr* South Australia

sau•té \sȯ-ˈtā, sō-\ *vb* **sau•téed** *or* **sau•téd; sau•té•ing** [F] : to fry lightly in a little fat — **sauté** *n*

sau•terne \sō-ˈtərn, sȯ-\ *n, often cap* : a usu. semisweet American white wine

¹sav•age \ˈsa-vij\ *adj* [ME *sauvage,* fr. MF, fr. ML *salvaticus,* alter. of L *silvaticus* of the woods, wild, fr. *silva* wood, forest] **1** : WILD, UNTAMED **2** : UNCIVILIZED, BARBAROUS **3** : CRUEL, FIERCE — **sav•age•ly** *adv* — **sav•age•ness** *n* — **sav•age•ry** \-rē\ *n*

²savage *n* **1** : a member of a primitive human society **2** : a rude, unmannerly, or brutal person

sa•van•na *or* **sa•van•nah** \sə-ˈva-nə\ *n* [Sp *zavana*] : grassland containing scattered trees

sa•vant \sa-ˈvänt, sə-, ˈsa-vənt\ *n* : a learned person : SCHOLAR

¹save \ˈsāv\ *vb* **saved; sav•ing 1** : to redeem from sin **2** : to rescue from danger **3** : to preserve or guard from destruction or loss **4** : to put aside as a store or reserve — **sav•er** *n*

²save *n* : a play that prevents an opponent from scoring or winning

³save *prep* : EXCEPT

⁴save *conj* : BUT

savings and loan association *n* : a cooperative association that holds savings of members in the form of dividend-bearing shares and that invests chiefly in mortgage loans

savings bank *n* : a bank that holds funds of individual depositors in interest-bearing accounts and makes long-term investments (as mortgage loans)

savings bond *n* : a registered U.S. bond issued in denominations of $50 to $10,000

sav•ior *or* **sav•iour** \ˈsāv-yər\ *n* **1** : one who saves **2** *cap* : Jesus Christ

sa•voir faire \ˌsav-ˌwär-ˈfar\ *n* [F *savoir-faire,* lit., knowing how to do] : sureness in social behavior

¹sa•vor *also* **sa•vour** \ˈsā-vər\ *n* **1** : the taste and odor of something **2** : a special flavor or quality — **sa•vory** *adj*

²savor *also* **savour** *vb* **1** : to have a specified taste, smell, or quality **2** : to taste with pleasure

sa•vo•ry \ˈsā-və-rē\ *n, pl* **-ries** : either of two aromatic mints used in cooking

¹sav•vy \ˈsa-vē\ *vb* **sav•vied; sav•vy•ing** : UNDERSTAND, COMPREHEND

²savvy *n* : practical know-how ⟨political ∼⟩ — **savvy** *adj*

¹saw *past of* SEE

²saw \ˈsȯ\ *n* : a cutting tool with a blade having a line of teeth along its edge

³saw *vb* **sawed** \ˈsȯd\; **sawed** *or* **sawn** \ˈsȯn\; **saw•ing** : to cut or shape with or as if with a saw

⁴saw *n* : a common saying : MAXIM

saw•dust \ˈsȯ-(ˌ)dəst\ *n* : fine particles made by a saw in cutting

saw•fly \-ˌflī\ *n* : any of numerous insects belonging to the same order as bees and wasps and including many whose larvae are plant-feeding pests

saw•horse \-ˌhȯrs\ *n* : a rack on which wood is rested while being sawed by hand

saw•mill \-ˌmil\ *n* : a mill for sawing logs

saw palmetto *n* : any of several shrubby palms with spiny-toothed petioles

saw•yer \ˈsȯ-yər\ *n* : a person who saws timber

sax \ˈsaks\ *n* : SAXOPHONE

sax•i•frage \ˈsak-sə-frij, -ˌfrāj\ *n* [ME, fr. MF, fr. LL *saxifraga,* fr. L, fem. of *saxifragus,* breaking rocks] : any of a genus of plants with showy flowers and usu. with leaves growing in tufts close to the ground

sax•o•phone \ˈsak-sə-ˌfōn\ *n* : a musical instrument having a conical metal tube with a reed mouthpiece and finger keys — **sax•o•phon•ist** \-ˌfō-nist\ *n*

¹say \ˈsā\ *vb* **said** \ˈsed\; **say•ing; says** \ˈsez\ **1** : to express in words ⟨∼ what you mean⟩ **2** : to state as opinion or belief **3** : PRONOUNCE; *also* : RECITE, REPEAT ⟨∼ your prayers⟩ **4** : INDICATE ⟨the clock ∼*s* noon⟩

²say *n, pl* **says** \ˈsāz\ **1** : an expression of opinion **2** : power of decision

say•ing *n* : a commonly repeated statement

say–so \ˈsā-(ˌ)sō\ *n* : an esp. authoritative assertion or decision; *also* : the right to decide

sb *abbr* substantive

Sb *symbol* [L *stibium*] antimony

SB *abbr* [NL *scientiae baccalaureus*] bachelor of science

SBA *abbr* Small Business Administration

sc *abbr* **1** scale **2** scene **3** science

Sc *symbol* scandium

SC *abbr* **1** South Carolina **2** supreme court

¹scab \ˈskab\ *n* **1** : scabies of domestic animals **2** : a protective crust over a sore or wound **3** : a worker who replaces a striker or works under conditions not authorized by a union **4** : any of various bacterial or fungus plant diseases marked by crusted spots on stems or leaves — **scab•by** *adj*

²scab *vb* **scabbed; scab•bing 1** : to become covered with a scab **2** : to work as a scab

scab•bard \ˈska-bərd\ *n* : a sheath for the blade of a weapon (as a sword)

sca•bies \ˈskā-bēz\ *n* [L] : contagious itch or mange caused by mites living as parasites under the skin

sca•brous \ˈska-brəs, ˈskā-\ *adj* **1** : DIFFICULT, KNOTTY **2** : rough to the touch : SCALY, SCURFY ⟨a ∼ leaf⟩ **3**

DICTIONARY

: dealing with suggestive, indecent, or scandalous themes; *also* : SQUALID

scad \ˈskad\ *n* : a large number or quantity — usu. used in pl.

scaf•fold \ˈska-fəld, -ˌfōld\ *n* **1** : a raised platform for workers to sit or stand on **2** : a platform on which a criminal is executed (as by hanging)

scaf•fold•ing *n* : a system of scaffolds; *also* : materials for scaffolds

scal•a•wag \ˈska-li-ˌwag\ *n* : RASCAL

¹scald \ˈskȯld\ *vb* **1** : to burn with or as if with hot liquid or steam **2** : to heat to just below the boiling point

²scald *n* : a burn caused by scalding

¹scale \ˈskāl\ *n* **1** : either pan of a balance **2** : BALANCE — usu. used in pl. **3** : a weighing instrument

²scale *vb* **scaled; scal•ing** : WEIGH

³scale *n* **1** : one of the small thin plates that cover the body esp. of a fish or reptile **2** : a thin plate or flake **3** : a thin coating, layer, or incrustation **4** : SCALE INSECT — **scaled** \ˈskāld\ *adj* — **scale•less** \ˈskāl-ləs\ *adj* — **scaly** *adj*

⁴scale *vb* **scaled; scal•ing** : to strip of scales

⁵scale *n* [ME, fr. LL *scala* ladder, staircase, fr. L *scalae*, pl., stairs, rungs, ladder] **1** : something divided into regular spaces as a help in drawing or measuring **2** : a graduated series **3** : the size of a sample (as a model) in proportion to the size of the actual thing **4** : a standard of estimation or judgment **5** : a series of musical tones going up or down in pitch according to a specified scheme

⁶scale *vb* **scaled; scal•ing 1** : to climb by or as if by a ladder **2** : to arrange in a graded series

scale insect *n* : any of numerous small insects with wingless scale-covered females that are related to aphids and live and are often pests on plants

scale•pan \ˈskāl-ˌpan\ *n* : ¹SCALE 1

scal•lion \ˈskal-yən\ *n* [ultim. fr. L *ascalonia* (*caepa*) onion of Ascalon (seaport in Palestine)] : an onion without an enlarged bulb

¹scal•lop \ˈskä-ləp, ˈska-\ *n* **1** : any of numerous marine bivalve mollusks with radially ridged shells; *also* : a large edible muscle of this mollusk **2** : one of a continuous series of rounded projections forming an edge

²scallop *vb* **1** : to bake in a casserole ⟨~*ed* potatoes⟩ **2** : to shape, cut, or finish in scallops ⟨~*ed* edges⟩

¹scalp \ˈskalp\ *n* : the part of the skin and flesh of the head usu. covered with hair

²scalp *vb* **1** : to remove the scalp from **2** : to resell at greatly increased prices ⟨~ tickets⟩ — **scalp•er** *n*

scal•pel \ˈskal-pəl\ *n* : a small straight knife with a thin blade used esp. in surgery

scam \ˈskam\ *n* : a fraudulent or deceptive act or operation

scamp \ˈskamp\ *n* : RASCAL

scam•per \ˈskam-pər\ *vb* : to run nimbly and playfully — **scamper** *n*

scam•pi \ˈskam-pē\ *n, pl* **scampi** [It] : SHRIMP; *esp* : large shrimp prepared with a garlic-flavored sauce

¹scan \ˈskan\ *vb* **scanned; scan•ning 1** : to read (verses) so as to show metrical structure **2** : to examine closely **3** : to examine with a sensing device esp. to obtain information **4** : to make a scan of (as the human body) — **scan•ner** *n*

²scan *n* **1** : the act or process of scanning **2** : a picture of the distribution of radioactive material in something; *also* : an image of a bodily part produced (as by computer) by combining radiographic data obtained from several angles or sections

Scand *abbr* Scandinavia; Scandinavian

scan•dal \ˈskand-ᵊl\ *n* [ME, fr. LL *scandalum* stumbling block, offense, fr. Gk *skandalon*] **1** : DISGRACE, DISHONOR **2** : malicious gossip : SLANDER — **scan•dal•ize** *vb* — **scan•dal•ous** *adj* — **scan•dal•ous•ly** *adv*

scan•dal•mon•ger \-ˌməŋ-gər, -ˌmäŋ-\ *n* : a person who circulates scandal

Scan•di•na•vian \ˌskan-də-ˈnā-vē-ən\ *n* : a native or inhabitant of Scandinavia — **Scandinavian** *adj*

scan•di•um \ˈskan-dē-əm\ *n* : a white metallic chemical element — see ELEMENT table

¹scant \ˈskant\ *adj* **1** : barely sufficient **2** : having scarcely enough **syn** scanty, skimpy, meager, sparse, exiguous

²scant *vb* **1** : SKIMP **2** : STINT

scant•ling \ˈskant-liŋ\ *n* : a small piece of lumber (as an upright in a house)

scanty \ˈskan-tē\ *adj* **scant•i•er; -est** : barely sufficient : SCANT — **scant•i•ly** \ˈskan-tə-lē\ *adv* — **scant•i•ness** \-tē-nəs\ *n*

scape•goat \ˈskāp-ˌgōt\ *n* : one that bears the blame for others

scape•grace \-ˌgrās\ *n* [*scape* (escape)] : an incorrigible rascal

scap•u•la \ˈska-pyə-lə\ *n, pl* **-lae** \-ˌlē\ *or* **-las** [L] : SHOULDER BLADE

scap•u•lar \-lər\ *n* : a pair of small cloth squares worn on the breast and back under the clothing esp. for religious purposes

scar \ˈskär\ *n* : a mark left after injured tissue has healed — **scar** *vb*

scar•ab \ˈskar-əb\ *n* [MF *scarabee*, fr. L *scarabaeus*] : any of a family of large stout beetles; *also* : an ornament (as a gem) representing such a beetle

scarce \ˈskers\ *adj* **scarc•er; scarc•est 1** : deficient in quantity or number : not plentiful **2** : intentionally absent ⟨made himself ~ at inspection time⟩ — **scar•ci•ty** \ˈsker-sə-tē\ *n*

scarce•ly \-lē\ *adv* **1** : BARELY **2** : almost not **3** : very probably not

¹scare \ˈsker\ *vb* **scared; scar•ing** : FRIGHTEN, STARTLE

²scare *n* : FRIGHT — **scary** *adj*

scare•crow \ˈsker-ˌkrō\ *n* : a crude figure set up to scare birds away from crops

¹scarf \ˈskärf\ *n, pl* **scarves** \ˈskärvz\ *or* **scarfs 1** : a broad band (as of cloth) worn about the shoulders, around the neck, over the head, or about the waist **2** : a long narrow cloth cover for a table or dresser top

²scarf *vb* [alter. of earlier *scoff* eat greedily] : to eat greedily

scar•i•fy \ˈskar-ə-ˌfī\ *vb* **-fied; -fy•ing 1** : to make scratches or small cuts in ⟨~ skin for vaccination⟩ ⟨~ seeds to help them germinate⟩ **2** : to lacerate the feelings of **3** : to break up and loosen the surface of (as a road) — **scar•i•fi•ca•tion** \ˌskar-ə-fə-ˈkā-shən\ *n*

scar•let \ˈskär-lət\ *n* : a bright red color — **scarlet** *adj*

scarlet fever *n* : an acute contagious disease marked by fever, sore throat, and red rash and caused by certain streptococci

scarp \ˈskärp\ *n* : a line of cliffs produced by faulting or erosion

scath•ing \ˈskā-thiŋ\ *adj* : bitterly severe ⟨a ~ condemnation⟩

scat•o•log•i•cal \ˌska-tə-ˈlä-ji-kəl\ *adj* : concerned with obscene matters

scat•ter \ˈska-tər\ *vb* **1** : to distribute or strew about irregularly **2** : DISPERSE

scat•ter•brain \ˈska-tər-ˌbrān\ *n* : a silly careless person — **scat•ter•brained** \-ˌbrānd\ *adj*

scav•enge \ˈska-vənj\ *vb* **scav•enged; scav•eng•ing** : to work or function as a scavenger

scav•en•ger \ˈska-vən-jər\ *n* [alter. of earlier *scavager*, fr. ME *skawager* customs collector, fr. *skawage* customs, fr. OF *escauwage* inspection] : a person or animal that collects, eats, or disposes of refuse or waste

sce•nar•io \sə-ˈnar-ē-ˌō\ *n, pl* **-i•os** : the plot or outline of a dramatic work; *also* : an account of a possible action

scene \ˈsēn\ *n* [MF, stage, fr. L *scena*, *scaena* stage, scene, prob. fr. Etruscan, fr. Gk *skēnē* temporary shelter, tent, building forming the background for a dramatic performance, stage] **1** : a division of one act of a play **2** : a single situation or sequence in a play or motion picture **3** : a stage setting **4** : VIEW, PROSPECT **5** : the place of an occurrence or action **6** : a display of strong feeling and esp. anger **7** : a sphere of activity ⟨the fashion ~⟩ — **sce•nic** \ˈsē-nik\ *adj*

scen•ery \ˈsē-nə-rē\ *n, pl* **-er•ies 1** : the painted scenes or hangings and accessories used on a theater stage **2** : a picturesque view or landscape

[1]**scent** \ˈsent\ *n* **1** : ODOR, SMELL **2** : sense of smell **3** : course of pursuit : TRACK **4** : PERFUME 2 — **scent•ed** \ˈsen-təd\ *adj* — **scent•less** *adj*

[2]**scent** *vb* **1** : SMELL **2** : to imbue or fill with odor

scep•ter \ˈsep-tər\ *n* : a staff borne by a sovereign as an emblem of authority

scep•tic \ˈskep-tik\ *var of* SKEPTIC

scep•tre *Brit var of* SCEPTER

sch *abbr* school

[1]**sched•ule** \ˈske-jül, *esp Brit* ˈshe-dyül\ *n* **1** : a list of items or details **2** : TIMETABLE

[2]**schedule** *vb* **sched•uled; sched•ul•ing 1** : to make a schedule of; *also* : to enter on a schedule **2** : to appoint, assign, or designate for a fixed time

sche•mat•ic \ski-ˈma-tik\ *adj* : of or relating to a scheme or diagram : DIAGRAMMATIC — **schematic** *n* — **sche•mat•i•cal•ly** \-ti-k(ə-)lē\ *adv*

[1]**scheme** \ˈskēm\ *n* **1** : a plan for doing something; *esp* : a crafty plot **2** : a systematic design

[2]**scheme** *vb* **schemed; schem•ing** : to form a plot : INTRIGUE — **schem•er** *n*

Schick test \ˈshik-\ *n* : a serological test for susceptibility to diphtheria

schil•ling \ˈshi-liŋ\ *n* — see MONEY table

schism \ˈsi-zəm, ˈski-\ *n* **1** : DIVISION, SPLIT; *also* : DISCORD, DISSENSION **2** : a formal division in or separation from a religious body

schis•mat•ic \siz-ˈma-tik, ski-\ *n* : one who creates or takes part in schism — **schismatic** *adj*

schist \ˈshist\ *n* : a metamorphic crystalline rock

schizo•phre•nia \ˌskit-sə-ˈfrē-nē-ə\ *n* [NL, fr. Gk *schizein* to split + *phrēn* diaphragm, mind] : a psychotic mental illness that is characterized by a twisted view of the real world, by a greatly reduced ability to carry out one's daily tasks, and by abnormal ways of thinking, feeling, and behaving — **schiz•oid** \ˈskit-ˌsȯid\ *adj or n* — **schizo•phren•ic** \ˌskit-sə-ˈfre-nik\ *adj or n*

schle•miel \shlə-ˈmēl\ *n* : an unlucky bungler : CHUMP

schlepp *or* **schlep** \ˈshlep\ *vb* [Yiddish *shlepn*] **1** : DRAG, HAUL **2** : to move slowly or awkwardly

schlock \ˈshläk\ *or* **schlocky** \ˈshlä-kē\ *adj* : of low quality or value — **schlock** *n*

schmaltz *also* **schmalz** \ˈshmȯlts, ˈshmälts\ *n* [Yiddish *shmalts,* lit., rendered fat] : sentimental or florid music or art — **schmaltzy** *adj*

schnau•zer \ˈshnau̇t-sər, ˈshnau̇-zər\ *n* [G, fr. *Schnauze* snout] : a dog of any of three breeds that are characterized by a wiry coat, long head, small ears, heavy eyebrows, and long hair on the muzzle

schol•ar \ˈskä-lər\ *n* **1** : STUDENT, PUPIL **2** : a learned person : SAVANT — **schol•ar•ly** *adj*

schol•ar•ship \-ˌship\ *n* **1** : the qualities or learning of a scholar **2** : money awarded to a student to help pay for further education

scho•las•tic \skə-ˈlas-tik\ *adj* : of or relating to schools, scholars, or scholarship

[1]**school** \ˈskül\ *n* **1** : an institution for teaching and learning; *also* : the pupils in attendance **2** : a body of persons of like opinions or beliefs ⟨the radical ~⟩

[2]**school** *vb* : TEACH, TRAIN, DRILL

[3]**school** *n* : a large number of one kind of water animal swimming and feeding together

school•boy \-ˌbȯi\ *n* : a boy attending school

school•fel•low \-ˌfe-lō\ *n* : SCHOOLMATE

school•girl \-ˌgərl\ *n* : a girl attending school

school•house \-ˌhau̇s\ *n* : a building used as a school

school•marm \-ˌmärm\ *or* **school•ma'am** \-ˌmäm, -ˌmam\ *n* **1** : a woman schoolteacher **2** : a person who exhibits characteristics popularly attributed to schoolteachers

school•mas•ter \-ˌmas-tər\ *n* : a male schoolteacher

school•mate \-ˌmāt\ *n* : a school companion

school•mis•tress \-ˌmis-trəs\ *n* : a woman schoolteacher

school•room \-ˌrüm, -ˌru̇m\ *n* : CLASSROOM

school•teach•er \-ˌtē-chər\ *n* : one who teaches in a school

schoo•ner \ˈskü-nər\ *n* : a fore-and-aft rigged sailing ship

schooner

schuss \ˈshu̇s, ˈshüs\ *vb* [G *Schuss,* n., lit., shot] : to ski down a slope at high speed — **schuss** *n*

sci *abbr* science; scientific

sci•at•i•ca \sī-ˈa-ti-kə\ *n* : pain in the region of the hips or along the course of the nerve at the back of the thigh

sci•ence \ˈsī-əns\ *n* [ME, fr. MF, fr. L *scientia,* fr. *scient-, sciens* having knowledge, fr. prp. of *scire* to know] **1** : an area of knowledge that is an object of study; *esp* : NATURAL SCIENCE **2** : knowledge covering general truths or the operation of general laws especially as obtained and tested through the scientific method — **sci•en•tif•ic** \ˌsī-ən-ˈti-fik\ *adj* — **sci•en•tif•i•cal•ly** \-fi-k(ə-)lē\ *adv* — **sci•en•tist** \ˈsī-ən-tist\ *n*

science fiction *n* : fiction dealing principally with the impact of actual or imagined science on society or individuals

scientific method *n* : the rules and methods for the pursuit of knowledge involving the finding and stating of a problem, the collection of facts through observation and experiment, and the making and testing of ideas that need to be proven right or wrong

scim•i•tar \ˈsi-mə-tər\ *n* : a curved sword used chiefly by Arabs and Turks

scin•til•la \sin-ˈti-lə\ *n* : SPARK, TRACE

scin•til•late \ˈsint-ᵊl-ˌāt\ *vb* **-lat•ed; -lat•ing** : SPARKLE, GLEAM — **scin•til•la•tion** \ˌsint-ᵊl-ˈā-shən\ *n*

sci•on \ˈsī-ən\ *n* **1** : a shoot of a plant joined to a stock in grafting **2** : DESCENDANT

scis•sors \ˈsi-zərz\ *n pl* : a cutting instrument like shears but usu. smaller

scissors kick *n* : a swimming kick in which the legs move like scissors

scle•ro•sis \sklə-ˈrō-səs\ *n* : abnormal hardening of tissue (as of an artery); *also* : a disease characterized by this — **scle•rot•ic** \-ˈrä-tik\ *adj*

scoff \ˈskäf\ *vb* : MOCK, JEER — **scoff•er** *n*

scoff•law \-ˌlȯ\ *n* : a contemptuous law violator

[1]**scold** \ˈskōld\ *n* : a person who scolds

[2]**scold** *vb* : to censure severely or angrily

sconce \ˈskäns\ *n* : a candlestick or an electric light fixture fastened to a wall

scone \ˈskōn, ˈskän\ *n* : a biscuit (as of oatmeal) baked on a griddle

[1]**scoop** \ˈsküp\ *n* **1** : a large shovel; *also* : a utensil with

a shovellike or rounded end **2** : an act of scooping **3** : information of immediate interest

[2]scoop *vb* **1** : to take out or up or empty with or as if with a scoop **2** : to make hollow **3** : to report a news item in advance of

scoot \ˈsküt\ *vb* : to move swiftly

scoot•er \ˈskü-tər\ *n* **1** : a child's vehicle consisting of a narrow board mounted between two wheels tandem with an upright steering handle attached to the front wheel **2** : MOTOR SCOOTER

[1]scope \ˈskōp\ *n* [It *scopo* purpose, goal, fr. Gk *skopos*] **1** : space or opportunity for action or thought **2** : extent covered : RANGE

[2]scope *n* : an instrument (as a microscope or radarscope) for viewing

scorch \ˈskȯrch\ *vb* : to burn the surface of; *also* : to dry or shrivel with heat ⟨~*ed* lawns⟩

[1]score \ˈskōr\ *n, pl* **scores 1** *or pl* **score** : TWENTY **2** : CUT, SCRATCH, SLASH **3** : a record of points made (as in a game) **4** : DEBT **5** : REASON, GROUND **6** : the music of a composition or arrangement with different parts indicated **7** : success in obtaining something (as drugs) esp. illegally

[2]score *vb* **scored; scor•ing 1** : RECORD **2** : to keep score in a game **3** : to mark with lines, grooves, scratches, or notches **4** : to gain or tally in or as if in a game ⟨*scored* a point⟩ **5** : to assign a grade or score to ⟨~ the tests⟩ **6** : to compose a score for **7** : SUCCEED — **score•less** *adj* — **scor•er** *n*

[1]scorn \ˈskȯrn\ *n* : an emotion involving both anger and disgust : CONTEMPT — **scorn•ful** \-fəl\ *adj* — **scorn•ful•ly** *adv*

[2]scorn *vb* : to hold in contempt : DISDAIN — **scorn•er** *n*

Scor•pio \ˈskȯr-pē-ˌō\ *n* [L, lit., scorpion] **1** : a zodiacal constellation between Libra and Sagittarius usu. pictured as a scorpion **2** : the 8th sign of the zodiac in astrology; *also* : one born under this sign

scor•pi•on \ˈskȯr-pē-ən\ *n* : any of an order of arthropods related to the spiders that have a poisonous stinger at the tip of a long jointed tail

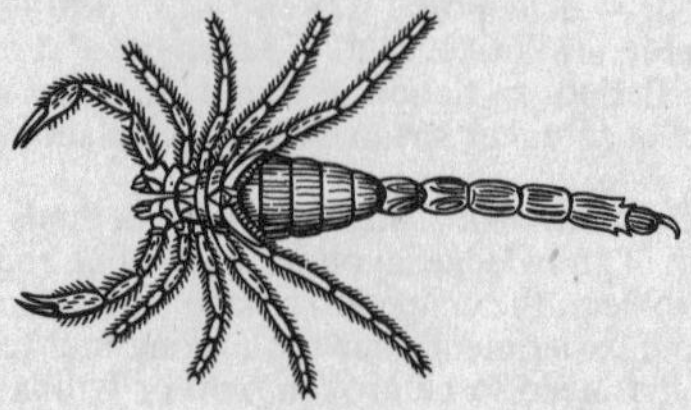

scorpion

[1]Scot \ˈskät\ *n* : a native or inhabitant of Scotland

[2]Scot *abbr* Scotland; Scottish

Scotch \ˈskäch\ *n* **1** : SCOTS **2 Scotch** *pl* : the people of Scotland **3** : a whiskey distilled in Scotland esp. from malted barley — **Scotch** *adj* — **Scotch•man** \-mən\ *n* — **Scotch•wom•an** \-ˌwu̇-mən\ *n*

Scotch pine *n* : a pine that is naturalized in the U.S. from northern Europe and Asia and is a valuable timber tree

Scotch terrier *n* : SCOTTISH TERRIER

scot–free \ˈskät-ˈfrē\ *adj* : free from obligation, harm, or penalty

Scots \ˈskäts\ *n* : the English language of Scotland

Scots•man \ˈskäts-mən\ *n* : SCOT

Scots•wom•an \-ˌwu̇-mən\ *n* : a woman who is a Scot

Scot•tie \ˈskä-tē\ *n* : SCOTTISH TERRIER

Scot•tish \ˈskä-tish\ *adj* : of, relating to, or characteristic of Scotland, Scots, or the Scots

Scottish terrier *n* : any of an old Scottish breed of terrier with short legs, a large head with small erect ears, a broad deep chest, and a thick rough coat

scoun•drel \ˈskau̇n-drəl\ *n* : a disreputable person : VILLAIN

[1]scour \ˈskau̇r\ *vb* **1** : to rub (as with a gritty substance) in order to clean **2** : to cleanse by or as if by rubbing

[2]scour *vb* **1** : to move rapidly through : RUSH **2** : to examine thoroughly

[1]scourge \ˈskərj\ *n* **1** : LASH, WHIP **2** : PUNISHMENT; *also* : a cause of affliction (as a plague)

[2]scourge *vb* **scourged; scourg•ing 1** : LASH, FLOG **2** : to punish severely

[1]scout \ˈskau̇t\ *vb* [ME, fr. MF *escouter* to listen, fr. L *auscultare*] **1** : to look around : RECONNOITER **2** : to inspect or observe to get information

[2]scout *n* **1** : a person sent out to get information; *also* : a soldier, airplane, or ship sent out to reconnoiter **2** : BOY SCOUT **3** : GIRL SCOUT — **scout•mas•ter** \-ˌmas-tər\ *n*

[3]scout *vb* : SCORN, SCOFF

scow \ˈskau̇\ *n* : a large flat-bottomed boat with square ends

scowl \ˈskau̇l\ *vb* : to make a frowning expression of displeasure — **scowl** *n*

SCPO *abbr* senior chief petty officer

scrab•ble \ˈskra-bəl\ *vb* **scrab•bled; scrab•bling 1** : SCRAPE, SCRATCH **2** : CLAMBER, SCRAMBLE **3** : to work hard and long **4** : SCRIBBLE — **scrabble** *n* — **scrab•bler** *n*

scrag•gly \ˈskra-glē\ *adj* : IRREGULAR; *also* : RAGGED, UNKEMPT

scram \ˈskram\ *vb* **scrammed; scram•ming** : to go away at once

scram•ble \ˈskram-bəl\ *vb* **scram•bled; scram•bling 1** : to clamber clumsily around **2** : to struggle for or as if for possession of something **3** : to spread irregularly **4** : to mix together **5** : to cook (eggs) by stirring during frying — **scramble** *n*

[1]scrap \ˈskrap\ *n* **1** : FRAGMENT, PIECE **2** : discarded material : REFUSE

[2]scrap *vb* **scrapped; scrap•ping 1** : to make into scrap ⟨~ a battleship⟩ **2** : to get rid of as useless

[3]scrap *n* : FIGHT

[4]scrap *vb* **scrapped; scrap•ping** : FIGHT, QUARREL — **scrap•per** *n*

scrap•book \ˈskrap-ˌbu̇k\ *n* : a blank book in which mementos are kept

[1]scrape \ˈskrāp\ *vb* **scraped; scrap•ing 1** : to remove by drawing a knife over; *also* : to clean or smooth by rubbing off the covering **2** : to damage or injure the surface of by contact with something rough **3** : to draw across a surface with a grating sound **4** : to get together (money) by strict economy **5** : to get along with difficulty — **scrap•er** *n*

[2]scrape *n* **1** : the act or the effect of scraping **2** : a bow accompanied by a drawing back of the foot **3** : an unpleasant predicament

[1]scrap•py \ˈskra-pē\ *adj* **scrap•pi•er; -est** : DISCONNECTED, FRAGMENTARY

[2]scrappy *adj* **scrap•pi•er; -est 1** : QUARRELSOME **2** : having an aggressive and determined spirit

[1]scratch \ˈskrach\ *vb* **1** : to scrape, dig, or rub with or as if with claws or nails ⟨a dog ~*ing* at the door⟩ ⟨~*ed* my arm⟩ **2** : SCRAPE 3 ⟨~*ed* his nails across the blackboard⟩ **3** : SCRAPE 4 **4** : to cancel or erase by or as if by drawing a line through **5** : to withdraw from a contest — **scratchy** *adj*

[2]scratch *n* **1** : a mark or injury made by or as if by scratching; *also* : a sound so made **2** : the starting line in a race **3** : a point at the beginning of a project at which nothing has been done ahead of time ⟨built from ~⟩

[3]scratch *adj* **1** : made as or used for a trial attempt ⟨~ paper⟩ **2** : made or done by chance ⟨a ~ hit⟩

scrawl \ˈskrȯl\ *vb* : to write hastily and carelessly — **scrawl** *n*

scraw•ny \ˈskrȯ-nē\ *adj* **scraw•ni•er; -est** : very thin : SKINNY

¹scream \ˈskrēm\ *vb* **:** to cry out loudly and shrilly
²scream *n* **:** a loud shrill cry
scream•ing *adj* **:** so striking as to attract notice as if by screaming ⟨~ headlines⟩
screech \ˈskrēch\ *vb* **:** SHRIEK — **screech** *n* — **screechy** \ˈskrē-chē\ *adj*
¹screen \ˈskrēn\ *n* **1 :** a device or partition used to hide, restrain, protect, or decorate ⟨a window ~⟩; *also* **:** something that shelters, protects, or conceals **2 :** a sieve or perforated material for separating finer from coarser parts (as of sand) **3 :** a surface on which an image is made to appear (as in television) **4 :** the motion-picture industry
²screen *vb* **1 :** to shield with or as if with a screen **2 :** to separate with or as if with a screen **3 :** to present (as a motion picture) on the screen
screen•ing \ˈskrē-niŋ\ *n* **1 :** metal or plastic mesh (as for window screens) **2 :** a showing of a motion picture
¹screw \ˈskrü\ *n* [ME, fr. MF *escroe* female screw, nut, fr. ML *scrofa*, fr. L, sow] **1 :** a machine consisting of a solid cylinder with a spiral groove around it and a corresponding hollow cylinder into which it fits **2 :** a naillike metal piece with a spiral groove and a head with a slot that is inserted into material by rotating and is used to fasten pieces of solid material together **3 :** PROPELLER
²screw *vb* **1 :** to fasten or close by means of a screw **2 :** to operate or adjust by means of a screw **3 :** to move or cause to move spirally; *also* **:** to close or set in position by such an action
screw•ball \ˈskrü-ˌbȯl\ *n* **1 :** a baseball pitch breaking in a direction opposite to a curve **2 :** a whimsical, eccentric, or crazy person
screw•driv•er \-ˌdrī-vər\ *n* **1 :** a tool for turning screws **2 :** a drink made of vodka and orange juice
screw•worm \ˈskrü-ˌwərm\ *n* **:** an American blowfly of warm regions whose larva matures in wounds or sores of mammals and may cause disease or death; *esp* **:** its larva
screwy \ˈskrü-ē\ *adj* **screw•i•er; -est 1 :** crazily absurd, eccentric, or unusual **2 :** CRAZY, INSANE
scrib•ble \ˈskri-bəl\ *vb* **scrib•bled; scrib•bling :** to write hastily or carelessly — **scribble** *n* — **scrib•bler** *n*
scribe \ˈskrīb\ *n* **1 :** a scholar of Jewish law in New Testament times **2 :** a person whose business is the copying of writing **3 :** JOURNALIST
scrim \ˈskrim\ *n* **:** a light loosely woven cotton or linen cloth
scrim•mage \ˈskri-mij\ *n* **:** the play between two football teams beginning with the snap of the ball; *also* **:** practice play between two teams — **scrimmage** *vb*
scrimp \ˈskrimp\ *vb* **:** to economize greatly ⟨~ and save⟩
scrim•shaw \ˈskrim-ˌshȯ\ *n* **:** carved or engraved articles made orig. by American whalers usu. from baleen or whale ivory — **scrimshaw** *vb*
scrip \ˈskrip\ *n* **1 :** a certificate showing its holder is entitled to something (as stock or land) **2 :** paper money issued for temporary use in an emergency
¹script \ˈskript\ *n* **1 :** written matter (as lines for a play or broadcast) **2 :** HANDWRITING
²script *abbr* scripture
scrip•ture \ˈskrip-chər\ *n* **1** *cap* **:** the books of the Bible — often used in pl. **2 :** the sacred writings of a religion — **scrip•tur•al** \ˈskrip-chə-rəl\ *adj* — **scrip•tur•al•ly** *adv*
scriv•en•er \ˈskri-və-nər\ *n* **:** SCRIBE, COPYIST, WRITER
scrod \ˈskräd\ *n* **:** a young fish (as a cod or haddock); *esp* **:** one split and boned for cooking
scrof•u•la \ˈskrȯ-fyə-lə\ *n* **:** tuberculosis of lymph nodes esp. in the neck
¹scroll \ˈskrōl\ *n* **:** a roll of paper or parchment for writing a document; *also* **:** a spiral or coiled ornamental form suggesting a loosely or partly rolled scroll
²scroll *vb* **:** to move or cause to move text or graphics up, down, or across a display screen
scroll saw *n* **:** JIGSAW
scro•tum \ˈskrō-təm\ *n, pl* **scro•ta** \-tə\ *or* **scrotums** [L] **:** a pouch that in most male mammals contains the testes
scrounge \ˈskraủnj\ *vb* **scrounged; scroung•ing :** to collect by or as if by foraging
¹scrub \ˈskrəb\ *n* **1 :** a thick growth of stunted trees or shrubs; *also* **:** an area of land covered with scrub **2 :** an inferior domestic animal **3 :** a person of insignificant size or standing **4 :** a player not on the first team — **scrub** *adj* — **scrub•by** *adj*
²scrub *vb* **scrubbed; scrub•bing 1 :** to clean or wash by rubbing ⟨~ clothes⟩ ⟨~ out a spot⟩ **2 :** CANCEL
³scrub *n* **:** an act or instance of scrubbing ⟨gave the clothes a good ~⟩
scrub•ber \ˈskrə-bər\ *n* **:** one that scrubs; *esp* **:** an apparatus for removing impurities esp. from gases
scruff \ˈskrəf\ *n* **:** the loose skin of the back of the neck **:** NAPE
scruffy \ˈskrə-fē\ *adj* **scruff•i•er; -est :** UNKEMPT, SLOVENLY
scrump•tious \ˈskrəmp-shəs\ *adj* **:** DELIGHTFUL, EXCELLENT; *esp* **:** DELICIOUS — **scrump•tious•ly** *adv*
¹scru•ple \ˈskrü-pəl\ *n* [ME *scrupul*, MF *scrupule*, fr. L *scrupulus*, dim. of *scrupus* source of uneasiness, lit., sharp stone] **1 :** a point of conscience or honor **2 :** hesitation due to ethical considerations
²scruple *vb* **scru•pled; scru•pling :** to be reluctant on grounds of conscience **:** HESITATE
scru•pu•lous \ˈskrü-pyə-ləs\ *adj* **1 :** having moral integrity **2 :** PAINSTAKING — **scru•pu•lous•ly** *adv* — **scru•pu•lous•ness** *n*
scru•ti•nise *Brit var of* SCRUTINIZE
scru•ti•nize \ˈskrü-tə-ˌnīz\ *vb* **-nized; -niz•ing :** to examine closely
scru•ti•ny \ˈskrüt-ᵊn-ē\ *n, pl* **-nies** [L *scrutinium*, fr. *scrutari* to search, examine, prob. fr. *scruta* trash] **:** a careful looking over **syn** inspection, examination, analysis
scu•ba \ˈskü-bə\ *n* [*s*elf-*c*ontained *u*nderwater *b*reathing *a*pparatus] **:** an apparatus for breathing while swimming underwater
scuba diver *n* **:** one who swims underwater with the aid of scuba gear
¹scud \ˈskəd\ *vb* **scud•ded; scud•ding :** to move speedily
²scud *n* **:** light clouds driven by the wind
¹scuff \ˈskəf\ *vb* **1 :** to scrape the feet while walking **:** SHUFFLE **2 :** to scratch or become scratched or worn away
²scuff *n* **1 :** a mark or injury caused by scuffing **2 :** a flat-soled slipper without heel strap
scuf•fle \ˈskə-fəl\ *vb* **scuf•fled; scuf•fling 1 :** to struggle confusedly at close quarters **2 :** to shuffle one's feet — **scuffle** *n*
¹scull \ˈskəl\ *n* **1 :** an oar for use in sculling; *also* **:** one of a pair of short oars for a single oarsman **2 :** a racing shell propelled by one or two persons using sculls
²scull *vb* **:** to propel (a boat) by an oar over the stern
scul•lery \ˈskə-lə-rē\ *n, pl* **-ler•ies** [ME, department of household in charge of dishes, fr. MF *escuelerie*, fr. *escuelle* bowl, fr. L *scutella* drinking bowl] **:** a small room near the kitchen used for cleaning dishes, cooking utensils, and vegetables
scul•lion \ˈskəl-yən\ *n* [ME *sculion*, fr. MF *escouillon* dishcloth, alter. of *escouvillon*, fr. *escouve* broom, fr. L *scopae*, lit., twigs bound together] **:** a kitchen helper
sculpt \ˈskəlpt\ *vb* **:** CARVE, SCULPTURE
sculp•tor \ˈskəlp-tər\ *n* **:** a person who produces works of sculpture
¹sculp•ture \ˈskəlp-chər\ *n* **:** the act, process, or art of carving or molding material (as stone, wood, or

DICTIONARY

plastic); *also* : work produced this way — **sculp·tur·al** \ˈskəlp-chə-rəl\ *adj*

2**sculpture** *vb* **sculp·tured; sculp·tur·ing** : to form or alter as or as if a work of sculpture

scum \ˈskəm\ *n* **1** : a slimy or filmy covering on the surface of a liquid **2** : waste matter **3** : RABBLE

scup·per \ˈskə-pər\ *n* : an opening in the side of a ship through which water on deck is drained overboard

scurf \ˈskərf\ *n* : thin dry scales of skin (as dandruff); *also* : a scaly deposit or covering — **scurfy** \ˈskər-fē\ *adj*

scur·ri·lous \ˈskər-ə-ləs\ *adj* : coarsely jesting : OBSCENE, VULGAR

scur·ry \ˈskər-ē\ *vb* **scur·ried; scur·ry·ing** : SCAMPER

1**scur·vy** \ˈskər-vē\ *n* : a disease marked by spongy gums, loosened teeth, and bleeding under the skin and caused by lack of vitamin C

2**scurvy** *adj* : MEAN, CONTEMPTIBLE — **scur·vi·ly** \ˈskər-və-lē\ *adv*

scutch·eon \ˈskə-chən\ *n* : ESCUTCHEON

1**scut·tle** \ˈskət-ᵊl\ *n* : a pail for carrying coal

2**scuttle** *n* : a small opening with a lid esp. in the deck, side, or bottom of a ship

3**scuttle** *vb* **scut·tled; scut·tling** : to cut a hole in the deck, side, or bottom of (a ship) in order to sink

4**scuttle** *vb* **scut·tled; scut·tling** : SCURRY, SCAMPER

scut·tle·butt \ˈskət-ᵊl-ˌbət\ *n* : GOSSIP

scythe \ˈsīth\ *n* : an implement for mowing (as grass or grain) by hand — **scythe** *vb*

SD *abbr* **1** South Dakota **2** special delivery

S Dak *abbr* South Dakota

SDI *abbr* Strategic Defense Initiative

Se *symbol* selenium

SE *abbr* southeast

sea \ˈsē\ *n* **1** : a large body of salt water **2** : OCEAN **3** : rough water; *also* : a large wave **4** : something likened to the sea esp. in vastness — **sea** *adj* — **at sea** : LOST, BEWILDERED

sea anemone *n* : any of numerous coelenterate polyps whose form, bright and varied colors, and cluster of tentacles superficially resemble a flower

sea·bird \ˈsē-ˌbərd\ *n* : a bird (as a gull) frequenting the open ocean

sea·board \-ˌbōrd\ *n* : SEACOAST; *also* : the land bordering a coast

sea·coast \-ˌkōst\ *n* : the shore of the sea

sea·far·er \-ˌfar-ər\ *n* : SEAMAN

sea·far·ing \-ˌfar-iŋ\ *n* : the use of the sea for travel or transportation — **seafaring** *adj*

sea·food \-ˌfüd\ *n* : edible marine fish and shellfish

sea·go·ing \-ˌgō-iŋ\ *adj* : OCEANGOING

sea horse *n* : any of a genus of small marine fishes with the head and forepart of the body sharply flexed like the head and neck of a horse

1**seal** \ˈsēl\ *n, pl* **seals** *also* **seal 1** : any of numerous large carnivorous sea mammals occurring chiefly in cold regions and having limbs adapted for swimming **2** : the pelt of a seal

2**seal** *vb* : to hunt seals

3**seal** *n* **1** : GUARANTEE, PLEDGE **2** : a device having a raised design that can be stamped on clay or wax; *also* : the impression made by stamping with such a device **3** : something that seals or closes up ⟨safety ~⟩

4**seal** *vb* **1** : to affix a seal to; *also* : AUTHENTICATE **2** : to fasten with or as if with a seal to prevent tampering **3** : to close or make secure against access, leakage, or passage **4** : to determine irrevocably ⟨~*ed* his fate⟩

sea–lane \ˈsē-ˌlān\ *n* : an established sea route

seal·ant \ˈsē-lənt\ *n* : a sealing agent

seal·er \ˈsē-lər\ *n* : a coat applied to prevent subsequent coats of paint or varnish from sinking in

sea level *n* : the level of the surface of the sea esp. at its mean midway between mean high and low water

sea lion *n* : any of several large Pacific seals with external ears

seal·skin \ˈsēl-ˌskin\ *n* **1** : 1SEAL 2 **2** : a garment of sealskin

1**seam** \ˈsēm\ *n* **1** : the line of junction of two edges and esp. of edges of fabric sewn together **2** : a layer of mineral matter **3** : WRINKLE — **seam·less** *adj*

2**seam** *vb* **1** : to join by or as if by sewing **2** : WRINKLE, FURROW

sea·man \ˈsē-mən\ *n* **1** : one who assists in the handling of ships : MARINER **2** : an enlisted man in the navy ranking next below a petty officer third class

seaman apprentice *n* : an enlisted man in the navy ranking next below a seaman

seaman recruit *n* : an enlisted man of the lowest rank in the navy

sea·man·ship \ˈsē-mən-ˌship\ *n* : the art or skill of handling a ship

sea·mount \ˈsē-ˌmau̇nt\ *n* : an underwater mountain

seam·stress \ˈsēm-strəs\ *n* : a woman who does sewing

seamy \ˈsē-mē\ *adj* **seam·i·er; -est 1** : UNPLEASANT **2** : DEGRADED, SORDID

sé·ance \ˈsā-ˌäns\ *n* [F] : a meeting to receive communications from spirits

sea·plane \ˈsē-ˌplān\ *n* : an airplane that can take off from and land on water

sea·port \-ˌpōrt\ *n* : a port for oceangoing ships

sear \ˈsir\ *vb* **1** : WITHER **2** : to burn or scorch esp. on the surface; *also* : BRAND — **sear** *n*

1**search** \ˈsərch\ *vb* [ME *cerchen,* fr. MF *cerchier* to go about, survey, search, fr. LL *circare* to go about, fr. L *circum* round about] **1** : to look through in trying to find something **2** : SEEK **3** : PROBE — **search·er** *n*

2**search** *n* : the act of searching

search·light \-ˌlīt\ *n* : an apparatus for projecting a powerful beam of light; *also* : the light projected

sea·scape \ˈsē-ˌskāp\ *n* **1** : a view of the sea **2** : a picture representing a scene at or of the sea

sea·shell \ˈsē-ˌshel\ *n* : the shell of a marine animal and esp. a mollusk

sea·shore \-ˌshōr\ *n* : the shore of a sea

sea·sick \-ˌsik\ *adj* : nauseated by or as if by the motion of a ship — **sea·sick·ness** *n*

sea·side \ˈsē-ˌsīd\ *n* : SEASHORE

1**sea·son** \ˈsē-zən\ *n* [ME, fr. OF *saison,* fr. L *sation-, satio* action of sowing, fr. *serere* to sow] **1** : one of the divisions of the year (as spring or summer) **2** : a special period ⟨the Easter ~⟩ — **sea·son·al** \-zə-nəl\ *adj* — **sea·son·al·ly** *adv*

2**season** *vb* **1** : to make pleasant to the taste by use of salt, pepper, or spices **2** : to make (as by aging or drying) suitable for use **3** : to accustom or habituate to something (as hardship) **syn** harden, inure, acclimatize, toughen — **sea·son·er** *n*

sea·son·able \ˈsē-zə-nə-bəl\ *adj* : occurring at a good or proper time **syn** timely, propitious, opportune — **sea·son·ably** \-blē\ *adv*

sea·son·ing *n* : something that seasons : CONDIMENT

1**seat** \ˈsēt\ *n* **1** : a chair, bench, or stool for sitting on **2** : a place which serves as a capital or center

2**seat** *vb* **1** : to place in or on a seat **2** : to provide seats for

seat belt *n* : straps designed to hold a person in a seat

SEATO \ˈsē-ˌtō\ *abbr* Southeast Asia Treaty Organization

seat–of–the–pants *adj* : employing or based on personal experience, judgment, and effort rather than technological aids ⟨~ navigation⟩

sea urchin *n* : any of numerous spiny marine echinoderms having thin brittle globular shells

sea·wall \ˈsē-ˌwȯl\ *n* : an embankment to protect the shore from erosion

1**sea·ward** \ˈsē-wərd\ *n* : the direction or side away from land and toward the open sea

2**seaward** *also* **sea·wards** \-wərdz\ *adv* : toward the sea

3**seaward** *adj* **1** : directed or situated toward the sea **2** : coming from the sea

sea•wa•ter \ˈsē-ˌwȯ-tər, -ˌwä-\ *n* : water in or from the sea

sea•way \-ˌwā\ *n* : an inland waterway that admits ocean shipping

sea•weed \-ˌwēd\ *n* : a marine alga (as a kelp); *also* : a mass of marine algae

sea•wor•thy \-ˌwər-t͟hē\ *adj* : fit for a sea voyage ⟨a ~ ship⟩

se•ba•ceous \si-ˈbā-shəs\ *adj* : of, relating to, or secreting fatty material

sec *abbr* **1** second; secondary **2** secretary **3** section **4** [L *secundum*] according to

SEC *abbr* Securities and Exchange Commission

se•cede \si-ˈsēd\ *vb* **se•ced•ed; se•ced•ing** : to withdraw from an organized body and esp. from a political body

se•ces•sion \si-ˈse-shən\ *n* : the act of seceding — **se•ces•sion•ist** *n*

se•clude \si-ˈklüd\ *vb* **se•clud•ed; se•clud•ing** : to keep or shut away from others

se•clu•sion \si-ˈklü-zhən\ *n* : the act of secluding : the state of being secluded — **se•clu•sive** \-siv\ *adj*

¹sec•ond \ˈse-kənd\ *adj* [ME, fr. OF, fr. L *secundus* second, following, favorable, fr. *sequi* to follow] **1** : being number two in a countable series **2** : next after the first **3** : ALTERNATE ⟨every ~ year⟩ — **second** *or* **sec•ond•ly** *adv*

²second *n* **1** : one that is second **2** : one who assists another (as in a duel) **3** : an inferior or flawed article (as of merchandise) **4** : the second forward gear in a motor vehicle

³second *n* [ME *secunde*, fr. ML *secunda*, fr. L, fem. of *secundus* second; fr. its being the second division of a unit into 60 parts, as a minute is the first] **1** : the 60th part of a minute of time or angular measure **2** : an instant of time

⁴second *vb* **1** : to encourage or give support to **2** : to act as a second to **3** : to support (a motion) by adding one's voice to that of a proposer

¹sec•ond•ary \ˈse-kən-ˌder-ē\ *adj* **1** : second in rank, value, or occurrence : LESSER **2** : belonging to a second or later stage of development **3** : coming after the primary or elementary ⟨~ schools⟩ **syn** subordinate, collateral, dependent

²secondary *n, pl* **-ar•ies** : the defensive backfield of a football team

secondary sex characteristic *n* : a physical characteristic that appears in members of one sex at puberty or in seasonal breeders at breeding season and is not directly concerned with reproduction

second fiddle *n* : one that plays a supporting or subservient role

sec•ond–guess \ˌse-kənd-ˈges\ *vb* **1** : to think out other strategies or explanations for after the event **2** : to seek to anticipate or predict

sec•ond•hand \-ˈhand\ *adj* **1** : not original **2** : not new : USED ⟨~ clothes⟩ **3** : dealing in used goods

second lieutenant *n* : a commissioned officer (as in the army) ranking next below a first lieutenant

sec•ond–rate \ˌse-kənd-ˈrāt\ *adj* : INFERIOR

second–story man *n* : a burglar who enters by an upstairs window

sec•ond–string \ˈse-kənd-ˈstriŋ\ *adj* : being a substitute (as on a team)

se•cre•cy \ˈsē-krə-sē\ *n, pl* **-cies 1** : the habit or practice of being secretive **2** : the condition of being hidden or concealed

¹se•cret \ˈsē-krət\ *adj* **1** : HIDDEN, CONCEALED ⟨a ~ staircase⟩ **2** : COVERT, STEALTHY; *also* : engaged in detecting or spying ⟨a ~ agent⟩ **3** : kept from general knowledge — **se•cret•ly** *adv*

²secret *n* **1** : MYSTERY **2** : something kept from the knowledge of others

sec•re•tar•i•at \ˌse-krə-ˈter-ē-ət\ *n* **1** : the office of a secretary **2** : the secretarial staff in an office **3** : the administrative department of a governmental organization ⟨the UN ~⟩

sec•re•tary \ˈse-krə-ˌter-ē\ *n, pl* **-tar•ies 1** : a person employed to handle records, correspondence, and routine work for another person **2** : an officer of a corporation or business who is in charge of correspondence and records **3** : an official at the head of a department of government **4** : a writing desk — **sec•re•tari•al** \ˌse-krə-ˈter-ē-əl\ *adj* — **sec•re•tary•ship** \ˈse-krə-ˌter-ē-ˌship\ *n*

¹se•crete \si-ˈkrēt\ *vb* **se•cret•ed; se•cret•ing** : to form and give off (a secretion)

²se•crete \si-ˈkrēt, ˈsē-krət\ *vb* **se•cret•ed; se•cret•ing** : HIDE, CONCEAL

se•cre•tion \si-ˈkrē-shən\ *n* **1** : the process of secreting something **2** : a product of glandular activity; *esp* : one (as a hormone) useful in the organism **3** : the act of hiding something — **se•cre•to•ry** \ˈsē-krə-ˌtōr-ē\ *adj*

se•cre•tive \ˈsē-krə-tiv, si-ˈkrē-\ *adj* : tending to keep secrets or to act secretly — **se•cre•tive•ly** *adv* — **se•cre•tive•ness** *n*

¹sect \ˈsekt\ *n* **1** : a dissenting religious body **2** : a religious denomination **3** : a group adhering to a distinctive doctrine or to a leader

²sect *abbr* section; sectional

¹sec•tar•i•an \sek-ˈter-ē-ən\ *adj* **1** : of or relating to a sect or sectarian **2** : limited in character or scope — **sec•tar•i•an•ism** *n*

²sectarian *n* **1** : an adherent of a sect **2** : a narrow or bigoted person

sec•ta•ry \ˈsek-tə-rē\ *n, pl* **-ries** : a member of a sect

¹sec•tion \ˈsek-shən\ *n* **1** : a part cut off or separated **2** : a distinct part **3** : the appearance that a thing has or would have if cut straight through

²section *vb* **1** : to separate or become separated into sections **2** : to represent in sections

sec•tion•al \ˈsek-shə-nəl\ *adj* **1** : of, relating to, or characteristic of a section **2** : local or regional rather than general in character **3** : divided into sections — **sec•tion•al•ism** *n*

sec•tor \ˈsek-tər\ *n* **1** : a part of a circle between two radii **2** : an area assigned to a military leader to defend **3** : a subdivision of society

sec•u•lar \ˈse-kyə-lər\ *adj* **1** : not sacred or ecclesiastical **2** : not bound by monastic vows ⟨a ~ priest⟩

sec•u•lar•ise *Brit var of* SECULARIZE

sec•u•lar•ism \ˈse-kyə-lə-ˌri-zəm\ *n* : indifference to or exclusion of religion — **sec•u•lar•ist** \-rist\ *n* — **secularist** *or* **sec•u•lar•is•tic** \ˌse-kyə-lə-ˈris-tik\ *adj*

sec•u•lar•ize \ˈse-kyə-lə-ˌrīz\ *vb* **-ized; -iz•ing 1** : to make secular **2** : to transfer from ecclesiastical to civil or lay use, possession, or control — **sec•u•lar•i•za•tion** \ˌse-kyə-lə-rə-ˈzā-shən\ *n* — **sec•u•lar•iz•er** \ˈse-kyə-lə-ˌrī-zər\ *n*

¹se•cure \si-ˈkyu̇r\ *adj* **se•cur•er; -est** [L *securus* safe, secure, fr. *se* without + *cura* care] **1** : easy in mind : free from fear **2** : free from danger or risk of loss : SAFE **3** : CERTAIN, SURE — **se•cure•ly** *adv*

²secure *vb* **se•cured; se•cur•ing 1** : to make safe : GUARD **2** : to assure payment of by giving a pledge or collateral **3** : to fasten safely ⟨~ a door⟩ **4** : GET, ACQUIRE

se•cu•ri•ty \si-ˈkyu̇r-ə-tē\ *n, pl* **-ties 1** : SAFETY **2** : freedom from worry **3** : something given as pledge of payment ⟨a ~ deposit⟩ **4** *pl* : bond or stock certificates **5** : PROTECTION

secy *abbr* secretary

se•dan \si-ˈdan\ *n* **1** : a covered chair borne on poles by two men **2** : an automobile seating four or more people and usu. having a permanent top

¹se•date \si-ˈdāt\ *adj* : quiet and dignified in behavior **syn** staid, sober, serious, solemn — **se•date•ly** *adv*

²sedate *vb* **se•dat•ed; se•dat•ing** : to dose with sedatives — **se•da•tion** \si-ˈdā-shən\ *n*

¹sed•a•tive \ˈse-də-tiv\ *adj* : serving or tending to relieve tension

[2]**sedative** *n* : a sedative drug

sed•en•tary \ˈsed-ᵊn-ˌter-ē\ *adj* : characterized by or requiring much sitting

sedge \ˈsej\ *n* : any of a family of plants esp. of marshy areas that differ from the related grasses esp. in having solid stems — **sedgy** \ˈse-jē\ *adj*

sed•i•ment \ˈse-də-mənt\ *n* **1** : the material that settles to the bottom of a liquid **2** : material (as stones and sand) deposited by water, wind, or a glacier — **sed•i•men•ta•ry** \ˌse-də-ˈmen-tə-rē\ *adj* — **sed•i•men•ta•tion** \-mən-ˈtā-shən, -ˌmen-\ *n*

se•di•tion \si-ˈdi-shən\ *n* : the causing of discontent, insurrection, or resistance against a government — **se•di•tious** \-shəs\ *adj*

se•duce \si-ˈdüs, -ˈdyüs\ *vb* **se•duced; se•duc•ing 1** : to persuade to disobedience or disloyalty **2** : to lead astray **3** : to entice to sexual intercourse **syn** tempt, entice, inveigle, lure — **se•duc•er** *n* — **se•duc•tion** \-ˈdək-shən\ *n* — **se•duc•tive** \-tiv\ *adj*

sed•u•lous \ˈse-jə-ləs\ *adj* [L *sedulus*, fr. *sedulo* sincerely, diligently, fr. *se* without + *dolus* guile] : DILIGENT, PAINSTAKING

[1]**see** \ˈsē\ *vb* **saw** \ˈsȯ\; **seen** \ˈsēn\; **see•ing 1** : to perceive by the eye; *also* : to have the power of sight **2** : EXPERIENCE **3** : UNDERSTAND **4** : to make sure ⟨~ that order is kept⟩ **5** : to meet with **6** : to keep company with esp. in dating **7** : ACCOMPANY, ESCORT **syn** behold, descry, espy, view, observe, note, discern

[2]**see** *n* : the authority or jurisdiction of a bishop

[1]**seed** \ˈsēd\ *n, pl* **seed** *or* **seeds 1** : the grains of plants used for sowing **2** : a ripened ovule of a flowering plant that may develop into a new plant; *also* : a plant structure (as a spore or small dry fruit) capable of producing a new plant **3** : DESCENDANTS **4** : SOURCE, ORIGIN — **seed•less** *adj* — **go to seed** *or* **run to seed 1** : to develop seed **2** : DECAY

[2]**seed** *vb* **1** : SOW, PLANT ⟨~ land to grass⟩ **2** : to bear or shed seeds **3** : to remove seeds from — **seed•er** *n*

seed•bed \-ˌbed\ *n* : soil or a bed of soil prepared for planting seed

seed•ling \ˈsēd-liŋ\ *n* **1** : a young plant grown from seed **2** : a young tree before it becomes a sapling

seed•time \ˈsēd-ˌtīm\ *n* : the season for sowing

seedy \ˈsē-dē\ *adj* **seed•i•er; -est 1** : containing or full of seeds **2** : SHABBY

seek \ˈsēk\ *vb* **sought** \ˈsȯt\; **seek•ing 1** : to search for **2** : to try to reach or obtain **3** : ATTEMPT — **seek•er** *n*

seem \ˈsēm\ *vb* **1** : to appear to the observation or understanding **2** : to give the impression of being : APPEAR

seem•ing *adj* : outwardly apparent — **seem•ing•ly** *adv*

seem•ly \ˈsēm-lē\ *adj* **seem•li•er; -est 1** : conventionally proper **2** : FIT

seep \ˈsēp\ *vb* : to flow or pass slowly through fine pores or cracks — **seep•age** \ˈsē-pij\ *n*

seer \ˈsir\ *n* : a person who foresees or predicts events : PROPHET

seer•suck•er \ˈsir-ˌsə-kər\ *n* [Hindi *śīrśaker*, fr. Per *shīr-o-shakar*, lit., milk and sugar] : a light fabric of linen, cotton, or rayon usu. striped and slightly puckered

see•saw \ˈsē-ˌsȯ\ *n* **1** : a contest in which now one side now the other has the lead **2** : a children's sport of riding up and down on the ends of a plank supported in the middle; *also* : the plank so used — **seesaw** *vb*

seethe \ˈsēth\ *vb* **seethed; seeth•ing** [archaic *seethe* boil] : to become violently agitated

seg•ment \ˈseg-mənt\ *n* **1** : a division of a thing : SECTION **2** : a part cut off from a geometrical figure (as a circle) by one or more points, lines, or planes — **seg•ment•ed** \-ˌmen-təd\ *adj*

seg•re•gate \ˈse-gri-ˌgāt\ *vb* **-gat•ed; -gat•ing** [L *segregare*, fr. *se-* apart + *greg-*, *grex* herd, flock] : to cut off from others; *esp* : to separate by races — **seg•re•ga•tion** \ˌse-gri-ˈgā-shən\ *n*

seg•re•ga•tion•ist \ˌse-gri-ˈgā-shə-nist\ *n* : one who believes in or practices the segregation of races

sei•gneur \sān-ˈyər\ *n, often cap* [MF, fr. ML *senior*, fr. L, adj., elder] : a feudal lord

[1]**seine** \ˈsān\ *n* : a large weighted fishing net

[2]**seine** *vb* **seined; sein•ing** : to fish or catch with a seine — **sein•er** *n*

seis•mic \ˈsīz-mik, ˈsīs-\ *adj* : of, relating to, resembling, or caused by an earthquake — **seis•mi•cal•ly** \-mik(ə-)lē\ *adv* — **seis•mic•i•ty** \sīz-ˈmi-sə-tē, sīs-\ *n*

seis•mo•gram \ˈsīz-mə-ˌgram, ˈsīs-\ *n* : the record of an earth tremor made by a seismograph

seis•mo•graph \-ˌgraf\ *n* : an apparatus to measure and record seismic vibrations — **seis•mo•graph•ic** \ˌsīz-mə-ˈgra-fik, ˌsīs-\ *adj* — **seis•mog•ra•phy** \sīz-ˈmä-grə-fē, sīs-\ *n*

seis•mol•o•gy \sīz-ˈmä-lə-jē, sīs-\ *n* : a science that deals with earthquakes — **seis•mo•log•i•cal** \ˌsīz-mə-ˈlä-ji-kəl, ˌsīs-\ *adj* — **seis•mol•o•gist** \sīz-ˈmä-lə-jist, sīs-\ *n*

seis•mom•e•ter \sīz-ˈmä-mə-tər, sīs-\ *n* : a seismograph measuring the actual movement of the ground

seize \ˈsēz\ *vb* **seized; seiz•ing 1** : to lay hold of or take possession of by force **2** : ARREST **3** : UNDERSTAND **4** : to attack or overwhelm physically : AFFLICT **syn** take, grasp, clutch, snatch, grab

sei•zure \ˈsē-zhər\ *n* **1** : the act of seizing : the state of being seized **2** : a sudden attack (as of disease)

sel *abbr* select; selected; selection

sel•dom \ˈsel-dəm\ *adv* : not often : RARELY

[1]**se•lect** \sə-ˈlekt\ *adj* **1** : CHOSEN, PICKED; *also* : CHOICE **2** : judicious or restrictive in choice : DISCRIMINATING

[2]**select** *vb* : to choose from a number or group : pick out

se•lec•tion \sə-ˈlek-shən\ *n* **1** : the act or process of selecting **2** : something selected : CHOICE **3** : a natural or artificial process that tends to favor the survival and reproduction of individuals with certain traits but not those with others

se•lec•tive \sə-ˈlek-tiv\ *adj* : of or relating to selection : selecting or tending to select ⟨~ shoppers⟩

selective service *n* : a system for calling men up for military service : DRAFT

se•lect•man \si-ˈlekt-ˌman, -mən\ *n* : one of a board of officials elected in towns of most New England states to administer town affairs

se•le•ni•um \sə-ˈlē-nē-əm\ *n* : a nonmetallic chemical element — see ELEMENT table

self \ˈself\ *n, pl* **selves** \ˈselvz\ **1** : the essential person distinct from all other persons in identity **2** : a particular side of a person's character **3** : personal interest : SELFISHNESS

self- *comb form* **1** : oneself : itself **2** : of oneself or itself **3** : by oneself or itself; *also* : automatic **4** : to, for, or toward oneself

self-abasement
self-absorbed
self-absorption
self-accusation
self-acting
self-addressed
self-adjusting
self-administer
self-advancement
self-aggrandizement
self-aggrandizing
self-analysis
self-appointed
self-asserting
self-assertion
self-assertive
self-assurance
self-assured
self-awareness
self-betrayal
self-closing
self-conceit
self-concern
self-condemned
self-confessed
self-confidence
self-confident
self-congratulation
self-congratulatory
self-constituted
self-contradiction
self-contradictory
self-control
self-correcting
self-created
self-criticism
self-cultivation
self-deceit
self-deception
self-defeating
self-definition
self-delusion
self-denial
self-denying

self-deprecating
self-deprecation
self-depreciation
self-despair
self-destruct
self-destruction
self-destructive
self-determination
self-discipline
self-distrust
self-doubt
self-educated
self-employed
self-employment
self-esteem
self-examination
self-explaining
self-explanatory
self-expression
self-forgetful
self-giving
self-governing
self-government
self-hate
self-help
self-hypnosis
self-identity
self-image
self-importance
self-important
self-imposed
self-improvement
self-incrimination
self-induced
self-indulgence
self-indulgent
self-inflicted
self-interest
self-knowledge
self-limiting
self-love
self-lubricating
self-luminous
self-operating
self-perception
self-perpetuating
self-pity
self-portrait
self-possessed
self-possession
self-preservation
self-proclaimed
self-propelled
self-propelling
self-protection
self-realization
self-referential
self-regard
self-reliance
self-reliant
self-reproach
self-respect
self-respecting
self-restraint
self-revelation
self-rule
self-sacrifice
self-sacrificing
self-satisfaction
self-satisfied
self-service
self-serving
self-starting
self-styled
self-sufficiency
self-sufficient
self-supporting
self-sustaining
self-taught
self-torment
self-winding
self-worth

self–cen•tered \ˈself-ˈsen-tərd\ *adj* : concerned only with one's own self — **self–cen•tered•ness** *n*

self–com•posed \ˌself-kəm-ˈpōzd\ *adj* : having control over one's emotions

self–con•scious \ˈself-ˈkän-chəs\ *adj* : uncomfortably conscious of oneself as an object of observation by others — **self–con•scious•ly** *adv* — **self–con•scious•ness** *n*

self–con•tained \ˌself-kən-ˈtānd\ *adj* **1** : complete in itself **2** : showing self-control; *also* : reserved in manner

self–de•fense \ˈself-di-ˈfens\ *n* **1** : a plea of justification for the use of force or for homicide **2** : the act of defending oneself, one's property, or a close relative

self–ef•fac•ing \-ə-ˈfā-siŋ\ *adj* : RETIRING, SHY

self–ev•i•dent \ˌself-ˈe-və-dənt\ *adj* : evident without proof or reasoning

self–fer•til•iza•tion \ˌself-ˌfərt-ᵊl-ə-ˈzā-shən\ *n* : fertilization of a plant or animal by its own pollen or sperm

self–ful•fill•ing \ˌself-fül-ˈfi-liŋ\ *adj* : becoming real or true by virtue of having been predicted or expected ⟨a ~ prophecy⟩

self•ish \ˈsel-fish\ *adj* : concerned with one's own welfare excessively or without regard for others — **self•ish•ly** *adv* — **self•ish•ness** *n*

self•less \ˈself-ləs\ *adj* : UNSELFISH — **self•less•ness** *n*

self–made \ˈself-ˈmād\ *adj* : having achieved success or prominance by one's own efforts ⟨a ~ man⟩

self–pol•li•na•tion \ˌself-ˌpä-lə-ˈnā-shən\ *n* : pollination of a flower by its own pollen or sometimes by pollen from another flower on the same plant

self–reg•u•lat•ing \ˈself-ˈre-gyə-ˌlā-tiŋ\ *adj* : AUTOMATIC

self–righ•teous \-ˈrī-chəs\ *adj* : strongly convinced of one's own righteousness — **self–righ•teous•ly** *adv*

self•same \ˈself-ˌsām\ *adj* : precisely the same : IDENTICAL

self–seal•ing \ˈself-ˈsē-liŋ\ *adj* : capable of sealing itself (as after puncture)

self–seek•ing \ˈself-ˈsē-kiŋ\ *adj* : seeking only to further one's own interests — **self–seeking** *n*

self–start•er \-ˈstär-tər\ *n* : a person who has initiative

self–will \ˈself-ˈwil\ *n* : OBSTINACY

sell \ˈsel\ *vb* **sold** \ˈsōld\; **sell•ing** **1** : to transfer (property) in return for money or something else of value **2** : to deal in as a business **3** : to be sold ⟨cars are ~*ing* well⟩ — **sell•er** *n*

sell out *vb* **1** : to dispose of entirely by sale; *esp* : to sell one's business **2** : BETRAY — **sell•out** \ˈsel-ˌau̇t\ *n*

selt•zer \ˈselt-sər\ *n* [modif. of G *Selterser (Wasser)* water of Selters, fr. Nieder *Selters,* Germany] : artificially carbonated water

sel•vage *or* **sel•vedge** \ˈsel-vij\ *n* : the edge of a woven fabric so formed as to prevent raveling

selves *pl of* SELF

sem *abbr* **1** semicolon **2** seminar **3** seminary

se•man•tic \si-ˈman-tik\ *also* **se•man•ti•cal** \-ti-kəl\ *adj* : of or relating to meaning in language

se•man•tics \si-ˈman-tiks\ *n sing or pl* : the study of meanings in language

sema•phore \ˈse-mə-ˌfōr\ *n* **1** : a visual signaling apparatus with movable arms **2** : signaling by hand-held flags

semaphore 2: alphabet; 3 positions following Z: error, end of word, numerals follow; numerals 1,2,3,4,5,6,7,8,9,0 same as A through J

sem•blance \ˈsem-bləns\ *n* **1** : outward appearance **2** : IMAGE, LIKENESS

se•men \ˈsē-mən\ *n* [NL, fr. L, seed] : a sticky whitish fluid of the male reproductive tract that contains the sperm

se•mes•ter \sə-ˈmes-tər\ *n* [G, fr. L *semestris* half-yearly, fr. *sex* six + *mensis* month] **1** : half a year **2** : one of the two terms into which many colleges divide the school year

semi- \ˈse-mi, -ˌmī\ *prefix* **1** : precisely half of **2** : half in quantity or value; *also* : half of or occurring halfway through a specified period **3** : partly : incompletely **4** : partial : incomplete **5** : having some of the characteristics of

semiannual
semiarid
semicentennial
semicircle
semicircular
semicivilized
semiclassical
semiconscious
semidarkness
semidivine
semiformal
semigloss
semi–independent
semiliquid
semiliterate
semimonthly
semiofficial
semipermanent
semipolitical
semiprecious
semiprivate
semiprofessional

semireligious
semiretired
semiskilled
semisoft
semisolid
semisweet
semitransparent
semiweekly
semiyearly

semi \ˈse-ˌmī\ *n, pl* **sem•is** : SEMITRAILER

semi•au•to•mat•ic \ˌse-mē-ˌȯ-tə-ˈma-tik\ *adj, of a firearm* : reloading by mechanical means but requiring release and another press of the trigger to fire again

semi•co•lon \ˈse-mi-ˌkō-lən\ *n* : a punctuation mark ; used esp. to separate major sentence elements

semi•con•duc•tor \ˌse-mi-kən-ˈdək-tər\ *n* : a substance whose electrical conductivity is between that of a conductor and an insulator — **semi•con•duct•ing** *adj*

[1]**semi•fi•nal** \ˌse-mi-ˈfīn-ᵊl\ *adj* : being next to the last in an elimination tournament

[2]**semi•fi•nal** \ˈse-mi-ˌfīn-ᵊl\ *n* : a semifinal round or match — **semi•fi•nal•ist** \-ist\ *n*

semi•lu•nar \-ˈlü-nər\ *adj* : shaped like a crescent

sem•i•nal \ˈse-mən-ᵊl\ *adj* **1** : of, relating to, or consisting of seed or semen **2** : containing or contributing the seeds of later development : CREATIVE, ORIGINAL — **sem•i•nal•ly** *adv*

sem•i•nar \ˈse-mə-ˌnär\ *n* **1** : a course of study pursued by a group of advanced students doing original research under a professor **2** : CONFERENCE

sem•i•nary \ˈse-mə-ˌner-ē\ *n, pl* **-nar•ies** [ME, seedbed, nursery, fr. L *seminarium,* fr. *semen* seed] : an educational institution; *esp* : one that gives theological training — **sem•i•nar•i•an** \ˌse-mə-ˈner-ē-ən\ *n*

Sem•i•nole \ˈse-mə-ˌnōl\ *n, pl* **Semi•noles** *or* **Seminole** : a member of an American Indian people of Florida

semi•per•me•able \ˌse-mi-ˈpər-mē-ə-bəl\ *adj* : partially but not freely or wholly permeable; *esp* : permeable to some usu. small molecules but not to other usu. larger particles ⟨a ~ membrane⟩ — **semi•per•me•abil•i•ty** \-ˌpər-mē-ə-ˈbi-lə-tē\ *n*

Sem•ite \ˈse-ˌmīt\ *n* : a member of any of a group of peoples (as the Hebrews or Arabs) of southwestern Asia — **Se•mit•ic** \sə-ˈmi-tik\ *adj*

semi•trail•er \ˈse-mi-ˌtrā-lər, -ˌmī-\ *n* : a freight trailer that when attached is supported at its forward end by the truck tractor; *also* : a semitrailer with attached tractor

semp•stress \ˈsemp-strəs\ *var of* SEAMSTRESS

[1]**sen** \ˈsen\ *n, pl* **sen** — see *yen* at MONEY table

[2]**sen** *n, pl* **sen** — see *dollar, ringgit, rupiah* at MONEY table

[3]**sen** *n, pl* **sen** — see *riel* at MONEY table

[4]**sen** *abbr* **1** senate; senator **2** senior

sen•ate \ˈse-nət\ *n* : the second of two chambers of a legislature

sen•a•tor \ˈse-nə-tər\ *n* : a member of a senate — **sen•a•to•ri•al** \ˌse-nə-ˈtōr-ē-əl\ *adj*

send \ˈsend\ *vb* **sent** \ˈsent\; **send•ing 1** : to cause to go **2** : EMIT **3** : to propel or drive esp. with force **4** : to put or bring into a certain condition — **send•er** *n*

send–off \ˈsend-ˌȯf\ *n* : a demonstration of goodwill and enthusiasm at the start of a new venture (as a trip)

se•ne \ˈsā-(ˌ)nā\ *n, pl* **sene** — see *tala* at MONEY table

Sen•e•ca \ˈse-ni-kə\ *n, pl* **Seneca** *or* **Senecas** : a member of an American Indian people of western New York

Sen•e•ga•lese \ˌse-ni-gə-ˈlēz, -ˈlēs\ *n, pl* **Senegalese** : a native or inhabitant of Senegal — **Senegalese** *adj*

se•nes•cence \si-ˈnes-ᵊns\ *n* : the state of being old; *also* : the process of becoming old — **se•nes•cent** \-ᵊnt\ *adj*

se•nile \ˈsē-ˌnīl, ˈse-\ *adj* : OLD, AGED; *esp* : exhibiting a loss of mental ability associated with old age — **se•nil•i•ty** \si-ˈni-lə-tē\ *n*

[1]**se•nior** \ˈsē-nyər\ *n* **1** : a person older or of higher rank than another **2** : a member of the graduating class of a high school or college

[2]**senior** *adj* [ME, fr. L, older, elder, compar. of *senex* old] **1** : ELDER **2** : more advanced in dignity or rank **3** : belonging to the final year of a school or college course

senior chief petty officer *n* : a petty officer in the navy or coast guard ranking next below a master chief petty officer

senior citizen *n* : an elderly person; *esp* : one who has retired

senior high school *n* : a school usu. including grades 10 to 12

se•nior•i•ty \sēn-ˈyȯr-ə-tē\ *n* **1** : the quality or state of being senior **2** : a privileged status owing to length of continuous service

senior master sergeant *n* : a noncommissioned officer in the air force ranking next below a chief master sergeant

sen•i•ti \ˈse-nə-tē\ *n, pl* **seniti** — see *pa'anga* at MONEY table

sen•na \ˈse-nə\ *n* **1** : CASSIA 2; *esp* : one used medicinally **2** : the dried leaflets or pods of a cassia used as a purgative

sen•sa•tion \sen-ˈsā-shən\ *n* **1** : awareness (as of noise or heat) or a mental process (as seeing or hearing) due to stimulation of a sense organ; *also* : an indefinite bodily feeling **2** : a condition of excitement; *also* : the thing that causes this condition

sen•sa•tion•al \-shə-nəl\ *adj* **1** : of or relating to sensation or the senses **2** : arousing an intense and usu. superficial interest or emotional reaction — **sen•sa•tion•al•ly** *adv*

sen•sa•tion•al•ise *Brit var of* SENSATIONALIZE

sen•sa•tion•al•ism \-nə-ˌli-zəm\ *n* : the use or effect of sensational subject matter or treatment — **sen•sa•tion•al•ist** \-nə-list\ *adj or n* — **sen•sa•tion•al•is•tic** \-ˌsā-shə-nə-ˈlis-tik\ *adj*

sen•sa•tion•al•ize \-nə-ˌlīz\ *vb* **-ized; -iz•ing** : to present in a sensational manner

[1]**sense** \ˈsens\ *n* **1** : semantic content : MEANING **2** : the faculty of perceiving by means of sense organs; *also* : a bodily function or mechanism (as sight, hearing, or smell) basically involving a stimulus and a sense organ **3** : SENSATION, AWARENESS **4** : INTELLIGENCE, JUDGMENT **5** : OPINION ⟨the ~ of the meeting⟩ — **sense•less** *adj* — **sense•less•ly** *adv*

[2]**sense** *vb* **sensed; sens•ing 1** : to be or become aware of ⟨~ danger⟩; *also* : to perceive by the senses **2** : to detect (as radiation) automatically

sense organ *n* : a bodily structure (as an eye or ear) that receives stimuli (as heat or light) which excite nerve cells to send information to the brain

sen•si•bil•i•ty \ˌsen-sə-ˈbi-lə-tē\ *n, pl* **-ties** : delicacy of feeling : SENSITIVITY

sen•si•ble \ˈsen-sə-bəl\ *adj* **1** : capable of being perceived by the senses or the mind; *also* : capable of receiving sense impressions **2** : AWARE, CONSCIOUS **3** : REASONABLE, RATIONAL — **sen•si•bly** \-blē\ *adv*

sen•si•tise *Brit var of* SENSITIZE

sen•si•tive \ˈsen-sə-tiv\ *adj* **1** : subject to excitation by or responsive to stimuli **2** : having power of feeling **3** : of such a nature as to be easily affected **4** : TOUCHY ⟨a ~ issue⟩ — **sen•si•tive•ness** *n* — **sen•si•tiv•i•ty** \ˌsen-sə-ˈti-və-tē\ *n*

sensitive plant *n* : any of several mimosas with leaves that fold or droop when touched

sen•si•tize \ˈsen-sə-ˌtīz\ *vb* **-tized; -tiz•ing** : to make or become sensitive or hypersensitive — **sen•si•ti•za•tion** \ˌsen-sə-tə-ˈzā-shən\ *n*

sen•sor \ˈsen-ˌsȯr, -sər\ *n* : a device that responds to a physical stimulus

sen•so•ry \ˈsen-sə-rē\ *adj* : of or relating to sensation or the senses

sen•su•al \ˈsen-shə-wəl\ *adj* **1** : relating to gratification of the senses **2** : devoted to the pleasures of the senses — **sen•su•al•ist** *n* — **sen•su•al•i•ty** \ˌsen-shə-ˈwa-lə-tē\ *n* — **sen•su•al•ly** *adv*

sen•su•ous \ˈsen-shə-wəs\ *adj* **1** : relating to the senses or to things that can be perceived by the senses **2**

: VOLUPTUOUS — **sen•su•ous•ly** *adv* — **sen•su•ous•ness** *n*

sent *past and past part of* SEND

sen•te \ˈsen-tē\ *n, pl* **li•cen•te** *or* **li•sen•te** \li-ˈsen-tē\ — see *loti* at MONEY table

[1]**sen•tence** \ˈsent-ᵊns, -ᵊnz\ *n* [ME, fr. MF, fr. L *sententia,* lit., feeling, opinion, fr. *sentire* to feel] **1 :** the punishment set by a court **2 :** a grammatically self-contained speech unit that expresses an assertion, a question, a command, a wish, or an exclamation

[2]**sentence** *vb* **sen•tenced; sen•tenc•ing :** to impose a sentence on

sen•ten•tious \sen-ˈten-chəs\ *adj* **:** using wise sayings or proverbs; *also* **:** using pompous language

sen•tient \ˈsen-chənt, -chē-ənt\ *adj* **:** capable of feeling **:** having perception

sen•ti•ment \ˈsen-tə-mənt\ *n* **1 :** FEELING; *also* **:** thought and judgment influenced by feeling **:** emotional attitude **2 :** OPINION, NOTION

sen•ti•men•tal \ˌsen-tə-ˈment-ᵊl\ *adj* **1 :** influenced by tender feelings **2 :** affecting the emotions **syn** bathetic, maudlin, mawkish, mushy — **sen•ti•men•tal•ism** *n* — **sen•ti•men•tal•ist** *n* — **sen•ti•men•tal•i•ty** \-ˌmen-ˈta-lə-tē, -mən-\ *n* — **sen•ti•men•tal•ly** *adv*

sen•ti•men•tal•ise *Brit var of* SENTIMENTALIZE

sen•ti•men•tal•ize \-ˈment-ᵊl-ˌīz\ *vb* **-ized; -iz•ing 1 :** to indulge in sentiment **2 :** to look upon or imbue with sentiment — **sen•ti•men•tal•i•za•tion** \-ˌment-ᵊl-ə-ˈzā-shən\ *n*

sen•ti•mo \sen-ˈtē-(ˌ)mō\ *n, pl* **-mos** — see *peso* at MONEY table

sen•ti•nel \ˈsent-ᵊn-əl\ *n* [MF *sentinelle,* fr. It *sentinella,* fr. *sentina* vigilance, fr. *sentire* to perceive, fr. L] **:** one that watches or guards

sen•try \ˈsen-trē\ *n, pl* **sentries :** SENTINEL, GUARD

sep *abbr* separate, separated

Sep *abbr* September

SEP *abbr* simplified employee pension

se•pal \ˈsē-pəl, ˈse-\ *n* **:** one of the modified leaves comprising a flower calyx

sep•a•ra•ble \ˈse-pə-rə-bəl\ *adj* **:** capable of being separated

[1]**sep•a•rate** \ˈse-pə-ˌrāt\ *vb* **-rat•ed; -rat•ing 1 :** to set or keep apart **:** DISCONNECT, SEVER **2 :** to keep apart by something intervening **3 :** to cease to be together **:** PART

[2]**sep•a•rate** \ˈse-prət, -pə-rət\ *adj* **1 :** not connected **2 :** divided from each other **3 :** SINGLE, PARTICULAR ⟨the ~ pieces of the puzzle⟩ — **sep•a•rate•ly** *adv*

[3]**sep•a•rate** *n* **:** an article of dress designed to be worn interchangeably with others to form various combinations

sep•a•ra•tion \ˌse-pə-ˈrā-shən\ *n* **1 :** the act or process of separating **:** the state of being separated **2 :** a point, line, means, or area of division **3 :** a formal separating of a married couple by agreement but without divorce

sep•a•rat•ist \ˈse-prə-tist, ˈse-pə-ˌrā-\ *n* **:** an advocate of separation (as from a political body) — **sep•a•rat•ism** \ˈse-prə-ˌti-zəm\ *n*

sep•a•ra•tive \ˈse-pə-ˌrā-tiv, ˈse-prə-tiv\ *adj* **:** tending toward, causing, or expressing separation

sep•a•ra•tor \ˈse-pə-ˌrā-tər\ *n* **:** one that separates; *esp* **:** a device for separating cream from milk

se•pia \ˈsē-pē-ə\ *n* **:** a brownish gray to dark brown color

sep•sis \ˈsep-səs\ *n, pl* **sep•ses** \ˈsep-ˌsēz\ **:** a toxic condition due to spread of bacteria or their products in the body

Sept *abbr* September

Sep•tem•ber \sep-ˈtem-bər\ *n* [ME *Septembre,* fr. OF & OE, both fr. L *September* (seventh month), fr. *septem* seven] **:** the 9th month of the year having 30 days

sep•tic \ˈsep-tik\ *adj* **1 :** PUTREFACTIVE **2 :** relating to or characteristic of sepsis

sep•ti•ce•mia \ˌsep-tə-ˈsē-mē-ə\ *n* **:** BLOOD POISONING

septic tank *n* **:** a tank in which sewage is disintegrated by bacteria

sep•tu•a•ge•nar•i•an \sep-ˌtü-ə-jə-ˈner-ē-ən, -ˌtyü-\ *n* **:** a person whose age is in the seventies — **septuagenarian** *adj*

Sep•tu•a•gint \sep-ˈtü-ə-jənt, -ˈtyü-\ *n* **:** a Greek version of the Old Testament prepared in the 3d and 2d centuries B.C. by Jewish scholars

sep•tum \ˈsep-təm\ *n, pl* **sep•ta** \-tə\ **:** a dividing wall or membrane esp. between bodily spaces or masses of soft tissue

se•pul•chral \sə-ˈpəl-krəl\ *adj* **1 :** relating to burial or the grave **2 :** GLOOMY

[1]**sep•ul•chre** *or* **sep•ul•cher** \ˈse-pəl-kər\ *n* **:** a burial vault **:** TOMB

[2]**sepulchre** *or* **sepulcher** *vb* **-chred** *or* **-chered; -chring** *or* **-cher•ing :** BURY, ENTOMB

sep•ul•ture \ˈse-pəl-ˌchu̇r\ *n* **1 :** BURIAL **2 :** SEPULCHRE

seq *abbr* [L *sequens, sequentes, sequentia*] the following

seqq *abbr* [L *sequentia*] the following ones

se•quel \ˈsē-kwəl\ *n* **1 :** logical consequence **2 :** a literary or cinematic work continuing a story begun in a preceding one

se•quence \ˈsē-kwəns\ *n* **1 :** SERIES **2 :** chronological order of events **3 :** RESULT, SEQUEL **syn** succession, chain, progression, train — **se•quen•tial** \si-ˈkwen-chəl\ *adj* — **se•quen•tial•ly** *adv*

se•quent \ˈsē-kwənt\ *adj* **1 :** SUCCEEDING, CONSECUTIVE **2 :** RESULTANT

se•ques•ter \si-ˈkwes-tər\ *vb* **:** to set apart **:** SEGREGATE

se•ques•trate \ˈsē-kwəs-ˌtrāt, si-ˈkwes-\ *vb* **-trat•ed; -trat•ing :** SEQUESTER — **se•ques•tra•tion** \ˌsē-kwəs-ˈtrā-shən, ˌse-\ *n*

se•quin \ˈsē-kwən\ *n* **1 :** an old gold coin of Turkey and Italy **2 :** a small metal or plastic plate used for ornamentation esp. on clothing

se•quoia \si-ˈkwȯi-ə\ *n* **:** either of two huge California coniferous trees

ser *abbr* **1** serial **2** series

sera *pl of* SERUM

se•ra•glio \sə-ˈral-yō\ *n, pl* **-glios** [It *serraglio*] **:** HAREM

se•ra•pe \sə-ˈrä-pē\ *n* **:** a colorful woolen shawl worn over the shoulders esp. by Mexican men

ser•aph \ˈser-əf\ *n, pl* **ser•a•phim** \-ə-ˌfim, -ˌfēm\ *or* **seraphs :** one of the 6-winged angels standing in the presence of God

ser•a•phim \ˈser-ə-ˌfim, -ˌfēm\ *n pl* **1 :** the highest order of angels **2** *sing, pl* **seraphim :** SERAPH — **se•raph•ic** \sə-ˈra-fik\ *adj*

Serb \ˈsərb\ *n* **:** a native or inhabitant of Serbia

Ser•bo–Cro•a•tian \ˌsər-(ˌ)bō-krō-ˈā-shən\ *n* **:** a Slavic language spoken in Croatia, Bosnia and Herzegovina, Serbia, and Montenegro

sere \ˈsir\ *adj* **:** DRY, WITHERED

[1]**ser•e•nade** \ˌser-ə-ˈnād\ *n* [F, fr. It *serenata,* fr. *sereno* clear, calm (of weather)] **:** music sung or played as a compliment esp. outdoors at night for a woman being courted

[2]**serenade** *vb* **-nad•ed; -nad•ing :** to entertain with or perform a serenade

ser•en•dip•i•ty \ˌser-ən-ˈdi-pə-tē\ *n* [fr. its possession by the heroes of the Persian fairy tale *The Three Princes of Serendip*] **:** the gift of finding valuable or agreeable things not sought for — **ser•en•dip•i•tous** \-təs\ *adj*

se•rene \sə-ˈrēn\ *adj* **1 :** CLEAR ⟨~ skies⟩ **2 :** QUIET, CALM **syn** tranquil, peaceful, placid — **se•rene•ly** *adv* — **se•ren•i•ty** \sə-ˈre-nə-tē\ *n*

serf \ˈsərf\ *n* **:** a member of a servile class bound to the land and subject to the will of the landowner — **serf•dom** \-dəm\ *n*

serg *or* **sergt** *abbr* sergeant

serge \ˈsərj\ *n* **:** a twilled woolen cloth

ser•geant \ˈsär-jənt\ *n* [ME, servant, attendant, sergeant, fr. OF *sergent, serjant,* fr. L *servient-, servi-*

ens, prp. of *servire* to serve] **1** : a noncommissioned officer (as in the army) ranking next below a staff sergeant **2** : an officer in a police force

sergeant first class *n* : a noncommissioned officer in the army ranking next below a master sergeant

sergeant major *n, pl* **sergeants major** *or* **sergeant majors** **1** : a senior staff noncommissioned officer in the army or marine corps serving as advisor in matters related to enlisted personnel **2** : a noncommissioned officer in the marine corps ranking above a first sergeant

[1]**se•ri•al** \ˈsir-ē-əl\ *adj* **1** : appearing in parts that follow regularly ⟨a ~ story⟩ **2** : effecting a series of similar acts over a period of time ⟨a ~ killer⟩; *also* : occurring in such a series — **se•ri•al•ly** *adv*

[2]**serial** *n* : a serial story or other writing — **se•ri•al•ist** \-ə-list\ *n*

se•ries \ˈsir-ēz\ *n, pl* **series** : a number of things or events arranged in order and connected by being alike in some way **syn** succession, progression, sequence, chain, train, string

seri•graph \ˈser-ə-ˌgraf\ *n* : an original silk-screen print — **se•rig•ra•pher** \sə-ˈri-grə-fər\ *n* — **se•rig•ra•phy** \-fē\ *n*

se•ri•ous \ˈsir-ē-əs\ *adj* **1** : thoughtful or subdued in appearance or manner : SOBER **2** : requiring much thought or work **3** : EARNEST, DEVOTED **4** : DANGEROUS, HARMFUL **5** : excessive or impressive in quantity or degree ⟨making ~ money⟩ **syn** grave, sedate, staid — **se•ri•ous•ly** *adv* — **se•ri•ous•ness** *n*

ser•mon \ˈsər-mən\ *n* [ME, fr. OF, fr. ML *sermon, sermo,* fr. L, speech, conversation, fr. *serere* to link together] **1** : a religious discourse esp. as part of a worship service **2** : a lecture on conduct or duty

se•rol•o•gy \sə-ˈrä-lə-jē\ *n* : a science dealing with serums and esp. their reactions and properties — **se•ro•log•i•cal** \ˌsir-ə-ˈlä-ji-kəl\ *or* **se•ro•log•ic** \-jik\ *adj*

se•rous \ˈsir-əs\ *adj* : of, relating to, resembling, or producing serum; *esp* : of thin watery constitution

ser•pent \ˈsər-pənt\ *n* : SNAKE

[1]**ser•pen•tine** \ˈsər-pən-ˌtēn, -ˌtīn\ *adj* **1** : SLY, CRAFTY **2** : WINDING, TURNING

[2]**ser•pen•tine** \-ˌtēn\ *n* : a dull-green mineral having a mottled appearance

ser•rate \ˈser-ˌāt\ *adj* : having a saw-toothed edge ⟨a ~ leaf⟩

ser•ried \ˈser-ēd\ *adj* : DENSE

se•rum \ˈsir-əm\ *n, pl* **serums** *or* **se•ra** \-ə\ [L, whey, wheylike fluid] : the clear yellowish antibody-containing fluid that can be separated from blood when it clots; *also* : a preparation of animal serum containing specific antibodies and used to prevent or cure disease

serv *abbr* service

ser•vant \ˈsər-vənt\ *n* : one that serves others; *esp* : a person employed for domestic or personal work

[1]**serve** \ˈsərv\ *vb* **served; serv•ing** **1** : to work as a servant **2** : to render obedience and worship to (God) **3** : to comply with the commands or demands of **4** : to work through or perform a term of service (as in the army) **5** : PUT IN ⟨*served* five years in jail⟩ **6** : to be of use : ANSWER ⟨pine boughs *served* for a bed⟩ **7** : BENEFIT **8** : to prove adequate or satisfactory for ⟨a pie that ~*s* eight people⟩ **9** : to make ready and pass out ⟨~ drinks⟩ **10** : to furnish or supply with something ⟨one power company *serving* the whole state⟩ **11** : to wait on ⟨~ a customer⟩ **12** : to treat or act toward in a specified way **13** : to put the ball in play (as in tennis) — **serv•er** *n*

[2]**serve** *n* : the act of serving a ball (as in tennis)

[1]**ser•vice** \ˈsər-vəs\ *n* **1** : the occupation of a servant **2** : HELP, BENEFIT **3** : a meeting for worship; *also* : a form followed in worship or in a ceremony ⟨burial ~⟩ **4** : the act, fact, or means of serving **5** : performance of official or professional duties **6** : SERVE **7** : a set of dishes or silverware **8** : a branch of public employment; *also* : the persons in it ⟨civil ~⟩ **9** : military or naval duty

[2]**service** *vb* **ser•viced; ser•vic•ing** : to do maintenance or repair work on or for

ser•vice•able \ˈsər-və-sə-bəl\ *adj* : prepared for service : USEFUL, USABLE

ser•vice•man \ˈsər-vəs-ˌman, -mən\ *n* **1** : a male member of the armed forces **2** : a man employed to repair or maintain equipment

service station *n* : a retail station for servicing motor vehicles

ser•vice•wom•an \ˈsər-vəs-ˌwu̇-mən\ *n* : a female member of the armed forces

ser•vile \ˈsər-vəl, -ˌvīl\ *adj* **1** : befitting a slave or servant **2** : behaving like a slave : SUBMISSIVE — **ser•vil•i•ty** \ˌsər-ˈvi-lə-tē\ *n*

serv•ing \ˈsər-viŋ\ *n* : HELPING

ser•vi•tor \ˈsər-və-tər\ *n* : a male servant

ser•vi•tude \ˈsər-və-ˌtüd, -ˌtyüd\ *n* : SLAVERY, BONDAGE

ser•vo \ˈsər-vō\ *n, pl* **servos** **1** : SERVOMOTOR **2** : SERVOMECHANISM

ser•vo•mech•a•nism \ˈsər-vō-ˌme-kə-ˌni-zəm\ *n* : a device for automatically correcting the performance of a mechanism

ser•vo•mo•tor \-ˌmō-tər\ *n* : a mechanism that supplements a primary control

ses•a•me \ˈse-sə-mē\ *n* : a widely cultivated annual herb of warm regions; *also* : its seeds that yield an edible oil (**sesame oil**) and are used in flavoring

ses•qui•cen•ten•ni•al \ˌses-kwi-sen-ˈte-nē-əl\ *n* [L *sesqui-* one and a half, half again] : a 150th anniversary or its celebration — **sesquicentennial** *adj*

ses•qui•pe•da•lian \ˌses-kwə-pə-ˈdāl-yən\ *adj* **1** : having many syllables : LONG **2** : using long words

ses•sile \ˈse-sīl, -səl\ *adj* : permanently attached and not free to move about

ses•sion \ˈse-shən\ *n* **1** : a meeting or series of meetings of a body (as a court or legislature) for the transaction of business **2** : a meeting or period devoted to a particular activity

[1]**set** \ˈset\ *vb* **set; set•ting** **1** : to cause to sit **2** : PLACE **3** : ARRANGE, ADJUST **4** : to cause to be or do **5** : SETTLE, DECREE **6** : to fix in a frame **7** : to fix at a certain amount **8** : WAGER, STAKE **9** : to make or become fast or rigid **10** : to adapt (as words) to something (as music) **11** : to become fixed or firm or solid **12** : to be suitable : FIT **13** : BROOD **14** : to have a certain direction **15** : to pass below the horizon **16** : to defeat in bridge — **set about** : to begin to do — **set forth** : to begin a trip — **set off** **1** : to start out on a course or a trip **2** : to cause to explode — **set out** : to begin a trip or undertaking — **set sail** : to begin a voyage — **set upon** : to attack usu. with violence

[2]**set** *n* **1** : a setting or a being set **2** : DIRECTION, COURSE; *also* : TENDENCY **3** : FORM, BUILD **4** : the fit of something (as a coat) **5** : an artificial setting for the scene of a play or motion picture **6** : a group of tennis games in which one side wins at least six **7** : a group of persons or things of the same kind or having a common characteristic usu. classed together **8** : a collection of things and esp. of mathematical elements (as numbers or points) **9** : an electronic apparatus ⟨a television ~⟩

[3]**set** *adj* **1** : DELIBERATE, INTENT **2** : fixed by authority or custom **3** : RIGID **4** : PERSISTENT

set•back \ˈset-ˌbak\ *n* : a temporary defeat : REVERSE

set back *vb* **1** : HINDER, DELAY; *also* : REVERSE **2** : COST

set piece **1** : a composition (as in literature or music) executed in fixed or ideal form often with brilliant effect **2** : a scene, depiction, speech, or event obviously designed to have an imposing effect

set•screw \ˈset-ˌskrü\ *n* : a screw screwed through one part tightly upon or into another part to prevent relative movement

set•tee \se-ˈtē\ *n* : a bench or sofa with a back and arms

set·ter \ˈse-tər\ *n* : a large long-coated hunting dog
set·ting \ˈse-tiŋ\ *n* **1** : the frame in which a gem is set **2** : the time, place, and circumstances in which something occurs or develops; *also* : SCENERY **3** : music written for a text (as of a poem) **4** : the eggs that a fowl sits on for hatching at one time
set·tle \ˈset-ᵊl\ *vb* **set·tled; set·tling** [ME *settlen* to seat, bring to rest, come to rest, fr. OE *setlan,* fr. *setl* seat] **1** : to place so as to stay **2** : to establish in residence; *also* : COLONIZE **3** : to make compact **4** : QUIET, CALM **5** : to establish or secure permanently **6** : to direct one's efforts **7** : to fix by agreement **8** : to give legally **9** : ADJUST, ARRANGE **10** : DECIDE, DETERMINE **11** : to make a final disposition of ⟨~ an account⟩ **12** : to come to rest **13** : to reach an agreement on **14** : to sink gradually to a lower level **15** : to become clear by depositing sediment — **set·tler** *n*
set·tle·ment \ˈset-ᵊl-mənt\ *n* **1** : the act or process of settling **2** : BESTOWAL ⟨a marriage ~⟩ **3** : payment or adjustment of an account **4** : COLONY **5** : a small village **6** : an institution providing various community services esp. to large city populations **7** : adjustment of doubts and differences
set–to \ˈset-ˌtü\ *n, pl* **set–tos** : FIGHT
set·up \ˈset-ˌəp\ *n* **1** : the manner or act of arranging **2** : glass, ice, and nonalcoholic beverage for mixing served to patrons who supply their own liquor **3** : something (as a plot) that has been constructed or contrived; *also* : FRAME-UP
set up *vb* **1** : to place in position; *also* : ASSEMBLE **2** : CAUSE **3** : FOUND, ESTABLISH **4** : FRAME 5
sev·en \ˈse-vən\ *n* **1** : one more than six **2** : the 7th in a set or series **3** : something having seven units — **seven** *adj or pron* — **sev·enth** \-vənth\ *adj or adv or n*
sev·en·teen \ˌse-vən-ˈtēn\ *n* : one more than 16 — **seventeen** *adj or pron* — **sev·en·teenth** \-ˈtēnth\ *adj or n*
seventeen–year locust *n* : a cicada of the U.S. that has in the North a life of 17 years and in the South of 13 years of which most is spent underground as a nymph and only a few weeks as a winged adult
sev·en·ty \ˈse-vən-tē\ *n, pl* **-ties** : seven times 10 — **sev·en·ti·eth** \-tē-əth\ *adj or n* — **seventy** *adj or pron*
sev·en·ty–eight \ˌse-vən-tē-ˈāt\ *n* : a phonograph record designed to be played at 78 revolutions per minute
sev·er \ˈse-vər\ *vb* **sev·ered; sev·er·ing** : DIVIDE; *esp* : to separate by or as if by cutting — **sev·er·ance** \ˈsev-rəns, ˈse-və-\ *n*
sev·er·al \ˈsev-rəl, ˈse-və-\ *adj* [ME, fr. MF, fr. ML *separalis,* fr. L *separ* separate, fr. *separare* to separate] **1** : INDIVIDUAL, DISTINCT ⟨federal union of the ~ states⟩ **2** : consisting of an indefinite number but yet not very many — **sev·er·al·ly** *adv*
severance pay *n* : extra pay given an employee upon termination of employment
se·vere \sə-ˈvir\ *adj* **se·ver·er; -est** **1** : marked by strictness or sternness : AUSTERE **2** : strict in discipline **3** : causing distress and esp. physical discomfort or pain ⟨~ weather⟩ ⟨a ~ wound⟩ **4** : hard to endure ⟨~ trials⟩ **5** : SERIOUS ⟨~ depression⟩ **syn** stern, ascetic, astringent — **se·vere·ly** *adv* — **se·ver·i·ty** \-ˈver-ə-tē\ *n*
sew \ˈsō\ *vb* **sewed; sewn** \ˈsōn\ *or* **sewed; sew·ing** **1** : to unite or fasten by stitches **2** : to engage in sewing
sew·age \ˈsü-ij\ *n* : waste materials carried off by sewers
[1]**sew·er** \ˈsō-ər\ *n* : one that sews
[2]**sew·er** \ˈsü-ər\ *n* : an artificial pipe or channel to carry off waste matter
sew·er·age \ˈsü-ə-rij\ *n* **1** : a system of sewers **2** : SEWAGE
sew·ing *n* **1** : the activity of one who sews **2** : material that has been or is to be sewed
sex \ˈseks\ *n* **1** : either of the two major forms that occur in many living things and are designated male or female according to their role in reproduction; *also* : the qualities by which these sexes are differentiated and which directly or indirectly function in reproduction involving two parents **2** : sexual activity or behavior; *also* : SEXUAL INTERCOURSE — **sexed** \ˈsekst\ *adj* — **sex·less** *adj*
sex·a·ge·nar·i·an \ˌsek-sə-jə-ˈner-ē-ən\ *n* : a person whose age is in the sixties — **sexagenarian** *adj*
sex cell *n* : an egg cell or sperm cell
sex chromosome *n* : one of usu. a pair of chromosomes that are usu. similar in one sex but different in the other sex and are concerned with the inheritance of sex
sex hormone *n* : a hormone (as from the gonads or adrenal cortex) that affects the growth or function of the reproductive organs or the development of secondary sex characteristics
sex·ism \ˈsek-ˌsi-zəm\ *n* : prejudice or discrimination based on sex; *esp* : discrimination against women — **sex·ist** \ˈsek-sist\ *adj or n*
sex·pot \ˈseks-ˌpät\ *n* : a conspicuously sexy woman
sex symbol *n* : a usu. renowned person (as an entertainer) noted and admired for conspicuous attractiveness
sex·tant \ˈsek-stənt\ *n* [NL *sextant-, sextans* sixth part of a circle, fr. L, sixth part, fr. *sextus* sixth] : a navigational instrument for determining latitude
sex·tet \sek-ˈstet\ *n* **1** : a musical composition for six voices or instruments; *also* : the performers of such a composition **2** : a group or set of six
sex·ton \ˈsek-stən\ *n* : one who takes care of church property
sex·u·al \ˈsek-shə-wəl\ *adj* : of, relating to, or involving sex or the sexes ⟨a ~ spore⟩ ⟨~ relations⟩ — **sex·u·al·i·ty** \ˌsek-shə-ˈwa-lə-tē\ *n* — **sex·u·al·ly** \ˈsek-shə-wə-lē\ *adv*
sexual intercourse *n* **1** : intercourse between a male and a female in which the penis is inserted into the vagina **2** : intercourse between individuals involving genital contact other than insertion of the penis into the vagina
sexually transmitted disease *n* : a disease (as syphilis, gonorrhea, AIDS, or the genital form of herpes simplex) that is caused by a microorganism or virus usu. or often transmitted by direct sexual contact
sexual relations *n pl* : SEXUAL INTERCOURSE
sexy \ˈsek-sē\ *adj* **sex·i·er; -est** : sexually suggestive or stimulating : EROTIC
SF *abbr* **1** sacrifice fly **2** science fiction
SFC *abbr* sergeant first class
SG *abbr* **1** senior grade **2** sergeant **3** solicitor general **4** surgeon general
sgd *abbr* signed
Sgt *abbr* sergeant
Sgt Maj *abbr* sergeant major
sh *abbr* share
shab·by \ˈsha-bē\ *adj* **shab·bi·er; -est** **1** : dressed in worn clothes **2** : threadbare and faded from wear **3** : DESPICABLE, MEAN; *also* : UNFAIR ⟨~ treatment⟩ — **shab·bi·ly** \ˈsha-bə-lē\ *adv* — **shab·bi·ness** \-bē-nəs\ *n*
shack \ˈshak\ *n* : HUT, SHANTY
[1]**shack·le** \ˈsha-kəl\ *n* **1** : something (as a manacle or fetter) that confines the legs or arms **2** : a check on free action made as if by fetters **3** : a device for making something fast or secure
[2]**shackle** *vb* **shack·led; shack·ling** : to bind or fasten with shackles
shad \ˈshad\ *n, pl* **shad** : any of several sea fishes related to the herrings that swim up rivers to spawn and include some important food fishes
[1]**shade** \ˈshād\ *n* **1** : partial obscurity **2** : space sheltered from the light esp. of the sun **3** : PHANTOM **4** : something that shelters from or intercepts light or heat;

also, pl : SUNGLASSES **5** : a dark color or a variety of a color **6** : a small difference

[2]**shade** *vb* **shad•ed; shad•ing 1** : to shelter from light and heat **2** : DARKEN, OBSCURE **3** : to mark with degrees of light or color **4** : to show slight differences esp. in color or meaning

shad•ing *n* : the color and lines representing darkness or shadow in a drawing or painting

[1]**shad•ow** \ˈsha-dō\ *n* **1** : partial darkness in a space from which light rays are cut off **2** : SHELTER **3** : shade cast upon a surface by something intercepting rays from a light ⟨the ~ of a tree⟩ **4** : PHANTOM **5** : a shaded portion of a picture **6** : a small portion or degree : TRACE ⟨a ~ of doubt⟩ **7** : a source of gloom or unhappiness — **shad•owy** *adj*

[2]**shadow** *vb* **1** : to cast a shadow on **2** : to represent faintly or vaguely **3** : to follow and watch closely : TRAIL

shad•ow•box \ˈsha-dō-ˌbäks\ *vb* : to box with an imaginary opponent esp. for training

shady \ˈshā-dē\ *adj* **shad•i•er; -est 1** : affording shade **2** : of questionable honesty or reputation

[1]**shaft** \ˈshaft\ *n, pl* **shafts 1** : the long handle of a spear or lance **2** : SPEAR, LANCE **3** *or pl* **shaves** \ˈshavz\ : POLE; *esp* : one of two poles between which a horse is hitched to pull a vehicle **4** : something (as a column) long and slender **5** : a bar to support a rotating piece or to transmit power by rotation **6** : an inclined opening in the ground (as for finding or mining ore) **7** : a vertical opening (as for an elevator) through the floors of a building **8** : harsh or unfair treatment — usu. used with *the*

[2]**shaft** *vb* **1** : to fit with a shaft **2** : to treat unfairly or harshly

shag \ˈshag\ *n* : a shaggy tangled mass or covering (as of wool) : long coarse or matted fiber, nap, or pile

shag•gy \ˈsha-gē\ *adj* **shag•gi•er; -est 1** : rough with or as if with long hair or wool **2** : tangled or rough in surface

shah \ˈshä, ˈshȯ\ *n, often cap* : a sovereign of Iran until 1979

Shak *abbr* Shakespeare

[1]**shake** \ˈshāk\ *vb* **shook** \ˈshu̇k\; **shak•en** \ˈshā-kən\; **shak•ing 1** : to move or cause to move jerkily or irregularly **2** : BRANDISH, WAVE ⟨*shaking* his fist⟩ **3** : to disturb emotionally ⟨*shaken* by her death⟩ **4** : WEAKEN ⟨*shook* his faith⟩ **5** : to bring or come into a certain position, condition, or arrangement by or as if by moving jerkily **6** : to clasp (hands) in greeting or as a sign of goodwill or agreement **syn** tremble, quake, quaver, shiver, quiver — **shak•able** \ˈshā-kə-bəl\ *adj*

[2]**shake** *n* **1** : the act or a result of shaking **2** : DEAL, TREATMENT ⟨a fair ~⟩

shake•down \ˈshāk-ˌdau̇n\ *n* **1** : an improvised bed **2** : EXTORTION **3** : a process or period of adjustment **4** : a test (as of a new ship or airplane) under operating conditions

shake down *vb* **1** : to take up temporary quarters **2** : to occupy a makeshift bed **3** : to become accustomed esp. to new surroundings or duties **4** : to settle down **5** : to give a shakedown test to **6** : to obtain money from in a deceitful or illegal manner **7** : to bring about a reduction of

shak•er \ˈshā-kər\ *n* **1** : one that shakes ⟨pepper ~⟩ **2** *cap* : a member of a religious sect founded in England in 1747

shake–up \ˈshāk-ˌəp\ *n* : an extensive often drastic reorganization

shaky \ˈshā-kē\ *adj* **shak•i•er; -est** : UNSOUND, WEAK — **shak•i•ly** \ˈshā-kə-lē\ *adv* — **shak•i•ness** \-kē-nəs\ *n*

shale \ˈshāl\ *n* : a finely layered rock formed from clay, mud, or silt

shall \shəl, ˈshal\ *vb, past* **should** \shəd, ˈshu̇d\; *pres sing & pl* **shall** — used as an auxiliary to express a command, what seems inevitable or likely in the future, simple futurity, or determination

shal•lop \ˈsha-ləp\ *n* : a light open boat

shal•lot \shə-ˈlät, ˈsha-lət\ *n* [modif. of F *échalote*] **1** : a small clustered bulb that is used in seasoning and is produced by a perennial herb belonging to a subspecies of the onion; *also* : this herb **2** : GREEN ONION

[1]**shal•low** \ˈsha-lō\ *adj* **1** : not deep **2** : not intellectually profound

[2]**shallow** *n* : a shallow place in a body of water — usu. used in pl.

[1]**sham** \ˈsham\ *n* **1** : an ornamental covering for a pillow **2** : COUNTERFEIT, IMITATION **3** : a person who shams

[2]**sham** *vb* **shammed; sham•ming** : FEIGN, PRETEND — **sham•mer** *n*

[3]**sham** *adj* : not genuine : FALSE, FEIGNED

sha•man \ˈshä-mən, ˈshā-\ *n* [ultim. fr. Evenki (a language of Siberia) *šamān*] : a priest or priestess who uses magic to cure the sick, to divine the hidden, and to control events

sham•ble \ˈsham-bəl\ *vb* **sham•bled; sham•bling** : to shuffle along — **sham•ble** *n*

sham•bles \ˈsham-bəlz\ *n* **1** : a scene of great slaughter **2** : a scene or state of great destruction or disorder; *also* : MESS

[1]**shame** \ˈshām\ *n* **1** : a painful sense of having done something wrong, improper, or immodest **2** : DISGRACE, DISHONOR **3** : a cause of feeling shame **4** : something to be regretted ⟨it's a ~ you'll miss the party⟩ — **shame•ful** \-fəl\ *adj* — **shame•ful•ly** *adv* — **shame•less** *adj* — **shame•less•ly** *adv*

[2]**shame** *vb* **shamed; sham•ing 1** : DISGRACE **2** : to make ashamed

shame•faced \ˈshām-ˌfāst\ *adj* : ASHAMED, ABASHED — **shame•faced•ly** \-ˌfā-səd-lē, -ˌfāst-lē\ *adv*

[1]**sham•poo** \sham-ˈpü\ *vb* [Hindi *cā̃po*, imper. of *cā̃pnā* to press, shampoo] : to wash (as the hair) with soap and water or with a special preparation; *also* : to clean (as a rug) similarly

[2]**shampoo** *n, pl* **shampoos 1** : the act or an instance of shampooing **2** : a preparation for use in shampooing

sham•rock \ˈsham-ˌräk\ *n* [Ir *seamróg*, dim. of *seamar* clover] : a plant of folk legend with leaves composed of three leaflets that is associated with St. Patrick and Ireland

shang•hai \shaŋ-ˈhī\ *vb* **shang•haied; shang•hai•ing** [*Shanghai*, China] : to force aboard a ship for service as a sailor; *also* : to trick or force into an undesirable position

Shan•gri–la \ˌshaŋ-gri-ˈlä\ *n* [*Shangri-La*, imaginary land depicted in the novel *Lost Horizon* (1933) by James Hilton] : a remote idyllic hideaway

shank \ˈshaŋk\ *n* **1** : the part of the leg between the knee and the human ankle or a corresponding part of a quadruped **2** : a cut of meat from the leg **3** : the narrow part of the sole of a shoe beneath the instep **4** : the part of a tool or instrument (as a key or anchor) connecting the functioning part with a part by which it is held or moved

shan•tung \ˌshan-ˈtəŋ\ *n* : a fabric in plain weave having a slightly irregular surface

shan•ty \ˈshan-tē\ *n, pl* **shanties** [prob. fr. CanF *chantier* lumber camp, hut, fr. F, gantry, fr. L *cantherius* rafter, trellis] : a small roughly built shelter or dwelling

[1]**shape** \ˈshāp\ *vb* **shaped; shap•ing 1** : to form esp. in a particular shape **2** : DESIGN **3** : ADAPT, ADJUST **4** : REGULATE **syn** make, fashion, fabricate, manufacture, frame, mold

[2]**shape** *n* **1** : APPEARANCE **2** : surface configuration : FORM **3** : bodily contour apart from the head and face : FIGURE **4** : PHANTOM **5** : CONDITION — **shaped** \ˈshāpt\ *adj*

shape•less \ˈshā-pləs\ *adj* **1** : having no definite shape **2** : not shapely — **shape•less•ly** *adv* — **shape•less•ness** *n*

shape•ly \ˈshā-plē\ *adj* **shape•li•er; -est** : having a pleasing shape — **shape•li•ness** *n*

shard \ˈshärd\ *also* **sherd** \ˈshərd\ *n* : a broken piece : FRAGMENT

[1]**share** \ˈshar\ *n* : PLOWSHARE

[2]**share** *n* **1** : a portion belonging to one person or group **2** : any of the equal interests into which the capital stock of a corporation is divided

[3]**share** *vb* **shared; shar•ing 1** : APPORTION **2** : to use or enjoy with others **3** : PARTICIPATE — **shar•er** *n*

share•crop•per \-ˌkrä-pər\ *n* : a farmer who works another's land in return for a share of the crop — **share•crop** *vb*

share•hold•er \-ˌhōl-dər\ *n* : STOCKHOLDER

[1]**shark** \ˈshärk\ *n* : any of various active, usu. predaceous, and mostly large marine cartilaginous fishes

[2]**shark** *n* : a greedy crafty person

shark•skin \-ˌskin\ *n* **1** : the hide of a shark or leather made from it **2** : a fabric (as of cotton or rayon) woven from strands of many fine threads and having a sleek appearance and silky feel

[1]**sharp** \ˈshärp\ *adj* **1** : having a thin cutting edge or fine point : not dull or blunt **2** : COLD, NIPPING ⟨a ~ wind⟩ **3** : keen in intellect, perception, or attention **4** : BRISK, ENERGETIC **5** : IRRITABLE ⟨a ~ temper⟩ **6** : causing intense distress ⟨a ~ pain⟩ **7** : HARSH, CUTTING ⟨a ~ rebuke⟩ **8** : affecting the senses as if cutting or piercing ⟨a ~ sound⟩ ⟨a ~ smell⟩ **9** : not smooth or rounded ⟨~ features⟩ **10** : involving an abrupt or extreme change ⟨a ~ turn⟩ **11** : CLEAR, DISTINCT ⟨mountains in ~ relief⟩; *also* : easy to perceive ⟨a ~ contrast⟩ **12** : higher than the true pitch; *also* : raised by a half step **13** : STYLISH ⟨a ~ dresser⟩ **syn** keen, acute, quick-witted, penetrative — **sharp•ly** *adv* — **sharp•ness** *n*

[2]**sharp** *adv* **1** : in a sharp manner **2** : EXACTLY, PRECISELY ⟨left at 8 ~⟩

[3]**sharp** *n* **1** : a sharp edge or point **2** : a character ♯ which indicates that a specified note is to be raised by a half step; *also* : the resulting note **3** : SHARPER

[4]**sharp** *vb* : to raise in pitch by a half step

sharp•en \ˈshär-pən\ *vb* : to make or become sharp — **sharp•en•er** *n*

sharp•er \ˈshär-pər\ *n* : SWINDLER; *esp* : a cheating gambler

sharp•ie *or* **sharpy** \ˈshär-pē\ *n, pl* **sharp•ies 1** : SHARPER **2** : a person who is exceptionally keen or alert

sharp•shoot•er \ˈshärp-ˌshü-tər\ *n* : a good marksman — **sharp•shoot•ing** *n*

shat•ter \ˈsha-tər\ *vb* : to dash or burst into fragments — **shat•ter•proof** \ˈsha-tər-ˌprüf\ *adj*

[1]**shave** \ˈshāv\ *vb* **shaved; shaved** *or* **shav•en** \ˈshā-vən\; **shav•ing 1** : to slice in thin pieces **2** : to make bare or smooth by cutting the hair from **3** : to cut or pare off by the sliding movement of a razor **4** : to skim along or near the surface of

[2]**shave** *n* **1** : any of various tools for cutting thin slices **2** : an act or process of shaving

shav•er \ˈshā-vər\ *n* **1** : an electric razor **2** : BOY, YOUNGSTER

shaves *pl of* SHAFT

shav•ing *n* **1** : the act of one that shaves **2** : something shaved off

shawl \ˈshȯl\ *n* : a square or oblong piece of fabric used esp. by women as a loose covering for the head or shoulders

Shaw•nee \shȯ-ˈnē, shä-\ *n, pl* **Shawnee** *or* **Shawnees** : a member of an American Indian people orig. of the central Ohio valley; *also* : their language

shd *abbr* should

she \ˈshē\ *pron* : that female one ⟨who is ~⟩; *also* : that one regarded as feminine ⟨~'s a fine ship⟩

sheaf \ˈshēf\ *n, pl* **sheaves** \ˈshēvz\ **1** : a bundle of stalks and ears of grain **2** : a group of things bound together

[1]**shear** \ˈshir\ *vb* **sheared; sheared** *or* **shorn** \ˈshōrn\; **shear•ing 1** : to cut the hair or wool from : CLIP, TRIM **2** : to deprive by or as if by cutting **3** : to cut or break sharply

[2]**shear** *n* **1** : any of various cutting tools that consist of two blades fastened together so that the edges slide one by the other — usu. used in pl. **2** *chiefly Brit* : the act, an instance, or the result of shearing **3** : an action or stress caused by applied forces that causes two parts of a body to slide on each other

sheath \ˈshēth\ *n, pl* **sheaths** \ˈshēthz, ˈshēths\ **1** : a case for a blade (as of a knife); *also* : an anatomical covering suggesting such a case **2** : a close-fitting dress usu. worn without a belt

sheathe \ˈshēth\ *also* **sheath** \ˈshēth\ *vb* **sheathed; sheath•ing 1** : to put into a sheath **2** : to cover with something that guards or protects

sheath•ing \ˈshē-thiŋ, -thiŋ\ *n* : material used to sheathe something; *esp* : the first covering of boards or of waterproof material on the outside wall of a frame house or on a timber roof

sheave \ˈshiv, ˈshēv\ *n* : a grooved wheel or pulley (as on a pulley block)

she•bang \shi-ˈbaŋ\ *n* : CONTRIVANCE, AFFAIR, CONCERN ⟨sold the whole ~⟩

[1]**shed** \ˈshed\ *vb* **shed; shed•ding 1** : to cause to flow from a cut or wound ⟨~ blood⟩ **2** : to pour down in drops ⟨~ tears⟩ **3** : to give out (as light) : DIFFUSE **4** : to throw off (as a natural covering) : DISCARD

[2]**shed** *n* : a slight structure built for shelter or storage

sheen \ˈshēn\ *n* : a subdued luster

sheep \ˈshēp\ *n, pl* **sheep 1** : any of various cud-chewing mammals that are stockier than the related goats and lack a beard in the male; *esp* : one raised for meat or for its wool or skin **2** : a timid or defenseless person **3** : SHEEPSKIN

sheep dog *n* : a dog used to tend, drive, or guard sheep

sheep•fold \ˈshēp-ˌfōld\ *n* : a pen or shelter for sheep

sheep•herd•er \-ˌhər-dər\ *n* : a worker in charge of sheep esp. on open range — **sheep•herd•ing** *n*

sheep•ish \ˈshē-pish\ *adj* : BASHFUL, TIMID; *esp* : embarrassed by consciousness of a fault — **sheep•ish•ly** *adv*

sheep•skin \ˈshēp-ˌskin\ *n* **1** : the hide of a sheep or leather prepared from it; *also* : PARCHMENT **2** : DIPLOMA

[1]**sheer** \ˈshir\ *vb* : to turn from a course

[2]**sheer** *adj* **1** : very thin or transparent **2** : UNQUALIFIED ⟨~ folly⟩ **3** : very steep **syn** pure, simple, absolute, unadulterated, unmitigated — **sheer** *adv*

[1]**sheet** \ˈshēt\ *n* **1** : a broad piece of cloth (as for a bed); *also* : SAIL 1 **2** : a single piece of paper **3** : a broad flat surface ⟨a ~ of ice⟩ **4** : something broad and long and relatively thin

[2]**sheet** *n* : a rope used to trim a sail

sheet•ing \ˈshē-tiŋ\ *n* : material in the form of sheets or suitable for forming into sheets

sheikh *or* **sheik** \ˈshēk, ˈshāk\ *n* : an Arab chief — **sheikh•dom** *or* **sheik•dom** \-dəm\ *n*

shek•el \ˈshe-kəl\ *n* — see MONEY table

shelf \ˈshelf\ *n, pl* **shelves** \ˈshelvz\ **1** : a thin flat usu. long and narrow structure fastened horizontally (as on a wall) above the floor to hold things **2** : something (as a sandbar) that suggests a shelf

shelf life *n* : the period of storage time during which a material will remain useful

[1]**shell** \ˈshel\ *n* **1** : a hard or tough often thin outer covering of an animal (as a beetle, turtle, or mollusk) or of an egg or a seed or fruit (as a nut); *also* : something that resembles a shell ⟨a pastry ~⟩ **2** : a light narrow racing boat propelled by oarsmen **3** : a case holding an explosive and designed to be fired from a cannon; *also* : a case holding the charge of powder and shot or bullet for small arms **4** : a plain usu. sleeveless blouse or sweater — **shelled** \ˈsheld\ *adj* — **shelly** \ˈshe-lē\ *adj*

[2]**shell** *vb* **1 :** to remove from a shell or husk **2 :** BOMBARD — **shell·er** *n*

[1]**shel·lac** \shə-ˈlak\ *n* **1 :** a purified lac **2 :** lac dissolved in alcohol and used as a wood filler or finish

[2]**shellac** *vb* **shel·lacked; shel·lack·ing 1 :** to coat or treat with shellac **2 :** to defeat decisively

shel·lack·ing *n* **:** a sound drubbing

shell bean *n* **:** a bean grown esp. for its edible seeds; *also* **:** its edible seed

shell·fish \-ˌfish\ *n* **:** an invertebrate water animal (as an oyster or lobster) with a shell

shell out *vb* **:** PAY

shell shock *n* **:** a psychological and nervous disorder of soldiers resulting from traumatic experience in combat — **shell–shocked** \ˈshel-ˌshäkt\ *adj*

[1]**shel·ter** \ˈshel-tər\ *n* **:** something that gives protection **:** REFUGE

[2]**shelter** *vb* **shel·tered; shel·ter·ing :** to give protection or refuge to

shelve \ˈshelv\ *vb* **shelved; shelv·ing 1 :** to slope gradually **2 :** to store on shelves **3 :** to dismiss from service or use **4 :** to put aside **:** DEFER ⟨~ a proposal⟩

shelv·ing \ˈshel-viŋ\ *n* **:** material for shelves; *also* **:** SHELVES

she·nan·i·gan \shə-ˈna-ni-gən\ *n* **1 :** an underhand trick **2 :** questionable conduct — usu. used in pl. **3 :** high-spirited or mischievous activity — usu. used in pl.

[1]**shep·herd** \ˈshe-pərd\ *n* **1 :** one who tends sheep **2 :** GERMAN SHEPHERD

[2]**shepherd** *vb* **:** to tend as or in the manner of a shepherd

shep·herd·ess \ˈshe-pər-dəs\ *n* **:** a woman who tends sheep

sheq·el \ˈshe-kəl\ *n, pl* **sheq·a·lim** \she-ˈkä-lim\ *var of* SHEKEL

sher·bet \ˈshər-bət\ *n* [Turk *şerbet*, fr. Per *sharbat*, fr. Ar *sharbah* drink] **1 :** a drink of sweetened diluted fruit juice **2** *or* **sher·bert** \-bərt\ **:** a frozen dessert of fruit juices, sugar, milk or water, and egg whites or gelatin

sherd *var of* SHARD

sher·iff \ˈsher-əf\ *n* [ME *shirreve*, fr. OE *scīrgerēfa*, lit., shire reeve (local official)] **:** a county officer charged with the execution of the law and the preservation of order

sher·ry \ˈsher-ē\ *n, pl* **sherries** [alter. of earlier *sherris* (taken as pl.), fr. *Xeres* (now *Jerez*), Spain] **:** a fortified wine with a nutty flavor

Shet·land pony \ˈshet-lənd-\ *n* **:** any of a breed of small stocky shaggy hardy ponies

shew \ˈshō\ *Brit var of* SHOW

shi·at·su *also* **shi·at·zu** \shē-ˈät-sü\ *n* [short for Jp *shiatsuryōhō*] **:** a finger massage of those bodily areas used in acupuncture

shib·bo·leth \ˈshi-bə-ləth\ *n* [Heb *shibbōleth* stream; fr. the use of this word as a test to distinguish the men of Gilead from members of the tribe of Ephraim, who pronounced it *sibbōleth* (Judges 12:5, 6)] **1 :** CATCHWORD 2 **2 :** language that is a criterion for distinguishing members of a group

[1]**shield** \ˈshēld\ *n* **1 :** a broad piece of defensive armor carried on the arm **2 :** something that protects or hides

[2]**shield** *vb* **:** to protect or hide with a shield **syn** protect, guard, safeguard

shier *comparative of* SHY

shiest *superlative of* SHY

[1]**shift** \ˈshift\ *vb* **1 :** EXCHANGE, REPLACE **2 :** to change place, position, or direction **:** MOVE; *also* **:** to change gears **3 :** GET BY, MANAGE

[2]**shift** *n* **1 :** SCHEME, TRICK **2 :** a woman's slip or loose-fitting dress **3 :** a change in direction, emphasis, or attitude **4 :** a group working together alternating with other groups **5 :** TRANSFER **6 :** GEARSHIFT

shift·less \ˈshift-ləs\ *adj* **:** LAZY, INEFFICIENT — **shift·less·ness** *n*

shifty \ˈshif-tē\ *adj* **shift·i·er; -est 1 :** TRICKY; *also* **:** ELUSIVE **2 :** indicative of a tricky nature ⟨~ eyes⟩

shih tzu \ˈshēd-ˈzü, ˈshēt-ˈsü\ *n, pl* **shih tzus** *also* **shih tzu** *often cap S&T* **:** any of a breed of small short-legged dogs of Chinese origin that have a short muzzle and a long dense coat

shill \ˈshil\ *n* **:** one who acts as a decoy (as for a pitchman) — **shill** *vb*

shil·le·lagh *also* **shil·la·lah** \shə-ˈlā-lē\ *n* [*Shillelagh*, town in Ireland] **:** CUDGEL, CLUB

shil·ling \ˈshi-liŋ\ *n* — see MONEY TABLE

shilly–shally \ˈshi-lē-ˌsha-lē\ *vb* **shilly–shall·ied; shilly–shally·ing 1 :** to show hesitation or lack of decisiveness **2 :** to waste time

shim \ˈshim\ *n* **:** a thin often tapered piece of wood, metal, or stone used (as in leveling) to fill in space

shim·mer \ˈshi-mər\ *vb* **:** to shine waveringly or tremulously **:** GLIMMER **syn** flash, gleam, glint, sparkle, glitter — **shimmer** *n* — **shim·mery** *adj*

shim·my \ˈshi-mē\ *n, pl* **shimmies :** an abnormal vibration esp. in the front wheels of a motor vehicle — **shimmy** *vb*

[1]**shin** \ˈshin\ *n* **:** the front part of the leg below the knee

[2]**shin** *vb* **shinned; shin·ning :** to climb (as a pole) by gripping alternately with arms or hands and legs

shin·bone \ˈshin-ˌbōn\ *n* **:** TIBIA

[1]**shine** \ˈshīn\ *vb* **shone** \ˈshōn\ *or* **shined; shin·ing 1 :** to give or cause to give light **2 :** GLEAM, GLITTER **3 :** to be eminent, conspicuous, or distinguished ⟨gave her a chance to ~⟩ **4 :** POLISH ⟨~ your shoes⟩

[2]**shine** *n* **1 :** BRIGHTNESS, RADIANCE **2 :** LUSTER, BRILLIANCE **3 :** fair weather **:** SUNSHINE ⟨rain or ~⟩ **4 :** LIKING, FANCY ⟨took a ~ to them⟩ **5 :** a polish given to shoes

shin·er \ˈshī-nər\ *n* **1 :** a small silvery fish; *esp* **:** any of numerous small freshwater American fishes related to the carp **2 :** a discoloration of the skin around the eye due to bruising

[1]**shin·gle** \ˈshiŋ-gəl\ *n* **1 :** a small thin piece of building material used in overlapping rows for covering a roof or outside wall **2 :** a small sign

[2]**shingle** *vb* **shin·gled; shin·gling :** to cover with shingles

[3]**shingle** *n* **:** a beach strewn with gravel; *also* **:** coarse gravel (as on a beach)

shin·gles \ˈshiŋ-gəlz\ *n* **:** an acute inflammation of the spinal and cranial nerves caused by reactivation of the chicken pox virus and associated with eruptions and pain along the course of the affected nerves

shin·ny \ˈshi-nē\ *vb* **shin·nied; shin·ny·ing :** SHIN

shin·splints \ˈshin-ˌsplints\ *n sing or pl* **:** a condition marked by pain and sometimes tenderness and swelling in the shin caused by repeated small injuries to muscles and associated tissue esp. from running

Shin·to \ˈshin-ˌtō\ *n* **:** the indigenous religion of Japan consisting esp. in reverence of the spirits of natural forces and imperial ancestors — **Shin·to·ism** *n* — **Shin·to·ist** *n or adj*

shiny \ˈshī-nē\ *adj* **shin·i·er; -est :** BRIGHT, RADIANT; *also* **:** POLISHED

[1]**ship** \ˈship\ *n* **1 :** a large oceangoing boat **2 :** a ship's officers and crew **3 :** AIRSHIP, AIRCRAFT, SPACECRAFT

[2]**ship** *vb* **shipped; ship·ping 1 :** to put or receive on board a ship for transportation **2 :** to have transported by a carrier **3 :** to take or draw into a boat ⟨~ oars⟩ ⟨~ water⟩ **4 :** to engage to serve on a ship — **ship·per** *n*

-ship \ˌship\ *n suffix* **1 :** state **:** condition **:** quality ⟨friend*ship*⟩ **2 :** office **:** dignity **:** profession ⟨lord*ship*⟩ ⟨clerk*ship*⟩ **3 :** art **:** skill ⟨horseman*ship*⟩ **4 :** something showing, exhibiting, or embodying a quality or state ⟨town*ship*⟩ **5 :** one entitled to a (specified) rank, title, or appellation ⟨his Lord*ship*⟩ **6 :** the body of persons engaged in a specified activity ⟨reader*ship*⟩

ship·board \ˈship-ˌbōrd\ *n* **:** SHIP

ship·build·er \-ˌbil-dər\ *n* **:** one who designs or builds ships

ship·fit·ter \-ˌfi-tər\ *n* **1 :** one who constructs ships **2 :** a naval enlisted man who works as a plumber
ship·mate \-ˌmāt\ *n* **:** a fellow sailor
ship·ment \-mənt\ *n* **:** the process of shipping; *also* **:** the goods shipped
ship·ping *n* **1 :** SHIPS; *esp* **:** ships in one port or belonging to one country **2 :** transportation of goods
ship·shape \ˈship-ˌshāp\ *adj* **:** TRIM, TIDY
ship·worm \-ˌwərm\ *n* **:** any of various wormlike marine clams that burrow in wood and damage wooden ships and wharves
[1]**ship·wreck** \-ˌrek\ *n* **1 :** a wrecked ship **2 :** destruction or loss of a ship **3 :** total loss or failure **:** RUIN
[2]**shipwreck** *vb* **:** to cause or meet disaster at sea through destruction or foundering
ship·wright \ˈship-ˌrīt\ *n* **:** a carpenter skilled in ship construction and repair
ship·yard \-ˌyärd\ *n* **:** a place where ships are built or repaired
shire \ˈshīr, *in place-name compounds* ˌshir, shər\ *n* **:** a county in Great Britain
shirk \ˈshərk\ *vb* **:** to avoid performing (duty or work) — **shirk·er** *n*
shirr \ˈshər\ *vb* **1 :** to make shirring in **2 :** to bake (eggs removed from the shell) until set
shirr·ing \ˈshər-iŋ\ *n* **:** a decorative gathering in cloth made by drawing up parallel lines of stitches

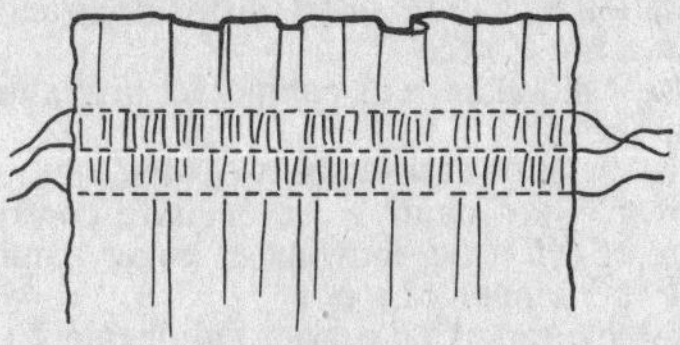

shirring

shirt \ˈshərt\ *n* **1 :** a loose cloth garment usu. having a collar, sleeves, a front opening, and a tail long enough to be tucked inside trousers or a skirt **2 :** UNDERSHIRT — **shirt·less** *adj*
shirt·ing \ˈshir-tiŋ\ *n* **:** cloth suitable for making shirts
shish ke·bab \ˈshish-kə-ˌbäb\ *n* [Turk *şiş kebabı*, fr. *şiş* spit + *kebap* roast meat] **:** kabob cooked on skewers
shiv \ˈshiv\ *n, slang* **:** KNIFE
[1]**shiv·er** \ˈshi-vər\ *vb* **:** TREMBLE, QUIVER **syn** shudder, quaver, shake, quake
[2]**shiver** *n* **:** an instance of shivering — **shiv·ery** *adj*
[1]**shoal** \ˈshōl\ *n* **1 :** SHALLOW **2 :** a sandbank or bar creating a shallow
[2]**shoal** *n* **:** a large group (as of fish)
shoat \ˈshōt\ *n* **:** a weaned young pig
[1]**shock** \ˈshäk\ *n* **:** a pile of sheaves of grain or cornstalks set up in a field
[2]**shock** *n* [MF *choc*, fr. *choquer* to strike against] **1 :** a sharp impact or violent shake or jar **2 :** a sudden violent mental or emotional disturbance **3 :** a state of bodily collapse caused esp. by crushing wounds, blood loss, or burns **4 :** the effect of a charge of electricity passing through the body **5 :** an attack of stroke or heart disease **6 :** SHOCK ABSORBER — **shock·proof** \-ˌprüf\ *adj*
[3]**shock** *vb* **1 :** to strike with surprise, horror, or disgust **2 :** to subject to the action of an electrical discharge
[4]**shock** *n* **:** a thick bushy mass (as of hair)
shock absorber *n* **:** any of several devices for absorbing the energy of sudden shocks in machinery
shock·er \ˈshä-kər\ *n* **:** one that shocks; *esp* **:** a sensational work of fiction or drama
shock·ing *adj* **:** extremely startling and offensive — **shock·ing·ly** *adv*
shock therapy *n* **:** the treatment of mental disorder by induction of coma or convulsions by drugs or electricity
shock wave *n* **:** a wave formed by the sudden violent compression of the medium through which it travels
[1]**shod·dy** \ˈshä-dē\ *n* **1 :** wool reclaimed from old rags; *also* **:** a fabric made from it **2 :** inferior or imitation material
[2]**shoddy** *adj* **shod·di·er; -est 1 :** made of shoddy **2 :** poorly done or made — **shod·di·ly** \ˈshä-də-lē\ *adv* — **shod·di·ness** \-dē-nəs\ *n*
[1]**shoe** \ˈshü\ *n* **1 :** a covering for the human foot **2 :** HORSESHOE **3 :** the part of a brake that presses on the wheel
[2]**shoe** *vb* **shod** \ˈshäd\ *also* **shoed** \ˈshüd\; **shoe·ing :** to put a shoe or shoes on
shoe·lace \ˈshü-ˌlās\ *n* **:** a lace or string for fastening a shoe
shoe·mak·er \-ˌmā-kər\ *n* **:** one who makes or repairs shoes
shoe·string \-ˌstriŋ\ *n* **1 :** SHOELACE **2 :** a small sum of money
sho·gun \ˈshō-gən\ *n* [Jp *shōgun* general] **:** any of a line of military governors ruling Japan until the revolution of 1867–68
shone *past and past part of* SHINE
shook *past of* SHAKE
shook–up \(ˌ)shu̇k-ˈəp\ *adj* **:** nervously upset **:** AGITATED
[1]**shoot** \ˈshüt\ *vb* **shot** \ˈshät\; **shoot·ing 1 :** to drive (as an arrow or bullet) forward quickly or forcibly **2 :** to hit, kill, or wound with a missile **3 :** to cause a missile to be driven forth or forth from ⟨∼ a gun⟩ **4 :** to send forth (as a ray of light) **5 :** to thrust forward or out **6 :** to pass rapidly along ⟨∼ the rapids⟩ **7 :** PHOTOGRAPH, FILM **8 :** to move swiftly **:** DART **9 :** to grow by or as if by sending out shoots; *also* **:** MATURE, DEVELOP — **shoot·er** *n*
[2]**shoot** *n* **1 :** a plant stem with its leaves and branches esp. when not yet mature **2 :** an act of shooting **3 :** a shooting match
shooting iron *n* **:** FIREARM
shooting star *n* **:** METEOR 2
shoot up *vb* **:** to inject a narcotic into a vein
[1]**shop** \ˈshäp\ *n* [ME *shoppe*, fr. OE *sceoppa* booth] **1 :** a place where things are made or worked on **:** FACTORY, MILL **2 :** a retail store ⟨dress ∼⟩
[2]**shop** *vb* **shopped; shop·ping :** to visit stores for purchasing or examining goods — **shop·per** *n*
shop·keep·er \ˈshäp-ˌkē-pər\ *n* **:** a retail merchant
shop·lift \-ˌlift\ *vb* **:** to steal goods on display from a store — **shop·lift·er** *n*
shop·talk \-tȯk\ *n* **:** talk about one's business or special interests
shop·worn \-ˌwōrn\ *adj* **:** soiled or frayed from much handling in a store
[1]**shore** \ˈshōr\ *n* **:** land along the edge of a body of water — **shore·less** *adj*
[2]**shore** *vb* **shored; shor·ing :** to give support to **:** BRACE
[3]**shore** *n* **:** [1]PROP
shore·bird \-ˌbərd\ *n* **:** any of a suborder of birds (as the plovers and sandpipers) mostly found along the seashore
shore patrol *n* **:** a branch of a navy that exercises guard and police functions
shor·ing \ˈshōr-iŋ\ *n* **:** a group of things that shore something up
shorn *past part of* SHEAR
[1]**short** \ˈshȯrt\ *adj* **1 :** not long or tall **2 :** not great in distance **3 :** brief in time **4 :** not coming up to standard or to an expected amount **5 :** CURT, ABRUPT **6 :** insufficiently supplied **7 :** made with shortening **:** FLAKY **8 :** consisting of or relating to a sale of securities or commodities that the seller does not possess or has not contracted for at the time of the sale ⟨∼ sale⟩ — **short·ness** *n*

²short *adv* **1 :** ABRUPTLY, CURTLY **2 :** at some point before a goal aimed at
³short *n* **1 :** something shorter than normal or standard **2** *pl* **:** drawers or trousers of less than knee length **3 :** SHORT CIRCUIT
⁴short *vb* **:** SHORT-CIRCUIT
short•age \ˈshȯr-tij\ *n* **:** LACK, DEFICIT
short•cake \ˈshȯrt-ˌkāk\ *n* **:** a dessert consisting of short biscuit spread with sweetened fruit
short•change \-ˈchānj\ *vb* **:** to cheat esp. by giving less than the correct amount of change
short circuit *n* **:** a connection made between points in an electric circuit where current is not intended to flow — **short–circuit** *vb*
short•com•ing \ˈshȯrt-ˌkə-miŋ\ *n* **:** FAULT 1, FAILING
short•cut \-ˌkət\ *n* **1 :** a route more direct than that usu. taken **2 :** a quicker way of doing something
short•en \ˈshȯrt-ᵊn\ *vb* **:** to make or become short **syn** curtail, abbreviate, abridge, retrench
short•en•ing \ˈshȯrt-ᵊn-iŋ\ *n* **:** a substance (as lard or butter) that makes pastry tender and flaky
short•hand \ˈshȯrt-ˌhand\ *n* **:** a method of writing rapidly by using symbols and abbreviations for letters, words, or phrases **:** STENOGRAPHY
short•hand•ed \ˌshȯrt-ˈhan-dəd\ *adj* **:** short of the needed number of people
short•horn \ˈshȯrt-ˌhȯrn\ *n, often cap* **:** any of a breed of red, roan, or white cattle of English origin
short hundredweight *n* — see WEIGHT table
short–lived \ˈshȯrt-ˌlivd, -ˈlīvd\ *adj* **:** of short life or duration
short•ly \ˈshȯrt-lē\ *adv* **1 :** in a few words **2 :** in a short time **:** SOON
short order *n* **:** an order for food that can be quickly cooked
short shrift *n* **1 :** a brief respite from death **2 :** little consideration
short•sight•ed \ˈshȯrt-ˌsī-təd\ *adj* **1 :** NEARSIGHTED **2 :** lacking foresight — **short•sight•ed•ness** *n*
short•stop \-ˌstäp\ *n* **:** a baseball player defending the area between second and third base
short story *n* **:** a short work of fiction usu. dealing with a few characters and a single event
short–tem•pered \ˌshȯrt-ˈtem-pərd\ *adj* **:** having a quick temper
short–term \ˈshȯrt-ˌtərm\ *adj* **1 :** occurring over or involving a relatively short period of time **2 :** of or relating to a financial transaction based on a term usu. of less than a year
short ton *n* — see WEIGHT table
short•wave \ˈshȯrt-ˌwāv\ *n* **:** a radio wave with a wavelength between 10 and 100 meters
Sho•sho•ne *or* **Sho•sho•ni** \shə-ˈshō-nē\ *n, pl* **Shoshones** *or* **Shoshoni :** a member of an American Indian people orig. ranging through California, Idaho, Nevada, Utah, and Wyoming
¹shot \ˈshät\ *n* **1 :** an act of shooting **2 :** a stroke or throw in some games **3 :** something that is shot **:** MISSILE, PROJECTILE; *esp* **:** small pellets forming a charge for a shotgun **4 :** a metal sphere that is thrown for distance in the shot put **5 :** RANGE, REACH **6 :** MARKSMAN **7 :** a single photographic exposure **8 :** a single sequence of a motion picture or a television program made by one camera **9 :** an injection (as of medicine) into the body **10 :** a small serving of undiluted liquor
²shot *past and past part of* SHOOT
shot•gun \ˈshät-ˌgən\ *n* **:** a gun with a smooth bore used to fire shot at short range
shot put *n* **:** a field event in which a shot is heaved for distance
should \ˈshu̇d, shəd\ *past of* SHALL — used as an auxiliary to express condition, obligation or propriety, probability, or futurity from a point of view in the past
¹shoul•der \ˈshōl-dər\ *n* **1 :** the part of the body of a person or animal where the arm or foreleg joins the body **2 :** either edge of a roadway **3 :** a rounded or sloping part (as of a bottle) where the neck joins the body
²shoulder *vb* **1 :** to push or thrust with the shoulder **2 :** to bear on the shoulder **3 :** to take the responsibility of
shoulder belt *n* **:** an automobile safety belt worn across the torso and over the shoulder
shoulder blade *n* **:** a flat triangular bone at the back of each shoulder
shout \ˈshau̇t\ *vb* **:** to utter a sudden loud cry — **shout** *n*
shove \ˈshəv\ *vb* **shoved; shov•ing :** to push along, aside, or away — **shove** *n*
¹shov•el \ˈshə-vəl\ *n* **1 :** a broad long-handled scoop used to lift and throw material **2 :** the amount a shovel will hold
²shovel *vb* **-eled** *or* **-elled; -el•ing** *or* **-el•ling 1 :** to take up and throw with a shovel **2 :** to dig or clean out with a shovel
¹show \ˈshō\ *vb* **showed** \ˈshōd\; **shown** \ˈshōn\ *or* **showed; show•ing 1 :** to cause or permit to be seen **:** EXHIBIT ⟨~ anger⟩ **2 :** CONFER, BESTOW ⟨~ mercy⟩ **3 :** REVEAL, DISCLOSE ⟨~*ed* courage in battle⟩ **4 :** INSTRUCT ⟨~ me how⟩ **5 :** PROVE ⟨~*s* he was guilty⟩ **6 :** APPEAR **7 :** to be noticeable **8 :** to be third in a horse race
²show *n* **1 :** a demonstrative display **2 :** outward appearance ⟨a ~ of resistance⟩ **3 :** SPECTACLE **4 :** a theatrical presentation **5 :** a radio or television program **6 :** third place in a horse race
¹show•case \ˈshō-ˌkās\ *n* **:** a cabinet for displaying items (as in a store)
²showcase *vb* **show•cased; show•cas•ing :** EXHIBIT
show•down \ˈshō-ˌdau̇n\ *n* **:** a decisive confrontation or contest; *esp* **:** the showing of poker hands to determine the winner of a pot
¹show•er \ˈshau̇-ər\ *n* **1 :** a brief fall of rain **2 :** a party given by friends who bring gifts **3 :** a bath in which water is showered on the person; *also* **:** a facility (as a stall) for such a bath — **show•ery** *adj*
²shower *vb* **1 :** to rain or fall in a shower **2 :** to bathe in a shower
show•man \ˈshō-mən\ *n* **:** one having a gift for dramatization and visual effectiveness — **show•man•ship** *n*
show–off \ˈshō-ˌȯf\ *n* **:** one that seeks to attract attention by conspicuous behavior
show off *vb* **1 :** to display proudly **2 :** to act as a show-off
show•piece \ˈshō-ˌpēs\ *n* **:** an outstanding example used for exhibition
show•place \-ˌplās\ *n* **:** an estate or building that is a showpiece
show up *vb* **:** ARRIVE
showy \ˈshō-ē\ *adj* **show•i•er; -est :** superficially impressive or striking — **show•i•ly** \ˈshō-ə-lē\ *adv* — **show•i•ness** \-ē-nəs\ *n*
shpt *abbr* shipment
shrap•nel \ˈshrap-nəl\ *n, pl* **shrapnel :** bomb, mine, or shell fragments
¹shred \ˈshred\ *n* **:** a narrow strip cut or torn off **:** a small fragment
²shred *vb* **shred•ded; shred•ding :** to cut or tear into shreds
shrew \ˈshrü\ *n* **1 :** any of a family of very small mammals with velvety fur that are related to the moles **2 :** a scolding woman
shrewd \ˈshrüd\ *adj* **:** CLEVER, ASTUTE — **shrewdly** *adv* — **shrewd•ness** *n*
shrew•ish \ˈshrü-ish\ *adj* **:** having an irritable disposition **:** ILL-TEMPERED
shriek \ˈshrēk\ *n* **:** a shrill cry **:** SCREAM, YELL — **shriek** *vb*
shrift \ˈshrift\ *n, archaic* **:** the act of shriving
shrike \ˈshrīk\ *n* **:** any of numerous usu. largely grayish

or brownish birds that often impale their usu. insect prey upon thorns before devouring it

[1]**shrill** \ˈshril\ *vb* : to make a high-pitched piercing sound

[2]**shrill** *adj* : high-pitched : PIERCING ⟨~ whistle⟩ — **shril•ly** *adv*

shrimp \ˈshrimp\ *n, pl* **shrimps** *or* **shrimp 1** : any of various small marine crustaceans related to the lobsters **2** : a small or puny person

shrine \ˈshrīn\ *n* [ME, receptacle for the relics of a saint, fr. OE *scrīn*, fr. L *scrinium* case, chest] **1** : the tomb of a saint; *also* : a place where devotion is paid to a saint or deity **2** : a place or object hallowed by its associations

[1]**shrink** \ˈshriŋk\ *vb* **shrank** \ˈshraŋk\ *also* **shrunk** \ˈshrəŋk\; **shrunk** *or* **shrunk•en** \ˈshrəŋ-kən\; **shrink•ing 1** : to draw back or away **2** : to become smaller or more compact **3** : to lessen in value **syn** contract, constrict, compress, condense — **shrink•able** *adj*

[2]**shrink** *n* : a clinical psychiatrist or psychologist

shrink•age \ˈshriŋ-kij\ *n* **1** : the act of shrinking **2** : the amount lost by shrinkage

shrive \ˈshrīv\ *vb* **shrived** *or* **shrove** \ˈshrōv\; **shriv•en** \ˈshri-vən\ *or* **shrived** [ME, fr. OE *scrīfan* to prescribe, allot, shrive, fr. L *scribere* to write] : to minister the sacrament of penance to

shriv•el \ˈshri-vəl\ *vb* **-eled** *or* **-elled; -el•ing** *or* **-el•ling** : to shrink and draw into wrinkles : DWINDLE

[1]**shroud** \ˈshraủd\ *n* **1** : something that covers or screens **2** : a cloth placed over a dead body **3** : any of the ropes leading from the masthead of a ship to the side to support the mast

[2]**shroud** *vb* : to veil or screen from view

shrub \ˈshrəb\ *n* : a low usu. several-stemmed woody plant — **shrub•by** *adj*

shrub•bery \ˈshrə-bə-rē\ *n, pl* **-ber•ies** : a planting or growth of shrubs

shrug \ˈshrəg\ *vb* **shrugged; shrug•ging** : to hunch (the shoulders) up to express aloofness, indifference, or uncertainty — **shrug** *n*

shrug off *vb* **1** : to brush aside : MINIMIZE **2** : to shake off **3** : to remove (a garment) by wriggling out

[1]**shuck** \ˈshək\ *n* : SHELL, HUSK

[2]**shuck** *vb* : to strip of shucks

shud•der \ˈshə-dər\ *vb* : TREMBLE, QUAKE — **shudder** *n*

shuf•fle \ˈshə-fəl\ *vb* **shuf•fled; shuf•fling 1** : to mix in a disorderly mass **2** : to rearrange the order of (cards in a pack) by mixing two parts of the pack together **3** : to shift from place to place **4** : to move with a sliding or dragging gait **5** : to dance in a slow lagging manner — **shuffle** *n*

shuf•fle•board \ˈshə-fəl-ˌbōrd\ *n* : a game in which players use long-handled cues to shove disks into scoring areas marked on a smooth surface

shun \ˈshən\ *vb* **shunned; shun•ning** : to avoid deliberately or habitually **syn** evade, elude, escape, duck

[1]**shunt** \ˈshənt\ *vb* [ME, to flinch] : to turn off to one side; *esp* : to switch (a train) from one track to another

[2]**shunt** *n* **1** : a method or device for turning or thrusting aside **2** : a conductor joining two points in an electrical circuit forming an alternate path through which a portion of the current may pass

shut \ˈshət\ *vb* **shut; shut•ting 1** : CLOSE **2** : to forbid entrance into **3** : to lock up **4** : to fold together ⟨~ a penknife⟩ **5** : to cease or suspend activity ⟨~ down an assembly line⟩

shut•down \-ˌdaủn\ *n* : a temporary cessation of activity (as in a factory)

shut–in \ˈshət-ˌin\ *n* : an invalid confined to home, a room, or bed

shut•out \ˈshət-ˌaủt\ *n* : a game or contest in which one side fails to score

shut out *vb* **1** : EXCLUDE **2** : to prevent (an opponent) from scoring in a game or contest

shut•ter \ˈshə-tər\ *n* **1** : a movable cover for a door or window : BLIND **2** : the part of a camera that opens and closes to expose the film

shut•ter•bug \ˈshə-tər-ˌbəg\ *n* : a photography enthusiast

[1]**shut•tle** \ˈshət-əl\ *n* **1** : an instrument used in weaving for passing the horizontal threads between the vertical threads **2** : a vehicle traveling back and forth over a short route ⟨a ~ bus⟩ **3** : SPACE SHUTTLE

[2]**shuttle** *vb* **shut•tled; shut•tling** : to move back and forth frequently

shut•tle•cock \ˈshət-əl-ˌkäk\ *n* : a light conical object (as of cork or plastic) used in badminton

shut up *vb* : to cease or cause to cease talking

[1]**shy** \ˈshī\ *adj* **shi•er** *or* **shy•er** \ˈshī-ər\; **shi•est** *or* **shy•est** \ˈshī-əst\ **1** : easily frightened : TIMID **2** : WARY **3** : BASHFUL **4** : DEFICIENT, LACKING — **shy•ly** *adv* — **shy•ness** *n*

[2]**shy** *vb* **shied; shy•ing 1** : to show a dislike : RECOIL **2** : to start suddenly aside through fright ⟨the horse *shied*⟩

shy•ster \ˈshīs-tər\ *n* : an unscrupulous lawyer or politician

Si *symbol* silicon

Si•a•mese \ˌsī-ə-ˈmēz, -ˈmēs\ *n, pl* **Sia•mese** : THAI — **Siamese** *adj*

Siamese twin *n* [fr. Chang †1874 and Eng †1874 twins born in Siam with bodies united] : one of a pair of twins with bodies joined together at birth

[1]**sib•i•lant** \ˈsi-bə-lənt\ *adj* : having, containing, or producing the sound of or a sound resembling that of the *s* or the *sh* in *sash* — **sib•i•lant•ly** *adv*

[2]**sibilant** *n* : a sibilant speech sound (as English \s\, \z\, \sh\, \zh\, \ch (=tsh)\, or \j (=dzh)\)

sib•ling \ˈsi-bliŋ\ *n* : a brother or sister considered irrespective of sex; *also* : one of two or more offspring having one common parent

sib•yl \ˈsi-bəl\ *n, often cap* : PROPHETESS — **sib•yl•line** \-bə-ˌlīn, -ˌlēn\ *adj*

sic \ˈsik, ˈsēk\ *adv* : intentionally so written — used after a printed word or passage to indicate that it exactly reproduces an original ⟨said he seed [~] it all⟩

sick \ˈsik\ *adj* **1** : not in good health : ILL; *also* : of, relating to, or intended for use in sickness ⟨~ pay⟩ **2** : NAUSEATED **3** : DISGUSTED **4** : PINING **5** : MACABRE, SADISTIC ⟨~ jokes⟩ — **sick•ly** *adj*

sick•bed \ˈsik-ˌbed\ *n* : a bed on which one lies sick

sick•en \ˈsi-kən\ *vb* : to make or become sick — **sick•en•ing•ly** *adv*

sick•le \ˈsi-kəl\ *n* : a cutting tool consisting of a curved metal blade with a short handle

sickle–cell anemia *n* : an inherited anemia in which red blood cells tend to become crescent-shaped and cannot carry oxygen properly and which occurs esp. in individuals of African, Mediterranean, or southwest Asian ancestry

sick•ness \ˈsik-nəs\ *n* **1** : ill health; *also* : a specific disease **2** : NAUSEA

side \ˈsīd\ *n* **1** : the right or left part of the trunk of a body **2** : a place away from a central point or line **3** : a border of an object; *esp* : one of the longer borders as contrasted with an end **4** : an outer surface of an object **5** : a position regarded as opposite to another **6** : a body of contestants — **side** *adj*

side•arm \-ˌärm\ *adj* : made with a sideways sweep of the arm — **sidearm** *adv*

side arm *n* : a weapon worn at the side or in the belt

side•bar \ˈsīd-ˌbär\ *n* : a short news story accompanying a major story and presenting related information

side•board \-ˌbōrd\ *n* : a piece of dining-room furniture for holding articles of table service

side•burns \-ˌbərnz\ *n pl* : whiskers on the side of the face in front of the ears

side by side *adv* **1** : beside one another **2** : in the same

DICTIONARY

place, time, or circumstance — **side–by–side** *adj*
side•car \-ˌkär\ *n* : a one-wheeled passenger car attached to the side of a motorcycle
side effect *n* : a secondary and usu. adverse effect (as of a drug)
side•kick \ˈsīd-ˌkik\ *n* : PAL, PARTNER
[1]**side•long** \ˈsīd-ˌlȯŋ\ *adv* : in the direction of or along the side : OBLIQUELY
[2]**sidelong** *adj* : directed to one side ⟨~ look⟩
side•man \ˈsīd-ˌman\ *n* : a member of a jazz or swing orchestra
side•piece \-ˌpēs\ *n* : a piece forming or contained in the side of something
si•de•re•al \sī-ˈdir-ē-əl, sə-\ *adj* [L *sidereus*, fr. *sider-, sidas* star, constellation] **1** : of or relating to the stars **2** : measured by the apparent motion of the stars
side•sad•dle \ˈsīd-ˌsad-ᵊl\ *n* : a saddle for women on which the rider sits with both legs on the same side of the horse — **sidesaddle** *adv*
side•show \ˈsīd-ˌshō\ *n* **1** : a minor show offered in addition to a main exhibition (as of a circus) **2** : an incidental diversion
side•step \-ˌstep\ *vb* **1** : to step aside **2** : AVOID, EVADE
side•stroke \-ˌstrōk\ *n* : a swimming stroke which is executed on the side and in which the arms are swept backward and downward and the legs do a scissors kick
side•swipe \-ˌswīp\ *vb* : to strike with a glancing blow along the side — **sideswipe** *n*
[1]**side•track** \-ˌtrak\ *n* : SIDING 1
[2]**sidetrack** *vb* **1** : to switch from a main railroad line to a siding **2** : to turn aside from a purpose
side•walk \ˈsīd-ˌwȯk\ *n* : a paved walk at the side of a road or street
side•wall \-ˌwȯl\ *n* **1** : a wall forming the side of something **2** : the side of an automobile tire
side•ways \-ˌwāz\ *adv or adj* **1** : from the side **2** : with one side to the front **3** : to, toward, or at one side
side•wind•er \-ˌwīn-dər\ *n* : a small pale-colored desert rattlesnake of the southwestern U.S.
sid•ing \ˈsī-diŋ\ *n* **1** : a short railroad track connected with the main track **2** : material (as boards) covering the outside of frame buildings
si•dle \ˈsīd-ᵊl\ *vb* **si•dled; si•dling** : to move sideways or with one side foremost
SIDS *abbr* sudden infant death syndrome
siege \ˈsēj\ *n* **1** : the placing of an army around or before a fortified place to force its surrender **2** : a persistent attack (as of illness)
sie•mens \ˈsē-mənz, ˈzē-\ *n* : a unit of conductance equivalent to one ampere per volt
si•er•ra \sē-ˈer-ə\ *n* [Sp, lit., saw, fr. L *serra*] : a range of mountains esp. with jagged peaks
si•es•ta \sē-ˈes-tə\ *n* [Sp, fr. L *sexta (hora)* noon, lit., sixth hour] : a midday rest or nap
sieve \ˈsiv\ *n* : a utensil with meshes or holes to separate finer particles from coarser or solids from liquids
sift \ˈsift\ *vb* **1** : to pass through a sieve **2** : to separate with or as if with a sieve **3** : to examine carefully **4** : to scatter by or as if by passing through a sieve — **sift•er** *n*
sig *abbr* **1** signal **2** signature
sigh \ˈsī\ *vb* **1** : to let out a deep audible breath (as in weariness or sorrow) **2** : GRIEVE, YEARN — **sigh** *n*
[1]**sight** \ˈsīt\ *n* **1** : something seen or worth seeing **2** : the process or power of seeing; *esp* : the sense of which the eye is the receptor and by which qualities of appearance (as position, shape, and color) are perceived **3** : INSPECTION **4** : a device (as a small bead on a gun barrel) that aids the eye in aiming **5** : VIEW, GLIMPSE **6** : the range of vision — **sight•less** *adj*
[2]**sight** *vb* **1** : to get sight of **2** : to aim by means of a sight
sight•ed \ˈsī-təd\ *adj* : having sight
sight•ly \-lē\ *adj* : pleasing to the sight
sight–see•ing \ˈsīt-ˌsē-iŋ\ *adj* : engaged in or used for seeing sights of interest — **sight•seer** \-ˌsē-ər\ *n*
sig•ma \ˈsig-mə\ *n* : the 18th letter of the Greek alphabet — Σ or σ or ς
[1]**sign** \ˈsīn\ *n* **1** : a gesture expressing a command, wish, or thought **2** : SYMBOL **3** : a notice publicly displayed for advertising purposes or for giving direction or warning **4** : OMEN, PORTENT **5** : TRACE, VESTIGE
[2]**sign** *vb* **1** : to mark with a sign **2** : to represent by a sign **3** : to make a sign or signal **4** : to write one's name on in token of assent or obligation **5** : to assign legally **6** : to use sign language — **sign•er** *n*
[1]**sig•nal** \ˈsig-nəl\ *n* **1** : a sign agreed on as the start of some joint action **2** : a sign giving warning or notice of something **3** : the message, sound, or image transmitted in electronic communication (as radio)
[2]**signal** *vb* **-naled** *or* **-nalled; -nal•ing** *or* **-nal•ling 1** : to notify by a signal **2** : to communicate by signals
[3]**signal** *adj* : DISTINGUISHED ⟨a ~ honor⟩ — **sig•nal•ly** *adv*
sig•nal•ise *Brit var of* SIGNALIZE
sig•nal•ize \ˈsig-nə-ˌlīz\ *vb* **-ized; -iz•ing** : to point out or make conspicuous — **sig•nal•i•za•tion** \ˌsig-nə-lə-ˈzā-shən\ *n*
sig•nal•man \ˈsig-nəl-mən, -ˌman\ *n* : a person who signals or works with signals
sig•na•to•ry \ˈsig-nə-ˌtōr-ē\ *n, pl* **-ries** : a person or government that signs jointly with others — **signatory** *adj*
sig•na•ture \ˈsig-nə-ˌchu̇r\ *n* **1** : the name of a person written by himself or herself **2** : the sign placed after the clef to indicate the key or the meter of a piece of music
sign•board \ˈsīn-ˌbōrd\ *n* : a board bearing a sign or notice
sig•net \ˈsig-nət\ *n* : a small intaglio seal (as in a ring)
sig•nif•i•cance \sig-ˈni-fi-kəns\ *n* **1** : something signified : MEANING **2** : SUGGESTIVENESS **3** : CONSEQUENCE, IMPORTANCE
sig•nif•i•cant \-kənt\ *adj* **1** : having meaning; *esp* : having a hidden or special meaning **2** : having or likely to have considerable influence or effect : IMPORTANT — **sig•nif•i•cant•ly** *adv*
sig•ni•fy \ˈsig-nə-ˌfī\ *vb* **-fied; -fy•ing 1** : to show by a sign **2** : MEAN, IMPORT **3** : to have significance — **sig•ni•fi•ca•tion** \ˌsig-nə-fə-ˈkā-shən\ *n*
sign in *vb* : to make a record of arrival (as by signing a register)
sign language *n* : a formal system of hand gestures used for communication (as by the deaf)
sign off *vb* : to announce the end (as of a program or broadcast)
sign of the cross : a gesture of the hand forming a cross (as to invoke divine blessing)
sign on *vb* **1** : ENLIST **2** : to announce the start of broadcasting for the day
sign out *vb* : to make a record of departure (as by signing a register)
sign•post \ˈsīn-ˌpōst\ *n* : a post bearing a sign
Sikh \ˈsēk\ *n* : an adherent of a religion of India marked by rejection of caste — **Sikh•ism** *n*
si•lage \ˈsī-lij\ *n* : fodder fermented (as in a silo) to produce a rich moist animal feed
[1]**si•lence** \ˈsī-ləns\ *n* **1** : the state of being silent **2** : STILLNESS **3** : SECRECY
[2]**silence** *vb* **si•lenced; si•lenc•ing 1** : to reduce to silence : STILL **2** : to cause to cease hostile firing or criticism
si•lenc•er \ˈsī-lən-sər\ *n* : a device for muffling the noise of a gunshot
si•lent \ˈsī-lənt\ *adj* **1** : not speaking : MUTE; *also* : TACITURN **2** : STILL, QUIET **3** : performed or borne without utterance **syn** reticent, reserved, closemouthed, close — **si•lent•ly** *adv*
[1]**sil•hou•ette** \ˌsi-lə-ˈwet\ *n* [F] **1** : a representation of the outlines of an object filled in with black or some other uniform color **2** : OUTLINE ⟨~ of a ship⟩

²silhouette *vb* **-ett•ed; -ett•ing :** to represent by a silhouette; *also* **:** to show against a light background

sil•i•ca \ˈsi-li-kə\ *n* **:** a mineral that consists of silicon and oxygen

sil•i•cate \ˈsi-lə-ˌkāt, ˈsi-li-kət\ *n* **:** a chemical salt that consists of a metal combined with silicon and oxygen

si•li•ceous *or* **si•li•cious** \sə-ˈli-shəs\ *adj* **:** of, relating to, or containing silica or a silicate

sil•i•con \ˈsi-li-kən, ˈsi-lə-ˌkän\ *n* **:** a nonmetallic chemical element that occurs in combination as the most abundant element next to oxygen in the earth's crust and is used esp. in electronics — see ELEMENT table

sil•i•cone \ˈsi-lə-ˌkōn\ *n* **:** an organic silicon compound used esp. for lubricants and varnishes

sil•i•co•sis \ˌsi-lə-ˈkō-səs\ *n* **:** a lung disease caused by prolonged inhaling of silica dusts

silk \ˈsilk\ *n* **1 :** a fine strong lustrous protein fiber produced by insect larvae usu. for their cocoons; *esp* **:** one from moth larvae (**silk•worms** \-ˌwərmz\) used for cloth **2 :** thread or cloth made from silk — **silk•en** \ˈsil-kən\ *adj* — **silky** *adj*

silk screen *n* **:** a stencil process in which coloring matter is forced through the meshes of a prepared silk or organdy screen; *also* **:** a print made by this process — **silk–screen** *vb*

sill \ˈsil\ *n* **:** a heavy crosspiece (as of wood or stone) that forms the bottom member of a window frame or a doorway; *also* **:** a horizontal supporting piece at the base of a structure

sil•ly \ˈsi-lē\ *adj* **sil•li•er; -est** [ME *sely, silly* happy, innocent, pitiable, feeble, fr. OE *sǣlig*] **:** FOOLISH, ABSURD, STUPID — **sil•li•ness** *n*

si•lo \ˈsī-lō\ *n, pl* **silos** [Sp] **1 :** a trench, pit, or esp. a tall cylinder for making and storing silage **2 :** an underground structure for housing a guided missile

¹silt \ˈsilt\ *n* **1 :** fine earth; *esp* **:** particles of such soil floating in rivers, ponds, or lakes **2 :** a deposit (as by a river) of silt — **silty** *adj*

²silt *vb* **:** to obstruct or cover with silt — **silt•ation** \sil-ˈtā-shən\ *n*

Si•lu•ri•an \sī-ˈlu̇r-ē-ən\ *adj* **:** of, relating to, or being the period of the Paleozoic era between the Ordovician and the Devonian marked by the appearance of the first land plants — **Silurian** *n*

¹sil•ver \ˈsil-vər\ *n* **1 :** a white ductile metallic chemical element that takes a high polish and is a better conductor of heat and electricity than any other substance — see ELEMENT table **2 :** coin made of silver **3 :** FLATWARE **4 :** a grayish white color — **sil•very** *adj*

²silver *adj* **1 :** relating to, made of, or coated with silver **2 :** SILVERY

³silver *vb* **sil•vered; sil•ver•ing :** to coat with or as if with silver — **sil•ver•er** *n*

silver bromide *n* **:** a light-sensitive compound used esp. in photography

sil•ver•fish \ˈsil-vər-ˌfish\ *n* **:** any of various small wingless insects found in houses and sometimes injurious esp. to sized paper and starched clothes

silver iodide *n* **:** a light-sensitive compound used in photography, rainmaking, and medicine

silver maple *n* **:** a No. American maple with deeply cut leaves that are green above and silvery white below

silver nitrate *n* **:** a soluble compound used in photography and as an antiseptic

sil•ver•ware \ˈsil-vər-ˌwar\ *n* **:** FLATWARE

sim•i•an \ˈsi-mē-ən\ *n* **:** MONKEY, APE — **simian** *adj*

sim•i•lar \ˈsi-mə-lər\ *adj* **:** marked by correspondence or resemblance **syn** alike, akin, comparable, parallel — **sim•i•lar•i•ty** \ˌsi-mə-ˈlar-ə-tē\ *n* — **sim•i•lar•ly** *adv*

sim•i•le \ˈsi-mə-(ˌ)lē\ *n* [ME, fr. L, likeness, comparison, fr. neut. of *similis* like, similar] **:** a figure of speech in which two dissimilar things are compared by the use of *like* or *as* (as in "cheeks like roses")

si•mil•i•tude \sə-ˈmi-lə-ˌtüd, -ˌtyüd\ *n* **:** LIKENESS, RESEMBLANCE

sim•mer \ˈsi-mər\ *vb* **sim•mered; sim•mer•ing 1 :** to stew at or just below the boiling point **2 :** to be on the point of bursting out with violence or emotional disturbance — **simmer** *n*

si•mo•nize \ˈsī-mə-ˌnīz\ *vb* **-nized; -niz•ing :** to polish with or as if with wax

si•mo•ny \ˈsī-mə-nē, ˈsi-\ *n* [ME *symonie,* fr. LL *simonia,* fr. *Simon* Magus sorcerer of Samaria in Acts 8:9–24] **:** the buying or selling of a church office

sim•pa•ti•co \sim-ˈpä-ti-ˌkō, -ˈpa-\ *adj* **:** CONGENIAL, LIKABLE

sim•per \ˈsim-pər\ *vb* **:** to smile in a silly manner — **simper** *n*

sim•ple \ˈsim-pəl\ *adj* **sim•pler** \-pə-lər\; **sim•plest** \-pə-ləst\ [ME, fr. OF, plain, uncomplicated, artless, fr. L *simplus, simplex,* lit., single; L *simplus* fr. *sim-* one + *-plus* multiplied by; L *simplex* fr. *sim-* + *-plex* -fold] **1 :** free from dishonesty or vanity **:** INNOCENT **2 :** free from ostentation **3 :** of humble origin or modest position **4 :** STUPID **5 :** not complex **:** PLAIN ⟨a ~ melody⟩ ⟨~ directions⟩ **6 :** lacking education, experience, or intelligence **7 :** developing from a single ovary ⟨a ~ fruit⟩ **syn** easy, facile, light, effortless — **sim•ple•ness** *n* — **sim•ply** *adv*

simple interest *n* **:** interest paid or computed on the original principal only of a loan or on the amount of an account

sim•ple•ton \ˈsim-pəl-tən\ *n* **:** FOOL

sim•plic•i•ty \sim-ˈpli-sə-tē\ *n* **1 :** lack of complication **:** CLEARNESS **2 :** CANDOR, ARTLESSNESS **3 :** plainness in manners or way of life **4 :** SILLINESS, FOLLY

sim•pli•fy \ˈsim-plə-ˌfī\ *vb* **-fied; -fy•ing :** to make less complex — **sim•pli•fi•ca•tion** \ˌsim-plə-fə-ˈkā-shən\ *n*

sim•plis•tic \sim-ˈplis-tik\ *adj* **:** excessively simple **:** tending to overlook complexities ⟨a ~ solution⟩

sim•u•late \ˈsim-yə-ˌlāt\ *vb* **-lat•ed; -lat•ing :** to give or create the effect or appearance of **:** IMITATE; *also* **:** to make a simulation of — **sim•u•la•tor** \ˈsim-yə-ˌlā-tər\ *n*

sim•u•la•tion \ˌsim-yə-ˈlā-shən\ *n* **1 :** the act or process of simulating **2 :** an object that is not genuine **3 :** the imitation by one system or process of the way in which another system or process works

si•mul•ta•ne•ous \ˌsī-məl-ˈtā-nē-əs, ˌsi-\ *adj* **:** occurring or operating at the same time — **si•mul•ta•ne•ous•ly** *adv* — **si•mul•ta•ne•ous•ness** *n*

¹sin \ˈsin\ *n* **1 :** an offense esp. against God **2 :** FAULT **3 :** a weakened state of human nature in which the self is estranged from God — **sin•less** *adj*

²sin *vb* **sinned; sin•ning :** to commit a sin — **sin•ner** *n*

¹since \ˈsins\ *adv* **1 :** from a past time until now **2 :** backward in time **:** AGO **3 :** after a time in the past

²since *conj* **1 :** from the time when **2 :** seeing that **:** BECAUSE

³since *prep* **1 :** in the period after ⟨changes made ~ the war⟩ **2 :** continuously from ⟨has been here ~ 1980⟩

sin•cere \sin-ˈsir\ *adj* **sin•cer•er; sin•cer•est 1 :** free from hypocrisy **:** HONEST **2 :** GENUINE, REAL — **sin•cere•ly** *adv* — **sin•cer•i•ty** \-ˈser-ə-tē\ *n*

si•ne•cure \ˈsī-ni-ˌkyu̇r, ˈsi-\ *n* **:** a paying job that requires little or no work

si•ne die \ˌsī-ni-ˈdī-ˌē, ˌsi-nā-ˈdē-ˌā\ *adv* [L, without day] **:** INDEFINITELY

si•ne qua non \ˌsi-ni-ˌkwä-ˈnän, -ˈnōn\ *n, pl* **sine qua nons** *also* **sine qui•bus non** \-ˌkwi-(ˌ)bu̇s-\ [LL, without which not] **:** something indispensable or essential

sin•ew \ˈsin-yü\ *n* **1 :** TENDON **2 :** physical strength — **sin•ewy** *adj*

sin•ful \ˈsin-fəl\ *adj* **:** marked by or full of sin **:** WICKED — **sin•ful•ly** *adv* — **sin•ful•ness** *n*

¹sing \ˈsiŋ\ *vb* **sang** \ˈsaŋ\ *or* **sung** \ˈsəŋ\; **sung; sing•ing 1 :** to produce musical tones with the voice; *also* **:** to utter with musical tones **2 :** to make a prolonged shrill sound ⟨locusts ~*ing*⟩ **3 :** to produce harmonious sustained sounds ⟨birds ~*ing*⟩ **4 :** CHANT, INTONE **5**

DICTIONARY

: to write poetry; *also* : to celebrate in song or verse **6** : to give information or evidence — **sing•er** *n*

[2]**sing** *abbr* singular

Sin•ga•por•ean \ˌsiŋ-ə-ˈpōr-ē-ən\ *n* : a native or inhabitant of Singapore — **Singaporean** *adj*

singe \ˈsinj\ *vb* **singed; singe•ing** : to scorch lightly the outside of; *esp* : to remove the hair or down from (a plucked fowl) with flame

[1]**sin•gle** \ˈsiŋ-gəl\ *adj* **1** : UNMARRIED **2** : being alone : being the only one **3** : having only one feature or part **4** : made for one person **syn** sole, unique, lone, solitary, separate, particular — **sin•gle•ness** *n* — **sin•gly** *adv*

[2]**single** *vb* **sin•gled; sin•gling 1** : to select (one) from a group **2** : to hit a single

[3]**single** *n* **1** : a separate person or thing; *also* : an unmarried person **2** : a hit in baseball that enables the batter to reach first base **3** *pl* : a tennis match with one player on each side

single bond *n* : a chemical bond in which one pair of electrons is shared by two atoms in a molecule

single–lens reflex *n* : a camera having a single lens that forms an image which is reflected to the viewfinder or recorded on film

sin•gle•tree \-ˌtrē\ *n* : WHIFFLETREE

sin•gu•lar \ˈsiŋ-gyə-lər\ *adj* **1** : of, relating to, or constituting a word form denoting one person, thing, or instance **2** : OUTSTANDING, EXCEPTIONAL **3** : of unusual quality **4** : ODD, PECULIAR — **singular** *n* — **sin•gu•lar•i•ty** \ˌsiŋ-gyə-ˈlar-ə-tē\ *n* — **sin•gu•lar•ly** *adv*

sin•is•ter \ˈsi-nəs-tər\ *adj* [ME, fr. L, on the left side, inauspicious] **1** : singularly evil or productive of evil **2** : accompanied by or leading to disaster **syn** baleful, malign, malefic, maleficent

[1]**sink** \ˈsiŋk\ *vb* **sank** \ˈsaŋk\ *or* **sunk** \ˈsəŋk\; **sunk; sink•ing 1** : SUBMERGE **2** : to descend lower and lower **3** : to grow less in volume or height **4** : to slope downward **5** : to penetrate downward **6** : to fail in health or strength **7** : LAPSE, DEGENERATE **8** : to cause (a ship) to descend to the bottom **9** : to make (a hole or shaft) by digging, boring, or cutting **10** : INVEST — **sink•able** *adj*

[2]**sink** *n* **1** : DRAIN, SEWER **2** : a basin connected with a drain **3** : an extensive depression in the land surface

sink•er \ˈsiŋ-kər\ *n* : a weight for sinking a fishing line or net

sink•hole \ˈsiŋk-ˌhōl\ *n* : a hollow place in which drainage collects

sin tax *n* : a tax on substances or activities considered sinful or harmful

sin•u•ous \ˈsin-yə-wəs\ *adj* : bending in and out : WINDING — **sin•u•os•i•ty** \ˌsin-yə-ˈwä-sə-tē\ *n*

si•nus \ˈsī-nəs\ *n* [ME, fr. ML, fr. L, curve, hollow] **1** : any of several cavities of the skull usu. connecting with the nostrils **2** : a space forming a channel (as for the passage of blood)

si•nus•itis \ˌsī-nə-ˈsī-təs\ *n* : inflammation of a sinus of the skull

Sioux \ˈsü\ *n, pl* **Sioux** *same or* ˈsüz\ [F] : DAKOTA

sip \ˈsip\ *vb* **sipped; sip•ping** : to drink in small quantities — **sip** *n*

[1]**si•phon** \ˈsī-fən\ *n* **1** : a bent tube through which a liquid can be transferred by means of air pressure up and over the edge of one container and into another container placed at a lower level **2** *usu* **sy•phon** : a bottle that ejects soda water through a tube when a valve is opened

[2]**siphon** *vb* **si•phoned; si•phon•ing** : to draw off by means of a siphon

sir \ˈsər\ *n* [ME *sire* sire, fr. OF, fr. L *senior,* compar. of *senex* old, old man] **1** : a man of rank or position — used as a title before the given name of a knight or baronet **2** — used as a usu. respectful form of address

Si•rach \ˈsī-rak, sə-ˈräk\ *n* — see BIBLE table

[1]**sire** \ˈsīr\ *n* **1** : FATHER; *also, archaic* : FOREFATHER **2** *archaic* : LORD — used as a form of address and a title **3** : the male parent of an animal (as a horse or dog)

siphon 1

[2]**sire** *vb* **sired; sir•ing** : BEGET

si•ren \ˈsī-rən\ *n* **1** : a seductive or alluring woman **2** : an electrically operated device for producing a loud shrill warning signal — **siren** *adj*

sir•loin \ˈsər-ˌlȯin\ *n* [alter. of earlier *surloin,* modif. of MF *surlonge,* fr. *sur* over (fr. L *super*) + *longe* loin] : a cut of beef taken from the part in front of the round

sirup *var of* SYRUP

si•sal \ˈsī-səl, -zəl\ *n* : a strong cordage fiber from an agave; *also* : this agave

sis•sy \ˈsi-sē\ *n, pl* **sissies** : an effeminate boy or man; *also* : a timid or cowardly person

sis•ter \ˈsis-tər\ *n* **1** : a female having one or both parents in common with another individual **2** : a member of a religious order of women : NUN **3** *chiefly Brit* : NURSE **4** : a woman regarded as a comrade — **sis•ter•ly** *adj*

sis•ter•hood \-ˌhu̇d\ *n* **1** : the state of being a sister **2** : a community or society of sisters **3** : the solidarity of women based on shared conditions

sis•ter–in–law \ˈsis-tə-rən-ˌlȯ\ *n, pl* **sisters–in–law** : the sister of one's spouse; *also* : the wife of one's brother

sit \ˈsit\ *vb* **sat** \ˈsat\; **sit•ting 1** : to rest upon the buttocks or haunches **2** : ROOST, PERCH **3** : to occupy a seat **4** : to hold a session **5** : to cover eggs for hatching : BROOD **6** : to pose for a portrait **7** : to remain quiet or inactive **8** : FIT **9** : to cause (oneself) to be seated **10** : to place in position **11** : to keep one's seat on ⟨~ a horse⟩ **12** : BABY-SIT — **sit•ter** *n*

si•tar \si-ˈtär\ *n* [Hindi *sitār*] : an Indian lute with a long neck and a varying number of strings

sit•com \ˈsit-ˌkäm\ *n* : SITUATION COMEDY

site \ˈsīt\ *n* : LOCATION

sit–in \ˈsit-ˌin\ *n* : an act of sitting in the seats or on the floor of an establishment as a means of organized protest

sit•u•at•ed \ˈsi-chə-ˌwā-təd\ *adj* : LOCATED, PLACED

sit•u•a•tion \ˌsi-chə-ˈwā-shən\ *n* **1** : LOCATION, SITE **2** : JOB **3** : CONDITION, CIRCUMSTANCES

situation comedy *n* : a radio or television comedy series that involves a continuing cast of characters in a succession of episodes

sit–up \ˈsit-ˌəp\ *n* : an exercise performed from a supine position by raising the trunk to a sitting position without lifting the feet and returning to the original position

six \ˈsiks\ *n* **1** : one more than five **2** : the 6th in a set or series **3** : something having six units — **six** *adj or pron* — **sixth** \ˈsiksth\ *adj or adv or n*

six–gun \ˈsiks-ˌgən\ *n* : a 6-chambered revolver

six–pack \-ˌpak\ *n* : six bottles or cans (as of beer) packaged and purchased together; *also* : the contents of a six-pack

six•pence \-pəns, *US also* -ˌpens\ *n* : the sum of six pence; *also* : an English silver coin of this value

six–shoot•er \ˈsiks-ˌshü-tər\ *n* : SIX-GUN

six·teen \ˌsiks-ˈtēn\ *n* : one more than 15 — **sixteen** *adj or pron* — **six·teenth** \-ˈtēnth\ *adj or n*
six·ty \ˈsiks-tē\ *n, pl* **sixties** : six times 10 — **six·ti·eth** \ˈsiks-tē-əth\ *adj or n* — **sixty** *adj or pron*
siz·able *or* **size·able** \ˈsī-zə-bəl\ *adj* : quite large — **siz·ably** \-blē\ *adv*
¹**size** \ˈsīz\ *n* : physical extent or bulk : DIMENSIONS; *also* : considerable proportions — **sized** \ˈsīzd\ *adj*
²**size** *vb* **sized; siz·ing 1** : to grade or classify according to size **2** : to form a judgment of ⟨~ up the situation⟩
³**size** *n* : a gluey material used for filling the pores in paper, plaster, or textiles — **siz·ing** *n*
⁴**size** *vb* **sized; siz·ing** : to cover, stiffen, or glaze with size
siz·zle \ˈsi-zəl\ *vb* **siz·zled; siz·zling** : to fry or shrivel up with a hissing sound — **sizzle** *n*
SJ *abbr* Society of Jesus
SK *abbr* Saskatchewan
ska \ˈskä\ *n* : popular music of Jamaican origin combining traditional Caribbean rhythms and jazz
¹**skate** \ˈskāt\ *n, pl* **skates** *also* **skate** : any of a family of rays with thick broad winglike fins
²**skate** *n* **1** : a metal frame and runner attached to a shoe and used for gliding over ice **2** : ROLLER SKATE — **skate** *vb* — **skat·er** *n*
skate·board \ˈskāt-ˌbōrd\ *n* : a short board mounted on small wheels — **skate·board·er** *n* — **skate·board·ing** *n*
skeet \ˈskēt\ *n* : trapshooting in which clay targets are thrown in such a way that their angle of flight simulates that of a flushed game bird
skein \ˈskān\ *n* : a loosely twisted quantity of yarn or thread wound on a reel
skel·e·ton \ˈske-lət-ᵊn\ *n* **1** : a usu. bony supporting framework of an animal body **2** : a bare minimum **3** : FRAMEWORK — **skel·e·tal** \-lət-ᵊl\ *adj*
skep·tic \ˈskep-tik\ *n* **1** : one who believes in skepticism **2** : a person disposed to skepticism esp. regarding religion — **skep·ti·cal** \-ti-kəl\ *adj*
skep·ti·cism \ˈskep-tə-ˌsi-zəm\ *n* **1** : a doubting state of mind **2** : a doctrine that certainty of knowledge cannot be attained **3** : doubt concerning religion
sketch \ˈskech\ *n* **1** : a rough drawing or outline **2** : a short or light literary composition (as a story or essay); *also* : a short comedy piece — **sketch** *vb* — **sketchy** *adj*
¹**skew** \ˈskyü\ *vb* : TWIST, SWERVE
²**skew** *n* : SLANT
skew·er \ˈskyü-ər\ *n* : a long pin for holding small pieces of meat and vegetables for broiling — **skewer** *vb*
¹**ski** \ˈskē\ *n, pl* **skis** [Norw, fr. ON *skīth* stick of wood, ski] : one of a pair of long strips (as of wood, metal or plastic) curving upward in front that are used for gliding over snow or water
²**ski** *vb* **skied** \ˈskēd\; **ski·ing** : to glide on skis — **ski·er** *n*
¹**skid** \ˈskid\ *n* **1** : a plank for supporting something above the ground **2** : a device placed under a wheel to prevent turning **3** : a timber or rail over or on which something is slid or rolled **4** : the act of skidding **5** : a runner on the landing gear of an aircraft **6** : ²PALLET
²**skid** *vb* **skid·ded; skid·ding 1** : to slide without rotating ⟨a *skidding* wheel⟩ **2** : to slide sideways on the road ⟨the car *skidded* on ice⟩ **3** : SLIDE, SLIP
skid row *n* : a district of cheap saloons frequented by vagrants and alcoholics
skiff \ˈskif\ *n* : a small boat
ski jump *n* : a jump made by a person wearing skis; *also* : a course or track prepared for such jumping — **ski jump** *vb* — **ski jumper** *n*
skil·ful *chiefly Brit var of* SKILLFUL
ski lift *n* : a mechanical device (as a chairlift) for carrying skiers up a long slope
skill \ˈskil\ *n* **1** : ability to use one's knowledge effectively in doing something **2** : developed or acquired ability **syn** art, craft, cunning, dexterity, expertise, know-how — **skilled** \ˈskild\ *adj*
skil·let \ˈski-lət\ *n* : a frying pan
skill·ful \ˈskil-fəl\ *adj* **1** : having or displaying skill : EXPERT **2** : accomplished with skill — **skill·ful·ly** *adv* — **skill·ful·ness** *n*
¹**skim** \ˈskim\ *vb* **skimmed; skim·ming 1** : to take off from the top of a liquid; *also* : to remove (scum or cream) from ⟨~ milk⟩ **2** : to read rapidly and superficially **3** : to pass swiftly over — **skim·mer** *n*
²**skim** *adj* : having the cream removed
skimp \ˈskimp\ *vb* : to give insufficient attention, effort, or funds; *also* : to save by skimping
skimpy \ˈskim-pē\ *adj* **skimp·i·er; -est** : deficient in supply or execution
¹**skin** \ˈskin\ *n* **1** : the outer limiting layer of an animal body; *also* : the usu. thin tough tissue of which this is made **2** : an outer or surface layer (as a rind or peel) — **skin·less** *adj* — **skinned** *adj*
²**skin** *vb* **skinned; skin·ning** : to free from skin : remove the skin of
³**skin** *adj* : devoted to showing nudes ⟨~ magazines⟩
skin diving *n* : the sport of swimming under water with a face mask and flippers and esp. without a portable breathing device — **skin–dive** *vb* — **skin diver** *n*
skin·flint \ˈskin-ˌflint\ *n* : a very stingy person
skin graft *n* : a piece of skin taken from one area to replace skin in another area — **skin grafting** *n*
¹**skin·ny** \ˈski-nē\ *adj* **skin·ni·er; -est 1** : resembling skin **2** : very thin
²**skinny** *n* : inside information
skin·ny–dip·ping \-ˌdi-piŋ\ *n* : swimming in the nude
skin·tight \ˈskin-ˈtīt\ *adj* : closely fitted to the figure
¹**skip** \ˈskip\ *vb* **skipped; skip·ping 1** : to move with leaps and bounds **2** : to leap lightly over **3** : to pass from point to point (as in reading) disregarding what is in between **4** : to pass over without notice or mention
²**skip** *n* : a light bouncing step; *also* : a gait of alternate hops and steps
skip·jack \ˈskip-ˌjak\ *n* : a small sailboat with vertical sides and a bottom similar to a flat V
skip·per \ˈski-pər\ *n* [ME, fr. MD *schipper*, fr. *schip* ship] : the master of a ship; *also* : the manager of a baseball team — **skipper** *vb*
skir·mish \ˈskər-mish\ *n* : a minor engagement in war; *also* : a minor dispute or contest — **skirmish** *vb*
¹**skirt** \ˈskərt\ *n* : a free-hanging garment or part of a garment extending from the waist down
²**skirt** *vb* **1** : to pass around the outer edge of **2** : BORDER **3** : EVADE
skit \ˈskit\ *n* : a brief dramatic sketch
ski tow *n* : SKI LIFT
skit·ter \ˈski-tər\ *vb* : to glide or skip lightly or quickly : skim along a surface
skit·tish \ˈski-tish\ *adj* **1** : CAPRICIOUS **2** : easily frightened ⟨a ~ horse⟩; *also* : WARY
ski·wear \ˈskē-ˌwar\ *n* : clothing suitable for wear while skiing
skosh \ˈskōsh\ *n* [Jp *sukoshi*] : a small amount : BIT
skul·dug·gery *or* **skull·dug·gery** \ˌskəl-ˈdə-gə-rē\ *n, pl* **-ger·ries** : underhanded or unscrupulous behavior
skulk \ˈskəlk\ *vb* : to move furtively : SNEAK, LURK — **skulk·er** *n*
skull \ˈskəl\ *n* : the skeleton of the head of a vertebrate that protects the brain and supports the jaws
skull and crossbones *n, pl* **skulls and crossbones** : a depiction of a human skull over crossbones usu. indicating a danger
skull·cap \ˈskəl-ˌkap\ *n* : a close-fitting brimless cap
¹**skunk** \ˈskəŋk\ *n, pl* **skunks** *also* **skunk 1** : any of various New World mammals related to the weasels that can forcibly eject an ill-smelling fluid when startled **2** : a contemptible person
²**skunk** *vb* : to defeat decisively; *esp* : to shut out in a game
skunk cabbage *n* : either of two No. American peren-

nial herbs related to the arums that occur in shaded wet to swampy areas and have a fetid odor suggestive of a skunk

sky \ˈskī\ *n, pl* **skies 1 :** the upper air **2 :** HEAVEN — **sky•ey** \ˈskī-ē\ *adj*

sky•cap \-ˌkap\ *n* **:** a person employed to carry luggage at an airport

sky•div•ing \-ˌdī-viŋ\ *n* **:** the sport of jumping from an airplane and executing various body maneuvers before opening a parachute — **sky diver** *n*

sky•jack \-ˌjak\ *vb* **:** to commandeer an airplane in flight by threat of violence — **sky•jack•er** *n* — **sky•jack•ing** *n*

¹**sky•lark** \-ˌlärk\ *n* **:** a European lark noted for singing in steep upward flight

²**skylark** *vb* **:** FROLIC, SPORT

sky•light \ˈskī-ˌlīt\ *n* **:** a window in a roof or ceiling — **sky•light•ed** \-ˌlī-təd\ *adj*

sky•line \-ˌlīn\ *n* **1 :** HORIZON **2 :** an outline against the sky

¹**sky•rock•et** \-ˌrä-kət\ *n* **:** ROCKET 1

²**skyrocket** *vb* **:** ROCKET 2

sky•scrap•er \-ˌskrā-pər\ *n* **:** a very tall building

sky•walk \-ˌwȯk\ *n* **:** an aerial walkway connecting two buildings

sky•ward \-wərd\ *adv* **:** toward the sky

sky•writ•ing \-ˌrī-tiŋ\ *n* **:** writing in the sky formed by smoke emitted from an airplane — **sky•writ•er** *n*

slab \ˈslab\ *n* **:** a thick flat piece or slice

¹**slack** \ˈslak\ *adj* **1 :** CARELESS, NEGLIGENT **2 :** SLUGGISH, LISTLESS **3 :** not taut **:** LOOSE **4 :** not busy or active **syn** lax, remiss, neglectful, delinquent, derelict — **slack•ly** *adv* — **slack•ness** *n*

²**slack** *vb* **1 :** to make or become slack **:** LOOSEN, RELAX **2 :** SLAKE 2

³**slack** *n* **1 :** cessation of movement or flow **:** LETUP **2 :** a part that hangs loose without strain ⟨~ of a rope⟩ **3 :** trousers esp. for casual wear — usu. used in pl.

slack•en \ˈsla-kən\ *vb* **:** to make or become slack

slack•er \ˈsla-kər\ *n* **:** one that shirks work or evades military duty

slag \ˈslag\ *n* **:** the waste left after the melting of ores and the separation of metal from them

slain *past part of* SLAY

slake \ˈslāk, *for 2 also* ˈslak\ *vb* **slaked; slak•ing 1 :** to relieve or satisfy with or as if with refreshing drink ⟨~ thirst⟩ **2 :** to cause (lime) to crumble by mixture with water

sla•lom \ˈslä-ləm\ *n* [Norw *slalåm,* lit., sloping track] **:** skiing in a zigzag course between obstacles

¹**slam** \ˈslam\ *n* **:** the winning of every trick or of all tricks but one in bridge

²**slam** *n* **:** a heavy jarring impact **:** BANG

³**slam** *vb* **slammed; slam•ming 1 :** to shut violently and noisily **2 :** to throw or strike with a loud impact

slam•mer \ˈsla-mər\ *n* **:** JAIL, PRISON

¹**slan•der** \ˈslan-dər\ *vb* **:** to utter slander against **:** DEFAME — **slan•der•er** *n*

²**slander** *n* [ME *sclaundre, slaundre,* fr. OF *esclandre,* fr. LL *scandalum* stumbling block, offense] **:** a false report maliciously uttered and tending to injure the reputation of a person — **slan•der•ous** *adj*

slang \ˈslaŋ\ *n* **:** an informal nonstandard vocabulary composed typically of invented words, arbitrarily changed words, and extravagant figures of speech — **slangy** *adj*

¹**slant** \ˈslant\ *n* **1 :** a sloping direction, line, or plane **2 :** a particular or personal viewpoint — **slant** *adj* — **slant•wise** \-ˌwīz\ *adv or adj*

²**slant** *vb* **1 :** SLOPE **2 :** to interpret or present in accordance with a special viewpoint or bias **syn** incline, lean, list, tilt, heel — **slant•ing•ly** *adv*

slap \ˈslap\ *vb* **slapped; slap•ping 1 :** to strike sharply with the open hand **2 :** REBUFF, INSULT — **slap** *n*

slap•stick \-ˌstik\ *n* **:** comedy stressing horseplay

¹**slash** \ˈslash\ *vb* **1 :** to cut with sweeping strokes **2 :** to cut slits in (a garment) **3 :** to reduce sharply

²**slash** *n* **1 :** GASH **2 :** an ornamental slit in a garment

slat \ˈslat\ *n* **:** a thin narrow flat strip

¹**slate** \ˈslāt\ *n* **1 :** a dense fine-grained rock that splits into thin layers **2 :** a roofing tile or a writing tablet made from this rock **3 :** a written or unwritten record ⟨start with a clean ~⟩ **4 :** a list of candidates for election

²**slate** *vb* **slat•ed; slat•ing 1 :** to cover with slate **2 :** to designate for action or appointment

slath•er \ˈsla-t͟hər\ *vb* **:** to spread with or on thickly or lavishly

slat•tern \ˈsla-tərn\ *n* **:** a slovenly woman — **slat•tern•ly** *adj*

¹**slaugh•ter** \ˈslȯ-tər\ *n* **1 :** the butchering of livestock for market **2 :** great destruction of lives esp. in battle

²**slaughter** *vb* **1 :** to kill (animals) for food **:** BUTCHER **2 :** to kill in large numbers or in a bloody way **:** MASSACRE

slaugh•ter•house \-ˌhau̇s\ *n* **:** an establishment where animals are butchered

Slav \ˈsläv, ˈslav\ *n* **:** a person speaking a Slavic language

¹**slave** \ˈslāv\ *n* [ME *sclave,* fr. OF or ML; OF *esclave,* fr. ML *sclavus,* fr. *Sclavus* Slav; fr. the enslavement of Slavs in eastern Europe in the Middle Ages] **1 :** a person held in servitude as property **2 :** a device (as the printer of a computer) that is directly responsive to another — **slave** *adj*

²**slave** *vb* **slaved; slav•ing :** to work like a slave **:** DRUDGE

¹**sla•ver** \ˈsla-vər, ˈslā-\ *n* **:** SLOBBER — **slaver** *vb*

²**slav•er** \ˈslā-vər\ *n* **:** a ship or a person engaged in transporting slaves

slav•ery \ˈslāv-rē, ˈslā-və-\ *n* **1 :** wearisome drudgery **2 :** the condition of being a slave **3 :** the practice of owning slaves **syn** servitude, bondage, enslavement

¹**Slav•ic** \ˈsla-vik, ˈslä-\ *n* **:** a branch of the Indo-European language family including various languages (as Russian or Polish) of eastern Europe

²**Slavic** *adj* **:** of or relating to the Slavs or their languages

slav•ish \ˈslā-vish\ *adj* **1 :** SERVILE **2 :** obeying or imitating with no freedom of judgment or choice — **slav•ish•ly** *adv*

slaw \ˈslȯ\ *n* **:** COLESLAW

slay \ˈslā\ *vb* **slew** \ˈslü\; **slain** \ˈslān\; **slay•ing :** KILL — **slay•er** *n*

sleaze \ˈslēz\ *n* **:** a sleazy quality, appearance, or behavior

slea•zy \ˈslē-zē\ *adj* **slea•zi•er; -est 1 :** FLIMSY, SHODDY **2 :** marked by cheapness of character or quality

¹**sled** \ˈsled\ *n* **:** a vehicle usu. on runners adapted esp. for sliding on snow

²**sled** *vb* **sled•ded, sled•ding :** to ride or carry on a sled

¹**sledge** \ˈslej\ *n* **:** SLEDGEHAMMER

²**sledge** *n* **:** a strong heavy sled

sledge•ham•mer \ˈslej-ˌha-mər\ *n* **:** a large heavy hammer wielded with both hands — **sledgehammer** *adj or vb*

¹**sleek** \ˈslēk\ *vb* **1 :** to make smooth or glossy **2 :** to gloss over

²**sleek** *adj* **:** having a smooth well-groomed look

¹**sleep** \ˈslēp\ *n* **1 :** the natural periodic suspension of consciousness during which bodily powers are restored **2 :** a state (as death or coma) suggesting sleep — **sleep•less** *adj* — **sleep•less•ness** *n*

²**sleep** *vb* **slept** \ˈslept\; **sleep•ing 1 :** to rest or be in a state of sleep; *also* **:** to spend in sleep **2 :** to have sexual intercourse — usu. used with *with* **3 :** to provide sleeping space for

sleep•er \ˈslē-pər\ *n* **1 :** one that sleeps **2 :** a horizontal beam to support something on or near ground level **3 :** SLEEPING CAR **4 :** someone or something unpromising or unnoticed that suddenly attains prominence or value

sleeping bag *n* : a warmly lined bag for sleeping esp. outdoors

sleeping car *n* : a railroad car with berths for sleeping

sleeping pill *n* : a drug in tablet or capsule form taken to induce sleep

sleeping sickness *n* : a serious disease of tropical Africa that is marked by fever, lethargy, tremors, and loss of weight and is caused by protozoans transmitted by the tsetse fly

sleep•over \ˈslēp-ˌō-vər\ *n* : an overnight stay (as at another's home)

sleep•walk•er \ˈslēp-ˌwȯ-kər\ *n* : one that walks while or as if while asleep — **sleep•walk** \-ˌwȯk\ *vb*

sleepy \ˈslē-pē\ *adj* **sleep•i•er; -est 1** : ready for sleep **2** : quietly inactive — **sleep•i•ly** \ˈslē-pə-lē\ *adv* — **sleep•i•ness** \-pē-nəs\ *n*

sleet \ˈslēt\ *n* : frozen or partly frozen rain — **sleet** *vb* — **sleety** *adj*

sleeve \ˈslēv\ *n* **1** : a part of a garment covering an arm **2** : a tubular part designed to fit over another part — **sleeved** *adj* — **sleeve•less** *adj*

¹sleigh \ˈslā\ *n* : an open usu. horse-drawn vehicle on runners for use on snow or ice

²sleigh *vb* : to drive or travel in a sleigh

sleight \ˈslīt\ *n* **1** : TRICK **2** : DEXTERITY

sleight of hand : a trick requiring skillful manual manipulation

slen•der \ˈslen-dər\ *adj* **1** : SLIM, THIN **2** : WEAK, SLIGHT **3** : MEAGER, INADEQUATE

slen•der•ize \-də-ˌrīz\ *vb* **-ized; -iz•ing** : to make slender

sleuth \ˈslüth\ *n* [short for *sleuthhound* bloodhound, fr. ME, fr. *sleuth* track of an animal or person, fr. ON *slōth*] : DETECTIVE

¹slew \ˈslü\ *past of* SLAY

²slew *vb* : TURN, VEER, SKID

¹slice \ˈslīs\ *vb* **sliced; slic•ing 1** : to cut a slice from; *also* : to cut into slices **2** : to hit (a ball) so that a slice results

²slice *n* **1** : a thin flat piece cut from something **2** : a flight of a ball (as in golf) that curves in the direction of the dominant hand of the player hitting it

¹slick \ˈslik\ *vb* : to make smooth or sleek

²slick *adj* **1** : very smooth : SLIPPERY **2** : CLEVER, SMART

³slick *n* **1** : a smooth patch of water covered with a film of oil **2** : a popular magazine printed on coated paper

slick•er \ˈsli-kər\ *n* **1** : a long loose raincoat **2** : a sly tricky person **3** : a city dweller esp. of natty appearance or sophisticated mannerisms

¹slide \ˈslīd\ *vb* **slid** \ˈslid\; **slid•ing** \ˈslī-diŋ\ **1** : to move smoothly along a surface **2** : to fall by a loss of support **3** : to pass unobtrusively **4** : to move or pass smoothly; *also* : to pass unnoticed ⟨let it ∼ by⟩ **5** : to fall or dive toward a base in baseball

²slide *n* **1** : an act or instance of sliding **2** : something (as a cover or fastener) that operates by sliding **3** : a fall of a mass of earth or snow down a hillside **4** : a surface on which something slides **5** : a glass plate on which a specimen is mounted for examination under a microscope **6** : a small transparent photograph that can be projected on a screen

slid•er \ˈslī-dər\ *n* **1** : one that slides **2** : a baseball pitch that looks like a fastball but curves slightly

slide rule *n* : a manual device for calculation consisting of a ruler and a movable middle piece graduated with logarithmic scales

slier *comparative of* SLY

sliest *superlative of* SLY

¹slight \ˈslīt\ *adj* **1** : SLENDER; *also* : FRAIL **2** : UNIMPORTANT **3** : SCANTY, MEAGER — **slight•ly** *adv*

²slight *vb* **1** : to treat as unimportant **2** : to ignore discourteously **3** : to perform or attend to carelessly

³slight *n* : a humiliating discourtesy

¹slim \ˈslim\ *adj* **slim•mer; slim•mest** [D, bad, inferior, fr. MD, *slimp* crooked, bad] **1** : SLENDER, SLIGHT, THIN **2** : SCANTY, MEAGER

²slim *vb* **slimmed; slim•ming** : to make or become slender

slime \ˈslīm\ *n* **1** : sticky mud **2** : a slippery substance (as on the skin of a slug or catfish) — **slimy** *adj*

¹sling \ˈsliŋ\ *vb* **slung** \ˈsləŋ\; **sling•ing 1** : to throw forcibly : FLING **2** : to hurl with or as if with a sling

²sling *n* **1** : a short strap with strings attached for hurling stones or shot **2** : something (as a rope or chain) used to hoist, lower, support, or carry; *esp* : a bandage hanging from the neck to support an arm or hand

sling•shot \ˈsliŋ-ˌshät\ *n* : a forked stick with elastic bands for shooting small stones or shot

slink \ˈsliŋk\ *vb* **slunk** \ˈsləŋk\ *also* **slinked** \ˈsliŋkt\; **slink•ing 1** : to move stealthily or furtively **2** : to move sinuously — **slinky** *adj*

¹slip \ˈslip\ *vb* **slipped; slip•ping 1** : to escape quietly or secretly **2** : to slide along or cause to slide along smoothly **3** : to make a mistake **4** : to pass unnoticed or undone **5** : to fall off from a standard or level

²slip *n* **1** : a ramp for repairing ships **2** : a ship's berth between two piers **3** : secret or hurried departure, escape, or evasion **4** : BLUNDER **5** : a sudden mishap **6** : a woman's one-piece garment worn under a dress **7** : PILLOWCASE

³slip *n* **1** : a shoot or twig from a plant for planting or grafting **2** : a long narrow strip; *esp* : one of paper used for a record ⟨deposit ∼⟩

⁴slip *vb* **slipped; slip•ping** : to take slips from (a plant)

slip•knot \ˈslip-ˌnät\ *n* : a knot that slips along the rope around which it is made

slipped disk *n* : a protrusion of one of the disks of cartilage between vertebrae with pressure on spinal nerves resulting esp. in low back pain

slip•per \ˈsli-pər\ *n* : a light low shoe that may be easily slipped on and off

slip•pery \ˈsli-pə-rē\ *adj* **slip•per•i•er; -est 1** : icy, wet, smooth, or greasy enough to cause one to fall or lose one's hold **2** : not to be trusted : TRICKY — **slip•per•i•ness** *n*

slip•shod \ˈslip-ˈshäd\ *adj* : SLOVENLY, CARELESS ⟨∼ work⟩

slip•stream \ˈslip-ˌstrēm\ *n* : a stream (as of air) driven aft by a propeller

slip•up \ˈslip-ˌəp\ *n* **1** : MISTAKE **2** : ACCIDENT

¹slit \ˈslit\ *vb* **slit; slit•ting 1** : SLASH **2** : to cut off or away

²slit *n* : a long narrow cut or opening

slith•er \ˈsli-t͟hər\ *vb* : to slip or glide along like a snake — **slith•ery** *adj*

sliv•er \ˈsli-vər\ *n* : SPLINTER

slob \ˈsläb\ *n* : a slovenly or boorish person

slob•ber \ˈslä-bər\ *vb* **slob•bered; slob•ber•ing** : to dribble saliva — **slobber** *n*

sloe \ˈslō\ *n* : the fruit of the blackthorn

slog \ˈsläg\ *vb* **slogged; slog•ging 1** : to hit hard : BEAT **2** : to work hard and steadily

slo•gan \ˈslō-gən\ *n* [alter. of earlier *slogorn*, fr. ScGael *sluagh-ghairm*, fr. *sluagh* army, host + *gairm* cry] : a word or phrase expressing the spirit or aim of a party, group, or cause

sloop \ˈslüp\ *n* : a single-masted sailboat with a jib and a fore-and-aft mainsail

¹slop \ˈsläp\ *n* **1** : thin tasteless drink or liquid food — usu. used in pl. **2** : food waste for animal feed : SWILL **3** : excreted body waste — usu. used in pl.

²slop *vb* **slopped; slop•ping 1** : SPILL **2** : to feed with slop ⟨∼ hogs⟩

¹slope \ˈslōp\ *vb* **sloped; slop•ing** : SLANT, INCLINE

²slope *n* **1** : upward or downward slant or degree of slant **2** : ground that forms an incline **3** : the part of a landmass draining into a particular ocean

slop•py \ˈslä-pē\ *adj* **slop•pi•er; -est 1** : MUDDY, SLUSHY **2** : SLOVENLY, MESSY

slosh \ˈsläsh\ *vb* **1** : to flounder through or splash about in or with water, mud, or slush **2 :** to move with a splashing motion

slot \ˈslät\ *n* **1 :** a long narrow opening or groove **2 :** a position in a sequence

slot car *n* **:** an electric toy racing car that runs on a grooved track

sloth \ˈslȯth\ *n, pl* **sloths** \ˈslȯths, ˈslȯt͟hz\ **1 :** LAZINESS, INDOLENCE **2 :** any of several slow-moving plant-eating arboreal mammals of So. and Central America — **sloth•ful** *adj*

sloth 2

slot machine *n* **1 :** a machine whose operation is begun by dropping a coin into a slot **2 :** a coin-operated gambling machine that pays off according to the matching of symbols on wheels spun by a handle

[1]slouch \ˈslau̇ch\ *n* **1 :** a lazy or incompetent person **2 :** a loose or drooping gait or posture

[2]slouch *vb* **:** to walk, stand, or sit with a slouch **:** SLUMP

[1]slough \ˈslü, *2 usu* ˈslau̇\ *n* **1 :** a wet and marshy or muddy place (as a swamp) **2 :** a discouraged state of mind

[2]slough \ˈsləf\ *also* **sluff** *n* **:** something that has been or may be shed or cast off

[3]slough \ˈsləf\ *also* **sluff** *vb* **:** to cast off

Slo•vak \ˈslō-ˌväk, -ˌvak\ *n* **:** a member of a Slavic people of Slovakia — **Slovak** *adj* — **Slo•va•ki•an** \slō-ˈvä-kē-ən, -ˈva-\ *adj or n*

slov•en \ˈslə-vən\ *n* [ME *sloveyn* rascal, perh. fr. D dial. *sloovin* woman of low character] **:** an untidy person

Slo•vene \ˈslō-ˌvēn\ *n* **:** a member of a Slavic people living largely in Slovenia — **Slovene** *adj* — **Slo•ve•nian** \slō-ˈvē-nē-ən\ *adj or n*

slov•en•ly \ˈslə-vən-lē\ *adj* **1 :** untidy in dress or person **2 :** lazily or carelessly done **:** SLIPSHOD

[1]slow \ˈslō\ *adj* **1 :** SLUGGISH; *also* **:** dull in mind **:** STUPID **2 :** moving, flowing, or proceeding at less than the usual speed **3 :** taking more than the usual time **4 :** registering behind the correct time **5 :** not lively **:** BORING **syn** dilatory, laggard, deliberate, leisurely — **slow** *adv* — **slow•ly** *adv* — **slow•ness** *n*

[2]slow *vb* **1 :** to make slow **:** hold back **2 :** to go slower

slow motion *n* **:** motion-picture action photographed so as to appear much slower than normal — **slow–motion** *adj*

SLR *abbr* single-lens reflex

sludge \ˈsləj\ *n* **:** a slushy mass **:** OOZE; *esp* **:** solid matter produced by sewage treatment processes

slue *var of* [2]SLEW

[1]slug \ˈsləg\ *n* **1 :** a small mass of metal; *esp* **:** BULLET **2 :** a metal disk for use (as in a slot machine) in place of a coin **3 :** any of numerous wormlike mollusks related to the snails **4 :** a quantity of liquor drunk

[2]slug *vb* **slugged; slug•ging :** to strike forcibly and heavily — **slug•ger** *n*

slug•gard \ˈslə-gərd\ *n* **:** a lazy person

slug•gish \ˈslə-gish\ *adj* **1 :** SLOTHFUL, LAZY **2 :** slow in movement or flow **3 :** STAGNANT, DULL — **slug•gish•ly** *adv* — **slug•gish•ness** *n*

[1]sluice \ˈslüs\ *n* **1 :** an artificial passage for water with a gate for controlling the flow; *also* **:** the gate so used **2 :** a channel that carries off surplus water **3 :** an inclined trough or flume for washing ore or floating logs

[2]sluice *vb* **sluiced; sluic•ing 1 :** to draw off through a sluice **2 :** to wash with running water **:** FLUSH

[1]slum \ˈsləm\ *n* **:** a thickly populated area marked by poverty and dirty or deteriorated houses

[2]slum *vb* **slummed; slum•ming :** to visit slums esp. out of curiosity; *also* **:** to go somewhere or do something that might be considered beneath one's station

[1]slum•ber \ˈsləm-bər\ *vb* **slum•bered; slum•ber•ing 1 :** DOZE; *also* **:** SLEEP **2 :** to be in a sluggish or torpid state

[2]slumber *n* **:** SLEEP

slum•ber•ous \ˈsləm-bə-rəs\ *or* **slum•brous** \-brəs\ *adj* **1 :** SLUMBERING, SLEEPY **2 :** PEACEFUL, INACTIVE

slum•lord \ˈsləm-ˌlȯrd\ *n* **:** a landlord who receives unusually large profits from substandard properties

slump \ˈsləmp\ *vb* **1 :** to sink down suddenly **:** COLLAPSE **2 :** SLOUCH **3 :** to decline sharply — **slump** *n*

slung *past and past part of* SLING

slunk *past and past part of* SLINK

[1]slur \ˈslər\ *vb* **slurred; slur•ring 1 :** to slide or slip over without due mention or emphasis **2 :** to perform two or more successive notes of different pitch in a smooth or connected way

[2]slur *n* **:** a curved line connecting notes to be slurred; *also* **:** a group of slurred notes

[3]slur *n* **:** a slighting remark **:** ASPERSION

slurp \ˈslərp\ *vb* **:** to eat or drink noisily — **slurp** *n*

slur•ry \ˈslər-ē\ *n, pl* **slur•ries :** a watery mixture of insoluble matter

slush \ˈsləsh\ *n* **1 :** partly melted or watery snow **2 :** soft mud — **slushy** *adj*

slut \ˈslət\ *n* **1 :** a slovenly woman **2 :** a lewd woman — **slut•tish** *adj*

sly \ˈslī\ *adj* **sli•er** *also* **sly•er** \ˈslī-ər\; **sli•est** *also* **sly•est** \ˈslī-əst\ **1 :** CRAFTY, CUNNING **2 :** SECRETIVE, FURTIVE **3 :** ROGUISH **syn** tricky, wily, artful, foxy, guileful — **sly•ly** *adv* — **sly•ness** *n*

sm *abbr* small

Sm *symbol* samarium

SM *abbr* sergeant major

SMA *abbr* sergeant major of the army

[1]smack \ˈsmak\ *n* **:** characteristic flavor; *also* **:** a slight trace

[2]smack *vb* **1 :** to have a taste **2 :** to have a trace or suggestion

[3]smack *vb* **1 :** to move (the lips) so as to make a sharp noise **2 :** to kiss or slap with a loud noise

[4]smack *n* **1 :** a sharp noise made by the lips **2 :** a noisy slap

[5]smack *adv* **:** squarely and sharply

[6]smack *n* **:** a sailing ship used in fishing

[7]smack *n, slang* **:** HEROIN

SMaj *abbr* sergeant major

[1]small \ˈsmȯl\ *adj* **1 :** little in size or amount **2 :** operating on a limited scale **3 :** little or close to zero (as in number or value) **4 :** made up of little things **5 :** TRIFLING, UNIMPORTANT **6 :** MEAN, PETTY **syn** diminutive, petite, wee, tiny, minute — **small•ish** *adj* — **small•ness** *n*

[2]small *n* **:** a small part or product ⟨the ~ of the back⟩

small•pox \ˈsmȯl-ˌpäks\ *n* **:** a contagious virus disease of humans formerly common but now eradicated

small–time \ˈsmȯl-ˈtīm\ *adj* **:** insignificant in performance and standing **:** MINOR — **small–tim•er** *n*

[1]smart \ˈsmärt\ *vb* **1 :** to cause or feel a stinging pain **2 :** to feel or endure distress — **smart** *n*

[2]smart *adj* **1 :** making one smart ⟨a ~ blow⟩ **2 :** mentally quick **:** BRIGHT **3 :** WITTY, CLEVER **4 :** STYLISH **5 :** being a guided missile **6 :** containing a microprocessor for limited computing capability ⟨~ terminal⟩

syn knowing, quick-witted, intelligent, brainy, sharp — **smart·ly** *adv* — **smart·ness** *n*

smart al·eck \ˈsmärt-ˌa-lik\ *n* : a person given to obnoxious cleverness

smart card *n* : a small plastic card that has a built-in microprocessor to store and handle data

¹smash \ˈsmash\ *n* **1** : a smashing blow **2** : a hard, overhand stroke in tennis **3** : the act or sound of smashing **4** : collision of vehicles : CRASH **5** : COLLAPSE, RUIN; *esp* : BANKRUPTCY **6** : a striking success : HIT — **smash** *adj*

²smash *vb* **1** : to break or be broken into pieces **2** : to move forward with force and shattering effect **3** : to destroy utterly : WRECK

smat·ter·ing \ˈsma-tə-riŋ\ *n* **1** : superficial knowledge **2** : a small scattered number or amount

¹smear \ˈsmir\ *n* **1** : a spot left by an oily or sticky substance **2** : material smeared on a surface (as of a microscope slide)

²smear *vb* **1** : to overspread esp. with something oily or sticky **2** : SMUDGE, SOIL **3** : to injure by slander or insults

¹smell \ˈsmel\ *vb* **smelled** \ˈsmeld\ *or* **smelt** \ˈsmelt\; **smell·ing** **1** : to perceive the odor of by sense organs of the nose; *also* : to detect or seek with or as if with these organs **2** : to have or give off an odor

²smell *n* **1** : ODOR, SCENT **2** : the process or power of perceiving odor; *also* : the special sense by which one perceives odor **3** : an act of smelling — **smelly** *adj*

smelling salts *n pl* : an aromatic preparation used as a stimulant and restorative (as to relieve faintness)

¹smelt \ˈsmelt\ *n, pl* **smelts** *or* **smelt** : any of a family of small food fishes of coastal or fresh waters that are related to the trouts and salmons

²smelt *vb* : to melt or fuse (ore) in order to separate the metal; *also* : REFINE

smelt·er \ˈsmel-tər\ *n* **1** : one that smelts **2** : an establishment for smelting

smid·gen *also* **smid·geon** *or* **smid·gin** \ˈsmi-jən\ *n* : a small amount : BIT

smi·lax \ˈsmī-ˌlaks\ *n* **1** : any of various mostly climbing and prickly plants related to the lilies **2** : an ornamental plant related to the asparagus

¹smile \ˈsmīl\ *vb* **smiled; smil·ing** **1** : to look with a smile **2** : to be favorable **3** : to express by a smile

²smile *n* : a change of facial expression to express amusement, pleasure, or affection

smirch \ˈsmərch\ *vb* **1** : to make dirty or stained **2** : to bring disgrace on — **smirch** *n*

smirk \ˈsmərk\ *vb* : to wear a self-conscious or conceited smile : SIMPER — **smirk** *n*

smite \ˈsmīt\ *vb* **smote** \ˈsmōt\; **smit·ten** \ˈsmit-ᵊn\ *or* **smote; smit·ing** \ˈsmī-tiŋ\ **1** : to strike heavily; *also* : to kill by striking **2** : to affect as if by a heavy blow

smith \ˈsmith\ *n* : a worker in metals; *esp* : BLACKSMITH

smith·er·eens \ˌsmi-t͟hə-ˈrēnz\ *n pl* [perh. fr. Ir *smidiríní*] : FRAGMENTS, BITS

smithy \ˈsmi-thē\ *n, pl* **smith·ies** : a smith's workshop

¹smock \ˈsmäk\ *n* : a loose garment worn over other clothes as a protection

²smock *vb* : to gather (cloth) in regularly spaced tucks — **smock·ing** *n*

smog \ˈsmäg, ˈsmȯg\ *n* [blend of *smoke* and *fog*] : a thick haze caused by the action of sunlight on air polluted by smoke and automobile exhaust fumes — **smog·gy** *adj*

¹smoke \ˈsmōk\ *n* **1** : the gas from burning material (as coal, wood, or tobacco) in which are suspended particles of soot **2** : a mass or column of smoke **3** : something (as a cigarette) to smoke; *also* : the act of smoking — **smoke·less** *adj* — **smoky** *adj*

²smoke *vb* **smoked; smok·ing** **1** : to emit smoke **2** : to inhale and exhale the fumes of burning tobacco; *also* : to use in smoking ⟨~ a pipe⟩ **3** : to stupefy or drive away by smoke **4** : to discolor with smoke **5** : to cure (as meat) with smoke — **smok·er** *n*

smoke detector *n* : an alarm that sounds automatically when it detects smoke

smoke jumper *n* : a forest firefighter who parachutes to locations otherwise difficult to reach

smoke·stack \ˈsmōk-ˌstak\ *n* : a pipe or funnel through which smoke and gases are discharged

smol·der *or* **smoul·der** \ˈsmōl-dər\ *vb* **smol·dered** *or* **smoul·dered; smol·der·ing** *or* **smoul·der·ing** **1** : to burn and smoke without flame **2** : to burn inwardly — **smolder** *n*

smooch \ˈsmüch\ *vb* : KISS, PET — **smooch** *n*

¹smooth \ˈsmüt͟h\ *adj* **1** : not rough or uneven **2** : not jarring or jolting **3** : BLAND, MILD **4** : fluent in speech and agreeable in manner — **smooth·ly** *adv* — **smooth·ness** *n*

²smooth *vb* **1** : to make smooth **2** : to free from trouble or difficulty

smooth muscle *n* : muscle with no cross striations that is typical of visceral organs (as the stomach and bladder) and is not under voluntary control

smor·gas·bord \ˈsmȯr-gəs-ˌbōrd\ *n* [Sw *smörgåsbord,* fr. *smörgås* open sandwich + *bord* table] : a luncheon or supper buffet consisting of many foods

smote *past and past part of* SMITE

¹smoth·er \ˈsmə-t͟hər\ *n* **1** : thick stifling smoke **2** : a dense cloud (as of fog or dust) **3** : a confused multitude of things

²smother *vb* **smoth·ered; smoth·er·ing** **1** : to be overcome by or die from lack of air **2** : to kill by depriving of air **3** : SUPPRESS **4** : to cover thickly

SMSgt *abbr* senior master sergeant

¹smudge \ˈsməj\ *vb* **smudged; smudg·ing** : to soil or blur by rubbing or smearing

²smudge *n* : a dirty or blurred spot — **smudgy** *adj*

smug \ˈsməg\ *adj* **smug·ger; smug·gest** : conscious of one's virtue and importance : SELF-SATISFIED — **smug·ly** *adv* — **smug·ness** *n*

smug·gle \ˈsmə-gəl\ *vb* **smug·gled; smug·gling** **1** : to import or export secretly, illegally, or without paying the duties required by law **2** : to convey secretly — **smug·gler** \ˈsmə-glər\ *n*

smut \ˈsmət\ *n* **1** : something (as soot) that smudges; *also* : SMUDGE, SPOT **2** : any of various destructive diseases of plants caused by fungi; *also* : a fungus causing smut **3** : indecent language or matter — **smut·ty** *adj*

smutch \ˈsməch\ *n* : SMUDGE

Sn *symbol* [LL *stannum*] tin

SN *abbr* seaman

snack \ˈsnak\ *n* : a light meal : BITE

snaf·fle \ˈsna-fəl\ *n* : a simple jointed bit for a horse's bridle

¹snag \ˈsnag\ *n* **1** : a stump or piece of a tree esp. when under water **2** : an unexpected difficulty **syn** obstacle, obstruction, impediment, bar

²snag *vb* **snagged; snag·ging** **1** : to become caught on or as if on a snag **2** : to seize quickly : SNATCH

snail \ˈsnāl\ *n* : any of numerous small gastropod mollusks with a spiral shell into which they can withdraw

snake \ˈsnāk\ *n* **1** : any of numerous long-bodied limbless reptiles : SERPENT **2** : a treacherous person **3** : something that resembles a snake — **snaky** *adj*

snake·bite \-ˌbīt\ *n* : the bite of a snake and esp. a venomous snake

¹snap \ˈsnap\ *vb* **snapped; snap·ping** **1** : to grasp or slash at something with the teeth **2** : to get or buy quickly **3** : to utter sharp or angry words **4** : to break suddenly with a sharp sound **5** : to give a sharp cracking noise **6** : to throw with a quick motion **7** : FLASH ⟨her eyes *snapped*⟩ **8** : to put a football into play — **snap·per** *n* — **snap·pish** *adj* — **snap·py** *adj*

²snap *n* **1** : the act or sound of snapping **2** : something very easy to do : CINCH **3** : a short period of cold weather **4** : a catch or fastening that closes with a

click **5 :** a thin brittle cookie **6 :** ENERGY, VIM; *also* **:** smartness of movement **7 :** the putting of the ball into play in football
snap bean *n* **:** a bean grown primarily for its young tender pods that are usu. broken in pieces for cooking
snap•drag•on \ˈsnap-ˌdra-gən\ *n* **:** any of a genus of herbs with long spikes of showy flowers
snapping turtle *n* **:** either of two large American turtles with powerful jaws and a strong musky odor
snap•shot \ˈsnap-ˌshät\ *n* **:** a photograph taken usu. with an inexpensive hand-held camera
snare \ˈsnar\ *n* **:** a trap often consisting of a noose for catching birds or mammals — **snare** *vb*
[1]**snarl** \ˈsnärl\ *vb* **:** to cause to become knotted and intertwined
[2]**snarl** *n* **:** TANGLE
[3]**snarl** *vb* **:** to growl angrily or threateningly
[4]**snarl** *n* **:** an angry ill-tempered growl
[1]**snatch** \ˈsnach\ *vb* **1 :** to try to grasp something suddenly **2 :** to seize or take away suddenly **syn** clutch, seize, grab, nab
[2]**snatch** *n* **1 :** a short period **2 :** an act of snatching **3 :** something brief or fragmentary ⟨~*es* of song⟩
[1]**sneak** \ˈsnēk\ *vb* **sneaked** \ˈsnēkt\ *or* **snuck** \ˈsnək\; **sneak•ing :** to move, act, or take in a furtive manner — **sneak•ing•ly** *adv*
[2]**sneak** *n* **1 :** one who acts in a furtive or shifty manner **2 :** a stealthy or furtive move or escape — **sneak•i•ly** \ˈsnē-kə-lē\ *adv* — **sneaky** *adj*
sneak•er \ˈsnē-kər\ *n* **:** a sports shoe with a pliable rubber sole
sneer \ˈsnir\ *vb* **:** to show scorn or contempt by curling the lip or by a jeering tone — **sneer** *n*
sneeze \ˈsnēz\ *vb* **sneezed; sneez•ing :** to force the breath out suddenly and violently as a reflex act — **sneeze** *n*
SNF *abbr* skilled nursing facility
snick•er \ˈsni-kər\ *n* **:** a partly suppressed laugh — **snicker** *vb*
snide \ˈsnīd\ *adj* **1 :** MEAN, LOW ⟨a ~ trick⟩ **2 :** slyly disparaging ⟨a ~ remark⟩
sniff \ˈsnif\ *vb* **1 :** to draw air audibly up the nose esp. for smelling **2 :** to show disdain or scorn **3 :** to detect by or as if by smelling — **sniff** *n*
snif•fle \ˈsni-fəl\ *n* **1** *pl* **:** a head cold marked by nasal discharge **2 :** SNUFFLE — **sniffle** *vb*
[1]**snip** \ˈsnip\ *n* **1 :** a fragment snipped off **2 :** a simple stroke of the scissors or shears
[2]**snip** *vb* **snipped; snip•ping :** to cut off by bits **:** CLIP; *also* **:** to remove by cutting off
[1]**snipe** \ˈsnīp\ *n, pl* **snipes** *or* **snipe :** any of several long-billed game birds esp. of marshy areas that belong to the same family as the sandpipers
[2]**snipe** *vb* **sniped; snip•ing :** to shoot at an exposed enemy from a concealed position — **snip•er** *n*
snip•py \ˈsni-pē\ *adj* **snip•pi•er; -est :** CURT, SNAPPISH
snips \ˈsnips\ *n pl* **:** hand shears used esp. for cutting sheet metal ⟨tin ~⟩
snitch \ˈsnich\ *vb* **1 :** INFORM, TATTLE **2 :** PILFER, SNATCH
sniv•el \ˈsni-vəl\ *vb* **-eled** *or* **-elled; -el•ing** *or* **-el•ling 1 :** to have a running nose; *also* **:** SNUFFLE **2 :** to whine in a snuffling manner — **snivel** *n*
snob \ˈsnäb\ *n* **:** one who seeks association with persons of higher social position and looks down on those considered inferior — **snob•bish** *adj* — **snob•bish•ly** *adv* — **snob•bish•ness** *n*
snob•bery \ˈsnä-bə-rē\ *n, pl* **-ber•ies :** snobbish conduct
[1]**snoop** \ˈsnüp\ *vb* [D *snoepen* to buy or eat on the sly] **:** to pry in a furtive or meddlesome way
[2]**snoop** *n* **:** a prying meddlesome person
snooty \ˈsnü-tē\ *adj* **snoot•i•er; -est :** DISDAINFUL, SNOBBISH
snooze \ˈsnüz\ *vb* **snoozed; snooz•ing :** to take a nap **:** DOZE — **snooze** *n*
snore \ˈsnōr\ *vb* **snored; snor•ing :** to breathe with a rough hoarse noise while sleeping — **snore** *n*
snor•kel \ˈsnȯr-kəl\ *n* [G *Schnorchel*] **:** a tube projecting above the water used by swimmers for breathing with the face under water — **snorkel** *vb*
snort \ˈsnȯrt\ *vb* **1 :** to force air violently and noisily through the nose ⟨his horse ~*ed*⟩ **2 :** INHALE — **snort** *n*
snot \ˈsnät\ *n* **:** nasal mucus
snout \ˈsnau̇t\ *n* **1 :** a long projecting muzzle (as of a pig) **2 :** a usu. large or grotesque nose
[1]**snow** \ˈsnō\ *n* **1 :** crystals of ice formed from water vapor in the air **2 :** a descent or shower of snow crystals
[2]**snow** *vb* **1 :** to fall or cause to fall in or as snow **2 :** to cover or shut in with or as if with snow
[1]**snow•ball** \ˈsnō-ˌbȯl\ *n* **:** a round mass of snow pressed into shape in the hand for throwing
[2]**snowball** *vb* **1 :** to throw snowballs at **2 :** to increase or expand at a rapidly accelerating rate
snow•bank \-ˌbaŋk\ *n* **:** a mound or slope of snow
snow•belt \-ˌbelt\ *n, often cap* **:** a region that receives an appreciable amount of annual snowfall
snow•blow•er \-ˌblō-ər\ *n* **:** a machine in which a rotating spiral blade picks up and propels snow aside
snow•board \-ˌbōrd\ *n* **:** a board like a wide ski ridden in a surfing position downhill over snow
snow•drift \-ˌdrift\ *n* **:** a bank of drifted snow
snow•drop \-ˌdräp\ *n* **:** a plant with narrow leaves and a nodding white flower that blooms early in the spring
snow•fall \-ˌfȯl\ *n* **:** a fall of snow
snow fence *n* **:** a fence across the path of prevailing winds to protect something (as a road) from drifting snow
snow•field \ˈsnō-ˌfēld\ *n* **:** a mass of perennial snow at the head of a glacier
snow•mo•bile \ˈsnō-mō-ˌbēl\ *n* **:** any of various automotive vehicles for travel on snow — **snow•mo•bil•er** \-ˌbē-lər\ *n* — **snow•mo•bil•ing** \-liŋ\ *n*
snow pea *n* **:** a cultivated pea with flat edible pods
snow•plow \ˈsnō-ˌplau̇\ *n* **1 :** a device for clearing away snow **2 :** a skiing maneuver in which the heels of both skis are slid outward for slowing down or stopping
[1]**snow•shoe** \-ˌshü\ *n* **:** a light frame of wood strung with thongs that is attached to a shoe or boot to prevent sinking down into soft snow
[2]**snowshoe** *vb* **snow•shoed; snow•shoe•ing :** to travel on snowshoes
snow•storm \-ˌstȯrm\ *n* **:** a storm of falling snow
snow thrower *n* **:** SNOWBLOWER
snowy \ˈsnō-ē\ *adj* **snow•i•er; -est 1 :** marked by snow **2 :** white as snow
snub \ˈsnəb\ *vb* **snubbed; snub•bing :** to treat with disdain **:** SLIGHT — **snub** *n*
snub–nosed \ˈsnəb-ˌnōzd\ *adj* **:** having a nose slightly turned up at the end
snuck *past and past part of* SNEAK
[1]**snuff** \ˈsnəf\ *vb* **1 :** to pinch off the charred end of (a candle) **2 :** to put out (a candle) — **snuff•er** *n*
[2]**snuff** *vb* **1 :** to draw forcibly into or through the nose **2 :** SMELL
[3]**snuff** *n* **:** SNIFF
[4]**snuff** *n* **:** pulverized tobacco
snuf•fle \ˈsnə-fəl\ *vb* **snuf•fled; snuf•fling 1 :** to snuff or sniff audibly and repeatedly **2 :** to breathe with a sniffing sound — **snuf•fle** *n*
snug \ˈsnəg\ *adj* **snug•ger; snug•gest 1 :** fitting closely and comfortably **2 :** CONCEALED — **snug•ly** *adv* — **snug•ness** *n*
snug•gle \ˈsnə-gəl\ *vb* **snug•gled; snug•gling :** to curl up or draw close comfortably **:** NESTLE
[1]**so** \ˈsō\ *adv* **1 :** in the manner indicated **2 :** in the same way **3 :** THUS **4 :** FINALLY **5 :** to the extent indicated **6 :** THEREFORE
[2]**so** *conj* **:** for that reason ⟨he wanted it, ~ he took it⟩
[3]**so** *pron* **1 :** the same ⟨became chairman and remained ~⟩ **2 :** approximately that ⟨a dozen or ~⟩

^{4}**so** *abbr* south; southern
SO *abbr* strikeout
^{1}**soak** \ˈsōk\ *vb* **1 :** to remain in a liquid **2 :** WET, SATURATE **3 :** to draw in by or as if by absorption **syn** drench, steep, impregnate
^{2}**soak** *n* **1 :** the act of soaking **2 :** the liquid in which something is soaked **3 :** DRUNKARD
soap \ˈsōp\ *n* **:** a cleansing substance made usu. by action of alkali on fat — **soap** *vb* — **soapy** *adj*
soap opera *n* [fr. its sponsorship by soap manufacturers] **:** a radio or television daytime serial drama
soap•stone \ˈsōp-ˌstōn\ *n* **:** a soft talc-containing stone with a soapy feel
soar \ˈsōr\ *vb* **:** to fly upward or at a height on or as if on wings
sob \ˈsäb\ *vb* **sobbed; sob•bing :** to weep with convulsive heavings of the chest or contractions of the throat — **sob** *n*
so•ber \ˈsō-bər\ *adj* **so•ber•er** \-bər-ər\; **so•ber•est** \-bə-rəst\ **1 :** temperate in the use of liquor **2 :** not drunk **3 :** serious or grave in mood or disposition **4 :** having a quiet tone or color **syn** solemn, earnest, staid, sedate — **so•ber•ly** *adv* — **so•ber•ness** *n*
so•bri•ety \sō-ˈbrī-ə-tē\ *n* **:** the quality or state of being sober
so•bri•quet \ˈsō-bri-ˌkā, -ˌket\ *n* [F] **:** NICKNAME
soc *abbr* **1** social; society **2** sociology
so–called \ˈsō-ˈkȯld\ *adj* **:** commonly but often inaccurately so termed
soc•cer \ˈsä-kər\ *n* [by shortening & alter. fr. *association football*] **:** a game played on a field by two teams with a round inflated ball advanced chiefly by kicking
^{1}**so•cia•ble** \ˈsō-shə-bəl\ *adj* **1 :** liking companionship **:** FRIENDLY **2 :** characterized by pleasant social relations **syn** gracious, cordial, affable, genial — **so•cia•bil•i•ty** \ˌsō-shə-ˈbi-lə-tē\ *n* — **so•cia•bly** \ˈsō-shə-blē\ *adv*
^{2}**sociable** *n* **:** SOCIAL
^{1}**so•cial** \ˈsō-shəl\ *adj* **1 :** marked by pleasant companionship with one's friends **2 :** naturally living and breeding in organized communities ⟨~ insects⟩ **3 :** of or relating to human society ⟨~ institutions⟩ **4 :** of, relating to, or based on rank in a particular society ⟨~ circles⟩; *also* **:** of or relating to fashionable society — **so•cial•ly** *adv*
^{2}**social** *n* **:** a social gathering
social disease *n* **:** VENEREAL DISEASE
so•cial•ise *Brit var of* SOCIALIZE
so•cial•ism \ˈsō-shə-ˌli-zəm\ *n* **:** any of various social systems based on shared or government ownership and administration of the means of production and distribution of goods — **so•cial•ist** \ˈsō-shə-list\ *n or adj* — **so•cial•is•tic** \ˌsō-shə-ˈlis-tik\ *adj*
so•cial•ite \ˈsō-shə-ˌlīt\ *n* **:** a person prominent in fashionable society
so•cial•ize \ˈsō-shə-ˌlīz\ *vb* **-ized; -iz•ing 1 :** to regulate according to the theory and practice of socialism **2 :** to adapt to social needs or uses **3 :** to participate actively in a social gathering — **so•cial•i•za•tion** \ˌsō-shə-lə-ˈzā-shən\ *n*
social science *n* **:** a science (as economics or political science) dealing with a particular aspect of human society — **social scientist** *n*
social work *n* **:** services, activities, or methods providing social services esp. to the economically underprivileged and socially maladjusted — **social worker** *n*
so•ci•e•ty \sə-ˈsī-ə-tē\ *n, pl* **-ties** [MF *societé*, fr. L *societat-, societas,* fr. *socius* companion] **1 :** COMPANIONSHIP **2 :** a voluntary association of persons for common ends **3 :** a part of a community bound together by common interests and standards; *esp* **:** the group or set of fashionable people
so•cio•eco•nom•ic \ˌsō-sē-ō-ˌe-kə-ˈnä-mik, ˌsō-shē-, -ˌē-kə-\ *adj* **:** of, relating to, or involving both social and economic factors
sociol *abbr* sociologist; sociology
so•ci•ol•o•gy \ˌsō-sē-ˈä-lə-jē, ˌsō-shē-\ *n* **:** the science of society, social institutions, and social relationships — **so•cio•log•i•cal** \ˌsō-sē-ə-ˈlä-ji-kəl, ˌsō-shē-\ *adj* — **so•ci•ol•o•gist** \-ˈä-lə-jist\ *n*
^{1}**sock** \ˈsäk\ *n, pl* **socks** *or* **sox** \ˈsäks\ **:** a stocking with a short leg
^{2}**sock** *vb* **:** to hit, strike, or apply forcefully
^{3}**sock** *n* **:** a vigorous blow **:** PUNCH
sock•et \ˈsä-kət\ *n* **:** an opening or hollow that forms a holder for something
socket wrench *n* **:** a wrench usu. in the form of a bar and removable socket made to fit a bolt or nut
^{1}**sod** \ˈsäd\ *n* **:** TURF 1
^{2}**sod** *vb* **sod•ded; sod•ding :** to cover with sod
so•da \ˈsō-də\ *n* **1 :** SODIUM CARBONATE **2 :** SODIUM BICARBONATE **3 :** SODIUM **4 :** SODA WATER **5 :** SODA POP **6 :** a sweet drink of soda water, flavoring, and often ice cream
soda pop *n* **:** a carbonated, sweetened, and flavored soft drink
soda water *n* **:** a beverage of water charged with carbon dioxide
sod•den \ˈsäd-ᵊn\ *adj* **1 :** lacking spirit **:** DULLED **2 :** SOAKED, DRENCHED **3 :** heavy or doughy from being improperly cooked ⟨~ biscuits⟩
so•di•um \ˈsō-dē-əm\ *n* **:** a soft waxy silver white metallic chemical element occurring in nature in combined form (as in salt) — see ELEMENT table
sodium bicarbonate *n* **:** a white weakly alkaline salt used esp. in baking powders, fire extinguishers, and medicine
sodium carbonate *n* **:** a carbonate of sodium used esp. in washing and bleaching textiles
sodium chloride *n* **:** SALT 1
sodium fluoride *n* **:** a salt used chiefly in tiny amounts to prevent tooth decay
sodium hydroxide *n* **:** a white brittle caustic substance used in making soap and rayon and in bleaching
sodium nitrate *n* **:** a crystalline salt used as a fertilizer and in curing meat
sodium thiosulfate *n* **:** a hygroscopic crystalline salt used as a photographic fixing agent
sod•omy \ˈsä-də-mē\ *n* **1 :** sexual intercourse with a member of the same sex or with an animal **2 :** noncoital and esp. anal or oral sexual intercourse with a member of the opposite sex — **sod•om•ize** \ˈsä-də-ˌmīz\ *vb*
so•ev•er \sō-ˈe-vər\ *adv* **1 :** in any degree or manner ⟨how bad ~⟩ **2 :** at all **:** of any kind ⟨any help ~⟩
so•fa \ˈsō-fə\ *n* [Ar *ṣuffah* long bench] **:** a couch usu. with upholstered back and arms
soft \ˈsȯft\ *adj* **1 :** not hard or rough **:** NONVIOLENT **2 :** RESTFUL, GENTLE, SOOTHING **3 :** emotionally susceptible **4 :** not prepared to endure hardship **5 :** not containing certain salts that prevent lathering ⟨~ water⟩ **6 :** occurring at such a speed as to avoid destructive impact ⟨~ landing of a spacecraft on the moon⟩ **7 :** BIODEGRADABLE ⟨a ~ detergent⟩ **8 :** not alcoholic ⟨~ drinks⟩ **9 :** less detrimental than a hard narcotic ⟨~ drugs⟩ — **soft•ly** *adv* — **soft•ness** *n*
soft•ball \ˈsȯft-ˌbȯl\ *n* **:** a game similar to baseball played with a ball larger and softer than a baseball; *also* **:** the ball used in this game
soft•bound \-ˌbau̇nd\ *adj* **:** not bound in hard covers ⟨~ books⟩
soft coal *n* **:** BITUMINOUS COAL
soft•en \ˈsȯ-fən\ *vb* **:** to make or become soft — **soft•en•er** *n*
soft palate *n* **:** the fold at the back of the hard palate that partially separates the mouth and the pharynx
soft•ware \ˈsȯft-ˌwar\ *n* **:** the entire set of programs, procedures, and related documentation associated with a system; *esp* **:** computer programs
soft•wood \-ˌwu̇d\ *n* **1 :** the wood of a coniferous tree as compared to that of a broad-leaved deciduous tree

2 : a tree that yields softwood — **softwood** *adj*
sog•gy \ˈsä-gē\ *adj* **sog•gi•er; -est** : heavy with water or moisture — **sog•gi•ly** \ˈsä-gə-lē\ *adv* — **sog•gi•ness** \-gē-nəs\ *n*
soi•gné *or* **soi•gnée** \swän-ˈyā\ *adj* : elegantly maintained; *esp* : WELL-GROOMED
¹**soil** \ˈsȯil\ *vb* **1** : CORRUPT, POLLUTE **2** : to make or become dirty **3** : STAIN, DISGRACE
²**soil** *n* **1** : STAIN, DEFILEMENT **2** : EXCREMENT, WASTE
³**soil** *n* **1** : firm land : EARTH **2** : the upper layer of earth in which plants grow **3** : COUNTRY, REGION
soi•ree *or* **soi•rée** \swä-ˈrā\ *n* [F *soirée* evening period, evening party, fr. MF, fr. *soir* evening, fr. L *sero* at a late hour] : an evening party
so•journ \ˈsō-ˌjərn, sō-ˈjərn\ *vb* : to dwell in a place temporarily — **so•journ** *n* — **so•journ•er** *n*
¹**sol** \ˈsäl, ˈsōl\ *n* — see MONEY table
²**sol** *n* : a fluid colloidal system
³**sol** *abbr* **1** solicitor **2** soluble **3** solution
Sol \ˈsäl\ *n* : SUN
¹**sol•ace** \ˈsä-ləs\ *n* : COMFORT
²**solace** *vb* **so•laced; so•lac•ing** : to give solace to : CONSOLE
so•lar \ˈsō-lər\ *adj* **1** : of, derived from, or relating to the sun **2** : measured by the earth's course in relation to the sun ⟨the ~ year⟩ **3** : operated by or using the sun's light or heat ⟨~ energy⟩
solar cell *n* : a photoelectric cell that converts light into electrical energy and is used as a power source
solar collector *n* : a device for the absorption of solar radiation for the heating of water or buildings or the production of electricity
solar flare *n* : a sudden temporary outburst of energy from a small area of the sun's surface
so•lar•i•um \sō-ˈlar-ē-əm\ *n, pl* **-ia** \-ē-ə\ *also* **-i•ums** : a room exposed to the sun; *esp* : a room (as in a hospital) for exposure of the body to sunshine
solar plexus *n* : the general area of the stomach below the sternum
solar system *n* : the sun together with the group of celestial bodies that revolve around it
solar wind *n* : plasma continuously ejected from the sun's surface
sold *past and past part of* SELL
sol•der \ˈsä-dər, ˈsȯ-\ *n* : a metallic alloy used when melted to mend or join metallic surfaces — **solder** *vb*
soldering iron *n* : a metal device for applying heat in soldering
¹**sol•dier** \ˈsōl-jər\ *n* [ME *soudier,* fr. MF, fr. *soulde* pay, fr. LL *solidus* a Roman coin, fr. L, solid] : a person in military service; *esp* : an enlisted man or woman — **sol•dier•ly** *adj or adv*
²**soldier** *vb* **sol•diered; sol•dier•ing 1** : to serve as a soldier **2** : to pretend to work while actually doing nothing
soldier of fortune : ADVENTURER 2
sol•diery \ˈsōl-jə-rē\ *n* : a body of soldiers
¹**sole** \ˈsōl\ *n* : any of various flatfishes marketed for food
²**sole** *n* **1** : the undersurface of the foot **2** : the bottom of a shoe
³**sole** *vb* **soled; sol•ing** : to furnish (a shoe) with a sole
⁴**sole** *adj* : SINGLE, ONLY — **sole•ly** \ˈsōl-lē\ *adv*
so•le•cism \ˈsä-lə-ˌsi-zəm, ˈsō-\ *n* **1** : a mistake in grammar **2** : a breach of etiquette
sol•emn \ˈsä-ləm\ *adj* **1** : marked by or observed with full religious ceremony **2** : FORMAL, CEREMONIOUS **3** : highly serious : GRAVE **4** : SOMBER, GLOOMY — **so•lem•ni•ty** \sə-ˈlem-nə-tē\ *n* — **sol•emn•ly** \ˈsä-ləm-lē\ *adv*
sol•em•nize \ˈsä-ləm-ˌnīz\ *vb* **-nized; -niz•ing 1** : to observe or honor with solemnity **2** : to celebrate (a marriage) with religious rites — **sol•em•ni•za•tion** \ˌsä-ləm-nə-ˈzā-shən\ *n*
so•le•noid \ˈsō-lə-ˌnȯid, ˈsä-\ *n* : a coil of wire usu. in cylindrical form that when carrying a current acts like a magnet
so•lic•it \sə-ˈli-sət\ *vb* **1** : ENTREAT, BEG **2** : to approach with a request or plea **3** : TEMPT, LURE — **so•lic•i•ta•tion** \-ˌli-sə-ˈtā-shən\ *n*
so•lic•i•tor \sə-ˈli-sə-tər\ *n* **1** : one that solicits **2** : LAWYER; *esp* : a legal official of a city or state
so•lic•i•tous \sə-ˈli-sə-təs\ *adj* **1** : WORRIED, CONCERNED **2** : EAGER, WILLING **syn** avid, impatient, keen, anxious — **so•lic•i•tous•ly** *adv*
so•lic•i•tude \sə-ˈli-sə-ˌtüd, -ˌtyüd\ *n* : CONCERN, ANXIETY
¹**sol•id** \ˈsä-ləd\ *adj* **1** : not hollow; *also* : written as one word without a hyphen ⟨a ~ compound⟩ **2** : having, involving, or dealing with three dimensions or with solids ⟨~ geometry⟩ **3** : not loose or spongy : COMPACT ⟨a ~ mass of rock⟩; *also* : neither gaseous nor liquid : HARD, RIGID ⟨~ ice⟩ **4** : of good substantial quality or kind ⟨~ comfort⟩ **5** : thoroughly dependable : RELIABLE ⟨a ~ citizen⟩; *also* : serious in purpose or character ⟨~ reading⟩ **6** : UNANIMOUS, UNITED ⟨~ for pay increases⟩ **7** : of one substance or character — **solid** *adv* — **so•lid•i•ty** \sə-ˈli-də-tē\ *n* — **sol•id•ly** *adv* — **sol•id•ness** *n*
²**solid** *n* **1** : a geometrical figure (as a cube or sphere) having three dimensions **2** : a solid substance
sol•i•dar•i•ty \ˌsä-lə-ˈdar-ə-tē\ *n* : unity based on shared interests, objectives, or standards
so•lid•i•fy \sə-ˈli-də-ˌfī\ *vb* **-fied; -fy•ing** : to make or become solid — **so•lid•i•fi•ca•tion** \-ˌli-də-fə-ˈkā-shən\ *n*
solid–state *adj* **1** : relating to the structure and properties of solid material **2** : using semiconductor devices rather than vacuum tubes
so•lil•o•quise *Brit var of* SOLILOQUIZE
so•lil•o•quize \sə-ˈli-lə-ˌkwīz\ *vb* **-quized; -quiz•ing** : to talk to oneself : utter a soliloquy
so•lil•o•quy \sə-ˈli-lə-kwē\ *n, pl* **-quies** [LL *soliloquium,* fr. L *solus* alone + *loqui* to speak] **1** : the act of talking to oneself **2** : a dramatic monologue that represents unspoken reflections by a character
sol•i•taire \ˈsä-lə-ˌtar\ *n* **1** : a single gem (as a diamond) set alone **2** : a card game for one person
sol•i•tary \ˈsä-lə-ˌter-ē\ *adj* **1** : being or living apart from others **2** : LONELY, SECLUDED **3** : SOLE, ONLY
sol•i•tude \ˈsä-lə-ˌtüd, -ˌtyüd\ *n* **1** : the state of being alone : SECLUSION **2** : a lonely place
soln *abbr* solution
¹**so•lo** \ˈsō-lō\ *n, pl* **solos** [It, fr. *solo* alone, fr. L *solus*] **1** : a piece of music for a single voice or instrument with or without accompaniment **2** : an action in which there is only one performer — **solo** *adj or vb* — **so•lo•ist** *n*
²**solo** *adv* : without a companion : ALONE
so•lon \ˈsō-lən\ *n* **1** : a wise and skillful lawgiver **2** : a member of a legislative body
sol•stice \ˈsäl-stəs, ˈsōl-\ *n* [ME, fr. OF, fr. L *solstitium,* fr. *sol* sun + *-stit-, -stes* standing] : the time of the year when the sun is farthest north of the equator (**summer solstice**) about June 22 or farthest south (**winter solstice**) about Dec. 22 — **sol•sti•tial** \säl-ˈsti-shəl, sōl-\ *adj*
sol•u•ble \ˈsäl-yə-bəl\ *adj* **1** : capable of being dissolved in or as if in a liquid **2** : capable of being solved or explained — **sol•u•bil•i•ty** \ˌsäl-yə-ˈbi-lə-tē\ *n*
sol•ute \ˈsäl-ˌyüt\ *n* : a dissolved substance
so•lu•tion \sə-ˈlü-shən\ *n* **1** : an action or process of solving a problem; *also* : an answer to a problem **2** : an act or the process by which one substance is homogenously mixed with another usu. liquid substance; *also* : a mixture thus formed
solve \ˈsälv\ *vb* **solved; solv•ing** : to find the answer to or a solution for — **solv•able** *adj*
sol•ven•cy \ˈsäl-vən-sē\ *n* : the condition of being solvent

¹sol•vent \-vənt\ *adj* **1** : able or sufficient to pay all legal debts **2** : dissolving or able to dissolve

²solvent *n* : a usu. liquid substance capable of dissolving or dispersing one or more other substances

So•ma•lian \sō-ˈmäl-yən\ *n* : a native or inhabitant of Somalia — **Somalian** *adj*

so•mat•ic \sō-ˈma-tik\ *adj* : of, relating to, or affecting the body in contrast to the mind or the sex cells and their precursors

som•ber *or* **som•bre** \ˈsäm-bər\ *adj* **1** : DARK, GLOOMY **2** : GRAVE, MELANCHOLY — **som•ber•ly** *adv*

som•bre•ro \səm-ˈbrer-ō\ *n, pl* **-ros** [Sp, fr. *sombra* shade] : a broad-brimmed felt hat worn esp. in the Southwest and in Mexico

sombrero

¹some \ˈsəm\ *adj* **1** : one unspecified ⟨~ man called⟩ **2** : an unspecified or indefinite number of ⟨~ berries are ripe⟩ **3** : at least a few or a little ⟨~ years ago⟩

²some *pron* : a certain number or amount ⟨~ of the berries are ripe⟩ ⟨~ of it is missing⟩

¹-some \səm\ *adj suffix* : characterized by a (specified) thing, quality, state, or action ⟨awe*some*⟩ ⟨burden*some*⟩

²-some *n suffix* : a group of (so many) members and esp. persons ⟨four*some*⟩

¹some•body \ˈsəm-ˌbä-dē, -bə-\ *pron* : some person

²somebody *n* : a person of importance

some•day \ˈsəm-ˌdā\ *adv* : at some future time

some•how \-ˌhau̇\ *adv* : by some means

some•one \-(ˌ)wən\ *pron* : some person

som•er•sault \ˈsə-mər-ˌsȯlt\ *n* [MF *sombresaut* leap, ultim. fr. L *super* over + *saltus* leap, fr. *salire* to jump] : a leap or roll in which a person turns heels over head — **somersault** *vb*

som•er•set \-ˌset\ *n or vb* : SOMERSAULT

some•thing \ˈsəm-thiŋ\ *pron* : some undetermined or unspecified thing

some•time \-ˌtīm\ *adv* **1** : at a future time **2** : at an unknown or unnamed time

some•times \-ˌtīmz\ *adv* : OCCASIONALLY

¹some•what \-ˌhwät, -ˌhwət\ *pron* : SOMETHING

²somewhat *adv* : in some degree

some•where \-ˌhwer\ *adv* : in, at, or to an unknown or unnamed place

som•nam•bu•lism \säm-ˈnam-byə-ˌli-zəm\ *n* : performance of motor acts (as walking) during sleep; *also* : an abnormal condition of sleep characterized by this — **som•nam•bu•list** \-list\ *n*

som•no•lent \ˈsäm-nə-lənt\ *adj* : SLEEPY, DROWSY — **som•no•lence** \-ləns\ *n*

son \ˈsən\ *n* **1** : a male offspring or descendant **2** *cap* : Jesus Christ **3** : a person deriving from a particular source (as a country, race, or school)

so•nar \ˈsō-ˌnär\ *n* [*so*und *n*avigation *a*nd *r*anging] : a method or device for detecting and locating submerged objects (as submarines) by sound waves

so•na•ta \sə-ˈnä-tə\ *n* [It] : an instrumental composition with three or four movements differing in rhythm and mood but related in key

son•a•ti•na \ˌsä-nə-ˈtē-nə\ *n* [It, dim. of *sonata*] : a short usu. simplified sonata

song \ˈsȯŋ\ *n* **1** : vocal music; *also* : a short composition of words and music **2** : poetic composition **3** : a distinctive or characteristic sound (as of a bird) **4** : a small amount ⟨sold for a ~⟩

song•bird \ˈsȯŋ-ˌbərd\ *n* : a bird that utters a series of musical tones

Song of Sol•o•mon \-ˈsä-lə-mən\ — see BIBLE table

Song of Songs — see BIBLE table

song•ster \ˈsȯŋ-stər\ *n* : one that sings

song•stress \-strəs\ *n* : a female singer

son•ic \ˈsä-nik\ *adj* : of or relating to sound waves or the speed of sound

sonic boom *n* : an explosive sound produced by an aircraft traveling at supersonic speed

son–in–law \ˈsən-ən-ˌlȯ\ *n, pl* **sons–in–law** : the husband of one's daughter

son•net \ˈsä-nət\ *n* : a poem of 14 lines usu. in iambic pentameter with a definite rhyme scheme

so•no•rous \sə-ˈnōr-əs, ˈsä-nə-rəs\ *adj* **1** : giving out sound when struck **2** : loud, deep, or rich in sound : RESONANT **3** : high-sounding : IMPRESSIVE — **so•nor•i•ty** \sə-ˈnȯr-ə-tē\ *n*

soon \ˈsün\ *adv* **1** : before long **2** : PROMPTLY, QUICKLY **3** *archaic* : EARLY **4** : WILLINGLY, READILY

soot \ˈsu̇t, ˈsət, ˈsüt\ *n* : a fine black powder consisting chiefly of carbon that is formed when something burns and that colors smoke — **sooty** *adj*

sooth \ˈsüth\ *n, archaic* : TRUTH

soothe \ˈsüth\ *vb* **soothed; sooth•ing** **1** : to please by flattery or attention **2** : to calm down : COMFORT — **sooth•er** *n* — **sooth•ing•ly** *adv*

sooth•say•er \ˈsüth-ˌsā-ər\ *n* : one who foretells events — **sooth•say•ing** *n*

¹sop \ˈsäp\ *n* : a conciliatory bribe, gift, or concession

²sop *vb* **sopped; sop•ping** **1** : to steep or dip in or as if in a liquid **2** : to wet thoroughly : SOAK; *also* : to mop up (a liquid)

SOP *abbr* standard operating procedure; standing operating procedure

soph *abbr* sophomore

soph•ism \ˈsä-ˌfi-zəm\ *n* **1** : an argument correct in form but embodying a subtle fallacy **2** : SOPHISTRY

soph•ist \ˈsä-fist\ *n* : PHILOSOPHER; *esp* : a captious or fallacious reasoner

so•phis•tic \sä-ˈfis-tik, sə-\ *or* **so•phis•ti•cal** \-ti-kəl\ *adj* : of or characteristic of sophists or sophistry **syn** fallacious, illogical, unreasonable, specious

so•phis•ti•cat•ed \sə-ˈfis-tə-ˌkā-təd\ *adj* **1** : COMPLEX ⟨~ instruments⟩ **2** : made worldly-wise by wide experience **3** : intellectually appealing ⟨~ novel⟩ — **so•phis•ti•ca•tion** \-ˌfis-tə-ˈkā-shən\ *n*

soph•ist•ry \ˈsä-fə-strē\ *n* : subtly deceptive reasoning or argument

soph•o•more \ˈsäf-ˌmōr, ˈsä-fə-\ *n* : a student in the second year of high school or college

soph•o•mor•ic \ˌsäf-ˈmōr-ik, ˌsä-fə-\ *adj* **1** : being overconfident of knowledge but poorly informed and immature **2** : of, relating to, or characteristic of a sophomore ⟨a ~ prank⟩

So•pho•ni•as \ˌsä-fə-ˈnī-əs, ˌsō-\ *n* : ZEPHANIAH

sop•o•rif•ic \ˌsä-pə-ˈri-fik\ *adj* **1** : causing sleep or drowsiness **2** : LETHARGIC

so•pra•no \sə-ˈpra-nō, -ˈprä-\ *n, pl* **-nos** [It, fr. *sopra* above, fr. L *supra*] **1** : the highest singing voice; *also* : a singer with this voice **2** : the highest part in a 4-part chorus — **soprano** *adj*

sor•bet \sȯr-ˈbā\ *n* : a fruit-flavored ice served for dessert or between courses as a palate refresher

sor•cery \ˈsȯr-sə-rē\ *n* [ME *sorcerie*, fr. OF, fr. *sorcier* sorcerer, fr. (assumed) VL *sortiarius*, fr. L *sort-*, *sors* chance, lot] : the use of magic : WITCHCRAFT — **sor•cer•er** \-rər\ *n* — **sor•cer•ess** \-rəs\ *n*

sor•did \ˈsȯr-dəd\ *adj* **1** : marked by baseness or grossness : VILE **2** : DIRTY, SQUALID — **sor•did•ly** *adv* — **sor•did•ness** *n*

[1]**sore** \ˈsōr\ *adj* **sor•er; sor•est 1** : causing pain or distress ⟨a ∼ bruise⟩ **2** : painfully sensitive ⟨∼ muscles⟩ **3** : SEVERE, INTENSE **4** : IRRITATED, ANGRY — **sore•ly** *adv* — **sore•ness** *n*

[2]**sore** *n* **1** : a sore spot on the body; *esp* : one (as an ulcer) with the tissues broken and usu. infected **2** : a source of pain or vexation

sore•head \ˈsōr-ˌhed, ˈsȯr-\ *n* : a person easily angered or discontented

sore throat *n* : painful throat due to inflammation

sor•ghum \ˈsȯr-gəm\ *n* : a tall variable Old World tropical grass grown widely for its edible seed, for forage, or for its sweet juice which yields a syrup

so•ror•i•ty \sə-ˈrȯr-ə-tē\ *n, pl* **-ties** [ML *sororitas* sisterhood, fr. L *soror* sister] : a club of girls or women esp. at a college

[1]**sor•rel** \ˈsȯr-əl\ *n* : a brownish orange to light brown color; *also* : a sorrel-colored animal (as a horse)

[2]**sorrel** *n* : any of various herbs having a sour juice

sor•row \ˈsär-ō\ *n* **1** : deep distress, sadness, or regret; *also* : resultant unhappy or unpleasant state **2** : a cause of grief or sadness **3** : a display of grief or sadness — **sorrow** *vb* — **sor•row•ful** \-fəl\ *adj* — **sor•row•ful•ly** \-f(ə-)lē\ *adv*

sor•ry \ˈsär-ē\ *adj* **sor•ri•er; -est 1** : feeling sorrow, regret, or penitence **2** : MOURNFUL, SAD **3** : causing sorrow, pity, or scorn : WRETCHED

[1]**sort** \ˈsȯrt\ *n* **1** : a group of persons or things that have similar characteristics : CLASS **2** : WAY, MANNER **3** : QUALITY, NATURE **4** : an instance of sorting — **out of sorts 1** : somewhat ill **2** : GROUCHY, IRRITABLE

[2]**sort** *vb* **1** : to put in a certain place according to kind, class, or nature **2** : to be in accord : AGREE — **sort•er** *n*

sor•tie \ˈsȯr-tē, sȯr-ˈtē\ *n* **1** : a sudden issuing of troops from a defensive position against the enemy **2** : one mission or attack by one airplane

sort of *adv* : to a moderate degree

SOS \ˌes-(ˌ)ō-ˈes\ *n* : a call or request for help or rescue

so–so \ˈsō-ˈsō\ *adv or adj* : PASSABLY

sot \ˈsät\ *n* : a habitual drunkard — **sot•tish** *adj* — **sot•tish•ly** *adv*

souf•flé \sü-ˈflā\ *n* [F, fr. *soufflé,* pp. of *souffler* to blow, puff up, fr. L *sufflare,* fr. *sub-* up + *flare* to blow] : a spongy dish made light in baking by stiffly beaten egg whites

sough \ˈsaů, ˈsəf\ *vb* : to make a moaning or sighing sound — **sough** *n*

sought *past and past part of* SEEK

[1]**soul** \ˈsōl\ *n* **1** : the immaterial essence of an individual life **2** : the spiritual principle embodied in human beings or the universe **3** : an active or essential part **4** : the moral and emotional nature of human beings **5** : spiritual or moral force **6** : PERSON ⟨a kindly ∼⟩ **7** : a strong, positive feeling (as of intense sensitivity and emotional fervor) conveyed esp. by black American performers; *also* : NEGRITUDE — **souled** \ˈsōld\ *adj* — **soul•less** \ˈsōl-ləs\ *adj*

[2]**soul** *adj* **1** : of, relating to, or characteristic of black Americans or their culture ⟨∼ food⟩ ⟨∼ music⟩ **2** : designed for or controlled by blacks ⟨∼ radio stations⟩

soul brother *n* : a black male

soul•ful \ˈsōl-fəl\ *adj* : full of or expressing deep feeling — **soul•ful•ly** *adv*

[1]**sound** \ˈsaůnd\ *adj* **1** : not diseased or sickly **2** : free from flaw or defect **3** : FIRM, STRONG **4** : free from error or fallacy : RIGHT **5** : LEGAL, VALID **6** : THOROUGH **7** : UNDISTURBED ⟨∼ sleep⟩ **8** : showing good judgment — **sound•ly** *adv* — **sound•ness** *n*

[2]**sound** *n* **1** : the sensation of hearing; *also* : mechanical energy transmitted by longitudinal pressure waves (**sound waves**) (as in air) that is the stimulus to hearing **2** : something heard : NOISE, TONE; *also* : hearing distance : EARSHOT **3** : a musical style — **sound•less** *adj* — **sound•less•ly** *adv* — **sound•proof** \-ˌprüf\ *adj or vb*

[3]**sound** *vb* **1** : to make or cause to make a sound **2** : to order or proclaim by a sound ⟨∼ the alarm⟩ **3** : to convey a certain impression : SEEM **4** : to examine the condition of by causing to give out sounds — **sound•able** \ˈsaůn-də-bəl\ *adj*

[4]**sound** *n* : a long passage of water wider than a strait often connecting two larger bodies of water ⟨Puget ∼⟩

[5]**sound** *vb* **1** : to measure the depth of (water) esp. by a weighted line dropped from the surface : FATHOM **2** : PROBE **3** : to dive down suddenly ⟨the hooked fish ∼*ed*⟩ — **sound•ing** *n*

sound bite *n* : a brief recorded statement broadcast esp. on a news program

sound•er \ˈsaůn-dər\ *n* : one that sounds; *esp* : a device for making soundings

sound•stage \ˈsaůnd-ˌstāj\ *n* : the part of a motion-picture studio in which a production is filmed

soup \ˈsüp\ *n* **1** : a liquid food with stock as its base and often containing pieces of solid food **2** : something having the consistency of soup **3** : an unfortunate predicament ⟨in the ∼⟩

soup•çon \süp-ˈsōⁿ\ *n* [F, lit., suspicion] : a little bit : [1]TRACE 2

soup up *vb* : to increase the power of

soupy \ˈsü-pē\ *adj* **soup•i•er; -est 1** : having the consistency of soup **2** : densely foggy or cloudy

[1]**sour** \ˈsaůr\ *adj* **1** : having an acid or tart taste ⟨∼ as vinegar⟩ **2** : SPOILED, PUTRID ⟨a ∼ odor⟩ **3** : UNPLEASANT, DISAGREEABLE ⟨∼ disposition⟩ — **sour•ish** *adj* — **sour•ly** *adv* — **sour•ness** *n*

[2]**sour** *vb* : to become or make sour

source \ˈsōrs\ *n* **1** : ORIGIN, BEGINNING **2** : a supplier of information **3** : the beginning of a stream of water

[1]**souse** \ˈsaůs\ *vb* **soused; sous•ing 1** : PICKLE **2** : to plunge into a liquid **3** : DRENCH **4** : to make drunk

[2]**souse** *n* **1** : something (as pigs' feet) steeped in pickle **2** : a soaking in liquid **3** : DRUNKARD

[1]**south** \ˈsaůth\ *adv* : to or toward the south; *also* : into a state of decline

[2]**south** *adj* **1** : situated toward or at the south **2** : coming from the south

[3]**south** *n* **1** : the direction to the right of one facing east **2** : the compass point directly opposite to north **3** *cap* : regions or countries south of a specified or implied point; *esp* : the southeastern part of the U.S. — **south•er•ly** \ˈsə-t͟hər-lē\ *adj or adv* — **south•ern** \ˈsə-t͟hərn\ *adj* — **South•ern•er** *n* — **south•ern•most** \-ˌmōst\ *adj* — **south•ward** \ˈsaůth-wərd\ *adv or adj* — **south•wards** \-wərdz\ *adv*

South African *n* : a native or inhabitant of the Republic of South Africa — **South African** *adj*

south•east \saů-ˈthēst, *naut* saů-ˈēst\ *n* **1** : the general direction between south and east **2** : the compass point midway between south and east **3** *cap* : regions or countries southeast of a specified or implied point — **southeast** *adj or adv* — **south•east•er•ly** *adv or adj* — **south•east•ern** \-ˈēs-tərn\ *adj*

south•paw \ˈsaůth-ˌpȯ\ *n* : a left-handed person; *esp* : a left-handed baseball pitcher — **southpaw** *adj*

south pole *n, often cap S&P* : the southernmost point of the earth

south•west \saůth-ˈwest, *naut* saů-ˈwest\ *n* **1** : the general direction between south and west **2** : the compass point midway between south and west **3** *cap* : regions or countries southwest of a specified or implied point — **southwest** *adj or adv* — **south•west•er•ly** *adv or adj* — **south•west•ern** \-ˈwes-tərn\ *adj*

sou•ve•nir \ˌsü-və-ˈnir\ *n* [F] : something serving as a reminder

sou'•west•er \saů-ˈwes-tər\ *n* : a long waterproof coat worn in storms at sea; *also* : a waterproof hat

[1]**sov•er•eign** \ˈsä-vrən, -və-rən\ *n* **1** : one possessing the

supreme power and authority in a state **2** : a gold coin of the United Kingdom

[2]**sovereign** *adj* **1** : EXCELLENT, FINE **2** : supreme in power or authority **3** : CHIEF, HIGHEST **4** : having independent authority

sov•er•eign•ty \-tē\ *n, pl* **-ties** **1** : supremacy in rule or power **2** : power to govern without external control **3** : the supreme political power in a state

so•vi•et \ˈsō-vē-ˌet, ˈsä-, -ət\ *n* **1** : an elected governmental council in a Communist country **2** *pl, cap* : the people and esp. the leaders of the U.S.S.R. — **soviet** *adj, often cap* — **so•vi•et•ize** *vb, often cap*

[1]**sow** \ˈsau̇\ *n* : an adult female swine

[2]**sow** \ˈsō\ *vb* **sowed; sown** \ˈsōn\ *or* **sowed; sow•ing** **1** : to plant seed esp. by scattering **2** : to strew with seed **3** : to scatter abroad — **sow•er** \ˈsō-ər\ *n*

sow bug \ˈsau̇-\ *n* : WOOD LOUSE

sox *pl of* SOCK

soy \ˈsȯi\ *n* : a sauce made from soybeans fermented in brine

soy•bean \ˈsȯi-ˌbēn\ *n* : an Asian legume widely grown for forage and for its edible seeds that yield a valuable oil (**soybean oil**); *also* : its seed

sp *abbr* **1** special **2** species **3** specimen **4** spelling **5** spirit

Sp *abbr* Spain

SP *abbr* **1** shore patrol; shore patrolman **2** shore police **3** specialist

spa \ˈspä\ *n* [*Spa,* watering place in Belgium] **1** : a resort with mineral springs **2** : a health and fitness facility **3** : a hot tub with a whirlpool device

[1]**space** \ˈspās\ *n* **1** : a period of time **2** : some small measurable distance, area, or volume **3** : the limitless area in which all things exist and move **4** : an empty place **5** : the region beyond the earth's atmosphere **6** : a definite place (as a seat on a train or ship)

[2]**space** *vb* **spaced; spac•ing** : to place at intervals — **spac•er** *n*

space–age \ˈspās-ˌāj\ *adj* : of or relating to the age of space exploration

space•craft \-ˌkraft\ *n* : a vehicle for travel beyond the earth's atmosphere

space•flight \-ˌflīt\ *n* : flight beyond the earth's atmosphere

space heater *n* : a usu. portable device for heating a relatively small area

space•man \ˈspās-ˌman, -mən\ *n* : one who travels outside the earth's atmosphere

space•ship \-ˌship\ *n* : a vehicle used for space travel

space shuttle *n* : a reusable spacecraft designed to transport people and cargo between earth and space

space station *n* : a large artificial satellite serving as a base (as for scientific observation)

space suit *n* : a suit equipped to make life in space possible for its wearer

space walk *n* : a period of activity outside a spacecraft by an astronaut in space — **space•walk** \ˈspās-ˌwȯk\ *vb* — **space•walk•er** *n*

spa•cious \ˈspā-shəs\ *adj* : very large in extent : ROOMY **syn** commodious, capacious, ample — **spa•cious•ly** *adv* — **spa•cious•ness** *n*

[1]**spade** \ˈspād\ *n* : a shovel with a blade for digging — **spade•ful** *n*

[2]**spade** *vb* **spad•ed; spad•ing** : to dig with a spade — **spad•er** *n*

[3]**spade** *n* : any of a suit of playing cards marked with a black figure resembling an inverted heart with a short stem at the bottom

spa•dix \ˈspā-diks\ *n, pl* **spa•di•ces** \ˈspā-də-ˌsēz\ : a floral spike with a fleshy or succulent axis usu. enclosed in a spathe

spa•ghet•ti \spə-ˈge-tē\ *n* [It, fr. pl. of *spaghetto,* dim. of *spago* cord, string] : thin solid pasta strings

[1]**span** \ˈspan\ *n* **1** : an English unit of length equal to nine inches (about 23 centimeters) **2** : a limited portion of time **3** : the spread (as of an arch) from one support to another

[2]**span** *vb* **spanned; span•ning** **1** : MEASURE **2** : to extend across

[3]**span** *n* : a pair of animals (as mules) driven together

Span *abbr* Spanish

span•dex \ˈspan-ˌdeks\ *n* : any of various elastic synthetic textile fibers

span•gle \ˈspaŋ-gəl\ *n* : a small disk of shining metal or plastic used esp. on a dress for ornament — **spangle** *vb*

Span•glish \ˈspaŋ-glish\ *n* : a combination of Spanish and English

Span•iard \ˈspan-yərd\ *n* : a native or inhabitant of Spain

span•iel \ˈspan-yəl\ *n* [ME *spaniell,* fr. MF *espaignol,* lit., Spaniard] : a dog of any of several breeds of mostly small and short-legged dogs usu. with long wavy hair and large drooping ears

spaniel

Span•ish \ˈspa-nish\ *n* **1** : the chief language of Spain and of the countries colonized by the Spanish **2** **Spanish** *pl* : the people of Spain — **Spanish** *adj*

Spanish American *n* : a resident of the U.S. whose native language is Spanish; *also* : a native or inhabitant of one of the countries of America in which Spanish is the national language — **Spanish–American** *adj*

Spanish fly *n* : a preparation of dried green European beetles noted as an aphrodisiac with often highly toxic side effects but not in reputable medical use

Spanish moss *n* : a plant related to the pineapple that grows in pendent tufts of grayish green filaments on trees from the southern U.S. to Argentina

Spanish rice *n* : rice cooked with onions, green peppers, and tomatoes

spank \ˈspaŋk\ *vb* : to hit on the buttocks with the open hand — **spank** *n*

spank•ing \ˈspaŋ-kiŋ\ *adj* : BRISK, LIVELY ⟨~ breeze⟩ — **spanking** *adv*

span•ner \ˈspan-ər\ *n, chiefly Brit* : WRENCH

[1]**spar** \ˈspär\ *n* **1** : a stout pole **2** : a rounded wood or metal piece (as a mast, yard, boom, or gaff) for supporting sail rigging

[2]**spar** *vb* **sparred; spar•ring** : to box for practice without serious hitting; *also* : SKIRMISH, WRANGLE

[1]**spare** \ˈspar\ *vb* **spared; spar•ing** **1** : to refrain from punishing or injuring : show mercy to ⟨~d the prisoners⟩ **2** : to exempt from something ⟨~ me the trouble⟩ **3** : to get along without ⟨can't ~ a dime⟩ **4** : to use frugally or rarely ⟨don't ~ the syrup⟩

[2]**spare** *adj* **spar•er; spar•est** **1** : held in reserve **2** : SUPERFLUOUS **3** : not liberal or profuse **4** : LEAN, THIN **5** : SCANTY **syn** meager, sparse, skimpy, exiguous, scant — **spare•ness** *n*

[3]**spare** *n* **1** : a duplicate kept in reserve; *esp* : a spare tire **2** : the knocking down of all the bowling pins with the first two balls

spar•ing \ˈspar-iŋ\ *adj* : SAVING, FRUGAL **syn** thrifty, economical, provident — **spar•ing•ly** *adv*

[1]**spark** \ˈspärk\ *n* **1** : a small particle of a burning substance or a hot glowing particle struck from a mass (as by steel on flint) **2** : a short bright flash of electricity between two points **3** : SPARKLE **4** : a particle capable of being kindled or developed : GERM

[2]**spark** *vb* **1** : to emit or produce sparks **2** : to stir to activity : INCITE

[3]**spark** *vb* : WOO, COURT

[1]**spar•kle** \ˈspär-kəl\ *vb* **spar•kled; spar•kling 1** : FLASH, GLEAM **2** : to perform brilliantly **3** : EFFERVESCE — **spar•kler** *n*

[2]**sparkle** *n* **1** : GLEAM **2** : ANIMATION

spark plug *n* **1** : a device that produces a spark to ignite the fuel mixture in an engine cylinder **2** : one that begins something or drives something forward

spar•row \ˈspar-ō\ *n* : any of several small dull-colored singing birds

sparse \ˈspärs\ *adj* **spars•er; spars•est** : thinly scattered : SCANTY **syn** meager, spare, skimpy, exiguous, scant — **sparse•ly** *adv* — **sparse•ness** *n*

spasm \ˈspa-zəm\ *n* **1** : a sudden involuntary and abnormal muscular contraction **2** : a sudden, violent, and temporary effort, feeling, or outburst

spas•mod•ic \spaz-ˈmä-dik\ *adj* **1** : relating to or affected or characterized by spasm ⟨~ movements⟩; *also* : resembling a spasm **2** : INTERMITTENT — **spas•mod•i•cal•ly** \-di-k(ə-)lē\ *adv*

spas•tic \ˈspas-tik\ *adj* : of, relating to, marked by, or affected with muscular spasm ⟨~ paralysis⟩ — **spastic** *n*

[1]**spat** \ˈspat\ *past and past part of* SPIT

[2]**spat** *n, pl* **spat** *or* **spats** : a young bivalve mollusk (as an oyster)

[3]**spat** *n* : a gaiter covering instep and ankle

spat

[4]**spat** *n* : a brief petty quarrel : DISPUTE

[5]**spat** *vb* **spat•ted; spat•ting** : to quarrel briefly

spate \ˈspāt\ *n* : a sudden outburst

spathe \ˈspāth\ *n* : a sheathing bract or pair of bracts enclosing an inflorescence (as of the calla lily) and esp. a spadix on the same axis

spa•tial \ˈspā-shəl\ *adj* : of or relating to space — **spa•tial•ly** *adv*

spat•ter \ˈspa-tər\ *vb* **1** : to splash with drops of liquid **2** : to sprinkle around — **spatter** *n*

spat•u•la \ˈspa-chə-lə\ *n* : a flexible knifelike implement for scooping, spreading, or mixing soft substances

spav•in \ˈspa-vən\ *n* : a bony enlargement of the hock of a horse — **spav•ined** \-vənd\ *adj*

[1]**spawn** \ˈspȯn\ *vb* [ME, fr. OF *espandre* to spread out, expand, fr. L *expandere*, fr. *ex-* out + *pandere* to spread] **1** : to produce eggs or offspring esp. in large numbers **2** : GENERATE — **spawn•er** *n*

[2]**spawn** *n* **1** : the eggs of water animals (as fishes or oysters) that lay many small eggs **2** : offspring esp. when produced in great quantities

spay \ˈspā\ *vb* **spayed; spay•ing** : to remove the ovaries of (a female animal)

SPCA *abbr* Society for the Prevention of Cruelty to Animals

SPCC *abbr* Society for the Prevention of Cruelty to Children

speak \ˈspēk\ *vb* **spoke** \ˈspōk\; **spo•ken** \ˈspō-kən\; **speak•ing 1** : to utter words **2** : to express orally **3** : to mention in speech or writing **4** : to address an audience **5** : to use or be able to use (a language) in talking

speak•easy \ˈspēk-ˌē-zē\ *n, pl* **-eas•ies** : an illicit drinking place

speak•er \ˈspē-kər\ *n* **1** : one that speaks **2** : the presiding officer of a deliberative assembly **3** : LOUDSPEAKER

[1]**spear** \ˈspir\ *n* **1** : a long-shafted weapon with a sharp point for thrusting or throwing **2** : a sharp-pointed instrument with barbs used in spearing fish — **spear•man** \-mən\ *n*

[2]**spear** *vb* : to strike or pierce with or as if with a spear — **spear•er** *n*

[3]**spear** *n* : a usu. young blade, shoot, or sprout (as of asparagus)

spear•head \-ˌhed\ *n* : a leading force, element, or influence — **spearhead** *vb*

spear•mint \-ˌmint\ *n* : a common highly aromatic garden mint

spec *abbr* **1** special **2** specifically

spe•cial \ˈspe-shəl\ *adj* **1** : UNCOMMON, NOTEWORTHY **2** : particularly favored **3** : INDIVIDUAL, UNIQUE **4** : EXTRA, ADDITIONAL **5** : confined to or designed for a definite field of action, purpose, or occasion — **special** *n*

special delivery *n* : delivery of mail by messenger for an extra fee

special effects *n pl* : images in a television or film production added after filming is completed to enhance believability

Special Forces *n pl* : a branch of the army composed of soldiers specially trained in guerrilla warfare

spe•cial•ise *Brit var of* SPECIALIZE

spe•cial•ist \ˈspe-shə-list\ *n* **1** : a person who specializes in a particular branch of learning or activity **2** : any of four enlisted ranks in the army corresponding to the grades of corporal through sergeant first class

spe•cial•ize \ˈspe-shə-ˌlīz\ *vb* **-ized; -iz•ing** : to concentrate one's efforts in a special activity or field; *also* : to change in an adaptive manner — **spe•cial•i•za•tion** \ˌspe-shə-lə-ˈzā-shən\ *n*

spe•cial•ly \ˈspe-shə-lē\ *adv* **1** : in a special manner **2** : for a special purpose : in particular

spe•cial•ty \ˈspe-shəl-tē\ *n, pl* **-ties 1** : a particular quality or detail **2** : a product of a special kind or of special excellence **3** : something (as a discipline) in which one specializes

spe•cie \ˈspē-shē, -sē\ *n* : money in coin

spe•cies \ˈspē-shēz, -sēz\ *n, pl* **spe•cies** [ME, fr. L, appearance, kind, species, fr. *specere* to look] **1** : SORT, KIND **2** : a category of biological classification ranking just below the genus or subgenus and comprising closely related organisms potentially able to breed with one another

specif *abbr* specific; specifically

[1]**spe•cif•ic** \spi-ˈsi-fik\ *adj* **1** : having a unique effect or influence or reacting in only one way or with only one thing ⟨~ antibodies⟩ ⟨~ enzymes⟩ **2** : DEFINITE, EXACT **3** : of, relating to, or constituting a species — **spe•cif•i•cal•ly** \-fi-k(ə-)lē\ *adv*

[2]**specific** *n* : something specific : DETAIL, PARTICULAR — usu. used in pl.

spec•i•fi•ca•tion \ˌspe-sə-fə-ˈkā-shən\ *n* **1** : the act or process of specifying **2** : a description of work to be done and materials to be used (as in building) — usu. used in pl.

specific gravity *n* : the ratio of the density of a substance to the density of some substance (as water) taken as a standard when both densities are obtained by weighing in air

spec•i•fy \ˈspe-sə-ˌfī\ *vb* **-fied; -fy•ing** : to mention or name explicitly

spec•i•men \ˈspe-sə-mən\ *n* : an item or part typical of a group or whole

spe•cious \ˈspē-shəs\ *adj* : seeming to be genuine, correct, or beautiful but not really so ⟨~ reasoning⟩

speck \ˈspek\ *n* **1** : a small spot or blemish **2** : a small particle — **speck** *vb*

speck•le \ˈspe-kəl\ *n* : a little speck — **speckle** *vb*

[1]**specs** \ˈspeks\ *n pl* : GLASSES

[2]**specs** *n pl* : SPECIFICATIONS

spec•ta•cle \ˈspek-ti-kəl\ *n* **1** : an unusual or impressive public display **2** *pl* : GLASSES — **spec•ta•cled** \-kəld\ *adj*

spec•tac•u•lar \spek-ˈta-kyə-lər\ *adj* : exciting to see : SENSATIONAL

spec•ta•tor \ˈspek-ˌtā-tər\ *n* : a person who looks on (as at a sports event) **syn** observer, witness, bystander, onlooker, eyewitness

spec•ter *or* **spec•tre** \ˈspek-tər\ *n* : a visible disembodied spirit : GHOST

spec•tral \ˈspek-trəl\ *adj* **1** : of, relating to, or resembling a specter **2** : of, relating to, or made by a spectrum

spec•tro•gram \ˈspek-trə-ˌgram\ *n* : a photograph or diagram of a spectrum

spec•tro•graph \-ˌgraf\ *n* : an instrument for dispersing radiation into a spectrum and photographing or mapping the spectrum — **spec•tro•graph•ic** \ˌspek-trə-ˈgra-fik\ *adj* — **spec•tro•graph•i•cal•ly** \-fi-k(ə-)lē\ *adv*

spec•trom•e•ter \spek-ˈträ-mə-tər\ *n* : an instrument for measuring spectra — **spec•tro•met•ric** \ˌspek-trə-ˈme-trik\ *adj* — **spec•trom•e•try** \spek-ˈträ-mə-trē\ *n*

spec•tro•scope \ˈspek-trə-ˌskōp\ *n* : an instrument that produces spectra esp. of visible electromagnetic radiation — **spec•tro•scop•ic** \ˌspek-trə-ˈskä-pik\ *adj* — **spec•tro•scop•i•cal•ly** \-pi-k(ə-)lē\ *adv* — **spec•tros•co•pist** \spek-ˈträs-kə-pist\ *n* — **spec•tros•co•py** \-pē\ *n*

spec•trum \ˈspek-trəm\ *n, pl* **spec•tra** \-trə\ *or* **spec•trums** [NL, fr. L, appearance, fr. *specere* to look] **1** : a series of colors formed when a beam of white light is dispersed (as by a prism) so that its parts are arranged in the order of their wavelengths **2** : a series of radiations arranged in regular order **3** : a continuous sequence or range ⟨a wide ~ of political opinions⟩

spec•u•late \ˈspe-kyə-ˌlāt\ *vb* **-lat•ed; -lat•ing** [L *speculari* to spy out, examine, fr. *specula* watchtower, fr. *specere* to look, look at] **1** : to think or wonder about a subject **2** : to take a business risk in hope of gain **syn** reason, think, deliberate, cogitate — **spec•u•la•tion** \ˌspe-kyə-ˈlā-shən\ *n* — **spec•u•la•tive** \ˈspe-kyə-ˌlā-tiv\ *adj* — **spec•u•la•tive•ly** *adv* — **spec•u•la•tor** \-ˌlā-tər\ *n*

speech \ˈspēch\ *n* **1** : the act of speaking **2** : TALK, CONVERSATION **3** : a public talk or lecture **4** : LANGUAGE, DIALECT **5** : an individual manner of speaking **6** : the power of speaking — **speech•less** *adj*

[1]**speed** \ˈspēd\ *n* **1** *archaic* : SUCCESS **2** : SWIFTNESS, RAPIDITY **3** : rate of motion or performance **4** : a transmission gear (as of a bicycle) **5** : METHAMPHETAMINE; *also* : a related drug **syn** haste, hurry, dispatch, celerity — **speed•i•ly** \ˈspē-də-lē\ *adv* — **speedy** *adj*

[2]**speed** *vb* **sped** \ˈsped\ *or* **speed•ed; speed•ing** **1** *archaic* : PROSPER; *also* : GET ALONG, FARE **2** : to go fast; *esp* : to go at an excessive or illegal speed **3** : to cause to go faster — **speed•er** *n*

speed•boat \-ˌbōt\ *n* : a fast motorboat

speed bump *n* : a low raised ridge across a roadway (as in a parking lot) to limit vehicle speed

speed•om•e•ter \spi-ˈdä-mə-tər\ *n* : an instrument for indicating speed

speed•up \ˈspēd-ˌəp\ *n* : ACCELERATION

speed•way \-ˌwā\ *n* : a racecourse for motor vehicles

speed•well \ˈspēd-ˌwel\ *n* : a low creeping plant that bears spikes of small usu. bluish flowers and is related to the snapdragon

[1]**spell** \ˈspel\ *vb* **spelled** \ˈspeld, ˈspelt\; **spell•ing** **1** : to name, write, or print in order the letters of a word **2** : MEAN

[2]**spell** *n* [ME, talk, tale, fr. OE] **1** : a magic formula : INCANTATION **2** : a controlling influence

[3]**spell** *n* **1** : one's turn at work or duty **2** : a stretch of a specified kind of weather **3** : a period of bodily or mental distress or disorder : ATTACK

[4]**spell** *vb* **spelled** \ˈspeld\; **spell•ing** : to take the place of for a time in work or duty : RELIEVE

spell•bind•er \-ˌbīn-dər\ *n* : a speaker of compelling eloquence

spell•bound \-ˌbau̇nd\ *adj* : held by or as if by a spell : FASCINATED

spell•er \ˈspe-lər\ *n* **1** : one who spells words **2** : a book with exercises for teaching spelling

spelt \ˈspelt\ *chiefly Brit past and past part of* [1]SPELL

spe•lunk•er \spi-ˈləŋ-kər, ˈspē-ˌləŋ-kər\ *n* [L *spelunca* cave, fr. Gk *spēlynx*] : one who makes a hobby of exploring caves — **spe•lunk•ing** *n*

spend \ˈspend\ *vb* **spent** \ˈspent\; **spend•ing** **1** : to pay out : EXPEND **2** : WEAR OUT, EXHAUST; *also* : to consume wastefully **3** : to cause or permit to elapse : PASS — **spend•er** *n*

spend•thrift \ˈspend-ˌthrift\ *n* : one who spends wastefully or recklessly

spent \ˈspent\ *adj* : drained of energy

sperm \ˈspərm\ *n, pl* **sperm** *or* **sperms** **1** : SEMEN **2** : a male gamete

sper•ma•to•zo•on \(ˌ)spər-ˌma-tə-ˈzō-ˌän, -ˈzō-ən\ *n, pl* **-zoa** \-ˈzō-ə\ : a motile male gamete of an animal usu. with a rounded or elongated head and a long posterior flagellum

sperm cell *n* : SPERM 2

sper•mi•cide \ˈspər-mə-ˌsīd\ *n* : a preparation or substance used to kill sperm — **sper•mi•cid•al** \ˌspər-mə-ˈsī-dəl\ *adj*

sperm whale *n* : a whale with conical teeth, no whalebone, and a large fluid-containing cavity in the head

spew \ˈspyü\ *vb* : VOMIT

SPF *abbr* sun protection factor

sp gr *abbr* specific gravity

sphag•num \ˈsfag-nəm\ *n* : any of a genus of atypical mosses that grow in wet acid areas where their remains become compacted with other plant debris to form peat; *also* : a mass of these mosses

sphere \ˈsfir\ *n* [ME *spere* globe, celestial sphere, fr. MF *espere*, fr. L *sphaera*, fr. Gk *sphaira*, lit., ball] **1** : a globe-shaped body : BALL **2** : a celestial body **3** : a solid figure so shaped that every point on its surface is an equal distance from the center **4** : range of action or influence — **spher•i•cal** \ˈsfir-i-kəl, ˈsfer-\ *adj* — **spher•i•cal•ly** \-i-k(ə-)lē\ *adv*

spher•oid \ˈsfir-ˌȯid, ˈsfer-\ *n* : a figure similar to a sphere but not perfectly round — **sphe•roi•dal** \sfir-ˈȯi-dəl\ *adj*

sphinc•ter \ˈsfiŋk-tər\ *n* : a muscular ring that closes a bodily opening

sphinx \ˈsfiŋks\ *n, pl* **sphinx•es** *or* **sphin•ges** \ˈsfin-ˌjēz\ **1** : a winged monster in Greek mythology having a woman's head and a lion's body and noted for killing anyone unable to answer its riddle **2** : an enigmatic or mysterious person **3** : an ancient Egyptian image having the body of a lion and the head of a man, ram, or hawk

spice \ˈspīs\ *n* **1** : any of various aromatic plant products (as pepper or nutmeg) used to season or flavor foods **2** : something that adds interest and relish — **spice** *vb* — **spicy** *adj*

spick–and–span *or* **spic–and–span** \ˌspik-ənd-ˈspan\ *adj* : quite new; *also* : spotlessly clean

spic•ule \ˈspi-kyül\ *n* : a slender pointed body esp. of calcium or silica ⟨sponge ∼*s*⟩

spi•der \ˈspī-dər\ *n* **1** : any of an order of arachnids that have a 2-part body, eight legs, and two or more pairs of abdominal organs for spinning threads of silk used esp. in making webs for catching prey **2** : a cast-iron frying pan — **spi•dery** *adj*

spider mite *n* : any of several small web-spinning mites that attack forage and crop plants

spider plant *n* : a houseplant of the lily family having long green leaves usu. striped with white and producing tufts of small plants on long hanging stems

spi•der•web \ˈspī-dər-ˌweb\ *n* : the web spun by a spider

spiel \ˈspēl\ *vb* : to talk in a fast, smooth, and usu. colorful manner — **spiel** *n*

spig•ot \ˈspi-gət, -kət\ *n* : FAUCET

[1]**spike** \ˈspīk\ *n* **1** : a very large nail **2** : any of various pointed projections (as on the sole of a shoe to prevent slipping) — **spiky** *adj*

[2]**spike** *vb* **spiked; spik•ing 1** : to fasten with spikes **2** : to put an end to : QUASH ⟨∼ a rumor⟩ **3** : to pierce with or impale on a spike **4** : to add alcoholic liquor to (a drink)

[3]**spike** *n* **1** : an ear of grain **2** : a long cluster of usu. stemless flowers

[1]**spill** \ˈspil\ *vb* **spilled** \ˈspild, ˈspilt\ *also* **spilt** \ˈspilt\; **spill•ing 1** : to cause or allow to fall, flow, or run out esp. unintentionally **2** : to cause (blood) to be lost by wounding **3** : to run out or over with resulting loss or waste **4** : to let out : DIVULGE — **spill•able** *adj*

[2]**spill** *n* **1** : an act of spilling; *also* : a fall from a horse or vehicle or an erect position **2** : something spilled

spill•way \-ˌwā\ *n* : a passage for surplus water to run over or around an obstruction (as a dam)

[1]**spin** \ˈspin\ *vb* **spun** \ˈspən\; **spin•ning 1** : to draw out (fiber) and twist into thread; *also* : to form (thread) by such means **2** : to form thread by extruding a sticky quickly hardening fluid; *also* : to construct from such thread ⟨spiders ∼ their webs⟩ **3** : to produce slowly and by degrees ⟨∼ a story⟩ **4** : TWIRL **5** : WHIRL, REEL ⟨my head is *spinning*⟩ **6** : to move rapidly along — **spin•ner** *n*

[2]**spin** *n* **1** : a rapid rotating motion **2** : an excursion in a wheeled vehicle **3** : a particular point of view, emphasis, or interpretation

spin•ach \ˈspi-nich\ *n* : a dark green herb grown for its edible leaves

spi•nal \ˈspīn-ᵊl\ *adj* : of or relating to the backbone or spinal cord — **spi•nal•ly** *adv*

spinal column *n* : BACKBONE

spinal cord *n* : the thick cord of nervous tissue that extends from the brain along the back in the cavity of the backbone and carries nerve impulses to and from the brain

spinal nerve *n* : any of the paired nerves which arise from the spinal cord and pass to various parts of the body and of which there are normally 31 pairs in human beings

spin•dle \ˈspind-ᵊl\ *n* **1** : a round tapering stick or rod by which fibers are twisted in spinning **2** : a turned part of a piece of furniture ⟨the ∼*s* of a chair⟩ **3** : a slender pin or rod which turns or on which something else turns

spin•dling \ˈspind-liŋ\ *adj* : SPINDLY

spin•dly \ˈspind-lē\ *adj* : being long or tall and thin and usu. weak

spin•drift \ˈspin-ˌdrift\ *n* : spray blown from waves

spine \ˈspīn\ *n* **1** : BACKBONE **2** : a stiff sharp process esp. on a plant or animal **3** : the part of a book where the pages are attached — **spiny** *adj*

spi•nel \spə-ˈnel\ *n* : a hard crystalline mineral of variable color used as a gem

spine•less \ˈspīn-ləs\ *adj* **1** : having no spines, thorns, or prickles **2** : lacking a backbone **3** : lacking courage or determination

spin•et \ˈspi-nət\ *n* **1** : an early harpsichord having a single keyboard and only one string for each note **2** : a small upright piano

spin•na•ker \ˈspi-ni-kər\ *n* : a large triangular sail set on a long light pole

spinning jen•ny \-ˈje-nē\ *n* : an early multiple-spindle machine for spinning wool or cotton

spinning wheel *n* : a small machine for spinning thread or yarn in which a large wheel drives a single spindle

spin–off \ˈspin-ˌȯf\ *n* **1** : a usu. useful by-product **2** : something (as a TV show) derived from an earlier work — **spin off** *vb*

spin•ster \ˈspin-stər\ *n* : an unmarried woman past the common age for marrying — **spin•ster•hood** \-ˌhu̇d\ *n*

spiny lobster *n* : any of several edible crustaceans differing from the related lobster in lacking the large front claws and in having a very spiny carapace

[1]**spi•ral** \ˈspī-rəl\ *adj* : winding or coiling around a center or axis and usu. getting closer to or farther away from it — **spi•ral•ly** *adv*

[2]**spiral** *n* **1** : something that has a spiral form; *also* : a single turn in a spiral object **2** : a continuously spreading and accelerating increase or decrease

[3]**spiral** *vb* **-raled** *or* **-ralled; -ral•ing** *or* **-ral•ling 1** : to move and esp. to rise or fall in a spiral course **2** : to form into a spiral

spi•rant \ˈspī-rənt\ *n* : a consonant (as \f\, \s\, \sh\) uttered with decided friction of the breath against some part of the oral passage — **spirant** *adj*

spire \ˈspīr\ *n* **1** : a slender tapering stalk (as of grass) **2** : a pointed tip (as of an antler) **3** : STEEPLE — **spiry** *adj*

spi•rea *or* **spi•raea** \spī-ˈrē-ə\ *n* : any of a genus of shrubs related to the roses with dense clusters of small white or pink flowers

[1]**spir•it** \ˈspir-ət\ *n* [ME, fr. OF or L; OF, fr. L *spiritus*, lit., breath, fr. *spirare* to blow, breathe] **1** : a life-giving force; *also* : the animating principle : SOUL **2** *cap* : HOLY SPIRIT **3** : SPECTER, GHOST **4** : PERSON **5** : DISPOSITION, MOOD **6** : VIVACITY, ARDOR **7** : essential or real meaning : INTENT **8** : distilled alcoholic liquor **9** : LOYALTY ⟨school ∼⟩ — **spir•it•less** *adj*

[2]**spirit** *vb* : to carry off secretly or mysteriously

spir•it•ed \ˈspir-ə-təd\ *adj* **1** : ANIMATED, LIVELY **2** : COURAGEOUS

[1]**spir•i•tu•al** \ˈspir-i-chəl, -chə-wəl\ *adj* **1** : of, relating to, consisting of, or affecting the spirit : INCORPOREAL **2** : of or relating to sacred matters **3** : ecclesiastical rather than lay or temporal — **spir•i•tu•al•i•ty** \ˌspir-i-chə-ˈwa-lə-tē\ *n* — **spir•i•tu•al•ize** \ˈspir-i-chə-ˌlīz, -chə-wə-\ *vb* — **spir•i•tu•al•ly** *adv*

[2]**spiritual** *n* : a religious song originating among blacks of the southern U.S.

spir•i•tu•al•ism \ˈspir-i-chə-ˌli-zəm, -chə-wə-\ *n* : a belief that spirits of the dead communicate with the living usu. through a medium — **spir•i•tu•al•ist** \-list\ *n*, *often cap* — **spir•i•tu•al•is•tic** \ˌspir-i-chə-ˈlis-tik, -chə-wə-\ *adj*

spir•i•tu•ous \ˈspir-i-chəs, -chə-wəs; ˈspir-ə-təs\ *adj* : containing alcohol

spi•ro•chete *also* **spi•ro•chaete** \ˈspī-rə-ˌkēt\ *n* : any of an order of spirally undulating bacteria including those causing syphilis and Lyme disease

spirt *var of* SPURT

[1]**spit** \ˈspit\ *n* **1** : a thin pointed rod for holding meat over a fire **2** : a point of land that runs out into the water

[2]**spit** *vb* **spit•ted; spit•ting** : to pierce with or as if with a spit

[3]**spit** *vb* **spit** *or* **spat** \ˈspat\; **spit•ting 1** : to eject (saliva) from the mouth **2** : to express by or as if by spitting **3** : to rain or snow lightly

[4]**spit** *n* **1** : SALIVA **2** : perfect likeness ⟨∼ and image of his father⟩

spit•ball \ˈspit-ˌbȯl\ *n* **1** : paper chewed and rolled into a ball to be thrown as a missile **2** : a baseball pitch delivered after the ball has been moistened with saliva or sweat

[1]spite \ˈspīt\ *n* : ill will with a wish to annoy, anger, or frustrate : petty malice **syn** malignity, spleen, grudge, malevolence — **spite•ful** \-fəl\ *adj* — **spite•ful•ly** *adv* — **spite•ful•ness** *n* — **in spite of** : in defiance or contempt of : NOTWITHSTANDING

[2]spite *vb* **spit•ed; spit•ing** : to treat maliciously : ANNOY, OFFEND

spit•tle \ˈspit-ᵊl\ *n* : SALIVA

spit•tle•bug \-ˌbəg\ *n* : any of a family of leaping insects with froth-secreting larvae that are related to aphids

spit•toon \spi-ˈtün\ *n* : a receptacle for spit

splash \ˈsplash\ *vb* **1** : to dash a liquid about **2** : to scatter a liquid on : SPATTER **3** : to fall or strike with a splashing noise **syn** sprinkle, bespatter, douse, splatter — **splash** *n*

splash•down \ˈsplash-ˌdaủn\ *n* : the landing of a manned spacecraft in the ocean — **splash down** *vb*

splat•ter \ˈspla-tər\ *vb* : SPATTER — **splatter** *n*

[1]splay \ˈsplā\ *vb* : to spread outward or apart — **splay** *n*

[2]splay *adj* **1** : spread out : turned outward **2** : AWKWARD, CLUMSY

spleen \ˈsplēn\ *n* **1** : a vascular organ located near the stomach in most vertebrates that is concerned esp. with the filtration and storage of blood, destruction of red blood cells, and production of lymphocytes **2** : SPITE, MALICE **syn** malignity, grudge, malevolence, ill will, spitefulness

splen•did \ˈsplen-dəd\ *adj* [L *splendidus*, fr. *splendēre* to shine] **1** : SHINING, BRILLIANT **2** : SHOWY, GORGEOUS **3** : ILLUSTRIOUS **4** : EXCELLENT **syn** resplendent, glorious, sublime, superb — **splen•did•ly** *adv*

splen•dor \ˈsplen-dər\ *n* **1** : BRILLIANCE **2** : POMP, MAGNIFICENCE

splen•dour *chiefly Brit var of* SPLENDOR

sple•net•ic \spli-ˈne-tik\ *adj* : marked by bad temper or spite

splen•ic \ˈsple-nik\ *adj* : of, relating to, or located in the spleen

splice \ˈsplīs\ *vb* **spliced; splic•ing 1** : to unite (as two ropes) by weaving the strands together **2** : to unite (as two lengths of film) by connecting the ends together — **splice** *n*

splint \ˈsplint\ *n* **1** : a thin strip of wood interwoven with others to make something (as a basket) **2** : material or a device used to protect and keep in place an injured body part (as a broken arm)

[1]splin•ter \ˈsplin-tər\ *n* : a thin piece of something split off lengthwise : SLIVER

[2]splinter *vb* : to split into splinters

split \ˈsplit\ *vb* **split; split•ting 1** : to divide lengthwise or along a grain or seam **2** : to burst or break in pieces **3** : to divide into parts or sections **4** : LEAVE **syn** rend, cleave, rip, tear — **split** *n*

split–lev•el \ˈsplit-ˈle-vəl\ *n* : a house divided so that the floor in one part is about halfway between two floors in the other

split personality *n* : SCHIZOPHRENIA; *also* : MULTIPLE PERSONALITY

split•ting *adj* : causing a piercing sensation ⟨∼ headache⟩

splotch \ˈsplăch\ *n* : BLOTCH

splurge \ˈsplərj\ *vb* **splurged; splurg•ing** : to spend more than usual esp. on oneself — **splurge** *n*

splut•ter \ˈsplə-tər\ *n* : SPUTTER — **splutter** *vb*

[1]spoil \ˈspȯil\ *n* : PLUNDER ⟨∼*s* of war⟩

[2]spoil *vb* **spoiled** \ˈspȯild, ˈspȯilt\ *or* **spoilt** \ˈspȯilt\; **spoil•ing 1** : ROB, PILLAGE **2** : to damage seriously : RUIN **3** : to impair the quality or effect of **4** : to damage the disposition of by pampering; *also* : INDULGE, CODDLE **5** : DECAY, ROT **6** : to have an eager desire ⟨∼*ing* for a fight⟩ **syn** injure, harm, hurt, mar — **spoil•age** \ˈspȯi-lij\ *n*

spoil•er \ˈspȯi-lər\ *n* **1** : one that spoils **2** : a device (as on an airplane or automobile) used to disrupt airflow and decrease lift

spoil•sport \ˈspȯil-ˌspōrt\ *n* : one who spoils the fun of others

[1]spoke \ˈspōk\ *past & archaic past part of* SPEAK

[2]spoke *n* : any of the rods extending from the hub of a wheel to the rim

spo•ken \ˈspō-kən\ *past part of* SPEAK

spokes•man \ˈspōks-mən\ *n* : a person who speaks as the representative of another or others

spokes•per•son \-ˌpər-sən\ *n* : SPOKESMAN

spokes•wom•an \-ˌwủ-mən\ *n* : a woman who speaks as the representative of another or others

spo•li•a•tion \ˌspō-lē-ˈā-shən\ *n* : the act of plundering : the state of being plundered

[1]sponge \ˈspənj\ *n* **1** : an elastic porous water-absorbing mass of fibers that forms the skeleton of various primitive sea animals; *also* : any of a phylum of chiefly marine sea animals that are the source of natural sponges **2** : a spongelike or porous mass or material — **spongy** \ˈspən-jē\ *adj*

[2]sponge *vb* **sponged; spong•ing 1** : to bathe or wipe with a sponge **2** : to live at another's expense **3** : to gather sponges — **spong•er** *n*

sponge cake *n* : a light cake made without shortening

sponge rubber *n* : a cellular rubber resembling natural sponge

spon•sor \ˈspăn-sər\ *n* [LL, fr. L, guarantor, surety, fr. *spondēre* to promise] **1** : one who takes the responsibility for some other person or thing : SURETY **2** : GODPARENT **3** : a business firm that pays the cost of a radio or television program usu. in return for advertising time during its course — **sponsor** *vb* — **spon•sor•ship** *n*

spon•ta•ne•ous \spăn-ˈtā-nē-əs\ *adj* [LL *spontaneus*, fr. L *sponte* of one's free will, voluntarily] **1** : done or produced freely or naturally **2** : acting or taking place without external force or cause **syn** impulsive, instinctive, automatic, unpremeditated — **spon•ta•ne•ity** \ˌspăn-tə-ˈnē-ə-tē, -ˈnā-\ *n* — **spon•ta•ne•ous•ly** *adv*

spontaneous combustion *n* : a bursting into flame of material through heat produced within itself by chemical action (as oxidation)

spoof \ˈspüf\ *vb* **1** : DECEIVE, HOAX **2** : to make good-natured fun of — **spoof** *n*

[1]spook \ˈspük\ *n* : GHOST, APPARITION — **spooky** *adj*

[2]spook *vb* : FRIGHTEN

spool \ˈspül\ *n* : a cylinder on which flexible material (as thread) is wound

spoon \ˈspün\ *n* [ME, fr. OE *spōn* splinter, chip] **1** : an eating or cooking implement consisting of a small shallow bowl with a handle **2** : a metal piece used on a fishing line as a lure — **spoon** *vb* — **spoon•ful** *n*

spoon•bill \ˈspün-ˌbil\ *n* : any of several wading birds related to the ibises that have a bill with a broad flat tip

spoon–feed \-ˌfēd\ *vb* **-fed** \-ˌfed\; **-feed•ing** : to feed by means of a spoon

spoor \ˈspủr, ˈspōr\ *n* : a track, a trail, a scent, or droppings esp. of a wild animal

spo•rad•ic \spə-ˈra-dik\ *adj* : occurring now and then **syn** occasional, rare, scarce, infrequent, uncommon — **spo•rad•i•cal•ly** \-di-k(ə-)lē\ *adv*

spore \ˈspōr\ *n* : a primitive usu. one-celled often environmentally resistant dormant or reproductive body produced by plants and some microorganisms

[1]sport \ˈspōrt\ *vb* [ME, to divert, disport, short for *disporten*, fr. MF *desporter*, fr. *des-* (fr. L *dis-* apart) + *porter* to carry, fr. L *portare*] **1** : to amuse oneself : FROLIC **2** : SHOW OFF 1 — **sport•ive** *adj*

[2]sport *n* **1** : a source of diversion : PASTIME **2** : physical activity engaged in for pleasure **3** : JEST **4** : MOCKERY

⟨make ∼ of his efforts⟩ **5** : BUTT, LAUGHINGSTOCK **6** : one who accepts results cheerfully whether favorable or not **7** : an individual exhibiting marked deviation from its normal type esp. as a result of mutation **syn** play, frolic, fun, recreation — **sporty** *adj*

[3]sport *or* **sports** *adj* : of, relating to, or suitable for sport or casual wear ⟨∼ coats⟩

sport fish *n* : a fish noted for the sport it affords anglers

sports•cast \ˈspōrts-ˌkast\ *n* : a broadcast dealing with sports events — **sports•cast•er** \-ˌkas-tər\ *n*

sports•man \ˈspōrts-mən\ *n* **1** : a person who engages in sports (as in hunting or fishing) **2** : one who plays fairly and wins or loses gracefully — **sports•man•like** \-ˌlīk\ *adj* — **sports•man•ship** *n*

sports•wom•an \-ˌwu̇-mən\ *n* : a woman who engages in sports

sports•writ•er \-ˌrī-tər\ *n* : one who writes about sports esp. for a newspaper — **sports•writ•ing** *n*

[1]spot \ˈspät\ *n* **1** : STAIN, BLEMISH **2** : a small part different (as in color) from the main part **3** : LOCATION, SITE — **spot•less** *adj* — **spot•less•ly** *adv* — **on the spot** **1** : at the place of action **2** : in difficulty or danger

[2]spot *vb* **spot•ted; spot•ting** **1** : to mark or disfigure with spots **2** : to pick out : RECOGNIZE, IDENTIFY

[3]spot *adj* **1** : being, done, or originating on the spot ⟨a ∼ broadcast⟩ **2** : paid upon delivery **3** : made at random or at a few key points ⟨a ∼ check⟩

spot–check \ˈspät-ˌchek\ *vb* : to make a spot check of

spot•light \-ˌlīt\ *n* **1** : a circle of brilliant light projected upon a particular area, person, or object (as on a stage); *also* : the device that produces this light **2** : public notice — **spotlight** *vb*

spotted owl *n* : a rare large dark brown dark-eyed owl of humid old growth forests and thickly wooded canyons from British Columbia to southern California and central Mexico

spot•ter \ˈspä-tər\ *n* **1** : one that keeps watch : OBSERVER **2** : one that removes spots

spot•ty \ˈspä-tē\ *adj* **spot•ti•er; -est** : uneven in quality; *also* : sparsely distributed ⟨∼ attendance⟩

spou•sal \ˈspau̇-zəl, -səl\ *n* : MARRIAGE 2, WEDDING — usu. used in pl.

spouse \ˈspau̇s\ *n* : one's husband or wife — **spou•sal** \ˈspau̇-zəl, -səl\ *adj*

[1]spout \ˈspau̇t\ *vb* **1** : to eject or issue forth forcibly and freely ⟨wells ∼*ing* oil⟩ **2** : to speak pompously

[2]spout *n* **1** : a pipe or hole through which liquid spouts **2** : a jet of liquid; *esp* : WATERSPOUT 2

spp *abbr, pl* species

[1]sprain \ˈsprān\ *n* : a sudden or severe twisting of a joint with stretching or tearing of ligaments; *also* : a sprained condition

[2]sprain *vb* : to subject to sprain

sprat \ˈsprat\ *n* **1** : a small European herring **2** : a young herring

sprawl \ˈsprȯl\ *vb* **1** : to lie or sit with limbs spread out awkwardly **2** : to spread out irregularly — **sprawl** *n*

[1]spray \ˈsprā\ *n* : a usu. flowering branch; *also* : a decorative arrangement of flowers and foliage

[2]spray *n* **1** : liquid flying in small drops like water blown from a wave **2** : a jet of fine vapor (as from an atomizer) **3** : an instrument (as an atomizer) for scattering fine liquid

[3]spray *vb* **1** : to scatter or let fall in a spray **2** : to discharge spray on or into — **spray•er** *n*

spray can *n* : a pressurized container from which aerosols are sprayed

spray gun *n* : a device for spraying liquids (as paint or insecticide)

[1]spread \ˈspred\ *vb* **spread; spread•ing** **1** : to scatter over a surface **2** : to flatten out : open out **3** : to distribute over a period of time or among many persons **4** : to cover something with ⟨∼ rugs on the floor⟩ **5** : to prepare for a meal ⟨∼ a table⟩ **6** : to pass on from person to person **7** : to stretch, force, or push apart — **spread•er** *n*

[2]spread *n* **1** : the act or process of spreading **2** : EXPANSE, EXTENT **3** : a prominent display in a periodical **4** : a food to be spread on bread or crackers **5** : a cloth cover for a bed **6** : distance between two points : GAP

spread•sheet \ˈspred-ˌshēt\ *n* : an accounting program for a computer

spree \ˈsprē\ *n* : an unrestrained outburst ⟨buying ∼⟩; *esp* : a drinking bout

sprig \ˈsprig\ *n* : a small shoot or twig

spright•ly \ˈsprīt-lē\ *adj* **spright•li•er; -est** : LIVELY, SPIRITED **syn** animated, vivacious, gay — **spright•li•ness** *n*

[1]spring \ˈspriŋ\ *vb* **sprang** \ˈspraŋ\ *or* **sprung** \ˈsprəŋ\; **sprung; spring•ing** **1** : to move suddenly upward or forward **2** : to grow quickly ⟨weeds *sprang* up overnight⟩ **3** : to come from by birth or descent **4** : to move quickly by elastic force **5** : WARP **6** : to develop (a leak) through the seams **7** : to cause to close suddenly ⟨∼ a trap⟩ **8** : to make known suddenly ⟨∼ a surprise⟩ **9** : to make lame : STRAIN

[2]spring *n* **1** : a source of supply; *esp* : an issuing of water from the ground **2** : SOURCE, ORIGIN; *also* : MOTIVE **3** : the season between winter and summer **4** : an elastic body or device that recovers its original shape when it is released after being distorted **5** : the act or an instance of leaping up or forward **6** : RESILIENCE — **springy** *adj*

spring•board \ˈspriŋ-ˌbōrd\ *n* : a springy board used in jumping or vaulting or for diving

spring fever *n* : a lazy or restless feeling often associated with the onset of spring

spring tide *n* : a tide of greater-than-average range that occurs at each new moon and full moon

spring•time \ˈspriŋ-ˌtīm\ *n* : the season of spring

[1]sprin•kle \ˈspriŋ-kəl\ *vb* **sprin•kled; sprin•kling** : to scatter in small drops or particles — **sprin•kler** *n*

[2]sprinkle *n* : a light rainfall

sprin•kling *n* : SMATTERING

[1]sprint \ˈsprint\ *vb* : to run at top speed esp. for a short distance — **sprint•er** *n*

[2]sprint *n* **1** : a short run at top speed **2** : a short distance race

sprite \ˈsprīt\ *n* **1** : GHOST, SPIRIT **2** : ELF, FAIRY

spritz *vb* : SPRAY

sprock•et \ˈsprä-kət\ *n* : a toothed wheel whose teeth engage the links of a chain

[1]sprout \ˈsprau̇t\ *vb* : to send out new growth ⟨∼*ing* seeds⟩

[2]sprout *n* : a usu. young and growing plant shoot (as from a seed)

[1]spruce \ˈsprüs\ *vb* **spruced; spruc•ing** : to make or become spruce

[2]spruce *adj* **spruc•er; spruc•est** : neat and smart in appearance **syn** stylish, fashionable, modish, dapper, natty

[3]spruce *n* : any of a genus of evergreen pyramid-shaped trees related to the pines and having soft light wood; *also* : the wood of a spruce

sprung *past and past part of* SPRING

spry \ˈsprī\ *adj* **spri•er** *or* **spry•er** \ˈsprī-ər\; **spri•est** *or* **spry•est** \ˈsprī-əst\ : NIMBLE, ACTIVE **syn** agile, brisk, lively, sprightly

spud \ˈspəd\ *n* **1** : a sharp narrow spade **2** : POTATO

spume \ˈspyüm\ *n* : frothy matter on liquids : FOAM — **spumy** \ˈspyü-mē\ *adj*

spu•mo•ni *also* **spu•mo•ne** \spu̇-ˈmō-nē\ *n* [It *spumone*, fr. *spuma* foam] : ice cream in layers of different colors, flavors, and textures often with candied fruits and nuts

spun *past and past part of* SPIN

spun glass *n* : FIBERGLASS

spunk \ˈspəŋk\ *n* [fr. *spunk* tinder, fr. ScGael *spong* sponge, tinder, fr. L *spongia* sponge] : PLUCK, COURAGE — **spunky** *adj*

[1]**spur** \ˈspər\ *n* **1 :** a pointed device fastened to a rider's boot and used to urge on a horse **2 :** something that urges to action **3 :** a stiff sharp spine (as on the leg of a cock); *also* **:** a hollow projecting appendage of a flower (as a columbine) **4 :** a ridge extending sideways from a mountain **5 :** a branch of railroad track extending from the main line **syn** goad, motive, impulse, incentive, inducement — **spurred** \ˈspərd\ *adj* — **on the spur of the moment :** on hasty impulse

[2]**spur** *vb* **spurred; spur•ring 1 :** to urge a horse on with spurs **2 :** INCITE

spurge \ˈspərj\ *n* **:** any of a genus of herbs and woody plants with bitter milky juice

spu•ri•ous \ˈspyůr-ē-əs\ *adj* [LL *spurius* false, fr. L, of illegitimate birth, fr. *spurius*, n., bastard] **:** not genuine **:** FALSE

spurn \ˈspərn\ *vb* **1 :** to kick away or trample on **2 :** to reject with disdain

[1]**spurt** \ˈspərt\ *vb* **:** to gush out **:** SPOUT

[2]**spurt** *n* **:** a sudden gushing or spouting

[3]**spurt** *n* **1 :** a sudden brief burst of effort or speed **2 :** a sharp increase of activity ⟨~ in sales⟩

[4]**spurt** *vb* **:** to make a spurt

sput•ter \ˈspə-tər\ *vb* **1 :** to spit small scattered particles **:** SPLUTTER **2 :** to utter words hastily or explosively in excitement or confusion **3 :** to make small popping sounds — **sputter** *n*

spu•tum \ˈspyü-təm\ *n, pl* **spu•ta** \-tə\ [L] **:** material that is spit or coughed up and consists of saliva and mucus

[1]**spy** \ˈspī\ *vb* **spied; spy•ing 1 :** to watch or search for information secretly **:** act as a spy **2 :** to get a momentary or quick glimpse of **:** SEE

[2]**spy** *n, pl* **spies 1 :** one who secretly watches others **2 :** a secret agent who tries to get information for one country in the territory of an enemy

spy•glass \ˈspī-ˌglas\ *n* **:** a small telescope

sq *abbr* **1** squadron **2** square

squab \ˈskwäb\ *n, pl* **squabs** *or* **squab :** a young bird and esp. a pigeon

squab•ble \ˈskwä-bəl\ *n* **:** a noisy altercation **:** WRANGLE **syn** quarrel, spat, row, tiff — **squabble** *vb*

squad \ˈskwäd\ *n* **1 :** a small organized group of military personnel **2 :** a small group engaged in a common effort

squad car *n* **:** a police car connected by two-way radio with headquarters

squad•ron \ˈskwä-drən\ *n* **:** any of several units of military organization

squal•id \ˈskwä-ləd\ *adj* **1 :** filthy or degraded through neglect or poverty **2 :** SORDID, DEBASED **syn** nasty, foul, dirty, grubby

squall \ˈskwȯl\ *n* **:** a sudden violent gust of wind often with rain or snow — **squally** *adj*

squa•lor \ˈskwä-lər\ *n* **:** the quality or state of being squalid

squan•der \ˈskwän-dər\ *vb* **:** to spend wastefully or foolishly

[1]**square** \ˈskwar\ *n* **1 :** an instrument used to lay out or test right angles **2 :** a rectangle with all four sides equal **3 :** something square **4 :** the product of a number multiplied by itself **5 :** an area bounded by four streets **6 :** an open area in a city where streets meet **7 :** a highly conventional person

[2]**square** *adj* **squar•er; squar•est 1 :** having four equal sides and four right angles **2 :** forming a right angle ⟨cut a ~ corner⟩ **3 :** multiplied by itself **:** SQUARED ⟨x^2 is the symbol for *x* ~⟩ **4 :** being a unit of square measure equal to a square each side of which measures one unit ⟨a ~ foot⟩ **5 :** being of a specified length in each of two dimensions ⟨an area 10 feet ~⟩ **6 :** exactly adjusted **7 :** JUST, FAIR ⟨a ~ deal⟩ **8 :** leaving no balance ⟨make accounts ~⟩ **9 :** SUBSTANTIAL ⟨a ~ meal⟩ **10 :** highly conservative or conventional — **squarely** *adv*

[3]**square** *vb* **squared; squar•ing 1 :** to form with four equal sides and right angles or with flat surfaces ⟨~ a timber⟩ **2 :** to multiply (a number) by itself **3 :** CONFORM, AGREE **4 :** BALANCE, SETTLE ⟨~ an account⟩

square dance *n* **:** a dance for four couples arranged to form a square

square measure *n* **:** a unit or system of units for measuring area — see METRIC SYSTEM table, WEIGHT table

square–rigged \ˈskwar-ˈrigd\ *adj* **:** having the chief sails extended on yards that are fastened to the masts horizontally and at their center

square–rig•ger \-ˌri-gər\ *n* **:** a square-rigged craft

square root *n* **:** either of the two numbers whose squares are equal to a given number ⟨the *square root* of 9 is +3 or −3⟩

[1]**squash** \ˈskwäsh, ˈskwȯsh\ *vb* **1 :** to beat or press into a pulp or flat mass **2 :** QUASH, SUPPRESS

[2]**squash** *n* **1 :** the impact of something soft and heavy; *also* **:** the sound of such impact **2 :** a crushed mass **3 :** a game played on a 4-wall court with a racket and rubber ball

[3]**squash** *n, pl* **squash•es** *or* **squash :** a fruit of any of various plants related to the gourds that is used esp. as a vegetable; *also* **:** a plant and esp. a vine bearing squashes

squash racquets *n* **:** SQUASH 3

[1]**squat** \ˈskwät\ *vb* **squat•ted; squat•ting 1 :** to sit down upon the hams or heels **2 :** to settle on land without right or title; *also* **:** to settle on public land with a view to acquiring title — **squat•ter** *n*

[2]**squat** *n* **:** the act or posture of squatting

[3]**squat** *adj* **squat•ter; squat•test :** low to the ground; *also* **:** short and thick in stature **syn** thickset, stocky, heavyset, stubby

squawk \ˈskwȯk\ *n* **:** a harsh loud cry; *also* **:** a noisy protest — **squawk** *vb*

squeak \ˈskwēk\ *vb* **1 :** to utter or speak in a weak shrill tone **2 :** to make a thin high-pitched sound — **squeak** *n* — **squeaky** *adj*

[1]**squeal** \ˈskwēl\ *vb* **1 :** to make a shrill sound or cry **2 :** to betray a secret or turn informer **3 :** COMPLAIN, PROTEST

[2]**squeal** *n* **:** a shrill sharp cry or noise

squea•mish \ˈskwē-mish\ *adj* **1 :** easily nauseated; *also* **:** NAUSEATED **2 :** easily disgusted **syn** fussy, nice, dainty, fastidious, persnickety — **squea•mish•ness** *n*

squee•gee \ˈskwē-ˌjē\ *n* **:** a blade set crosswise on a handle and used for spreading or wiping liquid on, across, or off a surface — **squeegee** *vb*

[1]**squeeze** \ˈskwēz\ *vb* **squeezed; squeez•ing 1 :** to exert pressure on the opposite sides or parts of **2 :** to obtain by pressure ⟨~ juice from a lemon⟩ **3 :** to force, thrust, or cause to pass by pressure — **squeez•er** *n*

[2]**squeeze** *n* **1 :** an act of squeezing **2 :** a quantity squeezed out

squeeze bottle *n* **:** a flexible plastic bottle that dispenses its contents when it is squeezed

squelch \ˈskwelch\ *vb* **1 :** to suppress completely **:** CRUSH **2 :** to move in soft mud — **squelch** *n*

squib \ˈskwib\ *n* **:** a brief witty writing or speech

squid \ˈskwid\ *n, pl* **squid** *or* **squids :** any of an order of long-bodied sea mollusks having eight arms and two longer tentacles and usu. a slender internal shell

squint \ˈskwint\ *vb* **1 :** to look or aim obliquely **2 :** to look or peer with the eyes partly closed **3 :** to be cross-eyed — **squint** *n or adj*

[1]**squire** \ˈskwīr\ *n* [ME *squier*, fr. OF *esquier*, fr. LL *scutarius*, fr. L *scutum* shield] **1 :** an armor-bearer of a knight **2 :** a man gallantly devoted to a lady **3 :** a member of the British gentry ranking below a knight and above a gentleman; *also* **:** a prominent landowner **4 :** a local magistrate

[2]**squire** *vb* **squired; squir•ing :** to attend as a squire or escort

squirm \ˈskwərm\ *vb* **:** to twist about like a worm **:** WRIGGLE

[1]**squir•rel** \ˈskwər-əl\ *n, pl* **squirrels** *also* **squirrel** [ME *squirel,* fr. MF *esquireul,* fr. (assumed) VL *scuriolus,* dim. of *scurius,* alter. of L *sciurus,* fr. Gk *skiouros,* prob. fr. *skia* shadow + *oura* tail] **:** any of various rodents usu. with a long bushy tail and strong hind legs; *also* **:** the fur of a squirrel

[2]**squirrel** *vb* **-reled** *or* **-relled; -rel•ing** *or* **-rel•ling :** to store up for future use

[1]**squirt** \ˈskwərt\ *vb* **:** to eject liquid in a thin spurt

[2]**squirt** *n* **1 :** an instrument (as a syringe) for squirting **2 :** a small forcible jet of liquid

[1]**Sr** *abbr* **1** senior **2** sister

[2]**Sr** *symbol* strontium

SR *abbr* seaman recruit

[1]**SRO** \ˌes-(ˌ)är-ˈō\ *n* [*s*ingle-*r*oom *o*ccupancy] **:** a house or apartment building in which low-income tenants live in single rooms

[2]**SRO** *abbr* standing room only

SS *abbr* **1** saints **2** Social Security **3** steamship **4** sworn statement

SSA *abbr* Social Security Administration

SSE *abbr* south-southeast

SSG *or* **SSgt** *abbr* staff sergeant

SSI *abbr* supplemental security income

SSM *abbr* staff sergeant major

SSN *abbr* Social Security Number

ssp *abbr* subspecies

SSR *abbr* Soviet Socialist Republic

SSS *abbr* Selective Service System

SST \ˌes-(ˌ)es-ˈtē\ *n* [*s*uper*s*onic *t*ransport] **:** a supersonic passenger airplane

SSW *abbr* south-southwest

st *abbr* **1** stanza **2** state **3** stitch **4** stone **5** street

St *abbr* saint

ST *abbr* **1** short ton **2** standard time

-st — see -EST

sta *abbr* station; stationary

[1]**stab** \ˈstab\ *n* **1 :** a wound produced by a pointed weapon **2 :** a quick thrust; *also* **:** a brief attempt

[2]**stab** *vb* **stabbed; stab•bing :** to pierce or wound with or as if with a pointed weapon; *also* **:** THRUST, DRIVE

sta•bile \ˈstā-ˌbēl\ *n* **:** an abstract sculpture or construction similar to a mobile but made to be stationary

sta•bi•lize \ˈstā-bə-ˌlīz\ *vb* **-lized; -liz•ing 1 :** to make stable **2 :** to hold steady ⟨~ prices⟩ — **sta•bi•li•za•tion** \ˌstā-bə-lə-ˈzā-shən\ *n* — **sta•bi•liz•er** \ˈstā-bə-ˌlī-zər\ *n*

[1]**sta•ble** \ˈstā-bəl\ *n* **:** a building in which domestic animals are sheltered and fed — **sta•ble•man** \-mən, -ˌman\ *n*

[2]**stable** *vb* **sta•bled; sta•bling :** to put or keep in a stable

[3]**stable** *adj* **sta•bler; sta•blest 1 :** firmly established; *also* **:** mentally and emotionally healthy **2 :** steady in purpose **:** CONSTANT **3 :** DURABLE, ENDURING **4 :** resistant to chemical or physical change **syn** lasting, permanent, perpetual, perdurable — **sta•bil•i•ty** \stə-ˈbi-lə-tē\ *n*

stac•ca•to \stə-ˈkä-tō\ *adj or adv* [It] **:** cut short so as not to sound connected ⟨~ notes⟩

[1]**stack** \ˈstak\ *n* **1 :** a large pile (as of hay or grain) **2 :** an orderly pile (as of poker chips) **3 :** a large quantity **4 :** a vertical pipe **:** SMOKESTACK **5 :** a rack with shelves for storing books

[2]**stack** *vb* **1 :** to pile up **2 :** to arrange (cards) secretly for cheating

stack up *vb* **:** MEASURE UP

sta•di•um \ˈstā-dē-əm\ *n, pl* **-dia** \-dē-ə\ *or* **-di•ums :** a structure with tiers of seats for spectators built around a field for sports events

[1]**staff** \ˈstaf\ *n, pl* **staffs** \ˈstafs, ˈstavz\ *or* **staves** \ˈstavz, ˈstāvz\ **1 :** a pole, stick, rod, or bar used for supporting, for measuring, or as a symbol of authority; *also* **:** CLUB, CUDGEL **2 :** something that sustains ⟨bread is the ~ of life⟩ **3 :** the five horizontal lines on which music is written **4 :** a body of assistants to an executive **5 :** a group of officers holding no command but having duties concerned with planning and managing

[2]**staff** *vb* **:** to supply with a staff or with workers

staff•er \ˈsta-fər\ *n* **:** a member of a staff (as of a newspaper)

staff sergeant *n* **:** a noncommissioned officer ranking in the army next below a sergeant first class, in the air force next below a technical sergeant, and in the marine corps next below a gunnery sergeant

[1]**stag** \ˈstag\ *n, pl* **stags** *or* **stag :** an adult male of various large deer

[2]**stag** *adj* **:** restricted to or intended for men ⟨a ~ party⟩ ⟨~ movies⟩

[3]**stag** *adv* **:** unaccompanied by a date

[1]**stage** \ˈstāj\ *n* **1 :** a raised platform on which an orator may speak or a play may be presented **2 :** the acting profession **:** THEATER **3 :** the scene of a notable action or event **4 :** a station or resting place on a traveled road **5 :** STAGECOACH **6 :** a degree of advance in an undertaking, process, or development **7 :** a propulsion unit in a rocket — **stagy** \ˈstā-jē\ *adj*

[2]**stage** *vb* **staged; stag•ing :** to produce or perform on or as if on a stage — **stage•able** *adj*

stage•coach \ˈstāj-ˌkōch\ *n* **:** a horse-drawn coach that runs regularly between stations

stag•fla•tion \ˌstag-ˈflā-shən\ *n* **:** inflation with stagnant economic activity and high unemployment

[1]**stag•ger** \ˈsta-gər\ *vb* **1 :** to reel from side to side **:** TOTTER **2 :** to begin to doubt **:** WAVER **3 :** to cause to reel or waver **4 :** to arrange in overlapping or alternating positions or times ⟨~ working hours⟩ **5 :** ASTONISH — **stag•ger•ing•ly** *adv*

[2]**stagger** *n* **1** *sing or pl* **:** an abnormal condition of domestic mammals and birds associated with damage to the central nervous system and marked by lack of coordination and a reeling unsteady gait **2 :** a reeling or unsteady gait or stance

stag•ing \ˈstā-jiŋ\ *n* **1 :** SCAFFOLDING **2 :** the assembling of troops and matériel in transit in a particular place

stag•nant \ˈstag-nənt\ *adj* **1 :** not flowing **:** MOTIONLESS ⟨~ water in a pond⟩ **2 :** DULL, INACTIVE ⟨~ business⟩

stag•nate \ˈstag-ˌnāt\ *vb* **stag•nat•ed; stag•nat•ing :** to be or become stagnant — **stag•na•tion** \stag-ˈnā-shən\ *n*

staid \ˈstād\ *adj* **:** SOBER, SEDATE **syn** grave, serious, earnest

[1]**stain** \ˈstān\ *vb* **1 :** DISCOLOR, SOIL **2 :** TAINT, CORRUPT **3 :** DISGRACE **4 :** to color (as wood, paper, or cloth) by processes affecting the material itself

[2]**stain** *n* **1 :** a small soiled or discolored area **2 :** a taint of guilt **:** STIGMA **3 :** a preparation (as a dye or pigment) used in staining — **stain•less** *adj*

stainless steel *n* **:** steel alloyed with chromium that is highly resistant to stain, rust, and corrosion

stair \ˈstar\ *n* **1 :** a series of steps or flights of steps for passing from one level to another — often used in pl. **2 :** one step of a stairway

stair•case \-ˌkās\ *n* **:** a flight of steps with their supporting framework, casing, and balusters

stair•way \-ˌwā\ *n* **:** one or more flights of stairs with connecting landings

stair•well \-ˌwel\ *n* **:** a vertical shaft in which stairs are located

[1]**stake** \ˈstāk\ *n* **1 :** a pointed piece of material (as of wood) driven into the ground as a marker or a support **2 :** a post to which a person is bound for death by burning; *also* **:** such a death **3 :** something that is staked for gain or loss **4 :** the prize in a contest

[2]**stake** *vb* **staked; stak•ing 1 :** to mark the limits of by or as if by stakes **2 :** to tie to a stake **3 :** to support or secure with stakes **4 :** BET, WAGER

stake•out \ˈstāk-ˌau̇t\ *n* **:** a surveillance by police (as of a suspected criminal)

sta•lac•tite \stə-ˈlak-ˌtīt\ *n* [NL *stalactites,* fr. Gk *sta-*

laktos dripping] : an icicle-shaped deposit hanging from the roof or sides of a cavern

sta•lag•mite \stə-ˈlag-ˌmīt\ *n* [NL *stalagmites*, fr. Gk *stalagma* drop or *stalagmos* dripping] : a deposit resembling an inverted stalactite rising from the floor of a cavern

stale \ˈstāl\ *adj* **stal•er; stal•est** **1** : having lost good taste and quality from age ⟨~ bread⟩ **2** : used or heard so often as to be dull ⟨~ news⟩ **3** : not as strong or effective as before ⟨~ from lack of practice⟩ — **staleness** *n*

stale•mate \ˈstāl-ˌmāt\ *n* : a drawn contest : DEADLOCK — **stalemate** *vb*

[1]**stalk** \ˈstȯk\ *n* : a plant stem; *also* : any slender usu. upright supporting or connecting part — **stalked** \ˈstȯkt\ *adj*

[2]**stalk** *vb* **1** : to pursue (game) stealthily **2** : to walk stiffly or haughtily

[1]**stall** \ˈstȯl\ *n* **1** : a compartment in a stable or barn for one animal **2** : a booth or counter where articles may be displayed for sale **3** : a seat in a church choir; *also* : a church pew **4** *chiefly Brit* : a front orchestra seat in a theater

[2]**stall** *vb* : to bring or come to a standstill unintentionally ⟨~ an engine⟩

[3]**stall** *n* : the condition of an airfoil or aircraft in which lift is lost and the airfoil or aircraft tends to drop

[4]**stall** *n* [alter. of *stale* lure] : a ruse to deceive or delay

[5]**stall** *vb* : to hold off, divert, or delay by evasion or deception

stal•lion \ˈstal-yən\ *n* : a male horse

stal•wart \ˈstȯl-wərt\ *adj* : STOUT, STRONG; *also* : BRAVE, VALIANT

sta•men \ˈstā-mən\ *n* : an organ of a flower that produces pollen

stam•i•na \ˈsta-mə-nə\ *n* [L, pl. of *stamen* warp, thread of life spun by the Fates] : VIGOR, ENDURANCE

sta•mi•nate \ˈstā-mə-nət, ˈsta-mə-, -ˌnāt\ *adj* **1** : having or producing stamens **2** : having stamens but no pistils

stam•mer \ˈsta-mər\ *vb* : to hesitate or stumble in speaking — **stammer** *n* — **stam•mer•er** *n*

[1]**stamp** \ˈstamp; *for 2 also* ˈstämp *or* ˈstȯmp\ *vb* **1** : to pound or crush with a heavy instrument **2** : to strike or beat with the bottom of the foot **3** : IMPRESS, IMPRINT **4** : to cut out or indent with a stamp or die **5** : to attach a postage stamp to

[2]**stamp** *n* **1** : a device or instrument for stamping **2** : the mark made by stamping; *also* : a distinctive mark or quality **3** : the act of stamping **4** : a stamped or printed paper affixed to show that a charge has been paid ⟨postage ~⟩ ⟨tax ~⟩

[1]**stam•pede** \stam-ˈpēd\ *n* : a wild headlong rush or flight esp. of frightened animals

[2]**stampede** *vb* **stam•ped•ed; stam•ped•ing** **1** : to flee or cause to flee in panic **2** : to act or cause to act together suddenly and heedlessly

stance \ˈstans\ *n* : a way of standing

[1]**stanch** \ˈstȯnch, ˈstänch\ *vb* : to check the flowing of (as blood); *also* : to cease flowing or bleeding

[2]**stanch** *var of* [2]STAUNCH

stan•chion \ˈstan-chən\ *n* : an upright bar, post, or support

[1]**stand** \ˈstand\ *vb* **stood** \ˈstu̇d\; **stand•ing** **1** : to take or be at rest in an upright or firm position **2** : to assume a specified position **3** : to remain stationary or unchanged **4** : to be steadfast **5** : to act in resistance ⟨~ against a foe⟩ **6** : to maintain a relative position or rank **7** : to gather slowly and remain ⟨tears *stood* in her eyes⟩ **8** : to set upright **9** : ENDURE, TOLERATE ⟨I won't ~ for that⟩ **10** : to submit to ⟨~ trial⟩ — **stand pat** : to oppose or resist change

[2]**stand** *n* **1** : an act of standing, staying, or resisting **2** : a stop made to give a performance **3** : POSITION, VIEWPOINT **4** : a place taken by a witness to testify in court **5** *pl* : tiered seats for spectators **6** : a raised platform (as for speakers) **7** : a structure for a small retail business **8** : a structure for supporting or holding something upright ⟨music ~⟩ **9** : a group of plants growing in a continuous area

stand–alone \ˈstan-də-ˌlōn\ *adj* : SELF-CONTAINED; *esp* : capable of operation independent of a computer system

stan•dard \ˈstan-dərd\ *n* **1** : a figure adopted as an emblem by a people **2** : the personal flag of a ruler; *also* : FLAG **3** : something set up as a rule for measuring or as a model to be followed **4** : an upright support ⟨lamp ~⟩ — **standard** *adj*

stan•dard–bear•er \-ˌbar-ər\ *n* : the leader of a cause

standard deviation *n* : a measure of dispersion in a set of data

stan•dard•ise *Brit var of* STANDARDIZE

stan•dard•ize \ˈstan-dər-ˌdīz\ *vb* **-ized; -iz•ing** : to make standard or uniform — **stan•dard•i•za•tion** \ˌstan-dər-də-ˈzā-shən\ *n*

standard of living : the necessities, comforts, and luxuries that a person or group is accustomed to

standard time *n* : the time established by law or by general usage over a region or country

[1]**stand•by** \ˈstand-ˌbī\ *n, pl* **stand•bys** \-ˌbīz\ **1** : one that can be relied on **2** : a substitute in reserve — **on standby** : ready or available for immediate action or use

[2]**standby** *adj* **1** : ready for use **2** : relating to airline travel in which the passenger must wait for an available unreserved seat — **standby** *adv*

stand–in \ˈstan-ˌdin\ *n* **1** : someone employed to occupy an actor's place while lights and camera are readied **2** : SUBSTITUTE

[1]**stand•ing** \ˈstan-diŋ\ *adj* **1** : ERECT **2** : not flowing : STAGNANT **3** : remaining at the same level or amount for an indefinite period ⟨~ offer⟩ **4** : PERMANENT **5** : done from a standing position ⟨a ~ jump⟩

[2]**standing** *n* **1** : length of service; *also* : relative position in society or in a profession : RANK **2** : DURATION

stand•off \ˈstan-ˌdȯf\ *n* : TIE, DRAW

stand•off•ish \stan-ˈdȯ-fish\ *adj* : somewhat cold and reserved

stand•out \ˈstan-ˌdau̇t\ *n* : something conspicuously excellent

stand•pipe \ˈstand-ˌpīp\ *n* : a high vertical pipe or reservoir for water used to produce a uniform pressure

stand•point \-ˌpȯint\ *n* : a position from which objects or principles are judged

stand•still \-ˌstil\ *n* : a state of rest

stand–up \ˈstan-ˌdəp\ *adj* : done or performing in a standing position ⟨a ~ comic⟩ ⟨~ comedy⟩

stank \ˈstaŋk\ *past of* STINK

stan•za \ˈstan-zə\ *n* [It] : a group of lines forming a division of a poem

sta•pes \ˈstā-ˌpēz\ *n, pl* **stapes** *or* **sta•pe•des** \ˈstā-pə-ˌdēz\ : the small innermost bone of the ear of mammals

staph \ˈstaf\ *n* : STAPHYLOCOCCUS

staph•y•lo•coc•cus \ˌsta-fə-lō-ˈkä-kəs\ *n, pl* **-coc•ci** \-ˈkä-ˌkī, -ˈkäk-ˌsī\ : any of various spherical bacteria including some pathogens of skin and mucous membranes — **staph•y•lo•coc•cal** \-ˈkä-kəl\ *adj*

[1]**sta•ple** \ˈstā-pəl\ *n* : a U-shaped piece of metal or wire with sharp points to be driven into a surface or through thin layers (as paper) for attaching or holding together — **staple** *vb* — **sta•pler** *n*

[2]**staple** *n* **1** : a chief commodity or product **2** : a chief part of something ⟨a ~ of their diet⟩ **3** : unmanufactured or raw material **4** : a textile fiber suitable for spinning into yarn

[3]**staple** *adj* **1** : regularly produced in large quantities **2** : PRINCIPAL, MAIN

[1]**star** \ˈstär\ *n* **1** : a celestial body that appears as a fixed point of light; *esp* : such a body that is gaseous, self-luminous, and of great mass **2** : a planet or configuration of planets that is held in astrology to influence

one's fortune — usu. used in pl. **3** *obs* : DESTINY, FORTUNE **4** : a conventional figure representing a star; *esp* : ASTERISK **5** : an actor or actress playing the leading role **6** : a brilliant performer — **star•dom** \ˈstär-dəm\ *n* — **star•less** *adj* — **star•like** *adj* — **star•ry** *adj*

[2]**star** *vb* **starred; star•ring 1** : to adorn with stars **2** : to mark with an asterisk **3** : to play the leading role

star•board \ˈstär-bərd\ *n* [ME *sterbord,* fr. OE *stēorbord,* fr. *stēor-* steering oar + *bord* ship's side] : the right side of a ship or airplane looking forward — **starboard** *adj*

[1]**starch** \ˈstärch\ *vb* : to stiffen with or as if with starch

[2]**starch** *n* : a complex carbohydrate that is stored in plants, is an important foodstuff, and is used in adhesives and sizes, in laundering, and in pharmacy — **starchy** *adj*

stare \ˈstar\ *vb* **stared; star•ing** : to look fixedly with wide-open eyes — **stare** *n* — **star•er** *n*

star•fish \ˈstär-ˌfish\ *n* : any of a class of echinoderms usu. having five arms arranged around a central disk and feeding largely on mollusks

star fruit *n* : CARAMBOLA 1

[1]**stark** \ˈstärk\ *adj* **1** : rigid as if in death; *also* : STRICT **2** *archaic* : STRONG, ROBUST **3** : SHEER, UTTER **4** : BARREN, DESOLATE ⟨~ landscape⟩; *also* : UNADORNED ⟨~ realism⟩ **5** : sharply delineated — **stark•ly** *adv*

[2]**stark** *adv* : WHOLLY, ABSOLUTELY ⟨~ naked⟩

star•light \ˈstär-ˌlīt\ *n* : the light given by the stars

star•ling \ˈstär-liŋ\ *n* : a dark brown or in summer glossy greenish black European bird related to the crows that is naturalized nearly worldwide and often considered a pest

[1]**start** \ˈstärt\ *vb* **1** : to give an involuntary twitch or jerk (as from surprise) **2** : BEGIN, COMMENCE **3** : to set going **4** : to enter or cause to enter a game or contest; *also* : to be in the starting lineup — **start•er** *n*

[2]**start** *n* **1** : a sudden involuntary motion : LEAP **2** : a spasmodic and brief effort or action **3** : BEGINNING; *also* : the place of beginning

star•tle \ˈstärt-ᵊl\ *vb* **star•tled; star•tling** : to frighten or surprise suddenly : cause to start

star•tling *adj* : causing sudden fear, surprise, or anxiety

starve \ˈstärv\ *vb* **starved; starv•ing** [ME *sterven* to die, fr. OE *steorfan*] **1** : to die or cause to die from hunger **2** : to suffer extreme hunger or deprivation ⟨*starving* for affection⟩ **3** : to subdue by famine — **star•va•tion** \stär-ˈvā-shən\ *n*

starve•ling \ˈstärv-liŋ\ *n* : one that is thin from lack of nourishment

stash \ˈstash\ *vb* : to store in a secret place for future use — **stash** *n*

stat *abbr* **1** [L *statim*] immediately **2** statute

[1]**state** \ˈstāt\ *n* [ME *stat,* fr. OF & L; OF *estat,* fr. L *status,* fr. *stare* to stand] **1** : mode or condition of being ⟨the four ~*s* of matter⟩ **2** : condition of mind **3** : social position **4** : a body of people occupying a territory and organized under one government; *also* : the government of such a body of people **5** : one of the constituent units of a nation having a federal government — **state•hood** \-ˌhu̇d\ *n*

[2]**state** *vb* **stat•ed; stat•ing 1** : FIX ⟨*stated* intervals⟩ **2** : to express in words

state•craft \ˈstāt-ˌkraft\ *n* : the art of conducting state affairs

state•house \-ˌhau̇s\ *n* : the building in which a state legislature meets

state•ly \ˈstāt-lē\ *adj* **state•li•er; -est 1** : having lofty dignity : HAUGHTY **2** : IMPRESSIVE, MAJESTIC **syn** magnificent, imposing, august — **state•li•ness** *n*

state•ment \ˈstāt-mənt\ *n* **1** : the act or result of presenting in words **2** : a summary of a financial account

state•room \ˈstāt-ˌrüm, -ˌru̇m\ *n* : a private room on a ship or railroad car

state•side \ˈstāt-ˌsīd\ *adj* : of or relating to the U.S. as regarded from outside its continental limits — **stateside** *adv*

states•man \ˈstāts-mən\ *n* : a person engaged in fixing the policies and conducting the affairs of a government; *esp* : one wise and skilled in such matters — **states•man•like** *adj* — **states•man•ship** *n*

[1]**stat•ic** \ˈsta-tik\ *adj* **1** : acting by mere weight without motion ⟨~ pressure⟩ **2** : relating to bodies at rest or forces in equilibrium **3** : not moving : not active **4** : of or relating to stationary charges of electricity **5** : of, relating to, or caused by radio static

[2]**static** *n* : noise produced in a radio or television receiver by atmospheric or other electrical disturbances

[1]**sta•tion** \ˈstā-shən\ *n* **1** : the place where a person or thing stands or is assigned to remain **2** : a regular stopping place on a transportation route : DEPOT **3** : a place where a fleet is assigned for duty **4** : a stock farm or ranch esp. in Australia or New Zealand **5** : social standing **6** : a complete assemblage of radio or television equipment for sending or receiving

[2]**station** *vb* : to assign to a station

sta•tion•ary \ˈstā-shə-ˌner-ē\ *adj* **1** : fixed in a station, course, or mode **2** : unchanging in condition

stationary front *n* : the boundary between two air masses neither of which is advancing

station break *n* : a pause in a radio or television broadcast to announce the identity of the network or station

sta•tio•ner \ˈstā-shə-nər\ *n* : one that sells stationery

sta•tio•nery \ˈstā-shə-ˌner-ē\ *n* : materials (as paper, pens, or ink) for writing; *esp* : letter paper with envelopes

station wagon *n* : an automobile having a passenger compartment which extends to the back of the vehicle and no trunk

sta•tis•tic \stə-ˈtis-tik\ *n* **1** : a single term or datum in a collection of statistics **2** : a quantity (as the mean) that is computed from a sample

sta•tis•tics \-tiks\ *n sing or pl* [G *Statistik* study of political facts and figures, fr. NL *statisticus* of politics, fr. L *status* state] : a branch of mathematics dealing with the collection, analysis, and interpretation of masses of numerical data; *also* : a collection of such numerical data — **sta•tis•ti•cal** \-ti-kəl\ *adj* — **sta•tis•ti•cal•ly** \-ti-k(ə-)lē\ *adv* — **stat•is•ti•cian** \ˌsta-tə-ˈsti-shən\ *n*

stat•u•ary \ˈsta-chə-ˌwer-ē\ *n, pl* **-ar•ies 1** : the art of making statues **2** : STATUES

stat•ue \ˈsta-chü\ *n* : a likeness (as of a person or animal) sculptured, modeled, or cast in a solid substance

stat•u•esque \ˌsta-chə-ˈwesk\ *adj* : tall and shapely

stat•u•ette \ˌsta-chə-ˈwet\ *n* : a small statue

stat•ure \ˈsta-chər\ *n* **1** : natural height (as of a person) **2** : quality or status gained (as by achievement)

sta•tus \ˈstā-təs, ˈsta-\ *n* **1** : the condition of a person in the eyes of others or of the law **2** : state of affairs

sta•tus quo \-ˈkwō\ *n* [L, state in which] : the existing state of affairs

stat•ute \ˈsta-chüt\ *n* : a law enacted by a legislative body

stat•u•to•ry \ˈsta-chə-ˌtōr-ē\ *adj* : imposed by statute : LAWFUL

statutory rape *n* : sexual intercourse with a person who is below the statutory age of consent

[1]**staunch** \ˈstȯnch\ *var of* [1]STANCH

[2]**staunch** *adj* **1** : WATERTIGHT ⟨a ~ ship⟩ **2** : FIRM, STRONG; *also* : STEADFAST, LOYAL **syn** resolute, constant, true, faithful — **staunch•ly** *adv*

[1]**stave** \ˈstāv\ *n* **1** : CUDGEL, STAFF **2** : any of several narrow strips of wood placed edge to edge to make something (as a barrel) **3** : STANZA

[2]**stave** *vb* **staved** *or* **stove** \ˈstōv\; **stav•ing 1** : to break in the staves of; *also* : to break a hole in **2** : to drive or thrust away ⟨~ off trouble⟩

staves *pl of* STAFF

[1]**stay** \ˈstā\ *n* **1** : a strong rope or wire used to support a mast **2** : [1]GUY

[2]**stay** *vb* **stayed** \ˈstād\ *also* **staid** \ˈstād\; **stay•ing 1** : PAUSE, WAIT **2** : REMAIN **3** : to stand firm **4** : LIVE, DWELL **5** : DELAY, POSTPONE **6** : to last out (as a race) **7** : STOP, CHECK **8** : to satisfy (as hunger) for a time **syn** remain, abide, linger, tarry

[3]**stay** *n* **1** : STOP, HALT **2** : a residence or sojourn in a place

[4]**stay** *n* **1** : PROP, SUPPORT **2** : CORSET — usu. used in pl.

[5]**stay** *vb* : to hold up : PROP

staying power *n* : STAMINA

stbd *abbr* starboard

std *abbr* standard

STD \ˌes-(ˌ)tē-ˈdē\ *n* : SEXUALLY TRANSMITTED DISEASE

Ste *abbr* [F *sainte*] saint (female)

stead \ˈsted\ *n* **1** : ADVANTAGE ⟨stood him in good ~⟩ **2** : the place or function ordinarily occupied or carried out by another ⟨acted in her brother's ~⟩

stead•fast \ˈsted-ˌfast\ *adj* **1** : firmly fixed in place **2** : not subject to change **3** : firm in belief, determination, or adherence : LOYAL **syn** resolute, true, faithful, staunch — **stead•fast•ly** *adv* — **stead•fast•ness** *n*

[1]**steady** \ˈste-dē\ *adj* **steadi•er; -est 1** : direct or sure in movement; *also* : CALM **2** : FIRM, FIXED **3** : STABLE **4** : CONSTANT, RESOLUTE **5** : REGULAR **6** : RELIABLE, SOBER **syn** uniform, even — **steadi•ly** \-də-lē\ *adv* — **steadi•ness** \-dē-nəs\ *n* — **steady** *adv*

[2]**steady** *vb* **stead•ied; steady•ing** : to make or become steady

steak \ˈstāk\ *n* : a slice of meat and esp. beef; *also* : a slice of a large fish

[1]**steal** \ˈstēl\ *vb* **stole** \ˈstōl\; **sto•len** \ˈstō-lən\; **steal•ing 1** : to take and carry away without right or permission **2** : to come or go secretly or gradually **3** : to get for oneself slyly or by skill and daring ⟨~ a kiss⟩ ⟨~ the ball in basketball⟩ **4** : to gain or attempt to gain a base in baseball by running without the aid of a hit or an error **syn** pilfer, filch, purloin, swipe

[2]**steal** *n* **1** : an act of stealing **2** : BARGAIN

stealth \ˈstelth\ *n* **1** : secret or unobtrusive procedure **2** : an aircraft design intended to produce a weak radar return

stealthy \ˈstel-thē\ *adj* **stealth•i•er; -est** : done by stealth : FURTIVE, SLY **syn** secret, covert, clandestine, surreptitious, underhanded — **stealth•i•ly** \ˈstel-thə-lē\ *adv*

[1]**steam** \ˈstēm\ *n* **1** : the vapor into which water is changed when heated to the boiling point **2** : water vapor when compressed so that it supplies heat and power **3** : POWER, FORCE, ENERGY — **steamy** *adj*

[2]**steam** *vb* **1** : to pass off as vapor **2** : to emit vapor **3** : to move by or as if by the agency of steam — **steam•er** *n*

steam•boat \ˈstēm-ˌbōt\ *n* : a boat driven by steam

steam engine *n* : a reciprocating engine having a piston driven by steam

steam•fit•ter \ˈstēm-ˌfi-tər\ *n* : a worker who puts in or repairs equipment (as steam pipes) for heating, ventilating, or refrigerating systems

steam•roll•er \-ˌrō-lər\ *n* : a machine for compacting roads or pavements — **steam•roll•er** *also* **steam•roll** \-ˌrōl\ *vb*

steam•ship \-ˌship\ *n* : a ship driven by steam

steed \ˈstēd\ *n* : HORSE

[1]**steel** \ˈstēl\ *n* **1** : iron treated with intense heat and mixed with carbon to make it hard and tough **2** : an article made of steel **3** : a quality (as hardness of mind) that suggests steel — **steel** *adj* — **steely** *adj*

[2]**steel** *vb* : to fill with courage or determination

steel wool *n* : long fine steel shavings used esp. for cleaning and polishing

[1]**steep** \ˈstēp\ *adj* **1** : having a very sharp slope : PRECIPITOUS **2** : too great or too high ⟨~ prices⟩ — **steep•ly** *adv* — **steep•ness** *n*

[2]**steep** *n* : a steep slope

[3]**steep** *vb* **1** : to soak in a liquid; *esp* : to extract the essence of by soaking ⟨~ tea⟩ **2** : SATURATE ⟨~*ed* in learning⟩

stee•ple \ˈstē-pəl\ *n* : a tall tapering structure built on top of a church tower; *also* : a church tower

stee•ple•chase \-ˌchās\ *n* [fr. the use of church steeples as landmarks to guide the riders] : a horse race across country; *also* : a race over a course obstructed by hurdles

[1]**steer** \ˈstir\ *n* : a male bovine animal castrated before sexual maturity and usu. raised for beef

[2]**steer** *vb* **1** : to direct the course of (as by a rudder or wheel) **2** : GUIDE, CONTROL **3** : to pursue a course of action **4** : to be subject to guidance or direction — **steers•man** \ˈstirz-mən\ *n*

steer•age \ˈstir-ij\ *n* **1** : DIRECTION, GUIDANCE **2** : a section in a passenger ship for passengers paying the lowest fares

stego•sau•rus \ˌste-gə-ˈsȯr-əs\ *n* : any of a genus of plant-eating armored dinosaurs with a series of bony plates along the backbone

stein \ˈstīn\ *n* : an earthenware mug

stel•lar \ˈste-lər\ *adj* : of or relating to stars : resembling a star

[1]**stem** \ˈstem\ *n* **1** : the main stalk of a plant; *also* : a plant part that supports another part (as a leaf or fruit) **2** : the bow of a ship **3** : a line of ancestry : STOCK **4** : that part of an inflected word which remains unchanged throughout a given inflection **5** : something resembling the stem of a plant — **stem•less** *adj* — **stemmed** \ˈstemd\ *adj*

[2]**stem** *vb* **stemmed; stem•ming** : to have a specified source : DERIVE

[3]**stem** *vb* **stemmed; stem•ming** : to make headway against ⟨~ the tide⟩

[4]**stem** *vb* **stemmed; stem•ming** : to stop or check by or as if by damming

stench \ˈstench\ *n* : STINK

sten•cil \ˈsten-səl\ *n* [ME *stanselen* to ornament with sparkling colors, fr. MF *estanceler,* fr. *estancele* spark, fr. (assumed) VL *stincilla,* alter. of L *scintilla*] : an impervious material (as metal or paper) perforated with lettering or a design through which a substance (as ink or paint) is applied to a surface to be printed — **stencil** *vb*

ste•nog•ra•phy \stə-ˈnä-grə-fē\ *n* : the art or process of writing in shorthand — **ste•nog•ra•pher** \-fər\ *n* — **steno•graph•ic** \ˌste-nə-ˈgra-fik\ *adj*

sten•to•ri•an \sten-ˈtōr-ē-ən\ *adj* : extremely loud and powerful

[1]**step** \ˈstep\ *n* **1** : a rest for the foot in ascending or descending : STAIR **2** : an advance made by raising one foot and putting it down elsewhere **3** : manner of walking **4** : a small space or distance **5** : a degree, rank, or plane in a series **6** : a sequential measure leading to a result

[2]**step** *vb* **stepped; step•ping 1** : to advance or recede by steps **2** : to go on foot : WALK **3** : to move along briskly **4** : to press down with the foot **5** : to measure by steps **6** : to construct or arrange in or as if in steps

step•broth•er \ˈstep-ˌbrə-t͟hər\ *n* : the son of one's stepparent by a former marriage

step•child \-ˌchīld\ *n* : a child of one's husband or wife by a former marriage

step•daugh•ter \-ˌdȯ-tər\ *n* : a daughter of one's wife or husband by a former marriage

step down *vb* **1** : RETIRE, RESIGN **2** : to lower (a voltage) by means of a transformer

step•fa•ther \-ˌfä-t͟hər\ *n* : the husband of one's mother by a subsequent marriage

step•lad•der \ˈstep-ˌla-dər\ *n* : a light portable set of steps in a hinged frame

step•moth•er \-ˌmə-t͟hər\ *n* : the wife of one's father by a subsequent marriage

step•par•ent \-ˌpar-ənt\ *n* : one's stepfather or stepmother
steppe \ˈstep\ *n* [Russ *step'*] : dry level grass-covered treeless land in regions of wide temperature range esp. in southeastern Europe and Asia
step•sis•ter \ˈstep-ˌsis-tər\ *n* : the daughter of one's stepparent by a former marriage
step•son \-ˌsən\ *n* : a son of one's wife or husband by a former marriage
step up *vb* **1** : to increase (a voltage) by means of a transformer **2** : INCREASE, ACCELERATE **3** : to come forward — **step–up** \ˈstep-ˌəp\ *n*
ster *abbr* sterling
ste•reo \ˈster-ē-ˌō, ˈstir-\ *n, pl* **ste•re•os 1** : stereophonic reproduction **2** : a stereophonic sound system — **stereo** *adj*
ste•reo•phon•ic \ˌster-ē-ə-ˈfä-nik, ˌstir-\ *adj* : of or relating to sound reproduction designed to create the effect of listening to the original — **ste•reo•phon•i•cal•ly** \-ˈfä-ni-k(ə-)lē\ *adv*
ster•e•o•scope \ˈster-ē-ə-ˌskōp, ˈstir-\ *n* [Gk *stereos* solid + *-skopion* means for viewing] : an optical instrument that blends two slightly different pictures of the same subject to give the effect of depth
ste•reo•scop•ic \ˌster-ē-ə-ˈskä-pik, ˌstir-\ *adj* **1** : of or relating to the stereoscope **2** : characterized by the seeing of objects in three dimensions ⟨~ vision⟩ — **ste•reo•scop•i•cal•ly** \-ˈskä-pi-k(ə-)lē\ *adv* — **ste•re•os•co•py** \ˌster-ē-ˈäs-kə-pē, ˌstir-\ *n*
ste•reo•type \ˈster-ē-ə-ˌtīp, ˈstir-\ *n* **1** : a metal printing plate cast from a mold made from set type **2** : something agreeing with a pattern; *esp* : an idea that many people have about a thing or a group and that may often be untrue or only partly true — **stereotype** *vb* — **ste•reo•typ•i•cal** \ˌster-ē-ə-ˈti-pi-kəl\ *adj* — **ste•reo•typ•i•cal•ly** \-pi-k(ə-)lē\ *adv*
ste•reo•typed \-ˌtīpt\ *adj* : lacking originality or individuality **syn** trite, clichéd, commonplace, hackneyed, stale, threadbare
ster•ile \ˈster-əl\ *adj* **1** : unable to bear fruit, crops, or offspring **2** : free from living things and esp. germs — **ste•ril•i•ty** \stə-ˈri-lə-tē\ *n*
ster•il•ize \ˈster-ə-ˌlīz\ *vb* **-ized; -iz•ing** : to make sterile; *esp* : to free from germs — **ster•il•i•za•tion** \ˌster-ə-lə-ˈzā-shən\ *n* — **ster•il•iz•er** \ˈster-ə-ˌlī-zər\ *n*
¹**ster•ling** \ˈstər-liŋ\ *n* **1** : British money **2** : sterling silver
²**sterling** *adj* **1** : of, relating to, or calculated in terms of British sterling **2** : having a fixed standard of purity represented by an alloy of 925 parts of silver with 75 parts of copper **3** : made of sterling silver **4** : EXCELLENT
¹**stern** \ˈstərn\ *adj* **1** : SEVERE, AUSTERE **2** : STOUT, STURDY ⟨~ resolve⟩ — **stern•ly** *adv* — **stern•ness** *n*
²**stern** *n* : the rear end of a boat
ster•num \ˈstər-nəm\ *n, pl* **sternums** *or* **ster•na** \-nə\ : a long flat bone or cartilage at the center front of the chest connecting the ribs of the two sides
ste•roid \ˈstir-ˌȯid\ *n* : any of numerous compounds including various hormones (as anabolic steroids) and sugar derivatives — **steroid** *or* **ste•roi•dal** \stə-ˈrȯid-ᵊl\ *adj*
stetho•scope \ˈste-thə-ˌskōp\ *n* : an instrument used to detect and listen to sounds produced in the body
ste•ve•dore \ˈstē-və-ˌdōr\ *n* [Sp *estibador,* fr. *estibar* to pack, fr. L *stipare* to press together] : one who works at loading and unloading ships
¹**stew** \ˈstü, ˈstyü\ *n* **1** : a dish of stewed meat and vegetables served in gravy **2** : a state of agitation, worry, or resentment
²**stew** *vb* **1** : to boil slowly : SIMMER **2** : to be in a state of agitation, worry, or resentment
stew•ard \ˈstü-ərd, ˈstyü-\ *n* [ME, fr. OE *stīweard,* fr. *stī, stig* hall, sty + *weard* ward] **1** : one employed on a large estate to manage domestic concerns **2** : one who supervises the provision and distribution of food (as on a ship); *also* : an employee on a ship or airplane who serves passengers **3** : one actively concerned with the direction of the affairs of an organization — **stew•ard•ship** *n*
stew•ard•ess \ˈstü-ər-dəs, ˈstyü-\ *n* : a woman who is a steward esp. on an airplane
stg *abbr* sterling
¹**stick** \ˈstik\ *n* **1** : a cut or broken branch or twig; *also* : a long slender piece of wood **2** : ROD, STAFF **3** : something resembling a stick **4** : a dull uninteresting person **5** *pl* : remote usu. rural areas
²**stick** *vb* **stuck** \ˈstək\; **stick•ing 1** : STAB, PRICK **2** : IMPALE **3** : ATTACH, FASTEN **4** : to thrust or project in some direction or manner **5** : to be unable to proceed or move freely **6** : to hold fast by or as if by gluing : ADHERE **7** : to hold to something firmly or closely : CLING **8** : to become jammed or blocked
stick•er \ˈsti-kər\ *n* : one that sticks (as a bur) or causes sticking (as glue); *esp* : an adhesive label
stick insect *n* : any of various usu. wingless insects with a long round body resembling a stick
stick•ler \ˈsti-klər, -kə-lər\ *n* : one who insists on exactness or completeness
stick shift *n* : a manually operated automobile gearshift usu. mounted on the floor
stick–to–it•ive•ness \stik-ˈtü-ə-tiv-nəs\ *n* : dogged perseverance : TENACITY
stick up *vb* : to rob at gunpoint — **stick•up** \ˈstik-ˌəp\ *n*
sticky \ˈsti-kē\ *adj* **stick•i•er; -est 1** : ADHESIVE **2** : VISCOUS, GLUEY **3** : tending to stick ⟨~ valve⟩ **4** : DIFFICULT
¹**stiff** \ˈstif\ *adj* **1** : not pliant : RIGID **2** : not limber ⟨~ joints⟩; *also* : TENSE, TAUT **3** : not flowing or working easily ⟨~ paste⟩ **4** : not natural and easy : FORMAL **5** : STRONG, FORCEFUL ⟨~ breeze⟩ **6** : HARSH, SEVERE **syn** inflexible, inelastic — **stiff•ly** *adv* — **stiff•ness** *n*
²**stiff** *vb* : to refuse to pay or tip
stiff•en \ˈsti-fən\ *vb* : to make or become stiff — **stiff•en•er** *n*
stiff–necked \ˈstif-ˈnekt\ *adj* : STUBBORN, HAUGHTY
sti•fle \ˈstī-fəl\ *vb* **sti•fled; sti•fling 1** : to kill by depriving of or die from lack of oxygen or air : SMOTHER **2** : to keep in check by effort : SUPPRESS ⟨~ a sneeze⟩ — **sti•fling•ly** *adv*
stig•ma \ˈstig-mə\ *n, pl* **stig•ma•ta** \stig-ˈmä-tə, ˈstig-mə-tə\ *or* **stigmas** [L] **1** : a mark of disgrace or discredit **2** *pl* : bodily marks resembling the wounds of the crucified Christ **3** : the upper part of the pistil of a flower that receives the pollen in fertilization — **stig•mat•ic** \stig-ˈma-tik\ *adj*
stig•ma•tize \ˈstig-mə-ˌtīz\ *vb* **-tized; -tiz•ing 1** : to mark with a stigma **2** : to characterize as disgraceful
stile \ˈstīl\ *n* : steps used for crossing a fence or wall
sti•let•to \stə-ˈle-tō\ *n, pl* **-tos** *or* **-toes** [It, dim. of *stilo* stylus, dagger] : a slender dagger
¹**still** \ˈstil\ *adj* **1** : MOTIONLESS **2** : making no sound : SILENT — **still•ness** *n*
²**still** *vb* : to make or become still
³**still** *adv* **1** : without motion ⟨sit ~⟩ **2** : up to and during this or that time **3** : in spite of that : NEVERTHELESS **4** : EVEN ⟨ran ~ faster⟩ **5** : BESIDES, YET
⁴**still** *n* **1** : STILLNESS, SILENCE **2** : a static photograph esp. from a motion picture
⁵**still** *n* **1** : DISTILLERY **2** : apparatus used in distillation
still•birth \ˈstil-ˌbərth\ *n* : the birth of a dead fetus
still•born \-ˈbȯrn\ *adj* : born dead
still life *n, pl* **still lifes** : a picture of inanimate objects
stilt \ˈstilt\ *n* : one of a pair of poles for walking with each having a step or loop for the foot to elevate the wearer above the ground; *also* : a polelike support of a structure above ground or water level
stilt•ed \ˈstil-təd\ *adj* : not easy and natural ⟨~ language⟩
Stil•ton \ˈstilt-ᵊn\ *n* : a blue cheese of English origin
stim•u•lant \ˈsti-myə-lənt\ *n* **1** : an agent (as a drug)

that temporarily increases the activity of an organism or any of its parts **2** : STIMULUS **3** : an alcoholic beverage — **stimulant** *adj*

stim•u•late \-ˌlāt\ *vb* **-lat•ed; -lat•ing** : to make active or more active : ANIMATE, AROUSE **syn** excite, provoke, motivate, quicken — **stim•u•la•tion** \ˌsti-myə-ˈlā-shən\ *n* — **stim•u•la•tive** \ˈsti-myə-ˌlā-tiv\ *adj*

stim•u•lus \ˈsti-myə-ləs\ *n, pl* **-li** \-ˌlī\ [L] **1** : something that moves to activity **2** : an agent that directly influences the activity of a living organism or one of its parts

¹sting \ˈstiŋ\ *vb* **stung** \ˈstəŋ\; **sting•ing 1** : to prick painfully esp. with a sharp or poisonous process **2** : to cause to suffer acutely — **sting•er** *n*

²sting *n* **1** : an act of stinging; *also* : a resultant wound, sore, or pain **2** : a pointed often venom-bearing organ (as of a bee) : STINGER **3** : an elaborate confidence game; *esp* : one worked by undercover police to trap criminals

stin•gy \ˈstin-jē\ *adj* **stin•gi•er; -est** : not generous : giving or spending as little as possible — **stin•gi•ness** *n*

stink \ˈstiŋk\ *vb* **stank** \ˈstaŋk\ *or* **stunk** \ˈstəŋk\; **stunk; stink•ing** : to give forth a strong and offensive smell; *also* : to be extremely bad in quality or repute — **stink** *n* — **stink•er** *n*

stink•bug \ˈstiŋk-ˌbəg\ *n* : any of various true bugs that emit a disagreeable odor

¹stint \ˈstint\ *vb* **1** : to be sparing or frugal **2** : to cut short in amount

²stint *n* **1** : an assigned amount of work **2** : RESTRAINT, LIMITATION **3** : a period of time spent at a particular activity

sti•pend \ˈstī-ˌpend, -pənd\ *n* [ME, alter. of *stipendy*, fr. L *stipendium*, fr. *stips* gift + *pendere* to weigh, pay] : a fixed sum of money paid periodically for services or to defray expenses

stip•ple \ˈsti-pəl\ *vb* **stip•pled; stip•pling 1** : to engrave by means of dots and light strokes **2** : to apply (as paint or ink) with small short touches — **stipple** *n*

stip•u•late \ˈsti-pyə-ˌlāt\ *vb* **-lat•ed; -lat•ing** : to make an agreement; *esp* : to make a special demand for something as a condition in an agreement — **stip•u•la•tion** \ˌsti-pyə-ˈlā-shən\ *n*

¹stir \ˈstər\ *vb* **stirred; stir•ring 1** : to move slightly **2** : AROUSE, EXCITE **3** : to mix, dissolve, or make by continued circular movement ⟨~ eggs into cake batter⟩ **4** : to move to activity (as by pushing, beating, or prodding)

²stir *n* **1** : a state of agitation or activity **2** : an act of stirring

stir–fry \ˈstər-ˌfrī\ *vb* : to fry quickly over high heat while stirring continuously — **stir–fry** *n*

stir•ring \ˈstər-iŋ\ *adj* **1** : ACTIVE, BUSTLING **2** : ROUSING, INSPIRING

stir•rup \ˈstər-əp\ *n* [ME *stirop*, fr. OE *stigrāp*, lit., mounting rope] **1** : a light frame hung from a saddle to support the rider's foot **2** : STAPES

¹stitch \ˈstich\ *n* **1** : a sudden sharp pain esp. in the side **2** : one of the series of loops formed by or over a needle in sewing

²stitch *vb* **1** : to fasten or join with stitches **2** : to decorate with stitches **3** : SEW

stk *abbr* stock

stoat \ˈstōt\ *n, pl* **stoats** *also* **stoat** : the common Old and New World ermine esp. in its brown summer coat

¹stock \ˈstäk\ *n* **1** *archaic* : a block of wood **2** : a stupid person **3** : a wooden part of a thing serving as its support, frame, or handle **4** *pl* : a device for publicly punishing offenders consisting of a wooden frame with holes in which the feet and hands can be locked **5** : the original from which others derive; *also* : a group having a common origin : FAMILY **6** : LIVESTOCK **7** : a supply of goods **8** : the ownership element in a corporation divided to give the owners an interest and usu. voting power **9** : a company of actors playing at a particular theater and presenting a series of plays **10** : liquid in which meat, fish, or vegetables have been simmered that is used as a basis for soup, gravy, or sauce

stocks 4

²stock *vb* : to provide with stock

³stock *adj* : kept regularly for sale or use; *also* : commonly used : STANDARD

stock•ade \stä-ˈkād\ *n* [Sp *estacada*, fr. *estaca* stake, pale] : an enclosure (as of posts and stakes) for defense or confinement

stock•bro•ker \-ˌbrō-kər\ *n* : one who executes orders to buy and sell securities

stock car *n* : a racing car that is similar to a regular car

stock exchange *n* : a place where the buying and selling of securities is conducted

stock•hold•er \ˈstäk-ˌhōl-dər\ *n* : one who owns corporate stock

stock•i•nette *or* **stock•i•net** \ˌstä-kə-ˈnet\ *n* : an elastic knitted fabric used esp. for infants' wear and bandages

stock•ing \ˈstä-kiŋ\ *n* : a close-fitting knitted covering for the foot and leg

stock market *n* **1** : STOCK EXCHANGE **2** : a market for stocks

stock•pile \ˈstäk-ˌpīl\ *n* : a reserve supply esp. of something essential — **stockpile** *vb*

stocky \ˈstä-kē\ *adj* **stock•i•er; -est** : being short and relatively thick : STURDY **syn** thickset, squat, heavyset, stubby

stock•yard \ˈstäk-ˌyärd\ *n* : a yard for stock; *esp* : one for livestock about to be slaughtered or shipped

stodgy \ˈstä-jē\ *adj* **stodg•i•er; -est 1** : HEAVY, DULL **2** : extremely old-fashioned

¹sto•ic \ˈstō-ik\ *n* [ME, fr. L *stoicus*, fr. Gk *stōïkos*, lit., of the portico, fr. *Stoa* (*Poikilē*) the Painted Portico, portico at Athens where the philosopher Zeno taught] : one who suffers without complaining

²stoic *or* **sto•i•cal** \-i-kəl\ *adj* : not affected by passion or feeling; *esp* : showing indifference to pain **syn** impassive, phlegmatic, apathetic, stolid — **sto•ical•ly** \-i-k(ə-)lē\ *adv* — **sto•icism** \ˈstō-ə-ˌsi-zəm\ *n*

stoke \ˈstōk\ *vb* **stoked; stok•ing 1** : to stir up a fire **2** : to tend and supply fuel to a furnace — **stok•er** *n*

STOL *abbr* short takeoff and landing

¹stole \ˈstōl\ *past of* STEAL

²stole *n* **1** : a long narrow band worn round the neck by some clergymen **2** : a long wide scarf or similar covering worn by women

stolen *past part of* STEAL

stol•id \ˈstä-ləd\ *adj* : not easily aroused or excited : showing little or no emotion **syn** phlegmatic, apathetic, impassive, stoic — **sto•lid•i•ty** \stä-ˈli-də-tē\ *n* — **stol•id•ly** *adv*

sto•lon \ˈstō-lən, -ˌlän\ *n* : RUNNER 6

¹stom•ach \ˈstə-mək\ *n* **1** : a saclike digestive organ of a vertebrate into which food goes from the mouth by way of the throat and which opens below into the intestine **2** : a cavity in an invertebrate animal that is analogous to a stomach **3** : ABDOMEN **4** : desire for food caused by hunger : APPETITE **5** : INCLINATION, DESIRE

[2]**stomach** *vb* : to bear without open resentment : put up with

stom•ach•ache \-ˌāk\ *n* : pain in or in the region of the stomach

stom•ach•er \ˈstə-mi-kər, -chər\ *n* : the front of a bodice often appearing between the laces of an outer garment (as in 16th century costume)

stomp \ˈstämp, ˈstȯmp\ *vb* : STAMP — **stomp** *n*

[1]**stone** \ˈstōn\ *n* **1** : hardened earth or mineral matter : ROCK **2** : a small piece of rock **3** : a precious stone : GEM **4** : CALCULUS 3 **5** : a hard stony seed (as of a date) or one (as of a plum) with a stony covering **6** *pl usu* **stone** : a British unit of weight equal to 14 pounds — **stony** *also* **ston•ey** \ˈstō-nē\ *adj*

[2]**stone** *vb* **stoned; ston•ing 1** : to pelt or kill with stones **2** : to remove the stones of (a fruit)

Stone Age *n* : the first known period of prehistoric human culture characterized by the use of stone tools

stoned \ˈstōnd\ *adj* **1** : DRUNK **2** : being under the influence of a drug

stone•wall \ˈstōn-ˌwȯl\ *vb* : to refuse to comply or cooperate with

stone•washed \ˈstōn-ˌwȯsht, -ˌwäsht\ *adj* : having been washed with stones during manufacture to create a softer fabric ⟨~ jeans⟩

stood *past and past part of* STAND

stooge \ˈstüj\ *n* **1** : a person who plays a subordinate or compliant role to a principal **2** : STRAIGHT MAN

stool \ˈstül\ *n* **1** : a seat usu. without back or arms **2** : FOOTSTOOL **3** : a seat used while urinating or defecating **4** : a discharge of fecal matter

stool pigeon *n* : DECOY, INFORMER

[1]**stoop** \ˈstüp\ *vb* **1** : to bend forward and downward **2** : CONDESCEND **3** : to lower oneself morally

[2]**stoop** *n* **1** : an act of bending forward **2** : a bent position of head and shoulders

[3]**stoop** *n* : a porch or platform at a house door

[1]**stop** \ˈstäp\ *vb* **stopped; stop•ping 1** : to close (an opening) by filling or covering closely **2** : BLOCK, HALT **3** : to cease to go on **4** : to bring activity or operation to an end **5** : STAY, TARRY **syn** quit, discontinue, desist, cease

[2]**stop** *n* **1** : END, CESSATION **2** : a set of organ pipes of one tone quality; *also* : a control knob for such a set **3** : OBSTRUCTION **4** : PLUG, STOPPER **5** : an act of stopping : CHECK **6** : a delay in a journey : STAY **7** : a place for stopping **8** *chiefly Brit* : any of several punctuation marks

stop•gap \ˈstäp-ˌgap\ *n* : something that serves as a temporary expedient

stop•light \-ˌlīt\ *n* : TRAFFIC LIGHT

stop•over \ˈstäp-ˌō-vər\ *n* **1** : a stop at an intermediate point in one's journey **2** : a stopping place on a journey

stop•page \ˈstä-pij\ *n* : the act of stopping : the state of being stopped

stop•per \ˈstä-pər\ *n* : something (as a cork) for sealing an opening

stop•watch \ˈstäp-ˌwäch\ *n* : a watch that can be started or stopped at will for exact timing

stor•age \ˈstōr-ij\ *n* **1** : space for storing; *also* : cost of storing **2** : MEMORY 6 **3** : the act of storing; *esp* : the safekeeping of goods (as in a warehouse)

storage battery *n* : a group of connected rechargeable electrochemical cells used to provide electric current

[1]**store** \ˈstōr\ *vb* **stored; stor•ing 1** : to place or leave in a safe location for preservation or future use **2** : to provide esp. for a future need

[2]**store** *n* **1** : something accumulated and kept for future use **2** : a large or ample quantity **3** : STOREHOUSE **4** : a retail business establishment

store•house \-ˌhau̇s\ *n* : a building for storing goods or supplies; *also* : an abundant source or supply

store•keep•er \-ˌkē-pər\ *n* : one who operates a retail store

store•room \-ˌrüm, -ˌru̇m\ *n* : a room for storing goods or supplies

sto•ried \ˈstōr-ēd\ *adj* : celebrated in story or history

stork \ˈstȯrk\ *n* : any of various large stout-billed Old World wading birds related to the herons and ibises

[1]**storm** \ˈstȯrm\ *n* **1** : a heavy fall of rain, snow, or hail with high wind **2** : a violent outbreak or disturbance **3** : a mass attack on a defended position — **storm•i•ly** \ˈstȯr-mə-lē\ *adv* — **storm•i•ness** \-mē-nəs\ *n* — **stormy** *adj*

[2]**storm** *vb* **1** : to blow with violence; *also* : to rain, snow, or hail heavily **2** : to make a mass attack against **3** : to be violently angry : RAGE **4** : to rush along furiously

[1]**sto•ry** \ˈstōr-ē\ *n, pl* **stories 1** : NARRATIVE, ACCOUNT **2** : REPORT, STATEMENT **3** : ANECDOTE **4** : SHORT STORY **5** : LIE, FALSEHOOD **6** : a news article or broadcast **syn** untruth, tale, canard

[2]**story** *also* **sto•rey** \ˈstōr-ē\ *n, pl* **stories** *also* **storeys** : a floor of a building or the space between two adjacent floor levels

sto•ry•tell•er \-ˌte-lər\ *n* : a teller of stories

sto•tin•ka \stō-ˈtiŋ-kə\ *n, pl* **-tin•ki** \-kē\ — see *lev* at MONEY table

[1]**stout** \ˈstau̇t\ *adj* **1** : BRAVE **2** : FIRM **3** : STURDY **4** : STAUNCH, ENDURING **5** : SOLID **6** : FORCEFUL, VIOLENT **7** : BULKY, THICKSET **syn** fleshy, fat, portly, corpulent, obese, plump — **stout•ly** *adv* — **stout•ness** *n*

[2]**stout** *n* : a dark heavy ale

[1]**stove** \ˈstōv\ *n* : an apparatus that burns fuel or uses electricity to provide heat (as for cooking or heating)

[2]**stove** *past and past part of* STAVE

stow \ˈstō\ *vb* **1** : HIDE, STORE **2** : to pack in a compact mass

stow•away \ˈstō-ə-ˌwā\ *n* : one who hides on a vehicle to ride free

STP *abbr* standard temperature and pressure

strad•dle \ˈstrad-ᵊl\ *vb* **strad•dled; strad•dling 1** : to stand, sit, or walk with legs spread apart **2** : to favor or seem to favor two apparently opposite sides — **straddle** *n*

strafe \ˈstrāf\ *vb* **strafed; straf•ing** [G *Gott strafe England* may God punish England, propaganda slogan during World War I] : to fire upon with machine guns from a low-flying airplane

strag•gle \ˈstra-gəl\ *vb* **strag•gled; strag•gling 1** : to wander from the direct course : ROVE, STRAY **2** : to become separated from others of the same kind — **strag•gler** *n* — **strag•gly** \ˈstra-g(ə-)lē\ *adj*

[1]**straight** \ˈstrāt\ *adj* **1** : free from curves, bends, angles, or irregularities **2** : not wandering from the main point or proper course ⟨~ thinking⟩ **3** : HONEST, UPRIGHT **4** : having the elements in correct order **5** : UNMIXED, UNDILUTED ⟨~ whiskey⟩ **6** : CONVENTIONAL, SQUARE; *also* : HETEROSEXUAL

[2]**straight** *adv* : in a straight manner

[3]**straight** *n* **1** : a straight line, course, or arrangement **2** : the part of a racetrack between the last turn and the finish **3** : a sequence of five cards in a poker hand

straight–arm \ˈstrāt-ˌärm\ *n* : an act of warding off a football tackler with the arm fully extended — **straight–arm** *vb*

straight•away \ˈstrā-tə-ˌwā\ *n* : a straight stretch (as at a racetrack)

straight•edge \ˈstrāt-ˌej\ *n* : a piece of material with a straight edge for testing straight lines and surfaces or drawing straight lines

straight•en \ˈstrāt-ᵊn\ *vb* : to make or become straight

straight flush *n* : a poker hand containing five cards of the same suit in sequence

straight•for•ward \strāt-ˈfȯr-wərd\ *adj* **1** : FRANK,

CANDID, HONEST **2 :** proceeding in a straight course or manner

straight man *n* **:** an entertainer who feeds lines to a comedian

straight•way \ˈstrāt-ˈwā, -ˌwā\ *adv* **:** IMMEDIATELY

[1]**strain** \ˈstrān\ *n* [ME *streen* progeny, lineage, fr. OE *strēon* gain, acquisition] **1 :** LINEAGE, ANCESTRY **2 :** a group (as of people or plants) of presumed common ancestry **3 :** an inherited or inherent character or quality ⟨a ~ of madness in the family⟩ **4 :** STREAK, TRACE **5 :** MELODY **6 :** the general style or tone

[2]**strain** *vb* [ME, fr. MF *estraindre,* fr. L *stringere* to bind or draw tight, press together] **1 :** to draw taut **2 :** to exert to the utmost **3 :** to strive violently **4 :** to injure by improper or excessive use **5 :** to filter or remove by filtering **6 :** to stretch beyond a proper limit — **strain•er** *n*

[3]**strain** *n* **1 :** excessive tension or exertion (as of body or mind) **2 :** bodily injury from excessive tension, effort, or use; *esp* **:** one in which muscles or ligaments are unduly stretched usu. from a wrench or twist **3 :** deformation of a material body under the action of applied forces

[1]**strait** \ˈstrāt\ *adj* [ME, fr. OF *estreit,* fr. L *strictus* strait, strict] **1** *archaic* **:** STRICT **2** *archaic* **:** NARROW **3** *archaic* **:** CONSTRICTED **4 :** DIFFICULT, STRAITENED

[2]**strait** *n* **1 :** a narrow channel connecting two bodies of water **2** *pl* **:** DISTRESS

strait•en \ˈstrāt-ᵊn\ *vb* **1 :** to hem in **:** CONFINE **2 :** to make distressing or difficult

strait•jack•et *also* **straight•jack•et** \ˈstrāt-ˌja-kət\ *n* **:** a cover or garment of strong material (as canvas) used to bind the body and esp. the arms closely in restraining a violent prisoner or patient — **straitjacket** *vb*

strait•laced *or* **straight•laced** \-ˈlāst\ *adj* **:** strict in manners, morals or opinion

[1]**strand** \ˈstrand\ *n* **:** SHORE, BEACH

[2]**strand** *vb* **1 :** to run, drift, or drive upon the shore ⟨a ~*ed* ship⟩ **2 :** to place or leave in a helpless position

[3]**strand** *n* **1 :** one of the fibers twisted or plaited together into a cord, rope, or cable; *also* **:** a cord, rope, or cable made up of such fibers **2 :** a twisted or plaited ropelike mass ⟨a ~ of pearls⟩ — **strand•ed** \ˈstrandəd\ *adj*

strange \ˈstrānj\ *adj* **strang•er; strang•est** [ME, fr. OF *estrange,* fr. L *extraneus,* lit., external, fr. *extra* outside] **1 :** of external origin, kind, or character **2 :** NEW, UNFAMILIAR **3 :** DISTANT 6 **4 :** UNACCUSTOMED, INEXPERIENCED **syn** singular, peculiar, eccentric, erratic, odd, queer, quaint, curious — **strange•ly** *adv* — **strange•ness** *n*

strang•er \ˈstrān-jər\ *n* **1 :** FOREIGNER **2 :** INTRUDER **3 :** a person with whom one is unacquainted

stran•gle \ˈstraŋ-gəl\ *vb* **stran•gled; stran•gling 1 :** to choke to death **:** THROTTLE **2 :** STIFLE, SUPPRESS — **stran•gler** *n*

stran•gu•late \ˈstraŋ-gyə-ˌlāt\ *vb* **-lat•ed; -lat•ing 1 :** STRANGLE, CONSTRICT **2 :** to become so constricted as to stop circulation

stran•gu•la•tion \ˌstraŋ-gyə-ˈlā-shən\ *n* **:** the act or process of strangling or strangulating; *also* **:** the state of being strangled or strangulated

[1]**strap** \ˈstrap\ *n* **:** a narrow strip of flexible material used esp. for fastening, holding together, or wrapping

[2]**strap** *vb* **strapped; strap•ping 1 :** to secure with a strap **2 :** BIND, CONSTRICT **3 :** to flog with a strap **4 :** STROP

strap•less \-ləs\ *adj* **:** having no straps; *esp* **:** having no shoulder straps

[1]**strap•ping** \ˈstra-piŋ\ *adj* **:** LARGE, STRONG, HUSKY

[2]**strap•ping** *n* **:** material for a strap

strat•a•gem \ˈstra-tə-jəm, -ˌjem\ *n* **1 :** a trick to deceive or outwit the enemy; *also* **:** a deceptive scheme **2 :** skill in deception

strat•e•gy \ˈstra-tə-jē\ *n, pl* **-gies** [Gk *stratēgia* generalship, fr. *stratēgos* general, fr. *stratos* camp, army + *agein* to lead] **1 :** the science and art of military command aimed at meeting the enemy under conditions advantageous to one's own force **2 :** a careful plan or method esp. for achieving an end — **stra•te•gic** \strə-ˈtē-jik\ *adj* — **strat•e•gist** \ˈstra-tə-jist\ *n*

strat•i•fy \ˈstra-tə-ˌfī\ *vb* **-fied; -fy•ing :** to form or arrange in layers — **strat•i•fi•ca•tion** \ˌstra-tə-fə-ˈkā-shən\ *n*

stra•tig•ra•phy \strə-ˈti-grə-fē\ *n* **:** geology that deals with rock strata — **strati•graph•ic** \ˌstra-tə-ˈgra-fik\ *adj*

strato•sphere \ˈstra-tə-ˌsfir\ *n* **:** the part of the earth's atmosphere between about 7 miles (11 kilometers) and 31 miles (50 kilometers) above the earth — **strato•spher•ic** \ˌstra-tə-ˈsfir-ik, -ˈsfer-\ *adj*

stra•tum \ˈstrā-təm, ˈstra-\ *n, pl* **stra•ta** \ˈstrā-tə, ˈstra-\ [NL, fr. L, spread, bed, fr. neut. of *stratus,* pp. of *sternere* to spread out] **1 :** a bed, layer, or sheetlike mass (as of one kind of rock lying between layers of other kinds of rock) **2 :** a level of culture; *also* **:** a group of people representing one stage in cultural development

[1]**straw** \ˈstrȯ\ *n* **1 :** stalks of grain after threshing; *also* **:** a single coarse dry stem (as of a grass) **2 :** a thing of small worth **:** TRIFLE **3 :** a tube (as of paper or plastic) for sucking up a beverage

[2]**straw** *adj* **1 :** made of straw **2 :** having no real force or validity ⟨a ~ vote⟩

straw•ber•ry \ˈstrȯ-ˌber-ē, -bə-rē\ *n* **:** an edible juicy usu. red pulpy fruit of any of serveral low herbs with white flowers and long slender runners; *also* **:** one of these herbs

strawberry

straw boss *n* **:** a foreman of a small group of workers

straw•flow•er \ˈstrȯ-ˌflau̇-ər\ *n* **:** any of several plants whose flowers can be dried with little loss of form or color

[1]**stray** \ˈstrā\ *n* **1 :** a domestic animal wandering at large or lost **2 :** WAIF

[2]**stray** *vb* **1 :** to wander or roam without purpose **2 :** DEVIATE

[3]**stray** *adj* **1 :** having strayed **:** separated from the group or the main body **2 :** occurring at random ⟨~ remarks⟩

[1]**streak** \ˈstrēk\ *n* **1 :** a line or mark of a different color or texture from its background **2 :** a narrow band of light; *also* **:** a lightning bolt **3 :** a slight admixture **:** TRACE **4 :** a brief run (as of luck); *also* **:** an unbroken series

[2]**streak** *vb* **1 :** to form streaks in or on **2 :** to move very swiftly

[1]**stream** \ˈstrēm\ *n* **1 :** a body of water (as a river) flowing on the earth; *also* **:** any body of flowing fluid (as water or gas) **2 :** a continuous procession ⟨a ~ of traffic⟩

[2]**stream** *vb* **1 :** to flow in or as if in a stream **2 :** to pour

out streams of liquid **3 :** to trail out in length **4 :** to move forward in a steady stream

stream•bed \ˈstrēm-ˌbed\ *n* **:** the channel occupied by a stream

stream•er \ˈstrē-mər\ *n* **1 :** a long narrow ribbonlike flag **2 :** a long ribbon on a dress or hat **3 :** a newspaper headline that runs across the entire sheet **4** *pl* **:** AURORA

stream•let \ˈstrēm-lət\ *n* **:** a small stream

stream•lined \-ˌlīnd\ *adj* **1 :** made with contours to reduce resistance to motion through water or air **2 :** SIMPLIFIED **3 :** MODERNIZED — **streamline** *vb*

street \ˈstrēt\ *n* [ME *strete*, fr. OE *strǣt*, fr. LL *strata* paved road, fr. L, fem. of *stratus*, pp. of *sternere* to spread out] **1 :** a thoroughfare esp. in a city, town, or village **2 :** the occupants of the houses on a street

street•car \-ˌkär\ *n* **:** a passenger vehicle running on rails on city streets

street railway *n* **:** a company operating streetcars or buses

street•walk•er \ˈstrēt-ˌwȯ-kər\ *n* **:** PROSTITUTE

strength \ˈstreŋth\ *n* **1 :** the quality of being strong **:** ability to do or endure **:** POWER **2 :** TOUGHNESS, SOLIDITY **3 :** power to resist attack **4 :** INTENSITY **5 :** force as measured in numbers ⟨the ~ of an army⟩

strength•en \ˈstreŋ-thən\ *vb* **:** to make or become stronger — **strength•en•er** *n*

stren•u•ous \ˈstren-yə-wəs\ *adj* **1 :** VIGOROUS, ENERGETIC **2 :** requiring energy or stamina — **stren•u•ous•ly** *adv*

strep \ˈstrep\ *n* **:** STREPTOCOCCUS

strep throat *n* **:** an inflammatory sore throat caused by streptococci and marked by fever, prostration, and toxemia

strep•to•coc•cus \ˌstrep-tə-ˈkä-kəs\ *n, pl* **-coc•ci** \-ˈkä-ˌkī, -ˈkäk-ˌsī, -ˈkä-ˌkē, -ˈkäk-ˌsē\ **:** any of various spherical bacteria that usu. grow in chains and include some causing serious diseases — **strep•to•coc•cal** \-kəl\ *adj*

strep•to•my•cin \-ˈmīs-ᵊn\ *n* **:** an antibiotic produced by soil bacteria and used esp. in treating tuberculosis

¹**stress** \ˈstres\ *n* **1 :** PRESSURE, STRAIN; *esp* **:** a force that tends to distort a body **2 :** a factor that induces bodily or mental tension; *also* **:** a state induced by such a stress **3 :** EMPHASIS **4 :** relative prominence of sound **5 :** ACCENT; *also* **:** any syllable carrying the accent — **stress•ful** \ˈstres-fəl\ *adj*

²**stress** *vb* **1 :** to put pressure or strain on **2 :** to put emphasis on **:** ACCENT

¹**stretch** \ˈstrech\ *vb* **1 :** to spread or reach out **:** EXTEND **2 :** to draw out in length or breadth **:** EXPAND **3 :** to make tense **:** STRAIN **4 :** EXAGGERATE **5 :** to become extended without breaking ⟨rubber ~*es* easily⟩

²**stretch** *n* **1 :** an act of extending or drawing out beyond ordinary or normal limits **2 :** a continuous extent in length, area, or time **3 :** the extent to which something may be stretched **4 :** either of the straight sides of a racecourse

³**stretch** *adj* **:** easily stretched ⟨~ pants⟩

stretch•er \ˈstre-chər\ *n* **1 :** one that stretches **2 :** a device for carrying a sick, injured, or dead person

strew \ˈstrü\ *vb* **strewed; strewed** *or* **strewn** \ˈstrün\; **strew•ing 1 :** to spread by scattering **2 :** to cover by or as if by scattering something over or on **3 :** DISSEMINATE

stria \ˈstrī-ə\ *n, pl* **stri•ae** \ˈstrī-ˌē\ **1 :** STRIATION 3 **2 :** a stripe or line (as in the skin)

stri•at•ed muscle \ˈstrī-ˌā-təd-\ *n* **:** muscle tissue made up of long thin cells with many nuclei and alternate light and dark stripes that includes esp. the muscle of the heart and muscle that moves the vertebrate skeleton and is mostly under voluntary control

stri•a•tion \strī-ˈā-shən\ *n* **1 :** the state of being marked with stripes or lines **2 :** arrangement of striations or striae **3 :** a minute groove, scratch, or channel esp. when one of a parallel series

strick•en \ˈstri-kən\ *adj* **1 :** afflicted by or as if by disease, misfortune, or sorrow **2 :** WOUNDED

strict \ˈstrikt\ *adj* **1 :** allowing no evasion or escape **:** RIGOROUS ⟨~ discipline⟩ **2 :** ACCURATE, PRECISE **syn** stringent, rigid — **strict•ly** *adv* — **strict•ness** *n*

stric•ture \ˈstrik-chər\ *n* **1 :** an abnormal narrowing of a bodily passage; *also* **:** the narrowed part **2 :** hostile criticism **:** a critical remark

¹**stride** \ˈstrīd\ *vb* **strode** \ˈstrōd\; **strid•den** \ˈstrid-ᵊn\; **strid•ing :** to walk or run with long regular steps — **strid•er** *n*

²**stride** *n* **1 :** a long step **2 :** a stage of progress **3 :** manner of striding **:** GAIT

stri•dent \ˈstrīd-ᵊnt\ *adj* **:** harsh sounding **:** GRATING, SHRILL

strife \ˈstrīf\ *n* **:** CONFLICT, FIGHT, STRUGGLE **syn** discord, contention, dissension

¹**strike** \ˈstrīk\ *vb* **struck** \ˈstrək\; **struck** *also* **strick•en** \ˈstri-kən\; **strik•ing 1 :** to take a course **:** GO ⟨*struck* off through the brush⟩ **2 :** to touch or hit sharply; *also* **:** to deliver a blow **3 :** to produce by or as if by a blow ⟨*struck* terror in the foe⟩ **4 :** to lower (as a flag or sail) **5 :** to collide with; *also* **:** to injure or destroy by collision **6 :** DELETE, CANCEL **7 :** to produce by impressing ⟨*struck* a medal⟩; *also* **:** COIN ⟨~ a new cent⟩ **8 :** to cause to sound ⟨~ a bell⟩ **9 :** to afflict suddenly **:** lay low ⟨*stricken* with a high fever⟩ **10 :** to appear to; *also* **:** to appear to as remarkable **:** IMPRESS **11 :** to reach by reckoning ⟨~ an average⟩ **12 :** to stop work in order to obtain a change in conditions of employment **13 :** to cause (a match) to ignite by rubbing **14 :** to come upon ⟨~ gold⟩ **15 :** TAKE ON, ASSUME ⟨~ a pose⟩ — **strik•er** *n*

²**strike** *n* **1 :** an act or instance of striking **2 :** a sudden discovery of rich ore or oil deposits **3 :** a pitched baseball that is swung at but not hit **4 :** the knocking down of all the bowling pins with the 1st ball **5 :** a military attack

strike•break•er \-ˌbrā-kər\ *n* **:** a person hired to replace a striking worker

strike•out \-ˌau̇t\ *n* **:** an out in baseball as a result of a batter's being charged with three strikes

strike out *vb* **1 :** to enter upon a course of action **2 :** to start out vigorously **3 :** to make an out in baseball by a strikeout

strike up *vb* **1 :** to begin or cause to begin to sing or play **2 :** BEGIN

strike zone *n* **:** the area over home plate through which a pitched baseball must pass to be called a strike

strik•ing \ˈstrī-kiŋ\ *adj* **:** attracting attention **:** very noticeable **syn** arresting, salient, conspicuous, outstanding, remarkable, prominent — **strik•ing•ly** *adv*

¹**string** \ˈstriŋ\ *n* **1 :** a line usu. composed of twisted threads **2 :** a series of things arranged as if strung on a cord **3 :** a plant fiber (as a leaf vein) **4** *pl* **:** the stringed instruments of an orchestra **syn** succession, progression, sequence, chain, train

²**string** *vb* **strung** \ˈstrəŋ\; **string•ing 1 :** to provide with strings ⟨~ a racket⟩ **2 :** to make tense **3 :** to thread on or as if on a string ⟨~ pearls⟩ **4 :** to hang, tie, or fasten by a string **5 :** to take the strings out of ⟨~ beans⟩ **6 :** to extend like a string

string bean *n* **:** a bean of one of the older varieties of kidney bean that have stringy fibers on the lines of separation of the pods; *also* **:** SNAP BEAN

stringed \ˈstriŋd\ *adj* **1 :** having strings ⟨~ instruments⟩ **2 :** produced by strings

strin•gen•cy \ˈstrin-jən-sē\ *n* **1 :** STRICTNESS, SEVERITY **2 :** SCARCITY ⟨~ of money⟩ — **strin•gent** \-jənt\ *adj*

string•er \ˈstriŋ-ər\ *n* **1 :** a long horizontal member in a framed structure or a bridge **2 :** a news correspondent paid by the amount of copy

stringy \ˈstriŋ-ē\ *adj* **string•i•er; -est 1 :** resembling string esp. in tough, fibrous, or disordered quality ⟨~ meat⟩ ⟨~ hair⟩ **2 :** lean and sinewy in build

¹**strip** \ˈstrip\ *vb* **stripped** \ˈstript\ *also* **stript; strip-**

ping 1 : to take the covering or clothing from **2 :** to take off one's clothes **3 :** to pull or tear off **4 :** to make bare or clear (as by cutting or grazing) **5 :** PLUNDER, PILLAGE **syn** divest, denude, deprive, dismantle — **strip•per** *n*

[2]**strip** *n* **1 :** a long narrow flat piece **2 :** AIRSTRIP

[1]**stripe** \ˈstrīp\ *vb* **striped** \ˈstrīpt\; **strip•ing :** to make stripes on

[2]**stripe** *n* **1 :** a line or long narrow division having a different color from the background **2 :** a strip of braid (as on a sleeve) indicating military rank or length of service **3 :** TYPE, CHARACTER — **striped** \ˈstrīpt, ˈstrī-pəd\ *adj*

striped bass *n* **:** a large marine bony fish of the Atlantic and Pacific coasts of the U.S. that is an excellent food and sport fish

strip•ling \ˈstri-pliŋ\ *n* **:** YOUTH, LAD

strip mine *n* **:** a mine that is worked from the earth's surface by the stripping of the topsoil — **strip–mine** *vb*

strip•tease \ˈstrip-ˌtēz\ *n* **:** a burlesque act in which a performer removes clothing piece by piece — **strip-teas•er** *n*

strive \ˈstrīv\ *vb* **strove** \ˈstrōv\ *also* **strived** \ˈstrīvd\; **striv•en** \ˈstri-vən\ *or* **strived; striv•ing 1 :** to make effort **:** labor hard **2 :** to struggle in opposition **:** CONTEND **syn** endeavor, attempt, try, assay

strobe \ˈstrōb\ *n* **1 :** STROBOSCOPE **2 :** a device for high-speed intermittent illumination (as in photography)

stro•bo•scope \ˈstrō-bə-ˌskōp\ *n* **:** an instrument for studying rapid motion by means of a rapidly flashing light

strode *past of* STRIDE

[1]**stroke** \ˈstrōk\ *vb* **stroked; strok•ing 1 :** to rub gently **2 :** to flatter in a manner designed to persuade

[2]**stroke** *n* **1 :** the act of striking **:** BLOW, KNOCK **2 :** a sudden action or process producing an impact ⟨~ of lightning⟩; *also* **:** an unexpected result **3 :** sudden weakening or loss of consciousness or the power to move or feel caused by rupture or obstruction (as by a clot) of an artery of the brain **4 :** one of a series of movements against air or water to get through or over it ⟨the ~ of a bird's wing⟩ **5 :** a rower who sets the pace for a crew **6 :** a vigorous effort **7 :** the sound of striking (as of a clock) **8 :** a single movement with or as if with a tool or implement (as a pen)

stroll \ˈstrōl\ *vb* **:** to walk in a leisurely or idle manner — **stroll** *n* — **stroll•er** *n*

strong \ˈstrȯŋ\ *adj* **stron•ger** \ˈstrȯŋ-gər\; **stron•gest** \ˈstrȯŋ-gəst\ **1 :** POWERFUL, VIGOROUS **2 :** HEALTHY, ROBUST **3 :** of a specified number ⟨an army 10 thousand ~⟩ **4 :** not mild or weak **5 :** VIOLENT ⟨~ wind⟩ **6 :** ZEALOUS **7 :** not easily broken **8 :** FIRM, SOLID **syn** stout, sturdy, stalwart, tough — **strong•ly** *adv*

strong–arm \ˈstrȯŋ-ˈärm\ *adj* **:** having or using undue force ⟨~ methods⟩

strong force *n* **:** the physical force responsible for binding together nucleons in the atomic nucleus

strong•hold \-ˌhōld\ *n* **:** a fortified place **:** FORTRESS

strong•man \-ˌman\ *n* **:** one who leads or controls by force of will and character or by military strength

stron•tium \ˈsträn-chē-əm, ˈsträn-tē-əm\ *n* **:** a soft malleable metallic chemical element — see ELEMENT table

[1]**strop** \ˈsträp\ *n* **:** STRAP; *esp* **:** one for sharpening a razor

[2]**strop** *vb* **stropped; strop•ping :** to sharpen a razor on a strop

stro•phe \ˈstrō-fē\ *n* [Gk *strophē*, lit., act of turning] **:** a division of a poem — **stroph•ic** \ˈsträ-fik\ *adj*

strove *past of* STRIVE

struck *past and past part of* STRIKE

[1]**struc•ture** \ˈstrək-chər\ *n* [ME, fr. L *structura*, fr. *structus*, pp. of *struere* to heap up, build] **1 :** the action of building **:** CONSTRUCTION **2 :** something built (as a house or a dam); *also* **:** something made up of interdependent parts in a definite pattern of organization **3 :** arrangement or relationship of elements (as particles, parts, or organs) in a substance, body, or system — **struc•tur•al** *adj*

[2]**structure** *vb* **struc•tured; struc•tur•ing :** to make into a structure

stru•del \ˈstrüd-ᵊl, ˈshtrüd-\ *n* [G, lit., whirlpool] **:** a pastry made of a thin sheet of dough rolled up with filling and baked ⟨apple ~⟩

[1]**strug•gle** \ˈstrə-gəl\ *vb* **strug•gled; strug•gling 1 :** to make strenuous efforts against opposition **:** STRIVE **2 :** to proceed with difficulty or with great effort **syn** endeavor, attempt, try, assay

[2]**struggle** *n* **1 :** CONTEST, STRIFE **2 :** a violent effort or exertion

strum \ˈstrəm\ *vb* **strummed; strum•ming :** to play on a stringed instrument by brushing the strings with the fingers ⟨~ a guitar⟩

strum•pet \ˈstrəm-pət\ *n* **:** PROSTITUTE

strung \ˈstrəŋ\ *past and past part of* STRING

[1]**strut** \ˈstrət\ *vb* **strut•ted; strut•ting :** to walk with an affectedly proud gait

[2]**strut** *n* **1 :** a bar or rod for resisting lengthwise pressure **2 :** a haughty or pompous gait

strych•nine \ˈstrik-ˌnīn, -nən, -ˌnēn\ *n* **:** a bitter poisonous plant alkaloid used as a poison (as for rats) and medicinally as a stimulant to the central nervous system

[1]**stub** \ˈstəb\ *n* **1 :** STUMP 2 **2 :** a short blunt end **3 :** a small part of each leaf (as of a checkbook) kept as a memorandum of the items on the detached part

[2]**stub** *vb* **stubbed; stub•bing :** to strike (as one's toe) against something

stub•ble \ˈstə-bəl\ *n* **1 :** the cut stem ends of herbs and esp. grasses left in the soil after harvest **2 :** a rough surface or growth resembling stubble — **stub•bly** \-b(ə-)lē\ *adj*

stub•born \ˈstə-bərn\ *adj* **1 :** FIRM, DETERMINED **2 :** done or continued in a willful, unreasonable, or persistent manner **3 :** not easily controlled or remedied ⟨a ~ cold⟩ — **stub•born•ly** *adv* — **stub•born•ness** *n*

stub•by \ˈstə-bē\ *adj* **:** short, blunt, and thick like a stub

stuc•co \ˈstə-kō\ *n, pl* **stuccos** *or* **stuccoes** [It] **:** plaster for coating exterior walls — **stuc•coed** \ˈstə-kōd\ *adj*

stuck *past and past part of* STICK

stuck–up \ˈstək-ˈəp\ *adj* **:** CONCEITED

[1]**stud** \ˈstəd\ *n* **:** a male animal and esp. a horse (**stud-horse** \-ˌhȯrs\) kept for breeding

[2]**stud** *n* **1 :** one of the smaller uprights in a building to which the wall materials are fastened **2 :** a removable device like a button used as a fastener or ornament ⟨shirt ~*s*⟩ **3 :** a projecting nail, pin, or rod

[3]**stud** *vb* **stud•ded; stud•ding 1 :** to supply with or adorn with studs **2 :** DOT

[4]**stud** *abbr* student

stud•book \ˈstəd-ˌbu̇k\ *n* **:** an official record of the pedigree of purebred animals (as horses or dogs)

stud•ding \ˈstə-diŋ\ *n* **:** the studs in a building or wall

stu•dent \ˈstüd-ᵊnt, ˈstyüd-\ *n* **:** SCHOLAR, PUPIL; *esp* **:** one who attends a school

stud•ied \ˈstə-dēd\ *adj* **:** INTENTIONAL ⟨a ~ insult⟩ **syn** deliberate, considered, premeditated, designed

stu•dio \ˈstü-dē-ˌō, ˈstyü-\ *n, pl* **-dios 1 :** a place where an artist works; *also* **:** a place for the study of an art **2 :** a place where motion pictures are made **3 :** a place equipped for the transmission of radio or television programs

stu•di•ous \ˈstü-dē-əs, ˈstyü-\ *adj* **:** devoted to study — **stu•di•ous•ly** *adv*

[1]**study** \ˈstə-dē\ *n, pl* **stud•ies 1 :** the use of the mind to gain knowledge **2 :** the act or process of learning about something **3 :** careful examination **4 :** INTENT, PURPOSE **5 :** a branch of learning **6 :** a room esp. for reading and writing

[2]**study** *vb* **stud•ied; study•ing 1 :** to engage in study or

the study of **2** : to consider attentively or in detail **syn** consider, contemplate, weigh

[1]stuff \ˈstəf\ *n* **1** : personal property **2** : raw material **3** : a finished textile fabric; *esp* : a worsted fabric **4** : writing, talk, or ideas of little or transitory worth **5** : an unspecified material substance or aggregate of matter **6** : fundamental material **7** : special knowledge or capability

[2]stuff *vb* **1** : to fill by packing things in : CRAM **2** : to eat greedily : GORGE **3** : to prepare (as meat) by filling with a stuffing **4** : to fill (as a cushion) with a soft material **5** : to stop up : PLUG

stuffed shirt \ˈstəft-\ *n* : a smug, conceited, and usu. pompous and inflexibly conservative person

stuff•ing *n* : material used to fill tightly; *esp* : a mixture of bread crumbs and spices used to stuff meat and poultry

stuffy \ˈstə-fē\ *adj* **stuff•i•er; -est 1** : STODGY **2** : lacking fresh air : CLOSE; *also* : blocked up ⟨a ~ nose⟩

stul•ti•fy \ˈstəl-tə-ˌfī\ *vb* **-fied; -fy•ing 1** : to cause to appear foolish or stupid **2** : to impair, invalidate, or make ineffective **3** : to have a dulling effect on — **stul•ti•fi•ca•tion** \ˌstəl-tə-fə-ˈkā-shən\ *n*

stum•ble \ˈstəm-bəl\ *vb* **stum•bled; stum•bling 1** : to blunder morally **2** : to trip in walking or running **3** : to walk unsteadily; *also* : to speak or act in a blundering or clumsy manner **4** : to happen by chance — **stumble** *n*

stumbling block *n* : an obstacle to belief, understanding, or progress

[1]stump \ˈstəmp\ *n* **1** : the base of a bodily part (as a leg or tooth) left after the rest is removed **2** : the part of a plant and esp. a tree remaining with the root after the trunk is cut off **3** : a place or occasion for political public speaking — **stumpy** *adj*

[2]stump *vb* **1** : BAFFLE, PERPLEX **2** : to clear (land) of stumps **3** : to tour (a region) making political speeches **4** : to walk clumsily and heavily

stun \ˈstən\ *vb* **stunned; stun•ning 1** : to make senseless or dizzy by or as if by a blow **2** : BEWILDER, STUPEFY

stung *past and past part of* STING

stunk *past and past part of* STINK

stun•ning *adj* **1** : causing astonishment or disbelief **2** : strikingly beautiful — **stun•ning•ly** *adv*

[1]stunt \ˈstənt\ *vb* : to hinder the normal growth or progress of

[2]stunt *n* : an unusual or spectacular feat

stu•pe•fy \ˈstü-pə-ˌfī, ˈstyü-\ *vb* **-fied; -fy•ing 1** : to make stupid, groggy, or insensible **2** : ASTONISH — **stu•pe•fac•tion** \ˌstü-pə-ˈfak-shən, ˌstyü-\ *n*

stu•pen•dous \stu̇-ˈpen-dəs, styu̇-\ *adj* : causing astonishment esp. because of great size or height **syn** tremendous, prodigious, monumental, monstrous — **stu•pen•dous•ly** *adv*

stu•pid \ˈstü-pəd, ˈstyü-\ *adj* [MF *stupide*, fr. L *stupidus*, fr. *stupēre* to be numb, be astonished] **1** : very dull in mind **2** : showing or resulting from dullness of mind — **stu•pid•i•ty** \stu̇-ˈpi-də-tē, styu̇-\ *n* — **stu•pid•ly** *adv*

stu•por \ˈstü-pər, ˈstyü-\ *n* **1** : a condition of greatly dulled or completely suspended sense or feeling **2** : a state of extreme apathy or torpor often following stress or shock — **stu•por•ous** *adj*

stur•dy \ˈstər-dē\ *adj* **stur•di•er; -est** [ME, brave, stubborn, fr. OF *estourdi* stunned, fr. pp. of *estourdir* to stun] **1** : RESOLUTE, UNYIELDING **2** : STRONG, ROBUST **syn** stout, stalwart, tough, tenacious — **stur•di•ly** \-də-lē\ *adv* — **stur•di•ness** \-dē-nəs\ *n*

stur•geon \ˈstər-jən\ *n* : any of a family of large bony fishes including some whose roe is made into caviar

stut•ter \ˈstə-tər\ *vb* : to speak with involuntary disruption or blocking of sounds — **stutter** *n*

[1]sty \ˈstī\ *n, pl* **sties** : a pen or housing for swine

[2]sty *or* **stye** *n, pl* **sties** *or* **styes** : an inflamed swelling of a skin gland on the edge of an eyelid

sturgeon

[1]style \ˈstīl\ *n* **1** : mode of address : TITLE **2** : a way of speaking or writing; *esp* : one characteristic of an individual, period, school, or nation ⟨ornate ~⟩ **3** : manner or method of acting, making, or performing; *also* : a distinctive or characteristic manner **4** : a slender pointed instrument or process; *esp* : STYLUS **5** : a fashionable manner or mode **6** : overall excellence, skill, or grace in performance, manner, or appearance **7** : the custom followed in spelling, capitalization, punctuation, and typography — **sty•lis•tic** \stī-ˈlis-tik\ *adj*

[2]style *vb* **styled; styl•ing 1** : NAME, DESIGNATE **2** : to make or design in accord with a prevailing mode

styl•ing \ˈstī-liŋ\ *n* : the way in which something is styled

styl•ise *Brit var of* STYLIZE

styl•ish \ˈstī-lish\ *adj* : conforming to current fashion **syn** modish, smart, chic — **styl•ish•ly** *adv* — **styl•ish•ness** *n*

styl•ist \ˈstī-list\ *n* **1** : one (as a writer) noted for a distinctive style **2** : a developer or designer of styles

styl•ize \ˈstī-ˌlīz, ˈstī-ə-\ *vb* **styl•ized; styl•iz•ing** : to conform to a style; *esp* : to represent or design according to a pattern or style rather than according to nature or tradition

sty•lus \ˈstī-ləs\ *n, pl* **sty•li** \ˈstī-ˌlī\ *also* **sty•lus•es** \ˈstī-lə-səz\ [L *stylus, stilus* spike, stylus] **1** : a pointed implement used by the ancients for writing on wax **2** : a phonograph needle

sty•mie \ˈstī-mē\ *vb* **sty•mied; sty•mie•ing** : BLOCK, FRUSTRATE

styp•tic \ˈstip-tik\ *adj* : tending to check bleeding — **styptic** *n*

suave \ˈswäv\ *adj* [MF, pleasant, sweet, fr. L *suavis*] : persuasively pleasing : smoothly agreeable **syn** urbane, smooth, bland — **suave•ly** *adv* — **sua•vi•ty** \ˈswä-və-tē\ *n*

[1]sub \ˈsəb\ *n* : SUBSTITUTE — **sub** *vb*

[2]sub *n* : SUBMARINE

[3]sub *abbr* **1** subtract **2** suburb

sub- \ˈsəb\ *prefix* **1** : under : beneath **2** : subordinate : secondary **3** : subordinate portion of : subdivision of **4** : with repetition of a process described in a simple verb so as to form, stress, or deal with subordinate parts or relations **5** : somewhat **6** : falling nearly in the category of : bordering on

subacute
subagency
subagent
subaqueous
subarctic
subarea
subatmospheric
subaverage
subbasement
subcategory
subcellular
subchapter
subclass
subclassify
subcommittee
subcontract
subcontractor
subculture
subcutaneous
subdiscipline
subentry
subfamily
subfield
subfreezing
subgenre
subgenus
subgroup
subhead
subheading
subhuman
subkingdom
sublethal
subliterate
subminimal
subminimum
suboptimal
suborder
subparagraph
subparallel
subphylum
subplot
subpopulation
subproblem
subprofessional
subprogram
subregion

subroutine
subsection
subsense
subsoil
subspecies
substage
substation
subsystem
subteen
subthreshold
subtopic
subtotal
subtreasury
subtype
subunit
subvariety
subvisible
subzero

sub·al·pine \ˌsəb-ˈal-ˌpīn\ *adj* **1 :** of or relating to the region about the foot and lower slopes of the Alps **2 :** of, relating to, or inhabiting high upland slopes esp. just below the timberline

sub·al·tern \sə-ˈbȯl-tərn\ *n* **:** SUBORDINATE; *esp* **:** a junior officer (as in the British army)

sub·as·sem·bly \ˌsəb-ə-ˈsem-blē\ *n* **:** an assembled unit to be incorporated with other units in a finished product

sub·atom·ic \ˌsəb-ə-ˈtä-mik\ *adj* **:** of or relating to the inside of the atom or to particles smaller than atoms

sub·clin·i·cal \ˌsəb-ˈkli-ni-kəl\ *adj* **:** not detectable by the usual clinical tests ⟨a ~ infection⟩

sub·com·pact \ˈsəb-ˈkäm-ˌpakt\ *n* **:** an automobile smaller than a compact

[1]**sub·con·scious** \ˌsəb-ˈkän-chəs, ˈsəb-\ *adj* **:** existing in the mind without entering conscious awareness — **sub·con·scious·ly** *adv* — **sub·con·scious·ness** *n*

[2]**subconscious** *n* **:** mental activities just below the threshold of consciousness

sub·con·ti·nent \ˌsəb-ˈkänt-ᵊn-ənt\ *n* **:** a major subdivision of a continent — **sub·con·ti·nen·tal** \ˌsəb-ˌkänt-ᵊn-ˈent-ᵊl\ *adj*

sub·di·vide \ˌsəb-də-ˈvīd, ˈsəb-də-ˌvīd\ *vb* **:** to divide the parts of into more parts; *esp* **:** to divide (a tract of land) into building lots — **sub·di·vi·sion** \-ˈvi-zhən, -ˌvi-\ *n*

sub·duc·tion \səb-ˈdək-shən\ *n* **:** the descent of the edge of one crustal plate beneath the edge of an adjacent plate

sub·due \səb-ˈdü, -ˈdyü\ *vb* **sub·dued; sub·du·ing 1 :** to bring into subjection **:** VANQUISH **2 :** to bring under control **:** CURB **3 :** to reduce the intensity of

subj *abbr* **1** subject **2** subjunctive

[1]**sub·ject** \ˈsəb-jikt\ *n* [ME, fr. MF, fr. L *subjectus* one under authority & *subjectum* subject of a proposition, fr. *subicere* to subject, lit., to throw under, fr. *sub-* under + *jacere* to throw] **1 :** a person under the authority of another **2 :** a person subject to a sovereign **3 :** an individual that is studied or experimented on **4 :** the person or thing discussed or treated **:** TOPIC, THEME **5 :** a word or word group denoting that of which something is predicated

[2]**subject** *adj* **1 :** being under the power or rule of another **2 :** LIABLE, EXPOSED ⟨~ to floods⟩ **3 :** dependent on some act or condition ⟨appointment ~ to senate approval⟩ **syn** subordinate, secondary, tributary, collateral, dependent

[3]**sub·ject** \səb-ˈjekt\ *vb* **1 :** to bring under control **:** CONQUER **2 :** to make liable **3 :** to cause to undergo or endure — **sub·jec·tion** \-ˈjek-shən\ *n*

sub·jec·tive \(ˌ)səb-ˈjek-tiv\ *adj* **1 :** of, relating to, or constituting a subject **2 :** of, relating to, or arising within one's self or mind in contrast to what is outside **:** PERSONAL — **sub·jec·tive·ly** *adv* — **sub·jec·tiv·i·ty** \-ˌjek-ˈti-və-tē\ *n*

subject matter *n* **:** matter presented for consideration, discussion, or study

sub·join \(ˌ)səb-ˈjȯin\ *vb* **:** APPEND

sub ju·di·ce \(ˌ)su̇b-ˈyü-di-ˌkā, ˈsəb-ˈjü-də-(ˌ)sē\ *adv* [L] **:** before a judge or court **:** not yet legally decided

sub·ju·gate \ˈsəb-ji-ˌgāt\ *vb* **-gat·ed; -gat·ing :** CONQUER, SUBDUE; *also* **:** ENSLAVE **syn** reduce, overcome, overthrow, vanquish, defeat, beat — **sub·ju·ga·tion** \ˌsəb-ji-ˈgā-shən\ *n*

sub·junc·tive \səb-ˈjəŋk-tiv\ *adj* **:** of, relating to, or constituting a verb form that represents an act or state as contingent or possible or viewed emotionally (as with desire) ⟨the ~ mood⟩ — **subjunctive** *n*

sub·lease \ˈsəb-ˈlēs, -ˌlēs\ *n* **:** a lease by a lessee of part or all of leased premises to another person with the original lessee retaining some right under the original lease — **sublease** *vb*

[1]**sub·let** \ˈsəb-ˈlet\ *vb* **-let; -let·ting :** to let all or a part of (a leased property) to another; *also* **:** to rent (a property) from a lessee

[2]**sublet** \-ˌlet\ *n* **:** property and esp. housing obtained by or available through a sublease

sub·li·mate \ˈsə-blə-ˌmāt\ *vb* **-mat·ed; -mat·ing 1 :** SUBLIME **2 :** to direct the expression of (as a desire or impulse) from a primitive to a more socially and culturally acceptable form — **sub·li·ma·tion** \ˌsə-blə-ˈmā-shən\ *n*

[1]**sub·lime** \sə-ˈblīm\ *vb* **sub·limed; sub·lim·ing :** to pass or cause to pass directly from the solid to the vapor state

[2]**sublime** *adj* **1 :** EXALTED, NOBLE **2 :** having awe-inspiring beauty or grandeur **syn** glorious, splendid, superb, resplendent, gorgeous — **sub·lime·ly** *adv* — **sub·lim·i·ty** \-ˈbli-mə-tē\ *n*

sub·lim·i·nal \(ˌ)səb-ˈli-mən-ᵊl, ˈsəb-\ *adj* **1 :** inadequate to produce a sensation or mental awareness ⟨~ stimuli⟩ **2 :** existing or functioning below the threshold of consciousness ⟨the ~ mind⟩ ⟨~ advertising⟩

sub·ma·chine gun \ˌsəb-mə-ˈshēn-ˌgən\ *n* **:** an automatic firearm fired from the shoulder or hip

[1]**sub·ma·rine** \ˈsəb-mə-ˌrēn, ˌsəb-mə-ˈrēn\ *adj* **:** UNDERWATER; *esp* **:** UNDERSEA

[2]**submarine** *n* **1 :** a naval vessel designed to operate underwater **2 :** a large sandwich made from a long split roll with any of a variety of fillings

sub·merge \səb-ˈmərj\ *vb* **sub·merged; sub·merg·ing 1 :** to put or plunge under the surface of water **2 :** INUNDATE — **sub·mer·gence** \-ˈmər-jəns\ *n*

sub·merse \səb-ˈmərs\ *vb* **sub·mersed; sub·mers·ing :** SUBMERGE — **sub·mer·sion** \-ˈmər-zhən\ *n*

[1]**sub·mers·ible** \səb-ˈmər-sə-bəl\ *adj* **:** capable of being submerged

[2]**submersible** *n* **:** something that is submersible; *esp* **:** a small underwater craft used for deep-sea research

sub·mi·cro·sco·pic \ˌsəb-ˌmī-krə-ˈskä-pik\ *adj* **:** too small to be seen in an ordinary light microscope

sub·min·ia·ture \ˌsəb-ˈmi-nē-ə-ˌchu̇r, ˈsəb-, -ˈmi-ni-ˌchu̇r, -chər\ *adj* **:** very small

sub·mit \səb-ˈmit\ *vb* **sub·mit·ted; sub·mit·ting 1 :** to commit to the discretion or decision of another or of others **2 :** YIELD, SURRENDER **3 :** to put forward as an opinion — **sub·mis·sion** \-ˈmi-shən\ *n* — **sub·mis·sive** \-ˈmi-siv\ *adj*

sub·nor·mal \ˌsəb-ˈnȯr-məl\ *adj* **:** falling below what is normal; *also* **:** having less of something and esp. intelligence than is normal — **sub·nor·mal·i·ty** \ˌsəb-nȯr-ˈma-lə-tē\ *n*

sub·or·bit·al \ˌsəb-ˈȯr-bət-ᵊl, ˈsəb-\ *adj* **:** being or involving less than one orbit

[1]**sub·or·di·nate** \sə-ˈbȯrd-ᵊn-ət\ *adj* **1 :** of lower class or rank **2 :** INFERIOR **3 :** submissive to authority **4 :** subordinated to other elements in a sentence **:** DEPENDENT ⟨~ clause⟩ **syn** secondary, subject, tributary, collateral

[2]**subordinate** *n* **:** one that is subordinate

[3]**sub·or·di·nate** \sə-ˈbȯrd-ᵊn-ˌāt\ *vb* **-nat·ed; -nat·ing 1 :** to place in a lower rank or class **2 :** SUBDUE — **sub·or·di·na·tion** \-ˌbȯrd-ᵊn-ˈā-shən\ *n*

sub·orn \sə-ˈbȯrn\ *vb* **1 :** to induce secretly to do an unlawful thing **2 :** to induce to commit perjury — **sub·or·na·tion** \ˌsə-ˌbȯr-ˈnā-shən\ *n*

[1]**sub·poe·na** \sə-ˈpē-nə\ *n* [ME *suppena*, fr. L *sub poena* under penalty] **:** a writ commanding the person named in it to attend court under penalty for failure to do so

[2]**subpoena** *vb* **-naed; -na·ing :** to summon with a subpoena

sub–Sa·ha·ran \ˌsəb-sə-ˈhar-ən\ *adj* : of, relating to, or being the part of Africa south of the Sahara

sub·scribe \səb-ˈskrīb\ *vb* **sub·scribed; sub·scrib·ing 1** : to sign one's name to a document **2** : to give consent by or as if by signing one's name **3** : to promise to contribute by signing one's name with the amount promised **4** : to place an order by signing **5** : to receive a periodical or service regularly on order **6** : FAVOR, APPROVE **syn** agree, acquiesce, assent, accede — **sub·scrib·er** *n*

sub·script \ˈsəb-ˌskript\ *n* : a symbol (as a letter or number) immediately below or below and to the right or left of another written character — **subscript** *adj*

sub·scrip·tion \səb-ˈskrip-shən\ *n* **1** : the act of subscribing : SIGNATURE **2** : a purchase by signed order

sub·se·quent \ˈsəb-si-kwənt, -sə-ˌkwent\ *adj* : following after : SUCCEEDING — **sub·se·quent·ly** *adv*

sub·ser·vi·ence \səb-ˈsər-vē-əns\ *n* **1** : a subordinate place or condition **2** : SERVILITY — **sub·ser·vi·en·cy** \-ən-sē\ *n* — **sub·ser·vi·ent** \-ənt\ *adj*

sub·set \ˈsəb-ˌset\ *n* : a set each of whose elements is an element of an inclusive set

sub·side \səb-ˈsīd\ *vb* **sub·sid·ed; sub·sid·ing** [L *subsidere*, fr. *sub-* under + *sidere* to sit down, sink] **1** : to settle to the bottom of a liquid **2** : to tend downward : DESCEND **3** : SINK, SUBMERGE **4** : to become quiet and tranquil **syn** abate, wane, moderate, slacken — **subsid·ence** \səb-ˈsīd-ᵊns, ˈsəb-sə-dəns\ *n*

¹sub·sid·iary \səb-ˈsi-dē-ˌer-ē\ *adj* **1** : furnishing aid or support **2** : of secondary importance **3** : of or relating to a subsidy **syn** auxiliary, contributory, subservient, accessory

²subsidiary *n, pl* **-iar·ies** : one that is subsidiary; *esp* : a company controlled by another

sub·si·dise *Brit var of* SUBSIDIZE

sub·si·dize \ˈsəb-sə-ˌdīz\ *vb* **-dized; -diz·ing** : to aid or furnish with a subsidy

sub·si·dy \ˈsəb-sə-dē\ *n, pl* **-dies** [ME, fr. L *subsidium* reserve troops, support, assistance, fr. *sub-* near + *sedēre* to sit] : a gift of public money to a private person or company or to another government

sub·sist \səb-ˈsist\ *vb* **1** : EXIST, PERSIST **2** : to have the means (as food and clothing) of maintaining life; *esp* : to nourish oneself

sub·sis·tence \səb-ˈsis-təns\ *n* **1** : EXISTENCE **2** : means of subsisting : the minimum (as of food and clothing) necessary to support life

sub·son·ic \ˌsəb-ˈsä-nik, ˈsəb-\ *adj* : being or relating to a speed less than that of sound; *also* : moving at such a speed

sub·species \ˈsəb-ˌspē-shēz, -sēz\ *n* : a subdivision of a species; *esp* : a category in biological classification ranking just below a species that designates a geographic population genetically distinct from other such populations and potentially able to breed with them where its range overlaps theirs

sub·stance \ˈsəb-stəns\ *n* **1** : essential nature : ESSENCE ⟨divine ~⟩; *also* : the fundamental or essential part or quality ⟨the ~ of the speech⟩ **2** : physical material from which something is made or which has discrete existence; *also* : matter of particular or definite chemical constitution **3** : material possessions : PROPERTY, WEALTH

substance abuse *n* : excessive use of a drug (as alcohol or cocaine) : use of a drug without medical justification

sub·stan·dard \ˌsəb-ˈstan-dərd\ *adj* : falling short of a standard or norm

sub·stan·tial \səb-ˈstan-chəl\ *adj* **1** : existing as or in substance : MATERIAL; *also* : not illusory : REAL **2** : IMPORTANT, ESSENTIAL **3** : NOURISHING, SATISFYING ⟨~ meal⟩ **4** : having means : WELL-TO-DO **5** : CONSIDERABLE ⟨~ profit⟩ **6** : STRONG, FIRM — **sub·stan·tial·ly** *adv*

sub·stan·ti·ate \səb-ˈstan-chē-ˌāt\ *vb* **-at·ed; -at·ing 1** : to give substance or body to **2** : VERIFY, PROVE — **sub·stan·ti·a·tion** \-ˌstan-chē-ˈā-shən\ *n*

sub·stan·tive \ˈsəb-stən-tiv\ *n* : NOUN; *also* : a word or phrase used as a noun

¹sub·sti·tute \ˈsəb-stə-ˌtüt, -ˌtyüt\ *n* : a person or thing replacing another — **substitute** *adj*

²substitute *vb* **-tut·ed; -tut·ing 1** : to put or use in the place of another **2** : to serve as a substitute — **sub·sti·tu·tion** \ˌsəb-stə-ˈtü-shən, -ˈtyü-\ *n*

sub·strate \ˈsəb-ˌstrāt\ *n* **1** : the base on which a plant or animal lives **2** : a substance acted upon (as by an enzyme)

sub·stra·tum \ˈsəb-ˌstrā-təm, -ˌstra-\ *n, pl* **-stra·ta** \-tə\ : the layer or structure (as subsoil) lying underneath

sub·struc·ture \ˈsəb-ˌstrək-chər\ *n* : FOUNDATION, GROUNDWORK

sub·sur·face \ˈsəb-ˌsər-fəs\ *n* : earth material near the surface of the ground — **subsurface** *adj*

sub·ter·fuge \ˈsəb-tər-ˌfyüj\ *n* : a trick or device used in order to conceal, escape, or evade **syn** fraud, deception, trickery

sub·ter·ra·nean \ˌsəb-tə-ˈrā-nē-ən\ *adj* **1** : lying or being underground **2** : SECRET, HIDDEN

sub·tile \ˈsət-ᵊl\ *adj* **sub·til·er** \ˈsət-lər, -ᵊl-ər\; **sub·til·est** \ˈsət-ləst, -ᵊl-əst\ : SUBTLE

sub·ti·tle \ˈsəb-ˌtīt-ᵊl\ *n* **1** : a secondary or explanatory title (as of a book) **2** : printed matter projected on a motion-picture screen during or between the scenes

sub·tle \ˈsət-ᵊl\ *adj* **sub·tler** \ˈsət-ᵊl-ər\; **sub·tlest** \ˈsət-ᵊl-əst\ **1** : hardly noticeable ⟨~ differences⟩ **2** : SHREWD, PERCEPTIVE **3** : CLEVER, SLY — **sub·tle·ty** \-tē\ *n* — **sub·tly** \ˈsət-ᵊl-ē\ *adv*

sub·tract \səb-ˈtrakt\ *vb* : to take away (as one part or number) from another; *also* : to perform the operation of deducting one number from another — **sub·trac·tion** \-ˈtrak-shən\ *n*

sub·tra·hend \ˈsəb-trə-ˌhend\ *n* : a number that is to be subtracted from another

sub·trop·i·cal \ˌsəb-ˈträ-pi-kəl, ˈsəb-\ *also* **sub·trop·ic** \-pik\ *adj* : of, relating to, or being regions bordering on the tropical zone — **sub·trop·ics** \-piks\ *n pl*

sub·urb \ˈsə-ˌbərb\ *n* **1** : an outlying part of a city; *also* : a small community adjacent to a city **2** *pl* : a residential area adjacent to a city — **sub·ur·ban** \sə-ˈbər-bən\ *adj or n* — **sub·ur·ban·ite** \sə-ˈbər-bə-ˌnīt\ *n*

sub·ur·bia \sə-ˈbər-bē-ə\ *n* **1** : SUBURBS **2** : suburban people or customs

sub·ven·tion \səb-ˈven-chən\ *n* : SUBSIDY, ENDOWMENT

sub·vert \səb-ˈvərt\ *vb* **1** : OVERTHROW, RUIN **2** : CORRUPT — **sub·ver·sion** \-ˈvər-zhən\ *n* — **sub·ver·sive** \-ˈvər-siv\ *adj*

sub·way \ˈsəb-ˌwā\ *n* : an underground way; *esp* : an underground electric railway

suc·ceed \sək-ˈsēd\ *vb* **1** : to follow next in order or next after another; *esp* : to inherit sovereignty, rank, title, or property **2** : to attain a desired object or end : be successful

suc·cess \sək-ˈses\ *n* **1** : favorable or desired outcome **2** : the gaining of wealth and fame **3** : one that succeeds — **suc·cess·ful** \-fəl\ *adj* — **suc·cess·ful·ly** *adv*

suc·ces·sion \sək-ˈse-shən\ *n* **1** : the order, act, or right of succeeding to a property, title, or throne **2** : the act or process of following in order **3** : a series of persons or things that follow one after another **syn** progression, sequence, chain, train, string

suc·ces·sive \sək-ˈse-siv\ *adj* : following in order : CONSECUTIVE — **suc·ces·sive·ly** *adv*

suc·ces·sor \sək-ˈse-sər\ *n* : one that succeeds (as to a throne, title, estate, or office)

suc·cinct \(ˌ)sək-ˈsiŋkt, sə-ˈsiŋkt\ *adj* : BRIEF, CONCISE **syn** terse, laconic, summary, curt, short — **suc·cinct·ly** *adv* — **suc·cinct·ness** *n*

suc·cor \ˈsə-kər\ *n* [ME *succur*, fr. earlier *sucurs*, taken as pl., fr. OF *sucors*, fr. ML *succursus*, fr. L *suc-*

currere to run up, run to help] : AID, HELP, RELIEF — **succor** *vb*
suc·co·tash \ˈsə-kə-ˌtash\ *n* [Narraganset (American Indian language of Rhode Island) *msíckquatash* boiled corn kernels] : beans and corn kernels cooked together
suc·cour *chiefly Brit var of* SUCCOR
[1]**suc·cu·lent** \ˈsə-kyə-lənt\ *adj* : full of juice : JUICY; *also* : having fleshy tissues that conserve moisture ⟨~ plants⟩ — **suc·cu·lence** \-ləns\ *n*
[2]**succulent** *n* : a succulent plant (as a cactus)
suc·cumb \sə-ˈkəm\ *vb* **1** : to yield to superior strength or force or overpowering appeal or desire **2** : DIE **syn** submit, capitulate, relent, defer
[1]**such** \ˈsəch, ˈsich\ *adj* **1** : of this or that kind **2** : having a quality just specified or to be specified
[2]**such** *pron* **1** : such a one or ones ⟨he's a star, and acted as ~⟩ **2** : that or those similar or related thereto ⟨boards and nails and ~⟩
[3]**such** *adv* : to that degree : so
such·like \ˈsəch-ˌlīk\ *adj* : SIMILAR
[1]**suck** \ˈsək\ *vb* **1** : to draw in liquid and esp. mother's milk with the mouth **2** : to draw liquid from by action of the mouth ⟨~ an orange⟩ **3** : to take in or up or remove by or as if by suction
[2]**suck** *n* **1** : a sucking movement or force **2** : the act of sucking
suck·er \ˈsə-kər\ *n* **1** : one that sucks **2** : a part of an animal's body used for sucking or for clinging **3** : a fish with thick soft lips for sucking in food **4** : a shoot from the roots or lower part of a plant **5** : a person easily deceived **6** — used as a generalized term of reference
suck·le \ˈsə-kəl\ *vb* **suck·led; suck·ling** : to give or draw milk from the breast or udder; *also* : NURTURE
suck·ling \ˈsə-kliŋ\ *n* : a young unweaned mammal
su·cre \ˈsü-(ˌ)krā\ *n* — see MONEY table
su·crose \ˈsü-ˌkrōs, -ˌkrōz\ *n* : a sweet sugar obtained commercially esp. from sugarcane or sugar beets
suc·tion \ˈsək-shən\ *n* **1** : the act of sucking **2** : the act or process of drawing something (as liquid or dust) into a space (as in a vacuum cleaner or a pump) by partially exhausting the air in the space — **suc·tion·al** \-shə-nəl\ *adj*
suction cup *n* : a cup-shaped device in which a partial vacuum is produced when applied to a surface
Su·da·nese \ˌsüd-ᵊn-ˈēz, -ˈēs\ *n* : a native or inhabitant of Sudan — **Sudanese** *adj*
sud·den \ˈsəd-ᵊn\ *adj* [ME *sodain,* fr. MF, fr. L *subitaneus,* fr. *subitus* sudden, fr. pp. of *subire* to come up] **1** : happening or coming unexpectedly ⟨~ shower⟩; *also* : changing angle or character all at once ⟨~ turn⟩ ⟨~ descent⟩ **2** : HASTY, RASH ⟨~ decision⟩ **3** : made or brought about in a short time : PROMPT ⟨~ cure⟩ **syn** precipitate, headlong, impetuous — **sud·den·ly** *adv* — **sud·den·ness** *n*
sudden infant death syndrome *n* : death due to unknown causes of an apparently healthy infant usu. before one year of age and esp. during sleep
suds \ˈsədz\ *n pl* : soapy water esp. when frothy — **sudsy** \ˈsəd-zē\ *adj*
sue \ˈsü\ *vb* **sued; su·ing 1** : PETITION, SOLICIT **2** : to seek justice or right by bringing legal action
suede *or* **suède** \ˈswād\ *n* [F *gants de Suède* Swedish gloves] **1** : leather with a napped surface **2** : a fabric with a suedelike nap
su·et \ˈsü-ət\ *n* : the hard fat from beef and mutton that yields tallow
suff *abbr* **1** sufficient **2** suffix
suf·fer \ˈsə-fər\ *vb* **suf·fered; suf·fer·ing 1** : to feel or endure pain **2** : EXPERIENCE, UNDERGO **3** : to bear loss, damage, or injury **4** : ALLOW, PERMIT **syn** endure, abide, tolerate, stand, brook, stomach — **suf·fer·able** \ˈsə-fə-rə-bəl\ *adj* — **suf·fer·er** *n*
suf·fer·ance \ˈsə-frəns, -fə-rəns\ *n* **1** : consent or approval implied by lack of interference or resistance **2** : ENDURANCE, PATIENCE
suf·fer·ing \ˈsə-friŋ, -fə-riŋ\ *n* : PAIN, MISERY, HARDSHIP
suf·fice \sə-ˈfīs\ *vb* **suf·ficed; suf·fic·ing 1** : to satisfy a need : be sufficient **2** : to be capable or competent
suf·fi·cien·cy \sə-ˈfi-shən-sē\ *n* **1** : a sufficient quantity to meet one's needs **2** : ADEQUACY
suf·fi·cient \sə-ˈfi-shənt\ *adj* : adequate to accomplish a purpose or meet a need — **suf·fi·cient·ly** *adv*
[1]**suf·fix** \ˈsə-ˌfiks\ *n* : an affix occurring at the end of a word
[2]**suf·fix** \ˈsə-fiks, (ˌ)sə-ˈfiks\ *vb* : to attach as a suffix — **suf·fix·ation** \ˌsə-ˌfik-ˈsā-shən\ *n*
suf·fo·cate \ˈsə-fə-ˌkāt\ *vb* **-cat·ed; -cat·ing** : STIFLE, SMOTHER, CHOKE — **suf·fo·cat·ing·ly** *adv* — **suf·fo·ca·tion** \ˌsə-fə-ˈkā-shən\ *n*
suf·fra·gan \ˈsə-fri-gən\ *n* : an assistant bishop; *esp* : one not having the right of succession — **suffragan** *adj*
suf·frage \ˈsə-frij\ *n* [L *suffragium*] **1** : VOTE **2** : the right to vote : FRANCHISE
suf·frag·ette \ˌsə-fri-ˈjet\ *n* : a woman who advocates suffrage for women
suf·frag·ist \ˈsəf-ri-jist\ *n* : one who advocates extension of the suffrage esp. to women
suf·fuse \sə-ˈfyüz\ *vb* **suf·fused; suf·fus·ing** : to spread over or through in the manner of a fluid or light **syn** infuse, imbue, ingrain, steep — **suf·fu·sion** \-ˈfyü-zhən\ *n*
[1]**sug·ar** \ˈshu̇-gər\ *n* **1** : a sweet substance that is colorless or white when pure and is chiefly sucrose from sugarcane or sugar beets **2** : a water-soluble compound (as glucose) similar to sucrose — **sug·ary** *adj*
[2]**sugar** *vb* **sug·ared; sug·ar·ing 1** : to mix, cover, or sprinkle with sugar **2** : SWEETEN ⟨~ advice with flattery⟩ **3** : to form sugar ⟨a syrup that ~*s*⟩ **4** : GRANULATE
sugar beet *n* : a large beet with a white root from which sugar is made
sug·ar·cane \ˈshu̇-gər-ˌkān\ *n* : a tall grass widely grown in warm regions for the sugar in its stalks
sugar daddy *n* **1** : a well-to-do usu. older man who supports or spends lavishly on a mistress or girlfriend **2** : a generous benefactor of a cause
sugar maple *n* : a maple with a sweet sap; *esp* : one of eastern No. America with sap that is the chief source of maple syrup and maple sugar
sugar pea *n* : SNOW PEA
sug·ar·plum \ˈshu̇-gər-ˌpləm\ *n* : a small ball of candy
sug·gest \səg-ˈjest, sə-\ *vb* **1** : to put (as a thought, plan, or desire) into a person's mind **2** : to remind or evoke by association of ideas **syn** imply, hint, intimate, insinuate, connote
sug·gest·ible \səg-ˈjes-tə-bəl, sə-\ *adj* : easily influenced by suggestion
sug·ges·tion \-ˈjes-chən\ *n* **1** : an act or instance of suggesting; *also* : something suggested **2** : a slight indication
sug·ges·tive \-ˈjes-tiv\ *adj* : tending to suggest something; *esp* : suggesting something improper or indecent — **sug·ges·tive·ly** *adv* — **sug·ges·tive·ness** *n*
sui·cide \ˈsü-ə-ˌsīd\ *n* **1** : the act of killing oneself purposely **2** : one that commits or attempts suicide — **sui·cid·al** \ˌsü-ə-ˈsīd-ᵊl\ *adj*
sui ge·ner·is \ˌsü-ˌī-ˈje-nə-rəs; ˌsü-ē-\ *adj* [L, of its own kind] : being in a class by itself : UNIQUE
[1]**suit** \ˈsüt\ *n* **1** : an action in court to recover a right or claim **2** : an act of suing or entreating; *esp* : COURTSHIP **3** : a number of things used together ⟨~ of clothes⟩ **4** : one of the four sets of playing cards in a pack
[2]**suit** *vb* **1** : to be appropriate or fitting **2** : to be becoming to **3** : to meet the needs or desires of : PLEASE
suit·able \ˈsü-tə-bəl\ *adj* : FITTING, PROPER, APPROPRIATE **syn** fit, meet, apt, happy — **suit·abil·i·ty** \ˌsü-tə-

ˈbi-lə-tē\ *n* — **suit•able•ness** \ˈsü-tə-bəl-nəs\ *n* — **suit•ably** \-tə-blē\ *adv*

suit•case \ˈsüt-ˌkās\ *n* **:** a bag or case carried by hand and designed to hold a traveler's clothing and personal articles

suite \ˈswēt, *for 4 also* ˈsüt\ *n* **1 :** RETINUE **2 :** a group of rooms occupied as a unit **3 :** a modern instrumental composition in several movements of different character; *also* **:** a long orchestral concert arrangement in suite form of material drawn from a longer work **4 :** a set of matched furniture for a room

suit•ing \ˈsü-tiŋ\ *n* **:** fabric for suits of clothes

suit•or \ˈsü-tər\ *n* **1 :** one who sues or petitions **2 :** one who seeks to marry a woman

su•ki•ya•ki \skē-ˈyä-kē, ˌsu̇-kē-ˈyä-\ *n* **:** thin slices of meat, bean curd, and vegetables cooked in soy sauce and sugar

sul•fa drug \ˈsəl-fə-\ *n* **:** any of various synthetic organic bacteria-inhibiting drugs

sul•fate \ˈsəl-ˌfāt\ *n* **:** a salt or ester of sulfuric acid

sul•fide \ˈsəl-ˈfīd\ *n* **:** a compound of sulfur

sul•fur *also* **sul•phur** \ˈsəl-fər\ *n* **:** a nonmetallic chemical element used esp. in the chemical and paper industries and in vulcanizing rubber — see ELEMENT table

sulfur di•ox•ide \-dī-ˈäk-sīd\ *n* **:** a heavy pungent toxic gas that is used esp. in bleaching, as a preservative, and as a refrigerant, and is a major air pollutant

sul•fu•ric \ˌsəl-ˈfyu̇r-ik\ *adj* **:** of, relating to, or containing sulfur

sulfuric acid *or* **sul•phu•ric acid** \ˌsəl-ˈfyu̇r-ik-\ *n* **:** a heavy corrosive oily strong acid

sul•fu•rous *also* **sul•phu•rous** \ˈsəl-fə-rəs, -fyə-, *also esp for 1* ˌsəl-ˈfyu̇r-əs\ *adj* **1 :** of, relating to, or containing sulfur **2 :** of or relating to brimstone or the fire of hell **:** INFERNAL **3 :** FIERY, INFLAMED ⟨~ sermons⟩

[1]**sulk** \ˈsəlk\ *vb* **:** to be or become moodily silent or irritable

[2]**sulk** *n* **:** a sulky mood or spell

[1]**sulky** \ˈsəl-kē\ *adj* **:** inclined to sulk **:** MOROSE, MOODY **syn** surly, glum, sullen, gloomy — **sulk•i•ly** \ˈsəl-kə-lē\ *adv* — **sulk•i•ness** \-kē-nəs\ *n*

[2]**sulky** *n, pl* **sulkies :** a light 2-wheeled horse-drawn vehicle with a seat for the driver and usu. no body

sul•len \ˈsə-lən\ *adj* **1 :** gloomily silent **:** MOROSE **2 :** DISMAL, GLOOMY ⟨a ~ sky⟩ **syn** glum, surly, dour, saturnine — **sul•len•ly** *adv* — **sul•len•ness** *n*

sul•ly \ˈsə-lē\ *vb* **sul•lied; sul•ly•ing :** SOIL, SMIRCH, DEFILE

sul•tan \ˈsəlt-ᵊn\ *n* **:** a sovereign esp. of a Muslim state — **sul•tan•ate** \-ˌāt\ *n*

sul•ta•na \ˌsəl-ˈta-nə\ *n* **1 :** a female member of a sultan's family **2 :** a pale seedless grape; *also* **:** a raisin of this grape

sul•try \ˈsəl-trē\ *adj* **sul•tri•er; -est** [obs. E *sulter* to swelter, alter. of E *swelter*] **:** very hot and moist **:** SWELTERING; *also* **:** exciting sexual desire

[1]**sum** \ˈsəm\ *n* [ME *summe,* fr. OF, fr. L *summa,* fr. fem. of *summus* highest] **1 :** a quantity of money **2 :** the whole amount **3 :** GIST **4 :** the result obtained by adding numbers **5 :** a problem in arithmetic

[2]**sum** *vb* **summed; sum•ming :** to find the sum of by adding or counting

su•mac *also* **su•mach** \ˈsü-ˌmak, ˈshü-\ *n* **:** any of a genus of trees, shrubs, and woody vines with feathery compound leaves and spikes of red or whitish berries

sum•ma•rise *Brit var of* SUMMARIZE

sum•ma•rize \ˈsə-mə-ˌrīz\ *vb* **-rized; -riz•ing :** to tell in a summary

[1]**sum•ma•ry** \ˈsə-mə-rē\ *adj* **1 :** covering the main points briefly **:** CONCISE **2 :** done without delay or formality ⟨~ punishment⟩ **syn** terse, succinct, laconic — **sum•mar•i•ly** \(ˌ)sə-ˈmer-ə-lē, ˈsə-mə-rə-lē\ *adv*

[2]**sum•ma•ry** *n, pl* **-ries :** a concise statement of the main points

sum•ma•tion \(ˌ)sə-ˈmā-shən\ *n* **:** a summing up; *esp* **:** a speech in court summing up the arguments in a case

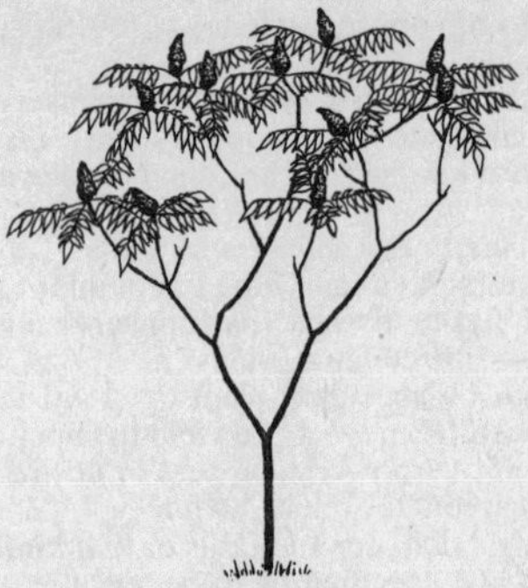

sumac

sum•mer \ˈsə-mər\ *n* **:** the season of the year in a region in which the sun shines most directly **:** the warmest period of the year — **sum•mery** *adj*

sum•mer•house \ˈsə-mər-ˌhau̇s\ *n* **:** a covered structure in a garden or park to provide a shady retreat

summer squash *n* **:** any of various garden squashes (as zucchini) used as a vegetable while immature

sum•mit \ˈsə-mət\ *n* **1 :** the highest point **2 :** a conference of highest-level officials

sum•mon \ˈsə-mən\ *vb* [ME *somonen,* fr. OF *somondre,* fr. (assumed) VL *summonere,* alter. of L *summonēre* to remind secretly] **1 :** to call to a meeting **:** CONVOKE **2 :** to send for; *also* **:** to order to appear in court **3 :** to evoke esp. by an act of the will ⟨~ up courage⟩ — **sum•mon•er** *n*

sum•mons \ˈsə-mənz\ *n, pl* **sum•mons•es 1 :** an authoritative call to appear at a designated place or to attend to a duty **2 :** a warning or citation to appear in court at a specified time to answer charges

sump•tu•ous \ˈsəmp-shə-wəs, -chə-\ *adj* **:** LAVISH, LUXURIOUS

sum up *vb* **:** SUMMARIZE

[1]**sun** \ˈsən\ *n* **1 :** the shining celestial body around which the earth and other planets revolve and from which they receive light and heat **2 :** a celestial body like the sun **3 :** SUNSHINE — **sun•less** *adj* — **sun•ny** *adj*

[2]**sun** *vb* **sunned; sun•ning 1 :** to expose to or as if to the rays of the sun **2 :** to sun oneself

Sun *abbr* Sunday

sun•bath \ˈsən-ˌbath, -ˌbȧth\ *n* **:** an exposure to sunlight or a sunlamp — **sun•bathe** \-ˌbāth\ *vb*

sun•beam \-ˌbēm\ *n* **:** a ray of sunlight

sun•block \ˈsən-ˌbläk\ *n* **:** a preparation for blocking out more of the sun's rays than a sunscreen

sun•bon•net \-ˌbä-nət\ *n* **:** a bonnet with a wide brim to shield the face and neck from the sun

[1]**sun•burn** \-ˌbərn\ *vb* **-burned** \-ˌbərnd\ *or* **-burnt** \-ˌbərnt\; **-burn•ing :** to cause or become affected with sunburn

[2]**sunburn** *n* **:** a skin inflammation caused by overexposure to sunlight

sun•dae \ˈsən-(ˌ)dā, -dē\ *n* **:** ice cream served with topping

Sun•day \ˈsən-dē, -ˌdā\ *n* **:** the 1st day of the week **:** the Christian Sabbath

sun•der \ˈsən-dər\ *vb* **:** to force apart **syn** sever, part, disjoin, disunite

sun•di•al \-ˌdī(-ə)l\ *n* **:** a device for showing the time of day from the shadow cast on a plate by an object with a straight edge

sun•down \-ˌdau̇n\ *n* **:** SUNSET 2

sun•dries \ˈsən-drēz\ *n pl* **:** various small articles or items

sun•dry \ˈsən-drē\ *adj* **:** SEVERAL, DIVERS, VARIOUS

sun•fish \ˈsən-ˌfish\ *n* **1 :** a huge marine fish with a deep flattened body **2 :** any of numerous often brightly colored American freshwater fishes related to the perches and usu. having the body flattened from side to side

sun•flow•er \-ˌflau̇-ər\ *n* : any of a genus of tall New World plants related to the daisies and often grown for the oil-rich seeds of their yellow-petaled dark-centered flower heads

sung *past and past part of* SING

sun•glasses \ˈsən-ˌgla-səz\ *n pl* : glasses to protect the eyes from the sun

sunk *past and past part of* SINK

sunk•en \ˈsəŋ-kən\ *adj* **1** : SUBMERGED **2** : fallen in : HOLLOW ⟨~ cheeks⟩ **3** : lying in a depression ⟨~ garden⟩; *also* : constructed below the general floor level ⟨~ living room⟩

sun•lamp \ˈsən-ˌlamp\ *n* : an electric lamp designed to emit radiation of wavelengths from ultraviolet to infrared

sun•light \-ˌlīt\ *n* : SUNSHINE

sun•lit \-ˌlit\ *adj* : lighted by or as if by the sun

sun•rise \-ˌrīz\ *n* **1** : the apparent rising of the sun above the horizon **2** : the time at which the sun rises

sun•roof \-ˌrüf, -ˌru̇f\ *n* : a panel in an automobile roof that can be opened

sun•screen \-ˌskrēn\ *n* : a substance used in suntan preparations to protect the skin

sun•set \-ˌset\ *n* **1** : the apparent descent of the sun below the horizon **2** : the time at which the sun sets

sun•shade \ˈsən-ˌshād\ *n* : something (as a parasol or awning) used as a protection from the sun's rays

sun•shine \-ˌshīn\ *n* : the direct light of the sun — **sun-shiny** *adj*

sun•spot \-ˌspät\ *n* : any of the dark spots that appear from time to time on the sun's surface

sun•stroke \-ˌstrōk\ *n* : heatstroke caused by direct exposure to the sun

sun•tan \-ˌtan\ *n* : a browning of the skin from exposure to the sun's rays

sun•up \-ˌəp\ *n* : SUNRISE 2

¹sup \ˈsəp\ *vb* **supped; sup•ping** : to take or drink in swallows or gulps

²sup *n* : a mouthful esp. of liquor or broth; *also* : a small quantity of liquid

³sup *vb* **supped; sup•ping 1** : to eat the evening meal **2** : to make one's supper ⟨*supped* on roast beef⟩

⁴sup *abbr* **1** superior **2** supplement; supplementary **3** supply **4** supra

¹su•per \ˈsü-pər\ *n* : SUPERINTENDENT

²super *adj* **1** : very fine : EXCELLENT **2** : EXTREME, EXCESSIVE

super- \ˌsü-pər\ *prefix* **1** : over and above : higher in quantity, quality, or degree than : more than **2** : in addition : extra **3** : exceeding a norm **4** : in excessive degree or intensity **5** : surpassing all or most others of its kind **6** : situated above, on, or at the top of **7** : next above or higher **8** : more inclusive than **9** : superior in status or position

superabsorbent
superachiever
superagency
superblock
superbomb
supercity
superclean
superexpensive
superfine
superheat
superheavy
superhero
superhuman
superhumanly
superindividual
superliner
superman
supermom
supernormal
superpatriot
superpatriotic
superpatriotism
superpremium
superrich
supersalesman
supersecret
supersize
supersized
supersmart
supersophisticated
superspy
superstar
superstate
superstore
superstratum
superstrength
superstrong
supersubtle
supersystem
supertanker
superthin
superwoman

su•per•abun•dant \ˌsü-pər-ə-ˈbən-dənt\ *adj* : more than ample — **su•per•abun•dance** \-dəns\ *n*

su•per•an•nu•ate \ˌsü-pər-ˈan-yə-ˌwāt\ *vb* **-at•ed; -at•ing 1** : to make out-of-date **2** : to retire and pension because of age or infirmity — **su•per•an•nu•at•ed** *adj*

su•perb \su̇-ˈpərb\ *adj* [L *superbus* excellent, proud, fr. *super* above] : marked to the highest degree by excellence, brilliance, or competence **syn** resplendent, glorious, gorgeous, sublime — **su•perb•ly** *adv*

su•per•charg•er \ˈsü-pər-ˌchär-jər\ *n* : a device for increasing the amount of air supplied to an internal combustion engine

su•per•cil•ious \ˌsü-pər-ˈsi-lē-əs\ *adj* [L *superciliosus,* fr. *supercilium* eyebrow, haughtiness] : haughtily contemptuous **syn** disdainful, overbearing, arrogant, lordly, superior

su•per•com•pu•ter \ˈsü-pər-kəm-ˌpyü-tər\ *n* : a large very fast mainframe

su•per•con•duc•tiv•i•ty \ˌsü-pər-ˌkän-ˌdək-ˈti-və-tē\ *n* : a complete disappearance of electrical resistance in a substance esp. at very low temperatures — **su•per•con•duc•tive** \-kən-ˈdək-tiv\ *adj* — **su•per•con•duc•tor** \-ˈdək-tər\ *n*

su•per•con•ti•nent \ˈsü-pər-ˌkänt-ᵊn-ənt\ *n* : a former large continent from which other continents are held to have broken off and drifted away

su•per•ego \ˌsü-pər-ˈē-gō\ *n* : the one of the three divisions of the psyche in psychoanalytic theory that functions to reward and punish through a system of moral attitudes, conscience, and a sense of guilt

su•per•fi•cial \ˌsü-pər-ˈfi-shəl\ *adj* **1** : of or relating to the surface or appearance only **2** : not thorough : SHALLOW — **su•per•fi•ci•al•i•ty** \-ˌfi-shē-ˈa-lə-tē\ *n* — **su•per•fi•cial•ly** *adv*

su•per•flu•ous \su̇-ˈpər-flə-wəs\ *adj* : exceeding what is sufficient or necessary : SURPLUS **syn** extra, spare, supernumerary — **su•per•flu•i•ty** \ˌsü-pər-ˈflü-ə-tē\ *n*

su•per•high•way \ˌsü-pər-ˈhī-ˌwā\ *n* : a broad highway designed for high-speed traffic

su•per•im•pose \-im-ˈpōz\ *vb* : to lay (one thing) over or above something else

su•per•in•tend \ˌsü-pə-rin-ˈtend\ *vb* : to have or exercise the charge and oversight of : DIRECT — **su•per•in•ten•dence** \-ˈten-dəns\ *n* — **su•per•in•ten•den•cy** \-dən-sē\ *n* — **su•per•in•ten•dent** \-dənt\ *n*

¹su•pe•ri•or \su̇-ˈpir-ē-ər\ *adj* **1** : situated higher up, over, or near the top; *also* : higher in rank or numbers **2** : of greater value or importance **3** : courageously indifferent (as to pain or misfortune) **4** : better than most others of its kind **5** : ARROGANT, HAUGHTY — **su•pe•ri•or•i•ty** \-ˌpir-ē-ˈȯr-ə-tē\ *n*

²superior *n* **1** : one who is above another in rank, office, or station; *esp* : the head of a religious house or order **2** : one higher in quality or merit

¹su•per•la•tive \su̇-ˈpər-lə-tiv\ *adj* **1** : of, relating to, or constituting the degree of grammatical comparison that denotes an extreme or unsurpassed level or extent **2** : surpassing others : SUPREME **syn** peerless, incomparable, superb — **su•per•la•tive•ly** *adv*

²superlative *n* **1** : the superlative degree or a superlative form in a language **2** : the utmost degree : ACME

su•per•mar•ket \ˈsü-pər-ˌmär-kət\ *n* : a self-service retail market selling foods and household merchandise

su•per•nal \su̇-ˈpər-nəl\ *adj* **1** : being or coming from on high **2** : of heavenly or spiritual character

su•per•nat•u•ral \ˌsü-pər-ˈna-chə-rəl\ *adj* : of or relating to phenomena beyond or outside of nature; *esp* : relating to or attributed to a divinity, ghost, or devil — **su•per•nat•u•ral•ly** *adv*

su•per•no•va \ˌsü-pər-ˈnō-və\ *n* : the explosion of a very large star

¹su•per•nu•mer•ary \-ˈnü-mə-ˌrer-ē, -ˈnyü-\ *adj* : exceeding the usual or required number : EXTRA **syn** surplus, superfluous, spare

[2]**supernumerary** *n, pl* **-ar•ies** : an extra person or thing; *esp* : an actor hired for a nonspeaking part

su•per•pose \ˌsü-pər-ˈpōz\ *vb* **-posed; -pos•ing** : SUPERIMPOSE — **su•per•po•si•tion** \-pə-ˈzi-shən\ *n*

su•per•pow•er \ˈsü-pər-ˌpau̇-ər\ *n* **1** : excessive or superior power **2** : one of a few politically and militarily dominant nations

su•per•sat•u•rat•ed \-ˈsa-chə-ˌrā-təd\ *adj* : containing an amount of a substance greater than that required for saturation

su•per•scribe \ˈsü-pər-ˌskrīb, ˌsü-pər-ˈskrīb\ *vb* **-scribed; -scrib•ing** : to write on the top or outside : ADDRESS — **su•per•scrip•tion** \ˌsü-pər-ˈskrip-shən\ *n*

su•per•script \ˈsü-pər-ˌskript\ *n* : a symbol (as a numeral or letter) written immediately above or above and to one side of another character

su•per•sede \ˌsü-pər-ˈsēd\ *vb* **-sed•ed; -sed•ing** [MF *superseder* to refrain from, fr. L *supersedēre* to be superior to, refrain from, fr. *super-* above + *sedēre* to sit] : to take the place of : REPLACE

su•per•son•ic \-ˈsä-nik\ *adj* **1** : ULTRASONIC **2** : being or relating to speeds from one to five times the speed of sound; *also* : capable of moving at such a speed ⟨a ~ airplane⟩

su•per•sti•tion \ˌsü-pər-ˈsti-shən\ *n* **1** : beliefs or practices resulting from ignorance, fear of the unknown, or trust in magic or chance **2** : an unreasoning fear of nature, the unknown, or God resulting from superstition — **su•per•sti•tious** \-shəs\ *adj*

su•per•struc•ture \ˈsü-pər-ˌstrək-chər\ *n* : something built on a base or as a vertical extension

su•per•vene \ˌsü-pər-ˈvēn\ *vb* **-vened; -ven•ing** : to occur as something additional or unexpected

su•per•vise \ˈsü-pər-ˌvīz\ *vb* **-vised; -vis•ing** : OVERSEE, SUPERINTEND — **su•per•vi•sion** \ˌsü-pər-ˈvi-zhən\ *n* — **su•per•vi•sor** \ˈsü-pər-ˌvī-zər\ *n* — **su•per•vi•so•ry** \ˌsü-pər-ˈvī-zə-rē\ *adj*

su•pine \su̇-ˈpīn\ *adj* **1** : lying on the back or with the face upward **2** : LETHARGIC, SLUGGISH; *also* : ABJECT **syn** inactive, inert, passive, idle

supp *or* **suppl** *abbr* supplement; supplementary

sup•per \ˈsə-pər\ *n* : the evening meal esp. when dinner is taken at midday — **sup•per•time** \-ˌtīm\ *n*

sup•plant \sə-ˈplant\ *vb* **1** : to take the place of (another) esp. by force or trickery **2** : REPLACE

sup•ple \ˈsə-pəl\ *adj* **sup•pler; sup•plest** **1** : COMPLIANT, ADAPTABLE **2** : capable of bending without breaking or creasing : LIMBER **syn** resilient, elastic, flexible

[1]**sup•ple•ment** \ˈsə-plə-mənt\ *n* **1** : something that supplies a want or makes an addition **2** : a continuation (as of a book) containing corrections or additional material — **sup•ple•men•tal** \ˌsə-plə-ˈment-ᵊl\ *adj* — **sup•ple•men•ta•ry** \-ˈmen-tə-rē\ *adj*

[2]**sup•ple•ment** \ˈsə-plə-ˌment\ *vb* : to fill up the deficiencies of : add to

sup•pli•ant \ˈsə-plē-ənt\ *n* : one who supplicates : PETITIONER, PLEADER

sup•pli•cant \ˈsə-pli-kənt\ *n* : SUPPLIANT

sup•pli•cate \ˈsə-plə-ˌkāt\ *vb* **-cat•ed; -cat•ing** **1** : to make a humble entreaty; *esp* : to pray to God **2** : to ask earnestly and humbly : BESEECH **syn** implore, beg, entreat, plead — **sup•pli•ca•tion** \ˌsə-plə-ˈkā-shən\ *n*

[1]**sup•ply** \sə-ˈplī\ *vb* **sup•plied; sup•ply•ing** [ME *supplien,* fr. MF *soupleier,* fr. L *supplēre* to fill up, supplement, supply, fr. *sub-* under, up to + *plēre* to fill] **1** : to add as a supplement **2** : to satisfy the needs of **3** : FURNISH, PROVIDE — **sup•pli•er** *n*

[2]**supply** *n, pl* **supplies** **1** : the quantity or amount (as of a commodity) needed or available; *also* : PROVISIONS, STORES — usu. used in pl. **2** : the act or process of filling a want or need : PROVISION **3** : the quantities of goods or services offered for sale at a particular time or at one price

sup•ply–side \sə-ˈplī-ˌsīd\ *adj* : of, relating to, or being an economic theory that recommends the reduction of tax rates to expand economic activity

[1]**sup•port** \sə-ˈpōrt\ *vb* **1** : BEAR, TOLERATE **2** : to take sides with : BACK, ASSIST **3** : to provide with food, clothing, and shelter **4** : to hold up or serve as a foundation for **syn** uphold, advocate, champion — **sup•port•able** *adj* — **sup•port•er** *n*

[2]**support** *n* **1** : the act of supporting : the state of being supported **2** : one that supports : PROP, BASE

support group *n* : a group of people with common experiences and concerns who provide emotional and moral support for one another

sup•pose \sə-ˈpōz\ *vb* **sup•posed; sup•pos•ing** **1** : to assume to be true (as for the sake of argument) **2** : EXPECT ⟨I am *supposed* to go⟩ **3** : to think probable — **sup•pos•al** *n*

sup•posed \sə-ˈpōzd, -ˈpō-zəd\ *adj* : BELIEVED; *also* : mistakenly believed — **sup•pos•ed•ly** \-ˈpō-zəd-lē, -ˈpōzd-lē\ *adv*

sup•pos•ing *conj* : if by way of hypothesis : on the assumption that

sup•po•si•tion \ˌsə-pə-ˈzi-shən\ *n* **1** : something that is supposed : HYPOTHESIS **2** : the act of supposing

sup•pos•i•to•ry \sə-ˈpä-zə-ˌtōr-ē\ *n, pl* **-ries** [ML *suppositorium,* fr. LL, neut. of *suppositorius* placed beneath] : a small easily melted mass of usu. medicated material for insertion (as into the rectum)

sup•press \sə-ˈpres\ *vb* **1** : to put down by authority or force : SUBDUE ⟨~ a revolt⟩ **2** : to keep from being known; *also* : to stop the publication or circulation of **3** : to hold back : REPRESS ⟨~ anger⟩ ⟨~ a cough⟩ — **sup•press•ible** \-ˈpre-sə-bəl\ *adj* — **sup•pres•sion** \-ˈpre-shən\ *n*

sup•pres•sant \sə-ˈpres-ᵊnt\ *n* : an agent (as a drug) suppressing rather than eliminating something ⟨a cough ~⟩

sup•pu•rate \ˈsə-pyə-ˌrāt\ *vb* **-rat•ed; -rat•ing** : to form or give off pus — **sup•pu•ra•tion** \ˌsə-pyə-ˈrā-shən\ *n*

su•pra \ˈsü-prə, -ˌprä\ *adv* : earlier in this writing : ABOVE

su•pra•na•tion•al \ˌsü-prə-ˈna-shə-nəl, -ˌprä-\ *adj* : going beyond national boundaries, authority, or interests ⟨~ organizations⟩

su•prem•a•cist \su̇-ˈpre-mə-sist\ *n* : an advocate of group supremacy

su•prem•a•cy \su̇-ˈpre-mə-sē\ *n, pl* **-cies** : supreme rank, power, or authority

su•preme \su̇-ˈprēm\ *adj* [L *supremus,* superl. of *superus* upper, fr. *super* over, above] **1** : highest in rank or authority **2** : highest in degree or quality ⟨~ among poets⟩ **3** : ULTIMATE ⟨the ~ sacrifice⟩ **syn** superlative, surpassing, peerless, incomparable — **su•preme•ly** *adv* — **su•preme•ness** *n*

Supreme Being *n* : GOD 1

supt *abbr* superintendent

sur•cease \ˈsər-ˌsēs\ *n* : CESSATION, RESPITE

[1]**sur•charge** \ˈsər-ˌchärj\ *vb* **1** : to fill to excess : OVERLOAD **2** : to apply a surcharge to (postage stamps)

[2]**surcharge** *n* **1** : an extra fee or cost **2** : an excessive load or burden **3** : something officially printed on a postage stamp esp. to change its value

sur•cin•gle \ˈsər-ˌsiŋ-gəl\ *n* : a band put around a horse's body to make something (as a saddle) fast

[1]**sure** \ˈshu̇r\ *adj* **sur•er; sur•est** [ME, fr. MF *sur,* fr. L *securus* secure] **1** : firmly established **2** : TRUSTWORTHY, RELIABLE **3** : CONFIDENT **4** : not to be disputed : UNDOUBTED **5** : bound to happen **6** : careful to remember or attend to something ⟨be ~ to lock the door⟩ **syn** certain, cocksure, positive — **sure•ness** *n*

[2]**sure** *adv* : SURELY

sure•fire \ˈshu̇r-ˈfīr\ *adj* : certain to get results : DEPENDABLE

sure•ly \ˈshu̇r-lē\ *adv* **1** : in a sure manner **2** : without doubt **3** : INDEED, REALLY

sure•ty \ˈshu̇r-ə-tē\ *n, pl* **-ties** **1** : SURENESS, CERTAINTY

DICTIONARY

2 : something that makes sure : GUARANTEE 3 : one who is a guarantor for another person

[1]**surf** \ˈsərf\ *n* : waves that break upon the shore; *also* : the sound or foam of breaking waves

[2]**surf** *vb* : to ride the surf (as on a surfboard) — **surf·er** *n* — **surf·ing** *n*

[1]**sur·face** \ˈsər-fəs\ *n* 1 : the outside of an object or body 2 : outward aspect or appearance — **surface** *adj*

[2]**surface** *vb* **sur·faced; sur·fac·ing** 1 : to give a surface to : make smooth 2 : to rise to the surface

surf·board \ˈsərf-ˌbōrd\ *n* : a buoyant board used in surfing

[1]**sur·feit** \ˈsər-fət\ *n* 1 : EXCESS, SUPERABUNDANCE 2 : excessive indulgence (as in food or drink) 3 : disgust caused by excess

[2]**surfeit** *vb* : to feed, supply, or indulge to the point of surfeit : CLOY

surg *abbr* surgeon; surgery; surgical

[1]**surge** \ˈsərj\ *vb* **surged; surg·ing** 1 : to rise and fall actively : TOSS 2 : to move in waves 3 : to rise suddenly to an excessive or abnormal value

[2]**surge** *n* 1 : a sweeping onward like a wave of the sea ⟨a ~ of emotion⟩ 2 : a large billow 3 : a transient sudden increase of current or voltage in an electrical circuit

sur·geon \ˈsər-jən\ *n* : a physician who specializes in surgery

sur·gery \ˈsər-jə-rē\ *n, pl* **-ger·ies** [ME *surgerie,* fr. OF *cirurgie, surgerie,* fr. L *chirurgia,* fr. Gk *cheirourgia,* fr. *cheirourgos* surgeon, fr. *cheirourgos* doing by hand, fr. *cheir* hand + *ergon* work] 1 : a branch of medicine concerned with the correction of physical defects, the repair of injuries, and the treatment of disease esp. by operations 2 : a room or area where surgery is performed 3 : the work done by a surgeon

sur·gi·cal \ˈsər-ji-kəl\ *adj* : of, relating to, or associated with surgeons or surgery — **sur·gi·cal·ly** \-k(ə-)lē\ *adv*

sur·ly \ˈsər-lē\ *adj* **sur·li·er; -est** [alter. of ME *sirly* lordly, imperious, fr. *sir*] : having a rude unfriendly disposition **syn** morose, glum, sullen, sulky, gloomy — **sur·li·ness** \-lē-nəs\ *n*

sur·mise \sər-ˈmīz\ *vb* **sur·mised; sur·mis·ing** : GUESS **syn** conjecture, presume, suppose — **surmise** *n*

sur·mount \sər-ˈmaůnt\ *vb* 1 : to prevail over : OVERCOME 2 : to get to or lie at the top of

sur·name \ˈsər-ˌnām\ *n* 1 : NICKNAME 2 : the name borne in common by members of a family

sur·pass \sər-ˈpas\ *vb* 1 : to be superior to in quality, degree, or performance : EXCEL 2 : to go beyond the reach or powers of **syn** transcend, outdo, outstrip, exceed — **sur·pass·ing·ly** *adv*

sur·plice \ˈsər-pləs\ *n* : a loose white outer garment worn at church services

sur·plus \ˈsər-(ˌ)pləs\ *n* 1 : quantity left over : EXCESS 2 : the excess of assets over liabilities **syn** superfluity, overabundance, surfeit

[1]**sur·prise** \sər-ˈprīz\ *n* 1 : an attack made without warning 2 : a taking unawares 3 : something that surprises 4 : AMAZEMENT, ASTONISHMENT

[2]**surprise** *also* **sur·prize** *vb* **sur·prised; sur·pris·ing** 1 : to come upon and attack unexpectedly 2 : to take unawares 3 : AMAZE 4 : to cause astonishment or surprise **syn** astonish, astound, dumbfound — **sur·pris·ing** *adj*

sur·pris·ing·ly \-ˈprī-ziŋ-lē\ *adv* 1 : in a surprising manner or degree 2 : it is surprising that

sur·re·al \sə-ˈrē-əl, -ˈrēl\ *adj* 1 : having the intense irrational reality of a dream 2 : of or relating to surrealism

sur·re·al·ism \sə-ˈrē-ə-ˌli-zəm\ *n* : art, literature, or theater characterized by fantastic or incongruous imagery or effects produced by unnatural juxtapositions and combinations — **sur·re·al·ist** \-list\ *n or adj* — **sur·re·al·is·tic** \sə-ˌrē-ə-ˈlis-tik\ *adj* — **sur·re·al·is·ti·cal·ly** \-ti-k(ə-)lē\ *adv*

[1]**sur·ren·der** \sə-ˈren-dər\ *vb* **-dered; -der·ing** 1 : to yield to the power of another : give up under compulsion 2 : RELINQUISH

[2]**surrender** *n* : the act of giving up or yielding oneself or the possession of something to another

sur·rep·ti·tious \ˌsər-əp-ˈti-shəs\ *adj* : done, made, or acquired by stealth : CLANDESTINE **syn** underhand, covert, furtive — **sur·rep·ti·tious·ly** *adv*

sur·rey \ˈsər-ē\ *n, pl* **surreys** : a 2-seated horse-drawn carriage

surrey

sur·ro·ga·cy \ˈsər-ə-gə-sē\ *n* : SURROGATE MOTHERHOOD

sur·ro·gate \ˈsər-ə-ˌgāt, -gət\ *n* 1 : DEPUTY, SUBSTITUTE 2 : a law officer in some states with authority in the probate of wills, the settlement of estates, and the appointment of guardians 3 : SURROGATE MOTHER

surrogate mother *n* : a woman who becomes pregnant (as by surgical implantation of a fertilized egg) in order to carry the fetus for another woman — **surrogate motherhood** *n*

sur·round \sə-ˈraůnd\ *vb* 1 : to enclose on all sides : ENCIRCLE 2 : to enclose so as to cut off retreat or escape

sur·round·ings \sə-ˈraůn-diŋz\ *n pl* : conditions by which one is surrounded

sur·tax \ˈsər-ˌtaks\ *n* : an additional tax over and above a normal tax

sur·tout \(ˌ)sər-ˈtü\ *n* [F, fr. *sur* over (fr. L *super*) + *tout* all, fr. L *totus* whole] : a man's long close-fitting overcoat

surv *abbr* survey; surveying; surveyor

sur·veil·lance \sər-ˈvā-ləns\ *n* [F] : close watch; *also* : SUPERVISION

[1]**sur·vey** \sər-ˈvā\ *vb* **sur·veyed; sur·vey·ing** 1 : to look over and examine closely 2 : to find and represent the contours, measurements, and position of a part of the earth's surface (as a tract of land) 3 : to view or study something as a whole **syn** scrutinize, examine, inspect, study — **sur·vey·or** \-ər\ *n*

[2]**sur·vey** \ˈsər-ˌvā\ *n, pl* **surveys** : the act or an instance of surveying; *also* : something that is surveyed

sur·vive \sər-ˈvīv\ *vb* **sur·vived; sur·viv·ing** 1 : to remain alive or existent 2 : OUTLIVE, OUTLAST — **sur·viv·al** *n* — **sur·vi·vor** \-ˈvī-vər\ *n*

sus·cep·ti·ble \sə-ˈsep-tə-bəl\ *adj* 1 : of such a nature as to permit ⟨words ~ of being misunderstood⟩ 2 : having little resistance to a stimulus or agency ⟨~ to colds⟩ 3 : IMPRESSIONABLE, RESPONSIVE **syn** sensitive, subject, exposed, prone, liable, open — **sus·cep·ti·bil·i·ty** \-ˌsep-tə-ˈbi-lə-tē\ *n*

su·shi \ˈsü-shē\ *n* [Jp] : cold rice formed into various shapes and garnished esp. with bits of raw fish or seafood

[1]**sus·pect** \ˈsəs-ˌpekt, sə-ˈspekt\ *adj* : regarded with suspicion; *also* : QUESTIONABLE

[2]**sus·pect** \ˈsəs-ˌpekt\ *n* : one who is suspected (as of a crime)

[3]**sus·pect** \sə-ˈspekt\ *vb* 1 : to have doubts of : MISTRUST 2 : to imagine to be guilty without proof 3 : SURMISE

sus·pend \sə-ˈspend\ *vb* **1** : to bar temporarily from a privilege, office, or function **2** : to stop temporarily : make inactive for a time **3** : to withhold (judgment) for a time **4** : HANG; *esp* : to hang so as to be free except at one point **5** : to keep from falling or sinking by some invisible support

sus·pend·er \sə-ˈspen-dər\ *n* : one of two supporting straps which pass over the shoulders and to which the trousers are fastened

sus·pense \sə-ˈspens\ *n* **1** : SUSPENSION **2** : mental uncertainty : ANXIETY **3** : excitement as to an outcome — **sus·pense·ful** *adj*

sus·pen·sion \sə-ˈspen-chən\ *n* **1** : the act of suspending : the state or period of being suspended **2** : the state of a substance when its particles are mixed with but undissolved in a fluid or solid; *also* : a substance in this state **3** : something suspended **4** : a device by which something is suspended

sus·pen·so·ry \sə-ˈspen-sə-rē\ *adj* **1** : SUSPENDED; *also* : fitted or serving to suspend something **2** : temporarily leaving undetermined

sus·pi·cion \sə-ˈspi-shən\ *n* **1** : the act or an instance of suspecting something wrong without proof **2** : TRACE, SOUPÇON **syn** mistrust, uncertainty, doubt, skepticism

sus·pi·cious \sə-ˈspi-shəs\ *adj* **1** : open to or arousing suspicion **2** : inclined to suspect **3** : showing suspicion — **sus·pi·cious·ly** *adv*

sus·tain \sə-ˈstān\ *vb* **1** : to provide with nourishment **2** : to keep going : PROLONG ⟨~*ed* effort⟩ **3** : to hold up : PROP **4** : to hold up under : ENDURE **5** : SUFFER ⟨~ a broken arm⟩ **6** : to support as true, legal, or valid **7** : PROVE, CORROBORATE — **sus·tain·able** \səs-ˈtā-nə-bəl\ *adj*

sus·te·nance \ˈsəs-tə-nəns\ *n* **1** : FOOD, NOURISHMENT **2** : a supplying with the necessities of life **3** : something that sustains or supports

su·ture \ˈsü-chər\ *n* **1** : material or a stitch for sewing a wound together **2** : a seam or line along which two things or parts are joined by or as if by sewing

su·zer·ain \ˈsü-zə-rən, -ˌrān\ *n* [F] **1** : a feudal lord **2** : a nation that has political control over the foreign relations of another nation — **su·zer·ain·ty** \-tē\ *n*

svc *or* **svce** *abbr* service

svelte \ˈsfelt\ *adj* [F, fr. It *svelto,* fr. pp. of *svellere* to pluck out, modif. of L *evellere,* fr. *e-* out + *vellere* to pluck] : SLENDER, LITHE

svgs *abbr* savings

SW *abbr* **1** shortwave **2** southwest

[1]**swab** \ˈswäb\ *n* **1** : MOP **2** : a wad of absorbent material esp. for applying medicine or for cleaning; *also* : a sample taken with a swab **3** : SAILOR

[2]**swab** *vb* **swabbed; swab·bing** : to use a swab on : MOP

swad·dle \ˈswäd-ᵊl\ *vb* **swad·dled; swad·dling** **1** : to bind (an infant) in bands of cloth **2** : to wrap up : SWATHE

swaddling clothes *n pl* : bands of cloth wrapped around an infant

swag \ˈswag\ *n* : stolen goods : LOOT

swag·ger \ˈswa-gər\ *vb* **1** : to walk with a conceited swing or strut **2** : BOAST, BRAG — **swagger** *n*

Swa·hi·li \swä-ˈhē-lē\ *n* : a language that is a trade and governmental language over much of East Africa and the Congo region

swain \ˈswān\ *n* [ME *swein* boy, servant, fr. ON *sveinn*] **1** : RUSTIC; *esp* : SHEPHERD **2** : ADMIRER, SUITOR

SWAK *abbr* sealed with a kiss

[1]**swal·low** \ˈswä-lō\ *n* : any of numerous small long-winged migratory birds that often have a deeply forked tail

[2]**swallow** *vb* **1** : to take into the stomach through the throat **2** : to envelop or take in as if by swallowing **3** : to accept or believe without question, protest, or anger

[3]**swallow** *n* **1** : an act of swallowing **2** : an amount that can be swallowed at one time

swal·low·tail \ˈswä-lō-ˌtāl\ *n* **1** : a deeply forked and tapering tail like that of a swallow **2** : TAILCOAT **3** : any of various large butterflies with the border of each hind wing usu. drawn out into a process resembling a tail — **swal·low–tailed** \-ˌtāld\ *adj*

swam *past of* SWIM

swa·mi \ˈswä-mē\ *n* [Hindi *svāmī,* fr. Skt *svāmin* owner, lord] : a Hindu ascetic or religious teacher

[1]**swamp** \ˈswämp\ *n* : a spongy wetland — **swamp** *adj* — **swampy** *adj*

[2]**swamp** *vb* **1** : to fill or become filled with or as if with water **2** : OVERWHELM 3

swamp·land \-ˌland\ *n* : SWAMP

swan \ˈswän\ *n, pl* **swans** *also* **swan** : any of various heavy-bodied long-necked mostly pure white swimming birds related to the geese

[1]**swank** \ˈswaŋk\ *or* **swanky** \ˈswaŋ-kē\ *adj* **swank·er** *or* **swank·i·er; -est** : showily smart and dashing; *also* : fashionably elegant

[2]**swank** *n* **1** : PRETENTIOUSNESS **2** : ELEGANCE

swans·down \ˈswänz-ˌdau̇n\ *n* **1** : the very soft down of a swan used esp. for trimming **2** : a soft thick cotton flannel

swan song *n* : a farewell appearance, act, or pronouncement

swap \ˈswäp\ *vb* **swapped; swap·ping** : TRADE, EXCHANGE — **swap** *n*

sward \ˈswȯrd\ *n* : the grassy surface of land

[1]**swarm** \ˈswȯrm\ *n* **1** : a great number of honeybees leaving together from a hive with a queen to start a new colony; *also* : a hive of bees **2** : a large crowd

[2]**swarm** *vb* **1** : to form in a swarm and depart from a hive **2** : to throng together : gather in great numbers

swart \ˈswȯrt\ *adj* : SWARTHY

swar·thy \ˈswȯr-thē, -thē\ *adj* **swar·thi·er; -est** : dark in color or complexion : dark-skinned

swash \ˈswäsh\ *vb* : to move about with a splashing sound — **swash** *n*

swash·buck·ler \-ˌbə-klər\ *n* : a swaggering or daring soldier or adventurer — **swash·buck·ling** *adj*

swas·ti·ka \ˈswäs-ti-kə\ *n* [Skt *svastika,* fr. *svasti* well-being, fr. *su-* well + *as-* to be] : a symbol or ornament in the form of a cross with the ends of the arms bent at right angles

swat \ˈswät\ *vb* **swat·ted; swat·ting** : to hit sharply ⟨~ a fly⟩ ⟨~ a ball⟩ — **swat** *n* — **swat·ter** *n*

SWAT *abbr* Special Weapons and Tactics

swatch \ˈswäch\ *n* : a sample piece (as of fabric) or a collection of samples

swath \ˈswäth, ˈswȯth\ *or* **swathe** \ˈswäth, ˈswȯth, ˈswāth\ *n* [ME, fr. OE *swæth* footstep, trace] **1** : a row of cut grass or grain **2** : the sweep of a scythe or mowing machine or the path cut in mowing

swathe \ˈswäth, ˈswȯth, ˈswāth\ *vb* **swathed; swath·ing** : to bind or wrap with or as if with a bandage

[1]**sway** \ˈswā\ *n* **1** : a gentle swinging from side to side **2** : controlling influence or power : DOMINION

[2]**sway** *vb* **1** : to swing gently from side to side **2** : RULE, GOVERN **3** : to cause to swing from side to side **4** : BEND, SWERVE; *also* : INFLUENCE **syn** oscillate, fluctuate, vibrate, waver

sway·backed \ˈswā-ˌbakt\ *also* **sway·back** \-ˌbak\ *adj* : having an abnormally sagging back ⟨a ~ mare⟩ — **swayback** *n*

swear \ˈswar\ *vb* **swore** \ˈswōr\; **sworn** \ˈswōrn\; **swear·ing** **1** : to make a solemn statement or promise under oath **2** : to assert or promise emphatically or earnestly **3** : to administer an oath to **4** : to bind by or as if by an oath **5** : to use profane or obscene language — **swear·er** *n*

swear in *vb* : to induct into office by administration of an oath

sweat \ˈswet\ *vb* **sweat** *or* **sweat·ed; sweat·ing** **1** : to excrete salty moisture from glands of the skin : PER-

SPIRE **2** : to form drops of moisture on the surface **3** : to work so that one sweats : TOIL **4** : to cause to sweat **5** : to draw out or get rid of by or as if by sweating **6** : to make a person overwork — **sweat** *n* — **sweaty** *adj*

sweat•er \ˈswe-tər\ *n* **1** : one that sweats **2** : a knitted or crocheted jacket or pullover

sweat•shirt \ˈswet-ˌshərt\ *n* : a loose collarless pullover usu. of heavy cotton jersey

sweat•shop \ˈswet-ˌshäp\ *n* : a shop or factory in which workers are employed for long hours at low wages and under unhealthy conditions

Swed *abbr* Sweden

swede \ˈswēd\ *n* **1** *cap* : a native or inhabitant of Sweden **2** *chiefly Brit* : RUTABAGA

Swed•ish \ˈswē-dish\ *n* **1** : the language of Sweden **2** **Swedish** *pl* : the people of Sweden — **Swedish** *adj*

[1]**sweep** \ˈswēp\ *vb* **swept** \ˈswept\; **sweep•ing** **1** : to remove or clean by or as if by brushing **2** : to destroy completely; *also* : to remove or take with a single swift movement **3** : to remove from sight or consideration **4** : to move over with speed and force ⟨the tide *swept* over the shore⟩ **5** : to win an overwhelming victory in; *also* : to win all the games or contests of **6** : to move or extend in a wide curve — **sweep•er** *n*

[2]**sweep** *n* **1** : something (as a long oar) that operates with a sweeping motion **2** : a clearing off or away **3** : a winning of all the contests or prizes in a competition **4** : a sweeping movement **5** : CURVE, BEND **6** : RANGE, SCOPE

sweep•ing *adj* : EXTENSIVE ⟨~ reforms⟩; *also* : indiscriminately inclusive ⟨~ generalities⟩

sweep•ings \ˈswē-piŋz\ *n pl* : things collected by sweeping

sweep–sec•ond hand \ˈswēp-ˌse-kənd-\ *n* : a hand marking seconds on a timepiece

sweep•stakes \ˈswēp-ˌstāks\ *also* **sweep•stake** \-ˌstāk\ *n, pl* **sweepstakes** **1** : a race or contest in which the entire prize may go to the winner **2** : any of various lotteries

[1]**sweet** \ˈswēt\ *adj* **1** : being or causing the one of the four basic taste sensations that is caused esp. by table sugar and is identified esp. by the taste buds at the front of the tongue; *also* : pleasing to the taste **2** : AGREEABLE **3** : pleasing to a sense other than taste ⟨a ~ smell⟩ ⟨~ music⟩ **4** : not stale or spoiled : WHOLESOME ⟨~ milk⟩ **5** : not salted ⟨~ butter⟩ — **sweet•ish** *adj* — **sweet•ly** *adv* — **sweet•ness** *n*

[2]**sweet** *n* **1** : something sweet : CANDY **2** : DARLING

sweet•bread \ˈswēt-ˌbred\ *n* : the pancreas or thymus of an animal (as a calf or lamb) used for food

sweet•bri•er *also* **sweet•bri•ar** \-ˌbrī-ər\ *n* : a thorny Old World rose with fragrant white to deep pink flowers

sweet clover *n* : any of a genus of erect legumes widely grown for soil improvement or hay

sweet corn *n* : an Indian corn with kernels rich in sugar and cooked as a vegetable while immature

sweet•en \ˈswē-tᵊn\ *vb* **sweet•ened; sweet•en•ing** : to make sweet — **sweet•en•er** *n* — **sweet•en•ing** *n*

sweet•heart \ˈswēt-ˌhärt\ *n* : one who is loved

sweet•meat \-ˌmēt\ *n* : CANDY

sweet pea *n* : a garden plant of the legume family with climbing stems and fragrant flowers of many colors; *also* : its flower

sweet pepper *n* : a large mild thick-walled fruit of a pepper; *also* : a plant related to the potato that bears sweet peppers

sweet potato *n* : a tropical vine related to the morning glory; *also* : its sweet yellow edible root

sweet–talk \ˈswēt-ˌtök\ *vb* : FLATTER, COAX — **sweet talk** *n*

sweet tooth *n* : a craving or fondness for sweet food

sweet wil•liam \ˌswēt-ˈwil-yəm\ *n, often cap W* : a widely cultivated Old World pink with small white to deep red or purple flowers often showily spotted, banded, or mottled

[1]**swell** \ˈswel\ *vb* **swelled; swelled** *or* **swol•len** \ˈswō-lən\; **swell•ing** **1** : to grow big or make bigger **2** : to expand or distend abnormally or excessively ⟨a *swollen* joint⟩; *also* : BULGE **3** : to fill or be filled with emotion (as pride) **syn** expand, amplify, distend, inflate, dilate — **swell•ing** *n*

[2]**swell** *n* **1** : a long crestless wave or series of waves in the open sea **2** : the condition of being protuberant **3** : a person dressed in the height of fashion; *also* : a person of high social position

[3]**swell** *adj* **1** : STYLISH; *also* : socially prominent **2** : EXCELLENT

swelled head *n* : an exaggerated opinion of oneself : SELF-CONCEIT

swell•head \ˈswel-ˌhed\ *n* : one who has a swelled head — **swell•head•ed** \-ˌhe-dəd\ *adj*

swel•ter \ˈswel-tər\ *vb* [ME *sweltren*, fr. *swelten* to die, be overcome by heat, fr. OE *sweltan* to die] **1** : to be faint or oppressed with the heat **2** : to become exceedingly hot

swept *past and past part of* SWEEP

swerve \ˈswərv\ *vb* **swerved; swerv•ing** : to move abruptly aside from a straight line or course — **swerve** *n*

[1]**swift** \ˈswift\ *adj* **1** : moving or capable of moving with great speed **2** : occurring suddenly **3** : READY, ALERT — **swift•ly** *adv* — **swift•ness** *n*

[2]**swift** *n* : any of numerous small insect-eating birds with long narrow wings

swig \ˈswig\ *vb* **swigged; swig•ging** : to drink in long drafts — **swig** *n*

[1]**swill** \ˈswil\ *vb* **1** : to swallow greedily : GUZZLE **2** : to feed (as hogs) on swill

[2]**swill** *n* **1** : food for animals composed of edible refuse mixed with liquid **2** : GARBAGE

[1]**swim** \ˈswim\ *vb* **swam** \ˈswam\; **swum** \ˈswəm\; **swim•ming** **1** : to propel oneself along in water by natural means (as by hands and legs, by tail, or by fins) **2** : to glide smoothly along **3** : FLOAT **4** : to be covered with or as if with a liquid **5** : to be dizzy ⟨his head *swam*⟩ **6** : to cross or go over by swimming — **swim•mer** *n*

[2]**swim** *n* **1** : an act of swimming **2** : the main current of activity ⟨in the ~⟩

swim•ming *n* : the action, art, or sport of swimming and diving

swimming pool *n* : a tank (as of concrete or plastic) designed for swimming

swim•suit \ˈswim-ˌsüt\ *n* : a suit for swimming or bathing

swin•dle \ˈswin-dᵊl\ *vb* **swin•dled; swin•dling** [fr. *swindler*, fr. G *Schwindler* giddy person, fr. *schwindeln* to be dizzy] : CHEAT, DEFRAUD — **swindle** *n* — **swindler** *n*

swine \ˈswīn\ *n, pl* **swine** **1** : any of a family of stout short-legged hoofed mammals with bristly skin and a long flexible snout; *esp* : one widely raised as a meat animal **2** : a contemptible person — **swin•ish** *adj*

[1]**swing** \ˈswiŋ\ *vb* **swung** \ˈswəŋ\; **swing•ing** **1** : to move or cause to move rapidly in an arc **2** : to sway or cause to sway back and forth **3** : to hang so as to move freely back and forth or in a curve **4** : to be executed by hanging **5** : to move or turn on a hinge or pivot **6** : to manage or handle successfully **7** : to march or walk with free swaying movements **8** : to have a steady pulsing rhythm; *also* : to play swing music **9** : to be lively and up-to-date; *also* : to engage freely in sex **syn** wield, manipulate, ply, maneuver — **swing•er** *n* — **swing•ing** *adj*

[2]**swing** *n* **1** : the act of swinging **2** : a swinging blow, movement, or rhythm **3** : the distance through which something swings : FLUCTUATION **4** : progression of an activity or process ⟨in full ~⟩ **5** : a seat suspended by a rope or chain for swinging back and forth for

pleasure **6 :** jazz music played esp. by a large band and marked by a steady lively rhythm, simple harmony, and a basic melody often submerged in improvisation

[3]**swing** *adj* **1 :** of or relating to swing music **2 :** that may swing often decisively either way (as on an issue) ⟨~ voters⟩

[1]**swipe** \ˈswīp\ *n* **:** a strong sweeping blow

[2]**swipe** *vb* **swiped; swip•ing 1 :** to strike or wipe with a sweeping motion **2 :** PILFER, SNATCH

swirl \ˈswərl\ *vb* **:** to move or cause to move with a whirling motion — **swirl** *n* — **swirly** \ˈswər-lē\ *adj*

swish \ˈswish\ *n* **1 :** a prolonged hissing sound **2 :** a light sweeping or brushing sound — **swish** *vb*

Swiss \ˈswis\ *n* **1** *pl* **Swiss :** a native or inhabitant of Switzerland **2 :** a hard cheese with large holes

Swiss chard *n* **:** a beet having large leaves and succulent stalks often cooked as a vegetable

[1]**switch** \ˈswich\ *n* **1 :** a slender flexible whip, rod, or twig **2 :** a blow with a switch **3 :** a shift from one thing to another; *also* **:** change from the usual **4 :** a device for adjusting the rails of a track so that a locomotive or train may be turned from one track to another; *also* **:** a railroad siding **5 :** a device for making, breaking, or changing the connections in an electrical circuit **6 :** a heavy strand of hair often used in addition to a person's own hair for some coiffures

[2]**switch** *vb* **1 :** to punish or urge on with a switch **2 :** WHISK ⟨a cow ~*ing* her tail⟩ **3 :** to shift or turn by operating a switch **4 :** CHANGE, EXCHANGE

switch•back \ˈswich-ˌbak\ *n* **:** a zigzag road, trail, or section of railroad tracks for climbing a steep hill

switch•blade \-ˌblād\ *n* **:** a pocket-knife with a spring-operated blade

switch•board \-ˌbōrd\ *n* **:** a panel for controlling the operation of a number of electric circuits; *esp* **:** one used to make and break telephone connections

switch–hit•ter \-ˈhi-tər\ *n* **:** a baseball player who bats either right-handed or left-handed — **switch–hit** \-ˈhit\ *vb*

switch•man \ˈswich-mən\ *n* **:** one who attends a railroad switch

Switz *abbr* Switzerland

[1]**swiv•el** \ˈswi-vəl\ *n* **:** a device joining two parts so that one or both can turn freely

[2]**swivel** *vb* **-eled** *or* **-elled; -el•ing** *or* **-el•ling :** to swing or turn on or as if on a swivel

swiv•et \ˈswi-vət\ *n* **:** an agitated state

swiz•zle stick \ˈswi-zəl-\ *n* **:** a stick used to stir mixed drinks

swollen *past part of* SWELL

swoon \ˈswün\ *vb* **:** FAINT — **swoon** *n*

swoop \ˈswüp\ *vb* **:** to move with a sweep ⟨the eagle ~*ed* down on its prey⟩ — **swoop** *n*

swop *chiefly Brit var of* SWAP

sword \ˈsȯrd\ *n* **1 :** a weapon with a long blade for cutting or thrusting **2 :** the use of force

sword•fish \-ˌfish\ *n* **:** a very large ocean fish used for food that has the upper jaw prolonged into a long swordlike beak

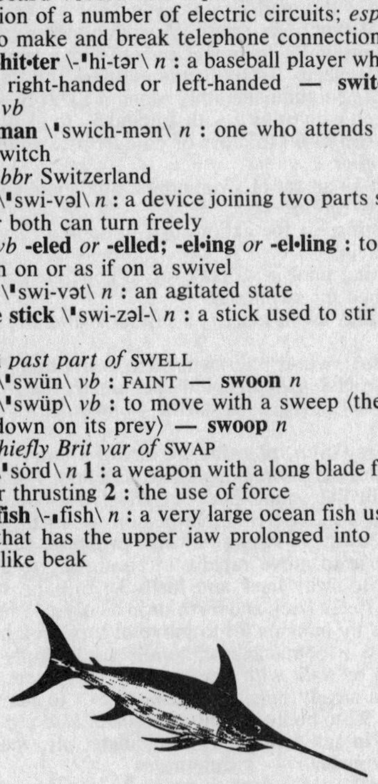

swordfish

sword•play \-ˌplā\ *n* **:** the art or skill of wielding a sword

swords•man \ˈsōrdz-mən\ *n* **:** one skilled in swordplay; *esp* **:** FENCER

sword•tail \ˈsōrd-ˌtāl\ *n* **:** a small brightly marked Central American fish

swore *past of* SWEAR

sworn *past part of* SWEAR

swum *past part of* SWIM

swung *past and past part of* SWING

syb•a•rite \ˈsi-bə-ˌrīt\ *n* **:** a lover of luxury **:** VOLUPTUARY — **syb•a•rit•ic** \ˌsi-bə-ˈri-tik\ *adj*

syc•a•more \ˈsi-kə-ˌmōr\ *n* **:** a large spreading tree of eastern and central No. America that has light brown flaky bark and small round fruits hanging on long stalks

sy•co•phant \ˈsi-kə-fənt\ *n* **:** a servile flatterer — **syc•o•phan•tic** \ˌsi-kə-ˈfan-tik\ *adj*

syl *or* **syll** *abbr* syllable

syl•lab•i•ca•tion \sə-ˌla-bə-ˈkā-shən\ *n* **:** the division of words into syllables

syl•lab•i•fy \sə-ˈla-bə-ˌfī\ *vb* **-fied; -fy•ing :** to form or divide into syllables — **syl•lab•i•fi•ca•tion** \-ˌla-bə-fə-ˈkā-shən\ *n*

syl•la•ble \ˈsi-lə-bəl\ *n* [ME, fr. MF *sillabe,* fr. L *syllaba,* fr. Gk *syllabē,* fr. *syllambanein* to gather together, fr. *syn* with + *lambanein* to take] **:** a unit of spoken language consisting of an uninterrupted utterance and forming either a whole word (as *cat*) or a commonly recognized division of a word (as *syl* in *syl-la-ble*); *also* **:** one or more letters representing such a unit — **syl•lab•ic** \sə-ˈla-bik\ *adj*

syl•la•bus \ˈsi-lə-bəs\ *n, pl* **-bi** \-ˌbī\ *or* **-bus•es :** a summary containing the heads or main topics of a speech, book, or course of study

syl•lo•gism \ˈsi-lə-ˌji-zəm\ *n* **:** a logical scheme of a formal argument consisting of a major and a minor premise and a conclusion which must logically be true if the premises are true — **syl•lo•gis•tic** \ˌsi-lə-ˈjis-tik\ *adj*

sylph \ˈsilf\ *n* **1 :** an imaginary being inhabiting the air **2 :** a slender graceful woman

syl•van \ˈsil-vən\ *adj* **1 :** living or located in a wooded area; *also* **:** of, relating to, or characteristic of forest **2 :** abounding in woods or trees

sym *abbr* **1** symbol **2** symmetrical

sym•bi•o•sis \ˌsim-ˌbī-ˈō-səs, -bē-\ *n, pl* **-o•ses** \-ˌsēz\ **:** the living together in close association of two dissimilar organisms esp. when mutually beneficial — **sym•bi•ot•ic** \-ˈä-tik\ *adj*

sym•bol \ˈsim-bəl\ *n* **1 :** something that stands for something else; *esp* **:** something concrete that represents or suggests another thing that cannot in itself be pictured ⟨the lion is a ~ of bravery⟩ **2 :** a letter, character, or sign used in writing or printing to represent operations, quantities, elements, sounds, or other ideas — **sym•bol•ic** \sim-ˈbä-lik\ *also* **sym•bol•i•cal** \-li-kəl\ *adj* — **sym•bol•i•cal•ly** \-k(ə-)lē\ *adv*

sym•bol•ise *Brit var of* SYMBOLIZE

sym•bol•ism \ˈsim-bə-ˌli-zəm\ *n* **:** representation of abstract or intangible things by means of symbols

sym•bol•ize \ˈsim-bə-ˌlīz\ *vb* **-ized; -iz•ing 1 :** to serve as a symbol of **2 :** to represent by symbols — **sym•bol•i•za•tion** \ˌsim-bə-lə-ˈzā-shən\ *n*

sym•me•try \ˈsi-mə-trē\ *n, pl* **-tries 1 :** an arrangement marked by regularity and balanced proportions **2 :** correspondence in size, shape, and position of parts that are on opposite sides of a dividing line or center — **sym•met•ri•cal** \sə-ˈme-tri-kəl\ *or* **sym•met•ric** \sə-ˈme-trik\ *adj* — **sym•met•ri•cal•ly** \-k(ə-)lē\ *adv*

sympathetic nervous system *n* **:** the part of the autonomic nervous system that is concerned esp. with preparing the body to react to situations of stress or emergency and that tends to decrease the tone and contractility of muscle not under direct voluntary control, increase the activity of the heart and the blood pressure, and cause the contraction of blood vessels

sym•pa•thise *chiefly Brit var of* SYMPATHIZE

sym•pa•thize \ˈsim-pə-ˌthīz\ *vb* **-thized; -thiz•ing** : to feel or show sympathy — **sym•pa•thiz•er** *n*

sym•pa•thy \ˈsim-pə-thē\ *n, pl* **-thies 1** : a relationship between persons or things wherein whatever affects one similarly affects the other **2** : harmony of interests and aims **3** : FAVOR, SUPPORT **4** : the capacity for entering into and sharing the feelings or interests of another; *also* : COMPASSION, PITY **5** : an expression of sorrow for another's loss, grief, or misfortune — **sym•pa•thet•ic** \ˌsim-pə-ˈthe-tik\ *adj* — **sym•pa•thet•i•cal•ly** \-ti-k(ə-)lē\ *adv*

sym•pho•ny \ˈsim-fə-nē\ *n, pl* **-nies 1** : harmony of sounds **2** : a large and complex composition for a full orchestra **3** : a large orchestra of a kind that plays symphonies — **sym•phon•ic** \sim-ˈfä-nik\ *adj*

sym•po•sium \sim-ˈpō-zē-əm\ *n, pl* **-sia** \-zē-ə\ *or* **-siums** : a conference at which a particular topic is discussed by various speakers; *also* : a collection of opinions about a subject

symp•tom \ˈsimp-təm\ *n* [LL *symptoma,* fr. Gk *symptōma* happening, attribute, symptom, fr. *sympiptein* to happen, fr. *syn* with + *piptein* to fall] **1** : something that indicates the presence of disease or abnormality; *esp* : something (as a headache) that can be sensed only by the individual affected **2** : SIGN, INDICATION — **symp•tom•at•ic** \ˌsimp-tə-ˈma-tik\ *adj*

syn *abbr* synonym; synonymous; synonymy

syn•a•gogue *or* **syn•a•gog** \ˈsi-nə-ˌgäg\ *n* [ME *synagoge,* fr. OF, fr. LL *synagoga,* fr. Gk *synagōgē* assembly, synagogue, fr. *synagein* to bring together] **1** : a Jewish congregation **2** : the house of worship of a Jewish congregation

syn•apse \ˈsi-ˌnaps, sə-ˈnaps\ *n* : the point at which a nervous impulse passes from one neuron to another

[1]**sync** *also* **synch** \ˈsiŋk\ *vb* **synced** *also* **synched** \ˈsiŋkt\; **sync•ing** *also* **synch•ing** \ˈsiŋ-kiŋ\ : SYNCHRONIZE

[2]**sync** *also* **synch** *n* : SYNCHRONIZATION, SYNCHRONISM — **sync** *adj*

syn•chro•nise *Brit var of* SYNCHRONIZE

syn•chro•nize \ˈsiŋ-krə-ˌnīz, ˈsin-\ *vb* **-nized; -niz•ing 1** : to occur or cause to occur at the same instant **2** : to represent, arrange, or tabulate according to dates or time **3** : to cause to agree in time **4** : to make synchronous in operation — **syn•chro•nism** \-ˌni-zəm\ *n* — **syn•chro•ni•za•tion** \ˌsiŋ-krə-nə-ˈzā-shən, ˌsin-\ *n* — **syn•chro•niz•er** *n*

syn•chro•nous \ˈsiŋ-krə-nəs, ˈsin-\ *adj* **1** : happening at the same time : CONCURRENT **2** : working, moving, or occurring together at the same rate and at the proper time

syn•co•pa•tion \ˌsiŋ-kə-ˈpā-shən, ˌsin-\ *n* : a shifting of the regular musical accent : occurrence of accented notes on the weak beat — **syn•co•pate** \ˈsiŋ-kə-ˌpāt, ˈsin-\ *vb*

syn•co•pe \ˈsiŋ-kə-(ˌ)pē, ˈsin-\ *n* : the loss of one or more sounds or letters in the interior of a word (as in *fo'c'sle* for *forecastle*)

[1]**syn•di•cate** \ˈsin-di-kət\ *n* **1** : a group of persons who combine to carry out a financial or industrial undertaking **2** : a loose association of racketeers **3** : a business concern that sells materials for publication in many newspapers and periodicals at the same time

[2]**syn•di•cate** \-də-ˌkāt\ *vb* **-cat•ed; -cat•ing 1** : to combine into or manage as a syndicate **2** : to publish through a syndicate — **syn•di•ca•tion** \ˌsin-də-ˈkā-shən\ *n*

syn•drome \ˈsin-ˌdrōm\ *n* : a group of signs and symptoms that occur together and characterize a particular abnormality

syn•er•gism \ˈsin-ər-ˌji-zəm\ *n* : interaction of discrete agencies (as industrial firms), agents (as drugs), or conditions such that the total effect is greater than the sum of the individual effects — **syn•er•gist** \-jist\ *n* — **syn•er•gis•tic** \ˌsi-nər-ˈjis-tik\ *adj* — **syn•er•gis•ti•cal•ly** \-ti-k(ə-)lē\ *adv*

syn•fuel \ˈsin-ˌfyül\ *n* [*syn*thetic] : a fuel derived esp. from a fossil fuel

syn•od \ˈsi-nəd\ *n* : COUNCIL, ASSEMBLY; *esp* : a religious governing body — **syn•od•al** \-nəd-ᵊl, -ˌnäd-ᵊl\ *adj* — **syn•od•ic** \-dik\ *or* **syn•od•i•cal** \sə-ˈnä-di-kəl\ *adj*

syn•onym \ˈsi-nə-ˌnim\ *n* : one of two or more words in the same language which have the same or very nearly the same meaning — **syn•on•y•mous** \sə-ˈnä-nə-məs\ *adj* — **syn•on•y•my** \-mē\ *n*

syn•op•sis \sə-ˈnäp-səs\ *n, pl* **-op•ses** \-ˌsēz\ : a condensed statement or outline (as of a treatise) : ABSTRACT

syn•op•tic \sə-ˈnäp-tik\ *also* **syn•op•ti•cal** \-ti-kəl\ *adj* : characterized by or affording a comprehensive view

syn•tax \ˈsin-ˌtaks\ *n* : the way in which words are put together to form phrases, clauses, or sentences — **syn•tac•tic** \sin-ˈtak-tik\ *or* **syn•tac•ti•cal** \-ti-kəl\ *adj*

syn•the•sis \ˈsin-thə-səs\ *n, pl* **-the•ses** \-ˌsēz\ : the combination of parts or elements into a whole; *esp* : the production of a substance by union of chemically simpler substances — **syn•the•size** \-ˌsīz\ *vb* — **syn•the•siz•er** *n*

syn•thet•ic \sin-ˈthe-tik\ *adj* : produced artificially esp. by chemical means; *also* : not genuine — **synthetic** *n* — **syn•thet•i•cal•ly** \-ti-k(ə-)lē\ *adv*

syph•i•lis \ˈsi-fə-ləs\ *n* [NL, fr. *Syphilus,* hero of the poem *Syphilis sive Morbus Gallicus* (*Syphilis or the French disease*) (1530) by Girolamo Fracastoro †1553 Ital. physician] : an infectious usu. venereal disease caused by a spirochete — **syph•i•lit•ic** \ˌsi-fə-ˈli-tik\ *adj or n*

sy•phon *var of* SIPHON

Syr•i•an \ˈsir-ē-ən\ *n* : a native or inhabitant of Syria — **Syrian** *adj*

[1]**sy•ringe** \sə-ˈrinj\ *n* : a device used esp. for injecting liquids into or withdrawing them from the body

[2]**syringe** *vb* **sy•ringed; sy•ring•ing** : to flush or cleanse with or as if with a syringe

syr•up \ˈsər-əp, ˈsir-əp\ *n* **1** : a thick sticky solution of sugar and water often flavored or medicated **2** : the concentrated juice of a fruit or plant — **syr•upy** *adj*

syst *abbr* system

sys•tem \ˈsis-təm\ *n* **1** : a group of units so combined as to form a whole and to operate in unison **2** : the body as a functioning whole; *also* : a group of bodily organs (as the nervous system) that together carry on some vital function **3** : a definite scheme or method of procedure or classification **4** : regular method or order — **sys•tem•at•ic** \ˌsis-tə-ˈma-tik\ *also* **sys•tem•at•i•cal** \-ti-kəl\ *adj* — **sys•tem•at•i•cal•ly** \-k(ə-)lē\ *adv*

sys•tem•a•tise *Brit var of* SYSTEMATIZE

sys•tem•a•tize \ˈsis-tə-mə-ˌtīz\ *vb* **-a•tized; -a•tiz•ing** : to make into a system : arrange methodically

[1]**sys•tem•ic** \sis-ˈte-mik\ *adj* **1** : of, relating to, or affecting the whole body ⟨~ disease⟩ **2** : of, relating to, or being a pesticide that when absorbed into the sap or bloodstream makes the entire plant or animal toxic to a pest (as an insect or fungus)

[2]**systemic** *n* : a systemic pesticide

systemic lupus erythematosus *n* : a systemic disease esp. of women characterized by fever, skin rash, and arthritis, often by anemia, by small hemorrhages of the skin and mucous membranes, and in serious cases by involvement of various internal organs

sys•tem•ize \ˈsis-tə-ˌmīz\ *vb* **-ized; -iz•ing** : SYSTEMATIZE

systems analyst *n* : a person who studies a procedure or business to determine its goals or purposes and to discover the best ways to accomplish them — **systems analysis** *n*

sys•to•le \ˈsis-tə-(ˌ)lē\ *n* : a rhythmically recurrent contraction of the heart — **sys•tol•ic** \sis-ˈtä-lik\ *adj*

T

¹t \ˈtē\ *n, pl* **t's** *or* **ts** \ˈtēz\ *often cap* **:** the 20th letter of the English alphabet

²t *abbr, often cap* **1** metric ton **2** tablespoon **3** teaspoon **4** temperature **5** ton **6** transitive **7** troy **8** true

T *abbr* **1** toddler **2** T-shirt

Ta *symbol* tantalum

TA *abbr* teaching assistant

¹tab \ˈtab\ *n* **1 :** a short projecting flap, loop, or tag; *also* **:** a small insert or addition **2 :** close surveillance **:** WATCH ⟨keep ~*s* on him⟩ **3 :** BILL, CHECK

²tab *vb* **tabbed; tab•bing :** DESIGNATE

tab•by \ˈta-bē\ *n, pl* **tabbies :** a usu. striped or mottled domestic cat; *also* **:** a female domestic cat

tab•er•na•cle \ˈta-bər-ˌna-kəl\ *n* [ME, fr. OF, fr. LL *tabernaculum,* fr. L, tent, fr. *taberna* hut] **1** *often cap* **:** a tent sanctuary used by the Israelites during the Exodus **2 :** a receptacle for the consecrated elements of the Eucharist **3 :** a house of worship

¹ta•ble \ˈtā-bəl\ *n* **1 :** a flat slab or plaque **:** TABLET **2 :** a piece of furniture consisting of a smooth flat top fixed on legs **3 :** a supply of food **:** BOARD, FARE **4 :** a group of people assembled at or as if at a table **5 :** an orderly arrangement of data usu. in rows and columns **6 :** a short list ⟨~ of contents⟩ **— ta•ble•top** \-ˌtäp\ *n*

²table *vb* **ta•bled; ta•bling 1** *Brit* **:** to place on the agenda **2 :** to remove (a parliamentary motion) from consideration indefinitely

tab•leau \ˈta-ˌblō\ *n, pl* **tab•leaux** \-ˌblōz\ *also* **tab•leaus** [F] **:** a scene or event usu. presented on a stage by costumed participants who remain silent and motionless

ta•ble•cloth \ˈtā-bəl-ˌklȯth\ *n* **:** a covering spread over a dining table before the table is set

ta•ble d'hôte \ˌtä-bəl-ˈdōt\ *n* [F, lit., host's table] **:** a complete meal of several courses offered at a fixed price

ta•ble•land \ˈtā-bəl-ˌland\ *n* **:** PLATEAU

ta•ble•spoon \-ˌspün\ *n* **1 :** a large spoon used esp. for serving **2 :** a unit of measure equal to ½ fluid ounce (15 milliliters)

ta•ble•spoon•ful \-ˌfu̇l\ *n, pl* **-spoonfuls** \-ˌfu̇lz\ *also* **-spoons•ful** \-ˌspünz-fu̇l\ **:** TABLESPOON 2

tab•let \ˈta-blət\ *n* **1 :** a flat slab suited for or bearing an inscription **2 :** a collection of sheets of paper glued together at one edge **3 :** a compressed or molded block of material; *esp* **:** a usu. disk-shaped medicated mass

table tennis *n* **:** a game resembling tennis played on a tabletop with wooden paddles and a small hollow plastic ball

ta•ble•ware \ˈtā-bəl-ˌwar\ *n* **:** utensils (as of china or silver) for table use

¹tab•loid \ˈta-ˌblȯid\ *adj* **:** condensed into small scope

²tabloid *n* **:** a newspaper marked by small pages, condensation of the news, and usu. many photographs; *esp* **:** one characterized by sensationalism

¹ta•boo *also* **ta•bu** \tə-ˈbü, ta-\ *adj* [Tongan (a Polynesian language) *tabu*] **:** prohibited by a taboo

²taboo *also* **tabu** *n, pl* **taboos** *also* **tabus 1 :** a prohibition against touching, saying, or doing something for fear of immediate harm from a supernatural force **2 :** a prohibition imposed by social custom

ta•bor *also* **ta•bour** \ˈtā-bər\ *n* **:** a small drum used to accompany a pipe or fife played by the same person

tab•u•lar \ˈta-byə-lər\ *adj* **1 :** having a flat surface **2 :** arranged in a table; *esp* **:** set up in rows and columns **3 :** computed by means of a table

tab•u•late \-ˌlāt\ *vb* **-lat•ed; -lat•ing :** to put into tabular form **— tab•u•la•tion** \ˌta-byə-ˈlā-shən\ *n* **— tab•u•la•tor** \ˈta-byə-ˌlā-tər\ *n*

TAC \ˈtak\ *abbr* Tactical Air Command

tach \ˈtak\ *n* **:** TACHOMETER

ta•chom•e•ter \ta-ˈkä-mə-tər, tə-\ *n* [ultim. fr. Gk *tachos* speed] **:** a device to indicate speed of rotation

tachy•car•dia \ˌta-ki-ˈkär-dē-ə\ *n* **:** relatively rapid heart action

tachy•on \ˈta-kē-ˌän\ *n* **:** a hypothetical particle held to travel faster than light

tac•it \ˈta-sət\ *adj* [F or L; F *tacite,* fr. L *tacitus* silent, fr. *tacēre* to be silent] **1 :** expressed without words or speech **2 :** implied or indicated but not actually expressed ⟨~ consent⟩ **— tac•it•ly** *adv* **— tac•it•ness** *n*

tac•i•turn \ˈta-sə-ˌtərn\ *adj* **:** disinclined to talk **syn** uncommunicative, reserved, reticent, closemouthed **— tac•i•tur•ni•ty** \ˌta-sə-ˈtər-nə-tē\ *n*

¹tack \ˈtak\ *vb* **1 :** to fasten with tacks; *also* **:** to add on **2 :** to change the direction of (a sailing ship) from one tack to another **3 :** to follow a zigzag course

²tack *n* **1 :** a small sharp nail with a broad flat head **2 :** the direction toward the wind that a ship is sailing ⟨starboard ~⟩; *also* **:** the run of a ship on one tack **3 :** a change of course from one tack to another **4 :** a zigzag course **5 :** a course of action

³tack *n* **:** gear for harnessing a horse

¹tack•le \ˈta-kəl, *naut often* ˈtā-\ *n* **1 :** GEAR, APPARATUS, EQUIPMENT **2 :** the rigging of a ship **3 :** an arrangement of ropes and pulleys for hoisting or pulling heavy objects **4 :** the act or an instance of tackling; *also* **:** a football lineman playing between guard and end

²tackle *vb* **tack•led; tack•ling 1 :** to attach and secure with or as if with tackle **2 :** to seize, grapple with, or throw down with the intention of subduing or stopping **3 :** to set about dealing with ⟨~ a problem⟩ **— tack•ler** *n*

¹tacky \ˈta-kē\ *adj* **tack•i•er; -est :** sticky to the touch

²tacky *adj* **tack•i•er; -est 1 :** SHABBY, SEEDY **2 :** marked by lack of style or good taste; *also* **:** cheaply showy

ta•co \ˈtä-kō\ *n, pl* **tacos** \-kōz\ [MexSp] **:** a usu. fried tortilla rolled up with or folded over a filling

tact \ˈtakt\ *n* [F, sense of touch, fr. L *tactus,* fr. *tangere* to touch] **:** a keen sense of what to do or say to keep good relations with others **— tact•ful** \-fəl\ *adj* **— tact•ful•ly** *adv* **— tact•less** *adj* **— tact•less•ly** *adv*

tac•tic \ˈtak-tik\ *n* **:** a planned action for accomplishing an end

tac•tics \ˈtak-tiks\ *n sing or pl* **1 :** the science of maneuvering forces in combat **2 :** the skill of using available means to reach an end **— tac•ti•cal** \-ti-kəl\ *adj* **— tac•ti•cian** \tak-ˈti-shən\ *n*

tac•tile \ˈtakt-ᵊl, ˈtak-ˌtīl\ *adj* **:** of, relating to, or perceptible through the sense of touch

tad•pole \ˈtad-ˌpōl\ *n* [ME *taddepol,* fr. *tode* toad + *polle* head] **:** an aquatic larva of a frog or toad that has a tail and gills

tae kwon do \ˈtī-ˈkwän-ˈdō\ *n* **:** a Korean martial art resembling karate

taf•fe•ta \ˈta-fə-tə\ *n* **:** a crisp lustrous fabric (as of silk or rayon)

taff•rail \ˈtaf-ˌrāl, -rəl\ *n* **:** the rail around a ship's stern

taf•fy \ˈta-fē\ *n, pl* **taffies :** a candy usu. of molasses or brown sugar stretched until porous and light-colored

¹tag \ˈtag\ *n* **1 :** a metal or plastic binding on an end of a shoelace **2 :** a piece of hanging or attached material **3 :** a hackneyed quotation or saying **4 :** a descriptive or identifying epithet

²tag *vb* **tagged; tag•ging 1 :** to provide or mark with or as if with a tag; *esp* **:** IDENTIFY **2 :** to attach as an addition **3 :** to follow closely and persistently ⟨~*s* along everywhere we go⟩ **4 :** to hold responsible for something

³tag *n* : a game in which one player chases others and tries to touch one of them

⁴tag *vb* **tagged; tag•ging 1** : to touch in or as if in a game of tag **2** : SELECT

TAG *abbr* the adjutant general

tag sale *n* : GARAGE SALE

Ta•hi•tian \tə-ˈhē-shən\ *n* **1** : a native or inhabitant of Tahiti **2** : the Polynesian language of the Tahitians — **Tahitian** *adj*

tai•ga \ˈtī-gə\ *n* [Russ *taĭga*] : a swampy coniferous subarctic forest extending south from the tundra

¹tail \ˈtāl\ *n* **1** : the rear end or a process extending from the rear end of an animal **2** : something resembling an animal's tail **3** *pl* : full evening dress for men **4** : the back, last, lower, or inferior part of something; *esp* : the reverse of a coin **5** : one who follows or keeps watch on someone — **tailed** \ˈtāld\ *adj* — **tail•less** \ˈtāl-ləs\ *adj*

²tail *vb* : FOLLOW; *esp* : to follow for the purpose of surveillance

tail•coat \-ˈkōt\ *n* : a coat with tails; *esp* : a man's full-dress coat with two long tapering skirts at the back

¹tail•gate \-ˌgāt\ *n* : a board or gate at the back end of a vehicle that can be let down (as for loading)

²tailgate *vb* **tail•gat•ed; tail•gat•ing 1** : to drive dangerously close behind another vehicle **2** : to hold a tailgate picnic

³tailgate *adj* : relating to or being a picnic set up on the tailgate esp. of a station wagon

tail•light \-ˌlīt\ *n* : a usu. red warning light mounted at the rear of a vehicle

¹tai•lor \ˈtā-lər\ *n* [ME *taillour,* fr. OF *tailleur,* fr. *taillier* to cut, fr. LL *taliare,* fr. L *talea* twig, cutting] : a person whose occupation is making or altering garments

²tailor *vb* **1** : to make or fashion as the work of a tailor **2** : to make or adapt to suit a special purpose

tail pipe *n* : an outlet by which the exhaust gases are removed from an engine (as of an automobile)

tail•spin \ˈtāl-ˌspin\ *n* : a rapid descent or downward spiral

tail wind *n* : a wind blowing in the same general direction as a course of movement (as of an aircraft)

¹taint \ˈtānt\ *vb* **1** : CORRUPT, CONTAMINATE **2** : to affect or become affected with something bad (as putrefaction)

²taint *n* : a contaminating mark or influence

Tai•wan•ese \ˌtī-wə-ˈnēz, -ˈnēs\ *n* : a native or inhabitant of Taiwan — **Taiwanese** *adj*

ta•ka \ˈtä-kə\ *n* — see MONEY table

¹take \ˈtāk\ *vb* **took** \ˈtu̇k\; **tak•en** \ˈtā-kən\; **tak•ing 1** : to get into one's hands or possession : GRASP, SEIZE **2** : CAPTURE; *also* : DEFEAT **3** : to obtain or secure for use **4** : to catch or attack through the effect of a sudden force or influence ⟨*taken* ill⟩ **5** : CAPTIVATE, DELIGHT **6** : to bring into a relation ⟨~ a wife⟩ **7** : REMOVE, SUBTRACT **8** : to pick out : CHOOSE **9** : ASSUME, UNDERTAKE **10** : RECEIVE, ACCEPT **11** : to use for transportation ⟨~ a bus⟩ **12** : to become impregnated with : ABSORB ⟨~*s* a dye⟩ **13** : to receive into one's body (as by swallowing) ⟨~ a pill⟩ **14** : ENDURE, UNDERGO **15** : to lead, carry, or cause to go along to another place **16** : NEED, REQUIRE **17** : to obtain as the result of a special procedure ⟨~ a snapshot⟩ **18** : to undertake and do, make, or perform ⟨~ a walk⟩ **19** : to take effect : ACT, OPERATE **syn** grab, clutch, snatch, seize, nab, grapple — **tak•er** *n* — **take advantage of 1** : to profit by **2** : EXPLOIT — **take after** : RESEMBLE — **take care** : to be careful — **take care of** : to care for : attend to — **take effect** : to become operative — **take exception** : OBJECT — **take for** : to suppose to be; *esp* : to mistake for — **take place** : HAPPEN — **take to 1** : to go to **2** : to apply or devote oneself to **3** : to conceive a liking for

²take *n* **1** : the number or quantity taken; *also* : PROCEEDS, RECEIPTS **2** : an act or the action of taking **3** : a television or movie scene filmed or taped at one time; *also* : a sound recording made at one time **4** : a distinct or personal point of view

take•off \ˈtā-ˌkȯf\ *n* **1** : IMITATION; *esp* : PARODY **2** : an act or instance of taking off

take off *vb* **1** : REMOVE **2** : DEDUCT **3** : to set out : go away **4** : to leave the surface; *esp* : to begin flight

take on *vb* **1** : to begin to perform or deal with; *also* : to contend with as an opponent **2** : ENGAGE, HIRE **3** : to assume or acquire as or as if one's own **4** : to make an unusual show of one's feelings esp. of grief or anger

take over *vb* : to assume control or possession of or responsibility for — **take•over** \ˈtā-ˌkō-vər\ *n*

take up *vb* **1** : PICK UP **2** : to begin to occupy **3** : to absorb or incorporate into itself ⟨plants *taking up* nutrients⟩ **4** : to begin to engage in ⟨*took up* jogging⟩ **5** : to make tighter or shorter ⟨*take up* the slack⟩

tak•ings \ˈtā-kiŋz\ *n pl* : receipts esp. of money

ta•la \ˈtä-lə\ *n, pl* **tala** — see MONEY table

talc \ˈtalk\ *n* : a soft mineral with a soapy feel used esp. in making toilet powder (**tal•cum powder** \ˈtal-kəm-\)

tale \ˈtāl\ *n* **1** : a relation of a series of events **2** : a report of a confidential matter **3** : idle talk; *esp* : harmful gossip **4** : a usu. imaginative narrative **5** : FALSEHOOD **6** : COUNT, TALLY

tal•ent \ˈta-lənt\ *n* **1** : an ancient unit of weight and value **2** : the natural endowments of a person **3** : a special often creative or artistic aptitude **4** : mental power : ABILITY **5** : a person of talent **syn** genius, gift, faculty, aptitude, knack — **tal•ent•ed** *adj*

ta•ler \ˈtä-lər\ *n* : any of numerous silver coins issued by German states from the 15th to the 19th centuries

tales•man \ˈtālz-mən\ *n* : a person summoned for jury duty

tal•is•man \ˈta-ləs-mən, -ləz-\ *n, pl* **-mans** [F *talisman* or Sp *talismán* or It *talismano,* fr. Ar *ṭilsam,* fr. MGk *telesma,* fr. Gk, consecration, fr. *telein* to initiate into the mysteries, complete, fr. *telos* end] : an object thought to act as a charm

¹talk \ˈtȯk\ *vb* **1** : to express in speech : utter words : SPEAK **2** : DISCUSS ⟨~ business⟩ **3** : to influence or cause by talking ⟨~*ed* him into going⟩ **4** : to use (a language) for communicating **5** : CONVERSE **6** : to reveal confidential information; *also* : GOSSIP **7** : to give a talk : LECTURE — **talk•er** *n* — **talk back** : to answer impertinently

²talk *n* **1** : the act of talking **2** : a way of speaking **3** : a formal discussion **4** : REPORT, RUMOR **5** : the topic of comment or gossip ⟨the ~ of the town⟩ **6** : an informal address or lecture

talk•ative \ˈtȯ-kə-tiv\ *adj* : given to talking **syn** loquacious, chatty, gabby, garrulous — **talk•ative•ly** *adv* — **talk•ative•ness** *n*

talk•ing–to \ˈtȯ-kiŋ-ˌtü\ *n* : REPRIMAND, REPROOF

talk radio *n* : radio programming consisting of call-in shows

tall \ˈtȯl\ *adj* **1** : high in stature; *also* : of a specified height ⟨six feet ~⟩ **2** : LARGE, FORMIDABLE ⟨a ~ order⟩ **3** : UNBELIEVABLE, IMPROBABLE ⟨a ~ story⟩ — **tall•ness** *n*

tal•low \ˈta-lō\ *n* : a hard white fat rendered usu. from cattle or sheep tissues and used esp. in candles

¹tal•ly \ˈta-lē\ *n, pl* **tallies** [ME *talye,* fr. ML *talea,* fr. L, twig, cutting] **1** : a device for visibly recording or accounting esp. business transactions **2** : a recorded account **3** : a corresponding part; *also* : CORRESPONDENCE

²tally *vb* **tal•lied; tal•ly•ing 1** : to mark on or as if on a tally **2** : to make a count of : RECKON; *also* : SCORE **3** : CORRESPOND, MATCH **syn** square, accord, harmonize, conform, jibe

tal•ly•ho \ˌta-lē-ˈhō\ *n, pl* **-hos** : a call of a huntsman at sight of the fox

Tal•mud \ˈtäl-ˌmu̇d, ˈtal-məd\ *n* [Late Heb *talmūdh,* lit., instruction] : the authoritative body of Jewish tradition — **Tal·mu·dic** \tal-ˈmü-dik, -ˈmyü-, -ˈmə-; täl-ˈmu̇-\ *adj* — **Tal·mud·ist** \ˈtäl-ˌmu̇-dist, ˈtal-mə-\ *n*

tal·on \ˈta-lən\ *n* : the claw of an animal and esp. of a bird of prey

ta·lus \ˈtā-ləs, ˈta-\ *n* : rock debris at the base of a cliff

tam \ˈtam\ *n* : TAM-O'-SHANTER

ta·ma·le \tə-ˈmä-lē\ *n* [MexSp *tamales*, pl. of *tamal* tamale, fr. Nahuatl (American Indian language) *tamalli* steamed cornmeal dough] : ground meat seasoned with chili, rolled in cornmeal dough, wrapped in corn husks, and steamed

tam·a·rack \ˈta-mə-ˌrak\ *n* : a larch of northern No. America; *also* : its hard resinous wood

tam·a·rind \ˈta-mə-rənd, -ˌrind\ *n* [Sp & Pg *tamarindo*, fr. Ar *tamr hindī*, lit., Indian date] : a tropical tree of the legume family with hard yellowish wood and feathery leaves; *also* : its acid fruit

tam·ba·la \täm-ˈbä-lə\ *n, pl* **-la** *or* **-las** — see *kwacha* at MONEY table

tam·bou·rine \ˌtam-bə-ˈrēn\ *n* : a small shallow drum with loose disks at the sides played by shaking or striking with the hand

[1]**tame** \ˈtām\ *adj* **tam·er; tam·est 1** : reduced from a state of native wildness esp. so as to be useful to humans : DOMESTICATED **2** : made docile : SUBDUED **3** : lacking spirit or interest : INSIPID **syn** submissive, domestic, domesticated — **tame·ly** *adv* — **tame·ness** *n*

[2]**tame** *vb* **tamed; tam·ing 1** : to make or become tame; *also* : to subject (land) to cultivation **2** : HUMBLE, SUBDUE — **tam·able** *or* **tame·able** \ˈtā-mə-bəl\ *adj* — **tame·less** *adj* — **tam·er** *n*

tam–o'–shan·ter \ˈta-mə-ˌshan-tər\ *n* [fr. poem *Tam o' Shanter* (1790) by Robert Burns †1796 Scot. poet] : a Scottish woolen cap with a wide flat circular crown and usu. a pom-pom in the center

tamp \ˈtamp\ *vb* : to drive down or in by a series of light blows

tam·per \ˈtam-pər\ *vb* **1** : to carry on underhand negotiations (as by bribery) ⟨~ with a witness⟩ **2** : to interfere so as to weaken or change for the worse ⟨~ with a document⟩ **3** : to try foolish or dangerous experiments

tam·pon \ˈtam-ˌpän\ *n* [F, lit., plug] : a plug (as of cotton) introduced into a body cavity usu. to absorb secretions (as from menstruation) or to arrest bleeding

[1]**tan** \ˈtan\ *vb* **tanned; tan·ning 1** : to change (hide) into leather esp. by soaking in a liquid containing tannin **2** : to make or become brown (as by exposure to the sun) **3** : WHIP, THRASH

[2]**tan** *n* **1** : a brown skin color induced by sun or weather **2** : a light yellowish brown color

[3]**tan** *abbr* tangent

tan·a·ger \ˈta-ni-jər\ *n* : any of numerous American birds that are often brightly colored

tan·bark \ˈtan-ˌbärk\ *n* : bark (as of oak or sumac) that is rich in tannin and used in tanning

[1]**tan·dem** \ˈtan-dəm\ *n* [L, at last, at length (taken to mean "lengthwise"), fr. *tam* so] **1** : a 2-seated carriage with horses hitched tandem; *also* : its team **2** : a bicycle for two persons sitting one behind the other — **in tandem** : in a tandem arrangement

[2]**tandem** *adv* : one behind another

[3]**tandem** *adj* **1** : consisting of things arranged one behind the other **2** : working in conjunction with each other

tang \ˈtaŋ\ *n* **1** : a part in a tool that connects the blade with the handle **2** : a sharp distinctive flavor; *also* : a pungent odor — **tangy** *adj*

[1]**tan·gent** \ˈtan-jənt\ *adj* [L *tangent-, tangens*, prp. of *tangere* to touch] : TOUCHING; *esp* : touching a circle or sphere at only one point

[2]**tangent** *n* **1** : a tangent line, curve, or surface **2** : an abrupt change of course — **tan·gen·tial** \tan-ˈjen-chəl\ *adj*

tan·ger·ine \ˈtan-jə-ˌrēn, ˌtan-jə-ˈrēn\ *n* : a deep orange loose-skinned citrus fruit; *also* : a tree that bears tangerines

[1]**tan·gi·ble** \ˈtan-jə-bəl\ *adj* **1** : perceptible esp. by the sense of touch : PALPABLE **2** : substantially real : MATERIAL ⟨~ rewards⟩ **3** : capable of being appraised **syn** appreciable, perceptible, sensible, discernible — **tan·gi·bil·i·ty** \ˌtan-jə-ˈbi-lə-tē\ *n*

[2]**tangible** *n* : something tangible; *esp* : a tangible asset

[1]**tan·gle** \ˈtaŋ-gəl\ *vb* **tan·gled; tan·gling 1** : to involve so as to hamper or embarrass; *also* : ENTRAP **2** : to unite or knit together in intricate confusion : ENTANGLE

[2]**tangle** *n* **1** : a tangled twisted mass **2** : a confusedly complicated state : MUDDLE

tan·go \ˈtaŋ-gō\ *n, pl* **tangos** : a dance of Latin-American origin — **tango** *vb*

tank \ˈtaŋk\ *n* **1** : a large artificial receptacle for liquids **2** : a heavily armed and armored combat vehicle that moves on tracks — **tank·ful** *n*

tan·kard \ˈtaŋ-kərd\ *n* : a tall one-handled drinking vessel

tank·er \ˈtaŋ-kər\ *n* : a vehicle equipped for transporting a liquid

tank top *n* : a sleeveless collarless pullover shirt with shoulder straps

tank town *n* : a small town

tan·ner \ˈta-nər\ *n* : one that tans hides

tan·nery \ˈta-nə-rē\ *n, pl* **-ner·ies** : a place where tanning is carried on

tan·nic acid \ˈta-nik-\ *n* : TANNIN

tan·nin \ˈta-nən\ *n* : any of various plant substances used esp. in tanning and dyeing, in inks, and as astringents

tan·sy \ˈtan-zē\ *n, pl* **tansies** [ME *tanesey*, fr. MF *tanesie*, fr. ML *athanasia*, fr. Gk, immortality, fr. *athanatos* immortal, fr. *a-* not + *thanatos* death] : a common weedy herb related to the daisies with an aromatic odor and bitter-tasting finely divided leaves

tan·ta·lise *Brit var of* TANTALIZE

tan·ta·lize \ˈtan-tə-ˌlīz\ *vb* **-lized; -liz·ing** [fr. *Tantalus*, king of Greek myth punished in Hades by having to stand up to his chin in water that receded as he bent to drink] : to tease or torment by presenting something desirable but keeping it out of reach — **tan·ta·liz·er** *n* — **tan·ta·liz·ing·ly** *adv*

tan·ta·lum \ˈtan-tə-ləm\ *n* : a hard ductile metallic chemical element — see ELEMENT table

tan·ta·mount \ˈtan-tə-ˌmau̇nt\ *adj* : equivalent in value or meaning

tan·trum \ˈtan-trəm\ *n* : a fit of bad temper

Tan·za·ni·an \ˌtan-zə-ˈnē-ən\ *n* : a native or inhabitant of Tanzania — **Tanzanian** *adj*

Tao·ism \ˈtau̇-ˌi-zəm, ˈdau̇-\ *n* : a Chinese mystical philosophy; *also* : a religion developed from Taoist philosophy and Buddhism — **Tao·ist** \-ist\ *adj or n*

[1]**tap** \ˈtap\ *n* **1** : FAUCET, COCK **2** : liquor drawn through a tap **3** : the removing of fluid from a container or cavity by tapping **4** : a tool for forming an internal screw thread **5** : a point in an electric circuit where a connection may be made

[2]**tap** *vb* **tapped; tap·ping 1** : to release or cause to flow by piercing or by drawing a plug from a container or cavity **2** : to pierce so as to let out or draw off a fluid **3** : to draw from ⟨~ resources⟩ **4** : to cut in on (a telephone wire) to get information; *also* : to cut in (an electrical circuit) on another circuit **5** : to form an internal screw thread in by means of a tap **6** : to connect (as a gas or water main) with a local supply — **tap·per** *n*

[3]**tap** *vb* **tapped; tap·ping 1** : to rap lightly **2** : to bring about by repeated light blows **3** : SELECT; *esp* : to elect to membership

[4]**tap** *n* **1** : a light blow or stroke; *also* : its sound **2** : a

small metal plate for the sole or heel of a shoe

ta•pa \ˈtä-pə, ˈta-\ *n* [Sp, lit., cover, lid] **:** an hors d'oeuvre served with drinks in Spanish bars — usu. used in pl.

[1]**tape** \ˈtāp\ *n* **1 :** a narrow band of woven fabric **2 :** a narrow flexible strip; *esp* **:** MAGNETIC TAPE

[2]**tape** *vb* **taped; tap•ing 1 :** to fasten or support with tape **2 :** to record on magnetic tape

tape deck *n* **:** a device used to play back magnetic tapes that usu. has to be connected to an audio system

tape measure *n* **:** a tape marked off in units (as inches) for measuring

[1]**ta•per** \ˈtā-pər\ *n* **1 :** a slender wax candle; *also* **:** a long waxed wick **2 :** a gradual lessening of thickness or width in a long object

[2]**taper** *vb* **ta•pered; ta•per•ing 1 :** to make or become gradually smaller toward one end **2 :** to diminish gradually

tape–re•cord \ˌtā-pri-ˈkȯrd\ *vb* **:** to make a recording of on magnetic tape — **tape recorder** *n* — **tape recording** *n*

tap•es•try \ˈta-pə-strē\ *n, pl* **-tries :** a heavy reversible textile that has designs or pictures woven into it and is used esp. as a wall hanging

tape•worm \ˈtāp-ˌwərm\ *n* **:** any of a class of long flat segmented worms parasitic in vertebrate intestines

tap•i•o•ca \ˌta-pē-ˈō-kə\ *n* **:** a usu. granular preparation of cassava starch used esp. in puddings; *also* **:** a dish (as pudding) that contains tapioca

ta•pir \ˈtā-pər\ *n, pl* **tapir** *or* **tapirs :** any of a genus of large harmless hoofed mammals of tropical America and Asia from Myanmar to Sumatra

tapir

tap•pet \ˈta-pət\ *n* **:** a lever or projection moved by some other piece (as a cam) or intended to move something else

tap•room \ˈtap-ˌrüm, -ˌru̇m\ *n* **:** BARROOM

tap•root \-ˌrüt, -ˌru̇t\ *n* **:** a large main root growing straight down and giving off small side roots

taps \ˈtaps\ *n sing or pl* **:** the last bugle call at night blown as a signal that lights are to be put out; *also* **:** a similar call blown at military funerals and memorial services

tap•ster \ˈtap-stər\ *n* **:** BARTENDER

[1]**tar** \ˈtär\ *n* **1 :** a thick dark sticky liquid distilled from organic material (as wood or coal) **2 :** SAILOR, SEAMAN

[2]**tar** *vb* **tarred; tar•ring :** to cover or smear with or as if with tar

tar•an•tel•la \ˌtar-ən-ˈte-lə\ *n* **:** a lively folk dance of southern Italy in 6/8 time

ta•ran•tu•la \tə-ˈran-chə-lə, -tə-lə\ *n, pl* **tarantulas** *also* **ta•ran•tu•lae** \-ˈran-chə-ˌlē, -tə-ˌlē\ **:** any of a family of large hairy American spiders with a sharp bite that is not very poisonous to human beings

tar•dy \ˈtär-dē\ *adj* **tar•di•er; -est 1 :** moving slowly **:** SLUGGISH **2 :** LATE **syn** behindhand, overdue, belated — **tar•di•ly** \-də-lē\ *adv* — **tar•di•ness** \-dē-nəs\ *n*

[1]**tare** \ˈtar\ *n* **:** a weed of grainfields

[2]**tare** *n* **:** a deduction from the gross weight of a substance and its container made in allowance for the weight of the container — **tare** *vb*

[1]**tar•get** \ˈtär-gət\ *n* [ME, fr. MF *targette,* dim. of *targe* light shield, of Gmc origin] **1 :** a mark to shoot at **2 :** an object of ridicule or criticism **3 :** a goal to be achieved

[2]**target** *vb* **:** to make a target of

tar•iff \ˈtar-əf\ *n* [It *tariffa,* fr. Ar *taʽrīf* notification] **1 :** a schedule of duties imposed by a government esp. on imported goods; *also* **:** a duty or rate of duty imposed in such a schedule **2 :** a schedule of rates or charges

tar•mac \ˈtär-ˌmak\ *n* **:** a surface paved with crushed stone covered with tar

tarn \ˈtärn\ *n* **:** a small mountain lake

tar•nish \ˈtär-nish\ *vb* **:** to make or become dull or discolored — **tarnish** *n*

ta•ro \ˈtär-ō, ˈtar-\ *n, pl* **taros :** a tropical plant related to the arums that is grown for its edible starchy fleshy root; *also* **:** this root

tar•ot \ˈtar-ō\ *n* **:** one of a set of usu. 78 playing cards used esp. for fortune-telling

tar•pau•lin \tär-ˈpȯ-lən, ˈtär-pə-\ *n* **:** a piece of material (as durable plastic) used for protecting exposed objects

tar•pon \ˈtär-pən\ *n, pl* **tarpon** *or* **tarpons :** a large silvery bony fish often caught for sport in the warm coastal waters of the Atlantic esp. off Florida

tar•ra•gon \ˈtar-ə-gən\ *n* **:** a small widely cultivated perennial wormwood with pungent leaves used as a flavoring; *also* **:** its leaves

[1]**tar•ry** \ˈtar-ē\ *vb* **tar•ried; tar•ry•ing 1 :** to be tardy **:** DELAY; *esp* **:** to be slow in leaving **2 :** to stay in or at a place **:** SOJOURN **syn** remain, wait, linger, abide

[2]**tar•ry** \ˈtär-ē\ *adj* **:** of, resembling, or smeared with tar

tar sand *n* **:** sand or sandstone that is naturally soaked with the heavy sticky portions of petroleum

tar•sus \ˈtär-səs\ *n, pl* **tar•si** \-ˌsī\ [NL] **:** the part of a vertebrate foot between the metatarsus and the leg; *also* **:** the small bones that support this part — **tarsal** \-səl\ *adj or n*

[1]**tart** \ˈtärt\ *adj* **1 :** agreeably sharp to the taste **:** PUNGENT **2 :** BITING, CAUSTIC — **tart•ly** *adv* — **tart•ness** *n*

[2]**tart** *n* **1 :** a small pie or pastry shell containing jelly, custard, or fruit **2 :** PROSTITUTE

tar•tan \ˈtärt-ᵊn\ *n* **:** a twilled woolen fabric with a plaid design of Scottish origin consisting of stripes of varying width and color usu. patterned to designate a distinctive clan

tar•tar \ˈtär-tər\ *n* **1 :** a substance in the juice of grapes deposited (as in wine casks) as a reddish crust or sediment **2 :** a hard crust of saliva, food debris, and calcium salts on the teeth

tar•tar sauce *or* **tar•tare sauce** \ˈtär-tər-\ *n* **:** mayonnaise with chopped pickles, olives, or capers

[1]**task** \ˈtask\ *n* [ME *taske,* fr. OF *tasque,* fr. ML *tasca* tax or service imposed by a feudal superior, fr. *taxare* to tax] **:** a piece of assigned work **syn** job, duty, chore, stint, assignment

[2]**task** *vb* **:** to oppress with great labor

task force *n* **:** a temporary grouping to accomplish a particular objective

task•mas•ter \ˈtask-ˌmas-tər\ *n* **:** one that imposes a task or burdens another with labor

[1]**tas•sel** \ˈta-səl, ˈtä-\ *n* **1 :** a hanging ornament made of a bunch of cords of even length fastened at one end **2 :** something suggesting a tassel; *esp* **:** a male flower cluster of Indian corn

[2]**tassel** *vb* **-seled** *or* **-selled; -sel•ing** *or* **-sel•ling :** to adorn with or put forth tassels

[1]**taste** \ˈtāst\ *vb* **tast•ed; tast•ing 1 :** EXPERIENCE, UNDERGO **2 :** to try or determine the flavor of by taking a bit into the mouth **3 :** to eat or drink esp. in small quantities **:** SAMPLE **4 :** to have a specific flavor

[2]**taste** *n* **1 :** a small amount tasted **2 :** BIT; *esp* **:** a sample

of experience **3** : the special sense that identifies sweet, sour, bitter, or salty qualities and is mediated by receptors in the taste buds of the tongue **4** : a quality perceptible to the sense of taste; *also* : a complex sensation involving true taste, smell, and touch **5** : individual preference **6** : critical judgment, discernment, or appreciation; *also* : aesthetic quality **syn** tang, relish, flavor, savor — **taste•ful** \-fəl\ *adj* — **taste•ful•ly** *adv* — **taste•less** *adj* — **taste•less•ly** *adv* — **tast•er** *n*

taste bud *n* : a sense organ mediating the sensation of taste

tasty \ˈtā-stē\ *adj* **tast•i•er; -est** : pleasing to the taste : SAVORY **syn** palatable, appetizing, toothsome, flavorsome — **tast•i•ness** \ˈtā-stē-nəs\ *n*

tat \ˈtat\ *vb* **tat•ted; tat•ting** : to work at or make by tatting

¹tat•ter \ˈta-tər\ *vb* : to make or become ragged

²tatter *n* **1** : a part torn and left hanging **2** *pl* : tattered clothing

tat•ter•de•ma•lion \ˌta-tər-di-ˈmāl-yən\ *n* : one that is ragged or disreputable

tat•ter•sall \ˈta-tər-ˌsȯl, -səl\ *n* : a pattern of colored lines forming squares on solid background; *also* : a fabric in a tattersall pattern

tat•ting \ˈta-tiŋ\ *n* : a delicate handmade lace formed usu. by looping and knotting with a single thread and a small shuttle; *also* : the act or process of making such lace

tat•tle \ˈtat-ᵊl\ *vb* **tat•tled; tat•tling 1** : CHATTER, PRATE **2** : to tell secrets; *also* : to inform against another — **tat•tler** *n*

tat•tle•tale \ˈtat-ᵊl-ˌtāl\ *n* : one that tattles : INFORMER

¹tat•too \ta-ˈtü\ *n, pl* **tattoos** [alter. of earlier *taptoo,* fr. D *taptoe,* fr. the phrase *tap toe!* taps shut!] **1** : a call sounded before taps as notice to go to quarters **2** : a rapid rhythmic rapping

²tattoo *vb* : to mark (the skin) with tattoos

³tattoo *n, pl* **tattoos** [Tahitian *tatau*] : an indelible figure fixed upon the body esp. by insertion of pigment under the skin

tau \ˈtau̇, ˈtȯ\ *n* : the 19th letter of the Greek alphabet— T or τ

taught *past and past part of* TEACH

¹taunt \ˈtȯnt\ *n* : a sarcastic challenge or insult

²taunt *vb* : to reproach or challenge in a mocking manner : jeer at **syn** mock, deride, ridicule, twit — **taunter** *n*

taupe \ˈtōp\ *n* : a brownish gray

Tau•rus \ˈtȯr-əs\ *n* [L, lit., bull] **1** : a zodiacal constellation between Aries and Gemini usu. pictured as a bull **2** : the 2d sign of the zodiac in astrology; *also* : one born under this sign

taut \ˈtȯt\ *adj* **1** : tightly drawn : not slack **2** : extremely nervous : TENSE **3** : TRIM, TIDY ⟨a ∼ ship⟩ — **tautly** *adv* — **taut•ness** *n*

tau•tol•o•gy \tȯ-ˈtä-lə-jē\ *n, pl* **-gies** : needless repetition of an idea, statement, or word; *also* : an instance of such repetition — **tau•to•log•i•cal** \ˌtȯt-ᵊl-ˈä-ji-kəl\ *adj* — **tau•to•log•i•cal•ly** \-ji-k(ə-)lē\ *adv* — **tau•tol•o•gous** \tȯ-ˈtä-lə-gəs\ *adj* — **tau•tol•o•gous•ly** *adv*

tav•ern \ˈta-vərn\ *n* [ME *taverne,* fr. OF, fr. L *taberna* hut, shop] **1** : an establishment where alcoholic liquors are sold to be drunk on the premises **2** : INN

taw \ˈtȯ\ *n* **1** : a marble used as a shooter **2** : the line from which players shoot at marbles

taw•dry \ˈtȯ-drē\ *adj* **taw•dri•er; -est** [*tawdry lace* a tie of lace for the neck, fr. *St. Audrey* (St. Etheldreda) †679 queen of Northumbria] : cheap and gaudy in appearance and quality **syn** garish, flashy, chintzy, meretricious — **taw•dri•ly** *adv*

taw•ny \ˈtȯ-nē\ *adj* **taw•ni•er; -est** : of a brownish orange color

¹tax \ˈtaks\ *vb* **1** : to levy a tax on **2** : CHARGE, ACCUSE **3** : to put under pressure — **tax•able** \ˈtak-sə-bəl\ *adj* — **tax•a•tion** \tak-ˈsā-shən\ *n*

²tax *n* **1** : a charge usu. of money imposed by authority on persons or property for public purposes **2** : a heavy charge : STRAIN

¹taxi \ˈtak-sē\ *n, pl* **tax•is** \-sēz\ *also* **tax•ies** : TAXICAB; *also* : a similarly operated boat or aircraft

²taxi *vb* **tax•ied; taxi•ing** *or* **taxy•ing; tax•is** *or* **taxies 1** : to move along the ground or on the water under an aircraft's own power when starting or after a landing **2** : to go by taxicab

taxi•cab \ˈtak-sē-ˌkab\ *n* : an automobile that carries passengers for a fare usu. based on the distance traveled

taxi•der•my \ˈtak-sə-ˌdər-mē\ *n* : the skill or occupation of preparing, stuffing, and mounting skins of animals — **taxi•der•mist** \-mist\ *n*

tax•on•o•my \tak-ˈsä-nə-mē\ *n* : classification esp. of animals or plants according to natural relationships — **tax•o•nom•ic** \ˌtak-sə-ˈnä-mik\ *adj* — **tax•on•o•mist** \tak-ˈsä-nə-mist\ *n*

tax•pay•er \ˈtaks-ˌpā-ər\ *n* : one who pays or is liable for a tax — **tax•pay•ing** *adj*

Tay–Sachs disease \ˈtā-ˈsaks-\ *n* : a hereditary disorder caused by the absence of an enzyme needed to break down fatty material, marked by buildup of lipids in nervous tissue, and causing death in childhood

tb *abbr* tablespoon; tablespoonful

Tb *symbol* terbium

TB \ˌtē-ˈbē\ *n* : TUBERCULOSIS

TBA *abbr, often not cap* to be announced

T–bar \ˈtē-ˌbär\ *n* : a ski lift with a series of T-shaped bars

tbs *or* **tbsp** *abbr* tablespoon; tablespoonful

Tc *symbol* technetium

TC *abbr* teachers college

T cell *n* : any of several lymphocytes (as a helper T cell) specialized esp. for activity in and control of immunity and the immune response

TD *abbr* **1** touchdown **2** Treasury Department

TDD *abbr* telecommunications device for the deaf

TDY *abbr* temporary duty

Te *symbol* tellurium

tea \ˈtē\ *n* **1** : the cured leaves and leaf buds of a shrub grown chiefly in China, Japan, India, and Sri Lanka; *also* : this shrub **2** : a drink made by steeping tea in boiling water **3** : refreshments usu. including tea served in late afternoon; *also* : a reception at which tea is served

teach \ˈtēch\ *vb* **taught** \ˈtȯt\; **teach•ing 1** : to cause to know something : act as a teacher **2** : to show how ⟨∼ a child to swim⟩ **3** : to make to know the disagreeable consequences of an action **4** : to guide the studies of **5** : to impart the knowledge of ⟨∼ algebra⟩ — **teachable** *adj* — **teach•er** *n*

teach•ing *n* **1** : the act, practice, or profession of a teacher **2** : something taught; *esp* : DOCTRINE

tea•cup \ˈtē-ˌkəp\ *n* : a small cup used with a saucer for hot beverages

teak \ˈtēk\ *n* : the hard durable yellowish brown wood of a tall East Indian timber tree related to the vervains; *also* : this tree

tea•ket•tle \ˈtē-ˌket-ᵊl\ *n* : a covered kettle with a handle and spout for boiling water

teal \ˈtēl\ *n, pl* **teal** *or* **teals 1** : any of various small short-necked wild ducks **2** : a dark greenish blue color

¹team \ˈtēm\ *n* [ME *teme,* fr. OE *tēam* offspring, lineage, group of draft animals] **1** : two or more draft animals harnessed to the same vehicle or implement **2** : a number of persons associated in work or activity; *esp* : a group on one side in a match

²team *vb* **1** : to haul with or drive a team **2** : to form a team : join forces

³team *adj* : of or performed by a team; *also* : marked by devotion to teamwork ⟨a ∼ player⟩

team•mate \-ˌmāt\ *n* : a fellow member of a team

teal 1

team•ster \ˈtēm-stər\ *n* : one that drives a team or truck

team•work \-ˌwərk\ *n* : the work or activity of a number of persons acting in close association as members of a unit

tea•pot \ˈtē-ˌpät\ *n* : a vessel with a spout for brewing and serving tea

[1]**tear** \ˈtir\ *n* : a drop of the salty liquid that moistens the eye and inner side of the eyelids; *also, pl* : an act of weeping or grieving — **tear•ful** \-fəl\ *adj* — **tear•ful•ly** *adv*

[2]**tear** \ˈtir\ *vb* : to fill with or shed tears ⟨eyes ~*ing* in the wind⟩

[3]**tear** \ˈtar\ *vb* **tore** \ˈtōr\; **torn** \ˈtōrn\; **tear•ing 1** : to separate parts of or pull apart by force : REND **2** : LACERATE **3** : to disrupt by the pull of contrary forces **4** : to remove by force : WRENCH **5** : to move or act with violence, haste, or force **syn** rip, split, cleave, rend

[4]**tear** \ˈtar\ *n* **1** : the act of tearing **2** : a hole or flaw made by tearing : RENT

tear gas \ˈtir-\ *n* : a substance that on dispersion in the atmosphere blinds the eyes with tears — **tear gas** *vb*

tear•jerk•er \ˈtir-ˌjər-kər\ *n* : an extravagantly pathetic story, song, play, movie, or broadcast

[1]**tease** \ˈtēz\ *vb* **teased; teas•ing 1** : to disentangle and lay parallel by combing or carding ⟨~ wool⟩ **2** : to scratch the surface of (cloth) so as to raise a nap **3** : to annoy persistently esp. in fun by goading, coaxing, or tantalizing **4** : to comb (hair) by taking a strand and pushing the short hairs toward the scalp with the comb **syn** harass, worry, pester, annoy

[2]**tease** *n* **1** : the act of teasing or state of being teased **2** : one that teases

tea•sel \ˈtē-zəl\ *n* : a prickly herb or its flower head covered with stiff bracts and used to raise the nap on cloth; *also* : an artificial device used for this purpose

tea•spoon \ˈtē-ˌspün\ *n* **1** : a small spoon suitable for stirring beverages **2** : a unit of measure equal to 1/6 fluid ounce (5 milliliters)

tea•spoon•ful \-ˌfu̇l\ *n, pl* **-spoonfuls** *also* **-spoons•ful** \-ˌspünz-ˌfu̇l\ : TEASPOON 2

teat \ˈtit, ˈtēt\ *n* : the protuberance through which milk is drawn from an udder or breast

tech *abbr* **1** technical; technically; technician **2** technological; technology

tech•ne•tium \tek-ˈnē-shē-əm\ *n* : a metallic chemical element produced in certain nuclear reactions — see ELEMENT table

tech•nic \ˈtek-nik, tek-ˈnēk\ *n* : TECHNIQUE 1

tech•ni•cal \ˈtek-ni-kəl\ *adj* [Gk *technikos* of art, skillful, fr. *technē* art, craft, skill] **1** : having special knowledge esp. of a mechanical or scientific subject ⟨~ experts⟩ **2** : of or relating to a particular and esp. a practical or scientific subject ⟨~ training⟩ **3** : according to a strict interpretation of the rules **4** : of or relating to technique — **tech•ni•cal•ly** \-k(ə-)lē\ *adv*

tech•ni•cal•i•ty \ˌtek-nə-ˈka-lə-tē\ *n, pl* **-ties 1** : a detail meaningful only to a specialist **2** : the quality or state of being technical

technical sergeant *n* : a noncommissioned officer in the air force ranking next below a master sergeant

tech•ni•cian \tek-ˈni-shən\ *n* : a person who has acquired the technique of a specialized skill or subject

tech•nique \tek-ˈnēk\ *n* [F] **1** : the manner in which technical details are treated or basic physical movements are used **2** : technical methods

tech•noc•ra•cy \tek-ˈnä-krə-sē\ *n* : management of society by technical experts — **tech•no•crat** \ˈtek-nə-ˌkrat\ *n* — **tech•no•crat•ic** \ˌtek-nə-ˈkra-tik\ *adj*

tech•nol•o•gy \tek-ˈnä-lə-jē\ *n, pl* **-gies** : ENGINEERING; *also* : a manner of accomplishing a task using technical methods or knowledge — **tech•no•log•i•cal** \ˌtek-nə-ˈlä-ji-kəl\ *adj*

tec•ton•ics \tek-ˈtä-niks\ *n sing or pl* **1** : geological structural features **2** : geology dealing esp. with the faulting and folding of a planet or moon — **tec•ton•ic** \-nik\ *adj*

ted•dy bear \ˈte-dē-ˌbar\ *n* [*Teddy* Roosevelt; fr. a cartoon depicting the president sparing the life of a bear cub while hunting] : a stuffed toy bear

te•dious \ˈtē-dē-əs\ *adj* : tiresome because of length or dullness **syn** boring, tiring, irksome — **te•dious•ly** *adv* — **te•dious•ness** *n*

te•di•um \ˈtē-dē-əm\ *n* : TEDIOUSNESS; *also* : BOREDOM

[1]**tee** \ˈtē\ *n* : a small mound or peg on which a golf ball is placed to be hit at the beginning of play on a hole; *also* : the area from which the ball is hit to begin play

[2]**tee** *vb* **teed; tee•ing** : to place (a ball) on a tee

teem \ˈtēm\ *vb* : to become filled to overflowing : ABOUND **syn** swarm, crawl, flow

teen *adj* : TEENAGE

teen•age \ˈtē-ˌnāj\ *or* **teen•aged** \-ˌnājd\ *adj* : of, being, or relating to people in their teens — **teen•ag•er** \-ˌnā-jər\ *n*

teens \ˈtēnz\ *n pl* : the numbers 13 to 19 inclusive; *esp* : the years 13 to 19 in a person's life

tee•ny \ˈtē-nē\ *adj* **tee•ni•er; -est** : TINY

tee•pee *var of* TEPEE

tee shirt *var of* T-SHIRT

tee•ter \ˈtē-tər\ *vb* **1** : to move unsteadily **2** : SEESAW — **teeter** *n*

teeth *pl of* TOOTH

teethe \ˈtēth\ *vb* **teethed; teeth•ing** : to grow teeth : cut one's teeth

teeth•ing *n* : growth of the first set of teeth through the gums with its accompanying phenomena

tee•to•tal \ˈtē-ˈtōt-ᵊl, -ˌtōt-\ *adj* : of or relating to the practice of complete abstinence from alcoholic drinks — **tee•to•tal•er** *or* **tee•to•tal•ler** \-ˈtōt-ᵊl-ər\ *n* — **tee•to•tal•ism** \-ᵊl-ˌi-zəm\ *n*

TEFL *abbr* teaching English as a foreign language

tek•tite \ˈtek-ˌtīt\ *n* : a glassy body of probably meteoric origin

tel *abbr* **1** telegram **2** telegraph **3** telephone

tele•cast \ˈte-li-ˌkast\ *vb* **-cast** *also* **-cast•ed; -cast•ing** : to broadcast by television — **telecast** *n* — **tele•cast•er** *n*

tele•com•mu•ni•ca•tion \ˌte-li-kə-ˌmyü-nə-ˈkā-shən\ *n* : communication at a distance (as by telephone or radio)

tele•com•mute \ˈte-li-kə-ˌmyüt\ *vb* : to work at home by the use of an electronic linkup with a central office

tele•con•fer•ence \ˈte-li-ˌkän-fə-rəns\ *n* : a conference among people remote from one another held using telecommunications — **tele•con•fer•enc•ing** *n*

teleg *abbr* telegraphy

tele•ge•nic \ˌte-lə-ˈje-nik, -ˈjē-\ *adj* : markedly attractive to television viewers

tele•gram \ˈte-lə-ˌgram\ *n* : a message sent by telegraph

[1]**tele•graph** \-ˌgraf\ *n* : an electric apparatus or system for sending messages by a code over wires — **tele•graph•ic** \ˌte-lə-ˈgra-fik\ *adj*

[2]**telegraph** *vb* : to send or communicate by or as if by telegraph — **te•leg•ra•pher** \tə-ˈle-grə-fər\ *n*

te•leg•ra•phy \tə-ˈle-grə-fē\ *n* : the use or operation of a telegraph apparatus or system

tele•mar•ket•ing \ˌte-lə-ˈmär-kə-tiŋ\ *n* : the marketing

DICTIONARY

of goods or services by telephone — **tele•mar•ket•er** \-tər\ *n*

te•lem•e•try \tə-ˈle-mə-trē\ *n* : the transmission esp. by radio of measurements made by automatic instruments to a distant station — **tele•me•ter** \ˈte-lə-ˌmē-tər\ *n*

te•lep•a•thy \tə-ˈle-pə-thē\ *n* : apparent communication from one mind to another by extrasensory means — **tele•path•ic** \ˌte-lə-ˈpa-thik\ *adj* — **tele•path•i•cal•ly** \-thi-k(ə-)lē\ *adv*

¹tele•phone \ˈte-lə-ˌfōn\ *n* : an instrument for sending and receiving sounds over long distances by electricity

²telephone *vb* **-phoned; -phon•ing** **1** : to send or communicate by telephone **2** : to speak to (a person) by telephone — **tele•phon•er** *n*

te•le•pho•ny \tə-ˈle-fə-nē, ˈte-lə-ˌfō-\ *n* : use or operation of apparatus for transmission of sounds between distant points — **tel•e•phon•ic** \ˌte-lə-ˈfä-nik\ *adj*

tele•pho•to \ˌte-lə-ˈfō-tō\ *adj* : being a camera lens giving a large image of a distant object — **tele•pho•tog•ra•phy** \-fə-ˈtä-grə-fē\ *n*

tele•play \ˈte-li-ˌplā\ *n* : a play written for television

tele•print•er \ˈte-lə-ˌprin-tər\ *n* : TELETYPEWRITER

¹tele•scope \ˈte-lə-ˌskōp\ *n* **1** : a cylindrical instrument equipped with lenses or mirrors for viewing distant objects **2** : RADIO TELESCOPE

²telescope *vb* **-scoped; -scop•ing** **1** : to slide or pass or cause to slide or pass one within another like the sections of a collapsible hand telescope **2** : COMPRESS, CONDENSE

tele•scop•ic \ˌte-lə-ˈskä-pik\ *adj* **1** : of or relating to a telescope **2** : seen only by a telescope **3** : able to discern objects at a distance **4** : having parts that telescope — **tele•scop•i•cal•ly** \-pi-k(ə-)lē\ *adv*

tele•text \ˈte-lə-ˌtekst\ *n* : a system for broadcasting text over a television signal and displaying it on a decoder-equipped television

tele•thon \ˈte-lə-ˌthän\ *n* : a long television program usu. to solicit funds for a charity

tele•type•writ•er \ˌte-lə-ˈtīp-ˌrī-tər\ *n* : a printing device resembling a typewriter used to send and receive signals over telephone lines

tele•vise \ˈte-lə-ˌvīz\ *vb* **-vised; -vis•ing** : to broadcast by television

tele•vi•sion \ˈte-lə-ˌvi-zhən\ *n* [F *télévision,* fr. Gk *tēle* far, at a distance + F *vision* vision] : a system for transmitting images and sound by converting them into electrical or radio waves which are converted back into images and sound by a receiver; *also* : a television receiving set

tell \ˈtel\ *vb* **told** \ˈtōld\; **tell•ing** **1** : COUNT, ENUMERATE **2** : to relate in detail : NARRATE **3** : SAY, UTTER **4** : to make known : REVEAL **5** : to report to : INFORM **6** : ORDER, DIRECT **7** : to find out by observing **8** : to have a marked effect **9** : to serve as evidence **syn** disclose, discover, betray

tell•er \ˈte-lər\ *n* **1** : one that relates : NARRATOR **2** : one that counts **3** : a bank employee handling money received or paid out

tell•ing \ˈte-liŋ\ *adj* : producing a marked effect : EFFECTIVE **syn** cogent, convincing, sound

tell off *vb* : REPRIMAND, SCOLD

tell•tale \ˈtel-ˌtāl\ *n* **1** : INFORMER, TATTLETALE **2** : something that serves to disclose : INDICATION — **telltale** *adj*

tel•lu•ri•um \tə-ˈlu̇r-ē-əm\ *n* : a chemical element used esp. in alloys — see ELEMENT table

tem•blor \ˈtem-blər\ *n* [Sp, lit., trembling] : EARTHQUAKE

te•mer•i•ty \tə-ˈmer-ə-tē\ *n, pl* **-ties** : rash or presumptuous daring : BOLDNESS **syn** audacity, effrontery, gall, nerve, cheek

¹temp \ˈtemp\ *n* **1** : TEMPERATURE **2** : a temporary worker

²temp *abbr* temporary

¹tem•per \ˈtem-pər\ *vb* **1** : to dilute or soften by the addition of something else ⟨~ justice with mercy⟩ **2** : to bring (as steel) to a desired hardness by reheating and cooling **3** : to toughen (glass) by gradual heating and cooling **4** : TOUGHEN **5** : TUNE

²temper *n* **1** : characteristic tone : TENDENCY **2** : the hardness or toughness of a substance ⟨~ of a knife blade⟩ **3** : a characteristic frame of mind : DISPOSITION **4** : calmness of mind : COMPOSURE **5** : state of feeling or frame of mind at a particular time **6** : heat of mind or emotion **syn** temperament, character, personality, makeup — **tem•pered** \ˈtem-pərd\ *adj*

tem•pera \ˈtem-pə-rə\ *n* [It] : a painting process using an albuminous or colloidal medium as a vehicle; *also* : a painting done in tempera

tem•per•a•ment \ˈtem-prə-mənt, -pər-mənt\ *n* **1** : characteristic or habitual inclination or mode of emotional response : DISPOSITION ⟨nervous ~⟩ **2** : excessive sensitiveness or irritability **syn** character, personality, nature, makeup — **tem•per•a•men•tal** \ˌtem-prə-ˈment-ᵊl, -pər-ˈment-\ *adj*

tem•per•ance \ˈtem-prəns, -pə-rəns\ *n* : habitual moderation in the indulgence of the appetites or passions; *esp* : moderation in or abstinence from the use of intoxicating drink

tem•per•ate \ˈtem-prət, -pə-rət\ *adj* **1** : not extreme or excessive : MILD **2** : moderate in indulgence of appetite or desire **3** : moderate in the use of intoxicating liquors **4** : having a moderate climate **syn** sober, continent, abstemious

temperate zone *n, often cap T&Z* : the region between the tropic of Cancer and the arctic circle or between the tropic of Capricorn and the antarctic circle

tem•per•a•ture \ˈtem-pər-ˌchu̇r, -prə-ˌchu̇r, -chər\ *n* **1** : degree of hotness or coldness of something (as air, water, or the body) as shown by a thermometer **2** : FEVER

tem•pest \ˈtem-pəst\ *n* [ME, fr. OF *tempeste,* ultim. fr. L *tempestas* season, weather, storm, fr. *tempus* time] : a violent storm

tem•pes•tu•ous \tem-ˈpes-chə-wəs\ *adj* : of, involving, or resembling a tempest : STORMY — **tem•pes•tu•ous•ly** *adv* — **tem•pes•tu•ous•ness** *n*

tem•plate *also* **tem•plet** \ˈtem-plət\ *n* : a gauge, mold, or pattern that functions as a guide to the form or structure of something being made

¹tem•ple \ˈtem-pəl\ *n* **1** : an edifice for the worship of a deity **2** : a place devoted to a special or exalted purpose

²temple *n* : the flattened space on each side of the forehead esp. of humans

tem•po \ˈtem-pō\ *n, pl* **tem•pi** \-(ˌ)pē\ *or* **tempos** [It, lit., time] **1** : the rate of speed of a musical piece or passage **2** : rate of motion or activity : PACE

¹tem•po•ral \ˈtem-pə-rəl\ *adj* **1** : of, relating to, or limited by time ⟨~ and spatial bounds⟩ **2** : of or relating to earthly life or secular concerns ⟨~ power⟩

²temporal *adj* : of or relating to the temples or the sides of the skull

¹tem•po•rary \ˈtem-pə-ˌrer-ē\ *adj* : lasting for a time only : TRANSITORY **syn** transient, ephemeral, momentary, impermanent — **tem•po•rar•i•ly** \ˌtem-pə-ˈrer-ə-lē\ *adv*

²temporary *n, pl* **-rar•ies** : one serving for a limited time

tem•po•rise *Brit var of* TEMPORIZE

tem•po•rize \ˈtem-pə-ˌrīz\ *vb* **-rized; -riz•ing** **1** : to adapt one's actions to the time or the dominant opinion : COMPROMISE **2** : to draw out matters so as to gain time — **tem•po•riz•er** *n*

tempt \ˈtempt\ *vb* **1** : to entice to do wrong by promise of pleasure or gain **2** : PROVOKE **3** : to risk the dangers of **4** : to induce to do something : INCITE **syn** inveigle, decoy, seduce, lure — **tempt•er** *n* — **tempt•ing•ly** *adv*

temp•ta•tion \temp-ˈtā-shən\ *n* **1** : the act of tempting

: the state of being tempted **2** : something that tempts
tempt•ress \ˈtemp-trəs\ *n* : a woman who tempts
ten \ˈten\ *n* **1** : one more than nine **2** : the 10th in a set or series **3** : something having 10 units — **ten** *adj or pron* — **tenth** \ˈtenth\ *adj or adv or n*
ten•a•ble \ˈte-nə-bəl\ *adj* : capable of being held, maintained, or defended — **ten•a•bil•i•ty** \ˌte-nə-ˈbi-lə-tē\ *n*
te•na•cious \tə-ˈnā-shəs\ *adj* **1** : not easily pulled apart : COHESIVE, TOUGH ⟨a ~ metal⟩ **2** : holding fast ⟨~ of his rights⟩ **3** : RETENTIVE ⟨a ~ memory⟩ — **te•na•cious•ly** *adv* — **te•nac•i•ty** \tə-ˈna-sə-tē\ *n*
ten•an•cy \ˈte-nən-sē\ *n, pl* **-cies** : the temporary possession or occupancy of something (as a house) that belongs to another; *also* : the period of a tenant's occupancy
ten•ant \ˈte-nənt\ *n* **1** : one who rents or leases (as a house) from a landlord **2** : DWELLER, OCCUPANT — **tenant** *vb* — **ten•ant•less** *adj*
tenant farmer *n* : a farmer who works land owned by another and pays rent either in cash or in shares of produce
ten•ant•ry \ˈte-nən-trē\ *n, pl* **-ries** : the body of tenants esp. on a great estate
Ten Commandments *n pl* : the commandments of God given to Moses on Mount Sinai
¹tend \ˈtend\ *vb* **1** : to apply oneself ⟨~ to your affairs⟩ **2** : to take care of ⟨~ a plant⟩ **3** : to manage the operations of ⟨~ a machine⟩
²tend *vb* **1** : to move or develop one's course in a particular direction **2** : to show an inclination or tendency
ten•den•cy \ˈten-dən-sē\ *n, pl* **-cies** **1** : DRIFT, TREND **2** : a proneness to or readiness for a particular kind of thought or action : PROPENSITY **syn** bent, leaning, disposition, inclination
ten•den•tious \ten-ˈden-chəs\ *adj* : marked by a tendency in favor of a particular point of view : BIASED — **ten•den•tious•ly** *adv* — **ten•den•tious•ness** *n*
¹ten•der \ˈten-dər\ *adj* **1** : having a soft texture : easily broken, chewed, or cut **2** : physically weak : DELICATE; *also* : IMMATURE **3** : expressing or responsive to love or sympathy : LOVING, COMPASSIONATE **4** : SENSITIVE, TOUCHY **syn** sympathetic, warm, warmhearted — **ten•der•ly** *adv* — **ten•der•ness** *n*
²tender *n* **1** : an offer or proposal made for acceptance; *esp* : an offer of a bid for a contract **2** : something (as money) that may be offered in payment
³tender *vb* : to present for acceptance
⁴tend•er \ˈten-dər\ *n* **1** : one that tends or takes care **2** : a boat carrying passengers and freight to a larger ship **3** : a car attached to a steam locomotive for carrying fuel and water
ten•der•foot \ˈten-dər-ˌfu̇t\ *n, pl* **-feet** \-ˌfēt\ *also* **-foots** \-ˌfu̇ts\ **1** : one not hardened to frontier or rough outdoor life **2** : an inexperienced beginner
ten•der•heart•ed \ˌten-dər-ˈhär-təd\ *adj* : easily moved to love, pity, or sorrow
ten•der•ize \ˈten-də-ˌrīz\ *vb* **-ized; -iz•ing** : to make (meat) tender — **ten•der•iz•er** \ˈten-də-ˌrī-zər\ *n*
ten•der•loin \ˈten-dər-ˌlȯin\ *n* **1** : a tender strip of beef or pork from near the backbone **2** : a district of a city largely devoted to vice
ten•di•ni•tis *or* **ten•don•itis** \ˌten-də-ˈnī-təs\ *n* : inflammation of a tendon
ten•don \ˈten-dən\ *n* : a tough cord of dense white fibrous tissue uniting a muscle with another part (as a bone) — **ten•di•nous** \-də-nəs\ *adj*
ten•dril \ˈten-drəl\ *n* : a slender coiling organ by which some climbing plants attach themselves to a support
ten•e•brous \ˈte-nə-brəs\ *adj* : shut off from the light : GLOOMY, OBSCURE
ten•e•ment \ˈte-nə-mənt\ *n* **1** : a house used as a dwelling **2** : a building divided into apartments for rent to families; *esp* : one meeting only minimum standards of safety and comfort **3** : APARTMENT, FLAT
te•net \ˈte-nət\ *n* [L, he holds, fr. *tenēre* to hold] : one of the principles or doctrines held in common by members of a group (as a church or profession) **syn** doctrine, dogma, belief
ten•fold \ˈten-ˌfōld, -ˈfōld\ *adj* : being 10 times as great or as many — **ten•fold** \-ˈfōld\ *adv*
ten–gallon hat *n* : a wide-brimmed hat with a large soft crown
Tenn *abbr* Tennessee
ten•nis \ˈte-nəs\ *n* : a game played with a ball and racket on a court divided by a net
ten•on \ˈte-nən\ *n* : a projecting part in a piece of material (as wood) for insertion into a mortise to make a joint
ten•or \ˈte-nər\ *n* **1** : the general drift of something spoken or written **2** : the highest natural adult male voice; *also* : a singer having this voice **3** : a continuing in a course, movement, or activity ⟨the ~ of my life⟩
ten•our *chiefly Brit var of* TENOR
ten•pen•ny \ˈten-ˈpe-nē\ *adj* : amounting to, worth, or costing 10 pennies
tenpenny nail *n* : a nail three inches (about 7.6 centimeters) long
ten•pin \ˈten-ˌpin\ *n* : a bottle-shaped bowling pin set in groups of 10 and bowled at in a game **(tenpins)**
¹tense \ˈtens\ *n* [ME *tens* time, tense, fr. MF, fr. L *tempus*] : distinction of form of a verb to indicate the time of the action or state
²tense *adj* **tens•er; tens•est** [L *tensus*, fr. pp. of *tendere* to stretch] **1** : stretched tight : TAUT **2** : feeling or showing nervous tension **syn** stiff, rigid, inflexible — **tense•ly** *adv* — **tense•ness** *n* — **ten•si•ty** \ˈten-sə-tē\ *n*
³tense *vb* **tensed; tens•ing** : to make or become tense
ten•sile \ˈten-səl, -ˌsīl\ *adj* : of or relating to tension ⟨~ strength⟩
ten•sion \ˈten-chən\ *n* **1** : the act of straining or stretching; *also* : the condition of being strained or stretched **2** : a state of mental unrest often with signs of bodily stress **3** : a state of latent hostility or opposition
ten–speed \ˈten-ˌspēd\ *n* : a bicycle with a derailleur having 10 possible combinations of gears
¹tent \ˈtent\ *n* **1** : a collapsible shelter of material stretched and supported by poles **2** : a canopy placed over the head and shoulders to retain vapors or oxygen given for medical reasons
²tent *vb* **1** : to lodge in tents **2** : to cover with or as if with a tent
ten•ta•cle \ˈten-ti-kəl\ *n* : any of various long flexible projections about the head or mouth (as of an insect, mollusk, or fish) — **ten•ta•cled** \-kəld\ *adj* — **ten•tac•u•lar** \ten-ˈta-kyə-lər\ *adj*
ten•ta•tive \ˈten-tə-tiv\ *adj* **1** : not fully worked out or developed ⟨~ plans⟩ **2** : HESITANT, UNCERTAIN ⟨a ~ smile⟩ — **ten•ta•tive•ly** *adv*
ten•u•ous \ˈten-yə-wəs\ *adj* **1** : not dense : RARE ⟨a ~ fluid⟩ **2** : not thick : SLENDER ⟨a ~ rope⟩ **3** : having little substance : FLIMSY, WEAK ⟨~ influences⟩ **4** : lacking stability : SHAKY ⟨~ reasoning⟩ — **te•nu•i•ty** \te-ˈnü-ə-tē, tə-, -ˈnyü-\ *n* — **ten•u•ous•ly** *adv* — **ten•u•ous•ness** *n*
ten•ure \ˈten-yər\ *n* : the act, right, manner, or period of holding something (as a landed property, an office, or a position)
ten•ured \ˈten-yərd\ *adj* : having tenure ⟨~ faculty members⟩
te•o•sin•te \ˌtā-ō-ˈsin-tē\ *n* : a tall annual grass of Mexico and Central America closely related to maize
te•pee \ˈtē-(ˌ)pē\ *n* [Dakota *tʰípi*, fr. *tʰi-* to dwell] : an American Indian conical tent usu. of skins
tep•id \ˈte-pəd\ *adj* **1** : moderately warm : LUKEWARM **2** : HALFHEARTED
te•qui•la \tə-ˈkē-lə, tā-\ *n* : a Mexican liquor made from mescal
ter *abbr* **1** terrace **2** territory

ter•bi•um \ˈtər-bē-əm\ *n* : a metallic chemical element — see ELEMENT table

ter•cen•te•na•ry \ˌtər-ˌsen-ˈte-nə-rē, tər-ˈsent-ᵊn-ˌer-ē\ *n, pl* **-ries** : a 300th anniversary or its celebration — **tercentenary** *adj*

ter•cen•ten•ni•al \ˌtər-ˌsen-ˈte-nē-əl\ *adj or n* : TERCENTENARY

te•re•do \tə-ˈrē-dō, -ˈrā-\ *n, pl* **teredos** *or* **te•red•i•nes** \-ˈred-ᵊn-ˌēz\ [L] : SHIPWORM

[1]**term** \ˈtərm\ *n* **1** : END, TERMINATION **2** : DURATION; *esp* : a period of time fixed esp. by law or custom **3** : a mathematical expression connected with another by a plus or minus sign; *also* : an element (as a numerator) of a fraction or proportion **4** : a word or expression that has a precise meaning in some uses or is limited to a particular subject or field **5** *pl* : PROVISIONS, CONDITIONS ⟨~*s* of a contract⟩ **6** *pl* : mutual relationship ⟨on good ~*s*⟩ **7** : AGREEMENT, CONCORD

[2]**term** *vb* : to apply a term to : CALL

ter•ma•gant \ˈtər-mə-gənt\ *n* : an overbearing or nagging woman : SHREW

[1]**ter•mi•nal** \ˈtər-mən-ᵊl\ *adj* **1** : of, relating to, or forming an end, limit, or terminus **2** : being or being in the final stages of a fatal disease ⟨a ~ patient⟩ ⟨~ illness⟩ **syn** final, concluding, last, latest — **ter•mi•nal•ly** *adv*

[2]**terminal** *n* **1** : EXTREMITY, END **2** : a device at the end of a wire or on electrical equipment for making a connection **3** : either end of a transportation line (as a railroad) with its offices and freight and passenger stations; *also* : a freight or passenger station **4** : a device (as in a computer system) for data entry and display

ter•mi•nate \ˈtər-mə-ˌnāt\ *vb* **-nat•ed; -nat•ing** : to bring or come to an end **syn** conclude, finish, complete — **ter•mi•na•ble** \-nə-bəl\ *adj* — **ter•mi•na•tion** \ˌtər-mə-ˈnā-shən\ *n* — **ter•mi•na•tor** \ˈtər-mə-ˌnā-tər\ *n*

ter•mi•nol•o•gy \ˌtər-mə-ˈnä-lə-jē\ *n, pl* **-gies** : the technical or special terms used in a business, art, science, or special subject

ter•mi•nus \ˈtər-mə-nəs\ *n, pl* **-ni** \-ˌnī\ *or* **-nus•es** [L] **1** : final goal : END **2** : either end of a transportation line or travel route; *also* : the station or city at such a place

ter•mite \ˈtər-ˌmīt\ *n* : any of numerous pale soft-bodied social insects that feed on wood

tern \ˈtərn\ *n* : any of various chiefly marine birds with narrow wings and often a forked tail

ter•na•ry \ˈtər-nə-rē\ *adj* **1** : of, relating to, or proceeding by threes **2** : having three elements or parts

terr *abbr* territory

[1]**ter•race** \ˈter-əs\ *n* **1** : a flat roof or open platform **2** : a level area next to a building **3** : an embankment with level top **4** : a bank or ridge on a slope to conserve moisture and soil **5** : a row of houses on raised land; *also* : a street with such a row of houses **6** : a strip of park in the middle of a street

[2]**terrace** *vb* **ter•raced; ter•rac•ing** : to form into a terrace or supply with terraces

ter•ra–cot•ta \ˌter-ə-ˈkä-tə\ *n* [It *terra cotta*, lit., baked earth] : a reddish brown earthenware

terra fir•ma \-ˈfər-mə\ *n* [NL] : solid ground

ter•rain \tə-ˈrān\ *n* : the surface features of an area of land ⟨a rough ~⟩

ter•ra in•cog•ni•ta \ˈter-ə-ˌin-ˌkäg-ˈnē-tə\ *n, pl* **ter•rae in•cog•ni•tae** \ˈter-ˌī-ˌin-ˌkäg-ˈnē-tī\ [L] : an unexplored area or field of knowledge

ter•ra•pin \ˈter-ə-pən\ *n* : any of various turtles of fresh or brackish water

ter•rar•i•um \tə-ˈrar-ē-əm\ *n, pl* **-ia** \-ē-ə\ *or* **-i•ums** : a usu. transparent enclosure for keeping or raising small plants and animals indoors

ter•res•tri•al \tə-ˈres-trē-əl\ *adj* **1** : of or relating to the earth or its inhabitants **2** : living or growing on land ⟨~ plants⟩ **syn** mundane, earthly, worldly

ter•ri•ble \ˈter-ə-bəl\ *adj* **1** : exciting terror : FEARFUL, DREADFUL ⟨~ weapons⟩ **2** : hard to bear : DISTRESSING ⟨a ~ situation⟩ **3** : extreme in degree : INTENSE ⟨~ heat⟩ **4** : of very poor quality : AWFUL ⟨a ~ play⟩ **syn** frightful, horrible, shocking, appalling — **ter•ri•bly** \-blē\ *adv*

ter•ri•er \ˈter-ē-ər\ *n* [F (*chien*) *terrier*, lit., earth dog, fr. *terrier* of earth, fr. ML *terrarius*, fr. L *terra* earth] : any of various usu. small dogs orig. used by hunters to drive small game animals from their holes

ter•rif•ic \tə-ˈri-fik\ *adj* **1** : exciting terror **2** : EXTRAORDINARY, ASTOUNDING ⟨~ speed⟩ **3** : unusually good ⟨makes ~ chili⟩

ter•ri•fy \ˈter-ə-ˌfī\ *vb* **-fied; -fy•ing** : to fill with terror : FRIGHTEN **syn** scare, terrorize, startle, alarm — **ter•ri•fy•ing•ly** *adv*

ter•ri•to•ry \ˈter-ə-ˌtōr-ē\ *n, pl* **-ries 1** : a geographical area belonging to or under the jurisdiction of a governmental authority **2** : a part of the U.S. not included within any state but organized with a separate legislature **3** : REGION, DISTRICT; *also* : a region in which one feels at home **4** : a field of knowledge or interest **5** : an assigned area **6** : an area occupied and defended by one or a group of animals — **ter•ri•to•ri•al** \ˌter-ə-ˈtōr-ē-əl\ *adj*

ter•ror \ˈter-ər\ *n* **1** : a state of intense fear : FRIGHT **2** : one that inspires fear **syn** panic, consternation, dread, alarm, dismay, horror, trepidation

ter•ror•ise *chiefly Brit var of* TERRORIZE

ter•ror•ism \ˈter-ər-ˌi-zəm\ *n* : the systematic use of terror esp. as a means of coercion — **ter•ror•ist** \-ist\ *adj or n*

ter•ror•ize \ˈter-ər-ˌīz\ *vb* **-ized; -iz•ing 1** : to fill with terror : SCARE **2** : to coerce by threat or violence **syn** terrify, frighten, alarm, startle

ter•ry \ˈter-ē\ *n, pl* **terries** : an absorbent fabric with a loose pile of uncut loops

terse \ˈtərs\ *adj* **ters•er; ters•est** [L *tersus* clean, neat, fr. pp. of *tergēre* to wipe off] : effectively brief : CONCISE — **terse•ly** *adv* — **terse•ness** *n*

ter•tia•ry \ˈtər-shē-ˌer-ē\ *adj* **1** : of third rank, importance, or value **2** *cap* : of, relating to, or being the earlier period of the Cenozoic era **3** : occurring in or being the third stage

Tertiary *n* : the Tertiary period

TESL *abbr* teaching English as a second language

TESOL *abbr* Teachers of English to Speakers of Other Languages

[1]**test** \ˈtest\ *n* [ME, vessel in which metals were assayed, fr. MF, fr. L *testum* earthen vessel] **1** : a critical examination or evaluation : TRIAL **2** : a means or result of testing

[2]**test** *vb* **1** : to put to test : TRY, EXAMINE **2** : to undergo or score on tests

tes•ta•ment \ˈtes-tə-mənt\ *n* **1** *cap* : either of two main divisions of the Bible **2** : EVIDENCE, WITNESS **3** : CREDO **4** : the legal instructions for the disposition of one's property after death : WILL — **tes•ta•men•ta•ry** \ˌtes-tə-ˈmen-tə-rē\ *adj*

tes•tate \ˈtes-ˌtāt, -tət\ *adj* : having left a valid will

tes•ta•tor \ˈtes-ˌtā-tər, tes-ˈtā-\ *n* : a person who dies leaving a valid will

tes•ta•trix \tes-ˈtā-triks\ *n* : a female testator

[1]**tes•ter** \ˈtē-stər, ˈtes-\ *n* : a canopy over a bed, pulpit, or altar

[2]**test•er** \ˈtes-tər\ *n* : one that tests

tes•ti•cle \ˈtes-ti-kəl\ *n* : TESTIS; *esp* : one of a higher mammal usu. with its enclosing structures

tes•ti•fy \ˈtes-tə-ˌfī\ *vb* **-fied; -fy•ing 1** : to make a statement based on personal knowledge or belief : bear witness **2** : to serve as evidence or proof

tes•ti•mo•ni•al \ˌtes-tə-ˈmō-nē-əl\ *n* **1** : a statement testifying to benefits received; *also* : a character reference **2** : an expression of appreciation : TRIBUTE — **testimonial** *adj*

tes•ti•mo•ny \ˈtes-tə-ˌmō-nē\ *n, pl* **-nies 1** : evidence based on observation or knowledge **2** : an outward sign : SYMBOL **3 :** a solemn declaration made by a witness under oath esp. in a court **syn** evidence, confirmation, proof, testament

tes•tis \ˈtes-təs\ *n, pl* **tes•tes** \ˈtes-ˌtēz\ [L, witness, testis] : a typically paired male reproductive gland that produces sperm and in most mammals is contained within the scrotum at sexual maturity

tes•tos•ter•one \te-ˈstäs-tə-ˌrōn\ *n* : a male sex hormone causing development of the male reproductive system and secondary sex characteristics

test tube *n* : a glass tube closed at one end and used esp. in chemistry and biology

tes•ty \ˈtes-tē\ *adj* **tes•ti•er; -est** [ME *testif,* fr. Anglo-French (the French of medieval England), headstrong, fr. OF *teste* head, fr. LL *testa* skull, fr. L, shell] : easily annoyed; *also* : marked by ill humor

tet•a•nus \ˈtet-ᵊn-əs\ *n* : an infectious disease caused by bacterial poisons and marked by muscle stiffness and spasms esp. of the jaws — **tet•a•nal** \-əl\ *adj*

tetchy \ˈte-chē\ *adj* **tetchi•er; -est** : irritably or peevishly sensitive

¹**tête–à–tête** \ˈtāt-ə-ˌtāt\ *n* [F, lit., head to head] : a private conversation between two persons

²**tête–à–tête** \ˌtāt-ə-ˈtāt\ *adv* : in private

³**tête–à–tête** \ˈtāt-ə-ˌtāt\ *adj* : being face-to-face : PRIVATE

¹**teth•er** \ˈte-thər\ *n* **1 :** something (as a rope) by which an animal is fastened **2 :** the limit of one's strength or resources

²**tether** *vb* : to fasten or restrain by or as if by a tether

tet•ra•eth•yl lead \ˌte-trə-ˈe-thəl-\ *n* : a heavy oily poisonous liquid used as an antiknock agent in gasoline

tet•ra•he•dron \-ˈhē-drən\ *n, pl* **-drons** *or* **-dra** \-drə\ : a polyhedron that has four faces — **tet•ra•he•dral** \-drəl\ *adj*

tet•ra•hy•dro•can•nab•i•nol \-ˌhī-drə-kə-ˈna-bə-ˌnȯl, -ˌnōl\ *n* : THC

te•tram•e•ter \te-ˈtra-mə-tər\ *n* : a line of verse consisting of four metrical feet

Teu•ton•ic \tü-ˈtä-nik, tyü-\ *adj* : GERMANIC

Tex *abbr* Texas

text \ˈtekst\ *n* **1 :** the actual words of an author's work **2 :** the main body of printed or written matter on a page **3 :** a scriptural passage chosen as the subject esp. of a sermon **4 :** THEME, TOPIC **5 :** TEXTBOOK — **tex•tu•al** \ˈteks-chə-wəl\ *adj*

text•book \ˈtekst-ˌbu̇k\ *n* : a book used in the study of a subject

tex•tile \ˈtek-ˌstīl, ˈtekst-ᵊl\ *n* : CLOTH; *esp* : a woven or knit cloth

tex•ture \ˈteks-chər\ *n* **1 :** the visual or tactile surface characteristics and appearance of something ⟨a coarse ∼⟩ **2 :** essential part **3 :** basic scheme or structure : FABRIC **4 :** overall structure

TGIF *abbr* thank God it's Friday

¹**Th** *abbr* Thursday

²**Th** *symbol* thorium

¹**-th** — see ¹-ETH

²**-th** *or* **-eth** *adj suffix* — used in forming ordinal numbers ⟨hundred*th*⟩

³**-th** *n suffix* **1 :** act or process **2 :** state or condition ⟨dear*th*⟩

Thai \ˈtī\ *n, pl* **Thai** *or* **Thais 1 :** a native or inhabitant of Thailand **2 :** the official language of Thailand — **Thai** *adj*

thal•a•mus \ˈtha-lə-məs\ *n, pl* **-mi** \-ˌmī\ [NL] : a subdivision of the brain that serves as a relay station to and from the cerebral cortex and functions in arousal and the integration of sensory information

thal•li•um \ˈtha-lē-əm\ *n* : a poisonous metallic chemical element — see ELEMENT table

¹**than** \ˈthən, ˈthan\ *conj* **1** — used after a comparative adjective or adverb to introduce the second part of a comparison expressing inequality ⟨older ∼ I am⟩ **2** — used after *other* or a word of similar meaning to express a difference of kind, manner, or identity ⟨adults other ∼ parents⟩

²**than** *prep* : in comparison with ⟨older ∼ me⟩

thane \ˈthān\ *n* **1 :** a free retainer of an Anglo-Saxon lord **2 :** a Scottish feudal lord

thank \ˈthaŋk\ *vb* : to express gratitude to ⟨∼*ed* them for the present⟩

thank•ful \ˈthaŋk-fəl\ *adj* **1 :** conscious of benefit received **2 :** expressive of thanks **3 :** GLAD — **thank•ful•ness** *n*

thank•ful•ly \-fə-lē\ *adv* **1 :** in a thankful manner **2 :** as makes one thankful

thank•less \ˈthaŋ-kləs\ *adj* **1 :** UNGRATEFUL **2 :** UNAPPRECIATED

thanks \ˈthaŋks\ *n pl* : an expression of gratitude

thanks•giv•ing \thaŋks-ˈgi-viŋ\ *n* **1 :** the act of giving thanks **2 :** a prayer expressing gratitude **3** *cap* : the 4th Thursday in November observed as a legal holiday for giving thanks for divine goodness

¹**that** \ˈthat, thət\ *pron, pl* **those** \ˈthōz\ **1 :** the one indicated, mentioned, or understood ⟨∼ is my house⟩ **2 :** the one farther away or first mentioned ⟨this is an elm, ∼'s a maple⟩ **3 :** what has been indicated or mentioned ⟨after ∼, we left⟩ **4 :** the one or ones : IT, THEY ⟨*those* who wish to leave may do so⟩

²**that** \thət, ˈthat\ *conj* **1 :** the following, namely ⟨he said ∼ he would⟩; *also* : which is, namely ⟨there's a chance ∼ it may fail⟩ **2 :** to this end or purpose ⟨shouted ∼ all might hear⟩ **3 :** as to result in the following, namely ⟨so heavy ∼ it can't be moved⟩ **4 :** for this reason, namely : BECAUSE ⟨we're glad ∼ you came⟩

³**that** *adj, pl* **those 1 :** being the one mentioned, indicated, or understood ⟨∼ boy⟩ ⟨*those* people⟩ **2 :** being the one farther away or less immediately under discussion ⟨this chair or ∼ one⟩

⁴**that** \thət, ˈthat\ *pron* **1 :** WHO, WHOM, WHICH ⟨the man ∼ saw you⟩ ⟨the man ∼ you saw⟩ ⟨the money ∼ was spent⟩ **2 :** in, on, or at which ⟨the way ∼ he drives⟩ ⟨the day ∼ it rained⟩

⁵**that** \ˈthat\ *adv* : to such an extent or degree ⟨I like it, but not ∼ much⟩

¹**thatch** \ˈthach\ *vb* : to cover with or as if with thatch — **thatch•er** *n*

²**thatch** *n* **1 :** plant material (as straw) for use as roofing **2 :** a mat of grass clippings accumulated next to the soil on a lawn **3 :** a covering of or as if of thatch ⟨a ∼ of white hair⟩

thaw \ˈthȯ\ *vb* **1 :** to melt or cause to melt **2 :** to become so warm as to melt ice or snow **3 :** to abandon aloofness or hostility — **thaw** *n*

THC \ˌtē-(ˌ)āch-ˈsē\ *n* [*tetrahydrocannabinol*] : a physiologically active chemical from hemp plant resin that is the chief intoxicant in marijuana

¹**the** \thə, *before vowel sounds usu* thē\ *definite article* **1 :** that in particular **2** — used before adjectives functioning as nouns ⟨a word to ∼ wise⟩

²**the** *adv* **1 :** to what extent ⟨∼ sooner, the better⟩ **2 :** to that extent ⟨the sooner, ∼ better⟩

theat *abbr* theater; theatrical

the•ater *or* **the•atre** \ˈthē-ə-tər\ *n* [ME *theatre,* fr. MF, fr. L *theatrum,* fr. Gk *theatron,* fr. *theasthai* to view, fr. *thea* act of seeing] **1 :** a building for dramatic performances; *also* : a building or area for showing motion pictures **2 :** a place of enactment of significant events ⟨∼ of war⟩ **3 :** a place (as a lecture room) resembling a theater **4 :** dramatic literature or performance

theater–in–the–round *n* : a theater with the stage in the center of the auditorium

the•at•ri•cal \thē-ˈa-tri-kəl\ *also* **the•at•ric** \-trik\ *adj* **1 :** of or relating to the theater **2 :** marked by artificiality of emotion : HISTRIONIC **3 :** marked by extravagant display : SHOWY

the•at•ri•cals \-kəlz\ *n pl* : the performance of plays

the·at·rics \thē-ˈa-triks\ *n pl* **1** : THEATRICALS **2** : staged or contrived effects
the·be \ˈthā-bā\ *n, pl* **thebe** — see *pula* at MONEY table
thee \ˈthē\ *pron, archaic objective case of* THOU
theft \ˈtheft\ *n* : the act of stealing
thegn \ˈthān\ *n* : THANE 1
their \thər, ˈther\ *adj* : of or relating to them or themselves
theirs \ˈtherz\ *pron* : their one : their ones
the·ism \ˈthē-ˌi-zəm\ *n* : belief in the existence of a god or gods — **the·ist** \-ist\ *n or adj* — **the·is·tic** \thē-ˈis-tik\ *adj*
them \thəm, ˈthem\ *pron, objective case of* THEY
theme \ˈthēm\ *n* **1** : a subject or topic of discourse or of artistic representation **2** : a written exercise : COMPOSITION **3** : a melodic subject of a musical composition or movement — **the·mat·ic** \thi-ˈma-tik\ *adj*
them·selves \thəm-ˈselvz, them-\ *pron pl* : THEY, THEM — used reflexively, for emphasis, or in absolute constructions ⟨they govern ~⟩ ⟨they ~ came⟩ ⟨~ busy, they sent me⟩
¹then \ˈthen\ *adv* **1** : at that time **2** : soon after that : NEXT **3** : in addition : BESIDES **4** : in that case **5** : CONSEQUENTLY
²then *n* : that time ⟨since ~⟩
³then *adj* : existing or acting at that time ⟨the ~ attorney general⟩
thence \ˈthens, ˈthens\ *adv* **1** : from that place **2** *archaic* : THENCEFORTH **3** : from that fact : THEREFROM
thence·forth \-ˌfōrth\ *adv* : from that time forward : THEREAFTER
thence·for·ward \thens-ˈfȯr-wərd, thens-\ *also* **thence·for·wards** \-wərdz\ *adv* : onward from that place or time
the·oc·ra·cy \thē-ˈä-krə-sē\ *n, pl* **-cies 1** : government by officials regarded as divinely inspired **2** : a state governed by a theocracy — **the·o·crat·ic** \ˌthē-ə-ˈkra-tik\ *adj*
theol *abbr* theological; theology
the·ol·o·gy \thē-ˈä-lə-jē\ *n, pl* **-gies 1** : the study of religious faith, practice, and experience; *esp* : the study of God and of God's relation to the world **2** : a theory or system of theology — **the·o·lo·gian** \ˌthē-ə-ˈlō-jən\ *n* — **the·o·log·i·cal** \-ˈlä-ji-kəl\ *adj*
the·o·rem \ˈthē-ə-rəm, ˈthir-əm\ *n* **1** : a statement esp. in mathematics that has been or is to be proved **2** : an idea accepted or proposed as a demonstrable truth : PROPOSITION
the·o·ret·i·cal \ˌthē-ə-ˈre-ti-kəl\ *also* **the·o·ret·ic** \-tik\ *adj* **1** : relating to or having the character of theory **2** : existing only in theory : HYPOTHETICAL — **the·o·ret·i·cal·ly** \-ti-k(ə-)lē\ *adv*
the·o·rise *Brit var of* THEORIZE
the·o·rize \ˈthē-ə-ˌrīz\ *vb* **-rized; -riz·ing** : to form a theory : SPECULATE — **the·o·rist** \-rist\ *n*
the·o·ry \ˈthē-ə-rē, ˈthir-ē\ *n, pl* **-ries 1** : abstract thought **2** : the general principles of a subject **3** : a plausible or scientifically acceptable general principle offered to explain observed facts **4** : HYPOTHESIS, CONJECTURE
theory of games : GAME THEORY
the·os·o·phy \thē-ˈä-sə-fē\ *n* : belief about God and the world held to be based on mystical insight — **theo·soph·i·cal** \ˌthē-ə-ˈsä-fi-kəl\ *adj* — **the·os·o·phist** \thē-ˈä-sə-fist\ *n*
ther·a·peu·tic \ˌther-ə-ˈpyü-tik\ *adj* [Gk *therapeutikos*, fr. *therapeuein* to attend, treat, fr. *theraps* attendant] : of, relating to, or dealing with healing and esp. with remedies for diseases — **ther·a·peu·ti·cal·ly** \-ti-k(ə-)lē\ *adv*
ther·a·peu·tics \ˌther-ə-ˈpyü-tiks\ *n* : a branch of medical or dental science dealing with the use of remedies
ther·a·py \ˈther-ə-pē\ *n, pl* **-pies** : treatment of bodily, mental, or behavioral disorders — **ther·a·pist** \-pist\ *n*
¹there \ˈthar, ˈther\ *adv* **1** : in or at that place — often used interjectionally **2** : to or into that place : THITHER **3** : in that matter or respect
²there \ˈthar, ˈther, thər\ *pron* — used as a function word to introduce a sentence or clause ⟨~'s a pen here⟩
³there \ˈthar, ˈther\ *n* **1** : that place ⟨get away from ~⟩ **2** : that point ⟨you take it from ~⟩
there·abouts \ˈthar-ə-ˈbau̇ts, ˌther-; ˈthar-ə-ˌbau̇ts, ˈther-\ *or* **there·about** \-ˈbau̇t, -ˌbau̇t\ *adv* **1** : near that place or time **2** : near that number, degree, or quantity
there·af·ter \thar-ˈaf-tər, ther-\ *adv* : after that : AFTERWARD
there·at \-ˈat\ *adv* **1** : at that place **2** : at that occurrence : on that account
there·by \thar-ˈbī, ther-, ˈthar-ˌbī, ˈther-ˌbī\ *adv* **1** : by that : by that means **2** : connected with or with reference to that
there·for \thar-ˈfȯr, ther-\ *adv* : for or in return for that
there·fore \ˈthar-ˌfōr, ˈther-\ *adv* : for that reason : CONSEQUENTLY
there·from \thar-ˈfrəm, ther-\ *adv* : from that or it
there·in \thar-ˈin, ther-\ *adv* **1** : in or into that place, time, or thing **2** : in that respect
there·of \-ˈəv, -ˈäv\ *adv* **1** : of that or it **2** : from that : THEREFROM
there·on \-ˈȯn, -ˈän\ *adv* **1** : on that **2** *archaic* : THEREUPON 3
there·to \thar-ˈtü, ther-\ *adv* : to that
there·un·to \thar-ˈən-(ˌ)tü; ˌthar-ən-ˈtü, ˌther-\ *adv, archaic* : THERETO
there·upon \ˈthar-ə-ˌpȯn, ˈther-, -ˌpän; ˌthar-ə-ˈpȯn, -ˈpän, ˌther-\ *adv* **1** : on that matter **2** : THEREFORE **3** : immediately after that : at once
there·with \thar-ˈwith, ther-, -with\ *adv* **1** : with that **2** *archaic* : THEREUPON, FORTHWITH
there·with·al \ˈthar-wi-ˌthȯl, ˈther-, -ˌthȯl\ *adv* **1** *archaic* : BESIDES **2** : THEREWITH
therm *abbr* thermometer
ther·mal \ˈthər-məl\ *adj* **1** : of, relating to, or caused by heat **2** : designed to prevent the loss of body heat ⟨~ underwear⟩ — **ther·mal·ly** *adv*
thermal pollution *n* : the discharge of heated liquid (as waste water from a factory) into natural waters at a temperature harmful to the environment
therm·is·tor \ˈthər-ˌmis-tər\ *n* : an electrical resistor whose resistance varies sharply with temperature
ther·mo·cline \ˈthər-mə-ˌklīn\ *n* : the region in a thermally stratified body of water that separates warmer surface water from cold deep water
ther·mo·cou·ple \ˈthər-mə-ˌkə-pəl\ *n* : a device for measuring temperature by measuring the temperature-dependent potential difference created at the junction of two dissimilar metals
ther·mo·dy·nam·ics \ˌthər-mə-dī-ˈna-miks\ *n* : physics that deals with the mechanical action or relations of heat — **ther·mo·dy·nam·ic** \-mik\ *adj* — **ther·mo·dy·nam·i·cal·ly** \-mi-k(ə-)lē\ *adv*
ther·mom·e·ter \thər-ˈmä-mə-tər\ *n* [F *thermomètre*, fr. Gk *thermē* heat + *metron* measure] : an instrument for measuring temperature typically by the rise or fall of a liquid (as mercury) in a thin glass tube — **ther·mo·met·ric** \ˌthər-mə-ˈme-trik\ *adj* — **ther·mo·met·ri·cal·ly** \-tri-k(ə-)lē\ *adv*
ther·mo·nu·cle·ar \ˌthər-mō-ˈnü-klē-ər, -ˈnyü-\ *adj* **1** : of or relating to changes in the nucleus of atoms of low atomic weight (as hydrogen) that require a very high temperature (as in the hydrogen bomb) **2** : utilizing or relating to a thermonuclear bomb ⟨~ war⟩
ther·mo·plas·tic \ˌthər-mə-ˈplas-tik\ *adj* : capable of softening when heated and of hardening again when cooled ⟨~ resins⟩ — **thermoplastic** *n*
ther·mos \ˈthər-məs\ *n* : a cylindrical container with a vacuum between an inner and an outer wall used to keep liquids hot or cold
ther·mo·sphere \ˈthər-mə-ˌsfir\ *n* : the part of the

earth's atmosphere that lies above the mesosphere and that is characterized by steadily increasing temperature with height

ther•mo•stat \ˈthər-mə-ˌstat\ *n* : a device that automatically controls temperature — **ther•mo•stat•ic** \ˌthər-mə-ˈsta-tik\ *adj* — **ther•mo•stat•i•cal•ly** \-ti-k(ə-)lē\ *adv*

the•sau•rus \thi-ˈsȯr-əs\ *n, pl* **-sau•ri** \-ˈsȯr-ˌī\ *or* **-sau•rus•es** \-ˈsȯr-ə-səz\ [NL, fr. L, treasure, collection, fr. Gk *thēsauros*] : a book of words and their synonyms — **the•sau•ral** \-ˈsȯr-əl\ *adj*

these *pl of* THIS

the•sis \ˈthē-səs\ *n, pl* **the•ses** \ˈthē-ˌsēz\ **1** : a proposition that a person advances and offers to maintain by argument **2** : an essay embodying results of original research; *esp* : one written for an academic degree

¹thes•pi•an \ˈthes-pē-ən\ *adj, often cap* [fr. *Thespis*, 6th cent. B.C. Greek poet and reputed originator of tragedy] : relating to the drama : DRAMATIC

²thespian *n* : ACTOR

Thess *abbr* Thessalonians

Thes•sa•lo•nians \ˌthe-sə-ˈlō-nyənz, -nē-ənz\ *n* — see BIBLE table

the•ta \ˈthā-tə\ *n* : the 8th letter of the Greek alphabet — Θ or *θ*

thew \ˈthü, ˈthyü\ *n* : MUSCLE, SINEW — usu. used in pl.

they \ˈt͟hā\ *pron* **1** : those individuals under discussion : the ones previously mentioned or referred to **2** : unspecified persons : PEOPLE

thi•a•mine \ˈthī-ə-mən, -ˌmēn\ *also* **thi•a•min** \-mən\ *n* : a vitamin of the vitamin B complex essential to normal metabolism and nerve function

¹thick \ˈthik\ *adj* **1** : having relatively great depth or extent from one surface to its opposite ⟨a ~ plank⟩; *also* : heavily built : THICKSET **2** : densely massed : CROWDED; *also* : FREQUENT, NUMEROUS **3** : dense or viscous in consistency ⟨~ syrup⟩ **4** : marked by haze, fog, or mist ⟨~ weather⟩ **5** : measuring in thickness ⟨one meter ~⟩ **6** : imperfectly articulated : INDISTINCT ⟨~ speech⟩ **7** : STUPID, OBTUSE **8** : associated on close terms : INTIMATE **9** : EXCESSIVE **syn** compact, close, tight — **thick•ly** *adv*

²thick *n* **1** : the most crowded or active part **2** : the part of greatest thickness

thick•en \ˈthi-kən\ *vb* : to make or become thick — **thick•en•er** *n*

thick•et \ˈthi-kət\ *n* : a dense growth of bushes or small trees

thick•ness \-nəs\ *n* **1** : the smallest of three dimensions ⟨length, width, and ~⟩ **2** : the quality or state of being thick **3** : LAYER, SHEET ⟨a single ~ of canvas⟩

thick•set \ˈthik-ˈset\ *adj* **1** : closely placed or planted **2** : having a thick body : BURLY

thick–skinned \-ˈskind\ *adj* **1** : having a thick skin **2** : not easily bothered by criticism or insult

thief \ˈthēf\ *n, pl* **thieves** \ˈthēvz\ : one that steals esp. secretly

thieve \ˈthēv\ *vb* **thieved; thiev•ing** : STEAL, ROB **syn** filch, pilfer, purloin, swipe

thiev•ery \ˈthē-və-rē\ *n, pl* **-er•ies** : the act of stealing : THEFT

thigh \ˈthī\ *n* : the part of the vertebrate hind limb between the knee and the hip

thigh•bone \ˈthī-ˌbōn\ *n* : FEMUR

thim•ble \ˈthim-bəl\ *n* : a cap or guard worn on the finger to push the needle in sewing — **thim•ble•ful** *n*

¹thin \ˈthin\ *adj* **thin•ner; thin•nest 1** : having little extent from one surface through to its opposite : not thick : SLENDER **2** : not closely set or placed : SPARSE ⟨~ hair⟩ **3** : not dense or not dense enough : more fluid or rarefied than normal ⟨~ air⟩ ⟨~ syrup⟩ **4** : lacking substance, fullness, or strength ⟨~ broth⟩ **5** : FLIMSY — **thin•ly** *adv* — **thin•ness** *n*

²thin *vb* **thinned; thin•ning** : to make or become thin

thine \ˈt͟hīn\ *pron, archaic* : one or the ones belonging to thee

thing \ˈthiŋ\ *n* **1** : a matter of concern : AFFAIR ⟨~*s* to do⟩ **2** *pl* : state of affairs ⟨~*s* are improving⟩ **3** : EVENT, CIRCUMSTANCE ⟨the crime was a terrible ~⟩ **4** : DEED, ACT ⟨expected great ~*s* of him⟩ **5** : a distinct entity : OBJECT **6** : an inanimate object distinguished from a living being **7** *pl* : POSSESSIONS, EFFECTS **8** : an article of clothing **9** : DETAIL, POINT **10** : IDEA, NOTION **11** : something one likes to do : SPECIALTY ⟨doing her ~⟩

think \ˈthiŋk\ *vb* **thought** \ˈthȯt\; **think•ing 1** : to form or have in the mind **2** : to have as an opinion : BELIEVE **3** : to reflect on : PONDER **4** : to call to mind : REMEMBER **5** : REASON **6** : to form a mental picture of : IMAGINE **7** : to devise by thinking ⟨*thought* up a plan to escape⟩ **syn** conceive, fancy, realize, envisage — **think•er** *n*

think tank *n* : an institute, corporation, or group organized for interdisciplinary research (as in technological or social problems)

thin•ner \ˈthi-nər\ *n* : a volatile liquid (as turpentine) used to thin paint

thin–skinned \ˈthin-ˈskind\ *adj* **1** : having a thin skin **2** : extremely sensitive to criticism or insult

¹third \ˈthərd\ *adj* : next after the second — **third** *or* **third•ly** *adv*

²third *n* **1** : one of three equal parts of something **2** : one that is number three in a countable series **3** : the 3d forward gear in an automotive vehicle

third degree *n* : the subjection of a prisoner to mental or physical torture to force a confession

third dimension *n* **1** : thickness, depth, or apparent thickness or depth that confers solidity on an object **2** : a quality that confers reality — **third–dimensional** *adj*

third world *n, often cap T&W* : the aggregate of the underdeveloped nations of the world

¹thirst \ˈthərst\ *n* **1** : a feeling of dryness in the mouth and throat associated with a desire to drink; *also* : a bodily condition producing this **2** : an ardent desire : CRAVING ⟨a ~ for knowledge⟩ — **thirsty** *adj*

²thirst *vb* **1** : to need drink : suffer thirst **2** : to have a strong desire : CRAVE

thir•teen \ˌthər-ˈtēn\ *n* : one more than 12 — **thirteen** *adj or pron* — **thir•teenth** \-ˈtēnth\ *adj or n*

thir•ty \ˈthər-tē\ *n, pl* **thirties** : three times 10 — **thir•ti•eth** \-tē-əth\ *adj or n* — **thirty** *adj or pron*

¹this \ˈt͟his\ *pron, pl* **these** \ˈt͟hēz\ **1** : the one close or closest in time or space ⟨~ is your book⟩ **2** : what is in the present or under immediate observation or discussion ⟨~ is a mess⟩; *also* : what is happening or being done now ⟨after ~ we'll leave⟩

²this *adj, pl* **these 1** : being the one near, present, just mentioned, or more immediately under observation ⟨~ book⟩ **2** : constituting the immediate past or future ⟨friends all *these* years⟩

³this *adv* : to such an extent or degree ⟨we need a book about ~ big⟩

this•tle \ˈthi-səl\ *n* : any of various tall prickly composite plants with often showy heads of tightly packed tubular flowers

this•tle•down \-ˌdau̇n\ *n* : the down from the ripe flower head of a thistle

¹thith•er \ˈthi-t͟hər\ *adv* : to that place

²thither *adj* : being on the farther side

thith•er•ward \-wərd\ *adv* : toward that place : THITHER

thole \ˈthōl\ *n* : a pin set in the gunwale of a boat to hold an oar in place

thong \ˈthȯŋ\ *n* **1** : a strip esp. of leather or hide **2** : a sandal held on the foot by a thong between the toes

tho•rax \ˈthōr-ˌaks\ *n, pl* **tho•rax•es** *or* **tho•ra•ces** \ˈthōr-ə-ˌsēz\ **1** : the part of the body of a mammal between the neck and the abdomen; *also* : its cavity containing the heart and lungs **2** : the middle of the three main divisions of the body of an insect — **tho·rac·ic** \thə-ˈra-sik\ *adj*

tho·ri·um \ˈthōr-ē-əm\ *n* **:** a radioactive metallic chemical element — see ELEMENT table

thorn \ˈthórn\ *n* **1 :** a woody plant bearing sharp processes **2 :** a sharp rigid plant process that is usu. a modified leafless branch **3 :** something that causes distress — **thorny** *adj*

thor·ough \ˈthər-ō\ *adj* **1 :** COMPLETE, EXHAUSTIVE ⟨a ~ search⟩ **2 :** very careful **:** PAINSTAKING ⟨a ~ scholar⟩ **3 :** having full mastery — **thor·ough·ly** *adv* — **thor·ough·ness** *n*

[1]**thor·ough·bred** \ˈthər-ə-ˌbred\ *adj* **1 :** bred from the best blood through a long line **2** *cap* **:** of or relating to the Thoroughbred breed of horses **3 :** marked by high-spirited grace

[2]**thoroughbred** *n* **1** *cap* **:** any of an English breed of light speedy horses kept chiefly for racing **2 :** one (as a pedigreed animal) of excellent quality

Thoroughbred 1

thor·ough·fare \-ˌfar\ *n* **:** a public road or street

thor·ough·go·ing \ˌthər-ə-ˈgō-iŋ\ *adj* **:** marked by thoroughness or zeal

thorp \ˈthórp\ *n, archaic* **:** VILLAGE

those *pl of* THAT

[1]**thou** \ˈt͟haü\ *pron, archaic* **:** the person addressed

[2]**thou** \ˈthaü\ *n, pl* **thou :** a thousand of something (as dollars)

[1]**though** \ˈt͟hō\ *conj* **1 :** despite the fact that ⟨~ the odds are hopeless, they fight on⟩ **2 :** granting that ⟨~ it may look bad, still, all is not lost⟩

[2]**though** *adv* **:** HOWEVER, NEVERTHELESS ⟨not for long, ~⟩

[1]**thought** \ˈthót\ *past and past part of* THINK

[2]**thought** *n* **1 :** the process of thinking **2 :** serious consideration **:** REGARD **3 :** reasoning power **4 :** the power to imagine **:** CONCEPTION **5 :** IDEA, NOTION **6 :** OPINION, BELIEF

thought·ful \ˈthót-fəl\ *adj* **1 :** absorbed in thought **2 :** marked by careful thinking ⟨a ~ essay⟩ **3 :** considerate of others ⟨a ~ host⟩ — **thought·ful·ly** *adv* — **thought·ful·ness** *n*

thought·less \-ləs\ *adj* **1 :** insufficiently alert **:** CARELESS ⟨a ~ worker⟩ **2 :** RECKLESS ⟨a ~ act⟩ **3 :** lacking concern for others **:** INCONSIDERATE ⟨~ remarks⟩ — **thought·less·ly** *adv* — **thought·less·ness** *n*

thou·sand \ˈthaüz-ᵊnd\ *n, pl* **thousands** *or* **thousand :** 10 times 100 — **thousand** *adj* — **thou·sandth** \-ᵊnth\ *adj or n*

thousands place *n* **:** the place four to the left of the decimal point in an Arabic number

thrall \ˈthról\ *n* **1 :** SLAVE, BONDMAN **2 :** a state of servitude — **thrall·dom** *or* **thral·dom** \ˈthról-dəm\ *n*

thrash \ˈthrash\ *vb* **1 :** THRESH 1 **2 :** BEAT, WHIP; *also* **:** DEFEAT **3 :** to move about violently **4 :** to go over again and again ⟨~ over the matter⟩; *also* **:** to hammer out ⟨~ out a plan⟩

[1]**thrash·er** \ˈthra-shər\ *n* **:** one that thrashes or threshes

[2]**thrasher** *n* **:** any of various long-tailed American songbirds related to the mockingbird

[1]**thread** \ˈthred\ *n* **1 :** a thin continuous strand of spun and twisted textile fibers **2 :** something resembling a textile thread **3 :** the ridge or groove that winds around a screw **4 :** a train of thought **5 :** a continuing element

[2]**thread** *vb* **1 :** to pass a thread through the eye of (a needle) **2 :** to pass (as film) through something **3 :** to make one's way through or between **4 :** to put together on a thread ⟨~ beads⟩ **5 :** to form a screw thread on or in

thread·bare \-ˌbar\ *adj* **1 :** having the nap worn off so that the thread shows **:** SHABBY **2 :** TRITE

thready \ˈthre-dē\ *adj* **1 :** consisting of or bearing fibers of filaments ⟨a ~ bark⟩ **2 :** lacking in fullness, body, or vigor

threat \ˈthret\ *n* **1 :** an expression of intent to do harm **2 :** one that threatens

threat·en \ˈthret-ᵊn\ *vb* **1 :** to utter threats against **2 :** to give signs or warning of **:** PORTEND **3 :** to hang over as a threat **:** MENACE — **threat·en·ing·ly** *adv*

threat·ened *adj* **:** having an uncertain chance of continued survival; *esp* **:** likely to become an endangered species

three \ˈthrē\ *n* **1 :** one more than two **2 :** the 3d in a set or series **3 :** something having three units — **three** *adj or pron*

3–D \ˈthrē-ˈdē\ *n* **:** three-dimensional form

three–dimensional *adj* **1 :** relating to or having three dimensions **2 :** giving the illusion of varying distances ⟨a ~ picture⟩

three·fold \ˈthrē-ˌfōld, -ˈfōld\ *adj* **1 :** having three parts **:** TRIPLE **2 :** being three times as great or as many — **three·fold** \-ˈfōld\ *adv*

three·pence \ˈthre-pəns, ˈthri-, ˈthrə-, *US also* ˈthrē-pens\ *n* **1** *pl* **threepence** *or* **three·penc·es :** a coin worth three pennies **2 :** the sum of three British pennies

three·score \ˈthrē-ˈskōr\ *adj* **:** being three times twenty **:** SIXTY

three·some \ˈthrē-səm\ *n* **:** a group of three persons or things

thren·o·dy \ˈthre-nə-dē\ *n, pl* **-dies :** a song of lamentation **:** ELEGY

thresh \ˈthrash, ˈthresh\ *vb* **1 :** to separate (as grain from straw) mechanically **2 :** THRASH — **thresh·er** *n*

thresh·old \ˈthresh-ˌhōld\ *n* **1 :** the sill of a door **2 :** a point or place of beginning or entering **:** OUTSET **3 :** a point at which a physiological or psychological effect begins to be produced

threw *past of* THROW

thrice \ˈthrīs\ *adv* **1 :** three times **2 :** in a threefold manner or degree

thrift \ˈthrift\ *n* [ME, fr. ON, prosperity, fr. *thrīfask* to thrive] **:** careful management esp. of money **:** FRUGALITY — **thrift·i·ly** \ˈthrif-tə-lē\ *adv* — **thrift·less** *adj* — **thrifty** *adj*

thrill \ˈthril\ *vb* [ME *thirlen, thrillen* to pierce, fr. OE *thyrlian,* fr. *thyrel* hole, fr. *thurh* through] **1 :** to have or cause to have sudden sharp feeling of excitement; *also* **:** TINGLE, SHIVER **2 :** TREMBLE, VIBRATE — **thrill** *n* — **thrill·er** *n* — **thrill·ing·ly** *adv*

thrive \ˈthrīv\ *vb* **throve** \ˈthrōv\ *or* **thrived; thriv·en** \ˈthri-vən\ *also* **thrived; thriv·ing 1 :** to grow luxuriantly **:** FLOURISH **2 :** to gain in wealth or possessions **:** PROSPER

throat \ˈthrōt\ *n* **:** the part of the neck in front of the spinal column; *also* **:** the passage through it to the stomach and lungs — **throat·ed** *adj*

throaty \ˈthrō-tē\ *adj* **throat·i·er; -est 1 :** uttered or produced from low in the throat ⟨a ~ voice⟩ **2 :** heavy, thick, or deep as if from the throat ⟨~ notes of a horn⟩ — **throat·i·ly** \-tə-lē\ *adv* — **throat·i·ness** \-tē-nəs\ *n*

[1]**throb** \ˈthräb\ *vb* **throbbed; throb·bing :** to pulsate or

pound esp. with abnormal force or rapidity : BEAT, VIBRATE

²throb *n* : BEAT, PULSE

throe \ˈthrō\ *n* **1** : PANG, SPASM **2** *pl* : a hard or painful struggle

throm•bo•sis \thräm-ˈbō-səs\ *n, pl* **-bo•ses** \-ˌsēz\ : the formation or presence of a clot in a blood vessel — **throm•bot•ic** \-ˈbä-tik\ *adj*

throm•bus \ˈthräm-bəs\ *n, pl* **throm•bi** \-ˌbī\ : a clot of blood formed within a blood vessel and remaining attached to its place of origin

throne \ˈthrōn\ *n* **1** : the chair of state of a sovereign or high dignitary **2** : royal power : SOVEREIGNTY

¹throng \ˈthrȯŋ\ *n* **1** : MULTITUDE **2** : a crowding together of many persons

²throng *vb* **thronged; throng•ing** : CROWD

¹throt•tle \ˈthrät-ᵊl\ *vb* **throt•tled; throt•tling** [ME *throtlen,* fr. *throte* throat] **1** : CHOKE, STRANGLE **2** : SUPPRESS **3** : to reduce the speed of (an engine) by closing the throttle — **throt•tler** *n*

²throttle *n* : a valve regulating the flow of steam or fuel to an engine; *also* : the lever controlling this valve

¹through \ˈthrü\ *prep* **1** : into at one side and out at the other side of ⟨go ~ the door⟩ **2** : by way of ⟨entered ~ a skylight⟩ **3** : in the midst of ⟨a path ~ the trees⟩ **4** : by means of ⟨succeeded ~ hard work⟩ **5** : over the whole of ⟨rumors swept ~ the office⟩ **6** : during the whole of ⟨~ the night⟩ **7** : to and including ⟨Monday ~ Friday⟩

²through *adv* **1** : from one end or side to the other **2** : from beginning to end : to completion ⟨see it ~⟩ **3** : to the core : THOROUGHLY ⟨he was wet ~⟩ **4** : into the open : OUT ⟨break ~⟩

³through *adj* **1** : permitting free passage ⟨a ~ street⟩ **2** : going from point of origin to destination without change or transfer ⟨a ~ train⟩ **3** : coming from or going to points outside a local area ⟨~ traffic⟩ **4** : FINISHED ⟨~ with the job⟩

¹through•out \thrü-ˈau̇t\ *adv* **1** : EVERYWHERE **2** : from beginning to end

²throughout *prep* **1** : in or to every part of **2** : during the whole period of

through•put \ˈthrü-ˌpu̇t\ *n* : OUTPUT, PRODUCTION ⟨the ~ of a computer⟩

throve *past of* THRIVE

¹throw \ˈthrō\ *vb* **threw** \ˈthrü\; **thrown** \ˈthrōn\; **throw•ing 1** : to propel through the air esp. with a forward motion of the hand and arm ⟨~ a ball⟩ **2** : to cause to fall or fall off **3** : to put suddenly in a certain position or condition ⟨~ into panic⟩ **4** : to put on or take off hastily ⟨~ on a coat⟩ **5** : to lose intentionally ⟨~ a game⟩ **6** : to move (a lever) so as to connect or disconnect parts of something (as a clutch) **7** : to act as host for ⟨~ a party⟩ **syn** toss, fling, pitch, sling — **throw•er** *n*

²throw *n* **1** : an act of throwing, hurling, or flinging; *also* : CAST **2** : the distance a missile may be thrown **3** : a light coverlet **4** : a woman's scarf or light wrap

throw•away \ˈthrō-ə-ˌwā\ *n* : something that is or is designed to be thrown away esp. after one use

throw•back \-ˌbak\ *n* : reversion to an earlier type or phase; *also* : an instance or product of this

throw up *vb* **1** : to build hurriedly **2** : VOMIT

thrum \ˈthrəm\ *vb* **thrummed; thrum•ming** : to play or pluck a stringed instrument idly : STRUM

thrush \ˈthrəsh\ *n* : any of numerous small or medium-sized songbirds that are mostly of a plain color often with spotted underparts

¹thrust \ˈthrəst\ *vb* **thrust; thrust•ing 1** : to push or drive with force : SHOVE **2** : STAB, PIERCE **3** : INTERJECT **4** : to press the acceptance of upon someone

²thrust *n* **1** : a lunge with a pointed weapon **2** : ATTACK **3** : the pressure of one part of a construction against another (as of an arch against an abutment) **4** : the force produced by a propeller or jet or rocket engine that drives a vehicle (as an aircraft) forward **5** : a violent push : SHOVE

thrust•er *also* **thrust•or** \ˈthrəs-tər\ *n* : one that thrusts; *esp* : a rocket engine

thru•way \ˈthrü-ˌwā\ *n* : EXPRESSWAY

¹thud \ˈthəd\ *n* **1** : BLOW **2** : a dull sound

²thud *vb* **thud•ded; thud•ding** : to move or strike so as to make a thud

thug \ˈthəg\ *n* [Hindi *ṭhag,* lit., thief] : a brutal ruffian or assassin — **thug•gish** *adj*

thu•li•um \ˈthü-lē-əm, ˈthyü-\ *n* : a rare metallic chemical element — see ELEMENT table

¹thumb \ˈthəm\ *n* **1** : the short thick first digit of the human hand or a corresponding digit of a lower animal **2** : the part of a glove or mitten that covers the thumb

²thumb *vb* **1** : to leaf through (pages) with the thumb **2** : to wear or soil with the thumb by frequent handling **3** : to request or obtain (a ride) in a passing automobile by signaling with the thumb

¹thumb•nail \ˈthəm-ˌnāl\ *n* : the nail of the thumb

²thumbnail *adj* : BRIEF, CONCISE ⟨a ~ description⟩

thumb•print \-ˌprint\ *n* : an impression made by the thumb

thumb•screw \-ˌskrü\ *n* **1** : a screw with a head that may be turned by the thumb and forefinger **2** : a device of torture for squeezing the thumb

thumb•tack \-ˌtak\ *n* : a tack with a broad flat head for pressing with one's thumb into a board or wall

¹thump \ˈthəmp\ *vb* **1** : to strike with or as if with something thick or heavy so as to cause a dull sound **2** : POUND

²thump *n* : a blow with or as if with something blunt or heavy; *also* : the sound made by such a blow

¹thun•der \ˈthən-dər\ *n* **1** : the sound following a flash of lightning; *also* : a noise like such a sound **2** : a loud utterance or threat

²thunder *vb* **1** : to produce thunder **2** : ROAR, SHOUT

thun•der•bolt \-ˌbōlt\ *n* : a flash of lightning with its accompanying thunder

thun•der•clap \-ˌklap\ *n* : a crash of thunder

thun•der•cloud \-ˌklau̇d\ *n* : a dark storm cloud producing lightning and thunder

thun•der•head \-ˌhed\ *n* : a large cumulus cloud often appearing before a thunderstorm

thun•der•ous \ˈthən-də-rəs\ *adj* : producing thunder; *also* : making a noise like thunder — **thun•der•ous•ly** *adv*

thun•der•show•er \ˈthən-dər-ˌshau̇-ər\ *n* : a shower accompanied by thunder and lightning

thun•der•storm \-ˌstȯrm\ *n* : a storm accompanied by thunder and lightning

thun•der•struck \-ˌstrək\ *adj* : stunned as if struck by a thunderbolt

Thurs *or* **Thu** *abbr* Thursday

Thurs•day \ˈthərz-dē, -ˌdā\ *n* [ME, fr. OE *thursdæg,* fr. ON *thōrsdagr,* lit., day of Thor (Norse god)] : the 5th day of the week

thus \ˈt͟həs\ *adv* **1** : in this or that manner **2** : to this degree or extent : SO **3** : because of this or that : HENCE

¹thwack \ˈthwak\ *vb* : to strike with or as if with something flat or heavy

²thwack *n* : a heavy blow : WHACK

¹thwart \ˈthwȯrt\ *vb* **1** : FOIL, BAFFLE **2** : BLOCK, DEFEAT **syn** balk, outwit, frustrate

²thwart \ˈthwȯrt, *naut often* ˈthȯrt\ *adv* : ATHWART

³thwart *adj* : situated or placed across something else

⁴thwart \ˈthwȯrt\ *n* : a rower's seat extending across a boat

thy \ˈt͟hī\ *adj, archaic* : of, relating to, or done by or to thee or thyself

thyme \ˈtīm, ˈthīm\ *n* [ME, fr. MF *thym,* fr. L *thymum,* fr. Gk *thymon,* prob. fr. *thyein* to make a burnt offering, sacrifice] : a garden mint with aromatic leaves used esp. in seasoning; *also* : its leaves so used

thy•mine \ˈthī-ˌmēn\ *n* : a pyrimidine base that is one of the four bases coding genetic information in the molecular chain of DNA

thy•mus \ˈthī-məs\ *n* : a glandular organ of the neck region that is composed largely of lymphoid tissue, functions esp. in the development of the immune system, and tends to atrophy in the adult

thy•ris•tor \thī-ˈris-tər\ *n* : a semiconductor device that acts as a switch, rectifier, or voltage regulator

thy•roid \ˈthī-ˌrȯid\ *also* **thy•roi•dal** \thī-ˈrȯid-ᵊl\ *adj* [NL *thyroides*, fr. Gk *thyreoeidēs* shield-shaped, thyroid, fr. *thyreos* shield shaped like a door, fr. *thyra* door] : of, relating to, or being a large endocrine gland that lies at the base of the neck and produces several iodine-containing hormones that affect growth, development, and metabolism — **thyroid** *n*

thy•rox•ine *or* **thy•rox•in** \thī-ˈräk-ˌsēn, -sən\ *n* : an iodine-containing hormone that is produced by the thyroid gland, increases metabolic rate, and is used to treat thyroid disorders

thy•self \th̲ī-ˈself\ *pron, archaic* : YOURSELF

Ti *symbol* titanium

ti•ara \tē-ˈar-ə, -ˈer-, -ˈär-\ *n* **1** : the pope's triple crown **2** : a decorative headband or semicircle for formal wear by women

Ti•bet•an \tə-ˈbet-ᵊn\ *n* : a native or inhabitant of Tibet — **Tibetan** *adj*

tib•ia \ˈti-bē-ə\ *n, pl* **-i•ae** \-bē-ˌē\ *also* **-i•as** [L] : the inner of the two bones of the vertebrate hind limb between the knee and the ankle

tic \ˈtik\ *n* : a local and habitual twitching of muscles esp. of the face

ti•cal \ti-ˈkäl, ˈti-kəl\ *n, pl* **ticals** *or* **tical** : BAHT

[1]**tick** \ˈtik\ *n* : any of a large group of small blood-sucking arachnids

[2]**tick** *n* : the fabric case of a mattress or pillow; *also* : a mattress consisting of a tick and its filling

[3]**tick** *n* **1** : a light rhythmic audible tap or beat **2** : a small mark used to draw attention to or check something

[4]**tick** *vb* **1** : to make the sound of a tick or series of ticks **2** : to mark, count, or announce by or as if by ticking beats **3** : to mark or check with a tick **4** : to function as an operating mechanism : RUN

[5]**tick** *n, chiefly Brit* : CREDIT; *also* : a credit account

tick•er \ˈti-kər\ *n* **1** : something (as a watch) that ticks **2** : a telegraph instrument that prints information (as stock prices) on paper tape **3** *slang* : HEART

ticker tape *n* : the paper ribbon on which a telegraphic ticker prints

[1]**tick•et** \ˈti-kət\ *n* [MF *etiquet, estiquette* notice attached to something, fr. *estiquier* to attach, fr. MD *steken* to stick] **1** : CERTIFICATE, LICENSE, PERMIT; *esp* : a certificate or token showing that a fare or admission fee has been paid **2** : TAG, LABEL **3** : SLATE 4 **4** : a summons issued to a traffic offender

[2]**ticket** *vb* **1** : to attach a ticket to **2** : to furnish or serve with a ticket

tick•ing \ˈti-kiŋ\ *n* : a strong fabric used in upholstering and as a mattress covering

tick•le \ˈti-kəl\ *vb* **tick•led; tick•ling 1** : to excite or stir up agreeably : PLEASE, AMUSE **2** : to have a tingling sensation **3** : to touch (as a body part) lightly so as to cause uneasiness, laughter, or spasmodic movements — **tickle** *n*

tick•lish \-kə-lish\ *adj* **1** : OVERSENSITIVE, TOUCHY **2** : UNSTABLE ⟨a ~ foothold⟩ **3** : requiring delicate handling ⟨~ subject⟩ **4** : sensitive to tickling — **tick•lish•ly** *adv* — **tick•lish•ness** *n*

tid•al wave \ˈtīd-ᵊl-\ *n* **1** : an unusually high sea wave that sometimes follows an earthquake **2** : an unusual rise of water alongshore due to strong winds

tid•bit \ˈtid-ˌbit\ *n* : a choice morsel

[1]**tide** \ˈtīd\ *n* [ME, time, fr. OE *tīd*] **1** : the alternate rising and falling of the surface of the ocean **2** : something that fluctuates like the tides of the sea — **tid•al** \ˈtīd-ᵊl\ *adj*

[2]**tide** *vb* **tid•ed; tid•ing** : to carry through or help along as if by the tide ⟨a loan to ~ us over⟩

tide•land \ˈtīd-ˌland, -lənd\ *n* **1** : land overflowed during flood tide **2** : land under the ocean within a nation's territorial waters — often used in pl.

tide•wa•ter \-ˌwȯ-tər, -ˌwä-\ *n* **1** : water overflowing land at flood tide **2** : low-lying coastal land

tid•ings \ˈtī-diŋz\ *n pl* : NEWS, MESSAGE

[1]**ti•dy** \ˈtī-dē\ *adj* **ti•di•er; -est 1** : well ordered and cared for : NEAT **2** : LARGE, SUBSTANTIAL ⟨a ~ sum⟩ — **ti•di•ness** \ˈtī-dē-nəs\ *n*

[2]**tidy** *vb* **ti•died; ti•dy•ing 1** : to put in order **2** : to make things tidy

[3]**tidy** *n, pl* **tidies** : a decorated covering used to protect the back or arms of a chair from wear or soil

[1]**tie** \ˈtī\ *n* **1** : a line, ribbon, or cord used for fastening, uniting, or closing **2** : a structural element (as a beam or rod) holding two pieces together **3** : one of the cross supports to which railroad rails are fastened **4** : a connecting link : BOND ⟨family ~*s*⟩ **5** : an equality in number (as of votes or scores); *also* : an undecided or deadlocked contest **6** : NECKTIE

[2]**tie** *vb* **tied; ty•ing** *or* **tie•ing 1** : to fasten, attach, or close by means of a tie **2** : to bring together firmly : UNITE **3** : to form a knot or bow in ⟨~ a scarf⟩ **4** : to restrain from freedom of action : CONSTRAIN **5** : to make or have an equal score with

tie•back \ˈtī-ˌbak\ *n* : a decorative strip for draping a curtain to the side of a window

tie–dye•ing \ˈtī-ˌdī-iŋ\ *n* : a method of producing patterns in textiles by tying parts of the fabric so that they will not absorb the dye — **tie–dyed** \-ˌdīd\ *adj*

tie–in \ˈtī-ˌin\ *n* : CONNECTION

tier \ˈtir\ *n* : ROW, LAYER; *esp* : one of two or more rows arranged one above another — **tiered** \ˈtird\ *adj*

tie–rod \ˈtī-ˌräd\ *n* : a rod used as a connecting member or brace

tie–up \-ˌəp\ *n* **1** : a slowing or stopping of traffic or business **2** : CONNECTION

tiff \ˈtif\ *n* : a petty quarrel — **tiff** *vb*

Tif•fa•ny \ˈti-fə-nē\ *adj* : made of pieces of stained glass ⟨a ~ lamp⟩

ti•ger \ˈtī-gər\ *n* : a very large tawny black-striped Asian cat — **ti•ger•ish** *adj*

tiger

[1]**tight** \ˈtīt\ *adj* **1** : so close in structure as to prevent passage of a liquid or gas **2** : strongly fixed or held : SECURE **3** : TAUT **4** : fitting usu. too closely ⟨~ shoes⟩ **5** : set close together : COMPACT ⟨a ~ formation⟩ **6** : DIFFICULT, TRYING ⟨get in a ~ spot⟩ **7** : STINGY, MISERLY **8** : evenly contested : CLOSE **9** : INTOXICATED **10** : low in supply : hard to get ⟨money is ~⟩ — **tight•ly** *adv* — **tight•ness** *n*

[2]**tight** *adv* **1** : TIGHTLY, FIRMLY **2** : SOUNDLY ⟨sleep ~⟩

tight•en \ˈtīt-ᵊn\ *vb* : to make or become tight

tight•fist•ed \ˈtīt-ˈfis-təd\ *adj* : STINGY

tight•rope \-ˌrōp\ *n* : a taut rope or wire for acrobats to perform on

tights \ˈtīts\ *n pl* : skintight garments covering the body esp. below the waist; *also, Brit* : PANTY HOSE

tight•wad \ˈtīt-ˌwäd\ *n* : a stingy person

ti•gress \ˈtī-grəs\ *n* : a female tiger

til•de \ˈtil-də\ *n* [Sp, fr. ML *titulus* tittle] : a mark ˜ placed esp. over the letter *n* (as in Spanish *señor* sir) to denote the sound \nʸ\ or over vowels (as in Portuguese *irmã* sister) to indicate nasal quality

¹tile \ˈtīl\ *n* **1** : a flat or curved piece of fired clay, stone, or concrete used for roofs, floors, or walls; *also* : a pipe of earthenware or concrete used for a drain **2** : a thin piece (as of linoleum) used for covering walls or floors — **til•ing** \ˈtī-liŋ\ *n*

²tile *vb* **tiled; til•ing** : to cover with tiles — **til•er** *n*

¹till \ˈtil\ *prep or conj* : UNTIL

²till *vb* : to work by plowing, sowing, and raising crops : CULTIVATE — **till•able** *adj*

³till *n* : DRAWER; *esp* : a money drawer in a store or bank

till•age \ˈti-lij\ *n* **1** : the work of tilling land **2** : cultivated land

¹til•ler \ˈti-lər\ *n* [OE *telgor, telgra* twig, shoot] : a sprout or stalk esp. from the base or lower part of a plant

²till•er \ˈti-lər\ *n* : one that tills

³til•ler \ˈti-lər\ *n* [ME *tiler* stock of a crossbow, fr. MF *telier*, lit., beam of a loom, fr. ML *telarium*, fr. L *tela* web] : a lever used for turning a boat's rudder from side to side

¹tilt \ˈtilt\ *n* **1** : a contest in which two combatants charging usu. with lances try to unhorse each other : JOUST; *also* : a tournament of tilts **2** : a verbal contest **3** : SLANT, TIP

²tilt *vb* **1** : to move or shift so as to incline : TIP **2** : to engage in or as if in combat with lances : JOUST, ATTACK

tilth \ˈtilth\ *n* **1** : TILLAGE 2 **2** : the state of a soil esp. in relation to the suitability of its particle size and structure for growing crops

Tim *abbr* Timothy

tim•ber \ˈtim-bər\ *n* [ME, fr. OE, building, wood] **1** : growing trees or their wood — often used interjectionally to warn of a falling tree **2** : wood for use in making something **3** : a usu. large squared or dressed piece of wood

tim•bered \ˈtim-bərd\ *adj* : having walls framed by exposed timbers

tim•ber•land \ˈtim-bər-ˌland\ *n* : wooded land

tim•ber•line \ˈtim-bər-ˌlīn\ *n* : the upper limit of tree growth in mountains or high latitudes

timber rattlesnake *n* : a widely distributed rattlesnake of the eastern U.S.

timber wolf *n* : GRAY WOLF

tim•bre *also* **tim•ber** \ˈtam-bər, ˈtim-\ *n* [F, fr. MF, bell struck by a hammer, fr. OF, drum, fr. MGk *tymbanon* kettledrum, fr. Gk *tympanon*] : the distinctive quality given to a sound by its overtones

tim•brel \ˈtim-brəl\ *n* : a small hand drum or tambourine

¹time \ˈtīm\ *n* **1** : a period during which an action, process, or condition exists or continues ⟨gone a long ~⟩ **2** : LEISURE ⟨found ~ to read⟩ **3** : a point or period when something occurs : OCCASION ⟨the last ~ we met⟩ **4** : a set or customary moment or hour for something to occur ⟨arrived on ~⟩ **5** : AGE, ERA **6** : state of affairs : CONDITIONS ⟨hard ~*s*⟩ **7** : a rate of speed : TEMPO **8** : a moment, hour, day, or year as indicated by a clock or calendar ⟨what ~ is it⟩ **9** : a system of reckoning time ⟨solar ~⟩ **10** : one of a series of recurring instances; *also, pl* : added or accumulated quantities or examples ⟨five ~*s* greater⟩ **11** : a person's experience during a particular period ⟨had a good ~⟩ **12** : the hours or days of one's work; *also* : an hourly pay rate ⟨straight ~⟩ **13** : TIME-OUT

²time *vb* **timed; tim•ing 1** : to arrange or set the time of : SCHEDULE ⟨~*s* his calls conveniently⟩ **2** : to set the tempo or duration of ⟨~ a performance⟩ **3** : to cause to keep time with **4** : to determine or record the time, duration, or rate of ⟨~ a sprinter⟩ — **tim•er** *n*

time bomb *n* **1** : a bomb so made as to explode at a predetermined time **2** : something with a potentially dangerous delayed reaction

time clock *n* : a clock that records the time workers arrive and depart

time frame *n* : a period of time esp. with respect to some action or project

time–hon•ored \ˈtīm-ˌä-nərd\ *adj* : honored because of age or long usage

time•keep•er \-ˌkē-pər\ *n* **1** : a clerk who keeps records of the time worked by employees **2** : one appointed to mark and announce the time in an athletic game or contest

time•less \-ləs\ *adj* **1** : ETERNAL **2** : not limited or affected by time ⟨~ works of art⟩ — **time•less•ly** *adv* — **time•less•ness** *n*

time•ly \-lē\ *adj* **time•li•er; -est 1** : coming early or at the right time ⟨a ~ arrival⟩ **2** : appropriate to the time ⟨a ~ book⟩ — **time•li•ness** *n*

time–out \ˈtīm-ˈau̇t\ *n* : a brief suspension of activity esp. in an athletic game

time•piece \-ˌpēs\ *n* : a device (as a clock) to show the passage of time

times \ˈtīmz\ *prep* : multiplied by ⟨2 ~ 2 is 4⟩

time–shar•ing \ˈtīm-ˌshar-iŋ\ *n* **1** : simultaneous use of a computer by many users **2** *or* **time–share** \-shar\ : joint ownership or rental of a vacation lodging by several persons with each taking turns using the place

times sign *n* : the symbol × used to indicate multiplication

time•ta•ble \ˈtīm-ˌtā-bəl\ *n* **1** : a table of the departure and arrival times (as of trains) **2** : a schedule showing a planned order or sequence

time warp *n* : an anomaly, discontinuity, or suspension held to occur in the progress of time

time•worn \-ˌwōrn\ *adj* **1** : worn by time **2** : HACKNEYED, STALE

tim•id \ˈti-məd\ *adj* : lacking in courage or self-confidence : FEARFUL — **ti•mid•i•ty** \tə-ˈmi-də-tē\ *n* — **tim•id•ly** *adv*

tim•o•rous \ˈti-mə-rəs\ *adj* : of a timid disposition : AFRAID — **tim•o•rous•ly** *adv* — **tim•o•rous•ness** *n*

tim•o•thy \ˈti-mə-thē\ *n* : a grass with long cylindrical spikes widely grown for hay

Tim•o•thy \ˈti-mə-thē\ *n* — see BIBLE table

tim•pa•ni \ˈtim-pə-nē\ *n sing or pl* [It] : a set of kettledrums played by one performer in an orchestra — **tim•pa•nist** \-nist\ *n*

¹tin \ˈtin\ *n* **1** : a soft white crystalline metallic chemical element malleable at ordinary temperatures that is used esp. in solders and alloys — see ELEMENT table **2** : a container (as a can) made of metal (as tinplate)

²tin *vb* **tinned; tin•ning 1** : to cover or plate with tin **2** : to pack in tins

TIN *abbr* taxpayer identification number

tinct \ˈtiŋkt\ *n* : TINCTURE, TINGE

¹tinc•ture \ˈtiŋk-chər\ *n* **1** *archaic* : a substance that colors **2** : a slight admixture : TRACE **3** : an alcoholic solution of a medicinal substance **syn** touch, suggestion, suspicion, tinge

²tincture *vb* **tinc•tured; tinc•tur•ing 1** : COLOR, TINGE **2** : AFFECT

tin•der \ˈtin-dər\ *n* **1** : a very flammable substance used as kindling **2** : something serving to incite or inflame

tin•der•box \ˈtin-dər-ˌbäks\ *n* **1** : a metal box for holding tinder and usu. flint and steel for striking a spark **2** : a highly flammable object or place

tine \ˈtīn\ *n* : a slender pointed part (as of a fork or an antler) : PRONG

tin•foil \ˈtin-ˌfȯil\ *n* : a thin metal sheeting usu. of aluminum or tin-lead alloy

¹tinge \ˈtinj\ *vb* **tinged; tinge•ing** *or* **ting•ing 1** : to color slightly : TINT **2** : to affect or modify esp. with a slight odor or taste

²tinge *n* : a slight coloring, flavor, or quality : TRACE **syn** touch, suggestion, suspicion, tincture, soupçon

tin•gle \ˈtiŋ-gəl\ *vb* **tin•gled; tin•gling 1 :** to feel a prickling or thrilling sensation **2 :** TINKLE — **tingle** *n*
[1]**tin•ker** \ˈtiŋ-kər\ *n* **1 :** a usu. itinerant mender of household utensils **2 :** an unskillful mender **:** BUNGLER
[2]**tinker** *vb* **:** to repair or adjust something in an unskillful or experimental manner — **tin•ker•er** *n*
[1]**tin•kle** \ˈtiŋ-kəl\ *vb* **tin•kled; tin•kling :** to make or cause to make a tinkle
[2]**tinkle** *n* **:** a series of short high ringing or clinking sounds
tin•ny \ˈti-nē\ *adj* **tin•ni•er; -est 1 :** abounding in or yielding tin **2 :** resembling tin; *also* **:** LIGHT, CHEAP **3 :** thin in tone ⟨a ~ voice⟩ — **tin•ni•ly** \-nə-lē\ *adv* — **tin•ni•ness** \-nē-nəs\ *n*
tin•plate \ˈtin-ˈplāt\ *n* **:** thin sheet iron or steel coated with tin — **tin–plate** *vb*
tin•sel \ˈtin-səl\ *n* [MF *etincelle* spark, glitter] **1 :** a thread, strip, or sheet of metal, paper, or plastic used to produce a glittering appearance **2 :** something superficially attractive but of little worth
tin•smith \ˈtin-ˌsmith\ *n* **:** one that works with sheet metal (as tinplate)
[1]**tint** \ˈtint\ *n* **1 :** a slight or pale coloration **:** HUE **2 :** any of various shades of a color
[2]**tint** *vb* **:** to impart a tint to **:** COLOR
tin•tin•nab•u•la•tion \ˌtin-tə-ˌna-byə-ˈlā-shən\ *n* **1 :** the ringing of bells **2 :** a tingling sound as if of bells
tin•ware \ˈtin-ˌwar\ *n* **:** articles and esp. utensils made of tinplate
ti•ny \ˈtī-nē\ *adj* **ti•ni•er; -est :** very small **:** MINUTE **syn** miniature, diminutive, wee, lilliputian
[1]**tip** \ˈtip\ *vb* **tipped; tip•ping 1 :** OVERTURN, UPSET **2 :** LEAN, SLANT; *also* **:** to raise and tilt forward ⟨*tipped* his hat⟩
[2]**tip** *n* **:** the act or an instance of tipping
[3]**tip** *vb* **tipped; tip•ping 1 :** to furnish with a tip **2 :** to cover or adorn the tip of
[4]**tip** *n* **1 :** the usu. pointed end of something **2 :** a small piece or part serving as an end, cap, or point
[5]**tip** *n* **:** a light touch or blow
[6]**tip** *vb* **tipped; tip•ping :** to strike lightly **:** TAP
[7]**tip** *n* **:** a piece of advice or expert or confidential information **:** HINT
[8]**tip** *vb* **tipped; tip•ping :** to impart a piece of information about or to
[9]**tip** *vb* **tipped; tip•ping :** to give a gratuity to
[10]**tip** *n* **:** a gift or small sum given for a service performed or anticipated
tip–off \ˈtip-ˌȯf\ *n* **:** WARNING, TIP
tip•pet \ˈti-pət\ *n* **:** a long scarf or shoulder cape
tip•ple \ˈti-pəl\ *vb* **tip•pled; tip•pling :** to drink intoxicating liquor esp. habitually or excessively — **tipple** *n* — **tip•pler** *n*
tip•ster \ˈtip-stər\ *n* **:** a person who gives or sells tips esp. for gambling
tip•sy \ˈtip-sē\ *adj* **tip•si•er; -est :** unsteady or foolish from the effects of alcohol — **tip•si•ly** \-sə-lē\ *adv*
[1]**tip•toe** \ˈtip-ˌtō\ *n* **:** the position of being balanced on the balls of the feet and toes with the heels raised; *also* **:** the ends of the toes
[2]**tiptoe** *adv or adj* **:** on or as if on tiptoe
[3]**tiptoe** *vb* **tip•toed; tip•toe•ing :** to walk or proceed on or as if on tiptoe
[1]**tip–top** \ˈtip-ˈtäp\ *n* **:** the highest point
[2]**tip–top** *adj* **:** EXCELLENT, FIRST-RATE
ti•rade \ˈtī-ˌrād\ *n* [F, shot, tirade, fr. MF, fr. It *tirata,* fr. *tirare* to draw, shoot] **:** a prolonged speech of abuse or condemnation
tir•a•mi•su \ˌtir-ə-ˈmē-sü, -mē-ˈsü\ *n* [It *tiramisù*] **:** a dessert made with ladyfingers, mascarpone, chocolate, and espresso
[1]**tire** \ˈtīr\ *vb* **tired; tir•ing 1 :** to make or become weary **:** FATIGUE **2 :** to wear out the patience of **:** BORE
[2]**tire** *n* **1 :** a metal hoop that forms the tread of a wheel **2 :** a rubber cushion usu. containing compressed air that encircles a wheel (as of a bike)
tired \ˈtīrd\ *adj* **1 :** WEARY, FATIGUED **2 :** HACKNEYED — **tired•ness** *n*
tire•less \ˈtīr-ləs\ *adj* **:** not tiring **:** UNTIRING, INDEFATIGABLE — **tire•less•ly** *adv* — **tire•less•ness** *n*
tire•some \-səm\ *adj* **:** tending to bore **:** WEARISOME, TEDIOUS — **tire•some•ly** *adv* — **tire•some•ness** *n*
ti•ro *chiefly Brit var of* TYRO
tis•sue \ˈti-shü\ *n* [ME *tissu,* a rich fabric, fr. OF, fr. *tistre* to weave, fr. L *texere*] **1 :** a fine lightweight often sheer fabric **2 :** NETWORK, WEB **3 :** a soft absorbent paper **4 :** a mass or layer of cells forming a basic structural material of an animal or plant
[1]**tit** \ˈtit\ *n* **:** TEAT
[2]**tit** *n* **:** TITMOUSE
Tit *abbr* Titus
ti•tan \ˈtīt-ᵊn\ *n* **1** *cap* **:** one of a family of giants overthrown by the gods of ancient Greece **2 :** one gigantic in size or power
ti•tan•ic \tī-ˈta-nik\ *adj* **:** enormous in size, force, or power **syn** immense, gigantic, giant, colossal, mammoth
ti•ta•ni•um \tī-ˈtā-nē-əm\ *n* **:** a gray light strong metallic chemical element used esp. in alloys — see ELEMENT table
tit•bit \ˈtit-ˌbit\ *var of* TIDBIT
tithe \ˈtīth\ *n* **:** a 10th part paid or given esp. for the support of a church — **tithe** *vb* — **tith•er** *n*
tit•il•late \ˈtit-ᵊl-ˌāt\ *vb* **-lat•ed; -lat•ing 1 :** to excite pleasurably **2 :** TICKLE — **tit•il•la•tion** \ˌtit-ᵊl-ˈā-shən\ *n*
tit•i•vate *or* **tit•ti•vate** \ˈti-tə-ˌvāt\ *vb* **-vat•ed; -vat•ing :** to dress up **:** spruce up — **tit•i•va•tion** \ˌti-tə-ˈvā-shən\ *n*
ti•tle \ˈtīt-ᵊl\ *n* **1 :** CLAIM, RIGHT; *esp* **:** a legal right to the ownership of property **2 :** the distinguishing name esp. of an artistic production (as a book) **3 :** an appellation of honor, rank, or office **4 :** CHAMPIONSHIP **syn** designation, denomination, appellation
ti•tled \ˈtīt-ᵊld\ *adj* **:** having a title esp. of nobility
title page *n* **:** a page of a book bearing the title and usu. the names of the author and publisher
tit•mouse \ˈtit-ˌmau̇s\ *n, pl* **tit•mice** \-ˌmīs\ **:** any of numerous small long-tailed insect-eating birds
ti•tra•tion \tī-ˈtrā-shən\ *n* **:** a process of finding the concentration of a solution (as of an acid) by adding small portions of a second solution of known concentration (as of a base) to a fixed amount of the first until an expected change (as in color) occurs
tit•ter \ˈti-tər\ *vb* **:** to laugh in an affected or in a nervous or half-suppressed manner **:** GIGGLE — **titter** *n*
tit•tle \ˈtit-ᵊl\ *n* **:** a tiny piece **:** JOT
tit•tle–tat•tle \ˈtit-ᵊl-ˌtat-ᵊl\ *n* **:** idle talk **:** GOSSIP — **tittle–tattle** *vb*
tit•u•lar \ˈti-chə-lər\ *adj* **1 :** existing in title only **:** NOMINAL ⟨~ ruler⟩ **2 :** of, relating to, or bearing a title ⟨~ role⟩
Ti•tus \ˈtī-təs\ *n* — see BIBLE table
tiz•zy \ˈti-zē\ *n, pl* **tizzies :** a highly excited and distracted state of mind
tk *abbr* **1** tank **2** truck
TKO \ˌtē-ˌkā-ˈō\ *n* [*t*echnical *k*nock*o*ut] **:** the termination of a boxing match when a boxer is declared unable to continue the fight
tkt *abbr* ticket
Tl *symbol* thallium
TLC *abbr* tender loving care
T lymphocyte *n* **:** T CELL
Tm *symbol* thulium
TM *abbr* trademark
T–man \ˈtē-ˌman\ *n* **:** a special agent of the U.S. Treasury Department
tn *abbr* **1** ton **2** town
TN *abbr* Tennessee
tng *abbr* training

tnpk *abbr* turnpike

TNT \ˌtē-(ˌ)en-ˈtē\ *n* : a flammable toxic compound used as a high explosive

¹to \tə, ˈtü\ *prep* **1** : in the direction of and reaching ⟨drove ~ town⟩ **2** : in the direction of : TOWARD **3** : ON, AGAINST ⟨apply salve ~ a burn⟩ **4** : as far as ⟨can pay up ~ a dollar⟩ **5** : so as to become or bring about ⟨beaten ~ death⟩ ⟨broken ~ pieces⟩ **6** : BEFORE ⟨it's five minutes ~ six⟩ **7** : UNTIL ⟨from May ~ December⟩ **8** : fitting or being a part of : FOR ⟨key ~ the lock⟩ **9** : with the accompaniment of ⟨sing ~ the music⟩ **10** : in relation or comparison with ⟨similar ~ that one⟩ ⟨won 10 ~ 6⟩ **11** : in accordance with ⟨add salt ~ taste⟩ **12** : within the range of ⟨~ my knowledge⟩ **13** : contained, occurring, or included in ⟨two pints ~ a quart⟩ **14** : as regards ⟨agreeable ~ everyone⟩ **15** : affecting as the receiver or beneficiary ⟨whispered ~ her⟩ ⟨gave it ~ me⟩ **16** : for no one except ⟨a room ~ myself⟩ **17** : into the action of ⟨we got ~ talking⟩ **18** — used for marking the following verb as an infinitive ⟨wants ~ go⟩ and often used by itself at the end of a clause in place of an infinitive suggested by the preceding context ⟨goes to town whenever he wants ~⟩ ⟨can leave if you'd like ~⟩

²to \ˈtü\ *adv* **1** : in a direction toward ⟨run ~ and fro⟩ **2** : into contact esp. with the frame of a door ⟨the door slammed ~⟩ **3** : to the matter in hand ⟨fell ~ and ate heartily⟩ **4** : to a state of consciousness or awareness ⟨came ~ hours after the accident⟩

TO *abbr* turn over

toad \ˈtōd\ *n* : any of numerous tailless leaping amphibians differing typically from the related frogs in having a shorter stockier build, rough dry warty skin, and less aquatic habits

toad

toad•stool \-ˌstül\ *n* : MUSHROOM; *esp* : one that is poisonous or inedible

toady \ˈtō-dē\ *n, pl* **toad•ies** : a person who flatters in the hope of gaining favors : SYCOPHANT — **toady** *vb*

to–and–fro \ˌtü-ən-ˈfrō\ *adj* : forward and backward — **to–and–fro** *n*

¹toast \ˈtōst\ *vb* **1** : to warm thoroughly **2** : to make (as bread) crisp, hot, and brown by heat **3** : to become toasted

²toast *n* **1** : sliced toasted bread **2** : someone or something in whose honor persons drink **3** : an act of drinking in honor of a toast

³toast *vb* : to propose or drink to as a toast

toast•er \ˈtō-stər\ *n* : an electrical appliance for toasting

toaster oven *n* : a portable electrical appliance that bakes, broils, and toasts

toast•mas•ter \ˈtōst-ˌmas-tər\ *n* : a person who presides at a banquet and introduces the after-dinner speakers

toast•mis•tress \-ˌmis-trəs\ *n* : a woman who acts as toastmaster

Tob *abbr* Tobit

to•bac•co \tə-ˈba-kō\ *n, pl* **-cos** [Sp *tabaco*] **1** : a tall broad-leaved herb related to the potato; *also* : its leaves prepared for smoking or chewing or as snuff **2** : manufactured tobacco products; *also* : smoking as a practice

to•bac•co•nist \tə-ˈba-kə-nist\ *n* : a dealer in tobacco

To•bi•as \tō-ˈbī-əs\ *n* : TOBIT

To•bit \ˈtō-bət\ *n* — see BIBLE table

¹to•bog•gan \tə-ˈbä-gən\ *n* : a long flat-bottomed light sled made of thin boards curved up at one end

²toboggan *vb* **1** : to coast on or as if on a toboggan **2** : to decline suddenly (as in value) — **to•bog•gan•er** *n*

toc•sin \ˈtäk-sən\ *n* **1** : an alarm bell **2** : a warning signal

¹to•day \tə-ˈdā\ *adv* **1** : on or for this day **2** : at the present time

²today *n* : the present day, time, or age

tod•dle \ˈtäd-ᵊl\ *vb* **tod•dled; tod•dling** : to walk with short tottering steps in the manner of a young child — **toddle** *n* — **tod•dler** *n*

tod•dy \ˈtä-dē\ *n, pl* **toddies** [Hindi *tāṛī* juice of a palm, fr. *tāṛ* a palm, fr. Skt *tāla*] : a drink made of liquor, sugar, spices, and hot water

to–do \tə-ˈdü\ *n, pl* **to–dos** \-ˈdüz\ : BUSTLE, STIR, FUSS

¹toe \ˈtō\ *n* **1** : one of the jointed parts of the front end of a vertebrate's foot **2** : the front part of a foot or hoof

²toe *vb* **toed; toe•ing** : to touch, reach, or drive with the toes

toea \ˈtoi-ə\ *n* — see *kina* at MONEY table

toe•hold \ˈtō-ˌhōld\ *n* **1** : a place of support for the toes **2** : a slight footing

toe•nail \ˈtō-ˌnāl\ *n* : a nail of a toe

tof•fee *or* **tof•fy** \ˈtò-fē, ˈtä-\ *n, pl* **toffees** *or* **toffies** : candy of brittle but tender texture made by boiling sugar and butter together

to•fu \ˈtō-(ˌ)fü\ *n* [Jp *tōfu*] : a soft vegetable cheese made from soybeans

tog \ˈtäg, ˈtòg\ *vb* **togged; tog•ging** : to put togs on : DRESS

to•ga \ˈtō-gə\ *n* : the loose outer garment worn in public by citizens of ancient Rome — **to•gaed** \-gəd\ *adj*

¹to•geth•er \tə-ˈge-thər\ *adv* **1** : in or into one place or group **2** : in or into contact or association ⟨mix ~⟩ **3** : at one time : SIMULTANEOUSLY ⟨talk and work ~⟩ **4** : in succession ⟨for days ~⟩ **5** : in or into harmony or coherence ⟨get ~ on a plan⟩ **6** : as a group : JOINTLY — **to•geth•er•ness** *n*

²together *adj* : composed in mind or manner

tog•gery \ˈtä-gə-rē, ˈtò-\ *n* : CLOTHING

tog•gle switch \ˈtä-gəl-\ *n* : an electric switch operated by pushing a projecting lever through a small arc

To•go•lese \ˌtō-gə-ˈlēz, -ˈlēs\ *n* : a native or inhabitant of Togo — **Togolese** *adj*

togs \ˈtägz, ˈtògz\ *n pl* : CLOTHING; *esp* : clothes for a specified use ⟨riding ~⟩

¹toil \ˈtòil\ *n* **1** : laborious effort **2** : long fatiguing labor : DRUDGERY — **toil•ful** \-fəl\ *adj* — **toil•some** *adj*

²toil *vb* [ME, to argue, struggle, fr. OF *toeillier* to stir, disturb, dispute, fr. L *tudiculare* to crush, grind, fr. *tudicula* machine for crushing olives, dim. of *tudes* hammer] **1** : to work hard and long **2** : to proceed with great effort : PLOD — **toil•er** *n*

³toil *n* [ME *toile* cloth, net, fr. L *tela* cloth on a loom] : NET, TRAP — usu. used in pl.

toi•let \ˈtòi-lət\ *n* **1** : the act or process of dressing and grooming oneself **2** : BATHROOM **3** : a fixture for use in urinating and defecating; *esp* : one consisting essentially of a water-flushed bowl and seat — **toilet** *vb*

toi•let•ry \ˈtòi-lə-trē\ *n, pl* **-ries** : an article or preparation used in making one's toilet — usu. used in pl.

toi•lette \twä-ˈlet\ *n* **1** : TOILET 1 **2** : formal attire; *also* : a particular costume

toilet training *n* : the process of training a child to control bladder and bowel movements and to use the toilet — **toilet train** *vb*

toil•worn \ˈtòil-ˌwōrn\ *adj* : showing the effects of toil

To•kay \tō-ˈkā\ *n* : naturally sweet wine from Hungary

toke \ˈtōk\ *n, slang* : a puff on a marijuana cigarette or pipe

[1]**to·ken** \ˈtō-kən\ *n* **1** : an outward sign **2** : SYMBOL, EMBLEM **3** : SOUVENIR, KEEPSAKE **4** : a small part representing the whole **5** : a piece resembling a coin issued as money or for use by a particular group on specified terms

[2]**token** *adj* **1** : done or given as a token esp. in partial fulfillment of an obligation **2** : representing only a symbolic effort : MINIMAL, PERFUNCTORY

to·ken·ism \ˈtō-kə-ˌni-zəm\ *n* : the policy or practice of making only a symbolic effort (as to desegregate)

told *past and past part of* TELL

tole \ˈtōl\ *n* : sheet metal and esp. tinplate for use in domestic and ornamental wares

tol·er·a·ble \ˈtä-lə-rə-bəl\ *adj* **1** : capable of being borne or endured **2** : moderately good : PASSABLE — **tol·er·a·bly** \-blē\ *adv*

tol·er·ance \ˈtä-lə-rəns\ *n* **1** : the act or practice of tolerating; *esp* : sympathy or indulgence for beliefs or practices differing from one's own **2** : the allowable deviation from a standard (as of size) **3** : the body's ability to become less responsive over time to something (as a drug) — **tol·er·ant** *adj* — **tol·er·ant·ly** *adv*

tol·er·ate \ˈtä-lə-ˌrāt\ *vb* **-at·ed; -at·ing 1** : to exhibit physiological tolerance for (as a drug) **2** : to allow to be or to be done without hindrance **syn** abide, bear, suffer, stand, brook — **tol·er·a·tion** \ˌtä-lə-ˈrā-shən\ *n*

[1]**toll** \ˈtōl\ *n* **1** : a tax paid for a privilege (as for passing over a bridge) **2** : a charge for a service (as for a long-distance telephone call) **3** : the cost in life, health, loss, or suffering

[2]**toll** *vb* **1** : to cause the slow regular sounding of (a bell) esp. by pulling a rope **2** : to give signal of : SOUND **3** : to sound with slow measured strokes **4** : to announce by tolling

[3]**toll** *n* : the sound of a tolling bell

toll·booth \ˈtōl-ˌbüth\ *n* : a booth where tolls are paid

toll·gate \-ˌgāt\ *n* : a point where vehicles stop to pay a toll

toll·house \-ˌhau̇s\ *n* : a house or booth where tolls are paid

tol·u·ene \ˈtäl-yə-ˌwēn\ *n* : a liquid hydrocarbon used esp. as a solvent

tom \ˈtäm\ *n* : the male of various animals (as a cat or turkey)

[1]**tom·a·hawk** \ˈtä-mə-ˌhȯk\ *n* : a light ax used as a missile and as a hand weapon esp. by No. American Indians

[2]**tomahawk** *vb* : to strike or kill with a tomahawk

to·ma·to \tə-ˈmā-tō, -ˈmä-\ *n, pl* **-toes** : a usu. large, rounded, and red or yellow pulpy edible berry of a widely grown tropical herb related to the potato; *also* : this herb

tomb \ˈtüm\ *n* **1** : a place of burial : GRAVE **2** : a house, chamber, or vault for the dead — **tomb** *vb*

tom·boy \ˈtäm-ˌbȯi\ *n* : a girl who behaves in a manner usu. considered boyish — **tom·boy·ish** *adj*

tomb·stone \ˈtüm-ˌstōn\ *n* : a stone marking a grave

tom·cat \ˈtäm-ˌkat\ *n* : a male domestic cat

Tom Col·lins \ˈtäm-ˈkä-lənz\ *n* : a tall iced drink with a base of gin

tome \ˈtōm\ *n* : BOOK; *esp* : a large or weighty one

tom·fool·ery \täm-ˈfü-lə-rē\ *n* : playful or foolish behavior

tom·my gun \ˈtä-mē-ˌgən\ *n* : SUBMACHINE GUN — **tommy-gun** *vb*

to·mog·ra·phy \tō-ˈmä-grə-fē\ *n* : a method of producing a three-dimensional image of the internal structures of a solid object (as the human body or the earth) — **to·mo·graph·ic** \ˌtō-mə-ˈgra-fik\ *adj*

to·mor·row \tə-ˈmär-ō\ *adv* : on or for the day after today — **tomorrow** *n*

tom·tit \ˈtäm-ˌtit, täm-ˈtit\ *n* : any of various small active birds

tom-tom \ˈtäm-ˌtäm\ *n* : a small-headed drum beaten with the hands

ton \ˈtən\ *n, pl* **tons** *also* **ton 1** — see WEIGHT table **2** : a unit equal to the volume of a long ton weight of seawater used in reckoning the displacement of ships and equal to 35 cubic feet

to·nal·i·ty \tō-ˈna-lə-tē\ *n, pl* **-ties** : tonal quality

[1]**tone** \ˈtōn\ *n* [ME, fr. L *tonus* tension, tone, fr. Gk *tonos*, lit., act of stretching; fr. the dependence of the pitch of a musical string on its tension] **1** : vocal or musical sound; *esp* : sound quality **2** : a sound of definite pitch **3** : WHOLE STEP **4** : accent or inflection expressive of an emotion **5** : the pitch of a word often used to express differences of meaning **6** : style or manner of expression **7** : color quality; *also* : SHADE, TINT **8** : the effect in painting of light and shade together with color **9** : healthy and vigorous condition of a living body or bodily part; *also* : the state of partial contraction characteristic of normal muscle **10** : general character, quality, or trend **syn** atmosphere, feeling, mood, vein — **ton·al** \ˈtōn-ᵊl\ *adj*

[2]**tone** *vb* **toned; ton·ing 1** : to give a particular intonation or inflection to **2** : to impart tone to **3** : SOFTEN, MELLOW **4** : to harmonize in color : BLEND

tone·arm *n* : the movable part of a record player that carries the pickup and the needle

tong \ˈtäŋ, ˈtȯŋ\ *n* : a Chinese secret society in the U.S.

tongs \ˈtäŋz, ˈtȯŋz\ *n pl* : a grasping device consisting of two pieces joined at one end by a pivot or hinged like scissors — **tong** *vb*

[1]**tongue** \ˈtəŋ\ *n* **1** : a fleshy movable process of the floor of the mouth used in tasting and in taking and swallowing food and in humans as a speech organ **2** : the flesh of a tongue (as of the ox) used as food **3** : the power of communication **4** : LANGUAGE 1 **5** : manner or quality of utterance; *also* : intended meaning **6** : ecstatic usu. unintelligible utterance accompanying religious excitation — usu. used in pl. **7** : something resembling an animal's tongue esp. in being elongated and fastened at one end only — **tongued** \ˈtəŋd\ *adj* — **tongue·less** *adj*

[2]**tongue** *vb* **tongued; tongu·ing 1** : to touch or lick with the tongue **2** : to articulate notes on a wind instrument

tongue-in-cheek *adj* : characterized by insincerity, irony, or whimsical exaggeration — **tongue in cheek** *adv*

tongue-lash \ˈtəŋ-ˌlash\ *vb* : CHIDE, REPROVE — **tongue-lash·ing** \-iŋ\ *n*

tongue-tied \-ˌtīd\ *adj* : unable or disinclined to speak clearly or freely (as from shyness or a tongue impairment)

tongue twister *n* : an utterance that is difficult to articulate because of a succession of similar consonants

[1]**ton·ic** \ˈtä-nik\ *adj* **1** : of, relating to, or producing a healthy physical or mental condition : INVIGORATING **2** : relating to or based on the 1st tone of a scale — **to·nic·i·ty** \tō-ˈni-sə-tē\ *n*

[2]**tonic** *n* **1** : something that invigorates, restores, or refreshes **2** : the 1st degree of a musical scale

tonic water *n* : a carbonated beverage flavored with a bit of quinine, lemon, and lime

[1]**to·night** \tə-ˈnīt\ *adv* : on this present night or the coming night

[2]**tonight** *n* : the present or the coming night

ton·nage \ˈtə-nij\ *n* **1** : a duty on ships based on tons carried **2** : ships in terms of the number of tons registered or carried **3** : total weight in tons shipped, carried, or mined

ton·sil \ˈtän-səl\ *n* : either of a pair of oval masses of lymphoid tissue that lie one on each side of the throat at the back of the mouth

ton·sil·lec·to·my \ˌtän-sə-ˈlek-tə-mē\ *n, pl* **-mies** : the surgical removal of the tonsils

ton·sil·li·tis \-ˈlī-təs\ *n* : inflammation of the tonsils

ton•so•ri•al \tän-ˈsōr-ē-əl\ *adj* : of or relating to a barber or a barber's work

ton•sure \ˈtän-chər\ *n* [ME, fr. ML *tonsura*, fr. L, act of shearing, fr. *tonsus*, pp. of *tondēre* to shear] **1** : the rite of admission to the clerical state by the clipping or shaving of the head **2** : the shaven crown or patch worn by clerics (as monks) — **tonsure** *vb*

too \ˈtü\ *adv* **1** : in addition : ALSO **2** : EXCESSIVELY **3** : to such a degree as to be regrettable **4** : VERY

took *past of* TAKE

¹tool \ˈtül\ *n* **1** : a hand instrument that aids in accomplishing a task **2** : the cutting or shaping part in a machine; *also* : a machine for shaping metal in any way **3** : something used in doing a job ⟨a scholar's books are his ~*s*⟩; *also* : a means to an end **4** : a person used by another : DUPE **5** *pl* : natural ability

²tool *vb* **1** : to shape, form, or finish with a tool; *esp* : to letter or decorate (as a book cover) by means of hand tools **2** : to equip a plant or industry with machines and tools for production **3** : DRIVE, RIDE ⟨~*ing* along at 60⟩

¹toot \ˈtüt\ *vb* **1** : to sound or cause to sound in short blasts **2** : to blow an instrument (as a horn) — **tooter** *n*

²toot *n* : a short blast (as on a horn)

tooth \ˈtüth\ *n, pl* **teeth** \ˈtēth\ **1** : one of the hard bony structures borne esp. on the jaws of vertebrates and used for seizing and chewing food and as weapons; *also* : a hard sharp structure esp. around the mouth of an invertebrate **2** : something resembling an animal's tooth **3** : any of the projections on the edge of a wheel that fits into corresponding projections on another wheel — **toothed** \ˈtütht\ *adj* — **tooth•less** *adj*

tooth•ache \ˈtüth-ˌāk\ *n* : pain in or about a tooth

tooth•brush \-ˌbrəsh\ *n* : a brush for cleaning the teeth

tooth•paste \-ˌpāst\ *n* : a paste for cleaning the teeth

tooth•pick \-ˌpik\ *n* : a pointed instrument for removing food particles caught between the teeth

tooth powder *n* : a powder for cleaning the teeth

tooth•some \ˈtüth-səm\ *adj* **1** : AGREEABLE, ATTRACTIVE **2** : pleasing to the taste : DELICIOUS **syn** palatable, appetizing, savory, tasty

toothy \ˈtü-thē\ *adj* **tooth•i•er; -est** : having or showing prominent teeth

¹top \ˈtäp\ *n* **1** : the highest part, point, or level of something **2** : the stalks and leaves of a plant with edible roots ⟨beet ~*s*⟩ **3** : the upper end, edge, or surface ⟨the ~ of a page⟩ **4** : an upper piece, lid, or covering **5** : the highest degree, pitch, or rank

²top *vb* **topped; top•ping 1** : to remove or trim the top of : PRUNE ⟨~ a tree⟩ **2** : to cover with a top or on the top : CROWN, CAP **3** : to be superior to : EXCEL, SURPASS **4** : to go over the top of **5** : to strike (a ball) above the center **6** : to make an end or conclusion ⟨~ off a meal with coffee⟩

³top *adj* **1** : of, relating to, or being at the top : HIGHEST **2** : CHIEF

⁴top *n* : a child's toy that has a tapering point on which it is made to spin

to•paz \ˈtō-ˌpaz\ *n* : a hard silicate of aluminum; *esp* : a yellow transparent topaz used as a gem

top•coat \ˈtäp-ˌkōt\ *n* **1** : a lightweight overcoat **2** : a protective coating (as of paint)

top dollar *n* : the highest amount being paid for a commodity or service

top–dress \-ˌdres\ *vb* : to apply material to (as land) without working it in; *esp* : to scatter fertilizer over

top•dress•ing \-ˌdre-siŋ\ *n* : a material used to top-dress soil

top•flight \ˈtäp-ˈflīt\ *adj* : of, relating to, or being the highest level of excellence or rank — **top flight** *n*

top hat *n* : a tall-crowned hat usu. of beaver or silk

top–heavy \ˈtäp-ˌhe-vē\ *adj* : having the top part too heavy for the lower part

top•ic \ˈtä-pik\ *n* **1** : a heading in an outlined argument **2** : the subject of a discourse or a section of it : THEME

top•i•cal \-pi-kəl\ *adj* **1** : designed to be applied to or to work on a part (as of the body) **2** : of, relating to, or arranged by topics ⟨a ~ outline⟩ **3** : relating to current or local events — **top•i•cal•ly** \-k(ə-)lē\ *adv*

top•knot \ˈtäp-ˌnät\ *n* **1** : an ornament (as a knot of ribbons) forming a headdress **2** : a crest of feathers or tuft of hair on the top of the head

top•less \-ləs\ *adj* **1** : wearing no clothing on the upper body **2** : featuring topless waitresses or entertainers

top•mast \ˈtäp-ˌmast, -məst\ *n* : the 2d mast above a ship's deck

top•most \ˈtäp-ˌmōst\ *adj* : highest of all : UPPERMOST

top–notch \-ˈnäch\ *adj* : of the highest quality : FIRST-RATE

to•pog•ra•phy \tə-ˈpä-grə-fē\ *n* **1** : the art of showing in detail on a map or chart the physical features of a place or region **2** : the outline of the form of a place showing its relief and the position of features (as rivers, roads, or cities) — **to•pog•ra•pher** \-fər\ *n* — **top•o•graph•ic** \ˌtä-pə-ˈgra-fik\ *or* **top•o•graph•i•cal** \-fi-kəl\ *adj*

top•ping \ˈtä-piŋ\ *n* : a food served on top of another to make it look or taste better

top•ple \ˈtä-pəl\ *vb* **top•pled; top•pling 1** : to fall from or as if from being top-heavy **2** : to push over : OVERTURN; *also* : OVERTHROW

tops \ˈtäps\ *adj* : topmost in quality or importance ⟨~ in his field⟩

top•sail \ˈtäp-ˌsāl, -səl\ *also* **top•s'l** \-səl\ *n* : the sail next above the lowest sail on a mast in a square-rigged ship

top secret *adj* : demanding complete secrecy among those concerned

top•side \ˈtäp-ˈsīd\ *adv or adj* **1** : to or on the top or surface **2** : on deck

top•sides \-ˈsīdz\ *n pl* : the top portion of the outer surface of a ship on each side above the waterline

top•soil \ˈtäp-ˌsȯil\ *n* : surface soil usu. including the organic layer in which plants have most of their roots

top•sy–tur•vy \ˌtäp-sē-ˈtər-vē\ *adv* **1** : in utter confusion **2** : UPSIDE DOWN — **topsy–turvy** *adj*

toque \ˈtōk\ *n* : a woman's small hat without a brim

tor \ˈtȯr\ *n* : a high craggy hill

To•rah \ˈtōr-ə\ *n* **1** : a scroll of the first five books of the Old Testament used in a synagogue; *also* : these five books **2** : the body of divine knowledge and law found in the Jewish scriptures and tradition

¹torch \ˈtȯrch\ *n* **1** : a flaming light made of something that burns brightly and usu. carried in the hand **2** : something that resembles a torch in giving light, heat, or guidance **3** *chiefly Brit* : FLASHLIGHT **4** : a portable burner for producing a hot flame

²torch *vb* : to set fire to

torch•bear•er \ˈtȯrch-ˌbar-ər\ *n* : one who carries a torch; *also* : one in the forefront (as of a political campaign)

torch•light \-ˌlīt\ *n* : light given by torches

torch song *n* : a popular sentimental song of unrequited love

tore *past of* TEAR

to•re•ador \ˈtȯr-ē-ə-ˌdȯr\ *n* : TORERO

to•re•ro \tə-ˈrer-ō\ *n, pl* **-ros** [Sp] : BULLFIGHTER

¹tor•ment \ˈtȯr-ˌment\ *n* **1** : extreme pain or anguish of body or mind **2** : a source of vexation or pain

²tor•ment \tȯr-ˈment\ *vb* **1** : to cause severe suffering of body or mind to **2** : DISTORT, TWIST **syn** rack, afflict, try, torture — **tor•men•tor** \-ˈmen-tər\ *n*

torn *past part of* TEAR

tor•na•do \tȯr-ˈnā-dō\ *n, pl* **-does** *or* **-dos** [modif of Sp *tronada* thunderstorm, fr. *tronar* to thunder, fr. L *tonare*] : a violent destructive whirling wind accompanied by a funnel-shaped cloud that moves over a narrow path

¹tor•pe•do \tȯr-ˈpē-dō\ *n, pl* **-does** : a thin cylindrical self-propelled underwater weapon

[2]**torpedo** *vb* **tor·pe·doed; tor·pe·do·ing** : to hit or destroy with or as if with a torpedo

torpedo boat *n* : a small very fast boat for firing torpedoes

tor·pid \ˈtȯr-pəd\ *adj* **1** : having lost motion or the power of exertion : DORMANT **2** : SLUGGISH **3** : lacking vigor : DULL — **tor·pid·i·ty** \tȯr-ˈpi-də-tē\ *n*

tor·por \ˈtȯr-pər\ *n* **1** : DULLNESS, APATHY **2** : extreme sluggishness : STAGNATION **syn** stupor, lethargy, languor, lassitude

[1]**torque** \ˈtȯrk\ *n* : a force that produces or tends to produce rotation or torsion

[2]**torque** *vb* **torqued; torqu·ing** : to impart torque to : cause to twist (as about an axis)

tor·rent \ˈtȯr-ənt\ *n* [F, fr. L *torrent-, torrens,* fr. *torrent-, torrens* burning, seething, rushing, fr. prp. of *torrēre* to parch, burn] **1** : a tumultuous outburst **2** : a rushing stream (as of water)

tor·ren·tial \tȯ-ˈren-chəl\ *adj* : relating to or resembling a torrent ⟨~ rains⟩

tor·rid \ˈtȯr-əd\ *adj* **1** : parched with heat esp. of the sun : HOT **2** : ARDENT

torrid zone *n* : the region of the earth between the tropic of Cancer and the tropic of Capricorn

tor·sion \ˈtȯr-shən\ *n* **1** : a wrenching by which one part of a body is under pressure to turn about a longitudinal axis while the other part is held fast or is under pressure to turn in the opposite direction **2** : a twisting of a bodily organ or part on its own axis — **tor·sion·al** \ˈtȯr-shə-nəl\ *adj* — **tor·sion·al·ly** *adv*

tor·so \ˈtȯr-sō\ *n, pl* **torsos** *or* **tor·si** \ˈtȯr-ˌsē\ [It, lit., stalk] : the trunk of the human body

tort \ˈtȯrt\ *n* : a wrongful act which does not involve a breach of contract and for which the injured party can recover damages in a civil action

tor·til·la \tȯr-ˈtē-ə\ *n* : a round thin cake of unleavened cornmeal or wheat flour bread

tor·toise \ˈtȯr-təs\ *n* : TURTLE; *esp* : any of a family of land turtles

tor·toise·shell \-ˌshel\ *n* : the mottled horny substance of the shell of some turtles used in inlaying and in making various ornamental articles — **tortoiseshell** *adj*

tor·to·ni \tȯr-ˈtō-nē\ *n* : rich ice cream often made with minced almonds and chopped cherries and flavored with rum

tor·tu·ous \ˈtȯr-chə-wəs\ *adj* **1** : marked by twists or turns : WINDING **2** : DEVIOUS, TRICKY

[1]**tor·ture** \ˈtȯr-chər\ *n* **1** : anguish of body or mind **2** : the infliction of severe pain esp. to punish or coerce

[2]**torture** *vb* **tor·tured; tor·tur·ing 1** : to cause intense suffering to : TORMENT **2** : to punish or coerce by inflicting severe pain **3** : TWIST, DISTORT **syn** rack, harrow, afflict, try — **tor·tur·er** *n*

To·ry \ˈtōr-ē\ *n, pl* **Tories 1** : a member of a chiefly 18th century British party upholding the established church and the traditional political structure **2** : an American supporter of the British during the American Revolution **3** *often not cap* : an extreme conservative — **Tory** *adj*

[1]**toss** \ˈtȯs, ˈtäs\ *vb* **1** : to fling to and fro or up and down **2** : to throw with a quick light motion; *also* : BANDY **3** : to fling or lift with a sudden motion ⟨~*ed* her head angrily⟩ **4** : to move restlessly or turbulently ⟨~*es* on the waves⟩ **5** : to twist and turn repeatedly **6** : FLOUNCE **7** : to accomplish readily ⟨~ off an article⟩ **8** : to decide an issue by flipping a coin

[2]**toss** *n* : an act or instance of tossing; *esp* : TOSS-UP 1

toss–up \-ˌəp\ *n* **1** : a deciding by flipping a coin **2** : an even chance **3** : something that offers no clear basis for choice

[1]**tot** \ˈtät\ *n* **1** : a small child **2** : a small drink of alcoholic liquor : SHOT

[2]**tot** *vb* **tot·ted; tot·ting** : to add up

[3]**tot** *abbr* total

[1]**to·tal** \ˈtōt-ᵊl\ *adj* **1** : making up a whole : ENTIRE ⟨~ amount⟩ **2** : COMPLETE, UTTER ⟨a ~ failure⟩ **3** : involving a complete and unified effort esp. to achieve a desired effect — **to·tal·ly** *adv*

[2]**total** *n* **1** : SUM 4 **2** : the entire amount **syn** aggregate, whole, gross, totality

[3]**total** *vb* **to·taled** *or* **to·talled; to·tal·ing** *or* **to·tal·ling 1** : to add up : COMPUTE **2** : to amount to : NUMBER **3** : to make a total wreck of (a car)

to·tal·i·tar·i·an \tō-ˌta-lə-ˈter-ē-ən\ *adj* : of, relating to, or advocating a political regime based on subordination of the individual to the state and strict control of all aspects of life esp. by coercive measures — **totalitarian** *n* — **to·tal·i·tar·i·an·ism** \-ē-ə-ˌni-zəm\ *n*

to·tal·i·ty \tō-ˈta-lə-tē\ *n, pl* **-ties 1** : an aggregate amount : SUM, WHOLE **2** : ENTIRETY, WHOLENESS

to·tal·iza·tor *or* **to·tal·isa·tor** \ˈtōt-ᵊl-ə-ˌzā-tər\ *n* : a machine for registering and indicating the number of bets and the odds on a horse or dog race

[1]**tote** \ˈtōt\ *vb* **tot·ed; tot·ing** : CARRY

[2]**tote** *vb* **tot·ed; tot·ing** : ADD, TOTAL — usu. used with *up*

to·tem \ˈtō-təm\ *n* : an object (as an animal or plant) serving as the emblem of a family or clan and often as a reminder of its ancestry; *also* : something usu. carved or painted to represent such an object

totem pole *n* : a pole that is carved with a series of totems and is erected before the houses of some northwest American Indians

tot·ter \ˈtä-tər\ *vb* **1** : to tremble or rock as if about to fall : SWAY **2** : to move unsteadily : STAGGER

tou·can \ˈtü-ˌkan\ *n* : any of a family of fruit-eating birds of tropical America with brilliant coloring and a very large beak

[1]**touch** \ˈtəch\ *vb* **1** : to bring a bodily part (as the hand) into contact with so as to feel **2** : to be or cause to be in contact **3** : to strike or push lightly esp. with the hand or foot **4** : DISTURB, HARM **5** : to make use of ⟨never ~*es* alcohol⟩ **6** : to induce to give or lend **7** : to get to : REACH **8** : to refer to in passing : MENTION **9** : to affect the interest of : CONCERN **10** : to leave a mark on; *also* : BLEMISH **11** : to move to sympathetic feeling **12** : to come close : VERGE **13** : to have a bearing : RELATE **14** : to make a usu. brief or incidental stop in port **syn** affect, influence, impress, strike, sway

[2]**touch** *n* **1** : a light stroke or tap **2** : the act or fact of touching or being touched **3** : the sense by which pressure or traction on the skin or mucous membrane is perceived; *also* : a particular sensation conveyed by this sense **4** : mental or moral sensitiveness : TACT **5** : a small quantity : HINT ⟨a ~ of spring in the air⟩ **6** : a manner of striking or touching esp. the keys of a keyboard instrument **7** : an improving detail ⟨add a few ~*es* to the painting⟩ **8** : distinctive manner or skill ⟨the ~ of a master⟩ **9** : the state of being in contact ⟨keep in ~⟩ **syn** suggestion, suspicion, tincture, tinge

touch·down \ˈtəch-ˌdau̇n\ *n* : the act of scoring six points in American football by being lawfully in possession of the ball on, above, or behind an opponent's goal line

tou·ché \tü-ˈshā\ *interj* [F] — used to acknowledge a hit in fencing or the success of an argument, an accusation, or a witty point

touch football *n* : football in which touching is substituted for tackling

touch·ing *adj* : capable of stirring emotions **syn** moving, impressive, poignant, affecting

touch off *vb* **1** : to describe with precision **2** : to start by or as if by touching with fire

touch·stone \ˈtəch-ˌstōn\ *n* : a test or criterion of genuineness or quality **syn** standard, gauge, benchmark, yardstick

touch up *vb* : to improve or perfect by small additional strokes or alterations — **touch–up** \ˈtəch-ˌəp\ *n*

touchy \ˈtə-chē\ *adj* **touch·i·er; -est 1** : easily offended

: PEEVISH **2** : calling for tact in treatment ⟨a ~ subject⟩ **syn** irascible, cranky, cross, tetchy, testy

[1]tough \ˈtəf\ *adj* **1** : strong or firm in texture but flexible and not brittle **2** : not easily chewed **3** : characterized by severity and determination ⟨a ~ policy⟩ **4** : capable of enduring strain or hardship : ROBUST **5** : hard to influence : STUBBORN **6** : difficult to accomplish, resolve, or cope with ⟨a ~ problem⟩ **7** : ROWDYISH **syn** tenacious, stout, sturdy, stalwart — **tough•ly** *adv* — **tough•ness** *n*

[2]tough *n* : a tough person : ROWDY

tough•en \ˈtə-fən\ *vb* **tough•ened; tough•en•ing** : to make or become tough

tou•pee \tü-ˈpā\ *n* [F *toupet* forelock] : a small wig for a bald spot

[1]tour \ˈtu̇r, *1 is also* ˈtau̇r\ *n* **1** : one's turn : SHIFT **2** : a journey in which one returns to the starting point

[2]tour *vb* : to make a tour

tour de force \ˌtu̇r-də-ˈfōrs\ *n, pl* **tours de force** *same*\ [F] : a feat of strength, skill, or ingenuity

tour•ist \ˈtu̇r-ist\ *n* : one that makes a tour for pleasure or culture

tourist class *n* : economy accommodations (as on a ship)

tour•ma•line \ˈtu̇r-mə-lən, -ˌlēn\ *n* : a mineral that when transparent is valued as a gem

tour•na•ment \ˈtu̇r-nə-mənt, ˈtər-\ *n* **1** : a medieval sport in which mounted armored knights contended with blunted lances or swords **2** : a championship series of games or athletic contests

tour•ney \-nē\ *n, pl* **tourneys** : TOURNAMENT

tour•ni•quet \ˈtu̇r-ni-kət, ˈtər-\ *n* : a device (as a tight bandage) for stopping bleeding or blood flow

tou•sle \ˈtau̇-zəl\ *vb* **tou•sled; tou•sling** : to disorder by rough handling : DISHEVEL, MUSS

tout \ˈtau̇t, *2 is also* ˈtüt\ *vb* **1** : to give a tip or solicit bets on a racehorse **2** : to praise or publicize loudly — **tout** *n*

[1]tow \ˈtō\ *vb* : to draw or pull along behind

[2]tow *n* **1** : an act of towing or condition of being towed **2** : something (as a barge) that is towed

[3]tow *n* : short or broken fiber (as of flax or hemp) used esp. for yarn, twine, or stuffing

to•ward \ˈtōrd, ˈtō-ərd, tə-ˈwȯrd\ *or* **to•wards** \ˈtōrdz, ˈtō-ərdz, tə-ˈwȯrdz\ *prep* **1** : in the direction of ⟨heading ~ the river⟩ **2** : along a course leading to ⟨efforts ~ reconciliation⟩ **3** : in regard to ⟨tolerance ~ minorities⟩ **4** : so as to face ⟨turn the chair ~ the window⟩ **5** : close upon ⟨it was getting along ~ sundown⟩ **6** : for part payment of ⟨here's $100 ~ your tuition⟩

tow•boat \ˈtō-ˌbōt\ *n* : TUGBOAT

tow•el \ˈtau̇-əl\ *n* : an absorbent cloth or paper for wiping or drying

tow•el•ing *or* **tow•el•ling** *n* : a cotton or linen fabric for making towels

[1]tow•er \ˈtau̇-ər\ *n* **1** : a tall structure either isolated or built upon a larger structure ⟨an observation ~⟩ **2** : a towering citadel — **tow•ered** *adj*

[2]tower *vb* : to reach or rise to a great height

tow•er•ing *adj* **1** : LOFTY ⟨~ pines⟩ **2** : reaching high intensity ⟨a ~ rage⟩ **3** : EXCESSIVE ⟨~ ambition⟩

tow•head \ˈtō-ˌhed\ *n* : a person having whitish blond hair — **tow•head•ed** \-ˌhe-dəd\ *adj*

to•whee \ˈtō-ˌhē, ˈtō-(ˌ)ē, tō-ˈhē\ *n* : a common finch of eastern No. America having the male black, white, and reddish; *also* : any of several closely related finches

to wit *adv* : NAMELY

town \ˈtau̇n\ *n* **1** : a compactly settled area usu. larger than a village but smaller than a city **2** : CITY **3** : the inhabitants of a town **4** : a New England territorial and political unit usu. containing both rural and urban areas; *also* : a New England community in which matters of local government are decided by a general assembly (**town meeting**) of qualified voters

town house *n* **1** : the city residence of a person having a country home **2** : a single-family house of two or sometimes three stories connected to another house by a common wall

town•ie *or* **towny** \ˈtau̇-nē\ *n, pl* **townies** : a permanent resident of a town as distinguished from a member of another group

towns•folk \ˈtau̇nz-ˌfōk\ *n pl* : TOWNSPEOPLE

town•ship \ˈtau̇n-ˌship\ *n* **1** : TOWN 4 **2** : a unit of local government in some states **3** : an unorganized subdivision of a county; *also* : an administrative division **4** : a division of territory in surveys of U.S. public land containing 36 square miles **5** : an area in the Republic of South Africa segregated for occupation by persons of non-European descent

towns•man \ˈtau̇nz-mən\ *n* **1** : a native or resident of a town or city **2** : a fellow citizen of a town

towns•peo•ple \-ˌpē-pəl\ *n pl* **1** : the inhabitants of a town or city **2** : town-bred persons

towns•wom•an \-ˌwu̇-mən\ *n* **1** : a woman who is a native or resident of a town or city **2** : a woman who is a fellow citizen of a town

tow•path \ˈtō-ˌpath, -ˌpȧth\ *n* : a path (as along a canal) traveled esp. by draft animals towing boats

tow truck *n* : a truck equipped for towing disabled vehicles

tox•emia \täk-ˈsē-mē-ə\ *n* : a bodily disorder associated with the presence of toxic substances in the blood

tox•ic \ˈtäk-sik\ *adj* [LL *toxicus*, fr. L *toxicum* poison, fr. Gk *toxikon* arrow poison, fr. neut. of *toxikos* of a bow, fr. *toxon* bow, arrow] : of, relating to, or caused by poison or a toxin : POISONOUS — **tox•ic•i•ty** \täk-ˈsi-sə-tē\ *n*

tox•i•col•o•gy \ˌtäk-si-ˈkä-lə-jē\ *n* : a science that deals with poisons and esp. with problems of their use and control — **tox•i•co•log•i•cal** \-kə-ˈlä-ji-kəl\ *or* **tox•i•co•log•ic** \-kə-ˈlä-jik\ *adj* — **tox•i•col•o•gist** \-ˈkä-lə-jist\ *n*

toxic shock syndrome *n* : an acute disease associated with the presence of a bacterium that is characterized by fever, diarrhea, nausea, diffuse erythema, and shock and occurs esp. in menstruating females using tampons

tox•in \ˈtäk-sən\ *n* : a poisonous substance produced by metabolic activities of a living organism that is usu. unstable, very toxic when introduced into the tissues, and usu. capable of inducing antibodies

[1]toy \ˈtȯi\ *n* **1** : something trifling **2** : a small ornament : BAUBLE **3** : something for a child to play with

[2]toy *vb* **1** : to deal with something lightly : TRIFLE **2** : FLIRT **3** : to amuse oneself as if with a plaything

[3]toy *adj* **1** : DIMINUTIVE **2** : designed for use as a toy

tp *abbr* **1** title page **2** township

tpk *or* **tpke** *abbr* turnpike

tr *abbr* **1** translated; translation; translator **2** transpose **3** troop

[1]trace \ˈtrās\ *n* **1** : a mark (as a footprint or track) left by something that has passed **2** : a minute or barely detectable amount

[2]trace *vb* **traced; trac•ing 1** : to mark out : SKETCH **2** : to form (as letters) carefully **3** : to copy (a drawing) by marking lines on transparent paper laid over the drawing to be copied **4** : to follow the trail of : track down **5** : to study out and follow the development of — **trace•able** *adj*

[3]trace *n* : either of two lines of a harness for fastening a draft animal to a vehicle

trac•er \ˈtrā-sər\ *n* **1** : one that traces **2** : ammunition containing a chemical to mark the flight of projectiles by a trail of smoke or fire

trac•ery \ˈtrā-sə-rē\ *n, pl* **-er•ies** : ornamental work having a design with branching or interlacing lines

tra•chea \ˈtrā-kē-ə\ *n, pl* **-che•ae** \-kē-ˌē\ *also* **-che•as** : the main tube by which air enters the lungs of vertebrates : WINDPIPE — **tra•che•al** \-kē-əl\ *adj*

tra•che•ot•o•my \ˌtrā-kē-ˈä-tə-mē\ *n, pl* **-mies** : the sur-

DICTIONARY

gical operation of cutting into the trachea esp. through the skin

trac•ing *n* **1** : the act of one that traces **2** : something that is traced **3** : a graphic record made by an instrument for measuring vibrations or pulsations

¹track \ˈtrak\ *n* **1** : a mark left in passing **2** : PATH, ROUTE, TRAIL **3** : a course laid out for racing; *also* : track-and-field sports **4** : one of a series of paths along which material (as music) is recorded (as on magnetic tape) **5** : the course along which something moves; *esp* : a way made by two parallel lines of metal rails **6** : awareness of a fact or progression ⟨lost ~ of time⟩ **7** : either of two endless metal belts on which a vehicle (as a bulldozer) travels

²track *vb* **1** : to follow the tracks or traces of : TRAIL **2** : to observe the moving path of (as a missile) **3** : to make tracks on **4** : to carry (as mud) on the feet and deposit — **track•er** *n*

track•age \ˈtra-kij\ *n* : lines of railway track

track–and–field *adj* : of or relating to athletic contests held on a running track or on the adjacent field

¹tract \ˈtrakt\ *n* **1** : an area without precise boundaries ⟨huge ~*s* of land⟩ **2** : a defined area of land **3** : a system of body parts or organs that act together to perform some function ⟨the digestive ~⟩

²tract *n* : a pamphlet of political or religious propaganda

trac•ta•ble \ˈtrak-tə-bəl\ *adj* : easily controlled : DOCILE **syn** amenable, obedient, biddable

tract house *n* : any of many similar houses built on a tract of land

trac•tion \ˈtrak-shən\ *n* **1** : the act of drawing : the state of being drawn **2** : the drawing of a vehicle by motive power; *also* : the particular form of motive power used **3** : the adhesive friction of a body on a surface on which it moves **4** : a pulling force applied to a skeletal structure (as a broken bone) by using a special device; *also* : a state of tension created by such a pulling force ⟨a leg in ~⟩ — **trac•tion•al** \-shə-nəl\ *adj* — **trac•tive** \ˈtrak-tiv\ *adj*

trac•tor \ˈtrak-tər\ *n* **1** : an automotive vehicle used esp. for drawing farm equipment **2** : a truck for hauling a trailer

¹trade \ˈtrād\ *n* **1** : one's regular business or work : OCCUPATION **2** : an occupation requiring manual or mechanical skill **3** : the persons engaged in a business or industry **4** : the business of buying and selling or bartering commodities **5** : an act of trading : TRANSACTION

²trade *vb* **trad•ed; trad•ing 1** : to give in exchange for another commodity : BARTER **2** : to engage in the exchange, purchase, or sale of goods **3** : to deal regularly as a customer — **trade on** : EXPLOIT ⟨*trades on* his family name⟩

trade–in \ˈtrād-ˌin\ *n* : an item of merchandise traded in

trade in *vb* : to turn in as part payment for a purchase

¹trade•mark \ˈtrād-ˌmärk\ *n* : a device (as a word or mark) that points distinctly to the origin or ownership of merchandise to which it is applied and that is legally reserved for the exclusive use of the owner; *also* : something that identifies a person or thing

²trademark *vb* : to secure the trademark rights for

trade name *n* : a name that is given by a manufacturer or merchant to a product to distinguish it as made or sold by him and that may be used and protected as a trademark

trad•er \ˈtrā-dər\ *n* **1** : a person whose business is buying or selling **2** : a ship engaged in trade

trades•man \ˈtrādz-mən\ *n* **1** : one who runs a retail store : SHOPKEEPER **2** : CRAFTSMAN

trades•peo•ple \-ˌpē-pəl\ *n pl* : people engaged in trade

trade union *n* : LABOR UNION

trade wind *n* : a wind blowing almost constantly in one direction

trading stamp *n* : a printed stamp given as a premium to a retail customer that when accumulated may be redeemed for merchandise

tra•di•tion \trə-ˈdi-shən\ *n* **1** : an inherited, established, or customary pattern of thought or action **2** : the handing down of beliefs and customs by word of mouth or by example without written instruction; *also* : a belief or custom thus handed down — **tra•di•tion•al** \-ˌdi-shə-nəl\ *adj* — **tra•di•tion•al•ly** *adv*

tra•duce \trə-ˈdüs, -ˈdyüs\ *vb* **tra•duced; tra•duc•ing** : to lower the reputation of : DEFAME, SLANDER **syn** malign, libel, calumniate — **tra•duc•er** *n*

¹traf•fic \ˈtra-fik\ *n* **1** : the business of bartering or buying and selling **2** : communication or dealings between individuals or groups **3** : the movement (as of vehicles) along a route; *also* : the vehicles, people, ships, or planes moving along a route **4** : the passengers or cargo carried by a transportation system

²traffic *vb* **traf•ficked; traf•fick•ing** : to carry on traffic — **traf•fick•er** *n*

traffic circle *n* : ROTARY 2

traffic light *n* : an electrically operated visual signal for controlling traffic

tra•ge•di•an \trə-ˈjē-dē-ən\ *n* **1** : a writer of tragedies **2** : an actor who plays tragic roles

tra•ge•di•enne \trə-ˌjē-dē-ˈen\ *n* [F] : an actress who plays tragic roles

trag•e•dy \ˈtra-jə-dē\ *n, pl* **-dies** [ME *tragedie,* fr. MF, fr. L *tragoedia,* fr. Gk *tragōidia,* fr. *tragos* goat + *aeidein* to sing] **1** : a serious drama with a sorrowful or disastrous conclusion **2** : a disastrous event : CALAMITY; *also* : MISFORTUNE **3** : tragic quality or element ⟨the ~ of life⟩

trag•ic \ˈtra-jik\ *also* **trag•i•cal** \-ji-kəl\ *adj* **1** : of, relating to, or expressive of tragedy **2** : appropriate to tragedy **3** : LAMENTABLE, UNFORTUNATE — **trag•i•cal•ly** \-ji-k(ə-)lē\ *adv*

¹trail \ˈtrāl\ *vb* **1** : to hang down so as to drag along or sweep the ground **2** : to draw or drag along behind **3** : to extend over a surface in a straggling manner **4** : to lag behind **5** : to follow the track of : PURSUE **6** : DWINDLE ⟨her voice ~*ed* off⟩

²trail *n* **1** : something that trails or is trailed ⟨a ~ of smoke⟩ **2** : a trace or mark left by something that has passed or been drawn along : SCENT, TRACK ⟨a ~ of blood⟩ **3** : a beaten path; *also* : a marked path through woods

trail bike *n* : a small motorcycle for off-road use

trail•blaz•er \-ˌblā-zər\ *n* : PATHFINDER, PIONEER — **trail•blaz•ing** *adj or n*

trail•er \ˈtrā-lər\ *n* **1** : one that trails; *esp* : a creeping plant (as an ivy) **2** : a vehicle that is hauled by another (as a tractor) **3** : a vehicle equipped to serve wherever parked as a dwelling or place of business

trailing arbutus *n* : a trailing spring-flowering plant of the heath family with fragrant pink or white flowers; *also* : its flower

¹train \ˈtrān\ *n* **1** : a part of a gown that trails behind the wearer **2** : RETINUE **3** : a moving file of persons, vehicles, or animals **4** : a connected series ⟨a ~ of thought⟩ **5** : AFTERMATH **6** : a connected line of railroad cars usu. hauled by a locomotive **syn** succession, sequence, procession, chain

²train *vb* **1** : to cause to grow as desired ⟨~ a vine on a trellis⟩ **2** : to form by instruction, discipline, or drill **3** : to make or become prepared (as by exercise) for a test of skill **4** : to aim or point at an object ⟨~ guns on a fort⟩ **syn** discipline, school, educate, instruct — **train•er** *n*

train•ee \trā-ˈnē\ *n* : one who is being trained esp. for a job

train•ing *n* **1** : the act, process, or method of one who trains **2** : the skill, knowledge, or experience gained by one who trains

train•man \-mən\ *n* : a member of a train crew

traipse \ˈtrāps\ *vb* **traipsed; traips•ing** : TRAMP, WALK

trait \ˈtrāt\ *n* **1** : a distinguishing quality (as of personality) : PECULIARITY **2** : an inherited characteristic

trai•tor \ˈtrā-tər\ *n* [ME *traitre*, fr. OF, fr. L *traditor*, fr. *tradere* to hand over, deliver, betray, fr. *trans-* across + *dare* to give] **1** : one who betrays another's trust or is false to an obligation **2** : one who commits treason — **trai•tor•ous** *adj*

tra•jec•to•ry \trə-ˈjek-tə-rē\ *n, pl* **-ries** : the curve that a body (as a planet in its orbit) describes in space

tram \ˈtram\ *n* **1** : a boxlike car running on a railway (**tram•way** \-ˌwā\) in a mine **2** *chiefly Brit* : STREETCAR **3** : an overhead cable car

¹tram•mel \ˈtra-məl\ *n* [ME *tramayle*, a kind of net, fr. MF *tremail*, fr. LL *tremaculum*, fr. L *tres* three + *macula* mesh, spot] : something impeding activity, progress, or freedom

²trammel *vb* **-meled** *or* **-melled; -mel•ing** *or* **-mel•ling** **1** : to catch and hold in or as if in a net **2** : HAMPER **syn** clog, fetter, shackle, hobble

¹tramp \ˈtramp, *1 & 3 are also* ˈträmp, ˈtrömp\ *vb* **1** : to walk, tread, or step heavily **2** : to walk about or through; *also* : HIKE **3** : to tread on forcibly and repeatedly

²tramp \ˈtramp, *5 is also* ˈträmp, ˈtrömp\ *n* **1** : a foot traveler **2** : a begging or thieving vagrant **3** : an immoral woman; *esp* : PROSTITUTE **4** : a walking trip : HIKE **5** : the succession of sounds made by the beating of feet on a road **6** : a ship that does not follow a regular course but takes cargo to any port

tram•ple \ˈtram-pəl\ *vb* **tram•pled; tram•pling** **1** : to tread heavily so as to bruise, crush, or injure **2** : to inflict injury or destruction **3** : to press down or crush by or as if by treading — **trample** *n* — **tram•pler** *n*

tram•po•line \ˌtram-pə-ˈlēn, ˈtram-pə-ˌlēn\ *n* [It *trampolino* springboard] : a resilient sheet or web (as of nylon) supported by springs in a metal frame and used as a springboard in tumbling — **tram•po•lin•ist** \-ˈlē-nist, -ˌlē-\ *n*

trance \ˈtrans\ *n* [ME, fr. MF *transe*, fr. *transir* to pass away, swoon, fr. L *transire* to pass, pass away, fr. *trans-* across + *ire* to go] **1** : a living state in which the vital bodily and mental activities slow down greatly **2** : a sleeplike state (as of deep hypnosis) **3** : a state of very deep absorption

tran•quil \ˈtraŋ-kwəl, ˈtran-\ *adj* : free from agitation or disturbance : QUIET **syn** serene, placid, peaceful — **tran•quil•li•ty** *or* **tran•quil•i•ty** \tran-ˈkwi-lə-tē, traŋ-\ *n* — **tran•quil•ly** *adv*

tran•quil•ize *also* **tran•quil•lize** \ˈtraŋ-kwə-ˌlīz, ˈtran-\ *vb* **-ized** *also* **-lized; -iz•ing** *also* **-liz•ing** : to make or become tranquil; *esp* : to relieve of mental tension and anxiety by means of drugs

tran•quil•iz•er *also* **tran•quil•liz•er** \-ˌlī-zər\ *n* : a drug used to relieve mental disturbance (as tension and anxiety)

trans *abbr* **1** transaction **2** transitive **3** translated; translation; translator **4** transmission **5** transportation **6** transverse

trans•act \tran-ˈzakt, -ˈsakt\ *vb* : CARRY OUT, PERFORM; *also* : CONDUCT

trans•ac•tion \-ˈzak-shən, -ˈsak-\ *n* **1** : something transacted; *esp* : a business deal **2** : an act or process of transacting **3** *pl* : the records of the proceedings of a society or organization

trans•at•lan•tic \ˌtrans-ət-ˈlan-tik, ˌtranz-\ *adj* : crossing or extending across or situated beyond the Atlantic Ocean

trans•ax•le \trans-ˈak-səl\ *n* : a unit combining the transmission and the front axle of a front-wheel-drive automobile

trans•ceiv•er \tran-ˈsē-vər\ *n* : a radio transmitter-receiver that uses many of the same components for both transmission and reception

tran•scend \tran-ˈsend\ *vb* **1** : to rise above the limits of **2** : SURPASS **syn** exceed, outdo, outshine, outstrip

tran•scen•dent \-ˈsen-dənt\ *adj* **1** : exceeding usual limits : SURPASSING **2** : transcending material existence **syn** superlative, supreme, peerless, incomparable

tran•scen•den•tal \ˌtran-ˌsen-ˈdent-ᵊl, -sən-\ *adj* **1** : TRANSCENDENT 2 **2** : of, relating to, or characteristic of transcendentalism; *also* : ABSTRUSE

tran•scen•den•tal•ism \-ᵊl-ˌi-zəm\ *n* : a philosophy holding that ultimate reality is unknowable or asserting the primacy of the spiritual over the material and empirical — **tran•scen•den•tal•ist** \-ᵊl-ist\ *adj or n*

trans•con•ti•nen•tal \ˌtrans-ˌkänt-ᵊn-ˈent-ᵊl\ *adj* : extending or going across a continent

tran•scribe \trans-ˈkrīb\ *vb* **tran•scribed; tran•scrib•ing** **1** : to write a copy of **2** : to make a copy of (dictated or recorded matter) in longhand or on a typewriter **3** : to represent (speech sounds) by means of phonetic symbols; *also* : to make a musical transcription of

tran•script \ˈtran-ˌskript\ *n* **1** : a written, printed, or typed copy **2** : an official copy esp. of a student's educational record

tran•scrip•tion \tran-ˈskrip-shən\ *n* **1** : an act or process of transcribing **2** : COPY, TRANSCRIPT **3** : an arrangement of a musical composition for some instrument or voice other than the original

tran•scrip•tion•ist \-shə-nist\ *n* : one that transcribes; *esp* : a typist who transcribes medical reports

trans•der•mal \trans-ˈdər-məl, ˈtranz-\ *adj* : relating to, being, or supplying a medication in a form for absorption through the skin ⟨~ nicotine patch⟩

trans•duc•er \trans-ˈdü-sər, tranz-, -ˈdyü-\ *n* : a device that is actuated by power from one system and supplies power usu. in another form to a second system

tran•sept \ˈtran-ˌsept\ *n* : the part of a cruciform church that crosses at right angles to the greatest length; *also* : either of the projecting ends

¹trans•fer \trans-ˈfər, ˈtrans-ˌfər\ *vb* **trans•ferred; trans•fer•ring** **1** : to pass or cause to pass from one person, place, or situation to another : TRANSPORT, TRANSMIT **2** : to make over the possession of : CONVEY **3** : to print or copy from one surface to another by contact **4** : to change from one vehicle or transportation line to another — **trans•fer•able** \trans-ˈfər-ə-bəl\ *adj* — **trans•fer•al** \-əl\ *n*

²trans•fer \ˈtrans-ˌfər\ *n* **1** : conveyance of right, title, or interest in property from one person to another **2** : an act or process of transferring **3** : one that transfers or is transferred **4** : a ticket entitling a passenger to continue a trip on another route

trans•fer•ence \trans-ˈfər-əns\ *n* : an act, process, or instance of transferring

trans•fig•ure \trans-ˈfi-gyər\ *vb* **-ured; -ur•ing** **1** : to change the form or appearance of **2** : EXALT, GLORIFY — **trans•fig•u•ra•tion** \ˌtrans-ˌfi-gyə-ˈrā-shən, -gə-\ *n*

trans•fix \trans-ˈfiks\ *vb* **1** : to pierce through with or as if with a pointed weapon **2** : to hold motionless by or as if by piercing

trans•form \trans-ˈförm\ *vb* : to change in structure, appearance, or character **syn** transmute, transfigure, transmogrify — **trans•for•ma•tion** \ˌtrans-fər-ˈmā-shən\ *n*

trans•form•er \trans-ˈför-mər\ *n* : one that transforms; *esp* : a device for converting variations of current in one circuit into variations of voltage and current in another circuit

trans•fuse \trans-ˈfyüz\ *vb* **trans•fused; trans•fus•ing** **1** : to cause to pass from one to another **2** : to diffuse into or through **3** : to transfer (as blood) into a vein of a person or animal — **trans•fu•sion** \-ˈfyü-zhən\ *n*

trans•gress \trans-ˈgres, tranz-\ *vb* [F *transgresser*, fr. L *transgressus*, pp. of *transgredi* to step beyond or across, fr. *trans-* across + *gradi* to step] **1** : to go beyond the limits set by ⟨~ the divine law⟩ **2** : to go beyond : EXCEED **3** : SIN — **trans•gres•sion** \-ˈgre-shən\ *n* — **trans•gres•sor** \-ˈgre-sər\ *n*

¹tran•sient \ˈtran-shənt; -sē-ənt, -shē-, -zē-\ *adj* **1** : not lasting long : SHORT-LIVED **2** : passing through a place with only a brief stay **syn** transitory, passing, momentary, fleeting — **tran•sient•ly** *adv*

[2]**transient** *n* : one that is transient; *esp* : a transient guest

tran•sis•tor \tran-ˈzis-tər, -ˈsis-\ *n* [*trans*fer + re*sistor*; fr. its transferring an electrical signal across a resistor] **1** : a small electronic semiconductor device used in electronic equipment **2** : a radio having transistors

tran•sis•tor•ized \-tə-ˌrīzd\ *adj* : having or using transistors

tran•sit \ˈtran-sət, -zət\ *n* **1** : a passing through, across, or over : PASSAGE **2** : conveyance of persons or things from one place to another **3** : usu. local transportation esp. of people by public conveyance **4** : a surveyor's instrument for measuring angles

tran•si•tion \tran-ˈsi-shən, -ˈzi-\ *n* : passage from one state, place, stage, or subject to another : CHANGE — **tran•si•tion•al** \-ˈsi-shə-nəl, ˈzi-\ *adj*

tran•si•tive \ˈtran-sə-tiv, -zə-\ *adj* **1** : having or containing an object required to complete the meaning **2** : TRANSITIONAL — **tran•si•tive•ly** *adv* — **tran•si•tive•ness** *n* — **tran•si•tiv•i•ty** \ˌtran-sə-ˈti-və-tē, -zə-\ *n*

tran•si•to•ry \ˈtran-sə-ˌtōr-ē, -zə-\ *adj* : of brief duration : SHORT-LIVED, TEMPORARY **syn** transient, passing, momentary, fleeting

transl *abbr* translated; translation

trans•late \trans-ˈlāt, tranz-\ *vb* **trans•lat•ed; trans•lat•ing 1** : to change from one place, state, or form to another **2** : to convey to heaven without death **3** : to turn into one's own or another language — **trans•lat•able** *adj* — **trans•la•tion** \-ˈlā-shən\ *n* — **trans•la•tor** \-ˈlā-tər\ *n*

trans•lit•er•ate \trans-ˈli-tə-ˌrāt, tranz-\ *vb* **-at•ed; -at•ing** : to represent or spell in the characters of another alphabet — **trans•lit•er•a•tion** \ˌtrans-ˌli-tə-ˈrā-shən, ˌtranz-\ *n*

trans•lu•cent \trans-ˈlüs-ᵊnt, tranz-\ *adj* : not transparent but clear enough to allow light to pass through — **trans•lu•cence** \-ᵊns\ *n* — **trans•lu•cen•cy** \-ᵊn-sē\ *n* — **trans•lu•cent•ly** *adv*

trans•mi•grate \-ˈmī-ˌgrāt\ *vb* : to pass at death from one body or being to another — **trans•mi•gra•tion** \ˌtrans-mī-ˈgrā-shən, ˌtranz-\ *n* — **trans•mi•gra•to•ry** \trans-ˈmī-grə-ˌtōr-ē\ *adj*

trans•mis•sion \-ˈmi-shən\ *n* **1** : an act or process of transmitting **2** : the passage of radio waves between transmitting stations and receiving stations **3** : the gears by which power is transmitted from the engine of an automobile to the axle that propels the vehicle **4** : something transmitted

trans•mit \-ˈmit\ *vb* **trans•mit•ted; trans•mit•ting 1** : to transfer from one person or place to another : FORWARD **2** : to pass on by or as if by inheritance **3** : to cause or allow to spread abroad or to another ⟨∼ a disease⟩ **4** : to cause (as light, electricity, or force) to pass through space or a medium **5** : to send out (radio or television signals) **syn** convey, communicate, impart — **trans•mis•si•ble** \-ˈmi-sə-bəl\ *adj* — **trans•mit•ta•ble** \-ˈmi-tə-bəl\ *adj* — **trans•mit•tal** \-ˈmit-ᵊl\ *n*

trans•mit•ter \-ˈmi-tər\ *n* : one that transmits; *esp* : an apparatus for transmitting telegraph, radio, or television signals

trans•mog•ri•fy \trans-ˈmä-grə-ˌfī, tranz-\ *vb* **-fied; -fy•ing** : to change or alter often with grotesque or humorous effect — **trans•mog•ri•fi•ca•tion** \-ˌmä-grə-fə-ˈkā-shən\ *n*

trans•mute \-ˈmyüt\ *vb* **trans•muted; trans•mut•ing** : to change or alter in form, appearance, or nature **syn** transform, convert, transfigure, metamorphose — **trans•mu•ta•tion** \ˌtrans-myu̇-ˈtā-shən, ˌtranz-\ *n*

trans•na•tion•al \-ˈna-shə-nəl\ *adj* : extending beyond national boundaries

trans•oce•an•ic \ˌtrans-ˌō-shē-ˈa-nik, ˌtranz-\ *adj* **1** : lying or dwelling beyond the ocean **2** : crossing or extending across the ocean

tran•som \ˈtran-səm\ *n* **1** : a piece (as a crossbar in the frame of a window or door) that lies crosswise in a structure **2** : a window above an opening (as a door) built on and often hinged to a horizontal crossbar

tran•son•ic *also* **trans–son•ic** \trans-ˈsä-nik\ *adj* : being or relating to speeds near that of sound in air or about 741 miles (1185 kilometers) per hour

trans•pa•cif•ic \ˌtrans-pə-ˈsi-fik\ *adj* : crossing, extending across, or situated beyond the Pacific Ocean

trans•par•ent \trans-ˈpar-ənt\ *adj* **1** : clear enough to be seen through **2** : SHEER, DIAPHANOUS ⟨a ∼ fabric⟩ **3** : readily understood : CLEAR; *also* : easily detected ⟨a ∼ lie⟩ **syn** lucid, translucent, lucent — **trans•par•en•cy** \-ən-sē\ *n* — **trans•par•ent•ly** *adv*

tran•spire \trans-ˈpīr\ *vb* **trans•pired; trans•pir•ing** [MF *transpirer,* fr. L *trans-* across + *spirare* to breathe] **1** : to pass or give off (as water vapor) through pores or a membrane **2** : to become known **3** : to take place : HAPPEN — **tran•spi•ra•tion** \ˌtrans-pə-ˈrā-shən\ *n*

[1]**trans•plant** \trans-ˈplant\ *vb* **1** : to dig up and plant elsewhere **2** : to remove from one place and settle or introduce elsewhere : TRANSPORT **3** : to transfer (an organ or tissue) from one part or individual to another — **trans•plan•ta•tion** \ˌtrans-ˌplan-ˈtā-shən\ *n*

[2]**trans•plant** \ˈtrans-ˌplant\ *n* **1** : a person or thing transplanted **2** : the act or process of transplanting

trans•po•lar \trans-ˈpō-lər\ *adj* : going or extending across either of the polar regions

transponder \tran-ˈspän-dər\ *n* [*trans*mitter + re*sponder*] : a radio or radar set that upon receiving a certain signal emits a signal of its own and that is used esp. for the identification and location of objects

[1]**trans•port** \trans-ˈpōrt\ *vb* **1** : to convey from one place to another : CARRY **2** : to carry away by strong emotion : ENRAPTURE **3** : to send to a penal colony overseas **syn** bear, ferry — **trans•por•ta•tion** \ˌtrans-pər-ˈtā-shən\ *n* — **trans•port•er** *n*

[2]**trans•port** \ˈtrans-ˌpōrt\ *n* **1** : an act of transporting **2** : strong or intensely pleasurable emotion ⟨∼*s* of joy⟩ **3** : a ship used in transporting troops or supplies; *also* : a vehicle (as a truck or plane) used to transport persons or goods

trans•pose \trans-ˈpōz\ *vb* **trans•posed; trans•pos•ing 1** : to change the position or sequence of ⟨∼ the letters in a word⟩ **2** : to write or perform (a musical composition) in a different key — **trans•po•si•tion** \ˌtrans-pə-ˈzi-shən\ *n*

trans•sex•u•al \(ˌ)trans-ˈsek-shə-wəl\ *n* : a person with a psychological urge to belong to the opposite sex that may be carried to the point of undergoing surgery to modify the sex organs to mimic the opposite sex

trans•ship \tran-ˈship, trans-\ *vb* : to transfer for further transportation from one ship or conveyance to another — **trans•ship•ment** *n*

tran•sub•stan•ti•a•tion \ˌtran-səb-ˌstan-chē-ˈā-shən\ *n* : the change in the eucharistic elements from the substance of bread and wine to the substance of the body of Christ with only the appearances of bread and wine remaining

trans•verse \trans-ˈvərs, tranz-\ *adj* : lying across : set crosswise — **transverse** \ˈtrans-ˌvərs, ˈtranz-\ *n* — **trans•verse•ly** *adv*

trans•ves•tite \trans-ˈves-ˌtīt, tranz-\ *n* : a person and esp. a male who adopts the dress and often the behavior of the opposite sex — **transvestite** *adj* — **trans•ves•tism** \-ˌti-zəm\ *n*

[1]**trap** \ˈtrap\ *n* **1** : a device for catching animals **2** : something by which one is caught unawares; *also* : a situation from which escape is difficult or impossible **3** : a machine for throwing clay pigeons into the air; *also* : SAND TRAP **4** : a light one-horse carriage on springs **5** : a device to allow some one thing to pass through while keeping other things out ⟨a ∼ in a

DICTIONARY

drainpipe⟩ **6** *pl* : a group of percussion instruments (as in a dance orchestra)

²trap *vb* **trapped; trap•ping 1 :** to catch in or as if in a trap; *also* : CONFINE **2 :** to provide or set (a place) with traps **3 :** to set traps for animals esp. as a business **syn** snare, entrap, ensnare, bag, lure, decoy — **trap•per** *n*

trap•door \ˈtrap-ˈdōr\ *n* : a lifting or sliding door covering an opening in a floor or roof

tra•peze \tra-ˈpēz\ *n* : a gymnastic apparatus consisting of a horizontal bar suspended by two parallel ropes

trap•e•zoid \ˈtra-pə-ˌzȯid\ *n* [NL *trapezoïdes*, fr. Gk *trapezoeidēs* trapezoidal, fr. *trapeza* table, fr. *tra*- four + *peza* foot] : a plane 4-sided figure with two and only two sides parallel — **trap•e•zoi•dal** \ˌtra-pə-ˈzȯid-ᵊl\ *adj*

trap•pings \ˈtra-piŋz\ *n pl* **1 :** CAPARISON 1 **2 :** outward decoration or dress; *also* : outward sign ⟨~ of success⟩

traps \ˈtraps\ *n pl* : personal belongings : LUGGAGE

trap•shoot•ing \ˈtrap-ˌshü-tiŋ\ *n* : shooting at clay pigeons sprung from a trap into the air away from the shooter

¹trash \ˈtrash\ *n* **1 :** something of little worth : RUBBISH **2 :** a worthless person; *also* : such persons as a group : RIFFRAFF — **trashy** *adj*

²trash *vb* **1 :** VANDALIZE, DESTROY **2 :** ATTACK **3 :** SPOIL, RUIN **4 :** to criticize or disparage harshly

trau•ma \ˈtrau̇-mə, ˈtrȯ-\ *n, pl* **traumas** *also* **trau•ma•ta** \-mə-tə\ [Gk] : a bodily or mental injury usu. caused by an external agent; *also* : a cause of trauma — **trau•mat•ic** \trə-ˈma-tik, trȯ-, trau̇-\ *adj*

¹tra•vail \trə-ˈvāl, ˈtra-ˌvāl\ *n* **1 :** painful work or exertion : TOIL **2 :** AGONY, TORMENT **3 :** CHILDBIRTH, LABOR

²travail *vb* : to labor hard : TOIL

¹trav•el \ˈtra-vəl\ *vb* **-eled** *or* **-elled; -el•ing** *or* **-el•ling** [ME *travailen* to labor, journey, fr. OF *travaillier* to torture, labor, fr. (assumed) VL *trepaliare* to torture, fr. LL *trepalium* instrument of torture] **1 :** to go on or as if on a trip or tour : JOURNEY **2 :** to move as if by traveling ⟨news *~s* fast⟩ **3 :** ASSOCIATE **4 :** to go from place to place as a sales representative **5 :** to move from point to point ⟨light waves ~ very fast⟩ **6 :** to journey over or through ⟨*~ing* the highways⟩ — **trav•el•er** *or* **trav•el•ler** *n*

²travel *n* **1 :** the act of traveling : PASSAGE **2 :** JOURNEY, TRIP — often used in pl. **3 :** the number traveling : TRAFFIC **4 :** the motion of a piece of machinery and esp. when to and fro

traveler's check *n* : a check paid for in advance that is signed when bought and signed again when cashed

traveling bag *n* : SUITCASE

trav•el•ogue *or* **trav•el•og** \ˈtra-və-ˌlȯg, -ˌläg\ *n* : a usu. illustrated lecture on travel

¹tra•verse \ˈtra-vərs\ *n* : something that crosses or lies across

²tra•verse \trə-ˈvərs, tra-ˈvərs *or* ˈtra-vərs\ *vb* **tra•versed; tra•vers•ing 1 :** to go or travel across or over **2 :** to move or pass along or through **3 :** to extend over **4 :** SWIVEL

³tra•verse \ˈtra-ˌvərs\ *adj* : TRANSVERSE

trav•er•tine \ˈtra-vər-ˌtēn, -tən\ *n* : a crystalline mineral formed by deposition from spring waters

¹trav•es•ty \ˈtra-və-stē\ *vb* **-tied; -ty•ing :** to make a travesty of

²travesty *n, pl* **-ties** [obs. E *travesty* disguised, parodied, fr. F *travesti*, pp. of *travestir* to disguise, fr. It *travestire*, fr. *tra-* across (fr. L *trans-*) + *vestire* to dress] : an imitation that makes crude fun of something; *also* : an inferior imitation

¹trawl \ˈtrȯl\ *vb* : to fish or catch with a trawl — **trawl•er** *n*

²trawl *n* **1 :** a large conical net dragged along the sea bottom in fishing **2 :** a long heavy fishing line equipped with many hooks in series

tray \ˈtrā\ *n* : an open receptacle with flat bottom and low rim for holding, carrying, or exhibiting articles

treach•er•ous \ˈtre-chə-rəs\ *adj* **1 :** characterized by treachery **2 :** UNTRUSTWORTHY, UNRELIABLE **3 :** providing insecure footing or support **syn** traitorous, faithless, false, disloyal — **treach•er•ous•ly** *adv*

treach•ery \ˈtre-chə-rē\ *n, pl* **-er•ies :** violation of allegiance or trust

trea•cle \ˈtrē-kəl\ *n* [ME *triacle* a medicinal compound, fr. MF, fr. L *theriaca*, fr. Gk *thēriakē* antidote against a poisonous bite, fr. *thērion* wild animal] *chiefly Brit* : MOLASSES — **trea•cly** \-k(ə-)lē\ *adj*

¹tread \ˈtred\ *vb* **trod** \ˈträd\; **trod•den** \ˈträd-ᵊn\ *or* **trod; tread•ing 1 :** to step or walk on or over **2 :** to move on foot : WALK; *also* : DANCE **3 :** to beat or press with the feet

²tread *n* **1 :** a mark made by or as if by treading **2 :** the manner or sound of stepping **3 :** the part of a wheel that makes contact with a road **4 :** the horizontal part of a step

trea•dle \ˈtred-ᵊl\ *n* : a lever device pressed by the foot to drive a machine — **treadle** *vb*

tread•mill \ˈtred-ˌmil\ *n* **1 :** a mill worked by persons who tread on steps around the edge of a wheel or by animals that walk on an endless belt **2 :** a device with an endless belt on which a person walks or runs in place **3 :** a wearisome routine

treas *abbr* treasurer; treasury

trea•son \ˈtrēz-ᵊn\ *n* : the offense of attempting to overthrow the government of one's country or of assisting its enemies in war — **trea•son•able** \-ᵊn-ə-bəl\ *adj* — **trea•son•ous** \-ᵊn-əs\ *adj*

¹trea•sure \ˈtre-zhər, ˈtrā-\ *n* **1 :** wealth stored up or held in reserve **2 :** something of great value

²treasure *vb* **trea•sured; trea•sur•ing 1 :** HOARD **2 :** to keep as precious : CHERISH **syn** prize, value, appreciate, esteem

trea•sur•er *n* : an officer of a club, business, or government who has charge of money taken in and paid out

treasure trove \-ˌtrōv\ *n* **1 :** treasure of unknown ownership found buried or hidden **2 :** a valuable discovery

trea•sury \ˈtre-zhə-rē, ˈtrā-\ *n, pl* **-sur•ies 1 :** a place in which stores of wealth are kept **2 :** the place where collected funds are stored and paid out **3** *cap* : a governmental department in charge of finances

¹treat \ˈtrēt\ *vb* **1 :** NEGOTIATE **2 :** to deal with esp. in writing; *also* : HANDLE **3 :** to pay for the food or entertainment of **4 :** to behave or act toward ⟨~ them well⟩ **5 :** to regard in a specified manner ⟨~ as inferiors⟩ **6 :** to give medical or surgical care to **7 :** to subject to some action ⟨~ soil with lime⟩

²treat *n* **1 :** an entertainment given free to those invited **2 :** a source of joy or amusement

trea•tise \ˈtrē-təs\ *n* : a systematic written exposition or argument

treat•ment \ˈtrēt-mənt\ *n* : the act or manner or an instance of treating someone or something; *also* : a substance or method used in treating

trea•ty \ˈtrē-tē\ *n, pl* **treaties :** an agreement made by negotiation or diplomacy esp. between two or more states or governments

¹tre•ble \ˈtre-bəl\ *n* **1 :** the highest of the four voice parts in vocal music : SOPRANO **2 :** a high-pitched or shrill voice or sound **3 :** the upper half of the musical pitch range

²treble *adj* **1 :** triple in number or amount **2 :** relating to or having the range of a musical treble **3 :** high-pitched : SHRILL — **tre•bly** *adv*

³treble *vb* **tre•bled; tre•bling :** to make or become three times the size, amount, or number

¹tree \ˈtrē\ *n* **1 :** a woody perennial plant usu. with a single main stem and a head of branches and leaves at the top **2 :** a piece of wood adapted to a particular use ⟨a shoe ~⟩ **3 :** something resembling a tree ⟨a genealogical ~⟩ — **tree•less** *adj*

[2]**tree** *vb* **treed; tree•ing :** to drive to or up a tree ⟨~ a raccoon⟩

tree farm *n* **:** an area of forest land managed to ensure continuous commercial production

tree line *n* **:** TIMBERLINE

tree of heaven : a Chinese ailanthus that is widely grown as a shade and ornamental tree

tree surgery *n* **:** operative treatment of diseased trees esp. for control of decay — **tree surgeon** *n*

tre•foil \ˈtrē-ˌfȯil, ˈtre-\ *n* **1 :** an herb (as clover) with leaves with three leaflets **2 :** a decorative design with three leaflike parts

[1]**trek** \ˈtrek\ *vb* **trekked; trek•king 1** *chiefly southern Africa* **:** to travel or migrate by ox wagon **2 :** to make one's way arduously

[2]**trek** *n* **1** *chiefly southern Africa* **:** a migration esp. of settlers by ox wagon **2 :** a slow or difficult journey

[1]**trel•lis** \ˈtre-ləs\ *n* [ME *trelis,* fr. MF *treliz* fabric of coarse weave, trellis, fr. (assumed) VL *trilicius* woven with triple thread, fr. L *tres* three + *licium* thread] **:** a frame of latticework used esp. for climbing plants

[2]**trellis** *vb* **:** to provide with a trellis; *esp* **:** to train (as a vine) on a trellis

trem•a•tode \ˈtre-mə-ˌtōd\ *n* **:** any of a class of parasitic worms

[1]**trem•ble** \ˈtrem-bəl\ *vb* **trem•bled; trem•bling 1 :** to shake involuntarily (as with fear or cold) **:** SHIVER **2 :** to move, sound, pass, or come to pass as if shaken or tremulous **3 :** to be affected with fear or doubt

[2]**tremble** *n* **:** a spell of shaking or quivering

tre•men•dous \tri-ˈmen-dəs\ *adj* **1 :** causing dread, awe, or terror **:** TERRIFYING **2 :** unusually large, powerful, great, or excellent **syn** stupendous, monumental, monstrous — **tre•men•dous•ly** *adv*

trem•o•lo \ˈtre-mə-ˌlō\ *n, pl* **-los** [It] **:** a rapid fluttering of a tone or alternating tones

trem•or \ˈtre-mər\ *n* **1 :** a trembling or shaking esp. from weakness, emotional stress, or disease **2 :** a quivering motion of the earth (as during an earthquake)

trem•u•lous \ˈtrem-yə-ləs\ *adj* **1 :** marked by trembling or tremors **:** QUIVERING **2 :** TIMOROUS, TIMID — **trem•u•lous•ly** *adv*

[1]**trench** \ˈtrench\ *n* [ME *trenche* track cut through a wood, fr. MF, act of cutting, fr. *trenchier* to cut, prob. fr. (assumed) VL *trinicare* to cut in three, fr. L *trini* three each] **1 :** a long narrow cut in the ground **:** DITCH; *esp* **:** a ditch protected by banks of earth and used to shelter soldiers **2** *pl* **:** a place or situation likened to trench warfare **3 :** a long narrow steep-sided depression in the ocean floor

[2]**trench** *vb* **1 :** to cut or dig trenches in **2 :** to protect (troops) with trenches **3 :** to come close **:** VERGE

tren•chant \ˈtren-chənt\ *adj* **1 :** vigorously effective; *also* **:** CAUSTIC **2 :** sharply perceptive **:** KEEN **3 :** CLEAR-CUT, DISTINCT

tren•cher \ˈtren-chər\ *n* **:** a wooden platter for serving food

tren•cher•man \ˈtren-chər-mən\ *n* **:** a hearty eater

trench foot *n* **:** a painful foot disorder resembling frostbite and resulting from exposure to cold and wet

trench mouth *n* **:** a progressive painful disease of the mouth and adjacent parts that is marked by ulceration and associated with a great increase in certain bacteria normally present in the mouth

[1]**trend** \ˈtrend\ *vb* **1 :** to have or take a general direction **:** TEND **2 :** to show a tendency **:** INCLINE

[2]**trend** *n* **1 :** a general direction taken (as by a stream or mountain range) **2 :** a prevailing tendency **:** DRIFT **3 :** a current style or preference **:** VOGUE

trendy \ˈtren-dē\ *adj* **trend•i•er; -est :** very fashionable; *also* **:** marked by superficial or faddish appeal or taste

trep•i•da•tion \ˌtre-pə-ˈdā-shən\ *n* **:** nervous agitation **:** APPREHENSION **syn** horror, terror, panic, consternation, dread, fright, dismay

[1]**tres•pass** \ˈtres-pəs, -ˌpas\ *n* **1 :** SIN, OFFENSE **2 :** unlawful entry on someone else's land **syn** transgression, violation, infraction, infringement

[2]**trespass** *vb* **1 :** to commit an offense **:** ERR, SIN **2 :** INTRUDE, ENCROACH; *esp* **:** to enter unlawfully upon the land of another — **tres•pass•er** *n*

tress \ˈtres\ *n* **:** a long lock of hair — usu. used in pl.

tres•tle *also* **tres•sel** \ˈtre-səl\ *n* **1 :** a supporting framework consisting usu. of a horizontal piece with spreading legs at each end **2 :** a braced framework of timbers, piles, or steel for carrying a road or railroad over a depression

trey \ˈtrā\ *n, pl* **treys :** a card or the side of a die with three spots

tri•ad \ˈtrī-ˌad, -əd\ *n* **:** a union or group of three usu. closely related persons or things

tri•age \trē-ˈäzh, ˈtrē-ˌäzh\ *n* [F, sorting] **:** the sorting of and allocation of treatment to patients and esp. battle or disaster victims according to a system of priorities designed to maximize the number of survivors

tri•al \ˈtrī-əl\ *n* **1 :** the action or process of trying or putting to the proof **:** TEST **2 :** the hearing and judgment of a matter in issue before a competent tribunal **3 :** a source of vexation or annoyance **4 :** an experiment to test quality, value, or usefulness **5 :** EFFORT, ATTEMPT **syn** cross, ordeal, tribulation, affliction — **trial** *adj*

tri•an•gle \ˈtrī-ˌaŋ-gəl\ *n* **1 :** a plane figure that has three sides and three angles **:** a polygon having three sides **2 :** something shaped like a triangle — **tri•an•gu•lar** \trī-ˈaŋ-gyə-lər\ *adj* — **tri•an•gu•lar•ly** *adv*

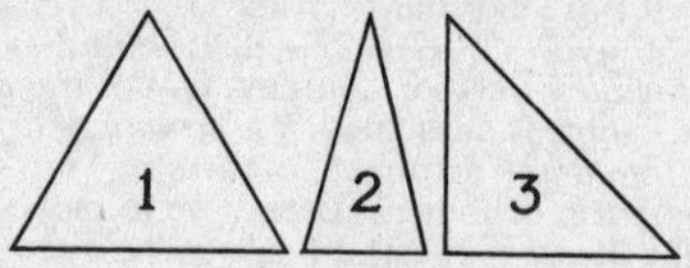

triangle 1: *1* equilateral, *2* isosceles, *3* right triangle

tri•an•gu•la•tion \(ˌ)trī-ˌaŋ-gyə-ˈlā-shən\ *n* **:** a method using trigonometry to find the location of a point using bearings from two fixed points a known distance apart — **tri•an•gu•late** \trī-ˈaŋ-gyə-ˌlāt\ *vb*

Tri•as•sic \trī-ˈa-sik\ *adj* **:** of, relating to, or being the earliest period of the Mesozoic era marked by the first appearance of the dinosaurs — **Triassic** *n*

trib *abbr* tributary

tribe \ˈtrīb\ *n* **1 :** a social group comprising numerous families, clans, or generations **2 :** a group of persons having a common character, occupation, or interest **3 :** a group of related plants or animals ⟨the cat ~⟩ — **trib•al** \ˈtrī-bəl\ *adj*

tribes•man \ˈtrībz-mən\ *n* **:** a member of a tribe

trib•u•la•tion \ˌtri-byə-ˈlā-shən\ *n* [ME *tribulacion,* fr. OF, fr. L *tribulatio,* fr. *tribulare* to press, oppress, fr. *tribulum* drag used in threshing] **:** distress or suffering resulting from oppression or persecution; *also* **:** a trying experience **syn** trial, affliction, cross, ordeal

tri•bu•nal \trī-ˈbyün-ᵊl, tri-\ *n* **1 :** the seat of a judge **2 :** a court of justice **3 :** something that decides or determines ⟨the ~ of public opinion⟩

tri•bune \ˈtri-ˌbyün, tri-ˈbyün\ *n* **1 :** an official in ancient Rome with the function of protecting the interests of plebeian citizens from the patricians **2 :** a defender of the people

[1]**trib•u•tary** \ˈtri-byə-ˌter-ē\ *adj* **1 :** paying tribute **:** SUBJECT **2 :** flowing into a larger stream or a lake **syn** subordinate, secondary, dependent

²tributary *n, pl* **-tar·ies 1 :** a ruler or state that pays tribute **2 :** a tributary stream

trib·ute \ˈtri-(ˌ)byüt, -byət\ *n* **1 :** a payment by one ruler or nation to another as an act of submission or price of protection **2 :** a usu. excessive tax, rental, or levy exacted by a sovereign or superior **3 :** a gift or service showing respect, gratitude, or affection; *also* **:** PRAISE **syn** eulogy, citation, encomium, panegyric

trice \ˈtrīs\ *n* **:** INSTANT, MOMENT

tri·ceps \ˈtrī-ˌseps\ *n, pl* **triceps :** a large muscle along the back of the upper arm that is attached at its upper end by three main parts and acts to extend the forearm at the elbow joint

tri·cer·a·tops \(ˌ)trī-ˈser-ə-ˌtäps\ *n, pl* **-tops** *also* **-tops·es** [NL, fr. Gk *tri-* three + *kerat-, keras* horn + *ōps* face] **:** any of a genus of large plant-eating Cretaceous dinosaurs with three horns, a bony crest on the neck, and hoofed toes

tri·chi·na \tri-ˈkī-nə\ *n, pl* **-nae** \-(ˌ)nē\ *also* **-nas :** a small slender nematode worm that in the larval state is parasitic in the voluntary muscles of flesh-eating mammals (as the hog and humans)

trich·i·no·sis \ˌtri-kə-ˈnō-səs\ *n* **:** infestation with or disease caused by trichinae and marked esp. by pain, fever, and swelling

¹trick \ˈtrik\ *n* **1 :** a crafty procedure meant to deceive **2 :** a mischievous action **:** PRANK **3 :** a childish action **4 :** a deceptive or ingenious feat designed to puzzle or amuse **5 :** PECULIARITY, MANNERISM **6 :** a quick or artful way of getting a result **:** KNACK **7 :** the cards played in one round of a card game **8 :** a tour of duty **:** SHIFT **syn** ruse, maneuver, artifice, wile, feint

²trick *vb* **1 :** to deceive by cunning or artifice **:** CHEAT **2 :** to dress ornately

trick·ery \ˈtri-kə-rē\ *n* **:** deception by tricks and stratagems

trick·le \ˈtri-kəl\ *vb* **trick·led; trick·ling 1 :** to run or fall in drops **2 :** to flow in a thin gentle stream — **trickle** *n*

trick·ster \ˈtrik-stər\ *n* **:** one who tricks or cheats

tricky \ˈtri-kē\ *adj* **trick·i·er; -est 1 :** inclined to trickery **2 :** requiring skill or caution ⟨a ~ situation to handle⟩ **3 :** UNRELIABLE ⟨a ~ lock⟩

tri·col·or \ˈtrī-ˌkə-lər\ *n* **:** a flag of three colors ⟨the French ~⟩

tri·cy·cle \ˈtrī-(ˌ)si-kəl\ *n* **:** a 3-wheeled vehicle usu. propelled by pedals

tri·dent \ˈtrīd-ᵊnt\ *n* [L *trident-, tridens,* fr. *tri-* three + *dent-, dens* tooth] **:** a 3-pronged spear

tried \ˈtrīd\ *adj* **1 :** found trustworthy through testing **2 :** subjected to trials

tri·en·ni·al \trī-ˈe-nē-əl\ *adj* **1 :** occurring or being done every three years **2 :** lasting for three years — **triennial** *n*

¹tri·fle \ˈtrī-fəl\ *n* **:** something of little value or importance

²trifle *vb* **tri·fled; tri·fling 1 :** to talk in a jesting or mocking manner **2 :** to treat someone or something as unimportant **3 :** DALLY, FLIRT **4 :** to handle idly **:** TOY — **tri·fler** *n*

tri·fling \ˈtrī-fliŋ\ *adj* **1 :** FRIVOLOUS **2 :** TRIVIAL, INSIGNIFICANT **syn** petty, paltry, measly, inconsequential

tri·fo·cals \trī-ˈfō-kəlz\ *n pl* **:** eyeglasses with lenses having one part for close focus, one for intermediate focus, and one for distant focus

tri·fo·li·ate \trī-ˈfō-lē-ət\ *adj* **:** having three leaves or leaflets

¹trig \ˈtrig\ *adj* **:** stylishly trim **:** SMART

²trig *n* **:** TRIGONOMETRY

¹trig·ger \ˈtri-gər\ *n* [alter. of earlier *tricker,* fr. D *trekker,* fr. MD *trecker* one that pulls, fr. *trecken* to pull] **:** a movable lever that activates a device when it is squeezed; *esp* **:** the part of a firearm lock moved by the finger to fire a gun — **trigger** *adj* — **trig·gered** *adj*

²trigger *vb* **1 :** to fire by pulling a trigger **2 :** to initiate, actuate, or set off as if by a trigger

tri·glyc·er·ide *n* **:** any of a group of fats and oils that are derived from glycerol and fatty acids and are widespread in animal tissue

trig·o·nom·e·try \ˌtri-gə-ˈnä-mə-trē\ *n* **:** the branch of mathematics dealing with the properties of triangles and esp. with finding unknown angles or sides given the size or length of some angles or sides — **trig·o·no·met·ric** \-nə-ˈme-trik\ *also* **trig·o·no·met·ri·cal** \-tri-kəl\ *adj*

trike \ˈtrīk\ *n* **:** TRICYCLE

¹trill \ˈtril\ *n* **1 :** the alternation of two musical tones a scale degree apart **2 :** WARBLE **3 :** the rapid vibration of one speech organ against another (as of the tip of the tongue against the teeth)

²trill *vb* **:** to utter as or with a trill

tril·lion \ˈtril-yən\ *n* **1 :** a thousand billions **2** *Brit* **:** a million billions — **trillion** *adj* — **tril·lionth** \-yənth\ *adj or n*

tril·li·um \ˈtri-lē-əm\ *n* **:** any of a genus of herbs of the lily family with an erect stem bearing a whorl of three leaves and a large solitary usu. spring-blooming flower with three petals

tril·o·gy \ˈtri-lə-jē\ *n, pl* **-gies :** a series of three dramas or literary or musical compositions that are closely related and develop one theme

¹trim \ˈtrim\ *vb* **trimmed; trim·ming** [OE *trymian, trymman* to strengthen, arrange, fr. *trum* strong, firm] **1 :** to put ornaments on **:** ADORN **2 :** to defeat esp. resoundingly **3 :** to make trim, neat, regular, or less bulky by or as if by cutting ⟨~ a beard⟩ ⟨~ a budget⟩ **4 :** to cause (a boat) to assume a desired position in the water by arrangement of the load; *also* **:** to adjust (as a submarine or airplane) esp. for horizontal motion **5 :** to adjust (a sail) to a desired position **6 :** to change one's views for safety or expediency — **trim·ly** *adv* — **trim·mer** *n* — **trim·ness** *n*

²trim *adj* **trim·mer; trim·mest :** showing neatness, good order, or compactness ⟨a ~ figure⟩ **syn** tidy, trig, smart, spruce, shipshape

³trim *n* **1 :** good condition **:** FITNESS **2 :** material used for ornament or trimming; *esp* **:** the woodwork in the finish of a house esp. around doors and windows **3 :** the position of a ship or boat esp. with reference to the horizontal; *also* **:** the relation between the plane of a sail and the direction of a ship **4 :** the position of an airplane at which it will continue in level flight with no adjustments to the controls **5 :** something that is trimmed off

tri·ma·ran \ˈtrī-mə-ˌran, ˌtrī-mə-ˈran\ *n* **:** a sailboat with three hulls

tri·mes·ter \trī-ˈmes-tər, ˈtrī-ˌmes-tər\ *n* **1 :** a period of three or about three months (as in pregnancy) **2 :** one of three terms into which an academic year is sometimes divided

trim·e·ter \ˈtri-mə-tər\ *n* **:** a line of verse consisting of three metrical feet

trim·ming \ˈtri-miŋ\ *n* **1 :** DEFEAT **2 :** the action of one that trims **3 :** something that trims, ornaments, or completes

tri·month·ly \trī-ˈmənth-lē\ *adj* **:** occurring every three months

trine \ˈtrīn\ *adj* **:** THREEFOLD, TRIPLE

Trin·i·da·di·an \ˌtri-nə-ˈdā-dē-ən, -ˈda-\ *n* **:** a native or inhabitant of the island of Trinidad — **Trinidadian** *adj*

Trin·i·tar·i·an \ˌtri-nə-ˈter-ē-ən\ *n* **:** a believer in the doctrine of the Trinity — **Trin·i·tar·i·an·ism** \-ē-ə-ˌni-zəm\ *n*

Trin·i·ty \ˈtri-nə-tē\ *n* **1 :** the unity of Father, Son, and Holy Spirit as three persons in one Godhead **2** *not cap* **:** TRIAD

trin·ket \ˈtriŋ-kət\ *n* **1 :** a small ornament (as a jewel or ring) **2 :** TRIFLE

DICTIONARY

trio \ˈtrē-ō\ *n, pl* **tri•os** **1** : a musical composition for three voices or three instruments **2** : the performers of a trio **3** : a group or set of three

[1]trip \ˈtrip\ *vb* **tripped; trip•ping** **1** : to move with light quick steps **2** : to catch the foot against something so as to stumble or cause to stumble **3** : to make a mistake : SLIP; *also* : to detect in a misstep : EXPOSE **4** : to release (as a spring or switch) by moving a catch; *also* : ACTIVATE **5** : to get high on a drug and esp. a hallucinatory drug

[2]trip *n* **1** : JOURNEY, VOYAGE **2** : a quick light step **3** : a false step : STUMBLE; *also* : ERROR **4** : the action of tripping mechanically; *also* : a device for tripping **5** : an intense drug-induced hallucinatory experience **6** : absorption in an attitude or state of mind ⟨an ego ~⟩

tri•par•tite \trī-ˈpär-ˌtīt\ *adj* **1** : divided into three parts **2** : having three corresponding parts or copies **3** : made between three parties ⟨a ~ treaty⟩

tripe \ˈtrīp\ *n* **1** : stomach tissue of a ruminant and esp. an ox used as food **2** : something poor, worthless, or offensive : TRASH

[1]tri•ple \ˈtri-pəl\ *vb* **tri•pled; tri•pling** **1** : to make or become three times as great or as many **2** : to hit a triple

[2]triple *n* **1** : a triple quantity **2** : a group of three **3** : a hit in baseball that lets the batter reach third base

[3]triple *adj* **1** : being three times as great or as many **2** : having three units or members **3** : repeated three times

triple bond *n* : a chemical bond in which three pairs of electrons are shared by two atoms in a molecule

triple point *n* : the condition of temperature and pressure under which the gaseous, liquid, and solid forms of a substance can exist in equilibrium

trip•let \ˈtri-plət\ *n* **1** : a unit of three lines of verse **2** : a group of three of a kind **3** : one of three offspring born at one birth

tri•plex \ˈtri-ˌpleks, ˈtrī-\ *adj* : THREEFOLD, TRIPLE

[1]trip•li•cate \ˈtri-pli-kət\ *adj* : made in three identical copies

[2]trip•li•cate \-plə-ˌkāt\ *vb* **-cat•ed; -cat•ing** **1** : TRIPLE **2** : to provide three copies of ⟨~ a document⟩

[3]trip•li•cate \-pli-kət\ *n* : three copies all alike — used with *in* ⟨typed in ~⟩

tri•ply \ˈtri-plē, ˈtri-pə-lē\ *adv* : in a triple degree, amount, or manner

tri•pod \ˈtrī-ˌpäd\ *n* : something (as a caldron, stool, or camera stand) that rests on three legs — **tripod** *or* **tri•po•dal** \ˈtri-pəd-ᵊl, ˈtrī-ˌpäd-\ *adj*

trip•tych \ˈtrip-tik\ *n* : a picture or carving in three panels side by side

tri•reme \ˈtrī-ˌrēm\ *n* : an ancient galley having three banks of oars

tri•sect \ˈtrī-ˌsekt, trī-ˈsekt\ *vb* : to divide into three usu. equal parts — **tri•sec•tion** \ˈtrī-ˌsek-shən\ *n*

trite \ˈtrīt\ *adj* **trit•er; trit•est** [L *tritus*, fr. pp. of *terere* to rub, wear away] : used so commonly that the novelty is worn off : STALE **syn** hackneyed, stereotyped, commonplace, clichéd

tri•ti•um \ˈtri-tē-əm, ˈtri-shē-\ *n* : a radioactive form of hydrogen with atoms of three times the mass of ordinary hydrogen atoms

tri•ton \ˈtrīt-ᵊn\ *n* : any of various large marine gastropod mollusks with a heavy elongated conical shell; *also* : the shell of a triton

trit•u•rate \ˈtri-chə-ˌrāt\ *vb* **-rat•ed; -rat•ing** : to rub or grind to a fine powder

[1]tri•umph \ˈtrī-əmf\ *n, pl* **tri•umphs** **1** : the joy or exultation of victory or success **2** : VICTORY, CONQUEST — **tri•um•phal** \trī-ˈəm-fəl\ *adj*

[2]triumph *vb* **1** : to obtain victory : PREVAIL **2** : to celebrate victory or success exultantly — **tri•um•phant** \trī-ˈəm-fənt\ *adj* — **tri•um•phant•ly** *adv*

tri•um•vir \trī-ˈəm-vər\ *n, pl* **-virs** *also* **-vi•ri** \-və-ˌrī\ : a member of a triumvirate

tri•um•vi•rate \-və-rət\ *n* : a ruling body of three persons

tri•une \ˈtrī-ˌün, -ˌyün\ *adj, often cap* : being three in one ⟨the ~ God⟩

triv•et \ˈtri-vət\ *n* **1** : a 3-legged stand : TRIPOD **2** : a usu. metal stand with short feet for use under a hot dish

triv•ia \ˈtri-vē-ə\ *n sing or pl* : unimportant matters : TRIFLES

triv•i•al \ˈtri-vē-əl\ *adj* [L *trivialis* found everywhere, commonplace, fr. *trivium* crossroads, fr. *tri-* three + *via* way] : of little importance — **triv•i•al•i•ty** \ˌtri-vē-ˈa-lə-tē\ *n*

triv•i•um \ˈtri-vē-əm\ *n, pl* **triv•ia** \-vē-ə\ : the three liberal arts of grammar, rhetoric, and logic in a medieval university

tri•week•ly \trī-ˈwē-klē\ *adj* **1** : occurring or appearing three times a week **2** : occurring or appearing every three weeks — **triweekly** *adv*

tro•che \ˈtrō-kē\ *n* : a medicinal lozenge

tro•chee \ˈtrō-(ˌ)kē\ *n* : a metrical foot of one accented syllable followed by one unaccented syllable — **tro•cha•ic** \trō-ˈkā-ik\ *adj*

trod *past and past part of* TREAD

trodden *past part of* TREAD

troi•ka \ˈtrȯi-kə\ *n* [Russ *troĭka*, fr. *troe* three] : a group of three; *esp* : an administrative or ruling body of three

[1]troll \ˈtrōl\ *vb* **1** : to sing the parts of (a song) in succession **2** : to fish by trailing a lure or baited hook from a moving boat **3** : to sing or play jovially

[2]troll *n* : a lure used in trolling; *also* : the line with its lure

[3]troll *n* : a dwarf or giant in Scandinavian folklore inhabiting caves or hills

trol•ley *also* **trol•ly** \ˈträ-lē\ *n, pl* **trolleys** *also* **trollies** **1** : a device (as a grooved wheel on the end of a pole) to carry current from a wire to an electrically driven vehicle **2** : a streetcar powered electrically through a trolley **3** : a wheeled carriage running on an overhead rail or track

trol•ley•bus \ˈträ-lē-ˌbəs\ *n* : a bus powered electrically through a trolley

trolley car *n* : TROLLEY 2

trol•lop \ˈträ-ləp\ *n* : a disreputable woman; *esp* : one who engages in sex promiscuously

trom•bone \träm-ˈbōn, ˈträm-ˌbōn\ *n* [It, lit., big trumpet, fr. *tromba* trumpet] : a brass wind instrument that consists of a long metal tube with two turns and a flaring end and that usu. has a movable slide to vary the pitch — **trom•bon•ist** \-ˈbō-nist, -ˌbō-\ *n*

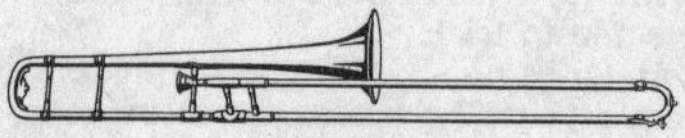

trombone

tromp \ˈträmp, ˈtrȯmp\ *vb* **1** : TRAMP, MARCH **2** : to stamp with the foot **3** : DEFEAT

[1]troop \ˈtrüp\ *n* **1** : a cavalry unit corresponding to an infantry company **2** *pl* : armed forces : SOLDIERS **3** : a collection of people or things **4** : a unit of Girl Scouts or Boy Scouts under an adult leader

[2]troop *vb* : to move or gather in crowds

troop•er \ˈtrü-pər\ *n* **1** : an enlisted cavalryman; *also* : a cavalry horse **2** : a mounted or a state police officer

troop•ship \ˈtrüp-ˌship\ *n* : a ship for carrying troops

trope \ˈtrōp\ *n* : a word or expression used in a figurative sense

tro•phy \ˈtrō-fē\ *n, pl* **trophies** : something gained or given in conquest or victory esp. when preserved or mounted as a memorial

trop•ic \ˈträ-pik\ *n* [ME *tropik*, fr. L *tropicus* of the solstice, fr. Gk *tropikos*, fr. *tropē* turn] **1** : either of the two parallels of latitude approximately 23½ degrees north (**tropic of Can•cer** \-ˈkan-sər\) or south (**tropic of Cap•ri•corn** \-ˈka-prə-ˌkȯrn\) of the equator where the sun is directly overhead when it reaches its most northerly or southerly point in the sky **2** *pl, often cap* : the region lying between the tropics — **trop•i•cal** \-pi-kəl\ *or* **tropic** *adj*

tro•pism \ˈtrō-ˌpi-zəm\ *n* : an automatic movement by an organism in response to a source of stimulation; *also* : a reflex reaction involving this

tro•po•sphere \ˈtrō-pə-ˌsfir, ˈträ-\ *n* : the part of the atmosphere between the earth's surface and the stratosphere in which most weather changes occur — **tro•po•spher•ic** \ˌtrō-pə-ˈsfir-ik, ˌträ-, -ˈsfer-\ *adj*

[1]**trot** \ˈträt\ *n* **1** : a moderately fast gait of a 4-footed animal (as a horse) in which the legs move in diagonal pairs **2** : a human jogging gait between a walk and a run

[2]**trot** *vb* **trot•ted; trot•ting 1** : to ride, drive, or go at a trot **2** : to proceed briskly : HURRY — **trot•ter** *n*

troth \ˈträth, ˈtrȯth, ˈtrōth\ *n* **1** : pledged faithfulness **2** : one's pledged word; *also* : BETROTHAL

trou•ba•dour \ˈtrü-bə-ˌdōr\ *n* [F, fr. OProv *trobador,* fr. *trobar* to compose] : any of a class of poet-musicians flourishing esp. in southern France and northern Italy during the 11th, 12th, and 13th centuries

[1]**trou•ble** \ˈtrə-bəl\ *vb* **trou•bled; trou•bling 1** : to agitate mentally or spiritually : DISTURB, WORRY **2** : to produce physical disorder in : AFFLICT **3** : to put to inconvenience **4** : RUFFLE ⟨~ the waters⟩ **5** : to make an effort **syn** distress, ail, upset — **trou•ble•some** *adj* — **trou•ble•some•ly** *adv* — **trou•blous** \-bə-ləs\ *adj*

[2]**trouble** *n* **1** : the quality or state of being troubled esp. mentally **2** : an instance of distress or annoyance **3** : DISEASE, AILMENT ⟨heart ~⟩ **4** : EXERTION, PAINS ⟨took the ~ to phone⟩ **5** : a cause of disturbance or distress

trou•ble•mak•er \-ˌmā-kər\ *n* : a person who causes trouble

trou•ble•shoot•er \-ˌshü-tər\ *n* **1** : a worker employed to locate trouble and make repairs in equipment **2** : an expert in resolving disputes or problems — **trou•ble•shoot** *vb*

trough \ˈtrȯf, ˈtrȯth, *by bakers often* ˈtrō\ *n, pl* **troughs** \ˈtrȯfs, ˈtrȯvz; ˈtrȯths, ˈtrȯt͟hz; ˈtrōz\ **1** : a long shallow open boxlike container esp. for water or feed for livestock **2** : a gutter along the eaves of a house **3** : a long channel or depression (as between waves or hills) **4** : an elongated area of low barometric pressure

trounce \ˈtrau̇ns\ *vb* **trounced; trounc•ing 1** : to thrash or punish severely **2** : to defeat decisively

troupe \ˈtrüp\ *n* : COMPANY; *esp* : a group of performers on the stage — **troup•er** *n*

trou•sers \ˈtrau̇-zərz\ *n pl* [alter. of earlier *trouse,* fr. ScGael *triubhas*] : an outer garment covering each leg separately and usu. extending from the waist to the ankle — **trouser** *adj*

trous•seau \ˈtrü-sō, trü-ˈsō\ *n, pl* **trousseaux** \-sōz, -ˈsōz\ *or* **trousseaus** [F] : the personal outfit of a bride

trout \ˈtrau̇t\ *n, pl* **trout** *also* **trouts** [ME, fr. OE *trūht,* fr. LL *tructa,* a fish with sharp teeth, fr. Gk *trōktēs,* lit., gnawer] : any of various mostly freshwater food and game fishes usu. smaller than the related salmons

trow \ˈtrō\ *vb, archaic* : THINK, SUPPOSE

trow•el \ˈtrau̇-əl\ *n* **1** : a hand tool used for spreading, shaping, or smoothing loose or plastic material (as mortar or plaster) **2** : a small flat or scooplike implement used in gardening — **trowel** *vb*

troy \ˈtrȯi\ *adj* : expressed in troy weight ⟨~ ounce⟩

troy weight *n* : a system of weights based on a pound of 12 ounces and an ounce of 480 grains (31 grams) — see WEIGHT table

tru•ant \ˈtrü-ənt\ *n* [ME, vagabond, idler, fr. OF, vagrant] : a student who stays out of school without permission — **tru•an•cy** \-ən-sē\ *n* — **truant** *adj*

truce \ˈtrüs\ *n* **1** : ARMISTICE **2** : a respite esp. from something unpleasant

[1]**truck** \ˈtrək\ *vb* **1** : EXCHANGE, BARTER **2** : to have dealings : TRAFFIC

[2]**truck** *n* **1** : BARTER **2** : small goods or merchandise; *esp* : vegetables grown for market **3** : DEALINGS

[3]**truck** *n* **1** : a wheeled vehicle (as a strong heavy automobile) designed for carrying heavy articles or hauling a trailer **2** : a swiveling frame with springs and one or more pairs of wheels used to carry and guide one end of a locomotive or railroad car

[4]**truck** *vb* **1** : to transport on a truck **2** : to be employed in driving a truck — **truck•er** *n*

truck farm *n* : a farm growing vegetables for market — **truck farmer** *n*

truck•le \ˈtrə-kəl\ *vb* **truck•led; truck•ling** : to yield slavishly to the will of another : SUBMIT **syn** fawn, toady, cringe, cower

truc•u•lent \ˈtrə-kyə-lənt\ *adj* **1** : feeling or showing ferocity : SAVAGE **2** : aggressively self-assertive : PUGNACIOUS — **truc•u•lence** \-ləns\ *n* — **truc•u•len•cy** \-lən-sē\ *n* — **truc•u•lent•ly** *adv*

trudge \ˈtrəj\ *vb* **trudged; trudg•ing** : to walk or march steadily and usu. laboriously

[1]**true** \ˈtrü\ *adj* **tru•er; tru•est 1** : STEADFAST, LOYAL **2** : agreeing with facts or reality ⟨a ~ description⟩ **3** : CONSISTENT ⟨~ to expectations⟩ **4** : properly so called ⟨~ love⟩ **5** : RIGHTFUL ⟨~ and lawful king⟩ **6** : conformable to a standard or pattern; *also* : placed or formed accurately **syn** constant, staunch, resolute, steadfast

[2]**true** *adv* **1** : TRUTHFULLY **2** : ACCURATELY ⟨the bullet flew straight and ~⟩; *also* : without variation from type ⟨breed ~⟩

[3]**true** *n* **1** : TRUTH, REALITY — usu. used with *the* **2** : the state of being accurate (as in alignment) ⟨out of ~⟩

[4]**true** *vb* **trued; true•ing** *also* **tru•ing** : to bring or restore to a desired precision

true–blue *adj* : marked by unswerving loyalty

true bug *n* : BUG 2

true•heart•ed \ˈtrü-ˈhär-təd\ *adj* : FAITHFUL, LOYAL

truf•fle \ˈtrə-fəl, ˈtrü-\ *n* **1** : the usu. dark and wrinkled edible fruit of any of several European underground fungi; *also* : one of these fungi **2** : a candy made of chocolate, butter, and sugar shaped into balls and coated with cocoa

tru•ism \ˈtrü-ˌi-zəm\ *n* : an undoubted or self-evident truth **syn** commonplace, platitude, bromide, cliché

tru•ly \ˈtrü-lē\ *adv* **1** : in all sincerity **2** : in agreement with fact **3** : ACCURATELY **4** : in a proper or suitable manner

[1]**trump** \ˈtrəmp\ *n* : TRUMPET

[2]**trump** *n* : a card of a designated suit any of whose cards will win over a card that is not of this suit; *also* : the suit itself — often used in pl.

[3]**trump** *vb* : to take with a trump

trumped–up \ˈtrəmpt-ˈəp\ *adj* : fraudulently concocted : SPURIOUS

trum•pery \ˈtrəm-pə-rē\ *n* **1** : NONSENSE **2** : trivial articles : JUNK

[1]**trum•pet** \ˈtrəm-pət\ *n* **1** : a wind instrument consisting of a long curved metal tube flaring at one end and with a cup-shaped mouthpiece at the other **2** : something that resembles a trumpet or its tonal quality **3** : a funnel-shaped instrument for collecting, directing, or intensifying sound

[2]**trumpet** *vb* **1** : to blow a trumpet **2** : to proclaim on or as if on a trumpet — **trum•pet•er** *n*

[1]**trun•cate** \ˈtrəŋ-ˌkāt, ˈtrən-\ *adj* : having the end square or blunt

[2]**truncate** *vb* **trun•cat•ed; trun•cat•ing** : to shorten by or as if by cutting : LOP — **trun•ca•tion** \ˌtrəŋ-ˈkā-shən\ *n*

trun•cheon \ˈtrən-chən\ *n* : a police officer's club

trun•dle \ˈtrənd-əl\ *vb* **trun•dled; trun•dling** : to roll along : WHEEL

trundle bed *n* : a low bed that can be stored under a higher bed

trunk \ˈtrəŋk\ *n* **1** : the main stem of a tree **2** : the body of a person or animal apart from the head and limbs **3** : the main or central part of something **4** : a box or chest used to hold usu. clothes or personal effects (as of a traveler); *also* : the enclosed luggage space in the rear of an automobile **5** : the long muscular nose of an elephant **6** *pl* : men's shorts worn chiefly for sports **7** : a usu. major channel or passage

trunk line *n* : a system handling long-distance through traffic

[1]**truss** \ˈtrəs\ *vb* **1** : to secure tightly : BIND **2** : to arrange for cooking by binding close the wings or legs of (a fowl) **3** : to support, strengthen, or stiffen by or as if by a truss

[2]**truss** *n* **1** : a collection of structural parts (as beams) forming a rigid framework (as in bridge or building construction) **2** : a device worn to reduce a hernia by pressure

[1]**trust** \ˈtrəst\ *n* **1** : assured reliance on the character, strength, or truth of someone or something **2** : a basis of reliance, faith, or hope **3** : confident hope **4** : financial credit **5** : a property interest held by one person for the benefit of another **6** : a combination of firms formed by a legal agreement; *esp* : one that reduces competition **7** : something entrusted to one to be cared for in the interest of another **8** : CARE, CUSTODY **syn** confidence, dependence, faith, reliance

[2]**trust** *vb* **1** : to place confidence : DEPEND **2** : to be confident : HOPE **3** : ENTRUST **4** : to permit to stay or go or to do something without fear or misgiving **5** : to rely on or on the truth of : BELIEVE **6** : to extend credit to

trust•ee \ˌtrəs-ˈtē\ *n* **1** : a person to whom property is legally committed in trust **2** : a country charged with the supervision of a trust territory

trust•ee•ship \ˌtrəs-ˈtē-ˌship\ *n* **1** : the office or function of a trustee **2** : supervisory control by one or more nations over a trust territory

trust•ful \ˈtrəst-fəl\ *adj* : full of trust : CONFIDING — **trust•ful•ly** *adv* — **trust•ful•ness** *n*

trust territory *n* : a non-self-governing territory placed under a supervisory authority by the Trusteeship Council of the United Nations

trust•wor•thy \-ˌwər-t͟hē\ *adj* : worthy of confidence : DEPENDABLE **syn** trusty, tried, reliable — **trust•wor•thi•ness** *n*

[1]**trusty** \ˈtrəs-tē\ *adj* **trust•i•er; -est** : TRUSTWORTHY, DEPENDABLE

[2]**trusty** \ˈtrəs-tē, ˌtrəs-ˈtē\ *n, pl* **trust•ies** : a trusted person; *esp* : a convict considered trustworthy and allowed special privileges

truth \ˈtrüth\ *n, pl* **truths** \ˈtrüt͟hz, ˈtrüths\ **1** : TRUTHFULNESS, HONESTY **2** : the real state of things : FACT **3** : the body of real events or facts : ACTUALITY **4** : a true or accepted statement or proposition ⟨the ∼*s* of science⟩ **5** : agreement with fact or reality : CORRECTNESS **syn** veracity, verity

truth•ful \ˈtrüth-fəl\ *adj* : telling or disposed to tell the truth — **truth•ful•ly** *adv* — **truth•ful•ness** *n*

truth serum *n* : a drug held to induce a subject under questioning to talk freely

[1]**try** \ˈtrī\ *vb* **tried; try•ing 1** : to examine or investigate judicially **2** : to conduct the trial of **3** : to put to test or trial **4** : to subject to strain, affliction, or annoyance **5** : to extract or clarify (as lard) by melting **6** : to make an effort to do something : ATTEMPT, ENDEAVOR **syn** essay, assay, strive, struggle

[2]**try** *n, pl* **tries** : an experimental trial

try•ing *adj* : severely straining the powers of endurance

try on *vb* : to put on (a garment) to test the fit and looks

try out *vb* : to participate in competition esp. for a position on an athletic team or a part in a play — **tryout** \ˈtrī-ˌau̇t\ *n*

tryst \ˈtrist\ *n* **1** : an agreement (as between lovers) to meet **2** : an appointed meeting or meeting place — **tryst** *vb* — **tryst•er** *n*

tsar \ˈzär, ˈtsär, ˈsär\ *var of* CZAR

tset•se fly \ˈtset-sē-, ˈtsēt-, ˈtet-, ˈtēt-, ˈset-, ˈsēt-\ *n* : any of several sub-Saharan African dipteran flies including the vector of sleeping sickness

TSgt *abbr* technical sergeant

T–shirt \ˈtē-ˌshərt\ *n* : a collarless short-sleeved or sleeveless cotton undershirt; *also* : an outer shirt of similar design — **T–shirt•ed** \-ˌshər-təd\ *adj*

tsp *abbr* teaspoon; teaspoonful

T square *n* : a ruler with a crosspiece at one end for making parallel lines

tsu•na•mi \su̇-ˈnä-mē, tsu̇-\ *n* [Jp] : a tidal wave caused by an underwater earthquake or volcanic eruption

TT *abbr* Trust Territories

TTY *abbr* teletypewriter

Tu *abbr* Tuesday

tub \ˈtəb\ *n* **1** : a wide low bucketlike vessel **2** : BATHTUB; *also* : BATH **3** : the amount that a tub will hold

tu•ba \ˈtü-bə, ˈtyü-\ *n* : a large low-pitched brass wind instrument

tub•al \ˈtü-bəl, ˈtyü-\ *adj* : of, relating to, or involving a tube and esp. a fallopian tube

tube \ˈtüb, ˈtyüb\ *n* **1** : any of various usu. cylindrical structures or devices; *esp* : one to convey fluids **2** : a slender hollow anatomical part (as a fallopian tube) functioning as a channel in a plant or animal body : DUCT **3** : a soft round container from which a paste is squeezed **4** : a tunnel for vehicular or rail travel **5** : INNER TUBE **6** : ELECTRON TUBE **7** : TELEVISION — **tubed** *adj* — **tube•less** *adj*

tu•ber \ˈtü-bər, ˈtyü-\ *n* : a short fleshy usu. underground stem (as of a potato plant) bearing minute scalelike leaves each with a bud at its base

tu•ber•cle \ˈtü-bər-kəl, ˈtyü-\ *n* **1** : a small knobby prominence or outgrowth esp. on an animal or plant **2** : a small abnormal lump in an organ or on the skin; *esp* : one caused by tuberculosis

tubercle bacillus *n* : a bacterium that is the cause of tuberculosis

tu•ber•cu•lar \tu̇-ˈbər-kyə-lər, tyu̇-\ *adj* **1** : TUBERCULOUS **2** : of, resembling, or being a tubercle

tu•ber•cu•lin \tu̇-ˈbər-kyə-lən, tyu̇-\ *n* : a sterile liquid extracted from the tubercle bacillus and used in the diagnosis of tuberculosis esp. in children and cattle

tu•ber•cu•lo•sis \tu̇-ˌbər-kyə-ˈlō-səs, tyu̇-\ *n, pl* **-lo•ses** \-ˌsēz\ : a communicable bacterial disease typically marked by wasting, fever, and formation of cheesy tubercles often in the lungs — **tu•ber•cu•lous** \-ˈbər-kyə-ləs\ *adj*

tube•rose \ˈtüb-ˌrōz, ˈtyüb-\ *n* : a bulbous herb related to the agaves and often grown for its spike of fragrant waxy-white flowers

tu•ber•ous \ˈtü-bə-rəs, ˈtyü-\ *adj* : of, resembling, or being a tuber

tub•ing \ˈtü-biŋ, ˈtyü-\ *n* **1** : material in the form of a tube; *also* : a length of tube **2** : a series or system of tubes

tu•bu•lar \ˈtü-byə-lər, ˈtyü-\ *adj* : having the form of or consisting of a tube; *also* : made with tubes

tu•bule \ˈtü-byül, ˈtyü-\ *n* : a small tube

[1]**tuck** \ˈtək\ *n* **1** : a fold stitched into cloth to shorten, decorate, or control fullness **2** : a cosmetic surgical operation for the removal of excess skin or fat ⟨a tummy ∼⟩

[2]**tuck** *vb* **1** : to pull up into a fold ⟨∼*ed* up her skirt⟩ **2** : to make tucks in **3** : to put into a snug often concealing place ⟨∼ a book under the arm⟩ **4** : to secure in place by pushing the edges under ⟨∼ in a blanket⟩ **5** : to cover by tucking in bedclothes

tuck•er \ˈtə-kər\ *vb* **tuck•ered; tuck•er•ing** : EXHAUST, FATIGUE

Tues *or* **Tue** *abbr* Tuesday
Tues•day \ˈtüz-dē, ˈtyüz-, -dā\ *n* : the 3d day of the week
tu•fa \ˈtü-fə, ˈtyü-\ *n* : a porous rock formed as a deposit from springs or streams
tuff \ˈtəf\ *n* : a rock composed of volcanic detritus
[1]**tuft** \ˈtəft\ *n* **1** : a small cluster of long flexible outgrowths (as hairs); *also* : a bunch of soft fluffy threads cut off short and used as ornament **2** : CLUMP, CLUSTER — **tuft•ed** *adj*
[2]**tuft** *vb* **1** : to provide or adorn with a tuft **2** : to make (as a mattress) firm by stitching at intervals and sewing on tufts — **tuft•er** *n*
[1]**tug** \ˈtəg\ *vb* **tugged; tug•ging 1** : to pull hard **2** : to struggle in opposition : CONTEND **3** : to move by pulling hard : HAUL **4** : to tow with a tugboat
[2]**tug** *n* **1** : a harness trace **2** : an act of tugging : PULL **3** : a straining effort **4** : a struggle between opposing people or forces **5** : TUGBOAT
tug•boat \-ˌbōt\ *n* : a strongly built boat used for towing or pushing
tug–of–war \ˌtəg-əv-ˈwȯr\ *n, pl* **tugs–of–war 1** : a struggle for supremacy **2** : an athletic contest in which two teams pull against each other at opposite ends of a rope
tu•grik *or* **tu•ghrik** \ˈtü-grik\ *n* — see MONEY table
tu•ition \tu̇-ˈi-shən, tyu̇-\ *n* : money paid for instruction ⟨college ∼⟩
tu•la•re•mia \ˌtü-lə-ˈrē-mē-ə, ˌtyü-\ *n* : an infectious bacterial disease esp. of wild rabbits, rodents, humans, and some domestic animals that in humans is marked by symptoms (as fever) of toxemia
tu•lip \ˈtü-ləp, ˈtyü-\ *n* [NL *tulipa*, fr. Turk *tülbent* turban] : any of a genus of Eurasian bulbous herbs related to the lilies and grown for their large showy erect cup-shaped flowers; *also* : a flower or bulb of a tulip
tulip tree *n* : a tall American timber tree with greenish tulip-shaped flowers and soft white wood that is related to the magnolias
tulle \ˈtül\ *n* : a sheer often stiffened silk, rayon, or nylon net ⟨a veil of ∼⟩
[1]**tum•ble** \ˈtəm-bəl\ *vb* **tum•bled; tum•bling** [ME, fr. *tumben* to dance, fr. OE *tumbian*] **1** : to fall or cause to fall suddenly and helplessly **2** : to fall into ruin **3** : to perform gymnastic feats of rolling and turning **4** : to roll over and over : TOSS **5** : to issue forth hurriedly and confusedly **6** : to come to understand **7** : to throw together in a confused mass
[2]**tumble** *n* **1** : a disorderly state **2** : an act or instance of tumbling
tum•ble•down \ˈtəm-bəl-ˈdau̇n\ *adj* : DILAPIDATED, RAMSHACKLE
tum•bler \ˈtəm-blər\ *n* **1** : one that tumbles; *esp* : ACROBAT **2** : a drinking glass without foot or stem **3** : a movable obstruction in a lock that must be adjusted to a particular position (as by a key) before the bolt can be thrown
tum•ble•weed \ˈtəm-bəl-ˌwēd\ *n* : a plant that breaks away from its roots in autumn and is driven about by the wind
tum•brel *or* **tum•bril** \ˈtəm-brəl\ *n* **1** : CART **2** : a vehicle carrying condemned persons (as during the French Revolution) to a place of execution
tu•mid \ˈtü-məd, ˈtyü-\ *adj* **1** : SWOLLEN, DISTENDED **2** : BOMBASTIC, TURGID
tum•my \ˈtə-mē\ *n, pl* **tummies** : BELLY, ABDOMEN, STOMACH
tu•mor \ˈtü-mər, ˈtyü-\ *n* : an abnormal and functionless mass of tissue that is not inflammatory and arises from preexistent tissue — **tu•mor•ous** *adj*
tu•mour *chiefly Brit var of* TUMOR
tu•mult \ˈtü-ˌməlt, ˈtyü-\ *n* **1** : UPROAR **2** : violent agitation of mind or feelings
tu•mul•tu•ous \tu̇-ˈməl-chə-wəs, tyu̇-, -chəs\ *adj* **1** : marked by tumult **2** : tending to incite a tumult **3** : marked by violent upheaval
tun \ˈtən\ *n* : a large cask
tu•na \ˈtü-nə, ˈtyü-\ *n, pl* **tuna** *or* **tunas** [Sp] : any of several mostly large marine fishes related to the mackerels and caught for food and sport; *also* : the flesh of a tuna

tuna

tun•able \ˈtü-nə-bəl, ˈtyü-\ *adj* : capable of being tuned — **tun•abil•i•ty** \ˌtü-nə-ˈbi-lə-tē, ˌtyü-\ *n*
tun•dra \ˈtən-drə\ *n* [Russ] : a treeless plain of arctic and subarctic regions
[1]**tune** \ˈtün, ˈtyün\ *n* **1** : a succession of pleasing musical tones : MELODY **2** : correct musical pitch **3** : harmonious relationship : AGREEMENT ⟨in ∼ with the times⟩ **4** : general attitude ⟨changed his ∼⟩ **5** : AMOUNT, EXTENT ⟨in debt to the ∼ of millions⟩
[2]**tune** *vb* **tuned; tun•ing 1** : to adjust in musical pitch **2** : to bring or come into harmony : ATTUNE **3** : to put in good working order **4** : to adjust a radio or television receiver so as to receive a broadcast **5** : to adjust the frequency of the output of (a device) to a chosen frequency — **tun•er** *n*
tune•ful \-fəl\ *adj* : MELODIOUS, MUSICAL — **tune•ful•ly** *adv* — **tune•ful•ness** *n*
tune•less \-ləs\ *adj* **1** : UNMELODIOUS **2** : not producing music — **tune•less•ly** *adv*
tune–up \ˈtün-ˌəp, ˈtyün-\ *n* : an adjustment to ensure efficient functioning ⟨an engine ∼⟩
tung•sten \ˈtəŋ-stən\ *n* [Sw, fr. *tung* heavy + *sten* stone] : a white hard heavy ductile metallic chemical element used esp. for electrical purposes and in alloys — see ELEMENT table
tu•nic \ˈtü-nik, ˈtyü-\ *n* **1** : a usu. knee-length belted under or outer garment worn by ancient Greeks and Romans **2** : a hip-length or longer blouse or jacket
tuning fork *n* : a 2-pronged metal implement that gives a fixed tone when struck and is useful for tuning musical instruments
Tu•ni•sian \tü-ˈnē-zhən, tyü-, -ˈni-\ *n* : a native or inhabitant of Tunisia — **Tunisian** *adj*
[1]**tun•nel** \ˈtən-ᵊl\ *n* : an enclosed passage (as a tube or conduit); *esp* : one underground (as in a mine)
[2]**tunnel** *vb* **-neled** *or* **-nelled; -nel•ing** *or* **-nel•ling** : to make a tunnel through or under
tun•ny \ˈtə-nē\ *n, pl* **tunnies** *also* **tunny** : TUNA
tuque \ˈtük, ˈtyük\ *n* [CanF] : a warm knitted cone-shaped cap
tur•ban \ˈtər-bən\ *n* **1** : a headdress worn esp. by Muslims and made of a cap around which is wound a long cloth **2** : a headdress resembling a turban; *esp* : a woman's close-fitting hat without a brim
tur•bid \ˈtər-bəd\ *adj* [L *turbidus* confused, turbid, fr. *turba* confusion, crowd] **1** : cloudy or discolored by suspended particles ⟨a ∼ stream⟩ **2** : CONFUSED, MUDDLED — **tur•bid•i•ty** \ˌtər-ˈbi-də-tē\ *n*
tur•bine \ˈtər-bən, -ˌbīn\ *n* [F, fr. L *turbin-*, *turbo* top, whirlwind, whirl] : an engine whose central driveshaft is fitted with curved vanes spun by the pressure of water, steam, or gas
tur•bo•fan \ˈtər-bō-ˌfan\ *n* : a jet engine having a fan driven by a turbine for supplying air for combustion
tur•bo•jet \-ˌjet\ *n* : an airplane powered by a jet engine (**turbojet engine**) having a turbine-driven air compressor supplying compressed air to the combustion chamber

tur•bo•prop \-ˌpräp\ *n* **:** an airplane powered by a jet engine (**turboprop engine**) having a turbine-driven propeller

tur•bot \ˈtər-bət\ *n, pl* **turbot** *also* **turbots :** a European flatfish that is a popular food fish; *also* **:** any of several similar flatfishes

tur•bu•lence \ˈtər-byə-ləns\ *n* **:** the quality or state of being turbulent

tur•bu•lent \-lənt\ *adj* **1 :** causing violence or disturbance **2 :** marked by agitation or tumult **:** TEMPESTUOUS **— tur•bu•lent•ly** *adv*

tu•reen \tə-ˈrēn, tyu̇-\ *n* [F *terrine,* fr. MF, fr. fem. of *terrin* of earth] **:** a deep bowl from which foods (as soup) are served at table

[1]**turf** \ˈtərf\ *n, pl* **turfs** \ˈtərfs\ *also* **turves** \ˈtərvz\ **1 :** the upper layer of soil bound by grass and roots into a close mat; *also* **:** a piece of this **2 :** an artificial substitute for turf (as on a playing field) **3 :** a piece of peat dried for fuel **4 :** a track or course for horse racing; *also* **:** horse racing as a sport or business

[2]**turf** *vb* **:** to cover with turf

tur•gid \ˈtər-jəd\ *adj* **1 :** being in a swollen state **2 :** excessively embellished in style or language **:** BOMBASTIC **— tur•gid•i•ty** \ˌtər-ˈji-də-tē\ *n*

Turk \ˈtərk\ *n* **:** a native or inhabitant of Turkey

tur•key \ˈtər-kē\ *n, pl* **turkeys** [*Turkey,* country in western Asia and southeastern Europe; fr. confusion with the guinea fowl, supposed to be imported from Turkish territory] **:** a large American bird related to the domestic chicken and widely raised for food; *also* **:** its flesh

turkey buzzard *n* **:** TURKEY VULTURE

turkey vulture *n* **:** an American vulture with a red head and whitish bill

Turk•ish \ˈtər-kish\ *n* **:** the language of Turkey **— Turkish** *adj*

tur•mer•ic \ˈtər-mə-rik\ *n* **:** a spice or dyestuff obtained from the large aromatic deep-yellow rhizome of an East Indian perennial herb related to the ginger; *also* **:** this herb

tur•moil \ˈtər-ˌmȯil\ *n* **:** an extremely confused or agitated condition

[1]**turn** \ˈtərn\ *vb* **1 :** to move or cause to move around an axis or center **:** ROTATE, REVOLVE ⟨~ a wheel⟩ **2 :** to effect a desired end by turning something ⟨~ the oven on⟩ **3 :** WRENCH ⟨~ an ankle⟩ **4 :** to change or cause to change position by moving through an arc of a circle ⟨~*ed* her chair to the fire⟩ **5 :** to cause to move around a center so as to show another side of ⟨~ a page⟩ **6 :** to revolve mentally **:** PONDER **7 :** to become dizzy **:** REEL **8 :** to reverse the sides or surfaces of ⟨~ a pancake⟩ **9 :** UPSET, DISORDER ⟨things were ~*ed* topsy-turvy⟩ **10 :** to set in another esp. contrary direction **11 :** to change one's course or direction **12 :** to go around ⟨~ a corner⟩ **13 :** BECOME ⟨my hair ~*ed* gray⟩ ⟨~*ed* twenty-one⟩ **14 :** to direct toward or away from something; *also* **:** DEVOTE, APPLY **15 :** to have recourse **16 :** to become or make hostile **17 :** to cause to become of a specified nature or appearance ⟨~*s* the leaves yellow⟩ **18 :** to make or become spoiled **:** SOUR **19 :** to pass from one state to another ⟨water ~*s* to ice⟩ **20 :** CONVERT, TRANSFORM **21 :** TRANSLATE, PARAPHRASE **22 :** to give a rounded form to; *esp* **:** to shape by means of a lathe **23 :** to gain by passing in trade ⟨~ a quick profit⟩ **— turn color 1 :** BLUSH **2 :** to become pale **— turn loose :** to set free

[2]**turn** *n* **1 :** a turning about a center or axis **:** REVOLUTION, ROTATION **2 :** the action or an act of giving or taking a different direction ⟨make a left ~⟩ **3 :** a change of course or tendency ⟨a ~ for the better⟩ **4 :** a place at which something turns **:** BEND, CURVE **5 :** a short walk or trip round about ⟨take a ~ around the block⟩ **6 :** an act affecting another ⟨did him a good ~⟩ **7 :** a place, time, or opportunity accorded in a scheduled order ⟨waited his ~ in line⟩ **8 :** a period of duty **:** SHIFT **9 :** a short act esp. in a variety show **10 :** a special purpose or requirement ⟨the job serves his ~⟩ **11 :** a skillful fashioning ⟨neat ~ of phrase⟩ **12 :** a single round (as of rope passed around an object) **13 :** natural or special aptitude **14 :** a usu. sudden and brief disorder of body or spirits; *esp* **:** a spell of nervous shock or faintness

turn•about \ˈtər-nə-ˌbau̇t\ *n* **1 :** a reversal of direction, trend, or policy **2 :** RETALIATION

turn•buck•le \ˈtərn-ˌbə-kəl\ *n* **:** a link with a screw thread at one or both ends for tightening a rod or stay

turn•coat \-ˌkōt\ *n* **:** one who switches to an opposing side or party **:** TRAITOR

turn down *vb* **:** to decline to accept **:** REJECT **— turn-down** \ˈtərn-ˌdau̇n\ *n*

turn•er \ˈtər-nər\ *n* **1 :** one that turns or is used for turning **2 :** one that forms articles with a lathe

turn•ery \ˈtər-nə-rē\ *n, pl* **-er•ies :** the work, products, or shop of a turner

turn in *vb* **1 :** to deliver up **2 :** to inform on **3 :** to acquit oneself of ⟨*turn in* a good job⟩ **4 :** to go to bed

turn•ing *n* **1 :** the act or course of one that turns **2 :** a place of a change of direction

tur•nip \ˈtər-nəp\ *n* **1 :** a garden herb related to the cabbage with a thick edible usu. white root **2 :** RUTABAGA **3 :** the root of a turnip

turn•key \ˈtərn-ˌkē\ *n, pl* **turnkeys :** one who has charge of a prison's keys

turn•off \ˈtərn-ˌȯf\ *n* **:** a place for turning off esp. from an expressway

turn off *vb* **1 :** to deviate from a straight course or a main road **2 :** to stop the functioning or flow of **3 :** to cause to lose interest; *also* **:** to evoke a negative feeling in

turn on *vb* **1 :** to cause to flow, function, or operate **2 :** to get high or cause to get high as a result of using a drug (as marijuana) **3 :** EXCITE, STIMULATE

turn•out \ˈtərn-ˌau̇t\ *n* **1 :** an act of turning out **2 :** the number of people who participate or attend an event **3 :** a widened place in a highway for vehicles to pass or park **4 :** manner of dress **5 :** net yield **:** OUTPUT

turn out *vb* **1 :** EXPEL, EVICT **2 :** PRODUCE **3 :** to come forth and assemble **4 :** to get out of bed **5 :** to prove to be in the end

[1]**turn•over** \ˈtər-ˌnō-vər\ *n* **1 :** UPSET **2 :** SHIFT, REVERSAL **3 :** a filled pastry made by turning half of the crust over the other half **4 :** the volume of business done **5 :** movement (as of goods or people) into, through, and out of a place **6 :** the number of persons hired within a period to replace those leaving or dropped **7 :** an instance of a team's losing possession of the ball esp. through error

[2]**turnover** *adj* **:** capable of being turned over

turn over *vb* **:** TRANSFER ⟨*turn* the job *over* to her⟩

turn•pike \ˈtərn-ˌpīk\ *n* [ME *turnepike* revolving frame bearing spikes and serving as a barrier, fr. *turnen* to turn + *pike*] **1 :** TOLLGATE; *also* **:** an expressway on which tolls are charged **2 :** a main road

turn•stile \-ˌstīl\ *n* **:** a post with arms pivoted on the top set in a passageway so that persons can pass through only on foot one by one

turn•ta•ble \-ˌtā-bəl\ *n* **:** a circular platform that revolves (as for turning a locomotive or a phonograph record)

turn to *vb* **:** to apply oneself to work

turn up *vb* **1 :** to come to light or bring to light **:** DISCOVER, APPEAR **2 :** to arrive at an appointed time or place **3 :** to happen unexpectedly

tur•pen•tine \ˈtər-pən-ˌtīn\ *n* **1 :** a mixture of oil and resin obtained from various cone-bearing trees (as pines) **2 :** an oil distilled from turpentine or pine wood and used as a solvent and paint thinner

tur•pi•tude \ˈtər-pə-ˌtüd, -ˌtyüd\ *n* **:** inherent baseness **:** DEPRAVITY

tur•quoise *also* **tur•quois** \ˈtər-ˌkȯiz, -ˌkwȯiz\ *n* [ME *turkeis, turcas,* fr. MF *turquoyse,* fr. fem. of *turquoys* Turkish, fr. OF, fr. *Turc* Turk] **1 :** a blue, bluish green, or greenish gray mineral that is valued as a gem **2** : a light greenish blue color

tur•ret \ˈtər-ət\ *n* **1** : a little tower often at an angle of a larger structure and merely ornamental **2** : a low usu. revolving structure (as on a tank or warship) in which one or more guns are mounted

¹tur•tle \ˈtərt-ᵊl\ *n, archaic* : TURTLEDOVE

²turtle *n, pl* **turtles** *also* **turtle** : any of an order of horny-beaked land, freshwater, or sea reptiles with the trunk enclosed in a bony shell

tur•tle•dove \ˈtərt-ᵊl-ˌdəv\ *n* : any of several small pigeons noted for plaintive cooing

tur•tle•neck \-ˌnek\ *n* : a high close-fitting turnover collar (as on a sweater); *also* : a sweater or shirt with a turtleneck — **tur•tle•necked** \-ˌnekt\ *adj*

turves *pl of* TURF

Tus•ca•ro•ra \ˌtəs-kə-ˈrōr-ə\ *n, pl* **Tuscarora** *or* **Tuscaroras** : a member of an American Indian people of No. Carolina and later of New York and Ontario

tusk \ˈtəsk\ *n* : a long enlarged protruding tooth (as of an elephant, walrus, or boar) used esp. to dig up food or as a weapon — **tusked** \ˈtəskt\ *adj*

tusk•er \ˈtəs-kər\ *n* : an animal with tusks; *esp* : a male elephant with two normally developed tusks

¹tus•sle \ˈtə-səl\ *n* **1** : a physical struggle : SCUFFLE **2** : an intense argument, controversy, or struggle

²tussle *vb* **tus•sled; tus•sling** : to struggle roughly

tus•sock \ˈtə-sək\ *n* : a dense tuft esp. of grass or sedge; *also* : a hummock in a marsh or bog bound together by roots — **tus•socky** *adj*

tu•te•lage \ˈtüt-ᵊl-ij, ˈtyüt-\ *n* **1** : an act of guarding or protecting **2** : the state of being under a guardian or tutor **3** : instruction esp. of an individual

tu•te•lary \ˈtüt-ᵊl-ˌer-ē, ˈtyüt-\ *adj* : acting as a guardian ⟨~ deity⟩

¹tu•tor \ˈtü-tər, ˈtyü-\ *n* **1** : a person charged with the instruction and guidance of another **2** : a private teacher

²tutor *vb* **1** : to have the guardianship of **2** : to teach or guide individually : COACH ⟨~*ed* her in Latin⟩ **3** : to receive instruction esp. privately

tu•to•ri•al \tü-ˈtōr-ē-əl, tyü-\ *n* : a class conducted by a tutor for one student or a small number of students

tut•ti \ˈtü-tē, ˈtu̇-, -ˌtē\ *adj or adv* [It, pl. of *tutto* all] : with all voices and instruments playing together — used as a direction in music

tut•ti–frut•ti \ˌtü-ti-ˈfrü-tē, ˌtu̇-\ *n* [It, lit., all fruits] : a confection or ice cream containing chopped usu. candied fruits

tux•e•do \ˌtək-ˈsē-dō\ *n, pl* **-dos** *or* **-does** [*Tuxedo* Park, N.Y.] **1** : a usu. black or blackish blue jacket **2** : semiformal evening clothes for men

TV \ˈtē-ˈvē\ *n* : TELEVISION

TVA *abbr* Tennessee Valley Authority

TV dinner *n* : a frozen packaged dinner that needs only heating before serving

twad•dle \ˈtwäd-ᵊl\ *n* : silly idle talk : DRIVEL — **twaddle** *vb*

twain \ˈtwān\ *n* **1** : TWO **2** : PAIR

¹twang \ˈtwaŋ\ *n* **1** : a harsh quick ringing sound like that of a plucked bowstring **2** : nasal speech or resonance **3** : the characteristic speech of a region

²twang *vb* **twanged; twang•ing 1** : to sound or cause to sound with a twang **2** : to speak with a nasal twang

tweak \ˈtwēk\ *vb* : to pinch and pull with a sudden jerk and twitch — **tweak** *n*

tweed \ˈtwēd\ *n* **1** : a rough woolen fabric made usu. in twill weaves **2** *pl* : tweed clothing; *esp* : a tweed suit

tweedy \ˈtwē-dē\ *adj* **tweed•i•er; -est 1** : of or resembling tweed **2** : given to wearing tweeds **3** : suggestive of the outdoors in taste or habits

tween \ˈtwēn\ *prep* : BETWEEN

tweet \ˈtwēt\ *n* : a chirping note — **tweet** *vb*

tweet•er \ˈtwē-tər\ *n* : a small loudspeaker that reproduces sounds of high pitch

twee•zers \ˈtwē-zərz\ *n pl* [obs. E *tweeze*, n., case for small implements, short for obs. E *etweese*, fr. pl. of obs. E *etwee*, fr. F *étui*] : a small pincerlike implement held between the thumb and forefinger for grasping something

twelve \ˈtwelv\ *n* **1** : one more than 11 **2** : the 12th in a set or series **3** : something having 12 units — **twelfth** \ˈtwelfth\ *adj or n* — **twelve** *adj or pron*

twelve•month \-ˌmənth\ *n* : YEAR

twen•ty \ˈtwen-tē\ *n, pl* **twenties** : two times 10 — **twen•ti•eth** \-tē-əth\ *adj or n* — **twenty** *adj or pron*

twenty–twenty *or* **20/20** \ˌtwen-tē-ˈtwen-tē\ *adj* : characterized by a visual capacity for seeing detail that is normal for the human eye ⟨~ vision⟩

twice \ˈtwīs\ *adv* **1** : on two occasions **2** : two times ⟨~ two is four⟩

¹twid•dle \ˈtwid-ᵊl\ *vb* **twid•dled; twid•dling 1** : to be busy with trifles; *also* : to play idly with something **2** : to rotate lightly or idly

²twiddle *n* : TURN, TWIST

twig \ˈtwig\ *n* : a small branch — **twig•gy** *adj*

twi•light \ˈtwī-ˌlīt\ *n* **1** : the light from the sky between full night and sunrise or between sunset and full night **2** : a state of imperfect clarity; *also* : a period of decline

twilight zone *n* **1** : TWILIGHT 2; *also* : an area just beyond ordinary legal or ethical limits **2** : a world of fantasy or unreality

twill \ˈtwil\ *n* [ME *twyll*, fr. OE *twilic* having a double thread, part trans. of L *bilic-*, *bilix*, fr. *bi-* two + *licium* thread] **1** : a fabric with a twill weave **2** : a textile weave that gives an appearance of diagonal lines

twilled \ˈtwild\ *adj* : made with a twill weave

¹twin \ˈtwin\ *n* **1** : either of two offspring produced at a birth **2** : one of two persons or things closely related to or resembling each other

²twin *vb* **twinned; twin•ning 1** : to be coupled with another **2** : to bring forth twins

³twin *adj* **1** : born with one another or as a pair at one birth ⟨~ brother⟩ ⟨~ girls⟩ **2** : made up of two similar or related members or parts **3** : being one of a pair ⟨~ city⟩

¹twine \ˈtwīn\ *n* **1** : a strong thread of two or three strands twisted together **2** : an act of entwining or interlacing — **twiny** *adj*

²twine *vb* **twined; twin•ing 1** : to twist together; *also* : to form by twisting **2** : INTERLACE, WEAVE **3** : to coil about a support **4** : to stretch or move in a sinuous manner — **twin•er** *n*

¹twinge \ˈtwinj\ *vb* **twinged; twing•ing** *or* **twinge•ing** : to affect with or feel a sharp sudden pain

²twinge *n* : a sudden sharp stab (as of pain or distress)

¹twin•kle \ˈtwiŋ-kəl\ *vb* **twin•kled; twin•kling 1** : to shine or cause to shine with a flickering or sparkling light **2** : to appear bright with merriment **3** : to flutter or flit rapidly — **twin•kler** *n*

²twinkle *n* **1** : a wink of the eyelids; *also* : the duration of a wink **2** : an intermittent radiance **3** : a rapid flashing motion — **twin•kly** \ˈtwiŋ-klē\ *adj*

twin•kling \ˈtwiŋ-kliŋ\ *n* : the time required for a wink : INSTANT

¹twirl \ˈtwərl\ *vb* : to turn or cause to turn rapidly ⟨~ a baton⟩ **syn** revolve, rotate, circle, spin, swirl, pirouette — **twirl•er** *n*

²twirl *n* **1** : an act of twirling **2** : COIL, WHORL — **twirly** \ˈtwər-lē\ *adj*

¹twist \ˈtwist\ *vb* **1** : to unite by winding one thread or strand round another **2** : WREATHE, TWINE **3** : to turn so as to hurt ⟨~*ed* her ankle⟩ **4** : to twirl into spiral shape **5** : to subject (as a shaft) to torsion **6** : to turn from the true form or meaning **7** : to pull off or break by torsion **8** : to follow a winding course **9** : to turn around

²twist *n* **1** : something formed by twisting or winding **2** : an act of twisting : the state of being twisted **3** : a spiral turn or curve; *also* : SPIN **4** : a turning aside **5** : ECCENTRICITY **6** : a distortion of meaning **7** : an unexpected turn or development **8** : DEVICE, TRICK **9** : a variant approach or method

twist•er \ˈtwis-tər\ *n* **1** : one that twists; *esp* : a ball with a forward and spinning motion **2** : TORNADO; *also* : WATERSPOUT 2

¹twit \ˈtwit\ *n* : FOOL

²twit *vb* **twit•ted; twit•ting** : to ridicule as a fault; *also* : TAUNT **syn** deride, mock, razz

¹twitch \ˈtwich\ *vb* **1** : to move or pull with a sudden motion : JERK **2** : to move jerkily : QUIVER

²twitch *n* **1** : an act or movement of twitching **2** : a short sharp contraction of muscle fibers

¹twit•ter \ˈtwi-tər\ *vb* **1** : to make a succession of chirping noises **2** : to talk in a chattering fashion **3** : to tremble with agitation : FLUTTER

²twitter *n* **1** : a slight agitation of the nerves **2** : a small tremulous intermittent noise (as made by a swallow) **3** : a light chattering

twixt \ˈtwikst\ *prep* : BETWEEN

two \ˈtü\ *n, pl* **twos 1** : one more than one **2** : the second in a set or series **3** : something having two units — **two** *adj or pron*

two cents *n* **1** : a sum or object of very small value **2** *or* **two cents worth** : an opinion offered on a topic under discussion

two–faced \ˈtü-ˈfāst\ *adj* **1** : DOUBLE-DEALING, FALSE **2** : having two faces

two•fold \ˈtü-ˌfōld, -ˈfōld\ *adj* **1** : having two units or members **2** : being twice as much or as many — **twofold** \-ˈfōld\ *adv*

2,4–D \ˌtü-ˌfōr-ˈdē\ *n* : an irritant compound used esp. as a weed killer

2,4,5–T \-ˌfīv-ˈtē\ *n* : an irritant compound used esp. as an herbicide and defoliant

two•pence \ˈtə-pəns, *US also* ˈtü-ˌpens\ *n* : the sum of two pence

two•pen•ny \ˈtə-pə-nē, *US also* ˈtü-ˌpe-nē\ *adj* : of the value of or costing twopence

two–ply \ˈtü-ˈplī\ *adj* **1** : woven as a double cloth **2** : consisting of two strands or thicknesses

two•some \ˈtü-səm\ *n* **1** : a group of two persons or things : COUPLE **2** : a golf match between two players

two–step \ˈtü-ˌstep\ *n* : a ballroom dance performed with a sliding step in march or polka time; *also* : a piece of music for this dance — **two–step** *vb*

two–time \ˈtü-ˌtīm\ *vb* : to betray (a spouse or lover) by secret lovemaking with another — **two–tim•er** *n*

two–way *adj* : involving two elements or allowing movement or use in two directions or manners

2WD *abbr* two-wheel drive

twp *abbr* township

TWX *abbr* teletypewriter exchange

TX *abbr* Texas

-ty *n suffix* : quality : condition : degree ⟨real*ty*⟩

ty•coon \tī-ˈkün\ *n* [Jp *taikun*] **1** : a masterful leader (as in politics) **2** : a powerful businessman or industrialist

tying *pres part of* TIE

tyke \ˈtīk\ *n* : a small child

tym•pan•ic membrane \tim-ˈpa-nik-\ *n* : EARDRUM

tym•pa•num \ˈtim-pə-nəm\ *n, pl* **-na** \-nə\ *also* **-nums** : EARDRUM; *also* : MIDDLE EAR — **tym•pan•ic** \tim-ˈpa-nik\ *adj*

¹type \ˈtīp\ *n* [ME, fr. LL *typus,* fr. L & Gk; L *typus* image, fr. Gk *typos* blow, impression, model, fr. *typtein* to strike, beat] **1** : a person, thing, or event that foreshadows another to come : TOKEN, SYMBOL **2** : MODEL, EXAMPLE **3** : a distinctive stamp, mark, or sign : EMBLEM **4** : rectangular blocks usu. of metal each having a face so shaped as to produce a character when printed **5** : the letters or characters printed from or as if from type **6** : general character or form common to a number of individuals and setting them off as a distinguishable class ⟨horses of draft ~⟩ **7** : a class, kind, or group set apart by common characteristics ⟨a seedless ~ of orange⟩; *also* : something distinguishable as a variety ⟨reactions of this ~⟩ **syn** sort, nature, character, description

²type *vb* **typed; typ•ing 1** : to represent beforehand as a type **2** : to produce a copy of; *also* : REPRESENT, TYPIFY **3** : to write with a typewriter **4** : to identify as belonging to a type **5** : TYPECAST

type•cast \-ˌkast\ *vb* **-cast; -cast•ing 1** : to cast (an actor) in a part calling for characteristics possessed by the actor **2** : to cast repeatedly in the same type of role

type•face \-ˌfās\ *n* : all type of a single design

type•script \ˈtīp-ˌskript\ *n* : typewritten matter

type•set \-ˌset\ *vb* **-set; -set•ting** : to set in type : COMPOSE — **type•set•ter** *n*

type•write \-ˌrīt\ *vb* **-wrote** \-ˌrōt\; **-writ•ten** \-ˌrit-ᵊn\ : TYPE 3

type•writ•er \-ˌrī-tər\ *n* **1** : a machine for writing in characters similar to those produced by printers' type by means of types striking a ribbon to transfer ink or carbon impressions onto paper **2** : TYPIST

type•writ•ing \-ˌrī-tiŋ\ *n* : the use of a typewriter ⟨teach ~⟩; *also* : writing produced with a typewriter

¹ty•phoid \ˈtī-ˌfȯid, tī-ˈfȯid\ *adj* : of, relating to, or being a communicable bacterial disease (**typhoid fever**) marked by fever, diarrhea, prostration, and intestinal inflammation

²typhoid *n* : TYPHOID FEVER

ty•phoon \tī-ˈfün\ *n* : a tropical cyclone in the region of the Philippines or the China sea

ty•phus \ˈtī-fəs\ *n* : a severe infectious disease transmitted esp. by body lice, caused by a rickettsia, and marked by high fever, stupor and delirium, intense headache, and a dark red rash

typ•i•cal \ˈti-pi-kəl\ *adj* **1** : being or having the nature of a type **2** : exhibiting the essential characteristics of a group **3** : conforming to a type — **typ•i•cal•i•ty** \ˌti-pə-ˈka-lə-tē\ *n* — **typ•i•cal•ness** *n*

typ•i•cal•ly \-pi-k(ə-)lē\ *adv* **1** : in a typical manner **2** : in typical circumstances

typ•i•fy \ˈti-pə-ˌfī\ *vb* **-fied; -fy•ing 1** : to represent by an image, form, model, or resemblance **2** : to embody the essential or common characteristics of

typ•ist \ˈtī-pist\ *n* : one who operates a typewriter

ty•po \ˈtī-pō\ *n, pl* **typos** : an error in typing or in setting type

ty•pog•ra•pher \tī-ˈpä-grə-fər\ *n* : one who designs or arranges printing

ty•pog•ra•phy \tī-ˈpä-grə-fē\ *n* : the art of printing with type; *also* : the style, arrangement, or appearance of printed matter — **ty•po•graph•ic** \ˌtī-pə-ˈgra-fik\ *or* **ty•po•graph•i•cal** \-fi-kəl\ *adj* — **ty•po•graph•i•cal•ly** *adv*

ty•ran•ni•cal \tə-ˈra-ni-kəl, tī-\ *also* **ty•ran•nic** \-nik\ *adj* : of or relating to a tyrant : DESPOTIC **syn** arbitrary, absolute, autocratic — **ty•ran•ni•cal•ly** \-ni-k(ə-)lē\ *adv*

tyr•an•nise *Brit var of* TYRANNIZE

tyr•an•nize \ˈtir-ə-ˌnīz\ *vb* **-nized; -niz•ing** : to act as a tyrant : rule with unjust severity — **tyr•an•niz•er** *n*

ty•ran•no•saur \tə-ˈra-nə-ˌsȯr\ *n* : a very large American flesh-eating dinosaur of the Cretaceous that had small forelegs and walked on its hind legs

ty•ran•no•sau•rus \tə-ˌra-nə-ˈsȯr-əs\ *n* : TYRANNOSAUR

tyr•an•nous \ˈtir-ə-nəs\ *adj* : TYRANNICAL — **tyr•an•nous•ly** *adv*

tyr•an•ny \ˈtir-ə-nē\ *n, pl* **-nies 1** : oppressive power **2** : the rule or authority of a tyrant : government in which absolute power is vested in a single ruler **3** : a tyrannical act

ty•rant \ˈtī-rənt\ *n* **1** : an absolute ruler : DESPOT **2** : a ruler who governs oppressively or brutally **3** : one who uses authority or power harshly

tyre *chiefly Brit var of* ²TIRE

ty•ro \ˈtī-rō\ *n, pl* **tyros** [ML, fr. L *tiro* young soldier, tyro] : a beginner in learning : NOVICE

tzar \ˈzär, ˈtsär, ˈsär\ *var of* CZAR

DICTIONARY

U

¹u \ˈyü\ *n, pl* **u's** *or* **us** \ˈyüz\ *often cap* : the 21st letter of the English alphabet
²u *abbr, often cap* unit
¹U \ˈyü\ *adj* : characteristic of the upper classes
²U *abbr* **1** [abbr. of *Union of Orthodox Hebrew Congregations*] kosher certification — often enclosed in a circle **2** university **3** unsatisfactory
³U *symbol* uranium
UAE *abbr* United Arab Emirates
UAR *abbr* United Arab Republic
UAW *abbr* United Automobile Workers
ubiq·ui·tous \yü-ˈbi-kwə-təs\ *adj* : existing or being everywhere at the same time : OMNIPRESENT — **ubiq·ui·tous·ly** *adv* — **ubiq·ui·ty** \-kwə-tē\ *n*
U–boat \ˈyü-ˌbōt\ *n* [trans. of G *U-boot,* short for *Unterseeboot,* lit., undersea boat] : a German submarine
UC *abbr* uppercase
ud·der \ˈə-dər\ *n* : an organ (as of a cow) consisting of two or more milk glands enclosed in a large hanging sac and each provided with a nipple
UFO \ˌyü-(ˌ)ef-ˈō\ *n, pl* **UFO's** *or* **UFOs** \-ˈōz\ : an unidentified flying object; *esp* : FLYING SAUCER
Ugan·dan \ü-ˈgan-dən, yü-, -ˈgän-\ *n* : a native or inhabitant of Uganda — **Ugandan** *adj*
ug·ly \ˈə-glē\ *adj* **ug·li·er; -est** [ME, fr. ON *uggligr,* fr. *uggr* fear] **1** : FRIGHTFUL, DIRE **2** : offensive to the sight : HIDEOUS **3** : offensive or unpleasant to any sense **4** : morally objectionable : REPULSIVE **5** : likely to cause inconvenience or discomfort **6** : SURLY, QUARRELSOME ⟨an ~ disposition⟩ — **ug·li·ness** \-glē-nəs\ *n*
UHF *abbr* ultrahigh frequency
UK *abbr* United Kingdom
ukase \yü-ˈkās, -ˈkāz\ *n* [F & Russ; F, fr. Russ *ukaz,* fr. *ukazat'* to show, order] : an edict esp. of a Russian emperor or government
Ukrai·ni·an \yü-ˈkrā-nē-ən\ *n* : a native or inhabitant of Ukraine — **Ukrainian** *adj*
uku·le·le *also* **uke·le·le** \ˌyü-kə-ˈlā-lē\ *n* [Hawaiian *'ukulele,* fr. *'uku* flea + *lele* jumping] : a small usu. 4-stringed guitar popularized in Hawaii
ul·cer \ˈəl-sər\ *n* **1** : an open eroded sore of skin or mucous membrane often discharging pus **2** : something that festers and corrupts like an open sore — **ul·cer·ous** *adj*
ul·cer·ate \ˈəl-sə-ˌrāt\ *vb* **-at·ed; -at·ing** : to become affected with an ulcer — **ul·cer·a·tive** \ˈəl-sə-ˌrā-tiv\ *adj*
ul·cer·a·tion \ˌəl-sə-ˈrā-shən\ *n* **1** : the process of forming or state of having an ulcer **2** : ULCER 1
ul·na \ˈəl-nə\ *n* : the bone on the little-finger side of the human forearm; *also* : a corresponding bone of the forelimb of vertebrates above fishes
ul·ster \ˈəl-stər\ *n* : a long loose overcoat
ult *abbr* **1** ultimate **2** ultimo
ul·te·ri·or \ˌəl-ˈtir-ē-ər\ *adj* **1** : lying farther away : more remote **2** : situated beyond or on the farther side **3** : going beyond what is openly said or shown : HIDDEN ⟨~ motives⟩
¹ul·ti·mate \ˈəl-tə-mət\ *adj* **1** : most remote in space or time : FARTHEST **2** : last in a progression : FINAL **3** : the best or most extreme of its kind **4** : arrived at as the last resort **5** : FUNDAMENTAL, ABSOLUTE, SUPREME ⟨~ reality⟩ **6** : incapable of further analysis or division : ELEMENTAL **7** : MAXIMUM **syn** concluding, eventual, latest, terminal — **ul·ti·mate·ly** *adv*
²ultimate *n* : something ultimate
ul·ti·ma·tum \ˌəl-tə-ˈmā-təm, -ˈmä-\ *n, pl* **-tums** *or* **-ta** \-tə\ : a final condition or demand whose rejection will bring about a resort to forceful action
ul·ti·mo \ˈəl-tə-ˌmō\ *adj* [L *ultimo mense* in the last month] : of or occurring in the month preceding the present
¹ul·tra \ˈəl-trə\ *adj* : going beyond others or beyond due limits : EXTREME
²ultra *n* : EXTREMIST
ul·tra·con·ser·va·tive \-kən-ˈsər-və-tiv\ *adj* : extremely conservative
ul·tra·high frequency \-ˈhī-\ *n* : a radio frequency between 300 and 3000 megahertz
¹ul·tra·light \ˈəl-trə-ˌlīt\ *adj* : extremely light esp. in weight
²ultralight *n* : a very light recreational aircraft typically carrying only one person
ul·tra·ma·rine \ˌəl-trə-mə-ˈrēn\ *n* **1** : a deep blue pigment **2** : a very bright deep blue color
ul·tra·mi·cro·scop·ic \-ˌmī-krə-ˈskä-pik\ *adj* : too small to be seen with an ordinary microscope
ul·tra·mod·ern \-ˈmä-dərn\ *adj* : extremely or excessively modern in idea, style, or tendency
ul·tra·mon·tane \-ˈmän-ˌtān, -ˌmän-ˈtān\ *adj* **1** : of or relating to countries or peoples beyond the mountains (as the Alps) **2** : favoring greater or absolute supremacy of papal over national or diocesan authority in the Roman Catholic Church — **ultramontane** *n, often cap* — **ul·tra·mon·tan·ism** \-ˈmänt-ᵊn-ˌi-zəm\ *n*
ul·tra·pure \-ˈpyu̇r\ *adj* : of the utmost purity
ul·tra·short \-ˈsho̊rt\ *adj* **1** : having a wavelength below 10 meters **2** : very short in duration
ul·tra·son·ic \ˌəl-trə-ˈsä-nik\ *adj* : having a frequency too high to be heard by the human ear — **ul·tra·son·i·cal·ly** \-ni-k(ə-)lē\ *adv*
ul·tra·son·ics \-ˈsä-niks\ *n sing or pl* **1** : ultrasonic vibrations **2** : the science of ultrasonic phenomena
ul·tra·sound \-ˌsau̇nd\ *n* **1** : ultrasonic vibrations **2** : the diagnostic or therapeutic use of ultrasound to form a two-dimensional image of internal body structures **3** : a diagnostic examination using ultrasound
ul·tra·vi·o·let \-ˈvī-ə-lət\ *adj* : having a wavelength shorter than those of visible light and longer than those of X rays ⟨~ radiation⟩; *also* : producing or employing ultraviolet radiation — **ultraviolet** *n*
ul·tra vi·res \ˈəl-trə-ˈvī-rēz\ *adv or adj* [NL, lit., beyond power] : beyond the scope of legal power or authority
ul·u·late \ˈəl-yə-ˌlāt\ *vb* **-lat·ed; -lat·ing** : HOWL, WAIL
um·bel \ˈəm-bəl\ *n* : a flat-topped or rounded flower cluster in which the individual flower stalks all arise near one point on the main stem
um·ber \ˈəm-bər\ *n* : a brown earthy substance valued as a pigment either in its raw state or burnt — **umber** *adj*
umbilical cord *n* : a cord containing blood vessels that connects the navel of a fetus with the placenta of its mother
um·bi·li·cus \ˌəm-ˈbi-li-kəs, ˌəm-bə-ˈlī-\ *n, pl* **um·bi·li·ci** \ˌəm-ˈbi-lə-ˌkī; ˌəm-bə-ˈlī-ˌkī, -ˌsī\ *or* **um·bi·li·cus·es** : NAVEL — **um·bil·i·cal** \ˌəm-ˈbi-li-kəl\ *adj*
um·bra \ˈəm-brə\ *n, pl* **umbras** *or* **um·brae** \-(ˌ)brē, -ˌbrī\ **1** : SHADE, SHADOW **2** : the conical part of the shadow of a celestial body from which the sun's light is completely blocked
um·brage \ˈəm-brij\ *n* **1** : SHADE; *also* : FOLIAGE **2** : RESENTMENT, OFFENSE ⟨take ~ at a remark⟩
um·brel·la \ˌəm-ˈbre-lə\ *n* **1** : a collapsible shade for protection against weather consisting of fabric stretched over hinged ribs radiating from a center pole **2** : something that resembles an umbrella in shape or purpose
umi·ak \ˈü-mē-ˌak\ *n* : an open Eskimo boat made of a wooden frame covered with skins

☞ For illustration, see next page.

umiak

um•pire \ˈəm-ˌpīr\ *n* [ME *oumpere,* alter. of *noumpere* (the phrase *a noumpere* being understood as *an oumpere*), fr. MF *nomper* not equal, not paired, fr. *non* not + *per* equal, fr. L *par*] **1 :** one having authority to decide finally a controversy or question between parties **2 :** an official in a sport who rules on plays — **umpire** *vb*
ump•teen \ˈəmp-ˌtēn\ *adj* **:** very many **:** indefinitely numerous — **ump•teenth** \-ˌtēnth\ *adj*
UN *abbr* United Nations
un- \ˌən, ˈən\ *prefix* **1 :** not **:** IN-, NON- **2 :** opposite of **:** contrary to

unabashed
unabated
unabsorbed
unabsorbent
unacademic
unaccented
unacceptable
unacclimatized
unaccommodating
unaccredited
unacknowledged
unacquainted
unadapted
unadjusted
unadorned
unadventurous
unadvertised
unaesthetic
unaffiliated
unafraid
unaggressive
unaided
unalike
unaltered
unambiguous
unambiguously
unambitious
unanchored
unannounced
unanswerable
unanswered
unanticipated
unapologetic
unapparent
unappealing
unappeased
unappetizing
unappreciated
unappreciative
unapproachable
unappropriated
unapproved
unarguable
unarguably
unarmored
unartistic
unashamed
unasked
unassertive
unassisted
unathletic
unattainable
unattended
unattested
unattractive
unauthentic
unauthorized
unavailable
unavowed
unawakened
unbaked
unbaptized
unbeloved
unbleached
unblemished
unblinking
unbound
unbranched
unbranded
unbreakable
unbridgeable
unbruised
unbrushed
unbudging
unburied
unburned
uncanceled
uncanonical
uncap
uncapitalized
uncared–for
uncataloged
uncaught
uncensored
uncensured
unchallenged
unchangeable
unchanged
unchanging
unchaperoned
uncharacteristic
unchaste
unchastely
unchasteness
unchastity
unchecked
unchivalrous
unchristened
unclad
unclaimed
unclassified
uncleaned
unclear
uncleared
unclouded
uncluttered
uncoated
uncollected
uncolored
uncombed
uncombined
uncomely
uncomic
uncommercial
uncompensated
uncomplaining
uncompleted
uncomplicated
uncomplimentary
uncompounded
uncomprehending
unconcealed
unconfined
unconfirmed
unconformable
uncongenial
unconnected
unconquered
unconsecrated
unconsidered
unconsolidated
unconstrained
unconsumed
unconsummated
uncontaminated
uncontested
uncontrolled
uncontroversial
unconverted
unconvincing
uncooked
uncooperative
uncoordinated
uncorrected
uncorroborated
uncountable
uncreative
uncredited
uncropped
uncrowded
uncrowned
uncrystallized
uncultivated
uncultured
uncured
uncurious
uncurtained
uncustomary
undamaged
undamped
undated
undecided
undecipherable
undeclared
undecorated
undefeated
undefended
undefiled
undefinable
undefined
undemanding
undemocratic
undenominational
undependable
undeserved
undeserving
undesired
undetected
undetermined
undeterred
undeveloped
undifferentiated
undigested
undignified
undiluted
undiminished
undimmed
undiplomatic
undirected
undisciplined
undisclosed
undiscovered
undiscriminating
undisguised
undismayed
undisputed
undissolved
undistinguished
undistributed
undisturbed
undivided
undocumented
undogmatic
undomesticated
undone
undoubled
undramatic
undraped
undreamed
undressed
undrinkable
undulled
undutiful
undyed
uneager
uneatable
uneaten
uneconomic
uneconomical
unedifying
unedited
uneducated
unembarrassed
unemotional
unemphatic
unenclosed
unencumbered
unendurable
unenforceable
unenforced
unenlightened
unenterprising
unenthusiastic
unenviable
unequipped
unessential
unethical
unexamined
unexcelled
unexceptional
unexcited
unexciting
unexpired
unexplained
unexploded
unexplored
unexposed
unexpressed
unexpurgated
unfading
unfaltering
unfashionable
unfashionably
unfathomable
unfavorable
unfavorably
unfeasible
unfeminine
unfenced
unfermented
unfertilized
unfilled
unfiltered
unfitted

unflagging
unflattering
unflavored
unfocused
unfolded
unforced
unforeseeable
unforeseen
unforgivable
unforgiving
unformulated
unfortified
unframed
unfree
unfulfilled
unfunded
unfunny
unfurnished
unfussy
ungentle
ungentlemanly
ungerminated
unglamorous
unglazed
ungoverned
ungraceful
ungracefully
ungraded
ungrammatical
unground
ungrudging
unguided
unhackneyed
unhampered
unhardened
unharmed
unharvested
unhatched
unhealed
unhealthful
unheated
unheeded
unhelpful
unheralded
unheroic
unhesitating
unhindered
unhistorical
unhonored
unhoused
unhurried
unhurt
unhygienic
unidentifiable
unidentified
unidiomatic
unimaginable
unimaginative
unimpaired
unimpassioned
unimpeded
unimportant
unimposing
unimpressed
unimpressive
unimproved
unincorporated
uninfected
uninfluenced
uninformative
uninformed
uninhabitable
uninhabited
uninitiated
uninjured
uninspired
uninstructed
uninstructive
uninsured
unintended
unintentional
unintentionally
uninteresting
uninvited
uninviting
unjointed
unjustifiable
unjustified
unkept
unknowable
unknowledgeable
unlabeled
unladylike
unlamented
unleavened
unlicensed
unlighted
unlikable
unlimited
unlined
unlit
unliterary
unlivable
unlovable
unloved
unloving
unmade
unmalicious
unmanageable
unmanned
unmapped
unmarked
unmarketable
unmarred
unmarried
unmasculine
unmatched
unmeant
unmeasurable
unmeasured
unmelodious
unmentioned
unmerited
unmilitary
unmilled
unmixed
unmodified
unmolested
unmotivated
unmounted
unmovable
unmoved
unmusical
unnameable
unnamed
unnecessary
unneeded
unnewsworthy
unnoticeable
unnoticed
unobjectionable
unobservant
unobserved
unobstructed
unobtainable
unofficial
unofficially
unopened
unopposed
unoriginal
unorthodox
unorthodoxy
unostentatious
unowned
unpaged
unpaid
unpainted
unpaired
unpalatable
unpardonable
unpasteurized
unpatriotic
unpaved
unpeeled
unperceived
unperceptive
unperformed
unpersuaded
unpersuasive
unperturbed
unplanned
unplanted
unpleasing
unplowed
unpoetic
unpolished
unpolitical
unpolluted
unposed
unpractical
unpredictable
unpredictability
unprejudiced
unpremeditated
unprepared
unpreparedness
unprepossessing
unpressed
unpretending
unpretty
unprivileged
unprocessed
unproductive
unprofessed
unprofessional
unprogrammed
unprogressive
unpromising
unprompted
unpronounceable
unpropitious
unprotected
unproven
unprovided
unprovoked
unpublished
unpunished
unquenchable
unquestioned
unraised
unrated
unratified
unreachable
unreadable
unready
unrealistic
unrealized
unrecognizable
unrecognized
unrecorded
unrecoverable
unredeemable
unrefined
unreflecting
unreflective
unregistered
unregulated
unrehearsed
unrelated
unreliable
unrelieved
unremarkable
unremembered
unremovable
unrepentant
unreported
unrepresentative
unrepresented
unrepressed
unresistant
unresisting
unresolved
unresponsive
unresponsiveness
unrestful
unrestricted
unreturnable
unrewarding
unrhymed
unrhythmic
unripened
unromantic
unromantically
unsafe
unsaid
unsalable
unsalted
unsanctioned
unsanitary
unsatisfactory
unsatisfied
unscented
unscheduled
unscholarly
unsealed
unseasoned
unseaworthy
unsegmented
unself–conscious
unself–consciously
unsensational
unsentimental
unserious
unserviceable
unsexual
unshaded
unshakable
unshaken
unshapely
unshaven
unshorn
unsifted
unsigned
unsinkable
unsmiling
unsociable
unsoiled
unsold
unsoldierly
unsolicited
unsolvable
unsolved
unsorted
unspecified
unspectacular
unspent
unspiritual
unspoiled
unspoken
unsportsmanlike
unstained
unstated
unsterile
unstructured

unstylish
unsubdued
unsubstantiated
unsubtle
unsuccessful
unsuccessfully
unsuitable
unsuited
unsullied
unsupervised
unsupportable
unsupported
unsure
unsurpassed
unsurprising
unsurprisingly
unsuspected
unsuspecting
unsuspicious
unsweetened
unsymmetrical
unsympathetic
unsystematic
untactful
untainted
untalented
untamed
untanned
untapped
untarnished
untaxed
unteachable
untenable
untenanted
untended
untested
unthrifty
untidy
untilled
untitled
untraceable
untraditional
untrained
untrammeled
untranslatable
untranslated
untraveled
untraversed
untreated
untrimmed
untrod
untroubled
untrustworthy
untruthful
untypical
unusable
unvaried
unvarying
unventilated
unverifiable
unverified
unversed
unvisited
unwanted
unwarranted
unwary
unwashed
unwavering
unweaned
unwearable
unwearied
unweathered
unwed
unwelcome
unwilling
unwillingly
unwillingness
unwomanly
unworkable
unworn
unworried
unwounded
unwoven

un•able \ˌən-ˈā-bəl\ *adj* **1** : not able **2** : UNQUALIFIED, INCOMPETENT

un•abridged \ˌən-ə-ˈbrijd\ *adj* **1** : not abridged ⟨an ~ edition of Shakespeare⟩ **2** : complete of its class : not based on one larger ⟨an ~ dictionary⟩

un•ac•com•pa•nied \ˌən-ə-ˈkəm-pə-nēd\ *adj* : not accompanied; *esp* : being without instrumental accompaniment

un•ac•count•able \ˌən-ə-ˈkau̇n-tə-bəl\ *adj* **1** : not to be accounted for : INEXPLICABLE **2** : not responsible — **un•ac•count•ably** \-blē\ *adv*

un•ac•count•ed \-ˈkau̇n-təd\ *adj* : not accounted ⟨the loss was ~ for⟩

un•ac•cus•tomed \ˌən-ə-ˈkəs-təmd\ *adj* **1** : not customary : not usual or common **2** : not accustomed or habituated ⟨~ to noise⟩

un•adul•ter•at•ed \ˌən-ə-ˈdəl-tə-ˌrā-təd\ *adj* : PURE, UNMIXED **syn** absolute, sheer, simple, unalloyed, undiluted, unmitigated

un•af•fect•ed \ˌən-ə-ˈfek-təd\ *adj* **1** : not influenced or changed mentally, physically, or chemically **2** : free from affectation : NATURAL, GENUINE — **un•af•fect•ed•ly** *adv*

un•alien•able \-ˈāl-yə-nə-bəl, -ˈā-lē-ə-\ *adj* : INALIENABLE

un•aligned \ˌən-ə-ˈlīnd\ *adj* : not associated with any one of competing international blocs ⟨~ nations⟩

un•al•loyed \ˌən-ə-ˈlȯid\ *adj* : UNMIXED, UNQUALIFIED, PURE ⟨~ happiness⟩

un•al•ter•able \ˌən-ˈȯl-tə-rə-bəl\ *adj* : not capable of being altered or changed — **un•al•ter•ably** \-blē\ *adv*

un–Amer•i•can \ˌən-ə-ˈmer-ə-kən\ *adj* : not characteristic of or consistent with American customs or principles

unan•i•mous \yu̇-ˈna-nə-məs\ *adj* [L *unanimus*, fr. *unus* one + *animus* mind] **1** : being of one mind : AGREEING **2** : formed with or indicating the agreement of all — **una•nim•i•ty** \yü-nə-ˈni-mə-tē\ *n* — **unan•i•mous•ly** *adv*

un•arm \ˌən-ˈärm\ *vb* : DISARM

un•armed \-ˈärmd\ *adj* : not armed or armored

un•as•sail•able \ˌən-ə-ˈsā-lə-bəl\ *adj* : not liable to doubt, attack, or question

un•as•sum•ing \ˌən-ə-ˈsü-miŋ\ *adj* : MODEST, RETIRING **syn** humble, lowly, meek

un•at•tached \ˌən-ə-ˈtacht\ *adj* **1** : not married or engaged **2** : not joined or united

un•avail•ing \ˌən-ə-ˈvā-liŋ\ *adj* : being of no avail — **un•avail•ing•ly** *adv*

un•avoid•able \ˌən-ə-ˈvȯi-də-bəl\ *adj* : not avoidable : INEVITABLE **syn** certain, ineluctable, inescapable, necessary — **un•avoid•ably** \-blē\ *adv*

[1]**un•aware** \ˌən-ə-ˈwar\ *adv* : UNAWARES

[2]**unaware** *adj* : not aware : IGNORANT — **un•aware•ness** *n*

un•awares \-ˈwarz\ *adv* **1** : without knowing : UNINTENTIONALLY **2** : without warning : by surprise ⟨taken ~⟩

un•bal•anced \ˌən-ˈba-lənst\ *adj* **1** : not in a state of balance **2** : mentally disordered **3** : not adjusted so as to make credits equal to debits

un•bar \-ˈbär\ *vb* : UNBOLT, OPEN

un•bear•able \ˌən-ˈbar-ə-bəl\ *adj* : greater than can be borne ⟨~ pain⟩ **syn** insufferable, insupportable, intolerable, unendurable, unsupportable — **un•bear•ably** \-blē\ *adv*

un•beat•able \-ˈbē-tə-bəl\ *adj* : not capable of being defeated **syn** indomitable, invincible, invulnerable, unconquerable

un•beat•en \-ˈbēt-ᵊn\ *adj* **1** : not pounded, beaten, or whipped **2** : UNTROD **3** : UNDEFEATED

un•be•com•ing \ˌən-bi-ˈkə-miŋ\ *adj* : not becoming : UNSUITABLE, IMPROPER **syn** indecorus, indecent, indelicate, unseemly — **un•be•com•ing•ly** *adv*

un•be•knownst \ˌən-bi-ˈnōnst\ *also* **un•be•known** \-ˈnōn\ *adj* : happening without one's knowledge

un•be•lief \ˌən-bə-ˈlēf\ *n* : the withholding or absence of belief : DOUBT — **un•be•liev•ing** \-ˈlē-viŋ\ *adj*

un•be•liev•able \-ˈlē-və-bəl\ *adj* : too improbable for belief; *also* : of such a superlative degree as to be hard to believe ⟨an ~ catch for a touchdown⟩ **syn** inconceivable, unimaginable, unthinkable — **un•be•liev•ably** \-blē\ *adv*

un•be•liev•er \-ˈlē-vər\ *n* **1** : DOUBTER **2** : INFIDEL

un•bend \-ˈbend\ *vb* **-bent** \-ˈbent\; **-bend•ing** **1** : to free from being bent : make or become straight **2** : UNTIE **3** : to make or become less stiff or more affable : RELAX

un•bend•ing *adj* : formal and distant in manner : INFLEXIBLE

un•bi•ased \ˌən-ˈbī-əst\ *adj* : free from bias; *esp* : UNPREJUDICED **syn** disinterested, dispassionate, impartial, nondiscriminatory, nonpartisan, objective, uncolored

un•bid•den \-ˈbid-ᵊn\ *also* **un•bid** \-ˈbid\ *adj* : not bidden : UNASKED

un•bind \-ˈbīnd\ *vb* **-bound** \-ˈbau̇nd\; **-bind•ing** **1** : to remove bindings from : UNTIE **2** : RELEASE

un•blessed *also* **un•blest** \ˌən-ˈblest\ *adj* **1** : not blessed **2** : EVIL

un•block \-ˈbläk\ *vb* : to free from being blocked

un•blush•ing \-ˈblə-shiŋ\ *adj* **1** : not blushing **2** : SHAMELESS — **un•blush•ing•ly** *adv*

un•bod•ied \-ˈbä-dēd\ *adj* **1** : having no body; *also* : DISEMBODIED **2** : FORMLESS

un•bolt \ˌən-ˈbōlt\ *vb* : to open or unfasten by withdrawing a bolt

un•bolt•ed \-ˈbōl-təd\ *adj* : not fastened by bolts

un•born \-ˈbȯrn\ *adj* : not yet born

un•bos•om \-ˈbu̇-zəm, -ˈbü-\ *vb* **1** : DISCLOSE, REVEAL **2**

: to disclose the thoughts or feelings of oneself

un•bound•ed \-ˈbau̇n-dəd\ *adj* : having no bounds or limits ⟨~ enthusiasm⟩ **syn** boundless, endless, immeasurable, limitless, measureless, unlimited

un•bowed \ˌən-ˈbau̇d\ *adj* **1** : not bowed down **2** : UNSUBDUED

un•bri•dled \-ˈbrīd-ᵊld\ *adj* **1** : UNRESTRAINED **2** : not confined by a bridle

un•bro•ken \-ˈbrō-kən\ *adj* **1** : not damaged **2** : not subdued or tamed **3** : not interrupted : CONTINUOUS

un•buck•le \-ˈbə-kəl\ *vb* : to loose the buckle of : UNFASTEN ⟨~ a belt⟩

un•bur•den \-ˈbərd-ᵊn\ *vb* **1** : to free or relieve from a burden **2** : to relieve oneself of (as cares or worries)

un•but•ton \-ˈbət-ᵊn\ *vb* : to unfasten the buttons of ⟨~ your coat⟩

un•called–for \ˌən-ˈkȯld-ˌfȯr\ *adj* : not called for, needed, or wanted

un•can•ny \-ˈka-nē\ *adj* **1** : GHOSTLY, MYSTERIOUS, EERIE **2** : suggesting superhuman or supernatural powers **syn** spooky, unearthly, weird — **un•can•ni•ly** \-ˈkan-ᵊl-ē\ *adv*

un•ceas•ing \-ˈsē-siŋ\ *adj* : never ceasing **syn** ceaseless, continuous, endless, interminable, unending, unremitting — **un•ceas•ing•ly** *adv*

un•cer•e•mo•ni•ous \ˌən-ˌser-ə-ˈmō-nē-əs\ *adj* : acting without or lacking ordinary courtesy : ABRUPT — **un•cer•e•mo•ni•ous•ly** *adv*

un•cer•tain \ˌən-ˈsərt-ᵊn\ *adj* **1** : not determined or fixed ⟨an ~ quantity⟩ **2** : subject to chance or change : not dependable ⟨~ weather⟩ **3** : not definitely known **4** : not sure ⟨~ of the truth⟩ — **un•cer•tain•ly** *adv*

un•cer•tain•ty \-ᵊn-tē\ *n* **1** : lack of certainty : DOUBT **2** : something that is uncertain **syn** concern, doubt, dubiety, incertitude, skepticism, suspicion

un•chain \ˌən-ˈchān\ *vb* : to free by or as if by removing a chain

un•charged \ˌən-ˈchärjd\ *adj* : having no electrical charge

un•char•i•ta•ble \-ˈchar-ə-tə-bəl\ *adj* : not charitable; *esp* : severe in judging others — **un•char•i•ta•ble•ness** *n* — **un•char•i•ta•bly** \-blē\ *adv*

un•chart•ed \-ˈchär-təd\ *adj* **1** : not recorded on a map, chart, or plan **2** : UNKNOWN

un•chris•tian \-ˈkris-chən\ *adj* **1** : not of the Christian faith **2** : contrary to the Christian spirit

un•churched \-ˈchərcht\ *adj* : not belonging to or connected with a church

un•cial \ˈən-shəl, -chəl; ˈən-sē-əl\ *adj* : relating to or written in a form of script with rounded letters used esp. in early Greek and Latin manuscripts — **uncial** *n*

un•cir•cu•lat•ed \ˌən-ˈsər-kyə-ˌlā-təd\ *adj* : issued for use as money but kept out of circulation

un•cir•cum•cised \ˌən-ˈsər-kəm-ˌsīzd\ *adj* : not circumcised; *also* : HEATHEN

un•civ•il \ˌən-ˈsi-vəl\ *adj* **1** : not civilized : BARBAROUS **2** : DISCOURTEOUS, ILL-MANNERED, IMPOLITE

un•civ•i•lized \-ˈsi-və-ˌlīzd\ *adj* **1** : not civilized : BARBAROUS **2** : remote from civilization : WILD

un•clasp \-ˈklasp\ *vb* : to open by or as if by loosing the clasp

un•cle \ˈəŋ-kəl\ *n* [ME, fr. OF, fr. L *avunculus* mother's brother] : the brother of one's father or mother; *also* : the husband of one's aunt

un•clean \ˌən-ˈklēn\ *adj* **1** : morally or spiritually impure **2** : prohibited by ritual law for use or contact **3** : DIRTY, SOILED — **un•clean•li•ness** \-lē-nəs\ *n* — **un•clean•ly** *adj* — **un•clean•ness** *n*

un•clench \-ˈklench\ *vb* : to open from a clenched position : RELAX

Uncle Tom \-ˈtäm\ *n* [fr. *Uncle Tom,* faithful slave in Harriet Beecher Stowe's novel *Uncle Tom's Cabin* (1851-52)] : a black eager to win the approval of whites

un•cloak \ˌən-ˈklōk\ *vb* **1** : to remove a cloak or cover from **2** : UNMASK, REVEAL

un•clog \-ˈkläg\ *vb* : to remove an obstruction from

un•close \-ˈklōz\ *vb* : OPEN — **un•closed** \-ˈklōzd\ *adj*

un•clothe \-ˈklōt͟h\ *vb* : to strip of clothes or a covering — **un•clothed** \-ˈklōt͟hd\ *adj*

un•coil \ˌən-ˈkȯil\ *vb* : to release or become released from a coiled state

un•com•fort•able \ˌən-ˈkəmf-tə-bəl, -ˈkəm-fər-tə-\ *adj* **1** : causing discomfort **2** : feeling discomfort — **un•com•fort•ably** \-blē\ *adv*

un•com•mit•ted \ˌən-kə-ˈmi-təd\ *adj* : not committed; *esp* : not pledged to a particular belief, allegiance, or program

un•com•mon \ˌən-ˈkä-mən\ *adj* **1** : not ordinarily encountered : UNUSUAL, RARE **2** : REMARKABLE, EXCEPTIONAL **syn** extraordinary, phenomenal, singular, unique — **un•com•mon•ly** *adv*

un•com•mu•ni•ca•tive \ˌən-kə-ˈmyü-nə-ˌkā-tiv, -ni-kə-\ *adj* : not inclined to talk or impart information : RESERVED **syn** closemouthed, reticent, silent, taciturn

un•com•pro•mis•ing \ˌən-ˈkäm-prə-ˌmī-ziŋ\ *adj* : not making or accepting a compromise : UNYIELDING **syn** adamant, inflexible, obdurate, rigid, unbending

un•con•cern \ˌən-kən-ˈsərn\ *n* **1** : lack of care or interest : INDIFFERENCE **2** : freedom from excessive concern

un•con•cerned \-ˈsərnd\ *adj* **1** : not having any part or interest **2** : not anxious or upset : free of worry **syn** aloof, detached, incurious, remote, uncurious, uninterested — **un•con•cern•ed•ly** \-ˈsər-nəd-lē\ *adv*

un•con•di•tion•al \ˌən-kən-ˈdi-shə-nəl\ *adj* : not limited in any way — **un•con•di•tion•al•ly** *adv*

un•con•di•tioned \-ˈdi-shənd\ *adj* **1** : not subject to conditions **2** : not acquired or learned : NATURAL ⟨~ responses⟩ **3** : producing an unconditioned response ⟨~ stimuli⟩

un•con•quer•able \ˌən-ˈkäŋ-kə-rə-bəl\ *adj* : incapable of being conquered or overcome : INDOMITABLE

un•con•scio•na•ble \-ˈkän-shə-nə-bəl\ *adj* **1** : not guided or controlled by conscience **2** : not in accordance with what is right or just **syn** unreasonable, undue, unjustifiable, unwarrantable, unwarranted — **un•con•scio•na•bly** \-blē\ *adv*

[1]**un•con•scious** \ˌən-ˈkän-chəs, -shəs\ *adj* **1** : not knowing or perceiving : not aware **2** : not done consciously or on purpose **3** : having lost consciousness **4** : of or relating to the unconscious — **un•con•scious•ly** *adv* — **un•con•scious•ness** *n*

[2]**unconscious** *n* : the part of one's mental life of which one is not ordinarily aware but which is often a powerful force in controlling behavior

un•con•sti•tu•tion•al \ˌən-ˌkän-stə-ˈtü-shə-nəl, -ˈtyü-\ *adj* : not according to or consistent with the constitution of a state or society — **un•con•sti•tu•tion•al•i•ty** \-tü-shə-ˈna-lə-tē, -ˈtyü-\ *n* — **un•con•sti•tu•tion•al•ly** \-ˈtü-shə-nə-lē, -ˈtyü-\ *adv*

un•con•trol•la•ble \ˌən-kən-ˈtrō-lə-bəl\ *adj* : incapable of being controlled : UNGOVERNABLE — **un•con•trol•la•bly** \-blē\ *adv*

un•con•ven•tion•al \-ˈven-chə-nəl\ *adj* : not conventional : being out of the ordinary — **un•con•ven•tion•al•i•ty** \-ˌven-chə-ˈna-lə-tē\ *n* — **un•con•ven•tion•al•ly** \-ˈven-chə-nə-lē\ *adv*

un•cork \ˌən-ˈkȯrk\ *vb* **1** : to draw a cork from **2** : to release from a sealed or pent-up state; *also* : to let go

un•count•ed \-ˈkau̇n-təd\ *adj* **1** : not counted **2** : INNUMERABLE

un•cou•ple \-ˈkə-pəl\ *vb* : DISCONNECT

un•couth \-ˈküth\ *adj* [ME, unfamiliar, fr. OE *uncūth,* fr. *un-* + *cūth* known] **1** : strange, awkward, and clumsy in shape or appearance **2** : vulgar in conduct or speech : RUDE **syn** discourteous, ill-mannered, impolite, ungracious, unmannered, unmannerly

un•cov•er \-ˈkə-vər\ *vb* **1** : to make known : DISCLOSE, REVEAL **2** : to expose to view by removing some covering **3** : to take the cover from **4** : to remove the hat from; *also* : to take off the hat as a token of respect — **un•covered** *adj*

un•crit•i•cal \ˌən-ˈkri-ti-kəl\ *adj* **1** : not critical : lacking in discrimination **2** : showing lack or improper use of critical standards or procedures — **un•crit•i•cal•ly** \-k(ə-)lē\ *adv*

un•cross \-ˈkrȯs\ *vb* : to change from a crossed position ⟨~*ed* his legs⟩

unc•tion \ˈəŋk-shən\ *n* **1** : the act of anointing as a rite of consecration or healing **2** : exaggerated or insincere earnestness of language or manner

unc•tu•ous \ˈəŋk-chə-wəs\ *adj* [ME, fr. MF or ML; MF *unctueux,* fr. ML *unctuosus,* fr. L *unctus* act of anointing, fr. *unguere* to anoint] **1** : FATTY, OILY **2** : insincerely smooth in speech and manner — **unc•tu•ous•ly** *adv*

un•curl \ˌən-ˈkərl\ *vb* : to make or become straightened out from a curled or coiled position

un•cut \ˌən-ˈkət\ *adj* **1** : not cut down or into **2** : not shaped by cutting ⟨an ~ diamond⟩ **3** : not having the folds of the leaves slit ⟨an ~ book⟩ **4** : not abridged or curtailed ⟨the ~ version of the film⟩ **5** : not diluted ⟨~ heroin⟩

un•daunt•ed \-ˈdȯn-təd\ *adj* : not daunted : not discouraged or dismayed **syn** bold, brave, dauntless, fearless, intrepid, valiant — **un•daunt•ed•ly** *adv*

un•de•ceive \ˌən-di-ˈsēv\ *vb* : to free from deception, illusion, or error

un•de•mon•stra•tive \ˌən-di-ˈmän-strə-tiv\ *adj* : restrained in expression of feeling : RESERVED

un•de•ni•able \ˌən-di-ˈnī-ə-bəl\ *adj* **1** : plainly true : INCONTESTABLE **2** : unquestionably excellent or genuine **syn** incontrovertible, indisputable, indubitable, unquestionable — **un•de•ni•ably** \-blē\ *adv*

¹un•der \ˈən-dər\ *adv* **1** : in or into a position below or beneath something **2** : below some quantity, level, or limit ⟨$10 or ~⟩ **3** : in or into a condition of subjection, subordination, or unconsciousness ⟨the ether put him ~⟩

²un•der \ˌən-dər, ˈən-\ *prep* **1** : lower than and overhung, surmounted, or sheltered by ⟨~ a tree⟩ **2** : subject to the authority or guidance of ⟨served ~ him⟩ ⟨was ~ contract⟩ **3** : subject to the action or effect of ⟨~ the influence of alcohol⟩ **4** : within the division or grouping of ⟨items ~ this heading⟩ **5** : less or lower than (as in size, amount, or rank) ⟨earns ~ $5000⟩

³under \ˈən-dər\ *adj* **1** : lying below, beneath, or on the ventral side **2** : facing or protruding downward **3** : SUBORDINATE **4** : lower than usual, proper, or desired in amount, quality, or degree

un•der•achiev•er \ˌən-dər-ə-ˈchē-vər\ *n* : one who performs below an expected level of proficiency

un•der•act \-ˈakt\ *vb* : to perform feebly or with restraint

un•der•ac•tive \-ˈak-tiv\ *adj* : characterized by abnormally low activity ⟨~ glands⟩ — **un•der•ac•tiv•i•ty** \-ˌak-ˈti-və-tē\ *n*

un•der•age \-ˈāj\ *adj* : of less than mature or legal age

un•der•arm \-ˈärm\ *adj* **1** : UNDERHAND 2 ⟨an ~ throw⟩ **2** : placed under or on the underside of the arms ⟨~ seams⟩ — **underarm** *adv or n*

un•der•bel•ly \ˈən-dər-ˌbe-lē\ *n* **1** : the underside of a body or mass **2** : a vulnerable area

un•der•bid \ˌən-dər-ˈbid\ *vb* **-bid; -bid•ding 1** : to bid less than another **2** : to bid too low

un•der•body \ˈən-dər-ˌbä-dē\ *n* : the lower parts of the body of a vehicle

un•der•bred \ˌən-dər-ˈbred\ *adj* : marked by lack of good breeding

un•der•brush \ˈən-dər-ˌbrəsh\ *n* : shrubs, bushes, or small trees growing beneath large trees

un•der•car•riage \-ˌkar-ij\ *n* **1** : a supporting framework (as of an automobile) **2** *chiefly Brit* : the landing gear of an airplane

un•der•charge \ˌən-dər-ˈchärj\ *vb* : to charge (as a person) too little — **undercharge** \ˈən-dər-ˌchärj\ *n*

un•der•class•man \ˌən-dər-ˈklas-mən\ *n* : a member of the freshman or sophomore class

un•der•clothes \ˈən-dər-ˌklōthz\ *n pl* : UNDERWEAR

un•der•cloth•ing \-ˌklō-thiŋ\ *n* : UNDERWEAR

un•der•coat \-ˌkōt\ *n* **1** : a coat worn under another **2** : a growth of short hair or fur partly concealed by the longer and usu. coarser hairs of a mammal **3** : a coat of paint under another

un•der•coat•ing \-ˌkō-tiŋ\ *n* : a special waterproof coating applied to the underside of a vehicle

un•der•cov•er \ˌən-dər-ˈkə-vər\ *adj* : acting or executed in secret; *esp* : employed or engaged in secret investigation ⟨an ~ agent⟩

un•der•croft \ˈən-dər-ˌkrȯft\ *n* [ME, fr. *under* + *crofte* crypt, fr. MD, fr. ML *crupta,* fr. L *crypta*] : a vaulted chamber under a church

un•der•cur•rent \-ˌkər-ənt\ *n* **1** : a current below the surface **2** : a hidden tendency of feeling or opinion

un•der•cut \ˌən-dər-ˈkət\ *vb* **-cut; -cut•ting 1** : to cut away the underpart of **2** : to offer to sell or to work at a lower rate than **3** : to strike (the ball) obliquely downward so as to give a backward spin or elevation to the shot — **un•der•cut** \ˈən-dər-ˌkət\ *n*

un•der•de•vel•oped \ˌən-dər-di-ˈve-ləpt\ *adj* **1** : not normally or adequately developed ⟨~ muscles⟩ **2** : having a relatively low level of economic development ⟨the ~ nations⟩

un•der•dog \ˈən-dər-ˌdȯg\ *n* : the loser or predicted loser in a struggle

un•der•done \ˌən-dər-ˈdən\ *adj* : not thoroughly done or cooked : RARE

un•der•draw•ers \ˈən-dər-ˌdrȯrz, -ˌdrȯ-ərz\ *n pl* : UNDERPANTS

un•der•em•pha•size \ˌən-dər-ˈem-fə-sīz\ *vb* : to emphasize inadequately — **un•der•em•pha•sis** \-səs\ *n*

un•der•em•ployed \-im-ˈplȯid\ *adj* : having less than full-time or adequate employment

un•der•es•ti•mate \-ˈes-tə-ˌmāt\ *vb* : to set too low a value on

un•der•ex•pose \-ik-ˈspōz\ *vb* : to expose (a photographic plate or film) for less time than is needed — **un•der•ex•po•sure** \-ˈspō-zhər\ *n*

un•der•feed \ˌən-dər-ˈfēd\ *vb* **-fed** \-ˈfed\; **-feed•ing** : to feed with too little food

un•der•foot \-ˈfu̇t\ *adv* **1** : under the feet ⟨flowers trampled ~⟩ **2** : close about one's feet : in the way

un•der•fur \ˈən-dər-ˌfər\ *n* : an undercoat of fur esp. when thick and soft

un•der•gar•ment \-ˌgär-mənt\ *n* : a garment to be worn under another

un•der•gird \ˌən-dər-ˈgərd\ *vb* : to brace up : STRENGTHEN

un•der•go \ˌən-dər-ˈgō\ *vb* **-went** \-ˈwent\; **-gone** \-ˈgȯn, -ˈgän\; **-go•ing 1** : to submit to : ENDURE **2** : to go through : EXPERIENCE

un•der•grad \ˈən-dər-ˌgrad\ *n* : UNDERGRADUATE

un•der•grad•u•ate \ˌən-dər-ˈgra-jə-wət, -jə-ˌwāt\ *n* : a student at a university or college who has not taken a first degree

¹un•der•ground \ˌən-dər-ˈgrau̇nd\ *adv* **1** : beneath the surface of the earth **2** : in or into hiding or secret operation

²un•der•ground \ˈən-dər-ˌgrau̇nd\ *n* **1** : a space under the surface of the ground; *esp* : SUBWAY **2** : a secret political movement or group; *esp* : an organized body working in secret to overthrow a government or an occupying power **3** : an avant-garde group or movement that operates outside the establishment

³underground \ˈən-dər-ˌgrau̇nd\ *adj* **1** : being, growing, operating, or located below the surface of the ground ⟨~ stems⟩ **2** : conducted by secret means **3** : produced or published by the underground ⟨~ publications⟩; *also* : of or relating to the avant-garde underground

un•der•growth \ˈən-dər-ˌgrōth\ *n* : low growth (as of herbs and shrubs) on the floor of a forest

[1]**un•der•hand** \ˈən-dər-ˌhand\ *adv* **1** : in an underhanded or secret manner **2** : with an underhand motion

[2]**underhand** *adj* **1** : UNDERHANDED **2** : made with the hand kept below the level of the shoulder

[1]**un•der•hand•ed** \ˌən-dər-ˈhan-dəd\ *adv* : UNDERHAND

[2]**underhanded** *adj* : marked by secrecy and deception — **un•der•hand•ed•ly** *adv* — **un•der•hand•ed•ness** *n*

un•der•lie \-ˈlī\ *vb* **-lay** \-ˈlā\; **-lain** \-ˈlān\; **-ly•ing** \-ˈlī-iŋ\ **1** : to lie or be situated under **2** : to be at the basis of : form the foundation of : SUPPORT

un•der•line \ˈən-dər-ˌlīn\ *vb* **1** : to draw a line under **2** : EMPHASIZE, STRESS — **underline** *n*

un•der•ling \ˈən-dər-liŋ\ *n* : SUBORDINATE, INFERIOR

un•der•lip \ˌən-dər-ˈlip\ *n* : the lower lip

un•der•ly•ing \ˌən-dər-ˌlī-iŋ\ *adj* **1** : lying under or below **2** : FUNDAMENTAL, BASIC ⟨~ principles⟩

un•der•mine \-ˈmīn\ *vb* **1** : to excavate beneath **2** : to weaken or wear away secretly or gradually

un•der•most \ˈən-dər-ˌmōst\ *adj* : lowest in relative position — **undermost** *adv*

[1]**un•der•neath** \ˌən-dər-ˈnēth\ *prep* **1** : directly under **2** : under subjection to

[2]**underneath** *adv* **1** : below a surface or object : BENEATH **2** : on the lower side

un•der•nour•ished \ˌən-dər-ˈnər-isht\ *adj* : supplied with insufficient nourishment — **un•der•nour•ish•ment** \-ˈnər-ish-mənt\ *n*

un•der•pants \ˈən-dər-ˌpants\ *n pl* : a usu. short undergarment for the lower trunk : DRAWERS

un•der•part \-ˌpärt\ *n* : a part lying on the lower side esp. of a bird or mammal

un•der•pass \-ˌpas\ *n* : a crossing of a highway and another way (as a road) at different levels; *also* : the lower level

un•der•pay \ˌən-dər-ˈpā\ *vb* : to pay too little

un•der•pin•ning \ˈən-dər-ˌpi-niŋ\ *n* : the material and construction (as a foundation) used for support of a structure — **un•der•pin** \ˌən-dər-ˈpin\ *vb*

un•der•play \ˌən-dər-ˈplā\ *vb* : to treat or handle with restraint; *esp* : to play a role with subdued force

un•der•pop•u•lat•ed \ˌən-dər-ˈpä-pyə-ˌlā-təd\ *adj* : having a lower than normal or desirable density of population

un•der•priv•i•leged \-ˈpriv-lijd, -ˈpri-və-lijd\ *adj* : having fewer esp. economic and social privileges than others

un•der•pro•duc•tion \ˌən-dər-prə-ˈdək-shən\ *n* : the production of less than enough to satisfy the demand or of less than the usual supply

un•der•rate \-ˈrāt\ *vb* : to rate or value too low

un•der•rep•re•sent•ed \-ˌre-pri-ˈzen-təd\ *adj* : inadequately represented

un•der•score \ˈən-dər-ˌskōr\ *vb* **1** : to draw a line under : UNDERLINE **2** : EMPHASIZE — **underscore** *n*

[1]**un•der•sea** \ˌən-dər-ˈsē\ *adj* : being, carried on, or used beneath the surface of the sea

[2]**undersea** *or* **un•der•seas** \-ˈsēz\ *adv* : beneath the surface of the sea

un•der•sec•re•tary \ˌən-dər-ˈse-krə-ˌter-ē\ *n* : a secretary immediately subordinate to a principal secretary ⟨~ of state⟩

un•der•sell \-ˈsel\ *vb* **-sold** \-ˈsōld\; **-sell•ing** : to sell articles cheaper than

un•der•sexed \-ˈsekst\ *adj* : deficient in sexual desire

un•der•shirt \ˈən-dər-ˌshərt\ *n* : a collarless undergarment with or without sleeves

un•der•shoot \ˌən-dər-ˈshüt\ *vb* **-shot** \-ˈshät\; **-shoot•ing 1** : to shoot short of or below (a target) **2** : to fall short of (a runway) in landing an airplane

un•der•shorts \ˈən-dər-ˌshȯrts\ *n pl* : SHORT 2

un•der•shot \ˈən-dər-ˌshät\ *adj* **1** : moved by water passing beneath ⟨an ~ waterwheel⟩ **2** : having the lower front teeth projecting beyond the upper when the mouth is closed

un•der•side \ˈən-dər-ˌsīd, ˌən-dər-ˈsīd\ *n* : the side or surface lying underneath

un•der•signed \ˈən-dər-ˌsīnd\ *n, pl* **undersigned** : one whose name is signed at the end of a document

un•der•sized \ˌən-dər-ˈsīzd\ *also* **un•der•size** \-ˈsīz\ *adj* : of a size less than is common, proper, or normal

un•der•skirt \ˈən-dər-ˌskərt\ *n* : a skirt worn under an outer skirt; *esp* : PETTICOAT

un•der•staffed \ˌən-dər-ˈstaft\ *adj* : inadequately staffed

un•der•stand \ˌən-dər-ˈstand\ *vb* **-stood** \-ˈstu̇d\; **-stand•ing 1** : to grasp the meaning of : COMPREHEND **2** : to have thorough or technical acquaintance with or expertness in ⟨~ finance⟩ **3** : to have reason to believe ⟨I ~ you are leaving tomorrow⟩ **4** : INTERPRET ⟨we ~ this to be a refusal⟩ **5** : to have a sympathetic attitude **6** : to accept as settled ⟨it is *understood* that he will pay the expenses⟩ — **un•der•stand•able** \-ˈstan-də-bəl\ *adj*

un•der•stand•ably \-blē\ *adv* : as can be easily understood

[1]**un•der•stand•ing** \ˌən-dər-ˈstan-diŋ\ *n* **1** : knowledge and ability to judge : INTELLIGENCE ⟨a person of ~⟩ **2** : agreement of opinion or feeling **3** : a mutual agreement informally or tacitly entered into

[2]**understanding** *adj* : endowed with understanding : TOLERANT, SYMPATHETIC

un•der•state \ˌən-dər-ˈstāt\ *vb* **1** : to represent as less than is the case **2** : to state with restraint esp. for effect — **un•der•state•ment** *n*

un•der•stood \ˌən-dər-ˈstu̇d\ *adj* **1** : agreed upon **2** : IMPLICIT

un•der•sto•ry \ˈən-dər-ˌstōr-ē, -ˌstȯr-\ *n* : the vegetative layer between the top layer of a forest and the ground cover

un•der•study \ˈən-dər-ˌstə-dē, ˌən-dər-ˈstə-dē\ *vb* : to study another actor's part in order to substitute in an emergency — **understudy** \ˈən-dər-ˌstə-dē\ *n*

un•der•sur•face \ˈən-dər-ˌsər-fəs\ *n* : UNDERSIDE

un•der•take \ˌən-dər-ˈtāk\ *vb* **-took** \-ˈtu̇k\; **-tak•en** \-ˈtā-kən\; **-tak•ing 1** : to take upon oneself : set about ⟨~ a task⟩ **2** : to put oneself under obligation **3** : GUARANTEE, PROMISE

un•der•tak•er \ˈən-dər-ˌtā-kər\ *n* : one whose business is to prepare the dead for burial and to arrange and manage funerals

un•der•tak•ing \ˈən-dər-ˌtā-kiŋ, ˌən-dər-ˈtā-kiŋ; *2 is* ˈən-dər-ˌtā-kiŋ *only*\ *n* **1** : the act of one who undertakes or engages in any project **2** : the business of an undertaker **3** : something undertaken **4** : PROMISE, GUARANTEE

under–the–counter *adj* : UNLAWFUL, ILLICIT ⟨~ sale of drugs⟩

un•der•tone \ˈən-dər-ˌtōn\ *n* **1** : a low or subdued tone or utterance **2** : a subdued color (as seen through and modifying another color)

un•der•tow \-ˌtō\ *n* : the current beneath the surface that flows seaward when waves are breaking upon the shore

un•der•trick \-ˌtrik\ *n* : a trick by which a declarer in bridge falls short of making the contract

un•der•val•ue \ˌən-dər-ˈval-yü\ *vb* **1** : to value or estimate below the real worth **2** : to esteem lightly

un•der•wa•ter \ˌən-dər-ˈwȯ-tər, -ˈwä-\ *adj* : lying, growing, worn, or operating below the surface of the water — **un•der•wa•ter** *adv*

under way \-ˈwā\ *adv* **1** : into motion from a standstill **2** : in progress

un•der•wear \ˈən-dər-ˌwar\ *n* : clothing or a garment worn next to the skin and under other clothing

un•der•weight \ˌən-dər-ˈwāt\ *n* : weight below what is normal, average, or necessary — **underweight** *adj*

un•der•world \ˈən-dər-ˌwərld\ *n* **1** : the place of departed souls : HADES **2** : the side of the world opposite to one **3** : the world of organized crime

un•der•write \ˈən-dər-ˌrīt, ˌən-dər-ˈrīt\ *vb* **-wrote**

\-ˌrōt, -ˈrōt\; **-writ·ten** \-ˌrit-ᵊn, -ˈrit-ᵊn\; **-writ·ing 1** : to write under or at the end of something else **2** : to set one's name to an insurance policy and thereby become answerable for a designated loss or damage **3** : to subscribe to : agree to **4** : to guarantee financial support of — **un·der·writ·er** *n*

un·de·sign·ing \ˌən-di-ˈzī-niŋ\ *adj* : having no artful, ulterior, or fraudulent purpose : SINCERE

un·de·sir·able \-ˈzī-rə-bəl\ *adj* : not desirable — **undesirable** *n*

un·de·vi·at·ing \ˌən-ˈdē-vē-ˌā-tiŋ\ *adj* : keeping a true course

un·dies \ˈən-dēz\ *n pl* : UNDERWEAR; *esp* : women's underwear

un·do \ˌən-ˈdü\ *vb* **-did** \-ˈdid\; **-done** \-ˈdən\; **-do·ing 1** : to make or become unfastened or loosened : OPEN **2** : to make null or as if not done : REVERSE **3** : to bring to ruin; *also* : UPSET

un·do·ing *n* : a cause of ruin

un·doubt·ed \-ˈdau̇-təd\ *adj* : not doubted or called into question : CERTAIN — **un·doubt·ed·ly** *adv*

[1]**un·dress** \ˌən-ˈdres\ *vb* : to remove the clothes or covering of : STRIP, DISROBE

[2]**undress** *n* **1** : informal dress; *esp* : a loose robe or dressing gown **2** : ordinary dress **3** : NUDITY

un·due \-ˈdü, -ˈdyü\ *adj* **1** : not due **2** : exceeding or violating propriety or fitness : EXCESSIVE

un·du·lant \ˈən-jə-lənt, ˈən-də-, -dyə-\ *adj* : UNDULATING

undulant fever *n* : a human disease caused by bacteria from infected domestic animals or their products and marked by intermittent fever, pain and swelling in the joints, and great weakness

un·du·late \-ˌlāt\ *vb* **-lat·ed; -lat·ing** [LL *undula* small wave, fr. L *unda* wave] **1** : to have a wavelike motion or appearance **2** : to rise and fall in pitch or volume

un·du·la·tion \ˌən-jə-ˈlā-shən, ˌən-də-, -dyə-\ *n* **1** : wavy or wavelike motion **2** : pulsation of sound **3** : a wavy appearance or outline — **un·du·la·to·ry** \ˈən-jə-lə-ˌtōr-ē, ˈən-də-, -dyə-\ *adj*

un·du·ly \ˌən-ˈdü-lē, ˈən-, -ˈdyü-\ *adv* : in an undue manner; *esp* : EXCESSIVELY

un·dy·ing \-ˈdī-iŋ\ *adj* : not dying : IMMORTAL, PERPETUAL

un·earned \-ˈərnd\ *adj* : not earned by labor, service, or skill ⟨~ income⟩

un·earth \ˌən-ˈərth\ *vb* **1** : to dig up out of or as if out of the earth ⟨~ buried treasure⟩ **2** : to bring to light : DISCOVER ⟨~ a secret⟩

un·earth·ly \-lē\ *adj* **1** : not of or belonging to the earth **2** : SUPERNATURAL, WEIRD; *also* : ABSURD

un·easy \ˌən-ˈē-zē\ *adj* **1** : AWKWARD, EMBARRASSED ⟨~ among strangers⟩ **2** : disturbed by pain or worry; *also* : RESTLESS **3** : UNSTABLE ⟨an ~ truce⟩ — **un·eas·i·ly** \-ˈē-zə-lē\ *adv* — **un·eas·i·ness** \-ˈē-zē-nəs\ *n*

un·em·ployed \ˌən-im-ˈplȯid\ *adj* : not being used; *also* : having no job

un·em·ploy·ment \-ˈplȯi-mənt\ *n* **1** : lack of employment **2** : money paid at regular intervals (as by a government agency) to an unemployed person

un·end·ing \ˌən-ˈen-diŋ\ *adj* : having no ending : ENDLESS

un·equal \ˌən-ˈē-kwəl\ *adj* **1** : not alike (as in size, amount, number, or value) **2** : not uniform : VARIABLE **3** : badly balanced or matched **4** : INADEQUATE, INSUFFICIENT ⟨~ to the task⟩ — **un·equal·ly** *adv*

un·equaled *or* **un·equalled** \-kwəld\ *adj* : not equaled : UNPARALLELED

un·equiv·o·cal \ˌən-i-ˈkwi-və-kəl\ *adj* : leaving no doubt : CLEAR — **un·equiv·o·cal·ly** *adv*

un·err·ing \ˌən-ˈer-iŋ, ˌən-ˈər-\ *adj* : making no errors : CERTAIN, UNFAILING — **un·err·ing·ly** *adv*

UNES·CO \yu̇-ˈnes-kō\ *abbr* United Nations Educational, Scientific, and Cultural Organization

un·even \ˌən-ˈē-vən\ *adj* **1** : ODD 3 **2** : not even : not level or smooth : RUGGED, RAGGED **3** : IRREGULAR; *also* : varying in quality — **un·even·ly** *adv* — **un·even·ness** *n*

un·event·ful \ˌən-i-ˈvent-fəl\ *adj* : lacking interesting or noteworthy incidents — **un·event·ful·ly** *adv*

un·ex·am·pled \ˌən-ig-ˈzam-pəld\ *adj* : UNPRECEDENTED, UNPARALLELED

un·ex·cep·tion·able \ˌən-ik-ˈsep-shə-nə-bəl\ *adj* : not open to exception or objection : beyond reproach

un·ex·pect·ed \ˌən-ik-ˈspek-təd\ *adj* : not expected : UNFORESEEN — **un·ex·pect·ed·ly** *adv*

un·fail·ing \ˌən-ˈfā-liŋ\ *adj* **1** : not failing, flagging, or waning : CONSTANT **2** : INEXHAUSTIBLE **3** : INFALLIBLE, SURE — **un·fail·ing·ly** *adv*

un·fair \-ˈfar\ *adj* **1** : marked by injustice, partiality, or deception : UNJUST **2** : not equitable in business dealings — **un·fair·ly** *adv* — **un·fair·ness** *n*

un·faith·ful \ˌən-ˈfāth-fəl\ *adj* **1** : not observant of vows, allegiance, or duty : DISLOYAL **2** : INACCURATE, UNTRUSTWORTHY — **un·faith·ful·ly** *adv* — **un·faith·ful·ness** *n*

un·fa·mil·iar \ˌən-fə-ˈmil-yər\ *adj* **1** : not well-known : STRANGE ⟨an ~ place⟩ **2** : not well acquainted ⟨~ with the subject⟩ — **un·fa·mil·iar·i·ty** \-ˌmi-lē-ˈar-, -ˈyar-\ *n*

un·fas·ten \ˌən-ˈfas-ᵊn\ *vb* : to make or become loose : UNDO, DETACH

un·feel·ing \-ˈfē-liŋ\ *adj* **1** : lacking feeling : INSENSATE **2** : HARDHEARTED, CRUEL — **un·feel·ing·ly** *adv*

un·feigned \-ˈfānd\ *adj* : not feigned : not hypocritical : GENUINE

un·fet·ter \-ˈfe-tər\ *vb* **1** : to free from fetters **2** : LIBERATE

un·fil·ial \ˌən-ˈfi-lē-əl, -ˈfil-yəl\ *adj* : not observing the obligations of a child to a parent : UNDUTIFUL

un·fin·ished \ˌən-ˈfi-nisht\ *adj* **1** : not brought to an end **2** : being in a rough or unpolished state

[1]**un·fit** \-ˈfit\ *adj* : not fit or suitable; *esp* : physically or mentally unsound — **un·fit·ness** *n*

[2]**unfit** *vb* : DISABLE, DISQUALIFY

un·fix \-ˈfiks\ *vb* **1** : to loosen from a fastening : DETACH **2** : UNSETTLE

un·flap·pa·ble \-ˈfla-pə-bəl\ *adj* : not easily upset or panicked — **un·flap·pa·bly** *adv*

un·fledged \ˌən-ˈflejd\ *adj* : not feathered or ready for flight; *also* : IMMATURE, CALLOW

un·flinch·ing \-ˈflin-chiŋ\ *adj* : not flinching or shrinking : STEADFAST — **un·flinch·ing·ly** *adv*

un·fold \-ˈfōld\ *vb* **1** : to open the folds of : open up **2** : to lay open to view : DISCLOSE **3** : BLOSSOM, DEVELOP

un·for·get·ta·ble \ˌən-fər-ˈge-tə-bəl\ *adj* : incapable of being forgotten — **un·for·get·ta·bly** \-blē\ *adv*

un·formed \-ˈfȯrmd\ *adj* : not regularly formed or ordered : UNDEVELOPED

un·for·tu·nate \-ˈfȯr-chə-nət\ *adj* **1** : not fortunate : UNLUCKY **2** : attended with misfortune **3** : UNSUITABLE — **unfortunate** *n*

un·for·tu·nate·ly \-nət-lē\ *adv* **1** : in an unfortunate manner **2** : it is unfortunate

un·found·ed \ˌən-ˈfau̇n-dəd\ *adj* : lacking a sound basis : GROUNDLESS

un·freeze \-ˈfrēz\ *vb* **-froze** \-ˈfrōz\; **-fro·zen** \-ˈfrōz-ᵊn\; **-freez·ing 1** : to cause to thaw **2** : to remove from a freeze ⟨~ prices⟩

un·fre·quent·ed \ˌən-frē-ˈkwen-təd; ˌən-ˈfrē-kwən-\ *adj* : seldom visited or traveled over

un·friend·ly \ˌən-ˈfrend-lē\ *adj* **1** : not friendly or kind : HOSTILE **2** : UNFAVORABLE — **un·friend·li·ness** \-lē-nəs\ *n*

un·frock \-ˈfräk\ *vb* : DEFROCK

un·fruit·ful \-ˈfrüt-fəl\ *adj* **1** : not producing fruit or offspring : BARREN **2** : yielding no valuable result : UNPROFITABLE — **un·fruit·ful·ness** *n*

un·furl \-ˈfərl\ *vb* : to loose from a furled state : UNFOLD

un·gain·ly \-ˈgān-lē\ *adj* [*un-* + obs. *gainly* proper, becoming, fr. *gain* direct, handy, fr. ME *geyn,* fr. OE *gēn,* fr. ON *gegn*] : CLUMSY, AWKWARD — **un•gain•li•ness** \-lē-nəs\ *n*

un•gen•er•ous \ˌən-ˈje-nə-rəs\ *adj* : not generous or liberal : STINGY

un•glued \ˌən-ˈglüd\ *adj* : UPSET, DISORDERED

un•god•ly \ˌən-ˈgäd-lē, -ˈgȯd-\ *adj* **1** : IMPIOUS, IRRELIGIOUS **2** : SINFUL, WICKED **3** : OUTRAGEOUS ⟨an ~ hour⟩ — **un•god•li•ness** \-lē-nəs\ *n*

un•gov•ern•able \-ˈgə-vər-nə-bəl\ *adj* : not capable of being governed, guided, or restrained : UNRULY

un•gra•cious \-ˈgrā-shəs\ *adj* **1** : not courteous : RUDE **2** : not pleasing : DISAGREEABLE

un•grate•ful \ˌən-ˈgrāt-fəl\ *adj* **1** : not thankful for favors **2** : DISAGREEABLE; *also* : THANKLESS — **un•grate•ful•ly** *adv* — **un•grate•ful•ness** *n*

un•guard•ed \-ˈgär-dəd\ *adj* **1** : UNPROTECTED **2** : DIRECT, INCAUTIOUS ⟨~ remarks⟩

un•guent \ˈəŋ-gwənt, ˈən-\ *n* : a soothing or healing salve : OINTMENT

[1]**un•gu•late** \ˈəŋ-gyə-lət, ˈən-, -ˌlāt\ *adj* [LL *ungulatus,* fr. L *ungula* hoof, fr. *unguis* nail, hoof] : having hoofs

[2]**ungulate** *n* : a hoofed mammal (as a cow, horse, or rhinoceros)

Unh *symbol* unnilhexium

un•hal•lowed \ˌən-ˈha-lōd\ *adj* **1** : not consecrated : UNHOLY **2** : IMPIOUS, PROFANE **3** : contrary to accepted standards : IMMORAL

un•hand \ˌən-ˈhand\ *vb* : to remove the hand from : let go

un•hand•some \-ˈhan-səm\ *adj* **1** : not beautiful or handsome : HOMELY **2** : UNBECOMING **3** : DISCOURTEOUS, RUDE

un•handy \-ˈhan-dē\ *adj* : INCONVENIENT; *also* : AWKWARD

un•hap•py \-ˈha-pē\ *adj* **1** : UNLUCKY, UNFORTUNATE **2** : SAD, MISERABLE **3** : INAPPROPRIATE — **un•hap•pi•ly** \-ˈha-pə-lē\ *adv* — **un•hap•pi•ness** \-pē-nəs\ *n*

un•har•ness \-ˈhär-nəs\ *vb* : to remove the harness from (as a horse)

un•healthy \-ˈhel-thē\ *adj* **1** : not conducive to health : UNWHOLESOME **2** : SICKLY, DISEASED

un•heard \-ˈhərd\ *adj* **1** : not heard **2** : not granted a hearing

unheard–of *adj* : previously unknown; *esp* : UNPRECEDENTED

un•hinge \ˌən-ˈhinj\ *vb* **1** : to take from the hinges **2** : to make unstable esp. mentally

un•hitch \-ˈhich\ *vb* : UNFASTEN, LOOSE

un•ho•ly \-ˈhō-lē\ *adj* : not holy : PROFANE, WICKED — **un•ho•li•ness** \-lē-nəs\ *n*

un•hook \-ˈhu̇k\ *vb* : to loose from a hook

un•horse \-ˈhȯrs\ *vb* : to dislodge from or as if from a horse

uni•cam•er•al \ˌyü-ni-ˈka-mə-rəl\ *adj* : having a single legislative house or chamber

UNI•CEF \ˈyü-nə-ˌsef\ *abbr* [*U*nited *N*ations *I*nternational *C*hildren's *E*mergency *F*und, its former name] United Nations Children's Fund

uni•cel•lu•lar \ˌyü-ni-ˈsel-yə-lər\ *adj* : having or consisting of a single cell

uni•corn \ˈyü-nə-ˌkȯrn\ *n* [ME *unicorne,* fr. OF, fr. LL *unicornis,* fr. L, having one horn, fr. *unus* one + *cornu* horn] : a mythical animal with one horn in the middle of the forehead

uni•cy•cle \ˈyü-ni-ˌsī-kəl\ *n* : a vehicle that has a single wheel and is usu. propelled by pedals

uni•di•rec•tion•al \ˌyü-ni-də-ˈrek-shə-nəl, -dī-\ *adj* : having, moving in, or responsive in a single direction

uni•fi•ca•tion \ˌyü-nə-fə-ˈkā-shən\ *n* : the act, process, or result of unifying : the state of being unified

[1]**uni•form** \ˈyü-nə-ˌfȯrm\ *adj* **1** : not varying **2** : of the same form with others ⟨~ procedures⟩ — **uni•form•ly** *adv*

[2]**uniform** *vb* : to clothe with a uniform

[3]**uniform** *n* : distinctive dress worn by members of a particular group (as an army or a police force)

uni•for•mi•ty \ˌyü-nə-ˈfȯr-mə-tē\ *n, pl* **-ties** : the state of being uniform

uni•fy \ˈyü-nə-ˌfī\ *vb* **-fied; -fy•ing** : to make into a coherent whole : UNITE

uni•lat•er•al \ˌyü-nə-ˈla-tə-rəl\ *adj* : of, having, affecting, or done by one side only — **uni•lat•er•al•ly** *adv*

un•im•peach•able \ˌən-im-ˈpē-chə-bəl\ *adj* : not liable to accusation : BLAMELESS, IRREPROACHABLE

un•in•hib•it•ed \ˌən-in-ˈhi-bə-təd\ *adj* : free from inhibition; *also* : boisterously informal — **un•in•hib•it•ed•ly** *adv*

un•in•tel•li•gent \-ˈte-lə-jənt\ *adj* : lacking intelligence

un•in•tel•li•gi•ble \-jə-bəl\ *adj* : not intelligible : OBSCURE — **un•in•tel•li•gi•bly** \-blē\ *adv*

un•in•ter•est•ed \ˌən-ˈin-trəs-təd, -tə-rəs-, -tə-ˌres-\ *adj* : not interested : not having the mind or feelings engaged or aroused

un•in•ter•rupt•ed \ˌən-ˌin-tə-ˈrəp-təd\ *adj* : not interrupted : CONTINUOUS

union \ˈyü-nyən\ *n* **1** : an act or instance of uniting two or more things into one : the state of being so united : COMBINATION, JUNCTION **2** : a uniting in marriage **3** : something formed by a combining of parts or members; *esp* : a confederation of independent individuals (as nations or persons) for some common purpose **4** : an organization of workers (as a labor union or a trade union) formed to advance its members' interests esp. in respect to wages and working conditions **5** : a device emblematic of union used on or as a national flag; *also* : the upper inner corner of a flag **6** : a device for connecting parts (as of a machine); *esp* : a coupling for pipes

union•ise *Brit var of* UNIONIZE

union•ism \ˈyü-nyə-ˌni-zəm\ *n* **1** : the principle or policy of forming or adhering to a union; *esp, cap* : adherence to the policy of a firm federal union before or during the U.S. Civil War **2** : the principles or system of trade unions — **union•ist** *n*

union•ize \ˈyü-nyə-ˌnīz\ *vb* **-ized; -iz•ing** : to form into or cause to join a labor union — **union•i•za•tion** \ˌyü-nyə-nə-ˈzā-shən\ *n*

union jack *n* **1** : a flag consisting of the part of a national flag that signifies union **2** *cap U&J* : the national flag of the United Kingdom

unique \yu̇-ˈnēk\ *adj* **1** : being the only one of its kind : SINGLE, SOLE **2** : very unusual : NOTABLE — **unique•ly** *adv* — **unique•ness** *n*

uni•sex \ˈyü-nə-ˌseks\ *adj* : not distinguishable as male or female; *also* : suitable or designed for both males and females — **unisex** *n*

uni•sex•u•al \ˌyü-nə-ˈsek-shə-wəl\ *adj* **1** : having only male or only female sex organs **2** : UNISEX

uni•son \ˈyü-nə-sən, -zən\ *n* [MF, fr. ML *unisonus* having the same sound, fr. L *unus* one + *sonus* sound] **1** : sameness or identity in musical pitch **2** : the condition of being tuned or sounded at the same pitch or in octaves ⟨sing in ~⟩ **3** : harmonious agreement or union : ACCORD

unit \ˈyü-nət\ *n* **1** : the smallest whole number greater than zero : ONE **2** : a definite amount or quantity used as a standard of measurement **3** : a single thing, person, or group that is a constituent of a whole; *also* : a part of a military establishment that has a prescribed organization — **unit** *adj*

Uni•tar•i•an \ˌyü-nə-ˈter-ē-ən\ *n* : a member of a religious denomination stressing individual freedom of belief — **Uni•tar•i•an•ism** *n*

uni•tary \ˈyü-nə-ˌter-ē\ *adj* **1** : of or relating to a unit **2** : not divided — **uni•tar•i•ly** \ˌyü-nə-ˈter-ə-lē\ *adv*

unite \yu̇-ˈnīt\ *vb* **unit•ed; unit•ing** **1** : to put or join together so as to make one : COMBINE, COALESCE **2** : to join by a legal or moral bond; *also* : to join in interest or fellowship **3** : AMALGAMATE, CONSOLIDATE **4** : to act in concert

unit•ed \yu̇-ˈnī-təd\ *adj* **1** : made one : COMBINED **2** : relating to or produced by joint action **3** : being in agreement : HARMONIOUS

unit•ize \ˈyü-nə-ˌtīz\ *vb* **-ized; -iz•ing** **1** : to form or convert into a unit **2** : to divide into units

uni•ty \ˈyü-nə-tē\ *n, pl* **-ties** **1** : the quality or state of being or being made one : ONENESS **2** : a definite quantity or combination of quantities taken as one or for which 1 is made to stand in calculation **3** : CONCORD, ACCORD, HARMONY **4** : continuity without change ⟨~ of purpose⟩ **5** : reference of all the parts of a literary or artistic composition to a single main idea **6** : totality of related parts **syn** solidarity, union, integrity

univ *abbr* **1** universal **2** university

uni•valve \ˈyü-ni-ˌvalv\ *n* : a mollusk having a shell with only one piece; *esp* : GASTROPOD — **univalve** *adj*

uni•ver•sal \ˌyü-nə-ˈvər-səl\ *adj* **1** : including, covering, or affecting the whole without limit or exception : UNLIMITED, GENERAL ⟨a ~ rule⟩ **2** : present or occurring everywhere **3** : used or for use among all ⟨a ~ language⟩ — **uni•ver•sal•ly** *adv*

uni•ver•sal•i•ty \-vər-ˈsa-lə-tē\ *n* : the quality or state of being universal

uni•ver•sal•ize \-ˈvər-sə-ˌlīz\ *vb* **-ized; -iz•ing** : to make universal : GENERALIZE — **uni•ver•sal•i•za•tion** \-ˌvər-sə-lə-ˈzā-shən\ *n*

universal joint *n* : a shaft coupling for transmitting rotation from one shaft to another not in a straight line with it

universal joint

Universal Product Code *n* : a combination of a bar code and numbers by which a scanner can identify a product and usu. assign a price

uni•verse \ˈyü-nə-ˌvərs\ *n* [L *universum,* fr. neut. of *universus* entire, whole, fr. *unus* one + *versus* turned toward, fr. pp. of *vertere* to turn] : the whole body of things observed or assumed : COSMOS

uni•ver•si•ty \ˌyü-nə-ˈvər-sə-tē\ *n, pl* **-ties** : an institution of higher learning authorized to confer degrees in various special fields (as theology, law, and medicine) as well as in the arts and sciences generally

un•just \ˌən-ˈjəst\ *adj* : characterized by injustice — **un•just•ly** *adv*

un•kempt \-ˈkempt\ *adj* **1** : lacking order or neatness; *also* : ROUGH, UNPOLISHED **2** : not combed : DISHEVELED

un•kind \-ˈkīnd\ *adj* : not kind or sympathetic ⟨an ~ remark⟩ — **un•kind•ly** *adv* — **un•kind•ness** *n*

un•kind•ly \-ˈkīnd-lē\ *adj* : UNKIND — **un•kind•li•ness** *n*

un•know•ing \ˌən-ˈnō-iŋ\ *adj* : not knowing — **un•know•ing•ly** *adv*

un•known \-ˈnōn\ *adj* : not known or not well-known — **unknown** *n*

un•lace \ˌən-ˈlās\ *vb* : to loose by undoing a lace

un•lade \-ˈlād\ *vb* **-lad•ed; -laded** *or* **-lad•en** \-ˈlād-ᵊn\; **-lad•ing** : to take the load or cargo from : UNLOAD

un•latch \-ˈlach\ *vb* **1** : to open or loose by lifting the latch **2** : to become loosed or opened

un•law•ful \ˌən-ˈlȯ-fəl\ *adj* **1** : not lawful : ILLEGAL **2** : ILLEGITIMATE — **un•law•ful•ly** *adv*

un•lead•ed \-ˈle-dəd\ *adj* : not treated or mixed with lead or lead compounds

un•learn \-ˈlərn\ *vb* : to put out of one's knowledge or memory; *also* : to discard the habit of

un•learned \-ˈlər-nəd *for 1;* -ˈlərnd *for 2*\ *adj* **1** : UNEDUCATED, ILLITERATE **2** : not gained by study or training

un•leash \-ˈlēsh\ *vb* : to free from or as if from a leash : let loose

un•less \ən-ˈles, ˈən-ˌles\ *conj* : except on condition that ⟨won't go ~ you do⟩

un•let•tered \ˌən-ˈle-tərd\ *adj* : not educated : ILLITERATE

[1]**un•like** \-ˈlīk\ *adj* **1** : not like : DISSIMILAR, DIFFERENT **2** : UNEQUAL — **un•like•ness** *n*

[2]**unlike** *prep* **1** : different from ⟨she's quite ~ her sister⟩ **2** : unusual for ⟨it's ~ you to be late⟩ **3** : differently from ⟨behaves ~ his brother⟩

un•like•li•hood \ˌən-ˈlī-klē-ˌhu̇d\ *n* : IMPROBABILITY

un•like•ly \-ˈlī-klē\ *adj* **1** : not likely : IMPROBABLE **2** : likely to fail

un•lim•ber \ˌən-ˈlim-bər\ *vb* : to get ready for action

un•list•ed \ˌən-ˈlis-təd\ *adj* **1** : not appearing on a list; *esp* : not appearing in a telephone book **2** : not listed on a stock exchange

un•load \-ˈlōd\ *vb* **1** : to take away or off : REMOVE ⟨~ cargo from a hold⟩; *also* : to get rid of **2** : to take a load from ⟨~ the ship⟩; *also* : to relieve or set free : UNBURDEN ⟨~ one's mind of worries⟩ **3** : to draw the charge from ⟨~*ed* the gun⟩ **4** : to sell in volume

un•lock \-ˈläk\ *vb* **1** : to open or unfasten through release of a lock **2** : RELEASE ⟨~ a flood of emotions⟩ **3** : DISCLOSE, REVEAL ⟨~ nature's secrets⟩

un•looked–for \-ˈlu̇kt-fȯr\ *adj* : UNEXPECTED

un•loose \ˌən-ˈlüs\ *vb* : to relax the strain of : set free; *also* : UNTIE

un•loos•en \-ˈlüs-ᵊn\ *vb* : UNLOOSE

un•love•ly \-ˈləv-lē\ *adj* : having no charm or appeal : not amiable

un•luck•i•ly \-ˈlə-kə-lē\ *adv* : UNFORTUNATELY

un•lucky \-ˈlə-kē\ *adj* **1** : UNFORTUNATE, ILL-FATED **2** : likely to bring misfortune : INAUSPICIOUS **3** : REGRETTABLE

un•man \ˌən-ˈman\ *vb* **1** : to deprive of manly courage **2** : CASTRATE

un•man•ly \-ˈman-lē\ *adj* : not manly : COWARDLY; *also* : EFFEMINATE

un•man•ner•ly \-ˈma-nər-lē\ *adj* : RUDE, IMPOLITE — **unmannerly** *adv*

un•mask \ˌən-ˈmask\ *vb* **1** : to strip of a mask or a disguise : EXPOSE **2** : to remove one's mask

un•mean•ing \-ˈmē-niŋ\ *adj* : having no meaning : SENSELESS

un•me•di•at•ed \ˌən-ˈmē-dē-ˌā-təd\ *adj* : not mediated : not communicated or transformed by an intervening agency

un•meet \-ˈmēt\ *adj* : not meet or fit : UNSUITABLE, IMPROPER

un•men•tion•able \-ˈmen-chə-nə-bəl\ *adj* : not fit or proper to be talked about

un•mer•ci•ful \-ˈmər-si-fəl\ *adj* : not merciful : CRUEL, MERCILESS — **un•mer•ci•ful•ly** *adv*

un•mind•ful \-ˈmīnd-fəl\ *adj* : not mindful : CARELESS, UNAWARE

un•mis•tak•able \ˌən-mə-ˈstā-kə-bəl\ *adj* : not capable of being mistaken or misunderstood : CLEAR, OBVIOUS — **un•mis•tak•ably** \-blē\ *adv*

un•mit•i•gat•ed \ˌən-ˈmi-tə-ˌgā-təd\ *adj* **1** : not softened or lessened **2** : ABSOLUTE, DOWNRIGHT ⟨an ~ liar⟩

un•moor \-ˈmu̇r\ *vb* : to loose from or as if from moorings

un•mor•al \-ˈmȯr-əl\ *adj* : having no moral perception or quality : AMORAL — **un•mo•ral•i•ty** \ˌən-mə-ˈra-lə-tē\ *n*

un•muz•zle \-ˈmə-zəl\ *vb* : to remove a muzzle from

un•nat•u•ral \ˌən-ˈna-chə-rəl\ *adj* : contrary to or acting contrary to nature or natural instincts; *also* : AB-

NORMAL — **un•nat•u•ral•ly** *adv* — **un•nat•u•ral•ness** *n*
un•nec•es•sar•i•ly \ˌən-ˌne-sə-ˈser-ə-lē\ *adv* **1** : not by necessity **2** : to an unnecessary degree ⟨~ harsh⟩
un•nerve \ˌən-ˈnərv\ *vb* : to deprive of courage, strength, or steadiness; *also* : UPSET
un•nil•hex•i•um \ˌyün-ᵊl-ˈhek-sē-əm\ *n* [NL, fr. *unnil-* (fr. L *unus* one + *nil* zero) + Gk *hex* six + NL *-ium*] : the chemical element of atomic number 106 — see ELEMENT table
un•nil•pen•ti•um \-ˈpen-tē-əm\ *n* : the chemical element of atomic number 105 — see ELEMENT table
un•nil•qua•di•um \-ˈkwä-dē-əm\ *n* : the chemical element of atomic number 104 — see ELEMENT table
un•num•bered \ˌən-ˈnəm-bərd\ *adj* : not numbered or counted : INNUMERABLE
un•ob•tru•sive \ˌən-əb-ˈtrü-siv\ *adj* : not obtrusive or forward : not bold : INCONSPICUOUS — **un•ob•tru•sive•ly** *adv*
un•oc•cu•pied \ˌən-ˈä-kyə-ˌpīd\ *adj* **1** : not busy : UNEMPLOYED **2** : not occupied : EMPTY, VACANT
un•or•ga•nized \-ˈȯr-gə-ˌnīzd\ *adj* **1** : not formed or brought into an integrated or ordered whole **2** : not organized into unions ⟨~ labor⟩
Unp *symbol* unnilpentium
un•pack \ˌən-ˈpak\ *vb* **1** : to separate and remove things packed **2** : to open and remove the contents of
un•par•al•leled \ˌən-ˈpar-ə-ˌleld\ *adj* : having no parallel; *esp* : having no equal or match
un•par•lia•men•ta•ry \ˌən-ˌpär-lə-ˈmen-tə-rē\ *adj* : contrary to parliamentary practice
un•peg \ˌən-ˈpeg\ *vb* **1** : to remove a peg from **2** : to unfasten by or as if by removing a peg
un•per•son \ˈən-ˈpərs-ᵊn, -ˌpərs-\ *n* : a person who usu. for political or ideological reasons is removed from recognition or consideration
un•pile \ˌən-ˈpīl\ *vb* : to take or disentangle from a pile
un•pin \-ˈpin\ *vb* : to remove a pin from : UNFASTEN
un•pleas•ant \-ˈplez-ᵊnt\ *adj* : not pleasant : DISAGREEABLE — **un•pleas•ant•ly** *adv* — **un•pleas•ant•ness** *n*
un•plug \ˌən-ˈpləg\ *vb* **1** : UNCLOG **2** : to remove (a plug) from a receptacle; *also* : to disconnect from an electric circuit by removing a plug
un•plumbed \-ˈpləmd\ *adj* **1** : not tested or measured with a plumb line **2** : not thoroughly explored
un•pop•u•lar \ˌən-ˈpä-pyə-lər\ *adj* : not popular : looked upon or received unfavorably — **un•pop•u•lar•i•ty** \ˌən-ˌpä-pyə-ˈlar-ə-tē\ *n*
un•prec•e•dent•ed \ˌən-ˈpre-sə-ˌden-təd\ *adj* : having no precedent : NOVEL
un•pre•ten•tious \ˌən-pri-ˈten-chəs\ *adj* : not pretentious : MODEST
un•prin•ci•pled \ˌən-ˈprin-sə-pəld\ *adj* : lacking sound or honorable principles : UNSCRUPULOUS
un•print•able \-ˈprin-tə-bəl\ *adj* : unfit to be printed
un•prof•it•able \ˌən-ˈprä-fə-tə-bəl\ *adj* : not profitable : USELESS, VAIN
Unq *symbol* unnilquadium
un•qual•i•fied \ˌən-ˈkwä-lə-ˌfīd\ *adj* **1** : not having requisite qualifications **2** : not modified or restricted by reservations : COMPLETE — **un•qual•i•fied•ly** \-ˌfī-əd-lē\ *adv*
un•ques•tion•able \-ˈkwes-chə-nə-bəl\ *adj* : not questionable : INDISPUTABLE — **un•ques•tion•ably** \-blē\ *adv*
un•ques•tion•ing \-chə-niŋ\ *adj* : not questioning : accepting without examination or hesitation — **un•ques•tion•ing•ly** *adv*
un•qui•et \-ˈkwī-ət\ *adj* **1** : not quiet : AGITATED, DISTURBED **2** : physically, emotionally, or mentally restless : UNEASY
un•quote \ˈən-ˌkwōt\ *n* — used orally to indicate the end of a direct quotation
un•rav•el \ˌən-ˈra-vəl\ *vb* **1** : to separate the threads of **2** : SOLVE ⟨~ a mystery⟩ **3** : to become unraveled
un•read \-ˈred\ *adj* **1** : not read; *also* : left unexamined **2** : lacking the benefits or the experience of reading
un•re•al \-ˈrēl\ *adj* : lacking in reality, substance, or genuineness — **un•re•al•i•ty** \ˌən-rē-ˈa-lə-tē\ *n*
un•rea•son•able \-ˈrēz-ᵊn-ə-bəl\ *adj* **1** : not governed by or acting according to reason; *also* : not conformable to reason : ABSURD **2** : exceeding the bounds of reason or moderation — **un•rea•son•able•ness** *n* — **un•rea•son•ably** *adv*
un•rea•soned \-ˈrēz-ᵊnd\ *adj* : not based on reason or reasoning
un•rea•son•ing \-ˈrēz-ᵊn-iŋ\ *adj* : not using or showing the use of reason as a guide or control
un•re•con•struct•ed \ˌən-ˌrē-kən-ˈstrək-təd\ *adj* : not reconciled to some political, economic, or social change; *esp* : holding stubbornly to a particular belief, view, place, or style
un•reel \ˌən-ˈrēl\ *vb* **1** : to unwind from or as if from a reel **2** : to perform successfully
un•re•gen•er•ate \ˌən-ri-ˈje-nə-rət\ *adj* : not regenerated or reformed
un•re•lent•ing \-ˈlen-tiŋ\ *adj* **1** : not yielding in determination : STERN ⟨~ leader⟩ **2** : not letting up or weakening in vigor or pace : CONSTANT — **un•re•lent•ing•ly** *adv*
un•re•mit•ting \-ˈmi-tiŋ\ *adj* : CONTINUOUS, INCESSANT, PERSEVERING — **un•re•mit•ting•ly** *adv*
un•re•quit•ed \ˌən-ri-ˈkwī-təd\ *adj* : not requited : not reciprocated or returned in kind ⟨~ love⟩
un•re•served \-ˈzərvd\ *adj* **1** : not limited or partial ⟨~ enthusiasm⟩ **2** : not cautious or reticent : FRANK, OPEN **3** : not set aside for special use — **un•re•serv•ed•ly** \-ˈzər-vəd-lē\ *adv*
un•rest \ˌən-ˈrest\ *n* : a disturbed or uneasy state : TURMOIL
un•re•strained \ˌən-ri-ˈstrānd\ *adj* **1** : IMMODERATE, UNCONTROLLED **2** : SPONTANEOUS
un•re•straint \-ri-ˈstrānt\ *n* : lack of restraint
un•rid•dle \ˌən-ˈrid-ᵊl\ *vb* : to find the explanation of : SOLVE
un•righ•teous \-ˈrī-chəs\ *adj* **1** : SINFUL, WICKED **2** : UNJUST — **un•righ•teous•ness** *n*
un•ripe \-ˈrīp\ *adj* : not ripe : IMMATURE
un•ri•valed *or* **un•ri•valled** \ˌən-ˈrī-vəld\ *adj* : having no rival : SUPREME
un•robe \-ˈrōb\ *vb* : DISROBE, UNDRESS
un•roll \-ˈrōl\ *vb* **1** : to unwind a roll of : open out **2** : DISPLAY, DISCLOSE **3** : to become unrolled or spread out
un•roof \-ˈrüf, -ˈru̇f\ *vb* : to strip off the roof or covering of
un•ruf•fled \ˌən-ˈrə-fəld\ *adj* **1** : not agitated or upset **2** : not ruffled : SMOOTH ⟨~ water⟩
un•ruly \-ˈrü-lē\ *adj* [ME *unreuly,* fr. *un-* + *reuly* disciplined, fr. *reule* rule, fr. OF, fr. L *regula* straightedge, rule, fr. *regere* to direct] : not submissive to rule or restraint : TURBULENT ⟨~ passions⟩ — **un•rul•i•ness** \-ˈrü-lē-nəs\ *n*
un•sad•dle \ˌən-ˈsad-ᵊl\ *vb* **1** : to remove the saddle from a horse **2** : UNHORSE
un•sat•u•rat•ed \-ˈsa-chə-ˌrā-təd\ *adj* **1** : capable of absorbing or dissolving more of something **2** : containing double or triple bonds between carbon atoms ⟨~ fats or oils⟩ — **un•sat•u•rate** \-rət\ *n*
un•saved \ˌən-ˈsāvd\ *adj* : not saved; *esp* : not rescued from eternal punishment
un•sa•vory \-ˈsā-və-rē\ *adj* **1** : TASTELESS **2** : unpleasant to taste or smell **3** : morally offensive
un•say \-ˈsā\ *vb* **-said** \-ˈsed\; **-say•ing** : to take back (something said) : RETRACT, WITHDRAW
un•scathed \-ˈskāt͟hd\ *adj* : wholly unharmed : not injured
un•schooled \-ˈsküld\ *adj* : not schooled : UNTAUGHT, UNTRAINED
un•sci•en•tif•ic \ˌən-ˌsī-ən-ˈti-fik\ *adj* : not scientific : not in accord with the principles and methods of science

un·scram·ble \ˌən-ˈskram-bəl\ *vb* **1** : RESOLVE, CLARIFY **2** : to restore (as a radio message) to intelligible form
un·screw \-ˈskrü\ *vb* **1** : to draw the screws from **2** : to loosen by turning
un·scru·pu·lous \-ˈskrü-pyə-ləs\ *adj* : not scrupulous : UNPRINCIPLED — **un·scru·pu·lous·ly** *adv* — **un·scru·pu·lous·ness** *n*
un·seal \-ˈsēl\ *vb* : to break or remove the seal of : OPEN
un·search·able \-ˈsər-chə-bəl\ *adj* : not capable of being searched or explored
un·sea·son·able \-ˈsēz-ᵊn-ə-bəl\ *adj* : not seasonable : happening or coming at the wrong time : UNTIMELY — **un·sea·son·ably** \-blē\ *adv*
un·seat \-ˈsēt\ *vb* **1** : to throw from one's seat esp. on horseback **2** : to remove from political office
un·seem·ly \-ˈsēm-lē\ *adj* : not according with established standards of good form or taste; *also* : not suitable — **un·seem·li·ness** *n*
un·seen \ˌən-ˈsēn\ *adj* : not seen : INVISIBLE
un·seg·re·gat·ed \-ˈse-gri-ˌgā-təd\ *adj* : not segregated; *esp* : free from racial segregation
un·self·ish \-ˈsel-fish\ *adj* : not selfish : GENEROUS — **un·self·ish·ly** *adv* — **un·self·ish·ness** *n*
un·set·tle \ˌən-ˈset-ᵊl\ *vb* : to move or loosen from a settled position : DISPLACE, DISTURB
un·set·tled \-ˈset-ᵊld\ *adj* **1** : not settled : not fixed (as in position or character) **2** : not calm : DISTURBED **3** : not decided in mind : UNDETERMINED **4** : not paid ⟨~ accounts⟩ **5** : not occupied by settlers
un·shack·le \-ˈsha-kəl\ *vb* : to free from shackles
un·shaped \-ˈshāpt\ *adj* : not shaped; *esp* : not being in finished, final, or perfect form ⟨~ ideas⟩ ⟨~ timber⟩
un·sheathe \ˌən-ˈshēth\ *vb* : to draw from or as if from a sheath
un·ship \-ˈship\ *vb* **1** : to remove from a ship **2** : to remove or become removed from position ⟨~ an oar⟩
un·shod \ˌən-ˈshäd\ *adj* : not wearing or provided with shoes
un·sight·ly \ˌən-ˈsīt-lē\ *adj* : unpleasant to the sight : UGLY
un·skilled \-ˈskild\ *adj* **1** : not skilled; *esp* : not skilled in a specified branch of work **2** : not requiring skill
un·skill·ful \-ˈskil-fəl\ *adj* : lacking in skill or proficiency — **un·skill·ful·ly** *adv*
un·sling \-ˈsliŋ\ *vb* **-slung** \-ˈsləŋ\; **-sling·ing** : to remove from being slung
un·snap \-ˈsnap\ *vb* : to loosen or free by or as if by undoing a snap
un·snarl \-ˈsnärl\ *vb* : to remove snarls from : UNTANGLE
un·so·phis·ti·cat·ed \ˌən-sə-ˈfis-tə-ˌkā-təd\ *adj* **1** : not worldly-wise : lacking sophistication **2** : SIMPLE
un·sought \ˌən-ˈsȯt\ *adj* : not sought : not searched for or asked for : not obtained by effort ⟨~ honors⟩
un·sound \-ˈsau̇nd\ *adj* **1** : not healthy or whole; *also* : not mentally normal **2** : not valid **3** : not firmly made or fixed — **un·sound·ly** *adv* — **un·sound·ness** *n*
un·spar·ing \-ˈspar-iŋ\ *adj* **1** : HARD, RUTHLESS **2** : not frugal : LIBERAL, PROFUSE
un·speak·able \-ˈspē-kə-bəl\ *adj* **1** : impossible to express in words **2** : extremely bad — **un·speak·ably** \-blē\ *adv*
un·spot·ted \-ˈspä-təd\ *adj* : not spotted or stained; *esp* : free from moral stain
un·sprung \-ˈsprəŋ\ *adj* : not sprung; *esp* : not equipped with springs
un·sta·ble \-ˈstā-bəl\ *adj* **1** : not stable **2** : FICKLE, VACILLATING; *also* : lacking effective emotional control **3** : readily changing (as by decomposing) in chemical or physical composition or in biological activity ⟨an ~ atomic nucleus⟩
un·steady \ˌən-ˈste-dē\ *adj* : not steady : UNSTABLE — **un·stead·i·ly** \-ˈsted-ᵊl-ē\ *adv* — **un·stead·i·ness** \-ˈste-dē-nəs\ *n*
un·stint·ing \-ˈstin-tiŋ\ *adj* **1** : not restricting or holding back **2** : giving or being given freely or generously ⟨~ praise⟩
un·stop \-ˈstäp\ *vb* **1** : UNCLOG **2** : to remove a stopper from
un·stop·pa·ble \ˌən-ˈstä-pə-bəl\ *adj* : incapable of being stopped
un·strap \-ˈstrap\ *vb* : to remove or loose a strap from
un·stressed \ˌən-ˈstrest\ *adj* : not stressed; *esp* : not bearing a stress or accent
un·strung \-ˈstrəŋ\ *adj* **1** : having the strings loose or detached **2** : nervously tired or anxious
un·stud·ied \-ˈstə-dēd\ *adj* **1** : not acquired by study **2** : NATURAL, UNFORCED ⟨moved with ~ grace⟩
un·sub·stan·tial \ˌən-səb-ˈstan-chəl\ *adj* : INSUBSTANTIAL
un·sung \ˌən-ˈsəŋ\ *adj* **1** : not sung **2** : not celebrated in song or verse ⟨~ heroes⟩
un·swerv·ing \ˌən-ˈswər-viŋ\ *adj* **1** : not swerving or turning aside **2** : STEADY
un·tan·gle \-ˈtaŋ-gəl\ *vb* **1** : DISENTANGLE **2** : to straighten out : RESOLVE ⟨~ a problem⟩
un·taught \-ˈtȯt\ *adj* **1** : not instructed or taught : IGNORANT **2** : NATURAL, SPONTANEOUS ⟨~ kindness⟩
un·think·able \-ˈthiŋ-kə-bəl\ *adj* : not to be thought of or considered as possible ⟨~ cruelty⟩
un·think·ing \ˌən-ˈthiŋ-kiŋ\ *adj* : not thinking; *esp* : THOUGHTLESS, HEEDLESS — **un·think·ing·ly** *adv*
un·thought \ˌən-ˈthȯt\ *adj* : not anticipated : UNEXPECTED — often used with *of* ⟨*unthought*-of developments⟩
un·tie \-ˈtī\ *vb* **-tied; -ty·ing** *or* **-tie·ing 1** : to free from something that ties, fastens, or restrains : UNBIND **2** : DISENTANGLE, RESOLVE **3** : to become loosened or unbound
[1]**un·til** \ˌən-ˈtil\ *prep* : up to the time of ⟨worked ~ 5 o'clock⟩
[2]**until** *conj* **1** : up to the time that ⟨wait ~ he calls⟩ **2** : to the point or degree that ⟨ran ~ she was breathless⟩
[1]**un·time·ly** \ˌən-ˈtīm-lē\ *adv* : at an inopportune time : UNSEASONABLY; *also* : PREMATURELY
[2]**untimely** *adj* : PREMATURE ⟨~ death⟩; *also* : INOPPORTUNE, UNSEASONABLE
un·tir·ing \ˌən-ˈtī-riŋ\ *adj* : not becoming tired : INDEFATIGABLE — **un·tir·ing·ly** *adv*
un·to \ˈən-ˌtü\ *prep* : TO
un·told \ˌən-ˈtōld\ *adj* **1** : not counted : VAST, NUMBERLESS **2** : not told : not revealed
[1]**un·touch·able** \ˌən-ˈtə-chə-bəl\ *adj* : forbidden to the touch
[2]**untouchable** *n* : a member of the lowest social class in India having in traditional Hindu belief the quality of defiling by contact a member of a higher caste
un·touched \ˌən-ˈtəcht\ *adj* **1** : not subjected to touching **2** : not described or dealt with **3** : not tasted **4** : being in a primeval state or condition **5** : UNAFFECTED
un·tow·ard \ˌən-ˈtōrd, -ˈtō-ərd; ˌən-tə-ˈwȯrd\ *adj* **1** : difficult to manage : STUBBORN, WILLFUL ⟨an ~ child⟩ **2** : INCONVENIENT, TROUBLESOME ⟨an ~ encounter⟩
un·tried \ˌən-ˈtrīd\ *adj* : not tested or proved by experience or trial; *also* : not tried in court
un·true \-ˈtrü\ *adj* **1** : not faithful : DISLOYAL **2** : not according with a standard of correctness **3** : FALSE
un·truth \ˌən-ˈtrüth, ˈən-ˌtrüth\ *n* **1** : lack of truthfulness **2** : FALSEHOOD
un·tune \-ˈtün, -ˈtyün\ *vb* **1** : to put out of tune **2** : DISARRANGE, DISCOMPOSE
un·tu·tored \-ˈtü-tərd, -ˈtyü-\ *adj* : UNTAUGHT, UNLEARNED, IGNORANT
un·twine \-ˈtwīn\ *vb* : UNWIND, DISENTANGLE
un·twist \ˌən-ˈtwist\ *vb* **1** : to separate the twisted parts of : UNTWINE **2** : to become untwined
un·used \-ˈyüst, -ˈyüzd *for 1;* -ˈyüzd *for 2*\ *adj* **1** : UNACCUSTOMED **2** : not used

un•usu•al \-ˈyü-zhə-wəl\ *adj* : not usual : UNCOMMON, RARE — **un•usu•al•ly** *adv*
un•ut•ter•able \ˌən-ˈə-tə-rə-bəl\ *adj* : being beyond the powers of description : INEXPRESSIBLE — **un•ut•ter•ably** \-blē\ *adv*
un•var•nished \-ˈvär-nisht\ *adj* **1** : not varnished **2** : not embellished : PLAIN ⟨the ~ truth⟩
un•veil \ˌən-ˈvāl\ *vb* **1** : to remove a veil or covering from : DISCLOSE **2** : to remove a veil : reveal oneself
un•voiced \-ˈvȯist\ *adj* **1** : not verbally expressed : UNSPOKEN **2** : VOICELESS 2
un•war•rant•able \-ˈwȯr-ən-tə-bəl\ *adj* : not justifiable : INEXCUSABLE — **un•war•rant•ably** \-blē\ *adv*
un•weave \-ˈwēv\ *vb* **-wove** \-ˈwōv\; **-wo•ven** \-ˈwō-vən\; **-weav•ing** : DISENTANGLE, RAVEL
un•well \ˌən-ˈwəl\ *adj* : SICK, AILING
un•whole•some \-ˈhōl-səm\ *adj* **1** : harmful to physical, mental, or moral well-being **2** : CORRUPT, UNSOUND; *also* : offensive to the senses : LOATHSOME
un•wieldy \-ˈwēl-dē\ *adj* : not easily managed, handled, or used (as because of bulk, weight, or complexity) : AWKWARD ⟨an ~ tool⟩
un•wind \-ˈwīnd\ *vb* **-wound** \-ˈwau̇nd\; **-wind•ing** **1** : to undo something that is wound : loose from coils **2** : to become unwound : be capable of being unwound **3** : RELAX
un•wise \ˌən-ˈwīz\ *adj* : not wise : FOOLISH — **un•wise•ly** *adv*
un•wit•ting \-ˈwi-tiŋ\ *adj* **1** : not knowing : UNAWARE **2** : not intended : INADVERTENT ⟨~ mistake⟩ — **un•wit•ting•ly** *adv*
un•wont•ed \-ˈwȯn-təd, -ˈwōn-\ *adj* **1** : RARE, UNUSUAL **2** : not accustomed by experience — **un•wont•ed•ly** *adv*
un•world•ly \-ˈwərld-lē\ *adj* **1** : not of this world; *esp* : SPIRITUAL **2** : NAIVE **3** : not swayed by worldly considerations — **un•world•li•ness** \-lē-nəs\ *n*
un•wor•thy \ˌən-ˈwər-t͟hē\ *adj* **1** : BASE, DISHONORABLE **2** : not meritorious : not worthy : UNDESERVING **3** : not deserved : UNMERITED ⟨~ treatment⟩ — **un•wor•thi•ly** \-t͟hə-lē\ *adv* — **un•wor•thi•ness** \-t͟hē-nəs\ *n*
un•wrap \-ˈrap\ *vb* : to remove the wrapping from : DISCLOSE
un•writ•ten \-ˈrit-ᵊn\ *adj* **1** : not in writing : ORAL, TRADITIONAL ⟨an ~ law⟩ **2** : containing no writing : BLANK
un•yield•ing \ˌən-ˈyēl-diŋ\ *adj* **1** : characterized by lack of softness or flexibility **2** : characterized by firmness or obduracy
un•yoke \-ˈyōk\ *vb* : to remove a yoke from; *also* : SEPARATE, DISCONNECT
un•zip \-ˈzip\ *vb* : to zip open : open by means of a zipper
[1]**up** \ˈəp\ *adv* **1** : in or to a higher position or level; *esp* : away from the center of the earth **2** : from beneath a surface (as ground or water) **3** : from below the horizon **4** : in or into an upright position; *esp* : out of bed **5** : with greater intensity ⟨speak ~⟩ **6** : in or into a better or more advanced state or a state of greater intensity or activity ⟨stir ~ a fire⟩ **7** : into existence, evidence, or knowledge ⟨the missing book turned ~⟩ **8** : into consideration ⟨brought the matter ~⟩ **9** : to or at bat **10** : into possession or custody ⟨gave himself ~⟩ **11** : ENTIRELY, COMPLETELY ⟨eat it ~⟩ **12** — used for emphasis ⟨clean ~ a room⟩ **13** : ASIDE, BY ⟨lay ~ supplies⟩ **14** : so as to arrive or approach ⟨ran ~ the path⟩ **15** : in a direction opposite to down **16** : in or into parts ⟨tear ~ paper⟩ **17** : to a stop ⟨pull ~ at the curb⟩ **18** : for each side ⟨the score was 15 ~⟩
[2]**up** *adj* **1** : risen above the horizon ⟨the sun is ~⟩ **2** : being out of bed ⟨~ by 6 o'clock⟩ **3** : relatively high ⟨prices are ~⟩ **4** : RAISED, LIFTED ⟨windows are ~⟩ **5** : BUILT, CONSTRUCTED ⟨the house is ~⟩ **6** : grown above a surface ⟨the corn is ~⟩ **7** : moving, inclining, or directed upward **8** : marked by agitation, excitement, or activity **9** : READY; *esp* : highly prepared **10** : going on : taking place ⟨find out what is ~⟩ **11** : EXPIRED, ENDED ⟨the time is ~⟩ **12** : well informed ⟨~ on the news⟩ **13** : being ahead or in advance of an opponent ⟨one hole ~ in a match⟩ **14** : presented for or being under consideration **15** : charged before a court ⟨~ for robbery⟩
[3]**up** *prep* **1** : to, toward, or at a higher point of ⟨~ a ladder⟩ **2** : to or toward the source of ⟨~ the river⟩ **3** : to or toward the northern part of ⟨~ the coast⟩ **4** : to or toward the interior of ⟨traveling ~ the country⟩ **5** : ALONG ⟨walk ~ the street⟩
[4]**up** *n* **1** : an upward course or slope **2** : a period or state of prosperity or success ⟨he had his ~*s* and downs⟩
[5]**up** *vb* **upped** \ˈəpt\ *or in 2* **up; upped; up•ping; ups** *or in 2* **up** **1** : to rise from a lying or sitting position **2** : to act abruptly or surprisingly ⟨she *upped* and left home⟩ **3** : to move or cause to move upward ⟨*upped* the prices⟩
Upa•ni•shad \ü-ˈpän-i-ˌshäd\ *n* : one of a set of Vedic philosophical treatises
[1]**up•beat** \ˈəp-ˌbēt\ *n* : an unaccented beat in a musical measure; *esp* : the last beat of the measure
[2]**upbeat** *adj* : OPTIMISTIC, CHEERFUL
up•braid \ˌəp-ˈbrād\ *vb* : to criticize, reproach, or scold severely
up•bring•ing \ˈəp-ˌbriŋ-iŋ\ *n* : the process of bringing up and training
UPC *abbr* Universal Product Code
up•chuck \ˈəp-ˌchək\ *vb* : VOMIT
up•com•ing \ˈəp-ˌkə-miŋ\ *adj* : FORTHCOMING, APPROACHING
up–coun•try \ˈəp-ˌkən-trē\ *adj* : of or relating to the interior of a country or a region — **up–country** \ˈəp-ˈkən-\ *adv*
up•date \ˌəp-ˈdāt\ *vb* : to bring up to date — **update** \ˈəp-ˌdāt\ *n*
up•draft \ˈəp-ˌdraft, -ˌdräft\ *n* : an upward movement of gas (as air)
up•end \ˌəp-ˈend\ *vb* : to set, stand, or rise on end; *also* : OVERTURN
up–front \ˈəp-ˌfrənt, ˌəp-ˈfrənt\ *adj* **1** : HONEST, CANDID **2** : ADVANCE ⟨~ payment⟩
up front *adv* : in advance ⟨paid *up front*⟩
[1]**up•grade** \ˈəp-ˌgrād\ *n* **1** : an upward grade or slope **2** : INCREASE, RISE
[2]**up•grade** \ˈəp-ˌgrād, ˌəp-ˈgrād\ *vb* : to raise to a higher grade or position; *esp* : to advance to a job requiring a higher level of skill
up•growth \ˈəp-ˌgrōth\ *n* : the process of growing upward : DEVELOPMENT; *also* : a product or result of this
up•heav•al \ˌəp-ˈhē-vəl\ *n* **1** : the action or an instance of uplifting esp. of part of the earth's crust **2** : a violent agitation or change
[1]**up•hill** \ˈəp-ˈhil\ *adv* : upward on a hill or incline; *also* : against difficulties
[2]**up•hill** \-ˌhil\ *adj* **1** : situated on elevated ground **2** : ASCENDING **3** : DIFFICULT, LABORIOUS
up•hold \ˌəp-ˈhōld\ *vb* **-held** \-ˈheld\; **-hold•ing** **1** : to give support to **2** : to support against an opponent **3** : to keep elevated — **up•hold•er** *n*
up•hol•ster \ˌəp-ˈhōl-stər\ *vb* : to furnish with or as if with upholstery — **up•hol•ster•er** *n*
up•hol•stery \-stə-rē\ *n, pl* **-ster•ies** [ME *upholdester* upholsterer, fr. *upholden* to uphold, fr. *up* + *holden* to hold] : materials (as fabrics, padding, and springs) used to make a soft covering esp. for a seat
UPI *abbr* United Press International
up•keep \ˈəp-ˌkēp\ *n* : the act or cost of keeping up or maintaining; *also* : the state of being maintained
up•land \ˈəp-lənd, -ˌland\ *n* : high land esp. at some distance from the sea — **upland** *adj*
[1]**up•lift** \ˌəp-ˈlift\ *vb* **1** : to lift or raise up : ELEVATE **2** : to improve the condition of esp. morally, socially, or intellectually
[2]**up•lift** \ˈəp-ˌlift\ *n* **1** : a lifting up; *esp* : an upheaval of

the earth's surface **2** : moral or social improvement; *also* : a movement to make such improvement
up•mar•ket \ˌəp-ˈmär-kət\ *adj* : appealing to wealthy consumers
up•most \ˈəp-ˌmōst\ *adj* : UPPERMOST
up•on \ə-ˈpȯn, -ˈpän\ *prep* : ON
¹up•per \ˈə-pər\ *adj* **1** : higher in physical position, rank, or order **2** : constituting the smaller and more restricted branch of a bicameral legislature **3** *cap* : being a later part or formation of a specific geological period **4** : being toward the interior ⟨the ~ Amazon⟩ **5** : NORTHERN ⟨~ New York State⟩
²upper *n* : one that is upper; *esp* : the parts of a shoe or boot above the sole
up•per•case \ˌə-pər-ˈkās\ *adj* : CAPITAL 1 — **uppercase** *n*
upper class *n* : a social class occupying a position above the middle class and having the highest status in a society — **upper–class** *adj*
up•per•class•man \ˌə-pər-ˈklas-mən\ *n* : a junior or senior in a college or high school
upper crust *n* : the highest social class or group; *esp* : the highest circle of the upper class
up•per•cut \ˈə-pər-ˌkət\ *n* : a short swinging punch delivered (as in boxing) in an upward direction usu. with a bent arm
upper hand *n* : MASTERY, ADVANTAGE
up•per•most \ˈə-pər-ˌmōst\ *adv* : in or into the highest or most prominent position — **uppermost** *adj*
up•pish \ˈə-pish\ *adj* : UPPITY
up•pi•ty \ˈə-pə-tē\ *adj* : ARROGANT, PRESUMPTUOUS
up•raise \ˌəp-ˈrāz\ *vb* : to lift up : ELEVATE
¹up•right \ˈəp-ˌrīt\ *adj* **1** : PERPENDICULAR, VERTICAL **2** : erect in carriage or posture **3** : morally correct : JUST — **upright** *adv* — **up•right•ly** *adv* — **up•right•ness** *n*
²upright *n* **1** : the state of being upright : a vertical position **2** : something that stands upright
upright piano *n* : a piano whose strings run vertically
up•ris•ing \ˈəp-ˌrī-ziŋ\ *n* : INSURRECTION, REVOLT, REBELLION
up•riv•er \ˈəp-ˈri-vər\ *adv or adj* : toward or at a point nearer the source of a river
up•roar \ˈəp-ˌrōr\ *n* [D *oproer,* fr. MD, fr. *op* up + *roer* motion] : a state of commotion, excitement, or violent disturbance
up•roar•i•ous \ˌəp-ˈrōr-ē-əs\ *adj* **1** : marked by uproar **2** : extremely funny — **up•roar•i•ous•ly** *adv*
up•root \ˌəp-ˈrüt, -ˈru̇t\ *vb* : to remove by or as if by pulling up by the roots
¹up•set \ˌəp-ˈset\ *vb* **-set; -set•ting 1** : to force or be forced out of the usual upright, level, or proper position **2** : to disturb emotionally : WORRY; *also* : to make somewhat ill **3** : UNSETTLE, DISARRANGE **4** : to defeat unexpectedly
²up•set \ˈəp-ˌset\ *n* **1** : an upsetting or being upset; *esp* : a minor illness **2** : a derangement of plans or ideas **3** : an unexpected defeat
³up•set \(ˌ)əp-ˈset\ *adj* : emotionally disturbed or agitated
up•shot \ˈəp-ˌshät\ *n* : the final result
¹up•side \ˈəp-ˌsīd\ *n* : the upper side
²up•side \ˌəp-ˈsīd\ *prep* : up on or against the side of ⟨knocked him ~ the head⟩
up•side down \ˌəp-ˌsīd-ˈdau̇n\ *adv* **1** : with the upper and the lower parts reversed in position **2** : in or into confusion or disorder — **upside–down** *adj*
up•si•lon \ˈüp-sə-ˌlän, ˈyüp-, ˈəp-\ *n* : the 20th letter of the Greek alphabet — Υ or υ
¹up•stage \ˈəp-ˈstāj\ *adv or adj* : toward or at the rear of a theatrical stage
²up•stage \ˌəp-ˈstāj\ *vb* : to draw attention away from (as an actor)
¹up•stairs \ˌəp-ˈstarz\ *adv* **1** : up the stairs : to or on a higher floor **2** : to or at a higher position
²up•stairs \ˈəp-ˈstarz\ *adj* : situated above the stairs esp. on an upper floor ⟨~ bedroom⟩
³up•stairs \ˈəp-ˈstarz, ˈəp-ˌstarz\ *n sing or pl* : the part of a building above the ground floor
up•stand•ing \ˌəp-ˈstan-diŋ, ˈəp-\ *adj* **1** : ERECT **2** : STRAIGHTFORWARD, HONEST
¹up•start \ˌəp-ˈstärt\ *vb* : to jump up suddenly
²up•start \ˈəp-ˌstärt\ *n* : one that has risen suddenly; *esp* : one that claims more personal importance than is warranted — **upstart** \-ˈstärt\ *adj*
up•state \ˈəp-ˈstāt\ *adj* : of, relating to, or characteristic of a part of a state away from a large city and esp. to the north — **upstate** *adv* — **upstate** *n*
up•stream \ˈəp-ˈstrēm\ *adv* : at or toward the source of a stream — **upstream** *adj*
up•stroke \ˈəp-ˌstrōk\ *n* : an upward stroke (as of a pen)
up•surge \-ˌsərj\ *n* : a rapid or sudden rise
up•swept \ˈəp-ˌswept\ *adj* : swept upward ⟨~ hairdo⟩
up•swing \ˈəp-ˌswiŋ\ *n* : an upward swing; *esp* : a marked increase or rise (as in activity)
up•take \ˈəp-ˌtāk\ *n* **1** : UNDERSTANDING, COMPREHENSION ⟨quick on the ~⟩ **2** : the process or an instance of absorbing and incorporating esp. into a living organism
up•thrust \ˈəp-ˌthrəst\ *n* : an upward thrust (as of the earth's crust) — **upthrust** *vb*
up•tight \ˈəp-ˈtīt\ *adj* **1** : TENSE, NERVOUS, UNEASY; *also* : ANGRY, INDIGNANT **2** : rigidly conventional
up–to–date *adj* **1** : extending up to the present time **2** : abreast of the times : MODERN — **up–to–date•ness** *n*
up•town \ˈəp-ˌtau̇n\ *n* : the upper part of a town or city; *esp* : the residential district — **up•town** \ˈəp-ˈtau̇n\ *adj or adv*
¹up•turn \ˈəp-ˌtərn, ˌəp-ˈtərn\ *vb* **1** : to turn (as earth) up or over **2** : to turn or direct upward
²up•turn \ˈəp-ˌtərn\ *n* : an upward turn esp. toward better conditions or higher prices
¹up•ward \ˈəp-wərd\ *or* **up•wards** \-wərdz\ *adv* **1** : in a direction from lower to higher **2** : toward a higher or better condition **3** : toward a greater amount or higher number, degree, or rate
²upward *adj* : directed or moving toward or situated in a higher place or level : ASCENDING — **up•ward•ly** *adv*
upwards of *also* **upward of** *adv* : more than : in excess of ⟨they cost *upwards of* $25 each⟩
up•well \ˌəp-ˈwel\ *vb* : to move or flow upward
up•well•ing \-ˈwe-liŋ\ *n* : a rising or an appearance of rising to the surface and flowing outward; *esp* : the movement of deep cold usu. nutrient-rich ocean water to the surface
up•wind \ˈəp-ˈwind\ *adv or adj* : in the direction from which the wind is blowing
ura•cil \ˈyu̇r-ə-ˌsil\ *n* : a pyrimidine base that is one of the four bases coding genetic information in the molecular chain of RNA
ura•ni•um \yu̇-ˈrā-nē-əm\ *n* : a silvery heavy radioactive metallic chemical element used as a source of atomic energy — see ELEMENT table
Ura•nus \ˈyu̇r-ə-nəs, yu̇-ˈrā-\ *n* [LL, the sky personified as a god, fr. Gk *Ouranos,* fr. *ouranos* sky, heaven] : the planet 7th in order from the sun — see PLANET table
ur•ban \ˈər-bən\ *adj* : of, relating to, characteristic of, or constituting a city
ur•bane \ˌər-ˈbān\ *adj* [L *urbanus* urban, urbane, fr. *urbs* city] : very polite and polished in manner : SUAVE
ur•ban•ise *Brit var of* URBANIZE
ur•ban•ite \ˈər-bə-ˌnīt\ *n* : a person who lives in a city
ur•ban•i•ty \ˌər-ˈba-nə-tē\ *n, pl* **-ties** : the quality or state of being urbane
ur•ban•ize \ˈər-bə-ˌnīz\ *vb* **-ized; -iz•ing** : to cause to

take on urban characteristics — **ur•ban•i•za•tion** \ˌər-bə-nə-ˈzā-shən\ *n*

ur•chin \ˈər-chən\ *n* [ME, hedgehog, fr. MF *herichon,* ultim. fr. L *ericius*] : a pert or mischievous youngster

Ur•du \ˈu̇r-dü, ˈər-\ *n* [Hindi *urdū,* fr. Per *zabān-e-urdū-e-muallā* language of the Exalted Comp (the imperial bazaar in Delhi)] : an official language of Pakistan that is widely used by Muslims in urban areas of India

urea \yu̇-ˈrē-ə\ *n* : a soluble nitrogenous compound that is the chief solid constituent of mammalian urine

ure•mia \yu̇-ˈrē-mē-ə\ *n* : accumulation in the blood of materials normally passed off in the urine resulting in a poisoned condition — **ure•mic** \-mik\ *adj*

ure•ter \ˈyu̇r-ə-tər\ *n* : a duct that carries the urine from a kidney to the bladder

ure•thra \yu̇-ˈrē-thrə\ *n, pl* **-thras** *or* **-thrae** \-(ˌ)thrē\ : the canal that in most mammals carries off the urine from the bladder and in the male also serves to carry semen from the body — **ure•thral** \-thrəl\ *adj*

ure•thri•tis \ˌyu̇r-i-ˈthrī-təs\ *n* : inflammation of the urethra

[1]urge \ˈərj\ *vb* **urged; urg•ing 1** : to present, advocate, or demand earnestly **2** : to try to persuade or sway ⟨~ a guest to stay⟩ **3** : to serve as a motive or reason for **4** : to impress or impel to some course or activity ⟨the dog *urged* the sheep onward⟩

[2]urge *n* **1** : the act or process of urging **2** : a force or impulse that urges or drives

ur•gent \ˈər-jənt\ *adj* **1** : calling for immediate attention : PRESSING **2** : urging insistently — **ur•gen•cy** \-jən-sē\ *n* — **ur•gent•ly** *adv*

uric \ˈyu̇r-ik\ *adj* : of, relating to, or found in urine

uric acid *n* : a nearly insoluble acid that is the chief nitrogenous excretory product of birds but is present in only small amounts in mammalian urine

uri•nal \ˈyu̇r-ən-ᵊl\ *n* **1** : a receptacle for urine **2** : a place for urinating

uri•nal•y•sis \ˌyu̇r-ə-ˈna-lə-səs\ *n* : chemical analysis of urine

uri•nary \ˈyu̇r-ə-ˌner-ē\ *adj* **1** : relating to, occurring in, or being organs for the formation and discharge of urine **2** : of, relating to, or for urine

urinary bladder *n* : a membranous sac in many vertebrates that serves for the temporary retention of urine and discharges by the urethra

uri•nate \ˈyu̇r-ə-ˌnāt\ *vb* **-nat•ed; -nat•ing** : to release or give off urine — **uri•na•tion** \ˌyu̇r-ə-ˈnā-shən\ *n*

urine \ˈyu̇r-ən\ *n* : a waste material from the kidneys that is usu. a yellowish watery liquid in mammals but is semisolid in birds and reptiles

urn \ˈərn\ *n* **1** : a vessel that typically has the form of a vase on a pedestal and often is used to hold the ashes of the dead **2** : a closed vessel usu. with a spout for serving a hot beverage

uro•gen•i•tal \ˌyu̇r-ō-ˈje-nət-ᵊl\ *adj* : of, relating to, or being the excretory and reproductive organs or functions

urol•o•gy \yu̇-ˈrä-lə-jē\ *n* : a branch of medical science dealing with the urinary or urogenital tract and its disorders — **uro•log•ic** \ˌyu̇r-ə-ˈlä-jik\ *or* **uro•log•i•cal** \-ji-kəl\ *adj* — **urol•o•gist** \yu̇-ˈrä-lə-jist\ *n*

Ur•sa Ma•jor \ˌər-sə-ˈmā-jər\ *n* [L, lit., greater bear] : the northern constellation that contains the stars which form the Big Dipper

Ursa Mi•nor \-ˈmī-nər\ *n* [L, lit., lesser bear] : the constellation including the north pole of the heavens and the stars that form the Little Dipper with the North Star at the tip of the handle

ur•sine \ˈər-ˌsīn\ *adj* : of, relating to, or resembling a bear

ur•ti•car•ia \ˌər-tə-ˈkar-ē-ə\ *n* [NL, fr. L *urtica* nettle] : HIVES

Uru•guay•an \ˌu̇r-ə-ˈgwī-ən, ˌyu̇r-ə-ˈgwā-\ *n* : a native or inhabitant of Uruguay — **Uruguayan** *adj*

us \ˈəs\ *pron, objective case of* WE

US *abbr* United States

USA *abbr* **1** United States Army **2** United States of America

us•able *also* **use•able** \ˈyü-zə-bəl\ *adj* : suitable or fit for use — **us•abil•i•ty** \ˌyü-zə-ˈbi-lə-tē\ *n*

USAF *abbr* United States Air Force

us•age \ˈyü-sij, -zij\ *n* **1** : habitual or customary practice or procedure **2** : the way in which words and phrases are actually used **3** : the action or mode of using **4** : manner of treating

USCG *abbr* United States Coast Guard

USDA *abbr* United States Department of Agriculture

[1]use \ˈyüs\ *n* **1** : the act or practice of using or employing something : EMPLOYMENT, APPLICATION **2** : the fact or state of being used **3** : the way of using **4** : USAGE, CUSTOM **5** : the privilege or benefit of using something **6** : the ability or power to use something (as a limb) **7** : the legal enjoyment of property that consists in its employment, occupation, or exercise; *also* : the benefit or profit esp. from property held in trust **8** : USEFULNESS, UTILITY; *also* : the end served : OBJECT, FUNCTION **9** : the occasion or need to employ ⟨he had no more ~ for it⟩ **10** : ESTEEM, LIKING ⟨had no ~ for modern art⟩

[2]use \ˈyüz\ *vb* **used** \ˈyüzd; "*used to*" *usu* ˈyüs-tə\; **us•ing 1** : to put into action or service : EMPLOY **2** : to consume or take (as drugs) regularly **3** : UTILIZE ⟨~ tact⟩; *also* : MANIPULATE ⟨*used* his friends to get ahead⟩ **4** : to expend or consume by putting to use **5** : to behave toward : TREAT ⟨*used* the horse cruelly⟩ **6** : to benefit from ⟨house could ~ a coat of paint⟩ **7** — used in the past with *to* to indicate a former practice, fact, or state ⟨we *used* to work harder⟩ — **us•er** *n*

used \ˈyüzd\ *adj* **1** : having been used by another : SECONDHAND ⟨~ cars⟩ **2** : ACCUSTOMED, HABITUATED ⟨~ to the heat⟩

use•ful \ˈyüs-fəl\ *adj* : capable of being put to use : ADVANTAGEOUS; *esp* : serviceable for a beneficial end — **use•ful•ly** *adv* — **use•ful•ness** *n*

use•less \-ləs\ *adj* : having or being of no use : WORTHLESS — **use•less•ly** *adv* — **use•less•ness** *n*

USES *abbr* United States Employment Service

use up *vb* : to consume completely

[1]ush•er \ˈə-shər\ *n* [ME *ussher,* fr. MF *ussier,* fr. (assumed) VL *ustiarius* doorkeeper, fr. L *ostium, ustium* door, mouth of a river] **1** : an officer who walks before a person of rank **2** : one who escorts people to their seats (as in a church or theater)

[2]usher *vb* **1** : to conduct to a place **2** : to precede as an usher, forerunner, or harbinger **3** : INAUGURATE, INTRODUCE ⟨~ in a new era⟩

ush•er•ette \ˌə-shə-ˈret\ *n* : a girl or woman who is an usher (as in a theater)

USIA *abbr* United States Information Agency

USMC *abbr* United States Marine Corps

USN *abbr* United States Navy

USO *abbr* United Service Organizations

USP *abbr* United States Pharmacopeia

USPS *abbr* United States Postal Service

USS *abbr* United States ship

USSR *abbr* Union of Soviet Socialist Republics

usu *abbr* usual; usually

usu•al \ˈyü-zhə-wəl\ *adj* **1** : accordant with usage, custom, or habit : NORMAL **2** : commonly or ordinarily used **3** : ORDINARY **syn** customary, habitual, accustomed, routine — **usu•al•ly** \ˈyü-zhə-wə-lē, ˈyü-zhə-lē\ *adv*

usu•fruct \ˈyü-zə-ˌfrəkt\ *n* [L *ususfructus,* fr. *usus et fructus* use and enjoyment] : the legal right to use and enjoy the benefits and profits of something belonging to another

usu•rer \ˈyü-zhər-ər\ *n* : one that lends money esp. at an exorbitant rate

usu•ri•ous \yü-ˈzhu̇r-ē-əs\ *adj* : practicing, involving, or constituting usury ⟨a ~ rate of interest⟩

usurp \yu̇-ˈsərp, -ˈzərp\ *vb* [ME, fr. MF *usurper,* fr. L *usurpare,* lit., to take possession of without legal claim, fr. *usu* (abl. of *usus* use) + *rapere* to seize] **:** to seize and hold by force or without right ⟨~ a throne⟩ **— usur·pa·tion** \ˌyü-sər-ˈpā-shən, -zər-\ *n* **— usurp·er** \yu̇-ˈsər-pər, -ˈzər-\ *n*

usu·ry \ˈyü-zhə-rē\ *n, pl* **-ries 1 :** the lending of money with an interest charge for its use **2 :** an excessive rate or amount of interest charged; *esp* **:** interest above an established legal rate

UT *abbr* Utah

Ute \ˈyüt\ *n, pl* **Ute** *or* **Utes :** a member of an American Indian people orig. ranging through Utah, Colorado, Arizona, and New Mexico

uten·sil \yu̇-ˈten-səl\ *n* [ME, vessels for domestic use, fr. MF *utensile,* fr. L *utensilia,* fr. neut. pl. of *utensilis* useful, fr. *uti* to use] **1 :** an instrument or vessel used in a household and esp. a kitchen **2 :** a useful tool

uter·ine tube \ˈyü-tə-ˌrīn-, -rən-\ *n* **:** FALLOPIAN TUBE

uter·us \ˈyü-tə-rəs\ *n, pl* **uteri** \ˈyü-tə-ˌrī\ *also* **uter·us·es :** the muscular organ of a female mammal in which the young develop before birth **— uter·ine** \-ˌrīn, -rən\ *adj*

utile \ˈyüt-ᵊl, ˈyü-ˌtīl\ *adj* **:** USEFUL

uti·lise *Brit var of* UTILIZE

[1]util·i·tar·i·an \yu̇-ˌti-lə-ˈter-ē-ən\ *n* **:** a person who believes in utilitarianism

[2]utilitarian *adj* **1 :** of or relating to utilitarianism **2 :** of or relating to utility **:** aiming at usefulness rather than beauty; *also* **:** serving a useful purpose

util·i·tar·i·an·ism \-ē-ə-ˌni-zəm\ *n* **:** a theory that the greatest good for the greatest number should be the main consideration in making a choice of actions

[1]util·i·ty \yü-ˈti-lə-tē\ *n, pl* **-ties 1 :** USEFULNESS **2 :** something useful or designed for use **3 :** a business organization performing a public service and subject to special governmental regulation **4 :** a public service or a commodity (as electricity or water) provided by a public utility; *also* **:** equipment to provide such or a similar service

[2]utility *adj* **1 :** capable of serving esp. as a substitute in various uses or positions ⟨a ~ outfielder⟩ ⟨a ~ knife⟩ **2 :** being of a usable but poor quality ⟨~ beef⟩

uti·lize \ˈyüt-ᵊl-ˌīz\ *vb* **-lized; -liz·ing :** to make use of **:** turn to profitable account or use **— uti·li·za·tion** \ˌyüt-ᵊl-ə-ˈzā-shən\ *n*

ut·most \ˈət-ˌmōst\ *adj* **1 :** situated at the farthest or most distant point **:** EXTREME **2 :** of the greatest or highest degree, quantity, number, or amount **— utmost** *n*

uto·pia \yu̇-ˈtō-pē-ə\ *n* [*Utopia,* imaginary island described in Sir Thomas More's *Utopia,* fr. Gk *ou* not, no + *topos* place] **1** *often cap* **:** a place of ideal perfection esp. in laws, government, and social conditions **2 :** an impractical scheme for social improvement

[1]uto·pi·an \-pē-ən\ *adj, often cap* **1 :** of, relating to, or resembling a utopia **2 :** proposing ideal social and political schemes that are impractical **3 :** VISIONARY

[2]utopian *n* **1 :** a believer in the perfectibility of human society **2 :** one that proposes or advocates utopian schemes

[1]ut·ter \ˈə-tər\ *adj* [ME, remote, fr. OE *ūtera* outer, compar. adj. fr. *ūt* out, adv.] **:** ABSOLUTE, TOTAL ⟨~ ruin⟩ **— ut·ter·ly** *adv*

[2]utter *vb* [ME *uttren,* fr. *utter* outside, adv., fr. OE *ūtor,* compar. of *ūt* out] **1 :** to send forth as a sound **:** express in usu. spoken words **:** PRONOUNCE, SPEAK **2 :** to put (as currency) into circulation **— ut·ter·er** *n*

ut·ter·ance \ˈə-tə-rəns\ *n* **1 :** something uttered; *esp* **:** an oral or written statement **2 :** the action of uttering with the voice **:** SPEECH **3 :** power, style, or manner of speaking

ut·ter·most \ˈə-tər-ˌmōst\ *adj* **:** EXTREME, UTMOST ⟨the ~ parts of the earth⟩ **— uttermost** *n*

U–turn \ˈyü-ˌtərn\ *n* **:** a turn resembling the letter U; *esp* **:** a 180-degree turn made by a vehicle in a road

UV *abbr* ultraviolet

uvu·la \ˈyü-vyə-lə\ *n, pl* **-las** *or* **-lae** \-ˌlē, -ˌlī\ **:** the fleshy lobe hanging at the back of the roof of the mouth **— uvu·lar** \-lər\ *adj*

UW *abbr* underwriter

ux·o·ri·ous \ˌək-ˈsōr-ē-əs, ˌəg-ˈzōr-\ *adj* **:** excessively devoted or submissive to a wife

V

[1]v \ˈvē\ *n, pl* **v's** *or* **vs** \ˈvēz\ *often cap* **:** the 22d letter of the English alphabet

[2]v *abbr, often cap* **1** vector **2** velocity **3** verb **4** verse **5** versus **6** very **7** victory **8** vide **9** voice **10** voltage **11** volume **12** vowel

V *symbol* **1** vanadium **2** volt

Va *abbr* Virginia

VA *abbr* **1** Veterans Administration **2** vice admiral **3** Virginia

va·can·cy \ˈvā-kən-sē\ *n, pl* **-cies 1 :** a vacating esp. of an office, position, or piece of property **2 :** a vacant office, position, or tenancy; *also* **:** the period during which it stands vacant **3 :** empty space **:** VOID **4 :** the state of being vacant

va·cant \ˈvā-kənt\ *adj* **1 :** not occupied ⟨~ seat⟩ ⟨~ room⟩ **2 :** EMPTY ⟨~ space⟩ **3 :** free from business or care ⟨a few ~ hours⟩ **4 :** devoid of thought, reflection, or expression ⟨a ~ smile⟩ **— va·cant·ly** *adv*

va·cate \ˈvā-ˌkāt\ *vb* **va·cat·ed; va·cat·ing 1 :** to make void **:** ANNUL **2 :** to make vacant (as an office or house); *also* **:** to give up the occupancy of

[1]va·ca·tion \vā-ˈkā-shən, və-\ *n* **:** a period of rest from work **:** HOLIDAY

[2]vacation *vb* **:** to take or spend a vacation **— va·ca·tion·er** *n*

va·ca·tion·ist \-shə-nist\ *n* **:** a person taking a vacation

va·ca·tion·land \-shən-ˌland\ *n* **:** an area with recreational attractions and facilities for vacationists

vac·ci·nate \ˈvak-sə-ˌnāt\ *vb* **-nat·ed; -nat·ing :** to administer a vaccine to usu. by injection; *also* **:** to produce immunity to smallpox by inoculating (a person) with the related cowpox virus

vac·ci·na·tion \ˌvak-sə-ˈnā-shən\ *n* **1 :** the act of vaccinating **2 :** the scar left by vaccinating

vac·cine \vak-ˈsēn, ˈvak-ˌsēn\ *n* [L *vaccinus* of or from cows, fr. *vacca* cow; so called from the derivation of smallpox vaccine from cows] **:** material (as a preparation of killed or weakened virus or bacteria) used in vaccinating to induce immunity to a disease

vac·cin·ia \vak-ˈsi-nē-ə\ *n* **:** COWPOX

vac·il·late \ˈva-sə-ˌlāt\ *vb* **-lat·ed; -lat·ing 1 :** SWAY, TOTTER; *also* **:** FLUCTUATE **2 :** to incline first to one course or opinion and then to another **:** WAVER **— vac·il·la·tion** \ˌva-sə-ˈlā-shən\ *n*

va·cu·ity \va-ˈkyü-ə-tē\ *n, pl* **-ities 1 :** an empty space **2 :** the state, fact, or quality of being vacuous **3 :** something that is vacuous

vac·u·ole \ˈva-kyə-ˌwōl\ *n* **:** a usu. fluid-filled cavity esp. in the cytoplasm of an individual cell **— vac·u·o·lar** \ˌva-kyə-ˈwō-lər, -ˌlär\ *adj*

vac·u·ous \ˈva-kyə-wəs\ *adj* **1 :** EMPTY, VACANT, BLANK **2 :** DULL, STUPID, INANE **— vac·u·ous·ly** *adv* **— vac·u·ous·ness** *n*

[1]vac·u·um \ˈva-(ˌ)kyüm, -kyəm\ *n, pl* **vacuums** *or* **vac·ua** \-kyə-wə\ [L, fr. neut. of *vacuus* empty] **1 :** a space entirely empty of matter **2 :** a space from which most of the air has been removed (as by a pump) **3** : VOID, GAP **4** : VACUUM CLEANER — **vacuum** *adj*

²vacuum *vb* : to use a vacuum device (as a vacuum cleaner) on

vacuum bottle *n* : THERMOS

vacuum cleaner *n* : a household appliance for cleaning (as floors or rugs) by suction

vacuum–packed *adj* : having much of the air removed before being hermetically sealed

vacuum tube *n* : an electron tube from which most of the air has been removed

va•de me•cum \ˌvā-dē-ˈmē-kəm, ˌvä-dē-ˈmā-\ *n, pl* **vade mecums** [L, go with me] : something (as a handbook or manual) carried as a constant companion

VADM *abbr* vice admiral

¹vag•a•bond \ˈva-gə-ˌbänd\ *adj* **1** : WANDERING, HOMELESS **2** : of, characteristic of, or leading the life of a vagrant or tramp **3** : leading an unsettled or irresponsible life

²vagabond *n* : one leading a vagabond life; *esp* : TRAMP

va•gar•i•ous \vā-ˈger-ē-əs\ *adj* : marked by vagaries : CAPRICIOUS — **va•gar•i•ous•ly** *adv*

va•ga•ry \ˈvā-gə-rē, və-ˈger-ē\ *n, pl* **-ries** : an odd or eccentric idea or action : WHIM, CAPRICE

va•gi•na \və-ˈjī-nə\ *n, pl* **-nae** \-(ˌ)nē\ *or* **-nas** [L, lit., sheath] : a canal that leads from the uterus to the external opening of the female sex organs — **vag•i•nal** \ˈva-jən-ᵊl\ *adj*

vag•i•ni•tis \ˌva-jə-ˈnī-təs\ *n* : inflammation of the vagina

va•gran•cy \ˈvā-grən-sē\ *n, pl* **-cies** **1** : the quality or state of being vagrant; *also* : a vagrant act or notion **2** : the offense of being a vagrant

¹va•grant \ˈvā-grənt\ *n* : a person who has no job and wanders from place to place

²vagrant *adj* **1** : of, relating to, or characteristic of a vagrant **2** : following no fixed course : RANDOM, CAPRICIOUS ⟨~ thoughts⟩ — **va•grant•ly** *adv*

vague \ˈvāg\ *adj* **vagu•er; vagu•est** [MF, fr. L *vagus*, lit., wandering] **1** : not clear, definite, or distinct **2** : not clearly felt or analyzed ⟨a ~ unrest⟩ **syn** obscure, dark, enigmatic, ambiguous, equivocal — **vague•ly** *adv* — **vague•ness** *n*

vain \ˈvān\ *adj* [ME, fr. MF, fr. L *vanus* empty, vain] **1** : of no real value : IDLE, WORTHLESS **2** : FUTILE, UNSUCCESSFUL **3** : proud of one's looks or abilities **syn** conceited, narcissistic, vainglorious — **vain•ly** *adv*

vain•glo•ri•ous \ˌvān-ˈglōr-ē-əs\ *adj* : marked by vainglory : BOASTFUL

vain•glo•ry \ˈvān-ˌglōr-ē\ *n* **1** : excessive or ostentatious pride esp. in one's own achievements **2** : vain display : VANITY

val *abbr* value; valued

va•lance \ˈva-ləns, ˈvā-\ *n* **1** : drapery hanging from an edge (as of an altar, table, or bed) **2** : a drapery or a decorative frame across the top of a window

vale \ˈvāl\ *n* : VALLEY, DALE

vale•dic•tion \ˌva-lə-ˈdik-shən\ *n* [L *valedicere* to say farewell, fr. *vale* farewell + *dicere* to say] : an act or utterance of leave-taking : FAREWELL

vale•dic•to•ri•an \-ˌdik-ˈtōr-ē-ən\ *n* : the student usu. of the highest rank in a graduating class who delivers the valedictory address at commencement

vale•dic•to•ry \-ˈdik-tə-rē\ *adj* : bidding farewell : delivered as a valediction ⟨a ~ address⟩ — **valedictory** *n*

va•lence \ˈvā-ləns\ *n* [LL *valentia* power, capacity, fr. L *valēre* to be strong] : the combining power of an atom as shown by the number of its electrons that are lost, gained, or shared in the formation of chemical bonds

Va•len•ci•ennes \və-ˌlen-sē-ˈen, ˌva-lən-sē-, -ˈenz\ *n* : a fine handmade lace

val•en•tine \ˈva-lən-ˌtīn\ *n* : a sweetheart chosen or complimented on St. Valentine's Day; *also* : a greeting card sent on this day

Valentine's Day *also* **Valentine Day** *n* : SAINT VALENTINE'S DAY

¹va•let \ˈva-lət, -(ˌ)lā; va-ˈlā\ *n* **1** : a male servant who takes care of a man's clothes and performs personal services **2** : an attendant in a hotel who performs personal services for customers

²valet *vb* : to serve as a valet

val•e•tu•di•nar•i•an \ˌva-lə-ˌtüd-ᵊn-ˈer-ē-ən, -ˌtyüd-\ *n* : a person of a weak or sickly constitution; *esp* : one whose chief concern is being or becoming an invalid — **val•e•tu•di•nar•i•an•ism** \-ē-ə-ˌni-zəm\ *n*

val•iant \ˈval-yənt\ *adj* : having or showing valor : BRAVE, HEROIC **syn** valorous, doughty, courageous, bold, audacious, dauntless, undaunted, intrepid — **val•iant•ly** *adv*

val•id \ˈva-ləd\ *adj* **1** : having legal force ⟨a ~ contract⟩ **2** : founded on truth or fact : capable of being justified or defended : SOUND ⟨a ~ argument⟩ ⟨~ reasons⟩ — **va•lid•i•ty** \və-ˈli-də-tē\ *n* — **val•id•ly** *adv*

val•i•date \ˈva-lə-ˌdāt\ *vb* **-dat•ed; -dat•ing** **1** : to make legally valid **2** : to confirm the validity of **3** : VERIFY — **val•i•da•tion** \ˌva-lə-ˈdā-shən\ *n*

va•lise \və-ˈlēs\ *n* [F] : SUITCASE

val•ley \ˈva-lē\ *n, pl* **valleys** : a long depression between ranges of hills or mountains

val•or \ˈva-lər\ *n* [ME, fr. MF *valour*, fr. ML *valor* value, valor, fr. L *valēre* to be strong] : personal bravery **syn** heroism, prowess, gallantry — **val•or•ous** \ˈva-lə-rəs\ *adj*

val•o•ri•za•tion \ˌva-lə-rə-ˈzā-shən\ *n* : the support of commodity prices by any of various forms of government subsidy — **val•o•rize** \ˈva-lə-ˌrīz\ *vb*

val•our *chiefly Brit var of* VALOR

valse \ˈväls\ *n* [F] : WALTZ; *esp* : a concert waltz

¹valu•able \ˈval-yə-bəl, -yə-wə-bəl\ *adj* **1** : having money value **2** : having great money value **3** : of great use or service **syn** invaluable, priceless, costly, expensive, dear, precious

²valuable *n* : a usu. personal possession of considerable value ⟨their ~*s* were stolen⟩

val•u•ate \ˈval-yə-ˌwāt\ *vb* **-at•ed; -at•ing** : to place a value on : APPRAISE — **val•u•a•tor** \-ˌwā-tər\ *n*

val•u•a•tion \ˌval-yə-ˈwā-shən\ *n* **1** : the act or process of valuing; *esp* : appraisal of property **2** : the estimated or determined market value of a thing

¹val•ue \ˈval-yü\ *n* **1** : a fair return or equivalent in money, goods, or services for something exchanged **2** : the monetary worth of a thing; *also* : relative worth, utility, or importance ⟨nothing of ~ to say⟩ **3** : an assigned or computed numerical quantity ⟨the ~ of *x* in an equation⟩ **4** : relative lightness or darkness of a color : LUMINOSITY **5** : the relative length of a tone or note **6** : something (as a principle or ideal) intrinsically valuable or desirable ⟨human rather than material ~*s*⟩ — **val•ue•less** *adj*

²value *vb* **val•ued; valu•ing** **1** : to estimate the monetary worth of : APPRAISE **2** : to rate in usefulness, importance, or general worth **3** : to consider or rate highly : PRIZE, ESTEEM — **val•u•er** *n*

val•ue–add•ed tax *n* : an incremental excise tax that is levied on the value added at each stage of the processing of a raw material or the production and distribution of a commodity

valve \ˈvalv\ *n* **1** : a structure (as in a vein) that temporarily closes a passage or that permits movement in one direction only **2** : a device by which the flow of a fluid material may be regulated by a movable part; *also* : the movable part of such a device **3** : a device in a brass wind instrument for quickly varying the tube length in order to change the fundamental tone by some definite interval **4** : one of the separate usu. hinged pieces of which the shell of some animals and esp. bivalve mollusks consists **5** : one of the pieces into which a ripe seed capsule or pod separates — **valved** \ˈvalvd\ *adj* — **valve•less** *adj*

val•vu•lar \ˈval-vyə-lər\ *adj* : of, relating to, or affecting a valve esp. of the heart ⟨~ heart disease⟩
va•moose \və-ˈmüs, va-\ *vb* **va•moosed; va•moos•ing** [Sp *vamos* let us go] : to leave or go away quickly
[1]**vamp** \ˈvamp\ *vb* **1** : to provide with a new vamp **2** : to patch up with a new part **3** : INVENT, IMPROVISE ⟨~ up an excuse⟩
[2]**vamp** *n* **1** : the part of a boot or shoe upper covering esp. the front part of the foot **2** : a short introductory musical passage often repeated
[3]**vamp** *n* : a woman who uses her charm or wiles to seduce and exploit men
[4]**vamp** *vb* : to practice seductive wiles on
vam•pire \ˈvam-ˌpīr\ *n* **1** : a night-wandering bloodsucking ghost **2** : a person who preys on other people; *esp* : a woman who exploits and ruins her lover **3** : VAMPIRE BAT
vampire bat *n* : any of various bats of Central and South America that feed on the blood of animals; *also* : any of several other bats that do not feed on blood but are sometimes reputed to do so
[1]**van** \ˈvan\ *n* : VANGUARD
[2]**van** *n* : a usu. enclosed wagon or motortruck for moving goods or animals; *also* : a versatile enclosed box-like motor vehicle
va•na•di•um \və-ˈnā-dē-əm\ *n* : a soft grayish ductile metallic chemical element used esp. to form alloys — see ELEMENT table
Van Al•len belt \van-ˈa-lən-\ *n* : a belt of intense radiation in the magnetosphere composed of charged particles trapped by earth's magnetic field
van•dal \ˈvand-ᵊl\ *n* **1** *cap* : a member of a Germanic people who sacked Rome in A.D. 455 **2** : a person who willfully mars or destroys property
van•dal•ise *Brit var of* VANDALIZE
van•dal•ism \-ˌi-zəm\ *n* : willful or malicious destruction or defacement of public or private property
van•dal•ize \-ˌīz\ *vb* **-ized; -iz•ing** : to subject to vandalism : DAMAGE
Van•dyke \van-ˈdīk\ *n* : a trim pointed beard
vane \ˈvān\ *n* [ME, fr. OE *fana* banner] **1** : a movable device attached to a high object for showing wind direction **2** : a thin flat or curved object that is rotated about an axis by a flow of fluid or that rotates to cause a fluid to flow or that redirects a flow of fluid ⟨the ~*s* of a windmill⟩
van•guard \ˈvan-ˌgärd\ *n* **1** : the troops moving at the front of an army **2** : the forefront of an action or movement
va•nil•la \və-ˈni-lə\ *n* [NL, genus name, fr. Sp *vainilla* vanilla (plant and fruit), dim. of *vaina* sheath, fr. L *vagina*] : a flavoring extract obtained from the long beanlike pods (**vanilla beans**) of a tropical American climbing orchid or made synthetically; *also* : this orchid
van•ish \ˈva-nish\ *vb* : to pass from sight or existence : disappear completely — **van•ish•er** *n*
van•i•ty \ˈva-nə-tē\ *n, pl* **-ties 1** : something that is vain, empty, or useless **2** : the quality or fact of being useless or futile : FUTILITY **3** : undue pride in oneself or one's appearance : CONCEIT **4** : a small case for cosmetics : COMPACT
vanity plate *n* : an automobile license plate bearing distinctive letters or numbers designated by the owner
van•quish \ˈvaŋ-kwish, ˈvan-\ *vb* **1** : to overcome in battle or in a contest **2** : to gain mastery over (as an emotion)
van•tage \ˈvan-tij\ *n* **1** : superiority in a contest **2** : a position giving a strategic advantage or a commanding perspective
va•pid \ˈva-pəd, ˈvā-\ *adj* : lacking spirit, liveliness, or zest : FLAT, INSIPID — **va•pid•i•ty** \va-ˈpi-də-tē\ *n* — **vap•id•ly** *adv* — **vap•id•ness** *n*
va•por \ˈvā-pər\ *n* **1** : fine separated particles (as fog or smoke) floating in the air and clouding it **2** : a substance in the gaseous state; *esp* : one that is liquid under ordinary conditions **3** : something insubstantial or fleeting **4** *pl* : a depressed or hysterical nervous condition
va•por•ing \ˈvā-pə-riŋ\ *n* : an idle, boastful, or high-flown expression or speech — usu. used in pl.
va•por•ise *Brit var of* VAPORIZE
va•por•ize \ˈvā-pə-ˌrīz\ *vb* **-ized; -iz•ing** : to convert into vapor — **va•por•i•za•tion** \ˌvā-pə-rə-ˈzā-shən\ *n*
va•por•iz•er \-ˌrī-zər\ *n* : a device that vaporizes something (as a medicated liquid)
vapor lock *n* : an interruption of flow of a fluid (as fuel in an engine) caused by the formation of vapor in the feeding system
va•por•ous \ˈvā-pə-rəs\ *adj* **1** : full of vapors : FOGGY, MISTY **2** : UNSUBSTANTIAL, VAGUE — **va•por•ous•ly** *adv* — **va•por•ous•ness** *n*
va•pory \ˈvā-pə-rē\ *adj* : MISTY
va•pour *chiefly Brit var of* VAPOR
va•que•ro \vä-ˈker-ō\ *n, pl* **-ros** [Sp, fr. *vaca* cow, fr. L *vacca*] : a ranch hand : COWBOY
var *abbr* **1** variable **2** variant; variation **3** variety **4** various
[1]**var•i•able** \ˈver-ē-ə-bəl\ *adj* **1** : able or apt to vary : CHANGEABLE **2** : FICKLE **3** : not true to type : ABERRANT ⟨a ~ wheat⟩ — **var•i•abil•i•ty** \ˌver-ē-ə-ˈbi-lə-tē, ˌvar-\ *n* — **var•i•ably** \-blē\ *adv*
[2]**variable** *n* **1** : a quantity that may take on any of a set of values; *also* : a mathematical symbol representing a variable **2** : something that is variable
var•i•ance \ˈver-ē-əns\ *n* **1** : variation or a degree of variation : DEVIATION **2** : DISAGREEMENT, DISPUTE **3** : a license to do something contrary to the usual rule ⟨a zoning ~⟩ **4** : the square of the standard deviation **syn** discord, contention, dissension, strife, conflict
[1]**var•i•ant** \ˈver-ē-ənt\ *adj* **1** : differing from others of its kind or class **2** : varying usu. slightly from the standard or type
[2]**variant** *n* **1** : one that exhibits variation from a type or norm **2** : one of two or more different spellings or pronunciations of a word
var•i•a•tion \ˌver-ē-ˈā-shən\ *n* **1** : the act, process, or an instance of varying : a change in form, position, or condition : MODIFICATION, ALTERATION **2** : extent of change or difference **3** : divergence in the characteristics of an organism from those typical or usual for its group; *also* : one exhibiting such variation **4** : repetition of a musical theme with modifications in rhythm, tune, harmony, or key
vari•col•ored \ˈver-i-ˌkə-lərd\ *adj* : having various colors : VARIEGATED
var•i•cose \ˈvar-ə-ˌkōs\ *adj* : abnormally swollen and dilated ⟨~ veins⟩ — **var•i•cos•i•ty** \ˌvar-ə-ˈkä-sə-tē\ *n*
var•ied \ˈver-ēd\ *adj* **1** : having many forms or types : DIVERSE **2** : VARIEGATED — **var•ied•ly** *adv*
var•ie•gat•ed \ˈver-ē-ə-ˌgā-təd\ *adj* **1** : having patches, stripes, or marks of different colors ⟨~ flowers⟩ **2** : VARIED 1 — **var•ie•gate** \-ˌgāt\ *vb* — **var•ie•ga•tion** \ˌver-ē-ə-ˈgā-shən\ *n*
[1]**va•ri•etal** \və-ˈrī-ət-ᵊl\ *adj* : of or relating to a variety; *esp* : of, relating to, or producing a varietal
[2]**varietal** *n* : a wine bearing the name of the principal grape from which it is made
va•ri•ety \və-ˈrī-ə-tē\ *n, pl* **-et•ies 1** : the state of being varied or various : DIVERSITY **2** : a collection of different things : ASSORTMENT **3** : something varying from others of the same general kind **4** : any of various groups of plants or animals within a species distinguished by characteristics insufficient to separate species : SUBSPECIES **5** : entertainment such as is given in a stage presentation comprising a series of performances (as songs, dances, or acrobatic acts)
var•i•o•rum \ˌver-ē-ˈōr-əm\ *n* : an edition or text of a work containing notes by various persons or variant readings of the text
var•i•ous \ˈver-ē-əs\ *adj* **1** : VARICOLORED **2** : of differ-

ing kinds : MULTIFARIOUS **3** : UNLIKE ⟨animals as ~ as the jaguar and the sloth⟩ **4** : having a number of different aspects **5** : NUMEROUS, MANY **6** : INDIVIDUAL, SEPARATE **syn** divergent, disparate, different, dissimilar, diverse, unalike — **var•i•ous•ly** *adv*

var•let \ˈvär-lət\ *n* **1** : ATTENDANT **2** : SCOUNDREL, KNAVE

var•mint \ˈvär-mənt\ *n* [alter. of *vermin*] **1** : an animal considered a pest; *esp* : one classed as vermin and unprotected by game law **2** : a contemptible person : RASCAL

¹var•nish \ˈvär-nish\ *n* **1** : a liquid preparation that is spread on a surface and dries into a hard glossy coating; *also* : the glaze of this coating **2** : something suggesting varnish by its gloss **3** : outside show : deceptive or superficial appearance

²varnish *vb* **1** : to cover with varnish **2** : to cover or conceal with something that gives a fair appearance : GLOSS

var•si•ty \ˈvär-sə-tē\ *n, pl* **-ties** [by shortening & alter. fr. *university*] **1** *Brit* : UNIVERSITY **2** : the principal team representing a college, school, or club

vary \ˈver-ē\ *vb* **var•ied; vary•ing 1** : ALTER, CHANGE **2** : to make or be of different kinds : introduce or have variety : DIVERSIFY, DIFFER **3** : DEVIATE, SWERVE **4** : to change in bodily structure or function away from what is usual for members of a group

vas•cu•lar \ˈvas-kyə-lər\ *adj* [NL *vascularis,* fr. L *vasculum* small vessel, dim. of *vas* vase, vessel] : of or relating to a channel or system of channels for the conveyance of a body fluid (as blood or sap); *also* : supplied with or containing such vessels and esp. blood vessels

vascular plant *n* : a plant having a specialized system for carrying fluids that includes xylem and phloem

vase \ˈvās, ˈvāz\ *n* : a usu. round vessel of greater depth than width used chiefly for ornament or for flowers

va•sec•to•my \və-ˈsek-tə-mē, vā-ˈzek-\ *n, pl* **-mies** : surgical excision of all or part of the sperm-carrying ducts of the testis usu. to induce sterility

va•so•con•stric•tion \ˌvas-ō-kən-ˈstrik-shən, ˌvāz-\ *n* : narrowing of the interior diameter of blood vessels

va•so•con•stric•tor \-tər\ *n* : an agent (as a nerve fiber or a drug) that initiates or induces vasoconstriction

vas•sal \ˈva-səl\ *n* **1** : a person under the protection of a feudal lord to whom he owes homage and loyalty : a feudal tenant **2** : one occupying a dependent or subordinate position — **vassal** *adj*

vas•sal•age \-sə-lij\ *n* **1** : the state of being a vassal **2** : the homage and loyalty due from a vassal **3** : SERVITUDE, SUBJECTION

¹vast \ˈvast\ *adj* : very great in size, amount, degree, intensity, or esp. extent **syn** enormous, huge, gigantic, colossal, mammoth — **vast•ly** *adv* — **vast•ness** *n*

²vast *n* : a great expanse : IMMENSITY

vasty \ˈvas-tē\ *adj* : VAST, IMMENSE

vat \ˈvat\ *n* : a large vessel (as a tub or barrel) esp. for holding liquids in manufacturing processes

VAT *abbr* value-added tax

vat•ic \ˈva-tik\ *adj* : PROPHETIC, ORACULAR

Vat•i•can \ˈva-ti-kən\ *n* **1** : the papal headquarters in Rome **2** : the papal government

vaude•ville \ˈvȯd-vəl, ˈväd-, ˈvōd-, -ˌvil\ *n* [F, fr. MF, satirical song, alter. of *vaudevire,* fr. *vau-de-Vire* valley of Vire, town in northwest France where such songs were composed] : a stage entertainment consisting of unrelated acts (as of acrobats, comedians, dancers, or singers)

¹vault \ˈvȯlt\ *n* **1** : an arched masonry structure usu. forming a ceiling or roof; *also* : something (as the sky) resembling a vault **2** : a room or space covered by a vault esp. when underground **3** : a room or compartment for the safekeeping of valuables **4** : a burial chamber; *also* : a usu. metal or concrete case in which a casket is enclosed at burial — **vaulty** *adj*

²vault *vb* : to form or cover with a vault

³vault *vb* : to leap vigorously esp. by aid of the hands or a pole — **vault•er** *n*

⁴vault *n* : an act of vaulting : LEAP

vault•ed *adj* **1** : built in the form of a vault : ARCHED **2** : covered with a vault

vault•ing *adj* : reaching for the heights ⟨~ ambition⟩

vaunt \ˈvȯnt\ *vb* [ME, fr. MF *vanter,* fr. LL *vanitare,* ultim. fr. L *vanus* vain] : BRAG, BOAST — **vaunt** *n*

vaunt•ed *adj* : much praised or boasted of

vb *abbr* verb; verbal

VCR \ˌvē-(ˌ)sē-ˈär\ *n* [*v*ideo*c*assette *r*ecorder] : a videotape recorder that uses videocassettes

VD *abbr* venereal disease

VDT *abbr* video display terminal

veal \ˈvēl\ *n* : the flesh of a young calf

vec•tor \ˈvek-tər\ *n* **1** : a quantity that has magnitude and direction **2** : an organism (as a fly or tick) that transmits disease germs

Ve•da \ˈvā-də\ *n* [Skt, lit., knowledge] : any of a class of Hindu sacred writings — **Ve•dic** \ˈvā-dik\ *adj*

Ve•dan•ta \vā-ˈdän-tə, və-, -ˈdan-\ *n* : an orthodox Hindu philosophy based on the Upanishads

vee•jay \ˈvē-ˌjā\ *n* : an announcer of a program featuring music videos

veep \ˈvēp\ *n* : VICE PRESIDENT

veer \ˈvir\ *vb* : to shift from one direction or course to another **syn** turn, avert, deflect, divert — **veer** *n*

veg•an \ˈvē-gən, ˈvā-; ˈve-jən, -ˌjan\ *n* : a strict vegetarian who consumes no animal food or dairy products — **veg•an•ism** \ˈvē-gə-ˌni-zəm, ˈvā-, ˈve-\ *n*

¹veg•e•ta•ble \ˈvej-tə-bəl, ˈve-jə-\ *adj* [ME, fr. ML *vegetabilis* vegetative, fr. *vegetare* to grow, fr. L, to animate, fr. *vegetus* lively, fr. *vegēre* to enliven] **1** : of, relating to, or growing like plants ⟨the ~ kingdom⟩ **2** : made or obtained from plants ⟨~ oils⟩ **3** : suggesting that of a plant (as in inertness) ⟨a ~ existence⟩

²vegetable *n* **1** : PLANT 1 **2** : a usu. herbaceous plant grown for an edible part that is usu. eaten as part of a meal; *also* : such an edible part

veg•e•tal \ˈve-jət-ᵊl\ *adj* **1** : VEGETABLE **2** : VEGETATIVE

veg•e•tar•i•an \ˌve-jə-ˈter-ē-ən\ *n* : one that believes in or practices living on a diet of vegetables, fruits, grains, nuts, and sometimes animal products (as milk and cheese) — **vegetarian** *adj* — **veg•e•tar•i•an•ism** \-ē-ə-ˌni-zəm\ *n*

veg•e•tate \ˈve-jə-ˌtāt\ *vb* **-tat•ed; -tat•ing** : to live or grow in the manner of a plant; *esp* : to lead a dull inert life

veg•e•ta•tion \ˌve-jə-ˈtā-shən\ *n* **1** : the act or process of vegetating; *also* : inert existence **2** : plant life or cover (as of an area) — **veg•e•ta•tion•al** \-shə-nəl\ *adj*

veg•e•ta•tive \ˈve-jə-ˌtā-tiv\ *adj* **1** : of or relating to nutrition and growth esp. as contrasted with reproduction **2** : of, relating to, or composed of vegetation **3** : VEGETABLE 3

veg out \ˈvej-\ *vb* **vegged out; vegging out** [short for *vegetate*] : to spend time idly or passively

ve•he•ment \ˈvē-ə-mənt\ *adj* **1** : marked by great force or energy **2** : marked by strong feeling or expression : PASSIONATE, FERVID — **ve•he•mence** \-məns\ *n* — **ve•he•ment•ly** *adv*

ve•hi•cle \ˈvē-ə-kəl, ˈvē-ˌhi-\ *n* **1** : a medium by which a thing is applied or administered ⟨linseed oil is a ~ for pigments⟩ **2** : a medium through or by means of which something is conveyed or expressed **3** : a means of transporting persons or goods **syn** instrument, agent, agency, organ, channel — **ve•hic•u•lar** \vē-ˈhi-kyə-lər\ *adj*

¹veil \ˈvāl\ *n* **1** : a piece of often sheer or diaphanous material used to screen or curtain something or to cover the head or face **2** : the state of becoming a nun ⟨take the ~⟩ **3** : something that hides or obscures like a veil

²veil *vb* : to cover with or as if with a veil : wear a veil

[1]**vein** \ˈvān\ *n* **1 :** a fissure in rock filled with mineral matter; *also* **:** a bed of useful mineral matter **2 :** any of the tubular branching vessels that carry blood from the capillaries toward the heart **3 :** any of the bundles of vascular vessels forming the framework of a leaf **4 :** any of the thickened ribs that stiffen the wings of an insect **5 :** something (as a wavy variegation in marble) suggesting veins **6 :** a distinctive style of expression **7 :** a distinctive element or quality **:** STRAIN **8 :** MOOD, HUMOR — **veined** \ˈvānd\ *adj*

[2]**vein** *vb* **:** to pattern with or as if with veins — **vein·ing** *n*

vel *abbr* velocity

ve·lar \ˈvē-lər\ *adj* **:** of or relating to a velum and esp. that of the soft palate

veld *or* **veldt** \ˈvelt, ˈfelt\ *n* [Afrikaans *veld,* fr. D, field] **:** an open grassland esp. in southern Africa usu. with few shrubs or trees

vel·lum \ˈve-ləm\ *n* [ME *velim,* fr. MF *veelin,* fr. *veelin,* adj., of a calf, fr. *veel* calf] **1 :** a fine-grained lambskin, kidskin, or calfskin prepared for writing on or for binding books **2 :** a strong cream-colored paper — **vellum** *adj*

ve·loc·i·pede \və-ˈlä-sə-ˌpēd\ *n* **:** an early bicycle

ve·loc·i·ty \və-ˈlä-sə-tē\ *n, pl* **-ties :** quickness of motion **:** SPEED ⟨the ∼ of light⟩

ve·lour *or* **ve·lours** \və-ˈlu̇r\ *n, pl* **velours** \-ˈlu̇rz\ **:** any of various textile fabrics with pile like that of velvet

ve·lum \ˈvē-ləm\ *n, pl* **ve·la** \-lə\ **:** a membranous body part (as the soft palate) resembling a veil

vel·vet \ˈvel-vət\ *n* [ME *veluet, velvet,* fr. MF *velu* shaggy, ultim. fr. L *villus* shaggy hair] **1 :** a fabric having a short soft dense warp pile **2 :** something resembling or suggesting velvet (as in softness or luster) **3 :** the soft skin covering the growing antlers of deer — **velvet** *adj* — **velvety** *adj*

vel·ve·teen \ˌvel-və-ˈtēn\ *n* **1 :** a fabric woven usu. of cotton in imitation of velvet **2** *pl* **:** clothes made of velveteen

Ven *abbr* venerable

ve·nal \ˈvēn-ᵊl\ *adj* **:** capable of being bought or bribed **:** MERCENARY, CORRUPT — **ve·nal·i·ty** \vi-ˈnal-ə-tē\ *n* — **ve·nal·ly** \ˈvēn-ᵊl-ē\ *adv*

ve·na·tion \ve-ˈnā-shən, vē-\ *n* **:** an arrangement or system of veins ⟨the ∼ of the hand⟩ ⟨leaf ∼⟩

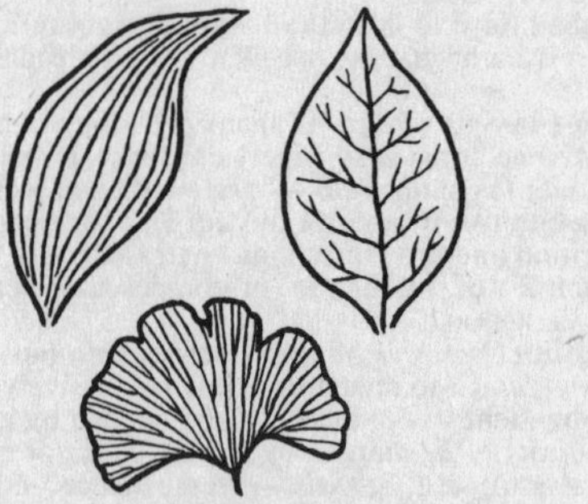

venation

vend \ˈvend\ *vb* **:** SELL; *esp* **:** to sell as a hawker or peddler — **vend·ible** *adj*

vend·ee \ven-ˈdē\ *n* **:** one to whom a thing is sold **:** BUYER

ven·det·ta \ven-ˈde-tə\ *n* **:** a feud marked by acts of revenge

vending machine *n* **:** a coin-operated machine for selling merchandise

ven·dor \ˈven-dər, *for 1 also* ven-ˈdȯr\ *n* **1 :** one that vends **:** SELLER **2 :** VENDING MACHINE

[1]**ve·neer** \və-ˈnir\ *n* [G *Furnier,* fr. *furnieren* to veneer, fr. F *fournir* to furnish] **1 :** a thin usu. superficial layer of material ⟨brick ∼⟩; *esp* **:** a thin layer of fine wood glued over a cheaper wood **2 :** superficial display **:** GLOSS

[2]**veneer** *vb* **:** to overlay with a veneer

ven·er·a·ble \ˈve-nə-rə-bəl\ *adj* **1 :** deserving to be venerated — often used as a religious title **2 :** made sacred by association

ven·er·ate \ˈve-nə-ˌrāt\ *vb* **-at·ed; -at·ing :** to regard with reverential respect **syn** adore, revere, reverence, worship — **ven·er·a·tion** \ˌve-nə-ˈrā-shən\ *n*

ve·ne·re·al \və-ˈnir-ē-əl\ *adj* **:** of or relating to sexual intercourse or to diseases transmitted by it ⟨a ∼ infection⟩

venereal disease *n* **:** a contagious disease (as gonorrhea or syphilis) usu. acquired by having sexual intercourse with someone who already has it

ve·ne·tian blind \və-ˈnē-shən-\ *n* **:** a blind having thin horizontal parallel slats that can be adjusted to admit a desired amount of light

Ven·e·zue·lan \ˌve-nə-ˈzwā-lən\ *n* **:** a native or inhabitant of Venezuela — **Venezuelan** *adj*

ven·geance \ˈven-jəns\ *n* **:** punishment inflicted in retaliation for an injury or offense **:** REVENGE

venge·ful \ˈvenj-fəl\ *adj* **:** filled with a desire for revenge **:** VINDICTIVE — **venge·ful·ly** *adv*

ve·nial \ˈvē-nē-əl\ *adj* **:** capable of being forgiven **:** EXCUSABLE ⟨∼ sin⟩

ve·ni·re \və-ˈnī-rē\ *n* **:** a panel from which a jury is drawn

ve·ni·re fa·ci·as \-ˈfā-shē-əs\ *n* [ME, fr. ML, you should cause to come] **:** a writ summoning persons to appear in court to serve as jurors

ve·ni·re·man \və-ˈnī-rē-mən, -ˈnir-ē-\ *n* **:** a member of a venire

ven·i·son \ˈven-ə-sən, -zən\ *n, pl* **venisons** *also* **venison** [ME, fr. OF *veneison* hunting, game, fr. L *venatio,* fr. *venari* to hunt, pursue] **:** the edible flesh of a deer

ven·om \ˈve-nəm\ *n* [ME *venim, venom,* fr. OF *venim,* ultim. fr. L *venenum* magic charm, drug, poison] **1 :** poisonous material secreted by some animals (as snakes, spiders, or bees) and transmitted usu. by biting or stinging **2 :** ILL WILL, MALEVOLENCE

ven·om·ous \ˈve-nə-məs\ *adj* **1 :** full of venom **:** POISONOUS **2 :** SPITEFUL, MALEVOLENT **3 :** secreting and using venom ⟨∼ snakes⟩ — **ven·om·ous·ly** *adv*

ve·nous \ˈvē-nəs\ *adj* **1 :** of, relating to, or full of veins **2 :** being purplish red oxygen-deficient blood rich in carbon dioxide that is present in most veins

[1]**vent** \ˈvent\ *vb* **1 :** to provide with a vent **2 :** to serve as a vent for **3 :** EXPEL, DISCHARGE **4 :** to give vigorous or emotional expression to

[2]**vent** *n* **1 :** an opportunity or way of escape or passage **:** OUTLET **2 :** an opening for the escape of a gas or liquid or for the relief of pressure

[3]**vent** *n* **:** a slit in a garment esp. in the lower part of a seam (as of a jacket or skirt)

ven·ti·late \ˈvent-ᵊl-ˌāt\ *vb* **-lat·ed; -lat·ing 1 :** to discuss freely and openly ⟨∼ a question⟩ **2 :** to give vent to ⟨∼ one's grievances⟩ **3 :** to cause fresh air to circulate through (as a room or mine) so as to replace foul air **4 :** to provide with a vent or outlet **syn** express, vent, air, utter, voice, broach — **ven·ti·la·tor** \-ᵊl-ˌā-tər\ *n*

ven·ti·la·tion \ˌvent-ᵊl-ˈā-shən\ *n* **1 :** the act or process of ventilating **2 :** circulation of air (as in a room) **3 :** a system or means of providing fresh air

ven·tral \ˈven-trəl\ *adj* **1 :** of or relating to the belly **:** ABDOMINAL **2 :** of, relating to, or located on or near the surface of the body that in humans is the front but in most other animals is the lower surface — **ven·tral·ly** *adv*

ven·tri·cle \ˈven-tri-kəl\ *n* **1 :** a chamber of the heart that receives blood from the atrium of the same side and pumps it into the arteries **2 :** any of the communicating cavities of the brain that are continuous with the central canal of the spinal cord

ven•tril•o•quism \ven-ˈtri-lə-ˌkwi-zəm\ *n* [LL *ventriloquus* ventriloquist, fr. L *venter* belly + *loqui* to speak; fr. the belief that the voice is produced from the ventriloquist's stomach] : the production of the voice in such a manner that the sound appears to come from a source other than the speaker — **ven•tril•o•quist** \-kwist\ *n*

ven•tril•o•quy \-kwē\ *n* : VENTRILOQUISM

[1]**ven•ture** \ˈven-chər\ *vb* **ven•tured; ven•tur•ing 1** : to expose to hazard : RISK **2** : to undertake the risks of : BRAVE **3** : to offer at the risk of rebuff, rejection, or censure ⟨~ an opinion⟩ **4** : to proceed despite danger : DARE

[2]**venture** *n* **1** : an undertaking involving chance or risk; *esp* : a speculative business enterprise **2** : something risked in a speculative venture : STAKE

ven•ture•some \ˈven-chər-səm\ *adj* **1** : involving risk : DANGEROUS, HAZARDOUS **2** : inclined to venture : BOLD, DARING **syn** adventurous, venturous, rash, reckless, foolhardy — **ven•ture•some•ly** *adv* — **ven•ture•some•ness** *n*

ven•tur•ous \ˈven-chə-rəs\ *adj* : VENTURESOME — **ven•tur•ous•ly** *adv* — **ven•tur•ous•ness** *n*

ven•ue \ˈven-yü\ *n* : the place in which the alleged events from which a legal action arises took place; *also* : the place from which the jury is taken and where the trial is held

Ve•nus \ˈvē-nəs\ *n* : the planet 2d in order from the sun — see PLANET table

Ve•nu•sian \vi-ˈnü-zhən, -ˈnyü-\ *adj* : of or relating to the planet Venus

Ve•nus's–fly•trap \ˈvē-nə-səz-ˈflī-ˌtrap\ *or* **Venus fly•trap** *n* : an insect-eating plant of the Carolina coast that has the leaf tip modified into an insect trap

ve•ra•cious \və-ˈrā-shəs\ *adj* **1** : TRUTHFUL, HONEST **2** : TRUE, ACCURATE — **ve•ra•cious•ly** *adv*

ve•rac•i•ty \və-ˈra-sə-tē\ *n, pl* **-ties 1** : devotion to truth : TRUTHFULNESS **2** : conformity with fact : ACCURACY **3** : something true

ve•ran•da *or* **ve•ran•dah** \və-ˈran-də\ *n* : a long open usu. roofed porch

verb \ˈvərb\ *n* : a word that is the grammatical center of a predicate and expresses an act, occurrence, or mode of being

[1]**ver•bal** \ˈvər-bəl\ *adj* **1** : of, relating to, or consisting of words; *esp* : having to do with words rather than with the ideas to be conveyed **2** : expressed in usu. spoken words : not written : ORAL ⟨a ~ contract⟩ **3** : of, relating to, or formed from a verb **4** : LITERAL, VERBATIM — **ver•bal•ly** *adv*

[2]**verbal** *n* : a word that combines characteristics of a verb with those of a noun or adjective

verbal auxiliary *n* : an auxiliary verb

ver•bal•ize \ˈvər-bə-ˌlīz\ *vb* **-ized; -iz•ing 1** : to speak or write in wordy or empty fashion **2** : to express something in words : describe verbally **3** : to convert into a verb — **ver•bal•i•za•tion** \ˌvər-bə-lə-ˈzā-shən\ *n*

verbal noun *n* : a noun derived directly from a verb or verb stem and in some uses having the sense and constructions of a verb

ver•ba•tim \(ˌ)vər-ˈbā-təm\ *adv or adj* : in the same words : word for word

ver•be•na \(ˌ)vər-ˈbē-nə\ *n* : VERVAIN; *esp* : any of several garden plants of hybrid origin with showy spikes of bright often fragrant flowers

ver•biage \ˈvər-bē-ij, -bij\ *n* **1** : superfluity of words usu. of little or obscure content **2** : DICTION, WORDING

ver•bose \(ˌ)vər-ˈbōs\ *adj* : using more words than are needed : WORDY **syn** prolix, diffuse, redundant, windy — **ver•bos•i•ty** \-ˈbä-sə-tē\ *n*

ver•bo•ten \vər-ˈbōt-ᵊn, fər-\ *adj* [G] : forbidden usu. by dictate

ver•dant \ˈvərd-ᵊnt\ *adj* : green with growing plants — **ver•dant•ly** *adv*

ver•dict \ˈvər-(ˌ)dikt\ *n* [alter. of ME *verdit,* fr. Anglo-French (the French of medieval England), fr. OF *ver* true (fr. L *verus*) + *dit* saying, dictum, fr. L *dictum,* fr. *dicere* to say] **1** : the finding or decision of a jury **2** : DECISION, JUDGMENT

ver•di•gris \ˈvər-də-ˌgrēs, -ˌgris\ *n* : a green or bluish deposit that forms on copper, brass, or bronze surfaces

ver•dure \ˈvər-jər\ *n* : the greenness of growing vegetation; *also* : such vegetation

[1]**verge** \ˈvərj\ *n* **1** : a staff carried as an emblem of authority or office **2** : something that borders or bounds : EDGE, MARGIN **3** : BRINK, THRESHOLD

[2]**verge** *vb* **verged; verg•ing 1** : to be contiguous **2** : to be on the verge

[3]**verge** *vb* **verged; verg•ing 1** : to move or extend in some direction or toward some condition : INCLINE **2** : to be in transition or change

verg•er \ˈvər-jər\ *n* **1** *chiefly Brit* : an attendant who carries a verge (as before a bishop) **2** : SEXTON

ve•rid•i•cal \və-ˈri-di-kəl\ *adj* **1** : TRUTHFUL **2** : not illusory : GENUINE

ver•i•fy \ˈver-ə-ˌfī\ *vb* **-fied; -fy•ing 1** : to confirm in law by oath **2** : to establish the truth, accuracy, or reality of **syn** authenticate, corroborate, substantiate, validate — **ver•i•fi•able** *adj* — **ver•i•fi•ca•tion** \ˌver-ə-fə-ˈkā-shən\ *n*

ver•i•ly \ˈver-ə-lē\ *adv* **1** : in very truth : CERTAINLY **2** : TRULY, CONFIDENTLY

veri•si•mil•i•tude \ˌver-ə-sə-ˈmi-lə-ˌtüd, -ˌtyüd\ *n* : the quality or state of appearing to be true

ver•i•ta•ble \ˈver-ə-tə-bəl\ *adj* : ACTUAL, GENUINE, TRUE — **ver•i•ta•bly** *adv*

ver•i•ty \ˈver-ə-tē\ *n, pl* **-ties 1** : the quality or state of being true or real : TRUTH, REALITY **2** : something (as a statement) that is true **3** : HONESTY, VERACITY

ver•meil *n* [MF] **1** \ˈvər-məl, -ˌmāl\ : VERMILION **2** \ver-ˈmā\ : gilded silver

ver•mi•cel•li \ˌvər-mə-ˈche-lē, -ˈse-\ *n* [It, fr. pl. of *vermicello,* dim. of *verme* worm] : a pasta made in thinner strings than spaghetti

ver•mic•u•lite \vər-ˈmi-kyə-ˌlīt\ *n* : any of various lightweight water-absorbent minerals derived from mica

ver•mi•form appendix \ˈvər-mə-ˌform-\ *n* : APPENDIX 2

ver•mil•ion *also* **ver•mil•lion** \vər-ˈmil-yən\ *n* : a bright reddish orange color; *also* : any of various red pigments

ver•min \ˈvər-mən\ *n, pl* **vermin 1** : small common harmful or objectionable animals (as lice or mice) that are difficult to get rid of **2** : birds and mammals that prey on game — **ver•min•ous** *adj*

ver•mouth \vər-ˈmüth\ *n* [F *vermout,* fr. G *Wermut* wormwood] : a dry or sweet wine flavored with herbs and often used in mixed drinks

[1]**ver•nac•u•lar** \vər-ˈna-kyə-lər\ *adj* [L *vernaculus* native, fr. *verna* slave born in the master's house, native] **1** : of, relating to, or being a language or dialect native to a region or country rather than a literary, cultured, or foreign language **2** : of, relating to, or being the normal spoken form of a language **3** : applied to a plant or animal in common speech as distinguished from biological nomenclature ⟨~ names⟩

[2]**vernacular** *n* **1** : a vernacular language **2** : the mode of expression of a group or class **3** : a vernacular name of a plant or animal

ver•nal \ˈvərn-ᵊl\ *adj* : of, relating to, or occurring in the spring

ver•ni•er \ˈvər-nē-ər\ *n* : a short scale made to slide along the divisions of a graduated instrument to indicate parts of divisions

ve•ron•i•ca \və-ˈrä-ni-kə\ *n* : SPEEDWELL

ver•sa•tile \ˈvər-sət-ᵊl\ *adj* : turning with ease from one thing or position to another; *esp* : having many aptitudes — **ver·sa·til·i·ty** \ˌvər-sə-ˈti-lə-tē\ *n*

[1]**verse** \ˈvərs\ *n* **1** : a line of poetry; *also* : STANZA **2** : metrical writing distinguished from poetry esp. by its lower level of intensity **3** : POETRY **4** : POEM **5** : one of the short divisions of a chapter in the Bible

[2]**verse** *vb* **versed; vers·ing** : to familiarize by experience, study, or practice ⟨well *versed* in the theater⟩

ver·si·cle \ˈvər-si-kəl\ *n* : a verse or sentence said or sung by a leader in public worship and followed by a response from the people

ver·si·fi·ca·tion \ˌvər-sə-fə-ˈkā-shən\ *n* **1** : the making of verses **2** : metrical structure

ver·si·fy \ˈvər-sə-ˌfī\ *vb* **-fied; -fy·ing 1** : to write verse **2** : to turn into verse — **ver·si·fi·er** \-ˌfī-ər\ *n*

ver·sion \ˈvər-zhən\ *n* **1** : TRANSLATION; *esp* : a translation of the Bible **2** : an account or description from a particular point of view esp. as contrasted with another **3** : a form or variant of a type or original

vers li·bre \ˌver-ˈlēbrᵊ\ *n, pl* **vers li·bres** *same*\ [F] : FREE VERSE

ver·so \ˈvər-sō\ *n, pl* **versos** : a left-hand page

ver·sus \ˈvər-səs\ *prep* **1** : AGAINST 1 ⟨the champion ~ the challenger⟩ **2** : in contrast or as an alternative to ⟨free trade ~ protection⟩

vert *abbr* vertical

ver·te·bra \ˈvər-tə-brə\ *n, pl* **-brae** \-ˌbrā, -(ˌ)brē\ *or* **-bras** [L] : one of the segments of bone or cartilage making up the backbone

ver·te·bral \(ˌ)vər-ˈtē-brəl, ˈvər-tə-\ *adj* : of, relating to, or made up of vertebrae : SPINAL

vertebral column *n* : BACKBONE

[1]**ver·te·brate** \ˈvər-tə-brət, -ˌbrāt\ *adj* **1** : having a backbone **2** : of or relating to the vertebrates

[2]**vertebrate** *n* : any of a large group of animals (as mammals, birds, reptiles, amphibians, or fishes) that have a backbone or in some primitive forms (as a lamprey) a flexible rod of cells and that have a tubular nervous system arranged along the back and divided into a brain and spinal cord

ver·tex \ˈvər-ˌteks\ *n, pl* **ver·ti·ces** \ˈvər-tə-ˌsēz\ *also* **ver·tex·es** [L *vertex, vortex* whirl, whirlpool, top of the head, summit, fr. *vertere* to turn] **1** : the point opposite to and farthest from the base of a geometrical figure **2** : the point where the sides of an angle or three or more edges of a polyhedron (as a cube) meet **3** : the highest point : TOP, SUMMIT

ver·ti·cal \ˈvər-ti-kəl\ *adj* **1** : of, relating to, or located at the vertex : directly overhead **2** : rising perpendicularly from a level surface : UPRIGHT — **vertical** *n* — **ver·ti·cal·i·ty** \ˌvər-tə-ˈka-lə-tē\ *n* — **ver·ti·cal·ly** \-k(ə-)lē\ *adv*

ver·tig·i·nous \(ˌ)vər-ˈti-jə-nəs\ *adj* : marked by, affected with, or tending to cause dizziness

ver·ti·go \ˈvər-ti-ˌgō\ *n, pl* **-goes** *or* **-gos** : DIZZINESS, GIDDINESS

ver·vain \ˈvər-ˌvān\ *n* : any of a genus of chiefly American herbs or low woody plants with often showy heads or spikes of tubular flowers

verve \ˈvərv\ *n* : liveliness of imagination; *also* : VIVACITY

[1]**very** \ˈver-ē\ *adj* **veri·er; -est** [ME *verray, verry,* fr. OF *verai,* ultim. fr. L *verax* truthful, fr. *verus* true] **1** : EXACT, PRECISE ⟨the ~ heart of the city⟩ **2** : exactly suitable ⟨the ~ tool for the job⟩ **3** : ABSOLUTE, UTTER ⟨the *veriest* nonsense⟩ **4** — used as an intensive esp. to emphasize identity ⟨before my ~ eyes⟩ **5** : MERE, BARE ⟨the ~ idea scared him⟩ **6** : SELFSAME, IDENTICAL ⟨the ~ man I saw⟩

[2]**very** *adv* **1** : in actual fact : TRULY **2** : to a high degree : EXTREMELY

very high frequency *n* : a radio frequency of between 30 and 300 megahertz

ves·i·cant \ˈve-si-kənt\ *n* : an agent that causes blistering — **vesicant** *adj*

ves·i·cle \ˈve-si-kəl\ *n* : a membranous and usu. fluid-filled cavity in a plant or animal; *also* : BLISTER — **ve·sic·u·lar** \və-ˈsi-kyə-lər\ *adj*

[1]**ves·per** \ˈves-pər\ *n* **1** *cap, archaic* : EVENING STAR **2** : a vesper bell **3** *archaic* : EVENING, EVENTIDE

[2]**vesper** *adj* : of or relating to vespers or the evening

ves·pers \-pərz\ *n pl, often cap* : a late afternoon or evening worship service

ves·sel \ˈve-səl\ *n* **1** : a container (as a barrel, bottle, bowl, or cup) for holding something **2** : a person held to be the recipient of a quality (as grace) **3** : a craft bigger than a rowboat **4** : a tube in which a body fluid (as blood or sap) is contained and circulated

[1]**vest** \ˈvest\ *vb* **1** : to place or give into the possession or discretion of some person or authority **2** : to grant or endow with a particular authority, right, or property **3** : to become legally vested **4** : to clothe with or as if with a garment; *esp* : to garb in ecclesiastical vestments

[2]**vest** *n* **1** : a man's sleeveless garment for the upper body usu. worn under a suit coat; *also* : a similar garment for women **2** *chiefly Brit* : a man's sleeveless undershirt **3** : a front piece of a dress resembling the front of a vest

[1]**ves·tal** \ˈvest-ᵊl\ *adj* : CHASTE

[2]**vestal** *n* : VESTAL VIRGIN

vestal virgin *n* **1** : a virgin consecrated to the Roman goddess Vesta and to the service of watching the sacred fire perpetually kept burning on her altar **2** : a chaste woman

vest·ed *adj* : fully and unconditionally guaranteed as a legal right, benefit, or privilege

vested interest *n* : an interest (as in an existing political, economic, or social arrangement) to which the holder has a strong commitment; *also* : one (as a corporation) having a vested interest

ves·ti·bule \ˈves-tə-ˌbyül\ *n* **1** : any of various bodily cavities forming or suggesting an entrance to some other cavity or space **2** : a passage or room between the outer door and the interior of a building — **ves·tib·u·lar** \ve-ˈsti-byə-lər\ *adj*

ves·tige \ˈves-tij\ *n* [F, fr. L *vestigium* footprint, track, vestige] : a trace or visible sign left by something lost or vanished; *also* : a minute remaining amount — **ves·ti·gial** \ve-ˈsti-jē-əl, -jəl\ *adj* — **ves·ti·gial·ly** *adv*

vest·ing \ˈves-tiŋ\ *n* : the conveying to an employee of inalienable rights to share in a pension fund; *also* : the right so conveyed

vest·ment \ˈvest-mənt\ *n* **1** : an outer garment; *esp* : a ceremonial or official robe **2** *pl* : CLOTHING, GARB **3** : a garment or insignia worn by a clergyman when officiating or assisting at a religious service

vest–pocket *adj* : very small ⟨a ~ park⟩

ves·try \ˈves-trē\ *n, pl* **vestries 1** : a room in a church for vestments, altar linens, and sacred vessels **2** : a room used for church meetings and classes **3** : a body administering the temporal affairs of an Episcopal parish

ves·try·man \-mən\ *n* : a member of a vestry

ves·ture \ˈves-chər\ *n* **1** : a covering garment **2** : CLOTHING, APPAREL

[1]**vet** \ˈvet\ *n* : VETERINARIAN

[2]**vet** *adj or n* : VETERAN

vetch \ˈvech\ *n* : any of a genus of twining herbs related to the garden pea including some grown for fodder and green manure

vet·er·an \ˈve-trən, -tə-rən\ *n* [L *veteranus,* fr. *veteranus* old, of long experience, fr. *veter-, vetus* old] **1** : an old soldier of long service **2** : a former member of the armed forces **3** : a person of long experience in an occupation or skill — **veteran** *adj*

Veterans Day *n* : November 11 observed as a legal holiday in commemoration of the end of hostilities in 1918 and 1945

vet·er·i·nar·i·an \ˌve-trə-ˈner-ē-ən, ˌve-tə-rə-\ *n* : one qualified and authorized to practice veterinary medicine

[1]vet·er·i·nary \ˈve-trə-ˌner-ē, ˈve-tə-rə-\ *adj* : of, relating to, or being the medical care of animals and esp. domestic animals

[2]veterinary *n, pl* **-nar·ies** : VETERINARIAN

[1]ve·to \ˈvē-tō\ *n, pl* **vetoes** [L, I forbid] **1** : an authoritative prohibition **2** : a power of one part of a government to forbid the carrying out of projects attempted by another part; *esp* : a power vested in a chief executive to prevent the carrying out of measures adopted by a legislature **3** : the exercise of the power of veto

[2]veto *vb* **1** : FORBID, PROHIBIT **2** : to refuse assent to (a legislative bill) so as to prevent enactment or cause reconsideration — **ve·to·er** *n*

vex \ˈveks\ *vb* **vexed** *also* **vext; vex·ing 1** : to bring trouble, distress, or agitation to **2** : to annoy continually with little irritations

vex·a·tion \vek-ˈsā-shən\ *n* **1** : the act of vexing **2** : the quality or state of being vexed : IRRITATION **3** : a cause of trouble or annoyance

vex·a·tious \-shəs\ *adj* **1** : causing vexation : ANNOYING **2** : full of distress or annoyance : TROUBLED — **vex·a·tious·ly** *adv* — **vex·a·tious·ness** *n*

vexed \ˈvekst\ *adj* : fully debated or discussed ⟨a ~ question⟩

VF *abbr* **1** video frequency **2** visual field

VFD *abbr* volunteer fire department

VFW *abbr* Veterans of Foreign Wars

VG *abbr* **1** very good **2** vicar-general

VHF *abbr* very high frequency

VI *abbr* Virgin Islands

via \ˈvī-ə, ˈvē-ə\ *prep* **1** : by way of **2** : by means of

vi·a·ble \ˈvī-ə-bəl\ *adj* **1** : capable of living; *esp* : capable of surviving outside the mother's womb without artificial support ⟨a ~ fetus⟩ **2** : capable of growing and developing ⟨~ seeds⟩ **3** : capable of being put into practice : WORKABLE **4** : having a reasonable chance of succeeding ⟨a ~ candidate⟩ — **vi·a·bil·i·ty** \ˌvī-ə-ˈbi-lə-tē\ *n* — **vi·a·bly** \ˈvī-ə-blē\ *adv*

via·duct \ˈvī-ə-ˌdəkt\ *n* : a long elevated roadway usu. consisting of a series of short spans supported on arches, piers, or columns

viaduct

vi·al \ˈvī-əl\ *n* : a small vessel for liquids

vi·and \ˈvī-ənd\ *n* : an article of food

vi·at·i·cum \vī-ˈa-ti-kəm, vē-\ *n, pl* **-cums** *or* **-ca** \-kə\ **1** : the Christian Eucharist given to a person in danger of death **2** : an allowance esp. in money for traveling needs and expenses

vibes \ˈvībz\ *n pl* **1** : VIBRAPHONE **2** : VIBRATIONS

vi·brant \ˈvī-brənt\ *adj* **1** : VIBRATING, PULSATING **2** : pulsating with vigor or activity **3** : readily set in vibration : RESPONSIVE **4** : sounding from vibration — **vi·bran·cy** \-brən-sē\ *n*

vi·bra·phone \ˈvī-brə-ˌfōn\ *n* : a percussion instrument like the xylophone but with metal bars and motor-driven resonators

vi·brate \ˈvī-ˌbrāt\ *vb* **vi·brat·ed; vi·brat·ing 1** : OSCILLATE **2** : to set in vibration **3** : to be in vibration **4** : WAVER, FLUCTUATE **5** : to respond sympathetically : THRILL

vi·bra·tion \vī-ˈbrā-shən\ *n* **1** : a rapid to-and-fro motion of the particles of an elastic body or medium (as a stretched cord) that produces sound **2** : an act of vibrating : a state of being vibrated : OSCILLATION **3** : a trembling motion **4** : VACILLATION **5** : a feeling or impression that someone or something gives off — usu. used in pl. ⟨good ~*s*⟩ — **vi·bra·tion·al** \-shə-nəl\ *adj*

vi·bra·to \vi-ˈbrä-tō\ *n, pl* **-tos** [It] : a slightly tremulous effect imparted to vocal or instrumental music

vi·bra·tor \ˈvī-ˌbrā-tər\ *n* : one that vibrates or causes vibration; *esp* : a vibrating electrical device used in massage or for sexual stimulation

vi·bra·to·ry \ˈvī-brə-ˌtōr-ē\ *adj* : consisting of, capable of, or causing vibration

vi·bur·num \vī-ˈbər-nəm\ *n* : any of a genus of widely distributed shrubs or trees related to the honeysuckle and bearing small usu. white flowers in broad clusters

vic *abbr* vicinity

Vic *abbr* Victoria

vic·ar \ˈvi-kər\ *n* **1** : an administrative deputy **2** : a minister in charge of a church who serves under the authority of another minister — **vi·car·i·ate** \vī-ˈker-ē-ət\ *n*

vic·ar·age \ˈvi-kə-rij\ *n* : a vicar's home

vicar–general *n, pl* **vicars–general** : an administrative deputy (as of a Roman Catholic or Anglican bishop)

vi·car·i·ous \vī-ˈker-ē-əs, -ˈkar-\ *adj* **1** : acting for another **2** : done or suffered by one person on behalf of another or others ⟨a ~ sacrifice⟩ **3** : sharing in someone else's experience through the use of the imagination or sympathetic feelings — **vi·car·i·ous·ly** *adv* — **vi·car·i·ous·ness** *n*

[1]vice \ˈvīs\ *n* **1** : DEPRAVITY, WICKEDNESS **2** : a moral fault or failing **3** : a habitual usu. trivial fault **4** : an undesirable behavior pattern in a domestic animal

[2]vice *chiefly Brit var of* VISE

[3]vi·ce \ˈvī-sē\ *prep* : in the place of; *also* : rather than

vice admiral *n* : a commissioned officer in the navy or coast guard ranking above a rear admiral

vice·ge·rent \ˈvīs-ˈjir-ənt\ *n* : an administrative deputy of a king or magistrate — **vice·ge·ren·cy** \-ən-sē\ *n*

vi·cen·ni·al \vī-ˈse-nē-əl\ *adj* : occurring once every 20 years

vice presidency *n* : the office of vice president

vice president *n* **1** : an officer ranking next to a president and usu. empowered to act for the president during an absence or disability **2** : any of several of a president's deputies

vice·re·gal \ˈvīs-ˈrē-gəl\ *adj* : of or relating to a viceroy

vice·roy \ˈvīs-ˌrȯi\ *n* : the governor of a country or province who rules as representative of the sovereign — **vice·roy·al·ty** \-əl-tē\ *n*

vice ver·sa \ˌvī-si-ˈvər-sə, ˈvīs-ˈvər-\ *adv* : with the order reversed

vi·chys·soise \ˌvi-shē-ˈswäz, ˌvē-\ *n* [F] : a soup made esp. from leeks or onions and potatoes, cream, and chicken stock and usu. served cold

vic·i·nage \ˈvis-ᵊn-ij\ *n* : a neighboring or surrounding district : VICINITY

vi·cin·i·ty \və-ˈsi-nə-tē\ *n, pl* **-ties** [MF *vicinité*, fr. L *vicinitas*, fr. *vicinus* neighboring, fr. *vicus* row of houses, village] **1** : NEARNESS, PROXIMITY **2** : a surrounding area : NEIGHBORHOOD

vi·cious \ˈvi-shəs\ *adj* **1** : having the quality of vice : WICKED, DEPRAVED **2** : DEFECTIVE, FAULTY; *also* : INVALID **3** : IMPURE, FOUL **4** : having a savage disposition; *also* : marked by violence or ferocity **5** : MALICIOUS, SPITEFUL **6** : worsened by internal causes that augment each other ⟨~ wage-price spiral⟩ — **vi·cious·ly** *adv* — **vi·cious·ness** *n*

vi•cis•si•tude \və-ˈsi-sə-ˌtüd, vī-, -ˌtyüd\ *n* : an irregular, unexpected, or surprising change

vic•tim \ˈvik-təm\ *n* **1** : a living being offered as a sacrifice in a religious rite **2** : an individual injured or killed (as by disease or accident) **3** : a person cheated, fooled, or injured ⟨a ~ of circumstances⟩

vic•tim•ise *Brit var of* VICTIMIZE

vic•tim•ize \ˈvik-tə-ˌmīz\ *vb* **-ized; -iz•ing** : to make a victim of — **vic•tim•i•za•tion** \ˌvik-tə-mə-ˈzā-shən\ *n* — **vic•tim•iz•er** \ˈvik-tə-ˌmī-zər\ *n*

vic•tim•less *adj* : having no victim ⟨considered gambling to be a ~ crime⟩

vic•tor \ˈvik-tər\ *n* : WINNER, CONQUEROR

vic•to•ria \vik-ˈtōr-ē-ə\ *n* : a low 4-wheeled carriage with a folding top and a raised driver's seat in front

[1]**Vic•to•ri•an** \vik-ˈtōr-ē-ən\ *adj* **1** : of or relating to the reign of Queen Victoria of England or the art, letters, or tastes of her time **2** : typical of the standards, attitudes, or conduct of the age of Victoria esp. when considered prudish or narrow

[2]**Victorian** *n* **1** : a person and esp. an author of the Victorian period **2** : a typically large ornate house built during Queen Victoria's reign

vic•to•ri•ous \vik-ˈtōr-ē-əs\ *adj* **1** : having won a victory **2** : of, relating to, or characteristic of victory — **vic•to•ri•ous•ly** *adv*

vic•to•ry \ˈvik-tə-rē\ *n, pl* **-ries 1** : the overcoming of an enemy or an antagonist **2** : achievement of mastery or success in a struggle or endeavor

[1]**vict•ual** \ˈvit-ᵊl\ *n* **1** : food fit for humans **2** *pl* : food supplies

[2]**victual** *vb* **-ualed** *or* **-ualled; -ual•ing** *or* **-ual•ling 1** : to supply with food **2** : to store up provisions

vict•ual•ler *or* **vict•ual•er** \ˈvit-ᵊl-ər\ *n* : one that supplies provisions (as to an army or a ship)

vi•cu•ña *or* **vi•cu•na** \vi-ˈkün-yə, vī-; vī-ˈkü-nə, -ˈkyü-\ *n* **1** : a So. American wild mammal related to the llama and alpaca; *also* : its wool **2** : a soft fabric woven from the wool of the vicuña; *also* : a sheep's wool imitation of this

vi•de \ˈvī-dē, ˈvē-ˌdā\ *vb imper* [L] : SEE — used to direct a reader to another item

vi•de•li•cet \və-ˈde-lə-ˌset, vī-; vi-ˈdā-li-ˌket\ *adv* [ME, fr. L, fr. *vidēre* to see + *licet* it is permitted] : that is to say : NAMELY

[1]**vid•eo** \ˈvi-dē-ˌō\ *n* **1** : TELEVISION **2** : VIDEOTAPE **3** : a videotaped performance ⟨music ~*s*⟩

[2]**video** *adj* **1** : relating to or used in transmission or reception of the television image **2** : relating to or being images on a television screen or computer display ⟨a ~ terminal⟩

vid•eo•cas•sette \ˌvi-dē-ō-kə-ˈset\ *n* **1** : a case containing videotape for use with a VCR **2** : a recording (as of a movie) on a videocassette

videocassette recorder *n* : VCR

vid•eo•disc *or* **vid•eo•disk** \ˈvi-dē-ō-ˌdisk\ *n* **1** : a disc similar in appearance and use to a phonograph record on which programs have been recorded for playback on a television set; *also* : OPTICAL DISK **2** : a recording (as of a movie) on a videodisc

video game *n* : an electronic game played on a video screen

vid•eo•phone \ˈvid-ē-ə-ˌfōn\ *n* : a telephone for transmitting both audio and video signals

[1]**vid•eo•tape** \ˈvid-ē-ō-ˌtāp\ *n* : a recording of visual images and sound made on magnetic tape; *also* : the magnetic tape used for such a recording

[2]**videotape** *vb* : to make a videotape of

videotape recorder *n* : a device for recording and playing back videotapes

vie \ˈvī\ *vb* **vied; vy•ing** \ˈvī-iŋ\ : to compete for superiority : CONTEND — **vi•er** \ˈvī-ər\ *n*

Viet•cong \vē-ˈet-ˈkäŋ, ˌvē-ət-, -ˈkȯŋ\ *n, pl* **Vietcong** : a guerrilla soldier of the Vietnamese communist movement

Viet•nam•ese \vē-ˌet-nə-ˈmēz, ˌvē-ət-, -ˈmēs\ *n, pl* **Vietnamese** : a native or inhabitant of Vietnam — **Vietnamese** *adj*

[1]**view** \ˈvyü\ *n* **1** : the act of seeing or examining : INSPECTION; *also* : SURVEY **2** : a way of looking at or regarding something **3** : ESTIMATE, JUDGMENT ⟨stated his ~*s*⟩ **4** : a sight (as of a landscape) regarded for its pictorial quality **5** : extent or range of vision ⟨within ~⟩ **6** : OBJECT, PURPOSE ⟨done with a ~ to promotion⟩ **7** : a picture of a scene

[2]**view** *vb* **1** : to look at attentively : EXAMINE **2** : SEE, WATCH **3** : to examine mentally : CONSIDER — **view•er** *n*

view•er•ship \ˈvyü-ər-ˌship\ *n* : a television audience esp. with respect to size or makeup

view•find•er \ˈvyü-ˌfīn-dər\ *n* : a device on a camera for showing the view to be included in the picture

view•point \-ˌpȯint\ *n* : POINT OF VIEW, STANDPOINT

vi•ges•i•mal \vī-ˈje-sə-məl\ *adj* : based on the number 20

vig•il \ˈvi-jəl\ *n* **1** : a religious observance formerly held on the night before a religious feast **2** : the day before a religious feast observed as a day of spiritual preparation **3** : evening or nocturnal devotions or prayers — usu. used in pl. **4** : an act or a time of keeping awake when sleep is customary; *esp* : WATCH 1

vig•i•lance \ˈvi-jə-ləns\ *n* : the quality or state of being vigilant

vigilance committee *n* : a committee of vigilantes

vig•i•lant \ˈvi-jə-lənt\ *adj* : alertly watchful esp. to avoid danger — **vig•i•lant•ly** *adv*

vig•i•lan•te \ˌvi-jə-ˈlan-tē\ *n* : a member of a volunteer committee organized to suppress and punish crime summarily (as when the processes of law appear inadequate); *also* : a self-appointed doer of justice — **vig•i•lan•tism** \-ˈlan-ˌti-zəm\ *n*

[1]**vi•gnette** \vin-ˈyet\ *n* [F, fr. MF *vignete*, fr. dim. of *vigne* vine] **1** : a small decorative design **2** : a picture (as an engraving or a photograph) that shades off gradually into the surrounding ground **3** : a short descriptive literary sketch

[2]**vignette** *vb* **vi•gnett•ed; vi•gnett•ing 1** : to finish (as a photograph) in the manner of a vignette **2** : to describe briefly

vig•or \ˈvi-gər\ *n* **1** : active strength or energy of body or mind **2** : INTENSITY, FORCE

vig•or•ous \ˈvi-gə-rəs\ *adj* **1** : having vigor : ROBUST **2** : done with force and energy — **vig•or•ous•ly** *adv* — **vig•or•ous•ness** *n*

vig•our *chiefly Brit var of* VIGOR

Vi•king \ˈvī-kiŋ\ *n* [ON *vīkingr*] : any of the pirate Norsemen who raided or invaded the coasts of Europe in the 8th to 10th centuries

vil *abbr* village

vile \ˈvīl\ *adj* **vil•er; vil•est 1** : morally despicable **2** : physically repulsive : FOUL **3** : of little worth **4** : DEGRADING, IGNOMINIOUS **5** : utterly bad or contemptible ⟨~ weather⟩ — **vile•ly** \ˈvīl-lē\ *adv* — **vile•ness** *n*

vil•i•fy \ˈvi-lə-ˌfī\ *vb* **-fied; -fy•ing** : to blacken the character of with abusive language : DEFAME **syn** malign, calumniate, slander, libel, traduce — **vil•i•fi•ca•tion** \ˌvi-lə-fə-ˈkā-shən\ *n* — **vil•i•fi•er** \ˈvi-lə-ˌfī-ər\ *n*

vil•la \ˈvi-lə\ *n* **1** : a country estate **2** : the rural or suburban residence of a wealthy person

vil•lage \ˈvi-lij\ *n* **1** : a settlement usu. larger than a hamlet and smaller than a town **2** : an incorporated minor municipality **3** : the people of a village

vil•lag•er \ˈvi-li-jər\ *n* : an inhabitant of a village

vil•lain \ˈvi-lən\ *n* **1** : VILLEIN **2** : an evil person : SCOUNDREL

vil•lain•ess \-lə-nəs\ *n* : a woman who is a villain

vil•lain•ous \-lə-nəs\ *adj* **1** : befitting a villain : WICKED, EVIL **2** : highly objectionable : DETESTABLE **syn** vicious, iniquitous, nefarious, infamous, corrupt, degenerate — **vil•lain•ous•ly** *adv* — **vil•lain•ous•ness** *n*

vil•lainy \-lə-nē\ *n, pl* **-lain•ies 1 :** villainous conduct; *also* **:** a villainous act **2 :** villainous character or nature

vil•lein \ˈvi-lən, -ˌlān\ *n* **1 :** a free villager of Anglo-Saxon times **2 :** an unfree peasant having the status of a slave to a feudal lord

vil•len•age \ˈvil-ə-nij\ *n* **1 :** the holding of land at the will of a feudal lord **2 :** the status of a villein

vil•lous \ˈvi-ləs\ *adj* **:** covered with fine hairs or villi

vil•lus \ˈvi-ləs\ *n, pl* **vil•li** \-ˌlī, -(ˌ)lē\ **:** a slender usu. vascular process; *esp* **:** one of the tiny projections of the mucous membrane of the small intestine that function in the absorption of food

vim \ˈvim\ *n* **:** robust energy and enthusiasm **:** VITALITY

VIN *abbr* vehicle identification number

vin•ai•grette \ˌvi-ni-ˈgret\ *n* [F] **:** a sauce made typically of oil and vinegar, onions, parsley, and herbs

vin•ci•ble \ˈvin-sə-bəl\ *adj* **:** capable of being overcome or subdued

vin•di•cate \ˈvin-də-ˌkāt\ *vb* **-cat•ed; -cat•ing 1 :** AVENGE **2 :** EXONERATE, ABSOLVE **3 :** CONFIRM, SUBSTANTIATE **4 :** to provide defense for **:** JUSTIFY **5 :** to maintain a right to **:** ASSERT — **vin•di•ca•tor** \-ˌkā-tər\ *n*

vin•di•ca•tion \ˌvin-də-ˈkā-shən\ *n* **:** a vindicating or being vindicated; *esp* **:** justification against denial or censure **:** DEFENSE

vin•dic•tive \vin-ˈdik-tiv\ *adj* **1 :** disposed to revenge **2 :** intended for or involving revenge **3 :** VICIOUS, SPITEFUL — **vin•dic•tive•ly** *adv* — **vin•dic•tive•ness** *n*

vine \ˈvīn\ *n* [ME, fr. OF *vigne,* fr. L *vinea* vine, vineyard, fr. fem. of *vineus* of wine, fr. *vinum* wine] **1 :** GRAPE 2 **2 :** a plant whose stem requires support and which climbs (as by tendrils) or trails along the ground; *also* **:** the stem of such a plant

vin•e•gar \ˈvi-ni-gər\ *n* [ME *vinegre,* fr. OF *vinaigre,* fr. *vin* wine + *aigre* keen, sour] **:** a sour liquid obtained by fermentation (as of cider, wine, or malt) and used in cookery and pickling

vin•e•gary \-gə-rē\ *adj* **1 :** resembling vinegar **:** SOUR **2 :** disagreeable in manner or disposition **:** CRABBED

vine•yard \ˈvin-yərd\ *n* **1 :** a field of grapevines esp. to produce grapes for wine production **2 :** a sphere of activity **:** field of endeavor

vi•nous \ˈvī-nəs\ *adj* **1 :** of, relating to, or made with wine ⟨~ medications⟩ **2 :** showing the effects of the use of wine ⟨~ bloodshot eyes⟩

¹vin•tage \ˈvin-tij\ *n* **1 :** a season's yield of grapes or wine **2 :** WINE; *esp* **:** a usu. superior wine which comes from a single year **3 :** the act or period of gathering grapes or making wine **4 :** a period of origin ⟨clothes of 1890 ~⟩

²vintage *adj* **1 :** of, relating to, or produced in a particular vintage **2 :** of old, recognized, and enduring interest, importance, or quality **:** CLASSIC ⟨~ cars⟩ **3 :** of the best and most characteristic — used with a proper noun

vint•ner \ˈvint-nər\ *n* **:** a dealer in wines

vi•nyl \ˈvīn-ᵊl\ *n* **1 :** a chemical derived from ethylene by the removal of one hydrogen atom **2 :** a polymer of a vinyl compound or a product (as a textile fiber) made from one

vinyl chloride *n* **:** a flammable gaseous carcinogenic compound used esp. to make vinyl resins

vi•ol \ˈvī-əl\ *n* **:** a bowed stringed instrument chiefly of the 16th and 17th centuries having a fretted neck and usu. six strings

¹vi•o•la \vī-ˈō-lə, ˈvī-ə-lə\ *n* **:** VIOLET 1; *esp* **:** any of various hybrid garden plants with white, yellow, purple, or variously colored flowers that resemble but are smaller than the related pansies

²vi•o•la \vē-ˈō-lə\ *n* **:** an instrument of the violin family slightly larger and tuned lower than a violin — **vi•o•list** \-list\ *n*

vi•o•la•ble \ˈvī-ə-lə-bəl\ *adj* **:** capable of being violated

vi•o•late \ˈvī-ə-ˌlāt\ *vb* **-lat•ed; -lat•ing 1 :** BREAK, DISREGARD ⟨~ a law⟩ ⟨~ a frontier⟩ **2 :** RAPE **3 :** PROFANE, DESECRATE **4 :** INTERRUPT, DISTURB ⟨*violated* his privacy⟩ — **vi•o•la•tor** \-ˌlā-tər\ *n*

vi•o•la•tion \ˌvī-ə-ˈlā-shən\ *n* **:** an act or instance of violating **:** the state of being violated **syn** breach, infraction, trespass, infringement, transgression

vi•o•lence \ˈvī-ləns, ˈvī-ə-\ *n* **1 :** exertion of physical force so as to injure or abuse **2 :** injury by or as if by infringement or profanation **3 :** intense or furious often destructive action or force **4 :** vehement feeling or expression **:** INTENSITY **5 :** jarring quality **:** DISCORDANCE **syn** compulsion, coercion, duress, constraint

vi•o•lent \-lənt\ *adj* **1 :** marked by extreme force or sudden intense activity **2 :** caused by or showing strong feeling ⟨~ words⟩ **3 :** EXTREME, INTENSE **4 :** emotionally agitated to the point of loss of self-control **5 :** caused by force **:** not natural ⟨~ death⟩ — **vi•o•lent•ly** *adv*

vi•o•let \ˈvī-ə-lət\ *n* **1 :** any of a genus of chiefly herbs usu. with heart-shaped leaves and both aerial and underground flowers; *esp* **:** one with small usu. solid-colored flowers **2 :** a reddish blue color

vi•o•lin \ˌvī-ə-ˈlin\ *n* **:** a bowed stringed instrument with four strings that has a shallow body, a fingerboard without frets, and a curved bridge — **vi•o•lin•ist** \-ˈli-nist\ *n*

violin

vi•o•lon•cel•lo \ˌvī-ə-lən-ˈche-lō\ *n* [It] **:** CELLO — **vi•o•lon•cel•list** \-list\ *n*

VIP \ˌvē-ˌī-ˈpē\ *n, pl* **VIPs** \-ˈpēz\ [*v*ery *i*mportant *p*erson] **:** a person of great influence or prestige; *esp* **:** a high official with special privileges

vi•per \ˈvī-pər\ *n* **1 :** a common stout-bodied Eurasian venomous snake having a bite only rarely fatal to humans; *also* **:** any snake (as a pit viper) of the same family as the viper **2 :** any venomous or reputedly venomous snake **3 :** a vicious or treacherous person — **vi•per•ine** \-pə-ˌrīn\ *adj*

vi•ra•go \və-ˈrä-gō, -ˈrā-\ *n, pl* **-goes** *or* **-gos** [ME, fr. L, strong or heroic woman, fr. *vir* man] **1 :** a loud overbearing woman **2 :** a woman of great strength and courage

vi•ral \ˈvī-rəl\ *adj* **:** of, relating to, or caused by a virus

vir•eo \ˈvir-ē-ˌō\ *n, pl* **-e•os** [L, a small bird, fr. *virēre* to be green] **:** any of various small insect-eating American songbirds mostly olive green and grayish in color

¹vir•gin \ˈvər-jən\ *n* **1 :** an unmarried woman devoted to religion **2 :** an unmarried girl or woman **3** *cap* **:** the mother of Jesus **4 :** a person who has not had sexual intercourse

²virgin *adj* **1 :** free from stain **:** PURE, SPOTLESS **2 :** CHASTE **3 :** befitting a virgin **:** MODEST **4 :** FRESH, UNSPOILED; *esp* **:** not altered by human activity ⟨~ forest⟩ **5 :** INITIAL, FIRST

¹vir•gin•al \ˈvər-jən-ᵊl\ *adj* **:** of, relating to, or characteristic of a virgin or virginity — **vir•gin•al•ly** *adv*

²virginal *n* **:** a small rectangular spinet without legs popular in the 16th and 17th centuries

Vir•gin•ia creeper \vər-ˈjin-yə-\ *n* **:** a No. American vine related to the grapes that has leaves with five leaflets and bluish black berries

Virginia reel *n* **:** an American country-dance

vir•gin•i•ty \vər-ˈji-nə-tē\ *n, pl* **-ties 1 :** the quality or state of being virgin; *esp* : MAIDENHOOD **2** : the unmarried life : CELIBACY

Vir•go \ˈvər-ˌgō\ *n* [L, lit., virgin] **1** : a zodiacal constellation between Leo and Libra usu. pictured as a young woman **2** : the 6th sign of the zodiac in astrology; *also* : one born under this sign

vir•gule \ˈvər-gyül\ *n* : a mark / used typically to denote "or" (as in *and/or*) or "per" (as in *feet/second*)

vir•i•des•cent \ˌvir-ə-ˈdes-ᵊnt\ *adj* : slightly green : GREENISH

vir•ile \ˈvir-əl\ *adj* **1** : having the nature, powers, or qualities of a man **2** : MASCULINE, MALE **3** : MASTERFUL, FORCEFUL — **vi•ril•i•ty** \və-ˈri-lə-tē\ *n*

vi•ri•on \ˈvī-rē-ˌän, ˈvir-ē-\ *n* : a complete virus particle consisting of an RNA or DNA core with a protein coat

vi•rol•o•gy \vī-ˈrä-lə-jē\ *n* : a branch of science that deals with viruses — **vi•rol•o•gist** \-jist\ *n*

vir•tu \ˌvər-ˈtü, vir-\ *n* [It *virtù*, lit., virtue] **1** : a love of or taste for objects of art **2** : objects of art (as curios and antiques)

vir•tu•al \ˈvər-chə-wəl\ *adj* : being in essence or in effect though not formally recognized or admitted ⟨a ~ dictator⟩

vir•tu•al•ly \ˈvər-chə-wə-lē\ *adv* **1** : almost entirely : NEARLY **2** : for all practical purposes

virtual reality *n* : an artificial environment that is experienced through sensory stimuli (as sights and sounds) provided by an interactive computer program

vir•tue \ˈvər-chü\ *n* [ME *virtu*, fr. OF, fr. L *virtus* strength, manliness, virtue, fr. *vir* man] **1** : conformity to a standard of right : MORALITY **2** : a particular moral excellence **3** : manly strength or courage : VALOR **4** : a commendable quality : MERIT **5** : active power to accomplish a given effect : POTENCY, EFFICACY **6** : chastity esp. in a woman

vir•tu•os•i•ty \ˌvər-chə-ˈwä-sə-tē\ *n, pl* **-ties** : great technical skill in the practice of a fine art

vir•tu•o•so \ˌvər-chə-ˈwō-sō, -zō\ *n, pl* **-sos** *or* **-si** \-sē, -zē\ [It] **1** : one skilled in or having a taste for the fine arts **2** : one who excels in the technique of an art; *esp* : a highly skilled musical performer **syn** expert, adept, artist, doyen, master — **virtuoso** *adj*

vir•tu•ous \ˈvər-chə-wəs\ *adj* **1** : having or showing virtue and esp. moral virtue **2** : CHASTE — **vir•tu•ous•ly** *adv*

vir•u•lent \ˈvir-ə-lənt, ˈvir-yə-\ *adj* **1** : highly infectious ⟨a ~ germ⟩; *also* : marked by a rapid, severe, and often deadly course ⟨a ~ disease⟩ **2** : extremely poisonous or venomous : NOXIOUS **3** : full of malice : MALIGNANT — **vir•u•lence** \-ləns\ *n* — **vir•u•lent•ly** *adv*

vi•rus \ˈvī-rəs\ *n* [L, venom, poisonous emanation] **1** : any of a large group of submicroscopic infectious agents that have an outside coat of protein around a core of RNA or DNA, that can grow and multiply only in living cells, and that cause important diseases in human beings, lower animals, and plants; *also* : a disease caused by a virus **2** : something (as a corrupting influence) that poisons the mind or spirit **3** : a computer program usu. hidden within another program that reproduces itself and inserts the copies into other programs and that usu. performs a malicious action (as destroying data)

vis *abbr* **1** visibility **2** visual

¹vi•sa \ˈvē-zə, -sə\ *n* [F] **1** : an endorsement by the proper authorities on a passport to show that it has been examined and the bearer may proceed **2** : a signature by a superior official signifying approval of a document

²visa *vb* **vi•saed** \-zəd, -səd\; **vi•sa•ing** \-zə-iŋ, -sə-\ : to give a visa to (a passport)

vis•age \ˈvi-zij\ *n* : the face or countenance of a person or sometimes an animal; *also* : LOOK, APPEARANCE

¹vis–à–vis \ˌvēz-ə-ˈvē, ˌvēs-\ *prep* [F, lit., face-to-face] **1** : face-to-face with : OPPOSITE **2** : in relation to **3** : as compared with

²vis–à–vis *n, pl* **vis–à–vis** *same or* -ˈvēz\ **1** : one that is face-to-face with another **2** : ESCORT **3** : COUNTERPART **4** : TÊTE-À-TÊTE

³vis–à–vis *adv* : in company : TOGETHER

viscera *pl of* VISCUS

vis•cer•al \ˈvi-sə-rəl\ *adj* **1** : felt in or as if in the viscera **2** : not intellectual : INSTINCTIVE **3** : of or relating to the viscera — **vis•cer•al•ly** *adv*

vis•cid \ˈvi-səd\ *adj* : VISCOUS — **vis•cid•i•ty** \vi-ˈsi-də-tē\ *n*

vis•cos•i•ty \vis-ˈkä-sə-tē\ *n, pl* **-ties** : the quality of being viscous; *esp* : the property of resistance to flow in a fluid

vis•count \ˈvī-ˌkaůnt\ *n* : a member of the British peerage ranking below an earl and above a baron

vis•count•ess \-ˌkaůn-təs\ *n* **1** : the wife or widow of a viscount **2** : a woman who holds the rank of viscount in her own right

vis•cous \ˈvis-kəs\ *adj* [ME *viscouse*, fr. LL *viscosus* full of birdlime, viscous, fr. L *viscum* mistletoe, birdlime] **1** : having the sticky consistency of glue **2** : having or characterized by viscosity

vis•cus \ˈvis-kəs\ *n, pl* **vis•cera** \ˈvi-sə-rə\ : an internal organ of the body; *esp* : one (as the heart or liver) located in the cavity of the trunk

vise \ˈvīs\ *n* [MF *vis* something winding, fr. L *vitis* vine] : a tool with two jaws for holding work that typically close by a screw or lever

vis•i•bil•i•ty \ˌvi-zə-ˈbi-lə-tē\ *n, pl* **-ties** **1** : the quality, condition, or degree of being visible **2** : the degree of clearness of the atmosphere

vis•i•ble \ˈvi-zə-bəl\ *adj* : capable of being seen ⟨~ stars⟩; *also* : MANIFEST, APPARENT ⟨has no ~ means of support⟩ — **vis•i•bly** \-blē\ *adv*

¹vi•sion \ˈvi-zhən\ *n* **1** : something seen otherwise than by ordinary sight (as in a dream or trance) **2** : a vivid picture created by the imagination **3** : the act or power of imagination **4** : unusual wisdom in foreseeing what is going to happen **5** : the act or power of seeing : SIGHT **6** : something seen; *esp* : a lovely sight

²vision *vb* : IMAGINE, ENVISION

¹vi•sion•ary \ˈvi-zhə-ˌner-ē\ *adj* **1** : of the nature of a vision : ILLUSORY, UNREAL **2** : not practical : UTOPIAN **3** : seeing or likely to see visions : given to dreaming or imagining **syn** imaginary, fantastic, chimerical, quixotic

²visionary *n, pl* **-ar•ies** **1** : one whose ideas or projects are impractical : DREAMER **2** : one who sees visions

¹vis•it \ˈvi-zət\ *vb* **1** : to go to see in order to comfort or help **2** : to call on either as an act of courtesy or friendship **3** : to dwell with for a time as a guest **4** : to come to or upon as a reward, affliction, or punishment **5** : INFLICT **6** : to make a visit or regular or frequent visits **7** : CHAT, CONVERSE — **vis•it•able** *adj*

²visit *n* **1** : a short stay : CALL **2** : a brief residence as a guest **3** : a journey to and stay at a place **4** : a formal or professional call (as by a doctor)

vis•i•tant \ˈvi-zə-tənt\ *n* : VISITOR

vis•i•ta•tion \ˌvi-zə-ˈtā-shən\ *n* **1** : VISIT; *esp* : an official visit **2** : a special dispensation of divine favor or wrath; *also* : a severe trial

visiting nurse *n* : a nurse employed to visit sick persons or perform public health services in a community

vis•i•tor \ˈvi-zə-tər\ *n* : one that visits

vi•sor \ˈvī-zər\ *n* **1** : the front piece of a helmet; *esp* : a movable upper piece **2** : VIZARD **3** : a projecting part (as on a cap) to shade the eyes — **vi•sored** \-zərd\ *adj*

vis•ta \ˈvis-tə\ *n* **1** : a distant view through or along an avenue or opening **2** : an extensive mental view over a series of years or events

VISTA *abbr* Volunteers in Service to America

¹vi•su•al \ˈvi-zhə-wəl\ *adj* **1** : of, relating to, or used in vision ⟨~ organs⟩ **2** : perceived by vision ⟨a ~ impression⟩ **3** : VISIBLE **4** : done by sight only ⟨~ navigation⟩ **5** : of or relating to instruction by means of sight ⟨~ aids⟩ — **vi·su·al·ly** *adv*

²**visual** *n* : something (as a picture, chart, or film) that appeals to the sight and is used for illustration, demonstration, or promotion — usu. used in pl.

vi·su·al·ise *Brit var of* VISUALIZE

vi·su·al·ize \ˈvi-zhə-wə-ˌlīz\ *vb* **-ized; -iz·ing** : to make visible; *esp* : to form a mental image of — **vi·su·al·i·za·tion** \ˌvi-zhə-wə-lə-ˈzā-shən\ *n* — **vi·su·al·iz·er** *n*

vi·ta \ˈvē-tə, ˈvī-\ *n, pl* **vi·tae** \ˈvē-ˌtī, ˈvī-tē\ [L, lit., life] : a brief autobiographical sketch

vi·tal \ˈvīt-ᵊl\ *adj* **1** : concerned with or necessary to the maintenance of life **2** : full of life and vigor : ANIMATED **3** : of, relating to, or characteristic of life or living beings **4** : FATAL, MORTAL ⟨~ wound⟩ **5** : FUNDAMENTAL, INDISPENSABLE — **vi·tal·ly** *adv*

vi·tal·i·ty \vī-ˈta-lə-tē\ *n, pl* **-ties** **1** : the property distinguishing the living from the nonliving **2** : mental and physical vigor **3** : enduring quality **4** : ANIMATION, LIVELINESS

vi·tal·ize \ˈvīt-ᵊl-ˌīz\ *vb* **-ized; -iz·ing** : to impart life or vigor to : ANIMATE — **vi·tal·i·za·tion** \ˌvīt-ᵊl-ə-ˈzā-shən\ *n*

vi·tals \ˈvīt-ᵊlz\ *n pl* **1** : vital organs (as the heart and brain) **2** : essential parts

vital signs *n pl* : the pulse rate, respiratory rate, body temperature, and often blood pressure of a person

vital statistics *n pl* : statistics dealing with births, deaths, marriages, health, and disease

vi·ta·min \ˈvī-tə-mən\ *n* : any of various organic substances that are essential in tiny amounts to the nutrition of most animals and some plants and are mostly obtained from foods

vitamin A *n* : any of several vitamins (as from egg yolk or fish-liver oils) required esp. for good vision

vitamin B *n* **1** : VITAMIN B COMPLEX **2** *or* **vitamin B_1** : THIAMINE

vitamin B complex *n* : a group of vitamins that are found widely in foods and are essential for normal function of certain enzymes and for growth

vitamin B_6 \-ˈbē-ˈsiks\ *n* : any of several compounds that are considered essential to vertebrate nutrition

vitamin B_{12} \-ˈbē-ˈtwelv\ *n* : a complex cobalt-containing compound that occurs esp. in liver and is essential to normal blood formation, neural function, and growth; *also* : any of several compounds of similar action

vitamin C *n* : a vitamin found esp. in fruits and vegetables that is needed by the body to prevent scurvy

vitamin D *n* : any or all of several vitamins that are needed for normal bone and tooth structure and are found esp. in fish-liver oils, egg yolk, and milk or are produced by the body in response to ultraviolet light

vitamin E *n* : any of various oily fat-soluble liquid vitamins whose absence in the body is associated with such ailments as infertility, the breakdown of muscles, and vascular problems and which are found esp. in leaves and in seed germ oils

vitamin K *n* [Dan *k*oagulation coagulation] : any of several vitamins needed for blood to clot properly

vi·ti·ate \ˈvi-shē-ˌāt\ *vb* **-at·ed; -at·ing** **1** : CONTAMINATE, POLLUTE; *also* : DEBASE, PERVERT **2** : to make legally ineffective : INVALIDATE — **vi·ti·a·tion** \ˌvi-shē-ˈā-shən\ *n* — **vi·ti·a·tor** \ˈvi-shē-ˌā-tər\ *n*

vi·ti·cul·ture \ˈvi-tə-ˌkəl-chər\ *n* : the growing of grapes — **vi·ti·cul·tur·al** \ˌvi-tə-ˈkəl-chə-rəl\ *adj* — **vi·ti·cul·tur·ist** \-rist\ *n*

vit·re·ous \ˈvi-trē-əs\ *adj* **1** : of, relating to, or resembling glass : GLASSY ⟨~ rocks⟩ **2** : of, relating to, or being the clear colorless transparent jelly (**vitreous humor**) behind the lens in the eyeball

vit·ri·ol \ˈvi-trē-əl\ *n* : something resembling acid in being caustic, corrosive, or biting — **vit·ri·ol·ic** \ˌvi-trē-ˈä-lik\ *adj*

vit·tles \ˈvit-ᵊlz\ *n pl* : VICTUALS

vi·tu·per·ate \vī-ˈtü-pə-ˌrāt, və-, -ˈtyü-\ *vb* **-at·ed; -at·ing** : to abuse in words : SCOLD **syn** revile, berate, rate, upbraid, rail, lash — **vi·tu·per·a·tive** \-ˈtü-pə-rə-tiv, -ˈtyü-, -ˌrā-\ *adj* — **vi·tu·per·a·tive·ly** *adv*

vi·tu·per·a·tion \(ˌ)vī-tü-pə-ˈrā-shən, və-, -tyü-\ *n* : lengthy harsh criticism or abuse

vi·va \ˈvē-və\ *interj* [It & Sp, long live] — used to express goodwill or approval

vi·va·ce \vē-ˈvä-chā\ *adv or adj* [It] : in a brisk spirited manner — used as a direction in music

vi·va·cious \və-ˈvā-shəs, vī-\ *adj* : lively in temper, conduct, or spirit : SPRIGHTLY — **vi·va·cious·ly** *adv* — **vi·va·cious·ness** *n*

vi·vac·i·ty \-ˈva-sə-tē\ *n* : the quality or state of being vivacious

vi·va vo·ce \ˌvī-və-ˈvō-sē, ˌvē-və-ˈvō-ˌchā\ *adj* [ML, with the living voice] : expressed or conducted by word of mouth : ORAL — **viva voce** *adv*

viv·id \ˈvi-vəd\ *adj* **1** : having the appearance of vigorous life **2** : BRILLIANT, INTENSE ⟨a ~ red⟩ **3** : producing a strong impression on the senses; *esp* : producing distinct mental pictures ⟨a ~ description⟩ — **viv·id·ly** *adv* — **viv·id·ness** *n*

viv·i·fy \ˈvi-və-ˌfī\ *vb* **-fied; -fy·ing** **1** : to put life into : ANIMATE **2** : to make vivid — **viv·i·fi·ca·tion** \ˌvi-və-fə-ˈkā-shən\ *n* — **viv·i·fi·er** *n*

vi·vip·a·rous \vī-ˈvi-pə-rəs, və-\ *adj* : producing living young from within the body rather than from eggs — **vi·vi·par·i·ty** \ˌvī-və-ˈpar-ə-tē, ˌvi-\ *n*

viv·i·sec·tion \ˌvi-və-ˈsek-shən, ˈvi-və-ˌsek-\ *n* : the cutting of or operation on a living animal; *also* : animal experimentation esp. if causing distress to the subject

vix·en \ˈvik-sən\ *n* **1** : an ill-tempered scolding woman **2** : a female fox

viz *abbr* videlicet

viz·ard \ˈvi-zərd\ *n* : a mask for disguise or protection

vi·zier \və-ˈzir\ *n* : a high executive officer of many Muslim countries

VJ *abbr* veejay

VOA *abbr* Voice of America

voc *abbr* **1** vocational **2** vocative

vocab *abbr* vocabulary

vo·ca·ble \ˈvō-kə-bəl\ *n* : TERM, NAME; *esp* : a word as such without regard to its meaning

vo·cab·u·lary \vō-ˈka-byə-ˌler-ē\ *n, pl* **-lar·ies** **1** : a list or collection of words usu. alphabetically arranged and defined or explained : LEXICON **2** : a stock of words in a language used by a class or individual or in relation to a subject

vocabulary entry *n* : a word (as the noun *book*), hyphened or open compound (as the verb *cross-refer* or the noun *boric acid*), word element (as the affix *-an*), abbreviation (as *agt*), verbalized symbol (as *Na*), or term (as *master of ceremonies*) entered alphabetically in a dictionary for the purpose of definition or identification or expressly included as an inflected form (as the noun *mice* or the verb *saw*) or as a derived form (as the noun *godlessness* or the adverb *globally*) or related phrase (as *in spite of*) run on at its base word and usu. set in a type (as boldface) readily distinguishable from that of the lightface running text which defines, explains, or identifies the entry

¹**vo·cal** \ˈvō-kəl\ *adj* **1** : uttered by the voice : ORAL **2** : relating to, composed or arranged for, or sung by the human voice ⟨~ music⟩ **3** : given to expressing oneself freely or insistently : OUTSPOKEN **4** : of or relating to the voice

²**vocal** *n* **1** : a vocal sound **2** : a vocal composition or its performance

vocal cords *n pl* : either of two pairs of elastic folds of mucous membrane that project into the cavity of the larynx and function in the production of vocal sounds

vo·cal·ic \vō-ˈka-lik\ *adj* : of, relating to, or functioning as a vowel

vo·cal·ise *Brit var of* VOCALIZE

vo•cal•ist \ˈvō-kə-list\ *n* : SINGER
vo•cal•ize \-ˌlīz\ *vb* **-ized; -iz•ing 1** : to give vocal expression to : UTTER; *esp* : SING **2** : to make voiced rather than voiceless — **vo•cal•iz•er** *n*
vo•ca•tion \vō-ˈkā-shən\ *n* **1** : a summons or strong inclination to a particular state or course of action ⟨religious ~⟩ **2** : regular employment : OCCUPATION, PROFESSION — **vo•ca•tion•al** \-shə-nəl\ *adj*
vo•ca•tion•al•ism \-shə-nə-ˌli-zəm\ *n* : emphasis on vocational training in education
voc•a•tive \ˈvä-kə-tiv\ *adj* : of, relating to, or constituting a grammatical case marking the one addressed — **vocative** *n*
vo•cif•er•ate \vō-ˈsi-fə-ˌrāt\ *vb* **-at•ed; -at•ing** [L *vociferari*, fr. *voc-, vox* voice + *ferre* to bear] : to cry out loudly : CLAMOR, SHOUT — **vo•cif•er•a•tion** \-ˌsi-fə-ˈrā-shən\ *n*
vo•cif•er•ous \vō-ˈsi-fə-rəs\ *adj* : making or given to loud outcry — **vo•cif•er•ous•ly** *adv* — **vo•cif•er•ous•ness** *n*
vod•ka \ˈväd-kə\ *n* [Russ, fr. *voda* water] : a colorless liquor distilled from a mash
vogue \ˈvōg\ *n* [MF, action of rowing, course, fashion, fr. It *voga*, fr. *vogare* to row] **1** : popular acceptance or favor : POPULARITY **2** : a period of popularity **3** : one that is in fashion at a particular time **syn** mode, fad, rage, craze, trend, fashion
vogu•ish \ˈvō-gish\ *adj* **1** : FASHIONABLE, SMART **2** : suddenly or temporarily popular
¹**voice** \ˈvȯis\ *n* **1** : sound produced through the mouth by vertebrates and esp. by human beings in speaking or shouting **2** : musical sound produced by the vocal cords : the power to produce such sound; *also* : one of the melodic parts in a vocal or instrumental composition **3** : the vocal organs as a means of tone production ⟨train the ~⟩ **4** : sound produced by vibration of the vocal cords as heard in vowels and some consonants **5** : the power of speaking **6** : a sound suggesting a voice ⟨the ~ of the sea⟩ **7** : an instrument or medium of expression **8** : a choice, opinion, or wish openly expressed; *also* : right of expression **9** : distinction of form of a verb to indicate the relation of the subject to the action expressed by the verb
²**voice** *vb* **voiced; voic•ing** : to give voice or expression to : UTTER ⟨~ a complaint⟩ **syn** express, vent, air, ventilate
voice box *n* : LARYNX
voiced \ˈvȯist\ *adj* **1** : having a voice ⟨soft-*voiced*⟩ **2** : uttered with voice ⟨a ~ consonant⟩ — **voiced•ness** \ˈvȯist-nəs, ˈvȯi-səd-nəs\ *n*
voice•less \ˈvȯis-ləs\ *adj* **1** : having no voice **2** : not pronounced with voice — **voice•less•ly** *adv* — **voice•less•ness** *n*
voice mail *n* : an electronic communication system in which spoken messages are recorded for later playback to the intended recipient
voice–over *n* : the voice in a film or television program of a person who is heard but not seen or not seen talking
voice•print \ˈvȯis-ˌprint\ *n* : an individually distinctive pattern of voice characteristics that is spectrographically produced
¹**void** \ˈvȯid\ *adj* **1** : UNOCCUPIED, VACANT **2** : containing nothing : EMPTY **3** : LACKING, DEVOID ⟨proposals ~ of sense⟩ **4** : VAIN, USELESS **5** : of no legal force or effect : NULL
²**void** *n* **1** : empty space : EMPTINESS, VACUUM **2** : a feeling of want or hollowness
³**void** *vb* **1** : to make or leave empty; *also* : VACATE, LEAVE **2** : DISCHARGE, EMIT ⟨~ urine⟩ **3** : to render void : ANNUL, NULLIFY ⟨~ a contract⟩ — **void•able** *adj* — **void•er** *n*
voi•là \vwä-ˈlä\ *interj* [F] — used to call attention or to express satisfaction or approval
voile \ˈvȯil\ *n* : a sheer fabric used for women's clothing and curtains
vol *abbr* **1** volume **2** volunteer
vol•a•tile \ˈvä-lət-ᵊl\ *adj* **1** : readily becoming a vapor at a relatively low temperature ⟨a ~ liquid⟩ **2** : likely to change suddenly ⟨a ~ temper⟩ — **vol•a•til•i•ty** \ˌvä-lə-ˈti-lə-tē\ *n* — **vol•a•til•ize** \ˈvä-lət-ᵊl-ˌīz\ *vb*
vol•ca•nic \väl-ˈka-nik\ *adj* **1** : of, relating to, or produced by a volcano **2** : explosively violent
vol•ca•nism \ˈväl-kə-ˌni-zəm\ *n* : volcanic action or activity
vol•ca•no \väl-ˈkā-nō\ *n, pl* **-noes** *or* **-nos** [It *vulcano*, fr. L *Volcanus, Vulcanus* Roman god of fire and metalworking] : an opening in the earth's crust from which molten rock and steam issue; *also* : a hill or mountain composed of the ejected material
vol•ca•nol•o•gy \ˌväl-kə-ˈnä-lə-jē\ *n* : a branch of geology that deals with volcanic phenomena — **vol•ca•nol•o•gist** \-kə-ˈnä-lə-jist\ *n*
vole \ˈvōl\ *n* : any of various small rodents that are closely related to the lemmings and muskrats
vo•li•tion \vō-ˈli-shən\ *n* **1** : the act or the power of making a choice or decision : WILL **2** : a choice or decision made — **vo•li•tion•al** \-ˈli-shə-nəl\ *adj*
¹**vol•ley** \ˈvä-lē\ *n, pl* **volleys 1** : a flight of missiles (as arrows) **2** : simultaneous discharge of a number of missile weapons **3** : an act of volleying **4** : a burst of many things at once ⟨a ~ of angry letters⟩
²**volley** *vb* **vol•leyed; vol•ley•ing 1** : to discharge or become discharged in or as if in a volley **2** : to hit an object of play in the air before it touches the ground
vol•ley•ball \-ˌbȯl\ *n* : a game played by volleying an inflated ball over a net; *also* : the ball used in this game
volt \ˈvōlt\ *n* : the meter-kilogram-second unit of electrical potential difference and electromotive force equal to the difference in potential between two points in a wire carrying a constant current of one ampere when the power dissipated between the points is equal to one watt
volt•age \ˈvōl-tij\ *n* : potential difference measured in volts
vol•ta•ic \väl-ˈtā-ik, vōl-\ *adj* : of, relating to, or producing direct electric current by chemical action
volte–face \ˌvȯlt-ˈfäs, ˌvȯl-tə-\ *n* : a reversal in policy : ABOUT-FACE
volt•me•ter \ˈvōlt-ˌmē-tər\ *n* : an instrument for measuring in volts the difference in potential between different points of an electrical circuit
vol•u•ble \ˈväl-yə-bəl\ *adj* : fluent and smooth in speech : GLIB **syn** garrulous, loquacious, talkative — **vol•u•bil•i•ty** \ˌväl-yə-ˈbi-lə-tē\ *n* — **vol•u•bly** \ˈväl-yə-blē\ *adv*
vol•ume \ˈväl-yəm\ *n* [ME, fr. MF, fr. L *volumen* roll, scroll, fr. *volvere* to roll] **1** : a series of printed sheets bound typically in book form; *also* : an arbitrary number of issues of a periodical **2** : space occupied as measured by cubic units ⟨the ~ of a cylinder⟩ **3** : sufficient matter to fill a book ⟨her glance spoke ~*s*⟩ **4** : AMOUNT ⟨increasing ~ of business⟩ **5** : the degree of loudness of a sound **syn** body, bulk, mass
vo•lu•mi•nous \və-ˈlü-mə-nəs\ *adj* : having or marked by great volume or bulk : LARGE — **vo•lu•mi•nous•ly** *adv* — **vo•lu•mi•nous•ness** *n*
¹**vol•un•tary** \ˈvä-lən-ˌter-ē\ *adj* **1** : done, made, or given freely and without compulsion ⟨a ~ sacrifice⟩ **2** : done on purpose : INTENTIONAL ⟨~ manslaughter⟩ **3** : of, relating to, or regulated by the will ⟨~ behavior⟩ **4** : having power of free choice **5** : provided or supported by voluntary action ⟨a ~ organization⟩ **syn** deliberate, willful, willing, witting — **vol•un•tar•i•ly** \ˌvä-lən-ˈter-ə-lē\ *adv*
²**voluntary** *n, pl* **-tar•ies** : an organ solo played in a religious service
voluntary muscle *n* : muscle (as most striated muscle) under voluntary control
¹**vol•un•teer** \ˌvä-lən-ˈtir\ *n* **1** : a person who voluntarily undertakes a service or duty **2** : a plant growing spon-

taneously esp. from seeds lost from a previous crop

²**volunteer** *vb* **1** : to offer or give voluntarily **2** : to offer oneself as a volunteer

vo•lup•tu•ary \və-ˈləp-chə-ˌwer-ē\ *n, pl* **-ar•ies** : a person whose chief interest in life is the indulgence of sensual appetites

vo•lup•tuous \-chə-wəs\ *adj* **1** : giving sensual gratification **2** : given to or spent in enjoyment of luxury or pleasure **syn** luxurious, epicurean, sensuous — **vo•lup•tuous•ly** *adv* — **vo•lup•tuous•ness** *n*

vo•lute \və-ˈlüt\ *n* : a spiral or scroll-shaped decoration

¹**vom•it** \ˈvä-mət\ *n* : an act or instance of throwing up the contents of the stomach through the mouth; *also* : the matter thrown up

²**vomit** *vb* **1** : to throw up the contents of the stomach through the mouth **2** : to belch forth : GUSH

voo•doo \ˈvü-dü\ *n, pl* **voodoos 1** : a religion that is derived from African polytheism and is practiced chiefly in Haiti **2** : a person who deals in spells and necromancy; *also* : ¹SPELL 1 **3** : a charm used in voodoo — **voodoo** *adj*

voo•doo•ism \-ˌi-zəm\ *n* **1** : VOODOO 1 **2** : the practice of witchcraft

vo•ra•cious \vȯ-ˈrā-shəs, və-\ *adj* **1** : having a huge appetite : RAVENOUS **2** : very eager ⟨a ~ reader⟩ **syn** gluttonous, ravening, rapacious — **vo•ra•cious•ly** *adv* — **vo•ra•cious•ness** *n* — **vo•rac•i•ty** \-ˈra-sə-tē\ *n*

vor•tex \ˈvȯr-ˌteks\ *n, pl* **vor•ti•ces** \ˈvȯr-tə-ˌsēz\ *also* **vor•tex•es** \ˈvȯr-ˌtek-səz\ : WHIRLPOOL; *also* : something resembling a whirlpool

vo•ta•ry \ˈvō-tə-rē\ *n, pl* **-ries 1** : ENTHUSIAST, DEVOTEE; *also* : a devoted adherent or admirer **2** : a devout or zealous worshiper

¹**vote** \ˈvōt\ *n* [ME, fr. L *votum* vow, wish, fr. *vovēre* to vow] **1** : a choice or opinion of a person or body of persons expressed usu. by a ballot, spoken word, or raised hand; *also* : the ballot, word, or gesture used to express a choice or opinion **2** : the decision reached by voting **3** : the right of suffrage **4** : a group of voters with some common characteristics ⟨the big city ~⟩ — **vote•less** *adj*

²**vote** *vb* **vot•ed; vot•ing 1** : to cast a vote **2** : to elect, decide, pass, defeat, grant, or make legal by a vote **3** : to declare by general agreement **4** : to offer as a suggestion : PROPOSE **5** : to cause to vote esp. in a given way — **vot•er** *n*

vo•tive \ˈvō-tiv\ *adj* : consisting of or expressing a vow, wish, or desire

vou *abbr* voucher

vouch \ˈvau̇ch\ *vb* **1** : PROVE, SUBSTANTIATE **2** : to verify by examining documentary evidence **3** : to give a guarantee **4** : to supply supporting evidence or testimony; *also* : to give personal assurance

vouch•er \ˈvau̇-chər\ *n* **1** : an act of vouching **2** : one that vouches for another **3** : a documentary record of a business transaction **4** : a written affidavit or authorization **5** : a form indicating a credit against future purchases or expenditures

vouch•safe \vau̇ch-ˈsāf\ *vb* **vouch•safed; vouch•saf•ing** : to grant or give as or as if a privilege or a special favor — **vouch•safe•ment** *n*

¹**vow** \ˈvau̇\ *n* : a solemn promise or statement; *esp* : one by which a person is bound to an act, service, or condition ⟨marriage ~*s*⟩

²**vow** *vb* **1** : to make a vow or as a vow **2** : to bind or commit by a vow — **vow•er** *n*

vow•el \ˈvau̇-əl\ *n* **1** : a speech sound produced without obstruction or friction in the mouth **2** : a letter representing such a sound

vox po•pu•li \ˈväks-ˈpä-pyə-ˌlī\ *n* [L, voice of the people] : popular sentiment

¹**voy•age** \ˈvȯi-ij\ *n* [ME, fr. OF *voiage*, fr. LL *viaticum*, fr. L, traveling money, fr. neut. of *viaticus* of a journey, fr. *via* way] : a journey esp. by water from one place or country to another

²**voyage** *vb* **voy•aged; voy•ag•ing** : to take or make a voyage — **voy•ag•er** *n*

voya•geur \ˌvȯi-ə-ˈzhər, ˌvwä-yä-\ *n* [CanF] : a person employed by a fur company to transport goods to and from remote stations esp. in the Canadian Northwest

voy•eur \vwä-ˈyər, vȯi-ˈər\ *n* : one who habitually seeks sexual stimulation by visual means — **voy•eur•ism** \-ˌi-zəm\ *n*

VP *abbr* **1** verb phrase **2** vice president

vs *abbr* **1** verse **2** versus

vss *abbr* **1** verses **2** versions

V/STOL *abbr* vertical or short takeoff and landing

Vt *or* **VT** *abbr* Vermont

VTOL *abbr* vertical takeoff and landing

VTR *abbr* videotape recorder

vul•ca•nise *Brit var of* VULCANIZE

vul•ca•nize \ˈvəl-kə-ˌnīz\ *vb* **-nized; -niz•ing** : to treat rubber or rubberlike material chemically to give useful properties (as elasticity and strength)

Vulg *abbr* Vulgate

vul•gar \ˈvəl-gər\ *adj* [ME, fr. L *vulgaris* of the mob, vulgar, fr. *vulgus* mob, common people] **1** : VERNACULAR ⟨the ~ tongue⟩ **2** : of or relating to the common people : GENERAL, COMMON **3** : lacking cultivation or refinement : BOORISH; *also* : offensive to good taste or refined feelings **syn** gross, obscene, ribald, dirty, indecent, profane — **vul•gar•ly** *adv*

vul•gar•i•an \ˌvəl-ˈgar-ē-ən\ *n* : a vulgar person

vul•gar•ism \ˈvəl-gə-ˌri-zəm\ *n* **1** : VULGARITY **2** : a word or expression originated or used chiefly by illiterate persons **3** : a coarse expression : OBSCENITY

vul•gar•i•ty \ˌvəl-ˈgar-ə-tē\ *n, pl* **-ties 1** : something vulgar **2** : the quality or state of being vulgar

vul•gar•ize \ˈvəl-gə-ˌrīz\ *vb* **-ized; -iz•ing** : to make vulgar — **vul•gar•i•za•tion** \ˌvəl-gə-rə-ˈzā-shən\ *n* — **vul•gar•iz•er** \ˈvəl-gə-ˌrī-zər\ *n*

Vul•gate \ˈvəl-ˌgāt\ *n* [ML *vulgata*, fr. LL *vulgata editio* edition in general circulation] : a Latin version of the Bible used by the Roman Catholic Church

vul•ner•a•ble \ˈvəl-nə-rə-bəl\ *adj* **1** : capable of being wounded : susceptible to wounds **2** : open to attack **3** : liable to increased penalties in contract bridge — **vul•ner•a•bil•i•ty** \ˌvəl-nə-rə-ˈbi-lə-tē\ *n* — **vul•ner•a•bly** \ˈvəl-nə-rə-blē\ *adv*

vul•pine \ˈvəl-ˌpīn\ *adj* : of, relating to, or resembling a fox esp. in cunning

vul•ture \ˈvəl-chər\ *n* **1** : any of various large birds (as a turkey vulture) related to the hawks, eagles, and falcons but having weaker claws and the head usu. naked and living chiefly on carrion **2** : a rapacious person

vul•va \ˈvəl-və\ *n, pl* **vul•vae** \-ˌvē\ [NL, fr. L, womb, female genitals] : the external parts of the female genital organs

vv *abbr* **1** verses **2** vice versa

vying *pres part of* VIE

W

¹**w** \ˈdə-bəl-(ˌ)yü\ *n, pl* **w's** *or* **ws** *often cap* : the 23d letter of the English alphabet

²**w** *abbr, often cap* **1** water **2** watt **3** week **4** weight **5** west; western **6** wide; width **7** wife **8** with

W *symbol* [G *Wolfram*] tungsten

WA *abbr* **1** Washington **2** Western Australia

wacky \ˈwa-kē\ *adj* **wack•i•er; -est** : ECCENTRIC, CRAZY

¹**wad** \ˈwäd\ *n* **1** : a little mass, bundle, or tuft ⟨~*s* of clay⟩ **2** : a soft mass of usu. light fibrous material **3** : a pliable plug (as of felt) used to retain a powder charge (as in a cartridge) **4** : a considerable amount (as of money) **5** : a roll of paper money

[2]wad *vb* **wad•ded; wad•ding 1 :** to push a wad into ⟨∼ a gun⟩ **2 :** to form into a wad **3 :** to hold in by a wad ⟨∼ a bullet in a gun⟩ **4 :** to stuff or line with a wad : PAD

wad•ding \ˈwä-diŋ\ *n* **1 :** WADS; *also* **:** material for making wads **2 :** a soft mass or sheet of short loose fibers used for stuffing or padding

wad•dle \ˈwäd-ᵊl\ *vb* **wad•dled; wad•dling :** to walk with short steps swaying from side to side like a duck — **waddle** *n*

wade \ˈwād\ *vb* **wad•ed; wad•ing 1 :** to step in or through a medium (as water) more resistant than air **2 :** to move or go with difficulty or labor and often with determination ⟨∼ through a dull book⟩ — **wad•able** *or* **wade•able** \ˈwā-də-bəl\ *adj* — **wade** *n*

wad•er \ˈwā-dər\ *n* **1 :** one that wades **2 :** SHOREBIRD; *also* **:** WADING BIRD **3** *pl* **:** a waterproof garment consisting of pants with attached boots for wading

wa•di \ˈwä-dē\ *n* [Ar *wādiy*] **:** a streambed of southwest Asia and northern Africa that is dry except in the rainy season

wading bird *n* **:** any of an order of long-legged birds (as sandpipers, cranes, or herons) that wade in water in search of food

wa•fer \ˈwā-fər\ *n* **1 :** a thin crisp cake or cracker **2 :** a thin round piece of unleavened bread used in the Eucharist **3 :** something (as a piece of candy) that resembles a wafer

waf•fle \ˈwä-fəl\ *n* **:** a soft but crisped cake of batter cooked in a special hinged metal utensil **(waffle iron)**

[1]waft \ˈwäft, ˈwaft\ *vb* **:** to cause to move or go lightly by or as if by the impulse of wind or waves

[2]waft *n* **1 :** a slight breeze **:** PUFF **2 :** the act of waving

[1]wag \ˈwag\ *vb* **wagged; wag•ging 1 :** to sway or swing shortly from side to side or to-and-fro ⟨the dog *wagged* his tail⟩ **2 :** to move in chatter or gossip ⟨scandal caused tongues to ∼⟩

[2]wag *n* **:** an act of wagging **:** a wagging movement

[3]wag *n* **:** WIT, JOKER

[1]wage \ˈwāj\ *n* **1 :** payment for labor or services usu. according to contract **2** *pl* **:** RECOMPENSE, REWARD

[2]wage *vb* **waged; wag•ing 1 :** to engage in **:** CARRY ON ⟨∼ a war⟩ **2 :** to be in process of being waged

[1]wa•ger \ˈwā-jər\ *n* **1 :** BET, STAKE **2 :** something on which bets are laid **:** GAMBLE

[2]wager *vb* **:** BET — **wa•ger•er** *n*

wag•gery \ˈwa-gə-rē\ *n, pl* **-ger•ies 1 :** mischievous merriment **:** PLEASANTRY **2 :** JEST, TRICK

wag•gish \ˈwa-gish\ *adj* **1 :** resembling or characteristic of a wag **:** MISCHIEVOUS **2 :** SPORTIVE, HUMOROUS

wag•gle \ˈwa-gəl\ *vb* **wag•gled; wag•gling :** to move backward and forward or from side to side **:** WAG — **waggle** *n*

wag•gon *chiefly Brit var of* WAGON

wag•on \ˈwa-gən\ *n* **1 :** a 4-wheeled vehicle; *esp* **:** one drawn by animals and used for freight or merchandise **2 :** PADDY WAGON **3 :** a child's 4-wheeled cart **4 :** STATION WAGON

wag•on•er \ˈwa-gə-nər\ *n* **:** the driver of a wagon

wag•on•ette \ˌwa-gə-ˈnet\ *n* **:** a light wagon with two facing seats along the sides behind a cross seat in front

wa•gon–lit \ˌvà-gōⁿ-ˈlē\ *n, pl* **wagons–lits** *or* **wagon–lits** *same or* -ˈlēz\ [F, fr. *wagon* railroad car + *lit* bed] **:** a railroad sleeping car

wagon train *n* **:** a column of wagons traveling overland

wag•tail \ˈwag-ˌtāl\ *n* **:** any of various slender-bodied mostly Old World birds with a long tail that jerks up and down

wa•hi•ne \wä-ˈhē-nē, -ˌnā\ *n* **1 :** a Polynesian woman **2 :** a female surfer

wa•hoo \ˈwä-ˌhü\ *n, pl* **wahoos :** a large vigorous food and sport fish related to the mackerel and found in warm seas

waif \ˈwāf\ *n* **1 :** something found without an owner and esp. by chance **2 :** a stray person or animal; *esp* **:** a homeless child

wail \ˈwāl\ *vb* **1 :** LAMENT, WEEP **2 :** to make a sound suggestive of a mournful cry **3 :** COMPLAIN — **wail** *n*

wail•ful \-fəl\ *adj* **:** SORROWFUL, MOURNFUL **syn** melancholy, doleful, lugubrious, lamentable, plaintive, woeful — **wail•ful•ly** *adv*

wain \ˈwān\ *n* **:** a usu. large heavy farm wagon

wain•scot \ˈwān-skət, -ˌskōt, -ˌskät\ *n* **1 :** a usu. paneled wooden lining of an interior wall of a room **2 :** the lower part of an interior wall when finished differently from the rest — **wainscot** *vb*

wain•scot•ing *or* **wain•scot•ting** \-ˌskō-tiŋ, -ˌskä-, -skə-\ *n* **:** material for a wainscot; *also* **:** WAINSCOT

waist \ˈwāst\ *n* **1 :** the narrowed part of the body between the chest and hips **2 :** a part resembling the human waist esp. in narrowness or central position ⟨the ∼ of a ship⟩ **3 :** a garment or part of a garment (as a blouse or bodice) for the upper part of the body

waist•band \-ˌband\ *n* **:** a band (as on trousers or a skirt) that fits around the waist

waist•coat \ˈwes-kət, ˈwāst-ˌkōt\ *n, chiefly Brit* **:** VEST 1

waist•line \ˈwāst-ˌlīn\ *n* **1 :** a line around the waist at its narrowest part; *also* **:** the length of this **2 :** the line at which the bodice and skirt of a dress meet

[1]wait \ˈwāt\ *vb* **1 :** to remain inactive in readiness or expectation **:** AWAIT ⟨∼ for orders⟩ **2 :** to delay serving (a meal) **3 :** to act as attendant or servant ⟨∼ on customers⟩ **4 :** to attend as a waiter **:** SERVE ⟨∼ tables⟩ ⟨∼ at a banquet⟩ **5 :** to be ready

[2]wait *n* **1 :** a position of concealment usu. with intent to attack or surprise ⟨lie in ∼⟩ **2 :** an act or period of waiting

wait•er \ˈwā-tər\ *n* **1 :** one that waits on another; *esp* **:** a person who waits tables **2 :** TRAY

waiting game *n* **:** a strategy in which one or more participants withhold action in the hope of an opportunity for more effective action later

waiting room *n* **:** a room (as at a doctor's office) for the use of persons who are waiting

wait•per•son \ˈwāt-ˌpər-sən\ *n* **:** a waiter or waitress

wait•ress \ˈwā-trəs\ *n* **:** a woman who waits tables

waive \ˈwāv\ *vb* **waived; waiv•ing** [ME *weiven,* fr. OF *weyver,* fr. *waif* lost, unclaimed] **1 :** to give up claim to ⟨*waived* his right to a trial⟩ **2 :** POSTPONE

waiv•er \ˈwā-vər\ *n* **:** the act of waiving right, claim, or privilege; *also* **:** a document containing a declaration of such an act

[1]wake \ˈwāk\ *vb* **woke** \ˈwōk\ *also* **waked** \ˈwākt\; **wo•ken** \ˈwō-kən\ *also* **waked** *or* **woke; wak•ing 1 :** to be or remain awake; *esp* **:** to keep watch (as over a corpse) **2 :** AWAKE, AWAKEN ⟨the baby *woke* up early⟩

[2]wake *n* **1 :** the state of being awake **2 :** a watch held over the body of a dead person prior to burial

[3]wake *n* **:** the track left by a ship in the water; *also* **:** a track left behind

wake•ful \ˈwāk-fəl\ *adj* **:** not sleeping or able to sleep **:** SLEEPLESS, ALERT — **wake•ful•ness** *n*

wak•en \ˈwā-kən\ *vb* **:** WAKE

wake–rob•in \ˈwāk-ˌrä-bən\ *n* **:** TRILLIUM

wak•ing \ˈwā-kiŋ\ *adj* **:** passed in a conscious or alert state ⟨every ∼ hour⟩

wale \ˈwāl\ *n* **:** a ridge esp. on cloth; *also* **:** the texture esp. of a fabric

[1]walk \ˈwȯk\ *vb* [partly fr. ME *walken,* fr. OE *wealcan* to roll, toss and partly fr. ME *walkien,* fr. OE *wealcian* to roll up, muffle up] **1 :** to move or cause to move on foot usu. at a natural unhurried gait ⟨∼ to town⟩ ⟨∼ a horse⟩ **2 :** to pass over, through, or along by walking ⟨∼ the streets⟩ **3 :** to perform or accomplish by walking ⟨∼ guard⟩ **4 :** to follow a course of action or way of life ⟨∼ humbly in the sight of God⟩ **5 :** WALK OUT **6 :** to receive a base on balls; *also* **:** to give a base on balls to — **walk•er** *n*

[2]walk *n* **1 :** a going on foot ⟨go for a ∼⟩ **2 :** a place, path, or course for walking **3** : distance to be walked ⟨a quarter-mile ~ from here⟩ **4** : manner of living : CONDUCT, BEHAVIOR **5** : social or economic status ⟨various ~*s* of life⟩ **6** : manner of walking : GAIT; *esp* : a slow 4-beat gait of a horse **7** : BASE ON BALLS

walk•away \ˈwȯ-kə-ˌwā\ *n* : an easily won contest

walk•ie–talk•ie \ˌwȯ-kē-ˈtȯ-kē\ *n* : a small portable radio transmitting and receiving set

¹walk–in \ˈwȯk-ˌin\ *adj* : large enough to be walked into ⟨a ~ refrigerator⟩

²walk–in *n* **1** : an easy election victory **2** : one that walks in

walking papers *n pl* : DISMISSAL, DISCHARGE

walking stick *n* **1** : a stick used in walking **2** *usu* **walk•ing•stick** : STICK INSECT; *esp* : one common in parts of the U.S.

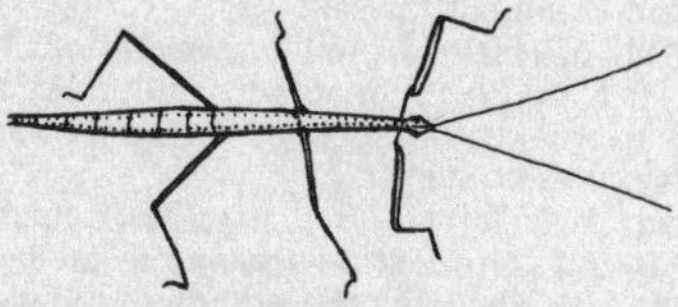

walking stick 2

walk–on \ˈwȯk-ˌȯn, -ˌän\ *n* : a small part in a dramatic production

walk•out \-ˌau̇t\ *n* **1** : a labor strike **2** : the action of leaving a meeting or organization as an expression of disapproval

walk out *vb* **1** : to leave suddenly often as an expression of disapproval **2** : to go on strike

walk•over \-ˌō-vər\ *n* : a one-sided contest : an easy victory

walk–up \ˈwȯk-ˌəp\ *n* : a building or apartment house without an elevator — **walk–up** *adj*

walk•way \-ˌwā\ *n* : a passage for walking

¹wall \ˈwȯl\ *n* [ME, fr. OE *weall,* fr. L *vallum* rampart, fr. *vallus* stake, palisade] **1** : a structure (as of stone or brick) intended for defense or security or for enclosing something **2** : one of the upright enclosing parts of a building or room **3** : the inside surface of a cavity or container ⟨the ~ of a boiler⟩ **4** : something like a wall in appearance, function, or effect ⟨a tariff ~⟩ — **walled** \ˈwȯld\ *adj*

²wall *vb* **1** : to provide, separate, or surround with or as if with a wall ⟨~ in a garden⟩ **2** : to close (an opening) with or as if with a wall ⟨~ up a door⟩

wal•la•by \ˈwä-lə-bē\ *n, pl* **wallabies** *also* **wallaby** : any of various small or medium-sized kangaroos

wall•board \ˈwȯl-ˌbōrd\ *n* : a structural material (as of wood pulp or plaster) made in large sheets and used for sheathing interior walls and ceilings

wal•let \ˈwä-lət\ *n* **1** : a bag or sack for carrying things on a journey **2** : a pocketbook with compartments (as for personal papers and usu. unfolded money) : BILLFOLD

wall•eye \ˈwȯ-ˌlī\ *n* **1** : an eye with a whitish iris or an opaque white cornea **2** : a large vigorous No. American food and sport fish related to the perches — **wall•eyed** \-ˌlīd\ *adj*

wall•flow•er \ˈwȯl-ˌflau̇-ər\ *n* **1** : any of several Old World plants related to the mustards; *esp* : one with showy fragrant flowers **2** : a person who usu. from shyness or unpopularity remains alone (as at a dance)

Wal•loon \wä-ˈlün\ *n* : a member of a people of southern and southeastern Belgium and adjacent parts of France — **Walloon** *adj*

¹wal•lop \ˈwä-ləp\ *vb* [ME *walopen* to gallop, fr. OF *waloper*] **1** : to beat soundly : TROUNCE **2** : to hit hard : SOCK **syn** batter, beat, lambaste, pound, pummel, thrash

²wallop *n* **1** : a powerful blow or impact **2** : the ability to hit hard **3** : emotional, sensory, or psychological force : IMPACT

wal•lop•ing \ˈwä-lə-piŋ\ *adj* **1** : LARGE, WHOPPING **2** : exceptionally fine or impressive

¹wal•low \ˈwä-lō\ *vb* **1** : to roll oneself about sluggishly in or as if in deep mud ⟨hogs ~*ing* in the mire⟩ **2** : to indulge oneself excessively ⟨~ in luxury⟩ **3** : to become or remain helpless ⟨~ in ignorance⟩ **syn** bask, indulge, luxuriate, revel, welter

²wallow *n* : a muddy or dust-filled area where animals wallow

wall•pa•per \ˈwȯl-ˌpā-pər\ *n* : decorative paper for the walls of a room — **wallpaper** *vb*

wall–to–wall *adj* **1** : covering the entire floor ⟨*wall-to-wall* carpeting⟩ **2** : covering or filling one entire space or time ⟨crowds of *wall-to-wall* people⟩

wal•nut \ˈwȯl-(ˌ)nət\ *n* [ME *walnot,* fr. OE *wealhhnutu,* lit., foreign nut, fr. *Wealh* Welshman, foreigner + *hnutu* nut] **1** : a nut with a furrowed usu. rough shell and an adherent husk from any of a genus of trees related to the hickories; *esp* : the large edible nut of a Eurasian tree **2** : a tree that bears walnuts **3** : the usu. reddish to dark brown wood of a walnut used esp. in cabinetwork and veneers

wal•rus \ˈwȯl-rəs, ˈwäl-\ *n, pl* **walrus** *or* **wal•rus•es** : a large mammal of northern seas related to the seals and having ivory tusks

¹waltz \ˈwȯlts\ *n* [G *Walzer,* fr. *walzen* to roll, dance] **1** : a gliding dance done to music having three beats to the measure **2** : music for or suitable for waltzing

²waltz *vb* **1** : to dance a waltz **2** : to move or advance easily, successfully, or conspicuously ⟨he ~*ed* off with the championship⟩

wam•ble \ˈwäm-bəl\ *vb* **wam•bled; wam•bling** : to progress unsteadily or with a lurching shambling gait

wam•pum \ˈwäm-pəm\ *n* [short for *wampumpeag,* fr. Massachuset (a North American Indian language) *wampompeag,* fr. *wampan* white + *api* string + *-ag,* pl. suffix] **1** : beads made of shells strung in strands, belts, or sashes and used by No. American Indians as money and ornaments **2** *slang* : MONEY

wan \ˈwän\ *adj* **wan•ner; wan•nest 1** : SICKLY, PALLID; *also* : FEEBLE **2** : DIM, FAINT **3** : LANGUID ⟨a ~ smile⟩ **syn** ashen, blanched, doughy, livid, pale, waxen — **wan•ly** *adv* — **wan•ness** *n*

wand \ˈwänd\ *n* **1** : a slender staff carried in a procession **2** : the staff of a fairy, diviner, or magician

wan•der \ˈwän-dər\ *vb* **1** : to move about aimlessly or without a fixed course or goal : RAMBLE **2** : to go astray in conduct or thought; *esp* : to become delirious **syn** gad, gallivant, meander, range, roam, rove — **wan•der•er** *n*

wandering Jew *n* : either of two trailing or creeping plants cultivated for their showy and often white-striped foliage

wan•der•lust \ˈwän-dər-ˌləst\ *n* : strong longing for or impulse toward wandering

¹wane \ˈwān\ *vb* **waned; wan•ing 1** : to grow gradually smaller or less ⟨the moon ~*s*⟩ ⟨his strength *waned*⟩ **2** : to lose power, prosperity, or influence **3** : to draw near an end ⟨summer is *waning*⟩ **syn** abate, ebb, moderate, relent, slacken, subside

²wane *n* : a waning (as in size or power); *also* : a period in which something is waning

wan•gle \ˈwaŋ-gəl\ *vb* **wan•gled; wan•gling 1** : to obtain by sly or devious means; *also* : to use trickery or questionable means to achieve an end **2** : MANIPULATE; *also* : FINAGLE

wan•na–be \ˈwä-nə-ˌbē\ *n* : a person who wants or aspires to be someone or something else or who tries to look or act like someone else

¹want \ˈwȯnt, ˈwänt\ *vb* **1** : to fail to possess : LACK ⟨they ~ the necessities of life⟩ **2** : to feel or suffer the need of **3** : NEED, REQUIRE ⟨the house ~*s* painting⟩ **4** : to desire earnestly : WISH

²want *n* **1** : a lack of a required or usual amount

: SHORTAGE **2** : dire need : DESTITUTION **3** : something wanted : DESIRE **4** : personal defect : FAULT

¹want•ing \ˈwȯn-tiŋ, ˈwän-\ *adj* **1** : not present or in evidence : ABSENT **2** : falling below standards or expectations **3** : lacking in ability or capacity : DEFICIENT ⟨~ in common sense⟩

²wanting *prep* **1** : LESS, MINUS ⟨a month ~ two days⟩ **2** : WITHOUT ⟨a book ~ a cover⟩

¹wan•ton \ˈwȯnt-ᵊn, ˈwänt-\ *adj* [ME, undisciplined, fr. *wan-* deficient, wrong + *towen*, pp. of *teen* to draw, train, discipline] **1** : UNCHASTE, LEWD, LUSTFUL; *also* : SENSUAL **2** : having no regard for justice or for other persons' feelings, rights, or safety : MERCILESS, INHUMANE ⟨~cruelty⟩ **3** : having no just cause ⟨a ~ attack⟩ — **wan•ton•ly** *adv* — **wan•ton•ness** *n*

²wanton *n* : a wanton individual; *esp* : a lewd or immoral person

³wanton *vb* **1** : to be wanton : act wantonly **2** : to pass or waste wantonly

wa•pi•ti \ˈwä-pə-tē\ *n, pl* **wapiti** *or* **wapitis** : ELK 2

¹war \ˈwȯr\ *n* **1** : a state or period of usu. open and declared armed fighting between states or nations **2** : the art or science of warfare **3** : a state of hostility, conflict, or antagonism **4** : a struggle between opposing forces or for a particular end ⟨~ against disease⟩ — **war•less** \-ləs\ *adj*

²war *vb* **warred; war•ring** : to engage in warfare : be in conflict

³war *abbr* warrant

¹war•ble \ˈwȯr-bəl\ *n* **1** : a melodious succession of low pleasing sounds **2** : a musical trill

²warble *vb* **war•bled; war•bling 1** : to sing or utter in a trilling manner or with variations **2** : to express by or as if by warbling

³warble *n* : a swelling under the hide esp. of the back of cattle, horses, and wild mammals caused by the maggot of a fly (**warble fly**); *also* : its maggot

war•bler \ˈwȯr-blər\ *n* **1** : SONGSTER **2** : any of various small slender-billed Old World singing birds related to the thrushes and noted for their song **3** : any of numerous small bright-colored American insect-eating birds with a usu. weak and unmusical song

war•bon•net \ˈwȯr-ˌbä-nət\ *n* : a feathered American Indian ceremonial headdress

war cry *n* **1** : a cry used by fighters in war **2** : a slogan used esp. to rally people to a cause

¹ward \ˈwȯrd\ *n* **1** : a guarding or being under guard or guardianship; *esp* : CUSTODY **2** : a body of guards **3** : a division of a prison **4** : a division in a hospital **5** : a division of a city for electoral or administrative purposes **6** : a person (as a child) under the protection of a guardian or a law court **7** : a person or body of persons under the protection or tutelage of a government **8** : a means of defense : PROTECTION

²ward *vb* : to turn aside : DEFLECT — usu. used with *off* ⟨~ off a blow⟩

¹-ward \wərd\ *also* **-wards** \wərdz\ *adj suffix* **1** : that moves, tends, faces, or is directed toward ⟨wind*ward*⟩ **2** : that occurs or is situated in the direction of ⟨sea*ward*⟩

²-ward *or* **-wards** *adv suffix* **1** : in a (specified) direction ⟨up*wards*⟩ ⟨after*ward*⟩ **2** : toward a (specified) point, position, or area ⟨sky*ward*⟩

war dance *n* : a dance performed (as by American Indians) before going to war or in celebration of victory

war•den \ˈwȯrd-ᵊn\ *n* **1** : GUARDIAN, KEEPER **2** : the governor of a town, district, or fortress **3** : an official charged with special supervisory or enforcement duties ⟨game ~⟩ ⟨air raid ~⟩ **4** : an official in charge of the operation of a prison **5** : one of two ranking lay officers of an Episcopal parish **6** : any of various British college officials

ward•er \ˈwȯr-dər\ *n* : WATCHMAN, WARDEN

ward heel•er \-ˌhē-lər\ *n* : a local worker for a political boss

ward•robe \ˈwȯr-ˌdrōb\ *n* [ME *warderobe*, fr. OF, fr. *warder* to guard + *robe* robe] **1** : a room or closet where clothes are kept; *also* : CLOTHESPRESS **2** : a collection of wearing apparel ⟨his summer ~⟩

ward•room \-ˌdrüm, -ˌdrům\ *n* : the dining area for officers aboard a warship

ward•ship \ˈwȯrd-ˌship\ *n* **1** : GUARDIANSHIP **2** : the state of being under care of a guardian

ware \ˈwar\ *n* **1** : manufactured articles or products of art or craft : GOODS ⟨glass*ware*⟩ **2** : an article of merchandise ⟨a peddler hawking his ~*s*⟩ **3** : items (as dishes) of fired clay : POTTERY

ware•house \-ˌhau̇s\ *n* : a place for the storage of merchandise or commodities : STOREHOUSE — **warehouse** *vb* — **ware•house•man** \-mən\ *n* — **ware•hous•er** \-ˌhau̇-zər, -sər\ *n*

ware•room \ˈwar-ˌrüm, -ˌrům\ *n* : a room in which goods are exhibited for sale

war•fare \ˈwȯr-ˌfar\ *n* **1** : military operations between enemies : WAR; *also* : an activity undertaken by one country to weaken or destroy another ⟨economic ~⟩ **2** : STRUGGLE, CONFLICT

war•fa•rin \ˈwȯr-fə-rən\ *n* : an anticoagulant compound used as a rodent poison and in medicine

war•head \ˈwȯr-ˌhed\ *n* : the section of a missile containing the charge

war•horse \-ˌhȯrs\ *n* **1** : a horse for use in war **2** : a veteran soldier or public person (as a politician)

war•like \-ˌlīk\ *adj* **1** : fond of war ⟨~ peoples⟩ **2** : of, relating to, or useful in war : MILITARY, MARTIAL ⟨~ supplies⟩ **3** : befitting or characteristic of war or of soldiers ⟨~ attitudes⟩

war•lock \-ˌläk\ *n* [ME *warloghe*, fr. OE *wǣrloga* one that breaks faith, the Devil, fr. *wǣr* faith, troth + *-loga* (fr. *lēogan* to lie)] : SORCERER, WIZARD

war•lord \-ˌlȯrd\ *n* **1** : a high military leader **2** : a military commander exercising local civil power by force ⟨former Chinese ~*s*⟩

¹warm \ˈwȯrm\ *adj* **1** : having or giving out heat to a moderate or adequate degree ⟨~ milk⟩ ⟨a ~ stove⟩ **2** : serving to retain heat ⟨~ clothes⟩ **3** : feeling or inducing sensations of heat ⟨~ from exercise⟩ ⟨a ~ climb⟩ **4** : showing or marked by strong feeling : ARDENT ⟨~ support⟩ **5** : marked by tense excitement or hot anger ⟨a ~ campaign⟩ **6** : giving a pleasant impression of warmth, cheerfulness, or friendliness ⟨~ colors⟩ ⟨a ~ tone of voice⟩ **7** : marked by or tending toward injury, distress, or pain ⟨made things ~ for the enemy⟩ **8** : newly made : FRESH ⟨a ~ scent⟩ **9** : near to a goal ⟨getting ~ in a search⟩ — **warm•ly** *adv*

²warm *vb* **1** : to make or become warm **2** : to give a feeling of warmth or vitality to **3** : to experience feelings of affection or pleasure ⟨she ~*ed* to her guest⟩ **4** : to reheat for eating ⟨~*ed* over the roast⟩ **5** : to make ready for operation or performance by preliminary exercise or operation ⟨~ up the motor⟩ **6** : to become increasingly ardent, interested, or competent ⟨the speaker ~*ed* to his topic⟩ — **warm•er** *n*

warm–blood•ed \-ˈblə-dəd\ *adj* : able to maintain a relatively high and constant body temperature relatively independent of that of the surroundings

warmed–over \ˈwȯrmd-ˈō-vər\ *adj* **1** : REHEATED ⟨~ cabbage⟩ **2** : not fresh or new ⟨~ ideas⟩

warm front *n* : an advancing edge of a warm air mass

warm•heart•ed \ˈwȯrm-ˈhär-təd\ *adj* : marked by warmth of feeling : CORDIAL — **warm•heart•ed•ness** *n*

warming pan *n* : a long-handled covered pan filled with live coals and formerly used to warm a bed

war•mon•ger \ˈwȯr-ˌməŋ-gər, -ˌmäŋ-\ *n* : one who urges or attempts to stir up war

warmth \ˈwȯrmth\ *n* **1** : the quality or state of being warm **2** : ZEAL, ARDOR, FERVOR

warm up *vb* : to engage in exercise or practice esp. be-

fore entering a game or contest — **warm–up** \ˈwȯrm-ˌəp\ *n*
warn \ˈwȯrn\ *vb* **1** : to put on guard : CAUTION; *also* : ADMONISH, COUNSEL **2** : to notify esp. in advance : INFORM **3** : to order to go or keep away
¹warn•ing \ˈwȯr-niŋ\ *n* **1** : the act of warning : the state of being warned **2** : something that warns or serves to warn
²warning *adj* : serving as an alarm, signal, summons, or admonition ⟨~ bell⟩ — **warn•ing•ly** *adv*
¹warp \ˈwȯrp\ *n* **1** : the lengthwise threads on a loom or in a woven fabric **2** : a twist out of a true plane or straight line ⟨a ~ in a board⟩
²warp *vb* [ME, fr. OE *weorpan* to throw] **1** : to turn or twist out of shape; *also* : to become so twisted **2** : to lead astray : PERVERT; *also* : FALSIFY, DISTORT
war paint *n* : paint put on the face and body by American Indians as a sign of going to war
war•path \ˈwȯr-ˌpath, -ˌpȧth\ *n* : the course taken by a party of American Indians going on a hostile expedition — **on the warpath** : ready to fight or argue
war•plane \-ˌplān\ *n* : a military airplane; *esp* : one armed for combat
¹war•rant \ˈwȯr-ənt, ˈwär-\ *n* **1** : AUTHORIZATION; *also* : JUSTIFICATION, GROUND **2** : evidence (as a document) of authorization; *esp* : a legal writ authorizing an officer to take action (as in making an arrest, seizure, or search) **3** : a certificate of appointment issued to an officer of lower rank than a commissioned officer
²warrant *vb* **1** : to guarantee security or immunity to : SECURE **2** : to declare or maintain positively ⟨I ~ this is so⟩ **3** : to assure (a person) of the truth of what is said **4** : to guarantee to be as it appears or as it is represented ⟨~ goods as of the first quality⟩ **5** : SANCTION, AUTHORIZE **6** : to give proof of : ATTEST; *also* : GUARANTEE **7** : JUSTIFY ⟨his need ~*s* the expenditure⟩
warrant officer *n* **1** : an officer in the armed forces ranking next below a commissioned officer **2** : a commissioned officer ranking below an ensign in the navy or coast guard and below a second lieutenant in the marine corps
war•ran•ty \ˈwȯr-ən-tē, ˈwär-\ *n, pl* **-ties** : an expressed or implied statement that some situation or thing is as it appears to be or is represented to be; *esp* : a usu. written guarantee of the integrity of a product and of the maker's responsibility for the repair or replacement of defective parts
war•ren \ˈwȯr-ən, ˈwär-\ *n* **1** : an area where rabbits breed; *also* : a structure where rabbits are bred or kept **2** : a crowded tenement or district
war•rior \ˈwȯr-yər; ˈwȯr-ē-ər, ˈwär-\ *n* : a man engaged or experienced in warfare
war•ship \ˈwȯr-ˌship\ *n* : a naval vessel
wart \ˈwȯrt\ *n* **1** : a small usu. horny projecting growth on the skin; *esp* : one caused by a virus **2** : a protuberance resembling a wart (as on a plant) — **warty** *adj*
wart•hog \ˈwȯrt-ˌhȯg, -ˌhäg\ *n* : a wild African hog which has large tusks and the males of which have two pairs of rough warty protuberances below the eyes
war•time \ˈwȯr-ˌtīm\ *n* : a period during which a war is in progress
wary \ˈwar-ē\ *adj* **war•i•er; -est** : very cautious; *esp* : careful in guarding against danger or deception
was *past 1st & 3d sing of* BE
¹wash \ˈwȯsh, ˈwäsh\ *vb* **1** : to clean with water and usu. soap or detergent ⟨~ clothes⟩ ⟨~ your hands⟩ **2** : to wet thoroughly : DRENCH **3** : to flow along the border of ⟨waves ~ the shore⟩ **4** : to pour or flow in a stream or current **5** : to move or remove by or as if by the action of water **6** : to cover or daub lightly with a liquid (as whitewash) **7** : to run water over (as gravel or ore) in order to separate valuable matter from refuse ⟨~ sand for gold⟩ **8** : to undergo laundering ⟨a dress that doesn't ~ well⟩ **9** : to stand a test ⟨that story will not ~⟩ **10** : to be worn away by water
²wash *n* **1** : the act or process or an instance of washing or being washed **2** : articles to be washed or being washed **3** : the flow or action of a mass of water (as a wave) **4** : erosion by waves (as of the sea) **5** *West* : the dry bed of a stream **6** : worthless esp. liquid waste : REFUSE, SWILL **7** : a thin coat of paint (as watercolor) **8** : a disturbance in the air caused by the passage of a wing or propeller
³wash *adj* : WASHABLE
Wash *abbr* Washington
wash•able \ˈwȯ-shə-bəl, ˈwä-\ *adj* : capable of being washed without damage
wash–and–wear *adj* : of, relating to, or being a fabric or garment that needs little or no ironing after washing
wash•ba•sin \ˈwȯsh-ˌbās-ᵊn, ˈwäsh-\ *n* : WASHBOWL
wash•board \-ˌbōrd\ *n* : a grooved board to scrub clothes on
wash•bowl \-ˌbōl\ *n* : a large bowl for water for washing hands and face
wash•cloth \-ˌklȯth\ *n* : a cloth used for washing one's face and body
washed–out \ˈwȯsht-ˈau̇t, ˈwäsht-\ *adj* **1** : faded in color **2** : EXHAUSTED ⟨felt ~ after working all night⟩
washed–up \-ˈəp\ *adj* : no longer successful, popular, skillful, or needed
wash•er \ˈwȯ-shər, ˈwä-\ *n* **1** : a ring or perforated plate used around a bolt or screw to ensure tightness or relieve friction **2** : one that washes; *esp* : a machine for washing
wash•er•wom•an \-ˌwu̇-mən\ *n* : a woman whose occupation is washing clothes
wash•house \ˈwȯsh-ˌhau̇s, ˈwäsh-\ *n* : a house or building for washing clothes
wash•ing \ˈwȯ-shiŋ, ˈwä-\ *n* **1** : material obtained by washing **2** : articles washed or to be washed
washing soda *n* : SODIUM CARBONATE
Wash•ing•ton's Birthday \ˈwȯ-shiŋ-tənz-, ˈwä-\ *n* : the 3d Monday in February observed as a legal holiday
wash•out \ˈwȯsh-ˌau̇t, ˈwäsh-\ *n* **1** : the washing away of earth (as from a road); *also* : a place where earth is washed away **2** : a complete failure
wash•room \-ˌrüm, -ˌru̇m\ *n* : BATHROOM
wash•stand \-ˌstand\ *n* **1** : a stand holding articles needed for washing face and hands **2** : LAVATORY 1
wash•tub \-ˌtəb\ *n* : a tub for washing or soaking clothes
wash•wom•an \ˈwȯsh-ˌwu̇-mən, ˈwäsh-\ *n* : WASHERWOMAN
washy \ˈwȯ-shē, ˈwä-\ *adj* **wash•i•er; -est** **1** : WEAK, WATERY **2** : PALLID **3** : lacking in vigor, individuality, or definiteness
wasp \ˈwäsp, ˈwȯsp\ *n* : any of numerous social or solitary winged insects related to the bees and ants with biting mouthparts and in females and workers an often formidable sting
WASP *or* **Wasp** *n* [*w*hite *A*nglo-*S*axon *P*rotestant] : an American of northern European and esp. British ancestry and of Protestant background
wasp•ish \ˈwäs-pish, ˈwȯs-\ *adj* **1** : SNAPPISH, IRRITABLE **2** : resembling a wasp in form; *esp* : slightly built **syn** fractious, fretful, huffy, peevish, petulant, querulous
wasp waist *n* : a very slender waist
¹was•sail \ˈwä-səl, wä-ˈsāl\ *n* [ME *wæs hæil,* fr. ON *ves heill* be well] **1** : an early English toast to someone's health **2** : a hot drink made with wine, beer, or cider, spices, sugar, and usu. baked apples and traditionally served at Christmas **3** : riotous drinking : REVELRY
²wassail *vb* **1** : CAROUSE **2** : to drink to the health of — **was•sail•er** *n*

Was•ser•mann test \ˈwä-sər-mən-, ˈvä-\ *n* : a blood test for infection with syphilis

wast•age \ˈwā-stij\ *n* : WASTE 3

¹waste \ˈwāst\ *n* **1** : a sparsely settled or barren region : DESERT; *also* : uncultivated land **2** : the act or an instance of wasting : the state of being wasted **3** : gradual loss or decrease by use, wear, or decay **4** : material left over, rejected, or thrown away; *also* : an unwanted by-product of a manufacturing or chemical process **5** : refuse (as garbage) that accumulates about habitations **6** : material (as feces) produced but not used by a living organism — **waste•ful** \-fəl\ *adj* — **waste•ful•ly** *adv* — **waste•ful•ness** *n*

²waste *vb* **wast•ed; wast•ing 1** : DEVASTATE **2** : to wear away or diminish gradually : CONSUME **3** : to spend or use carelessly or uselessly : SQUANDER **4** : to lose or cause to lose weight, strength, or energy ⟨*wasting* away from fever⟩ **5** : to become diminished in bulk or substance : DWINDLE **syn** depredate, desolate, despoil, ravage, spoil, strip — **wast•er** *n*

³waste *adj* **1** : being wild and uninhabited : BARREN, DESOLATE; *also* : UNCULTIVATED **2** : being in a ruined condition **3** : discarded as worthless after being used ⟨~ water⟩ **4** : excreted from or stored in inert form in a living organism as a by-product of vital activity ⟨~ matter from birds⟩

waste•bas•ket \ˈwāst-ˌbas-kət\ *n* : a receptacle for refuse

waste•land \-ˌland, -lənd\ *n* : land that is barren or unfit for cultivation

waste•pa•per \-ˈpā-pər\ *n* : paper thrown away as used, not needed, or not fit for use

wast•rel \ˈwā-strəl\ *n* : one that wastes : SPENDTHRIFT

¹watch \ˈwäch, ˈwȯch\ *vb* **1** : to be or stay awake intentionally : keep vigil ⟨~*ed* by the patient's bedside⟩ ⟨~ and pray⟩ **2** : to be on the lookout for danger : be on one's guard **3** : to keep guard ⟨~ outside the door⟩ **4** : OBSERVE ⟨~ a game⟩ **5** : to keep in view so as to prevent harm or warn of danger ⟨~ a brush fire carefully⟩ **6** : to keep oneself informed about ⟨~ his progress⟩ **7** : to lie in wait for esp. so as to take advantage of ⟨~*ed* her opportunity⟩ — **watch•er** *n*

²watch *n* **1** : the act of keeping awake to guard, protect, or attend; *also* : a state of alert and continuous attention **2** : a public weather alert ⟨tornado ~⟩ **3** : close observation **4** : LOOKOUT, WATCHMAN, GUARD **5** : a period during which a part of a ship's crew is on duty; *also* : the part of a crew on duty during a watch **6** : a portable timepiece carried on the person

watch•band \ˈwäch-ˌband, ˈwȯch-\ *n* : the bracelet or strap of a wristwatch

watch•dog \-ˌdȯg\ *n* **1** : a dog kept to guard property **2** : one that guards or protects

watch•ful \-fəl\ *adj* : steadily attentive and alert esp. to danger : VIGILANT — **watch•ful•ly** *adv* — **watch•ful•ness** *n*

watch•mak•er \-ˌmā-kər\ *n* : one that makes or repairs watches — **watch•mak•ing** \-ˌmā-kiŋ\ *n*

watch•man \-mən\ *n* : a person assigned to watch : GUARD

watch night *n* : a devotional service lasting until after midnight esp. on New Year's Eve

watch•tow•er \ˈwäch-ˌtau̇-ər, ˈwȯch-\ *n* : a tower for a lookout

watch•word \-ˌwərd\ *n* **1** : a secret word used as a signal or sign of recognition **2** : a word or motto used as a slogan or rallying cry

¹wa•ter \ˈwȯ-tər, ˈwä-\ *n* **1** : the liquid that descends as rain and forms rivers, lakes, and seas **2** : a natural mineral water — usu. used in pl. **3** *pl* : the water occupying or flowing in a particular bed; *also* : a band of seawater bordering on and under the control of a country ⟨sailing Canadian ~*s*⟩ **4** : any of various liquids containing or resembling water; *esp* : a watery fluid (as tears, urine, or sap) formed or circulating in a living organism **5** : a specified degree of thoroughness or completeness ⟨a scoundrel of the first ~⟩

²water *vb* **1** : to supply with or get or take water ⟨~ horses⟩ ⟨the ship ~*ed* at each port⟩ **2** : to treat (as cloth) so as to give a lustrous appearance in wavy lines **3** : to dilute by or as if by adding water to **4** : to form or secrete water or watery matter ⟨her eyes ~*ed*⟩ ⟨my mouth ~*ed*⟩

water bed *n* : a bed whose mattress is a watertight bag filled with water

wa•ter•borne \-ˌbōrn\ *adj* : supported or carried by water

water buffalo *n* : a common oxlike often domesticated Asian bovine

water buffalo

water chestnut *n* : a whitish crunchy vegetable used esp. in Chinese cooking that is the peeled tuber of a widely cultivated Asian sedge; *also* : the tuber or the sedge itself

water closet *n* : a compartment or room with a toilet bowl : BATHROOM; *also* : a toilet bowl along with its accessories

wa•ter•col•or \ˈwȯ-tər-ˌkə-lər, ˈwä-\ *n* **1** : a paint whose liquid part is water **2** : the art of painting with watercolors **3** : a picture made with watercolors

wa•ter•course \-ˌkōrs\ *n* : a stream of water; *also* : the bed of a stream

wa•ter•craft \-ˌkraft\ *n* : a craft for water transport : SHIP, BOAT

wa•ter•cress \-ˌkres\ *n* : a perennial European cress with white flowers that is naturalized in the U.S. and is used esp. in salads

wa•ter•fall \-ˌfȯl\ *n* : a very steep descent of the water of a stream

wa•ter•fowl \ˈwȯ-tər-ˌfau̇l, ˈwä-\ *n* **1** : a bird that frequents water **2 waterfowl** *pl* : wild ducks and geese hunted as game

wa•ter•front \-ˌfrənt\ *n* : land or a section of a town fronting or abutting on a body of water

water gap *n* : a pass in a mountain ridge through which a stream runs

water glass *n* : a drinking glass

water hyacinth *n* : a showy floating aquatic plant of tropical America that often clogs waterways (as in the southern U.S.)

watering place *n* : a resort that features mineral springs or bathing

water lily *n* : any of various aquatic plants with floating roundish leaves and showy solitary flowers

wa•ter•line \ˈwȯ-tər-ˌlīn, ˈwä-\ *n* : a line that marks the level of the surface of water on something (as a ship or the shore)

wa•ter•logged \-ˌlȯgd, -ˌlägd\ *adj* : so filled or soaked with water as to be heavy or unmanageable ⟨a ~ boat⟩

wa•ter•loo \ˌwȯ-tər-ˈlü, ˌwä-\ *n, pl* **-loos** [*Waterloo*, Belgium, scene of Napoleon's defeat in 1815] : a decisive or final defeat or setback

¹wa•ter•mark \ˈwȯ-tər-ˌmärk, ˈwä-\ *n* **1** : a mark indicating height to which water has risen **2** : a marking

in paper visible when the paper is held up to the light
[2]**watermark** *vb* : to mark (paper) with a watermark
wa•ter•mel•on \-ˌme-lən\ *n* : a large roundish or oblong fruit with sweet juicy usu. red pulp; *also* : a widely grown African vine related to the squashes that produces watermelons
water moccasin *n* : a venomous pit viper chiefly of the southeastern U.S. that is related to the copperhead
water ou•zel \-ˈü-zəl\ *n* : DIPPER 1
water pipe *n* : a pipe for smoking that has a long flexible tube whereby the smoke is cooled by passing through water
water polo *n* : a team game played in a swimming pool with a ball resembling a soccer ball
wa•ter•pow•er \ˈwȯ-tər-ˌpau̇-ər, ˈwä-\ *n* : the power of moving water used to run machinery
[1]**wa•ter•proof** \ˈwȯ-tər-ˌprüf, ˈwä-\ *adj* : not letting water through; *esp* : covered or treated with a material to prevent permeation by water — **wa•ter•proof•ing** *n*
[2]**waterproof** *n* **1** : a waterproof fabric **2** *chiefly Brit* : RAINCOAT
[3]**waterproof** *vb* : to make waterproof
wa•ter–re•pel•lent \ˌwȯ-tər-ri-ˈpe-lənt, ˌwä-\ *adj* : treated with a finish that is resistant to water penetration
wa•ter–re•sis•tant \-ri-ˈzis-tənt\ *adj* : WATER-REPELLENT
wa•ter•shed \ˈwȯ-tər-ˌshed, ˈwä-\ *n* **1** : a dividing ridge between two drainage areas **2** : the region or area drained by a particular body of water
wa•ter•side \-ˌsīd\ *n* : the land bordering a body of water
water ski *n* : a ski used on water when the wearer is towed — **wa•ter–ski** *vb* — **wa•ter–ski•er** \-ˌskē-ər\ *n*
wa•ter•spout \ˈwȯ-tər-ˌspau̇t, ˈwä-\ *n* **1** : a pipe for carrying water from a roof **2** : a funnel-shaped cloud extending from a cloud down to a spray torn up by whirling winds from an ocean or lake
water strider *n* : any of various long-legged bugs that move about swiftly on the surface of water
water table *n* : the upper limit of the portion of the ground wholly saturated with water
wa•ter•tight \ˌwȯ-tər-ˈtīt, ˌwä-\ *adj* **1** : constructed so as to keep water out **2** : allowing no possibility for doubt or uncertainty ⟨a ~ case against the accused⟩
wa•ter•way \ˈwȯ-tər-ˌwā, ˈwä-\ *n* : a navigable body of water
wa•ter•wheel \-ˌhwēl\ *n* : a wheel made to turn by water flowing against it
water wings *n pl* : an air-filled device to give support to a person's body esp. when learning to swim
wa•ter•works \ˈwȯ-tər-ˌwərks, ˈwä-\ *n pl* : a system for supplying water (as to a city)
wa•tery \ˈwȯ-tə-rē, ˈwä-\ *adj* **1** : containing, full of, or giving out water ⟨~ clouds⟩ **2** : being like water : THIN, WEAK ⟨~ lemonade⟩; *also* : being soft and soggy ⟨~ turnips⟩
WATS \ˈwäts\ *abbr* Wide-Area Telecommunications Service
watt \ˈwät\ *n* [James *Watt* †1819 Scottish engineer and inventor] : the metric unit of power equal to the work done at the rate of one joule per second or to the power produced by a current of one ampere across a potential difference of one volt
watt•age \ˈwä-tij\ *n* : amount of power expressed in watts
wat•tle \ˈwät-ᵊl\ *n* **1** : a framework of rods with flexible branches or reeds interlaced used esp. formerly in building; *also* : material for this framework **2** : a naked fleshy process hanging usu. from the head or neck (as of a bird) — **wat•tled** \-ᵊld\ *adj*
W Aust *abbr* Western Australia
[1]**wave** \ˈwāv\ *vb* **waved; wav•ing 1** : FLUTTER ⟨flags *waving* in the breeze⟩ **2** : to motion with the hands or with something held in them in signal or salute **3** : to become moved or brandished to-and-fro; *also* : BRANDISH, FLOURISH ⟨~ a sword⟩ **4** : to move before the wind with a wavelike motion ⟨fields of *waving* grain⟩ **5** : to curve up and down like a wave : UNDULATE
[2]**wave** *n* **1** : a moving ridge or swell on the surface of water **2** : a wavelike formation or shape ⟨a ~ in the hair⟩ **3** : the action or process of making wavy or curly **4** : a waving motion; *esp* : a signal made by waving something **5** : FLOW, GUSH ⟨a ~ of anger swept over her⟩ **6** : a peak of activity ⟨a ~ of selling⟩ **7** : a disturbance that transfers energy progressively from point to point in a medium ⟨light travels in ~*s*⟩ ⟨a sound ~⟩ **8** : a period of hot or cold weather — **wave•like** *adj*
wave•length \ˈwāv-ˌleŋth\ *n* **1** : the distance in the line of advance of a wave from any one point (as a crest) to the next corresponding point **2** : a line of thought that reveals a common understanding
wave•let \-lət\ *n* : a little wave : RIPPLE
wa•ver \ˈwā-vər\ *vb* **1** : to fluctuate in opinion, allegiance, or direction **2** : REEL, TOTTER; *also* : QUIVER, FLICKER ⟨~*ing* flames⟩ **3** : FALTER **4** : to give an unsteady sound : QUAVER **syn** falter, hesitate, shilly-shally, vacillate — **waver** *n* — **wa•ver•er** *n* — **wa•ver•ing•ly** *adv*
wavy \ˈwā-vē\ *adj* **wav•i•er; -est** : having waves : moving in waves
[1]**wax** \ˈwaks\ *n* **1** : a yellowish plastic substance secreted by bees for constructing the honeycomb **2** : any of various substances like beeswax
[2]**wax** *vb* : to treat or rub with wax
[3]**wax** *vb* **1** : to increase in size, numbers, strength, volume, or duration **2** : to increase in apparent size ⟨the moon ~*es* toward the full⟩ **3** : to take on a quality or state : BECOME ⟨~*ed* indignant⟩ ⟨the party ~*ed* merry⟩
wax bean *n* : a kidney bean with pods that turn creamy yellow to bright yellow when mature enough to use as snap beans
wax•en \ˈwak-sən\ *adj* **1** : made of or covered with wax **2** : resembling wax (as in color or consistency)
wax myrtle *n* : any of a genus of shrubs or trees with aromatic leaves; *esp* : an evergreen shrub of the eastern U.S. that produces small hard berries with a thick coating of white wax used for candles
wax•wing \ˈwaks-ˌwiŋ\ *n* : any of a genus of chiefly brown to gray singing birds with a showy crest and red waxy material on the tips of some wing feathers
wax•work \-ˌwərk\ *n* **1** : an effigy usu. of a person in wax **2** *pl* : an exhibition of wax figures
waxy \ˈwak-sē\ *adj* **wax•i•er; -est 1** : made of or full of wax **2** : WAXEN 2
way \ˈwā\ *n* **1** : a thoroughfare for travel or passage : ROAD, PATH, STREET **2** : ROUTE **3** : a course of action ⟨chose the easy ~⟩; *also* : opportunity, capability, or fact of doing as one pleases ⟨always had your own ~⟩ **4** : a possible course : POSSIBILITY ⟨no two ~*s* about it⟩ **5** : METHOD, MODE ⟨this ~ of thinking⟩ ⟨a new ~ of painting⟩ **6** : FEATURE, RESPECT ⟨a good worker in many ~*s*⟩ **7** : the usual or characteristic state of affairs ⟨as is the ~ with old people⟩; *also* : individual characteristic or peculiarity ⟨used to her ~*s*⟩ **8** : DISTANCE ⟨a short ~ from here⟩ ⟨a long ~ from success⟩ **9** : progress along a course ⟨working my ~ through college⟩ **10** : something having direction : LOCALITY ⟨out our ~⟩ **11** : STATE, CONDITION ⟨the ~ things are⟩ **12** *pl* : an inclined structure upon which a ship is built or is supported in launching **13** : CATEGORY, KIND ⟨get what you need in the ~ of supplies⟩ **14** : motion or speed of a boat through the water — **by the way** : by way of interjection or digression — **by way of 1** : for the purpose of ⟨*by way of* illustration⟩ **2** : by the route through : VIA — **out of the way 1** : WRONG, IMPROPER **2** : SECLUDED, REMOTE
way•bill \ˈwā-ˌbil\ *n* : a paper that accompanies a

freight shipment and gives details of goods, route, and charges

way·far·er \ˈwā-ˌfar-ər\ *n* **:** a traveler esp. on foot — **way·far·ing** \-ˌfar-iŋ\ *adj*

way·lay \ˈwā-ˌlā\ *vb* **-laid** \-ˌlād\; **-lay·ing :** to lie in wait for or attack from ambush

way–out \ˈwā-ˈau̇t\ *adj* **:** FAR-OUT

-ways \ˌwāz\ *adv suffix* **:** in (such) a way, course, direction, or manner ⟨side*ways*⟩

ways and means *n pl* **:** methods and resources esp. for raising revenues needed by a state; *also* **:** a legislative committee concerned with this function

way·side \ˈwā-ˌsīd\ *n* **:** the side of or land adjacent to a road or path

way station *n* **:** an intermediate station on a line of travel (as a railroad)

way·ward \ˈwā-wərd\ *adj* [ME, short for *awayward* turned away, fr. *away,* adv. + *-ward* directed toward] **1 :** following one's own capricious or wanton inclinations ⟨~ children⟩ **2 :** UNPREDICTABLE, IRREGULAR ⟨a ~ act⟩

WBC *abbr* white blood cells

WC *abbr* **1** water closet **2** without charge

WCTU *abbr* Women's Christian Temperance Union

we \ˈwē\ *pron* **1** — used of a group that includes the speaker or writer **2** — used for the singular *I* by a monarch, editor, or writer

weak \ˈwēk\ *adj* **1 :** lacking strength or vigor **:** FEEBLE **2 :** not able to sustain or resist much weight, pressure, or strain **3 :** deficient in vigor of mind or character; *also* **:** resulting from or indicative of such deficiency ⟨a ~ policy⟩ ⟨a ~ will⟩ ⟨*weak*-minded⟩ **4 :** not supported by truth or logic ⟨a ~ argument⟩ **5 :** lacking skill or proficiency; *also* **:** indicative of a lack of skill or aptitude **6 :** lacking vigor of expression or effect **7 :** of less than usual strength ⟨~ tea⟩ **8 :** not having or exerting authority ⟨~ government⟩; *also* **:** INEFFECTIVE, IMPOTENT **9 :** of, relating to, or constituting a verb or verb conjugation that forms the past tense and past participle by adding *-ed* or *-d* or *-t* — **weak·ly** *adv*

weak·en \ˈwē-kən\ *vb* **:** to make or become weak **syn** enfeeble, debilitate, undermine, sap, cripple, disable

weak·fish \ˈwēk-ˌfish\ *n* [obs. D *weekvis,* fr. D *week* soft + *vis* fish; fr. its tender flesh] **:** a common marine fish of the Atlantic coast of the U.S. caught for food and sport; *also* **:** any of several related food fishes

weak force *n* **:** the physical force responsible for particle decay processes in radioactivity

weak–kneed \ˈwēk-ˈnēd\ *adj* **:** lacking willpower or resolution

weak·ling \ˈwē-kliŋ\ *n* **:** a person who is physically, mentally, or morally weak

weak·ly \ˈwē-klē\ *adj* **:** FEEBLE, WEAK

weak·ness \ˈwēk-nəs\ *n* **1 :** the quality or state of being weak; *also* **:** an instance or period of being weak ⟨in a moment of ~ he agreed to go⟩ **2 :** FAULT, DEFECT **3 :** an object of special desire or fondness ⟨chocolate is her ~⟩

[1]**weal** \ˈwēl\ *n* **:** WELL-BEING, PROSPERITY

[2]**weal** *n* **:** WELT

weald \ˈwēld\ *n* [The *Weald,* wooded district in England, fr. ME *Weeld* the Weald, fr. OE *weald* forest] **1 :** FOREST **2 :** WOLD

wealth \ˈwelth\ *n* [ME *welthe* welfare, prosperity, fr. *wele* weal] **1 :** abundance of possessions or resources **:** AFFLUENCE, RICHES **2 :** abundant supply **:** PROFUSION ⟨a ~ of detail⟩ **3 :** all property that has a money or an exchange value; *also* **:** all objects or resources that have economic value **syn** fortune, property, substance, worth

wealthy \ˈwel-thē\ *adj* **wealth·i·er; -est :** having wealth **:** RICH

wean \ˈwēn\ *vb* **1 :** to accustom (a young mammal) to take food by means other than nursing **2 :** to free from a source of dependence; *also* **:** to free from a usu. unwholesome habit or interest

weap·on \ˈwe-pən\ *n* **1 :** something (as a gun, knife, or club) used to injure, defeat, or destroy **2 :** a means of contending against another — **weap·on·less** \-ləs\ *adj*

weap·on·ry \-rē\ *n* **:** WEAPONS

[1]**wear** \ˈwar\ *vb* **wore** \ˈwōr\; **worn** \ˈwōrn\; **wear·ing 1 :** to use as an article of clothing or adornment ⟨~ a coat⟩ ⟨~*s* earrings⟩; *also* **:** to carry on the person ⟨~ a gun⟩ **2 :** EXHIBIT, PRESENT ⟨~ a smile⟩ **3 :** to impair, diminish, or decay by use or by scraping or rubbing ⟨clothes *worn* to shreds⟩; *also* **:** to produce gradually by friction, rubbing, or wasting away ⟨~ a hole in the rug⟩ **4 :** to exhaust or lessen the strength of **:** WEARY, FATIGUE ⟨*worn* by care and toil⟩ **5 :** to endure use **:** last under use or the passage of time ⟨this cloth ~*s* well⟩ **6 :** to diminish or fail with the passage of time ⟨the day ~*s* on⟩ ⟨the effect of the drug *wore* off⟩ **7 :** to grow or become by attrition, use, or age ⟨the coin was *worn* thin⟩ — **wear·able** \ˈwar-ə-bəl\ *adj* — **wear·er** *n*

[2]**wear** *n* **1 :** the act of wearing **:** the state of being worn ⟨clothes for everyday ~⟩ **2 :** clothing usu. of a particular kind or for a special occasion or use ⟨children's ~⟩ **3 :** wearing or lasting quality ⟨the coat still has lots of ~ in it⟩ **4 :** the result of wearing or use **:** impairment due to use ⟨the suit shows ~⟩

wear and tear *n* **:** the loss, injury, or stress to which something is subjected in the course of use; *esp* **:** normal depreciation

wear down *vb* **:** to weary and overcome by persistent resistance or pressure

wea·ri·some \ˈwir-ē-səm\ *adj* **:** causing weariness **:** TIRESOME — **wea·ri·some·ly** *adv* — **wea·ri·some·ness** *n*

wear out *vb* **1 :** TIRE **2 :** to make or become useless by wear

[1]**wea·ry** \ˈwir-ē\ *adj* **wea·ri·er; -est 1 :** worn out in strength, energy, or freshness **2 :** expressing or characteristic of weariness ⟨a ~ sigh⟩ **3 :** having one's patience, tolerance, or pleasure exhausted ⟨~ of war⟩ — **wea·ri·ly** \ˈwir-ə-lē\ *adv* — **wea·ri·ness** \-ē-nəs\ *n*

[2]**weary** *vb* **wea·ried; wea·ry·ing :** to become or make weary **:** TIRE

[1]**wea·sel** \ˈwē-zəl\ *n, pl* **weasels :** any of various small slender flesh-eating mammals related to the minks

weasel

[2]**weasel** *vb* **wea·seled; wea·sel·ing 1 :** to use weasel words **:** EQUIVOCATE **2 :** to escape from or evade a situation or obligation — often used with *out*

weasel word *n* [fr. the weasel's reputed habit of sucking the contents out of an egg while leaving the shell superficially intact] **:** a word used to avoid a direct or forthright statement or position

[1]**weath·er** \ˈwe-t͟hər\ *n* **1 :** the state of the atmosphere with respect to heat or cold, wetness or dryness, calm or storm, clearness or cloudiness **2 :** a particular and esp. a disagreeable atmospheric state **:** RAIN, STORM

[2]**weather** *vb* **1 :** to expose to or endure the action of weather; *also* **:** to alter (as in color or texture) by such exposure **2 :** to bear up against successfully ⟨~ a storm⟩ ⟨~ troubles⟩

[3]**weather** *adj* : WINDWARD

weath•er–beat•en \ˈwe-t͟hər-ˌbēt-ᵊn\ *adj* : worn or damaged by exposure to the weather; *also* : toughened or tanned by the weather ⟨~ face⟩

weath•er•cock \-ˌkäk\ *n* : a weather vane shaped like a rooster

weath•er•ing \ˈwe-t͟hə-riŋ\ *n* : the action of the weather in altering the color, texture, composition, or form of exposed objects; *also* : alteration thus effected

weath•er•ize \ˈwe-t͟hə-ˌrīz\ *vb* **-ized; -iz•ing** : to make (as a house) better protected against winter weather (as by adding insulation)

weath•er•man \-ˌman\ *n* : one who reports and forecasts the weather : METEOROLOGIST

weath•er•per•son \-ˌpər-sən\ *n* : a person who reports and forecasts the weather : METEOROLOGIST

weath•er•proof \ˈwe-t͟hər-ˌprüf\ *adj* : able to withstand exposure to weather — **weatherproof** *vb*

weather stripping *n* : material used to seal a door or window at the edges

weather vane *n* : VANE 1

weath•er•worn \ˈwe-t͟hər-ˌwōrn\ *adj* : worn by exposure to the weather

[1]**weave** \ˈwēv\ *vb* **wove** \ˈwōv\ *or* **weaved; wo•ven** \ˈwō-vən\ *or* **weaved; weav•ing 1** : to form by interlacing strands of material; *esp* : to make on a loom by interlacing warp and filling threads ⟨~ cloth⟩ **2** : to interlace (as threads) into a fabric and esp. cloth **3** : SPIN 2 **4** : to make as if by weaving together parts **5** : to insert as a part : work in **6** : to move in a winding or zigzag course esp. to avoid obstacles ⟨we *wove* our way through the crowd⟩ — **weav•er** *n*

[2]**weave** *n* : something woven; *also* : a pattern or method of weaving ⟨a loose ~⟩

[1]**web** \ˈweb\ *n* **1** : a fabric on a loom or coming from a loom **2** : COBWEB; *also* : SNARE, ENTANGLEMENT ⟨caught in a ~ of deceit⟩ **3** : an animal or plant membrane; *esp* : one uniting the toes (as in many birds) **4** : NETWORK ⟨a ~ of highways⟩ **5** : the series of barbs on each side of the shaft of a feather — **webbed** \ˈwebd\ *adj*

[2]**web** *vb* **webbed; web•bing 1** : to make a web **2** : to cover or provide with webs or a network **3** : ENTANGLE, ENSNARE

web•bing \ˈwe-biŋ\ *n* : a strong closely woven tape designed for bearing weight and used esp. for straps, harness, or upholstery

web–foot•ed \ˈweb-ˈfu̇-təd\ *adj* : having webbed feet

wed \ˈwed\ *vb* **wed•ded** *also* **wed; wed•ding 1** : to take, give, enter into, or join in marriage : MARRY **2** : to unite firmly

Wed *abbr* Wednesday

wed•ding \ˈwe-diŋ\ *n* **1** : a marriage ceremony usu. with accompanying festivities : NUPTIALS **2** : a joining in close association **3** : a wedding anniversary or its celebration

[1]**wedge** \ˈwej\ *n* **1** : a piece of wood or metal that tapers to a thin edge and is used to split logs or rocks or to raise heavy weights **2** : something (as an action or policy) that serves to open up a way for a breach, change, or intrusion **3** : a wedge-shaped object or part ⟨a ~ of pie⟩

[2]**wedge** *vb* **wedged; wedg•ing 1** : to hold firm by or as if by driving in a wedge **2** : to force (something) into a narrow space

wed•lock \ˈwed-ˌläk\ *n* [ME *wedlok*, fr. OE *wedlāc* marriage bond, fr. *wedd* pledge + *-lāc*, suffix denoting activity] : the state of being married : MARRIAGE, MATRIMONY

Wednes•day \ˈwenz-dē, -(ˌ)dā\ *n* [ME, fr. OE *wōdensdæg*, lit., day of Woden (supreme god of the pagan Anglo-Saxons)] : the 4th day of the week

wee \ˈwē\ *adj* [ME *we*, fr. *we*, n., little bit, fr. OE *wæge* weight] **1** : very small : TINY **2** : very early ⟨~ hours of the morning⟩

[1]**weed** \ˈwēd\ *n* : a plant that tends to grow thickly where it is not wanted and to choke out more desirable plants

[2]**weed** *vb* **1** : to clear of or remove weeds or something harmful, inferior, or superfluous ⟨~ a garden⟩ **2** : to get rid of ⟨~ out the troublemakers⟩ — **weed•er** *n*

[3]**weed** *n* : mourning clothes — usu. used in pl. ⟨widow's ~*s*⟩

weedy \ˈwē-dē\ *adj* **1** : full of weeds **2** : resembling a weed esp. in vigor of growth or spread **3** : noticeably lean and scrawny : LANKY

week \ˈwēk\ *n* **1** : seven successive days; *esp* : a calendar period of seven days beginning with Sunday and ending with Saturday **2** : the working or school days of the calendar week

week•day \ˈwēk-ˌdā\ *n* : a day of the week except Sunday or sometimes except Saturday and Sunday

[1]**week•end** \-ˌend\ *n* : the period between the close of one working or business or school week and the beginning of the next

[2]**weekend** *vb* : to spend the weekend

[1]**week•ly** \ˈwē-klē\ *adj* **1** : occurring, appearing, or done every week **2** : computed in terms of one week — **weekly** *adv*

[2]**weekly** *n, pl* **weeklies** : a weekly publication

ween \ˈwēn\ *vb, archaic* : SUPPOSE 3

wee•ny \ˈwē-nē\ *also* **ween•sy** \ˈwēn-sē\ *adj* : exceptionally small

weep \ˈwēp\ *vb* **wept** \ˈwept\; **weep•ing 1** : to express emotion and esp. sorrow by shedding tears : BEWAIL, CRY **2** : to give off fluid slowly : OOZE — **weep•er** *n*

weep•ing *adj* **1** : TEARFUL **2** : having slender drooping branches

weeping willow *n* : a willow with slender drooping branches

weepy \ˈwē-pē\ *adj* : inclined to weep

wee•vil \ˈwē-vəl\ *n* : any of a large group of mostly small beetles with a long head usu. curved into a snout and larvae that feed esp. in fruits or seeds — **wee•vily** *or* **wee•vil•ly** \ˈwē-və-lē\ *adj*

weft \ˈweft\ *n* **1** : a filling thread or yarn in weaving **2** : WEB, FABRIC; *also* : something woven

[1]**weigh** \ˈwā\ *vb* [ME *weyen*, fr. OE *wegan* to move, carry, weigh] **1** : to find the heaviness of **2** : to have weight or a specified weight **3** : to consider carefully : PONDER **4** : to merit consideration as important : COUNT ⟨evidence ~*ing* against him⟩ **5** : to raise before sailing ⟨~ anchor⟩ **6** : to press down with or as if with a heavy weight

[2]**weigh** *n* [alter. of *way*] : WAY — used in the phrase *under weigh*

[1]**weight** \ˈwāt\ *n* **1** : the amount that something weighs; *also* : the standard amount that something should weigh **2** : a quantity or object weighing a usu. specified amount **3** : a unit (as a pound or kilogram) of weight or mass; *also* : a system of such units **4** : a heavy object for holding or pressing something down; *also* : a heavy object for throwing or lifting in an athletic contest **5** : a mental or emotional burden **6** : IMPORTANCE; *also* : INFLUENCE ⟨threw his ~ around⟩ **7** : overpowering force **8** : relative thickness (as of a textile) ⟨summer-*weight* clothes⟩ **syn** significance, moment, consequence, import, authority, prestige, credit

☞ For table, see next page.

[2]**weight** *vb* **1** : to load with or as if with a weight **2** : to oppress with a burden ⟨~*ed* down with cares⟩

weight•less \ˈwāt-ləs\ *adj* : having little weight : lacking apparent gravitational pull — **weight•less•ly** *adv* — **weight•less•ness** *n*

weighty \ˈwā-tē\ *adj* **weight•i•er; -est 1** : of much importance or consequence : MOMENTOUS, SERIOUS ⟨~ problems⟩ **2** : SOLEMN ⟨a ~ manner⟩ **3** : HEAVY **4** : POWERFUL, TELLING ⟨~ arguments⟩

weir \ˈwar, ˈwir\ *n* **1** : a fence set in a waterway for catching fish **2** : a dam in a stream to raise the water level or divert its flow

WEIGHTS AND MEASURES[1]

UNIT	ABBREVIATION OR SYMBOL	EQUIVALENT IN OTHER U.S. UNITS	METRIC EQUIVALENT
		WEIGHT	
		avoirdupois (ordinary commodities)	
ton			
short ton		20 short hundredweight, 2000 pounds	0.907 metric ton
long ton		20 long hundredweight, 2240 pounds	1.016 metric tons
hundredweight	cwt		
short hundredweight		100 pounds, 0.05 short ton	45.359 kilograms
long hundredweight		112 pounds, 0.05 long ton	50.802 kilograms
pound	lb *or* lb avdp *also* #	16 ounces, 7000 grains (1.215 apothecaries' or troy pound)	0.454 kilogram
ounce	oz *or* oz avdp	16 drams, 437.5 grains (0.911 apothecaries' or troy ounce)	28.350 grams
dram	dr *or* dr avdp	27.344 grains, 0.0625 ounce	1.772 grams
grain	gr	0.037 dram, 0.002286 ounce	0.0648 gram
		troy (precious metals, jewels)	
pound	lb t	12 ounces, 240 pennyweight, 5760 grains (0.823 avoirdupois pound, 1.0 apothecaries' pound)	0.373 kilogram
ounce	oz t	20 pennyweight, 480 grains (1.097 avoirdupois ounce, 1.0 apothecaries' ounce)	31.103 grams
pennyweight	dwt *also* pwt	24 grains, 0.05 ounce	1.555 grams
grain	gr	0.042 pennyweight, 0.002083 ounce	0.0648 gram
		apothecaries' (drugs)	
pound	lb ap	12 ounces, 5760 grains (0.822 avoirdupois pound, 1.0 troy pound)	0.373 kilogram
ounce	oz ap *or* ℥	8 drams, 480 grains (1.097 avoirdupois ounce, 1.0 troy ounce)	31.103 grams
dram	dr ap *or* ʒ	0.125 ounce, 60 grains	3.888 grams
grain	gr	0.0166 dram, 0.002083 ounce	0.0648 gram
		CAPACITY	
		U.S. liquid measure	
gallon	gal	4 quarts (231 cubic inches)	3.785 liters
quart	qt	2 pints (57.75 cubic inches)	0.946 liter
pint	pt	4 gills (28.875 cubic inches)	0.473 liter
gill	gi	4 fluid ounces (7.219 cubic inches)	118.294 milliliters
fluid ounce	fl oz *or* *f* ℥	8 fluid drams (1.805 cubic inches)	29.573 milliliters
fluid dram	fl dr *or* *f* ʒ	60 minims (0.226 cubic inch)	3.697 milliliters
minim	min *or* ♍	1/60 fluid dram (0.003760 cubic inch)	0.061610 milliliter
		U.S. dry measure	
bushel	bu	4 pecks (2150.42 cubic inches)	35.239 liters
peck	pk	8 quarts (537.605 cubic inches)	8.810 liters
quart	qt	2 pints (67.201 cubic inches)	1.101 liters
pint	pt	½ quart (33.600 cubic inches)	0.551 liter
		LENGTH	
mile	mi	5280 feet, 320 rods, 1760 yards	1.609 kilometers
rod	rd	5.50 yards, 16.5 feet	5.029 meters
yard	yd	3 feet, 36 inches	0.9144 meter
foot	ft *or* ′	12 inches, 0.333 yard	30.48 centimeters
inch	in *or* ″	0.083 foot, 0.028 yard	2.54 centimeters
		AREA	
square mile	sq mi *or* mi^2	640 acres, 102,400 square rods	2.590 square kilometers
acre		4840 square yards, 43,560 square feet	4047 square meters
square rod	sq rd *or* rd^2	30.25 square yards, 0.00625 acre	25.293 square meters
square yard	sq yd *or* yd^2	1296 square inches, 9 square feet	0.836 square meter
square foot	sq ft *or* ft^2	144 square inches, 0.111 square yard	0.093 square meter
square inch	sq in *or* in^2	0.0069 square foot, 0.00077 square yard	6.452 square centimeters
		VOLUME	
cubic yard	cu yd *or* yd^3	27 cubic feet, 46.656 cubic inches	0.765 cubic meter
cubic foot	cu ft *or* ft^3	1728 cubic inches, 0.0370 cubic yard	0.028 cubic meter
cubic inch	cu in *or* in^3	0.00058 cubic foot, 0.000021 cubic yard	16.387 cubic centimeters

[1]For U.S. equivalents of metric units see Metric System table

weird \ˈwird\ *adj* [ME *wird, werd* fate, destiny, fr. OE *wyrd*] **1** : MAGICAL **2** : UNEARTHLY, MYSTERIOUS **3** : ODD, UNUSUAL **syn** eerie, uncanny, spooky — **weird•ly** *adv* — **weird•ness** *n*

weirdo \ˈwir-(ˌ)dō\ *n, pl* **weird•os** : a person who is extraordinarily strange or eccentric

Welch \ˈwelch\ *var of* WELSH

1wel•come \ˈwel-kəm\ *vb* **wel•comed; wel•com•ing 1** : to greet cordially or courteously **2** : to accept, meet, or face with pleasure ⟨he ~*s* criticism⟩

2welcome *adj* **1** : received gladly into one's presence ⟨a ~ visitor⟩ **2** : giving pleasure : PLEASING ⟨~ news⟩ **3** : willingly permitted or admitted ⟨all are ~ to use the books⟩ **4** — used in the phrase "You're welcome" as a reply to an expression of thanks

3welcome *n* **1** : a cordial greeting or reception **2** : the state of being welcome ⟨overstayed their ~⟩

1weld \ˈweld\ *vb* **1** : to unite (metal or plastic parts) either by heating and allowing the parts to flow together or by hammering or pressing together **2** : to unite closely or intimately ⟨~*ed* together in friendship⟩ — **weld•er** *n*

2weld *n* **1** : a welded joint **2** : union by welding

wel•fare \ˈwel-ˌfar\ *n* **1** : the state of doing well esp. in respect to happiness, well-being, or prosperity **2** : aid in the form of money or necessities for those in need; *also* : the agency through which the aid is given

welfare state *n* : a nation or state that assumes primary responsibility for the individual and social welfare of its citizens

wel•kin \ˈwel-kən\ *n* : SKY; *also* : AIR

1well \ˈwel\ *n* **1** : a spring with its pool : FOUNTAIN; *also* : a source of supply ⟨a ~ of information⟩ **2** : a hole sunk in the earth to obtain a natural deposit (as of water, oil, or gas) **3** : an open space (as for a staircase) extending vertically through floors of a structure **4** : something suggesting a well

2well *vb* : to rise up and flow out

3well *adv* **bet•ter** \ˈbe-tər\; **best** \ˈbest\ **1** : in a good or proper manner : RIGHTLY; *also* : EXCELLENTLY, SKILLFULLY **2** : SATISFACTORILY, FORTUNATELY ⟨the party turned out ~⟩ **3** : ABUNDANTLY ⟨eat ~⟩ **4** : with reason or courtesy : PROPERLY ⟨I cannot ~ refuse⟩ **5** : COMPLETELY, FULLY, QUITE ⟨~ worth the price⟩ ⟨*well*-hidden⟩ **6** : INTIMATELY, CLOSELY ⟨I know him ~⟩ **7** : CONSIDERABLY, FAR ⟨~ over a million⟩ ⟨~ ahead⟩ **8** : without trouble or difficulty ⟨we could ~ have gone⟩ **9** : EXACTLY, DEFINITELY ⟨remember it ~⟩

4well *adj* **1** : PROSPEROUS; *also* : being in satisfactory condition or circumstances **2** : SATISFACTORY, PLEASING ⟨all is ~⟩ **3** : ADVISABLE, DESIRABLE ⟨it is not ~ to anger him⟩ **4** : free or recovered from ill health : HEALTHY **5** : FORTUNATE ⟨it is ~ that this has happened⟩

well–ad•just•ed \ˌwel-ə-ˈjəs-təd\ *adj* : WELL-BALANCED 2

well–ad•vised \-əd-ˈvīzd\ *adj* **1** : PRUDENT **2** : resulting from, based on, or showing careful deliberation or wise counsel ⟨~ plans⟩

well–ap•point•ed \-ə-ˈpȯin-təd\ *adj* : properly fitted out

well–ba•lanced \ˈwel-ˈba-lənst\ *adj* **1** : nicely or evenly balanced or arranged **2** : emotionally or psychologically untroubled

well–be•ing \-ˈbē-iŋ\ *n* : the state of being happy, healthy, or prosperous

well•born \-ˈbȯrn\ *adj* : born of noble or wealthy lineage

well–bred \-ˈbred\ *adj* : having or indicating good breeding : REFINED

well–de•fined \-di-ˈfīnd\ *adj* : having clearly distinguishable limits or boundaries

well–dis•posed \-di-ˈspōzd\ *adj* : disposed to be friendly, favorable, or sympathetic

well–done \ˈwel-ˈdən\ *adj* **1** : rightly or properly performed **2** : cooked thoroughly

well–fa•vored \-ˈfā-vərd\ *adj* : GOOD-LOOKING, HANDSOME

well–fixed \-ˈfikst\ *adj* : WELL-HEELED

well–found•ed \-ˈfau̇n-dəd\ *adj* : based on good reasons

well–groomed \-ˈgrümd, -ˈgru̇md\ *adj* : neatly dressed or cared for

well–ground•ed \-ˈgrau̇n-dəd\ *adj* **1** : having a firm foundation **2** : WELL-FOUNDED

well•head \-ˌhed\ *n* **1** : the source of a spring or a stream **2** : principal source **3** : the top of or a structure built over a well

well–heeled \-ˈhēld\ *adj* : financially well-off

well–known \-ˈnōn\ *adj* : fully or widely known

well–mean•ing \-ˈmē-niŋ\ *adj* : having or based on good intentions

well•ness \-nəs\ *n* : good health esp. as an actively sought goal ⟨~ clinics⟩ ⟨lifestyles that promote ~⟩

well–nigh \-ˈnī\ *adv* : ALMOST, NEARLY

well–off \-ˈȯf\ *adj* : being in good condition or circumstances; *esp* : WELL-TO-DO

well–or•dered \-ˈȯr-dərd\ *adj* : having an orderly procedure or arrangement

well–read \-ˈred\ *adj* : well informed through reading

well–round•ed \-ˈrau̇n-dəd\ *adj* **1** : broadly trained, educated, and experienced **2** : COMPREHENSIVE ⟨a ~ program of activities⟩

well–spo•ken \ˈwel-ˈspō-kən\ *adj* **1** : speaking well and esp. courteously **2** : spoken with propriety ⟨~ words⟩

well•spring \-ˌspriŋ\ *n* : a source of continuous supply

well–timed \-ˈtīmd\ *adj* : TIMELY

well–to–do \ˌwel-tə-ˈdü\ *adj* : having more than adequate financial resources : PROSPEROUS

well–turned \ˈwel-ˈtərnd\ *adj* **1** : pleasingly shaped ⟨a ~ ankle⟩ **2** : pleasingly expressed ⟨a ~ phrase⟩

well–wish•er \ˈwel-ˌwi-shər\ *n* : one that wishes well to another — **well–wish•ing** *adj or n*

welsh \ˈwelsh, ˈwelch\ *vb* **1** : to avoid payment **2** : to break one's word ⟨~*ed* on his promises⟩

Welsh \ˈwelsh\ *n* **1 Welsh** *pl* : the people of Wales **2** : the Celtic language of Wales — **Welsh** *adj* — **Welsh•man** \-mən\ *n*

Welsh cor•gi \-ˈkȯr-gē\ *n* [W *corgi*, fr. *cor* dwarf + *ci* dog] : a short-legged long-backed dog with foxy head of either of two breeds of Welsh origin

Welsh rabbit *n* : melted often seasoned cheese served over toast or crackers

Welsh rare•bit \-ˈrar-bət\ *n* : WELSH RABBIT

1welt \ˈwelt\ *n* **1** : the narrow strip of leather between a shoe upper and sole to which other parts are stitched **2** : a doubled edge, strip, insert, or seam for ornament or reinforcement **3** : a ridge or lump raised on the skin usu. by a blow; *also* : a heavy blow

2welt *vb* **1** : to furnish with a welt **2** : to hit hard

1wel•ter \ˈwel-tər\ *vb* **1** : WRITHE, TOSS; *also* : WALLOW **2** : to rise and fall or toss about in or with waves **3** : to become deeply sunk, soaked, or involved **4** : to be in turmoil

2welter *n* **1** : TURMOIL **2** : a chaotic mass or jumble

wel•ter•weight \ˈwel-tər-ˌwāt\ *n* : a boxer weighing more than 135 but not over 147 pounds

wen \ˈwen\ *n* : an abnormal growth or a cyst protruding from a surface esp. of the skin

wench \ˈwench\ *n* [ME *wenche*, short for *wenchel* child, fr. OE *wencel*] **1** : a young woman **2** : a female servant

wend \ˈwend\ *vb* : to direct one's course : proceed on (one's way)

went *past of* GO

wept *past and past part of* WEEP

were *past 2d sing, past pl, or past subjunctive of* BE

were•wolf \ˈwer-ˌwu̇lf, ˈwir-, ˈwər-\ *n, pl* **were•wolves** \-ˌwu̇lvz\ [ME, fr. OE *werwulf*, fr. *wer* man + *wulf* wolf] : a person transformed into a wolf or capable of assuming a wolf's form

wes•kit \ˈwes-kət\ *n* : VEST 1

DICTIONARY

[1]**west** \ˈwest\ *adv* : to or toward the west

[2]**west** *adj* **1** : situated toward or at the west **2** : coming from the west

[3]**west** *n* **1** : the general direction of sunset **2** : the compass point directly opposite to east **3** *cap* : regions or countries west of a specified or implied point **4** *cap* : Europe and the Americas — **west•er•ly** \ˈwes-tər-lē\ *adv or adj* — **west•ward** *adv or adj* — **west•wards** *adv*

[1]**west•ern** \ˈwes-tərn\ *adj* **1** : lying toward or coming from the west **2** *cap* : of, relating to, or characteristic of a region conventionally designated West **3** *cap* : of or relating to the Roman Catholic or Protestant segment of Christianity — **West•ern•er** *n*

[2]**western** *n, often cap* : a novel, story, film, or radio or television show about life in the western U.S. during the latter half of the 19th century

west•ern•ise *Brit var of* WESTERNIZE

west•ern•ize \ˈwes-tər-ˌnīz\ *vb* **-ized; -iz•ing** : to give western characteristics to

[1]**wet** \ˈwet\ *adj* **wet•ter; wet•test 1** : consisting of or covered or soaked with liquid (as water) **2** : RAINY **3** : not dry ⟨~ paint⟩ **4** : permitting or advocating the manufacture and sale of alcoholic beverages ⟨a ~ town⟩ ⟨a ~ candidate⟩ **syn** damp, dank, moist, humid — **wet•ly** *adv* — **wet•ness** *n*

[2]**wet** *n* **1** : WATER; *also* : WETNESS, MOISTURE **2** : rainy weather : RAIN **3** : an advocate of a wet liquor policy

[3]**wet** *vb* **wet** *or* **wet•ted; wet•ting** : to make or become wet

wet blanket *n* : one that quenches or dampens enthusiasm or pleasure

weth•er \ˈwe-t͟hər\ *n* : a castrated male sheep or goat

wet•land \ˈwet-ˌland, -lənd\ *n* : land or areas (as swamps) containing much soil moisture — usu. used in pl.

wet nurse *n* : a woman who cares for and suckles children not her own

wet suit *n* : a rubber suit for swimmers that acts to retain body heat by keeping a layer of water against the body as insulation

wh *abbr* **1** which **2** white

[1]**whack** \ˈhwak\ *vb* **1** : to strike with a smart or resounding blow **2** : to cut with or as if with a whack

[2]**whack** *n* **1** : a smart or resounding blow; *also* : the sound of such a blow **2** : PORTION, SHARE **3** : CONDITION, STATE ⟨the machine is out of ~⟩ **4** : an opportunity or attempt to do something : CHANCE **5** : a single action or occasion ⟨made three pies at a ~⟩

[1]**whale** \ˈhwāl\ *n, pl* **whales 1** *or pl* **whale** : CETACEAN; *esp* : one (as a sperm whale or killer whale) of large size **2** : a person or thing impressive in size or quality ⟨a ~ of a story⟩

[2]**whale** *vb* **whaled; whal•ing** : to fish or hunt for whales

[3]**whale** *vb* **whaled; whal•ing 1** : THRASH **2** : to strike or hit vigorously

whale•boat \-ˌbōt\ *n* : a long narrow rowboat originally used by whalers

whale•bone \-ˌbōn\ *n* : BALEEN

whal•er \ˈhwā-lər\ *n* **1** : a person or ship that hunts whales **2** : WHALEBOAT

wham•my \ˈhwa-mē\ *n, pl* **wham•mies** : JINX, HEX

wharf \ˈhwȯrf\ *n, pl* **wharves** \ˈhwȯrvz\ *also* **wharfs** : a structure alongside which ships lie to load and unload

[1]**what** \ˈhwät, ˈhwət\ *pron* **1** — used to inquire about the identity or nature of a being, an object, or some matter or situation ⟨~ is he, a salesman⟩ ⟨~*'s* that⟩ ⟨~ happened⟩ **2** : that which ⟨I know ~ you want⟩ **3** : WHATEVER 1 ⟨take ~ you want⟩

[2]**what** *adv* **1** : in what respect : HOW ⟨~ does he care⟩ **2** — used with *with* to introduce a prepositional phrase that expresses cause ⟨kept busy ~ with school and work⟩

[3]**what** *adj* **1** — used to inquire about the identity or nature of a person, object, or matter ⟨~ books do you read⟩ **2** : how remarkable or surprising ⟨~ an idea⟩ **3** : WHATEVER

[1]**what•ev•er** \hwät-ˈe-vər\ *pron* **1** : anything or everything that ⟨does ~ he wants to⟩ **2** : no matter what ⟨~ you do, don't cheat⟩ **3** : WHAT 1 — used as an intensive ⟨~ do you mean⟩

[2]**whatever** *adj* : of any kind at all ⟨no food ~⟩

[1]**what•not** \ˈhwät-ˌnät\ *pron* : any of various other things that might also be mentioned ⟨needles, pins, and ~⟩

[2]**whatnot** *n* : a light open set of shelves for small ornaments

what•so•ev•er \ˌhwät-sō-ˈe-vər\ *pron or adj* : WHATEVER

wheal \ˈhwēl\ *n* : a rapidly formed flat slightly raised itching or burning patch on the skin; *also* : WELT

wheat \ˈhwēt\ *n* : a cereal grain that yields a fine white flour and is the chief breadstuff of temperate regions; *also* : any of several grasses yielding wheat — **wheat•en** *adj*

wheat germ *n* : the vitamin-rich wheat embryo separated in milling

whee•dle \ˈhwēd-ᵊl\ *vb* **whee•dled; whee•dling 1** : to entice by flattery **2** : to gain or get by wheedling

[1]**wheel** \ˈhwēl\ *n* **1** : a disk or circular frame that turns on a central axis **2** : a device whose main part is a wheel **3** : something resembling a wheel in shape or motion **4** : a curving or circular movement **5** : machinery that imparts motion : moving power ⟨the ~*s* of government⟩ **6** : a person of importance **7** *pl, slang* : AUTOMOBILE — **wheeled** \ˈhwēld\ *adj* — **wheel•less** *adj*

[2]**wheel** *vb* **1** : ROTATE, REVOLVE **2** : to change direction as if turning on a pivot **3** : to convey or move on wheels or in a vehicle

wheel•bar•row \-ˌbar-ō\ *n* : a vehicle with handles and usu. one wheel for carrying small loads

wheel•base \-ˌbās\ *n* : the distance in inches between the front and rear axles of an automotive vehicle

wheel•chair \-ˌcher\ *n* : a chair mounted on wheels esp. for the use of disabled persons

wheel•er \ˈhwē-lər\ *n* **1** : one that wheels **2** : WHEELHORSE **3** : something that has wheels — used in combination ⟨a side-*wheeler*⟩

wheel•er–deal•er \ˌhwē-lər-ˈdē-lər\ *n* : a shrewd operator esp. in business or politics

wheel•horse \ˈhwēl-ˌhȯrs\ *n* **1** : a horse in a position nearest the front wheels of a wagon **2** : a steady and effective worker esp. in a political body

wheel•house \-ˌhau̇s\ *n* : PILOTHOUSE

wheel–thrown \ˈhwēl-ˌthrōn\ *adj* : made on a potter's wheel

wheel•wright \-ˌrīt\ *n* : a maker and repairer of wheels and wheeled vehicles

[1]**wheeze** \ˈhwēz\ *vb* **wheezed; wheez•ing** : to breathe with difficulty usu. with a whistling sound

[2]**wheeze** *n* **1** : a sound of wheezing **2** : an often repeated and well-known joke **3** : a trite saying

wheezy \ˈhwē-zē\ *adj* **wheez•i•er; -est 1** : inclined to wheeze **2** : having a wheezing sound — **wheez•i•ly** \-zə-lē\ *adv* — **wheez•i•ness** \-zē-nəs\ *n*

whelk \ˈhwelk\ *n* : a large sea snail; *esp* : one much used as food in Europe

whelm \ˈhwelm\ *vb* : to overcome or engulf completely : OVERWHELM

[1]**whelp** \ˈhwelp\ *n* : any of the young of various carnivorous mammals (as a dog)

[2]**whelp** *vb* : to give birth to (whelps); *also* : bring forth young

[1]**when** \ˈhwen\ *adv* **1** : at what time ⟨~ will you return⟩ **2** : at or during which time ⟨a time ~ things were better⟩

[2]**when** *conj* **1** : at or during the time that ⟨leave ~ I do⟩ **2** : every time that ⟨they all clapped ~ he sang⟩ **3** : in the event that : IF ⟨disqualified ~ you cheat⟩ **4** : AL-

THOUGH ⟨quit politics ~ he might have had a great career in it⟩

[3]**when** *pron* : what or which time ⟨since ~ have you been the boss⟩

[4]**when** *n* : the time of a happening

whence \ˈhwens\ *adv or conj* : from what place, source, or cause

when•ev•er \hwe-ˈne-vər, hwə-\ *conj or adv* : at whatever time

when•so•ev•er \ˈhwen-sō-ˌe-vər\ *conj* : at whatever time

[1]**where** \ˈhwer\ *adv* **1** : at, in, or to what place ⟨~ is it⟩ ⟨~ will we go⟩ **2** : at, in, or to what situation, position, direction, circumstances, or respect ⟨~ does this road lead⟩

[2]**where** *conj* **1** : at, in, or to what place ⟨knows ~ the house is⟩ **2** : at, in, or to what situation, position, direction, circumstances, or respect ⟨shows ~ the road leads⟩ **3** : WHEREVER ⟨goes ~ she likes⟩ **4** : at, in, or to which place ⟨the town ~ we live⟩ **5** : at, in, or to the place at, in, or to which ⟨stay ~ you are⟩ **6** : in a case, situation, or respect in which ⟨outstanding ~ endurance is called for⟩

[3]**where** *n* : PLACE, LOCATION ⟨the ~ and how of the accident⟩

[1]**where•abouts** \-ə-ˌbau̇ts\ *also* **where•about** \-ˌbau̇t\ *adv* : about where : near what place ⟨~ does he live⟩

[2]**whereabouts** *n sing or pl* : the place where a person or thing is ⟨his present ~ are unknown⟩

where•as \hwer-ˈaz\ *conj* **1** : while on the contrary; *also* : ALTHOUGH **2** : in view of the fact that : SINCE

where•at \-ˈat\ *conj* **1** : at or toward which **2** : in consequence of which : WHEREUPON

where•by \-ˈbī\ *conj* : by, through, or in accordance with which ⟨the means ~ we achieved our goals⟩

[1]**where•fore** \ˈhwer-ˌfōr\ *adv* **1** : for what reason or purpose : WHY **2** : THEREFORE

[2]**wherefore** *n* : an answer or statement giving an explanation : REASON

[1]**where•in** \hwer-ˈin\ *adv* : in what : in what respect ⟨~ was I wrong⟩

[2]**wherein** *conj* **1** : in which : WHERE ⟨the city ~ we live⟩ **2** : during which **3** : in what way : HOW ⟨showed me ~ I was wrong⟩

where•of \-ˈəv, -ˈäv\ *conj* **1** : of what ⟨knows ~ he speaks⟩ **2** : of which or whom ⟨books ~ the best are lost⟩

where•on \-ˈȯn, -ˈän\ *conj* : on which ⟨the base ~ it rests⟩

where•so•ev•er \ˈhwer-sō-ˌe-vər\ *conj* : WHEREVER

where•to \ˈhwer-ˌtü\ *conj* : to which

where•up•on \ˈhwer-ə-ˌpȯn, -ˌpän\ *conj* **1** : on which **2** : closely following and in consequence of which

[1]**wher•ev•er** \hwer-ˈe-vər\ *adv* : where in the world ⟨~ did he get that tie⟩

[2]**wherever** *conj* **1** : at, in, or to whatever place **2** : in any circumstance in which

where•with \ˈhwer-ˌwith, -ˌwith\ *conj* : with or by means of which

where•with•al \ˈhwer-wi-ˌthȯl, -ˌthȯl\ *n* : MEANS, RESOURCES; *esp* : MONEY

wher•ry \ˈhwer-ē\ *n, pl* **wherries** : a long light rowboat sharp at both ends

whet \ˈhwet\ *vb* **whet•ted; whet•ting 1** : to sharpen by rubbing on or with something abrasive (as a whetstone) **2** : to make keen : STIMULATE ⟨~ the appetite⟩

wheth•er \ˈhwe-thər\ *conj* **1** : if it is or was true that ⟨ask ~ he is going⟩ **2** : if it is or was better ⟨uncertain ~ to go or stay⟩ **3** : whichever is or was the case, namely that ⟨~ we succeed or fail, we must try⟩ **4** : EITHER ⟨turned out well ~ by accident or design⟩

whet•stone \ˈhwet-ˌstōn\ *n* : a stone for sharpening blades

whey \ˈhwā\ *n* : the watery part of milk that separates after the milk sours and thickens

[1]**which** \ˈhwich\ *adj* **1** : being what one or ones out of a group ⟨~ shirt should I wear⟩ **2** : WHICHEVER

[2]**which** *pron* **1** : which one or ones ⟨~ is yours⟩ ⟨~ are his⟩ ⟨it's in May or June, I'm not sure ~⟩ **2** : WHICHEVER ⟨we have all kinds; take ~ you like⟩ **3** — used to introduce a relative clause and to serve as a substitute therein for the noun modified by the clause ⟨the money ~ is coming to me⟩

[1]**which•ev•er** \hwich-ˈe-vər\ *adj* : no matter which ⟨~ way you go⟩

[2]**whichever** *pron* : whatever one or ones

which•so•ev•er \ˌhwich-sō-ˈe-vər\ *pron or adj* : WHICHEVER

whick•er \ˈhwi-kər\ *vb* : NEIGH, WHINNY — **whicker** *n*

[1]**whiff** \ˈhwif\ *n* **1** : a quick puff or slight gust (as of air) **2** : an inhalation of odor, gas, or smoke **3** : a slight trace **4** : STRIKEOUT

[2]**whiff** *vb* **1** : to expel, puff out, or blow away in or as if in whiffs **2** : to inhale an odor **3** : STRIKE OUT 3

whif•fle•tree \ˈhwi-fəl-(ˌ)trē\ *n* : the pivoted swinging bar to which the traces of a harness are fastened

Whig \ˈhwig\ *n* [short for *Whiggamore,* member of a Scottish group that marched to Edinburgh in 1648 to oppose the court party] **1** : a member or supporter of a British political group of the late 17th through early 19th centuries seeking to limit royal authority and increase parliamentary power **2** : an American favoring independence from Great Britain during the American Revolution **3** : a member or supporter of an American political party formed about 1834 to oppose the Democrats

[1]**while** \ˈhwīl\ *n* **1** : a period of time ⟨stay a ~⟩ **2** : the time and effort used : TROUBLE ⟨worth your ~⟩

[2]**while** *conj* **1** : during the time that ⟨she called ~ you were out⟩ **2** : AS LONG AS ⟨~ there's life there's hope⟩ **3** : ALTHOUGH ⟨~ he's respected, he's not liked⟩

[3]**while** *vb* **whiled; whil•ing** : to cause to pass esp. pleasantly ⟨~ away an hour⟩

[1]**whi•lom** \ˈhwī-ləm\ *adv* [ME, lit., at times, fr. OE *hwīlum,* dat. pl. of *hwīl* time, while] *archaic* : FORMERLY

[2]**whilom** *adj* : FORMER ⟨his ~ friends⟩

whilst \ˈhwīlst\ *conj, chiefly Brit* : WHILE

whim \ˈhwim\ *n* : a sudden wish, desire, or change of mind

whim•per \ˈhwim-pər\ *vb* : to make a low whining plaintive or broken sound — **whimper** *n*

whim•si•cal \ˈhwim-zi-kəl\ *adj* **1** : full of whims : CAPRICIOUS **2** : resulting from or characterized by whim or caprice : ERRATIC — **whim•si•cal•i•ty** \ˌhwim-zə-ˈka-lə-tē\ *n* — **whim•si•cal•ly** \ˈhwim-zi-k(ə-)lē\ *adv*

whim•sy *or* **whim•sey** \ˈhwim-zē\ *n, pl* **whimsies** *or* **whimseys 1** : WHIM, CAPRICE **2** : a fanciful or fantastic device, object, or creation esp. in writing or art

whine \ˈhwīn\ *vb* **whined; whin•ing** [ME, fr. OE *hwīnan* to whiz] **1** : to utter a usu. high-pitched plaintive or distressed cry; *also* : to make a sound similar to such a cry **2** : to complain with or as if with a whine — **whine** *n* — **whin•er** *n* — **whiny** *also* **whin•ey** \ˈhwī-nē\ *adj*

[1]**whin•ny** \ˈhwi-nē\ *vb* **whin•nied; whin•ny•ing** : to neigh usu. in a low or gentle manner

[2]**whinny** *n, pl* **whinnies** : NEIGH

[1]**whip** \ˈhwip\ *vb* **whipped; whip•ping 1** : to move, snatch, or jerk quickly or forcefully ⟨~ out a gun⟩ **2** : to strike with a slender lithe implement (as a lash) esp. as a punishment; *also* : SPANK **3** : to drive or urge on by or as if by using a whip **4** : to bind or wrap (as a rope or rod) with cord in order to protect and strengthen; *also* : to wind or wrap around something **5** : DEFEAT **6** : to stir up : INCITE ⟨~ up enthusiasm⟩ **7** : to produce in a hurry ⟨~ up a meal⟩ **8** : to beat (as eggs or cream) into a froth **9** : to proceed nimbly or briskly; *also* : to flap about forcefully ⟨flags *whipping*

in the wind⟩ — **whip•per** *n* — **whip into shape** : to bring forcefully to a desired state or condition

²whip *n* **1** : a flexible instrument used for whipping **2** : a stroke or cut with or as if with a whip **3** : a dessert made by whipping a portion of the ingredients ⟨prune ~⟩ **4** : a person who handles a whip **5** : a member of a legislative body appointed by a party to enforce party discipline **6** : a whipping or thrashing motion

whip•cord \-ˌkȯrd\ *n* **1** : a thin tough braided cord **2** : a strong cloth with fine diagonal cords or ribs

whip hand *n* : positive control : ADVANTAGE

whip•lash \ˈhwip-ˌlash\ *n* **1** : the lash of a whip **2** : injury resulting from a sudden sharp movement of the neck and head (as of a person in a vehicle that is struck from the rear)

whip•per•snap•per \ˈhwi-pər-ˌsna-pər\ *n* : a small, insignificant, or presumptuous person

whip•pet \ˈhwi-pət\ *n* : any of a breed of small swift slender dogs that are used for racing

whipping boy *n* : SCAPEGOAT

whip•ple•tree \ˈhwi-pəl-(ˌ)trē\ *n* : WHIFFLETREE

whip•poor•will \ˈhwi-pər-ˌwil\ *n* : an American insect-eating bird with dull variegated plumage whose call at nightfall and just before dawn is suggestive of its name

whippoorwill

whip•saw \ˈhwip-ˌsȯ\ *vb* : to beset with two or more adverse conditions or situations at once

¹whir *also* **whirr** \ˈhwər\ *vb* **whirred; whir•ring** : to move, fly, or revolve with a whir

²whir *also* **whirr** *n* : a continuous fluttering or vibratory sound made by something in rapid motion

¹whirl \ˈhwərl\ *vb* **1** : to move or drive in a circle or curve esp. with force or speed **2** : to turn or cause to turn rapidly in circles **3** : to turn abruptly : WHEEL **4** : to move or go quickly **5** : to become dizzy or giddy : REEL

²whirl *n* **1** : a rapid rotating or circling movement; *also* : something whirling **2** : COMMOTION, BUSTLE ⟨the social ~⟩ **3** : a state of mental confusion **4** : TRY ⟨gave it a ~⟩

whirl•i•gig \ˈhwər-li-ˌgig\ *n* [ME *whirlegigg,* fr. *whirlen* to whirl + *gigg* top] **1** : a child's toy having a whirling motion **2** : something that continuously whirls or changes

whirl•pool \ˈhwərl-ˌpül\ *n* : water moving rapidly in a circle so as to produce a depression in the center into which floating objects may be drawn

whirl•wind \-ˌwind\ *n* **1** : a small whirling windstorm **2** : a confused rush **3** : a violent or destructive force

whirly•bird \ˈhwər-lē-ˌbərd\ *n* : HELICOPTER

¹whish \ˈhwish\ *vb* : to move with a whish or swishing sound

²whish *n* : a rushing sound : SWISH

¹whisk \ˈhwisk\ *n* **1** : a quick light sweeping or brushing motion **2** : a usu. wire kitchen implement for beating food by hand **3** : WHISK BROOM

²whisk *vb* **1** : to move nimbly and quickly **2** : to move or convey briskly ⟨~*ed* the children off to bed⟩ **3** : to beat or whip lightly ⟨~ eggs⟩ **4** : to brush or wipe off lightly ⟨~ a coat⟩

whisk broom *n* : a small broom with a short handle used esp. as a clothes brush

whis•ker \ˈhwis-kər\ *n* **1** : one hair of the beard **2** *pl* : the part of the beard that grows on the sides of the face or on the chin **3** : one of the long bristles or hairs growing near the mouth of an animal (as a cat or mouse) — **whis•kered** \-kərd\ *adj*

whis•key *or* **whis•ky** \ˈhwis-kē\ *n, pl* **whiskeys** *or* **whiskies** [Ir *uisce beathadh* & ScGael *uisge beatha,* lit., water of life] : a liquor distilled from the fermented mash of grain (as rye, corn, or barley)

¹whis•per \ˈhwis-pər\ *vb* **1** : to speak very low or under the breath; *also* : to tell or utter by whispering ⟨~ a secret⟩ **2** : to make a low rustling sound ⟨~*ing* leaves⟩

²whisper *n* **1** : something communicated by or as if by whispering : HINT, RUMOR **2** : an act or instance of whispering

whist \ˈhwist\ *n* : a card game played by four players in two partnerships with a deck of 52 cards

¹whis•tle \ˈhwi-səl\ *n* **1** : a device by which a shrill sound is produced ⟨steam ~⟩ ⟨tin ~⟩ **2** : a shrill clear sound made by forcing breath out or air in through the puckered lips **3** : the sound or signal produced by a whistle or as if by whistling **4** : the shrill clear note of an animal (as a bird)

²whistle *vb* **whis•tled; whis•tling** **1** : to utter a shrill clear sound by blowing or drawing air through the puckered lips **2** : to utter a shrill note or call resembling a whistle **3** : to make a shrill clear sound esp. by rapid movements ⟨the wind *whistled*⟩ **4** : to blow or sound a whistle **5** : to signal or call by a whistle **6** : to produce, utter, or express by whistling ⟨~ a tune⟩ — **whis•tler** *n*

whis•tle–blow•er \ˈhwi-səl-ˌblō-ər\ *n* : INFORMER

whis•tle–stop \-ˌstäp\ *n* : a brief personal appearance by a political candidate orig. on the rear platform of a touring train

whit \ˈhwit\ *n* [prob. alter. of ME *wiht, wight* creature, thing, fr. OE *wiht*] : the smallest part or particle : BIT

¹white \ˈhwīt\ *adj* **whit•er; whit•est** **1** : free from color **2** : of the color of new snow or milk; *esp* : of the color white **3** : light or pallid in color ⟨lips ~ with fear⟩ **4** : SILVERY; *also* : made of silver **5** : of, relating to, or being a member of a group or race characterized by light-colored skin **6** : free from spot or blemish : PURE, INNOCENT **7** : BLANK 2 ⟨~ space in printed matter⟩ **8** : not intended to cause harm ⟨a ~ lie⟩ **9** : wearing white ⟨~ friars⟩ **10** : marked by snow ⟨~ Christmas⟩ **11** : consisting of a wide range of frequencies ⟨~ light⟩ — **white•ness** \-nəs\ *n* — **whit•ish** \ˈhwī-tish\ *adj*

²white *n* **1** : the color of maximal lightness that characterizes objects which both reflect and transmit light : the opposite of black **2** : a white or light-colored part or thing ⟨the ~ of an egg⟩; *also, pl* : white garments **3** : the light-colored pieces in a 2-player board game; *also* : the person by whom these are played **4** : one that is or approaches the color white **5** : a person of a light-skinned race

white ant *n* : TERMITE

white blood cell *n* : a colorless blood cell (as a lymphocyte) that does not contain hemoglobin but does have a nucleus

white–bread \ˈhwīt-ˈbred\ *adj* : being, typical of, or having qualities (as blandness) associated with the white middle class

white•cap \ˈhwīt-ˌkap\ *n* : a wave crest breaking into white foam

white chocolate *n* : a whitish chocolate candy

white–col•lar \ˈhwīt-ˈkä-lər\ *adj* : of, relating to, or constituting the class of salaried workers whose duties do not require the wearing of work clothes or protective clothing

white dwarf *n* : a small very dense whitish star of low luminosity

white elephant *n* **1** : an Indian elephant of a pale color that is sometimes venerated in India, Sri Lanka, Thailand, and Myanmar **2** : something requiring much care and expense and giving little profit or enjoyment

white feather *n* [fr. the superstition that a white feather in the plumage of a gamecock is a mark of a poor fighter] : a mark or symbol of cowardice

white•fish \ˈhwīt-ˌfish\ *n* : any of various freshwater food fishes related to the salmons and trouts

white flag *n* : a flag of pure white used to signify truce or surrender

white gold *n* : a pale alloy of gold resembling platinum in appearance

white goods *n pl* : white fabrics or articles (as sheets or towels) typically made of cotton or linen

White•hall \ˈhwīt-ˌhȯl\ *n* : the British government

white•head \-ˌhed\ *n* : a small whitish lump in the skin due to retention of secretion in an oil gland duct

white heat *n* : a temperature higher than red heat at which a body becomes brightly incandescent

white–hot *adj* **1** : being at or radiating white heat **2** : FERVID

White House \-ˌhau̇s\ *n* **1** : the executive department of the U.S. government **2** : a residence of the president of the U.S.

white lead *n* : a heavy white poisonous carbonate of lead used esp. as a pigment in exterior paints

white matter *n* : whitish nerve tissue that consists largely of nerve-cell processes enclosed in a fatty material and that lies under the gray matter of the brain and spinal cord or is collected into nerves

whit•en \ˈhwīt-ᵊn\ *vb* : to make or become white **syn** blanch, bleach — **whit•en•er** *n*

white pine *n* : a tall-growing pine of eastern No. America with needles in clusters of five; *also* : its wood

white sale *n* : a sale on white goods

white shark *n* : GREAT WHITE SHARK

white slave *n* : a woman or girl held unwillingly for purposes of prostitution — **white slavery** *n*

white•tail \ˈhwīt-ˌtāl\ *n* : WHITE-TAILED DEER

white–tailed deer *n* : a No. American deer with a rather long tail white on the underside the males of which have forward-arching antlers

white•wall \ˈhwīt-ˌwȯl\ *n* : an automobile tire having a white band on the sidewall

[1]**white•wash** \-ˌwȯsh, -ˌwäsh\ *vb* **1** : to whiten with whitewash **2** : to clear of a charge of wrongdoing by offering excuses, hiding facts, or conducting a perfunctory investigation **3** : SHUT OUT 2

[2]**whitewash** *n* **1** : a liquid mixture (as of lime and water) for whitening a surface **2** : a clearing of wrongdoing by whitewashing

white•wood \-ˌwu̇d\ *n* : any of various trees and esp. a tulip tree having light-colored wood; *also* : such wood

[1]**whith•er** \ˈhwi-t͟hər\ *adv* **1** : to what place **2** : to what situation, position, degree, or end ⟨~ will this drive him⟩

[2]**whither** *conj* **1** : to the place at, in, or to which; *also* : to which place **2** : to whatever place

whith•er•so•ev•er \ˌhwi-t͟hər-sō-ˈe-vər\ *conj* : to whatever place

[1]**whit•ing** \ˈhwī-tiŋ\ *n* : any of several usu. light or silvery food fishes (as a hake) found mostly near seacoasts

[2]**whiting** *n* : calcium carbonate in powdered form used esp. as a pigment and in putty

whit•low \ˈhwit-ˌlō\ *n* : a deep inflammation of a finger or toe with pus formation

Whit•sun•day \ˈhwit-ˈsən-dē, -sən-ˌdā\ *n* [ME *Whitsonday,* fr. OE *hwīta sunnandæg,* lit., white Sunday; prob. fr. the custom of wearing white robes by those newly baptized at this season] : PENTECOST

whit•tle \ˈhwit-ᵊl\ *vb* **whit•tled; whit•tling 1** : to pare or cut off chips from the surface of (wood) with a knife; *also* : to cut or shape by such paring **2** : to reduce as if by paring down ⟨~ down expenses⟩

[1]**whiz** *or* **whizz** \ˈhwiz\ *vb* **whizzed; whiz•zing** : to hum, whir, or hiss like a speeding object (as an arrow or ball) passing through air

[2]**whiz** *or* **whizz** *n, pl* **whiz•zes** : a hissing, buzzing, or whizzing sound

[3]**whiz** *n, pl* **whiz•zes** : WIZARD 2

who \ˈhü\ *pron* **1** : what or which person or persons ⟨~ did it⟩ ⟨~ is he⟩ ⟨~ are they⟩ **2** : the person or persons that ⟨knows ~ did it⟩ **3** — used to introduce a relative clause and to serve as a substitute therein for the substantive modified by the clause ⟨the man ~ lives there is rich⟩

WHO *abbr* World Health Organization

whoa \ˈwō, ˈhwō, ˈhō\ *vb imper* — a command to an animal to stand still

who•dun•it *also* **who•dun•nit** \hü-ˈdə-nət\ *n* : a detective or mystery story

who•ev•er \hü-ˈe-vər\ *pron* : whatever person : no matter who

[1]**whole** \ˈhōl\ *adj* [ME *hool* healthy, unhurt, entire, fr. OE *hāl*] **1** : being in healthy or sound condition : free from defect or damage **2** : having all its proper parts or elements ⟨~ milk⟩ **3** : constituting the total sum of : ENTIRE ⟨owns the ~ island⟩ **4** : each or all of the ⟨the ~ family⟩ **5** : not scattered or divided : CONCENTRATED ⟨gave me his ~ attention⟩ **6** : seemingly complete or total ⟨the ~ idea is to help, not hinder⟩ **syn** perfect, intact, sound — **whole•ness** *n*

[2]**whole** *n* **1** : a complete amount or sum **2** : something whole or entire — **on the whole 1** : in view of all the circumstances or conditions **2** : in general

whole•heart•ed \ˈhōl-ˈhär-təd\ *adj* : undivided in purpose, enthusiasm, or will : HEARTY, ZESTFUL, SINCERE

whole note *n* : a musical note equal to one measure of four beats

whole number *n* : any of the set of nonnegative integers; *also* : INTEGER

[1]**whole•sale** \ˈhōl-ˌsāl\ *n* : the sale of goods in quantity usu. for resale by a retail merchant

[2]**wholesale** *adj* **1** : performed on a large scale without discrimination ⟨~ slaughter⟩ **2** : of, relating to, or engaged in wholesaling — **wholesale** *adv*

[3]**wholesale** *vb* **whole•saled; whole•sal•ing** : to sell at wholesale — **whole•sal•er** *n*

whole•some \ˈhōl-səm\ *adj* **1** : promoting mental, spiritual, or bodily health or well-being ⟨a ~ environment⟩ **2** : sound in body, mind, or morals : HEALTHY **3** : PRUDENT ⟨~ respect for the law⟩ — **whole•some•ness** *n*

whole step *n* : a musical interval comprising two half steps (as C–D or F♯–G♯)

whole wheat *adj* : made of ground entire wheat kernels

whol•ly \ˈhōl-lē\ *adv* **1** : COMPLETELY, TOTALLY **2** : SOLELY, EXCLUSIVELY

whom \ˈhüm\ *pron, objective case of* WHO

whom•ev•er \hü-ˈme-vər\ *pron, objective case of* WHOEVER

whom•so•ev•er \ˌhüm-sō-ˈe-vər\ *pron, objective case of* WHOSOEVER

[1]**whoop** \ˈhwüp, ˈhwu̇p, ˈhüp, ˈhu̇p\ *vb* **1** : to shout or call loudly and vigorously **2** : to make the characteristic whoop of whooping cough **3** : to go or pass with a loud noise **4** : to utter or express with a whoop; *also* : to urge, drive, or cheer with a whoop

[2]**whoop** *n* **1** : a whooping sound or utterance : SHOUT, HOOT **2** : a crowing intake of breath after a fit of coughing in whooping cough

whooping cough *n* : an infectious bacterial disease esp. of children marked by convulsive coughing fits often followed by a shrill gasping intake of breath

whooping crane *n* : a large white nearly extinct No. American crane noted for its loud whooping call

☞ For illustration, see next page.

whoop•la \ˈhwüp-ˌlä, ˈhwu̇p-\ *n* **1** : HOOPLA **2** : boisterous merrymaking

whooping crane

whop•per \ˈhwä-pər\ *n* : something unusually large or extreme of its kind; *esp* : a monstrous lie
whop•ping \ˈhwä-piŋ\ *adj* : extremely large
whore \ˈhōr\ *n* : PROSTITUTE
whorl \ˈhwȯrl, ˈhwərl\ *n* **1** : a group of parts (as leaves or petals) encircling an axis and esp. a plant stem **2** : something that whirls or coils around a center : COIL, SPIRAL **3** : one of the turns of a snail shell
whorled \ˈhwȯrld, ˈhwərld\ *adj* : having or arranged in whorls
[1]**whose** \ˈhüz\ *adj* : of or relating to whom or which esp. as possessor or possessors, agent or agents, or object or objects of an action ⟨asked ~ bag it was⟩
[2]**whose** *pron* : whose one or ones ⟨~ is this car⟩ ⟨~ are those books⟩
who•so \ˈhü-ˌsō\ *pron* : WHOEVER
who•so•ev•er \ˌhü-sō-ˈe-vər\ *pron* : WHOEVER
whs *or* **whse** *abbr* warehouse
whsle *abbr* wholesale
[1]**why** \ˈhwī\ *adv* : for what reason, cause, or purpose ⟨~ did you do it?⟩
[2]**why** *conj* **1** : the cause, reason, or purpose for which ⟨that is ~ you did it⟩ **2** : for which : on account of which ⟨knows the reason ~ you did it⟩
[3]**why** *n, pl* **whys** : REASON, CAUSE ⟨the ~*s* of racial prejudice⟩
[4]**why** \ˈwī, ˈhwī\ *interj* — used to express surprise, hesitation, approval, disapproval, or impatience ⟨~, here's what I was looking for⟩
WI *abbr* **1** West Indies **2** Wisconsin
WIA *abbr* wounded in action
wick \ˈwik\ *n* : a loosely bound bundle of soft fibers that draws up oil, tallow, or wax to be burned in a candle, oil lamp, or stove
wick•ed \ˈwi-kəd\ *adj* **1** : morally bad : EVIL, SINFUL **2** : FIERCE, VICIOUS **3** : ROGUISH ⟨a ~ glance⟩ **4** : REPUGNANT, VILE ⟨a ~ odor⟩ **5** : HARMFUL, DANGEROUS ⟨a ~ attack⟩ **6** : impressively excellent ⟨throws a ~ fastball⟩ — **wick•ed•ly** *adv* — **wick•ed•ness** *n*
wick•er \ˈwi-kər\ *n* **1** : a small pliant branch (as an osier or a withe) **2** : WICKERWORK — **wicker** *adj*
wick•er•work \-ˌwərk\ *n* : work made of osiers, twigs, or rods : BASKETRY
wick•et \ˈwi-kət\ *n* **1** : a small gate or door; *esp* : one forming a part of or placed near a larger one **2** : a window-like opening usu. with a grille or grate (as at a ticket office) **3** : a set of three upright rods topped by two crosspieces bowled at in cricket **4** : an arch or hoop in croquet
wick•i•up \ˈwi-kē-ˌəp\ *n* : a hut used by nomadic Indians of the western and southwestern U.S. with a usu. oval base and a rough frame covered with reed mats, grass, or brushwood
wid *abbr* widow, widower
[1]**wide** \ˈwīd\ *adj* **wid•er; wid•est 1** : covering a vast area **2** : measured across or at right angles to the length **3** : not narrow : BROAD; *also* : ROOMY **4** : opened to full width ⟨eyes ~ with wonder⟩ **5** : not limited : EXTENSIVE ⟨~ experience⟩ **6** : far from the goal, mark, or truth ⟨a ~ guess⟩ — **wide•ly** *adv*
[2]**wide** *adv* **wid•er; wid•est 1** : over a great distance or extent : WIDELY ⟨searched far and ~⟩ **2** : over a specified distance, area, or extent **3** : so as to leave a wide space between ⟨~ apart⟩ **4** : so as to clear by a considerable distance ⟨ran ~ around left end⟩ **5** : COMPLETELY, FULLY ⟨opened her eyes ~⟩
wide–awake \ˌwīd-ə-ˈwāk\ *adj* : fully awake; *also* : KNOWING, ALERT
wide–body \ˈwīd-ˌbä-dē\ *n* : a large jet aircraft
wide–eyed \ˈwīd-ˈīd\ *adj* **1** : having the eyes wide open esp. with wonder or astonishment **2** : NAIVE
wide•mouthed \-ˈmau̇t͟hd, -ˈmau̇tht\ *adj* **1** : having one's mouth opened wide (as in awe) **2** : having a wide mouth ⟨~ jars⟩
wid•en \ˈwīd-ᵊn\ *vb* : to increase in width, scope, or extent
wide•spread \ˈwīd-ˈspred\ *adj* **1** : widely scattered or prevalent **2** : widely extended or spread out ⟨~ wings⟩
[1]**wid•ow** \ˈwi-dō\ *n* : a woman who has lost her husband by death and has not married again — **wid•ow•hood** *n*
[2]**widow** *vb* : to cause to become a widow or widower
wid•ow•er \ˈwi-də-wər\ *n* : a man who has lost his wife by death and has not married again
width \ˈwidth\ *n* **1** : a distance from side to side : the measurement taken at right angles to the length : BREADTH **2** : largeness of extent or scope; *also* : FULLNESS **3** : a measured and cut piece of material ⟨a ~ of calico⟩
wield \ˈwēld\ *vb* **1** : to use or handle esp. effectively ⟨~ a broom⟩ **2** : to exert authority by means of : EMPLOY ⟨~ influence⟩ — **wield•er** *n*
wie•ner \ˈwē-nər\ *n* [short for *wienerwurst,* fr. G, lit., Vienna sausage] : FRANKFURTER
wife \ˈwīf\ *n, pl* **wives** \ˈwīvz\ **1** *dial* : WOMAN **2** : a woman acting in a specified capacity — used in combination **3** : a female partner in a marriage — **wife•hood** *n* — **wife•less** *adj* — **wife•ly** *adj*
wig \ˈwig\ *n* [short for *periwig,* fr. MF *perruque,* fr. It *parrucca, perrucca* hair, wig] : a manufactured covering of natural or synthetic hair for the head; *also* : TOUPEE
wi•geon *or* **wid•geon** \ˈwi-jən\ *n, pl* **wigeon** *or* **wigeons** *or* **widgeon** *or* **widgeons** : any of several medium-sized freshwater ducks
wig•gle \ˈwi-gəl\ *vb* **wig•gled; wig•gling 1** : to move to and fro with quick jerky or shaking movements : JIGGLE **2** : WRIGGLE — **wiggle** *n*
wig•gler \ˈwi-glər, -gə-lər\ *n* **1** : a larva or pupa of a mosquito **2** : one that wiggles
wig•gly \ˈwi-glē, -gə-lē\ *adj* **1** : tending to wiggle ⟨a ~ worm⟩ **2** : WAVY ⟨~ lines⟩
wight \ˈwīt\ *n* : a living being : CREATURE
wig•let \ˈwi-glət\ *n* : a small wig used esp. to enhance a hairstyle
[1]**wig•wag** \ˈwig-ˌwag\ *vb* **1** : to signal by or as if by a flag or light waved according to a code **2** : to make or cause to make a signal (as with the hand or arm)
[2]**wigwag** *n* : the art or practice of wigwagging
wig•wam \ˈwig-ˌwäm\ *n* : a hut of the Indians of the eastern U.S. having typically an arched framework of poles overlaid with bark, rush mats, or hides
[1]**wild** \ˈwīld\ *adj* **1** : living in a state of nature and not ordinarily tamed ⟨~ ducks⟩ **2** : growing or produced without human aid or care ⟨~ honey⟩ ⟨~ plants⟩ **3** : WASTE, DESOLATE ⟨~ country⟩ **4** : UNCONTROLLED, UNRESTRAINED, UNRULY ⟨~ passions⟩ ⟨a ~ young stallion⟩ **5** : TURBULENT, STORMY ⟨a ~ night⟩ **6** : EXTRAVAGANT, FANTASTIC, CRAZY ⟨~ ideas⟩ **7** : indicative of strong passion, desire, or emotion ⟨a ~ stare⟩ **8** : UNCIVILIZED, SAVAGE **9** : deviating from the natural or expected course : ERRATIC ⟨a ~ throw⟩ **10** : having a denomination determined by the holder ⟨deuces ~⟩ — **wild•ly** *adv* — **wild•ness** *n*
[2]**wild** *adv* **1** : WILDLY **2** : without regulation or control ⟨running ~⟩
[3]**wild** *n* **1** : WILDERNESS **2** : a natural or undomesticated state or existence

wild boar *n* : an Old World wild hog from which most domestic swine have been derived

wild carrot *n* : QUEEN ANNE'S LACE

[1]**wild•cat** \ˈwīld-ˌkat\ *n, pl* **wildcats 1** : any of various small or medium-sized cats (as a lynx or ocelot) **2** : a quick-tempered hard-fighting person

[2]**wildcat** *adj* **1** : not sound or safe ⟨~ schemes⟩ **2** : initiated by a group of workers without formal union approval ⟨~ strike⟩

[3]**wildcat** *vb* **wild•cat•ted; wild•cat•ting** : to drill an oil or gas well in a region not known to be productive

wil•de•beest \ˈwil-də-ˌbēst\ *n, pl* **wildebeests** *also* **wildebeest** [Afrikaans *wildebees,* fr. *wilde* wild + *bees* ox] : GNU

wil•der•ness \ˈwil-dər-nəs\ *n* [ME, fr. *wildern* wild, fr. OE *wilddēoren* of wild beasts] : an uncultivated and uninhabited region

wild•fire \ˈwīld-ˌfīr\ *n* : an uncontrollable fire — **like wildfire** : very rapidly

wild•fowl \-ˌfau̇l\ *n* : a bird and esp. a waterfowl (as a wild duck or goose) hunted as game

wild–goose chase *n* : the pursuit of something unattainable

wild•life \ˈwīld-ˌlīf\ *n* : nonhuman living things and esp. wild animals living in their natural environment

wild oat *n* **1** : any of several wild grasses **2** *pl* : offenses and indiscretions attributed to youthful exuberance — usu. used in the phrase *sow one's wild oats*

wild rice *n* : a No. American aquatic grass; *also* : its edible seed

wild•wood \ˈwīld-ˌwu̇d\ *n* : a wood unaltered or unfrequented by humans

[1]**wile** \ˈwīl\ *n* **1** : a trick or stratagem intended to ensnare or deceive; *also* : a playful trick **2** : TRICKERY, GUILE

[2]**wile** *vb* **wiled; wil•ing** : LURE, ENTICE

[1]**will** \ˈwil\ *vb, past* **would** \ˈwu̇d\; *pres sing & pl* **will 1** : WISH, DESIRE ⟨call it what you ~⟩ **2** — used as an auxiliary verb to express (1) desire, willingness, or in negative constructions refusal ⟨~ you have another⟩ ⟨he *won't* do it⟩, (2) customary or habitual action ⟨~ get angry over nothing⟩, (3) simple futurity ⟨tomorrow we ~ go shopping⟩, (4) capability or sufficiency ⟨the back seat ~ hold three⟩, (5) determination or willfulness ⟨I ~ go despite them⟩, (6) probability ⟨that ~ be the mailman⟩, (7) inevitability ⟨accidents ~ happen⟩, or (8) a command ⟨you ~ do as I say⟩

[2]**will** *n* **1** : wish or desire often combined with determination ⟨the ~ to win⟩ **2** : something desired; *esp* : a choice or determination of one having authority or power **3** : the act, process, or experience of willing : VOLITION **4** : the mental powers manifested as wishing, choosing, desiring, or intending **5** : a disposition to act according to principles or ends **6** : power of controlling one's own actions or emotions ⟨a leader of iron ~⟩ **7** : a legal document in which a person declares to whom his or her possessions are to go after death

[3]**will** *vb* **1** : to dispose of by or as if by a will : BEQUEATH **2** : to determine by an act of choice; *also* : DECREE, ORDAIN **3** : INTEND, PURPOSE; *also* : CHOOSE

will•ful *or* **wil•ful** \ˈwil-fəl\ *adj* **1** : governed by will without regard to reason : OBSTINATE **2** : INTENTIONAL ⟨~ murder⟩ — **will•ful•ly** *adv*

wil•lies \ˈwi-lēz\ *n pl* : a fit of nervousness : JITTERS — used with *the*

will•ing \ˈwi-liŋ\ *adj* **1** : inclined or favorably disposed in mind : READY ⟨~ to go⟩ **2** : prompt to act or respond ⟨~ workers⟩ **3** : done, borne, or accepted voluntarily or without reluctance **4** : of or relating to the will : VOLITIONAL — **will•ing•ly** *adv* — **will•ing•ness** *n*

wil•li•waw \ˈwi-lē-ˌwȯ\ *n* : a sudden violent gust of cold land air common along mountainous coasts of high latitudes

will–o'–the–wisp \ˌwil-ə-t͟hə-ˈwisp\ *n* **1** : a light that appears at night over marshy grounds **2** : a misleading or elusive goal or hope

wil•low \ˈwi-lō\ *n* **1** : any of a genus of quick-growing shrubs and trees with tough pliable shoots **2** : an object made of willow wood

wil•low•ware \-ˌwar\ *n* : dinnerware that is usu. blue and white and that is decorated with a story-telling design featuring a large willow tree by a little bridge

wil•lowy \ˈwi-lə-wē\ *adj* : PLIANT; *also* : gracefully tall and slender

will•pow•er \ˈwil-ˌpau̇-ər\ *n* : energetic determination : RESOLUTENESS

wil•ly–nil•ly \ˌwi-lē-ˈni-lē\ *adv or adj* [alter. of *will I nill I* or *will ye nill ye* or *will he nill he*; *nill* fr. archaic *nill* to be unwilling, fr. ME *nilen,* fr. OE *nyllan,* fr. *ne* not + *wyllan* to wish] : without regard for one's choice : by compulsion ⟨they rushed us along ~⟩

[1]**wilt** \ˈwilt\ *vb* **1** : to lose or cause to lose freshness and become limp esp. from lack of water : DROOP **2** : to grow weak or faint : LANGUISH

[2]**wilt** *n* : any of various plant disorders marked by wilting and often shriveling

wily \ˈwī-lē\ *adj* **wil•i•er; -est** : full of guile : TRICKY — **wil•i•ness** \-lē-nəs\ *n*

wimp \ˈwimp\ *n* : a weak, cowardly, or ineffectual person — **wimpy** \ˈwim-pē\ *adj*

[1]**wim•ple** \ˈwim-pəl\ *n* : a cloth covering worn over the head and around the neck and chin by women esp. in the late medieval period and by some nuns

[2]**wimple** *vb* **wim•pled; wim•pling 1** : to cover with or as if with a wimple **2** : to ripple or cause to ripple

[1]**win** \ˈwin\ *vb* **won** \ˈwən\; **win•ning** [ME *winnen,* fr. OE *winnan* to struggle] **1** : to get possession of esp. by effort : GAIN; *also* : to obtain by work : EARN **2** : to gain in or as if in battle or contest; *also* : to be the victor in ⟨*won* the war⟩ **3** : to solicit and gain the favor of; *esp* : to induce to accept oneself in marriage

[2]**win** *n* : VICTORY; *esp* : 1st place at the finish (as of a horse race)

wince \ˈwins\ *vb* **winced; winc•ing** : to shrink back involuntarily (as from pain) : FLINCH — **wince** *n*

winch \ˈwinch\ *n* : a machine that has a drum on which is wound a rope or cable for hauling or hoisting — **winch** *vb*

[1]**wind** \ˈwind\ *n* **1** : a movement of the air **2** : a prevailing force or influence : TENDENCY, TREND **3** : BREATH ⟨he had the ~ knocked out of him⟩ **4** : gas produced in the stomach or intestines **5** : something insubstantial; *esp* : idle words **6** : air carrying a scent (as of game) **7** : INTIMATION ⟨they got ~ of our plans⟩ **8** : WIND INSTRUMENTS; *also, pl* : players of wind instruments

[2]**wind** *vb* **1** : to get a scent of ⟨the dogs ~*ed* the game⟩ **2** : to cause to be out of breath ⟨he was ~*ed* from the climb⟩ **3** : to allow (as a horse) to rest so as to recover breath

[3]**wind** \ˈwīnd, ˈwind\ *vb* **wind•ed** \ˈwīn-dəd, ˈwin-\ *or* **wound** \ˈwau̇nd\; **wind•ing** : to sound by blowing ⟨~ a horn⟩

[4]**wind** \ˈwīnd\ *vb* **wound** \ˈwau̇nd\ *also* **wind•ed; wind•ing 1** : ENTANGLE, INVOLVE **2** : to introduce stealthily : INSINUATE **3** : to encircle or cover with something pliable : WRAP, COIL, TWINE ⟨~ a bobbin⟩ **4** : to hoist or haul by a rope or chain and a winch **5** : to tighten the spring of; *also* : CRANK **6** : to raise to a high level (as of excitement) **7** : to cause to move in a curving line or path **8** : to have a curving course or shape ⟨a river ~*ing* through the valley⟩ **9** : to move or lie so as to encircle

[5]**wind** \ˈwīnd\ *n* : COIL, TURN

wind•age \ˈwin-dij\ *n* : the influence of the wind in deflecting the course of a projectile through the air; *also* : the amount of such deflection

wind•bag \ˈwind-ˌbag\ *n* : an overly talkative person

wind•blown \-ˌblōn\ *adj* : blown by the wind; *also*

: having the appearance of being blown by the wind

wind•break \-ˌbrāk\ *n* : a growth of trees or shrubs serving to break the force of the wind; *also* : a shelter from the wind

wind•break•er \-ˌbrā-kər\ *n* : a light jacket made of material that can resist the wind

wind–bro•ken \-ˌbrō-kən\ *adj* : having the power of breathing impaired by disease — used of a horse

wind•burned \-ˌbərnd\ *adj* : irritated and inflamed by exposure to the wind — **wind•burn** \-ˌbərn\ *n*

wind•chill \-ˌchil\ *n* : a still-air temperature that would have the same cooling effect on exposed human skin as a given combination of temperature and wind speed

windchill factor *n* : WINDCHILL

wind•er \ˈwīn-dər\ *n* : one that winds

wind•fall \ˈwind-ˌfȯl\ *n* **1** : something (as a tree or fruit) blown down by the wind **2** : an unexpected or sudden gift, gain, or advantage

wind•flow•er \-ˌflau̇-ər\ *n* : ANEMONE

[1]**wind•ing** \ˈwīn-diŋ\ *n* : material (as wire) wound or coiled about an object

[2]**winding** *adj* **1** : having a pronounced curve or spiral ⟨~ stairs⟩ **2** : having a course that winds ⟨a ~ road⟩

wind•ing–sheet \-ˌshēt\ *n* : SHROUD

wind instrument *n* : a musical instrument (as a flute or horn) sounded by wind and esp. by the breath

wind•jam•mer \ˈwind-ˌja-mər\ *n* : a sailing ship; *also* : one of its crew

wind•lass \ˈwind-ləs\ *n* [ME *wyndlas*, alter. of *wyndas*, fr. ON *vindāss*, fr. *vinda* to wind + *āss* pole] : a winch used esp. on ships for hoisting or hauling

wind•mill \ˈwind-ˌmil\ *n* : a mill or machine worked by the wind turning sails or vanes that radiate from a central shaft

win•dow \ˈwin-dō\ *n* [ME *windowe*, fr. ON *vindauga*, fr. *vindr* wind + *auga* eye] **1** : an opening in the wall of a building to let in light and air; *also* : the framework with fittings that closes such an opening **2** : WINDOWPANE **3** : an opening resembling or suggesting that of a window in a building **4** : an interval of time during which certain conditions or an opportunity exists **5** : an area of a computer display on which different information may be displayed independently — **win•dow•less** *adj*

window box *n* : a box for growing plants in or by a window

window dressing *n* **1** : display of merchandise in a store window **2** : a showing made to create a deceptively favorable impression

win•dow•pane \ˈwin-dō-ˌpān\ *n* : a pane in a window

win•dow–shop \-ˌshäp\ *vb* : to look at the displays in store windows without going inside the stores to make purchases — **win•dow–shop•per** *n*

win•dow•sill \-ˌsil\ *n* : the horizontal member at the bottom of a window

wind•pipe \ˈwind-ˌpīp\ *n* : the passage for the breath from the larynx to the lungs

wind•proof \-ˈprüf\ *adj* : impervious to wind ⟨a ~ jacket⟩

wind•row \ˈwind-ˌrō\ *n* **1** : hay raked up into a row to dry **2** : a row of something (as dry leaves) swept up by or as if by the wind

wind shear *n* : a radical shift in wind speed and direction that occurs over a very short distance

wind•shield \ˈwind-ˌshēld\ *n* : a transparent screen (as of glass) in front of the occupants of a vehicle

wind sock *n* : an open-ended truncated cloth cone mounted in an elevated position to indicate wind direction

wind•storm \-ˌstȯrm\ *n* : a storm with high wind and little or no rain

wind•surf•ing \-ˌsər-fiŋ\ *n* : the sport or activity of riding a sailboard — **wind•surf** \-ˌsərf\ *vb* — **wind•surf•er** *n*

wind•swept \ˈwind-ˌswept\ *adj* : swept by or as if by wind ⟨~ plains⟩

wind tunnel *n* : an enclosed passage through which air is blown to investigate air flow around an object

wind•up \ˈwīn-ˌdəp\ *n* **1** : CONCLUSION, FINISH **2** : a series of regular and distinctive motions made by a pitcher preliminary to delivering a pitch

wind up *vb* **1** : to bring or come to a conclusion : END **2** : to put in order for the purpose of bringing to an end **3** : to arrive in a place, situation, or condition at the end or as a result of a course of action ⟨*wound up* as paupers⟩ **4** : to make a pitching windup

[1]**wind•ward** \ˈwin-dwərd\ *n* : the side or direction from which the wind is blowing

[2]**windward** *adj* : being in or facing the direction from which the wind is blowing

windy \ˈwin-dē\ *adj* **wind•i•er; -est** **1** : having wind : exposed to winds ⟨a ~ day⟩ ⟨a ~ prairie⟩ **2** : STORMY **3** : FLATULENT **4** : indulging in or characterized by useless talk : VERBOSE

[1]**wine** \ˈwīn\ *n* **1** : fermented grape juice used as a beverage **2** : the usu. fermented juice of a plant product (as fruit) used as a beverage ⟨rice ~⟩

[2]**wine** *vb* **wined; win•ing** : to treat to or drink wine

wine cellar *n* : a room for storing wines; *also* : a stock of wines

wine•grow•er \-ˌgrō-ər\ *n* : one that cultivates a vineyard and makes wine

wine•press \-ˌpres\ *n* : a vat in which juice is pressed from grapes

[1]**wing** \ˈwiŋ\ *n* **1** : one of the movable feathered or membranous paired appendages by means of which a bird, bat, or insect flies **2** : something suggesting a wing; *esp* : an airfoil that develops the lift which supports an aircraft in flight **3** : a plant or animal appendage or part likened to a wing **4** : a turned-back or extended edge on an article of clothing **5** : a means of flight or rapid progress **6** : the act or manner of flying : FLIGHT **7** *pl* : the area at the side of the stage out of sight **8** : one of the positions or players on either side of a center position or line **9** : either of two opposing groups within an organization : FACTION **10** : a unit in military aviation consisting of two or more squadrons — **wing•less** *adj* — **on the wing** : in flight : FLYING — **under one's wing** : in one's charge or care

[2]**wing** *vb* **1** : to fit with wings; *also* : to enable to fly easily **2** : to pass through in flight : FLY ⟨~ the air⟩ ⟨swallows ~*ing* southward⟩ **3** : to let fly : DISPATCH **4** : to wound in the wing ⟨~ a bird⟩; *also* : to wound without killing **5** : to perform without preparation : IMPROVISE ⟨~*ing* it⟩

wing•ding \ˈwiŋ-ˌdiŋ\ *n* : a wild, lively, or lavish party

winged \ˈwiŋd, ˈwiŋ-əd, *in compounds* ˈwiŋd\ *adj* **1** : having wings esp. of a specified character **2** : soaring with or as if with wings : ELEVATED **3** : SWIFT, RAPID

wing•span \ˈwiŋ-ˌspan\ *n* : the distance between the tips of a pair of wings

wing•spread \-ˌspred\ *n* : the spread of the wings; *esp* : the distance between the tips of the fully extended wings of a winged animal

[1]**wink** \ˈwiŋk\ *vb* **1** : to close and open one eye quickly as a signal or hint **2** : to close and open the eyes quickly : BLINK **3** : to avoid seeing or noticing something ⟨~ at a traffic violation⟩ **4** : TWINKLE, FLICKER — **wink•er** \ˈwiŋ-kər\ *n*

[2]**wink** *n* **1** : a brief period of sleep : NAP **2** : an act of winking; *esp* : a hint or sign given by winking **3** : INSTANT ⟨dries in a ~⟩

win•ner \ˈwi-nər\ *n* : one that wins

[1]**win•ning** \ˈwi-niŋ\ *n* **1** : VICTORY **2** : something won; *esp* : money won at gambling ⟨large ~*s*⟩

[2]**winning** *adj* **1** : successful esp. in competition **2** : ATTRACTIVE, CHARMING

win•now \ˈwi-nō\ *vb* **1** : to remove (as chaff) by a current of air; *also* : to free (as grain) from waste in this manner **2** : to sort or separate as if by winnowing

wino \ˈwī-nō\ *n, pl* **win•os** : one who is addicted to drinking wine

win•some \ˈwin-səm\ *adj* [ME *winsum,* fr. OE *wynsum,* fr. *wynn* joy] **1** : generally pleasing and engaging **2** : CHEERFUL, GAY — **win•some•ly** *adv* — **win•some•ness** *n*

[1]**win•ter** \ˈwin-tər\ *n* : the season of the year in any region in which the noonday sun shines most obliquely : the coldest period of the year

[2]**winter** *adj* : sown in autumn for harvesting in the following spring or summer ⟨~ wheat⟩

win•ter•green \ˈwin-tər-ˌgrēn\ *n* **1** : a low evergreen plant of the heath family with white bell-shaped flowers and spicy red berries **2** : an aromatic oil from the common wintergreen or its flavor or something flavored with it

win•ter•ize \ˈwin-tə-ˌrīz\ *vb* **-ized; -iz•ing** : to make ready for winter

win•ter–kill \ˈwin-tər-ˌkil\ *vb* : to kill or die by exposure to winter weather

winter squash *n* : any of various hard-shelled squashes that keep well in storage

win•ter•tide \-ˌtīd\ *n* : WINTER

win•ter•time \-ˌtīm\ *n* : WINTER

win•try \ˈwin-trē\ *also* **win•tery** \ˈwin-tə-rē\ *adj* **win•tri•er; -est 1** : of, relating to, or characteristic of winter ⟨~ weather⟩ **2** : CHILLING, CHEERLESS ⟨a ~ welcome⟩

[1]**wipe** \ˈwīp\ *vb* **wiped; wip•ing 1** : to clean or dry by rubbing ⟨~ dishes⟩ **2** : to remove by or as if by rubbing ⟨~ away tears⟩ **3** : to erase completely : OBLITERATE **4** : to pass or draw over a surface ⟨*wiped* his hand across his face⟩ — **wip•er** *n*

[2]**wipe** *n* **1** : an act or instance of wiping; *also* : BLOW, STRIKE, SWIPE **2** : something used for wiping

wipe out *vb* : to destroy completely

[1]**wire** \ˈwīr\ *n* **1** : metal in the form of a thread or slender rod; *also* : a thread or rod of metal **2** : hidden or secret influences controlling the action of a person or organization — usu. used in pl. ⟨pull ~*s*⟩ **3** : a line of wire for conducting electric current **4** : a telegraph or telephone wire or system **5** : TELEGRAM, CABLEGRAM **6** : the finish line of a race

[2]**wire** *vb* **wired; wir•ing 1** : to provide or equip with wire ⟨~ a house⟩ **2** : to bind, string, or mount with wire **3** : to send or send word to by telegraph

wire•hair \ˈwīr-ˌhar\ *n* : a wirehaired dog or cat

wire•haired \-ˈhard\ *adj* : having a stiff wiry outer coat of hair

[1]**wire•less** \-ləs\ *adj* **1** : having no wire or wires **2** *chiefly Brit* : RADIO

[2]**wireless** *n* **1** : wireless telegraphy **2** *chiefly Brit* : RADIO

wire–pull•er \-ˌpu̇-lər\ *n* : one who uses secret or underhanded means to influence the acts of a person or organization — **wire–pull•ing** *n*

wire service *n* : a news agency that sends out syndicated news copy to subscribers by wire or satellite

wire•tap \-ˌtap\ *n* : the act or an instance of tapping a telephone or telegraph wire to get information; *also* : an electrical connection used for such tapping — **wiretap** *vb* — **wire•tap•per** \-ˌta-pər\ *n*

wire•worm \-ˌwərm\ *n* : any of various slender hard-coated beetle larvae esp. destructive to plant roots

wir•ing \ˈwīr-iŋ\ *n* : a system of wires

wiry \ˈwīr-ē\ *adj* **wir•i•er** \ˈwī-rē-ər\; **-est 1** : made of or resembling wire **2** : slender yet strong and sinewy — **wir•i•ness** \ˈwī-rē-nəs\ *n*

Wis *or* **Wisc** *abbr* Wisconsin

Wisd *abbr* Wisdom

wis•dom \ˈwiz-dəm\ *n* [ME, fr. OE *wīsdom,* fr. *wīs* wise] **1** : accumulated philosophic or scientific learning : KNOWLEDGE; *also* : INSIGHT **2** : good sense : JUDGMENT **3** : a wise attitude or course of action

Wisdom *n* — see BIBLE table

wisdom of Sol•o•mon \-ˈsä-lə-mən\ — see BIBLE table

wisdom tooth *n* : the last tooth of the full set on each half of each human jaw

[1]**wise** \ˈwīz\ *n* : WAY, MANNER, FASHION ⟨in no ~⟩ ⟨in this ~⟩

[2]**wise** *adj* **wis•er; wis•est 1** : having wisdom : SAGE **2** : having or showing good sense or good judgment **3** : aware of what is going on : KNOWING; *also* : CRAFTY, SHREWD **4** : possessing inside information — **wise•ly** *adv*

-wise \-ˌwīz\ *adv comb form* : in the manner or direction of ⟨slant*wise*⟩

wise•acre \ˈwī-ˌzā-kər\ *n* [MD *wijssegger* soothsayer] : SMART ALECK

[1]**wise•crack** \ˈwīz-ˌkrak\ *n* : a clever, smart, or flippant remark

[2]**wisecrack** *vb* : to make a wisecrack

[1]**wish** \ˈwish\ *vb* **1** : to have a desire : long for ⟨~ you were here⟩ ⟨~ for a puppy⟩ **2** : to form or express a wish concerning ⟨~*ed* him a happy birthday⟩ **3** : BID ⟨he ~*ed* me good morning⟩ **4** : to request by expressing a desire ⟨I ~ you to go now⟩

[2]**wish** *n* **1** : an act or instance of wishing or desire : WANT; *also* : GOAL **2** : an expressed will or desire

wish•bone \-ˌbōn\ *n* : a forked bone in front of the breastbone in most birds

wish•ful \ˈwish-fəl\ *adj* **1** : expressive of a wish; *also* : having a wish **2** : according with wishes rather than fact ⟨~ thinking⟩

wishy–washy \ˈwi-shē-ˌwȯ-shē, -ˌwä-\ *adj* : WEAK, INSIPID; *also* : morally feeble

wisp \ˈwisp\ *n* **1** : a small handful (as of hay or straw) **2** : a thin strand, strip, or fragment ⟨a ~ of hair⟩; *also* : a thready streak ⟨a ~ of smoke⟩ **3** : something frail, slight, or fleeting ⟨a ~ of a smile⟩ — **wispy** *adj*

wis•te•ria \wis-ˈtir-ē-ə\ *or* **wis•tar•ia** \-ˈtir-ē-ə *also* -ˈter-\ *n* : any of a genus of chiefly Asian mostly woody vines related to the peas and widely grown for their long showy clusters of blue, white, purple, or rose flowers

wist•ful \ˈwist-fəl\ *adj* : feeling or showing a timid desire — **wist•ful•ly** *adv* — **wist•ful•ness** *n*

wit \ˈwit\ *n* **1** : reasoning power : INTELLIGENCE **2** : mental soundness : SANITY — usu. used in pl. **3** : RESOURCEFULNESS, INGENUITY; *esp* : quickness and cleverness in handling words and ideas **4** : a talent for making clever remarks; *also* : a person noted for making witty remarks — **wit•ted** \ˈwi-təd\ *adj* — **at one's wit's end** : at a loss for a means of solving a problem

[1]**witch** \ˈwich\ *n* **1** : a person believed to have magic power; *esp* : SORCERESS **2** : an ugly old woman : HAG **3** : a charming or alluring girl or woman

[2]**witch** *vb* : BEWITCH

witch•craft \ˈwich-ˌkraft\ *n* : the power or practices of a witch : SORCERY

witch doctor *n* : a person in a primitive society who uses magic to treat sickness and to fight off evil spirits

witch•ery \ˈwi-chə-rē\ *n, pl* **-er•ies 1** : SORCERY **2** : FASCINATION, CHARM

witch•grass \ˈwich-ˌgras\ *n* : any of several grasses that are weeds in cultivated areas

witch ha•zel \ˈwich-ˌhā-zəl\ *n* **1** : a shrub of eastern No. America bearing small yellow flowers in the fall **2** : a soothing alcoholic lotion made from witch hazel bark

witch–hunt \ˈwich-ˌhənt\ *n* **1** : a searching out and persecution of persons accused of witchcraft **2** : the searching out and deliberate harassment esp. of political opponents

witch•ing \ˈwi-chiŋ\ *adj* : of, relating to, or suitable for sorcery or supernatural occurrences

with \ˈwith, ˈwith\ *prep* **1** : AGAINST ⟨a fight ~ his brother⟩ **2** : FROM ⟨parting ~ friends⟩ **3** : in mutual relation to ⟨talk ~ a friend⟩ **4** : in the company of ⟨went there ~ her⟩ **5** : AS REGARDS, TOWARD ⟨is patient ~

children⟩ **6** : compared to ⟨on equal terms ~ another⟩ **7** : in support of ⟨I'm ~ you all the way⟩ **8** : in the presence of : CONTAINING ⟨tea ~ sugar⟩ **9** : in the opinion of : as judged by ⟨their arguments had weight ~ her⟩ **10** : BECAUSE OF, THROUGH ⟨pale ~ anger⟩; *also* : by means of ⟨hit him ~ a club⟩ **11** : in a manner indicating ⟨work ~ a will⟩ **12** : GIVEN, GRANTED ⟨~ your permission I'll leave⟩ **13** : HAVING ⟨came ~ good news⟩ ⟨stood there ~ his mouth open⟩ **14** : at the time of : right after ⟨~ that we left⟩ **15** : DESPITE ⟨~ all her cleverness, she failed⟩ **16** : in the direction of ⟨swim ~ the tide⟩

with•al \wi-ˈthȯl, -ˈthȯl\ *adv* **1** : together with this : BESIDES **2** : on the other hand : NEVERTHELESS

with•draw \with-ˈdrȯ, with-\ *vb* **-drew** \-ˈdrü\; **-drawn** \-ˈdrȯn\; **-draw•ing** \-ˈdrȯ-iŋ\ **1** : to take back or away : REMOVE **2** : to call back (as from consideration); *also* : RETRACT **3** : to go away : RETREAT, LEAVE **4** : to terminate one's participation in or use of something

with•draw•al \-ˈdrȯ-əl\ *n* **1** : an act or instance of withdrawing **2** : the discontinuance of the use or administration of a drug and esp. an addicting drug; *also* : the period following such discontinuance marked by often painful physiological and psychological symptoms **3** : a pathological retreat from the real world (as in some schizophrenic states)

with•drawn \with-ˈdrȯn\ *adj* **1** : ISOLATED, SECLUDED **2** : socially detached and unresponsive

withe \ˈwith\ *n* : a slender flexible twig or branch

with•er \ˈwi-thər\ *vb* **1** : to shrivel from or as if from loss of bodily moisture and esp. sap **2** : to lose or cause to lose vitality, force, or freshness **3** : to cause to feel shriveled ⟨~*ed* him with a glance⟩

with•ers \ˈwi-thərz\ *n pl* : the ridge between the shoulder bones of a horse; *also* : the corresponding part in other 4-footed animals

with•hold \with-ˈhōld, with-\ *vb* **-held** \-ˈheld\; **-hold•ing** **1** : to hold back : RESTRAIN; *also* : RETAIN **2** : to refrain from granting, giving, or allowing ⟨~ permission⟩ ⟨~ names⟩

withholding tax *n* : a tax on income withheld at the source

[1]**with•in** \wi-ˈthin, -ˈthin-\ *adv* **1** : in or into the interior : INSIDE **2** : inside oneself : INWARDLY

[2]**within** *prep* **1** : inside the limits or influence of ⟨~ call⟩ **2** : in the limits or compass of ⟨~ a mile⟩ **3** : in or to the inner part of ⟨~ the room⟩

with–it \ˈwi-thət, -thət\ *adj* : socially or culturally up-to-date

[1]**with•out** \wi-ˈthau̇t, -ˈthau̇t\ *prep* **1** : OUTSIDE **2** : LACKING ⟨~ hope⟩; *also* : not accompanied by or showing ⟨spoke ~ thinking⟩

[2]**without** *adv* **1** : on the outside : EXTERNALLY **2** : with something lacking or absent ⟨has learned to do ~⟩

with•stand \with-ˈstand, with-\ *vb* **-stood** \-ˈstu̇d\; **-stand•ing** : to stand against : RESIST; *esp* : to oppose (as an attack) successfully

wit•less \ˈwit-ləs\ *adj* : lacking wit or understanding : FOOLISH — **wit•less•ly** *adv* — **wit•less•ness** *n*

[1]**wit•ness** \ˈwit-nəs\ *n* [ME *witnesse*, fr. OE *witnes* knowledge, testimony, witness, fr. *wit* mind, intelligence] **1** : TESTIMONY ⟨bear ~ to the fact⟩ **2** : one that gives evidence; *esp* : one who testifies in a cause or before a court **3** : one present at a transaction so as to be able to testify that it has taken place **4** : one who has personal knowledge or experience of something **5** : something serving as evidence or proof : SIGN

[2]**witness** *vb* **1** : to bear witness : TESTIFY **2** : to act as legal witness of **3** : to furnish proof of : BETOKEN **4** : to be a witness of **5** : to be the scene of ⟨this region has ~*ed* many wars⟩

wit•ti•cism \ˈwi-tə-ˌsi-zəm\ *n* : a witty saying or phrase

wit•ting \ˈwi-tiŋ\ *adj* : done knowingly : INTENTIONAL — **wit•ting•ly** *adv*

wit•ty \ˈwi-tē\ *adj* **wit•ti•er; -est** : marked by or full of wit : AMUSING ⟨a ~ writer⟩ ⟨a ~ remark⟩ **syn** humorous, facetious, jocular, jocose — **wit•ti•ly** \-tə-lē\ *adv* — **wit•ti•ness** \-tē-nəs\ *n*

wive \ˈwīv\ *vb* **wived; wiv•ing** : to take a wife

wives *pl of* WIFE

wiz•ard \ˈwi-zərd\ *n* [ME *wysard* wise man, fr. *wys* wise] **1** : MAGICIAN, SORCERER **2** : a very clever or skillful person ⟨a ~ at chess⟩

wiz•ard•ry \ˈwi-zər-drē\ *n, pl* **-ries** **1** : magic skill : SORCERY **2** : great skill or cleverness in an activity

wiz•en \ˈwiz-ᵊn, ˈwēz-\ *vb* : to become or cause to become dry, shrunken, or wrinkled

wk *abbr* **1** week **2** work

WL *abbr* wavelength

wmk *abbr* watermark

WNW *abbr* west-northwest

WO *abbr* warrant officer

w/o *abbr* without

woad \ˈwōd\ *n* : a European herb related to the mustards; *also* : a blue dyestuff made from its leaves

wob•ble \ˈwä-bəl\ *vb* **wob•bled; wob•bling** **1** : to move or cause to move with an irregular rocking or side-to-side motion **2** : TREMBLE, QUAVER **3** : WAVER, VACILLATE — **wobble** *n* — **wob•bly** \-bə-lē\ *adj*

woe \ˈwō\ *n* **1** : deep suffering from misfortune, affliction, or grief **2** : TROUBLE, MISFORTUNE ⟨economic ~*s*⟩

woe•be•gone \ˈwō-bi-ˌgȯn\ *adj* : exhibiting woe, sorrow, or misery; *also* : being in a sorry condition

woe•ful *also* **wo•ful** \ˈwō-fəl\ *adj* **1** : full of woe : AFFLICTED **2** : involving, bringing, or relating to woe **3** : DEPLORABLE — **woe•ful•ly** *adv*

wok \ˈwäk\ *n* : a bowl-shaped cooking utensil used esp. in stir-frying

woke *past of* WAKE

woken *past part of* WAKE

wold \ˈwōld\ *n* : an upland plain or stretch of rolling land without woods

[1]**wolf** \ˈwu̇lf\ *n, pl* **wolves** \ˈwu̇lvz\ **1** : any of several large erect-eared bushy-tailed doglike predatory mammals that live and hunt in packs; *esp* : GRAY WOLF **2** : a fierce or destructive person — **wolf•ish** *adj*

[2]**wolf** *vb* : to eat greedily : DEVOUR

wolf•hound \-ˌhau̇nd\ *n* : any of several large dogs orig. used in hunting wolves

wol•fram \ˈwu̇l-frəm\ *n* : TUNGSTEN

wol•ver•ine \ˌwu̇l-və-ˈrēn\ *n, pl* **wolverines** *also* **wolverine** : a dark shaggy-coated flesh-eating mammal of northern forests and associated tundra that is related to the weasels

wom•an \ˈwu̇-mən\ *n, pl* **wom•en** \ˈwi-mən\ [ME, fr. OE *wīfman*, fr. *wīf* woman, wife + *man* human being, man] **1** : an adult female person **2** : WOMANKIND **3** : feminine nature : WOMANLINESS **4** : a female servant or attendant

wom•an•hood \ˈwu̇-mən-ˌhu̇d\ *n* **1** : the state of being a woman : the distinguishing qualities of a woman or of womankind **2** : WOMEN, WOMANKIND

wom•an•ish \ˈwu̇-mə-nish\ *adj* **1** : of, relating to, or characteristic of a woman **2** : suitable to a woman rather than to a man : EFFEMINATE

wom•an•kind \ˈwu̇-mən-ˌkīnd\ *n* : the females of the human race : WOMEN

wom•an•like \-ˌlīk\ *adj* : WOMANLY

wom•an•ly \-lē\ *adj* : having qualities characteristic of a woman — **wom•an•li•ness** \-lē-nəs\ *n*

woman suffrage *n* : possession and exercise of suffrage by women

womb \ˈwüm\ *n* **1** : UTERUS **2** : a place where something is generated

wom•bat \ˈwäm-ˌbat\ *n* : any of several stocky burrowing Australian marsupials that resemble small bears

wom•en•folk \ˈwi-mən-ˌfōk\ *also* **wom•en•folks** \-ˌfōks\ *n pl* : WOMEN

[1]**won** \ˈwən\ *past and past part of* WIN

[2]**won** \ˈwȯn\ *n, pl* **won** — see MONEY table

[1]**won·der** \ˈwən-dər\ *n* **1** : a cause of astonishment or surprise : MARVEL; *also* : MIRACLE **2** : the quality of exciting wonder ⟨the charm and ~ of the scene⟩ **3** : a feeling (as of awed astonishment or uncertainty) aroused by something extraordinary or affecting

[2]**wonder** *vb* **1** : to feel surprise or amazement **2** : to feel curiosity or doubt

wonder drug *n* : MIRACLE DRUG

won·der·ful \ˈwən-dər-fəl\ *adj* **1** : exciting wonder : MARVELOUS, ASTONISHING **2** : unusually good : ADMIRABLE — **won·der·ful·ly** \-f(ə-)lē\ *adv* — **won·der·ful·ness** *n*

won·der·land \-ˌland, -lənd\ *n* **1** : an imaginary place of delicate beauty or magical charm **2** : a place that excites admiration or wonder

won·der·ment \-mənt\ *n* **1** : ASTONISHMENT, SURPRISE **2** : a cause of or occasion for wonder **3** : curiosity about something

won·drous \ˈwən-drəs\ *adj* : WONDERFUL, MARVELOUS — **won·drous·ly** *adv* — **won·drous·ness** *n*

[1]**wont** \ˈwȯnt, ˈwōnt\ *adj* [ME *woned, wont,* fr. pp. of *wonen* to dwell, be used to, fr. OE *wunian*] **1** : ACCUSTOMED, USED ⟨as we are ~ to do⟩ **2** : INCLINED, APT

[2]**wont** *n* : CUSTOM, USAGE, HABIT ⟨according to her ~⟩

won't \ˈwōnt\ : will not

wont·ed \ˈwȯn-təd, ˈwōn-\ *adj* : ACCUSTOMED, CUSTOMARY ⟨his ~ courtesy⟩

woo \ˈwü\ *vb* **1** : to try to gain the love of : COURT **2** : SOLICIT, ENTREAT **3** : to try to gain or bring about ⟨~ public favor⟩ — **woo·er** *n*

[1]**wood** \ˈwu̇d\ *n* **1** : a dense growth of trees usu. larger than a grove and smaller than a forest — often used in pl. **2** : a hard fibrous substance that is basically xylem and forms the bulk of trees and shrubs beneath the bark; *also* : this material fit or prepared for some use (as burning or building) **3** : something made of wood

[2]**wood** *adj* **1** : WOODEN **2** : suitable for holding, cutting, or working with wood **3** *or* **woods** \ˈwu̇dz\ : living or growing in woods

[3]**wood** *vb* **1** : to supply or load with wood esp. for fuel **2** : to cover with a growth of trees

wood alcohol *n* : METHANOL

wood·bine \ˈwu̇d-ˌbīn\ *n* : any of several honeysuckles; *also* : VIRGINIA CREEPER

wood·block \-ˌbläk\ *n* : WOODCUT

wood·chop·per \-ˌchä-pər\ *n* : one engaged esp. in chopping down trees

wood·chuck \-ˌchək\ *n* : a thickset grizzled marmot of Alaska, Canada, and the northeastern U.S.

wood·cock \ˈwu̇d-ˌkäk\ *n, pl* **woodcocks** : a brown eastern No. American game bird with a short neck and long bill that is related to the snipe; *also* : a related and similar Old World bird

wood·craft \-ˌkraft\ *n* **1** : skill and practice in matters relating to the woods and esp. in how to take care of oneself in them **2** : skill in shaping or constructing articles from wood

wood·cut \-ˌkət\ *n* **1** : a relief printing surface engraved on a block of wood **2** : a print from a woodcut

wood·cut·ter \-ˌkə-tər\ *n* : a person who cuts wood

wood·ed \ˈwu̇-dəd\ *adj* : covered with woods or trees ⟨~ slopes⟩

wood·en \ˈwu̇d-ᵊn\ *adj* **1** : made of wood **2** : lacking flexibility : awkwardly stiff — **wood·en·ly** *adv* — **wood·en·ness** *n*

wood·en·ware \ˈwu̇d-ᵊn-ˌwar\ *n* : articles made of wood for domestic use

wood·land \ˈwu̇d-lənd, -ˌland\ *n* : land covered with trees : FOREST — **woodland** *adj*

wood·lot \ˈwu̇d-ˌlät\ *n* : a restricted area of woodland usu. privately kept to meet fuel and timber needs ⟨a farm ~⟩

wood louse *n* : any of various small flat crustaceans that live esp. in ground litter and under stones and bark

wood·man \ˈwu̇d-mən\ *n* : WOODSMAN

wood·note \-ˌnōt\ *n* : verbal expression that is natural and artless

wood nymph *n* : a nymph living in the woods

wood·peck·er \ˈwu̇d-ˌpe-kər\ *n* : any of numerous usu. brightly marked climbing birds with stiff spiny tail feathers and a chisellike bill used to drill into trees for insects

wood·pile \-ˌpīl\ *n* : a pile of wood and esp. firewood

wood·shed \-ˌshed\ *n* : a shed for storing wood and esp. firewood

woods·man \ˈwu̇dz-mən\ *n* : a person who frequents or works in the woods; *esp* : one skilled in woodcraft

woodsy \ˈwu̇d-zē\ *adj* : relating to or suggestive of woods

wood·wind \ˈwu̇d-ˌwind\ *n* : one of a group of wind instruments including flutes, clarinets, oboes, bassoons, and sometimes saxophones

wood·work \-ˌwərk\ *n* : work made of wood; *esp* : interior fittings (as moldings or stairways) of wood

woody \ˈwu̇-dē\ *adj* **wood·i·er; -est** **1** : abounding or overgrown with woods **2** : of or containing wood or wood fibers **3** : characteristic or suggestive of wood — **wood·i·ness** \ˈwu̇-dē-nəs\ *n*

woof \ˈwu̇f\ *n* [alter. of ME *oof,* fr. OE *ōwef,* fr. *ō-* (fr. *on* on) + *wefan* to weave] **1** : WEFT 1 **2** : a woven fabric; *also* : its texture

woof·er \ˈwu̇-fər\ *n* : a loudspeaker that reproduces sounds of low pitch

wool \ˈwu̇l\ *n* **1** : the soft wavy or curly hair of some mammals and esp. the domestic sheep; *also* : something (as a textile or garment) made of wool **2** : material that resembles a mass of wool — **wooled** \ˈwu̇ld\ *adj*

[1]**wool·en** *or* **wool·len** \ˈwu̇-lən\ *adj* **1** : made of wool **2** : of or relating to the manufacture or sale of woolen products ⟨~ mills⟩

[2]**woolen** *or* **woollen** *n* **1** : a fabric made of wool **2** : garments of woolen fabric — usu. used in pl.

wool·gath·er·ing \-ˌga-t͟hə-riŋ\ *n* : idle daydreaming

[1]**wool·ly** *also* **wooly** \ˈwu̇-lē\ *adj* **wool·li·er; -est** **1** : of, relating to, or bearing wool **2** : consisting of or resembling wool **3** : mentally confused ⟨~ thinking⟩ **4** : marked by a lack of order or restraint ⟨the wild and ~ West⟩

[2]**wool·ly** *also* **wool·ie** *or* **wooly** \ˈwu̇-lē\ *n, pl* **woollies** : a garment made from wool; *esp* : underclothing of knitted wool — usu. used in pl.

woolly bear *n* : any of numerous very hairy moth caterpillars

woo·zy \ˈwü-zē\ *adj* **woo·zi·er; -est** **1** : BEFUDDLED **2** : somewhat dizzy, nauseated, or weak — **woo·zi·ness** \ˈwü-zē-nəs\ *n*

[1]**word** \ˈwərd\ *n* **1** : something that is said; *esp* : a brief remark **2** : a speech sound or series of speech sounds that communicates a meaning; *also* : a graphic representation of such a sound or series of sounds **3** : ORDER, COMMAND **4** *often cap* : the 2d person of the Trinity; *also* : GOSPEL **5** : NEWS, INFORMATION **6** : PROMISE **7** *pl* : QUARREL, DISPUTE **8** : a verbal signal : PASSWORD — **word·less** *adj*

[2]**word** *vb* : to express in words : PHRASE

word·age \ˈwər-dij\ *n* **1** : WORDS **2** : number of words **3** : WORDING

word·book \ˈwərd-ˌbu̇k\ *n* : VOCABULARY, DICTIONARY

word·ing \ˈwər-diŋ\ *n* : verbal expression : PHRASEOLOGY

word of mouth : oral communication

word·play \ˈwərd-ˌplā\ *n* : verbal wit

word processing *n* : the production of typewritten documents with automated and usu. computerized text-editing equipment — **word process** *vb*

word processor *n* : a keyboard-operated terminal for

use in word processing; *also* : software to perform word processing

wordy \ˈwər-dē\ *adj* **word•i•er; -est** : using many words : VERBOSE **syn** prolix, diffuse, redundant — **word•i•ness** \-dē-nəs\ *n*

wore *past of* WEAR

[1]**work** \ˈwərk\ *n* **1** : TOIL, LABOR; *also* : EMPLOYMENT ⟨out of ~⟩ **2** : TASK, JOB ⟨have ~ to do⟩ **3** : the energy used when a force is applied over a given distance **4** : DEED, ACHIEVEMENT **5** : a fortified structure **6** *pl* : engineering structures **7** *pl* : a place where industrial labor is done : PLANT, FACTORY **8** *pl* : the moving parts of a mechanism **9** : something produced by mental effort or physical labor; *esp* : an artistic production (as a book or needlework) **10** : WORKMANSHIP ⟨careless ~⟩ **11** : material in the process of manufacture **12** *pl* : everything possessed, available, or belonging ⟨the whole ~*s* went overboard⟩; *also* : drastic treatment ⟨gave him the ~*s*⟩ **syn** occupation, employment, business, pursuit, calling — **in the works** : in process of preparation

[2]**work** *adj* **1** : used for work ⟨~ elephants⟩ **2** : suitable or styled for wear while working ⟨~ clothes⟩

[3]**work** *vb* **worked** \ˈwərkt\ *or* **wrought** \ˈrȯt\; **working 1** : to bring to pass : EFFECT **2** : to fashion or create a useful or desired product through labor or exertion **3** : to prepare for use (as by kneading) **4** : to bring into a desired form by a manufacturing process ⟨~ cold steel⟩ **5** : to set or keep in operation : OPERATE ⟨a pump ~*ed* by hand⟩ **6** : to solve by reasoning or calculation ⟨~ out a problem⟩ **7** : to cause to toil or labor ⟨~*ed* the men hard⟩; *also* : to make use of ⟨~ a mine⟩ **8** : to pay for with labor or service ⟨~ off a debt⟩ **9** : to bring or get into some position or condition by stages ⟨the stream ~*ed* itself clear⟩ ⟨the knot ~*ed* loose⟩ **10** : CONTRIVE, ARRANGE ⟨~ it so you can leave early⟩ **11** : to practice trickery or cajolery on ⟨~*ed* the management for a free ticket⟩ **12** : EXCITE, PROVOKE ⟨~*ed* himself into a rage⟩ **13** : to exert oneself physically or mentally; *esp* : to perform work regularly for wages **14** : to function according to plan or design **15** : to produce a desired effect : SUCCEED ⟨the plan ~*ed*⟩ **16** : to make way slowly and with difficulty ⟨he ~*ed* forward through the crowd⟩ **17** : to permit of being worked ⟨this wood ~*s* easily⟩ **18** : to be in restless motion; *also* : FERMENT 1 — **work on 1** : AFFECT **2** : to try to influence or persuade — **work upon** : to have effect upon : operate on : INFLUENCE

work•able \ˈwər-kə-bəl\ *adj* **1** : capable of being worked **2** : PRACTICABLE, FEASIBLE — **work•able•ness** *n*

work•a•day \ˈwər-kə-ˌdā\ *adj* **1** : relating to or suited for working days **2** : PROSAIC, ORDINARY

work•a•hol•ic \ˌwər-kə-ˈhȯ-lik, -ˈhä-\ *n* : a compulsive worker

work•bench \-ˌbench\ *n* : a bench on which work esp. of mechanics, machinists, and carpenters is performed

work•book \-ˌbu̇k\ *n* **1** : a worker's manual **2** : a student's book of problems to be answered directly on the pages

work•day \ˈwərk-ˌdā\ *n* **1** : a day on which work is done as distinguished from a day off **2** : the period of time in a day when work is performed

work•er \ˈwər-kər\ *n* **1** : one that works; *esp* : a person who works for wages **2** : any of the sexually undeveloped individuals of a colony of social insects (as bees, ants, or termites) that perform the work of the community

workers' compensation *n* : a system of insurance that reimburses an employer for damages paid to an employee who was injured while working

work ethic *n* : belief in work as a moral good

work farm *n* : a farm on which persons guilty of minor law violations are confined

work•horse \ˈwərk-ˌhȯrs\ *n* **1** : a horse used for hard work **2** : a person who does most of the work of a group task **3** : a strong useful machine or vehicle

work•house \-ˌhau̇s\ *n* **1** *Brit* : POORHOUSE **2** : a house of correction for persons guilty of minor law violations

[1]**work•ing** \ˈwər-kiŋ\ *n* **1** : manner of functioning — usu. used in pl. **2** *pl* : an excavation made in mining or tunneling

[2]**working** *adj* **1** : engaged in work ⟨a ~ journalist⟩ **2** : adequate to allow work to be done ⟨a ~ majority⟩ ⟨a ~ knowledge of French⟩ **3** : adopted or assumed to help further work or activity ⟨a ~ model of the car⟩ **4** : spent at work ⟨~ life⟩

work•ing•man \ˈwər-kiŋ-ˌman\ *n* : WORKER 1

work•man \ˈwərk-mən\ *n* **1** : WORKER 1 **2** : ARTISAN, CRAFTSMAN

work•man•like \-ˌlīk\ *adj* : worthy of a good workman : SKILLFUL

work•man•ship \-ˌship\ *n* : the art or skill of a workman : CRAFTSMANSHIP; *also* : the quality of a piece of work ⟨a vase of exquisite ~⟩

work•out \ˈwərk-ˌau̇t\ *n* **1** : a practice or exercise to test or improve one's fitness, ability, or performance **2** : a test or trial to determine ability or capacity or suitability

work out *vb* **1** : to bring about esp. by resolving difficulties **2** : DEVELOP, ELABORATE **3** : to prove effective, practicable, or suitable **4** : to amount to a total or calculated figure — used with *at* **5** : to engage in a workout

work•room \ˈwərk-ˌrüm, -ˌru̇m\ *n* : a room used for work

work•shop \-ˌshäp\ *n* **1** : a shop where manufacturing or handicrafts are carried on **2** : a seminar emphasizing exchange of ideas and practical methods

work•sta•tion \-ˌstā-shən\ *n* : an area with equipment for the performance of a specialized task; *also* : an intelligent terminal or personal computer usu. connected to a computer network

world \ˈwərld\ *n* [ME, fr. OE *woruld* human existence, this world, age, fr. a prehistoric compound whose first constituent is represented by OE *wer* man and whose second constituent is akin to OE *eald* old] **1** : the earth with its inhabitants and all things upon it **2** : people in general : MANKIND **3** : human affairs ⟨withdraw from the ~⟩ **4** : UNIVERSE, CREATION **5** : a state of existence : scene of life and action ⟨the ~ of the future⟩ **6** : a distinctive class of persons or their sphere of interest ⟨the musical ~⟩ **7** : a part or section of the earth or its inhabitants by itself **8** : a great number or quantity ⟨a ~ of troubles⟩ **9** : a celestial body

world–beat•er \-ˌbē-tər\ *n* : one that excels all others of its kind : CHAMPION

world•ling \-liŋ\ *n* : a person absorbed in the concerns of the present world

world•ly \-lē\ *adj* **1** : of, relating to, or devoted to this world and its pursuits rather than to religion or spiritual affairs **2** : WORLDLY-WISE, SOPHISTICATED — **world•li•ness** \-lē-nəs\ *n*

world•ly–wise \-ˌwīz\ *adj* : possessing a practical and often shrewd understanding of human affairs

world•wide \ˈwərld-ˈwīd\ *adj* : extended throughout the entire world — **worldwide** *adv*

[1]**worm** \ˈwərm\ *n* **1** : any of various small long usu. naked and soft-bodied round or flat invertebrate animals (as an earthworm, nematode, tapeworm, or maggot) **2** : a human being who is an object of contempt, loathing, or pity : WRETCH **3** : something that inwardly torments or devours **4** *pl* : infestation with or disease caused by parasitic worms **5** : a spiral or wormlike thing (as the thread of a screw) — **wormy** *adj*

[2]**worm** *vb* **1** : to move or cause to move or proceed slowly and deviously **2** : to insinuate or introduce (oneself) by devious or subtle means **3** : to obtain or extract by artful or insidious pleading, asking, or per-

suading ⟨~*ed* the truth out of him⟩ **4 :** to treat (an animal) with a drug to destroy or expel parasitic worms

worm–eat•en \ˈwərm-ˌēt-ᵊn\ *adj* **:** eaten or burrowed by worms

worm gear *n* **:** a mechanical linkage consisting of a short rotating screw whose threads mesh with the teeth of a gear wheel

worm•hole \ˈwərm-ˌhōl\ *n* **:** a hole or passage burrowed by a worm

worm•wood \-ˌwu̇d\ *n* **1 :** any of a genus of aromatic woody plants (as a sagebrush); *esp* **:** one of Europe used in absinthe **2 :** something bitter or grievous **:** BITTERNESS

worn *past part of* WEAR

worn–out \ˈwōrn-ˈau̇t\ *adj* **:** exhausted or used up by or as if by wear

wor•ri•some \ˈwər-ē-səm\ *adj* **1 :** causing distress or worry **2 :** inclined to worry or fret

[1]wor•ry \ˈwər-ē\ *vb* **wor•ried; wor•ry•ing 1 :** to shake and mangle with the teeth ⟨a terrier ~*ing* a rat⟩ **2 :** to make anxious or upset ⟨her poor health *worries* me⟩ **3 :** to feel or express great care or anxiety **:** FRET — **wor•ri•er** *n*

[2]worry *n, pl* **worries 1 :** ANXIETY **2 :** a cause of anxiety **:** TROUBLE

wor•ry•wart \ˈwər-ē-ˌwȯrt\ *n* **:** one who is inclined to worry unduly

[1]worse \ˈwərs\ *adj, comparative of* BAD *or of* ILL **1 :** bad or evil in a greater degree **:** less good **2 :** more unfavorable, unpleasant, or painful; *also* **:** SICKER

[2]worse *n* **1 :** one that is worse **2 :** a greater degree of ill or badness ⟨a turn for the ~⟩

[3]worse *adv, comparative of* BAD *or of* ILL **:** in a worse manner **:** to a worse extent or degree

wors•en \ˈwərs-ᵊn\ *vb* **:** to make or become worse

[1]wor•ship \ˈwər-shəp\ *n* [ME *worshipe* worthiness, respect, reverence paid to a divine being, fr. OE *weorthscipe* worthiness, respect, fr. *weorth* worthy, worth + *-scipe* -ship, suffix denoting quality or condition] **1** *chiefly Brit* **:** a person of importance — used as a title for officials **2 :** reverence toward a divine being or supernatural power; *also* **:** the expression of such reverence **3 :** extravagant respect or admiration or devotion ⟨~ of the dollar⟩

[2]worship *vb* **-shiped** *or* **-shipped; -ship•ing** *or* **-ship•ping 1 :** to honor or reverence as a divine being or supernatural power **2 :** IDOLIZE **3 :** to perform or take part in worship — **wor•ship•er** *or* **wor•ship•per** *n*

wor•ship•ful \ˈwər-shəp-fəl\ *adj* **1** *archaic* **:** NOTABLE, DISTINGUISHED **2** *chiefly Brit* — used as a title for various persons or groups of rank or distinction **3 :** VENERATING, WORSHIPING

[1]worst \ˈwərst\ *adj, superlative of* BAD *or of* ILL **1 :** most bad, evil, ill, or corrupt **2 :** most unfavorable, unpleasant, or painful; *also* **:** most unsuitable, faulty, or unattractive **3 :** least skillful or efficient

[2]worst *adv, superlative of* ILL *or of* BAD *or* BADLY **1 :** to the extreme degree of badness or inferiority **:** in the worst manner **2 :** MOST ⟨those who need help ~⟩

[3]worst *n* **:** one that is worst

[4]worst *vb* **:** DEFEAT

wor•sted \ˈwu̇s-təd, ˈwər-stəd\ *n* [ME, fr. *Worsted* (now *Worstead*), England] **:** a smooth compact yarn from long wool fibers; *also* **:** a fabric made from such yarn

wort \ˈwərt, ˈwȯrt\ *n* **:** a solution obtained by infusion from malt and fermented to form beer

[1]worth \ˈwərth\ *n* **1 :** monetary value; *also* **:** the equivalent of a specified amount or figure ⟨$5 ~ of gas⟩ **2 :** the value of something measured by its qualities **3 :** MERIT, EXCELLENCE

[2]worth *prep* **1 :** equal in value to; *also* **:** having possessions or income equal to **2 :** deserving of ⟨well ~ the effort⟩

worth•less \ˈwərth-ləs\ *adj* **1 :** lacking worth **:** VALUELESS; *also* **:** USELESS **2 :** LOW, DESPICABLE — **worth•less•ness** *n*

worth•while \ˈwərth-ˈhwīl\ *adj* **:** being worth the time or effort spent

[1]wor•thy \ˈwər-t͟hē\ *adj* **wor•thi•er; -est 1 :** having worth or value **:** ESTIMABLE **2 :** HONORABLE, MERITORIOUS **3 :** having sufficient worth ⟨~ of the honor⟩ — **wor•thi•ly** \ˈwər-t͟hə-lē\ *adv* — **wor•thi•ness** \-t͟hē-nəs\ *n*

[2]worthy *n, pl* **worthies :** a worthy person

would \ˈwu̇d\ *past of* WILL **1** *archaic* **:** wish for **:** WANT **2 :** strongly desire **:** WISH ⟨I ~ I were young again⟩ **3** — used as an auxiliary to express (1) preference ⟨~ rather run than fight⟩, (2) wish, desire, or intent ⟨those who ~ forbid gambling⟩, (3) habitual action ⟨we ~ meet often for lunch⟩, (4) a contingency or possibility ⟨if he were coming, he ~ be here by now⟩, (5) probability ⟨~ have won if he hadn't tripped⟩, or (6) a request ⟨~ you help us⟩ **4 :** COULD **5 :** SHOULD

would–be \ˈwu̇d-ˈbē\ *adj* **:** desiring or pretending to be ⟨a ~ artist⟩

[1]wound \ˈwünd\ *n* **1 :** an injury involving cutting or breaking of bodily tissue (as by violence, accident, or surgery) **2 :** an injury or hurt to feelings or reputation

[2]wound *vb* **:** to inflict a wound to or in

[3]wound \ˈwau̇nd\ *past and past part of* WIND

wove *past of* WEAVE

woven *past part of* WEAVE

[1]wow \ˈwau̇\ *n* **:** a striking success **:** HIT

[2]wow *vb* **:** to arouse enthusiastic approval

WP *abbr* word processing; word processor

WPM *abbr* words per minute

wpn *abbr* weapon

wrack \ˈrak\ *n* [ME, fr. OE *wræc* misery, punishment, something driven by the sea] **:** violent or total destruction

wraith \ˈrāth\ *n, pl* **wraiths** \ˈrāths, ˈrāt͟hz\ **1 :** GHOST, SPECTER **2 :** an insubstantial appearance **:** SHADOW

[1]wran•gle \ˈraŋ-gəl\ *vb* **wran•gled; wran•gling 1 :** to quarrel angrily or peevishly **:** BICKER **2 :** ARGUE **3 :** to obtain by persistent arguing **4 :** to herd and care for (livestock) on the range — **wran•gler** *n*

[2]wrangle *n* **:** an angry, noisy, or prolonged dispute; *also* **:** CONTROVERSY

[1]wrap \ˈrap\ *vb* **wrapped; wrap•ping 1 :** to cover esp. by winding or folding **2 :** to envelop and secure for transportation or storage **3 :** to enclose wholly **:** ENFOLD **4 :** to coil, fold, draw, or twine about something **5 :** SURROUND, ENVELOP ⟨*wrapped* in mystery⟩ **6 :** INVOLVE, ENGROSS ⟨*wrapped* up in a hobby⟩ **7 :** to complete filming or videotaping

[2]wrap *n* **1 :** WRAPPER, WRAPPING **2 :** an article of clothing that may be wrapped around a person **3** *pl* **:** SECRECY ⟨kept under ~*s*⟩ **4 :** completion of filming or videotaping

wrap•around \ˈra-pə-ˌrau̇nd\ *n* **:** a garment (as a dress) adjusted to the figure by wrapping around

wrap•per \ˈra-pər\ *n* **1 :** that in which something is wrapped **2 :** one that wraps **3 :** an article of clothing worn wrapped around the body

wrap•ping \ˈra-piŋ\ *n* **:** something used to wrap an object **:** WRAPPER

wrap–up \ˈrap-ˌəp\ *n* **:** SUMMARY

wrap up *vb* **1 :** SUMMARIZE, SUM UP **2 :** to bring to a usu. successful conclusion

wrasse \ˈras\ *n* **:** any of a large family of usu. brightly colored marine fishes including many food fishes

wrath \ˈrath\ *n* **1 :** violent anger **:** RAGE **2 :** divine punishment **syn** indignation, ire, fury, anger

wrath•ful \-fəl\ *adj* **1 :** filled with wrath **:** very angry **2 :** showing, marked by, or arising from anger — **wrath•ful•ly** *adv* — **wrath•ful•ness** *n*

wreak \ˈrēk\ *vb* **1 :** to exact as a punishment **:** INFLICT ⟨~ vengeance on an enemy⟩ **2 :** to give free scope or rein to ⟨~*ed* his wrath⟩ **3 :** BRING ABOUT, CAUSE ⟨~ havoc⟩

wreath \ˈrēth\ *n, pl* **wreaths** \ˈrēt͟hz, ˈrēths\ : something (as boughs or flowers) intertwined into a circular shape
wreathe \ˈrēt͟h\ *vb* **wreathed; wreath•ing 1** : to shape or take on the shape of a wreath **2** : to crown, decorate, or cover with or as if with a wreath ⟨a face *wreathed* in smiles⟩
[1]**wreck** \ˈrek\ *n* **1** : something (as goods) cast up on the land by the sea after a shipwreck **2** : SHIPWRECK **3** : the action of breaking up or destroying something **4** : broken remains (as of a vehicle after a crash) **5** : something disabled or in a state of ruin; *also* : an individual broken in health or strength
[2]**wreck** *vb* **1** : SHIPWRECK **2** : to ruin or damage by breaking up : involve in disaster or ruin
wreck•age \ˈre-kij\ *n* **1** : the act of wrecking : the state of being wrecked : RUIN **2** : the remains of a wreck
wreck•er \ˈre-kər\ *n* **1** : one that searches for or works upon the wrecks of ships **2** : TOW TRUCK **3** : one that wrecks; *esp* : one whose work is the demolition of buildings
wren \ˈren\ *n* : any of a family of small mostly brown singing birds with short wings and often a tail that points upward
[1]**wrench** \ˈrench\ *vb* **1** : to move with a violent twist **2** : to pull, strain, or tighten with violent twisting or force **3** : to injure or disable by a violent twisting or straining **4** : to snatch forcibly : WREST
[2]**wrench** *n* **1** : a forcible twisting; *also* : an injury (as to one's ankle) by twisting **2** : a tool for holding, twisting, or turning (as nuts or bolts)
[1]**wrest** \ˈrest\ *vb* **1** : to pull or move by a forcible twisting movement **2** : to gain with difficulty by or as if by force or violence ⟨~ control of the government from the dictator⟩
[2]**wrest** *n* : a forcible twist : WRENCH
[1]**wres•tle** \ˈre-səl, ˈra-\ *vb* **wres•tled; wres•tling 1** : to scuffle with and try to throw down an opponent **2** : to compete against in wrestling **3** : to struggle for control (as of something difficult) ⟨~ with a problem⟩ — **wres•tler** \ˈres-lər, ˈras-\ *n*
[2]**wrestle** *n* : the action or an instance of wrestling : STRUGGLE
wres•tling \ˈres-liŋ\ *n* : the sport in which two opponents wrestle each other
wretch \ˈrech\ *n* [ME *wrecche,* fr. OE *wrecca* outcast, exile] **1** : a miserable unhappy person **2** : a base, despicable, or vile person
wretch•ed \ˈre-chəd\ *adj* **1** : deeply afflicted, dejected, or distressed : MISERABLE **2** : WOEFUL, GRIEVOUS ⟨a ~ accident⟩ **3** : DESPICABLE ⟨a ~ trick⟩ **4** : poor in quality or ability : INFERIOR ⟨~ workmanship⟩ — **wretch•ed•ly** *adv* — **wretch•ed•ness** *n*
wrig•gle \ˈri-gəl\ *vb* **wrig•gled; wrig•gling 1** : to twist or move to and fro like a worm : SQUIRM ⟨*wriggled* in his chair⟩ ⟨~ your toes⟩; *also* : to move along by twisting and turning ⟨a snake *wriggled* along the path⟩ **2** : to extricate oneself as if by wriggling ⟨~ out of difficulty⟩ — **wriggle** *n*
wrig•gler *n* **1** : one that wriggles **2** : WIGGLER 1
wring \ˈriŋ\ *vb* **wrung** \ˈrəŋ\; **wring•ing** \ˈriŋ-iŋ\ **1** : to squeeze or twist esp. so as to make dry or to extract moisture or liquid ⟨~ wet clothes⟩ **2** : to get by or as if by twisting or pressing ⟨~ the truth out of him⟩ **3** : to twist so as to strain or sprain : CONTORT ⟨~ his neck⟩ **4** : to twist together as a sign of anguish ⟨*wrung* her hands⟩ **5** : to affect painfully as if by wringing : TORMENT ⟨her plight *wrung* my heart⟩
wring•er \ˈriŋ-ər\ *n* : one that wrings; *esp* : a device for squeezing out liquid or moisture ⟨clothes ~⟩
[1]**wrin•kle** \ˈriŋ-kəl\ *n* **1** : a crease or small fold on a surface (as in the skin or in cloth) **2** : a clever or new method, trick, or idea — **wrin•kly** \-k(ə-)lē\ *adj*
[2]**wrinkle** *vb* **wrin•kled; wrin•kling** : to develop or cause to develop wrinkles
wrist \ˈrist\ *n* : the joint or region between the hand and the arm; *also* : a corresponding part in a lower animal
wrist•band \-ˌband\ *n* : a band or the part of a sleeve encircling the wrist
wrist•let \-lət\ *n* : WRISTBAND; *esp* : a close-fitting knitted band attached to the top of a glove or the end of a sleeve
wrist•watch \-ˌwäch\ *n* : a small watch attached to a bracelet or strap to fasten about the wrist
writ \ˈrit\ *n* **1** : something written **2** : a written legal order signed by a court officer
write \ˈrīt\ *vb* **wrote** \ˈrōt\; **writ•ten** \ˈrit-ᵊn\ *also* **writ** \ˈrit\; **writ•ing** \ˈrī-tiŋ\ [ME, fr. OE *wrītan* to scratch, draw, inscribe] **1** : to form characters, letters, or words on a surface ⟨learn to read and ~⟩ **2** : to form the letters or the words of ⟨~ your name⟩ ⟨~ a check⟩ **3** : to put down on paper : express in writing **4** : to make up and set down for others to read ⟨~ a book⟩ ⟨~ music⟩ **5** : to write a letter to **6** : to communicate by letter : CORRESPOND
write–in \ˈrīt-ˌin\ *n* : a vote cast by writing in the name of a candidate; *also* : a candidate whose name is written in
write in *vb* : to insert (a name not listed on a ballot) in an appropriate space; *also* : to cast (a vote) in this manner
write off *vb* **1** : to reduce the estimated value of : DEPRECIATE **2** : CANCEL ⟨*write off* a bad debt⟩
writ•er \ˈrī-tər\ *n* : one that writes esp. as a business or occupation : AUTHOR
writer's cramp *n* : a painful spasmodic cramp of muscles of the hand or fingers brought on by excessive writing
write–up \ˈrīt-ˌəp\ *n* : a written account (as in a newspaper); *esp* : a flattering article
writhe \ˈrīt͟h\ *vb* **writhed; writh•ing 1** : to twist and turn this way and that ⟨~ in pain⟩ **2** : to suffer with shame or confusion
writ•ing *n* **1** : the act of one that writes; *also* : HANDWRITING **2** : something that is written or printed **3** : a style or form of composition **4** : the occupation of a writer
wrnt *abbr* warrant
[1]**wrong** \ˈrȯŋ\ *n* **1** : an injurious, unfair, or unjust act **2** : a violation of the legal rights of another person **3** : something that is wrong : wrong principles, practices, or conduct ⟨know right from ~⟩ **4** : the state, position, or fact of being wrong
[2]**wrong** *adj* **wrong•er** \ˈrȯŋ-ər\; **wrong•est** \ˈrȯŋ-əst\ **1** : SINFUL, IMMORAL **2** : not right according to a standard or code : IMPROPER **3** : INCORRECT ⟨a ~ solution⟩ **4** : UNSATISFACTORY **5** : UNSUITABLE, INAPPROPRIATE **6** : constituting a surface that is considered the back, bottom, inside, or reverse of something ⟨iron only on the ~ side of the fabric⟩ **syn** false, erroneous, incorrect, inaccurate, untrue — **wrong•ly** *adv*
[3]**wrong** *adv* **1** : INCORRECTLY **2** : in a wrong direction, manner, or relation
[4]**wrong** *vb* **wronged; wrong•ing** \ˈrȯŋ-iŋ\ **1** : to do wrong to : INJURE, HARM **2** : to treat unjustly : DISHONOR, MALIGN **syn** oppress, persecute, aggrieve
wrong•do•er \ˈrȯŋ-ˌdü-ər\ *n* : a person who does wrong and esp. moral wrong — **wrong•do•ing** \-ˌdü-iŋ\ *n*
wrong•ful \ˈrȯŋ-fəl\ *adj* **1** : WRONG, UNJUST **2** : UNLAWFUL — **wrong•ful•ly** *adv* — **wrong•ful•ness** *n*
wrong•head•ed \-ˈhe-dəd\ *adj* : stubborn in clinging to wrong opinion or principles — **wrong•head•ed•ly** *adv* — **wrong•head•ed•ness** *n*
wrote *past of* WRITE
wroth \ˈrȯth, ˈrōth\ *adj* : filled with wrath : ANGRY
wrought \ˈrȯt\ *adj* [ME, fr. pp. of *worken* to work] **1** : FASHIONED, FORMED ⟨carefully ~ essays⟩ **2** : ORNAMENTED **3** : beaten into shape by tools : HAMMERED ⟨~ metals⟩ **4** : deeply stirred : EXCITED ⟨gets easily ~ up⟩

wrought iron *n* : a commercial form of iron that is tough, malleable, and relatively soft — **wrought–iron** *adj*
wrung *past and past part of* WRING
wry \ˈrī\ *adj* **wry•er** \ˈrī-ər\; **wry•est** \ˈrī-əst\ **1** : having a bent or twisted shape ⟨a ~ smile⟩; *esp* : turned abnormally to one side : CONTORTED ⟨a ~ neck⟩ **2** : cleverly and often ironically humorous — **wry•ly** *adv* — **wry•ness** *n*
wry•neck \ˈrī-ˌnek\ *n* **1** : either of two Old World woodpeckers that differ from typical woodpeckers in having a peculiar manner of twisting the head and neck **2** : an abnormal twisting of the neck and head to one side caused by muscle spasms
WSW *abbr* west-southwest
wt *abbr* weight
wurst \ˈwərst, ˈwu̇rst\ *n* : SAUSAGE
wuss \ˈwu̇s\ *n* : WIMP — **wussy** \ˈwu̇-sē\ *adj*
WV *or* **W Va** *abbr* West Virginia
WW *abbr* World War
w/w *abbr* wall-to-wall
WY *or* **Wyo** *abbr* Wyoming
WYS•I•WYG \ˈwi-zē-ˌwig\ *adj* [*w*hat *y*ou *s*ee *i*s *w*hat *y*ou *g*et] : of, relating to, or being a computer display that shows a document exactly as it will appear when printed out

X

[1]**x** \ˈeks\ *n, pl* **x's** *or* **xs** \ˈek-səz\ *often cap* **1** : the 24th letter of the English alphabet **2** : an unknown quantity
[2]**x** *vb* **x-ed** *also* **x'd** *or* **xed** \ˈekst\; **x-ing** *or* **x'ing** \ˈek-siŋ\ : to cancel or obliterate with a series of *x*'s — usu. used with *out*
[3]**x** *abbr* **1** ex **2** experimental
[4]**x** *symbol* **1** times ⟨3 *x* 2 is 6⟩ **2** by ⟨a 3 *x* 5 index card⟩ **3** *often cap* power of magnification
Xan•a•du \ˈza-nə-ˌdü, -ˌdyü\ *n* [fr. *Xanadu*, locality in *Kubla Khan* (1798), poem by Eng. poet Samuel Taylor Coleridge †1834] : an idyllic, exotic, or luxurious place
Xan•thip•pe \zan-ˈthi-pē, -ˈti-\ *or* **Xan•tip•pe** \-ˈti-pē\ *n* [Gk *Xanthippē*, shrewish wife of Socrates] : an ill-tempered woman
x–ax•is \ˈeks-ˌak-səs\ *n* : the axis of a graph or of a system of coordinates in a plane parallel to which abscissas are measured
X–C *abbr* cross-country
X chromosome *n* : a sex chromosome that usually occurs paired in each female cell and single in each male cell in organisms (as human beings) in which the male normally has two unlike sex chromosomes
Xe *symbol* xenon
xe•non \ˈzē-ˌnän, ˈze-\ *n* [Gk, neut. of *xenos* strange] : a heavy gaseous chemical element occurring in minute quantities in air — see ELEMENT table
xe•no•pho•bia \ˌze-nə-ˈfō-bē-ə, ˌzē-\ *n* : fear and hatred of strangers or foreigners or of what is strange or foreign — **xe•no•phobe** \ˈze-nə-ˌfōb, ˈzē-\ *n* — **xe•no•pho•bic** \ˌze-nə-ˈfō-bik, ˌzē-\ *adj*
xe•ric \ˈzir-ik, ˈzer-\ *adj* : characterized by or requiring only a small amount of moisture ⟨a ~ habitat⟩
xe•rog•ra•phy \zə-ˈrä-grə-fē\ *n* : a process for copying printed matter by the action of light on an electrically charged surface in which the latent image usu. is developed with a powder — **xe•ro•graph•ic** \ˌzir-ə-ˈgra-fik\ *adj*
xe•ro•phyte \ˈzir-ə-ˌfīt\ *n* : a plant adapted for growth with a limited water supply — **xe•ro•phyt•ic** \ˌzir-ə-ˈfi-tik\ *adj*
xi \ˈzī, ˈksī\ *n* : the 14th letter of the Greek alphabet — Ξ or ξ
XL *abbr* **1** extra large **2** extra long
Xmas \ˈkris-məs *also* ˈeks-məs\ *n* [*X* (symbol for *Christ*, fr. the Gk letter chi (X), initial of *Christos* Christ) + *-mas* (in *Christmas*)] : CHRISTMAS
XO *abbr* executive officer
x–ra•di•a•tion \ˌeks-ˌrā-dē-ˈā-shən\ *n, often cap* **1** : exposure to X rays **2** : radiation consisting of X rays
x–ray \ˈeks-ˌrā\ *vb, often cap* : to examine, treat, or photograph with X rays
X ray \ˈeks-ˌrā\ *n* **1** : a radiation of the same nature as light rays but of extremely short wavelength that is able to penetrate through various thicknesses of solids and to act on photographic film **2** : a photograph taken with X rays — **X–ray** *adj*
XS *abbr* extra small
xu \ˈsü\ *n, pl* **xu** — see *dong* at MONEY table
xy•lem \ˈzī-ləm, -ˌlem\ *n* : a woody tissue of vascular plants that transports water and dissolved materials upward, functions in support and storage, and lies central to the phloem
xy•lo•phone \ˈzī-lə-ˌfōn\ *n* [Gk *xylon* wood + *phōnē* voice, sound] : a musical instrument consisting of a series of wooden bars graduated in length to produce the musical scale, supported on belts of straw or felt, and sounded by striking with two small wooden hammers — **xy•lo•phon•ist** \-ˌfō-nist\ *n*

Y

[1]**y** \ˈwī\ *n, pl* **y's** *or* **ys** \ˈwīz\ *often cap* : the 25th letter of the English alphabet
[2]**y** *abbr* **1** yard **2** year
[1]**Y** \ˈwī\ *n* : YMCA, YWCA
[2]**Y** *symbol* yttrium
[1]**-y** *also* **-ey** \ē\ *adj suffix* **1** : characterized by : full of ⟨dirt*y*⟩ ⟨clay*ey*⟩ **2** : having the character of : composed of ⟨ic*y*⟩ **3** : like : like that of ⟨hom*ey*⟩ ⟨wintr*y*⟩ ⟨stag*y*⟩ **4** : tending or inclined to ⟨sleep*y*⟩ ⟨chatt*y*⟩ **5** : giving occasion for (specified) action ⟨tear*y*⟩ **6** : performing (specified) action ⟨curl*y*⟩
[2]**-y** \ē\ *n suffix, pl* **-ies** **1** : state : condition : quality ⟨beggar*y*⟩ **2** : activity, place of business, or goods dealt with ⟨laundr*y*⟩ **3** : whole body or group ⟨soldier*y*⟩
[3]**-y** *n suffix, pl* **-ies** : instance of a (specified) action ⟨entreat*y*⟩ ⟨inquir*y*⟩
YA *abbr* young adult
[1]**yacht** \ˈyät\ *n* [obs. D *jaght*, fr. Middle Low German *jacht*, short for *jachtschip*, lit., hunting ship] : a usu. large recreational watercraft
[2]**yacht** *vb* : to race or cruise in a yacht
yacht•ing *n* : the sport of racing or cruising in a yacht
yachts•man \ˈyäts-mən\ *n* : a person who owns or sails a yacht
ya•hoo \ˈyā-hü, ˈyä-\ *n, pl* **yahoos** [fr. *Yahoo*, one of a race of brutes having the form of men in Jonathan Swift's *Gulliver's Travels*] : a boorish, crass, or stupid person
Yah•weh \ˈyä-ˌwā\ *also* **Yah•veh** \-ˌvā\ *n* : GOD 1 — used esp. by the Hebrews
[1]**yak** \ˈyak\ *n, pl* **yaks** *also* **yak** : a large long-haired wild or domesticated ox of Tibet and adjacent Asian uplands
☞ For illustration, see next page.
[2]**yak** *also* **yack** \ˈyak\ *n* : persistent or voluble talk — **yak** *also* **yack** *vb*
yam \ˈyam\ *n* **1** : the edible starchy root of a twining

yak

vine that largely replaces the potato as food in the tropics; *also* : a plant that produces yams **2** : a usu. deep orange sweet potato

yam•mer \ˈya-mər\ *vb* [ME *yameren*, alter. of *yomeren* to murmur, be sad, fr. OE *gēomrian*] **1** : WHIMPER **2** : CHATTER — **yammer** *n*

¹yank \ˈyaŋk\ *n* : a strong sudden pull : JERK

²yank *vb* : to pull with a quick vigorous movement

Yank \ˈyaŋk\ *n* : YANKEE

Yan•kee \ˈyaŋ-kē\ *n* **1** : a native or inhabitant of New England; *also* : a native or inhabitant of the northern U.S. **2** : AMERICAN 2

yan•qui \ˈyäŋ-kē\ *n, often cap* [Sp] : a citizen of the U.S. as distinguished from a Latin American

¹yap \ˈyap\ *vb* **yapped; yap•ping 1** : BARK, YELP **2** : GAB

²yap *n* **1** : a quick sharp bark **2** : CHATTER

¹yard \ˈyärd\ *n* [ME, fr. OE *geard* enclosure, yard] **1** : a small enclosed area open to the sky and adjacent to a building **2** : the grounds of a building **3** : the grounds surrounding a house usu. covered with grass **4** : an enclosure for livestock **5** : an area set aside for a particular business or activity **6** : a system of railroad tracks for storing cars and making up trains

²yard *n* [ME *yarde*, fr. OE *gierd* twig, measure, yard] **1** — see WEIGHT table **2** : a long spar tapered toward the ends that supports and spreads the head of a sail — **the whole nine yards** : all of a set of circumstances, conditions, or details

yard•age \ˈyär-dij\ *n* : an aggregate number of yards; *also* : the length, extent, or volume of something as measured in yards

yard•arm \ˈyärd-ˌärm\ *n* : either end of the yard of a square-rigged ship

yard•man \-mən, -ˌman\ *n* : a person employed in or about a yard

yard•mas•ter \-ˌmas-tər\ *n* : the person in charge of a railroad yard

yard•stick \-ˌstik\ *n* **1** : a graduated measuring stick three feet long **2** : a standard for making a critical judgment : CRITERION **syn** gauge, touchstone, benchmark, measure

yar•mul•ke *also* **yar•mel•ke** \ˈyä-mə-kə, ˈyär-, -məl-\ *n* : a skullcap worn esp. by Jewish males in the synagogue and the home

yarn \ˈyärn\ *n* **1** : a continuous often plied strand composed of fibers or filaments and used in weaving and knitting to form cloth **2** : STORY; *esp* : a tall tale

yar•row \ˈyar-ō\ *n* : a strong-scented herb related to the daisies that has white or pink flowers in flat clusters

yaw \ˈyȯ\ *vb* : to deviate erratically from a course ⟨the ship ~*ed* in the heavy seas⟩ — **yaw** *n*

yawl \ˈyȯl\ *n* : a 2-masted sailboat with the shorter mast aft of the rudder

¹yawn \ˈyȯn\ *vb* : to open wide; *esp* : to open the mouth wide usu. as an involuntary reaction to fatigue or boredom — **yawn•er** *n*

²yawn *n* : a deep usu. involuntary intake of breath through the wide-open mouth

yawp *or* **yaup** \ˈyȯp\ *vb* **1** : to make a raucous noise : SQUAWK **2** : CLAMOR, COMPLAIN — **yawp•er** *n*

yaws \ˈyȯz\ *n pl* : an infectious tropical disease caused by a spirochete closely resembling the causative agent of syphilis

y–ax•is \ˈwī-ˌak-səs\ *n* : the axis of a graph or of a system of coordinates in a plane parallel to which the ordinates are measured

Yb *symbol* ytterbium

YB *abbr* yearbook

Y chromosome *n* : a sex chromosome that is characteristic of male cells in organisms (as humans) in which the male typically has two unlike sex chromosomes

yd *abbr* yard

¹ye \ˈyē\ *pron* : YOU 1

²ye \yē, yə, *originally same as* THE\ *definite article, archaic* : THE — used by early printers to represent the manuscript word *þe* (*the*)

¹yea \ˈyā\ *adv* **1** : YES — used in oral voting **2** : INDEED, TRULY

²yea *n* : an affirmative vote; *also* : a person casting such a vote

year \ˈyir\ *n* **1** : the period of about 365¼ solar days required for one revolution of the earth around the sun **2** : a cycle of 365 or 366 days beginning with January 1; *also* : a calendar year specified usu. by a number **3** *pl* : a time of special significance ⟨their glory ~*s*⟩ **4** *pl* : AGE ⟨advanced in ~*s*⟩ **5** : a period of time other than a calendar year ⟨the school ~⟩

year•book \-ˌbu̇k\ *n* **1** : a book published annually esp. as a report **2** : a school publication recording the history and activities of a graduating class

year•ling \ˈyir-liŋ, ˈyər-lən\ *n* **1** : one that is a year old **2** : a racehorse between January 1st of the year after the year in which it was born and the next January 1st

year•long \ˈyir-ˈlȯŋ\ *adj* : lasting through a year

¹year•ly \ˈyir-lē\ *adj* : ANNUAL

²yearly *adv* : every year

yearn \ˈyərn\ *vb* **1** : to feel a longing or craving **2** : to feel tenderness or compassion **syn** long, pine, hanker, hunger, thirst

yearn•ing *n* : a tender or urgent longing

year–round \ˈyir-ˈrau̇nd\ *adj* : effective, employed, or operating for the full year : not seasonal ⟨a ~ resort⟩

yeast \ˈyēst\ *n* **1** : a surface froth or a sediment in sugary liquids (as fruit juices) that consists largely of cells of a tiny fungus and is used in making alcoholic liquors and as a leaven in baking **2** : a commercial product containing yeast plants in a moist or dry medium **3** : a minute one-celled fungus present and functionally active in yeast that reproduces by budding; *also* : any of several similar fungi **4** *archaic* : the foam of waves : SPUME **5** : something that causes ferment or activity

yeasty \ˈyē-stē\ *adj* **yeast•i•er; -est 1** : of, relating to, or resembling yeast **2** : UNSETTLED **3** : full of vitality; *also* : FRIVOLOUS

yegg \ˈyeg\ *n* : one that breaks open safes to steal; *also* : ROBBER

¹yell \ˈyel\ *vb* : to utter a loud cry or scream : SHOUT

²yell *n* **1** : SHOUT **2** : a cheer used esp. to encourage an athletic team (as at a college)

¹yel•low \ˈye-lō\ *adj* **1** : of the color yellow **2** : having a yellow complexion or skin **3** : SENSATIONAL ⟨~ journalism⟩ **4** : COWARDLY — **yel•low•ish** \ˈye-lə-wish\ *adj*

²yellow *n* **1** : a color between green and orange in the spectrum : the color of ripe lemons or sunflowers **2** : something yellow; *esp* : the yolk of an egg **3** *pl* : any of several plant diseases marked by stunted growth and yellowing of foliage

³yellow *vb* : to make or turn yellow

yellow birch *n* : a No. American birch with thin lustrous gray or yellow bark; *also* : its strong hard wood

yellow fever *n* : an acute destructive virus disease marked by prostration, jaundice, fever, and often hemorrhage and transmitted by a mosquito

yellow jack *n* : YELLOW FEVER

yellow jacket *n* **:** any of various small social wasps having the body barred with bright yellow

yelp \ˈyelp\ *vb* [ME, to boast, cry out, fr. OE *gielpan* to boast, exult] **:** to utter a sharp quick shrill cry — **yelp** *n*

Ye•me•ni \ˈye-mə-nē\ *n* **:** YEMENITE — **Yemeni** *adj*

Ye•men•ite \ˈye-mə-ˌnīt\ *n* **:** a native or inhabitant of Yemen — **Yemenite** *adj*

[1]**yen** \ˈyen\ *n, pl* **yen** — see MONEY table

[2]**yen** *n* [obs. E argot *yen-yen* craving for opium, fr. Chin (Guangdong dial.) *yīn-yáhn,* fr. *yīn* opium + *yáhn* craving] **:** a strong desire **:** LONGING

yeo•man \ˈyō-mən\ *n* **1 :** an attendant or officer in a royal or noble household **2 :** a naval petty officer who performs clerical duties **3 :** a person who owns and cultivates a small farm; *esp* **:** one of a class of English freeholders below the gentry

yeo•man•ry \-rē\ *n* **:** the body of yeomen and esp. of small landed proprietors

-yer — see -ER

[1]**yes** \ˈyes\ *adv* — used as a function word esp. to express assent or agreement or to introduce a more emphatic or explicit phrase

[2]**yes** *n* **:** an affirmative reply

ye•shi•va *or* **ye•shi•vah** \yə-ˈshē-və\ *n, pl* **yeshivas** *or* **ye•shi•voth** \-ˌshē-ˈvōt, -ˈvōth\ **:** a Jewish school esp. for religious instruction

yes–man \ˈyes-ˌman\ *n* **:** a person who endorses uncritically every opinion or proposal of a superior

[1]**yes•ter•day** \ˈyes-tər-dē, -ˌdā\ *adv* **1 :** on the day preceding today **2 :** only a short time ago

[2]**yesterday** *n* **1 :** the day last past **2 :** time not long past

yes•ter•year \ˈyes-tər-ˌyir\ *n* **1 :** last year **2 :** the recent past

[1]**yet** \ˈyet\ *adv* **1 :** in addition **:** BESIDES; *also* **:** EVEN 6 **2 :** up to now; *also* **:** STILL **3 :** so soon as now ⟨not time to go ~⟩ **4 :** EVENTUALLY **5 :** NEVERTHELESS, HOWEVER

[2]**yet** *conj* **:** but nevertheless **:** BUT

ye•ti \ˈye-tē, ˈyā-\ *n* [Tibetan] **:** ABOMINABLE SNOWMAN

yew \ˈyü\ *n* **1 :** any of a genus of evergreen trees and shrubs with dark stiff poisonous needles and fleshy fruits **2 :** the wood of a yew; *esp* **:** that of an Old World yew

Yid•dish \ˈyi-dish\ *n* [Yiddish *yidish,* short for *yidish daytsh,* lit., Jewish German] **:** a language derived from medieval German and spoken by Jews esp. of eastern European origin — **Yiddish** *adj*

[1]**yield** \ˈyēld\ *vb* **1 :** to give as fitting, owed, or required **2 :** GIVE UP; *esp* **:** to give up possession of on claim or demand **3 :** to bear as a natural product **4 :** PRODUCE, SUPPLY **5 :** to bring in **:** RETURN **6 :** to give way (as to force or influence) **7 :** to give place **syn** relinquish, cede, waive, surrender

[2]**yield** *n* **:** something yielded; *esp* **:** the amount or quantity produced or returned

yield•ing \ˈyēl-diŋ\ *adj* **1 :** not rigid or stiff **:** FLEXIBLE **2 :** SUBMISSIVE, COMPLIANT

yikes \ˈyīks\ *interj* — used to express fear or astonishment

yip \ˈyip\ *vb* **yipped; yip•ping :** YAP

YMCA \ˌwī-ˌem-(ˌ)sē-ˈā\ *n* **:** Young Men's Christian Association

YMHA \ˌwī-ˌem-ˌāch-ˈā\ *n* **:** Young Men's Hebrew Association

yo \ˈyō\ *interj* — used to call attention, indicate attentiveness, or express affirmation

YOB *abbr* year of birth

yo•del \ˈyōd-ᵊl\ *vb* **yo•deled** *or* **yo•delled; yo•del•ing** *or* **yo•del•ling :** to sing by suddenly changing from chest voice to falsetto and back; *also* **:** to shout or call in this manner — **yodel** *n* — **yo•del•er** *n*

yo•ga \ˈyō-gə\ *n* [Skt, lit., yoking, fr. *yunakti* he yokes] **1** *cap* **:** a Hindu theistic philosophy teaching the suppression of all activity of body, mind, and will in order that the self may realize its distinction from them and attain liberation **2 :** a system of exercises for attaining bodily or mental control and well-being

yo•gi \ˈyō-gē\ *also* **yo•gin** \-gən, -ˌgin\ *n* **1 :** a person who practices yoga **2** *cap* **:** an adherent of Yoga philosophy

yo•gurt *also* **yo•ghurt** \ˈyō-gərt\ *n* [Turk *yoğurt*] **:** a soured slightly acid often flavored semisolid milk food made of skimmed cow's milk and milk solids to which cultures of bacteria have been added

[1]**yoke** \ˈyōk\ *n, pl* **yokes 1 :** a wooden bar or frame by which two draft animals (as oxen) are coupled at the heads or necks for working together; *also* **:** a frame fitted to a person's shoulders to carry a load in two equal portions **2 :** a clamp that embraces two parts to hold or unite them in position **3** *pl usu* **yoke :** two animals yoked together **4 :** SERVITUDE, BONDAGE **5 :** TIE, LINK ⟨the ~ of matrimony⟩ **6 :** a fitted or shaped piece esp. at the shoulder of a garment **syn** couple, pair, brace

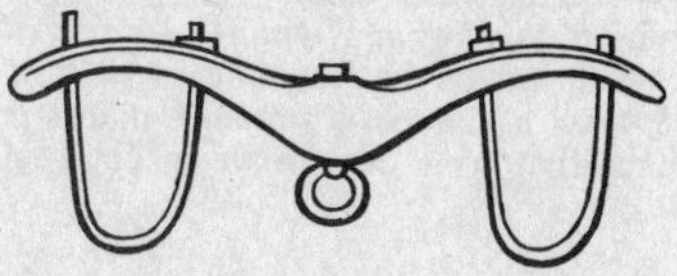

yoke 1

[2]**yoke** *vb* **yoked; yok•ing 1 :** to put a yoke on **:** couple with a yoke **2 :** to attach a draft animal to ⟨~ a plow⟩ **3 :** JOIN; *esp* **:** MARRY

yo•kel \ˈyō-kəl\ *n* **:** a naive or gullible country person

yolk \ˈyōk\ *n* **1 :** the yellow rounded inner mass of the egg of a bird or reptile **2 :** the stored food material of an egg consisting chiefly of proteins, lecithin, and cholesterol — **yolked** \ˈyōkt\ *adj*

Yom Kip•pur \ˌyōm-ki-ˈpu̇r, ˌyäm-, -ˈki-pər\ *n* [Heb *yōm kippūr,* lit., day of atonement] **:** a Jewish holiday observed in September or October with fasting and prayer as a day of atonement

[1]**yon** \ˈyän\ *adj* **:** YONDER

[2]**yon** *adv* **1 :** YONDER **2 :** THITHER ⟨ran hither and ~⟩

[1]**yon•der** \ˈyän-dər\ *adv* **:** at or to that place

[2]**yonder** *adj* **1 :** more distant ⟨the ~ side of the river⟩ **2 :** being at a distance within view ⟨~ hills⟩

yore \ˈyōr\ *n* [ME, fr. *yore,* adv., long ago, fr. OE *geāra,* fr. *gēar* year] **:** time long past ⟨in days of ~⟩

York•ie \ˈyȯr-kē\ *n* **:** YORKSHIRE TERRIER

York•shire terrier \ˈyȯrk-ˌshir-, -shər-\ *n* **:** any of a breed of compact toy terriers with long straight silky hair

you \ˈyü\ *pron* **1 :** the person or persons addressed ⟨~ are a nice person⟩ ⟨~ are nice people⟩ **2 :** ONE 2 ⟨~ turn this knob to open it⟩

[1]**young** \ˈyəŋ\ *adj* **youn•ger** \ˈyəŋ-gər\; **youn•gest** \ˈyəŋ-gəst\ **1 :** being in the first or an early stage of life, growth, or development **2 :** having little experience **3 :** recently come into being **4 :** YOUTHFUL **5** *cap* **:** belonging to or representing a new or revived usu. political group or movement — **young•ish** \ˈyəŋ-ish\ *adj*

[2]**young** *n, pl* **young :** young persons; *also* **:** young animals

young•ling \ˈyəŋ-liŋ\ *n* **:** one that is young — **youngling** *adj*

young•ster \-stər\ *n* **1 :** a young person **2 :** CHILD

your \ˈyu̇r, ˈyōr, yər\ *adj* **:** of or relating to you or yourself

yours \ˈyu̇rz, ˈyōrz\ *pron* **:** one or the ones belonging to you

your•self \yər-ˈself\ *pron, pl* **yourselves** \-ˈselvz\ **:** YOU — used reflexively, for emphasis, or in absolute constructions ⟨you'll hurt ~⟩ ⟨do it ~⟩

youth \ˈyüth\ *n, pl* **youths** \ˈyüt͟hz, ˈyüths\ **1 :** the pe-

riod of life between childhood and maturity **2** : a young man; *also* : young persons **3** : YOUTHFULNESS
youth•ful \ˈyüth-fəl\ *adj* **1** : of, relating to, or appropriate to youth **2** : being young and not yet mature **3** : FRESH, VIGOROUS — **youth•ful•ly** *adv* — **youth•ful•ness** *n*
youth hostel *n* : HOSTEL 2
yowl \ˈyau̇l\ *vb* : to utter a loud long mournful cry : WAIL — **yowl** *n*
yo–yo \ˈyō-(ˌ)yō\ *n, pl* **yo–yos** : a thick grooved double disk with a string attached to its center which is made to fall and rise to the hand by unwinding and rewinding on the string
yr *abbr* **1** year **2** your
yrbk *abbr* yearbook
YT *abbr* Yukon Territory
yt•ter•bi•um \i-ˈtər-bē-əm\ *n* : a rare metallic chemical element — see ELEMENT table
yt•tri•um \ˈi-trē-əm\ *n* : a rare metallic chemical element — see ELEMENT table
yu•an \ˈyü-ən, yu̇-ˈän\ *n, pl* **yuan 1** — see MONEY table **2** : the dollar of the Republic of China (Taiwan)
yuc•ca \ˈyə-kə\ *n* : any of a genus of plants related to the agaves that grow esp. in warm dry regions and bear large clusters of white cup-shaped flowers atop a long stiff stalk
yuck \ˈyək\ *interj* — used to express rejection or disgust
Yu•go•slav \ˌyü-gō-ˈsläv, -ˈslav\ *n* : a native or inhabitant of Yugoslavia — **Yugoslav** *adj* — **Yu•go•sla•vi•an** \-ˈslä-vē-ən\ *adj or n*
yule \ˈyül\ *n, often cap* : CHRISTMAS
Yule log *n* : a large log formerly put onthe hearth on Christmas Eve as the foundation of the fire
yule•tide \ˈyül-ˌtīd\ *n, often cap* : CHRISTMASTIDE
yum•my \ˈyə-mē\ *adj* **yum•mi•er; -est** : highly attractive or pleasing
yup•pie \ˈyə-pē\ *n* [prob. fr. young *u*rban *p*rofessional + *-ie* (as in hipp*ie*)] : a young college-educated adult employed in a well-paying profession and living and working in or near a large city
yurt \ˈyu̇rt\ *n* : a light round tent of skins or felt stretched over a lattice framework used by pastoral peoples of inner Asia
YWCA \ˌwī-ˌdə-bəl-yu̇-(ˌ)sē-ˈā\ *n* : Young Women's Christian Association
YWHA \-ˌāch-ˈā\ *n* : Young Women's Hebrew Association

Z

[1]z \ˈzē\ *n, pl* **z's** *or* **zs** *often cap* : the 26th letter of the English alphabet
[2]z *abbr* **1** zero **2** zone
Z *symbol* atomic number
Zach *abbr* Zacharias
Zach•a•ri•as \ˌza-kə-ˈrī-əs\ *n* : ZECHARIAH
zaire \ˈzīr, zä-ˈir\ *n, pl* **zaires** *or* **zaire** — see MONEY table
Zair•ian \zä-ˈir-ē-ən\ *n* : a native or inhabitant of Zaire — **Zairian** *adj*
Zam•bi•an \ˈzam-bē-ən\ *n* : a native or inhabitant of Zambia — **Zambian** *adj*
[1]za•ny \ˈzā-nē\ *n, pl* **zanies** [It *zanni,* a traditional masked clown, fr. It dial. *Zanni,* nickname for It *Giovanni* John] **1** : CLOWN, BUFFOON **2** : a silly or foolish person
[2]zany *adj* **za•ni•er; -est 1** : characteristic of a zany **2** : CRAZY, FOOLISH — **za•ni•ly** \ˈzā-nə-lē, ˈzān-ᵊl-ē\ *adv* — **za•ni•ness** \ˈzā-nē-nəs\ *n*
zap \ˈzap\ *vb* **zapped; zap•ping 1** : DESTROY, KILL **2** : to irradiate esp. with microwaves
zeal \ˈzēl\ *n* : eager and ardent interest in the pursuit of something : FERVOR **syn** enthusiasm, passion, ardor
zeal•ot \ˈze-lət\ *n* : a zealous person; *esp* : a fanatical partisan **syn** enthusiast, bigot
zeal•ous \ˈze-ləs\ *adj* : filled with, characterized by, or due to zeal — **zeal•ous•ly** *adv* — **zeal•ous•ness** *n*
ze•bra \ˈzē-brə\ *n, pl* **zebras** *also* **zebra** : any of several African mammals related to the horse but conspicuously striped with black or brown and white or buff
ze•bu \ˈzē-bü, -byü\ *n* : an ox of any of various breeds developed in India that have a large fleshy hump over the shoulders, a dewlap, drooping ears, and marked resistance to heat and to insect attack
Zech *abbr* Zechariah
Zech•a•ri•ah \ˌze-kə-ˈrī-ə\ *n* — see BIBLE table
zed \ˈzed\ *n, chiefly Brit* : the letter *z*
zeit•geist \ˈtsīt-ˌgīst, ˈzīt-\ *n* [G, fr. *Zeit* time + *Geist* spirit] : the general intellectual, moral, and cultural state of an era
Zen \ˈzen\ *n* : a Japanese Buddhist sect that teaches self-discipline, meditation, and attainment of enlightenment through direct intuitive insight
ze•na•na \zə-ˈnä-nə\ *n* : HAREM
ze•nith \ˈzē-nəth\ *n* **1** : the point in the heavens directly overhead **2** : the highest point : ACME **syn** culmination, pinnacle, apex

zebu

ze•o•lite \ˈzē-ə-ˌlīt\ *n* : any of various feldsparlike silicates used esp. as water softeners
Zeph *abbr* Zephaniah
Zeph•a•ni•ah \ˌze-fə-ˈnī-ə\ *n* — see BIBLE table
zeph•yr \ˈze-fər\ *n* : a breeze from the west; *also* : a gentle breeze
zep•pe•lin \ˈze-plən, -pə-lən\ *n* [Count Ferdinand von *Zeppelin* †1917 Ger. airship manufacturer] : a cylindrical rigid blimplike airship
[1]ze•ro \ˈzē-rō, ˈzir-ō\ *n, pl* **zeros** *also* **zeroes** [ultim. fr. Ar *ṣifr*] **1** : the numerical symbol 0 **2** : the number represented by the symbol 0 **3** : the point at which the graduated degrees or measurements on a scale (as of a thermometer) begin **4** : the lowest point
[2]zero *adj* **1** : of, relating to, or being a zero **2** : having no magnitude or quantity **3** : ABSENT, LACKING; *esp* : having no modified inflectional form
[3]zero *vb* : to adjust the sights of a firearm to hit the point aimed at ⟨~ in⟩
zero hour *n* : the time at which an event (as a military operation) is scheduled to begin
zest \ˈzest\ *n* **1** : a quality of enhancing enjoyment : PIQUANCY **2** : keen enjoyment : GUSTO — **zest•ful** \-fəl\ *adj* — **zest•ful•ly** *adv* — **zest•ful•ness** *n*
ze•ta \ˈzā-tə, ˈzē-\ *n* : the 6th letter of the Greek alphabet — Z or ζ
zi•do•vu•dine \zi-ˈdō-vyü-ˌdēn\ *n* : AZT

[1]**zig•zag** \ˈzig-ˌzag\ *n* : one of a series of short sharp turns, angles, or alterations in a course; *also* : something marked by such a series
[2]**zigzag** *adv* : in or by a zigzag path
[3]**zigzag** *adj* : having short sharp turns or angles
[4]**zigzag** *vb* **zig•zagged; zig•zag•ging** : to form into or proceed along a zigzag
zil•lion \ˈzil-yən\ *n* : a large indeterminate number
Zim•ba•bwe•an \zim-ˈbä-bwē-ən\ *n* : a native or inhabitant of Zimbabwe — **Zimbabwean** *adj*
zinc \ˈziŋk\ *n* : a bluish white crystalline metallic chemical element that is commonly found in minerals and is used esp. as a protective coating for iron and steel — see ELEMENT table
zinc ointment *n* : ZINC OXIDE OINTMENT
zinc oxide *n* : a white solid used esp. as a pigment, in compounding rubber, and in ointments
zinc oxide ointment *n* : an ointment containing zinc oxide and used for skin disorders
zing \ˈziŋ\ *n* **1** : a shrill humming noise **2** : VITALITY 4 — **zing** *vb*
zing•er \ˈziŋ-ər\ *n* : a pointed witty remark or retort
zin•nia \ˈzi-nē-ə, ˈzēn-yə\ *n* : any of a small genus of tropical American herbs related to the daisies and widely grown for their showy long-lasting flower heads
Zi•on \ˈzī-ən\ *n* **1** : the Jewish people **2** : the Jewish homeland as a symbol of Judaism or of Jewish national aspiration **3** : HEAVEN **4** : UTOPIA
Zi•on•ism \ˈzī-ə-ˌni-zəm\ *n* : an international movement orig. for the establishment of a Jewish national or religious community in Palestine and later for the support of modern Israel — **Zi•on•ist** \-nist\ *adj or n*
[1]**zip** \ˈzip\ *vb* **zipped; zip•ping** : to move, act, or function with speed or vigor
[2]**zip** *n* **1** : a sudden sharp hissing sound **2** : ENERGY, VIM
[3]**zip** *n* : NOTHING, ZERO
[4]**zip** *vb* **zipped; zip•ping** : to close or open with a zipper
zip code *n, often cap Z&I&P* [zone *i*mprovement *p*lan] : a number that identifies each postal delivery area in the U.S.
zip•per \ˈzi-pər\ *n* : a fastener consisting of two rows of metal or plastic teeth on strips of tape and a sliding piece that closes an opening by drawing the teeth together
zip•py \ˈzi-pē\ *adj* **zip•pi•er; -est** : BRISK, SNAPPY
zir•con \ˈzər-ˌkän\ *n* : a zirconium-containing mineral transparent varieties of which are used as gems
zir•co•ni•um \ˌzər-ˈkō-nē-əm\ *n* : a gray corrosion-resistant metallic chemical element used esp. in alloys and ceramics — see ELEMENT table
zit \ˈzit\ *n* : PIMPLE
zith•er \ˈzi-thər, -thər\ *n* : a musical instrument having 30 to 40 strings played with plectrum and fingers
zi•ti \ˈzē-tē\ *n, pl* **ziti** [It] : medium-size tubular pasta
zlo•ty \ˈzlò-tē\ *n, pl* **zlo•tys** \-tēz\ *or* **zloty** — see MONEY table
Zn *symbol* zinc
zo•di•ac \ˈzō-dē-ˌak\ *n* [ME, fr. MF *zodiaque,* fr. L *zodiacus,* fr. Gk *zōidiakos,* fr. *zōidion* carved figure, sign of the zodiac, fr. dim. of *zōion* living being, figure] **1** : an imaginary belt in the heavens that encompasses the paths of most of the planets and that is divided into 12 constellations or signs **2** : a figure representing the signs of the zodiac and their symbols — **zo•di•a•cal** \zō-ˈdī-ə-kəl\ *adj*
zom•bie *also* **zom•bi** \ˈzäm-bē\ *n* : a person who is believed to have died and been brought back to life without speech or free will
zon•al \ˈzōn-ᵊl\ *adj* : of, relating to, or having the form of a zone — **zon•al•ly** *adv*
[1]**zone** \ˈzōn\ *n* [ME, fr. L *zona* belt, zone, fr. Gk *zōnē*] **1** : any of five great divisions of the earth's surface made according to latitude and temperature and including the torrid zone about the equator, the two temperate zones lying between the torrid zone and the polar circles, and the two frigid zones lying between the polar circles and the poles **2** : an encircling band or girdle ⟨a ~ of trees⟩ **3** : a section of an area or territory created for a particular purpose ⟨business ~⟩ ⟨postal ~⟩
[2]**zone** *vb* **zoned; zon•ing 1** : ENCIRCLE **2** : to arrange in or mark off into zones; *esp* : to divide (as a city) into sections reserved for different purposes
zonked \ˈzäŋkt\ *adj* : being or acting as if under the influence of alcohol or a drug : HIGH
zoo \ˈzü\ *n, pl* **zoos** : a zoological garden or collection of living animals usu. for public display
zoo•ge•og•ra•phy \ˌzō-ə-jē-ˈä-grə-fē\ *n* : a branch of biogeography concerned with the geographical distribution of animals — **zoo•ge•og•ra•pher** \-fər\ *n* — **zoo•geo•graph•ic** \-ˌjē-ə-ˈgra-fik\ *also* **zoo•geo•graph•i•cal** \-fi-kəl\ *adj*
zoo•keep•er \ˈzü-ˌkē-pər\ *n* : a person who cares for animals in a zoo
zool *abbr* zoological; zoology
zoological garden *n* : a garden or park where wild animals are kept for exhibition
zo•ol•o•gy \zō-ˈä-lə-jē\ *n* : a branch of biology that deals with the classification and the properties and vital phenomena of animals — **zo•o•log•i•cal** \ˌzō-ə-ˈlä-ji-kəl\ *adj* — **zo•ol•o•gist** \zō-ˈä-lə-jist\ *n*
zoom \ˈzüm\ *vb* **1** : to move with a loud hum or buzz **2** : to gain altitude quickly **3** : to focus a camera or microscope using a special lens that permits the apparent distance of the object to be varied — **zoom** *n*
zoom lens *n* : a camera lens in which the image size can be varied continuously while the image remains in focus
zoo•mor•phic \ˌzō-ə-ˈmòr-fik\ *adj* **1** : having the form of an animal **2** : of, relating to, or being the representation of a deity in the form or with the attributes of an animal
zoo•plank•ton \ˌzō-ə-ˈplaŋk-tən, -ˌtän\ *n* : animal life of the plankton
zoo•spore \ˈzō-ə-ˌspōr\ *n* : a motile spore
zoot suit \ˈzüt-\ *n* : a flashy suit of extreme cut typically consisting of a thigh-length jacket with wide padded shoulders and trousers that are wide at the top and narrow at the bottom — **zoot•suit•er** \-ˌsü-tər\ *n*
Zo•ro•as•tri•an•ism \ˌzōr-ə-ˈwas-trē-ə-ˌni-zəm\ *n* : a religion founded by the Persian prophet Zoroaster — **Zo•ro•as•tri•an** \-trē-ən\ *adj or n*
Zou•ave \zü-ˈäv\ *n* : a member of a French infantry unit orig. composed of Algerians wearing a brilliant uniform and conducting a quick spirited drill; *also* : a member of a military unit modeled on the Zouaves
zounds \ˈzaủndz\ *interj* [euphemism for *God's wounds*] — used as a mild oath
zoy•sia \ˈzòi-shə, -zhə, -sē-ə, -zē-ə\ *n* : any of a genus of creeping perennial grasses having fine wiry leaves and including some used as lawn grasses
ZPG *abbr* zero population growth
Zr *symbol* zirconium
zuc•chet•to \zü-ˈke-tō, tsü-\ *n, pl* **-tos** [It] : a small round skullcap worn by Roman Catholic ecclesiastics
zuc•chi•ni \zủ-ˈkē-nē\ *n, pl* **-ni** *or* **-nis** [It] : a summer squash of bushy growth with smooth cylindrical dark green fruits; *also* : its fruit
Zu•lu \ˈzü-ˌlü\ *n, pl* **Zulu** *or* **Zulus** : a member of a Bantu-speaking people of South Africa; *also* : the Bantu language of the Zulus
Zu•ni \ˈzü-nē\ *or* **Zu•ñi** \-nyē\ *n, pl* **Zuni** *or* **Zunis** *or* **Zuñi** *or* **Zuñis** : a member of an American Indian people of western New Mexico; *also* : the language of the Zuni people
zwie•back \ˈswē-ˌbak, ˈswī-, ˈzwē-, ˈzwī-, -ˌbäk\ *n* [G, lit., twice baked, fr. *zwie-* twice + *backen* to

DICTIONARY

bake] : a usu. sweetened bread that is baked and then sliced and toasted until dry and crisp

Zwing•li•an \ˈzwiŋ-glē-ən, ˈswiŋ-, -lē-; ˈtsfiŋ-lē-\ *adj* : of or relating to the Swiss religious reformer Ulrich Zwingli or his teachings — **Zwinglian** *n*

zy•de•co \ˈzī-də-ˌkō\ *n* : popular music of southern Louisiana that combines tunes of French origin with elements of Caribbean music and the blues

zy•gote \ˈzī-ˌgōt\ *n* : a cell formed by the union of two sexual cells; *also* : the developing individual produced from such a cell — **zy•got•ic** \zī-ˈgä-tik\ *adj*

Common English Given Names

The following vocabulary presents given names that are most frequent in English use. The list is not exhaustive either of the names themselves or the variant spellings of those names which are entered. Compound or double names and surnames used as given names are not entered except in cases where long-continued or common use gives them an independent character.

Besides the pronunciations of the names, the list usually provides at least one of the following kinds of information at each entry: (1) etymology, indicating the language source but not the original form of the name, and (2) meaning where known or ascertainable with reasonable certainty.

Names of Men

Aar•on \ˈar-ən, ˈer-\ [Heb]
Abra•ham \ˈā-brə-ˌham\ [Heb]
Ad•am \ˈad-əm\ [Heb] man
Ad•di•son \ˈad-ə-sən\ [fr. a surname]
Adolph \ˈad-ˌälf, ˈā-ˌdälf\ [Gmc] noble wolf, *i.e.*, noble hero
Adri•an \ˈā-drē-ən\ [L] of Hadria, ancient town in central Italy
Al \al\ *dim of* ALAN, ALBERT, *etc.*
Al•an \ˈal-ən\ [Celt]
Al•bert \ˈal-bərt\ [Gmc] illustrious through nobility
Al•den \ˈȯl-dən\ [OE] old friend
Al•ex \ˈal-iks\ *or* **Al•ec** \ˈal-ik\ *dim of* ALEXANDER
Al•ex•an•der \ˌal-ig-ˈzan-dər\ [Gk] a defender of men
Al•fred \ˈal-frəd, -fərd\ [OE] elf counsel, *i.e.*, good counsel
Al•len *or* **Al•lan** *or* **Al•lyn** \ˈal-ən\ *var of* ALAN
Al•ton \ˈȯlt-ᵊn, ˈalt-\ [prob. fr. a surname]
Al•va *or* **Al•vah** \ˈal-və\ [Heb]
Al•vin \ˈal-vən\ [Gmc]
Amos \ˈā-məs\ [Heb]
An•dre \ˈän-(ˌ)drā\ [F] *var of* ANDREW
An•drew \ˈan-(ˌ)drü\ [Gk] manly
An•dy \ˈan-dē\ *dim of* ANDREW
An•ge•lo \ˈan-jə-ˌlō\ [It, fr. Gk] angel, messenger
An•gus \ˈaŋ-gəs\ [Celt]
An•tho•ny \ˈan(t)-thə-nē, *chiefly Brit* ˈan-tə-\ [L]
An•ton \ˈant-ᵊn, ˈan-ˌtän\ [G & Slav] *var of* ANTHONY
An•to•nio \an-ˈtō-nē-ˌō\ [It] *var of* ANTHONY
Ar•chi•bald \ˈär-chə-ˌbȯld, -bəld\ [Gmc]
Ar•chie \ˈär-chē\ *dim of* ARCHIBALD
Ar•den \ˈärd-ᵊn\ [prob. fr. a surname]
Ar•len *or* **Ar•lin** \ˈär-lən\ [prob. fr. a surname]
Ar•lo \ˈär-(ˌ)lō\
Ar•mand \ˈär-ˌmänd, -mənd\ [F] *var of* HERMAN
Arne \ˈärn\ [Scand] eagle
Ar•nold \ˈärn-ᵊld\ [Gmc] power of an eagle
Art \ˈärt\ *dim of* ARTHUR
Ar•thur \ˈär-thər\ [prob. L]
Au•brey \ˈȯ-brē\ [Gmc] elf ruler
Au•gust \ˈȯ-gəst\ [L] August, majestic
Aus•tin \ˈȯs-tən, ˈäs-\ *alter of* Augustine

Bai•ley \ˈbā-lē\ [fr. a surname]
Bar•clay \ˈbär-klē\ [fr. a surname]
Bar•net *or* **Bar•nett** \bär-ˈnet\ [fr. a surname]
Bar•ney \ˈbär-nē\ *dim of* BERNARD
Bar•rett \ˈbar-ət\ [fr. a surname]
Bar•ry *or* **Bar•rie** \ˈbar-ē\ [Ir]
Bart \ˈbärt\ *dim of* Bartholomew
Bar•ton \ˈbärt-ᵊn\ [fr. a surname]
Ba•sil \ˈbaz-əl, ˈbäs-, ˈbās-, ˈbāz-\ [Gk] kingly, royal
Ben \ˈben\ *or* **Ben•nie** *or* **Ben•ny** \ˈben-ē\ *dim of* BENJAMIN
Ben•e•dict \ˈben-ə-ˌdikt\ [L] blessed
Ben•ja•min \ˈbenj-(ə-)mən\ [Heb] son of the right hand
Ben•nett \ˈben-ət\ [OF] *var of* BENEDICT
Ben•ton \ˈbent-ᵊn\ [fr. a surname]
Ber•nard \ˈbər-nərd, (ˌ)bər-ˈnärd\ *or* **Bern•hard** \ˈbərn-ˌhärd\ [Gmc] bold as a bear
Ber•nie \ˈbər-nē\ *dim of* BERNARD
Bert *or* **Burt** \ˈbərt\ *dim of* BERTRAM, ALBERT, etc.
Ber•tram \ˈbər-trəm\ [Gmc] bright raven
Bill \ˈbil\ *or* **Bil•ly** *or* **Bil•lie** \ˈbil-ē\ *dim of* WILLIAM
Blaine \ˈblān\ [fr. a surname]
Blair \ˈbla(ə)r, ˈble(ə)r\ [fr. a surname]
Bob•by \ˈbäb-ē\ *or* **Bob** \ˈbäb\ *dim of* ROBERT
Bo•ris \ˈbōr-əs, ˈbȯr-, ˈbär-\ [Russ]
Boyd \ˈbȯid\ [fr. a surname]
Brad•ford \ˈbrad-fərd\ [fr. a surname]
Brad•ley \ˈbrad-lē\ [fr. a surname]
Bran•don \ˈbran-dən\ [fr. a surname]
Bren•dan \ˈbren-dən\ [Celt]
Brent \ˈbrent\ [fr. a surname]
Brett *or* **Bret** \ˈbret\ [IrGael]
Bri•an *or* **Bry•an** \ˈbrī-ən\ [Celt]
Brooks \ˈbrůks\ [fr. a surname]
Bruce \ˈbrüs\ [fr. a surname]
Bru•no \ˈbrü-(ˌ)nō\ [It, fr. Gmc] brown
Bryce *or* **Brice** \ˈbrīs\ [fr. a surname]
Bud•dy \ˈbəd-ē\ [prob. alter. of *brother*]
Bu•ford \ˈbyü-fərd\ [fr. a surname]
Burke \ˈbərk\ [fr. a surname]
Bur•ton \ˈbərt-ᵊn\ [fr. a surname]
By•ron \ˈbī-rən\ [fr. a surname]

Cal•vin \ˈkal-vən\ [fr. a surname]
Cam•er•on \ˈkam-(ə-)rən\ [fr. a surname]
Carl \ˈkär(-ə)l\ *var of* KARL
Car•los \ˈkär-ləs, -ˌlōs\ [Sp] *var of* CHARLES
Carl•ton *or* **Carle•ton** \ˈkär(-ə)l-tən, ˈkärlt-ᵊn\ [fr. a surname]
Car•lyle \kär-ˈlī(ə)l, ˈkär-ˌ\ [fr. a surname]
Car•men \ˈkär-mən\ [Sp, fr. L] song
Car•roll \ˈkar-əl\ [fr. a surname]
Car•son \ˈkärs-ᵊn\ [fr. a surname]
Car•ter \ˈkärt-ər\ [fr. a surname]
Cary *or* **Car•ey** \ˈka(ə)r-ē, ˈke(ə)r-ē\ [fr. a surname]
Ce•cil \ˈsē-səl, ˈses-əl\ [L]
Chad \ˈchad\ [Gmc]
Charles \ˈchär(-ə)lz\ [Gmc] man of the common people
Ches•ter \ˈches-tər\ [fr. a surname]
Chris \ˈkris\ *dim of* CHRISTOPHER
Chris•tian \ˈkris(h)-chən\ [Gk] Christian (the believer)
Chris•to•pher \ˈkris-tə-fər\ [Gk] Christ bearer
Clar•ence \ˈklar-ən(t)s\ [fr. the English dukedom]
Clark *or* **Clarke** \ˈklärk\ [fr. a surname]
Claude *or* **Claud** \ˈklȯd\ [L]
Clay \ˈklā\ *dim of* CLAYTON
Clay•ton \ˈklāt-ᵊn\ [fr. a surname]
Clem \ˈklem\ *dim of* CLEMENT
Clem•ent \ˈklem-ənt\ [L] mild, merciful
Clif•ford \ˈklif-ərd\ [fr. a surname]
Clif•ton \ˈklif-tən\ [fr. a surname]
Clint \ˈklint\ *dim of* CLINTON
Clin•ton \ˈklint-ᵊn\ [fr. a surname]
Clyde \ˈklīd\ [fr. a surname]

Cole \ˈkōl\ [fr. a surname]
Co·lin \ˈkäl-ən, ˈkō-lən\ *or* **Col·lin** \ˈkäl-ən\ *dim of* NICHOLAS
Con·rad \ˈkän-ˌrad, -rəd\ [Gmc] bold counsel
Con·stan·tine \ˈkän(t)-stən-ˌtēn, -ˌtīn\ [L]
Cor·ey \ˈkȯr-ē\ [fr. a surname]
Cor·ne·lius \kȯr-ˈnēl-yəs\ [L]
Craig \ˈkrāg\ [fr. a surname]
Cur·tis \ˈkərt-əs\ [OF] courteous
Cyr·il \ˈsir-əl\ [Gk] lordly
Cy·rus \ˈsī-rəs\ [OPer]

Dale \ˈdā(ə)l\ [fr. a surname]
Dal·las \ˈdal-əs\ [fr. a surname]
Dal·ton \ˈdȯlt-ᵊn\ [fr. a surname]
Dan \ˈdan\ [Heb] judge
Da·na \ˈdā-nə\ [fr. a surname]
Dan·iel \ˈdan-yəl *also* ˈdan-ᵊl\ [Heb] God has judged
Dan·ny \ˈdan-ē\ *dim of* DANIEL
Dar·old \ˈdar-əld\ *perh alter of* DARRELL
Dar·rell *or* **Dar·rel** *or* **Dar·ryl** *or* **Dar·yl** \ˈdar-əl\ [fr. a surname]
Dar·win \ˈdär-wən\ [fr. a surname]
Dave \ˈdāv\ *dim of* DAVID
Da·vid \ˈdā-vəd\ [Heb] beloved
Da·vis \ˈdā-vəs\ [fr. a surname]
Dean *or* **Deane** \ˈdēn\ [fr. a surname]
Del·a·no \ˈdel-ə-ˌnō\ [fr. a surname]
Del·bert \ˈdel-bərt\ *dim of* Adalbert
Del·mar \ˈdel-mər, -ˌmär\ *or* **Del·mer** \-mər\ [fr. a surname]
Den·nis *or* **Den·is** \ˈden-əs\ [OF, fr. Gk] belonging to Dionysus, god of wine
Den·ny \ˈden-ē\ *dim of* DENNIS
Den·ton \ˈdent-ᵊn\ [fr. a surname]
Der·ek \ˈder-ik\ [Middle Dutch, fr. Gmc] ruler of the people
Dew·ey \ˈd(y)ü-ē\ [fr. a surname]
De·witt \di-ˈwit\ [fr. a surname]
Dex·ter \ˈdek-stər\ [L] on the right hand, fortunate
Dick \ˈdik\ *dim of* RICHARD
Dirk \ˈdərk\ [Dutch] *var of* DEREK
Dom·i·nic *or* **Dom·i·nick** \ˈdäm-ə-(ˌ)nik\ [L] belonging to the Lord
Don *or* **Donn** \ˈdän\ *dim of* DONALD
Don·al \ˈdän-ᵊl\ *var of* DONALD
Don·ald \ˈdän-ᵊld\ [ScGael] world ruler
Don·nie \ˈdän-ē\ *dim of* DON
Don·o·van \ˈdän-ə-vən, ˈdən-\ [fr. a surname]
Doug \ˈdəg\ *dim of* DOUGLAS
Doug·las *or* **Doug·lass** \ˈdəg-ləs\ [fr. a surname]
Duane \dŭ-ˈān, ˈdwān\ [fr. a surname]
Dud·ley \ˈdəd-lē\ [fr. a surname]
Dun·can \ˈdəŋ-kən\ [ScGael] brown head
Dur·ward \ˈdər-wərd\ [fr. a surname]
Dwayne *or* **Dwaine** \ˈdwān\ [fr. a surname]
Dwight \ˈdwīt\ [fr. a surname]
Dy·lan \ˈdil-ən\ [W]

Earl *or* **Earle** \ˈər(-ə)l\ [OE] warrior, noble
Ed \ˈed\ *dim of* EDWARD, EDGAR, etc.
Ed·die *or* **Ed·dy** \ˈed-ē\ *dim of* ED
Ed·gar \ˈed-gər\ [OE] spear of wealth
Ed·mund *or* **Ed·mond** \ˈed-mənd\ [OE] protector of wealth
Ed·son \ˈed-sən\ [fr. a surname]
Ed·ward \ˈed-wərd\ [OE] guardian of wealth
Ed·win \ˈed-wən\ [OE] friend of wealth
El·bert \ˈel-bərt\ *var of* ALBERT
Eli \ˈē-ˌlī\ [Heb] high
E·li·as \i-ˈlī-əs\ [Gk] *var of* Elijah
El·liott *or* **El·liot** *or* **El·iot** \ˈel-ē-ət, ˈel-yət\ [fr. a surname]
El·lis \ˈel-əs\ *var of* ELIAS
Ells·worth \ˈelz-(ˌ)wərth\ [fr. a surname]
El·mer \ˈel-mər\ [fr. a surname]
El·mo \ˈel-(ˌ)mō\ [It, fr. Gk] lovable
El·ton \ˈelt-ᵊn\ [fr. a surname]
El·vin \ˈel-vən\ [fr. a surname]
El·wood *or* **Ell·wood** \ˈel-ˌwu̇d\ [fr. a surname]
Em·man·u·el *or* **Eman·u·el** \i-ˈman-yə(-wə)l\ [Heb] God with us
Em·er·son \ˈem-ər-sən\ [fr. a surname]
Emil \ˈā-məl\ *or* **Emile** \ā-ˈmē(ə)l\ [L]
Em·mett \ˈem-ət\ [fr. a surname]
Em·o·ry *or* **Em·ery** \ˈem-(ə-)rē\ [Gmc]
Er·ic *or* **Er·ich** *or* **Er·ik** \ˈer-ik\ [Scand]
Er·nest *or* **Ear·nest** \ˈər-nəst\ [G] earnestness
Er·nie \ˈər-nē\ *dim of* ERNEST
Ernst \ˈərn(t)st, ˈe(ə)rn(t)st\ [G] *var of* ERNEST
Er·rol \ˈer-əl\ [prob. fr. a surname]
Ethan \ˈē-thən\ [Heb] strength
Eu·gene \yü-ˈjēn, ˈyü-ˌ\ [Gk] wellborn
Ev·an \ˈev-ən\ [W] *var of* JOHN
Ev·er·ett \ˈev-(ə-)rət\ [fr. a surname]

Fe·lix \ˈfē-liks\ [L] happy, prosperous
Fer·di·nand \ˈfərd-ᵊn-ˌand\ [Gmc]
Fer·nan·do \fər-ˈnan-(ˌ)dō\ [Sp] *var of* FERDINAND
Fletch·er \ˈflech-ər\ [fr. a surname]
Floyd \ˈflȯid\ [fr. a surname]
For·rest *or* **For·est** \ˈfȯr-əst, ˈfär-\ [fr. a surname]
Fos·ter \ˈfȯs-tər, ˈfäs-\ [fr. a surname]
Fran·cis \ˈfran(t)-səs\ [OIt & OF] Frenchman
Fran·cis·co \fran-ˈsis-(ˌ)kō\ [Sp] *var of* FRANCIS
Frank \ˈfraŋk\ [Gmc] freeman, Frank
Frank·lin *or* **Frank·lyn** \ˈfraŋ-klən\ [fr. a surname]
Fred \ˈfred\ *dim of* FREDERICK, ALFRED
Fred·die \ˈfred-ē\ *dim of* FREDERICK
Fred·er·ick *or* **Fred·er·ic** *or* **Fred·rick** *or* **Fred·ric** \ˈfred-(ə-)rik\ [Gmc] peaceful ruler
Free·man \ˈfrē-mən\ [fr. a surname]
Fritz \ˈfrits\ [G] *dim of* Friedrich

Ga·bri·el \ˈgā-brē-əl\ [Heb] man of God
Gar·land \ˈgär-lənd\ [fr. a surname]
Gar·rett \ˈgar-ət\ [fr. a surname]
Garth \ˈgärth\ [fr. a surname]
Gary \ˈgar-ē, ˈger-ē\ *or* **Gar·ry** \ˈgar-\ [prob. fr. a surname]
Gay·lord \ˈgā-ˌlȯ(ə)rd\ [fr. a surname]
Gene \ˈjēn\ *dim of* EUGENE
Geof·frey \ˈjef-rē\ [OF, fr. Gmc]
George \ˈjȯ(ə)rj\ [Gk] of or relating to a farmer
Ger·ald \ˈjer-əld\ [Gmc] spear dominion
Ge·rard \jə-ˈrärd, *chiefly Brit* ˈjer-ˌärd, -ərd\ *or* **Ger·hard** \ˈge(ə)r-ˌhärd\ [Gmc] strong with the spear
Ger·ry \ˈjer-ē\ *var of* JERRY
Gil·bert \ˈgil-bərt\ [Gmc] *prob* illustrious through hostages
Giles \ˈjī(ə)lz\ [OF, fr. LL]
Glenn *or* **Glen** \ˈglen\ [fr. a surname]
Gor·don \ˈgȯrd-ᵊn\ [fr. a surname]
Gra·ham \ˈgrā-əm, ˈgra(-ə)m\ [fr. a surname]
Grant \ˈgrant\ [fr. a surname]
Gran·ville \ˈgran-ˌvil\ [fr. a surname]
Gray \ˈgrā\ [fr. a surname]
Gregg *or* **Greg** \ˈgreg\ *dim of* GREGORY
Greg·o·ry \ˈgreg-(ə-)rē\ [LGk] vigilant
Gro·ver \ˈgrō-vər\ [fr. a surname]
Gus \ˈgəs\ *dim of* Gustav *or* Augustus
Guy \ˈgī\ [OF, fr. Gmc]

Hal \ˈhal\ *dim of* HENRY
Hall \ˈhȯl\ [fr. a surname]
Ham·il·ton \ˈham-əl-tən, -əlt-ᵊn\ [fr. a surname]
Hans \ˈhanz, ˈhän(t)s\ [G] *dim of* Johannes
Har·lan \ˈhär-lən\ *or* **Har·land** \-lənd\ [fr. a surname]
Har·ley \ˈhär-lē\ [fr. a surname]
Har·low \ˈhär-(ˌ)lō\ [fr. a surname]
Har·mon \ˈhär-mən\ [fr. a surname]
Har·old \ˈhar-əld\ [OE] army dominion

Har•ris \ˈhar-əs\ [fr. a surname]
Har•ri•son \ˈhar-ə-sən\ [fr. a surname]
Har•ry \ˈhar-ē\ *dim of* HENRY
Har•vey \ˈhär-vē\ [fr. a surname]
Hec•tor \ˈhek-tər\ [Gk] holding fast
Hel•mut \ˈhel-mət, -ˌmüt\ [G] helmet courage
Hen•ry \ˈhen-rē\ [Gmc] ruler of the home
Her•bert \ˈhər-bərt\ [Gmc] illustrious by reason of an army
Her•man *or* **Her•mann** \ˈhər-mən\ [Gmc] warrior
Her•schel *or* **Her•shel** \ˈhər-shəl\ [fr. a surname]
Hi•ram \ˈhī-rəm\ [Phoenician]
Ho•bart \ˈhō-bərt, -ˌbärt\ [fr. a surname]
Hol•lis \ˈhäl-əs\ [fr. a surname]
Ho•mer \ˈhō-mər\ [Gk]
Hor•ace \ˈhȯr-əs, ˈhär-\ [L]
How•ard \ˈhau̇(-ə)rd\ [fr. a surname]
How•ell \ˈhau̇(-ə)l\ [W]
Hu•bert \ˈhyü-bərt\ [Gmc] bright in spirit
Hud•son \ˈhəd-sən\ [fr. a surname]
Hugh \ˈhyü\ *or* **Hu•go** \ˈhyü-(ˌ)gō\ [Gmc] *prob* mind, spirit

Ian \ˈē-ən\ [ScGael] *var of* JOHN
Ira \ˈī-rə\ [Heb]
Ir•ving \ˈər-viŋ\ *or* **Ir•vin** \-vən\ [fr. a surname]
Ir•win \ˈər-wən\ [fr. a surname]
Isaac \ˈī-zik, -zək\ [Heb] he laughs
Ivan \ˈī-vən\ [Russ] *var of* JOHN

Jack \ˈjak\ *dim of* JOHN
Jack•son \ˈjak-sən\ [fr. a surname]
Ja•cob \ˈjā-kəb, -kəp\ [Heb] one who supplants
Jacques *or* **Jacque** \ˈzhäk\ [F] *var of* JAMES
Jake \ˈjāk\ *dim of* JACOB
James \ˈjāmz\ [OF, fr. LL *Jacobus*] *var of* JACOB
Ja•mie \ˈjā-mē\ *dim of* JAMES
Jan \ˈjan\ [Dutch & LG] *var of* JOHN
Jar•ed \ˈjar-əd, ˈjer-\ [Heb] descent
Ja•son \ˈjās-ᵊn\ [Gk]
Jay \ˈjā\ [prob. fr. a surname]
Jed \ˈjed\ *dim of* Jedidiah
Jef•frey *or* **Jeff•ery** *or* **Jef•fry** \ˈjef-(ə-)rē\ *var of* GEOFFREY
Jer•ald *or* **Jer•old** *or* **Jer•rold** \ˈjer-əld\ *var of* GERALD
Jer•e•my \ˈjer-ə-mē\ *or* **Jer•e•mi•ah** \ˌjer-ə-ˈmī-ə\ [Heb] *prob* Yahweh exalts
Je•rome \jə-ˈrōm, *Brit also* ˈjer-əm\ [Gk] bearing a holy name
Jer•ry *or* **Jere** \ˈjer-ē\ *dim of* GERALD
Jes•se \ˈjes-ē\ [Heb]
Jim \ˈjim\ *or* **Jim•my** *or* **Jim•mie** \ˈjim-ē\ *dim of* JAMES
Jo•dy \ˈjō-dē\ *perh alter of* JOSEPH
Joe \ˈjō\ *dim of* JOSEPH
Jo•el \ˈjō-əl\ [Heb] Yahweh is God
John \ˈjän\ [Heb] Yahweh is gracious
Jon \ˈjän\ *var of* JOHN
Jo•nah \ˈjō-nə\ [Heb]
Jon•a•than \ˈjän-ə-thən\ [Heb] Yahweh has given
Jor•dan \ˈjȯrd-ᵊn\ [fr. a surname]
Jo•seph *or* **Jo•sef** \ˈjō-zəf *also* -səf\ [Heb] he shall add
Josh•ua \ˈjäsh-(ə-)wə\ [Heb] Yahweh saves
Judd \ˈjəd\ [fr. a surname]
Jud•son \ˈjəd-sən\ [fr. a surname]
Jules \ˈjülz\ [F] *var of* JULIUS
Ju•lian *or* **Ju•lien** \ˈjül-yən\ [L] sprung from or belonging to Julius
Ju•lius \ˈjül-yəs\ *or* **Ju•lio** \-(ˌ)yō\ [L]
Jus•tin \ˈjəs-tən\ *or* **Jus•tus** \-təs\ [L] just

Karl \ˈkär(-ə)l\ [G & Scand] *var of* CHARLES
Keith \ˈkēth\ [fr. a surname]
Kel•ly \ˈkel-ē\ [fr. a surname]
Ken \ˈken\ *dim of* KENNETH
Ken•dall \ˈken-dᵊl\ [fr. a surname]
Ken•neth \ˈken-əth\ [ScGael]
Kent \ˈkent\ [prob. fr. a surname]
Ken•ton \ˈkent-ᵊn\ [fr. a surname]
Ker•mit \ˈkər-mət\ [prob. fr. a surname]
Ker•ry \ˈker-ē\ [prob. fr. the county of Ireland]
Kev•in \ˈkev-ən\ [OIr]
Kir•by \ˈkər-bē\ [fr. a surname]
Kirk \ˈkərk\ [fr. a surname]
Klaus \ˈklau̇s, ˈklȯs\ [G] *dim of* Nikolaus
Kurt \ˈkərt, ˈku̇(ə)rt\ [G] *dim of* CONRAD
Kyle \ˈkī(ə)l\ [Celt]

La•mar \lə-ˈmär\ [fr. a surname]
Lance \ˈlan(t)s\ *dim of* Lancelot
Lane \ˈlān\ [fr. a surname]
Lan•ny \ˈlan-ē\ *prob dim of* LAWRENCE
Lar•ry \ˈlar-ē\ *dim of* LAWRENCE
Lars \ˈlärz\ [Sw] *var of* LAWRENCE
Law•rence *or* **Lau•rence** \ˈlȯr-ən(t)s, ˈlär-\ [L] of Laurentum, ancient city in central Italy
Lee *or* **Leigh** \ˈlē\ [fr. a surname]
Leigh•ton *or* **Lay•ton** \ˈlāt-ᵊn\ [fr. a surname]
Le•land \ˈlē-lənd\ [fr. a surname]
Len \ˈlen\ *dim of* LEONARD
Leo \ˈle-(ˌ)ō\ [L] lion
Le•on \ˈlē-ˌän, -ən\ [Sp] *var of* LEO
Leon•ard \ˈlen-ərd\ [G] strong or brave as a lion
Le•roy \li-ˈrȯi, ˈlē-ˌ\ [OF] royal
Les•lie \ˈles-lē, ˈlez-\ [fr. a surname]
Les•ter \ˈles-tər\ [fr. a surname]
Lew•is \ˈlü-əs\ *var of* LOUIS
Li•am \ˈlē-əm\ [Ir]
Lin•coln \ˈliŋ-kən\ [fr. a surname]
Li•o•nel \ˈlī-ən-ᵊl, -ə-ˌnel\ [OF] young lion
Lloyd *or* **Loyd** \ˈlȯid\ [W] gray
Lo•gan \ˈlō-gən\ [fr. a surname]
Lon \ˈlän\ *dim of* Alonzo
Lon•nie *or* **Lon•ny** \ˈlän-ē\ *dim of* LON
Lo•ren \ˈlōr-ən, ˈlȯr-\ *dim of* Lorenzo
Lou•ie \ˈlü-ē\ *var of* LOUIS
Lou•is *or* **Lu•is** \ˈlü-əs, ˈlü-ē\ [Gmc] famous warrior
Low•ell \ˈlō-əl\ [fr. a surname]
Lu•cian \ˈlü-shən\ [Gk]
Lud•wig \ˈləd-(ˌ)wig, ˈlüd-\ [G] *var of* LOUIS
Luke \ˈlük\ [Gk] *prob dim of* LUCIUS
Lu•ther \ˈlü-thər\ [fr. a surname]
Lyle \ˈlī(ə)l\ [fr. a surname]
Ly•man \ˈlī-mən\ [fr. a surname]
Lynn \ˈlin\ [fr. a surname]

Mack *or* **Mac** \ˈmak\ [fr. surnames beginning with *Mc* or *Mac*, fr. Gael *mac* son]
Mal•colm \ˈmal-kəm\ [ScGael] servant of (St.) Columba
Man•fred \ˈman-frəd\ [Gmc] peace among men
Man•u•el \ˈman-yə(-wə)l\ [Sp & Pg] *var of* EMMANUEL
Mar•cus \ˈmär-kəs\ [L]
Ma•rio \ˈmär-ē-ˌō\ [It] *var of* MARIUS
Mar•i•on \ˈmer-ē-ən, ˈmar-\ [fr. a surname]
Mark *or* **Marc** \ˈmärk\ *var of* MARCUS
Mar•lin \ˈmär-lən\ [prob. fr. a surname]
Mar•shall *or* **Mar•shal** \ˈmär-shəl\ [fr. a surname]
Mar•tin \ˈmärt-ᵊn\ [LL] of Mars
Mar•vin \ˈmär-vən\ [prob. fr. a surname]
Ma•son \ˈmās-ᵊn\ [fr. a surname]
Matt \ˈmat\ *dim of* MATTHEW
Mat•thew \ˈmath-(ˌ)yü *also* ˈmath-(ˌ)ü\ [Heb] gift of Yahweh
Mau•rice \ˈmȯr-əs, ˈmär-; mȯ-ˈrēs\ [LL] *prob* Moorish
Max \ˈmaks\ *dim of* MAXIMILIAN
Max•well \ˈmak-ˌswel, -swəl\ [fr. a surname]
May•nard \ˈmā-nərd\ [Gmc] bold in strength
Mel•ville \ˈmel-ˌvil\ [fr. a surname]
Mel•vin *or* **Mel•vyn** \ˈmel-vən\ [prob. fr. a surname]
Mer•e•dith \ˈmer-əd-əth\ [W]
Merle \ˈmər(-ə)l\ [F] blackbird

Mer•lin *or* **Mer•lyn** \ˈmər-lən\ [Celt]
Mer•rill \ˈmer-əl\ [fr. a surname]
Mi•chael \ˈmī-kəl\ [Heb] who is like God?
Mick•ey \ˈmik-ē\ *dim of* MICHAEL
Mike \ˈmīk\ *dim of* MICHAEL
Mi•lan \ˈmī-lən\ [prob. fr. the city in Italy]
Miles *or* **Myles** \ˈmī(ə)lz\ [Gmc]
Mil•ford \ˈmil-fərd\ [fr. a surname]
Mil•lard \ˈmil-ərd, mil-ˈärd\ [fr. a surname]
Mi•lo \ˈmī-(ˌ)lō\ [prob. L]
Mil•ton \ˈmilt-ᵊn\ [fr. a surname]
Mitch•ell \ˈmich-əl\ [fr. a surname]
Mon•roe \mən-ˈrō, ˈmən-ˌ\ [fr. a surname]
Mon•te *or* **Mon•ty** \ˈmänt-ē\ *dim of* MONTAGUE
Mor•gan \ˈmȯr-gən\ [W] *prob* dweller on the sea
Mor•ris \ˈmȯr-əs, ˈmär-\ *var of* MAURICE
Mor•ton \ˈmȯrt-ᵊn\ [fr. a surname]
Mur•ray \ˈmər-ē, ˈmə-rē\ [fr. a surname]
My•ron \ˈmī-rən\ [Gk]

Na•than \nā-thən\ [Heb] given, gift
Na•than•iel \nə-ˈthan-yəl\ [Heb] gift of God
Ned \ˈned\ *dim of* EDWARD, EDWIN
Neil *or* **Neal** \ˈnē(ə)l\ [Celt]
Nel•son \ˈnel-sən\ [fr. a surname]
Nev•ille \ˈnev-əl\ [fr. a surname]
Nev•in \ˈnev-ən\ [fr. a surname]
New•ell \ˈn(y)ü-əl\ [fr. a surname]
New•ton \ˈn(y)üt-ᵊn\ [fr. a surname]
Nich•o•las \ˈnik-(ə-)ləs\ [Gk] victorious among the people
Nick \ˈnik\ *dim of* NICHOLAS
Niles \ˈnī(ə)lz\ [fr. a surname]
Nils \ˈnils, ˈnē(ə)ls\ [Scand]
No•ah \ˈnō-ə\ [Heb] rest
No•el \ˈnō-əl\ [F, fr. L] Christmas
No•lan \ˈnō-lən\ [fr. a surname]
Nor•man \ˈnȯr-mən\ [Gmc] Norseman, Norman
Nor•ris \ˈnȯr-əs, ˈnär-\ [fr. a surname]
Nor•ton \ˈnȯrt-ᵊn\ [fr. a surname]

Ol•i•ver \ˈäl-ə-vər\ [OF]
Ol•lie \ˈäl-ē\ *dim of* OLIVER
Or•lan•do \ȯr-ˈlan-(ˌ)dō\ [It] *var of* ROLAND
Or•rin \ˈȯr-ən, ˈär-\ *or* **Orin** *or* **Oren** \ˈȯr-, ˈär-, ˈōr-\ [prob. fr. a surname]
Or•ville *or* **Or•val** \ˈȯr-vəl\ [prob. fr. a surname]
Os•car \ˈäs-kər\ [OE] spear of a deity
Otis \ˈōt-əs\ [fr. a surname]
Ot•to \ˈät-(ˌ)ō\ [Gmc]
Ow•en \ˈō-ən\ [OW]

Palm•er \ˈpäm-ər, ˈpäl-mər\ [fr. a surname]
Par•ker \ˈpär-kər\ [fr. a surname]
Pat \ˈpat\ *dim of* PATRICK
Pat•rick \ˈpa-trik\ [L] patrician
Paul \ˈpȯl\ [L] little
Pe•dro \ˈpē-(ˌ)drō, ˈpā-\ [Sp] *var of* PETER
Per•cy \ˈpər-sē\ [fr. a surname]
Per•ry \ˈper-ē\ [fr. a surname]
Pete \ˈpēt\ *dim of* PETER
Pe•ter \ˈpēt-ər\ [Gk] rock
Phil \ˈfil\ *dim of* PHILIP
Phil•ip *or* **Phil•lip** \ˈfil-əp\ [Gk] lover of horses
Pierre \pē-ˈe(ə)r\ [F] *var of* PETER
Por•ter \ˈpōrt-ər, ˈpȯrt-\ [fr. a surname]
Pres•ton \ˈpres-tən\ [fr. a surname]

Quen•tin \ˈkwent-ᵊn\ [LL] of or relating to the fifth

Ra•fa•el *or* **Ra•pha•el** \ˈraf-ē-əl, ˈrā-fē-\ [Heb] God has healed
Ra•leigh \ˈrȯl-ē, ˈräl-\ [fr. a surname]
Ralph \ˈralf, *Brit also* ˈrāf\ [Gmc] wolf in counsel
Ra•mon \rə-ˈmōn, ˈrā-mən\ [Sp] *var of* RAYMOND
Ran•dall *or* **Ran•dal** \ˈran-dᵊl\ *var of* RANDOLPH
Ran•dolph \ˈran-ˌdälf\ [Gmc] shield wolf
Ran•dy \ˈran-dē\ *dim of* RANDOLPH
Ray \ˈrā\ *dim of* RAYMOND
Ray•mond \ˈrā-mənd\ [Gmc] wise protection
Reed *or* **Reid** \ˈrēd\ [fr. a surname]
Reg•gie \ˈrej-ē\ *dim of* REGINALD
Reg•i•nald \ˈrej-ən-ᵊld\ [Gmc] wise dominion
Re•gis \ˈrē-jəs\ [fr. a proper name]
Re•ne \ˈren-(ˌ)ā, rə-ˈnā, ˈrā-nē, ˈrē-nē\ [F, fr. L] reborn
Reu•ben *or* **Ru•ben** \ˈrü-bən\ [Heb]
Rex \ˈreks\ [L] king
Reyn•old \ˈren-ᵊld\ *var of* REGINALD
Rich•ard \ˈrich-ərd\ [Gmc] strong in rule
Rob•ert \ˈräb-ərt\ [Gmc] bright in fame
Ro•ber•to \rə-ˈbərt-(ˌ)ō, rō-, -ˈbert-\ [Sp & It] *var of* ROBERT
Rob•in \ˈräb-ən\ *dim of* ROBERT
Rod•er•ick \ˈräd-(ə-)rik\ [Gmc] famous ruler
Rod•ney \ˈräd-nē\ [fr. a surname]
Rog•er *or* **Rod•ger** \ˈräj-ər\ [Gmc] famous spear
Rog•ers \ˈräj-ərz\ [fr. a surname]
Ro•land \ˈrō-lənd\ *or* **Rol•land** \ˈräl-ənd\ *or* **Row•land** \ˈrō-lənd\ [Gmc] famous land
Rolf \ˈrälf\ *var of* RUDOLPH
Rol•lin \ˈräl-ən\ *var of* ROLAND
Ron \ˈrän\ *dim of* RONALD
Ron•al \ˈrän-ᵊl\ *var of* RONALD
Ron•ald \ˈrän-ᵊld\ [ON] *var of* REGINALD
Ron•nie *or* **Ron•ny** \ˈrän-ē\ *dim of* RONALD
Ros•coe \ˈräs-(ˌ)kō, ˈrȯs-\ [fr. a surname]
Ross \ˈrȯs\ [fr. a surname]
Roy \ˈrȯi\ [ScGael]
Roy•al \ˈrȯi(-ə)l\ [prob. fr. a surname]
Royce \ˈrȯis\ [fr. a surname]
Ru•dolph *or* **Ru•dolf** \ˈrü-ˌdälf\ [Gmc] famous wolf
Ru•dy \ˈrüd-ē\ *dim of* RUDOLPH
Ru•fus \ˈrü-fəs\ [L] red, red-haired
Ru•pert \ˈrü-pərt\ *var of* ROBERT
Rus•sell *or* **Rus•sel** \ˈrəs-əl\ [fr. a surname]
Ry•an \ˈrī-ən\ [IrGael]

Sal•va•tore \ˈsal-və-ˌtō(ə)r, -ˌtȯ(ə)r; ˌsal-və-ˈtōr-ē, -ˈtȯr-\ [It] savior
Sam \ˈsam\ *dim of* SAMUEL
Sam•my *or* **Sam•mie** \ˈsam-ē\ *dim of* SAM
Sam•u•el \ˈsam-yə(-wə)l\ [Heb] name of God
San•ford \ˈsan-fərd\ [fr. a surname]
Saul \ˈsȯl\ [Heb] asked for
Scott \ˈskät\ [fr. a surname]
Sean \ˈshȯn\ [Ir] *var of* JOHN
Seth \ˈseth\ [Heb]
Sey•mour \ˈsē-ˌmō(ə)r, -ˌmȯ(ə)r\ [fr. a surname]
Shel•by \ˈshel-bē\ [fr. a surname]
Shel•don \ˈshel-dən\ [fr. a surname]
Sher•i•dan \ˈsher-əd-ᵊn\ [fr. a surname]
Sher•man \ˈshər-mən\ [fr. a surname]
Sher•win \ˈshər-wən\ [fr. a surname]
Sher•wood \ˈshər-ˌwu̇d, ˈshe(ə)r-\ [fr. a surname]
Sid•ney *or* **Syd•ney** \ˈsid-nē\ [fr. a surname]
Sieg•fried \ˈsig-ˌfrēd, ˈsēg-\ [Gmc] victorious peace
Sig•mund \ˈsig-mənd\ [Gmc] victorious protection
Si•mon \ˈsī-mən\ [Heb]
Sol•o•mon \ˈsäl-ə-mən\ [Heb] peaceable
Spen•cer \ˈspen(t)-sər\ [fr. a surname]
Sta•cy *or* **Sta•cey** \ˈstā-sē\ [ML]
Stan \ˈstan\ *dim of* STANLEY
Stan•ford \ˈstan-fərd\ [fr. a surname]
Stan•ley \ˈstan-lē\ [fr. a surname]
Stan•ton \ˈstant-ᵊn\ [fr. a surname]
Ste•fan \ˈstef-ən, -ˌän\ [Pol] *var of* STEPHEN
Ste•phen *or* **Ste•ven** *or* **Ste•phan** \ˈstē-vən\ [Gk] crown
Ster•ling \ˈstər-liŋ\ [fr. a surname]
Steve \ˈstēv\ *dim of* STEVEN
Stu•art *or* **Stew•art** \ˈst(y)ü-ərt, ˈst(y)ü(-ə)rt\ [fr. a surname]

Syl·ves·ter \sil-ˈves-tər\ [L] woodsy, of the woods

Tay·lor \ˈtā-lər\ [fr. a surname]
Ted \ˈted\ *or* **Ted·dy** \ˈted-ē\ *dim of* EDWARD, THEODORE
Ter·ence *or* **Ter·rance** *or* **Ter·rence** \ˈter-ən(t)s\ [L]
Ter·rell *or* **Ter·rill** \ˈter-əl\ [fr. a surname]
Ter·ry \ˈter-ē\ *dim of* TERENCE
Thad \ˈthad\ *dim of* THADDEUS
Thad·de·us \ˈthad-ē-əs\ [Gk]
The·o·dore \ˈthē-ə-ˌdō(ə)r, -ˌdȯ(ə)r, -əd-ər\ [Gk] gift of God
Thom·as \ˈtäm-əs\ [Aram] twin
Thur·man \ˈthər-mən\ [fr. a surname]
Tim \ˈtim\ *dim of* TIMOTHY
Tim·o·thy \ˈtim-ə-thē\ [Gk] revering God
To·by \ˈtō-bē\ *dim of* TOBIAS
Todd \ˈtäd\ [prob. fr. a surname]
Tom \ˈtäm\ *or* **Tom·my** *or* **Tom·mie** \ˈtäm-ē\ *dim of* THOMAS
To·ny \ˈtō-nē\ *dim of* ANTHONY
Tra·cy \ˈtrā-sē\ [fr. a surname]
Trav·is \ˈtrav-əs\ [fr. a surname]
Trent \ˈtrent\ [fr. a surname]
Tre·vor \ˈtrev-ər\ [Celt]
Troy \ˈtrȯi\ [prob. fr. a surname]
Tru·man \ˈtrü-mən\ [fr. a surname]
Ty·ler \ˈtī-lər\ [fr. a surname]
Ty·rone \ˈtī-ˌrōn, tī-ˈ; tir-ˈōn\ [prob. fr. the county in Ireland]

Val \ˈval\ *dim of* VALENTINE
Van \ˈvan\ [fr. surnames beginning with *Van,* fr. Dutch *van* of]
Vance \ˈvan(t)s\ [fr. a surname]
Vaughn \ˈvȯn, ˈvän\ [fr. a surname]
Verne *or* **Vern** \ˈvərn\ *prob alter of* VERNON
Ver·non \ˈvər-nən\ [prob. fr. a surname]
Vic·tor \ˈvik-tər\ [L] conqueror
Vin·cent \ˈvin(t)-sənt\ [LL] of or relating to the conquering one
Vir·gil \ˈvər-jəl\ [L]

Wade \ˈwād\ [fr. a surname]
Wal·lace *or* **Wal·lis** \ˈwäl-əs\ [fr. a surname]
Walt \ˈwȯlt\ *dim of* WALTER
Wal·ter \ˈwȯl-tər\ [Gmc] army of dominion
Wal·ton \ˈwȯlt-ᵊn\ [fr. a surname]
Ward \ˈwȯ(ə)rd\ [fr. a surname]
War·ner \ˈwȯr-nər\ [fr. a surname]
War·ren \ˈwȯr-ən, ˈwär-\ [fr. a surname]
Wayne \ˈwān\ [fr. a surname]
Wel·don \ˈwel-dən\ [fr. a surname]
Wen·dell \ˈwen-dᵊl\ [fr. a surname]
Wer·ner \ˈwər-nər, ˈwe(ə)r-\ [Gmc] army of the Varini, a Germanic people
Wes·ley \ˈwes-lē *also* ˈwez-\ [fr. a surname]
Wil·bur *or* **Wil·ber** \ˈwil-bər\ [fr. a surname]
Wi·ley *or* **Wy·lie** \ˈwī-lē\ [fr. a surname]
Wil·ford \ˈwil-fərd\ [fr. a surname]
Wil·fred \ˈwil-frəd\ [OE] desired peace
Will \ˈwil\ *or* **Wil·lie** \-ē\ *dim of* WILLIAM
Wil·lard \ˈwil-ərd\ [fr. a surname]
Wil·liam \ˈwil-yəm\ [Gmc] desired helmet
Wil·lis \ˈwil-əs\ [fr. a surname]
Wil·mer \ˈwil-mər\ [fr. a surname]
Wil·son \ˈwil-sən\ [fr. a surname]
Wil·ton \ˈwilt-ᵊn\ [fr. a surname]
Win·field \ˈwin-ˌfēld\ [fr. a surname]
Win·fred \ˈwin-frəd\ [OE] *prob* joyous peace
Win·ston \ˈwin(t)-stən\ [fr. a surname]
Win·ton \ˈwint-ᵊn\ [fr. a surname]
Wood·row \ˈwu̇d-(ˌ)rō\ [fr. a surname]
Wy·att \ˈwī-ət\ [fr. a surname]

Yale \ˈyā(ə)l\ [fr. a surname]

Zach·a·ry \ˈzak-ə-rē\ *dim of* ZACHARIAH
Zane \ˈzān\ [fr. a surname]

Names of Women

Ab·by \ˈab-ē\ *dim of* ABIGAIL
Ab·i·gail \ˈab-ə-ˌgāl\ [Heb] *prob* source of joy
Ada \ˈād-ə\ [Heb] *prob* ornament
Ad·di·son \ˈad-ə-sən\ [fr. a surname]
Ad·e·laide \ˈad-ᵊl-ˌād\ [Gmc] of noble rank
Adele \ə-ˈdel\ [Gmc] noble
Adri·enne \ˈā-drē-ˌen, -ən\ [F] *fem of* ADRIEN
Ag·nes \ˈag-nəs\ [LL]
Ai·leen \ī-ˈlēn\ [IrGael] *var of* HELEN
Al·ber·ta \al-ˈbərt-ə\ *fem of* ALBERT
Al·ex·an·dra \ˌal-ig-ˈzan-drə\ [Gk] *fem of* ALEXANDER
Alex·is \ə-ˈlek-səs\ [Gk]
Al·ice *or* **Al·yce** \ˈal-əs\ [OF] *var of* ADELAIDE
Ali·cia \ə-ˈlish-ə\ [ML] *var of* ADELAIDE
Al·i·son *or* **Al·li·son** \ˈal-ə-sən\ [OF] *dim of* ALICE
Al·ma \ˈal-mə\ [L] nourishing, cherishing
Al·va \ˈal-və\ [Sp, fr. L] white
Aman·da \ə-ˈman-də\ [L] worthy to be loved
Am·ber \ˈam-bər\ [E]
Ame·lia \ə-ˈmēl-yə\ [Gmc]
Amy \ˈā-mē\ [L] beloved
An·as·ta·sia \ˌan-ə-ˈstā-zh(ē-)ə\ [LGk] of the resurrection
An·drea \ˈan-drē-ə, an-ˈdrā-ə\ *fem of* ANDREW
An·ge·la \ˈan-jə-lə\ [It, fr. Gk] angel
An·gel·i·ca \an-ˈjel-i-kə\ *var of* ANGELA
An·ge·line \ˈan-jə-ˌlīn, -ˌlēn\ *dim of* ANGELA
Ani·ta \ə-ˈnēt-ə\ [Sp] *dim of* ANN
Ann *or* **Anne** \ˈan\ *or* **An·na** \ˈan-ə\ [Heb] grace
An·na·belle \ˈan-ə-ˌbel\ *prob var of* MABEL
An·nette \a-ˈnet, ə-\ *or* **An·net·ta** \-ˈnet-ə\ [F] *dim of* ANN
An·nie \ˈan-ē\ *dim of* ANN
An·toi·nette \ˌan-t(w)ə-ˈnet\ [F] *dim of* ANTONIA
April \ˈā-prəl\ [E] April (the month)
Ar·dell *or* **Ar·delle** \är-ˈdel\ *var of* ADELE
Ar·lene *or* **Ar·leen** *or* **Ar·line** \är-ˈlēn\
Ash·ley \ˈash-lē\ [OE] ash-tree meadow
As·trid \ˈas-trəd\ [Scand] beautiful as a deity
Au·dra \ˈȯ-drə\ *var of* AUDREY
Au·drey \ˈȯ-drē\ [OE] noble strength

Ba·bette \ba-ˈbet\ [F] *dim of* ELIZABETH
Bar·ba·ra \ˈbär-b(ə-)rə\ [Gk] foreign
Be·atrice \ˈbē-ə-trəs\ [It, fr. ML] she that makes happy
Becky \ˈbek-ē\ *dim of* REBECCA
Ber·na·dette \ˌbər-nə-ˈdet\ [F] *fem of* BERNARD
Ber·na·dine \ˈbər-nə-ˌdēn\ *fem of* BERNARD
Ber·nice \(ˌ)bər-ˈnēs, ˈbər-nəs\ [Gk] bringing victory
Ber·tha \ˈbər-thə\ [Gmc] bright
Ber·yl \ˈber-əl\ [Gk] beryl (the mineral)
Bes·sie \ˈbes-ē\ *dim of* ELIZABETH
Beth \ˈbeth\ *dim of* ELIZABETH
Bet·sy *or* **Bet·sey** \ˈbet-sē\ *dim of* ELIZABETH
Bet·ty *or* **Bet·te** *or* **Bet·tye** *or* **Bet·tie** \ˈbet-ē\ *dim of* ELIZABETH
Beu·lah \ˈbyü-lə\ [Heb] married
Bev·er·ly *or* **Bev·er·ley** \ˈbev-ər-lē\ [prob. fr. a surname]
Bil·lie \ˈbil-ē\ *fem of* BILLY
Blair \ˈble(ə)r\ [fr. a surname]
Blake \ˈblāk\ [fr. a surname]
Blanche \ˈblanch\ [OF, fr. Gmc] white
Bob·bie \ˈbäb-ē\ *dim of* ROBERTA
Bo·ni·ta \bə-ˈnēt-ə\ [Sp] pretty
Bon·nie \ˈbän-ē\ [ME] pretty
Bran·dy \ˈbran-dē\ [E]

Bren•da \ˈbren-də\ [Scand]
Bri•gitte \ˈbrij-ət, brə-ˈjit\ [G] *var of* BRIDGET
Brit•tany \ˈbrit-ᵊn-ē\ [E]
Brooke \ˈbrŭk\ [OE] brook

Cait•lin \ˈkāt-lin\ [Ir] *var of* CATHERINE
Ca•mil•la \kə-ˈmil-ə\ [L] freeborn girl attendant at a sacrifice
Ca•mille \kə-ˈmē(ə)l\ [F] *var of* CAMILLA
Can•da•ce \ˈkan-dəs, kan-ˈdā-sē\ [Gk]
Car•la \ˈkär-lə\ [It] *fem of* Carlo
Car•lene \kär-ˈlēn\ *var of* CARLA
Car•lot•ta \kär-ˈlät-ə\ [It] *var of* CHARLOTTE
Car•men \ˈkär-mən\ *or* **Car•mine** \kär-ˈmēn, ˈkär-mən\ [Sp, fr. L] song
Car•ol *or* **Car•ole** *or* **Car•yl** \ˈkar-əl\ *dim of* CAROLYN
Car•o•lyn \ˈkar-ə-lən\ *or* **Car•o•line** \-lən, -ˌlīn\ [It] *fem of* CHARLES
Car•rie \ˈkar-ē\ *dim of* CAROLINE
Cath•er•ine *or* **Cath•a•rine** \ˈkath-(ə-)rən\ [LGk]
Cath•leen \kath-ˈlēn\ [IrGael] *var of* CATHERINE
Cath•ryn \ˈkath-rən\ *var of* CATHERINE
Cathy *or* **Cath•ie** \ˈkath-ē\ *dim of* CATHERINE
Ce•cile \sə-ˈsē(ə)l\ *var of* CECILIA
Ce•ci•lia \sə-ˈsēl-yə, -ˈsil-\ *or* **Ce•ce•lia** \-ˈsēl-\ [L] *fem of* CECIL
Ce•leste \sə-ˈlest\ [L] heavenly
Ce•lia \ˈsēl-yə\ *dim of* CECILIA
Char•lene \shär-ˈlēn\ *fem of* CHARLES
Char•lotte \ˈshär-lət\ [F] *fem dim of* CHARLES
Cher•ie \ˈsher-ē\ [F] dear
Cher•ry \ˈcher-ē\ [E] cherry
Cher•yl \ˈcher-əl, ˈsher-\ *prob var of* CHERRY
Chloe \ˈklō-ē\ [Gk] young verdure
Chris•tie \ˈkris-tē\ *dim of* CHRISTINE
Chris•tine \kris-ˈtēn\ *or* **Chris•ti•na** \-ˈtē-nə\ [Gk] Christian
Cin•dy \ˈsin-dē\ *dim of* LUCINDA
Claire *or* **Clare** \ˈkla(ə)r, ˈkle(ə)r\ *var of* CLARA
Clara \ˈklar-ə\ [L] bright
Cla•rice \ˈklar-əs, klə-ˈrēs\ *dim of* CLARA
Clau•dette \klȯ-ˈdet\ [F] *fem of* CLAUDE
Clau•dia \ˈklȯd-ē-ə\ [L] *fem of* CLAUDE
Clau•dine \klȯ-ˈdēn\ [F] *fem of* CLAUDE
Cleo \ˈklē-(ˌ)ō\ *dim of* Cleopatra
Co•lette \kä-ˈlet\ [OF] *fem dim of* NICHOLAS
Col•leen \kä-ˈlēn\ [IrGael] girl
Con•nie \ˈkän-ē\ *dim of* CONSTANCE
Con•stance \ˈkän(t)-stən(t)s\ [L] constancy
Co•ra \ˈkōr-ə, ˈkȯr-\ [Gk] maiden
Cor•ey \ˈkȯr-ē\ [Ir]
Co•rinne *or* **Cor•rine** \kə-ˈrin, -ˈrēn\ [Gk] *dim of* CORA
Cor•ne•lia \kȯr-ˈnēl-yə\ [L] *fem of* CORNELIUS
Court•ney \ˈkō(ə)rt-nē, ˈkȯ(ə)rt-\ [OE] of the court
Crys•tal \ˈkris-tᵊl\ [E]
Cyn•thia \ˈsin(t)-thē-ə\ [Gk] she of Mount Cynthus on the island of Delos

Dai•sy \ˈdā-zē\ [E] daisy
Dale \ˈdā(ə)l\ [E] valley
Da•na \ˈdā-nə\ [fr. a surname]
Dan•ielle \dăn-ˈyel\ [F] *fem of* DANIEL
Daph•ne \ˈdaf-nē\ [Gk] laurel
Dar•la \ˈdär-lə\ [deriv. of *darling*]
Dar•lene \där-ˈlēn\ [deriv. of *darling*]
Dawn \ˈdȯn, ˈdän\ [E] dawn
De•an•na \dē-ˈan-ə\ *or* **De•anne** \-ˈan\ *var of* DIANA
Deb•bie *or* **Deb•by** \ˈdeb-ē\ *dim of* DEBORAH
Deb•o•rah *or* **Deb•o•ra** \ˈdeb-(ə-)rə\ [Heb] bee
Deb•ra \ˈdeb-rə\ *var of* DEBORAH
Dee \ˈdē\ *prob dim of* EDITH
Deir•dre \ˈdi(ə)r-drē, ˈde(ə)r-\ [IrGael]
De•lia \ˈdēl-yə\ [Gk] she of Delos (i.e. the goddess Artemis)
Del•la \ˈdel-ə\ *dim of* ADELAIDE, DELIA
De•lo•res \də-ˈlōr-əs, -ˈlȯr-\ *var of* DOLORES
De•na *or* **Dee•na** \ˈdē-nə\ *dim of* GERALDINE
De•nise \də-ˈnēz, -ˈnēs\ [F] *fem of* DENIS
Di•ana *or* **Di•an•na** \dī-ˈan-ə\ [L]
Di•ane *or* **Di•anne** *or* **Di•an** *or* **Di•ann** \dī-ˈan\ [F] *var of* DIANA
Di•na *or* **Di•nah** \ˈdī-nə\ [Heb] judged
Dix•ie \ˈdik-sē\ [E] *prob* Dixie (nickname for the southern states of the U.S.)
Do•lo•res \də-ˈlōr-əs, -ˈlȯr-\ [Sp, fr. L] sorrows (i.e. those of the Virgin Mary)
Don•na \ˈdän-ə\ *or* **Do•na** \ˈdän-ə, ˈdō-nə\ [It, fr. L] lady
Do•ra \ˈdōr-ə, ˈdȯr-\ *dim of* THEODORA, Eudora
Do•reen \dȯ-ˈrēn, də-\ [IrGael]
Dor•is \ˈdȯr-əs, ˈdär-\ [Gk] *prob* Dorian (a member of an ancient Hellenic race)
Dor•o•thy \ˈdȯr-ə-thē, ˈdär-\ *or* **Dor•o•thea** \ˌdȯr-ə-ˈthē-ə, ˌdär-\ [LGk] goddess of gifts
Dot•tie *or* **Dot•ty** \ˈdät-ē\ *dim of* DOROTHY

Edith *or* **Edythe** \ˈēd-əth\ [OE]
Ed•na \ˈed-nə\ [Aram]
Ed•wi•na \e-ˈdwē-nə, -ˈdwin-ə\ *fem of* EDWIN
Ef•fie \ˈef-ē\ *dim of* Euphemia
Ei•leen \ī-ˈlēn\ [IrGael] *var of* HELEN
Elaine \i-ˈlān\ [OF] *var of* HELEN
El•ea•nor *or* **El•i•nor** *or* **El•ea•nore** \ˈel-ə-nər, -ˌnȯ(ə)r, -ˌnō(ə)r\ [OProv] *var of* HELEN
Ele•na \ˈel-ə-nə, ə-ˈlē-nə\ [It] *var of* HELEN
Elise \ə-ˈlēz, -ˈlēs\ [F] *var of* ELIZABETH
Eliz•a•beth *or* **Elis•a•beth** \i-ˈliz-ə-bəth\ [Heb] God has sworn
El•la \ˈel-ə\ [OF]
El•len *or* **El•lyn** \ˈel-ən\ *var of* HELEN
El•o•ise \ˈel-ə-ˌwēz, ˌel-ə-ˈ\ [OF, fr. Gmc]
El•sa \ˈel-sə\ [G] *dim of* ELIZABETH
El•sie \ˈel-sē\ *dim of* ELIZABETH
El•va \ˈel-və\ [Gmc] elf
Em•i•ly *or* **Em•i•lie** \ˈem-(ə-)lē\ [L] *fem of* EMIL
Em•ma \ˈem-ə\ [Gmc] *var of* ERMA
Enid \ˈē-nəd\ [W]
Er•i•ka \ˈer-i-kə\ *fem of* ERIC
Er•in \ˈer-ən\ [IrGael]
Er•ma \ˈər-mə\ [Gmc]
Er•nes•tine \ˈər-nə-ˌstēn\ *fem of* ERNEST
Es•telle \e-ˈstel\ *or* **Es•tel•la** \e-ˈstel-ə\ [OProv, fr. L] star
Es•ther \ˈes-tər\ [prob. fr. Per] *prob* star
Eth•el \ˈeth-əl\ [OE] noble
Et•ta \ˈet-ə\ *dim of* HENRIETTA
Eu•ge•nia \yŭ-ˈjēn-yə\ *or* **Eu•ge•nie** \-ˈjē-nē\ *fem of* EUGENE
Eu•nice \ˈyü-nəs\ [Gk] having (i.e. bringing) happy victory
Eva \ˈē-və\ *var of* EVE
Evan•ge•line \i-ˈvan-jə-lən, -ˌlēn, -ˌlīn\ [Gk] bringing good news
Eve \ˈēv\ [Heb] life, living
Ev•e•lyn \ˈev-(ə-)lən, *chiefly Brit* ˈēv-\ [OF, fr. Gmc]

Faith \ˈfāth\ [E] faith
Faye *or* **Fay** \ˈfā\ *dim of* FAITH
Fe•lice \fə-ˈlēs\ [L] happiness
Fern *or* **Ferne** \ˈfərn\ [E] fern
Flo•ra \ˈflōr-ə, ˈflȯr-\ [L] goddess of flowers
Flor•ence \ˈflȯr-ən(t)s, ˈflär-\ [L] bloom, prosperity
Fran•ces \ˈfran(t)-səs, -səz\ *fem of* FRANCIS
Fran•cine \fran-ˈsēn\ [F] *prob dim of* FRANCES
Fre•da *or* **Frie•da** \ˈfrēd-ə\ *dim of* WINIFRED
Fred•er•ic•ka *or* **Fred•er•i•ca** \ˌfred-(ə-)ˈrē-kə, -ˈrik-ə\ *fem of* FREDERICK

Gail *or* **Gayle** *or* **Gale** \ˈgā(ə)l\ *dim of* ABIGAIL
Gay \ˈgā\ [E] gay
Ge•ne•va \jə-ˈnē-və\ *var of* GENEVIEVE
Gen•e•vieve \ˈjen-ə-ˌvēv\ [prob. fr. Celt]

George•ann \jȯr-ˈjan\ [*George + Ann*]
Geor•gette \jȯr-ˈjet\ *fem of* GEORGE
Geor•gia \ˈjȯr-jə\ *fem of* GEORGE
Geor•gi•na \jȯr-ˈjē-nə\ *fem of* GEORGE
Ger•al•dine \ˈjer-əl-ˌdēn\ *fem of* GERALD
Ger•trude \ˈgər-ˌtrüd\ [Gmc] spear strength
Gil•li•an \ˈjil-ē-ən\ *var of* JULIANA
Gin•ger \ˈjin-jər\ [E] ginger
Gi•sela \jə-ˈsel-ə, -ˈzel-\ [Gmc] pledge
Gi•selle \jə-ˈzel\ *var of* GISELA
Glad•ys \ˈglad-əs\ [W]
Glen•da \ˈglen-də\ *prob var of* GLENNA
Glen•na \ˈglen-ə\ *fem of* GLENN
Glo•ria \ˈglōr-ē-ə, ˈglȯr-\ [L] glory
Grace \ˈgrās\ [L] favor, grace
Gre•ta \ˈgrēt-ə, ˈgret-\ *dim of* MARGARET
Gretch•en \ˈgrech-ən\ [G] *dim of* MARGARET
Gwen \ˈgwen\ *dim of* GWENDOLYN
Gwen•do•lyn \ˈgwen-də-lən\ [W]

Han•nah \ˈhan-ə\ [Heb] *var of* ANN
Har•ri•et *or* **Har•ri•ett** *or* **Har•ri•ette** \ˈhar-ē-ət\ *var of* HENRIETTA
Hat•tie \ˈhat-ē\ *dim of* HARRIET
Ha•zel \ˈhā-zəl\ [E] hazel
Heath•er \ˈheth-ər\ [ME] heather (the shrub)
Hei•di \ˈhīd-ē\ [G] *dim of* ADELAIDE
He•laine \hə-ˈlān\ *var of* HELEN
Hel•en \ˈhel-ən\ *or* **He•le•na** \ˈhel-ə-nə, hə-ˈlē-nə\ [Gk]
He•lene \hə-ˈlēn\ [F] *var of* HELEN
Hel•ga \ˈhel-gə\ [Scand] holy
Hen•ri•et•ta \ˌhen-rē-ˈet-ə\ [MF] *fem of* HENRY
Her•mine \ˈhər-ˌmēn\ [G] *prob fem of* HERMAN
Hes•ter \ˈhes-tər\ *var of* ESTHER
Hil•ary *or* **Hil•la•ry** \ˈhil-ə-rē\ [L] cheerful
Hil•da \ˈhil-də\ [OE] battle
Hil•de•gard *or* **Hil•de•garde** \ˈhil-də-ˌgärd\ [Gmc] *prob* battle enclosure
Hol•ly \ˈhäl-ē\ [E] holly
Hope \ˈhōp\ [E] hope

Ida \ˈīd-ə\ [Gmc]
Ilene \ī-ˈlēn\ *var of* EILEEN
Imo•gene \ˈim-ə-ˌjēn, ˈī-mə-\
Ina \ˈī-nə\
Inez \ī-ˈnez, ˈī-nəz\ [Sp] *var of* AGNES
In•grid \ˈiŋ-grəd\ [Scand] beautiful as Ing (an ancient Germanic god)
Irene \ī-ˈrēn\ [Gk] peace
Iris \ˈī-rəs\ [Gk] rainbow
Ir•ma \ˈər-mə\ *var of* ERMA
Is•a•bel *or* **Is•a•belle** \ˈiz-ə-ˌbel\ [OProv] *var of* ELIZABETH

Jack•ie *or* **Jacky** \ˈjak-ē\ *dim of* JACQUELINE
Jac•que•line *or* **Jac•que•lyn** *or* **Jac•que•lin** \ˈjak-(w)ə-lən, -ˌlēn\ [OF] *fem of* JACOB
Ja•mie \ˈjā-mē\ *fem of* JAMES
Jan \ˈjan\ *dim of* JANET
Jane *or* **Jayne** \ˈjān\ [OF] *var of* JOAN
Ja•net *or* **Ja•nette** \ˈjan-ət, jə-ˈnet\ *dim of* JANE
Ja•nice \ˈjan-əs, jə-ˈnēs\ *or* **Jan•is** \ˈjan-əs\ *prob dim of* JANE
Ja•nie \ˈjā-nē\ *dim of* JANE
Jean *or* **Jeanne** \ˈjēn\ [OF] *var of* JOAN
Jea•nette *or* **Jean•nette** \jə-ˈnet\ [F] *dim of* JEANNE
Jean•nie *or* **Jean•ie** \ˈjē-nē\ *dim of* JEAN
Jean•nine *or* **Jea•nine** \jə-ˈnēn\ [F] *dim of* JEANNE
Jen•nie *or* **Jen•ny** \ˈjen-ē\ *dim of* JANE
Jen•ni•fer \ˈjen-ə-fər\ [Celt]
Jer•al•dine \ˈjer-əl-ˌdēn\ *var of* GERALDINE
Jer•i•lyn \ˈjer-ə-lən\ *var of* GERALDINE
Jer•ry *or* **Jeri** *or* **Jer•rie** \ˈjer-ē\ *dim of* GERALDINE
Jes•si•ca \ˈjes-i-kə\ [prob. Heb]
Jes•sie \ˈjes-ē\ [Sc] *dim of* JANET
Jew•el *or* **Jew•ell** \ˈjü(-ə)l\ [E] jewel

Jill \ˈjil\ *dim of* JULIANA
Jo \ˈjō\ *dim of* JOSEPHINE
Joan *or* **Joann** *or* **Joanne** \ˈjō(-ə)n, jō-ˈan\ [Gk] *fem of* JOHN
Jo•an•na \jō-ˈan-ə\ *or* **Jo•han•na** \-ˈ(h)an-ə\ *var of* JOAN
Joc•e•lyn \ˈjäs-(ə-)lən\ [OF, fr. Gmc]
Jo•dy *or* **Jo•die** \ˈjō-dē\ *alter of* JUDITH
Jo•lene \jō-ˈlēn\ *prob dim of* JO
Jo•se•phine \ˈjō-zə-ˌfēn *also* ˈjō-sə-\ *fem of* JOSEPH
Joy \ˈjȯi\ [E] joy
Joyce \ˈjȯis\ [OF]
Jua•ni•ta \wä-ˈnēt-ə\ [Sp] *fem dim of* JOHN
Ju•dith \ˈjüd-əth\ [Heb] Jewess
Ju•dy *or* **Ju•di** *or* **Ju•die** \ˈjüd-ē\ *dim of* JUDITH
Ju•lia \ˈjül-yə\ [L] *fem of* JULIUS
Ju•li•ana \ˌjü-lē-ˈan-ə\ [LL] *fem of* JULIAN
Ju•li•anne *or* **Ju•li•ann** \ˌjü-lē-ˈan, jül-ˈyan\ *var of* JULIANA
Ju•lie \ˈjü-lē\ [MF] *var of* JULIA
Ju•liet \ˈjül-yət, -ē-ˌet, -ē-ət; ˌjül-ē-ˈet, jül-ˈyet, ˈjül-ˌyet\ [It] *dim of* JULIA
June \ˈjün\ [E] June (the month)
Jus•tine \ˌjəs-ˈtēn\ [F] *fem of* JUSTIN

Ka•ra \ˈkär-ə, ˈkar-ə\ *var of* CATHERINE
Kar•en *or* **Kar•in** *or* **Kaa•ren** \ˈkar-ən, ˈkär-\ [Scand] *var of* CATHERINE
Kar•la \ˈkär-lə\ *var of* CARLA
Kar•ol \ˈkar-əl\ *var of* CAROL
Kar•o•lyn \ˈkar-ə-lən\ *var of* CAROLYN
Kate \ˈkāt\ *dim of* CATHERINE
Kath•er•ine *or* **Kath•a•rine** *or* **Kath•ryn** \ˈkath-(ə-)rən\ *var of* CATHERINE
Kath•leen \kath-ˈlēn\ [IrGael] *var of* CATHERINE
Kathy \ˈkath-ē\ *dim of* CATHERINE
Ka•tie \ˈkāt-ē\ *dim of* KATE
Kay *or* **Kaye** \ˈkā\ *dim of* CATHERINE
Kel•ly \ˈkel-ē\ [fr. a surname]
Ker•ry \ˈker-ē\ [prob. fr. the county of Ireland]
Kim \ˈkim\ *prob dim of* KIMBERLY
Kim•ber•ly \ˈkim-bər-lē\ [OE]
Kit•ty \ˈkit-ē\ *dim of* CATHERINE
Kris•tin \ˈkris-tən\ [Scand] *var of* CHRISTINE
Kris•tine \kris-ˈtēn\ *var of* CHRISTINE

La•na \ˈlan-ə, ˈlän-ə, ˈlā-nə\
Lau•ra \ˈlȯr-ə, ˈlär-\ [ML] *prob fem dim of* LAWRENCE
Lau•rel \ˈlȯr-əl, ˈlär-\ [E] laurel
Lau•ren \ˈlȯr-ən, ˈlär-\ *var of* LAURA
Lau•rie \ˈlȯr-ē, ˈlär-\ *dim of* LAURA
La•verne *or* **La•vern** \lə-ˈvərn\
Le•ah \ˈlē-ə\ [Heb] *prob* wild cow
Le•anne \lē-ˈan\ [prob. fr. *Lee + Ann*]
Lee \ˈlē\ [fr. a surname]
Leigh \ˈlē\ *var of* LEE
Lei•la *or* **Le•la** \ˈlē-lə\ [Per] dark as night
Le•lia \ˈlēl-yə\ [L]
Le•na \ˈlē-nə\ [G] *dim of* HELENA, Magdalena
Le•nore \lə-ˈnō(ə)r, -ˈnȯ(ə)r\ *or* **Le•no•ra** \lə-ˈnōr-ə, -ˈnȯr-\ *var of* LEONORA
Le•o•na \lē-ˈō-nə\ *fem of* LEON
Le•o•no•ra \ˌlē-ə-ˈnōr-ə, -ˈnȯr-\ *var of* ELEANOR
Les•lie *or* **Les•ley** \ˈles-lē *also* ˈlez-\ [fr. a surname]
Le•ti•tia \li-ˈtish-ə, -ˈtē-shə\ [L] gladness
Lib•by \ˈlib-ē\ *dim of* ELIZABETH
Li•la \ˈlī-lə\ *var of* LEILA
Lil•lian \ˈlil-yən, ˈlil-ē-ən\ *prob dim of* ELIZABETH
Lil•lie \ˈlil-ē\ *dim of* LILLIAN
Lily \ˈlil-ē\ [E] lily
Lin•da *or* **Lyn•da** \ˈlin-də\ *dim of* MELINDA, Belinda
Lind•sey *or* **Lind•say** \ˈlin-zē\ [OE] linden isle
Li•sa \ˈlē-sə, ˈlī-zə\ *dim of* ELIZABETH
Lo•is \ˈlō-əs\ [Gk]
Lo•la \ˈlō-lə\ [Sp] *dim of* DOLORES
Lon•na \ˈlän-ə\ *fem of* LON

Lo•ra \ˈlōr-ə, ˈlȯr-\ *var of* LAURA
Lo•re•lei \ˈlōr-ə-ˌlī, ˈlȯr-\ [G]
Lo•rene \lȯ-ˈrēn\ *dim of* LORA
Lo•ret•ta \lə-ˈret-ə, lȯ-\ [ML] *var of* Lauretta
Lo•ri \ˈlōr-ē, ˈlȯr-\ *var of* LAURA
Lor•na \ˈlȯr-nə\
Lor•raine *or* **Lo•raine** \lə-ˈrān, lȯ-\ [prob. fr. *Lorraine*, region in northeast France]
Lou \ˈlü\ *dim of* LOUISE
Lou•ise \lu̇-ˈēz\ *or* **Lou•i•sa** \-ˈē-zə\ *fem of* LOUIS
Lu•anne \lü-ˈan\ [*Lu-* + *Anne*]
Lu•cille *or* **Lu•cile** \lü-ˈsē(ə)l\ [L] *prob dim of* LUCIA
Lu•cin•da \lü-ˈsin-də\ [L] *var of* LUCY
Lu•cre•tia \lü-ˈkrē-shə\ [L]
Lu•cy \ˈlü-sē\ *or* **Lu•cia** \ˈlü-shə\ [L] *fem of* Lucius
Lu•el•la \lu̇-ˈel-ə\ [prob. fr. *Lou* (dim. of *Louise*) + *Ella*]
Lyd•ia \ˈlid-ē-ə\ [Gk] woman of Lydia, ancient country in Asia Minor
Ly•nette \lə-ˈnet\ [W]
Lynne *or* **Lynn** \ˈlin\ *dim of* CAROLYN, JACQUELYN, etc.

Ma•bel \ˈmā-bəl\ [L] lovable
Mac•ken•zie \mə-ˈken-zē\ [fr. a surname]
Mad•e•line *or* **Mad•e•leine** *or* **Mad•e•lyn** \ˈmad-ᵊl-ən\ [Gk] woman of Magdala, ancient town in northern Palestine
Madge \ˈmaj\ *dim of* MARGARET
Mal•lory \ˈmal-(ə-)rē\ [fr. a surname]
Ma•mie \ˈmā-mē\ *dim of* MARGARET
Ma•ra \ˈmär-ə\ *var of* MARY
Mar•cel•la \mär-ˈsel-ə\ [L] *fem of* Marcellus
Mar•cia \ˈmär-shə\ [L] *fem of* MARCUS
Mar•ga•ret \ˈmär-g(ə-)rət\ [Gk] pearl
Mar•gery \ˈmärj-(ə-)rē\ [OF] *var of* MARGARET
Mar•gie \ˈmär-jē\ *dim of* MARGARET
Mar•go \ˈmär-(ˌ)gō\ *var of* MARGOT
Mar•got \ˈmär-(ˌ)gō, -gət\ *dim of* MARGARET
Mar•gue•rite \ˌmär-g(y)ə-ˈrēt\ [OF] *var of* MARGARET
Ma•ria \mə-ˈrē-ə *also* -ˈrī-\ *var of* MARY
Mar•i•an \ˈmer-ē-ən, ˈmar-\ *var of* MARIANNE
Mar•i•anne \ˌmer-ē-ˈan, ˌmar-\ *or* **Mar•i•an•na** \-ˈan-ə\ [F] *dim of* MARY
Ma•rie \mə-ˈrē\ [OF] *var of* MARY
Mar•i•et•ta \ˌmer-ē-ˈet-ə, ˌmar-\ *dim of* MARY
Mar•i•lee \ˈmer-ə-(ˌ)lē, ˈmar-\ [prob. fr. *Mary* + *Lee*]
Mar•i•lyn *or* **Mar•i•lynn** *or* **Mar•y•lyn** \ˈmer-ə-lən, ˈmar-\ [prob. fr. *Mary* + *-lyn*]
Ma•ri•na \mə-ˈrē-nə\ [LGk]
Mar•i•on \ˈmer-ē-ən, ˈmar-\ *dim of* MARY
Mar•jo•rie *or* **Mar•jo•ry** \ˈmärj-(ə-)rē\ *var of* MARGERY
Mar•la \ˈmär-lə\ *prob dim of* MARLENE
Mar•lene \mär-ˈlēn(-ə), -ˈlā-nə\ [G] *dim of* Magdalene
Mar•lyn \ˈmär-lən\ *prob var of* MARLENE
Mar•sha \ˈmär-shə\ *var of* MARCIA
Mar•ta \ˈmärt-ə\ [It] *var of* MARTHA
Mar•tha \ˈmär-thə\ [Aram] lady
Mar•va \ˈmär-və\ *prob fem of* MARVIN
Mary \ˈme(ə)r-ē, ˈmā-rē\ [Gk, fr. Heb]
Mary•ann *or* **Mary•anne** \ˌmer-ē-ˈan, ˌmā-rē-\ [*Mary* + *Ann*]
Mary•el•len \ˌmer-ē-ˈel-ən, ˌmā-rē-\ [*Mary* + *Ellen*]
Mar•y•lon \ˈmer-ə-lən, ˈmar-\ *var of* MARILYN
Maude \ˈmȯd\ [OF] *var of* Matilda
Mau•reen *or* **Mau•rine** \mȯ-ˈrēn\ [Ir] *dim of* MARY
Max•ine \mak-ˈsēn\ [F] *fem dim of* Maximilian
May *or* **Mae** \ˈmā\ *dim of* MARY
Me•gan \ˈmeg-ən, ˈmē-gən\ [Ir]
Mel•a•nie \ˈmel-ə-nē\ [Gk] blackness
Mel•ba \ˈmel-bə\ [E] woman of Melbourne, Australia
Me•lin•da \mə-ˈlin-də\ *prob alter of* Belinda
Me•lis•sa \mə-ˈlis-ə\ [Gk] bee
Mel•va \ˈmel-və\ *prob fem of* MELVIN
Mer•e•dith \ˈmer-əd-əth\ [W]
Merle \ˈmər(-ə)l\ [F] blackbird
Mer•ri•ly \ˈmer-ə-lē\ *alter of* MARILEE
Mer•ry \ˈmer-ē\ [E] merry
Mia \ˈmē-ə\ [It]
Mi•chele *or* **Mi•chelle** \mi-ˈshel\ [F] *fem of* MICHAEL
Mil•dred \ˈmil-drəd\ [OE] gentle strength
Mil•li•cent \ˈmil-ə-sənt\ [Gmc]
Mil•lie \ˈmil-ē\ *dim of* MILDRED
Min•nie \ˈmin-ē\ [Sc] *dim of* MARY
Mir•an•da \mə-ˈran-də\ [L] admirable
Mir•i•am \ˈmir-ē-əm\ [Heb] *var of* MARY
Mit•zi \ˈmit-sē\ *prob dim of* MARGARET
Mol•ly *or* **Mol•lie** \ˈmäl-ē\ *dim of* MARY
Mo•na \ˈmō-nə\ [IrGael]
Mon•i•ca \ˈmän-i-kə\ [LL]
Mu•ri•el \ˈmyu̇r-ē-əl\ [prob. Celt]
My•ra \ˈmī-rə\
Myr•na \ˈmər-nə\
Myr•tle \ˈmərt-ᵊl\ [Gk] myrtle

Na•dine \nā-ˈdēn, nə-\ [F, fr. Russ] hope
Nan \ˈnan\ *dim of* ANN
Nan•cy \ˈnan(t)-sē\ *dim of* ANN
Nan•nette *or* **Na•nette** \na-ˈnet, nə-\ [F] *dim of* ANN
Na•o•mi \nā-ˈō-mē\ [Heb] pleasant
Nat•a•lie \ˈnat-ᵊl-ē\ [LL] of or relating to Christmas
Nel•lie \ˈnel-ē\ *or* **Nell** \ˈnel\ *dim of* ELLEN, HELEN, ELEANOR
Net•tie \ˈnet-ē\ [Sc] *dim of* JANET
Ni•cole \nē-ˈkȯl\ [F] *fem of* NICHOLAS
Ni•na \ˈnē-nə\ [Russ] *dim of* ANN
Ni•ta \ˈnēt-ə\ [Sp] *dim of* JUANITA
No•na \ˈnō-nə\ [L] ninth
No•ra \ˈnōr-ə, ˈnȯr-\ *dim of* LEONORA, ELEANOR, Honora
No•reen \nȯ-ˈrēn\ [IrGael] *dim of* NORA
Nor•ma \ˈnȯr-mə\ [It]

Ol•ga \ˈäl-gə, ˈōl-\ [Russ] *var of* HELGA
Ol•ive \ˈäl-iv, -əv\ *or* **O•liv•ia** \ə-ˈliv-ē-ə, ō-\ [L] olive
Opal \ˈō-pəl\ [E] opal

Pam \ˈpam\ *dim of* PAMELA
Pa•me•la \ˈpam-ə-lə; pə-ˈmē-lə, pa-\
Pa•tri•cia \pə-ˈtrish-ə, -ˈtrē-shə\ [L] *fem of* PATRICK
Pat•sy \ˈpat-sē\ *dim of* PATRICIA
Pat•ty *or* **Pat•ti** *or* **Pat•tie** \ˈpat-ē\ *dim of* PATRICIA
Pau•la \ˈpȯ-lə\ [L] *fem of* PAUL
Pau•lette \pȯ-ˈlet\ *fem dim of* PAUL
Pau•line \pȯ-ˈlēn\ *fem dim of* PAUL
Pearl \ˈpər(-ə)l\ [E] pearl
Peg•gy \ˈpeg-ē\ *dim of* MARGARET
Pe•nel•o•pe \pə-ˈnel-ə-pē\ [Gk]
Pen•ny \ˈpen-ē\ *dim of* PENELOPE
Phoe•be \ˈfē-bē\ [Gk] shining
Phyl•lis \ˈfil-əs\ [Gk] green leaf
Pol•ly \ˈpäl-ē\ *dim of* MARY
Por•tia \ˈpōr-shə, ˈpȯr-\ [L]
Pris•cil•la \prə-ˈsil-ə\ [L]
Pru•dence \ˈprüd-ᵊn(t)s\ [E] prudence

Ra•chel \ˈrā-chəl\ [Heb] ewe
Rae \ˈrā\ *dim of* RACHEL
Ra•mo•na \rə-ˈmō-nə\ [Sp] *fem of* RAMON
Re•ba \ˈrē-bə\ *dim of* REBECCA
Re•bec•ca \ri-ˈbek-ə\ [Heb]
Re•gi•na \ri-ˈjē-nə, -ˈjī-\ [L] queen
Re•nee \rə-ˈnā, ˈren-(ˌ)ā, ˈrā-nē, ˈrē-nē\ [F] reborn
Rhea \ˈrē-ə\ [Gk]
Rho•da \ˈrōd-ə\ [Gk] rose
Ri•ta \ˈrēt-ə\ [It] *dim of* MARGARET
Ro•ber•ta \rə-ˈbərt-ə, rō-\ *fem of* ROBERT
Rob•in *or* **Rob•yn** \ˈräb-ən\ [E] robin
Ro•chelle \rō-ˈshel\ [prob. fr. a surname]
Ro•na *or* **Rho•na** \ˈrō-nə\
Ron•da \ˈrän-də\ *var of* Rhonda
Ron•nie \ˈrän-ē\ *dim of* VERONICA

Ro•sa•lie \ˈrō-zə-(ˌ)lē, ˈräz-ə-\ [L] festival of roses
Ro•sa•lind \ˈräz-(ə-)lənd, ˈrō-zə-lənd\ [Sp]
Rose \ˈrōz\ *or* **Ro•sa** \ˈrō-zə\ [L] rose
Rose•anne \rō-ˈzan\ [*Rose* + *Anne*]
Rose•mary \ˈrōz-ˌmer-ē\ *or* **Rose•ma•rie** \ˌrōz-mə-ˈrē\ [E] rosemary
Ro•set•ta \rō-ˈzet-ə\ *dim of* ROSE
Ros•lyn \ˈräz-lən\ *or* **Ro•sa•lyn** *or* **Ro•se•lyn** \ˈräz-(ə-)lən, ˈrō-zə-lən\ *var of* ROSALIND
Ro•we•na \rə-ˈwē-nə\ [perh. fr. OE]
Rox•anne \räk-ˈsan\ [OPer]
Ru•by \ˈrü-bē\ [E] ruby
Ruth \ˈrüth\ [Heb]
Ruth•ann \rü-ˈthan\ [*Ruth* + *Ann*]

Sa•bra \ˈsā-brə\ *dim of* Sabrina
Sa•die \ˈsād-ē\ *dim of* SARA
Sal•ly *or* **Sal•lie** \ˈsal-ē\ *dim of* SARA
Sa•man•tha \sə-ˈman-thə\ [Aram]
San•dra \ˈsan-drə, ˈsän-\ *dim of* ALEXANDRA
San•dy \ˈsan-dē\ *dim of* ALEXANDRA
Sar•ah *or* **Sara** \ˈser-ə, ˈsar-ə, ˈsā-rə\ [Heb] princess
Sara•lee \ˈser-ə-(ˌ)lē, ˈsar-\ [prob. fr. *Sara* + *Lee*]
Saun•dra \ˈsȯn-drə, ˈsän-\ *var of* SANDRA
Sel•ma \ˈsel-mə\ [Sw] *fem dim of* Anselm
Shari \ˈsha(ə)r-ē, ˈshe(ə)r-\ *dim of* SHARON
Shar•lene \shär-ˈlēn\ *var of* CHARLENE
Shar•on *or* **Shar•ron** \ˈshar-ən, ˈsher-\ [Heb]
Shei•la \ˈshē-lə\ [IrGael] *var of* CECILIA
She•lia \ˈshēl-yə\ *var of* SHEILA
Shel•ley \ˈshel-ē\ [fr. a surname]
Sher•rill *or* **Sher•yl** \ˈsher-əl\ [prob. fr. a surname]
Sher•ry *or* **Sher•rie** *or* **Sheri** \ˈsher-ē\
Shir•ley \ˈshər-lē\ [fr. a surname]
Sig•rid \ˈsig-rəd\ [Scand] beautiful as victory
Son•dra \ˈsän-drə\ *var of* SANDRA
So•nia *or* **So•nya** *or* **So•nja** \ˈsō-nyə, ˈsȯ-\ [Russ] *dim of* SOPHIA
So•phia \sə-ˈfē-ə, -ˈfī-\ *or* **So•phie** \ˈsō-fē\ [Gk] wisdom
Sta•cy *or* **Sta•cey** \ˈstā-sē\ *dim of* ANASTASIA
Stel•la \ˈstel-ə\ [L] star
Steph•a•nie \ˈstef-ə-nē\ *fem of* STEPHEN
Sue \ˈsü\ *or* **Su•sie** \ˈsü-zē\ *dim of* SUSAN
Su•el•len \sü-ˈel-ən\ [*Sue* + *Ellen*]
Su•san *or* **Su•zan** \ˈsüz-ᵊn\ *dim of* SUSANNA
Su•san•na *or* **Su•san•nah** \sü-ˈzan-ə\ [Heb] lily
Su•zanne *or* **Su•sanne** *or* **Su•zann** \sü-ˈzan\ [F] *var of* SUSAN
Syb•il \ˈsib-əl\ [Gk] sibyl
Syl•via \ˈsil-vē-ə\ [L] she of the forest

Ta•mara \tə-ˈmar-ə\ [prob. fr. Georgian (language of the Republic of Georgia)]
Tan•ya \ˈtan-yə\ [Russ] *dim of* TATIANA
Ta•ra \ˈtăr-ə\ [IrGael]
Tat•i•ana \ˌtät-ē-ˈän-ə\ [Russ]
Te•re•sa \tə-ˈrē-sə\ *var of* THERESA
Ter•ry *or* **Ter•ri** \ˈter-ē\ *dim of* THERESA
Thel•ma \ˈthel-mə\
The•o•do•ra \ˌthē-ə-ˈdōr-ə, -ˈdȯr-\ [LGk] *fem of* THEODORE
The•re•sa *or* **Te•re•sa** \tə-ˈrē-sə\ [LL]
The•rese \tə-ˈrēs\ *var of* THERESA
Tif•fa•ny \ˈtif-ə-nē\ [Gk]
Ti•na \ˈtē-nə\ *dim of* CHRISTINA
To•by \ˈtō-bē\
To•ni \ˈtō-nē\ *dim of* Antonia
Tra•cy \ˈtrā-sē\ [fr. a surname]
Tru•dy \ˈtrüd-ē\ *dim of* GERTRUDE

Ur•su•la \ˈər-sə-lə\ [LL] little she-bear

Val•er•ie \ˈval-ə-rē\ [L] *prob* strong
Van•es•sa \və-ˈnes-ə\
Vel•ma \ˈvel-mə\
Ve•ra \ˈvir-ə\ [Russ] faith
Ver•na \ˈvər-nə\ *prob fem of* VERNON
Ve•ron•i•ca \və-ˈrän-i-kə\ [LL]
Vicki *or* **Vicky** *or* **Vick•ie** \ˈvik-ē\ *dim of* VICTORIA
Vic•to•ria \vik-ˈtōr-ē-ə, -ˈtȯr-\ [L] victory
Vi•da \ˈvēd-ə, ˈvīd-\ *fem dim of* DAVID
Vi•o•la \vī-ˈō-lə, vē-ˈō-, ˈvī-ə-, ˈvē-ə-\ [L] violet
Vi•o•let \ˈvī-ə-lət\ [OF, fr. L] violet
Vir•gin•ia \vər-ˈjin-yə, -ˈjin-ē-ə\ [L]
Viv•i•an \ˈviv-ē-ən\ [LL]

Wan•da \ˈwän-də\ [Pol]
Wen•dy \ˈwen-dē\
Whit•ney \ˈhwit-nē, ˈwit-\ [OE]
Wil•da \ˈwil-də\ *var of* WILLA
Wil•la \ˈwil-ə\ *or* **Wil•lie** \ˈwil-ē\ *prob fem dim of* WILLIAM
Wil•ma \ˈwil-mə\ *prob fem dim of* WILLIAM
Win•i•fred \ˈwin-ə-frəd\ [W]

Yvette \i-ˈvet\ [F]
Yvonne \i-ˈvän\ [F]

Zel•da \ˈzel-də\ *dim of* Griselda

DICTIONARY

Foreign Words and Phrases

ab·eunt stu·dia in mo·res \ˈä-be-ˌůnt-ˈstü-dē-ˌä-ˌin-ˈmō-ˌrās\ [L] : practices zealously pursued pass into habits

à bien·tôt \à-bya^{n}-tō\ [F] : so long

ab in·cu·na·bu·lis \ˌäb-ˌiŋ-ků-ˈnä-bů-ˌlēs\ [L] : from the cradle : from infancy

à bon chat, bon rat \à-bō^{n}-ˈshà-bō^{n}-ˈrà\ [F] : to a good cat, a good rat : retaliation in kind

à bouche ou·verte \à-bü-shü-vert\ [F] : with open mouth : eagerly : uncritically

ab ovo us·que ad ma·la \äb-ˈō-vō-ˌůs-kwe-ˌäd-ˈmä-lä\ [L] : from egg to apples : from soup to nuts : from beginning to end

à bras ou·verts \à-brà-zü-ver\ [F] : with open arms : cordially

ab·sit in·vi·dia \ˈäb-ˌsit-in-ˈwi-dē-ˌä\ [L] : let there be no envy or ill will

ab uno dis·ce om·nes \äb-ˈü-nō-ˌdis-ke-ˈȯm-ˌnās\ [L] : from one learn to know all

ab ur·be con·di·ta \äb-ˈůr-be-ˈkȯn-di-ˌtä\ [L] : from the founding of the city (Rome, founded 753 B.C.) — used by the Romans in reckoning dates

ab·usus non tol·lit usum \ˈä-ˌbü-sůs-ˌnōn-ˌtȯ-lit-ˈü-sům\ [L] : abuse does not take away use, i.e., is not an argument against proper use

à compte \à-kō^{n}t\ [F] : on account

à coup sûr \à-kü-sueͣr\ [F] : with sure stroke : surely

acte gra·tuit \àk-tə-grà-tw^{y}ē\ [F] : gratuitous impulsive act

ad ar·bi·tri·um \ˌad-är-ˈbi-trē-ům\ [L] : at will : arbitrarily

ad as·tra per as·pe·ra \ad-ˈas-trə-ˌpər-ˈas-pə-rə\ [L] : to the stars by hard ways — motto of Kansas

ad ex·tre·mum \ˌad-ik-ˈstrē-məm\ [L] : to the extreme : at last

ad ka·len·das Grae·cas \ˌäd-kä-ˈlen-däs-ˈgrī-ˌkäs\ [L] : at the Greek calends : never (since the Greeks had no calends)

ad ma·jo·rem Dei glo·ri·am \ˌäd-mä-ˈyōr-ˌem-ˈde-ˌē-ˈglōr-ē-ˌäm\ [L] : to the greater glory of God — motto of the Society of Jesus

ad pa·tres \äd-ˈpä-ˌtrās\ [L] : (gathered) to his fathers : deceased

ad re·fe·ren·dum \ˌäd-ˌre-fe-ˈren-dům\ [L] : for reference : for further consideration by one having the authority to make a final decision

à droite \à-drwät\ [F] : to or on the right hand

ad un·guem \äd-ˈůŋ-ˌgwem\ [L] : to the fingernail : to a nicety : exactly (from the use of the fingernail to test the smoothness of marble)

ad utrum·que pa·ra·tus \ˌäd-ů-ˈtrům-kwe-pä-ˈrä-tůs\ [L] : prepared for either (event)

ad vi·vum \äd-ˈwē-ˌwům\ [L] : to the life

ae·gri som·nia \ˈī-grē-ˈsȯm-nē-ˌä\ [L] : a sick man's dreams

ae·quam ser·va·re men·tem \ˈī-ˌkwäm-ser-ˈwä-rā-ˈmen-ˌtem\ [L] : to preserve a calm mind

ae·quo ani·mo \ˈī-ˌkwō-ˈä-ni-ˌmō\ [L] : with even mind : calmly

ae·re per·en·ni·us \ī-rā-pe-ˈre-nē-ˌůs\ [L] : more lasting than bronze

à gauche \à-gōsh\ [F] : to or on the left hand

age quod agis \ˈä-ge-ˌkwȯd-ˈä-gis\ [L] : do what you are doing : to the business at hand

à grands frais \à-grä^{n}-fre\ [F] : at great expense

à huis clos \à-w^{y}ē-klō\ [F] : with closed doors

aide–toi, le ciel t'ai·dera \ed-twà-lə-ˈsyel-te-drà\ [F] : help yourself (and) heaven will help you

aî·né \e-nā\ [F] : elder : senior (masc.)

aî·née \e-nā\ [F] : elder : senior (fem.)

à l'aban·don \à-là-bä^{n}-dō^{n}\ [F] : carelessly : in disorder

à la belle étoile \à-là-bel-ā-twál\ [F] : under the beautiful star : in the open air at night

à la bonne heure \à-là-bȯ-nœr\ [F] : at a good time : well and good : all right

à la fran·çaise \à-là-frä^{n}-sez\ [F] : in the French manner

à l'amé·ri·caine \à-là-mā-rē-ken\ [F] : in the American manner : of the American kind

à l'an·glaise \à-lä^{n}-glez\ [F] : in the English manner

à la page \à-là-päzh\ [F] : at the page : up-to-the-minute

à la russe \à-là-rueͣs\ [F] : in the Russian manner

alea jac·ta est \ˈä-lē-ˌä-ˌyäk-tä-ˈest\ [L] : the die is cast

à l'im·pro·viste \à-la^{n}-prȯ-vēst\ [F] : unexpectedly

ali·quan·do bo·nus dor·mi·tat Ho·me·rus \ˌä-li-ˈkwän-dō-ˈbȯ-nůs-dȯr-ˈmē-tät-hō-ˈmer-ůs\ [L] : sometimes (even) good Homer nods

alis vo·lat pro·pri·is \ˈä-ˌlēs-ˈwȯ-ˌlät-ˈprō-prē-ˌēs\ [L] : she flies with her own wings — motto of Oregon

al–ki \ˈal-ˌkī\ [Chinook Jargon] : by and by — motto of Washington

alo·ha oe \ä-ˌlō-hä-ˈȯi, -ˈō-ē\ [Hawaiian] : love to you : greetings : farewell

al·ter idem \ˌȯl-tər-ˈī-ˌdem, ˌäl-ter-ˈē-\ [L] : second self

a max·i·mis ad mi·ni·ma \ä-ˈmäk-si-ˌmēs-ˌäd-ˈmi-ni-ˌmä\ [L] : from the greatest to the least

ami·cus hu·ma·ni ge·ne·ris \ä-ˈmē-kůs-hü-ˈmä-nē-ˈge-ne-ris\ [L] : friend of the human race

ami·cus us·que ad aras \-ˌůs-kwe-ˌäd-ˈär-ˌäs\ [L] : a friend as far as to the altars, i.e., except in what is contrary to one's religion; *also* : a friend to the last extremity

ami de cour \à-mē-də-kůr\ [F] : court friend : insincere friend

amor pa·tri·ae \ˈä-ˌmȯr-ˈpä-trē-ˌī\ [L] : love of one's country

amor vin·cit om·nia \ˈä-ˌmȯr-ˈwiŋ-kit-ˈȯm-nē-ä\ [L] : love conquers all things

an·cienne no·blesse \ä^{n}-syen-nȯ-bles\ [F] : old-time nobility : the French nobility before the Revolution of 1789

an·guis in her·ba \ˈäŋ-gwis-in-ˈher-ˌbä\ [L] : snake in the grass

ani·mal bi·pes im·plu·me \ˈä-ni-ˌmäl-ˈbi-ˌpās-im-ˈplü-me\ [L] : two-legged animal without feathers (i.e., the human race)

ani·mis opi·bus·que pa·ra·ti \ˈä-ni-ˌmēs-ˌȯ-pi-ˈbůs-kwe-pä-ˈrä-tē\ [L] : prepared in mind and resources — one of the mottoes of South Carolina

an·no ae·ta·tis su·ae \ˈä-nō-ī-ˈtä-tis-ˈsü-ˌī\ [L] : in the (specified) year of his or her age

an·no mun·di \ˈä-nō-ˈmůn-dē\ [L] : in the year of the world — used in reckoning dates from the supposed period of the creation of the world, esp. as fixed by James Ussher at 4004 B.C. or by the Jews at 3761 B.C.

an·no ur·bis con·di·tae \ˈä-nō-ˈůr-bis-ˈkȯn-di-ˌtī\ [L] : in the year of the founded city (Rome, founded 753 B.C.)

an·nu·it coep·tis \ˈä-nů-ˌwit-ˈkȯip-ˌtēs\ [L] : He (God)

has approved our beginnings — motto on the reverse of the Great Seal of the United States
à peu près \à-pœ-pre\ [F] : nearly : approximately
à pied \à-pyā\ [F] : on foot
après moi le dé•luge \à-pre-mwä-lə-dā-lüezh\ *or* **après nous le déluge** \à-pre-nü-\ [F] : after me the deluge — attributed to Louis XV
à pro•pos de bottes \à-prə-pō-də-bȯt\ [F] : apropos of boots — used to change the subject
à pro•pos de rien \-ryaⁿ\ [F] : apropos of nothing
aqua et ig•ni in•ter•dic•tus \ˈäk-wä-et-ˈig-nē-ˌin-ter-ˈdik-tu̇s\ [L] : forbidden to be furnished with water and fire : outlawed
Ar•ca•des am•bo \ˈär-kä-ˌdes-ˈäm-bō\ [L] : both Arcadians : two persons of like occupations or tastes; *also* : two rascals
ar•rec•tis au•ri•bus \ä-ˈrek-ˌtēs-ˈau̇-ri-ˌbu̇s\ [L] : with ears pricked up : attentively
ar•ri•ve•der•ci \ä-ˌrē-ve-ˈder-chē\ [It] : till we meet again : farewell
ars est ce•la•re ar•tem \ˈärs-ˌest-kä-ˈlär-ā-ˈär-ˌtem\ [L] : it is (true) art to conceal art
ars lon•ga, vi•ta bre•vis \ˈärs-ˈlȯŋ-ˌgä-ˈwē-ˌtä-ˈbre-wis\ [L] : art is long, life is short
a ter•go \ä-ˈter-(ˌ)gō\ [L] : from behind
à tort et à tra•vers \à-tȯr-ā-à-trà-ver\ [F] : wrong and crosswise : at random : without rhyme or reason
au bout de son la•tin \ō-bü-də-sōⁿ-là-taⁿ\ [F] : at the end of one's Latin : at the end of one's mental resources
au con•traire \ō-kōⁿ-trer\ [F] : on the contrary
au•de•mus ju•ra nos•tra de•fen•de•re \au̇-ˈdā-mu̇s-ˈyu̇r-ä-ˈnȯ-strä-dā-ˈfen-de-rā\ [L] : we dare defend our rights — motto of Alabama
au•den•tes for•tu•na ju•vat \au̇-ˈden-ˌtās-fȯr-ˈtü-nä-ˈyü-ˌwät\ [L] : fortune favors the bold
au•di al•ter•am par•tem \ˈau̇-ˌdē-ˈäl-te-ˌräm-ˈpär-ˌtem\ [L] : hear the other side
au fait \ō-fet, -fe\ [F] : to the point : fully competent : fully informed : socially correct
au fond \ō-fōⁿ\ [F] : at bottom : fundamentally
au grand sé•rieux \ō-gräⁿ-sā-ryœ\ [F] : in all seriousness
au pays des aveugles les borgnes sont rois \ō-pā-ē-dā-zà-vœglᵊ-lā-bȯrnʸ-ə-sōⁿ-rwä\ [F] : in the country of the blind the one-eyed men are kings
au•rea me•di•o•cri•tas \ˈau̇-rē-ä-ˌme-dē-ˈȯ-kri-ˌtäs\ [L] : the golden mean
au reste \ō-rest\ [F] : for the rest : besides
aus•si•tôt dit, aus•si•tôt fait \ō-sē-tō-dē-ō-sē-tō-fe\ [F] : no sooner said than done
aut Cae•sar aut ni•hil \ˌau̇t-ˈkī-sär-ˌau̇t-ˈni-ˌhil\ [L] : either a Caesar or nothing
aut Caesar aut nul•lus \-ˈnu̇-lu̇s\ [L] : either a Caesar or a nobody
au•tres temps, au•tres mœurs \ō-trə-täⁿ-ō-trə-mœrs\ [F] : other times, other customs
aut vin•ce•re aut mo•ri \ˌau̇t-ˈwiŋ-ke-rā-ˌau̇t-ˈmȯ-ˌrē\ [L] : either to conquer or to die
aux armes \ō-zärm\ [F] : to arms
avant la lettre \à-väⁿ-lä-letrᵊ\ [F] : before the letter : before a (specified) name existed
ave at•que va•le \ˈä-ˌwā-ˌät-kwe-ˈwä-ˌlā\ [L] : hail and farewell
à vo•tre san•té \à-vȯt-säⁿ-tā, -vȯ-trə-\ [F] : to your health — used as a toast
beaux yeux \bō-zyœ\ [F] : beautiful eyes : beauty of face
bel•la fi•gu•ra \ˈbel-lä-fē-ˈgü-rä\ [It] : fine appearance or impression
belle laide \bel-led\ [F] : beautiful ugly woman : a woman who is attractive though not conventionally beautiful
bien en•ten•du \byaⁿ-näⁿ-täⁿ-dūe\ [F] : well understood : of course
bien–pen•sant \byaⁿ-päⁿ-säⁿ\ [F] : right-minded : one who holds orthodox views
bien•sé•ance \byaⁿ-sā-äⁿs\ [F] : propriety
bis dat qui ci•to dat \ˈbis-ˌdät-kwē-ˈki-tō-ˌdät\ [L] : he or she gives twice who gives promptly
bon ap•pé•tit \bȯ-nà-pā-tē\ [F] : good appetite : enjoy your meal
bon gré, mal gré \ˈbōⁿ-ˌgrā-ˈmàl-ˌgrā\ [F] : whether with good grace or bad : willy-nilly
bo•nis avi•bus \ˈbȯ-ˌnēs-ˈä-wi-ˌbu̇s\ [L] : under good auspices
bon•jour \bōⁿ-zhür\ [F] : good day : good morning
bonne foi \bȯn-fwä\ [F] : good faith
bon•soir \bōⁿ-swär\ [F] : good evening
bru•tum ful•men \ˈbrü-tu̇m-ˈfu̇l-men\ [L] : insensible thunderbolt : a futile threat or display of force
buon gior•no \bwȯn-ˈjȯr-nō\ [It] : good day
ca•dit quae•stio \ˈkä-dit-ˈkwī-stē-ˌō\ [L] : the question drops : the argument collapses
cau•sa si•ne qua non \ˈkau̇-ˌsä-ˌsi-nā-kwä-ˈnōn\ [L] : an indispensable cause or condition
ça va sans dire \sà-và-säⁿ-dēr\ [F] : it goes without saying
ca•ve ca•nem \ˈkä-wā-ˈkä-ˌnem\ [L] : beware the dog
ce•dant ar•ma to•gae \ˈkā-ˌdänt-ˈär-mə-ˈtō-ˌgī\ [L] : let arms yield to the toga : let military power give way to civil power — motto of Wyoming
ce n'est que le pre•mier pas qui coûte \snek-lə-prə-myā-pä-kē-küt\ [F] : it is only the first step that costs
c'est–à–dire \se-tà-dēr\ [F] : that is to say : namely
c'est au•tre chose \se-tōt-shōz, -tō-trə-\ [F] : that's a different thing
c'est la guerre \se-là-ger\ [F] : that's war : it cannot be helped
c'est la vie \se-là-vē\ [F] : that's life : that's how things happen
c'est plus qu'un crime, c'est une faute \se-plūe-kœⁿ-krēm-se-tūen-fōt\ [F] : it is worse than a crime, it is a blunder
ce•te•ra de•sunt \ˈkā-te-ˌrä-ˈdā-ˌsu̇nt\ [L] : the rest is missing
cha•cun à son goût \shà-kœⁿ-nà-sōⁿ-gü\ [F] : everyone to his or her taste
châ•teau en Es•pagne \shä-tō-äⁿ-nes-pànʸ\ [F] : castle in Spain : a visionary project
cher•chez la femme \sher-shā-là-fàm\ [F] : look for the woman
che sa•rà, sa•rà \ˌkā-sä-ˌrä-sä-ˈrä\ [It] : what will be, will be
che•val de ba•taille \shə-vàl-də-bà-täʸ\ [F] : war-horse : argument constantly relied on : favorite subject
co•gi•to, er•go sum \ˈkō-gi-ˌtō-ˌer-gō-ˈsu̇m\ [L] : I think, therefore I exist
co•mé•die hu•maine \kȯ-mā-dē-ūe-men\ [F] : human comedy : the whole variety of human life
comme ci, comme ça \kȯm-sē-kȯm-sà\ [F] : so-so
com•pa•gnon de voy•age \kōⁿ-pà-nʸōⁿ-də-vwà-yàzh\ [F] : traveling companion
compte ren•du \kōⁿt-räⁿ-dūe\ [F] : report (as of proceedings in an investigation)
con•cor•dia dis•cors \kȯn-ˈkȯr-dē-ä-ˈdis-ˌkōrs\ [L] : discordant harmony
cor•rup•tio op•ti•mi pes•si•ma \kȯ-ˈru̇p-tē-ˌō-ˈäp-ti-ˌmē-ˈpe-si-ˌmä\ [L] : the corruption of the best is the worst of all
coup de maî•tre \küd-metrᵊ, kü-də-\ [F] : masterstroke
coup d'es•sai \kü-dā-se\ [F] : experiment : trial
coûte que coûte \küt-kə-küt\ [F] : cost what it may
cre•do quia ab•sur•dum est \ˈkrā-dō-ˈkwē-ä-äp-ˈsu̇r-du̇m-ˈest\ [L] : I believe it because it is absurd
cres•cit eun•do \ˈkres-kit-ˈeu̇n-dō\ [L] : it grows as it goes — motto of New Mexico
crise de nerfs *or* **crise des nerfs** \krēz-də-ner\ [F] : crisis of nerves : nervous collapse : hysterical fit
crux cri•ti•co•rum \ˈkru̇ks-ˌkri-ti-ˈkōr-u̇m\ [L] : crux of critics

cuj·us re·gio, ej·us re·li·gio \ˈkü-yu̇s-ˈre-gē-ˌō-ˈe-yu̇s-re-ˈli-gē-ˌō\ [L] : whose region, his or her religion : subjects are to accept the religion of their ruler
cum gra·no sa·lis \ku̇m-ˈgrä-nō-ˈsä-lis\ [L] : with a grain of salt
cur·sus ho·no·rum \ˈku̇r-su̇s-hȯ-ˈnō-ru̇m\ [L] : course of honors : succession of offices of increasing importance
cus·tos mo·rum \ˈku̇s-tōs-ˈmōr-u̇m\ [L] : guardian of manners or morals : censor
d'ac·cord \dȧ-kȯr\ [F] : in accord : agreed
dame d'hon·neur \dȧm-dȯ-nœr\ [F] : lady-in-waiting
dam·nant quod non in·tel·li·gunt \ˈdäm-ˌnänt-ˌkwȯd-ˈnōn-in-ˈte-li-ˌgu̇nt\ [L] : they condemn what they do not understand
de bonne grâce \də-bȯn-gräs\ [F] : with good grace : willingly
de gus·ti·bus non est dis·pu·tan·dum \dā-ˈgu̇s-ti-ˌbu̇s-ˈnōn-ˌest-ˌdis-pu̇-ˈtän-ˌdu̇m\ [L] : there is no disputing about tastes
Dei gra·tia \ˈde-ˌē-ˈgrä-tē-ˌä\ [L] : by the grace of God
de in·te·gro \dā-ˈin-te-ˌgrō\ [L] : anew : afresh
de l'au·dace, en·core de l'au·dace, et tou·jours de l'au·dace \də-lō-dȧs-äⁿ-kȯr-də-lō-dȧs-ā-tü-zhür-də-lō-dȧs\ [F] : audacity, more audacity, and ever more audacity
de·len·da est Car·tha·go \dā-ˈlen-dä-ˌest-kär-ˈtä-gō\ [L] : Carthage must be destroyed
de·li·ne·a·vit \dā-ˌlē-nā-ˈä-wit\ [L] : he or she drew it
de mal en pis \də-mȧ-läⁿ-pē\ [F] : from bad to worse
de mi·ni·mis non cu·rat lex \dā-ˈmi-ni-ˌmēs-ˌnōn-ˈkü-ˌrät-ˈleks\ [L] : the law takes no account of trifles
de mor·tu·is nil ni·si bo·num \dā-ˈmȯr-tu̇-ˌwēs-ˌnēl-ˌni-sē-ˈbȯ-ˌnu̇m\ [L] : of the dead (say) nothing but good
de nos jours \də-nō-zhür\ [F] : of our time : contemporary — used postpositively esp. after a proper name
Deo fa·ven·te \ˌdā-ō-fä-ˈven-tā\ [L] : with God's favor
Deo gra·ti·as \ˌdā-ō-ˈgrä-tē-ˌäs\ [L] : thanks (be) to God
de pro·fun·dis \ˌdā-prō-ˈfu̇n-dēs\ [L] : out of the depths
der Geist der stets ver·neint \dər-ˈgīst-dər-ˌshtāts-fer-ˈnīnt\ [G] : the spirit that ever denies — applied originally to Mephistopheles
de·si·pe·re in lo·co \dā-ˈsi-pe-rā-in-ˈlȯ-kō\ [L] : to indulge in trifling at the proper time
Deus vult \ˈdā-u̇s-ˈwu̇lt\ [L] : God wills it — rallying cry of the First Crusade
di·es fau·stus \ˈdē-ˌās-ˈfau̇-stu̇s\ [L] : lucky day
dies in·fau·stus \-ˈin-ˌfau̇-stu̇s\ [L] : unlucky day
dies irae \-ˈē-ˌrī\ [L] : day of wrath — used of the Judgment Day
Dieu et mon droit \dyœ̄-ā-mȯⁿ-drwä\ [F] : God and my right — motto on the British royal arms
Dieu vous garde \dyœ̄-vü-gȧrd\ [F] : God keep you
di·ri·go \ˈdē-ri-ˌgō\ [L] : I direct — motto of Maine
dis ali·ter vi·sum \ˈdēs-ˈä-li-ˌter-ˈwē-ˌsu̇m\ [L] : the Gods decreed otherwise
di·tat De·us \ˈdē-ˌtät-ˈdā-ˌu̇s\ [L] : God enriches — motto of Arizona
di·vi·de et im·pe·ra \ˈdē-wi-ˌde-ˌet-ˈim-pe-ˌrä\ [L] : divide and rule
do·cen·do dis·ci·mus \dȯ-ˌken-dō-ˈdis-ki-ˌmu̇s\ [L] : we learn by teaching
Do·mi·ne di·ri·ge nos \ˈdȯ-mi-ˌne-ˈdē-ri-ge-ˈnōs\ [L] : Lord, direct us — motto of the City of London
Do·mi·nus vo·bis·cum \ˈdȯ-mi-ˌnu̇s-wō-ˈbēs-ˌku̇m\ [L] : the Lord be with you
dul·ce et de·co·rum est pro pa·tria mo·ri \ˈdu̇l-ˌkā-et-de-ˈkōr-u̇m-ˌest-prō-ˈpä-trē-ˌä-ˈmȯ-ˌrē\ [L] : it is sweet and seemly to die for one's country
dum spi·ro, spe·ro \du̇m-ˈspē-rō-ˈspā-rō\ [L] : while I breathe I hope — one of the mottoes of South Carolina
dum vi·vi·mus vi·va·mus \du̇m-ˈwē-wē-ˌmu̇s-wē-ˈwä-mu̇s\ [L] : while we live, let us live
d'un certain âge \dœⁿ-ser-te-näzh\ [F] : of a certain age : no longer young
dux fe·mi·na fac·ti \ˈdu̇ks-ˈfā-mi-nä-ˈfäk-ˌtē\ [L] : a woman was leader of the exploit
ec·ce sig·num \ˈe-ke-ˈsig-ˌnu̇m\ [L] : behold the sign : look at the proof
e con·tra·rio \ˌā-kȯn-ˈträr-ē-ˌō\ [L] : on the contrary
écra·sez l'in·fâme \ā-krä-zā-laⁿ-fäm\ [F] : crush the infamous thing
eheu fu·ga·ces la·bun·tur an·ni \ˈā-ˌheu̇-fü-ˈgä-ˌkās-lä-ˌbu̇n-ˌtu̇r-ˈän-ˌē\ [L] : alas! the fleeting years glide on
ein' fes·te Burg ist un·ser Gott \īn-ˌfes-tə-ˈbu̇rk-ist-ˌu̇n-zər-ˈgȯt\ [G] : a mighty fortress is our God
em·bar·ras de ri·chesses *or* **embarras de ri·chesse** \äⁿ-bȧ-rä-də-rē-shes\ [F] : embarrassing surplus of riches : confusing abundance
em·bar·ras de choix \äⁿ-bȧ-rä-də-shwȧ\ *or* **embarras du choix** \-dǖ-shwä\ [F] : embarrassing variety of choice
en ami \äⁿ-nȧ-mē\ [F] : as a friend
en ef·fet \äⁿ-nā-fe\ [F] : in fact : indeed
en fa·mille \äⁿ-fä-mēy\ [F] : in or with one's family : at home : informally
en·fant ché·ri \äⁿ-fäⁿ-shā-rē\ [F] : loved or pampered child : one that is highly favored
en·fant gâ·té \äⁿ-fäⁿ-gä-tā\ [F] : spoiled child
en·fants per·dus \äⁿ-fäⁿ-per-dǖ\ [F] : lost children : soldiers sent to a dangerous post
en·fin \äⁿ-faⁿ\ [F] : in conclusion : in a word
en gar·çon \äⁿ-gȧr-sōⁿ\ [F] : as or like a bachelor
en garde \äⁿ-gȧrd\ [F] : on guard
en pan·tou·fles \äⁿ-päⁿ-tüflᵊ\ [F] : in slippers : at ease : informally
en plein air \äⁿ-ple-ner\ [F] : in the open air
en plein jour \äⁿ-plaⁿ-zhür\ [F] : in broad day
en règle \äⁿ-reglᵊ\ [F] : in order : in due form
en re·tard \äⁿ-rə-tȧr\ [F] : behind time : late
en re·traite \äⁿ-rə-tret\ [F] : in retreat : in retirement
en re·vanche \äⁿ-rə-väⁿsh\ [F] : in return : in compensation
en se·condes noces \äⁿ-sə-gōⁿd-nȯs\ [F] : in a second marriage
en·se pe·tit pla·ci·dam sub li·ber·ta·te qui·e·tem \ˈen-se-ˈpe-tit-ˈplä-ki-ˌdäm-su̇b-ˈlē-ber-ˌtä-te-kwē-ˈā-ˌtem\ [L] : with the sword she seeks calm repose under liberty : by the sword we seek peace, but peace only under liberty — motto of Massachusetts
eo ip·so \ˌā-ō-ˈip-(ˌ)sō\ [L] : by that itself : by that fact alone
épa·ter le bour·geois \ā-pȧ-tā-lə-bür-zhwȧ\ [F] : to shock the middle classes
e plu·ri·bus unum \ˌē-ˈplu̇r-ə-bəs-ˈyü-nəm, ˌā-ˈplu̇r-i-bu̇s-ˈü-nu̇m\ [L] : one out of many — used on the Great Seal of the U.S. and on several U.S. coins
ep·pur si muo·ve \āp-ˈpür-sē-ˈmwȯ-vā\ [It] : and yet it does move — attributed to Galileo after recanting his assertion of the earth's motion
Erin go bragh \ˈer-ən-gə-ˈbrȯ, -gō-ˈbrä\ [Ir *go brách* or *go bráth*, lit., till doomsday] : Ireland forever
er·ra·re hu·ma·num est \e-ˈrär-e-hü-ˈmä-nu̇m-ˈest\ [L] : to err is human
es·prit de l'es·ca·lier \es-prēd-les-kȧ-lyā\ *or* **es·prit d'es·ca·lier** \-prē-des-\ [F] : staircase wit : repartee thought of only too late
es·se quam vi·de·ri \ˈe-sā-ˌkwäm-wi-ˈdā-rē\ [L] : to be rather than to seem — motto of North Carolina
est mo·dus in re·bus \est-ˈmȯ-ˌdu̇s-in-ˈrā-ˌbu̇s\ [L] : there is a proper measure in things, i.e., the golden mean should always be observed
es·to per·pe·tua \ˈes-ˌtō-per-ˈpe-tu̇-ˌwä\ [L] : may she endure forever — motto of Idaho
et hoc ge·nus om·ne \et-ˈhōk-ˈge-nu̇s-ˈȯm-ne\ *or* **et id genus omne** \et-ˌid-\ [L] : and everything of this kind

et in Ar•ca•dia ego \ˌet-in-är-ˈkä-dē-ä-ˈe-gō\ [L] : I too (lived) in Arcadia
et sic de si•mi•li•bus \et-ˈsēk-dā-si-ˈmi-li-ˌbu̇s\ [L] : and so of like things
et tu Bru•te \et-ˈtü-ˈbrü-te\ [L] : thou too, Brutus — exclamation attributed to Julius Caesar on seeing his friend Brutus among his assassins
eu•re•ka \yu̇-ˈrē-kə\ [Gk] : I have found it — motto of California
Ewig–Weib•li•che \ˌā-vik-ˈvīp-li-kə\ [G] : eternal feminine
ex•al•té \eg-zäl-tā\ [F] : emotionally excited or elated : fanatic
ex ani•mo \eks-ˈä-ni-ˌmō\ [L] : from the heart : sincerely
ex•cel•si•or \ik-ˈsel-sē-ər, eks-ˈkel-sē-ˌȯr\ [L] : still higher — motto of New York
ex•cep•tio pro•bat re•gu•lam de re•bus non ex•cep•tis \eks-ˈkep-tē-ˌō-ˈprō-bät-ˈrā-gü-ˌläm-dā-ˈrā-ˌbu̇s-ˈnōn-eks-ˈkep-ˌtēs\ [L] : an exception establishes the rule as to things not excepted
ex•cep•tis ex•ci•pi•en•dis \eks-ˈkep-ˌtēs-eks-ˌki-pē-ˈen-ˌdēs\ [L] : with the proper or necessary exceptions
ex•i•tus ac•ta pro•bat \ˈek-si-ˌtu̇s-ˈäk-tä-ˈprō-ˌbät\ [L] : the outcome justifies the deed
ex li•bris \eks-ˈlē-bris\ [L] : from the books of — used on bookplates
ex me•ro mo•tu \ˌeks-ˈmer-ō-ˈmō-tü\ [L] : out of mere impulse : of one's own accord
ex ne•ces•si•ta•te rei \ˌeks-ne-ˌke-si-ˈtä-te-ˈrā-ˌē\ [L] : from the necessity of the case
ex ni•hi•lo ni•hil fit \eks-ˈni-hi-ˌlō-ˈni-ˌhil-ˈfit\ [L] : from nothing nothing is produced
ex pe•de Her•cu•lem \eks-ˈpe-de-ˈher-ku̇-ˌlem\ [L] : from the foot (we may judge of the size of) Hercules : from a part we may judge of the whole
ex•per•to cre•de \eks-ˈper-tō-ˈkrā-de\ *or* **experto cre•di•te** \-ˈkrā-di-ˌte\ [L] : believe one who has had experience
ex un•gue le•o•nem \eks-ˈu̇ŋ-gwe-le-ˈō-ˌnem\ [L] : from the claw (we may judge of) the lion : from a part we may judge of the whole
ex vi ter•mi•ni \eks-ˈwē-ˈter-mi-ˌnē\ [L] : from the force of the term
fa•ci•le prin•ceps \ˈfä-ki-le-ˈpriŋ-ˌkeps\ [L] : easily first
fa•ci•lis de•scen•sus Aver•no \ˈfä-ki-ˌlis-dā-ˈskān-ˌsu̇s-ä-ˈwer-nō\ *or* **facilis descensus Aver•ni** \-(ˌ)nē\ [L] : the descent to Avernus is easy : the road to evil is easy
fa•çon de par•ler \fà-sō^{n}-də-pȧr-lā\ [F] : manner of speaking : figurative or conventional expression
faire suivre \fer-sw^{y}ēvr^{ə}\ [F] : have forwarded : please forward
fas est et ab ho•ste do•ce•ri \ˌfäs-ˈest-et-äb-ˈhȯ-ste-dȯ-ˈkā-(ˌ)rē\ [L] : it is right to learn even from an enemy
Fa•ta vi•am in•ve•ni•ent \ˈfä-tä-ˈwē-ˌäm-in-ˈwe-nē-ˌent\ [L] : the Fates will find a way
fat•ti mas•chii, pa•ro•le fe•mi•ne \ˈfät-tē-ˈmäs-ˌkē-pä-ˈrȯ-lä-ˈfā-mē-ˌnā\ [It] : deeds are males, words are females : deeds are more effective than words — motto of Maryland, where it is generally interpreted as meaning "manly deeds, womanly words"
faux bon•homme \fō-bȯ-nȯm\ [F] : pretended good fellow
faux–naïf \fœ-nȧ-ēf\ [F] : spuriously or affectedly childlike : artfully simple
fe•lix cul•pa \ˈfā-liks-ˈku̇l-pä\ [L] : fortunate fault — used esp. of original sin in relation to the consequent coming of Christ
femme de cham•bre \fäm-də-shä^{n}br^{ə}\ [F] : chambermaid : lady's maid
fe•sti•na len•te \fe-ˈstē-nä-ˈlen-ˌtā\ [L] : make haste slowly
feux d'ar•ti•fice \fœ-dȧr-tē-fēs\ [F] : fireworks : display of wit
fi•at ex•pe•ri•men•tum in cor•po•re vi•li \ˈfē-ˌät-ek-ˌsper-ē-ˈmen-ˌtu̇m-in-ˈkȯr-pȯ-re-ˈwē-lē\ [L] : let experiment be made on a worthless body
fi•at ju•sti•tia, ru•at cae•lum \ˈfē-ät-yu̇s-ˈti-tē-ä-ˈrü-ˌät-ˈkī-ˌlu̇m\ [L] : let justice be done though the heavens fall
fi•at lux \ˈfē-ˌät-ˈlu̇ks\ [L] : let there be light
Fi•dei De•fen•sor \ˈfi-de-ˌē-dā-ˈfān-ˌsȯr\ [L] : Defender of the Faith — a title of the sovereigns of England
fi•dus Acha•tes \ˌfē-du̇s-ä-ˈkä-ˌtās\ [L] : faithful Achates : trusty friend
fille de cham•bre \fēy-də-shä^{n}br^{ə}\ [F] : lady's maid
fille d'hon•neur \fēy-dȯ-nœr\ [F] : maid of honor
fils \fēs\ [F] : son — used orig. after French and now also after other family names to distinguish a son from his father
fi•nem re•spi•ce \ˈfē-ˌnem-ˈrā-spi-ˌke\ [L] : consider the end
fi•nis co•ro•nat opus \ˌfē-nis-kȯ-ˈrō-ˌnät-ˈō-ˌpu̇s\ [L] : the end crowns the work
flo•re•at \ˈflō-rē-ˌät\ [L] : may (he, she, or it) flourish — usu. followed by a name
fluc•tu•at nec mer•gi•tur \ˈflu̇k-tü-ˌwät-ˌnek-ˈmer-gi-ˌtu̇r\ [L] : it is tossed by the waves but does not sink — motto of Paris
fo•lie de gran•deur *or* **fo•lie des gran•deurs** \fȯ-lē-də-grä^{n}-dœr\ [F] : delusion of greatness : megalomania
force de frappe \fȯrs-də-fràp\ [F] : military striking force esp. with nuclear weapons
fors•an et haec olim me•mi•nis•se ju•va•bit \ˈfȯr-ˌsän-ˌet-ˈhīk-ˈō-lim-ˌme-mi-ˈni-se-yu̇-ˈwä-bit\ [L] : perhaps this too will be a pleasure to look back on one day
for•tes for•tu•na ju•vat \ˈfȯr-ˌtās-fȯr-ˈtü-nä-ˈyu̇-ˌwät\ [L] : fortune favors the brave
fron•ti nul•la fi•des \ˈfrȯn-ˌtē-ˈnu̇-lä-ˈfi-ˌdās\ [L] : no reliance can be placed on appearance
fu•it Ili•um \ˈfu̇-it-ˈi-lē-u̇m\ [L] : Troy has been (i.e., is no more)
fu•ror lo•quen•di \ˈfu̇r-ˌȯr-lȯ-ˈkwen-(ˌ)dē\ [L] : rage for speaking
furor po•e•ti•cus \-pȯ-ˈā-ti-ku̇s\ [L] : poetic frenzy
furor scri•ben•di \-skrē-ˈben-(ˌ)dē\ [L] : rage for writing
Gal•li•ce \ˈgä-li-ˌke\ [L] : in French : after the French manner
gar•çon d'hon•neur \gȧr-sō^{n}-dȯ-nœr\ [F] : bridegroom's attendant
garde du corps \gȧrd-dᵫ-kȯr\ [F] : bodyguard
gar•dez la foi \gȧr-dā-lȧ-fwä\ [F] : keep faith
gau•de•a•mus igi•tur \ˌgau̇-dē-ˈä-mu̇s-ˈi-gi-ˌtu̇r\ [L] : let us then be merry
gens d'é•glise \zhä^{n}-dā-glēz\ [F] : church people : clergy
gens de guerre \zhä^{n}-də-ger\ [F] : military people : soldiery
gens du monde \zhä^{n}-dᵫ-mō^{n}d\ [F] : people of the world : fashionable people
gno•thi se•au•ton \ˈgnō-thē-ˌse-au̇-ˈtȯn\ [Gk] : know thyself
grand monde \grä^{n}-mō^{n}d\ [F] : great world : high society
gros•so mo•do \ˈgrȯs-(ˌ)sō-ˈmō-(ˌ)dō\ [It] : roughly
guerre à ou•trance \ger-ȧ-ü-trä^{n}s\ [F] : war to the uttermost
gu•ten Tag \ˈgüt-^{ə}n-ˈtäk\ [G] : good day
has•ta la vis•ta \ˈäs-tä-lä-ˈvēs-tä\ [Sp] : good-bye
haut goût \ō-gü\ [F] : high flavor : slight taint of decay
hic et nunc \ˈhēk-et-ˈnu̇ŋk\ [L] : here and now
hic et ubi•que \ˈhēk-et-u̇-ˈbē-kwe\ [L] : here and everywhere
hic ja•cet \hik-ˈjā-sət, hēk-ˈyä-ket\ [L] : here lies — used preceding a name on a tombstone
hinc il•lae la•cri•mae \ˈhiŋk-ˈi-ˌlī-ˈlä-kri-ˌmī\ [L] : hence those tears

hoc age \hō-ˈäg-e\ [L] : do this : apply yourself to what you are about

hoc opus, hic la·bor est \ˌhōk-ˈō-ˌpu̇s-ˌhēk-ˈlä-ˌbȯr-ˈest\ [L] : this is the hard work, this is the toil

homme d'af·faires \ȯm-dȧ-fer\ [F] : man of business : business agent

homme d'es·prit \-des-prē\ [F] : man of wit

homme moyen sen·suel \ȯm-mwȧ-ya^{n}-sä^{n}-sw^{y}el\ [F] : the average nonintellectual man

ho·mo sum: hu·ma·ni nil a me ali·e·num pu·to \ˈhȯ-mō-ˌsu̇m-hü-ˈmä-nē-ˈnēl-ä-ˌmā-ˌä-lē-ˈā-nu̇m-ˈpu̇-tō\ [L] : I am a human being : I regard nothing of human concern as foreign to my interests

ho·ni soit qui mal y pense \ȯ-nē-swȧ-kē-mȧl-ē-pä^{n}s\ [F] : shamed be he who thinks evil of it — motto of the Order of the Garter

hu·ma·num est er·ra·re \hü-ˈmä-nu̇m-ˌest-e-ˈrär-e\ [L] : to err is human

ich dien \ik-ˈdēn\ [G] : I serve — motto of the Prince of Wales

ici on parle fran·cais \ē-sē-ō^{n}-pȧrl-frä^{n}-se\ [F] : French is spoken here

idées re·çues \ē-dā-rə-sue̅\ [F] : received ideas : conventional opinions

id est \id-ˈest\ [L] : that is

ig·no·ran·tia ju·ris ne·mi·nem ex·cu·sat \ˌig-nə-ˈrän-tē-ä-ˈyu̇r-is-ˈnā-mi-ˌnem-eks-ˈkü-ˌsät\ [L] : ignorance of the law excuses no one

ig·no·tum per ig·no·ti·us \ig-ˈnō-tu̇m-ˌper-ig-ˈnō-tē-ˌu̇s\ [L] : (explaining) the unknown by means of the more unknown

il faut cul·ti·ver no·tre jar·din \ēl-fō-kue̅l-tē-vā-nȯt-zhȧr-da^{n}, -nȯ-trə-zhȧr-\ [F] : we must cultivate our garden : we must tend to our own affairs

in ae·ter·num \ˌin-ī-ˈter-ˌnu̇m\ [L] : forever

in du·bio \in-ˈdu̇b-ē-ˌō\ [L] : in doubt : undetermined

in fu·tu·ro \ˌin-fü-ˈtu̇r-ō\ [L] : in the future

in hoc sig·no vin·ces \ˌin-ˌhōk-ˈsig-nō-ˈwiŋ-ˌkās\ [L] : by this sign (the Cross) you will conquer

in li·mi·ne \in-ˈlē-mi-ˌne\ [L] : on the threshold : at the beginning

in om·nia pa·ra·tus \in-ˈȯm-nē-ä-pä-ˈrä-ˌtu̇s\ [L] : ready for all things

in par·ti·bus in·fi·de·li·um \in-ˈpär-ti-ˌbu̇s-ˌin-fə-ˈdā-lē-ˌu̇m\ [L] : in the regions of the infidels — used of a titular bishop having no diocesan jurisdiction, usu. in non-Christian countries

in prae·sen·ti \ˌin-prī-ˈsen-ˌtē\ [L] : at the present time

in sae·cu·la sae·cu·lo·rum \in-ˈsī-ku̇-ˌlä-ˌsī-ku̇-ˈlōr-u̇m, -ˈsā-ku̇-ˌlä-ˌsā-\ [L] : for ages of ages : forever and ever

insh·al·lah \ˌin-shä-ˈlä\ [Ar] : if Allah wills : God willing

in sta·tu quo an·te bel·lum \in-ˈstä-ˌtü-kwō-ˈän-te-ˈbe-lu̇m\ [L] : in the same state as before the war

in·te·ger vi·tae sce·le·ris·que pu·rus \ˈin-te-ˌger-ˈwē-ˌtī-ˌske-le-ˈris-kwe-ˈpü-ru̇s\ [L] : upright of life and free from wickedness

in·ter nos \ˌin-tər-ˈnōs\ [L] : between ourselves

in·tra mu·ros \ˌin-trä-ˈmü-ˌrōs\ [L] : within the walls

in usum Del·phi·ni \in-ˈü-su̇m-del-ˈfē-nē\ [L] : for the use of the Dauphin : expurgated

in utrum·que pa·ra·tus \ˌin-ü-ˈtru̇m-kwe-pä-ˈrä-ˌtu̇s\ [L] : prepared for either (event)

in·ve·nit \in-ˈwā-nit\ [L] : he or she devised it

in vi·no ve·ri·tas \in-ˈwē-nō-ˈwā-ri-ˌtäs\ [L] : there is truth in wine

in·vi·ta Mi·ner·va \in-ˈwē-ˌtä-mi-ˈner-ˌwä\ [L] : Minerva being unwilling : without natural talent or inspiration

ip·sis·si·ma ver·ba \ip-ˈsi-si-ˌmä-ˈwer-ˌbä\ [L] : the very words

ira fu·ror bre·vis est \ˈē-rä-ˈfu̇r-ˌȯr-ˈbre-wis-ˈest\ [L] : anger is a brief madness

j'ac·cuse \zhȧ-kue̅z\ [F] : I accuse : bitter denunciation

jac·ta alea est \ˈyäk-ˌtä-ˈä-lē-ˌä-ˈest\ [L] : the die is cast

j'adoube \zhȧ-düb\ [F] : I adjust — used in chess when touching a piece without intending to move it

ja·nu·is clau·sis \ˌyä-nu̇-ˌwēs-ˈklau̇-ˌsēs\ [L] : behind closed doors

je main·tien·drai \zhə-ma^{n}-tya^{n}-drā\ [F] : I will maintain — motto of the Netherlands

jeu de mots \zhœ̄-də-mō\ [F] : play on words : pun

Jo·an·nes est no·men eius \yō-ˈä-nās-est-ˈnō-men-ˈā-yu̇s\ [L] : John is his name — motto of Puerto Rico

jo·lie laide \zhȯ-lē-led\ [F] : good-looking ugly woman : woman who is attractive though not conventionally pretty

jour·nal in·time \zhür-nȧl-a^{n}-tēm\ [F] : intimate journal : private diary

jus di·vi·num \ˈyüs-di-ˈwē-ˌnu̇m\ [L] : divine law

jus·ti·tia om·ni·bus \yu̇s-ˈti-tē-ˌä-ˈȯm-ni-ˌbu̇s\ [L] : justice for all — motto of the District of Columbia

j'y suis, j'y reste \zhē-sw^{y}ē-zhē-rest\ [F] : here I am, here I remain

la belle dame sans mer·ci \lȧ-bel-dȧm-sä^{n}-mer-sē\ [F] : the beautiful lady without mercy

la·bo·ra·re est ora·re \ˌlä-bō-ˈrär-ā-ˌest-ˈō-ˌrär-ā\ [L] : to work is to pray

la·bor om·nia vin·cit \ˈlä-ˌbȯr-ˌȯm-nē-ˌä-ˈwiŋ-kit\ [L] : labor conquers all things — motto of Oklahoma

la·cri·mae re·rum \ˈlä-kri-ˌmī-ˈrā-ˌru̇m\ [L] : tears for things : pity for misfortune; *also* : tears in things : tragedy in life

lais·sez–al·ler *or* **lais·ser–al·ler** \le-sā-ȧ-lā\ [F] : letting go : lack of restraint

lap·sus ca·la·mi \ˈläp-su̇s-ˈkä-lä-ˌmē\ [L] : slip of the pen

lap·sus lin·guae \-ˈliŋ-ˌgwī\ [L] : slip of the tongue

la reine le veut \lȧ-ren-lə-vœ̄\ [F] : the queen wills it

la·scia·te ogni spe·ran·za, voi ch'en·tra·te \läsh-ˈshä-tā-ˌō-n^{y}ē-spā-ˈrän-tsä-ˌvō-ē-kān-ˈträ-tā\ [It] : abandon all hope, ye who enter

lau·da·tor tem·po·ris ac·ti \lau̇-ˈdä-ˌtȯr-ˌtem-pȯ-ris-ˈäk-ˌtē\ [L] : one who praises past times

laus Deo \lau̇s-ˈdā-ō\ [L] : praise (be) to God

Le·bens·welt \ˈlā-bəns-ˌvelt\ [G] : life world : world of lived experience

le cœur a ses rai·sons que la rai·son ne con·naît point \lə-kœr-ȧ-sā-re-zō^{n}k-lȧ-re-zō^{n}-nə-kȯ-ne-pwa^{n}\ [F] : the heart has its reasons that reason knows nothing of

le roi est mort, vive le roi \lə-rwä-e-mȯr-vēv-lə-rwä\ [F] : the king is dead, long live the king

le roi le veut \-lə-vœ̄\ [F] : the king wills it

le roi s'avi·se·ra \-sȧ-vēz-rȧ\ [F] : the king will consider

le style, c'est l'homme \lə-stēl-se-lȯm\ [F] : the style is the man

l'état, c'est moi \lā-tȧ-se-mwȧ\ [F] : the state, it is I

l'étoile du nord \lā-twȧl-due̅-nȯr\ [F] : the star of the north — motto of Minnesota

Lie·der·kranz \ˈlē-dər-ˌkränts\ [G] : wreath of songs : German singing society

lit·tera scrip·ta ma·net \ˈli-te-ˌrä-ˈskrip-tä-ˈmä-net\ [L] : the written letter abides

lo·cus in quo \ˈlō-ku̇s-in-ˈkwō\ [L] : place in which

l'union fait la force \lue̅-nyō^{n}-fe-lȧ-fȯrs\ [F] : union makes strength — motto of Belgium

lu·sus na·tu·rae \ˈlü-su̇s-nä-ˈtu̇r-ē, -ˈtu̇r-ˌī\ [L] : freak of nature

ma foi \mȧ-fwä\ [F] : my faith! : indeed

mag·na est ve·ri·tas et prae·va·le·bit \ˈmäg-nä-ˌest-ˈwā-ri-ˌtäs-et-ˌprī-wä-ˈlā-bit\ [L] : truth is mighty and will prevail

mag·ni no·mi·nis um·bra \ˈmäg-nē-ˈnō-mi-nis-ˈu̇m-brä\ [L] : the shadow of a great name

ma·ha·lo \ˈmä-hä-lō\ [Hawaiian] : thank you

mai·son de san·té \mā-zō^{n}-də-sä^{n}-tā\ [F] : private hospital : asylum

ma·lade ima·gi·naire \må-låd-ē-må-zhē-ner\ [F] : imaginary invalid : hypochondriac
ma·lis avi·bus \ˈmä-ˌlēs-ˈä-wi-ˌbu̇s\ [L] : under evil auspices
ma·no a ma·no \ˈmä-nō-ä-ˈmä-nō\ [Sp] : hand to hand : in direct competition or confrontation
man spricht Deutsch \ˌmän-ˌshprikt-ˈdȯich\ [G] : German spoken
ma·riage de con·ve·nance \må-ryåzh-də-kō^{n}v-nä^{n}s\ [F] : marriage of convenience
mau·vaise honte \mō-vez-ō^{n}t\ [F] : bad shame : bashfulness
mau·vais quart d'heure \mō-ve-kår-dœr\ [F] : bad quarter hour : an uncomfortable though brief experience
me·dio tu·tis·si·mus ibis \ˈme-dē-ˌō-tü-ˈti-si-mu̇s-ˈē-bis\ [L] : you will go most safely by the middle course
me ju·di·ce \mā-ˈyü-di-ke\ [L] : I being judge : in my judgment
mens sa·na in cor·po·re sa·no \māns-ˈsä-nä-in-ˈkȯr-pȯ-re-ˈsä-nō\ [L] : a sound mind in a sound body
me·um et tu·um \ˈmē-u̇m-ˌet-ˈtü-u̇m, ˈmā-u̇m-\ [L] : mine and thine : distinction of private property
mi·ra·bi·le vi·su \mi-ˈrä-bi-lā-ˈwē-sü\ [L] : wonderful to behold
mi·ra·bi·lia \ˌmir-ä-ˈbi-lē-ä\ [L] : wonders : miracles
mœurs \mœr, mœrs\ [F] : mores : attitudes, customs, and manners of a society
mo·le ru·it sua \ˈmō-le-ˈru̇-it-ˈsu̇-ä\ [L] : it collapses from its own bigness
monde \mō^{n}d\ [F] : world : fashionable world : society
mon·ta·ni sem·per li·be·ri \mȯn-ˈtä-nē-ˈsem-per-ˈlē-be-ˌrē\ [L] : mountaineers are always free — motto of West Virginia
mo·nu·men·tum ae·re per·en·ni·us \ˌmȯ-nu̇-ˈmen-tu̇m-ˌī-re-pe-ˈre-nē-u̇s\ [L] : a monument more lasting than bronze — used of an immortal work of art or literature
mo·ri·tu·ri te sa·lu·ta·mus \ˌmȯr-i-ˈtu̇r-ē-ˌtā-ˌsä-lü-ˈtä-mu̇s\ *or* **morituri te sa·lu·tant** \-ˈsä-lü-ˌtänt\ [L] : we (or those) who are about to die salute thee
mul·tum in par·vo \ˈmu̇l-tu̇m-in-ˈpär-vō\ [L] : much in little
mu·ta·to no·mi·ne de te fa·bu·la nar·ra·tur \mü-ˈtä-tō-ˈnō-mi-ne-ˌdā-ˈtā-ˈfä-bu̇-lä-nä-ˈrä-ˌtu̇r\ [L] : with the name changed the story applies to you
my·ster·i·um tre·men·dum \mi-ˈster-ē-ˌu̇m-tre-ˈmen-du̇m\ [L] : overwhelming mystery
na·tu·ram ex·pel·las fur·ca, ta·men us·que re·cur·ret \nä-ˈtü-ˌräm-ek-ˌspe-läs-ˈfu̇r-ˌkä-ˌtä-men-ˈu̇s-kwe-re-ˈku̇r-et\ [L] : you may drive nature out with a pitchfork, but she will keep coming back
na·tu·ra non fa·cit sal·tum \nä-ˈtü-rä-ˌnōn-ˈfä-kit-ˈsäl-ˌtu̇m\ [L] : nature makes no leap
ne ce·de ma·lis \nā-ˈkā-de-ˈmä-ˌlēs\ [L] : yield not to misfortunes
ne·mo me im·pu·ne la·ces·sit \ˈnā-mō-ˈmā-im-ˈpü-nā-lä-ˈke-sit\ [L] : no one attacks me with impunity — motto of Scotland and of the Order of the Thistle
ne quid ni·mis \ˌnā-ˌkwid-ˈni-mis\ [L] : not anything in excess
n'est–ce pas? \nes-pä\ [F] : isn't it so?
nicht wahr? \nikt-ˈvär\ [G] : not true? : isn't it so?
nil ad·mi·ra·ri \ˈnēl-ˌäd-mi-ˈrär-ē\ [L] : to be excited by nothing : equanimity
nil de·spe·ran·dum \ˈnēl-ˌdā-spā-ˈrän-du̇m\ [L] : never despair
nil si·ne nu·mi·ne \ˈnēl-ˌsi-nā-ˈnü-mi-ne\ [L] : nothing without the divine will — motto of Colorado
n'im·porte \na^{n}-pȯrt\ [F] : it's no matter
no·lens vo·lens \ˈnō-ˌlenz-ˈvō-ˌlenz\ [L] : unwilling (or) willing : willy-nilly
non om·nia pos·su·mus om·nes \nōn-ˈȯm-nē-ä-ˌpȯ-su̇-mu̇s-ˈȯm-ˌnās\ [L] : we can't all (do) all things
non om·nis mo·ri·ar \nōn-ˈȯm-nis-ˈmȯr-ē-ˌär\ [L] : I shall not wholly die
non sans droict \nō^{n}-sä^{n}-drwä\ [OF] : not without right — motto on Shakespeare's coat of arms
non sum qua·lis eram \ˌnōn-ˌsu̇m-ˈkwä-lis-ˈer-ˌäm\ [L] : I am not what I used to be
nos·ce te ip·sum \ˈnȯs-ke-ˌtā-ˈip-ˌsu̇m\ [L] : know thyself
nos·tal·gie de la boue \nȯs-tål-zhē-də-lå-bü\ [F] : yearning for the mud : attraction to what is unworthy, crude, or degrading
nous avons chan·gé tout ce·la \nü-zå-vō^{n}-shä^{n}-zhā-tü-sə-lå\ [F] : we have changed all that
nous ver·rons ce que nous ver·rons \nü-ve-rō^{n}-sə-kə-nü-ve-rō^{n}\ [F] : we shall see what we shall see
no·vus ho·mo \ˈnȯ-wu̇s-ˈhȯ-mō\ [L] : new man : man newly ennobled : upstart
no·vus or·do se·clo·rum \-ˈȯr-ˌdō-sā-ˈklōr-u̇m\ [L] : a new cycle of the ages — motto on the reverse of the Great Seal of the United States
nu·gae \ˈnü-ˌgī\ [L] : trifles
nuit blanche \nw^{y}ē-blä^{n}sh\ [F] : white night : a sleepless night
nyet \ˈnyet\ [Russ] : no
ob·iit \ˈō-bē-ˌit\ [L] : he or she died
ob·scu·rum per ob·scu·ri·us \ȯb-ˈskyu̇r-u̇m-ˌper-ȯb-ˈskyu̇r-ē-u̇s\ [L] : (explaining) the obscure by means of the more obscure
ode·rint dum me·tu·ant \ˈō-de-ˌrint-ˌdu̇m-ˈme-tü-ˌwänt\ [L] : let them hate, so long as they fear
odi et amo \ˈō-ˌdē-et-ˈä-(ˌ)mō\ [L] : I hate and I love
omer·tà \ō-ˈmer-tä\ [It] : submission : code chiefly among members of the criminal underworld that enjoins private vengeance and the refusal to give information to outsiders (as the police)
om·ne ig·no·tum pro mag·ni·fi·co \ˈȯm-ne-ig-ˈnō-ˌtu̇m-prō-mäg-ˈni-fi-ˌkō\ [L] : everything unknown (is taken) as grand : the unknown tends to be exaggerated in importance or difficulty
om·nia mu·tan·tur, nos et mu·ta·mur in il·lis \ˈȯm-nē-ä-mü-ˈtän-ˌtu̇r-ˌnōs-ˌet-mü-ˈtä-mu̇r-in-ˈi-ˌlēs\ [L] : all things are changing, and we are changing with them
om·nia vin·cit amor \ˈȯm-nē-ä-ˈwiŋ-kit-ˈä-ˌmȯr\ [L] : love conquers all
onus pro·ban·di \ˈō-nu̇s-prō-ˈban-ˌdī, -dē\ [L] : burden of proof
ora pro no·bis \ˈō-rä-prō-ˈnō-ˌbēs\ [L] : pray for us
ore ro·tun·do \ˈōr-ā-rō-ˈtu̇n-dō\ [L] : with round mouth : eloquently
oro y pla·ta \ˈōr-ō-ē-ˈplä-tä\ [Sp] : gold and silver — motto of Montana
o tem·pora! o mo·res! \ō-ˈtem-pȯ-rä-ō-ˈmō-ˌrās\ [L] : oh the times! oh the manners!
oti·um cum dig·ni·ta·te \ˈō-tē-ˌu̇m-ku̇m-ˌdig-ni-ˈtä-te\ [L] : leisure with dignity
où sont les neiges d'an·tan? \ü-sō^{n}-lā-nezh-dä^{n}-tä^{n}\ [F] : where are the snows of yesteryear?
outre–mer \ütrᵊ-mer\ [F] : overseas : distant lands
pal·li·da Mors \ˈpa-li-də-ˈmȯrz\ [L] : pale Death
pa·nem et cir·cen·ses \ˈpän-ˌem-et-kir-ˈkān-ˌsās\ [L] : bread and circuses : provision of the means of life and recreation by government to appease discontent
pan·ta rhei \ˌpän-ˌtä-ˈrā\ [Gk] : all things are in flux
par avance \pår-å-vä^{n}s\ [F] : in advance : by anticipation
par avion \pår-å-vyō^{n}\ [F] : by airplane — used on airmail
par ex·em·ple \pår-āg-zä^{n}plᵊ\ [F] : for example
pars pro to·to \ˈpärs-ˌprō-ˈtō-(ˌ)tō\ [L] : part (taken) for the whole
par·tu·ri·unt mon·tes, nas·ce·tur ri·di·cu·lus mus \pär-ˈtu̇r-ē-ˌu̇nt-ˈmȯn-ˌtās-näs-ˈkā-ˌtu̇r-ri-ˈdi-ku̇-lu̇s-ˈmüs\ [L] : the mountains are in labor, and a ridiculous mouse will be brought forth
pa·ter pa·tri·ae \ˈpä-ˌter-ˈpä-trē-ˌī\ [L] : father of his country

pau·cis ver·bis \ˈpau̇-ˌkēs-ˈwer-ˌbēs\ [L] : in a few words

pax vo·bis·cum \ˈpäks-vō-ˈbēs-ˌku̇m\ [L] : peace (be) with you

peine forte et dure \pen-fȯr-tä-dɯ̄r\ [F] : strong and hard punishment : torture

per an·gus·ta ad au·gus·ta \per-ˈän-ˌgu̇s-tä-äd-ˈau̇-ˌgu̇s-tä\ [L] : through difficulties to honors

père \per\ [F] : father — used orig. after French and now also after other family names to distinguish a father from his son

per·eant qui an·te nos nos·tra dix·e·runt \ˈper-e-ˌänt-kwē-ˌän-te-ˈnōs-ˈnȯs-trä-dēk-ˈsā-ˌru̇nt\ [L] : may they perish who have expressed our bright ideas before us

per·fide Al·bion \per-fēd-ȧl-byō^{n}\ [F] : perfidious Albion (England)

peu à peu \pœ̄-ȧ-pœ̄\ [F] : little by little

peu de chose \pœ̄-də-shōz\ [F] : a trifle

pièce d'oc·ca·sion \pyes-dȯ-kä-zyō^{n}\ [F] : piece for a special occasion

pinx·it \ˈpiŋk-sit\ [L] : he or she painted it

place aux dames \plȧs-ō-dȧm\ [F] : (make) room for the ladies

ple·no ju·re \ˈplā-nō-ˈyu̇r-e\ [L] : with full right

plus ça change, plus c'est la même chose \plɯ̄-sȧ-shä^{n}zh-plɯ̄-se-lȧ-mem-shōz\ [F] : the more that changes, the more it's the same thing — often shortened to *plus ça change*

plus roy·a·liste que le roi \plɯ̄-rwȧ-yȧ-lēst-kəl-rwȧ\ [F] : more royalist than the king

po·cas pa·la·bras \ˈpō-käs-pä-ˈlä-vräs\ [Sp] : few words

po·eta nas·ci·tur, non fit \pȯ-ˈā-tä-ˈnäs-ki-ˌtu̇r-nōn-ˈfit\ [L] : a poet is born, not made

pol·li·ce ver·so \ˈpȯ-li-ke-ˈver-sō\ [L] : with thumb turned : with a gesture or expression of condemnation

post hoc, er·go prop·ter hoc \ˈpȯst-ˌhōk-ˌer-gō-ˈprȯp-ter-ˌhōk\ [L] : after this, therefore on account of it (a fallacy of argument)

post ob·itum \pȯst-ˈō-bi-ˌtu̇m\ [L] : after death

pour ac·quit \pu̇r-ȧ-kē\ [F] : received payment

pour le mé·rite \pu̇r-lə-mā-rēt\ [F] : for merit

pri·mum non no·ce·re \ˌprē-mu̇m-ˌnōn-nȯ-ˈkā-re\ [L] : the first thing (is) to do no harm

pro aris et fo·cis \prō-ˈä-ˌrēs-et-ˈfō-ˌkēs\ [L] : for altars and firesides

pro bo·no pu·bli·co \prō-ˈbȯ-nō-ˈpü-bli-ˌkō\ [L] : for the public good

pro hac vi·ce \prō-ˈhäk-ˈwi-ke\ [L] : for this occasion

pro pa·tria \prō-ˈpä-trē-ˌä\ [L] : for one's country

pro re·ge, le·ge, et gre·ge \prō-ˈrā-ˌge-ˈlā-ˌge-et-ˈgre-ˌge\ [L] : for the king, the law, and the people

pro re na·ta \ˌprō-ˈrā-ˈnä-tä\ [L] : for an occasion that has arisen : as needed — used in medical prescriptions

quand même \kä^{n}-mem\ [F] : even so : all the same

quan·tum mu·ta·tus ab il·lo \ˈkwän-tu̇m-mü-ˈtä-tis-äb-ˈi-lō\ [L] : how changed from what he once was

quan·tum suf·fi·cit \ˈkwän-tu̇m-ˈsə-fi-ˌkit\ [L] : as much as suffices : a sufficient quantity — used chiefly in medical prescriptions

¿quién sa·be? \kyān-ˈsä-vā\ [Sp] : who knows?

qui fa·cit per ali·um fa·cit per se \kwē-ˈfä-kit-ˌper-ˈä-lē-ˌu̇m-ˈfä-kit-ˌper-ˈsā\ [L] : he who does (something) through another does it through himself

quis cus·to·di·et ip·sos cus·to·des? \ˌkwis-ku̇s-ˈtō-dē-ˌet-ip-ˌsōs-ku̇s-ˈtō-ˌdās\ [L] : who will keep the keepers themselves?

qui s'ex·cuse s'ac·cuse \kē-sek-skɯ̄z-sȧ-kɯ̄z\ [F] : he who excuses himself accuses himself

quis se·pa·ra·bit? \ˌkwis-ˌsā-pä-ˈrä-bit\ [L] : who shall separate (us)? — motto of the Order of St. Patrick

qui trans·tu·lit sus·ti·net \kwē-ˈträns-tu̇-ˌlit-ˈsu̇s-ti-ˌnet\ [L] : He who transplanted sustains (us) — motto of Connecticut

qui va là? \kē-vȧ-lȧ\ [F] : who goes there?

quo·ad hoc \ˌkwȯ-ˌäd-ˈhōk\ [L] : as far as this : to this extent

quod erat de·mon·stran·dum \ˌkwȯd-ˈer-ˌät-ˌde-mȯn-ˈsträn-du̇m\ [L] : which was to be proved

quod erat fa·ci·en·dum \-ˌfä-kē-ˈen-ˌdu̇m\ [L] : which was to be done

quod sem·per, quod ubi·que, quod ab om·ni·bus \kwȯd-ˈsem-ˌper-kwȯd-ˈu̇-bi-ˌkwā-ˌkwȯd-äb-ˈȯm-ni-ˌbu̇s\ [L] : what (has been held) always, everywhere, by everybody

quod vi·de \kwȯd-ˈwi-ˌde\ [L] : which see

quo·rum pars mag·na fui \ˈkwōr-u̇m-ˌpärs-ˈmäg-nə-ˈfu̇-ē\ [L] : in which I played a great part

quos de·us vult per·de·re pri·us de·men·tat \kwōs-ˈde-u̇s-ˌwu̇lt-ˈper-de-ˌre-ˈprē-u̇s-dā-ˈmen-ˌtät\ [L] : those whom a god wishes to destroy he first drives mad

quot ho·mi·nes, tot sen·ten·ti·ae \kwȯt-ˈhȯ-mi-ˌnās-ˌtȯt-sen-ˈten-tē-ˌī\ [L] : there are as many opinions as there are men

quo va·dis? \kwō-ˈvä-dis, -ˈwä-\ [L] : whither are you going?

rai·son d'état \re-zō^{n}-dā-tȧ\ [F] : reason of state

re·cu·ler pour mieux sau·ter \rə-kɯ̄-lā-pu̇r-myœ̄-sō-tā\ [F] : to draw back in order to make a better jump

reg·nat po·pu·lus \ˈreg-ˌnät-ˈpȯ-pu̇-ˌlu̇s\ [L] : the people rule — motto of Arkansas

re in·fec·ta \ˈrā-in-ˈfek-ˌtä\ [L] : the business being unfinished : without accomplishing one's purpose

re·li·gio lo·ci \re-ˈli-gē-ˌō-ˈlȯ-ˌkē\ [L] : religious sanctity of a place

rem acu te·ti·gis·ti \ˌrem-ˈä-ˌkü-te-ti-ˈgis-tē\ [L] : you have touched the point with a needle : you have hit the nail on the head

ré·pon·dez s'il vous plaît \rā-pō^{n}-dā-sēl-vü-ple\ [F] : reply, if you please

re·qui·es·cat in pa·ce \ˌre-kwē-ˈes-ˌkät-in-ˈpä-ˌke, ˌrā-kwē-ˈes-ˌkät-in-ˈpä-ˌchā\ [L] : may he or she rest in peace — used on tombstones

re·spi·ce fi·nem \ˈrā-spi-ˌke-ˈfē-ˌnem\ [L] : look to the end : consider the outcome

re·sur·gam \re-ˈsu̇r-ˌgäm\ [L] : I shall rise again

re·te·nue \rət-nɯ̄\ [F] : self-restraint : reserve

re·ve·nons à nos mou·tons \rəv-nō^{n}-ȧ-nō-mü-tō^{n}\ [F] : let us return to our sheep : let us get back to the subject

ruse de guerre \rɯ̄z-də-ger\ [F] : war stratagem

rus in ur·be \ˈrüs-in-ˈu̇r-ˌbe\ [L] : country in the city

sae·va in·dig·na·tio \ˈsī-wä-ˌin-dig-ˈnä-tē-ō\ [L] : fierce indignation

sal At·ti·cum \ˈsal-ˈa-ti-kəm\ [L] : Attic salt : wit

salle à man·ger \sȧl-ȧ-mä^{n}-zhā\ [F] : dining room

sa·lon des re·fu·sés \sȧ-lō^{n}-dā-rə-fɯ̄-zā\ [F] : salon of the refused : exhibition of art that has been rejected by an official body

sa·lus po·pu·li su·pre·ma lex es·to \ˈsäl-ˌüs-ˈpȯ-pu̇-ˌlē-su̇-ˈprā-mä-ˌleks-ˈes-tō\ [L] : let the welfare of the people be the supreme law — motto of Missouri

sanc·ta sim·pli·ci·tas \ˌsäŋk-tä-sim-ˈpli-ki-ˌtäs\ [L] : holy simplicity — often used ironically in reference to another's naïveté

sans doute \sä^{n}-düt\ [F] : without doubt

sans gêne \sä^{n}-zhen\ [F] : without embarrassment or constraint

sans peur et sans re·proche \sä^{n}-pœr-ā-sä^{n}-rə-prȯsh\ [F] : without fear and without reproach

sans sou·ci \sä^{n}-sü-sē\ [F] : without worry

sa·yo·na·ra \ˌsä-yō-ˈnär-ä\ [Jp] : good-bye

sculp·sit \ˈsku̇lp-sit\ [L] : he or she carved it

scu·to bo·nae vo·lun·ta·tis tu·ae co·ro·nas·ti nos \ˈskü-ˌtō-ˈbȯ-ˌnī-ˌvȯ-lu̇n-ˈtä-tis-ˈtü-ˌī-ˌkȯr-ō-ˈnäs-tē-ˈnōs\ [L] : Thou hast crowned us with the shield of Thy good will — a motto on the Great Seal of Maryland

se·cun·dum ar·tem \se-ˈku̇n-du̇m-ˈär-ˌtem\ [L] : according to the art : according to the accepted practice of a profession or trade
secundum na·tu·ram \-nä-ˈtü-ˌräm\ [L] : according to nature : naturally
se de·fen·den·do \ˈsā-ˌdā-ˌfen-ˈden-dō\ [L] : in self-defense
se ha·bla es·pa·ñol \sā-ˌäb-lä-ˌās-pä-ˈnʸōl\ [Sp] : Spanish spoken
sem·per ea·dem \ˈsem-ˌper-ˈe-ä-ˌdem\ [L] : always the same (fem.) — motto of Queen Elizabeth I
sem·per fi·de·lis \ˈsem-pər-fi-ˈdā-lis\ [L] : always faithful — motto of the U.S. Marine Corps
sem·per idem \ˈsem-ˌper-ˈē-ˌdem\ [L] : always the same (masc.)
sem·per pa·ra·tus \ˌsem-pər-pä-ˈrä-təs\ [L] : always prepared — motto of the U.S. Coast Guard
se non è ve·ro, è ben tro·va·to \sā-ˌnōn-e-ˈvā-rō-e-ˌben-trō-ˈvä-tō\ [It] : even if it is not true, it is well conceived
sic itur ad as·tra \ˌsēk-ˈi-ˌtu̇r-ˌäd-ˈäs-trä\ [L] : thus one goes to the stars : such is the way to immortality
sic sem·per ty·ran·nis \ˌsik-ˈsem-pər-ti-ˈra-nis\ [L] : thus ever to tyrants — motto of Virginia
sic trans·it glo·ria mun·di \ˌsēk-ˈträn-sit-ˈglōr-ē-ä-ˈmu̇n-dē\ [L] : so passes away the glory of the world
si jeu·nesse sa·vait, si vieil·lesse pou·vait! \sē-zhœ-nes-sȧ-ve-sē-vye-yes-pü-ve\ [F] : if youth only knew, if age only could!
si·lent le·ges in·ter ar·ma \ˈsi-ˌlent-ˈlā-ˌgās-ˌin-ter-ˈär-mä\ [L] : the laws are silent in the midst of arms
s'il vous plaît \sēl-vü-ple\ [F] : if you please
si·mi·lia si·mi·li·bus cu·ran·tur \si-ˈmi-lē-ä-si-ˈmi-li-bu̇s-kü-ˈrän-ˌtu̇r\ [L] : like is cured by like
si·mi·lis si·mi·li gau·det \ˈsi-mi-lis-ˈsi-mi-lē-ˈgau̇-ˌdet\ [L] : like takes pleasure in like
si mo·nu·men·tum re·qui·ris, cir·cum·spi·ce \ˌsē-ˌmō-nü-ˈmen-tu̇m-re-ˈkwē-ris-kir-ˈku̇m-spi-ke\ [L] : if you seek his monument, look around — epitaph of Sir Christopher Wren in St. Paul's, London, of which he was architect
sim·pliste \saⁿ-plēst\ [F] : simplistic : overly simple or naive
si quae·ris pen·in·su·lam amoe·nam, cir·cum·spi·ce \sē-ˈkwī-ris-pā-ˈnin-su̇-ˌläm-ä-ˈmȯi-ˌnäm-kir-ˈku̇m-spi-ke\ [L] : if you seek a beautiful peninsula, look around — motto of Michigan
sis·te vi·a·tor \ˈsis-te-wē-ˈä-ˌtȯr\ [L] : stop, traveler — used on Roman roadside tombs
si vis pa·cem, pa·ra bel·lum \ˌsē-ˈwēs-ˈpä-ˌkem-ˌpä-rä-ˈbe-ˌlu̇m\ [L] : if you wish peace, prepare for war
sol·vi·tur am·bu·lan·do \ˈsȯl-wi-ˌtu̇r-ˌäm-bu̇-ˈlän-dō\ [L] : it is solved by walking : the problem is solved by a practical experiment
splen·di·de men·dax \ˈsplen-di-ˌdā-ˈmen-ˌdäks\ [L] : nobly untruthful
spo·lia opi·ma \ˈspȯ-lē-ä-ō-ˈpē-mä\ [L] : rich spoils : the arms taken by the victorious from the vanquished general
sta·tus in quo \ˈstä-tu̇s-ˌin-ˈkwō\ [L] : state in which : the existing state
status quo an·te bel·lum \-kwō-ˌän-te-ˈbe-lu̇m\ [L] : the state existing before the war
sua·vi·ter in mo·do, for·ti·ter in re \ˈswä-wi-ˌter-in-ˈmȯ-dō-ˈfȯr-ti-ˌter-in-ˈrā\ [L] : gently in manner, strongly in deed
sub ver·bo \ˌsu̇b-ˈwer-bō\ *or* **sub vo·ce** \ˌsu̇b-ˈwō-ke\ [L] : under the word — introducing a cross-reference in a dictionary or index
sunt la·cri·mae re·rum \ˌsu̇nt-ˌlä-kri-ˌmī-ˈrā-ru̇m\ [L] : there are tears for things : tears attend trials
suo ju·re \ˌsu̇-ō-ˈyu̇r-e\ [L] : in his or her own right
suo lo·co \-ˈlȯ-kō\ [L] : in its proper place
suo Mar·te \-ˈmär-te\ [L] : by one's own exertions
su·um cui·que \ˌsu̇-u̇m-ˈkwi-kwe\ [L] : to each his own
tant mieux \täⁿ-myœ̄\ [F] : so much the better
tant pis \-pē\ [F] : so much the worse : too bad
tem·po·ra mu·tan·tur, nos et mu·ta·mur in il·lis \ˈtem-pȯ-rä-mü-ˈtän-ˌtu̇r-ˈnōs-ˌet-mü-ˈtä-mu̇r-in-ˈi-ˌlēs\ [L] : the times are changing, and we are changing with them
tem·pus edax re·rum \ˈtem-pu̇s-ˌe-ˌdäks-ˈrā-ru̇m\ [L] : time, that devours all things
tem·pus fu·git \ˈtem-pəs-ˈfyü-jət, ˈtem-pu̇s-ˈfü-git\ [L] : time flies
ti·meo Da·na·os et do·na fe·ren·tes \ˈti-mē-ˌō-ˈdä-nä-ˌōs-ˌet-ˈdō-nä-fe-ˈren-ˌtās\ [L] : I fear the Greeks even when they bring gifts
to·ti·dem ver·bis \ˈtȯ-ti-ˌdem-ˈwer-ˌbēs\ [L] : in so many words
to·tis vi·ri·bus \ˈtō-ˌtēs-ˈwē-ri-ˌbu̇s\ [L] : with all one's might
to·to cae·lo \ˈtō-tō-ˈkī-lō\ *or* **toto coe·lo** \-ˈkȯi-lō\ [L] : by the whole extent of the heavens : diametrically
tou·jours per·drix \tü-zhür-per-drē\ [F] : always partridge : too much of a good thing
tour d'ho·ri·zon \tür-dȯ-rē-zōⁿ\ [F] : circuit of the horizon : general survey
tous frais faits \tü-fre-fe\ [F] : all expenses defrayed
tout à fait \tü-tȧ-fe\ [F] : altogether : quite
tout au con·traire \tü-tō-kōⁿ-trer\ [F] : quite the contrary
tout à vous \tü-tȧ-vü\ [F] : wholly yours : at your service
tout bien ou rien \tü-byaⁿ-nü-ryaⁿ\ [F] : everything well (done) or nothing (attempted)
tout com·pren·dre c'est tout par·don·ner \tü-kōⁿ-präⁿ-drə-se-tü-pȧr-dȯ-nā\ [F] : to understand all is to forgive all
tout court \tü-kür\ [F] : quite short : and nothing more : simply : just; *also* : brusquely
tout de même \tüt-mem\ [F] : all the same : nevertheless
tout de suite \tüt-swʸēt\ [F] : immediately; *also* : all at once : consecutively
tout en·sem·ble \tü-täⁿ-säⁿblᵊ\ [F] : all together : general effect
tout est per·du fors l'hon·neur \tü-te-per-dᵫ-fȯr-lȯ-nœr\ *or* **tout est perdu hors l'honneur** \-dᵫ-ȯr-\ [F] : all is lost save honor
tout le monde \tül-mōⁿd\ [F] : all the world : everybody
tra·hi·son des clercs \trȧ-ē-zōⁿ-dā-klerk\ [F] : treason of the intellectuals
tranche de vie \träⁿsh-də-vē\ [F] : slice of life
trist·esse \trē-stes\ [F] : melancholy
tru·di·tur di·es die \ˈtrü-di-ˌtu̇r-ˈdi-ˌās-ˈdi-ˌā\ [L] : day is pushed forth by day : one day hurries on another
tu·e·bor \tü-ˈā-ˌbȯr\ [L] : I will defend — a motto on the Great Seal of Michigan
ua mau ke ea o ka ai·na i ka po·no \ˌu̇-ä-ˈmä-u̇-ke-ˈe-ä-ō-kä-ˈä-ē-nä-ˌē-kä-ˈpō-nō\ [Hawaiian] : the life of the land is established in righteousness — motto of Hawaii
über alles [G] : above everything else
ue·ber·mensch \ˈᵫ-bər-ˌmensh\ [G] : superman
ul·ti·ma ra·tio re·gum \ˈu̇l-ti-mä-ˌrä-tē-ō-ˈrā-gu̇m\ [L] : the final argument of kings, i.e., war
und so wei·ter \ˌu̇nt-zō-ˈvī-tər\ [G] : and so on
uno ani·mo \ˈü-nō-ˈä-ni-ˌmō\ [L] : with one mind : unanimously
ur·bi et or·bi \ˈu̇r-bē-ˌet-ˈȯr-bē\ [L] : to the city (Rome) and the world : to everyone
uti·le dul·ci \ˈü-ti-le-ˈdu̇l-ˌkē\ [L] : the useful with the agreeable
ut in·fra \u̇t-ˈin-frä\ [L] : as below
ut su·pra \u̇t-ˈsü-prä\ [L] : as above
va·de re·tro me, Sa·ta·na \ˈwä-de-ˈrā-trō-ˌmā-ˈsä-tä-ˌnä\ [L] : get thee behind me, Satan
vae vic·tis \wī-ˈwik-ˌtēs\ [L] : woe to the vanquished
va·ria lec·tio \ˈwär-ē-ä-ˈlek-tē-ˌō\ *pl* **va·ri·ae lec·ti-**

o·nes \ˈwär-ē-ˌī-ˌlek-tē-ˈō-ˌnās\ [L] : variant reading
va·ri·um et mu·ta·bi·le sem·per fe·mi·na \ˈwär-ē-u̇m-ˌet-ˌmü-ˈtä-bi-le-ˈsem-ˌper-ˈfā-mi-nä\ [L] : woman is ever a fickle and changeable thing
ve·di Na·po·li e poi mo·ri \ˈvā-dē-ˈnä-pō-lē-ā-ˌpȯ-ē-ˈmȯ-rē\ [It] : see Naples and then die
ve·ni, vi·di, vi·ci \ˈwā-nē-ˈwē-dē-ˈwē-kē\ [L] : I came, I saw, I conquered
ven·tre à terre \vän-trà-ter\ [F] : belly to the ground : at very great speed
ver·ba·tim ac lit·te·ra·tim \wer-ˈbä-tim-ˌäk-ˌli-te-ˈrä-tim\ [L] : word for word and letter for letter
ver·bum sat sa·pi·en·ti est \ˈwer-bu̇m-ˈsät-ˌsä-pē-ˈen-tē-ˈest\ [L] : a word to the wise is sufficient
vieux jeu \vyœ̄-zhœ̄\ [F] : old game : old hat
vin·cit om·nia ve·ri·tas \ˈwiŋ-ket-ˈȯm-nē-ä-ˈwā-ri-ˌtäs\ [L] : truth conquers all things
vin·cu·lum ma·tri·mo·nii \ˈwiŋ-ku̇-lu̇m-ˌmä-tri-ˈmō-nē-ˌē\ [L] : bond of marriage
vin du pays \van-dü̅-pā-ē\ *or* **vin de pays** \van-də-\ [F] : wine of the locality
vir·gi·ni·bus pu·e·ris·que \wir-ˈgi-ni-bu̇s-ˌpu̇-e-ˈrēs-kwe\ [L] : for girls and boys
vir·go in·tac·ta \ˈvīr-ˌgō-in-ˈtäk-tä\ [L] : untouched virgin
vir·tu·te et ar·mis \wir-ˈtü-te-ˌet-ˈär-mēs\ [L] : by valor and arms — motto of Mississippi
vis me·di·ca·trix na·tu·rae \ˈwēs-ˌme-di-ˈkä-triks-nä-ˈtü-ˌrī\ [L] : the healing power of nature
vive la dif·fé·rence \vēv-lä-dē-fā-räns\ [F] : long live the difference (between the sexes)
vive la reine \vēv-là-ren\ [F] : long live the queen
vive le roi \vēv-lə-rwä\ [F] : long live the king
vix·e·re for·tes an·te Aga·mem·no·na \wik-ˈsā-re-ˈfȯr-ˌtās-ˌän-te-ˌä-gä-ˈmem-nȯ-ˌnä\ [L] : brave men lived before Agamemnon
vogue la ga·lère \vȯg-là-gà-ler\ [F] : let the galley be kept rowing : keep on, whatever may happen
voi·là tout \vwà-là-tü\ [F] : that's all
vox et prae·te·rea ni·hil \ˈwōks-et-prī-ˈter-e-ä-ˈni-ˌhil\ [L] : voice and nothing more
vox po·pu·li vox Dei \ˈwōks-ˈpȯ-pu̇-ˌlē-ˈwōks-ˈde-ē\ [L] : the voice of the people is the voice of God
Wan·der·jahr \ˈvän-dər-ˌyär\ [G] : year of wandering
wie geht's? \vē-ˈgāts\ [G] : how goes it?
wun·der·bar \ˈvu̇n-dər-ˌbär\ [G] : wonderful

Biographical, Biblical, and Mythological Names

This section is a listing of the names of important figures from recorded history, biblical tradition, classical mythology, popular legend, and current events. Figures from the Bible, myth, or legend are clearly identified as such. In cases where figures have alternate names, they are entered under the name by which they are best known. The part of the name shown in boldface type is either the family name or the common shorter name for that figure. The dates following the name or pronunciation are the birth and death dates. Other dates in the entry refer to the dates of a particular office, honor, or achievement. Italicized names within an entry refer to a person's nickname, original name, title, or other name.

Aar•on \ˈar-ən, ˈer-\ brother of Moses and first high priest of the Hebrews in the Bible

Abel \ˈā-bəl\ son of Adam and Eve and brother of Cain in the Bible

Abra•ham \ˈā-brə-ˌham\ patriarch and founder of the Hebrew people in the Bible

Achil•les \ə-ˈkil-ēz\ Greek hero in the Trojan War in mythology

Ad•am \ˈad-əm\ the first man in the Bible

Ad•ams \ˈad-əmz\ Abigail 1744–1818 American writer; wife of John Adams

Adams John 1735–1826 2d president of the U.S. (1797–1801)

Adams John Quin•cy \ˈkwin-zē, ˈkwin(t)-sē\ 1767–1848 6th president of the U.S. (1825–29); son of John and Abigail Adams

Adams Samuel 1722–1803 patriot in the American Revolutionary War

Ad•dams \ˈad-əmz\ Jane 1860–1935 American social worker; Nobel Prize winner (1931)

Ado•nis \ə-ˈdän-əs, -ˈdō-nəs\ beautiful youth in Greek mythology who is loved by Aphrodite

Ae•ne•as \i-ˈnē-əs\ Trojan hero in Greek and Roman mythology

Ae•o•lus \ˈē-ə-ləs\ god of the winds in Greek mythology

Aes•chy•lus \ˈes-kə-ləs, ˈēs-\ 525–456 B.C. Greek dramatist

Aes•cu•la•pi•us \ˌes-kyə-ˈlā-pē-əs\ god of medicine in Roman mythology — compare ASCLEPIUS

Ae•sop \ˈē-ˌsäp, -səp\ legendary Greek writer of fables

Ag•a•mem•non \ˌag-ə-ˈmem-ˌnän, -nən\ leader of the Greeks during the Trojan War in Greek mythology

Ag•nes \ˈag-nəs\ Saint *died* 304 A.D. Christian martyr

Ahab \ˈā-ˌhab\ king of Israel in the 9th century B.C. and husband of Jezebel

Ajax \ˈā-ˌjaks\ hero in Greek mythology who kills himself because the armor of Achilles is awarded to Odysseus during the Trojan War

Alad•din \ə-ˈlad-ᵊn\ youth in the *Arabian Nights' Entertainments* who comes into possession of a magic lamp and ring

Al•cott \ˈȯl-kət, ˈal-, -ˌkät\ Louisa May 1832–1888 American author

Al•ex•an•der \ˌal-ig-ˈzan-der, ˌel-\ name of eight popes: especially **VI** (Rodrigo Borgia) 1431–1503 (pope 1492–1503)

Alexander III of Macedon 356–323 B.C. *the Great* king (336–323)

Al•fred \ˈal-frəd, -fərd\ 849–899 *the Great* king of the West Saxons (871–899)

Ali Ba•ba \ˌal-ē-ˈbäb-ə\ a woodcutter in the *Arabian Nights' Entertainments* who enters the cave of the Forty Thieves by using the password *Sesame*

Al•len \ˈal-ən\ Ethan 1738–1789 American Revolutionary soldier

Amerigo Vespucci — see VESPUCCI

Am•herst \ˈam-(ˌ)ərst\ Jeffrey 1717–1797 *Baron Amherst* British general in America

Amund•sen \ˈäm-ən-sən\ Roald 1872–1928 Norwegian explorer and discoverer of the South Pole (1911)

An•a•ni•as \ˌan-ə-ˈnī-əs\ early Christian struck dead for lying

An•der•sen \ˈan-dər-sən\ Hans Christian 1805–1875 Danish writer of fairy tales

An•der•son \ˈan-dər-sən\ Marian 1897–1993 American contralto

Anne \ˈan\ 1665–1714 queen of Great Britain (1702–14)

An•tho•ny \ˈan(t)-thə-nē\ Susan Brownell 1820–1906 American suffragist

An•tig•o•ne \an-ˈtig-ə-nē\ daughter of Oedipus and Jocasta in Greek mythology

An•to•ni•us \an-ˈtō-nē-əs\ Marcus *about* 82–30 B.C. *Mark* or *Marc An•to•ny* or *An•tho•ny* \ˈan(t)-thə-nē, *chiefly British* ˈan-tə-nē\ Roman general

Aph•ro•di•te \ˌaf-rə-ˈdīt-ē\ goddess of love and beauty in Greek mythology — compare VENUS

Apol•lo \ə-ˈpäl-ō\ god of sunlight, prophecy, music, and poetry in Greek and Roman mythology

Aqui•nas \ə-ˈkwī-nəs\ Saint Thomas 1224 (or 1225)–1274 Italian theologian

Ar•chi•me•des \ˌär-kə-ˈmēd-ēz\ *about* 287–212 B.C. Greek mathematician

Ares \ˈa(ə)r-ēz, ˈe(ə)r-\ god of war in Greek mythology — compare MARS

Ar•is•toph•a•nes \ˌar-ə-ˈstäf-ə-ˌnēz\ *about* 450–*about* 388 B.C. Greek dramatist

Ar•is•tot•le \ˈar-ə-ˌstät-ᵊl\ 384–322 B.C. Greek philosopher

Arm•strong \ˈärm-ˌstrȯŋ\ Louis 1901–1971 *Satchmo* \ˈsach-ˌmō\ American jazz musician

Armstrong Neil Alden 1930– American astronaut and first man on the moon (1969)

Ar•nold \ˈärn-ᵊld\ Benedict 1741–1801 American Revolutionary general and traitor

Ar•te•mis \ˈärt-ə-məs\ goddess of the moon, wild animals, and hunting in Greek mythology — compare DIANA

Ar•thur \ˈär-thər\ legendary king of the Britons whose story is based on traditions of a 6th century military leader — **Ar•thu•ri•an** \är-ˈth(y)u̇r-ē-ən\ *adj*

Arthur Chester Alan 1829–1886 21st president of the U.S. (1881–85)

As•cle•pi•us \ə-ˈsklē-pē-əs\ god of medicine in Greek mythology — compare AESCULAPIUS

As•tor \ˈas-tər\ John Jacob 1763–1848 American (German-born) fur trader and capitalist

Athe•na \ə-ˈthē-nə\ *or* **Athe•ne** \-nē\ goddess of wisdom in Greek mythology — compare MINERVA

At•las \ˈat-ləs\ Titan in Greek mythology forced to bear the heavens on his shoulders

At•ti•la \ə-ˈtil-ə, ˈat-ᵊl-ə\ 406?–453 A.D. *the Scourge of God* king of the Huns

At·tucks \ˈat-əks\ Crispus 1723?–1770 American patriot; one of five men killed in Boston Massacre

Au·du·bon \ˈȯd-ə-ˌbän, -bən\ John James 1785–1851 American (Haitian-born) artist and naturalist

Au·gus·tine \ˈȯ-gə-ˌstēn; ȯ-ˈgəs-tən, ə-\ Saint 354–430 A.D. church father; bishop of Hippo (396–430)

Au·gus·tus \ȯ-ˈgəs-təs, ə-\ *or* **Augustus Caesar** *or* **Oc·ta·vi·an** \äk-ˈtā-vē-ən\ 63 B.C.–14 A.D. 1st Roman emperor (27 B.C.–14 A.D.)

Aus·ten \ˈȯs-tən, ˈäs-\ Jane 1775–1817 English author

Bac·chus \ˈbak-əs\ — see DIONYSUS

Bach \ˈbäk, ˈbäk\ Johann Sebastian 1685–1750 German composer and organist

Ba·con \ˈbā-kən\ Francis 1561–1626 English philosopher and author

Ba·den–Pow·ell \ˌbād-ᵊn-ˈpō-əl\ Robert Stephenson Smyth 1857–1941 English founder of Boy Scout movement

Baf·fin \ˈbaf-ən\ William *about* 1584–1622 English navigator

Bal·boa, de \bal-ˈbō-ə\ Vasco Núñez 1475–1519 Spanish explorer and first European to sight Pacific Ocean (1513)

Bal·ti·more \ˈbȯl-tə-ˌmō(ə)r, -ˌmȯ(ə)r\ Lord — see George CALVERT

Bal·zac, de \ˈbȯl-ˌzak, ˈbal-\ Honoré 1799–1850 French author

Ba·rab·bas \bə-ˈrab-əs\ prisoner released in preference to Jesus at the demand of the multitude

Bar·num \ˈbär-nəm\ Phineas Taylor 1810–1891 American show-business manager

Bar·rie \ˈbar-ē\ Sir James Matthew 1860–1937 Scottish author

Bar·thol·di \bär-ˈtäl-dē, -ˈtȯl-, -ˈthäl-, -ˈthȯl-\ Frédéric-Auguste 1834–1904 French sculptor who designed the Statue of Liberty

Bar·ton \ˈbärt-ᵊn\ Clara 1821–1912 founder of American Red Cross Society

Beau·re·gard \ˈbōr-ə-ˌgärd, ˈbȯr-\ Pierre Gustave Toutant 1818–1893 American Confederate general

Beck·et, à \ə-ˈbek-ət, ä-\ Saint Thomas *about* 1118–1170 archbishop of Canterbury (1162–1170)

Bee·tho·ven \ˈbā-ˌtō-vən\ Ludwig van 1770–1827 German composer

Bell \ˈbel\ Alexander Graham 1847–1922 American (Scottish-born) inventor of the telephone

Ben·e·dict \ˈben-ə-ˌdikt\ name of 15 popes: especially **XIV** (*Prospero Lambertini*) 1675–1758 (pope 1740–58); **XV** (*Giacomo della Chiesa*) 1854–1922 (pope 1914–22)

Be·nét \bə-ˈnā\ Stephen Vincent 1898–1943 American author

Ben·ja·min \ˈbenj-(ə-)mən\ youngest son of Jacob and ancestor of one of the 12 tribes of Israel in the Bible

Ben·ton \ˈbent-ᵊn\ Thomas Hart 1889–1975 American painter

Be·o·wulf \ˈbā-ə-ˌwu̇lf\ legendary warrior and hero of the Old English poem *Beowulf*

Be·ring \ˈbi(ə)r-iŋ, ˈbe(ə)r-\ Vitus 1681–1741 Danish navigator; explored Bering sea and strait for Russia

Ber·lin \(ˌ)bər-ˈlin\ Irving 1888–1989 American (Russian-born) composer

Ber·ni·ni \bər-ˈnē-nē\ Gian Lorenzo 1598–1680 Italian sculptor, architect, and painter

Bes·se·mer \ˈbes-ə-mər\ Sir Henry 1813–1898 English engineer and inventor

Be·thune \bə-ˈth(y)ün\ Mary 1875–1955 née *McLeod* American educator

Bi·zet \bē-ˈzā\ Alexandre-César-Léopold 1838–1875 called *Georges* French composer

Black Hawk \ˈblak-ˌhȯk\ 1767–1838 American Indian chief

Black·well \ˈblak-ˌwel, -wəl\ Elizabeth 1821–1910 American (English-born) physician

Blake \ˈblāk\ William 1757–1827 English poet and artist

Bloom·er \ˈblü-mər\ Amelia Jenks 1818–1894 American social reformer

Boc·cac·cio \bō-ˈkäch-(ē-ˌ)ō\ Giovanni 1313–1375 Italian author

Bohr \ˈbō(ə)r, ˈbȯ(ə)r\ Niels 1885–1962 Danish physicist; Nobel prize winner (1922)

Bo·leyn \bu̇-ˈlin, ˈbu̇l-ən\ Anne 1507?–1536 2d wife of Henry VIII and mother of Elizabeth I of England

Bo·lí·var Si·món \sē-ˌmōn-bə-ˈlē-ˌvär, ˌsī-mən-ˈbäl-ə-vər\ 1783–1830 South American liberator

Bon·i·face \ˈbän-ə-fəs, -ˌfās\ name of nine popes: especially **VIII** (*Benedetto Caetani*) *about* 1235 (or 1240)–1303 (pope 1294–1303)

Boone \ˈbün\ Daniel 1734–1820 American pioneer

Booth \ˈbüth\ John Wilkes 1838–1865 assassin of Abraham Lincoln

Bo·re·as \ˈbōr-ē-əs, ˈbȯr-\ god of the north wind in Greek mythology

Bot·ti·cel·li \ˌbät-ə-ˈchel-ē\ Sandro 1445–1510 Italian painter

Bow·ie \ˈbü-ē, ˈbō-\ James 1796–1836 hero of Texas revolution

Boyle \ˈbȯi(ə)l\ Robert 1627–1691 English physicist and chemist

Brad·bury \ˈbrad-ˌber-ē, -b(ə-)rē\ Ray Douglas 1920– American author

Brad·dock \ˈbrad-ək\ Edward 1695–1755 British general in America

Brad·ford \ˈbrad-fərd\ William 1590–1657 Pilgrim leader

Brad·street \ˈbrad-ˌstrēt\ Anne *about* 1612–1672 American poet

Bra·dy \ˈbrād-ē\ Mathew B. 1823?–1896 American photographer

Brah·ma \ˈbräm-ə\ creator god of the Hindu sacred triad — compare SIVA, VISHNU

Brahms \ˈbrämz\ Johannes 1833–1897 German composer

Braille \ˈbrā(ə)l, ˈbrī\ Louis 1809–1852 French blind teacher of the blind

Braun \ˈbrau̇n\ Wernher von 1912–1977 American (German-born) engineer

Brezh·nev \ˈbrezh-ˌnef\ Leonid Ilyich 1906–1982 Russian politician; 1st secretary of Communist party (1964–82); president of the U.S.S.R. (1960–64; 1977–82)

Brid·ger \ˈbrij-ər\ James 1804–1881 American pioneer and scout

Bron·të \ˈbränt-ē, ˈbrän-ˌtā\ family of English writers: Charlotte 1816–1855 and her sisters Emily 1818–1848 and Anne 1820–1849

Brooks \ˈbru̇ks\ Gwendolyn Elizabeth 1917– American poet

Brown \ˈbrau̇n\ John *Old Brown of Osa·wat·o·mie* \ˌō-sə-ˈwät-ə-mē\ 1800–1859 American abolitionist

Brow·ning \ˈbrau̇-niŋ\ Elizabeth Barrett 1806–1861 English poet; wife of Robert

Browning Robert 1812–1889 English poet; husband of Elizabeth

Bru·tus \ˈbrüt-əs\ Marcus Junius 85–42 B.C. Roman politician; one of Julius Caesar's assassins

Bry·an \ˈbrī-ən\ William Jennings 1860–1925 American lawyer and politician

Bu·chan·an \byü-ˈkan-ən, bə-\ James 1791–1868 15th president of the U.S. (1857–61)

Buck \ˈbək\ Pearl 1892–1973 American author; Nobel Prize winner (1938)

Buddha — see GAUTAMA BUDDHA

Buffalo Bill — see William Frederick CODY

Bun·yan \ˈbən-yən\ John 1628–1688 English preacher and author

Bur·bank \ˈbər-ˌbaŋk\ Luther 1849–1926 American horticulturist

Bur·goyne \(ˌ)bər-ˈgȯin, ˈbər-ˌgȯin\ John 1722–1792 British general in America

Burns \ˈbərnz\ Robert 1759–1796 Scottish poet

Burn•side \ˈbərn-ˌsīd\ Ambrose Everett 1824–1881 American general
Burr \ˈbər\ Aaron 1756–1836 vice president of the U.S. (1801–05)
Bush \ˈbu̇sh\ George Herbert Walker 1924– 41st president of the U.S. (1989–93)
By•ron \ˈbī-rən\ Lord 1788–1824 *George Gordon Byron* English poet
Cab•ot \ˈkab-ət\ John *about* 1450–*about* 1499 Italian navigator; explored coast of North America for England
Cabot Sebastian 1476?–1557 English navigator; son of John Cabot
Ca•bri•ni \kə-ˈbrē-nē\ Saint Frances Xavier 1850–1917 *Mother Cabrini* first American (Italian-born) saint (1946)
Cae•sar \ˈsē-zər\ Gaius Julius 100–44 B.C. Roman general, political leader, and writer
Cain \ˈkān\ brother of Abel in the Bible
Cal•houn \kal-ˈhün\ John Caldwell 1782–1850 vice president of the U.S. (1825–32)
Ca•lig•u•la \kə-ˈlig-yə-lə\ 12–41 A.D. *Gaius Caesar* Roman emperor (37–41)
Cal•li•ope \kə-ˈlī-ə-ˌpē\ muse of heroic poetry in Greek mythology
Cal•vert \ˈkal-vərt\ George 1580?–1632 1st Baron *Baltimore* English colonist in America
Cal•vin \ˈkal-vən\ John 1509–1564 French theologian and reformer
Ca•nute \kə-ˈn(y)üt\ *died* 1035 *the Great* king of England (1016–35); of Denmark (1018–35); of Norway (1028–35)
Car•ne•gie \ˈkär-nə-gē, kär-ˈneg-ē\ Andrew 1835–1919 American (Scottish-born) industrialist and philanthropist
Carroll Lewis — see Charles Lutwidge DODGSON
Car•son \ˈkärs-ᵊn\ Christopher 1809–1868 *Kit* American soldier and guide
Carson Rachel Louise 1907–1964 American scientist
Car•ter \ˈkärt-ər\ James Earl, Jr. 1924– *Jimmy* 39th president of the U.S. (1977–81)
Car•tier \kär-ˈtyā, ˈkärt-ē-ˌā\ Jacques 1491–1557 French navigator; explored Saint Lawrence river
Ca•ru•so \kə-ˈrü-sō, -zō\ **En•ri•co** \en-ˈrē-kō\ 1873–1921 Italian tenor
Car•ver \ˈkär-vər\ George Washington *about* 1864–1943 American botanist
Ca•sa•no•va \ˌkaz-ə-ˈnō-və, ˌkas-\ Giovanni Giacomo 1725–1798 Italian adventurer
Cas•san•dra \kə-ˈsan-drə\ daughter of Priam in Greek mythology who is endowed with the gift of prophecy but fated never to be believed
Cas•satt \kə-ˈsat\ Mary 1845–1926 American painter
Cas•tro \ˈkas-trō, ˈkäs-\ **(Ruz)** \ˈrüs\ **Fi•del** \fē-ˈdel\ 1926– Cuban premier (1959–)
Cath•er \ˈkath-ər\ Willa Sibert 1873–1947 American author
Cath•er•ine \ˈkath-(ə-)rən\ name of 1st, 5th, and 6th wives of Henry VIII of England: Catherine of Aragon 1485–1536; Catherine Howard 1520?–1542; Catherine Parr 1512–1548
Catherine I 1684–1727 wife of Peter the Great; empress of Russia (1725–27)
Catherine II 1729–1796 *the Great* empress of Russia (1762–96)
Cav•en•dish \ˈkav-ən-(ˌ)dish\ Henry 1731–1810 English scientist
Ce•ci•lia \sə-ˈsēl-yə, -ˈsil-\ Saint 2d or 3d century A.D. Roman martyr; patron saint of music
Ce•res \ˈsi(ə)r-ˌēz\ the goddess of agriculture in Roman mythology — compare DEMETER
Cer•van•tes \sər-ˈvan-ˌtēz\ Miguel de 1547–1616 Spanish author
Cé•zanne \sā-ˈzan\ Paul 1839–1906 French painter
Cha•gall \shə-ˈgäl, -ˈgal\ Marc 1887–1985 Russian painter
Cham•plain \(ˈ)sham-ˈplān\ Samuel de *about* 1567–1635 French explorer in America; founder of Quebec
Chap•lin \ˈchap-lən\ Sir Charles Spencer 1889–1977 British actor and producer
Chap•man \ˈchap-mən\ John 1774–1845 *Johnny Appleseed* \ˈap-əl-ˌsēd\ American pioneer
Char•le•magne \ˈshär-lə-ˌmān\ 742–814 A.D. *Charles the Great* or *Charles I* Frankish king (768–814); emperor of the West (800–814)
Charles \ˈchär(-ə)lz\ name of 10 kings of France: especially **I** 823–877 A.D. (reigned 840–77) *the Bald*; Holy Roman emperor as *Charles II* (875–77); **IV** 1294–1328 (reigned 1322–28) *the Fair*; **V** 1337–1380 (reigned 1364–80) *the Wise*; **VI** 1368–1422 (reigned 1380–1422) *the Mad* or *the Beloved*; **VII** 1403–1461 (reigned 1422–61) *the Victorious*; **IX** 1550–1574 (reigned 1560–74); **X** 1757–1836 (reigned 1824–30)
Charles name of two kings of Great Britain: **I** 1600–1649 (reigned 1625–49) *Charles Stuart*; **II** 1630–1685 (reigned 1660–85) son of Charles I
Charles V 1500–1558 Holy Roman emperor (1519–56); king of Spain as *Charles I* (1516–56)
Charles Edward Stuart 1720–1788 *the Young Pretender*; *(Bonnie) Prince Charlie* English prince
Charles Mar•tel \mär-ˈtel\ *about* 688–741 A.D. Frankish ruler (719–41); grandfather of Charlemagne
Cha•ryb•dis \kə-ˈrib-dəs, shə-, chə-\ a whirlpool off the coast of Sicily personified in Greek mythology as a female monster
Chau•cer \ˈchȯ-sər\ Geoffrey *about* 1342–1400 English poet
Che•khov \ˈchek-ˌȯf, -ˌȯv\ Anton Pavlovich 1860–1904 Russian author
Cheops — see KHUFU
Ches•ter•ton \ˈches-tərt-ᵊn\ Gilbert Keith 1874–1936 English author
Cho•pin \ˈshō-ˌpan\ Frédéric François 1810–1849 Polish pianist and composer
Chou En–lai \ˈjō-ˈen-ˈlī\ 1898–1976 Chinese Communist politician; premier (1949–76)
Christ Jesus — see JESUS
Chris•tie \ˈkris-tē\ Agatha 1890–1976 English author
Chur•chill \ˈchər-ˌchil, ˈchərch-ˌhil\ Sir Winston Leonard Spencer 1874–1965 British prime minister (1940–45; 1951–55)
Clark \ˈklärk\ George Rogers 1752–1818 American soldier and pioneer
Clark William 1770–1838 American explorer
Clay \ˈklā\ Henry 1777–1852 American politician and orator
Clem•ens \ˈklem-ənz\ Samuel Langhorne 1835–1910 pseudonym *Mark Twain* \ˈtwān\ American author
Cle•o•pa•tra \ˌklē-ə-ˈpa-trə, -ˈpā-, -ˈpä-\ 69–30 B.C. queen of Egypt (51–30)
Cleve•land \ˈklēv-lənd\ (Stephen) Grover 1837–1908 22d and 24th president of the U.S. (1885–89; 1893–97)
Clin•ton \ˈklin-tᵊn\ William Jefferson 1946– 42d president of the U.S. (1993–)
Cly•tem•nes•tra \ˌklīt-əm-ˈnes-trə\ wife of Agamemnon in Greek mythology
Cobb \ˈkäb\ Tyrus Raymond 1886–1961 *Ty* American baseball player
Co•chise \kō-ˈchēs\ 1812?–1874 Apache chief
Co•dy \ˈkōd-ē\ William Frederick 1846–1917 *Buffalo Bill* American hunter, guide, and entertainer
Co•han \ˈkō-ˌhan\ George Michael 1878–1942 American actor and composer
Cole•ridge \ˈkōl-rij, ˈkō-lə-rij\ Samuel Taylor 1772–1834 English poet
Co•lette \kȯ-ˈlet\ Sidonie-Gabrielle 1873–1954 French author
Co•lum•bus \kə-ˈləm-bəs\ Christopher 1451–1506 Genoese navigator; discovered America for Spain (1492)
Con•fu•cius \kən-ˈfyü-shəs\ 551–479 B.C. Chinese philosopher

Con•rad \ˈkän-ˌrad\ Joseph 1857–1924 British (Ukrainian-born of Polish parents) author

Con•sta•ble \ˈkən(t)-stə-bəl, ˈkän(t)-\ John 1776–1837 English painter

Con•stan•tine \ˈkän(t)-stən-ˌtēn, -ˌtīn\ *died* 337 A.D. *the Great* Roman emperor (306–37)

Cook \ˈku̇k\ Captain James 1728–1779 English navigator

Coo•lidge \ˈkü-lij\ (John) Calvin 1872–1933 30th president of the U.S. (1923–29)

Coo•per \ˈkü-pər, ˈku̇p-ər\ James Fen•i•more \ˈfen-ə-ˌmō(ə)r, -ˌmȯ(ə)r\ 1789–1851 American author

Co•per•ni•cus \kō-ˈpər-ni-kəs\ Nicolaus 1473–1543 Polish astronomer

Cop•land \ˈkō-plənd\ Aaron 1900–1990 American composer

Cop•ley \ˈkäp-lē\ John Sin•gle•ton \ˈsiŋ-gəl-tən\ 1738–1815 American portrait painter

Corn•wal•lis \kȯrn-ˈwäl-əs\ 1st Marquis 1738–1805 *Charles Cornwallis* British general in America

Co•ro•na•do \ˌkȯr-ə-ˈnäd-ō, ˌkär-\ Francisco Vásquez de *about* 1510–1554 Spanish explorer of southwestern U.S.

Cor•tés \kȯr-ˈtez, ˈkȯr-ˌtez\ Hernán *or* Hernando 1485–1547 Spanish conqueror of Mexico

Cous•teau \kü-ˈstō\ Jacques-Yves 1910– French marine explorer

Crane \ˈkrān\ Stephen 1871–1900 American author

Crazy Horse \ˈkrā-zē-ˌhȯrs\ 1842–1877 Sioux chief

Crock•ett \ˈkräk-ət\ David 1786–1836 *Davy* American pioneer

Crom•well \ˈkräm-ˌwel, ˈkrəm-, -wəl\ Oliver 1599–1658 English general and political leader; lord protector of England (1653–58)

Cro•nus \ˈkrō-nəs, ˈkrän-əs\ a Titan in Greek mythology overthrown by his son Zeus

Cum•mings \ˈkəm-iŋz\ Edward Estlin 1894–1962 known as *e. e. cummings* American poet

Cu•pid \ˈkyü-pəd\ god of love in Roman mythology — compare EROS

Cu•rie \kyu̇-ˈrē, ˈkyu̇(ə)r-ē\ Marie 1867–1934 French (Polish-born) chemist; Nobel Prize winner (1903, 1911)

Curie Pierre 1859–1906 French chemist; Nobel Prize winner (1903)

Cus•ter \ˈkəs-tər\ George Armstrong 1839–1876 American general

Cy•ra•no de Ber•ge•rac \ˌsir-ə-ˌnō-də-ˈber-zhə-ˌrak\ Savinien de 1619–1655 French poet and soldier

Dae•da•lus \ˈded-ᵊl-əs, ˈdēd-\ builder in Greek mythology of the Cretan labyrinth and inventor of wings by which he and his son Icarus escape from it

Dal•ton \ˈdȯlt-ᵊn\ John 1766–1844 English chemist and physicist

Da•na \ˈdā-nə\ Richard Henry 1815–1882 American author

Dan•iel \ˈdan-yəl\ a prophet in the Bible who is held captive in Babylon and delivered by God from a den of lions

Dan•te \ˈdän-tā, ˈdan-, -tē\ 1265–1321 Italian poet

Dare \ˈda(ə)r, ˈde(ə)r\ Virginia 1587–? first child born in America of English parents

Da•ri•us I \də-ˈrī-əs\ 550–486 B.C. *the Great* king of Persia (522–486)

Dar•row \ˈdar-ō\ Clarence Seward 1857–1938 American lawyer

Dar•win \ˈdär-wən\ Charles Robert 1809–1882 English naturalist

Da•vid \ˈdā-vəd\ a youth in the Bible who slays Goliath and succeeds Saul as king of Israel

Da•vis \ˈdā-vəs\ Jefferson 1808–1889 president of the Confederate States of America (1861–65)

Dawes \ˈdȯz\ William 1745–1799 American patriot

Debs \ˈdebz\ Eugene Victor 1855–1926 American socialist

De•bus•sy \ˌdeb-yu̇-ˈsē, ˌdāb-; də-ˈbyü-sē\ (Achille-) Claude 1862–1918 French composer

De•ca•tur \di-ˈkāt-ər\ Stephen 1779–1820 American naval officer

De•foe \di-ˈfō\ Daniel 1660–1731 English author

De•gas \də-ˈgä\ (Hilaire-Germain-) Edgar 1834–1917 French painter

de Gaulle \di-ˈgōl, -ˈgȯl\ Charles-André-Joseph-Marie 1890–1970 French general; president of Fifth Republic (1958–69)

De•li•lah \di-ˈlī-lə\ mistress and betrayer of Samson in the Bible

De•me•ter \di-ˈmēt-ər\ goddess of agriculture in Greek mythology — compare CERES

de Mille \də-ˈmil\ Agnes George 1905–1993 American dancer and choreographer

Des•cartes \dā-ˈkärt\ René 1596–1650 French mathematician and philosopher

de So•to \di-ˈsōt-ō\ Hernando 1496 (or 1499 or 1500)–1542 Spanish explorer in America

Dew•ey \ˈd(y)ü-ē\ George 1837–1917 American admiral

Dewey John 1859–1952 American philosopher and educator

Dewey Melvil 1851–1931 American librarian

Di•ana \dī-ˈan-ə\ goddess of the forest and of childbirth in ancient Italian mythology who was identified with Artemis by the Romans

Dick•ens \ˈdik-ənz\ Charles John Huffam 1812–1870 pseudonym *Boz* \ˈbäz, ˈbōz\ English author

Dick•in•son \ˈdik-ən-sən\ Emily Elizabeth 1830–1886 American poet

Di•do \ˈdīd-ō\ legendary queen of Carthage who falls in love with Aeneas and kills herself when he leaves her

Di•o•ny•sus \ˌdī-ə-ˈnī-səs, -ˈnē-\ god of wine and ecstasy in Greek mythology — called also *Bacchus* — **Di•o•ny•sian** \dī-ə-ˈnizh-ē-ən\ *adj*

Dis•ney \ˈdiz-nē\ Walter Elias 1901–1966 American film producer

Dis•rae•li \diz-ˈrā-lē\ Benjamin 1804–1881 1st Earl of *Bea•cons•field* \ˈbē-kənz-ˌfēld\ British prime minister (1868; 1874–80)

Dix \ˈdiks\ Dorothea Lynde 1802–1887 American social reformer

Dodg•son \ˈdäj-sən, ˈdäd-\ Charles Lut•widge \ˈlət-wij\ 1832–1898 pseudonym *Lewis Car•roll* \ˈkar-əl\ English author and mathematician

Donne \ˈdən\ John 1572–1631 English poet and minister

Don Qui•xote \ˌdän-kē-ˈ(h)ōt-ē, ˌdäŋ-; dän-ˈkwik-sət\ the idealistic and impractical hero of Cervantes' *Don Quixote*

Dos•to•yev•ski \ˌdäs-tə-ˈyef-skē, -ˈyev-\ Fyodor Mikhaylovich 1821–1881 Russian novelist

Doug•las \ˈdəg-ləs\ Stephen Arnold 1813–1861 American politician

Doug•lass \ˈdəg-ləs\ Frederick 1817–1895 American abolitionist

Doyle \ˈdȯi(ə)l\ Sir Arthur Co•nan \ˈkō-nən\ 1859–1930 British physician, novelist, and detective-story writer

Drake \ˈdrāk\ Sir Francis 1540 (or 1543)–1596 English navigator and admiral

Drei•ser \ˈdrī-sər, -zər\ Theodore 1871–1945 American author

Du Bois \d(y)ü-ˈbȯis\ William Edward Burghardt 1868–1963 American educator and writer

Du•mas \d(y)ü-ˈmä, ˈd(y)ü-ˌmä\ Alexandre 1802–1870 *Dumas père* \ˈpe(ə)r\ French author

Dumas Alexandre 1824–1895 *Dumas fils* \ˈfēs\ French author

Dun•can \ˈdəŋ-kən\ Isadora 1877–1927 American dancer

Dü•rer \ˈd(y)u̇r-ər\ Albrecht 1471–1528 German painter and engraver

Ea•kins \ˈā-kənz\ Thomas 1844–1916 American artist

Ear•hart \ˈe(ə)r-ˌhärt, ˈi(ə)r-\ Amelia 1897–1937 American aviator

Ed•dy \ˈed-ē\ Mary Baker 1821–1910 American founder of the Christian Science Church

Ed•i•son \ˈed-ə-sən\ Thomas Alva 1847–1931 American inventor

Ed•ward \ˈed-wərd\ name of eight post-Norman kings of England: **I** 1239–1307 (reigned 1272–1307) *Longshanks*; **II** 1284–1327 (reigned 1307–27); **III** 1312–1377 (reigned 1327–77); **IV** 1442–1483 (reigned 1461–70; 1471–83); **V** 1470–1483 (reigned 1483); **VI** 1537–1553 (reigned 1547–53) son of Henry VIII and Jane Seymour; **VII** 1841–1910 (reigned 1901–10) *Albert Edward* son of Queen Victoria; **VIII** 1894–1972 (reigned 1936; abdicated) *Duke of Windsor* son of George V

Ein•stein \ˈīn-ˌstīn\ Albert 1879–1955 American (German-born) physicist; Nobel Prize winner (1921)

Ei•sen•how•er \ˈīz-ᵊn-ˌhau̇(-ə)r\ Dwight David 1890–1969 American general; 34th president of the U.S. (1953–61)

Elec•tra \i-ˈlek-trə\ sister of Orestes in Greek mythology who with her brother avenges their father's murder

Eli•jah \i-ˈlī-jə\ Hebrew prophet of the 9th century B.C.

El•iot \ˈel-ē-ət, ˈel-yət\ George 1819–1880 pseudonym of *Mary Ann Evans* English author

Eliot Thomas Stearns 1888–1965 British (American-born) poet and critic

Eliz•a•beth I \i-ˈliz-ə-bəth\ 1533–1603 daughter of Henry VIII and Anne Boleyn; queen of England (1558–1603)

Elizabeth II 1926– queen of the United Kingdom (1952–)

Em•er•son \ˈem-ər-sən\ Ralph Waldo 1803–1882 American essayist and poet

En•dym•i•on \en-ˈdim-ē-ən\ beautiful youth in Greek mythology loved by the goddess of the moon

Ep•i•cu•rus \ˌep-i-ˈkyu̇r-əs\ 341–270 B.C. Greek philosopher

Er•ik \ˈer-ik\ *the Red* 10th century Norwegian navigator; explored Greenland coast

Eriksson Leif — see LEIF ERIKSSON

Eros \ˈe(ə)r-ˌäs, ˈi(ə)r-\ god of love in Greek mythology — compare CUPID

Esau \ˈē-(ˌ)sȯ\ son of Isaac and Rebekah and elder twin brother of Jacob in the Bible

Es•ther \ˈes-tər\ Hebrew woman in the Bible who as the queen of Persia delivers her people from destruction

Eu•clid \ˈyü-kləd\ *flourished about* 300 B.C. Greek mathematician

Eu•rip•i•des \yu̇-ˈrip-ə-ˌdēz\ *about* 484–406 B.C. Greek dramatist

Eu•ro•pa \yu̇-ˈrō-pə\ a princess in Greek mythology who was carried off by Zeus disguised as a white bull

Eu•ryd•i•ce \yu̇-ˈrid-ə-sē\ the wife of Orpheus whom he attempts to bring back from Hades

Eve \ˈēv\ the first woman in the Bible

Eze•kiel \i-ˈzē-kyəl, -kē-əl\ Hebrew prophet of the 6th century B.C.

Fahr•en•heit \ˈfar-ən-ˌhīt, ˈfär-\ Daniel Gabriel 1686–1736 German physicist

Far•a•day \ˈfar-ə-ˌdā, -əd-ē\ Michael 1791–1867 English chemist and physicist

Far•ra•gut \ˈfar-ə-gət\ David Glasgow 1801–1870 American admiral

Faulk•ner \ˈfȯk-nər\ William 1897–1962 American author; Nobel Prize winner (1949)

Faust \ˈfau̇st\ *or* **Fau•stus** \ˈfau̇-stəs, ˈfȯ-\ a legendary German magician who sells his soul to the devil

Fawkes \ˈfȯks\ Guy 1570–1606 English conspirator

Fer•di•nand \ˈfərd-ᵊn-ˌand\ **II** of Aragon *or* **V** of Castile 1452–1516 *the Catholic* king of Castile (1474–1504); of Aragon (1479–1516); of Naples (1504–16); founder of the Spanish monarchy

Fer•mi \ˈfe(ə)r-mē\ Enrico 1901–1954 American (Italian-born) physicist; Nobel Prize winner (1938)

Fiel•ding \ˈfē(ə)l-diŋ\ Henry 1707–1754 English author

Fill•more \ˈfil-ˌmō(ə)r, -ˌmȯ(ə)r\ Millard 1800–1874 13th president of the U.S. (1850–53)

Fitz•ger•ald \fits-ˈjer-əld\ Francis Scott Key 1896–1940 American author

Flem•ing \ˈflem-iŋ\ Sir Alexander 1881–1955 British bacteriologist; Nobel Prize winner (1945)

Flo•ra \ˈflōr-ə, ˈflȯr-\ goddess of flowers in Roman mythology

Flying Dutchman legendary Dutch mariner condemned to sail the seas until Judgment Day

Ford \ˈfō(ə)rd, ˈfȯ(ə)rd\ Gerald Rudolph 1913– 38th president of the U.S. (1974–77)

Ford Henry 1863–1947 American automobile manufacturer

Fos•ter \ˈfȯs-tər, ˈfäs-\ Stephen Collins 1826–1864 American songwriter

Francis \ˈfran(t)-səs\ **of As•si•si** \ə-ˈsis-ē, -ˈsē-zē, -ˈsē-sē, -ˈsiz-ē\ Saint 1181 (or 1182)–1226 Italian friar; founder of Franciscan order

Frank•lin \ˈfraŋ-klən\ Benjamin 1706–1790 American patriot, author, and inventor

Fred•er•ick I \ˈfred-(ə-)rik\ *about* 1123–1190 *Frederick Bar•ba•ros•sa* \ˌbär-bə-ˈräs-ə, -ˈrȯs-\ Holy Roman emperor (1152–90)

Frederick II 1712–1786 *the Great* king of Prussia (1740–86)

Fré•mont \ˈfrē-ˌmänt\ John Charles 1813–1890 American general and explorer

French \ˈfrench\ Daniel Chester 1850–1931 American sculptor

Freud \ˈfrȯid\ Sigmund 1856–1939 Austrian neurologist; founder of psychoanalysis

Frig•ga \ˈfrig-ə\ wife of Odin and goddess of married love and the hearth in Norse mythology

Frost \ˈfrȯst\ Robert Lee 1874–1963 American poet

Ful•ler \ˈfu̇l-ər\ (Richard) Buckminster 1895–1983 American engineer

Fuller (Sarah) Margaret 1810–1850 American author and reformer

Ful•ton \ˈfu̇lt-ᵊn\ Robert 1765–1815 American inventor

Ga•bri•el \ˈgā-brē-əl\ one of the four archangels named in Hebrew tradition — compare MICHAEL, RAPHAEL, URIEL

Ga•ga•rin \gə-ˈgär-ən\ Yu•ry \ˈyu̇(ə)r-ē\ Alekseyevich 1934–1968 Russian astronaut; first man in space

Gage \ˈgāj\ Thomas 1721–1787 British general in America

Gal•a•had \ˈgal-ə-ˌhad\ knight of the Round Table who finds the Holy Grail

Gal•a•tea \ˌgal-ə-ˈtē-ə\ a female figure sculpted by Pygmalion in Greek mythology and given life by Aphrodite in answer to the sculptor's prayer

Ga•len \ˈgā-lən\ 129–*about* 199 A.D. Greek physician and writer

Ga•li•lei \ˌgal-ə-ˈlā-ˌē\ Ga•li•leo \ˌgal-ə-ˈlē-ō, -ˈlā-\ 1564–1642 usually called *Galileo* Italian astronomer and physicist — **Gal•i•le•an** \ˌgal-ə-ˈlē-ən\ *adj*

Gall \ˈgȯl\ 1840?–1894 Sioux leader

Ga•ma, da \ˈgam-ə, ˈgäm-\ Vasco *about* 1460–1524 Portuguese navigator

Gan•dhi \ˈgän-dē, ˈgan-\ Mohandas Karamchand 1869–1948 *Ma•hat•ma* \mə-ˈhät-mə, -ˈhat-\ Indian leader

Gar•field \ˈgär-ˌfēld\ James Abram 1831–1881 20th president of the U.S. (1881)

Gar•i•bal•di \ˌgar-ə-ˈbȯl-dē\ Giuseppe 1807–1882 Italian patriot

Gar•ri•son \ˈgar-ə-sən\ William Lloyd 1805–1879 American abolitionist

Gau•guin \gō-gan\ (Eugène-Henri-) Paul 1848–1903 French painter

Gau•ta•ma Bud•dha \ˌgau̇t-ə-mə-ˈbüd-ə, -ˈbu̇d-\ *about*

563–*about* 483 B.C. *The Buddha* Indian philosopher; founder of Buddhism

Gen•ghis Khan \ˌjeŋ-gə-ˈskän, ˌgeŋ-\ *about* 1162–1227 Mongol conqueror

George \ˈjȯ(ə)rj\ name of six kings of Great Britain: **I** 1660–1727 (reigned 1714–27); **II** 1683–1760 (reigned 1727–60); **III** 1738–1820 (reigned 1760–1820); **IV** 1762–1830 (reigned 1820–30); **V** 1865–1936 (reigned 1910–36); **VI** 1895–1952 (reigned 1936–52)

Ge•ron•i•mo \jə-ˈrän-ə-ˌmō\ 1829–1909 Apache leader

Gersh•win \ˈgərsh-wən\ George 1898–1937 American composer

Gid•e•on \ˈgid-ē-ən\ Hebrew hero in the Bible

Gil•bert \ˈgil-bərt\ Sir William Schwenck 1836–1911 English librettist and poet; collaborator with Sir Arthur Sullivan

Glad•stone \ˈglad-ˌstōn, *chiefly British* -stən\ William Ewart 1809–1898 British prime minister (1868–74; 1880–85; 1886; 1892–94)

Glenn \ˈglen\ John Herschel 1921– American astronaut and politician; first American to orbit the earth (1962)

Go•di•va \gə-ˈdī-və\ an English gentlewoman who in legend rode naked through Coventry to save its citizens from a tax

Goe•thals \ˈgō-thəlz\ George Washington 1858–1928 American general and engineer

Goe•the \ˈgə(r)-tə\ Johann Wolfgang von 1749–1832 German author

Gogh, van \van-ˈgō, -ˈgäk, -ˈkȯk\ Vincent Willem 1853–1890 Dutch painter

Go•li•ath \gə-ˈlī-əth\ Philistine giant who is killed by David in the Bible

Gom•pers \ˈgäm-pərz\ Samuel 1850–1924 American (British-born) labor leader

Good•year \ˈgu̇d-ˌyi(ə)r, ˈgu̇j-ˌi(ə)r\ Charles 1800–1860 American inventor

Gor•gas \ˈgȯr-gəs\ William Crawford 1854–1920 American army surgeon

Gra•ham \ˈgrā-əm, ˈgra(-ə)m\ Martha 1893–1991 American dancer and choreographer

Grant \ˈgrant\ Ulysses 1822–1885 originally *Hiram Ulysses Grant* American general; 18th president of the U.S. (1869–77)

Gre•co, El \el-ˈgrek-ō\ 1541–1614 *Doménikos Theotokópoulos* Spanish (Cretan-born) painter

Gree•ley \ˈgrē-lē\ Horace 1811–1872 American journalist and politician

Greene \ˈgrēn\ Graham 1904–1991 British novelist

Greene Nathanael 1742–1786 American Revolutionary general

Greg•o•ry \ˈgreg-(ə-)rē\ name of 16 popes: especially **I** Saint *about* 540–604 *the Great* (pope 590–604); **VII** Saint *about* 1020–1085 (pope 1073–85); **XIII** 1502–1585 (pope 1572–85)

Grey \ˈgrā\ Lady Jane 1537–1554 English noblewoman beheaded as a possible rival for the throne of Mary I

Grey Zane 1875–1939 American novelist

Grimm \ˈgrim\ Jacob 1785–1863 and his brother Wilhelm 1786–1859 German philologists and folklorists

Guin•e•vere \ˈgwin-ə-ˌvi(ə)r\ wife of King Arthur and lover of Lancelot

Gu•ten•berg \ˈgüt-ᵊn-ˌbərg\ Johannes *about* 1390–1468 German inventor of printing from movable type

Ha•des \ˈhād-ˌēz\ — see PLUTO

Ha•dri•an \ˈhā-drē-ən\ 76–138 A.D. Roman emperor (117–138)

Ha•gar \ˈhā-ˌgär, -gər\ mistress of Abraham and mother of Ishmael in the Bible

Hai•le Se•las•sie \ˌhī-lē-sə-ˈlas-ē, -ˈläs-\ 1892–1975 emperor of Ethiopia (1930–36; 1941–74)

Hale \ˈhā(ə)l\ Edward Everett 1822–1909 American minister and author

Hale Nathan 1755–1776 American Revolutionary hero

Hal•ley \ˈhal-ē, ˈhā-lē\ Edmond *or* Edmund 1656–1742 English astronomer

Hal•sey \ˈhȯl-sē, -zē\ William Frederick 1882–1959 American admiral

Ham•il•ton \ˈham-əl-tən\ Alexander 1755–1804 American political leader

Ham•mu•ra•bi \ˌham-ə-ˈräb-ē\ *or* **Ham•mu•ra•pi** \-ˈräp-ē\ *died* 1750 B.C. king of Babylon (1792–50)

Han•cock \ˈhan-ˌkäk\ John 1737–1793 American Revolutionary patriot

Han•del \ˈhan-dᵊl\ George Frideric 1685–1759 British (German-born) composer

Han•dy \ˈhan-dē\ William Christopher 1873–1958 American blues musician

Han•ni•bal \ˈhan-ə-bəl\ 247–183 B.C. Carthaginian general

Har•ding \ˈhärd-iŋ\ Warren Gamaliel 1865–1923 29th president of the U.S. (1921–23)

Har•dy \ˈhärd-ē\ Thomas 1840–1928 English author

Har•ri•son \ˈhar-ə-sən\ Benjamin 1833–1901 23d president of the U.S. (1889–93)

Harrison William Henry 1773–1841 9th president of the U.S. (1841)

Harte \ˈhärt\ Francis Brett 1836–1902 known as *Bret* American author

Har•vey \ˈhär-vē\ William 1578–1657 English physician and anatomist

Haw•thorne \ˈhȯ-ˌthȯ(ə)rn\ Nathaniel 1804–1864 American author

Hayes \ˈhāz\ Rutherford Birchard 1822–1893 19th president of the U.S. (1877–81)

Hearst \ˈhərst\ William Randolph 1863–1951 American newspaper publisher

Hec•tor \ˈhek-tər\ son of Priam and Trojan hero slain by Achilles in Greek mythology

Hec•u•ba \ˈhek-yə-bə\ wife of Priam in Greek mythology

Hel•en of Troy \ˌhel-ə-nəv-ˈtrȯi\ wife of Menelaus whose abduction by Paris in Greek mythology caused the Trojan War

He•li•os \ˈhē-lē-əs, -ōs\ god of the sun in Greek mythology

Hem•ing•way \ˈhem-iŋ-ˌwā\ Ernest Miller 1899–1961 American author; Nobel Prize winner (1954)

Hen•ry \ˈhen-rē\ name of eight kings of England: **I** 1068–1135 (reigned 1100–35); **II** 1133–1189 (reigned 1154–89); **III** 1207–1272 (reigned 1216–72); **IV** 1367–1413 (reigned 1399–1413); **V** 1387–1422 (reigned 1413–22); **VI** 1421–1471 (reigned 1422–61; 1470–71); **VII** 1457–1509 (reigned 1485–1509); **VIII** 1491–1547 (reigned 1509–47)

Henry name of 4 kings of France: **I** 1008–1060 (reigned 1031–60); **II** 1519–1559 (reigned 1547–59); **III** 1551–1589 (reigned 1574–89); **IV** 1553–1610 *Henry of Navarre* (reigned 1589–1610)

Henry O. — see William Sydney PORTER

Henry Patrick 1736–1799 American patriot and orator

He•phaes•tus \hi-ˈfes-təs, -ˈfēs-\ god of fire and of metalworking in Greek mythology — compare VULCAN

He•ra \ˈhir-ə, ˈhē-rə\ sister and wife of Zeus and goddess of women and marriage in Greek mythology — compare JUNO

Her•cu•les \ˈhər-kyə-ˌlēz\ *or* **Her•a•cles** \ˈher-ə-ˌklēz\ hero in Greek mythology noted for his strength and for performing 12 labors imposed on him by Hera

Her•maph•ro•di•tus \(ˌ)hər-ˌmaf-rə-ˈdīt-əs\ son of Hermes and Aphrodite who in Greek mythology is joined with a nymph into one body

Her•mes \ˈhər-mēz\ god of commerce, eloquence, invention, travel, and theft who serves as herald and messenger of the other gods in Greek mythology

Her•od \ˈher-əd\ 73–4 B.C. *the Great* Roman king of Judea (37–4)

Herod An•ti•pas \ˈant-ə-ˌpas, -pəs\ 21 B.C.–39 A.D. Roman governor of Galilee (4 B.C.–39 A.D.); son of Herod the Great

Hey•er•dahl \ˈhā-ər-ˌdäl, ˈhī-\ Thor 1914– Norwegian explorer and author

Hi·a·wa·tha \ˌhī-ə-ˈwȯ-thə, ˌhē-ə-, -ˈwäth-ə\ legendary Iroquois chief

Hick·ok \ˈhik-ˌäk\ James Butler 1837–1876 *Wild Bill* American scout and United States marshal

Hil·ton \ˈhilt-ᵊn\ James 1900–1954 English novelist

Hip·poc·ra·tes \hip-ˈäk-rə-ˌtēz\ *about* 460–*about* 377 B.C. *founder of medicine* Greek physician

Hi·ro·hi·to \ˌhir-ō-ˈhē-tō\ 1901–1989 emperor of Japan (1926–89)

Hit·ler \ˈhit-lər\ Adolf 1889–1945 German (Austrian-born) chancellor (1933–45)

Holmes \ˈhōmz, ˈhōlmz\ Oliver Wendell 1809–1894 American physician and author

Holmes Oliver Wendell 1841–1935 American jurist; son of the preceding

Ho·mer \ˈhō-mər\ 9th–8th? century B.C. Greek epic poet — **Ho·mer·ic** \hō-ˈmer-ik\ *adj*

Homer Winslow 1836–1910 American painter

Hooke \ˈhu̇k\ Robert 1635–1703 English scientist

Hook·er \ˈhu̇k-ər\ Thomas 1586?–1647 English colonist; a founder of Connecticut

Hoo·ver \ˈhü-vər\ Herbert Clark 1874–1964 31st president of the U.S. (1929–33)

Hoover John Edgar 1895–1972 American criminologist; director of the Federal Bureau of Investigation (1924–72)

Hou·di·ni \hü-ˈdē-nē\ Harry 1874–1926 originally *Ehrich Weiss* American magician

Hous·ton \ˈ(h)yü-stən\ Samuel 1793–1863 *Sam* American general; president of the Republic of Texas (1836–38; 1841–44)

Howe \ˈhau̇\ Elias 1819–1867 American inventor

Howe Julia 1819–1910 née *Ward* American suffragist and reformer

Hud·son \ˈhəd-sən\ Henry *died* 1611 English navigator and explorer

Hughes \ˈhyüz *also* ˈyüz\ (James) Langston 1902–1967 American author

Hus·sein I \hü-ˈsān\ 1935– king of Jordan (1952–)

Hutch·in·son \ˈhəch-ə(n)-sən\ Anne 1591–1643 religious leader in America

Hutchinson Thomas 1711–1780 American colonial administrator

Hux·ley \ˈhək-slē\ Aldous Leonard 1894–1963 English author

Hy·men \ˈhī-mən\ god of marriage in Greek mythology

Ib·sen \ˈib-sən, ˈip-\ Henrik 1828–1906 Norwegian dramatist and poet

Ic·a·rus \ˈik-ə-rəs\ son of Daedalus who in Greek mythology falls into the sea when the wax of his artificial wings melts as he flies too near the sun

Ig·na·tius \ig-ˈnā-sh(ē-)əs\ *Saint Ignatius of Loy·o·la* \lȯi-ˈō-lə\ 1491–1556 Spanish soldier and priest; founded the Society of Jesus

In·no·cent \ˈin-ə-sənt\ name of 13 popes: especially **II** *died* 1143 (pope 1130–43); **III** 1160 (or 1161)–1216 (pope 1198–1216); **IV** *died* 1254 (pope 1243–54); **XI** 1611–1689 (pope 1676–89)

Ir·ving \ˈər-viŋ\ Washington 1783–1859 American author

Isaac \ˈī-zik, -zək\ son of Abraham and father of Jacob in the Bible

Is·a·bel·la I \ˌiz-ə-ˈbel-ə\ 1451–1504 queen of Castile (1474–1504) and of Aragon (1479–1504); wife of Ferdinand V of Castile

Isa·iah \ī-ˈzā-ə\ Hebrew prophet of the 8th century B.C.

Ish·ma·el \ˈish-(ˌ)mā-əl, -mē-\ outcast son of Abraham and Hagar in the Bible

Ives \ˈīvz\ Charles Edward 1874–1954 American composer

Jack·son \ˈjak-sən\ Andrew 1767–1845 American general; 7th president of the U.S. (1829–37)

Jackson Thomas Jonathan 1824–1863 *Stonewall* American Confederate general

Ja·cob \ˈjā-kəb\ son of Isaac and Rebekah and younger twin brother of Esau in the Bible

James \ˈjāmz\ one of the 12 apostles in the Bible

James *the Less* one of the 12 apostles in the Bible

James name of two kings of Great Britain: **I** 1566–1625 (reigned 1603–25); king of Scotland as *James VI* (reigned 1567–1603); **II** 1633–1701 (reigned 1685–88)

James Henry 1843–1916 British (American-born) author

Ja·nus \ˈjā-nəs\ god of gates and doors and of beginnings and endings in Roman mythology who is usually pictured as having two opposite faces

Ja·son \ˈjās-ᵊn\ hero in Greek mythology noted for his successful quest of the Golden Fleece

Jay \ˈjā\ John 1745–1829 American jurist and political leader; 1st chief justice of the U.S. Supreme Court (1789–95)

Jef·fer·son \ˈjef-ər-sən\ Thomas 1743–1826 3d president of the U.S. (1801–09) — **Jef·fer·so·nian** \ˌjef-ər-ˈsō-nē-ən, -nyən\ *adj*

Jer·e·mi·ah \ˌjer-ə-ˈmī-ə\ Hebrew prophet of the 6th and 7th centuries B.C.

Je·sus \ˈjē-zəs, -zəz\ *or* **Jesus Christ** \ˈkrīst\ *or* **Christ Jesus** *about* 6 B.C.–*about* 30 A.D. source of the Christian religion and Savior in the Christian faith

Jez·e·bel \ˈjez-ə-ˌbel\ queen of Israel and wife of Ahab who was noted for her wickedness

Joan of Arc \ˌjō-nə-ˈvärk\ Saint *about* 1412–1431 *the Maid of Orleans* French national heroine

Job \ˈjōb\ man in the Bible who has many sufferings but keeps his faith

Jo·cas·ta \jō-ˈkas-tə\ queen of Thebes in Greek mythology who unknowingly marries her son Oedipus

John \ˈjän\ *the Baptist* prophet and baptizer of Jesus in the Bible

John one of the 12 apostles believed to be the author of the fourth Gospel, three Epistles, and the Book of Revelation

John name of 21 popes: especially **XXIII** 1881–1963 (pope 1958–63)

John 1167–1216 *John Lack·land* \ˈlak-ˌland\ king of England (1199–1216)

John·son \ˈjän(t)-sən\ Andrew 1808–1875 17th president of the U.S. (1865–69)

Johnson Lyndon Baines 1908–1973 36th president of the U.S. (1963–69)

Johnson Samuel 1709–1784 *Dr. Johnson* English lexicographer and author

Jol·liet *or* **Jo·liet** \zhȯl-ˈyā, ˌjō-lē-ˈet\ Louis 1645–1700 French explorer in America

Jo·nah \ˈjō-nə\ Hebrew prophet who in the Bible spends three days in the belly of a great fish

Jones \ˈjōnz\ John Paul 1747–1792 American (Scottish-born) naval officer

Jop·lin \ˈjäp-lən\ Scott 1868–1917 American pianist and composer

Jo·seph \ˈjō-zəf *also* -səf\ a son of Jacob in the Bible who rose to high office in Egypt after being sold into slavery by his brothers

Joseph *about* 1840–1904 Nez Percé Indian chief

Joseph Saint husband of Mary, the mother of Jesus, in the Bible

Josh·ua \ˈjäsh-(ə-)wə\ Hebrew leader in the Bible who succeeds Moses during the settlement of the Israelites in Canaan

Ju·dah \ˈjüd-ə\ son of Jacob and ancestor of one of the 12 tribes of Israel in the Bible

Ju·das \ˈjüd-əs\ or **Judas Is·car·i·ot** \-is-ˈkar-ē-ət\ one of the 12 apostles and the betrayer of Jesus in the Bible

Ju·no \ˈjü-nō\ the queen of heaven in Roman mythology, wife of Jupiter, and goddess of light, birth, women, and marriage — compare HERA

Ju·pi·ter \ˈjü-pət-ər\ the chief god in Roman mythology, husband of Juno, and the god of light, of the sky and weather, and of the state

Kalb \ˈkälp, ˈkalb\ Johann 1721–1780 Baron *de Kalb*

DICTIONARY

\di-ˈkalb\ German general in American Revolutionary army
Keats \ˈkēts\ John 1795–1821 English poet
Kel•ler \ˈkel-ər\ Helen Adams 1880–1968 American deaf and blind lecturer
Kel•vin \ˈkel-vən\ 1st Baron 1824–1907 *William Thomson* British mathematician and physicist
Ken•ne•dy \ˈken-əd-ē\ John Fitzgerald 1917–1963 35th president of the U.S. (1961–63)
Kennedy Robert Francis 1925–1968 American politician; attorney general of the U.S. (1961–64); brother of John F. Kennedy
Ke•o•kuk \ˈkē-ə-ˌkək\ 1788?–?1848 American Indian chief
Key \ˈkē\ Francis Scott 1779–1843 American lawyer; author of "The Star-Spangled Banner"
Khayyám Omar — see OMAR KHAYYÁM
Khru•shchev \krüsh-ˈ(ch)öf, -ˈ(ch)öv, -ˈ(ch)ef\ Ni•ki•ta \nə-ˈkēt-ə\ Sergeyevich 1894–1971 premier of U.S.S.R. (1958–64)
Khu•fu \ˈkü-fü\ *or Greek* **Che•ops** \ˈkē-ˌäps\ 26th century B.C. king of Egypt and pyramid builder
Kidd \ˈkid\ William *about* 1645–1701 *Captain Kidd* Scottish pirate
King \ˈkiŋ\ Martin Luther, Jr. 1929–1968 American minister and civil rights leader; Nobel Prize winner (1964)
Kip•ling \ˈkip-liŋ\ Rud•yard \ˈrəd-yərd, ˈrəj-ərd\ 1865–1936 English author
Kis•sin•ger \ˈkis-ᵊn-jər\ Henry Alfred 1923– American (German-born) scholar and government official; U.S. secretary of state (1973–77); Nobel Prize winner (1973)
Knox \ˈnäks\ John *about* 1514–1572 Scottish religious reformer
Koch \ˈkök, ˈkȯk\ Robert 1843–1910 German bacteriologist; Nobel Prize winner (1905)
Kos̍•ciusz•ko \ˌkäs-ē-ˈəs-ˌkō, kösh-ˈchüsh-kō\ Tadeusz 1746–1817 Polish patriot and general in American Revolutionary army
Krish•na \ˈkrish-nə\ god worshipped in later Hinduism
Kriss Kringle — see SANTA CLAUS
Ku•blai Khan \ˌkü-blə-ˈkän, -ˌblī-\ 1215–1294 founder of Mongol dynasty in China
La•fa•yette \ˌläf-ē-ˈet, ˌlaf-\ Marquis de 1757–1834 French general in American Revolutionary army
La•ius \ˈlā-(y)əs, ˈlī-əs\ king of Thebes who in Greek mythology is killed by his son Oedipus
Lan•ce•lot \ˈlan(t)-sə-ˌlät\ legendary knight of the Round Table and lover of Queen Guinevere
La Salle \lə-ˈsal\ Sieur de 1643–1687 French explorer in America
La•voi•sier \ləv-ˈwäz-ē-ˌā\ Antoine-Laurent 1743–1794 French chemist
Law•rence \ˈlör-ən(t)s, ˈlär-\ Thomas Edward 1888–1935 *Lawrence of Arabia* later surnamed *Shaw* British archaeologist, soldier, and author
Laz•a•rus \ˈlaz-(ə-)rəs\ brother of Mary and Martha who in the Bible is raised by Jesus from the dead
Lazarus beggar in the biblical parable of the rich man and the beggar
Le•da \ˈlēd-ə\ a queen of Sparta in Greek mythology who is courted by Zeus in the form of a swan
Lee \ˈlē\ Ann 1736–1784 English mystic; founder of Shaker society in the U.S.
Lee Henry 1756–1818 *Light-Horse Harry* American general
Lee Robert Edward 1807–1870 American Confederate general
Leeu•wen•hoek \ˈlā-vən-ˌhük\ Antonie van 1632–1723 Dutch naturalist
Leif Er•iks•son \ˌlā-ˈver-ik-sən, ˌlē-ˈfer-\ *or* **Er•ics•son** *flourished* 1000 Norwegian explorer; son of Erik the Red
Le•nin \ˈlen-ən\ 1870–1924 originally *Vladimir Ilyich Ul•ya•nov* \ül-ˈyän-əf, -ˌöf, -ˌöv\ Russian Communist leader
Leo \ˈlē-ō\ name of 13 popes: especially **I** Saint *died* 461 (pope 440–61); **III** Saint *died* 816 (pope 795–816); **XIII** 1810–1903 (pope 1878–1903)
Le•o•nar•do da Vin•ci \ˌlē-ə-ˈnärd-ˌōd-ə-ˈvin-chē, ˌlā-, -ˈvēn-\ 1452–1519 Italian painter, sculptor, architect, and engineer
Lew•is \ˈlü-əs\ John Llewellyn 1880–1969 American labor leader
Lewis Meriwether 1774–1809 American explorer (with William Clark)
Lewis (Harry) Sinclair 1885–1951 American author; Nobel Prize winner (1930)
Lin•coln \ˈliŋ-kən\ Abraham 1809–1865 16th president of the U.S. (1861–65)
Lind•bergh \ˈlin(d)-ˌbərg\ Charles Augustus 1902–1974 American aviator
Lin•nae•us \lə-ˈnē-əs, -ˈnā-\ Carolus 1707–1778 Swedish *Carl von Lin•né* \lə-ˈnā\ Swedish botanist
Lis•ter \ˈlis-tər\ Joseph 1827–1912 English surgeon
Liszt \ˈlist\ Franz 1811–1886 Hungarian pianist and composer
Liv•ing•stone \ˈliv-iŋ-stən\ David 1813–1873 Scottish explorer in Africa
Long•fel•low \ˈlöŋ-ˌfel-ō\ Henry Wads•worth \ˈwädz-(ˌ)wərth\ 1807–1882 American poet
Lou•is \ˈlü-ē, ˈlü-əs\ name of 18 kings of France: especially **IX** Saint 1214–1270 (reigned 1226–70); **XI** 1423–1483 (reigned 1461–83); **XII** 1462–1515 (reigned 1498–1515); **XIII** 1601–1643 (reigned 1610–43); **XIV** 1638–1715 (reigned 1643–1715); **XV** 1710–1774 (reigned 1715–74); **XVI** 1754–1793 (reigned 1774–92; guillotined); **XVII** 1785–1795 (reigned in name 1793–95); **XVIII** 1755–1824 (reigned 1814–15; 1815–24)
Low \ˈlō\ Juliette Gordon 1860–1927 American founder of the Girl Scouts
Low•ell \ˈlō-əl\ Amy 1874–1925 American poet
Lowell James Russell 1819–1891 American author
Luke \ˈlük\ physician and companion of the apostle Paul believed to be the author of the third Gospel and the Book of Acts
Lu•ther \ˈlü-thər\ Martin 1483–1546 German Reformation leader
Ly•on \ˈlī-ən\ Mary 1797–1849 American educator
Mac•Ar•thur \mə-ˈkär-thər\ Douglas 1880–1964 American general
Mc•Car•thy \mə-ˈkär-thē\ Joseph Raymond 1908–1957 American politician
Mc•Clel•lan \mə-ˈklel-ən\ George Brinton 1826–1885 American general
Mc•Cor•mick \mə-ˈkör-mik\ Cyrus Hall 1809–1884 American inventor
Mc•Kin•ley \mə-ˈkin-lē\ William 1843–1901 25th president of the U.S. (1897–1901)
Ma•cy \ˈmā-sē\ Anne Sullivan 1866–1936 American educator; teacher of Helen Keller
Mad•i•son \ˈmad-ə-sən\ James 1751–1836 4th president of the U.S. (1809–17)
Ma•gel•lan \mə-ˈjel-ən\ Ferdinand *about* 1480–1521 Portuguese navigator
Mal•colm X \ˌmal-kə-ˈmeks\ 1925–1965 American civil rights leader
Ma•net \ma-ˈnā, mä-\ Édouard 1832–1883 French painter
Mann \ˈman\ Horace 1796–1859 American educator
Mao Tse-tung \ˌmaü(d)-zə-ˈdüŋ, ˌmaüt-sə-\ 1893–1976 Chinese Communist; leader of People's Republic of China (1949–76)
Mar•co•ni \mär-ˈkō-nē\ Guglielmo 1874–1937 Italian physicist and inventor; Nobel Prize winner (1909)
Ma•rie An•toi•nette \mə-ˈrē-ˌan-t(w)ə-ˈnet\ 1755–1793 wife of Louis XVI
Mar•i•on \ˈmer-ē-ən, ˈmar-ē-\ Francis 1732?–1795 *the Swamp Fox* American commander in Revolution

Mark \ˈmärk\ evangelist believed to be the author of the second Gospel
Mar•quette \mär-ˈket\ Jacques 1637–1675 French-born Jesuit missionary and explorer in America
Mars \ˈmärz\ the god of war in Roman mythology
Mar•shall \ˈmär-shəl\ George Catlett 1880–1959 American general and diplomat
Marshall John 1755–1835 American jurist; chief justice of the U.S. Supreme Court (1801–35)
Mar•tha \ˈmär-thə\ sister of Lazarus and Mary and friend of Jesus in the Bible
Mar•tin \ˈmärt-ᵊn\ Saint *about* 316–397 *Martin of Tours* \-ˈtu̇(ə)r\ patron saint of France
Marx \ˈmärks\ Karl 1818–1883 German political philosopher and socialist
Mary \ˈme(ə)r-ē, ˈma(ə)r-ē, ˈmā-rē\ mother of Jesus
Mary sister of Lazarus and Martha in the Bible
Mary I 1516–1558 *Mary Tudor; Bloody Mary* queen of England (1553–58)
Mary II 1662–1694 joint British sovereign with William III (1689–94)
Mary Mag•da•lene \-ˈmag-də-ˌlən, -ˌlēn\ woman in the Bible who was healed of evil spirits by Jesus and who later saw the risen Christ
Mary Stuart 1542–1587 *Mary, Queen of Scots* queen of Scotland (1542–87)
Mas•sa•soit \ˌmas-ə-ˈsȯit\ *died* 1661 Indian chief in eastern Massachusetts
Math•er \ˈmat͟h-ər, ˈmath-\ Cotton 1663–1728 American religious leader and author
Mather Increase 1639–1723 American minister and author; father of Cotton Mather
Mat•thew \ˈmath-yü\ apostle believed to be the author of the first Gospel
Mau•pas•sant \ˌmō-pə-ˈsänt\ (Henri-René-Albert-) Guy de 1850–1893 French short-story writer
Mead \ˈmēd\ Margaret 1901–1978 American anthropologist
Meade \ˈmēd\ George Gordon 1815–1872 American general
Mea•ny \ˈmē-nē\ George 1894–1980 American labor leader
Me•dea \mə-ˈdē-ə\ woman with magic powers in Greek mythology who helps Jason to win the Golden Fleece and who kills her children when he leaves her
Me•di•ci, de' \ˈmed-ə-chē\ Catherine 1519–1589 French *Catherine de Médicis* \ˌmād-ə-ˈsē(s)\ queen of Henry II of France
Me•ir \me-ˈi(ə)r\ Golda 1898–1978 prime minister of Israel (1969–74)
Mel•ville \ˈmel-ˌvil\ Herman 1819–1891 American author
Men•del \ˈmen-dᵊl\ Gregor Johann 1822–1884 Austrian botanist
Men•e•la•us \ˌmen-ᵊl-ˈā-əs\ king of Sparta, brother of Agamemnon, and husband of Helen of Troy in Greek mythology
Meph•is•toph•e•les \ˌmef-ə-ˈstäf-ə-ˌlēz\ chief devil in the Faust legend
Mer•ca•tor \(ˌ)mər-ˈkāt-ər\ Gerardus 1512–1594 Flemish mapmaker
Mer•cu•ry \ˈmər-kyə-rē, -k(ə-)rē\ god of commerce, eloquence, travel, and theft who serves as herald and messenger of the other gods in Roman mythology
Mer•lin \ˈmər-lən\ prophet and magician in the legend of King Arthur
Mi•chael \ˈmī-kəl\ one of the four archangels named in Hebrew tradition — compare GABRIEL, RAPHAEL, URIEL
Mi•chel•an•ge•lo \ˌmī-kə-ˈlan-jə-ˌlō, ˌmik-ə-ˈlan-, ˌmē-kə-ˈlän-\ 1475–1564 Italian sculptor, painter, architect, and poet
Mi•das \ˈmīd-əs\ legendary king who was given the power to turn everything he touched into gold
Mil•lay \mil-ˈā\ Edna St. Vincent 1892–1950 American poet
Mil•ler \ˈmil-ər\ Arthur 1915– American author
Mil•ton \ˈmilt-ᵊn\ John 1608–1674 English poet
Mi•ner•va \mə-ˈnər-və\ goddess of wisdom in Roman mythology — compare ATHENA
Mi•no•taur \ˈmin-ə-ˌtȯ(ə)r, ˈmī-nə-\ monster in Greek mythology shaped half like a man and half like a bull
Min•u•it \ˈmin-yə-wət\ Peter 1580–1638 Dutch colonial administrator in America
Mitch•ell \ˈmich-əl\ Maria 1818–1889 American astronomer
Mo•lière \mōl-ˈye(ə)r, ˈmōl-ˌye(ə)r\ 1622–1673 originally *Jean-Baptiste Poquelin* French actor and dramatist
Mo•net \mō-ˈnā\ Claude 1840–1926 French painter
Mon•roe \mən-ˈrō\ James 1758–1831 5th president of the U.S. (1817–25)
Mont•calm de Saint-Vé•ran \mänt-ˈkäm-də-ˌsan-vā-ˈrän, -ˈkälm-\ Marquis de 1712–1759 French field marshal in Canada
Mon•tes•so•ri \ˌmänt-ə-ˈsōr-ē, -ˈsȯr-\ Maria 1870–1952 Italian physician and educator
Mon•te•zu•ma II \ˌmänt-ə-ˈzü-mə\ 1466–1520 last Aztec emperor of Mexico (1502–20)
Moore \ˈmō(ə)r, ˈmȯ(ə)r, ˈmu̇(ə)r\ Marianne Craig 1887–1972 American poet
More \ˈmō(ə)r, ˈmȯ(ə)r\ Sir Thomas 1478–1535 *Saint* English public official and author
Mor•gan \ˈmȯr-gən\ John Pierpont 1837–1913 American financier
Mor•ri•son \ˈmȯr-ə-sən, ˌmär-\ Toni 1931– American author
Morse \ˈmȯ(ə)rs\ Samuel Finley Breese 1791–1872 American artist and inventor
Mo•ses \ˈmō-zəz *also* -zəs\ Hebrew prophet and lawgiver who in the Bible freed the Israelites from slavery in Egypt
Mott \ˈmät\ Lucretia 1793–1880 American reformer
Mo•zart \ˈmōt-ˌsärt\ Wolfgang Amadeus 1756–1791 Austrian composer
Mu•ham•mad \mō-ˈham-əd, -ˈhäm- *also* mü-\ *about* 570–632 Arab prophet and founder of Islam
Mus•so•li•ni \ˌmü-sə-ˈlē-nē, ˌmu̇s-ə-\ Be•ni•to \bə-ˈnēt-ō\ 1883–1945 *Il Du•ce* \ēl-ˈdü-chā\ Italian fascist premier (1922–43)
Na•po•léon I \nə-ˈpōl-yən, -ˈpō-lē-ən\ *or* **Napoléon Bo•na•parte** \ˈbō-nə-ˌpärt\ 1769–1821 emperor of the French (1804–15) — **Na•po•le•on•ic** \nə-ˌpō-lē-ˈän-ik\ *adj*
Nar•cis•sus \när-ˈsis-əs\ a beautiful youth in Greek mythology who pines away for love of his own reflection and is then turned into the narcissus flower
Nash \ˈnash\ Ogden 1902–1971 American poet
Na•tion \ˈnā-shən\ Car•ry \ˈkar-ē\ Amelia 1846–1911 American social reformer
Neb•u•cha•drez•zar II \ˌneb-(y)ə-kə-ˈdrez-ər\ *also* **Neb•u•chad•nez•zar** \-kəd-ˈnez-\ *about* 630–562 B.C. Chaldean king of Babylon (605–562)
Neh•ru \ˈne(ə)r-ˌü, ˈnā-rü\ Ja•wa•har•lal \jə-ˈwä-hər-ˌläl\ 1889–1964 Indian nationalist; 1st prime minister (1947–64)
Nel•son \ˈnel-sən\ Horatio 1758–1805 Viscount *Nelson* British admiral
Nem•e•sis \ˈnem-ə-səs\ the goddess of reward and punishment in Greek mythology
Nep•tune \ˈnep-ˌt(y)ün\ the god of the sea in Roman mythology
Ne•ro \ˈnē-ˌrō, ˈni(ə)r-ō\ 37–68 A.D. Roman emperor (54–68)
New•ton \ˈn(y)üt-ᵊn\ Sir Isaac 1642–1727 English mathematician and physicist
Nich•o•las \ˈnik-(ə-)ləs\ Saint 4th century Christian bishop
Nicholas I 1796–1855 czar of Russia (1825–55)
Nicholas II 1868–1918 czar of Russia (1894–1917)
Night•in•gale \ˈnīt-ᵊn-ˌgāl, -iŋ-\ Florence 1820–1910 English nurse and philanthropist

Ni•ke \ˈnī-kē\ the goddess of victory in Greek mythology

Ni•o•be \ˈnī-ə-bē\ a daughter of Tantalus in Greek mythology who while weeping for her slain children is turned into a stone from which her tears continue to flow

Nix•on \ˈnik-sən\ Richard Mil•hous \ˈmil-ˌhau̇s\ 1913–1994 37th president of the U.S. (1969–74)

No•ah \ˈnō-ə\ Old Testament builder of the ark in which he, his family, and living creatures of every kind survived the Flood

No•bel \nō-ˈbel\ Alfred Bernhard 1833–1896 Swedish manufacturer, inventor, and philanthropist

Oce•anus \ō-ˈsē-ə-nəs\ a Titan who rules over a great river encircling the earth in Greek mythology

Odin \ˈōd-ᵊn\ *or* **Wo•den** \ˈwōd-ᵊn\ god of war and patron of heroes in Norse mythology

Odys•seus \ō-ˈdis-ē-əs, -ˈdis-yəs, -ˈdish-əs, -ˈdish-ˌüs\ or **Ulys•ses** \yu̇-ˈlis-ēz\ king of Ithaca and hero in Greek mythology who after the Trojan war wanders for 10 years before reaching home

Oe•di•pus \ˈed-ə-pəs, ˈēd-\ son of Laius and Jocasta who in Greek mythology kills his father and marries his mother not knowing their identity

Ogle•thorpe \ˈō-gəl-ˌthȯrp\ James Edward 1696–1785 English general and philanthropist; founder of Georgia

O'•Keeffe \ō-ˈkēf\ Georgia 1887–1986 American painter

Omar Khay•yám \ˌō-ˌmär-ˌkī-ˈ(y)äm, ˌō-mər-, -ˈ(y)am\ 1048?–1122 Persian poet and astronomer

O'•Neill \ō-ˈnē(ə)l\ Eugene Gladstone 1888–1953 American dramatist; Nobel Prize winner (1936)

Or•pheus \ˈȯr-ˌfyüs, -fē-əs\ poet and musician in Greek mythology who almost rescues his wife Eurydice from Hades by charming Pluto and Persephone with his lyre

Or•well \ˈȯr-ˌwel, -wəl\ George 1903–1950 pseudonym of *Eric Blair* English author — **Or•well•ian** \ȯr-ˈwel-ē-ən\ *adj*

Osce•o•la \ˌäs-ē-ˈō-lə, ˌō-sē-\ *about* 1800–1838 Seminole chief

Otis \ˈōt-əs\ James 1725–1783 American Revolutionary patriot

Ov•id \ˈäv-əd\ 43 B.C.–17 A.D.? Roman poet

Ow•en \ˈō-ən\ Robert 1771–1858 Welsh social reformer

Ow•ens \ˈō-ənz\ Jesse 1913–1980 originally *James Cleveland* American athlete

Paine \ˈpān\ Thomas 1737–1809 American (English-born) political philosopher and author

Pan \ˈpan\ god of forests, pastures, flocks, and shepherds in Greek mythology who is represented as having the legs, ears, and horns of a goat

Pan•do•ra \pan-ˈdōr-ə, -ˈdȯr-\ woman in Greek mythology who out of curiosity opened a box and let loose all of the evils that trouble humans

Par•is \ˈpar-əs\ son of Priam whose abduction of Helen of Troy in Greek mythology led to the Trojan War

Park•man \ˈpärk-mən\ Francis 1823–1893 American historian

Pas•cal \pas-ˈkal\ Blaise 1623–1662 French mathematician and philosopher

Pas•ter•nak \ˈpas-tər-ˌnak\ Boris Leonidovich 1890–1960 Russian author; Nobel Prize winner (1958)

Pas•teur \pas-ˈtər\ Louis 1822–1895 French chemist and microbiologist

Pat•rick \ˈpa-trik\ Saint 5th century apostle and patron saint of Ireland

Pat•ton \ˈpat-ᵊn\ George Smith 1885–1945 American general

Paul \ˈpȯl\ Saint *died between* 62 *and* 68 A.D. author of several New Testament epistles — **Pau•line** \ˈpȯ-ˌlīn\ *adj*

Paul name of six popes: especially **III** 1468–1549 (pope 1534–49); **V** 1552–1621 (pope 1605–21); **VI** 1897–1978 (pope 1963–78)

Paul Bun•yan \ˈpȯl-ˈbən-yən\ giant lumberjack in American folklore

Pau•ling \ˈpȯ-liŋ\ Linus Carl 1901–1994 American chemist; Nobel Prize winner (1954, 1962)

Pav•lov \ˈpäv-ˌlȯf, ˈpav-, -ˌlȯv\ Ivan Petrovich 1849–1936 Russian physiologist; Nobel Prize winner (1904)

Pa•vlo•va \ˈpav-lə-və, pav-ˈlō-və\ Anna 1882–1931 Russian ballerina

Pea•ry \ˈpi(ə)r-ē\ Robert Edwin 1856–1920 American arctic explorer

Pe•cos Bill \ˌpā-kəs-ˈbil\ a cowboy in American folklore known for his extraordinary feats

Peg•a•sus \ˈpeg-ə-səs\ winged horse in Greek mythology

Penn \ˈpen\ William 1644–1718 English Quaker; founder of Pennsylvania

Per•i•cles \ˈper-ə-ˌklēz\ *about* 495–429 B.C. Athenian political leader

Per•ry \ˈper-ē\ Matthew Calbraith 1794–1858 American commodore

Perry Oliver Hazard 1785–1819 American naval officer

Per•seph•o•ne \pər-ˈsef-ə-nē \ daughter of Zeus and Demeter who in Greek mythology is abducted by Pluto to rule with him over the underworld

Per•shing \ˈpər-shiŋ, -zhiŋ\ John Joseph 1860–1948 American general

Pe•ter \ˈpēt-ər\ Saint *died about* 64 A.D. *Si•mon Peter* \ˈsī-mən-\ one of the 12 apostles in the Bible

Peter I 1672–1725 *the Great* czar of Russia (1682–1725)

Phil•ip \ˈfil-əp\ one of the 12 apostles in the Bible

Philip 1639?–1676 American Indian chief

Philip name of six kings of France: especially **II** *or* **Philip Augustus** 1165–1223 (reigned 1179–1223); **IV** 1268–1314 (reigned 1285–1314) *the Fair*; **VI** 1293–1350 (reigned 1328–50)

Philip name of five kings of Spain: especially **II** 1527–1598 (reigned 1556–98); **V** 1683–1746 (reigned 1700–46)

Philip II 382–336 B.C. king of Macedon (359–336); father of Alexander the Great

Pi•cas•so \pi-ˈkäs-ō, -ˈkas-\ Pablo 1881–1973 Spanish painter and sculptor in France

Pick•ett \ˈpik-ət\ George Edward 1825–1875 American Confederate general

Pierce \ˈpi(ə)rs\ Franklin 1804–1869 14th president of the U.S. (1853–57)

Pi•late \ˈpī-lət\ Pon•tius \ˈpän-chəs, ˈpən-chəs\ *died* after 36 A.D. Roman governor of Judea

Pitt \ˈpit\ William 1759–1806 English prime minister (1783–1801; 1804–6)

Pi•us \ˈpī-əs\ name of 12 popes: especially **VII** 1742–1823 (pope 1800–23); **IX** 1792–1878 (pope 1846–78); **X** 1835–1914 (pope 1903–14); **XI** 1857–1939 (pope 1922–39); **XII** 1876–1958 (pope 1939–58)

Pi•zar•ro \pə-ˈzär-ō\ Francisco *about* 1475–1541 Spanish conqueror of Peru

Pla•to \ˈplāt-ō\ *about* 428–348 (*or* 347) B.C. Greek philosopher

Plu•to \ˈplüt-ō\ god of the dead and the underworld in Greek mythology

Po•ca•hon•tas \ˌpō-kə-ˈhänt-əs\ *about* 1595–1617 American Indian princess

Poe \ˈpō\ Edgar Allan 1809–1849 American author

Polk \ˈpōk\ James Knox 1795–1849 11th president of the U.S. (1845–49)

Po•lo \ˈpō-lō\ Mar•co \ˈmär-kō\ 1254–1324 Venetian traveler

Poly•phe•mus \ˌpäl-ə-ˈfē-məs\ a Cyclops in Greek mythology who is blinded by Odysseus

Ponce de Le•ón \ˌpän(t)-sə-ˌdā-lē-ˈōn, ˌpän(t)s-də-ˈlē-ən\ Juan 1460–1521 Spanish explorer and discoverer of Florida (1513)

Pon•ti•ac \ˈpänt-ē-ˌak\ *about* 1720–1769 Ottawa chief

Por·ter \ˈpōrt-ər, ˈpȯrt-\ Cole Albert 1891–1964 American composer and songwriter

Porter David Dixon 1813–1891 American admiral

Porter Katherine Anne 1890–1980 American author

Porter William Sydney 1862–1910 pseudonym *O. Henry* \(ˈ)ō-ˈhen-rē\ American author

Po·sei·don \pə-ˈsīd-ᵊn\ god of the sea in Greek mythology — compare NEPTUNE

Pot·ter \ˈpät-ər\ Beatrix 1866–1943 British author and illustrator

Pow·ha·tan \ˌpau̇-ə-ˈtan, pau̇-ˈhat-ᵊn\ 1550?–1618 American Indian chief

Pri·am \ˈprī-əm, -ˌam\ king of Troy during the Trojan War in Greek mythology

Pro·me·theus \prə-ˈmē-th(y)üs, -thē-əs\ a Titan in Greek mythology who is punished by Zeus for stealing fire from heaven and giving it to human beings

Pro·teus \ˈprō-ˌt(y)üs, ˈprōt-ē-əs\ sea god in Greek mythology who is capable of assuming different forms

Puc·ci·ni \pü-ˈchē-nē\ Giacomo 1858–1924 Italian composer

Pu·las·ki \pə-ˈlas-kē, pyü-\ Kazimierz 1747–1779 Polish soldier in American Revolutionary army

Pu·lit·zer \ˈpu̇l-ət-sər, ˈpyü-lət-sər\ Joseph 1847–1911 American (Hungarian-born) journalist

Pyg·ma·lion \pig-ˈmāl-yən, -ˈmā-lē-ən\ a sculptor in Greek mythology who falls in love with a statue which is then brought to life

Py·thag·o·ras \pə-ˈthag-ə-rəs, pī-\ *about* 580–*about* 500 B.C. Greek philosopher and mathematician

Ra \ˈrä, ˈrȯ\ god of the sun and chief deity of ancient Egypt

Ra·leigh *or* **Ra·legh** \ˈrȯl-ē, ˈräl- *also* ˈral-\ Sir Walter 1554–1618 English navigator and historian

Ram·ses \ˈram-ˌsēz\ *or* **Ram·e·ses** \ˈram-ə-ˌsēz\ name of 12 kings of Egypt: especially **II** (reigned 1304–1237 B.C.); **III** (reigned 1198–66 B.C.)

Ran·dolph \ˈran-ˌdälf\ Asa Philip 1889–1979 American labor leader

Ra·pha·el \ˈraf-ē-əl, ˈrā-fē-\ one of the four archangels named in Hebrew tradition — compare GABRIEL, MICHAEL, URIEL

Ra·pha·el \ˈraf-ē-əl, ˈrā-fē-, ˈräf-ē-\ 1483–1520 Italian painter

Ras·pu·tin \ra-ˈsp(y)üt-ᵊn, -ˈspu̇t-\ Grigory Yefimovich 1872–1916 Russian mystic

Rea·gan \ˈrā-gən *also* ˈrē-\ Ronald Wilson 1911– 40th president of the U.S. (1981–89)

Re·bek·ah *or* **Re·bec·ca** \ri-ˈbek-ə\ wife of Isaac in the Bible

Red Cloud \ˈred-ˌklau̇d\ 1822–1909 American Indian chief

Reed \ˈrēd\ Walter 1851–1902 American army surgeon

Rem·brandt \ˈrem-ˌbrant *also* -ˌbränt\ 1606–1669 Dutch painter

Re·mus \ˈrē-məs\ son of Mars who in Roman mythology is killed by his twin brother Romulus

Re·noir \ˈren-ˌwär, rən-ˈwär\ Pierre-Auguste 1841–1919 French painter

Re·vere \ri-ˈvi(ə)r\ Paul 1735–1818 American patriot and silversmith

Rich·ard \ˈrich-ərd\ name of three kings of England: **I** 1157–1199 (reigned 1189–99) *the Lion-Hearted*; **II** 1367–1400 (reigned 1377–99); **III** 1452–1485 (reigned 1483–85)

Rob·in Good·fel·low \ˌräb-ən-ˈgu̇d-ˌfel-ō\ mischievous elf in English folklore

Rob·in·son \ˈräb-ən-sən\ Edwin Arlington 1869–1935 American poet

Rob·in·son Cru·soe \ˌräb-ə(n)-sən-ˈkrü-sō\ a shipwrecked sailor in Daniel Defoe's *Robinson Crusoe* who lives for many years on a desert island

Ro·cham·beau \ˌrō-ˌsham-ˈbō\ Comte de 1725–1807 French general in American Revolution

Rocke·fel·ler \ˈräk-i-ˌfel-ər, ˈräk-ˌfel-\ John Davison father 1839–1937 and son 1874–1960 American oil magnates and philanthropists

Ro·ma·nov *or* **Ro·ma·noff** \rō-ˈmän-əf, ˈrō-mə-ˌnäf\ Michael 1596–1645 1st czar (1613–45) of Russian Romanov dynasty (1613–1917)

Rom·u·lus \ˈräm-yə-ləs\ son of Mars in Roman mythology who was the twin brother of Remus and the founder of Rome

Rönt·gen *or* **Roent·gen** \ˈrent-gən, ˈrənt-, -jən\ Wilhelm Conrad 1845–1923 German physicist; Nobel Prize winner (1901)

Roo·se·velt \ˈrō-zə-vəlt (*Roosevelts' usual pronunciation*), -ˌvelt *also* ˈrü-\ (Anna) Eleanor 1884–1962 American lecturer and writer; wife of Franklin Delano Roosevelt

Roosevelt Franklin Del·a·no \ˈdel-ə-ˌnō\ 1882–1945 32d president of the U.S. (1933–45)

Roosevelt Theodore 1858–1919 26th president of the U.S. (1901–09); Nobel Prize winner (1906)

Ross \ˈrȯs\ Betsy 1752–1836 reputed maker of first American flag

Ros·si·ni \rō-ˈsē-nē, rə-\ Gioacchino Antonio 1792–1868 Italian composer

Ru·bens \ˈrü-bənz\ Peter Paul 1577–1640 Flemish painter

Rus·sell \ˈrəs-əl\ Bertrand Arthur William 1872–1970 English mathematician and philosopher; Nobel Prize winner (1950)

Ruth \ˈrüth\ woman in the Bible who was one of the ancestors of King David

Ruth George Herman 1895–1948 *Babe* American baseball player

Ruth·er·ford \ˈrət͟h-ə(r)-fərd, ˈrəth-\ Ernest 1871–1937 1st Baron *Rutherford of Nelson* British physicist

Sa·bin \ˈsā-bin\ Albert Bruce 1906–1993 American physician

Sac·a·ga·wea \ˌsak-ə-jə-ˈwē-ə, -ˈwä-ə\ 1786?–1812 Shoshone interpreter and guide to Lewis and Clark

Sā·dāt \sə-ˈdat, -ˈdät\ Anwar el- 1918–1981 president of Egypt (1970–81)

Saint Nicholas — see NICHOLAS, SANTA CLAUS

Sal·in·ger \ˈsal-ən-jər\ Jerome David 1919– American author

Salk \ˈsȯk, ˈsȯlk\ Jonas Edward 1914–1995 American physician

Sa·lo·me \sə-ˈlō-mē\ niece of Herod Antipas who in the Bible is given the head of John the Baptist as a reward for her dancing

Sa·mo·set \ˈsam-ə-ˌset, sə-ˈmäs-ət\ *died about* 1653 Abenaki leader

Sam·son \ˈsam(p)-sən\ powerful Hebrew hero in the Bible who fought against the Philistines

Sam·u·el \ˈsam-yə(-wə)l\ Hebrew judge in the Bible who appointed Saul and then David king

Sand·burg \ˈsan(d)-ˌbərg\ Carl 1878–1967 American author

San·ta Claus \ˈsant-ē-ˌklȯz, ˈsant-ə-\ *or* **Saint Nich·o·las** \sānt-ˈnik-(ə-)ləs, sənt-\ *or* **Kriss Krin·gle** \ˈkris-ˈkriŋ-gəl\ a fat jolly old man in modern folklore who delivers presents to good children at Christmastime

Sap·pho \ˈsaf-ō\ *flourished about* 610–*about* 580 B.C. Greek poet

Sa·rah \ˈser-ə, ˈsar-ə, ˈsā-rə\ wife of Abraham and mother of Isaac in the Bible

Sar·gent \ˈsär-jənt\ John Singer 1856–1925 American painter

Sat·urn \ˈsat-ərn\ a god of agriculture in Roman mythology

Saul \ˈsȯl\ first king of Israel in the Bible

Saul *or* **Saul of Tar·sus** \-ˈtär-səs\ the apostle Paul

Sche·her·a·zade \shə-ˌher-ə-ˈzäd(-ə), -ˈzäd(-ē)\ fictional oriental queen and narrator of the tales in the *Arabian Nights' Entertainments*

Schu·bert \ˈshü-bərt, -ˌbərt\ Franz Peter 1797–1828 Austrian composer

Schweit·zer \ˈshwīt-sər, ˈswīt-, ˈshvīt-\ Albert 1875–

1965 French Protestant minister, philosopher, physician, and music scholar; Nobel Prize winner (1952)
Scott \ˈskät\ Dred \ˈdred\ 1795?–1858 American slave
Scott Sir Walter 1771–1832 Scottish author
Scott Winfield 1786–1866 American general
Scyl•la \ˈsil-ə\ a nymph in Greek mythology who is changed into a monster and inhabits a cave opposite the whirlpool Charybdis off the coast of Sicily
Se•quoya \si-ˈkwȯi-ə\ *about* 1760–1843 Cherokee linguist
Ser•ra \ˈser-ə\ Junípero 1713–1784 Spanish missionary in Mexico and California
Se•ton \ˈsēt-ᵊn\ Saint Elizabeth Ann Bayley 1774–1821 *Mother Seton* American religious leader
Sew•ard \ˈsü-ərd, ˈsu̇(-ə)rd\ William Henry 1801–1872 American politician; secretary of state (1861–69)
Shake•speare \ˈshāk-ˌspi(ə)r\ William 1564–1616 English dramatist and poet
Shaw \ˈshȯ\ George Bernard 1856–1950 British author
Shel•ley \ˈshel-ē\ Mary Woll•stone•craft \ˈwu̇l-stən-ˌkraft\ 1797–1851 English novelist; wife of Percy Bysshe Shelley
Shelley Percy Bysshe \ˈbish\ 1792–1822 English poet
Shep•ard \ˈshep-ərd\ Alan Bartlett 1923– American astronaut; first American in space (1961)
Sher•i•dan \ˈsher-əd-ᵊn\ Philip Henry 1831–1888 American general
Sher•lock Holmes \ˈshər-ˌläk-ˈhōmz, -ˈhōlmz\ detective in stories by Sir Arthur Conan Doyle
Sher•man \ˈshər-mən\ John 1823–1900 American politician
Sherman William Tecumseh 1820–1891 American general
Sieg•fried \ˈsig-ˌfrēd, ˈsēg-\ hero in Germanic legend who kills a dragon guarding a gold hoard
Si•mon \ˈsī-mən\ *or* **Simon the Zealot** one of the 12 apostles
Sind•bad the Sailor \ˈsin-ˌbad-\ citizen of Baghdad whose adventures are narrated in the *Arabian Nights' Entertainments*
Sis•y•phus \ˈsis-ə-fəs\ king of Corinth who in Greek mythology is condemned to roll a heavy stone up a hill in Hades only to have it roll down again as it nears the top
Sit•ting Bull \ˌsit-iŋ-ˈbu̇l\ *about* 1831–90 Sioux Indian leader
Si•va \ˈshiv-ə, ˈsiv-; ˈshē-və, ˈsē-\ god of destruction in the Hindu sacred triad — compare BRAHMA, VISHNU
Smith \ˈsmith\ Bessie 1894 (or 1898)–1937 American blues singer
Smith John *about* 1580–1631 English colonist in America
Smith Joseph 1805–1844 American founder of the Mormon Church
Soc•ra•tes \ˈsäk-rə-ˌtēz\ *about* 470–399 B.C. Greek philosopher
Sol•o•mon \ˈsäl-ə-mən\ son of David and 10th-century B.C. king of Israel noted for his wisdom
Soph•o•cles \ˈsäf-ə-ˌklēz \ *about* 496–406 B.C. Greek dramatist
Sou•sa \ˈsü-zə, ˈsü-sə\ John Philip 1854–1932 American bandmaster and composer
Spar•ta•cus \ˈspärt-ə-kəs\ *died* 71 B.C. Roman slave and gladiator; leader of a slave rebellion
Sphinx \ˈsfiŋ(k)s\ monster in Greek mythology having a lion's body, wings, and the head and bust of a woman
Squan•to \ˈskwän-tō\ *died* 1622 Indian friend of the Pilgrims
Sta•lin \ˈstäl-ən, ˈstal-, -ˌēn\ Joseph 1879–1953 Soviet leader
Stan•dish \ˈstan-dish\ Myles *or* Miles 1584?–1656 American colonist
Stan•ley \ˈstan-lē\ Sir Henry Morton 1841–1904 British explorer in Africa
Stan•ton \ˈstant-ᵊn\ Elizabeth Cady 1815–1902 American suffragist
Stein \ˈstīn\ Gertrude 1874–1946 American author
Stein•beck \ˈstīn-ˌbek\ John Ernst 1902–1968 American author; Nobel Prize winner (1962)
Steu•ben, von \ˈst(y)ü-bən, ˈshtȯi-\ Baron Friedrich Wilhelm Ludolf Gerhard Augustin 1730–1794 Prussian-born general in American Revolution
Ste•ven•son \ˈstē-vən-sən\ Adlai Ewing 1900–1965 American politician
Stevenson Robert Louis Balfour 1850–1894 Scottish author
Stowe \ˈstō\ Harriet Elizabeth Beecher 1811–1896 American author
Stra•di•va•ri \ˌstrad-ə-ˈvär-ē, -ˈvar-, -ˈver-\ Antonio 1644–1737 Latin *Antonius Strad•i•var•i•us* \ˌstrad-ə-ˈvar-ē-əs, -ˈver-\ Italian violin maker
Strauss \ˈstrau̇s, ˈshtrau̇s\ Johann father 1804–1849 and his sons Johann 1825–1899 and Josef 1827–1870 Austrian composers
Stu•art \ˈst(y)ü-ərt, ˈst(y)u̇(-ə)rt\ — see CHARLES I, MARY STUART
Stuart Charles—CHARLES EDWARD STUART
Stuart Gilbert Charles 1755–1828 American painter
Stuart James Ewell Brown 1833–1864 *Jeb* American Confederate general
Stuy•ve•sant \ˈstī-və-sənt\ Peter *about* 1610–1672 Dutch colonial administrator in America
Sul•li•van \ˈsəl-ə-vən\ Sir Arthur Seymour 1842–1900 English composer; collaborator with Sir William Gilbert
Sullivan Louis Henri 1856–1924 American architect
Sum•ner \ˈsəm-nər\ Charles 1811–1874 American politician
Swift \ˈswift\ Jonathan 1667–1745 English author
Taft \ˈtaft\ William Howard 1857–1930 27th president of the U.S. (1909–13); chief justice of the U.S. Supreme Court (1921–30)
Ta•ney \ˈtȯ-nē\ Roger Brooke 1777–1864 American jurist; chief justice of the U.S. Supreme Court (1836–64)
Tan•ta•lus \ˈtant-ᵊl-əs\ king in Greek mythology who is condemned to stand up to his chin in a pool of water in Hades and beneath fruit-laden boughs only to have the water or fruit go out of reach at each attempt to drink or eat
Tay•lor \ˈtā-lər\ Zachary 1784–1850 12th president of the U.S. (1849–50)
Tchai•kov•sky \chī-ˈkȯf-skē, chə-, -ˈkȯv-\ Pyotr Ilich 1840–1893 Russian composer
Te•cum•seh \tə-ˈkəm(p)-sə, -sē\ 1768–1813 Shawnee chief
Ten•ny•son \ˈten-ə-sən\ Alfred 1809–1892 known as *Alfred, Lord Tennyson* English poet
Te•re•sa \tə-ˈrā-zə, -ˈrē-sə\ **of Ávi•la** \ˈäv-i-lə\ Saint 1515–1582 Spanish nun and mystic
The•seus \ˈthē-ˌsüs, -sē-əs\ hero in Greek mythology who kills the Minotaur and conquers the Amazons
Thom•as \ˈtäm-əs\ apostle in the Bible who demanded proof of Christ's resurrection
Thomas à Becket — see BECKET, À
Thor \ˈthȯ(ə)r\ god of thunder, weather, and crops in Norse mythology
Tho•reau \thə-ˈrō, thȯ-; ˈthȯr-ō\ Henry David 1817–1862 American author
Thur•ber \ˈthər-bər\ James Grover 1894–1961 American author
Ti•be•ri•us \tī-ˈbir-ē-əs\ 42 B.C.–37 A.D. Roman emperor (14–37)
Tocque•ville \ˈtōk-ˌvil, ˈtȯk-, ˈtäk-, -ˌvēl, -vəl\ Alexis-Charles-Henri Clérel de 1805–1859 French politician and author
Tol•kien \ˈtȯl-ˌkēn, ˈtōl-, ˈtäl-\ John Ronald Reuel 1892–1973 English author
Tol•stoy \tȯl-ˈstȯi, tōl-ˈstȯi, täl-ˈstȯi, ˈtȯl-ˌstȯi, ˈtōl-

ˌstȯi, ˈtäl-ˌstȯi\ Count Lev Nikolayevich 1828–1910 Russian author

Tri•ton \ˈtrīt-ᵊn\ sea god in Greek mythology who is half man and half fish

Trots•ky \ˈträt-skē, ˈtrȯt-\ Leon 1879–1940 originally *Lev Davidovich Bronstein* Russian Communist

Tru•man \ˈtrü-mən\ Harry S. 1884–1972 33d president of the U.S. (1945–53)

Truth \ˈtrüth\ Sojourner 1797?–1883 American abolitionist

Tub•man \ˈtəb-mən\ Harriet *about* 1820–1913 American abolitionist

Tut•ankh•a•men \ˌtü-ˌtaŋ-ˈkäm-ən, -ˌtäŋ-\ *or* **Tut•ankh•a•ten** \-ˈkät-ᵊn\ *about* 1370–1352 B.C. king of Egypt (1361–1352 B.C.)

Twain Mark — see CLEMENS

Tweed \ˈtwēd\ William Marcy 1823–1878 *Boss Tweed* American politician

Ty•ler \ˈtī-lər\ John 1790–1862 10th president of the U.S. (1841–45)

Ulysses — see ODYSSEUS

Ura•nus \ˈyu̇r-ə-nəs, yu̇-ˈrā-\ the sky personified as a god and father of the Titans in Greek mythology

Ur•ban \ˈər-bən\ name of eight popes: especially **II** *about* 1035–1099 (pope 1088–99)

Uri•el \ˈyu̇r-ē-əl\ one of the four archangels named in Hebrew tradition — compare GABRIEL, MICHAEL, RAPHAEL

Val•en•tine \ˈval-ən-ˌtīn\ Saint 3d century Christian martyr

Van Bu•ren \van-ˈbyu̇r-ən, vən-\ Martin 1782–1862 8th president of the U.S. (1837–41)

Van Dyck *or* **Van•dyke** \van-ˈdīk, vən-\ Sir Anthony 1599–1641 Flemish painter

Ve•láz•quez \və-ˈlas-kəs\ Diego Rodríguez de Silva 1599–1660 Spanish painter

Ve•nus \ˈvē-nəs\ the goddess of love and beauty in Roman mythology — compare APHRODITE

Ver•di \ˈve(ə)rd-ē\ Giuseppe Fortunio Francesco 1813–1901 Italian composer

Ver•meer \vər-ˈme(ə)r, -ˈmi(ə)r\ Jan 1632–1675 also called *Jan van der Meer van Delft* Dutch painter

Verne Jules \ˈjülz-ˈvərn\ 1828–1905 French author

Ves•puc•ci \ve-ˈspü-chē\ Ame•ri•go \ˌäm-ə-ˈrē-gō\ 1454–1512 Latin *Amer•i•cus Ves•pu•cius* \ə-ˈmer-ə-kəs-ˌves-ˈpyü-sh(ē-)əs\ Italian navigator for whom America was named

Vic•to•ria \vik-ˈtōr-ē-ə, -ˈtȯr-\ 1819–1901 *Alexandrina Victoria* queen of Great Britain (1837–1901)

Vinci, da Leonardo — see LEONARDO DA VINCI

Vir•gil *also* **Ver•gil** \ˈvər-jəl\ 70–19 B.C. Roman poet

Vish•nu \ˈvish-nü\ god of preservation in the Hindu sacred triad — compare BRAHMA, SIVA

Vol•ta \ˈvōl-tə, ˈväl-, ˈvȯl-\ Count Alessandro Giuseppe Antonio Anastasio 1745–1827 Italian physicist

Vol•taire \vōl-ˈta(ə)r, vȯl-, väl-, -ˈte(ə)r\ 1694–1778 originally *François-Marie Arouet* French author

Vul•can \ˈvəl-kən\ the god of fire and metalworking in Roman mythology — compare HEPHAESTUS

Wag•ner \ˈväg-nər\ (Wilhelm) Ri•chard \ˈrik-ˌärt, ˈrik-\ 1813–1883 German composer

Walk•er \ˈwȯ-kər\ Alice Malsenior 1944– American author

War•ren \ˈwȯr-ən, ˈwär-\ Earl 1891–1974 American jurist; chief justice of the U.S. Supreme Court (1953–69)

Wash•ing•ton \ˈwȯsh-iŋ-tən, ˈwäsh-\ Book•er \ˈbu̇k-ər\ Tal•ia•ferro \ˈtäl-ə-vər\ 1856–1915 American educator

Washington George 1732–1799 American general; 1st president of the U.S. (1789–97)

Watt \ˈwät\ James 1736–1819 Scottish inventor

Wayne \ˈwān\ Anthony 1745–1796 *Mad Anthony* American general

Web•ster \ˈweb-stər\ Daniel 1782–1852 American politician

Webster Noah 1758–1843 American lexicographer

Wel•ling•ton \ˈwel-iŋ-tən\ 1st Duke of 1769–1852 *Arthur Wellesley; the Iron Duke* British general and politician

Wells \ˈwelz\ Herbert George 1866–1946 English author and historian

Wes•ley \ˈwes-lē, ˈwez-\ John 1703–1791 English founder of Methodism

Wes•ting•house \ˈwes-tiŋ-ˌhau̇s\ George 1846–1914 American inventor

Whar•ton \ˈhwȯrt-ᵊn, ˈwȯrt-\ Edith Newbold 1862–1937 American author

Whis•tler \ˈhwis-lər, ˈwis-\ James Abbott McNeill 1834–1903 American artist

Whit•man \ˈhwit-mən, ˈwit-\ Walt 1819–1892 American poet

Whit•ney \ˈhwit-nē, ˈwit-\ Eli 1765–1825 American inventor

Whit•ti•er \ˈhwit-ē-ər, ˈwit-\ John Greenleaf 1807–1892 American poet

Wilde \ˈwī(ə)ld\ Oscar Fingal O'Flahertie Wills 1854–1900 Irish author

Wil•der \ˈwīl-dər\ Thornton Niven 1897–1975 American author

Wil•liam \ˈwil-yəm\ name of four kings of England: **I** *(the Conqueror) about* 1028–1087 (reigned 1066–87); **II** *(Rufus* \ˈrü-fəs\) *about* 1056–1100 (reigned 1087–1100); **III** 1650–1702 (reigned 1689–1702); **IV** 1765–1837 (reigned 1830–37)

Wil•liam Tell \ˌwil-yəm-ˈtel\ legendary Swiss patriot commanded to shoot an apple from his son's head

Wil•liams \ˈwil-yəmz\ Roger 1603?–1683 English colonist; founder of Rhode Island

Williams Tennessee 1911–1983 originally *Thomas Lanier Williams* American dramatist

Wil•son \ˈwil-sən\ (Thomas) Wood•row \ˈwu̇d-ˌrō\ 1856–1924 28th president of the U.S. (1913–21); Nobel Prize winner (1919)

Win•throp \ˈwin(t)-thrəp\ John 1588–1649 1st governor of Massachusetts Bay Colony

Woden — see ODIN

Woolf \ˈwu̇lf\ Virginia 1882–1941 English author

Words•worth \ˈwərdz-(ˌ)wərth\ William 1770–1850 English poet

Wren \ˈren\ Sir Christopher 1632–1723 English architect

Wright \ˈrīt\ Frank Lloyd 1867–1959 American architect

Wright Or•ville \ˈȯr-vəl\ 1871–1948 and his brother Wilbur 1867–1912 American pioneers in aviation

Wright Richard 1908–1960 American author

Wy•eth \ˈwī-əth\ Andrew Newell 1917– American painter

Yeats \ˈyāts\ William Butler 1865–1939 Irish author

Young \ˈyəŋ\ Brig•ham \ˈbrig-əm\ 1801–1877 American Mormon leader

Zech•a•ri•ah \ˌzek-ə-ˈrī-ə\ Hebrew prophet of the 6th century B.C.

Zeng•er \ˈzeŋ-(g)ər\ John Peter 1697–1746 American (German-born) journalist and printer

Zeph•y•rus \ˈzef-ə-rəs\ god of the west wind in Greek mythology

Zeus \ˈzüs\ chief god, ruler of the sky and weather (as lightning and rain), and husband of Hera in Greek mythology

Presidents of the United States

no.	name (pronunciation)	life dates	birthplace	term dates
1	George Washington \'wȯsh-ing-tən, 'wäsh-\	1732–1799	Va.	1789–1797
2	John Adams \'ad-əmz\	1735–1826	Mass.	1797–1801
3	Thomas Jefferson \'jef-ər-sən\	1743–1826	Va.	1801–1809
4	James Madison \'mad-ə-sən\	1751–1836	Va.	1809–1817
5	James Monroe \mən-'rō\	1758–1831	Va.	1817–1825
6	John Quincy Adams \'ad-əmz\	1767–1848	Mass.	1825–1829
7	Andrew Jackson \'jak-sən\	1767–1845	S. C.	1829–1837
8	Martin Van Buren \van-'byu̇r-ən\	1782–1862	N. Y.	1837–1841
9	William Henry Harrison \'har-ə-sən\	1773–1841	Va.	1841
10	John Tyler \'tī-lər\	1790–1862	Va.	1841–1845
11	James Knox Polk \'pōk\	1795–1849	N. C.	1845–1849
12	Zachary Taylor \'tā-lər\	1784–1850	Va.	1849–1850
13	Millard Fillmore \'fil-'mōr\	1800–1874	N. Y.	1850–1853
14	Franklin Pierce \'piərs\	1804–1869	N. H.	1853–1857
15	James Buchanan \byü-'kan-ən\	1791–1868	Penn.	1857–1861
16	Abraham Lincoln \'ling-kən\	1809–1865	Ky.	1861–1865
17	Andrew Johnson \'jän-sən\	1808–1875	N. C.	1865–1869
18	Ulysses S. Grant \'grant\	1822–1885	Ohio	1869–1877
19	Rutherford B. Hayes \'hāz\	1822–1893	Ohio	1877–1881
20	James A. Garfield \'gär-'fēld\	1831–1881	Ohio	1881
21	Chester A. Arthur \'är-thər\	1830–1886	Vt.	1881–1885
22	Grover Cleveland \'klēv-lənd\	1837–1908	N. J.	1885–1889
23	Benjamin Harrison \'har-ə-sən\	1833–1901	Ohio	1889–1893
24	Grover Cleveland \'klēv-lənd\	1837–1908	N. J.	1893–1897
25	William McKinley \mə-'kin-lē\	1843–1901	Ohio	1897–1901
26	Theodore Roosevelt \'rō-zə-'velt\	1858–1919	N. Y.	1901–1909
27	William Howard Taft \'taft\	1857–1930	Ohio	1909–1913
28	Woodrow Wilson \'wil-sən\	1856–1924	Va.	1913–1921
29	William G. Harding \'härd-ing\	1865–1923	Ohio	1921–1923
30	Calvin Coolidge \'kü-lij\	1872–1933	Vt.	1923–1929
31	Herbert C. Hoover \'hü-vər\	1874–1964	Iowa	1929–1933
32	Franklin D. Roosevelt \'rō-zə-'velt\	1882–1945	N. Y.	1933–1945
33	Harry S Truman \'trü-mən\	1884–1972	Mo.	1945–1953
34	Dwight D. Eisenhower \'īz-n-'hau̇-ər\	1890–1969	Texas	1953–1961
35	John F. Kennedy \'ken-ə-dē\	1917–1963	Mass.	1961–1963
36	Lyndon B. Johnson \'jän-sən\	1908–1973	Texas	1963–1969
37	Richard M. Nixon \'nik-sən\	1913–1994	Calif.	1969–1974
38	Gerald R. Ford \'fōrd\	1913–	Neb.	1974–1977
39	Jimmy Carter \'kärt-ər\	1924–	Ga.	1977–1981
40	Ronald W. Reagan \'rā-gən\	1911–	Ill.	1981–1989
41	George H. W. Bush \'bu̇sh\	1924–	Mass.	1989–1993
42	William J. Clinton \'klin-tən\	1946–	Ark.	1993–2001
43	George W. Bush \'bu̇sh\	1946–	Conn.	2001–

Prime Ministers of Canada

no.	name (pronunciation)	life dates	term dates
1	John A. Macdonald \mək-ˈdän-^{ə}ld\	1815–1891	1867–1873
2	Alexander Mackenzie \mə-ˈken-zē\	1822–1892	1873–1878
3	John A. Macdonald \mək-ˈdän-^{ə}ld\	1815–1891	1878–1891
4	John J. C. Abbott \ˈab-ət\	1821–1893	1891–1892
5	John S. D. Thompson \ˈtäm(p)-sən\	1844–1894	1892–1894
6	Mackenzie Bowell \ˈbō(-ə)l\	1823–1917	1894–1896
7	Charles Tupper \ˈtəp-ər\	1821–1915	1896
8	Wilfrid Laurier \lȯr-yā, ˈlȯr-ē-ˌā\	1841–1919	1896–1911
9	Robert L. Borden \ˈbȯrd-^{ə}n\	1854–1937	1911–1920
10	Arthur Meighen \ˈmē-ən\	1874–1960	1920–1921
11	W. L. Mackenzie King \ˈkiŋ\	1874–1950	1921–1926
12	Arthur Meighen \ˈmē-ən\	1874–1960	1926
13	W. L. Mackenzie King \ˈkiŋ\	1874–1950	1926–1930
14	Richard B. Bennett \ˈben-ət\	1870–1947	1930–1935
15	W. L. Mackenzie King \ˈkiŋ\	1874–1950	1935–1948
16	Louis Stephen St. Laurent \sa^{n}-lȯ-rä^{n}\	1882–1973	1948–1957
17	John Goerge Diefenbaker \ˈdē-fən-ˌbā-kər\	1895–1979	1957–1963
18	Lester B. Pearson \ˈpi(ə)rs-^{ə}n\	1897–1972	1963–1968
19	Pierre Elliott Trudeau \ˈtrü-(ˌ)dō, trü-ˈ\	1919–	1968–1979
20	Joe Clark \ˈklärk\	1939–	1979–1980
21	Pierre Elliott Trudeau \ˈtrü-(ˌ)dō, trü-ˈ\	1919–	1980–1984
22	John Turner \ˈtərn-ər\	1929–	1984
23	Brian Mulroney \məl-ˈrü-nē\	1939–	1984–1993
24	Kim Campbell \ˈkam-bəl\	1947–	1993
25	Jean Chrétien \krā-tya^{n}\	1934–	1993–

Nations of the World

name and pronunciation	population
Afghanistan \af-ˈga-nə-ˌstan\	20,269,000
Albania \al-ˈbā-nē-ə\	3,422,000
Algeria \al-ˈjir-ē-ə\	27,029,000
Andorra \an-ˈdȯr-ə\	61,900
Angola \aŋ-ˈgō-lə, an-\	10,916,000
Antigua and Barbuda \an-ˈtē-gə...bär-ˈbü-də\	66,000
Argentina \ˌär-jen-ˈtē-nə\	33,507,000
Armenia \är-ˈmē-nē-ə\	3,550,000
Australia \ȯ-ˈstrāl-yə\	17,729,000
Austria \ˈȯs-trē-ə\	7,938,000
Azerbaijan \ˌä-zər-ˌbī-ˈjän\	7,398,000
Bahamas \bə-ˈhä-məz\	266,000
Bahrain \bä-ˈrān\	486,000
Bangladesh \ˌbäŋ-glə-ˈdesh, -ˈdāsh\	115,075,000
Barbados \bär-ˈbā-dəs, -(ˌ)dōz, -(ˌ)däs\	260,000
Belarus \ˌbye-lə-ˈrüs\	10,353,000
Belgium \ˈbel-jəm\	10,072,000
Belize \bə-ˈlēz\	204,000
Benin \bə-ˈnin\	5,091,000
Bhutan \bü-ˈtan, -ˈtän\	1,546,000
Bolivia \bə-ˈli-vē-ə\	7,715,000
Bosnia and Herzegovina \ˈbäz-nē-ə...ˌhert-sə-gō-ˈvē-nə, -ˈgō-və-nə\	4,422,000
Botswana \bät-ˈswä-nə\	1,406,000
Brazil \brə-ˈzil\	156,493,000
Brunei \brü-ˈnī, ˈbrü-ˌnī\	275,000
Bulgaria \ˌbəl-ˈgar-ē-ə, bu̇l-\	8,466,000
Burkina Faso \bu̇r-ˈkē-nə-ˈfä-sō\	9,780,000
Burundi \bu̇-ˈrün-dē\	5,665,000
Cambodia \kam-ˈbō-dē-ə\	9,287,000
Cameroon \ˌka-mə-ˈrün\	13,103,000
Canada \ˈka-nə-də\	28,846,761
Cape Verde \ˌkāp-ˈvərd\	350,000
Central African Republic	2,998,000
Chad \ˈchad\	6,118,000
Chile \ˈchi-lē\	13,542,000
China, People's Republic of \-ˈchī-nə\	1,179,467,000
Colombia \kə-ˈləm-bē-ə\	33,951,000
Comoro Islands \ˈkä-mə-ˌrō-\	516,000
Congo, Republic of \ˈkäŋ-gō\	2,775,000
Congo, Democratic Republic of	42,473,000
Costa Rica \ˌkäs-tə-ˈrē-kə\	3,199,000
Croatia \krō-ˈā-shə\	4,821,000
Cuba \ˈkyü-bə\	10,892,000
Cyprus \ˈsī-prəs\	764,000
Czech Republic \ˈchek-\	10,332,000
Denmark \ˈden-ˌmärk\	5,187,000
Djibouti \jə-ˈbü-tē\	565,000
Dominica \ˌdä-mə-ˈnē-kə\	74,000
Dominican Republic \də-ˈmi-ni-kən-\	7,634,000
Ecuador \ˈe-kwə-ˌdȯr\	10,985,000
Egypt \ˈē-jəpt\	57,109,000
El Salvador \el-ˈsal-və-ˌdȯr\	5,517,000
Equatorial Guinea \-ˈgi-nē\	377,000
Eritrea \ˌer-ə-ˈtrā-ə\	3,317,611
Estonia \e-ˈstō-nē-ə\	1,536,000
Ethiopia \ˌē-thē-ˈō-pē-ə\	52,078,000
Fiji \ˈfē-(ˌ)jē\	762,000
Finland \ˈfin-lənd\	5,058,000
France \ˈfrans\	57,690,000
Gabon \ga-ˈbōn\	1,280,000
Gambia \ˈgam-bē-ə\	1,033,000
Georgia \ˈjȯr-jə\	5,493,000
Germany \ˈjər-mə-nē\	81,187,000
Ghana \ˈgä-nə\	15,636,000
Greece \ˈgrēs\	10,310,000
Grenada \grə-ˈnā-də\	91,000
Guatemala \ˌgwä-tə-ˈmä-lə\	9,713,000
Guinea \ˈgi-nē\	7,418,000
Guinea-Bissau \-bi-ˈsau̇\	1,036,000
Guyana \gī-ˈa-nə\	755,000
Haiti \ˈhā-tē\	6,902,000
Honduras \hän-ˈdu̇r-əs\	5,148,000
Hungary \ˈhəŋ-gə-rē\	10,296,000
Iceland \ˈīs-lənd, -ˌland\	264,000
India \ˈin-dē-ə\	896,567,000
Indonesia \ˌin-də-ˈnē-zhə\	188,216,000
Iran \i-ˈran, -ˈrän\	60,768,000
Iraq \i-ˈräk, -ˈrak\	19,435,000
Ireland \ˈīr-lənd\	3,516,000
Israel \ˈiz-rē-əl\	5,451,000
Italy \ˈi-tə-lē\	57,235,000
Ivory Coast	13,459,000
Jamaica \jə-ˈmā-kə\	2,472,000
Japan \jə-ˈpan\	124,670,000
Jordan \ˈjȯr-dən\	3,764,000
Kazakhstan \ˌkä-ˌzäk-ˈstän\	17,186,000
Kenya \ˈken-yə, ˈkēn-\	28,113,000
Kiribati \ˈkir-ə-ˌbas\	76,900
Kuwait \kə-ˈwāt\	1,433,000
Kyrgyzstan \ˌkir-gi-ˈstän\	4,526,000
Laos \ˈlau̇s, ˈlä-ōs\	4,533,000
Latvia \ˈlat-vē-ə\	2,596,000
Lebanon \ˈle-bə-nən\	2,909,000
Lesotho \lə-ˈsü-ˌtü\	1,903,000
Liberia \lī-ˈbir-ē-ə\	2,844,000
Libya \ˈli-bē-ə\	4,573,000
Liechtenstein \ˈlik-tən-ˌshtīn\	30,100
Lithuania \ˌli-thə-ˈwā-nē-ə\	3,753,000
Luxembourg \ˈlək-səm-ˌbərg, ˈlu̇k-səm-ˌbu̇rg\	392,000
Macedonia \ˌma-sə-ˈdō-nē-ə\	2,063,000
Madagascar \ˌma-də-ˈgas-kər\	13,255,000
Malawi \mə-ˈlä-wē\	10,581,000
Malaysia \mə-ˈlā-zhə\	19,077,000
Maldives \ˈmȯl-ˌdēvz, -ˌdīvz\	237,000
Mali \ˈmä-lē\	8,646,000
Malta \ˈmȯl-tə\	363,000
Mauritania \ˌmȯr-ə-ˈtā-nē-ə\	2,171,000
Mauritius \mȯ-ˈri-shē-əs\	1,103,000
Mexico \ˈmek-si-ˌkō\	89,955,000
Moldova \mäl-ˈdō-və\	4,362,000
Monaco \ˈmä-nə-ˌkō\	30,500
Mongolia \män-ˈgōl-yə\	2,256,000
Morocco \mə-ˈrä-kō\	26,494,000
Mozambique \ˌmō-zəm-ˈbēk\	15,243,000
Myanmar \ˈmyän-ˌmär\	44,613,000
Namibia \na-ˈmi-bē-ə\	1,537,000
Nauru \nä-ˈü-(ˌ)rü\	10,000
Nepal \nə-ˈpȯl\	19,264,000
Netherlands \ˈne-t͟hər-ləndz\	15,302,000
New Zealand \-ˈzē-lənd\	3,520,000

Nicaragua \ˌni-kə-ˈrä-gwə\	4,265,000
Niger \ˈnī-jər\	8,516,000
Nigeria \nī-ˈjir-ē-ə\	91,549,000
North Korea \-kə-ˈrē-ə\	22,646,000
Norway \ˈnȯr-ˌwā\	4,308,000
Oman \ō-ˈmän\	1,698,000
Pakistan \ˈpa-ki-ˌstan, ˌpä-ki-ˈstän\	127,962,000
Panama \ˈpa-nə-ˌmä\	2,563,000
Papua New Guinea \ˈpä-pə-wə-\	3,918,000
Paraguay \ˈpar-ə-ˌgwī, -ˌgwā\	4,613,000
Peru \pə-ˈrü\	22,916,000
Philippines \ˌfi-lə-ˈpēnz, ˈfi-lə-ˌpēnz\	64,954,000
Poland \ˈpō-lənd\	38,521,000
Portugal \ˈpōr-chi-gəl\	9,823,000
Qatar \ˈkä-tər\	539,000
Romania \rü-ˈmā-nē-ə\	22,789,000
Russia \ˈrə-shə\	148,000,000
Rwanda \rü-ˈän-də\	7,584,000
St. Kitts-Nevis \-ˈkits-ˈnē-vəs\	41,800
St. Lucia \-ˈlü-shə\	136,000
St. Vincent and the Grenadines \-ˈvin-sənt... ˌgre-nə-ˈdēnz\	109,000
Samoa \sə-ˈmō-ə\	163,000
San Marino \ˌsan-mə-ˈrē-nō\	24,100
Sao Tome and Principe \ˌsau̇-tə-ˈmā... ˈprin-sə-pə\	125,000
Saudi Arabia \ˌsau̇-dē-ə-ˈrā-bē-ə, sä-ˌü-dē-\	17,419,000
Senegal \ˌse-ni-ˈgȯl\	7,899,000
Seychelles \sā-ˈchelz\	71,000
Sierra Leone \sē-ˌer-ə-lē-ˈōn\	4,491,000
Singapore \ˈsiŋ-ə-ˌpōr\	2,876,000
Slovakia \slō-ˈvä-kē-ə\	5,329,000
Slovenia \slō-ˈvē-nē-ə\	1,997,000
Solomon Islands \ˈsä-lə-mən-\	349,000
Somalia \sō-ˈmä-lē-ə\	8,050,000
South Africa, Republic of	33,071,000
South Korea \-kə-ˈrē-ə\	44,042,000
Spain \ˈspān\	39,141,000
Sri Lanka \srē-ˈläŋ-kə, shrē-\	17,616,000
Sudan \sü-ˈdan\	25,000,000
Suriname \ˌsu̇r-ə-ˈnä-mə\	405,000
Swaziland \ˈswä-zē-ˌland\	814,000
Sweden \ˈswē-dən\	8,727,000
Switzerland \ˈswit-sər-lənd\	6,996,000
Syria \ˈsir-ē-ə\	13,398,000
Taiwan (Republic of China) \tī-ˈwän\	20,926,000
Tajikistan \tä-ˌji-ki-ˈstän\	5,705,000
Tanzania \ˌtan-zə-ˈnē-ə\	26,542,000
Thailand \ˈtī-ˌland, -lənd\	57,829,000
Togo \ˈtō-gō\	3,810,000
Tonga \ˈtäŋ-gə\	99,100
Trinidad and Tobago \ˈtrin-ə-ˌdad... tə-ˈbā-gō\	1,249,000
Tunisia \tü-ˈnē-zhə\	8,530,000
Turkey \ˈtər-kē\	59,869,000
Turkmenistan \ˌtərk-ˌme-nə-ˈstän\	4,294,000
Tuvalu \tü-ˈvä-lü\	9,500
Uganda \yü-ˈgan-də\	17,741,000
Ukraine \ˈyü-ˌkrān, ˌyü-ˈkrān\	52,344,000
United Arab Emirates	1,986,000
United Kingdom of Great Britain and Northern Ireland \-ˈbri-tən...ˈīr-lənd\	55,500,000
England \ˈiŋ-glənd\	46,161,000
Northern Ireland	1,583,000
Scotland \ˈskät-lənd\	4,957,000
Wales \ˈwālz\	2,799,000
United States of America \-ə-ˈmer-i-kə\	249,632,692
Uruguay \ˈür-ə-ˌgwī, ˈyu̇r-ə-ˌgwā\	3,149,000
Uzbekistan \ˌu̇z-ˌbe-ki-ˈstän\	21,901,000
Vanuatu \ˌvan-ˌwä-ˈtü\	160,000
Vatican City State \ˈva-ti-kən-\	1,800
Venezuela \ˌve-nə-ˈzwā-lə\	20,609,000
Vietnam \vē-ˈet-ˈnäm\	70,902,000
Yemen \ˈye-mən\	12,519,000
Yugoslavia \ˌyü-gō-ˈslä-vē-ə\	10,561,000
Zambia \ˈzam-bē-ə\	8,504,000
Zimbabwe \zim-ˈbäb-wā\	10,123,000

Population of Places in the United States

Having 19,000 or More Inhabitants in 2000

A

Aberdeen, S. Dak.	24,658
Abilene, Tex.	115,930
Acton, Mass.	20,331
Addison, Ill.	35,914
Adrian, Mich.	21,574
Agawam, Mass.	28,144
Agoura Hills, Calif.	20,537
Aiken, S.C.	25,337
Akron, Ohio	217,074
Alameda, Calif.	72,259
Alamogordo, N. Mex.	35,582
Albany, Ga.	76,939
Albany, N.Y.	95,658
Albany, Oreg.	40,852
Albert Lea, Minn.	18,356
Albuquerque, N. Mex.	448,607
Alexandria, La.	46,342
Alexandria, Va.	128,283
Alhambra, Calif.	85,804
Alice, Tex.	19,010
Allen, Tex.	43,554
Allen Park, Mich.	29,376
Allentown, Pa.	106,632
Alliance, Ohio	23,253
Alsip, Ill.	19,725
Altamonte Springs, Fla.	41,200
Alton, Ill.	30,496
Altoona, Pa.	49,523
Altus, Okla.	21,447
Alvin, Tex.	21,413
Amarillo, Tex.	173,627
Ames, Iowa	50,731
Amherst, Mass.	34,874
Amsterdam, N.Y.	18,355
Anaheim, Calif.	328,014
Anchorage, Alaska	260,283
Anderson, Ind.	59,734
Anderson, S.C.	25,514
Andover, Mass.	31,247
Ankeny, Iowa	27,117
Annapolis, Md.	35,838
Ann Arbor, Mich.	114,024
Anniston, Ala.	24,276
Ansonia, Conn.	18,554
Antioch, Calif.	90,532
Apache Junction, Ariz.	31,814
Appleton, Wis.	70,087
Apple Valley, Calif.	54,239
Apple Valley, Minn.	45,527
Arcadia, Calif.	53,054
Ardmore, Okla.	23,711
Arlington, Mass.	42,389
Arlington, Tex.	332,969
Arlington Heights, Ill.	76,031
Arnold, Mo.	19,965
Arvada, Colo.	102,153
Asheville, N.C.	68,889
Ashland, Ky.	21,981
Ashland, Ohio	21,249
Ashtabula, Ohio	20,962
Atascadero, Calif.	26,411
Athens, Ga.	100,266
Athens, Ohio	21,342
Atlanta, Ga.	416,474
Atlantic City, N.J.	40,517
Attleboro, Mass.	42,068
Atwater, Calif.	23,113
Auburn, Ala.	42,987
Auburn, Me.	23,203
Auburn, N.Y.	28,574
Auburn, Wash.	40,314
Augusta, Ga.	195,182
Augusta, Me.	18,560
Aurora, Colo.	276,393
Aurora, Ill.	142,990
Austin, Minn.	23,314
Austin, Tex.	656,562
Azusa, Calif.	44,712

B

Bakersfield, Calif.	247,057
Baldwin, Pa.	19,999
Baldwin Park, Calif.	75,837
Ballwin, Mo.	31,283
Baltimore, Md.	651,154
Bangor, Me.	31,473
Banning, Calif.	23,567
Barberton, Ohio	27,899
Barnstable, Mass.	47,821
Barstow, Calif.	21,119
Bartlesville, Okla.	34,748
Bartlett, Ill.	36,706
Bartlett, Tenn.	40,543
Baton Rouge, La.	227,818
Battle Creek, Mich.	53,364
Bay City, Mich.	36,817
Bay City, Tex.	18,667
Bayonne, N.J.	61,842
Baytown, Tex.	66,430
Beaumont, Tex.	113,866
Beavercreek, Ohio	37,984
Beaverton, Oreg.	76,129
Bedford, Tex.	47,152
Bell, Calif.	36,664
Belleville, Ill.	41,410
Belleville, N.J.	35,928
Bellevue, Nebr.	44,382
Bellevue, Wash.	109,569
Bellflower, Calif.	72,878
Bell Gardens, Calif.	44,054
Bellingham, Wash.	67,171
Bellwood, Ill.	20,535
Belmont, Calif.	25,123
Belmont, Mass.	24,194
Beloit, Wis.	35,775
Belton, Mo.	21,730
Benbrook, Tex.	20,208
Bend, Oreg.	52,029
Benicia, Calif.	26,865
Bensenville, Ill.	20,703
Benton, Ark.	21,906
Berea, Ohio	18,970
Bergenfield, N.J.	26,247
Berkeley, Calif.	102,743
Berwyn, Ill.	54,016
Bessemer, Ala.	29,672
Bethany, Okla.	20,307
Bethel, Conn.	18,067
Bethel Park, Pa.	33,556

Bethesda, Md.	55,277
Bethlehem, Pa.	71,329
Bettendorf, Iowa	31,275
Beverly, Mass.	39,862
Beverly Hills, Calif.	33,784
Biddeford, Me.	20,942
Big Spring, Tex.	25,233
Billerica, Mass.	38,981
Billings, Mont.	89,847
Biloxi, Miss.	50,644
Binghamton, N.Y.	47,380
Birmingham, Ala.	242,820
Birmingham, Mich.	19,291
Bismarck, N. Dak.	55,532
Blacksburg, Va.	39,573
Blaine, Minn.	44,942
Bloomfield, N.J.	47,683
Bloomington, Ill.	64,808
Bloomington, Ind.	69,291
Bloomington, Minn.	85,172
Blue Island, Ill.	23,463
Blue Springs, Mo.	48,080
Blytheville, Ark.	18,272
Boca Raton, Fla.	74,764
Boise, Idaho	185,787
Bolingbrook, Ill.	56,321
Bossier City, La.	56,461
Boston, Mass.	589,141
Boulder, Colo.	94,673
Bountiful, Utah	41,301
Bowie, Md.	50,269
Bowling Green, Ky.	49,296
Bowling Green, Ohio	29,636
Boynton Beach, Fla.	60,389
Bozeman, Mont.	27,509
Bradenton, Fla.	49,504
Braintree, Mass.	33,828
Branford, Conn.	28,683
Brawley, Calif.	22,052
Brea, Calif.	35,410
Bremerton, Wash.	37,259
Bridgeport, Conn.	139,529
Bridgeton, N.J.	22,771
Bristol, Conn.	60,062
Bristol, R.I.	22,469
Bristol, Tenn.	24,821
Brockton, Mass.	94,304
Broken Arrow, Okla.	74,859
Brookfield, Ill.	19,085
Brookfield, Wis.	38,649
Brookline, Mass.	57,107
Brooklyn Center, Minn.	29,172
Brooklyn Park, Minn.	67,388
Brook Park, Ohio	21,218
Broomfield, Colo.	38,272
Brownsville, Tex.	139,722
Brownwood, Tex.	18,813
Brunswick, Me.	21,172
Brunswick, Ohio	33,388
Bryan, Tex.	65,660
Buena Park, Calif.	78,282
Buffalo, N.Y.	292,648
Buffalo Grove, Ill.	42,909
Bullhead City, Ariz.	33,769
Burbank, Calif.	100,316
Burbank, Ill.	27,902
Burlingame, Calif.	28,158
Burlington, Iowa	26,839
Burlington, Mass.	22,876
Burlington, N.C.	44,917
Burlington, Vt.	38,889
Burnsville, Minn.	60,220
Burton, Mich.	30,308
Butte, Mont.	33,892

C

Caldwell, Idaho	25,967
Calexico, Calif.	27,109
Calumet City, Ill.	39,071
Camarillo, Calif.	57,077
Cambridge, Mass.	101,355
Camden, N.J.	79,904
Campbell, Calif.	38,138
Canton, Mass.	20,775
Canton, Ohio	80,806
Cape Coral, Fla.	102,286
Cape Girardeau, Mo.	35,349
Carbondale, Ill.	20,681
Carlsbad, Calif.	78,247
Carlsbad, N. Mex.	25,625
Carmel, Ind.	37,733
Carol Stream, Ill.	40,438
Carpentersville, Ill.	30,586
Carrollton, Tex.	109,576
Carson City, Nev.	52,457
Carson, Calif.	89,730
Carteret, N.J.	20,709
Cary, N.C.	94,536
Casa Grande, Ariz.	25,224
Casper, Wyo.	49,644
Casselberry, Fla.	22,629
Cathedral City, Calif.	42,647
Cedar Falls, Iowa	36,145
Cedar Hill, Tex.	32,093
Cedar Rapids, Iowa	120,758
Centerville, Ohio	23,024
Central Falls, R.I.	18,928
Ceres, Calif.	34,609
Cerritos, Calif.	51,488
Champaign, Ill.	67,518
Chandler, Ariz.	176,581
Chapel Hill, N.C.	48,715
Charleston, Ill.	21,039
Charleston, S.C.	96,650
Charleston, W. Va.	53,421
Charlotte, N.C.	540,828
Charlottesville, Va.	45,049
Chattanooga, Tenn.	155,554
Chelmsford, Mass.	33,858
Chelsea, Mass.	35,080
Chesapeake, Va.	199,184
Cheshire, Conn.	28,543
Chester, Pa.	36,854
Chesterfield, Mo.	46,802
Cheyenne, Wyo.	53,011
Chicago, Ill.	2,896,016
Chicago Heights, Ill.	32,776
Chico, Calif.	59,954
Chicopee, Mass.	54,653
Chillicothe, Ohio	21,796
Chino, Calif.	67,168
Chula Vista, Calif.	173,556
Cicero, Ill.	85,616
Cincinnati, Ohio	331,285
Claremont, Calif.	33,998
Clarksdale, Miss.	20,645
Clarksville, Ind.	21,400
Clarksville, Tenn.	103,455
Clearfield, Utah	25,974
Clearwater, Fla.	108,787
Cleburne, Tex.	26,005
Cleveland, Ohio	478,403
Cleveland, Tenn.	37,192
Cleveland Heights, Ohio	49,958
Cliffside Park, N.J.	23,007
Clifton, N.J.	78,672
Clinton, Iowa	27,772
Clinton, Miss.	23,347
Clovis, Calif.	68,468
Clovis, N. Mex.	32,667
Coconut Creek, Fla.	43,566

Coeur d'Alene, Idaho	34,514
College Park, Ga.	20,382
College Park, Md.	24,657
College Station, Tex.	67,890
Collinsville, Ill.	24,707
Colorado Springs, Colo.	360,890
Colton, Calif.	47,662
Columbia, Mo.	84,531
Columbia, S.C.	116,278
Columbia, Tenn.	33,055
Columbia Heights, Minn.	18,520
Columbus, Ga.	185,781
Columbus, Ind.	39,059
Columbus, Miss.	25,944
Columbus, Nebr.	20,971
Columbus, Ohio	711,470
Compton, Calif.	93,493
Concord, Calif.	121,780
Concord, N.C.	55,977
Concord, N.H.	40,687
Conroe, Tex.	36,811
Conway, Ark.	43,167
Cookeville, Tenn.	23,923
Coon Rapids, Minn.	61,607
Cooper City, Fla.	27,939
Copperas Cove, Tex.	29,592
Coral Gables, Fla.	42,249
Coral Springs, Fla.	117,549
Corona, Calif.	124,966
Coronado, Calif.	24,100
Corpus Christi, Tex.	277,454
Corsicana, Tex.	24,485
Cortland, N.Y.	18,740
Corvallis, Oreg.	49,322
Costa Mesa, Calif.	108,724
Cottage Grove, Minn.	30,582
Council Bluffs, Iowa	58,268
Coventry, R.I.	33,668
Covina, Calif.	46,837
Covington, Ky.	43,370
Cranston, R.I.	79,269
Crown Point, Ind.	19,806
Crystal, Minn.	22,698
Crystal Lake, Ill.	38,000
Cudahy, Calif.	24,208
Cudahy, Wis.	18,429
Culver City, Calif.	38,816
Cumberland, Md.	21,518
Cumberland, R.I.	31,840
Cupertino, Calif.	50,546
Cuyahoga Falls, Ohio	49,374
Cypress, Calif.	46,229

D

Dallas, Tex.	1,188,580
Dalton, Ga.	27,912
Daly City, Calif.	103,621
Dana Point, Calif.	35,110
Danbury, Conn.	74,848
Danvers, Mass.	25,212
Danville, Calif.	41,715
Danville, Ill.	33,904
Danville, Va.	48,411
Darien, Conn.	19,607
Darien, Ill.	22,860
Dartmouth, Mass.	30,666
Davenport, Iowa	98,359
Davie, Fla.	75,720
Davis, Calif.	60,308
Daytona Beach, Fla.	64,112
Dayton, Ohio	166,179
Dearborn, Mich.	97,775
Dearborn Heights, Mich.	58,264
Decatur, Ala.	53,929
Decatur, Ill.	81,860
Dedham, Mass.	23,464
Deerfield Beach, Fla.	64,583
Deer Park, Tex.	28,520
De Kalb, Ill.	39,018
Delano, Calif.	38,824
Delaware, Ohio	25,243
Del City, Okla.	22,128
Delray Beach, Fla.	60,020
Del Rio, Tex.	33,867
Denison, Tex.	22,773
Denton, Tex.	80,537
Denver, Colo.	554,636
Derry, N.H.	34,021
Des Moines, Iowa	198,682
De Soto, Tex.	37,646
Des Plaines, Ill.	58,720
Detroit, Mich.	951,270
Diamond Bar, Calif.	56,287
Dodge City, Kans.	25,176
Dolton, Ill.	25,614
Dothan, Ala.	57,737
Dover, Del.	32,135
Dover, N.H.	26,884
Downers Grove, Ill.	48,724
Downey, Calif.	107,323
Dracut, Mass.	28,562
Duarte, Calif.	21,486
Dublin, Calif.	29,973
Dubuque, Iowa	57,686
Duluth, Minn.	86,918
Duncan, Okla.	22,505
Duncanville, Tex.	36,081
Dunedin, Fla.	35,691
Durham, N.C.	187,035

E

Eagan, Minn.	63,557
Eagle Pass, Tex.	22,413
East Chicago, Ind.	32,414
East Cleveland, Ohio	27,217
East Hartford, Conn.	49,575
East Haven, Conn.	28,189
Eastlake, Ohio	20,255
East Lansing, Mich.	46,525
East Moline, Ill.	20,333
Easton, Mass.	22,299
Easton, Pa.	26,263
East Orange, N.J.	69,824
East Palo Alto, Calif.	29,506
East Peoria, Ill.	22,638
East Point, Ga.	39,595
Eastpointe, Mich.	34,077
East Providence, R.I.	48,688
East Ridge, Tenn.	20,640
East St. Louis, Ill.	31,542
Eau Claire, Wis.	61,704
Eden Prairie, Minn.	54,901
Edina, Minn.	47,425
Edinburg, Tex.	48,465
Edmond, Okla.	68,315
Edmonds, Wash.	39,515
El Cajon, Calif.	94,869
El Centro, Calif.	37,835
El Cerrito, Calif.	23,171
El Dorado, Ark.	21,530
Elgin, Ill.	94,487
Elizabeth, N.J.	120,568
Elizabethtown, Ky.	22,542
Elk Grove Village, Ill.	34,727
Elkhart, Ind.	51,874
Elmhurst, Ill.	42,762
Elmira, N.Y.	30,940
El Monte, Calif.	115,965
Elmwood Park, Ill.	25,405
Elmwood Park, N.J.	18,925
El Paso, Tex.	563,662
El Paso de Robles, Calif.	24,297

Elyria, Ohio	55,953
Emporia, Kans.	26,760
Bronx, N.Y.	1,332,650
Brooklyn, N.Y.	2,465,326
Manhattan, N.Y.	1,537,195
Queens, N.Y.	2,229,379
Richmond, N.Y.	443,728
Encinitas, Calif.	58,014
Enfield, Conn.	45,212
Englewood, Colo.	31,727
Englewood, N.J.	26,203
Enid, Okla.	47,045
Enterprise, Ala.	21,178
Erie, Pa.	103,717
Escondido, Calif.	133,559
Euclid, Ohio	52,717
Eugene, Oreg.	137,893
Euless, Tex.	46,005
Eureka, Calif.	26,128
Evanston, Ill.	74,239
Evansville, Ind.	121,582
Everett, Mass.	38,037
Everett, Wash.	91,488
Evergreen Park, Ill.	20,821

F

Fairbanks, Alaska	30,224
Fairborn, Ohio	32,052
Fairfax, Va.	21,498
Fairfield, Calif.	96,178
Fairfield, Conn.	57,340
Fairfield, Ohio	42,097
Fair Lawn, N.J.	31,637
Fairmont, W. Va.	19,097
Fall River, Mass.	91,938
Falmouth, Mass.	32,660
Fargo, N. Dak.	90,599
Farmers Branch, Tex.	27,508
Farmington, N. Mex.	37,844
Farmington Hills, Mich.	82,111
Fayetteville, Ark.	58,047
Fayetteville, N.C.	121,015
Ferguson, Mo.	22,406
Ferndale, Mich.	22,105
Findlay, Ohio	38,967
Fitchburg, Mass.	39,102
Flagstaff, Ariz.	52,849
Flint, Mich.	124,943
Florence, Ala.	36,264
Florence, Ky.	23,551
Florence, S.C.	30,248
Florissant, Mo.	50,497
Folsom, Calif.	51,884
Fond du Lac, Wis.	42,203
Fontana, Calif.	128,929
Forest Park, Ohio	19,463
Fort Collins, Colo.	118,652
Fort Dodge, Iowa	25,136
Fort Lauderdale, Fla.	152,397
Fort Lee, N.J.	35,461
Fort Myers, Fla.	48,208
Fort Pierce, Fla.	37,516
Fort Smith, Ark.	80,268
Fort Walton Beach, Fla.	19,973
Fort Wayne, Ind.	205,727
Fort Worth, Tex.	534,694
Foster City, Calif.	28,803
Fountain Valley, Calif.	54,978
Framingham, Mass.	66,910
Frankfort, Ky.	27,741
Franklin, Mass.	29,560
Franklin, Tenn.	41,842
Franklin, Wis.	29,494
Franklin Park, Ill.	19,434
Frederick, Md.	52,767
Fredericksburg, Va.	19,279
Freeport, Ill.	26,443
Freeport, N.Y.	43,783
Fremont, Calif.	203,413
Fremont, Nebr.	25,174
Fresno, Calif.	427,652
Fridley, Minn.	27,449
Friendswood, Tex.	29,037
Fullerton, Calif.	126,003

G

Gadsden, Ala.	38,978
Gahanna, Ohio	32,636
Gainesville, Fla.	95,447
Gainesville, Ga.	25,578
Gaithersburg, Md.	52,613
Galesburg, Ill.	33,706
Gallatin, Tenn.	23,230
Gallup, N. Mex.	20,209
Galveston, Tex.	57,247
Gardena, Calif.	57,746
Garden City, Kans.	28,451
Garden City, Mich.	30,047
Garden City, N.Y.	21,672
Garden Grove, Calif.	165,196
Gardner, Mass.	20,770
Garfield, N.J.	29,786
Garfield Heights, Ohio	30,734
Garland, Tex.	215,768
Gary, Ind.	102,746
Gastonia, N.C.	66,277
Germantown, Tenn.	37,348
Gilbert, Ariz.	109,697
Gillette, Wyo.	19,646
Gilroy, Calif.	41,464
Gladstone, Mo.	26,365
Glastonbury, Conn.	31,876
Glen Cove, N.Y.	26,622
Glendale, Ariz.	218,812
Glendale, Calif.	194,973
Glendale Heights, Ill.	31,765
Glendora, Calif.	49,415
Glen Ellyn, Ill.	26,999
Glenview, Ill.	41,847
Gloucester, Mass.	30,273
Golden Valley, Minn.	20,281
Goldsboro, N.C.	39,043
Goose Creek, S.C.	29,208
Goshen, Ind.	29,383
Grand Forks, N. Dak.	49,321
Grand Island, Nebr.	42,940
Grand Junction, Colo.	41,986
Grand Prairie, Tex.	127,427
Grand Rapids, Mich.	197,800
Grandview, Mo.	24,881
Granite City, Ill.	31,301
Grapevine, Tex.	42,059
Great Falls, Mont.	56,690
Greeley, Colo.	76,930
Greenacres City, Fla.	27,569
Green Bay, Wis.	102,313
Greenbelt, Md.	21,456
Greenfield, Mass.	18,168
Greenfield, Wis.	35,476
Greensboro, N.C.	223,891
Greenville, Miss.	41,633
Greenville, N.C.	60,476
Greenville, S.C.	56,002
Greenville, Tex.	23,960
Greenwich, Conn.	61,101
Greenwood, Ind.	36,037
Greenwood, Miss.	18,425
Greenwood, S.C.	22,071
Gresham, Oreg.	90,205
Griffin, Ga.	23,451
Groton, Conn.	39,907
Grove City, Ohio	27,075

Guilford, Conn.	21,398
Gulfport, Miss.	71,127

H

Hackensack, N.J.	42,677
Hagerstown, Md.	36,687
Hallandale, Fla.	34,282
Haltom City, Tex.	39,018
Hamden, Conn.	56,913
Hamilton, Ohio	60,690
Hammond, Ind.	83,048
Hampton, Va.	146,437
Hamtramck, Mich.	22,976
Hanford, Calif.	41,686
Hanover Park, Ill.	38,278
Harlingen, Tex.	57,564
Harrisburg, Pa.	48,950
Harrisonburg, Va.	40,468
Harrison, N.Y.	24,154
Hartford, Conn.	121,578
Harvey, Ill.	30,000
Hastings, Nebr.	24,064
Hattiesburg, Miss.	44,779
Havelock, N.C.	22,442
Haverhill, Mass.	58,969
Hawthorne, Calif.	84,112
Hays, Kans.	20,013
Hayward, Calif.	140,030
Hazel Park, Mich.	18,963
Hazleton, Pa.	23,329
Helena, Mont.	25,780
Hemet, Calif.	58,812
Hempstead, N.Y.	56,554
Henderson, Ky.	27,373
Henderson, Nev.	175,381
Hendersonville, Tenn.	40,620
Hermosa Beach, Calif.	18,566
Hesperia, Calif.	62,582
Hialeah, Fla.	226,419
Hickory, N.C.	37,222
Highland, Calif.	44,605
Highland, Ind.	23,546
Highland Park, Ill.	31,365
High Point, N.C.	85,839
Hillsboro, Oreg.	70,186
Hilo, Hawaii	40,759
Hilton Head Island, S.C.	33,862
Hinesville, Ga.	30,392
Hingham, Mass.	19,882
Hobart, Ind.	25,363
Hobbs, N. Mex.	28,657
Hoboken, N.J.	38,577
Hoffman Estates, Ill.	49,495
Holland, Mich.	35,048
Hollister, Calif.	34,413
Hollywood, Fla.	139,357
Holyoke, Mass.	39,838
Homestead, Fla.	31,909
Homewood, Ala.	25,043
Homewood, Ill.	19,543
Honolulu, Hawaii	371,657
Hoover, Ala.	62,742
Hopewell, Va.	22,354
Hopkinsville, Ky.	30,089
Hot Springs, Ark.	35,750
Houma, La.	32,393
Houston, Tex.	1,953,631
Huber Heights, Ohio	38,212
Huntington Beach, Calif.	189,594
Huntington, W. Va.	51,475
Huntington Park, Calif.	61,348
Huntsville, Ala.	158,216
Huntsville, Tex.	35,078
Hurst, Tex.	36,273
Hutchinson, Kans.	40,787

I

Idaho Falls, Idaho	50,730
Imperial Beach, Calif.	26,992
Independence, Mo.	113,288
Indianapolis, Ind.	781,870
Indio, Calif.	49,116
Inglewood, Calif.	112,580
Inkster, Mich.	30,115
Inver Grove Heights, Minn.	29,751
Iowa City, Iowa	62,220
Irvine, Calif.	143,072
Irving, Tex.	191,615
Ithaca, N.Y.	29,287

J

Jackson, Mich.	36,316
Jackson, Miss.	184,256
Jackson, Tenn.	59,643
Jacksonville Beach, Fla.	20,990
Jacksonville, Ark.	29,916
Jacksonville, Fla.	735,617
Jacksonville, Ill.	18,940
Jacksonville, N.C.	66,715
Jamestown, N.Y.	31,730
Janesville, Wis.	59,498
Jefferson City, Mo.	39,636
Jeffersontown, Ky.	26,633
Jeffersonville, Ind.	27,362
Jersey City, N.J.	240,055
Johnson City, Tenn.	55,469
Johnston, R.I.	28,195
Johnstown, Pa.	23,906
Joliet, Ill.	106,221
Jonesboro, Ark.	55,515
Joplin, Mo.	45,504
Junction City, Kans.	18,886
Juneau, Alaska	30,711
Jupiter, Fla.	39,328

K

Kailua, Hawaii	36,513
Kalamazoo, Mich.	77,145
Kaneohe, Hawaii	34,970
Kankakee, Ill.	27,491
Kannapolis, N.C.	36,910
Kansas City, Kans.	146,866
Kansas City, Mo.	441,545
Kearney, Nebr.	27,431
Kearny, N.J.	40,513
Keene, N.H.	22,563
Keizer, Oreg.	32,203
Kenner, La.	70,517
Kennewick, Wash.	54,693
Kenosha, Wis.	90,352
Kent, Ohio	27,906
Kent, Wash.	79,524
Kentwood, Mich.	45,255
Kettering, Ohio	57,502
Key West, Fla.	25,478
Killeen, Tex.	86,911
Kingsport, Tenn.	44,905
Kingston, N.Y.	23,456
Kingsville, Tex.	25,575
Kinston, N.C.	23,688
Kirkland, Wash.	45,054
Kirkwood, Mo.	27,324
Kissimmee, Fla.	47,814
Klamath Falls, Oreg.	19,462
Knoxville, Tenn.	173,890
Kokomo, Ind.	46,113

L

La Canada Flintridge, Calif.	20,318
Lacey, Wash.	31,226

Lackawanna, N.Y.	19,064
La Crosse, Wis.	51,818
Lafayette, Calif.	23,908
Lafayette, Ind.	56,397
Lafayette, La.	110,257
La Grange, Ga.	25,998
Laguna Beach, Calif.	23,727
Laguna Niguel, Calif.	61,891
La Habra, Calif.	58,974
Lake Charles, La.	71,757
Lake Elsinore, Calif.	28,928
Lake Forest, Ill.	20,059
Lake Havasu City, Ariz.	41,938
Lake Jackson, Tex.	26,386
Lakeland, Fla.	78,452
Lake Oswego, Oreg.	35,278
Lakeville, Minn.	43,128
Lakewood, Calif.	79,345
Lakewood, Colo.	144,126
Lakewood, Ohio	56,646
Lake Worth, Fla.	35,133
La Mesa, Calif.	54,749
La Mirada, Calif.	46,783
Lancaster, Calif.	118,718
Lancaster, Ohio	35,335
Lancaster, Pa.	56,348
Lancaster, Tex.	25,894
Lansing, Ill.	28,332
Lansing, Mich.	119,128
La Porte, Ind.	21,621
La Porte, Tex.	31,880
La Puente, Calif.	41,063
Laramie, Wyo.	27,204
Laredo, Tex.	176,576
Largo, Fla.	69,371
Las Cruces, N. Mex.	74,267
Las Vegas, Nev.	478,434
Lauderdale Lakes, Fla.	31,705
Lauderhill, Fla.	57,585
Laurel, Md.	19,960
Laurel, Miss.	18,393
La Verne, Calif.	31,638
Lawndale, Calif.	31,711
Lawrence, Ind.	38,915
Lawrence, Kans.	80,098
Lawrence, Mass.	72,043
Lawton, Okla.	92,757
Layton, Utah	58,474
League City, Tex.	45,444
Leavenworth, Kans.	35,420
Leawood, Kans.	27,656
Lebanon, Pa.	24,461
Lee's Summit, Mo.	70,700
Lemon Grove, Calif.	24,918
Lenexa, Kans.	40,238
Leominster, Mass.	41,303
Lewiston, Idaho	30,904
Lewiston, Me.	35,690
Lewisville, Tex.	77,737
Lexington, Ky.	260,512
Lexington, Mass.	30,355
Liberty, Mo.	26,232
Libertyville, Ill.	20,742
Lima, Ohio	40,081
Lincoln, Nebr.	225,581
Lincoln, R.I.	20,898
Lincoln Park, Mich.	40,008
Linden, N.J.	39,394
Lindenhurst, N.Y.	27,819
Lisle, Ill.	21,182
Little Rock, Ark.	183,133
Littleton, Colo.	40,340
Livermore, Calif.	73,345
Livonia, Mich.	100,545
Lockport, N.Y.	22,279
Lodi, Calif.	56,999
Lodi, N.J.	23,971
Logan, Utah	42,670
Lombard, Ill.	42,322
Lomita, Calif.	20,046
Lompoc, Calif.	41,103
Long Beach, Calif.	461,522
Long Beach, N.Y.	35,462
Long Branch, N.J.	31,340
Longmont, Colo.	71,093
Longview, Tex.	73,344
Longview, Wash.	34,660
Lorain, Ohio	68,652
Los Altos, Calif.	27,693
Los Angeles, Calif.	3,694,820
Los Gatos, Calif.	28,592
Louisville, Ky.	256,231
Loveland, Colo.	50,608
Lowell, Mass.	105,167
Lubbock, Tex.	199,564
Ludlow, Mass.	21,209
Lufkin, Tex.	32,709
Lumberton, N.C.	20,795
Lynbrook, N.Y.	19,911
Lynchburg, Va.	65,269
Lynn, Mass.	89,050
Lynnwood, Wash.	33,847
Lynwood, Calif.	69,845

M

Machesney Park, Ill.	20,759
Macomb, Ill.	18,558
Macon, Ga.	97,255
Madera, Calif.	43,207
Madison, Wis.	208,054
Madison Heights, Mich.	31,101
Malden, Mass.	56,340
Manassas, Va.	35,135
Manchester, Conn.	54,740
Manchester, N.H.	107,006
Manhattan Beach, Calif.	33,852
Manhattan, Kans.	44,831
Manitowoc, Wis.	34,053
Mankato, Minn.	32,427
Mansfield, Conn.	20,720
Mansfield, Ohio	49,346
Manteca, Calif.	49,258
Maple Grove, Minn.	50,365
Maple Heights, Ohio	26,156
Maplewood, Minn.	34,947
Marblehead, Mass.	20,377
Margate, Fla.	53,909
Marietta, Ga.	58,748
Marina, Calif.	25,101
Marion, Ind.	31,320
Marion, Iowa	26,294
Marion, Ohio	35,318
Marlborough, Mass.	36,255
Marquette, Mich.	19,661
Marshall, Tex.	23,935
Marshalltown, Iowa	26,009
Marshfield, Mass.	24,324
Marshfield, Wis.	18,800
Martinez, Calif.	35,866
Maryland Heights, Mo.	25,756
Maryville, Tenn.	23,120
Mason City, Iowa	29,172
Massillon, Ohio	31,325
Mattoon, Ill.	18,291
Mayfield Heights, Ohio	19,386
Maywood, Calif.	28,083
Maywood, Ill.	26,987
McAllen, Tex.	106,414
McKeesport, Pa.	24,040
McKinney, Tex.	54,369
McMinnville, Oreg.	26,499
Medford, Mass.	55,765
Medford, Oreg.	63,154

Melbourne, Fla.	71,382
Melrose, Mass.	27,134
Melrose Park, Ill.	23,171
Memphis, Tenn.	650,100
Menlo Park, Calif.	30,785
Menomonee Falls, Wis.	32,647
Mentor, Ohio	50,278
Merced, Calif.	63,893
Mercer Island, Wash.	22,036
Meriden, Conn.	58,244
Meridian, Miss.	39,968
Merrillville, Ind.	30,560
Mesa, Ariz.	396,375
Mesquite, Tex.	124,523
Methuen, Mass.	43,789
Miami Beach, Fla.	87,933
Miami, Fla.	362,470
Miamisburg, Ohio	19,489
Michigan City, Ind.	32,900
Middleborough, Mass.	19,941
Middletown, Conn.	43,167
Middletown, N.Y.	25,388
Middletown, Ohio	51,605
Midland, Mich.	41,685
Midland, Tex.	94,996
Midwest City, Okla.	54,088
Milford, Conn.	52,305
Milford, Mass.	26,799
Mililani Town, Hawaii	28,608
Millbrae, Calif.	20,718
Milledgeville, Ga.	18,757
Millville, N.J.	26,847
Milpitas, Calif.	62,698
Milton, Mass.	26,062
Milwaukee, Wis.	596,974
Milwaukie, Oreg.	20,490
Mineola, N.Y.	19,234
Minneapolis, Minn.	382,618
Minnetonka, Minn.	51,301
Minot, N. Dak.	36,567
Miramar, Fla.	72,739
Mishawaka, Ind.	46,557
Mission, Tex.	45,408
Mission Viejo, Calif.	93,102
Missoula, Mont.	57,053
Missouri City, Tex.	52,913
Mobile, Ala.	198,915
Modesto, Calif.	188,856
Moline, Ill.	43,768
Monroe, La.	53,107
Monroe, Mich.	22,076
Monrovia, Calif.	36,929
Montclair, Calif.	33,049
Montclair, N.J.	38,977
Montebello, Calif.	62,150
Monterey, Calif.	29,674
Monterey Park, Calif.	60,051
Montgomery, Ala.	201,568
Moore, Okla.	41,138
Moorhead, Minn.	32,177
Moorpark, Calif.	31,415
Moreno Valley, Calif.	142,381
Morgan Hill, Calif.	33,556
Morgantown, W. Va.	26,809
Morristown, Tenn.	24,965
Morton Grove, Ill.	22,451
Moscow, Idaho	21,291
Mountain Brook, Ala.	20,604
Mountain View, Calif.	70,708
Mountlake Terrace, Wash.	20,362
Mount Pleasant, Mich.	25,946
Mount Pleasant, S.C.	47,609
Mount Prospect, Ill.	56,265
Mount Vernon, N.Y.	68,381
Mount Vernon, Wash.	26,232
Muncie, Ind.	67,430
Mundelein, Ill.	30,935
Munster, Ind.	21,511
Murfreesboro, Tenn.	68,816
Murray, Utah	34,024
Muscatine, Iowa	22,697
Muskegon, Mich.	40,105
Muskogee, Okla.	38,310
Myrtle Beach, S.C.	22,759

N

Nacogdoches, Tex.	29,914
Nampa, Idaho	51,867
Napa, Calif.	72,585
Naperville, Ill.	128,358
Naples, Fla.	20,976
Nashua, N.H.	86,605
Nashville, Tenn.	545,524
Natchez, Miss.	18,464
Natick, Mass.	32,170
National City, Calif.	54,260
Naugatuck, Conn.	30,989
Needham, Mass.	28,911
Neenah, Wis.	24,507
New Albany, Ind.	37,603
Newark, Calif.	42,471
Newark, Del.	28,547
Newark, N.J.	273,546
Newark, Ohio	46,279
New Bedford, Mass.	93,768
New Berlin, Wis.	38,220
New Braunfels, Tex.	36,494
New Brighton, Minn.	22,206
New Britain, Conn.	71,538
New Brunswick, N.J.	48,573
Newburgh, N.Y.	28,259
New Canaan, Conn.	19,395
New Castle, Pa.	26,309
New Haven, Conn.	123,626
New Hope, Minn.	20,873
New Iberia, La.	32,623
Newington, Conn.	29,306
New London, Conn.	25,671
New Milford, Conn.	27,121
New Orleans, La.	484,674
Newport Beach, Calif.	70,032
Newport, R.I.	26,475
Newport News, Va.	180,150
New Rochelle, N.Y.	72,182
Newton, Mass.	83,829
Newtown, Conn.	25,031
New York City, N.Y.	8,008,278
Niagara Falls, N.Y.	55,593
Niles, Ill.	30,068
Niles, Ohio	20,932
Noblesville, Ind.	28,590
Nogales, Ariz.	20,878
Norco, Calif.	24,157
Norfolk, Nebr.	23,516
Norfolk, Va.	234,403
Normal, Ill.	45,386
Norman, Okla.	95,694
Norristown, Pa.	31,282
Northampton, Mass.	28,978
North Andover, Mass.	27,202
North Attleboro, Mass.	27,143
Northbrook, Ill.	33,435
North Charleston, S.C.	79,641
North Chicago, Ill.	35,918
Northglenn, Colo.	31,575
North Haven, Conn.	23,035
North Kingstown, R.I.	26,326
North Las Vegas, Nev.	115,488
North Lauderdale, Fla.	32,264
North Little Rock, Ark.	60,433
North Miami Beach, Fla.	40,786
North Miami, Fla.	59,880
North Olmsted, Ohio	34,113

North Plainfield, N.J.	21,103
North Platte, Nebr.	23,878
North Providence, R.I.	32,411
North Richland Hills, Tex.	55,635
North Ridgeville, Ohio	22,338
North Royalton, Ohio	28,648
North Tonawanda, N.Y.	33,262
Norton Shores, Mich.	22,527
Norwalk, Calif.	103,298
Norwalk, Conn.	82,951
Norwich, Conn.	36,117
Norwood, Mass.	28,587
Norwood, Ohio	21,675
Novato, Calif.	47,630
Novi, Mich.	47,386
Nutley, N.J.	27,362

O

Oak Creek, Wis.	28,456
Oakdale, Minn.	26,653
Oak Forest, Ill.	28,051
Oakland, Calif.	399,484
Oakland Park, Fla.	30,966
Oak Lawn, Ill.	55,245
Oak Park, Ill.	52,524
Oak Park, Mich.	29,793
Oak Ridge, Tenn.	27,387
Ocala, Fla.	45,943
Oceanside, Calif.	161,029
Odessa, Tex.	90,943
O'Fallon, Mo.	46,169
Ogden, Utah	77,226
Oklahoma City, Okla.	506,132
Olathe, Kans.	92,962
Olympia, Wash.	42,514
Omaha, Nebr.	390,007
Ontario, Calif.	158,007
Opelika, Ala.	23,498
Opelousas, La.	22,860
Orange, Calif.	128,821
Orange, N.J.	32,868
Orange, Tex.	18,643
Oregon, Ohio	19,355
Orem, Utah	84,324
Orlando, Fla.	185,951
Orland Park, Ill.	51,077
Ormond Beach, Fla.	36,301
Oshkosh, Wis.	62,916
Ossining, N.Y.	24,010
Ottumwa, Iowa	24,998
Overland Park, Kans.	149,080
Owatonna, Minn.	22,434
Owensboro, Ky.	54,067
Oxford, Ohio	21,943
Oxnard, Calif.	170,358

P

Pacifica, Calif.	38,390
Paducah, Ky.	26,307
Palatine, Ill.	65,479
Palm Bay, Fla.	79,413
Palm Springs, Calif.	42,807
Palo Alto, Calif.	58,598
Panama City, Fla.	36,417
Paradise, Calif.	26,408
Paragould, Ark.	22,017
Paramount, Calif.	55,266
Paramus, N.J.	25,737
Paris, Tex.	25,898
Parkersburg, W. Va.	33,099
Park Forest, Ill.	23,462
Park Ridge, Ill.	37,775
Parma, Ohio	85,655
Parma Heights, Ohio	21,659
Pasadena, Calif.	133,936
Pasadena, Tex.	141,674
Pascagoula, Miss.	26,200
Pasco, Wash.	32,066
Passaic, N.J.	67,861
Paterson, N.J.	149,222
Pawtucket, R.I.	72,958
Peabody, Mass.	48,129
Peachtree City, Ga.	31,580
Pearland, Tex.	37,640
Pearl City, Hawaii	30,976
Pearl, Miss.	21,961
Peekskill, N.Y.	22,441
Pekin, Ill.	33,857
Pembroke Pines, Fla.	137,427
Pensacola, Fla.	56,255
Peoria, Ariz.	108,346
Peoria, Ill.	112,936
Perris, Calif.	36,189
Perth Amboy, N.J.	47,303
Petaluma, Calif.	54,548
Petersburg, Va.	33,740
Pharr, Tex.	46,660
Phenix City, Ala.	28,265
Philadelphia, Pa.	1,517,550
Phoenix, Ariz.	1,321,045
Pico Rivera, Calif.	63,428
Pine Bluff, Ark.	55,085
Pinellas Park, Fla.	45,658
Piqua, Ohio	20,612
Pittsburg, Calif.	56,769
Pittsburg, Kans.	19,243
Pittsburgh, Pa.	334,563
Pittsfield, Mass.	45,793
Placentia, Calif.	46,488
Plainfield, N.J.	47,829
Plainview, Tex.	22,336
Plano, Tex.	222,030
Plantation, Fla.	82,934
Plant City, Fla.	29,915
Plattsburgh, N.Y.	18,816
Pleasant Hill, Calif.	32,837
Pleasanton, Calif.	63,654
Plum, Pa.	26,940
Plymouth, Mass.	51,701
Plymouth, Minn.	65,894
Pocatello, Idaho	51,466
Point Pleasant, N.J.	19,306
Pomona, Calif.	149,473
Pompano Beach, Fla.	78,191
Ponca City, Okla.	25,919
Pontiac, Mich.	66,337
Portage, Ind.	33,496
Portage, Mich.	44,897
Port Angeles, Wash.	18,397
Port Arthur, Tex.	57,755
Port Chester, N.Y.	27,867
Porterville, Calif.	39,615
Port Hueneme, Calif.	21,845
Port Huron, Mich.	32,338
Portland, Me.	64,249
Portland, Oreg.	529,121
Port Orange, Fla.	45,823
Portsmouth, N.H.	20,784
Portsmouth, Ohio	20,909
Portsmouth, Va.	100,565
Port St. Lucie, Fla.	88,769
Pottstown, Pa.	21,859
Poughkeepsie, N.Y.	29,871
Poway, Calif.	48,044
Prairie Village, Kans.	22,072
Prattville, Ala.	24,303
Prescott, Ariz.	33,938
Prichard, Ala.	28,633
Providence, R.I.	173,618
Provo, Utah	105,166
Pueblo, Colo.	102,121
Pullman, Wash.	24,675
Puyallup, Wash.	33,011

Q

Quincy, Ill.	40,366
Quincy, Mass.	88,025

R

Racine, Wis.	81,855
Radcliff, Ky.	21,961
Rahway, N.J.	26,500
Raleigh, N.C.	276,093
Rancho Cucamonga, Calif.	127,743
Rancho Palos Verdes, Calif.	41,145
Randolph, Mass.	30,963
Rapid City, S. Dak.	59,607
Raytown, Mo.	30,388
Reading, Mass.	23,708
Reading, Pa.	81,207
Redding, Calif.	80,865
Redlands, Calif.	63,591
Redmond, Wash.	45,256
Redondo Beach, Calif.	63,261
Redwood City, Calif.	75,402
Reno, Nev.	180,480
Renton, Wash.	50,052
Revere, Mass.	47,283
Reynoldsburg, Ohio	32,069
Rialto, Calif.	91,873
Richardson, Tex.	91,802
Richfield, Minn.	34,439
Richland, Wash.	38,708
Richmond, Calif.	99,216
Richmond, Ind.	39,124
Richmond, Ky.	27,152
Richmond, Va.	197,790
Ridgecrest, Calif.	24,927
Ridgefield, Conn.	23,643
Ridgewood, N.J.	24,936
Rio Rancho, N. Mex.	51,765
Riverside, Calif.	255,166
Riviera Beach, Fla.	29,884
Roanoke, Va.	94,911
Rochester, Minn.	85,806
Rochester, N.H.	28,461
Rochester, N.Y.	219,773
Rochester Hills, Mich.	68,825
Rockford, Ill.	150,115
Rock Hill, S.C.	49,765
Rock Island, Ill.	39,684
Rocklin, Calif.	36,330
Rock Springs, Wyo.	18,708
Rockville Centre, N.Y.	24,568
Rockville, Md.	47,388
Rocky Mount, N.C.	55,893
Rocky River, Ohio	20,735
Rogers, Ark.	38,829
Rohnert Park, Calif.	42,236
Rolling Meadows, Ill.	24,604
Rome, Ga.	34,980
Rome, N.Y.	34,950
Romulus, Mich.	22,979
Roselle, Ill.	23,115
Roselle, N.J.	21,274
Rosemead, Calif.	53,505
Rosenberg, Tex.	24,043
Roseville, Calif.	79,921
Roseville, Mich.	48,129
Roseville, Minn.	33,690
Roswell, Ga.	79,334
Roswell, N. Mex.	45,293
Round Rock, Tex.	61,136
Rowlett, Tex.	44,503
Royal Oak, Mich.	60,062
Roy, Utah	32,885
Russellville, Ark.	23,682
Ruston, La.	20,546
Rutherford, N.J.	18,110

S

Sacramento, Calif.	407,018
Saginaw, Mich.	61,799
Salem, Mass.	40,407
Salem, N.H.	28,112
Salem, Oreg.	136,924
Salem, Va.	24,747
Salina, Kans.	45,679
Salinas, Calif.	151,060
Salisbury, Md.	23,743
Salisbury, N.C.	26,462
Salt Lake City, Utah	181,743
San Angelo, Tex.	88,439
San Antonio, Tex.	1,144,646
San Benito, Tex.	23,444
San Bernardino, Calif.	185,401
San Bruno, Calif.	40,165
San Carlos, Calif.	27,718
San Clemente, Calif.	49,936
San Diego, Calif.	1,223,400
San Dimas, Calif.	34,980
Sandusky, Ohio	27,844
Sandy, Utah	88,418
San Fernando, Calif.	23,564
Sanford, Fla.	38,291
Sanford, Me.	20,806
San Francisco, Calif.	776,733
San Gabriel, Calif.	39,804
San Jose, Calif.	894,943
San Juan Capistrano, Calif.	33,826
San Leandro, Calif.	79,452
San Luis Obispo, Calif.	44,174
San Marcos, Calif.	54,977
San Marcos, Tex.	34,733
San Mateo, Calif.	92,482
San Pablo, Calif.	30,215
San Rafael, Calif.	56,063
San Ramon, Calif.	44,722
Santa Ana, Calif.	337,977
Santa Barbara, Calif.	92,325
Santa Clara, Calif.	102,361
Santa Clarita, Calif.	151,088
Santa Cruz, Calif.	54,593
Santa Fe, N. Mex.	62,203
Santa Maria, Calif.	77,423
Santa Monica, Calif.	84,084
Santa Paula, Calif.	28,598
Santa Rosa, Calif.	147,595
Santee, Calif.	52,975
Sapulpa, Okla.	19,166
Sarasota, Fla.	52,715
Saratoga, Calif.	29,843
Saratoga Springs, N.Y.	26,186
Saugus, Mass.	26,078
Savannah, Ga.	131,510
Sayreville, N.J.	40,377
Schaumburg, Ill.	75,386
Schenectady, N.Y.	61,821
Schererville, Ind.	24,851
Scottsdale, Ariz.	202,705
Scranton, Pa.	76,415
Seal Beach, Calif.	24,157
Seaside, Calif.	31,696
Seattle, Wash.	563,374
Sedalia, Mo.	20,339
Seguin, Tex.	22,011
Selma, Ala.	20,512
Shaker Heights, Ohio	29,405
Shawnee, Kans.	47,996
Shawnee, Okla.	28,692
Sheboygan, Wis.	50,792
Shelton, Conn.	38,101
Sherman, Tex.	35,082
Sherwood, Ark.	21,511
Shoreview, Minn.	25,924
Shreveport, La.	200,145
Shrewsbury, Mass.	31,640

Sidney, Ohio	20,211
Sierra Vista, Ariz.	37,775
Simi Valley, Calif.	111,351
Simsbury, Conn.	23,234
Sioux City, Iowa	85,013
Sioux Falls, S. Dak.	123,975
Skokie, Ill.	63,348
Slidell, La.	25,695
Smithfield, R.I.	20,613
Smyrna, Ga.	40,999
Socorro, Tex.	27,152
Solon, Ohio	21,802
Somerset, Mass.	18,234
Somerville, Mass.	77,478
Southaven, Miss.	28,977
South Bend, Ind.	107,789
South El Monte, Calif.	21,144
South Euclid, Ohio	23,537
Southfield, Mich.	78,296
South Gate, Calif.	96,375
Southgate, Mich.	30,136
South Holland, Ill.	22,147
Southington, Conn.	39,728
South Kingstown, R.I.	27,921
South Lake Tahoe, Calif.	23,609
South Milwaukee, Wis.	21,256
South Pasadena, Calif.	24,292
South Plainfield, N.J.	21,810
South Portland, Me.	23,324
South San Francisco, Calif.	60,552
South St. Paul, Minn.	20,167
South Windsor, Conn.	24,412
Sparks, Nev.	66,346
Spartanburg, S.C.	39,673
Spokane, Wash.	195,629
Springdale, Ark.	45,798
Springfield, Ill.	111,454
Springfield, Mass.	152,082
Springfield, Mo.	151,580
Springfield, Ohio	65,358
Springfield, Oreg.	52,864
Spring Valley, N.Y.	25,464
Stamford, Conn.	117,083
Stanton, Calif.	37,403
Starkville, Miss.	21,869
State College, Pa.	38,420
Statesville, N.C.	23,320
Staunton, Va.	23,853
St. Charles, Ill.	27,896
St. Charles, Mo.	60,321
St. Clair Shores, Mich.	63,096
St. Cloud, Minn.	59,107
Sterling Heights, Mich.	124,471
Steubenville, Ohio	19,015
Stevens Point, Wis.	24,551
St. George, Utah	49,663
Stillwater, Okla.	39,065
St. Joseph, Mo.	73,990
St. Louis, Mo.	348,189
St. Louis Park, Minn.	44,126
Stockton, Calif.	243,771
Stoneham, Mass.	22,219
Stoughton, Mass.	27,149
Stow, Ohio	32,139
St. Paul, Minn.	287,151
St. Petersburg, Fla.	248,232
St. Peters, Mo.	51,381
Stratford, Conn.	49,976
Streamwood, Ill.	36,407
Strongsville, Ohio	43,858
Suffolk, Va.	63,677
Sugar Land, Tex.	63,328
Suisun City, Calif.	26,118
Sulphur, La.	20,512
Summerville, S.C.	27,752
Summit, N.J.	21,131
Sumter, S.C.	39,643
Sunnyvale, Calif.	131,760
Sunrise, Fla.	85,779
Superior, Wis.	27,368
Syracuse, N.Y.	147,306

T

Tacoma, Wash.	193,556
Tallahassee, Fla.	150,624
Tamarac, Fla.	55,588
Tampa, Fla.	303,447
Tarpon Springs, Fla.	21,003
Taunton, Mass.	55,976
Taylor, Mich.	65,868
Temecula, Calif.	57,716
Tempe, Ariz.	158,625
Temple City, Calif.	33,377
Temple, Tex.	54,514
Terre Haute, Ind.	59,614
Tewksbury, Mass.	28,851
Texarkana, Ark.	26,448
Texarkana, Tex.	34,782
Texas City, Tex.	41,521
The Colony, Tex.	26,531
Thornton, Colo.	82,384
Thousand Oaks, Calif.	117,005
Tiffin, Ohio	18,135
Tigard, Oreg.	41,223
Tinley Park, Ill.	48,401
Titusville, Fla.	40,670
Toledo, Ohio	313,619
Topeka, Kans.	122,377
Torrance, Calif.	137,946
Torrington, Conn.	35,202
Tracy, Calif.	56,929
Trenton, Mich.	19,584
Trenton, N.J.	85,403
Troy, Mich.	80,959
Troy, N.Y.	49,170
Troy, Ohio	21,999
Trumbull, Conn.	34,243
Tucson, Ariz.	486,699
Tulare, Calif.	43,994
Tulsa, Okla.	393,049
Tupelo, Miss.	34,211
Turlock, Calif.	55,810
Tuscaloosa, Ala.	77,906
Tustin, Calif.	67,504
Twin Falls, Idaho	34,469
Tyler, Tex.	83,650

U

Union City, Calif.	66,869
Union City, N.J.	67,088
University City, Mo.	37,428
University Park, Tex.	23,324
Upland, Calif.	68,393
Upper Arlington, Ohio	33,686
Urbana, Ill.	36,395
Urbandale, Iowa	29,072
Utica, N.Y.	60,651

V

Vacaville, Calif.	88,625
Valdosta, Ga.	43,724
Vallejo, Calif.	116,760
Valley Stream, N.Y.	36,368
Valparaiso, Ind.	27,428
Vancouver, Wash.	143,560
Ventura (San Buenaventura), Calif.	100,916
Vernon, Conn.	28,063
Vestavia Hills, Ala.	24,476
Vicksburg, Miss.	26,407
Victoria, Tex.	60,603
Victorville, Calif.	64,029
Villa Park, Ill.	22,075

Vincennes, Ind.	18,701
Vineland, N.J.	56,271
Virginia Beach, Va.	425,257
Visalia, Calif.	91,565
Vista, Calif.	89,857

W

Waco, Tex.	113,726
Waipahu, Hawaii	33,108
Wakefield, Mass.	24,804
Walla Walla, Wash.	29,686
Wallingford, Conn.	43,026
Walnut, Calif.	30,004
Walnut Creek, Calif.	64,296
Walpole, Mass.	22,824
Waltham, Mass.	59,226
Wareham, Mass.	20,335
Warner Robins, Ga.	48,804
Warren, Mich.	138,247
Warren, Ohio	46,832
Warwick, R.I.	85,808
Washington, D.C.	572,059
Watauga, Tex.	21,908
Waterbury, Conn.	107,271
Waterford, Conn.	19,152
Waterloo, Iowa	68,747
Watertown, Conn.	21,661
Watertown, Mass.	32,986
Watertown, N.Y.	26,705
Watertown, S. Dak.	20,237
Watertown, Wis.	21,598
Watsonville, Calif.	44,265
Waukegan, Ill.	87,901
Waukesha, Wis.	64,825
Wausau, Wis.	38,426
Wauwatosa, Wis.	47,271
Waxahachie, Tex.	21,426
Wayne, Mich.	19,051
Waynesboro, Va.	19,520
Webster Groves, Mo.	23,230
Weirton, W. Va.	20,411
Wellesley, Mass.	26,613
Wenatchee, Wash.	27,856
Weslaco, Tex.	26,935
West Allis, Wis.	61,254
West Bend, Wis.	28,152
West Covina, Calif.	105,080
West Des Moines, Iowa	46,403
Westerly, R.I.	22,966
Westerville, Ohio	35,318
Westfield, Mass.	40,072
Westfield, N.J.	29,644
West Hartford, Conn.	63,589
West Haven, Conn.	52,360
West Hollywood, Calif.	35,716
West Jordan, Utah	68,336
West Lafayette, Ind.	28,778
Westlake, Ohio	31,719
Westland, Mich.	86,602
West Memphis, Ark.	27,666
West Mifflin, Pa.	22,464
Westminster, Calif.	88,207
Westminster, Colo.	100,940
Westmont, Ill.	24,554
West New York, N.J.	45,768
West Orange, N.J.	44,943
West Palm Beach, Fla.	82,103
Westport, Conn.	25,749
West Sacramento, Calif.	31,615
West Springfield, Mass.	27,899
West St. Paul, Minn.	19,405
West Valley City, Utah	108,896
West Warwick, R.I.	29,581
Wethersfield, Conn.	26,271
Weymouth, Mass.	53,988
Wheaton, Ill.	55,416
Wheat Ridge, Colo.	32,913
Wheeling, Ill.	34,496
Wheeling, W. Va.	31,419
White Bear Lake, Minn.	24,325
Whitehall, Ohio	19,201
White Plains, N.Y.	53,077
Whittier, Calif.	83,680
Wichita, Kans.	344,284
Wichita Falls, Tex.	104,197
Wilkes-Barre, Pa.	43,123
Wilkinsburg, Pa.	19,196
Williamsport, Pa.	30,706
Willmar, Minn.	18,351
Willoughby, Ohio	22,621
Wilmette, Ill.	27,651
Wilmington, Del.	72,664
Wilmington, Mass.	21,363
Wilmington, N.C.	75,838
Wilson, N.C.	44,405
Winchester, Mass.	20,810
Winchester, Va.	23,585
Windham, Conn.	22,857
Windsor, Conn.	28,237
Winona, Minn.	27,069
Winston-Salem, N.C.	185,776
Winter Haven, Fla.	26,487
Winter Park, Fla.	24,090
Winter Springs, Fla.	31,666
Winthrop, Mass.	18,303
Wisconsin Rapids, Wis.	18,435
Woburn, Mass.	37,258
Woodbury, Minn.	46,463
Woodland, Calif.	49,151
Woodridge, Ill.	30,934
Woonsocket, R.I.	43,224
Wooster, Ohio	24,811
Worcester, Mass.	172,648
Wyandotte, Mich.	28,006
Wyoming, Mich.	69,368

X

Xenia, Ohio	24,164

Y

Yakima, Wash.	71,845
Yarmouth, Mass.	24,807
Yonkers, N.Y.	196,086
Yorba Linda, Calif.	58,918
York, Pa.	40,862
Youngstown, Ohio	82,026
Ypsilanti, Mich.	22,362
Yuba City, Calif.	36,758
Yucaipa, Calif.	41,207
Yukon, Okla.	21,043
Yuma, Ariz.	77,515

Z

Zanesville, Ohio	25,586
Zion, Ill.	22,866

Population of the United States

SUMMARY BY STATES AND DEPENDENCIES

(Figures in parentheses give rank of states in population; population figures based on 2000 census.)

THE STATES AND THE DISTRICT OF COLUMBIA

Alabama	(23)	4,447,100
Alaska	(48)	626,932
Arizona	(20)	5,130,632
Arkansas	(33)	2,673,400
California	(1)	33,871,648
Colorado	(24)	4,301,261
Connecticut	(29)	3,405,565
Delaware	(45)	783,600
District of Columbia		572,059
Florida	(4)	15,982,378
Georgia	(10)	8,186,453
Hawaii	(42)	1,211,537
Idaho	(39)	1,293,953
Illinois	(5)	12,419,293
Indiana	(14)	6,080,485
Iowa	(30)	2,926,324
Kansas	(32)	2,688,418
Kentucky	(25)	4,041,769
Louisiana	(22)	4,468,976
Maine	(40)	1,274,923
Maryland	(19)	5,296,486
Massachusetts	(13)	6,349,097
Michigan	(8)	9,938,444
Minnesota	(21)	4,919,479
Mississippi	(31)	2,844,658
Missouri	(17)	5,595,211
Montana	(44)	902,195
Nebraska	(38)	1,711,263
Nevada	(35)	1,998,257
New Hampshire	(41)	1,235,786
New Jersey	(9)	8,414,350
New Mexico	(36)	1,819,046
New York	(3)	18,976,457
North Carolina	(11)	8,049,313
North Dakota	(47)	642,200
Ohio	(7)	11,353,140
Oklahoma	(27)	3,450,654
Oregon	(28)	3,421,399
Pennsylvania	(6)	12,281,054
Rhode Island	(43)	1,048,319
South Carolina	(26)	4,012,012
South Dakota	(46)	754,844
Tennessee	(16)	5,689,283
Texas	(2)	20,851,820
Utah	(34)	2,233,169
Vermont	(49)	608,827
Virginia	(12)	7,078,515
Washington	(15)	5,894,121
West Virginia	(37)	1,808,344
Wisconsin	(18)	5,363,675
Wyoming	(50)	493,782
Total		281,421,906

DEPENDENCIES

American Samoa	57,291
Guam	154,805
Northern Mariana Islands	69,221
Puerto Rico	3,808,610
Virgin Islands of the U.S.	108,612

Population of Places in Canada

Having 21,500 or More Inhabitants (population figures based on 1996 census)

Abbotsford, B.C.	105,403
Ajax, Ont.	64,430
Alma, Que.	26,127
Ancaster, Ont.	23,403
Anjou, Que.	37,308
Aurora, Ont.	34,857
Aylmer, Que.	34,901
Baie-Comeau, Que.	25,554
Barrie, Ont.	79,191
Beauport, Que.	72,920
Belleville, Ont.	37,083
Blainville, Que.	29,603
Boisbriand, Que.	25,227
Boucherville, Que.	34,989
Brampton, Ont.	268,251
Brandon, Man.	39,175
Brantford, Ont.	84,764
Brockville, Ont.	21,752
Brossard, Que.	65,927
Burlington, Ont.	136,976
Burnaby, B.C.	179,209
Caledon, Ont.	39,893
Calgary, Alta.	768,082
Cambridge, Ont.	101,429
Cap-de-la-Madeleine, Que.	33,438
Cape Breton, N.S.	114,733
Charlesbourg, Que.	70,942
Châteauguay, Que.	41,423
Chatham, Ont.	43,409
Chicoutimi, Que.	63,061
Chilliwack, B.C.	60,186
Clarington, Ont.	60,615
Coquitlam, B.C.	101,820
Corner Brook, Nfld.	21,893

Cornwall, Ont.	47,403
Côte-St-Luc, Que.	29,705
Cumberland, Ont.	47,367
Dartmouth, N.S.	65,629
Delta, B.C.	95,411
Dollard-des-Ormeaux, Que.	47,826
Drummondville, Que.	44,882
Dundas, Ont.	23,125
East York, Ont.	107,822
Edmonton, Alta.	616,306
Etobicoke, Ont.	328,718
Flamborough, Ont.	34,037
Fort Erie, Ont.	27,183
Fredericton, N.B.	46,507
Gatineau, Que.	100,702
Georgina, Ont.	34,777
Gloucester, Ont.	104,022
Granby, Que.	43,316
Grande Prairie, Alta.	31,140
Guelph, Ont.	95,821
Halifax, N.S.	113,910
Halton Hills, Ont.	42,390
Hamilton, Ont.	322,352
Hull, Que.	62,339
Innisfil, Ont.	24,711
Jonquière, Que.	56,503
Kamloops, B.C.	76,394
Kanata, Ont.	47,909
Kelowna, B.C.	89,442
Kingston, Ont.	55,947
Kitchener, Ont.	178,420
Lachine, Que.	35,171
Langley, B.C.	22,523
LaSalle, Que.	72,029
Laval, Que.	330,393
Lethbridge, Alta.	63,053
Lévis, Que.	40,407
London, Ont.	325,646
Longueuil, Que.	127,977
Maple Ridge, B.C.	56,173
Markham, Ont.	173,383
Mascouche, Que.	28,097
Medicine Hat, Alta.	46,783
Milton, Ont.	32,104
Mission, B.C.	30,519
Mississauga, Ont.	544,382
Moncton, N.B.	59,313
Montreal, Que.	1,016,376
Montreal North, Que.	81,581
Moose Jaw, Sask.	32,973
Mount Pearl, Nfld.	25,519
Nanaimo, B.C.	70,130
Nanticoke, Ont.	23,485
Nepean, Ont.	115,100
Newmarket, Ont.	57,125
New Westminster, B.C.	49,350
Niagara Falls, Ont.	76,917
North Bay, Ont.	54,332
North Vancouver, B.C.	41,475
North York, Ont.	589,653
Oakville, Ont.	128,405
Orillia, Ont.	27,846
Oshawa, Ont.	134,364
Ottawa, Ont.	323,340
Outremont, Que.	22,571
Owen Sound, Ont.	21,390
Penticton, B.C.	30,987
Peterborough, Ont.	69,535
Pickering, Ont.	78,989
Pierrefonds, Que.	52,986
Pointe-Claire, Que.	28,435
Port Coquitlam, B.C.	46,682
Prince Albert, Sask.	34,777
Prince George, B.C.	75,150
Quebec, Que.	167,264
Red Deer, Alta.	60,075
Regina, Sask.	180,400
Repentigny, Que.	53,824
Richmond, B.C.	148,867
Richmond Hill, Ont.	101,725
Rimouski, Que.	31,773
Rouyn-Noranda, Que.	28,819
Saanich, B.C.	101,388
St. Albert, Alta.	46,888
St-Bruno-de-Montarville, Que.	23,714
St. Catharines, Ont.	130,926
Ste-Foy, Que.	72,330
Ste-Thérèse, Que.	23,477
St. Eustache, Que.	39,848
St-Hubert, Que.	77,042
St-Hyacinthe, Que.	38,981
St-Jean-sur-Richelieu, Que.	36,435
St-Jerôme, Que.	23,916
Saint John, N.B.	72,494
St. John's, Nfld.	101,936
St-Laurent, Que.	74,240
St-Léonard, Que.	71,327
St. Thomas, Ont.	32,275
Salaberry-de-Valleyfield, Que.	26,600
Sarnia, Ont.	72,738
Saskatoon, Sask.	193,647
Sault Ste. Marie, Ont.	80,054
Scarborough, Ont.	558,960
Sept-Iles, Que.	25,224
Sherbrooke, Que.	76,786
Stoney Creek, Ont.	54,318
Stratford, Ont.	28,987
Sudbury, Ont.	92,059
Surrey, B.C.	304,477
Terrebonne, Que.	42,214
Thunder Bay, Ont.	113,662
Timmins, Ont.	47,499
Toronto, Ont.	653,734
Trois-Rivières, Que.	48,419
Val-d'Or, Que.	24,285
Valley East, Ont.	23,537
Vancouver, B.C.	514,008
Vaughan, Ont.	132,549
Verdun, Que.	59,714
Vernon, B.C.	31,817
Victoria, B.C.	73,504
Victoriaville, Que.	38,174
Waterloo, Ont.	77,949
Welland, Ont.	48,411
West Vancouver, B.C.	40,882
Whitby, Ont.	73,794
Windsor, Ont.	197,694
Winnipeg, Man.	618,477
Wood Buffalo, Alta.	35,213
Woodstock, Ont.	32,086
York, Ont.	146,534

Population of Canada

*Summary by Provinces and Territories (population figures based in 1996 census)**

Alberta	2,696,826	Ontario	10,753,573
British Columbia	3,724,500	Prince Edward Island	134,557
Manitoba	1,113,898	Quebec	7,138,795
New Brunswick	738,133	Saskatchewan	990,237
Newfoundland	551,792	Yukon Territory	30,766
Northwest Territories	64,402	*Nunavut	27,000
Nova Scotia	909,282	TOTAL	28,846,761

*Nunavut officially became a territory in 1999, created out of part of Northwest Territories. The population figure given is a 1999 estimate and is not calculated in the 1996 census total.

Signs and Symbols

Astronomy

☉	the sun; Sunday
◐, ☾, *or* ☽	the moon; Monday
●	new moon
☽, ◐, ☽, ☽	first quarter
○ *or* ☺	full moon
☾, ◑, ☾, ☾	last quarter
☿	Mercury; Wednesday
♀	Venus; Friday
⊕, ⊖, *or* ♁	the earth
♂	Mars; Tuesday
♃	Jupiter; Thursday
♄ *or* ♄	Saturn; Saturday
⛢, ♅, *or* ♅	Uranus
♆, ♆, *or* ♆	Neptune
♇	Pluto
☄	comet
✳ *or* ✶	fixed star

Business

a/c	account ⟨in a/c with⟩
@	at; each ⟨4 apples @ 5¢ = 20¢⟩
/ *or* ℘	per
c/o	care of
#	number if it precedes a numeral ⟨track #3⟩; pounds if it follows ⟨a 5# sack of sugar⟩
℔	pound; pounds
%	percent
‰	per thousand
$	dollars
¢	cents
£	pounds
/	shillings
©	copyrighted
®	registered trademark

Mathematics

+	plus; positive ⟨a+b=c⟩—used also to indicate omitted figures or an approximation
−	minus; negative
±	plus or minus ⟨the square root of $4a^2$ is ± 2a⟩
×	multiplied by; times ⟨6×4=24⟩—also indicated by placing a dot between the factors ⟨6·4=24⟩ or by writing the factors one after the other, often enclosed in parentheses, without explicitly indicating multiplication ⟨(4)(5)(3)=60⟩ ⟨−4*abc*⟩
÷ *or* :	divided by ⟨24÷6=4⟩—also indicated by writing the divisor under the dividend with a line between ⟨$\frac{24}{6}$=4⟩ or by writing the divisor after the dividend with an oblique line between ⟨3/8⟩
=	equals ⟨6+2=8⟩
≠ *or* ∓	is not equal to
>	is greater than ⟨6>5⟩
<	is less than ⟨3<4⟩
≧ *or* ≥	is greater than or equal to
≦ *or* ≤	is less than or equal to
∝	varies directly as; is proportional to
:	is to; the ratio of
∴	therefore
∞	infinity
∠	angle; the angle ⟨∠ABC⟩
∟	right angle ⟨∟ABC⟩
⊥	the perpendicular; is perpendicular to ⟨AB⊥CD⟩

$\parallel$	parallel; is parallel to ⟨AB $\parallel$ CD⟩
$\odot$ *or* ○	circle
⌒	arc of a circle
$\triangle$	triangle
$\square$	square
▭	rectangle
$\sqrt{\ }$ *or* $\surd$	root—used without a figure to indicate a square root (as in $\sqrt{4}=2$) or with an index above the sign to indicate a higher degree (as in $\sqrt[3]{3}, \sqrt[5]{7}$); also denoted by a fractional index at the right of a number whose denominator expresses the degree of the root ⟨$3^{1/3}=\sqrt[3]{3}$⟩
( )	parentheses } indicate that the quantities enclosed by them are to be taken together
[ ]	brackets
{ }	braces
s	standard deviation of a sample taken from a population
σ	standard deviation of a population
$\bar{x}$	arithmetic mean of a sample of a variable x
μ	arithmetic mean of a population
μ_2 *or* σ^2	variance
π	pi; the number 3.14159265+; the ratio of the circumference of a circle to its diameter
°	degree ⟨60°⟩
′	minute; foot ⟨30′⟩—used also to distinguish between different values of the same variable or between different variables (as a', a'', a''', usually read *a* prime, *a* double prime, *a* triple prime)
″	second; inch ⟨30″⟩
^{0}, ^{1}, ^{2}, ^{3}, etc.	—used as exponents placed above and at the right of an expression to indicate that it is raised to a power whose degree is indicated by the figure ⟨a^0 equals 1⟩ ⟨a^1 equals a⟩ ⟨a^2 is the square of a⟩
$^{-1}$, $^{-2}$, $^{-3}$, etc.	—used as exponents placed above and at the right of an expression to indicate that the reciprocal of the expression is raised to the power whose degree is indicated by the figure ⟨a^{-1} equals $1/a$⟩ ⟨a^{-2} equals $1/a^2$⟩
!	factorial ⟨$n! = n\,(n\text{-}1)(n\text{-}2)\ldots 1$⟩
n	an unspecified number esp. when an integer
$\subset$	is included in, is a subset of
$\supset$	contains as a subset
$\in$ *or* ϵ	is an element of
$\notin$	is not an element of

Medicine

$\overline{AA}$, $\bar{A}$, *or* $\bar{a}\bar{a}$	of each
℞	take—used on prescriptions; prescription; treatment
☠	poison

Miscellaneous

&	and
&c	et cetera; and so forth
" *or* "	ditto marks
/	virgule; used to mean "or" (as in *and/or*), "and/or" (as in *dead/wounded*), "per" (as in *feet/second*), indicates end of a line of verse; separates the figures of a date (4/8/74)
☞	index *or* fist

<	derived from	used in linguistics
>	whence derived	
+	and	
*	hypothetical, ungrammatical	
†	died—used esp. in genealogies	
✚	cross	
☧	monogram from Greek XP signifying Christ	
✡	Judaism	
☥	ankh	
℣	versicle	
℟	response	
∗	—used in Roman Catholic and Anglican service books to divide each verse of a psalm, indicating where the response begins	
✠ *or* +	—used in some service books to indicate where the sign of the cross is to be made; also used by certain Roman Catholic and Anglican prelates as a sign of the cross preceding their signatures	
LXX	Septuagint	
f/ or f:	relative aperture of a photographic lens	
	civil defense	
☮	peace	
卐	swastika	

Reference marks

*	asterisk *or* star	§	section *or* numbered clause
†	dagger	‖	parallels
‡	double dagger	¶ *or* ⁋	paragraph

Stamps and stamp collecting

★ *or* *	unused
★★ *or* **	unused with original gum intact and never mounted with a stamp hinge
⊙ *or* ○ *or* 0	used
⊞	block of four or more
⊠	entire cover or card

Weather

H *or* Ⓗ	high pressure region	∞	haze
L *or* Ⓛ	low pressure region		hurricane
◎	calm		tropical storm
○	clear	●	rain
◐	cloudy (partly)		rain and snow
●	cloudy (completely overcast)		frost
	drifting or blowing snow		sandstorm or dust storm
	drizzle	▽	shower(s)
≡	fog		shower of rain
	freezing rain		shower of hail
▲▲▲▲	cold front	△	sleet
	warm front	✱	snow
	stationary front		thunderstorm
][	funnel clouds		visibility reduced by smoke

A Handbook of Style

Punctuation

The English writing system uses punctuation marks to separate groups of words for meaning and emphasis; to convey an idea of the variations of pitch, volume, pauses, and intonations of speech; and to help avoid contextual ambiguity. The use of the standard English punctuation marks is discussed in the following pages; examples are provided to illustrate the general rules.

Apostrophe ’

1. Indicates the possessive case of nouns and indefinite pronouns. The possessive case of almost all singular nouns may be formed by adding ’s. Traditionally, however, only the apostrophe is added when the s would not be pronounced in normal speech. The possessive case of plural nouns ending in s or in an \s\ or \z\ sound is generally formed by adding an apostrophe only; the possessive of irregular plurals is formed by adding ’s.

her mother-in-law’s car
anyone’s guess
the boy’s mother
the boys’ mothers
Degas’s drawings
Knox’s products
Aristophanes’ play
for righteousness’ sake
the Stephenses’ house
children’s laughter

2. Marks omission of letters in contracted words.

didn’t
o’clock
hang ’em up

3. Marks omission of digits in numbers.

class of ’83

4. Is often used to form plurals of letters, figures, punctuated abbreviations, symbols, and words referred to as words.

Dot your *i*’s and cross your *t*’s.
Two of the junior faculty have Ph.D’s.
She has trouble pronouncing her *the*’s.

Brackets [ ]

1. Set off interpolated editorial matter within quoted material.

He wrote, “I ain’t [sic] going.”

Vaulting ambition, which o’erleaps itself
And falls on the other [side].
—Shakespeare

2. Function as parentheses within parentheses.

Bowman Act (22 Stat., ch. 4, § [or sec.] 4, p. 50)

3. Set off phonetic symbols and transcriptions.

[t] in British *duty*
the word is pronounced [ˈek-sə-jənt]

Colon :

1. Introduces a clause or phrase that explains, illustrates, amplifies, or restates what has gone before.

The sentence was poorly constructed: it lacked both unity and coherence.

2. Directs attention to an appositive.

He had only one pleasure: eating.

3. Introduces a series.

Three abstained: England, France, and Belgium.

4. Introduces lengthy quoted material set off from the rest of a text by indentation but not by quotation marks.

I quote from the text of Chapter One:

5. Separates elements in page references, in bibliographical and biblical citations, and in set formulas used to express ratios and time.

Journal of the American Medical Association 48:356
Stendhal, *Love* (New York: Penguin, 1975)
John 4:10
a ratio of 3:5
8:30 a.m.

6. Separates titles and subtitles (as of books).

DICTIONARY

Battle Cry of Freedom: The Era of the Civil War

7. Follows the salutation in formal correspondence.

Dear Sir or Madam:

Ladies and Gentlemen:

8. Punctuates headings in memorandums and formal correspondence.

TO:	VIA:
SUBJECT:	REFERENCE:

, Comma

1. Separates main clauses joined by a coordinating conjunction (such as *and, but, or, nor*, or *for*) and sometimes short parallel clauses not joined by conjunctions.

She knew very little about him, and he volunteered nothing.

I came, I saw, I conquered.

2. Sets off an adverbial clause or a long adverbial phrase that precedes or interrupts the main clause.

When she discovered the answer, she reported it to us.

The report, after being read aloud, was put up for consideration.

3. Sets off transitional words and expressions (such as *on the contrary, on the other hand*), conjunctive adverbs (such as *consequently, furthermore, however*), and expressions that introduce an illustration or example (such as *namely, for example*).

My partner, on the other hand, remains unconvinced.

The regent's whim, however, threw the negotiations into chaos.

She responded as completely as she could; that is, she answered each individual question specifically.

4. Sets off contrasting and opposing expressions within sentences.

The cost is not $65.00, but $56.65.

He changed his style, not his ethics.

5. Separates words, phrases, or clauses in series. (Many omit the comma before the conjunction introducing the last item in a series when no ambiguity results.)

He was young, eager, and restless.

It requires one to travel constantly, to have no private life, and to live on almost nothing.

Be sure to pack a flashlight, a sweater and an extra pair of socks.

6. Separates coordinate adjectives modifying a noun. However, a comma is not used between two adjectives when the first modifies the combination of the second adjective and the word or phrase it modifies.

The harsh, damp, piercing wind cut through his jacket.

a low common denominator

7. Sets off parenthetical elements such as nonrestrictive clauses and phrases.

Our guide, who wore a blue beret, was an experienced traveler.

We visited Gettysburg, site of the famous battle.

The book's author, Marie Jones, was an accomplished athlete.

8. Introduces a direct quotation, terminates a direct quotation that is neither a question nor an exclamation, and sets off split quotations. The comma is not used with quotations that are tightly integrated into the sentences in which they appear (e.g., as subject or predicate nominatives) or those that do not represent actual dialogue.

Mary said, "I am leaving."

"I am leaving," Mary said.

"I am leaving," Mary said with determination, "even if you want me to stay."

"The computer is down" was the reply she feared.

The fact that he said he was about to "faint from hunger" doesn't mean he actually fainted.

9. Sets off words in direct address, absolute phrases, and mild interjections.

You may go, John, if you wish.

I fear their encounter, his temper being what it is.

Ah, that's my idea of an excellent dinner.

10. Separates a tag question from the rest of the sentence.

It's a fine day, isn't it?

11. Indicates the omission of a word or words used in a parallel construction earlier in the sentence. When the meaning of the sentence is quite clear without the comma, the comma is omitted.

Common stocks are preferred by some investors; bonds, by others.

He was in love with her and she with him.

12. Is used to avoid ambiguity that might arise from adjacent words.

To Mary, Jane was someone special.

13. Is used to to divide digits in numbers into groups of three; however, it is generally not used in pagination, in dates, or in street numbers, and sometimes not used in numbers with four digits.

Smithville, pop. 100,000

4,550 cars

but

page 1411	4507 Main St.
3600 rpm	the year 1983

14. Punctuates an inverted name.

Morton, William A.

15. Separates a surname from a following title or degree and often from the words "Junior" and "Senior" and their abbreviations.

Sandra H. Cobb, Vice President

Jesse Ginsburg, D.D.M.

16. Sets off geographical names (such as state or country from city), elements of dates, and addresses. When just the month and the year are given in a date, the comma is usually omitted.

Shreveport, Louisiana, is the site of a large air base.

On Sunday, June 23, 1940, he was wounded.

Number 10 Downing Street, London, is a famous address.

She began her career in April 1993 at a modest salary.

17. Follows the salutation in informal correspondence, and follows the complimentary close of a letter.

Dear Mark,

Affectionately,

Very truly yours,

Dash —

1. Usually marks an abrupt change or break in the continuity of a sentence.

When in 1960 the stockpile was sold off—indeed, dumped as surplus—natural rubber sales were hard hit.—Barry Commoner.

2. Is sometimes used in place of commas or parentheses when special emphasis is required.

The presentations—and especially the one by Ms. Dow—impressed the audience.

3. Introduces a statement that explains, summarizes, or expands on what precedes it.

Oil, steel, and wheat—these are the sinews of industrialization.

The motion was then tabled—that is, removed indefinitely from consideration.

4. Often precedes the attribution of a quotation.

My foot is on my native heath. . .
—Sir Walter Scott

5. Sets off an interrupting clause or phrase. The dash takes the place of a comma that would ordinarily set off the clause, but an exclamation point or question mark is retained.

If we don't succeed—and the critics say we won't—then the whole project is in jeopardy.

They are demanding that everything—even the marshland!—be transferred to the new trust.

Your question—it was *your* question, wasn't it, Mr. Jones?—just can't be answered.

Ellipsis (or Suspension Points) . . . .

1. Indicates the omission of one or more words within a quoted passage. When four dots are used, the ellipsis indicates the omission of one or more sentences within the passage or the omission of words at the end of a sentence. The first or the last of the four dots is a period.

In the little world in which children have their existence, . . . there is nothing so finely perceived and so finely felt as injustice.—Charles Dickens

Security is mostly a superstition. . . . Avoiding danger is no safer in the long run than outright exposure. . . . Life is either a daring adventure or nothing.—Helen Keller

2. Usually indicates omission of one or more lines of poetry when ellipsis is extended the length of the line.

I think that I shall never see
A poem lovely as a tree
. . . .
Poems are made by fools like me,
But only God can make a tree.
—Joyce Kilmer

3. Indicates halting speech or an unfinished sentence in dialogue.

"I'd like to. . . that is. . . if you don't mind. . . ."

Exclamation Point !

1. Ends an emphatic phrase or sentence.

Get out of here!

Her notorious ostentation—she flew her friends to Bangkok for her birthday parties!—was feasted on by the popular press.

2. Ends an emphatic interjection.

Encore!

All of this proves—at long last!—that we were right from the start.

Hyphen -

The hyphen is often used between parts of a compound. The styling of such words varies; when in doubt, see the entry in the dictionary at its own place or in a list of undefined words at an individual prefix. For unentered compounds, advice will be found in *Webster's Standard American Style Manual* or a comparable guide.

1. Is often used between a prefix and root, especially whenever the root is capitalized, when two identical vowels come together, or when the resulting word could be confused with another identically spelled word.

pre-Renaissance co-opted
anti-inflationary
re-cover a sofa
but
recover from an illness

2. Is used in some compounds, especially those containing prepositions.

president-elect sister-in-law
good-for-nothing over-the-counter
falling-out write-off

3. Is often used in compound modifiers in attributive position.

traveling in a fast-moving van
She has gray-green eyes.
a come-as-you-are party

4. Suspends the first element of a hyphenated compound or a prefix (hyphenated or not) when the second element or base word is part of a following hyphenated compound or derived form.

a six- or eight-cylinder engine
pre- and postadolescent trauma

5. Marks division of a word at the end of a line.

The ruling pas-
sion of his life

6. Is used in writing out compound numbers between 21 and 99.

thirty-four
one hundred and thirty-eight

7. Is often used between the numerator and the denominator in writing out fractions, especially when they are used as modifiers. However, fractions used as nouns are often written as open compounds, especially when either the numerator or the denominator already contains a hyphen.

a two-thirds majority of the vote
three fifths of her paycheck
one seventy-second of an inch

8. Serves as an equivalent of *through* or (*up*) *to and including* when used between indicators of range such as numbers and dates. (In typeset material the longer en dash is used.)

pages 40–98
the years 1980–89

9. Serves as the equivalent of *to, and,* or *versus* in indicating linkage or opposition. (In typeset material the longer en dash is used.)

the New York–Paris flight
the Hardy–Weinberg law
the Lincoln–Douglas Debates
The final score was 7–2.

= Hyphen, Double

Is used at the end-of-line division of a hyphenated compound to indicate that the compound is hyphenated and not closed.

self= [end of line] seeker
but
self- [end of line] same

( ) Parentheses

1. Enclose words, numbers, phrases, or clauses that provide examples, explanations, or supplementary material that does not essentially alter the meaning of the sentence.

Three old destroyers (all now out of commission) will be scrapped.

He has followed the fortunes of the modern renaissance (*al-Nahdad*) in the Arabic-speaking world.

2. Enclose numerals that confirm a written number in a text.

Delivery will be made in thirty (30) days.

3. Enclose numbers or letters in a series.

We must set forth (1) our long-term goals, (2) our immediate objectives, and (3) the means at our disposal.

4. Enclose abbreviations that follow their spelled-out forms or spelled-out forms that follow their abbreviations.

a ruling by the Federal Communications Commission (FCC)

the manufacture and disposal of PVC (polyvinyl chloride)

5. Indicate alternative terms.

Please indicate the lecture(s) you would like to attend.

6. Enclose publication data in footnotes and endnotes.

Marguerite Yourcenar, *The Dark Brain of Piranesi and Other Essays* (New York: Farrar, Straus and Giroux, 1985), p. 9.

7. Are used with other punctuation marks in the following ways:

If the parenthetic expression is an independent sentence standing alone, its first word is capitalized and a period is included *inside* the last parenthesis. However, if the parenthetic expression, even if it could stand alone as a sentence, occurs within a sentence, it is uncapitalized and has no sentence period but may have an exclamation point, a question mark, a period for an abbreviation, or quotation marks within the closing parenthesis.

The discussion was held in the boardroom. (The results are still confidential.)

Although we liked the restaurant (their Italian food was the best), we seldom went there.

After waiting in line for an hour (why do we do these things?), we finally left.

Years ago, someone (I wish I could remember who!) told me about it.

What was once informally known as A.B.D. status is now often recognized by the degree of Master of Philosophy (M. Phil.).

He was depressed ("I must resign") and refused to do anything.

No punctuation mark should be placed directly before parenthetical material in a sentence; if a break is required, punctuation should be placed *after* the final parenthesis.

I'll get back to you tomorrow (Friday), when I have more details.

Period .

1. Ends sentences or sentence fragments that are neither interrogatory nor exclamatory.

Not bad.

Give it your best.

I gave it my best.

He asked if she had given it her best.

2. Follows some abbreviations and contractions.

Dr.	A.D.	ibid.	i.e.
Jr.	etc.	cont.	

3. Is normally used with an individual's initials.

F. Scott Fitzgerald

T. S. Eliot

4. Is used after numerals and letters in vertical enumerations and outlines.

Required skills are:
1. Shorthand
2. Typing
3. Transcription

I. Objectives
  A. Economy
    1. low initial cost
    2. low maintenance cost
  B. Ease of operation

Question Mark ?

1. Ends a direct question.

How did she do it?

"How did she do it?" he asked.

2. Ends a question that is part of a larger sentence, but not an indirect question.

How did she do it? was the question on each person's mind.

He wondered, Will it work?

He wondered whether it would work.

3. Indicates the writer's ignorance or uncertainty.

Geoffrey Chaucer, English poet (1342?–1400)

Quotation Marks, Double " "

1. Enclose direct quotations but not indirect quotations.

She said, "I am leaving."

She said that she was leaving.

2. Enclose words or phrases borrowed from others, words used in a special way, and words of marked informality when introduced into formal writing.

Much of the population in the hellish future he envisions is addicted to "derms," patches that deliver potent drug doses instantaneously through the skin.

He called himself "emperor," but he was really just a dictator.

He was arrested for smuggling "smack."

3. Enclose titles of poems, short stories, articles, lectures, chapters of books, short musical compositions, and radio and TV programs.

Robert Frost's "After Apple-Picking"

Cynthia Ozick's "Rosa"

The third chapter of *Treasure Island* is entitled "The Black Spot."

"All the Things You Are"

Debussy's "Clair de lune"

NBC's "Today Show"

4. Are used with other punctuation marks in the following ways:

The period and the comma fall *within* the quotation marks.

"I am leaving," she said.

It was unclear how she maintained such an estate on "a small annuity."

The colon and semicolon fall *outside* the quotation marks.

There was only one thing to do when he said, "I may not run": promise him a large campaign contribution.

He spoke of his "little cottage in the country"; he might better have called it a mansion.

The dash, the question mark, and the exclamation point fall *within* the quotation marks when they refer to the quoted matter only; they fall *outside* when they refer to the whole sentence.

"I can't see how—" he started to say.

He asked, "When did she leave?"

What is the meaning of "the open door"?

The sergeant shouted "Halt!"

Save us from his "mercy"!

5. Are not used with *yes* or *no* except in direct discourse.

She said yes to all our requests.

6. Are not used with lengthy quotations set off from the text.

He took the title for his biography of Thoreau from a passage in *Walden*:

> I long ago lost a hound, a bay horse, and a turtledove, and am still on their trail. . . . I have met one or two who had heard the hound, and the tramp of the horse, and even seen the dove disappear behind a cloud, and they seemed as anxious to recover them as if they had lost them themselves.

However, the title *A Hound, a Bay Horse, and a Turtle-Dove* probably puzzled some readers.

' ' Quotation Marks, Single

1. Enclose a quotation within a quotation in American usage. When both single and double quotation marks occur at the end of a sentence, the period typically falls within *both* sets of marks.

The witness said, "I distinctly heard him say, 'Don't be late,' and then heard the door close."

The witness said, "I distinctly heard him say, 'Don't be late.'"

2. Are sometimes used in place of double quotation marks especially in British usage. In this case a quotation within a quotation is set off by double quotation marks.

The witness said, 'I distinctly heard him say, "Don't be late," and then heard the door close.'

Semicolon ;

1. Links independent clauses not joined by a coordinating conjunction.

Some people have the ability to write well; others do not.

2. Links clauses joined by a conjunctive adverb (such as *consequently, furthermore, however*).

Speeding is illegal; furthermore, it is very dangerous.

3. Often occurs before expressions that introduce expansions or series (such as *for example, for instance, that is, e.g.,* or *i.e.).*

As a manager she tried to do the best job she could; that is, to keep her project on schedule and under budget.

4. Separates phrases that contain commas.

The country's resources consist of large ore deposits; lumber, waterpower, and fertile soils; and a strong, rugged people.

Send copies to our offices in Portland, Maine; Springfield, Illinois; and Savannah, Georgia.

5. Is placed outside quotation marks and parentheses.

They again demanded "complete autonomy"; the demand was again rejected.

/ Virgule (or Slash)

1. Separates alternatives.

high-heat and/or high-speed applications

. . . sit hour after hour. . . and finally year after year in a catatonic/frenzied trance rewriting the Bible —William Saroyan

2. Replaces the word *to* or *and* between related terms that are compounded.

the fiscal year 1983/1984

in the May/June issue

3. Divides run-in lines of poetry.

Say, sages, what's the charm on earth/Can turn death's dart aside?—Robert Burns

4. Divides elements in dates and divides numerators and denominators in fractions.

offer expires 5/19/94

Fifteen and 44/100 dollars

5. Often represents *per* or *to* when used with units of measure or to indicate the terms of a ratio.

9 ft/sec

risk/reward trade-off

6. Sets off phonemes of phonemic transcription.

/b/ as in *but*

Capitalization

Capitals are used for two broad purposes in English: they mark a beginning (as of a sentence) and they signal a proper noun, pronoun, or adjective. The following principles, each with examples, describe the most common uses of capital letters.

Beginnings

1. The first word of a sentence or sentence fragment is capitalized.

The play lasted nearly three hours.

How are you feeling?

Bravo!

2. The first word of a sentence contained within parentheses is capitalized if it does not occur within another sentence. The first word of a parenthetical sentence within another sentence is not capitalized.

The discussion was held in the boardroom. (The results are still confidential.)

Although we liked the restaurant (their Italian food was the best), we seldom ate there.

After waiting in line for an hour (why do we do these things?), we finally left.

3. The first word of a direct quotation is capitalized. However, if the quotation is interrupted in the middle of a sentence, the second part does not begin with a capital. When a quotation, whether a sentence fragment or a complete sentence, is syntactically dependent on the sentence in which it occurs, the quotation does not begin with a capital.

The President said, "We have rejected this report entirely."

"We have rejected this report entirely," the President said, "and we will not comment on it further."

The President made it clear that "there is no room for compromise."

4. The first word of a sentence within a sentence is usually capitalized when it represents a direct question, a motto or aphorism, or spoken or unspoken dialogue. The first word following a colon may be either lowercased or capitalized if it introduces a complete sentence. While the former is more usual, the latter is common when the sentence is fairly lengthy and distinctly separate from the preceding clause.

That question, as Disraeli said, is this: Is man an ape or an angel?

My first thought was, How can I avoid this assignment?

The advantage of this particular system is clear: it's inexpensive.

The situation is critical: This company cannot hope to recoup the fourth-quarter losses that were sustained in five operating divisions.

5. The first word of a line of poetry is traditionally capitalized; however, in much twentieth-century poetry the line beginnings are lowercased.

The best lack all conviction, while the worst
Are full of passionate intensity.
—W. B. Yeats

6. The first words of run-in enumerations that form complete sentences are capitalized, as are usually the first words of vertical lists and enumerations. However, enumerations of words or phrases run in with the introductory text are generally lowercased.

Do the following tasks at the end of the day: 1. Clear your desktop of papers. 2. Cover office machines. 3. Straighten the contents of your desk drawers, cabinets, and bookcases.

This is the agenda:
Call to order
Roll call
Minutes of the previous meeting
Treasurer's report

On the agenda will be (1) call to order, (2) roll call, (3) minutes of the previous meeting, (4) treasurer's report. . . .

7. The first word in an outline heading is capitalized.

I. Editorial tasks
II. Production responsibilities
A. Cost estimates
B. Bids

8. The first word of the salutation of a letter and the first word of a complimentary close are capitalized.

Dear Mary,

Ladies and Gentlemen:

Sincerely yours,

Proper Nouns, Pronouns, and Adjectives

Capitals are used with almost all proper nouns—that is, nouns that name particular persons, places, or things (including abstract entities), distinguishing them from others of the same class—and proper adjectives—that is, adjectives that take their meaning from what is named by the proper noun. The essential distinction in the use of capitals and lowercase letters at the beginnings of words lies in this individualizing significance of capitals as against the generalizing significance of lowercase. The following subject headings are in alphabetical order.

ARMED FORCES

1. Branches and units of the armed forces are capitalized, as are easily recognized short forms of full branch and unit designations. However, the words *army, navy*, etc., are lowercased when used in their plural forms or when they are not part of an official title.

United States Army
a contract with the Army
Corps of Engineers
a bridge built by the Engineers
allied armies

AWARDS

2. Names of awards and prizes are capitalized.

the Nobel Prize in Chemistry
Distinguished Service Cross
Academy Award

DERIVATIVES OF PROPER NAMES

3. Derivatives of proper names are capitalized when used in their primary sense. However, if the derived term has taken on a specialized meaning, it is usually not capitalized.

Roman customs
Shakespearean comedies
Edwardian era
but
quixotic
herculean
bohemian tastes

GEOGRAPHICAL REFERENCES

4. Divisions of the earth's surface and names of distinct areas, regions, places, or districts are capitalized, as are most derivative adjectives and some derivative nouns and verbs.

The Eastern Hemisphere
Midwest
Tropic of Cancer
Springfield, Massachusetts
the Middle Eastern situation
an Americanism
but
french fries
a japan finish
manila envelope

5. Popular names of localities are capitalized.

the Corn Belt	the Loop
The Big Apple	the Gold Coast
the Pacific Rim	

6. Words designating global, national, regional, or local political divisions are capitalized when they are essential elements of specific names. However, they are usually lowercased when they precede a proper name or stand alone. (In legal documents, these words are often capitalized regardless of position.)

the British Empire	Washington State
New York City	Ward 1
but	
the fall of the empire	the state of Washington
the city of New York	fires in three wards

7. Generic geographical terms (such as *lake, mountain, river, valley*) are capitalized if they are part of a specific proper name.

Hudson Bay	Long Island
Niagara Falls	Crater Lake
the Shenandoah Valley	

8. Generic terms preceding names are usually capitalized.

Lakes Michigan and Superior
Mounts Whitney and Rainier

9. Generic terms following names are usually lowercased, as are singular or plural generic terms that are used descriptively or alone.

the Himalaya and Andes mountains
the Atlantic coast of Labrador
the Hudson valley
the river valley
the valley

10. Compass points are capitalized when they refer to a geographical region or when they are part of a street name, but they are lowercased when they refer to simple direction.

up North
back East
the Northwest
West Columbus Avenue
Park Avenue South
but
west of the Rockies
the east coast of Florida

11. Adjectives derived from compass points and nouns designating the inhabitants of some geographical regions are capitalized. When in doubt, see the entry in the dictionary.

a Southern accent
Northerners

12. Terms designating public places are capitalized if they are part of a proper name.

Brooklyn Bridge
Lincoln Park

the St. Regis Hotel

Independence Hall

but

Wisconsin and Connecticut avenues

the Plaza and St. Regis hotels

GOVERNMENTAL AND JUDICIAL BODIES

13. Full names of legislative, deliberative, executive, and administrative bodies are capitalized, as are short forms of these names. However, nonspecific noun and adjective references to them are usually lowercased.

the U.S. House of Representatives

the House

the Federal Bureau of Investigation

but

both houses of Congress

a federal agency

14. Names of international courts, the U.S. Supreme Court, and other higher courts are capitalized. However, names of city and county courts are usually lowercased.

The International Court of Arbitration

the Supreme Court of the United States

the Supreme Court

the United States Court of Appeals for the Second Circuit

the Michigan Court of Appeals

Lawton municipal court

Newark night court

HISTORICAL PERIODS AND EVENTS

15. Names of congresses, councils, and expositions are capitalized.

the Yalta Conference

the Republican National Convention

16. Names of historical events, some historical periods, and some cultural periods and movements are capitalized. When in doubt, consult the entry in the dictionary, especially for periods.

the Boston Tea Party

Renaissance

Prohibition

the Augustan Age

the Enlightenment

but

the space age

neoclassicism

17. Numerical designations of historical time periods are capitalized when they are part of a proper name; otherwise they are lowercased.

the Third Reich

the Roaring Twenties

but

the eighteenth century

the eighties

18. Names of treaties, laws, and acts are capitalized.

Treaty of Versailles

The Clear Air Act of 1990

ORGANIZATIONS

19. Names of firms, corporations, schools, and organizations and their members are capitalized. However, common nouns occurring after the names of two or more organizations are lowercased. The word *the* at the beginning of such names is only capitalized when the full legal name is used.

Thunder's Mouth Press

University of Wisconsin

European Community

Rotary International

Kiwanians

American and United airlines

20. Words such as *group, division, department, office*, or *agency* that designate a corporate and organizational unit are capitalized only when used with its specific name.

in the Editorial Department of Merriam-Webster

but

a notice to all department heads

PEOPLE

21. Names of persons are capitalized. However, the capitalization of particles such as *de, della, der, du, l', la, ten,* and *van* varies widely, especially in names of people in English-speaking countries.

Noah Webster

W.E.B. Du Bois

Daphne du Maurier

Werner Von Braun

Anthony Van Dyck

22. Titles preceding the name of a person and epithets used instead of a name are capitalized. However, titles following a name or used alone are usually lowercased.

President Roosevelt

Professor Kaiser

Queen Elizabeth

Old Hickory

the Iron Chancellor

but

Henry VIII, king of England

23. Corporate titles are capitalized when used with an individual's name; otherwise, they are lowercased.

Lisa Dominguez, Vice President

The sales manager called me.

24. Words of family relationship preceding or used in place of a person's name are capitalized; how-

ever, these words are lowercased if they are part of a noun phrase used in place of a name.

Cousin Julia

I know when Mother's birthday is.

but

I know when my mother's birthday is.

25. Words designating peoples, nationalities, religious groups, tribes, races, and languages are capitalized. Other terms used to refer to groups of people are often lowercased. Designations based on color are usually lowercased.

Canadians	Iroquois
Ibo	African-American
Latin	Indo-European

highlander (an inhabitant of a highland)

Highlander (an inhabitant of the Highlands of Scotland)

black	white

PERSONIFICATIONS

26. Personifications are capitalized.

She dwells with Beauty—Beauty, that must die;
And Joy, whose hand is ever at his lips
Bidding adieu.
—John Keats

obey the commands of Nature

PRONOUNS

27. The pronoun *I* is capitalized. For pronouns referring to the Deity, see rule 29 below.

. . . no one but I myself had yet printed any of my work.—Paul Bowles

RELIGIOUS TERMS

28. Words designating the Deity are capitalized.

An anthropomorphic, vengeful Jehovah became a spiritual, benevolent Supreme Being.—A. R. Katz

29. Personal pronouns referring to the Deity are usually capitalized, even when they closely follow their antecedent. However, many writers never capitalize such pronouns.

All Thy works, O Lord, shall bless Thee.
—*Oxford American Hymnal*

God's in his heaven—
All's right with the world!
—Robert Browning

30. Traditional designations of revered persons, such as prophets, apostles, and saints, are often capitalized.

our Lady

the Prophet

the Lawgiver

31. Names of religions, creeds and confessions, denominations, and religious orders are capitalized, as is the word *Church* when used as part of a proper name.

Judaism

Apostles' Creed

the Thirty-nine Articles of the Church of England

Society of Jesus

Hunt Memorial Church

but

the local Baptist church

32. Names for the Bible or parts, versions, or editions of it and names of other sacred books are capitalized but not italicized. Adjectives derived from the names of sacred books are irregularly capitalized or lowercased; when in doubt, see the entry in the dictionary.

Authorized Version	New English Bible
Old Testament	Pentateuch
Apocrypha	Gospel of Saint Mark
Talmud	Koran
biblical	Koranic

SCIENTIFIC TERMS

33. Names of planets and their satellites, asteroids, stars, constellations and groups of stars, and other unique celestial objects are capitalized. However, the words *sun, earth*, and *moon* are usually lowercased unless they occur with other astronomical names.

Venus	Ganymede
Sirius	Pleiades

the Milky Way

enjoying the beauty of the moon

probes heading for the Moon and Mars

34. New Latin genus names in zoology and botany are capitalized; the second term in binomial scientific names, identifying the species, is not.

a cabbage butterfly *(Pieris rapae)*

a common buttercup *(Ranunculus acris)*

35. New Latin names of all groups above genus in zoology and botany (such as class or family) are capitalized; however, their derivative adjectives and nouns are not.

Gastropoda *but* gastropod

Mantidae *but* mantid

36. Names of geological eras, periods, epochs, and strata and names of prehistoric divisions are capitalized.

Silurian period	Pleistocene epoch
Age of Reptiles	Neolithic age

SEASONS, MONTHS, DAYS

37. Names of months, days of the week, and holidays and holy days are capitalized.

January	Ramadan
Tuesday	Thanksgiving
Yom Kippur	Easter

38. Names of seasons are not capitalized except when personified.

last spring

the sweet breath of Spring

TITLES OF PRINTED MATTER AND WORKS OF ART

39. Words in titles are capitalized, with the exception of internal conjunctions, prepositions, and articles. In some publications, prepositions of five or more letters are capitalized also.

Of Mice and Men

"The Man Who Would Be King"

"To His Coy Mistress"

Slouching Toward Bethlehem

40. Capitalization of the titles of movies, plays, paintings, sculpture, and musical compositions follow similar conventions. For more details, see the Italicization section below.

41. Major sections of books, long articles, or reports are capitalized when they are referred to within the same material.

See the Appendix for further information.

The Introduction explains the scope of this book.

discussed later in Chapter 4

42. Nouns used with numbers or letters to designate major reference headings are capitalized. Nouns designating minor elements are typically lowercased.

Volume V	Table 3
page 101	note 10

TRADEMARKS

43. Registered trademarks and service marks are capitalized.

Express Mail	Orlon
Kleenex	Walkman

VEHICLES

44. Names of ships, aircraft, and spacecraft are capitalized.

Titanic

Lindbergh's *Spirit of St. Louis*

Apollo 13

Italicization

The following are usually italicized in print and underlined in manuscript and typescript.

1. Words and passages that are to be emphasized.

This was their fatal error: there *was* no cache of supplies in the now-abandoned depot.

2. Titles of books, magazines, newspapers, plays, long poems, movies, paintings, sculpture, and long musical compositions (but not musical compositions identified by the name of their genre).

Dickens's *Bleak House*

National Geographic

Christian Science Monitor

Shakespeare's *Othello*

Eliot's *The Waste Land*

the movie *Back to the Future*

Gainsborough's *Blue Boy*

Mozart's *Don Giovanni*

but

Schubert's Sonata in B-flat Major, D. 960

NOTE: In the plurals of such italicized titles, the *s* or *es* endings are usually in roman type.

hidden under a stack of *New Yorker*s

3. Names of ships, aircraft, and spacecraft.

Titanic

Lindbergh's *Spirit of St. Louis*

Apollo 13

4. Words, letters, and figures when referred to as such.

The *g* in *align* is silent.

The first *2* and the last *0* are barely legible.

5. Unfamiliar words when first introduced and defined in a text.

Heart failure is often accompanied by *edema*, an accumulation of fluid which tends to produce swelling of the lower extremities.

6. Foreign words and phrases that have not been naturalized in English. In general, any word entered in the main A–Z vocabulary of this dictionary need not be italicized.

c'est la vie

aere perennius

che sarà, sarà

sans peur et sans reproche

but

pasta ad hoc ex officio

7. New Latin scientific names of genera, species, subspecies, races, and varieties (but not groups of higher rank, such as phyla, classes, or orders) in botanical or zoological names.

a thick-shelled American clam *(Mercenaria mercenaria)*

a mallard *(Anas platyrhynchos)*

but

the family Hominidae

8. Case titles in legal citations, both in full and shortened form; "v" for "versus" is set in either roman or italic.

Jones v. *Ohio*

Smith et al v. Jones

the *Jones* case

Jones

Documentation of Sources

Writers and editors use various methods to indicate the source of a quotation or piece of information borrowed from another work. In works published for the general public and traditionally in scholarly works in the humanities, footnotes or endnotes have been preferred. In this system, sequential numbers within the text refer the reader to notes at the bottom of the page or at the end of the article, chapter, or book; these notes contain full bibliographical information of the works cited. In scholarly works in the social and natural sciences, and increasingly in the humanities as well, parenthetical references within the text refer the reader to an alphabetically arranged list of sources at the end of the work. The system of footnotes or endnotes is the more flexible, in that it allows for commentary on the work or subject and can also be used for brief peripheral discussions not tied to any specific work. However, style manuals tend to encourage the use of parenthetical references in addition to or instead of footnotes or endnotes, since for most kinds of material they are efficient and convenient for both writer and reader. In a carefully documented work, a bibliography or list of sources normally follows the entire text (including any endnotes) regardless of which system is used.

Though different publishers and journals have adopted slightly varying styles, the following examples illustrate standard styles for references, notes, and bibliographic entries. For more extensive treatment than can be provided here, *Webster's Standard American Style Manual, The Chicago Manual of Style, The MLA Style Manual,* or the *Publication Manual of the American Psychological Association* may be consulted.

Footnotes and Endnotes

Footnotes and endnotes are indicated by superscript Arabic numerals placed immediately after the material to be documented. The numbering is consecutive throughout an article or monograph; in a book, it usually starts over with each new chapter or section. Footnotes appear at the bottom of the page; endnotes, which take the same form as footnotes, are gathered at the end of the article, chapter, or book. Endnotes are generally preferred over footnotes by writers and publishers because they are easier to handle when preparing both manuscript and printed pages, though they can be less convenient for the reader. All of the examples shown reflect humanities citation style. All of the cited works appear again in the Lists of Sources section below.

Books

One author

[1]Elizabeth Bishop, *The Complete Poems: 1927–1979* (New York: Farrar, Straus & Giroux, 1983), 46.

Two or more authors

[2]Bert Holldobler and Edward O. Wilson, *The Ants* (Cambridge, Mass.: Belknap–Harvard Univ. Press, 1990), 119.

[3]Randolph Quirk et al., *A Comprehensive Grammar of the English Language* (London: Longman, 1985), 135.

Edition and/or translation

[4]Arthur S. Banks, ed. *Political Handbook of the World: 1992* (Binghamton, N.Y.: CSA Publications, 1992), 293–95.

[5]Simone de Beauvoir, *The Second Sex,* trans. and ed. H.M. Parshley (New York: Knopf, 1953; Random House, 1974), 446.

Second or later edition

[6]Albert C. Baugh and Thomas Cable, *A History of the English Language*, 3d ed. (Englewood Cliffs, N.J.: Prentice Hall, 1978), 14.

Article in a collection or festschrift

[7]Ernst Mayr, "Processes of Speciation in Animals," in *Mechanisms of Speciation*, ed. C. Barigozzi (New York: Alan R. Liss, 1982), 1–3.

Work in two or more volumes

[8]Ronald M. Nowak, *Walker's Mammals of the World,* 5th ed. (Baltimore: Johns Hopkins Univ. Press, 1991), 2:661.

Corporate author

[9]Commission of the Humanities. *The Humanities in American Life* (Berkeley: Univ. of California Press, 1980), 46.

Book lacking publication data

[10]*Photographic View Album of Cambridge* [England], n.p., n.d., n.pag.

Subsequent reference

[11]Baugh and Cable, 18–19.

Articles

Journal paginated consecutively throughout annual volume

[12]Stephen Jay Gould and Niles Eldredge, "Punctuated Equilibria: The Tempo and Mode of Evolution Reconsidered," *Paleobiology* 3 (1977): 121.

Journal paginated consecutively only within each issue

[13]Roseann Duenas Gonzalez, "Teaching Mexican American Students to Write: Capitalizing on the Culture," *English Journal* 71.7 (Nov. 1982): 22–24.

Monthly magazine

[14]John Lukacs, "The End of the Twentieth Century," *Harper's*, Jan. 1993: 40.

Weekly magazine

[15]Richard Preston, "A Reporter at Large: Crisis in the Hot Zone," *New Yorker*, 26 Oct. 1992: 58.

Newspaper

[16]William J. Broad, "Big Science Squeezes Small-Scale Researchers," *New York Times*, 29 Dec. 1992: C1.

Signed review

[17]George Steiner, review of *Oeuvres en Prose Complètes, Tome 3,* by Charles Péguy, *Times Literary Supplement,* 25 Dec. 1992: 3.

Parenthetical References

Parenthetical references are highly abbreviated bibliographical citations that appear within the text itself, enclosed in parentheses. Such references direct the reader to a detailed bibliography or list of sources at the end of the work, often removing the need for footnotes or endnotes. The parenthetical references usually include only the author's last name and a page reference. (In the social and natural sciences, the year of publication is included after the author's name, and the page number is often omitted.) Any element of the reference that is clear from the context may be omitted. To distinguish among cited works published by the same author, the author's name may be followed by the specific work's title, which is usually shortened. (If the author-date system is being used, a lowercase letter can be added after the year—e.g., 1992a, 1992b—to distinguish between works published in the same year.) Each of the following references is keyed to an entry in the Lists of Sources section below.

Humanities style

(Quirk et al., 135)
(Baugh and Cable, *History*, 14)
(Commission on the Humanities, 46)

Sciences style

(Mayr 1982, 1–3)
(Nowak 1991, 2:661)
(Gould and Eldredge 1977)

Lists of Sources

A bibliography or list of sources in alphabetical order usually appears at the end of the work. The following lists of cited works illustrate standard styles employed in, respectively, the humanities and the social and natural sciences. The principal differences between the two styles are these. In the sciences, (1) an initial is generally used instead of the author's first name, (2) the date is placed directly after the author's name, (3) all words in titles are lowercased except the first word and the first word of any subtitle as well as proper nouns and adjectives, and (4) article titles are not set off by quotation marks. (In some scientific publications, book and journal titles are not italicized.)

Humanities style

Baugh, Albert C., and Thomas Cable. *A History of the English Language*. 3d ed. Englewood Cliffs, N.J.: Prentice Hall, 1978.

Beauvoir, Simone de. *The Second Sex*. Trans. and ed. H. M. Parshley. New York: Alfred A. Knopf, 1953. Reprint. New York: Random House, 1974.

Bishop, Elizabeth. *The Complete Poems: 1927–1979*. New York: Farrar, Straus & Giroux, 1983.

Commission on the Humanities. *The Humanities in American Life*. Berkeley: University of California Press, 1980.

Gonzalez, Roseann Duenas. "Teaching Mexican American Students to Write: Capitalizing on the Culture." *English Journal* 71.7 (November 1982): 22–24.

Lukacs, John. "The End of the Twentieth Century." *Harper's*, January 1993: 39–58.

Photographic View Album of Cambridge [England]. N.d., n.p., n. pag.

Quirk, Randolph, Sidney Greenbaum, Geoffrey Leech, and Jan Svartvik. *A Comprehensive Grammar of the English Language*. London: Longman, 1985.

Steiner, George. Review of *Oeuvres en Prose Complètes, Tome 3*, by Charles Péguy. *Times Literary Supplement*, 25 December 1992: 3–4.

Sciences style

Banks, A. S., ed. 1992. *Political handbook of the world: 1992*. Binghamton, N.Y.: CSA Publications.

Broad, W. J. 1992. Big science squeezes small-scale researchers. *New York Times*, 29 Dec.: C1 +.

Gould, S. J., and N. Eldredge. 1977. Punctuated equilibria: The tempo and mode of evolution reconsidered. *Paleobiology* 3: 115–151.

Holldobler, B., and E. O. Wilson. 1990. *The ants*. Cambridge, Mass.: Belknap–Harvard Univ. Press.

Mayr, E. 1982. Processes of speciation in animals. In C. Barigozzi, ed., *Mechanisms of speciation*. New York: Alan R. Liss: 1–19.

Nowak, R.M. 1991. *Walker's mammals of the world*. 5th ed. 2 vols. Baltimore: Johns Hopkins Univ. Press.

Preston, R. 1992. A reporter at large: Crisis in the hot zone. *New Yorker*, 26 Oct.: 58–81.

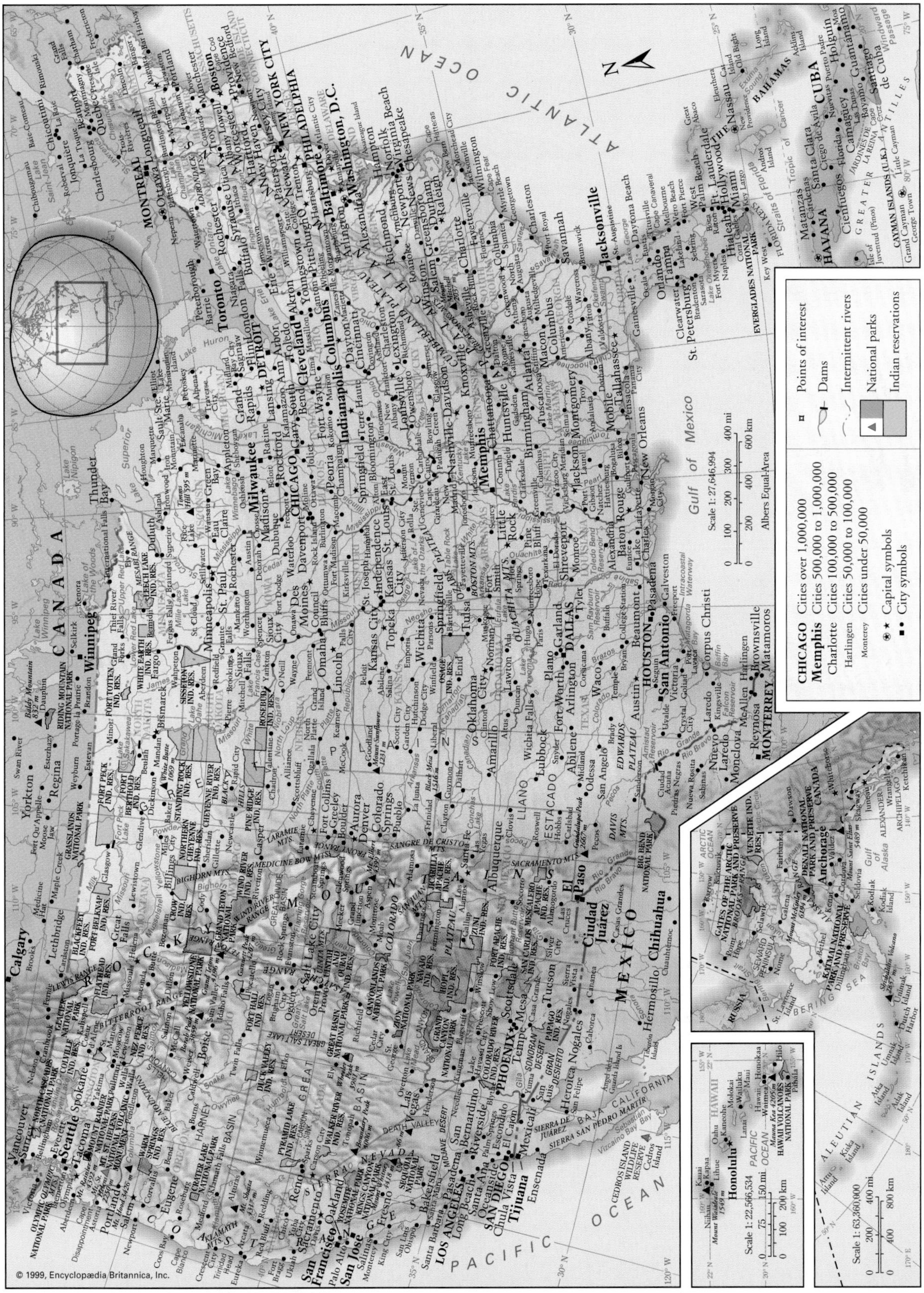
CANADA
UNITED STATES
MEXICO
PACIFIC OCEAN
ATLANTIC OCEAN
Gulf of Mexico
CHICAGO Cities over 1,000,000
Memphis Cities 500,000 to 1,000,000
Charlotte Cities 100,000 to 500,000
Harlingen Cities 50,000 to 100,000
Monterey Cities under 50,000
Capital symbols
City symbols
Points of interest
Dams
Intermittent rivers
National parks
Indian reservations
Scale 1: 27,646,994
Albers Equal-Area
Scale 1: 22,566,534
Scale 1: 63,360,000
© 1999, Encyclopædia Britannica, Inc.

WORLD

ARCTIC
150° W
120° W
90° W
60° W
30° W
QUEEN ELIZABETH ISLANDS
Greenland (Denmark)
GREENLAND SEA
Baffin Bay
Baffin I.
Victoria I.
CHUKCHI SEA
BEAUFORT SEA
BROOKS RANGE
Arctic Circle
Alaska (U.S.)
Yukon
Fairbanks
ALASKA RANGE
Mt. Denali
Anchorage
BERING SEA
60° N
Mackenzie
Great Bear L.
Great Slave L.
Peace
Hudson Bay
LABRADOR SEA
Reykjavík
ICELAND
Gulf of Alaska
ROCKY MOUNTAINS
GREAT PLAINS
CANADA
Edmonton
Saskatoon
Calgary
Winnipeg
ALEUTIAN ISLANDS
Vancouver
Seattle
Portland
Snake
Missouri
L. Superior
L. Huron
L. Michigan
Minneapolis
Chicago
Detroit
Toronto
Ottawa
Montreal
Quebec
Boston
Halifax
Island of Newfoundland
St. Johns
Gulf of St. Lawrence
IRELAND
Dublin
U.K.
London
FRANCE
UNITED STATES
APPALACHIAN MTS.
Ohio
New York City
Philadelphia
Washington, D.C.
San Francisco
Las Vegas
Colorado
Denver
Arkansas
Kansas City
St. Louis
Mississippi
Memphis
Atlanta
Los Angeles
San Diego
Phoenix
Oklahoma City
Dallas
ATLANTIC OCEAN
AZORES (Portugal)
PORTUGAL
Lisbon
Madrid
SPAIN
Bermuda (U.K.)
MADEIRA IS. (Portugal)
Rabat
Casablanca
MOROCCO
ATLAS
30° N
Baja California
Juárez
Rio Grande
Houston
Gulf of Mexico
Miami
CANARY IS. (Spain)
El Aaiún
Western Sahara (Morocco)
SIERRA MADRE OCCIDENTAL
MEXICO
Monterrey
Nassau
THE BAHAMAS
TURKS AND CAICOS (U.K.)
Santo Domingo
Tropic of Cancer
HAWAIIAN IS. (U.S.)
Bay of Campeche
Havana
CUBA
Puerto Rico (U.S.)
VIRGIN IS. (U.S.-U.K.)
ANTIGUA AND BARBUDA
ST. KITTS AND NEVIS
Guadeloupe (Fr.)
DOMINICA
Martinique (Fr.)
MAURITANIA
MALI
Guadalajara
Mexico City
JAMAICA
HAITI
Port-au-Prince
Kingston
DOMINICAN REPUBLIC
ST. LUCIA
BARBADOS
Belmopan
BELIZE
Tegucigalpa
HONDURAS
Guatemala City
GUATEMALA
San Salvador
EL SALVADOR
Managua
NICARAGUA
CARIBBEAN SEA
ST. VINCENT AND THE GRENADINES
GRENADA
TRINIDAD AND TOBAGO
Nouakchott
CAPE VERDE
Praia
THE GAMBIA
Dakar
SENEGAL
Banjul
Bamako
BURKINA FASO
Niger
Bissau
Ouagadougou
GUINEA-BISSAU
Conakry
GUINEA
Freetown
SIERRA LEONE
Monrovia
LIBERIA
CÔTE D'IVOIRE
GHANA
Abidjan
Accra
N
PACIFIC OCEAN
Barranquilla
San José
COSTA RICA
Panama City
PANAMA
LLANOS
Maracaibo
Caracas
Orinoco
VENEZUELA
GUYANA
Georgetown
SURINAME
Paramaribo
Cayenne
French Guiana (FR.)
GUIANA HIGHLANDS
Palmyra Atoll (U.S.)
Cali
Bogotá
COLOMBIA
Equator
0°
GALÁPAGOS IS. (Ecuador)
Quito
ECUADOR
Guayaquil
Iquitos
Manaus
Amazon
Belém
Fortaleza
Gulf of Guinea
KIRIBATI
PERU
ANDES
Madeira
Tapajós
Xingu
Recife
BRAZIL
Tocantins
São Francisco
COOK IS. (N.Z.)
SAMOA
AMERICAN SAMOA (U.S.)
FRENCH POLYNESIA (France)
Lima
Ucayali
L. Titicaca
La Paz
BRAZILIAN HIGHLANDS
Brasília
Bahia
Arequipa
BOLIVIA
Sucre
Belo Horizonte
TONGA
Tropic of Capricorn
ATACAMA DESERT
PARAGUAY
Paraná
Rio de Janeiro
São Paulo
Antofagasta
GRAN CHACO
Asunción
San Felix I.
San Ambrosia I.
30° S
Córdoba
Rosario
Porto Alegre
Mt. Aconcagua
PAMPA
URUGUAY
Montevideo
JUAN FERNÁNDEZ ISLANDS
Santiago
Buenos Aires
Concepción
ARGENTINA
CHILE
ATLANTIC OCEAN
Scale at equator
1: 119,240,000
0 500 1000 1500 2000 mi
0 1000 2000 3000 km
Robinson
Chiloé I.
PATAGONIA
FALKLAND IS. (U.K.)
SOUTH GEORGIA (U.K.)
Tierra del Fuego
Cape Horn
60° S
Antarctic Circle
Alexander I.
ANTARCTIC PEN.
WEDDELL SEA
MARIE BYRD LAND
Berkner I.
TRANSANTARCTIC MOUNTAINS

OCEAN
30° E
60° E
90° E
120° E
150° E
FRANZ JOSEF LAND
SVALBARD (Norway)
NORWEGIAN SEA
NOVAYA ZEMLYA
KARA SEA
NEW SIBERIAN IS.
EAST SIBERIAN SEA
Arctic Circle
NORWAY
SWEDEN
FINLAND
Arkhangelsk
Helsinki
St. Petersburg
Stockholm
Oslo
Tallinn
EST.
LAT.
LITH.
Riga
Vilnius
Moscow
NORTH SEA
DEN.
Copenhagen
BALTIC SEA
NETH.
BEL.
Berlin
GER.
POL.
Warsaw
Minsk
BELARUS
Kiev
UKRAINE
Paris
CZ. REP.
SLVK.
AUS.
HUN.
MOL.
SW.
SL.
CR.
B.-H.
YUGO.
ROM.
BUL.
Bucharest
ITALY
Rome
ALB.
MAC.
GREECE
Athens
Ankara
TURKEY
BLACK SEA
GEORGIA
Tbilisi
ARMENIA
AZERBAIJAN
Nizhniy Novgorod
Kazan
Ufa
Perm
Samara
Volgograd
URAL MOUNTAINS
Yekaterinburg
Chelyabinsk
Omsk
Novosibirsk
Novokuznetsk
Barnaul
Krasnoyarsk
WEST SIBERIAN PLAIN
RUSSIA
Ob
Yenisey
Lower Tunguska
Lena
VERKHOYANSK MTS.
Yakutsk
Kolyma
KOLYMA MTS.
60° N
BERING SEA
KAMCHATKA PEN.
SEA OF OKHOTSK
STANOVOY MTS.
Lake Baikal
Irkutsk
Chita
Amur
Khabarovsk
Sakhalin
Astana
KAZAKSTAN
L. Balkhash
ARAL SEA
CASPIAN SEA
UZBEKISTAN
TURKMENISTAN
Ashkhabad
Tashkent
Bishkek
Almaty
KYRGYZSTAN
TAJIKISTAN
TIAN SHAN
Ulaanbaatar
MONGOLIA
GOBI DESERT
Harbin
Vladivostok
Hokkaido
Shenyang
Beijing
NORTH KOREA
P'yongyang
Seoul
SOUTH KOREA
Pusan
JAPAN
Honshu
Tokyo
Osaka
Shikoku
Kyushu
PACIFIC OCEAN
Tianjin
YELLOW SEA
CHINA
KUNLUN MTS.
Huang He
Lanzhou
Xi'an
Nanjing
Yangtze
Wuhan
Shanghai
Chongqing
Lhasa
PLATEAU OF TIBET
MIDWAY IS. (U.S.)
30° N
Algiers
MEDITERRANEAN SEA
Tunis
TUNISIA
Tripoli
MTNS.
CYPRUS
SYRIA
Damascus
LEBANON
Beirut
ISRAEL
Jerusalem
Alexandria
JORDAN
Cairo
IRAQ
Baghdad
Tehran
IRAN
ZAGROS MOUNTAINS
KUWAIT
Kuwait
BAHRAIN
Persian Gulf
Riyadh
QATAR
U.A.E.
Muscat
OMAN
SAUDI ARABIA
Jiddah
RUB 'AL KHALI DESERT
AFGHANISTAN
Kabul
Islamabad
PAKISTAN
Lahore
Indus
Karachi
Delhi
New Delhi
NEPAL
Mount Everest
Kathmandu
BHUTAN
Thimphu
Ganges
BANGLADESH
Dhaka
Calcutta
INDIA
Ahmadabad
Nagpur
Bombay
Hyderabad
Bangalore
Madras
ARABIAN SEA
Bay of Bengal
ALGERIA
SAHARA
LIBYA
EGYPT
L. Nasser
Nile
RED SEA
AHAGGAR MTS.
TIBESTI MTS.
NIGER
SAHEL
CHAD
L. Chad
Niamey
N'Djamena
Khartoum
THE SUDAN
Asmara
ERITREA
Sanaa
YEMEN
Gulf of Aden
Socotra (Yemen)
DJIBOUTI
Djibouti
Cape Gwardafuy
NIGERIA
Abuja
BENIN
TOGO
Porto-Novo
CAMEROON
Yaoundé
Malabo
EQ. GUINEA
C.A.R.
Bangui
Addis Ababa
ETHIOPIA
ETHIOPIAN PLATEAU
SOMALIA
White Nile
GABON
Libreville
REP. OF THE CONGO
Congo
Brazzaville
UGANDA
Kampala
KENYA
Nairobi
Mogadishu
RWANDA
Kigali
BURUNDI
Bujumbura
Lake Victoria
Kilimanjaro
TANZANIA
Dar es Salaam
Cabinda (ANGOLA)
Kinshasa
DEM. REP. OF THE CONGO
Lake Tanganyika
Luanda
ANGOLA
MALAWI
Lake Malawi
SEYCHELLES
Victoria
Moroni
COMOROS
ZAMBIA
Lusaka
Lilongwe
Kubango
Harare
ZIMBABWE
MOZAMBIQUE
Mozambique Channel
Antananarivo
MADAGASCAR
NAMIBIA
Windhoek
NAMIB DESERT
BOTSWANA
Gaborone
Pretoria
Johannesburg
Maputo
Mbabane
SWAZILAND
Maseru
LESOTHO
Orange
SOUTH AFRICA
Cape Town
Cape of Good Hope
MAURITIUS
Port Louis
Réunion (Fr.)
BRITISH INDIAN OCEAN TERRITORY (U.K.)
INDIAN OCEAN
ANDAMAN IS. (India)
NICOBAR IS. (India)
Colombo
SRI LANKA
MALDIVES
Male
KEELING IS. (Austl.)
MYANMAR
Yangon
LAOS
Vientiane
Hanoi
THAILAND
Bangkok
VIETNAM
CAMBODIA
Phnom Penh
Ho Chi Minh City
SOUTH CHINA SEA
Guangzhou
HONG KONG
TAIWAN
Taipei
Kaohsiung
Tropic of Cancer
PHILIPPINE SEA
Luzon
Manila
PHILIPPINES
Mindanao
NORTHERN MARIANA IS. (U.S.)
Guam (U.S.)
Koror
PALAU
FEDERATED STATES OF MICRONESIA
Palikir
MARSHALL IS.
Majuro
Medan
Kuala Lumpur
MALAYSIA
BRUNEI
Bandar Seri Begawan
SINGAPORE
Sumatra
Borneo
Celebes
Palembang
INDONESIA
Jakarta
Bandung
Semarang
Surabaya
Java
Timor
New Guinea
PAPUA NEW GUINEA
Port Moresby
Equator
Bairiki
KIRIBATI
0°
SOLOMON ISLANDS
Honiara
TUVALU
Funafuti
ARAFURA SEA
ARNHEM LAND
CORAL SEA
Great Barrier Reef
GREAT DIVIDING RANGE
VANUATU
Port-Vila
Éfaté
FIJI
Suva
New Caledonia (Fr.)
Tropic of Capricorn
GREAT SANDY DESERT
GREAT ARTESIAN BASIN
AUSTRALIA
Brisbane
GREAT VICTORIA DESERT
Darling
Perth
30° S
Great Australian Bight
Adelaide
Sydney
Canberra
Melbourne
Auckland
NEW ZEALAND
Wellington
Tasmania
Hobart
TASMAN SEA
Amsterdam I. (Fr.)
Saint Paul I. (Fr.)
CROZET IS. (Fr.)
PRINCE EDWARD IS. (South Africa)
Kerguelen I. (Fr.)
AUCKLAND IS. (N.Z.)
60° S
Antarctic Circle
ENDERBY LAND
QUEEN MAUD LAND
WILKES LAND
VICTORIA LAND
ROSS SEA
ANTARCTICA
© 1999, Encyclopædia Britannica, Inc.

NORTH AMERICA

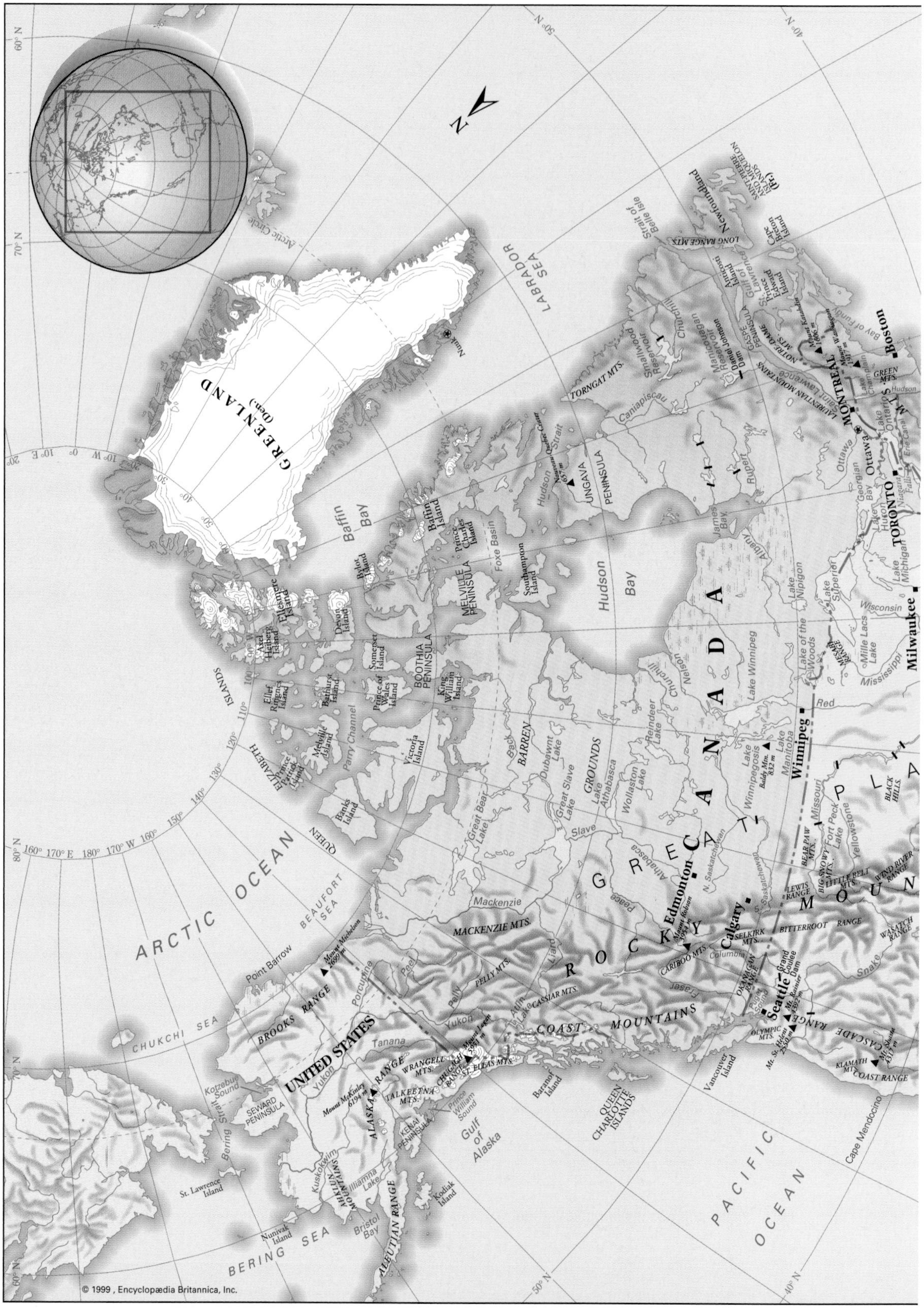

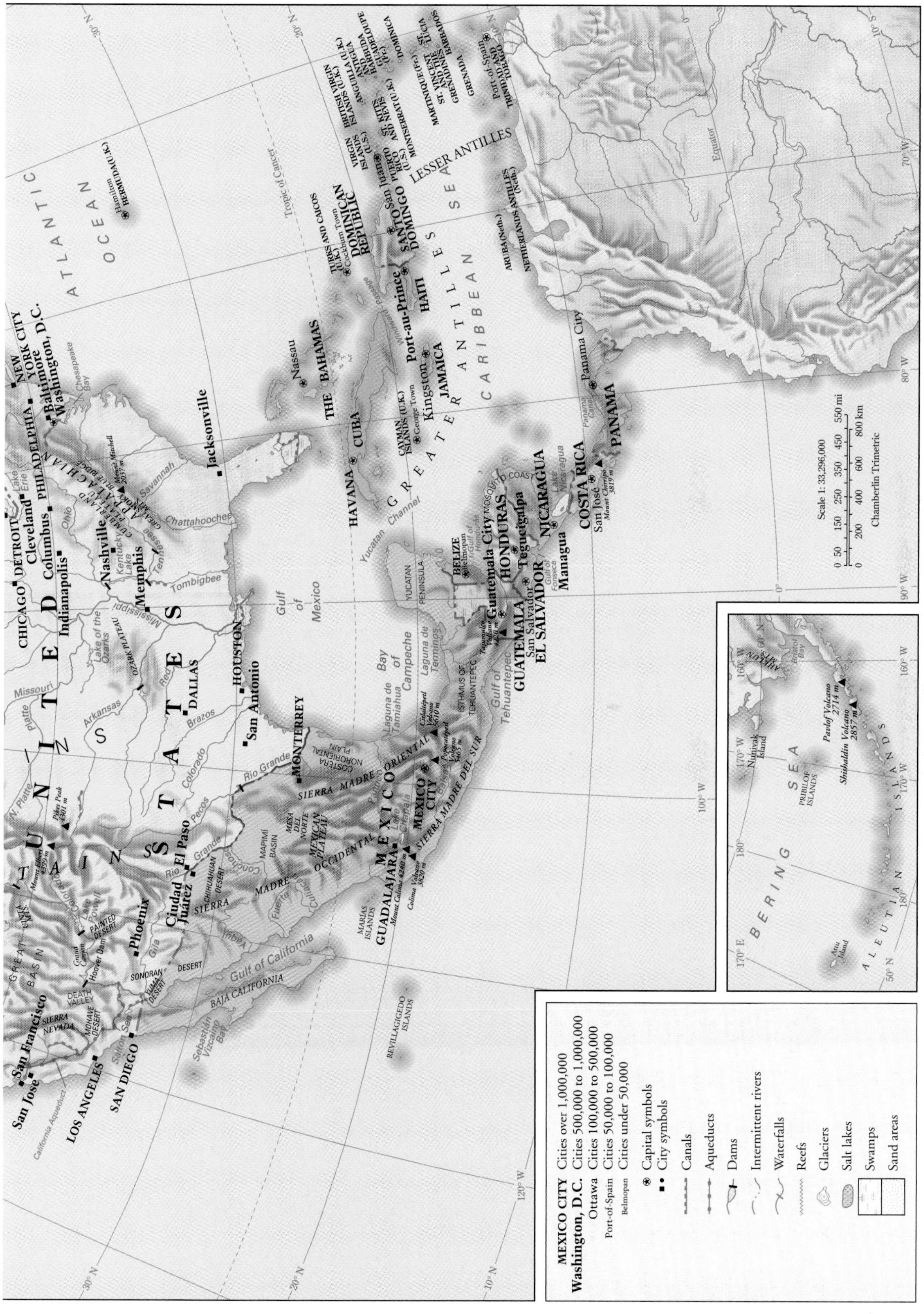
MEXICO CITY Cities over 1,000,000
Washington, D.C. Cities 500,000 to 1,000,000
Ottawa Cities 100,000 to 500,000
Port-of-Spain Cities 50,000 to 100,000
Belmopan Cities under 50,000
Capital symbols
City symbols
Canals
Aqueducts
Dams
Intermittent rivers
Waterfalls
Reefs
Glaciers
Salt lakes
Swamps
Sand areas
Scale 1: 33,296,000
0 50 150 250 350 450 550 mi
0 200 400 600 800 km
Chamberlin Trimetric
UNITED STATES
MEXICO
ATLANTIC OCEAN
CARIBBEAN SEA
Gulf of Mexico
Bay of Campeche
Gulf of California
BAJA CALIFORNIA
GREATER ANTILLES
LESSER ANTILLES
Tropic of Cancer
Equator
BERING SEA
ALEUTIAN ISLANDS
PRIBILOF ISLANDS
Nunivak Island
Attu Island
Bristol Bay
Pavlof Volcano 2714 m
Shishaldin Volcano 2857 m
NEW YORK CITY
Washington, D.C.
Baltimore
PHILADELPHIA
CHICAGO
DETROIT
Cleveland
Columbus
Indianapolis
Nashville
Memphis
Jacksonville
HOUSTON
San Antonio
DALLAS
El Paso
Ciudad Juárez
Phoenix
SAN DIEGO
LOS ANGELES
San Francisco
San Jose
MONTERREY
GUADALAJARA
MEXICO CITY
HAVANA
CUBA
THE BAHAMAS
Nassau
JAMAICA
Kingston
HAITI
Port-au-Prince
DOMINICAN REPUBLIC
SANTO DOMINGO
San Juan
BERMUDA (U.K.)
BELIZE
Belmopan
GUATEMALA
Guatemala City
HONDURAS
Tegucigalpa
EL SALVADOR
San Salvador
NICARAGUA
Managua
COSTA RICA
San José
PANAMA
Panama City
Port-of-Spain
TRINIDAD AND TOBAGO
ARUBA (Neth.)
NETHERLANDS ANTILLES (Neth.)
SIERRA MADRE ORIENTAL
SIERRA MADRE OCCIDENTAL
SIERRA MADRE DEL SUR
YUCATAN PENINSULA
ISTHMUS OF TEHUANTEPEC
Rio Grande
Mississippi
Missouri
Arkansas
Colorado
Pikes Peak 4301 m
Mount Mitchell 2037 m

CANADA

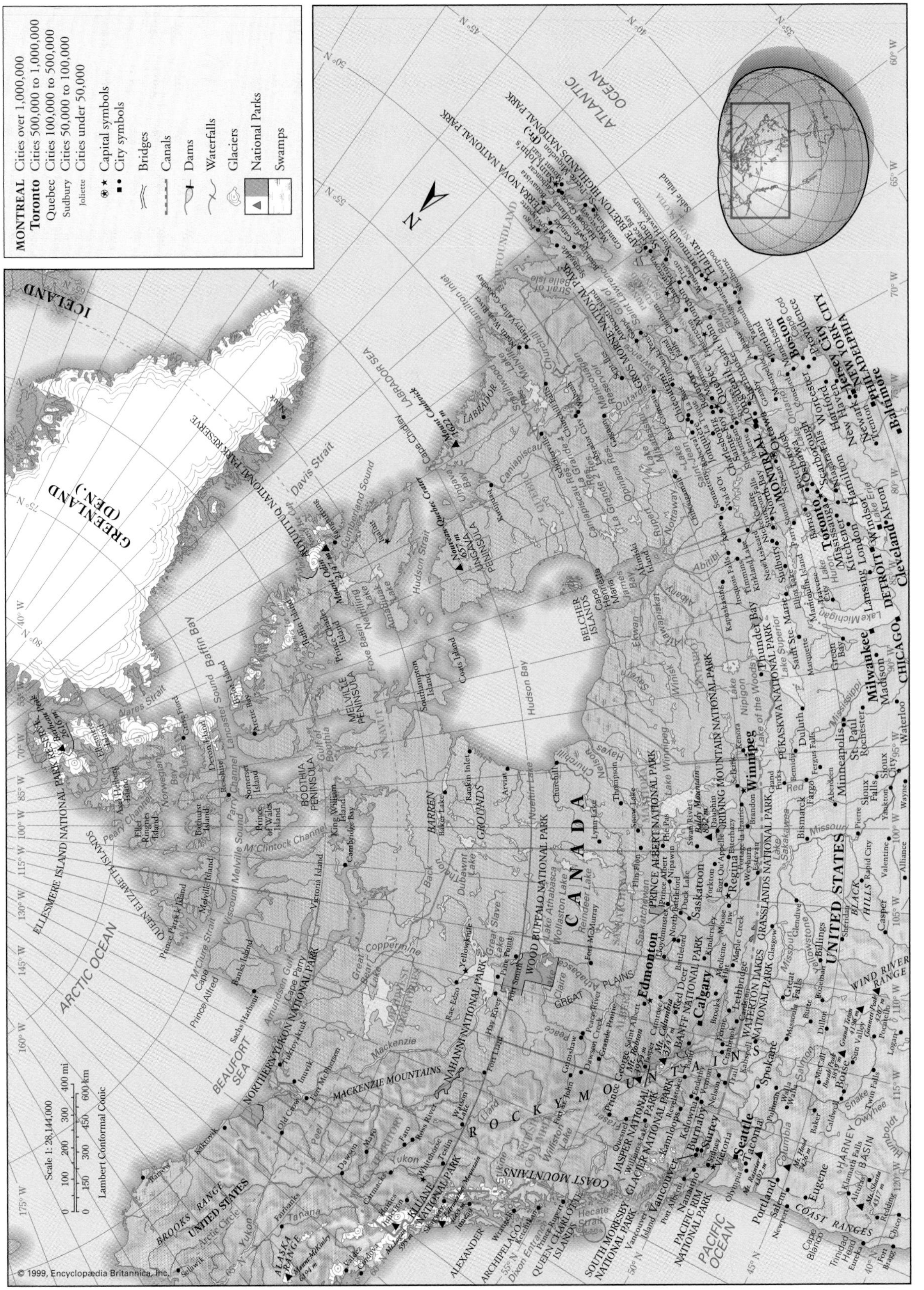

MONTREAL Cities over 1,000,000
Toronto Cities 500,000 to 1,000,000
Quebec Cities 100,000 to 500,000
Sudbury Cities 50,000 to 100,000
Joliette Cities under 50,000
Capital symbols
City symbols
Bridges
Canals
Dams
Waterfalls
Glaciers
National Parks
Swamps
Scale 1: 28,144,000
Lambert Conformal Conic
ATLANTIC OCEAN
ARCTIC OCEAN
PACIFIC OCEAN
GREENLAND (DEN.)
ICELAND
UNITED STATES
CANADA
Hudson Bay
Baffin Bay
Davis Strait
LABRADOR SEA
BEAUFORT SEA
© 1999, Encyclopædia Britannica, Inc.

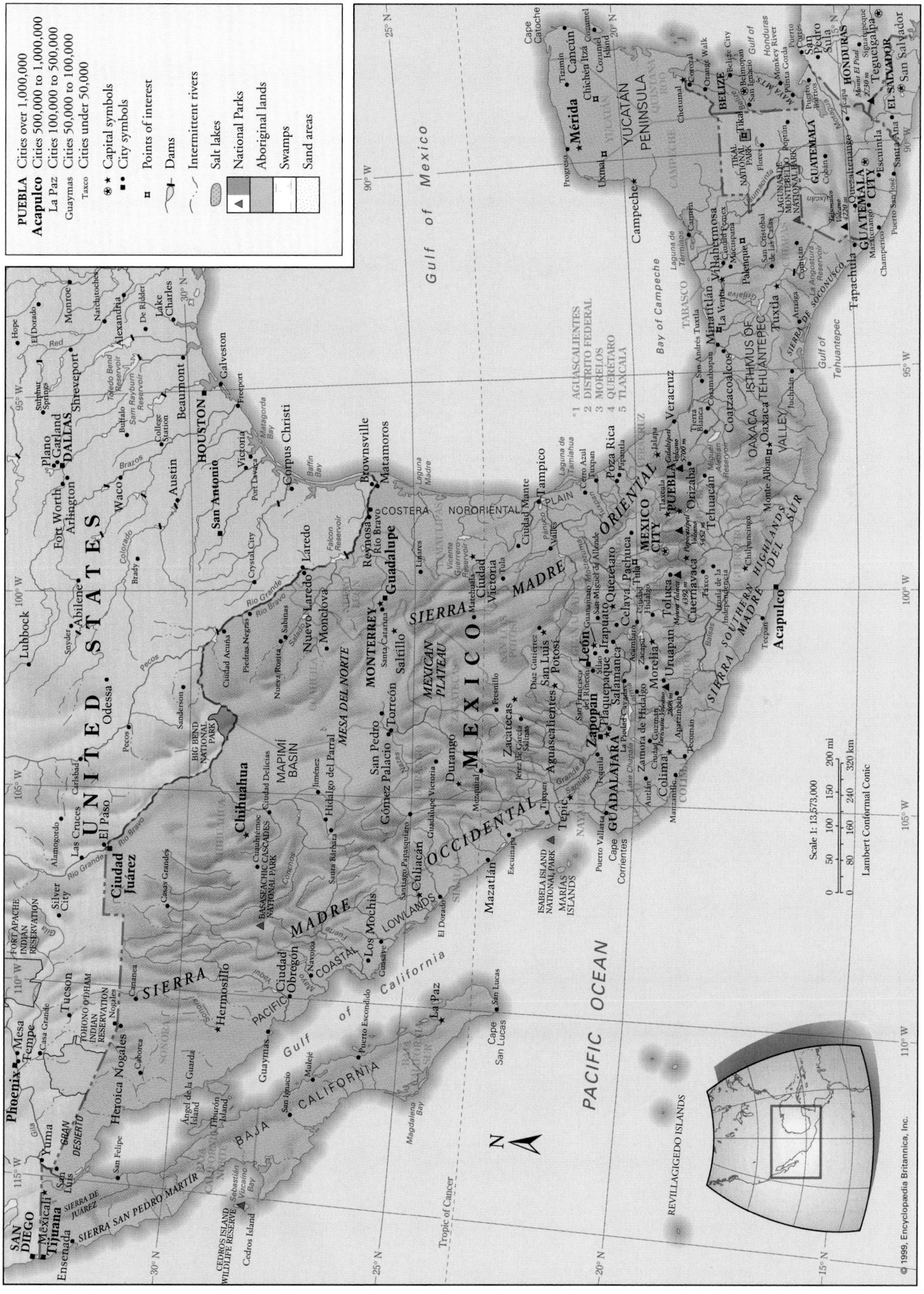
PUEBLA Cities over 1,000,000
Acapulco Cities 500,000 to 1,000,000
La Paz Cities 100,000 to 500,000
Guaymas Cities 50,000 to 100,000
Taxco Cities under 50,000
Capital symbols
City symbols
Points of interest
Dams
Intermittent rivers
Salt lakes
National Parks
Aboriginal lands
Swamps
Sand areas
UNITED STATES
MEXICO
Gulf of Mexico
PACIFIC OCEAN
Gulf of California
BAJA CALIFORNIA
SIERRA MADRE OCCIDENTAL
SIERRA MADRE ORIENTAL
SIERRA MADRE DEL SUR
MEXICAN PLATEAU
MESA DEL NORTE
MAPIMÍ BASIN
YUCATÁN PENINSULA
ISTHMUS OF TEHUANTEPEC
Bay of Campeche
Gulf of Tehuantepec
Gulf of Honduras
MEXICO CITY
GUADALAJARA
MONTERREY
PUEBLA
BELIZE
GUATEMALA
HONDURAS
EL SALVADOR
GUATEMALA CITY
REVILLAGIGEDO ISLANDS
Tropic of Cancer
1 AGUASCALIENTES
2 DISTRITO FEDERAL
3 MORELOS
4 QUERÉTARO
5 TLAXCALA
Scale 1: 13,573,000
Lambert Conformal Conic
© 1999, Encyclopædia Britannica, Inc.

THE CARIBBEAN

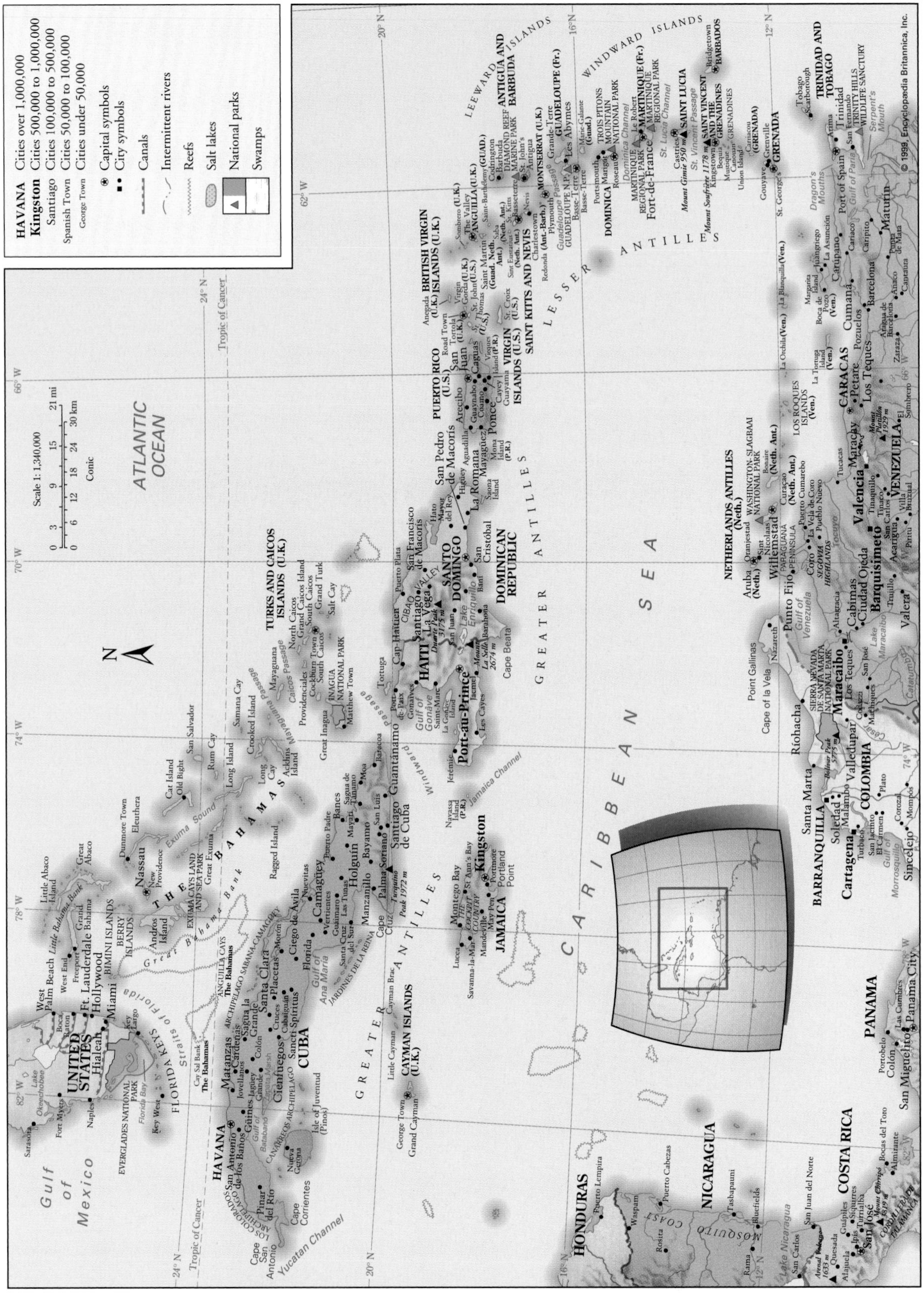

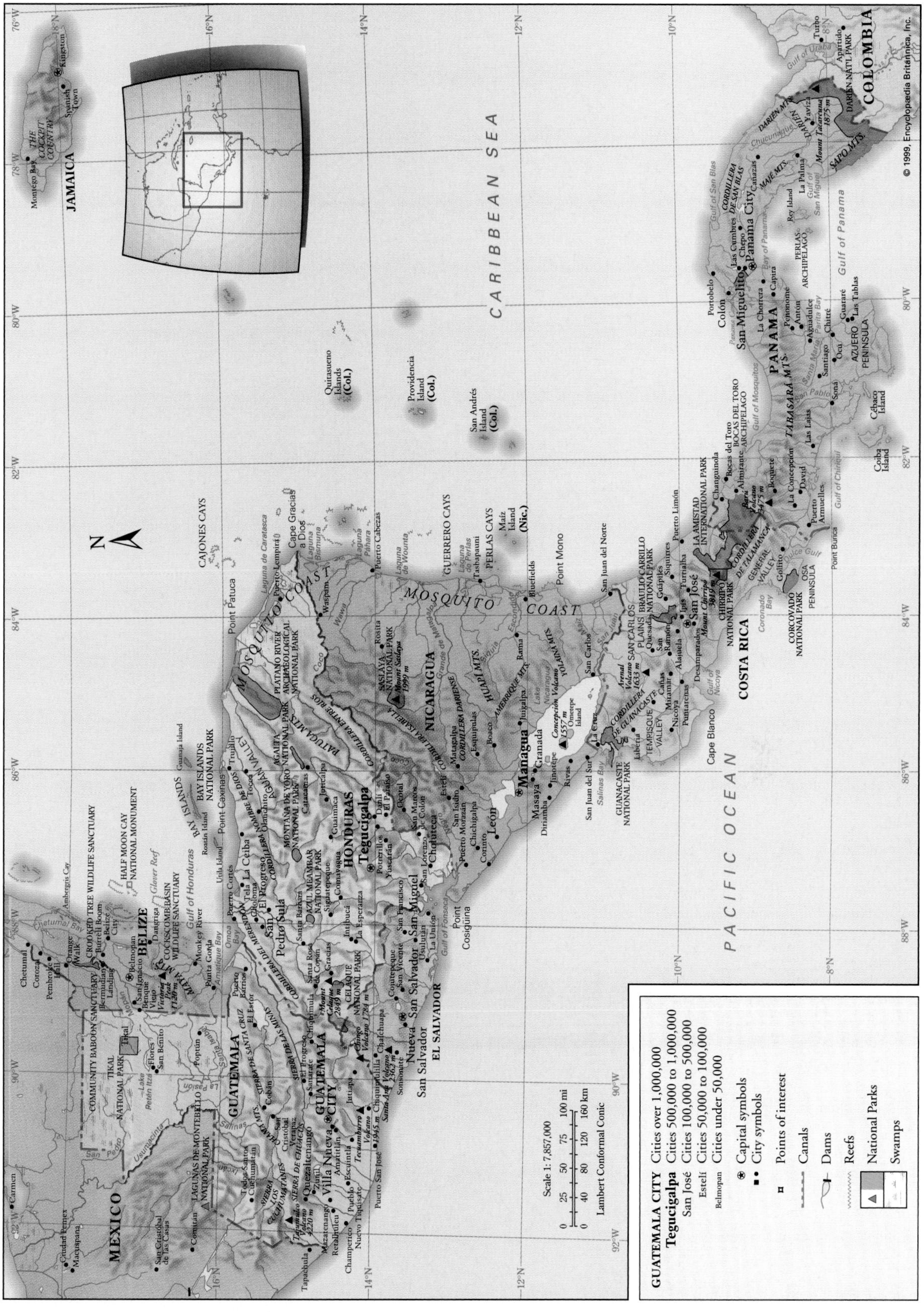
MEXICO
BELIZE
GUATEMALA
HONDURAS
EL SALVADOR
NICARAGUA
COSTA RICA
PANAMA
COLOMBIA
JAMAICA
CARIBBEAN SEA
PACIFIC OCEAN
MOSQUITO COAST
Gulf of Honduras
Gulf of Fonseca
Gulf of Panama
GUATEMALA CITY
Tegucigalpa
San Salvador
Managua
San José
Panama City
Belmopan
Kingston
GUATEMALA CITY Cities over 1,000,000
Tegucigalpa Cities 500,000 to 1,000,000
San José Cities 100,000 to 500,000
Estelí Cities 50,000 to 100,000
Belmopan Cities under 50,000
Capital symbols
City symbols
Points of interest
Canals
Dams
Reefs
National Parks
Swamps
Scale 1: 7,857,000
0 25 50 75 100 mi
0 40 80 120 160 km
Lambert Conformal Conic
© 1999, Encyclopædia Britannica, Inc.

SOUTH AMERICA

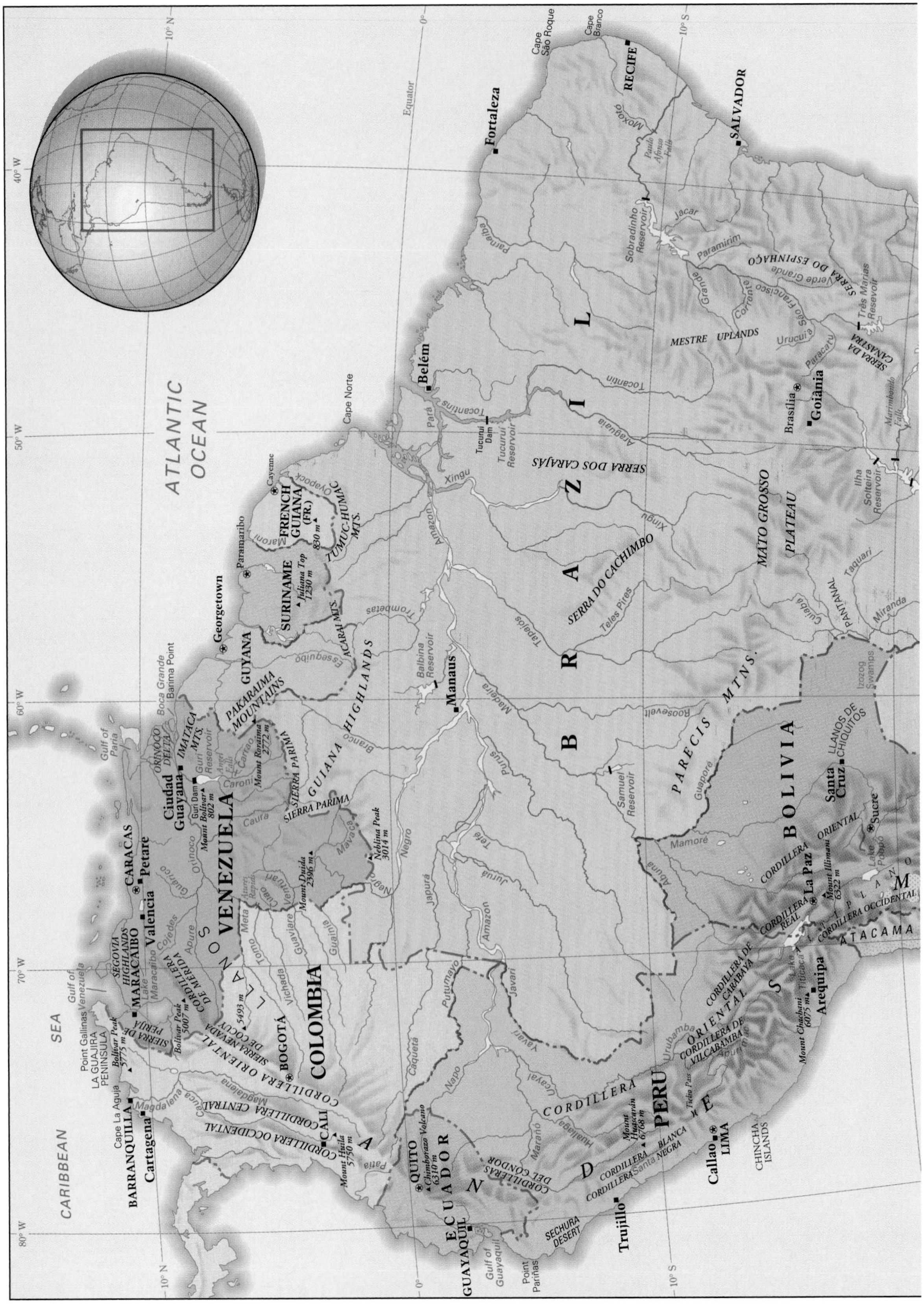

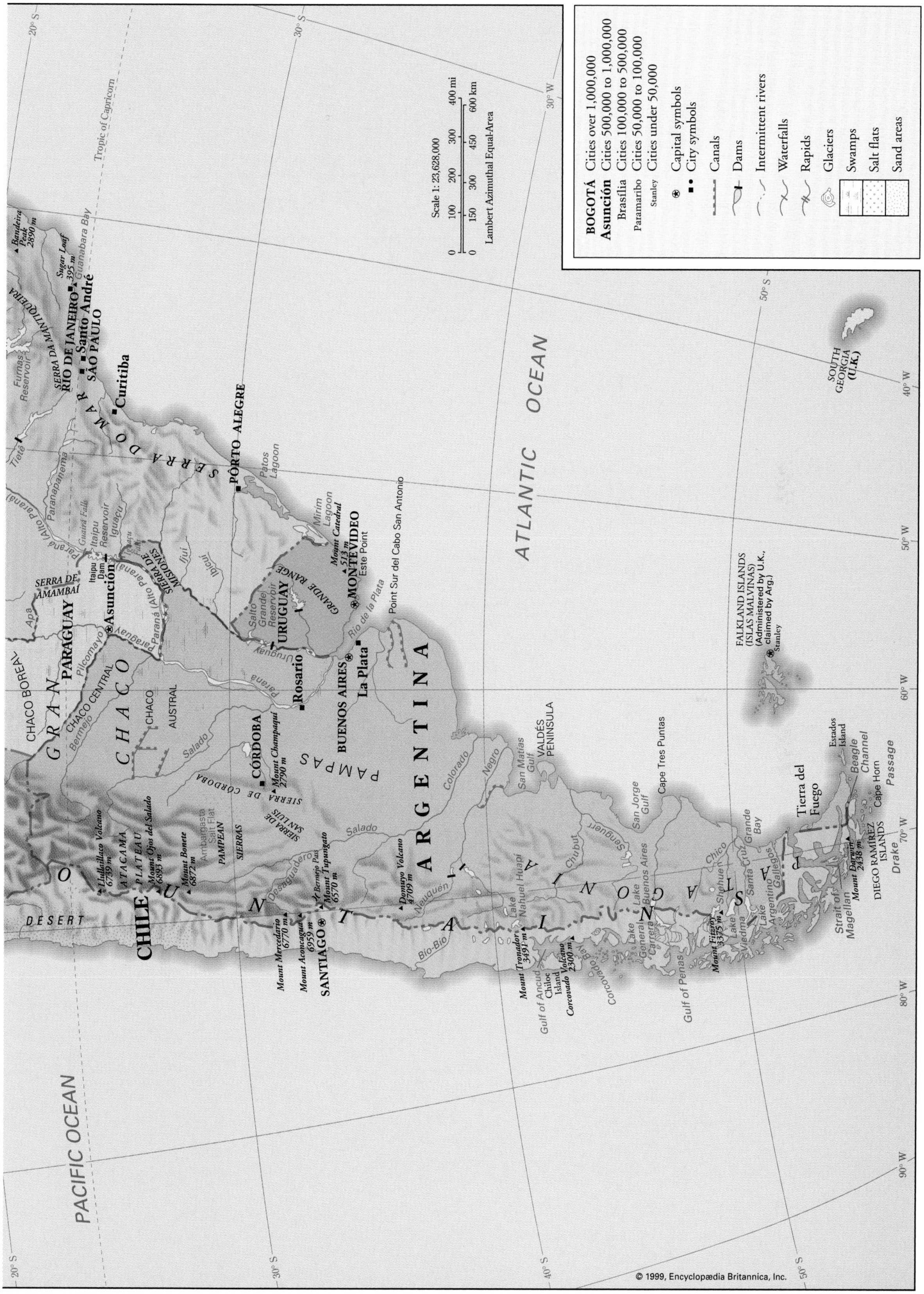

BOGOTÁ Cities over 1,000,000
Asunción Cities 500,000 to 1,000,000
Brasília Cities 100,000 to 500,000
Paramaribo Cities 50,000 to 100,000
Stanley Cities under 50,000
Capital symbols
City symbols
Canals
Dams
Intermittent rivers
Waterfalls
Rapids
Glaciers
Swamps
Salt flats
Sand areas
Scale 1: 23,628,000
0 100 200 300 400 mi
0 150 300 450 600 km
Lambert Azimuthal Equal-Area
PACIFIC OCEAN
ATLANTIC OCEAN
Tropic of Capricorn
CHILE
ARGENTINA
PARAGUAY
URUGUAY
SANTIAGO
BUENOS AIRES
MONTEVIDEO
Asunción
Córdoba
Rosario
La Plata
PÔRTO ALEGRE
Curitiba
SÃO PAULO
Santo André
RIO DE JANEIRO
GRAN CHACO
PAMPAS
PATAGONIA
ATACAMA DESERT
PUNA DE ATACAMA
SERRA DO MAR
Mount Aconcagua 6959 m
Mount Mercedario 6770 m
Mount Tupungato 6570 m
Mount Bonete 6872 m
Llullaillaco Volcano 6739 m
Mount Ojos del Salado 6893 m
Domuyo Volcano 4709 m
Mount Champaquí 2790 m
Mount Tronador 3491 m
Corcovado Volcano 2300 m
Mount Fitzroy 3375 m
Mount Darwin 2438 m
Mount Catedral 513 m
Sugar Loaf 395 m
Bandeira Peak 2890 m
VALDÉS PENINSULA
San Matías Gulf
San Jorge Gulf
Cape Tres Puntas
Gulf of Penas
Gulf of Ancud
Chiloe Island
Tierra del Fuego
Estados Island
Beagle Channel
Cape Horn
Drake Passage
Strait of Magellan
DIEGO RAMÍREZ ISLANDS
FALKLAND ISLANDS (ISLAS MALVINAS) (Administered by U.K., claimed by Arg.)
Stanley
SOUTH GEORGIA (U.K.)
Río de la Plata
Point Sur del Cabo San Antonio
Este Point
Mirim Lagoon
Patos Lagoon
Itaipu Dam
Itaipu Reservoir
Salto Grande Reservoir
Furnas Reservoir
Paraná
Uruguay
Paraguay
Pilcomayo
Bermejo
Salado
Colorado
Negro
Chubut
Santa Cruz
20° S
30° S
40° S
50° S
30° W
40° W
50° W
60° W
70° W
80° W
90° W

BRAZIL, BOLIVIA, AND PARAGUAY

BRAZIL, BOLIVIA, AND PARAGUAY

ARGENTINA, CHILE, AND URUGUAY

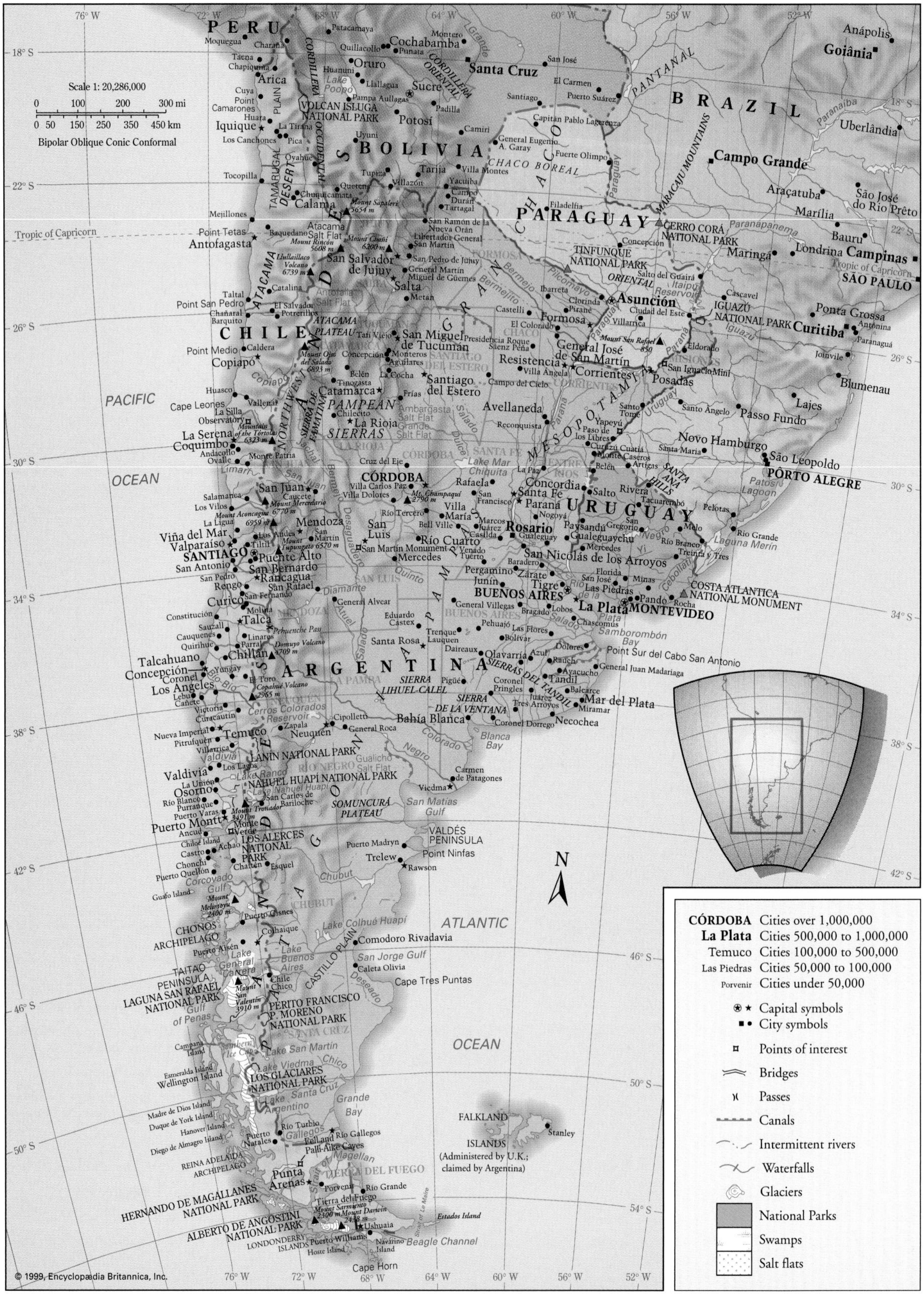

ECUADOR AND PERU

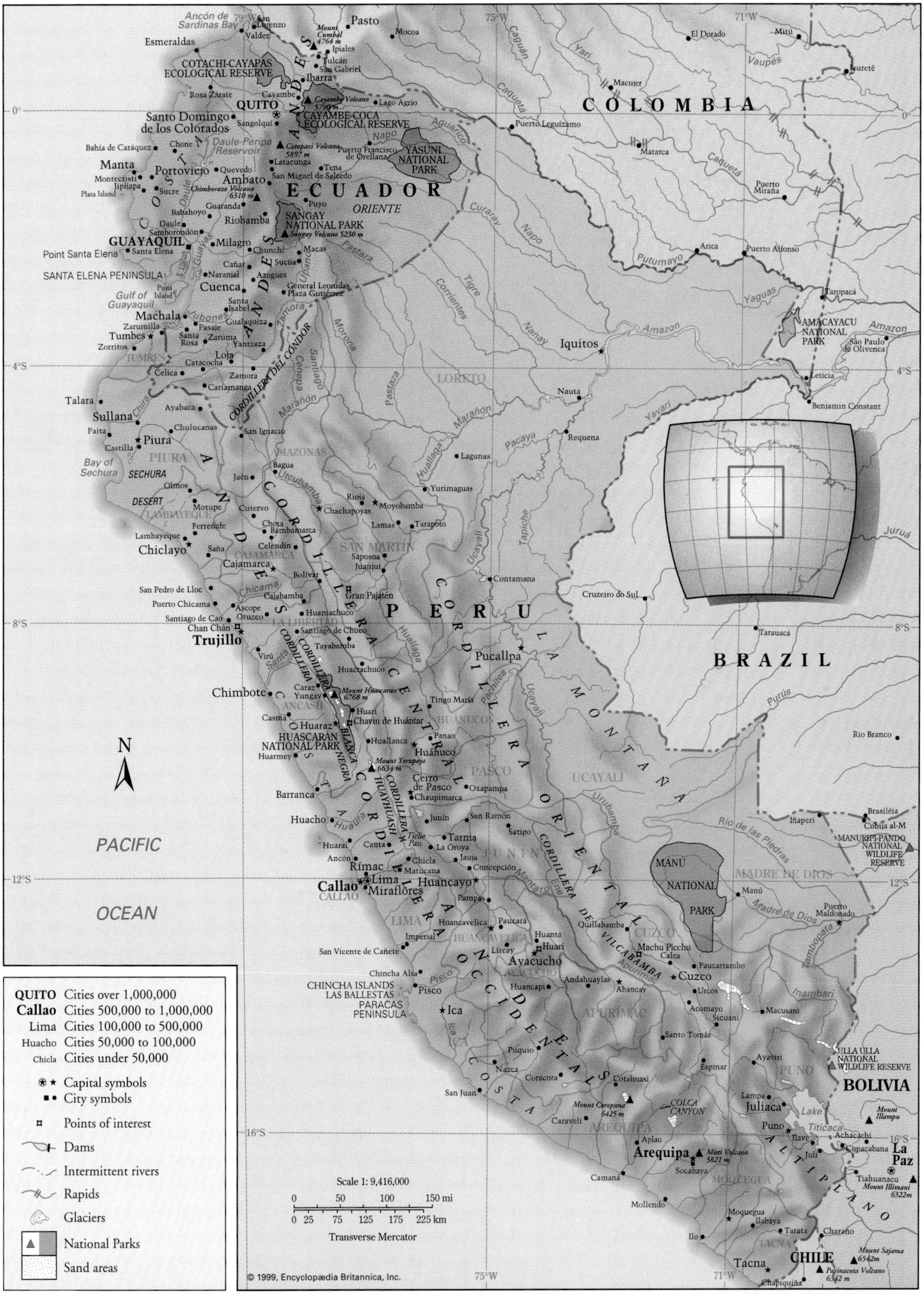

COLOMBIA AND VENEZUELA

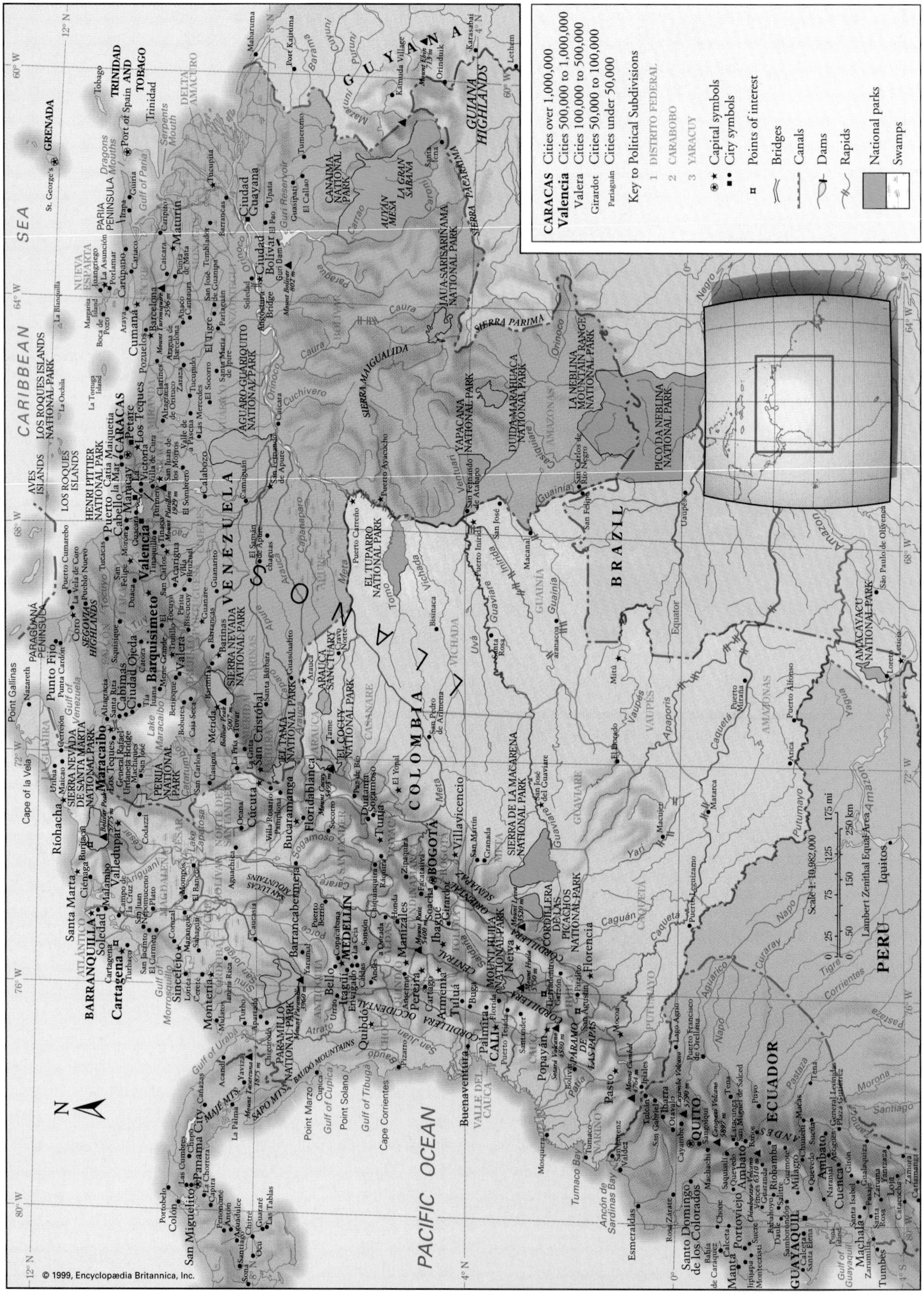
CARACAS Cities over 1,000,000
Valencia Cities 500,000 to 1,000,000
Valera Cities 100,000 to 500,000
Girardot Cities 50,000 to 100,000
Pariaguán Cities under 50,000
Key to Political Subdivisions
1 DISTRITO FEDERAL
2 CARABOBO
3 YARACUY
Capital symbols
City symbols
Points of interest
Bridges
Canals
Dams
Rapids
National parks
Swamps
Scale 1:10,982,000
Lambert Zenithal Equal-Area
CARIBBEAN SEA
PACIFIC OCEAN
COLOMBIA
VENEZUELA
BRAZIL
PERU
ECUADOR
GUYANA
© 1999, Encyclopædia Britannica, Inc.

UNITED KINGDOM AND IRELAND

EUROPE

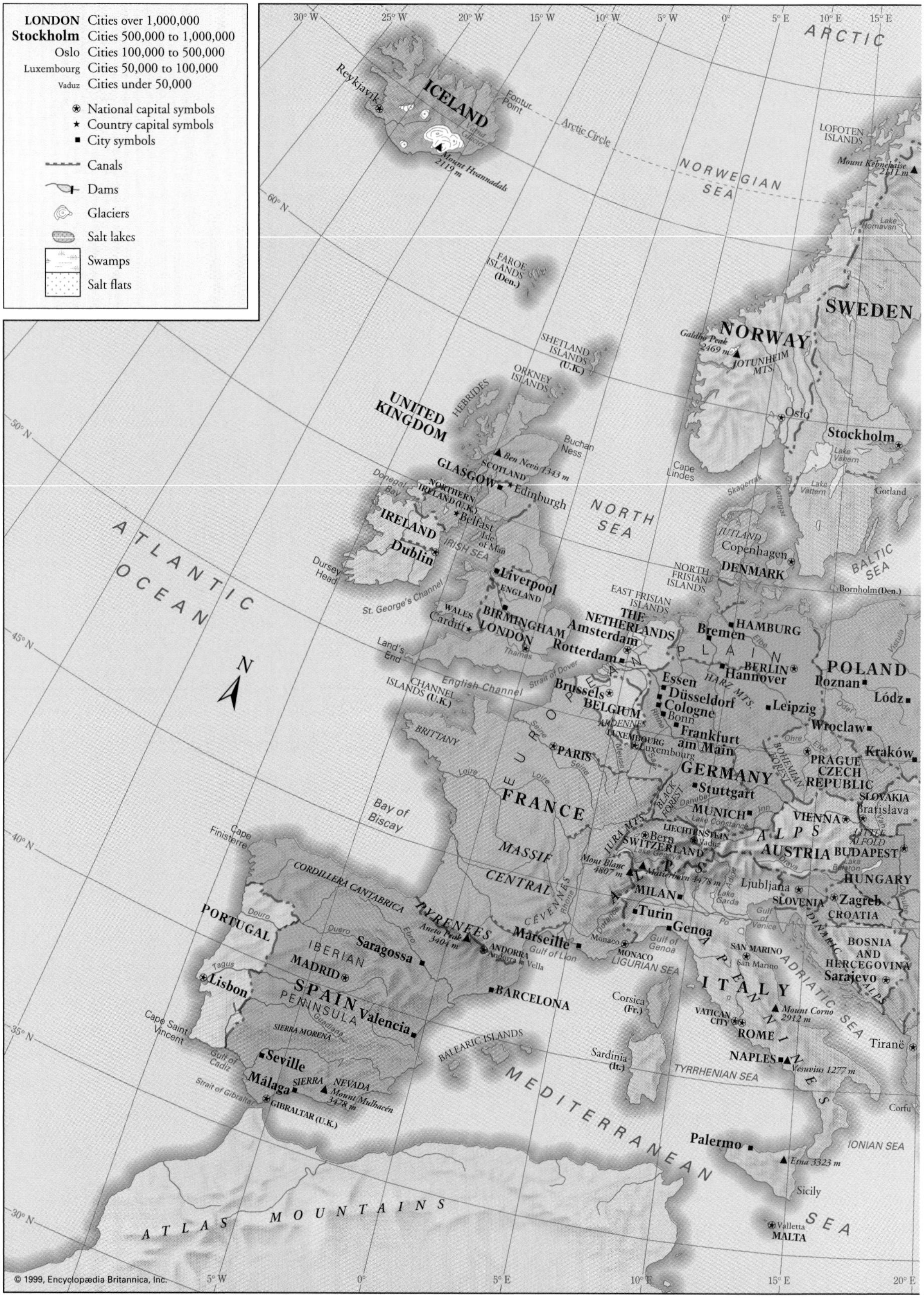

LONDON Cities over 1,000,000
Stockholm Cities 500,000 to 1,000,000
Oslo Cities 100,000 to 500,000
Luxembourg Cities 50,000 to 100,000
Vaduz Cities under 50,000
National capital symbols
Country capital symbols
City symbols
Canals
Dams
Glaciers
Salt lakes
Swamps
Salt flats
ARCTIC
ICELAND
Reykjavík
Fontur Point
Arctic Circle
Mount Hvannadals 2119 m
NORWEGIAN SEA
LOFOTEN ISLANDS
Mount Kebnekaise 2111 m
Lake Hornavan
FAROE ISLANDS (Den.)
SWEDEN
NORWAY
Galdhø Peak 2469 m
JOTUNHEIM MTS.
SHETLAND ISLANDS (U.K.)
ORKNEY ISLANDS
HEBRIDES
UNITED KINGDOM
Oslo
Stockholm
Lake Vänern
Lake Vättern
Gotland
Buchan Ness
Ben Nevis 1343 m
SCOTLAND
Cape Lindes
Skagerrak
Kattegat
GLASGOW
Edinburgh
NORTHERN IRELAND (U.K.)
Belfast
Donegal Bay
NORTH SEA
IRELAND
Dublin
IRISH SEA
Isle of Man
JUTLAND
Copenhagen
DENMARK
BALTIC SEA
ATLANTIC OCEAN
Dursey Head
Liverpool
ENGLAND
NORTH FRISIAN ISLANDS
Bornholm (Den.)
St. George's Channel
WALES
Cardiff
BIRMINGHAM
LONDON
Thames
EAST FRISIAN ISLANDS
THE NETHERLANDS
Amsterdam
Bremen
HAMBURG
Elbe
Rotterdam
Land's End
Strait of Dover
English Channel
CHANNEL ISLANDS (U.K.)
N
Brussels
BELGIUM
Essen
Düsseldorf
Cologne
Bonn
HARZ MTS.
BERLIN
Hannover
POLAND
Poznan
Lódz
Leipzig
Oder
Wroclaw
Kraków
BRITTANY
ARDENNES
LUXEMBOURG
Luxembourg
Frankfurt am Main
PARIS
Seine
Loire
GERMANY
PRAGUE
CZECH REPUBLIC
BOHEMIAN FOREST
SLOVAKIA
Bratislava
Stuttgart
BLACK FOREST
Danube
MUNICH
Inn
VIENNA
FRANCE
Bay of Biscay
NORTH EUROPEAN PLAIN
Lake Constance
LIECHTENSTEIN
Vaduz
Bern
SWITZERLAND
Lake Geneva
JURA MTS.
ALPS
AUSTRIA
LITTLE ALFOLD
BUDAPEST
Lake Balaton
Mont Blanc 4807 m
Matterhorn 4478 m
HUNGARY
Drava
MASSIF CENTRAL
Cape Finisterre
CORDILLERA CANTABRICA
MILAN
Lake Garda
Ljubljana
SLOVENIA
Zagreb
CROATIA
CÉVENNES
Rhône
Turin
Po
Gulf of Venice
DINARIC ALPS
PORTUGAL
Douro
PYRENEES
Aneto Peak 3404 m
Marseille
Monaco
MONACO
Genoa
Gulf of Genoa
SAN MARINO
San Marino
BOSNIA AND HERCEGOVINA
Sarajevo
Ebro
Saragossa
ANDORRA
Andorra la Vella
Gulf of Lion
LIGURIAN SEA
ADRIATIC SEA
IBERIAN PENINSULA
Tagus
MADRID
Lisbon
SPAIN
BARCELONA
Corsica (Fr.)
ITALY
APENNINES
VATICAN CITY
ROME
Mount Corno 2912 m
Valencia
Cape Saint Vincent
SIERRA MORENA
Guadiana
BALEARIC ISLANDS
Sardinia (It.)
Tiranë
NAPLES
Vesuvius 1277 m
TYRRHENIAN SEA
Gulf of Cadiz
Seville
Málaga
SIERRA NEVADA
Mount Mulhacén 3478 m
Strait of Gibraltar
GIBRALTAR (U.K.)
MEDITERRANEAN SEA
Corfu
IONIAN SEA
Palermo
Etna 3323 m
Sicily
ATLAS MOUNTAINS
Valletta
MALTA
© 1999, Encyclopædia Britannica, Inc.

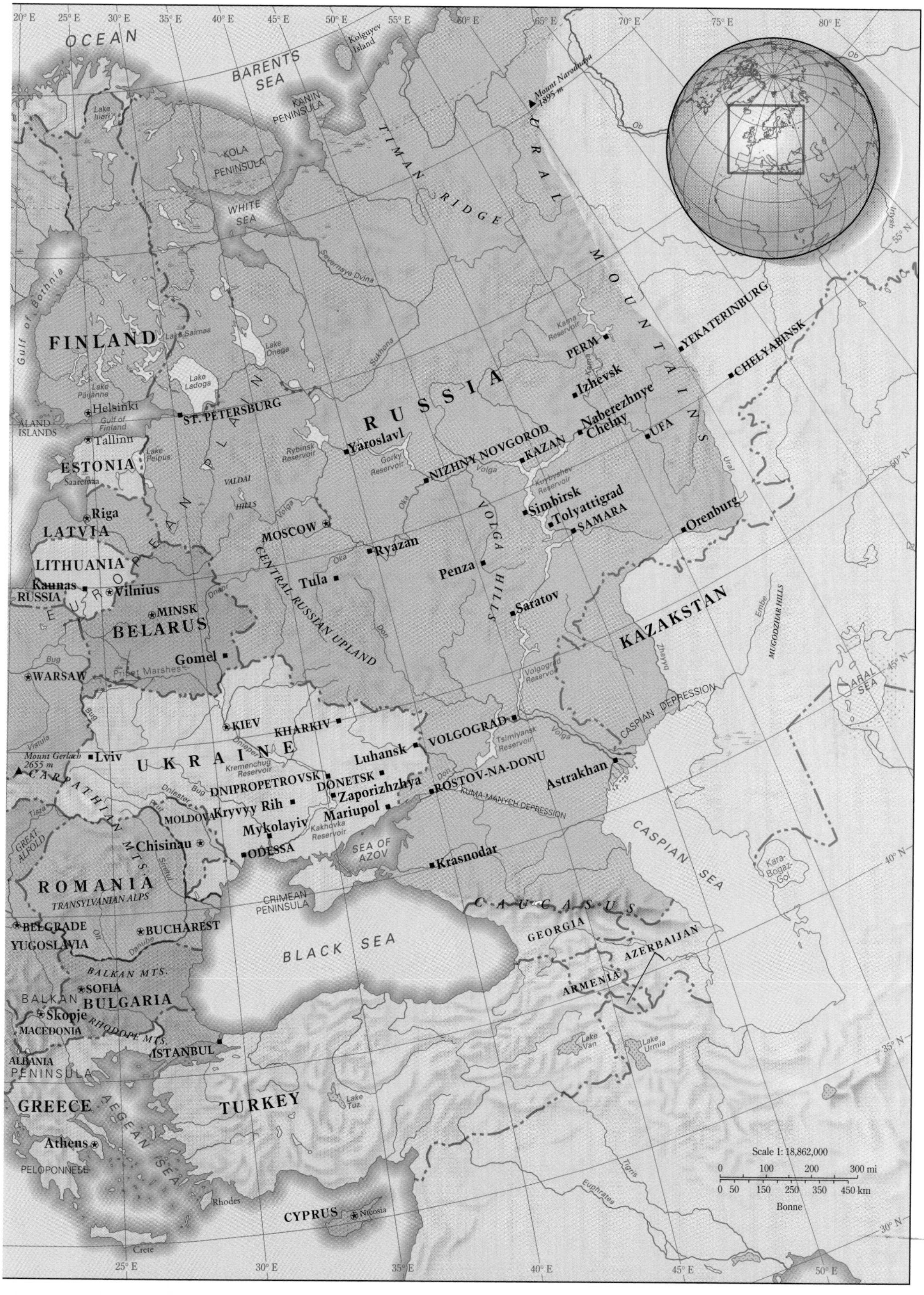

OCEAN
BARENTS SEA
Kolguyev Island
KANIN PENINSULA
KOLA PENINSULA
WHITE SEA
Lake Inari
TIMAN RIDGE
URAL MOUNTAINS
Mount Narodnaya 1895 m
FINLAND
Gulf of Bothnia
Lake Saimaa
Lake Onega
Lake Ladoga
Lake Päijänne
Helsinki
ÅLAND ISLANDS
Gulf of Finland
ST. PETERSBURG
Tallinn
ESTONIA
Saaremaa
Lake Peipus
Riga
LATVIA
LITHUANIA
Kaunas
Vilnius
RUSSIA
MINSK
BELARUS
Gomel
WARSAW
Pripet Marshes
EUROPEAN PLAIN
VALDAI HILLS
RUSSIA
Yaroslavl
Rybinsk Reservoir
Gorky Reservoir
NIZHNY NOVGOROD
KAZAN
MOSCOW
Ryazan
Tula
CENTRAL RUSSIAN UPLAND
Penza
VOLGA HILLS
Saratov
Simbirsk
Tolyattigrad
SAMARA
Kuybyshev Reservoir
PERM
Kama Reservoir
Izhevsk
Naberezhnye Chelny
UFA
YEKATERINBURG
CHELYABINSK
Orenburg
KAZAKSTAN
MUGODZHAR HILLS
Emba
ARAL SEA
CASPIAN DEPRESSION
Volgograd Reservoir
VOLGOGRAD
Tsimlyansk Reservoir
Astrakhan
KUMA-MANYCH DEPRESSION
CASPIAN SEA
Kara-Bogaz-Gol
Severnaya Dvina
Sukhona
Volga
Oka
Don
Dnepr
Ural
Ob
Irtysh
Zhayyq
KIEV
KHARKIV
UKRAINE
Lviv
Mount Gerlach 2655 m
CARPATHIAN MTS.
Kremenchug Reservoir
DNIPROPETROVSK
DONETSK
Luhansk
Zaporizhzhya
Mariupol
ROSTOV-NA-DONU
Kryvyy Rih
Mykolayiv
ODESSA
Kakhovka Reservoir
Dnieper
Dniester
Bug
Vistula
Tisza
Siretul
Olt
Danube
MOLDOVA
Chisinau
GREAT ALFOLD
ROMANIA
TRANSYLVANIAN ALPS
BELGRADE
YUGOSLAVIA
BUCHAREST
SEA OF AZOV
CRIMEAN PENINSULA
Krasnodar
BLACK SEA
CAUCASUS
GEORGIA
AZERBAIJAN
ARMENIA
BALKAN MTS.
SOFIA
BULGARIA
BALKAN PENINSULA
Skopje
MACEDONIA
RHODOPE MTS.
ISTANBUL
ALBANIA
GREECE
AEGEAN SEA
Athens
PELOPONNESE
Rhodes
Crete
TURKEY
Lake Tuz
Lake Van
Lake Urmia
Tigris
Euphrates
CYPRUS
Nicosia
Scale 1: 18,862,000
0 100 200 300 mi
0 50 150 250 350 450 km
Bonne
20° E
25° E
30° E
35° E
40° E
45° E
50° E
55° E
60° E
65° E
70° E
75° E
80° E
55° N
50° N
45° N
40° N
35° N
30° N

SPAIN AND PORTUGAL

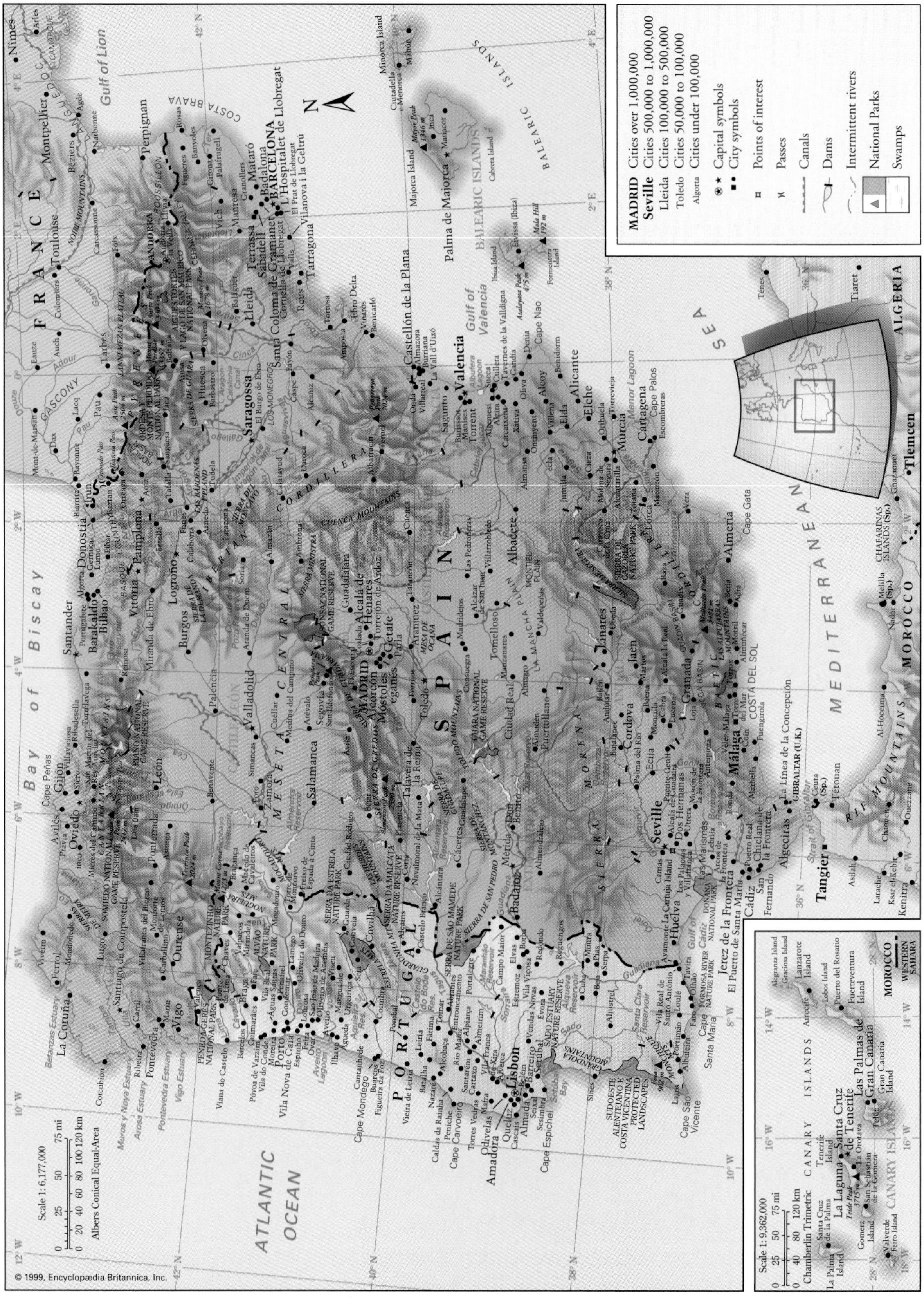

Scale 1: 6,123,000
0 25 50 75 mi
0 20 40 60 80 100 120 km
Albers Conical Equal-Area
PARIS Cities over 1,000,000
Marseille Cities 500,000 to 1,000,000
Orléans Cities 100,000 to 500,000
Créteil Cities 50,000 to 100,000
Évry Cities under 50,000
Capital symbols
City symbols
Canals
Glaciers
National parks
© 1999, Encyclopædia Britannica, Inc.
ATLANTIC OCEAN
English Channel
CELTIC SEA
Bay of Biscay
Gulf of Lion
MEDITERRANEAN SEA
FRANCE
UNITED KINGDOM
BELGIUM
LUXEMBOURG
GERMANY
SWITZERLAND
ITALY
SPAIN
ANDORRA
MONACO
Corsica
PARIS
Marseille
Lyon
Toulouse
Nice
Nantes
Strasbourg
Montpellier
Bordeaux
Rennes
Le Havre
Reims
Lille
Saint-Étienne
Toulon
Grenoble
Dijon
Angers
Brest
Le Mans
Clermont-Ferrand
Limoges
Tours
Amiens
Metz
Besançon
Perpignan
Orléans
Rouen
Caen
Mulhouse
Nancy
Brussels
Geneva
Zürich
Basel
Turin
Genoa
MILAN
Cologne
Stuttgart
Frankfurt am Main
Pamplona
Bilbao
Donostia
Vitoria
Santander
Logroño
N

ITALY, SLOVENIA, AND CROATIA

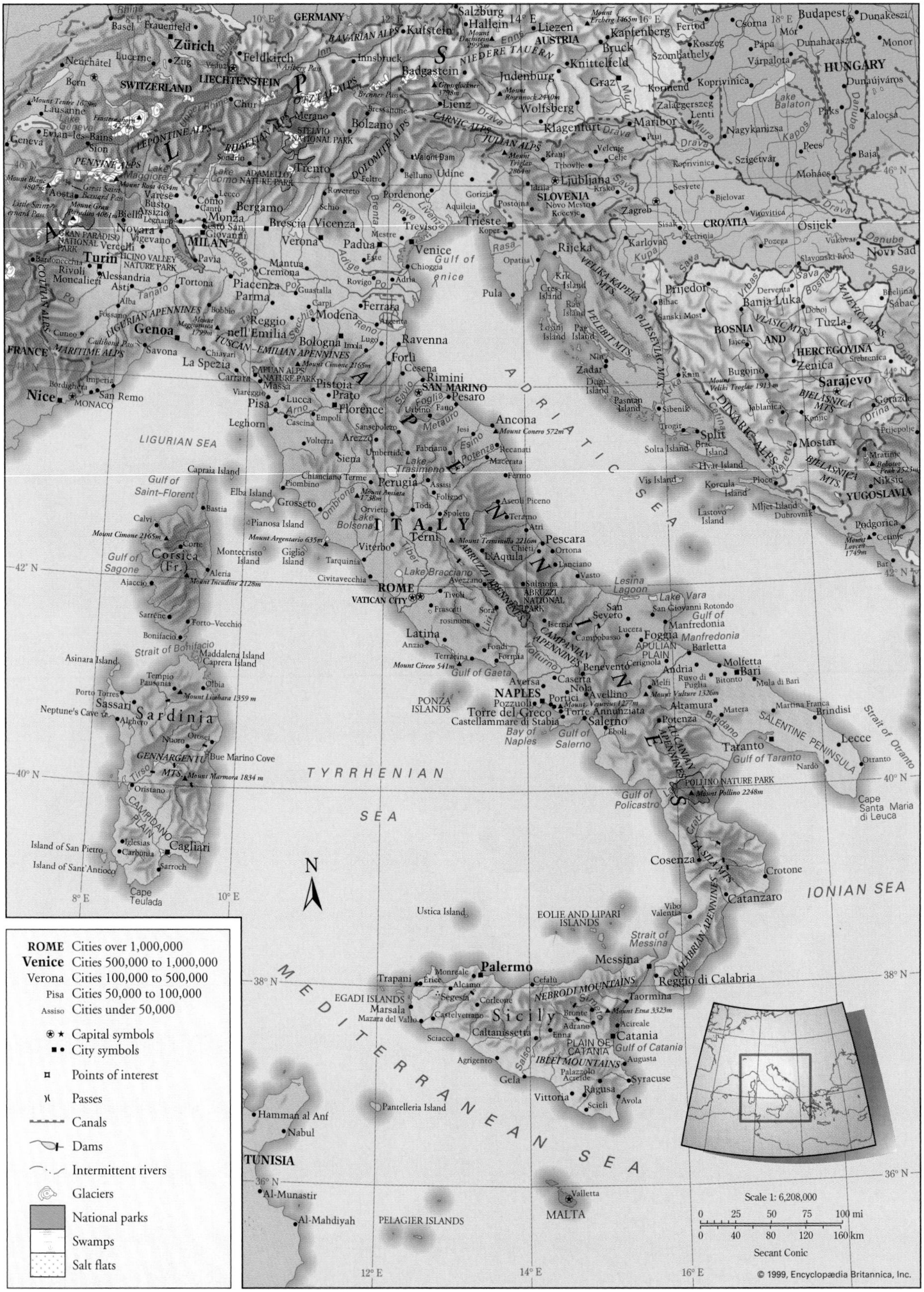

SCANDINAVIA

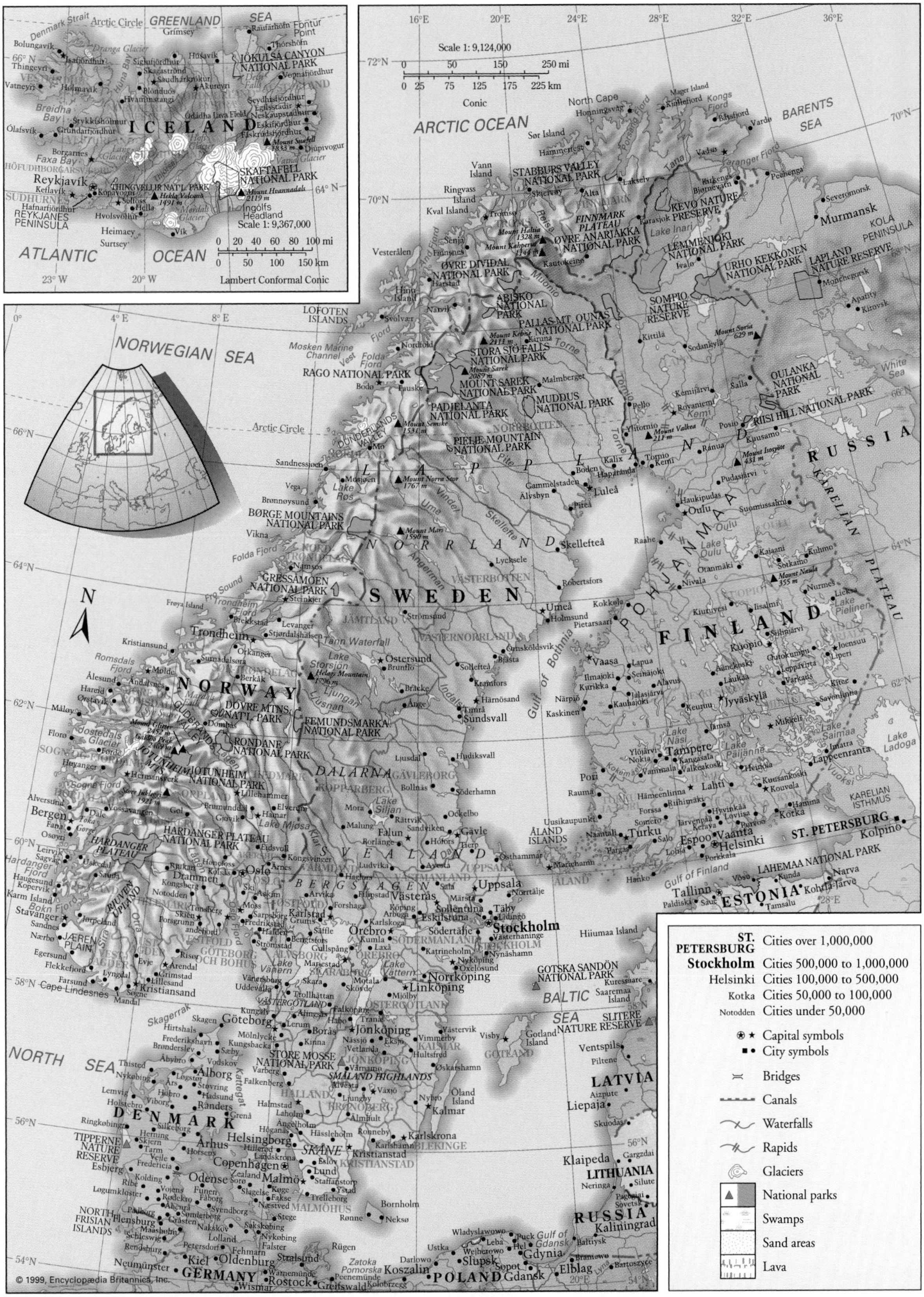

WESTERN AND CENTRAL EUROPE

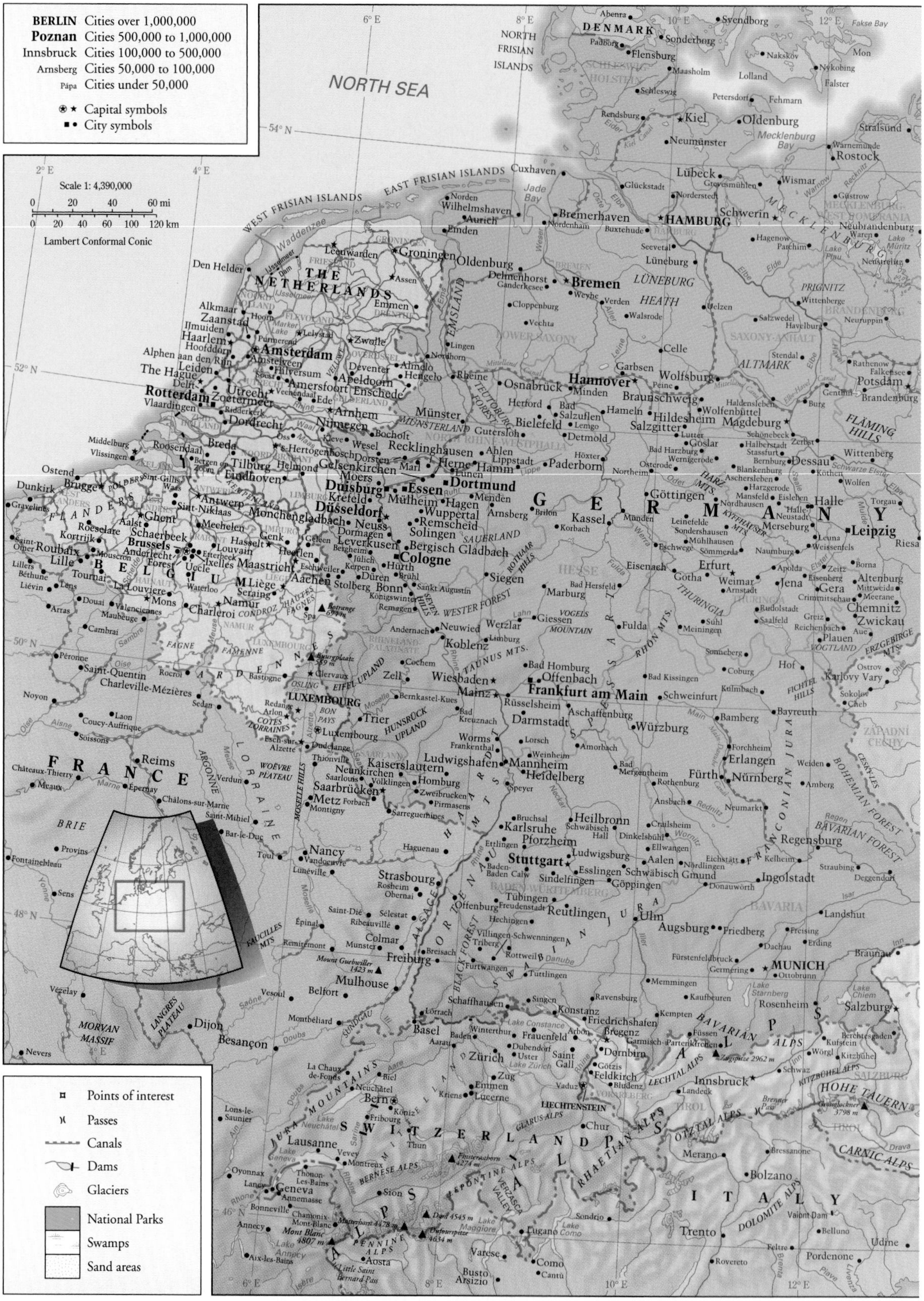

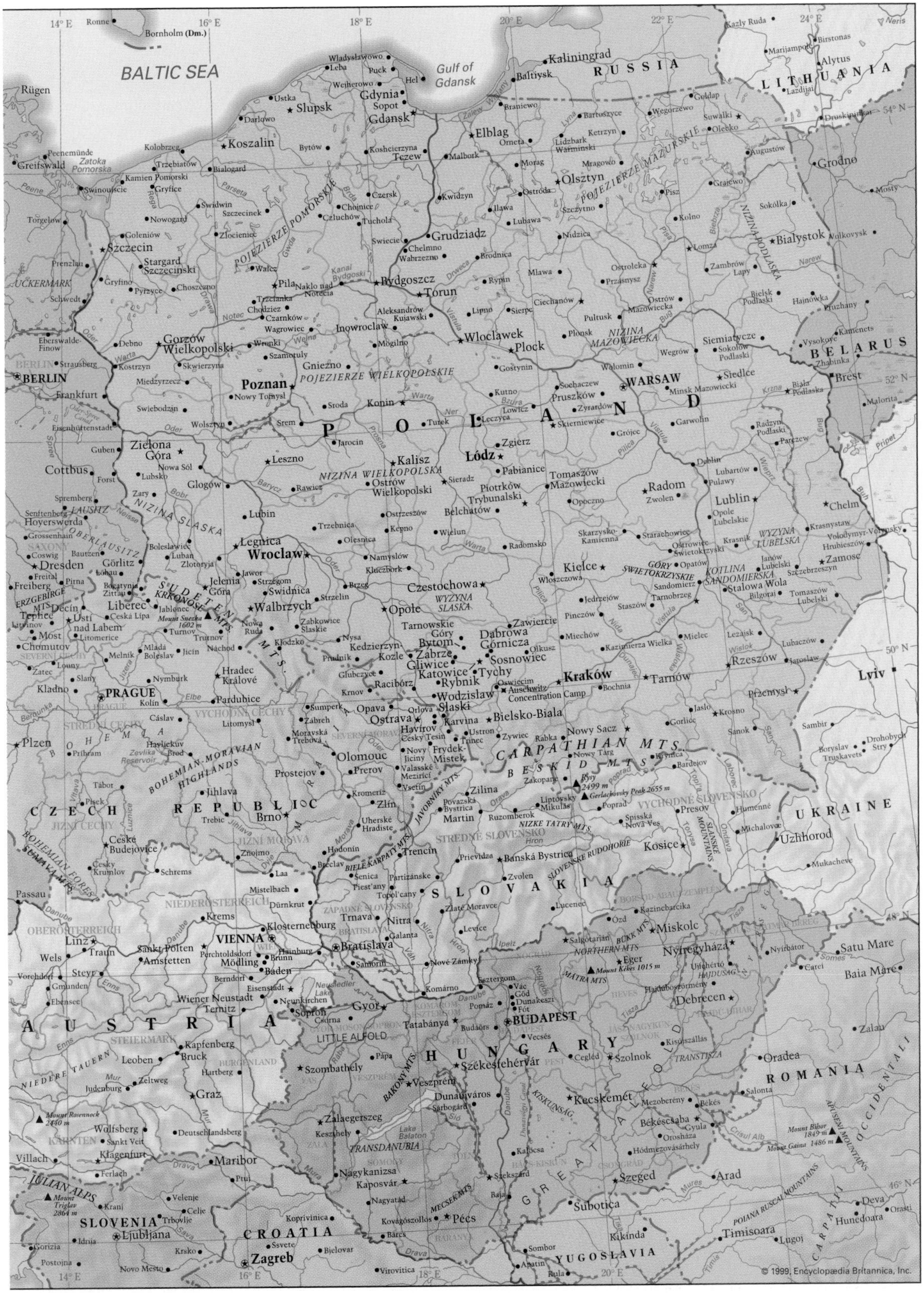
BALTIC SEA
Gulf of Gdansk
RUSSIA
LITHUANIA
BELARUS
POLAND
UKRAINE
CZECH REPUBLIC
SLOVAKIA
AUSTRIA
HUNGARY
ROMANIA
SLOVENIA
CROATIA
YUGOSLAVIA
BERLIN
WARSAW
PRAGUE
VIENNA
BUDAPEST
Bratislava
Ljubljana
Zagreb
Gdansk
Gdynia
Kaliningrad
Szczecin
Poznan
Wroclaw
Lódz
Kraków
Lublin
Bialystok
Grodno
Brest
Lviv
Dresden
Ostrava
Brno
Olomouc
Kosice
Miskolc
Debrecen
Szeged
Pécs
Graz
Linz
Maribor
Timisoara
Arad
Oradea
POJEZIERZE POMORSKIE
POJEZIERZE MAZURSKIE
POJEZIERZE WIELKOPOLSKIE
NIZINA MAZOWIECKA
NIZINA PODLASKA
NIZINA SLASKA
SUDETEN MTS.
CARPATHIAN MTS
BESKID MTS
BOHEMIAN-MORAVIAN HIGHLANDS
LITTLE ALFOLD
GREAT ALFOLD
TRANSDANUBIA
Lake Balaton
JULIAN ALPS
Mount Sneżka 1602 m
Rysy 2499 m
Gerlachovsky Peak 2655 m
Mount Kékes 1015 m
Mount Triglav 2864 m
Mount Bihor 1849 m
14° E
16° E
18° E
20° E
22° E
24° E
54° N
52° N
50° N
48° N
46° N
© 1999, Encyclopædia Britannica, Inc.

SOUTHEASTERN EUROPE

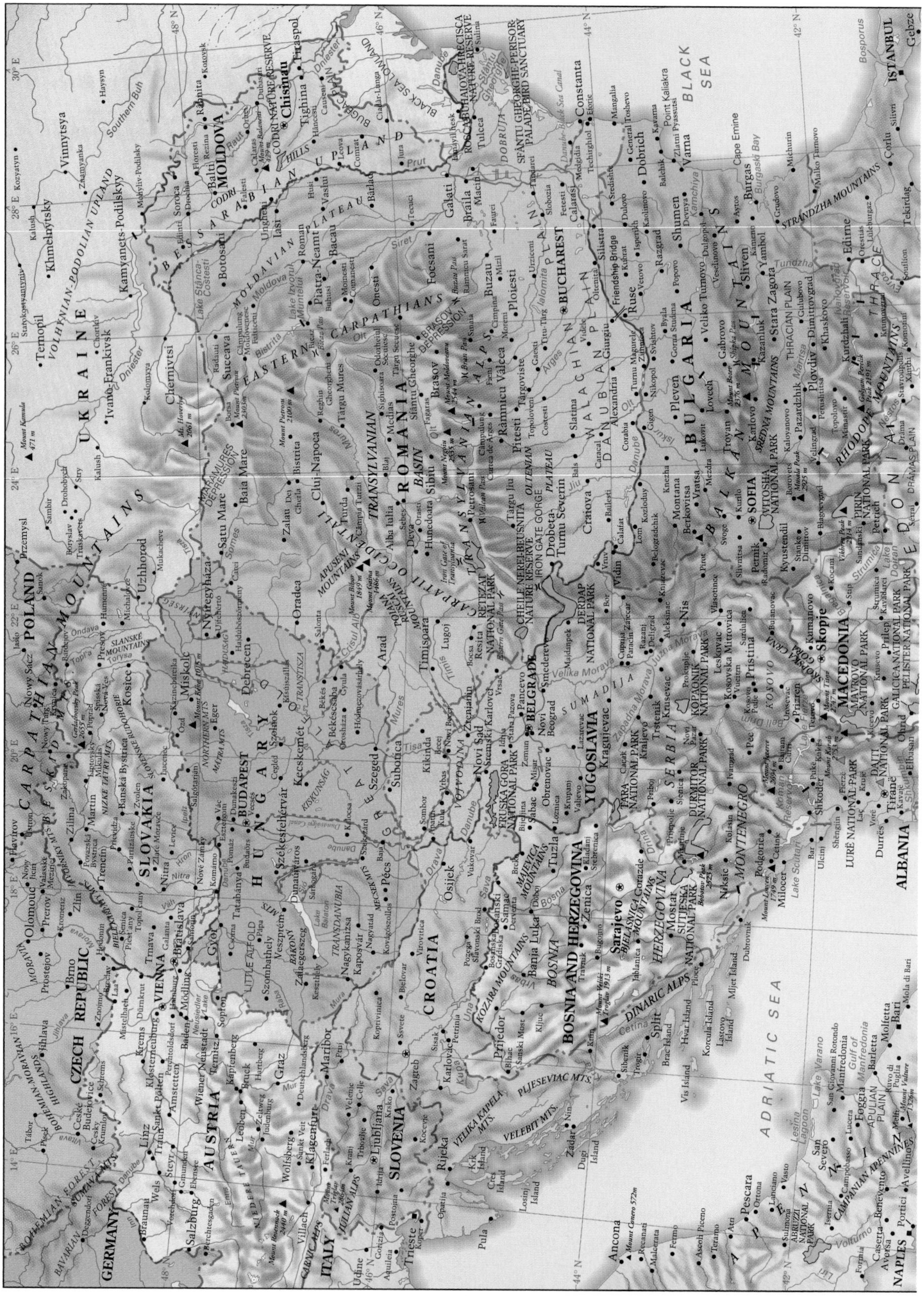

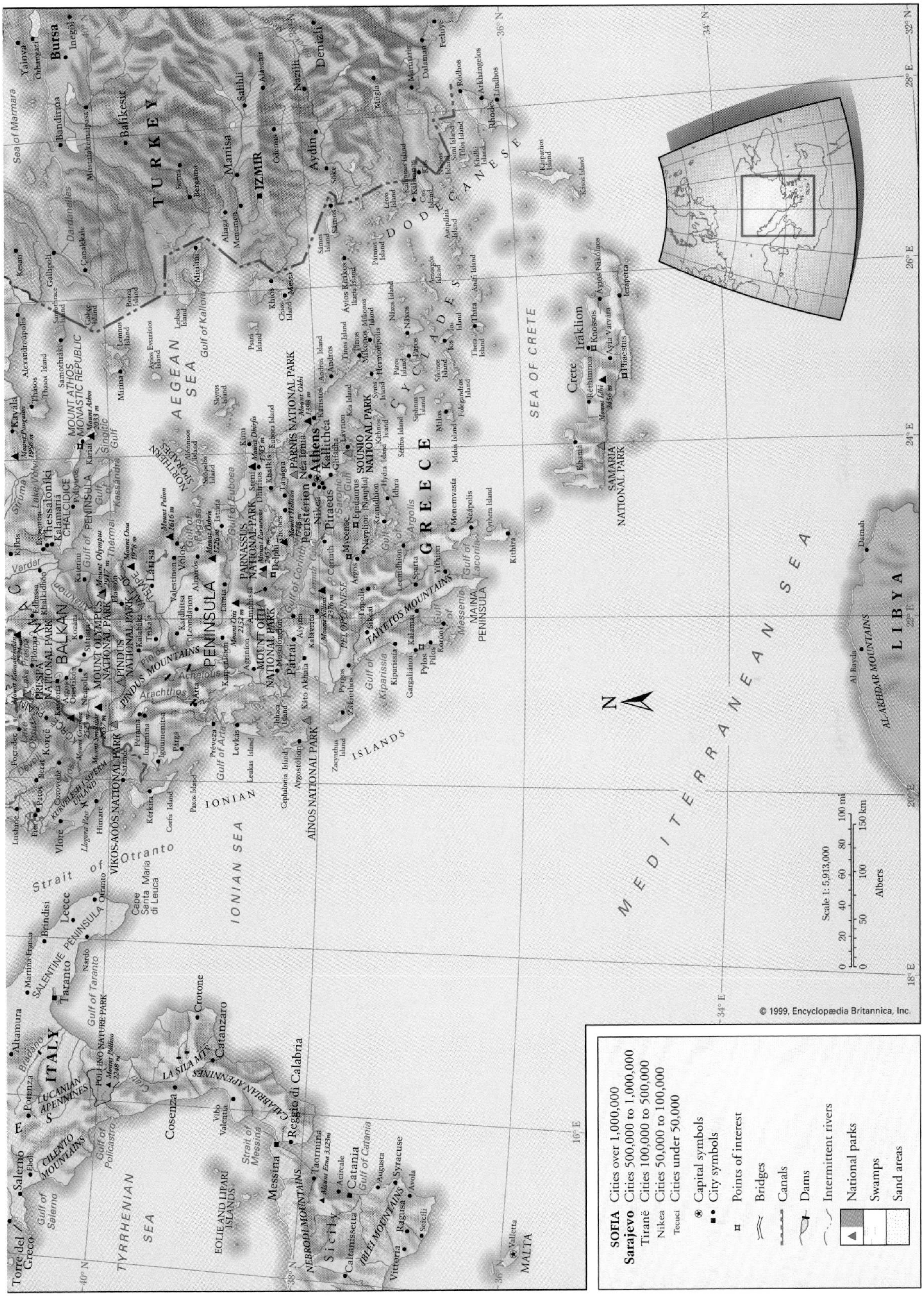

SOFIA Cities over 1,000,000
Sarajevo Cities 500,000 to 1,000,000
Tiranë Cities 100,000 to 500,000
Nikea Cities 50,000 to 100,000
Tecuci Cities under 50,000
Capital symbols
City symbols
Points of interest
Bridges
Canals
Dams
Intermittent rivers
National parks
Swamps
Sand areas
Scale 1: 5,913,000
0 20 40 60 80 100 mi
0 50 100 150 km
Albers
© 1999, Encyclopædia Britannica, Inc.
TURKEY
GREECE
ITALY
LIBYA
MALTA
BALKAN PENINSULA
PELOPONNESE
AEGEAN SEA
IONIAN SEA
TYRRHENIAN SEA
MEDITERRANEAN SEA
SEA OF CRETE
Sea of Marmara
Strait of Otranto
IONIAN ISLANDS
CYCLADES
DODECANESE
NORTHERN SPORADES
Crete
Sicily
Athens
Piraeus
Thessaloniki
Larisa
Patrai
Iráklion
IZMIR
Bursa
Balıkesir
Manisa
Aydın
Denizli
Taranto
Brindisi
Lecce
Catanzaro
Reggio di Calabria
Messina
Catania
Syracuse
Valletta
PINDUS MOUNTAINS
TAYGETOS MOUNTAINS
CALABRIAN APENNINES
LUCANIAN APENNINES
AL-AKHDAR MOUNTAINS

RUSSIA AND KAZAKSTAN

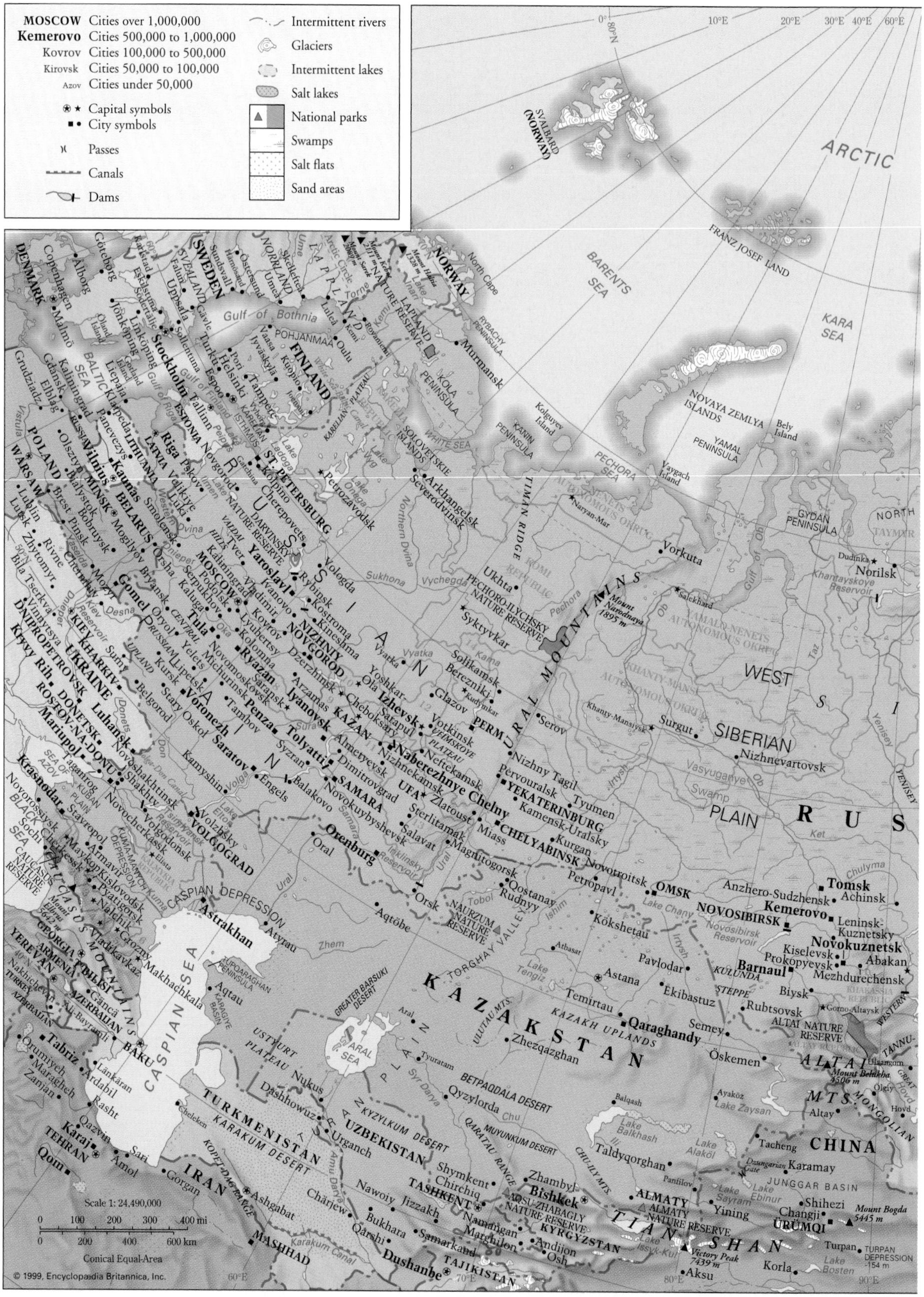

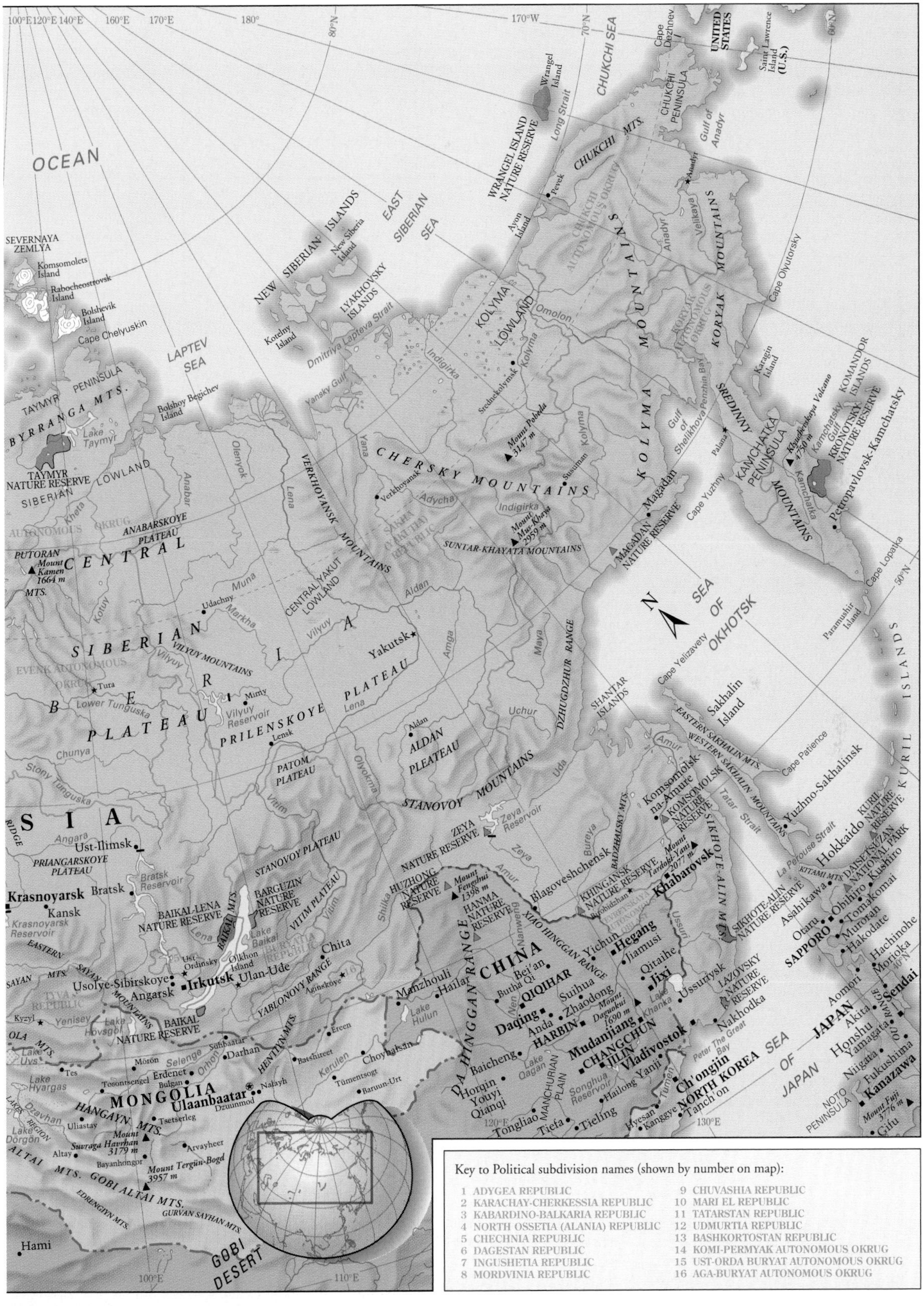
OCEAN
SEVERNAYA ZEMLYA
Komsomolets Island
Rabocheostrovsk Island
Bolshevik Island
Cape Chelyuskin
LAPTEV SEA
TAYMYR PENINSULA
BYRRANGA MTS.
Lake Taymyr
TAYMYR NATURE RESERVE
NORTH SIBERIAN LOWLAND
NEW SIBERIAN ISLANDS
New Siberia Island
LYAKHOVSKY ISLANDS
Kotelny Island
Dmitriya Lapteva Strait
EAST SIBERIAN SEA
Wrangel Island
WRANGEL ISLAND NATURE RESERVE
Long Strait
CHUKCHI SEA
Cape Dezhnev
UNITED STATES
Saint Lawrence Island (U.S.)
CHUKCHI PENINSULA
Gulf of Anadyr
CHUKCHI MTS.
CHUKCHI AUTONOMOUS OKRUG
Pevek
Ayon Island
Anadyr
KOLYMA LOWLAND
Omolon
Srednekolymsk
KORYAK MOUNTAINS
KORYAK AUTONOMOUS OKRUG
Cape Olyutorsky
Karagin Island
KOMANDOR ISLANDS
SREDINNY
Klyuchevskaya Volcano 4750 m
KRONOTSKY NATURE RESERVE
Kamchatsky Gulf
KAMCHATKA PENINSULA
Petropavlovsk-Kamchatsky
Palana
Gulf of Shelikhova
Penzhin Bay
KOLYMA MOUNTAINS
Mount Pobeda 3147 m
CHERSKY MOUNTAINS
Verkhoyansk
Adycha
Indigirka
Mount Mus-Khaya 2959 m
SUNTAR-KHAYATA MOUNTAINS
SAKHA (YAKUTIA) REPUBLIC
VERKHOYANSK MOUNTAINS
Magadan
MAGADAN NATURE RESERVE
Cape Yuzhny
Anabar
Olenyok
Lena
Yana
Kheta
ANABARSKOYE PLATEAU
PUTORAN MTS.
Mount Kamen 1664 m
CENTRAL SIBERIAN PLATEAU
Udachny
Muna
Markha
CENTRAL YAKUT LOWLAND
Vilyuy
VILYUY MOUNTAINS
Yakutsk
Aldan
Amga
Mirny
Vilyuy Reservoir
Tura
EVENK AUTONOMOUS OKRUG
Lower Tunguska
PRILENSKOYE PLATEAU
Lensk
Chunya
Stony Tunguska
PATOM PLATEAU
ALDAN PLATEAU
Uchur
Maya
DZHUGDZHUR RANGE
SEA OF OKHOTSK
Cape Yelizavety
Paramushir Island
Cape Lopatka
KURIL ISLANDS
SHANTAR ISLANDS
Sakhalin Island
EASTERN SAKHALIN MTS.
WESTERN SAKHALIN MOUNTAINS
Cape Patience
Yuzhno-Sakhalinsk
Tatar Strait
La Perouse Strait
Amur
STANOVOY MOUNTAINS
Olyokma
Vitim
Uda
Zeya Reservoir
ZEYA NATURE RESERVE
Zeya
Bureya
BADZHALSKY MTS.
Komsomolsk-na-Amure
KOMSOMOLSK NATURE RESERVE
Mount Tardoki-Yani 2077 m
SIKHOTE-ALIN MTS.
SIKHOTE-ALIN NATURE RESERVE
Khabarovsk
KHINGANSK NATURE RESERVE
Birobidzhan
Blagoveshchensk
Angara
Ust-Ilimsk
PRIANGARSKOYE PLATEAU
Bratsk Reservoir
Bratsk
Krasnoyarsk
Kansk
Krasnoyarsk Reservoir
EASTERN SAYAN MTS.
BAIKAL-LENA NATURE RESERVE
BARGUZIN NATURE RESERVE
STANOVOY PLATEAU
VITIM PLATEAU
Lake Baikal
Olkhon Island
Ust-Ordinsky
Irkutsk
Ulan-Ude
Usolye-Sibirskoye
Angarsk
Chita
Aginskoye
YABLONOVY RANGE
BAIKAL NATURE RESERVE
TUVA REPUBLIC
Kyzyl
Yenisey
Lake Hovsgol
Lake Uvs
Lake Hyargas
Sühbaatar
Darhan
Mörön
Selenge
Orhon
Erdenet
MONGOLIA
Ulaanbaatar
Nalayh
Dzuunmod
HANGAYN MTS.
Tsetserleg
Uliastay
Mount Suvraga Havrhan 3179 m
Bulgan
Arvayheer
Bayanhongor
Mount Tergün-Bogd 3957 m
GOBI ALTAI MTS.
GURVAN SAYHAN MTS.
Hami
GOBI DESERT
HENTIYN MTS.
Ereen
Batshireet
Kerulen
Choybalsan
Tümentsogt
Baruun-Urt
Manzhouli
Hailar
Lake Hulun
HUZHONG NATURE RESERVE
Mount Fenghui 1398 m
HANMA NATURE RESERVE
DA HINGGAN RANGE
XIAO HINGGAN RANGE
CHINA
Bei'an
QIQIHAR
Suihua
Zhaodong
Daqing
Anda
HARBIN
Yichun
Hegang
Jiamusi
Qitaihe
Jixi
Mount Daguokui 1690 m
Mudanjiang
CHANGCHUN
JILIN
Baicheng
Horqin Youyi Qianqi
Tongliao
Tiefa
Tieling
Songhua Reservoir
Hailong
Yanji
Lake Khanka
Ussuriysk
LAZOVSKY NATURE RESERVE
Nakhodka
Vladivostok
Peter The Great Bay
Ch'ongjin
NORTH KOREA
Tanch'on
Hyesan
Kanggye
SEA OF JAPAN
JAPAN
Hokkaido
KITAMI MTS.
DAISETSUZAN NATIONAL PARK
Asahikawa
Obihiro
Kushiro
Tomakomai
Otaru
SAPPORO
Muroran
Hakodate
Aomori
Hachinohe
Morioka
Akita
Honshu
OU RANGE
Sendai
Yamagata
Niigata
Fukushima
NOTO PENINSULA
Kanazawa
Mount Fuji 3776 m
Gifu
Key to Political subdivision names (shown by number on map):
1 ADYGEA REPUBLIC
2 KARACHAY-CHERKESSIA REPUBLIC
3 KABARDINO-BALKARIA REPUBLIC
4 NORTH OSSETIA (ALANIA) REPUBLIC
5 CHECHNIA REPUBLIC
6 DAGESTAN REPUBLIC
7 INGUSHETIA REPUBLIC
8 MORDVINIA REPUBLIC
9 CHUVASHIA REPUBLIC
10 MARI EL REPUBLIC
11 TATARSTAN REPUBLIC
12 UDMURTIA REPUBLIC
13 BASHKORTOSTAN REPUBLIC
14 KOMI-PERMYAK AUTONOMOUS OKRUG
15 UST-ORDA BURYAT AUTONOMOUS OKRUG
16 AGA-BURYAT AUTONOMOUS OKRUG

EASTERN EUROPE

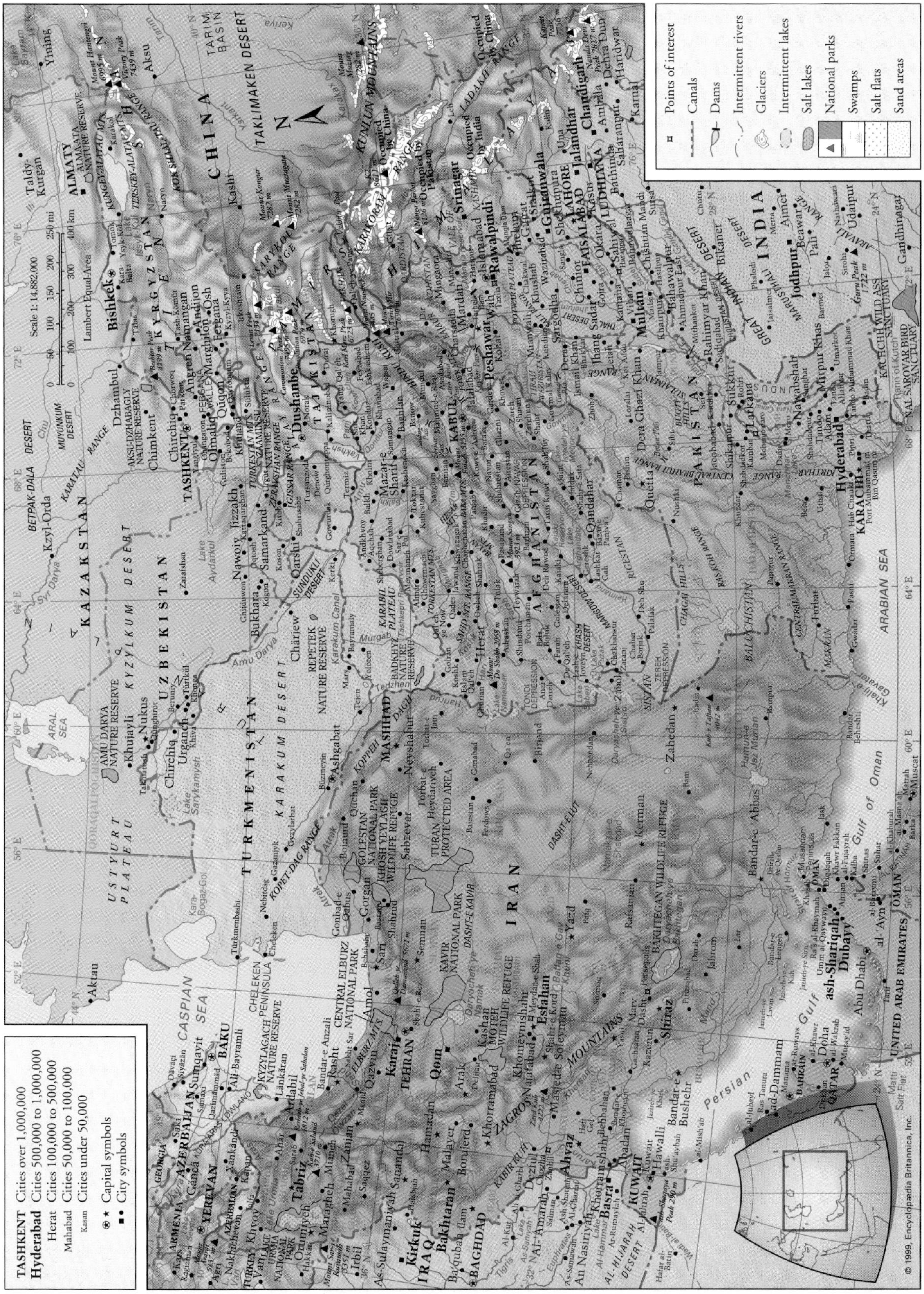
TASHKENT Cities over 1,000,000
Hyderabad Cities 500,000 to 1,000,000
Herat Cities 100,000 to 500,000
Mahabad Cities 50,000 to 100,000
Kasan Cities under 50,000
Capital symbols
City symbols
Points of interest
Canals
Dams
Intermittent rivers
Glaciers
Intermittent lakes
Salt lakes
National parks
Swamps
Salt flats
Sand areas
Scale 1: 14,882,000
Lambert Equal-Area
© 1999, Encyclopædia Britannica, Inc.

ASIA

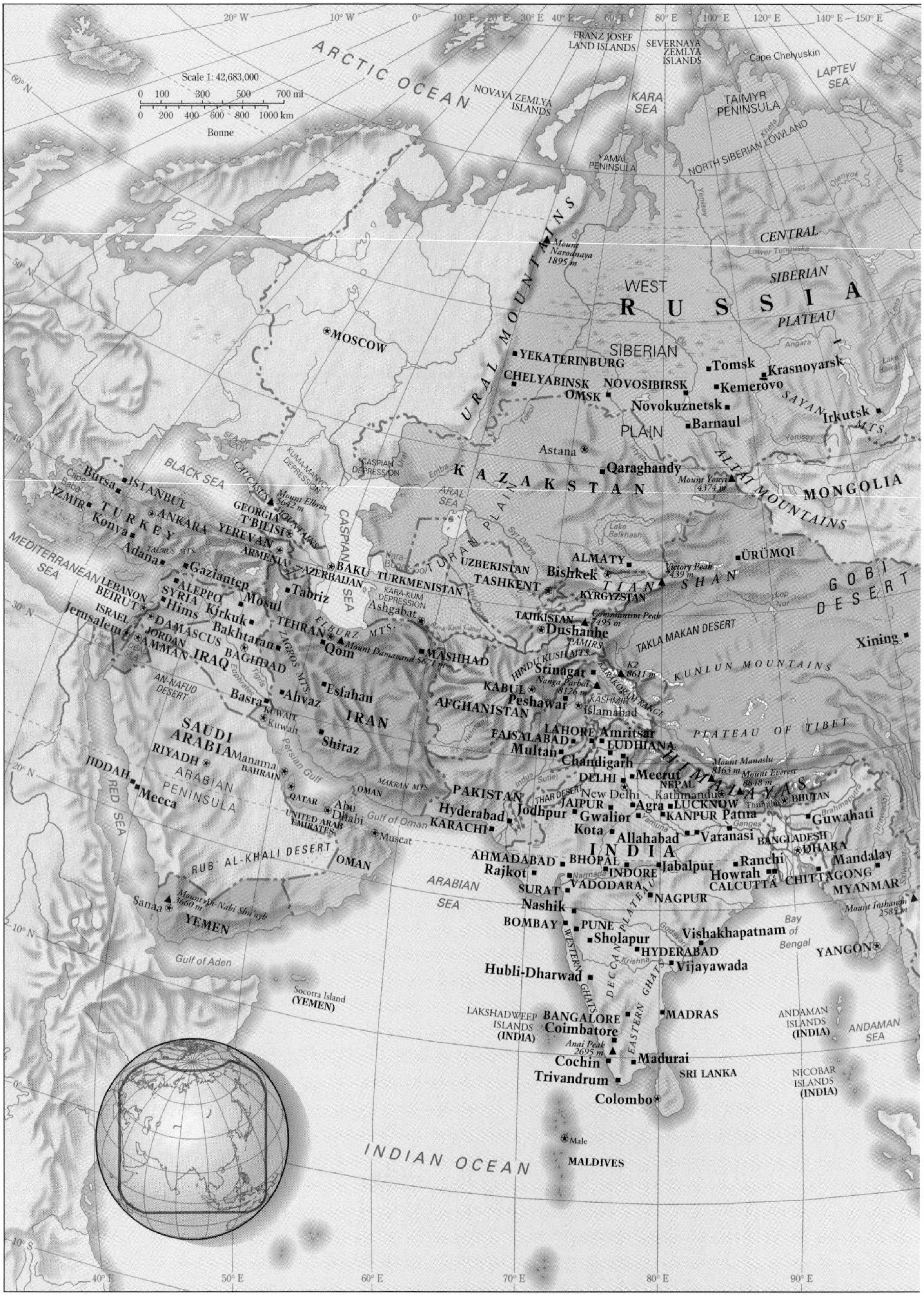

Scale 1: 42,683,000
0 100 300 500 700 mi
0 200 400 600 800 1000 km
Bonne
ARCTIC OCEAN
NOVAYA ZEMLYA ISLANDS
FRANZ JOSEF LAND ISLANDS
SEVERNAYA ZEMLYA ISLANDS
Cape Chelyuskin
LAPTEV SEA
KARA SEA
TAIMYR PENINSULA
NORTH SIBERIAN LOWLAND
YAMAL PENINSULA
URAL MOUNTAINS
Mount Narodnaya 1895 m
CENTRAL SIBERIAN PLATEAU
WEST SIBERIAN PLAIN
RUSSIA
MOSCOW
YEKATERINBURG
CHELYABINSK
NOVOSIBIRSK
OMSK
Tomsk
Krasnoyarsk
Kemerovo
Novokuznetsk
Barnaul
Irkutsk
SAYAN MTS.
Lake Baikal
Astana
Qaraghandy
KAZAKHSTAN
Mount Youyi 4374 m
ALTAI MOUNTAINS
MONGOLIA
SEA OF AZOV
BLACK SEA
KUMA-MANYCH DEPRESSION
CASPIAN DEPRESSION
CAUCASUS MOUNTAINS
Mount Elbrus 5642 m
CASPIAN SEA
ARAL SEA
TURAN PLAIN
Lake Balkhash
Bursa
ISTANBUL
IZMIR
TURKEY
ANKARA
Konya
Adana
TAURUS MTS.
GEORGIA
T'BILISI
YEREVAN
ARMENIA
BAKU
AZERBAIJAN
MEDITERRANEAN SEA
LEBANON
BEIRUT
ISRAEL
Jerusalem
JORDAN
AMMAN
DAMASCUS
SYRIA
Hims
ALEPPO
Gaziantep
Mosul
Kirkuk
Tabriz
TEHRAN
Qom
ELBURZ MTS.
Mount Damavand 5671 m
Bakhtaran
BAGHDAD
IRAQ
ZAGROS MTS.
Esfahan
Ahvaz
Basra
KUWAIT
Kuwait
IRAN
Shiraz
MASHHAD
TURKMENISTAN
KARA-KUM DEPRESSION
Ashgabat
UZBEKISTAN
TASHKENT
ALMATY
Bishkek
KYRGYZSTAN
TIAN SHAN
Victory Peak 7439 m
ÜRÜMQI
GOBI DESERT
TAJIKISTAN
Communism Peak 7495 m
Dushanbe
PAMIRS
TAKLA MAKAN DESERT
Xining
HINDU KUSH MTS.
KABUL
Peshawar
Islamabad
AFGHANISTAN
Srinagar
KASHMIR
K2 8611 m
Nanga Parbat 8126 m
KARAKORAM RANGE
KUNLUN MOUNTAINS
PLATEAU OF TIBET
AN-NAFUD DESERT
SAUDI ARABIA
RIYADH
Manama
BAHRAIN
Persian Gulf
QATAR
Abu Dhabi
UNITED ARAB EMIRATES
Gulf of Oman
Muscat
OMAN
MAKRAN MTS.
JIDDAH
Mecca
RED SEA
ARABIAN PENINSULA
RUB' AL-KHALI DESERT
Sanaa
Mount an-Nabi Shu'ayb 3660 m
YEMEN
Gulf of Aden
Socotra Island (YEMEN)
ARABIAN SEA
PAKISTAN
Hyderabad
KARACHI
LAHORE
Amritsar
FAISALABAD
LUDHIANA
Multan
Chandigarh
DELHI
New Delhi
Meerut
THAR DESERT
JAIPUR
Jodhpur
Agra
LUCKNOW
Gwalior
KANPUR
Patna
Kota
Allahabad
Varanasi
NEPAL
Kathmandu
HIMALAYAS
Mount Manaslu 8165 m
Mount Everest 8848 m
Thimphu
BHUTAN
Guwahati
BANGLADESH
DHAKA
INDIA
AHMADABAD
BHOPAL
INDORE
Jabalpur
Ranchi
Rajkot
SURAT
VADODARA
Howrah
CALCUTTA
CHITTAGONG
Mandalay
MYANMAR
Nashik
NAGPUR
BOMBAY
PUNE
Sholapur
Vishakhapatnam
HYDERABAD
Vijayawada
Hubli-Dharwad
WESTERN GHATS
DECCAN PLATEAU
EASTERN GHATS
Bay of Bengal
YANGON
Mount Inthanon 2585 m
LAKSHADWEEP ISLANDS (INDIA)
BANGALORE
Coimbatore
MADRAS
Anai Peak 2695 m
Cochin
Madurai
Trivandrum
SRI LANKA
Colombo
ANDAMAN ISLANDS (INDIA)
ANDAMAN SEA
NICOBAR ISLANDS (INDIA)
Male
MALDIVES
INDIAN OCEAN

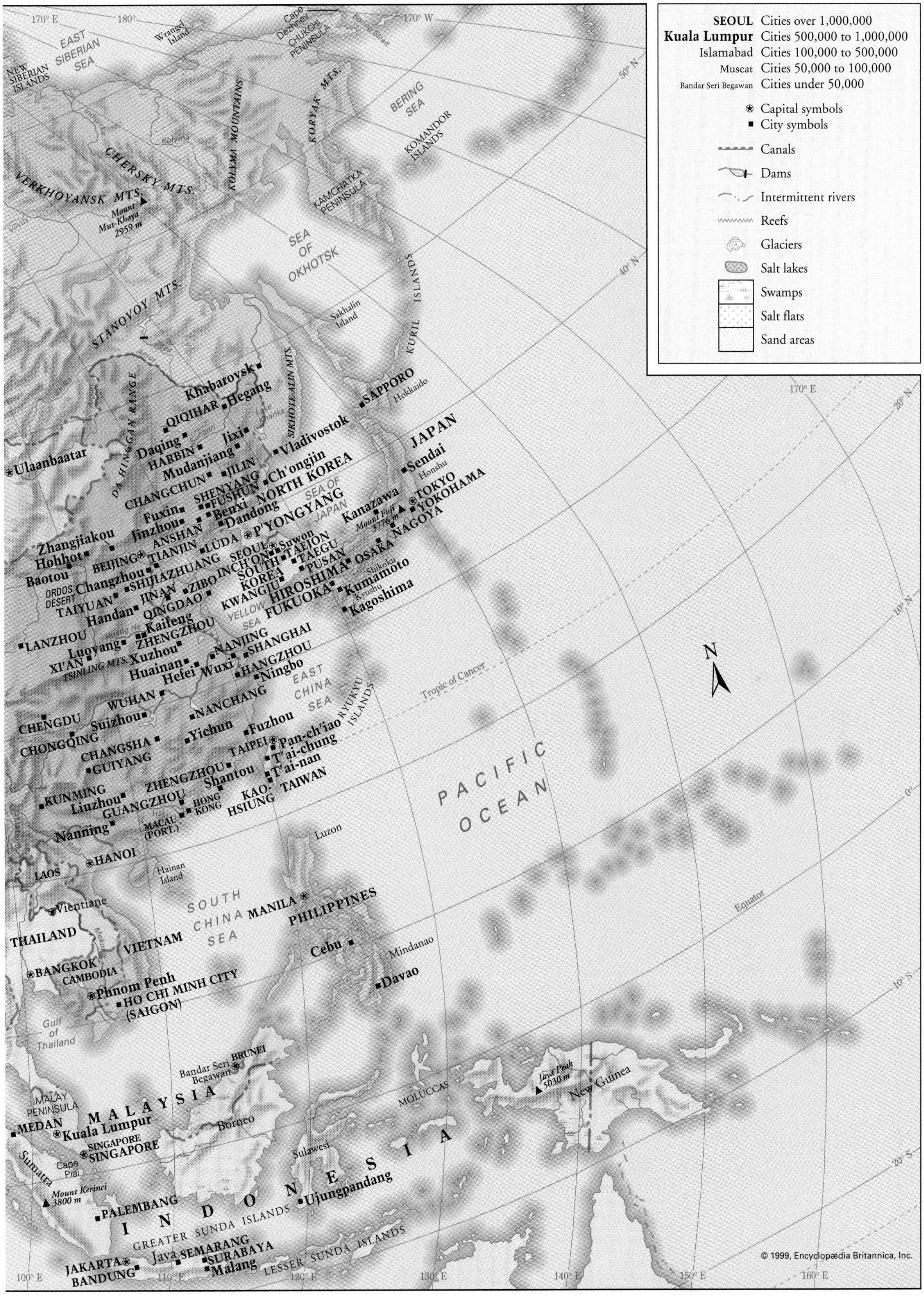
SEOUL Cities over 1,000,000
Kuala Lumpur Cities 500,000 to 1,000,000
Islamabad Cities 100,000 to 500,000
Muscat Cities 50,000 to 100,000
Bandar Seri Begawan Cities under 50,000
Capital symbols
City symbols
Canals
Dams
Intermittent rivers
Reefs
Glaciers
Salt lakes
Swamps
Salt flats
Sand areas
170° E
180°
170° W
Wrangel Island
Cape Dezhnev
CHUKCHI PENINSULA
Bering Strait
EAST SIBERIAN SEA
NEW SIBERIAN ISLANDS
50° N
40° N
20° N
10° N
0°
10° S
20° S
KOLYMA MOUNTAINS
KORYAK MTS.
BERING SEA
KOMANDOR ISLANDS
Indigirka
Kolyma
CHERSKY MTS.
VERKHOYANSK MTS.
Mount Mus-Khaya 2959 m
Vilyuy
Aldan
KAMCHATKA PENINSULA
SEA OF OKHOTSK
KURIL ISLANDS
STANOVOY MTS.
Sakhalin Island
Zeya
Amur
Shilka
Argun
DA HINGGAN RANGE
SIKHOTE-ALIN MTS.
Khabarovsk
Hegang
QIQIHAR
Lake Khanka
Sungari
SAPPORO
Hokkaido
Daqing
HARBIN
Jixi
Mudanjiang
Vladivostok
JAPAN
Ulaanbaatar
JILIN
Ch'ongjin
Sendai
Honshu
CHANGCHUN
SHENYANG
FUSHUN
NORTH KOREA
SEA OF JAPAN
TOKYO
YOKOHAMA
Fuxin
Benxi
Dandong
Kanazawa
Mount Fuji 3776 m
NAGOYA
Jinzhou
P'YONGYANG
Zhangjiakou
ANSHAN
Suwon
Hohhot
BEIJING
TIANJIN
LÜDA
SEOUL
TAEJON
TAEGU
OSAKA
Baotou
SHIJIAZHUANG
INCH'ON
SOUTH KOREA
PUSAN
Shikoku
ORDOS DESERT
Changzhou
ZIBO
HIROSHIMA
Kumamoto
TAIYUAN
JINAN
KWANGJU
Kyushu
Handan
QINGDAO
YELLOW SEA
FUKUOKA
Kagoshima
LANZHOU
Huang He
Kaifeng
ZHENGZHOU
Luoyang
NANJING
SHANGHAI
XI'AN
TSINLING MTS.
Xuzhou
HANGZHOU
Huainan
Hefei
Wuxi
Ningbo
EAST CHINA SEA
Tropic of Cancer
Yangtze
WUHAN
RYUKYU ISLANDS
CHENGDU
Suizhou
NANCHANG
CHONGQING
Fuzhou
CHANGSHA
Yichun
Pan-ch'iao
TAIPEI
T'ai-chung
GUIYANG
T'ai-nan
ZHENGZHOU
Shantou
KUNMING
TAIWAN
Liuzhou
GUANGZHOU
KAO-HSIUNG
HONG KONG
PACIFIC OCEAN
Hsi
Nanning
MACAU (PORT.)
Red
Luzon
HANOI
LAOS
Hainan Island
Vientiane
SOUTH CHINA SEA
MANILA
PHILIPPINES
THAILAND
Mekong
VIETNAM
Equator
Cebu
Mindanao
BANGKOK
CAMBODIA
Phnom Penh
HO CHI MINH CITY (SAIGON)
Davao
Gulf of Thailand
BRUNEI
Bandar Seri Begawan
Jaya Peak 5030 m
New Guinea
MALAY PENINSULA
MALAYSIA
MOLUCCAS
MEDAN
Kuala Lumpur
Borneo
SINGAPORE
Sumatra
Cape Piai
Sulawesi
INDONESIA
Mount Kerinci 3800 m
Ujungpandang
PALEMBANG
GREATER SUNDA ISLANDS
JAKARTA
Java
SEMARANG
SURABAYA
LESSER SUNDA ISLANDS
BANDUNG
Malang
100° E
110° E
120° E
130° E
140° E
150° E
160° E
N
© 1999, Encyclopædia Britannica, Inc.

CHINA, MONGOLIA, KOREA, AND JAPAN

CHINA, MONGOLIA, KOREA, AND JAPAN

SOUTHEASTERN ASIA

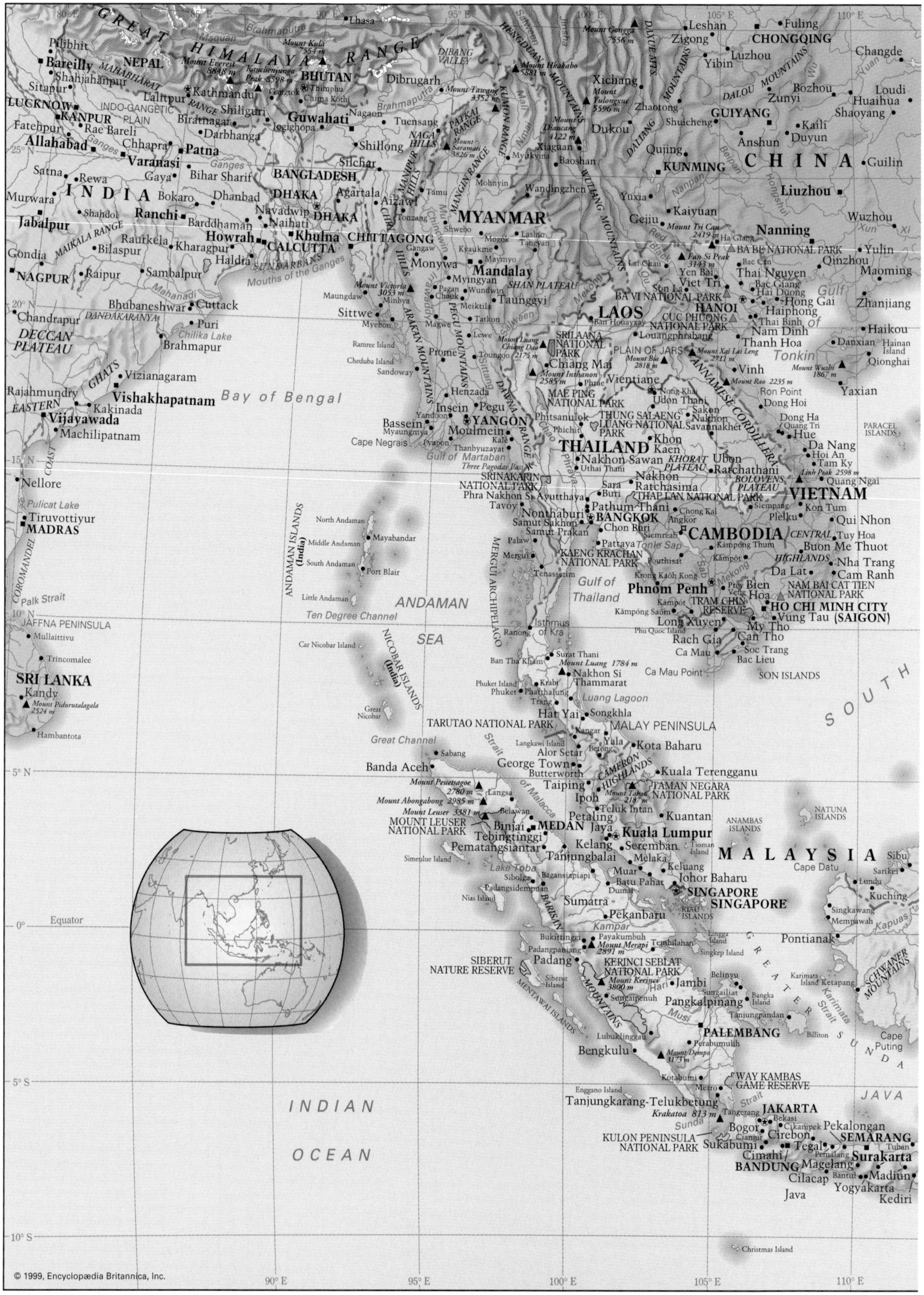

SOUTHEASTERN ASIA

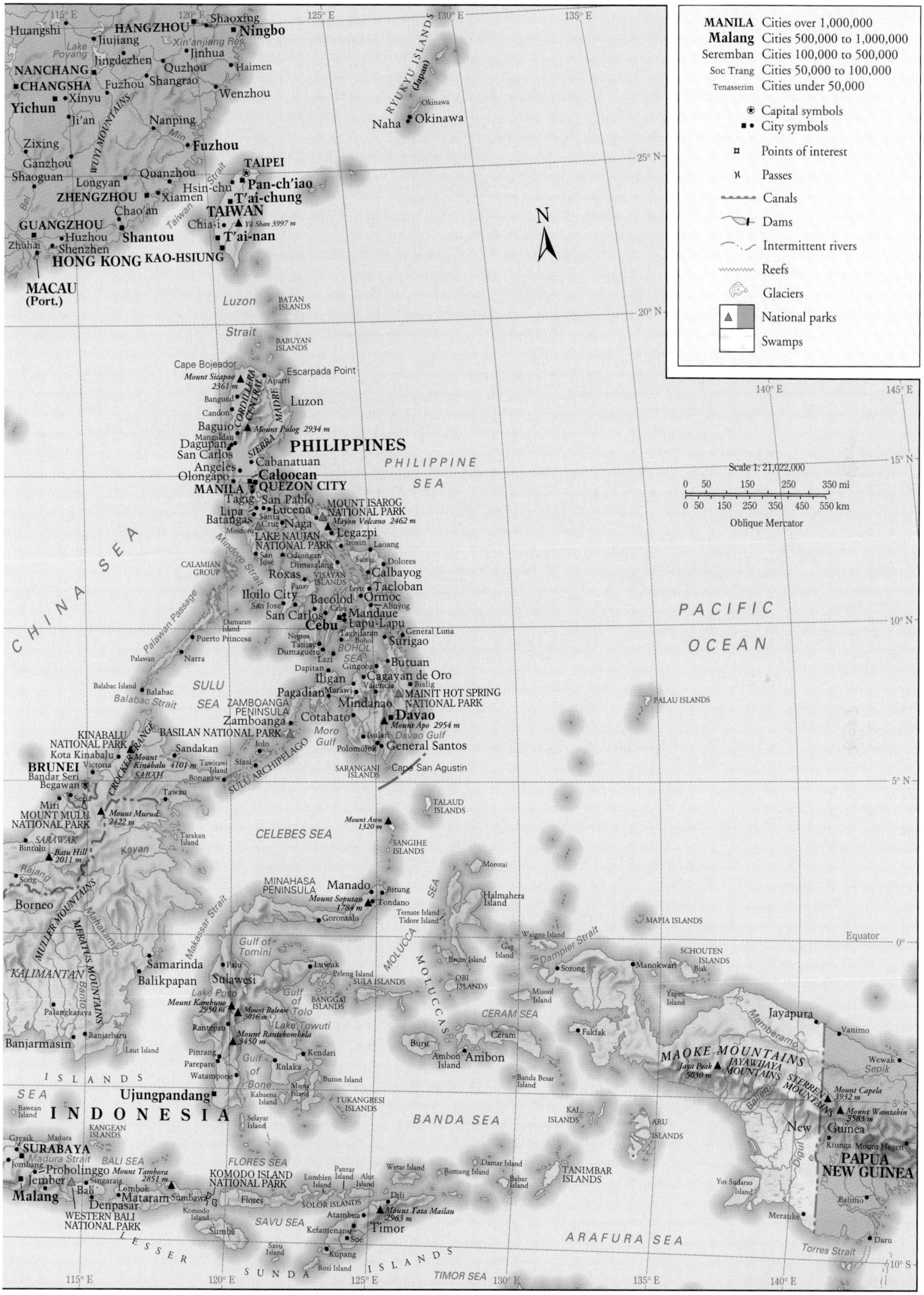

INDIA

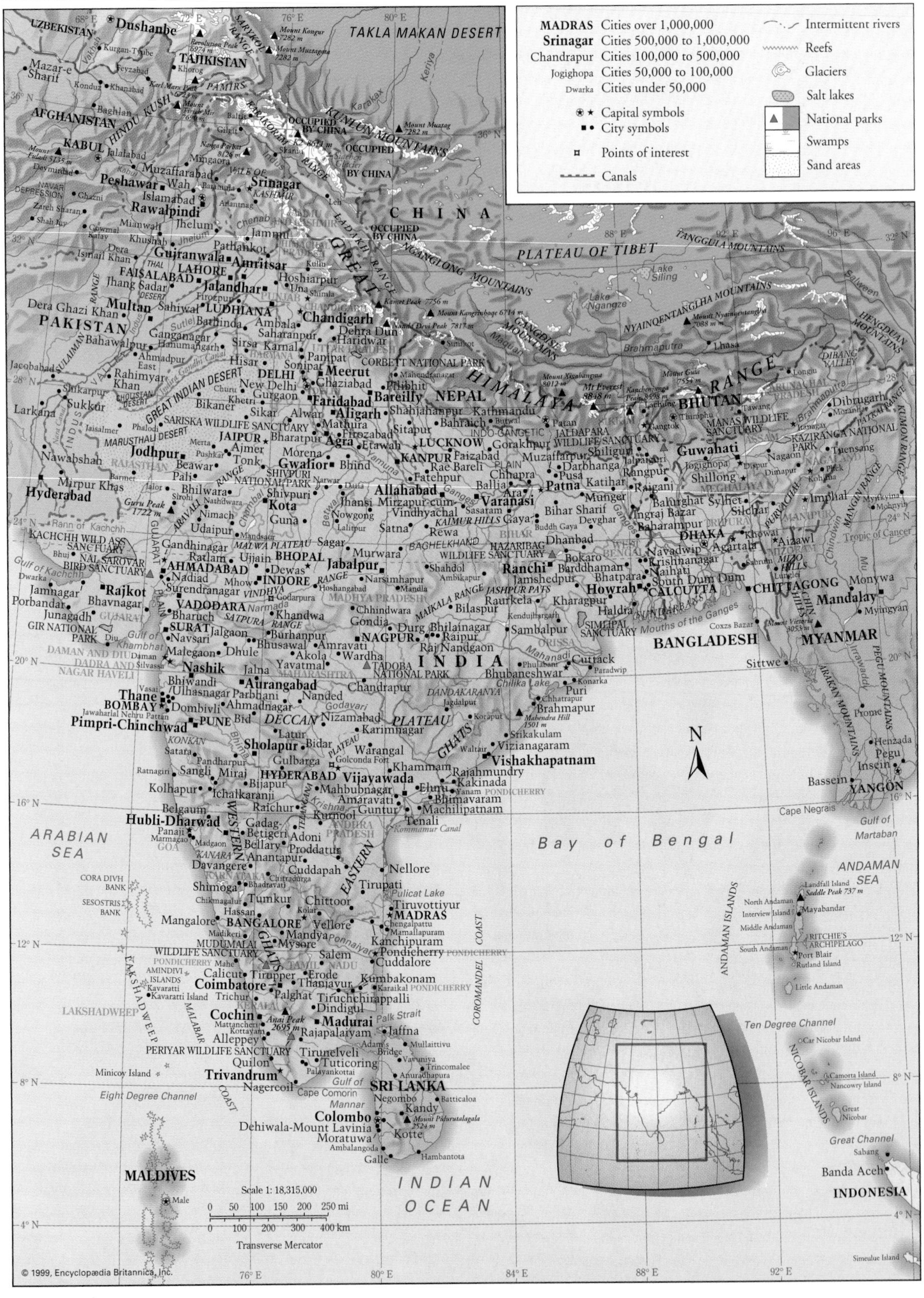
MADRAS Cities over 1,000,000
Srinagar Cities 500,000 to 1,000,000
Chandrapur Cities 100,000 to 500,000
Jogighopa Cities 50,000 to 100,000
Dwarka Cities under 50,000
Capital symbols
City symbols
Points of interest
Canals
Intermittent rivers
Reefs
Glaciers
Salt lakes
National parks
Swamps
Sand areas
TAKLA MAKAN DESERT
UZBEKISTAN
Dushanbe
TAJIKISTAN
AFGHANISTAN
HINDU KUSH
KABUL
PAMIRS
KARAKORAM RANGE
KUNLUN MOUNTAINS
OCCUPIED BY CHINA
Peshawar
Islamabad
Rawalpindi
Srinagar
C H I N A
PLATEAU OF TIBET
TANGGULA MOUNTAINS
NYAINQENTANGLHA MOUNTAINS
HENGDUAN MOUNTAINS
Lhasa
Gujranwala
Amritsar
LAHORE
FAISALABAD
Jalandhar
Multan
LUDHIANA
Chandigarh
PAKISTAN
GREAT HIMALAYA RANGE
Dehra Dun
Meerut
DELHI
New Delhi
Faridabad
Aligarh
Bareilly
NEPAL
Kathmandu
Mt Everest 8848 m
BHUTAN
Thimphu
GREAT INDIAN DESERT
Hyderabad
Jodhpur
JAIPUR
Agra
Gwalior
LUCKNOW
KANPUR
Allahabad
Varanasi
Patna
Guwahati
Shillong
Imphal
Kota
BHOPAL
Jabalpur
AHMADABAD
INDORE
Ranchi
Jamshedpur
Howrah
CALCUTTA
DHAKA
CHITTAGONG
Mandalay
BANGLADESH
MYANMAR
Rajkot
VADODARA
SURAT
Gulf of Kachchh
Gulf of Khambhat
NAGPUR
Raipur
I N D I A
Cuttack
Bhubaneshwar
Nashik
Aurangabad
Thane
BOMBAY
PUNE
Pimpri-Chinchwad
DECCAN PLATEAU
Sholapur
HYDERABAD
Vijayawada
Vishakhapatnam
EASTERN GHATS
WESTERN GHATS
Hubli-Dharwad
ARABIAN SEA
Bay of Bengal
Nellore
Tirupati
MADRAS
BANGALORE
Mysore
Coimbatore
Cochin
Madurai
Trivandrum
COROMANDEL COAST
MALABAR COAST
LAKSHADWEEP
Palk Strait
Gulf of Mannar
SRI LANKA
Colombo
Kandy
Jaffna
MALDIVES
Male
INDIAN OCEAN
ANDAMAN SEA
ANDAMAN ISLANDS
NICOBAR ISLANDS
Ten Degree Channel
Great Channel
Banda Aceh
INDONESIA
Sittwe
YANGON
Bassein
Gulf of Martaban
Scale 1: 18,315,000
0 50 100 150 200 250 mi
0 100 200 300 400 km
Transverse Mercator
© 1999, Encyclopædia Britannica, Inc.

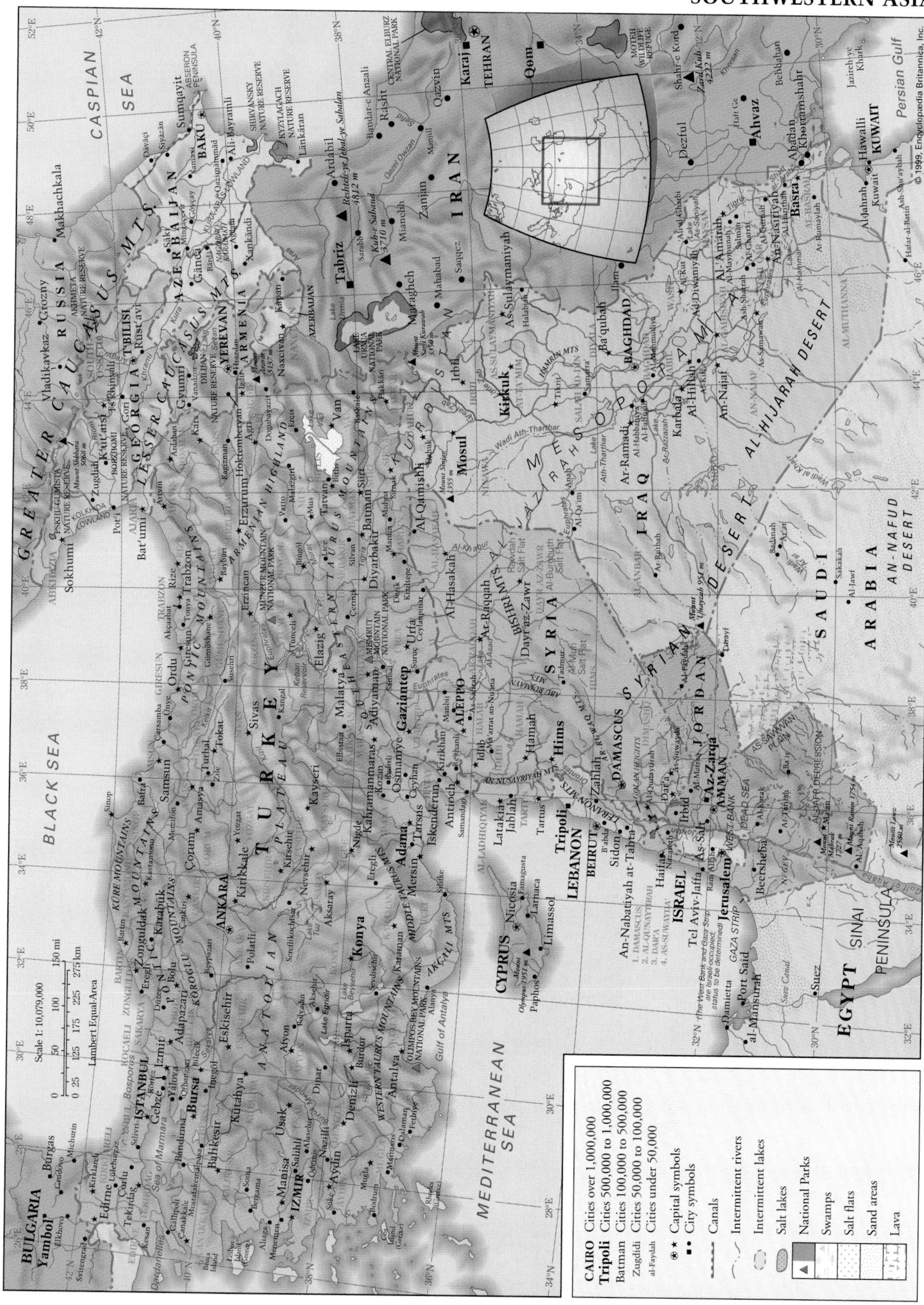
CAIRO Cities over 1,000,000
Tripoli Cities 500,000 to 1,000,000
Batman Cities 100,000 to 500,000
Zugdidi Cities 50,000 to 100,000
al-Faydah Cities under 50,000
Capital symbols
City symbols
Canals
Intermittent rivers
Intermittent lakes
Salt lakes
National Parks
Swamps
Salt flats
Sand areas
Lava
Scale 1: 10,079,000
Lambert Equal-Area
© 1999, Encyclopædia Britannica, Inc.
BLACK SEA
CASPIAN SEA
MEDITERRANEAN SEA
Persian Gulf
TURKEY
IRAN
IRAQ
SYRIA
JORDAN
ISRAEL
LEBANON
CYPRUS
EGYPT
SAUDI ARABIA
KUWAIT
GEORGIA
ARMENIA
AZERBAIJAN
RUSSIA
BULGARIA
GREATER CAUCASUS
LESSER CAUCASUS MTS.
ANATOLIAN PLATEAU
PONTIC MOUNTAINS
SOUTHEASTERN TAURUS MOUNTAINS
KURDISTAN
MESOPOTAMIA
SYRIAN DESERT
AL-HIJARAH DESERT
AN-NAFUD DESERT
SINAI PENINSULA
ANKARA
ISTANBUL
IZMIR
BAGHDAD
DAMASCUS
BEIRUT
AMMAN
TEHRAN
BAKU
YEREVAN
TBILISI
Jerusalem
ALEPPO

AFRICA

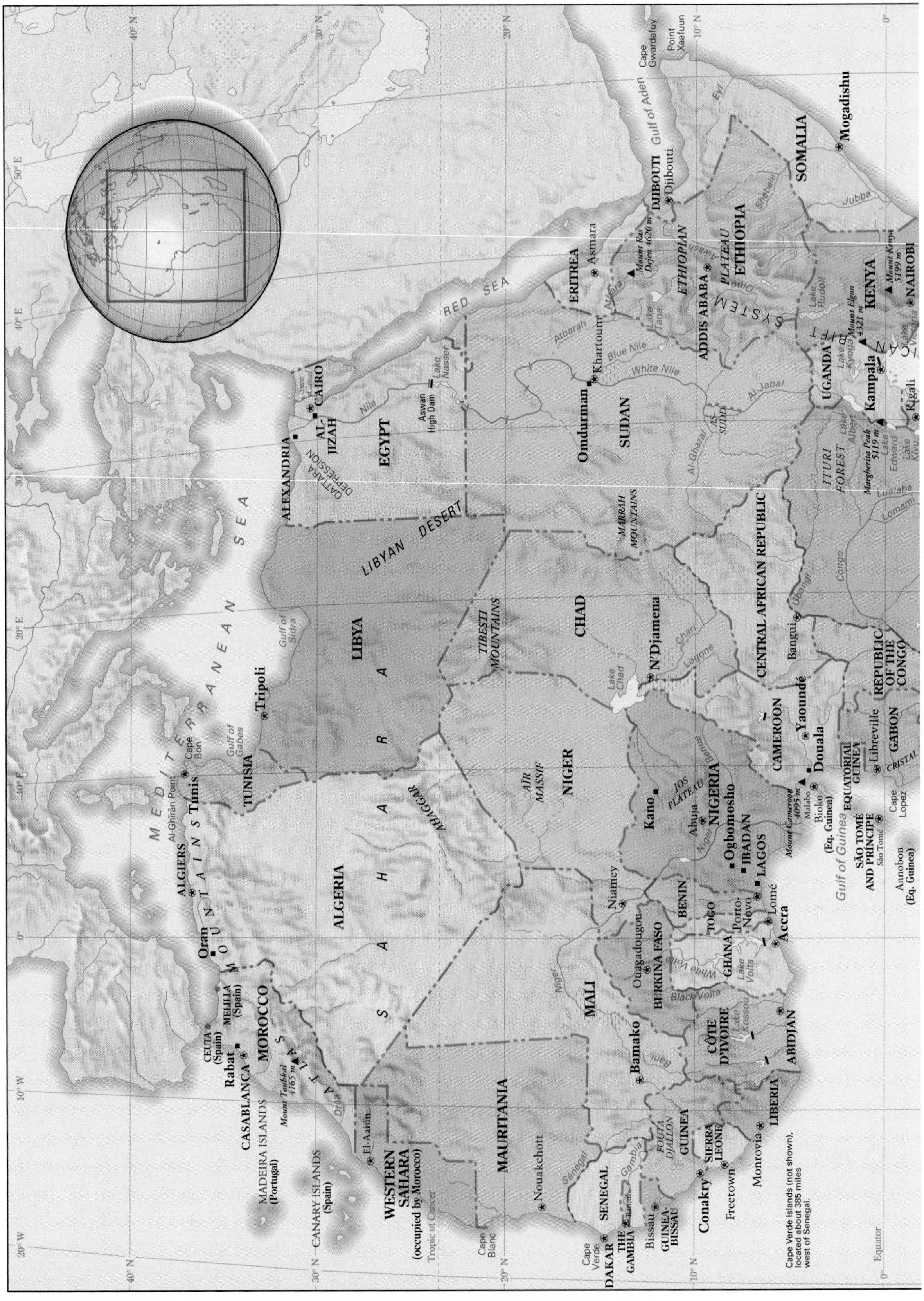
MEDITERRANEAN SEA
RED SEA
Gulf of Aden
Gulf of Guinea
SAHARA
LIBYAN DESERT
ATLAS MOUNTAINS
TIBESTI MOUNTAINS
AHAGGAR
AÏR MASSIF
MARRAH MOUNTAINS
QATTARA DEPRESSION
ETHIOPIAN PLATEAU
RIFT SYSTEM
ITURI FOREST
JOS PLATEAU
FOUTA DJALLON
AS-SUDD
Tropic of Cancer
Equator
MOROCCO
ALGERIA
TUNISIA
LIBYA
EGYPT
SUDAN
ERITREA
DJIBOUTI
ETHIOPIA
SOMALIA
KENYA
UGANDA
CHAD
NIGER
MALI
MAURITANIA
WESTERN SAHARA (occupied by Morocco)
SENEGAL
THE GAMBIA
GUINEA-BISSAU
GUINEA
SIERRA LEONE
LIBERIA
CÔTE D'IVOIRE
BURKINA FASO
GHANA
TOGO
BENIN
NIGERIA
CAMEROON
CENTRAL AFRICAN REPUBLIC
EQUATORIAL GUINEA
GABON
REPUBLIC OF THE CONGO
SÃO TOMÉ AND PRÍNCIPE
CANARY ISLANDS (Spain)
MADEIRA ISLANDS (Portugal)
CEUTA (Spain)
MELILLA (Spain)
Rabat
CASABLANCA
Oran
ALGIERS
Tunis
Tripoli
ALEXANDRIA
CAIRO
AL-JIZAH
Aswan High Dam
Lake Nasser
Khartoum
Omdurman
Asmara
Djibouti
ADDIS ABABA
Mogadishu
NAIROBI
Kampala
Kigali
El-Aaiún
Nouakchott
DAKAR
Banjul
Bissau
Conakry
Freetown
Monrovia
Bamako
ABIDJAN
Ouagadougou
Niamey
Accra
Lomé
Porto-Novo
LAGOS
IBADAN
Ogbomosho
Abuja
Kano
N'Djamena
Yaoundé
Douala
Malabo
Bioko (Eq. Guinea)
Libreville
São Tomé
Bangui
Annobon (Eq. Guinea)
Cape Blanc
Cape Verde
Cape Bon
Cape Lopez
Cape Gwardafuy
Point Xaafuun
Al-Ghirān Point
Gulf of Sidra
Gulf of Gabes
Suez Canal
Mount Toubkal 4165 m
Mount Cameroon 4095 m
Mount Ras Dejen 4620 m
Mount Elgon 4321 m
Mount Kenya 5199 m
Margherita Peak 5119 m
Lake Chad
Lake Volta
Lake Kossou
Lake Tana
Lake Rudolf
Lake Kyoga
Lake Albert
Lake Edward
Lake Kivu
Lake Victoria
Nile
Blue Nile
White Nile
Atbarah
Al-Jabal
Al-Ghazal
Niger
Benue
Senegal
Gambia
Draa
Bani
Black Volta
White Volta
Chari
Logone
Ubangi
Congo
Lualaba
Lomami
Shebele
Jubba
Awash
Omo
CRISTAL
Cape Verde Islands (not shown), located about 385 miles west of Senegal.
40° N
30° N
20° N
10° N
0°
20° W
10° W
10° E
20° E
30° E
40° E
50° E

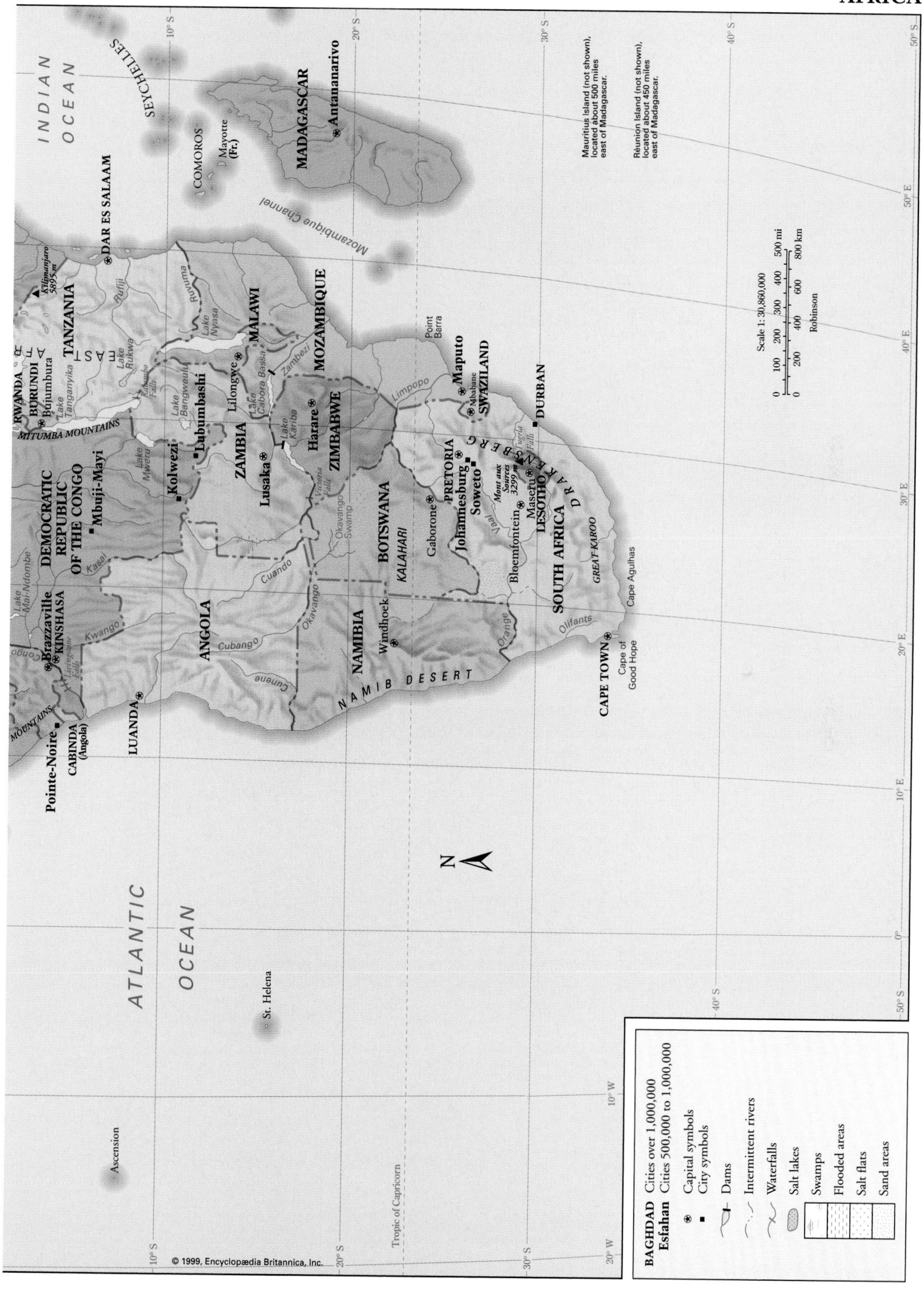
INDIAN OCEAN
ATLANTIC OCEAN
SEYCHELLES
COMOROS
Mayotte (Fr.)
MADAGASCAR
Antananarivo
Mozambique Channel
DAR ES SALAAM
Kilimanjaro 5895 m
TANZANIA
EAST AFR
RWANDA
BURUNDI
Bujumbura
Lake Tanganyika
Lake Rukwa
Rufiji
Ruvuma
Lake Nyasa
MALAWI
Lilongwe
MOZAMBIQUE
Lake Cabora Bassa
Zambezi
Kalambo Falls
Lake Bangweulu
Lake Mweru
MITUMBA MOUNTAINS
DEMOCRATIC REPUBLIC OF THE CONGO
Mbuji-Mayi
Kolwezi
Lubumbashi
ZAMBIA
Lusaka
Lake Kariba
Harare
ZIMBABWE
Victoria Falls
Okavango Swamp
BOTSWANA
KALAHARI
Gaborone
Limpopo
Point Barra
Maputo
Mbabane
SWAZILAND
DURBAN
PRETORIA
Johannesburg
Soweto
Mont aux Sources 3299 m
Tugela Falls
DRAKENSBERG
Maseru
LESOTHO
Bloemfontein
Vaal
SOUTH AFRICA
GREAT KAROO
Cape Agulhas
Olifants
Orange
CAPE TOWN
Cape of Good Hope
NAMIBIA
Windhoek
NAMIB DESERT
Cunene
Cubango
Okavango
Cuando
ANGOLA
Kasai
Kwango
Lake Mai-Ndombe
Brazzaville
KINSHASA
Livingstone Falls
Congo
MOUNTAINS
Pointe-Noire
CABINDA (Angola)
LUANDA
St. Helena
Ascension
Tropic of Capricorn
10° S
20° S
30° S
40° S
50° S
20° W
10° W
0°
10° E
20° E
30° E
40° E
50° E
N
Mauritius Island (not shown), located about 500 miles east of Madagascar.
Réunion Island (not shown), located about 450 miles east of Madagascar.
Scale 1: 30,860,000
0 100 200 300 400 500 mi
0 200 400 600 800 km
Robinson
© 1999, Encyclopædia Britannica, Inc.
BAGHDAD Cities over 1,000,000
Esfahan Cities 500,000 to 1,000,000
Capital symbols
City symbols
Dams
Intermittent rivers
Waterfalls
Salt lakes
Swamps
Flooded areas
Salt flats
Sand areas

NORTHERN AFRICA

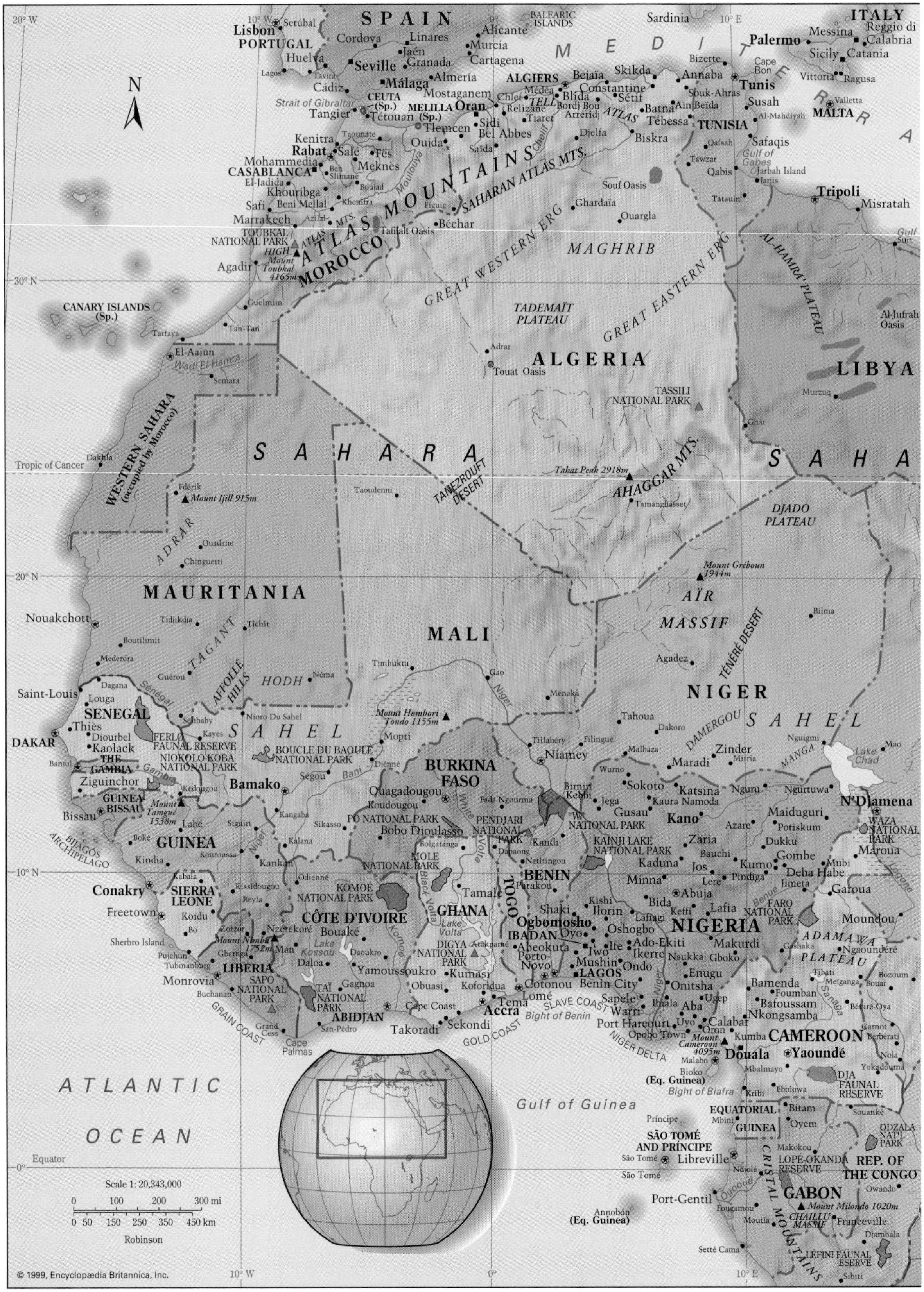

NORTHERN AFRICA

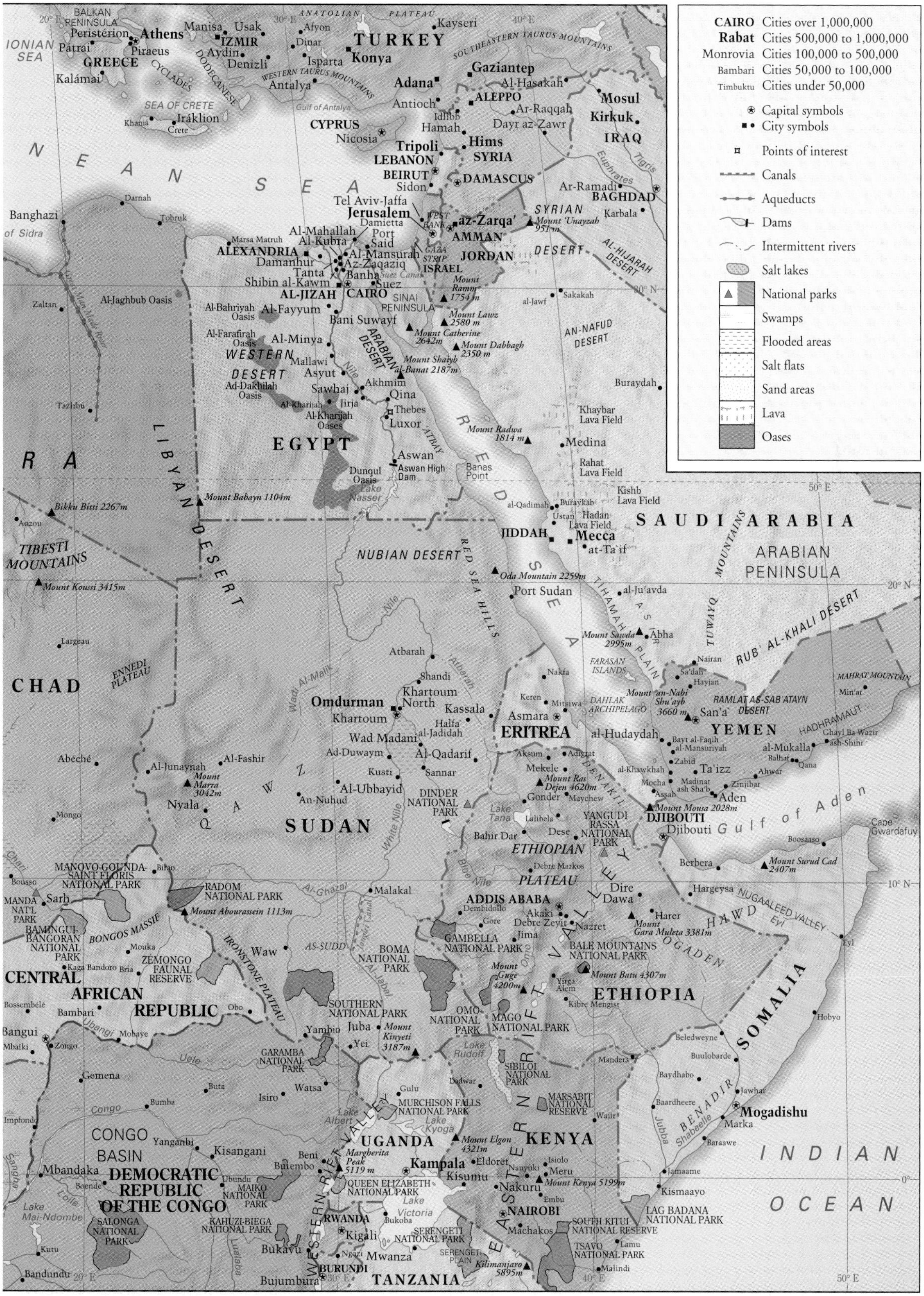

SOUTHERN AFRICA

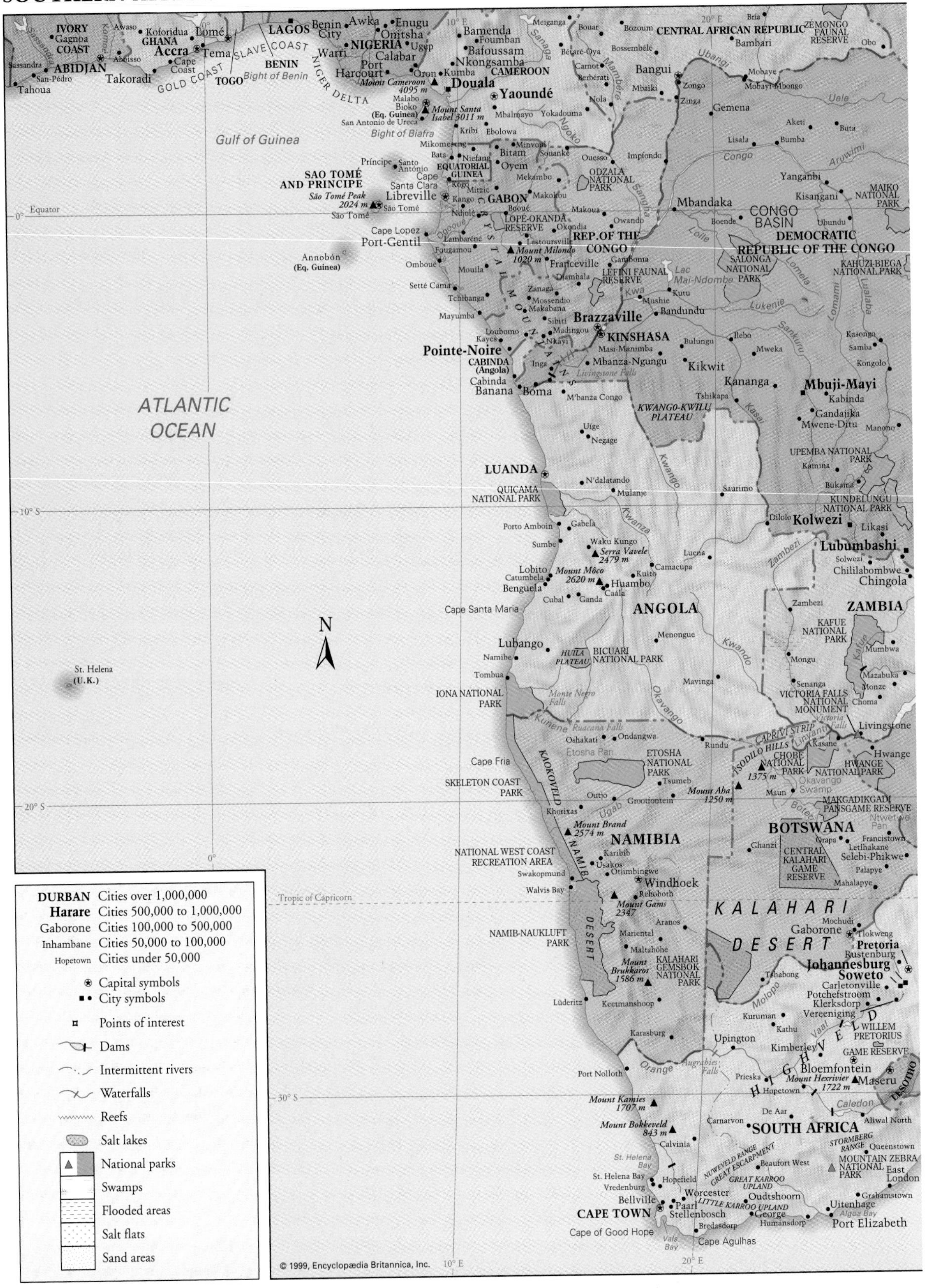

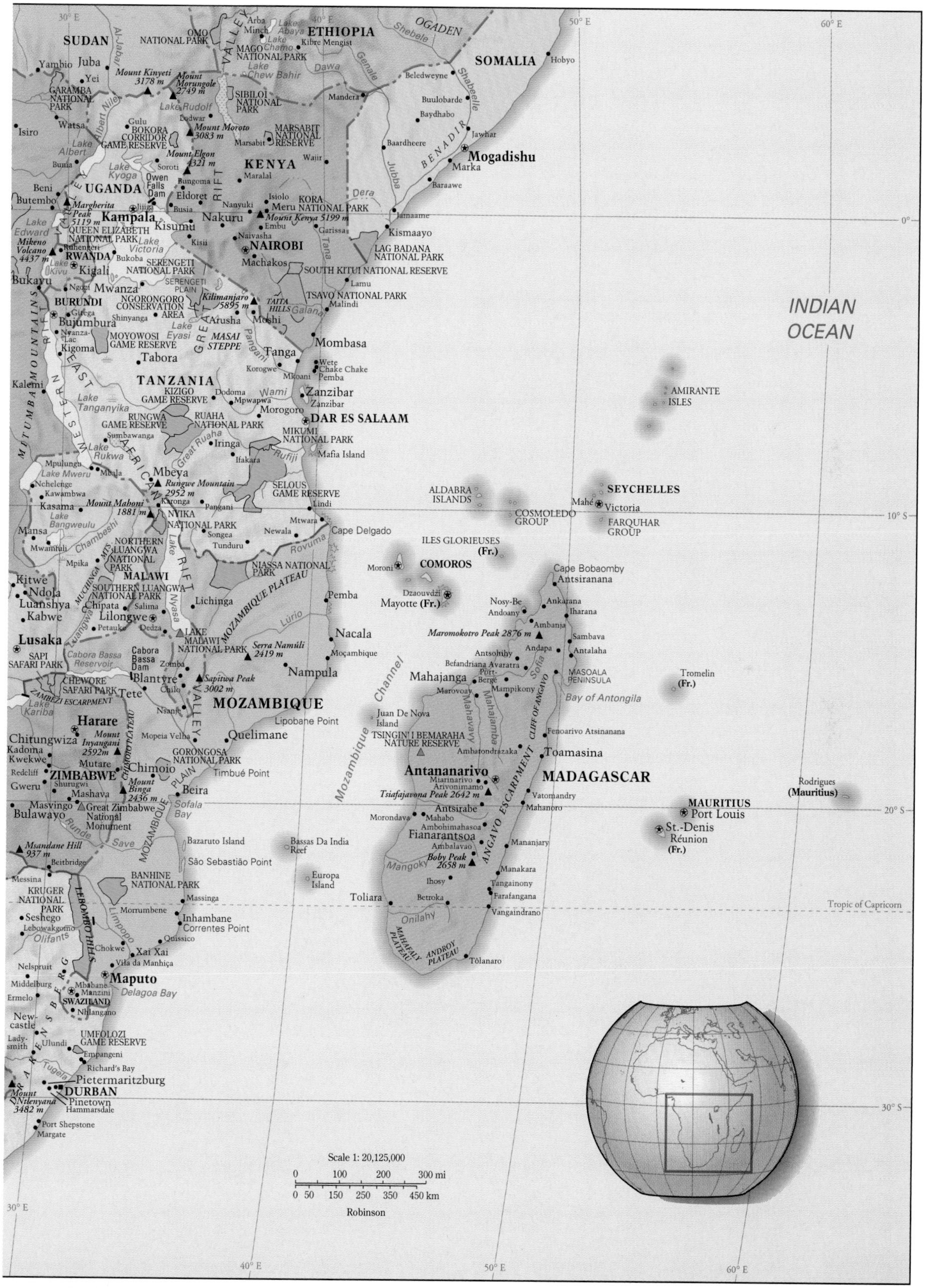

SUDAN
ETHIOPIA
SOMALIA
KENYA
UGANDA
RWANDA
BURUNDI
TANZANIA
MALAWI
MOZAMBIQUE
ZIMBABWE
SWAZILAND
MADAGASCAR
COMOROS
SEYCHELLES
MAURITIUS
INDIAN OCEAN
OGADEN
BENADIR
Yambio
Juba
Yei
Isiro
Watsa
Bunia
Beni
Butembo
Gulu
Lodwar
Soroti
Owen Falls Dam
Jinja
Kampala
Busia
Bungoma
Eldoret
Kisumu
Kisii
Nakuru
Naivasha
NAIROBI
Machakos
Nanyuki
Meru
Isiolo
Embu
Garissa
Maralal
Marsabit
Wajir
Mandera
Arba Minch
Kibre Mengist
Hobyo
Beledweyne
Buulobarde
Baydhabo
Jawhar
Baardheere
Mogadishu
Marka
Baraawe
Jamaame
Kismaayo
Lamu
Malindi
Mombasa
Tanga
Wete
Chake Chake
Pemba
Mkoani
Zanzibar
DAR ES SALAAM
Morogoro
Dodoma
Mpwapwa
Iringa
Ifakara
Mafia Island
Korogwe
Moshi
Arusha
Shinyanga
Mwanza
Bukoba
Ngozi
Gitega
Bujumbura
Kigali
Bukavu
Rubengeri
Nyanza-Lac
Kigoma
Tabora
Kalemi
Sumbawanga
Mpulungu
Mbala
Mbeya
Nchelenge
Kawambwa
Kasama
Karonga
Mansa
Mwamfuli
Mpika
Pangani
Songea
Tunduru
Newala
Mtwara
Lindi
Cape Delgado
Kitwe
Ndola
Luanshya
Kabwe
Lusaka
Chipata
Salima
Lilongwe
Petauke
Dedza
Lichinga
Pemba
Nacala
Moçambique
Nampula
Blantyre
Zomba
Chilo
Tete
Nsanje
Mopeia Velha
Quelimane
Lipobane Point
Harare
Chitungwiza
Kadoma
Kwekwe
Redcliff
Gweru
Shurugwi
Mutare
Chimoio
Mashava
Masvingo
Bulawayo
Beira
Timbué Point
Beitbridge
Messina
Seshego
Lebowakgomo
Nelspruit
Middelburg
Ermelo
Mbabane
Manzini
Nhlangano
Maputo
Xai Xai
Vila da Manhiça
Chokwe
Quissico
Inhambane
Correntes Point
Massinga
Morrumbene
Bazaruto Island
São Sebastião Point
Newcastle
Ladysmith
Ulundi
Empangeni
Richard's Bay
Pietermaritzburg
DURBAN
Pinetown
Hammarsdale
Port Shepstone
Margate
Delagoa Bay
Sofala Bay
Moroni
Dzaouvdzi
Mayotte (Fr.)
Cape Bobaomby
Antsiranana
Nosy-Be
Andoany
Ambanja
Ankarana
Iharana
Sambava
Antalaha
Andapa
Antsohihy
Befandriana Avaratra
Port-Bergé
Mahajanga
Marovoay
Mampikony
MASOALA PENINSULA
Bay of Antongila
Fenoarivo Atsinanana
Toamasina
Ambatondrazaka
Antananarivo
Miarinarivo
Arivonimamo
Vatomandry
Mahanoro
Antsirabe
Morondava
Mahabo
Ambohimahasoa
Fianarantsoa
Ambalavao
Mananjary
Manakara
Ihosy
Tangainony
Farafangana
Vangaindrano
Betroka
Toliara
Tôlanaro
Victoria
Mahé
Port Louis
St.-Denis
Réunion (Fr.)
Rodrigues (Mauritius)
Tromelin (Fr.)
AMIRANTE ISLES
ALDABRA ISLANDS
COSMOLEDO GROUP
FARQUHAR GROUP
ILES GLORIEUSES (Fr.)
Juan De Nova Island
Bassas Da India Reef
Europa Island
Mozambique Channel
Lake Albert
Lake Kyoga
Lake Edward
Lake Kivu
Lake Victoria
Lake Rudolf
Lake Chew Bahir
Lake Abaya
Lake Chamo
Lake Eyasi
Lake Tanganyika
Lake Rukwa
Lake Mweru
Lake Bangweulu
Lake Nyasa
Lake Kariba
Cabora Bassa Reservoir
Cabora Bassa Dam
Albert Nile
Al Jabal
Shebele
Genale
Dawa
Shabeelle
Jubba
Dera
Tana
Galana
Pangani
Wami
Great Ruaha
Rufiji
Ruvuma
Lurio
Luangwa
Chambeshi
Zambezi
Save
Runde
Limpopo
Olifants
Tugela
Mangoky
Onilahy
Mahavavy
Mahajamba
Sofia
Mount Kinyeti 3178 m
Mount Morungole 2749 m
Mount Moroto 3083 m
Mount Elgon 4321 m
Margherita Peak 5119 m
Mikeno Volcano 4437 m
Mount Kenya 5199 m
Kilimanjaro 5895 m
Rungwe Mountain 2952 m
Mount Mahoni 1881 m
Serra Namúli 2419 m
Sapitwa Peak 3002 m
Mount Inyangani 2592m
Mount Binga 2436 m
Msandane Hill 937 m
Mount Ntlenyana 3482 m
Maromokotro Peak 2876 m
Tsiafajavona Peak 2642 m
Boby Peak 2658 m
OMO NATIONAL PARK
MAGO NATIONAL PARK
GARAMBA NATIONAL PARK
SIBILOI NATIONAL PARK
BOKORA CORRIDOR GAME RESERVE
MARSABIT NATIONAL RESERVE
KORA NATIONAL PARK
QUEEN ELIZABETH NATIONAL PARK
LAG BADANA NATIONAL PARK
SERENGETI NATIONAL PARK
SERENGETI PLAIN
SOUTH KITUI NATIONAL RESERVE
TSAVO NATIONAL PARK
TAITA HILLS
NGORONGORO CONSERVATION AREA
MOYOWOSI GAME RESERVE
MASAI STEPPE
KIZIGO GAME RESERVE
RUNGWA GAME RESERVE
RUAHA NATIONAL PARK
MIKUMI NATIONAL PARK
SELOUS GAME RESERVE
NYIKA NATIONAL PARK
NORTHERN LUANGWA NATIONAL PARK
NIASSA NATIONAL PARK
SOUTHERN LUANGWA NATIONAL PARK
LAKE MALAWI NATIONAL PARK
SAPI SAFARI PARK
CHEWORE SAFARI PARK
ZAMBEZI ESCARPMENT
GORONGOSA NATIONAL PARK
Great Zimbabwe National Monument
BANHINE NATIONAL PARK
KRUGER NATIONAL PARK
UMFOLOZI GAME RESERVE
TSINGIN' I BEMARAHA NATURE RESERVE
MITUMBA MOUNTAINS
WESTERN RIFT
EAST AFRICAN RIFT
GREAT RIFT VALLEY
RIFT VALLEY
MUCHINGA MTS.
MOZAMBIQUE PLATEAU
CHIMANIMANI PLATEAU
MOZAMBIQUE PLAIN
LEBOMBO HILLS
DRAKENSBERG
CLIFF OF ANGAVO
ANGAVO ESCARPMENT
MAHAFALY PLATEAU
ANDROY PLATEAU
Tropic of Capricorn
30° E
40° E
50° E
60° E
0°
10° S
20° S
30° S
Scale 1: 20,125,000
0 100 200 300 mi
0 50 150 250 350 450 km
Robinson

ARABIAN PENINSULA

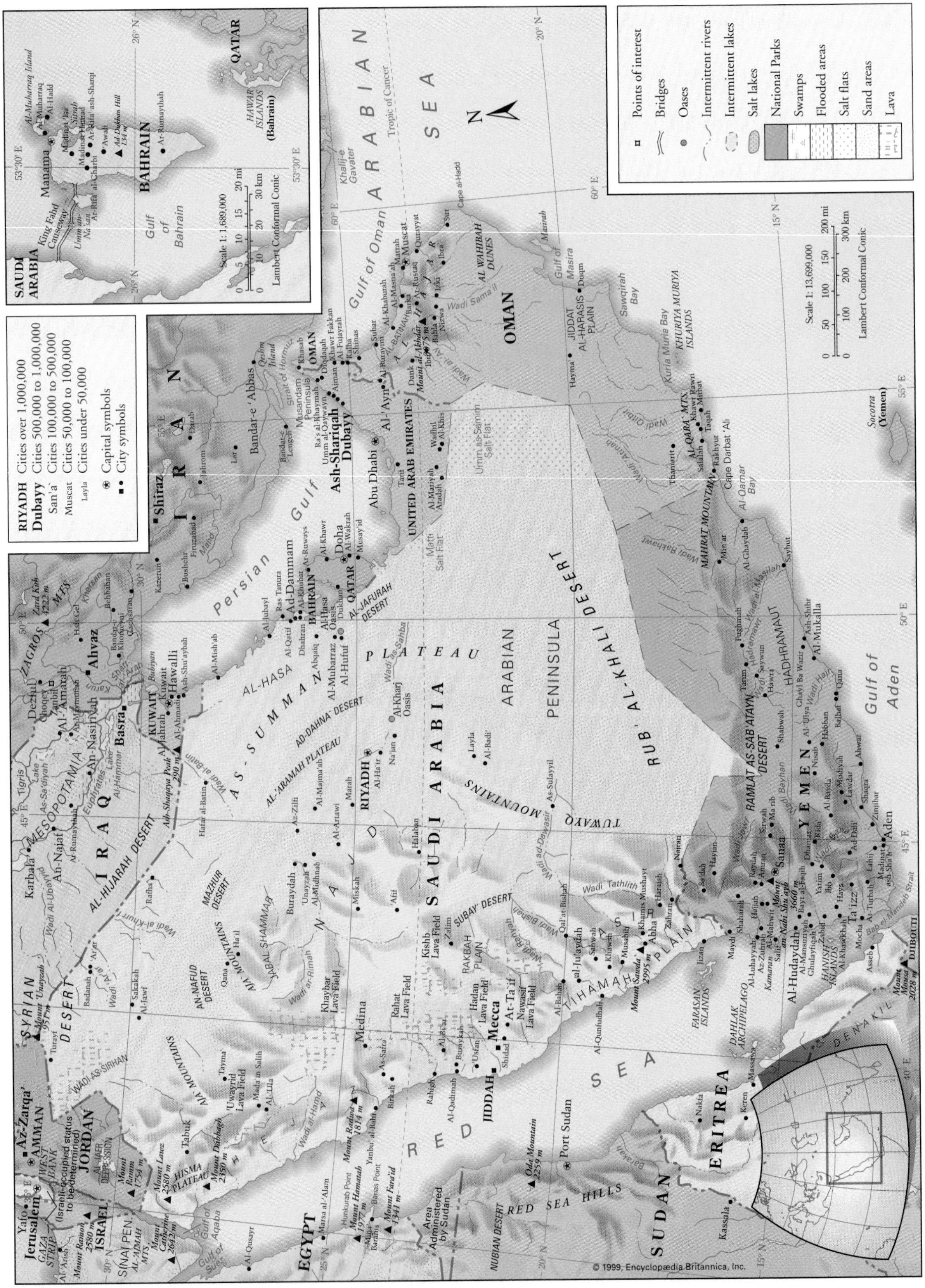

AUSTRALIA AND NEW ZEALAND

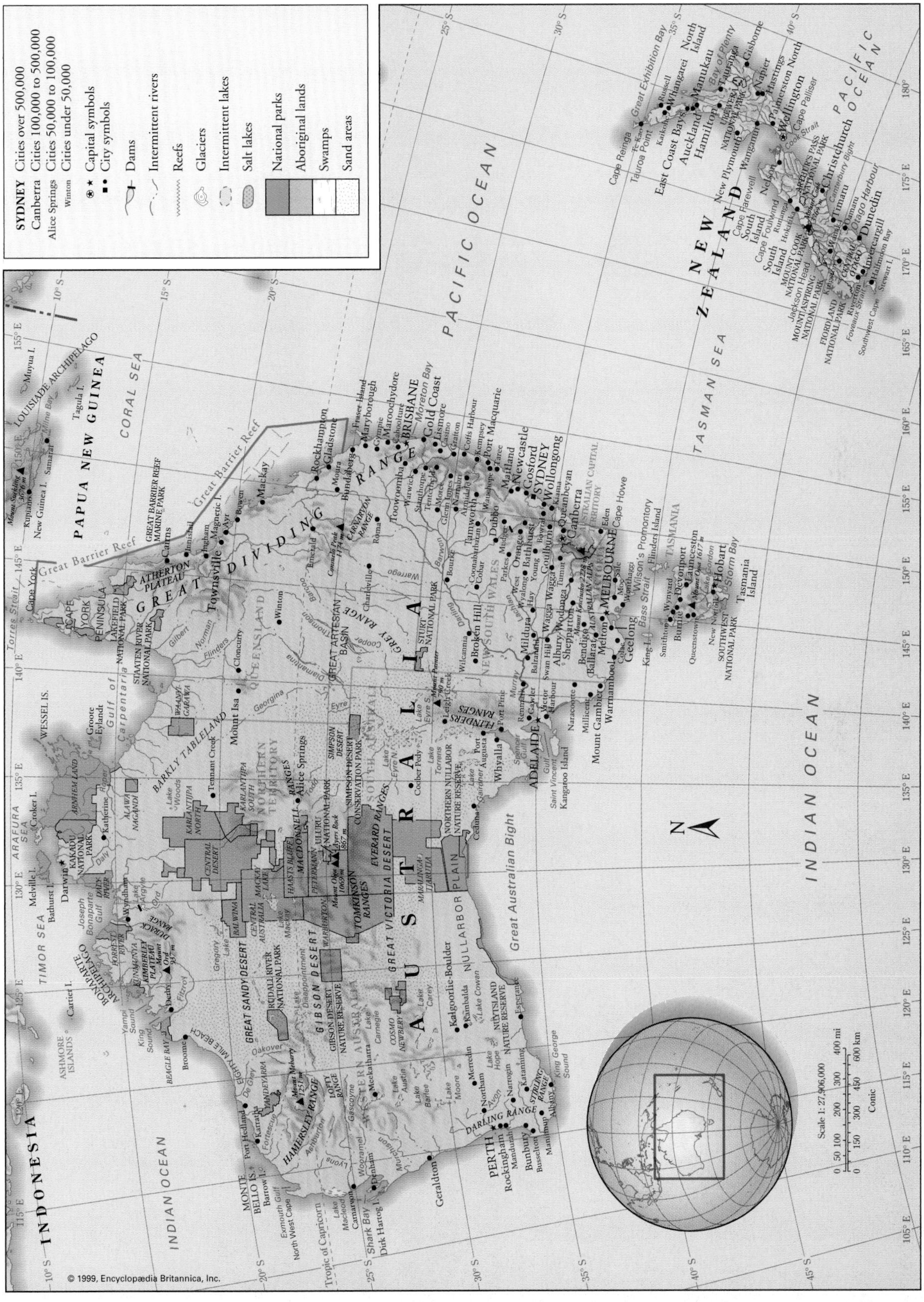

OCEANIA

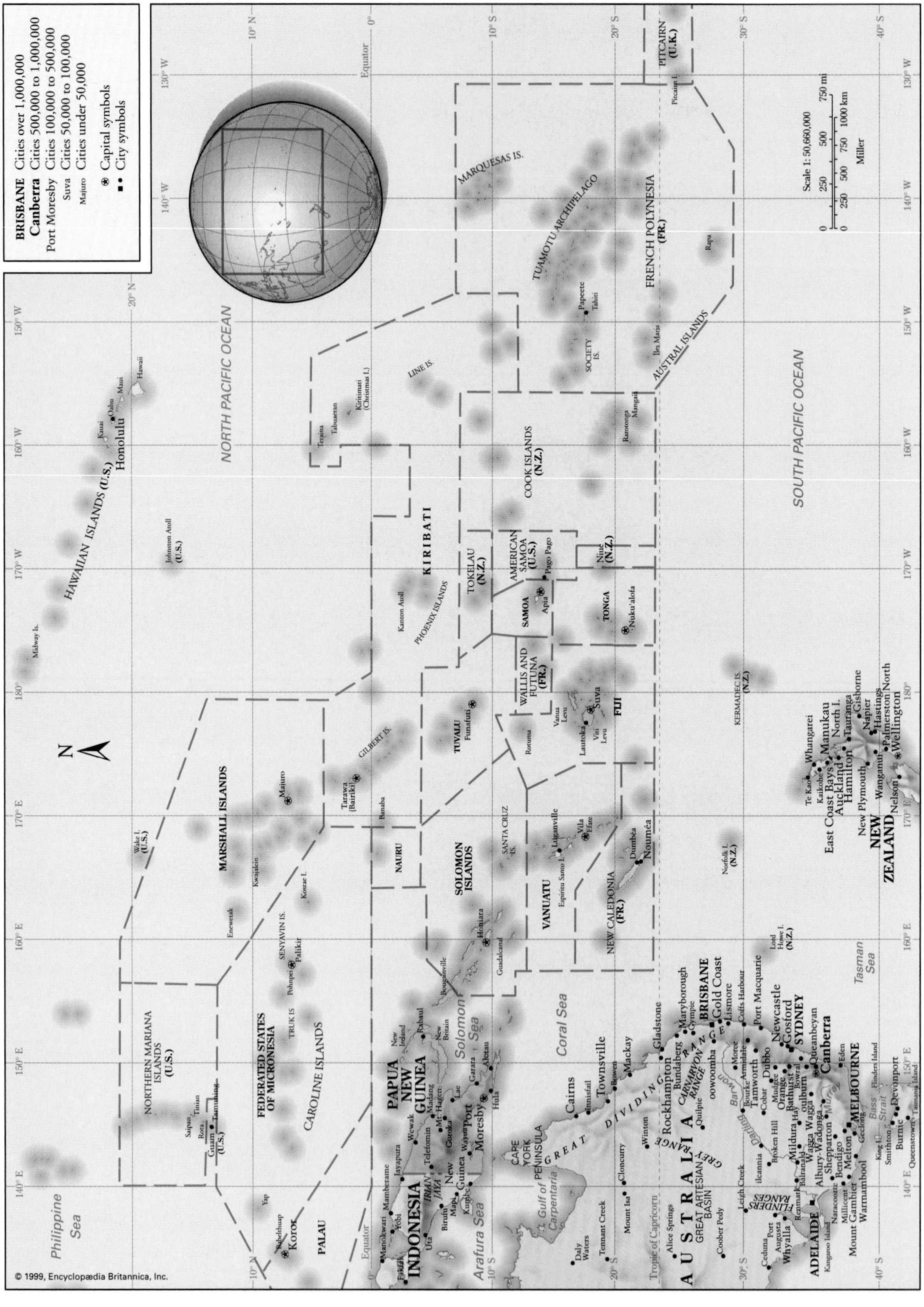
BRISBANE Cities over 1,000,000
Canberra Cities 500,000 to 1,000,000
Port Moresby Cities 100,000 to 500,000
Suva Cities 50,000 to 100,000
Majuro Cities under 50,000
Capital symbols
City symbols
Scale 1: 50,660,000
0 250 500 750 mi
0 250 500 750 1000 km
Miller
NORTH PACIFIC OCEAN
SOUTH PACIFIC OCEAN
Philippine Sea
Coral Sea
Solomon Sea
Arafura Sea
Tasman Sea
Gulf of Carpentaria
Bass Strait
Equator
Tropic of Capricorn
HAWAIIAN ISLANDS (U.S.)
Honolulu
Kauai
Oahu
Maui
Hawaii
Midway Is.
Johnston Atoll (U.S.)
Wake I. (U.S.)
NORTHERN MARIANA ISLANDS (U.S.)
Saipan
Tinian
Rota
Guam (U.S.)
Tamuning
MARSHALL ISLANDS
Majuro
Kwajalein
Enewetak
FEDERATED STATES OF MICRONESIA
CAROLINE ISLANDS
Palikir
Pohnpei
SENYAVIN IS.
TRUK IS.
Kosrae I.
Yap
PALAU
Koror
Babelthuap
KIRIBATI
GILBERT IS.
Tarawa (Bairiki)
Banaba
PHOENIX ISLANDS
Kanton Atoll
LINE IS.
Kiritimati (Christmas I.)
Tabuaeran
Teraina
NAURU
TUVALU
Funafuti
TOKELAU (N.Z.)
AMERICAN SAMOA (U.S.)
Pago Pago
SAMOA
Apia
WALLIS AND FUTUNA (FR.)
COOK ISLANDS (N.Z.)
Rarotonga
Mangaia
Niue (N.Z.)
TONGA
Nuku'alofa
FIJI
Suva
Lautoka
Vanua Levu
Viti Levu
Rotuma
KERMADEC IS. (N.Z.)
MARQUESAS IS.
TUAMOTU ARCHIPELAGO
FRENCH POLYNESIA (FR.)
SOCIETY IS.
Papeete
Tahiti
AUSTRAL ISLANDS
Îles Maria
Rapa
PITCAIRN (U.K.)
Pitcairn I.
SOLOMON ISLANDS
Honiara
Guadalcanal
Bougainville
SANTA CRUZ IS.
VANUATU
Espiritu Santo I.
Luganville
Vila
Efate
NEW CALEDONIA (FR.)
Nouméa
Dumbéa
Norfolk I. (N.Z.)
Lord Howe I. (N.Z.)
PAPUA NEW GUINEA
Port Moresby
New Britain
New Ireland
Rabaul
Lae
Madang
Wewak
Mt. Hagen
Goroka
Garara
Alotau
Hula
Kiunga
INDONESIA
IRIAN JAYA
New Guinea
Jayapura
Manokwari
Sorong
Biak
Yobi
Mamberamo
Uta
Biruta
Merauke
CAPE YORK PENINSULA
GREAT DIVIDING RANGE
AUSTRALIA
GREAT ARTESIAN BASIN
CARNARVON RANGE
GREY RANGE
FLINDERS RANGES
Darling
Murray
Cairns
Innisfail
Townsville
Bowen
Mackay
Rockhampton
Gladstone
Bundaberg
Maryborough
Gympie
BRISBANE
Gold Coast
Lismore
Coffs Harbour
Port Macquarie
Newcastle
Gosford
SYDNEY
Wollongong
Queanbeyan
Canberra
Eden
MELBOURNE
Geelong
Bendigo
Ballarat
Shepparton
Albury-Wodonga
Wagga Wagga
Goulburn
Orange
Bathurst
Dubbo
Tamworth
Armidale
Moree
Toowoomba
Quilpie
Bourke
Cobar
Broken Hill
Mildura
Mount Gambier
Warrnambool
Naracoorte
Millicent
ADELAIDE
Whyalla
Port Augusta
Ceduna
Coober Pedy
Leigh Creek
Alice Springs
Tennant Creek
Daly Waters
Mount Isa
Cloncurry
Winton
Kangaroo Island
Flinders Island
King I.
Devonport
Burnie
Queenstown
Smithton
Tasmania
NEW ZEALAND
North I.
Whangarei
Auckland
Manukau
East Coast Bays
Hamilton
Tauranga
Gisborne
Napier
Hastings
Palmerston North
Wanganui
New Plymouth
Wellington
Nelson
Te Kao
Kaikohe
© 1999, Encyclopædia Britannica, Inc.

THESAURUS

Preface

The thesaurus section of the *Webster's New Explorer Dictionary and Thesaurus* is based on the idea that people use such a resource to find a more appropriate word for the meaning they want to express. It is designed to make it as easy as possible for users to find just the right word.

The main entries for synonyms are arranged in alphabetical order. In addition to a list of synonyms, main entries include a brief, straightforward statement of the meaning shared by the group of synonyms, along with lists of antonyms, related and contrasted words, and idiomatic expressions (common words or phrases that have a meaning similar to that of the entry word). These lists are presented to help users recognize slight differences in meaning or tone that may affect word choice and are organized to make the search for an appropriate term as easy as possible. The Explanatory Notes that follow the Introduction should be read carefully. They contain an explanation of how the book is organized and discuss the kinds of information that may be found at each entry.

This thesaurus was created in cooperation with the editors of Merriam-Webster Inc., a company that has been publishing dictionaries for over 150 years.

Introduction

The word *thesaurus* derives from the Greek *thesauros* meaning "a storehouse or treasury." As you become familiar with this book, you will find it to be a storehouse of useful words waiting to give precision and sparkle to your speech and writing. This Introduction and the following Explanatory Notes describe the features of your new thesaurus and will guide you in understanding and using this valuable reference.

The Synonym

English is a very complex language. With its intricate interweaving of strands of Celtic, earlier Roman and later churchly Latin, northern and western Germanic tongues, and, through Norman-French, the whole body of Romance languages, it is not surprising that it is a language peculiarly rich in synonyms.

Synonyms lend character and flexibility to writing and speech. They relieve monotony and enhance expressiveness. But just what are synonyms? To the earlier writers the meaning was clear; they viewed synonyms as words meaning the same thing. Unfortunately, during the last century or so this simple, clearcut meaning has become blurred. To many, the term *synonym* has come to mean little more than words that are somewhat similar in meaning. We feel this loose definition to be unsuitable for the selection of terms in a thesaurus since it deprives you of the guidance you have a right to expect.

As a result, we looked for a new approach and were soon convinced that to identify synonyms we had to isolate a segment of meaning that two or more words had in common. In order to analyze each word carefully, then, we had to think of synonymy not just as a relationship between words, nor even between dictionary senses of words. We had to look for separate objective denotations not marked by such peripheral aspects of meaning as connotations, implications, or quirks of idiomatic usage. Only by taking apart senses could we reach the word's ultimate meaning, which for the sake of simplicity we call an *elementary meaning*. Perhaps if we explain this approach by using an example, it will be clearer to you. In Webster's Third New International Dictionary, a sense of the noun *input* reads:

> : power or energy put into a machine or system for storage (as into a storage battery) or for conversion in kind (as into a mechanically driven electric generator or a radio receiver) or conversion of characteristics (as into a transformer or electric amplifier) usu. with the intent of sizable recovery in the form of output

Much of this definition contains peripheral matter, and from the dictionary point of view it is necessary to include it because it helps guide and orient you in knowing how and when to use the word. However, the fundamental meaning of this sense, its denotation, may be restated as:

> power or energy put into a machine or system for storage or for conversion in kind or conversion of characteristics

When we express this graphically

power		machine		storage
	put into a		for	conversion in kind
energy		system		conversion of characteristics

you can see that there are twelve simple statements of denotation or individual elementary meanings associated in this single sense of *input*. Of these twelve only one, "energy put into a system for storage," can reasonably be considered a synonym of *charge* as applied to a storage battery. If we were compiling a list of synonyms for *charge* as applied to a storage battery, we would consider *input* a synonym because of this shared elementary meaning. For the purposes of this thesaurus then, we consider a word to be a synonym only if it or one of its senses shares with another word or a sense of another word one or more such elementary meanings.

When we look at the synonymous relationship of words in terms of elementary meanings, the process of choosing synonyms is simpler and more exact. For example, it is easy to see that no term more restricted in definition than the pertinent meaning of the headword can be its synonym, i.e., *station wagon* cannot be a synonym of *automobile,* and *biceps* cannot be a synonym of *muscle.* Even though a very definite relationship exists between the members of each pair, *station wagon* is a type of automobile and *biceps* is a type of muscle, and so are narrower in their range of application. On the other hand, a word more broadly defined than another word in the dictionary may be considered a synonym of the other word so long as the two words share one or more elementary meanings. In order to pin down the area of shared meaning for you, each main entry in this thesaurus contains before its synonym list a *meaning core* (see p. 9a) which states the elementary meaning or meanings that are shared by all the words in that particular synonym group.

The Antonym

Like *synonym, antonym* has been used by some writers with a great deal of vagueness and often applied loosely to words which show no real oppositeness when compared one to another. We feel that a reappraisal of the antonym concept is long overdue. As in the case of synonyms, the relation needs to be seen as one between segments of meaning which can be isolated, rather than between words or dictionary senses of words. For the purpose of this book, we consider a word to be an antonym when one or more of its elementary meanings precisely opposes or negates the same area of meaning of another word. This definition excludes from consideration as antonyms several classes of words that are sometimes treated as antonyms but that actually contain words which neither directly oppose nor directly negate the words with which they are said to be antonymous. Three such groups seem worth a little attention.

1. *Relative terms* have such a relationship to each other that one can scarcely be used without suggesting the other (as *husband* and *wife, father* and *son, buyer* and *seller*), yet there is no real opposition or real negation between such pairs. Their relation is reciprocal or correlative rather than antonymous.

2. *Complementary terms* in a similar way are usually paired and have a reciprocal relationship to the point that one seems incomplete without the other (as in such pairs as *question* and *answer, seek* and *find*). This relation which involves no negation is better seen as sequential than antonymous.

3. *Contrastive terms* differ sharply from their "opposites" only in some parts of their meaning. They neither oppose nor negate fully, since they are significantly different in range of meaning and applicability, in emphasis, and in the suggestions they convey. For example, *destitute* (a strong word carrying suggestions of misery and distress) is contrastive rather than antonymous with respect to *rich* (a rather neutral and matter-of-fact term), while *poor* (another neutral and matter-of-fact term) is the appropriate antonym of *rich.* Basically, contrastive words are only opposed incidentally; they do not meet head on.

In this thesaurus such words, where appropriate, appear as contrasted words.

What then do we consider antonyms? In this thesaurus three classes of words have been accepted as truly antonymous and as sources from which antonyms may reasonably be drawn. These are:

1. *Opposites without intermediates.* These are words that are so opposed that they are mutually exclusive and leave no middle ground between them. Each denies, point by point and item by item, whatever its opposite affirms. Thus, what is *perfect* can be in no way *imperfect* and what is *imperfect,* to however slight a degree, cannot be viewed as *perfect;* you cannot at the same time *accept* and *reject* or *agree* and *disagree.*

2. *Opposites with intermediates.* Such words make up the extremes in a range of difference and are so completely opposed that the language allows no wider difference. Thus, a scale of excellence might include *superiority, adequacy, mediocrity,* and *inferiority,* but only *superiority* and *inferiority* are so totally opposed that each exactly negates what its opposite affirms.

3. *Reverse opposites.* These are words that are opposed in such a way that each means the

undoing or nullification of what the other affirms. Such reverse opposites exactly oppose and fully negate the special features of their opposites. Thus, *disprove* and its synonym *refute* so perfectly oppose and so clearly negate the implications of *prove* that they fit the concept of antonyms as well as does *unkind* with respect to *kind,* or *come* with respect to *go.*

Related and Contrasted Words

What if you are not looking for an exact synonym or antonym, but are looking for a word somewhat similar or somewhat opposed to a known word? To meet such needs, this thesaurus includes lists of related and contrasted words wherever these seem appropriate and likely to be helpful. We can thus offer a wider range of material for use in word finding and vocabulary building without doing violence to our rather strict interpretation of the synonym and antonym. Related words (near-synonyms) and contrasted words (near-antonyms) are so closely related to, or so clearly contrastable with, the members of a synonym group that you have a right to expect them under the appropriate headings.

Phrases and Idiomatic Equivalents

In the search for longer synonym lists, synonymists increasingly have included phrases among their synonyms. These phrases fall into three classes:

1. *Word equivalents.* These are phrases that act as if they were single words. More often than not they are combinations of noun and attributive noun (as *county agent*) or noun and adjective (as *hard sell*) or of verb and adverb (as *make up*). However, such phrases may be made up of any kinds of word elements and may act as any part-of-speech (as in *passing,* adverb; *except for,* preposition; ||*half-seas over,* adjective; *as long as,* conjunction). These fixed combinations that act as if they were single words cannot be entirely excluded from word lists. This thesaurus includes such combinations when they are so firmly fixed in usage that they are entered in major modern dictionaries with part-of-speech labels.

2. *Glosses.* These are phrases that say the meaning of a word in another way. Essentially, they are brief definitions. There is no definition of synonym that reasonably can be used to justify including these restatements or definitions in synonym lists. Thus "do heavy menial service" is a gloss rather than a synonym of *drudge,* "have an opinion" is a gloss of *opine,* and "in a state of inferiority to" is a gloss of *under.* Such glosses are excluded from this thesaurus since they add nothing useful to the vocabulary of the user of a thesaurus.

3. *Idioms.* These are phrases that have a meaning different from the overall meaning of the words that make them up. For example, there are no literal meanings of *compare* and *note* that allow the phrase "compare notes" to mean "to exchange observations and views"; yet, this is what it does mean. There are no literal meanings of the words that allow the phrase "come a long way" to mean "make progress, succeed"; yet, it does mean this. When idiomatic phrases mean the same thing as particular words it is difficult not to include them in relevant synonym lists. Such phrases, however, do not have the qualities that allow word equivalents to be included in synonym lists — they do not function as words but, rather, as different ways of conveying the same meaning as particular words do. As in the case of glosses there is no definition of synonym that justifies including idioms in a synonym list. Still, we think that such idiomatic equivalents can be helpful to you since they can add force and variety to your expression. This thesaurus has arrived at a compromise and included selected idiomatic equivalents of synonym groups or of particular words in synonym lists in separate lists that follow the relevant lists of synonyms or related words.

Explanatory Notes

How to use this thesaurus

If you expect to make effective use of this thesaurus, you should read and study these Explanatory Notes. In the paragraphs that follow you will find brief explanations of the order of entries, the kinds of entries, and how each entry is put together. The explanations are illustrated with the actual examples taken from the book. In addition you will find a keyline at the foot of every other page of the main vocabulary to serve as a reminder of the information contained in these Explanatory Notes.

A thesaurus consists mostly of lists of words. It is often difficult for the user to be sure what meaning of a word the editor intended when including it in a list. This thesaurus has been edited with features — such as the meaning cores and verbal illustrations — which will help keep you aware of the meaning intended. But because the English language has so many different ways of combining words and so many subtle shades of meaning, you should always use this thesaurus along with an adequate dictionary. Most of the time you will find that a good desk-size dictionary will be extremely helpful.

Scope of this thesaurus

This thesaurus is concerned with the general vocabulary of English. Most obsolete and archaic words and highly technical terms have been left out. Since the vocabulary of this thesaurus is based on Webster's Third New International Dictionary, its editors feel that enough unusual words have been retained to satisfy the student in search of a sprinkling of out-of-the-ordinary terms to use. Some of these words will not be found in a desk-size dictionary and it then may be necessary for you to use an unabridged dictionary to check the suitability of a particular term. If you do not have ready access to an unabridged dictionary, you may not be able to be sure about some of the rarer words. You should use rare or unusual terms, therefore, with caution. Most of you will find that the words entered in a good desk-size dictionary will provide adequate stimulus for the growth of your vocabulary.

Entry Order

The body of the book consists of main entries and secondary entries. These entries are arranged in alphabetical order. Each main and secondary entry is introduced by a boldface headword, as seen in the following examples:

> **hang** *n* the special method of doing, using, or dealing with something <can't get the *hang* of this gadget>
> ***syn*** knack, swing, trick
> ***rel*** art, craft, skill
>
> **hang around** *vb* ***syn*** see FREQUENT
> **hanger-on** *n* ***syn*** see PARASITE
> ***rel*** bystander, follower, spectator, syncophant

In the above examples, *hang, hang around, hanger-on* are the headwords introducing either a main entry, as **hang** *n* does, or a secondary entry, as **hang around** *vb* or **hanger-on** *n* do.

Homograph headwords, that is words which are spelled alike, are entered in historical order. The one first used in English is entered first, as:

> **till** *prep*
> **till** *conj*
> **till** *vb*

Verbs used frequently with one or two prepositions or adverbs may be headwords introducing main entries or secondary entries. If they are used as headwords, they are entered with the verb part

THESAURUS

in boldface type followed by the preposition or adverb in parentheses in lightface type. Such combinations immediately follow the base verb in alphabetical order. In the following example, you can see that the base verb **put** comes first and is followed in alphabetical order by the entries with preposition or adverb in parentheses, **put** (back), **put** (on), and **put** (on or upon):

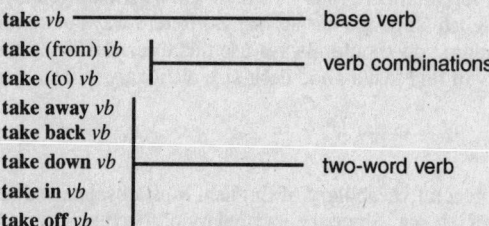

put *vb*	base-verb homograph
put (back) *vb* **put** (on) *vb* **put** (on *or* upon) *vb*	verb combinations
put *n*	noun homograph

All of these verb entries are then followed by the noun **put**. Two-word verbs (verbs regularly followed by an adverb) that are commonly entered in dictionaries have been entered in boldface at their own alphabetical places in this book. However, they follow in alphabetical order all of those entries showing a verb with a preposition or adverb in parentheses. You can see this in the following example:

take *vb*	base verb
take (from) *vb* **take** (to) *vb*	verb combinations
take away *vb* **take back** *vb* **take down** *vb* **take in** *vb* **take off** *vb*	two-word verb

Headwords are entered according to normal dictionary practices. This means that nouns appear in the singular and verbs in the infinitive form. Special situations such as those showing plural usage or variant spellings are signaled by showing them in boldface subheads, as at the following entries:

crossroad *n, usu* **crossroads** *pl but sing or pl in constr* ***syn*** see JUNCTURE 2

woe *n* **3** *usu* **woes** *pl* ***syn*** see DISASTER

catercorner *or* **catty-corner** *or* **kitty-corner** *adv* ***syn*** see DIAGONALLY

In the above, **crossroads** and **woes** are subheads indicating plural usage of the headwords. **Catty-corner** and **kitty-corner** are subheads showing variant spellings of the headword.

The Main Entry and Its Elements

Each main entry is made up of a boldface headword followed by a part-of-speech label, a sense number when needed, a meaning core with a short verbal illustration, and a list of synonyms. Nearly all the time, the main entry also has lists of related words, idiomatic equivalents, contrasted words, and antonyms. A typical main entry is:

calm *adj* **1** free from storm or rough activity <the wind died and the sea became *calm*>
syn halcyon, hushed, placid, quiet, still, stilly, untroubled
rel inactive, quiescent, reposing, resting; pacific, smooth, tranquil, unruffled
idiom calm as a millpond, still as death
con agitated, disturbed, perturbed, restless, turbulent, uneasy
ant stormy

The headword **calm** is followed by the italic part-of-speech label *adj* which indicates that this word is an adjective. Other part-of-speech labels used in the book are *adv* (adverb), *conj* (conjunction), *interj* (interjection), *n* (noun), *prep* (preposition), *pron* (pronoun), and *vb* (verb).

Individual senses of entries such as **calm** *adj* with more than one sense are introduced by a boldface sense number.

The meaning core indicates the area of meaning in which a group of words are synonymous. At **calm 1**, for example, this reads "free from storm or rough activity". This is the meaning in which the words *calm, halcyon, hushed, placid, quiet, still, stilly,* and *untroubled* can be viewed as synonyms. In other words, the meaning core pinpoints the exact relationship between the main-entry headword and its synonyms.

Material showing a typical or occasionally a single object of reference is enclosed in parentheses, as in the meaning core of **express** *vb* **2**

to give expression to (as a thought, an opinion, or an emotion)

The parenthesized material is included to alert you to the fact that when this sense of **express** is used, it is usually in connection with "a thought, an opinion, or an emotion".

A meaning core also may have a usage note introduced by a lightface dash. This is used when more information or comments on usage are needed, as in the following example:

yet *adv* **1** beyond this — used as an intensive to stress the comparative degree

Some interjections express feelings but cannot be translated into a simple meaning; in such cases, the meaning core itself may be replaced by a usage note which describes the function of the interjection:

good-bye *interj* — used as a conventional expression of good wishes at parting

Each meaning core is followed by a verbal illustration enclosed by angle brackets, as

<the wind died and the sea became *calm*>

Here, the verbal illustration shows a typical use of the headword calm in the sense expressed by the meaning core.

The verbal illustration has another use. You can use it as a frame in which to test the suitability of a synonym or a related term in this particular context. At **calm 1** , for instance, you might want to see if the synonym *hushed* can be used exactly the same way *calm* can be. If you substitute *hushed* for *calm* in the verbal illustration, you will get:

<the wind died and the sea became *hushed*>

You will probably notice at once that this sounds a bit odd. Apparently *hushed* cannot always be used where *calm* can be used. English is full of similar slight differences in meaning and it is for this reason that you are urged to consult the more specific definitions in a good dictionary for any case that seems doubtful to you.

The boldface italic abbreviation ***syn*** introduces a synonym list that appears at each main entry on a line below the meaning core and the verbal illustration. In the Introduction on page 4a, you read about the aspects which governed the choosing of synonyms. The ***syn*** list may have only one synonym, as at the entry **hitherto** *adv* **2**, where *here* is the only synonym, or the list may have many synonyms, as *halcyon, hushed, placid, quiet, still, stilly*, and *untroubled* which are shown at **calm** *adj* **1**. Each synonym in a main-entry list is entered in boldface at its own alphabetical place.

A compare cross-reference may appear at the end of a main-entry ***syn*** list. This cross-reference is introduced by the italic word *compare*. You will find it when two or more groups of synonyms are very closely related and the editors felt that the user looking at one list should know of the existence of the other list. Examples of compare cross-references are found at the entries **assassin** and **murderer:**

assassin ***n*** a person hired or hirable to commit murder <found out who paid the *assassin*> ***syn*** bravo, cutthroat, gun, gunman, ||gunsel, gunslinger, hatchet man, hit man, torpedo, triggerman; *compare* MURDERER

murderer *n* one who kills a human being <a *murderer* who wouldn't hesitate to kill in cold blood>
syn homicide, killer, manslayer, slayer; *compare* ASSASSIN

You will notice that although the headwords are related, there are differences between **assassin** and **murderer** and their respective synonyms. It will help you, then, to find exactly the word you are looking for if you check out these compare cross-references when you see them.

The compare cross-reference is also used when closely related entries such as **ration** and

share 1 both include some of the same words as synonyms. This results from the way language tends to change, sometimes narrowing, sometimes broadening or even subdividing meanings. When this has happened the compare cross-reference warns you of words that, though appropriate to more than one synonym list, may in some contexts blur fine distinctions that you would like to make. A comparison of the main entries of **ration** *n* and **share** *n* **1** will point this up:

> **ration** *n* an amount allotted or made available especially from a limited supply <saved up their gasoline *ration* for a vacation trip>
> ***syn*** allotment, allowance, apportionment, measure, need, part, portion, quantum, quota, share; *compare* SHARE 1
>
> **share** *n* **1** something belonging to, assumed by, or falling to one (as in division or apportionment) <wanted his *share* of the prize money>
> ***syn*** allotment, allowance, bite, cut, lot, part, partage, portion, quota, slice; *compare* RATION

You will see that the synonyms *allotment, allowance, part, portion, quota,* and *share* are found in both lists. By taking these synonyms and substituting them in the verbal illustrations, you will find that they sound right, and can be interchanged. If, on the other hand, you take a synonym found in one list, but not in the other, for instance *cut* from the list at **share,** and substitute it in the verbal illustration at **ratio** *n,* you will find that the differences between the meaning cores become more obvious. If you say <wanted his *cut* of the prize money>, you are choosing a word which fits the context. If you try using *cut* in the verbal illustration at *ration,* <saved up their gasoline *cut* for a vacation trip> you will find that *cut* doesn't sound right. So, even though some of the same synonyms appear in both lists, you must be careful to distinguish among all the synonyms in every list. Don't forget to keep a good dictionary on hand to help you do this.

Many main entries include lists of related words, idiomatic equivalents, contrasted words, and antonyms. If an entry has all of these lists, they are shown in the order mentioned above. The boldface italic abbreviation ***rel*** introduces a list of related words. The related words are ones that are almost but not quite synonymous with the headword. These come immediately after the ***syn*** list. For example, at the main entry:

> **splendid** *adj* . . . **2** extraordinary or transcendently impressive <a *splendid* new city>
> ***syn*** glorious, gorgeous, magnificent, proud, resplendent, splendiferous, splendorous, sublime, superb
> ***rel*** eminent, illustrious; grand, impressive, lavish, luxurious, royal, sumptuous; divine, exquisite, lovely; incomparable, matchless, peerless, superlative, supreme, unparalleled, unsurpassed; surpassing, transcendent

the ***rel*** list is made up of twenty words separated by semicolons into five subgroups. Each of these subgroups shares a common relation to the headword and its synonyms. Related words are not entered in boldface at their own alphabetical places unless they are synonyms in other lists or head their own main entries.

The boldface italic abbreviation ***idiom*** introduces a list of idiomatic phrases that are essentially the same in meaning as the words of a synonym group. For a more detailed discussion of these phrases, you might look again at pages 5a & 6a in the Introduction. An ***idiom*** list at a main entry includes phrases that are generally pertinent to the entire ***syn*** list and the headword, as the ones at:

> **speak** *vb* **1** to articulate words in order to express thoughts <always *speak* clearly>
> ***syn*** talk, utter, verbalize, vocalize, voice
> ***rel*** . . .
> ***idiom*** break silence, give voice (*or* tongue *or* utterance) to, let fall, make public (*or* known), open one's mouth (*or* lips), put in (*or* into) words, say one's say, speak one's piece

Some idiomatic expressions may be used in more than one form. Such variation is shown in this thesaurus by including the variant word in parentheses. At **slavery** *n* **2**

> ***idiom*** the yoke (*or* chains) of slavery

gives you the choice of using either *yoke* or *chains* in the phrase.

Idiomatic phrases, including those fixed verb plus preposition combinations that act as idioms rather than as literal meanings of the verb are not entered in boldface at their own alphabetical places in this book.

The boldface italic abbreviation ***con*** introduces a list of contrasted words. This category contains terms that may be strongly contrasted with the headword, but are not quite antonyms of the headword. An example of a ***con*** list is:

> **watchful** *adj* paying close attention usually with a view to anticipating approaching danger or opportunity <adopted a policy of *watchful* waiting>
> ***syn*** alert, open-eyed, unsleeping, vigilant, wakeful, wide-awake
> ***rel*** . . .
> ***idiom*** . . .
> ***con*** careless, heedless, thoughless; inadvertent; absentminded, abstracted, faraway
> ***ant*** . . .

At this main entry, the ***con*** list is made up of seven words separated by semicolons into three subgroups. Each of these words may be contrasted with the headword *watchful* and with the words in its ***syn*** list. Contrasted words are not entered in boldface at their own alphabetical places unless they are synonyms in other lists or head their own main entries.

The boldface italic abbreviation ***ant*** introduces the last possible part of an entry. This is an antonym, as at the entry:

> **perfect** *adj* . . . **2** . . .
> ***ant*** imperfect

where *imperfect* is the antonym of **perfect 2**, or a list of antonyms as at the entry

> **quiet** *adj*. . . **4** not showy or obtrusive
> ***ant*** gaudy, loud

In the Introducton to this book on page 5a, you learned about the different classes of opposites to which antonyms belong. When antonyms come from different classes of opposites, they are separated by a semicolon, as at:

> **assistance** *n*
> ***syn*** see HELP 1
> ***rel*** backing, supporting, upholding; advantage, avail, profit, use; appropriation, grant, subsidy, subvention
> ***con*** checking, hampering, hindering, hindrance; balking, foiling, frustrating, thwarting
> ***ant*** impediment, impeding; obstructing, obstruction

In the above, *impediment* and *impeding* belong to the class of antonyms that are opposites with intermediates. If you study the ***rel*** and ***con*** lists at **assistance** you will see that the first sets of each group form a continuous series:

> backing, supporting, upholding *and* checking, hampering, hindering, hindrance

of which *assistance* forms one extreme and *impeding* (or *impediment*) forms the other. The second pair of antonyms are separated from the first by a semicolon because they belong to a different class — that of antonyms that are reverse opposites. The difference should be plain; *obstruction* (or *obstructing*) amounts to the undoing of whatever is implied by *assistance*.

You may find material in parentheses following antonyms, as at **abrogate** *vb* **2**:

> ***ant*** establish, fix (*as a right, a quality, or a custom*)

In such cases an antonym or group of antonyms is associated with a particular object or objects of reference. This information will help orient you in choosing the best word possible. Like related and contrasted words, antonyms are not entered in boldface at their own alphabetical places unless they are synonyms in other lists or head their own main entries.

The Secondary Entry

A secondary entry consists of a boldface headword followed by a part-of-speech label, a boldface sense number when needed, and most importantly, a ***syn*** see cross-reference in small capital letters directing you to the appropriate main entry in whose ***syn*** list the secondary entry appears. If this main entry has more than one sense, a lightface number follows the see cross-reference to tell you the sense to look for at the main entry.

Like the main entry, the secondary entry may also have lists of related words, idiomatic phrases, contrasted words, and antonyms. If it does, as at:

short *adj* . . . **7**
syn see CONCISE
rel compact; pointed
idiom to the point
con extended, protracted, spun-out
ant lengthy, long-drawn-out

the terms in the lists apply only to the boldface headword and not necessarily to all of the synonyms at the main entry to which there is a cross-reference. Normally, only a few related words, idiomatic phrases, contrasted words, and antonyms found at the main entry are repeated at the secondary entry. For this reason you should check the main entry for the most complete collection of terms.

Main and Secondary Entries: the One Arbitrary Rule

There is one rule in particular which the editors have followed in working with both main and secondary entries: *no word may appear in more than one list at any single sense of a main or a secondary entry.* For example, *nice* is a synonym at **pleasant** *adj* **1,** which has the meaning core "highly acceptable to the mind or senses". You might reasonably consider other senses of *nice* to qualify it as a related word at **pleasant** *adj* **1,** in addition to its entry as a synonym. This could be the sense meaning "mild", in <the *nice* weather of late spring> or that meaning "suitable", as in <the *nice* clothes she wears>. Further, there is even a sense of *nice* which means "unpleasant", as in <got into a *nice* fix> which could qualify it as a contrasted word or even as an antonym. You can see how confusing the entry would have looked with *nice* shown at three or four places. In order to be as clear as possible, then, each entry shows a word in only one list at any one sense.

Labels

As we mentioned earlier, the part-of-speech label found at each entry is one of the following: *adj* (adjective), *adv* (adverb), *conj* (conjunction), *interj* (interjection), *n* (noun), *prep* (preposition), *pron* (pronoun), and *vb* (verb).

Words that are labeled *cap* or *usu[ally] cap* in Webster's Third New International Dictionary are capitalized in this book:

Gehenna *n*
syn see HELL

If only one entered sense of a word is capitalized, an italic cap label followed by the boldface capitalized form is shown at the appropriate sense:

pandemonium *n* **1** *cap* **Pandemonium** ***syn*** see HELL
2 ***syn*** see SINK 1
3 ***syn*** see DIN 1

Pandemonium should be capitalized when it is used as a synonym of *hell*. When *pandemonium* is used as a synonym of *sink* (sense 1) or *din* (sense 1), it is not capitalized. In addition to the part-of-speech label, an italic label *pl* may be present to indicate that a word or a sense of a word is used in the plural.

Some words are always used in the plural. A typical example is:

years *n pl* ***syn*** see OLD AGE

The *pl* label shows that the headword **years** is plural in form and takes a plural verb when used to mean *old age*.

Some words are often used in the plural and are so labeled:

> **road** *n* **1** *often* **roads** *pl* ***syn*** see HARBOR 3
> **2** ***syn*** see WAY 1
> **3** ***syn*** see WAY 2

This label means that about half the time the word is used in the plural and about half the time it is used in the singular. In the above example, only sense 1 of the headword is often used in the plural.

Some words are usually used in the plural and are so labeled. This means that more often than not, the word will be found in the plural:

> **minutia** *n, usu* **minutiae** *pl* **1** ***syn*** see INS AND OUTS
> **2** ***syn*** see TRIVIA

The placing of the label before both senses indicates that the headword **minutia** is usually but not always used in the plural in both senses.

There are words which are plural in form, but which may sometimes take a singular verb in construction. An example is:

> **trivia** *n pl but sometimes sing in constr* . . .

Other words are plural in form but are as likely to take a plural verb as a singular one. The first entered sense of **common** is such a case:

> **common** *n* **1** **commons** *pl but sing or pl in constr*
> ***syn*** see COMMONALTY

The label shows that in this use *common* occurs only in plural form but may take either a plural or a singular verb.

Finally, there are nouns which are plural in form and always take a singular verb:

> **outdoors** *n pl but sing in constr* the space where air is unconfined <every night he let the dog run in the *outdoors*>

One other label which you will see used a few times in this thesaurus is an italic subject guide phrase. The subject guide phrase precedes the meaning core and indicates that the meaning core is limited in application. At **set** *vb*

> **set** *vb* **11** *of a fowl* to incubate eggs by crouching upon them . . .

the phrase *of a fowl* indicates that in this sense **set** is used of a fowl (and not, for instance, of people or crocodiles).

Symbol

One warning symbol is used in this book: double bars ‖. This is placed before a word to alert you that its usage is in some way restricted. Whenever this symbol appears you should check the word in a good dictionary if you are unfamiliar with it. A double-barred word might be slang, as ‖*fat cat* at the entry **notable** *n*. A word may be used by only one segment of the English-speaking population, as ‖*nipper* at **kid** *n* which is chiefly British, or ‖*swarf* at **faint** *vb* which is Scottish. The word might also be an American regional term, such as the Western word ‖*Rocky Mountain Canary* which is a synonym of **donkey** *n*, or the Southern word ‖*glade* which is a related word at **swamp** *n*. These words have been included in this thesaurus to introduce you to the extensive range of the English language and to help you stretch your vocabulary. In order to know exactly which restriction the double bars for each term carries, you are urged to consult a good dictionary.

All double-barred words in this thesaurus follow the labels shown in Webster's Third New International Dictionary.

A

abaft *adv* **syn** see UNAWARES

abaft *adv* toward or at the stern (of a vessel) <headed *abaft* for a smoke>
syn aft, astern
rel after, back, behind
ant forward

abaft *prep* to the rear of <huddled in a nook *abaft* the chimney>
syn back of, behind

abalienate *vb* **syn** see TRANSFER 4

abandon *vb* **1** to give up without intent to return or reclaim <*abandoned* his family>
syn chuck, desert, forsake, quit, renounce, throw over
rel cast (off), discard, disuse, drop, junk, scrap; reject, repudiate
idiom have done with, leave flat, quit cold, run out on, turn one's back on (*or* upon), walk out on
con hold, keep, possess, retain; redeem, rescue, save; acquire, gain, get, procure, win; cherish, foster
ant reclaim
2 syn see RELINQUISH
ant retain

abandon *n* **1 syn** see UNCONSTRAINT
2 carefree disregard for consequences <behave with *abandon*>
syn impulsiveness, uninhibitedness, unrestraint; *compare* UNCONSTRAINT
rel freedom, liberty, license; exuberance, heedlessness, laxity, laxness, looseness, unruliness, wildness; incontinence, licentiousness, wantonness; fun, games, play, sport
con constraint, inhibitedness, inhibition, restraint; repression, suppression
ant self-restraint

abandoned *adj* **1 syn** see DERELICT 1
2 free from moral restraint <led a thoroughly *abandoned* life>
syn dissolute, licentious, profligate, reprobate, self-abandoned, unprincipled
rel debased, debauched, depraved, perverted, riotous; incorrigible; lascivious, lecherous, lewd, wanton; corrupt, degenerate
idiom dead to honor, gone to the bad, lost to shame, rotten (to *or* at) the core
con ethical, high-principled, moral, reputable, virtuous; correct, decent, decorous, proper, seemly
ant scrupulous, upright

abase *vb* **syn** see HUMBLE
rel demote, diminish, downgrade, reduce; fawn, grovel, toady; cower, cringe, truckle
con elevate, lift, raise
ant exalt; extol

abash *vb* **syn** see EMBARRASS 1
rel abase, demean, humble, humiliate
idiom make one eat humble pie
ant embolden, reassure

abashment *n* **syn** see EMBARRASSMENT

abate *vb* **1 syn** see ABOLISH 1
2 syn see ANNIHILATE 2
3 syn see DECREASE
4 to lessen in force or intensity <the storm *abated* slowly>
syn ‖bate, die (down *or* away), ease off, ebb, fall, let up, lull, moderate, relent, slacken, subside, wane
rel decrease, diminish, dwindle, lessen, weaken
idiom run its course
con augment, expand, extend, increase; mount, rage, soar, surge
ant revive; rise

abatement *n* **syn** see DEDUCTION 1
con enlargement, increase
ant addition

abbreviate *vb* **syn** see SHORTEN
rel attenuate, extenuate
con enlarge, increase; amplify, dilate, expand
ant lengthen; extend

ABC *n* **1** *usu* **ABC's** *pl* **syn** see ALPHABET 1
2 *often* **ABC's** *pl* **syn** see ALPHABET 2

abdicate *vb* **1** to part formally or definitely with a position of honor or power <the king *abdicated* the throne in order to marry a commoner>
syn demit, renounce, resign; *compare* RELINQUISH
rel abandon, leave, relinquish, surrender; drop; withdraw
con appropriate, arrogate, confiscate; grab, seize, take over, wrest
ant assume, usurp
2 syn see DISCARD
con keep, retain, treasure

abdomen *n* the part of the body between the chest and the pelvis <intense pain in the lower *abdomen*>
syn belly, ‖gut, paunch, stomach, tummy, venter
rel bay window, ‖breadbasket, corporation, pod, pot, potbelly; middle, midriff, midsection

abduct *vb* **syn** see KIDNAP
rel grab, seize

abecedarian *n* **syn** see AMATEUR 2

aberrant *adj* **1 syn** see ABNORMAL 1
rel different, disparate, divergent; eccentric, odd, peculiar, strange; exceptional, unusual
con natural, normal, regular, typical; customary, usual, wonted

---

syn synonym(s) **rel** related word(s)
ant antonym(s) **con** contrasted word(s)
idiom idiomatic equivalent(s)
‖ use limited; if in doubt, see a dictionary

ant true (*to a type*)
2 ***syn*** see ERRANT 2

aberration *n* **1** ***syn*** see DEVIATION 1
rel abnormality; mistake, slip; curiosity, oddity, prodigy, rarity
con average, mean, norm; normality
ant conformity; regularity
2 ***syn*** see INSANITY 1
ant soundness (*of mind*)

abet *vb* **1** ***syn*** see INCITE
rel egg, exhort, goad, prod, spur, urge; advocate, countenance, encourage, endorse
con forbid, prevent, prohibit; debar, deter, discourage
2 ***syn*** see HELP 1

abettor *n* ***syn*** see CONFEDERATE

abeyance *n* a state of temporary inactivity <the warm dry weather kept his asthma in *abeyance*>
syn abeyancy, cold storage, doldrums, dormancy, intermission, interruption, latency, quiescence, quiescency, suspension
rel break, interval, pause, respite
con activeness, activity, stir
ant continuance

abeyancy *n* ***syn*** see ABEYANCE
ant continuancy

abeyant *adj* ***syn*** see LATENT
rel deferred, intermitted, postponed, stayed, suppressed; repressed
con refreshed, renewed, restored
ant active, operative; revived

abhor *vb* **1** ***syn*** see HATE
2 ***syn*** see DESPISE
con dote (on *or* upon), like, love
ant admire

abhorrence *n* ***syn*** see ABOMINATION 2
rel distaste, repellency; dismay, horror
con affection, attachment, love
ant admiration; enjoyment

abhorrent *adj* **1** ***syn*** see HATEFUL 2
ant admirable
2 ***syn*** see REPUGNANT 1
rel antipathetic; uncongenial, unsympathetic
con alluring, attractive, captivating; enticing, seductive, tempting
ant congenial

abide *vb* **1** ***syn*** see STAY 2
rel adhere, cleave, cling, stick; dwell, live, reside
con go, leave, quit; move, remove, shift
ant depart
2 ***syn*** see CONTINUE 1
rel linger; exist, subsist
con avoid, elude, escape, evade
ant pass
3 ***syn*** see BEAR 10
rel accept, receive; accede, consent
idiom put up with
4 ***syn*** see RESIDE 1

abiding *adj* ***syn*** see SURE 2
rel durable, lasting, perdurable, persistent
con ephemeral, impermanent, short-lived, transient, transitory

ability *n* **1** physical, mental, or legal power to perform <he has the *ability* to accomplish whatever he sets his mind to>
syn adequacy, capability, capacity, competence, might, qualification, qualifiedness
rel address, adroitness, cleverness, dexterity; aptitude, aptness, facility, knack
idiom what it takes
con impotence, inadequacy, incapability, incompetence
ant inability
2 natural or acquired proficiency especially in a particular activity <he has unusual *ability* in planning and designing>
syn command, expertise, expertism, expertness, knack, know-how, mastership, mastery, skill
rel adroitness, deftness, efficiency, handiness, proficiency; ingenuity, resourcefulness; talent
con inadequacy, incompetence, ineffectualness, unfitness; fatuity, futility, inanity

abject *adj* ***syn*** see DOWNTRODDEN

abjure *vb* to give up (something formerly adhered to) irrevocably and usually solemnly or formally <an immigrant solemnly *abjuring* allegiance to his former country>
syn forswear, palinode, recall, recant, retract, take back, unsay, withdraw
rel disavow, disown, renounce, repudiate; abandon, desert, forsake; cede, relinquish, surrender
idiom eat one's words

ablaze *adj* **1** ***syn*** see BURNING 1
2 ***syn*** see ALIGHT 2

able *adj* possessed of or marked by a high level of efficiency and ability <an *able* student always near the head of his class>
syn au fait, capable, competent, good, proper, qualified, wicked
rel effective, effectual, efficient; expert, proficient, skilled, skillful; alert, clever, keen, sharp; brainy, brilliant, intelligent, smart; enterprising, go-ahead, up-and-coming
con ineffective, ineffectual, inefficient; incapable, incompetent, unqualified; fair, indifferent, mediocre; lackluster, maladroit
ant inept; unable

abnegation *n* ***syn*** see RENUNCIATION

abnormal *adj* **1** departing significantly from the normal or a norm <the *abnormal* rains caused flooding>
syn aberrant, anomalous, atypical, deviant, deviative, heteroclite, preternatural, unrepresentative, untypical
rel divergent, offtype; irregular, unnatural; uncustomary, unusual, unwonted; heteromorphic; paratypic
con common, familiar, natural, ordinary, regular, typical; customary, usual, wonted
ant normal
2 ***syn*** see IRREGULAR 1

abode *n* ***syn*** see HABITATION 2

abolish *vb* **1** to bring to an end often by formal or concerted action <*abolish* a tax>
syn abate, abrogate, annihilate, annul, circumduct, invalidate, negate, nullify, quash, undo, vitiate

rel cancel, disallow, disannul, repeal, rescind, revoke, vacate
idiom bring to naught, make void, set aside
con conserve, preserve, save; keep, retain
2 ***syn*** see ANNIHILATE 2
con found, institute
ant establish

abominable *adj* ***syn*** see HATEFUL 2
rel accursed, cursed; loathsome, offensive, repugnant, revolting
con applaudable, commendable
ant laudable (*as practices, customs*); delightful, enjoyable

abominate *vb* ***syn*** see HATE
rel curse, damn, objurgate
idiom hold in abomination, take an aversion to
con admire, regard
ant enjoy; esteem

abomination *n* **1** one that is a source of utter disgust or intense dislike <found the new tax form an *abomination* of confused complexity>
syn anathema, bête noire, black beast, bugbear, detestation, hate
rel annoyance, pest, plague, trial; bogey, bugaboo, incubus
con delectation, delight, joy, pleasure; treasure
2 a feeling of extreme disgust and dislike <they hold every indulgence in *abomination*>
syn abhorrence, aversion, detestation, hate, hatred, horror, loathing, repugnance, repugnancy, repulsion, revulsion
rel contempt, despite, disdain, scorn; disfavor, dislike, disrelish, distaste
con admiration, regard, respect; fondness, liking, relish, taste; approbation, approval, countenance, favor; acceptance, tolerance
ant esteem; enjoyment

aboriginal *adj* ***syn*** see NATIVE 2
rel primeval, primitive, primordial, pristine; barbarian, barbaric, barbarous, savage
con advanced, progressive; civilized, cultured; sequent, successive

abort *vb* ***syn*** CANCEL 2
rel end, terminate; scrap, scratch

abortion *n* ***syn*** see FREAK 2

abortive *adj* ***syn*** see FUTILE
rel unformed; immature, unmatured, unripe
con accomplished, completed, concluded, finished
ant consummated

abound *vb* ***syn*** see TEEM

abounding *adj* ***syn*** see ALIVE 5
rel full, jammed, packed, stuffed

about *adv* **1** in every direction <looked carefully *about*>
syn around, round, round about
2 in a circuitous way or course <took the long way *about*>
syn circuitously, round about
3 ***syn*** see NEARLY
4 here or there without plan or order <left his tools lying *about*>
syn anyhow, any which way, anywise, around, at random, haphazard, haphazardly, helter-skelter, random, randomly
rel back and forth, hither and thither, to and fro; aimlessly, carelessly, casually
5 in the vicinity <talked to the people standing *about*>
syn near, near-at-hand, nearby
idiom close by
6 in the opposite direction <he turned *about* and saw her>
syn again, around, back, backward, in reverse, round, round about
idiom in one's course

about *prep* **1** in the vicinity of <*about* five miles to go>
syn around, circa, close on, near, nearby, nigh
idiom hard by, not far from
2 ***syn*** see APROPOS
idiom in point of, with regard to
3 ***syn*** see OVER 3
4 here and there upon or within <traveled *about* the country>
syn round, through, throughout
idiom all over

about–face *n* ***syn*** see REVERSAL 1

above *adv* **1** ***syn*** see OVER 4
ant below
2 higher on the same page or on a preceding page <earlier examples appear *above*>
syn supra
ant below, infra

above *prep* **1** ***syn*** see OVER 1
ant below
2 ***syn*** see BEYOND 2

aboveboard *adj* ***syn*** see STRAIGHTFORWARD 2
rel open, scrupulous; artless, ingenuous, unsophisticated
con clandestine, covert, furtive, secret, surreptitious; deceitful; crooked, devious, oblique
ant underhand, underhanded

abracadabra *n* ***syn*** see GIBBERISH 3
rel mystification; argot, cant, jargon

abrade *vb* **1** to injure or flaw by frictional action <wind-driven sand *abraded* the glass>
syn chafe, corrade, erode, gall, graze, rub, ruffle, wear
rel corrode, eat away, fret; grate, rasp, scrape
2 ***syn*** see CHAFE 3
rel burn
3 ***syn*** see ANNOY 1
rel disorganize, disturb, flurry, rattle; confuse, distract, perturb
con calm, relieve, soothe

Abraham's bosom *n* ***syn*** see HEAVEN 2

abreast *adj* **1** ***syn*** see UP-TO-DATE
2 ***syn*** see FAMILIAR 3

abridge *vb* **1** to make less by in some manner restricting <laws that *abridge* freedom of speech>
syn curtail, diminish, lessen, minify
rel limit, narrow, reduce, restrict; minimize
con augment, broaden, enlarge, extend

---

syn synonym(s) ***rel*** related word(s)
ant antonym(s) ***con*** contrasted word(s)
idiom idiomatic equivalent(s)
‖ use limited; if in doubt, see a dictionary

ant amplify
2 *syn* see SHORTEN
con amplify, augment, enlarge, increase
ant expand, extend

abridgment *n* a shortened version of a larger work or treatment produced by condensing and omitting without basic alteration of intent and language <an *abridgment* of a dictionary>
syn abstract, boildown, breviary, breviate, brief, condensation, conspectus, epitome, synopsis
rel aperçu, compendium, digest, outline, précis, sketch, syllabus; capsule, summary; sum, summation, summing-up
con elaboration; paraphrase
ant expansion

abroad *adv syn* see OVERSEAS

abrogate *vb* **1** *syn* see ANNUL 4
rel abate, extinguish
con establish, found; confirm, ratify
ant institute (*as by enacting or decreeing*)
2 *syn* see ABOLISH 1
rel extinguish; blot out, cancel, obliterate; ruin, wreck
con support, uphold
ant establish, fix (*as a right, a quality, or a custom*)

abrupt *adj* **1** *syn* see PRECIPITATE 1
rel hastened; casual, informal, unceremonious; quick, speedy
con dilatory, laggard; easy, relaxed
ant deliberate, leisurely
2 *syn* see BLUFF
rel brisk, crisp, sharp; impetuous, quick, ready
con calm, easy, relaxed
3 *syn* see STEEP 1
rel perpendicular, plumb, vertical
con inclined, slanting; flat, level, plane, smooth
ant sloping

abruptly *adv syn* see SHORT 1

abscess *n* a localized swollen area of infection containing pus <had an *abscess* on his leg>
syn boil, carbuncle, furuncle, pimple, pustule
rel lesion, sore, trauma; botch, ulcer

abscond *vb syn* see ESCAPE 1
rel go, leave, quit, withdraw
idiom do the disappearing act, skip out, take French leave
con render, surrender, yield
ant give (oneself) up

absence *n* the state of being absent or missing <the *absence* of news was disturbing>
syn dearth, default, defect, lack, ‖miss, privation, want; *compare* FAILURE 3
rel deficiency, drought, inadequacy, insufficiency; exigency, necessity, need; vacuum, void; nonappearance, nonattendance
con abundance, copiousness, plenty
ant presence

absent *adj* **1** not now present <all missed their *absent* friend>
syn away, gone, lacking, missing, omitted, wanting
ant present
2 *syn* see ABSTRACTED
rel absorbed; forgetful, heedless
con attending, hearkening, listening; considerate, thoughtful
ant attentive

absentminded *adj syn* see ABSTRACTED
rel unnoticing, unobserving, unperceiving, unseeing; heedless, inattentive
idiom lost in thought
con alert; aware
ant wide-awake

absolute *adj* **1** *syn* see PERFECT 2
rel pure, sheer, simple
con circumscribed, limited, partial, restricted
2 *syn* see PURE 2
rel abstract, ideal; real, true
con imperfect, incomplete
ant mixed, qualified
3 *syn* see UTTER
4 exercising power or authority without external restraint <an *absolute* monarch>
syn arbitrary, autarchic, autocratic, despotic, monocratic, tyrannical, tyrannous; *compare* TOTALITARIAN 1
rel dictatorial, magisterial; authoritarian, totalitarian; domineering, imperious, masterful; plenipotential, plenipotentiary, unlimited
con circumscribed, limited, restrained, restricted; constitutional, lawful
5 *syn* see ACTUAL 2
6 *syn* see ULTIMATE 3
rel ideal, transcendent, transcendental; autonomous, free, independent, sovereign; boundless, eternal, infinite
con circumscribed, limited, restricted; conditional, contingent, dependent

absolutely *adv syn* see EASILY 2

absolution *n syn* see PARDON
rel condonation
con censure, reprehension, reprobation
ant condemnation

absolve *vb* **1** *syn* see EXEMPT
2 *syn* see EXCULPATE
rel discharge, free, release
con condemn, doom, sentence; chasten, discipline, punish
ant charge (with), hold (to)

absorb *vb* **1** to take in and make a part of one's being <*absorb* knowledge from reading>
syn assimilate, imbibe, incorporate, inhaust, insorb
rel embody, imbue, impregnate, infuse, permeate
con disgorge, eject, expel, vomit; discharge, eliminate, emit, give off, pass
ant exude, give out
2 *syn* see MONOPOLIZE
rel concern, engage, immerse, involve, preoccupy
con diffuse, disperse, scatter
ant dissipate (*as time, attention*)

absorbed *adj syn* see INTENT
rel involved
idiom caught up in, up to the elbows (*or* ears) in
con apathetic, disinterested, indifferent, unconcerned; uninterested; absent, abstracted

ant distracted

absorbing *adj* ***syn*** see ENGROSSING
ant irksome

abstain *vb* **1** ***syn*** see DENY 3
rel abnegate, eschew, forgo; decline, refuse, reject, spurn
idiom dispense with, do without, let alone
con pamper; gratify, regale; sate, satiate, surfeit
ant indulge
2 ***syn*** see REFRAIN 1

abstemious *adj* marked by restraint in satisfying desires (as for food, drink, or pleasure) <an *abstemious* man, little given to self-indulgence>
syn abstentious, abstinent, continent, self-restraining, sober, temperate; *compare* SOBER 3
rel self-abnegating, self-denying; ascetic, austere; sparing
con greedy, rapacious, voracious; epicurean, sybaritic, voluptuous
ant gluttonous

abstentious *adj* ***syn*** see ABSTEMIOUS
ant gluttonous

abstinence *n* ***syn*** see TEMPERANCE 2
rel renunciation
con gorging, sating, surfeiting; immoderateness, overdoing, unrestraint; crapulence, excess, extravagance
ant self-indulgence

abstinent *adj* ***syn*** see ABSTEMIOUS
ant gluttonous

abstract *adj* **1** having conceptual rather than concrete existence <the *abstract* perfect society>
syn hypothetical, ideal, theoretical, transcendent, transcendental
rel academic, impractical, utopian, visionary; speculative, undemonstrable; conceptual, notional; inconcrete
con corporeal, material, objective, phenomenal, physical; actual, factual, real
ant concrete
2 ***syn*** see NEUTRAL

abstract *n* ***syn*** see ABRIDGMENT
con enlargement, expansion
ant amplification

abstract *vb* **1** ***syn*** see DETACH
rel divide, part, separate
con insinuate, interpolate, interpose
ant insert, introduce
2 ***syn*** see STEAL 1

abstracted *adj* withdrawn in mind and inattentive to external matters <seemed *abstracted* and remote>
syn absent, absentminded, bemused, distrait, faraway, inconscient, lost, preoccupied
rel engrossed, intent, rapt; oblivious, unmindful, unminding; heedless, inattentive
idiom in a brown study, lost in thought, lost to the world
con attentive, vigilant, watchful, wide-awake; noticing, noting, observant, seeing
ant alert

abstruse *adj* ***syn*** see RECONDITE
rel complex, complicated, intricate, knotty; abstract, hypothetical, ideal
con clear, evident, manifest, palpable; clear, lucid, perspicuous; easy, facile, simple
ant obvious, plain

absurd *adj* ***syn*** see FOOLISH 2
rel comic, droll, funny; asinine, fatuous, simple; irrational, unreasonable
con logical, ratiocinative, subtle
ant rational, sensible

absurdity *n* ***syn*** see FOOLISHNESS

abundance *n* ***syn*** see PROSPERITY 2
rel adequacy, competence, enough, plenty, sufficiency; lavishness, prodigality
idiom enough and to spare
con deficiency, inadequacy, insufficiency, lack, paucity

abundant *adj* ***syn*** see PLENTIFUL
rel lavish, lush, luxuriant, profuse; crammed, crowded, thick; common
idiom in good supply
con infrequent, rare, uncommon; inadequate, scanty
ant scarce

abuse *vb* **1** ***syn*** see DECRY 2
ant praise
2 to put to a bad or improper use <*abuse* the prerogatives of office>
syn misapply, misemploy, mishandle, misimprove, misuse, pervert, prostitute
rel mar, spoil; corrupt, debase, desecrate, profane
idiom make ill use of
con esteem, honor, respect
3 ***syn*** see EXPLOIT 2
4 to treat without compassion and usually in a hurtful manner <parents who *abuse* children>
syn ill-treat, ill-use, maltreat, mistreat, misuse, outrage
rel damage, harm, hurt, impair, injure; oppress, persecute, wrong; manhandle, mess (up)
idiom do one dirt, do violence to
con cherish, prize, treasure; esteem, revere, reverence, venerate
ant honor, respect

abuse *n* vehemently and usually coarsely expressed condemnation or disapproval <had an unequaled vocabulary of *abuse*>
syn billingsgate, contumely, invective, obloquy, scurrility, vituperation
rel calumny, defamation, malignment, mud, vilification; cursing, profanity, swearing; berating, railing, rating, reviling
con acclaim, laudation, praise; applause, commendation, compliment
ant adulation

abusive *adj* coarse, insulting, and contemptuous in character or utterance <an *abusive* denunciation>

---

syn synonym(s) — *rel* related word(s)
ant antonym(s) — *con* contrasted word(s)
idiom idiomatic equivalent(s)
‖ use limited; if in doubt, see a dictionary

THESAURUS

syn contumelious, invective, opprobrious, scurrile, scurrilous, truculent, vituperative, vituperatory, vituperous
rel affronting, insulting, offending, outraging; dirty, odious, offensive; aspersing, maligning, vilifying
con acclaiming, extolling, lauding, praising; eulogistic, panegyrical; flattering
ant complimentary; respectful

abut *vb syn* see ADJOIN

abutting *adj syn* see ADJACENT 3
rel connecting, joining; impinging
con detached, disengaged; disassociated, disconnected, disjoined, parted, separated

abysm *n syn* see GULF 2

abysmal *adj* **1** *syn* see BOTTOMLESS 2
2 *syn* see DEEP 1
rel illimitable, infinite

abyss *n* **1** *syn* see HELL
2 *syn* see GULF 2
3 *syn* see DEPTH 2

academic *adj* **1** *syn* see PEDANTIC
con ignorant, illiterate, unlettered; down-to-earth, everyday, practical, realistic, straightforward
2 *syn* see THEORETICAL 1
rel impractical, utopian, visionary; chimerical, imaginary

accede *vb syn* see ASSENT
rel concur, cooperate; allow, let, permit
con decline; balk, shy, stick; expostulate, kick, object, protest; fight, oppose, resist, withstand
ant demur

accelerate *vb syn* see SPEED 3
rel drive, impel
idiom get going, make up for lost time
con clog, hamper; delay, detain, slow
ant decelerate; retard

accent *n* **1** *syn* see INFLECTION
2 *syn* see EMPHASIS
rel cadence, meter, rhythm; beat, pulsation, pulse, throb

accentuation *n syn* see EMPHASIS
con evenness, sameness, steadiness, uniformity
ant inaccentuation

accept *vb* **1** *syn* see APPROVE 1
rel fancy, like, relish; admire, esteem
con discountenance, disesteem, dislike, disrelish
ant reject
2 to take or sustain without protest or repining <a losing candidate must *accept* the decision of the electorate>
syn bear (with), endure, pocket, swallow, tolerate, tough (out); *compare* BEAR 10
rel acquiesce (in), agree (to *or* with), assent (to), subscribe (to); respect; bow, capitulate, yield
idiom abide by, put up with
con disavow, disown; brush (aside), deny, reject, repudiate
3 *syn* see BELIEVE 1
4 *syn* see APPREHEND 1

acceptable *adj syn* see DECENT 4
rel average, commonplace, ordinary; bearable, endurable, supportable
con insupportable, intolerable, unbearable, unendurable
ant unacceptable

acceptably *adv syn* see WELL 4

acceptant *adj syn* see RECEPTIVE 1

acceptation *n syn* see MEANING 1

accepted *adj* **1** *syn* see USUAL 1
rel conventional, established, recognized; correct, orthodox, proper, right
idiom according to custom (*or* use)
con irregular, questionable, unacceptable, unconventional; incongruent, unconformable, unorthodox
2 *syn* see ORTHODOX 1

acceptive *adj syn* see RECEPTIVE 1

access *n* **1** *syn* see ATTACK 3
rel onset; taking; pang, stitch, twinge
2 *syn* see OUTBURST 1
3 *syn* see DOOR 2
rel passage, route
con departure, retreat, withdrawal
ant egress; outlet

accessible *adj* **1** *syn* see OPEN 4
rel approachable
con limited, restricted; remote
2 *syn* see OPEN 5
ant inaccessible

accession *n syn* see ADDITION
ant discard

accessory *n* **1** *syn* see APPENDAGE
rel accompaniment, concomitant; accretion, addition, increment
2 *syn* see CONFEDERATE
ant principal

accessory *adj syn* see AUXILIARY
rel secondary, subordinate, tributary; coincident, concomitant, concurrent; adventitious, incidental
con constitutional, ingrained, inherent, intrinsic; cardinal, fundamental, vital; essential, indispensable, necessary
ant constituent, integral

accident *n* **1** absence of positive plan or intent <we stopped there by *accident*>
syn chance, fortuity, hap, luck
rel fluke, fortune, hazard
con design, premeditation
ant intent
2 a chance event bringing injury, loss, or distress <the school was closed by an *accident* to the heating system>
syn casualty, misadventure, mischance, mishap
rel calamity, catastrophe, disaster, tragedy; misfortune; chance, destiny, fate, kismet
con foreordination, predestination

accidental *adj* resulting from chance <an *accidental* meeting>
syn casual, chance, contingent, fluky, fortuitous, incidental, odd; *compare* RANDOM, UNINTENTIONAL
rel conditional, dependent; coincident, coincidental; inadvertent, undesigned, unintended, unintentional, unmeant, unplanned, unpurposed, unwitting

con designed, intended, purposed; constitutional, inherent, intrinsic; innate
ant planned; essential

accidentally *adv* ***syn*** see INCIDENTALLY 1

acclaim *vb* ***syn*** see COMMEND 2
rel cheer, root (for); exalt, magnify; glorify, honor
con berate, rate, revile; damn, execrate, objurgate; censure, denounce
ant vituperate

acclaim *n* ***syn*** see APPLAUSE
rel homage, honor, reverence; éclat, glory
con abuse, invective, obloquy; censure, condemnation, denunciation, reprobation
ant vituperation

acclamation *n* ***syn*** see APPLAUSE

acclimate *vb* ***syn*** see HARDEN 2

acclimatize *vb* ***syn*** see HARDEN 2

accolade *n* ***syn*** see HONOR 2

accommodate *vb* **1** ***syn*** see ADAPT
rel bow, defer, submit, yield; alter, change, modify, vary
con alienate, estrange
ant constrain
2 ***syn*** see HARMONIZE 3
3 ***syn*** see OBLIGE 2
rel cater (to), humor, indulge
con annoy, harass, harry; irk, vex, worry
ant incommode
4 ***syn*** see CONTAIN 2
rel encase, enclose
5 ***syn*** see HARBOR 2

accommodations *n pl* shelter, food, and services (as at a hotel) <searched for *accommodations* as night drew near>
syn lodging, lodgment, room and board
rel bed, room; keep; housing, shelter
idiom bed and breakfast

accompaniment *n* **1** something added to a principal thing usually to increase its impact or effectiveness <her song had a soft orchestral *accompaniment*>
syn augmentation, complement, enhancement, enrichment
rel accessory, addition, supplement; aid, assistance, help
2 an accompanying individual, situation, or occurrence <smog is an inevitable *accompaniment* of excessive numbers of automobiles>
syn associate, companion, concomitant, consort, fellow, mate
rel attendant, colleague, comrade, partner; corollary, equivalent

accompany *vb* to go or be together with <*accompanied* his wife to the theater>
syn attend, bear, ||bring, ||carry, chaperon, companion, company, conduct, consort (with), convoy, escort
rel associate, combine, join, link; defend, guard, protect, safeguard, shield; guide, lead, pilot, steer
idiom bear one company, go along with, go hand in hand with
con leave, quit, withdraw; abandon, forsake

accompanying *adj* ***syn*** see CONCOMITANT

accomplice *n* ***syn*** see CONFEDERATE
rel aider, assistant, helper; flunky, stooge

accomplish *vb* ***syn*** see GAIN 1

accomplished *adj* ***syn*** see CONSUMMATE 1
rel adept, expert, masterly, proficient; all-around, many-sided, versatile

accomplishment *n* **1** ***syn*** see ACQUIREMENT
rel art, craft, skill; adeptness, expertise, expertness, proficiency
2 ***syn*** see ACTION 1

accord *vb* **1** ***syn*** see AGREE 4
rel coincide, concur; blend, coalesce, fuse, merge
con differ, disagree; compare, contrast
ant conflict
2 ***syn*** see GRANT 1
rel allot
con deny, gainsay; refuse; detain, hold, reserve
ant withhold
3 ***syn*** see GIVE 2

accord *n* **1** ***syn*** see HARMONY 2
rel affinity, attraction, empathy, sympathy; solidarity, union
idiom community of interest(s)
con conflict, contention, difference; animosity, antipathy, hostility
ant dissension, strife; antagonism
2 ***syn*** see AGREEMENT 2
3 ***syn*** see HARMONY 1

accordant *adj* ***syn*** see HARMONIOUS 2

accordingly *adv* ***syn*** see THEREFORE
idiom by reason of that (*or* this), for that (*or* this) reason

according to *prep* ***syn*** see BY 5

accost *vb* **1** ***syn*** see ADDRESS 7
rel buttonhole
con ignore, overlook, slight; avoid, elude, evade, shun
2 to approach boldly or in a challenging or sometimes a defensive manner <*accosted* by a beggar who demanded money>
syn confront, face, front
rel affront, insult, offend, outrage; annoy, bother; challenge, dare, outface
idiom come face to face with, meet face to face
3 ***syn*** see ADDRESS 4
rel call (to), hail, halloo; buttonhole; dog, hound, pester, worry

accouchement *n* ***syn*** see CONFINEMENT 2

account *n* **1** ***syn*** see BILL 1
2 ***syn*** see USE 3
con immateriality, inconsequence, insignificance, unimportance; bootlessness, fruitlessness, futility
3 ***syn*** see WORTH 1
4 ***syn*** see REGARD 4
rel consequence, dignity, distinction, note; reputation, repute

---

syn synonym(s) ***rel*** related word(s)
ant antonym(s) ***con*** contrasted word(s)
idiom idiomatic equivalent(s)
|| use limited; if in doubt, see a dictionary

5 *syn* see EXPLANATION 2
6 *syn* see SCORE 4
7 a statement of real or purported events, occurrences, or conditions <wrote an *account* of his travels>
syn chronicle, history, narrative, report, story, version; *compare* STORY 2

account *vb* **1** *syn* see CONSIDER 3
rel appraise, assess, estimate, evaluate, rate; esteem
con underestimate, underrate, undervalue
2 *syn* see EXPLAIN 3
rel answer, elucidate, expound, interpret

accountable *adj syn* see RESPONSIBLE
con absolute, arbitrary, autocratic; imperious, magisterial, masterful
ant unaccountable

accouter *vb syn* see FURNISH 1
rel attire, dress; adorn, deck, decorate, embellish; fix (up), prepare, ready

accouterment *n, usu* **accouterments** *pl syn* see EQUIPMENT
rel appointment(s); furnishing(s); bravery, regalia, trappings

accredit *vb* **1** *syn* see APPROVE 2
rel commend, recommend; attest, certify, vouch (for)
con belittle, deprecate, depreciate, disapprove; reject, repudiate
2 *syn* see ASCRIBE
3 *syn* see AUTHORIZE 1
rel introduce, present

accretion *n syn* see ADDITION
rel enlargement; attachment, joining, uniting; adjunct, appendage

accroach *vb* **1** *syn* see ARROGATE 1
2 *syn* see APPROPRIATE 1

accumulate *vb* to bring together and form a store of <*accumulate* knowledge>
syn amass, cumulate, garner, hive, lay up, roll up, stockpile, store (up), uplay; *compare* HOARD
rel assemble, collect, gather, lay by, lay down, lay in; heap, mass, pile, stock; fund, hoard, treasure
idiom squirrel away
con decrease, diminish, lessen; deal, dispense, distribute, dole (out); dispel, disperse, scatter; consume, expend, spend, use, use up
ant dissipate

accumulation *n* a mass, quantity, or number that has accumulated <an *accumulation* of rubbish>
syn agglomeration, aggregation, amassment, collection, conglomeration, cumulation, hoard, trove
rel bank, heap, mass, pile; cumulus, reserve, stock, store
con dispersal, dispersion, scattering

accumulative *adj syn* see CUMULATIVE
rel aggregative, conglomerative; augmentative, multiplicative
con contractile, contractive, reducing, reductive; dispelling, dispersing, dispersive, dissipative, scattering

accuracy *n syn* see PRECISION

accurate *adj* **1** *syn* see CORRECT 2
con slipshod, slovenly; careless, heedless, lax
ant inaccurate
2 *syn* see CERTAIN 3

accurately *adv syn* see JUST 1

accursed *adj syn* see EXECRABLE 1
rel abhorrent, abominable, detestable, hateful, odious; offensive, repugnant, revolting
con admirable, estimable; honorable; divine, holy, sacred
ant blessed

accuse *vb* to declare one guilty of a fault or offense <*accused* her daughter of neglecting her children>
syn arraign, charge, criminate, impeach, incriminate, inculpate, indict, tax
rel blame, censure, criticize, denounce, reprobate; complain
idiom bring charges (against), point the finger at, prefer charges (against)
con absolve, acquit, exonerate, vindicate; accept, approve, endorse, sanction
ant exculpate

accustom *vb* to make something familiar or acceptable through use or experience <*accustom* oneself to city life>
syn familiarize, habituate, inure, use, wont
rel accommodate, adapt, adjust; acclimatize, harden, season
con alienate, estrange, wean; abjure, reject, repudiate; rebuff, repel, repulse, scorn
ant disaccustom

accustomed *adj* **1** *syn* see HABITUAL 2
2 *syn* see USUAL 1
rel commonplace, everyday; conventional, regulation, standard
con infrequent, occasional, uncommon; erratic, odd, peculiar, queer, singular
ant unaccustomed

ace *n* **1** *syn* see HAIR
2 *syn* see PARTICLE

acedia *n syn* see SLOTH 2

acerb *adj* **1** *syn* see SOUR 1
2 *syn* see SARCASTIC

acerbate *vb syn* see EXACERBATE

acerbic *adj* **1** *syn* see SOUR 1
2 *syn* see SARCASTIC

acerbity *n* **1** *syn* see ACRIMONY
rel acidity, sourness, tartness; crabbedness, dourness, saturninity, surliness; acridity, bitterness; harshness, roughness
con blandness, gentleness, mildness, smoothness; amiability, complaisance, good nature
ant mellowness
2 *syn* see SARCASM

acetose *adj syn* see SOUR 1

ache *vb* **1** *syn* see HURT 4
2 *syn* see COMPASSIONATE
rel deplore; sorrow (over); comfort, console, solace
3 *syn* see LONG

ache *n syn* see PAIN 1
rel injury; rack
con alleviation, assuagement, mitigation, relief; comfort, ease

acheronian *adj syn* see GLOOMY 3
acherontic *adj syn* see GLOOMY 3
achieve *vb* **1** *syn* see PERFORM 2
rel complete, conclude, finish; conquer, overcome, surmount
idiom bring to a happy issue, bring to pass
con begin, commence, start
ant fail (in *or* to do)
2 *syn* see GAIN 1
rel acquire, get, obtain, secure; actualize; arrive, come
idiom gain one's end
con depart, deviate, swerve; avoid, elude, escape, shun
ant miss
achievement *n* **1** *syn* see FEAT 2
con omission, slighting
ant failure
2 *syn* see ACQUIREMENT
Achilles' heel *n syn* see SOFT SPOT 2
aching *adj syn* see PAINFUL 1
rel achy
acicular *adj syn* see POINTED 1
aciculate *adj syn* see POINTED 1
acid *adj syn* see SOUR 1
con bland, mild, neutral
ant sweet; alkaline, basic
acidulous *adj syn* see SOUR 1
rel biting, cutting, sharp; piquant, pungent
con bland, mild, neutral; mellow, smooth, suave
ant saccharine
acknowledge *vb* **1** to show often grudgingly by word or deed that one knows of and agrees to or with something <*acknowledge* the justice of a complaint>
syn admit, allow, avow, concede, confess, fess (up), grant, let on, own, own up
rel disclose, divulge, reveal, tell; announce, declare, proclaim, publish
con disallow, disavow, disown, ‖nix, reject; contradict, gainsay, impugn, negate, negative
ant deny
2 to take notice of and accept as being as stated <he is generally *acknowledged* to be the leader in his profession>
syn admit, agree, recognize
rel accept, receive; concede, consider, deem, hold, view
con disregard, neglect, slight; reject, repudiate, spurn
ant ignore
acknowledgment *n syn* see CREDIT 4
acme *n syn* see APEX 2
acoustic *adj syn* see AUDITORY
acquaint *vb* **1** *syn* see INTRODUCE 4
idiom make acquainted
2 *syn* see INFORM 2
rel disclose, divulge, reveal; accustom, habituate
con hold, hold back, reserve, withhold; conceal, hide
acquaintance *n* **1** knowledge of something based on personal exposure <had a considerable *acquaintance* with modern poetry>
syn experience, familiarity, intimacy, inwardness
rel apprehension, grasp, ken; appreciation, awareness, consciousness
con inexperience, unfamiliarity; greenness, verdancy
2 *syn* see FRIEND
rel associate, companion, comrade, crony
con outsider, stranger
acquainted *adj syn* see FAMILIAR 3
acquiesce *vb syn* see ASSENT
rel accommodate, adapt, adjust, reconcile; bow, coincide, concur
con balk, demur, shy (away); kick, protest, remonstrate; differ, dissent
ant object
acquiescence *n* weak or passive agreement to what is asked or demanded <his childish *acquiescence* to all claims on his time>
syn compliance, conformity, resignation
rel complaisance; submissiveness; deference
con contumaciousness, insubordination; independence, self-assurance
ant rebellion, rebelliousness
acquiescent *adj syn* see PASSIVE 2
acquire *vb* **1** *syn* see GET 1
rel achieve, reach; add
con alienate, convey, transfer; abandon, relinquish, surrender, yield
ant forfeit
2 *syn* see EARN 1
rel accumulate, amass, collect, cumulate, garner
3 *syn* see DEVELOP 4
acquirement *n* a power or skill that results from persistent endeavor and cultivation <proud of his scholastic *acquirements*>
syn accomplishment, achievement, acquisition, attainment, finish
rel accretion, addition; advance, advancement; education, erudition, knowledge
con dearth, defect, lack, privation, want
acquisition *n syn* see ACQUIREMENT
rel accession, increment; assets, belongings, means, possessions
acquisitive *adj syn* see COVETOUS
rel demanding, exacting, exigent
con eschewing, forbearing, forgoing; sacrificing
ant abnegating, self-denying
acquit *vb* **1** *syn* see EXCULPATE
rel discharge, free, liberate, release; justify
con condemn, damn, doom, proscribe, sentence
ant convict
2 *syn* see BEHAVE 1
acres *n pl syn* see ESTATE 3
acrid *adj* having or being a noticeable, persistent, and usually unpleasant flavor or sometimes odor <the tonic had an *acrid* aftertaste>
syn amaroidal, astringent, austere, bitter, harsh, sharp

---

syn synonym(s) *rel* related word(s)
ant antonym(s) *con* contrasted word(s)
idiom idiomatic equivalent(s)
‖ use limited; if in doubt, see a dictionary

rel biting, caustic, cutting; piquant, pungent; cloying, oversweet, saccharine
con palatable, sapid, tasty, toothsome; delectable, delicious, luscious
ant savory

acrimonious *adj* ***syn*** see ANGRY
rel cranky, cross, irascible, splenetic, testy; belligerent, contentious, quarrelsome
con benign, benignant, kind, kindly
ant irenic, peaceable

acrimony *n* sharpness or rancor manifested in words, manner, or disposition <the dispute was renewed with increasing *acrimony*>
syn acerbity, asperity, mordancy
rel bitterness, ill will, malevolence, malice, malignity, spite, spleen; animosity, animus, antipathy, rancor
con civility, courtesy, graciousness, politeness; diplomacy, urbanity
ant suavity

acroamatic *adj* ***syn*** see RECONDITE

across *adv* **1** so as to intersect the length of something <cut the board *across*>
syn athwart, crossways, crosswise
2 ***syn*** see OVER 1

across *prep* from one side to the other <drew the curtain *across* the window>
syn athwart, cross, over

act *vb* **1** to present a role or performance on or as if on the stage <*acted* the part of Hamlet's father>
syn discourse, do, enact, impersonate, perform, personate, play, playact
rel characterize, portray, represent; masquerade; counterfeit, feign, sham, simulate
2 ***syn*** see ASSUME 4
idiom act a part, put on an act (of)
3 ***syn*** see BEHAVE 1
rel perform
4 to perform the duties or function of <he *acted* as president for over a year>
syn function, officiate, serve
idiom do duty (as), discharge the office (of), serve in the office (*or* capacity) of
5 to perform especially in an indicated way <the laxative *acted* quickly>
syn behave, function, operate, perform, react, take, work
idiom take effect
6 ***syn*** see FUNCTION 3

act *n* ***syn*** see ACTION 1
rel exploit, feat

actify *vb* ***syn*** see VITALIZE

acting *adj* ***syn*** see TEMPORARY

action *n* **1** something done or effected <a kindly *action*>
syn accomplishment, act, deed, doing, thing
rel discharge, effectuation, execution, fulfillment, performance; activity, behavior, operation, reaction, work; procedure, proceeding, process
2 ***syn*** see BATTLE
rel affray, combat, conflict, fray
3 ***syn*** see SERVICE 1
4 ***syn*** see SUIT 1

activate *vb* ***syn*** see VITALIZE
rel arouse, awaken, rally, rouse, stir, wake, waken
ant arrest

active *adj* **1** being at work or in effective operation <marginal mines that are *active* only when prices are high>
syn alive, dynamic, functioning, live, operative, running, working
rel assiduous, busy, diligent, industrious; energetic, strenuous, vigorous; alert, wide-awake; rushing
con dormant, latent, quiescent; idle, inert, passive, supine; dead, dull, slow
ant inactive; abeyant
2 ***syn*** see AGILE
rel animated, spirited, vivacious; flexible, graceful, supple
con inert, lumpish, torpid
ant inactive
3 ***syn*** see ENERGETIC 2
rel expeditious, prompt, ready
con disinterested, indifferent, unconcerned

actively *adv* ***syn*** see SERIOUSLY 1

activity *n* ***syn*** see EXERCISE 2

activize *vb* ***syn*** see VITALIZE

actor *n* **1** one who takes part in an exhibition simulating happenings in real life <had been an *actor* on the stage and in television>
syn impersonator, mime, mimic, mummer, performer, playactor, player, thespian, trouper
2 ***syn*** see PARTICIPANT
rel mainstay, supporter, sustainer, upholder
con abettor, backer, patron, promoter

actual *adj* **1** existing in act <our *actual* intentions>
syn existent, extant
ant possible, potential
2 existing in or based on fact <problems of *actual* life>
syn absolute, factual, genuine, hard, positive, sure-enough
rel commonplace, everyday, ordinary, routine, usual; concrete, real, tangible
con conjectural, hypothetical, theoretical; putative, reputed, supposititious
ant apparent, nominal
3 ***syn*** see REAL 3
rel material, objective, phenomenal, physical; authentic, bona fide, legitimate
con abstract, transcendent, transcendental; academic, speculative, theoretical; fabulous, fictitious, mythical
ant ideal; imaginary

actuality *n* **1** ***syn*** see EXISTENCE 1
rel actualization, externalization, incarnation, materialization; achievement, attainment
con abstraction, ideality, transcendence
ant possibility, potentiality
2 something that has existence <a predicted downturn in the stock market was received as if it were an *actuality*>
syn materiality, reality
rel basis, essence, substance; embodiment, incarnation

3 ***syn*** see FACT 1
actually *adv* ***syn*** see VERY 2
actuate *vb* **1** ***syn*** see MOVE 5
2 ***syn*** see MOBILIZE 1
rel excite, galvanize, provoke; arouse, rouse, stir; vitalize
act up *vb* ***syn*** see CUT UP 2
acumen *n* ***syn*** see WIT 3
rel acuteness, sharpness
con denseness, density, slowness
ant obtuseness, obtusity
acuminate *adj* ***syn*** see POINTED 1
acuminous *adj* ***syn*** see POINTED 1
acute *adj* **1** ***syn*** see POINTED 1
rel barbed, prickly, spiky, spined, spiny
ant blunt
2 ***syn*** see SHARP 4
rel cutting, incisive, trenchant; piercing
con crass, dense, dull, slow, stupid
ant obtuse
3 perceiving clearly and sensitively <an *acute* ear>
syn keen, perceptive, sensitive, sharp
rel observant, penetrating, probing; accurate, meticulous, precise
con imperceptive, insensitive; imprecise, inaccurate; inexact, uncritical
ant dull
4 elevated in pitch <an *acute* note>
syn argute, high, piercing, piping, sharp, shrill, thin, treble
rel penetrating; reedy, screechy, shrieky, shrilly, squeaky; tinny
con bass, deep, low
ant grave
5 ***syn*** see SHARP 8
6 serious to the point of approaching a crisis <an *acute* housing shortage>
syn climacteric, critical, crucial, desperate, dire
rel afflictive, grave, serious; aggravated, intensified; dangerous, hazardous, menacing, perilous, precarious, threatening; exigent, urgent
adage *n* ***syn*** see SAYING
adamant *adj* ***syn*** see INFLEXIBLE 2
rel immobile, immovable; unsubmitting
con placable, relenting, submitting; complaisant, obliging; subdued, submissive
ant yielding
adamantine *adj* ***syn*** see INFLEXIBLE 2
rel immobile, immovable; unsubmitting
con placable, relenting, submitting; complaisant, obliging; subdued, submissive
ant yielding
adapt *vb* to bring into correspondence or make suitable <*adapted* himself easily to the company he found himself with>
syn accommodate, adjust, conform, fit, quadrate, reconcile, square, suit, tailor, tailor-make
rel qualify, temper; acclimate, acclimatize
ant unfit
adaptable *adj* **1** ***syn*** see VERSATILE
2 ***syn*** see PLASTIC
con intractable, irreconcilable, nonconforming, refractory, unaccommodating
ant inadaptable, unadaptable
adapted *adj* ***syn*** see ASSORTED 2
add *vb* **1** to bring in or join on something more so as to form a larger or more inclusive whole <*added* music to his accomplishments>
syn annex, append, subjoin, superadd, take on
rel affix, attach, fasten, superimpose, tack (on); augment, enlarge, increase; burden, clutter, cumber, encumber, saddle
con abstract, detach; curtail, decrease, diminish, lessen, reduce
ant deduct, subtract
2 to combine numbers or quantities into one sum <*add* up a column of figures>
syn cast, figure, foot, sum, summate, tot, total, totalize, tote
rel calculate, compute, estimate, reckon; score, tally
added *adj* ***syn*** see ADDITIONAL
addendum *n, sometimes* **addenda** *pl but sing or pl in constr* ***syn*** see APPENDIX 1
addict *vb* ***syn*** see HABITUATE 2
rel bias, dispose, incline, predispose; address, apply, direct
con alienate, estrange; detach, disengage, disincline, indispose
ant wean
addict *n* a person who by habit or strong inclination indulges in something <a science fiction *addict*>
syn aficionado, buff, devotee, fan, habitué, hound, lover, votary
rel enthusiast, fanatic, zealot; hobbyist, putterer, tinkerer
addition *n* something that tends to increase something else (as in size, number, or content) <there are several new *additions* to our staff>
syn accession, accretion, augmentation, increase, increment, raise, rise
rel accessory, adjunct, appanage, appurtenance, supplement; continuation, extension, rider; accrual, accruement, accumulation
con deduction, lessening, reduction
additional *adj* being or coming by way of addition <gave *additional* reasons to justify his position>
syn added, another, else, farther, fresh, further, more, new, other
rel accessory, adscititious, collateral, extra, supplemental, supplementary
additionally *adv* **1** ***syn*** see ALSO 2
2 ***syn*** see AGAIN 4
additive *adj* ***syn*** see CUMULATIVE
rel component, constituent, elemental
additory *adj* ***syn*** see CUMULATIVE
addle *vb* ***syn*** see CONFUSE 2
rel confound, dumbfound, nonplus; amaze, astound, flabbergast
idiom addle one's wits
con animate, enliven, quicken, vivify

---

syn synonym(s) ***rel*** related word(s)
ant antonym(s) ***con*** contrasted word(s)
idiom idiomatic equivalent(s)
‖ use limited; if in doubt, see a dictionary

ant refresh (*mentally*)

address *vb* **1** ***syn*** see DIRECT 2
2 ***syn*** see SEND 1
3 to occupy (oneself or one's attention or efforts) with something <*addressed* himself to the job and soon finished it>
syn apply, bend, buckle (down), devote, direct, give, throw, turn
rel associate, connect, couple, link, relate; aim, level, point
idiom bring (oneself) into relation with something, tax (one's energies) with something
con disregard, ignore, overlook
4 to communicate directly to or with <*addressed* the governor with his petition>
syn accost, apply (to), approach, bespeak, memorialize
rel speak (to), talk (with); appeal (to); apostrophize; petition
con ignore, overlook, pass up, slight; avoid, cut, disregard
5 ***syn*** see TALK 7
6 to affix directions for delivery <*address* a letter>
syn direct, superscribe
7 to seek the attention of usually orally and in order to gain recognition <*address* a stranger to ask directions>
syn accost, call (to), greet, hail, salute
rel converse, speak, talk
idiom attract one's attention
8 to direct one's attention to in the role of a suitor <ready to marry the first man that *addressed* her>
syn court, make up (to), pursue, spark, sue, sweetheart, woo
rel attend, escort, squire; neck, pet, romance, rush, smooch, spoon
idiom make a play for, pay (one's) addresses to, run after

address *n* **1** the quality or state of being ready or skillful <to bring off such a coup requires *address*>
syn adroitness, deftness, dexterity, dexterousness, prowess, readiness, skill, sleight; *compare* TACT
rel competence, efficiency, expertise, know-how, proficiency; craft, finesse; ingeniousness, ingenuity, resourcefulness
con inadequacy, ineptitude, ineptness, unskillfulness; awkwardness, clumsiness, gawkiness, lubberliness, stupidity
2 ***syn*** see TACT
rel dexterity, ease, facility; cleverness, readiness; affability, graciousness
con awkwardness, clumsiness, gaucheness; boorishness, churlishness
ant maladroitness
3 ***syn*** see BEARING 1
4 ***syn*** see SPEECH 2

adduce *vb* to bring forward for consideration <*adduce* evidence in support of a hypothesis>
syn advance, allege, cite, lay, offer, present
rel animadvert, comment, commentate, remark; document, exemplify, illustrate; prefer, proffer, propose, submit, suggest, tender

add up *vb* ***syn*** see AMOUNT 1
add up (to) *vb* ***syn*** see MEAN 2
adept *n* ***syn*** see EXPERT
ant bungler, incompetent
adept *adj* ***syn*** see PROFICIENT
rel clever; adroit, deft, dexterous
con amateurish, dabbling, dilettantish; awkward, clumsy, maladroit
ant bungling, inapt, inept
adequacy *n* **1** ***syn*** see ABILITY 1
rel equality, satisfactoriness, sufficiency
idiom enough on the ball
ant inadequacy, inadequateness
2 ***syn*** see ENOUGH
adequate *adj* **1** ***syn*** see SUFFICIENT 1
con meager, scanty, sparse
ant inadequate, unadequate
2 ***syn*** see DECENT 4
adequately *adv* **1** ***syn*** see ENOUGH 1
2 ***syn*** see WELL 4
adequation *n* ***syn*** see EQUIVALENCE
adhere *vb* ***syn*** see STICK 2
rel combine, join, link, unite
con disjoin, disunite
adherence *n* **1** a physical adhering <the close *adherence* of scales to a plant bud>
syn adhesion, bond, cling, clinging, coherence, cohesion, stickage, sticking
rel agglutination, cementation, concretion, conglutination; congelation, set, setting, solidification
con detachment, disjunction, parting, separation
2 ***syn*** see ATTACHMENT 1
con fickleness, inconstancy
adherent *n* ***syn*** see FOLLOWER
rel backer, champion, upholder
con apostate, recreant; deserter, forsaker; adversary, antagonist, opponent
ant renegade
adhesion *n* **1** ***syn*** see ADHERENCE 1
ant nonadhesion
2 ***syn*** see ATTACHMENT 1
con fickleness, inconstancy
adhesive *adj* ***syn*** see STICKY 1
adieu *interj* ***syn*** see GOOD-BYE
adieu *n* ***syn*** see PARTING
ad interim *adj* ***syn*** see TEMPORARY
ant permanent
adipose *adj* ***syn*** see FATTY 1
adiposity *n* ***syn*** see OBESITY
adit *n* ***syn*** see DOOR 2
adjacent *adj* **1** ***syn*** see NEIGHBORING
ant remote
2 ***syn*** see CONVENIENT 2
3 having a common border <the brothers built on *adjacent* lots>
syn abutting, adjoining, approximal, bordering, conterminous, contiguous, juxtaposed, touching
rel closest, nearest, next; consecutive, successive; attached, connected, joined, linked

con distant, far, remote, removed; parted, separated
ant nonadjacent

adjoin *vb* to be contiguous or adjacent to <the new suburb *adjoins* farmland>
syn abut, border, butt (on *or* against), communicate, join, line, march, neighbor, touch, verge
rel meet, run (into); end

adjoining *adj* ***syn*** see ADJACENT 3
ant detached

adjourn *vb* **1** ***syn*** see DEFER
rel curb, hold back, restrain
con advance, expedite, further, promote
2 to bring to a formal close <*adjourn* the legislature>
syn dissolve, prorogate, prorogue, recess, rise, terminate
rel break up, close, disband, discontinue, disperse; stay, suspend
con open; mobilize, muster, rally
ant convene, convoke

adjudge *vb* ***syn*** see JUDGE 1
rel accord, allot, assign, award, grant

adjudicate *vb* ***syn*** see JUDGE 1

adjunct *n* ***syn*** see APPENDAGE
rel accretion, addition; appanage; affix, attachment, fixture

adjust *vb* **1** ***syn*** see ADAPT
rel accord, correspond; attune, harmonize
2 to alter so as to make efficient or more efficient <*adjust* a carburetor>
syn fix, regulate, tune (up)
rel correct, rectify, right; balance, stabilize, steady, trim, true; arrange, order, rig
idiom make right, put (*or* set) in order, put right (*or* to rights), set right (*or* to rights)
con disarrange, disorder, disturb, upset
ant derange
3 ***syn*** see HABITUATE 2

adjuvant *adj* ***syn*** see AUXILIARY
rel synergistic
con antagonistic, negating, negativing, neutralizing; hindering, impeding, obstructing
ant counteractive

ad–lib *vb* ***syn*** see IMPROVISE

admeasure *vb* ***syn*** see ALLOT

admeasurement *n* ***syn*** see SIZE 1

adminicular *adj* ***syn*** see CORROBORATIVE

administer *vb* **1** to supervise the affairs or the provision, use, or conduct of especially in the capacity of an agent or steward <*administer* justice>
syn administrate, carry out, execute, govern, render
rel conduct, direct, manage, run, supervise
2 to provide in appropriate amount <*administer* a laxative>
syn apportion, deal (out), dispense, dole (out), mete (out), portion (out), share out
rel distribute, give, give out, issue; allot, assign, consign; allocate, ration
3 ***syn*** see GIVE 10

administrate *vb* ***syn*** see ADMINISTER 1

administrator *n* ***syn*** see EXECUTIVE

admirable *adj* ***syn*** see WORTHY 1

admiration *n* **1** ***syn*** see WONDER 2
rel surprise; ecstasy, rapture, transport
con aloofness, indifference, unconcern
2 ***syn*** see REGARD 4
rel appreciation; adoration, reverence, veneration, worship
con detestation, hate, hatred, loathing; dislike, disrelish, distaste
ant abhorrence

admire *vb* **1** to view with an elevated feeling of pleasure <*admired* the scene that spread out before them>
syn appreciate, cherish, delight (in), relish; *compare* APPRECIATE 1
rel adore, revere, reverence, venerate, worship
idiom go into raptures over, take delight in
con disesteem, disfavor, dislike, disrelish, mislike
ant disdain
2 to hold in high esteem <*admired* his ability to get things done>
syn consider, esteem, regard, respect
rel appreciate, cherish, prize, treasure, value
idiom have (*or* hold) a high opinion of, rate highly, set (great) store by, think much (*or* highly) of
con abominate, detest, hate, loathe; contemn, despise, disdain, scorn
ant abhor

admirer *n* ***syn*** see AMATEUR 1

admissible *adj* ***syn*** see PERMISSIBLE

admission *n* ***syn*** see DOOR 2

admit *vb* **1** ***syn*** see TAKE 10
rel allow, permit, suffer; entertain, harbor, house, lodge, shelter
con debar, exclude, shut out; bar, block, hinder, obstruct
ant eject, expel
2 ***syn*** see ACKNOWLEDGE 1
rel acquiesce, agree, assent, subscribe
ant gainsay
3 ***syn*** see ENTER 2
rel induct, initiate, install; insert, interject, interpose
con debar, shut out; eject, expel, oust
ant exclude
4 ***syn*** see ACKNOWLEDGE 2

admittance *n* ***syn*** see DOOR 2

admix *vb* ***syn*** see MIX 1

admixture *n* **1** an added ingredient that alters the character of something <her love had a marring *admixture* of selfishness>
syn adulterant, alloy, denaturant
rel doctor, fortification, taint; accretion, addition; bit, dash, shade, smack, spice, tinge
2 ***syn*** see MIXTURE

admonish *vb* ***syn*** see REPROVE
rel caution, forewarn, warn
idiom have a word with

---

syn synonym(s) ***rel*** related word(s)
ant antonym(s) ***con*** contrasted word(s)
idiom idiomatic equivalent(s)
‖ use limited; if in doubt, see a dictionary

con applaud, approve, compliment
ant commend
admonishing *adj* *syn* see MONITORY
admonishment *n* *syn* see REBUKE
admonition *n* **1** *syn* see REBUKE
2 *syn* see WARNING
admonitory *adj* *syn* see MONITORY
ado *n* *syn* see STIR 1
rel effort, exertion, pains, trouble; confusion, hurly-burly, turmoil, uproar
con calm, peace, serenity, tranquillity; quiet, silence, stillness
adolescence *n* *syn* see YOUTH 1
ant senescence
adopt *vb* to make one's own what in some fashion one owes to another <*adopt* a new style>
syn embrace, espouse, take on, take up
rel affect, assume; appropriate, arrogate, take, usurp; domesticate, naturalize
idiom adapt to one's own ends, go in for
con reject, spurn; abjure, forswear, renounce
ant discard; repudiate
adoption *n* *syn* see ESPOUSAL 4
adorable *adj* **1** *syn* see LOVABLE
2 *syn* see DELIGHTFUL
adoration *n* deep, ardent, and often excessive attachment or love <the *adoration* given popular heroes>
syn idolatry, idolization, worship
rel affection, attachment, devotion, love; crush, infatuation, passion, weakness
con antipathy, aversion; disfavor, dislike, distaste
ant detestation
adore *vb* **1** *syn* see REVERE
rel extol, laud, praise
con curse, execrate
2 *syn* see LOVE 2
3 to love, admire, or enjoy excessively <she *adores* and spoils her grandchildren>
syn dote (on *or* upon), idolize, worship
rel admire, esteem, love; coddle, indulge, pamper, spoil
idiom be silly over
con abhor, abominate, hate, loathe; contemn, despise, disdain, scorn
ant detest
4 *syn* see LOVE 1
adorn *vb* to add something nonessential to enhance the appearance or beauty of <a hat *adorned* with feathers>
syn beautify, bedeck, deck, decorate, dress (up), embellish, garnish, ornament, prank, trim
rel enrich, furbish, smarten, spruce (up); bedizen, dandify, fancy up; enhance, heighten, intensify
con clear, divest, expose, strip, uncover; deface, mar, scar, spoil
ant disfigure
ad rem *adj* *syn* see RELEVANT
adroit *adj* **1** *syn* see DEXTEROUS 1
ant maladroit
2 *syn* see SKILLFUL 2
3 *syn* see CLEVER 4
rel astute, perspicacious, shrewd; intelligent, quick-witted, smart; artful, subtle
con dense, dull, stupid; apathetic, heavy, impassive, phlegmatic, stodgy
ant stolid
adroitness *n* **1** *syn* see ADDRESS 1
2 *syn* see ART 1
adscititious *adj* *syn* see ADVENTITIOUS
adulation *n* *syn* see FLATTERY
rel acclaim, applause
ant abuse
adult *adj* *syn* see MATURE 1
rel aged
con adolescent, pubescent
ant juvenile, puerile
adulterant *n* *syn* see ADMIXTURE 1
adulterate *vb* to alter fraudulently usually for profit <sausage *adulterated* with cereal products>
syn debase, doctor, dope (up), load, sophisticate, weight
rel cut, dilute; denaturalize, denature, manipulate, tamper (with); defile, impurify, pollute, taint; deacon
con better, improve; augment, fortify, supplement
ant refine
adumbrate *vb* **1** to give a hint or indication of something to come <social unrest that *adumbrated* the revolt>
syn foreshadow, hint, prefigurate, prefigure, shadow (forth); *compare* SUGGEST 5
rel augur, bode, forebode, foretell, portend, presage; lower, menace, threaten; symbolize, typify
idiom cast its shadow before
2 *syn* see FORETELL
rel argue, bespeak, betoken, indicate
3 *syn* see SKETCH
4 *syn* see SUGGEST 5
rel denote, mean, signify
5 *syn* see OBSCURE
adumbration *n* *syn* see SHADE 1
rel hint, intimation, suggestion; sign, symptom, token; emblem, symbol, type
con disclosure, discovery, divulgence
ant revelation
advance *vb* **1** to cause to proceed or progress toward a goal <warm rains *advanced* the crops>
syn encourage, forward, foster, further, promote, serve
rel aid, assist, help; accelerate, quicken, speed
con hinder, impede; delay, slow; curb, restrain
ant retard; check
2 to raise in rank or position <was *advanced* to the presidency>
syn elevate, prefer, promote, upgrade
rel aggrandize, exalt, raise, uplift; glorify, immortalize, magnify
ant hold back; reduce (*in rank*)
3 *syn* see LEND
4 *syn* see ADDUCE
rel air, broach, expose
5 to go forward in space or time or toward an objective <prices *advanced* sharply>

syn get along, get on, march, move, proceed, progress

rel heighten, increase, intensify; develop, mature

idiom forge ahead, gain ground, get ahead, make headway (*or* progress), make one's way, make rapid strides

con retire, retreat, retrograde, withdraw

ant recede

advance *n* **1** ***syn*** see PROGRESS 2

2 forward movement especially on a course of action or development <the recent *advance* of technology>

syn advancement, anabasis, headway, march, ongoing, proficiency, progress

rel betterment, furtherance, improvement; development, evolution; breakthrough

con retreat, retrogression; ebbing, retiring, withdrawal

ant recession

3 ***syn*** see OVERTURE 1

rel offer, proffer

advanced *adj* **1** ***syn*** see PRECOCIOUS

con retrograde, retrogressive

ant backward

2 ***syn*** see LIBERAL 3

rel adventurous, daring, venturesome

ant conservative

advancement *n* **1** the act of raising or the status of being raised in grade, rank, or dignity <his *advancement* in his profession was rapid>

syn elevation, preference, preferment, prelation, promotion, upgrading

rel aggrandizement, dignification, magnification, raising, uplifting

con demotion, downgrading, reduction

ant degradation

2 ***syn*** see ADVANCE 2

advantage *n* **1** ***syn*** see BETTER 2

2 ***syn*** see WELFARE

3 something giving one person or side a position of superiority (as in a contest) <he had the *advantage* of greater height>

syn allowance, bulge, ‖deadwood, draw, edge, handicap, head start, odds, ‖overhand, start, vantage; *compare* BETTER 2

rel drop, jump, lead, running start; ascendancy, domination, leadership; mastery, superiority, upper hand, whip hand

idiom ace in the hole, inside track

con embarrassment, hamper, hindrance, impediment, inconvenience

ant disadvantage

4 ***syn*** see USE 3

rel betterment, improvement; enhancement; heightening

con damage, harm, hurt, injury

ant detriment

5 ***syn*** see GOOD 1

advantage *vb* ***syn*** see BENEFIT

advantageous *adj* **1** yielding a profit <sold on very *advantageous* terms>

syn gainful, good, lucrative, moneymaking, paying, profitable, remunerative, well-paying, worthwhile

rel acceptable, agreeable, desirable, pleasing, satisfactory, satisfying

idiom in the black, paying its (own) way

con disadvantageous, unfavorable, unprofitable; damaging, hurtful

2 ***syn*** see GOOD 1

rel remedial, salutary; conducive, contributory, implemental, instrumental; advisable, expedient

con unfavorable; inconvenient; deleterious, detrimental

ant disadvantageous

advenient *adj* ***syn*** see ADVENTITIOUS

advent *n* ***syn*** see ARRIVAL 1

rel approach, nearing

ant exit

advential *adj* ***syn*** see ADVENTITIOUS

adventitious *adj* coming from without and not participating in the fundamental nature of something <*adventitious* notions that have corrupted the primitive doctrine>

syn adscititious, advenient, advential, supervenient

rel accidental, casual, contingent, fortuitous, incidental

con constitutional, essential, intrinsic; inborn, inbred, innate

ant inherent

adventure *n* an undertaking or experience that involves hazard and requires boldness <recounted the *adventures* of his solitary voyage>

syn emprise, enterprise, exploit, feat, gest, venture

rel hazard, peril, risk; quest; achievement

adventure *vb* ***syn*** see VENTURE 1

adventuresome *adj* ***syn*** see ADVENTUROUS

ant unadventurous; cautious

adventurous *adj* courting danger or exposing oneself to danger beyond the call of duty or courage <*adventurous* boys scrambled over the cliff face>

syn adventuresome, audacious, daredevil, daring, foolhardy, rash, reckless, temerarious, venturesome, venturous

rel bold, doughty, intrepid; brash, harebrained, hotheaded, impetuous, imprudent, madcap, overconfident

con shrinking, timid, timorous; afraid, alarmed, fearful, scared; apprehensive, uneasy

ant unadventurous; cautious

adversary *n* ***syn*** see OPPONENT

rel assaulter, attacker

con backer, supporter, upholder

ant ally

adverse *adj* **1** acting against or in a contrary direction <hindered by *adverse* forces>

syn antagonistic, anti, antipathetic, opposed, opposing, oppugnant

rel contrary, counter, counteractive; hindering, impeding, obstructive; hostile, unfriendly

---

syn synonym(s) ***rel*** related word(s)
ant antonym(s) ***con*** contrasted word(s)
idiom idiomatic equivalent(s)
‖ use limited; if in doubt, see a dictionary

con coactive, collaborative, cooperative; adjuvant, synergistic; favorable, propitious
2 being opposed to one's interests <an *adverse* balance of trade>
syn detrimental, negative, unfavorable
rel deleterious, harmful, hurtful, injurious; disadvantageous, prejudicial, unpropitious, unsatisfactory
con advantageous, favorable, positive, propitious, satisfactory

adversity *n* ***syn*** see MISFORTUNE
rel distress, misery, suffering; deprivation, destitution, indigence, poverty
con bliss, felicity, happiness; comfort, ease
ant prosperity

advert *vb* ***syn*** see REFER 3
rel animadvert, note, notice, observe, remark
con disregard, ignore, neglect, overlook

advertent *adj* ***syn*** see ATTENTIVE 1

advertise *vb* **1** ***syn*** see DECLARE 1
rel recount, relate, report; communicate, impart; ballyhoo, promote, propagandize, publicize
con conceal, repress, suppress; bury, hide, obscure
2 ***syn*** see PUBLICIZE
3 ***syn*** see PROMOTE 3

advertisement *n* ***syn*** see DECLARATION
rel ballyhoo, promotion, propaganda, publicity

advertising *n* ***syn*** see PUBLICITY

advice *n* **1** recommendation regarding a decision or course of conduct <benefited from his *advice* on study habits>
syn advisement, counsel
rel direction, guidance, instruction, teaching; input; admonition; caution, cautioning, forewarning, warning
2 ***syn*** see NEWS

advisable *adj* ***syn*** see EXPEDIENT
rel commendable, desirable; becoming, seemly, suitable; sensible
ant inadvisable

advise *vb* **1** ***syn*** see COUNSEL
rel caution, forewarn, warn; coax, induce, persuade, win (over)
con bedazzle, misadvise, mislead
2 ***syn*** see CONFER 2
rel deliberate
3 ***syn*** see INFORM 2
rel disclose, let out, reveal; communicate, impart

advised *adj* ***syn*** see DELIBERATE 1
rel intended, intentional, meant; knowing, purposeful, willful

advisement *n* ***syn*** see ADVICE 1

advocate *n* ***syn*** see EXPONENT

advocate *vb* **1** ***syn*** see ENCOURAGE 2
2 ***syn*** see SUPPORT 2
rel justify, vindicate; advance, forward, promote
idiom hold a brief for
con assail, attack; combat, fight, oppose
ant impugn

aegis *n* **1** ***syn*** see DEFENSE 1
2 ***syn*** see BACKING

aeneous *adj* ***syn*** see BRAZEN 4

aeon *n* ***syn*** see AGE 2

aerial *adj* **1** ***syn*** see AIRY 1
2 ***syn*** see LOFTY 6
3 ***syn*** see AIRY 3
rel immaterial, incorporeal; impalpable, imperceptible, imponderable

aesthete *n* ***syn*** see CONNOISSEUR
rel perfectionist, stickler; fussbudget, old maid
con barbarian; clod, lout, oaf

affable *adj* **1** ***syn*** see GRACIOUS 1
rel courteous, polite; suave, urbane; loquacious, talkative
con crabbed, glum, surly; reticent, withdrawn; silent, taciturn, uncommunicative
ant reserved
2 ***syn*** see GENTLE 2

affair *n* **1** something done or dealt with <trying to get at the truth of the *affair*>
syn business, concern, matter, shooting match, thing
rel care, lookout, responsibility; pie, proceeding
idiom cup of tea
2 ***syn*** see BUSINESS 8
3 ***syn*** see LOVE AFFAIR
4 ***syn*** see AMOUR 2

affect *vb* **1** ***syn*** see ASSUME 4
2 ***syn*** see FREQUENT

affect *vb* to produce a usually mental or emotional effect on one capable of reaction <much *affected* by the touching scene>
syn carry, get, impress, influence, inspire, move, strike, sway, touch
rel actuate, draw, drive, impel; penetrate, pierce
idiom work on

affectation *n* ***syn*** see POSE 2
rel ostentation, pretentiousness
con ingenuousness, naiveté, naturalness, simplicity, unsophistication
ant artlessness

affected *adj* **1** ***syn*** see INTERESTED
2 ***syn*** see SELF-CONSCIOUS
3 ***syn*** see GENTEEL 3
4 ***syn*** see PRECIOUS 4
5 ***syn*** see ARTIFICIAL 3

affecting *adj* ***syn*** see MOVING 2
rel piteous, pitiable, pitiful; distressful, distressing, disturbing, troubling

affection *n* **1** ***syn*** see FEELING 3
rel leaning, penchant, propensity; bias, predilection; bent, faculty, turn
con aversion, hate, hatred; dislike, distaste
ant antipathy
2 ***syn*** see LOVE 1
rel sympathy, tenderness, warmth; attention, concern, interest; doting, enjoying
con coolness, frigidity
ant coldness

affection *vb* ***syn*** see LOVE 2

affection *n* **1** ***syn*** see DISEASE 1
rel access, attack, paroxysm, spell; derangement, disordering, disturbance
2 ***syn*** see QUALITY 1

affectionate *adj* ***syn*** see LOVING
rel sympathetic, tender, warm
con apathetic, impassive, stolid; remote, uninterested, withdrawn
ant cold; undemonstrative
affective *adj* ***syn*** see EMOTIONAL 2
affectivity *n* ***syn*** see FEELING 3
affianced *adj* ***syn*** see ENGAGED 2
affianced *n* ***syn*** see BETROTHED
affiche *n* ***syn*** see POSTER
affiliated *adj* ***syn*** see RELATED
con autonomous, free, independent
ant unaffiliated
affiliation *n* ***syn*** see ASSOCIATION 1
affinity *n* **1** ***syn*** see ATTRACTION 2
con antipathy, aversion; dislike, distaste; repugnance, repellency, repulsion
2 ***syn*** see LIKENESS
rel accord
affirm *vb* ***syn*** see ASSERT 1
rel attest, certify, guarantee, vouch, witness; say, state
con debate
affirmative *adj* ***syn*** see POSITIVE 6
affix *vb* ***syn*** see FASTEN 1
rel add, annex, append, subjoin
con disengage, disjoin
ant detach
afflation *n* ***syn*** see INSPIRATION
afflatus *n* ***syn*** see INSPIRATION
afflict *vb* to inflict upon one something hard to endure <he was *afflicted* with boils>
syn agonize, crucify, excruciate, harrow, martyr, martyrize, rack, smite, strike, torment, torture, try, wring
rel annoy, harass, harry, pester, plague, press, worry; bother, irk, vex; lacerate, wound
con console, delight, gladden, please, rejoice; ease, relieve, solace
ant comfort
afflicted *adj* ***syn*** see WOEFUL 1
affliction *n* **1** ***syn*** see TRIAL 1
rel mischance, mishap
con alleviation, assuagement, easement, relief
ant consolation, solace
2 ***syn*** see SORROW
3 ***syn*** see SICKNESS 1
afflictive *adj* **1** ***syn*** see PAINFUL 1
2 ***syn*** see DEPLORABLE
3 ***syn*** see BITTER 2
affluent *adj* ***syn*** see RICH 1
rel acquisitive, grasping
con poor; bankrupt, impoverished
ant impecunious; straitened
affranchise *vb* ***syn*** see ENFRANCHISE
affray *n* **1** ***syn*** see BRAWL 2
2 ***syn*** see CLASH 2
affright *vb* ***syn*** see FRIGHTEN
rel bewilder, confound
con animate, fire, inspire
ant embolden, nerve
affront *vb* **1** ***syn*** see OFFEND 3
rel criticize, dispraise
con compliment; laud, praise; dignify, honor
2 ***syn*** see CONFRONT 1
affront *n* a speech or an action designed to impugn the honor or worth of someone or something <her costume was an *affront* to the solemnity of the occasion>
syn contumely, despite, indignity, insult, slap
rel dishonor, flouting, offense, outrage, slight; aspersion, barb, defamation, dig
idiom slap in the face
con deference, homage, honor; adulation, compliment, flattery
aficionado *n* ***syn*** see ADDICT
afield *adj* ***syn*** see AMISS 2
afire *adj* **1** ***syn*** see BURNING 1
2 ***syn*** see ALIGHT 2
aflame *adj* **1** ***syn*** see BURNING 1
2 ***syn*** see ALIGHT 2
aflicker *adj* ***syn*** ALIGHT 2, ablaze, afire, aflame, aglow
à fond *adv* ***syn*** see WELL 3
aforementioned *adj* ***syn*** see SUCH 1
aforesaid *adj* ***syn*** see SUCH 1
aforethought *adj* ***syn*** see DELIBERATE 1
afraid *adj* **1** suffering the effects of apprehension, fear, or terror <too *afraid* to even cry for help>
syn aghast, anxious, ||ascared, fearful, frightened, scared, scary, terrified; *compare* FEARFUL 2
rel shrinking, shy, timid, timorous; cautious, chary, wary; jumpy, skittish
idiom frightened out of one's wits, in a (blue) funk, scared to death, terror stricken
con confident, dauntless, fearless; assured, collected, poised, self-possessed
ant unafraid
2 ***syn*** see FEARFUL 2
idiom all of a twitter (*or* flutter)
ant unafraid; sanguine
3 ***syn*** see DISINCLINED
afresh *adv* **1** ***syn*** see OVER 7
2 ***syn*** see NEW
||African dominoes *n pl* ***syn*** see DICE
aft *adv* ***syn*** see ABAFT
rel hind, posterior
con ahead, before, forward
ant fore
after *adv* so as to follow in time or space <*after,* we turned toward home>
syn afterward, afterwhile, behind, by and by, infra, later, latterly, next, subsequently
rel abaft, aft, astern
idiom after a time (*or* while), in the wake of
con ahead, forward
ant before
after *prep* **1** so as to resemble or follow in some respect <named *after* his father>
syn for, from
2 later in time or lower in place or rank <*after* our discussion>

---

syn synonym(s) ***rel*** related word(s)
ant antonym(s) ***con*** contrasted word(s)
idiom idiomatic equivalent(s)
|| use limited; if in doubt, see a dictionary

syn behind, below, following, next, since, subsequent to
con ante, ere, in advance of, preceding, prior to
ant before
3 *syn* see BEYOND 1
after *adj* 1 *syn* see SUBSEQUENT 1
2 *syn* see POSTERIOR 2
con antecedent, preceding, prior
after all *adv syn* see HOWEVER
aftereffect *n syn* see EFFECT 1
rel remainder, residual, residuum
afterlife *n* 1 *syn* see ETERNITY 2
2 *syn* see HEREAFTER 2
afterlight *n syn* see REVIEW 5
aftermath *n syn* see EFFECT 1
rel remainder, residual, residuum
aftertime *n syn* see FUTURE
afterward *adv syn* see AFTER
afterward *n syn* see FUTURE
afterwhile *adv syn* see AFTER
afterword *n syn* see EPILOGUE 1
afterworld *n syn* see HEREAFTER 2
again *adv* 1 *syn* see ABOUT 6
2 *syn* see OVER 7
3 *syn* see THEN 1
4 as another point, fact, or instance <*again*, consider taxes>
syn additionally, also, besides, further, in addition, then; *compare* ALSO 2
idiom by the same token, into the bargain, on top of that
5 as an alternative and especially a converse <he may win and *again* he may not>
syn contra, contrariwise, contrary, contrawise, conversely, oppositely, vice versa; *compare* HOWEVER
idiom at the same time, be that as it may, just the same, on the other hand
again and again *adv syn* see OFTEN
against *prep* 1 directly opposite <stood *against* the crowd and shouted for order>
syn contra, facing, fronting, over against, toward, vis-à-vis
idiom counter to, face to face with
2 so as to touch <vines trained *against* the wall>
syn to, touching
idiom in contact with, next to
3 *syn* see VERSUS 1
4 without being prevented or obstructed by <succeeded *against* grave handicaps>
syn despite, in spite of, notwithstanding, regardless of
idiom in the face of
5 *syn* see FROM 2
6 *syn* see APROPOS
agape *adj syn* see AGHAST 2
age *n* 1 *syn* see OLD AGE
ant youth
2 *often* **ages** *pl* a long or seemingly long period of time <haven't seen her for *ages*>
syn aeon, blue moon, coon's age, dog's age, donkey's years, eternity, long
idiom month of Sundays, ‖right smart spell
con flash, instant, minute, moment, second, split second, trice
3 *syn* see PERIOD 2
age *vb syn* see MATURE
aged *adj* 1 being in the declining phase of life <*aged* pensioners>
syn ancient, elderly, old, olden
rel pensioned (off), retired, superannuated; senior; hoary, patriarchal, venerable; doddering, senescent, senile, tottery
idiom along in years, getting on, getting on (*or* along) in years, gray with age, on one's last legs, stricken with years
con juvenile, puerile
ant youthful
2 *syn* see ANCIENT 1
3 *syn* see RIPE 3
ageless *adj syn* see ETERNAL 4
agency *n syn* see MEAN 2
rel antecedent, cause, determinant; gear
agenda *n syn* see PROGRAM 1
agent *n* 1 *syn* see MEAN 2
rel doer, executive, executor, performer; actor, worker; activator, energizer
2 one who acts for another <diplomatic *agents* serving abroad>
syn assignee, attorney, deputy, factor, proxy; *compare* DELEGATE
rel go-between, middleman; instrument, minister, tool; commissioner, proctor, procurator, representative, steward; buyer, commissionaire
ant principal
3 *syn* see SPY
age-old *adj syn* see ANCIENT 1
agglomerate *n syn* see AGGREGATE 1
rel heap, mass, pile
agglomeration *n* 1 *syn* see ACCUMULATION
rel association, combination
2 *syn* see AGGREGATE 1
aggrandize *vb* 1 *syn* see INCREASE 1
rel amplify, build up
2 *syn* see EXALT 1
ant belittle
aggrandizement *n syn* see APOTHEOSIS 2
aggravate *vb* 1 *syn* see INTENSIFY
rel augment, enlarge, increase, multiply; aggrandize
con extenuate, palliate
ant alleviate
2 *syn* see IRRITATE
rel disturb, perturb, upset; annoy, bedevil
con calm, tranquilize
ant appease
aggravation *n syn* see ANNOYANCE 2
aggregate *vb syn* see AMOUNT 1
aggregate *n* 1 a mass or body formed of particles or parts that retain their individuality <an *aggregate* of ill-planned arguments>
syn agglomerate, agglomeration, aggregation, conglomerate, conglomeration; *compare* ACCUMULATION
ant constituent, element
2 *syn* see BODY 5
ant individual, unit; particular
3 *syn* see WHOLE 1
aggregation *n* 1 *syn* see AGGREGATE 1

ant constituent, element
2 *syn* see ACCUMULATION
rel backlog, reserve, stockpile
3 *syn* see GATHERING 2

aggress *vb* ***syn*** see ATTACK 1

aggression *n* **1 *syn*** see ATTACK 1
2 *syn* see ATTACK 2
rel incursion, inroad, invasion, raid; irruption
ant resistance

aggressive *adj* marked by bold determination and readiness for conflict <an *aggressive* fighter>
syn assertive, assertory, militant, pushful, pushing, pushy, self-assertive
rel belligerent, combative, contentious, scrappy; domineering, imperious, masterful, tough; energetic, hard-hitting, strenuous, vigorous
con passive, unassertive; meek, submissive, yielding

aggressiveness *n* ***syn*** see ATTACK 2

aggrieve *vb* **1 *syn*** see DISTRESS 2
rel abuse, misuse, outrage; pain
con delight, gladden, please
2 *syn* see WRONG
rel afflict, torment, try; annoy, harass, harry, plague, worry
con benefit, profit

aghast *adj* **1 *syn*** see AFRAID 1
rel appalled, horrified, horror-struck; undone, unmanned
idiom scared stiff (*or* white)
2 struck by an intense emotional reaction (as surprise, disgust, or bewilderment) <*aghast* at the lack of discipline>
syn agape, confounded, dismayed, dumbfounded, overwhelmed, shocked, thunderstruck
rel agog, amazed, startled; awed, awestricken; astonished, flabbergasted, surprised
idiom struck all of a heap, taken aback, unable to believe one's eyes (*or* senses)
con acceptant, acquiescent, tolerant

agile *adj* acting or moving with easy alacrity <an *agile* athlete with superior flexibility>
syn active, brisk, brisky, catty, lively, nimble, sprightly, spry, volant, yare, zippy
rel adroit, deft, dexterous; fleet, quick, speedy; limber, lissome, lithe, supple; light-footed, tripping
con inactive, inert, passive; heavy, lethargic, logy; dull, slow, sluggish
ant torpid

agitable *adj* ***syn*** see EXCITABLE

agitate *vb* **1 *syn*** see SHAKE 4
rel bounce, joggle, jounce; actuate, drive, impel, move
con lull, quiet, still
2 *syn* see DISCOMPOSE 1
rel exasperate, irritate, peeve, provoke, rile, ruffle
ant calm, tranquilize
3 *syn* see DISCUSS 1
rel air, broach, ventilate; consider; assail, attack

agitation *n* ***syn*** see COMMOTION 2
rel ado, bustle, disturbance, stir
ant tranquillity

agitator *n* ***syn*** see INSTIGATOR

aglow *adj* ***syn*** see ALIGHT 2
rel gleaming, glowing, shining; lucent, luminous, radiant

agnate *adj* **1 *syn*** see RELATED
2 *syn* see LIKE

agog *adj* ***syn*** see EAGER
rel aroused, roused, stirred; excited, galvanized, stimulated; restive; zestful
ant aloof

agonize *vb* **1 *syn*** see AFFLICT
rel distress, trouble; chafe, fret, gall
2 *syn* see WRITHE 1
rel bear, endure, suffer

agonizing *adj* ***syn*** see EXCRUCIATING
rel exquisite, fierce, intense, vehement, violent

agony *n* ***syn*** see DISTRESS
con repose, rest

agrarian *adj* ***syn*** see WILD 1

agree *vb* **1 *syn*** see ACKNOWLEDGE 2
rel allow, concede, grant, own
con except, exclude
ant deny
2 *syn* see ASSENT
rel allow, concede, grant; receive; acknowledge, admit
con expostulate, kick, object, remonstrate; balk, demur, jib; oppose, resist, withstand
ant protest (against); differ (with)
3 to achieve harmony (as of opinion, feeling, or purpose) <they *agreed* finally on all major issues>
syn coincide, concert, concord, concur, harmonize
rel coact, cooperate, unite
idiom fall in with, hit it off with
con bicker, quarrel, squabble, wrangle; argue, debate, dispute, hassle
ant differ; disagree
4 to exist or go together without conflict or incongruity <his conclusion *agrees* with the evidence>
syn accord, check, check out, cohere, comport, conform, consist, consort, correspond, dovetail, fit (in), ‖gee, go, harmonize, jibe, march, quadrate, rhyme, square, suit, tally
rel approach, equal, match, rival, touch; complete, fulfill, round out, supplement
idiom go hand in hand
con negate, negative, nullify; clash, conflict, jar
ant differ (from)

agree (with) *vb* ***syn*** see SUIT 4

agreeability *n* ***syn*** see AMENITY 1

agreeable *adj* **1 *syn*** see PLEASANT 1
rel delectable, delightful
ant disagreeable
2 *syn* see CONSONANT 1

---

syn synonym(s) ***rel*** related word(s)
ant antonym(s) ***con*** contrasted word(s)
idiom idiomatic equivalent(s)
‖ use limited; if in doubt, see a dictionary

con conflicting, inharmonious, jarring, uncongenial
agreeableness *n* ***syn*** see AMENITY 1
agreed *adv* ***syn*** see YES 1
agreement *n* **1** ***syn*** see HARMONY 2
ant disagreement
2 a settlement reached by parties to a dispute or negotiation <the company has reached an *agreement* with the striking workers>
syn accord, deal, understanding; *compare* CONTRACT
rel cartel, concordat, convention, entente, pact; compact, contract, covenant, treaty; engagement; consensus
3 ***syn*** see TREATY
4 ***syn*** see CONTRACT
agrestal *adj* ***syn*** see WILD 1
agrestic *adj* ***syn*** see RURAL
agriculture *n* the science or business of raising useful plants and animals <opening the country for *agriculture*>
syn farming, husbandry
aground *adj* being or becoming forced onto the ground or shore <the boat is *aground* and breaking up>
syn beached, grounded, stranded
idiom high and dry, on the rocks
ant afloat
ahead *adv* **1** ***syn*** see BEFORE 1
con after
ant behind
2 further on in the direction in question <the road stretched *ahead* toward the west>
syn alee, forth, forward, onward
ahead of *prep* ***syn*** see BEFORE 1
aid *vb* ***syn*** see HELP 1
rel alleviate, lighten, mitigate, relieve
ant impede
aid *n* **1** ***syn*** see HELP 1
2 ***syn*** see HELP 2
rel alleviation, assuagement, mitigation; backing, support
idiom a leg up
con check, curb, restraint; bar, obstacle, obstruction
ant impediment
3 ***syn*** see HELPER
4 ***syn*** see ASSISTANT 2
rel aider, befriender, benefactor, ministrant, succorer; striker
aidant *adj* ***syn*** see HELPFUL 1
aide *n* ***syn*** see ASSISTANT 2
aide–de–camp *n* ***syn*** see ASSISTANT 2
aiding *adj* ***syn*** see HELPFUL 1
ail *vb* ***syn*** see TROUBLE 1
rel afflict, try
idiom be the matter (with), give one trouble
con alleviate, ease, relieve; comfort, console, solace
ailing *adj* ***syn*** see UNWELL
rel debilitated, enfeebled, gone, strengthless, weak; droopy, limp, sapless, spiritless
con hale, lusty, robust, rugged, vigorous
ailment *n* **1** ***syn*** see DISEASE
2 ***syn*** see UNREST
aim *vb* **1** ***syn*** see DIRECT 2
rel concentrate, fix, focus
idiom draw a bead on, take aim
2 to have as a controlling desire something that transcends one's present capacity for attainment <from a boy he had *aimed* at high office>
syn aspire, pant
rel attempt, endeavor, essay, strive, try; design, intend, propose, purpose; covet, crave, yearn (for)
idiom have an eye to, reach for the stars, set one's eyes upon
3 ***syn*** see INTEND 2
rel choose, desire, want, wish; expect
idiom have (*or* keep) in view, promise oneself (to)
4 ***syn*** see SLANT 2
aim *n* ***syn*** see AMBITION 2
rel desideratum, desire, idol, urge
idiom end in view
aimless *adj* ***syn*** see RANDOM
air *n* **1** ***syn*** see BEARING 1
rel manner, style
2 *usu* **airs** *pl* ***syn*** see POSE 2
rel loftiness, ostentation, pretentiousness, show; complacency, self-importance, vainglory, vanity
3 a pervading influence that colors outward appearance or apparent character <the village had an *air* of decay>
syn atmosphere, aura, feel, feeling, mood, semblance
rel character, property, quality
con basis, essence, reality
4 ***syn*** see MELODY
air *vb* ***syn*** see EXPRESS 2
rel discover, divulge, reveal; broadcast, declare, proclaim, publish
idiom make public, noise (*or* sound) abroad, spread far and wide
airless *adj* ***syn*** see STUFFY 1
airman *n* ***syn*** see PILOT 2
airy *adj* **1** of or relating to air <clouds drifting on *airy* currents>
syn aerial, atmospheric, pneumatic
rel gaseous, vaporous
2 ***syn*** see LOFTY 6
rel exposed, windswept; supernal
3 resembling or suggesting air especially in lightness or lack of substance <*airy* persiflage>
syn aerial, ethereal, vaporous, vapory
rel frivolous, light, volatile; rare, rarefied, tenuous, thin; dainty, delicate, diaphanous, exquisite, spirituel
con corporeal, material, physical; bulky, massive, massy
ant substantial
4 ***syn*** see ELASTIC 2
rel animated, high-spirited, spirited
5 ***syn*** see WINDY 1
akin *adj* **1** ***syn*** see RELATED
2 ***syn*** see LIKE
rel kindred; according, agreeing, conforming, harmonizing

con extraneous, foreign
ant alien

alacrity *n* promptness in responding or acting <accepted the invitation with *alacrity*>
syn dispatch, expedition, goodwill, promptitude, readiness
rel briskness, eagerness; enthusiasm, fervor, heartiness, zeal; promptness, quickness
con hesitation, procrastination, temporization, vacillation; apathy, indifference, lethargy, phlegm, sluggishness
ant dilatoriness

a la mode *adj* ***syn*** see STYLISH

alarm *n* **1** a signal that warns or calls to action <the *alarm* consisted of two quick flashes of light>
syn alert, SOS, tocsin
rel caution, forewarning, prenotice, warning
2 ***syn*** see FEAR 1
rel upset; strain, stress, tension
con calm, calmness, serenity, tranquillity; equanimity, sangfroid
ant assurance; composure

alarm *vb* ***syn*** see FRIGHTEN
rel amaze, astonish, surprise
idiom give one a turn
con comfort, console, solace
ant assure, relieve

alarmable *adj* ***syn*** see EXCITABLE

albeit *conj* ***syn*** see THOUGH

album *n* ***syn*** see ANTHOLOGY

alcohol *n* ***syn*** see LIQUOR 2

alcoholic *adj* ***syn*** see SPIRITUOUS

alcoholized *adj* ***syn*** see INTOXICATED 1

alcove *n* ***syn*** see SUMMERHOUSE

alee *adv* ***syn*** see AHEAD 2

alehouse *n* an establishment serving primarily beer and ale <an *alehouse* specializing in beers actually brewed on the premises>
syn beer garden, beer hall, ‖beerhouse, bierstube, mughouse, stube; *compare* BAR 5
rel barrelhouse, bistro, bottle club, brasserie, cabaret, café, honky-tonk, nightclub, rathskeller, roadhouse, wineshop

alembicated *adj* ***syn*** see PRECIOUS 4

alert *adj* **1** ***syn*** see WATCHFUL
rel attentive, heedful, mindful; careful
idiom all eyes and ears, on (one's) guard, on the alert
con inattentive, unmindful; aloof, detached, indifferent, unconcerned
2 ***syn*** see INTELLIGENT 2
rel apt, prompt, quick, ready
con lackadaisical, languid, listless
3 ***syn*** see LIVELY 1
rel frisky; mercurial
idiom full of life
con inactive, indolent
ant inert

alert *n* ***syn*** see ALARM 1

alfresco *adj* ***syn*** see OUTDOOR

algetic *adj* ***syn*** see PAINFUL 1

alias *n* ***syn*** see PSEUDONYM

alibi *n* ***syn*** see EXCUSE 1

alien *adj* ***syn*** see EXTRINSIC
rel exotic, outlandish, strange; incompatible, incongrous, inconsonant
con cognate, kindred, related; compatible, congenial, congruous, consonant; germane, material, pertinent, relevant
ant akin; assimilable

alien *n* ***syn*** see STRANGER
con national, subject
ant citizen

alien *vb* **1** ***syn*** see ESTRANGE
rel alter, change, convert
con accommodate, adjust, conform, reconcile
ant unite; reunite
2 ***syn*** see TRANSFER 4
rel give up, hand over, relinquish

alienate *vb* **1** ***syn*** see TRANSFER 4
rel give up, hand over, relinquish
2 ***syn*** see ESTRANGE
rel alter, change, convert
con accommodate, adjust, conform, reconcile
ant unite; reunite

alienation *n* **1** ***syn*** see ESTRANGEMENT
2 ***syn*** see INSANITY 1

alight *vb* to come to rest after or as if after a flight, a descent, or a fall <snowflakes *alighting* on the bare trees>
syn land, light, perch, roost, set down, settle, sit down, touch down
rel drop, fall, tumble
con arise, ascend, rise, soar

alight *adj* **1** ***syn*** see BURNING 1
2 made bright by or as if by fire <her face *alight* with joy>
syn ablaze, afire, aflame, aflicker, aglow
rel bright, effulgent, fulgent, refulgent; blazing, flaming, flaring, glowing
con dark, dusky, gloomy, heavy, lowery, shadowed, shadowy

align *vb* ***syn*** see LINE 1
rel adjust, fix, regulate
con unsettle

alike *adj* ***syn*** see LIKE
con separate
ant unlike; different

alikeness *n* ***syn*** see LIKENESS

aliment *n* ***syn*** see FOOD 2

alimentary *adj* ***syn*** see NUTRITIVE 1

alimentation *n* ***syn*** see LIVING

alimentative *adj* ***syn*** see NUTRITIVE 1

alimony *n* ***syn*** see LIVING

alive *adj* **1** ***syn*** see LIVING 1
con inactive, inert
ant dead, defunct
2 ***syn*** see EXTANT 1
3 ***syn*** see ACTIVE 1
rel fresh, green, verdant
con dormant, inactive, quiescent
ant dead, extinct

---

syn synonym(s) ***rel*** related word(s)
ant antonym(s) ***con*** contrasted word(s)
idiom idiomatic equivalent(s)
‖ use limited; if in doubt, see a dictionary

4 ***syn*** see AWARE
rel vigilant, watchful, wide-awake; intelligent, quick, quick-witted
con heedless, inattentive, oblivious, unmindful; careless, neglectful, negligent
ant blind (to)
5 full of vigorous life, animation, or activity <the streets were *alive* with shoppers>
syn abounding, overflowing, replete, rife, swarming, teeming, thronged
rel crowded, populous, thick; filled, flush, full
con barren, empty, vacant, void; unoccupied, unpopulated, untenanted

all *adj* **1** ***syn*** see WHOLE 4
rel full, plenary
2 each member or individual of <*all* my friends came with me>
syn each, every
ant no

all *adv* **1** without exception <the money was *all* spent>
syn all in all, altogether, exactly, in toto, just, purely, quite, stick, totally, utterly, wholly
idiom in its entirety
2 ***syn*** see APIECE

all *pron* **1** ***syn*** see EVERYTHING
2 ***syn*** see EVERYBODY

all *n* ***syn*** see WHOLE 1

all–around *adj* **1** ***syn*** see VERSATILE
rel complete, consummate
2 not narrowly particularized <taking an *all-around* view of the problem>
syn comprehensive, general, global, inclusive, overall, sweeping
rel broad, extensive, panoramic, wide; all-inclusive, unexcluding, unexclusive, wide-ranging; synoptic
con express, particular, specific; narrow, precise, restricted; individual, singular

allay *vb* **1** ***syn*** see RELIEVE 1
con arouse, rouse, stir; excite, provoke, stimulate; aggravate, enhance
ant intensify
2 ***syn*** see CALM
rel ease, soften, subdue; deaden, dull, temper; disburden, disembarrass, disencumber; deliver, free, release
con aggravate, enhance, heighten, magnify, worsen
ant intensify

all but *adv* **1** ***syn*** see NEARLY
2 ***syn*** see ALMOST 2

allege *vb* ***syn*** see ADDUCE
rel affirm, assert, avouch, avow, declare, profess; recite, recount, rehearse, state
con contradict, deny, gainsay, impugn, negate, negative; controvert, disprove, rebut, refute
ant contravene

alleged *adj* of questionable truth or genuineness <had doubts of the *alleged* miracle>
syn ostensible, pretended, professed, purported, so-called, supposed; *compare* SUPPOSED 1
rel credible, plausible, specious; doubtful, dubious, questionable; self-styled, soi-disant, would-be
idiom in name only
con authentic, bona fide, genuine, veritable; actual, real, true; delusory, erroneous, fallacious, false, illusory, imaginary, unreal

allegiance *n* ***syn*** see FIDELITY 1
rel firmness; consecration, dedication; deference, homage, honor
con alienation, disaffection; disloyalty, treason

allegiant *adj* ***syn*** see FAITHFUL 1

allegory *n* **1** a method of indirect representation (as in literature or art) of ideas or truths <by *allegory* such abstractions as love and fear can be depicted>
syn figuration, symbolism, symbolization, typification
2 a literary form that tells a story to present a truth or enforce a moral <Orwell's *Animal Farm* is a well-known English *allegory*>
syn apologue, fable, myth, parable; *compare* MYTH 1

allergy *n* ***syn*** see ANTIPATHY 2
rel rejection, repulsion, revulsion
con affinity, attraction, sympathy

alleviate *vb* ***syn*** see RELIEVE 1
rel cure, remedy
idiom temper the wind to the shorn lamb
con augment, heighten, intensify
ant aggravate

alleviation *n* ***syn*** see EASE 3

all–fired *adj* ***syn*** see UTTER

alliance *n* **1** ***syn*** see ASSOCIATION 1
2 an association (as of nations) for a common object <a world *alliance* in support of peace>
syn anschluss, coalition, confederacy, confederation, federation, league, union; *compare* UNIFICATION
rel association, club, order, society

allied *adj* ***syn*** see RELATED
rel linked, united; parallel, similar
con alien, extraneous, foreign; discrete, separate, several
ant unallied

all in *adj* ***syn*** see EFFETE 2
idiom at last gasp

all in all *adv* **1** ***syn*** see ALL 1
2 ***syn*** see ALTOGETHER 3

allineate *vb* ***syn*** see LINE 1

allness *n* ***syn*** see ENTIRETY 1

allocate *vb* **1** ***syn*** see ALLOT
con reserve, sequester, stockpile
2 ***syn*** see DESIGNATE 3

allocution *n* ***syn*** see SPEECH 2

allot *vb* to give as one's share, portion, role, or place <*allotted* himself a daily hour for exercise>
syn admeasure, allocate, allow, apportion, assign, give, lot, mete (out)
rel deal (out), dispense, distribute, dole (out); equip, fit out, furnish; accord, grant, vouchsafe; appoint, ordain, prescribe
con detain, hold, hold back, keep, retain, withhold; appropriate, arrogate, confiscate

allotment *n* **1** ***syn*** see SHARE 1
2 ***syn*** see RATION

all–out *adj* ***syn*** see TOTAL 5

all over *adv* ***syn*** see EVERYWHERE 1
allover *adj* ***syn*** see OMNIPRESENT
‖**all–overs** *n pl* ***syn*** see JITTERS
allow *vb* **1** ***syn*** see ALLOT
rel bestow, confer
con refuse
2 ***syn*** see ACKNOWLEDGE 1
rel accede, acquiesce, assent
con confute, refute, reject
ant disallow
3 ***syn*** see LET 2
rel brook, endure, stand, tolerate; defer, submit, yield
con avert, prevent, ward (off)
ant inhibit
allowable *adj* ***syn*** see PERMISSIBLE
allowance *n* **1** ***syn*** see RATION
rel assignment; appropriation, grant, subsidy
2 ***syn*** see SHARE 1
3 ***syn*** see ADVANTAGE 3
rel aid, assistance, help; bounty, grant, subsidy
4 ***syn*** see PERMISSION
rel countenance, favor; indulgence, toleration
con refusal, rejection; contradiction, contravention, negation
5 a taking into account of extenuating circumstances or of contingencies <we must make *allowance* for the inexperience of youth>
syn concession
rel accommodation, adaptation, adjustment; extenuation, mitigation, palliation
alloy *n* **1** ***syn*** see ADMIXTURE 1
2 ***syn*** see MIXTURE
all–powerful *adj* ***syn*** see OMNIPOTENT
all right *adv* ***syn*** see YES 1
all right *adj* ***syn*** see DECENT 4
all round (*or* **all around**) *adv* ***syn*** see EVERYWHERE 1
all there *adj* ***syn*** see SANE 2
all told *adv* ***syn*** see ALTOGETHER 3
allude *vb* ***syn*** see REFER 3
rel hint, imply, intimate, suggest
allure *vb* **1** ***syn*** see ATTRACT 1
rel delude; woo
con avoid, elude, eschew, shun; alienate, disaffect, estrange, wean
2 ***syn*** see LURE
allure *n* ***syn*** see CHARM 3
allurement *n* **1** ***syn*** see ATTRACTION 1
2 ***syn*** see LURE 2
alluring *adj* ***syn*** see ATTRACTIVE 1
rel appetizing; beguiling, delusive
con repellent; disagreeable, displeasing, uninviting, unlikable, unpleasant
ant repulsive
almighty *adj* ***syn*** see OMNIPOTENT
almost *adv* **1** ***syn*** see NEARLY
2 not actually but in effect <he paid *almost* nothing for it>
syn all but, as good as, as much as, essentially, practically, well-nigh; *compare* VIRTUALLY
idiom for all practical purposes, in effect, just about, to all intents and purposes
alms *n pl* ***syn*** see DONATION
aloft *adv* ***syn*** see OVER 4
rel high; skyward, upward
idiom in the clouds
alone *adj* **1** separated from others <the house was *alone* on a windy ridge>
syn apart, detached, isolate, isolated, removed, unaccompanied
rel out-of-the-way, private, remote, retired, secluded, withdrawn
idiom off the beaten track
con adjacent, close-by, near-at-hand, nearly, neighboring, nigh
2 ***syn*** see LONE 1
3 having no equal or rival and being single in kind or excellence <a drug *alone* in its curative powers>
syn matchless, only, peerless, unequaled, unique, unmatched, unparalleled, unrivaled; *compare* SUPREME
rel inimitable; incomparable, unexcelled, unsurpassed; excellent, good, superior
idiom second to none
con common, commonplace, everyday, ordinary, usual; accustomed, conventional, customary, regular
4 ***syn*** see ONLY 2
alone *adv* ***syn*** see ONLY 1
aloneness *n* ***syn*** see SOLITUDE
along *adv* **1** so as to make forward progress <hurrying *along* toward town>
syn forth, forward, on, onward; *compare* AHEAD 2
2 ***syn*** see ALSO 2
alongside *prep* ***syn*** see BESIDE 1
aloof *adj* **1** ***syn*** see INDIFFERENT 2
rel arrogant, disdainful, haughty, proud; chilly, cold, cool, frigid; constrained, reserved, restrained, reticent, standoffish
con affable, companionable, gregarious, sociable, social; friendly, neighborly
ant familiar; outgoing
2 ***syn*** see UNSOCIABLE
alp *n* ***syn*** see MOUNTAIN 1
alpha *n* ***syn*** see BEGINNING
ant omega
alphabet *n* **1** a set of characters in which a language can be written <the Greek *alphabet*>
syn ABC(s), christcross-row, letters
2 the simplest fundamental part or level <learning the *alphabet* of computer science>
syn ABC's, elements, fundamentals, grammar, principles, rudiments
rel beginning, commencement, start; outset
idiom first steps
con entirety, total, whole; details, minutiae, trivia
already *adv* **1** ***syn*** see BEFORE 2
2 ***syn*** see EVEN 2
also *adv* **1** in the same manner <they *also* serve who nurse the wounded soldiers>

---

syn synonym(s) ***rel*** related word(s)
ant antonym(s) ***con*** contrasted word(s)
idiom idiomatic equivalent(s)
‖ use limited; if in doubt, see a dictionary

syn correspondingly, likewise, similarly, so
idiom in like manner
2 in addition to that <he was stern but *also* just>
syn additionally, along, as well, besides, furthermore, item, likewise, more, moreover, still, too, withal, yea, yet
idiom into the bargain, on top of that, to boot
3 ***syn*** see AGAIN 4

alter *vb* **1** ***syn*** see CHANGE 1
rel accommodate, adapt, adjust, moderate, modulate, temper; doctor
idiom work a change (in)
con conserve, keep, preserve, retain
ant fix
2 ***syn*** see STERILIZE

alteration *n* **1** ***syn*** see CHANGE 1
rel accommodation, adaptation, adjustment; conversion, metamorphosis, transformation; fluctuation, shilly-shally, vacillation, wavering
con perdurability, permanence, stability; continuance, endurance, persistence
ant fixation, fixity
2 ***syn*** see TRANSITION
3 ***syn*** see CONVERSION 2

altercate *vb* ***syn*** see QUARREL
rel agitate, argue, debate, dispute
con accord, get along; accommodate, adapt, adjust, conform
ant concur

altercation *n* ***syn*** see QUARREL
rel argument; combat, contest
con agreement, concord, consonance, harmony; empathy, like-mindedness, sympathy, understanding
ant accord; concurrence

alterity *n* ***syn*** see DISSIMILARITY

alternate *adj* **1** ***syn*** see INTERMITTENT
rel alternant, alternating, rotating; complementary, corresponding, reciprocal
con sequent, successive
ant consecutive
2 ***syn*** see SUBSTITUTE 1
rel equivalent, proxy, replacing; exchangeable, interchangeable; makeshift, provisional, tentative

alternate *vb* ***syn*** see ROTATE 2
rel fluctuate, oscillate, sway, waver; recur, return, revert
con follow, succeed

alternate *n* ***syn*** see SUBSTITUTE

alternately *adv* ***syn*** see INSTEAD

alternation *n* ***syn*** see SUCCESSION 2
rel recurrence, return, reversion; reappearance, repetition

alternative *adj* ***syn*** see SUBSTITUTE 1
rel equivalent, proxy, replacing; exchangeable, interchangeable; makeshift, provisional, tentative

alternative *n* ***syn*** see CHOICE 1
rel attainable, contingency, possibility

alternatively *adv* ***syn*** see INSTEAD

although *conj* ***syn*** see THOUGH

altitude *n* ***syn*** see HEIGHT
rel apex, eminence, peak, summit
con depth

altitudinous *adj* ***syn*** see HIGH 1

altogether *adv* **1** ***syn*** see WELL 3
2 ***syn*** see ALL 1
3 as a total <*altogether* it cost over a thousand dollars>
syn all told, in all, quite
idiom taken together
4 with minor exceptions or flaws <*altogether* the party was a success>
syn all in all, by and large, en masse, generally, on the whole
idiom all things considered, as a whole, for the most part, generally speaking, in the main

altruistic *adj* ***syn*** see CHARITABLE 1
rel considerate, kind, unselfish; bounteous, bountiful, generous, liberal, openhanded; bighearted, magnanimous, noble-minded
con egotistic, self-centered, selfish, self-seeking; illiberal, mean, niggardly, stingy, ungenerous
ant egoistic

always *adv* **1** on every relevant occasion <*always* made the same mistake>
syn constantly, continuously, ever, invariably, perpetually
rel frequently, often, regularly, usually
idiom in every case (*or* instance), without exception
con rarely, seldom
ant never
2 ***syn*** see EVER 2

‖amah *n* ***syn*** see NURSEMAID

amalgam *n* ***syn*** see MIXTURE

amalgamate *vb* ***syn*** see MIX 1
rel compact, consolidate, unify
con crumble, decompose, disintegrate; disperse, dissipate, scatter

amalgamation *n* **1** ***syn*** see MIXTURE
2 ***syn*** see CONSOLIDATION 2

amaranthine *adj* ***syn*** see EVERLASTING 1

amaroidal *adj* ***syn*** see ACRID

amass *vb* ***syn*** see ACCUMULATE
ant distribute

amassment *n* ***syn*** see ACCUMULATION

amateur *n* **1** one having a marked and usually informed taste or liking for something <an *amateur* of fine fabrics>
syn admirer, devotee, fan, fancier, votary
rel crank, enthusiast, faddist, infatuate, ‖nut, zealot; aesthete, cognoscente, connoisseur, dilettante; illuminato, illuminist
con abecedarian, dabbler, tyro; adept, expert
2 one who follows a pursuit without attaining mastery or professional status <a nation handicapped by *amateurs* in high office>
syn abecedarian, dabbler, dilettante, nonprofessional, smatterer, tyro, uninitiate
rel beginner, greenhorn, neophyte; apprentice, novice, probationer; potterer, putterer, tinker
con adept, virtuoso, wizard
ant expert, master; professional

amateurish *adj* lacking or marked by lack of expert skill or finish <an *amateurish* actor>

syn dabbling, dilettante, dilettantish, dilettantist, jackleg, unaccomplished, unfinished, ungifted, unskilled
rel clumsy, crude, green, raw, untutored; defective, deficient, faulty, flawed
con accomplished, expert, gifted, skilled
ant professional

amative *adj syn* see EROTIC

amatory *adj syn* see EROTIC
rel admiring, attracted, yearning

amaze *vb syn* see SURPRISE 2
rel affect, impress, move, strike, touch

amaze *n syn* see WONDER 2
rel confoundment; surprise

amazement *n syn* see WONDER 2
rel confoundment; surprise

amazing *adj syn* see MARVELOUS 1

amazon *n syn* see VIRAGO

ambidextrous *adj* **1** *syn* see TWO-HANDED 2
2 *syn* see VERSATILE
3 *syn* see INSINCERE

ambience *n syn* see ENVIRONMENT

ambient *n syn* see ENVIRONMENT

ambiguity *n* expression or an expression obscure because subject to more than one interpretation <a speech full of *ambiguities*>
syn amphibology, double entendre, double meaning, equivocality, equivocation, equivoque, tergiversation
rel dodge, evasion, hedge, quibble, shift, subterfuge; cavil, haggling, hairsplitting, quibbling; obscurity, uncertainty, vagueness
con definiteness, expressness, specificity; clearness, exactness, precision
ant explicitness; lucidity

ambiguous *adj* **1** *syn* see OBSCURE 3
rel doubtful, dubious, questionable
con clear, lucid, perspicuous; categorical, express, specific
ant explicit
2 *syn* see DOUBTFUL 1

ambit *n* **1** *syn* see CIRCUMFERENCE
2 *syn* see RANGE 2

ambition *n* **1** strong desire for advancement <a life ruled by *ambition*>
syn ambitiousness, aspiration, pretension
rel drive, go-ahead, push; anxiety, avidity, eagerness, keenness; energy, enterprise, spirit; goad, incentive, motive, spur
con contentment, satisfaction; faineance, indolence, lethargy, sloth
2 an object of desire or intent <his *ambition* was to have enough to live on without working>
syn aim, goal, mark, objective, quaesitum, target; *compare* INTENTION
rel design, intent, purpose; desire, fancy, hope, wish; dream, ideal, nirvana
3 *syn* see ENTERPRISE 4

ambitious *adj* **1** marked by intense desire for advancement (as in power, fame, or wealth) <a ruthlessly *ambitious* politician>
syn aspiring, emulous, vaulting
rel aggressive, enterprising, go-ahead, pushing, up-and-doing; energetic, hardworking, indefatigable; anxious, avid, eager, keen
con apathetic, phlegmatic, stolid; faineant, indolent, lazy, slothful
2 of a kind to try or exceed one's powers of performance <an *ambitious* scheme to corner the gold market>
syn grandiose, lofty, pretentious, utopian, visionary
rel audacious, bold, daring; chimerical, extravagant, high-flown, impractical, quixotic, unrealistic
con easy, plain, straightforward; feasible, practicable, realistic; unpretentious
ant modest

ambitiousness *n syn* see AMBITION 1

ambivalent *adj syn* see EQUIVOCAL 2

amble *vb syn* see SAUNTER
rel dally, dawdle, dillydally, loiter

ambrosial *adj* **1** *syn* see DELIGHTFUL
2 *syn* see SWEET 2

ambulant *adj syn* see ITINERANT
ant bedfast, bedridden

ambulate *vb syn* see WALK 1

ambulatory *adj syn* see ITINERANT

ambuscade *n syn* see AMBUSH

ambush *vb syn* see SURPRISE 1
rel assail, assault, attack; ensnare, entrap, snare, trap

ambush *n* a device to entrap an enemy by lying in hiding until a surprise attack is feasible <planned an *ambush* on the cliff above the trail>
syn ambuscade, ambushment
rel lure, snare, trap; blind, cover, hideout, retreat

ambushment *n syn* see AMBUSH

ameliorate *vb* **1** *syn* see IMPROVE 1
rel alleviate, lighten, mitigate, relieve
con damage, harm, hurt, impair, injure, mar, spoil; aggravate, intensify
ant worsen; deteriorate
2 *syn* see IMPROVE 3

amenable *adj* **1** *syn* see RESPONSIBLE
rel open, subject; dependent, subordinate
con autarchic, free
ant independent (of); autonomous
2 *syn* see OBEDIENT
rel subdued, tame; receptive, responsive, willing; adaptable, impressionable, malleable, plastic, pliable, pliant
con fierce, mulish, obstinate, stubborn, truculent
ant recalcitrant, refractory

amend *vb* **1** *syn* see CORRECT 1
rel repair; elevate, lift, raise
con corrupt, debauch, deprave, pervert, vitiate
ant debase
2 *syn* see IMPROVE 1
rel advance, forward, promote
ant worsen; impair

amends *n pl syn* see REPARATION

---

syn synonym(s) *rel* related word(s)
ant antonym(s) *con* contrasted word(s)
idiom idiomatic equivalent(s)
|| use limited; if in doubt, see a dictionary

amenity *n* **1** the quality of being pleasant or agreeable <a discussion conducted in perfect *amenity*><the *amenity* of the climate>
syn agreeability, agreeableness, amiability, cordiality, enjoyableness, geniality, gratefulness, pleasance, pleasantness, sweetness and light
rel attractiveness, charm, delightfulness; fascination, pleasingness
con disagreeableness, distastefulness, unattractiveness, unpleasantness
2 a feature that makes for pleasantness or ease <among the *amenities* of the house is central air-conditioning>
syn comfort, convenience, facility
rel betterment, enhancement, enrichment, improvement; excellence, merit, quality, virtue
con difficulty, hardship, trial, vicissitude
3 *pl* **amenities** *syn* see MANNER 5
4 *syn* see LUXURY
5 *syn* see COURTESY 1
rel civility, courteousness, politeness; affability, cordiality, geniality, graciousness, sociability
con discourtesy, impoliteness, incivility; affront, indignity, insult; acrimony
ant rudeness
ament *n* *syn* see FOOL 4
amerce *vb* *syn* see PENALIZE
amercement *n* *syn* see FINE
amiability *n* *syn* see AMENITY 1
amiable *adj* **1** of a generally agreeable nature especially in social interaction <the meeting ended on an *amiable* note>
syn complaisant, easy, good-humored, good-natured, good-tempered, lenient, mild, obliging
rel affable, cordial, genial, gracious; courteous, mannerly; benign, benignant, kind, kindly; responsive, warm, warmhearted
idiom easy to get along with
con discourteous, ill-mannered, ill-natured, impolite, rude; crabbed, dour, unsociable
ant unamiable; surly
2 *syn* see GENTLE 2
amicable *adj* **1** characterized by peaceableness and goodwill <the negotiators joined in *amicable* discussion>
syn friendly, neighborly
rel empathic, like-minded, sympathetic, understanding; accordant, agreeing, concordant, frictionless, harmonious; pacific, peaceable, peaceful
con bellicose, belligerent, combative, contentious, pugnacious, quarrelsome; antipathetic, hostile, suspicious, uncooperative
2 *syn* see HARMONIOUS 3
amical *adj* *syn* see HARMONIOUS 3
amid *prep* **1** in or into the central part of <the bomb burst *amid* the crowd>
syn among, mid, midst
idiom in (*or* into) the middle of, in (*or* into) the midst of, in (*or* into) the thick of
2 *syn* see AMONG 1
3 *syn* see DURING
amigo *n* *syn* see FRIEND
amiss *adv* **1** in a mistaken, inappropriate, or reprehensible way <I feel you judge him *amiss*>
syn faultily, incorrectly, wrongly
rel inaccurately; indiscreetly, unwisely
con accurately, correctly, properly, rightly; cleverly, wisely
ant right
2 out of the proper course <our planning had gone *amiss*>
syn afield, astray, awry, badly, unfavorably, wrong; *compare* HARD 5
idiom beside (*or* off) the mark
con auspiciously, famously, favorably, promisingly, propitiously, well
ant aright
amiss *adj* **1** *syn* see BAD 1
2 *syn* see FAULTY
3 *syn* see BLAMEWORTHY
amity *n* *syn* see GOODWILL 1
rel accord, agreement, concord, harmony; amicableness, neighborliness
con animosity, antagonism, antipathy, hostility; conflict, contention, discord, dissension, strife
ant enmity
amnesty *n* *syn* see PARDON
among *prep* **1** surrounded by <the valley nestled *among* high mountains>
syn amid, mid, midst
2 *syn* see AMID 1
3 *syn* see BETWEEN
amorist *n* *syn* see GALLANT 2
amorous *adj* *syn* see EROTIC
rel enamored, infatuated; lustful
con aloof, detached, indifferent; cold, cool; apathetic, impassive, unconcerned
ant frigid
amorousness *n* *syn* see LOVE 2
amorphous *adj* *syn* see FORMLESS
amount *vb* **1** to make up as a total <their expenses *amounted* to just a hundred dollars>
syn add up, aggregate, come, number, run (to *or* into), sum (to *or* into), total
rel comprehend, comprise, embody, include, incorporate, reach, subsume
2 to be essentially equivalent <that utter terror that *amounts* to madness>
syn approach, correspond (to), equal, match, partake (of), rival, touch
rel hint, imply, intimate, smack (of), suggest
idiom be near to, come to the same thing as, have all the earmarks (*or* features) of
amount *n* **1** *syn* see BODY 5
2 *syn* see SUBSTANCE 2
amour *n* **1** *syn* see LOVE AFFAIR
2 an illicit or informal sexual relation <memoirs devoted to accounts of his *amours*>
syn affair, intrigue, liaison
rel entanglement, intimacy, relationship; love affair, romance
3 *syn* see LOVE 2
amour propre *n* **1** *syn* see PRIDE 2
2 *syn* see CONCEIT 2
rel complacency, self-complacency, self-satisfaction, smugness; pride
amphibological *adj* *syn* see OBSCURE 3
amphibology *n* *syn* see AMBIGUITY

ample *adj* **1** ***syn*** see SPACIOUS
rel distended, expanded, inflated, swollen
con scant, skimpy, spare; cramped, exiguous, narrow, strait
ant meager; circumscribed
2 ***syn*** see PLENTIFUL
rel lavish, prodigal, profuse; handsome
idiom enough and to spare
con scrimpy, spare, sparse; beggarly, miserable, niggardly
ant meager, scant

amplify *vb* **1** ***syn*** see EXPAND 4
rel augment, extend, increase; unfold
con abbreviate, shorten
ant abridge, condense
2 ***syn*** see EXPAND 3

amplitude *n* **1** ***syn*** see SIZE 2
2 ***syn*** see BREADTH 2
con closeness, limitation, restriction, straitness
ant narrowness
3 ***syn*** see EXPANSE
rel bigness, greatness, largeness; capaciousness, commodiousness, roominess, spaciousness
con circumscription, restriction
ant straitness; limitation

amply *adv* ***syn*** see WELL 4

amulet *n* ***syn*** see CHARM 2
rel lucky piece, rabbit-foot

amuse *vb* to pass or cause to pass time in pleasant or agreeable activity <simple toys to *amuse* children on long trips>
syn divert, entertain, recreate
rel absorb, distract, engross; animate, enliven, fleet, quicken; beguile, charm, delight, enchant, fascinate, wile; while
con fatigue, irk, jade, pall (on), tire, wear (on), weary; bore, ennui

amusement *n* ***syn*** see ENTERTAINMENT

ana *n* ***syn*** see ANTHOLOGY

anabasis *n* ***syn*** see ADVANCE 2

anachronism *n* **1** a chronological error <*anachronisms* of several centuries mar some earlier chronicles>
syn misdate, misdating, mistiming, parachronism
rel antedate, anticipation, prochronism, prolepsis; postdate
2 one that is inappropriately situated especially in time <born centuries too late, he was an *anachronism* in modern urban society>
syn solecism
rel faux pas, gaffe; defect, flaw, mistake, slip

anagogic *adj* ***syn*** see MYSTICAL 1
rel esoteric, occult, recondite; allegorical, symbolical

analects *n pl* ***syn*** see ANTHOLOGY

analgesic *n* ***syn*** see ANODYNE 1
ant irritant

analogous *adj* ***syn*** see LIKE
rel convertible, corresponding, interchangeable; kindred

analogue *n* ***syn*** see PARALLEL
rel cognate, congener

analogy *n* **1** ***syn*** see LIKENESS
2 expression or an expression involving explicit or implied comparison of things basically unlike but with some striking similarities <God can be described only by *analogy*>
syn metaphor, simile, similitude
rel ambiguity, equivocation, equivoque, tergiversation
con demonstration, description, formulation

analphabet *n* ***syn*** see ILLITERATE

analysis *n* **1** separation of a whole into its fundamental elements or constituent parts <*analysis* of a problem>
syn breakdown, breakup, dissection, resolution
rel division, separation; decomposition, disintegration
con combination, union; concatenation, integration, unification
ant synthesis
2 ***syn*** see EXAMINATION

analytic *adj* ***syn*** see LOGICAL 2
rel deep, profound; acute, keen, sharp; penetrating, piercing
con constructive, creative, inventive

analytical *adj* ***syn*** see LOGICAL 2

analyze *vb* to divide a complex whole into its constituent parts or elements <*analyze* the plot of a novel>
syn anatomize, break down, decompose, decompound, dissect, resolve
rel divide, part, separate; assort, classify, pigeonhole; examine, inspect, investigate, scrutinize
con articulate, concatenate, integrate
ant compose, compound; construct

anamnesis *n* ***syn*** see MEMORY 2

Ananias *n* ***syn*** see LIAR

anarch *n* ***syn*** see REBEL

anarchism *n* **1** a political theory opposed to all forms of government and advocating voluntary cooperation and interaction of individuals and groups in satisfying their common needs <the doubtful premises of *anarchism* about human nature>
syn anarchy
rel utopianism; communism, Marxism, syndicalism
con absolutism, authoritarianism, dictatorship; elitism
2 ***syn*** see DISORDER 2

anarchist *n* ***syn*** see REBEL

anarchy *n* **1** absence of effective government or the resulting social disorder <complete *anarchy* followed the breakdown of communications>
syn chaos, lawlessness, mobocracy, ochlocracy
rel confusion, disorder, disorganization
idiom mob rule (*or* law), reign of terror
2 ***syn*** see ANARCHISM
3 ***syn*** see DISORDER 2

anastomose *vb* ***syn*** see INTERJOIN

---

syn synonym(s) ***rel*** related word(s)
ant antonym(s) ***con*** contrasted word(s)
idiom idiomatic equivalent(s)
‖ use limited; if in doubt, see a dictionary

anathema *n* **1** ***syn*** see CURSE 1
rel censure, condemnation, denunciation, reprehension, reprobation, reproof
con eulogy, laudation, praise
2 ***syn*** see ABOMINATION 1
rel leper, pariah, outcast, untouchable

anathematize *vb* ***syn*** see EXECRATE 1
rel impugn, reproach
con approbate, approve, countenance, endorse, favor

anatomize *vb* ***syn*** see ANALYZE

ancestor *n* **1** a person from whom one is descended <proud of his pioneer *ancestors*>
syn antecedent (s), ascendant, forebear, forefather, primogenitor, progenitor
ant descendant
2 ***syn*** see FORERUNNER 2

ancestry *n* one's progenitors or their character or quality as a whole <a man of noble *ancestry*>
syn blood, descent, extraction, lineage, origin, pedigree
rel family, kindred, line, race, stock; derivation, source; breed, breeding
ant descendants; posterity

anchor *vb* ***syn*** see FASTEN 2
rel imbed, plant
idiom make fast (*or* secure)

anchorage *n* ***syn*** see HARBOR 3

ancient *adj* **1** persisting from the distant past <an *ancient* monument>
syn aged, age-old, antediluvian, antique, hoary, Noachian, old, timeworn, venerable; *compare* OBSOLETE
rel primal, primeval, primordial, pristine; forgotten, immemorial, remote, traditional; ageless, dateless
idiom old as time, older than God (*or* the hills), out of the dim past
con current, fresh, new, novel, prevailing, up-to-date
ant modern
2 ***syn*** see AGED 1
rel doddering, doting, fading, sinking, waning, wasting
idiom old as Methuselah (*or* the hills)

ancient *n* ***syn*** see OLDSTER

ancilla *n* ***syn*** see HELPER

ancillary *adj* **1** ***syn*** see AUXILIARY
2 ***syn*** see CONCOMITANT

androgynous *adj* ***syn*** see BISEXUAL

android *n* ***syn*** see ROBOT 1

anecdote *n* ***syn*** see STORY 2
rel recital, relation; episode, event, incident

anemic *adj* ***syn*** see PALE 2

anent *prep* ***syn*** see APROPOS

anesthetic *adj* ***syn*** see INSENSIBLE 5
rel impenetrable, impermeable, impervious; obtuse
con responsive, sensitive

anesthetic *n* ***syn*** see ANODYNE 1
ant stimulant

anesthetized *adj* ***syn*** see NUMB 1

anew *adv* **1** ***syn*** see OVER 7
2 ***syn*** see NEW

anfractuous *adj* ***syn*** see WINDING

angel *n* ***syn*** see SPONSOR
rel ‖butter-and-egg man

angelic *adj* ***syn*** see SAINTLY

anger *n* emotional excitement induced by intense displeasure <a man easily aroused to *anger*>
syn fury, indignation, ire, mad, rage, wrath
rel ‖dander, dudgeon, ‖Dutch, huff, ‖monkey, pet, pique, temper; annoyance, exasperation, infuriation, irritation
ant forbearance

anger *vb* **1** to make angry <their constant heedless interruptions *angered* her>
syn enrage, incense, infuriate, ire, mad, madden, steam up, umbrage
rel annoy, irk, vex; aggravate, exasperate, irritate, nettle, provoke, rile; affront, offend, outrage
idiom burn one up, make one hot under the collar, put (*or* get) one's dander up, set one by the ears
con appease, conciliate, mollify, placate, propitiate, soothe
ant gratify; pacify
2 to be or become angry <he *angers* easily>
syn blow up, boil, boil over, bristle, burn, flare (up), fume, rage, seethe
rel chafe, fret, stew; rant, rave, storm
idiom breathe fire, fly into a rage, get hot under the collar, get one's blood (*or* dander) up, hit the ceiling, lose one's temper, see red
ant calm (down)

angle *vb* ***syn*** see HINT 4

angle *n* **1** ***syn*** see VIEWPOINT 2
2 ***syn*** see PHASE
rel detail, item, particular
3 ***syn*** see TURN 4

angle *vb* **1** ***syn*** see SLANT 2
2 ***syn*** see SLANT 3

angry *adj* feeling or showing strong displeasure or bad temper <*angry* at the children's lack of consideration>
syn acrimonious, choleric, heated, indignant, irate, ireful, mad, shirty, waxy, wrathful, wrathy, wroth, wrothful, wrothy
rel aggravated, exasperated, perturbed, put out, riley, upset, uptight, worked up, wrought (up); angered, enraged, incensed, infuriate, infuriated, maddened, sore, vexed; orey-eyed, red-faced, wild-eyed
idiom foaming at the mouth, hot under the collar, in a taking, in a temper (*or* rage), mad as a hornet (*or* wet hen)
con calm, placid, tolerant; content, pleased, satisfied

anguish *n* ***syn*** see SORROW
rel anxiety, worry; ache, pain, pang, throe; torment, torture
con comfort, consolation, solace; alleviation, assuagement, mitigation
ant relief

angular *adj* **1** ***syn*** see RUDE 1
2 ***syn*** see LEAN
rel lathy, ribby, weedy

con chubby, chuffy
ant rotund

anima *n* ***syn*** see SOUL 1

animadversion *n* a remark or statement that constitutes an adverse and usually uncharitable criticism <her spiteful *animadversions* on her neighbors' children>
syn aspersion, obloquy, reflection, slam, slur, stricture
rel censure, criticism, reprehension; accusation, imputation, insinuation; captiousness, carping, caviling, faultfinding
con acclaim, extolling, laudation, praise; approbation, approval
ant commendation

animadvert *vb* ***syn*** see REMARK 2
rel declare, say, state, tell, utter; descant, dilate, expatiate, perorate; adduce, offer, present
con disregard, ignore, overlook

animal *n* ***syn*** see BEAST

animal *adj* **1** ***syn*** see BRUTISH
2 ***syn*** see CARNAL 2
rel bestial, brutal, brutish
con intellectual, mental, psychic; reasoning, thinking; nonphysical, spiritual
ant rational

animalism *n* ***syn*** see ANIMALITY
rel lasciviousness, lecherousness, lechery, licentiousness, lustfulness, unchastity; sensualism, sensuality, voluptuousness

animality *n* the animal aspect or quality of human beings or human nature <his violent reaction was sheer *animality*>
syn animalism, carnality, fleshliness
rel maleness, masculinity, virility; sensuality; brutishness, coarseness, grossness
ant spirituality

animalize *vb* ***syn*** see DEBASE 1

animate *adj* **1** ***syn*** see LIVING 1
rel breathing, viable
ant inanimate
2 ***syn*** see LIVELY 1
rel active, dynamic, live; activated, energized, vitalized
con dead, inanimate, lifeless; passive
ant inert

animate *vb* **1** ***syn*** see ENCOURAGE 1
rel invigorate, refresh, renew; fortify, reinforce, strengthen
idiom give a lift (to), put on (*or* upon) one's mettle, raise the spirits of
2 ***syn*** see QUICKEN 1
3 ***syn*** see FIRE 2
rel activate, actuate, motivate; drive, impel, move
con check, curb, restrain; frustrate, thwart
ant inhibit

animated *adj* **1** ***syn*** see LIVING 1
rel activated, energized, vitalized
con passive
ant inert
2 ***syn*** see LIVELY 1
rel exuberant, high-spirited, zestful
con enervated, spiritless; comatose
ant dejected, depressed

animating *adj* ***syn*** see INVIGORATING

animation *n* ***syn*** see SPIRIT 5

animosity *n* ***syn*** see ENMITY
con amity; esteem
ant goodwill

animus *n* **1** ***syn*** see INTENTION
2 ***syn*** see SOUL 1
3 ***syn*** see ENMITY
rel grudge; bias, discrimination, prejudice
con partiality, predilection; sympathy
ant favor

annals *n pl* ***syn*** see HISTORY 2

annex *vb* **1** ***syn*** see ADD 1
rel associate, connect, join, link, unite
con disengage; divorce, part, separate
2 ***syn*** see GET 1
3 ***syn*** see APPROPRIATE 1
4 ***syn*** see STEAL 1

annex *n* a subsidiary structure associated with a main building <built an *annex* to the museum to hold a new collection>
syn arm, block, ell, extension, wing
rel addition, continuation

annihilate *vb* **1** ***syn*** see ABOLISH 1
2 to destroy utterly <matter cannot be *annihilated*>
syn abate, abolish, blot out, eradicate, exterminate, extinguish, extirpate, murder, root out, uncreate, uproot, wipe (out)
rel cancel, efface, erase, expunge, obliterate
con renew, restore; create, discover, invent; fashion, forge, form, make, shape
3 ***syn*** see DESTROY 1
4 ***syn*** see SLAUGHTER 3
rel rout
5 ***syn*** see CRUSH 5

annihilative *adj* ***syn*** see DESTRUCTIVE

annotate *vb* to add or append comment <*annotate* a volume of poems>
syn gloss
rel construe, elucidate, explain, expound; comment, commentate, remark

announce *vb* **1** ***syn*** see DECLARE 1
rel communicate, impart
con hush (up), smother, stifle, suppress
2 to point to as a future occurrence or development <the shortening days *announce* the coming of winter>
syn forerun, foreshow, harbinger, herald, preindicate, presage
rel augur, forebode, forecast, foretell, predict
3 ***syn*** see INDICATE 2
rel present, set forth, show (forth)

announcement *n* ***syn*** see DECLARATION
rel affirmation, assertion, averment, statement

annoy *vb* **1** to disturb and upset nervously <her persistent prying soon *annoyed* her hostess>

---

syn synonym(s) ***rel*** related word(s)
ant antonym(s) ***con*** contrasted word(s)
idiom idiomatic equivalent(s)
‖ use limited; if in doubt, see a dictionary

syn abrade, bother, ‖bug, chafe, exercise, fret, gall, irk, provoke, ruffle, vex; *compare* IRRITATE
rel agitate, disturb, perturb, upset
idiom get in one's hair
con comfort, console, solace; content, gratify, please, satisfy
ant soothe
2 ***syn*** see WORRY 1
rel badger, bait, chivy, heckle, hector; chafe, distress, gall, rub
idiom get (*or* grate) on one's nerves, rub one the wrong way
con disregard, ignore, overlook; appease, calm, dulcify, mollify; cool, lull, subdue

annoyance *n* **1** the act of annoying <devoted himself to the *annoyance* of his patient wife>
syn bothering, harassment, irking, provocation, provoking, vexation, vexing
rel pestering, teasing
2 the state or feeling of being annoyed <her *annoyance* increased as he continued to pester her>
syn aggravation, bother, botheration, exasperation, pother
rel anger, indignation, ire, wrath; aversion, repugnance, repulsion, revulsion; disgust, dislike, distaste
con appreciation, enjoyment, liking, pleasure
3 something that causes an annoyed state or feeling <his constant baiting was an *annoyance* to her>
syn besetment, bother, botheration, botherment, exasperation, irritant, nuisance, pest, pester, ‖pesterment, plague
rel affliction, aggravation, distress, provocation, trial; riding

annual *n* ***syn*** see YEARBOOK

annuary *n* ***syn*** see YEARBOOK

annul *vb* **1** ***syn*** see ERASE
rel abstract, dispose (of), eliminate, remove
2 ***syn*** see NEUTRALIZE
rel outweigh, overbalance
3 ***syn*** see ABOLISH 1
rel counteract, negative, neutralize; blot out, cancel, efface, obliterate; extinguish
idiom make void, set aside
con enact, ordain, pass
4 to deprive of legal validity, force, or authority <*annul* a marriage>
syn abrogate, discharge, dissolve, quash, vacate, void
rel abolish, cancel, countermand, invalidate, nullify, undo
idiom make void

annunciate *vb* ***syn*** see DECLARE 1
rel affirm, assert, asseverate, aver; profess, protest; pronounce, state

anodyne *n* **1** something used to relieve or prevent pain <opium and its derivatives are still our most potent *anodynes*>
syn analgesic, anesthetic, pain-killer
rel calmative, depressant, sedative, tranquilizer; hypnotic, somnifacient, soporific, stupefacient
2 something that soothes or, often, dulls or deadens the senses or sensibilities <the kind of religion that is no more than an *anodyne*>
syn narcotic, nepenthe, opiate
ant energizer, stimulant; irritant

anomalous *adj* **1** ***syn*** see IRREGULAR 1
rel monstrous, prodigious
2 ***syn*** see ABNORMAL 1
rel foreign, peculiar, singular, strange; monstrous, prodigious
con accustomed, customary, usual, wonted

anon *adv* **1** ***syn*** see PRESENTLY 1
2 ***syn*** see THEN 1

anonym *n* ***syn*** see PSEUDONYM

anonymous *adj* not identified by name <saved by an *anonymous* hero>
syn innominate, nameless, undesignated, unnamed
rel incognito, unidentified, unknown, unrecognized, unspecified
ant named, onymous

another *adj* **1** ***syn*** see THAT 1
2 ***syn*** see ADDITIONAL
rel second

anschauung *n* ***syn*** see INTUITION

anschluss *n* ***syn*** see ALLIANCE 2

answer *n* **1** something spoken or written by way of return to a question or demand <a sullen *answer*>
syn antiphon, rejoinder, reply, respond, response, retort, return
rel comment, observation, remark; defense, justification; rebuttal, refutation; replication
con inquiry, interrogation, query, question, quiz
2 something attained by mental effort and especially by computation <got the *answer* by trial-and-error methods>
syn result, solution

answer *vb* **1** to say, write, or do something in response (as to a question) <*answered* his critics with documented facts>
syn come in, rejoin, reply, respond, retort, return
rel acknowledge, recognize; disprove, rebut, refute; countercharge, recriminate
idiom come back (at), make reply (to)
con ask, inquire, interrogate, query, question, quiz
2 ***syn*** see SATISFY 5

answerable *adj* ***syn*** see RESPONSIBLE
rel bound, compelled, constrained, duty-bound, obligated, obliged

Antaean *adj* ***syn*** see HUGE

antagonism *n* **1** ***syn*** see ENMITY
rel opposition, oppugnancy, resistance, withstanding; clashing, conflict, difference, disagreement, discord, friction
con concord, consonance, harmony; agreement, understanding
ant accord; comity
2 an opposing state, action, or position <the natural *antagonism* of predators and prey>
syn antithesis, con, contradistinction, contraposition, contrariety, opposition, opposure
rel disagreement, discrepancy, disparity, incongruity; annulling, negation, nullification; counteraction

con agreement, congruity; alliance, association, rapport; empathy, sympathy
antagonist *n* ***syn*** see OPPONENT
con adherent, henchman, partisan
ant supporter
antagonistic *adj* **1** ***syn*** see BITTER 3
2 ***syn*** see ADVERSE 1
rel discordant, incompatible, inconsonant; averse, disinclined, indisposed, unwilling; conflicting, hostile
con advantageous, beneficial; auspicious, benign, propitious
ant favorable
3 ***syn*** see ANTIPATHETIC 1
rel adverse, counter, counteractive, reactive; discordant; antonymous, opposing, oppugnant
ante *adv* ***syn*** see BEFORE 1
ante *prep* ***syn*** see BEFORE 1
ante *n* ***syn*** see BET
antecede *vb* ***syn*** see PRECEDE 2
antecedence *n* ***syn*** see PRIORITY
antecedent *n* **1** ***syn*** see CAUSE 1
rel forebear, forerunner, precursor; agency, instrumentality, means
con sequel; upshot
ant consequence
2 ***syn*** see FORERUNNER 2
3 antecedents *pl* ***syn*** see ANCESTOR 1
antecedent *adj* ***syn*** see PRECEDING
ant consequent; subsequent
antecedently *adv* ***syn*** see BEFORE 1
antecessor *n* ***syn*** see FORERUNNER 2
antedate *vb* ***syn*** see PRECEDE 2
antediluvian *adj* ***syn*** see ANCIENT 1
antediluvian *n* ***syn*** see FOGY
anterior *adj* ***syn*** see PRECEDING
con after, back, hind, hinder, rear
ant posterior
anthology *n* a collection of selected artistic and especially literary pieces or passages <an *anthology* of sacred music>
syn album, ana, analects, florilegium, garland, miscellany, omnibus, posy
rel collection, compilation; delectus, treasure-house, treasury
anthropoid *adj* resembling man <*anthropoid* extraterrestrials>
syn anthropomorphic, anthropomorphous, humanoid, manlike
anthropomorphic *adj* ***syn*** see ANTHROPOID
anthropomorphous *adj* ***syn*** see ANTHROPOID
anti *n* ***syn*** see OPPONENT
anti *adj* ***syn*** see ADVERSE 1
ant pro
antic *n* ***syn*** see PRANK
rel artifice, wile; romp
antic *adj* **1** ***syn*** see FANTASTIC 2
rel foolish; comic, comical, farcical, laughable, ludicrous
con prudent, sensible, wise; conventional, formal; grave, sedate, serious, solemn, somber
2 characterized by a light gay quality <a briskly *antic* and delightful tale>
syn frolicsome, playful, rollicking, sprightly
rel gay, lively, spirited; light, whimsical; casual, easy, suave
con constrained, controlled, curbed, guarded, inhibited, restrained
3 ***syn*** see PLAYFUL 1
anticipant *adj* ***syn*** see EXPECTANT 1
anticipate *vb* **1** ***syn*** see PREVENT 1
rel forecast, foretell, presage
idiom be one step ahead of
con disregard, ignore, neglect, overlook, slight
2 ***syn*** see FORESEE
rel await, contemplate, expect; foretaste
idiom be on the lookout (*or* watch) for, look forward to, look (*or* watch) out for
anticipation *n* ***syn*** see EXPECTANCY 1
anticipative *adj* ***syn*** see EXPECTANT 1
anticipatory *adj* ***syn*** see EXPECTANT 1
antidote *n* ***syn*** see REMEDY 2
rel negator, neutralizer, nullifier, offset; backfire
antipasto *n* ***syn*** see APPETIZER
antipathetic *adj* **1** having a natural or inherent opposition <national needs *antipathetic* to peace>
syn antagonistic, clashing, conflicting, contrariant, contrary, discordant
rel antipodal, antithetical, antonymous, contradictory, opposite
idiom at cross purposes, at daggers drawn, at war with one another
con agreeing, consonant, correspondent, harmonious; coactive, collaborative, cooperative
ant concordant
2 arousing marked aversion or dislike <found his sister's husband in every way *antipathetic*>
syn aversive, kindless, repellent, repugnant, uncongenial, ungenial, unsympathetic
rel abhorrent, obnoxious; disgustful, disgusting, distasteful, loathsome, repulsive
con compatible, consonant, sympathetic; alluring, attractive, charming; agreeable, pleasant, pleasing, satisfying, soothing
ant congenial
3 ***syn*** see ADVERSE 1
antipathy *n* **1** ***syn*** see ENMITY
rel disrelish, distaste, repellency, repugnance; avoidance, escape, eschewal, evasion
con liking, partiality, predilection, prepossession; attachment, love; attraction, taste (for)
ant affection (for)
2 the state of mind induced by what is antipathetic <a strong *antipathy* to modern art>
syn allergy, aversion, dyspathy
rel abhorrence, dislike, disrelish, distaste, repellency, repugnance; avoidance, escape, eschewal, evasion
con liking, partiality, predilection, prepossession; affection, attachment, love; attraction
ant taste (for)
antiphon *n* ***syn*** see ANSWER 1
antipodal *adj* ***syn*** see OPPOSITE

---

syn synonym(s) *rel* related word(s)
ant antonym(s) *con* contrasted word(s)
idiom idiomatic equivalent(s)
|| use limited; if in doubt, see a dictionary

THESAURUS

antipode *n* ***syn*** see OPPOSITE
antipodean *adj* ***syn*** see OPPOSITE
antipole *n* ***syn*** see OPPOSITE
antiquate *vb* ***syn*** see OUTDATE
antiquated *adj* ***syn*** see OLD-FASHIONED
con modern, new, novel
ant modernistic
antique *adj* **1** ***syn*** see ANCIENT 1
rel ancestral, dateless, immemorial, legendary, time-honored, traditional
con advanced, current, recent
2 ***syn*** see OLD-FASHIONED
antisocial *adj* averse to the society of others <a pure scholar, remote and *antisocial*>
syn eremitic, misanthropic, reclusive, reserved, solitary, standoffish
rel ascetic, austere, cold, remote; cynical, introverted, withdrawn
con affable, friendly, gregarious; communicative, outgoing, sociable
ant social
antithesis *n* **1** ***syn*** see ANTAGONISM 2
2 ***syn*** see OPPOSITE
antithetical *adj* ***syn*** see OPPOSITE
anxiety *n* ***syn*** see CARE 2
rel doubt, mistrust, uncertainty; distress, misery, suffering; dread; panic
con composure, equanimity, sangfroid; aplomb, confidence, self-possession; certainty, certitude, faith, trust
ant security
anxious *adj* **1** ***syn*** see AFRAID 1
rel agitated, apprehensive, jittery, perturbed, upset, worried; alarmed, bothered, disquieted, troubled, uneasy
idiom ill at ease
con calm, collected, cool, easy, imperturbable, unruffled; assured, confident, sanguine, sure
2 ***syn*** see EAGER
rel importunate, pressing, urgent
idiom all agog, bursting to
con averse, disinclined, hesitant, indisposed, reluctant
ant loath
anyhow *adv* ***syn*** see ABOUT 4
anytime *adv* ***syn*** see EVER 4
anyway *adv* ***syn*** see EVER 5
any which way *adv* ***syn*** see ABOUT 4
anywise *adv* **1** ***syn*** see ABOUT 4
2 ***syn*** see EVER 5
A1 *adj* ***syn*** see EXCELLENT
apace *adv* ***syn*** see FAST 2
apart *adv* **1** as a discrete item <taken *apart,* his view seemed sound enough>
syn independently, individually, one by one, separately, severally, singly
idiom one at a time
2 excluded from consideration <these slips *apart,* he had done very well>
syn aside
idiom to one side
3 in or into parts <tore the sheets *apart*>
syn asunder, sky-high
idiom all to pieces, to bits (*or* flinders)
apart *adj* ***syn*** see ALONE 1
apart from *prep* ***syn*** see EXCEPT
apartheid *n* ***syn*** see SEGREGATION
apartment *n* **1** a set of rooms (as in a private house or a block) rented or leased for use as a dwelling place <had a tiny top-floor *apartment*>
syn ‖chambers, flat, lodging(s), rental, rooms, suite, tenement
2 ***syn*** see ROOM 1
apathetic *adj* ***syn*** see IMPASSIVE 1
rel dull, inert, languid, sluggish, torpid; anesthetic, impassible, insensible, insensitive; callous, unmoved, untouched; limp, spiritless
con aroused, awake, aware, conscious, impressionable, perceptive, receptive; vigilant, watchful, wide-awake
ant alert
apathy *n* **1** lack of emotional responsiveness <hid her sorrow behind a dull brooding *apathy*>
syn impassivity, insensibility, phlegm, stoicism, stolidity, unresponsiveness
rel inertness, passivity, supineness; aloofness, detachment, indifference, unconcern; lethargy, torpidity, torpor; listlessness, numbness, stupefaction, stupor
con ardor, fervor, passion, responsiveness, warmth; alertness, awareness, concern, solicitude
ant zeal; enthusiasm
2 lack of interest or concern <public *apathy* toward the school crisis>
syn disinterest, disregard, heedlessness, indifference, insouciance, lassitude, lethargy, listlessness, unconcern, unmindfulness
rel callousness, hardness, insensitivity, obduracy, unawareness; coldness, halfheartedness, lukewarmness; calmness, dispassion, dispassionateness
con attentiveness, concern, heedfulness, interest; awareness, mindfulness, sensitivity, solicitude; ardency, fervency, passion, warmth, zeal
ape *vb* ***syn*** see MIMIC
rel caricature; emulate, rival
idiom make like
aperçu *n* ***syn*** see COMPENDIUM 1
aperitive *adj* ***syn*** see PALATABLE
aperture *n* a discontinuity allowing passage <the mouse squeezed through a narrow *aperture* in the wall>
syn hole, opening, orifice, outlet, vent
rel discontinuity, gap, hiatus, interstice; bore, perforation, pinhole, prick, puncture; chasm, cleft, cut, gash, slash, slit; breach, break, rupture
apery *n* ***syn*** see MIMICRY
apex *n* **1** ***syn*** see TOP 1
rel extremity, limit, spire
ant nadir
2 the culminating point <the *apex* of his career>
syn acme, apogee, capsheaf, capstone, climax, comble, crescendo, crest, crown, culmen, culmination, meridian, ne plus ultra, noon, noontide, peak, pinnacle, sublimity, summit, zenith
rel last word, prime, quintescence, ultimate; achievement, attainment, consummation, realization

ant nadir
3 *syn* see POINT 9
rel cap, crest, peak, prominence, spire
aphorism *n syn* see MAXIM
aphrodisia *n syn* see LUST 2
aphrodisiac *adj syn* see EROTIC
ant anaphrodisiac
apiarist *n syn* see BEEKEEPER
apical *adj syn* see TOP 1
apiculturist *n syn* see BEEKEEPER
apiece *adv* by, for, or to each one <gave the boys a dollar *apiece*>
syn all, aside, each, ‖per, per capita, per caput
rel individually, one by one, respectively, severally, singly, successively
apish *adj syn* see SLAVISH 3
aplomb *n syn* see CONFIDENCE 2
rel poise, savoir faire; coolness, imperturbability, levelheadedness, nonchalance; composure, ease, easiness, equanimity, sangfroid
idiom presence of mind
con bewilderment, distraction, perplexity; befuddlement, confusion, fluster, fuddlement; discomfiture, embarrassment, perturbation
ant shyness
apocalypse *n syn* see REVELATION
rel envisioning, foresight, precognition, prevision
apocalyptic *adj* 1 *syn* see PROPHETIC
2 *syn* see OMINOUS
apocryphal *adj syn* see SPURIOUS 3
rel false, erroneous, inaccurate, incorrect, untrue, wrong; doubtful, dubious, questionable
idiom open to question
con accurate, correct, established, factual, true, truthful, veracious; authentic
apogee *n syn* see APEX 2
Apollyon *n syn* see DEVIL 1
apologetic *adj syn* see REMORSEFUL
apologetic *n syn* see APOLOGY 1
apologia *n syn* see APOLOGY 1
rel clarification, elucidation, explanation, interpretation
apologue *n syn* see ALLEGORY 2
apology *n* 1 a presentation intended to justify or defend something <the white paper is essentially an *apology* for recent foreign policy>
syn apologetic, apologia, defense, justification; *compare* EXCUSE 1
rel excuse, extenuation, mitigation, palliation; advocating, advocation, championing, espousal, espousing, support
idiom pleading one's cause, putting in a good word for, speaking up for
con blame, censure, condemnation, decrial, reprehension, reprobation
2 an acknowledgment expressing regret for a wrong, improper, or discommoding act <murmured a brief *apology* for her lateness>
syn excuse, regrets; *compare* EXCUSE 1
rel amends, atonement; acknowledgment, admission, concession, confession, mea culpa; reparation, redress, satisfaction
3 *syn* see EXCUSE 3
aporetic *adj syn* see INCREDULOUS
apostasy *n syn* see DEFECTION
rel perfidy, treacherousness
apostate *n syn* see RENEGADE
rel bolter; dissenter, nonconformist, recusant
con adherent, follower, partisan; convert, proselyte
apostatize *vb syn* see DEFECT
a posteriori *adj syn* see INDUCTIVE
apostle *n syn* see MISSIONARY
apothecary *n syn* see DRUGGIST
apothegm *n syn* see MAXIM
apotheosis *n* 1 the consummate form, example, or instance (as of a quality) <the *apotheosis* of vulgarity>
syn epitome, last word, quintessence, ultimate; *compare* EMBODIMENT
rel acme, culmination, height, peak, summit
idiom ‖the living end
2 a raising to a state of eminent triumph or glory <the *apotheosis* of a folk hero>
syn aggrandizement, deification, dignification, exaltation, glorification
rel elevation, ennoblement, enshrinement, idolization, immortalization, lionization
con debasement, defamation, degradation, denigration, sullying
appall *vb syn* see DISMAY 1
rel awe, faze, overawe
con brace (up), buck up, cheer (up); assure, hearten, inspire, inspirit
ant embolden, nerve
appalling *adj syn* see FEARFUL 3
rel daunting, dismaying, horrifying; bewildering, confounding, dumbfounding
con assuring, heartening, inspiriting
ant reassuring
appanage *n syn* see RIGHT 2
apparatus *n syn* see EQUIPMENT
rel implement, instrument, tool, utensil; furnishings, provisions, supplies
apparel *vb syn* see CLOTHE
rel appoint
con bare, denude
ant divest
apparel *n syn* see CLOTHES
apparent *adj* 1 *syn* see CLEAR 5
rel ponderable; noticeable, prominent; discernible, observable, perceivable
idiom plain as day, plain to be seen
con ambiguous, hidden, obscure
ant inapparent
2 being other than seems to be the case <her *apparent* goodwill masked an inner loathing>
syn Barmecidal, illusive, illusory, ostensible, seeming, semblant
rel deceptive, delusive, delusory, misleading; credible, plausible, specious; factitious, fake, false, pseudo, sham, suppositious, supposititious

---

syn synonym(s) *rel* related word(s)
ant antonym(s) *con* contrasted word(s)
idiom idiomatic equivalent(s)
‖ use limited; if in doubt, see a dictionary

con genuine, true, valid; basic, essential, fundamental, inherent, intrinsic
ant actual, real

apparently *adv* ***syn*** see OSTENSIBLY

apparition *n* a visible appearance of something not present and especially of a dead person <illusions that the superstitious see as *apparitions*>
syn bogey, eidolon, ghost, ‖haunt, phantasm, phantom, revenant, shade, shadow, specter, spectrum, spirit, ‖spook, umbra, wraith
rel delusion, hallucination, illusion; corposant, fox fire, ignis fatuus, jack-o'-lantern, marshfire, Saint Elmo's fire, will-o'- the-wisp

appeal *n* **1** ***syn*** see PRAYER
rel asking, requesting, solicitation
con claim, demand, exaction; kick, objection, protest
2 ***syn*** see ATTRACTION 1
3 ***syn*** see CHARM 3
rel draw; pleasantness
con disagreeableness, unpleasantness

appeal *vb* **1** ***syn*** see BEG
2 ***syn*** see PETITION
3 ***syn*** see INTEREST

appealing *adj* ***syn*** see ATTRACTIVE 1

appear *vb* **1** to become visible <the sun *appeared* from behind a cloud>
syn emerge, loom, show
rel arrive, come; arise, emanate, issue, materialize, outcrop, rise, spring
idiom come in sight, come into view, meet (*or* strike) the eye, show one's face
con go, leave; depart, retire, withdraw
ant disappear, vanish
2 ***syn*** see SEEM
idiom give an appearance of, strike one as

appearance *n* **1** the state or form in which one appears <his disheveled *appearance* surprised his guests>
syn aspect, look, mien, seeming
rel air, bearing, countenance, demeanor, manner
2 *usu* **appearances** *pl* outward and often deceptive indication or look <to all *appearances* he was guilty>
syn face, guise, seeming, semblance, show, showing, simulacrum; *compare* MASK
rel fiction, make-believe, pretense, pretension; disguise, facade, front, masquerade, outside, pose
idiom outward show
con fact, reality, truth

appease *vb* **1** ***syn*** see PACIFY
rel calm (down), ease, soothe; extenuate, gloss (over), palliate, whitewash
con annoy, bother, irk, vex; anger, enrage, incense, infuriate; discompose, disturb, perturb, upset
ant exasperate
2 ***syn*** see SATISFY 3
rel ease, relieve; cater (to), coddle, pamper, spoil
ant aggravate

appellation *n* ***syn*** see NAME 1

appellative *n* ***syn*** see NAME 1

append *vb* ***syn*** see ADD 1

appendage *n* something accompanying or attached to another thing to which it is usually subordinate or nonessential <people to whom culture is a mere *appendage* to life>
syn accessory, adjunct, appendix, appurtenance
rel auxiliary, incidental, subsidiary, supplement; collateral, extra, nonessential

appendix *n* **1** additional material subjoined to a writing and especially a book <a dictionary with an *appendix* of new words>
syn addendum, codicil, rider, supplement
2 ***syn*** see APPENDAGE

apperception *n* ***syn*** see RECOGNITION 1
rel apprehension, grasp, perception; comprehension, understanding

appertain *vb* **1** ***syn*** see BELONG 2
2 ***syn*** see BEAR (on *or* upon)

appetence *n* ***syn*** see APPETITE 1

appetent *adj* ***syn*** see EAGER
rel craving, desirous, lusting, yearning
idiom consumed with desire

appetite *n* **1** a natural enjoyment of food <all fell to with a hearty *appetite*>
syn appetence, stomach, taste
rel gluttony, greed, hunger, voracity; epicurism, gourmandise
2 ***syn*** see DESIRE 1
rel cupidity, greed, urgency
con abnegation, asceticism, renunciation, self-denial; distaste, revulsion
3 an attraction toward something <had a great *appetite* for gossip>
syn fondness, inclination, liking, soft spot, taste, weakness
rel bent, bias, flair, leaning, penchant, proclivity, propensity
con disinclination, dislike, distaste; disinterest, unconcern

appetition *n* ***syn*** see DESIRE 1

appetizer *n* food or drink served before a meal to stimulate appetite <*appetizers* such as cocktails and canap>
syn antipasto, hors d'oeuvre, whet, zakuska
rel dainty, delicacy, goody, tidbit; savory

appetizing *adj* ***syn*** see PALATABLE
ant disgusting, nauseating

applaud *vb* **1** ***syn*** see COMMEND 2
rel boost, plug
ant admonish; censure
2 to express enthusiastic approval <*applauded* wildly when his team won a point>
syn cheer, rise (to), root
rel acclaim, extol, laud, praise; eulogize, glorify, magnify, panegyrize
con deride, mock, ridicule, taunt; contemn, disdain, scorn, scout
ant boo, hiss

applause *n* public expression of approbation <her appearance was greeted with *applause*>
syn acclaim, acclamation, plaudit(s)
rel cheers, hand, ovation, round; cheering, clapping, rooting
con derision, mockery, ridicule, taunting; Bronx cheer, raspberry

ant booing, hissing

‖**apple knocker** *n* ***syn*** see RUSTIC

apple–polish *vb* ***syn*** see FAWN

apple–polisher *n* ***syn*** see SYCOPHANT

‖**applesauce** *n* ***syn*** see NONSENSE 2

appliance *n* ***syn*** see USE 1

applicability *n* ***syn*** see USE 3
con irrelevance, unsuitability
ant inapplicability

applicable *adj* **1** ***syn*** see RELEVANT
rel alliable, associable, compatible, congenial, connective
con incompatible, uncongenial; inappropriate, unfit, unsuitable
ant inapplicable
2 ***syn*** see FIT 1
rel correct, good, seemly
idiom as it ought to be, as it should be
con improper, incorrect

applicant *n* ***syn*** see CANDIDATE

application *n* **1** ***syn*** see ATTENTION 1
rel busyness, zeal; energy, indefatigability
con bemusement, wool-gathering; faineance, laziness, sloth
ant indolence
2 ***syn*** see USE 1
3 ***syn*** see EXERCISE 1
4 ***syn*** see PRAYER

applicative *adj* ***syn*** see RELEVANT

applicatory *adj* ***syn*** see RELEVANT

apply *vb* **1** ***syn*** see ADDRESS 3
rel set about, take on, undertake; drudge, grind, toil
idiom burn the midnight oil, keep one's nose to the grindstone, work like a horse (*or* dog); concern (oneself) with something, set (one's hand) to something
con let slide, neglect, pass over, slight
2 ***syn*** see BEAR (on *or* upon)
idiom come into relation with
3 ***syn*** see RESORT 2
rel appeal, petition; beg, beseech, entreat, implore, supplicate; importune, press, urge
idiom make application to
4 ***syn*** see USE 2

apply (to) *vb* ***syn*** see ADDRESS 4

appoint *vb* **1** ***syn*** see DESIGNATE 2
rel accredit, authorize, commission
con cashier, discharge, dismiss; debar, exclude, reject
2 ***syn*** see FURNISH 1
rel embellish, enrich, furbish, garnish; dress up, set off, spruce (up)
con denude, dismantle, divest, strip

appointment *n* **1** ***syn*** see JOB 2
2 ***syn*** see ENGAGEMENT 3

apportion *vb* **1** ***syn*** see ALLOT
rel divide, partition, share
con assemble, collect, gather
2 to separate something into shares with care and accuracy and distribute it among a number <Christ *apportioned* the loaves and fishes>
syn divide, ‖divvy, parcel, portion, prorate, quota, ration, share, ‖shift
rel accord, award, bestow, distribute; give, grant, present; part, separate, split
3 ***syn*** see ADMINISTER 2
rel dish out, serve

apportionment *n* ***syn*** see RATION

apposite *adj* ***syn*** see RELEVANT
rel felicitous, happy; opportune, pat, seasonable, timely
idiom to the point (*or* purpose)
con awkward, inept; casual, haphazard, hit-or-miss, random
ant inapposite, inapt

appositeness *n* ***syn*** see ORDER 11

appraisal *n* **1** ***syn*** see ESTIMATE 1
2 ***syn*** see ESTIMATION 1

appraise *vb* ***syn*** see ESTIMATE 1
rel adjudge, deem, esteem, judge; audit, examine, inspect, scrutinize
idiom set (*or* place) a value on, take the measure of

appraisement *n* **1** ***syn*** see ESTIMATE 1
2 ***syn*** see ESTIMATION 1

appreciable *adj* ***syn*** see PERCEPTIBLE
rel noticeable; apparent, clear, evident, manifest, obvious, plain; concrete, material, real, substantial
con impalpable, imperceptible, imponderable, insensible, intangible
ant inappreciable

appreciate *vb* **1** to hold in high estimation <*appreciate* the kindness of a friend>
syn apprize, cherish, esteem, prize, treasure, value; *compare* ADMIRE 1
rel admire, regard, respect; adore, ‖eat up, enjoy, like, love, relish
idiom rate highly, set great store by, think much (*or* well) of
con contemn, disapprove, disdain, scorn; decry, depreciate, disparage
ant despise
2 ***syn*** see ADMIRE 1
rel enjoy, like, savor
con contemn, disdain, scorn
3 ***syn*** see KNOW 1
rel catch, seize, take in

appreciation *n* ***syn*** see TESTIMONIAL 2

apprehend *vb* **1** to recognize the existence or meaning of <as a child learns to *apprehend* the relation between naughtiness and punishment>
syn accept, catch, compass, comprehend, conceive, cotton (to *or* on to), ‖dig, follow, grasp, make out, see, take, take in, tumble (to), twig, understand
rel realize, recognize, sense; absorb, digest, seize; catch on, wise (up); penetrate
idiom catch (*or* get) the drift of, get the idea, get through one's head, make head or tail of
ant misapprehend
2 ***syn*** see ARREST 2

---

syn synonym(s) ***rel*** related word(s)
ant antonym(s) ***con*** contrasted word(s)
idiom idiomatic equivalent(s)
‖ use limited; if in doubt, see a dictionary

3 ***syn*** see FORESEE
rel dread, fear
idiom be on pins and needles, have one's heart in one's mouth, wait with bated breath
4 ***syn*** see KNOW 1
idiom be acquainted with, be cognizant of

apprehensible *adj* ***syn*** see UNDERSTANDABLE

apprehension *n* **1** ***syn*** see IDEA
2 ***syn*** see ARREST
3 fear that something is going or will go wrong <had the strongest *apprehension* about her sister's health>
syn apprehensiveness, foreboding, misgiving, premonition, prenotion, presage, presentiment
rel agitation, angst, anxiety, care, concern, disquiet, disquietude, solicitude, unease, uneasiness, worry; alarm, dread, fear, panic
idiom the anxious seat
con assurance, composure, equanimity, sangfroid, self-possession; faith, reliance, trust
ant confidence

apprehensive *adj* **1** ***syn*** see AWARE
2 ***syn*** see FEARFUL 2
ant confident

apprehensiveness *n* ***syn*** see APPREHENSION 3

apprentice *n* ***syn*** see NOVICE
rel starter; amateur
con adept, expert, specialist

apprenticed *adj* ***syn*** see BOUND 2

apprise *vb* ***syn*** see INFORM 2
rel announce, communicate, declare, proclaim, publish; disclose, discover, divulge, reveal, tell
idiom make known to, serve (one) notice

apprize *vb* ***syn*** see APPRECIATE 1

approach *vb* **1** to come or go near or nearer <as a boy *approaches* manhood>
syn approximate, near, nigh
rel achieve, arrive (at), attain, gain, hit, make, reach; draw on
idiom come to close quarters with
con recede, retire, retreat, withdraw; depart, go, leave
2 ***syn*** see ADDRESS 4
rel advise, confer, consult, counsel, negotiate, parley; beg, beseech, entreat, implore, plead, supplicate
3 ***syn*** see REACH 3
4 ***syn*** see AMOUNT 2
con depart, deviate, digress; differ, disaccord, disharmonize, vary
5 ***syn*** see BORDER 3

approach *n* ***syn*** see OVERTURE 1
rel attempt, endeavor, essay, try; call, invitation
ant withdrawal

approaching *adj* ***syn*** see FORTHCOMING

approbate *vb* ***syn*** see APPROVE 1

approbation *n* warmly commending acceptance or agreement <expressed *approbation* of their progress>
syn approval, benediction, blessing, favor, OK (*or* okay)
rel commendation, countenance, goodwill, sanction; admiration, esteem, liking, regard, respect; pleasure, satisfaction
con censure, condemnation, criticism, disapproval, disfavor, reprehension; annoyance, disgust, irritation; distress, regret, sorrow
ant disapprobation

approbative *adj* ***syn*** see FAVORABLE 1

approbatory *adj* ***syn*** see FAVORABLE 1

appropinquity *n* ***syn*** see PROXIMITY

appropriate *vb* **1** to take over as if by preeminent right <limitations on the right of the state to *appropriate* private property>
syn accroach, annex, arrogate, commandeer, confiscate, expropriate, preempt, seize, sequester, take; *compare* ARROGATE 1
rel grab, grasp, snatch; claim, exact, extort, wrench; conscript, draft, press
idiom help oneself to, lay hold of, make free with, take possession of
2 ***syn*** see STEAL 1
rel despoil, spoil; forage, raid
3 ***syn*** see ARROGATE 1

appropriate *adj* **1** ***syn*** see FIT 1
rel apposite, germane, pertinent, relevant; opportune, pat, seasonable, timely
con incompatible, incongruous, inconsonant
ant inappropriate
2 ***syn*** see GOOD 2
rel agreeable, desirable, enjoyable, pleasant; acceptable, admissible, eligible, entitled, right, worthy
con disagreeable undesirable, unpleasant; inadmissible, ineligible, unworthy, wrong
ant inappropriate
3 ***syn*** see JUST 3
con unfair, unjustified, unmerited, unreasonable; unsuitable
ant inappropriate
4 ***syn*** see TRUE 7
ant inappropriate

appropriately *adv* ***syn*** see WELL 4

appropriateness *n* **1** ***syn*** see USE 3
2 ***syn*** see ORDER 11

appropriation *n* property (as money) set apart or given by official or formal action for a predetermined use by others <an increased *appropriation* for public housing>
syn grant, subsidy, subvention
rel allotment, allowance, stipend; aid, assistance, grant-in-aid, help

approval *n* ***syn*** see APPROBATION
rel applause, commendation, compliment; acceptance, endorsement, sanction, suffrage
con depreciation, derogation, disparagement
ant disapproval

approve *vb* **1** to find acceptable <they don't *approve* of their daughter's life-style>
syn accept, approbate, countenance, favor, go (for), hold (with)
rel back (up), stand by, support, sustain, uphold; bear, endure, put up (with), tolerate
idiom be in favor of, pat on the back, take kindly to, think well (*or* highly) of, view with approval (*or* favor)
con deprecate, disfavor, dislike, frown (on *or* upon); object (to), oppose

ant disapprove

2 to give an often formal expression of approval and support <the committee *approved* the plans for the new clubhouse>

syn accredit, certify, endorse, OK (*or* okay), sanction

rel applaud, commend, compliment; confirm, initial, ratify; clear

con refuse, reject, repudiate, spurn; censure, condemn, criticize, reprehend, reprobate

ant disapprove

approving *adj* ***syn*** see FAVORABLE 1

approximal *adj* ***syn*** see ADJACENT 3

approximate *adj* **1** ***syn*** see COMPARATIVE

2 ***syn*** see RUDE 3

approximate *vb* **1** ***syn*** see APPROACH 1

idiom be in the neighborhood of

2 ***syn*** see ESTIMATE 3

approximately *adv* ***syn*** see NEARLY

idiom in round numbers, right about

ant exactly, precisely

appulse *n* ***syn*** see IMPACT 1

appurtenance *n* ***syn*** see APPENDAGE

rel appointment (*usu* appointments *pl*), equipment, furnishings, furniture

appurtenant *adj* ***syn*** see AUXILIARY

a priori *adj* ***syn*** see DEDUCTIVE

apriorism *n* ***syn*** see ASSUMPTION 2

apropos *adj* ***syn*** see RELEVANT

rel meet, proper

con clumsy, gauche, inappropriate, inept

ant malapropos

apropos *prep* in reference to <it is impossible to reach a decision *apropos* this matter at present>

syn about, against, anent, as for, as regards, as respects, as to, concerning, in re, in respect to, re, regarding, respecting, touching, toward, with respect to

apt *adj* **1** having a tendency or inclination <it is *apt* to be cool late in the evening>

syn given, inclined, liable, likely, prone

rel disposed, minded, predisposed

con averse, disinclined, indisposed, loath; doubtful, improbable, unlikely

2 ***syn*** see FIT 1

rel apposite, apropos, pertinent, relevant; compelling, convincing, telling; exact, nice, precise

con awkward, clumsy, maladroit

ant inapt, inept

3 ***syn*** see QUICK 2

rel alert, brainy, bright; gifted, talented

con laggard

aptness *n* **1** ***syn*** see ORDER 11

rel helpfulness, propitiousness

2 ***syn*** see GIFT 2

‖**apurpose** *adv* ***syn*** see INTENTIONALLY

apyrous *adj* ***syn*** see NONCOMBUSTIBLE

aquake *adj* ***syn*** see TREMULOUS

aqua vitae *n* ***syn*** see LIQUOR 2

aqueduct *n* ***syn*** see CHANNEL 1

aquiculture *n* ***syn*** see HYDROPONICS

aquiver *adj* ***syn*** see TREMULOUS

arab *n* **1** ***syn*** see VAGABOND

‖2 ***syn*** see PEDDLER

arable *adj* suitable for tilling and for growing crops <used their *arable* land intensively>

syn cultivable, cultivatable, tillable

rel fat, fertile, fruitful, productive

con barren, sterile, unfertile, unfruitful, unproductive

arbiter *n* ***syn*** see JUDGE 1

rel moderator

arbitrary *adj* **1** characterized by or given to willful and often unwise or irrational choices and demands <a proud fitful *arbitrary* nature>

syn capricious, erratic, freakish, vagarious, wayward, whimsical, whimsied

rel undisciplined, unruly, wild, willful; arrogant, unconstrained, unreasonable; careless, heedless, impetuous, indiscreet, precipitate, rash; kooky, screwball, zany

con circumspect, discreet, heedful, judicious, politic, reflective; calculating, discriminative, judicial, prudent, well-advised

2 ***syn*** see ABSOLUTE 4

rel authoritarian, dictatorial, magisterial, oracular

con lawful, legal, licit, rightful

ant legitimate

arbitrate *vb* ***syn*** see JUDGE 1

rel intermediate, intervene, mediate; appease, placate, soothe

arbitrator *n* **1** ***syn*** see MODERATOR

2 ***syn*** see JUDGE 1

arbor *n* a shelter (as in a garden) formed of vines or branches or of latticework covered with climbing shrubs or vines <the children picnicked under the *arbor*>

syn bower, pergola

rel belvedere, casino, gazebo, summerhouse

arc *n* ***syn*** see CURVE

arcadia *n* ***syn*** see UTOPIA

arcane *adj* ***syn*** see MYSTERIOUS

rel eerie, uncanny, weird; anagogic, mystical

arced *adj* ***syn*** see CURVED

arch *n* ***syn*** see CURVE

arch *adj* **1** ***syn*** see FIRST 3

rel conspicuous, notable, noteworthy; extraordinary, extreme

2 ***syn*** see SAUCY 1

rel impish, mischievous, playful, roguish, waggish; bold, cheeky, cocky, flippant, fresh; derisive, mocking, twitting

con modest, quiet, respectful, submissive

3 ***syn*** see COY 2

archaic *adj* **1** ***syn*** see OLD-FASHIONED

idiom behind the times, of the old school

con fresh, modern, new, novel; fashionable

ant up-to-date

2 ***syn*** see PRIMITIVE 3

arched *adj* ***syn*** see CURVED

archetypal *adj* ***syn*** see TYPICAL 1

archetype *n* **1** ***syn*** see ORIGINAL 1

---

syn synonym(s) ***rel*** related word(s)
ant antonym(s) ***con*** contrasted word(s)
idiom idiomatic equivalent(s)
‖ use limited; if in doubt, see a dictionary

2 ***syn*** see MODEL 2
archfiend *n* ***syn*** see DEVIL 2
archilochian *adj* ***syn*** see SARCASTIC
archimage *n* ***syn*** see MAGICIAN 1
architect *n* ***syn*** see FATHER 2
architecture *n* ***syn*** see MAKEUP 1
archive *n, usu* **archives** *pl* **1** ***syn*** see LIBRARY
2 ***syn*** see DOCUMENT 1
rel papers, parchments, scrolls, writings; clippings, cuttings, excerpts, extracts, fragments, gleanings, remains
arciform *adj* ***syn*** see CURVED
arctic *adj* ***syn*** see COLD 1
rel bitter, boreal, hyperborean; numbing, rigorous; hibernal, hiemal
idiom cold as charity, cold enough to freeze a brass monkey
ant torrid
ardent *adj* **1** ***syn*** see IMPASSIONED
rel enthusiastic, urgent; avid, desirous, eager, keen
con calm, composed, imperturbable, nonchalant; apathetic, impassive, phlegmatic; disinterested, dispassionate, impartial, uninterested
ant cool
2 very deep or moving <had an *ardent* longing for knowledge>
syn extreme, intense
rel crying, importunate, insistent, urgent; great, mighty, powerful, strong
con feeble, minimal, slight, trivial
3 ***syn*** see EAGER
rel hasty, impetuous, impulsive, precipitate; fervid, fiery, hectic, hot; uncontrolled, ungoverned; earnest, intent, urgent, vehement
con dull, heavy, inert, leaden, lumpish; languid, lethargic, listless; apathetic, impassive, phlegmatic
ant easygoing
4 ***syn*** see FAITHFUL 1
5 ***syn*** see HOT 1
6 ***syn*** see SPIRITUOUS
ardor *n* **1** ***syn*** see PASSION 6
rel avidity; gusto, spirit, verve, zest; excitement, galvanization, quickening, stimulation
con aloofness, detachment, disinterest, unconcern; apathy, lackadaisy, languor, listlessness
ant coolness; indifference
2 ***syn*** see EAGERNESS
rel ardency, fervor, warmth
3 ***syn*** see FIDELITY 1
rel adoration, love, worship
arduous *adj* **1** ***syn*** see HARD 6
2 ***syn*** see STEEP 1
3 ***syn*** see TIGHT 4
arduously *adv* ***syn*** see HARD 8
con easily, facilely
ant effortlessly
area *n* **1** a distinguishable extent of surface and especially of the earth's surface <a large wooded *area*>
syn belt, region, territory, tract, zone
rel expanse, stretch; district, locality, place; lot, plot, section; terrain; circuit
2 ***syn*** see LOCALITY 1
arena *n* ***syn*** see SCENE 4
arete *n* ***syn*** see EXCELLENCE
argent *adj* ***syn*** see SILVERY
argentate *adj* ***syn*** see SILVERY
argenteous *adj* ***syn*** see SILVERY
argentine *adj* ***syn*** see SILVERY
argot *n* ***syn*** see DIALECT 2
arguable *adj* ***syn*** see MOOT
argue *vb* **1** ***syn*** see DISCUSS 1
rel analyze, investigate, review, sift, study, ventilate; expostulate, object, protest, remonstrate
2 to contend in words <*arguing* about who should answer the phone>
syn argufy, bicker, dispute, hassle, quibble, squabble, wrangle; *compare* QUARREL
rel differ, disaccord, disagree, dissent; balk, demur, jib; clash, conflict
idiom bandy words, have it out, join (*or* take) issue
con accord, agree, concur
3 ***syn*** see INDICATE 2
4 ***syn*** see MAINTAIN 2
argue (into) *vb* ***syn*** see INDUCE 1
argufy *vb* ***syn*** see ARGUE 2
argument *n* **1** ***syn*** see REASON 3
rel basis, foundation; position, posture, stance, standpoint
2 a vigorous often heated discussion of a moot question <their continuing *argument* over household expenses>
syn contention, controversy, dispute, hurrah, rumpus
rel argumentation, debate, disputation, polemic; disagreement, dissension, squabbling; embroilment, fuss, hassle, wrangle
3 ***syn*** see SUBJECT 2
rel position, proposition, statement, thesis
argumentation *n* the act or art or an exercise of one's powers of argument <noted for his skill in *argumentation*>
syn debate, dialectic, disputation, forensic, mooting
rel argument, controversy, dispute; declamation, elocution, eloquence, oratory, rhetoric
argumentative *adj* ***syn*** see CONTENTIOUS 2
argute *adj* **1** ***syn*** see SHREWD
2 ***syn*** see ACUTE 4
aria *n* ***syn*** see SONG 2
arid *adj* **1** ***syn*** see DRY 1
rel barren, infertile, sterile, unfruitful
con fecund, fertile, fruitful
2 lacking in interest or liveliness <some of the most *arid* prose ever written>
syn bromidic, dry, dryasdust, dull, dusty, insipid, tedious, uninteresting, weariful, wearisome; *compare* TEPID 2, UNORIGINAL
rel drab, dreary, flat, heavy, lackluster, leaden, unanimated, unlively; academic, bookish, pedantic; boring, humdrum, monotonous, unimaginative, uninspired
con appealing, bright, lively, sparkling, stimulating, vigorous, vivid
aright *adv* ***syn*** see WELL 1

arise *vb* **1** ***syn*** see RISE 4
ant recline; slump
2 ***syn*** see ROLL OUT
3 ***syn*** see SPRING 1
rel ensue, follow, succeed
4 ***syn*** see BEGIN 2
aristarch *n* ***syn*** see CRITIC
‖**aristo** *n* ***syn*** see GENTLEMAN 1
aristocracy *n* the highest stratum of a society <the self-centered attitude of some *aristocracies*>
syn aristoi, blue blood, carriage trade, crème de la crème, elite, flower, gentility, gentry, haut monde, optimacy, patriciate, quality, society, upper class, upper crust, who's who
rel nobility, noblesse, patricians; county; beau monde, bon ton, jet set, smart set
con canaille, mob, rabble, riffraff; commoners, commons, masses, people, plebeians
aristocrat *n* ***syn*** see GENTLEMAN 1
ant commoner
aristoi *n* ***syn*** see ARISTOCRACY
arithmetic *n* ***syn*** see COMPUTATION
arm *n* **1** ***syn*** see INLET
2 ***syn*** see ANNEX
3 ***syn*** see POWER 4
arm *vb* ***syn*** see FURNISH 1
rel prepare, ready
idiom put in (*or* into) shape
ant disarm
armament *n* ***syn*** see DEFENSE 1
armamentarium *n* ***syn*** see SUPPLY
armed forces *n pl* ***syn*** see TROOP 2
armistice *n* ***syn*** see TRUCE
armor *n* ***syn*** see DEFENSE 1
rel cloak, mantle, shroud, veil; buckler, cover, screen, shelter
armory *n* a place where military arms and supplies are stored <the problem of weapon theft from *armories*>
syn arsenal, depot, dump, magazine
army *n* ***syn*** see MULTITUDE 1
rel crush, horde, mob, press, throng
aroma *n* **1** ***syn*** see FRAGRANCE
2 ***syn*** see SMELL 1
rel fetor, mephitis, reek, stench, stink
aromal *adj* ***syn*** see SWEET 2
rel penetrating, piquant, pungent
ant acrid
aromatic *adj* ***syn*** see SWEET 2
ant acrid
aromatize *vb* ***syn*** see SCENT 2
around *adv* **1** ***syn*** see ABOUT 1
2 ***syn*** see THROUGH 1
3 ***syn*** see ABOUT 4
4 ***syn*** see ABOUT 6
around *prep* ***syn*** see ABOUT 1
around *adj* ***syn*** see EXTANT 1
around–the–clock *adj* ***syn*** see CONTINUAL
arouse *vb* ***syn*** see STIR 1
rel alert, excite, work up; electrify, thrill; fire, inflame
idiom fan the fire (*or* flame), raise to fever heat, set on fire, stir one's blood (*or* feelings)
con allay, alleviate, assuage, ease, mitigate, relieve; mollify, pacify, placate
ant calm, quiet
arraign *vb* ***syn*** see ACCUSE
rel cite, summon; test, try
idiom bring to book, call to account
con absolve, acquit, exculpate, exonerate, vindicate; defend, justify
arrange *vb* **1** ***syn*** see ORDER 1
rel assort, categorize, pigeonhole, sort
con disorder, disorganize, disturb, unsettle; confuse, jumble, muddle, tumble; disperse, scatter
ant derange, disarrange
2 ***syn*** see DESIGN 3
3 ***syn*** see PLAN 2
4 ***syn*** see NEGOTIATE 1
rel design, plan, project, scheme
5 ***syn*** see HARMONIZE 4
arrangement *n* ***syn*** see ORDER 3
rel layout, lineup, setup; method, system
ant disarrangement
arrant *adj* **1** ***syn*** see UTTER
rel plain, pure, regular, sheer
2 ***syn*** see SHAMELESS
array *vb* **1** ***syn*** see ORDER 1
ant disarray
2 ***syn*** see CLOTHE
array *n* **1** ***syn*** see GROUP 3
2 ***syn*** see DISPLAY 2
rel exhibition, exposing, showing; arranging, marshaling, ordering
arrear *n, usu* **arrears** *pl* ***syn*** see DEBT 3
arrearage *n* **1** ***syn*** see DEBT 3
2 ***syn*** see INDEBTEDNESS 1
arrect *adj* **1** ***syn*** see ERECT
2 ***syn*** see ATTENTIVE 1
arrest *vb* **1** to bring to a halt <science cannot yet *arrest* the process of aging>
syn check, halt, interrupt, stall, stay; *compare* STOP 3
rel balk, frustrate, thwart; choke, obstruct, stop (up); delay, detain, hamper, hinder, restrain, retard; interfere, interpose, intervene; contain, stem, withstand
idiom bring to a halt (*or* stand *or* standstill), bring up short, check in full career, cut short
con advance, forward, further, promote; expedite, hasten, quicken, speed
2 to take and hold in custody under authority of the law <*arrested* for murder>
syn apprehend, ‖bust, detain, nab, pick up, pinch, pull in, run in; *compare* CATCH 1
rel immure, imprison, incarcerate, jail, lock (up), ‖slough; attach
idiom lay by the heels, lay hands on
con discharge, free, liberate, release
arrest *n* the taking and holding of a person in custody under authority of the law <unwilling to submit to *arrest*>

syn synonym(s) ***rel*** related word(s)
ant antonym(s) ***con*** contrasted word(s)
idiom idiomatic equivalent(s)
‖ use limited; if in doubt, see a dictionary

syn apprehension, arrestation, arrestment, ‖bust, detention, ‖nab, pickup, pinch
rel capture, catch, collar, seizure, taking
con discharge, freeing, liberation, release
arrestation *n* ***syn*** see ARREST
arresting *adj* ***syn*** see NOTICEABLE
rel attractive, enchanting, fascinating; affective, appealing, impressive, moving, touching
idiom enough to make one stop and take notice
con common, familiar, ordinary, run-of-the-mill; hackneyed, stereotyped, trite
arrestive *adj* ***syn*** see NOTICEABLE
arrestment *n* ***syn*** see ARREST
arride *vb* ***syn*** see PLEASE 2
rel beguile, divert, entertain, recreate
idiom tickle one's fancy
con bore, ennui, jade, weary
arrival *n* **1** the reaching of a destination <the train was late in its *arrival*>
syn advent, coming
rel appearance, emergence, entrance, issuance, manifestation
con disappearance, going, leaving, withdrawal; recession, retirement, retreat
ant departure
2 ***syn*** see SUCCESS
arrive *vb* **1** ***syn*** see COME 1
con get away, go, retire
ant depart
2 ***syn*** see SUCCEED 3
arriviste *n* ***syn*** see UPSTART
arrogance *n* ***syn*** see PRIDE 3
ant humility
arrogant *adj* **1** ***syn*** see PROUD 1
rel domineering, imperative, peremptory; affected, artificial, highfalutin, mannered, showy
idiom too big for one's britches
con humble; deferential, submissive; abject, obsequious, subservient, truckling
ant meek
2 ***syn*** see POMPOUS 1
arrogate *vb* **1** to claim or take over in a high-handed manner <*arrogated* to himself the right to make all decisions>
syn accroach, appropriate, assume, commandeer, preempt, usurp; *compare* APPROPRIATE 1
rel annex, preempt, preoccupy, sequester; grab, seize, take, take over
idiom help oneself to, make free with, take into one's own hands
con cede, relinquish, resign, surrender, yield
ant renounce
2 ***syn*** see APPROPRIATE 1
arrondi *adj* ***syn*** see CURVED
arroyo *n* ***syn*** see RAVINE
arsenal *n* **1** ***syn*** see ARMORY
2 ***syn*** see DEPOT 2
arsonist *n* ***syn*** see INCENDIARY
arsy–varsy *adj* ***syn*** see UPSIDE-DOWN 2
art *n* **1** a usually acquired proficiency in doing or performing <there's an *art* to competent public speaking>
syn adroitness, craft, cunning, dexterity, expertise, know-how, skill
rel capability, competence, handiness, proficiency; address, finesse, ‖savvy
con clumsiness, maladroitness
2 ***syn*** see CUNNING 2
rel acuteness, astuteness
con candor, frankness, sincerity; directness, straightforwardness, bluffness, bluntness
3 ***syn*** see TRADE 1
artery *n* ***syn*** see WAY 1
artful *adj* ***syn*** see SLY 2
rel diplomatic, oily, politic, smooth, suave; facile, specious, superficial; adroit, dexterous
ant artless
artfulness *n* ***syn*** see CUNNING 2
article *n* **1** ***syn*** see POINT 1
rel division, section, segment
2 ***syn*** see ESSAY 2
rel critique, manifesto, report, statement, study, survey
3 ***syn*** see THING 3
rel detail, particular
articled *adj* ***syn*** see BOUND 2
articulate *adj* **1** ***syn*** see VOCAL 1
rel clear, distinct, intelligible
ant inarticulate; dumb
2 ***syn*** see VOCAL 3
rel meaningful, significant; garrulous, prolix, talkative; uttering, venting
ant inarticulate
articulate *vb* **1** ***syn*** see INTEGRATE 3
rel connect, join, relate; methodize, order, organize, systematize; adjust, coordinate, harmonize, regulate; assemble, collect, gather; unify
con dissect, resolve; divide, part, separate
2 to form speech sounds <regional differences in *articulating* the letter *r*>
syn enunciate, phonate, pronounce, say
rel sound, utter
articulation *n* ***syn*** see VOCALIZATION
artifice *n* **1** ***syn*** see CUNNING 2
rel ingenuity, inventiveness, originality; adroitness, cleverness, keenness, quickness, shrewdness; adeptness, proficiency
2 ***syn*** see TRICK 1
rel chicane, chicanery, trickery; knavery, rascality, skulduggery; deceit, dissimulation, duplicity, guile
artificial *adj* **1** ***syn*** see SYNTHETIC
rel fabricated, fashioned, made
con native
ant natural
2 taking the place of something else and especially of something finer or more costly <*artificial* diamonds>
syn dummy, ersatz, false, imitation, mock, sham, simulated, spurious, substitute; *compare* FICTITIOUS 2, SPURIOUS 3
rel fake, papier-mâché, ‖pretend, unreal; hollow, painted
con authentic, bona fide, genuine, real, sure-enough, true, veritable
3 lacking in spontaneity and genuineness <exchanged *artificial* smiles>
syn affected, assumed, feigned, put-on, spurious

rel histrionic, insincere, overdone, quaint, stagy, theatrical, unnatural; cute, cutesy, goody-goody, mincing, overrefined, simpering; contrived, forced, labored
con genuine, sincere, spontaneous, unaffected

artist *n syn* see EXPERT
rel ace, crackerjack, first-rater, shark, topnotcher; genius, prodigy, wonder

artiste *n syn* see EXPERT

artless *adj syn* see NATURAL 5
rel free, relaxed; aboveboard, forthright, straightforward; childlike, trusting, unsuspicious; untouched, virginal
con cunning, insidious, sly, wily; calculating, designing, intriguing, scheming; artificial, insincere
ant artful; affected

arty *adj syn* see PRETENTIOUS 3

arty–crafty *adj syn* see PRETENTIOUS 3

as *conj syn* see BECAUSE

as a rule *adv syn* see USUALLY 2

‖**ascared** *adj syn* see AFRAID 1

ascend *vb* **1** to move upward to or toward a summit <*ascend* a mountain>
syn climb, escalade, escalate, mount, scale, upclimb, upgo
rel clamber, get up, scramble, shin; crest, surmount, top
idiom scale the heights, work one's way up
ant descend
2 *syn* see RISE 4

ascendancy *n syn* see SUPREMACY

ascendant *n* **1** *syn* see SUPREMACY
2 *syn* see ANCESTOR 1
rel forerunner, precursor, predecessor
ant descendant

ascendant *adj syn* see DOMINANT 1

ascension *n syn* see ASCENT

ascent *n* a moving upward or an upward movement <the slow *ascent* of the creaky old elevator>
syn ascension, rise, rising
rel elevation, raising, uplifting
ant descent

ascertain *vb syn* see DISCOVER 3
rel ask, inquire, interrogate, query, question; appraise, inspect, observe, survey, view; consider, contemplate, study, weigh
con assume, presume; conjecture, guess, surmise

ascetic *adj syn* see SEVERE 1
rel abstemious, abstinent, forbearing; self-abasing, self-abnegating, self-denying, self-forgetful, selfless; disciplined, restrained, schooled, trained
con epicurean, sensual, sensuous, sybaritic; abandoned, dissolute, licentious, self-indulgent
ant luxurious, voluptuous

ascribe *vb* to refer especially to a supposed cause, source, or author <a manuscript commonly *ascribed* to Saint Augustine>
syn accredit, assign, attribute, charge, credit, impute, lay, refer
rel attach (to), connect (with), fix (on *or* upon), pin (on), saddle (on *or* upon *or* with); affix, fasten; conjecture, guess, surmise; adduce, advance, allege, cite

aseptic *adj syn* see UNDEMONSTRATIVE

as for *prep syn* see APROPOS

as good as *adv* **1** *syn* see NEARLY
2 *syn* see ALMOST 2

ash *n* the residue left when material is consumed by fire <cold whitened *ash* on the hearth>
syn ashes, cinders, clinkers
rel dross, scoria, slag; charcoal, coal(s), coke, ember(s); fumes, smoke, soot

ashake *adj syn* see TREMULOUS

ashamed *adj* humiliated or disconcerted usually by feelings of guilt, disgrace, or impropriety <*ashamed* of her brother's noisy boasting>
syn chagrined, mortified, shamed
rel abashed, discomfited, embarrassed; abased, humbled, humiliated; abject, hangdog, mean; contrite, penitent, repentant
idiom unable to show one's face
con arrogant, assured, overbearing, self-assured; vain, vainglorious
ant proud

ashen *adj syn* see PALE 1
rel corpselike, ghostly, macabre; blanched, bleached, decolorized, faded

ashes *n pl syn* see ASH

ashiver *adj syn* see TREMULOUS

ashy *adj syn* see PALE 1

aside *adv* **1** in a slanting or sloping direction <his head hung *aside* as if he lacked the strength to hold it up>
syn aslant, aslope, obliquely, sideways, sidewise, slant, slantingly, slantingways, slantly, slantways, slantwise, ‖slaunchways, slopeways; *compare* SIDEWAYS 1
rel askance, askant, askew, awry; downgrade, downhill
con erectly, uprightly, vertically
2 *syn* see APART 2
3 *syn* see APIECE

‖**aside** *prep syn* see NEAR 2

aside *n syn* see DIGRESSION

aside from *prep syn* see EXCEPT

asinine *adj syn* see SIMPLE 3
rel puerile; absurd, irrational, unreasonable
con prudent, sage, sane, sapient, wise; clever, intelligent, knowing, smart; rational, reasonable
ant judicious, sensible

ask *vb* **1** to call upon for an answer or information <*asked* him to explain his behavior>
syn catechize, examine, inquire, interrogate, query, question, quiz
rel argue, canvass, debate, deliberate, discuss, review, talk (over)
con answer, rejoin, reply, respond, retort
2 to seek to obtain by making one's needs or desires known <*asked* for time to consider the problem>

---

syn synonym(s) *rel* related word(s)
ant antonym(s) *con* contrasted word(s)
idiom idiomatic equivalent(s)
‖ use limited; if in doubt, see a dictionary

syn bespeak, desire, request, solicit
rel claim, demand, exact, require; beg, beseech, entreat, implore, importune
idiom put in for
3 ***syn*** see DEMAND 2
4 ***syn*** see INVITE
rel canvass, request, seek
askance *adv* **1** ***syn*** see AWRY 1
ant directly
2 with absence of approval or trust <a proceeding one must view more than a little *askance*>
syn distrustfully, doubtfully, mistrustfully, skeptically, suspiciously
rel captiously, critically, cynically, doubtingly; deprecatingly, depreciatively, disparagingly
con approvingly, favorably
askant *adv* ***syn*** see AWRY 1
ant directly
asker *n* ***syn*** see SUPPLIANT
askew *adv* ***syn*** see AWRY 1
ant straight
aslant *adv* ***syn*** see ASIDE 1
asleep *adj* **1** ***syn*** see DEAD 1
2 ***syn*** see NUMB 1
3 ***syn*** see INACTIVE
as long as *conj* ***syn*** see BECAUSE
aslope *adv* ***syn*** see ASIDE 1
as much as *adv* ***syn*** see ALMOST 2
asomatous *adj* ***syn*** see IMMATERIAL 1
aspect *n* **1** ***syn*** see APPEARANCE 1
rel countenance, face, visage; air, bearing, port, presence
2 ***syn*** see PHASE
rel point of view, slant, standpoint
asperity *n* **1** ***syn*** see DIFFICULTY 1
rel austerity, bitterness, grimness, harshness, inclemency, severity, stringency
con blandness, gentleness, mildness, softness
2 ***syn*** see INEQUALITY 1
3 ***syn*** see ACRIMONY
rel harshness, keenness, roughness, sharpness; irritability, snappishness, tartness, waspishness
con blandness, smoothness, suavity, urbanity; courtesy, gallantry
ant amenity
asperous *adj* ***syn*** see ROUGH 1
asperse *vb* **1** ***syn*** see MALIGN
rel deride, mock, taunt; affront, insult, offend
con applaud, commend, compliment
2 ***syn*** see BAPTIZE
aspersion *n* ***syn*** see ANIMADVERSION
rel abuse, invective, muck, vituperation; backbiting, calumny, detraction, scandal, slander; lampoon, libel, pasquinade, skit, squib
con eulogy, extolling, laudation, praise; acclaim, acclamation, applause, plaudits; commendation, compliment
asphyxiate *vb* ***syn*** see SUFFOCATE
aspirant *n* ***syn*** see CANDIDATE
aspiration *n* ***syn*** see AMBITION 1
rel aim, direction, goal, objective; desire, lust, passion, urge
aspire *vb* **1** ***syn*** see AIM 2
rel hunger, long, pine, thirst; bid (for), strain (for *or* after), struggle (for), try (for)
idiom cry for the moon, have at heart, have one's heart set on, reach for (*or* keep one's eyes on) the stars
con condescend, deign, look down (on); grovel, stoop, wallow
2 ***syn*** see RISE 4
aspiring *adj* ***syn*** see AMBITIOUS 1
rel desirous, impassioned, urgent; wanting, wishful, yearning
as regards *prep* ***syn*** see APROPOS
as respects *prep* ***syn*** see APROPOS
ass *n* **1** ***syn*** see DONKEY 1
2 ***syn*** see FOOL 1
assail *vb* ***syn*** see ATTACK 1
rel beat, belabor, buffet, pound, pummel
idiom round on
assailment *n* ***syn*** see ATTACK 1
assassin *n* a person hired or hirable to commit murder <found out who paid the *assassin*>
syn bravo, cutthroat, gun, gunman, ‖gunsel, gunslinger, hatchet man, hit man, torpedo, triggerman; *compare* MURDERER
rel apache, desperado, goon, ‖gorilla, highbinder, strong arm, thug
assassinate *vb* ***syn*** see MURDER 1
assault *n* ***syn*** see ATTACK 1
rel brush, clash, invasion, melee, skirmish; brawl, contest, fracas, set-to
assault *vb* ***syn*** see ATTACK 1
rel battle, fight, war; clash, collide, encounter, engage; skirmish
assay *vb* **1** ***syn*** see TRY 5
rel venture
idiom make an effort to
2 ***syn*** see ESTIMATE 1
rel demonstrate, prove, test, try; analyze, resolve; calculate, compute, reckon
assemblage *n* ***syn*** see GATHERING 1
assemble *vb* **1** ***syn*** see CONVOKE
2 ***syn*** see GATHER 6
rel associate, combine, unite; convene, convoke
con dispel, dissipate, scatter; leave, part, quit, separate
ant disperse
3 ***syn*** see GROUP 1
rel accumulate, aggregate, amass, garner; bunch, clump; bank, heap, mound, pile, stack
con dispel, dissipate, scatter; leave, part, quit, separate; break up, disband
ant disperse
4 ***syn*** see MAKE 3
assembly *n* **1** ***syn*** see GATHERING 2
rel association, band, conclave, party, troupe
2 ***syn*** see GROUP 1
rel crowd, push; faction, interest, sect, wing; brotherhood, fellowship, fraternity
con masses, multitude; canaille, rabble, riffraff, ruck, trash
assent *vb* to give or express one's consent or concurrence <*assented* grudgingly to her plans for the evening>
syn accede, acquiesce, agree, consent, subscribe, yes
rel adopt, embrace, espouse; accept; abide, bear (with), endure, stand, suffer, tolerate; down,

stomach, swallow, take; defer, relent, submit, yield
idiom be at one with, cast one's vote for, give the nod of approval, go along with, see eye to eye with
con rebuff, refuse, reject, scorn, scout, spurn; deny, gainsay
ant dissent

assert *vb* **1** to state firmly, positively, or assuredly <he continued to *assert* his innocence>
syn affirm, aver, avouch, avow, constate, declare, depose, predicate, profess, protest
rel adduce, advance, allege, cite, claim, pretend; announce, broadcast, disseminate, proclaim, promulgate, publish, spread
idiom have it
con contradict, contravene, dispute, gainsay, negate, negative, traverse; confute, disprove, rebut, refute
ant deny; controvert
2 ***syn*** see MAINTAIN 2
rel declare, express, utter, voice; advance, state, stipulate, submit

assertive *adj* **1** ***syn*** see EMPHATIC
2 ***syn*** see AGGRESSIVE
rel affirmative; arbitrary, dogmatic, peremptory, positive; assured, certain, cocksure, opinionated, opinionative, self-assured, sure; confident, presumptuous, sanguine, self-confident
con bashful, diffident, modest, shy; amenable, biddable, docile, submissive
ant retiring; acquiescent

assertory *adj* ***syn*** see AGGRESSIVE

assess *vb* **1** ***syn*** see LEVY
2 ***syn*** see ESTIMATE 1
rel calculate, compute; account, consider, deem, reckon, weigh

assessment *n* **1** ***syn*** see ESTIMATION 1
2 ***syn*** see ESTIMATE 1
3 ***syn*** see TAX 1

asset *n* **1 assets** *pl* ***syn*** see MEAN 3
rel bankroll, money; equity; principal
ant liabilities
2 ***syn*** see CREDIT 3
rel distinction, glory, honor, ornament
con detriment, disadvantage, discredit, liability
ant handicap

asshead *n* ***syn*** see FOOL 1

assiduous *adj* marked by careful attention or persistent application <learned to speak French fluently by *assiduous* practice>
syn diligent, industrious, operose, sedulous; *compare* BUSY 1
rel hardworking, laborious, moiling; indefatigable, tireless, untiring, unwearied, zealous
idiom hard at it
con casual, haphazard, happy-go-lucky, hit-or-miss, intermittent, random; careless, lax, remiss, slack, sloppy, slovenly; indolent, lazy, slothful
ant desultory

assiduously *adv* ***syn*** see HARD 3

assign *vb* **1** ***syn*** see TRANSFER 4
2 ***syn*** see ALLOT
rel establish, fix, set, settle
3 ***syn*** see ASCRIBE
rel associate, link, relate; classify, pigeonhole
4 ***syn*** see PRESCRIBE 2
rel decide, determine; commit, consign, entrust, relegate

assignation *n* ***syn*** see ENGAGEMENT 3
rel agreement, arrangement, understanding; get-together

assignee *n* ***syn*** see AGENT 2

assignment *n* ***syn*** see TASK 1
rel incumbency, liability, obligation, responsibility

assimilate *vb* **1** ***syn*** see ABSORB 1
rel imbue, infuse, ingrain, inoculate, leaven, suffuse; adopt, embrace, espouse; corner, engross, monopolize
2 ***syn*** see EQUATE 2

assimilation *n* ***syn*** see RECOGNITION 1
rel awareness, consciousness, mindfulness

assist *vb* ***syn*** see HELP 1
rel accompany, attend, escort; concur, cooperate
con clog, fetter, trammel; forestall, prevent; burden, encumber, handicap, tax, weigh down
ant hamper; impede

assist *n* ***syn*** see HELP 1

assistance *n* ***syn*** see HELP 1
rel backing, supporting, upholding; advantage, avail, profit, use; appropriation, grant, subsidy, subvention
con checking, hampering, hindering, hindrance; balking, foiling, frustration, thwarting
ant impediment, impeding; obstructing, obstruction

assistant *n* **1** ***syn*** see HELPER
2 a person who takes over part of the duties of a superior <started as *assistant* to the secretary>
syn aid, aide, aide-de-camp, coadjutant, coadjutor, lieutenant
rel acolyte, attendant, second; flunky, henchman, minion, stooge; girl Friday, right-hand man; agent, attorney, deputy, factor, proxy; fall guy, patsy; co-worker, workfellow, yokemate

assistive *adj* ***syn*** see HELPFUL 1

assize *n* **1** ***syn*** see LAW 1
2 ***syn*** see STANDARD 4

associate *vb* ***syn*** see JOIN 1
rel amalgamate, blend, coalesce, merge, mingle, mix; ally, confederate, federate, league
con alienate, estrange; divide, divorce, part

associate *n* **1** ***syn*** see PARTNER
rel affiliate, ally, confederate, leaguer; abettor, accomplice, collaborator
2 ***syn*** see COLLEAGUE
3 a person regularly frequenting the company of another <a man is judged by the *associates* he keeps>

syn synonym(s) ***rel*** related word(s)
ant antonym(s) ***con*** contrasted word(s)
idiom idiomatic equivalent(s)
‖ use limited; if in doubt, see a dictionary

syn buddy, chum, comate, companion, comrade, crony, ‖cully, pal, running mate; *compare* FRIEND
rel acquaintance, friend, sympathizer; confidant, familiar, intimate; brother-in-arms, comrade-in-arms
4 ***syn*** see ACCOMPANIMENT 2
rel complement, correlate, correlative, counterpart, match; correspondent
con competitor, rival; adversary, antagonist, opponent

association *n* **1** the quality or state of being associated <worked in close *association* with the courts>
syn affiliation, alliance, cahoots, combination, conjointment, conjunction, connection, hookup, partnership, tie-up, togetherness
rel coaction, collaboration, concert, cooperation, teamwork; conviviality, gaiety, joviality, sociability
con aloofness, apartness, disjunction, disunion, isolation, separation
ant disassociation, dissociation
2 an organization of persons sharing a common interest or purpose <a buyers' *association*>
syn brotherhood, club, congress, fellowship, fraternity, guild, league, order, society, sodality, union
rel alliance, axis, bloc, coalition, federation, organization; faction, interest, sect, wing; combine, gang, machine, ring
3 ***syn*** see LEAGUE 4
4 something (as a feeling or recollection) associated in the mind with a particular person or thing <the thought of her childhood home always carried an *association* of loving warmth>
syn connotation, hint, implication, overtone, suggestion, undertone
rel image, picture, vision; appearance, fantasy, illusion, mirage

assort *vb* to arrange systematically <*assort* yarn by color>
syn categorize, class, classify, group, pigeonhole
rel arrange, methodize, order, systematize; distribute, divide, separate; screen, sift; stratify
con derange, disarrange, disorder, disorganize; commingle, jumble, mingle, mix, scramble

assorted *adj* **1** ***syn*** see MISCELLANEOUS
con chosen, picked, preferred, selected
2 corresponding in such manner or degree as to be appropriately associated <they made a well-*assorted* pair>
syn adapted, conformable, fitted, matched, suited
rel chosen, picked, preferred, selected; associated, bracketed, coupled, linked
con confused, disordered, fouled-up, haywire, jumbled, muddled, scrambled

assortment *n* **1** ***syn*** see VARIETY 2
2 ***syn*** see MISCELLANY 1

assuage *vb* **1** ***syn*** see RELIEVE 1
rel placate
con augment, increase, recruit, reinforce; enhance, exaggerate, heighten, intensify, magnify, strengthen
ant exacerbate
2 ***syn*** see PACIFY
rel calm, ease, relax, slack, slacken, soothe
con annoy, inflame, nettle, provoke, ruffle, vex

as such *adv* ***syn*** see PER SE

assumably *adv* ***syn*** see PRESUMABLY

assume *vb* **1** ***syn*** see DON 2
2 ***syn*** see DON 1
3 ***syn*** see ARROGATE 1
rel grab, seize, snatch, take
idiom take over the helm, take possession (*or* command)
4 to take on or present a false or deceptive appearance <their gaiety was *assumed*>
syn act, affect, bluff, counterfeit, fake, feign, pretend, put on, sham, simulate
rel camouflage, cloak, conceal, disguise, dissemble, hide, mask
idiom make believe
5 ***syn*** see PRESUPPOSE
rel affirm, assert, aver, predicate, profess; allow, concede, grant
6 ***syn*** see UNDERSTAND 3

assumed *adj* ***syn*** see ARTIFICIAL 3
rel factitious, synthetic; deceptive, delusory, illusory, insubstantial, unreal
con authentic, bona fide, genuine, veritable; real, true

assumption *n* **1** ***syn*** see PRESUPPOSITION
2 something that is taken for granted or advanced as fact <decisions based on *assumptions* about the nature of society>
syn apriorism, posit, postulate, postulation, premise, presumption, presupposition, supposition, thesis
rel conjecture, guess, surmise; hypothesis, theory; axiom, fundamental, law, principle, theorem

assurance *n* **1** ***syn*** see WORD 8
rel parole, promise, troth; plight; agreement, compact, covenant, pact, understanding
2 ***syn*** see CERTAINTY
rel credit; dependence, reliance, trust
con suspicion, uncertainty; disbelief, incredulity, unbelief
ant mistrust; dubiousness
3 ***syn*** see SAFETY
4 ***syn*** see CONFIDENCE 2
rel composure, equanimity, sangfroid
con agitation, disquiet, jumpiness, nervousness, shakiness, skittishness; anxiety, doubt, foreboding, funk, perturbation, trepidation
ant alarm
5 ***syn*** see TEMERITY
rel brazenness, cockiness, presumption; conceit, self-conceit, self-importance, vanity
con diffidence, modesty, shyness, timidity; self-depreciation, self-effacement, unassumingness, unpretentiousness

assure *vb* **1** ***syn*** see ENSURE
con abash, discomfit, embarrass; buffalo, bulldoze, cow, daunt, intimidate, shake; demoralize, disquiet, unman, unnerve
ant alarm

2 to make one sure or certain of something <pinched his arm to *assure* himself he was awake>
syn convince, persuade, satisfy
idiom bring (*or* drive) home to, lead one to believe, sell one on something
assured *adj* **1** ***syn*** see CONFIDENT 1
rel collected, composed, cool, imperturbable, unflappable, unruffled; game, plucky, resolute, spunky
con abashed, discomfited, disconcerted, embarrassed, rattled; hesitant, insecure, reluctant, uncertain; apprehensive, timorous
2 ***syn*** see DECIDED 1
rel certain, fixed, set
con ambiguous, uncertain; enigmatic, mysterious, obscure
assuredness *n* ***syn*** see CERTAINTY
astern *adv* ***syn*** see ABAFT
rel rear
con ahead, before, forward
as to *prep* **1** ***syn*** see APROPOS
2 ***syn*** see BY 5
astonish *vb* ***syn*** see SURPRISE 2
rel overwhelm; affright, alarm, terrify
astonishing *adj* ***syn*** see MARVELOUS 1
astound *vb* ***syn*** see SURPRISE 2
astounding *adj* ***syn*** see MARVELOUS 1
astral *adj* **1** ***syn*** see STELLAR 1
2 ***syn*** see DREAMY 1
3 ***syn*** see EXALTED 1
astray *adv* ***syn*** see AMISS 2
astricted *adj* ***syn*** see CONSTIPATED
astringent *adj* **1** ***syn*** see ACRID
rel puckery
con bland, mellow, mild
2 ***syn*** see SEVERE 1
rel biting, cutting, incisive, penetrating, piercing, stabbing; brisk, caustic, keen, sharp
con lax, loose, relaxed, slack, weak; unexacting
3 ***syn*** see TONIC 1
astucious *adj* ***syn*** see SHREWD
astucity *n* ***syn*** see WIT 3
astute *adj* **1** ***syn*** see SHREWD
rel discreet, foresighted, prudent; cunning, sly, wily
con ingenuous, naive, simple, unsophisticated; dull, heavy, obtuse, slow; arid, barren, staid, stuffy, uninspired
ant gullible
2 ***syn*** see SLY 2
rel subtile, subtle; keen, knowing, sharp
idiom slippery as an eel, too clever by half
con aboveboard, forthright, straightforward; ingenuous, naive, simple, unsophisticated
astuteness *n* ***syn*** see WIT 3
asudden *adv* ***syn*** see SHORT 1
asunder *adv* ***syn*** see APART 3
idiom all to pieces, one part from the other, to shreds
as usual *adv* ***syn*** see USUALLY 1
asweat *adj* ***syn*** see SWEATY
as well *adv* **1** ***syn*** see ALSO 2
idiom over and above
2 ***syn*** see EVEN 1
as well as *prep* ***syn*** see BESIDES 1
as yet *adv* ***syn*** see HITHERTO 1
asylum *n* **1** ***syn*** see SHELTER 1
2 ***syn*** see REFUGE 1
rel inviolability; security
3 an institution for the care of the insane <demand for improved *asylums*>
syn booby hatch, ||bughouse, crazy house, ||funny farm, loony bin, madhouse, ||nuthouse
rel farm, home, institution, sanatorium
idiom insane (*or* lunatic) asylum, mental hospital (*or* institution), state hospital
asymmetric *adj* ***syn*** see LOPSIDED
at all *adv* **1** ***syn*** see EVER 5
2 ***syn*** see EVER 4
ataraxy *n* ***syn*** see EQUANIMITY
atavism *n* ***syn*** see REVERSION 1
ataxia *n* ***syn*** see CONFUSION 3
at close hand *adv* ***syn*** see CLOSE
atelier *n* ***syn*** see STUDIO
athenaeum *n* ***syn*** see LIBRARY
athirst *adj* **1** ***syn*** see THIRSTY 1
rel dehydrated, desiccated, dried up
2 ***syn*** see EAGER
con lackadaisical, languid, listless; autistic, withdrawn
athletic *adj* ***syn*** see MUSCULAR 2
rel active, energetic, strenuous, vigorous
con delicate; decadent, effete, flabby, soft
athletics *n pl* physical activities engaged in for exercise or pleasure <went in heavily for *athletics*>
syn games, sports
rel calisthenics, exercise, gymnastics; drill, practice, workout; amusement, diversion, entertainment, pastime, recreation
athwart *adv* **1** ***syn*** see ACROSS 1
2 ***syn*** see OVER 1
athwart *prep* ***syn*** see ACROSS
atiptoe *adj* ***syn*** see EXPECTANT 1
atmosphere *n* **1** ***syn*** see AIR 3
rel character, flavor, property, quality; characteristic, individuality, peculiarity; impression, suggestion
2 ***syn*** see ENVIRONMENT
atmospheric *adj* ***syn*** see AIRY 1
atom *n* ***syn*** see PARTICLE
rel dash, touch, trace; shade, smack, spice, soupçon, suggestion, suspicion, tincture, tinge
atomize *vb* ***syn*** see DESTROY 1
at once *adv* **1** ***syn*** see TOGETHER 1
2 ***syn*** see AWAY 3
atone *vb* ***syn*** see EXPIATE
rel compensate, pay, recompense, satisfy; appease, conciliate, propitiate
idiom set one's house in order
atone (for) *vb* ***syn*** see COMPENSATE 1
atramentous *adj* ***syn*** see BLACK 1
at random *adv* ***syn*** see ABOUT 4

---

syn synonym(s) ***rel*** related word(s)
ant antonym(s) ***con*** contrasted word(s)
idiom idiomatic equivalent(s)
|| use limited; if in doubt, see a dictionary

atrocious *adj* **1** ***syn*** see OUTRAGEOUS 2
rel flagitious, infamous, iniquitous, vicious; barbarous, savage; glaring, rank; abominable, contemptible, despicable, execrable, odious, vile
con fine, righteous, upright, virtuous; benign, gentle, kindly
ant humane
2 ***syn*** see OFFENSIVE
rel displeasing, distasteful
con alluring, magnetic

atrociousness *n* ***syn*** see ENORMITY 1

atrocity *n* ***syn*** see ENORMITY 1

atrophy *n* ***syn*** see DETERIORATION 1

attach *vb* ***syn*** see FASTEN 1
rel associate; add, annex, append; bind, tie
con disassociate, dissociate; disembarrass, disencumber, disengage, disentangle
ant detach

attachment *n* **1** the state of being firmly attached to someone or something (as by affection, sympathy, or self-interest) <his *attachment* to an outworn code>
syn adherence, adhesion, constancy, faithfulness, fidelity, loyalty
rel firmness, staunchness, steadfastness; allegiance, devotion, fealty
con disloyalty, faithlessness, infidelity, unfaithfulness; aloofness, distance, remoteness; disinterest, disregard, unconcern, unmindfulness
ant detachment
2 ***syn*** see LOVE 1
rel piety; devotedness
con antipathy, disinclination, dislike; alienation, disaffection, estrangement
ant aversion

attack *vb* **1** to act in violent opposition <cavalry *attacked* the Indian camp>
syn aggress, assail, assault, beset, fall (on *or* upon), storm, strike
rel invade, irrupt; charge, raid, rush; besiege, blockade, encompass, invest; beleaguer, beset, harass, harry, press; turn (on)
idiom gang up on, light into, sail into, set upon, take the offensive
con defend, guard, protect, shield; combat, oppose, resist, withstand
2 to begin to work vigorously (as at a task) <*attack* a problem>
syn bang away (at), tackle
rel buckle (to *or* down *or* down to), fall to, pitch in, wade (in *or* into)
idiom address (*or* apply *or* devote) oneself to, give oneself up to
con dawdle, lag, poke, putter

attack *n* **1** an act of attacking especially in the form of an attempt to injure, destroy, or defame <insecticides that are essential for successful *attack* on insect pests>
syn aggression, assailment, assault, offense, offensive, onfall, onset, onslaught
rel charge, descent, drive, foray, push, raid, sally, sortie; blitz, incursion, inroad, surprise; action, battle
con championing, justification, protection, support, vindication; opposition, resistance; defending, guarding, protecting, sheltering
ant defense
2 action or an attitude in a struggle that calls for or is opposed by defense <his policy had always been one of *attack*>
syn aggression, aggressiveness, belligerence, combativeness, fight, pugnacity
rel bellicosity, chauvinism, jingoism, warmongering; activation, militarization, mobilization, muster
con submissiveness, yielding
3 an episode of bodily or mental disorder <a sudden *attack* of dizziness>
syn access, fit, seizure, spell, throe, turn; *compare* SIEGE
rel outbreak, paroxysm, spasm; affection, ailment, complaint, disease, disorder

attain *vb* ***syn*** see GAIN 1
idiom gain one's end, make good

attainable *adj* ***syn*** see AVAILABLE 1

attainment *n* ***syn*** see ACQUIREMENT

attempt *vb* ***syn*** see TRY 5
rel begin, commence, inaugurate, initiate, start; venture
idiom give (something) a try, take a crack (*or* whack) at
con accomplish, achieve, effect, execute, fulfill, perform; attain, compass, gain, reach
ant succeed

attempt *n* an effort made to do or accomplish something <made a determined *attempt* to improve her writing>
syn endeavor, essay, hassle, striving, struggle, trial, try, undertaking
rel care, effort, pains, trouble; beginning, commencement, initiation, offer, shy, start
con accomplishment, achievement, attainment, finish, fulfillment

attend *vb* **1** ***syn*** see LISTEN
idiom be attentive (to), give heed (to)
2 ***syn*** see TEND 2
rel govern, oversee, supervise; direct, handle, manage, regulate, run; aid, assist, help
3 ***syn*** see ACCOMPANY
rel associate, fraternize, join, mingle, mix

attendant *adj* ***syn*** see CONCOMITANT

attendant *n* ***syn*** see HELPER

attending *adj* ***syn*** see CONCOMITANT

attention *n* **1** a focusing of the mind on something <gave the problem careful *attention*>
syn application, concentration, consideration, debate, deliberation, heed, study
rel assiduity, diligence, industry, sedulity, sedulousness; notice, observation, regard, remark; absorption, engrossment, immersion, intentness
con absence, absentmindedness, abstraction, detachment, remoteness, withdrawal; disinterest, indifference, unconcern, unmindfulness
ant inattention
2 ***syn*** see NOTICE 1
rel awareness, consciousness, mindfulness, sensibility

con disregard, heedlessness, insensibility, unawareness, unconsciousness
3 ***syn*** see COURTESY 1
rel deference, homage, honor, reverence; benignity; considerateness, consideration, kindliness, solicitude
con neglect, negligence; aloofness, indifference, unconcern; discourtesy

attentive *adj* **1** concentrating one's attention on something <listeners *attentive* to the speaker's appeal>
syn advertent, arrect, heedful, intentive, observant, regardful
rel alert, aware, mindful; agog, eager, interested, keen; concentrating, earnest, intent; open-eared, open-eyed
idiom all ears (*or* eyes), on the ball, paying attention
con absorbed, abstracted, bemused, preoccupied; absentminded, daydreaming, faraway, oblivious, wandering, woolgathering
ant absent; inattentive
2 ***syn*** see THOUGHTFUL 3
con aloof, indifferent
ant inattentive; neglectful

attenuate *vb* **1** ***syn*** see THIN 1
rel lessen; sap; dissipate; constrict, contract, deflate, shrink
con amplify, dilate, distend, expand, inflate, swell; augment, enlarge, increase; enrich
2 ***syn*** see WEAKEN 1
3 ***syn*** see THIN 2

attenuate *adj* **1** ***syn*** see THIN 1
2 ***syn*** see THIN 2

attenuated *adj* ***syn*** see THIN 2

attest *vb* **1** ***syn*** see CERTIFY 1
rel confirm, corroborate, substantiate, verify; support, sustain, uphold, warrant; affirm, asseverate, depone, swear, testify
con confute, controvert, disprove, refute; contradict, deny, gainsay
2 ***syn*** see INDICATE 2
rel authenticate, confirm, substantiate
con falsify, misrepresent; distort, garble, pervert, twist, warp
ant belie
3 ***syn*** see TESTIFY 1

attestation *n* ***syn*** see TESTIMONY

at times *adv* ***syn*** see SOMETIMES

attire *vb* ***syn*** see CLOTHE
rel accouter, appoint, arm, equip, outfit
con bare, denude, dismantle, strip
ant divest

attire *n* ***syn*** see CLOTHES

attirement *n* ***syn*** see CLOTHES

attitude *n* **1** ***syn*** see POSTURE 1
rel air, demeanor, port, presence
2 ***syn*** see POSITION 1
rel point of view; bias, predilection, prejudice, prepossession

attitudinize *vb* ***syn*** see POSE 4

attorney *n* **1** ***syn*** see AGENT 2
rel alternate, locum tenens, stand-in, substitute, supply
2 ***syn*** see LAWYER

attorney-at-law *n* ***syn*** see LAWYER

attract *vb* **1** to exert an irresistible or compelling influence on <her beauty *attracted* all eyes>
syn allure, bewitch, captivate, charm, draw, enchant, fascinate, magnetize, take, wile
rel entice, lure, seduce, tempt; beguile, draw (in), intrigue, inveigle, suck (in); enrapture, entrance; court, invite, solicit
con fend (off), hold (off *or* away), rebuff, repulse; disgust, offend, revolt
ant repel
2 ***syn*** see INTEREST

attracting *adj* ***syn*** see ATTRACTIVE 1

attraction *n* **1** a quality that elicits admiration or pleased responsiveness <yielding to the *attraction* of the balmy afternoon>
syn allurement, appeal, attractiveness, call, draw, drawing power, lure, pull, seduction
rel charm, glamour, interest; delight, pleasure; bait, hook, snare
con offensiveness, repulsiveness, ugliness
2 a relationship characteristic of individuals that are drawn together naturally or involuntarily and exert a degree of influence on one another <the *attraction* between iron and the magnet>
syn affinity, sympathy
rel accord, concord, harmony
idiom drawing together
con conflict, discord, friction, tension

attractive *adj* **1** having the power to attract <an area *attractive* to wildlife>
syn alluring, appealing, attracting, bewitching, captivating, charming, drawing, enchanting, engaging, fascinating, glamorous, magnetic, mesmeric, prepossessing, seductive, siren
rel beautiful, bonny, comely, fair, lovely, pretty; Circean, enticing, fetching, luring, tempting; interesting, taking, winning; beckoning, come-hither, inviting, provocative, tantalizing, teasing; likable, simpatico
con abhorrent, distasteful, obnoxious, repugnant; loathsome, offensive, repulsive, revolting; antipathetic, unsympathetic
ant repellent, repelling; forbidding
2 ***syn*** see BEAUTIFUL
rel agreeable, goodly, ||likely, pleasing, sightly
con homely, ill-favored, plain, uncomely, unprepossessing
ant unattractive

attractiveness *n* ***syn*** see ATTRACTION 1

attribute *n* **1** ***syn*** see QUALITY 1
rel particularity, singularity, specialty; brand, earmark, impress, stamp
2 ***syn*** see SYMBOL 1

attribute *vb* ***syn*** see ASCRIBE
rel calendar, chronologize, date, place

attrition *n* ***syn*** see PENITENCE

attritional *adj* ***syn*** see REMORSEFUL

---

syn synonym(s) ***rel*** related word(s)
ant antonym(s) ***con*** contrasted word(s)
idiom idiomatic equivalent(s)
|| use limited; if in doubt, see a dictionary

attune *vb* ***syn*** see HARMONIZE 3
rel balance, compensate, counterbalance; accord, agree; fix, rectify, regulate
idiom put in tune, set to rights (*or* in order)
con divide, separate, wean

‖atween *prep* ***syn*** see BETWEEN 2

‖atwixt *prep* ***syn*** see BETWEEN 2

atypical *adj* ***syn*** see ABNORMAL 1
rel irregular, unnatural; different, divergent; exceptional, odd, peculiar, queer, strange
con customary, usual
ant typical; representative

auberge *n* ***syn*** see HOTEL

au courant *adj* **1** ***syn*** see AWARE
2 ***syn*** see UP-TO-DATE
3 ***syn*** see FAMILIAR 3

audacious *adj* **1** ***syn*** see BRAVE 1
rel adventurous, daredevil, daring, foolhardy, rash, reckless, venturesome; brash, brazen, shameless
con calculating, cautious, chary, wary; judicious, prudent, sane, wise; careful, circumspect, discreet
2 ***syn*** see ADVENTUROUS
rel fearless, valiant, valorous
con careful, circumspect, discreet; calculating, cautious, chary, wary
3 ***syn*** see INSOLENT 2
4 free from constraint and formality <found life an *audacious* ever-changing adventure>
syn uncurbed, ungoverned, unhampered, uninhibited, unrestrained, untrammeled
rel emancipated, free, independent; easy, relaxed; careless, heedless, thoughtless; self-absorbed, self-centered, selfish
con checked, curbed, governed, hampered, inhibited, restrained, trammeled; careful, cautious, heedful, mindful, thoughtful; considerate, generous, self-abnegating, self-effacing; drab, dull, pedestrian

audacity *n* ***syn*** see TEMERITY
rel cheek, effrontery, face, gall; brass, brazenness, cockiness; forwardness, impudence, resolution; courage, mettle, spirit
con calculation, caution, wariness; shyness, timidity, timorousness; agitation, disquiet, nervousness, perturbation, trepidation
ant circumspection

audible *adj* ***syn*** see AURAL 1
ant inaudible

audience *n* **1** ***syn*** see HEARING 2
rel attention, consideration, ear
2 ***syn*** see FOLLOWING 2
rel admirers, devotees, fanciers, fans, votaries

audile *adj* ***syn*** see AUDITORY

audit *n* ***syn*** see EXAMINATION
rel investigation, probe; check, control, corrective

audition *n* ***syn*** see HEARING 2

auditory *adj* of, relating to, or experienced through the sense of hearing <*auditory* disorders>
syn acoustic, audile, aural; *compare* AURAL 1

au fait *adj* **1** ***syn*** see ABLE
2 ***syn*** see FAMILIAR 3
3 ***syn*** see DECOROUS 1

au fond *adv* ***syn*** see ESSENTIALLY 1

Augean stable *n* ***syn*** see SINK 1

aught (*or* **ought**) *n* ***syn*** see ZERO 1

augment *vb* **1** ***syn*** see INCREASE 1
2 ***syn*** see INCREASE 2

augment *n* ***syn*** see INCREASE 1
rel exalt, hike, raise
con attenuate, decrease, dwindle; abridge; alleviate, assuage, relieve
ant abate

augmentation *n* **1** ***syn*** see ACCOMPANIMENT 1
rel adjunct, annex, attachment, fixture, reinforcement; bonus, boot, extra, plus
2 ***syn*** see ADDITION
con subtraction

augur *n* ***syn*** see PROPHET

augur *vb* **1** ***syn*** see FORETELL
rel argue, bespeak, indicate
2 to indicate or suggest a future probability <their enthusiasm *augurs* well for the success of the enterprise>
syn betoken, bode, forebode, foreshadow, foreshow, foretoken, omen, portend, presage, promise
rel hint, imply, intimate, suggest; prefigure, shadow (forth)
idiom bid fair to, give promise (*or* fair promise) of, hold out hope of, lead one to believe (*or* expect)

augury *n* ***syn*** see FORETOKEN
rel anticipation, premonition, presentiment
con accomplishment, effecting, effectuation, fulfillment; actualization, materialization, realization; appearance, emergence, forthcoming, issuance

august *adj* ***syn*** see GRAND 1
rel splendid, sublime, superb; impressive, moving, striking; awe-inspiring, awful, fearful, overwhelming

au naturel *adj* ***syn*** see NUDE 2

aura *n* ***syn*** see AIR 3
rel appearance, aspect, suggestion; aureole, radiance

aural *adj* **1** heard or perceived with the ear <responded to *aural* stimuli>
syn audible, auricular; *compare* AUDITORY
2 ***syn*** see AUDITORY

aureate *adj* ***syn*** see RHETORICAL
rel baroque, rococo
con moderate, quiet, restrained, sober, temperate
ant austere

auricular *n* ***syn*** see AURAL 1

aurora *n* ***syn*** see DAWN 1

auslander *n* ***syn*** see STRANGER

auspex *n* ***syn*** see PROPHET

auspices *n pl* ***syn*** see BACKING

auspicious *adj* **1** ***syn*** see FAVORABLE 5
rel hopeful; golden, halcyon, roseate, rosy
con ominous, portentous, unpropitious; adverse, antagonistic
ant inauspicious; ill-omened

2 ***syn*** see TIMELY 1

austere *adj* **1** ***syn*** see SEVERE 1
rel bald, bare, simple, unadorned, undecorated, unembellished, unornamented; earnest, grave, serious, sober, somber
con complicated, elaborate, fancy, flamboyant, fussy, ornate; frivolous, light, light-minded, shallow, superficial
2 ***syn*** see ACRID
rel biting, keen, rough
con bland, mellow, smooth, soft
3 ***syn*** see GRIM 2

autarchic *adj* **1** ***syn*** see ABSOLUTE 4
rel commanding, dogmatic, imperious; nonconstitutional, undemocratic
2 ***syn*** see FREE 1
rel self-dependent, self-reliant, self-sufficient

autarkic *adj* ***syn*** see FREE 1
rel self-dependent, self-reliant, self-sufficient

authentic *adj* **1** worthy of acceptance because of accuracy <an *authentic* portrayal of ancient customs>
syn convincing, credible, faithful, trustworthy, trusty
rel accurate, dependable, factual, reliable, sure; solid, sound, straight, valid; authoritative, cathedral, official, standard
idiom all wool and a yard wide; to be depended (*or* relied) on
con incredible, unconvincing, untrustworthy; equivocal, obscure, uncertain, vague; hypothetical, purported, putative, supposed, supposititious; debatable, doubtful, questionable; nonstandard
ant inauthentic
2 being exactly as appears or is claimed <an *authentic* masterpiece>
syn blown-in-the-bottle, bona fide, genuine, indubitable, pukka, questionless, real, right, simon-pure, sure-enough, true, undoubted, undubitable, unquestionable, veritable, very
rel cognizable, identifiable, knowable, recognizable; honest, pure, unadulterated, unalloyed
con deceptive, delusive, delusory, false, misleading, wrong; unidentifiable, unrecognizable
ant spurious
3 ***syn*** see CERTAIN 3

authenticate *vb* **1** ***syn*** see CONFIRM 2
rel accredit, approve, endorse; demonstrate, prove, test, try; avouch, vouch (for)
con reject, repudiate, spurn; contradict, deny, negate
ant impugn

author *n* ***syn*** see FATHER 2
rel origin, source; ancestor, parent, procreator

authoritarian *adj* **1** ***syn*** see DICTATORIAL
rel heavy-handed, high-handed, oppressive, strict, stringent
ant libertarian; anarchistic
2 ***syn*** see TOTALITARIAN 1
rel fascistic, nazi; patriarchal
ant democratic

authoritative *adj* **1** ***syn*** see OFFICIAL
2 ***syn*** see TRUE 9
rel attested, authenticated, circumstantiated, confirmed, proven, validated, verified; convincing, indisputable, irrefutable, sure, unrefutable; cathedral, cathedratic
con contestable, controversial, debatable, disputable, refutable; dubious, questionable, suspect, unreliable
3 ***syn*** see DICTATORIAL
4 ***syn*** see ORTHODOX 1

authority *n* **1** ***syn*** see EXPERT
2 ***syn*** see POWER 1
rel governance, government, rule
3 ***syn*** see INFLUENCE 1
rel example, exemplar, ideal, model, pattern, standard; force, power, pressure

authorization *n* ***syn*** see PERMISSION

authorize *vb* **1** to invest with power or the right to act <I did not *authorize* him to speak for me>
syn accredit, commission, empower, enable, license
rel approve, countenance, endorse; aid, assist, help, support, subserve; advance, facilitate, forward, further, promote
con bar, disallow, enjoin, forbid, interdict, prohibit
2 ***syn*** see ENTITLE 2
rel allow, let, permit; approve, countenance, endorse
idiom give one the right to
3 ***syn*** see INVEST 2

auto *n* ***syn*** see CAR

auto *vb* **1** ***syn*** see DRIVE 5
2 ***syn*** see RIDE 1

autobiographer *n* ***syn*** see BIOGRAPHER

autobiographist *n* ***syn*** see BIOGRAPHER

autobiography *n* ***syn*** see BIOGRAPHY
rel diary, journal, letters

autocar *n* ***syn*** see CAR

autochthonous *adj* ***syn*** see NATIVE 2
con alien, extraneous, extrinsic, foreign; imported, introduced
ant naturalized

autocracy *n* ***syn*** see TYRANNY

autocratic *adj* ***syn*** see ABSOLUTE 4
rel arrogant, haughty, overbearing, overweening
con deferential, submissive, yielding; forbearing, indulgent, lenient, tolerant

autodidactic *adj* ***syn*** see SELF-TAUGHT

autograph *vb* ***syn*** see SIGN 1

autognosis *n* ***syn*** see SELF-KNOWLEDGE

autoist *n* ***syn*** see MOTORIST

automatic *adj* **1** ***syn*** see SPONTANEOUS
rel prompt, quick, ready; accustomed, confirmed, habitual, habituated
2 ***syn*** see PERFUNCTORY

automaton *n* **1** ***syn*** see ROBOT 1
2 ***syn*** see ROBOT 2

automobile *n* ***syn*** see CAR

---

syn synonym(s) ***rel*** related word(s)
ant antonym(s) ***con*** contrasted word(s)
idiom idiomatic equivalent(s)
‖ use limited; if in doubt, see a dictionary

THESAURUS

automobilist *n* ***syn*** see MOTORIST

autonomous *adj* ***syn*** see FREE 1
rel self-governed; unconstrained, uncontrolled, unsubordinated
con controlled, subordinated; governed, ruled; affiliated, allied

autopsy *n* examination of the body after death usually to determine the cause of death <the *autopsy* of a murder victim>
syn necropsy, ‖post, postmortem, postmortem examination

autoschediasm *n* ***syn*** see IMPROVISATION

autoschediastic *adj* ***syn*** see EXTEMPORANEOUS

auxiliary *adj* capable of supplying or intended to supply aid or support <an *auxiliary* police unit>
syn accessory, adjuvant, ancillary, appurtenant, collateral, contributory, subservient, subsidiary
rel complementary, supplementary; peripheral, secondary, subordinate, tributary; backing, supporting, upholding; aiding, assisting, helping
con chief, leading, main, principal; sole, solitary, unique

avail *vb* ***syn*** see BENEFIT
rel answer, fill, fulfill, meet, satisfy
con damage, harm, hurt, injure

avail *n* ***syn*** see USE 3
rel interest; appositeness, suitability
con inappropriateness, unsuitableness

available *adj* **1** that is accessible or may be obtained <the best pen *available* at the present time>
syn attainable, disponible, gettable, obtainable, procurable, securable
rel accessible, convenient, handy
idiom to be had
con unattainable, unobtainable; absent, deficient, lacking, missing
ant unavailable
2 ***syn*** see PURCHASABLE 1

avarice *n* ***syn*** see CUPIDITY
rel frugality, parsimony, thrift; miserliness, niggardliness, parsimoniousness, stinginess; acquisitiveness, covetousness, graspingness, piggishness
con extravagance; bountifulness, bounty, generosity, liberality, munificence, openhandedness
ant prodigality

avariciousness *n* ***syn*** see CUPIDITY

avenge *vb* to inflict punishment by way of repayment for <*avenge* an insult>
syn redress, revenge, venge, vindicate
rel compensate, pay (back), pay out, recompense, repay, requite, retaliate, retribute; chasten, chastise, punish; correct, right
idiom get an eye for an eye, get even with, settle accounts, wreak one's vengeance
con condone, disregard, ignore, overlook; absolve, amnesty, forgive, pardon, remit; bear, endure, stand, suffer, tolerate

avengement *n* ***syn*** see RETALIATION

avenging *n* ***syn*** see RETALIATION

avenue *n* **1** ***syn*** see WAY 1
‖**2** ***syn*** see DRIVEWAY

aver *vb* ***syn*** see ASSERT 1
rel defend, hold, justify, maintain
con deny

average *n* something (as a number, quantity, or condition) that represents a middle point between extremes <somewhat sweeter than *average*>
syn mean, median, norm, par
ant maximum; minimum

average *adj* ***syn*** see MEDIUM
rel common, familiar, ordinary; customary, usual
idiom common or garden variety
con choice, excellent, exceptional, prime, superior; conspicuous, noticeable, outstanding, prominent; bad, inferior, low-grade, poor, punk

averagely *adv* ***syn*** see ENOUGH 2

avernal *adj* ***syn*** see INFERNAL 2

averse *adj* ***syn*** see DISINCLINED
rel balky, contrary, perverse; flinching, quailing, recoiling, resistant, shrinking; uncongenial, unsympathetic
ant avid (of *or* for)

aversion *n* **1** ***syn*** see DISLIKE
rel antagonism, antipathy, hostility; dread, fear, horror
con bias, partiality; leaning, propensity, taste
ant predilection
2 ***syn*** see ANTIPATHY 2
rel abhorrence, distaste, repellency, repugnance, repulsion, revulsion; disgust, dread, loathing
con bias, partiality, penchant; flair, inclination, leaning, taste
ant attachment; predilection
3 ***syn*** see ABOMINATION 2
ant delight

aversive *adj* ***syn*** see ANTIPATHETIC 2

avert *vb* **1** ***syn*** see TURN 6
rel remove, transfer
2 ***syn*** see PREVENT 2
rel anticipate; balk, foil, frustrate, thwart; check, halt, stay, stop
con advance, further, promote

aviary *n* a house, enclosure, or large cage for confining live birds <the zoo's *aviary*>
syn birdhouse
rel dovecote, dovehouse; columbary, pigeon house

aviator *n* ***syn*** see PILOT 2

avid *adj* ***syn*** see EAGER
rel covetous, craving, desirous, wanting, wishful; importunate, insistent, pressing, urgent; gluttonous, omnivorous
con aloof, disinterested, uninterested; disinclined, indisposed, loath
ant indifferent; averse

avidity *n* ***syn*** see CUPIDITY

avoid *vb* ***syn*** see ESCAPE 2
rel avert, deflect, divert, obviate, prevent, ward (off); debar, exclude, preclude; forbid, prohibit
idiom give a miss (*or* a wide berth), have no truck with, set one's face against, steer clear of, turn one's back on
con court, invite, solicit

ant face; meet
avoidance *n* ***syn*** see ESCAPE 2
avouch *vb* ***syn*** see ASSERT 1
rel confirm, corroborate; acknowledge, admit, confess, own
con deny, impugn
avow *vb* **1** ***syn*** see ASSERT 1
rel defend, maintain, vindicate; asseverate, swear, testify
2 ***syn*** see ACKNOWLEDGE 1
con repudiate, withdraw
avowry *n* ***syn*** see PATRON SAINT
await *vb* ***syn*** see EXPECT 1
rel abide, stay, wait
idiom bide one's time, sweat (*or* tough) it out
awake *vb* ***syn*** see WAKE 1
awake *adj* ***syn*** see AWARE
rel vigilant, watchful; aroused, awakened, roused, stirred up; excited
con drowsy, sleepy, slumberous, somnolent; inactive, inert, supine
awaken *vb* **1** ***syn*** see WAKE 1
2 ***syn*** see STIR 1
rel fire, inflame; alert
idiom stir the feelings (*or* blood) of
con arrest, check, retard, subdue; calm, compose, restrain
awanting *prep* ***syn*** see WITHOUT 2
award *vb* **1** ***syn*** see GRANT 1
rel allocate, allot, apportion, assign; dower, endow, endue
2 ***syn*** see GIVE 2
award *n* ***syn*** see HONOR 2
aware *adj* marked by realization, perception, or knowledge often of something not generally realized, perceived, or known <*aware* of her own inner weakness>
syn alive, apprehensive, au courant, awake, cognizant, conscious, conversant, knowing, mindful, sensible, sentient, ware, witting
rel acquainted, apprised, informed; alert, heedful; impressionable, perceptive, receptive
con anesthetic, impassible, insensible, insensitive; ignorant, unknowing
ant unaware
awash *adj* ***syn*** see FULL 1
away *adv* **1** from this or that place <come *away* at once>
syn hence, thence
rel forth, out, therefrom
2 at some distance from a place expressed or implied <he lived several blocks *away*>
syn off, over
rel afar, far; apart, aside
3 without hesitation or delay <fire *away* when you see the target>
syn at once, directly, first off, forthwith, immediately, instanter, instantly, now, PDQ, right, right away, right off, straight, straight away, straight off, straightway
rel momentarily, promptly, ‖pronto, punctually; expeditiously, quickly, speedily, swiftly
away *adj* ***syn*** see ABSENT 1
awe *n* ***syn*** see REVERENCE 2
rel esteem, regard, respect, veneration, worship; admiration, amazement, wonder, wonderment
con despite, scorn; arrogance, insolence, superciliousness
awe *vb* ***syn*** see FRIGHTEN
aweless *adj* ***syn*** see BRAVE 1
awful *adj* ***syn*** see FEARFUL 3
rel impressive, moving; august, imposing, majestic; splendid, superb; grave, serious, solemn; ominous, portentous
‖**awful** *adv* ***syn*** see VERY 1
awfully *adv* ***syn*** see VERY 1
awkward *adj* **1** ***syn*** see CLUMSY 1
rel blundering, bumbling, bungling; clownish, lubberly, oafish; cumbrous, hulking, ponderous
idiom all thumbs
2 marked by a lack of grace, ease, skill, or fitness (as in action or speech) <his *awkward* approach to the problem>
syn bumbling, clumsy, gauche, halting, ham-handed, heavy-handed, inept, lumbering, maladroit, unhandy, unhappy, wooden; *compare* CLUMSY 1
rel rigid, stiff; discomfited, disconcerted, embarrassed; bunglesome, bungling, inefficient, inexpert, unskillful
con adept, adroit, dexterous, expert, finished, polished, proficient, skilled, skillful, smooth; easy, effortless, facile, simple
ant deft; graceful
3 ***syn*** see INCONVENIENT
4 ***syn*** see INFELICITOUS
awry *adv* (*or adj*) **1** deviating from a straight line or direction <the coverlet was pulled *awry*>
syn askance, askant, askew, ‖cam, cock-a-hoop, cockeyed, crookedly
rel aside, aslant, obliquely, slantways
con even, straight, true; directly, undeviatingly
2 ***syn*** see AMISS 2
rel erroneously, faultily, untruly; aside
ax *vb* ***syn*** see DISMISS 3
axiom *n* **1** ***syn*** see PRINCIPLE 1
2 ***syn*** see MAXIM
‖**ayah** *n* ***syn*** see NURSEMAID
aye *adv* ***syn*** see YES 1

---

syn synonym(s) ***rel*** related word(s)
ant antonym(s) ***con*** contrasted word(s)
idiom idiomatic equivalent(s)
‖ use limited; if in doubt, see a dictionary

B

Babbitt *n* ***syn*** see PHILISTINE

babblative *adj* ***syn*** see TALKATIVE

babble *vb* **1** ***syn*** see GIBBER
2 to talk nonsensically <silly people *babbling* on about trivia>
syn blabber, blather, drivel, drool, gabble, prate, prattle, twaddle, ‖waffle
rel clack, jaw, rattle, run on, yak, yammer, yap
idiom run off at the mouth
3 ***syn*** see CHAT 1

babble *n* **1** ***syn*** see CHATTER
2 ***syn*** see GIBBERISH 1

babe *n* ***syn*** see BABY 1

babel *n* ***syn*** see DIN
con hush, noiselessness; peace, quiet, silence

babushka *n* ***syn*** see KERCHIEF 1

baby *n* **1** a very young child especially in the first year of life <the love of a mother for her *baby*>
syn babe, bantling, infant, neonate, newborn
rel bambino, little one, toddler, tot; nursling, suckling, weanling; bratling
idiom babe in arms
2 ***syn*** see WEAKLING
‖**3** ***syn*** see GIRL FRIEND 2

baby *vb* to treat with special, excessive, or fond care <*baby* a sick husband>
syn cater (to), cocker, coddle, cosset, cotton, humor, indulge, mollycoddle, pamper, spoil
rel dry-nurse, wet-nurse; dote (on *or* upon), favor; gratify, please, satisfy
con control, discipline, restrain; abuse, ill-treat, ill-use, mistreat, oppress; neglect, overlook, slight

baby buggy *n* ***syn*** see BABY CARRIAGE

baby carriage *n* a four-wheeled push carriage with a folding top for a baby <a park popular with young mothers pushing *baby carriages*>
syn baby buggy, bassinet, ‖perambulator, ‖pram

babyhood *n* ***syn*** see INFANCY 1

babyish *adj* ***syn*** see CHILDISH

bacchanal *n* ***syn*** see ORGY 2

bacchanalia *n* ***syn*** see ORGY 2

back *n* **1** the surface or part most remote from the front <the *back* of his neck>
syn posterior, rear, rearward
rel extremity, tail; reverse
con anterior
ant front
2 ***syn*** see SPINE

back *adv* ***syn*** see ABOUT 6

back *adj* **1** distant from settled areas <*back* regions in the hill country>
syn frontier, outlandish, remote, unsettled
rel uncultivated, uninhabited, unoccupied, unpopulated, wild
con built-up, settled, urban
2 ***syn*** see POSTERIOR 2
ant front

back *vb* **1** ***syn*** see SUPPORT 2
rel aid, assist, help; abet
2 ***syn*** see CAPITALIZE
3 ***syn*** see MOUNT 5
4 ***syn*** see RECEDE 1
con advance, progress

back answer *n* ***syn*** see RETORT 2

backbiting *n* ***syn*** see DETRACTION
rel animadversion, reflection, stricture; abuse, invective, obloquy, vituperation
con accolade, commendation, encomium, eulogy, laudation, paean, panegyric, praise, tribute; adulation, blarney, compliment, flattery, soft soap

backbiting *adj* ***syn*** see LIBELOUS

backbone *n* **1** ***syn*** see SPINE
2 ***syn*** see FORTITUDE
rel hardihood; heart
con irresoluteness, irresolution
ant backbonelessness, spinelessness
3 ***syn*** see MAINSTAY

backchat *n* ***syn*** see BANTER

backcountry *n* ***syn*** see FRONTIER 2

‖**backdoor trots** *n pl but sing or pl in constr* ***syn*** see DIARRHEA

back down *vb* to withdraw from a previous agreement or stand <a politician *backing down* on an earlier promise>
syn back off, back out, backpedal, backwater, cop out, crawfish (out), cry off, declare off, renege, resile, welsh
rel disavow, recall, recant, retract, take back, withdraw; backtrack; beg off, weasel (out); balk, demur, hold back, stickle
idiom get out of, go back on

backer *n* ***syn*** see SPONSOR
rel ally, protagonist; bankroller, ‖grubstaker, ‖meal ticket, promoter

backer–up *n* ***syn*** see SPONSOR

backfire *vb* to have the reverse of the desired effect <the new policy *backfired* disastrously>
syn backlash, boomerang, bounce (back), kick back
rel fall (through), fizzle, miscarry, miss, ricochet
idiom come to grief, go on the rocks, ‖lay an egg
con come off, succeed, work out

backhouse *n* ***syn*** see PRIVY 1

backing *n* aid or support given to an undertaking <the project had the *backing* of the city fathers>
syn aegis, auspices, patronage, sponsorship
rel championship, cooperation, fosterage; guidance, tutelage; encouragement; assistance, help, support

backland *n* ***syn*** see FRONTIER 2

backlash *vb* ***syn*** see BACKFIRE

backlog *n* ***syn*** see RESERVE

back of *prep* ***syn*** see ABAFT

back off *vb* ***syn*** see BACK DOWN

back out *vb* ***syn*** see BACK DOWN

backpack *n* a carrying case (as of canvas or nylon) held on the back by shoulder straps <carried his supplies in a *backpack*>
syn haversack, knapsack, pack, packsack, rucksack

backpedal *vb* ***syn*** see BACK DOWN
rel dodge, duck, elude, evade, get around, shirk, sidestep

backset *n* ***syn*** see SETBACK

backside *n* ***syn*** see BUTTOCKS

backslide *vb* ***syn*** see LAPSE
rel regress, retrovert, return, revert; defect, desert, tergiversate, turn
idiom fall away, fall (*or* sink *or* slide *or* slip) back into, give in to

backsliding *n* ***syn*** see LAPSE 2

backstabbing *n* ***syn*** see DETRACTION

backstage *adj or adv* off or away from the part of the stage visible to the audience <*backstage* sounds that gave the impression of a storm>
syn offstage
idiom behind the scenes
ant onstage

backstop *vb* ***syn*** see SUPPORT 2

back talk *n* impudent and insolent talk <do as you're told and no *back talk*>
syn guff, ||jaw, ||lip, mouth, sass, sauce
rel cheek, impudence, insolence

backup *n* ***syn*** see SUBSTITUTE 1

backup *adj* ***syn*** see SUBSTITUTE 1

||**backveld** *n* ***syn*** see FRONTIER 2

backward *adv* ***syn*** see ABOUT 6

backward *adj* **1** directed, turned, or executed backward <the *backward* swimming of the crayfish>
syn retral, retrograde
rel inverted, reversed
ant advance, forward
2 ***syn*** see DISINCLINED
rel bashful, diffident
3 ***syn*** see SHY 1
4 ***syn*** see RETARDED
5 holding to outworn or traditional views, ideas, or principles <had a *backward* attitude toward social inferiors>
syn benighted, ignorant, unenlightened, unprogressive
rel conservative, reactionary; obtuse, stupid, thickheaded; bigoted, hidebound, narrow; blind; unenlightened, uninformed
con advanced, aware, enlightened, forward-looking, progressive, unbenighted
6 not developing or progressing especially in economic and social areas <*backward* nations using primitive farming methods>
syn behindhand, underdeveloped, undeveloped, unprogressive
rel poor, struggling; medieval; benighted, retarded, uncultivated, uncultured
idiom behind the times
con forward-looking, progressive; civilized, cultivated, cultured; modern
ant advanced

backwash *n* ***syn*** see FRONTIER 2

backwater *n* ***syn*** see FRONTIER 2

backwater *vb* ***syn*** see BACK DOWN
rel dodge, duck, elude, evade, get around, shirk, sidestep

backwoods *n pl but sing or pl in constr* ***syn*** see FRONTIER 2

||**backwoodser** *n* ***syn*** see RUSTIC

backwoodsman *n* ***syn*** see RUSTIC

bad *adj* **1** falling short of a standard of what is satisfactory <a *bad* repair job>
syn amiss, ||bum, ||crappy, dissatisfactory, poor, ||punk, rotten, unsatisfactory, up, wrong
rel deficient, inadequate, inferior; careless, slipshod; defective, disordered, off, unsound; execrable, ||lousy, miserable, wretched; inadmissible, objectionable, unacceptable; insufferable, intolerable
idiom below par, not up to snuff (*or* scratch)
con excellent, fine, meritorious; acceptable, adequate, sound
2 ***syn*** see WRONG 1
rel arrant, peccant; graceless, improper, indecorous, untoward; disorderly, misbehaving, naughty, rowdy, ruffianly, unruly; froward, perverse
ant good
3 ***syn*** see EVIL 5
4 ***syn*** see EVIL 6
5 having undergone decay <one *bad* apple can spoil the barrel>
syn decayed, putrid, rotten, spoiled
rel fusty, stale; mildewed, moldered, moldy, moth-eaten, musty, rancid, worm-eaten, decomposed, putrefied, putrifacted; tainted, turned
con crisp, dewy, fresh, sweet, unspoiled; choice, picked, prime
ant good
6 ***syn*** see NAUGHTY 1
7 ***syn*** see TOUGH 8
8 arousing discomfort or distaste <a *bad* smell>
syn ||chiselly, disagreeable, displeasing, rotten, sour, unhappy, unpleasant
rel disgusting, foul, nauseating, noisome, noxious, offensive, repulsive, sickening; abhorrent, hateful, loathsome, obnoxious; uneasy; thankless, ungrateful; distasteful, distressing, sticky; ungracious, unhandsome
con agreeable, pleasant, pleasing, refreshing, soothing; unoffensive
9 ***syn*** see HARMFUL
10 ***syn*** see DOWNCAST
11 ***syn*** see NULL

bad actor *n* ***syn*** see TROUBLEMAKER

bad books *n pl* ***syn*** see DISLIKE

badge *n* **1** ***syn*** see INSIGNIA
2 ***syn*** see HONOR 2

badger *vb* ***syn*** see BAIT 2

---

syn synonym(s) ***rel*** related word(s)
ant antonym(s) ***con*** contrasted word(s)
idiom idiomatic equivalent(s)
|| use limited; if in doubt, see a dictionary

rel plague, tease, worry
badinage *n* ***syn*** see BANTER
rel chaffing, guying, japery, joshing, kidding, sport
badland *n* ***syn*** see WASTE 1
||bad lot *n* ***syn*** see WASTREL 1
badly *adv* **1** ***syn*** see HARD 5
2 ***syn*** see AMISS 2
ant well
badman *n* ***syn*** see OUTLAW
rel criminal, villain; hood, hoodlum, hooligan, thug; blackguard, devil, knave, rapscallion, rascal, rascallion, rogue, scoundrel
bad–mouth *vb* ***syn*** see DECRY 2
bad–tempered *adj* ***syn*** see ILL-TEMPERED
rel cantankerous, cranky, crusty, temperamental, touchy
con forbearing, long-suffering, patient
ant good-tempered
Baedeker *n* ***syn*** see HANDBOOK
baffle *vb* ***syn*** see FRUSTRATE 1
rel confound, dumbfound, flummox, mystify, nonplus, puzzle; addle, ball up, befuddle, confuse, fog, mix up, muddle; discomfit, disconcert, embarrass, faze, rattle
con enlighten, illuminate
bag *n* **1** a container made of a flexible material and open or opening at the top <a grocery *bag*>
syn ||poke, pouch, sack
||**2** ***syn*** see HAG 2
bag *vb* ***syn*** see CATCH 1
rel clench, ||cop, ||glom, hook, land, nab, net, sack, scoop
idiom lay by the heels
baggage *n* ***syn*** see WANTON
||bagged *adj* ***syn*** see INTOXICATED 1
bagnio *n* ***syn*** see BROTHEL
bail *n* ***syn*** see GUARANTEE 1
bail *vb* ***syn*** see DIP 2
bailiwick *n* ***syn*** see FIELD
rel district, jurisdiction, neighborhood, place, quarter, realm; beat, circuit, round, walk
bait *vb* **1** ***syn*** see MOLEST
2 to persist in tormenting or harassing another <*baiting* him with gibes about his humble origin>
syn badger, bullyrag, chivy, heckle, hector, hound, ride
rel annoy, bother, bedevil, devil, rag, worry; harass, harry, haze, vex; ||bug, nag, pester, push around
3 ***syn*** see LURE
bait *n* **1** ***syn*** see LURE 2
||**2** ***syn*** see SNACK
bake *vb* **1** ***syn*** see BURN 3
2 ***syn*** see FIRE 6
baking *adj* ***syn*** see HOT 1
balance *n* **1** the stability resulting from the equalization of opposing forces <keeping his emotional *balance* when under stress>
syn counterpoise, equilibrium, equipoise, poise, stasis
rel collectedness, composure, cool, coolness, coolth, equanimity, repose, sangfroid; aplomb, assurance, self-assurance, self-possession; control, self-control, stability, steadiness; stagnancy, stagnation
con imbalance, unbalance; instability, nervousness, shakiness, uncontrol, unsteadiness
2 ***syn*** see SYMMETRY
rel congruity, consistency, correspondence, sameness
con disbalance, disharmony, disproportion, incongruity, inconsistency, irregularity, overbalance, unbalance
ant imbalance
3 ***syn*** see REMAINDER
balance *vb* ***syn*** see COMPENSATE 1
rel adjust, attune, harmonize, tune; accord, agree, correspond; even, level, square
idiom strike a balance
bald *adj* **1** ***syn*** see HAIRLESS
rel bobbed, clipped, cropped, polled, shaven, sheared
con bushy, hairy, hirsute, shaggy; unshaven, unshorn; fleecy, furry, woolly; downy, fuzzy, pilose, pubescent
2 ***syn*** see BARE 1
rel austere, severe; plain, unadorned, undecorated, unembellished, ungarnished, unornamented; colorless, lackluster, lifeless, lusterless, uncolored
balderdash *n* ***syn*** see NONSENSE 2
baldhead *n* one who has a bald head
syn baldpate, ||baldy, ||skinhead
baldpate *n* ***syn*** see BALDHEAD
||baldy *n* ***syn*** see BALDHEAD
balefire *n* ***syn*** see BEACON 1
baleful *adj* ***syn*** see SINISTER
rel deadly, evil, harmful, pernicious; bodeful, foreboding; unfavorable, unpromising
con auspicious, benign, favorable, promising, propitious; advantageous, beneficial
ant beneficent
2 ***syn*** see OMINOUS
balk *n* ***syn*** see TIMBER 2
balk *vb* **1** ***syn*** see FRUSTRATE 1
idiom stand in the way of
con back, support, uphold; aid, assist, help
ant forward
2 ***syn*** see DEMUR
rel decline, refuse, turn down; flinch, hang back, quail, recoil, shrink
con capitulate, give in
balky *adj* ***syn*** see CONTRARY 3
rel immovable, inflexible, unbending, unmanageable; averse, disinclined, hesitant, indisposed, loath, reluctant
con subdued, submissive, tame
ball *n* a more or less spherical body or mass <a *ball* of string>
syn globe, orb, rondure, round, sphere
rel egg, oval, ovoid
ball *vb* to form into a more or less spherical body or mass <*balled* the cookie dough with her hands>
syn conglobate, conglobe, ensphere, round, sphere
rel bead, pill; clot, wad

balladmonger *n* ***syn*** see POETASTER
ball and chain *n* **1** ***syn*** see RESTRICTION 1
‖**2** ***syn*** see WIFE
ballast *vb* ***syn*** see STABILIZE
ballerina *n* ***syn*** see DANCER
ballet girl *n* ***syn*** see DANCER
ballot *n* **1** a piece of paper used to cast a vote in an election <deliberately spoiled his *ballot*>
syn ticket, vote
rel Australian ballot, Indiana ballot, Massachusetts ballot, office-block ballot, office-group ballot, party-column ballot, secret ballot
2 ***syn*** see SUFFRAGE
ballot *vb* ***syn*** see ELECT 2
‖**ballup** *n* ***syn*** see CONFUSION 3
ball up *vb* ***syn*** see CONFUSE 2
ballyhoo *vb* ***syn*** see TOUT
balm *n* **1** ***syn*** see OINTMENT
2 ***syn*** see FRAGRANCE
balm *vb* ***syn*** see CALM
balmy *adj* **1** ***syn*** see SWEET 2
rel musky; refreshing, rejuvenating, restorative; pleasant, pleasing
2 ***syn*** see GENTLE 1
rel agreeable, delightful, gratifying, pleasant, pleasing; allaying, assuaging, balsamic, easing, lightening, relieving, soothing
con annoying, bothering, bothersome, irking, irksome, vexing
‖**3** ***syn*** see FOOLISH 2
‖**baloney** *n* ***syn*** see NONSENSE 2
balustrade *n* ***syn*** see RAILING
bamboozle *vb* ***syn*** see DUPE
rel bilk, diddle, swindle
ban *vb* ***syn*** see FORBID
rel illegalize, outlaw
con approve, authorize; suffer, tolerate
ban *n* ***syn*** see TABOO
banal *adj* ***syn*** see INSIPID 3
rel hackneyed, pedestrian, trite, warmed-over; bromidic, commonplace, corny, platitudinous, stock; bewhiskered, hoary, old; asinine, fatuous, silly, simple
con fresh, new, novel; different, uncommon, unusual; stimulating, zesty; choice, rare, recherché
ant original
banality *n* ***syn*** see COMMONPLACE
bananas *adj* ***syn*** see INSANE 1
banausic *adj* **1** ***syn*** see DULL 9
2 ***syn*** see MATERIALISTIC
band *n* ***syn*** see STRIP 1
rel belt, border, edge, line; tape; fascia, taenia; streak, vein
band *vb* **1** ***syn*** see BELT 1
2 ***syn*** see UNITE 2
rel amalgamate, unionize; consociate; club, team (up)
con disintegrate, disperse, dissolve, separate
ant break up, disband
band *n* **1** ***syn*** see COMPANY 4
rel assembly, bevy, body, bunch, covey, group; detachment, detail
2 ***syn*** see GROUP 1
3 ***syn*** see ORCHESTRA
bandage *vb* to cover with a bandage <*bandage* wounds>
syn bind, dress
bandanna *n* ***syn*** see KERCHIEF 1
bandar–log *n* ***syn*** see CHATTERBOX
bandbox *adj* ***syn*** see DAPPER
bandeau *n* ***syn*** see STRIP 1
banderole *n* ***syn*** see FLAG
‖**bandido** *n* ***syn*** see OUTLAW
rel brigand, footpad, highwayman, holdup man; bravo, cutthroat, gunman, villain; gangster, mobster, racketeer
banding *n* ***syn*** see STRIP 1
bandit *n* **1** ***syn*** see OUTLAW
rel brigand, footpad, highwayman, holdup man; bravo, cutthroat, villain; gangster, mobster, racketeer; jayhawker
2 ***syn*** see MARAUDER
bandwagon *n* ***syn*** see FASHION 3
bandy *vb* ***syn*** see EXCHANGE 3
rel chuck, flip, pitch, throw, toss; banter; answer, repay, retort
idiom bat (*or* beat) back and forth
bandy *adj* ***syn*** see BOWLEGGED
bandy–legged *adj* ***syn*** see BOWLEGGED
bane *n* **1** ***syn*** see POISON
2 ***syn*** see DOWNFALL 2
baneful *adj* **1** ***syn*** see PERNICIOUS
rel injurious; insalubrious, noisome, unhealthy, unwholesome
con benign, favorable, propitious; advantageous, helpful, profitable; healthful, salubrious, salutary, wholesome
ant beneficial
2 ***syn*** see OMINOUS
‖**bang** *vb* ***syn*** see SURPASS 1
bang *n* **1** ***syn*** see BLOW 1
2 a loud percussive or explosive noise <slammed the book shut with a *bang*>
syn blast, boom, burst, clap, crack, crash, slam, smash, wham
rel noise, report, sound; discharge, explosion, pop, shot; howl, roar, roll, rumble, thunder
3 ***syn*** see THRILL
4 ***syn*** see SMASH 6
5 ***syn*** see VIGOR 2
bang *adv* ***syn*** see JUST 1
bang away (at) *vb* ***syn*** see ATTACK 2
bang–up *adj* ***syn*** see EXCELLENT
banish *vb* to eject by force or authority from a country, state, or sovereignty <*banish* an enemy of the king>
syn cast out, deport, displace, exile, expatriate, expel, expulse, ‖lag, ostracize, oust, relegate, run out, transport; *compare* EJECT 1
rel disfellowship, excommunicate, rusticate; debar, exclude, shut out; drive out, eject, evict, turn out; bump, can, cashier, discharge, dismiss, fire, put out, sack; blackball, blacklist, boycott

---

syn synonym(s) ***rel*** related word(s)
ant antonym(s) ***con*** contrasted word(s)
idiom idiomatic equivalent(s)
‖ use limited; if in doubt, see a dictionary

banishment *n syn* see EXILE 1

banister *n syn* see RAILING

bank *n* **1** *syn* see PILE 1
rel snowbank, snowdrift; cloudage, fogbank
2 *syn* see SHORE
rel bankside, levee, riverfront, streamside; lakefront, lakeshore, lakeside, margin; oceanfront, seabank, seabeach, seaboard, seafront, sea frontage, sea line, sea sands, shingle
idiom water's edge

bank *vb syn* see HEAP 1
rel compact, concentrate

bank *vb* to place money in a bank <*banks* half his paycheck every week>
syn deposit
rel invest, lay aside, lay away, salt away, salt down, save, set aside, sock away; cache, coffer, hoard, squirrel (away), stash
con draw out, take out, withdraw; disburse, expend, fork (over *or* out), lay out, pay (out), spend

bank (on *or* upon) *vb syn* see RELY (on *or* upon)
rel intend, plan; bet (on), gamble (on), stake, venture, wager
idiom bank the rent on, bet one's bottom dollar on, go bail on, lay money on

bankroll *vb syn* see CAPITALIZE

bankrupt *vb* **1** *syn* see DEPLETE
rel break, impair, incapacitate
con rebuild, repair, restore, revive; augment, bolster, fortify, strengthen
2 *syn* see STRIP 2
3 *syn* see RUIN 3
4 *syn* see RUIN 2

banned *adj* **1** *syn* see FORBIDDEN
2 *syn* see CONTRABAND

banner *n syn* see FLAG
rel banneret

banner *adj syn* see EXCELLENT

bannerol *n syn* see FLAG

banquet *n syn* see DINNER
rel bridale, feed, ‖gaudy, harvest home, repast, ‖tuck, ‖tuck-in, ‖tuck-out

bantam *adj* **1** *syn* see SMALL 1
2 *syn* see SAUCY 1

banter *vb* **1** to make fun of good-naturedly <the students resented their teacher's *bantering* them about mistakes>
syn chaff, fool, fun, jest, ‖jive, joke, jolly, josh, kid, rag, razz, rib
rel deride, guy, mock, quiz, rally, ridicule, satirize, taunt, tease, twit
idiom make fun of, make merry with, poke fun at
‖**2** *syn* see FACE 3
‖**3** *syn* see COAX

banter *n* animated back-and-forth exchange of remarks <entertained the group with their jolly *banter*>
syn backchat, badinage, ‖cross talk, persiflage, repartee, snip-snap
rel chitchat, gossip, gossipry, small talk; rallying, teasing; exchange, give-and-take
con debate, deliberation, discussion

bantling *n syn* see BABY 1

baptismal name *n syn* see GIVEN NAME

baptize *vb* **1** to administer the rite of baptism <a child *baptized* in the Catholic Church>
syn asperse, christen, immerse, sprinkle
rel cleanse, purify, regenerate
2 *syn* see NAME 1

bar *n* **1** a solid piece of material usually rectangular and considerably longer than it is wide <a *bar* of gold>
syn billet, ingot, rod, slab, stick, strip
2 something that stands in the way of some objective <his religion was a *bar* to membership in that exclusive club>
syn barricade, barrier, blank wall, block, blockade, fence, roadblock, stop, wall
rel clog, encumbrance, hamper, hindrance, impediment; hurdle, obstacle, obstruction, stumbling block; check, checkrein, control, curb; bamboo curtain, iron curtain; difficulty, hardship, vicissitude
3 *syn* see OBSTACLE
rel check, checkrein, control, curb
con accommodation, convenience, facility, service
ant advantage
4 *syn* see COURT 2
5 a room or public establishment where alcoholic beverages are served <nightly discussions in the *bar*>
syn barroom, ‖boozer, ‖bucket shop, buvette, cantina, cocktail lounge, drinkery, drunkery, ‖gin mill, ‖groggery, ‖grogshop, lounge, pothouse, pub, ‖public house, ‖rum-hole, rummery, ‖rum-mill, rumshop, saloon, tap, taproom, tavern, watering hole, watering place; *compare* ALEHOUSE
rel barrelhouse, bistro, bottle club, cabaret, café, dive, honky-tonk, nightclub, rathskeller, roadhouse, wineshop

bar *vb* **1** *syn* see LIMIT 2
2 *syn* see EXCLUDE
rel block, hinder; leave out, omit, pass over; banish, deport, exile, ostracize
con accept, receive, welcome; allow, let, permit
ant admit, include
3 *syn* see HINDER
rel halt, stop
con back, support, uphold

bar *prep syn* see EXCEPT

barathrum *n syn* see HELL

barb *n syn* see SHAFT 2

barbarian *adj* **1** of, relating to, or characteristic of people that are not fully civilized <the *barbarian* tribes that sacked Rome>
syn barbaric, barbarous, Gothic, Hunnic, Hunnish, rude, savage, uncivil, uncivilized, uncultivated, wild
rel heathenish, vandal, vandalic; backward, coarse, crude, ill-mannered, primitive, rough; untamed; uncouth, uncultured; beastish, bloodthirsty, brutal, cruel, ferocious, inhuman
con gentle, peaceful, subdued, submissive, tame; cultured, enlightened, humane, sophisticated; genteel, refined, well-bred, well-mannered

ant civilized
2 *syn* see BARBARIC 1

barbaric *adj* **1** marked by a lack of restraint, cultivated taste, and refinement <the *barbaric* use of color and ornament>
syn barbarian, barbarous, graceless, outlandish, tasteless, vulgar, wild
rel coarse, crude, rough, rude, uncouth; flamboyant, florid, ornate, ostentatious, showy; blatant, flashy, garish, gaudy, loud, tawdry; cacophonous, harsh, raucous; aggressive
con quiet, restrained, soft, subdued; concinnous, cultivated, elegant, polished, refined; smooth, sophisticated, urbane
2 *syn* see BARBARIAN 1

barbarism *n* a word or expression which in form or use offends against contemporary standards of correctness or purity in a language <many writers consider *irregardless* a *barbarism*>
syn corruption, impropriety, slangism, solecism, vernacularism, vernacularity, vulgarism
rel neologism; colloquialism, foreignism; shibboleth; Goldwyn- ism, Irish bull, malaprop, malapropism, spoonerism; caconym; error, lapse, misuse, slip

barbarous *adj* **1** *syn* see BARBARIAN 1
2 *syn* see OUTRAGEOUS 1
3 *syn* see BARBARIC 1
rel backward, benighted, cretinous, ignorant, illiterate, lowbrow, philistine, uneducated, unlettered, unread, unschooled, untaught, untutored
con aware, informed, sophisticated, with-it; finished, polished, rounded; well-bred, well-mannered; educated, intelligent, learned, schooled; erudite, well-read
4 *syn* see FIERCE 1
rel heartless, uncompassionate, unmerciful; atrocious, monstrous, outrageous; bloody, butcherly, sanguinary; fiendish, sadistic
con forbearing, lenient, merciful, tolerant; compassionate, sympathetic, tender; benevolent, humane, humanitarian
ant clement

barbate *adj* *syn* see BEARDED

barber *n* one whose occupation is primarily cutting hair
syn haircutter
rel coiffeur, coiffeuse, friseur, hairdresser, hair stylist; beautician, cosmetologist; clipper, cropper, shaver

bard *n* **1** a poet-singer who sang or recited verse to the accompaniment of a stringed instrument (as a harp) <*bards* were the theater of olden times>
syn jongleur, minstrel, troubadour
rel meistersinger, minnesinger, rhapsodist; gleeman; skald; conteur
2 *syn* see POET

bardlet *n* *syn* see POETASTER

bardling *n* *syn* see POETASTER

bare *adj* **1** lacking a natural or usual cover or finish <the room looked *bare* without curtains and pictures>
syn bald, naked, nude
rel denuded, dismantled, divested, peeled, stripped, uncovered; baldish, depilated, hairless; unattired, unclad, unclothed, undressed, unrobed; arid, bleak, desert, desolate
con attired, clad, clothed, dressed, garbed; furry, hairy; green, leafy, luxuriant, verdant; complete, consummate, finished, perfect
ant covered
2 *syn* see OPEN 2
3 *syn* see EMPTY 1
rel barren, depleted, destitute, dried-up, emptied, exhausted; unfilled, unstocked, unsupplied
con bountiful, bursting, chock-full, complete, crammed, laden, overflowing, overfull, replete, stuffed; full, stocked, supplied
4 *syn* see VERY 4

bare *vb* *syn* see STRIP 2
rel disclose, exhibit, expose, reveal, show, unveil
con camouflage, cloak, disguise, dissemble, mask; apparel, attire, dress, garb, invest, robe
ant cover

barefaced *adj* *syn* see SHAMELESS
rel blunt, candid, frank, open, plain, temerarious; indecent, indecorous, unseemly
con covert, secret, secretive, stealthy; cautious, circumspect, discreet, tactful
ant furtive

barefisted *adj or adv* *syn* see BARE-HANDED

barefoot *adj* **1** wearing no shoes or stockings <always went *barefoot* in the summer>
syn shoeless, unsandaled, unshod
con socked, stockinged; sockless; booted, sandaled, shod
2 *syn* see DISCALCED

bare–handed *adj or adv* without covering on the hands <box *bare-handed*>
syn barefisted, bareknuckle
ant gloved

bareknuckle *adj or adv* *syn* see BARE-HANDED

barely *adv* *syn* see JUST 2
con amply; adequately, enough, sufficiently

barf *vb* *syn* see VOMIT

bargain *n* **1** an advantageous purchase <at that price the car is a *bargain*>
syn buy, closeout, pennyworth, steal
rel deal; giveaway
con cheat, flimflam, gouge, sticking, sting
2 *syn* see CONTRACT

bargain *vb* **1** *syn* see HAGGLE 2
rel arrange, confer, negotiate; compromise
2 *syn* see TRADE 1

barge *vb* *syn* see LUMBER

bark *vb* *syn* see SNAP 1

barkeeper *n* **1** *syn* see SALOONKEEPER
2 *syn* see BARTENDER

barmaid *n* *syn* see BARTENDER

barman *n* *syn* see BARTENDER

Barmecidal *adj* *syn* see APPARENT 2

barnacle *n* *syn* see PARASITE

---

syn synonym(s) *rel* related word(s)
ant antonym(s) *con* contrasted word(s)
idiom idiomatic equivalent(s)
‖ use limited; if in doubt, see a dictionary

‖**barney** *n* ***syn*** see QUARREL
barnyard *adj* ***syn*** see OBSCENE 2
baron *n* ***syn*** see MAGNATE
baronial *adj* ***syn*** see GRAND 1
baroque *adj* ***syn*** see ORNATE
rel embellished, gilt, ornamented, scrolled
con austere, gray
barrage *n* a vigorous expulsion or projection of many things at once <the announcement was met with a *barrage* of protests>
syn bombardment, broadside, burst, cannonade, drumfire, fusillade, hail, salvo, shower, storm, volley
rel burst, eruption, flare, outburst, stream, surge, tornado
barrel *n* **1** ***syn*** see CASK
2 ***syn*** see MUCH
barrel *vb* ***syn*** see HURRY 2
barrelhouse *n* ***syn*** see DIVE
barrelhouse *vb* ***syn*** see HURRY 2
barren *adj* **1** ***syn*** see STERILE 1
rel childless, fallow, heirless, issueless
con pregnant; fertile
ant fecund
2 deficient in production of vegetation and especially crops <*barren* deserts and wastelands>
syn hardscrabble, infertile, unbearing, unfertile, unproductive
rel fallow; irreclaimable, uncultivable, unhusbanded, untillable, wild; bleak, depleted, impoverished, poor, worn-out; vegetationless, verdureless; arid, desert, dry, parched
con arable, fruitful, productive; fat, rich; lush, luxuriant; green, verdant, verdurous
ant fertile
barren *n* ***syn*** see WASTE 1
barricade *n* ***syn*** see BAR 2
barrier *n* ***syn*** see BAR 2
barring *prep* ***syn*** see EXCEPT
barroom *n* ***syn*** see BAR 5
bar sinister *n* ***syn*** see STIGMA
bartender *n* one who serves alcoholic beverages at a bar <worked for some years as a *bartender*>
syn barkeeper, barmaid, barman, mixologist, tapster; *compare* SALOONKEEPER
barter *vb* ***syn*** see TRADE 1
basal *adj* **1** ***syn*** see FUNDAMENTAL 1
rel pedimental; bottommost, lowermost, lowest, nethermost, undermost
con highest, uppermost
2 ***syn*** see ELEMENTARY 1
base *n* **1** something on which another thing is reared or built or by which it is supported or fixed in place <the *base* of a lamp>
syn basement, basis, bed, bedrock, bottom, footing, foundation, ground, groundwork, hardpan, infrastructure, rest, seat, seating, substratum, substruction, substructure, underpinning, understructure; *compare* BASIS 1
rel bolster, buttress, framework, prop, stand, stay, support; foot
2 ***syn*** see BASIS 1
3 ***syn*** see BOTTOM 3
base *vb* to supply or to serve as a basis <*based* his accusation on sound evidence>
syn bottom, establish, found, ground, predicate, rest, stay
rel build, construct, fix, plant, seat, set up
base *adj* **1** ***syn*** see IGNOBLE 1
2 ***syn*** see CHEAP 2
3 contemptible because beneath minimal standards of human decency <a *base* lying cheat>
syn despicable, ignoble, low, low-down, servile, sordid, squalid, ugly, vile, wretched; *compare* CONTEMPTIBLE
rel beggarly, lousy, sorry; abominable, disgraceful, loathsome; bad, evil, wicked; base-minded, low-minded, meanspirited; caitiff, cowardly, dastardly, recreant; unworthy; dirty, filthy; degrading, humiliating, ignominious
con honest, honorable, upright; virtuous; ethical, moral, righteous; fair, forbearing, open-minded, patient, reasonable, tolerant, understanding
ant noble
baseborn *adj* **1** ***syn*** see IGNOBLE 1
2 ***syn*** see ILLEGITIMATE 1
baseless *adj* being without cause or occasion <anxious old ladies with their *baseless* fears>
syn bottomless, foundationless, gratuitous, groundless, un-called-for, unfounded, ungrounded, unwarranted
rel false, wrong; indefensible, reasonless, unjustifiable, unsolid, unsupported, unsustained, untenable; empty, idle, vain; needless, pointless, senseless, unnecessary, unneeded
con actual, real, reasonable, true; authentic, bona fide, genuine, valid
basement *n* ***syn*** see BASE 1
bash *n* **1** ***syn*** see BLOW 1
2 ***syn*** see SHINDIG 1
bashful *adj* ***syn*** see SHY 1
rel timorous; recoiling, shrinking; mousy; abashed, embarrassed; blushful
con assured, bold, intrepid; arrogant, barefaced, brazen, impudent, shameless; loquacious, talkative
ant brash, forward
basic *adj* **1** ***syn*** see FUNDAMENTAL 1
rel capital, chief, main, principal
2 ***syn*** see ELEMENTAL 1
basic *n* ***syn*** see ESSENTIAL 1
basically *adv* ***syn*** see ESSENTIALLY 1
basin *n* ***syn*** see DEPRESSION 2
basis *n* **1** something that supports or sustains anything immaterial <his argument rested on a *basis* of conjecture>
syn base, bedrock, footing, foundation, ground, groundwork, infrastructure, root, substratum, underpinning; *compare* BASE 1
rel axiom, fundamental, law, principle, theorem; assumption, postulate, premise, presumption, presupposition; essence, heart
2 ***syn*** see BASE 1
3 something serving as a reason or justification for an action or opinion <resented such a challenge without *basis* or reason>
syn foundation, warrant
rel call, justification, right; ground(s), reason

bask *vb* **1** ***syn*** see SUN
2 ***syn*** see WALLOW 3
bassinet *n* ***syn*** see BABY CARRIAGE
bastard *n* **1** one born out of wedlock <bore a *bastard* before she was fifteen>
syn by-blow, catch colt, chance child, come-by-chance, filius nullius, filius populi, illegitimate, love child, mamzer (*or* momzer *or* momser), natural child, whoreson, woods colt
2 ***syn*** see HYBRID
bastard *adj* **1** ***syn*** see ILLEGITIMATE 1
2 ***syn*** see SPURIOUS 3
bastardize *vb* ***syn*** see DEBASE 1
bastardy *n* ***syn*** see ILLEGITIMACY 1
baste *vb* **1** ***syn*** see BEAT 1
rel clobber, ||larrup, mill, whip
2 ***syn*** see SCOLD 1
bastille *n* ***syn*** see JAIL
bastille *vb* ***syn*** see IMPRISON
bastinado *n* ***syn*** see BLOW 1
bastion *n* ***syn*** see BULWARK
bat *n* **1** ***syn*** see BLOW 1
2 ***syn*** see CUDGEL
||**3** ***syn*** see SPEED 2
4 ***syn*** see BINGE 1
||**bat** *n* ***syn*** see HAG 2
bat *vb* ***syn*** see WANDER 1
bat *vb* ***syn*** see WINK
batch *n* ***syn*** see GROUP 3
bate *vb* ||**1** ***syn*** see ABATE 4
||**2** ***syn*** see DECREASE
3 ***syn*** see EXCLUDE
bath *n, usu* **baths** *pl* ***syn*** see SPA 1
||**bath** *vb* ***syn*** see BATHE 1
bathe *vb* **1** to clean oneself with a bath <*bathed* only on Saturday nights>
syn ||bath, shower, tub, wash
rel soap; douse, soak
2 to flow or splash against <waves *bathed* the rocky shore>
syn lap, lave, lip, wash
rel drench, soak, sop, souse; flush
bathetic *adj* **1** ***syn*** see TRITE
2 ***syn*** see SENTIMENTAL
bathtub gin *n* ***syn*** see MOONSHINE 2
bating *prep* ***syn*** see EXCEPT
baton *n* ***syn*** see CUDGEL
batter *vb* **1** to affect (as by repeated blows) so severely as to disfigure or damage <so *battered* in the fight he couldn't even crawl away> <a boat *battered* to pieces by stormy seas>
syn ||bung up, mangle, maul
rel disable, disfigure; maim, mutilate; cripple, lame; bruise, contuse, lacerate; baste, clobber, pummel; shatter, wreck
idiom beat black and blue, beat to pieces (*or* shreds), beat within an inch of one's life
2 ***syn*** see BEAT 1
battery *n* ***syn*** see GROUP 3
battle *n* a hostile meeting between opposing military forces <the *battle* continued until nightfall>
syn action, engagement
rel brush, clash, encounter, pitched battle, scrimmage, skirmish; assault, attack, onset, onslaught, sortie; combat, conflict, contest, fight; hostilities
battle *vb* ***syn*** see CONTEND 1
rel clash, scrimmage; assail, assault, attack, bombard
battle cry *n* a word or phrase used as a slogan by a faction <"death to the invader" was the *battle cry*>
syn cry, motto, rallying cry, war cry; *compare* CATCHWORD
battlesome *adj* ***syn*** see QUARRELSOME 2
||**batty** *adj* ***syn*** see INSANE 1
bauble *n* ***syn*** see KNICKKNACK
bavardage *n* ***syn*** see SMALL TALK
bawd *n* ***syn*** see PROSTITUTE
bawdy house *n* ***syn*** see BROTHEL
bawl *vb* **1** ***syn*** see ROAR
rel holler, scream, screech, shout, shriek, squall, yammer, yell
2 to cry and weep loudly or lustily especially from distress <the baby *bawled* and kicked when its bottle was taken away>
syn howl, squall, wail, yowl; *compare* CRY 2, ROAR
rel blubber, boohoo, cry, sob, weep
bawl out *vb* ***syn*** see SCOLD 1
rel condemn, denounce
idiom read a lecture (*or* lesson)
bay *n, usu* **bays** *pl* ***syn*** see HONOR 2
bay *vb* ***syn*** see HOWL 1
bay *n* ***syn*** see INLET
baygall *n* ***syn*** see SWAMP
bayou *n* ***syn*** see INLET
bay window *n* ***syn*** see POTBELLY
bazoo *n* ||**1** ***syn*** see MOUTH 1
2 ***syn*** see RASPBERRY
be *vb* to have actuality or reality <I think, therefore I *am*>
syn breathe, exist, live, move, subsist
rel hold, obtain, stand; abide, continue, endure, go on, persist, prevail, remain; come
beach *n* ***syn*** see SHORE
rel oceanfront; lakeshore, lakeside
beach *vb* ***syn*** see SHIPWRECK 1
beached *adj* ***syn*** see AGROUND
beacon *n* **1** a signal fire usually on an elevated place <a *beacon* on the hill to warn of danger>
syn balefire, watchfire
rel flare; bonfire
2 ***syn*** see LIGHTHOUSE
beak *n* **1** ***syn*** see BILL 1
2 ***syn*** see NOSE 1
3 ***syn*** see PROMONTORY
||**4** ***syn*** see JUDGE 2
beak *vb* ***syn*** see PECK 1
be–all and end–all *n* **1** ***syn*** see ESSENCE 2
2 ***syn*** see WHOLE 1
beam *n* **1** ***syn*** see TIMBER 2
2 ***syn*** see RAY 1

---

syn synonym(s) ***rel*** related word(s)
ant antonym(s) ***con*** contrasted word(s)
idiom idiomatic equivalent(s)
|| use limited; if in doubt, see a dictionary

3 ***syn*** see BUTTOCKS
beam *vb* **1** ***syn*** see SHINE 1
2 ***syn*** see SMILE
beaming *adj* ***syn*** see BRIGHT 1
‖**bean** *n* ***syn*** see HEAD 1
beanery *n* ***syn*** see EATING HOUSE
beany *adj* ***syn*** see SPIRITED 2
bear *vb* **1** ***syn*** see CARRY 1
rel shoulder
2 ***syn*** see BEHAVE 1
3 to have attached to one <the bottle *bears* the label "poisonous">
syn carry, have, possess
rel display, exhibit, show
con lack, need, want
4 ***syn*** see ACCOMPANY
5 to give birth to offspring <she has *borne* several children>
syn ‖birth, ‖born, bring forth, deliver
idiom bring abed, bring to bed, bring to birth, give birth to, have a baby
con abort, miscarry
6 ***syn*** see PRESS 8
7 ***syn*** see PRESS 1
8 ***syn*** see PROCREATE 1
9 to bring forth a product <the apple trees *bear* every year>
syn produce, turn out, yield
rel breed, engender, generate, propagate, reproduce; fructify, fruit; fabricate, fashion, form, make, shape; create, invent
10 to put up with something trying or difficult <can't *bear* the tension of the work>
syn abide, brook, digest, endure, go, lump, stand, ‖stick, stick out, stomach, suffer, support, sustain, swallow, sweat out, take, tolerate; *compare* ACCEPT 2
rel afflict, torment, torture, try; allow, condone, countenance, permit; acquiesce, bow, defer, submit, yield
idiom make do, put up with, take lying down
con decline, refuse, reject, spurn; avoid, bypass, elude, evade, shun
11 ***syn*** see HEAD 3
bear (on *or* upon) *vb* to have a connection especially logically <this situation *bears* directly upon the question under discussion>
syn appertain, apply, pertain, relate
rel refer; affect, concern, involve, touch; correspond, parallel
idiom have to do with, tie in with
bear (with) *vb* ***syn*** see ACCEPT 2
bearable *adj* capable of being borne <his outrageous behavior is hardly *bearable*>
syn endurable, livable, sufferable, supportable, sustainable, tolerable
rel acceptable, admissible, allowable, satisfactory
con insufferable, insupportable, intolerable, unendurable, unsupportable
ant unbearable
beard *n* the natural growth of hair on a man's face <some men look better with *beards*>
syn beaver, whiskers; *compare* SIDE-WHISKERS
rel charley, galways, goatee, imperial, spade beard, Vandyke; fuzz
beard *vb* ***syn*** see FACE 3
idiom beard the lion in his den
bearded *adj* having a beard <an old *bearded* philosopher>
syn barbate, bewhiskered, whiskered
rel beardy; goateed; hairy; stubbed, stubbly, unshaven
con barefaced, clean-faced, clean-shaven, shaven, smooth-faced, whiskerless
ant beardless
bear down *vb* ***syn*** see CONQUER 1
bearer *n* **1** ***syn*** see MESSENGER
2 a man who carries baggage and supplies for travelers <native *bearers* serving the safari>
syn carrier, drogher, porter
rel boy, cargador, coolie; redcap, skycap
bearing *n* **1** the way in which or the quality by which a person outwardly manifests his personality <a dowager with a regal *bearing*>
syn address, air, comportment, demeanor, deportment, mien, port, presence, set
rel aspect, brow, look; attitude, carriage, pose, posture, stand; poise; display, front; behavior, conduct
2 ***syn*** see BIRTH 1
bearish *adj* ***syn*** see CANTANKEROUS
bear out *vb* ***syn*** see CONFIRM 2
bear up *vb* ***syn*** see SUPPORT 4
beast *n* a lower animal as distinguished from man <*beasts* of the field>
syn animal, brute, creature, ‖critter
rel beastie, varmint; quadruped
beastly *adj* ***syn*** see BRUTISH
beat *vb* **1** to strike repeatedly <robbed and *beaten* by thugs>
syn baste, batter, belabor, buffet, drub, ‖dump, hammer, lam, lambaste, paste, pelt, pound, pummel, thrash, tromp, wallop, whop
rel bastinado, baton, bludgeon, cudgel, fustigate, pistol-whip; flog, lace, lash, tan, whip; lay on, maul, muss up, rough (up)
idiom give one beans, rain blows on
2 ***syn*** see WHIP 2
3 ***syn*** see SCOUR 2
4 ***syn*** see WHIP 3
5 ***syn*** see WAG
6 ***syn*** see HAMMER 1
7 ***syn*** see SURPASS 1
idiom beat (all) hollow
8 ***syn*** see NONPLUS 1
9 ***syn*** see CHEAT
10 ***syn*** see FRUSTRATE 1
11 ***syn*** see SCOOP 3
12 ***syn*** see PULSATE
13 ***syn*** see WIN 1
beat *n* **1** ***syn*** see RHYTHM
2 ***syn*** see SCOOP
beat down *vb* ***syn*** see CONQUER 1
beating *n* ***syn*** see DEFEAT 1
rel lump(s)
beatitude *n* ***syn*** see HAPPINESS
rel ecstasy, rapture, transport

con affliction, trial, tribulation; anguish, grief, sorrow, woe; agony, suffering
ant despair, dolor
beau *n* **1** ***syn*** see BOYFRIEND 1
2 ***syn*** see BOYFRIEND 2
Beau Brummel *n* ***syn*** see FOP
beau ideal *n* ***syn*** see MODEL 2
idiom shining example
||**beaut** *n* ***syn*** see BEAUTY
beauteous *adj* ***syn*** see BEAUTIFUL
beautiful *adj* very pleasing or delightful to look at <the most *beautiful* woman in the world>
syn attractive, beauteous, ||bonny, comely, dishy, fair, foxy, good-looking, handsome, lovely, pretty, pulchritudinous, stunning, well-favored
rel choice, elegant, exquisite; glorious, resplendent, splendid, sublime, superb; eye-appealing, eye-filling, ||proper; personable, pleasing
con offensive, repugnant, repulsive, revolting; homely, ordinary, plain, unattractive, unbeauteous, uncomely, unhandsome, unlovely, unpretty
ant ugly, unbeautiful
beautiful people *n pl* ***syn*** see SMART SET
beautify *vb* ***syn*** see ADORN
rel glamorize, prettify
con deface, disfigure; damage, mar, spoil
ant uglify
beauty *n* a physically attractive woman <a charming woman and a *beauty* to boot>
syn ||beaut, bunny, eyeful, knockout, looker, lovely, stunner
rel charmer, dazzler, dream, eye-opener, good-looker, peach; belle, toast
idiom raving beauty
con dog, gorgon, hag, slattern, witch
beaver *n* ***syn*** see BEARD
becalm *vb* ***syn*** see CALM
because *conj* for the reason that <I left *because* I was bored>
syn as, as long as, ||being, 'cause, considering, for, inasmuch as, now, seeing, since, whereas
idiom in view of the fact
because of *prep* ***syn*** see OVER 6
becloud *vb* **1** ***syn*** see OBSCURE
rel befuddle, confuse, perplex, puzzle
con illuminate
2 ***syn*** see CONFUSE 4
become *vb* **1** to commence to be <*became* sick yesterday>
syn come, ||come over, get, go, grow, run, turn, wax
rel arise, mount, rise, soar
idiom get to be, turn out to be
2 ***syn*** see SUIT 4
3 ***syn*** see FLATTER
becoming *adj* ***syn*** see DECOROUS 1
rel attractive, flattering; tasteful
con unattractive, unflattering; distasteful; inappropriate, unfitting, unrespectable, unsuitable
ant unbecoming
becomingly *adv* ***syn*** see WELL 4
becrush *vb* ***syn*** see CRUSH 2
bed *n* ***syn*** see BASE 1
bed *vb* **1** to put to bed <getting the children *bedded*>
syn tuck (in)
rel cradle
2 ***syn*** see RETIRE 4
bedamn *vb* ***syn*** see SWEAR 3
bedaub *vb* ***syn*** see SMEAR 1
bedaze *vb* ***syn*** see DAZE 2
bedazzle *vb* ***syn*** see DAZE 1
bedcover *n* ***syn*** see BEDSPREAD
bedeck *vb* ***syn*** see ADORN
rel bedaub, bedizen
bedevil *vb* ***syn*** see WORRY 1
bedfast *adj* ***syn*** see BEDRIDDEN
bedim *vb* ***syn*** see OBSCURE
con highlight, illuminate
bedlamite *n* ***syn*** see LUNATIC 1
bedlamite *adj* ***syn*** see INSANE 1
bedog *vb* ***syn*** see TAIL
bedraggled *adj* ***syn*** see SHABBY 1
bedridden *adj* confined to one's bed by illness or injury <a *bedridden* invalid>
syn bedfast
rel confined, incapacitated, laid up; feeble, infirm, sickly, weak
idiom flat on one's back
con healed, well; hale, healthy, whole
ant ambulant, ambulatory
bedrock *n* **1** ***syn*** see BASE 1
2 ***syn*** see BASIS 1
bedspread *n* an often ornamental outer covering for a bed <an appliquéd *bedspread*>
syn bedcover, counterpane, coverlet, ||coverlid, spread
bee *n* ***syn*** see CAPRICE
rel idea; impulse
beef *n* **1** ***syn*** see MUSCLE 1
2 ***syn*** see POWER 4
3 ***syn*** see QUARREL
||**beef** *vb* ***syn*** see GRIPE
beef (up) *vb* ***syn*** see INCREASE 1
beefheaded *adj* ***syn*** see STUPID 1
beef-witted *adj* ***syn*** see STUPID 1
beefy *adj* ***syn*** see HUSKY 1
beekeeper *n* one who engages in the production of and caring for bees and honey <special masks and gloves for *beekeepers*>
syn apiarist, apiculturist, beeman, beemaster
beeline *vb* ***syn*** see HURRY 2
Beelzebub *n* ***syn*** see DEVIL 1
beeman *n* ***syn*** see BEEKEEPER
beemaster *n* ***syn*** see BEEKEEPER
beer garden *n* ***syn*** see ALEHOUSE
beer hall *n* ***syn*** see ALEHOUSE
||**beerhouse** *n* ***syn*** see ALEHOUSE
beetle *vb* **1** ***syn*** see HANG 4
2 ***syn*** see BULGE
beetlehead *n* ***syn*** see DUNCE
beetleheaded *adj* ***syn*** see STUPID 1

syn synonym(s) ***rel*** related word(s)
ant antonym(s) ***con*** contrasted word(s)
idiom idiomatic equivalent(s)
|| use limited; if in doubt, see a dictionary

‖**beezer** *n* ***syn*** see NOSE 1
befall *vb* ***syn*** see HAPPEN 1
befit *vb* ***syn*** see SUIT 4
befitting *adj* **1** ***syn*** see FIT 1
ant unbefitting
2 ***syn*** see DECOROUS 1
befittingly *adv* ***syn*** see WELL 1
befog *vb* **1** ***syn*** see OBSCURE
2 ***syn*** see CONFUSE 4
3 ***syn*** see PUZZLE
befool *vb* ***syn*** see DUPE
before *adv* **1** so as to precede something in order or time <racing on *before* to give warning>
syn ahead, ante, antecedently, beforehand, fore, forward, in advance, precedently, previous
con behind; abaft, aft, astern
ant after
2 in time past <had heard that joke *before*>
syn already, earlier, erstwhile, formerly, heretofore, once, previously; *compare* THEN 1
ant after
3 until now or then <you'll get it tomorrow and not *before*>
syn beforehand, earlier, sooner
before *prep* **1** coming before in space or time <be home *before* dark>
syn ahead of, ante, ere, in advance of, preceding, prior to, to; *compare* UNTIL
con since, subsequent to
ant after
2 in the presence of <stood *before* the court>
syn confronting, facing
idiom face to face with
3 ***syn*** see UNTIL
beforehand *adv* **1** ***syn*** see BEFORE 1
2 ***syn*** see BEFORE 3
befoul *vb* **1** ***syn*** see CONTAMINATE 2
2 ***syn*** see MALIGN
befuddle *vb* ***syn*** see CONFUSE 2
rel daze
befuddlement *n* ***syn*** see HAZE 2
rel confusion, mix-up
con clearheadedness, lucidness
beg *vb* to ask for or ask one for something urgently <*beg* one's life from an attacker><*beg* a stranger for help>
syn appeal, beseech, brace, conjure, crave, entreat, implore, importune, invoke, plead, pray, supplicate
rel ask, call (on), request, solicit; petition, sue; besiege, demand, press; nag, worry
idiom throw oneself at the feet of (*or* on the mercy of)
con hint, intimate, suggest
‖**begats** *n pl* **1** ***syn*** see GENEALOGY
2 ***syn*** see OFFSPRING
begem *vb* ***syn*** see BEJEWEL
beget *vb* **1** ***syn*** see FATHER
2 ***syn*** see PROCREATE 1
beggar *n* **1** one who begs especially habitually or as a livelihood <*beggars* crying out to tourists>
syn bummer, cadger, moocher, panhandler, ‖schnorrer
rel deadbeat, freeloader, sponge, sponger; ‖bindle stiff, hobo, tramp
2 ***syn*** see SUPPLIANT
3 ***syn*** see PAUPER
beggared *adj* ***syn*** see POOR 1
beggarly *adj* ***syn*** see CONTEMPTIBLE
rel wretched; ‖cheesy, trashy; measly, paltry
beggary *n* **1** ***syn*** see POVERTY 1
2 ***syn*** see MENDICANCY
begin *vb* **1** to carry out the first act or step of an action or operation <*began* his lecture with a joke>
syn commence, embark (on *or* upon), enter, get off, inaugurate, initiate, jump (off), kick off, launch, lead off, open, set to, start, take up, tee off
rel establish, found, institute; introduce, usher in; broach; attack, tackle; prepare; break in; dig in
idiom get the show on the road, get to work, get underway
con cease, desist, discontinue, quit, stop; close, complete, conclude, finish, terminate; abandon, forsake, leave, quit; back out, renege, withdraw
ant end
2 to come into existence <not since civilization *began* has there been such distress>
syn arise, commence, originate, start; *compare* SPRING 1
rel spring; open
idiom raise its head
con end, finish, terminate
beginner *n* ***syn*** see NOVICE
beginning *n* the first part or stage of a process or development <the first few chapters at the *beginning* of the novel>
syn alpha, birth, commencement, dawn, dawning, day spring, genesis, onset, opening, opening gun, outset, outstart, setout, start
rel creation, inception, origin, origination, root, source, spring; anlage, rudiment, sprout; prologue; appearance, emergence, rise; incipiency, infancy
idiom the word go
con consummation, termination; closing, completion, conclusion; omega
ant end, ending
beginning *adj* **1** ***syn*** see INITIAL 1
2 ***syn*** see ELEMENTARY 1
begird *vb* **1** ***syn*** see BELT 1
2 ***syn*** see SURROUND 1
begirdle *vb* ***syn*** see BELT 1
begone *vb* ***syn*** see GET OUT 1
begrime *vb* ***syn*** see SOIL 2
begrudge *vb* ***syn*** see ENVY
beguile *vb* **1** ***syn*** see MANIPULATE 2
2 ***syn*** see DECEIVE
rel entice, lure, seduce
3 ***syn*** see WHILE
beguiling *adj* ***syn*** see MISLEADING
béguin *n* ***syn*** see INFATUATION
behave *vb* **1** to act in a specified way <*behave* as people of good breeding should>
syn acquit, act, bear, carry, comport, conduct, demean, deport, disport, do, go on, move, quit
rel control, direct, manage

idiom make as if (*or* as though); be on one's best behavior, mind one's p's and q's
ant misbehave, misconduct
2 *syn* see ACT 5

behavior *n* one's actions in general or on a particular occasion <his flustered *behavior* before women>
syn comportment, conduct, deportment, tenue
rel bearing, demeanor, mien; action, manner, way
con misbehavior, misconduct

behead *vb* to sever the head <nobles *beheaded* for treason>
syn decapitate, decollate, guillotine, head, neck
idiom bring to the block

behemoth *n syn* see GIANT

behemothic *adj syn* see HUGE

behest *n syn* see COMMAND 1
rel demand; prompting, request, solicitation

behind *adv syn* see AFTER

behind *prep* **1** *syn* see ABAFT
2 *syn* see AFTER 2

behind *n syn* see BUTTOCKS

behindhand *adj* **1** *syn* see NEGLIGENT
2 *syn* see BACKWARD 6
3 *syn* see TARDY
ant beforehand

behold *vb syn* see SEE 1

beholden *adj syn* see INDEBTED

beholder *n syn* see SPECTATOR

being *n* **1** *syn* see EXISTENCE 1
rel character, individuality, personality
ant nonbeing
2 *syn* see THING 5
3 *syn* see ENTITY 1
4 *syn* see ESSENCE 1
5 *syn* see HUMAN

||**being** *conj syn* see BECAUSE

bejewel *vb* to ornament with or as if with jewels <a *bejeweled* headdress> <cobwebs all *bejeweled* with glittering morning dew>
syn begem, beset, enjewel, gem, jewel
rel bespangle, spangle; diamond; encrust

belabor *vb syn* see BEAT 1

belated *adj* **1** *syn* see TARDY
2 *syn* see OLD-FASHIONED

belch *vb* **1** to expel gas suddenly from the stomach through the mouth <ate and ate until he *belched*>
syn burp, eruct, eructate
2 *syn* see ERUPT 1

beldam *n* **1** a woman of advanced years <a crotchety *beldam* hunched over the fire>
syn dame, gammer, grandam; *compare* GAFFER, OLDSTER
rel grandmother, granny; grand dame; matron; matriarch
idiom old girl
con damsel, lass, maid, miss
2 *syn* see HAG 2

beleaguer *vb* **1** *syn* see BESIEGE
rel siege, storm
idiom set upon from all sides
2 *syn* see WORRY 1

belfry *n* **1** *syn* see BELL TOWER
||**2** *syn* see HEAD 1

belie *vb syn* see MISREPRESENT
rel contradict, contravene, negative; controvert, disprove; conceal, disguise, hide
con bespeak, betoken, indicate; disclose, discover, reveal
ant attest

belief *n* **1** the act of assenting intellectually to something proposed as true or the state of mind of one who so assents <offered ready *belief* to anyone he trusted>
syn credence, credit, faith
rel assurance, certainty, certitude, conviction, sureness; acquiescence, assent; trust; credibility, trustworthiness
con distrust, doubt, mistrust, uncertainty; incredulity; question
ant disbelief, unbelief
2 *syn* see OPINION
rel doctrine, dogma, fundamental, law, precept, principle; concept, idea

believable *adj* worthy of belief <the author's bizarre characterizations are hardly *believable*>
syn colorable, credible, creditable, plausible
rel likely, possible, probable, tenable; conceivable, rational, reasonable; presumable, supposable; unquestionable; convincing, impressive, persuasive, satisfying; meaningful, solid, substantial
con improbable, unlikely; doubtable, doubtful, dubious, fishy, questionable, specious; implausible, incredible; inconceivable, untenable; fabulous, mythological
ant unbelievable

believe *vb* **1** to have a firm conviction in the reality of something <*believes* in ghosts>
syn accept, ||buy, swallow
rel accredit, credit, trust; admit
idiom have no doubts about, hold the belief that, take (*or* accept) as gospel, take at one's word, take one's word for
con discredit, distrust, doubt, mistrust, question, suspect; challenge, dispute; reject, turn down
ant disbelieve, misbelieve
2 *syn* see FEEL 3
3 *syn* see UNDERSTAND 3

belittle *vb syn* see DECRY 2
rel criticize, discredit; underestimate, underrate, undervalue
con intensify; boast, crow
ant aggrandize; magnify

belittlement *n syn* see DETRACTION

bell *vb syn* see RING

||**bell cow** *n syn* see LEADER 1

bellicose *adj syn* see BELLIGERENT
rel aggressive, assertive; factious, fighting, rebellious

---

syn synonym(s) *rel* related word(s)
ant antonym(s) *con* contrasted word(s)
idiom idiomatic equivalent(s)
|| use limited; if in doubt, see a dictionary

idiom full of fight
con gentle, moderate, temperate
ant amicable; pacific
belligerence *n syn* see ATTACK 2
belligerent *adj* having or taking an aggressive or fighting attitude <a *belligerent* reply to a diplomatic note>
syn bellicose, combative, contentious, gladiatorial, militant, pugnacious, quarrelsome, ‖ructious, scrappy, truculent, warlike; *compare* QUARRELSOME 2
rel battling, fighting, warring; attacking, invading; aggressive, antagonistic, fierce, hostile; ardent, hot, hot-tempered
con neutral; pacific, pacifist, peaceable, peaceful; conciliatory; amicable
ant friendly
‖**belling** *n syn* see SHIVAREE
bellow *vb syn* see ROAR
rel bark, bay, yelp; cry, wail; low, moo
bell ringer *n syn* see SMASH 6
bell tower *n* a tower that supports or shelters a bell or group of bells <a *bell tower* stood free from the church>
syn belfry, campanile, carillon
bellwether *n syn* see LEADER 1
belly *n syn* see ABDOMEN
bellyache *n syn* see STOMACHACHE
‖**bellyache** *vb syn* see GRIPE
‖**bellyacher** *n syn* see GROUCH
belong *vb* **1** to be suitable, appropriate, or advantageous or to be in a proper or fitting place or situation <the boxes *belong* in the attic>
syn fit, go, set
rel become, befit, suit; accord, agree, chime, harmonize; correspond, match, tally
idiom have one's place
2 to be the property of (a person or thing) <the books *belong* to the library>
syn appertain, pertain, vest
3 to be an attribute, part, adjunct, or function (of a person or thing) <good humor and wit *belong* to his personality>
syn indwell, inhere
idiom run in one's blood (*or* family)
belongings *n pl syn* see POSSESSION 2
beloved *adj syn* see FAVORITE 1
beloved *n* **1** *syn* see SWEETHEART 1
2 *syn* see GIRL FRIEND 2
3 *syn* see BOYFRIEND 2
below *adv* **1** in or at a lower position than something expressed or implied <several business establishments were situated *below*>
syn beneath, under, underneath
ant above
2 lower on the same page or on a following page <for additional examples see *below*>
syn infra
ant above, supra
below *prep* **1** in a lower position relative to some other object or place <lives just *below* me>
syn beneath, under, underneath
con over
ant above
2 *syn* see AFTER 2
belt *n* **1** a strip of flexible material worn around the waist <a leather *belt*>
syn ceinture, cincture, girdle, sash, waistband
rel baldric, cummerbund; band
2 *syn* see AREA 1
rel stretch, strip
belt *vb* **1** to bind about or around with or as if with a belt <gold lamé *belting* the gown>
syn band, begird, begirdle, cincture, encincture, engird, engirdle, gird, girdle
rel tie (up); loop; sash; circle, encircle, ring
2 *syn* see SLAM 1
belt *n syn* see BLOW 1
belvedere *n syn* see SUMMERHOUSE
bemean *vb syn* see HUMBLE
bemedaled *adj* having or wearing decorations especially as awarded by the military <the general's *bemedaled* uniform>
syn beribboned, decorated
bemired *adj syn* see MUDDY 1
bemoan *vb syn* see DEPLORE 1
rel regret; complain
con applaud, cheer, huzzah; delight, jubilate, rejoice
ant exult
bemuse *vb syn* see DAZE 2
rel addle; perplex, puzzle
con enlighten, illuminate
bemused *adj syn* see ABSTRACTED
benchmark *n syn* see STANDARD 3
bend *vb* **1** *syn* see CURVE
rel arch, curl, double, hook
ant straighten
2 *syn* see GIVE 12
3 *syn* see INCLINE 3
4 *syn* see ADDRESS 3
bend (over) *vb syn* see HANG 4
bend *n* **1** *syn* see TURN 2
2 *syn* see TURN 4
3 *syn* see CURVE
bender *n syn* see BINGE 1
bending *adj syn* see CROOKED 1
beneath *adv syn* see BELOW 1
beneath *prep syn* see BELOW 1
ant above, over
benediction *n* **1** *syn* see BLESSING 1
2 *syn* see GRACE 1
3 *syn* see APPROBATION
4 *syn* see GOOD 1
benefact *vb syn* see HELP 1
benefaction *n syn* see DONATION
benefic *adj syn* see GOOD 1
rel desirable, pleasing, satisfying
con damaging, harmful, injurious
ant malefic
beneficence *n syn* see DONATION
beneficial *adj syn* see GOOD 1
rel salutary, wholesome
con baneful, deleterious, noxious, pernicious
ant detrimental, harmful
benefit *n* **1** *syn* see GOOD 1
2 *syn* see WELFARE
rel account, behalf, sake; gain, profit

con catastrophe, disaster, misfortune; detriment
ant harm, ill

benefit *vb* to be useful or profitable to <medicines that *benefit* mankind>
syn advantage, avail, profit, serve, work (for)
rel advance, ameliorate, better, contribute (to), favor, improve; relieve, succor; build, further, promote; aid, assist, help
idiom do a world of good
con hinder, impede; damage, impair, injure; distress, upset; afflict, anguish; oppose
ant harm, hurt

benet *vb* ***syn*** see CATCH 3

benevolence *n* **1** ***syn*** see GOODWILL 1
con animosity, bitterness, ill will; antagonism, hostility; inimicality, unkindliness; stinginess
2 ***syn*** see GIFT 1

benevolent *adj* **1** ***syn*** see GENEROUS 1
rel beneficent; charitable; humane; compassionate, tenderhearted
con cruel, inhuman, malicious, spiteful
ant malevolent
2 ***syn*** see CHARITABLE 1
rel bighearted, freehearted, generous, greathearted, largehearted, liberal, openhanded; public-spirited; do-good
con niggardly, stingy; callous, indifferent, insensitive, unconcerned, unfeeling

benighted *adj* **1** ***syn*** see IGNORANT 1
rel backward, unenlightened; uninformed
idiom in the dark
con informed, intelligent
2 ***syn*** see BACKWARD 5

benightedness *n* ***syn*** see IGNORANCE 1

benign *adj* **1** ***syn*** see KIND
rel gracious
con malevolent, malicious, malignant, spiteful; acrid, caustic, mordant
ant malign
2 ***syn*** see FAVORABLE 5
rel gentle, mild; benevolent, charitable, humane; clement, forbearing, merciful
con menacing, threatening
ant malign

benignant *adj* ***syn*** see KIND
rel mild; gracious
con malevolent, malicious, spiteful; relentless
ant malignant

benison *n* ***syn*** see BLESSING 1

bent *n* **1** ***syn*** see LEANING 2
2 ***syn*** see GIFT 2
con antipathy, aversion; inability, incapacity

bent *adj* **1** ***syn*** see CURVED
2 ***syn*** see DECIDED 2

benumb *vb* **1** ***syn*** see DEADEN 1
2 ***syn*** see DAZE 2

benumbed *adj* ***syn*** see NUMB 1

bequeath *vb* **1** ***syn*** see WILL
con disinherit, exheridate
2 ***syn*** see HAND DOWN

bequest *n* ***syn*** see LEGACY 1

berate *vb* ***syn*** see SCOLD 1
con acclaim, praise; applaud; commend, compliment

berceuse *n* ***syn*** see LULLABY

bereave *vb* ***syn*** see DEPRIVE 2

bereaved *adj* suffering the death of a loved one <the *bereaved* family>
syn bereft
rel distressed, sorrowing

bereft *adj* ***syn*** see BEREAVED

beribboned *adj* ***syn*** see BEMEDALED

berth *n* **1** ***syn*** see WHARF
2 ***syn*** see JOB 2

beseech *vb* ***syn*** see BEG

beset *vb* **1** ***syn*** see BEJEWEL
2 ***syn*** see ATTACK 1
3 ***syn*** see BESIEGE
4 ***syn*** see INFEST 1
5 ***syn*** see SURROUND 1
idiom come at from all directions (*or* sides)

besetment *n* ***syn*** see ANNOYANCE 3

beside *prep* **1** at or by the side of <left the car *beside* the road>
syn alongside, by, ‖fornent, next to
rel near, opposite
2 ***syn*** see NEAR 2
3 ***syn*** see BESIDES 1
4 ***syn*** see EXCEPT

besides *adv* **1** ***syn*** see ALSO 2
idiom at that
2 ***syn*** see AGAIN 4

besides *prep* **1** in addition to <*besides* being tall, he's thin>
syn as well as, beside, beyond, over and above
idiom along with, together with
2 ***syn*** see EXCEPT

besides *adj* ***syn*** see ADDITIONAL

besiege *vb* to surround an enemy in a fortified or strong position so as to prevent ingress and egress <Troy was *besieged* by Greeks for ten years>
syn beleaguer, beset, blockade, invest
rel encircle, encompass, hem (in), surround; trap; assail, assault, attack

besmear *vb* **1** ***syn*** see SMEAR 1
2 ***syn*** see TAINT 1

besmirch *vb* ***syn*** see TAINT 1

besoil *vb* ***syn*** see SOIL 2

besotted *adj* ***syn*** see INFATUATED

bespangle *vb* ***syn*** see SPANGLE 1

bespatter *vb* **1** ***syn*** see SPOT 1
2 ***syn*** see MALIGN

bespeak *vb* **1** ***syn*** see RESERVE 2
2 ***syn*** see ADDRESS 4
3 ***syn*** see ASK 2
idiom put in for
4 ***syn*** see INDICATE 2

bespeckle *vb* ***syn*** see SPECKLE 1

bespectacled *adj* having or wearing glasses <*bespectacled* thesaurists>
syn spectacled

bespot *vb* ***syn*** see SPOT 1

---

syn synonym(s) ***rel*** related word(s)
ant antonym(s) ***con*** contrasted word(s)
idiom idiomatic equivalent(s)
‖ use limited; if in doubt, see a dictionary

besprinkle *vb* ***syn*** see SPRINKLE 1
best *adj* much more than half <passed the *best* part of a month at the shore>
syn better, ‖bettermost, greater, largest, most
best *vb* **1** ***syn*** see CONQUER 2
2 ***syn*** see SURPASS 1
3 ***syn*** see DEFEAT 2
best *n* the choicest one or part <always gave the *best* that she had>
syn choice, cream, elite, fat, flower, pick, pride, prime, primrose, prize, top
rel gem; nonesuch, nonpareil; exemplar, model, paragon, pattern
idiom cock of the walk, flower of the flock, one in a thousand (*or* million)
ant worst
bestain *vb* ***syn*** see STAIN 1
‖best bib and tucker *n* ***syn*** see FINERY
best girl *n* ***syn*** see GIRL FRIEND 1
bestial *adj* ***syn*** see BRUTISH
bestialize *vb* ***syn*** see DEBASE 1
bestir *vb* ***syn*** see STIR 1
bestow *vb* **1** ***syn*** see USE 2
2 ***syn*** see STOW
3 ***syn*** see HARBOR 2
4 ***syn*** see GIVE 1
bestower *n* ***syn*** see DONOR
bestrew *vb* ***syn*** see STREW 1
bestride *vb* **1** ***syn*** see MOUNT 5
2 to sit with one leg on each side <boys *bestriding* a fallen log>
syn straddle, ‖striddle, stride
bet *n* something of value (as money) staked on a winner-take-all basis on the outcome of an uncertainty <laid a *bet* at three to one on the champion>
syn ante, pot, stake, wager
bet *vb* ***syn*** see GAMBLE 1
bête noire *n* ***syn*** see ABOMINATION 1
bethink *vb* ***syn*** see REMEMBER
betide *vb* ***syn*** see HAPPEN 1
betimes *adv* **1** ***syn*** see EARLY 1
2 ***syn*** see EARLY 2
‖**3** ***syn*** see SOMETIMES
betoken *vb* **1** ***syn*** see INDICATE 2
2 ***syn*** see AUGUR 2
betray *vb* **1** ***syn*** see DECEIVE
rel ensnare, entrap, snare, trap
2 to prove faithless or treacherous <*betrayed* his own people by going over to the enemy>
syn cross, double-cross, sell, sell out, ‖split
rel desert, renegade; give away, inform, turn in; collaborate; apostatize
idiom act (*or* play) the traitor, break faith, round on, sell down the river
3 ***syn*** see REVEAL 1
rel demonstrate, evidence, evince, manifest, show; betoken, indicate
con defend, guard, protect, safeguard, shield
betrayer *n* ***syn*** see INFORMER
betrothal *n* ***syn*** see ENGAGEMENT 2
betrothed *n* either member of a couple engaged to be married
syn affianced, intended
rel fiancé, husband-to-be; bride-to-be, fiancée, wife-to-be
betrothed *adj* ***syn*** see ENGAGED 2
betrothing *n* ***syn*** see ENGAGEMENT 2
betrothment *n* ***syn*** see ENGAGEMENT 2
better *adj* **1** ***syn*** see BEST
2 more worthy or pleasing than an alternative <it is *better* to lose gracefully than to win arrogantly>
syn ‖bettermost, preferable, superior; *compare* GOOD
rel exceeding, exceptional, surpassing; choice, desirable, excellent
idiom more than a match for
ant worse
better *adv* ***syn*** see MORE 2
ant worse
better *n* **1** ***syn*** see SUPERIOR
2 a superior or winning position <had the *better* of the argument>
syn advantage, superiority, upper hand, victory, whip hand; *compare* ADVANTAGE 3
rel success, triumph, win
con collapse, defeat, disadvantage, loss; beating, drubbing, licking
ant worse
better *vb* **1** ***syn*** see IMPROVE 1
ant worsen
2 ***syn*** see SURPASS 1
‖**bettermost** *adj* **1** ***syn*** see BETTER 2
2 ***syn*** see BEST
between *prep* **1** in common to (as in position, in a distribution, or in participation) <a treaty *between* three powers>
syn among
2 in the time, space, or interval that separates <*between* the ages 12 and 20>
syn ‖atween, ‖atwixt, ‖betwixt, in between, tween, twixt
‖**betwixt** *prep* ***syn*** see BETWEEN 2
bevel *adj* ***syn*** see DIAGONAL
beveled *adj* ***syn*** see DIAGONAL
‖**bever** *n* ***syn*** see SNACK
beverage *n* ***syn*** see DRINK 1
bevy *n* ***syn*** see GROUP 1
bewail *vb* ***syn*** see DEPLORE 1
ant rejoice
beware *vb* to be cautious <*beware* of the dog>
syn look out, mind, watch out
rel attend, heed, notice, watch
idiom be on one's guard, be on the lookout (*or* watch), keep at a safe distance, take care (*or* heed)
con disregard, ignore, neglect
bewhiskered *adj* ***syn*** see BEARDED
bewilder *vb* **1** ***syn*** see PUZZLE
rel baffle, fuddle, muddle
2 ***syn*** see CONFUSE 2
bewitch *vb* **1** to practice witchcraft on <medicine men who *bewitch* ignorant tribesmen>
syn charm, enchant, ensorcell, hex, spell, voodoo, witch
rel bedevil, demonize, overlook, possess, sorcerize; beglamour, dazzle, trick

idiom cast a spell on (*or* over), give (*or* cast) the evil eye, put a curse on
2 *syn* see ATTRACT 1
rel beglamour, ||snow
bewitched *adj* ***syn*** see ENAMORED 3
bewitching *adj* ***syn*** see ATTRACTIVE 1
con forbidding, grim
bewitchment *n* ***syn*** see MAGIC 1
beyond *adv* **1** on or to the farther side <a house with mountains *beyond*>
syn farther, further, ||yon, yonder
2 *syn* see OVER 1
beyond *prep* **1** on or to the farther side of <the store is just *beyond* the next house>
syn after, outside, past, without
2 out of the reach, sphere, or comprehension of <it's *beyond* me how he did it>
syn above, past
idiom beyond one's depth (*or* power), over (*or* above) one's head, too deep (*or* much) for
3 *syn* see BESIDES 1
beyond *adj* ***syn*** see ADDITIONAL
beyond *n* ***syn*** see HEREAFTER 2
||**b'hoy** *n* ***syn*** see TOUGH
bias *n* **1 *syn*** see LEANING 2
2 *syn* see PREJUDICE
rel inclination, predisposition; slant, standpoint, viewpoint
con dispassionateness; fairness, justness
bias *adj* ***syn*** see DIAGONAL
bias *vb* **1 *syn*** see SLANT 3
2 *syn* see INCLINE 3
3 *syn* see PREJUDICE 2
biased *adj* **1 *syn*** see DIAGONAL
2 exhibiting or characterized by a highly personal and unreasoned distortion of judgment <a *biased* estimate of the book's worth>
syn colored, jaundiced, one-sided, partial, partisan, prejudiced, prepossessed, tendentious, unindifferent, unneutral, warped
rel bent, disposed, inclined, predisposed; influenced, interested, swayed; opinionated
con detached, dispassionate, impartial, neutral, open-minded; fair, honest, just
ant unbiased
bibber *n* ***syn*** see DRUNKARD
bibble–babble *n* ***syn*** see CHATTER
bibelot *n* ***syn*** see KNICKKNACK
Bible *n* the sacred volume of Christians <students of the *Bible*>
syn Book, Holy Writ, Sacred Writ, Scripture
idiom Book of Books, Good Book, Word of God
bibliopole *n* ***syn*** see BOOKDEALER
bicker *vb* **1 *syn*** see ARGUE 2
rel battle, contend, fight, war
2 *syn* see QUARREL
3 *syn* see RATTLE 1
bickering *n* ***syn*** see QUARREL
bicycle *n* a pedal-propelled vehicle with two wheels tandem, a steering handle, and a saddle seat <ten-speed *bicycles*>
syn bike, cycle, two-wheeler, velocipede
bid *vb* **1 *syn*** see COMMAND
rel summon
con interdict, prohibit
ant forbid
2 *syn* see INVITE
rel request
biddable *adj* ***syn*** see OBEDIENT
rel amiable, good-natured, obliging
con mulish, obstinate, stiff-necked, stubborn
ant recalcitrant
bidding *n* ***syn*** see COMMAND 1
rel call, summoning
biddy *n* **1 *syn*** see MAID 2
2 *syn* see HAG 2
bide *vb* **1 *syn*** see STAY 2
rel continue
2 *syn* see RESIDE 1
bierstube *n* ***syn*** see ALEHOUSE
biff *n* ***syn*** see BLOW 1
||**biff** *vb* ***syn*** see STRIKE 2
||**biffy** *n* ***syn*** see PRIVY 1
bifold *adj* ***syn*** see TWOFOLD 1
big *adj* **1** of significant size or scope <a *big* expanse of mud> <*big* plans>
syn considerable, extensive, hefty, large, large-scale, major, sizable
rel bumper, hulking, whacking, whopping; clumsy, unwieldy; ample, biggish, capacious, commodious, comprehensive, copious, roomy, spacious, voluminous; distended, inflated, swollen
con paltry, piddling, trivial; slight, small; insignificant; minute, tiny, wee
ant little
2 *syn* see LARGE 1
3 *syn* see PREGNANT 1
4 *syn* see FULL 1
rel flushed, overflowing; cloyed, glutted, sated, satiated, satisfied
idiom full to bursting (*or* overflowing), full to the ears, stuffed to the gills
con empty
5 *syn* see IMPORTANT 1
6 *syn* see PRETENTIOUS 3
7 *syn* see GENEROUS 1
||**big** *adv* ***syn*** see VERY 1
big *n* ***syn*** see NOTABLE 1
big boy *n* ***syn*** see NOTABLE 1
||**big bug** *n* ***syn*** see NOTABLE 1
||**big cheese** *n* ***syn*** see NOTABLE 1
||**big chief** *n* ***syn*** see NOTABLE 1
||**biggety** *adj* ***syn*** see WISE 5
||**biggie** *n* ***syn*** see NOTABLE 1
big gun *n* ***syn*** see NOTABLE 1
||**big house** *n* ***syn*** see JAIL
bight *n* ***syn*** see INLET
big name *n* ***syn*** see CELEBRITY 2
bigness *n* ***syn*** see SIZE 2
||**big noise** *n* ***syn*** see NOTABLE 1
bigot *n* ***syn*** see ENTHUSIAST

syn synonym(s) ***rel*** related word(s)
ant antonym(s) ***con*** contrasted word(s)
idiom idiomatic equivalent(s)
|| use limited; if in doubt, see a dictionary

THESAURUS

rel approver, liker, relisher; mumpsimus, racist, segregationist
con depreciator, disparager, knocker; disliker, disrelisher, hater, loather, misliker

bigoted *adj syn* see ILLIBERAL
rel lily-white; conservative

big shot *n syn* see NOTABLE 1

big-timer *n syn* see NOTABLE 1

‖**big wheel** *n syn* see NOTABLE 1

bigwig *n syn* see NOTABLE 1

bike *n syn* see BICYCLE

bilge *n syn* see NONSENSE 2

bilk *vb* **1** *syn* see FRUSTRATE 1
con fulfill
2 *syn* see CHEAT
3 *syn* see ESCAPE 2
rel dodge, shake

bill *n* **1** the jaws of a bird with their projecting horny covering <the huge *bill* of the toucan>
syn beak, neb, nib, pecker
2 *syn* see PROMONTORY
3 *syn* see VISOR 1

bill *n* **1** a statement of the amount due a creditor <*bills* from the grocer and doctor>
syn account, invoice, reckoning, score, statement, tab
rel charges, damage
idiom statement of account
2 *syn* see CHECK 2
3 *syn* see POSTER
4 *syn* see DOLLAR

billet *n syn* see JOB 2

billet *vb* **1** to assign quarters to soldiers <the troops were *billeted* in private homes>
syn canton, quarter
rel bed, house, lodge, put up; bestow
2 *syn* see HARBOR 2

billet *n syn* see BAR 1

billet-doux *n syn* see LOVE LETTER

billingsgate *n syn* see ABUSE

billy *n syn* see CUDGEL

billy club *n syn* see CUDGEL

‖**bim** *n syn* see WANTON

bimanal *adj syn* see TWO-HANDED 2

bimanual *adj syn* see TWO-HANDED 1

‖**bimbo** *n syn* see WANTON

binary *adj syn* see TWOFOLD 1

bind *vb* **1** *syn* see TIE 1
con release
ant unloose
2 *syn* see BANDAGE

‖**bindle stiff** *n syn* see VAGABOND

‖**bing** *n syn* see PILE 1

binge *n* **1** a drunken revel <hung over after a weekend *binge*>
syn bat, bender, blowoff, booze, brannigan, bum, bust, carousal, carouse, compotation, drunk, jag, orgy, ran-tan, rowdydow, soak, souse, spree, tear, ‖time, toot, wassail
rel bacchanal, bacchanalia, debauch; blast, ‖blowout; ‖bun
2 *syn* see SPREE 1

bio *n syn* see BIOGRAPHY

biocide *n syn* see PESTICIDE

biographer *n* one who writes a biography <irresponsible *biographers* whose work is more fiction than fact>
syn autobiographer, autobiographist, Boswell, memoirist

biography *n* a more or less detailed account of the events and circumstances of a person's life <wrote a *biography* of his grandfather>
syn autobiography, bio, confessions, life, memoir
rel diary, journal, letters; adventures, history, story; profile; obit, obituary

biologic *n syn* see DRUG 1

bird *n* **1** *syn* see RASPBERRY
‖**2** *syn* see GIRL 1

birdbrain *n syn* see SCATTERBRAIN

birdhouse *n syn* see AVIARY

birdman *n syn* see PILOT 2

bird-witted *adj syn* see GIDDY 1

birr *n syn* see ENERGY 2

birth *n* **1** the act or process of bringing forth young from the womb <had a very hard *birth* after a prolonged labor>
syn bearing, ‖birthing, childbearing, childbirth, delivery, parturition
rel abortion, miscarriage, slip
2 *syn* see BEGINNING

birth *vb* ‖**1** *syn* see BEAR 5
2 *syn* see SPRING 1

birth control *n* control of the number of children born especially by preventing or lessening the frequency of conception <cultural and religious aspects of *birth control*>
syn contraception
rel rhythm method; planned parenthood; vasectomy; (the) pill

‖**birthing** *n syn* see BIRTH 1

birthmark *n* **1** a congenital pigmented area on the skin <*birthmarks* often appear on the neck>
syn mole, nevus
2 *syn* see CHARACTERISTIC 1

birth pang *n, usu* **birth pangs** *pl syn* see LABOR 2

birthright *n* **1** *syn* see RIGHT 2
2 *syn* see HERITAGE 1

bisexual *adj* being structurally and functionally both male and female <many lower animals are *bisexual*>
syn androgynous, hermaphrodite, hermaphroditic

bistered *adj syn* see DARK 3

bistro *n syn* see NIGHTCLUB

bit *n* **1** *syn* see MORSEL 1
2 *syn* see PARTICLE
3 *syn* see END 4
4 *syn* see WHILE 1

bit *vb syn* see RESTRAIN 1

bit by bit *adv syn* see GRADUALLY

bite *vb* **1** to seize with the teeth so that they enter <*bite* into a pear>
syn champ, chomp
rel gnaw, nibble, tooth; ‖chaw, chew, crunch, masticate, munch, scrunch; eat
idiom sink one's teeth into
2 *syn* see EAT 3

3 *syn* see SMART
bite *n* **1** *syn* see MORSEL 1
2 *syn* see SNACK
3 *syn* see SHARE 1
biting *adj* *syn* see INCISIVE
||**bitsy** *adj* *syn* see TINY
bitter *adj* **1** *syn* see ACRID
rel acerb, acid, bitterish
con delicious; bland, flat, insipid
2 difficult to accept mentally <the *bitter* truth>
syn afflictive, distasteful, galling, grievous, painful, unpalatable
rel annoying, distressing, disturbing, woeful; bad, disagreeable, displeasing, offensive, unpleasant; galling, provoking, vexatious
con agreeable, gratifying, satisfying
3 marked by intense animosity <*bitter* contempt>
syn antagonistic, hostile, rancorous, virulent, vitriolic
rel alienated, divided, estranged; irreconcilable
4 *syn* see SEVERE 3
con mild, springlike, summery
bitter–ender *n* *syn* see DIEHARD 1
bitterly *adv* *syn* see HARD 6
bivouac *vb* *syn* see CAMP
||**bivvy** *vb* *syn* see CAMP
bizarre *adj* **1** *syn* see STRANGE 4
2 *syn* see FANTASTIC 2
con normal, ordinary, regular
blab *n* *syn* see CHATTER
blab *vb* *syn* see GOSSIP
blab (out) *vb* *syn* see REVEAL 1
blabber *vb* *syn* see BABBLE 2
blabber *n* *syn* see CHATTER
blabber *n* *syn* see CHATTERBOX
blabbermouth *n* *syn* see CHATTERBOX
blabmouth *n* *syn* see CHATTERBOX
black *adj* **1** having the color of soot or coal <a *black* hearse>
syn atramentous, ebon, ebony, inky, jet, jetty, onyx, pitch-black, pitch-dark, pitchy, raven, sable
rel blackish; charcoal, slate; piceous; dusky, swart, swarthy; brunet
idiom black as a crow (*or* a shoe *or* the ace of spades), black as hell (*or* night)
ant white
2 *syn* see DIRTY 1
3 *syn* see GLOOMY 3
4 *syn* see UTTER
black *vb* *syn* see BRUISE 1
black (out) *vb* *syn* see ERASE
black and white *n* *syn* see PRINT 2
black–a–vised *adj* *syn* see DARK 3
black beast *n* *syn* see ABOMINATION 1
||**blackcoat** *n* *syn* see CLERGYMAN
black dog *n* *syn* see SADNESS
blacken *vb* *syn* see MALIGN
idiom blacken one's good name, give one a black eye, throw mud at
black eye *n* **1** a bruise about the eye <got a *black eye* in a fight>
syn mouse, shiner
rel contusion
2 *syn* see STIGMA
blackguard *n* *syn* see VILLAIN 1
black out *vb* *syn* see FAINT
blackout *n* *syn* see FAINT
blague *n* *syn* see NONSENSE 2
blah *n* *syn* see NONSENSE 2
blah *adj* *syn* see DULL 9
blamable *adj* *syn* see BLAMEWORTHY
blame *vb* *syn* see CRITICIZE
rel accuse, charge; impute
idiom lay at one's door (*or* doorstep), lay (*or* put) the blame on
con exculpate, vindicate; praise
blame *n* responsibility for misdeed or delinquency <accepted the *blame* for his foolish act>
syn culpability, fault, guilt, onus
rel accountability, answerability, liability; accusation, charge, imputation; censure, condemnation, denunciation, reprehension
idiom burden of guilt
con commendation, compliment; acclaim, applause, praise
blamed *adj* **1** *syn* see DAMNED 2
2 *syn* see UTTER
blameful *adj* *syn* see BLAMEWORTHY
blameless *adj* **1** *syn* see INNOCENT 2
2 *syn* see GOOD 11
rel unimpeachable
ant blameworthy
blameworthy *adj* deserving reproach and punishment <though not criminal, his behavior was certainly *blameworthy*>
syn amiss, blamable, blameful, censurable, culpable, demeritorious, guilty, reprehensible, sinful, unholy
rel illaudable, uncommendable, unpraiseworthy, unpretty; delinquent, faultful; punishable; foolish, irresponsible, reckless
idiom at fault, to blame
con faultless, flawless, impeccable, irreproachable, unimpeachable; guiltless, innocent, sinless; creditable, high-principled, upright
ant blameless; unblamable
blanch *vb* *syn* see WHITEN 1
blanch (over) *vb* *syn* see PALLIATE
blanch *vb* *syn* see RECOIL
blanched *adj* *syn* see PALE 1
bland *adj* **1** *syn* see SUAVE
rel good-natured, ingratiating
con bluff, crusty, gruff
ant brusque
2 *syn* see GENTLE 1
3 *syn* see INSIPID 3
con pungent, savory, spicy, zestful
blandish *vb* *syn* see COAX
rel flatter; beguile, charm
con threaten
blandishment *n* *syn* see FLATTERY

---

syn synonym(s) *rel* related word(s)
ant antonym(s) *con* contrasted word(s)
idiom idiomatic equivalent(s)
|| use limited; if in doubt, see a dictionary

THESAURUS

blank *adj* **1** ***syn*** see EXPRESSIONLESS
2 ***syn*** see UTTER
blank *n* ***syn*** see OMISSION
blank check *n* ***syn*** see CARTE BLANCHE
blanket *vb* ***syn*** see COVER 3
blankety–blank *adj* **1** ***syn*** see DAMNED 2
2 ***syn*** see UTTER
blankness *n* ***syn*** see VACUITY 2
blank wall *n* ***syn*** see BAR 2
blare *vb* **1** ***syn*** see BLAZE
2 ***syn*** see SCREAM 4
blaring *adj* ***syn*** see LOUD 1
blarney *vb* ***syn*** see COAX
blarney *n* ***syn*** see FLATTERY
blasé *adj* ***syn*** see SOPHISTICATED 2
con awed, wide-eyed; artless, naive, natural, unsophisticated
blasphemous *adj* ***syn*** see SACRILEGIOUS
blasphemy *n* **1** impious or irreverent language <cursing God is *blasphemy*>
syn cursing, cussing, execration, imprecation, profanity, swearing
rel affront, indignity, insult; abuse, billingsgate, scurrility, vituperation
con reverence, veneration, worship
ant adoration
2 ***syn*** see PROFANATION
rel abuse, befouling, shaming
blast *n* ***syn*** see BANG 2
blast *vb* **1** to ruin or to injure severely, suddenly, or surprisingly <we'll have no peaches; frost *blasted* the blossoms this year>
syn blight, dash, nip
rel destroy, ruin, wreck; damage, injure, spoil; shrivel, stunt, wither
2 ***syn*** see SLAM 1
3 ***syn*** see WHIP 2
blasted *adj* **1** ***syn*** see DAMNED 2
2 ***syn*** see UTTER
blat *vb* ***syn*** see EXCLAIM
blatant *adj* **1** ***syn*** see VOCIFEROUS
rel screaming; obtrusive
con modest, soft-spoken
2 ***syn*** see GAUDY
3 ***syn*** see SHAMELESS
blather *vb* ***syn*** see BABBLE 2
blather *n* ***syn*** see NONSENSE 2
blatherskite *n* ***syn*** see NONSENSE 2
‖**blatter** *n* ***syn*** see CHATTER
blaze *vb* to burn or appear to burn brightly <the hot sun *blazed* down>
syn blare, flame, flare, glare, glow
rel illuminate, illumine, light; radiate, shine; coruscate, fulgurate, scintillate, sparkle; incandesce
blaze (abroad) *vb* ***syn*** see DECLARE 1
blazes *n pl* ***syn*** see HELL
blazing *adj* **1** ***syn*** see BURNING 1
2 ***syn*** see IMPASSIONED
blazon *vb* ***syn*** see DECLARE 1
bleach *vb* ***syn*** see WHITEN 1
bleak *adj* **1** ***syn*** see GRIM 2
2 ***syn*** see GLOOMY 3
blear *vb* ***syn*** see DULL 4
blear *adj* ***syn*** see FAINT 2
blear–eyed *adj* ***syn*** see STUPID 1
blear–witted *adj* ***syn*** see STUPID 1
bleary *adj* **1** ***syn*** see FAINT 2
2 ***syn*** see EFFETE 2
bleat *vb* ***syn*** see GRIPE
bleed *vb* **1** ***syn*** see EXUDE
2 ***syn*** see FLEECE 1
bleeding *adj* **1** ***syn*** see DAMNED 2
2 ***syn*** see UTTER
blemish *vb* ***syn*** see INJURE 1
blemish *n* an imperfection (as a spot or crack) <a *blemish* on the face>
syn defect, flaw, vice
rel fault, scar; blister, blotch, disfigurement, pockmark, wart; catch, snag, tear
blench *vb* ***syn*** see RECOIL
blench *vb* ***syn*** see WHITEN 1
blend *vb* **1** ***syn*** see MIX 1
rel combine, integrate
con resolve, separate
2 ***syn*** see HARMONIZE 4
blend *n* ***syn*** see MIXTURE
blending *adj* ***syn*** see HARMONIOUS 1
bless *vb* **1** to make holy by religious rite or word <the priest *blessed* the water and wine>
syn consecrate, hallow, sanctify
rel dedicate
con defile, desecrate, profane
2 ***syn*** see PRAISE 2
blessed *adj* **1** ***syn*** see HOLY 1
2 ***syn*** see DAMNED 2
3 ***syn*** see UTTER
blessedness *n* ***syn*** see HAPPINESS
con agony, suffering
ant misery
blessing *n* **1** an expression or utterance of good wishes <on departing, he received his father's *blessing*>
syn benediction, benison
rel Godspeed, valediction
2 ***syn*** see APPROBATION
3 ***syn*** see GOOD 1
4 ***syn*** see GRACE 1
‖**bless out** *vb* ***syn*** see SCOLD 1
blight *vb* ***syn*** see BLAST 1
blighted *adj* **1** ***syn*** see DAMNED 2
2 ***syn*** see UTTER
‖**blighter** *n* ***syn*** see WRETCH 1
blimp *n* **1** ***syn*** see FATTY
2 *cap* ***syn*** see REACTIONARY
3 *cap* ***syn*** see STUFFED SHIRT
blind *adj* **1** lacking the power to see <kittens are *blind* at birth>
syn ‖dark, eyeless, sightless, stone-blind, visionless
rel dim-sighted, purblind, short-sighted; blindish; blindfolded; unseeing
idiom blind as a bat
con seeing, sighted; keen, sharp
2 ***syn*** see INTOXICATED 1
3 ***syn*** see DULL 7
blind *vb* ***syn*** see DAZE 1
blind *n* **1** ***syn*** see FRONT 3

2 ***syn*** see DECOY 2
blind alley *n* ***syn*** see DEAD END
blinding *adj* **1** ***syn*** see DAMNED 2
2 ***syn*** see UTTER
blink *vb* **1** ***syn*** see WINK
2 to shine intermittently <we'll signal by *blinking* the headlights>
syn flash, flicker, twinkle
rel glimmer, scintillate, shimmer
blink (at) *vb* ***syn*** see CONNIVE 1
blink (at *or* away) *vb* ***syn*** see NEGLECT
‖**blinking** *adj* **1** ***syn*** see DAMNED 2
2 ***syn*** see UTTER
blip *vb* **1** ***syn*** see SLAP 1
2 ***syn*** see CENSOR
bliss *n* **1** ***syn*** see HAPPINESS
con dolor, misery, woe
ant anguish
2 ***syn*** see HEAVEN 2
blissfulness *n* ***syn*** see HAPPINESS
rel ecstasy, euphoria, exaltation; heaven, paradise
blister *vb* ***syn*** see LAMBASTE 3
blistering *adj* **1** ***syn*** see HOT 1
‖**2** ***syn*** see DAMNED 2
blithe *adj* **1** ***syn*** see CHEERFUL 1
2 ***syn*** see MERRY
ant atrabilious, morose
blithering *adj* ***syn*** see UTTER
blithesome *adj* ***syn*** see MERRY
blitz *vb* ***syn*** see BOMBARD
‖**bloat** *n* ***syn*** see DRUNKARD
bloated *adj* ***syn*** see POMPOUS 1
bloc *n* ***syn*** see COMBINATION 2
block *n* **1** ***syn*** see BAR 2
2 ***syn*** see ANNEX
block *vb* **1** ***syn*** see HINDER
2 ***syn*** see INTERCEPT
3 ***syn*** see FILL 1
block (out) *vb* ***syn*** see SKETCH
blockade *n* **1** ***syn*** see BAR 2
‖**2** ***syn*** see MOONSHINE 2
blockade *vb* ***syn*** see BESIEGE
block and block *adj* ***syn*** see FULL 1
blockhead *n* ***syn*** see DUNCE
blockheaded *adj* ***syn*** see STUPID 1
blockish *adj* ***syn*** see STUPID 1
block out *vb* ***syn*** see SCREEN 3
‖**bloke** *n* ***syn*** see MAN 3
blond *adj* **1** of a pale soft yellow color <*blond* hair>
syn flaxen, golden, straw
rel blondish; platinum; champagne, towheaded
con dark; brunet
2 ***syn*** see FAIR 3
blood *n* **1** the fluid that circulates in the heart, arteries, capillaries, and veins of a vertebrate animal <*blood* covered the battlefield>
syn ‖claret, gore
rel ichor; humor
2 ***syn*** see ANCESTRY
3 ***syn*** see MURDER
4 ***syn*** see FOP
blood–and–guts *adj* ***syn*** see INTENSIVE
bloodbath *n* ***syn*** see MASSACRE
bloodless *adj* **1** ***syn*** see PALE 2
rel colorless; lifeless
con alive; vigorous; florid
ant plethoric; sanguine
2 ***syn*** see INSENSIBLE 5
bloodshed *n* ***syn*** see MASSACRE
bloodstained *adj* ***syn*** see BLOODY 1
bloodsucker *n* ***syn*** see PARASITE
bloodthirsty *adj* ***syn*** see MURDEROUS
bloody *adj* **1** affected by or involving the shedding of blood <a *bloody* knife> <when will this long and *bloody* conflict cease?>
syn bloodstained, ensanguined, gory, imbrued, sanguinary, sanguine, sanguineous
rel bloodthirsty, grim, murderous, slaughterous; cutthroat, red-handed
2 ***syn*** see MURDEROUS
bloom *n* **1** ***syn*** see FLOWER 1
2 a state or time of beauty, freshness, and vigor <the *bloom* of youth>
syn blossom, flush
rel glow
3 a rosy appearance of the cheeks <recovered all her health and *bloom*>
syn blossom, blush, flush, glow
bloom *vb* ***syn*** see BLOSSOM
‖**blooming** *adj* **1** ***syn*** see DAMNED 2
2 ***syn*** see UTTER
blooper *n* **1** ***syn*** see ERROR 2
2 ***syn*** see FAUX PAS
blossom *n* **1** ***syn*** see FLOWER 1
rel capitulum, corymb, cyme, inflorescence, panicle, raceme, spike, umbel
2 ***syn*** see BLOOM 2
3 ***syn*** see BLOOM 3
blossom *vb* to produce flowers or be in flower <lilacs *blossom* in the spring>
syn bloom, blow, burgeon, effloresce, flower, outbloom
rel bud; leaf; shoot; open, unfold
idiom burst into bloom, come into flower, put forth blossoms (*or* flowers *or* bloom)
con fade, fall, wither
blot *n* ***syn*** see STIGMA
rel blemish, flaw, defect
blot *vb* ***syn*** see STAIN 1
blotch *vb* ***syn*** see SPLOTCH
blot out *vb* **1** ***syn*** see ERASE
2 ***syn*** see ANNIHILATE 2
‖**blotter** *n* ***syn*** see DRUNKARD
‖**blotto** *adj* ***syn*** see INTOXICATED 1
bloviate *vb* ***syn*** see ORATE
blow *vb* **1** to produce a current of air on <let the wind *blow* your hair dry>
syn fan, ruffle, wind, winnow
2 ***syn*** see BOAST
3 ***syn*** see PANT 1
4 ***syn*** see WASTE 2

---

syn synonym(s) ***rel*** related word(s)
ant antonym(s) ***con*** contrasted word(s)
idiom idiomatic equivalent(s)
‖ use limited; if in doubt, see a dictionary

5 ***syn*** see TREAT 3
‖6 ***syn*** see BOTCH
‖7 ***syn*** see GO 2
blow *n* ***syn*** see BREAK 4
blow *vb* ***syn*** see BLOSSOM
blow *n* **1** a forceful sharp stroke (as with the fist or an instrument) <struck him a sudden *blow*>
syn bang, bash, bastinado, bat, belt, biff, bop, crack, ‖ding, ‖douse, pound, slam, slosh, smack, smash, sock, ‖swap, thwack, wallop, ‖welt, whack, whop; *compare* CUFF, HIT 1
rel recumbentibus, slug, ‖souse; clip, pelt, plug, punch, swat
2 ***syn*** see IMPACT 1
blow–by–blow *adj* ***syn*** see CIRCUMSTANTIAL
blowen *n* ***syn*** see HARLOT 1
blower *n* ***syn*** see BRAGGART
blowhard *n* ***syn*** see BRAGGART
‖**blow in** *vb* ***syn*** see COME 1
blown–in–the–bottle *adj* ***syn*** see AUTHENTIC 2
‖**blow off** *vb* ***syn*** see GRIPE
blowoff *n* ***syn*** see BINGE 1
‖**blowout** *n* ***syn*** see SHINDIG 1
blowsy *adj* ***syn*** see SLATTERNLY
ant spruce
blow up *vb* **1** ***syn*** see EXPLODE 1
2 ***syn*** see DISCREDIT 2
3 ***syn*** see ANGER 2
blowy *adj* ***syn*** see WINDY 1
blub *vb* ***syn*** see CRY 2
blubber *vb* ***syn*** see CRY 2
bludgeon *n* ***syn*** see CUDGEL
bludgeon *vb* ***syn*** see INTIMIDATE
blue *adj* **1** ***syn*** see DOWNCAST
2 ***syn*** see RISQUÉ
3 ***syn*** see UTTER
blue *n* ***syn*** see OCEAN
blue blood *n* **1** ***syn*** see GENTLEMAN 1
2 ***syn*** see ARISTOCRACY
‖**bluebottle** *n* ***syn*** see POLICEMAN
bluecoat *n* ***syn*** see POLICEMAN
blue–eyed *adj* ***syn*** see FAVORITE 1
blue moon *n* ***syn*** see AGE 2
bluenose *n* ***syn*** see PRUDE
bluenosed *adj* ***syn*** see PRIM 1
blueprint *n* ***syn*** see PLAN 1
rel outline, sketch
blueprint *vb* ***syn*** see PLAN 2
blue–ribbon *adj* ***syn*** see EXCELLENT
blues *n pl but sometimes sing in constr* ***syn*** see SADNESS
bluff *adj* direct and unceremonious in speech or manner <*bluff* aggressive questions>
syn abrupt, blunt, breviloquent, brief, brusque, crusty, curt, gruff, rough, short, short-spoken, snippety, snippy
rel hearty, honest, sincere; barefaced, candid, direct, forthright, frank, no-nonsense, outspoken, plainspoken, straightforward; bearish, rude, tactless; sharp, tart; laconic, terse
idiom to the point
con civil, courteous, courtly, gallant, polite; diplomatic, urbane
ant smooth, suave
bluff *vb* **1** ***syn*** see DECEIVE
rel fool, joke, trick
2 ***syn*** see ASSUME 4
blunder *vb* **1** ***syn*** see STUMBLE 3
2 ***syn*** see WALLOW 2
3 ***syn*** see BOTCH
blunder (away) *vb* ***syn*** see WASTE 2
blunder *n* ***syn*** see ERROR 2
blunderbuss *n* ***syn*** see STUMBLEBUM
blunderer *n* ***syn*** see STUMBLEBUM
blunt *adj* **1** ***syn*** see DULL 6
rel unpointed, unsharp; insensitive
con acuminate, acute
ant keen, sharp
2 ***syn*** see BLUFF
con politic, smooth, suave
ant subtle; tactful
blunt *vb* **1** ***syn*** see DULL 3
2 ***syn*** see DEADEN 1
3 ***syn*** see DULL 5
4 ***syn*** see WEAKEN 1
‖**blunt** *n* ***syn*** see MONEY
blur *n* ***syn*** see STIGMA
blur *vb* **1** ***syn*** see TAINT 1
2 ***syn*** see CONFUSE 4
3 ***syn*** see DULL 4
blurb *n* ***syn*** see PUFF 3
blurt (out) *vb* ***syn*** see EXCLAIM
blush *vb* to turn or glow red in the face <*blushed* from embarrassment>
syn color, crimson, flush, glow, mantle, pink, pinken, redden, rose, rouge
blush *n* ***syn*** see BLOOM 3
bluster *vb* **1** ***syn*** see ROAR
rel blast, storm, rage
2 ***syn*** see INTIMIDATE
blustering *adj* ***syn*** see WILD 6
blustery *adj* ***syn*** see WILD 6
board *vb* **1** to get aboard of <*boarded* the wrong bus>
syn embark
rel embus, emplane, entrain
idiom get on
con debus, deplane, detrain; land
ant debark, disembark, get off
2 ***syn*** see HARBOR 2
rel care (for), cherish, nurture, tend
board *n* **1 boards** *pl* ***syn*** see DRAMA
2 ***syn*** see TABLE 1
boast *vb* to express pride in oneself or one's accomplishments <*boasting* about all the girl friends he had>
syn blow, brag, cock-a-doodle-doo, crow, gasconade, mouth, prate, puff, rodomontade, vaunt
rel pique, plume, preen, pride, quack; gush, vapor; aggrandize, exalt, glory, triumph; bluster, ‖bounce, bully, ruffle, swash, swashbuckle, swagger; flaunt, parade, show off
idiom blow one's horn, congratulate oneself, hug oneself, pat oneself on the back
con belittle, decry, degrade, disparage, knock, minimize, run down
ant depreciate
boaster *n* ***syn*** see BRAGGART

boastful *adj* given to or characterized by boasting <a *boastful* old windbag>
syn braggadocian, braggart, braggy, rodomontade, self-glorifying, vaunting
rel arrogant, pretentious; cock-a-hoop, exultant; big-headed, conceited, swelled-headed; self-aggrandizing, self-applauding, self-flattering, vainglorious
idiom having a high opinion of oneself, seeing oneself larger than life
con self-depreciating, self-effacing, unassuming; bashful, demure, sheepish, shy, timid; quiet, reserved, restrained, retiring
ant modest

bob *vb syn* see TAP 1
bobbery *n syn* see BRAWL 2
bobble *vb syn* see BOTCH
‖**bobby** *n syn* see POLICEMAN
‖**bodacious** *adj syn* see NOTEWORTHY
bode *vb syn* see AUGUR 2
bodement *n syn* see FORETOKEN
bodiless *adj syn* see IMMATERIAL 1

bodily *adj* of or relating to the human body <*bodily* pain>
syn carnal, corporal, corporeal, fleshly, physical, somatic
rel animal, sensual
con intellectual, mental, psychic, psychological; spiritual, unworldly

boding *n syn* see FORETOKEN

body *n* **1** *syn* see HUMAN
2 *syn* see CORPSE
3 the main, central, or essential part <the *body* of the discussion dealt with ways to ensure equal opportunities for all>
syn bulk, core, corpus, mass, staple, substance; *compare* ESSENCE 2, SUBSTANCE 2, TENOR 1
rel majority; sum, total, whole; basis, crux, fundamental, gravamen; gist, pith
con angle, aspect, facet, feature, side; accessory, extension, offshoot, side issue
4 a discrete portion of matter <unknown *bodies* in space>
syn bulk, mass, object, volume
5 a determinable or measurable whole <collected a large *body* of evidence>
syn aggregate, amount, budget, bulk, quantity, quantum, total
rel input; extent, range; number, stock, sum, whole
6 *syn* see GROUP 3
7 *syn* see SUBSTANCE 2

body (forth) *vb syn* see REPRESENT 2
boeotian *n syn* see PHILISTINE
bog *n syn* see SWAMP
bog (down) *vb syn* see DELAY 1
bogey *n syn* see APPARITION
boggle *vb* **1** *syn* see DEMUR
2 *syn* see BOTCH
3 *syn* see STAGGER 5
bogus *adj syn* see COUNTERFEIT
rel forged; imitation
con bona fide, good
ant authentic, genuine, real

Bohemian *n* a person (as an artist) who has an unconventional life-style that often reflects protest against or indifference to convention <a gathering place for radicals and *Bohemians*>
syn maverick, nonconformist
rel beat, beatnik, dropout, hippie; iconoclast; eccentric, original; recusant
con conformer, conventionalist, formalist, pedant

bohunk *n syn* see OAF 2
boil *n syn* see ABSCESS
boil *vb* **1** *syn* see SEETHE 4
2 to prepare (as food) in a liquid heated to the point that it begins to give off steam <*boil* eggs>
syn parboil, seethe, simmer, stew
rel coddle, poach; decoct; steam
3 *syn* see ANGER 2
4 *syn* see RUSH 1
boil down *vb syn* see SIMPLIFY
boildown *n syn* see ABRIDGMENT
‖**boiled** *adj syn* see INTOXICATED 1
boiling *adj syn* see HOT 1
boil over *vb syn* see ANGER 2
boisterous *adj* **1** *syn* see TURBULENT 1
2 *syn* see VOCIFEROUS
rel brawling, noisy, riotous, rollicking, rowdy
con sedate, sober, staid; noiseless
‖**boko** *n syn* see NOSE 1
bold *adj* **1** *syn* see BRAVE 1
con pusillanimous, shrinking, timid, timorous
ant cowardly
2 *syn* see WISE 5
rel audacious; bluff
con mousy, quiet, shy
3 *syn* see INSOLENT 2
‖**boldacious** *adj syn* see INSOLENT 2
bold–faced *adj syn* see WISE 5
boldhearted *adj syn* see BRAVE 1
boldness *n syn* see INSOLENCE
bollix *vb syn* see BOTCH
Bolshevik *n syn* see COMMUNIST
‖**Bolshie** *n syn* see COMMUNIST
bolster *vb* **1** *syn* see SUPPORT 4
rel reinforce, strengthen
2 *syn* see SUPPORT 5
bolt *n syn* see THUNDERBOLT
bolt *vb* **1** *syn* see START 1
2 *syn* see RUSH 1
3 *syn* see RUN 2
4 *syn* see EXCLAIM
5 *syn* see GULP
bomb *n* **1** *syn* see FAILURE 5
‖**2** *syn* see FORTUNE 4
bomb *vb* **1** *syn* see BOMBARD
2 *syn* see FAIL 4

bombard *vb* to assault with bombs or shells <cities *bombarded* by planes and artillery>
syn blitz, bomb, cannonade, shell
rel barrage, strafe, strike

---

syn synonym(s) *rel* related word(s)
ant antonym(s) *con* contrasted word(s)
idiom idiomatic equivalent(s)
‖ use limited; if in doubt, see a dictionary

THESAURUS

idiom open up on, pour a broadside into
bombardment *n syn* see BARRAGE
bombast *n* pretentious inflated speech or writing <adolescent *bombast* about Youth and Destiny>
syn fustian, highfalutin, rant, rhapsody, rhetoric, rodomontade
rel grandiloquence, magniloquence; flatulence, orotundity, tumidity, turgidity; heroics, pyrotechnics, sesquipedality; Johnsonese; spread-eagleism; nonsense
idiom purple prose
bombastic *adj syn* see RHETORICAL
rel flatulent
con unimpassioned; unaffected
‖**bombed** *adj syn* see INTOXICATED 1
bombinate *vb syn* see HUM
bona fide *adj syn* see AUTHENTIC 2
bona fides *n syn* see GOOD FAITH
bonanza *n* a place of great abundance or a source of great wealth or opportunity <the town proved to be a *bonanza* for entrepreneurs>
syn eldorado, Golconda, gold mine, mine, treasure-house, treasure trove, treasury
bond *n* **1** *usu* **bonds** *pl syn* see SHACKLE
2 *syn* see CONTRACT
3 a uniting or binding element or force <the *bonds* of friendship>
syn knot, ligament, ligature, link, nexus, tie, vinculum, yoke
rel bridge, connection, connective, liaison; interrelationship, relationship
4 *syn* see ADHERENCE 1
5 *syn* see GUARANTEE 1
bondage *n* the state of subjection to an owner or master <prisoners sold into *bondage*>
syn enslavement, helotry, peonage, serfage, serfdom, servility, servitude, slavery, thrall, thralldom, villenage, yoke
rel subjection, subjugation
con freedom, independence, liberty
bondman *n syn* see SLAVE 1
bondslave *n syn* see SLAVE 1
bondsman *n syn* see SLAVE 1
bone *n* **1** **bones** *pl syn* see DICE
‖**2** *syn* see DOLLAR
bone (up) *vb syn* see CRAM 4
bone–dry *adj* **1** *syn* see DRY 1
2 *syn* see DRY 3
bonehead *n syn* see DUNCE
boneless *adj syn* see WEAK 4
boner *n* **1** *syn* see ERROR 2
2 *syn* see FAUX PAS
‖**boneyard** *n syn* see CEMETERY
bong *vb syn* see RING
boniface *n syn* see SALOONKEEPER
‖**bonkers** *adj syn* see INSANE 1
bonne bouche *n syn* see DELICACY
‖**bonnet** *n syn* see DECOY 2
‖**bonny** *adj syn* see BEAUTIFUL
bon vivant *n syn* see EPICURE
rel bon viveur, boulevardier, high liver, high roller, man-about-town, sport
bony *adj syn* see LEAN
boo *n syn* see RASPBERRY
boo *n syn* see MARIJUANA
boob *n* **1** *syn* see DUNCE
2 *syn* see PHILISTINE
‖**boo–boo** *n syn* see FAUX PAS
boob tube *n syn* see TELEVISION
booby *n syn* see DUNCE
booby hatch *n syn* see ASYLUM 3
booby trap *n syn* see PITFALL
boodle *n* **1** *syn* see FORTUNE 4
2 *syn* see SPOIL
boodle *vb syn* see CHEAT
boohoo *vb syn* see CRY 2
book *n* **1** a collection of folded, cut, bound, and usually printed sheets <a *book* of poems>
syn tome, volume
rel publication, work, writing; scroll; booklet, brochure, folder, leaflet, magazine, pamphlet; compendium, handbook, manual, monograph, textbook, tract, treatise; codex; novel
2 *cap* **Book** *syn* see BIBLE
book *vb* **1** *syn* see LIST 3
2 *syn* see TIME 1
3 *syn* see RESERVE 2
bookdealer *n* one who deals in books <sold his library to a *bookdealer*>
syn bibliopole, bookman, bookseller
rel bouquiniste
bookie *n syn* see BOOKMAKER
bookish *adj syn* see PEDANTIC
rel booksy, highbrow
book–learned *adj syn* see PEDANTIC
bookmaker *n* one who determines odds and receives and pays off bets <*bookmakers* who welsh on paying off winners>
syn bookie, layer
rel pricemaker; runner
bookman *n syn* see BOOKDEALER
bookseller *n syn* see BOOKDEALER
booky *adj syn* see PEDANTIC
boom *n* **1** *syn* see BANG 2
2 *syn* see PROSPERITY 4
boomerang *vb syn* see BACKFIRE
booming *adj syn* see FLOURISHING
boon *n* **1** *syn* see GIFT 1
2 *syn* see GOOD 1
boon *adj syn* see MERRY
‖**boondocks** *n pl syn* see FRONTIER 2
‖**boonies** *n pl syn* see FRONTIER 2
boor *n* an uncouth ungainly fellow <an ill-mannered *boor*>
syn ‖bosthoon, chuff, churl, clodhopper, clown, grobian, mucker
rel barbarian, vulgarian; looby, lubber; farmer, loon, rustic, swain; ‖carl; bohunk; boob, buffoon, oaf
con slicker, smoothy; gentleman; cosmopolitan, cosmopolite, sophisticate
boorish *adj* uncouth in manner or appearance <a *boorish* fellow lacking all grace>
syn churlish, cloddish, clodhopping, clownish, ill-bred, loutish, lowbred, lubberly, lumpish, robustious, rugged, swainish, uncivilized, uncultured, unpolished, unrefined; *compare* COARSE 3

rel barbarian, barbaric, outlandish, tasteless, vulgar; bucolic, countrified, inurbane, provincial, rustic, yokelish; ill-mannered, impolite, rude, uncivil, ungracious; graceless, unpoised
con cultivated, cultured, refined; suave, urbane; courteous, courtly, genteel, polite, well-bred; graceful, gracious, poised

boost *vb* **1** *syn* see RAISE 9
2 *syn* see INCREASE 1
3 *syn* see PROMOTE 3
‖**4** *syn* see SHOPLIFT

boost *n syn* see RISE 3

‖**booster** *n syn* see DECOY 2

boot *n* **1** *syn* see THRILL
2 *syn* see NOVICE

boot (out) *vb* **1** *syn* see EJECT 1
2 *syn* see DISMISS 3

‖**boot hill** *n syn* see CEMETERY

bootleg *n syn* see MOONSHINE 2

bootleg *vb syn* see SMUGGLE

bootless *adj syn* see FUTILE
rel frustrating; profitless, worthless

bootlick *vb syn* see FAWN

bootlick *n syn* see SYCOPHANT

bootlicker *n syn* see SYCOPHANT

bootlicking *adj syn* see FAWNING

booty *n syn* see SPOIL

booze *vb syn* see DRINK 3

booze *n* **1** *syn* see LIQUOR 2
2 *syn* see BINGE 1

‖**boozed** *adj syn* see INTOXICATED 1

boozehound *n syn* see DRUNKARD

boozer *n* **1** *syn* see DRUNKARD
‖**2** *syn* see BAR 5

‖**boozy** *adj syn* see INTOXICATED 1

bop *n syn* see BLOW 1

borasca *n syn* see POVERTY 1

bordello *n syn* see BROTHEL

border *n* **1** a line or relatively narrow space that marks the outermost bound of something <the *border* of the rug>
syn brim, brink, edge, fringe, hem, margin, perimeter, periphery, rim, selvage, skirt, verge; *compare* CIRCUMFERENCE
rel butts and bounds, lines, metes and bounds; bound, circumference, confine, end, extremity, limit, termination; boundary, frontier, march, pale; beginning, door, entrance, threshold; sideline; lip
con inside, interior; recesses; center; body, bulk, mass, whole
2 *syn* see FRONTIER 1

border *vb* **1** to form a border to <hedges *border* the park>
syn bound, define, edge, fringe, hem, margin, outline, rim, skirt, surround, verge
rel circumscribe, encircle, enclose, frame; contour, delineate, mark (off), outline, set off; flank, line, side; trim
2 *syn* see ADJOIN
3 to come to be closely similiar to a specified thing <ideas that *border* on the absurd>
syn approach, trench, verge
rel approximate, compare, near
idiom come close (*or* near) to

bordering *adj syn* see ADJACENT 3

borderland *n syn* see FRONTIER 1

borderline *adj syn* see DOUBTFUL 1

bore *vb* **1** *syn* see PERFORATE
2 *syn* see GAZE 1

bore *vb* to induce a state of boredom in <*bored* to death by his endless sermon>
syn ennui, pall, tire, weary
rel jade; fatigue, wear; annoy, irk, irritate; afflict, bother, discomfort
idiom put one to sleep
con amuse, entertain; excite, fascinate, intrigue; absorb, beguile, engross, enthrall, grip; enliven, freshen, invigorate, quicken, stimulate
ant interest

bore *n* someone or something that is boring <cocktail parties frequented mainly by *bores*>
syn drag, ‖dullsville, ‖pill
rel bad news; downer; soporific
idiom crashing bore

boreal *adj syn* see COLD 1

boredom *n syn* see TEDIUM
rel fatigue, weariness; disgust, distaste
con amusement, diversion, entertainment; excitement, fascination; engrossment, enthrallment

boresome *adj syn* see IRKSOME
rel deadly, dreary, dull, humdrum, monotonous
con amusing, entertaining; exciting, fascinating, intriguing; absorbing, engrossing, enthralling, gripping, stimulating
ant interesting

boring *adj syn* see IRKSOME

born *adj syn* see INHERENT

‖**born** *vb syn* see BEAR 5

borné *adj syn* see LITTLE 2

bosh *n syn* see NONSENSE 2

bosom *n syn* see HEART 1

bosomy *adj syn* see BUXOM

boss *n syn* see LEADER 2

‖**boss** *adj syn* see EXCELLENT

boss *vb syn* see SUPERVISE

bossy *adj syn* see MASTERFUL 1

‖**bosthoon** *n syn* see BOOR

Boswell *n syn* see BIOGRAPHER

botch *vb* to do or proceed ineffectively or badly through clumsiness, stupidity, or lack of ability <a complete incompetent —*botches* everything he puts his hand to>
syn ‖blow, blunder, bobble, boggle, bollix, bugger up, bumble, bungle, cobble, dub, flub, fluff, foozle, fumble, goof (up), gum (up), louse up, mess, ‖muck, mucker, muff, ‖screw (up)
rel butcher, mangle, murder, mutilate; mar, ruin, spoil; destroy, wreck; hash; tinker; misconduct, mishandle, mismanage; confuse, disorder
idiom ‖drop a clanger, play (*or* wreak) havoc with, play hell with, pull a boner (*or* rock)

---

syn synonym(s) *rel* related word(s)
ant antonym(s) *con* contrasted word(s)
idiom idiomatic equivalent(s)
‖ use limited; if in doubt, see a dictionary

botch *n syn* see MESS 3
botchery *n syn* see MESS 3
botchy *adj syn* see SLIPSHOD 3
bother *vb* **1** *syn* see DISCOMPOSE 1
2 *syn* see ANNOY 1
bother *n* **1** *syn* see ANNOYANCE 2
2 *syn* see ANNOYANCE 3
3 *syn* see INCONVENIENCE
botheration *n* **1** *syn* see ANNOYANCE 2
2 *syn* see ANNOYANCE 3
bothering *n syn* see ANNOYANCE 1
botherment *n syn* see ANNOYANCE 3
bothersomeness *n syn* see INCONVENIENCE
bottega *n syn* see STUDIO
bottle (up) *vb* **1** *syn* see RESTRAIN
2 *syn* see CORNER
bottom *n* **1** the under surface as opposed to the top surface <gum was stuck to the *bottom* of her shoe>
syn sole, underneath, underside, undersurface
rel belly, underbelly, underbody; base, floor, foot, ground
con acme, apex, cap, crest, crown, tip, upper
ant top
2 *syn* see BUTTOCKS
3 the lower or lowest point <the *bottom* of the page>
syn base, foot, nadir
rel basement, floor, ground; end; low
con acme, apex, pinnacle, zenith
ant top
4 *syn* see BASE 1
5 *syn* see ESSENCE 2
bottom *vb syn* see BASE
bottom *adj* **1** *syn* see BOTTOMMOST
2 *syn* see FUNDAMENTAL 1
bottom dog *n syn* see VICTIM 2
bottomless *adj* **1** *syn* see BASELESS
rel reasonless, unjustifiable, unsupportable
2 extremely deep <the *bottomless* sea>
syn abysmal, fathomless, plumbless, plummetless, soundless, unfathomable; *compare* DEEP 1
rel endless, infinite
bottommost *adj* that is at the very bottom <the ladder's *bottommost* rung>
syn bottom, lowermost, lowest, nethermost, rock-bottom, undermost
con top, upper, uppermost
ant topmost
bough *n syn* see LIMB
bought *adj syn* see READY-MADE
‖**boughten** *adj syn* see READY-MADE
boulevard *n syn* see WAY 1
bounce *vb* **1** *syn* see JUMP 1
2 *syn* see DISMISS 3
‖**3** *syn* see INTIMIDATE
bounce (back) *vb* **1** *syn* see RECOVER 3
2 *syn* see BACKFIRE
bouncer *n* ‖**1** *syn* see LIE
rel exaggeration, hyperbole, overstatement
idiom tall tale
2 a person employed to restrain or eject disorderly persons (as at a bar) <tossed out by the *bouncer*>
syn chucker, ‖chucker-out, houseman
rel goon, muscleman, strong arm
bouncy *adj syn* see ELASTIC 2
bound *n* **1** *usu* **bounds** *pl syn* see ENVIRONS 1
2 *syn* see LIMIT 1
bound *vb* **1** *syn* see DEMARCATE 1
2 *syn* see BORDER 1
bound *adj* **1** *syn* see FINITE
2 obliged to serve a master or in a clearly defined capacity for a certain length of time by the terms of a contract or mutual agreement <brought to the American colonies as a *bound* servant>
syn apprenticed, articled, indentured
rel contracted; enslaved
con free, freed
3 *syn* see CONSTIPATED
bound *vb syn* see JUMP 1
boundary *n syn* see ENVIRONS 1
bounded *adj syn* see FINITE
ant unbounded
bounder *n syn* see CAD
boundless *adj syn* see LIMITLESS
bounteous *adj* **1** *syn* see LIBERAL 1
con cheap, illiberal, scant
ant niggardly
2 *syn* see PLENTIFUL
con insufficient, scant, sparse
bountiful *adj* **1** *syn* see LIBERAL 1
2 *syn* see PLENTIFUL
bouquet *n* **1** cut flowers arranged for wear or display <a *bouquet* of spring flowers>
syn nosegay, posy
rel arrangement; boutonniere, corsage; spray; wreath; garland, festoon; lei
2 *syn* see COMPLIMENT 1
3 *syn* see FRAGRANCE
Bourbon *n syn* see REACTIONARY
bout *n* **1** *syn* see SPELL 1
2 *syn* see SIEGE
boutade *n syn* see CAPRICE
bow *vb syn* see YIELD 2
bow *n* **1** *syn* see CURVE
2 *syn* see TURN 4
bow *vb syn* see CURVE
bowdlerize *vb syn* see CENSOR
bowed *adj* **1** *syn* see CURVED
2 *syn* see BOWLEGGED
bowel *vb syn* see EVISCERATE
bower *n syn* see ARBOR
bowery *n syn* see SKID ROW
bowl *n syn* see STADIUM
‖**bowl** (down *or* out) *vb syn* see WHIP 2
bowl (down *or* over) *vb syn* see FELL 1
bowlegged *adj* having legs bent outward <a *bowlegged* cowboy>
syn bandy, bandy-legged, bowed
rel bent, crooked, curved, misshapen
bowwow *n syn* see DOG 1
box *n* ‖**1** *syn* see HUT
‖**2** *syn* see PREDICAMENT
3 *syn* see TELEVISION
box *n syn* see CUFF
box *vb syn* see SLAP 1

boxing *n* the art of attack and defense with the fists practiced as a sport <he liked *boxing* —at least as a spectator sport>
syn fisticuffs, prizefighting, pugilism, ring

boy *n* **1** a male person not fully matured <a *boy* of nine>
syn lad, laddie, shaveling, son, stripling, tad
rel gamin, ragamuffin, street arab, urchin; hobbledehoy, whippersnapper; schoolboy
idiom little shaver, small fry
2 *syn* see MAN 3

boyfriend *n* **1** a man who is a woman's usual or preferred escort or companion <went to the movies with her *boyfriend*>
syn beau, gentleman friend, swain, young man
rel admirer
2 a man who shares with a woman a strong and usually sexually oriented mutual attraction <this was the *boyfriend* she hoped to marry>
syn beau, beloved, flame, inamorato, lover, steady, sweetheart, truelove
rel crush, heartthrob; fiancé
3 *syn* see LOVER 1

brabble *vb* *syn* see QUARREL

brabble *n* **1** *syn* see QUARREL
2 *syn* see CHATTER

brace *n* **1** *syn* see COUPLE
2 *syn* see SUPPORT 3
3 braces *pl* *syn* see SUSPENDERS

brace *vb* **1** *syn* see GIRD 3
2 *syn* see SUPPORT 4
3 *syn* see BEG

bracing *adj* *syn* see INVIGORATING

bracket *vb* **1** *syn* see JOIN 1
2 *syn* see COMPARE 2

brag *vb* *syn* see BOAST
con apologize, deprecate

braggadocian *adj* *syn* see BOASTFUL

braggadocio *n* *syn* see BRAGGART

braggart *n* one who boasts <too much of a *braggart* about his strength>
syn blower, blowhard, boaster, braggadocio, bragger, ‖gasbag, puckfist, rodomont, rodomontade, vaunter
rel bluffer, blusterer, loudmouth, miles gloriosus, ranter, raver, windbag
con Milquetoast

braggart *adj* *syn* see BOASTFUL

bragger *n* *syn* see BRAGGART

braggy *adj* *syn* see BOASTFUL

Brahmin *n* *syn* see INTELLECTUAL 2

brain *n* **1** *syn* see MIND 1
2 *syn* see INTELLECT 2
3 *often* **brains** *pl* *syn* see INTELLIGENCE 1

brainchild *n* *syn* see INVENTION

brainless *adj* *syn* see SIMPLE 3

brainpower *n* *syn* see INTELLIGENCE 1

brainsick *adj* *syn* see INSANE 1

brainwork *n* *syn* see THOUGHT 1

brainy *adj* *syn* see INTELLIGENT 2

brake *vb* *syn* see HINDER
rel slow, stop

branch *n* **1** *syn* see LIMB
rel branchlet
2 *syn* see CREEK 2

brand *n* **1** *syn* see MARK 7
2 *syn* see STIGMA

brandish *vb* *syn* see SHOW 4

brand name *n* *syn* see MARK 7

brand–new *adj* conspicuously new and unused <a *brand-new* car right out of the showroom>
syn fire-new, mint, spang-new, spanking-new, span-new, spick-and-span
rel untouched, unused; clean, fresh, pristine
con hand-me-down, secondhand, used; outworn, shabby, worn, worn-out
ant old

brannigan *n* **1** *syn* see BINGE 1
2 *syn* see QUARREL

brash *adj* **1** *syn* see RASH 1
2 *syn* see EXUBERANT 1
3 *syn* see TACTLESS
4 *syn* see PRESUMPTUOUS
rel bold, brazen; rash, reckless; headlong, impetuous; cocksure

brashness *n* **1** *syn* see TEMERITY
2 *syn* see EFFRONTERY

brass *n* ‖**1** *syn* see MONEY
2 *syn* see EFFRONTERY

brassbound *adj* **1** *syn* see ILLIBERAL
2 *syn* see INFLEXIBLE 2
3 *syn* see PRESUMPTUOUS

brass hat *n* *syn* see SUPERIOR

brassy *adj* **1** *syn* see SHAMELESS
2 *syn* see BRAZEN 4

brave *adj* **1** having or showing no fear when faced with something dangerous, difficult, or unknown <made a *brave* attempt to save the burning house>
syn audacious, aweless, bold, boldhearted, bravehearted, chin-up, courageous, dauntless, doughty, fearless, gallant, game, greathearted, ‖gutsy, heroic, intrepid, lionhearted, manful, manly, ‖plucked, plucky, soldierly, spunky, stalwart, stout, stouthearted, unafraid, unblenched, unblenching, undauntable, undaunted, unfearful, unfearing, valiant, valorous
rel daring, defiant, gritty, hardy, mettlesome, resolute, spirited, steadfast, unapprehensive, undismayed, unflinching, unfrightened, unquailing, unshrinking, unswerving, unwincing, unyielding, venturesome; chivalrous, noble, preux; confident
con cringing, flinching, frightened, pusillanimous, scared, shrinking, timid; chickenhearted, fainthearted, lily-livered, nerveless, soft, spineless, unmanly, weakhearted, weak-kneed, yellow
ant cowardly, craven
2 *syn* see COLORFUL
3 *syn* see GOOD 1

brave *vb* *syn* see FACE 3
con avoid

bravehearted *adj* *syn* see BRAVE 1

---

syn synonym(s) *rel* related word(s)
ant antonym(s) *con* contrasted word(s)
idiom idiomatic equivalent(s)
‖ use limited; if in doubt, see a dictionary

bravery *n* ***syn*** see FINERY
bravo *n* ***syn*** see ASSASSIN
brawl *vb* ***syn*** see QUARREL
brawl *n* **1** ***syn*** see QUARREL
2 a rough, noisy, and often prolonged hand-to-hand fight usually involving several people <windows and furniture were broken in the barroom *brawl*>
syn affray, bobbery, broil, dogfight, donnybrook, fight, fracas, fray, free-for-all, knock-down-and-drag-out, maul, melee, mellay, ||muss, rough-and-tumble, row, rowdydow, ruction, scrap, scrimmage, scuffle, set-to; *compare* QUARREL
rel fistfight, fisticuffs, slugfest; struggle, tussle; conflict, contention, contest, riot; altercation, embroilment, imbroglio, quarrel, wrangle; commotion, disturbance, eruption, hubbub, pandemonium, ruckus, rumpus, turn-to, ||turnup, upheaval, uproar; incident, ||rumble
idiom a coming to blows, exchange of blows
brawling *adj* ***syn*** see QUARRELSOME 2
brawlsome *adj* ***syn*** see QUARRELSOME 2
brawly *adj* ***syn*** see QUARRELSOME 2
brawn *n* ***syn*** see MUSCLE 1
brawny *adj* ***syn*** see MUSCULAR 2
rel lusty, red-blooded, vigorous, vital; tough
con lanky, lean, rawboned, skinny, thin
ant scrawny
bray *vb* ***syn*** see PULVERIZE 1
brazen *adj* **1** ***syn*** see INSOLENT 2
2 ***syn*** see SHAMELESS
3 ***syn*** see GAUDY
4 of the color of polished brass <a *brazen* sky at sunset>
syn aeneous, brassy
rel bronze
brazenfaced *adj* ***syn*** see SHAMELESS
breach *n* **1** the act or offense of failing to keep the law or to do what law, duty, or obligation requires <sued for *breach* of contract> <his behavior was a gross *breach* of good manners>
syn contravention, infraction, infringement, transgression, trespass, violation
rel disregard, nonobservance; delinquency, dereliction, neglect
con conformance, conformity, observance
ant observance
2 ***syn*** see GAP 1
3 an interruption of accustomed friendly relations <a trivial misunderstanding caused a *breach* between the brothers>
syn break, fissure, fracture, rent, rift, rupture, schism, split; *compare* SCHISM 3
rel division, separation, severance; alienation, estrangement; difference, discord, disharmony, dissension, disunity, strife, variance; secession, withdrawal; falling-out, quarrel
idiom parting of ways
con integrity, solidarity, union, unity; communion, community; accord, concord, harmony
4 ***syn*** see GAP 2
breach *vb* **1** ***syn*** see OPEN 3
rel bore, penetrate
2 ***syn*** see VIOLATE 1
bread *n* **1** ***syn*** see FOOD 1
2 ***syn*** see LIVING
||**3** ***syn*** see MONEY
bread and butter *n* ***syn*** see LIVING
breadth *n* **1** ***syn*** see EXPANSE
2 spaciousness of extent <the *breadth* of his knowledge on the subject is awesome>
syn amplitude, comprehensiveness, fullness, scope, wideness
rel compass, gamut, orbit, range, reach, sweep; expanse, spread, stretch
con limitation, restriction
ant narrowness
breadthen *vb* ***syn*** see BROADEN
break *vb* **1** ***syn*** see GIVE 12
2 ***syn*** see PLOW
3 ***syn*** see VIOLATE 1
ant observe
4 ***syn*** see ESCAPE 1
5 ***syn*** see FAIL 5
idiom go broke
6 ***syn*** see RUIN 3
7 ***syn*** see DEGRADE 1
8 ***syn*** see DISPROVE 1
9 ***syn*** see COMMUNICATE 1
10 ***syn*** see SOLVE 2
11 ***syn*** see DECODE
12 ***syn*** see HAPPEN 1
13 ***syn*** see GET OUT 2
||**14** ***syn*** see CLEAR 9
break *n* **1** ***syn*** see GAP 1
2 ***syn*** see GAP 3
3 ***syn*** see INTERLUDE
4 a usually short rest period <took a *break* for coffee>
syn blow, breath, breather, breathing space (*or* spell), respite, ten; *compare* PAUSE
5 ***syn*** see BREACH 3
6 ***syn*** see FAUX PAS
7 ***syn*** see OPPORTUNITY
breakable *adj* ***syn*** see FRAGILE 1
break down *vb* **1** ***syn*** see ANALYZE
2 ***syn*** see DECAY
3 ***syn*** see COLLAPSE 2
breakdown *n* **1** ***syn*** see NERVOUS BREAKDOWN
2 ***syn*** see COLLAPSE 2
3 ***syn*** see ANALYSIS 1
break in *vb* **1** ***syn*** see HOUSEBREAK
idiom break and enter
2 ***syn*** see INTERRUPT 2
breakneck *adj* ***syn*** see FAST 3
break out *vb* ***syn*** see ERUPT 2
breakout *n* ***syn*** see ESCAPE 1
breakthrough *n* ***syn*** see RISE 3
break up *vb* **1** ***syn*** see SEPARATE 1
2 ***syn*** see DISBAND
breakup *n* ***syn*** see ANALYSIS 1
breast *n* ***syn*** see HEART 1
breast-feed *vb* ***syn*** see NURSE 1
breastwork *n* ***syn*** see BULWARK
breath *n* **1** ***syn*** see HINT 2
2 ***syn*** see BREAK 4
breathe *vb* **1** ***syn*** see BE

2 ***syn*** see REST 3
3 to draw (as air) into and expel from the lungs <*breathe* clean air>
syn respire
rel exhale, inhale
4 ***syn*** see CONFIDE 1
breathe (in) *vb* ***syn*** see INHALE
breathe (out) *vb* ***syn*** see EXHALE
breather *n* ***syn*** see BREAK 4
breathing *n* ***syn*** see INSTANT 1
breathing space (*or* **spell**) *n* ***syn*** see BREAK 4
breathless *adj* **1** ***syn*** see EAGER
2 ***syn*** see STUFFY 1
bred–in–the–bone *adj* ***syn*** see INVETERATE 1
breech *n* ***syn*** see BUTTOCKS
breed *vb* **1** ***syn*** see PROCREATE 1
2 ***syn*** see FATHER 1
3 ***syn*** see GENERATE 3
4 ***syn*** see GROW 1
breed *n* ***syn*** see TYPE
breeding *n* ***syn*** see CULTURE
rel civility, courtesy, gentility, grace
con barbarism, boorishness; coarseness, grossness; discourtesy, rudeness
ant vulgarity
breeding ground *n* a place or environment which favors growth <the slum was a *breeding ground* for crime>
syn forcing bed, forcing house, hotbed, hothouse
breeze *n* ***syn*** see SNAP 1
breeze *vb* to proceed quickly and easily <*breezed* through customs>
syn waltz, zip
rel skim, slide, slip
con drag, falter, flag, lag, trail
breezy *adj* **1** ***syn*** see WINDY 1
2 ***syn*** see EASYGOING 3
breviary *n* ***syn*** see ABRIDGMENT
breviate *n* ***syn*** see ABRIDGMENT
breviloquent *adj* **1** ***syn*** see CONCISE
2 ***syn*** see BLUFF
brew *vb* ***syn*** see LOOM 2
brew *n* ***syn*** see MISCELLANY 1
bribable *adj* ***syn*** see VENAL 1
bribe *vb* to give or promise money or favor to a person in a position of trust to influence his judgment or conduct <*bribed* a building inspector>
syn buy, buy off, fix, have, ‖lubricate, sop, square, tamper (with)
rel approach; corrupt, instigate, suborn; soften (up), sweeten
idiom grease the palm (*or* hand), oil the palm (*or* hand), tickle the palm
bridal *n* ***syn*** see WEDDING
bridewell *n* ***syn*** see JAIL
bridle *vb* ***syn*** see RESTRAIN 1
rel repress, suppress; control, manage; govern, rule
con air, express, utter, ventilate, voice
ant vent
brief *adj* **1** ***syn*** see SHORT 1
rel fleeting, momentary, passing, transient
ant long
2 ***syn*** see CONCISE
3 ***syn*** see BLUFF
brief *n* ***syn*** see ABRIDGMENT
briefly *adv* in a few words <he answered *briefly* and to the point>
syn concisely, in brief, in short, laconically, shortly, succinctly, tersely
rel accurately, crisply, exactly, precisely
idiom in a capsule, in a nutshell, in a word, to make a long story short
con diffusely, long-windedly, profusely, prolixly, protractedly, verbosely, wordily; at length, comprehensively, fully
‖**brig** *n* ***syn*** see JAIL
brigand *n* ***syn*** see MARAUDER
bright *adj* **1** shining or glowing with light <the *bright* sun>
syn beaming, brilliant, effulgent, fulgent, incandescent, lambent, lucent, lucid, luminous, lustrous, radiant, refulgent
rel clear, light, undimmed; illuminated, lighted; coruscating, flashing, gleaming, glistening, glittering, scintillating, shimmering, sparkling; blazing, flaming, glowing; burnished, polished, shiny; sunshiny
con dark, dusky, gloomy, murky, tenebrous; colorless, drab, dreary, lackluster, leaden; somber; cloudy, gray, overcast, shadowy; moonless, starless, sunless; faint, pale, weak
ant dim; dull
2 ***syn*** see COLORFUL
3 ***syn*** see GLAD 2
4 ***syn*** see FAVORABLE 5
5 ***syn*** see INTELLIGENT 2
rel advanced, precocious
con retarded
ant dense, dull
6 ***syn*** see LIVELY 1
brilliant *adj* **1** ***syn*** see BRIGHT 1
ant subdued
2 ***syn*** see INTELLIGENT 2
rel erudite, learned; sage, wise
brim *n* ***syn*** see BORDER 1
brimful *adj* **1** ***syn*** see FULL 1
2 ***syn*** see BIG 3
brimming *adj* **1** ***syn*** see FULL 1
2 ***syn*** see BIG 3
brine *n* ***syn*** see OCEAN
bring *vb* **1** ***syn*** see CONVERT 1
‖2 ***syn*** see ACCOMPANY
3 ***syn*** see SELL 4
bring about *vb* ***syn*** see EFFECT 1
bring around *vb* ***syn*** see INDUCE 1
bring down *vb* ***syn*** see FELL 1
bring forth *vb* ***syn*** see BEAR 5
bring in *vb* **1** ***syn*** see YIELD 5
2 ***syn*** see SELL 4
3 ***syn*** see EARN 1

syn synonym(s) ***rel*** related word(s)
ant antonym(s) ***con*** contrasted word(s)
idiom idiomatic equivalent(s)
‖ use limited; if in doubt, see a dictionary

bring off *vb* ***syn*** see EFFECT 2
bring out *vb* ***syn*** see SAY 1
bring up *vb* **1** to give a child a parent's fostering care <the orphan was *brought up* by his aunt>
syn ‖fetch up, raise, rear
rel breed, cultivate, foster, nurture; feed, nourish, provide (for); discipline, educate, train
con abuse, ill-use, maltreat; neglect
2 ***syn*** see STOP 4
3 ***syn*** see REFER 3
4 ***syn*** see BROACH
5 ***syn*** see VOMIT
brink *n* **1** ***syn*** see BORDER 1
2 ***syn*** see VERGE 2
‖**briny** *n* ***syn*** see OCEAN
brio *n* ***syn*** see SPIRIT 5
brisk *adj* ***syn*** see AGILE
rel adroit; quick
con inactive, torpid
ant sluggish
brisky *adj* ***syn*** see AGILE
bristle *vb* ***syn*** see ANGER 2
brittle *adj* ***syn*** see SHORT 6
broach *n* ***syn*** see BROOCH
broach *vb* to open up (a subject) for discussion <would be awkward to *broach* the matter now>
syn bring up, introduce, moot, ventilate
rel interject, interpose; mention, speak (about); propose, suggest
con hush (up), quash, stifle, suppress; black out, censor
broad *adj* **1** ***syn*** see LIBERAL 3
2 ***syn*** see EXTENSIVE 1
3 ***syn*** see RISQUÉ
broadcast *n* ***syn*** see DECLARATION
broadcast *vb* **1** ***syn*** see STREW 1
2 ***syn*** see DECLARE 1
rel communicate, radio, televise, transmit
idiom spread a report, spread far and wide
broaden *vb* to grow or become broad or broader <the street *broadens* into an avenue>
syn breadthen, widen
rel expand; spread (out); open
con contract, shrink; slim, thin
ant narrow
broad-minded *adj* ***syn*** see LIBERAL 3
broadside *n* ***syn*** see BARRAGE
Brobdingnagian *adj* ***syn*** see HUGE
brocard *n* ***syn*** see MAXIM
‖**brogue** *vb* ***syn*** see IDLE
broil *vb* ***syn*** see BURN 3
broil *n* ***syn*** see BRAWL 2
broiling *adj* ***syn*** see HOT 1
broke *adj* ***syn*** see POOR 1
broken-down *adj* ***syn*** see SHABBY 1
broker *n* ***syn*** see GO-BETWEEN 2
bromide *n* ***syn*** see COMMONPLACE
bromidic *adj* ***syn*** see ARID 2
‖**Bronx cheer** *n* ***syn*** see RASPBERRY
brooch *n* an ornament with a pin or clasp now worn usually by women <a diamond *brooch*>
syn broach, clip, pin
brood *n* ***syn*** see OFFSPRING
brood *vb* **1** ***syn*** see SET 11
2 ***syn*** see MOPE 1
brook *vb* ***syn*** see BEAR 10
brook *n* ***syn*** see CREEK 2
brothel *n* an establishment where prostitutes ply their trade <madam of the local *brothel*>
syn bagnio, bawdy house, bordello, call house, cathouse, crib, disorderly house, fancy house, ‖hookshop, ‖joyhouse, lupanar, parlor house, seraglio, sporting house, stew, whorehouse
idiom house of ill fame (*or* repute), house of prostitution
brotherhood *n* ***syn*** see ASSOCIATION 2
brouhaha *n* **1** ***syn*** see DIN
2 ***syn*** see COMMOTION 3
brow *n* ***syn*** see FOREHEAD
browbeat *vb* ***syn*** see INTIMIDATE
browbeater *n* ***syn*** see BULLY 1
brownie *n* ***syn*** see FAIRY
‖**brownnose** *vb* ***syn*** see FAWN
‖**brownnose** *n* ***syn*** see SYCOPHANT
‖**brownnoser** *n* ***syn*** see SYCOPHANT
brown study *n* ***syn*** see REVERIE
browse *vb* to read through, study, or examine cursorily <*browsed* through the book looking for illustrations>
syn dip (into), flip (through), glance (at *or* over), leaf (through), riff (through), riffle (through), run (through *or* over), scan, skim (through), thumb (through)
rel go (through *or* over), look (over), peruse, skip (through)
idiom give the once over, run the eye over
con examine, study; delve (into), dig (into)
ant pore (over)
bruise *n* an injury involving rupture of small blood vessels and discoloration without break in the overlying skin <got an ugly *bruise* when he fell>
syn contusion; *compare* BLACK EYE
rel ‖boo-boo; abrasion, scrape, scratch
idiom black-and-blue spot (*or* mark)
bruise *vb* **1** to inflict a bruise on <fell down and *bruised* his hip>
syn black, contuse
rel batter, ‖bung up
2 ***syn*** see CRUSH 2
bruit (about) *vb* ***syn*** see DECLARE 1
rel hint, intimate, rumor, suggest
bruja *n* ***syn*** see WITCH 1
brume *n* ***syn*** see HAZE 1
brummagem *adj* ***syn*** see COUNTERFEIT
brunet *adj* ***syn*** see DARK 3
brush *vb* to touch or strike lightly (as in passing) <they *brushed* fenders but no real damage was done>
syn glance, graze, kiss, shave, skim
rel bump, clash, collide, sideswipe; clip, contact, scrape, touch
brush *n* **1** ***syn*** see ENCOUNTER
rel clash, engagement
2 ***syn*** see CLASH 2
brush up *vb* ***syn*** see TOUCH UP
brusque *adj* ***syn*** see BLUFF
brutal *adj* **1** ***syn*** see BRUTISH

2 ***syn*** see SEVERE 3
brutalize *vb* ***syn*** see DEBASE 1
brute *adj* ***syn*** see BRUTISH
brute *n* ***syn*** see BEAST
brutish *adj* marked by animal traits and by a lack of man's dignity or refinement <a graceless *brutish* hulk of a man>
syn animal, beastly, bestial, brutal, brute, feral, ferine, swinish
rel animalistic; coarse, crude; base, low, mean, scurvy, vile
bubble *vb* **1** ***syn*** see SLOSH 1
2 ***syn*** see SEETHE 4
bubble *n* ***syn*** see PIPE DREAM
buccaneer *n* ***syn*** see PIRATE
buck *n* **1** ***syn*** see MAN 3
2 ***syn*** see FOP
‖**3** ***syn*** see DOLLAR
4 ***syn*** see SAWHORSE
buck *vb* **1** ***syn*** see RESIST
2 ***syn*** see CARRY 1
3 ***syn*** see PASS 9
buck (off) *vb* ***syn*** see THROW 2
buck *vb* ***syn*** see PULVERIZE 1
‖**bucket** *n* ***syn*** see JAIL
bucket *vb* ***syn*** see HURRY 2
‖**bucket shop** *n* ***syn*** see BAR 5
buckle (down) *vb* **1** ***syn*** see ADDRESS 3
2 ***syn*** see PITCH IN 1
buckle (under) *vb* ***syn*** see YIELD 2
buckram *adj* ***syn*** see STIFF 4
buck up *vb* ***syn*** see COMFORT
bucolic *adj* ***syn*** see RURAL
ant urbane
bucolic *n* ***syn*** see RUSTIC
bud *n* **1** ***syn*** see CHILD 1
2 ***syn*** see SEED 2
buddy *n* ***syn*** see ASSOCIATE 3
‖**buddy–buddy** *adj* ***syn*** see INTIMATE 4
‖**budge** *n* ***syn*** see LIQUOR 2
budget *n* ***syn*** see BODY 5
budtime *n* ***syn*** see SPRING 5
buff *n* ***syn*** see ADDICT
buff *vb* ***syn*** see POLISH 1
buffalo *vb* **1** ***syn*** see FRUSTRATE 1
2 ***syn*** see NONPLUS 1
buff–bare *adj* ***syn*** see NUDE 2
buffet *n* ***syn*** see CUFF
buffet *vb* **1** ***syn*** see SLAP 1
2 ***syn*** see BEAT 1
‖**buffet** *n* ***syn*** see EATING HOUSE
‖**bufflehead** *n* ***syn*** see DUNCE
‖**buffle–headed** *adj* ***syn*** see SIMPLE 3
buffoon *n* ***syn*** see CLOWN 3
‖**buffy** *adj* ***syn*** see INTOXICATED 1
bug *n* ***syn*** see ENTHUSIAST
‖**bug** *vb* ***syn*** see ANNOY 1
bugbear *n* ***syn*** see ABOMINATION 1
‖**bugger** *n* ***syn*** see SNOT 1
‖**bugger** *vb* ***syn*** see EXHAUST 4
bugger up *vb* ***syn*** see BOTCH
‖**buggy** *adj* **1** ***syn*** see ENTHUSIASTIC
2 ***syn*** see INSANE 1
‖**buggy** *n* ***syn*** see CAR
‖**bughouse** *n* ***syn*** see ASYLUM 3
‖**bughouse** *adj* ***syn*** see INSANE 1
bug off *vb* ***syn*** see GET OUT 1
‖**bugs** *adj* **1** ***syn*** see INSANE 1
2 ***syn*** see ENTHUSIASTIC
build *vb* **1** to form or fashion a structure <will *build* either a garage or carport>
syn construct, erect, put up, raise, rear, uprear; *compare* ERECT 3, MAKE 3
rel fabricate, fashion, frame, manufacture; run up, throw up; prefabricate
con demolish, destroy, dismantle, level, pull down, raze, take down, tear down, wreck
2 ***syn*** see MAKE 3
3 ***syn*** see INCREASE 1
4 ***syn*** see INCREASE 2
build (on) *vb* ***syn*** see RELY (on *or* upon)
build *n* ***syn*** see PHYSIQUE
rel conformation
building *n* a usually roofed and walled structure built for permanent use <a *building* with four apartments>
syn fabric, structure; *compare* EDIFICE, HUT
build up *vb* **1** ***syn*** see ERECT 5
2 ***syn*** see PUBLICIZE
buildup *n* ***syn*** see PUBLICITY
‖**built** *adj* **1** ***syn*** see CURVACEOUS
2 ***syn*** see BUXOM
built–in *adj* ***syn*** see INHERENT
bulge *vb* to extend outward beyond the usual or normal line <the box was so full that the sides *bulged*>
syn beetle, jut, overhang, poke, pouch, pout, project, protrude, protuberate, stand out, stick out
rel bag, belly, dilate, distend, expand, swell
bulge *n* **1** ***syn*** see PROJECTION 1
rel bump, lump, swelling
con depression, hollow, pit
2 ***syn*** see ADVANTAGE 3
bulk *n* **1** a body of usually material substance that constitutes a thing or unit <his industry was proven by the *bulk* of his accomplishment> <a great dark *bulk* blocked the alley>
syn mass, volume
rel bigness, greatness, largeness, magnitude, quantity, totality
2 ***syn*** see BODY 4
3 ***syn*** see BODY 5
4 ***syn*** see BODY 3
bulk *vb* ***syn*** see LOOM 3
bull *n* **1** ***syn*** see ERROR 2
‖**2** ***syn*** see NONSENSE 2
‖**3** ***syn*** see POLICEMAN
bull *adj* ***syn*** see LARGE 1
‖**bull band** *n* ***syn*** see SHIVAREE
bulldoze *vb* **1** ***syn*** see INTIMIDATE
rel menace, threaten; harass, harry
2 ***syn*** see PUSH 2

---

syn synonym(s) ***rel*** related word(s)
ant antonym(s) ***con*** contrasted word(s)
idiom idiomatic equivalent(s)
‖ use limited; if in doubt, see a dictionary

bulldozer *n* ***syn*** see BULLY 1
bullet *vb* ***syn*** see HURRY 2
bullfighter *n* one who fights bulls <moved with the grace of an experienced *bullfighter*>
syn matador, toreador, torero
rel banderillero; cuadrillero, picador; cuadrilla
bullheaded *adj* ***syn*** see OBSTINATE
bullwork *n* ***syn*** see WORK 2
bully *n* **1** an insolent, overbearing person who persists in tormenting another <a big *bully* who picked on little kids>
syn browbeater, bulldozer, harasser, harrier, hector, intimidator; *compare* TOUGH
rel annoyer, antagonizer, heckler, persecutor, pest, tease, tormenter
2 ***syn*** see PIMP 1
bully *adj* ***syn*** see EXCELLENT
bully *vb* ***syn*** see INTIMIDATE
rel torment, torture; menace, threaten
ant coax
bullyboy *n* ***syn*** see TOUGH
bullyrag *vb* **1** ***syn*** see INTIMIDATE
2 ***syn*** see BAIT 2
bulwark *n* an aboveground defensive structure that forms part of a fortification <the *bulwarks* were woefully undermanned>
syn bastion, breastwork, parapet, rampart
rel citadel, fort, fortress, stronghold
con bunker, dugout
bulwark *vb* ***syn*** see DEFEND 1
||**bum** *vb* ***syn*** see HUM
bum *vb* ***syn*** see IDLE
bum *n* **1** ***syn*** see VAGABOND
2 ***syn*** see SLUGGARD
||**bum** *adj* ***syn*** see BAD 1
bum *n* ***syn*** see BINGE 1
bumble *vb* ***syn*** see HUM
bumble *vb* **1** ***syn*** see BOTCH
2 ***syn*** see STUMBLE 3
bumbling *adj* ***syn*** see AWKWARD 2
||**bumfuzzle** *vb* ***syn*** see CONFUSE 2
bummel *vb* ***syn*** see SAUNTER
bummer *n* **1** ***syn*** see BEGGAR 1
2 ***syn*** see MARAUDER
3 ***syn*** see FAILURE 5
bumming *n* ***syn*** see MENDICANCY
bump *vb* **1** to meet with or come up against forcibly <the two cars *bumped* with a great crumpling of fenders>
syn clash, collide, ||prang
rel bang, carom, crash, hit, knock, slam, strike; impinge; jar, jolt
idiom whang together
2 ***syn*** see HAPPEN 2
3 ***syn*** see DEGRADE 1
bump *n* **1** ***syn*** see IMPACT 1
2 a swelling of tissue usually resulting from a blow <fell and got a *bump* on his head>
syn bunch, knot, lump, ||pumpknot
rel protuberance, swelling
3 a marked unevenness in a road surface likely to jolt a passing vehicle
syn ||cahot, thank-you-ma'am
rel chuckhole, mudhole, pothole, rut
4 ***syn*** see GIFT 2
bumpkin *n* ***syn*** see RUSTIC
bump off *vb* ***syn*** see MURDER 1
||**bump–off** *n* ***syn*** see MURDER
bunch *n* **1** ***syn*** see BUMP 2
2 ***syn*** see GROUP 3
3 ***syn*** see SET 5
4 ***syn*** see GROUP 1
bunco steerer *n* ***syn*** see SWINDLER
bundle *n* **1** ***syn*** see GROUP 3
2 ***syn*** see FORTUNE 4
bundle up *vb* to dress warmly <*bundle up*, it's cold outside>
syn ||hap, muffle, wrap (up)
rel envelop, mummify, swaddle, swathe
||**bung** *vb* ***syn*** see THROW 1
bung–full *adj* ***syn*** see FULL 1
bungle *vb* ***syn*** see BOTCH
bungle *n* ***syn*** see ERROR 2
bungler *n* ***syn*** see STUMBLEBUM
||**bung up** *vb* ***syn*** see BATTER 1
bunk *vb* ***syn*** see HARBOR 2
||**bunk** *vb* ***syn*** see ESCAPE 1
||**bunk** *n* ***syn*** see NONSENSE 2
||**bunk** *vb* ***syn*** see DECEIVE
bunkum *n* ***syn*** see NONSENSE 2
||**bunkum** *adj* **1** ***syn*** see EXCELLENT
2 ***syn*** see HEALTHY 1
bunny *n* ***syn*** see BEAUTY
rel bimbo
buns *n pl* ***syn*** see BUTTOCKS
Bunyanesque *adj* ***syn*** see HUGE
buoy (up) *vb* ***syn*** see SUPPORT 5
buoyancy *n* ***syn*** see EBULLIENCE
buoyant *adj* ***syn*** see ELASTIC 2
burble *vb* **1** ***syn*** see SLOSH 1
2 ***syn*** see CHAT 1
burden *n* **1** ***syn*** see LOAD 1
2 ***syn*** see LOAD 3
burden *vb* to lay a heavy load on or to lie like a heavy load on a person or thing <*burdened* his men with needless heavy work><I won't *burden* you with this lengthy story>
syn charge, clog, cumber, encumber, lade, load, lumber, saddle, task, tax, weigh, weight
rel overburden, overload, overweigh; handicap; afflict, oppress
idiom bear down on (*or* upon)
con alleviate, ease, lighten, relieve, unload; disburden, disencumber
ant unburden
burden *n* ***syn*** see SUBSTANCE 2
burdensome *adj* ***syn*** see ONEROUS
burdensomely *adv* ***syn*** see HARD 8
bureaucrat *n* a member of a bureaucracy <*bureaucrats* were blamed for the error>
syn mandarin
rel civil servant, functionary, official
burg *n* a small, insignificant, remote town <the *burg* had only two stores and one gas station>
syn hick town, jerkwater town, mudhole, one-horse town, Podunk, tank town, whistle-stop
rel cowtown; crossroads; jumping-off place; hamlet, village

con city, metropolis
burgee *n syn* see FLAG
burgeon *vb* **1** *syn* see INCREASE 2
2 *syn* see BLOSSOM
burghal *adj syn* see URBAN
burgher *n syn* see TOWNSMAN
burglarize *vb* to commit an act of breaking open and entering with a felonious purpose the dwelling house of another by night <that night several homes were *burglarized*>
syn burgle; *compare* HOUSEBREAK, ROB 1
rel knock over, rob; ransack, rifle; screw
burgle *vb syn* see BURGLARIZE
burial *n* **1** *syn* see GRAVE
2 the act or ceremony of burying <his *burial* took place yesterday>
syn entombment, inhumation, interment, sepulture
rel burying, exequies, funeral, obsequies; deposition; deep six
con disinterment, exhumation
burial ground *n syn* see CEMETERY
buried *adj syn* see ULTERIOR
burke *vb* **1** *syn* see SUPPRESS 3
2 *syn* see SKIRT 3
burlesque *n* **1** *syn* see MOCKERY 2
2 *syn* see CARICATURE 2
burlesque *vb syn* see MIMIC
burly *adj syn* see HUSKY 1
||**burn** *n syn* see CREEK 2
burn *vb* **1** *syn* see SHINE 1
2 to undergo combustion <the wood is too green to *burn*>
syn combust
rel fire, flame, ignite, incinerate, kindle, light; consume, use; smolder, sputter
3 to be hot as if on fire <sand *burning* in the blazing sun>
syn bake, broil, cook, melt, roast, scorch, swelter
rel parch, toast, warm; char
con chill, cool, freeze
4 *syn* see ANGER 2
5 *syn* see SMART
6 *syn* see FIRE 6
||**7** *syn* see CHEAT
burn (up) *vb syn* see IRRITATE
burnable *adj syn* see COMBUSTIBLE 1
burning *adj* **1** on fire <the *burning* house>
syn ablaze, afire, aflame, alight, blazing, conflagrant, fiery, flaming, flaring, ignited, lighted
rel aglow, glowing, incandescent
idiom in flames
con burned-out, cold
2 *syn* see HOT 1
ant icy
3 *syn* see FEVERISH 2
4 *syn* see IMPASSIONED
5 *syn* see PRESSING
burnish *vb syn* see POLISH 1
burnished *adj syn* see LUSTROUS 1
burn off *vb syn* see CLEAR 9
burnsides *n pl syn* see SIDE-WHISKERS
burp *vb syn* see BELCH 1
burro *n syn* see DONKEY 1
burrow *n* **1** *syn* see LAIR 1
2 *syn* see HOVEL
burrow *vb syn* see SNUGGLE
burst *vb* **1** *syn* see EXPLODE 1
2 *syn* see SHATTER 1
3 *syn* see PLUNGE 2
burst (forth) *vb syn* see ERUPT 2
burst *n* **1** *syn* see OUTBREAK 1
2 *syn* see OUTBURST 1
3 *syn* see BANG 2
4 *syn* see BARRAGE
bury *vb* **1** to deposit (a corpse) in or as if in the earth <the pharaohs were *buried* in pyramids> <*buried* at sea>
syn entomb, inhume, inter, lay away, plant, put away, sepulcher, sepulture, tomb; *compare* ENTOMB 1
rel inurn; coffin
idiom consign to the grave, lay to rest, put six feet under
con dig (up), disentomb, disinter, exhume, untomb; burn, cremate
2 *syn* see HIDE
burying ground *n syn* see CEMETERY
||**bus** *n syn* see CAR
bush *n syn* see FRONTIER 2
bush *adj syn* see MINOR 2
bush–league *adj syn* see MINOR 2
||**bush up** *vb syn* see HIDE
bushwa *n syn* see NONSENSE 2
business *n* **1** *syn* see FUNCTION 1
2 *syn* see PATRONAGE 2
3 *syn* see WORK 1
4 activity concerned with the supplying and distribution of commodities <the lumber *business* depends heavily on the housing *business*>
syn commerce, industry, trade, traffic
5 *syn* see ENTERPRISE 3
6 *syn* see AFFAIR 1
7 *syn* see DOODAD
8 something personal to oneself <that is none of your *business*>
syn affair, concern, lookout, occasions, palaver
businessman *n syn* see MERCHANT
buss *vb syn* see KISS 1
bust *vb* **1** *syn* see RUIN 3
2 *syn* see DEGRADE 1
ant promote
3 *syn* see FAIL 5
||**4** *syn* see ARREST 2
bust *n* ||**1** *syn* see CUFF
2 *syn* see FAILURE 5
3 *syn* see BINGE 1
4 *syn* see RAID 2
||**5** *syn* see ARREST
||**busthead** *n syn* see MOONSHINE 2
bustle *vb syn* see HURRY 2
bustle *n* **1** *syn* see STIR 1

---

syn synonym(s) *rel* related word(s)
ant antonym(s) *con* contrasted word(s)
idiom idiomatic equivalent(s)
|| use limited; if in doubt, see a dictionary

2 ***syn*** see COMMOTION 4
bustling *adj* full of activity <a *bustling* frontier town>
syn busy, fussy, hopping, humming, hustling, lively, popping
rel active, brisk, energetic
idiom on its way, on the go (*or* move), up and doing
busty *adj* ***syn*** see BUXOM
busy *adj* **1** engaged in activity <I can't stop to talk. I'm *busy*>
syn employed, engaged, occupied, working; *compare* ASSIDUOUS
idiom at work, on the fly
con idle, inactive
ant free
2 ***syn*** see BUSTLING
3 ***syn*** see IMPERTINENT 2
busy *vb* ***syn*** see ENGAGE 4
busybody *n* one who concerns himself with affairs not his own <a meddlesome *busybody* who saw all and tattled all she saw>
syn butt-in, ‖buttinsky, intermeddler, kibitzer, meddler, Meddlesome Mattie, nose, nosey Parker, Paul Pry, polypragmatist, pragmatic, pragmatist, prier (*or* pryer), quidnunc, rubber, rubberneck, snoop, ‖stickybeak; *compare* GOSSIP 1, INFORMER
rel gossip, gossipmonger, newsmonger, rumormonger, scandalmonger, tabby, talebearer, telltale
idiom curiosity shop, question box
busybody *vb* **1** ***syn*** see SNOOP
2 ***syn*** see MEDDLE
but *conj* **1** ***syn*** see ONLY
2 ***syn*** see EXCEPT 1
but *prep* ***syn*** see EXCEPT
but *adv* **1** ***syn*** see ONLY 1
2 ***syn*** see JUST 3
butcher *vb* **1** ***syn*** see SLAUGHTER 1
2 ***syn*** see SLAUGHTER 2
butchery *n* ***syn*** see MASSACRE
butt *n* **1** ***syn*** see TARGET 1
2 ***syn*** see LAUGHINGSTOCK
3 ***syn*** see FOOL 3
butt (on *or* against) *vb* ***syn*** see ADJOIN
‖**butt** *n* **1** ***syn*** see BUTTOCKS
2 ***syn*** see CIGARETTE
butt *n* ***syn*** see CASK
butterball *n* ***syn*** see FATTY
butt in *vb* **1** ***syn*** see INTRUDE 1
con abstain, forbear, restrain
2 ***syn*** see MEDDLE
butt-in *n* ***syn*** see BUSYBODY
‖**buttinsky** *n* ***syn*** see BUSYBODY
buttocks *n pl* the part of the back on which a person sits <gave the boy a whack across the *buttocks*>
syn backside, beam, behind, bottom, breech, buns, ‖butt, ‖can, cheeks, derriere, ‖duff, fanny, fundament, hams, haunches, heinie (*or* hiney), hind end, ‖hinder, hunkers, ‖keister, nates, podex, posterior, rear, rear end, rump, seat, ‖stern, tail, tail end, ‖tokus
idiom seat of one's pants
button-down *adj* ***syn*** see CONVENTIONAL 1
buttress *n* ***syn*** see SUPPORT 3
buttress *vb* ***syn*** see SUPPORT 4
buvette *n* ***syn*** see BAR 4
buxom *adj* having an amply developed bosom <a *buxom* young woman>
syn bosomy, ‖built, busty, chesty, full-bosomed, ‖stacked; *compare* CURVACEOUS
rel full-figured, Junoesque, shapely, well-developed, well-proportioned
buy *vb* **1** to acquire something for money or the equivalent <*bought* a new car>
syn purchase, take
rel acquire, get, obtain, procure
ant sell
2 ***syn*** see RANSOM
3 ***syn*** see BRIBE
‖**4** ***syn*** see BELIEVE 1
buy *n* ***syn*** see BARGAIN 1
buyable *adj* ***syn*** see VENAL 1
buyer *n* ***syn*** see PURCHASER
buy off *vb* ***syn*** see BRIBE
buzz *vb* **1** ***syn*** see HUM
2 ***syn*** see HISS
‖**3** ***syn*** see TELEPHONE
buzz *n* ***syn*** see REPORT 1
‖**buzzed** *adj* ***syn*** see INTOXICATED 1
buzz off *vb* ***syn*** see GET OUT 1
by *prep* **1** ***syn*** see BESIDE 1
2 ***syn*** see NEAR 2
3 ***syn*** see VIA 1
4 ***syn*** see VIA 2
5 with reference to <sorted *by* color>
syn according to, as to
by *adv* ***syn*** see OVER 5
by *interj* ***syn*** see GOOD-BYE
by all odds *adv* ***syn*** see FAR AND AWAY
by a long shot *adv* ***syn*** see FAR AND AWAY
by and by *adv* **1** ***syn*** see AFTER
2 ***syn*** see PRESENTLY 1
by-and-by *n* ***syn*** see FUTURE
by and large *adv* ***syn*** see ALTOGETHER 3
by-blow *n* ***syn*** see BASTARD 1
by dint of *prep* ***syn*** see VIA 2
bye-bye *interj* ***syn*** see GOOD-BYE
by far *adv* ***syn*** see FAR AND AWAY
bygone *adj* **1** ***syn*** see FORMER 2
2 ***syn*** see OLD-FASHIONED
3 ***syn*** see EXTINCT 2
by long odds *adv* ***syn*** see FAR AND AWAY
by means of *prep* ***syn*** see VIA 2
byname *n* ***syn*** see NICKNAME
by odds *adv* ***syn*** see FAR AND AWAY
by ordinary *adv* ***syn*** see USUALLY 2
bypass *vb* **1** ***syn*** see SKIRT 2
2 ***syn*** see SKIRT 3
byplace *n* ***syn*** see NOOK
by-product *n* ***syn*** see OUTGROWTH 2
by-sitter *n* ***syn*** see SPECTATOR
bystander *n* ***syn*** see SPECTATOR
by stealth *adv* ***syn*** see SECRETLY
by-talk *n* ***syn*** see SMALL TALK
by the bye *adv* ***syn*** see INCIDENTALLY 2

by the way *adv* ***syn*** see INCIDENTALLY 2
by–the–way *adj* ***syn*** see INDIFFERENT 2
by virtue of *prep* ***syn*** see VIA 2
by way of *prep* **1** ***syn*** see VIA 1
2 ***syn*** see VIA 2

byword *n* **1** ***syn*** see SAYING
2 ***syn*** see CATCHWORD
3 ***syn*** see NICKNAME
Byzantine *adj* ***syn*** see COMPLEX 2

syn synonym(s)
rel related word(s)
ant antonym(s)
con contrasted word(s)
idiom idiomatic equivalent(s)
‖ use limited; if in doubt, see a dictionary

C

cab *n* ***syn*** see TAXICAB
||**cab** *n* ***syn*** see CRUD
cabal *n* **1** ***syn*** see CLIQUE
2 ***syn*** see PLOT 2
cabalistic *adj* ***syn*** see MYSTERIOUS
cabaret *n* ***syn*** see NIGHTCLUB
||**cabbage** *n* ***syn*** see MONEY
cabbage *vb* ***syn*** see STEAL 1
cabbagehead *n* ***syn*** see DUNCE
cabin *n* ***syn*** see HUT
||**caboose** *n* ***syn*** see HUT
||**caboose** *n* ***syn*** see JAIL
||**ca' canny** *n* ***syn*** see SLOWDOWN 2
cache *vb* ***syn*** see HIDE
con discover, unearth
cachet *n* ***syn*** see STATUS 2
||**cack** *vb* ***syn*** see VOMIT
cackle *vb* ***syn*** see CHAT 1
cackle *n* ***syn*** see CHATTER
cacophonic *adj* ***syn*** see DISSONANT 1
cacophonous *adj* ***syn*** see DISSONANT 1
cad *n* a person without gentlemanly instincts <gloated over his rival's distress like the *cad* that he was>
syn bounder, cur, rotter, yellow dog
rel boor, churl, clown, lout; guttersnipe, mucker, vulgarian; ||creep; bastard, heel, louse, rat, stinker
idiom Jack Nasty
ant gentleman
cadaver *n* ***syn*** see CORPSE
cadaverous *adj* **1** ***syn*** see GHASTLY 2
2 ***syn*** see EMACIATED
rel careworn, haggard, pinched, worn
cadence *n* ***syn*** see RHYTHM
rel accent, accentuation, emphasis, stress; pulsation, pulse, throb
cadency *n* ***syn*** see RHYTHM
||**cadet** *n* ***syn*** see PIMP 1
cadger *n* ***syn*** see BEGGAR 1
cadging *n* ***syn*** see MENDICANCY
caducity *n* ***syn*** see OLD AGE
rel dotage, dotingness, second childhood
café *n* **1** ***syn*** see EATING HOUSE
2 ***syn*** see NIGHTCLUB
||**caff** *n* ***syn*** see EATING HOUSE
cage *vb* ***syn*** see ENCLOSE 1
rel imprison, incarcerate, jail
cagey *adj* ***syn*** see SHREWD
cageyness *n* ***syn*** see CUNNING 2
cahoots *n pl* ***syn*** see ASSOCIATION 1
||**cahot** *n* ***syn*** see BUMP 3
cajole *vb* ***syn*** see COAX
rel beguile, deceive, delude; tantalize; crowd, push
cake *vb* **1** to cover with a surface layer <the floor was *caked* with filth>
syn crust, encrust (*or* incrust), incrustate, rime
rel besmear, coat, smear, spread; cover, daub
2 ***syn*** see HARDEN 1
rel compress, condense, contract, shrink
cakewalk *n* ***syn*** see RUNAWAY
||**calaboose** *n* ***syn*** see JAIL
calamitous *adj* **1** ***syn*** see FATAL 2
2 ***syn*** see DEPLORABLE
calamity *n* ***syn*** see DISASTER
rel collapse, ruin, wreck; affliction, cross, trial, tribulation, visitation
con fortune, luck; benefaction; favor, gift
ant boon
calamity howler *n* ***syn*** see PESSIMIST
calculate *vb* to determine or approximate a mathematical value (as speed, cost, or quantity) <*calculate* the cost of a new car>
syn cipher, compute, estimate, figure, reckon
rel consider, study, weigh; ascertain, determine, discover; appraise, evaluate, price, value; assess, prize, rate
con conjecture, guess, surmise
calculate (on *or* upon) *vb* ***syn*** see RELY (on *or* upon)
calculating *adj* ***syn*** see CAUTIOUS
rel artful, crafty, cunning, guileful, sly, wily
con improvident, imprudent, indiscreet
ant rash, reckless
calculation *n* ***syn*** see COMPUTATION
calembour *n* ***syn*** see PUN
calendar *n* ***syn*** see PROGRAM 1
calenture *n* ***syn*** see PASSION 6
caliber *n* **1** ***syn*** see QUALITY 2
rel ability, capability, capacity; force, power
2 ***syn*** see QUALITY 3
caliginous *adj* ***syn*** see DARK 1
call *vb* **1** to speak or utter in a loud distinct carrying voice <*call* for help>
syn cry, hallo, holler, hollo, shout, vociferate, yell; *compare* SHOUT 1
rel bawl, bellow, hoot, howl, roar, scream, screech, shriek, shrill, whoop, yowl
con murmur, whisper
2 ***syn*** see DEMAND 1
3 ***syn*** see SUMMON 2
rel assemble, collect, gather, round up; bid, invite
4 ***syn*** see CONVOKE
5 ***syn*** see TELEPHONE
6 ***syn*** see NAME 1
7 ***syn*** see PREDICT 2
8 ***syn*** see ESTIMATE 3
9 ***syn*** see FORETELL
10 ***syn*** see VISIT 2
call (for) *vb* ***syn*** see DEMAND 2
call (to) *vb* ***syn*** see ADDRESS 7
call *n* **1** the natural vocal sound of an animal and especially a bird <the clear *call* of a bellbird>
syn cry, note, song

rel cheep, chirp, peep, twitter, warble
2 ***syn*** see ATTRACTION 1
3 ***syn*** see OCCASION 3
4 ***syn*** see VISIT 1

call down *vb* ***syn*** see REPROVE

caller *n* ***syn*** see VISITOR 1

‖callet *n* ***syn*** see PROSTITUTE

call girl *n* ***syn*** see PROSTITUTE

call house *n* ***syn*** see BROTHEL

calligraphy *n* ***syn*** see HANDWRITING

call in *vb* ***syn*** see SUMMON 2

calling *n* **1** ***syn*** see MISSION
2 ***syn*** see TRADE 1
3 ***syn*** see WORK 1

‖callithump *n* ***syn*** see SHIVAREE

call off *vb* ***syn*** see CANCEL 2

callous *adj* ***syn*** see UNFEELING 2
rel indurated, set

callow *adj* **1** ***syn*** see YOUNG 1
2 ***syn*** see INEXPERIENCED

callowness *n* ***syn*** see INEXPERIENCE

call up *vb* to summon for active military duty <*called up* the army reserves>
syn order up; *compare* DRAFT 1
rel mobilize
idiom call to the colors
ant discharge, muster out

calm *n* ***syn*** see QUIET 1

calm *adj* **1** free from storm or rough activity <the wind died and the sea became *calm*>
syn halcyon, hushed, placid, quiet, still, stilly, untroubled
rel inactive, quiescent, reposing, resting; pacific, smooth, tranquil, unruffled
idiom calm as a millpond, still as death
con agitated, disturbed, perturbed, restless, turbulent, uneasy
ant stormy
2 free from mental or emotional distress or agitation <a man who remained *calm* under stress>
syn collected, composed, easy, easygoing, placid, poised, possessed, self-composed, self-possessed, serene, tranquil
rel cool, imperturbable, laid-back, nonchalant, unflappable, unruffled; even-tempered, impassive, phlegmatic, steady; firm, stable, staunch
con discomposed, disturbed, perturbed, upset; anxious, bothered, confused, nervous; fidgety, jittery, jumpy, shaky, tense
ant agitated

calm *vb* to relieve from or bring to an end whatever distresses, agitates, or disturbs <that inner faith that *calms* the troubled spirit>
syn allay, balm, becalm, compose, lull, quiet, ‖quieten, settle, soothe, ‖soother, still, tranquilize
rel alleviate, assuage, mitigate, relieve; appease, mollify, pacify, placate; relax, steady
con bother, discompose, disquiet, disturb, flurry, perturb, stir up, upset
ant agitate; arouse

calmant *n* ***syn*** see SEDATIVE

calmative *n* ***syn*** see SEDATIVE

calmness *n* ***syn*** see EQUANIMITY

calumniate *vb* ***syn*** see MALIGN
ant eulogize; vindicate

calumnious *adj* ***syn*** see LIBELOUS

calumny *n* ***syn*** see DETRACTION
rel animadversion, reflection, stricture
con encomium, panegyric, tribute; adulation, compliment, flattery
ant eulogy; vindication

calvary *n* ***syn*** see TRIAL 1

‖cam *adv* ***syn*** see AWRY 1

camaraderie *n* a spirit of friendly goodwill typical of comrades <the easy *camaraderie* of a cozy neighborhood bar>
syn comradery, good-fellowship
rel affability, friendliness, gregariousness, sociability; cheer, conviviality, jollity
con aloofness, coldness, frigidity, inaccessibility, reclusiveness, remoteness, self-containment; exclusiveness, self-sufficiency, unsociability

camarilla *n* ***syn*** see CLIQUE

cameraman *n* ***syn*** see PHOTOGRAPHER

camerist *n* ***syn*** see PHOTOGRAPHER

camouflage *vb* ***syn*** see DISGUISE
rel becloud, befog, dim

camp *n* **1** a place where a number of people (as vacationers or soldiers) live temporarily together in usually more or less casual housing <planned to summer at a fishing *camp* in Maine>
syn campground, encampment
2 ***syn*** see CLIQUE
3 ***syn*** see HUT

camp *vb* to live temporarily in a camp or the outdoors <*camped* under the trees for the night>
syn bivouac, ‖bivvy, encamp, ‖laager, ‖maroon, tent
idiom rough it
con decamp

campanile *n* ***syn*** see BELL TOWER

camper *n* ***syn*** see TRAILER

campestral *adj* ***syn*** see RURAL

camp follower *n* ***syn*** see PROSTITUTE

campground *n* ***syn*** see CAMP 1

‖cample *vb* ***syn*** see SCOLD 1

‖can *n* **1** ***syn*** see JAIL
2 ***syn*** see TOILET
3 ***syn*** see BUTTOCKS

‖can *vb* ***syn*** see DISMISS 3

Canaan *n* ***syn*** see HEAVEN 2

canaille *n* ***syn*** see RABBLE 2

canal *n* ***syn*** see CHANNEL 1

canard *n* ***syn*** see LIE
rel hoax, humbug, mare's nest, sell, spoof; artifice, dodge, trick

‖canary *n* ***syn*** see INFORMER

cancel *vb* **1** ***syn*** see ERASE
2 to give up something previously arranged or agreed on <decided to *cancel* his appointment with the dentist>
syn abort, call off, drop, scrub

---

syn synonym(s) ***rel*** related word(s)
ant antonym(s) ***con*** contrasted word(s)
idiom idiomatic equivalent(s)
‖ use limited; if in doubt, see a dictionary

THESAURUS

rel end, terminate; annul, invalidate, rescind, revoke; give up, relinquish, surrender

cancel (out) *vb* ***syn*** see NEUTRALIZE

candid *adj* **1** ***syn*** see FAIR 4

rel aboveboard, forthright, straightforward; honest, scrupulous, upright

2 ***syn*** see FRANK

ant evasive

candidate *n* one who seeks an office, honor, position, or award <examining *candidates* for editorial positions>

syn applicant, aspirant, hopeful, seeker

rel nominee; dark horse; also-ran, has-been; campaigner, electioneerer, stumper, whistle-stopper

candy *vb* ***syn*** see SUGARCOAT 1

canine *n* ***syn*** see DOG 1

canker *vb* ***syn*** see DEBASE 1

cankered *adj* ***syn*** see CANTANKEROUS

cannabis *n* ***syn*** see MARIJUANA

canned *adj* **1** ***syn*** see CONDENSED

‖**2** ***syn*** see INTOXICATED 1

cannibalic *adj* ***syn*** see FIERCE 1

canniness *n* **1** ***syn*** see PRUDENCE 1

2 ***syn*** see CUNNING 2

‖**cannon** *n* ***syn*** see PICKPOCKET

cannonade *n* ***syn*** see BARRAGE

cannonade *vb* ***syn*** see BOMBARD

canny *adj* **1** ***syn*** see CLEVER 4

2 ***syn*** see SPARING

3 ***syn*** see WISE 4

canon *n* **1** ***syn*** see LAW 1

2 ***syn*** see DOCTRINE

canonical *adj* ***syn*** see ORTHODOX 1

‖**cant** *adj* ***syn*** see LIVELY 1

cant *vb* ***syn*** see SLANT 1

cant *n* **1** ***syn*** see DIALECT 2

rel diction, language, phraseology, vocabulary; idiom, speech

2 ***syn*** see TERMINOLOGY

3 ***syn*** see HYPOCRISY

cantankerous *adj* habitually ill-humored, irritable, and disagreeable <one of our more *cantankerous* fellow workers>

syn bearish, cankered, cranky, cross-grained, crotchety, ornery, rantankerous, vinegarish, vinegary, waspish, waspy; *compare* IRASCIBLE, IRRITABLE

rel dour, morose, sour; crabbed, cross, crusty, huffy, petulant, prickly, snappish; dyspeptic, ill-conditioned, ill-natured; liverish

idiom like a bear with a sore paw

con benign, kindly, mellow, mild; amiable, congenial, friendly, pleasant, well-disposed; benevolent, gracious, kind

canter *n* ***syn*** see VAGABOND

cantina *n* ***syn*** see BAR 5

canting *adj* ***syn*** see HYPOCRITICAL

canton *vb* ***syn*** see BILLET 1

‖**canty** *adj* ***syn*** see LIVELY 1

canvass *vb* **1** ***syn*** see SCRUTINIZE 1

2 ***syn*** see DISCUSS 1

3 ***syn*** see SOLICIT 1

cap *vb* **1** ***syn*** see SURMOUNT 3

‖**2** ***syn*** see PUZZLE

3 ***syn*** see COVER 3

4 ***syn*** see SURPASS 1

5 ***syn*** see CLIMAX

capability *n* **1** ***syn*** see ABILITY 1

rel art, craft, cunning, skill

con inability, disability

ant incapability, incompetence

2 ***syn*** see EFFICACY 1

capable *adj* ***syn*** see ABLE

ant incapable

capacious *adj* ***syn*** see SPACIOUS

rel dilatable, distensible, expandable, expansive, extensile; abundant, copious, plentiful

ant exiguous

capacity *n* **1** ***syn*** see ABILITY 1

rel bent, faculty, gift, knack, talent, twin; caliber, stature

con impotence, ineffectiveness, powerlessness

ant incapacity

2 ***syn*** see STATUS 1

cape *n* ***syn*** see PROMONTORY

caper *vb* ***syn*** see GAMBOL

idiom cut capers

caper *n* **1** ***syn*** see ESCAPADE

2 ***syn*** see PRANK

rel devilment, impishness, mischief, roguery, waggishness

‖**capernoited** *adj* ***syn*** see INTOXICATED 1

capital *adj* **1** ***syn*** see EGREGIOUS

2 ***syn*** see CHIEF 2

rel cardinal, essential, vital; basic, fundamental, underlying

3 ***syn*** see EXCELLENT

capital *n* ***syn*** see MEAN 3

capitalize *vb* to supply capital for or to <agreed to *capitalize* the venture>

syn back, bankroll, finance, grubstake, stake

rel aid, assist, help, subsidize, support; fund; promote, sponsor

capitulate *vb* ***syn*** see YIELD 2

capitulation *n* ***syn*** see SURRENDER

capper *n* ***syn*** see DECOY 2

caprice *n* an arbitrary, impulsive, and often illogical notion or change of mind <given to sudden *caprices* and random fancies>

syn bee, boutade, conceit, crank, crotchet, fancy, freak, humor, maggot, megrim, notion, vagary, whigmaleerie, whim, whimsy

rel mood, temper, vein; contrariety, inconsistency, perversity; characteristic, foible, habit, mannerism, peculiarity, trait, trick

capricious *adj* **1** ***syn*** see ARBITRARY 1

2 ***syn*** see INCONSTANT 1

rel humorsome, moody; effervescent

con constant, steady

ant steadfast

3 ***syn*** see UNCERTAIN 1

capsheaf *n* ***syn*** see APEX 2

capstone *n* ***syn*** see APEX 2

capsule *adj* ***syn*** see CONDENSED

caption *n* an explanatory or identifying comment accompanying a pictorial illustration <the *captions* were under the wrong figures>

syn legend, underline

captious *adj* ***syn*** see CRITICAL 1
rel demanding, exacting, finicky; contrary, perverse; irritable, peevish, petulant, snappish, snappy, testy
con judicious, sensible, wise; rational, reasonable; knowing, knowledgeable
ant appreciative

captivate *vb* ***syn*** see ATTRACT 1
rel delight, gratify, please; enthrall, grip, hold, mesmerize, spellbind
ant repulse

captivated *adj* ***syn*** see ENAMORED 3

captivating *adj* ***syn*** see ATTRACTIVE 1

capture *vb* ***syn*** see CATCH 1

Capuan *adj* ***syn*** see LUXURIOUS 3

car *n* a usually private passenger-carrying automotive vehicle <drove a shabby old *car*>
syn auto, autocar, automobile, buggy, ‖bus, machine, motor, motorcar
rel beach wagon, coach, compact, convertible, coupe, fastback, hardtop, hatchback, limousine, notchback, phaeton, roadster, runabout, sedan, station wagon, subcompact, touring car; ‖clunker, ‖crate, ‖heap, ‖jalopy, junker, ‖wreck

‖**caravan** *n* ***syn*** see TRAILER

caravansary *n* ***syn*** see HOTEL

carbon *n* ***syn*** see REPRODUCTION

carbon copy *n* ***syn*** see REPRODUCTION

carbuncle *n* ***syn*** see ABSCESS

carcass *n* ***syn*** see CORPSE

‖**carcel** *n* ***syn*** see JAIL

card *n* **1** ***syn*** see WAG 1
2 ***syn*** see PROGRAM 1
3 ***syn*** see MENU

card *vb* ***syn*** see SCHEDULE 1

cardboard *adj* ***syn*** see STIFF 4
rel unlifelike, unreal, unrealistic

cardinal *adj* **1** ***syn*** see ESSENTIAL 2
2 ***syn*** see CENTRAL 1

care *n* **1** ***syn*** see SORROW
rel strain, stress, tension
2 a burdened or disquieted state of mind <a mind full of *care* and sadness>
syn anxiety, concern, concernment, disquiet, disquietude, solicitude, unease, uneasiness, worry
rel apprehension, foreboding, misgiving, suspense; agitation, disturbance, perturbation; alarm, consternation, dismay, fear
con calm, ease, peace, quietude; assurance, comfort, easiness
3 ***syn*** see TRIAL 2
4 serious and heedful attentiveness <attended his words with *care*>
syn carefulness, concern, consciousness, heed, heedfulness, regard; *compare* ATTENTION 1
rel curiosity; enthusiasm, interest; consideration, solicitude, thoughtfulness; effort, exertion, pains, trouble; alertness, vigilance, watchfulness
con carelessness, disregard, heedlessness, unconcern; boredom, disinterest, ennui
5 ***syn*** see OVERSIGHT 1
6 ***syn*** see CUSTODY

care (for) *vb* **1** ***syn*** see TEND 2
2 ***syn*** see MINISTER (to)
idiom take care of

careen *vb* ***syn*** see LURCH 2

career *vb* ***syn*** see COURSE

carefree *adj* **1** ***syn*** see HAPPY-GO-LUCKY
2 ***syn*** see IRRESPONSIBLE

careful *adj* **1** ***syn*** see CAUTIOUS
rel attentive, heedful, observant
2 closely attentive to details or showing such attention <*careful* workmanship>
syn conscientious, conscionable, exact, fussy, heedful, meticulous, painstaking, punctilious, punctual, scrupulous
rel accurate, nice, precise; deliberate, studied; foresighted, provident, prudent; critical, discriminating, finical, finicky; observant, particular, religious; duteous, dutiful, intent
con disorderly, lax, negligent, slack, slipshod, slovenly; heedless, neglectful, remiss
ant careless

carefulness *n* ***syn*** see CARE 4

careless *adj* **1** lacking in or showing lack of care and attention <*careless* of the harm his neglect might do to others> <unwilling to accept such *careless* shoddy work>
syn feckless, heedless, inadvertent, irreflective, thoughtless, uncaring, unheeding, unrecking, unreflective, unthinking; *compare* INCAUTIOUS, RASH 1
rel forgetful, inattentive, oblivious, unmindful; lax, neglectful, negligent, slack, unconcerned, uninterested; inadequate, incapable, unfit, unqualified
con careful, heedful, thoughtful; concerned, considerate, punctilious, scrupulous
ant careful
2 ***syn*** see IRRESPONSIBLE
3 ***syn*** see NEGLIGENT
4 ***syn*** see SLIPSHOD 3
5 ***syn*** see SLOVENLY 1

caress *vb* to express interest, affection, or love by touching or handling <*caress* a frightened child>
syn cosset, cuddle, dandle, fondle, love, pet
rel cocker, coddle, indulge, pamper; coquet, dally, flirt, toy, trifle; nuzzle, pat, stroke

careworn *adj* ***syn*** see HAGGARD
rel distressed, troubled; exhausted, fagged, jaded, tuckered
ant carefree

cargo *n* ***syn*** see LOAD 1

caricature *n* **1** ***syn*** see MOCKERY 2
2 a grotesque or bizarre imitation <a doting attentiveness that was a sickly *caricature* of motherhood>
syn burlesque, parody, takeoff, travesty

---

syn synonym(s) ***rel*** related word(s)
ant antonym(s) ***con*** contrasted word(s)
idiom idiomatic equivalent(s)
‖ use limited; if in doubt, see a dictionary

rel lampoon, libel, pasquinade; laughingstock, mockery; cheat, fake, imitation, phony, sham; bosh, bunk, gammon, hokum, moonshine; clinquant, pinchbeck, shoddy, tinsel

carillon *n* ***syn*** see BELL TOWER

caritas *n* ***syn*** see MERCY

cark *vb* **1** ***syn*** see TROUBLE 1
2 ***syn*** see WORRY 3

carnage *n* ***syn*** see MASSACRE

carnal *adj* **1** ***syn*** see BODILY
rel material, substantial; earthly, earthy
2 characterized by physical rather than intellectual or spiritual day-to-day <giving too much heed to the *carnal* aspects of day-to-day life>
syn animal, fleshly, sensual; *compare* SENSUOUS
rel bodily, corporal, corporeal, physical; coarse, gross, obscene, vulgar; earthly, earthy, mundane, temporal, worldly; lascivious, lewd, lustful, wanton; Pandemic, sensuous
con ethical, moral, noble, righteous, virtuous; aerial, ethereal, otherworldly, supernal; chaste, decent, modest, pure
ant spiritual; intellectual

carnality *n* ***syn*** see ANIMALITY

carom *vb* ***syn*** see GLANCE 1

carousal *n* ***syn*** see BINGE 1

carouse *n* ***syn*** see BINGE 1

carouse *vb* ***syn*** see REVEL 1

carp (at) *vb* ***syn*** see NAG

carper *n* ***syn*** see CRITIC

‖**carpet** *vb* ***syn*** see SCOLD 1
idiom call on the carpet, take to task

carpet knight *n* ***syn*** see HEDONIST

carping *adj* ***syn*** see CRITICAL 1
rel blaming, criticizing, reprehending, reprobating; jawing, railing, upbraiding; blameful, condemnatory, damnatory, objurgatory, reproachful, reprobatory
con applauding, commendatory, complimentary; approving, endorsing; extolling, laudatory, praiseful
ant fulsome

carriage *n* **1** ***syn*** see TRANSPORTATION 1
2 ***syn*** see POSTURE 1

carriageable *adj* ***syn*** see PORTABLE

carriage trade *n* ***syn*** see ARISTOCRACY

carrier *n* **1** ***syn*** see BEARER 2
2 ***syn*** see MESSENGER
3 ***syn*** see VECTOR

carrot *n* ***syn*** see REWARD

carry *vb* **1** to be the agent or means by which someone or something is shifted from one place to another <*carried* the child on his shoulder>
syn bear, buck, convey, ferry, ‖hump, ‖jag, lug, pack, tote, transport
rel bring, fetch, take; move, remove, shift, transfer; send, transmit
‖**2** ***syn*** see ACCOMPANY
3 ***syn*** see AFFECT
4 ***syn*** see BEAR 3
5 ***syn*** see CONDUCT 4
6 ***syn*** see BEHAVE 1
7 ***syn*** see SUPPORT 4
8 ***syn*** see STOCK

carrying *n* ***syn*** see TRANSPORTATION 1

carry off *vb* ***syn*** see KILL 1

carry on *vb* **1** ***syn*** see CONDUCT 3
2 ***syn*** see CUT UP 2
3 ***syn*** see PERSEVERE

carry out *vb* **1** ***syn*** see ADMINISTER 1
rel complete, finalize; discharge, effect, effectuate, fulfill; prosecute, transact
idiom put in force (*or* into effect); sign, seal, and deliver
2 ***syn*** see EFFECT 2

carrytale *n* ***syn*** see GOSSIP 1

carry through *vb* **1** ***syn*** see EFFECT 2
2 ***syn*** see CONTINUE 1

carte blanche *n* full discretionary power <was given *carte blanche* to build, landscape, and furnish the house>
syn blank check, free hand
rel license, prerogative, right; authority, power; say, say-so
idiom power of attorney

carte d'entrée *n* ***syn*** see TICKET 2

carte du jour *n* ***syn*** see MENU

cartel *n* **1** ***syn*** see DEFIANCE 1
rel gage, gauntlet, glove; blow, slap
2 ***syn*** see SYNDICATE
rel corporation; multinational; consortium, merger

carve *vb* **1** ***syn*** see CUT 5
2 ***syn*** see SCULPTURE

Casanova *n* **1** ***syn*** see GALLANT 2
2 ***syn*** see WOLF

cascade *n* ***syn*** see WATERFALL

‖**cascade** *vb* ***syn*** see VOMIT

case *n* **1** ***syn*** see EVENT 4
2 ***syn*** see ORDER 9
3 ***syn*** see SUIT 1
4 ***syn*** see INSTANCE
rel circumstance, episode, event, incident, occurrence; condition, situation, state
5 ***syn*** see ECCENTRIC

case *n* ***syn*** see HULL

‖**case** *vb* ***syn*** see SCRUTINIZE 1

case history *n* ***syn*** see INSTANCE

cash *n* ***syn*** see MONEY

cashier *vb* **1** ***syn*** see DISMISS 3
rel eject, expel, oust; bar, eliminate, exclude; pass over, shelve
con appoint, designate, elect, name; employ, engage, hire
2 ***syn*** see DISCARD

cash in *vb* ***syn*** see DIE 1

cask *n* a vessel made of staves, headings, and hoops <a *cask* of cider>
syn barrel, butt, hogshead, keg, pipe, tun

Cassandra *n* ***syn*** see PESSIMIST

cassock *n* ***syn*** see CLERGYMAN

cast *vb* **1** ***syn*** see THROW 1
rel broadcast, disperse, distribute, scatter
2 ***syn*** see DIRECT 2
3 ***syn*** see DISCARD
rel abandon, leave, relinquish, surrender, yield; dismiss, drop
‖**4** ***syn*** see VOMIT

5 ***syn*** see ADD 2
6 ***syn*** see PLAN 2
cast *n* **1** ***syn*** see LOOK 2
2 ***syn*** see PREDICTION
3 ***syn*** see COLOR 1
4 ***syn*** see HINT 2
5 ***syn*** see TYPE
6 ***syn*** see FORM 1
cast about *vb* ***syn*** see SEEK 1
cast away *vb* **1** ***syn*** see WASTE 2
2 ***syn*** see SHIPWRECK 1
castaway *n* ***syn*** see OUTCAST
cast down *vb* ***syn*** see HUMBLE
cast down *adj* ***syn*** see DOWNCAST
castigate *vb* **1** ***syn*** see PUNISH 1
rel baste, beat, belabor, drub, pummel, thrash; berate, rail, rate, tongue-lash, upbraid, wig; penalize
2 ***syn*** see LAMBASTE 3
castigation *n* ***syn*** see PUNISHMENT
castigatory *adj* ***syn*** see PUNITIVE
castle *n* ***syn*** see MANSION
castle-builder *n* ***syn*** see DREAMER
cast out *vb* **1** ***syn*** see BANISH
‖2 ***syn*** see QUARREL
castrate *vb* **1** ***syn*** see STERILIZE
2 ***syn*** see UNNERVE
rel bleed, drain, empty, exhaust
casual *adj* **1** ***syn*** see ACCIDENTAL
rel unplanned, unpremeditated; extemporaneous, extempore, impromptu, improvised, offhand; impulsive, spontaneous
con advised, considered, deliberate, intentional, planned, premeditated, studied
ant deliberate
2 ***syn*** see INDIFFERENT 2
3 ***syn*** see EASYGOING 3
con ceremonial, conventional, formal
4 ***syn*** see LITTLE 3
casually *adv* ***syn*** see INCIDENTALLY 1
casualty *n* **1** ***syn*** see ACCIDENT 2
2 ***syn*** see FATALITY 2
3 ***syn*** see VICTIM 2
casuistry *n* ***syn*** see FALLACY 2
‖**cat** *n* ***syn*** see MAN 3
‖**cat** *vb* ***syn*** see VOMIT
cataclysm *n* **1** ***syn*** see FLOOD 2
2 ***syn*** see DISASTER
cataclysmic *adj* ***syn*** see FATAL 2
catacomb *n* ***syn*** see CRYPT
catalog *n* ***syn*** see LIST
rel program, prospectus, syllabus
catalog *vb* **1** ***syn*** see INVENTORY
2 ***syn*** see LIST 3
rel admit, enter, introduce; count, enumerate, number
catalyst *n* ***syn*** see STIMULUS
cataplasm *n* ***syn*** see POULTICE
cataract *n* **1** ***syn*** see WATERFALL
2 ***syn*** see FLOOD 2
catastrophe *n* ***syn*** see DISASTER
catastrophic *adj* ***syn*** see FATAL 2
catcall *n* ***syn*** see RASPBERRY
catch *vb* **1** to obtain physical mastery and possession of <the cat *caught* a mouse>
syn bag, capture, collar, ‖cotch, get, nail, prehend, secure, take; *compare* ARREST 2, SEIZE 2
rel clutch, grab, snatch; clasp, grasp, grip; ensnare, entangle, entrap, snare, tangle, trap
con free, release
ant miss
2 ***syn*** see SEIZE 2
3 to put at a disadvantage or bring under control by or as if by enmeshing in a net <*caught* in the fallacy of his own argument>
syn benet, catch up, ensnare, entangle, entrap, snare, tangle, trap; *compare* ENTANGLE 3
rel baffle, confound, nonplus, perplex, stick, stump; abash, disturb, embarrass, put out; confuse, flurry, fluster, rattle
4 ***syn*** see DUPE
5 ***syn*** see FIND 1
6 ***syn*** see MARRY 1
7 to come up with often unexpectedly <the storm *caught* them unawares>
syn ‖cotch, overhaul, overtake, take
rel reach
idiom come upon
8 ***syn*** see SEIZE 3
9 ***syn*** see INTERCEPT
10 ***syn*** see CONTRACT 1
idiom fall ill (of *or* with), fall victim to
11 ***syn*** see FASTEN 2
12 ***syn*** see STRIKE 2
13 ***syn*** see APPREHEND 1
catch colt *n* ***syn*** see BASTARD
catching *adj* **1** ***syn*** see INFECTIOUS 2
2 ***syn*** see INFECTIOUS 3
catch on *vb* ***syn*** see DISCOVER 3
catchphrase *n* ***syn*** see CATCHWORD
catchpole *n* ***syn*** see DELEGATE
catch up *vb* **1** ***syn*** see CATCH 3
2 ***syn*** see ENTHRALL 2
catchword *n* a word or phrase that catches the eye or ear and is repeated so often that it becomes representative of a political party, school of thought, or point of view <"new deal" became the *catchword* of supporters and critics of Franklin Roosevelt>
syn byword, catchphrase, phrase, shibboleth, slogan, watchword; *compare* BATTLE CRY
rel household word; maxim, motto
catchy *adj* ***syn*** see FITFUL
catechize *vb* ***syn*** see ASK 1
categorical *adj* **1** ***syn*** see ULTIMATE 3
con conjectural, hypothetical, supposititious; conditional, contingent, dependent, relative
2 ***syn*** see EXPLICIT
rel certain, positive, sure; direct, downright, forthright
con ambiguous; doubtful, dubious, problematic, questionable
3 ***syn*** see POSITIVE 1
categorically *adv* ***syn*** see EXPRESSLY 1

---

syn synonym(s) ***rel*** related word(s)
ant antonym(s) ***con*** contrasted word(s)
idiom idiomatic equivalent(s)
‖ use limited; if in doubt, see a dictionary

categorize *vb* ***syn*** see ASSORT
rel identify, nail down, peg, put down
category *n* ***syn*** see CLASS 1
cater (to) *vb* **1** ***syn*** see BABY
idiom make much of
2 ***syn*** see INDULGE 1
cateran *n* ***syn*** see MARAUDER
catercorner (*or* **catty-corner** *or* **kitty-corner**) *adv*
syn see DIAGONALLY
cater–cousin *n* ***syn*** see FRIEND
caterwaul *vb* ***syn*** see QUARREL
catharsis *n* ***syn*** see PURIFICATION
catholic *adj* **1** ***syn*** see UNIVERSAL 2
rel comprehensive, inclusive; general, generic, indeterminate; extensive, large-scale
ant parochial; provincial
2 ***syn*** see ECLECTIC 2
catholicon *n* ***syn*** see PANACEA
cathouse *n* ***syn*** see BROTHEL
catlike *adj* ***syn*** see STEALTHY 2
catnap *n* ***syn*** see NAP
catnap *vb* ***syn*** see NAP
||**catouse** *n* ***syn*** see COMMOTION 3
cat's–paw *n* ***syn*** see TOOL 2
catty *adj* **1** ***syn*** see STEALTHY 2
2 ***syn*** see AGILE
3 ***syn*** see MALICIOUS
||**caulk** (off) *vb* ***syn*** see NAP
||**caulker** *n* ***syn*** see DRAM
causatum *n* ***syn*** see EFFECT 1
cause *n* **1** that (as a person, fact, or condition) which is responsible for an effect <the storm was the *cause* of all our difficulties>
syn antecedent, determinant, occasion, reason
rel goad, impulse, incentive, inducement, motive, spring; origin, prime mover, root, source; author, creator, generator, originator
con consequence, effect, issue, outcome, result
2 ***syn*** see MOTIVE 1
3 ***syn*** see OCCASION 3
4 ***syn*** see SUIT 1
cause *vb* **1** ***syn*** see GENERATE 3
2 ***syn*** see EFFECT 1
rel elicit, evoke, provoke
idiom be at the root of, give origin to, set on foot
'cause *conj* ***syn*** see BECAUSE
causerie *n* ***syn*** see CHAT 2
caustic *adj* **1** marked by sharp and often witty incisiveness <a *caustic* critic>
syn mordacious, mordant, salty, scathing, trenchant; *compare* SARCASTIC
rel biting, cutting, incisive; acrid, bitter, pungent, tart; acute, keen, sharp; ironic, sarcastic, satiric, stinging; harsh, rough, severe, stringent; crisp, pithy, succinct, terse
con gentle, mild; cordial, gracious; bland, diplomatic, suave, urbane
ant genial
2 ***syn*** see SARCASTIC
causticity *n* ***syn*** see SARCASM
caution *n* **1** ***syn*** see WARNING
2 ***syn*** see PRUDENCE 1
caution *vb* ***syn*** see WARN 1
cautionary *adj* ***syn*** see MONITORY
cautioning *adj* ***syn*** see MONITORY
cautious *adj* marked by careful prudence especially in reducing or avoiding risk or danger <a *cautious* approach to marriage>
syn calculating, careful, chary, circumspect, considerate, discreet, gingerly, guarded, safe, wary
rel alert, vigilant, watchful; cagey, canny, cozy, foresighted, precautious, shrewd; forethoughtful, prethoughtful, provident, prudent; calculating, scheming, shrewd; expedient, judicious, politic
idiom on one's guard, on the safe side, playing it safe
con daring, rash, reckless, venturesome; headlong, impetuous, precipitate
ant adventurous, temerarious
cavalier *adj* ***syn*** see PROUD 1
cave *n* a usually natural underground chamber <the limestone *caves* of Kentucky>
syn cavern, grotto, subterrane, subterranean
cave *vb* **1** ***syn*** see GIVE 12
2 ***syn*** see YIELD 2
cave (in) *vb* ***syn*** see COLLAPSE 2
caveat *n* ***syn*** see WARNING
cavern *n* ***syn*** see CAVE
cavernous *adj* **1** suggestive of a cave <a *cavernous* fireplace that gulped in wood>
syn chasmal, gaping, yawning
rel commodious, vast
2 ***syn*** see HOLLOW 1
cavil *vb* ***syn*** see QUIBBLE 1
caviler *n* ***syn*** see CRITIC
caviling *adj* ***syn*** see CRITICAL 1
rel contrary, perverse; demanding, exacting; finicky, fussy, picky; mean, petty, small; hairsplitting, niggling, nitpicking
con amiable, complaisant, good-natured, tolerant; accommodating, easy, obliging
cavillous *adj* ***syn*** see CRITICAL 1
cavity *n* ***syn*** see HOLE 3
cavort *vb* ***syn*** see GAMBOL
rel carry on, cut up, horse (around), horseplay, roughhouse
caw *vb* ***syn*** see SQUALL 1
cease *vb* ***syn*** see STOP 3
rel close, conclude, end, finish, terminate; intermit
con continue, persist; extend, prolong, protract; arise, originate, rise, spring
cease *n* ***syn*** see END 2
cease-fire *n* ***syn*** see TRUCE
ceaseless *adj* **1** ***syn*** see CONTINUAL
2 ***syn*** see EVERLASTING 1
cede *vb* **1** ***syn*** see RELINQUISH
rel accord, concede, grant, vouchsafe
con hold, hold back, keep back, retain, withhold
2 ***syn*** see TRANSFER 4
ceinture *n* ***syn*** see BELT 1
||**celeb** *n* ***syn*** see CELEBRITY 2
celebrate *vb* **1** ***syn*** see KEEP 2
2 ***syn*** see PRAISE 2
celebrated *adj* ***syn*** see FAMOUS 2
celebrious *adj* ***syn*** see FAMOUS 2

celebrity *n* **1** ***syn*** see FAME 2
ant obscurity
2 a widely known and popularly esteemed person <youngsters making a great to-do over sports *celebrities*>
syn big name, ‖celeb, luminary, name, notability, notable, somebody
rel hero, immortal, mahatma, star, superstar; lion; personage, worthy; cynosure
idiom center of attraction, person of note (*or* mark)
con back number; nobody

celerity *n* **1** ***syn*** see HASTE 1
rel alacrity, briskness, legerity
2 ***syn*** see SPEED 2

celestial *adj* of, relating to, or befitting heaven or the heavens <*celestial* music from an angelic choir>
syn empyreal, empyrean, heavenly
rel ethereal, supernal, transcendental; otherworldly, unearthly, transmundane; beatific, blessed, elysian, Olympian
con earthly, earthy, mundane, sublunary, worldly; chthonian, hellish, infernal
ant terrestrial, uncelestial

cemetery *n* a piece of land used for burying the dead <the quiet peace of a country *cemetery*>
syn ‖boneyard, ‖boot hill, burial ground, burying ground, God's acre, graveyard, memorial park, necropolis, polyandrium, potter's field
rel churchyard; catacomb
idiom city of the dead

censor *vb* to remove matter considered objectionable by expurgation or alteration <*censor* a movie>
syn blip, bowdlerize, expurgate, screen
rel cut out, excise, exscind; blue-pencil, delete, edit, red-pencil; bleach, clean (up), purge, purify; narrow, restrain, restrict

censorious *adj* ***syn*** see CRITICAL 1
rel chiding, reproachful, reproaching; condemnatory, condemning, denouncing, denunciatory, reprehending; accusatory, culpatory
con acclaiming, acclamatory, extolling, laudatory, lauding, praising; adulatory, complimentary, flattering
ant eulogistic

censurable *adj* ***syn*** see BLAMEWORTHY
rel improper, incorrect, objectionable, wrong, wrongful; discreditable, doubtful, questionable; inadmissible, unacceptable
con correct, proper, right; acceptable, admissible; creditable
ant uncensurable

censure *vb* ***syn*** see CRITICIZE
rel rebuke, reprimand, reproach, reprove; contemn, disdain, scorn, scout, strafe; disallow, disapprove, oppose, reject, stigmatize
con applaud, compliment, recommend; allow, approve, support
ant commend

center *n* **1** a point or part in a surface or solid more or less equidistant from the periphery <the *center* of the earth>
syn core, middle, midpoint, midst
rel inside, interior
con circumference, compass, perimeter, periphery; bounds, confines, limits
2 one eminent in or central to a particular activity, condition, or interest <a *center* of international trade>
syn focal point, focus, heart, hub, nerve center, polestar, seat; *compare* ESSENCE 2
3 a source or point of origin (as of an influence, pressure, or effect) <the group proved a *center* of discontent>
syn core, heart, pith, quick, root
rel activator, dynamo, energizer, stimulant

center *adj* **1** ***syn*** see MIDDLE 1
2 ***syn*** see MIDDLE 2

centermost *adj* ***syn*** see MIDDLE 1

central *adj* **1** occupying a dominant or supremely important position <the *central* theme of American foreign policy>
syn cardinal, overriding, overruling, pivotal, ruling
rel dominant, paramount, predominant, preponderant; important, significant; outstanding, salient, signal; chief, essential, foremost, leading, main; all-absorbing, controlling, master; focal, key; basic, fundamental, primary, radical
con insignificant, minor, trivial, unimportant; borderline, marginal
ant peripheral
2 ***syn*** see MIDDLE 2

centralizing *adj* ***syn*** see INTEGRATIVE

centripetal *adj* ***syn*** see INTEGRATIVE

‖**cep** *prep* ***syn*** see EXCEPT

cerate *n* ***syn*** see OINTMENT

cerberus *n* ***syn*** see CUSTODIAN

cerebral *adj* **1** ***syn*** see MENTAL 1
2 ***syn*** see INTELLECTUAL 2

cerebrate *vb* ***syn*** see THINK 5

cerebration *n* ***syn*** see THOUGHT 1

ceremonial *adj* stressing or concerned with careful attention to form and detail <his *ceremonial* approach to everyday life>
syn ceremonious, conventional, formal, solemn, stately
rel mannered, studied, stylized; liturgical, ritual, ritualistic; august, courtly, imposing, lofty; fixed, rigid, set, starchy, stiff
con casual, easy, informal, relaxed; artless, ingenuous, open, sincere

ceremonial *n* **1** ***syn*** see FORM 2
2 ***syn*** see RITE 2

ceremonious *adj* ***syn*** see CEREMONIAL
rel decorous, proper, seemly; impressive, moving, striking; grandiose, imposing, majestic
ant unceremonious

ceremony *n* **1** ***syn*** see FORM 2
2 ***syn*** see RITE 2

certain *adj* **1** ***syn*** see FIRM 4

---

rel assured, certified, guaranteed, warranted; ensured, insured, sure
2 constituting an indeterminate and otherwise unidentified part of a group or whole <*certain* students dispute this finding>
syn some, various
rel a, an, one; many, numerous; divers, several, sundry
con no; all
3 being such beyond a doubt <no *certain* likeness of this saint survives>
syn accurate, authentic, dependable, reliable
rel credible, plausible, well-grounded
con counterfeit, false, spurious; controversial, doubtful, dubious, questionable
ant uncertain
4 ***syn*** see INFALLIBLE 2
5 ***syn*** see POSITIVE 3
rel confirmable, demonstrable, establishable, provable, verifiable; doubtless, trustworthy, unerring
con controversial, iffy
ant uncertain
6 ***syn*** see INEVITABLE
rel indefeasible, irrevocable, unalterable, written; fated, predestinated, predetermined
ant uncertain
7 ***syn*** see SURE 5
rel assured, confident, sanguine
con hesitant, indecisive, vague, wavering; doubtful, dubious, questionable
ant uncertain

certainty *n* a state of mind in which one is free from doubt <answered with complete *certainty*>
syn assurance, assuredness, certitude, confidence, conviction, sureness, surety
rel belief, credence, faith; absoluteness, definiteness, dogmatism, positiveness, positivism; firmness, staunchness, steadiness
con doubt, mistrust, skepticism, unsureness; fluctuation, irresolution, shifting, trimming, vacillation, wavering; obscurity, vagueness
ant uncertainty

certification *n* ***syn*** see CREDENTIALS

certify *vb* **1** to testify usually formally and in writing to the truth or genuineness of something <*certify* a student's college transcript>
syn attest, vouch, witness
rel assert, aver, avouch, avow, profess
2 ***syn*** see WARRANT 2
3 ***syn*** see APPROVE 2
rel authorize, commission, license
con antagonize, counter, oppose

certitude *n* ***syn*** see CERTAINTY
rel cocksureness
con uncertainty
ant doubt

‖**cess** *n* ***syn*** see TAX 1

cessation *n* ***syn*** see END 2

cesspit *n* ***syn*** see SINK 1

cesspool *n* ***syn*** see SINK 1

‖**chack** *n* ***syn*** see SNACK

chafe *vb* **1** ***syn*** see ANNOY 1
2 ***syn*** see ABRADE 1
3 to make sore or raw through friction <the high stiff collar *chafed* his neck>
syn abrade, excoriate, fret, gall, rub
rel damage, hurt, impair, injure; flay, peel, skin; inflame, irritate; graze, scrape, scratch
con ease, relieve, soothe

chaff *vb* ***syn*** see BANTER 1
idiom make merry over

chaffer *vb* ***syn*** see HAGGLE 2
rel beg, coax, plead

chafing *adj* ***syn*** see IMPATIENT 1

chagrined *adj* ***syn*** see ASHAMED
rel crushed, disconcerted; discomposed, perturbed, upset
idiom put out of countenance

chain *n* **1 chains** *pl* ***syn*** see SHACKLE
2 ***syn*** see SUCCESSION 2
3 ***syn*** see SYNDICATE

chain *adj* **1** ***syn*** see CUMULATIVE
2 ***syn*** see TRITE

chair *vb* ***syn*** see PRESIDE

chair car *n* ***syn*** see PARLOR CAR

chalk (out) *vb* ***syn*** see SKETCH

chalk up *vb* ***syn*** see GET 1

challenge *vb* **1** ***syn*** see DEMAND 1
2 ***syn*** see QUESTION 2
3 ***syn*** see FACE 3
rel question; dispute; strive, struggle, try
idiom throw down the (*or* one's) gage
con bypass, evade
4 ***syn*** see STIR 1

challenge *n* **1** ***syn*** see DEMUR 2
2 ***syn*** see DEFIANCE 1
rel calling, claiming, demanding, exacting; importuning, insistence

chamber *n* **1** ***syn*** see ROOM 1
‖**2 chambers** *pl* ***syn*** see APARTMENT 1

chamber *vb* ***syn*** see HARBOR 1

champ *vb* **1** ***syn*** see CHEW 1
rel crush, macerate, mash, smash
2 ***syn*** see BITE 1
rel nibble, nip; gum, mouth, mumble; peck, pick

champaign *n* ***syn*** see FIELD

champion *n* ***syn*** see EXPONENT

champion *vb* ***syn*** see SUPPORT 2
rel battle, contend, fight (for)
idiom put in a good word for, stand behind (*or* back of), stand up for
con condemn, denounce
ant combat

champion *adj* **1** ***syn*** see EXCELLENT
rel distinguished, illustrious, outstanding, splendid
2 ***syn*** see FIRST 3

chance *n* **1** ***syn*** see ACCIDENT 1
con certainty, inevitability, necessity; destiny, fate, foreordination, predestination
ant law
2 an unpurposed, unpredictable, and uncontrollable master force <the folly of depending on *chance* for success in life>
syn fortune, hazard, luck
rel advantage, break, fluke; fate, lot; contingency

3 ***syn*** see OPPORTUNITY
rel likelihood, possibility, probability; outlook, prospect

chance *vb* **1** ***syn*** see HAPPEN 1
2 ***syn*** see HAPPEN 2
3 ***syn*** see GAMBLE 2
4 ***syn*** see VENTURE 1
idiom put at (*or* in) hazard
con cherish, protect, safeguard, secure

chance *adj* ***syn*** see ACCIDENTAL
rel careless, heedless, offhand

chance child *n* ***syn*** see BASTARD 1

chancy *adj* **1** ***syn*** see UNCERTAIN 1
rel hazardous, risky, speculative, unsound; precarious, ticklish, touchy, tricky
idiom hanging by a thread, on thin ice (*or* slippery ground)
con safe, secure, sound, stable
2 ***syn*** see DANGEROUS 1

change *vb* **1** to make or become different <*changed* her will again and again> <our needs *change* as we grow older>
syn alter, modify, mutate, refashion, turn, vary; *compare* TRANSFORM
rel convert, metamorphose, transform, transmute; diversify, variegate; exchange, interchange
idiom go (*or* pass through) a change
con establish, fix, set
2 ***syn*** see TRANSFORM
3 ***syn*** see REVERSE 1
4 ***syn*** see STERILIZE
5 to make substitution for or among <it's time to *change* the subject>
syn replace, shift
rel exchange, swap, trade; substitute
6 ***syn*** see EXCHANGE 2

change *n* **1** a making different <saw a gradual *change* of attitude in the community>
syn alteration, modification, mutation, turn, variation
rel aberration, deviation, divergence; diversification; shift; innovation
ant uniformity
2 a result of such change <amazed at the *changes* in the town>
syn innovation, mutation, novelty, permutation, sport, vicissitude
rel conversion, metamorphosis, transformation, transmutation; shift, substitute, surrogate; avatar

changeable *adj* **1** alterable or changing under slight provocation <*changeable* April weather>
syn changeful, fluid, mobile, mutable, protean, unsettled, unstable, unsteady, variable, weathery; *compare* INCONSTANT 1, MUTABLE 2
rel adaptable, impressionable, plastic, pliant; ever-changing, kaleidoscopic; restless, unfixed; inconstant, uncertain, vicissitudinous
con constant, invariable, permanent; certain, fixed, immutable, unalterable, unmodifiable; abiding, enduring, persistent
ant unchangeable; unchanging
2 ***syn*** see MUTABLE 2
3 ***syn*** see INCONSTANT 1

changeabout *n* ***syn*** see REVERSAL 1

changeful *adj* ***syn*** see CHANGEABLE 1
rel active, dynamic, live; lively, vigorous
con durable, lasting, perdurable, stable; steady, uniform
ant changeless, unchanging

changeover *n* ***syn*** see CONVERSION 2

channel *n* **1** passage through which a fluid (as water) flows or is led <the river cut a new *channel* to the sea>
syn aqueduct, canal, conduit, course, duct, watercourse
rel pass, passage, way
2 ***syn*** see MEAN 2
3 ***syn*** see PIPELINE

channel *vb* ***syn*** see CONDUCT 4

chant *vb* ***syn*** see SING 1

chaos *n* **1** ***syn*** see CONFUSION 3
2 ***syn*** see ANARCHY 1
rel misrule, unruliness

chap *n* ***syn*** see MAN 3

chaperon *vb* **1** ***syn*** see ACCOMPANY
rel guide, overlook, oversee, supervise
2 ***syn*** see SUPERVISE

chapfallen *adj* ***syn*** see DOWNCAST

chaplet *n* ***syn*** see WREATH

character *n* **1** an arbitrary or conventional device used in writing or printing <an inscription in runic *characters*>
syn mark, sign, symbol
rel cipher, device, monogram; letter
2 ***syn*** see CHARACTERISTIC 1
3 ***syn*** see QUALITY 1
rel distinction, uniqueness, uniquity
4 ***syn*** see TYPE
5 ***syn*** see DISPOSITION 3
rel soul, spirit; courage, mettle, resolution; intellect, intelligence, mind
6 ***syn*** see ROLE 1
7 ***syn*** see STATUS 1
8 ***syn*** see NOTABLE 1
9 ***syn*** see ECCENTRIC
‖**10** ***syn*** see HUMAN
11 ***syn*** see REPUTATION 2

character assassination *n* ***syn*** see DETRACTION

characteristic *adj* being or revealing a quality specific or identifying to an individual or group <her *characteristic* down-to-earth approach to a problem>
syn diacritic, diagnostic, distinctive, idiosyncratic, individual, peculiar, proper
rel especial, particular, special, specific; natural, normal, regular, typical
con general, generic, universal
ant uncharacteristic

characteristic *n* **1** something that marks or sets apart <*characteristics* that distinguish man from lower primates>

---

syn synonym(s) ***rel*** related word(s)
ant antonym(s) ***con*** contrasted word(s)
idiom idiomatic equivalent(s)
‖ use limited; if in doubt, see a dictionary

THESAURUS

syn birthmark, character, feature, point, trait; *compare* QUALITY 1
rel badge, mark, sign, token; flavor, odor, savor, smack, tang; differentia; singularity
2 *syn* see QUALITY 1

characterize *vb* 1 *syn* see SKETCH
2 to be a peculiar or significant quality or feature of something <a man *characterized* by quiet dignity>
syn distinguish, individualize, individuate, mark, qualify, signalize, singularize
rel define, describe, differentiate, identify; peculiarize, personalize
idiom be a feature of

characterless *adj* lacking in character or solid qualities <a drab *characterless* little man that no one ever seemed to notice>
syn namby-pamby, pantywaist, wishy-washy
rel childish, infantile; sissified, sissy, unmanly; futile, weak; impotent, powerless
con manly, strong, vigorous, virile

charade *n syn* see PRETENSE 2

chare *n syn* see TASK 1

charge *vb* 1 *syn* see BURDEN
2 *syn* see LOAD 3
3 *syn* see PERMEATE
4 *syn* see ENTRUST 1
5 *syn* see COMMAND
rel ask, request, solicit; adjure
6 *syn* see ACCUSE
rel impugn, reprehend, reproach
idiom bring (*or* prefer) charges
con excuse, forgive, pardon, remit; acquit
ant absolve
7 *syn* see ASCRIBE
8 *syn* see RUSH 1

charge *n* 1 *syn* see LOAD 3
rel business, devoir, place
2 *syn* see OBLIGATION 2
3 *syn* see OVERSIGHT 1
4 *syn* see COMMAND 1
5 *syn* see PRICE 1

chargeless *adj syn* see FREE 5

charger *n syn* see COURSER

charioteer *vb syn* see DRIVE 5

charisma *n syn* see CHARM 3

charitable *adj* 1 having or showing interest in or concern for the welfare of others <spent generously for *charitable* aid to the needy>
syn altruistic, benevolent, eleemosynary, good, humane, humanitarian, philanthropic
rel accommodating, helpful, obliging; benign, kindhearted, kindly, sympathetic
2 *syn* see FORBEARING
rel benevolent, considerate, kindly, thoughtful
con cold, harsh, heartless, unfeeling
ant uncharitable

charity *n* 1 *syn* see MERCY
rel affection, attachment, love; altruism, benevolence, humaneness; kindliness; amity, friendliness, goodwill
con malevolence, malignancy, malignity, spite, spleen
ant ill will, malice
2 *syn* see DONATION

charivari *n syn* see SHIVAREE

charlatan *n* one who pretends unscrupulously to knowledge or skill <the medical establishment called him a *charlatan*>
syn mountebank, quack, quacksalver, quackster, saltimbanque; *compare* IMPOSTOR
rel bluff, four-flusher, sham

Charlie McCarthy *n syn* see STOOGE 1

charm *n* 1 *syn* see SPELL
2 an object worn or cherished to ward off evil or attract good fortune <the American Indian medicine bag is essentially a *charm*>
syn amulet, fetish, juju, luck, mascot, periapt, phylactery, talisman, zemi
3 a quality or combination of qualities that is wholly attractive and irresistible <the *charm* of her smile>
syn allure, appeal, charisma, fascination, glamour, magnetism, witchcraft, witchery
rel allurement, attraction, attractiveness, lure; agreeableness, delightfulness, gratefulness
con hatefulness, obnoxiousness, odiousness, repulsiveness; distastefulness, unpleasantness

charm *vb* 1 *syn* see ATTRACT 1
2 *syn* see BEWITCH 1

charmed *adj syn* see ENAMORED 3

charmer *n syn* see MAGICIAN 1

charming *adj syn* see ATTRACTIVE 1
ant charmless

chart *n* 1 a stylized or symbolic depiction of something incapable of direct verbal or pictorial representation (as because of complexity or abstractness) <a *chart* of anticipated economic progress>
syn graph, map
rel plan, plat, plot, scheme
2 *syn* see TABLE 2

chart *vb syn* see PLAN 2

charter *n syn* see DEED 3

charter *vb syn* see HIRE 1

chary *adj* 1 *syn* see CAUTIOUS
rel disinclined, hesitant, loath, reluctant; economical, frugal, sparing, thrifty; constrained, inhibited, restrained
2 *syn* see SPARING

chase *vb* 1 *syn* see FOLLOW 2
con flee, fly
2 *syn* see HUNT 1
3 *syn* see EJECT 1
4 *syn* see RUSH 1
5 *syn* see COURSE

chase *n syn* see HUNTING
2 *syn* see GAME 3

chaser *n syn* see WOLF

chasm *n* 1 *syn* see GULF 2
2 *syn* see RAVINE
3 *syn* see OMISSION
4 *syn* see SCHISM 3

chasmal *adj syn* see CAVERNOUS 1

chaste *adj* free from every trace of the lewd or salacious <was as *chaste* in language as in conduct>

syn clean, decent, immaculate, modest, pure, spotless, stainless, unblemished, undefiled, unsullied
rel ethical, moral, righteous, virtuous; maidenly, virgin, virginal; becoming, decorous, proper, seemly; abstinent, continent
con coarse, gross, obscene, ribald, vulgar; lascivious, lecherous, licentious, lustful; gluttonous, incontinent, self-indulgent
ant unchaste

chasten *vb syn* see PUNISH 1
rel abase, humble, humiliate; afflict, try
con baby, humor, indulge, spoil
ant pamper

chastise *vb syn* see PUNISH 1
rel baste, beat, belabor, pummel, thrash

chastisement *n syn* see PUNISHMENT

chat *vb* **1** to emit a ready flow of inconsequential talk <*chats* on the phone for hours>
syn babble, burble, cackle, chatter, chin-chin, clack, clatter, ‖dish, dither, gab, gabble, ‖gas, jaw, ‖natter, patter, prate, prattle, rattle, run on, smatter, talk, tinkle, twaddle, twiddle, twitter, yak, yakety-yak, yammer, yatter; *compare* CONVERSE
rel yap; blab, gossip; gush, lallygag; confabulate
idiom beat one's gums, ‖chew the fat (*or* rag), ‖shoot (*or* bat) the breeze, ‖shoot (*or* sling) the bull
con discourse, expound; declaim, harangue, hold forth, orate, preach
2 *syn* see CONVERSE

chat *n* **1** *syn* see CHATTER
2 an informal conversation <had a satisfactory little *chat* with the new assistant>
syn causerie, chin, prose, rap, talk, yarn; *compare* CONVERSATION 2
rel gossip, tête-à-tête
idiom bull session, rap session
con debate, deliberation, discussion
3 *syn* see CONVERSATION 1

chateau *n syn* see MANSION

chattel *n* **1 chattels** *pl syn* see POSSESSION 2
2 *syn* see SLAVE 1

chatter *vb* **1** *syn* see GIBBER
2 *syn* see CHAT 1

chatter *n* idle and often loud and incessant talk <schoolgirl *chatter*>
syn babble, bibble-babble, blab, blabber, ‖blatter, brabble, cackle, chat, chin-chin, ‖chin music, chitchat, chitter-chatter, clack, gab, gabble, gibble-gabble, jabber, palaver, prate, prattle, stultiloquence, talkee-talkee, tittle-tattle, yak, yakety-yak, yak-yak, yatter
rel ‖bull, gossip, small talk
idiom tongue wagging

chatterbox *n* one who engages in chatter <that old *chatterbox* will talk your arm off>
syn bandar-log, blabber, blabbermouth, blabmouth, chatterer, chewet, gabber, jabberer, magpie, prater, prattler
rel busybody, gossip, newsmonger, quidnunc, scandalmonger, tabby, tattletale

chatterer *n syn* see CHATTERBOX

chatty *adj syn* see TALKATIVE

‖**chaw** *vb* **1** *syn* see CHEW 1
2 *syn* see PONDER 2

chawbacon *n syn* see RUSTIC

cheap *adj* **1** costing little <produce is usually *cheaper* in summer>
syn inexpensive, low, low-cost, low-priced, popular, reasonable, uncostly, undear
rel bargain-basement, bargain-counter, cut-rate, reduced; dirt-cheap
con dear, high, high-priced
ant costly, expensive
2 of inferior quality <*cheap* furniture is never a bargain>
syn base, cheesy, common, mean, ‖ornery, paltry, poor, rubbishing, rubbishly, rubbishy, shoddy, sleazy, tatty, trashy, trumpery; *compare* INFERIOR 2
rel cheap-jack, valueless, worthless; flashy, garish, meretricious, tawdry; brummagem, fake, phony, sham; bad, rotten, terrible
con capital, excellent, fine, good; first-class, first-rate, high-class, high-grade, superior, tip-top, top-notch
ant precious
3 *syn* see CONTEMPTIBLE
rel wrong; base, low, vile; measly, paltry, petty, trifling
ant noble
4 *syn* see STINGY

cheapen *vb syn* see DEPRECIATE 1

cheap–jack (*or* **cheap–john**) *n syn* see PEDDLER

cheapskate *n syn* see MISER

cheat *n* **1** *syn* see DECEPTION 1
2 *syn* see IMPOSTURE
rel bamboozlement, cozening, hoaxing; chicane, chicanery, trickery
3 *syn* see SWINDLER

cheat *vb* to obtain something (as money) from or an advantage over by dishonesty and trickery <*cheated* out of his inheritance by a grasping lawyer>
syn beat, bilk, boodle, ‖burn, chisel, chouse, cozen, ‖crook, defraud, diddle, do, ‖doodle, ‖dry-shave, ‖duff, flimflam, gyp, ‖mace, ‖mump, overreach, ream, ‖screw, sucker, swindle, take; *compare* EXTORT 1, FLEECE 1
rel befool, dupe, fool, gull, slick; bunco, con, fudge, short; beguile, deceive, delude, double-cross, mislead

cheater *n syn* see SWINDLER

check *vb* **1** *syn* see ARREST 1
rel cease, desist, discontinue, stop; repress, suppress; circumvent, foil, frustrate, thwart
ant expedite
2 *syn* see RESTRAIN 1
rel baffle, balk; obviate, preclude, prevent
ant accelerate (*of speed*); advance (*as of hopes, plans*); release (*of feelings, energies*)

---

syn synonym(s) *rel* related word(s)
ant antonym(s) *con* contrasted word(s)
idiom idiomatic equivalent(s)
‖ use limited; if in doubt, see a dictionary

3 ***syn*** see TRY 1
4 ***syn*** see AGREE 4
check *n* **1** ***syn*** see SETBACK
2 a statement of charges for food and drink consumed (as at a restaurant) <shocked at the size of the *check*>
syn bill, tab
rel damage, score
check out *vb* ‖**1** ***syn*** see DIE 1
2 ***syn*** see AGREE 4
check over *vb* ***syn*** see SCRUTINIZE 1
check–over *n* ***syn*** see EXAMINATION
check up *vb* ***syn*** see SCRUTINIZE 1
checkup *n* ***syn*** see EXAMINATION
cheek *n* **1 cheeks** *pl* ***syn*** see BUTTOCKS
2 ***syn*** see EFFRONTERY
cheeky *adj* ***syn*** see WISE 5
cheep *vb* ***syn*** see CHIRP
cheer *vb* **1** ***syn*** see COMFORT
2 ***syn*** see ENCOURAGE 1
3 ***syn*** see APPLAUD 2
cheerful *adj* **1** marked by or suggestive of lighthearted ease of mind and spirit <a *cheerful* smile>
syn blithe, cheery, ‖chirk, chirpy, chirrupy, lightsome, sunbeamy, sunny; *compare* LIVELY 1
rel airy, carefree, debonair, jaunty; animated, gay, lighthearted, lively, vivacious; buoyant, corky
idiom in good (*or* high) spirits, of good cheer
con blue, dejected, depressed, melancholy; dispirited, heavyhearted; joyless, mournful, sorrowful, woeful; dour, morose, saturnine, sullen; doleful, lugubrious; austere, forbidding, grim, stern
ant gloomy, glum
2 ***syn*** see GLAD 2
ant cheerless
‖**cheerio** *interj* ***syn*** see GOOD-BYE
cheerless *adj* ***syn*** see GLOOMY 3
rel dejecting
ant cheerful
cheery *adj* **1** ***syn*** see GLAD 2
2 ***syn*** see CHEERFUL 1
cheeseparer *n* ***syn*** see MISER
cheeseparing *adj* ***syn*** see STINGY
rel cheap, grudging, mean, shabby; illiberal
cheesy *adj* ***syn*** see CHEAP 2
chef d'oeuvre *n* **1** ***syn*** see MASTERPIECE 1
2 ***syn*** see SHOWPIECE
‖**chemist** *n* ***syn*** see DRUGGIST
cherish *vb* **1** ***syn*** see NURSE 2
rel conserve, preserve, save; entertain, harbor, keep, shelter; defend, guard, safeguard, shield
con reject, repudiate, scorn
ant abandon
2 ***syn*** see APPRECIATE 1
rel revere, reverence, venerate
idiom hold in high esteem
con disregard, forget, ignore, overlook, slight
ant neglect
3 ***syn*** see ADMIRE 1
chest *n* ***syn*** see TREASURY 2
chesty *adj* ***syn*** see BUXOM
chew *vb* **1** to crush or grind with the teeth <*chew* your food well>
syn champ, ‖chaw, chomp, ‖chonk, chumble, chump, crunch, masticate, munch, ruminate, scrunch
rel bite; gnaw, nibble; consume, devour, eat; gum, mumble
‖**2** ***syn*** see SCOLD 1
chewet *n* ***syn*** see CHATTERBOX
‖**chew out** *vb* ***syn*** see SCOLD 1
chiaus *n* ***syn*** see SWINDLER
chic *n* ***syn*** see FASHION 3
chic *adj* ***syn*** see STYLISH
chicane *vb* **1** ***syn*** see QUIBBLE 1
2 ***syn*** see DUPE
chicane *n* ***syn*** see DECEPTION 1
rel artifice, feint, gambit, maneuver, ploy, ruse, stratagem, trick, wile; furtiveness, surreptitiousness, underhandedness
con forthrightness, straightforwardness
chicanery *n* ***syn*** see DECEPTION 1
rel intrigue, machination, plot; furtiveness, surreptitiousness, underhandedness
con forthrightness, straightforwardness; honesty, honor, integrity, probity
chichi *adj* **1** ***syn*** see SHOWY
2 ***syn*** see PRECIOUS 4
chick *n* **1** ***syn*** see CHILD 1
‖**2** ***syn*** see GIRL FRIEND 1
chickabiddy *n* ***syn*** see CHILD 1
chicken *n* ***syn*** see COWARD
‖**chicken** *adj* ***syn*** see COWARDLY
chide *vb* ***syn*** see REPROVE
rel berate, rate, scold, upbraid
con applaud, compliment; approve, endorse, sanction
ant commend
chiding *n* ***syn*** see REBUKE
chief *n* **1** ***syn*** see LEADER 2
rel dictator, duce, führer
2 ***syn*** see NOTABLE 1
chief *adj* **1** ***syn*** see FIRST 3
2 standing apart by reason of superior importance, significance, or influence <his *chief* claim to consideration is his unquestionable uprightness>
syn capital, ‖cock, dominant, main, major, number one, outstanding, predominant, preeminent, principal, star, stellar
rel primal, primary, prime; important, prominent, significant; consequential, momentous, weighty; effective, potent, telling; controlling, master, ruling
con inconsequential, minor, trivial, unimportant; collateral, contingent, secondary
chiefly *adv* ***syn*** see GENERALLY 1
chieftain *n* ***syn*** see LEADER 2
chiffer *n* ***syn*** see NUMBER
child *n* **1** a young person <a movie for both *children* and adults>
syn bud, chick, chickabiddy, chit, juvenile, kid, moppet, ‖nipper, puss, youngling, young one, youngster, youth

rel minor; adolescent, teenager, teener, teenybopper; brat, bratling, dickens, runabout; cherub, innocent, lamb, sweetling
idiom a slip of a boy (*or* girl), small fry, young hopeful
ant adult, grown-up
2 children *pl syn* see OFFSPRING
childbearing *n* **1** *syn* see BIRTH 1
2 *syn* see LABOR 2
childbed *n syn* see CONFINEMENT 2
childbirth *n* **1** *syn* see BIRTH 1
2 *syn* see LABOR 2
childing *adj* **1** *syn* see PREGNANT 1
2 *syn* see FERTILE
childish *adj* significantly deficient in maturity <a *childish* and spiteful attitude>
syn babyish, immature, infantile, infantine, prekindergarten, puerile
rel asinine, fatuous, foolish, silly, simple; naive, unsophisticated; arrested, backward, moronic, retarded, slow, ||wanting
ant adult
child's play *n syn* see SNAP 1
chill *vb syn* see DISCOURAGE 1
chill *adj* **1** *syn* see COLD 1
2 *syn* see COLD 2
rel distant, formal, reserved, solitary, standoffish, uncompanionable, withdrawn; abstracted, disinterested, uninterested
con easy, gregarious, informal; sociable
chiller *n syn* see THRILLER
chillsome *adj syn* see COLD 1
chilly *adj syn* see COLD 1
chime *n syn* see HARMONY 2
chime *vb syn* see RING
chime in *vb* **1** *syn* see INTERRUPT 2
2 *syn* see SAY 1
chimera *n syn* see PIPE DREAM
chimerical *adj syn* see FICTITIOUS 1
rel ambitious, pretentious, utopian; deceptive, delusive, delusory; fabulous, mythical; absurd, preposterous
con believable, plausible, rational, reasonable; possible, practicable
ant feasible
chiming *adj syn* see HARMONIOUS 1
chin *n syn* see CHAT 2
chin *vb syn* see CONVERSE
chin–chin *vb syn* see CHAT 1
chin–chin *n syn* see CHATTER
||**chinchy** *adj syn* see STINGY
chine *n syn* see RIDGE 1
Chinese puzzle *n syn* see MYSTERY
Chinese wall *n syn* see OBSTACLE
chink *n syn* see CRACK 3
rel interruption
chink *vb syn* see JINGLE
||**chink** *n syn* see MONEY
chinkle *vb syn* see JINGLE
||**chin music** *n syn* see CHATTER
chintzy *adj* **1** *syn* see GAUDY
2 *syn* see STINGY
chin–up *adj syn* see BRAVE 1
chip *vb syn* see CHIRP
chip in *vb* **1** *syn* see CONTRIBUTE 1
2 *syn* see INTERRUPT 2
chipper *vb syn* see CHIRP
chipper *adj* **1** *syn* see LIVELY 1
2 *syn* see NEAT 2
||**chippy** *n syn* see DOXY 1
||**chips** *n pl syn* see MONEY
||**chirk** *adj* **1** *syn* see LIVELY 1
2 *syn* see CHEERFUL 1
chirk (up) *vb syn* see ENCOURAGE 1
||**chirm** *n syn* see DIN
||**chirm** *vb syn* see CHIRP
chirography *n syn* see HANDWRITING
chirp *vb* to make a short, sharp, and usually repetitive sound <sparrows *chirping* on the lawn>
syn cheep, chip, chipper, ||chirm, chirrup, clutter, peep, tweedle, tweet, twitter
chirpy *adj syn* see CHEERFUL
chirrup *vb syn* see CHIRP
chirrupy *adj syn* see CHEERFUL 1
chisel *vb* **1** *syn* see SCULPTURE
2 *syn* see CHEAT
chisel (in) *vb syn* see INTRUDE 1
||**chiselly** *adj syn* see BAD 8
chit *n syn* see CHILD 1
chit *n syn* see NOTE 2
chitchat *n* **1** *syn* see CHATTER
2 *syn* see SMALL TALK
chitter *vb syn* see CHIRP
chitter–chatter *n* **1** *syn* see CHATTER
2 *syn* see SMALL TALK
chivalrous *adj syn* see GENEROUS 1
rel knightly, manly, noble
con churlish common, low
chivy *vb* **1** *syn* see FOLLOW 2
2 *syn* see BAIT 2
rel afflict, torment, try; chase, pursue, trail
choate *adj syn* see WHOLE 3
chockablock *adj syn* see FULL 1
chock–full *adj syn* see FULL 1
choice *n* **1** the act, right, opportunity, or faculty of choosing or deciding <the *choice* lies with the electorate>
syn alternative, ||druthers, election, option, preference, selection
rel decision, determination, finding, judgment, verdict; appraisal, evaluation, rating
2 *syn* see BEST
choice *adj* having qualities that appeal to a fine or highly refined taste <a few *choice* spirits gathered nightly to discuss the day's events>
syn dainty, delicate, elegant, exquisite, rare, recherché, select, superior
rel incomparable, peerless, preeminent, prime, superlative, supreme, surpassing, transcendent, unsurpassed; chosen, culled, picked, selected
con common, ordinary; average, fair, mediocre, medium, middling, run-of-the-mill, second-rate; drab, dull, lackluster, lusterless

---

syn synonym(s) *rel* related word(s)
ant antonym(s) *con* contrasted word(s)
idiom idiomatic equivalent(s)
|| use limited; if in doubt, see a dictionary

ant indifferent
||**choicy** *adj* ***syn*** see NICE 1
choke *vb* **1** to check normal breathing especially by compressing or obstructing the windpipe <*choked* by a bone in the throat>
syn strangle, throttle; *compare* SUFFOCATE
2 ***syn*** see SUFFOCATE
3 ***syn*** see FILL 1
4 ***syn*** see LOAD 3
choke (off) *vb* ***syn*** see SILENCE
||**chokey** *n* ***syn*** see JAIL
choking *n* ***syn*** see REPRESSION 1
choleric *adj* **1** ***syn*** see IRASCIBLE
rel acrimonious, angry, fiery, indignant, irate, mad, spunky, wrathful, wroth; captious, carping, faultfinding
con calm, serene, tranquil; composed, cool, nonchalant
ant placid
2 ***syn*** see ANGRY
chomp *vb* **1** ***syn*** see CHEW 1
2 ***syn*** see BITE 1
||**chonk** *vb* ***syn*** see CHEW 1
choose *vb* **1** to fix upon one among alternatives as the one to be taken, accepted, or adopted <*chose* the largest apple but found it sour>
syn cull, elect, mark, opt (for), optate, pick, pick out, prefer, select, single (out), take
rel adopt, embrace, espouse; crave, desire, love, want, wish
con decline, refuse, repudiate, spurn; abnegate, forbear, forgo
ant reject; eschew
2 ***syn*** see WILL
rel favor, prefer
||**3** ***syn*** see DESIRE 1
choosy *adj* ***syn*** see NICE 1
chop *vb* **1** ***syn*** see FELL 2
2 to cut into fragments by repeated strokes <*chop* meat and onions for hash>
syn hash, mince
rel cut up, dice, fragment
idiom cut to bits, make mincemeat of
chop *n* ***syn*** see CUFF
chop–chop *adv* ***syn*** see FAST 2
chore *n* **1** ***syn*** see TASK 1
2 ***syn*** see TASK 2
rel trial, tribulation
chortle *vb* ***syn*** see LAUGH
chorus *n* ***syn*** see HARMONY 1
chosen *adj* ***syn*** see SELECT 1
chouse *n* ***syn*** see TRICK 1
chouse *vb* ***syn*** see CHEAT
||**chow** *n* **1** ***syn*** see FOOD 1
2 ***syn*** see MEAL
chowchow *adj* ***syn*** see MISCELLANEOUS
chowchow *n* ***syn*** see MISCELLANY 1
chowderhead *n* ***syn*** see DUNCE
chrism *n* ***syn*** see OINTMENT
christcross–row *n* ***syn*** see ALPHABET 1
christen *vb* **1** ***syn*** see BAPTIZE
2 ***syn*** see NAME 1
Christian *adj* ***syn*** see DECOROUS 1
Christian name *n* ***syn*** see GIVEN NAME
Christmas *n* a festival or holiday commemorating the birth of Christ <gave presents on *Christmas*>
syn Nativity, noel, Xmas, yule, yuletide
chronic *adj* **1** ***syn*** see HABITUAL 2
2 ***syn*** see USUAL 1
chronicle *n* **1** ***syn*** see HISTORY 2
2 ***syn*** see ACCOUNT 7
rel narration, recital, recountal
chthonian *adj* ***syn*** see INFERNAL 1
chthonic *adj* ***syn*** see INFERNAL 1
chubby *adj* ***syn*** see ROTUND 2
ant slim
chuck *vb* **1** ***syn*** see DISCARD
2 ***syn*** see EJECT 1
3 ***syn*** see ABANDON 1
4 ***syn*** see THROW 1
||**chuck** *n* ***syn*** see HARBOR 3
chucker *n* ***syn*** see BOUNCER 2
||**chucker–out** *n* ***syn*** see BOUNCER 2
chuckhole *n* ***syn*** see POTHOLE
chuckle *vb* ***syn*** see LAUGH
chucklehead *n* ***syn*** see DUNCE
chuckleheaded *adj* ***syn*** see STUPID 1
chuff *n* **1** ***syn*** see BOOR
2 ***syn*** see MISER
||**chuff** *adj* ***syn*** see SULLEN
||**chuffy** *adj* ***syn*** see STOCKY
||**chuffy** *adj* ***syn*** see SULLEN
chum *n* ***syn*** see ASSOCIATE 3
chumble *vb* ***syn*** see CHEW 1
chummy *adj* **1** ***syn*** see FAMILIAR 1
2 ***syn*** see INTIMATE 4
chump *n* ||**1** ***syn*** see HEAD 1
2 ***syn*** see DUNCE
3 ***syn*** see FOOL 3
chump *vb* ***syn*** see CHEW 1
||**chumpy** *adj* ***syn*** see STOCKY
chunk *n* ***syn*** see LUMP 1
chunky *adj* ***syn*** see STOCKY
rel chubby, rotund
||**chunter** *vb* ***syn*** see MUMBLE
church *n* **1** ***syn*** see HOUSE OF WORSHIP
2 ***syn*** see RELIGION 2
church *adj* ***syn*** see ECCLESIASTICAL
churchly *adj* ***syn*** see ECCLESIASTICAL
churchman *n* ***syn*** see CLERGYMAN
churchmanly *adj* ***syn*** see ECCLESIASTICAL
churl *n* ***syn*** see BOOR
ant aristocrat, gentleman
churlish *adj* ***syn*** see BOORISH
rel crude, discourteous; blunt, brusque, crusty, curt, gruff; dour, surly; naive, unschooled
con bland, politic, smooth; polished, sophisticated
ant courtly
churn *vb* ***syn*** see SEETHE 4
chute *n* ***syn*** see WATERFALL
chutzpah *n* ***syn*** see EFFRONTERY
cicatrix *n* ***syn*** see SCAR
cicatrize *vb* ***syn*** see SCAR
||**cig** *n* ***syn*** see CIGARETTE
cigarette *n* a paper-wrapped tube of finely cut smoking tobacco <dependence on *cigarettes*>

syn ‖butt, ‖cig, ‖coffin nail, fag, ‖gasper, ‖pill, ‖skag, smoke

cimmerian *adj* ***syn*** see INFERNAL 2

cinch *n* ***syn*** see SNAP 1

cinch *vb* ***syn*** see ENSURE

cincture *n* ***syn*** see BELT 1

cincture *vb* ***syn*** see BELT 1

cinders *n pl* ***syn*** see ASH

cine *n* ***syn*** see MOVIE

‖**cinema** *n* ***syn*** see MOVIE

cipher *n* **1** ***syn*** see ZERO 1
2 ***syn*** see NUMBER
3 ***syn*** see MONOGRAM
4 ***syn*** see NONENTITY

cipher *vb* **1** ***syn*** see CALCULATE
‖**2** ***syn*** see SOLVE 2

ciphering *n* ***syn*** see COMPUTATION

circa *prep* ***syn*** see ABOUT 1

Circean *adj* ***syn*** see ENTICING

circle *n* **1** ***syn*** see RANGE 2
2 ***syn*** see CYCLE 1
3 ***syn*** see SET 5
rel acquaintance; cronies, friends, intimates; associates, companions, comrades
4 ***syn*** see CLIQUE

circle *vb* **1** ***syn*** see SURROUND 1
2 ***syn*** see TURN 1

circuit *n* **1** ***syn*** see CIRCUMFERENCE
rel course, route, way; journey, tour, travels, trip
2 ***syn*** see REVOLUTION 1
3 ***syn*** see TOUR 2
4 ***syn*** see LEAGUE 4

circuitous *adj* ***syn*** see INDIRECT 1
ant straight

circuitously *adv* ***syn*** see ABOUT 2

circular *adj* **1** ***syn*** see ROUND 1
2 ***syn*** see INDIRECT 1

circulate *vb* **1** ***syn*** see SPREAD 1
rel exchange, interchange; flow; revolve, rotate
2 ***syn*** see MOBILIZE 1

circulation *n* ***syn*** see REVOLUTION 1

circulator *n* ***syn*** see GOSSIP 1

circumambages *n pl* ***syn*** see VERBIAGE 1

circumambulate *vb* ***syn*** see WANDER 1

circumbendibus *n* ***syn*** see VERBIAGE 1

circumduct *vb* **1** ***syn*** see TURN 1
2 ***syn*** see ABOLISH 1

circumference *n* a continuous line or course about an area <strolled along the *circumference* of the reservoir>
syn ambit, circuit, compass, perimeter, periphery; *compare* BORDER 1
rel boundary, bounds, confines, limits; border, margin, rim

circumlocution *n* ***syn*** see VERBIAGE 1
con conciseness, concision, pithiness, succinctness, terseness; compactness

circumnavigate *vb* ***syn*** see SKIRT 2

circumscribe *vb* ***syn*** see LIMIT 2
rel fetter, hamper, trammel
con amplify, distend, inflate, swell; enlarge
ant dilate, expand

circumscribed *adj* ***syn*** see DEFINITE 1
rel bound, bounded, finite; confined, cramped, strait

circumscription *n* **1** ***syn*** see RESTRICTION 1
2 ***syn*** see RESTRICTION 2

circumspect *adj* ***syn*** see CAUTIOUS
rel meticulous, punctilious, scrupulous
con adventurous, daredevil, foolhardy; careless, heedless; bold
ant audacious

circumstance *n* **1** ***syn*** see OCCURRENCE
rel detail, item, particular; component, constituent, element, factor
2 ***syn*** see FATE

circumstantial *adj* marked by careful attention to relevant details <gave a *circumstantial* account of his adventure>
syn blow-by-blow, clocklike, detailed, full, itemized, minute, particular, particularized, thorough
rel accurate, exact, nice, precise; complete, replete; close, strict
con compendious, concise, laconic, pithy, short, succinct, terse; abbreviated, curtailed, cut, pruned, shortened, trimmed
ant abridged; summary

circumvent *vb* **1** ***syn*** see FRUSTRATE 1
rel befool, dupe, hoodwink, trick; avoid, elude, escape, evade
ant conform (*to laws, orders*); cooperate (*with persons*)
2 ***syn*** see SKIRT 2
3 ***syn*** see SKIRT 3

circumvolution *n* ***syn*** see REVOLUTION 1

cit *n* ***syn*** see TOWNSMAN

citadel *n* ***syn*** see FORT

citation *n* ***syn*** see ENCOMIUM
rel award, guerdon, reward

cite *vb* **1** ***syn*** see REMEMBER
2 ***syn*** see MENTION
3 ***syn*** see ADDUCE
rel count, enumerate, number, tell

citizen *n* **1** ***syn*** see TOWNSMAN
2 a person regarded as a member of a sovereign state, entitled to its protection, and subject to its laws <the subtle bond between the *citizen* and the nation>
syn national, subject
con foreigner, stranger
ant alien

city *adj* ***syn*** see URBAN

civic *adj* ***syn*** see PUBLIC 1

civil *adj* **1** ***syn*** see PUBLIC 1
2 adequate in courtesy <made a *civil* inquiry about their health>
syn courteous, genteel, mannerly, polite, well-mannered; *compare* COURTLY
rel cultivated, refined, well-bred; accommodating, affable, cordial, obliging; bland, diplomatic, gracious, politic, suave, urbane

---

syn synonym(s) ***rel*** related word(s)
ant antonym(s) ***con*** contrasted word(s)
idiom idiomatic equivalent(s)
‖ use limited; if in doubt, see a dictionary

con boorish, churlish, loutish, uncouth; discourteous, ill-mannered, impolite, ungracious
ant uncivil; rude
civilities *n pl* ***syn*** see MANNER 5
civilized *adj* **1** ***syn*** see DECOROUS 1
2 ***syn*** see SUAVE
Civitas Dei *n* ***syn*** see HEAVEN 2
‖**clabber** *vb* ***syn*** see CURDLE
clack *vb* **1** ***syn*** see CHAT 1
2 ***syn*** see RATTLE 1
clack *n* **1** ***syn*** see CHATTER
2 ***syn*** see GOSSIP 1
clad *vb* **1** ***syn*** see CLOTHE
2 ***syn*** see SHEATHE
‖**claggy** *adj* **1** ***syn*** see STICKY 1
2 ***syn*** see MUDDY 1
claim *vb* **1** ***syn*** see DEMAND 1
rel adduce, advance, allege; assert, defend, justify, maintain, vindicate
con abnegate, forgo; refuse, reject, repudiate; disavow, disown
ant disclaim; renounce
2 ***syn*** see MAINTAIN 2
claim *n* **1** a real or assumed right to demand something as one's own or one's due <his genial wit was his greatest *claim* to fame>
syn ‖dibs, pretense, pretension, title
rel birthright, prerogative, privilege, right; affirmation, assertion, declaration, protestation
2 ***syn*** see INTEREST 1
clamant *adj* ***syn*** see PRESSING
clamber *vb* ***syn*** see SCRAMBLE 1
clamor *n* **1** ***syn*** see COMMOTION 4
2 ***syn*** see DIN
3 ***syn*** see COMMOTION 1
clamor *vb* ***syn*** see ROAR
rel claim, demand; agitate, debate, dispute
idiom make the welkin ring, raise the roof
clamorous *adj* **1** ***syn*** see VOCIFEROUS
rel articulate, eloquent, vocal, voluble; adjuring, begging, imploring, importunate
ant taciturn
2 ***syn*** see PRESSING
clamp *n* ***syn*** see HOLD
clampdown *n* ***syn*** see REPRESSION 2
clan *n* **1** ***syn*** see FAMILY 1
2 ***syn*** see CLIQUE
clandestine *adj* ***syn*** see SECRET 1
rel illegitimate, illicit; artful, foxy, sly
con aboveboard, forthright, straightforward
ant open
clandestinely *adv* ***syn*** see SECRETLY
‖**clanger** *n* ***syn*** see ERROR 2
clangorous *adj* ***syn*** see NOISY
clap *n* ***syn*** see BANG 2
‖**clapped–out** *adj* **1** ***syn*** see EFFETE 2
2 ***syn*** see TIRED 1
claptrap *n* ***syn*** see NONSENSE 2
‖**claret** *n* ***syn*** see BLOOD 1
clarify *vb* **1** ***syn*** see PURIFY 1
2 to make clear and understandable <felt a need to *clarify* his position on the question>
syn clear, clear up, elucidate, explain, illuminate, illustrate; *compare* EXPLAIN 1
rel settle, straighten out; define, delineate, formulate; analyze, break down, simplify
idiom make plain
con befog, cloud, obfuscate, obscure; confuse, foul up, muddle, ‖snafu
clarion *adj* ***syn*** see FAIR 2
clarity *n* notable precision of thought or expression <*clarity* of expression depends on use of exactly the right words in precisely the right way>
syn clearness, limpidity, lucidity, perspicuity, plainness
rel articulateness, articulation; care, exactitude, fussiness, meticulousness, nicety, precision; accuracy, correctitude, propriety
con haziness, imprecision, indefiniteness, unclearness, vagueness; inexactness, laxity, looseness, sloppiness, slovenliness
ant obscurity
‖**clarty** *adj* **1** ***syn*** see MUDDY 1
2 ***syn*** see STICKY 1
clash *vb* **1** ***syn*** see BUMP 1
2 to be markedly out of harmony <garish colors that *clashed* almost painfully>
syn conflict, disaccord, discord, disharmonize, jangle, jar, mismatch
rel fret, gall, grate, try
idiom swear at one another
con accord, blend, conform, correspond; fit, meet, suit
ant harmonize
clash *n* **1** ***syn*** see IMPACT 1
2 a sharp and usually brief conflict especially between military units <recurrent border *clashes*>
syn affray, brush, fray, melee, mellay, scrimmage, skirmish
rel brawl, broil, fracas, riot, row, rumpus, scrap, set-to; action, battle, conflict, engagement; embroilment, encounter
idiom clash of arms, passage at (*or* of) arms
clashing *adj* ***syn*** see ANTIPATHETIC 1
clasp *n* ***syn*** see HOLD
clasp *vb* **1** ***syn*** see EMBRACE 1
2 ***syn*** see TAKE 4
class *n* **1** a unit or a subunit of a larger whole made up of members sharing one or more characteristics <miniaturization of circuitry made possible a whole new *class* of small computers and calculators>
syn category, grade, group, grouping, league, pigeonhole, tier
rel brand, color, description, feather, genre, grain, ilk, kidney, kind, nature, order, sort, stamp, style, type; bracket, branch, denomination, division, head, section; genus, species
2 ***syn*** see QUALITY 3
3 ***syn*** see TYPE
class *vb* **1** ***syn*** see ASSORT
2 to put into an appropriate class <he is generally *classed* among our leading theoretical physicists>
syn classify, evaluate, grade, rank, rate
rel appraise, gauge, judge; divide, part, separate; allot, assign; account, assess, consider, hold, reckon, regard; mark, score

classic *adj* **1** ***syn*** see EXCELLENT
2 ***syn*** see VINTAGE 1
3 ***syn*** see TYPICAL 1
classic *n* ***syn*** see MASTERPIECE 1
classical *adj* **1** ***syn*** see EXCELLENT
2 ***syn*** see VINTAGE 1
3 ***syn*** see TYPICAL 1
classify *vb* **1** ***syn*** see ASSORT
2 ***syn*** see CLASS 2
‖**classy** *adj* ***syn*** see STYLISH
clatter *vb* **1** ***syn*** see RATTLE 1
2 ***syn*** see CHAT 1
clatter *n* ***syn*** see COMMOTION 4
clattery *adj* ***syn*** see NOISY
claviger *n* ***syn*** see CUSTODIAN
‖**clawback** *n* ***syn*** see SYCOPHANT
clean *adj* **1** free from dirt <kept a *clean* house in a dirty neighborhood>
syn cleanly, immaculate, spotless, taintless, unsoiled, unsullied
rel bright, shining, sparkling; fresh, pure, untainted, wholesome
idiom clean as a whistle (*or* new penny)
con dingy, grimy, grubby, messy, mussy, slovenly; filthy, foul, noisome
ant dirty, unclean
2 ***syn*** see INNOCENT 2
3 ***syn*** see CHASTE
ant unclean
4 ***syn*** see FAIR 5
clean *vb* **1** ***syn*** see PURIFY 1
2 to make clean <*cleaned* his car every week>
syn cleanse, clean up
rel do, neaten, order, police, spruce, straighten (up), tidy, trim; brighten, freshen, furbish, recondition; renew, renovate
idiom make spick-and-span
con begrime, daub, dirty, sully; besmirch, defile, foul, pollute
ant soil
3 ***syn*** see DRESS 3
clean-cut *adj* ***syn*** see EXPLICIT
clean-limbed *adj* ***syn*** see SHAPELY
cleanly *adj* ***syn*** see CLEAN 1
rel neat, orderly, spick-and-span, tidy, trim; dainty, fastidious, fussy, nice
con disheveled, disorderly, slipshod, sloppy, slovenly, unkempt
ant uncleanly
cleanse *vb* **1** ***syn*** see CLEAN 2
rel disinfect, sanitize, sterilize
2 ***syn*** see PURIFY 1
3 ***syn*** see PURIFY 2
cleansing *n* ***syn*** see PURIFICATION
clean up *vb* **1** ***syn*** see CLEAR 6
2 ***syn*** see CLEAN 2
3 ***syn*** see SETTLE 7
‖**clean up** (on) *vb* ***syn*** see WHIP 2
clear *adj* **1** ***syn*** see FAIR 2
2 ***syn*** see TRANSPARENT 1
3 ***syn*** see TRANSLUCENT 3
rel milky, opalescent
4 free from obscurity or ambiguity <his account of the accident was perfectly *clear*>
syn clear-cut, crystal, lucent, lucid, luculent, luminous, pellucid, perspicuous, translucent, transparent, transpicuous, unambiguous, unblurred; *compare* UNDERSTANDABLE
rel apprehensible, comprehensible, graspable, knowable, understandable; plain, simple, straightforward, uncomplicated, unperplexed; defined, definite
idiom clear as day (*or* crystal), plain as the nose on one's face
con clouded, dark, mysterious, unclear; hazy, ill-defined, vague
ant obscure
5 readily perceived or apprehended <a *clear* case of embezzlement>
syn apparent, conspicuous, distinct, evident, manifest, obvious, open-and-shut, openhanded, palpable, patent, plain, straightforward, unambiguous, unequivocal, univocal, unmistakable; *compare* SELF-EXPLANATORY, UNDERSTANDABLE
rel appreciable, perceptible, recognizable, sensible, tangible; overt, public, published, unhidden, unobscured; exact, precise
con dim, dusky, gloomy, murky; cryptic, dark, enigmatic, equivocal, indistinct, vague; arcane, esoteric, mysterious, occult
ant obscure
6 ***syn*** see EMPTY 1
clear *adv* ***syn*** see WELL 3
clear *vb* **1** ***syn*** see EXCULPATE
2 ***syn*** see CLARIFY 2
3 ***syn*** see VACATE 2
4 ***syn*** see RID
rel eliminate, rule out; clean, cleanse
5 to make right by presenting what is due <*clear* one's accounts>
syn clear off, discharge, liquidate, pay, pay up, quit, satisfy, settle, square
rel close, pay off, repay, sink, solve
6 to obtain as a profit or return <he *cleared* several thousand on the deal>
syn clean up, gain, make, net
rel acquire, get, obtain, secure; earn, win; accumulate, gather, glean, pick up
7 ***syn*** see EXTRICATE 2
8 to pass over or by <*cleared* the hurdle with perfect form>
syn hurdle, leap, negotiate, over, overleap, surmount, vault
9 to become fair <the weather *cleared* later in the day>
syn ‖break, burn off
rel ameliorate, better, improve, meliorate; settle, stabilize
10 ***syn*** see VANISH
clear away *vb* **1** ***syn*** see REMOVE 4
2 ***syn*** see EXTRICATE 2
clear-cut *adj* **1** ***syn*** see CLEAR 4
2 ***syn*** see EXPLICIT

---

syn synonym(s) ***rel*** related word(s)
ant antonym(s) ***con*** contrasted word(s)
idiom idiomatic equivalent(s)
‖ use limited; if in doubt, see a dictionary

3 ***syn*** see INCISIVE
rel clear, distinct, manifest, plain; definite, explicit, express; exact, nice, precise
con fogged, hazy, misty; confused, muddled; obscured, overcast
4 ***syn*** see DECIDED 1
rel indubitable, undisputed, undoubted, unquestioned
idiom beyond a shade (*or* shadow) of doubt, past dispute

clearness *n* ***syn*** see CLARITY
clear off *vb* ***syn*** see CLEAR 5
clear out *vb* ***syn*** see GET OUT 1
clear–sightedness *n* ***syn*** see WIT 3
clear up *vb* **1** ***syn*** see CLARIFY 2
2 ***syn*** see SOLVE 2
cleavage *n* ***syn*** see SCHISM 3
cleave *vb* ***syn*** see STICK 2
rel associate, combine, conjoin, join, link, unite
con alienate, disaffect, disunite, estrange, separate
cleave *vb* **1** ***syn*** see CUT 5
2 ***syn*** see TEAR 1
rel divide, divorce, separate; chop, hew
con join, link, unite; attach, fasten
cleft *n* **1** ***syn*** see CRACK 3
2 ***syn*** see RAVINE
3 ***syn*** see SCHISM 3
clemency *n* **1** ***syn*** see MERCY
rel gentleness, mildness; equitableness, fairness, justness
con austerity, severity, sternness; rigidity, rigorousness, strictness; inexorableness, inflexibility, obduracy
ant harshness
2 ***syn*** see FORBEARANCE 2
rel endurance, sufferance
con firmness, hardness, inflexibility, obdurateness, relentlessness, rigidity
ant harshness
clement *adj* ***syn*** see FORBEARING
rel compassionate, sympathetic, tender; benign, benignant, kind, kindly; benevolent, charitable, humane
con austere, severe, stern; rigid, rigorous, strict, stringent
ant harsh; barbarous
clench *n* ***syn*** see HOLD
clergyman *n* one duly ordained to the service of God in the Christian church <the responsibility of the *clergyman* to the whole community>
syn ‖blackcoat, cassock, churchman, cleric, clerical, clerk, ‖devil-dodger, divine, ‖dominie, ecclesiast, ecclesiastic, ‖Holy Joe, minister, parson, preacher, pulpitarian, pulpiteer, pulpiter, reverend, sermonizer, sky pilot
rel evangelist, missionary; chaplain, curate, pastor, vicar; father, priest, shepherd; predicant
idiom man of God, man of the cloth
cleric *n* ***syn*** see CLERGYMAN
clerical *n* ***syn*** see CLERGYMAN
clerisy *n* ***syn*** see INTELLIGENTSIA
clerk *n* ***syn*** see CLERGYMAN
clerkish *adj* ***syn*** see NICE 1

clever *adj* **1** ***syn*** see SKILLFUL 2
2 ***syn*** see DEXTEROUS 1
3 ***syn*** see INTELLIGENT 2
rel apt, prompt, quick, ready; able, capable, competent; all-around, many-sided, versatile
idiom quick as a flash, sharp (*or* smart) as a whip
con asinine, fatuous, foolish, simple
ant dull
4 highly skilled in devising or contriving <very *clever* about getting her own way>
syn adroit, canny, ‖coony, cunning, dexterous, ingenious, ‖sleighty, slim, sly; *compare* SKILLFUL 2
rel able, adept, expert, handy, masterly, proficient, skilled, skillful; capable, competent, qualified; crafty, deceitful, slick, tricky
con awkward, clumsy, gauche, inept, maladroit; dilatory, laggard, slow, sluggish; incapable, incompetent, inept, unqualified
5 pleasing because of aptness, sparkle, and usually wit <delighted her audience with a series of *clever* comparisons>
syn good, scintillating, smart, sprightly
rel bright, brilliant, coruscating, dazzling, sparkling; piquant, racy, salty; fanciful, whimsical; amusing, entertaining, pleasing; facetious, funny, humorous, witty; laughable, risible
con drab, dull, humdrum, monotonous, stodgy; barren, empty, inane; fatuous, pointless; absurd, foolish, nonsensical, ridiculous
ant stupid
‖**cleverly** *adv* ***syn*** see WELL 3
cliché *n* ***syn*** see COMMONPLACE
cliché *adj* ***syn*** see TRITE
clichéd *adj* ***syn*** see TRITE
click *vb* ***syn*** see SUCCEED 2
client *n* ***syn*** see CUSTOMER
clientage *n* ***syn*** see FOLLOWING 2
clientele *n* ***syn*** see FOLLOWING 2
climacteric *adj* ***syn*** see ACUTE 6
climate *n* ***syn*** see ENVIRONMENT
climatize *vb* ***syn*** see HARDEN 2
climax *n* ***syn*** see APEX 2
climax *vb* to bring to or come to a satisfying termination <the feast was *climaxed* by a glorious plum pudding>
syn cap, crown, culminate, finish off, round off, top off
rel content, please, satisfy; conclude, end, finish, terminate
climb *vb* ***syn*** see ASCEND 1
‖**clinch** *vb* ***syn*** see EMBRACE 1
clinch *n* ***syn*** see HOLD
clincher *n* ***syn*** see TRUMP CARD
cling *vb* ***syn*** see STICK 2
cling *n* ***syn*** see ADHERENCE 1
clinging *n* ***syn*** see ADHERENCE 1
clink *vb* ***syn*** see JINGLE
‖**clink** *n* ***syn*** see JAIL
clinkers *n pl* ***syn*** see ASH
‖**clip** *vb* ***syn*** see EMBRACE 1
clip *n* ***syn*** see BROOCH
clip *vb* **1** ***syn*** see CUT 6

2 ***syn*** see MOW
3 ***syn*** see REDUCE 2
4 ***syn*** see OVERCHARGE 1
clique *n* a narrowly exclusive group of people usually held together by a common often selfish interest or purpose <there was a politically minded *clique* on the campus>
syn cabal, camarilla, camp, circle, clan, coterie, in-group, mob, ring; *compare* SET 5
clitter *vb* ***syn*** see RATTLE 1
cloak *n* ***syn*** see MASK 2
cloak *vb* ***syn*** see DISGUISE
rel blanket, curtain, screen, shroud, veil
ant uncloak
clobber *vb* ‖**1** ***syn*** see WHIP 2
2 ***syn*** see SLAM 1
clochard *n* ***syn*** see VAGABOND
clock *vb* ***syn*** see TIME 2
‖**clock** *vb* ***syn*** see SET 11
clocklike *adj* ***syn*** see CIRCUMSTANTIAL
clockwise *adj* ***syn*** see RIGHT-HANDED
clod *n* **1** ***syn*** see LUMP 1
2 ***syn*** see DUNCE
cloddish *adj* ***syn*** see BOORISH
clodhopper *n* **1** ***syn*** see RUSTIC
2 ***syn*** see BOOR
clodhopping *adj* ***syn*** see BOORISH
clodpate *n* ***syn*** see DUNCE
clodpoll *n* ***syn*** see DUNCE
clog *n* ***syn*** see ENCUMBRANCE
clog *vb* **1** ***syn*** see BURDEN
2 ***syn*** see HAMPER
3 ***syn*** see FILL 1
cloggy *adj* ***syn*** see STICKY 1
cloister *vb* ***syn*** see SECLUDE
cloistered *adj* ***syn*** see SECLUDED
clonk *vb* ***syn*** see THUD
‖**Cloot** *n, usu* **Cloots** *pl* ***syn*** see DEVIL 1
‖**Clootie** *n* ***syn*** see DEVIL 1
close *vb* **1** to fill an opening with an appropriate closure <be sure to *close* the gate>
syn ‖put to, shut
rel bang, clap, slam; block, choke, clog, obstruct, occlude, stop; debar, exclude
ant open
2 ***syn*** see SCREEN 3
3 to bring or come to a limit or to a natural or appropriate stopping point <*closed* the meeting as soon as the discussion was over>
syn complete, conclude, consummate, determine, do, end, finish, halt, terminate, ultimate, wind up, wrap up
rel cease, desist, quit, stop; finalize, write off
idiom call it a day, set a period to
con begin, commence, enter (on *or* upon), inaugurate, initiate, start
4 ***syn*** see FILL 1
5 ***syn*** see DECREASE
6 ***syn*** see MEET 6
close *n* **1** ***syn*** see END 2
2 ***syn*** see FINALE
ant opening
‖**close** *n* ***syn*** see COURT 1
close *adj* **1** ***syn*** see SILENT 3
idiom close as a clam
con candid, frank, plain
ant open
2 ***syn*** see STUFFY 1
rel humid, muggy, sticky
3 ***syn*** see STINGY
ant liberal
4 having the constituent parts massed closely together <a paper of fine *close* texture>
syn compact, crowded, dense, thick, tight
rel compacted, compressed, condensed, consolidated, constricted, contracted; firm, solid, substantial; impenetrable, impermeable; close-grained
con lax, loose, slack; unconsolidated
5 ***syn*** see TIGHT 3
6 not far removed (as in space, time, or relationship) from something stipulated or understood <true and veritable are *close* synonyms> <the park is very *close* to the river> <it is *close* to closing time>
syn immediate, near, near-at-hand, nearly, nigh, proximate; *compare* NEIGHBORING
rel abutting, adjacent, adjoining, contiguous; convenient, handy; nearest, nearmost, next
idiom at hand, at one's fingers' ends (*or* fingertips), under one's nose
con distant, far, faraway, far-off, removed
ant remote
7 ***syn*** see FAMILIAR 1
con cool, remote, withdrawn
ant aloof
close *adv* into proximity with respect to space, time, or approach <hoping to come *closer* to the truth of the matter>
syn at close hand, hard, near, nearby, nigh
rel almost, nearabout, nearly
idiom as near as no matter (*or* never mind), in hailing (*or* spitting) distance, within an inch (*or* an ace) of, within a stone's throw
con afar, distantly, far
ant remotely
close–at–hand *adj* **1** ***syn*** see NEIGHBORING
2 ***syn*** see CONVENIENT 2
close–by *adj* **1** ***syn*** see NEIGHBORING
2 ***syn*** see CONVENIENT 2
closed *adj* ***syn*** see SELF-SUFFICIENT
closed book *n* ***syn*** see MYSTERY
closed–minded *adj* ***syn*** see OBSTINATE
closefisted *adj* ***syn*** see STINGY
rel clinging, clutching, grasping, keeping, tenacious
close in *vb* ***syn*** see ENCLOSE 1
close–lipped *adj* ***syn*** see SILENT 3
closely *adv* ***syn*** see HARD 4
rel carefully, heedfully, mindfully, thoughtfully; meticulously, minutely, punctiliously, scrupulously
con carelessly, heedlessly, thoughtlessly

syn synonym(s) ***rel*** related word(s)
ant antonym(s) ***con*** contrasted word(s)
idiom idiomatic equivalent(s)
‖ use limited; if in doubt, see a dictionary

closemouthed *adj* ***syn*** see SILENT 3
close off *vb* ***syn*** see ISOLATE
close on *prep* ***syn*** see ABOUT 1
close out *vb* ***syn*** see SELL OUT 1
closeout *n* ***syn*** see BARGAIN 1
‖**closet** *n* ***syn*** see PRIVY 1
closet *adj* **1** ***syn*** see PRIVATE 2
2 ***syn*** see THEORETICAL 1
close–tongued *adj* ***syn*** see SILENT 3
closing *n* ***syn*** see END 2
closing *adj* ***syn*** see LAST
closure *n* ***syn*** see END 2
clot *n* ***syn*** see GROUP 3
clot *vb* ***syn*** see COAGULATE
clothe *vb* to cover with or as if with garments <forests *clothe* the rocky slopes>
syn apparel, array, attire, clad, dress, enclothe, garb, garment, raiment
rel costume, do up, dress up, tog (up *or* out); cloak, mantle, robe; accouter, equip, outfit, rig (out); bedrape, drape, swathe; endue, invest
con dismantle, divest, strip
ant unclothe
clothes *n pl* a person's garments as a whole <dressed in new *clothes* from the skin out>
syn apparel, attire, attirement, clothing, dress, duds, habiliment(s), rags, raiment, rigging, things, togs
rel array, garb, toggery, vestments, vesture; costume, getup, outfit, rig
clothing *n* **1** ***syn*** see CLOTHES
2 ***syn*** see ROLE 1
cloud *n* ***syn*** see MULTITUDE 1
cloud *vb* **1** ***syn*** see OBSCURE
rel addle, befuddle, confuse, muddle; distract, perplex, puzzle
2 ***syn*** see CONFUSE 4
3 ***syn*** see TAINT 1
clouded *adj* ***syn*** see DOUBTFUL 1
cloudless *adj* ***syn*** see FAIR 2
cloudy *adj* **1** ***syn*** see OVERCAST
2 ***syn*** see HAZY
3 ***syn*** see MURKY 3
clough *n* ***syn*** see RAVINE
clout *n* **1** ***syn*** see CUFF
2 ***syn*** see PULL 2
clout *vb* **1** ***syn*** see STRIKE 2
‖**2** ***syn*** see STEAL 1
clove *n* ***syn*** see RAVINE
clown *n* **1** ***syn*** see RUSTIC
2 ***syn*** see BOOR
3 a performer (as in a circus) who entertains by grotesque appearance and actions <children delighted by the antics of the *clowns*>
syn buffoon, harlequin, merry-andrew, zany
rel comedian; fool, jester, mountebank; mime, mummer
4 ***syn*** see ZANY 2
clownish *adj* ***syn*** see BOORISH
rel awkward, clumsy, gauche; green, raw, rough, rude, uncouth
ant urbane
cloy *vb* ***syn*** see SATIATE
con excite, pique, provoke, stimulate
ant whet
club *n* **1** ***syn*** see CUDGEL
2 ***syn*** see ASSOCIATION 2
club car *n* ***syn*** see PARLOR CAR
‖**cluck** *n* ***syn*** see DUNCE
clue *n* ***syn*** see HINT 1
clue (*or* **clew**) *vb* ***syn*** see INFORM 2
clump *n* **1** ***syn*** see GROUP 3
rel clutter, hodgepodge, jumble, omnium-gatherum
2 ***syn*** see LUMP 1
clump *vb* ***syn*** see LUMBER
clumsy *adj* **1** lacking in physical ease and grace usually because of coarse cumbersome build or poor coordination <a *clumsy* boy constantly stumbling over his own feet> <the *clumsy* gait of a young puppy>
syn awkward, gawky, lumbering, lumpish, splathering, splay, ungainly; *compare* AWKWARD 2
rel butterfingered, heavy-handed, left-handed, unhandy; graceless, inelegant, uncouth; bulky, hulking, unwieldy
idiom all thumbs, fingers all thumbs
con comely, shapely, well-formed, well-proportioned; apt, deft, handy, quick, ready
2 ***syn*** see AWKWARD 2
clunk *vb* ***syn*** see THUD
clunker *n* ***syn*** see JALOPY
cluster *n* **1** ***syn*** see GROUP 3
2 ***syn*** see GROUP 1
cluster *vb* ***syn*** see GROUP 1
rel accumulate, aggregate, associate, cumulate; bundle, package, parcel
clutch *vb* ***syn*** see SEIZE 2
rel clench, clinch, gripe; cherish, harbor, hold, keep
clutch *n* ***syn*** see HOLD
clutch *n* ***syn*** see GROUP 3
clutter *n* **1** ***syn*** see CONFUSION 3
2 a disordered nondescript mass or group <a *clutter* of ornaments on the mantel>
syn hash, hugger-mugger, jumble, jungle, litter, mash, mishmash, muddle, rummage, scramble, shuffle, tumble
rel hodgepodge, macédoine, medley, mélange; disarray, mess, muss, ruck
con arrangement, array, order; grouping, ordering, pigeonholing, ranking, sorting
‖**cly** *vb* ***syn*** see STEAL 1
coact *vb* ***syn*** see INTERACT
coacting *adj* ***syn*** see COOPERATIVE
coactive *adj* ***syn*** see COOPERATIVE
coadjutant *n* ***syn*** see ASSISTANT 2
coadjute *vb* ***syn*** see UNITE 2
coadjutor *n* ***syn*** see ASSISTANT 2
coadunate *vb* ***syn*** see JOIN 1
coadunation *n* ***syn*** see UNIFICATION
coagment *vb* ***syn*** see JOIN 1
coagulate *vb* to alter by chemical reaction from a liquid to a more or less firm jelly <the blood *coagulated* and closed the wound>
syn clot, congeal, gel, gelate, gelatinize, jell, jellify, jelly, set

rel concrete, harden, solidify; curdle, inspissate; compact, concentrate, consolidate; coalesce; freeze; dehydrate, dry; condense, thicken
con deliquesce, fluidify, liquefy, liquesce; flux, fuse, melt, run
coalesce *vb* ***syn*** see JOIN 1
rel adhere, cleave, cling, stick; blend, fuse, merge, mingle, mix
coalition *n* **1** ***syn*** see UNIFICATION
2 ***syn*** see COMBINATION 2
3 ***syn*** see ALLIANCE 2
coarct *vb* ***syn*** see RESTRAIN 1
coarse *adj* **1** made up of relatively large particles <*coarse* sand>
syn grainy, granular
rel caked, cakey, lumpy, particulate
2 ***syn*** see CRUDE 5
3 deficient in refinement of manner and delicacy of feeling <a *coarse* practical man lacking all social graces>
syn crass, crude, gross, incult, inelegant, low, raw, rough, rude, uncouth, uncultivated, uncultured, unrefined, vulgar; *compare* BOORISH
rel raffish, roughneck, rowdy, vulgarian; common, tacky
con considerate, courtly, gracious; cultivated, polished, refined
4 ***syn*** see OBSCENE 2
‖**5** ***syn*** see WILD 6
coast *n* ***syn*** see SHORE
coast *vb* ***syn*** see SLIDE 6
coax *vb* to influence or persuade by artful ingratiation <*coaxed* her friend to help her with her work>
syn ‖barter, blandish, blarney, cajole, con, soft-soap, sweet-talk, wheedle
rel pester, plague, tease; importune, press, urge; get, induce, persuade, prevail; entice, inveigle, lure, tempt; butter (up)
con coerce, compel, constrain, force, oblige; browbeat, bulldoze, cow, intimidate
ant bully
cob *vb* ***syn*** see SURPASS 1
cobble *vb* ***syn*** see BOTCH
rel confuse, foul up, snafu, snarl (up)
‖**cobblers** *n* ***syn*** see NONSENSE 2
cobweb *n* ***syn*** see WEB 2
cock *n* **1** ***syn*** see FAUCET
2 ***syn*** see LEADER 2
‖**3** ***syn*** see NONSENSE 2
‖**cock** *adj* ***syn*** see CHIEF 2
cock *vb* ***syn*** see LORD
cock *n* ***syn*** see PILE 1
cock *vb* ***syn*** see HEAP 1
cock-a-doodle-doo *vb* ***syn*** see BOAST
cock-a-hoop *adj* **1** ***syn*** see EXULTANT
2 ***syn*** see AWRY 1
Cockaigne *n* ***syn*** see UTOPIA
cockamamie *adj* ***syn*** see FOOLISH 2
cock-and-bull story *n* ***syn*** see LIE
cock-a-whoop *adj* ***syn*** see EXULTANT
cockcrow *n* ***syn*** see DAWN 1
cockcrowing *n* ***syn*** see DAWN 1
cocker *vb* ***syn*** see BABY
‖**cocket** *adj* ***syn*** see SAUCY 1
cockeyed *adj* **1** ***syn*** see AWRY 1
2 ***syn*** see INTOXICATED 1
cockle *vb* ***syn*** see RIPPLE
cocksure *adj* ***syn*** see SURE 5
cocktail lounge *n* ***syn*** see BAR 5
‖**coco** *n* ***syn*** see HEAD 1
coconspirator *n* ***syn*** see CONFEDERATE
‖**coconut** *n* ***syn*** see HEAD 1
cocotte *n* ***syn*** see PROSTITUTE
coddle *vb* ***syn*** see BABY
codicil *n* ***syn*** see APPENDIX 1
‖**codswallop** *n* ***syn*** see NONSENSE 2
coefficient *adj* ***syn*** see COOPERATIVE
coerce *vb* ***syn*** see FORCE 2
rel beset, push, urge; browbeat, bulldoze, bully, cow, intimidate; menace, terrorize, threaten
coercion *n* ***syn*** see FORCE 4
rel menace, menacing, threat, threatening
coetaneous *adj* ***syn*** see CONTEMPORARY 1
coeval *adj* ***syn*** see CONTEMPORARY 1
coexistent *adj* ***syn*** see CONTEMPORARY 1
coexisting *adj* ***syn*** see CONTEMPORARY 1
coffee shop *n* ***syn*** see EATING HOUSE
coffer *n* ***syn*** see TREASURY 2
‖**coffin nail** *n* ***syn*** see CIGARETTE
cogency *n* ***syn*** see POINT 3
rel pertinence, relevance; bearing, concern, connection
cogent *adj* **1** ***syn*** see VALID
rel compelling, constraining, forceful, forcible, potent, powerful, puissant; inducing, persuasive; justified, well-founded, well-grounded
con ineffective, ineffectual, inefficacious; feeble, forceless, impotent, powerless, weak
2 ***syn*** see WELL-FOUNDED
rel consequential, influential, momentous, weighty; meaningful, significant
cogitable *adj* ***syn*** see THINKABLE 1
cogitate *vb* **1** ***syn*** see THINK 5
rel conceive, envisage, envision, imagine
2 ***syn*** see PLOT
cogitation *n* ***syn*** see THOUGHT 1
cogitative *adj* ***syn*** see THOUGHTFUL 1
cognate *adj* ***syn*** see RELATED
rel common, general, generic, universal
con different, disparate, divergent, diverse, various
cognizance *n* ***syn*** see NOTICE 1
cognizant *adj* ***syn*** see AWARE
con forgetful, oblivious, unmindful; heedless, ignoring, neglectful, slighting, unmindful
ant ignorant
cognize *vb* ***syn*** see KNOW 1
cognomen *n* ***syn*** see NAME 1
cognoscente *n* ***syn*** see CONNOISSEUR
rel ‖dab, proficient, specialist; authority, critic, judge
cohere *vb* **1** ***syn*** see STICK 2

---

syn synonym(s) *rel* related word(s)
ant antonym(s) *con* contrasted word(s)
idiom idiomatic equivalent(s)
‖ use limited; if in doubt, see a dictionary

THESAURUS

rel blend, coalesce, fuse, merge; associate, combine, connect, join, unite
con disembarrass, disentangle, untangle
2 *syn* see AGREE 4

coherence *n* 1 *syn* see ADHERENCE 1
rel integrity, solidarity, union, unity
ant incoherence
2 *syn* see CONSISTENCY

cohesion *n* 1 *syn* see ADHERENCE 1
ant incohesion
2 *syn* see SOLIDARITY

cohort *n* 1 *syn* see PARTNER
2 *syn* see FOLLOWER

coil *n* *syn* see COMMOTION 3

coil *vb* *syn* see WIND 2
rel revolve, rotate, turn

‖**coin** *n* *syn* see MONEY
idiom coin of the realm

coinage *n* *syn* see INVENTION

coincide *vb* *syn* see AGREE 3
rel accord, correspond, jibe, tally; equal, match
con deviate, divagate, divaricate, diverge; bias, skew, twist, warp
ant differ

coincident *adj* *syn* see CONCOMITANT

coincidentally *adv* *syn* see TOGETHER 1

coincidently *adv* *syn* see TOGETHER 1

coinstantaneously *adv* *syn* see TOGETHER 1

cold *adj* 1 marked by a deficiency of warmth <a *cold* day>
syn arctic, chill, chillsome, chilly, cool, freezing, frigid, frore, frosty, gelid, glacial, icy, nippy, shivery
rel biting, bleak, chilling, cutting, nipping, polar, raw, sharp; frozen, iced, wintry; bracing, brisk, crisp, snappy
con genial, mild
ant warm
2 lacking cordiality or emotional warmth <a *cold* greeting>
syn chill, emotionless, frigid, glacial, icy, indifferent, unemotional
rel unenthusiastic, unresponsive, unsympathetic
con cordial, friendly, genial, hearty, warm; empathic, sympathetic
3 *syn* see MATTER-OF-FACT 3
4 *syn* see FRIGID 3
ant hot
5 *syn* see GLOOMY 3
6 *syn* see DEAD 1
7 *syn* see INSENSIBLE 2

cold–blooded *adj* 1 *syn* see UNFEELING 2
2 *syn* see MATTER-OF-FACT 3

cold feet *n* *syn* see FEAR 1

coldhearted *adj* *syn* see UNFEELING 2
ant warmhearted

‖**cold meat** *n* *syn* see CORPSE

cold–shoulder *vb* *syn* see CUT 7

cold storage *n* *syn* see ABEYANCE

colic *n* *syn* see STOMACHACHE

coliseum *n* *syn* see STADIUM

‖**coll** *vb* *syn* see EMBRACE 1

collapse *vb* 1 *syn* see GIVE 12
rel break up, disintegrate, shatter
idiom fall to pieces
2 to lose energy, stamina, or control under stress <exhausted to the point of *collapsing* helplessly on the bed>
syn break down, cave (in), drop, ‖flake out, give out, peg out, succumb, wilt
rel droop, fail, languish, weaken; exhaust, fag, flag, play out, tire, weary
con enliven, invigorate, stimulate

collapse *n* 1 *syn* see NERVOUS BREAKDOWN
2 a sudden and grave failure <the *collapse* of an overextended market>
syn breakdown, crack-up, crash, debacle, smash, smashup, wreck
rel breakup, disorganization, disruption, undoing; cataclysm, catastrophe; destruction, ruination, ruining; failure

collar *vb* 1 *syn* see CORNER
2 *syn* see CATCH 1
3 *syn* see STEAL 1

collate *vb* *syn* see COMPARE 2

collateral *adj* 1 *syn* see CONCOMITANT
2 *syn* see INDIRECT 1
3 *syn* see CORROBORATIVE
4 *syn* see SUBORDINATE
rel allied, cognate, kindred, related; complementary, corresponding, reciprocal
con major, prominent
5 *syn* see AUXILIARY

‖**collateral** *n* *syn* see REFUSE

colleague *n* one affiliated with another usually through a common office or profession <he claims to speak for his *colleagues* in the Senate>
syn associate, compatriot, compeer, confrere
rel consociate, copartner, fellow, partner; coworker, workfellow; buddy, chum, companion, crony, pal; aide, assistant, helper

collect *vb* 1 *syn* see GATHER 6
con assort, sort; sever, sunder; deal, dispense, divide, dole
ant disperse; distribute
2 *syn* see INFER
3 *syn* see COMPOSE 4
4 *syn* see GROUP 1
rel align, array, dispose, marshal, order, rank
con broadcast, disperse, distribute, scatter

collected *adj* 1 *syn* see CALM 2
rel peaceful, quiet, still
ant distraught
2 *syn* see COOL 2
rel assured, confident, sanguine, sure; complacent, self-satisfied, smug
con disordered, troubled

collection *n* 1 *syn* see GATHERING 2
rel band, crew, outfit, party
2 *syn* see ACCUMULATION
rel assortment, medley, miscellany, variety; bunch, clump, cluster, group; armamentarium; caboodle, kit, lot

‖**college** *n* *syn* see JAIL

collide *vb* *syn* see BUMP 1
rel atomize, fragment, pulverize, shatter, smash, splinter; break up, crunch, scrap

collimate *vb syn* see PARALLEL 2

collision *n syn* see IMPACT 1
rel dilapidation, ruin, wreck; demolishment, destruction

collocate *vb syn* see PARALLEL 2

collogue *vb* ‖**1** *syn* see PLOT
2 *syn* see CONFER 2

colloque *vb syn* see CONVERSE

colloquial *adj syn* see VERNACULAR

colloquial *n syn* see VERNACULAR 3

colloquium *n syn* see CONFERENCE 2

colloquy *n* **1** *syn* see CONVERSATION 1
2 *syn* see CONVERSATION 2
3 *syn* see CONFERENCE 2

collude *vb syn* see PLOT

collusion *n syn* see COMPLICITY

colluvies *n syn* see MISCELLANY 1

collywobbles *n pl but sing or pl in constr syn* see STOMACHACHE

Colonel Blimp *n* **1** *syn* see STUFFED SHIRT
2 *syn* see REACTIONARY

color *n* **1** a property of a visible thing recognizable only when rays of light fall upon it and serving to distinguish things otherwise visually identical (as in size, shape, or texture) <the green *color* of foliage turns red and gold in autumn>
syn cast, hue, shade, tinge, tint, tone
2 *syn* see MASK 2
3 *syn* see VERISIMILITUDE
4 *syn* see POSITION 1
5 *syn* see FLAG
6 something used to impart visible color to something <dyed her curtains with one of the new easy-to-use *colors*>
syn colorant, dye, dyestuff, pigment, stain, tincture

color *vb* **1** *syn* see EMBROIDER
rel disguise, distort, fake, misrepresent
con constrain, minimize, reduce, soften, temper; blue-pencil, censor, edit
2 *syn* see MISREPRESENT
3 *syn* see BLUSH

colorable *adj syn* see BELIEVABLE
rel cogent, compelling, convincing, sound, telling, valid

colorant *n syn* see COLOR 6

colored *adj syn* see BIASED 2

colorful *adj* making a fine display of usually showy color <a *colorful* bed of asters>
syn brave, bright, colory, gay, vivid
rel blatant, florid, garish, gaudy, loud; flashy, showy, splashy
con blanched, bleached, pallid, wan; dim, dull, faint, pale, weak
ant colorless

coloring *n* **1** *syn* see MASK 2
2 *syn* see EXAGGERATION

colorless *adj* **1** *syn* see PALE 1
2 lacking in sparkle and vitality <an accurate but *colorless* recital of facts>
syn drab, dull, flat, lackluster, lifeless, lusterless, prosaic, prosy
rel blurry, hazy, obscure, vague; feeble, insipid, milk-and-water, namby-pamby, weak, wishy-washy; unimaginative, uninspired
con clear, concise, exact, precise; exciting, provocative, rousing, stimulating, stirring
ant colorful
3 *syn* see NEUTRAL
rel aloof, remote, withdrawn

colory *adj syn* see COLORFUL

colossal *adj syn* see HUGE

colporteur *n syn* see MISSIONARY

colt *n syn* see NOVICE

coltish *adj syn* see PLAYFUL 1

columbary *n syn* see DOVECOTE

column *n* **1** *syn* see PILLAR 1
2 *syn* see SUPPORT 3

coma *n* **1** *syn* see FAINT
2 *syn* see LETHARGY 1

comate *n syn* see ASSOCIATE 3

comatose *adj* **1** *syn* see INSENSIBLE 2
2 *syn* see LETHARGIC
rel anesthetic, impassible, insensitive
ant awake

comb *vb* **1** *syn* see SORT 2
2 *syn* see SCOUR 2
rel examine, inspect, scrutinize; investigate, probe, sift

combat *vb syn* see RESIST
rel battle, contend, war

combat *n syn* see SERVICE 1

combative *adj syn* see BELLIGERENT
rel energetic, strenuous, vigorous; manful, manly, virile
ant pacifistic

combativeness *n syn* see ATTACK 2

‖**combe** *n syn* see VALLEY

combination *n* **1** *syn* see UNIFICATION
2 individuals or organized interests banded together to further a common end <a *combination* of citizens devoted to holding down taxes>
syn bloc, coalition, combine, faction, party, ring
rel cartel, pool, syndicate, trust; cabal, circle, clique, coterie, set
3 *syn* see ASSOCIATION 1

combine *vb* **1** *syn* see JOIN 1
rel amalgamate, blend, commingle, fuse, mingle, mix; consolidate, unify
con divide, divorce, part
ant separate
2 *syn* see EMBODY 2
3 *syn* see UNITE 2
rel agree, coincide; merge, pool

combine *n* **1** *syn* see COMBINATION 2
2 *syn* see SYNDICATE

comble *n syn* see APEX 2

combust *vb syn* see BURN 2

combustible *adj* **1** capable of catching or being set on fire <*combustible* materials should be stored away from open fire>
syn burnable, flammable, ignitable, inflammable

---

syn synonym(s) *rel* related word(s)
ant antonym(s) *con* contrasted word(s)
idiom idiomatic equivalent(s)
‖ use limited; if in doubt, see a dictionary

rel comburent, combustive; burning, firing, igniting, kindling
con fireproof; flameproof, nonflammable; fire-resistant, fire-resistive, fire-retardant
ant incombustible, noncombustible
2 *syn* see EXCITABLE

come *vb* **1** to attain to a destination <when will they *come*>
syn arrive, ‖blow in, get, get in, reach, show, show up, turn up
rel approach, near, nigh
con depart, leave, quit, retreat, withdraw
ant go
2 *syn* see AMOUNT 1
3 *syn* see HAPPEN 1
4 *syn* see BECOME 1

come (from) *vb* **1** *syn* see SPRING
2 *syn* see ORIGINATE 5

come (in) *vb syn* see ENTER 1

comeback *n syn* see RETORT 2

come by *vb syn* see VISIT 2

come–by–chance *n syn* see BASTARD 1

comedian *n* **1** *syn* see HUMORIST 2
2 *syn* see WAG 1

come down (with) *vb syn* see CONTRACT 1

comedown *n* a loss of status <bitter over their *comedown* in the world>
syn descent, discomfiture, down; *compare* SETBACK
rel collapse, crash, downfall, fall, ruin, smash, undoing, wreck
con advance, headway, progress
ant rise

comedy *n syn* see HUMOR 4

come in *vb syn* see ANSWER 1

comely *adj* **1** *syn* see BEAUTIFUL
ant homely
2 *syn* see DECOROUS 1

come off *vb* **1** *syn* see SUCCEED 2
2 *syn* see HAPPEN 1

come–off *n syn* see ESCAPE 2

come–on *n* **1** *syn* see LURE 2
‖**2** *syn* see FOOL 3
3 *syn* see SWINDLER

come out *vb* **1** *syn* see GET OUT 2
2 *syn* see DEBUT

come out (with) *vb syn* see SAY 1

come over *vb* **1** *syn* see VISIT 2
2 *syn* see BECOME 1

come round *vb syn* see RECOVER 2

comestible *adj syn* see EDIBLE

comestibles *n pl syn* see FOOD 1

come through *vb* **1** *syn* see SURVIVE 2
2 *syn* see CONTRIBUTE 1

comeuppance *n syn* see DUE 1

comfort *n* **1** *syn* see HELP 1
2 *syn* see AMENITY 2

comfort *vb* to cheer or try to cheer a person overcome by grief or misery <*comforting* her widowed sister with words of hope>
syn buck up, cheer, console, solace, upraise
rel brighten, gladden, lighten; allay, alleviate, assuage, mitigate, relieve; refresh, renew, restore; reassure; commiserate, condole, sympathize
idiom give a lift to
con torment, torture, try; distress, trouble, worry; annoy, irk, vex
ant afflict; bother

comfortable *adj* **1** *syn* see SUFFICIENT 1
2 enjoying or providing conditions that make for comfort and security <lived in a *comfortable* home on a quiet street>
syn comfy, cozy, cushy, easeful, easy, snug, soft
rel agreeable, grateful, gratifying, welcome; pleasant, pleasing; restful; comforting, consoling, solacing; content, pleased, satisfied
con distressing, perturbing, troubling; annoying, bothering, irking, vexing; inferior, miserable, poor, substandard, wretched
ant uncomfortable
3 *syn* see PROSPEROUS 3
idiom in comfortable circumstances

‖**comfortable** *n syn* see QUILT

comforter *n syn* see QUILT

comfortless *adj syn* see UNCOMFORTABLE

comfy *adj syn* see COMFORTABLE 2

comic *adj syn* see LAUGHABLE
rel antic, fantastic, grotesque; mocking, ridiculing
ant tragic

comic *n syn* see HUMORIST 2

comical *adj syn* see LAUGHABLE
rel absurd, foolish, silly; impish, roguish, sportive, waggish
con doleful, dolorous, lugubrious, melancholy
ant pathetic

comicality *n syn* see HUMOR 4

comicalness *n syn* see HUMOR 4

coming *n syn* see ARRIVAL 1

coming *adj* **1** *syn* see FORTHCOMING
2 *syn* see NEXT

coming in *n, usu* **comings in** *pl syn* see REVENUE

comingle *vb syn* see MIX 1

comity *n syn* see GOODWILL 1
rel accord, concord, harmony; camaraderie, companionship, comradeship, good-fellowship

comma *n syn* see PAUSE

command *vb* to issue orders or an order to <the general *commanded* the troops to advance>
syn bid, charge, direct, enjoin, instruct, order, tell, warn
rel demand, exact, require; coerce, compel, constrain, force, oblige; conduct, control, manage; ask, call (on), request, say
ant comply, obey

command *n* **1** a direction that must or should be obeyed <failure to obey a direct *command* subjects the soldier to grave penalties>
syn behest, bidding, charge, dictate, injunction, mandate, order, word
rel direction, directive, instruction; canon, law, ordinance, precept, rule, statute; devoir, duty, obligation, responsibility
2 *syn* see POWER 1
rel rule
3 *syn* see ABILITY 2
rel aplomb, assurance, confidence, poise
con incertitude, insecurity, uncertainty, unsureness; indecisiveness, vagueness

commandeer *vb* **1** ***syn*** see APPROPRIATE 1
2 ***syn*** see ARROGATE 1
comme il faut *adj* ***syn*** see DECOROUS 1
commemorate *vb* **1** ***syn*** see KEEP 2
2 ***syn*** see MEMORIALIZE 2
commemorative *adj* ***syn*** see MEMORIAL
commemoratory *adj* ***syn*** see MEMORIAL
commence *vb* **1** ***syn*** see BEGIN 1
2 ***syn*** see BEGIN 2
idiom come into being (*or* existence)
commencement *n* ***syn*** see BEGINNING
commend *vb* **1** ***syn*** see COMMIT 1
rel resign, yield; proffer, tender
2 to indicate one's warm approval <the teacher *commended* her pupils' studious attitude>
syn acclaim, applaud, compliment, hail, kudize, praise, recommend, ‖roose
rel eulogize, extol; approve, countenance, endorse, support
con blame, criticize, reprehend, reprobate; chide, rebuke, reprimand, reproach, reprove
ant censure; admonish
commendable *adj* ***syn*** see WORTHY 1
commensurable *adj* ***syn*** see PROPORTIONAL
commensurate *adj* ***syn*** see PROPORTIONAL
comment *n* **1** ***syn*** see REMARK 2
2 ***syn*** see CRITICISM 1
comment *vb* ***syn*** see REMARK 2
rel construe, elucidate, explain, explicate, expound; annotate, gloss
commentary *n* ***syn*** see REMARK 2
commentate *vb* ***syn*** see REMARK 2
commerce *n* **1** ***syn*** see CONTACT 2
2 a situation characterized by mutual exchange (as of ideas) <those who feel that art should have no *commerce* with morality>
syn communion, dealings, intercourse, traffic, truck
rel communication, congress, contact, exchange, interchange, intercommunication; basis, common ground, takeoff
3 ***syn*** see BUSINESS 4
commie *n* ***syn*** see COMMUNIST
commination *n* ***syn*** see CURSE 1
commingle *vb* ***syn*** see MIX 1
rel integrate, unify
comminute *vb* ***syn*** see PULVERIZE 1
commiserable *adj* ***syn*** see PITIFUL 1
commiserate *vb* ***syn*** see COMPASSIONATE
commiseration *n* ***syn*** see PITY
commission *vb* **1** ***syn*** see AUTHORIZE 1
rel appoint, designate, name, nominate; bid, charge, command, enjoin, instruct, order
2 ***syn*** see DELEGATE
commit *vb* **1** to assign (as to a person) especially for use or safekeeping <it is unwise to *commit* all power and authority to one man> <sainted beings who *commit* their spirits to God>
syn commend, confide, consign, entrust, hand over, relegate, turn over
rel allocate, allot, assign, destine, ordain; move, remove, shift, transfer; deliver, give, offer, submit; delegate, deputize
idiom give into the charge (*or* hands) of
2 to be responsible for or guilty of (an offense or wrongdoing) <*commit* a crime>
syn perpetuate, pull
rel accomplish, achieve, do, effectuate, execute, perform, pull off; contravene, transgress, trespass, violate; offend, scandalize, sin
commitment *n* ***syn*** see OBLIGATION 2
committal *n* ***syn*** see OBLIGATION 2
commix *vb* ***syn*** see MIX 1
commixture *n* ***syn*** see MIXTURE
commodious *adj* ***syn*** see SPACIOUS
con cramped, narrow, strait
ant incommodious
commodities *n pl* ***syn*** see MERCHANDISE
rel articles, items, things
common *adj* **1** generally shared in or participated in by members of a community <our *common* civic responsibilities>
syn communal, conjoint, conjunct, intermutual, joint, mutual, public, shared
rel general, generic, universal; like, reciprocal, similar; corporate
con personal, private, restricted
ant individual
2 ***syn*** see GENERAL 2
rel popular, public
3 ***syn*** see IMPURE 3
4 taking place often <a *common* occurrence>
syn customary, everyday, familiar, frequent
rel repetitious, routine, usual
con infrequent, occasional, unfrequent; casual, chance, incidental
ant rare, uncommon
5 ***syn*** see GENERAL
6 conforming to a type without noteworthy excellences or faults <just a *common* everyday sort trying to get by in life>
syn commonplace, ordinary, prosaic, uneventful, unexceptional, unnoteworthy
rel down-to-earth, matter-of-fact, prosy, unexciting; dull, flat, trite, stale, uninteresting
con exceptional, noteworthy, remarkable; excellent, marvelous, prodigious, wonderful; aberrant, divergent, eccentric
ant extraordinary
7 ***syn*** see DECENT 4
8 ***syn*** see CHEAP 2
9 ***syn*** see INFERIOR 2
‖**10** ***syn*** see EASYGOING 3
common *n* **1 commons** *pl but sing or pl in constr*
syn see COMMONALTY
2 an often improved and ornamentally planted open space for public use in a built-up area <in summer a band played on the village *common*>
syn green, plaza, square
rel garden, park, pleasance, pleasure ground
commonage *n* ***syn*** see COMMONALTY
commonalty *n* persons without rank or authority or the political estate made up of these <laws

syn synonym(s) ***rel*** related word(s)
ant antonym(s) ***con*** contrasted word(s)
idiom idiomatic equivalent(s)
‖ use limited; if in doubt, see a dictionary

that both the gentles and the *commonalty* recognized as just>
syn commonage, commoners, common men, commune, people, plebeians, plebes, plebs, populace, rank and file, third estate
rel masses, mob, multitude, proletariat, public
con aristocracy, elite, gentility, nobility; classes, gentry, nobs

commoners *n pl* ***syn*** see COMMONALTY

commonition *n* ***syn*** see WARNING

commonly *adv* ***syn*** see USUALLY 2
idiom more often than not

common men *n pl* ***syn*** see COMMONALTY

commonplace *n* an idea or expression deficient in originality or freshness <lazily exchanging *commonplaces* over their beer>
syn banality, bromide, cliché, platitude, prosaicism, prosaism, rubber stamp, shibboleth, tag, truism
rel chestnut, corn, prose, stereotype; inanity, shallowness, wishy-washiness; threadbareness, triteness
ant profundity

commonplace *adj* **1** ***syn*** see COMMON 6
2 ***syn*** see GENERAL 1
3 ***syn*** see PROSAIC 3
4 ***syn*** see TRITE
idiom a dime a dozen, as everyday as breakfast

common sense *n* ***syn*** see SENSE 6

commorancy *n* ***syn*** see HABITATION 2

commotion *n* **1** a state of often disorderly civic unrest <the whole city was in *commotion* over the new restrictions>
syn clamor, convulsion, ferment, outcry, tumult, upheaval, upturn
rel insurgence, insurrection, mutiny, rebellion, revolt, riot, uprising
2 a state of usually mental or emotional excitement <this challenge threw him into great *commotion* of mind>
syn agitation, confusion, dither, flap, lather, pother, stew, tumult, turbulence, turmoil
rel discomposure, disquiet, flurry, fluster, perturbation, upset; annoyance, bother, irritation, vexation; strain, tension
con calm, placidity, quietude, relaxation, serenity
3 a noisy and often unruly disturbance <the children created a *commotion* over missing the circus>
syn brouhaha, ‖catouse, coil, foofaraw, furore, fuss, hurrah, ruckus, rumpus, shindig, shindy, to-do, uproar
rel din, hubbub, hullabaloo, pandemonium, racket; fracas, ruction, row
4 a state of noisy confusion <never saw such *commotion* as the time the old sow got out and knocked the preacher into the midden>
syn bustle, clamor, clatter, hassle, hubbub, hurly-burly, lather, moil, pother, rowdydow, ruction, storm, to-do, tow-row, tumult, turmoil, uproar, whirl, whoopla; *compare* DIN, STIR 1
con calmness, order, peace, quiet

commove *vb* ***syn*** see ELATE

communal *adj* ***syn*** see COMMON 1

commune *n* ***syn*** see COMMONALTY

communicable *adj* **1** ***syn*** see INFECTIOUS 2
2 ***syn*** see COMMUNICATIVE

communicate *vb* **1** to make known <*communicated* the whole story under a pledge of secrecy>
syn break, convey, impart, pass on, transmit
rel betray, disclose, discover, divulge, ‖let out, reveal, tell; hint, imply, let on, suggest; broadcast, disseminate, publicize
con conceal, hide, obscure, screen, veil; dissemble; distort, garble, twist, warp; camouflage, disguise
2 ***syn*** see ADJOIN

communication *n* **1** ***syn*** see MESSAGE 1
2 ***syn*** see CONTACT 2
3 interchange of thoughts or opinions through shared symbols <the difficulties of *communication* between people of different cultural backgrounds>
syn communion, converse, intercommunication, intercourse
rel exchange, interchange; conversing, discussing, talking; conversation, discussion, talk; advice, intelligence, news, tidings

communicative *adj* inclined to talk freely and sometimes indiscreetly <too *communicative* to be trusted with a secret>
syn communicable, expansive; *compare* FRANK
rel garrulous, loquacious, talkative, voluble; conversational; demonstrative, effusive, gushing
con constrained, guarded, inhibited, restrained; bridled, controlled, curbed

communion *n* **1** ***syn*** see COMMERCE 2
2 ***syn*** see COMMUNICATION 3
3 ***syn*** see CONTACT 2
4 ***syn*** see RELIGION 2

Communist *n* a member of the Russian Communist party <restructuring of Russia by the *Communists*>
syn Bolshevik, ‖Bolshie, commie, comrade, Red
rel fellow traveler, pink, pinko; Leninist, Marxist, Stalinist, Trotskyist; apparatchik

community *n* ***syn*** see SOCIETY 3

commutable *adj* ***syn*** see INTERCHANGEABLE

commute *vb* ***syn*** see TRANSFORM

compact *adj* **1** ***syn*** see PITHY
2 ***syn*** see CLOSE 4
rel hard; appressed, bunched, packed
con loose, slack, unconstrained; rare, tenuous, thin

compact *vb* ***syn*** see UNIFY 1
rel compress, condense, contract; combine, unite; set, solidify
con disperse, dissipate; fluff, loosen

compact *n* ***syn*** see CONTRACT

compacting *adj* ***syn*** see INTEGRATIVE

companion *n* **1** ***syn*** see ASSOCIATE 3
rel colleague, fellow, partner; chaperon, escort
2 ***syn*** see MATE 5
3 ***syn*** see ACCOMPANIMENT 2

companion *vb* ***syn*** see ACCOMPANY

companionable *adj* ***syn*** see SOCIAL 1
rel amiable, complacent, good-natured

con uncongenial, unsympathetic; reserved, taciturn, uncommunicative

companionship *n* ***syn*** see COMPANY 1

company *n* **1** association between individuals especially on pleasant or intimate terms <we always enjoyed his *company*>
syn companionship, fellowship, society
rel camaraderie, comradeship, consociation
2 persons visiting especially in one's house <invited *company* for dinner>
syn guests, visitors; *compare* VISITOR 1
3 ***syn*** see GATHERING 2
4 a group of persons associated in a joint effort or for a common purpose <a *company* of thieves lay in wait by the highway>
syn band, corps, outfit, party, troop, troupe; *compare* GROUP 1
rel crew, gang, pack, team; circle, clique, coterie, set; association, club, order, society; crowd, horde, mob, throng; group
5 ***syn*** see ENTERPRISE 3

company *vb* ***syn*** see ACCOMPANY

comparable *adj* ***syn*** see LIKE
ant disparate

comparative *adj* being such in comparison with an expressed or implied standard or absolute <living in *comparative* poverty>
syn approximate, near, relative
rel equivalent, like, similar
con genuine, real, true
ant absolute

compare *vb* **1** ***syn*** see EQUATE 2
2 to examine side by side or point by point in order to establish likenesses and differences <*compare* the effects of two diets on weight loss>
syn bracket, collate, contrast
rel approach, equal, match, rival, touch; examine, inspect, observe, scan, scrutinize, size (up); consider, contemplate, ponder, study, weigh

comparison *n* ***syn*** see LIKENESS

compass *vb* **1** ***syn*** see SURROUND 1
2 ***syn*** see GET 1
3 ***syn*** see APPREHEND 1

compass *n* **1** ***syn*** see CIRCUMFERENCE
rel domain, field, sphere; enclosure
2 ***syn*** see ENVIRONS 1
3 ***syn*** see RANGE 2
rel bounds, limits; circumscription, limitation, restriction

compassion *n* **1** ***syn*** see SYMPATHY 2
rel charity, clemency, grace, lenity, mercy; benevolence, humaneness, humanity
con aloofness, indifference, unconcern; cruelty, harshness, mercilessness; implacability, relentlessness
2 ***syn*** see PITY

compassionate *adj* ***syn*** see TENDER
rel clement, forbearing; piteous, pitiful
con grim, implacable, merciless, relentless, unrelenting; adamant, inexorable, inflexible, obdurate

compassionate *vb* to feel or express compassion for <a kindly man who *compassionated* all human misery>
syn ache, commiserate, feel (for), pity, sympathize (with)
rel grieve (over), regret, repine; lament, mourn, sorrow (for *or* over); deplore
con accept, endure, tolerate; disregard, ignore, overlook, pass over

compassionless *adj* ***syn*** see UNFEELING 2

compatible *adj* ***syn*** see CONSONANT 1
rel appropriate, fit, fitting, meet, proper, suitable
ant incompatible

compatriot *n* ***syn*** see COLLEAGUE

compeer *n* ***syn*** see COLLEAGUE

compel *vb* ***syn*** see FORCE 2

compellation *n* ***syn*** see NAME 1

compendiary *adj* ***syn*** see CONCISE

compendious *adj* ***syn*** see CONCISE
rel close, compact
con amplified, elaborated, expanded, inflated; complete, full

compendium *n* **1** a condensed treatment of a subject <prepared a *compendium* of the state laws dealing with education>
syn aperçu, digest, pandect, précis, sketch, survey, syllabus, sylloge
rel abridgment, abstract, brief, conspectus, epitome; overview
con elaboration, expansion
2 ***syn*** see HANDBOOK

compenetrate *vb* ***syn*** see PERMEATE

compensate *vb* **1** to make good the defects of <her kind heart *compensated* for her nosy ways>
syn atone (for), balance, counterbalance, counterpoise, countervail, make up, offset, outweigh, redeem, set off
rel abrogate, annul, invalidate, negate, nullify; counteract, negative, neutralize; better, fix (up), improve, repair; redress
idiom make amends (*or* reparations), make matters right
2 ***syn*** see PAY 1
3 to make proper payment to (as for injury, loss, or damage) <*compensated* a worker injured on the job>
syn indemnify, pay, recompense, reimburse, remunerate, repay, requite
rel recoup, refund
idiom make restitution (*or* reparation)

compensation *n* ***syn*** see REPARATION

compete *vb* **1** to strive to gain mastery or obtain a prize <students *competing* for a scholarship>
syn contend, contest, rival, vie
rel dispute; battle, fight, strive, struggle; attempt, essay, try
2 ***syn*** see RIVAL 2
rel approach, equal, match, touch

competence *n* **1** ***syn*** see ENOUGH
2 ***syn*** see ABILITY 1
rel appropriateness, fitness, suitability

---

syn synonym(s) ***rel*** related word(s)
ant antonym(s) ***con*** contrasted word(s)
idiom idiomatic equivalent(s)
‖ use limited; if in doubt, see a dictionary

ant incompetence
competent *adj* **1** *syn* see ABLE
rel adept, finished, masterly, polished
ant incompetent
2 *syn* see SUFFICIENT 1
competition *n* **1** *syn* see CONTEST 1
2 *syn* see CONTEST 2
3 *syn* see RIVAL
competitor *n* *syn* see RIVAL
complacence *n* *syn* see CONCEIT 2
complacency *n* *syn* see CONCEIT 2
complacent *adj* feeling or showing an often excessive or unjustified satisfaction and pleasure in one's status, possessions, or attainments <had the *complacent* air of superiority that often mars an ignorant self-made man>
syn priggish, self-complacent, self-contented, self-pleased, self-satisfied, smug
rel assured, confident, self-assured, self-confident, self-possessed; conceited, egoistic, egotistic
con humble, modest; diffident, shy
complain *vb* to express discontent, resentment, or regret usually peaceably and as if seeking sympathy <a nice girl but given to *complaining* over trifles>
syn fuss, kick, murmur, repine, wail, whine; *compare* GRIPE 2, GRUMBLE 1
rel fret, worry; nag, pester
idiom air a grievance, find fault, register a complaint, sing (*or* cry) the blues
con accept, condone, countenance, tolerate
complainer *n* *syn* see GROUCH
complaint *n* *syn* see DISEASE 1
complaisant *adj* *syn* see AMIABLE 1
rel accommodating, agreeable, generous, indulgent; submissive
con harsh, rigorous, stern; determined, firm, masterful
complement *n* **1** something that makes up a deficiency in another thing <bought the farm with its *complement* of equipment and livestock>
syn supplement
rel correlate, counterpart; makeweight
2 *syn* see ACCOMPANIMENT 1
3 *syn* see COUNTERPART 1
complete *adj* **1** *syn* see WHOLE 3
2 *syn* see UNABRIDGED
3 *syn* see WHOLE 4
4 brought to completion <each *complete* revolution of the earth>
syn completed, concluded, done, down, ended, finished, terminated, through
rel accomplished, achieved, effected, executed, realized; attained, compassed
idiom all over, done with, set at rest
ant incomplete
5 *syn* see EXHAUSTIVE
ant incomplete
6 *syn* see UTTER
complete *vb* **1** *syn* see CLOSE 3
rel accomplish, achieve, discharge, effect, execute, fulfill, perform
idiom carry through, go through with
2 *syn* see FULFILL 1
completed *adj* *syn* see COMPLETE 4
completely *adv* **1** *syn* see DOWN 2
idiom down to the ground
2 *syn* see THOROUGHLY 2
3 *syn* see WELL 3
completeness *n* **1** *syn* see ENTIRETY 1
2 *syn* see INTEGRITY 2
complex *adj* **1** made up of two or more separable or identifiable elements <the *complex* vascular system of higher plants>
syn composite, compound
rel blended, compounded, mingled, mixed; heterogeneous, varied; elaborate, intricate, involved; complicated, confused, mixed-up
con homogeneous, uniform
ant simple
2 difficult to comprehend because of a multiplicity of interrelated elements <a *complex* plot to undermine the government by discrediting its leaders>
syn Byzantine, complicated, daedal, elaborate, gordian, intricate, involved, knotty, labyrinthine, sophisticated
rel bewildering, confusing, distracting, disturbing; baffling, confounding, mysterious, mystifying, perplexing, puzzling; equivocal, obscure, vague; involute, involuted, reticular
con clear, defined, definite, distinct, plain, recognizable, uncomplicated, uninvolved; comprehensible, explicable, intelligible, knowable
ant simple
complex *n* *syn* see SYSTEM 1
con constituent, element, factor; member, part, piece, portion; detail, item, particular
ant component
complexion *n* *syn* see DISPOSITION 3
rel kind, sort, style, type
complexion *vb* *syn* see TINT
complexionless *adj* *syn* see PALE 1
compliance *n* *syn* see ACQUIESCENCE
rel amenability, docility, obedience, tractability; deference, submission, submissiveness
con contumacy, obstinacy, stubbornness
ant frowardness
complicate *vb* to make complex, involved, or difficult <a disagreement *complicated* by intense personal animosities>
syn entangle, ‖muck, muddle, perplex, ravel, snarl, tangle
rel jumble, ‖snafu; derange, disarrange, disorder, mix up, upset
con arrange, order; disentangle, straighten (out), untangle
ant simplify
complicated *adj* **1** *syn* see ELABORATE 2
2 *syn* see COMPLEX 2
rel arduous, difficult, hard; abstruse, recondite
con easy, facile, light; clear-cut, precise, straightforward
ant simple
complicity *n* association with an improper or unlawful activity <failed to prove his *complicity* in the cover-up>
syn collusion, connivance

rel implication, involvement; engineering, machination, manipulation, wire-pulling

compliment *n* **1** an expression of regard or praise <a man meriting the *compliments* and homage of his fellows>
syn bouquet, kudo, orchid(s)
rel trade-last; laud, laudation, praise; accolade, commendation, honor; blessing(s), congratulation(s), felicitation(s); encomium, eulogy, tribute
con dig, gibe, jeer, slam
ant taunt
‖**2** *syn* see GIFT 1

compliment *vb syn* see COMMEND 2
idiom take off one's hat to
con belittle, decry, denigrate, depreciate, disparage, run down

complimentary *adj syn* see FREE 5

comply *vb syn* see OBEY

component *n syn* see ELEMENT 2
con admixture, amalgam, blend, compound, mixture
ant composite; complex

comport *vb* **1** *syn* see AGREE 4
2 *syn* see BEHAVE 1

comportment *n* **1** *syn* see BEARING 1
2 *syn* see BEHAVIOR

compose *vb* **1** *syn* see CONSTITUTE 1
rel consist (of)
2 to bring into being by mental and especially artistic effort <*compose* a ballad or a history of England>
syn create
rel devise, invent, make up, originate; dream up
3 *syn* see CALM
rel ease, lessen, soften; comfort, console, solace
con agitate, embroil, trouble, unsettle
ant discompose
4 to bring oneself or one's emotions under control <*composed* himself and turned to face the new attack>
syn collect, contain, control, cool, re-collect, rein, repress, restrain, simmer down, smother, suppress
rel down, mitigate, moderate, modulate, pocket, temper, tune down; bottle (up), check, hold in; ease (off *or* up), let up, relax, slacken
idiom calm down, control one's feelings (*or* emotions), get hold of oneself, master one's feelings, pull oneself together

composed *adj* **1** *syn* see CALM 2
2 *syn* see COOL 2
rel quiet, still; sedate, serious, staid; repressed, suppressed
con concerned, worried
ant discomposed, ruffled

composite *adj syn* see COMPLEX 1

composite *n syn* see MIXTURE
rel combination, union

composition *n* **1** *syn* see MAKEUP 1
2 *syn* see COMPROMISE
3 *syn* see ESSAY 2

compos mentis *adj syn* see SANE 2

compost *n syn* see MIXTURE

composure *n syn* see EQUANIMITY
ant discomposure, perturbation

compotation *n syn* see BINGE 1

compound *vb* **1** *syn* see JOIN 1
2 *syn* see MIX 1
3 *syn* see INCREASE 1

compound *adj syn* see COMPLEX 1

compound *n syn* see MIXTURE

comprehend *vb* **1** *syn* see APPREHEND 1
2 *syn* see KNOW 1
rel envisage, envision, see
3 *syn* see INCLUDE

comprehendible *adj syn* see UNDERSTANDABLE
ant incomprehensible

comprehensible *adj syn* see UNDERSTANDABLE
ant incomprehensible

comprehensive *adj* **1** *syn* see ENCYCLOPEDIC
2 *syn* see ALL-AROUND 2
idiom in depth

comprehensiveness *n syn* see BREADTH 2

compress *vb* **1** *syn* see CONTRACT 3
rel compact, consolidate; cram, crowd, press, squeeze
con disperse, dissipate, scatter
ant stretch; spread
2 *syn* see PRESS 1

comprise *vb syn* see CONSTITUTE 1

compromise *n* a settlement reached by mutual concession <the company and the union agreed to a *compromise* on fringe benefits>
syn composition
rel golden mean, mean, middle ground, middle way; agreement, compact, contract, pact; arrangement, bargain, understanding
idiom happy medium

compromise *vb syn* see ENDANGER
rel blast, blight, mar, queer, ruin, spoil
idiom cook one's goose; play havoc (*or* hob) with, settle one's hash

compulsatory *adj syn* see MANDATORY

compulsion *n syn* see FORCE 4
rel driving, impelling, pressing; exigency, necessity, need; pressure, stress
con coaxing, inducing, persuasion; choice, election, option, preference

compulsory *adj syn* see MANDATORY

compunction *n* **1** *syn* see PENITENCE
rel conscience, conscientiousness, punctiliousness, scrupulosity, scrupulousness
con brazenness, callousness, hardness, insensitivity; disinterest, indifference, unconcern; obduracy, recalcitrance
2 *syn* see QUALM
rel disinclination; hesitancy, hesitation

compunctious *adj syn* see REMORSEFUL

computation *n* the act or action of calculating mathematically <by his *computation* they could not possibly afford a new car>
syn arithmetic, calculation, ciphering, estimation, figuring, reckoning

---

syn synonym(s) *rel* related word(s)
ant antonym(s) *con* contrasted word(s)
idiom idiomatic equivalent(s)
‖ use limited; if in doubt, see a dictionary

compute *vb* ***syn*** see CALCULATE
comrade *n* **1** ***syn*** see ASSOCIATE 3
rel consort, fellow, mate; adjunct, ally, auxiliary
2 ***syn*** see COMMUNIST
comradery *n* ***syn*** see CAMARADERIE
comstock *n* ***syn*** see PRUDE
con *vb* **1** ***syn*** see SCRUTINIZE 1
2 ***syn*** see MEMORIZE
con *n* **1** ***syn*** see OPPONENT
ant pro
2 ***syn*** see ANTAGONISM 2
con *vb* **1** ***syn*** see DUPE
2 ***syn*** see COAX
||**con** *n* ***syn*** see CONVICT
concatenate *vb* ***syn*** see INTEGRATE 3
concavity *n* ***syn*** see DEPRESSION 2
conceal *vb* ***syn*** see HIDE
rel camouflage, disguise, dissemble
idiom keep (something) dark
con betray, divulge; evidence, evince, manifest
ant reveal
concealed *adj* ***syn*** see ULTERIOR
concede *vb* **1** ***syn*** see ACKNOWLEDGE 1
rel cede, relinquish, waive
con agitate, argue, debate, discuss; answer, confute, refute; controvert
ant dispute
2 ***syn*** see GRANT 1
con refuse, reject
ant deny
conceit *n* **1** ***syn*** see IDEA
2 an attitude of regarding oneself with favor <his constant boasting was an indication of *conceit*>
syn amour propre, complacence, complacency, conceitedness, consequence, egoism, egotism, narcissism, outrecuidance, pride, self-admiration, self-complacency, self-conceit, self-consequence, self-esteem, self-exaltation, self-glory, self-importance, self-love, self-opinion, self-pride, swelled head, swellheadedness, vainglory, vainness, vanity
rel assurance, pomposity, self-partiality, smugness, stuffiness
con humbleness, humility, self-depreciation, unpretentiousness
ant modesty
3 ***syn*** see CAPRICE
||**conceit** *vb* ***syn*** see UNDERSTAND 3
conceited *adj* ***syn*** see VAIN 3
conceitedness *n* ***syn*** see CONCEIT 2
||**conceity** *adj* ***syn*** see VAIN 3
conceivable *adj* **1** ***syn*** see THINKABLE 2
2 ***syn*** see PROBABLE
conceive *vb* **1** ***syn*** see THINK 1
rel excogitate; cogitate, speculate; meditate, ponder, ruminate
2 ***syn*** see APPREHEND 1
rel heed, mark, note, notice, observe, remark
3 ***syn*** see UNDERSTAND 3
rel judge; deem, feel
concenter *vb* **1** ***syn*** see FASTEN 3
2 ***syn*** see CONVERGE
concentrate *vb* **1** ***syn*** see FASTEN 3
rel establish, set, settle
2 ***syn*** see UNIFY 1
rel assemble, collect, gather; heap, mass, pile
con dispel, disperse; attenuate, dilute, extenuate, rarefy, thin; dispense, distribute
ant dissipate
3 ***syn*** see CONTRACT 3
4 ***syn*** see CONVERGE
concentrated *adj* **1** ***syn*** see STRONG 3
2 ***syn*** see WHOLE 5
rel complete, entire, total
3 ***syn*** see INTENSE 1
concentrating *adj* ***syn*** see INTEGRATIVE
concentration *n* ***syn*** see ATTENTION 1
rel enthrallment, raptness
ant distraction
concept *n* ***syn*** see IDEA
con percept, sensation, sense-datum, sensum
conception *n* ***syn*** see IDEA
conceptual *adj* existing or dealing with what exists only in the mind <*conceptual* analysis of a problem>
syn ideal, ideational, notional
rel abstract, transcendent, transcendental; absolute, categorical, ultimate; obscure, remote; fanciful, imaginary, visionary
con practical, pragmatic, realistic; concrete, material, substantial, tangible
concern *n* **1** ***syn*** see INTEREST 3
2 ***syn*** see AFFAIR 1
3 ***syn*** see BUSINESS 8
4 ***syn*** see CARE 4
5 ***syn*** see CONSIDERATION 3
6 ***syn*** see UNCERTAINTY
rel faltering, irresolution; apprehension, misgiving; inquietude, suspense
7 ***syn*** see CARE 2
rel attention, consideration, thoughtfulness
con aloofness, incuriousness, indifference
ant unconcern
8 ***syn*** see ENTERPRISE 3
9 ***syn*** see GADGET 1
concerned *adj* ***syn*** see INTERESTED
concerning *prep* ***syn*** see APROPOS
concernment *n* ***syn*** see CARE 2
concert *vb* **1** ***syn*** see NEGOTIATE 1
rel argue, debate, discuss; concur, cooperate, unite
2 ***syn*** see AGREE 3
concert *n* ***syn*** see HARMONY 1
concession *n* ***syn*** see ALLOWANCE 5
conciliate *vb* ***syn*** see PACIFY
rel intervene, mediate; persuade, prevail; calm, quiet, soothe, tranquilize
con alienate, disaffect, estrange; foment, incite; excite, pique, provoke, stimulate
ant antagonize
concise *adj* presented with or given to brevity of expression <a *concise* statement of the problem> <a very *concise* thinker>
syn breviloquent, brief, compendiary, compendious, curt, laconic, short, short and sweet, succinct, summary, terse; *compare* PITHY
rel abridged, compressed, condensed; marrowy, meaty, pithy; lean

con diffuse, long-winded, prolix, rambling, voluble, wordy
ant redundant; verbose
concisely *adv syn* see BRIEFLY
conclude *vb* **1** *syn* see DECIDE
2 *syn* see CLOSE 3
idiom ring down the curtain
ant open
3 *syn* see INFER
concluded *adj syn* see COMPLETE 4
concluding *adj syn* see LAST
ant opening
conclusion *n* **1** *syn* see INFERENCE 2
2 *syn* see FINALE
3 *syn* see END 2
4 *syn* see DECISION 1
conclusive *adj* putting an end to debate or question usually by reason of irrefutability <the evidence was *conclusive* and no defense was possible>
syn definitive
rel cogent, compelling, convincing, telling; incontrovertible, irrefragable, irrefrangible, irrefutable, unanswerable; deciding, decisive, determinant, determinate, determinative; clear, precise, unambiguous
con doubtful, dubious, problematic, questionable; credible, plausible, specious; ambiguous, cryptic, enigmatic, obscure
ant inconclusive
concoct *vb syn* see CONTRIVE 2
rel conceive, envisage, envision; create, discover, originate
concomitant *adj* occurring in company with <good manners are likely to be *concomitant* with good behavior>
syn accompanying, ancillary, attendant, attending, coincident, collateral, incident, satellite
rel accessory, adjuvant, supplementary; correlative, corresponding
concomitant *n syn* see ACCOMPANIMENT 2
concord *n* **1** *syn* see HARMONY 2
rel amity, comity, friendship, goodwill; calmness, peace, placidity, serenity, tranquillity
con conflict, contention, difference, dissension, strife, variance
ant discord
2 *syn* see HARMONY 3
3 *syn* see HARMONY 1
4 *syn* see TREATY
concord *vb syn* see AGREE 3
concordance *n syn* see HARMONY 2
concordant *adj syn* see HARMONIOUS 2
concours *n syn* see CONTEST 2
concourse *n* a coming, flocking, or flowing together <they doubt the universe originated in a chance *concourse* of atoms>
syn concursion, confluence, gathering, junction, meeting
rel association, joining, linkage
con disassociation, parting, separation
concrete *vb* **1** *syn* see HARDEN 1
2 *syn* see JOIN 1
concupiscence *n syn* see LUST 2
concupiscent *adj syn* see LUSTFUL 2
concur *vb* **1** *syn* see UNITE 2
rel accord, agree, harmonize, jibe
2 *syn* see AGREE 3
rel accede, acquiesce, assent, consent
ant contend; altercate
concurrent *adj syn* see CONTEMPORARY 1
concurrently *adv syn* see TOGETHER 1
concursion *n syn* see CONCOURSE
concuss *vb* **1** *syn* see SHAKE 4
2 *syn* see FORCE 2
concussion *n syn* see IMPACT 1
rel beating, buffeting, jarring, jolting, pounding, shaking; blow, clip, clout
condemn *vb* **1** *syn* see CRITICIZE
rel belittle, decry, depreciate, disparage; deprecate, disapprove
idiom damn with faint praise, find fault with
con applaud, commend, compliment; acclaim, eulogize, extol, laud, praise; condone, excuse, forgive, pardon
2 *syn* see SENTENCE
con deliver, redeem, rescue, save
condemned *adj syn* see DAMNED 1
rel fallen, fated
condensation *n syn* see ABRIDGMENT
condense *vb* **1** *syn* see CONTRACT 3
rel compact, consolidate; curtail, minimize
con amplify
2 *syn* see EPITOMIZE 1
con broaden, expand, extend, widen
ant amplify
condensed *adj* made shorter and typically simpler <a *condensed* biography>
syn canned, capsule, epitomized, pocket, potted
rel abbreviated, abridged, bobbed, bobtail, bobtailed, curtailed, shortened
con elaborated, polished, refined; amplified, enlarged, expanded
condescend *vb syn* see STOOP 1
condign *adj syn* see JUST 3
rel grim, rigorous, stern, strict, stringent; atrocious, awful, dreadful, horrible
condition *n* **1** something that limits or qualifies an agreement or offer <included the *condition* that any heir contesting the will would be automatically disinherited>
syn provision, proviso, reservation, stipulation, strings, terms
rel prerequisite, requirement, requisite; exception, exemption, limitation, modification, qualification, restriction, saving clause
2 *syn* see ESSENTIAL 2
3 *syn* see STATE 1
4 *syn* see ORDER 9
5 *syn* see ORDER 10
6 *syn* see DISEASE 1

---

syn synonym(s) *rel* related word(s)
ant antonym(s) *con* contrasted word(s)
idiom idiomatic equivalent(s)
‖ use limited; if in doubt, see a dictionary

conditional *adj* **1** containing or dependent on a condition <our agreement is *conditional* on your raising the needed funds>
syn provisional, provisionary, provisory, tentative
rel iffy, obscure, uncertain; limited, modified, qualified, restricted
con fixed, set, sure
ant unconditional
2 ***syn*** see DEPENDENT 1
rel provisional, tentative; problematic, questionable; fortuitous, incidental
ant unconditional

condonable *adj* ***syn*** see JUSTIFIABLE
rel acceptable, tolerable

condone *vb* ***syn*** see EXCUSE 1
rel disregard, forget, ignore, overlook
con deplore, deprecate, disapprove; impugn, reproach

conduce *vb* ***syn*** see CONTRIBUTE 2

conduct *n* **1** ***syn*** see OVERSIGHT 1
2 ***syn*** see BEHAVIOR
rel bearing, demeanor, mien, posture, stance

conduct *vb* **1** ***syn*** see GUIDE
2 ***syn*** see ACCOMPANY
rel convey, transmit
3 to have the direction of and responsibility for <he had *conducted* a small market for many years>
syn carry on, direct, keep, manage, operate, ordain, run
rel administer, handle, head, oversee, supervise; arrange, control, keep up, order, regulate, rule; engineer, lead, pilot, steer
4 to act as a conduit for <shady transactions that *conducted* profits away from the stockholders>
syn carry, channel, convey, funnel, pipe, siphon, traject, transmit
rel remove, separate, take away, withdraw
5 ***syn*** see BEHAVE 1

conduit *n* **1** ***syn*** see CHANNEL 1
2 ***syn*** see PIPELINE

confab *vb* ***syn*** see CONFER 2

confabulate *vb* ***syn*** see CONFER 2

confabulation *n* **1** ***syn*** see CONVERSATION 1
2 ***syn*** see CONVERSATION 2
3 ***syn*** see CONFERENCE 1

confederacy *n* ***syn*** see ALLIANCE 2

confederate *n* one associated with another or others in a wrong or unlawful act <conspiring with his *confederates* to overthrow the government>
syn abettor, accessory, accomplice, coconspirator, conspirator
rel collaborator, fellow traveler; associate, colleague, fellow, partner

confederation *n* ***syn*** see ALLIANCE 2

confer *vb* **1** ***syn*** see GIVE 2
rel allot, provide; vouchsafe
2 to carry on a conversation or discussion usually directed toward reaching a decision or settlement <the President *conferred* with his cabinet about the scandal>
syn advise, collogue, confab, confabulate, consult, huddle, parley, powwow, treat
rel bargain, chaffer, deal, negotiate; argue, debate, discuss; converse, speak, talk
idiom put one's head together with

conference *n* **1** an interchanging of views <took several hours of *conference* to find a solution to the problem>
syn confabulation, deliberation, discussion, rap, ventilation
2 a meeting for the purpose of serious discussion and interchange of views <the association held a *conference* on the problems of aging>
syn colloquium, colloquy, palaver, rap session, seminar
rel round robin, round table
3 ***syn*** see TALK 4
4 ***syn*** see LEAGUE 4

conferrer *n* ***syn*** see DONOR

confess *vb* ***syn*** see ACKNOWLEDGE 1
idiom make a clean breast, open one's heart

confessions *n pl* ***syn*** see BIOGRAPHY

confidant *n* ***syn*** see FRIEND

confide *vb* **1** to tell confidentially <shyly *confided* her secret>
syn breathe, whisper
rel hint, insinuate, intimate, suggest
con advertise, broadcast, proclaim, publish
2 ***syn*** see COMMIT 1
rel bestow, present

confidence *n* **1** ***syn*** see TRUST 1
con distrust, mistrust; despair, hopelessness
ant doubt; apprehension
2 a feeling or showing of adequacy and reliance on oneself and one's powers <had serene *confidence* in his own ability to win>
syn aplomb, assurance, self-assurance, self-assuredness, self-confidence, self-trust; *compare* EQUANIMITY
rel courage, mettle, resolution, spirit, tenacity; brashness, impudence, presumption
con apprehension, incertitude, misgiving, self-depreciation, self-doubt, uncertitude
ant diffidence
3 ***syn*** see CERTAINTY
4 ***syn*** see EFFRONTERY

confidence man *n* ***syn*** see SWINDLER

confident *adj* **1** marked by a strong, fearless, and bold belief in oneself and one's capacities <faced his accusers with a *confident* air>
syn assured, sanguine, secure, self-assured, self-confident, undoubtful
rel certain, cocksure, cocky, perky, positive, sure; self-possessed, self-reliant; bold, brave, courageous, dauntless, fearless, intrepid, unafraid, undaunted, valiant
con jittery, nervous, uneasy; afraid, daunted, fearful; doubtful, dubious
ant apprehensive
2 ***syn*** see SURE 5
3 ***syn*** see PRESUMPTUOUS

confidential *adj* **1** ***syn*** see PRIVATE 2
2 ***syn*** see FAMILIAR 1
rel secret; tried, trustworthy, trusty

configuration *n* ***syn*** see FORM 1

confine *vb* **1** ***syn*** see LIMIT 2

2 ***syn*** see IMPRISON

confine *n, usu* **confines** *pl* **1** ***syn*** see ENVIRONS 1

2 ***syn*** see LIMIT 1

rel circumference, compass, periphery

3 ***syn*** see RANGE 2

confined *adj* ***syn*** see CRAMPED

confinement *n* **1** ***syn*** see RESTRICTION 2

2 the state attending and consequent to childbirth <had a long difficult *confinement*>

syn accouchement, childbed, lying-in

rel parturition; labor, travail

confirm *vb* **1** ***syn*** see RATIFY

rel accede, acquiesce, assent, consent, subscribe; validate

idiom make good

con decline, refuse, reject

2 to attest to the truth, genuineness, accuracy, or validity of something <a surprise witness *confirmed* his account of the incident>

syn authenticate, bear out, corroborate, justify, substantiate, validate, verify

rel attest, certify, vouch, witness; back, support, underpin, uphold, warrant; check, check out

con confute, controvert, disprove, refute; contravene, gainsay, impugn, negative, traverse

ant deny; contradict

confirm (in) *vb* ***syn*** see HABITUATE 2

confirmation *n* ***syn*** see TESTIMONY

confirmative *adj* ***syn*** see CORROBORATIVE

confirmatory *adj* ***syn*** see CORROBORATIVE

confirmed *adj* **1** ***syn*** see HABITUAL 2

2 ***syn*** see INVETERATE 1

confiscate *vb* ***syn*** see APPROPRIATE 1

confiture *n* ***syn*** see JAM

conflagrant *adj* ***syn*** see BURNING 1

conflagration *n* ***syn*** see FIRE 1

conflict *n* **1** ***syn*** see CONTEST 1

rel argument, controversy, dispute

2 ***syn*** see CONTEST 2

3 ***syn*** see DISCORD

conflict *vb* ***syn*** see CLASH 2

rel differ, disagree, vary; disturb, interfere

idiom run against the tide

conflicting *adj* **1** ***syn*** see ANTIPATHETIC 1

2 ***syn*** see INCONSONANT 1

confluence *n* ***syn*** see CONCOURSE

conform *vb* **1** ***syn*** see ADAPT

rel attune, harmonize, tune

2 ***syn*** see AGREE 4

con conflict, differ, disagree

ant diverge

3 ***syn*** see HARMONIZE 3

4 ***syn*** see OBEY

idiom toe the line

conformable *adj* ***syn*** see ASSORTED 2

rel appropriate, fitting, suitable; applicable, usable

conformation *n* ***syn*** see FORM 1

conforming *adj* ***syn*** see DECOROUS 1

conformity *n* **1** ***syn*** see CONSISTENCY

2 ***syn*** see ACQUIESCENCE

confound *vb* **1** ***syn*** see PUZZLE

idiom take aback

2 ***syn*** see MISTAKE 1

ant discriminate, distinguish

3 ***syn*** see EMBARRASS

4 ***syn*** see DISPROVE 1

confounded *adj* **1** ***syn*** see AGHAST 2

2 ***syn*** see DAMNED 2

3 ***syn*** see UTTER

confoundedly *adv* ***syn*** see EVER 6

confrere *n* **1** ***syn*** see COLLEAGUE

2 ***syn*** see PARTNER

confront *vb* **1** to stand over against in the role of an adversary or enemy <he *confronted* his accusers with perfect aplomb>

syn affront, encounter, face, meet; *compare* MEET 6

rel beard, brave, challenge, defy; flout, scorn, scout; oppose, resist, withstand

idiom come to close quarters with, come up against

con avoid, elude, evade

2 ***syn*** see ACCOST 2

confronting *prep* ***syn*** see BEFORE 2

confuse *vb* **1** ***syn*** see EMBARRASS

2 to make unclear in mind or purpose <found the city hustle and noise very *confusing*>

syn addle, ball up, befuddle, bewilder, ||bumfuzzle, discombobulate, distract, dizzy, fluster, fuddle, mix up, ||mizzle, ||momble, muddle, mull, throw off, throw out

rel misguide, mislead; agitate, bother, discompose, disquiet, flurry, perturb, upset

3 ***syn*** see PUZZLE

4 to make indistinct the elements or true character of (as a discussion) <*confuse* an issue in a debate>

syn becloud, befog, blur, cloud, fog, muddy

rel complicate, confound, involve, mix up

idiom lose in a fog

con clarify, elucidate; simplify

5 to throw into disorder <surging waves *confused* the waters> <her accounts were totally *confused*>

syn foul up, jumble, mix up, muddle, ||snafu, snarl up, tumble; *compare* DISORDER 1

rel derange, disarrange, disorder, disorganize, disturb, mess (up), unsettle

idiom put in a flutter, throw into confusion

6 ***syn*** see MISREPRESENT

7 ***syn*** see MISTAKE 1

ant differentiate

confusion *n* **1** ***syn*** see RUIN 3

2 ***syn*** see EMBARRASSMENT

3 a condition in which things are out of their normal or proper places or relationships <the room was in complete *confusion*>

syn ataxia, ||ballup, chaos, clutter, disarray, disorder, huddle, misorder, muddle, ||mullock, pell-mell, snarl, topsy-turviness

rel derangement, disarrangement, disturbance; foul-up, mess, mix-up, muck, ||mux, ||snafu; babel, din, hullabaloo, pandemonium
con methodization, ordering, organization, systematization; method, order, system
4 ***syn*** see COMMOTION 2
rel disorder, disorganization, disturbance; discomfiture, embarrassment

confute *vb* ***syn*** see DISPROVE 1

congé *n* ***syn*** see PARTING

congeal *vb* **1** ***syn*** see HARDEN 1
rel chill, cool, freeze
2 ***syn*** see COAGULATE

congenial *adj* **1** ***syn*** see HARMONIOUS 3
ant uncongenial
2 ***syn*** see CONSONANT 1
rel companionable, cooperative, social; affable, cordial, genial, gracious, sociable; pleasant, pleasing
ant uncongenial; antipathetic (*of persons*); abhorrent (*of tasks, responsibilities*)
3 ***syn*** see PLEASANT 1
4 ***syn*** see GRACIOUS 1

congenital *adj* **1** ***syn*** see INNATE 1
2 ***syn*** see INHERENT

congeries *n* ***syn*** see GATHERING 2

congest *vb* ***syn*** see FILL 1

conglobate *vb* ***syn*** see BALL

conglobe *vb* ***syn*** see BALL

conglomerate *adj* ***syn*** see MISCELLANEOUS

conglomerate *n* **1** ***syn*** see AGGREGATE 1
2 ***syn*** see SYNDICATE

conglomeration *n* **1** ***syn*** see ACCUMULATION
2 ***syn*** see AGGREGATE 1

congratulate *vb* to express to another one's pleasure in his good fortune or success <*congratulate* a friend when she wins a race>
syn felicitate
rel applaud, laud, praise; bless, compliment
idiom pat one on the back, tender (*or* offer) congratulation, wish one joy, wish one well
con belittle, depreciate, disparage, knock, run down, slur

congregate *vb* ***syn*** see GATHER 6
rel swarm, teem
ant disperse

congregation *n* ***syn*** see GATHERING 2
rel audience, disciples, following, public

congress *n* ***syn*** see ASSOCIATION 2

congress *vb* ***syn*** see GATHER 6

congruity *n* ***syn*** see CONSISTENCY

congruous *adj* **1** ***syn*** see CONSONANT 1
rel appropriate, fit, fitting, meet; proper, seemly
ant incongruous
2 ***syn*** see HARMONIOUS 2

conjectural *adj* ***syn*** see SUPPOSED 1
con demonstrated; unquestionable

conjecture *n* ***syn*** see THEORY 2
ant fact

conjecture *vb* to draw an inference from slight or inadequate evidence <when he failed to arrive on time she *conjectured* that he was drinking again>
syn guess, presume, pretend, suppose, surmise, think; *compare* INFER, UNDERSTAND 3
rel assume, expect, suspect; believe, deem, feel; conceive, fancy, imagine; conclude, estimate, gather, glean, infer, judge
idiom hazard a guess, take for granted
con demonstrate, prove, test, try; ascertain, determine, discover, learn

conjoin *vb* **1** ***syn*** see JOIN 1
2 ***syn*** see UNITE 2

conjoint *adj* **1** ***syn*** see COMMON 1
2 ***syn*** see COOPERATIVE

conjointly *adv* ***syn*** see TOGETHER 3

conjointment *n* ***syn*** see ASSOCIATION 1

conjugal *adj* ***syn*** see MATRIMONIAL

conjugality *n* ***syn*** see MARRIAGE 1

conjugate *vb* ***syn*** see JOIN 1

conjunct *adj* ***syn*** see COMMON 1

conjunction *n* ***syn*** see ASSOCIATION 1

conjuration *n* ***syn*** see SPELL

conjure *vb* ***syn*** see BEG

conjurer *n* **1** ***syn*** see MAGICIAN 1
2 ***syn*** see MAGICIAN 2

conjuring *n* **1** ***syn*** see MAGIC 1
2 ***syn*** see MAGIC 2

conjury *n* ***syn*** see MAGIC 1

||conk *n* **1** ***syn*** see NOSE 1
2 ***syn*** see HEAD 1

||conk *n* ***syn*** see HIT 1

conk *vb* ***syn*** see DIE 1

con man *n* ***syn*** see SWINDLER
rel shill
con mark, sucker, victim; greenhorn

connate *adj* **1** ***syn*** see INNATE 1
2 ***syn*** see INHERENT
3 ***syn*** see RELATED

connatural *adj* **1** ***syn*** see INNATE 1
2 ***syn*** see RELATED

connect *vb* ***syn*** see JOIN 1
ant disconnect

connection *n* **1** ***syn*** see ASSOCIATION 1
2 ***syn*** see JOINT 1
3 ***syn*** see JOB 2
4 ***syn*** see RELIGION 2

connivance *n* ***syn*** see COMPLICITY

connive *vb* **1** to secretly favor or sympathize with something improper or illicit <*connive* at treason>
syn blink (at), wink (at)
rel condone, disregard, ignore, overlook, tolerate
idiom close (*or* shut) one's eyes to, let go by (*or* get by) one's eye, regard with indulgence
con disapprove, disfavor, frown (at *or* upon); disallow, reject, repudiate; disdain, scorn, scout, spurn
2 ***syn*** see PLOT

connoisseur *n* a person who enjoys with discrimination and appreciation of subtleties and details especially in matters of culture or art <a *connoisseur* of fine wines>
syn aesthete, cognoscente, dilettante
rel bon vivant, epicure, gourmet; adept, authority, critic, expert
con abecedarian, amateur, dabbler, tyro

connotation *n* ***syn*** see ASSOCIATION 4

connote *vb* **1** ***syn*** see MEAN 2
2 ***syn*** see SUGGEST 1
connubial *adj* ***syn*** see MATRIMONIAL
connubiality *n* ***syn*** see MARRIAGE 1
conquer *vb* **1** to overcome or gain dominion over by force of arms <leaders who have tried and failed to *conquer* the world>
syn bear down, beat down, crush, defeat, overpower, reduce, subdue, subjugate, vanquish; *compare* DEFEAT 2, OVERTHROW 2, WHIP 2, WIN 1
rel baffle, balk, circumvent, foil, frustrate, outwit, override, thwart; bend, control, master, overmaster, subject, worst
idiom bring one to one's knees, trample in the dust, trample underfoot
con bow, cave, give up, succumb, yield; capitulate, submit, surrender
2 to gain mastery over something by getting the better of obstacles and difficulties <trials faced by the men who *conquered* Mount Everest>
syn best, master, overcome, prevail, triumph; *compare* OVERCOME 1
3 ***syn*** see OVERCOME 1
conqueror *n* ***syn*** see VICTOR 1
conquest *n* ***syn*** see VICTORY 1
rel defeating, overthrow, rout, routing, subdual
consanguine *adj* ***syn*** see RELATED
‖**consarned** *adj* **1** ***syn*** see DAMNED 2
2 ***syn*** see UTTER
conscience *n* ***syn*** see QUALM
conscienceless *adj* ***syn*** see UNSCRUPULOUS
rel devious, shifty, tricky, unfair
ant conscientious
conscientious *adj* **1** ***syn*** see UPRIGHT 2
ant conscienceless
2 ***syn*** see CAREFUL 2
conscionable *adj* ***syn*** see CAREFUL 2
conscious *adj* **1** ***syn*** see AWARE
rel noticing, noting, observing, perceiving, remarking; vigilant, watchful
con forgetful, oblivious, unmindful; disregarding, ignoring, overlooking
ant unconscious
2 ***syn*** see SELF-CONSCIOUS
consciousness *n* ***syn*** see CARE 4
conscribe *vb* ***syn*** see DRAFT 1
conscript *vb* ***syn*** see DRAFT 1
consecrate *vb* **1** ***syn*** see DEVOTE 1
con desecrate, profane; defile, pollute
2 ***syn*** see BLESS 1
consecrated *adj* ***syn*** see HOLY 1
consecution *n* **1** ***syn*** see ORDER 5
2 ***syn*** see SUCCESSION 2
consecutive *adj* following one after another in orderly fashion <it rained for five *consecutive* days>
syn sequent, sequential, serial, subsequent, subsequential, succedent, succeeding, successional, successive; *compare* NEXT
rel after, ensuing, following, later; enlarging, increasing, progressive
con antecedent, preceding, prior
consecutively *adv* ***syn*** see TOGETHER 2
consent *vb* ***syn*** see ASSENT
rel allow, let, permit; approve, sanction; concur
con decline; balk, demur, stick, stickle
consent *n* **1** ***syn*** see PERMISSION
2 ***syn*** see AGREEMENT 2
consentaneous *adj* ***syn*** see UNANIMOUS
consentient *adj* ***syn*** see UNANIMOUS
consequence *n* **1** ***syn*** see EFFECT 1
con origin, root, source
ant antecedent
2 ***syn*** see IMPORTANCE
rel exigency, need; fame, honor, renown, reputation, repute
3 ***syn*** see STATUS 2
4 ***syn*** see CONCEIT 2
consequent *adj* ***syn*** see RATIONAL
consequential *adj* ***syn*** see IMPORTANT 1
consequently *adv* ***syn*** see THEREFORE
conservancy *n* ***syn*** see CONSERVATION 1
conservation *n* **1** a deliberate planned guarding and protecting of something felt as precious <*conservation* of our natural resources>
syn conservancy, husbanding, preserval, preservation, salvation, saving
rel attention, care, cherishing, protection; control, directing, governing, management, managing, supervising, supervision
con neglect, squandering, waste
2 ***syn*** see PRESERVATION 1
conservative *adj* **1** tending to resist or oppose change <took a very *conservative* stance politically>
syn die-hard, fogyish, old-line, orthodox, reactionary, right, tory, traditionalistic
con modern, progressive, radical
ant advanced
2 kept or keeping within bounds <equally *conservative* in speech and action>
syn controlled, discreet, moderate, reasonable, restrained, temperate, unexcessive, unextreme
rel cautious, chary, wary; circumspect, politic, proper, prudent
con expansive, unconstrained; excessive, freewheeling, uncontrolled, unrestrained
conservative *n* ***syn*** see DIEHARD 1
conservatory *n* ***syn*** see GREENHOUSE
conserve *vb* ***syn*** see SAVE 3
rel keep up, maintain, support, sustain
con dissipate, fritter, squander, waste
conserve *n* ***syn*** see JAM
consider *vb* **1** to give serious thought to <*consider* the risk you would be taking>
syn contemplate, excogitate, mind, perpend, ponder, study, think (out *or* over), weigh
rel meditate, muse, ruminate; cogitate, reason, reflect, speculate, think; examine, inspect, look (at), scan, scrutinize, see
idiom bestow thought to, chew the cud over, revolve (*or* turn over) in one's mind
con disregard, ignore, neglect, overlook, slight

---

2 ***syn*** see EYE 1
rel envisage, envision
3 to come to view, judge, or classify <he *considered* thrift essential to success>
syn account, deem, reckon, regard, view; *compare* FEEL 3
rel conceive, fancy, imagine, think; conclude, gather, infer, judge, rule
4 ***syn*** see ADMIRE 2
5 ***syn*** see FEEL 3

considerable *adj* **1** ***syn*** see IMPORTANT 1
2 tending more to the large than the small <buckled down with his ax and made a *considerable* impression on the woodpile>
syn good, respectable, ‖right smart, sensible, sizable, ‖smart
rel able, capable, competent; active, effective, efficacious; important, notable, significant; goodly, pretty, substantial, tidy
con insignificant, meager, slight, trivial; big, grand, great, huge
3 ***syn*** see BIG 1

considerably *adv* ***syn*** see WELL 8

considerate *adj* **1** ***syn*** see CAUTIOUS
2 ***syn*** see THOUGHTFUL 3
rel kind, kindly; compassionate, sympathetic, tender, warmhearted; amiable, complaisant, obliging
ant inconsiderate
3 ***syn*** see GENEROUS 1

considerately *adv* ***syn*** see WELL 2
rel solicitously, tenderly; altruistically, benevolently, charitably
con austerely, harshly, severely, strictly

considerateness *n* ***syn*** see CONSIDERATION 3

consideration *n* **1** ***syn*** see ATTENTION 1
2 ***syn*** see MOTIVE 1
3 thoughtful and sympathetic attention <showed great *consideration* to the needs of others>
syn concern, considerateness, regard, solicitude
rel awareness, heed, heedfulness, mindfulness; forbearance, mercy, quarter
con disregard, heedlessness, unconcern, unmindfulness; inconsiderateness; contempt, despite, disdain, disinterest, scorn
4 ***syn*** see REGARD 4

considered *adj* ***syn*** see DELIBERATE 1
rel intentional, voluntary, willful
con impulsive, instinctive, spontaneous; headlong, impetuous, precipitate
ant unconsidered

considering *conj* ***syn*** see BECAUSE

consign *vb* **1** ***syn*** see COMMIT 1
rel resign, surrender, yield
2 ***syn*** see SEND 1

consist *vb* **1** to have existence or a place <our national strength *consists* not solely in military readiness>
syn dwell, exist, inhere, lie, reside
rel be, subsist; abide, repose, rest
idiom have one's (*or* a) place
2 ***syn*** see AGREE 4

consistency *n* agreement or harmony of parts, traits, or features <his adversary had to admit the *consistency* of his position>
syn coherence, conformity, congruity, correspondence; *compare* HARMONY 2
rel agreement, concord, consonance; likeness, similarity; apposition, aptness, felicity, fitness, suitability
con incoherence, incongruity; impropriety, inappropriateness, unsuitability
ant inconsistency

consistent *adj* **1** ***syn*** see SAME 3
2 ***syn*** see CONSONANT 1

consistently *adv* ***syn*** see USUALLY 1

consociate *n* ***syn*** see PARTNER

console *vb* ***syn*** see COMFORT
rel calm, relieve, tranquilize; animate, hearten, inspirit
idiom lift the spirits of
con agitate, discompose, disquiet, disturb, perturb, upset

consolidate *vb* ***syn*** see UNIFY 1
rel amalgamate, blend, fuse, merge; set, solidify
con part, sever, sunder; liquefy, melt

consolidating *adj* ***syn*** see INTEGRATIVE

consolidation *n* **1** ***syn*** see UNIFICATION
2 a union of two or more businesses <*consolidation* is often accompanied by a new corporate name>
syn amalgamation, merger
ant dissolution

consonance *n* **1** ***syn*** see HARMONY 2
con discrepancy, incompatibility, incongruousness
ant discord
2 ***syn*** see HARMONY 1
ant dissonance

consonant *adj* **1** conforming (as to a pattern, a standard, or a relationship) without discord or difficulty <his performance was seldom *consonant* with his very real abilities>
syn agreeable, compatible, congenial, congruous, consistent, sympathetic; *compare* HARMONIOUS 2
rel accordant, conformable, harmonious; coincident, concurrent; en rapport
con discordant, discrepant; incompatible, incongruous, inconsistent
ant inconsonant
2 ***syn*** see HARMONIOUS 1
ant dissonant
3 ***syn*** see LIKE
4 ***syn*** see RESONANT

consort *n* **1** ***syn*** see ACCOMPANIMENT 2
2 ***syn*** see SPOUSE

consort *vb* ***syn*** see AGREE 4

consort (with) *vb* ***syn*** see ACCOMPANY

consortium *n* ***syn*** see ASSOCIATION 2

conspectus *n* ***syn*** see ABRIDGMENT

conspicuous *adj* **1** ***syn*** see CLEAR 5
2 ***syn*** see NOTICEABLE
rel celebrated, eminent, illustrious; showy
con common, everyday, ordinary; covert, secret; concealed, hidden

ant inconspicuous
conspiracy *n* ***syn*** see PLOT 2
rel sedition, treason; disloyalty, faithlessness, falsity, perfidiousness, perfidy, treacherousness, treachery
con faith, faithfulness, fealty, loyalty
conspirator *n* ***syn*** see CONFEDERATE
conspire *vb* ***syn*** see PLOT
‖**constable** *n* ***syn*** see POLICEMAN
constancy *n* ***syn*** see ATTACHMENT 1
constant *adj* **1** ***syn*** see FAITHFUL 1
rel abiding, clinging, enduring, lasting, persistent, persisting
con capricious, mercurial
ant fickle, inconstant
2 ***syn*** see INFLEXIBLE 3
con fluctuant, fluctuating, fluctuational, unstable
ant inconstant, variable
3 ***syn*** see SAME 3
4 ***syn*** see STEADY 2
5 ***syn*** see CONTINUAL
rel chronic, confirmed, inveterate; dogged, obstinate, pertinacious; persevering
con alternate, intermittent, recurrent; infrequent, occasional, sporadic
ant fitful
constantly *adv* ***syn*** see ALWAYS 1
idiom day after day, day in, day out
ant occasionally
constate *vb* ***syn*** see ASSERT 1
consternate *vb* ***syn*** see DISMAY 1
consternation *n* ***syn*** see FEAR 1
rel confusion, muddle, muddlement; bewilderment, distraction, perplexity
con composure, equanimity, phlegm, sangfroid; aplomb, poise, self-command, self-possession
constipate *vb* ***syn*** see STULTIFY
constipated *adj* being unable to defecate regularly and without difficulty <complained that she was constantly *constipated*>
syn astricted, bound, costive, obstipated
constituent *n* ***syn*** see ELEMENT 2
rel division, fraction, part, portion
con complex, economy, organism, system; amalgam, blend, composite, compound
ant aggregate, whole
constitute *vb* **1** to be all or a fundamental part of the substance of <water *constitutes* the greater part of the human body>
syn compose, comprise, form, make, make up
rel embody, incorporate, integrate; complement, complete, fill out, flesh (out)
2 ***syn*** see ENACT 1
3 ***syn*** see FOUND 2
constitution *n* **1** ***syn*** see PHYSIQUE
2 ***syn*** see MAKEUP 1
constitutional *adj* ***syn*** see INHERENT
con anomalous, irregular, unnatural
ant advenient
constitutional *n* ***syn*** see WALK 1
rel ambulation, footwork, legwork, perambulation
constitutive *adj* ***syn*** see ESSENTIAL 2
constrain *vb* **1** ***syn*** see FORCE 2
2 ***syn*** see RESTRAIN 1
3 ***syn*** see DENY 3
rel abridge, curtail, deprive; ban, bar, disallow, enjoin
4 ***syn*** see IMPRISON
5 ***syn*** see PRESS 1
6 ***syn*** see DISTRESS 2
constrained *adj* ***syn*** see RESERVED 1
constrainment *n* ***syn*** see RESTRICTION 2
constraint *n* **1** ***syn*** see FORCE 4
rel repression, suppression; driving, impelling, impulsion; goad, motive, spring, spur
2 ***syn*** see RESTRICTION 2
constrict *vb* **1** ***syn*** see CONTRACT 3
rel curb, restrain; circumscribe, confine, limit, restrict
con enlarge, expand, increase, maximize
2 to make narrow or narrower <the muscles that *constrict* the sphincter>
syn constringe, narrow
rel gather, plait, pucker; compress, constrain, squeeze; astringe
con broaden, dilate, distend, widen
ant expand
constringe *vb* ***syn*** see CONSTRICT 2
construal *n* ***syn*** see EXPLANATION 1
construct *vb* **1** ***syn*** see MAKE 3
2 ***syn*** see BUILD 1
3 ***syn*** see ERECT 5
construction *n* **1** ***syn*** see MAKEUP 1
2 ***syn*** see EXPLANATION 1
constructive *adj* ***syn*** see IMPLICIT 2
rel inferential, ratiocinative; construable, interpretable, renderable
con clear, evident, obvious, patent
ant manifest
construe *vb* ***syn*** see EXPLAIN 1
consuetude *n* ***syn*** see HABIT 1
consult *vb* ***syn*** see CONFER 2
rel cogitate, counsel, deliberate; consider, examine, review
consume *vb* **1** to bring to an end by or as if by the action of a destroying force <the village was *consumed* by fire>
syn devour, eat, eat up, exhaust, use up
rel destroy, raze, ruin, wreck; annihilate, extinguish; crush, overwhelm, suppress
con bolster, brace, buttress, hold up, prop, stay, support, sustain; build, construct, create, make, produce; renew, restore
2 ***syn*** see WASTE 2
3 ***syn*** see GO 4
4 ***syn*** see EAT 1
5 to eat or drink usually gluttonously or without measure <*consumed* dozens of burgers and a case of beer>
syn polish off, punish, put away, put down, shift, swill; *compare* EAT 1

---

syn synonym(s) *rel* related word(s)
ant antonym(s) *con* contrasted word(s)
idiom idiomatic equivalent(s)
‖ use limited; if in doubt, see a dictionary

rel absorb, ingest; devour, gobble (up), gorge, wolf; down, gulp, guzzle, inhale, swallow
idiom dispose of
6 *syn* see MONOPOLIZE
consumedly *adv syn* see EVER 6
consuming *adj syn* see ENGROSSING
consummate *adj* 1 brought to the highest possible point of perfection <the difficult allegro passages displayed her *consummate* skill>
syn accomplished, finished, perfected, ripe, virtuosic; *compare* PERFECT 2
rel faultless, flawless, impeccable, perfect; practiced, skilled, trained; able, gifted, talented; inimitable, peerless, superb, superlative, supreme, transcendent, unsurpassable
con callow, crude, green, raw, rough, uncouth; defective, deficient, inadequate
2 *syn* see UTTER
consummate *vb syn* see CLOSE 3
consumption *n syn* see TUBERCULOSIS
contact *n* 1 the state of being in or coming into close association or connection <shuddered at the *contact* of his icy hand>
syn contingence, touch
rel closeness, contiguity, nearness, propinquity, proximity; impingement, taction, touching; association, connection, relation; oneness, union, unity
con breach, break, rift, rupture, split; insularity, isolation, seclusion, segregation, separation; distance, farness, remoteness
2 a situation permitting exchange of ideas and opinions <tried for several days to get in *contact* with her brother>
syn commerce, communication, communion, intercommunication, intercourse
rel association, companionship, fellowship; oneness, union, unity; accord, concord, harmony, rapport; empathy, sympathy, understanding
contact *vb syn* see REACH 4
contagion *n syn* see POISON
rel contamination, corruption, pollution, taint; miasma
contagious *adj* 1 *syn* see INFECTIOUS 2
2 *syn* see INFECTIOUS 3
contain *vb* 1 *syn* see COMPOSE 4
2 to have or be capable of having within <the box *contained* family papers> <a mug that will *contain* a quart of ale>
syn accommodate, hold
rel harbor, house, lodge, shelter; admit, receive, take, take in
3 *syn* see INCLUDE
contaminate *vb* 1 to debase by making impure or unclean <feared her child's morals would be *contaminated* by others>
syn defile, pollute, soil, taint; *compare* TAINT 1
rel corrupt, debase, debauch, deprave, pervert, vitiate; harm, injure, spoil
con better, elevate, improve
ant purify
2 to render unfit for use by the introduction of unwholesome or undesirable elements <water *contaminated* by sewage>
syn befoul, foul, pollute
rel infect; poison; dirty, soil
ant purify
contemn *vb syn* see DESPISE
contemplate *vb* 1 *syn* see EYE 1
rel ponder, reflect, study; examine, inspect, scan, scrutinize
2 *syn* see CONSIDER 1
rel drift, roam
3 *syn* see INTEND 2
idiom have in view
contemplative *adj syn* see THOUGHTFUL 1
rel musing, weighing; reasoning
idiom in a brown study
contemporaneous *adj syn* see CONTEMPORARY 1
contemporary *adj* 1 existing or occurring at the same time <the story has come down from several *contemporary* sources>
syn coetaneous, coeval, coexistent, coexisting, concurrent, contemporaneous, simultaneous, synchronal, synchronic, synchronous
rel accompanying, attendant, attending, coincident, concomitant; current, existing, present; associated, connected, linked, related
con antecedent, foregoing, preceding, previous, prior; ensuing, following, succeeding
2 *syn* see PRESENT
3 *syn* see UP-TO-DATE
contempt *n* 1 *syn* see DESPITE 1
rel antipathy, aversion; distaste, repugnance
con awe, fear, reverence
ant regard
2 *syn* see DISGRACE
3 *syn* see DEFIANCE 2
contemptible *adj* arousing or meriting scorn or disdain <a *contemptible* attempt to blame his wife for his failure>
syn beggarly, cheap, despicable, despisable, mean, pitiable, pitiful, scummy, scurvy, shabby, sorry; *compare* BASE 3
rel abhorrent, abominable, detestable, hateful, odious; abject, ignoble, sordid; bad, inferior, poor, sad; disgusting, scrimy, shameful; outcast
con creditable, estimable, honorable, noble; high-minded, high-principled, principled, true, upright; honest, square, straight
ant admirable
contend *vb* 1 to strive in opposition to someone or something <*contending* against the temptation to look behind him>
syn battle, fight, oppugn, tug, war
rel combat, oppose, resist, withstand; contest, cope (with), vie
2 *syn* see MAINTAIN 2
rel report, say, tell; charge, enjoin, urge; dictate, prescribe
3 *syn* see COMPETE 1
rel combat, oppose, resist, withstand; confront, encounter, face, meet, stand
content *vb syn* see SATISFY 3
rel delight, thrill, tickle; bewitch, captivate, charm, enrapture
con disappoint, dishearten, displease
ant discontent

contention *n* **1** ***syn*** see DISCORD
rel altercation, quarrel, squabble, wrangle; argument, controversy, dispute
con agreement, coincidence, concurrence
2 ***syn*** see ARGUMENT 2
3 ***syn*** see THESIS 1
contentious *adj* **1** ***syn*** see BELLIGERENT
rel contrary, froward, perverse; captious, carping, caviling, faultfinding
con calm, serene, tranquil; amiable, complaisant, good-natured, obliging
ant peaceable
2 prone to wordy contention <a *contentious* old chap, always ready for an argument>
syn argumentative, controversial, disputatious, litigious, polemical
rel fiery, hasty, hotheaded, impetuous, peppery; bellicose, belligerent, scrappy
con amiable, complaisant, good-natured, obliging; agreeable, cooperative, understanding
conterminous *adj* ***syn*** see ADJACENT 3
contest *vb* **1** ***syn*** see COMPETE 1
rel endeavor
2 ***syn*** see RESIST
contest *n* **1** an earnest struggle for superiority or victory <the rival factions continued in *contest* for several years>
syn competition, conflict, emulation, rivalry, strife, striving, tug-of-war, warfare
rel brush, encounter, skirmish; action, battle, engagement
2 a competitive encounter between groups or individuals <there were *contests* of skill and endurance>
syn competition, concours, conflict, meet, meeting, rencontre
rel proving, testing, trial, trying
contestation *n* ***syn*** see THESIS 1
contiguity *n* ***syn*** see PROXIMITY
contiguous *adj* **1** ***syn*** see ADJACENT 3
rel close, near, nearby, nigh
con apart, separate; distant, remote
2 ***syn*** see NEIGHBORING
contiguously *adv* ***syn*** see IMMEDIATELY 1
contiguousness *n* ***syn*** see PROXIMITY
continence *n* ***syn*** see TEMPERANCE 2
rel self-restraint; moderation, temperateness; chasteness, chastity, purity
con self-indulgence; excessiveness, inordinateness; lasciviousness, lecherousness, lewdness, licentiousness, wantonness
ant incontinence
continent *adj* ***syn*** see ABSTEMIOUS
rel bridled, curbed, inhibited, restrained; chaste, pure
con self-indulgent, spoiled
ant incontinent
contingence *n* ***syn*** see CONTACT 1
contingency *n* ***syn*** see JUNCTURE 2
rel break, chance, occasion, opportunity
contingent *adj* **1** ***syn*** see ACCIDENTAL
rel unanticipated, unforeseeable, unforeseen; likely, possible, probable
con certain, inevitable, necessary
2 ***syn*** see DEPENDENT 1
continual *adj* continuing without intermission and seemingly without end <they were tired of her *continual* nagging>
syn around-the-clock, ceaseless, constant, continuous, endless, everlasting, incessant, interminable, minutely, perpetual, timeless, unceasing, unending, unintermitted, unintermittent, uninterrupted, unremitting
rel abiding, enduring, persistent, persisting, staying; unvarying; unchanging, unfailing, unflagging, unwaning; relentless, running, steady
con ephemeral, evanescent, impermanent, short-lived, temporary, transient, transitory
continually *adv* ***syn*** see TOGETHER 2
continuance *n* ***syn*** see RUN 2
rel constancy, longevity, permanence; survival
continuation *n* **1** uninterrupted existence or succession <the *continuation* of political disorder in Northern Ireland>
syn continuity, duration, endurance, persistence
rel extension, prolongation, protraction
ant termination
2 ***syn*** see RUN 2
ant cessation
continue *vb* **1** to remain indefinitely in existence or in a particular state or course <many traditional beliefs still *continue*> <do you expect to *continue* in school for the rest of your life?>
syn abide, carry through, endure, last, perdure, persist
rel carry on, carry over, ride, run on; outlast, outlive, survive; remain, stay
con cease, desist, discontinue, quit; arrest, check, interrupt; defer, intermit, postpone, stay, suspend
ant discontinue
2 ***syn*** see RESUME 2
continuing *adj* ***syn*** see OLD 2
continuity *n* ***syn*** see CONTINUATION 1
continuous *adj* ***syn*** see CONTINUAL
ant discontinuous
continuously *adv* **1** ***syn*** see TOGETHER 2
2 ***syn*** see ALWAYS 1
contort *vb* ***syn*** see DEFORM
rel bend, curve, twist
contour *n* ***syn*** see OUTLINE
contra *prep* ***syn*** see AGAINST 1
contra *adv* ***syn*** see AGAIN 5
contra *n* ***syn*** see OPPOSITE
contraband *adj* prohibited or excluded by law or treaty <fur or feathers from endangered species are *contraband* in advanced nations>
syn banned, hot
rel disapproved, proscribed, taboo; forbidden, prohibited; excluded, shut out
contraband *vb* ***syn*** see SMUGGLE
contraception *n* ***syn*** see BIRTH CONTROL

---

syn synonym(s) ***rel*** related word(s)
ant antonym(s) ***con*** contrasted word(s)
idiom idiomatic equivalent(s)
‖ use limited; if in doubt, see a dictionary

contract *n* a usually legally enforceable arrangement between two or more parties <a *contract* for a new roof>
syn agreement, bargain, bond, compact, convention, covenant, pact, transaction; *compare* AGREEMENT 2, TREATY
contract *vb* **1** to become affected by a disease or disorder <*contracted* a severe cold that later turned into pneumonia>
syn catch, come down (with), get, sicken (with *or* of), take
rel acquire, obtain; decline, fail, sink, weaken; afflict, derange, disorder, indispose, upset; bring on, cause, induce; succumb (to)
idiom be laid by the heels by, fall (a) victim to
2 ***syn*** see INCUR
3 to make or become smaller in bulk or volume <*contract* a muscle>
syn compress, concentrate, condense, constrict, shrink
rel decrease, diminish, dwindle, lessen, reduce
con dilate, distend, inflate, swell
ant expand
contracted *adj* ***syn*** see ENGAGED 2
contradict *vb* ***syn*** see DENY 4
rel dispute; belie, falsify, garble
con authenticate, substantiate, verify
ant corroborate; confirm
contradiction *n* ***syn*** see DENIAL 2
contradictory *n* ***syn*** see OPPOSITE
contradictory *adj* ***syn*** see OPPOSITE
rel negating, nullifying; adverse, antagonistic, counteractive
con agreeing, jibing, squaring, tallying
ant corroboratory; confirmatory
contradistinction *n* ***syn*** see ANTAGONISM 2
contraposition *n* ***syn*** see ANTAGONISM 2
contraption *n* ***syn*** see DEVICE 2
contrariant *n* ***syn*** see ANTIPATHETIC 1
contrariety *n* ***syn*** see ANTAGONISM 2
contrariwise *adv* ***syn*** see AGAIN 5
idiom on (*or* to) the contrary
contrary *n* ***syn*** see OPPOSITE
contrary *adj* **1** ***syn*** see OPPOSITE
2 ***syn*** see ANTIPATHETIC 1
3 obstinately self-willed in refusing to concur, conform, or submit <why be *contrary* about something that you cannot change>
syn balky, cross-grained, froward, ornery, perverse, restive, wayward, wrongheaded
rel headstrong, intractable, recalcitrant, refractory, unruly; contumacious, insubordinate, rebellious; dissentient, dissident, nonconforming, nonconformist, recusant; obstinate, stubborn
con amenable, biddable, docile, obedient, tractable; amiable, obliging; acquiescent, compliant; forbearing, long-suffering, tolerant
ant complaisant
contrary *adv* ***syn*** see AGAIN 5
contrast *vb* ***syn*** see COMPARE 2
contravene *vb* **1** ***syn*** see VIOLATE 1
rel encroach, intrude, overstep, trespass
2 ***syn*** see DENY 4
rel combat, fight, oppose, resist; abjure, disclaim, disown, exclude, reject, repudiate, spurn
con accept, agree, subscribe (to); admit, allow, own
ant uphold (*as a principle*); allege (*as a right or claim*)
contravention *n* ***syn*** see BREACH 1
rel crime, offense, sin, vice
contrawise *adv* ***syn*** see AGAIN 5
contretemps *n* ***syn*** see MISFORTUNE
contribute *vb* **1** to give in common with others <*contribute* to a fund for handicapped children>
syn chip in, come through, kick in, pitch in, subscribe; *compare* GIVE 1
idiom put something in the pot, sweeten the kitty
2 to have a share in something (as an act or effect) <careful planning *contributed* greatly to the success of the project>
syn conduce, redound, tend
rel aid, help, assist; add (to), augment, supplement; fortify, recruit, reinforce, strengthen
idiom do one's bit, have a hand in
con detract, minus, subtract, take away
contribution *n* ***syn*** see DONATION
contributory *adj* ***syn*** see AUXILIARY
contrite *adj* ***syn*** see REMORSEFUL
contriteness *n* ***syn*** see PENITENCE
contrition *n* ***syn*** see PENITENCE
contriturate *vb* ***syn*** see PULVERIZE 1
contrivance *n* **1** ***syn*** see DEVICE 2
2 ***syn*** see INVENTION
contrive *vb* **1** ***syn*** see PLOT
rel develop, elaborate, work out
2 to use ingenuity in making or doing or achieving an end <*contrived* a useful camp stove from a few bricks and a piece of screen>
syn concoct, cook (up), devise, dream up, formulate, frame, hatch (up), invent, make up, vamp (up)
rel plan, plot, project, scheme; fabricate, fashion, make, manufacture; handle, manipulate, move; rig
control *vb* **1** ***syn*** see COMPOSE 4
rel adjust, regulate; curb, master, quell, subdue
2 ***syn*** see GOVERN 3
rel regulate, supervise; discipline
idiom put through the mill (*or* a course of sprouts), take in hand
control *n* ***syn*** see POWER 1
controlled *adj* ***syn*** see CONSERVATIVE 2
controversial *adj* ***syn*** see CONTENTIOUS 2
controversy *n* **1** ***syn*** see ARGUMENT 2
2 ***syn*** see QUARREL
controvert *vb* ***syn*** see DISPROVE 1
rel challenge, oppugn, question
contumacious *adj* ***syn*** see INSUBORDINATE
rel contrary, froward, perverse; alienated, disaffected, estranged, irreconcilable
con acquiescent, compliant, resigned
ant obedient
contumacy *n* ***syn*** see DEFIANCE 2
contumelious *adj* **1** ***syn*** see ABUSIVE
2 ***syn*** see INSOLENT 2
ant obsequious
contumely *n* **1** ***syn*** see ABUSE

rel animadversion, aspersion, reflection, stricture
idiom hard (*or* bitter) words
2 *syn* see AFFRONT
contuse *vb syn* see BRUISE 1
contusion *n syn* see BRUISE
conundrum *n syn* see MYSTERY
convalesce *vb syn* see IMPROVE 3
convenance *n syn* see FORM 3
convene *vb* 1 to begin a session (as of a legislature or conference) <the council *convened* at 10 o'clock>
syn meet, open, sit
idiom hold a meeting (*or* session)
2 *syn* see SUMMON 2
rel convoke, muster
3 *syn* see CONVOKE
convenience *n* 1 *syn* see AMENITY 2
2 *syn* see TOILET
convenience *vb syn* see OBLIGE 2
convenient *adj* 1 *syn* see GOOD 2
2 situated within easy reach <left his glasses *convenient* to his book>
syn adjacent, close-at-hand, close-by, handy, near-at-hand, nearby
rel close, near, nigh; immediate, next
idiom at one's beck and call, at one's fingertips, in one's immediate neighborhood, under one's nose
ant inconvenient
convention *n* 1 *syn* see TREATY
2 *syn* see CONTRACT
rel accord, understanding
3 *syn* see FORM 3
rel canon, law, precept, rule; custom, practice
conventional *adj* 1 according with or based on generally accepted and well-established usage <took a very *conventional* view of his duty>
syn button-down, orthodox, square, straight; *compare* TRADITIONAL 1
rel moderate, sober, temperate; constrained, restrained; dependable, reliable, responsible; conscientious, fastidious, nice, punctilious, scrupulous; conservative, traditionalistic
ant unconventional
2 *syn* see TRADITIONAL 1
3 *syn* see CEREMONIAL
rel decent, decorous, proper, seemly; correct, precise, right
con lax, negligent, remiss, slack; artless, ingenuous, naive, natural, simple, unsophisticated
ant unconventional
converge *vb* to come to or trend toward a common point <the main streets *converge* on a central square>
syn concenter, concentrate, focus, meet
idiom come to a center, come (*or* run) together
conversant *adj* 1 *syn* see AWARE
ant ignorant
2 *syn* see FAMILIAR 3
rel sensible; up-to-date; apprehending, comprehending, perceptive, percipient
con unfamiliar; nescient
ant unconversant

conversation *n* 1 oral exchange of information or ideas <leaned against the fence in casual *conversation*>
syn chat, colloquy, confabulation, converse, dialogue, parley
rel discussion; discourse, speech, talk
2 an instance of conversational exchange <had a long *conversation* about family problems>
syn colloquy, confabulation, dialogue, talk; *compare* CHAT 2
rel debate, deliberation, discussion, ventilation; comment, observation, remark; cross talk, repartee
conversation piece *n syn* see CURIOSITY 2
converse *vb* to engage in conversation <they *conversed* quietly while waiting for their friend>
syn chat, chin, colloque, talk, visit, yarn; *compare* CHAT 1
converse (in) *vb syn* see SPEAK 3
converse *n* 1 *syn* see CONVERSATION 1
2 *syn* see COMMUNICATION 3
converse *adj syn* see OPPOSITE
converse *n syn* see OPPOSITE
conversely *adv syn* see AGAIN 5
conversion *n* 1 fundamental alteration in one's system of beliefs <Judaism does not encourage *conversion* of gentiles>
syn metanoia, rebirth
rel about-face, reversal, turning; reclamation, regeneration
idiom change of heart
2 change of one thing to another usually by substitution <*conversion* of locomotives from steam to diesel power>
syn alteration, changeover, shift, transformation
rel change, modification, qualification; metamorphosis, mutation, permutation, transmutation; innovation, novelty
convert *vb* 1 to induce (another or others) to accept the validity of something (as a belief, course of action, or point of view) <Chinese missionaries *converted* many Japanese to Buddhism>
syn bring, lead, move, persuade
rel redeem, reform, save; bend, bias, incline, sway; actuate, budge, impel; proselyte, proselytize
2 *syn* see TRANSFORM
rel fabricate, forge, make, manufacture; apply, employ, use, utilize
convey *vb* 1 *syn* see CARRY 1
2 *syn* see COMMUNICATE 1
rel project, put across
3 *syn* see TRANSFER 4
rel commit, consign, relegate
4 *syn* see CONDUCT 4
conveyance *n* 1 *syn* see TRANSPORTATION 1
2 *syn* see DEED 3
3 *syn* see VEHICLE 3

---

syn synonym(s) *rel* related word(s)
ant antonym(s) *con* contrasted word(s)
idiom idiomatic equivalent(s)
|| use limited; if in doubt, see a dictionary

convict *n* a person serving time in prison after conviction as a criminal <mixing hardened *convicts* with juvenile offenders>
syn ‖con, jailbird, ‖lag, loser, prison bird
rel long-termer, longtimer; ‖stir bug; recidivist, repeater
conviction *n* **1** *syn* see CERTAINTY
con dubiety, dubiosity, uncertainty; disbelief, incredulity, unbelief
2 *syn* see OPINION
rel doctrine, dogma, tenet
convince *vb* **1** *syn* see ASSURE 2
2 *syn* see INDUCE 1
convincing *adj* **1** *syn* see AUTHENTIC 1
2 *syn* see VALID
convivial *adj* *syn* see SOCIAL 1
rel lively, vivacious; jocund, jolly, merry
con grave, sedate, serious, sober, solemn, somber; reserved, reticent, silent
ant taciturn; stolid
convoke *vb* to bring together by or as if by summons <the ruler *convoked* his council>
syn assemble, call, convene, summon; *compare* SUMMON 2
rel collect, congregate, gather; ask, bid, invite, request; meet, sit
con adjourn, close, dissolve, prorogue, recess, suspend; disperse, scatter
convoluted *adj* *syn* see WINDING
convoy *vb* *syn* see ACCOMPANY
rel defend, guard, protect, safeguard, shield
convulse *vb* *syn* see SHAKE 4
convulsion *n* *syn* see COMMOTION 1
rel cataclysm, disaster; quaking, rocking, shaking, tottering, trembling
cook *vb* **1** to make ready or fit for eating by the use of heat <liked everything well-*cooked*>
syn do
2 *syn* see BURN 3
cook (up) *vb* *syn* see CONTRIVE 2
cookshop *n* *syn* see EATING HOUSE
cool *adj* **1** *syn* see COLD 1
ant warm
2 freed or giving the impression of freedom from all agitation or excitement <they looked *cool* and very formidable>
syn collected, composed, disimpassioned, imperturbable, nonchalant, unflappable, unruffled; *compare* HAPPY-GO-LUCKY
rel calm, placid, serene, tranquil; aloof, detached, indifferent; impassive, phlegmatic, stolid; assured, confident, self-possessed
con fervent, fervid, impassioned, passionate, perfervid; discomposed, disturbed, flurried, flustered, perturbed, upset
ant ardent; agitated
3 *syn* see UNSOCIABLE
‖**4** *syn* see MARVELOUS 2
cool *vb* **1** *syn* see COMPOSE 4
2 *syn* see MURDER 1
cooler *n* *syn* see JAIL
coolness *n* *syn* see EQUANIMITY
‖**coon** *vb* *syn* see STEAL 1
coon's age *n* *syn* see AGE 2
‖**coony** *adj* *syn* see CLEVER 4
coop *n* *syn* see JAIL
coop *vb* *syn* see ENCLOSE 1
rel bar, block, hinder, impede, obstruct
cooperate *vb* *syn* see UNITE 2
rel agree, coincide
con annul, negate, nullify; negative, neutralize
ant counteract
cooperative *adj* involving joint action in producing a result <the need of *cooperative* efforts to effect lasting social change>
syn coacting, coactive, coefficient, conjoint, synergetic, synergic
rel collaborative, concerted; noncompetitive, uncompetitive
con competitive, emulous, rivaling, vying; antagonistic, conflicting, oppugnant
ant counteractive
coordinate *vb* *syn* see HARMONIZE 3
coordinate *n* **1** *syn* see OPPOSITE NUMBER
2 *syn* see MATE 5
‖**cop** *vb* *syn* see STEAL 1
cop *n* *syn* see POLICEMAN
copartner *n* *syn* see PARTNER
copious *adj* *syn* see PLENTIFUL
rel exuberant, lush, luxuriant
con exiguous, scant, scanty, scrimpy, spare, sparse; slender, slight, slim, tenuous, thin
ant meager
cop out *vb* ‖**1** *syn* see DIE 1
2 *syn* see BACK DOWN
‖**copper** *n* *syn* see POLICEMAN
copy *n* **1** *syn* see IMITATION
2 *syn* see REPRODUCTION
rel counterpart, parallel; impress, impression, imprint, print; effigy, image, likeness
ant original
copy *vb* to make a copy of <*copied* the speech word for word>
syn duplicate, imitate, reduplicate, replicate, reproduce
rel ditto, repeat; counterfeit, fake, sham, simulate; ape, burlesque, mock, parody, take off, travesty
ant originate
coquet *vb* *syn* see TRIFLE 1
coquette *n* *syn* see FLIRT
coquettish *adj* *syn* see COY 2
cordial *adj* *syn* see GRACIOUS 1
rel responsive, sympathetic, tender, warm, warmhearted; heartfelt, hearty, sincere, wholehearted
con cold, cool, frigid, frosty; aloof, detached, disinterested, indifferent; reserved, silent, taciturn
cordiality *n* *syn* see AMENITY 1
rel responsiveness, sympathy, understanding, warmth; mutuality, reciprocity; approbation, approval, favor
con cross-purposes, difference, disagreement, misunderstanding, odds, variance; disapprobation, disapproval, disfavor
core *n* **1** *syn* see CENTER 1
2 *syn* see BODY 3

3 ***syn*** see SUBSTANCE 2
rel consequence, import, importance, significance
4 ***syn*** see CENTER 3
rel base, basis, foundation; beginning, commencement, origin, start

‖**corker** *n* ***syn*** ‖DILLY, crackerjack, ‖daisy, dandy, humdinger, jim-dandy, knockout, ‖lalapalooza, ‖lulu, nifty

corkscrew *vb* ***syn*** see WIND 2

corner *n* **1** ***syn*** see PREDICAMENT
2 ***syn*** see MONOPOLY

corner *vb* to get into one's control or a position from which escape is difficult <*cornered* him at a party and tried to borrow a hundred dollars>
syn bottle (up), collar, tree
rel bother, disturb, put out, trouble; capture, catch, nab, seize, trap
idiom chase up a tree, drive (*or* run) into a corner, get (*or* have) on the ropes

cornerwise *adv* ***syn*** see DIAGONALLY

corny *adj* ***syn*** see TRITE

corollary *n* ***syn*** see EFFECT 1

coronal *n* ***syn*** see WREATH

coronet *n* ***syn*** see WREATH

corporal *adj* ***syn*** see BODILY

corporation *n* ***syn*** see POTBELLY

corporeal *adj* **1** ***syn*** see BODILY
2 ***syn*** see MATERIAL 1

corps *n* ***syn*** see COMPANY 4

corpse *n* a dead body especially of a human being <concealed the *corpse* under some rubbish>
syn body, cadaver, carcass, ‖cold meat, ‖deader, mort, remains, stiff
rel carrion; bones

corpselike *adj* **1** ***syn*** see DEATHLY 1
2 ***syn*** see GHASTLY 2

corpsy *adj* ***syn*** see DEATHLY 1

corpulence *n* ***syn*** see OBESITY

corpulent *adj* ***syn*** see FAT 2

corpus *n* **1** ***syn*** see BODY 3
2 ***syn*** see OEUVRE

corrade *vb* ***syn*** see ABRADE 1

corral *vb* ***syn*** see ENCLOSE 1

correct *vb* **1** to set right something that is wrong <*correct* a misstatement>
syn amend, emend, mend, rectify, right
rel ameliorate, better, improve; redress, remedy, revise; make over, reform; adjust, fix, regulate
con damage, harm, hurt, impair, injure, mar, spoil
2 ***syn*** see PUNISH 1
con baby, coddle, cosset, humor, indulge, pamper, spoil

correct *adj* **1** ***syn*** see DECOROUS 1
rel careful, meticulous, punctilious, scrupulous
2 conforming to or agreeing with fact <the *correct* solution to the problem>
syn accurate, exact, nice, precise, proper, right, rigorous
rel faithful, true, undistorted, veracious, veridical; faultless, flawless, impeccable, perfect
con fallacious, false, wrong; defective, faulty, flawed, imperfect
ant incorrect

correction *n* ***syn*** see PUNISHMENT

correctitude *n* ***syn*** see ORDER 7

corrective *n* ***syn*** see REMEDY 2

correctly *adv* ***syn*** see WELL 1

correctness *n* **1** ***syn*** see ORDER 7
2 ***syn*** see PRECISION

correlate *n* **1** ***syn*** see COUNTERPART 1
2 ***syn*** see PARALLEL

correspond *vb* ***syn*** see AGREE 4

correspond (to) *vb* ***syn*** see AMOUNT 2

correspondence *n* ***syn*** see CONSISTENCY
ant divergence

correspondent *n* ***syn*** see PARALLEL

corresponding *adj* ***syn*** see LIKE

correspondingly *adv* ***syn*** see ALSO 1

corridor *n* ***syn*** see PASSAGE 4

corrival *n* ***syn*** see RIVAL

corroborate *vb* ***syn*** see CONFIRM 2
con invalidate, negate, nullify
ant contradict

corroborative *adj* serving or tending to corroborate <*corroborative* evidence>
syn adminicular, collateral, confirmative, confirmatory, corroboratory, verificatory
rel ancillary, auxiliary, supplementary, supportive; assisting, helping
con confutative, refutative, refutatory; contradictory, negatory

corroboratory *adj* ***syn*** see CORROBORATIVE

corrode *vb* ***syn*** see EAT 3

corrosive *adj* ***syn*** see SARCASTIC

corrosiveness *n* ***syn*** see SARCASM

corrugation *n* ***syn*** see WRINKLE

corrupt *vb* **1** ***syn*** see DEBASE 1
rel abase, degrade; ruin, wreck
con amend, correct, reform
2 ***syn*** see DECAY
rel befoul, defile, foul; smirch, tarnish

corrupt *adj* **1** ***syn*** see VICIOUS 2
rel crooked, devious, oblique; baneful, deleterious, detrimental, noxious, pernicious; abased, degraded, low
2 seeking sordid advantage with little regard to moral or legal bars <a *corrupt* politician>
syn mercenary, praetorian, unethical, unprincipled, unscrupulous, venal; *compare* CROOKED 2, VENAL 1
rel undependable, unreliable, untrustworthy; faithless, inconstant, unfaithful; double-dealing, perfidious, treacherous, two-faced; bribable, corruptible; blackguardly, knavish, reprobate
con ethical, principled, scrupulous, upright; dependable, reliable, trustworthy, trusty
3 ***syn*** see CROOKED 2

corrupted *adj* ***syn*** see DEBASED

corruptible *adj* ***syn*** see VENAL 1

corruption *n* **1** ***syn*** see VICE 1
2 ***syn*** see BARBARISM

---

syn synonym(s) ***rel*** related word(s)
ant antonym(s) ***con*** contrasted word(s)
idiom idiomatic equivalent(s)
‖ use limited; if in doubt, see a dictionary

corsair *n* ***syn*** see PIRATE

coruscate *vb* ***syn*** see FLASH 1

coruscation *n* ***syn*** see FLASH 1

corybantic *adj* ***syn*** see FURIOUS 2

coryphée *n* ***syn*** see DANCER

cosmic *adj* ***syn*** see UNIVERSAL 2

cosmopolitan *adj* **1** exhibiting or characterized by a sophistication and savoir faire arising from cultured urban life and wide travel <had a thoroughly *cosmopolitan* outlook on life>
syn metropolitan, urbane; *compare* SOPHISTICATED 2
rel civilized, polished, smooth; sophisticated, worldly-wise; cultivated, cultured
con boorish, cloddish, rude, rustic; insular, parochial, provincial
2 ***syn*** see UNIVERSAL 2

cosmos (*or* **kosmos**) *n* ***syn*** see UNIVERSE

cosset *vb* **1** ***syn*** see CARESS
2 ***syn*** see BABY

cost *n* **1** ***syn*** see PRICE 1
2 ***syn*** see EXPENSE 1
3 ***syn*** see EXPENSE 2

costive *adj* **1** ***syn*** see CONSTIPATED
2 ***syn*** see STINGY

costless *adj* ***syn*** see FREE 5

costly *adj* **1** commanding or being a large price <the scarcer an item becomes the more *costly* it is>
syn dear, expensive, high; *compare* PRECIOUS 1
rel excessive, exorbitant, extravagant, inordinate, steep, stiff; fancy, premium, top
con inexpensive, low, low-priced, reasonable
ant cheap
2 ***syn*** see PRECIOUS 1

costume *n* style of clothing and adornment <her *costume* was always suitable to the occasion>
syn dress, getup, guise, outfit, rig, setout, turnout
rel fashion, mode, style

cot *n* ***syn*** see HUT

||**cotch** *vb* **1** ***syn*** see SEIZE 2
2 ***syn*** see CATCH 1
3 ***syn*** see CATCH 7

coterie *n* ***syn*** see CLIQUE

cottage *n* ***syn*** see HUT

cotton *vb* **1** ***syn*** see BABY
2 ***syn*** see FAWN

cotton (to *or* on to) *vb* ***syn*** see APPREHEND 1

cottony *adj* ***syn*** see SOFT 3

couch *vb* **1** ***syn*** see WORD
2 ***syn*** see LOWER 3

couch *n* ***syn*** see LAIR 1

couleur de rose *adj* ***syn*** see HOPEFUL 2

couloir *n* ***syn*** see PASSAGE 4

counsel *n* ***syn*** see ADVICE 1

counsel *vb* to give advice to or about <*counseled* him to wait for a more propitious occasion>
syn advise, recommend
rel admonish, reprehend, warn; direct, order, prescribe; charge, enjoin, prompt, urge; advocate, suggest

count *vb* **1** to ascertain the total of units in a collection by noting one after another <*counted* the sheep in the pasture>
syn enumerate, number, numerate, tale, tally, tell
rel add, cast, figure, foot, sum, tot, total; calculate, compute, estimate, reckon; tell off
2 ***syn*** see MATTER
3 ***syn*** see WEIGH 3

count (on) *vb* ***syn*** see RELY (on *or* upon)

count (on *or* upon) *vb* ***syn*** see EXPECT 1

countenance *n* **1** ***syn*** see LOOK 2
idiom (the) cut of one's jib
2 ***syn*** see FACE 1

countenance *vb* **1** ***syn*** see ENCOURAGE 2
rel applaud, commend; back, champion, support, uphold
con deride, ridicule; criticize, reprehend, reprobate; reproach, reprove
ant discountenance
2 ***syn*** see APPROVE 1

counter *vb* ***syn*** see OPPOSE 1
rel baffle, balk, beat, bilk, circumvent, dash, disappoint, foil, frustrate, ruin

counter *n* ***syn*** see OPPOSITE

counter *adj* ***syn*** see OPPOSITE
rel hostile, inimical; adverse, antagonistic, anti, oppugnant; hindering, impeding, obstructive

counteract *vb* ***syn*** see NEUTRALIZE
rel correct, fix, rectify, right
con cooperate, coordinate, synergize; back, reinforce, support

counteractant *n* ***syn*** see REMEDY 2

counteractive *n* ***syn*** see REMEDY 2

counteragent *n* ***syn*** see REMEDY 2

counterbalance *vb* ***syn*** see COMPENSATE 1
rel amend, correct, rectify
con overbalance, unbalance

counterblow *n* ***syn*** see RETALIATION

countercheck *vb* ***syn*** see NEUTRALIZE

counterfactual *adj* ***syn*** see FALSE 1

counterfeit *vb* ***syn*** see ASSUME 4
rel ape, copy, imitate, mimic

counterfeit *adj* being an imitation intended to mislead or deceive <*counterfeit* money> <*counterfeit* sympathy>
syn bogus, brummagem, fake, false, phony, pinchbeck, pseudo, sham, snide, spurious; *compare* SPURIOUS 3
rel feigned, pretended, simulated; deceptive, delusive, delusory, misleading; fraudulent
con authentic, veritable; actual, real, true; unquestionable, valid
ant bona fide, genuine

counterfeit *n* ***syn*** see IMPOSTURE
rel copy, facsimile, reproduction; dummy, simulacrum

countermeasure *n* ***syn*** see REMEDY 2

counterpane *n* ***syn*** see BEDSPREAD

counterpart *n* **1** something that completes or complements <export controls as a *counterpart* of domestic distribution controls>
syn complement, correlate, pendant; *compare* PARALLEL
rel analogue, correlate, correspondent; equal, equivalent, like, match
con counterpoint, opposite

2 ***syn*** see PARALLEL
3 ***syn*** see EQUAL
4 ***syn*** see OPPOSITE NUMBER

counterpoise *n* ***syn*** see BALANCE 1

counterpoise *vb* ***syn*** see COMPENSATE 1
rel ballast, poise, stabilize, steady, trim
con capsize, overturn, upset

counterpole *n* ***syn*** see OPPOSITE

countersign *n* ***syn*** see PASSWORD 1

counterstep *n* ***syn*** see REMEDY 2

countertype *n* ***syn*** see PARALLEL

countervail *vb* ***syn*** see COMPENSATE 1
rel amend, correct, rectify; foil, frustrate, thwart; overcome, surmount

countless *adj* ***syn*** see INNUMERABLE

count out *vb* ***syn*** see EXCLUDE

countrified *adj* ***syn*** see RURAL

country *n* the nation-state to which one belongs or from which one originated <returned to his own *country* after years of exile>
syn fatherland, home, homeland, land, mother country, motherland, soil

country *adj* ***syn*** see RURAL

country jake *n* ***syn*** see RUSTIC

countryman *n* ***syn*** see RUSTIC

couple *vb* **1** ***syn*** see JOIN 1
2 ***syn*** see HITCH 2
rel hook up, ‖inspan

couple *n* two individuals of the same or a similar kind that occur, function, or are considered together <a *couple* of ideas for improving the book> <the happiest *couple* I know>
syn brace, doublet, duo, dyad, pair, twosome
rel span, team, yoke

coupling *n* ***syn*** see JOINT 1

courage *n* a quality of mind or temperament that enables one to stand fast in the face of opposition, hardship, or danger <had the kind of *courage* that could appreciate a danger yet steadfastly face it>
syn dauntlessness, guts, heart, mettle, ‖moxie, pluck, resolution, spirit, spunk; *compare* FORTITUDE
rel audacity, boldness, bravery, doughtiness, fearlessness, intrepidity; gallantry, heroism, valor; backbone, fortitude, grit, sand; assurance, determination, firmness, persistence, tenacity
con chickenheartedness, faintheartedness, unmanliness, yellowness; baseness, cravenness, poltroonery, pusillanimity; timidity, timorousness
ant cowardice

courageous *adj* ***syn*** see BRAVE 1
rel fiery, high-spirited; strong, tenacious
con afraid, apprehensive, fearful
ant pusillanimous

courier *n* ***syn*** see MESSENGER

course *n* **1** ***syn*** see WAY 2
rel circuit, orbit, range, scope
2 ***syn*** see CHANNEL 1
3 way of acting or proceeding <hard to decide on the best *course* to follow>
syn line, policy, polity, procedure, program
rel design, pattern, plan, platform, scheme; manner, system, way
idiom course of action
4 ***syn*** see PROGRESS 2
5 ***syn*** see SUCCESSION 2

course *vb* to proceed with great celerity (as in pursuing or competing) <the fox *coursed* after the hare>
syn career, chase, race, rush, speed, tear; *compare* RUSH 1
rel hasten, hurry, hustle; dart, dash, scamper, scoot, scurry; run, sprint
idiom step on the gas, stir one's stumps

courser *n* a strong vigorous horse formerly used in mounted combat <heroes mounted on great fiery *coursers*>
syn charger, war-horse

court *n* **1** an open space wholly or partly enclosed (as by buildings or walls) <the apartment overlooks the *court*>
syn ‖close, courtyard, curtilage, enclosure, quad, quadrangle, yard
2 a place or the persons assembled for the administration of justice <the *court* was called to order>
syn bar, lawcourt, tribunal
3 ***syn*** see JUDGE 2

court *vb* ***syn*** see ADDRESS 8
rel allure, attract, captivate, charm

courteous *adj* ***syn*** see CIVIL 2
rel attentive, considerate, thoughtful
con blunt, brusque, curt, gruff; insolent, overbearing, supercilious
ant discourteous

courtesan *n* ***syn*** see HARLOT 1

courtesy *n* **1** courteous behavior or a courteous act <noted for her *courtesy* and graciousness> <such little *courtesies* take little time but often brighten lonely lives>
syn amenity, attention, gallantry
rel affability, cordiality, geniality, graciousness; comity, complaisance; chivalry, civility, courteousness, courtliness; attentiveness, considerateness, consideration, thoughtfulness
con boorishness, churlishness; impoliteness, incivility, rudeness, ungraciousness
ant discourtesy
2 ***syn*** see FAVOR 4

courtly *adj* marked by elaborate and often ceremonious courtesy <a *courtly* gentleman of the old school>
syn gallant, gracious, preux, stately; *compare* CIVIL 2
rel august, dignified, imposing, lofty; prim, starchy, stiff, stilted, studied; ceremonious, conventional, formal; civilized
con discourteous, ill-mannered, impolite, rude, uncivil, ungracious; boorish, coarse, gross, loutish, uncouth, vulgar
ant churlish

courtyard *n* ***syn*** see COURT 1

---

syn synonym(s) ***rel*** related word(s)
ant antonym(s) ***con*** contrasted word(s)
idiom idiomatic equivalent(s)
‖ use limited; if in doubt, see a dictionary

cousinage *n* ***syn*** see KIN 2
cousinhood *n* ***syn*** see KIN 2
cove *n* ***syn*** see INLET
covenant *n* ***syn*** see CONTRACT
covenant *vb* ***syn*** see VOW
rel agree, concur
cover *vb* **1** ***syn*** see DEFEND 1
2 ***syn*** see HIDE
3 to spread over or put something over <fog *covered* the ground> <*covered* the bed with a quilt>
syn blanket, cap, crown, overcast, overlay, overspread
rel conceal, hide, screen; defend, protect, shield; enclose, enfold, envelop, shroud, wrap; superimpose, superpose
con display, exhibit, expose
ant bare, uncover
4 ***syn*** see TRAVEL 2
5 ***syn*** see SET 11
cover *n* **1** ***syn*** see SHELTER 1
rel concealment, hiding, screen; safety, security
ant exposure
2 ***syn*** see MASK 2
coverlet *n* ***syn*** see BEDSPREAD
‖**coverlid** *n* ***syn*** see BEDSPREAD
covert *adj* **1** ***syn*** see SECRET 1
rel camouflaged, cloaked, disguised, dissembled, masked
con candid, frank, open
ant overt
2 ***syn*** see ULTERIOR
con direct, forthright; honest, square, straight
covert *n* ***syn*** see SHELTER 1
covertly *adv* ***syn*** see SECRETLY
covet *vb* ***syn*** see DESIRE 1
con abjure, forswear
ant renounce
covetous *adj* having or marked by an urgent and often unscrupulous desire for possessions <the *covetous* eye of an avid collector>
syn acquisitive, desirous, grabby, grasping, greedy, itchy, prehensile
rel esurient, gluttonous, rapacious, ravenous, voracious; hoggish, lickerish, piggish, swinish; avid, eager, keen; envious, jealous; grudging, selfish
con generous, liberal, munificent; ungrudging, unselfish; abstemious, abstinent, ascetic, austere; moderate, restrained, temperate
covey *n* ***syn*** see GROUP 1
covin *n* ***syn*** see PLOT 2
cow *vb* ***syn*** see INTIMIDATE
rel appall, daunt, dismay; abash, discomfit, disconcert, embarrass, faze, rattle
con cower, cringe, fawn, toady, truckle
coward *n* one who shows or yields to ignoble fear <a treacherous *coward* who betrayed his friends to save his own skin>
syn chicken, craven, dastard, funk, funker, poltroon, quitter, yellowbelly
rel baby, fraidycat, invertebrate, jellyfish, milksop, scaredy-cat; caitiff, recreant
con gallant, hero, palladin, stalwart; ideal, model, pattern, standard
coward *adj* ***syn*** see COWARDLY
cowardly *adj* marked by or arising from a base lack of courage <a *cowardly* desertion>
syn ‖chicken, coward, cowhearted, craven, gutless, lily-livered, milk-livered, poltroon, poltroonish, poor-spirited, pusillanimous, spunkless, unmanly, white-livered, yellow
rel afraid, chickenhearted, fainthearted, fearful, timid, timorous; funky, panicky; caitiff, dastardly, recreant, vile, worthless
con courageous, fearless, intrepid, valiant; daring, reckless, temerarious
ant brave
cower *vb* ***syn*** see FAWN
rel blench, flinch, quail, recoil, shrink, wince
con browbeat, bulldoze, bully, cow, intimidate; bristle, strut, swagger
cowering *adj* ***syn*** see FAWNING
cowhearted *adj* ***syn*** see COWARDLY
coxcomb *n* ***syn*** see FOP
coy *adj* **1** ***syn*** see SHY 1
rel decent, decorous, nice, proper, seemly
con brash, brazen, impudent
2 marked by a light playful artlessness <glanced up with a *coy* twinkle in her eye>
syn arch, coquettish, roguish
rel capricious, kittenish, lively, mischievous, playful, skittish
con serious, sober, thoughtful
cozen *vb* **1** ***syn*** see CHEAT
2 ***syn*** see DECEIVE
cozy *adj* **1** ***syn*** see COMFORTABLE 2
rel safe, secure
2 ***syn*** see INTIMATE 4
crab *vb* ***syn*** see GRIPE
idiom fret and fume
crab *n* ***syn*** see GROUCH
crabbed *adj* ***syn*** see SULLEN
rel blunt, brusque, crusty, gruff; choleric, cranky, splenetic, testy; huffy, irascible, irritable, snappish
con amiable, complaisant, good-natured, obliging; benign, benignant, kind, kindly; agreeable, pleasing; affable, genial, gracious
crabber *n* ***syn*** see GROUCH
crabby *adj* ***syn*** see SULLEN
crabwise *adv* ***syn*** see SIDEWAYS 1
crack *vb* ***syn*** see DECODE
rel puzzle out
crack *n* **1** ***syn*** see BANG 2
rel splintering, splitting; percussion
2 ***syn*** see JOKE 1
rel dig, fling, potshot
idiom flash of wit
3 a usually narrow opening, break, or discontinuity made by splitting and rupture <a *crack* in the ice>
syn chink, cleft, fissure, rift, rima, rimation, rime, split
rel rent; discontinuity, interstice, interval; cranny, niche; crevasse, crevice
4 ***syn*** see INSTANT 1
idiom flash of lightning
5 ***syn*** see BLOW 1

6 *syn* see FLING 1
crack *adj syn* see PROFICIENT
rel excellent, superior
crackbrain *n syn* see CRACKPOT
idiom cracked wit
crackbrained *adj syn* see INSANE 1
crackdown *n syn* see REPRESSION 2
rel quashing
idiom lowering the boom
cracked *adj syn* see INSANE 1
idiom ||off in the upper story
crackerjack *n syn* see ||DILLY
crackerjack *adj syn* see PROFICIENT
||**crackers** *adj syn* see INSANE 1
cracking *adj syn* see MONSTROUS 1
crackpot *n* one given to extremely eccentric or lunatic ideas or actions <a *crackpot* who wrote threatening letters to public figures>
syn crackbrain, crank, cuckoo, ding-a-ling, harebrain, kook, lunatic, nut, screwball
rel case, character, ||dingbat, eccentric, oddball, oddity, ||wack; loon, loony, madman, maniac
crack–up *n* 1 *syn* see NERVOUS BREAKDOWN
2 *syn* see CRASH 3
3 *syn* see COLLAPSE 2
rel decline, deterioration
||**cracky** *adj syn* see INSANE 1
cradlesong *n syn* see LULLABY
craft *n* 1 *syn* see ART 1
2 *syn* see TRADE 1
rel job
3 *syn* see CUNNING 2
craftiness *n syn* see CUNNING 2
crafty *adj syn* see SLY 2
rel adroit, clever, tidy; acute, keen, sharp; deceitful, fawning, ||sleekit, ||sleeky
cragged *adj syn* see ROUGH 1
craggy *adj syn* see ROUGH 1
cram *vb* 1 to fill (a limited space) forcibly with more than is practicable or fitting <*crammed* the suitcase chock-full and had to sit on it to close it>
syn jam, jam-pack, ||pang, ram, stuff, tamp; *compare* LOAD 3, PRESS 7
rel pack, stive; fill, heap; chock, choke; press, shove, thrust; drive, force; squeeze, wedge
2 *syn* see PRESS 7
3 *syn* see GULP
rel overeat
idiom pack it in
4 to study intensively or under pressure <had to *cram* all night before the exam>
syn bone (up), ||mug (up)
rel study; review
idiom burn the midnight oil
cram–full *adj syn* see FULL 1
crammed *adj syn* see FULL 1
idiom crammed full, crammed to the bursting point, fit (*or* ready) to burst
ant emptied
cramp *n* 1 *syn* see RESTRICTION 1
rel shackle
2 *syn* see RESTRICTION 2
rel constipation, stultification
cramp *adj syn* see CRAMPED
cramped *adj* having insufficient size or capacity <a *cramped* cubbyhole of an office>
syn confined, cramp, incommodious, squeezy, ||tucked up
rel close, narrow, tight, two-by-four; little, minute, small, tiny
con commodious, unconfined
ant spacious
crank *n* 1 *syn* see CAPRICE
2 *syn* see CRACKPOT
rel freak
3 *syn* see GROUCH
cranky *adj* 1 *syn* see INSANE 1
2 *syn* see CANTANKEROUS
rel contrary, difficult, froward, perverse
3 *syn* see IRASCIBLE
rel bad-humored, ill-humored; disagreeable; ugly
idiom out of sorts
cranny *n syn* see NOOK
||**crap** *n syn* see NONSENSE 2
||**crap out** *vb syn* see FAINT
||**crappy** *adj syn* see BAD 1
crash *vb syn* see FAIL 5
ant skyrocket
crash *n* 1 *syn* see BANG 2
2 *syn* see IMPACT 1
3 a wrecking or smashing especially of a vehicle <an air *crash*>
syn crack-up, pileup, ||prang, smash, smashup, ||stramash, wreck
rel accident; collision
4 *syn* see COLLAPSE 2
crashing *adj syn* see UTTER
crass *adj syn* see COARSE 3
rel churlish, loutish
ant refined
crate *n syn* see JALOPY
crave *vb* 1 *syn* see BEG
2 *syn* see DESIRE 1
con contemn, despise, disdain, scorn
ant spurn
3 *syn* see LONG
idiom have a craving for
4 *syn* see DEMAND 2
craven *adj syn* see COWARDLY
craven *n syn* see COWARD
craving *n syn* see DESIRE 1
crawfish (out) *vb syn* see BACK DOWN
crawl *vb* 1 *syn* see CREEP 1
rel grovel; worm
2 *syn* see TEEM
||3 *syn* see LAMBASTE 3
craze *vb syn* see MADDEN 1
craze *n syn* see FASHION 3
rel enthusiasm, fever
crazed *adj syn* see INSANE 1
craziness *n syn* see FOOLISHNESS

---

syn synonym(s) *rel* related word(s)
ant antonym(s) *con* contrasted word(s)
idiom idiomatic equivalent(s)
|| use limited; if in doubt, see a dictionary

crazy *adj* **1** ***syn*** see INSANE 1
rel doting, gaga, moonstruck; beeheaded, silly; erratic, possessed
idiom as crazy as a loon, having a screw loose, having bats in one's belfry, not having all one's marbles (*or* buttons)
ant sane
2 ***syn*** see FOOLISH 2
rel goofy, senseless
idiom beyond the realm of reason, out of all reason
con practical, reasonable, reasoned, sensible
ant sane

‖**crazy** *adv* ***syn*** see VERY 1

crazy house *n* ***syn*** see ASYLUM 3

cream *n* **1** ***syn*** see OINTMENT
2 ***syn*** see BEST
idiom (the) top cream

‖**cream** *vb* ***syn*** see WHIP 2

crease *n* ***syn*** see WRINKLE

create *vb* **1** ***syn*** see GENERATE 1
idiom call into being
2 ***syn*** see FOUND 2
3 ***syn*** see COMPOSE 2
rel conceive, formulate; imagine

creation *n* ***syn*** see UNIVERSE

creative *adj* ***syn*** see INVENTIVE
rel causal, institutive, occasional; Promethean
ant uncreative

creator *n* ***syn*** see FATHER 2
rel brain(s), brainpower, mastermind

creature *n* **1** ***syn*** see BEAST
2 ***syn*** see HUMAN
3 ***syn*** see SYCOPHANT

credence *n* ***syn*** see BELIEF 1
rel acceptance, accepting, admission, admitting; confidence, reliance, trust
con skepticism; distrust, mistrust; disbelief, incredulity, unbelief

credentials *n pl* something presented or held by one as proof that he is what or who he claims to be <her academic *credentials* were excellent>
syn certification, document(s), documentation, paper(s)
rel voucher; accreditation, endorsement, sanction; character, recommendation, reference, testimonial

credible *adj* **1** ***syn*** see BELIEVABLE
rel satisfactory, satisfying; solid, sound, straight, valid
idiom to be believed
con unsatisfactory; preposterous, ridiculous
ant incredible
2 ***syn*** see AUTHENTIC 1
rel likely, probable; rational, reasonable; conclusive, determinative
ant incredible

credit *n* **1** ***syn*** see BELIEF 1
rel confidence, reliance, trust
2 ***syn*** see INFLUENCE 1
rel fame, renown, reputation, repute
con disrepute, ignominy, obloquy, opprobrium
ant discredit
3 one that enhances another <he is a *credit* to his family>
syn asset
rel honor
4 favorable notice or attention resulting from an action or achievement <took all the *credit* for the idea>
syn acknowledgment, recognition
rel attention, notice; distinction, fame, honor; glory, kudos

credit *vb* **1** ***syn*** see FEEL 3
con disbelieve, pooh-pooh
ant discredit
2 ***syn*** see ASCRIBE

creditable *adj* **1** ***syn*** see BELIEVABLE
ant discreditable
2 ***syn*** see RESPECTABLE 1
rel satisfactory; suitable
ant discreditable

credo *n* ***syn*** see IDEOLOGY

credulous *adj* ready or inclined to believe especially on slight or insufficient evidence <deceiving the *credulous* young girls>
syn unsuspecting, unsuspicious, unwary
rel believing; accepting, unquestioning; trustful, trusting; green, inexperienced; naive, simple, unsophisticated; dupable, gullible
con mistrustful, suspecting, suspicious; careful, wary; doubtful, doubting, questioning
ant incredulous, skeptical

creed *n* **1** ***syn*** see RELIGION 1
2 ***syn*** see RELIGION 2
3 ***syn*** see IDEOLOGY

creek *n* ‖**1** ***syn*** see INLET
rel ria
2 a natural stream of water normally smaller than and often tributary to a river <went wading in the *creek*>
syn ‖branch, brook, ‖burn, ‖crick, gill, race, ‖rindle, ‖rithe, rivulet, ‖run, runnel, stream
rel ‖beck, brooklet, ‖rigolet, rill, rillet, runlet, streamlet; freshet; ditch, watercourse; wadi

creep *vb* **1** to move along a surface in a prone or crouching position <a cat *creeping* through the grass>
syn crawl, slide, snake
rel glide, slither; sneak, steal, tiptoe; edge, inch; sniggle, wriggle
2 ***syn*** see STEAL 3
3 ***syn*** see SNEAK

crème de la crème *n* ***syn*** see ARISTOCRACY

crepehanger *n* ***syn*** see PESSIMIST

crescendo *n* ***syn*** see APEX 2

crest *n* **1** ***syn*** see TOP 1
rel cap
2 ***syn*** see RIDGE 1
3 ***syn*** see APEX 2

crest *vb* ***syn*** see SURMOUNT 3

crestfallen *adj* ***syn*** see DOWNCAST
idiom ‖in a funk
ant elated

cretin *n* ***syn*** see FOOL 4
rel zombie

crew *n* ***syn*** see GROUP 1
rel aggregation, collection, congregation; gang, retinue, set

crib *n* **1** ***syn*** see BROTHEL
2 ***syn*** see PONY
rel plagiarism
‖**crib** *vb* ***syn*** see GRIPE
‖**crick** *n* ***syn*** see CREEK 2
crime *n* **1** a serious breach of the public law <armed robbery is a *crime*>
syn misdeed, offense
rel criminality, illegality, lawlessness; delict, delictum; breach, break, infringement, transgression, violation; wrong, wrongdoing; felony
2 ***syn*** see EVIL 3
crimeless *adj* ***syn*** see INNOCENT 2
criminal *adj* ***syn*** see UNLAWFUL
criminal *n* one who has committed a usually serious offense <car thieves and other *criminals*>
syn felon, lawbreaker, malefactor, offender
rel scofflaw; transgressor, trespasser, wrongdoer; crook, ‖twicer; gangster, hood, mobster, racketeer, thug; fugitive, outlaw; convict, jailbird
criminate *vb* ***syn*** see ACCUSE
ant exonerate
crimp *vb* **1** ***syn*** see CRUMPLE 1
2 ***syn*** see RESTRAIN 1
crimp *n* ***syn*** see OBSTACLE
crimple *vb* ***syn*** see CRUMPLE 1
crimson *vb* ***syn*** see BLUSH
ant blanch
cringe *vb* ***syn*** see FAWN
rel blench, flinch, quail, recoil, wince; ‖croodle, crouch, shrink
idiom bow and scrape, eat dirt
cringing *adj* ***syn*** see FAWNING
rel obeisant, prostrate
idiom bowing and scraping, eating dirt, eating humble pie, on one's hands and knees
crinkle *vb* ***syn*** see CRUMPLE 1
crinkle *n* ***syn*** see WRINKLE
rel crimp
cripple *vb* **1** ***syn*** see MAIM
rel lame
2 ***syn*** see PARALYZE 1
3 ***syn*** see WEAKEN 1
crisis *n* ***syn*** see JUNCTURE 2
crisp *adj* **1** ***syn*** see SHORT 6
con flabby, flaccid, limp
2 ***syn*** see INCISIVE
rel piquing, provoking, stimulating
crisscross *vb* ***syn*** see INTERSECT
criterion *n* ***syn*** see STANDARD 3
rel adjudgment, judgment
critic *n* one given to harsh or captious judgment <chronic *critics* of the administration>
syn aristarch, carper, caviler, criticizer, faultfinder, knocker, momus, smellfungus, Zoilus
rel Monday morning quarterback; nitpicker, quibbler; belittler, disparager; complainer; censurer; muckraker, mudslinger
con backer, supporter; partisan; advocate, champion, protagonist
critic *adj* ***syn*** see CRITICAL 1
critical *adj* **1** exhibiting the spirit of one who looks for and points out faults and defects <constant *critical* comments about her attire>
syn captious, carping, caviling, cavillous, censorious, critic, faultfinding, hypercritical, overcritical
rel discerning, discriminating, penetrating; finicky, fussy, particular; belittling, demeaning, disparaging, humbling, lowering
con cursory, shallow, superficial; encouraging, flattering, praising
ant uncritical
2 ***syn*** see ACUTE 6
rel conclusive, decisive, determinative; consequential, important, momentous, significant, weighty
criticism *n* **1** a discourse that evaluates or analyzes something (as a work of art or literature) <read every *criticism* of the new play>
syn comment, critique, notice, review, reviewal
rel analysis, examination, study; commentary, observation; opinion; appraisal, assessment, estimate, rating
2 an unfavorable observation or commentary <her recent theatrical offerings have met only with *criticism*>
syn flak, knock, ‖pan, rap, swipe
rel cavil, nit-picking, quibble; aspersion, censure, denunciation; blast; roast
idiom bad press
con blurb, puff; hype, plug, promo
ant commendation
criticize *vb* to make adverse comments about (someone or something) openly, often publicly, and with varying severity <*criticized* his opponent's liberal views>
syn blame, censure, condemn, cut up, denounce, denunciate, knock, pan, rap, reprehend, reprobate, skin; *compare* LAMBASTE 3, REPROVE, SCOLD 1
rel blast, castigate, fulminate (against), fustigate, roast, scathe
idiom find fault with, pull (*or* pick *or* tear) to pieces, take to task
con approve, countenance, endorse, OK (*or* okay)
ant praise
criticizer *n* ***syn*** CRITIC, aristarch, carper, caviler, faultfinder, knocker, momus, smellfungus, Zoilus
critique *n* ***syn*** see CRITICISM 1
‖**critter** *n* ***syn*** see BEAST
croak *vb* **1** ***syn*** see GRUMBLE 1
rel complain, quarrel
‖**2** ***syn*** see DIE 1
‖**croaker** *n* ***syn*** see PHYSICIAN
croaking *adj* ***syn*** see HOARSE 1
croaky *adj* ***syn*** see HOARSE 1
crock *n* ***syn*** see NONSENSE 2
‖**crocked** *adj* ***syn*** see INTOXICATED 1
crone *n* ***syn*** see HAG 2
rel frump, slattern, sloven
crony *n* ***syn*** see ASSOCIATE 3

---

syn synonym(s) ***rel*** related word(s)
ant antonym(s) ***con*** contrasted word(s)
idiom idiomatic equivalent(s)
‖ use limited; if in doubt, see a dictionary

idiom bosom buddy

‖**crooch** *vb syn* see CROUCH

‖**croodle** *vb syn* see SNUGGLE

crook *vb* **1** *syn* see CURVE
‖**2** *syn* see STEAL 1
‖**3** *syn* see CHEAT

crooked *adj* **1** departing from a straight line or course <a *crooked* road>
syn bending, curving, devious, twisting; *compare* CURVED, WINDING
rel oblique; circuitous, indirect, roundabout; errant, meandering, rambling, serpentine, snaky, tortuous, winding; zigzag
con direct, undeviating
ant straight
2 deviating from rectitude <*crooked* police officers on the take>
syn corrupt, dishonest, snide; *compare* CORRUPT 2, VENAL 1
rel devious, indirect, shifty, underhand; double-dealing, fraudulent; deceitful, lying, untruthful; ruthless, unscrupulous
con aboveboard, forthright, straightforward; conscientious, honorable, just, proper, righteous, scrupulous, upright
ant honest, straight

crookedly *adv syn* see AWRY 1
ant straight

crop *n syn* see HARVEST 2

crop *vb* **1** *syn* see TOP 1
rel chop, hew, slash; detach, disengage
2 *syn* see MOW
3 *syn* see CUT 6
rel snip

cropping *n syn* see HARVEST 1

cross *n* **1** *syn* see TRIAL 1
idiom a cross to bear
2 *syn* see HYBRID

cross *vb* **1** *syn* see DENY 4
2 *syn* see BETRAY 2
idiom bite the hand that feeds one, stab in the back
3 *syn* see TRAVERSE 4
4 to cause (an animal or plant) to breed with one of a different kind <*crossing* a horse with an ass results in a mule>
syn crossbreed, cross-mate, hybridize, interbreed, intercross
rel mongrelize
5 *syn* see INTERSECT
idiom lie (*or* be) athwart

cross *adj syn* see IRASCIBLE
rel captious, carping, caviling, faultfinding
idiom cross as a bear

cross *prep syn* see ACROSS

crossbred *n syn* see HYBRID

crossbreed *vb syn* see CROSS 4

crossbreed *n syn* see HYBRID

crosscut *vb syn* see INTERSECT

cross–examination *n* a thorough, typically formal questioning for full information <*cross-examination* of a hostile witness>
syn grill, grilling, interrogation, third degree
rel debriefing; questioning

cross–grained *adj* **1** *syn* see CANTANKEROUS
2 *syn* see CONTRARY 3
rel difficult

crossing *adj syn* see TRANSVERSE

cross–mate *vb syn* see CROSS 4

crosspatch *n syn* see GROUCH

crossroad *n, usu* **crossroads** *pl but sing or pl in constr syn* see JUNCTURE 2

‖**cross talk** *n syn* see BANTER

crossways *adv syn* see ACROSS 1
rel transversely; askew, awry, crisscross
con lengthwise
ant longways

crosswise *adv syn* see ACROSS 1
con longways
ant lengthwise

crosswise *adj syn* see TRANSVERSE
ant lengthwise

crotchet *n syn* see CAPRICE
rel eccentricity, kink, kinkiness, quirk, twist
idiom bee in one's bonnet (*or* brain), flea in one's nose, kink in one's horn, maggot in one's brain

crotchety *adj syn* see CANTANKEROUS

crouch *vb* to stoop low with the limbs close to the body <*crouched* behind a rock and watched>
syn ‖crooch, huddle, hunch, scrooch (down); *compare* SQUAT
rel bend, bow, dip, duck; hunker (down), ‖quat, squat, stoop, ‖swat; cower, cringe, flinch, quail, wince; grovel

crow *vb syn* see BOAST
rel cry, exult, jubilate

crowd *vb* **1** *syn* see PRESS 1
rel ram, shove
2 *syn* see PRESS 7
rel bunch, cluster

crowd *n* **1** a usually large group of people <a *crowd* gathered before the palace>
syn crush, drove, horde, multitude, press, push, squash, throng; *compare* MULTITUDE 1
rel army, host, legion; flock, gaggle, herd, swarm; mob, rabble, rout
2 *syn* see GATHERING 2
rel huddle, parley; troop; herd; rally
3 *syn* see MULTITUDE 1
4 *syn* see SET 5

crowded *adj* **1** *syn* see FULL 1
rel overcharged, overloaded
ant uncrowded
2 *syn* see CLOSE 4
ant uncrowded

crown *n* **1** *syn* see TOP 1
2 *syn* see WREATH
rel diadem, tiara
3 *syn* see APEX 2

crown *vb* **1** *syn* see SURMOUNT 3
2 *syn* see COVER 3
3 *syn* see CLIMAX

crown (with) *vb syn* see ENDOW 1

crucial *adj syn* see ACUTE 6
rel deciding, decisive, important; necessary, vital; clamorous, compelling, crying, imperative, insistent, pressing

crucible *n syn* see TRIAL 1

crucify *vb* ***syn*** see AFFLICT
rel bedevil, bother, browbeat
idiom kill by inches, nail to the cross, put on the rack

crud *n* a deposit or incrustation of something filthy, greasy, or sticky <machinery all covered with *crud*>
syn ‖cab, goo, gook, gunk; *compare* GOO 1
rel filth, muck, slime, sludge; debris, junk, rubbish, trash

‖**cruddle** *vb* ***syn*** see CURDLE

crude *adj* **1** ***syn*** see UNREFINED 3
2 ***syn*** see COARSE 3
rel backward, ignorant, unenlightened; boorish, cloddish, clodhopping, ill-bred, loutish, low-bred; savage; insensible
3 ***syn*** see RUDE 1
rel immature, unmatured; coarse, graceless
con cultivated, cultured, refined; developed, matured, ripened
ant consummate, finished
4 ***syn*** see OBSCENE 2
rel blue, risqué
idiom rated X
5 rough in plan or execution <*crude* imitations, completely lacking in the original artistry>
syn coarse, inexpert, prentice; *compare* RUDE 1
rel amateurish, unproficient, unskilled, untaught, untrained; raw, rough, rude, unfinished, unpolished; inadequate, ineffective, inferior, poor
con finished, perfected, polished
ant expert

cruel *adj* ***syn*** see FIERCE 1
rel atrocious, heinous, monstrous, outrageous; bestial, bloodthirsty, brutish; heartless, implacable, relentless; impiteous, unpitying
con compassionate, sympathetic, tender; clement, forbearing, lenient, merciful; humane, kindly

‖**cruise** *vb* ***syn*** see GO 1

cruise *n* ***syn*** see VOYAGE
rel sail

‖**cruiser** *n* ***syn*** see PROSTITUTE

crumb *n* ***syn*** see PARTICLE

crumble *vb* ***syn*** see DECAY
rel mush, squash

crumbly *adj* ***syn*** see SHORT 6
rel rubbery

‖**crump** *adj* ***syn*** see SHORT 6

crumple *vb* **1** to press or twist into folds or wrinkles <*crumple* a piece of paper>
syn crimp, crimple, crinkle, ‖crunkle, rimple, ruck (up), ‖ruckle, rumple, screw, scrunch, wrinkle
rel crease, fold; buckle, cockle; wad
ant smooth
2 ***syn*** see GIVE 12

crunch *vb* ***syn*** see CHEW 1

crunchy *adj* ***syn*** see SHORT 6

‖**crunkle** *vb* ***syn*** see CRUMPLE 1

crusading *adj* ***syn*** see EVANGELICAL

crush *vb* **1** ***syn*** see PRESS 3
rel ‖scruze, squeeze
2 to reduce or be reduced to a pulpy or broken mass <*crushed* rose petals>
syn becrush, bruise, mash, ‖mush (up), pulp, squash
rel press, squeeze; contuse; batter, maim; beat, pound; dash, quash, ‖quat, smash; comminute, powder, pulverize, triturate
3 ***syn*** see PULVERIZE 1
4 ***syn*** see PRESS 1
5 to bring to an end by destroying or defeating <the police *crushed* the rebellion>
syn annihilate, extinguish, put down, quash, quell, quench, squash, suppress; *compare* SUPPRESS 2
rel ‖quelch, repress, squelch, strangle; beat down, conquer, defeat, subdue, subjugate; ruin, wreck; abolish, demolish, destroy; blot out, obliterate
idiom crush (*or* grind) under one's heel, ride down into the dust, roll (*or* trample) in the dust
6 ***syn*** see CONQUER 1
idiom bring one to his knees
7 ***syn*** see PRESS 7

crush *n* **1** ***syn*** see CROWD 1
2 ***syn*** see INFATUATION
rel calf love, puppy love

‖**crust** *n* ***syn*** see EFFRONTERY

crust *vb* ***syn*** see CAKE 1

crusty *adj* **1** ***syn*** see BLUFF
rel irritable, snappish, waspish; choleric, cranky, irascible, splenetic, testy; crabbed, dour, saturnine, surly
2 ***syn*** see OBSCENE 2

crux *n* ***syn*** see SUBSTANCE 2

cry *vb* **1** ***syn*** see CALL 1
rel bleat
2 to show distress, grief, or pain by tears and usually incoherent utterances <the little girl *cried* when she fell down>
syn blub, blubber, boohoo, ‖pipe, sob, wail, weep; *compare* BAWL 2, WHIMPER
rel sniff, snivel, whimper, whine; break down, choke up; groan, moan, sigh; bemoan, bewail, keen, lament, mourn, sorrow; bawl, howl, squall, yowl
idiom cry one's eyes (*or* heart) out, ‖pipe one's eye, shed tears
3 ***syn*** see SHOUT 1
4 ***syn*** see PUBLICIZE

cry *n* **1** ***syn*** see BATTLE CRY
rel slogan
2 ***syn*** see REPORT 1
3 ***syn*** see FASHION 3
4 ***syn*** see CALL 1
rel screech, squawk; squeak; caw

cry down *vb* ***syn*** see DECRY 2
ant cry up

crying *adj* **1** ***syn*** see PRESSING
rel necessary, needed

---

syn synonym(s) ***rel*** related word(s)
ant antonym(s) ***con*** contrasted word(s)
idiom idiomatic equivalent(s)
‖ use limited; if in doubt, see a dictionary

2 ***syn*** see OUTRAGEOUS 2
cry off *vb* ***syn*** see BACK DOWN
cry out *vb* ***syn*** see EXCLAIM
crypt *n* a subterranean chamber <a burial *crypt*>
syn catacomb, undercroft, vault
rel cell; chamber, compartment, room; cave, cavern, grotto
cryptanalyze *vb* ***syn*** see DECODE
cryptic *adj* being intentionally obscure and mysterious <the senator made some *cryptic* statements about intelligence operations>
syn dark, Delphian, enigmatic, mystifying; *compare* OBSCURE 3
rel equivocal, murky, obscure, opaque, tenebrous, unclear, uninformative, vague; incomprehensible, inexplicable, strange, unfathomable; abstruse, mysterious; evasive, secretive
crystal *adj* ***syn*** see CLEAR 4
idiom clear as crystal, crystal clear
cry up *vb* ***syn*** see PRAISE 2
idiom beat the drum for, praise to the skies
ant cry down
cubby *n* ***syn*** see CUBBYHOLE
cubbyhole *n* an excessively small room or place <a cramped *cubbyhole* of an office>
syn cubby, mousehole, pigeonhole
rel recess; niche; cubicle
idiom hole in the wall
||**cubes** *n pl* ***syn*** see DICE
cuckoo *n* ***syn*** see CRACKPOT
cuckoo *adj* ***syn*** see INSANE 1
cuddle *vb* **1** ***syn*** see CARESS
rel embrace, enfold, hold
2 ***syn*** see SNUGGLE
cudgel *n* a short solid stick used as a weapon or an instrument of punishment <beat the prisoner with a *cudgel*>
syn bat, baton, billy, billy club, bludgeon, club, knobkerrie, mace, nightstick, ||shillelagh, spontoon, truncheon, war club
rel birch, cane, ferule, hickory, paddle, rattan, rod, switch; blackjack; quarterstaff; bastinado
cue *n* ***syn*** see HINT 1
cuff *vb* ***syn*** see SLAP 1
cuff *n* a sharp blow typically delivered with the hand <gave him a good *cuff* in the face>
syn box, buffet, ||bust, chop, clout, haymaker, ||paste, poke, punch, slap, smack, sock, spank, ||spat, ||swack; *compare* BLOW 1, HIT 1
rel bat, blow, clip, wallop
cul–de–sac *n* ***syn*** see DEAD END
rel stalemate
cull *vb* **1** ***syn*** see GLEAN
rel accumulate, amass, collect, round up
2 ***syn*** see CHOOSE 1
rel discriminate
idiom separate the sheep from the goats, separate the wheat from the chaff
||**cull** *n* ***syn*** see FOOL 3
||**cully** *n* ***syn*** see ASSOCIATE 3
culmen *n* ***syn*** see APEX 2
culminate *vb* ***syn*** see CLIMAX
culmination *n* ***syn*** see APEX 2
rel extremity, limit, maximum
culpability *n* ***syn*** see BLAME
con blamelessness, innocence
ant inculpability
culpable *adj* ***syn*** see BLAMEWORTHY
rel impeachable, indictable
ant inculpable
cult *n* **1** ***syn*** see RELIGION 1
2 ***syn*** see RELIGION 2
cultivable *adj* ***syn*** see ARABLE
ant uncultivable
cultivatable *adj* ***syn*** see ARABLE
ant uncultivatable
cultivate *vb* **1** ***syn*** see TILL
rel crop, farm, manage
2 ***syn*** see NURSE 2
rel raise, rear; educate, instruct, teach, train; ameliorate, better, improve
con disregard, ignore, neglect, slight
3 ***syn*** see GROW 1
rel develop, mature, ripen
cultivated *adj* ***syn*** see GENTEEL 1
rel courteous, polite
ant uncultivated
cultivation *n* ***syn*** see CULTURE
culture *n* enlightenment and excellence of taste acquired by intellectual and aesthetic training <a man of *culture* is known by his reading>
syn breeding, cultivation, polish, refinement
rel education, enlightenment, erudition, learning; gentility, manners; discrimination, taste; savoir-faire, sophistication, urbanity; class, elegance
con greenness, ignorance, inexperience, verdancy; crudeness, vulgarity
cultured *adj* ***syn*** see GENTEEL 1
rel educated, enlightened, erudite, learned, literate; civilized
ant uncultured
culverhouse *n* ***syn*** see DOVECOTE
cumber *vb* ***syn*** see BURDEN
cumbersome *adj* ***syn*** see UNWIELDY
rel irksome, tiresome, wearisome
cumbrance *n* ***syn*** see ENCUMBRANCE
rel burden, charge, pressure
cumbrous *adj* ***syn*** see UNWIELDY
rel clogging, hampering, hindering, impeding
cumshaw *n* ***syn*** see GRATUITY
cumulate *vb* ***syn*** see ACCUMULATE
rel obtain, secure
ant dissipate
cumulation *n* ***syn*** see ACCUMULATION
rel stockpile; snowball
cumulative *adj* increasing or produced by addition of like or similar things <the *cumulative* effect of several drugs>
syn accumulative, additive, additory, chain, summative
rel accumulated, amassed; augmenting, increasing, multiplying; advancing, heightening, intensifying, magnifying, snowballing
con dispersed, dissipated, scattered
cunning *adj* **1** ***syn*** see CLEVER 4
rel well-devised, well-laid, well-planned; crackerjack, masterful

idiom too clever by half
2 ***syn*** see SLY 2
rel acute, keen, sharp; knowing, smart; wary
idiom not to be caught with chaff
con artless, naive, unsophisticated

cunning *n* 1 ***syn*** see ART 1
rel deftness, dexterousness; adeptness, expertness; cleverness, ingeniousness, ingenuity
2 skill in devising or using indirect or subtle methods <a woman able to maneuver people with great *cunning*>
syn art, artfulness, artifice, cageyness, canniness, craft, craftiness, foxiness, slyness, wiliness
rel savvy, sharpness, shrewdness; cleverness, ingeniousness, ingenuity; agility, facility, finesse, slickness; subtlety; insidiousness, shiftiness, trickiness
3 ***syn*** see DECEIT 1
idiom satanic cunning, the cunning of the serpent

cupidity *n* intense desire for possessions and wealth <the sight of so much money aroused his *cupidity*>
syn avarice, avariciousness, avidity, greed, rapacity
rel acquisitiveness, greediness, possessiveness, rapaciousness; eagerness, voracity; craving, desire; lust; infatuation, passion

cur *n* 1 ***syn*** see SNOT 1
rel riffraff
2 ***syn*** see CAD

curative *adj* restoring or tending to restore to a state of normalcy or health <a *curative* drug>
syn curing, healing, remedial, remedying, restorative, sanative, sanatory, vulnerary, wholesome
rel medicable, medicative, medicinal; corrective, therapeutic; invigorating, tonic; beneficial, helpful, salutary, wholesome

curb *vb* 1 ***syn*** see HAMPER
2 ***syn*** see DENY 3
rel repress, suppress
ant goad
3 ***syn*** see RESTRAIN 1
rel fetter, hamper, hog-tie, manacle, shackle
idiom hold in leash, keep a tight rein on
con unbridle, unleash
ant spur

curd *vb* ***syn*** see CURDLE

curdle *vb* to cause to become coagulated or thickened and often sour <hot weather will *curdle* milk>
syn ||clabber, ||cruddle, curd, ||lopper, turn
rel clot, coagulate, condense, thicken; ferment; go off, sour, spoil

cure *n* 1 ***syn*** see REMEDY 1
2 ***syn*** see REMEDY 2

cure *vb* to rectify an unhealthy or undesirable condition <aspirin *cured* his headache>
syn heal, remedy
rel doctor, medicate; restore; ameliorate, better, improve

cure–all *n* ***syn*** see PANACEA

cureless *adj* ***syn*** see HOPELESS 2

curing *adj* ***syn*** see CURATIVE

curio *n* ***syn*** see KNICKKNACK

curiosity *n* 1 ***syn*** see INTEREST 3
rel inquisitiveness, questioning
ant disinterest
2 something that arouses interest especially because of uncommon or exotic characteristics <an architectural *curiosity*>
syn conversation piece, oddity
rel exception, nonesuch, rarity; marvel, prodigy, wonder; anomaly; freak, monstrosity
idiom something to write home about

curious *adj* 1 ***syn*** see INQUISITIVE 1
rel searching; analytical; prurient
ant incurious
2 interested in what is not one's personal or proper concern <a *curious* old woman prying into her neighbors' affairs>
syn inquisitive, inquisitorial, inquisitory, ||nibby, nosy, peery, prying, snoopy
rel interfering, intermeddling, meddling, tampering; examining, inspecting, scrutinizing; impertinent, intrusive, meddlesome
idiom consumed (*or* burning *or* eaten up) with curiosity, curious as a cat (*or* monkey)
con aloof, detached, disinterested, indifferent, unconcerned, uninterested; apathetic, impassive, phlegmatic, stolid
ant incurious
3 ***syn*** see STRANGE 4

curl *vb* ***syn*** see WIND 2
rel crook; roll; ringlet; kink
con straighten, unkink, unwind
ant uncurl

currency *n* ***syn*** see MONEY

current *adj* 1 ***syn*** see PRESENT
rel topical, up-to-date
con antiquated, antique, obsolete
2 ***syn*** see PREVAILING
rel accustomed, customary; a la mode, fashionable, modern, popular
ant antique

current *n* 1 ***syn*** see FLOW
2 ***syn*** see TENDENCY 1

curry *vb* ***syn*** see WHIP 2

curse *n* 1 a denunciation that conveys a wish or threat of evil <the dying man's *curse* against his family>
syn anathema, commination, imprecation, malediction, malison
rel execration, objurgation; damning, denunciation; blasphemy, profanation, profanity, sacrilege
ant blessing
2 ***syn*** see SWEARWORD
3 ***syn*** see PLAGUE 1

curse *vb* 1 ***syn*** see EXECRATE 1
rel blaspheme; blight; doom

---

syn synonym(s) ***rel*** related word(s)
ant antonym(s) ***con*** contrasted word(s)
idiom idiomatic equivalent(s)
|| use limited; if in doubt, see a dictionary

idiom call down curses on the head of, call down evil on
ant bless
2 *syn* see SWEAR 3
idiom ‖curse up a storm
cursed *adj* 1 *syn* see DAMNED 2
rel hateful
2 *syn* see EXECRABLE 1
rel disgusting; odious
ant blessed
cursing *n syn* see BLASPHEMY 1
cursive *adj syn* see EASY 9
cursory *adj syn* see SUPERFICIAL 2
rel fast, hasty, hurried, quick, rapid, speedy, swift; brief, short; casual, desultory, haphazard, random
con careful, meticulous, scrupulous
ant painstaking
curt *adj* 1 *syn* see CONCISE
2 *syn* see BLUFF
rel imperious, peremptory
ant voluble
curtail *vb* 1 *syn* see SHORTEN
ant prolong, protract
2 *syn* see ABRIDGE 1
ant extend
curtains *n pl but sing in constr syn* see DEATH 1
curtilage *n syn* see COURT 1
curvaceous *adj* having a shapely figure marked by pronounced curves <*curvaceous* bikini-clad girls swarmed over the beach>
syn ‖built, curvesome, curvilinear, curvy, Junoesque, rounded, ‖stacked, well-developed; *compare* BUXOM, SHAPELY
rel shapeful, shapely, statuesque, well-proportioned; attractive, charming, pleasing
curvation *n syn* see CURVE
curvature *n syn* see CURVE
curve *vb* to swerve or cause to swerve from a straight line or course <the road *curves* to the right>
syn bend, bow, crook, round; *compare* WIND 2
rel deflect, divert, turn; deviate, swerve, veer; coil, curl, spiral, twist, wind; incurve
ant straighten
curve *n* something (as a line or surface) that curves or is curved <a slight *curve* to her eyebrows>
syn arc, arch, bend, bow, curvation, curvature, round
rel incurvation, incurvature; inflection; rondure; circuit, circumference, compass
curved *adj* having or characterized by a curve or curves <a *curved* vault>
syn arced, arched, arciform, arrondi, bent, bowed, curvilinear, round, rounded; *compare* CROOKED 1
rel declinate; embowed, incurvate, incurved; excurved; bending, twisted, twisting
ant straight
curvesome *adj syn* see CURVACEOUS
curvilinear *adj* 1 *syn* see CURVED
2 *syn* see CURVACEOUS
curving *adj syn* see CROOKED 1
curvy *adj syn* see CURVACEOUS
cushy *adj syn* see COMFORTABLE 2
cusp *n syn* see POINT 9
cuspidate *adj syn* see POINTED 1
cuss *n* 1 *syn* see SWEARWORD
2 *syn* see MAN 3
cuss *vb syn* see SWEAR 3
idiom ‖cuss up a blue streak
cussed *adj syn* see DAMNED 2
cussing *n syn* see BLASPHEMY 1
cussword *n syn* see SWEARWORD
custodian *n* one that guards, protects, or maintains (as property or records) <was the *custodian* of the manor for many years>
syn cerberus, claviger, ‖custodier, custos, guardian, keeper, warden, watchdog
rel curator, steward; castellan, governor; overseer, supervisor
‖**custodier** *n syn* see CUSTODIAN
custody *n* the act or duty of guarding and preserving <the government has *custody* of all state gifts>
syn care, guardianship, keeping, safekeeping, trust, ward
rel caretaking; charge, management, supervision; protection
custom *n* 1 *syn* see HABIT 1
rel precedent; ritual; mold; fixture, institution; prescription, rubric; canon, law, precept, rule
idiom matter of course
con departure, deviation, shift; exception; irregularity
2 *syn* see PATRONAGE 2
custom *adj syn* see CUSTOM-MADE
customarily *adv syn* see USUALLY 1
rel conventionally, traditionally; normally, ordinarily; routinely
idiom as a matter of course
con rarely; never
ant occasionally
customary *adj* 1 *syn* see USUAL 1
rel acknowledged, recognized, understood; standard; conventional, orthodox, traditional; prescriptive, regulation, stipulated
idiom being the customary (*or* usual) thing
con occasional; infrequent, inhabitual, sporadic, uncommon; irregular
ant uncustomary
2 *syn* see COMMON 4
rel household, popular; general, universal
ant uncustomary
custom–built *adj syn* see CUSTOM-MADE
customer *n* one that patronizes or uses the services of something (as a store or restaurant) <many *customers* in the shop>
syn client, patron
rel buyer, consumer, purchaser, shopper
customized *adj syn* see CUSTOM-MADE
custom–made *adj* made according to personal order and individual specifications <he always wore a *custom-made* suit>
syn custom, custom-built, customized, custom-tailored, made-to-order, tailor-made
ant mass-produced
custom–tailored *adj syn* see CUSTOM-MADE

custos *n* ***syn*** see CUSTODIAN

cut *vb* **1** to penetrate with or as if with a sharp edge <*cut* his hand on a broken bottle>
syn gash, incise, pierce, slash, slice, slit
rel cleave, dissever, sever, sunder; rend, rip, rive, tear; lacerate, wound
2 ***syn*** see SHORTEN
3 ***syn*** see REDUCE 2
4 ***syn*** see MOW
5 to penetrate and divide with an edged tool or instrument <*cut* the melon into slices>
syn carve, cleave, dissect, dissever, sever, slice, split, sunder
rel divide, part, separate; chop, dice, hash, mince, mow
idiom lay open
6 to reduce by severing parts <the barber *cut* his hair too short>
syn clip, crop, pare, prune, shave, shear, skive, trim
rel cut back, dock, lop, poll, pollard, shrub; amputate; curtail
7 to refuse social recognition especially by way of rebuke <his friends *cut* him after the scandal broke>
syn cold-shoulder, ostracize, snob, snub
rel disdain, ignore, rebuff, reject, slight, turn away; affront, insult, offend
idiom give the cold shoulder (to), show one his place, slam the door in one's face, slam the door on, slap one in the face, turn aside (*or* away) from, turn one's back (on *or* upon)
8 ***syn*** see DILUTE
9 ***syn*** see FELL 2
10 ***syn*** see OPERATE 2

cut *n* **1** ***syn*** see PART 1
2 ***syn*** see SHARE 1
3 ***syn*** see TRENCH
4 ***syn*** see TYPE

cut *adj* ***syn*** see INTOXICATED 1

cut back *vb* **1** ***syn*** see SHORTEN
2 ***syn*** see REDUCE 2

cut down *vb* ***syn*** see REDUCE 2

cut in *vb* ***syn*** see INTRUDE 1

cut off *vb* **1** ***syn*** see KILL 1
2 ***syn*** see INTERCEPT
3 ***syn*** see ISOLATE
4 ***syn*** see DISINHERIT 1

cutoff *n* ***syn*** see SHORTCUT

cut out *vb* **1** ***syn*** see EXCISE
2 ***syn*** see SUPPLANT 1

cutpurse *n* ***syn*** see PICKPOCKET

cutthroat *n* ***syn*** see ASSASSIN

cutting *adj* ***syn*** see INCISIVE
rel piercing, probing

cut up *vb* **1** ***syn*** see CRITICIZE
2 to behave in a boisterously comic or unruly manner <children *cutting up* in front of company>
syn act up, carry on, horse, horseplay
rel caper, cavort, romp; clown; show off; roughhouse; misbehave
idiom cut a dido (*or* shine), cut up rough, ‖kick up a shindy, raise Cain (*or* Ned), whoop it up

cutup *n* ***syn*** see ZANY 2

cycle *n* **1** a complete course of recurrent operations or events <a 24-hour *cycle* of medication>
syn circle, round, wheel; *compare* SUCCESSION 2
rel chain, sequel, sequence, series; course, run; circuit, loop, ring
2 ***syn*** see BICYCLE

cyclone *n* ***syn*** see TORNADO

cyclopean *adj* ***syn*** see HUGE
ant lilliputian

cynical *adj* ***syn*** see SARDONIC

cyprian *n* ***syn*** see WANTON

czar *n* ***syn*** see MAGNATE

---

syn synonym(s) ***rel*** related word(s)
ant antonym(s) ***con*** contrasted word(s)
idiom idiomatic equivalent(s)
‖ use limited; if in doubt, see a dictionary

D

dab *vb* ***syn*** see SMEAR 1

‖**dab** *n* ***syn*** see EXPERT

dabbler *n* ***syn*** see AMATEUR 2
con adept, artist, connoisseur; expert, master, professional

dabbling *adj* ***syn*** see AMATEURISH
rel sciolistic, shallow, sophomoric, superficial
con adept, capable, competent

‖**dabster** *n* ***syn*** see EXPERT

dad *n* ***syn*** see FATHER 1

dada *n* ***syn*** see FATHER 1

dad–blamed *adj* **1** ***syn*** see DAMNED 2
2 ***syn*** see UTTER

dad–blasted *adj* **1** ***syn*** see DAMNED 2
2 ***syn*** see UTTER

dad–burned *adj* **1** ***syn*** see DAMNED 2
2 ***syn*** see UTTER

daddy *n* ***syn*** see FATHER 1

daedal *adj* ***syn*** see COMPLEX 2

daffy *adj* **1** ***syn*** see INSANE 1
2 ***syn*** see FOOLISH 2

daft *adj* ***syn*** see INSANE 1

daily *adj* of each or every day <*daily* prayers for the dead>
syn diurnal, quotidian
con nocturnal; alternate, intermittent, periodic, recurrent, spasmodic; erratic, fitful, fluctuating, infrequent, irregular; occasional, sporadic
ant nightly

dainty *n* ***syn*** see DELICACY

dainty *adj* **1** ***syn*** see CHOICE
rel beautiful, bonny, fair, lovely, pretty; delectable, delicious, delightful; airy, diaphanous, ethereal, light
con coarse, vulgar
ant gross
2 ***syn*** see NICE 1
rel acute, penetrative, perceptive
con careless, neglectful, negligent, thoughtless

‖**daisy** *n* ***syn*** ‖DILLY, ‖corker, crackerjack, dandy, humdinger, jim-dandy, knockout, ‖lalapalooza, ‖lulu, nifty

dale *n* ***syn*** see VALLEY

dally *vb* **1** ***syn*** see TRIFLE 1
rel frolic, gambol, play, rollick, romp, sport; caress, cosset, cuddle, dandle, fondle, pet
2 ***syn*** see DELAY 2
con fleet, rush, scurry, skedaddle
ant hasten

dam *vb* ***syn*** see HINDER
rel repress, suppress
con air, express, utter, vent

damage *n* ***syn*** see INJURY 1
rel impairment, marring; deterioration, dilapidation, disrepair, ruining, wrecking; deleteriousness, disadvantage, drawback
con amelioration, betterment, improvement; benefit, profit; advantage, service, use
ant repair

damage *vb* ***syn*** see INJURE 1
rel demolish, destroy, raze, ruin, wreck; deteriorate, dilapidate; abuse, ill-treat, maltreat, mistreat, misuse, outrage
con ameliorate, amend, better, improve; mend
ant repair

damaged *adj* having been injured <*damaged* merchandise>
syn flawed, impaired, marred, spoiled
rel blemished, broken, imperfect, injured, unsound
con flawless, good, intact, unbroken, unhurt, unimpaired, uninjured, unmarred, whole; corrected, improved, rectified, repaired
ant undamaged

damaging *adj* ***syn*** see HARMFUL

dame *n* **1** ***syn*** see MATRIARCH
2 ***syn*** see BELDAM 1
‖**3** ***syn*** see WOMAN 1

damn *vb* **1** ***syn*** see SENTENCE
rel castigate, discipline, penalize, punish; banish, cast out, expel
con deliver, ransom, redeem, rescue; reward
ant save
2 ***syn*** see EXECRATE 1
rel abominate; vituperate
3 ***syn*** see SWEAR 3

damn *n* ***syn*** see PARTICLE

damnable *adj* **1** ***syn*** see EXECRABLE 1
rel abhorrent, abominable, detestable, hateful, odious; damned
con admirable, commendable, estimable; laudable, praiseworthy
2 ***syn*** see DAMNED 2
3 ***syn*** see UTTER

damned *adj* **1** being doomed to eternal punishment <a *damned* soul>
syn condemned, doomed, lost
rel anathematized, cursed, reprobate; done for
idiom gone to blazes, hell bound
con delivered, ransomed, redeemed
ant saved
2 deserving censure or strong disapproval — often used as a generalized expression of annoyance <this *damned* door won't open>
syn blamed, blankety-blank, blasted, bleeding, blessed, blighted, blinding, ‖blinking, ‖blistering, ‖blooming, confounded, ‖consarned, cursed, cussed, dad-blamed, dad-blasted, dad-burned, damnable, dang, darn (*or* durn), dashed, doggone, dratted, execrable, goldarn, infernal, perishing, so-and-so
3 ***syn*** see UTTER

damned *adv* ***syn*** see VERY 1

damp *adj* slightly or relatively wet <her dress was still *damp*>
syn dampish, dank, moist, moisty, wettish

rel drenched, saturated, soaked, soaking; soggy, water-logged
con arid, dry

dampen *vb* ***syn*** see MUFFLE 2

dampish *adj* ***syn*** see DAMP

damsel *n* ***syn*** see GIRL 1

dance *vb* **1** to perform a rhythmic and patterned succession of steps usually to music <the band was good enough to *dance* to>
syn foot (it), hoof (it), prance, step, tread
rel shuffle, trip, truck
idiom ||cut a rug, trip the light fantastic
2 ***syn*** see FLIT 2
rel quaver, quiver, shake, tremble, wobble

dancer *n* a professional performer of dances <*dancers* performing a ballet>
syn ballerina, ballet girl, coryphée, dancing girl, danseur, danseuse, figurant, figurante, hoofer
rel chorine, chorus boy, chorus girl, chorus man; danseur noble, premier danseur, premiere danseuse, prima ballerina

dancing girl *n* ***syn*** see DANCER

dandle *vb* ***syn*** see CARESS
rel disport, play, sport

dandy *n* **1** ***syn*** see FOP
con clod, lout, lump, oaf, slob, slouch
ant sloven
2 ***syn*** ||DILLY, ||corker, crackerjack, ||daisy, humdinger, jim-dandy, ||lalapalooza, ||lulu, nifty, peach

||**dandy** *adj* **1** ***syn*** see MARVELOUS 2
2 ***syn*** see EXCELLENT
rel grand, hunky-dory, keen, nifty, swell
idiom fine and dandy
con ||bum, ||crummy, grim, ||lousy, ||putrid, rotten
ant blah

dang *adj* **1** ***syn*** see DAMNED 2
2 ***syn*** see UTTER

danger *n* the state of being exposed to injury, pain, or loss <they are seeking a place where children can play without *danger*>
syn hazard, jeopardy, peril, risk
rel menace, precariousness, threat; emergency, exigency, pass; precipice
idiom dangerous ground, thin ice
con safety; exemption, immunity; defense, guard, protection, safeguard, shield
ant security

dangerous *adj* **1** attended by or involving the possibility of injury, pain, or loss <a *dangerous* crossing>
syn chancy, ||dangersome, hairy, hazardous, jeopardous, parlous, perilous, risky, treacherous, unhealthy, unsound, wicked; *compare* GRAVE 3
rel insecure, precarious, uncertain, unsafe; chance, haphazard, hit-or-miss, random; critical, menacing, serious, threatening
idiom beset (*or* fraught) with danger, on a collision course
con certain, reliable; harmless, innocent
ant safe, secure
2 ***syn*** see GRAVE 3

||**dangersome** *adj* ***syn*** see DANGEROUS 1

dangle *vb* ***syn*** see HANG 1

dank *adj* ***syn*** see DAMP

danseur *n* ***syn*** see DANCER

danseuse *n* ***syn*** see DANCER

dap *vb* ***syn*** see GLANCE 1

dapper *adj* trimly neat and tidy <a *dapper* dresser, always neat as a pin>
syn bandbox, doggish, doggy, natty, sassy, sparkish, spiffy, spruce, sprucy, well-groomed; *compare* NEAT 2, STYLISH
rel chichi; jaunty, rakish; showy
con dowdy, drab, unstylish; disheveled, disordered, slipshod, sloppy, slovenly, unkempt, untidy; blowsy, dowdy, frowsy, shabby, slatternly

dappled *adj* ***syn*** see VARIEGATED
con pure, smooth, spotless, unbroken, uniform

dare *vb* ***syn*** see FACE 3
rel change, hazard, risk
idiom take the bull by the horns
con avoid, evade; flee, run

dare *n* ***syn*** see DEFIANCE 1

daredevil *adj* ***syn*** see ADVENTUROUS
con timid, timorous; cautious, chary, circumspect, wary; discreet, judicious, prudent, sane, sensible

daring *adj* ***syn*** see ADVENTUROUS

dark *adj* **1** deficient in light <a *dark* room>
syn caliginous, dim, dun, dusk, dusky, gloomy, lightless, murky, obscure, somber, tenebrous, unilluminated
rel cloudy, dull, shadowy, shady; pitch-black, pitch-dark
con bright, brilliant, luminous, radiant; enlightened, illuminated, illumined, lighted
ant light
2 ***syn*** see CRYPTIC
rel abstruse, esoteric, hidden, occult, recondite; anagogic, cabalistic, darkling, mystic, mystical; complicated, intricate, knotty
con clear, perspicuous; easy, facile, light, simple
ant lucid
3 of dark complexion <her *dark* good looks>
syn bistered, black-a-vised, brunet, dark-skinned, dusky, swart, swarth, swarthy
con blond, fair, light; ruddy, tawny
||**4** ***syn*** see BLIND 1

darken *vb* ***syn*** see OBSCURE
ant illuminate

dark-skinned *adj* ***syn*** see DARK 3

darling *n* ***syn*** see SWEETHEART 1

darling *adj* **1** ***syn*** see FAVORITE 1
2 ***syn*** see DELIGHTFUL

darn (*or* **durn**) *adj* **1** ***syn*** see DAMNED 2
2 ***syn*** see UTTER

dart *n* ***syn*** see SHAFT 2

dart *vb* ***syn*** see FLY 1
rel hasten, hurry, precipitate, speed; run, scamper, scoot, scurry, sprint, spurt

---

syn synonym(s) ***rel*** related word(s)
ant antonym(s) ***con*** contrasted word(s)
idiom idiomatic equivalent(s)
|| use limited; if in doubt, see a dictionary

con dally, dawdle, delay, linger, tarry; lumber, plod, slog, trudge

dash *vb* **1** ***syn*** see RUSH 1
rel run, scamper, scoot, scurry, sprint
con dally, dawdle, delay, linger, tarry; lumber, plod, slog, trudge
2 ***syn*** see RUN 1
3 ***syn*** see BLAST 1
4 ***syn*** see FRUSTRATE 1

dash *n* **1** ***syn*** see SPIRIT 5
rel energy, force, might, power, strength; intensity, vehemence; impressiveness
con apathy, dullness, languor, lethargy, listlessness, sluggishness, stagnation, torpor
2 ***syn*** see HINT 2
rel impress, impression, stamp

dashed *adj* **1** ***syn*** see DAMNED 2
2 ***syn*** see UTTER

dashing *adj* **1** ***syn*** see LIVELY 1
2 ***syn*** see STYLISH
rel flashy, flaunting; dapper, jaunty, spiffy, spruce
idiom cutting a fine figure
con unfashionable, unstylish; modest, unostentatious, unpretentious
ant drab

dastard *n* ***syn*** see COWARD

date *vb* to go or take on a date <he *dated* her several times that winter>
syn see, take out
rel accompany, escort; court, woo
idiom go out with

date *n* **1** ***syn*** see ENGAGEMENT 3
2 ***syn*** see ESCORT 1

dated *adj* ***syn*** see OLD-FASHIONED
ant up-to-the-minute

dateless *adj* ***syn*** see ETERNAL 4
ant ephemeral

daub *vb* ***syn*** see SMEAR 1
rel spatter, speckle, spot; dapple, fleck, variegate

daunt *vb* ***syn*** see DISMAY 1
rel browbeat, bully, cow, intimidate; baffle, foil, frustrate, thwart
con arouse, awaken, rally, rouse, stir, waken; actuate, drive, impel, move; activate, energize, vitalize
ant enhearten

dauntless *adj* ***syn*** see BRAVE 1
rel indomitable, invincible, unconquerable
con hesitant, reluctant
ant poltroon

dauntlessness *n* ***syn*** see COURAGE
ant poltroonery

dawdle *vb* **1** ***syn*** see IDLE
2 ***syn*** see DELAY 2
rel amble, saunter, stroll; stay, wait; toy, trifle; fritter, waste
idiom fritter away time
con arouse, rally, rouse, stir; hasten, hurry, speed

dawdler *n* ***syn*** see LAGGARD

dawn *n* **1** the first appearance of light in the morning <birds which sing at *dawn*>
syn aurora, cockcrow, cockcrowing, dawning, daybreak, daylight, light, morn, morning, sunrise, sunup
rel prime
idiom break of day, crack of dawn, first blush (*or* flush) of day, first light, peep of day, the wee small hours
2 ***syn*** see BEGINNING
ant sunset

dawning *n* **1** ***syn*** see DAWN 1
2 ***syn*** see BEGINNING
ant sunset

day *n* **1** the time of light between one night and the next <waiting for *day* to dawn>
syn daylight, daytime
rel light, sunlight, sunshine
con dark, nighttime
ant night
2 *usu* **days** *pl* ***syn*** see PERIOD 2

daybreak *n* ***syn*** see DAWN 1

daydream *n* ***syn*** see FANCY 4
rel conceiving, fancying, imagination, imagining
con substantiality, tangibility; authenticity, truth, verity

daydreaming *adj* ***syn*** see DREAMY 1

daydreamy *adj* ***syn*** see DREAMY 1

daylight *n* **1** ***syn*** see DAWN 1
syn see DAY 1

dayspring *n* ***syn*** see BEGINNING

daystar *n* ***syn*** see SUN 1

daytime *n* ***syn*** see DAY 1

daze *vb* **1** to confuse with light <the bright sunlight *dazed* him>
syn bedazzle, blind, dazzle
rel overcome, overpower, overwhelm; dizzy
2 to dull or deaden the powers of the mind through some disturbing experience or influence <*dazed* by the news of the accident>
syn bedaze, bemuse, benumb, paralyze, petrify, stun, stupefy
rel bewilder, confound, disorder, distract, dumbfound, mystify; befuddle, confuse, fuddle, muddle; dazzle, dizzy; rock
con enhance, expand, heighten, sharpen; alert, arouse, waken

daze *n* ***syn*** see HAZE 2

dazzle *vb* ***syn*** see DAZE 1

dead *adj* **1** devoid of life <a *dead* person>
syn asleep, cold, deceased, defunct, departed, exanimate, extinct, inanimate, late, lifeless, spiritless, unanimated
rel bloodless, breathless; gone, reposing; inactive, inert; belowground, buried
idiom dead as a doornail, gone the way of all flesh, out of one's misery, pushing up daisies
con animate, animated, living, vital; being, existing; active, live
ant alive
2 ***syn*** see DEATHLY 1
rel insensible, insentient, numb, unfeeling, unresponsive; inanimate, unconscious
con feeling, responsive, sensitive, sentient; animate, animated, living, spirited, vivacious

ant alive
3 ***syn*** see NUMB 1
4 ***syn*** see OBSOLETE
ant living; viable
5 ***syn*** see EXTINCT 2
6 ***syn*** see DULL 7
rel bleak, dismal
con glorious, resplendent
7 ***syn*** see UTTER

dead *adv* ***syn*** see DIRECTLY 1

deaden *vb* **1** to impair in vigor, force, activity, or sensation <the news *deadened* his distress>
syn benumb, blunt, desensitize, dull, mull, numb
rel anesthetize, paralyze, unnerve; stun, stupefy
con animate, vivify; energize, invigorate; activate, vitalize
ant enliven
2 ***syn*** see MUFFLE 2

dead end *n* a course which leads to nothing further <had reached a *dead end* in negotiations>
syn blind alley, cul-de-sac, impasse, pocket
rel corner, hole; deadlock, halt, standstill; bottleneck

deadened *adj* **1** ***syn*** see DEATHLY 1
2 ***syn*** see NUMB 1

||**deader** *n* ***syn*** see CORPSE

deadfall *n* ***syn*** see PITFALL

deadliness *n* ***syn*** see FATALITY 1

deadlock *n* ***syn*** see DRAW 4
rel condition, posture, situation, state; dilemma, plight, predicament, quandary
con decision, determination, resolution, solution

deadly *adj* **1** causing or causative of death <a *deadly* disease>
syn deathly, fatal, lethal, mortal, mortiferous, pestilent, pestilential; *compare* PERNICIOUS
rel destroying, destructive; killing, slaying; internecine; baneful, noxious, pernicious; poisonous, toxic, virulent
con healthful, healthy, wholesome; advantageous, beneficial, restorative, sanative
2 ***syn*** see PERNICIOUS
con harmless, innocuous, inoffensive, unoffending
3 ***syn*** see DEATHLY 1

deadpan *adj* ***syn*** see EXPRESSIONLESS

dead to rights *adv* ***syn*** see RED-HANDED

deadweight *n* ***syn*** see LOAD 3

||**deadwood** *n* ***syn*** see ADVANTAGE 3

deaf *adj* ***syn*** see OBSTINATE

deal *vb* **1** ***syn*** see DISTRIBUTE 1
rel partake, participate, share
con receive, take; detain, hold, hold back, keep, retain, withhold; appropriate, arrogate, confiscate
2 ***syn*** see GIVE 10
rel impart, mete, render
con annul, cancel, remove, rescind, revoke

deal (out) *vb* ***syn*** see ADMINISTER 2
rel dish, dish out, help, serve; offer, present, proffer, tender
con hold, hold back, keep, retain, withhold

deal (with) *vb* ***syn*** see TREAT 2
rel control, direct; clear, rid, unburden
con misconduct, misdirect, mishandle, mismanage; disregard, ignore, neglect; burden, cumber, encumber

deal *n* **1** ***syn*** see AGREEMENT 2
2 treatment received in a transaction from another <a fair *deal*>
syn shake

dealer *n* ***syn*** see MERCHANT

dealings *n pl* ***syn*** see COMMERCE 1
rel affairs, business, concerns, doings, matters, things; proceedings

deambulatory *adj* ***syn*** see ITINERANT

dean *n* ***syn*** see LEADER 1

dear *adj* **1** ***syn*** see FAVORITE 1
2 ***syn*** see LOVING
3 ***syn*** see COSTLY 1
con inexpensive, low, moderate, modest, nominal
ant cheap

dear *n* ***syn*** see SWEETHEART 1

dearth *n* ***syn*** see ABSENCE
rel infrequency, rareness, scarcity, uncommonness; exiguousness, meagerness, scantiness, scantness; insufficiency, paucity
con superfluity, surplus; lavishness, prodigality, profusion
ant excess

death *n* **1** the end or the ending of life <*death* of a man><*death* of an enterprise>
syn curtains, decease, defunction, demise, dissolution, grim reaper, (the) Pale Horse, passing, quietus, silence, sleep
rel annihilation, ending, expiration, extinction, grave, termination
idiom crossing the bar
ant life
2 ***syn*** see FATALITY 2

deathful *adj* ***syn*** see DEATHLY 1

deathless *adj* ***syn*** see IMMORTAL 1
rel eternal; abiding, lasting, persisting

deathlike *adj* **1** ***syn*** see DEATHLY 1
2 ***syn*** see GHASTLY 2

deathly *adj* **1** suggesting death (as in inertness or appearance) <fell in a *deathly* faint>
syn corpselike, corpsy, dead, deadened, deadly, deathful, deathlike
rel cadaverous, haggard, wasted; ghastly, grisly, gruesome, macabre; appalling, dreadful, horrible
con healthy, hearty, robust; stout, sturdy; energetic, strenuous, vigorous
2 ***syn*** see DEADLY 1

debacle *n* **1** ***syn*** see DEFEAT 1
2 ***syn*** see COLLAPSE 2

debar *vb* ***syn*** see EXCLUDE
rel forbid, interdict; block, hinder, impede, obstruct

---

syn synonym(s) ***rel*** related word(s)
ant antonym(s) ***con*** contrasted word(s)
idiom idiomatic equivalent(s)
|| use limited; if in doubt, see a dictionary

con accept, receive; allow, let, permit
ant admit
debark *vb* *syn* see DISEMBARK
debase *vb* **1** to cause to become impaired in quality or character <vulgarly outrageous movies that *debase* the taste of the people>
syn animalize, bastardize, bestialize, brutalize, canker, corrupt, debauch, demoralize, deprave, pervert, poison, rot, stain, vitiate, warp; *compare* ADULTERATE
rel damage, harm, impair, injure, mar, spoil; contaminate, defile, dishonor, pollute, taint; commercialize
con enhance, heighten; lift, raise; ameliorate, better, improve
ant elevate; amend
2 *syn* see HUMBLE
rel cripple, debilitate, disable, enfeeble, sap, undermine, weaken
con acclaim, laud, praise; refresh, rejuvenate, renew, restore
3 *syn* see ADULTERATE
rel damage, impair, worsen; corrupt, defile, spoil
idiom play the devil (*or* the mischief) with
con amend, upgrade
debased *adj* being lowered in quality or character <became *debased* in his greed for money>
syn corrupted, debauched, depraved, perverted, vitiate, vitiated
rel decadent, degenerate, degenerated, deteriorated; abandoned, dissolute, profligate, reprobate
con ameliorated, bettered, improved; elevated, lifted, raised
ant elevated
debatable *adj* *syn* see MOOT
ant undebatable
debate *n* **1** *syn* see ARGUMENTATION
rel controverting, rebutting, refuting
2 *syn* see ATTENTION 1
debate *vb* *syn* see DISCUSS 1
rel altercate, quarrel, wrangle; confute, controvert, disprove, rebut, refute; demonstrate, prove; contend, contest
con agree, coincide, concur; affirm, aver, maintain, profess
debauch *vb* **1** *syn* see DEBASE 1
rel decoy, inveigle, lure, seduce, tempt
con amend, remedy; clean, cleanse, purge, purify; preserve, reclaim, save
2 *syn* see SEDUCE 2
debauch *n* *syn* see ORGY 2
debauched *adj* *syn* see DEBASED
rel lascivious, lecherous, lewd, libertine, libidinous, licentious, wanton
con delivered, reclaimed, redeemed, rescued, saved; chaste, decent, pure; moral, virtuous; continent, temperate
debilitate *vb* *syn* see WEAKEN 1
rel devitalize; attenuate, extenuate; harm, hurt, mar, spoil
con energize, vitalize; fortify, reinforce, strengthen; refresh, rejuvenate, renew, restore; rally, rouse, stir
ant invigorate
debility *n* *syn* see INFIRMITY 1
debris *n* *syn* see REFUSE
rel dregs, dross, rubble
debt *n* **1** *syn* see EVIL 2
2 *syn* see INDEBTEDNESS 1
3 something (as money) that is owed <struggling to keep ahead of his *debts*>
syn arrear(s), arrearage, due, indebtedness, liability; *compare* INDEBTEDNESS 1
rel default, deficit, delinquency, nonpayment, outstandings; debit, demurrage
con asset, credit; compensation, refund, reimbursement, remuneration
debunk *vb* *syn* see EXPOSE 4
debut *vb* to make one's formal entrance into society <she *debuted* on her 20th birthday>
syn come out
idiom make one's bow
decadence *n* *syn* see DETERIORATION 1
rel regress, regression, regressiveness, retrogradation, retrograding, retrogression, retrogressiveness; debasement, degradation
con advance, progress, progression; amelioration, bettering, betterment, improvement
ant rise; flourishing
decadent *adj* *syn* see EFFETE 3
decamp *vb* **1** *syn* see GET OUT 1
2 *syn* see ESCAPE 1
rel exit, go, leave, quit, retire, withdraw; avoid, elude, evade, shun
con arrive, come
decapitate *vb* **1** *syn* see BEHEAD
2 *syn* see DESTROY 1
decay *vb* to undergo or to cause to undergo destructive changes <apples *decaying* in the basket>
syn break down, corrupt, crumble, decompose, disintegrate, molder, ||perish, putrefy, putresce, rot, spoil, taint, turn
rel deteriorate; debilitate, enfeeble, sap, undermine, weaken; contaminate, defile, pollute; dilapidate, ruin, wreck; curdle, ferment, sour, work; dry-rot
idiom go bad, go to pot, go to seed, go to wrack and ruin
con mature, ripen; refresh, renew, restore; activate, energize, vitalize; cleanse, purify; galvanize, quicken, stimulate, strengthen
decayed *adj* **1** *syn* see EFFETE 3
2 *syn* see BAD 5
decease *n* *syn* see DEATH 1
decease *vb* *syn* see DIE 1
deceased *adj* *syn* see DEAD 1
deceit *n* **1** the act or practice of imposing upon the credulity of others by dishonesty, fraud, or trickery <he was full of *deceit* in his business dealings>
syn cunning, dissemblance, dissimulation, duplicity, guile
rel chicane, chicanery, deception, double-dealing, fraud, trickery; artifice, craft; cheating, cozening, defrauding, entrapping, overreaching, trapping

con honesty, scrupulosity, scrupulousness, uprightness; candidness, candor, frankness, openness; forthrightness, straightforwardness
2 ***syn*** see IMPOSTURE

deceitful *adj* ***syn*** see DISHONEST 1
rel artful, crafty, cunning, foxy, guileful, insidious, sly, tricky, wily; clandestine, furtive, stealthy, underhand, underhanded; deceptive, delusive, delusory, misleading
con assuring, convincing, reassuring
ant trustworthy

deceive *vb* to lead astray or frustrate by underhandedness <advertising that *deceives* the public>
syn beguile, betray, bluff, ||bunk, cozen, delude, double-cross, four-flush, humbug, illude, juggle, mislead, mock, sell out, suck in, take in, two-time
rel cheat, defraud, do, overreach; circumvent, outwit; bamboozle, befool, dupe, gull, hoax, hoodwink, spoof, trick, victimize; throw off
idiom pull one's leg, pull the wool over one's eyes, put something over (*or* across), take for a ride, take into camp, throw off the scent (*or* track)
con correct, disabuse, rectify, unblind; acquaint, advise, apprise, inform
ant undeceive; enlighten

deceiving *adj* ***syn*** see MISLEADING
ant undeceiving; enlightening

decelerate *vb* ***syn*** see DELAY 1
ant accelerate

decency *n* ***syn*** see DECORUM 1
rel appropriateness, fitness, fittingness, suitability; ceremoniousness, conventionality, formality
con impropriety, indecorousness, unseemliness; inappropriateness, unfitness, unsuitability; discourteousness, impoliteness, rudeness
ant indecency

decent *adj* **1** ***syn*** see DECOROUS 1
con awkward, clumsy, gauche, inept, maladroit; discomfiting, disconcerting, embarrassing; crude, rough, rude, uncouth
2 ***syn*** see CHASTE
rel noble; good, right; rigid, strict; ascetic, austere, severe
con lewd; libertine, wanton; abandoned, dissolute, profligate, reprobate
ant indecent; obscene
3 ***syn*** see RESPECTABLE 5
4 better than mediocre but less than excellent <the accommodations were *decent*>
syn acceptable, adequate, all right, common, good, respectable, right, satisfactory, sufficient, tolerable, unexceptionable, unexceptional, unimpeachable, unobjectionable; *compare* RESPECTABLE 5, SUFFICIENT 1
rel average, fair, mediocre, middling
con imperfect, inadequate, unacceptable, unsatisfactory; excellent, fine, superior
5 ***syn*** see SUFFICIENT 1

decently *adv* ***syn*** see WELL 1

deception *n* **1** the act of deliberately deceiving <resort to falsehood and *deception* in avoiding the tax>
syn cheat, chicane, chicanery, dipsy-doodle, dirt, dishonesty, double-dealing, dupery, fourberie, fraud, hanky-panky, highbinding, indirection, sharp practice, subterfuge, ||suck-in, trickery
rel cunning, deceit, dissimulation, duplicity, guile; cheating, cozening, defrauding, overreaching; bamboozling, befooling, duping, gulling, hoaxing, hoodwinking; manipulation; ride, ||snow job
con candidness, frankness, openness; honesty, integrity, probity; artlessness, ingenuousness, naiveté
2 ***syn*** see IMPOSTURE
rel delusion, hallucination, illusion, mirage
3 ***syn*** see FALLACY 2

deceptive *adj* ***syn*** see MISLEADING
rel colorable, plausible, specious; apparent, illusory, ostensible, seeming
con authentic, bona fide, genuine, veritable; actual, real, true; dependable, reliable, trustworthy

deceptiveness *n* ***syn*** see FALLACY 2

decide *vb* to come or to cause to come to a conclusion <he *decided* how to solve the problem>
syn conclude, determine, figure, resolve, rule, settle
rel gather; adjudge, adjudicate, judge; conjecture, guess, surmise; establish, fix, set
idiom cast the die, make up one's mind, settle in one's mind
con falter, hesitate, vacillate, waver; fluctuate, oscillate; balk, demur, scruple, shy

decided *adj* **1** beyond any doubt or ambiguity <a *decided* advantage over her opponent>
syn assured, clear-cut, definite, pronounced
rel determined, resolved; certain, positive, sure; categorical, explicit, express, unequivocal; clear, obvious, runaway, unmistakable
con doubtful, dubious, problematic, uncertain; equivocal, obscure, vague
ant questionable
2 free from doubt or wavering <he had a *decided* manner>
syn bent, decisive, determined, intent, resolute, resolved, set, settled
rel certain, cocksure, positive, sure; iron-jawed; established, fixed; earnest, purposeful, serious; unfaltering, unhesitating, unwavering
con doubtful, dubious, irresolute, uncertain; faltering, hesitant, vacillating, wavering; undetermined, unresolved, unsettled, unsure
ant undecided
3 ***syn*** see POSITIVE 1

decidedness *n* ***syn*** see DECISION 2

decimate *vb* **1** ***syn*** see DESTROY 1
2 ***syn*** see SLAUGHTER 3

decipher *vb* **1** ***syn*** see DECODE
ant cipher, encipher
2 ***syn*** see SOLVE 2

---

syn synonym(s) ***rel*** related word(s)
ant antonym(s) ***con*** contrasted word(s)
idiom idiomatic equivalent(s)
|| use limited; if in doubt, see a dictionary

rel paraphrase, translate; analyze, break down
idiom find the key of
con misconstrue, misinterpret, misunderstand; confuse, muddle; bewilder, confound, mystify, puzzle; jumble, mix, scramble

decision *n* **1** a position arrived at after consideration <the *decision* of the committee remains firm>
syn conclusion, determination, resolution, settlement
rel accord, agreement, understanding; accommodation, adjustment, arrangement; compromise, reconciliation; choice, preference, selection
con deadlock, draw, stalemate, standoff, tie
2 freedom from doubt or wavering <a man of unusual *decision*>
syn decidedness, determination, firmness, purposefulness, purposiveness, resoluteness, resolution, resolve
rel doggedness, obstinacy, obstinance, perseverance, persistence, stubbornness; earnestness, seriousness; backbone, fortitude, grit, pluck
con changeableness, indetermination, irresolution; uncertainty, unsureness; faltering, fluctuation, hesitation, vacillation, wavering
ant indecision

decisive *adj* ***syn*** see DECIDED 2
rel imperative, imperious, masterful, peremptory; assured, self-assured, self-confident; steadfast, unswerving, unwavering
con fluctuating, oscillating; hesitant, reluctant; doubtful, dubious, irresolute, uncertain, undecided
ant indecisive

deck *vb* ***syn*** see ADORN
rel apparel, array, attire, clothe, dress; accouter, appoint, furnish
con deface, disfigure; impair, mar, spoil; contort, deform, distort; dismantle, divest, strip

deck (out) *vb* ***syn*** see DRESS UP 1

declaim *vb* ***syn*** see ORATE

declamatory *adj* ***syn*** see RHETORICAL

declaration *n* the act of declaring, proclaiming, or publicly announcing <a *declaration* of war>
syn advertisement, announcement, broadcast, proclamation, promulgation, pronouncement, pronunciamento, publication
rel information, notice, notification; communication; disclosure, revelation; report, statement; acknowledgment, avowal
con concealment, hiding; denial, disaffirmation; recall, recantation, retraction, revocation

declare *vb* **1** to make known openly or publicly <*declared* his intention to run for the senate>
syn advertise, announce, annunciate, blaze (abroad), blazon, broadcast, bruit (about), disseminate, proclaim, promulgate, publish, sound, toot, vend
rel acquaint, advise, apprise, inform, notify; communicate, impart; pronounce; disclose, discover, divulge, reveal; report
idiom declare oneself, make public (*or* known)
con hold, hold back, keep back, reserve, withhold; recall, recant, retract, revoke
2 ***syn*** see ASSERT 1
rel air, broach, express, utter, vent, ventilate, voice; acknowledge, admit, own
idiom have one's say
con controvert; deny; repress, suppress; conceal, hide
3 ***syn*** see SAY 1
rel broach, express, voice
idiom speak one's piece

declare off *vb* ***syn*** see BACK DOWN

declass *vb* ***syn*** see DEGRADE 1
rel disbar, exclude, rule out; abash, discomfit, disconcert
con aggrandize, exalt, magnify

déclassé *adj* ***syn*** see INFERIOR 2

declension *n* ***syn*** see DETERIORATION 1
rel regression, regressiveness, retrogression, retrogressiveness; dilapidation, ruination
con ascension, ascent; rise, rising; advance, progress, progression; development, maturation

declination *n* **1** ***syn*** see DETERIORATION 1
2 ***syn*** see FAILURE 4

decline *vb* **1** ***syn*** see SET 12
ant ascend
2 ***syn*** see FAIL 1
rel backslide, lapse, relapse; slide; return, revert; recede, retrograde; abate, ebb, subside, wane
idiom go downhill, take a turn for the worse
con advance, progress; develop, mature; gain, recover
3 ***syn*** see DETERIORATE 1
4 to turn away by not accepting, receiving, or considering <he *declined* the invitation>
syn disapprove, dismiss, refuse, reject, reprobate, repudiate, spurn, turn down
rel balk, boggle, demur, jib, scruple, shy, stick, stickle; abstain, forbear, refrain; deny, gainsay; abjure, renounce; bypass
idiom send regrets
con receive, take; accede, acquiesce, assent, consent; choose, select; adopt, embrace, espouse
ant accept

decline *n* **1** ***syn*** see FAILURE 4
rel devitalization, weakening
con advancement, progress; recovery; development, maturation
2 ***syn*** see DETERIORATION 1
rel comedown, descent, drop, fall, falling off, slump; ebb, wane; backsliding, lapse, relapse
con development, evolution
3 a downward movement (as in price or value) <stocks suffered a *decline* in the market>
syn dip, downslide, downswing, downtrend, downturn, drop, falloff, sag, slide, slip, slump
rel lapse, loss, lowering; depression; decrease, drop-off, sell-off
con upswing, uptrend, upturn
4 ***syn*** see DESCENT 4

declivate *adj* ***syn*** see INCLINED 3

declivitous *adj* ***syn*** see INCLINED 3

declivity *n* ***syn*** see DESCENT 4
ant acclivity

decode *vb* to convert code into ordinary language <*decode* a message>

syn break, crack, cryptanalyze, decipher, decrypt
rel anagram; render, translate; ‖dope out, figure out, make out; resolve, solve, unfold, unravel, unriddle, work, work out; elucidate, explain, interpret
con cipher, codify, encipher; anagrammatize
ant code, encode, encrypt

decollate *vb* ***syn*** see BEHEAD

decolor *vb* ***syn*** see WHITEN 1
rel wash out; achromatize, fume, peroxide
con blacken; dye, imbue, stain, tinge, tint; paint, shade
ant color

decolorize *vb* ***syn*** see WHITEN 1
ant color

decompose *vb* **1** ***syn*** see ANALYZE
con combine, join, link, write; synthesize, unify; amalgamate, merge, mix
ant compound
2 ***syn*** see DECAY
rel deliquesce, liquefy, melt; break up, dissolve

decompound *vb* ***syn*** see ANALYZE
ant compound

decorate *vb* ***syn*** see ADORN
rel accouter, appoint, equip, furnish, outfit
con impair, injure, mar, spoil; blot, blotch, foul, mutilate, scar, uglify; dismantle, divest, strip

decorated *adj* ***syn*** see BEMEDALED

decoration *n* ***syn*** see HONOR 2

decorous *adj* **1** conforming to an accepted standard of propriety or good form <*decorous* behavior seems regrettably out of fashion>
syn au fait, becoming, befitting, Christian, civilized, comely, conforming, correct, decent, de rigueur, done, nice, proper, respectable, right, seemly
rel ceremonial, ceremonious, conventional, formal; dignified, elegant; appropriate, fit, fitting, meet, seasonable, suitable; prim, punctilious, rigid, stiff, stuffy
con blatant, clamorous, obstreperous, strident; aggressive, assertive, pushing, pushy; coarse, gross, vulgar; easy, fast, loose; improper, incorrect, unbecoming
ant indecorous
2 ***syn*** see GOOD 13

decorously *adv* ***syn*** see WELL 1

decorousness *n* ***syn*** see ORDER 7
rel ceremoniousness, conventionality, formality, solemnity; convenance, convention, form, usage
con inappropriateness, incorrectness; unfitness, unsuitability, unsuitableness; disorder, misbehavior, misconduct, misdeed, misdemeanor
ant indecorousness

decorticate *vb* ***syn*** see SKIN 2
rel bark; scalp; denude, divest

decorum *n* **1** socially acceptable behavior or accepted standards of this <they found his conduct quite lacking in *decorum*>
syn decency, dignity, etiquette, propriety, seemliness
rel convenance, convention, form, usage
con laxity, laxness, license, slackness; carelessness, heedlessness, inconsiderateness, mannerlessness; inappropriateness, incorrectness
ant indecorum
2 ***syn*** see ORDER 7
rel ceremoniousness, conventionality, formality, solemnity; convenance, convention, form, usage
con inappropriateness, incorrectness; unfitness, unsuitability, unsuitableness; disorder, misbehavior, misconduct, misdeed, misdemeanor
ant indecorum; license
3 *usu* **decorums** ***syn*** see MANNER 3

decoy *n* **1** ***syn*** see LURE 2
rel chicane, chicanery, deception, trickery; drawing card
con rebuff, repellence, repellency, repellent, repugnance, repulse, repulsion
2 a person used as a lure <used the detective as a *decoy* to catch the pushers>
syn blind, ‖bonnet, ‖booster, capper, shill, shillaber, stick
rel lugger, roper, steerer; come-on, front, plant, stall

decoy *vb* ***syn*** see LURE
rel deceive, delude, mislead; ensorcell, wile
con disgust, repel, sicken; offend, repulse, revolt

decrease *vb* to grow less especially gradually <his influence *decreased* as a new generation grew up>
syn abate, bate, close, diminish, drain (away), dwindle, lessen, peak (out), peter (out), rebate, recede, reduce, taper, taper off
rel abbreviate, abridge, clip, curtail, retrench, shorten, trim; contract, shrink; allay, alleviate, ease, lighten, mitigate; ebb, subside; cut, cut back, cut down, lower; deduct, subtract
con augment, enlarge, multiply; elongate, extend, lengthen, prolong, protract; amplify, dilate, distend, expand, swell; accumulate, amass
ant increase

decree *n* **1** ***syn*** see EDICT 1
2 ***syn*** see LAW 1
rel behest, bidding, injunction, order; charge, charging, direction, instruction; announcement, declaration, proclamation, promulgation, pronouncement

decree *vb* ***syn*** see DICTATE
rel compel, constrain, force, oblige; demand, require

decrepit *adj* **1** ***syn*** see WEAK 1
rel haggard, wasted, worn; aged, old, superannuated; creaky, quavering, shaking, tottering
con strong; lusty; hale, healthy, hearty, robust, sound, well
ant sturdy
2 ***syn*** see SHABBY 1

---

syn synonym(s) *rel* related word(s)
ant antonym(s) *con* contrasted word(s)
idiom idiomatic equivalent(s)
‖ use limited; if in doubt, see a dictionary

rel damaged, impaired, injured, marred, spoiled; cast-off, ragged, used; slipshod, sloppy, unkempt

decrepitude *n* ***syn*** see INFIRMITY 1
ant vigor

decretum *n* ***syn*** see LAW 1

decry *vb* **1** ***syn*** see DEPRECIATE 1
2 to indicate one's low opinion of something <*decrying* his opponent's character>
syn abuse, bad-mouth, belittle, cry down, depreciate, derogate, detract (from), diminish, discount, disparage, dispraise, downcry, ‖low-rate, minimize, opprobriate, put down, run down, take (from), take away, write off
rel deprecate, disapprove; censure, condemn, criticize, denounce, reprehend, reprobate; asperse, calumniate, defame, malign, traduce, vilify; discredit, disgrace
idiom bring into discredit, cast a slur upon, cast blame upon, dump on, throw stones at
con acclaim, eulogize, laud, praise; aggrandize, exalt, magnify; applaud, commend, compliment, recommend; endorse, sanction; approve, countenance, favor
ant extol, puff

decrypt *vb* ***syn*** see DECODE

decumbent *adj* ***syn*** see PRONE 4

decussate *vb* ***syn*** see INTERSECT

dedicate *vb* ***syn*** see DEVOTE 1
rel address, apply, direct, give, surrender; commit, confide, consign, entrust; allot, appropriate, assign, set (aside)
idiom give over to

dedition *n* ***syn*** see SURRENDER

deduce *vb* ***syn*** see INFER
rel cogitate; consider, deem, regard; conceive, fancy, imagine; assume, presume, presuppose; read (into)
idiom take to mean

deducible *adj* ***syn*** see DEDUCTIVE

deduct *vb* **1** to take away one quantity from another <*deduct* the cost from his bill>
syn discount, draw back, knock off, substract, subtract, take, take away, take off, take out
rel decrease, diminish, lessen, reduce; roll back
con cast, figure, sum, tot, total
ant add
2 ***syn*** see INFER

deduction *n* **1** an amount subtracted from a sum <*deductions* from gross income>
syn abatement, discount, rebate, reduction, subtraction
rel allowance, credit, cut; decrease, decrement, depreciation, diminution; charge-off, offtake, takeoff, write-off; dockage
con accession, accretion, augmentation, increase, increment, raise, rise; appreciation
ant addition
2 ***syn*** see INFERENCE 1
3 ***syn*** see INFERENCE 2
rel cogitation, deliberation, reasoning, reflection, speculation, thinking; consideration, contemplation; meditation, mulling, musing, pondering, rumination

deductive *adj* that can be deduced or developed from premises <*deductive* laws>
syn a priori, deducible, derivable, dogmatic, reasoned
rel illative, inferential, ratiocinative; conjectural, hypothetical, purported, putative, supposed, suppositious; academic, speculative, theoretical
con categorical, definite, explicit, express; instinctive, intuitive

deed *n* **1** ***syn*** see ACTION 1
2 ***syn*** see FEAT 2
rel gaining, securing, winning; adventure, enterprise, quest; cause, crusade
idiom bold stroke
3 a written, signed, and usually sealed instrument that spells out some bargain, transfer, or contract <the *deed* to the property>
syn charter, conveyance
rel bargain, compact, contract, covenant, pact

deed *vb* ***syn*** see TRANSFER 4

deem *vb* **1** ***syn*** see CONSIDER 3
rel conjecture, guess, surmise, suspect, ‖suspicion, understand; ‖allow, assume, believe, ‖calculate, daresay, divine, expect, presume, suppose
idiom hold to be true
2 ***syn*** see FEEL 3
idiom take for granted

de–emphasize *vb* ***syn*** see SOFT-PEDAL

deep *adj* **1** having great extension downward or inward <a *deep* well><a *deep* closet>
syn abysmal, profound; *compare* BOTTOMLESS 2
con depthless, shallow, superficial, unprofound; flat, level, plain, plane
ant shallow
2 ***syn*** see INTENSIVE
3 ***syn*** see RECONDITE
rel complex, complicated, intricate; arcane, mysterious; concealed, hidden
con easy, facile, simple; apparent, clear, distinct, evident, manifest, obvious; lucid, perspicuous; depthless, shallow, superficial, unprofound
4 ***syn*** see SLY 2
rel shrewd; acute, keen, knowing, sharp; contriving, intriguing, plotting
con ingenuous, naive, simple, unsophisticated; aboveboard, forthright, straightforward
5 ***syn*** see INTENT
rel abstracted, concentrated; centered, fixed, focused, set
con distracted, diverted; detached, disinterested, indifferent, unconcerned, uninterested

deep *n* ***syn*** see OCEAN

deep–dyed *adj* ***syn*** see INVETERATE 1

deepen *vb* ***syn*** see INTENSIFY

deepness *n* **1** ***syn*** see DEPTH 1
ant shallowness
2 ***syn*** see DEPTH 2

deep–rooted *adj* ***syn*** see INVETERATE 1

deep–seated *adj* **1** ***syn*** see INHERENT
2 ***syn*** see INVETERATE 1
rel constitutional, immanent, indwelling, ingrained, inherent, intrinsic; deep, profound; inner, internal, inward; implanted; infixed

con peripheral, shallow, superficial, surface; adventitious, casual, chance, incidental
ant skin-deep

‖**deep–six** *vb* ***syn*** see DISCARD

deep water *n* ***syn*** see PREDICAMENT

deface *vb* to mar the appearance of <*deface* the wall with graffiti>
syn disfashion, disfeature, disfigure
rel blemish, damage, harm, impair, injure, mar, spoil; contort, deform, distort, misshape; batter, mangle, mutilate; demolish, destroy; dilapidate, ruin, wreck
con mend, patch, repair; freshen, improve, refurbish, renew, restore; adorn, beautify, deck, decorate, embellish, ornament

defacer *n* ***syn*** see VANDAL

de facto *adv* ***syn*** see VERY 2

defalcation *n* ***syn*** see FAILURE 3
rel laxness, negligence, remissness, slackness; failing, fault
con discharge, effectuation, execution, fulfillment; completion, conclusion

defamation *n* ***syn*** see DETRACTION
ant puffery

defamatory *adj* ***syn*** see LIBELOUS

defame *vb* ***syn*** see MALIGN
rel belie, misrepresent
idiom cast a slur on, throw mud at
con applaud, commend, compliment; exalt, magnify; back, champion, support, uphold
ant laud; puff

default *n* **1** ***syn*** see FAILURE 1
rel deficiency, fault, imperfection, shortcoming; lapse, weakness; disregard, omission, overlooking, slight
2 ***syn*** see ABSENCE

defeasance *n* ***syn*** see DEFEAT 1

defeat *vb* **1** ***syn*** see CONQUER 1
rel bar, block, hinder, impede, obstruct; repress, suppress
idiom beat all hollow, get the better of, grind into the dust
con capitulate, defer, give in, submit; back down, withdraw
2 to win a victory over <*defeated* his opponent in the race>
syn best, down, outdo, ‖pip, worst; *compare* CONQUER 1, WHIP 2
rel outfight, outgame; nose out
idiom get the better of

defeat *n* **1** an overthrow especially of an army in battle <the brigade suffered a *defeat*>
syn beating, debacle, defeasance, discomfiture, downcast, downthrow, drubbing, ‖dusting, licking, overthrow, rout, shellacking, thrashing, trouncing, vanquishment, warming
rel bafflement, check, foil, frustration; rebuff, repulse, reversal, reverse, setback; ‖cleaning, ‖cleanup, clobbering, lambasting
con conquest, triumph; gaining, securing, winning; ascendancy, supremacy
ant victory
2 ***syn*** see FAILURE 2

defeater *n* ***syn*** see VICTOR 1
ant defeated

defect *n* **1** ***syn*** see BLEMISH
rel failing, fault, foible, frailty; infirmity, weakness; deficiency, imperfection, shortcoming
con excellence, faultlessness, impeccability; merit, perfection, virtue
2 ***syn*** see ABSENCE
rel scantiness, scarceness, scarcity, shortage
con overage, overplus, superfluity, surplus, surplusage
ant excess

defect *vb* to desert a cause or party often in order to espouse another <he *defected* from the Communist party>
syn apostatize, desert, rat, renounce, repudiate, tergiversate, tergiverse, turn
rel abandon, forsake; back out, renege, withdraw; depart, go, leave, quit; reject, spurn
idiom change sides, go back on, go over, turn one's coat, walk (*or* run) out on
con adhere (to), cling (to), hang on, stick (to *or* with); cherish, cultivate, foster

defection *n* conscious abandonment of allegiance or duty <*defection* from family responsibilities in times of trouble>
syn apostasy, desertion, falseness, recreancy, tergiversation
rel alienation, disaffection, estrangement; disloyalty, faithlessness; abandonment, forsaking; divorce, parting, runout, separation, sundering; disownment, rejection, repudiation
idiom running out on, ‖taking a runout powder
con constancy, faithfulness, loyalty, resoluteness, staunchness, steadfastness; allegiance, fealty, fidelity; dependability, reliability, trustworthiness

defective *adj* **1** ***syn*** see FAULTY
rel broken, damaged, impaired, injured
con faultless, flawless, impeccable, unblemished, undamaged
ant defectless
2 ***syn*** see DEFICIENT 1
rel corrupted, debased, vitiated; deranged, disordered, disturbed, unsettled; unhealthy, unsound
con entire, perfect, whole; complete, full, plenary; healthy, sound
ant intact; defectless

defector *n* ***syn*** see RENEGADE

defend *vb* **1** to keep safe (as from danger or against attack) <*defend* the country from aggression>
syn bulwark, cover, fend, guard, protect, safeguard, screen, secure, shield
rel avert, prevent, ward; oppose, resist, withstand; battle, contend, fight, war; conserve, preserve, save
idiom stand on the defensive, stave off from

---

syn synonym(s) ***rel*** related word(s)
ant antonym(s) ***con*** contrasted word(s)
idiom idiomatic equivalent(s)
‖ use limited; if in doubt, see a dictionary

con aggress, assail, assault, fall (on *or* upon); bombard, storm; beset, besiege, overrun; capitulate, cave, submit, yield
ant attack
2 ***syn*** see MAINTAIN 2
rel air, express, utter, vent, voice; account, explain, justify, rationalize; back, champion, support, uphold
idiom speak (*or* stand *or* stick) up for
con contradict, deny, gainsay, traverse; confute, controvert, disprove, rebut, refute

defendable *adj* ***syn*** see TENABLE 1
ant undefendable

defense *n* **1** means or method of defending <the skunk's powerful *defense* against attackers>
syn aegis, armament, armor, guard, protection, safeguard, security, shield, ward
rel arms, munitions, weaponry, weapons; fastness, fort, fortress, stronghold
con aggression, offense, offensive
ant attack
2 ***syn*** see APOLOGY 1
rel answer, rejoinder, reply, response, retort, return; exculpation, excuse, explanation, rationalization
con censure, condemnation, criticism, decrial, reprehension, reprobation, reproof; assault, attack, onset, onslaught

defenseless *adj* ***syn*** see HELPLESS 1

defensible *adj* **1** ***syn*** see TENABLE 1
ant indefensible
2 ***syn*** see JUSTIFIABLE
ant indefensible

defer *vb* to delay an action or proceeding <decided to *defer* voting until the next meeting>
syn adjourn, delay, hold off, hold over, hold up, intermit, lay over, postpone, prorogue, put off, put over, remit, shelve, stand over, stay, suspend, waive
rel detain, retard, slow; block, hinder, impede, obstruct; stall; extend, lengthen, prolong, protract
idiom hold up on, lay to one side, put on ice, set aside
con accelerate, hasten, hurry, speed; expedite, further, promote
ant advance

defer *vb* ***syn*** see YIELD 2
rel accede, acquiesce, agree, assent; accommodate, adapt, adjust, conform; cringe, fawn, truckle
con combat, fight, oppose, resist; object, remonstrate; balk, demur, stickle, strain
ant withstand

deference *n* ***syn*** see HONOR 1
rel acquiescence, compliance; submission, submissiveness
con insolence, irreverence; disesteem, disfavor; discourtesy, incivility, rudeness
ant disrespect

deferential *adj* **1** ***syn*** see RESPECTFUL
2 ***syn*** see INGRATIATING

defi *n* ***syn*** see DEFIANCE 1

defiance *n* **1** the act or an instance of defying <presented a *defiance* to his rival>
syn cartel, challenge, dare, defi, defy, stump
rel call, muster, summons; command, enjoinder, order
con capitulation, submission, surrender
2 disposition to resist or unwillingness to brook opposition <exhibited *defiance* toward his teacher>
syn contempt, contumacy, despite, recalcitrance, stubbornness
rel factiousness, insubordination, insurgency, rebelliousness; headstrongness, intractableness, unruliness; boldness, bravado, brazenness, impudence, insolence; audacity, effrontery, hardihood, temerity; contrariness, perversity
con acquiescence, compliance; amenableness, docility, obedience, tractableness; submissiveness

deficiency *n* **1** ***syn*** see FAILURE 3
rel absence, default, defect, want
con copiousness, plenty; great deal, heap, lot, much
2 ***syn*** see IMPERFECTION
rel dearth, defect, lack, privation, want; default, dereliction, miscarriage, neglect
ant excess

deficient *adj* **1** showing lack of something necessary <*deficient* in judgment>
syn defective, inadequate, incomplete, insufficient, lacking, uncomplete, wanting
rel faulty, flawed, imperfect, unsound; damaged, impaired, injured, marred; amiss, bad, unsatisfactory
idiom in want of
con complete, entire, intact, whole; acceptable, adequate, sufficient
2 ***syn*** see SHORT 3
rel infrequent, rare, uncommon
idiom found wanting
con excessive, extravagant, immoderate, inordinate; enough, satisfactory, sufficing
ant adequate, sufficient

deficit *n* ***syn*** see FAILURE 3
con copiousness, plenty; excess, surplus, surplusage

defile *vb* **1** ***syn*** see CONTAMINATE 1
rel desecrate, profane; befoul, dirty, foul, sully, tarnish
con consecrate, hallow
ant cleanse; purify
2 ***syn*** see RAPE
rel dishonor, shame, soil, sully
3 ***syn*** see TAINT 1

defiled *adj* ***syn*** see IMPURE

define *vb* **1** ***syn*** see PRESCRIBE 2
rel circumscribe, limit, mark (off), mark (out); designate; delineate, describe
con confound, confuse, mistake
2 ***syn*** see BORDER 1
3 ***syn*** see ETCH 2
rel explain, expound, interpret

definite *adj* **1** having distinct or certain limits <*definite* dimensions>
syn circumscribed, determinate, fixed, limited, narrow, precise, restricted

rel assigned, defined, prescribed; established, set; decided, determined, settled
con ambiguous, obscure, vague; unconditional, unlimited, unqualified, unrestricted; indeterminate, uncircumscribed; imprecise, loose, undefined
ant indefinite
2 *syn* see EXPLICIT
rel complete, full; downright, forthright; incisive
con doubtful, dubious, questionable; ambiguous
ant indefinite; equivocal
3 *syn* see POSITIVE 1
4 *syn* see DECIDED 1
ant uncertain

definitely *adv* **1** *syn* see EXPRESSLY 1
2 *syn* see EASILY 2

definiteness *n syn* see PRECISION
ant indefiniteness

definitive *adj* **1** *syn* see CONCLUSIVE
rel determining, settling; concluding, final, last, terminal, ultimate; closing, completing, ending, finishing, terminating; absolute, categorical
con inconclusive, indecisive; temporary, transitory
ant provisional, tentative
2 *syn* see EXPLICIT
rel actual, real
con doubtful, dubious, questionable; ambiguous
ant indefinitive

definitiveness *n syn* see PRECISION
ant indefinitiveness, indefinitude

definitude *n syn* see PRECISION
ant indefinitiveness, indefinitude

deflect *vb* **1** *syn* see TURN 6
rel disperse, swerve; hook, skew
2 *syn* see WARD 1
rel hold off, keep off

deflection *n* **1** *syn* see DEVIATION 1
rel bending, curving, twisting; departing, swerve, swerving, veer, veering
2 *syn* see TURN 2

deflorate *vb syn* see RAPE

deflower *vb* **1** *syn* see RAPE
2 *syn* see RAVAGE

deform *vb* to mar or spoil by or as if by twisting <a face *deformed* by bitterness>
syn contort, distort, misshape, torture, warp, wind
rel batter, cripple, maim, mangle, mutilate; deface, disfigure; damage, impair, injure, mar, spoil; blemish, flaw; screw (up), squinch

deformity *n* a physical blemish or disfigurement <the dwarf's humpback *deformity*>
syn distortion, malconformation, malformation, misshape
rel defacement, deformation, disfigurement; damage, impairment, injury; aberration, abnormality; irregularity, unnaturalness

defraud *vb syn* see CHEAT
rel bamboozle, hoax, trick; circumvent, foil, outwit; fleece, milk, stick; take in
idiom do out of, put over a fast one, take to the cleaner's

defrauder *n syn* see SWINDLER

deft *adj syn* see DEXTEROUS 1
rel agile, brisk, fleet; apt, prompt, quick, ready; adept, crack, crackerjack; ingenious, neat
con heavy-handed, unskillful; blundering, bungling, butterfingered; rigid, stiff, wooden
ant awkward, unhandy

deftness *n syn* see ADDRESS 1
rel agility, fleetness, nimbleness; assuredness, confidence
con incompetence, inefficiency; clumsiness, heavy-handedness, maladroitness
ant awkwardness

defunct *adj* **1** *syn* see DEAD 1
rel inactive, inert
ant alive; live
2 *syn* see EXTINCT 2
ant surviving

defunction *n syn* see DEATH 1

defy *vb syn* see FACE 3
rel deride, mock, ridicule; gibe, flout; scorn, scout, spurn; disregard, ignore
idiom fling (*or* throw) down the gauntlet, hurl defiance at
con blench, flinch, quail, shrink
ant recoil

defy *n syn* see DEFIANCE 1

dégagé *adj syn* see EASYGOING 3
ant mannered

degeneracy *n syn* see DETERIORATION 1

degenerate *adj* **1** *syn* see EFFETE 3
rel deteriorating, retrograde, retrogressive, worsening; failing, sinking
2 *syn* see VICIOUS 2
rel degraded, demeaned
con ethical, moral, virtuous; honorable, just, upright
ant regenerate

degenerate *vb syn* see DETERIORATE 1
rel corrupt, deprave, vitiate; backslide, lapse; return, revert
con improve, upgrade; lift, uplift

degeneration *n syn* see DETERIORATION 1
rel regression, regressiveness, retrogression, retrogressiveness; depreciation; corruption, depravation, depravedness, depravity, perversion
con regeneracy, regenerateness; progress, progression
ant regeneration

degradation *n syn* see DEMOTION
ant advancement; elevation

degrade *vb* **1** to lower in station, rank, or grade <*degraded* in rank for misconduct>
syn break, bump, bust, declass, demerit, demote, disgrade, disrate, downgrade, put down, reduce

---

syn synonym(s) *rel* related word(s)
ant antonym(s) *con* contrasted word(s)
idiom idiomatic equivalent(s)
|| use limited; if in doubt, see a dictionary

THESAURUS

rel abase, debase, humble, humiliate, lower; disbar, rule out
con advance, further; boost, lift, raise; enhance, heighten
ant elevate
2 ***syn*** see HUMBLE
rel belittle, decry, derogate, detract, disparage; diminish, lessen, reduce
con elevate, raise; acclaim, extol, laud, praise
ant uplift

degree *n* **1** a unitary component of a process, course, or order of classification <advanced by *degrees*>
syn grade, notch, rung, stage, step
2 relative size or character of the parts or components in a complex whole compared with other like things <the *degree* of difference between the two jobs> <his work demands a high *degree* of intelligence>
syn proportion, rate, ratio, scale
rel dimension; extent, magnitude, measure, size

dégringolade *n* ***syn*** see DETERIORATION 1

dehydrate *vb* ***syn*** see DRY 1
ant hydrate; rehydrate

deific *adj* **1** ***syn*** see DIVINE 1
2 ***syn*** see DIVINE 2

deification *n* ***syn*** see APOTHEOSIS 2

deign *vb* ***syn*** see STOOP 1

deject *vb* ***syn*** see DISCOURAGE 1
ant exhilarate; cheer

dejected *adj* ***syn*** see DOWNCAST
idiom down in the dumps (*or* mouth), in the dumps
ant animated

dejection *n* ***syn*** see SADNESS
rel despair, desperation
ant exhilaration

‖**dekko** *vb* ***syn*** see SEE 2

delay *vb* **1** to cause to be late or behind in movement or progress <was *delayed* by traffic>
syn bog (down), decelerate, detain, embog, hang up, mire, retard, set back, slacken, slow (up *or* down)
rel block, hinder, impede, obstruct; defer, hold over, hold up, intermit, postpone, put off, stay, suspend; arrest, check, interrupt
idiom hang fire
con accelerate, hasten, hurry, precipitate, quicken, speed; advance, forward, further, promote
ant expedite
2 to move or act slowly so that progress or work is retarded <their landlord kept *delaying* in making repairs>
syn dally, dawdle, dilly, dillydally, drag, lag, linger, loiter, mull, poke, procrastinate, put off, tarry, trail
rel hang back, idle, wait; drone; falter, hesitate, vacillate, waver
idiom take one's own sweet (*or* good) time
ant hasten, hurry
3 ***syn*** see DEFER

delectable *adj* ***syn*** see DELIGHTFUL
rel choice, dainty, delicate, exquisite, rare; palatable, sapid, savory, tasty, toothsome
con loathsome, offensive, repulsive, revolting
ant distasteful

delectate *vb* ***syn*** see PLEASE 2

delectation *n* **1** ***syn*** see PLEASURE 2
rel gratification, gratifying, regalement, regaling; enjoyment, relish
ant distaste
2 ***syn*** see ENJOYMENT 1

‖**deleerit** *adj* ***syn*** see INTOXICATED 1

delegate *n* a person standing in the place of another or others <was a *delegate* to the convention>
syn catchpole, deputy, representant, representative; *compare* AGENT 2
rel agent, factor, proxy; alternate, replacement, stand-in, substitute, surrogate; mouthpiece, spokesman; emissary, envoy

delegate *vb* to appoint as one's representative <*delegated* her to watch the children>
syn commission, depute, deputize
rel ascribe, assign, charge; appoint, designate, name; choose, pick, select

delete *vb* ***syn*** see ERASE
rel eliminate, exclude, rule out; omit

deleterious *adj* ***syn*** see HARMFUL
rel destroying, destructive; ruining, ruinous
con advantageous, profitable; healthful, healthy, salubrious, wholesome
ant salutary

deliberate *adj* **1** arrived at after due thought <a *deliberate* judgment>
syn advised, aforethought, considered, designed, premeditated, prepense, studied, studious, thought-out
rel planned, projected, schemed; calculated; careful, meticulous, scrupulous; foresighted, forethoughtful, provident, prudent
con chance, chancy, desultory, haphazard, happy-go-lucky, hit-or-miss, random; aimless, designless, purposeless; hasty, hurried; abrupt, impetuous, sudden; automatic, instinctive, spontaneous
ant casual
2 ***syn*** see VOLUNTARY
rel intended, meant, meditated, purposed; determined, purposeful; aware, cognizant, conscious
con careless, heedless, inadvertent, thoughtless; unintended, unpurposed
ant impulsive
3 ***syn*** see SLOW 2
rel calculating, cautious, chary, circumspect, wary; careful, heedful; collected, composed, cool, imperturbable
con hasty, headlong, impetuous, sudden
ant abrupt, precipitate

deliberate *vb* **1** ***syn*** see PONDER 2
2 ***syn*** see THINK 5
rel excogitate, study, weigh; argue, debate, discuss, talk over

deliberately *adv* ***syn*** see INTENTIONALLY

deliberation *n* **1** ***syn*** see ATTENTION 1
2 ***syn*** see THOUGHT 1
3 ***syn*** see CONFERENCE 1

delicacy *n* something special and delicious to eat <fresh fruit in the winter was once an uncommon *delicacy*>
syn bonne bouche, dainty, goody, kickshaw, morsel, tidbit (*or* titbit), treat
rel banquet, feast, regale; cosseting, indulgence, luxury
idiom choice bit, dish fit for a king

delicate *adj* **1** ***syn*** see CHOICE
rel delectable, delicious, delightful; balmy, gentle, lenient, mild, soft; aerial, airy, ethereal
con coarse, crude, vulgar
ant gross
2 ***syn*** see FINE 1
3 ***syn*** see NICE 1
rel perceptive, sensitive
con insensitive, undiscriminating, unperceptive
4 ***syn*** see FRAGILE 1
5 lacking in strength or substance <a *delicate* constitution>
syn flimsy, slight
rel feeble, fragile, frail, weak; sickly, unhealthy; decrepit, infirm
con stalwart, stout, strong, sturdy, tenacious, tough; hale, healthy, robust, sound, well, wholesome
6 ***syn*** see TACTFUL
rel adept, expert, masterly, proficient; discreet, foresighted, prudent; careful, heedful; cautious, wary
con impolitic; imprudent, indiscreet; awkward, clumsy, gauche, inept, maladroit; unskillful
7 marked by or requiring tact <a *delicate* situation>
syn precarious, sensitive, ticklish, touchy, tricky
rel uncertain, unpredictable; hair-trigger, volatile; sticky

delicatesse *n* ***syn*** see TACT
ant indelicacy

delicious *adj* ***syn*** see DELIGHTFUL
rel appetizing, palatable, sapid, savory, toothsome; choice, dainty, delicate, exquisite, rare
con banal, flat, inane, insipid, jejune, wishy-washy

delight *vb* **1** ***syn*** see EXULT
2 ***syn*** see PLEASE 2
rel amuse, divert, entertain; allure, attract, charm, enchant, fascinate; enrapture, entrance, transport
con aggrieve, distress, pain, trouble; afflict, try; grieve; bother, irk; bore

delight (in) *vb* **1** ***syn*** see ADMIRE 1
rel enjoy, like, savor; eat up, luxuriate (in)
con abhor, abominate, hate, loathe
2 ***syn*** see LOVE 1

delight *n* ***syn*** see PLEASURE 2
rel glee, hilarity, jollity, mirth; ecstasy, rapture, transport; contentment, satisfaction; relish
con abhorrence, detestation, hate, hatred; dislike, distaste; discontent, dissatisfaction
ant aversion; disappointment

delightful *adj* highly pleasing to the senses or to aesthetic taste <a *delightful* view>
syn adorable, ambrosial, darling, delectable, delicious, heavenly, luscious, lush, scrumptious, yummy
rel charming, enchanting, fascinating; alluring, attractive; beautiful, fair, lovely; ineffable; agreeable, gratifying, pleasant, pleasing; satisfying
con miserable, wretched; distasteful, obnoxious, repellent, repugnant; abhorrent, detestable, hateful, odious; boring, irksome, tedious; distressing, troubling
ant abominable, horrid

delimit *vb* **1** ***syn*** see DEMARCATE 1
rel decide
2 ***syn*** see LIMIT 2

delimitate *vb* **1** ***syn*** see DEMARCATE 1
2 ***syn*** see LIMIT 2

delineate *vb* **1** ***syn*** see REPRESENT 1
rel design, plan; evoke, paint
2 ***syn*** see ETCH 2

delineation *n* **1** ***syn*** see REPRESENTATION
rel design, plan; evocation, painting; account, story, version
2 ***syn*** see OUTLINE

delinquency *n* ***syn*** see FAILURE 1
rel nonobservance; nonfulfillment; lapse, weakness

delinquent *adj* ***syn*** see NEGLIGENT

deliquesce *vb* ***syn*** see LIQUEFY
rel decay, decompose, disintegrate
con cake, harden, indurate, set, solidify

delirious *adj* **1** disordered in mind especially temporarily <*delirious* from the fever>
syn raving, wandering
rel deranged, disarranged, disordered, disturbed, unsettled; bewildered, confused, distracted; rambling; irrational, unreasonable; crazed, crazy, demented, insane, lunatic, mad, maniac
idiom out of one's head (*or* mind)
con rational, reasonable; sane, sensible; comatose, unconscious
2 ***syn*** see FURIOUS 2
rel overexcited, overwrought; ecstatic, rapturous, transported; delighted, enthused, thrilled
idiom all agog, beside oneself
con collected, composed, easy, relaxed; unexcited, unmoved, unstimulated

delirium *n* frenzied excitement or wild enthusiasm <in a *delirium* of patriotic feeling>
syn frenzy, furor
rel ardor, enthusiasm, fervor, passion, zeal; ecstasy, rapture, transport
con nonchalance, sangfroid; indifference, unconcern
ant apathy

deliver *vb* **1** ***syn*** see RESCUE
con immure, imprison, incarcerate, intern, jail; capture, catch, ensnare, entrap, snare, trap; condemn, damn, doom

---

syn synonym(s) ***rel*** related word(s)
ant antonym(s) ***con*** contrasted word(s)
idiom idiomatic equivalent(s)
‖ use limited; if in doubt, see a dictionary

2 ***syn*** see GIVE 3
rel relinquish, resign, surrender, yield
con keep, retain
3 ***syn*** see BEAR 5
4 ***syn*** see SAY 1
rel broach, express, vent, voice; communicate, impart
5 ***syn*** see GIVE 10
rel dispatch, send, transmit; fling, hurl, pitch, throw
delivery *n* ***syn*** see BIRTH 1
Delphian *adj* **1** ***syn*** see PROPHETIC
2 ***syn*** see CRYPTIC
delude *vb* ***syn*** see DECEIVE
idiom play tricks (*or* a trick) on
con enlighten, illume, illuminate, illustrate, light, lighten; elucidate, explain
deluding *adj* ***syn*** see MISLEADING
deluge *n* ***syn*** see FLOOD 2
rel flux; overrunning
deluge *vb* **1** to flow over so as to submerge or enclose <the lowlands were completely *deluged*>
syn drown, engulf, flood, inundate, overflow, overwhelm, submerge, swamp, whelm
rel overrun; flush, gush, pour, sluice, stream
2 ***syn*** see WET
con dehydrate, desiccate, dry, parch
3 to affect overwhelmingly as if by a deluge of water <he was *deluged* by telephone calls>
syn flood, overwhelm, swamp, whelm
rel overcome; oversupply; abound, teem
delusion *n* **1** something accepted as true that is actually false or unreal <people who suffer from *delusions* of persecution>
syn hallucination, ignis fatuus, illusion, mirage, phantasm
rel chicane, chicanery, deception, trickery; cheat, counterfeit, deceit, fake, fraud, humbug, imposture, sham; daydream, dream, fancy, fantasy, figment, vision; apparition, eidolon, ghost, phantom, shade
ant reality
2 ***syn*** see FALLACY 2
ant verity
delusive *adj* ***syn*** see MISLEADING
rel chimerical, fanciful, fantastic, imaginary, quixotic, visionary; apparent, illusory, ostensible, seeming
con authentic, bona fide, genuine, veritable; actual, real, true
delusory *adj* ***syn*** see MISLEADING
deluxe *adj* ***syn*** see LUXURIOUS 3
rel choice, dainty, delicate, elegant, exquisite, rare, recherché
con coarse, common, ordinary; inelegant
delve *vb* ‖**1** ***syn*** see DIG 1
rel gouge (out), hollow (out), quarry (out), scoop (out); burrow, tunnel; comb, ferret out, search, seek
2 ***syn*** see MINE
delve (into) *vb* ***syn*** see EXPLORE
delve *n* ***syn*** see HOLE 1
delving *n* ***syn*** see INQUIRY 1
demagogue *n* a leader who makes use of popular prejudices and false claims especially for political advantage <*demagogues* who endanger the orderly processes of democratic government>
syn rabble-rouser
rel fomenter, inciter, instigator; agitator, firebrand, hothead, incendiary, inflamer; troublemaker
demand *n* **1** ***syn*** see REQUIREMENT 1
2 ***syn*** see NEED 3
demand *vb* **1** to ask for something as or as if one's right or due <the physician *demanded* payment of his bill>
syn call, challenge, claim, exact, postulate, require, requisition, solicit
rel ask, request; bid, charge, command, direct, enjoin, order; cite, summon, summons; coerce, compel, constrain, force, oblige; necessitate
con cede, relinquish, resign, waive; allow, concede, grant; give, offer, tender
2 to have as a need or requirement <it *demands* considerable practice to master the piano>
syn ask, call (for), crave, necessitate, require, take
rel fail, lack, need, want
idiom need (*or* want), doing, stand in need of
demanding *adj* ***syn*** see ONEROUS
rel rigid, rigorous, severe, stern, strict, stringent; crying, imperative, importunate, instant, pressing, urgent
ant undemanding
demarcate *vb* **1** to mark the limits of <*demarcate* the boundary between two countries>
syn bound, delimit, delimitate, determine, limit, mark (out), measure
rel establish, fix, set; assign, define, prescribe; circumscribe, confine, restrict
2 ***syn*** see DISTINGUISH
rel insulate, isolate, seclude, segregate, sequester
demean *vb* ***syn*** see BEHAVE 1
demean *vb* ***syn*** see HUMBLE
rel belittle, decry, derogate, detract, disparage; contemn, despise, scorn
con elevate, enhance, heighten
demeanor *n* ***syn*** see BEARING 1
rel behavior, conduct
dement *n* ***syn*** see LUNATIC 1
demented *adj* ***syn*** see INSANE 1
rel delirious, frenzied, hysterical
demerit *n* ***syn*** see IMPERFECTION
demerit *vb* ***syn*** see DEGRADE 1
demeritorious *adj* ***syn*** see BLAMEWORTHY
ant meritorious
demesne *n* ***syn*** see FIELD
demigod *n* ***syn*** see SUPERMAN
demimondaine *n* ***syn*** see HARLOT 1
demimonde *n* ***syn*** see HARLOT 1
demirep *n* ***syn*** see HARLOT 1
demise *vb* ***syn*** see DIE 1
demise *n* ***syn*** see DEATH 1
rel annihilation, ending, expiration, extinction
demit *vb* ***syn*** see ABDICATE 1
demit *vb* ***syn*** see LOWER 3
demiurgic *adj* ***syn*** see INVENTIVE
‖**demob** *vb* ***syn*** see DISCHARGE 7

ant mobilize

demobilize *vb syn* see DISCHARGE 7
rel break up, disband, dispel, disperse, scatter; retire, withdraw
ant mobilize

democratic *adj* of or relating to a political system in which the supreme power is held and exercised by the people <a *democratic* government>
syn popular, self-governing, self-ruling
rel representative; libertarian
con totalitarian; absolute, arbitrary, autocratic, despotic; tyrannical, tyrannous; fascistic, nazi, patriarchal
ant authoritarian; undemocratic

démodé *adj syn* see OLD-FASHIONED
ant a la mode

demoded *adj syn* see OLD-FASHIONED
ant a la mode

demolish *vb syn* see DESTROY 1
rel dilapidate; crush, smash; break, burst, crack
con build, erect, frame, raise, rear
ant construct; rebuild
2 *syn* see TOTAL 3

demon *n syn* see DEVIL 2

demoniac *adj syn* see FIENDISH
rel crazed, crazy, insane, maniac; fired, inspired
con celestial, heavenly
ant angelic

demonian *adj syn* see FIENDISH
rel crazed, crazy, insane, maniac; fired, inspired
con celestial, heavenly
ant angelic

demonic *adj syn* see FIENDISH
rel crazed, crazy, insane, maniac; fired, inspired
con celestial, heavenly
ant angelic

demonstrate *vb* **1** *syn* see SHOW 2
rel display, exhibit, expose, flaunt, parade; explain, set forth
idiom go to show
con conceal, hide, secrete; camouflage, cloak, disguise, dissemble, mask
2 *syn* see PROVE 1
rel authenticate, validate
3 *syn* see ESTABLISH 6

demonstration *n syn* see EXHIBITION 1

demonstrative *adj* marked by display of feeling <was *demonstrative* in his welcome>
syn expansive, outgoing, unconstrained, unreserved, unrestrained
rel affectionate, loving; effusive, outpouring, profuse; candid, frank, open, outspoken, plain
con constrained, reserved, restrained, reticent, taciturn; bashful, shy; retiring, shrinking; introverted; aloof, detached, indifferent, unconcerned; chilly, cold, frigid, glacial, icy
ant undemonstrative

demoralize *vb* **1** *syn* see DEBASE 1
rel debilitate, undermine, weaken; damp, dampen
2 *syn* see DISCOURAGE 1
rel agitate, disturb, upset; disarrange, disorder, disorganize, unsettle; confuse, jumble, muddle, snarl; debilitate, undermine, weaken; unman, unnerve
con arrange, order, organize; energize, fortify, invigorate, strengthen

demote *vb syn* see DEGRADE 1
rel demean, lower
ant promote

demotion *n* the action or an instance of demoting <received a *demotion* from sergeant to corporal>
syn degradation, downgrading, reduction
rel debasement, humbling, humiliation; blackballing, disbarment, exclusion, suspension
con advancement, preferment, upgrading; aggrandizement; boost, elevation, lift, raise
ant promotion

demur *vb* to object or have scruples <he *demurred* at any horseplay>
syn balk, boggle, gag, jib, scruple, shy, stick, stickle, strain, stumble
rel falter, hesitate, vacillate, waver; combat, fight, oppose, resist; expostulate, object, protest, remonstrate; deprecate, disapprove
con accept, admit, receive, take; acquiesce, agree, assent, consent, subscribe, yes; concur; defer, relent, submit, succumb, yield
ant accede

demur *n* **1** *syn* see QUALM
rel faltering, hesitancy, hesitation; aversion, disinclination, loathness; expostulation, protest
con promptness, quickness, readiness
2 the act of objecting or taking exception <accepted without *demur*>
syn challenge, demurral, demurrer, difficulty, objection, protest, question, remonstrance, remonstration
rel reluctance, unwillingness; faltering, hesitancy, hesitation; deprecation, disapproval; protestation; difference, disagreement, dissent, variance
con acquiescence, agreement, assent, consent; concurrence; submission

demure *adj syn* see SHY 1
rel decent, decorous, nice, proper, seemly; prim; earnest, serious, solemn; close, reserved, reticent, silent
con impertinent, intrusive, meddlesome, obtrusive, officious; brash, forward, unbashful, unretiring

demurral *n syn* see DEMUR 2

demurrer *n syn* see DEMUR 2

den *n* **1** *syn* see LAIR 1
2 *syn* see HIDEOUT
3 *syn* see SINK 1

denaturant *n syn* see ADMIXTURE 1

denial *n* **1** refusal to satisfy a request or desire <*denial* of his visiting privileges>
syn disallowance, refusal, rejection
rel declination, nonacceptance
con allowing, conceding, grant, letting; leave, permission, sufferance

---

syn synonym(s) *rel* related word(s)
ant antonym(s) *con* contrasted word(s)
idiom idiomatic equivalent(s)
‖ use limited; if in doubt, see a dictionary

2 refusal to admit the truth <his *denial* that he took the money>
syn contradiction, gainsaying, negation
rel controversion, disproof, rebuttal, refutal, refutation; refusal, rejection, repudiation
con acknowledgment, avowal, confession; affirmation, assertion, confirmation
ant admission
3 ***syn*** see RENUNCIATION
rel abstaining, refraining
con indulgence, self-indulgence; overdoing, overindulgence

denigrate *vb* ***syn*** see MALIGN

denizen *n* **1** ***syn*** see INHABITANT
rel citizen, national, subject
2 ***syn*** see HABITUÉ 1

denominate *vb* ***syn*** see NAME 1

denomination *n* **1** ***syn*** see NAME 1
2 ***syn*** see RELIGION 2

denotative *adj* ***syn*** see INDICATIVE

denote *vb* ***syn*** see MEAN 2
rel insinuate; announce, argue, bespeak, prove

denotive *adj* ***syn*** see INDICATIVE

denounce *vb* ***syn*** see CRITICIZE
rel accuse, arraign, charge, impeach, incriminate, indict, tax; revile, vituperate; delate, inform
idiom cry harrow (*or* haro)
con panegyrize, praise
ant eulogize

de novo *adv* ***syn*** see OVER 7

dense *adj* **1** ***syn*** see CLOSE 4
rel heaped, massed, piled; crammed, crowded, jam-packed
con dispersed, dissipated, scattered; rare, thin; exiguous, meager, scant, scanty, spare
ant sparse; tenuous
2 ***syn*** see STUPID 1
rel obtuse; impassive, phlegmatic, stolid; lethargic, sluggish, torpid
ant subtle; bright

denticulate *adj* ***syn*** see SERRATE

denudate *vb* ***syn*** see STRIP 2

denude *vb* **1** ***syn*** see STRIP 1
2 ***syn*** see STRIP 2

denuded *adj* ***syn*** see OPEN 2

denunciate *vb* ***syn*** see CRITICIZE
rel delate, inform; menace, threaten
ant eulogize

deny *vb* **1** ***syn*** see DISCLAIM
rel abandon, desert, forsake
con adopt, embrace, espouse; recognize
ant acknowledge; admit
2 to refuse to grant <he was unwilling to *deny* the child's request>
syn disallow, keep back, refuse, withhold
idiom say no to, turn thumbs down on
con allow, concede, let, permit; afford, give
ant grant
3 to restrain (as oneself) from or forgo what is pleasant or satisfying <decided to *deny* himself a second piece of pie>
syn abstain, constrain, curb, hold back, refrain
rel eschew, forbear, forgo, sacrifice; inhibit, restrain; avoid, shun
con overdo, overindulge
ant indulge
4 to refuse to accept as true, valid, or worthy of consideration <*denying* the existence of witches>
syn contradict, contravene, cross, disaffirm, gainsay, impugn, negate, negative, traverse
rel decline, refuse, reject, repudiate; confute, controvert, disprove, rebut, refute; downface
con affirm, assert, aver; allow, grant; authenticate, corroborate, substantiate, validate, verify; avow, confess; claim, submit
ant concede; confirm

depart *vb* **1** ***syn*** see GO 2
rel set out, start, strike out, toddle
con linger, stay, tarry, wait; come; approach, near
ant arrive; abide, remain
2 ***syn*** see DIE 1
con exist, live, survive
3 ***syn*** see SWERVE 2
rel abandon, desert, forsake; reject, repudiate; cast, discard; differ, disagree, dissent, vary
4 ***syn*** see DIGRESS 2

departed *adj* **1** ***syn*** see DEAD 1
idiom called home, gone to a better land
2 ***syn*** see EXTINCT 2

departing *adj* ***syn*** see PARTING

departure *n* **1** the act of going, coming out, or leaving a place <the hasty *departure* of the refugees>
syn egress, egression, exit, exiting, exodus, offgoing, setting-out, withdrawal
rel going, leaving, quitting, retreat; decampment, flight; farewell, leave-taking
con coming, entering, ingress
ant arrival
2 ***syn*** see DEVIATION 1
rel rambling, straying, wandering

depend *vb* ***syn*** see HANG 1

depend (on *or* upon) *vb* **1** to rest or to be contingent upon something uncertain, variable, or indeterminable <our trip *depends* upon the weather>
syn hang (on *or* upon), hinge (on *or* upon), ‖pend, stand (on *or* upon), turn (on *or* upon)
rel base, bottom, found, ground, rest, stay
idiom hang in the balance
2 ***syn*** see RELY (on *or* upon)
rel incline, lean

dependable *adj* **1** ***syn*** see RELIABLE 1
rel assured, confident, sure; responsible; constant, faithful, loyal, staunch, steadfast, steady
idiom as good as one's word, to be counted on
con capricious, fickle, inconstant, mercurial, unstable; dishonest, lying, mendacious, untruthful
ant independable, undependable
2 ***syn*** see TRUE 9
3 ***syn*** see CERTAIN 3

dependence *n* ***syn*** see TRUST 1

dependent *adj* **1** determined or conditioned by another <a conclusion that is *dependent* on a premise>

syn conditional, contingent, relative, reliant
rel exposed, liable, open, subject, susceptible; iffy, provisional, provisory; uncertain; circumscribed, limited, restricted
con categorical, ultimate; boundless, eternal, illimitable, uncircumscribed; basal, basic, fundamental, primary, underived
ant absolute; infinite; original
2 *syn* see SUBORDINATE
rel counting, depending, reckoning, relying, trusting; accessory, ancillary, appurtenant; abased, debased, humbled
con principal; paramount, predominant, preponderant, preponderating, sovereign
ant independent

depict *vb syn* see REPRESENT 1
rel narrate, recite, recount, rehearse, relate, report, state; outline, sketch

depiction *n syn* see REPRESENTATION

deplete *vb* to bring to a low estate by depriving of something essential <an epidemic which *depletes* an army of manpower>
syn bankrupt, drain, draw, draw down, exhaust, impoverish, use up
rel cripple, debilitate, disable, enfeeble, sap, undermine, weaken; decrease, diminish, lessen, reduce; bleed, draw off, dry up, empty, milk; consume, expend, finish, spend, wash up
idiom dig into
con augment, enlarge, increase; bolster, fortify, strengthen; rebuild, repair, restore, revive
ant renew, replace

depleted *adj syn* see EFFETE 2
rel sapped, weakened
con augmented, enlarged, increased

deplorable *adj* of a kind to cause great distress <a *deplorable* loss of life>
syn afflictive, calamitous, dire, distressing, dolorous, grievous, heartbreaking, heartrending, lamentable, mournful, regrettable, unfortunate, woeful
rel awful, dreadful, terrible; horrifying, intolerable, overwhelming, sickening, unbearable; miserable, wretched; disastrous
idiom as bad as bad can be, as bad as can be
con beneficial, helpful, salutary; advantageous, favorable, propitious

deplore *vb* **1** to manifest grief or sorrow for something <*deplore* the death of a close friend>
syn bemoan, bewail, grieve, lament, moan, weep
rel deprecate, disapprove; mourn, sorrow; cry, keen, wail
con boast, brag, crow, vaunt; rejoice
2 *syn* see REGRET

depone *vb syn* see TESTIFY 2

deport *vb* **1** *syn* see BEHAVE 1
2 *syn* see BANISH

deportation *n syn* see EXILE 1

deportment *n* **1** *syn* see BEHAVIOR
2 *syn* see BEARING 1

depose *vb* **1** to remove from a throne or other high position <trying to *depose* the king in favor of his brother> <*deposed* industrial leaders>
syn dethrone, discrown, disenthrone, displace, disthrone, uncrown, unmake
rel overthrow, subvert, upset; chuck, dismiss, eject, oust, throw out
con inaugurate, induct, install, instate, invest; crown, enthrone, throne
2 *syn* see ASSERT 1
3 *syn* see TESTIFY 2

deposit *vb syn* see BANK
rel put by, store, stow

deposit *n syn* see SEDIMENT

depository *n syn* see DEPOT 2

depot *n* **1** *syn* see ARMORY
2 a place where something is deposited or stored <a gasoline *depot*>
syn arsenal, depository, magazine, repository, store, storehouse
rel storeroom, warehouse
3 *syn* see RAILROAD STATION
rel terminal, terminus

deprave *vb syn* see DEBASE 1
con elevate, ennoble, exalt, raise, uplift

depraved *adj* **1** *syn* see DEBASED
rel degenerate, infamous, vicious, villainous; degraded; twisted, warped
con scrupulous, upright
2 *syn* see VICIOUS 2

depravity *n syn* see VICE 1

deprecate *vb syn* see DISAPPROVE 1
rel bemoan, bewail, deplore, lament; derogate, detract
ant endorse

depreciate *vb* **1** to reduce the value of <*depreciate* the dollar>
syn cheapen, decry, devalorize, devaluate, devalue, downgrade, lower, mark down, soften, underprize, underrate, undervalue, write down, write off
rel depress; abate, decrease, diminish, dwindle, lessen, reduce; erode
con augment, increase; bloat, blow up, expand, inflate; amplify, magnify
ant appreciate
2 *syn* see DECRY 2
rel underestimate, underrate, undervalue; discountenance, disesteem, disfavor
con cherish, prize, treasure, value; comprehend, understand
ant appreciate

depreciation *n syn* see DETRACTION

depreciative *adj syn* see DEROGATORY
rel underestimating, underrating, undervaluing
ant appreciative

depreciatory *adj syn* see DEROGATORY
rel underestimating, underrating, undervaluing
ant appreciative

depredate *vb syn* see RAVAGE

depredator *n syn* see MARAUDER

depress *vb* **1** *syn* see LOWER 3
2 to lower in spirit or mood <the thought of all his debts *depressed* him>

---

syn synonym(s) *rel* related word(s)
ant antonym(s) *con* contrasted word(s)
idiom idiomatic equivalent(s)
|| use limited; if in doubt, see a dictionary

THESAURUS

syn oppress, press, sadden, weigh down
rel ail, distress, trouble; afflict, torment, try; contrist, deject, discourage, dishearten, dispirit; bother, disturb, perturb, upset
con delight, gladden, gratify, please, rejoice; excite, inspire, stimulate; brighten, cheer up, encourage; buoy, elevate
ant elate, exhilarate; cheer

depressant *adj syn* see GLOOMY 3

depressed *adj* **1** *syn* see DOWNCAST
rel lugubrious, melancholy
ant exhilarated; animated
2 *syn* see UNDERPRIVILEGED

depressing *adj* **1** *syn* see GLOOMY 3
con cheering, elevating, uplifting; exciting, inspiring
ant exhilarating
2 *syn* see SAD 2

depression *n* **1** *syn* see SADNESS
rel boredom, doldrums, ennui, tedium
con glee, hilarity, mirth
ant buoyancy; elation
2 a low spot <a *depression* in the land>
syn basin, concavity, dip, hollow, sag, sink, sinkage, sinkhole; *compare* NOTCH 1
rel cavity, hole, pocket, vacuity, vacuum, void; crater, pit; scoop
3 a period of lowered economic activity and extensive unemployment <indicators that warn of a coming *depression*>
syn recession, slump, stagnation
rel crash, decline, dislocation, drop; sag; paralysis; ‖stagflation
con expansion; booming, development, growth; advancement, progress
ant boom

depressive *adj syn* see GLOOMY 3

deprivation *n syn* see PRIVATION 2

deprive *vb* **1** *syn* see STRIP 2
2 to prevent one from possessing <to *deprive* a person of his civil rights>
syn bereave, disinherit, dispossess, divest, lose, oust, rob; *compare* STRIP 2
rel dock; bare, denude, dismantle, strip
con furnish, give, supply; clothe, endow, equip, fit (out), invest, outfit
ant provide

deprived *adj syn* see UNDERPRIVILEGED

deprivement *n syn* see PRIVATION 2

depth *n* **1** the perpendicular extent or measurement downward from a surface <measured the *depth* of the river>
syn deepness, drop
rel profoundness, profundity; lowness; sounding; draft
con shallowness; altitude, elevation
2 the quality of being profound (as in insight) or full (as of knowledge) <her answer showed she had great *depth* in that subject>
syn abyss, deepness, profoundness, profundity
rel sense, wisdom, wiseness; brain, intellect, intelligence; keenness, sharpness
con shallowness, superficiality, unprofoundness; sciolism, smatter, smattering

depthless *adj syn* see SUPERFICIAL 2

depurate *vb syn* see PURIFY 1

depute *vb syn* see DELEGATE

deputize *vb syn* see DELEGATE

deputy *n* **1** *syn* see AGENT 2
rel substitute, surrogate; replacement
2 *syn* see DELEGATE

derange *vb* **1** *syn* see DISORDER 1
rel perturb; discommode, incommode, inconvenience
con compose, settle
ant arrange; adjust
2 *syn* see UPSET 5
3 *syn* see MADDEN 1

deranged *adj syn* see INSANE 1
rel disarranged, disordered, disturbed

derangement *n syn* see INSANITY 1
rel disarrangement, disorder; confusion; disturbance; unsoundness

derelict *adj* **1** given up especially by the owner or occupant <a *derelict* old home>
syn abandoned, deserted, desolate, forsaken, lorn, solitary, uncouth
rel dilapidated, dingy, faded, run-down, seedy, shabby, threadbare
con cherished, prized, treasured; attended, kept up, maintained
2 *syn* see NEGLIGENT
rel irresponsible, undependable, unreliable, untrustworthy
con dependable, reliable, responsible, trustworthy; careful, heedful, thoughtful
ant faithful

derelict *n* **1** *syn* see OUTCAST
2 *syn* see VAGABOND

dereliction *n syn* see FAILURE 1
rel abuse, misuse, outrage
ant faithfulness

deride *vb syn* see RIDICULE
rel banter, chaff, jolly, kid, rag, rib

de rigueur *adj syn* see DECOROUS 1

derision *n syn* see LAUGHINGSTOCK

derivable *adj syn* see DEDUCTIVE

derivate *adj syn* see SECONDARY 2

derivation *n syn* see SOURCE

derivational *adj syn* see SECONDARY 2

derivative *adj syn* see SECONDARY 2
ant underivative

derivative *n syn* see OUTGROWTH 2

derive *vb* **1** to reach (as a conclusion) as an end point of reasoning and observation <evidence from which he *derived* a startling new set of axioms>
syn educe, evolve, excogitate
rel conclude, deduce, gather, infer, judge; arrive (at), elicit, extract, reach; develop, elaborate, formulate, put (together), work out
2 *syn* see INFER
3 *syn* see TAKE 14

derive (from) *vb syn* see SPRING 1

derived *adj syn* see SECONDARY 2

dernier cri *n syn* see FASHION 3

dernier ressort *n syn* see RESOURCE 3

derogate *vb syn* see DECRY 2

rel decrease, lessen, reduce; discredit, disgrace
con enhance, heighten, intensify

derogatory *adj* designed or tending to belittle <*derogatory* comments about the actor's performance>
syn depreciative, depreciatory, detracting, disadvantageous, disparaging, dyslogistic, pejorative, slighting, uncomplimentary
rel belittling, decrying, minimizing; aspersing, calumnious, defamatory, maligning, vilifying; degrading, demeaning, humiliating; despiteful, malevolent, malicious, spiteful; contumelious, disdainful, scornful
con admiring, esteeming; acclaiming, laudatory, praising; appreciative
ant complimentary

derout *vb syn* see ROUT 1

derriere *n syn* see BUTTOCKS

descant *n* **1** *syn* see MELODY
2 *syn* see SONG 2

descant *vb syn* see DISCOURSE 1

descend *vb* **1** *syn* see FALL 1
ant rise
2 *syn* see STOOP 2
3 *syn* see DETERIORATE 1

descendant *n* **1 descendants** *pl syn* see OFFSPRING
ant ancestors, ascendants
2 *syn* see OUTGROWTH 2

descent *n* **1** the act or process of passing from a higher to a lower level or state <a parachute *descent*><his slow *descent* to the gutter>
syn drop, fall
rel plummeting, plunging, sinking
con rise, upswing, upturn; advance, headway, progress, progression; betterment, improvement
ant ascent
2 *syn* see COMEDOWN
3 *syn* see ANCESTRY
4 an inclination downward <the steep *descent* of the mountain>
syn decline, declivity, dip, drop, fall
rel downgrade, grade, gradient, incline, slope; drop, drop-off
con acclivity, upgrade, uphill
ant ascent, rise

describe *vb* **1** *syn* see RELATE 1
rel communicate, impart; transmit; construe, elucidate, explain, explicate, expound; exemplify, illustrate; characterize, distinguish
2 *syn* see REPRESENT 1

description *n* **1** *syn* see REPRESENTATION
2 a descriptive statement <a fascinating *description* of his adventures>
syn narration, recital, recountal, recounting
rel anecdote, narrative, story, tale, yarn; account, chronicle, version; report, statement
3 *syn* see TYPE

descry *vb* **1** *syn* see SEE 1
2 *syn* see FIND 1
rel appreciate, comprehend, understand; realize

desecrate *vb syn* see RAVAGE

desecrated *adj syn* see IMPURE 3

desecration *n syn* see PROFANATION
ant consecration

desensitize *vb syn* see DEADEN 1
ant sensitize

desert *n syn* see WASTE 1

desert *n usu* **deserts** *pl syn* see DUE 1
rel chastening, chastisement, discipline, discipling, punishment
idiom just deserts

desert *vb* **1** *syn* see ABANDON 1
rel depart, go, leave
con adhere, cohere
ant cleave (to), stick (to)
2 *syn* see DEFECT
rel abscond, decamp, escape, flee, fly
idiom go over the hill
con abide, remain, stay

deserted *adj syn* see DERELICT 1
rel empty, vacant; uninhabited, unoccupied; bare, barren

desertion *n syn* see DEFECTION
rel perfidiousness, perfidy, treacherousness, treachery

deserve *vb syn* see EARN 2
rel gain, get, win; demand
idiom have it coming

deserved *adj syn* see JUST 3
ant undeserved

deserving *n syn* see DUE 1

deserving *adj syn* see WORTHY 1
ant undeserving

desexualize *vb syn* see STERILIZE

desiccate *vb* **1** *syn* see DRY 1
2 to drain or be drained of emotional or intellectual vitality <this book is *desiccated* by undue concentration on statistics>
syn devitalize, dry up
rel deplete, drain, exhaust; divest; decay, fade, shrivel, wither, wizen
con brighten, enliven

desiderate *vb syn* see DESIRE 1

desight *n syn* see EYESORE

design *vb* **1** *syn* see INTEND 2
2 *syn* see PLAN 2
rel delineate, diagram; create, invent; construct, fashion, form, frame, produce; contrive
con accomplish, achieve, effect, execute, fulfill, perform
3 to work out the arrangement of the parts of <*design* an urban center>
syn arrange, lay out, map (out), plan, set out; *compare* PLAN 2
rel delineate, diagram, draft, outline, sketch

design *n* **1** *syn* see PLAN 1
rel delineation, diagram, draft, outline, sketch, tracing; creation, invention
con accomplishment, achievement, execution, fulfillment, performance
2 *syn* see INTENTION

---

syn synonym(s) *rel* related word(s)
ant antonym(s) *con* contrasted word(s)
idiom idiomatic equivalent(s)
|| use limited; if in doubt, see a dictionary

rel conation, volition, will; deliberation, reflection, thinking, thought; intrigue, machination, plot
con accident, chance, fortuity, hap; impulse
3 *syn* see FIGURE 3
4 *syn* see MAKEUP 1

designate *vb* **1** *syn* see NAME 1
2 to declare a person one's choice <*designated* him to fill the position>
syn appoint, finger, make, name, nominate, tap
rel choose, elect, opt, pick, select, single; assign, delegate, depute; dictate
con disapprove, disfavor, object (to), oppose; disallow, reject, turn down
3 to set aside (as funds) for a specific use <*designated* the income to be used for charity>
syn allocate, earmark
rel specify; appropriate, reserve; stipulate; allot, apportion, mete (out)

designation *n syn* see NAME 1
rel identification, recognition; classification, pigeonhole, pigeonholing

designative *adj syn* see INDICATIVE

designed *adj syn* see DELIBERATE 1
rel decided, determined, resolved
con casual, chance, contingent, fluky, fortuitous, incidental; impulsive, spontaneous; natural, normal, regular, typical
ant accidental

designedly *adv syn* see INTENTIONALLY

designless *adj syn* see RANDOM

desire *n* **1** a longing for something that promises enjoyment or satisfaction <he had a strong *desire* for fame and fortune>
syn appetite, appetition, craving, itch, lust, passion, urge
rel hankering, hunger, hungering, longing, pining, thirst, thirsting, yearning; desideratum, desiderium; avarice, cupidity, greed, rapacity; concupiscence, eros
con abhorrence, repellency, repugnance, repulsion; aversion, disfavor, dislike
ant distaste
2 *syn* see LUST 2

desire *vb* **1** to have a longing for something <women who *desire* success>
syn ||choose, covet, crave, desiderate, want, wish
rel hanker, hunger, long, pine, thirst, yearn; enjoy, fancy, like; aim, aspire, pant
idiom set one's eyes (*or* heart) upon
con abhor, abominate, detest, hate, loath; decline, refuse, reject, repudiate, spurn
2 *syn* see ASK 2

desired *adj syn* see TRUE 7

desirous *adj syn* see COVETOUS

desist *vb syn* see STOP 3
rel abstain, forbear; abandon, relinquish, resign, yield
idiom have done with
con continue; persevere
ant persist

desistance *n syn* see END 2

desk *n* a table, frame, or case with a sloping or horizontal surface especially for writing <sat meditating at her *desk*>
syn escritoire, secretaire, secretary, writing desk
rel lectern, reading desk

desolate *adj* **1** *syn* see DERELICT 1
rel empty, vacant; uninhabited, unoccupied
2 *syn* see INCONSOLABLE
3 *syn* see GLOOMY 3
rel bare, barren; destitute, poor, poverty-stricken; dark, murky

desolate *vb syn* see RAVAGE

despair *vb* to lose all hope or confidence <*despaired* of winning>
syn despond, give up
rel abandon, drop, relinquish, renounce, resign, surrender, yield
idiom lose heart (*or* courage *or* faith *or* hope)
con await, count (on), depend (on), hope, look (for); trust (in *or* to)
ant expect

despairing *adj syn* see DESPONDENT
rel atrabilious, melancholic, melancholy; cynical, misanthropic, pessimistic; depressed, oppressed, weighed down
con optimistic, roseate, rose-colored; assured, confident, sanguine, sure
ant hopeful

desperado *n syn* see OUTLAW
rel convict, criminal, lawbreaker

desperate *adj* **1** *syn* see DESPONDENT
rel foolhardy, rash, reckless, venturesome; headlong, precipitate; baffled, balked, circumvented, foiled, frustrated, outwitted, thwarted
con collected, composed, cool, nonchalant; assured, confident, sanguine, sure
2 *syn* see ACUTE 6
3 *syn* see INTENSE 1
4 *syn* see OUTRAGEOUS 2

despicable *adj* **1** *syn* see CONTEMPTIBLE
rel disgraceful, disreputable, ignominious, infamous, loathsome
con applaudable, commendable
ant laudable, praiseworthy
2 *syn* see BASE 3

despisable *adj syn* see CONTEMPTIBLE

despisal *n syn* see DESPITE 1

despise *vb* to regard as beneath one's notice and unworthy of consideration or interest <he had always *despised* the weak>
syn abhor, contemn, disdain, look down, scorn, scout
rel abominate, detest, execrate, hate, loathe; reject, repudiate, spurn; avoid, eschew, renounce, shun; disregard, ignore, overlook, slight, snub
idiom have no use for, look down one's nose at
con apprize, cherish, prize, treasure, value; admire, regard, respect
ant appreciate, esteem

despisement *n syn* see DESPITE 1

despite *n* **1** the feeling or attitude of despising <felt *despite* toward the lowly>
syn contempt, despisal, despisement, disdain, disparagement, scorn
rel disdainfulness, insolence, superciliousness; abhorrence, abomination, detestation, hate, hatred, loathing; rejection, repudiation, spurning;

aversion, disfavor, dislike, distaste; cold shoulder, rebuff, slight, snub; disgust, loathing
con admiration, esteem, honor, regard, respect; attraction, liking
2 ***syn*** see MALICE
rel contempt, disdain, scorn; abhorrence, abomination, detestation, hate, hatred, loathing
con admiration, esteem, respect; awe, fear, reverence
ant appreciation
3 ***syn*** see DEFIANCE 2
rel harm, hurt, injury
4 ***syn*** see AFFRONT
rel cut, discourtesy, incivility; rebuff, slight, snub

despite *prep* ***syn*** see AGAINST 4

despiteful *adj* ***syn*** see MALICIOUS

despitefulness *n* ***syn*** see MALICE

despoil *vb* ***syn*** see RAVAGE

despoiler *n* **1** ***syn*** see MARAUDER
2 ***syn*** see VANDAL

despond *vb* **1** ***syn*** see DESPAIR
rel droop, sag; languish
idiom reach the depths
con expect, hope, look
2 ***syn*** see MOPE 1

despondent *adj* having lost all or nearly all hope <*despondent* about his health>
syn despairing, desperate, desponding, forlorn, hopeless
rel grieving, mourning, sorrowful; dejected, depressed, melancholy, sad; disconsolate, dispirited, downcast, woebegone; discouraged, disheartened
con cheerful, glad, happy, joyful, joyous; buoyant, elastic, resilient, volatile; hopeful, optimistic
ant lighthearted

desponding *adj* ***syn*** see DESPONDENT

despot *n* ***syn*** see TYRANT

despotic *adj* ***syn*** see ABSOLUTE 4

despotism *n* ***syn*** see TYRANNY

despotize *vb* ***syn*** see TYRANNIZE

desquamate *vb* ***syn*** see SCALE 2

destine *vb* ***syn*** see PREDESTINE 1

destiny *n* ***syn*** see FATE
rel design, goal, intent, intention, objective

destitute *adj* **1** ***syn*** see DEVOID
rel deficient; bankrupt, bankrupted, depleted, drained, exhausted; divested, stripped
con complete, full, replete
2 ***syn*** see POOR 1
rel depleted, drained, exhausted
idiom on one's uppers, on the rocks
con comfortable, prosperous, well-fixed, well-off, well-to-do
ant opulent

destituteness *n* ***syn*** see POVERTY 1
rel absence, dearth, lack; adversity, misfortune
con competence, sufficiency
ant opulence

destitution *n* ***syn*** see POVERTY 1
rel absence, dearth, lack, privation, want; adversity, misfortune
con competence, sufficiency
ant opulence

destroy *vb* **1** to bring to ruin <the army *destroyed* the enemy village><his health was finally *destroyed* by drink>
syn annihilate, atomize, decapitate, decimate, demolish, destruct, discreate, dismantle, dissolve, dynamite, pull down, pulverize, quench, raze, rub out, ruin, ‖ruinate, shatter, shoot, smash, tear down, unbuild, undo, unframe, unmake, wrack, wreck; *compare* TOTAL 3
rel abolish, extinguish; devastate, pillage, ravage, sack, waste; eradicate, exterminate, extirpate, wipe; mangle, mutilate; rubble; doom
idiom blow to bits, bring to an end, dispose of, tear to shreds
con establish, found, institute, organize; fabricate, fashion, forge, form, make, manufacture, shape; conserve, preserve, protect, save
2 ***syn*** see KILL 1

destroyer *n* **1** ***syn*** see VANDAL
2 ***syn*** see DOWNFALL 2

destruct *vb* ***syn*** see DESTROY 1

destruction *n* **1** ***syn*** see DOWNFALL 2
2 ***syn*** see RUIN 3

destructive *adj* having the capability, property, or effect of destroying <a *destructive* windstorm> <his brother was a *destructive* influence in his life>
syn annihilative, ruinous, shattering, wrackful, wreckful
rel calamitous, deadly, disastrous, fatal, lethal, mortal; consumptive; internecine; baneful, deleterious, detrimental
con creative, formative; harmless, innocuous, inoffensive; helpful, improving
ant constructive

desuetude *n* **1** ***syn*** see END 2
2 ***syn*** see DISUSE

desultory *adj* **1** ***syn*** see FITFUL
rel erratic; shifting, vagrant, wavering
con constant, invariable, unchanging, unfailing
ant steady
2 ***syn*** see RANDOM
rel fitful, spasmodic; disorderly, unmethodical, unsystematic; capricious, fickle, inconstant, mercurial
con orderly, systematic
ant assiduous; methodical

detach *vb* to remove one thing from another with which it is in union or association <*detach* sheets from a loose-leaf book>
syn abstract, disassociate, disconnect, disengage, dissociate, uncouple, unfix
rel cut off, divorce, part, separate, sever, sunder; disjoin, disunite; disassemble, dismantle, dismember, dismount; disaffiliate
idiom take apart
con fasten, fix; bind, tie; combine, conjoin, unite
ant affix, attach

---

syn synonym(s) ***rel*** related word(s)
ant antonym(s) ***con*** contrasted word(s)
idiom idiomatic equivalent(s)
‖ use limited; if in doubt, see a dictionary

detached *adj* **1** ***syn*** see ALONE 1
rel separate, unconnected
con abutting, adjacent; connected, joined, linked
ant adjoining; attached
2 ***syn*** see INDIFFERENT 2
con anxious, concerned, solicitous; self-centered, selfish
ant interested
3 ***syn*** see NEUTRAL
rel distant, remote, removed

detachment *n* ***syn*** see SEPARATION 1

detail *n* ***syn*** see POINT 1
con anatomy, framework, skeleton, structure; bulk, mass; design, plan

detail *vb* ***syn*** see SPECIFY 3

detailed *adj* ***syn*** see CIRCUMSTANTIAL
rel abundant, copious; exhausting, exhaustive, thoroughgoing

detailedly *adv* ***syn*** see THOROUGHLY 2

detain *vb* **1** ***syn*** see ARREST 2
rel buttonhole, hold, restrain
2 ***syn*** see KEEP 5
3 ***syn*** see DELAY 1
rel check, curb, inhibit, restrain

detect *vb* ***syn*** see FIND 1

detectable *adj* ***syn*** see PERCEPTIBLE

detection *n* ***syn*** see DISCOVERY

detective *n* one employed or engaged in detecting lawbreakers or in getting information that is not readily or publicly accessible <used *detectives* to locate the missing witness>
syn dick, ‖eye, gumshoe, hawkshaw, investigator, plainclothesman, Sherlock, Sherlock Holmes, sleuth, ‖tec; *compare* INFORMER, PRIVATE DETECTIVE
rel G-man; roper; shoofly; ‖nare

detention *n* ***syn*** see ARREST
rel imprisonment, incarceration, internment

deter *vb* **1** ***syn*** see DISSUADE
rel prevent; block, hinder, impede, obstruct; debar, shut out; frighten, scare; inhibit, restrain
con abet, incite, instigate; excite, provoke, stimulate; actuate, motivate
2 ***syn*** see PREVENT 2

deteriorate *vb* **1** to pass from a higher to a lower type or condition <the road quickly *deteriorated* into a bumpy path>
syn decline, degenerate, descend, disimprove, disintegrate, retrograde, rot, sink, worsen
rel crumble, decay, decompose; impair, mar, spoil; debilitate, undermine, weaken; depreciate, lessen
idiom be the worse for wear, go downhill, go to pot (*or* the dogs)
con better, improve; advance, progress; enhance, heighten
ant ameliorate
2 ***syn*** see FAIL 1

deterioration *n* **1** a falling from a higher to a lower level (as of quality or character) <the *deterioration* of business during the depression>
syn atrophy, decadence, declension, declination, decline, degeneracy, degeneration, dégringolade, devaluation, devolution, downfall, downgrade, ruin
rel impairment, spoiling; crumbling, decay, decaying, decomposition, disintegration, dissolution, dry rot, rotting; debasement, degradation; depreciation, lessening; dislocation, disruption
con betterment, help; enhancement, heightening, improvement
ant amelioration
2 ***syn*** see FAILURE 4
con convalescence, recovering, recuperation
ant improvement

determinable *adj* ***syn*** see TERMINABLE

determinant *n* ***syn*** see CAUSE 1
rel factor; authority, influence, weight

determinate *adj* **1** ***syn*** see INFLEXIBLE 3
2 ***syn*** see DEFINITE 1
ant indeterminate

determinate *vb* ***syn*** see IDENTIFY

determination *n* **1** ***syn*** see DECISION 1
2 ***syn*** see DECISION 2
ant indetermination

determine *vb* **1** ***syn*** see ESTABLISH 6
rel fix, set; settle
2 ***syn*** see PREDESTINE 1
3 ***syn*** see DEMARCATE 1
4 ***syn*** see DECIDE
rel bias, dispose, incline, predispose; actuate, drive, impel, move; induce, persuade
5 ***syn*** see CLOSE 3
6 ***syn*** see DISCOVER 3

determined *adj* ***syn*** see DECIDED 2
rel earnest, purposeful, serious; unfaltering, unhesitating, unwavering
con unresolved, unsettled; hesitant, hesitating, wavering
ant undetermined

detest *vb* ***syn*** see HATE
rel reject, repudiate, spurn
con love; appreciate, treasure, value
ant adore

detestable *adj* ***syn*** see HATEFUL 2
rel sorry; atrocious, heinous, monstrous, outrageous
ant adorable

detestation *n* **1** ***syn*** see ABOMINATION 2
rel antipathy, disgust
con affection, attachment, love; forbearance, indulgence, tolerance
ant adoration
2 ***syn*** see ABOMINATION 1
ant adoration

dethrone *vb* ***syn*** see DEPOSE 1
ant enthrone, throne

detonate *vb* ***syn*** see EXPLODE 1

detour *n* an indirect course often temporarily replacing part of a usual route <a *detour* around road construction> <took a *detour* to show him the lake>
syn roundabout, runaround
rel bypass

detour *vb* ***syn*** see SKIRT 2

detract (from) *vb* ***syn*** see DECRY 2

rel libel, slander; decrease, lessen, reduce
con enhance, heighten, intensify
detracting *adj* **1** *syn* see DEROGATORY
2 *syn* see LIBELOUS
detraction *n* the expression of damaging or malicious opinions <his persistent *detraction* of his rival's motives was wholly unfair>
syn backbiting, backstabbing, belittlement, calumny, character assassination, defamation, depreciation, disparagement, scandal, slander, sycophancy, tale
rel damage, harm, hurt, injury; injustice, wrong; aspersion, calumniation, libel, libeling, maligning, slandering, traducing, vilification
con enhancement, heightening, laudation, praise; approbation, approval
ant commendation
detractive *adj syn* see LIBELOUS
detractory *adj syn* see LIBELOUS
detriment *n syn* see DISADVANTAGE
rel damage, harm, hurt, injury, mischief; impairment, marring, spoiling
ant advantage, benefit
detrimental *adj syn* see HARMFUL
con aiding, helpful, helping; harmless
ant beneficial
2 *syn* see ADVERSE 2
de trop *adj syn* see SUPERFLUOUS
detruncate *vb syn* see TOP 1
deuced *adj syn* see UTTER
||**deval** *vb syn* see STOP 3
devalorize *vb syn* see DEPRECIATE 1
devaluate *vb syn* see DEPRECIATE 1
devaluation *n syn* see DETERIORATION 1
devalue *vb syn* see DEPRECIATE 1
devast *vb syn* see RAVAGE
devastate *vb syn* see RAVAGE
devastation *n syn* see RUIN 3
||**devel** *vb syn* see STRIKE 2
develop *vb* **1** *syn* see EXPAND 4
2 *syn* see UNFOLD 3
rel actualize, materialize, realize
3 *syn* see MATURE
rel dilate, expand; enroot, establish; flourish, prosper, thrive
con shrivel, wither, wizen
4 to come to have usually gradually <*develop* a taste for dry wine>
syn acquire, form
rel gain, get, obtain; achieve, attain, reach
5 *syn* see HAPPEN 1
development *n* progressive advance from a lower or simpler to a higher or more complex form <*development* of a seed into a plant><*development* of an industry>
syn evolution, evolvement, flowering, growth, progress, progression, unfolding, upgrowth
rel advance, advancement, ongoing
con decadence, declension, degeneration, deterioration, devolution
ant decline
deviant *adj* **1** *syn* see ABNORMAL 1
con normal; natural
2 *syn* see IRREGULAR 1
deviate *vb* **1** *syn* see SWERVE 2
2 *syn* see ERR
idiom deviate from the path of virtue
deviation *n* **1** departure from a course or procedure or from a norm or standard <no *deviation* from traditional methods was permitted>
syn aberration, deflection, departure, divergence, diversion, turning
rel alteration, change, modification, variation; breach, transgression, violation; anomaly, failing, fault; blunder, error, lapse
con accordance, agreement, conformance, conformity, correspondence
2 *syn* see TURN 2
deviative *adj syn* see ABNORMAL 1
device *n* **1** *syn* see TRICK 1
2 something (as a mechanical device) that performs a function or effects a desired end <invented many handy household *devices*>
syn contraption, contrivance; *compare* GADGET 1
rel appliance, implement, instrument, tool, utensil; apparatus, machine, mechanism; expedient, makeshift, resort, resource, shift; creation, invention; dingus, doohickey, hickey, thingumbob
3 *syn* see FIGURE 3
rel attribute, emblem, symbol, type; insignia, motto
deviceful *adj syn* see INVENTIVE
devil *n* **1** *often cap* the personal supreme spirit of evil and unrighteousness in Jewish and Christian theology
syn Apollyon, Beelzebub, ||Cloot(s), ||Clootie, diablo, fiend, Lord Harry, Lucifer, Old Gooseberry, Old Nick, Old Scratch, Satan, serpent
rel cacodemon; dybbuk
idiom Prince of Darkness
2 an extremely and malignantly wicked person <he was a *devil* who would stop at nothing to get what he wanted>
syn Archfiend, demon, fiend, Satan, succubus; *compare* SCAMP, VILLAIN 1
rel blackguard, caitiff, knave; scoundrel, villain; beast, brute
3 *syn* see SCAMP
||**devil–devil** *n syn* see SPELL
||**devil–dodger** *n syn* see CLERGYMAN
deviling *n syn* see IMP 1
devilish *adj* **1** *syn* see FIENDISH
rel iniquitous, nefarious, villainous; accursed, cursed, damnable, execrable; bad, evil, wicked
ant angelic
2 *syn* see SATANIC 1
devilkin *n syn* see IMP 1
devil–may–care *adj syn* see WILD 7
rel rash, reckless
con careful, heedful, responsible, thoughtful
devilment *n syn* see MISCHIEVOUSNESS
devilry *n syn* see MISCHIEVOUSNESS

---

syn synonym(s) *rel* related word(s)
ant antonym(s) *con* contrasted word(s)
idiom idiomatic equivalent(s)
|| use limited; if in doubt, see a dictionary

‖**devil's–bones** *n pl* ***syn*** see DICE
deviltry *n* ***syn*** see MISCHIEVOUSNESS
devious *adj* **1** ***syn*** see OBSCURE 2
2 ***syn*** see CROOKED 1
rel deviating, digressing, diverting
ant straightforward
3 ***syn*** see ERRATIC 1
4 ***syn*** see ERRANT 2
rel artful, crafty, cunning, foxy, insidious, sly, tricky
5 ***syn*** see UNDERHAND
ant straightforward
devise *n* ***syn*** see LEGACY 1
devise *vb* **1** ***syn*** see PLAN 2
2 ***syn*** see CONTRIVE 2
rel create, discover; forge, form, shape; design
3 ***syn*** see PLOT
4 ***syn*** see WILL
devitalize *vb* ***syn*** see DESICCATE 2
rel deprive; eviscerate, weaken
ant vitalize
devoid *adj* showing a want or lack <a poem *devoid* of worth>
syn destitute, empty, innocent, void
rel bare, barren; lacking, wanting; deficient
con filled, full; furnished, provided, supplied
ant replete
devoir *n* **1** ***syn*** see OBLIGATION 2
2 ***syn*** see TASK 1
devolution *n* ***syn*** see DETERIORATION 1
rel regression, regressiveness, retrogression, retrogressiveness; receding, recession, retrogradation, retrograding
con development; progress, progression
ant evolution
devote *vb* **1** to set apart for a particular and often a better or higher use or end <a woman who *devotes* her life to helping others>
syn consecrate, dedicate, hallow
rel sanctify, vow; commit, confide, consign, entrust
idiom set apart
2 ***syn*** see GIVE 1
3 ***syn*** see ADDRESS 3
rel attempt, endeavor, strive, struggle, try; employ, use, utilize
devote (to) *vb* ***syn*** see HABITUATE 2
rel attach, wrap (up)
devoted *adj* ***syn*** see LOVING
rel constant, faithful, loyal, true; thoughtful; fervid, zealous
devotee *n* **1** ***syn*** see ADDICT
2 ***syn*** see AMATEUR 1
devotion *n* **1** ***syn*** see FIDELITY 1
rel enthusiasm, fervor, passion, zeal; affection, attachment, love; consecration, dedication, devotement
2 ***syn*** see LOVE 1
devour *vb* **1** ***syn*** see EAT 1
2 ***syn*** see EAT UP 1
idiom eat like a horse, eat one's head off
3 ***syn*** see CONSUME 1
4 ***syn*** see RAVAGE
rel demolish, destroy; ruin, wreck; dissipate, squander
5 to exhibit avid interest in or enjoyment of <the crowd *devoured* the lurid scene>
syn ‖eat up
rel delight (in), enjoy, rejoice (in), relish, revel (in); feast (on), gloat (over *or* on)
con avoid, eschew, shun
devout *adj* showing fervor in the practice of religion <a *devout* churchgoer>
syn godly, holy, pietistic, pious, prayerful, religious
rel ardent, fervent, fervid, zealous; adoring, revering, venerating, worshiping
con impious, irreligious, ungodly, unholy; irreverent; apostate, backsliding
ant undevout
dexter *adj* ***syn*** see FAVORABLE 5
ant sinister
dexterity *n* **1** ***syn*** see ADDRESS 1
rel adeptness, skillfulness; effortlessness, smoothness
con awkwardness, maladroitness
ant clumsiness
2 ***syn*** see ART 1
dexterous *adj* **1** ready and skilled in physical movements <a *dexterous* worker>
syn adroit, clever, deft, handy, neat-handed, nimble
rel agile; adept, expert, masterly, proficient, skilled, skillful; easy, effortless, facile, smooth
con awkward, gauche, inept, maladroit
ant clumsy
2 ***syn*** see CLEVER 4
dexterousness *n* ***syn*** see ADDRESS 1
ant clumsiness
dextrorotatory *adj* ***syn*** see RIGHT-HANDED
ant levorotatory
diablerie *n* **1** ***syn*** see MISCHIEVOUSNESS
2 ***syn*** see EVIL 3
diablo *n* ***syn*** see DEVIL 1
diabolic *adj* **1** ***syn*** see SATANIC 1
2 ***syn*** see FIENDISH
rel evil, ill, wicked
ant angelic
diabolism *n* ***syn*** see SATANISM
diabolonian *adj* ***syn*** see FIENDISH
diacritic *adj* ***syn*** see CHARACTERISTIC
diagnose *vb* ***syn*** see IDENTIFY
diagnostic *adj* ***syn*** see CHARACTERISTIC
diagnosticate *vb* ***syn*** see IDENTIFY
diagonal *adj* between horizontal and vertical in direction <cloth with a *diagonal* stripe>
syn bevel, beveled, bias, biased, slanted, slanting; *compare* INCLINED 3
diagonally *adv* in a line running across from corner to corner <decided to place the couch *diagonally* at the end of the room>
syn catercorner (*or* catty-corner *or* kitty-corner), cornerwise, slantingways, slantways, slantwise, ‖slaunchways
idiom on the bias
con parallelly, square, straight
‖**dial** *n* ***syn*** see FACE 1
dial *vb* ***syn*** see TUNE 3
dialect *n* **1** ***syn*** see LANGUAGE 1

2 a form of language that is not recognized as standard <the Doric *dialect* of ancient Greece>
syn argot, cant, jargon, lingo, patois, patter, slang, vernacular; *compare* TERMINOLOGY, VERNACULAR 3
rel localism, provincialism, regionalism

dialectic *n* ***syn*** see ARGUMENTATION

dialogue *n* **1** ***syn*** see CONVERSATION 1
2 ***syn*** see CONVERSATION 2

diametric *adj* ***syn*** see OPPOSITE

diapason *n* **1** ***syn*** see MELODY
2 ***syn*** see RANGE 5

diaphanous *adj* ***syn*** see FILMY

diarrhea *n* abnormally frequent intestinal evacuations with more or less fluid stools <they were taken with severe *diarrhea*>
syn ‖backdoor trots, dysentery, flux, Montezuma's revenge, ‖runs, scour(s), ‖squirts, summer complaint, ‖trots
idiom Montezuma's revenge, summer complaint

diatribe *n* ***syn*** see TIRADE

‖**dibs** *n pl* **1** ***syn*** see MONEY
2 ***syn*** see CLAIM 1

dice *n pl, sing* **die** a pair or set of small cubes marked on each face with from one to six spots and used in various games and in gambling by being shaken and thrown to come to rest at random <staked everything on a cast of the *dice*>
syn ‖African dominoes, bones, ‖cubes, ‖devil's bones, ‖ivory, ‖tats

dice *vb* ***syn*** see DISCARD

dicey *adj* ***syn*** see UNCERTAIN 1

dichotomize *vb* ***syn*** see SEPARATE 1

dick *n* **1** ***syn*** see DETECTIVE

dicker *vb* ***syn*** see HAGGLE 2

dickey *adj* ***syn*** see WEAK 2

dictate *vb* to promulgate expressly something to be followed, observed, obeyed, or accepted <the commission *dictated* the policies to be followed>
syn decree, impose, lay down, ordain, prescribe, set
rel control, direct, manage; guide, lead; govern, rule; say, tell, utter; bid, charge, command, enjoin, instruct, order

dictate *n* ***syn*** see COMMAND 1

dictative *adj* ***syn*** see DICTATORIAL

dictator *n* ***syn*** see TYRANT

dictatorial *adj* imposing one's will or opinions on others <the chief was inclined to be *dictatorial* with his subordinates>
syn authoritarian, authoritative, dictative, doctrinaire, dogmatic, magisterial; *compare* TOTALITARIAN 1
rel bossy, domineering, imperative, imperious, masterful, peremptory; absolute, arbitrary, autocratic, despotic, tyrannical; arrogant, haughty, overbearing, proud; firm, stern
con amenable, biddable, docile, obedient, tractable; menial, obsequious, servile, slavish, subservient

dictatorship *n* ***syn*** see TYRANNY

diction *n* ***syn*** see WORDING

dictionary *n* ***syn*** see TERMINOLOGY

dictum *n* ***syn*** see MAXIM

‖**dicty** *adj* ***syn*** see SNOBBISH

didactic *adj* overburdened with instruction and the proprieties <his speech to the new freshmen was painfully *didactic*>
syn moral, moralizing, preachy, schoolmasterish, sermonic, sermonizing, teachy
rel advisory, exhortative, hortative; preceptive
ant undidactic

‖**didder** *vb* ***syn*** see SHAKE 1

diddle *vb* **1** ***syn*** see IDLE
2 ***syn*** see CHEAT

diddle–daddle *vb* ***syn*** see IDLE

diddler *n* ***syn*** see SWINDLER

dido *n* **1** *usu* **didoes** *pl* ***syn*** see PRANK
2 ***syn*** see KNICKKNACK

die *vb* **1** to pass from physical life <he *died* at an advanced age>
syn cash in, ‖check out, conk, ‖cop out, ‖croak, decease, demise, depart, drop, expire, go, ‖kick in, ‖kick off, pass, pass away, pass out, peg out, perish, pip, pop off, ‖snuff (out), succumb, ‖swelt
idiom be gathered to one's fathers, bite the dust (*or* ground), breathe one's last, cash in one's checks (*or* chips), give up the ghost, ‖kick the bucket, ‖kick up one's heels, meet one's end, shuffle off this mortal coil, ‖snuff it, turn up one's toes (to the daisies)
con be, exist, subsist; flourish, thrive
ant live
2 ***syn*** see PERISH 2

die (down *or* away) *vb* ***syn*** see ABATE 4
rel recede; disappear
con ascend, mount, rise
ant come up

die *n* **1** *see* DICE
‖**2** ***syn*** see TOY 2

die–away *adj* ***syn*** see LANGUID

diehard *n* **1** an irreconcilable opponent of change <party *diehards* who would make no concessions>
syn bitter-ender, conservative, fundamentalist, old liner, praetorian, pullback, right, rightist, right wing, right-winger, standpat, standpatter, tory; *compare* REACTIONARY
rel mossback, old fogy, stick-in-the-mud; intransigent; true blue; right-center
con liberal, progressive, radical
2 ***syn*** see REACTIONARY

die–hard *adj* ***syn*** see CONSERVATIVE 1

differ *vb* **1** to be unlike or distinct in nature, form, or characteristics <the houses *differ* only in a few minor details>
syn disagree, vary
rel depart, deviate, diverge
con accord, conform, correspond
ant agree
2 to be of unlike or opposite opinion <men who *differ* on religious matters>

---

syn synonym(s) ***rel*** related word(s)
ant antonym(s) ***con*** contrasted word(s)
idiom idiomatic equivalent(s)
‖ use limited; if in doubt, see a dictionary

syn disaccord, disagree, discord, dissent, divide, vary
rel clash, conflict, jar; bicker, quarrel, squabble; argue, debate, dispute; oppose, protest (against)
idiom differ in opinion, hold opposite views
con coincide, concert, concur, harmonize; accord, conform, correspond
ant agree

difference *n* **1** *syn* see DISSIMILARITY
rel modification, variation
con equivalence, equivalency, sameness
ant resemblance
2 *syn* see DISCORD
rel clash, conflict
3 *syn* see VARIANCE 1

difference *vb* *syn* see KNOW 4

different *adj* **1** unlike in kind or character <could hardly be more *different*>
syn disparate, dissimilar, distant, divergent, diverse, other, otherwise, unalike, unequal, unlike, unsimilar, various
rel particular, single; distinctive, individual, peculiar; divers, sundry
con akin, analogous, comparable, like, parallel, similar, uniform; equal, equivalent, self-same
ant alike, identical, same
2 *syn* see DISTINCT 1

differential *adj* *syn* see DISCRIMINATORY

differentiate *vb* *syn* see KNOW 4
rel comprehend, understand
con confound, mistake
ant confuse

differently *adv* *syn* see OTHERWISE 1

difficile *adj* *syn* see HARD 6

difficult *adj* *syn* see HARD 6
rel problem, problematic
idiom easier said than done, no picnic, tough sledding
ant simple

difficultly *adv* *syn* see HARD 8

difficulty *n* **1** something obstructing one's course and demanding effort and endurance if one's end is to be attained <she encountered great *difficulties* on her way to success>
syn asperity, hardness, hardship, rigor, vicissitude
rel impediment, obstacle, obstruction, snag; dilemma, fix, jam, pickle, plight, predicament, quandary, scrape; emergency, exigency, pass, pinch, strait; bother, inconvenience, problem, trouble
idiom hard nut to crack, hard row to hoe, heavy sledding
2 *syn* see DEMUR 2
3 *syn* see QUARREL

diffident *adj* *syn* see SHY 1
rel blenching, flinching, shrinking; hesitant, reluctant
con assured, presumptuous, sanguine, sure; self-assured, self-confident, self-possessed, self-reliant; brazen, impudent, shameless
ant confident

difform *adj* *syn* see LOPSIDED

diffuse *adj* *syn* see WORDY
rel exuberant, lavish, profuse; casual, desultory, random; lax, loose, slack; lengthy, long
con concentrated; condensed
ant succinct

diffuse *vb* **1** *syn* see SPREAD 1
rel extend; expand
con compact, consolidate; center, centralize, focus
ant concentrate
2 *syn* see INTERFUSE 2

dig *vb* **1** to loosen and turn over or remove (as soil) with or as if with a spade <*dig* for potatoes> <*dug* through her drawer looking for the scarf>
syn ‖delve, excavate, grub, shovel, spade
rel quarry; enter, penetrate, pierce, probe; dig up, root, rootle, root out
2 to form by digging <*dig* a trench>
syn dig out, excavate, scoop, shovel, spade
3 *syn* see THRUST 2
‖**4** *syn* see RESIDE 1
5 *syn* see POKE 1
‖**6** *syn* see APPREHEND 1
7 *syn* see ENJOY 1

dig (into) *vb* *syn* see EXPLORE

dig *n* **1** *syn* see POKE 1
2 *syn* see SITE 3

digest *n* *syn* see COMPENDIUM 1
rel abridgment, synopsis

digest *vb* **1** *syn* see BEAR 10
2 *syn* see EPITOMIZE 1

digit *n* *syn* see NUMBER

dignification *n* *syn* see APOTHEOSIS 2

dignify *vb* *syn* see EXALT 1
con abase, debase
ant demean

dignitary *n* *syn* see NOTABLE 1

dignity *n* **1** *syn* see STATUS 2
2 *syn* see DECORUM 1
rel excellence, merit, perfection, virtue; ethicalness, ethics, morality, nobility, nobleness
con impropriety, indecency, indecorum, unseemliness
3 *syn* see ELEGANCE
rel augustness, grandeur, grandness, magnificence, majesty, nobility, nobleness; address, poise

dig out *vb* **1** *syn* see DIG 2
2 *syn* see RUMMAGE 3

digress *vb* **1** *syn* see SWERVE 2
2 to turn aside from the main subject of attention or course of argument <he *digressed* into too many side issues>
syn depart, divagate, diverge, excurse, ramble, stray, wander
rel drift, roam
idiom get off the subject, go off on a tangent
con advance, proceed, progress

digression *n* a departure from a subject or theme <a *digression* from the main point of the speech>
syn aside, discursion, divagation, excursion, excursus, parenthesis
rel episode, excurse, incident, underaction; deflection, deviation, divergence; departure; drifting, rambling, straying, wandering

‖**dike** (out *or* up) *vb* ***syn*** see DRESS UP 1
dilapidate *vb* ***syn*** see RUIN 2
rel crumble, decay, decompose, disintegrate; disregard, forget, ignore, neglect, overlook, slight
con mend, rebuild, repair; rejuvenate, renew, renovate, restore
dilapidated *adj* ***syn*** see SHABBY 1
rel damaged, impaired, injured, marred; crumbled, decayed
dilate *vb* ***syn*** see EXPAND 3
rel augment, enlarge, increase; extend, lengthen, prolong, protract; broaden, widen
con compress, condense, contract, shrink; attenuate
ant circumscribe; constrict
dilate (on *or* upon) *vb* ***syn*** see DISCOURSE 1
rel describe, narrate, recite, recount, rehearse, relate
con abbreviate, abridge, curtail, shorten
dilatory *adj* ***syn*** see SLOW 2
rel lax, neglectful, negligent, remiss, slack
con assiduous, busy, industrious, sedulous; prompt, quick, ready; hasty, impetuous, precipitate
ant diligent
dilemma *n* ***syn*** see PREDICAMENT
rel bewilderment, mystification, perplexity
idiom horns of a dilemma
dilettante *n* **1** ***syn*** see CONNOISSEUR
2 ***syn*** see AMATEUR 2
dilettante *adj* ***syn*** see AMATEURISH
dilettantish *adj* ***syn*** see AMATEURISH
dilettantist *adj* ***syn*** see AMATEURISH
diligent *adj* ***syn*** see ASSIDUOUS
rel persevering, persistent, persisting; unflagging
con deliberate, laggard, leisurely, slow; desultory
ant dilatory
‖**dilly** *adj* ***syn*** see FOOLISH 2
‖**dilly** *n* one that is remarkable or extraordinary of its kind <came up with a *dilly* of an idea to sell the product>
syn ‖corker, crackerjack, ‖daisy, dandy, ‖dinger, ‖doozer, humdinger, jim-dandy, knockout, ‖lalapalooza, ‖lulu, nifty, peach, ‖pip, pippin, ripper, ripsnorter, rouser
dilly *vb* ***syn*** see DELAY 2
dillydally *vb* ***syn*** see DELAY 2
dilute *vb* to make less strong or concentrated <*dilute* acid>
syn cut, thin, weaken
rel moderate, qualify, temper; deliquesce, liquefy; alter, modify
con enrich, fortify, richen, upgrade; condense, densify, evaporate, thicken
ant concentrate
dilute *adj* of relatively low strength or concentration <*dilute* acid>
syn diluted, thin, washy, watered-down, waterish, watery, weak
rel reduced; adulterated, sophisticated; impaired, impoverished, weakened
con condensed, densified, thickened
ant concentrated
diluted *adj* ***syn*** see DILUTE
ant concentrated
dim *adj* **1** ***syn*** see DARK 1
ant bright
2 ***syn*** see DULL 7
‖**3** ***syn*** see DULL 9
4 ***syn*** see FAINT 2
con manifest, plain
ant distinct
dim *vb* **1** ***syn*** see OBSCURE
2 ***syn*** see DULL 1
3 ***syn*** see DULL 4
dime novel *n* a usually paperback melodramatic novel <read mostly *dime novels*>
syn dreadful, penny dreadful, shilling shocker, shocker, yellowback
rel bloodcurdler, chiller, ‖killer-diller; thriller; pulp
dimension *n* **1** *usu* **dimensions** *pl* ***syn*** see SIZE 1
2 *usu* **dimensions** *pl* ***syn*** see RANGE 2
dimensionality *n* ***syn*** see SIZE 1
diminish *vb* **1** ***syn*** see ABRIDGE 1
2 ***syn*** see DECREASE
rel ebb, subside, wane; moderate, temper; attenuate, extenuate
con aggravate, enhance, heighten, intensify
3 ***syn*** see DECRY 2
diminutive *adj* ***syn*** see TINY
‖**dimmet** *n* ***syn*** see EVENING 1
dimple *vb* ***syn*** see RIPPLE
‖**dimps** *n* ***syn*** see EVENING 1
‖**dimpsy** *n* ***syn*** see EVENING 1
dim–sighted *adj* ***syn*** see PURBLIND
dimwit *n* ***syn*** see DUNCE
dim–witted *adj* ***syn*** see RETARDED
con alert, keen
din *n* a welter of discordant sounds <the *din* of a machine shop>
syn babel, brouhaha, ‖chirm, clamor, hubbub, hullabaloo, jangle, music, pandemonium, racket, racketry, tintamarre, tumult, uproar; *compare* COMMOTION 4
rel blatancy, boisterousness, clamorousness, stridency; bedlam; clangor, clatter, rattle; clash, percussion; ‖row; noise, sound
con calm, lull, quietude, stillness; concord, consonance, harmony; melody, musicality, tunefulness
diner *n* ***syn*** see EATING HOUSE
‖**dinero** *n* ***syn*** see MONEY
ding *vb* **1** ***syn*** see STRIKE 2
2 ***syn*** see SURPASS 1
‖**ding** *n* ***syn*** see BLOW 1
ding–a–ling *n* ***syn*** see CRACKPOT
dingdong *adv* ***syn*** see HARD 3
dinge *n* ***syn*** see SADNESS

‖**dinger** *n* ***syn*** ‖DILLY, ‖corker, crackerjack, ‖daisy, dandy, humdinger, jim-dandy, knockout, ‖lalapalooza, ‖lulu

dingus *n* ***syn*** see DOODAD

dingy *adj* ***syn*** see SHABBY 1
rel grimed, smirched, soiled, sullied, tarnished; dull; dusky, gloomy, murky
con bright, brilliant, luminous, shining; clean, cleanly

dining table *n* ***syn*** see TABLE 1

dinky *adj* ***syn*** see MINOR 2

‖**dinky–di** *adj* ***syn*** see FAITHFUL 1

dinner *n* a usually elaborate meal served to guests or a group often to mark an occasion or honor an individual <the annual club *dinner*>
syn banquet, feast, regale, spread
rel ‖blowout, festival, fete, junket; breakfast, collation, luncheon

dinner table *n* ***syn*** see TABLE 1

dinosauric *adj* ***syn*** see HUGE

‖**dinsome** *adj* ***syn*** see VOCIFEROUS

dint *n* ***syn*** see POWER 4

dip *vb* **1** to plunge or thrust momentarily or partially under the surface of a liquid <*dip* a dress in cleansing fluid>
syn douse, duck, dunk, immerse, souse, submerge, submerse
rel pitch, plunge
2 to lift a portion of by reaching below the surface with something shaped to hold liquid <*dip* drinking water from a spring>
syn bail, lade, ladle, scoop
rel dish, spoon; bucket (up *or* out), draw
‖**3** ***syn*** see PAWN
4 ***syn*** see DUCK 2
5 ***syn*** see PLUMMET
6 ***syn*** see SET 12
7 ***syn*** see SWERVE 1

dip (into) *vb* ***syn*** see BROWSE

dip *n* **1** ***syn*** see DESCENT 4
2 ***syn*** see DECLINE 3
3 ***syn*** see DEPRESSION 2
‖**4** ***syn*** see PICKPOCKET

diplomacy *n* ***syn*** see TACT

diplomatic *adj* ***syn*** see TACTFUL
rel bland, smooth; courteous, polite; astute, shrewd; artful, crafty, guileful, wily
ant undiplomatic

‖**dippy** *adj* ***syn*** see FOOLISH 2

‖**dipsy–doodle** *n* ***syn*** see DECEPTION 1

dire *adj* **1** ***syn*** see FEARFUL 3
2 ***syn*** see DEPLORABLE
rel depressing, oppressing
3 ***syn*** see OMINOUS
4 ***syn*** see PRESSING
5 ***syn*** see ACUTE 6

direct *vb* **1** ***syn*** see ADDRESS 6
2 to turn something toward its appointed or intended mark or goal <*directed* her eyes to the door>
syn address, aim, cast, head, incline, lay, level, point, present, set, train, turn, zero (in)
rel beam; divert; fasten, focus
3 ***syn*** see ADDRESS 3
rel fix, set, settle
con deflect, divert; deviate, digress, diverge, swerve
4 ***syn*** see GUIDE
ant misdirect
5 ***syn*** see GOVERN 3
6 ***syn*** see CONDUCT 3
7 ***syn*** see COMMAND
rel assign, define, prescribe

direct *adj* **1** being or passing in a straight line of descent from parent to offspring <*direct* ancestors>
syn lineal
2 admitting free or continuous passage <a *direct* route to the beach>
syn straight, straightforward, through, uninterrupted
rel linear; continuous, unbroken, undeviating, unswerving
con circuitous, roundabout
ant indirect
3 ***syn*** see FRANK
ant devious
4 marked by absence of an intervening agency, instrumentality, or influence <he had no *direct* knowledge of the crime>
syn firsthand, immediate, primary
rel contiguous, next, proximate
ant indirect

direct *adv* **1** ***syn*** see DIRECTLY 1
2 ***syn*** see VERBATIM

direction *n* **1** ***syn*** see VIEWPOINT 2

directive *n* **1** ***syn*** see EDICT 1
2 ***syn*** see MEMORANDUM 2
3 ***syn*** see MESSAGE 1

directly *adv* **1** without deviation of course <the turnpike runs *directly* east and west>
syn dead, direct, due, right, straight, straightly, undeviatingly
idiom as the crow flies, in a beeline
con circuitously, deviously, round about; discursively, ramblingly
ant indirectly
2 ***syn*** see VERBATIM
3 ***syn*** see IMMEDIATELY 1
4 ***syn*** see AWAY 3
5 ***syn*** see PRESENTLY 1

direful *adj* **1** ***syn*** see FEARFUL 3
2 ***syn*** see OMINOUS

dirt *n* **1** ***syn*** see EARTH 2
2 ***syn*** see DECEPTION 1

dirt poor *adj* ***syn*** see POOR 1

dirty *adj* **1** soiled or begrimed with dirt <wash those *dirty* hands>
syn black, dungy, filthy, foul, grimy, grubby, grungy, impure, mucky, murky, nasty, soily, sordid, squalid, unclean, uncleanly
rel contaminated, defiled, polluted, tainted; dreggy; draggled, draggletailed, draggly
idiom dirty as a pig
con immaculate, spotless; unsoiled, unspotted, unsullied
ant clean
2 ***syn*** see IMPURE 1

ant clean
3 syn see OBSCENE 2
4 syn see WILD 6
dirty *vb* **1 syn** see SOIL 2
ant clean
2 syn see TAINT 1
idiom dirty one's hands
disability *n* **syn** see DISADVANTAGE
disable *vb* **1 syn** see DISQUALIFY
2 syn see PARALYZE 1
3 syn see WEAKEN 1
rel harm, hurt, mar, spoil; batter, maim, mangle, mutilate; ruin, wreck
con restore, resuscitate, revive, revivify
ant rehabilitate
disabuse *vb* to set free from mistakes (as in reasoning or judgment) <he was *disabused* of the notion that he was indispensable to the company>
syn purge, undeceive, undelude
rel amend, correct, emend, rectify, redress; disillude, disillusion, unblind; enlighten, illuminate; free, liberate, release
idiom open one's eyes, prick the (*or* one's) bubble, puncture one's balloon, set (*or* put) right (*or* straight)
con deceive, delude, mislead; dupe, gull
disaccord *vb* **1 syn** see CLASH 2
2 syn see DIFFER 2
ant accord
disaccord *n* **syn** see DISCORD
ant accord
disacknowledge *vb* **syn** see DISCLAIM
disadvantage *n* an unfavorable or prejudicial quality or circumstance <the machine has two serious *disadvantages*>
syn detriment, disability, drawback, handicap
rel bar, impediment, obstacle, obstruction; blocking, hamper, hindrance, imposition
con aid, assistance, help; service, usefulness, utility, value, worth
ant advantage
disadvantaged *adj* **syn** see UNDERPRIVILEGED
ant advantaged
disadvantageous *adj* **syn** see DEROGATORY
disadvise *vb* **syn** see DISSUADE
disaffect *vb* **syn** see ESTRANGE
rel agitate, discompose, disquiet, disturb, upset
ant win (over)
disaffection *n* **syn** see ESTRANGEMENT
disaffirm *vb* **syn** see DENY 4
disagree *vb* **1 syn** see DIFFER 1
ant agree
2 syn see DIFFER 2
ant agree
disagreeable *adj* **1 syn** see BAD 8
rel annoying, distressing, disturbing, woeful
ant agreeable
2 syn see IRRITABLE
ant agreeable
disallow *vb* **1 syn** see DENY 2
con accede, acquiesce, assent
ant allow
2 syn see DISCLAIM
rel debar, exclude, shut out
ant allow
disallowance *n* **syn** see DENIAL 1
disappear *vb* **syn** see VANISH
rel go, leave
ant appear
disappoint *vb* **syn** see FRUSTRATE 1
disapprove *vb* **1** to feel or express an objection <*disapprove* of his actions>
syn deprecate, discommend, discountenance, disesteem, disfavor, frown, object
rel blame, censure, condemn, criticize, denounce, reprehend, reprobate; decry, depreciate, detract, disparage, dispraise; expostulate, remonstrate
idiom look askance at, make a wry face at, not go for, take a dim view of, take exception to
con applaud, commend, compliment, recommend; accredit, certify, endorse, sanction; approbate, countenance, favor
ant approve
2 syn see DECLINE 4
disarm *vb* **1 syn** see PARALYZE 1
2 to influence favorably by persuasive words or acts <*disarmed* by her smile>
syn unarm, unsteel, win (over)
rel allure, attract, bewitch, captivate, charm, enchant, fascinate
con alert, caution, tip (off), warn
ant arm
disarming *adj* **syn** ingratiating, deferential, ingratiatory, insinuating, insinuative, saccharine, silken, silky
disarrange *vb* **syn** see DISORDER 1
rel mislay, misplace; displace, replace; overturn
ant arrange
disarray *n* **syn** see CONFUSION 3
con arrangement, marshaling
disarray *vb* **syn** see DISORDER 1
ant array
disassemble *vb* **syn** see DISMOUNT
disassociate *vb* **syn** see DETACH
disaster *n* a sudden calamitous event bringing great damage, loss, or destruction <a flood *disaster* struck the valley>
syn calamity, cataclysm, catastrophe, misadventure, tragedy, woe(s)
rel accident, casualty, fatality, mishap; adversity, distress, misadventure, mischance, misfortune; rock(s)
disastrous *adj* **syn** see FATAL 2
rel hapless, luckless, unfortunate; destructive
con fortunate, happy, lucky, providential
disavow *vb* **syn** see DISCLAIM
rel impugn, negate, negative
con allow, concede, grant; assert, justify, maintain
ant avow
disband *vb* to cease to exist as a unit <the dance group *disbanded* after a farewell concert>

---

syn synonym(s) **rel** related word(s)
ant antonym(s) **con** contrasted word(s)
idiom idiomatic equivalent(s)
‖ use limited; if in doubt, see a dictionary

syn break up, disperse, dissolve
rel dispel, dissipate, scatter; dichotomize, disjoin, disjoint, dissect, dissever, disunite, divide, divorce, part, separate, sever, sunder
idiom go their several ways, part company
con combine, concur, conjoin, cooperate, unite; assemble, collect, congregate, gather; call up, summon
ant band

disbelief *n* ***syn*** see UNBELIEF
rel atheism, deism; rejection, repudiation, spurning
con credence, credit, faith
ant belief

disbelieve *vb* to hold not to be true or real <*disbelieved* his professions of sincerity>
syn discredit, unbelieve
rel distrust, doubt, mistrust, question, suspect; eschew, reject, scorn, scout
con accept, ‖buy, swallow
ant believe

disbelieving *adj* ***syn*** see INCREDULOUS

disbodied *adj* ***syn*** see IMMATERIAL 1

disburden *vb* ***syn*** see UNLOAD

disburse *vb* **1** ***syn*** see SPEND 1
2 ***syn*** see DISTRIBUTE 1

disbursement *n* ***syn*** see EXPENSE 1

discalceate *adj* ***syn*** see DISCALCED

discalced *adj* wearing only sandals on the feet <*discalced* monks>
syn barefoot, discalceate
con calced, shod

discard *vb* to get rid of <*discard* old clothes> <people who *discard* traditional values>
syn abdicate, cashier, cast, chuck, ‖deep-six, ‖dice, ditch, dump, jettison, junk, lay aside, reject, scrap, shed, ‖shoot, shuck (off), slough, throw away, throw out, wash out
rel abandon, desert, forsake; repudiate, spurn; dismiss, eject, oust
idiom do away with, let go by the board
con adopt, embrace, espouse, take on, take up; employ, use, utilize; hold, hold back, keep, retain; cherish, esteem, nurture

discarding *n* ***syn*** see DISPOSAL 2

discarnate *adj* ***syn*** see IMMATERIAL 1
ant carnate, incarnate

discept *vb* ***syn*** see DISCUSS 1

discern *vb* **1** ***syn*** see SEE 1
rel ascertain, discover; anticipate, apprehend, divine, foresee
2 ***syn*** see KNOW 4

discernible *adj* ***syn*** see PERCEPTIBLE
ant indiscernible

discerning *adj* ***syn*** see WISE 1
ant undiscerning

discernment *n* ***syn*** see WIT 3
rel intuition, reason; sagaciousness, sagacity
con crassness, density, slowness; blindness

discharge *vb* **1** ***syn*** see UNLOAD
2 ***syn*** see EXEMPT
3 ***syn*** see SHOOT 1
4 ***syn*** see FREE
rel dismiss, eject, expel, oust; eliminate, exclude
5 to give outlet to <the river *discharges* its waters into the bay>
syn disembogue, emit, flow, give off, pour, void
rel eject, exude, release
6 ***syn*** see DISMISS 3
rel displace, replace, supersede, supplant
con hire; contract
ant engage
7 to release from service with the armed forces <*discharged* from the army with the rank of sergeant>
syn ‖demob, demobilize, muster out, separate
rel disenroll; deactivate, inactivate; bounce, cashier, dismiss, drop, fire, sack
8 ***syn*** see CLEAR 5
9 ***syn*** see ANNUL 4

discinct *adj* ***syn*** see NEGLIGENT

disciple *n* ***syn*** see FOLLOWER
rel enthusiast, fanatic, zealot

disciplinary *adj* ***syn*** see PUNITIVE

discipline *n* **1** ***syn*** see PUNISHMENT
2 ***syn*** see WILL 3

discipline *vb* **1** ***syn*** see PUNISH 1
rel overcome, reduce, subdue, subjugate; bridle, check, curb, inhibit, restrain
2 ***syn*** see TEACH
rel guide, lead; conduct, control, direct, manage

disclaim *vb* to refuse to admit, accept, or approve <the senator *disclaimed* the comment attributed to him> <*disclaim* responsibility for a subordinate's mistake>
syn deny, disacknowledge, disallow, disavow, disown, repudiate
rel contradict, contravene, gainsay, traverse; refuse, reject, spurn; deprecate; belittle, disparage, minimize; abjure, forswear, recant, renounce, retract; challenge, criticize
idiom turn one's back on, wash one's hands of
con acknowledge, avow, own; accept, admit, receive, take
ant claim

disclose *vb* **1** ***syn*** see OPEN 2
2 ***syn*** see REVEAL 1
rel acknowledge, admit, avow, confess, own
idiom make public
con conceal, hide; camouflage, cloak, disguise, dissemble, mask

discolor *vb* **1** ***syn*** see TAINT 1
2 ***syn*** see STAIN 1

discolor *adj* ***syn*** see VARIEGATED

discombobulate *vb* **1** ***syn*** see DISCOMPOSE 1
2 ***syn*** see CONFUSE 2

discomfit *vb* ***syn*** see EMBARRASS
rel annoy, bother, irk, vex; disturb, perturb, upset

discomfiture *n* **1** ***syn*** see DEFEAT 1
2 ***syn*** see COMEDOWN
3 ***syn*** see EMBARRASSMENT
rel agitation, disquiet, perturbation, upset; commotion; prickles

discomforting *adj* ***syn*** see UNCOMFORTABLE
ant comforting

discommend *vb* ***syn*** see DISAPPROVE 1
rel admonish; criticize, reprehend; censure

con approve, endorse, sanction
ant commend; recommend
discommode *vb* ***syn*** see INCONVENIENCE
rel flurry, fluster, perturb, upset; bother, irk, vex
discommoding *adj* ***syn*** see INCONVENIENT
discommodious *adj* ***syn*** see INCONVENIENT
discompose *vb* **1** to destroy or impair one's capacity for collected thought or decisive action <*discomposed* by the rudeness of his friend>
syn agitate, bother, discombobulate, dismay, disquiet, disturb, flurry, fluster, perturb, unhinge, unsettle, untune, upset; *compare* EMBARRASS
rel disagree; annoy, irk, vex; harass, harry, pester, plague, worry
con calm, quiet, settle, soothe, tranquilize; allay, alleviate, assuage; appease, conciliate, mollify, pacify, placate, propitiate
ant compose
2 ***syn*** see DISORDER 1
ant compose
discomposure *n* ***syn*** see EMBARRASSMENT
ant composure
disconcert *vb* ***syn*** see EMBARRASS
rel bewilder, nonplus, perplex, puzzle
disconcertion *n* ***syn*** see EMBARRASSMENT
disconcertment *n* ***syn*** see EMBARRASSMENT
disconfirm *vb* ***syn*** see DISPROVE 1
disconnect *vb* ***syn*** see DETACH
ant connect
disconnected *adj* ***syn*** see INCOHERENT 2
ant connected
disconsolate *adj* **1** ***syn*** see DOWNCAST
rel comfortless, inconsolable; sorrowful, woeful; doleful, melancholy; unhappy
ant cheerful
2 ***syn*** see INCONSOLABLE
3 ***syn*** see GLOOMY 3
ant cheerful, cheery
disconsonant *adj* ***syn*** see INCONSONANT 1
discontent *adj* ***syn*** see DISCONTENTED
ant content
discontented *adj* showing or expressing a sense of grievance or thwarted aspirations or desires <*discontented* with his position>
syn discontent, disgruntled, dissatisfied, malcontent, malcontented, uncontent, uncontented, ungratified
rel disquieted, disturbed, perturbed, restless, upset; displeased; unhappy
con satisfied; gratified, pleased; happy; elated, exultant, jubilant, triumphant
ant contented
discontinuance *n* ***syn*** see END 2
ant continuance, continuation
discontinuation *n* ***syn*** see END 2
ant continuance, continuation
discontinue *vb* ***syn*** see STOP 3
ant continue
discontinuity *n* ***syn*** see GAP 1
ant continuity
discontinuous *adj* ***syn*** see INCOHERENT 2
ant continuous

||**disconvenience** *n* ***syn*** see INCONVENIENCE
ant convenience
||**disconvenience** *vb* ***syn*** see INCONVENIENCE
ant convenience
discord *n* the state of those who disagree and lack harmony <a household full of turmoil and *discord*>
syn conflict, contention, difference, disaccord, disharmony, dispeace, dissension, dissent, dissidence, dissonance, disunion, disunity, division, inharmony, mischief, strife, unpeace, variance
rel discrepancy, incompatibility, incongruity, inconsistency, inconsonance, uncongeniality; animosity, antagonism, antipathy, enmity, hostility, rancor; polarization; collision
con accord, consonance; agreement, concordance, concurrence
ant concord, harmony
discord *vb* **1** ***syn*** see CLASH 2
ant concord, harmonize
2 ***syn*** see DIFFER 2
ant accord
discordant *adj* **1** ***syn*** see INHARMONIOUS 2
2 ***syn*** see INCONSONANT 1
con according, agreeing, congenial, harmonious, harmonizing
ant concordant
3 ***syn*** see ANTIPATHETIC 1
ant concordant
4 ***syn*** see DISSONANT 1
discotheque *n* ***syn*** see NIGHTCLUB
discount *n* ***syn*** see DEDUCTION 1
discount *vb* **1** ***syn*** see DEDUCT 1
con boost, hike, increase, mark up, raise
2 ***syn*** see NEGLECT
3 ***syn*** see DECRY 2
discountenance *vb* **1** ***syn*** see EMBARRASS
idiom put out of countenance
2 ***syn*** see DISAPPROVE 1
rel reproach, reprove
con encourage, favor
ant countenance
discourage *vb* **1** to weaken the stamina, interest, or zeal of <the long winter and lack of fuel *discouraged* the settlers>
syn chill, deject, demoralize, dishearten, disparage, dispirit
rel depress, weigh; afflict, try; damp, dampen, droop; distress, trouble; bother, irk, vex
idiom take the heart out of
con cheer, embolden, hearten, inspirit, nerve, steel
ant encourage
2 ***syn*** see DISSUADE
rel check, inhibit, restrain; prevent; frighten, scare
idiom lay a wet blanket on, throw cold water on
con advocate, countenance, favor; approve, back, endorse

---

syn synonym(s) ***rel*** related word(s)
ant antonym(s) ***con*** contrasted word(s)
idiom idiomatic equivalent(s)
|| use limited; if in doubt, see a dictionary

THESAURUS

ant encourage
discouraging *adj syn* see GLOOMY 3
rel deterring; hindering
ant encouraging
discourse *n* **1** *syn* see SPEECH 1
2 a systematic, serious, and often learned exposition of a subject or topic <his *discourses* during the seminar were long remembered>
syn disquisition, dissertation, memoir, monograph, monography, thesis, tractate, treatise
rel article, essay, paper; lecture, sermon; rhetoric, speech, talk
discourse *vb* **1** to express oneself especially formally and at length <*discourses* knowledgeably about the laws of nature>
syn descant, dilate (on *or* upon), discuss, dissert, dissertate, expatiate, sermonize
rel converse, speak, talk, voice; argue, dispute; harangue, lecture, orate, perorate; amplify, develop, elaborate, enlarge, expand; explain, expound; comment, commentate, remark
2 *syn* see ACT 1
discourteous *adj syn* see RUDE 6
con chivalrous, civil, courtly, gallant
ant courteous
discover *vb* **1** *syn* see EXPOSE 4
2 *syn* see REVEAL 1
rel advertise, proclaim, publish
con repress, suppress
3 to become or be made aware of something not previously known <*discover* a secret>
syn ascertain, catch on, determine, find out, hear, learn, see, tumble, unearth
rel descry, detect, encounter, espy, hit (on *or* upon), meet (with), spot; discern, note, observe, perceive
idiom get wise to
con miss, overlook; disregard, ignore
discovery *n* the gaining knowledge of or ascertaining the existence of something previously unknown or unrecognized <the *discovery* of a new chemical element>
syn detection, espial, find, strike, unearthing
rel disclosure, exposition, exposure, revelation, uncovering
discreate *vb syn* see DESTROY 1
discredit *vb* **1** *syn* see DISBELIEVE
ant credit
2 to deprive of credibility <he *discredited* the rumor immediately>
syn blow up, disprove, explode, puncture, shoot
rel expose, show up; destroy, ruin
idiom bring to naught, knock the bottom out of, not leave a leg to stand on
con accept, believe, credit
discredit *n syn* see DISGRACE
ant credit
discreditable *adj syn* see DISREPUTABLE 1
discreet *adj* **1** *syn* see CAUTIOUS
con foolhardy
ant indiscreet
2 *syn* see PLAIN 1
3 *syn* see CONSERVATIVE 2
discreetness *n syn* see PRUDENCE 1
ant indiscreetness
discrepancy *n syn* see DISSIMILARITY
discrepant *adj syn* see INCONSONANT 1
rel different, disparate, divergent, diverse; disagreeing, varying
con agreeing, conforming, corresponding, jibing, squaring, tallying; alike, identical, like, parallel, similar, uniform
discrepate *vb syn* see KNOW 4
discrete *adj syn* see DISTINCT 1
con blended, fused, merged, mingled
ant indiscrete
discretion *n syn* see PRUDENCE 1
rel moderation, restraint; gumption, judgment, sense, wisdom
con asininity, fatuousness, foolishness, simplicity; foolhardiness, rashness, recklessness
ant indiscretion
discretionary *adj syn* see OPTIONAL
discriminate *vb syn* see KNOW 4
rel note, perceive, remark; collate, compare, contrast
ant confound
discriminating *adj syn* see ECLECTIC 1
rel careful; judicious, prudent, wise
ant undiscriminating
discrimination *n syn* see WIT 3
rel judgment, sense
con crassness, density, slowness
discriminative *adj syn* see DISCRIMINATORY
ant undiscriminative
discriminatory *adj* applying or favoring discrimination in treatment <*discriminatory* employment practices against women>
syn discriminative
rel biased, inequitable, partial, partisan, prejudiced, prepossessed, unfair, unjust
con dispassionate, equal, equitable, fair, impartial, just, objective, unbiased, uncolored, unprejudiced
ant nondiscriminatory
discrown *vb syn* see DEPOSE 1
disculpate *vb syn* see EXCULPATE
ant inculpate
discumber *vb syn* see EXTRICATE 2
discursion *n syn* see DIGRESSION
discuss *vb* **1** to exchange views about something in order to arrive at the truth or to convince others <met to *discuss* community needs>
syn agitate, argue, canvass, debate, discept, dispute, ||kick around, moot, pro-and-con, thrash out, toss (around)
rel deliberate, hash over, reason (out), talk over; consider, weigh
idiom consider pro and con, go into, reason the point
2 *syn* see DISCOURSE 1
rel elucidate, explicate, interpret
discussion *n syn* see CONFERENCE 1
disdain *n* **1** *syn* see DESPITE 1
rel antipathy, aversion; arrogance, haughtiness, insolence, superciliousness
con awe, fear, reverence
2 *syn* see PRIDE 3

disdain *vb* ***syn*** see DESPISE
con accept, receive, take; acknowledge, admit, own; esteem, respect
ant admire
disdainful *adj* ***syn*** see PROUD 1
rel rejecting, repudiating, spurning; contemning, despising, scorning, scouting; antipathetic, averse, unsympathetic
ant admiring; respectful
disdainfulness *n* ***syn*** see PRIDE 3
disease *n* **1** a kind or instance of impairment of a living being that interferes with normal bodily function <tuberculosis has become a controllable *disease*>
syn affection, ailment, complaint, condition, disorder, ill, infirmity, malady, sickness, syndrome; *compare* INFIRMITY 1, SICKNESS 1
rel bug, ‖epizootic, ‖misery, virus
2 ***syn*** see INFIRMITY 1
ant health
diseasedness *n* ***syn*** see SICKNESS 1
disedge *vb* ***syn*** see DULL 3
disembark *vb* to go ashore out of a ship <*disembark* at the next port>
syn debark, land
rel put in
con board, get on
ant embark
disembarrass *vb* ***syn*** see EXTRICATE 2
rel clear, rid, unburden
ant embarrass
disembodied *adj* ***syn*** see IMMATERIAL 1
disembogue *vb* ***syn*** see DISCHARGE 5
disembowel *vb* ***syn*** see EVISCERATE
disembroil *vb* ***syn*** see EXTRICATE 2
ant embroil
disemploy *vb* ***syn*** see DISMISS 3
disenable *vb* ***syn*** see DISQUALIFY
disenchanted *adj* ***syn*** see SOPHISTICATED 2
disencumber *vb* ***syn*** see EXTRICATE 2
rel alleviate, lighten, relieve
con depress, oppress, weigh
ant encumber
disenfranchise *vb* ***syn*** see DISFRANCHISE
disengage *vb* **1** ***syn*** see DETACH
rel free, liberate, release
con associate, connect, join, link, unite
ant engage
2 ***syn*** see LOOSE 3
disentangle *vb* ***syn*** see EXTRICATE 2
rel detach, disengage; part, separate, sever, sunder
con enmesh, involve
ant entangle, tangle
disenthrall *vb* ***syn*** see FREE
disenthrone *vb* ***syn*** see DEPOSE 1
disentranced *adj* ***syn*** see SOPHISTICATED 2
disentwine *vb* ***syn*** see EXTRICATE 2
disesteem *vb* ***syn*** see DISAPPROVE 1
disesteem *n* ***syn*** see DISGRACE
ant esteem
disfashion *vb* ***syn*** see DEFACE
disfavor *n* **1** ***syn*** see DISLIKE
rel distrust, mistrust
con approbation, approval; admiration, esteem, liking, regard, respect
ant favor
2 ***syn*** see DISGRACE
disfavor *vb* ***syn*** see DISAPPROVE 1
con accept, approbate, approve, countenance, go (for), hold (with)
ant favor
disfeature *vb* ***syn*** see DEFACE
disfigure *vb* ***syn*** see DEFACE
ant adorn
disfranchise *vb* to deprive of a legal right and especially of the right to vote <people subtly *disfranchised* by community apathy>
syn disenfranchise
rel deprive, take away
ant affranchise, enfranchise, franchise
disgorge *vb* **1** ***syn*** see VOMIT
2 ***syn*** see ERUPT 1
disgrace *n* the state of one who has lost esteem and good repute <retired in *disgrace* after the scandal became public>
syn contempt, discredit, disesteem, disfavor, dishonor, disrepute, ignominy, infamy, obloquy, odium, opprobrium, shame
rel abasement, debasement, debasing, degradation, humbling, humiliation; black eye, blot, brand, spot, stain, stigma
con admiration, regard; awe, fear, reverence; fame, glory, honor, renown, repute
ant esteem, respect
disgraceful *adj* ***syn*** see DISREPUTABLE 1
ant respectable; respectworthy
disgracious *adj* ***syn*** see RUDE 6
ant gracious
disgrade *vb* ***syn*** see DEGRADE 1
disgruntled *adj* ***syn*** see DISCONTENTED
disguise *vb* to alter so as to hide the true appearance or character of <*disguised* herself with a wig> <*disguised* his anger behind a false geniality>
syn camouflage, cloak, dissemble, dissimulate, dress up, mask
rel conceal, hide; obfuscate, obscure; belie, falsify, garble, misrepresent; affect, assume, counterfeit, feign, pretend, sham, simulate
con display, exhibit, expose, flaunt, parade, show; betray, disclose, discover, reveal
disguise *n* **1** ***syn*** see MASK 2
rel deception, delusion; speciousness
2 ***syn*** see PRETENSE 2
disguised *adj* ***syn*** see INTOXICATED 1
disguisement *n* ***syn*** see MASK 2
disgust *vb* to be offensive to the taste or sensibilities of <the sight of filth *disgusted* him>
syn nauseate, reluct, repel, repulse, revolt, sicken
rel offend, outrage

---

syn synonym(s) ***rel*** related word(s)
ant antonym(s) ***con*** contrasted word(s)
idiom idiomatic equivalent(s)
‖ use limited; if in doubt, see a dictionary

idiom make one sick, stick in one's craw (*or* crop *or* gizzard), turn one's stomach
con charm, entice, tempt; delight, gratify, please, rejoice, tickle
disgusted *adj* ***syn*** see FED UP
disgusting *adj* ***syn*** see OFFENSIVE
‖**dish** *vb* ***syn*** see CHAT 1
disharmonic *adj* ***syn*** see DISSONANT 1
ant harmonic, harmonious
disharmonious *adj* ***syn*** see DISSONANT 1
ant harmonic, harmonious
disharmonize *vb* ***syn*** see CLASH 2
ant harmonize
disharmony *n* ***syn*** see DISCORD
ant harmony
dishearten *vb* ***syn*** see DISCOURAGE 1
ant hearten
disheartening *adj* ***syn*** see GLOOMY 3
rel despondent, pessimistic
con encouraging, optimistic
ant heartening
disheveled *adj* ***syn*** see SLOVENLY 1
dishonest *adj* **1** unworthy of trust or belief <made a *dishonest* report on their progress>
syn deceitful, knavish, lying, mendacious, roguish, shifty, unhonest, untruthful
rel crooked, devious, furtive, oblique; faithless, false, perfidious, untrustworthy; cheating, cozening, ‖cronk, defrauding, double-dealing, fraudulent, swindling, two-faced; insidious, tricky
con conscientious, honorable, just, scrupulous, upright; aboveboard, forthright, straightforward; candid, fair, frank, open, plain; dependable, reliable, sure, trustworthy, trusty
ant honest
2 ***syn*** see CROOKED 2
dishonesty *n* ***syn*** see DECEPTION 1
dishonor *n* ***syn*** see DISGRACE
con reverence, veneration; authority, credit, influence, prestige, weight
ant honor
dishonorable *adj* ***syn*** see DISREPUTABLE 1
ant honorable
dish out *vb* ***syn*** see GIVE 3
dishy *adj* ***syn*** see BEAUTIFUL
disillusioned *adj* ***syn*** see SOPHISTICATED 2
con beguiled, deceived, deluded, misled
disimpassioned *adj* ***syn*** see COOL 2
ant heated, impassioned
disimprison *vb* ***syn*** see FREE
ant imprison
disimprove *vb* ***syn*** see DETERIORATE 1
ant improve
disinclination *n* ***syn*** see DISLIKE
ant inclination
disinclined *adj* lacking the will or desire to do something <*disinclined* to accept her story>
syn afraid, averse, backward, hesitant, indisposed, loath, reluctant, shy, uneager, unwilling, unwishful
rel antipathetic, unsympathetic; doubtful, dubious; opposing, resisting; balking, boggling, shying, sticking, stickling; objecting, protesting
con anxious, avid, eager, keen; disposed, predisposed, ready, willing
ant inclined
disingenuous *adj* lacking in candor and often giving a false appearance of simple frankness <had a *disingenuous* way of asking for advice when he really wanted help>
syn uncandid, unfrank
rel false, feigned, insincere, left-handed; artful, crafty, cunning, foxy, guileful, insidious, sly, tricky, wily; devious, indirect, oblique
con artless, naive, natural, simple, unsophisticated; candid, frank, open, plain; sincere, unfeigned; aboveboard, direct, straightforward
ant ingenuous
disinherit *vb* **1** to deprive (an heir apparent) of the right to inherit <the father *disinherited* his wayward son in his will>
syn cut off
rel disown, repudiate; dispossess
idiom cut off without a cent
2 ***syn*** see DEPRIVE 2
disinhume *vb* ***syn*** see EXHUME
ant inhume
disintegrate *vb* **1** ***syn*** see DECAY
rel deliquesce; disperse, dissipate, scatter
con articulate, concatenate; blend, coalesce, fuse, merge; associate, combine, conjoin, connect, join, link, unite
2 ***syn*** see DETERIORATE 1
disinter *vb* ***syn*** see EXHUME
ant inter
disinterest *n* ***syn*** see APATHY 2
ant interest
disinterested *adj* **1** ***syn*** see INDIFFERENT 2
rel negative, neutral
con concerned, curious; fervent, impassioned, passionate
ant interested
2 ***syn*** see NEUTRAL
rel fair, just, impartial, unbiased
con biased, prejudiced; involved
ant concerned
disject *vb* ***syn*** see STREW 1
disjoin *vb* ***syn*** see SEPARATE 1
disjoint *vb* **1** ***syn*** see SEPARATE 1
2 ***syn*** see DISORDER 1
disjointed *adj* ***syn*** see INCOHERENT 2
dislike *n* a state of mind or feeling marked by an inner avoidance of something usually felt as unpleasant or repugnant <a pronounced *dislike* for mathematics>
syn aversion, bad books, disfavor, disinclination, disliking, displeasure, disrelish, dissatisfaction, distaste, indisposition
rel detestation, hate, hatred; deprecation, disapproval; prejudice, scunner
idiom ‖a derry on
con affection, attachment, love; partiality, predilection, preference
ant liking
disliking *n* ***syn*** see DISLIKE
ant liking
dislimb *vb* ***syn*** see MAIM

dislimn *vb* ***syn*** see OBSCURE
dislocate *vb* **1** ***syn*** see DISORDER 1
2 ***syn*** see MOVE 4
disloyal *adj* ***syn*** see FAITHLESS
rel alienated, disaffected, estranged
ant loyal
disloyalty *n* **1** ***syn*** see INFIDELITY
ant loyalty
2 ***syn*** see TREACHERY
ant loyalty
dismal *adj* ***syn*** see GLOOMY 3
con animated, gay, lively; cheerful
dismals *n pl, used with* the ***syn*** see SADNESS
dismantle *vb* **1** ***syn*** see STRIP 2
con appoint, equip, outfit
2 ***syn*** see DESTROY 1
3 ***syn*** see REVOKE 2
4 ***syn*** see DISMOUNT
dismay *n* ***syn*** see FEAR 1
con aplomb, assurance, confidence, self-possession; mettle, resolution, spirit
dismay *vb* **1** to unnerve and check by arousing fear, apprehension, or aversion <*dismayed* by the task that lay ahead>
syn appall, consternate, daunt, horrify, shake
rel bewilder, confound, dumbfound, mystify, nonplus, perplex, puzzle; abash, discomfit, disconcert, embarrass, faze, rattle; discourage, dishearten; affright, alarm, frighten, scare, terrify
idiom set one back on one's heels, take aback
con assure, ensure, secure; excite, galvanize, pique, provoke, quicken, stimulate
2 ***syn*** see DISCOMPOSE 1
dismayed *adj* ***syn*** see AGHAST 2
rel discomfited, disconcerted, fazed, rattled
ant undismayed
dismember *vb* **1** ***syn*** see MAIM
rel part, separate, sever, sunder
2 ***syn*** see DISMOUNT
dismiss *vb* **1** ***syn*** see DIVORCE 2
2 ***syn*** see DECLINE 4
3 to let go from one's employ or service <during the recession thousands of employees were *dismissed*>
syn ax, boot (out), bounce, ‖can, cashier, discharge, disemploy, drop, fire, kick out, let out, sack, terminate, turn off
rel depose, deselect, displace, furlough, lay off, remove, retire, suspend, unseat; reject, turn away; riff
idiom give one the gate (*or* one's walking papers), let go; give the ax (*or* the can) to
con hire; contract, engage; get, obtain, procure, secure
ant employ
4 ***syn*** see EJECT 1
rel cast, discard, shed, slough
idiom send one to Coventry
5 to refuse to consider seriously <*dismisses* the other performers as mere amateurs>
syn kiss off, pooh-pooh
rel deride, mock, rally, ridicule, taunt, twit; flout, gibe, gird, jeer, scoff; contemn, despise, disdain, scorn, scout; reject
dismissive *adj* ***syn*** see PROUD 1
dismount *vb* to take down or apart from an assembled position <*dismount* a revolver for cleaning>
syn disassemble, dismantle, dismember, take down
rel detach, disengage; disconnect, disjoin, disunite, separate
idiom take apart, take to pieces
con assemble, construct, put together; combine, unite
disobedient *adj* refusing or neglecting to obey <the *disobedient* child refused to come in>
syn naughty, obstreperous, unruly; *compare* CONTRARY 3, NAUGHTY 1
rel headstrong, recalcitrant, willful; contumacious, insubordinate, rebellious
con amenable, biddable, docile, tractable; decorous, good, well-behaved
ant obedient
disoblige *vb* ***syn*** see INCONVENIENCE
con accommodate, convenience, favor
ant oblige
disorder *n* **1** ***syn*** see CONFUSION 3
con orderliness; pattern, plan
ant order
2 breach of public order <the overthrow of the government caused *disorder* in the country>
syn anarchism, anarchy, distemper, misrule, riot
rel anomie; agitation, commotion, convulsion, tumult, turbulence, turmoil, upheaval
ant order
3 ***syn*** see DISEASE 1
4 ***syn*** see SICKNESS 1
disorder *vb* **1** to undo the fixed or proper order of something <*disorder* the carefully arranged contents of a drawer>
syn derange, disarrange, disarray, discompose, disjoint, dislocate, disorganize, disrupt, distemper, disturb, jumble, ‖mammock, mess (up), mix up, muddle, muss (up), ‖mux, rummage, shuffle, tumble, unsettle, upset; *compare* CONFUSE 5
rel ball up, embroil; dishevel, rumple
idiom make hay of
con arrange, marshal, methodize, organize, systematize; align, array, line, line up, range; adjust, fix, regulate
ant order
2 ***syn*** see UPSET 5
disordered *adj* **1** ***syn*** see INCOHERENT 2
2 ***syn*** see INSANE 1
disorderly *adj* ***syn*** see TURBULENT 1
disorderly house *n* ***syn*** see BROTHEL
disorganize *vb* ***syn*** see DISORDER 1
ant organize
disown *vb* ***syn*** see DISCLAIM
ant own
disparage *vb* **1** ***syn*** see DECRY 2

---

syn synonym(s) ***rel*** related word(s)
ant antonym(s) ***con*** contrasted word(s)
idiom idiomatic equivalent(s)
‖ use limited; if in doubt, see a dictionary

ant applaud
2 ***syn*** see DISCOURAGE 1

disparagement *n* **1** ***syn*** see DETRACTION
rel animadversion, aspersion, reflection, stricture
2 ***syn*** see DESPITE 1

disparaging *adj* ***syn*** see DEROGATORY
rel underestimating, underrating, undervaluing
con acclaiming, extolling, praising; exalting, magnifying

disparate *adj* ***syn*** see DIFFERENT 1
rel discordant, discrepant, incompatible, inconsistent, inconsonant; distinct, separate
ant analogous, comparable

disparity *n* the state of being different (as in degree, rank, excellence, or number) <the *disparity* between the rich and the poor> <their stories showed significant *disparity*>
syn disproportion, imparity, inequality, unevenness
rel alterity, difference, dissemblance, dissimilarity, dissimilitude, distinction, divergence, divergency, otherness, unlikeness
con adequation, equality, equatability, equivalence, equivalency, sameness; correlation, correspondence, likeness; evenness
ant parity

dispassionate *adj* **1** ***syn*** see NEUTRAL
rel imperturbable, unflappable, unruffled
con fervent, vehement; intemperate
2 ***syn*** see FAIR 4
rel aloof, indifferent; frank, open; aboveboard, straightforward

dispatch *vb* **1** ***syn*** see SEND 1
rel hasten, quicken, speed
2 ***syn*** see KILL 1
3 ***syn*** see EAT UP 1

dispatch *n* **1** ***syn*** see HASTE 1
con dawdling, loitering, procrastination
ant delay
2 ***syn*** see ALACRITY
rel diligence, industriousness

dispeace *n* ***syn*** see DISCORD

dispel *vb* ***syn*** see SCATTER 1
rel dismiss, eject, expel, oust; crumble, disintegrate

dispensable *adj* capable of being dispensed with <many household gadgets are readily *dispensable*>
syn nonessential, unessential, unrequired
rel needless, unnecessary, unneeded; minor, trivial, unimportant
con essential, imperative, necessary, necessitous, required; vital
ant indispensable

dispensation *n* ***syn*** see FAVOR 4

dispense *vb* **1** ***syn*** see DISTRIBUTE 1
2 ***syn*** see GIVE 3
rel portion, prorate
3 ***syn*** see ADMINISTER 2
4 ***syn*** see HANDLE 2
5 ***syn*** see EXEMPT

disperse *vb* **1** ***syn*** see SCATTER 1
rel discharge, dismiss
con call, cite, convene, convoke, summon
ant assemble, congregate; collect
2 ***syn*** see DISTRIBUTE 1
3 ***syn*** see SPREAD 1
4 ***syn*** see DISBAND

dispirit *vb* ***syn*** see DISCOURAGE 1
idiom dampen (*or* lower) one's spirits
ant inspirit

dispirited *adj* ***syn*** see DOWNCAST
rel melancholy, sad
ant high-spirited, inspirited

dispiriting *adj* ***syn*** see GLOOMY 3
rel dejecting, distressing; oppressing
ant inspiriting

displace *vb* **1** ***syn*** see BANISH
2 ***syn*** see DEPOSE 1
3 ***syn*** see SUPPLANT 1

displaced person *n* ***syn*** see REFUGEE

displacement *n* ***syn*** see EXILE 1

display *vb* **1** ***syn*** see OPEN 2
rel demonstrate, evidence, evince, lay out, manifest, show
con camouflage, cloak, disguise, dissemble, mask; conceal, hide, secrete
2 ***syn*** see SHOW 4
3 ***syn*** see SHOW 1

display *n* **1** ***syn*** see EXHIBITION 1
2 a striking or spectacular exhibition <a parvenu's *display* of wealth>
syn array, fanfare, panoply, parade, pomp, shine, show
rel ostentation, ostentatiousness, pretension, pretentiousness, showiness; setout

displeasing *adj* ***syn*** see BAD 8
rel annoying, bothersome, irksome, vexing
con agreeable, gratifying, pleasant
ant pleasing

displeasure *n* ***syn*** see DISLIKE
rel anger; vexation
con delight, enjoyment
ant pleasure

disponible *adj* ***syn*** see AVAILABLE 1

disport *n* ***syn*** see PLAY 1
rel jollity, merriment

disport *vb* **1** ***syn*** see SHOW 4
2 ***syn*** see BEHAVE 1
3 ***syn*** see PLAY 1

disposal *n* **1** ***syn*** see ORDER 3
2 the act of ridding oneself of something <incinerators used for the *disposal* of trash>
syn discarding, disposition, dumping, jettison, junking, relegation, riddance, scrapping, throwing away
rel chucking, clearance; demolishing, demolition, destroying, destruction
con acquirement, acquisition; accumulation, collection, cumulation, deposit, hoard, trove

dispose *vb* **1** ***syn*** see INCLINE 3
ant indispose
2 ***syn*** see ORDER 1

disposed *adj* ***syn*** see WILLING 1
ant indisposed

disposition *n* **1** ***syn*** see DISPOSAL 2
rel control, controlling, direction, management

2 ***syn*** see ORDER 3

3 the complex of especially mental and emotional qualities that distinguish an individual <a man of irritable *disposition*>

syn character, complexion, humor, individualism, individuality, makeup, nature, personality, temper, temperament

rel mood, tone, vein; cast, stamp, tenor, type; being; identity

idiom frame of mind

4 ***syn*** see LEANING 2

dispossess *vb* ***syn*** see DEPRIVE 2

con provide, supply

dispossession *n* ***syn*** see PRIVATION 2

dispraise *vb* ***syn*** see DECRY 2

ant praise

disproportion *n* ***syn*** see DISPARITY

disproportional *adj* ***syn*** see LOPSIDED

disproportionate *adj* ***syn*** see LOPSIDED

ant proportionate

disprove *vb* **1** to show by presenting evidence that something is not true <the defendant's claims were *disproved* by the testimony>

syn break, confound, confute, controvert, disconfirm, evert, rebut, refute

rel contravene, impugn, negative, traverse; overthrow, overturn

con evidence, show; demonstrate, display, illustrate, manifest; argue, bespeak, tell

ant prove

2 ***syn*** see DISCREDIT 2

disputable *adj* ***syn*** see MOOT

disputation *n* ***syn*** see ARGUMENTATION

disputatious *adj* ***syn*** see CONTENTIOUS 2

dispute *vb* **1** ***syn*** see ARGUE 2

con give in, surrender

2 ***syn*** see DISCUSS 1

rel confute, controvert, disprove, rebut, refute

con allow, grant

ant concede

3 ***syn*** see QUESTION 2

4 ***syn*** see RESIST

dispute *n* **1** ***syn*** see ARGUMENT 2

rel conflict, discord, dissension, strife

2 ***syn*** see QUARREL

disqualified *adj* ***syn*** see UNFIT 2

ant qualified

disqualify *vb* to deprive of a power, right, or privilege <a conviction of perjury *disqualified* him from being a witness>

syn disable, disenable, incapacitate

rel bar, bate, debar, eliminate, except, exclude, rule out, suspend

con empower, enable

ant qualify

disquiet *vb* ***syn*** see DISCOMPOSE 1

rel distress, trouble

con calm, compose, lull, still

ant quiet, soothe, tranquilize

disquiet *n* **1** ***syn*** see CARE 2

ant quiet

2 ***syn*** see UNREST

ant quiet

disquietude *n* **1** ***syn*** see CARE 2

2 ***syn*** see UNREST

ant quietness, quietude

disquisition *n* ***syn*** see DISCOURSE 2

rel inquiry, investigation; argumentation, debate, disputation

disquisitive *adj* ***syn*** see INQUISITIVE 1

disrate *vb* ***syn*** see DEGRADE 1

disregard *vb* ***syn*** see NEGLECT

con attend, mind, tend, watch; note, notice, observe, remark

ant regard

disregard *n* ***syn*** see APATHY 2

rel forgetting, ignoring, neglecting, omission, omitting, overlooking, slighting

con consideration, thoughtfulness

disregardful *adj* ***syn*** see NEGLIGENT

ant regardful

disrelish *n* ***syn*** see DISLIKE

ant relish

disremember *vb* ***syn*** see FORGET 1

disreputable *adj* **1** not reputable or decent <was punished for his *disreputable* conduct>

syn discreditable, disgraceful, dishonorable, ignominious, inglorious, shabby, shady, shameful, shoddy, unrespectable

rel abject, mean, sordid; beggarly, cheap, contemptible, despicable, pitiable, scurvy, sorry

con admirable, creditable, estimable, honorable, respectable

ant reputable

2 ***syn*** see SHABBY 1

disrepute *n* ***syn*** see DISGRACE

ant repute

disrespect *n* ***syn*** see INSOLENCE

ant respect

disrespectful *adj* ***syn*** see RUDE 6

ant respectful

disrobe *vb* **1** ***syn*** see STRIP 1

2 ***syn*** see STRIP 2

disrupt *vb* **1** ***syn*** see OPEN 3

2 ***syn*** see DISORDER 1

dissatisfaction *n* ***syn*** see DISLIKE

ant satisfaction

dissatisfactory *adj* ***syn*** see BAD 1

ant satisfactory

dissatisfied *adj* ***syn*** see DISCONTENTED

rel annoyed, bothered, irked, vexed

con content, contented, gratified

ant satisfied

dissect *vb* **1** ***syn*** see SEPARATE 1

2 ***syn*** see CUT 5

rel penetrate, pierce, probe

3 ***syn*** see ANALYZE

dissection *n* ***syn*** see ANALYSIS 1

rel examination, inspection, review, scrutiny; criticism, critique

dissemblance *n* ***syn*** see DISSIMILARITY

ant resemblance, semblance

dissemblance *n* ***syn*** see DECEIT 1

---

syn synonym(s) ***rel*** related word(s)

ant antonym(s) ***con*** contrasted word(s)

idiom idiomatic equivalent(s)

‖ use limited; if in doubt, see a dictionary

dissemble *vb* ***syn*** see DISGUISE
con demonstrate, evidence, evince, manifest, show
dissembler *n* ***syn*** see HYPOCRITE
disseminate *vb* **1** ***syn*** see SPREAD 1
2 ***syn*** see DECLARE 1
3 ***syn*** see STREW 1
dissension *n* ***syn*** see DISCORD
rel altercation, bickering, quarrel, wrangle; argument, controversy, dispute
con amity, friendship, goodwill
ant accord; comity
dissent *vb* ***syn*** see DIFFER 2
rel balk, boggle, demur, shy, stickle
con accede, acquiesce, agree, subscribe
ant assent; concur
dissent *n* **1** ***syn*** see DISCORD
2 ***syn*** see HERESY
rel disagreement, nonagreement, nonconcurrence
dissenter *n* ***syn*** see HERETIC
dissert *vb* ***syn*** see DISCOURSE 1
dissertate *vb* ***syn*** see DISCOURSE 1
dissertation *n* ***syn*** see DISCOURSE 2
rel exposition; argumentation, disputation
dissever *vb* **1** ***syn*** see SEPARATE 1
2 ***syn*** see CUT 5
dissidence *n* **1** ***syn*** see DISCORD
2 ***syn*** see HERESY
dissident *adj* ***syn*** see HERETICAL
dissident *n* ***syn*** see HERETIC
dissimilar *adj* ***syn*** see DIFFERENT 1
rel antithetical, antonymous, contradictory, contrary, opposite
ant similar
dissimilarity *n* lack of agreement or correspondence or an instance of this <the *dissimilarities* in the cultures of the two countries>
syn alterity, difference, discrepancy, dissemblance, dissimilitude, distance, distinction, divarication, divergence, divergency, otherness, unlikeness
rel disparity, diversity; discordance, incongruity, inconsistency, inconsonance; discord, variance; severance; offset; margin
con affinity, analogy, likeness, resemblance, similitude; accordance, congruity, consistency, consonance; agreement, conformity, correspondence
ant similarity
dissimilitude *n* ***syn*** see DISSIMILARITY
ant similitude
dissimulate *vb* ***syn*** see DISGUISE
dissimulation *n* ***syn*** see DECEIT 1
rel camouflaging, cloaking, disguising, dissembling, masking; concealing, hiding, secreting; feigning, pretending, pretense, shamming; hypocrisy, pharisaism, sanctimony
dissimulator *n* ***syn*** see HYPOCRITE
dissipate *vb* **1** ***syn*** see SCATTER 1
rel crumble, disintegrate
ant accumulate; concentrate (*as efforts, thoughts*)
2 ***syn*** see WASTE 2
rel disappear, evanesce, evaporate, vanish
ant absorb (*as time, attention*)
dissipation *n* ***syn*** see ENTERTAINMENT
dissociate *vb* ***syn*** see DETACH
rel alienate, estrange
ant associate
dissolute *adj* ***syn*** see ABANDONED 2
rel lax, light, loose, slack, wanton, wayward; fast, raffish, rakish, wild
dissolution *n* **1** ***syn*** see SEPARATION 1
2 ***syn*** see DEATH 1
dissolve *vb* **1** ***syn*** see DESTROY 1
2 ***syn*** see ADJOURN 2
3 ***syn*** see ANNUL 4
4 ***syn*** see LIQUEFY
5 ***syn*** see SOLVE 2
6 ***syn*** see DISBAND
dissonance *n* ***syn*** see DISCORD
dissonant *adj* **1** marked by a mingling of discordant sounds <the two bands playing different pieces at the same time sounded *dissonant*>
syn cacophonic, cacophonous, discordant, disharmonic, disharmonious, immusical, inharmonic, inharmonious, rude, unharmonious, unmusical
rel grating, harsh, hoarse, jarring, raucous, rugged, strident
con blending, chiming, concerted, harmonic, symphonious; euphonious, harmonious, mellifluous, mellow, melodious, musical; agreeable, pleasing
ant consonant
2 ***syn*** see INCONSONANT 1
dissuade *vb* to turn one aside from a purpose, a project, or a plan <they tried to *dissuade* a friend from making a mistake>
syn deter, disadvise, discourage, divert
rel derail, throw off; advise, counsel; exhort, prick, urge
idiom talk out of
con get, induce, prevail; affect, influence, touch
ant persuade
distance *n* **1** an extent of areal or linear measure <he did not know the *distance* he had walked>
syn length, stretch
rel area, extent; ambit, compass, extension, orbit, purview, radius, range, reach, scope, sweep
2 the length of a literal or figurative course traversed or to be traversed <she had come a long *distance* from her pitiful beginnings>
syn way, ways
rel extent, size; piece, spell
3 ***syn*** see EXPANSE
4 ***syn*** see DISSIMILARITY
distance *vb* ***syn*** see OUTSTRIP 1
distant *adj* **1** not close in space, time, or relationship <traveling to a more *distant* place> <the *distant* days of the Pilgrim fathers> <a *distant* cousin>
syn far, faraway, far-flung, far-off, off-lying, outlying, remote, removed
rel apart, isolated, obscure, out-of-the-way, retired, secret; secluded, sequestered
idiom at a distance

con close, near, nearby, next, nigh; adjacent, adjoining, contiguous
2 ***syn*** see DIFFERENT 1
3 ***syn*** see UNSOCIABLE
rel arrogant, haughty, proud; modest, retiring, shy
con forward, presuming, ||pushy, self-assertive

distaste *n* ***syn*** see DISLIKE
rel abhorrence, repugnance, repulsion, revulsion; antipathy, hostility
con relish, zest; appetite, desire; enjoyment
ant taste

distasteful *adj* **1** ***syn*** see UNPALATABLE 1
ant tasteful, tasty
2 ***syn*** see BITTER 2
rel obnoxious, repellent, repugnant, repulsive; abominable, detestable, hateful, odious
con agreeable, grateful, gratifying, pleasant, pleasing, welcome

distemper *vb* ***syn*** see DISORDER 1

distemper *n* ***syn*** see DISORDER 2

distend *vb* ***syn*** see EXPAND 3
rel augment, enlarge, increase; extend, lengthen
ant constrict

disthrone *vb* ***syn*** see DEPOSE 1

distill *vb* ***syn*** see DRIP

distinct *adj* **1** capable of being distinguished as differing <the novel has two related, but nevertheless *distinct,* plots>
syn different, discrete, diverse, separate, several, various
rel distinctive, individual, peculiar; particular, single, sole; especial, individual, special, specific; disparate, dissimilar, divergent
con identical, same, selfsame; corresponding, equivalent, like, similar
ant indistinguishable
2 ***syn*** see CLEAR 5
rel defined, prescribed; categorical, definite, explicit, express, specific; lucid, perspicuous; clear-cut, incisive, trenchant
con faint, obscure
ant indistinct; nebulous

distinction *n* **1** ***syn*** see DISSIMILARITY
con affinity, analogy, likeness, similarity, similitude
ant indistinction, resemblance
2 ***syn*** see EMINENCE 1
3 ***syn*** see HONOR 2

distinctive *adj* ***syn*** see CHARACTERISTIC
rel separate, single, unique; discrete, distinct, several
con common, familiar, ordinary, popular, vulgar; alike, analogous, comparable, identical, like, parallel; equal, equivalent, same

distinctively *adv* ***syn*** see ESPECIALLY 1

distinctiveness *n* ***syn*** see INDIVIDUALITY 3

distingué *adj* ***syn*** see GENTEEL 1

distinguish *vb* **1** ***syn*** see KNOW 4
rel divide, part; detach, disengage; demarcate, set off
con confuse, mistake
ant confound
2 ***syn*** see EXALT 1
3 ***syn*** see CHARACTERIZE 2
idiom set apart
4 ***syn*** see SEE 1
5 ***syn*** see IDENTIFY

distinguished *adj* ***syn*** see FAMOUS 2
rel courtly, dignified, grand, imposing, stately
ant undistinguished

distort *vb* **1** ***syn*** see MISREPRESENT
rel misconstrue, misinterpret; alter, change
2 ***syn*** see DEFORM
rel bend, curve, twist

distortion *n* ***syn*** see DEFORMITY

distract *vb* **1** ***syn*** see CONFUSE 2
2 ***syn*** see MADDEN 1

distracted *adj* ***syn*** see DISTRAUGHT

distraction *n* **1** ***syn*** see INSANITY 1
2 ***syn*** see ENTERTAINMENT

distrait *adj* **1** ***syn*** see ABSTRACTED
2 ***syn*** see DISTRAUGHT

distraught *adj* **1** agitated with doubt or mental conflict <*distraught* over the health of her child>
syn distracted, distrait, distressed, harassed, tormented, troubled, worried
rel agitated, concerned, discomposed, flustered, perturbed, upset; addled, confused, muddled; bewildered, nonplussed
idiom beside oneself
con composed, cool, imperturbable, nonchalant, unflappable, unruffled; calm, tranquil; unconcerned, undisturbed, unworried
ant collected
2 ***syn*** see INSANE 1

distress *n* the state of being in serious trouble or in mental or physical anguish <in great *distress* over the decision she had to make>
syn agony, dolor, misery, passion, suffering
rel affliction, cross, trial, tribulation, visitation; anguish, grief, heartbreak, sorrow, woe; exigency, pass, pinch, strait; difficulty, hardship, rigor, vicissitude; ache, pain, pang, throe, twinge
con comfort, comforting, consolation, solace, solacing; allaying, alleviation, assuagement, ease, relief, relieving; peace, security, tranquility

distress *vb* **1** ***syn*** see TRY 2
rel afflict, rack, torment, torture
con allay, alleviate, assuage, lighten, mitigate, relieve
2 to cause pain or suffering to <the death of his longtime friend *distressed* him deeply>
syn aggrieve, constrain, grieve, hurt, injure, pain
rel harass, strain, stress, try, trouble; depress, oppress, weigh
con comfort, console, solace; aid, assist, help
3 ***syn*** see TROUBLE 1
rel annoy, harry, pester, plague

distressed *adj* ***syn*** see DISTRAUGHT

distressing *adj* ***syn*** see DEPLORABLE

---

syn synonym(s) ***rel*** related word(s)
ant antonym(s) ***con*** contrasted word(s)
idiom idiomatic equivalent(s)
|| use limited; if in doubt, see a dictionary

THESAURUS

distribute *vb* **1** to give out, usually in shares, to each member of a group <*distributed* his possessions among his heirs>
syn deal, disburse, dispense, disperse, divide, ||divvy, dole (out), lot (out), measure (out), partition
rel allocate, allot, apportion, assign, mete (out); parcel, portion, prorate, ration; administer; dribble; bestow, donate, give, present
con assemble, gather; accumulate, hoard
ant amass; collect
2 *syn* see SPREAD 1
distribution *n* *syn* see ORDER 3
district *n* **1** *syn* see QUARTER 2
2 *syn* see LOCALITY 1
rel division, parcel
distrust *vb* to have no trust or confidence in <he *distrusted* most politicians>
syn doubt, misdoubt, mistrust, suspect, ||suspicion
rel disbelieve, discredit, unbelieve
con bank, count, depend, reckon, rely; commit, confide, consign, entrust
ant trust
distrustful *adj* *syn* see SUSPICIOUS 2
distrustfully *adv* *syn* see ASKANCE 2
disturb *vb* **1** *syn* see MOVE 4
2 *syn* see DISCOMPOSE 1
rel alarm, frighten, scare, terrify; bewilder, distract, perplex, puzzle; discommode, incommode, inconvenience, trouble
3 *syn* see DISORDER 1
rel displace, replace; move, remove, shift; interfere, intermeddle, meddle, tamper
con establish, fix, set, settle; adjust, regulate
disunify *vb* *syn* see ESTRANGE
disunion *n* **1** *syn* see SEPARATION 1
2 *syn* see DISCORD
disunite *vb* **1** *syn* see SEPARATE 1
2 *syn* see ESTRANGE
disunity *n* *syn* see DISCORD
disusage *n* *syn* see DISUSE
disuse *n* cessation of use, practice, or exercise <to keep the mind from falling into *disuse,* one must exercise one's reading abilities> <his muscles became atrophied from *disuse*>
syn desuetude, disusage
con appliance, application, employment, operation, play, usance; exercise
ant use
disused *adj* *syn* see OBSOLETE
ditch *n* *syn* see TRENCH
ditch *vb* **1** *syn* see DISCARD
||**2** *syn* see HIDE
||**dite** *n* *syn* see PARTICLE
dither *vb* **1** *syn* see SHAKE 1
2 *syn* see HESITATE
3 *syn* see CHAT 1
dither *n* **1** *syn* see JITTERS
2 *syn* see COMMOTION 2
dithyrambic *adj* *syn* see IMPASSIONED
ditto *n* *syn* see REPRODUCTION
ditty *n* *syn* see SONG 2
diurnal *adj* *syn* see DAILY
ant nocturnal
diuturnal *adj* *syn* see LASTING
divagate *vb* *syn* see DIGRESS 2
divagation *n* *syn* see DIGRESSION
divarication *n* *syn* see DISSIMILARITY
dive *vb* *syn* see PLUNGE 2
rel bound, jump, leap, spring; impel, move
dive *n* a shabby or disreputable place for drinking or entertainment <got a schooner of beer at the *dive* down the street>
syn barrelhouse, hangout, honky-tonk, joint
rel dump, hole; bar, barroom, lounge, pothouse, pub, saloon, taproom, tavern
||**diver** *n* *syn* see PICKPOCKET
diverge *vb* **1** *syn* see SWERVE 2
rel differ, disagree, vary; divide, part, separate
ant converge; conform
2 *syn* see DIGRESS 2
divergence *n* **1** *syn* see DISSIMILARITY
rel diversity, variety
con accord, concord, consonance, harmony
ant conformity, correspondence
2 *syn* see DEVIATION 1
rel division, parting, separation; differing, disagreeing, varying
con agreement, coincidence, concurrence
ant convergence
divergency *n* *syn* see DISSIMILARITY
divergent *adj* **1** *syn* see DIFFERENT 1
rel antithetical, contradictory, contrary, opposite; aberrant, abnormal, atypical
con alike, identical, parallel, same
ant convergent
2 *syn* see IRREGULAR 1
divers *adj* *syn* see SEVERAL 3
divers *pron, pl in constr* *syn* see SUNDRY
diverse *adj* **1** *syn* see DIFFERENT 1
rel contrasted, contrasting, contrastive; contradictory, contrary, opposite
con equal, equivalent, same
ant identical, selfsame
2 *syn* see DISTINCT 1
idiom of every description
3 *syn* see MANIFOLD
diversely *adv* *syn* see OTHERWISE 1
diverseness *n* *syn* see VARIETY 1
diversiform *adj* *syn* see MANIFOLD
diversion *n* **1** *syn* see DEVIATION 1
2 *syn* see PLAY 1
3 *syn* see ENTERTAINMENT
rel frivolity, levity
4 *syn* see ENJOYMENT 1
diversity *n* *syn* see VARIETY 1
rel difference, dissimilarity, distinction, divergence, divergency, unlikeness
ant uniformity; identity
divert *vb* **1** *syn* see TURN 6
rel swerve; alter, change, modify
con fix, set, settle
2 *syn* see DISSUADE
rel abstract, detach, disengage
3 *syn* see AMUSE
rel delight, gladden, please, regale, tickle
divertissement *n* *syn* see ENTERTAINMENT

divest *vb* **1** ***syn*** see STRIP 2
ant invest, vest; apparel, attire, clothe
2 ***syn*** see DEPRIVE 2
rel despoil, plunder, spoil
ant invest, vest
divestiture *n* ***syn*** see PRIVATION 2
divide *vb* **1** ***syn*** see SEPARATE 1
rel carve, chop, cut
ant unite
2 ***syn*** see DISTRIBUTE 1
3 ***syn*** see APPORTION 2
rel allocate, allot, assign
4 ***syn*** see DIFFER 2
rel part, separate
con combine, concur, conjoin, cooperate
ant unite
dividend *n* ***syn*** see REWARD
divine *n* ***syn*** see CLERGYMAN
divine *vb* ***syn*** see FORESEE
divine *adj* **1** of or relating to God or a god <the *divine* will>
syn deific, godly
rel chthonian
2 like or like that of God or a god <men who aspire to *divine* honors>
syn deific, godlike
rel extramundane, superhuman, superphysical, transmundane
3 ***syn*** see MARVELOUS 2
division *n* **1** ***syn*** see PART 1
2 ***syn*** see SEPARATION 1
3 ***syn*** see DISCORD
divorce *n* ***syn*** see SEPARATION 1
divorce *vb* **1** ***syn*** see SEPARATE 1
rel disaffect, wean
2 to end a marriage by legal action <unable to agree, they decided to *divorce*><*divorced* his wife>
syn dismiss, put away, unmarry
rel break up, separate, split; annul, cancel
divorcement *n* ***syn*** see SEPARATION 1
divulge *vb* ***syn*** see REVEAL 1
rel proclaim; gossip, tattle
‖**divvy** *vb* **1** ***syn*** see DISTRIBUTE 1
2 ***syn*** see APPORTION 2
‖**dizzard** *n* ***syn*** see DUNCE
dizzy *adj* **1** ***syn*** see GIDDY 1
rel asinine, fatuous, foolish; inane
2 affected by a sensation of being whirled about or around <the speed with which she dispatched her tasks made the onlookers *dizzy*>
syn giddy, light, light-headed, swimming, swimmy, vertiginous
rel reeling, whirling; bewildered, confounded, distracted, puzzled; addled, befuddled, confused, dazed, dazzled, fuddled, muddled
idiom with spots before one's eyes
3 ***syn*** see EXCESSIVE 1
dizzy *vb* ***syn*** see CONFUSE 2
do *vb* **1** ***syn*** see PERFORM 2
2 ***syn*** see CLOSE 3
3 ***syn*** see ACT 1
4 ***syn*** see CHEAT
idiom do out of, sell one a bill of goods
5 ***syn*** see COOK 1
6 ***syn*** see BEHAVE 1
7 ***syn*** see SHIFT 5
8 ***syn*** see HAPPEN 1
9 ***syn*** see TRAVEL 2
10 ***syn*** see SERVE 3
11 ***syn*** see SERVE 5
‖**do** *n* ***syn*** see SUCCESS
doable *adj* ***syn*** see POSSIBLE 1
doc *n* ***syn*** see PHYSICIAN
docile *adj* ***syn*** see OBEDIENT
rel adaptable, pliable, pliant
con obstinate, self-willed, stubborn, willful
ant indocile; ungovernable, unruly
‖**docious** *adj* ***syn*** see OBEDIENT
dock *n* ***syn*** see WHARF
docket *n* ***syn*** see PROGRAM 1
doctor *n* ***syn*** see PHYSICIAN
doctor *vb* **1** ***syn*** see TREAT 4
2 ***syn*** see MEND 2
3 ***syn*** see ADULTERATE
doctrinaire *adj* ***syn*** see DICTATORIAL
rel bullheaded, dogged, mulish, obstinate, pertinacious, pigheaded, stiff-necked, stubborn
ant undoctrinaire
doctrine *n* a principle accepted as valid and authoritative <the *doctrine* of evolution>
syn canon, dogma, tenet
rel instruction, teaching; axiom, basic, fundamental, principle
idiom article of belief (*or* faith)
document *n* **1** something preserved and serving as evidence (as of an event, a situation, or the culture of a period) <ceramic and flint artifacts provide our only *document* of this ancient people>
syn archive(s), monument, record
rel evidence, testimony
2 *usu* **documents** *pl* ***syn*** see CREDENTIALS
documentation *n* ***syn*** see CREDENTIALS
doddering *adj* ***syn*** see SENILE
doddery *adj* ***syn*** see SENILE
dodge *vb* **1** to avoid or evade by some maneuver or shift <*dodging* in and out among the crowd> <*dodged* his pursuer with ease>
syn duck, fence, parry, shirk, sidestep
rel malinger; avoid, elude, escape, evade, skirt; slide, slip; short-circuit
idiom fight shy of
con ‖banter, beard, brave, challenge, dare, defy, front, venture; confront, encounter, meet
ant face
2 ***syn*** see EQUIVOCATE 2
dodo *n* ***syn*** see DUNCE
‖**dods** *n pl* ***syn*** see SULK
‖**dodunk** *n* ***syn*** see DUNCE
doff *vb* ***syn*** see REMOVE 3
do for *vb* ***syn*** see HELP 1
dofunny *n* ***syn*** see DOODAD

syn synonym(s) ***rel*** related word(s)
ant antonym(s) ***con*** contrasted word(s)
idiom idiomatic equivalent(s)
‖ use limited; if in doubt, see a dictionary

dog *n* **1** a highly variable carnivorous domesticated mammal <many households have *dogs* as pets>
syn bowwow, canine, hound, ||pooch, tyke
rel pup, puppy; cur, ||feist, mongrel, mutt
2 *syn* see SNOT 1
3 *syn* see FRANKFURTER
4 *syn* see JALOPY
dog *vb syn* see TAIL
Dogberry *n syn* see POLICEMAN
dogfall *n syn* see DRAW 4
dogfight *n syn* see BRAWL 2
dogged *adj* **1** *syn* see INFLEXIBLE 2
2 *syn* see PERSISTENT 1
doggery *n syn* see RABBLE 2
doggish *adj syn* see DAPPER
doggone *adj* **1** *syn* see DAMNED 2
2 *syn* see UTTER
doggy *adj syn* see DAPPER
dogma *n syn* see DOCTRINE
rel belief, conviction, persuasion, view
dogmatic *adj* **1** *syn* see DICTATORIAL
2 *syn* see DEDUCTIVE
dog nap *n syn* see NAP
dog's age *n syn* see AGE 2
||**dogsbody** *n syn* see SLAVE 2
do in *vb* **1** *syn* see RUIN 2
2 *syn* see MURDER 1
3 *syn* see EXHAUST 4
doing *n syn* see ACTION 1
doit *n syn* see PARTICLE
doldrums *n pl* **1** *syn* see TEDIUM
rel blues, dejection, depression, dumps, gloom; apathy, disinterest, indifference, listlessness
con high spirits, spirits
2 *syn* see ABEYANCE
rel depression, retardation, slump, stagnation; inactivity
dole (out) *vb* **1** *syn* see ADMINISTER 2
2 *syn* see DISTRIBUTE 1
||**dole** *n* **1** *syn* see SORROW
2 *syn* see MISFORTUNE
doleful *adj* **1** *syn* see DOWNCAST
2 *syn* see WOEFUL 1
3 *syn* see MELANCHOLY 2
rel grieving, mourning, sorrowing; piteous, pitiful
con blithe, blithesome, radiant, sparkling, sunny
ant cheerful, cheery
dolefuls *n pl, used with* the *syn* see SADNESS
dolent *adj syn* see WOEFUL 1
dolesome *adj syn* see MELANCHOLY 2
dolittle *n syn* see SLUGGARD
||**doll** *n syn* see WOMAN 1
dollar *n* a currency bill representing one hundred cents <had a single *dollar* left>
syn bill, ||bone, ||buck, ||fish, ||frogskin, ||iron man, oner, rock, ||skin, ||smacker, ||smackeroo
dollop *n syn* see DRAM 1
doll out *vb syn* see DRESS UP 1
doll up *vb syn* see DRESS UP 1
dolor *n syn* see DISTRESS
con blessedness, bliss, felicity, happiness
ant beatitude
dolorous *adj* **1** *syn* see DEPLORABLE
2 *syn* see WOEFUL 1
3 *syn* see MELANCHOLY 2
dolt *n syn* see DUNCE
dolthead *n syn* see DUNCE
doltish *adj syn* see STUPID 1
domain *n syn* see FIELD
||**dome** *n syn* see HEAD 1
domestic *adj* **1** of or relating to the household or family <*domestic* chores required to maintain a home>
syn family, home, household
con civic, public; personal, private; business, occupational, professional
2 of, relating to, or carried on within an indicated or implied country <charts of *domestic* as well as foreign waters>
syn home, ||inland, internal, intestine, municipal, national, native
ant foreign
3 *syn* see TAME
domesticate *vb* to adapt (an animal or plant) to life in intimate association with and to the advantage of man <the man who *domesticated* the first dog>
syn domesticize, domiciliate, master, tame
rel gentle, subdue; housebreak; break, bust, train
domesticated *adj syn* see TAME
domesticize *vb syn* see DOMESTICATE
domicile *n syn* see HABITATION 2
domicile *vb syn* see HARBOR 2
domiciliate *vb* **1** *syn* see HARBOR 2
2 *syn* see DOMESTICATE
dominance *n syn* see SUPREMACY
dominant *adj* **1** superior to all others in power, influence, or importance <the Sumerians were a *dominant* race of ancient times>
syn ascendant, master, outweighing, overbalancing, overbearing, overweighing, paramount, predominant, predominate, preponderant, prevalent, regnant, sovereign
rel prevailing; preeminent, supreme, surpassing, transcendent; chief, first, foremost, leading, main, principal; governing, ruling
con collateral, dependent, secondary, subject, tributary; unimportant
ant subordinate
2 *syn* see CHIEF 2
dominate *vb* **1** *syn* see GOVERN 3
2 *syn* see RULE 2
3 *syn* see OVERLOOK 2
domination *n* **1** *syn* see SUPREMACY
2 *syn* see POWER 1
dominator *n syn* see LEADER 2
domineer *vb syn* see RULE 2
domineering *adj syn* see MASTERFUL 1
rel arrogant, insolent, lordly
con obsequious, servile, slavish; bootlicking, groveling, sycophantic, toadying
ant subservient; fawning
||**dominie** *n syn* see CLERGYMAN
dominion *n* **1** *syn* see SUPREMACY

2 ***syn*** see FIELD
3 ***syn*** see OWNERSHIP
domino *n* ***syn*** see MASK 1
domitae naturae *adj* ***syn*** see TAME
don *vb* **1** to place on one's person (an article of clothing) <*donned* a raincoat for his trip>
syn assume, draw on, get on, huddle (on), put on, slip (on), throw
rel apparel, array, attire, clad, clothe, dress, enclothe, garb, garment, raiment
con cast, pull (off), remove, take off, throw off; unclothe, undress; disrobe
ant doff
2 to clothe or envelop oneself in <able to *don* a new personality at will>
syn assume, pull, put on, strike, take on
rel camouflage, color, disguise; belie, falsify, garble, misrepresent
donate *vb* ***syn*** see GIVE 1
donation *n* a gift of money or its equivalent to a charity, humanitarian cause, or public institution <sought *donations* for victims of the flood>
syn alms, benefaction, beneficence, charity, contribution, offering
rel aid, assistance, help, relief; philanthropy; bequest, endowment; appropriation, grant, subsidy, subvention; allowance, dole, pittance, ration
donator *n* ***syn*** see DONOR
done *adj* **1** ***syn*** see DECOROUS 1
2 ***syn*** see COMPLETE 4
3 ***syn*** see EFFETE 2
4 ***syn*** see THROUGH 4
done for *adj* ***syn*** see THROUGH 3
done in *adj* ***syn*** see EFFETE 2
||**doney** *n* ***syn*** see GIRL FRIEND 1
||**donicker** *n* ***syn*** see TOILET
Don Juan *n* **1** ***syn*** see GALLANT 2
2 ***syn*** see WOLF
donk *n* ***syn*** see DONKEY 1
donkey *n* **1** the domestic ass <the *donkey,* a typical pack animal>
syn ass, burro, donk, jackass, ||moke, ||neddy, ||Rocky Mountain canary
rel ||dickey, jack; hinny, mule; jennet, jenny, jenny ass
2 ***syn*** see FOOL 1
donkeyish *adj* ***syn*** see FOOLISH 2
donkey's years *n pl* ***syn*** see AGE 2
donkeywork *n* ***syn*** see WORK 2
donnybrook *n* ***syn*** see BRAWL 2
donor *n* one that gives something to another <a *donor* of funds to research foundations>
syn bestower, conferrer, donator, giver, presenter
rel contributor, subscriber
do–nothing *n* ***syn*** see SLUGGARD
||**donsie** *adj* ***syn*** see UNWELL
doodad *n* something trivial which is hard to classify or whose name is unknown <wondered what the little round *doodad* was for>
syn business, dingus, dofunny, doohickey, gadget, gizmo, ||hootenanny, jigger, rigamajig, thingum, thingumajig, thingumbob, thingummy; *compare* GADGET 1, WHAT-DO-YOU-CALL-IT
doodle *n* ***syn*** see FOOL 1
||**doodle** *vb* ***syn*** see CHEAT
doodle *vb* ***syn*** see FIDDLE 2
doohickey *n* ***syn*** see DOODAD
doom *n* ***syn*** see FATE
rel calamity, cataclysm, catastrophe, disaster, tragedy
doom *vb* ***syn*** see SENTENCE
doom (to) *vb* ***syn*** see PREDESTINE 1
doomed *adj* ***syn*** see DAMNED 1
doomful *adj* ***syn*** see OMINOUS
door *n* **1** an opening by which one can enter or leave a structure and especially a building <looked through the front *door*>
syn doorway, entrance, entranceway, entry, entryway, portal
2 a means or right of entering, approaching, or participating <viewed education as the *door* to success>
syn access, adit, admission, admittance, entrance, entrée, entry, ingress, way
doormat *n* ***syn*** see WEAKLING
doorway *n* ***syn*** see DOOR 1
||**doozer** *n* ***syn*** ||DILLY, ||corker, ||daisy, dandy, ||dinger, humdinger, jim-dandy, ||lalapalooza, ||lulu, peach
dope *n* **1** ***syn*** see DRUG 2
2 ***syn*** see DUNCE
dope (up) *vb* ***syn*** see ADULTERATE
doped *adj* ***syn*** see DRUGGED
||**dope out** *vb* **1** ***syn*** see SOLVE 2
2 ***syn*** see INFER
3 ***syn*** see PLAN 2
dopey *adj* ***syn*** see LETHARGIC
||**do–re–mi** *n* ***syn*** see MONEY
||**dorm** *vb* ***syn*** see DOZE
dormancy *n* ***syn*** see ABEYANCE
dormant *adj* ***syn*** see LATENT
ant active
||**dort** *vb* ***syn*** see SULK
||**dorts** *n pl* ***syn*** see SULK
||**dorty** *adj* ***syn*** see SULLEN
||**doss** *n* ***syn*** see SLEEP 1
||**doss** *vb* ***syn*** see SLEEP
dot *n* ***syn*** see POINT 11
dot *vb* **1** ***syn*** see SPECKLE 1
2 ***syn*** see SPOT 2
dot *n* ***syn*** see DOWRY
dotage *n* advanced age accompanied by a decline of mental poise and alertness <a doddering eighty-year-old entering his *dotage*>
syn second childhood, senility; *compare* OLD AGE
rel decrepitude, feebleness, infirmity; age, elderliness, senectitude
con adolescence, youth; maturity
dote (on *or* upon) *vb* ***syn*** see ADORE 3
rel enjoy, fancy, like
idiom be sweet on
ant loathe

---

syn synonym(s) ***rel*** related word(s)
ant antonym(s) ***con*** contrasted word(s)
idiom idiomatic equivalent(s)
|| use limited; if in doubt, see a dictionary

‖**doted** *adj* ***syn*** see SENILE

doting *adj* **1** ***syn*** see SENILE
2 ***syn*** see LOVING
rel asinine, fatuous, foolish, silly, simple

dottiness *n* ***syn*** see FOOLISHNESS

dotty *adj* **1** ***syn*** see INFATUATED
2 ***syn*** see FOOLISH 2

double *adj* **1** ***syn*** see TWOFOLD 1
2 ***syn*** see TWIN
3 ***syn*** see TWOFOLD 2
4 ***syn*** see INSINCERE

double *n* **1** ***syn*** see MATE 5
2 ***syn*** see IMAGE 1
3 ***syn*** see TURN 2
rel departure, digression, divergence, swerving, veering

double *vb* **1** to make twice as great or as many <*doubled* the amount of his salary>
syn dualize, dupe, duplicate
rel replicate; amplify, augment, enlarge, increase, magnify; supplement
con decrease, lessen, minimize
ant halve
2 to make of two thicknesses by turning or bending usually in the middle <he *doubled* the towel for better absorbency>
syn fold
rel pleat, plicate, turn over
3 ***syn*** see ESCAPE 2
4 ***syn*** see DUB

double-barreled *adj* **1** ***syn*** see TWOFOLD 2
2 ***syn*** see TWOFOLD 1

double-cross *vb* **1** ***syn*** see DECEIVE
2 ***syn*** see BETRAY 2

double-dealer *n* ***syn*** see SWINDLER

double-dealing *n* ***syn*** see DECEPTION 1

double-dealing *adj* ***syn*** see INSINCERE

double-distilled *adj* ***syn*** see UTTER

‖**double-dog dare** *vb* ***syn*** see FACE 3

double-dome *n* ***syn*** see INTELLECTUAL 2

double-dyed *adj* ***syn*** see UTTER

double-edged *adj* ***syn*** see OBSCURE 3

double entendre *n* ***syn*** see AMBIGUITY

double-faced *adj* **1** ***syn*** see OBSCURE 3
2 ***syn*** see INSINCERE

doublehearted *adj* ***syn*** see INSINCERE

double meaning *n* ***syn*** see AMBIGUITY

double-minded *adj* **1** ***syn*** see VACILLATING 2
idiom of two minds
2 ***syn*** see INSINCERE

doublet *n* ***syn*** see COUPLE

double-talk *n* **1** ***syn*** see NONSENSE 2
2 ***syn*** see GOBBLEDYGOOK

double-tongued *adj* ***syn*** see INSINCERE

doubt *vb* **1** ***syn*** see QUESTION 2
2 ***syn*** see DISTRUST
con accredit, credit, trust; accept, believe, ‖buy, swallow

doubt *n* ***syn*** see UNCERTAINTY
rel dubiousness, questionableness; disbelief, incredulity, unbelief
con dependence, faith, reliance, trust
ant certitude; confidence

doubtable *adj* ***syn*** see DOUBTFUL 1
ant undoubtable

doubter *n* ***syn*** see SKEPTIC

doubtful *adj* **1** not having or affording assurance of the certainty or soundness of something or someone <their chance of success is *doubtful*>
syn ambiguous, borderline, clouded, doubtable, dubious, dubitable, equivocal, fishy, impugnable, indecisive, open, precarious, problematic, queasy, shady, shaky, suspect, suspicious, uncertain, unclear, undecided, uneasy, unsettled, unstable, unsure; *compare* MOOT
rel question-begging; touch-and-go; chancy, insecure, questionable, speculative; hazy, obscure; unlikely; contingent, iffy
idiom at issue, in dispute, in doubt, in question
con decisive, open-and-shut, positive, sure; inarguable, incontestable, unarguable, undeniable, undoubted, unquestionable
ant indubitable
2 ***syn*** see MOOT
3 ***syn*** see IMPROBABLE 1

doubtfully *adv* ***syn*** see ASKANCE 2

doubtfulness *n* ***syn*** see UNCERTAINTY

doubting Thomas *n* ***syn*** see SKEPTIC

doubtless *adv* **1** ***syn*** see EASILY 2
2 ***syn*** see PRESUMABLY

doubtlessly *adv* **1** ***syn*** see WELL 7
ant doubtfully
2 ***syn*** see EASILY 2

dough *n* ***syn*** see MONEY

doughface *n* ***syn*** see MASK 1

‖**doughhead** *n* ***syn*** see DUNCE

doughty *adj* ***syn*** see BRAVE 1

doughy *adj* ***syn*** see PALE 1

do up *vb* ***syn*** see MEND 2

dour *adj* **1** ***syn*** see GRIM 2
rel rigid, rigorous, strict; implacable
2 ***syn*** see SULLEN

‖**douse** *n* ***syn*** see BLOW 1

douse *vb* ***syn*** see REMOVE 3

douse *vb* **1** ***syn*** see DIP 1
2 ***syn*** see WET
con bake, dehydrate, desiccate, dry, parch
3 ***syn*** see SPLASH
4 ***syn*** see EXTINGUISH 1

‖**dout** *vb* ***syn*** see EXTINGUISH 1

dove *n* ***syn*** see PACIFIST
ant hawk

dovecote *n* a small compartmented raised house or box for domestic pigeons <old countryseats with elaborate stone *dovecotes*>
syn columbary, culverhouse, dovehouse, pigeon house, pigeonry
rel aviary, birdhouse; perch, roost

dovehouse *n* ***syn*** see DOVECOTE

‖**dover** *n* ***syn*** see NAP

dovetail *vb* ***syn*** see AGREE 4

dowager *n* ***syn*** see MATRIARCH

dowd *n* ***syn*** see SLATTERN 1

dowdy *n* ***syn*** see SLATTERN 1

dowdy *adj* **1** ***syn*** see SLATTERNLY
con chic, fashionable, modish, stylish; flashy, garish, gaudy
ant smart

2 ***syn*** see TACKY 2
ant smart
3 ***syn*** see OLD-FASHIONED

dower *n* ***syn*** see DOWRY

dower *vb* ***syn*** see ENDOW 1
rel accouter, appoint, equip, furnish, outfit

||**dowly** *adj* ***syn*** see OVERCAST

down *adv* **1** from a higher to a lower level <the land sloped *down* toward the sea>
syn downward, downwardly, downwards, netherwards
rel below, earthward, groundward; downgrade, downhill, downslope
con aloft, upward, upwardly, upwards
ant up
2 to completion <wash *down* the car>
syn completely, fully, through-and-through
idiom from top to bottom
3 ***syn*** see SERIOUSLY 1

down *adj* **1** ***syn*** see SLOW 3
2 ***syn*** see DOWNCAST
ant up
3 ***syn*** see SICK 1
4 ***syn*** see LOWER
ant up
5 ***syn*** see COMPLETE 4

down *n* ***syn*** see COMEDOWN

down *vb* **1** ***syn*** see SWALLOW 1
2 ***syn*** see DEFEAT 2
3 ***syn*** see FELL 1
4 ***syn*** see KILL 1
5 ***syn*** see OVERCOME 1

down *n* a soft fluffy material or covering <the *down* on a peach>
syn floss, flue, fluff, fur, fuzz, lint, pile

down–and–out *n* ***syn*** see PAUPER

down–at–heel *adj* ***syn*** see SHABBY 1

downcast *n* ***syn*** see DEFEAT 1

downcast *adj* low in spirits <felt *downcast* by the rejection>
syn bad, blue, cast down, chapfallen, crestfallen, dejected, depressed, disconsolate, dispirited, doleful, down, downhearted, down-in-the-mouth, downthrown, droopy, dull, heartsick, heartsore, hipped, low, low-spirited, mopey, soul-sick, spiritless, sunk, woebegone; *compare* SAD 1
rel discouraged, disheartened; oppressed, weighed down; distressed, troubled; despondent, forlorn; listless; broody, moody; gloomy, glum, morose
idiom in the depths
con cheerful, happy, joyous, lighthearted; excited, exhilarated, intoxicated; buoyed up, gladdened; encouraged, heartened; animated, gay, lively, sprightly, vivacious; delighted, pleased
ant elated

downcry *vb* ***syn*** see DECRY 2

downfall *n* **1** ***syn*** see DETERIORATION 1
rel comedown, descent, discomfiture, down
2 something that causes a downfall <drink was his *downfall*>
syn bane, destroyer, destruction, ruin, ruination, undoing
rel headache, problem, trouble
idiom road to ruin
con aid, help, support

downgrade *n* ***syn*** see DETERIORATION 1
ant upgrade

downgrade *vb* **1** ***syn*** see DEPRECIATE 1
ant upgrade
2 ***syn*** see DEGRADE 1
ant upgrade

downgrading *n* ***syn*** see DEMOTION
ant upgrading

downhearted *adj* ***syn*** see DOWNCAST

down–in–the–mouth *adj* ***syn*** see DOWNCAST

downright *adj* **1** ***syn*** see UTTER
2 being what is stated beyond any possibility of doubt <a *downright* lie>
syn flat, indubitable, unquestionable, up-and-down; *compare* POSITIVE 3
rel out-and-out, sure-enough; absolute, positive; certain, clear

downside–up *adj* ***syn*** see UPSIDE-DOWN 2

downslide *n* ***syn*** see DECLINE 3

downswing *n* ***syn*** see DECLINE 3

downthrow *n* ***syn*** see DEFEAT 1

downthrown *adj* ***syn*** see DOWNCAST

down–to–date *adj* ***syn*** see UP-TO-DATE

down–to–earth *adj* ***syn*** see REALISTIC

downtrend *n* ***syn*** see DECLINE 3

downtrodden *adj* oppressed by superior power <the *downtrodden* peasants>
syn abject, underfoot
rel oppressed, persecuted; abused, maltreated, mistreated

downturn *n* ***syn*** see DECLINE 3

downward *adv* ***syn*** see DOWN 1
ant upward

downwardly *adv* ***syn*** see DOWN 1
ant upwardly

downwards *adv* ***syn*** see DOWN 1
ant upwards

||**downy** *adj* ***syn*** see SLY 2

dowry *n* the money, goods, or estate that a woman brings to her husband in marriage <from a poor family, she came to her marriage with no *dowry*>
syn dot, dower, marriage portion
con bride-price, bridewealth; settlement

doxy *n* **1** a usually young woman who is sexually promiscuous <a *doxy* who frequented singles bars>
syn ||chippy, floozy, grisette, light-o'-love, nymph, nymphet, party girl, tart, ||tootsie
rel groupie
idiom woman of easy virtue
||**2** ***syn*** see MISTRESS

doyen *n* **1** ***syn*** see LEADER 1
2 ***syn*** see EXPERT

doze *vb* to sleep lightly <he was inclined to *doze* at his desk>

---

syn synonym(s) ***rel*** related word(s)
ant antonym(s) ***con*** contrasted word(s)
idiom idiomatic equivalent(s)
|| use limited; if in doubt, see a dictionary

syn ‖dorm, drowse, ‖sloom, slumber, ‖snoozle, ‖sog; *compare* NAP, SLEEP
doze (off) *vb* to fall into a light sleep <*dozed* off while sitting before the fire>
syn drop off, drowse (off)
idiom drift off
doze *n* a light sleep <was caught in a *doze* at her desk>
syn drowse, ‖sloom, slumber; *compare* NAP, SLEEP 1
dozy *adj* ***syn*** see SLEEPY 1
DP *n* ***syn*** see REFUGEE
drab *n* **1** ***syn*** see HAG 2
2 ***syn*** see SLATTERN 1
3 ***syn*** see PROSTITUTE
drab *adj* **1** ***syn*** see DULL 8
2 ***syn*** see COLORLESS 2
rel bleak, desolate, dismal, dispiriting, dreary; dingy, faded
con bright, brilliant, luminous
draconian *adj* ***syn*** see RIGID 3
draffy *adj* ***syn*** see WORTHLESS 1
draft *n* DRINK 3, drag, drain, drench, ‖peg, swig, swill
draft *vb* **1** to enroll in the armed forces by compulsion <*drafted* when he was barely eighteen>
syn conscribe, conscript; *compare* CALL UP
rel induct; enlist, enroll, muster (in *or* out); impress, press
2 ***syn*** see SKETCH
3 to formulate and produce <*drafting* plans to meet an emergency>
syn draw up, formulate, frame, make, prepare
rel concoct, contrive, devise, invent; fabricate, fashion, forge, form, manufacture, shape; plan, project; outline, sketch
4 ***syn*** see DRAIN 1
drag *n* **1** ***syn*** see DRAW 1
2 ***syn*** see DRINK 3
‖**3** ***syn*** see PULL 2
‖**4** ***syn*** see WAY 1
5 ***syn*** see BORE
drag *vb* **1** ***syn*** see PULL 2
con propel, push, shove, thrust; drive, impel, move
2 ***syn*** see DELAY 2
idiom drag one's feet (*or* heels)
con hasten, hurry
3 to hang down and be drawn behind <her dress *dragged* in the dust>
syn draggle, trail, traipse
rel droop, hang, sag
‖**drag down** *vb* ***syn*** see EARN 1
dragging *adj* ***syn*** see LONG 2
draggle *vb* ***syn*** see DRAG 3
draggle–tail *n* ***syn*** see SLATTERN 1
draggletailed *adj* ***syn*** see SLATTERNLY
dragoon *vb* ***syn*** see INTIMIDATE
drain *vb* **1** to draw off (liquid) by degrees <*drain* the water from the swimming pool>
syn draft, draw, draw off, pump, siphon, tap
rel milk; bleed; suck; empty, exhaust
2 ***syn*** see TIRE 1
3 ***syn*** see DEPLETE
idiom bleed white
drain (away) *vb* ***syn*** see DECREASE
drain *n* ***syn*** see DRINK 3
drained *adj* ***syn*** see EFFETE 2
dram *n* **1** a small quantity of something (as alcoholic liquor) to drink <a *dram* of brandy helped to break his chill>
syn ‖caulker, dollop, drop, jolt, nip, shot, slug, snifter, snort, snorter, spot, toothful, tot, ‖wet
rel draft, drink, ‖peg, potation, pull, swig, swill; finger; jigger; dash; ‖splash; snack; quick one
2 ***syn*** see PARTICLE
drama *n* dramatic art, literature, or affairs <was interested in *drama* during her college years>
syn boards, footlights, (the) stage, theater
rel show business
dramatic *adj* **1** of or relating to drama <made no objections to his son's *dramatic* ambitions>
syn dramaturgic, histrionic, theatral, theatric, theatrical, thespian
2 ***syn*** see THEATRICAL 2
ant undramatic
dramatist *n* ***syn*** see PLAYWRIGHT
dramatizer *n* ***syn*** see PLAYWRIGHT
dramaturge *n* ***syn*** see PLAYWRIGHT
dramaturgic *adj* ***syn*** see DRAMATIC 1
drape *vb* **1** ***syn*** see SWATHE
2 ***syn*** see SPRAWL 1
dratted *adj* ***syn*** see DAMNED 2
draw *vb* **1** ***syn*** see PULL 2
rel bring, fetch; educe, elicit, evoke, extract
con propel, push, shove, thrust; drive, impel, move
2 ***syn*** see DRAIN 1
3 ***syn*** see ATTRACT 1
4 ***syn*** see INDUCE 1
5 ***syn*** see TAKE 14
6 ***syn*** see INFER
7 ***syn*** see EXTEND 3
8 ***syn*** see DEPLETE
9 ***syn*** see EVISCERATE
draw *n* **1** a sucking pull on something (as a sipping straw or cigarette) <took a long *draw* on his pipe before answering>
syn drag, puff, pull
rel smoke; inhale
2 ***syn*** see ADVANTAGE 3
3 ***syn*** see ATTRACTION 1
4 an indecisive ending to a contest or competition <the prizefight ended in a *draw*>
syn deadlock, dogfall, stalemate, standoff, tie
rel dead heat, photo finish; standstill
con loss; win
draw back *vb* ***syn*** see DEDUCT 1
drawback *n* ***syn*** see DISADVANTAGE
rel evil, ill; inconvenience, trouble
con advantage, edge
draw down *vb* **1** ***syn*** see EARN 1
2 ***syn*** see DEPLETE
draw in *vb* ***syn*** see INDUCE 1
drawing *adj* ***syn*** see ATTRACTIVE 1
drawing power *n* ***syn*** see ATTRACTION 1
drawing room *n* ***syn*** see SALON 1
drawn *adj* ***syn*** see HAGGARD

con hale, robust
drawn–out *adj* ***syn*** see LONG 2
draw off *vb* ***syn*** see DRAIN 1
rel abstract; withdraw; move, remove, shift, transfer
draw on *vb* **1** ***syn*** see EFFECT 1
2 ***syn*** see INDUCE 1
3 ***syn*** see DON 1
draw out *vb* ***syn*** see EXTEND 3
draw up *vb* **1** ***syn*** see DRAFT 3
2 ***syn*** see STOP 4
dray horse *n* ***syn*** see SLAVE 2
dread *n* ***syn*** see FEAR 1
dreadful *adj* ***syn*** see FEARFUL 3
‖**dreadful** *adv* ***syn*** see VERY 1
dreadful *n* ***syn*** see DIME NOVEL
dreadfully *adv* ***syn*** see VERY 1
dream *n* **1** ***syn*** see FANCY 4
2 ***syn*** see PIPE DREAM
dream *vb* ***syn*** see LONG
dreamer *n* one whose conduct is guided more by ideals than practicalities <a *dreamer* proposing glorious plans impossible to make work>
syn castle-builder, idealist, ideologue, utopian, visionary
rel daydreamer, illusionist, lotus-eater, wishful thinker; Don Quixote; theorist
con pragmatist, realist; Babbitt, Philistine; pedant
dream up *vb* ***syn*** see CONTRIVE 2
dreamy *adj* **1** given to dreaming, reverie, or fancy <a *dreamy* and most impractical person>
syn astral, daydreaming, daydreamy, otherworldly, unworldly, visionary
rel fanciful, idealistic, romantic, whimsical
con down-to-earth, practical, pragmatic, realistic; actual, factual
2 ***syn*** see MARVELOUS 2
drear *adj* ***syn*** see GLOOMY 3
dreary *adj* **1** ***syn*** see GLOOMY 3
2 ***syn*** see DULL 9
dreck *n* ***syn*** see REFUSE
dreg *n, usu* **dregs** *pl* **1** ***syn*** see SEDIMENT
2 ***syn*** see RABBLE 2
‖**dreich** *adj* ***syn*** see LONG 2
drench *n* ***syn*** see DRINK 3
drench *vb* **1** ***syn*** see WET
rel dip, duck, dunk, immerse, submerge
2 ***syn*** see SOAK 1
3 ***syn*** see POUR 3
drenched *adj* ***syn*** see WET 1
dress *vb* **1** ***syn*** see CLOTHE
ant undress
2 ***syn*** see BANDAGE
3 to remove the entrails from <*dress* fish, fowl, or game>
syn clean, gut
rel butcher, slaughter
4 ***syn*** see TILL
rel fertilize, topdress
dress (up) *vb* ***syn*** see ADORN
dress *n* **1** ***syn*** see CLOTHES
2 ***syn*** see COSTUME
dress down *vb* ***syn*** see SCOLD 1
dress up *vb* **1** to attire in best or formal clothes <*dressed up* to go to the theater>
syn deck (out), ‖dike (out *or* up), doll out, doll up, ‖dude up, fix up, gussy up, prank, ‖prick (up), primp, prink (up), slick, smarten (up), smug, spiff, spruce (up), tog (out *or* up), ‖toggle, trick (off, out, *or* up)
rel prettify, pretty (up); apparel, array, attire, clad, clothe, dress, enclothe, garb, garment, raiment; overdress; preen; prim (up)
idiom dress fit to kill, dress to the nines, put on the dog
2 ***syn*** see DISGUISE
drib *vb* ***syn*** see DRIP
drib *n* ***syn*** see DROP 1
dribble *vb* **1** ***syn*** see DRIP
2 ***syn*** see DROOL 2
dribble (away) *vb* ***syn*** see WASTE 2
dribble *n* ***syn*** see PITTANCE
driblet *n* **1** ***syn*** see PITTANCE
2 ***syn*** see DROP 1
drift *n* **1** ***syn*** see FLOW
2 ***syn*** see PILE 1
rel array, batch, bunch, bundle, clump, cluster, clutch, group, lot, parcel, set
‖**3** ***syn*** see DROVE 2
4 ***syn*** see TENDENCY 1
rel motion, movement, progress, progression; aim, intent, intention, purpose
5 ***syn*** see LEANING 2
6 ***syn*** see TENOR 1
rel direction, line, set
drift *vb* **1** to become carried or floated along <cakes of ice *drifting* along the stream>
syn float, ride, wash
rel dart, fly, sail, scud, shoot, skim; dance, flicker, flit, flitter, flutter, hover
2 ***syn*** see SAUNTER
3 ***syn*** see WANDER 1
4 ***syn*** see SLIDE 6
5 ***syn*** see HEAP 1
drifter *n* **1** ***syn*** see ROVER
2 ***syn*** see VAGABOND
driftwood *n* vagrant impoverished people <the *driftwood* of skid row>
syn flotsam, jetsam, wreckage
drill *vb* **1** ***syn*** see PERFORATE
2 ***syn*** see EXERCISE 3
rel accustom, habituate
drill *n* ***syn*** see EXERCISE 3
drilling *n* ***syn*** see EXERCISE 3
drink *vb* **1** to take in (potable liquid) <the boys *drank* all the soda>
syn imbibe, quaff, sip, sup (off *or* up), swallow, toss
rel drain, gulp, guzzle, slosh, slurp, swig, swill; wash down
idiom wet one's whistle

---

syn synonym(s) ***rel*** related word(s)
ant antonym(s) ***con*** contrasted word(s)
idiom idiomatic equivalent(s)
‖ use limited; if in doubt, see a dictionary

2 to salute and wish honor and health to (a person) by raising and then drinking from a vessel <*drink* to the bride and groom>
syn pledge, toast
rel honor, salute; wet
3 to partake of alcoholic liquors especially habitually or to excess <he *drinks* but does not smoke>
syn booze, guzzle, imbibe, liquor (up), ‖lush (up), nip, soak, swig, swill, swizzle, tank up, tipple, tope
idiom bend the elbow, cheer the inner man, drink like a fish, go on a binge, hit the bottle, take a nip

drink *n* **1** liquid suitable for swallowing <able to make palatable *drink* from seawater>
syn beverage, drinkable, liquor, potable
rel liquid; brew; potion
2 *syn* see LIQUOR 2
3 a portion of potable liquid <took a *drink* from the cup>
syn draft, drag, drain, drench, ‖peg, swig, swill
rel draw, pull; finger, jigger; libation
4 *syn* see OCEAN

drinkable *adj syn* see POTABLE

drinkable *n syn* see DRINK 1

drinkery *n syn* see BAR 5

drip *vb* to let fall drops of moisture or liquid <trees *dripping* after the rain>
syn distill, drib, dribble, drop, trickle, trill, weep
rel spatter, sprinkle, spurtle; gush, pour, sluice, stream

‖**drip** *n* **1** *syn* see NONSENSE 2
2 *syn* see DUNCE

dripping *adj syn* see WET 1

drippy *adj syn* see SENTIMENTAL

drive *vb* **1** *syn* see MOVE 5
rel coerce, compel, force; incite, instigate
con check, curb, inhibit, restrain; guide, lead, pilot, steer
2 *syn* see PUSH 1
3 to urge along (as cattle) <cowboys *driving* the great herds north>
syn ‖drove, herd, run
rel shepherd; wrangle; egg, exhort, goad, prick, prod, punch, sic, spur, urge
4 *syn* see THRUST 2
5 to operate and steer (a motor vehicle) <*drive* a car>
syn auto, charioteer, motor, pilot, tool, wheel
rel operate, run, work; guide, steer; roll; chauffeur
6 *syn* see IMPRESS 3
7 *syn* see PLUNGE 2
8 *syn* see LABOR 1

drive *n* **1** a short trip in a vehicle <took a *drive* around town>
syn ride, spin, turn; *compare* TRIP 1
rel whirl; joyride; excursion, outing
2 *syn* see DRIVEWAY
3 *syn* see ENTERPRISE 4
4 *syn* see VIGOR 2
rel impetus, momentum, speed, velocity

drivel *vb* **1** *syn* see DROOL 2
2 *syn* see BABBLE 2
3 *syn* see WASTE 2

drivel *n* **1** *syn* see NONSENSE 2
2 *syn* see GIBBERISH 1

driveling *adj syn* see INSIPID 3

driver *n syn* see MOTORIST

driveway *n* a private road giving access from a public way <the *driveway* to a house>
syn ‖avenue, drive
rel court, place, row, street

driving *adj syn* see ENERGETIC 2

drizzle *vb syn* see SPRINKLE 5

drogher *n syn* see BEARER 2

drôlerie *n syn* see JOKE 1

droll *adj syn* see LAUGHABLE
rel absurd, preposterous

droll *n syn* see HUMORIST 2

drollery *n* **1** *syn* see JOKE 1
2 *syn* see HUMOR 4

drollness *n syn* see HUMOR 4

drone *vb* **1** *syn* see HUM
2 *syn* see IDLE

drony *adj syn* see LAZY

drool *vb* **1** to secrete or become filled with saliva usually in anticipation of food <mouths *drooled* as we waited for dinner>
syn water
idiom water at the mouth
2 to let saliva or some other substance flow from the mouth <babies often *drool* uncontrollably>
syn dribble, drivel, salivate, slabber, slaver, slobber
3 *syn* see ENTHUSE 2
4 *syn* see BABBLE 2

drool *n syn* see NONSENSE 2

droop *vb* **1** *syn* see SLOUCH
2 *syn* see LOWER 3
3 to become literally or figuratively limp through loss of vigor or freshness <he walked along, his shoulders *drooping* from exhaustion>
syn flag, sag, swag, wilt
rel drop, fall, sink, slump, subside; dangle, hang, loll, lop, sling, suspend; decline, deteriorate, ‖dwine, fade, fail, languish, weaken

droopy *adj syn* see DOWNCAST

drop *n* **1** the quantity of fluid that falls in one spherical mass <a *drop* of rain>
syn drib, driblet, droplet, globule, gobbet
rel dribble, drip, trickle
2 *syn* see PARTICLE
3 *syn* see DRAM
4 *syn* see DESCENT 4
5 *syn* see DESCENT 1
6 *syn* see DECLINE 3
7 *syn* see DEPTH 1

drop *vb* **1** *syn* see FALL 2
2 *syn* see FALL 1
ant mount
3 *syn* see PLUMMET
rel slide, slip
con rally, rebound; ascend, climb; soar
ant mount
4 *syn* see COLLAPSE 2
rel backslide, lapse, relapse

5 ***syn*** see DIE 1
6 ***syn*** see DRIP
7 ***syn*** see FELL 1
8 ***syn*** see QUIT 6
9 ***syn*** see CANCEL 2
10 ***syn*** see DISMISS 3
11 ***syn*** see LOSE 2
12 ***syn*** see LOSE 1

drop (in *or* by) *vb* ***syn*** see VISIT 2

drop (off) *vb* ***syn*** see SLIP 6

droplet *n* ***syn*** see DROP 1

drop off *vb* ***syn*** see DOZE (off)

dropsical *adj* ***syn*** see INFLATED

dropsied *adj* ***syn*** see INFLATED

drossy *adj* ***syn*** see WORTHLESS 1

droughty *adj* ***syn*** see DRY 1

‖**drouk** *vb* ***syn*** see SOAK 1

drove *n* **1** ***syn*** see CROWD 1
2 a group of domestic animals reared or handled as a unit <a *drove* of cattle>
syn ‖drift, flock, herd
rel drive; pack; school

‖**drove** *vb* ***syn*** see DRIVE 3

drown *vb* **1** ***syn*** see OVERWHELM 4
2 ***syn*** see DELUGE 1
3 ***syn*** see WET

drowse *vb* ***syn*** see DOZE

drowse (off) *vb* ***syn*** see DOZE (off)

drowse *n* ***syn*** see DOZE

drowsy *adj* ***syn*** see SLEEPY 1
rel lackadaisical, languid, languorous
con alert, vigilant, watchful; active, dynamic, live; animated, lively, vivacious

drub *vb* **1** ***syn*** see BEAT 1
2 ***syn*** see LAMBASTE 3
3 ***syn*** see WHIP 2

drubbing *n* ***syn*** see DEFEAT 1

drudge *vb* to perform hard, menial, or monotonous work <*drudged* all day washing floors>
syn grind, grub, ‖muck, plod, slave, slog, toil
rel hammer, peg (away *or* at *or* on), plow, plug, pound (away); perform, work
idiom keep one's nose to the grindstone
con idle, laze, loaf, lounge; dally, dawdle, potter, putter; cheat, chisel

drudge *n* **1** ***syn*** see SLAVE 2
2 ***syn*** see WORK 2
3 ***syn*** see HACK 2

drudgery *n* ***syn*** see WORK 2

drudging *adj* ***syn*** see IRKSOME

drug *n* **1** a substance used by itself or in a mixture in the treatment or diagnosis of disease <a life-sustaining *drug*>
syn biologic, medicinal, pharmaceutic, pharmaceutical
rel cure, medicament, medication, medicine, physic, remedy, specific; simple
2 a narcotic substance or preparation <depended on *drugs* to make life bearable>
syn dope, ‖hop, narcotic, opiate

drugged *adj* being under the influence of a drug taken for nonmedical purposes <was *drugged* on LSD>
syn doped, high, hopped-up, spaced-out, stoned, tripped out, turned on, ‖wiped out, zonked
idiom on a trip
ant straight

druggist *n* one who deals in medicinal drugs
syn apothecary, ‖chemist, pharmacist
rel pharmacologist

drum *vb* ***syn*** see SOLICIT 1

drumfire *n* ***syn*** see BARRAGE

drumhead *adj* ***syn*** see SUMMARY 2

drum up *vb* ***syn*** see SOLICIT 1

drunk *adj* ***syn*** see INTOXICATED 1
rel drinking, drinky
idiom roaring drunk
con bone-dry, dry
ant sober

drunk *n* **1** ***syn*** see BINGE 1
2 ***syn*** see DRUNKARD

drunkard *n* one who drinks alcoholic liquors to excess <*drunkards* lurching homeward when the bar finally closes>
syn bibber, ‖bloat, ‖blotter, boozehound, boozer, drunk, fuddler, guzzler, inebriate, lush, ‖lusher, rumdum, rummy, ‖rumpot, ‖shicker, soak, soaker, sot, sponge, stiff, swillbowl, swiller, tippler, toper, tosspot
rel alcoholic, dipsomaniac; wino; drammer
idiom elbow bender (*or* crooker)
ant teetotaler

drunken *adj* ***syn*** see INTOXICATED 1

drunkery *n* ***syn*** see BAR 5

‖**druthers** *n* ***syn*** see CHOICE 1

dry *adj* **1** devoid of or deficient in moisture <preferred a *dry* climate>
syn arid, bone-dry, droughty, moistureless, sere, thirsty, unwatered, waterless
rel baked, dehydrated, desiccated, parched; bald, bare, barren; depleted, drained, exhausted, impoverished; juiceless, sapless, sapped
con drenched, dripping, saturated, soaked, soaking, sodden, sopping, soppy, soused, wringing-wet; damp, dank, humid, moist; exuberant, lush, luxuriant, prodigal, profuse
ant wet
2 ***syn*** see THIRSTY 1
3 marked by the absence of or abstention from alcoholic beverages <a *dry* party>
syn bone-dry, teetotal
ant wet
4 ***syn*** see IMPASSIVE 1
5 ***syn*** see ARID 2
6 ***syn*** see PLAIN 1
7 ***syn*** see SOUR 1
ant sweet
8 ***syn*** see HARSH 3

dry *vb* **1** to treat or affect so as to deprive of moisture <clothes *dried* in the wind>
syn dehydrate, desiccate, exsiccate, parch, sear

THESAURUS

rel evaporate; anhydrate; deplete, drain, exhaust; shrivel, wither, wizen
con deluge, douse, drench, soak, sop, souse; damp, dampen, moisten
ant wet
2 *syn* see HARDEN 1
dryasdust *adj syn* see ARID 2
dry land *n syn* see EARTH 2
‖**dry–shave** *vb syn* see CHEAT
dry up *vb* **1** *syn* see DESICCATE 2
2 *syn* see WITHER
3 *syn* see SHUT UP 2
dual *adj* **1** *syn* see TWOFOLD 1
2 *syn* see TWIN
dualistic *adj syn* see TWOFOLD 1
dualize *vb syn* see DOUBLE 1
dub *vb* **1** *syn* see NAME 1
2 *syn* see BOTCH
dub *vb* to provide (a motion-picture film) with a new sound track (as by substituting dialogue in a foreign language) <*dubbed* the Italian movie into English>
syn double
dubiety *n syn* see UNCERTAINTY
rel hesitancy; faltering, vacillation, wavering
con decidedness, decisiveness
ant decision
dubiosity *n syn* see UNCERTAINTY
rel addlement, confusion, muddlement; faltering, vacillation, wavering
con cocksureness, positiveness
ant decidedness
dubious *adj* **1** *syn* see MOOT
2 *syn* see DOUBTFUL 1
rel skeptical; mistrustful; disinclined, hesitant, reluctant
con dependable, tried, trustworthy, trusty; certain, positive, sure
ant cocksure; reliable
3 *syn* see IMPROBABLE 1
4 *syn* see UNRELIABLE 1
ant trustworthy
dubitable *adj syn* see DOUBTFUL 1
ant indubitable
dubitancy *n syn* see UNCERTAINTY
duce *n syn* see TYRANT
‖**duck** *n syn* see ECCENTRIC
duck *vb* **1** *syn* see DIP 1
2 to lower (as the head or body) quickly <had to *duck* his head to get through the door>
syn dip, stoop
rel bend; bow
3 *syn* see DODGE 1
rel avert, prevent, ward
4 *syn* see ESCAPE 2
duck soup *n syn* see SNAP 1
duct *n syn* see CHANNEL 1
ductile *adj syn* see PLASTIC
rel responsive; submitting; fluid, liquid
con intractable, refractory; adamant, obdurate
ductus *n syn* see HANDWRITING
dud *n syn* see FAILURE 5
dude *n syn* see FOP
‖**dude up** *vb syn* see DRESS UP 1
dudgeon *n syn* see OFFENSE 2
rel fury, ire, rage, wrath; humor, mood, temper
duds *n pl* **1** *syn* see CLOTHES
‖**2** *syn* see RAGS 1
due *adj* **1** *syn* see JUST 3
rel good, right; equitable, fair, just; coming, earned
con excessive, exorbitant, extravagant, immoderate, inordinate; deficient
ant undue
2 having reached the date at which payment is required <a note that would become *due* after eighteen months>
syn mature, payable
3 *syn* see UNPAID 2
due *n* **1** what one fairly has coming <the artist has finally been accorded her *due*>
syn comeuppance, desert(s), deserving, lumps, merit, right(s)
rel deservedness, dueness, entitlement; compensation, payment, recompense, recompensing, repayment, satisfaction; reprisal, retaliation, retribution, revenge, vengeance; guerdon, need, reward
idiom what is coming to one
2 *syn* see DEBT 3
due *adv syn* see DIRECTLY 1
duel *vb syn* see RESIST
due to *prep syn* see OVER 6
‖**duff** *vb syn* see CHEAT
‖**duff** *n syn* see BUTTOCKS
duffer *n* ‖**1** *syn* see PEDDLER
2 *syn* see DUNCE
dulcet *adj* **1** *syn* see MELODIOUS 1
con grinding, rasping, scraping, scratching
ant grating
2 *syn* see SWEET 1
dull *adj* **1** *syn* see STUPID 1
ant sharp
2 *syn* see RETARDED
con advanced, precocious
3 *syn* see INSENSIBLE 5
4 *syn* see DOWNCAST
5 *syn* see COLORLESS 2
ant bright
6 lacking sharpness of edge or point <a knife with a *dull* blade>
syn blunt, obtuse
rel blunted, dulled, unsharpened
con honed, keen, razor-sharp, unblunted, whetted
ant sharp
7 lacking warmth, luster, or brilliance <a smooth *dull* finish>
syn blind, dead, dim, flat, lackluster, lusterless, mat, muted
rel cold, dingy, drab, dun, leaden, somber; deadened, lifeless
con beaming, bright, brilliant, effulgent, fulgent, incandescent, lambent, lucent, lucid, luminous, lustrous, radiant, refulgent; burnished, polished, shiny
8 cloudy in color <a *dull* brown>
syn drab, muddy, murky, subfusc

rel blurry, cloudy, hazy; flat, lackluster, lifeless, lusterless; mousy
ant clear; rich
9 being so unvaried or uninteresting as to provoke boredom or tedium <any routine constantly repeated can become *dull*>
syn banausic, blah, ‖dim, dreary, humdrum, monotone, monotonous, pedestrian, plodding, poky, stodgy
rel boring, irksome, tedious, tiring, wearisome; brainless; exhausting, fagging, fatiguing
con animating, exciting, stimulating; gay, spritely
ant lively
10 *syn* see OVERCAST
11 *syn* see ARID 2
rel matter-of-fact, prosaic, prosy; bloodless
idiom dull as ditchwater
con exciting, stimulating
ant lively

dull *vb* **1** to make less clear, distinct, or bright <colors *dulled* by the sun>
syn dim, fade, muddy, pale, tarnish
rel discolor, wash out; blur
con brighten, freshen, intensify
2 *syn* see DEADEN 1
ant sharpen
3 to deprive of sharpness (as of edge or point) <*dull* a spade>
syn blunt, disedge, obtund, turn
idiom take the edge off
con edge, hone
ant sharpen
4 to impair one or more of the senses <age had *dulled* his hearing>
syn blear, blur, dim
rel debilitate, enfeeble, weaken; darken; retard, slow
ant sharpen
5 to make slow or obtuse <his mind had been *dulled* by drink>
syn blunt, hebetate, stupefy
rel becloud, befog, cloud, darken, dim; benumb, deaden, numb; retard, slow
con quicken, stimulate, whet
ant sharpen

dullard *n* *syn* see DUNCE

dullhead *n* *syn* see DUNCE

dullness *n* *syn* see LETHARGY 1
rel denseness, stupidity
con edge, incisiveness, keenness
ant sharpness

‖**dullsville** *n* **1** *syn* see BORE
rel burg, hick town, jerkwater town, mudhole, one-horse town, Podunk, tank town, whistle-stop
2 *syn* see TEDIUM

dumb *adj* **1** lacking the power to speak <deaf and *dumb* from birth>
syn inarticulate, mute, silent, speechless, unarticulate, voiceless; *compare* SILENT 2
ant articulate
2 *syn* see SILENT 2
rel incoherent, indistinct, maundering, tongue-tied
3 *syn* see SILENT 3
con speaking, talking; talkative, verbose
4 *syn* see STUPID 1
idiom dumb as an ox

dumb (up) *vb* *syn* see SHUT UP 2

dumbbell *n* *syn* see DUNCE

‖**dumb bunny** *n* *syn* see DUNCE

‖**dumb cluck** *n* *syn* see DUNCE

dumbfound *vb* **1** *syn* see SURPRISE 2
2 *syn* see STAGGER 5

dumbfounded *adj* *syn* see AGHAST 2

‖**dumbhead** *n* *syn* see DUNCE

‖**dummkopf** *n* *syn* see DUNCE

dummy *n* **1** *syn* see DUNCE
2 *syn* see STOOGE 1

dummy *adj* *syn* see ARTIFICIAL 2

‖**dummy** (up) *vb* *syn* see SHUT UP 2

dump *vb* **1** *syn* see DISCARD
‖2 *syn* see BEAT 1

dump *n* **1** *syn* see ARMORY
2 *syn* see STY 1

dumping *n* *syn* see DISPOSAL 2

dumpling *n* *syn* see FATTY

dumps *n pl* *syn* see SADNESS
idiom low spirits

dumpy *adj* *syn* see STOCKY
rel formless, shapeless, unformed

dun *adj* *syn* see DARK 1

dun *vb* *syn* see WORRY 1

dunce *n* a dull-witted person <the traditional *dunce* in pointed cap>
syn beetlehead, blockhead, bonehead, boob, booby, ‖bufflehead, cabbagehead, chowderhead, chucklehead, chump, clod, clodpate, clodpoll, ‖cluck, dimwit, ‖dizzard, dodo, ‖dodunk, dolt, dolthead, dope, ‖doughhead, ‖drip, duffer, dullard, dullhead, dumbbell, ‖dumb bunny, ‖dumb cluck, ‖dumbhead, ‖dummkopf, dummy, dunderhead, dunderpate, fathead, featherweight, goof, ‖goon, hammerhead, idiot, ignoramus, ironhead, knothead, knucklehead, lackwit, lame-brain, lunk, lunkhead, ‖moonraker, moron, muddlehead, mug, muggins, mutt, muttonhead, nitwit, noddy, noodle, numskull, oaf, pinhead, poke, prune, pumpkin head, put, ‖schnook, simp, simpleton, ‖spoon, squarehead, ‖stunpoll, ‖stupe, stupid, thickhead, thickskull, turnip, wantwit, woodenhead, zombie
rel lightweight; ass, donkey, fool, imbecile, jackass, jerk, nincompoop, ninny, ‖schmo, ‖schmuck; birdbrain, featherbrain, scatterbrain
idiom dumb ox, Simple Simon
con brain, highbrow, intellectual, thinker, wit; pundit, sage, savant, scholar, wise man; prodigy, wizard; genius, mastermind

duncical *adj* *syn* see STUPID 1

dunderhead *n* *syn* see DUNCE

dunderpate *n* *syn* see DUNCE

dundrearies *n pl* *syn* see SIDE-WHISKERS

---

dungeon *n* a close dark prison or vault commonly underground <the prisoners were kept in lightless *dungeons*>
syn oubliette
rel vault; black hole; cell; jail, prison
dungy *adj* ***syn*** see DIRTY 1
dunk *vb* ***syn*** see DIP 1
rel saturate, soak, sop
duo *n* ***syn*** see COUPLE
dupe *n* ***syn*** see FOOL 3
dupe *vb* to delude by underhand methods <the public is easily *duped* by extravagant claims in advertising>
syn bamboozle, befool, catch, chicane, con, dust, flimflam, fool, gull, hoax, hoodwink, hornswoggle, job, kid, pigeon, ‖rig, spoof, trick, victimize
rel beguile, betray, deceive, delude, double-cross, mislead; cheat, cozen, defraud, overreach; baffle, circumvent, outwit
idiom pull one's leg, put something over (*or* across)
con enlighten, inform, wise (up)
dupe *vb* ***syn*** see DOUBLE 1
dupery *n* ***syn*** see DECEPTION 1
duple *adj* ***syn*** see TWOFOLD 1
duplex *adj* ***syn*** see TWOFOLD 1
duplicate *adj* ***syn*** see SAME 2
duplicate *n* **1** ***syn*** see REPRODUCTION
rel analogue, counterpart, parallel
2 ***syn*** see MATE 5
duplicate *vb* **1** ***syn*** see DOUBLE 1
2 ***syn*** see COPY
duplicitous *adj* ***syn*** see UNDERHAND
duplicity *n* ***syn*** see DECEIT 1
rel faithlessness, perfidiousness, perfidy, treacherousness, treachery
durable *adj* ***syn*** see LASTING
rel stout, strong, tenacious
con feeble, fragile, frail, weak
duration *n* **1** ***syn*** see CONTINUATION 1
2 ***syn*** see RUN 2
3 ***syn*** see TERM 2
duress *n* ***syn*** see FORCE 4
during *prep* in the course of <*during* the disorder some men kept their heads>
syn amid, mid, midst, over, throughout
dusk *adj* ***syn*** see DARK 1
dusk *n* ***syn*** see EVENING 1
‖**dusk dark** *n* ***syn*** see EVENING 1
dusky *adj* **1** ***syn*** see DARK 3
2 ***syn*** see DARK 1
3 ***syn*** see GLOOMY 3
4 ***syn*** see OBSCURE 3
dust *n* **1** ***syn*** see DUSTING
2 ***syn*** see QUARREL
‖**3** ***syn*** see REFUSE
dust *vb* **1** ***syn*** see SPRINKLE 1
2 ***syn*** see WHIP 2
3 ***syn*** see DUPE
idiom throw dust in one's eyes
‖**4** ***syn*** see HURRY 2
dusting *n* **1** a small quantity lightly applied to or sprinkled on <a *dusting* of sugar on the cake>
syn dust, powdering, sprinkling
‖**2** ***syn*** see DEFEAT 1
‖**dust off** *vb* ***syn*** see MURDER 1
dustup *n* ***syn*** see QUARREL
dusty *adj* ***syn*** see ARID 2
Dutch *n* ***syn*** see TROUBLE 3
duteous *adj* ***syn*** see RESPECTFUL
dutiful *adj* ***syn*** see RESPECTFUL
duty *n* **1** ***syn*** see OBLIGATION 2
rel accountability, amenability, answerability, liability
2 ***syn*** see FUNCTION 1
3 ***syn*** see LOAD 3
4 ***syn*** see TAX 1
5 ***syn*** see TASK 1
6 ***syn*** see USE 4
dwarf *n* a very small person <she was a tiny little thing, almost a *dwarf*>
syn homunculus, hop-o'-my-thumb, Lilliputian, manikin, midge, midget, peewee, pygmy, runt, Tom Thumb
rel half-pint, ‖ribe, ‖shrimp, wart; dwarfling; minimus
ant giant
dwarf *vb* ***syn*** see STUNT
dwarf *adj* ***syn*** see TINY
dwarfish *adj* ***syn*** see TINY
dwell *vb* **1** ***syn*** see RESIDE 1
2 ***syn*** see CONSIST 1
dweller *n* ***syn*** see INHABITANT
dwelling *n* ***syn*** see HABITATION 2
dwindle *vb* **1** ***syn*** see DECREASE
rel ebb, subside, wane; attenuate, extenuate, thin; moderate; disappear
2 ***syn*** see FAIL 3
‖**dwine** *vb* ***syn*** see FAIL 1
dyad *n* ***syn*** see COUPLE
dye *n* ***syn*** see COLOR 6
dyed-in-the-wool *adj* ***syn*** see INVETERATE 1
dyestuff *n* ***syn*** see COLOR 6
dying *adj* ***syn*** see MORIBUND
dynamic *adj* **1** ***syn*** see ACTIVE 1
rel activating, energizing, vitalizing
ant static
2 ***syn*** see VIGOROUS
rel forceful, forcible; intense, vehement, violent
con idle, inactive, passive
ant inert
dynamite *vb* ***syn*** see DESTROY 1
dynamo *n* ***syn*** see HUSTLER 1
dysentery *n* ***syn*** see DIARRHEA
dyslogistic *adj* ***syn*** see DEROGATORY
ant eulogistic
dyspathy *n* ***syn*** see ANTIPATHY 2
dyspeptic *adj* ***syn*** see ILL-TEMPERED
dysphoria *n* ***syn*** see SADNESS

E

each *adj* ***syn*** see ALL 2
rel any, several, various; particular, respective, specific

each *adv* ***syn*** see APIECE
idiom a shot, a throw, a whack

eager *adj* moved by a strong and urgent desire or interest <young executives *eager* to succeed>
syn agog, anxious, appetent, ardent, athirst, avid, breathless, impatient, keen, raring, solicitous, thirsty
rel enthusiastic, gung ho, heated, hot; ambitious, intent; acquisitive, covetous, craving, desirous, hankering, ||honing, hungry, longing, pining, wishful, yearning; impatient, restive, restless
idiom champing at the bit, ready and willing
con aloof, disinterested, incurious, indifferent, unconcerned, uninterested; apathetic, detached, impassive, stolid
ant listless

eagerness *n* a strong and urgent desire or interest <an *eagerness* to learn>
syn ardor, enthusiasm, zing
rel alacrity, avidity, keenness, quickness; ambition; gusto, ||mustard, zest
con lackadaisicality, languor, lethargy; aloofness, disinterest; apathy, deliberation, detachment, impassivity, stolidity
ant listlessness

eagle eye *n* ***syn*** see EYE 3

eagle–eyed *adj* ***syn*** see SHARP-EYED

ear *n* ***syn*** see NOTICE 1

earlier *adv* **1** ***syn*** see BEFORE 2
2 ***syn*** see HITHERTO 1
3 ***syn*** see BEFORE 3

earliest *adj* ***syn*** see FIRST 2
con final, terminal, ultimate
ant latest

early *adv* **1** at or nearly at the beginning of a period, course, process, or series <it is much too *early* to guess the outcome>
syn betimes, seasonably, soon, timely
rel first
2 in advance of the expected or usual time <these apples bear *early* and heavy>
syn betimes, oversoon, prematurely
rel beforehand
idiom ahead of time, bright and early

early *adj* **1** of, relating to, or occurring near the beginning of a period of time, a development, or a series <*early* Renaissance><*early* art forms>
syn primitive, primordial
rel original, pristine; ancient, antediluvian, antiquated, primal, primeval; antecedent, preceding, prevenient, prior
con conclusive, final, last, terminal, ultimate; eventual; intermediate, middle, midmost
ant late
2 occurring before the expected or usual time <an *early* death><an *early* peach>
syn overearly, oversoon, premature, previous, ||soon, untimely; *compare* PRECOCIOUS
rel anticipative, anticipatory, precipitant, precocious; unanticipated, unexpected
con slow, tardy; anticipated, expected
ant late

earmark *vb* ***syn*** see DESIGNATE 3

earn *vb* **1** to receive as return for effort <*earn* a living wage>
syn acquire, bring in, ||drag down, draw down, gain, get, knock down, make, win
rel attain, effect, obtain, procure, realize, receive, secure
2 to be or make worthy of <his devotion to duty *earned* him a promotion>
syn deserve, merit, rate
rel bag, come by, harvest, net, reap, score

earnest *n* ***syn*** see EARNESTNESS
rel attention, interest; enthusiasm, warmth, zeal
ant jest, play

earnest *adj* ***syn*** see SERIOUS 1
rel ardent, enthusiastic, passionate, pressing, warm, zealous; assiduous, busy, diligent, industrious, perseverant, sedulous; sincere, wholehearted, whole-souled
con buoyant, effervescent, elastic, flippant, light
ant frivolous

earnest *n* ***syn*** see PLEDGE 1

earnestly *adv* **1** ***syn*** see HARD 3
rel seriously, soberly, solemnly, thoughtfully; zealously
2 ***syn*** see SERIOUSLY 1

earnestness *n* a state of freedom from all jesting or trifling <he studied with great *earnestness*>
syn earnest, intentness, serious-mindedness, seriousness
rel doggedness, perseverance, persistence; decision, determination, firmness, purposefulness, resolve; absorption, attentiveness, concentration, engrossment; deliberation; gravity, sobriety
con levity, lightness; shallowness, superficiality; carelessness, slackness
ant frivolity

earnings *n pl* ***syn*** see PROFIT

earshot *n* the range within which something (as a voice) may be heard <the gossips were still within *earshot* of her>
syn hearing, sound
idiom carrying (*or* hearing) distance

---

syn synonym(s) ***rel*** related word(s)
ant antonym(s) ***con*** contrasted word(s)
idiom idiomatic equivalent(s)
|| use limited; if in doubt, see a dictionary

earsplitting *adj* ***syn*** see LOUD 1
rel penetrating, shrill

earth *n* **1** the entire area in which man lives and acts <expect the destruction of the *earth*>
syn globe, (the) planet, world
rel orb, sphere; cosmos, creation, macrocosm, universe, vale
2 areas of land as distinguished from sea and air <clayey *earth*, difficult to drain>
syn dirt, dry land, ground, land, soil, terra firma
rel clay, gravel, humus, loam, mud, sand; fill, subsoil; terrain, turf; clod

earthlike *adj* ***syn*** see EARTHY 1

earthly *adj* **1** of, relating to, or characteristic of this earth or man's life on earth <*earthly* pursuits>
syn earthy, mundane, sublunary, tellurian, telluric, terrene, terrestrial, uncelestial, worldly
rel carnal, corporeal, earthbound, physical; material, temporal; unspiritual
con celestial, empyreal, empyrean, heavenly; ideal, utopian; divine, spiritual
2 ***syn*** see PROBABLE
rel imaginable, potential

earthquake *n* a shaking or trembling of the earth that is volcanic or tectonic in origin <homes destroyed by *earthquakes*>
syn quake, ‖quaker, shake, shock, temblor (*or* tremblor), tremor

earthy *adj* **1** consisting of, resembling, or suggesting earth <a stale *earthy* smell>
syn earthlike, terrene, terrestrial
rel clayey, dusty, muddy, sandy
2 ***syn*** see EARTHLY 1
3 ***syn*** see MATERIALISTIC
4 ***syn*** see REALISTIC
ant impractical

ease *n* **1** ***syn*** see REST 1
rel idleness, inactivity, inertia, inertness, passivity, supinity; calmness, security
con labor, toil, travail; adversity, difficulty; burden, care, worry
2 ***syn*** see UNCONSTRAINT
3 freedom from or mitigation of pain <medication brought him instant *ease*>
syn alleviation, easement, mitigation, relief
rel decrease, diminishment, moderation, reduction; calming, soothing
con discomfort, unrest; agony, pain
4 ***syn*** see READINESS 3
rel adroitness, artfulness, cleverness, deftness, effortlessness, expertise, expertness, fluency, knack, poise, skillfulness, smoothness; dispatch, efficiency
con awkwardness, clumsiness, maladroitness, stiffness, woodenness; constraint; inconvenience, pains; exertion
ant effort
5 ***syn*** see PROSPERITY 2

ease *vb* **1** ***syn*** see RELIEVE 1
rel deaden, dull; ameliorate, help
con afflict, torment
2 ***syn*** see LOOSE 5
rel disengage, free, release
con bind, restrain, tighten
3 to make less difficult <new laws that will *ease* voting requirements>
syn facilitate
rel aid, assist, better, help, improve; forward, further, promote, speed
idiom clear (*or* prepare) the way (for), grease the wheels, open the door (to *or* for)
con hinder, impede, retard

easeful *adj* ***syn*** see COMFORTABLE 2

easement *n* ***syn*** see EASE 3
rel allayment, appeasement, assuagement, mollification

ease off *vb* **1** ***syn*** see LOOSE 5
2 ***syn*** see ABATE 4
3 ***syn*** see RELAX 2

easily *adv* **1** without discomfort, difficulty, or reluctance <*easily* translated the document>
syn effortlessly, facilely, freely, lightly, readily, smoothly, well
rel competently, dexterously, efficiently, fluently, handily, simply
idiom hands down, slick as a whistle
con awkwardly, clumsily, ineptly, stiffly; arduously, wearily
ant laboriously
2 without question <this is *easily* the best course of action>
syn absolutely, definitely, doubtless, doubtlessly, positively, unequivocally, unquestionably
rel actually, assuredly, certainly, clearly, decidedly, indeed, really, truly, undoubtedly
idiom no doubt
con apparently, perhaps, probably, seemingly; doubtfully, equivocally, questionably
3 ***syn*** see WELL 7

easy *adj* **1** causing or involving little or no difficulty <an *easy* solution>
syn effortless, facile, light, royal, simple, smooth, untroublesome
rel apparent, clear, distinct, evident, manifest, obvious, plain; clear-cut, straightforward, uncomplicated, uncompounded, uninvolved
idiom easy as falling off a log, easy as pie, nothing to it
con arduous, difficult, troublesome; abstruse, complex, complicated, intricate, knotty
ant hard
2 ***syn*** see FORBEARING
rel compassionate, condoning, excusing, forgiving, pardoning, sympathetic; benign, kindly; lax, moderate, soft; humoring, mollycoddling, pampering, spoiling
con austere, exacting, rigid, severe, stern, strict, stringent
3 easily taken advantage of or imposed upon <he was *easy* prey to her wiles>
syn fleeceable, gullible, naive, susceptible
rel credulous, trusting, unmistrusting, unsuspicious; deceivable, deludable, dupable, exploitable; artless, dewy-eyed, green, simple, unsophisticated
con critical, cynical, disbelieving, mistrustful, scoffing, skeptical, suspicious, unbelieving

4 *syn* see FAST 7
5 *syn* see COMFORTABLE 2
rel secure
con discontented, dissatisfied; miserable
ant uncomfortable
6 *syn* see AMIABLE 1
rel familiar, gregarious, informal; courtly, diplomatic, pleasant, polite, sociable; smooth, suave, urbane
con brusque, curt, unfriendly, unpleasant; constrained, embarrassed, formal, restrained; discourteous, impolite, undiplomatic, ungracious; stiff, unsocial, withdrawn, wooden
ant ill at ease
7 *syn* see CALM 2
rel relaxed; lethargic, unambitious
con agitated, tense, troubled, uptight
8 *syn* see PROSPEROUS 3
rel successful, thriving
idiom in easy circumstances, on easy street
con straitened
9 marked by ready facility (as of expression) <an *easy* style of writing>
syn cursive, effortless, flowing, fluent, running, smooth
rel facile; graceful
con effortful, labored
ant difficult

easygoing *adj* **1** *syn* see CALM 2
con agitated, flurried, flustered, harassed; anxious, concerned, upset, worried
ant uptight
2 *syn* see LAZY
rel apathetic, careless, indifferent, unconcerned; unambitious
con active, ambitious, diligent, dynamic, energetic, industrious, live, vigorous
3 not constrained or bound by rigid standards <enjoyed the *easygoing* morality of a commune>
syn breezy, casual, ‖common, dégagé, hang-loose, informal, low-pressure, relaxed, ‖sonsy, unconstrained, unfussy, unreserved
rel affable, folksy; flexible, lax, moderate, offhand, off-handed, unaffected; carefree, devil-may-care, happy-go-lucky; outgiving; uninhibited
idiom free and easy
con ceremonious, decorous, formal, proper, stuffy; constrained, inflexible, inhibited, restrained, rigid, starchy, stiff

easy mark *n* **1** *syn* see FOOL 3
2 *syn* see SOFT TOUCH 1

‖**easy rider** *n* **1** *syn* see SYCOPHANT
2 *syn* see PIMP 1

easy street *n syn* see PROSPERITY 2

eat *vb* **1** to take in as food <they quickly *ate* a light breakfast>
syn consume, devour, feed (on), ingest, meal, partake (of), take; *compare* CONSUME 5
rel banquet, feast, gormandize; eat up, gobble (up *or* down), gorge (on), ‖mop (up), polish off, scoff; breakfast, dine, lunch, nosh, snack, sup; mouth, ‖muckamuck; nibble, pick
idiom break bread, get away with, have (*or* take) a bite, take nourishment, ‖put on the feed bag
2 *syn* see CONSUME 1
3 to consume gradually <the acid *ate* the surface of the copper>
syn bite, corrode, eat away, erode, gnaw, scour, wear (away)
rel nibble (away); consume, decompose, disintegrate, dissolve

eatable *adj syn* see EDIBLE

eat away *vb syn* see EAT 3

eating house *n* a cheap often small restaurant <grabbed a quick sandwich at a local *eating house*>
syn beanery, ‖buffet, café, ‖caff, coffee shop, cookshop, diner, ‖greasy spoon, ‖hashery, ‖hash house, lunch counter (*or* bar), luncheonette, lunchroom, lunch wagon (*or* cart), quick-lunch, sandwich shop, snack bar (*or* counter)
rel cafeteria, eatery, tearoom; trattoria

‖**eats** *n pl syn* see FOOD 1

eat up *vb* **1** to eat completely and without delay <*eat up* your dinner before it gets cold>
syn devour, dispatch, polish off
rel down, eat; bolt, gobble (up *or* down), gorge (on), ‖mop (up), wolf
2 *syn* see CONSUME 1
‖3 *syn* see DEVOUR 5
rel luxuriate (in), riot (in), wallow (in)
idiom be beside oneself over, be thrilled to death by, smack one's lips over, take delight in
‖4 *syn* see LOVE 1

ebb *vb syn* see ABATE 4
rel decline, peter (out); recede, retreat, retrograde
con ascend, increase, mount, rise; advance, progress
ant flow

ebbing *n syn* see FAILURE 4
rel declining, sinking

ebon *adj syn* see BLACK 1

ebony *adj syn* see BLACK 1

ebullience *n* lively or enthusiastic expression of thoughts or feelings <her bubbling *ebullience* was infectious>
syn buoyancy, effervescence, exuberance, exuberancy
rel animation, enthusiasm, gaiety, high-spiritedness, liveliness, vitality, vivaciousness, vivacity; agitation, excitement, exhilaration, ferment
con apathy, impassivity, languor, lethargy, listlessness, passivity, sluggishness, stolidity, torpidity, torpor; enervation, inactivity, inertia, lifelessness; disinterest, unconcern, uninterest

ebullient *adj syn* see EXUBERANT 1

eccentric *adj* **1** not having the same center <not concentric but *eccentric* circles>
syn off-center
rel uncentered; off-balance, unbalanced
con centered; balanced
ant concentric

---

syn synonym(s) *rel* related word(s)
ant antonym(s) *con* contrasted word(s)
idiom idiomatic equivalent(s)
‖ use limited; if in doubt, see a dictionary

2 ***syn*** see STRANGE 4

rel anomalous, irregular, unnatural; exceptionable, exceptional, quirky, quizzical; beeheaded, ‖dippy, wacky; fantastic, grotesque

con customary, habitual; natural, normal, regular, typical

eccentric *n* one who deviates from established patterns especially in odd or whimsical ways <an *eccentric* who filled his house with statues of himself>

syn case, character, ‖duck, oddball, oddity, original, quiz, ‖spook, ‖wack, zombie

rel bohemian, maverick, nonconformist, unconformist; dissenter, heretic; caution, coot, ‖geezer; crackpot, crank, freak, kook, screwball

idiom queer duck (*or* potato)

con conformer, conformist, conventionalist, traditionalist; bore, bromide, dullard

ecclesiast *n* ***syn*** see CLERGYMAN

ecclesiastic *n* ***syn*** see CLERGYMAN

ecclesiastical *adj* of, relating to, or belonging to a church especially as an established institution <*ecclesiastical* law>

syn church, churchly, churchmanly, spiritual

rel apostolic, canonical, episcopal, episcopalian, evangelistic, theological; clerical, ministerial, papal, pastoral, patriarchal, pontifical, prelatial, priestly, rabbinical, sacerdotal; cathedralesque, churchlike, pantheonic, synagogal, synagogical, tabernacular, templelike

con lay, secular

ecdysiast *n* ***syn*** see STRIPTEASER

echelon *n* ***syn*** see LINE 5

echoic *adj* ***syn*** see ONOMATOPOEIC

éclat *n* ***syn*** see FAME 2

rel bang, brilliance, brilliancy, display, luster, noticeableness, prominence, remarkableness; distinction, standing; kudos

con oblivion, obscurity; contempt, derision, scorn

eclectic *adj* **1** selecting what appears to be the best from various doctrines, methods, or styles <an *eclectic* taste in music>

syn discriminating, select, selective

rel elective, selecting; choosing, choosy, discerning, fastidious, finicky, fussy, particular, picky

2 composed of elements drawn from various sources <an *eclectic* art incorporating romanticism and impressionism>

syn catholic

rel broad, comprehensive, inclusive; assorted, mingled, mixed; diverse, diversified, heterogeneous, multifarious, multiform, varied; derived, unoriginal

con distinctive, narrow; new, original

eclipse *vb* ***syn*** see OBSCURE

economical *adj* ***syn*** see SPARING

rel careful, forehanded, prudent; economizing, penny-wise; cheeseparing, close, mean, miserly, niggardly, penny-pinching, penurious, scrimping, skimping, spare, stingy

con generous, lavish, wasteful

ant extravagant

economic poison *n* ***syn*** see PESTICIDE

economize *vb* to avoid unnecessary waste or expense <*economize* on food by using leftovers>

syn save

rel conserve; scrimp, skimp

con dissipate, scatter, waste

ant squander, throw away

economy *n* careful management of material resources <retired people often must learn to practice *economy*>

syn forehandedness, frugality, husbandry, providence, prudence, thrift, thriftiness

rel meanness, miserliness, niggardliness, parcity, parsimony, scrimping, skimping, stinginess; carefulness, discretion

con improvidence, lavishness, prodigality, squandering, thriftlessness, wastefulness

ant extravagance

ecstasy *n* intense exaltation of mind and feelings <was in *ecstasy* over flying>

syn heaven, rapture, rhapsody, seventh heaven, transport; *compare* EXHILARATION

rel beatitude, blessedness, bliss, blissfulness, felicity, gladness, happiness; delectation, delight, elation, joy, joyfulness, overjoyfulness, pleasure; enchantment, euphoria, intoxication, madness; exaltation, inspiration; paradise; afflatus, frenzy, fury

idiom cloud nine

con dejection, downheartedness, lowness, low-spiritedness, oppression; blues, dumps, melancholy

ant depression

ecumenical *adj* ***syn*** see UNIVERSAL 2

rel heaven-wide; all-comprehending, all-comprehensive, all-covering, all-including, all-pervading; comprehensive, general, inclusive

con diocesan, local, parochial, provincial; circumscribed, insular, limited, narrow, restricted

edacious *adj* ***syn*** see VORACIOUS

eddy *n* a swirling mass especially of water <dark *eddies* in the flooded stream>

syn maelstrom, vortex, whirl, whirlpool

rel gurge, surge, swirl, twirl, whirl; back current, back stream, countercurrent, counterflow, counterflux; backwash, backwater

eddy *vb* ***syn*** see SWIRL

edge *n* **1** ***syn*** see BORDER 1

rel end, extremity; ledge, side

con area, surface

2 a cutting quality <there was an *edge* to his voice as he answered>

syn incisiveness, keenness, sharpness

rel bite, cut, sting; knife-edge, razor-edge; acerbity, acidity, acridity, causticity; astringency, stringency; acuteness, penetration, shrillness, thinness

3 ***syn*** see VERGE 2

4 ***syn*** see ADVANTAGE 3

con bar, encumbrance, obstacle; disadvantage

edge *vb* **1** ***syn*** see SHARPEN

2 ***syn*** see BORDER 1

3 ***syn*** see SIDLE

edge in *vb* ***syn*** see INSINUATE 3

edgy *adj* **1** ***syn*** see TENSE 2
rel skittish; excitable, excited, high-strung, overstrung; irritable, touchy; impatient, restless
idiom on edge
con detached; peaceful, placid; patient
2 ***syn*** see EXCITABLE

edible *adj* suitable for use as food <*edible* plant products>
syn comestible, eatable, esculent
rel digestible; nourishing, nutritious, nutritive; palatable, savory, succulent, tasty, toothsome
ant inedible

edibles *n pl* ***syn*** see FOOD 1

edict *n* **1** a publicly proclaimed order or rule of conduct by a competent authority <a government *edict* regarding curfew enforcement>
syn decree, directive, ruling, ukase
rel instrument; order; manifesto, proclamation, pronouncement, pronunciamento; bull
2 ***syn*** see LAW 1

edifice *n* a large, magnificent, or massive building <a marble *edifice* now used as a museum>
syn erection, pile, structure; *compare* BUILDING, HUT

edify *vb* ***syn*** see ILLUMINATE 2
rel better, enhance; elucidate; educate, instruct, teach
con debase, deprave

edition *n* the total number of copies of the same work printed during a stretch of time <the initial *edition* of 50,000 copies was exhausted in a month>
syn impression, printing, reissue, reprinting

educate *vb* ***syn*** see TEACH
rel cultivate, nurture; brief, explain, inform

education *n* **1** the act or process of educating <devoted herself to the *education* of illiterate adults>
syn instruction, schooling, teaching, training, tuition, tutelage
rel coaching, pedagogy, tutorage, tutoring, tutorship; direction, guidance
2 the product or result of being educated <obtained his *education* in local schools and in college>
syn erudition, knowledge, learning, scholarship, science
rel culture, edification, enlightenment, learnedness, literacy
con ignorance, illiteracy

educational *adj* ***syn*** see INFORMATIVE

educative *adj* ***syn*** see INFORMATIVE

educe *vb* **1** to draw out something hidden, latent, or reserved <*educed* important information from the witness>
syn elicit, evince, evoke, extort, extract, milk
rel drag, draw, draw out, pull, wrest, wring; gain, get, obtain, procure, secure; distill
con miss, overlook, pass over
2 ***syn*** see DERIVE 1
rel reason (out), think (out)

eerie *adj* ***syn*** see WEIRD 1
rel bizarre, fantastic, grotesque; arcane; crawly

efface *vb* ***syn*** see ERASE
rel eradicate, extirpate; eliminate, exclude, rule out

effect *n* **1** a condition or occurrence traceable to a cause <the *effect* of the medicine was dizziness>
syn aftereffect, aftermath, causatum, consequence, corollary, end product, event, eventuality, issue, outcome, precipitate, result, sequel, sequence, upshot
rel pursuance; development, fruit, outgrowth, ramification; denouement, repercussion; conclusion, end; side effect
con antecedent, determinant, occasion, reason; base, basis, foundation, ground, groundwork
ant cause
2 effects *pl* ***syn*** see POSSESSION 2
3 the force of impression of one thing on another <had a profound *effect* on our lives>
syn impact, imprint, influence, mark, repercussion
rel backlash, backwash; recoil, reflex, response; aftereffect, aftermath

effect *vb* **1** to induce to come into being <specific genes *effect* specific bodily characters>
syn bring about, cause, draw on, make, produce, secure
rel conceive, create, generate; bring on, induce; enact, render, turn out, yield
con impede, limit, restrict; repress, suppress
2 to carry to a successful conclusion <found a pass that allowed them to *effect* passage through the mountains>
syn bring off, carry out, carry through, effectuate; *compare* FULFILL 1, PERFORM 2
rel actualize, realize; achieve, procure
con fail, fall down
3 ***syn*** see ENFORCE

effective *adj* producing or capable of producing a result <an *effective* rebuke>
syn effectual, efficacious, efficient, virtuous
rel adequate, capable, competent; cogent, compelling, convincing, sound, telling, valid; able, active, dynamic; operative, useful; direct
con abortive, bootless, fruitless, futile, vain; empty, hollow, idle, nugatory, otiose, pointless; inoperative, useless, worthless
ant ineffective

effectiveness *n* **1** ***syn*** see POINT 3
rel forcefulness, potency, power, strength, verve, vigor
con impotence, weakness
ant ineffectiveness
2 ***syn*** see EFFICIENCY 1
3 ***syn*** see EFFICACY 1

effectual *adj* ***syn*** see EFFECTIVE
rel accomplishing, achieving, effecting, fulfilling; practicable, sound, useful, valid, workable; conclusive, decisive, determinative, influential; authoritative, potent, powerful, strong, toothy
con impotent, weak

---

syn synonym(s) ***rel*** related word(s)
ant antonym(s) ***con*** contrasted word(s)
idiom idiomatic equivalent(s)
|| use limited; if in doubt, see a dictionary

ant ineffectual

effectuate *vb* ***syn*** see EFFECT 2

effeminate *adj* lacking manly strength and purpose <a young man with extravagant and *effeminate* mannerisms>
syn epicene, Miss-Nancyish, pansified, prissy, sissified, sissy, unmanly
rel chichi, old-maidish, overnice, precious; foppish, sappy, silken
ant manly, masculine

effervescence *n* ***syn*** see EBULLIENCE
rel bubbling, ebullition, fizzing, foaming
con deadness, flatness, staleness

effervescent *adj* **1** ***syn*** see EXUBERANT 1
2 ***syn*** see ELASTIC 2
rel animated, boiling, bubbly, excited, gay, lively, sparkling, sprightly, vivacious; gleeful, hilarious, jolly, mirthful
con lifeless, listless, subdued; earnest, sedate, serious, solemn

effete *adj* **1** ***syn*** see STERILE 1
2 having lost energy or drive <*effete*, weary, burned-out revolutionaries>
syn all in, bleary, ‖clapped-out, depleted, done, done in, drained, exhausted, far-gone, spent, used up, washed-out, worn-out
rel consumed; debilitated, enfeebled, fatigued
idiom on one's last legs, out on one's feet
con alive, lively, vigorous, vital
3 having lost character <a soft, *effete* society>
syn decadent, decayed, degenerate, overripe
rel decaying, declining; soft, weak; dissolute, immoral

efficacious *adj* ***syn*** see EFFECTIVE
rel active, operative, productive; influential, potent, powerful, puissant, strong
con abortive; impotent, powerless, useless, vain, weak
ant inefficacious

efficacy *n* **1** the power to produce an effect <*efficacy* of the drug>
syn capability, effectiveness, efficiency, potency
rel capableness, productiveness, use; adequacy, capacity, sufficiency
con ineffectiveness, inefficiency; uselessness, worthlessness
ant inefficacy
2 ***syn*** see EFFICIENCY 1

efficiency *n* **1** the capacity to produce desired results with a minimum expenditure of energy, time, or resources <demands a high degree of *efficiency* on the job>
syn effectiveness, efficacy, performance
rel ability, address, adeptness, competence, expertise, know-how, proficiency, prowess, skill; capability, resourcefulness; productivity
con inadequacy, incompetence, ineffectiveness; unproductiveness
ant inefficiency
2 ***syn*** see EFFICACY 1

efficient *adj* ***syn*** see EFFECTIVE
rel able, capable, competent, fitted, qualified; adept, expert, masterly, proficient, skilled, skillful
con incapable, incompetent, inexpert, unadept, unproficient, unqualified, unsuitable; unproductive; ineffectual
ant inefficient

effloresce *vb* ***syn*** see BLOSSOM

effort *n* **1** the active use of energy in producing a result <thought the job wasn't worth the *effort*>
syn elbow grease, exertion, pains, trouble, while
rel labor, toil, travail, work; energy, force, might, power, puissance; attempt, endeavor, essay
idiom sweat of one's brow
con adroitness, facility, smoothness; do-nothingness, inaction, indolence, inertia, lackadaisicalness, languor, laziness
ant ease
2 ***syn*** see TASK 2

effortful *adj* ***syn*** see HARD 6

effortless *adj* **1** ***syn*** see EASY 1
rel adept, expert, masterly, proficient, ready, skilled, skillful
con laborious, toilsome, trying
ant painstaking
2 ***syn*** see EASY 9

effortlessly *adv* ***syn*** see EASILY 1
rel adeptly, adroitly, efficiently, expertly, proficiently, skillfully
con painstakingly
ant arduously, laboriously

effrontery *n* flagrant disregard of courtesy or propriety and an arrogant assumption of privilege <had the *effrontery* to insult her father>
syn brashness, brass, cheek, chutzpah, confidence, ‖crust, face, gall, nerve, presumption; *compare* INSOLENCE
rel audacity, hardihood, temerity; assurance, self-assurance, self-confidence; brazenness, impudence; impertinence, insolence
con courtesy, grace, propriety

effulgent *adj* ***syn*** see BRIGHT 1
rel vivid; glorious, resplendent, splendid
con dark, dusky, gloomy, murky

effusive *adj* unduly demonstrative <*effusive* assurances of undying love>
syn gushing, gushy, slobbering, slobbery, sloppy
rel expansive, fulsome, outpouring, profuse; demonstrative, unconstrained, unreserved, unrestrained; cloying, slushy; smarmy
con close, restrained, reticent, taciturn; bashful, modest, shy
ant reserved

egg (on) *vb* ***syn*** see URGE
rel agitate, excite, pique, stimulate; instigate; arouse, drive, rally, stir up, whip (on *or* up)
con arrest, bridle

egghead *n* ***syn*** see INTELLECTUAL 2

egocentric *adj* **1** concerned with the individual person rather than society <an *egocentric* approach to world problems>
syn individualist, individualistic
rel self-centered, selfish
2 concerned only with one's own activities or needs and usually tending to self-assertion or

self-satisfaction <an *egocentric* man, lacking feeling for others>
syn egoistic, egomaniacal, egotistic, self-absorbed, self-centered, self-concerned, self-interested, self-involved, selfish, self-seeking, self-serving; *compare* POMPOUS 1
rel conceited, narcissistic, self-affected, self-applauding, self-conceited, self-concentered, self-indulgent, self-loving, stuck-up, vainglorious; megalomaniac
idiom wrapped up in oneself

egoism *n* **1** ***syn*** see EGOTISM 1
rel self-assurance, self-confidence, self-possession
ant altruism
2 ***syn*** see CONCEIT 2
rel self-satisfaction
con meekness, modesty
ant humility

egoistic *adj* ***syn*** see EGOCENTRIC 2
rel individualistic; self-satisfied, swellheaded
con humble, modest
ant altruistic

egomaniacal *adj* ***syn*** see EGOCENTRIC 2
rel self-exalting, self-glorifying, vainglorious

egotism *n* **1** an exaggerated sense of one's own importance <in believing that he was indispensable, he exhibited consummate *egotism*>
syn egoism, self-importance
rel conceit, conceitedness, narcissism, self-esteem, self-love, vainness; boastfulness, boasting, bragging, gasconade, gasconism, megalomania, vaunting
con humility, lowliness; bashfulness, diffidence, shyness; modesty
ant altruism
2 ***syn*** see CONCEIT 2
rel arrogance, superiority; contempt
con humbleness, self-effacement
ant humility

egotistic *adj* ***syn*** see EGOCENTRIC 2
rel boastful, cocky, inflated, pretentious, proud, puffed up, self-satisfied; conceited, stuck-up
idiom in love with oneself, stuck on oneself
con humble, modest; self-effacing, shy

egregious *adj* conspicuously bad or objectionable <an *egregious* mistake>
syn capital, flagrant, glaring, gross, rank
rel arrant, outright, stark; infamous, nefarious, notorious; atrocious, deplorable, heinous, monstrous, outrageous, preposterous
con measly, minor, petty, piddling, slender, slight, trifling, trivial

egress *n* **1** ***syn*** see DEPARTURE 1
rel emergence, emerging
con coming, entering; arrival
ant ingress
2 a place or means of going out <a gate providing *egress* from the pasture>
syn exit, outlet
rel opening, passage; escape
idiom way out
con entrance, entry, entryway
ant access, ingress

egression *n* ***syn*** see DEPARTURE 1
con entrance, entering
ant ingression

eidolon *n* ***syn*** see APPARITION

ejaculate *vb* ***syn*** see EXCLAIM
rel call (out), shout, vociferate, yell

eject *vb* **1** to drive or force (somebody) out <*eject* an intruder from one's home>
syn boot (out), chase, chuck, dismiss, evict, extrude, kick out, out, throw out; *compare* BANISH
rel displace, dispossess; drive off, rout, run off; debar, disbar, eliminate, exclude, rule out, shut out; bump, cashier, discharge, fire, sack; discard, shed; reject, repudiate, spurn
idiom give one his walking papers, send packing, show one the door
con accept, admit, install, receive; entertain, harbor, house, lodge, shelter
2 ***syn*** see ERUPT 1

elaborate *adj* **1** ***syn*** see COMPLEX 2
2 marked by complexity of detail or ornament <an *elaborate* coiffure>
syn complicated, fancy, intricate
rel detailed, highly-wrought; decorated, dressy, embellished, ornate; elegant; busy, overdone, overworked, overwrought
con common, ordinary, plain, unpolished; inartificial, inornate, natural
ant simple

elaborate *vb* **1** ***syn*** see EXPAND 4
rel comment, discuss, dwell (upon); clarify, explain, expound, interpret
2 ***syn*** see UNFOLD 3

élan *n* ***syn*** see SPIRIT 5
rel impetus

élan vital *n* ***syn*** see SOUL 1

elapse *vb* ***syn*** see PASS 3
rel flow, glide, pass (by), slide, slip (by); lapse, run out

elastic *adj* **1** able to withstand strain without being permanently affected or injured <a rubber band is *elastic*>
syn flexible, resilient, springy, stretch, stretchy, supple, whippy
rel ductile, malleable, pliable, pliant, plastic, rubberlike, rubbery; adaptable, moldable, stretchable, yielding; bouncy, limber, lithe
con brittle; inflexible, stiff, tense
ant rigid
2 able to recover quickly from depression and maintain high spirits <had an *elastic* optimistic nature>
syn airy, bouncy, buoyant, effervescent, expansive, resilient, volatile
rel animated, gay, lively, sprightly, vivacious; ebullient, high-spirited, mettlesome, soaring, spirited; adaptable, recuperative
con blue, dejected, depressed, gloomy, melancholy, sad; flaccid, limp

---

syn synonym(s) ***rel*** related word(s)
ant antonym(s) ***con*** contrasted word(s)
idiom idiomatic equivalent(s)
|| use limited; if in doubt, see a dictionary

elate *vb* to elevate the spirits of <the phenomenal sales record *elated* him>
syn commove, excite, exhilarate, inspire, set up, spirit (up), stimulate
rel brighten, cheer, cheer up, encourage; delight, gladden, gratify, overjoy; buoy, elevate, exalt, uplift
con distress; oppress, weigh; weary
ant depress

elated *adj* ***syn*** see INTOXICATED 2
rel enchanted, enraptured, exalted, transported; delighted, ecstatic, euphoric, exultant, jubilant, overjoyed
idiom in heaven, in seventh heaven, on cloud nine
con blue, deflated, unhappy

elation *n* **1** the quality or state of being elated <felt great *elation* when he won the presidential nomination>
syn euphoria, exaltation, exhilaration
rel buoyancy; happiness, joy; excitement; rapture, transport
idiom stars in one's eyes
con blues, depression; distress, misery, sadness, unhappiness
ant deflation
2 ***syn*** see EUPHORIA 2
ant depression

elbow *vb* ***syn*** see PUSH 2

elbowroom *n* ***syn*** see ROOM 3
rel space

elder *n* **1** ***syn*** see SENIOR 2
2 ***syn*** see OLDSTER
3 ***syn*** see SUPERIOR

elderliness *n* ***syn*** see OLD AGE

elderly *adj* ***syn*** see AGED 1
rel aging, declining
con juvenile, young
ant youthful

eldorado *n* ***syn*** see BONANZA

elect *adj* ***syn*** see SELECT 1
rel choice, rare; hand-picked, singled out; designated, destined, ordained; delivered, redeemed, saved
con refused, rejected, repudiated, spurned; disdained, scorned; damned, doomed, reprobate

elect *vb* **1** ***syn*** see CHOOSE 1
rel decide, determine, resolve, settle; conclude, judge; accept, admit, receive
con reject; dismiss, eject, expel, oust
ant abjure
2 to select by or as if by ballot <the board of directors *elected* a new chairman>
syn ballot, vote (in)
rel choose, designate, name, opt, pick, select, single; nominate; appoint
3 ***syn*** see WILL

election *n* ***syn*** see CHOICE 1

elective *adj* ***syn*** see OPTIONAL

electrify *vb* ***syn*** see THRILL
rel provoke; jar, stagger, stun

eleemosynary *adj* ***syn*** see CHARITABLE 1
rel beneficent, generous, liberal, munificent, openhanded
con close, parsimonious, tight

elegance *n* impressive beauty of form, appearance, or behavior <the sumptuous *elegance* of the furnishings>
syn dignity, grace
rel beauty, charm; cultivation, culture, polish, refinement, sophistication, style, taste, tastefulness; lushness, magnificence, ornateness, poshness, richness, splendor, sumptuousness
con grotesqueness, ugliness; clumsiness, crudeness, roughness, rudeness; austerity, bareness, inornateness, severity

elegant *adj* ***syn*** see CHOICE
rel august, grand, majestic, noble, stately; beautiful, graceful, handsome, lovely; cultivated, cultured, finished, polished, refined, tasteful; luxurious, opulent, sumptuous
con crude, rough, rude, uncouth; grotesque

element *n* **1** ***syn*** see ESSENTIAL 1
2 one of the parts, substances, or principles that make up a compound or complex whole <analyzed the various *elements* of the problem>
syn component, constituent, factor, ingredient; *compare* POINT 1
rel fundamental, principle; item, member, part, particle, piece, portion; detail, particular; aspect, facet, feature, view
con bulk, mass, volume; entirety, whole; sum, total, totality
ant composite, compound
3 elements *pl* ***syn*** see ALPHABET 2
rel basics, basis, foundations, groundwork; outlines
4 ***syn*** see POINT 1
rel division, member, section, sector, segment

elemental *adj* **1** of, relating to, or being an ultimate and irreducible element <such *elemental* aspects of life as sex and nutrition>
syn basic, elementary, essential, fundamental, primitive, substratal, underlying
rel primary, prime, primordial; inherent, intrinsic, radical
con secondary, subordinate; casual, incidental, trivial, unimportant
2 ***syn*** see ELEMENTARY 1
3 ***syn*** see INHERENT

elementary *adj* **1** of, relating to, or dealing with the simplest principles of something <can't handle the most *elementary* decision-making>
syn basal, beginning, elemental, rudimental, rudimentary, simplest
rel introductory, prefatory, preliminary; easy, simple; rude, unsubtle
con complex, complicated, elaborate, intricate, labyrinthine; sophisticated
ant advanced
2 ***syn*** see ELEMENTAL 1

elephantine *adj* **1** ***syn*** see HUGE
con slender, slight, slim, thin; dainty
2 ***syn*** see PONDEROUS 2
rel awkward, clumsy, graceless, maladroit, ungraceful
con graceful, nimble, quick

elevate *vb* **1** ***syn*** see LIFT 1

rel ensky, erect
con cut (down), deflate, depress, scale (down)
ant lower
2 *syn* see ADVANCE 2
rel boost; enhance, glorify, heighten
con demote, downgrade, lower, reduce; abase, debase, degrade

elevated *adj* **1** being positioned above a surface <an *elevated* monorail>
syn lifted, raised, upheaved, uplifted, upraised, uprisen
rel high; aerial
con ground-level, low, lowered, low-lying, unelevated
ant sunken
2 being on a high moral or intellectual plane <*elevated* ideas>
syn high-minded, moral, noble
rel ethical, honorable, righteous, upright, upstanding, virtuous
con base, ignoble, mean; immoral, low, unethical; intolerable, unacceptable
3 *syn* see GRAND 3
4 being exceedingly dignified in form, tone, or style <an *elevated* prose style>
syn eloquent, high, lofty
rel dignified, formal; grand, grandiloquent, grandiose, high-flown, majestic, stately, towering
con informal; lowly, unassuming

elevation *n* **1** *syn* see HEIGHT
rel acclivity, ascent, rise
con depression, descent; flatness, levelness
2 *syn* see ADVANCEMENT 1
rel advance, boost, raise; ennoblement, exaltation, glorification, lionization; apotheosis, deification, immortalization, magnification
con downgrading; depreciation, detraction, disparagement
ant degradation

elf *n syn* see FAIRY

elicit *vb syn* see EDUCE 1
rel bring, fetch
con eschew, forego; abandon

elide *vb syn* see NEGLECT

eligible *adj* qualified to be or worthy of being chosen <an *eligible* bachelor>
syn fit, suitable
rel acceptable, desirable, likely, preferable, seemly; capable, fitted, qualified, suited, worthy; marriageable, nubile; visitable
con undesirable; disqualified, unfit, unqualified, unsuitable, unworthy
ant ineligible

eliminate *vb* **1** *syn* see EXCLUDE
rel freeze out, shut out; dismiss, ||dump, eject, evict, expel, oust; delete, erase, expunge
con accept, receive
2 *syn* see REMOVE 4
3 *syn* see PURGE 3

elite *n* **1** *syn* see BEST
rel elect, pink, select; ||hoi polloi
idiom cream of the crop, crème de la crème, pick of the bunch
2 *syn* see ARISTOCRACY
rel drawing rooms; Four Hundred; beautiful people, jet set, smart set
idiom high society, horsey set
con hoi polloi, (the) masses, mob, peasantry, people, proletariat, rabble

elixir *n syn* see PANACEA
rel balm, cure, therapy, therapeutic

ell *n syn* see ANNEX

elocution *n syn* see ORATORY

elongate *vb syn* see EXTEND 3
rel drag (out); string
con contract, draw in; compress; curtail, retrench; shrink
ant abbreviate, shorten

elongate *adj syn* see LONG 1
rel lengthened
ant abbreviated, shortened

elongated *adj syn* see LONG 1
rel drawn (out), lengthened, prolongated, prolonged, protracted, stretched
con contracted, drawn (in), shrunken
ant shortened

elongation *n syn* see EXTENSION 1

elope *vb* to go away secretly usually with the intention of marrying <decided to *elope* rather than endure a big wedding>
syn run away
idiom go to Gretna Green

eloquence *n* discourse marked by force and persuasiveness suggesting strong feeling <read the poem with *eloquence*>
syn expression, expressiveness, expressivity, facundity
rel meaningfulness, persuasiveness; fervor, force, forcefulness, passion, power, spirit, vigor

eloquent *adj* **1** *syn* see VOCAL 3
rel forceful, potent, powerful; ardent, fervent, fervid, impassioned, passionate; glib, silver-tongued, voluble
con inarticulate, ineffective, weak
2 *syn* see EXPRESSIVE
rel graphic, indicative, revealing, suggestive, telling; affecting, impressive, moving, poignant, touching
3 *syn* see ELEVATED 4

else *adv syn* see OTHERWISE 2

else *adj syn* see ADDITIONAL

||**elseways** *adv syn* see OTHERWISE 2

elsewise *adv syn* see OTHERWISE 2

elucidate *vb syn* see CLARIFY 2
rel exemplify; demonstrate, prove; annotate, spell out; enlighten
con confuse; darken

elude *vb syn* see ESCAPE 2
rel baffle, circumvent, foil, frustrate, outwit, thwart; flee, fly
idiom give the slip

---

syn synonym(s) *rel* related word(s)
ant antonym(s) *con* contrasted word(s)
idiom idiomatic equivalent(s)
|| use limited; if in doubt, see a dictionary

con accost, face; chase, follow, pursue, tag, tail, trail
elusion *n* ***syn*** see ESCAPE 2
elusive *adj* not easily perceived, grasped, comprehended, pinned down, or isolated <inspiration need not be forever *elusive* > <they finally isolated the *elusive* virus that caused the disease>
syn elusory, evasive, intangible
rel evanescent, fleeting, fugitive; baffling, imponderable, incomprehensible, mysterious; insubstantial, phantom
elusory *adj* ***syn*** see ELUSIVE
rel nebulous, vague
elvish *adj* ***syn*** see PLAYFUL 1
elysium *n* ***syn*** see HEAVEN 2
emaciated *adj* being very lean through loss of flesh (as from hunger or disease) <*emaciated* bony hands clutched at him>
syn cadaverous, gaunt, skeletal, wasted
rel bony, lean, scrawny, skinny, wizened; starved, underfed, undernourished
idiom all skin and bones, thin as a rail
con fit, husky, solid, well-fed, well-nourished; chubby, plump, portly, rotund, stocky, stout; corpulent, obese
ant fleshy
emanate *vb* ***syn*** see SPRING 1
rel initiate; emit, exude, radiate
emancipate *vb* ***syn*** see FREE
ant enslave
emasculate *vb* ***syn*** see UNNERVE
rel debilitate, devitalize
con energize, vitalize
emasculate *adj* ***syn*** see WEAK 4
embark *vb* ***syn*** see BOARD 1
embark (on *or* upon) *vb* ***syn*** see BEGIN 1
embarrass *vb* to throw into a state of self-conscious distress <bawdy stories *embarrassed* her>
syn abash, confound, confuse, discomfit, disconcert, discountenance, faze, rattle; *compare* DISCOMPOSE 1
rel agitate, bother, discompose, flurry, fluster, perturb; nonplus; chagrin, distress, vex; queer
idiom put on the spot, put to the blush
con calm, relieve, soothe
embarrassing *adj* ***syn*** see INCONVENIENT
embarrassment *n* the quality, state, or condition of being embarrassed <felt great *embarrassment* when she fell down>
syn abashment, confusion, discomfiture, discomposure, disconcertion, disconcertment, unease, uneasiness
rel constraint, strain; agitation, discombobulation, perturbation; chagrin, distress, vexation; humiliation, mortification; difficulty, Queer Street
con assurance, calm, imperturbability, savoir faire
embed *vb* ***syn*** see ENTRENCH 1
embellish *vb* **1** ***syn*** see ADORN
rel apparel, array, ‖doll up, dress up, emblaze, embroider, enrich, furbish
con bare, denude, divest, strip
2 ***syn*** see EMBROIDER
embellishment *n* ***syn*** see EXAGGERATION
rel floridity, ostentation
embezzle *vb* to appropriate dishonestly and fraudulently to one's own use <*embezzled* a trust fund>
syn misappropriate, peculate
rel loot, pilfer, steal, thieve
embitter *vb* ***syn*** see EXACERBATE
rel bitter, sour
emblem *n* **1** ***syn*** see SYMBOL 1
2 ***syn*** see INSIGNIA
emblematize *vb* ***syn*** see REPRESENT 2
embodiment *n* a concrete or actual entity in which something (as an idea, principle, or type) is embodied <he is the *embodiment* of all our hopes>
syn incarnation, personification; *compare* APOTHEOSIS 1
rel manifestation; prosopopoeia; archetype; apotheosis, epitome, quintessence
embody *vb* **1** to make an abstraction concrete or perceptible often by representation in human or animal form <Dickens *embodied* hypocrisy in his Uriah Heep>
syn exteriorize, externalize, incarnate, manifest, materialize, objectify, personalize, personify, personize, substantiate; *compare* REPRESENT 2
rel actualize, hypostatize, realize, reify, symbolize, typify; demonstrate, evince, exemplify, exhibit, illustrate, show (forth)
ant disembody
2 to cause to become a body or part of another body <*embodied* a revenue provision in the new law>
syn combine, incorporate, integrate
rel absorb, amalgamate, assimilate, blend, consolidate, fuse, merge, unify
3 ***syn*** see INCLUDE
rel compose, consist (of), constitute
4 ***syn*** see REPRESENT 2
embog *vb* ***syn*** see DELAY 1
embolden *vb* ***syn*** see ENCOURAGE 1
rel impel; inspire; chance, hazard, venture
con deter, discourage
ant abash
embouchement *n* ***syn*** see MOUTH 5
embouchure *n* ***syn*** see MOUTH 5
embowel *vb* ***syn*** see EVISCERATE
embrace *vb* **1** to gather into one's arms usually as a gesture of affection <*embraced* his wife>
syn clasp, ‖clinch, ‖clip, ‖coll, enfold, hug, press, squeeze
rel cling, grip, hold; encircle, entwine, envelop, enwind, fold, lock, twine, wrap; cuddle, fondle, nuzzle, snuggle; cradle, hold
idiom ‖go into a clinch
2 ***syn*** see ADOPT
rel accept, accommodate, admit, incorporate, receive, take (over), take in; seize (upon), welcome
con reject; abjure, deny, forswear, renounce
ant spurn
3 ***syn*** see INCLUDE
rel compose, cover, enclose, hold
embracement *n* ***syn*** see ESPOUSAL 4

embracing *n* ***syn*** see ESPOUSAL 4
embrangle *vb* ***syn*** see ENTANGLE 3
embroider *vb* to give an elaborate account of, often with florid language and fictitious details <*embroidered* the story of his adventures in the army>
syn color, embellish, exaggerate, fudge, magnify, overcharge, overdraw, overpaint, overstate, pad, stretch
rel aggrandize, amplify, build up, distend, elaborate, enhance, enlarge (upon), expand; dramatize, hyperbolize, overdo, overelaborate, overembellish, overemphasize, overestimate
idiom lay it on thick, stretch (*or* strain) the truth
con deemphasize, minimize, play (down), underestimate, understate
embroidering *n* ***syn*** see EXAGGERATION
embroil *vb* ***syn*** see INVOLVE 1
embroilment *n* **1** ***syn*** see QUARREL
2 ***syn*** see ENTANGLEMENT 1
embryo *n* ***syn*** see SEED 2
emend *vb* ***syn*** see CORRECT 1
rel alter, edit, emendate; polish, retouch
emerge *vb* ***syn*** see APPEAR 1
rel derive, originate, spring, stem; arise, materialize, rise; come (forth), come out, emanate, flow, issue (forth); proceed
idiom appear on the horizon, come on the scene, come out in the open, come to light, make its appearance
con disappear, fade, fade (out); evaporate; dissolve
emergency *n* ***syn*** see JUNCTURE 2
rel difficulty, extremity; clutch, fix, hole, pinch, push, squeeze, vicissitude; climax
idiom turn of events
emigrant *n* one that leaves one place to settle in another <a city teeming with *emigrants* from many lands>
syn immigrant, migrant
rel alien, displaced person, DP, émigré, evacuee, exile, expatriate, fugitive, refugee; migrator, migratory
con aborigine, native
emigrate *vb* ***syn*** see MIGRATE
émigré *n* **1** a person forced to immigrate usually for political reasons <a city filled with White Russian *émigrés*>
syn exile, expatriate, expellee
rel emigrant, immigrant; alien, displaced person, DP, evacuee, fugitive, refugee
2 ***syn*** see REFUGEE
eminence *n* **1** a condition, position, or state of great importance or superiority <the *eminence* of the presidency>
syn distinction, illustriousness, kudos, preeminence, prestige, prominence, prominency, renown
rel greatness, loftiness, prepotency, significance, superiority; authority, credit, dignity, importance, influence, power, weight; fame, famousness, glory, honor, reputation, repute
con insignificance, unimportance; obscurity
2 ***syn*** see NOTABLE 1
3 a natural elevation <the house stood on an *eminence* overlooking the river>
syn projection, prominence
rel peak, raise, rise, uprise; altitude, elevation, height; highness, loftiness
con cavity, depression, dip
eminency *n* ***syn*** see FORTE
eminent *adj* ***syn*** see FAMOUS 2
rel well-known; august, dominant, exalted, important, lofty, noble, preeminent; big league, big-name, big-time
con uncelebrated, unremarkable, unrenowned; common, lowly
eminently *adv* ***syn*** see VERY 1
emissary *n* ***syn*** see MESSENGER
emit *vb* **1** ***syn*** see DISCHARGE 5
2 to discharge something such as moisture, vapor, or fumes <a smokestack *emitting* effluents>
syn give off, give out, issue, release, throw off, vent
rel discharge, evacuate, expel; let out, loose, pass (off); pour (out), reek; drip, emanate, excrete, extrude, exude, ooze, secrete; exhale, expire
emolument *n* ***syn*** see WAGE
rel guerdon
emote *vb* to give expression to emotion especially on or as if on the stage <she *emotes,* postures, and harangues at the slightest provocation>
syn emotionalize
rel gush, sentimentalize; carry on, rage, rant, storm, take on
emotion *n* ***syn*** see FEELING 3
rel excitability, responsiveness, sensibility, sensitiveness, sensitivity, susceptibilities; sensation
con coldness, detachment, reserve, unfeelingness
emotionable *adj* ***syn*** see EMOTIONAL 1
emotional *adj* **1** dominated by, prone to, or moved by emotion <an irritable *emotional* woman who was easily upset by trivialities>
syn emotionable, feeling, sensitive, sentient
rel responsive, susceptible, susceptive; softhearted, sympathetic; ardent, fervent, passionate; rhapsodic, rhapsodical
con cold, detached, insensitive, reserved, taciturn, unfeeling
ant emotionless, unemotional
2 appealing to or arousing emotion <an *emotional* sermon>
syn affective, emotive, moving; *compare* MOVING 2
rel affecting, stirring, touching
emotionalize *vb* ***syn*** see EMOTE
emotionless *adj* **1** ***syn*** see COLD 2
rel nonemotional, undemonstrative; cool, dispassionate, distant, immovable, impassive, remote, reserved; heartless, unfeeling

---

syn synonym(s) ***rel*** related word(s)
ant antonym(s) ***con*** contrasted word(s)
idiom idiomatic equivalent(s)
|| use limited; if in doubt, see a dictionary

con responsive, softhearted, sympathetic; ardent, fervent, passionate
ant emotional
2 *syn* see MATTER-OF-FACT 3
emotive *adj syn* see EMOTIONAL 2
empathy *n syn* see SYMPATHY 2
rel accord, affinity, communion, compatibility, concord, congeniality, fellow feeling, rapport, responsiveness, warmth; appreciation, comprehension, understanding
idiom community of interests
con animosity, animus, antagonism, antipathy, enmity
emphasis *n* force brought to bear on something to bring out what is important <the school's *emphasis* on discipline>
syn accent, accentuation, stress
rel attention; force, insistence; weight
emphasize *vb* to give emphasis to especially by displaying more or less prominently <the papers *emphasized* crime stories>
syn feature, italicize, play (up), stress, underline, underscore
rel accent, accentuate, charge, highlight, mark, pinpoint, point (up), punctuate, spotlight; assert, press
idiom bear down on (*or* upon)
con depreciate, minimize, play (down), shrug off, underrate, understate
ant de-emphasize
emphatic *adj* marked by, uttered with, or made prominent by stress or emphasis <made his point in an *emphatic* argument>
syn assertive, forceful, insistent, resounding
rel aggressive, energetic, insistive, vigorous; accented, accentuated, assertative, decided, emphasized, marked, pointed, stressed, underlined
con insipid, milk-and-water, unaggressive, unassertive, weak, wishy-washy; de-emphasized, played (down), understated
ant unemphatic
empirical *adj* originating in, relying on, or based on factual information, observation, or direct sense experience <an *empirical* basis for an ethical theory>
syn experient, experiential, experimental
rel observational; factual
con conjectural, speculative, unproved, unsubstantiated; ideal, imagined
ant theoretical
employ *vb* **1** *syn* see USE 2
rel avail, exert, practice, work; devote, engross, monopolize
2 to provide with a job that pays wages <*employed* a new draftsman>
syn engage, hire, put on, take on
rel add, contract (for), obtain, procure, retain, secure, sign (on *or* up)
employable *adj syn* see OPEN 5
employed *adj syn* see BUSY 1
employment *n* **1** *syn* see USE 1
rel purpose; disposition, exercise, exploitation, handling, utilization
2 *syn* see EXERCISE 1
3 *syn* see WORK 1
rel assignment, mission; office, position, post, situation; function
4 the act of employing for wages <handled the *employment* of new workers>
syn engagement, engaging, hiring
rel enlistment, enrollment, recruitment, signing on
empower *vb* **1** *syn* see INVEST 2
2 *syn* see AUTHORIZE 1
3 *syn* see ENABLE 2
rel endow, invest; authorize, charge, commission, entitle, entrust, license, privilege, sanction
con debar, disallow, disbar, exclude, rule out, shut out
emprise *n syn* see ADVENTURE
emptiness *n syn* see VACUITY 2
emptor *n syn* see PURCHASER
empty *adj* **1** lacking contents that could or should be present <an *empty* apartment> <the whole book is *empty* of meaning>
syn bare, clear, stark, vacant, vacuous, void
rel barren, blank; abandoned, deserted, emptied, forsaken, godforsaken, unfilled, unfurnished, uninhabited, untenanted, vacated; destitute, devoid; depleted, drained, exhausted
con complete, replete; filled, occupied, packed, teeming
ant full
2 *syn* see VAIN 1
rel paltry, petty, trifling, trivial; banal, flat, inane, ineffectual, insipid, jejune, vapid; dumb, fatuous, foolish, ignorant, silly, simple
con meaningful, pregnant, significant; authentic, bona fide, genuine, veritable
3 *syn* see EXPRESSIONLESS
4 *syn* see DEVOID
empty *vb syn* see VACATE 2
empty–headed *adj* **1** *syn* see GIDDY 1
rel brainless, rattleheaded; ignorant, simple
2 *syn* see VACUOUS 2
3 *syn* see IGNORANT 1
empyreal *adj syn* see CELESTIAL
rel aerial, airy; extraterrestrial; divine, holy, spiritual, sublime
ant terrestrial
empyrean *adj syn* see CELESTIAL
empyrean *n* **1** *syn* see HEAVEN 2
2 *syn* see SKY
emulate *vb syn* see RIVAL 2
rel challenge, outvie
emulation *n syn* see CONTEST 1
emulative *adj syn* see SLAVISH 3
emulous *adj syn* see AMBITIOUS 1
rel aiming, striving; agog, athirst; competitive, vying
con unambitious, unaspiring; detached, disinterested, uninterested
enable *vb* **1** *syn* see AUTHORIZE 1
rel allow, let, permit, sanction
2 to render able often by giving power, strength, or competence to <her education *enabled* her to find an excellent job>
syn empower

rel allow, let, permit; condition, fit, prepare, qualify, ready
con inhibit, preclude, prevent; disallow, enjoin, forbid, prohibit
enact *vb* **1** to cause to be by legal and authoritative act <*enact* a law>
syn constitute, establish, make
rel bring about, institute; authorize, decree, proclaim; accomplish, carry (through), effect, effectuate, execute, legislate, pass, put (through), ratify
con abolish, abrogate, annul, cancel, invalidate, nullify, rescind, revoke; overturn
ant repeal
2 *syn* see ACT 1
rel depict, portray, represent
enamored *adj* **1** moved by intense sexual attraction <became more desperately *enamored* of the man every day>
syn mashed, smitten, soft (on), spoony (over *or* on)
rel infatuated; crazy (over *or* about), mad (about), nuts (about), silly (over *or* about), wild (about); amorous, devoted, loving
idiom head over heels in love, stuck on, sweet on
2 *syn* see INFATUATED
3 taking great pleasure in something <found herself *enamored* of those huge English teas>
syn bewitched, captivated, charmed, enchanted, entranced, fascinated
rel fond
encamp *vb syn* see CAMP
encampment *n syn* see CAMP 1
enceinte *adj syn* see PREGNANT 1
enchant *vb* **1** *syn* see BEWITCH 1
2 *syn* see ATTRACT 1
rel delight, enthrall, please, send, thrill; mesmerize
idiom carry away, knock dead
con disillusion, dissatisfy, let down
ant disenchant
enchanted *adj syn* see ENAMORED 3
rel delighted, pleased; pixilated
ant disenchanted
enchanter *n syn* see MAGICIAN 1
enchanting *adj syn* see ATTRACTIVE 1
rel attractive, pleasing; delectable, delightful; beguiling, enthralling, entrancing, intriguing, witching; exciting, sirenic
con repellent
enchantment *n syn* see MAGIC 1
enchantress *n syn* see WITCH 1
enchiridion *n syn* see HANDBOOK
rel book, text
encincture *vb syn* see BELT 1
encircle *vb syn* see SURROUND 1
rel band, cincture, circuit, enring; halo, wreathe
enclose *vb* **1** to shut up or confine by or as if by barriers <a valley *enclosed* by mountains>
syn cage, close in, coop, corral, envelop, fence, hedge, hem, immure, mew, mure, pen, shut in, wall
rel bound, circumscribe, confine, contain, limit, restrict; circle, compass, encircle, encompass, surround; environ; enlock
2 *syn* see ENFOLD 1
enclosure *n syn* see COURT 1
enclothe *vb syn* see CLOTHE
encomiastic *adj syn* see EULOGISTIC
encomium *n* a formal expression of praise <an unstinted *encomium* of a national hero>
syn citation, eulogy, panegyric, salutation, tribute
rel approval, kudos, laud, laudation, magnification, praise; acclaim, acclamation, applause, plaudits; accolade, commendation, compliment
con abuse, invective, obloquy, vituperation; criticism, critique, faultfinding
encompass *vb* **1** *syn* see SURROUND 1
rel bound, delimit
2 *syn* see INCLUDE
encounter *vb* **1** *syn* see CONFRONT 1
rel clash, collide, conflict
2 *syn* see ENGAGE 5
3 *syn* see MEET 6
rel ‖bump (into), come (across), run (across), run (into)
idiom cross the path of, fall in with, meet up with
con miss, pass (by)
4 *syn* see FIND 1
encounter *n* a sudden, hostile, and usually brief confrontation or dispute between factions or persons <a sharp courtroom *encounter* between opposing lawyers>
syn brush, run-in, set-to, skirmish, velitation
rel conflict, contest; scrap; fight, fray; battle; argument, contention, quarrel
encourage *vb* **1** to fill with courage or strength of purpose especially in preparation for a hard task <the teacher's praise *encouraged* the student to try harder>
syn animate, cheer, chirk (up), embolden, enhearten, hearten, inspirit, nerve, ‖pearten (up), steel, strengthen; *compare* SUPPORT 5
rel assure, reassure; boost, excite, galvanize, pique, provoke, quicken, stimulate; buck up, buoy (up), energize, fortify, invigorate; rally, stir
idiom give a shot in the arm
con deject, depress, discourage, dishearten, dispirit; affright, caution, frighten
ant discourage
2 to give the support of one's approval to <the government openly *encouraged* East-West détente>
syn advocate, countenance, favor
rel approve, back, endorse, go (for), sanction, subscribe (to); abet, assist, reinforce, support, sustain; incite, instigate; induce, prevail
idiom lend one's countenance to, lend one's favor (*or* support) to, smile upon
con deter, dissuade, divert, hinder; inhibit, restrain; disapprove
ant discourage

---

syn synonym(s) *rel* related word(s)
ant antonym(s) *con* contrasted word(s)
idiom idiomatic equivalent(s)
‖ use limited; if in doubt, see a dictionary

3 ***syn*** see ADVANCE 1
rel patronize, push, support; develop, improve, subsidize
con weaken; check, retard, slow
ant discourage
encouraging *adj* ***syn*** see HOPEFUL 2
encroach *vb* ***syn*** see TRESPASS 2
rel barge (in), ‖bust (in), butt (in), chisel (in), horn (in), muscle (in), worm (in); interfere, interpose, intervene, meddle; overstep
idiom foist oneself upon, stick one's nose in (*or* into)
con ignore, let (alone), pass over; avoid
encrust (*or* **incrust**) *vb* ***syn*** see CAKE 1
encumber *vb* ***syn*** see BURDEN
rel freight; discommode, incommode, inconvenience; fetter, hamper, handicap; block, impede, obstruct; oppress, overburden
encumbrance *n* something that impedes and makes action difficult <told his story simply without the *encumbrance* of unnecessary details>
syn clog, cumbrance, hindrance, impedance, impediment
rel disadvantage, handicap, load; difficulty, hardship, inconvenience
con aid; catalyst, impetus, stimulus
ant assist, assistance
encyclopedic *adj* embracing, comprehensively treating, or informed in a wide range of subjects <an *encyclopedic* article on world history>
syn comprehensive, inclusive
rel all-comprehensive, all-embracing, all-inclusive, complete; extensive, general; discursive
end *n* **1** ***syn*** see LIMIT 1
rel borderline, tip; extreme, extremity
con center, hub, middle
2 ceasing of a course (as of action or activity) or the point at which something ceases <the *end* of the war>
syn cease, cessation, close, closing, closure, conclusion, desistance, desuetude, discontinuance, discontinuation, ending, finish, period, stop, termination, terminus; *compare* FINALE
rel consummation, culmination; expiration; coda, curtains, finale, finality, finis, terminal, windup
idiom cutoff point, end of the line, stopping point
con genesis, inception
ant beginning
3 ***syn*** see FINALE
4 something residual <melted down candle *ends*>
syn bit, fragment, scrap
rel butt end, fag end, leaving, remainder, remnant, residue; part, particle, piece
end *vb* ***syn*** see CLOSE 3
ant begin
endable *adj* ***syn*** see TERMINABLE
endanger *vb* to bring into peril (as of harm or disaster) <conspirators who were *endangering* the cause of freedom>
syn compromise, hazard, imperil, jeopard, jeopardize, jeopardy, menace, peril, risk
rel expose, lay (open); chance, venture
con guard, protect, shelter, shield; preserve, save
endeavor *vb* ***syn*** see TRY 5
rel determine, intend, purpose; address, apply, bid (for), drive (at), go (for); strain
endeavor *n* ***syn*** see ATTEMPT
rel exertion, push; labor, toil, travail, work
ended *adj* ***syn*** see COMPLETE 4
endemic *adj* ***syn*** see NATIVE 2
rel home-bred, native-born
con pandemic; extraneous, extrinsic
ant exotic
ending *n* **1** ***syn*** see END 2
ant beginning
2 ***syn*** see FINALE
endless *adj* **1** ***syn*** see LIMITLESS
2 ***syn*** see EVERLASTING 1
rel constant, continuous; deathless, immortal, undying; boundless, limitless, unbounded, unlimited; self-perpetuating
3 ***syn*** see CONTINUAL
rel overlong
endorse *vb* ***syn*** see APPROVE 2
rel attest, authenticate, pass (on *or* upon), vouch, witness; command, recommend; advocate, back (up), champion, stand by, support, uphold
con deprecate, disapprove; anathematize, denounce
endorsement *n* ***syn*** see SANCTION
endow *vb* **1** to furnish or provide with a gift, talent, or good quality <poets *endowed* with genius>
syn crown (with), dower, endue
rel bestow, confer; accord, award, grant; empower, enable; enhance, enrich, heighten
con bare, denude, divest, strip; despoil, ravage, spoliate; deplete, drain, exhaust
2 to furnish, (as an institution) with a store of capital <*endowed* a hospital>
syn finance, fund, subsidize
rel found, organize; bequeath, contribute, donate, subscribe, support; award, grant; back, promote, sponsor; provide, supply
con beggar, impoverish, pauperize; drain, draw (on)
end product *n* ***syn*** see EFFECT 1
endue *vb* ***syn*** see ENDOW 1
rel clothe, invest, vest; accouter, equip, furnish, outfit
endurable *adj* ***syn*** see BEARABLE
endurance *n* **1** ***syn*** see CONTINUATION 1
2 ***syn*** see TOLERANCE 1
endure *vb* **1** ***syn*** see CONTINUE 1
rel bide, linger
con crumble, decay, disintegrate; collapse, fall
ant perish
2 ***syn*** see ACCEPT 2
rel stand, submit (to), suffer, sustain; undergo
con break, collapse, give in, resign
3 ***syn*** see BEAR 10
enduring *adj* **1** ***syn*** see LASTING
ant fleeting
2 ***syn*** see OLD 2

3 ***syn*** see SURE 2
rel durable, resolute, solid, sound, stable, staunch, sturdy, substantial
con capricious, changeable, fickle, inconstant, mercurial, unstable, variable

endways *adv* ***syn*** see LENGTHWISE

endwise *adv* ***syn*** see LENGTHWISE

enemy *n* an individual or group that is hostile toward another <the senator was blackmailed by a political *enemy*>
syn foe
rel adversary, antagonist, opponent; assailant, attacker, combatant, invader; competitor, contender, emulator, rival
con benefactor, friend, supporter; ally, collaborator, colleague, confederate, friendly; adherent, follower, partisan, upholder

energetic *adj* **1** ***syn*** see VIGOROUS
rel aggressive, emphatic, vibrant; indefatigable
con easygoing; faineant, idle, languorous, lethargic
2 disposed to or having a capacity for action <an *energetic* campaign worker>
syn active, driving, enterprising, lively
rel animated, breezy, brisk, fresh, kinetic, peppy, spirited, sprightly, spry, vivacious, zippy
idiom full of go (*or* life *or* pep *or* zip)
con apathetic, inert; lethargic, limp, listless, passive, phlegmatic, spiritless, spunkless
ant inactive

energetically *adv* ***syn*** see HARD 1
rel firmly, strenuously; busily, industriously, zealously
idiom at full tilt
con idly, lazily, lethargically, listlessly; slowly
ant unenergetically

energize *vb* **1** ***syn*** see VITALIZE
idiom put pep (*or* zip) into
con emasculate, enervate; debilitate, enfeeble
2 ***syn*** see STRENGTHEN 2
rel arm, empower, enable; build (up), sustain
con daunt

energy *n* **1** ***syn*** see POWER 4
rel activity, operativeness; forcefulness, mightiness, powerfulness
con impotence; decrepitude, feebleness, weakness; powerlessness
ant inertia
2 vigorous and effectual application and operation of power <work with *energy*>
syn birr, go, hardihood, ‖moxie, pep, potency, tuck, vigor; *compare* VIGOR 2
rel application, effectiveness, efficacy; effort, operativeness; toughness
con kef, languor, lethargy, listlessness, sluggishness; ergophobia

enervate *vb* ***syn*** see UNNERVE
rel debilitate, devitalize, disable; exhaust, fatigue, jade, tire, weary
con activate, energize, vitalize; galvanize, quicken, stimulate

enervated *adj* ***syn*** see LANGUID
rel debilitated, devitalized, enfeebled, undermined, weakened; exhausted, fatigued, run-down, tired, weary; decadent, degenerate, degenerated, deteriorated
con active, animated, energetic, lusty, strenuous, vigorous, vital; strong, sturdy, tenacious, tough

enfant terrible *n* ***syn*** see SCAMP

enfeeble *vb* ***syn*** see WEAKEN 1
rel devitalize, exhaust
con galvanize; harden, strengthen
ant fortify

enfold *vb* **1** to surround or cover closely <a heavy fog *enfolded* the ships>
syn enclose, enshroud, envelop, enwrap, invest, shroud, veil, wrap; *compare* SWATHE
rel cover, drape; encase, ensheathe; encircle, encompass, environ, gird, girdle, surround
2 ***syn*** see EMBRACE 1

enforce *vb* to put something into effect or operation <*enforce* a law>
syn effect, implement, invoke
rel accomplish, administer, carry (out *or* through), discharge, execute, fulfill, perform; compel, force, oblige
con disregard, forget, ignore, neglect; relax

enfranchise *vb* to admit to full political rights as a freeman or citizen <slaves were emancipated in 1863 but were not *enfranchised* until the Fifteenth Amendment went into effect in 1870>
syn affranchise, franchise
rel emancipate, free, liberate, release; deliver, extricate, rescue
con enslave, oppress, subject
ant disenfranchise, disfranchise

engage *vb* **1** to come into contact and interlock with <the teeth of one gear wheel *engaging* those of another>
syn intermesh, mesh
rel interact, interlace, interlock, interplay
con free, release
ant disengage
2 ***syn*** see PROMISE 1
rel commit; bind, tie; affiance, betroth, troth
3 ***syn*** see EMPLOY 2
con dismiss, eject, fire
ant discharge
4 to hold the attention of <the puzzle *engaged* him all evening>
syn busy, engross, immerse, occupy, soak
rel absorb, imbue, involve; arrest, captivate, enthrall, fascinate, grip; monopolize, preengage, preoccupy
5 to enter into contest or conflict with <ordered to seek out and *engage* the enemy fleet>
syn encounter, face, meet, take on
rel assault, attack, strike; battle, fight
idiom do battle with, join battle with
con elude, escape, evade

engaged *adj* **1** ***syn*** see BUSY 1
ant unengaged

---

syn synonym(s) ***rel*** related word(s)
ant antonym(s) ***con*** contrasted word(s)
idiom idiomatic equivalent(s)
‖ use limited; if in doubt, see a dictionary

2 pledged in marriage <the *engaged* couple made a charming pair>
syn affianced, betrothed, contracted, intended, plighted, ‖promised
rel committed, pledged
con free, uncommitted, unpledged
ant unengaged
3 ***syn*** see INTENT

engagement *n* **1** ***syn*** see PROMISE
2 the act or state of being engaged to be married <the couple recently announced their *engagement*>
syn betrothal, betrothing, betrothment, espousal, troth
rel pledge, plight, promise
ant disengagement
3 a promise to be in an agreed place at a specified time, usually for a particular purpose <had an *engagement* with him for nine that evening>
syn appointment, assignation, date, rendezvous, tryst
rel arrangement, invitation; interview; get-together, meeting, visit
4 ***syn*** see EMPLOYMENT 4
5 ***syn*** see BATTLE

engaging *adj* **1** ***syn*** see ATTRACTIVE 1
2 ***syn*** see SWEET 1
rel alluring, appealing, attractive, captivating, charming, enchanting, entrancing, fetching; fascinating, interesting, intriguing
con repellent, repelling, repulsive; unappealing, unattractive, uninteresting
ant loathsome

engaging *n* ***syn*** see EMPLOYMENT 4

engender *vb* ***syn*** see GENERATE 3
rel develop; excite, stimulate; arouse, quicken, rouse, stir

engineer *vb* to contrive or plan out usually with subtle skill or craft <*engineered* an agreement between the two rival governments>
syn finagle, machinate, maneuver, wangle; *compare* MANIPULATE 2
rel arrange, contrive, devise, mastermind, plan (out), set up; intrigue, plot, scheme; manage, manipulate, negotiate; put (over), put (through), swing
idiom pull strings (*or* wires)

engird *vb* ***syn*** see BELT 1

engirdle *vb* ***syn*** see BELT 1

englut *vb* ***syn*** see GULP

engrave *vb* **1** to cut into a surface usually with a graving tool in order to form an inscription or a pictorial illustration <*engraved* a banknote design on the copper plate>
syn etch, grave, incise
rel chase, enchase; carve; inscribe
2 to impress deeply <the incident was *engraved* in his memory>
syn etch, impress, imprint, inscribe
rel carve; fix; instill; print; embed, entrench, infix, ingrain, root

engross *vb* **1** ***syn*** see WRITE
rel enscroll, scroll; superscribe
2 ***syn*** see MONOPOLIZE
rel apply, fill, occupy, preoccupy; assimilate, take up; arrest, engage, grip, ‖hog, hold, immerse, involve; attract, captivate, enthrall
con bewilder, distract; disperse, dissipate, scatter
3 ***syn*** see ENGAGE 4

engrossed *adj* ***syn*** see INTENT
rel consumed, monopolized, occupied; submerged; assiduous, busy, diligent, industrious, sedulous
idiom caught up in, lost in, taken up with
con detached, disinterested, indifferent, unconcerned, uninterested

engrossing *adj* gripping the attention completely so as to exclude everything else <the *engrossing* nature of his task made the time pass quickly>
syn absorbing, consuming, monopolizing
rel all-consuming, controlling, gripping; interesting, intriguing; exciting, provoking, stimulating; obsessing, preoccupying
con boring, drab, dull, monotonous; unentertaining, unexciting, uninteresting

engulf *vb* ***syn*** see DELUGE 1

enhance *vb* **1** ***syn*** see INTENSIFY
rel elevate, lift, raise; enlarge (upon), exaggerate, strengthen; augment, build (up), increase; adorn, beautify, embellish, embroider
con belittle, deprecate, detract, minimize
2 ***syn*** see FLATTER

enhancement *n* ***syn*** see ACCOMPANIMENT 1
rel improvement, intensification

enhearten *vb* ***syn*** see ENCOURAGE 1

enigma *n* ***syn*** see MYSTERY
rel crux, knot, puzzler, sticker; bewilderment, perplexity, question, question mark
idiom hard nut to crack

enigmatic *adj* ***syn*** see CRYPTIC

enisle *vb* ***syn*** see ISOLATE

enjewel *vb* ***syn*** see BEJEWEL

enjoin *vb* **1** ***syn*** see COMMAND
rel decree, dictate, impose, prescribe, rule; adjure, advise, counsel; admonish, caution, forewarn
con acquiesce, agree, comply, conform, obey, submit, yield
2 ***syn*** see FORBID
rel deny, disallow

enjoy *vb* **1** to take pleasure in or receive satisfaction from <*enjoyed* the meal>
syn ‖dig, go, like, ‖mind, relish
rel cotton (to); take (to); appreciate, dote (on *or* upon), fancy, love; delight (in), drink (in), eat up, luxuriate (in), savor
con abhor, abominate, detest, hate, loathe; condemn, despise, scorn
2 ***syn*** see HAVE 1
rel fill, occupy, maintain; boast, command

enjoyableness *n* ***syn*** see AMENITY 1
rel attractiveness, pleasingness, pleasurableness; niceness

enjoyment *n* **1** an attitude, circumstance, or favorable response to a stimulus that tends to make one gratified or happy <gave himself up to vigorous *enjoyment* of his pipe>

syn delectation, diversion, pleasure, relish; *compare* PLEASURE 2
rel delight, joy; amusement, entertainment; indulgence, savor; recreation, relaxation; gratification, satisfaction
con abhorrence, antipathy, aversion; repugnance, repulsion
2 *syn* see PLEASURE 2

enkindle *vb* ***syn*** see LIGHT 1

enlarge *vb* **1 *syn*** see INCREASE 1
rel add (to), embroider, exaggerate; grow, stretch, widen
con attenuate; abridge; compress
2 *syn* see EXPAND 4
3 *syn* see INCREASE 2

enlargement *n* ***syn*** see EXPANSION 2

enlighten *vb* ***syn*** see ILLUMINATE 2
rel direct, educate, guide, inform, instruct, school, teach, train; acquaint, advise, apprise, inform
con bewilder, confuse, mystify, perplex, puzzle; addle, fuddle, muddle

enlightening *adj* tending to dissipate ignorance or increase knowledge and awareness <an *enlightening* glimpse of government in action>
syn illuminant, illuminating, illuminative, illumining
rel broadening, edifying, educational, instructive; clarifying, elucidative, explanatory
con unedifying, uninstructive; confusing, obfuscatory, obscuring

enlist *vb* ***syn*** see ENTER 3

enliven *vb* ***syn*** see QUICKEN 1
rel refresh, rejuvenate, renew, restore; excite, galvanize, invigorate, jazz (up), pep (up), provoke, stimulate; amuse, cheer, divert, entertain, recreate; exhilarate, fire, inspire
idiom give (new) life to
con depress, oppress, weigh
ant subdue

en masse *adv* ***syn*** see ALTOGETHER 3

enmesh *vb* ***syn*** see ENTANGLE 3
rel drag (into), draw (in), hook, tangle; embarrass, implicate
idiom make party to
con disembarrass, disentangle
ant extricate

enmeshment *n* ***syn*** see ENTANGLEMENT 1

enmity *n* deep-seated dislike or ill will or a manifestation of such feeling <the country had experienced generations of racial *enmity*>
syn animosity, animus, antagonism, antipathy, hostility, rancor
rel uncordiality, unfriendliness; alienation, dead set, disaffection, estrangement; abhorrence, detestation, dislike, hate, hatred, loathing; aversion; bad blood, bitterness, daggers, gall, ill will, malevolence, malice, malignancy, malignity, spite, spleen
con amicability, cordiality, friendliness, neighborliness; comity, empathy, friendship, goodwill, sympathy, understanding
ant amity

ennoble *vb* ***syn*** see EXALT 1

ennui *n* ***syn*** see TEDIUM
rel blues, dejection, depression, dumps, melancholy, sadness; fatigue, languidness, languor, listlessness, spiritlessness, tiredness, weariness; satiety, surfeit

ennui *vb* ***syn*** see BORE
con enliven, stimulate, vitalize

enormity *n* **1** the quality or state of being abnormally, monstrously, or outrageously evil <the utter *enormity* of the crime>
syn atrociousness, atrocity, heinousness, monstrousness
rel grossness, outrage, outrageousness, rankness; depravity; flagrancy
con excusableness, remissibility, veniality; bearableness, tolerability
2 the quality or state of being huge <the *enormity* of the task confounded him>
syn enormousness, hugeness, immensity, magnitude, tremendousness, vastness
rel bigness, greatness, massiveness; graveness, seriousness, weightiness
con diminutiveness, minuteness, smallness, tininess; triviality, unimportance

enormous *adj* ***syn*** see HUGE
rel stupendous
ant tiny

enormousness *n* ***syn*** see ENORMITY 2
rel monstrousness, prodigiousness, stupendousness

enough *adj* ***syn*** see SUFFICIENT 1

enough *adv* **1** in or to a degree or quantity that satisfies some condition <unstable *enough* to react with water>
syn adequately, sufficiently
rel abundantly, amply; acceptably, admissibly, satisfactorily; commensurately, proportionately
2 in a tolerable degree <she sang well *enough*>
syn averagely, fairly, moderately, passably, rather, so-so, tolerably
rel acceptably, decently, satisfactorily

enough *n* as much as is needed or wanted <we have *enough* for all of our needs>
syn adequacy, competence, sufficiency, sufficient
rel abundance, ampleness, plenty
con inadequateness; deficiency, deficit, lack, shortage, want; outage, ullage, wantage
ant inadequacy, insufficiency

enounce *vb* ***syn*** see ENUNCIATE 1

enrage *vb* ***syn*** see ANGER 1
idiom make one's blood boil, work up into a passion
ant placate

enrapture *vb* ***syn*** see TRANSPORT 2
rel elate, gladden, gratify, please, rejoice; allure, attract, captivate, charm, enchant, enthrall, fascinate

enravish *vb* ***syn*** see TRANSPORT 2

---

enrich *vb* to make financially rich or richer <*enriched* himself through speculation>
syn richen

enrichment *n* *syn* see ACCOMPANIMENT 1

enroll *vb* **1** to take in (as a person) by entering identification in a list, catalog, or roll <the school *enrolls* about 800 students>
syn list, register
rel enter, insert; catalog, inscribe, record; enlist, line (up), recruit, sign (up); join, matriculate
con discard, omit, reject
2 *syn* see LIST 3
3 *syn* see ENTER 3

ensample *n* **1** *syn* see MODEL 2
2 *syn* see EXAMPLE 3

ensanguined *adj* *syn* see BLOODY 1

ensconce *vb* **1** *syn* see HIDE
2 to establish or place firmly, comfortably, or snugly <was happily *ensconced* on the sofa before the fire>
syn install, settle
rel establish, fix, locate, place, plant, seat, set, situate, station

ensepulcher *vb* *syn* see ENTOMB 1

enshroud *vb* *syn* see ENFOLD 1
rel cloak, conceal, curtain, hide
con disclose, display, illustrate, open (up), reveal, show, uncover, unveil

ensign *n* *syn* see FLAG

enslave *vb* to reduce to and hold in a state of servitude <free peasants reduced to serfdom or *enslaved*>
syn enthrall, subjugate
rel disenfranchise, disfranchise; subject; oppress, shackle, yoke
con affranchise, enfranchise; free, liberate
ant emancipate

enslavement *n* *syn* see BONDAGE

ensnare *vb* *syn* see CATCH 3
rel decoy, entice, inveigle, lure; hook, net, snag; bag, capture

ensnarl *vb* **1** *syn* see ENTANGLE 1
2 *syn* see ENTANGLE 3

ensorcell *vb* *syn* see BEWITCH 1

ensorcellment *n* *syn* see MAGIC 1

ensphere *vb* *syn* see BALL

ensue *vb* *syn* see FOLLOW 1
rel derive, emanate, issue, proceed, stem; attend, result
idiom be subsequent (to), come next
con antecede, forerun, preface

ensuing *adj* **1** *syn* see SUBSEQUENT 1
2 *syn* see NEXT

ensure *vb* to make something certain or sure <provisions *ensuring* that the rank and file have a voice in union policy-making>
syn assure, cinch, insure, secure
rel certify, guarantee, warrant; arrange, establish, provide, set out

enswathe *vb* *syn* see SWATHE

entangle *vb* **1** to twist or interweave so as to make separation difficult <*entangled* the yarn>
syn ensnarl, intertangle, perplex, snarl, tangle
rel intertwine, interweave, ‖snirl, twist; ball up
2 *syn* see COMPLICATE
3 to catch or hold as if in a net from which escape is difficult <a firm hopelessly *entangled* in financial difficulties>
syn embrangle, enmesh, ensnarl, trammel; *compare* CATCH 3, INVOLVE 1
rel burden, clog, fetter, hamper, impede; bag, capture, catch, ensnare, entrap, snare, trap; discomfit, embarrass, embroil
con extricate, untangle; detach, disengage; clear, free; disburden, unfetter
ant disentangle
4 *syn* see CATCH 3

entanglement *n* **1** the condition of being deeply involved or closely linked often in an embarrassing or compromising way <*entanglements* with underworld figures tarnished his reputation>
syn embroilment, enmeshment, involvement; *compare* WEB 2
rel ensnarement; affair, intrigue, liaison; association, contact
2 *syn* see WEB 2

enter *vb* **1** to come or go into some place or thing <he *entered* the room>
syn come (in), go in, ingress, penetrate
rel pierce, probe
idiom set foot in
con egress, exit, go out, leave; come out, emerge, sally; escape, flee
ant issue
2 to cause or permit to go in or into <*enter* synonyms in a thesaurus>
syn admit, introduce
rel inject, insert, intercalate, interpolate, put (in), set down; docket, inscribe, list, post, record, register; enroll
3 to make or become a member of <decided to *enter* the army>
syn enlist, enroll, join (up), muster, sign on, sign up
rel come (into), go (into)
idiom get oneself into, take up (*or* out) membership (in)
4 *syn* see BEGIN 1

enterprise *n* **1** *syn* see ADVENTURE
rel attempt, effort, endeavor, striving, struggle; campaign, cause, project, pursuit, task, undertaking; deed
2 *syn* see PROJECT 2
rel speculation
3 a unit of economic or business organization or activity <an economy encouraging the expansion of small, privately owned *enterprises*>
syn business, company, concern, establishment, firm, house, outfit
rel interest; organization; corporation; industry
4 readiness to attempt or engage in what requires energy or daring <complained about his brother's lack of *enterprise*>
syn ambition, drive, get-up-and-go, initiative, push; *compare* VIGOR 2
rel ambitiousness, eagerness, energy, enthusiasm, ‖hustle, vigor; boldness, courage, daring, venturesomeness; inventiveness, self-reliance

con languor, lethargy; indolence, laziness, sloth; apathy, inertia

enterprising *adj* **1** ***syn*** see ENERGETIC 2
rel aggressive, ambitious, busy, eager, hustling, pushing, up-and-coming; adventurous, venturesome
2 showing initiative, resolution, and determined effort (as in pursuing a course or a career) <an *enterprising* young woman likely to go far>
syn go-ahead, gumptious, up-and-coming
rel aggressive, pushing; diligent, hardworking, industrious, zealous; ambitious, aspiring, craving, hungry, itching, lusting, yearning; audacious, daring, dashing, venturesome
idiom on one's toes
ant unenterprising

entertain *vb* **1** ***syn*** see HARBOR 2
rel invite; admit, receive; cherish, cultivate, foster; feed, nourish
con banish, eject, throw out; ignore, neglect
2 ***syn*** see AMUSE
rel delight, enliven, gladden, gratify, please, regale, rejoice

entertainment *n* something diverting, amusing, or entertaining <staged a floor show as *entertainment* for her guests>
syn amusement, dissipation, distraction, diversion, divertissement, recreation
rel disport, play, sport; enjoyment, gaiety, pleasure; relaxation, relief

enthrall *vb* **1** ***syn*** see ENSLAVE
rel master, subdue
con emancipate
2 to hold spellbound <told mystery stories that *enthralled* his playmates>
syn catch up, fascinate, grip, hold, mesmerize, spellbind
rel absorb, engage, preoccupy; charm, enchant, engross, intrigue
con bore, ennui, weary

enthuse *vb* **1** ***syn*** see THRILL
2 to show great enthusiasm <tourists *enthusing* over the medieval towns>
syn drool, rave, rhapsodize, rhapsody
con censure, criticize; belittle, depreciate, disparage, dispraise, knock, undervalue

enthusiasm *n* **1** ***syn*** see PASSION 6
rel craze, fascination, infatuation, mania
con impassivity, phlegm, stolidity; aloofness, detachment, indifference, unconcern
ant apathy
2 ***syn*** see EAGERNESS
rel earnest, interest; ebullience, élan

enthusiast *n* a person who manifests extreme and often uncritical ardor, fervor, or devotion in an attachment <an increasing number of ecology *enthusiasts*>
syn bigot, bug, fanatic, fiend, freak, maniac, nut, zealot
rel addict, aficionado, buff, bum, devotee, fan, habitué, lover, votary; partisan, supporter; bear, extremist
con depreciator, detractor, disparager, knocker

enthusiastic *adj* filled with or marked by enthusiasm <was *enthusiastic* about golf>
syn ‖buggy, ‖bugs, gung ho, keen, nutty, warm, zealous
rel ardent, devoted, eager, fervent, hearty, spirited; gaga, ‖gone (on), hopped-up; hipped, obsessed; passionate, vascular; rabid
con apathetic, detached, indifferent, reluctant, uninterested
ant unenthusiastic

entice *vb* ***syn*** see LURE
con alarm, fright, frighten (off), terrify
ant scare (off)

enticement *n* ***syn*** see LURE 2

enticing *adj* being extremely and often dangerously attractive <she looked at him with an *enticing* smile>
syn Circean, fetching, luring, tempting
rel attractive, beguiling, bewitching, enchanting, fascinating, intriguing, inviting, siren, witching; captivating; likable, pleasant, pleasing

entify *vb* ***syn*** see MATERIALIZE 2

entire *adj* **1** ***syn*** see WHOLE 3
rel all, gross; plenary
con incomplete, unfinished; limited, qualified
ant partial
2 ***syn*** see WHOLE 1
rel concatenated, integrated; compacted, consolidated, unified
con broken (up); faulty
ant impaired
3 ***syn*** see WHOLE 4

entirely *adv* **1** ***syn*** see WELL 3
2 ***syn*** see ONLY 1

entireness *n* **1** ***syn*** see ENTIRETY 1
con incompleteness
2 ***syn*** see INTEGRITY 2

entirety *n* **1** the state of being complete <the striking *entirety* and self-sufficiency of the feudal community>
syn allness, completeness, entireness, oneness, totality, wholeness
rel collectiveness, unity; integrity, plenitude; comprehensiveness, omneity, universality
con disunity, division, separateness; fragmentation, incompleteness
2 ***syn*** see WHOLE 1
rel collectivity, complex, everything
con component, detail, element, item, part
ant particular

entitle *vb* **1** ***syn*** see NAME 1
2 to furnish with proper authority or grounds for seeking or claiming something <this ticket *entitles* the bearer to free admission>
syn authorize, qualify
rel empower, license; allow, enable, let, permit

entity *n* **1** one that has real and independent existence <each *entity* of the series requires separate study>
syn being, existence, existent, individual, something, thing

THESAURUS

rel body, object
2 *syn* see THING 5
3 *syn* see WHOLE 2

entomb *vb* **1** to deposit in or as if in a tomb <relics *entombed* in pyramids>
syn ensepulcher, sepulcher, sepulture, tomb; *compare* BURY 1
rel bury, inhume, inter, ‖plant; inurn; enshrine, shrine
con dig (up), disinhume, disinter, exhume, unbury
ant disentomb
2 *syn* see BURY 1

entombment *n* *syn* see BURIAL 2

entourage *n* one's attendants or subordinates <the queen's *entourage*>
syn following, retinue, suite, train
rel associates, attendants, courtiers, followers, retainers; hangers-on, sycophants, toadies

entrails *n pl* the internal organs of the body <some of the *entrails* are valued as food>
syn gut(s), innards, insides, internals, inwards, ‖pudding(s), stuffing, tripes, viscera
rel bowels, intestines; vitals; giblets, pluck, purtenance

entrammel *vb* *syn* see HAMPER
con assist, expedite, facilitate; extricate

entrance *n* **1** the act or fact of going in or coming in <awaited the *entrance* of the army into the city>
syn entry, ingress, ingression
rel arrival, coming, incoming, ingoing; penetration
con departure, egress, emergence, emerging, emigration, exit
ant egression, exiting
2 *syn* see DOOR 1
rel access, aperture, opening, threshold
ant exit
3 *syn* see DOOR 2
rel open door

entrance *vb* *syn* see TRANSPORT 2
rel gladden, please, rejoice; attract, bewitch, captivate, charm, enchant, fascinate; enthrall, hypnotize, spellbind
con disappoint, disgust, repel, repulse; bore

entranced *adj* *syn* see ENAMORED 3

entranceway *n* *syn* see DOOR 1

entrap *vb* **1** *syn* see CATCH 3
2 *syn* see LURE

entreat *vb* *syn* see BEG
rel blandish, coax, wheedle; pester, plague, press, urge

entreaty *n* *syn* see PRAYER

entrée *n* *syn* see DOOR 2
rel introduction; open door

entrench *vb* **1** to establish so solidly or strongly as to make dislodgment or change extremely difficult <prejudices *entrenched* for generations>
syn embed, fix, infix, ingrain, lodge, root
rel found, ground; implant; confirm, define, establish, settle, strengthen
con eliminate, eradicate, root out, uproot; banish, cast out, eject, expel; remove
ant dislodge
2 *syn* see TRESPASS 2
rel interfere, intervene
idiom break in upon, stick one's nose into

entrenched *adj* *syn* see INVETERATE 1

entrepreneur *n* **1** one who owns, launches, manages, and assumes the risks of an economic venture <theatrical *entrepreneurs* making fortunes from successful shows>
syn undertaker
rel organizer; backer, impresario; contractor; administrator, manager; producer; promoter
2 *syn* see GO-BETWEEN 2

entrust *vb* **1** to confer a trust upon <*entrusted* him with responsibility for completing the work>
syn charge, trust
rel confer, impose; delegate, relegate; allocate, allot, assign
2 *syn* see COMMIT 1
rel deliver, deposit, leave, trust; bank, count, depend, reckon, rely
idiom give in trust

entry *n* **1** *syn* see ENTRANCE 1
2 *syn* see DOOR 1
rel access, opening, threshold
con egress
ant exit
3 *syn* see DOOR 2

entryway *n* *syn* see DOOR 1
rel threshold
con egress
ant exit

entwine *vb* *syn* see WIND 2
rel entangle, entwist, interlace, interplait, intertwine, interweave; enmesh
con uncoil, undo, unravel, untwine, untwist, unwind, unwrap; straighten (out)

enumerate *vb* **1** *syn* see COUNT 1
2 to specify one after the other <*enumerated* the advantages of his position>
syn list, numerate, tick off
rel run (over), tell off; identify, mention, recite, recount, relate, specify
3 *syn* see ITEMIZE 1

enunciate *vb* **1** to make a definite or systematic statement of <was the first to *enunciate* the modern principle of inertia>
syn enounce, state
rel develop, formulate, outline, postulate; advance, lay down, submit; announce, declare, proclaim; affirm; show
idiom set forth
2 *syn* see ARTICULATE 2
rel express, intone, modulate, vocalize, voice

envelop *vb* **1** *syn* see ENFOLD 1
rel cloak, hide, mask
2 *syn* see SWATHE
3 *syn* see ENCLOSE 1
rel guard, protect, shield

envenom *vb* *syn* see EXACERBATE

envious *adj* maliciously grudging another's advantages <*envious* of her rival's charm>
syn envying, green-eyed, invidious, jealous

rel coveting, covetous, grasping, greedy; begrudging, grudging; appetent, desirous, longing, yearning; resentful, umbrageous
idiom green with envy
con benign, benignant; generous, kind; tolerant; unconcerned, uninterested

enviousness *n* ***syn*** see ENVY

environ *vb* ***syn*** see SURROUND 1
rel enclose, fence, go (around)

environment *n* surrounding or associated matters that influence or modify a course of development <the socioeconomic *environment* in Germany that produced Hitler>
syn ambience, ambient, atmosphere, climate, medium, milieu, mise-en-scène, surroundings
rel habitat; backdrop, background, context, setting; situation, status

environs *n pl* **1** an enclosing line or margin <several thousand businesses located within the *environs* of the city>
syn bound(s), boundary, compass, confine(s), limits, precinct(s), purlieus; *compare* LIMIT 1
rel fringes
2 the suburban areas or districts around a city or heavily populated area <a new system of parks for the national capital and its *environs*>
syn outskirt(s), purlieus, suburbs
rel locality, neighborhood, vicinity; surroundings

envisage *vb* ***syn*** see THINK 1
rel behold, grasp, look (upon), picture, regard, survey, view; externalize, materialize, objectify; foresee
idiom form a mental picture of, have a picture of, picture to oneself, view in the mind's eye

envision *vb* ***syn*** see THINK 1
rel call up, conjure up, summon up; picture, view; foresee
idiom have a mental picture of, picture to oneself, view in the mind's eye

envoy *n* **1** a representative with a rank between an ambassador and a minister resident who is accredited to a foreign government <the President received the *envoy* from Spain>
syn envoy extraordinary, minister plenipotentiary
rel ambassador, attaché, chargé d'affaires, consul, councillor, internuncio, legate, minister, nuncio; diplomat
2 ***syn*** see MESSENGER

envoy extraordinary *n* ***syn*** see ENVOY 1

envy *n* spiteful malice and resentment over another's advantage <his lavish life-style provoked *envy* among his colleagues>
syn enviousness, invidiousness, jealousy
rel covetousness; grudging; resentment

envy *vb* to experience envy <while she outwardly criticized her sister's looks, she secretly *envied* them>
syn begrudge, grudge
rel covet, crave, desire, hanker, long, want, yearn
idiom be green with envy

envying *adj* ***syn*** see ENVIOUS

enwrap *vb* **1** ***syn*** see SWATHE
2 ***syn*** see ENFOLD 1
rel enswathe, swaddle, swathe; sheathe

ephemeral *adj* ***syn*** see TRANSIENT
rel brief, short, temporary, unenduring; episodic
idiom here today and gone tomorrow
con endless, enduring, eternal, everlasting, lasting
ant perpetual

epicene *adj* ***syn*** see EFFEMINATE

epicure *n* one who takes great and fastidious pleasure in eating and drinking <was a real *epicure,* and his dinners were excellent>
syn bon vivant, gastronome, gastronomer, gastronomist, gourmand, gourmet
rel amateur, connoisseur, epicurean; glutton, ravener; high liver

epicurean *adj* ***syn*** see SENSUOUS

epidemic *n* the sudden widespread occurrence of something felt to resemble an epidemic disease <an *epidemic* of art forgeries>
syn outbreak, plague, rash; *compare* OUTBREAK 1

epigrammatic *adj* ***syn*** see PITHY

epilogue *n* **1** the final part that rounds out or completes the design of a nondramatic literary work <the author wrote an *epilogue* to his book explaining that some of his earlier impressions were wrong>
syn afterword
rel postlude; conclusion, ending
con prelude; foreword, introduction, preface
ant prologue
2 something that resembles an epilogue in rounding out or giving point to something else <an incident that can be regarded as an *epilogue* to the history of Roman Britain>
syn sequel
rel follow-up, postscript
ant prologue

episode *n* ***syn*** see OCCURRENCE

epistle *n* ***syn*** see LETTER 2
rel communication

epitaph *n* an inscription on a tombstone in memory of the one buried there
syn hic jacet

epitome *n* **1** ***syn*** see ABRIDGMENT
2 ***syn*** see SUMMARY
3 ***syn*** see APOTHEOSIS 1

epitomize *vb* **1** to make or give an epitome of <a report which *epitomizes* one of the most complex theories of all time>
syn condense, digest, inventory, nutshell, sum, summarize, summate, sum up, synopsize
rel boil down, capsulize; outline, tabulate
con elaborate, enlarge (on), expand
2 to serve as the typical representation or ideal expression of <he *epitomized* safe, dull conservatism>

---

syn synonym(s) ***rel*** related word(s)
ant antonym(s) ***con*** contrasted word(s)
idiom idiomatic equivalent(s)
‖ use limited; if in doubt, see a dictionary

syn exemplify, typify
rel embody, incarnate, incorporate, personify, represent, symbolize
3 *syn* see REPRESENT 2
epitomized *adj syn* see CONDENSED
epoch *n syn* see PERIOD 2
rel interval, term
epochal *adj* uniquely or highly significant <had to make an *epochal* decision: whether or not to declare war>
syn momentous
rel consequential, far-reaching, important; unmatched, unparalleled
con inconsequential, minor, petty, small-time, trivial, unimportant
equable *adj syn* see STEADY 2
rel methodical, orderly, regular, systematic; immutable, invariable, unchangeable; equal, equivalent, same
con variable; fitful, spasmodic
ant inequable, unequable
equal *adj* **1** *syn* see SAME 2
rel equable, even, uniform; alike, like; commensurate, corresponding, proportionate
idiom one and the same
con different, disparate, divergent, diverse, varied; unalike, unequable, uneven; irregular
ant unequal
2 *syn* see FAIR 4
idiom without distinction
con discriminating, discriminative, unfair
ant inequitable
3 *syn* see EVEN 3
4 *syn* see EVEN 4
5 *syn* see PROPORTIONAL
equal *n* one that is equal to another in status, achievement, value, meaning, or effect <he has no *equal* in common sense and honesty>
syn counterpart, equivalent, like, match; *compare* OPPOSITE NUMBER, PARALLEL
rel companion, fellow, mate, peer; alter ego, double, twin; competitor, rival; similar
equal *vb* **1** *syn* see AMOUNT 2
rel compare, parallel; accord, agree, square, tally; reach
idiom amount to the same thing
2 *syn* see EVEN 2
3 to make or produce something equal to (as in quality or value) <*equal* that if you can>
syn match, measure up, meet, rival, tie, touch
rel beat, top
equality *n syn* see EQUIVALENCE
equalize *vb* **1** to make equal in amount, degree, or status <*equalize* educational opportunities>
syn equate, even
rel balance, level, square
2 *syn* see EVEN 2
equally *adv* **1** *syn* see EVENLY 1
2 *syn* see EVENLY 2
equanimity *n* the characteristic quality of one who is self-possessed and not easily disturbed or perturbed <faced disaster with bland *equanimity*>
syn ataraxy, calmness, composure, coolness, imperturbability, phlegm, sangfroid, self-possession; *compare* CONFIDENCE 2
rel balance, equilibrium, equipoise, poise; aplomb, assurance, confidence, self-assurance; detachment; placidity, serenity, tranquillity
con alarm, anxiety, apprehension; excitability, nervousness; agitation, discomposure, disquiet, disturbance, perturbation
equatability *n syn* see EQUIVALENCE
equate *vb* **1** *syn* see EQUALIZE 1
2 to treat, represent, or regard as equal, equivalent, or comparable <*equated* retreat with cowardice>
syn assimilate, compare, liken, match, paragon, parallel
rel associate, relate, similize; consider, hold, regard, represent, treat
equidistant *adj syn* see MIDDLE 1
equilibrium *n syn* see BALANCE 1
rel stabilization, steadiness, steadying; counterbalance, counterpoise
con top-heaviness
equip *vb syn* see FURNISH 1
rel provide, supply; fit (out), rig (up *or* out), turn (out); gear, prepare, qualify
equipment *n* items needed for the performance of a task or useful in effecting an end <the *equipment* for the polar expedition included ships, instruments, sleds, dogs, and supplies>
syn accouterment(s), apparatus, gear, habiliments, machinery, material(s), matériel, outfit, paraphernalia, tackle, tackling
rel accessories, appurtenances, attachments, fittings, trappings; baggage, belonging(s), impedimenta, rig, things, traps; equipage, provisioning, provisions
equipoise *n syn* see BALANCE 1
rel counterbalance, counterpoise, counterweight
equitable *adj* **1** *syn* see FAIR 4
rel level, stable; equivalent, identical, same
idiom fair and square
con discriminatory
ant inequitable, unfair
2 *syn* see EVEN 3
equity *n syn* see JUSTICE 1
rel equitableness, justness
con bias, discrimination, partiality, unfairness
ant inequity
equivalence *n* the state or property of being equivalent or the result of making equivalent <the *equivalence* of paper money and coins>
syn adequation, equality, equatability, equivalency, par, parity, sameness
rel likeness; compatibility, correlation, correspondence; exchangeability, interchangeability
con discrepancy, disparity, divergence, incompatibility, inequality, unlikeness
ant difference
equivalency *n syn* see EQUIVALENCE
equivalent *adj* **1** *syn* see SAME 2
rel commensurate, proportionate; convertible, correlative, corresponding, parallel, reciprocal, substitute
con disparate, divergent, diverse, various; discordant, discrepant, incompatible, inconsonant

ant different
2 ***syn*** see LIKE
equivalent *n* ***syn*** see EQUAL
rel obverse, reciprocal, substitute; parallel
equivocal *adj* **1** ***syn*** see OBSCURE 3
rel hazy, indistinct; doubtful, dubious, questionable; indeterminate, multivocal
idiom clear as mud
con clear, distinct, understandable; categorical, explicit, unambiguous, univocal; certain, conclusive
ant unequivocal
2 characterized by a mixture of opposing feelings <an *equivocal* attitude toward the expensive proposal>
syn ambivalent
rel uncertain, undecided
idiom having mixed (*or* divided) feelings
con assured, certain, decided, sure
3 ***syn*** see DOUBTFUL 1
rel disreputable
idiom open to question
con credible
equivocality *n* ***syn*** see AMBIGUITY
equivocate *vb* **1** ***syn*** see LIE
rel elude, escape, evade
2 to avoid committing oneself by speaking evasively <he'd rather be brutally frank with them than *equivocate* on that issue>
syn dodge, evade, hedge, pussyfoot, shuffle, sidestep, tergiversate, tergiverse, weasel; *compare* SKIRT 3
rel cavil, prevaricate, quibble; fence, parry; avoid, elude, eschew
idiom beat around (*or* about) the bush, beg the question, mince words
equivocating *adj* ***syn*** see EVASIVE 1
rel deceptive, delusive, misleading
equivocation *n* **1** ***syn*** see AMBIGUITY
rel hedging; coloring, distortion, misrepresentation; deceit, dissimulation, duplicity
ant explicitness
2 ***syn*** see FALLACY 2
rel haggling, quibbling; fib, fibbing, lie, lying
equivoque *n* ***syn*** see AMBIGUITY
era *n* ***syn*** see PERIOD 2
rel term; stage
eradicate *vb* ***syn*** see ANNIHILATE 2
rel demolish, destroy, raze; liquidate, purge
con establish, fix, set; implant, inculcate, instill; breed, engender, generate, propagate
erase *vb* to eliminate or neutralize with or as if with a stroke of the pen <time has *erased* their sad memories> <*erase* an error>
syn annul, black (out), blot out, cancel, delete, efface, expunge, obliterate, wipe (out), x (out)
rel disannul, negate, nullify; abolish, blank (out), cross (off *or* out), cut out, dele, eliminate, excise, extirpate, rub out, scrape, sponge (out), strike (out); neutralize; remove, take out, withdraw
con impress, imprint, print, stamp; insert; reinstate, renew, restore
ere *prep* ***syn*** see BEFORE 1
erect *adj* standing up straight <the dog's *erect* ears pricked forward>
syn arrect, raised, stand-up, straight-up, upright, upstanding
rel erectile; elevated, lifted, upraised; perpendicular, standing, vertical
con decumbent, flat, prostrate, recumbent; drooping, hanging, pendent
erect *vb* **1** ***syn*** see BUILD 1
2 ***syn*** see MAKE 3
rel compose, create; make up, run up
con demolish, destroy, tear up, unbuild, wreck
3 to fix in an upright position <*erected* a flagpole>
syn put up, raise, rear, set up; *compare* BUILD 1
rel elevate, heighten, hoist, lift, upraise, uprear; upend
4 ***syn*** see EXALT 1
idiom put on a pedestal
ant abase
5 to bring into existence as if by raising a building <*erect* social barriers along religious lines>
syn build up, construct, establish, hammer (out), set up
rel fabricate, fashion, forge, form, shape; bring about, effect
con break down, tear down; liquidate, purge; dispose (of), eliminate, remove
erection *n* ***syn*** see EDIFICE
eremitic *adj* ***syn*** see ANTISOCIAL
ergo *adv* ***syn*** see THEREFORE
erode *vb* **1** ***syn*** see EAT 3
rel crumble, decay, deteriorate, disintegrate; consume
2 ***syn*** see ABRADE 1
rel grate, rub (off *or* away), scrape (off *or* away)
erotic *adj* of, devoted to, affected by, or tending to arouse sexual love or desire <*erotic* art>
syn amative, amatory, amorous, aphrodisiac
rel ardent, fervent, fervid, impassioned, lovesome, passionate; earthy; carnal, epicurean, fleshly, voluptuous; bawdy, sexy, spicy; concupiscent, lecherous; lascivious, lewd, lickerish, prurient, salacious, sensual
eroticism *n* ***syn*** see LUST 2
err *vb* to depart from a standard (as of wisdom or morality) <the human tendency to *err*>
syn deviate, stray, wander
rel miscalculate; lapse, slip (up), stumble, trip; transgress, trespass; offend; sin
idiom go astray (*or* amiss *or* wrong), leave the straight and narrow
errable *adj* ***syn*** see FALLIBLE
errant *adj* **1** ***syn*** see ERRATIC 1
rel drifting, itinerant, meandering, rambling, ranging, roaming, roving, shifting, straying
con static, unmoving
2 deviating from an accepted pattern or standard <a parent scolding her *errant* child>

---

syn synonym(s) ***rel*** related word(s)
ant antonym(s) ***con*** contrasted word(s)
idiom idiomatic equivalent(s)
|| use limited; if in doubt, see a dictionary

syn aberrant, devious, erring
rel deviating, straying, wandering; misbehaving, mischievous, naughty
idiom off the straight and narrow
3 *syn* see FALLIBLE
rel aberrant, erring; unreliable
con perfect, trustworthy
ant inerrant

erratic *adj* 1 moving about aimlessly or irregularly without a fixed course <an *erratic* breeze barely stirred the leaves of the tree>
syn devious, errant, stray, wandering
rel curving, meandering, roundabout, winding; shifting, undirected
con fixed, stable, unmoving; active, animated, brisk, lively, sprightly
ant static
2 *syn* see UNCERTAIN 1
rel doubtful, dubious
ant stable
3 *syn* see ARBITRARY 1
rel changeable, inconsistent, inconstant, unpredictable, variable; mercurial, unstable, volatile
con consistent, conventional, predictable, stable
4 *syn* see STRANGE 4
rel anomalous, irregular, unnatural
con natural, normal, regular, typical; customary, usual

erring *adj syn* see ERRANT 2

erroneous *adj* 1 *syn* see FALSE 1
rel amiss, askew, awry, off; defective; mistaken
idiom all off, all wrong, way off the mark
con right, true
ant accurate, correct
2 *syn* see MISTAKEN

erroneousness *n syn* see FALLACY 1
rel inaccurateness, mistakenness
con accuracy, accurateness, rightness
ant correctness

error *n* 1 an often unintentional deviation from truth or accuracy <made an *error* in adding the figures>
syn mistake, x
rel inaccuracy; miscalculation, miscomputation; oversight, slip
2 something (as an act, statement, or belief) that departs from what is or is generally held to be acceptable <spying on the opposing party proved to be a grave *error*>
syn blooper, blunder, boner, bull, bungle, ‖clanger, fluff, goof, lapse, miscue, misstep, mistake, rock, slip, slipup, trip; *compare* FAUX PAS
rel fault, misdoing, misjudgment, stumble; ‖boo-boo, botch, fumble, muff; howler, screamer; impropriety, indecorum
3 *syn* see FALLACY 1
rel misreading, misunderstanding; delusion, illusion

errorless *adj syn* see IMPECCABLE 1
con imprecise, inaccurate, incorrect, unexact, wrong

ersatz *adj syn* see ARTIFICIAL 2
rel factitious, synthetic; fake

ersatz *n syn* see IMITATION

erstwhile *adv syn* see BEFORE 2

erstwhile *adj syn* see FORMER 2

eruct *vb* 1 *syn* see BELCH 1
idiom bring up gas
2 *syn* see ERUPT 1

eructate *vb syn* see BELCH 1

erudite *adj syn* see LEARNED
rel lettered, well-read; studious
ant illiterate

eruditeness *n syn* see ERUDITION 2

erudition *n* 1 *syn* see EDUCATION 2
2 the quality or state of being erudite <a scholar of great cultivation and *erudition*>
syn eruditeness, learnedness, scholarliness, scholarship
rel cultivation, culture, education, intellectuality, literacy; bookishness, pedantry, studiousness
ant illiteracy

erupt *vb* 1 to give off or release (as something pent up) forcefully <the volcano *erupted* gouts of lava>
syn belch, disgorge, eject, eruct, expel, irrupt, spew
rel cast (out *or* up), hurl, throw off; boil, discharge, emit; jet, spout, spurt; extravasate
2 to break away or burst from limits or restraint <riots *erupted* in the ghetto>
syn break out, burst (forth), explode
rel detonate, touch off; go off

eruption *n* 1 *syn* see OUTBURST 1
2 *syn* see OUTBREAK 1

escalade *vb syn* see ASCEND 1
con clamber (down), climb (down); go (down)

escalate *vb* 1 *syn* see ASCEND 1
2 to increase in extent, volume, amount, number, intensity, or scope <a little war threatens to *escalate* into a huge, ugly one>
syn expand, grow
rel broaden, enlarge, heighten, increase, intensify, spread, widen
con decrease, limit, minimize; constrict, contract, narrow; collapse, shrink, shrivel
ant de-escalate

escapade *n* a usually adventurous action that runs counter to approved or conventional conduct <childish *escapades* on Halloween>
syn caper, lark, rollick; *compare* PRANK
rel antic, frolic, vagary; prank; fling, spree; mischief, roguery

escape *vb* 1 to run away especially from something that limits one's freedom and threatens one's well-being <trying to *escape* from prison>
syn abscond, break, ‖bunk, decamp, flee, fly, scape
rel get away, make off, mosey, run away; bail out, ‖ditch, double, duck out, flit, jump, skip; depart; disappear, vanish
idiom cut and run, cut loose, fly the coop, take it on the lam
con come back, return; abide, remain, stay; chase, follow, pursue, tag, trail
2 to get away or keep away from what one does not wish to incur, endure, or encounter <made every effort to *escape* suspicion>

syn avoid, bilk, double, duck, elude, eschew, evade, shun, shy; *compare* SHAKE 5, SKIRT 3
rel burke, bypass, circumvent; dodge, shake, shun, skit; miss
idiom fight shy of, give the slip
con catch, contract, incur; abide, bear, brook, endure, stand, suffer, tolerate; dare, face, meet

escape *n* **1** the act or fact of escaping or having escaped physically <succeeded in making his *escape* from the prison>
syn breakout, escapement, escaping, flight, getaway, lam, ‖scape, slip
rel departure; deliverance, liberation, release
con return; grasp, grip, hold, retention; imprisonment, incarceration
2 the act or fact of escaping or having escaped what one does not wish to incur, encounter, or endure <sought *escape* from responsibility>
syn avoidance, come-off, elusion, escaping, eschewal, evasion, runaround, shunning
rel bypassing, circumvention, dodging, ducking, sidestepping; elusiveness, evasiveness
con abidance, abiding, bearing, endurance, enduring, submission, submitting, toleration; facing

escapement *n* ***syn*** see ESCAPE 1

escaping *n* **1** ***syn*** see ESCAPE 1
2 ***syn*** see ESCAPE 2

eschew *vb* **1** ***syn*** see ESCAPE 2
idiom shy away from, steer clear of
con adopt, embrace, espouse
ant choose
2 ***syn*** see FORGO
rel abstain, refrain
idiom let well enough alone

eschewal *n* ***syn*** see ESCAPE 2
rel shirking; shying

escort *n* **1** a boy or man who goes on a date with a girl or woman <had her pick of *escorts* to the dance>
syn date
rel beau, boyfriend, fellow; cavalier, gallant, squire, vis-à-vis
2 a person who leads or directs another or others in a way or course (as through difficult terrain) <served as our *escort* when we drove through the desert>
syn guide
rel attendant, companion, guard

escort *vb* **1** ***syn*** see ACCOMPANY
2 ***syn*** see GUIDE
rel bring; squire

escritoire *n* ***syn*** see DESK

esculent *adj* ***syn*** see EDIBLE

esoteric *adj* ***syn*** see RECONDITE

especial *adj* **1** ***syn*** see SPECIAL 1
rel preeminent, supreme, surpassing; dominant, paramount, predominant, preponderant; exceptional, notable, singular, unusual
con unexceptional, usual
ant general
2 ***syn*** see EXPRESS 2

especially *adv* **1** in a special way <was *especially* good at math>
syn distinctively, particularly, special, specially, specifically
rel remarkably, unusually; exceptionally, markedly, peculiarly, singularly, uniquely; eminently, notably, preeminently, supremely
idiom before all else
2 ***syn*** see EXPRESSLY 2

espial *n* ***syn*** see DISCOVERY

espionage *n* systematic secret observation in order to accumulate information <agents engaged in industrial *espionage*>
syn spying
rel observation, reconnaissance, sleuthing, surveillance, watching

espousal *n* **1** ***syn*** see ENGAGEMENT 2
2 *often* **espousals** *pl* ***syn*** see WEDDING
3 ***syn*** see MARRIAGE
rel mating; union
idiom getting hitched, taking on the ball and chain, tying the knot
con estrangement, separation
4 ready acceptance of or the taking up of a cause or belief <his wholehearted *espousal* of left-wing philosophies worried his family>
syn adoption, embracement, embracing
rel acceptance, approval; advocacy; aid, promotion, support
con denial, rejection; disapproval, dislike, distaste; antipathy, aversion, intolerance
ant repudiation

espouse *vb* **1** ***syn*** see MARRY 1
2 ***syn*** see ADOPT
rel accept, approve; advocate, back, champion, support, uphold
con abandon, desert, forsake; deny, reject; disapprove, dislike
ant repudiate

esprit *n* **1** ***syn*** see SPIRIT 5
rel acumen, acuteness, brains, brightness, cleverness, intelligence, mind, quick-wittedness, sharpness, wit; courage, mettle, tenacity; fervor, passion
2 ***syn*** see MORALE
rel camaraderie, fellowship; devotion, loyalty; enthusiasm, fervor, passion
3 ***syn*** see WIT 5

esprit de corps *n* ***syn*** see MORALE
rel camaraderie, comradeship, fellowship; partisanism, partisanship; devotion, loyalty; enthusiasm, spirit

espy *vb* **1** ***syn*** see SEE 1
rel recognize, take in; sight, spot, spy; witness
idiom catch sight of, get a load of
2 ***syn*** see FIND 1
rel spy; make out; notice

essay *vb* ***syn*** see TRY 5
rel venture; labor, toil, travail, work
idiom give it a try (*or* fling *or* go), have at it, make a stab at, take a crack (*or* whack) at

---

syn synonym(s) *rel* related word(s)
ant antonym(s) *con* contrasted word(s)
idiom idiomatic equivalent(s)
‖ use limited; if in doubt, see a dictionary

essay *n* **1** ***syn*** see ATTEMPT
rel exertion; labor, toil, travail, work; go, venture
2 a relatively brief discourse written for others' reading or consideration <an *essay* on free will>
syn article, composition, paper, theme
rel discourse, discussion, explication, exposition, study; piece; tract, treatise; dissertation, thesis

essence *n* **1** a basic underlying or constituting entity, substance, or form <succeeds in conveying completely the cruel *essence* of loneliness>
syn being, essentia, essentiality, nature, texture
rel entity, form, substance
2 the most basic, significant, and indispensable element, attribute, quality, property, or aspect of a thing <the very *essence* of Machiavellianism is the belief that in politics there is neither good nor evil>
syn be-all and end-all, bottom, essentiality, marrow, pith, quintessence, quintessential, rock bottom, root, soul, stuff, substance, virtuality; *compare* BODY 3, CENTER 2, SUBSTANCE 2
rel timber; element, fiber, property; aspect, attribute, quality, spirit; inwardness, significance; crux, gist, kernel, nub, nubbin; distillate, distillation

essentia *n* ***syn*** see ESSENCE 1

essential *adj* **1** ***syn*** see INHERENT
con conditional, contingent, dependent
ant accidental
2 so important to the nature and essence of a thing as to be indispensable <the *essential* ingredient in this medicine is a new drug>
syn cardinal, constitutive, fundamental, vital
rel basal, basic, underlying; capital, chief, foremost, leading, main, principal; primal, primary, prime
con dependent, secondary, subordinate; accessory, auxiliary, contributory, subsidiary
3 ***syn*** see ELEMENTAL 1
4 urgently required <raw materials *essential* to industry>
syn imperative, indispensable, necessary, necessitous, prerequisite
rel needed, needful; required, requisite, wanted; right-hand; vital
con dispensable, unnecessary, unneeded, unrequired, unwanted
ant nonessential

essential *n* **1** something that forms part of the minimal body, character, or structure of a thing <prosperity is an *essential* of the good life>
syn basic, element, fundamental, part and parcel, rudiment
rel essence, stuff, substance; must, necessary, prerequisite, sine qua non
2 something necessary, required, or unavoidable <work was an *essential* to survival>
syn condition, must, necessity, precondition, prerequisite, requirement, requisite, sine qua non
idiom name of the game

essentiality *n* **1** ***syn*** see ESSENCE 1
2 ***syn*** see ESSENCE 2

essentially *adv* **1** in regard to the essential points <*essentially* the problem is this: he is unreliable>
syn au fond, basically, fundamentally, in essence
rel actually, really
idiom at bottom
2 ***syn*** see ALMOST 2
rel substantially, virtually
idiom in the main

establish *vb* **1** ***syn*** see SET 1
rel enroot, entrench, implant, inculcate, infix, instill, root; set down, set up; moor, rivet, secure; found, ground
con eradicate, exterminate, extirpate, uproot, wipe (out)
ant abrogate
2 ***syn*** see BASE
idiom lay the foundation for (*or* of)
3 ***syn*** see ENACT 1
rel formulate; authorize, decree, legislate, prescribe
ant repeal
4 ***syn*** see FOUND 2
rel endow, provide; originate; build
con disestablish; demolish, tear down
ant abolish
5 ***syn*** see ERECT 5
6 to make clear beyond a reasonable doubt <*established* an alibi for the time of the crime>
syn demonstrate, determine, make out, prove, show
rel authenticate, confirm, corroborate, document, substantiate, verify; attest; clarify
idiom afford (*or* offer) proof of
con discredit, expose, show up; confute, invalidate, parry, rebut, refute
ant disprove

established *adj* ***syn*** see FIRM 3

establishment *n* **1** ***syn*** see ENTERPRISE 3
rel workplace; institute, institution; foundation
2 *often cap* a group of influential leaders who represent an established order of society <the literary *establishment*>
syn Old Guard
rel conservative(s), diehard(s)
con liberal(s)

estate *n* **1** ***syn*** see ORDER 9
rel form, state
2 a class of people in a community distinguishable by social or political duties or privileges <a party platform appealing to people of every *estate*>
syn grade, rank
rel bracket, category; footing, level, order, standing; place, position, station; caste, class
3 an extensive landed property <spent the weekend at his country *estate*>
syn acres, land, manor, quinta
rel farm, ranch; plantation; villa

esteem *n* ***syn*** see REGARD 4
rel approval, liking; appreciation, valuation
ant abomination

esteem *vb* **1** ***syn*** see APPRECIATE 1
rel idolize, revere, worship
idiom hold dear, think the world of
ant despise
2 ***syn*** see ADMIRE 2
rel revere, venerate
idiom hold in esteem (*or* high regard)
con abhor
ant abominate

estimable *adj* **1** ***syn*** see WORTHY 1
2 ***syn*** see RESPECTABLE 1
rel admired, esteemed, respected
con disreputable, unworthy; bad
3 ***syn*** see HONORABLE 1

estimate *vb* **1** to judge something with respect to its worth <*estimated* the value of the jewels>
syn appraise, assay, assess, evaluate, rate, set (at), survey, valuate, value
rel adjudge, adjudicate, judge; ascertain, determine, discover; price, prize; decide, settle
2 ***syn*** see CALCULATE
rel cast, sum; count, enumerate
3 to fix some value (as size, distance, or composition) more or less accurately <*estimated* the rainfall at over six inches>
syn approximate, call, judge, place, put, reckon
rel round, round off; conjecture, guess, suppose, surmise; fancy, imagine; deduce, infer
con calculate, compute; measure

estimate *n* **1** the act of appraising or valuing the nature, character, quality, status, or worth of something <his influence as President is beyond *estimate*>
syn appraisal, appraisement, assessment, estimation, evaluation, valuation
rel calculation, measurement, reckoning; sizing up; projection
2 ***syn*** see ESTIMATION 1
idiom point of view

estimation *n* **1** the result of evaluating something <his *estimation* of the man's ability proved incorrect>
syn appraisal, appraisement, assessment, estimate, evaluation, judgment, stock
rel impression; opinion
2 ***syn*** see COMPUTATION
3 ***syn*** see ESTIMATE 1
4 ***syn*** see REGARD 4

estrange *vb* to cause one to break a bond or tie of affection or loyalty <her arrogance *estranged* her children and friends>
syn alien, alienate, disaffect, disunify, disunite, wean
rel break up, divide, divorce, part, separate, sever, split, sunder
idiom set at odds
con appease, conciliate, pacify, propitiate; associate, espouse, join, link, unite
ant reconcile

estrangement *n* the act of estranging or the condition of being estranged <a petty dispute resulted in total *estrangement*>
syn alienation, disaffection
rel division, divorce, schism; withdrawal
con appeasement, conciliation, propitiation
ant reconciliation

etceteras *n pl* ***syn*** see SUNDRIES

etch *vb* **1** ***syn*** see ENGRAVE 1
2 to set forth in a sharp, clear-cut manner with minute attention to detail <the most sharply *etched* character in the novel>
syn define, delineate
rel outline, set forth; depict, describe, picture, portray, represent
3 ***syn*** see ENGRAVE 2

eternal *adj* **1** ***syn*** see INFINITE 1
rel endless, interminable, unceasing, unending; lasting, permanent, perpetual; deathless, immortal, undying
con ephemeral, evanescent, momentary, passing, short-lived, temporary, transient
ant mortal
2 ***syn*** see EVERLASTING 1
rel deathless, undying
3 ***syn*** see CONTINUAL
con interrupted, sporadic
4 valid or existing unaltered at all times <right and wrong are *eternal* verities that cannot be changed>
syn ageless, dateless, intemporal, timeless
rel immemorial, lasting, perdurable, permanent, perpetual; immutable, inalterable, unalterable, unchangeable, unchanging
con alterable, changeable, changing, fluctuating, varying; debatable, questionable, suspect

eternalize *vb* ***syn*** see PERPETUATE

eternally *adv* ***syn*** see EVER 2

eternity *n* **1** a totality of infinite time <in *eternity* there is no change or passing away>
syn infinity, sempiternity
rel endlessness, infiniteness, infinitude, perpetuity, timelessness
con ephemerality, impermanence, transience; limitedness, restrictedness
ant finiteness
2 unending existence after death <belief in the *eternity* of our spiritual nature>
syn afterlife, everlastingness, eviternity, immortality, world-without-end
3 ***syn*** see AGE 2
idiom forever and a day, forever and ever

eternize *vb* ***syn*** see PERPETUATE

ethereal *adj* ***syn*** see AIRY 3
rel celestial, empyreal, empyrean, heavenly; vaporish, vaporlike, unsubstantial; filmy, gossamer; delicate, fragile, light
con heavy, thick
ant substantial

ethic *n* **1 ethics** *pl but usu sing in constr* the discipline dealing with what is good and bad and with moral duty and obligation <*ethics* has been called the science of the ideal of human character>

---

syn morals
2 a group of moral principles or set of values <the Christian *ethic*>
syn morality, morals, mores
3 ethics *pl* the code of conduct or behavior governing an individual or a group (as the members of a profession) <medical *ethics*>
syn principles
rel moralities, morals, mores; criteria, standards
4 the complex of ideals, beliefs, or standards that characterizes or pervades a group, community, or people <the American work *ethic*>
syn ethos
rel belief, ideal, standard, value

ethical *adj* ***syn*** see MORAL 1
rel high-principled; elevated; upright, upstanding
con flagitious, iniquitous, nefarious; improper, indecent, indecorous, unbecoming, unseemly; immoral, low

ethnic *adj* **1** ***syn*** see HEATHEN
rel non-Christian, unchristian
2 of, relating to, or originating from the traits shared by members of a group as a product of their common heredity and cultural tradition <only a person thoroughly familiar with Yiddish can recognize the *ethnic* quality of the pun> <*ethnic* cookery>
syn racial
rel national; tribal

ethos *n* ***syn*** see ETHIC 4

etiquette *n* **1** ***syn*** see MANNER 5
2 ***syn*** see DECORUM 1
rel behavior, conduct, deportment, manners; amenities, civilities, formalities; convention, form, protocol
idiom social graces

eulogistic *adj* of, relating to, characterized by, or bestowing praise <the speaker made *eulogistic* remarks on the group's accomplishment>
syn encomiastic, laudative, laudatory, panegyrical, praiseful
rel approbatory, approving, commendatory, complimentary
con uncomplimentary; critical, disapproving, disparaging; abusive
ant dyslogistic

eulogize *vb* ***syn*** see PRAISE 2
rel applaud; belaud, bepraise
idiom praise to the skies, sing the praises of
ant vilify

eulogy *n* ***syn*** see ENCOMIUM
rel adulation, glorification
con calumny, slander
ant vilification

euphemism *n* an agreeable or inoffensive expression that is substituted for one that might offend or suggest unpleasantness <vandalism that goes under the *euphemism* of souvenir hunting>
syn nice Nelly, nice-nellyism
ant dysphemism

euphonic *adj* ***syn*** see MELODIOUS 1

euphonious *adj* ***syn*** see MELODIOUS 1

euphoria *n* **1** ***syn*** see ELATION 1
ant deflation, dysphoria
2 an often groundless or excessive feeling of well-being and happiness <drug-induced *euphoria*>
syn elation, exaltation, intoxication
rel ecstasy, frenzy; madness; glee
con anxiety, unease, uneasiness
ant depression

euphuistic *adj* ***syn*** see RHETORICAL
rel elaborate; colorful; verbose; elevated
con concise, simple, straightforward; lean

evacuee *n* ***syn*** see REFUGEE

evade *vb* **1** ***syn*** see ESCAPE 2
rel flee, fly, slip (away); foil, outwit, thwart
idiom keep (*or* know) one's distance
con accost, confront, dare, face
2 ***syn*** see EQUIVOCATE 2
rel bypass, circumvent, duck; parry, turn (aside)
idiom give (someone) the runaround
con confront, face; elucidate, explain

evaluate *vb* **1** ***syn*** see ESTIMATE 1
rel appreciate; class, gauge, rank; criticize
2 ***syn*** see CLASS 2

evaluation *n* **1** ***syn*** see ESTIMATE 1
rel interpreting; judging, rating
2 ***syn*** see ESTIMATION 1
rel appreciation; interpretation; decision

evanesce *vb* ***syn*** see VANISH
rel disintegrate, dispel, disperse, dissipate, dissolve, scatter
idiom go up in smoke, vanish into thin air
con appear; coalesce
ant materialize

evanescent *adj* ***syn*** see TRANSIENT
rel temporary; flying; dissolving, fading, melting; disappearing, vanishing

evangelical *adj* characterized by or reflecting a missionary, reforming, or redeeming impulse or purpose <a mood of *evangelical* nationalism>
syn crusading, evangelistic
rel ardent, fervid, impassioned, militant, zealous; missionary, propagandizing, proselytizing

evangelist *n* ***syn*** see MISSIONARY

evangelistic *adj* ***syn*** see EVANGELICAL
rel missionary, reforming

evangelize *vb* ***syn*** see PREACH 1

evanish *vb* ***syn*** see VANISH
idiom pass out of the picture

evaporate *vb* ***syn*** see VANISH
rel escape, pass (away *or* off); weaken; vaporize
idiom go pouf

evasion *n* ***syn*** see ESCAPE 2
rel dodging, equivocating, equivocation, evading, excuse, subterfuge; haggling, quibbling; escapism
con confrontation, confronting; daring
ant facing

evasive *adj* **1** tending to evade or avoid confrontation <his answers were ambiguous and *evasive*>
syn equivocating, prevaricative, prevaricatory, shifty, shuffling
rel ambiguous, equivocal, unclear, vague; sliding, slippery, sly
con categorical, definite, explicit, unambiguous, univocal; candid, forthright

ant direct
2 ***syn*** see ELUSIVE

even *adj* **1** ***syn*** see LEVEL
con bent, crooked, curved, twisted
ant uneven
2 ***syn*** see STEADY 2
rel equal, identical, same; consistent, continual, continuous, undeviating, unvaried
3 giving no advantage to either side <an *even* exchange>
syn equal, equitable, fair
rel balanced, fair and square, square; honest, straightforward, unprejudiced
con inequitable, unequal, unfair
ant uneven
4 being nicely in balance <his chances for success or failure are *even*>
syn equal, even-up, fifty-fifty
rel balanced, comparable, proportionate
con disproportionate, unbalanced
ant uneven
5 being neither more nor less than the named or understood amount, extent, or number <an *even* mile>
syn exact, square
con approximate, imprecise, inaccurate

even *adv* **1** in a like manner <they can learn *even* as others do>
syn as well, exactly, expressly, just, precisely
2 at the very time <perhaps *even* now the moment has come to consider a retreat>
syn already
3 not this merely but also — used as an intensive to emphasize the identity or character of something <a huge, *even* monstrous animal>
syn indeed, nay, truly, verily, yea
rel absolutely, positively; quite, really
4 — used as an intensive to indicate an extreme, hypothetical, or unlikely case or instance <refused *even* to look at her> <*even* if this were so, it should not change our plans>
syn so much as
idiom even so much as
5 ***syn*** see YET 1

even *vb* **1** to make (as a surface) smooth, even, level, or flat <*even* the soil with a spade>
syn flatten, flush, lay, level, plane, smooth, smoothen
rel grade, roll; align; symmetrize; uniform; pancake
con rough, roughen
2 to make even or balanced in advantage <hoped to *even* the odds by training>
syn equal, equalize
rel balance, square
con unbalance, unequalize, upset; derange, disarrange
3 ***syn*** see EQUALIZE 1

evening *n* **1** the closing part of day and the early part of night <the last light of *evening*>
syn ‖dimmet, ‖dimps, ‖dimpsy, dusk, ‖dusk dark, eventide, gloaming, nightfall, owl-light, twilight
rel afternoon; sundown, sunset; duskiness, duskness
con sunrise; dawn
ant morning
2 a latter portion or a period of decline <in the *evening* of life>
syn sunset, twilight
3 a party taking place in the evening <their *evenings* were notable affairs>
syn soiree
rel reception; salon; party

evenly *adv* **1** in equal parts <a career divided *evenly* between stage and screen>
syn equally, fifty-fifty, squarely
rel commensurably, proportionately
con disproportionately, unequally
ant unevenly
2 in a just or fair manner <she was *evenly* polite to everyone>
syn equally, impartially
rel fairly, justly
con unfairly, unjustly
3 without variation or fluctuation <spread the paint *evenly*>
syn flatly, smooth, smoothly, uniformly
con irregularly, roughly
ant unevenly

event *n* **1** ***syn*** see OCCURRENCE
rel act, action, deed; achievement, exploit, feat; accident, chance, fortune
2 a matter worthy of remark <the trip was an *event* in their dull routine>
syn milepost, milestone, occasion
rel affair, landmark; delight, treat
idiom historic event
con insignificancy, trifle, triviality
3 ***syn*** see EFFECT 1
rel offshoot, outgrowth; product, resultant, sequent
idiom end result
4 a postulated outcome, condition, or contingency <in the *event* of rain, we will not meet>
syn case, eventuality
rel chance, fortuity, hap, happenstance
5 any of the contests in a sports program <track-and-field *events*>
syn match, meet
rel competition, contest
6 ***syn*** see FACT 2

eventide *n* ***syn*** see EVENING 1

eventual *adj* ***syn*** see LAST
rel consequent, ensuing, inevitable, succeeding; ending, endmost
con antecedent, beginning, inceptive, initial, original

eventuality *n* **1** ***syn*** see EVENT 4
rel contingency, possibility
2 ***syn*** see EFFECT 1
con antecedent, beginning, root

eventually *adv* ***syn*** see YET 2
idiom in the long run

---

syn synonym(s) ***rel*** related word(s)
ant antonym(s) ***con*** contrasted word(s)
idiom idiomatic equivalent(s)
‖ use limited; if in doubt, see a dictionary

even–up *adj* ***syn*** see EVEN 4
ever *adv* **1** ***syn*** see ALWAYS 1
2 through all or an indefinite time <a name that will *ever* be respected>
syn always, eternally, evermore, forever, forevermore, in perpetuum
3 in each and every case <war and suffering have *ever* gone hand in hand>
syn invariably
rel consistently, regularly, usually
4 at any time or on any occasion <he is seldom if *ever* absent>
syn anytime, at all
5 in any way <nor was it *ever* important>
syn anyway, anywise, at all, once
6 — used as an intensive after an inverted verb-subject construction <is he *ever* proud of himself>
syn confoundedly, consumedly, excessively, extremely, immensely, inordinately, over, overfull, overly, overmuch, super, too, unduly
rel annoyingly, plaguey; grievously, mortally; consummately
ever and again *adv* ***syn*** see SOMETIMES
ever and anon *adv* ***syn*** see SOMETIMES
everlasting *adj* **1** lasting or enduring through all time <*everlasting* laws governing the physical universe>
syn amaranthine, ceaseless, endless, eternal, immortal, never-ending, unending, world-without-end; *compare* IMMORTAL 1
rel lasting, perdurable, permanent, perpetual; boundless, infinite, limitless, termless
con ephemeral, evanescent, momentary, short-lived, transitory
2 ***syn*** see CONTINUAL
con interrupted, off-and-on, periodic, sporadic
everlastingness *n* ***syn*** see ETERNITY 2
evermore *adv* ***syn*** see EVER 2
evert *vb* ***syn*** see DISPROVE 1
every *adj* ***syn*** see ALL 2
everybody *pron* every person <*everybody* must do what his conscience dictates>
syn all, everyman, everyone
idiom all and sundry
ant nobody
everyday *adj* **1** ***syn*** see COMMON 4
con distinctive, singular, unique; uncommon, unusual
ant exceptional
2 ***syn*** see PROSAIC 3
3 ***syn*** see ORDINARY 1
everyman *pron* ***syn*** see EVERYBODY
idiom the man in the street
everyone *pron* ***syn*** see EVERYBODY
ant no one
everyplace *adv* ***syn*** see EVERYWHERE 1
idiom all over the place
everything *pron* the whole amount <lost *everything* in the fire>
syn all
idiom all in all, the lot, the whole ball of wax, the whole bit (*or* shebang), the whole kit and kaboodle, the works
everywhere *adv* **1** in every place or in all places <poverty anywhere is a danger to peace and prosperity *everywhere* >
syn all over, all round (*or* all around), everyplace, far and near, far and wide, high and low, overall, throughout
idiom in all quarters, in every quarter
2 ***syn*** see WHEREVER
evict *vb* ***syn*** see EJECT 1
rel dislodge, dispossess, force (out), put out, shut out, turn out
idiom turn (*or* put) out bag and baggage, turn out of doors, turn out of house and home
con harbor, house, lodge, shelter
evidence *n* **1** ***syn*** see INDICATION 3
2 ***syn*** see TESTIMONY
evidence *vb* ***syn*** see SHOW 2
rel display, expose; attest, bespeak, betoken, confirm, indicate, prove, testify
evident *adj* ***syn*** see CLEAR 5
rel noticeable, prominent, pronounced
idiom as plain as the nose on one's face, plain as day
con inconspicuous; ambiguous, unapparent, unrecognizable; concealed, hidden
ant inevident
evidently *adv* ***syn*** see OSTENSIBLY
evil *n* **1** whatever is harmful, distressing, or disastrous <attempts to grasp the nature of *evil* >
syn ill
rel bad, badness, devilry, diablerie, diabolism, evilness, satanism, satanity, wickedness, wrong
con goodness, virtue
ant good
2 whatever is morally unacceptable <return good for *evil*>
syn debt, sin, wickedness, wrong
rel evildoing, misconduct, sinfulness, wrongdoing
con rectitude, righteousness, virtue
ant good
3 a particular thing (as an act) that is evil <choose the lesser of two *evils*>
syn crime, diablerie, iniquity, sin, tort, wrong, wrongdoing
rel badness, evilness, maleficence, vice, wickedness; misdeed, offense
evil *adj* **1** ***syn*** see WRONG 1
rel base, low, vile; flagitious, nefarious; baneful, pernicious; black, damnable, execrable
con high, noble; exemplary, salutary
ant good
2 ***syn*** see OFFENSIVE
rel distasteful, repellent; fetid, putrid, stinking
3 ***syn*** see MALICIOUS
rel angry, disagreeable, ugly, unpleasant, wrathful; harmful, hurtful, injurious, mischievous; destructive
4 ***syn*** see HARMFUL
rel calamitous, destructive, disastrous
con harmless, noninjurious
ant innocuous
5 reporting or predicting harm or misfortune <messengers bearing *evil* tidings>

syn bad, ill, unfavorable; *compare* OMINOUS
rel baleful, baneful, inauspicious; ill-boding, ill-omened, ominous
con auspicious, favorable
ant good
6 marked by misfortune or calamity <the family fell upon *evil* times>
syn bad, inauspicious
rel unfavorable, unfortunate, unlucky; difficult, hard, trying; calamitous, disastrous
con favorable; lucky; easy, prosperous; auspicious, halcyon, happy
ant good

evince *vb* **1** *syn* see SHOW 2
rel argue, attest, bespeak, betoken, confirm, indicate, prove; display, exhibit, expose, illustrate, signify
con repress, suppress; conceal, hide
2 *syn* see EDUCE 1
rel bring (about), cause; provoke, stimulate

eviscerate *vb* to take out the entrails of <*eviscerate* a turkey>
syn bowel, disembowel, draw, embowel, exenterate, gut, paunch

eviternity *n* *syn* see ETERNITY 2

evocative *adj* serving or tending to call something (as a mood) forth <conduct *evocative* of the utmost contempt>
syn evocatory, suggestive
rel meaningful, pregnant, weighty; arousing, moving, stimulating, stirring; causing, effecting, inducing, producing

evocatory *adj* *syn* see EVOCATIVE

evoke *vb* *syn* see EDUCE 1
rel excite, provoke, stimulate; arouse, awaken, rally, rouse, stir, waken; call forth, call up, conjure (up), raise, summon (forth *or* up)

evolution *n* *syn* see DEVELOPMENT
rel change, transformation

evolve *vb* **1** *syn* see DERIVE 1
rel get (at), obtain; advance
2 *syn* see UNFOLD 3
rel advance, progress; mature, open (up), ripen

evolvement *n* *syn* see DEVELOPMENT
rel metamorphosis, transformation

evulse *vb* *syn* see EXTRACT 1

exacerbate *vb* to cause to become increasingly bitter or severe <foolish words that only *exacerbated* the quarrel>
syn acerbate, embitter, envenom
rel annoy, exasperate, irritate, provoke; aggravate, heighten, intensify; inflame
idiom add fuel to the flame, fan the flames, feed the fire, pour oil on the fire
con appease, mollify, pacify, placate, quell; lessen, moderate
ant assuage

exact *vb* **1** *syn* see EXTORT 1
2 *syn* see LEVY
3 *syn* see DEMAND 1
rel coerce, compel, constrain, force, oblige; extort, extract, squeeze, wrest, wring

exact *adj* **1** *syn* see CORRECT 2
idiom on the money
2 *syn* see EVEN 5
ant imprecise, inexact
3 *syn* see SAME 1
4 *syn* see CAREFUL 2
5 *syn* see PRECISE 4

exacting *adj* *syn* see ONEROUS
rel rigid, rigorous, severe, stern, strict, stringent; finicky, fussy, particular; critical, hypercritical
con laissez-faire, lenient
ant unexacting

exactitude *n* *syn* see PRECISION

exactly *adv* **1** *syn* see JUST 1
rel ||plumb, plunk; specifically
idiom on the dot (*or* nose), right on the nail
con about, around, more or less, roughly
ant approximately
2 *syn* see ALL 1
rel absolutely, expressly, positively; completely
3 as you say or state — used to express agreement or concurrence <"You are accusing me of lying?" he asked. "*Exactly,*" she replied.>
syn precisely, yes
idiom quite so, (that's) for sure (*or* certain)
4 *syn* see EVEN 1

exactness *n* *syn* see PRECISION

exaggerate *vb* *syn* see EMBROIDER
rel hyperbolize, overcolor, romance, romanticize
idiom blow up out of (all) proportion, draw the long bow, make the eagle scream
ant understate

exaggeration *n* an overstepping of the bounds of truth <the passage shows the author's penchant for grotesque *exaggeration*>
syn coloring, embellishment, embroidering, hyperbole, overstatement
rel aggrandizement, amplification, enlargement; overcoloring, overdrawing, romance, stretching
idiom flight of fancy, tall talk
con minimizing, underestimation
ant understatement

exalt *vb* **1** to enhance the status of <propaganda that *exalts* nationalism to the level of religion>
syn aggrandize, dignify, distinguish, ennoble, erect, glorify, honor, magnify, pedestal, stellify, sublime, uprear
rel boost, build up, elevate, lift, promote, raise, upgrade, uplift; enhance, heighten, intensify; acclaim, enhalo, extol, laud, praise; apotheosize
con debase, degrade, demean, humble, humiliate; belittle, decry, depreciate, derogate, detract, disparage, downgrade, minimize
ant abase
2 *syn* see FIRE 2
rel pique, quicken, stimulate; deepen, enhance, sharpen; encourage, inspirit, spirit (up), uplift

exaltation *n* **1** *syn* see APOTHEOSIS 2

---

syn synonym(s) *rel* related word(s)
ant antonym(s) *con* contrasted word(s)
idiom idiomatic equivalent(s)
|| use limited; if in doubt, see a dictionary

rel upgrading, uplifting; extolment, laudation, praise
con debasement, degradation, demeanment, humiliation; belittlement, depreciation, derogation, disparagement, downgrading
ant abasement
2 *syn* see ELATION 1
rel delectation, delight; bliss, joy, rapture
ant deflation
3 *syn* see EUPHORIA 2
ant depression

exalted *adj* **1** raised to or having high rank <moved in *exalted* circles> <Alexander was *exalted* to the papal throne in 1492>
syn astral, highest, highest-ranking, top-drawer, top-ranking
rel august, noble; eminent, illustrious, prominent; high, high-ranking; foremost, number one; first, leading, outstanding
con low, lowly, low-ranking, unimportant; minor; humble, plebeian
ant abject
2 *syn* see GRAND 3
ant abject

examination *n* a careful, detailed, and often formal study designed to uncover pertinent information <the doctor gave him a physical *examination*>
syn analysis, audit, check-over, checkup, inspection, perlustration, review, scan, scrutiny, survey, view
rel assay, breakdown, diagnosis, dissection; sifting, winnowing; canvass, catechization, inquiry, questioning, quizzing, testing

examine *vb* **1** *syn* see SCRUTINIZE 1
rel check (out), go (over), investigate, look (into); contemplate, look (at *or* over), observe
idiom give a going over, give the once-over, go over with a fine-toothed comb
2 *syn* see TRY 1
3 *syn* see ASK 1
rel cross-examine; grill; pump
idiom give the third degree to, put to the question

example *n* **1** *syn* see INSTANCE
2 *syn* see MODEL 2
idiom shining example
3 an instance that illustrates a rule or provides practice in its application <worked out his arithmetic *examples*>
syn ensample, illustration, problem
idiom case in point

exanimate *adj syn* see DEAD 1

exasperate *vb syn* see IRRITATE
rel agitate, work up
idiom try one's temper (*or* patience)
ant appease; mollify

exasperation *n* **1** *syn* see ANNOYANCE 2
rel irritation, vexation; displeasure; resentment
2 *syn* see ANNOYANCE 3

ex cathedra *adj syn* see OFFICIAL

excavate *vb* **1** *syn* see DIG 1
rel gouge (out), hollow (out), scoop (out), scrape (out), quarry (out)
2 *syn* see DIG 2

exceed *vb* **1** to go or be beyond a natural or set limit <the policeman *exceeded* his authority> <this task *exceeds* my powers>
syn outstep, overrun, overstep, surpass
rel outreach, overreach; dare, presume, venture
2 *syn* see SURPASS 1

exceedingly *adv syn* see VERY 1

excel *vb syn* see SURPASS 1

excellence *n* something that gives especial worth or value <the particular *excellence* of this cake is its lightness>
syn arete, excellency, merit, perfection, quality, virtue
rel value, worth; distinction, fineness, superiority; goodness, niceness, superbness; class
con blemish, defect, flaw; failing, foible, frailty, vice
ant fault

excellency *n syn* see EXCELLENCE

excellent *adj* meritoriously near the standard or model and eminently good of its kind <an *excellent* restaurant specializing in French cuisine>
syn A1, bang-up, banner, blue-ribbon, ‖boss, bully, ‖bunkum, capital, champion, classic, classical, ‖dandy, famous, fine, first-class, first-rate, first-string, five-star, front-rank, Grade A, number one, par excellence, prime, quality, royal, skookum, ‖slap-up, sovereign, stunning, superior, ‖swingeing, top, top-notch, whiz-bang; *compare* MARVELOUS 2, SUPREME
rel high-class, high-grade, proper; ‖rum; distinguished, exceptional, premium; brag, incomparable, magnificent, nobby, sensational, smart, superb, superlative, terrific, tip-top, unsurpassed
idiom all wool and a yard wide, beyond compare, out of this world
con mediocre; bad, inadequate, inferior, low, low-grade, low-quality, substandard; fourth-rate, second-class, second-rate; poor, shoddy, sorry, unsatisfactory, wretched; commonplace, mediocre, ordinary
ant execrable

except *vb* **1** *syn* see EXCLUDE
rel omit, pass over; exempt; reject
con incorporate, receive, work in
ant admit
2 *syn* see OBJECT 1

except *prep* with the exclusion or exception of <*except* Christmas, we had no long holiday>
syn apart from, aside from, bar, barring, bating, beside, besides, but, ‖cep, except for, excluding, exclusive of, outside, outside of, save, saving

except *conj* **1** on any other condition than that <wouldn't go near that woman *except* I had to>
syn but, save, saving, unless, ‖without
2 *syn* see ONLY

except for *prep syn* see EXCEPT

exceptionable *adj syn* see OBJECTIONABLE
con unimpeachable; exemplary
ant unexceptionable

exceptional *adj* **1** being out of the ordinary <an *exceptional* opportunity>
syn extraordinary, phenomenal, rare, remarkable, singular, uncommon, uncustomary, un-

imaginable, unique, unordinary, unthinkable, unusual, unwonted; *compare* STRANGE 4
rel infrequent, scarce; distinct, notable, noteworthy
con frequent; common, commonplace, familiar, ordinary, usual
ant unexceptional
2 ***syn*** see SUPERIOR 4
rel good; excellent, marvelous, outstanding, phenomenal, wonderful; extraordinary, singular, special
con common, ordinary, run-of-the-mill
ant average

exceptionally *adv* ***syn*** see VERY 1
rel especially, particularly; extraordinarily, unusually; marvelously, phenomenally, stupendously, wonderfully

excerpt *vb* to select (passages or details) as typical of a larger store <quotations *excerpted* from many authors>
syn extract
rel cull, glean; choose, pick, pick out, select, single; cite, quote

excess *n* **1** whatever exceeds a limit, measure, bound, or accustomed degree <the proper balance between sufficiency and *excess*>
syn fat, overabundance, overflow, overkill, overmuch, overplus, plethora, superfluity, surfeit, surplus, surplusage
rel overbalance, overspill; oversupply; profusion; superabundance
idiom enough and then some, enough and to spare, too much of a good thing
con insufficiency, lack, scarcity
ant deficiency; dearth
2 the amount or degree by which a thing or number exceeds another <an *excess* of 10 bushels over what was needed>
syn overage, overstock, oversupply, plus, surplus, surplusage
rel overproduction; overmeasure
ant deficit, shortfall
3 *often* **excesses** *pl* undue or immoderate personal indulgence especially in eating and drinking <*excess* at table is seldom healthful> <his *excesses* led to his failure in business>
syn immoderation, inordinateness, intemperance, overindulgence
rel extravagance, overdoing; indulgence, self-indulgence; immoderacy, immoderateness; dissipation, prodigality, saturnalia
con moderation; sobriety, temperateness; restraint, self-discipline, self-restraint
ant temperance

excess *adj* ***syn*** see SUPERFLUOUS
rel redundant; unessential

excessive *adj* **1** going beyond a normal or acceptable limit <spend an *excessive* amount on clothes>
syn dizzy, exorbitant, extravagant, extreme, immoderate, inordinate, sky-high, steep, stiff, stratospheric, supernatural, towering, unconscionable, undue, unmeasurable
rel boundless, limitless, unbounded; over, overboard, overmuch, overweening; super
idiom out of bounds
con exiguous, meager, narrow, scant, scanty, skimpy, sparse, tight
ant deficient
2 given to personal excesses <an *excessive* drinker, often drunk and never quite sober>
syn immoderate, inordinate, intemperate, overindulgent, unrestrained, untempered
rel extravagant; indulgent, self-indulgent; dissipated, prodigal
con conservative, moderate, sober, temperate
ant restrained

excessively *adv* ***syn*** see EVER 6

exchange *vb* **1** ***syn*** see TRADE 1
2 to give up, taking in return something else <*exchanged* his uniform for civilian clothes>
syn change, substitute, swap, switch, trade; *compare* TRADE 1
rel displace, replace
3 to give and receive reciprocally <*exchanged* a few words with her neighbor>
syn bandy, interchange
rel pay back, reciprocate
idiom give as much as one takes, give tit for tat, return the compliment

exchangeable *adj* ***syn*** see INTERCHANGEABLE

exchequer *n* ***syn*** see TREASURY 2

excise *vb* to remove by or as if by dissecting <*excise* a tumor> <*excised* some wordy passages>
syn cut out, exsect, extirpate, resect
rel amputate, cut off; elide, remove, strike out; eradicate, root out; delete, expurgate, exscind, slash

excitable *adj* easily excited <an *excitable* child who needs a firm hand>
syn agitable, alarmable, combustible, edgy, skittery, skittish, startlish, volatile
rel high-strung, mercurial, temperamental, unstable; touchy
idiom like a bundle of nerves, likely to go off at half cock, on edge, on the ragged edge
con calm, collected, cool, easy, easygoing, phlegmatic, placid, quiet
ant unexcitable

excite *vb* **1** ***syn*** see PROVOKE 4
rel agitate, discompose, disquiet, disturb, perturb, stir up; impassion; charge (up), energize, touch off, turn on
idiom set astir, set on fire, stir the blood
con allay, placate, soothe
ant quiet
2 ***syn*** see ELATE
rel move; fire
con depress, dishearten
3 ***syn*** see INTEREST

excited *adj* ***syn*** see INTOXICATED 2
rel animated, atwitter; agitated, charged (up), inflamed, pink; delighted, enthusiastic
idiom all fired up, all of a twitter, beside oneself

---

con apathetic, unmoved; deflated
ant unexcited

exciting *adj* absorbingly interesting <the most *exciting* day of her life><an *exciting* personality>
syn exhilarant, exhilarating, exhilarative, eye-popping, inspiring, intoxicating, rousing, stimulating, stirring
rel arresting, interesting, intriguing; moving, provocative; heady, thrilling
con blah, dull, uninteresting, unintriguing; humdrum, monotonous, tedious
ant unexciting

exclaim *vb* to speak or utter suddenly and usually sharply, vehemently, or passionately <*exclaimed* in delight at the sight of the toy>
syn blat, blurt (out), bolt, cry out, ejaculate
rel burst (out); roar, snort

exclude *vb* to prevent the participation, consideration, or inclusion of <*excluded* that subject from discussion>
syn bar, bate, count out, debar, eliminate, except, rule out, suspend
rel ban; close out, estop, obviate, preclude, prevent, prohibit, ward (off); blackball, blacklist, ostracize; block; disbar; lock out, put out, shut out
idiom close (*or* shut) the door on
con comprehend, involve; embrace, take in
ant admit; include

excluding *prep* ***syn*** see EXCEPT

exclusionary *adj* ***syn*** see EXCLUSIVE 1

exclusive *adj* **1** having or exercising the power to limit or exclude <a tangle of *exclusive* laws>
syn exclusionary, exclusory
rel barring, debarring, excluding; limitative, limiting, restrictive; preclusive, prohibitive
con free, unlimited, unrestricted, unrestrictive
ant admissive
2 ***syn*** see SELECT 1
rel aristocratic, elite, preferred, privileged, tony; aloof, clannish, cliquey, cliquish; high-hat, snobbish, standoffish
con catholic, cosmopolitan, universal; common, familiar, ordinary, popular, vulgar
ant inclusive
3 ***syn*** see STYLISH
con tasteless; frumpy, unfashionable
4 ***syn*** see SOLE 4
rel individual, lone, only
con common, general, public
5 ***syn*** see WHOLE 5
con divided, partial

exclusive *n* ***syn*** see SCOOP

exclusively *adv* ***syn*** see ONLY 1
rel completely, wholly; particularly

exclusive of *prep* ***syn*** see EXCEPT

exclusory *adj* ***syn*** see EXCLUSIVE 1

excogitate *vb* **1** ***syn*** see CONSIDER 1
2 ***syn*** see DERIVE 1
rel contrive, invent, think (up); develop, think (out)

excoriate *vb* **1** ***syn*** see CHAFE 3
2 ***syn*** see LAMBASTE 3
idiom tear into

excorticate *vb* ***syn*** see SKIN 2

excrescence *n* ***syn*** see OUTGROWTH 1

excrescency *n* ***syn*** see OUTGROWTH 1

excruciate *vb* ***syn*** see AFFLICT
rel inflame, irritate; hurt, pain, wound; convulse
idiom prolong the agony

excruciating *adj* intensely or unbearably painful <his suffering was *excruciating*>
syn agonizing, harrowing, racking, tearing, tormenting, torturing, torturous
rel acute, extreme; piercing, sharp, shooting, stabbing; consuming, rending

exculpate *vb* to free from alleged fault or guilt <the court *exculpated* him after a thorough investigation>
syn absolve, acquit, clear, disculpate, exonerate, vindicate
rel explain, justify, rationalize; condone, excuse, forgive, pardon, remit; amnesty, free, let off
idiom clear the (*or* one's) record, wipe the slate clean
con blame, censure, denounce, reprehend, reprobate; incriminate; accuse, charge; arraign, indict; impeach; convict
ant inculpate

excurse *vb* ***syn*** see DIGRESS 2

excursion *n* **1** a trip not involving a prolonged or definite separation from one's usual abode or way of life <an afternoon *excursion* to the city>
syn jaunt, junket, outing, roundabout, sally
rel expedition, journey, trek, trip, safari; circuit, tour; one-way trip, pleasure trip, round trip; ‖pasear, paseo, walk, ‖walkabout
2 ***syn*** see DIGRESSION

excursus *n* ***syn*** see DIGRESSION

excusable *adj* **1** ***syn*** see VENIAL
2 ***syn*** see JUSTIFIABLE

excuse *vb* **1** to exact neither punishment nor redress for or from <she was much too ready to *excuse* her children's faults>
syn condone, forgive, pardon, remit
rel alibi, apologize (for), explain, justify, pretext, rationalize; absolve, acquit, clear, exculpate, exonerate, vindicate; extenuate, gloss (over), gloze, overlook, palliate, pass over, shrug off, whitewash, wink (at)
con blame, censure, criticize, reprehend, reprobate; castigate, chasten, chastise, correct, discipline; admonish, chide, rebuke, reprimand
ant punish
2 ***syn*** see EXEMPT

excuse *n* **1** a justifying explanation of a fault or defect <what's your *excuse* for being late>
syn alibi, plea, pretext, ‖right; *compare* APOLOGY 1, 2
rel defense; explanation, justification, rationalization; reason
2 ***syn*** see APOLOGY 2
3 an inferior example of a specified kind <this heap is a sorry *excuse* for a car>
syn apology
rel makeshift, shift, stopgap, substitute
idiom a sorry specimen

con nonpareil, paragon; gem, jewel, treasure

exec *n* ***syn*** see EXECUTIVE

execrable *adj* **1** so odious as to be utterly detestable <an *execrable* crime>
syn accursed, cursed, damnable
rel atrocious, heinous, horrific, horrifying, monstrous; base, despicable, foul, low, vile; detestable, loathsome, nauseating, repulsive, revolting
idiom beneath (*or* below) contempt, not to be put up with (*or* endured)
2 ***syn*** see DAMNED 2

execrate *vb* **1** to denounce violently <*execrated* those responsible for the concentration camps>
syn anathematize, curse, damn, objurgate
rel censure, condemn, denounce, reprehend, reprobate, reprove; ban; revile; accurse, imprecate
con applaud, commend, compliment; acclaim, extol, laud, praise; admire
ant eulogize
2 ***syn*** see HATE
3 ***syn*** see SWEAR 3

execration *n* ***syn*** see BLASPHEMY 1

execute *vb* **1** ***syn*** see PERFORM 2
rel act; bring about, cause; carry out, complete, discharge, transact
2 ***syn*** see ADMINISTER 1
rel discharge, dispatch, transact; conduct, handle
3 ***syn*** see FULFILL 1
rel put through
4 ***syn*** see MURDER 1
rel eliminate, purge
idiom put to death

executive *n* one who holds an administrative or managerial position <a senior sales *executive*>
syn administrator, exec, manager, officer, official
rel businessman, businesswoman; entrepreneur; higher-up; director, leader, supervisor

exegesis *n* ***syn*** see EXPLANATION 1

exegetic *adj* ***syn*** see EXPLANATORY

exemplar *n* ***syn*** see MODEL 2
rel soul; exponent, illustration; prototype

exemplary *adj* **1** ***syn*** see GOOD 11
rel ideal, model; admirable, commendable, praiseworthy, worthy
con evil, corrupt; unworthy
2 ***syn*** see TYPICAL 1

exemplify *vb* **1** to use examples in order to clarify <a good teacher *exemplifies* each complex point>
syn illustrate, instance
rel clarify, clear up, spell out; cite, quote; enlighten, illuminate
2 ***syn*** see EPITOMIZE 2
rel demonstrate; illustrate
3 ***syn*** see REPRESENT 2

exempt *vb* to free from a liability or requirement <*exempt* a man from military service>
syn absolve, discharge, dispense, excuse, let off, privilege (from), relieve, spare
rel except; free
idiom give (one) exemption

exemption *n* freeing or the state of being free or freed from a charge or obligation to which others are subject <received a tax *exemption*>
syn immunity, impunity
rel exception; discharge, freedom, release

exenterate *vb* ***syn*** see EVISCERATE

exercise *n* **1** the act of bringing into play or realizing in action <one can usually avoid accidents by the *exercise* of foresight>
syn application, employment, exercising, exertion, operation, use; *compare* USE 1
con dereliction, disregard, neglect; carelessness, heedlessness, inattention, laxity
2 regular or repeated appropriate use of a faculty, power, or bodily organ <muscular atrophy from lack of *exercise*>
syn activity, exercising, exertion
rel action, movement; practice, use, workout
con inactiveness, inactivity; idleness, unemployment
3 something practiced or performed in order to develop, improve, or display a specific power or skill <spelling *exercises*>
syn drill, drilling, practice
4 a performance having a strongly marked secondary or ulterior aspect <his writing is an *exercise* in confusion>
syn lesson, study

exercise *vb* **1** ***syn*** see USE 2
idiom put into practice
2 ***syn*** see EXERT
3 to use repeatedly in order to master or strengthen <beginning swimmers *exercising* their new skill> <games that *exercise* the muscles>
syn drill, practice, rehearse
rel break in, condition, groom, prepare, train; cultivate, develop, foster, improve; fix, set
4 ***syn*** see ANNOY 1

exercising *n* **1** ***syn*** see EXERCISE 1
2 ***syn*** see EXERCISE 2

exert *vb* to bring to bear especially with sustained effort or lasting effect <*exerted* tremendous influence over his son's development>
syn exercise, ply, put out, throw, wield
rel apply, employ, use
idiom put forth

exertion *n* **1** ***syn*** see EXERCISE 1
2 ***syn*** see EFFORT 1
rel strain, striving, struggle
idiom hard (*or* long) pull
con ease, leisure, relaxation, repose, rest; inactivity, idleness
ant inertia
3 ***syn*** see EXERCISE 2

exfoliate *vb* ***syn*** see SCALE 2

exhale *vb* to let or force out of the lungs <*exhaled* a cloud of cigarette smoke>
syn breathe (out), expire, outbreathe

---

syn synonym(s) ***rel*** related word(s)
ant antonym(s) ***con*** contrasted word(s)
idiom idiomatic equivalent(s)
‖ use limited; if in doubt, see a dictionary

rel emit, let (out); blow
ant inhale, inspire
exhaust *vb* **1** *syn* see DEPLETE
rel dispel, disperse, dissipate, scatter; run out
idiom suck dry
con conserve, preserve, save; renew, restore
2 *syn* see CONSUME 1
3 *syn* see GO 4
4 to tire utterly
syn ‖bugger, do in, fag, frazzle, knock out, out-tire, outwear, ‖poop, prostrate, sew up, tucker, wear out; *compare* TIRE 1
rel overdo, overdrive, overexert, overextend, overply, overwork; debilitate, enfeeble, weaken
idiom run one ragged, tire to death
con relax, rest, unlax
exhausted *adj* *syn* see EFFETE 2
rel run-down, weak, weakened; ‖beat, dog-tired, tired, ‖tucked up; limp; dead
idiom all done in (*or* for)
exhaustion *n* *syn* see FATIGUE
rel collapse, prostration
exhaustive *adj* testing all possibilities or considering all the elements of <an *exhaustive* search>
syn complete, full-dress, thorough, thoroughgoing, whole-hog
rel all-encompassing, all-out, comprehensive, full-blown, full-scale, out-and-out, profound, total; intensive, radical, sweeping
con cursory, shallow; incomplete, partial; slipshod, unthorough
ant superficial
exhaustively *adv* **1** *syn* see HARD 3
con cursorily, superficially; incompletely, partially
2 *syn* see THOROUGHLY 2
exhibit *vb* **1** *syn* see SHOW 2
2 *syn* see LOOK 4
3 *syn* see SHOW 4
idiom parade one's wares, strut one's stuff
exhibit *n* *syn* see EXHIBITION 2
exhibition *n* **1** an act or instance of showing, evincing, or showing off <she gave an incredible *exhibition* of bad manners>
syn demonstration, display, show, spectacle
rel manifestation, sight
2 a public display of objects of interest <a trade *exhibition*>
syn exhibit, exposition, fair, show
rel demonstration, display, offering, presentation, showing
exhibitive *adj* *syn* see INDICATIVE
exhilarant *adj* *syn* see EXCITING
exhilarate *vb* *syn* see ELATE
rel animate, enliven, invigorate, vitalize; boost, buoy, exalt, inspirit, lift, pep (up), uplift; cheer, delight, gladden, ‖send, thrill
idiom send into ecstasies
con deject, dishearten, dispirit, weigh down
ant depress
exhilarated *adj* *syn* see INTOXICATED 2
rel buoyed up, exalted, gladdened, pepped up, uplifted
idiom in ecstasies, on cloud nine
con blue, dispirited, down, low, unhappy, weighed down
ant depressed
exhilarating *adj* **1** *syn* see EXCITING
rel animating, animative, enlivening, inspiriting, invigorating, quickening; cheering, elevating, uplifting; breathtaking, electric
con deflating, disheartening, dispiriting
ant depressing
2 *syn* see INVIGORATING
exhilaration *n* *syn* see ELATION 1 *compare* ECSTASY
rel animation, enlivenment, firing, invigoration, quickening, stimulation, vitalization, vivification; electrification, excitation, excitement, galvanization; elevation, inspiration, uplift
ant dejection
exhilarative *adj* **1** *syn* see EXCITING
2 *syn* see INVIGORATING
exhort *vb* *syn* see URGE
rel admonish, plead; call upon, insist; stimulate
con block, deter, discourage, impede
exhumate *vb* *syn* see EXHUME
exhume *vb* to take out of a place of burial <the body was *exhumed* and burned>
syn disinhume, disinter, exhumate, unbury, uncharnel
rel dig up, disentomb, unearth; disembalm
con bury, entomb, inter, ‖plant
ant inhume
exigency *n* **1** *syn* see JUNCTURE 2
rel difficulty, hardship, rigor, vicissitude; dilemma, fix, jam, pickle, scrape; pressure, urgency
2 *syn* see NEED 4
rel demand, imperativeness, insistence, requirement; coercion, compulsion, constraint; duress, pressure, urgency
idiom matter of life and death
exigent *adj* **1** *syn* see PRESSING
rel acute; necessary; menacing, threatening
2 *syn* see ONEROUS
exiguous *adj* *syn* see MEAGER 2
rel diminutive, little, small, tiny; slender, slight, tenuous, thin; confined, limited, narrow, restricted, straitened
ant ample
exile *n* **1** forced removal from one's native country <a deposed king living in *exile* in Rome>
syn banishment, deportation, displacement, expulsion, ostracism, relegation
rel exclusion; extradition; expatriation; diaspora, dispersion, migration, scattering
con recall, restoration
2 *syn* see ÉMIGRÉ
rel nonperson, outcast, unperson
idiom man without a country
exile *vb* *syn* see BANISH
rel dispossess; evacuate; extradite; drive out
idiom turn out of house and home
con recall, restore
exist *vb* **1** *syn* see BE
2 *syn* see CONSIST 1
existence *n* **1** the state or fact of having independent reality <customs that have recently come into *existence*>

syn actuality, being
rel life; presence; reality; perseity
ant nonexistence
2 ***syn*** see ENTITY 1
rel essence; individuality
existent *adj* **1** ***syn*** see ACTUAL 1
rel existing; present
2 ***syn*** see EXTANT 1
3 ***syn*** see PRESENT
existent *n* ***syn*** see ENTITY 1
existing *adj* ***syn*** see EXTANT 1
exit *n* **1** ***syn*** see DEPARTURE 1
ant entry
2 ***syn*** see EGRESS 2
ant entrance, entry
exit *vb* ***syn*** see GO 2
idiom make an (*or* one's) exit
con arrive, come
ant enter
exiting *n* ***syn*** see DEPARTURE 1
ant entering
exodus *n* ***syn*** see DEPARTURE 1
rel emigration, migration; flight
con immigration; ingress
ant influx
ex officio *adj* ***syn*** see OFFICIAL
exonerate *vb* ***syn*** see EXCULPATE
rel disburden, free
ant incriminate
exorbitant *adj* ***syn*** see EXCESSIVE 1
rel overboard, overmuch; unwarranted; outrageous, preposterous; exacting, extortionate
idiom out of sight
con equitable, fair, just; rational, reasonable
exordium *n* ***syn*** see INTRODUCTION
rel preliminary
con afterword, conclusion, epilogue, postscript
exotic *adj* **1** not native to the place where found <*exotic* fish>
syn foreign
rel imported, introduced, naturalized; alien, extrinsic, strange
con aboriginal, autochthonous, endemic, native; domestic, local
ant indigenous
2 excitingly or enticingly different or unusual <he was moved by her *exotic* beauty>
syn romanesque, romantic, strange
rel different, unusual; alluring, enticing, fascinating, glamorous, mysterious
expand *vb* **1** ***syn*** see OPEN 4
2 ***syn*** see INCREASE 1
3 to increase or become increased in bulk, volume, or size <water *expands* when heated>
syn amplify, dilate, distend, inflate, swell
rel grow; bulk (up), enlarge, fill (out); bolster; mushroom, ‖plim, puff (up)
con condense, decrease, deflate, shrink, shrivel; dwindle, lessen
ant contract
4 to express more fully and in greater detail <*expanded* his notes into an essay>
syn amplify, develop, elaborate, enlarge
rel detail, explicate; augment; discourse, expatiate
con compress, condense, contract
ant abridge
5 ***syn*** see INCREASE 2
6 ***syn*** see ESCALATE 2
rel prolong, protract
con de-escalate; circumscribe
ant limit, restrict
expanse *n* a significantly large area or range <a trackless *expanse* of moor>
syn amplitude, breadth, distance, expansion, space, spread, stretch
rel compass, extent, orbit, range, reach, scope, sweep; area, domain, field, sphere, territory; immensity, magnitude
expansion *n* **1** ***syn*** see EXPANSE
2 the act or process of increasing in some way <the recent *expansion* of science>
syn enlargement, extension, spread
con contraction, decrease, shrinking
expansive *adj* **1** ***syn*** see ELASTIC 2
rel communicative, demonstrative, extroverted, gregarious, unconstrained, unreserved, unrestrained; effusive, gushy, lavish; generous, liberal, openhanded
con austere, severe, stern; reserved, reticent, silent, taciturn
2 ***syn*** see DEMONSTRATIVE
ant withdrawn
3 ***syn*** see COMMUNICATIVE
4 ***syn*** see EXTENSIVE 1
rel ample, large; big, great
ant limited
expatiate *vb* ***syn*** see DISCOURSE 1
rel narrate, recite, recount, rehearse, relate; ramble
expatriate *vb* ***syn*** see BANISH
ant repatriate
expatriate *n* ***syn*** see ÉMIGRÉ
ant repatriate
expect *vb* **1** to anticipate in the mind <did not *expect* him for dinner>
syn await, count (on *or* upon), hope, look
rel anticipate, apprehend, divine, foreknow, foresee
idiom bargain on (*or* for), look for
ant despair (of)
2 ***syn*** see UNDERSTAND 3
rel feel, sense; presume, presuppose
expectancy *n* **1** the state of one who looks forward to something <had an air of wistful *expectancy*>
syn anticipation, expectation
rel presensation, presentiment
2 ***syn*** see EXPECTATION 2
expectant *adj* **1** characterized by expectation <an *expectant* crowd>
syn anticipant, anticipative, anticipatory, atiptoe, expecting
rel open-eyed, openmouthed; hopeful; eager; alert, watchful

---

syn synonym(s) ***rel*** related word(s)
ant antonym(s) ***con*** contrasted word(s)
idiom idiomatic equivalent(s)
‖ use limited; if in doubt, see a dictionary

con apathetic, indifferent, uninterested; unconcerned, unimpressed, unmoved
2 *syn* see PREGNANT 1
idiom anticipating a blessed event, waiting for the stork

expectation *n* 1 *syn* see EXPECTANCY 1
2 something that is expected <each had his own dreams and *expectations*>
syn expectancy
rel design, hope, intention, motive, notion; prospect

expecting *adj* 1 *syn* see EXPECTANT 1
2 *syn* see PREGNANT 1

expediency *n* 1 *syn* see ORDER 11
rel propitiousness; convenience
2 *syn* see RESOURCE 3
rel design, strategy, tactic; measure, step
idiom card up one's sleeve, means to an end

expedient *adj* dictated by practical or prudential motives <decided it was not *expedient* to interfere yet>
syn advisable, politic, prudent, tactical, wise
rel advantageous, beneficial, convenient, practical, profitable, useful, utilitarian; opportune, seasonable, timely, well-timed; feasible, possible, practicable; appropriate, fit, fitting, suitable; judicious
con deleterious, detrimental; harmful, hurtful, injurious; fruitless, futile, vain; inappropriate, uncalled-for, unfitting, unsuitable; impolite, imprudent, inadvisable, injudicious, unwise
ant inexpedient

expedient *n syn* see RESOURCE 3
rel agency, instrument, instrumentality, means, medium

expedition *n* 1 *syn* see JOURNEY
rel campaign; entrada, exploration
2 *syn* see HASTE 1
rel alacrity, promptitude
con delay, retardation, slackening, slowing
ant procrastination
3 *syn* see ALACRITY
rel expeditiousness, speediness, swiftness; punctuality
con dawdling, delaying, faltering, hesitation

expeditious *adj syn* see FAST 3
rel effective, effectual, efficacious, efficient; prompt, ready
con ineffective, ineffectual, inefficacious, inefficient; dilatory, laggard, leisurely, slow
ant sluggish

expeditiously *adv syn* see FAST 2
rel effectively, efficaciously; punctually
con ineffectively; deliberately, dilatorily, leisurely, slowly
ant sluggishly

expeditiousness *n syn* see HASTE 1

expeditive *adj syn* see FAST 3

expel *vb* 1 *syn* see ERUPT 1
rel blow off, blow out, ejaculate, exhaust
2 *syn* see BANISH
rel drum out, read out; eliminate, turn out; ||bounce
idiom give (one) the boot, give the bum's rush, give the old heave-ho, send to Coventry, throw out on one's ear
ant admit

expellee *n syn* see ÉMIGRÉ

expend *vb* 1 *syn* see SPEND 1
rel dispense, distribute; blow, exhaust, use up
idiom loose (*or* untie) the purse strings, open one's purse
con hoard, lay up, save
2 *syn* see GO 4

expenditure *n syn* see EXPENSE 1

expense *n* 1 something expended to secure a benefit or bring about a result <spared no *expense* in furnishing their home>
syn cost, disbursement, expenditure, outlay
2 a loss incurred in the course of gaining something <won the war at the *expense* of many lives>
syn cost, price, toll
rel decrement, forfeit, forfeiture, sacrifice; deprivation, loss

expensive *adj syn* see COSTLY 1
rel immoderate, uneconomical; big-ticket, high-priced
con economical, moderate; bargain, low-cost, low-priced, thrifty; cheap
ant inexpensive

experience *n syn* see ACQUAINTANCE 1
rel background; observation; know-how, practice, skill; savoir faire, sophistication; wisdom
ant inexperience

experience *vb* 1 to meet with directly (as through participation or observation) <*experience* pain> <trying to *experience* the problems of a different culture>
syn have, know, see, suffer, sustain, undergo
rel encounter, meet; accept, receive
2 *syn* see FEEL 2
rel behold, see, survey, view

experienced *adj* made skillful or wise through practice <an *experienced* sales executive>
syn old, old-time, practical, practiced, seasoned, skilled, versed, vet, veteran; *compare* PROFICIENT
rel broken in; accomplished, skillful; expert, qualified; old-line, wise
idiom having been around, knowing the score (*or* the ropes)
con apprentice, beginning, freshman, green, new, novice, raw, untested, untried
ant experienceless, inexperienced

experient *adj syn* see EMPIRICAL

experiential *adj syn* see EMPIRICAL

experiment *n* an operation or process carried out to resolve an uncertainty <*experiments* that added much to our understanding of nutritional needs>
syn experimentation, test, trial, trial and error, trial run
rel probe, research, search; examination, investigation; analysis, study

experiment *vb* to engage in experimentation <*experimenting* with regional solutions to urban problems>

syn experimentalize, experimentize, test (out), try (out), try on
rel investigate, probe, research, search; analyze, scrutinize, study, weigh
idiom play around with
experimental *adj* **1** ***syn*** see EMPIRICAL
2 of, relating to, or having the characteristics of experiment <*experimental* missile flights>
syn experimentative, test, trial
rel preliminary, preparatory; developmental; provisional, temporary, tentative
con tested, tried; permanent, proved; accepted, established, standard
experimentalize *vb* ***syn*** see EXPERIMENT
experimentation *n* ***syn*** see EXPERIMENT
experimentative *adj* ***syn*** see EXPERIMENTAL 2
experimentize *vb* ***syn*** see EXPERIMENT
expert *adj* ***syn*** see PROFICIENT
rel schooled, trained; adroit, deft, dexterous; pro, professional
con unpracticed; unschooled
ant amateur, inexpert
expert *n* one who has acquired special skill in or knowledge and mastery of something <a fingerprint *expert*>
syn adept, artist, artiste, authority, ‖dab, ‖dabster, doyen, master, master-hand, maven, passed master, past master, pro, professional, proficient, swell, virtuoso, whiz, wiz, wizard
rel ‖darb; specialist
con dabbler, dilettante, tyro; apprentice, novice, probationer
ant amateur
expertise *n* **1** ***syn*** see ABILITY 2
rel readiness; competence; skillfulness
2 ***syn*** see ART 1
rel quickness; cleverness, ingeniousness; finesse; savvy
expertism *n* ***syn*** see ABILITY 2
expertness *n* ***syn*** see ABILITY 2
rel prowess; facility
expiate *vb* to make amends or give satisfaction for wrong done <*expiated* his crime with his life>
syn atone
rel amend, compensate (for), correct, rectify, redress, remedy
idiom make up for, put right
expiative *adj* ***syn*** see PURGATIVE
expiatory *adj* ***syn*** see PURGATIVE
expire *vb* **1** ***syn*** see DIE 1
idiom draw one's last breath; give up the breath of life
con live, thrive
2 ***syn*** see PASS 3
3 ***syn*** see EXHALE
ant inspire
explain *vb* **1** to make something comprehensible or more comprehensible <a commentary that *explains* the allegory>
syn construe, explicate, expound, interpret, spell out; *compare* CLARIFY 2
rel decipher, disentangle, undo, unravel, unriddle, unscramble, untangle; analyze, break down; clear up, resolve, solve
idiom put into plain English
con confound, confuse, puzzle
ant obfuscate
2 ***syn*** see CLARIFY 2
3 to give the reason for or cause of <unable to *explain* his strange conduct>
syn account, explain away, justify, rationalize
rel condone, excuse; absolve, acquit, exculpate, exonerate, vindicate
explain away *vb* ***syn*** see EXPLAIN 3
explanation *n* **1** something that makes clear what is obscure <sought some *explanation* of the difficult passage>
syn construal, construction, exegesis, explication, exposé, exposition, interpretation
rel disentanglement, unscrambling; enlightenment, illumination; definition, meaning; resolution, solution; demonstration, example, exemplification, illustration
2 a statement of causes, grounds, or motives <refused an *explanation* for her act>
syn account, justification, rationale, rationalization, reason
rel grounds; motive
explanative *adj* ***syn*** see EXPLANATORY
explanatory *adj* serving to explain <*explanatory* notes in a book>
syn exegetic, explanative, explicative, explicatory, expositional, expositive, expository, interpretive
rel enlightening, illuminating; discursive; demonstrative, illustrative
con baffling, bewildering, confusing, misleading, mystifying, puzzling
ant obfuscatory
expletive *n* ***syn*** see SWEARWORD
explicate *vb* ***syn*** see EXPLAIN 1
rel amplify, develop, dilate, enlarge (upon), expand, expatiate; demonstrate
idiom dot the *i*'s (and cross the *t*'s)
explication *n* ***syn*** see EXPLANATION 1
rel amplification, development, enlargement, expansion, expatiation
explicative *adj* ***syn*** see EXPLANATORY
rel annotative, exemplificative, scholiastic
explicatory *adj* ***syn*** see EXPLANATORY
explicit *adj* characterized by full precise expression <gave the guard *explicit* orders about whom to admit>
syn categorical, clean-cut, clear-cut, definite, definitive, express, specific, unambiguous
rel certain, clear, distinct, lucid, perspicuous, plain, sure, understandable, unequivocal; accurate, correct, exact, precise
con cryptic, dark, enigmatic, equivocal, obscure, unclear, vague; implicit, implied, inferred; imprecise, inaccurate, incorrect, inexact
ant ambiguous
explicitly *adv* ***syn*** see EXPRESSLY 1

---

syn synonym(s) ***rel*** related word(s)
ant antonym(s) ***con*** contrasted word(s)
idiom idiomatic equivalent(s)
‖ use limited; if in doubt, see a dictionary

explode *vb* **1** to burst violently and noisily usually due to pressure within <the bomb *exploded*>
syn blow up, burst, detonate, go off, mushroom
rel blast, discharge
idiom blow sky-high, blow to kingdom come
con fail, fizzle, peter (out)
2 ***syn*** see ERUPT 2
rel flame (up), flare (up)
idiom blow a fuse (*or* gasket)
3 ***syn*** see DISCREDIT 2
rel invalidate; deflate
idiom shoot full of holes

exploit *n* **1** ***syn*** see ADVENTURE
rel effort, job; maneuver
2 ***syn*** see FEAT 2
rel do, performance, stunt; blow, coup, stroke
idiom bold stroke

exploit *vb* **1** ***syn*** see USE 2
rel cultivate, work
2 to take unfair advantage of <*exploits* his friend's good nature>
syn abuse, impose (on *or* upon), use
rel manipulate; bleed, fleece, skin, soak, stick
3 ***syn*** see MANIPULATE 2

explore *vb* to search through or into <*explored* the possibilities of reaching an agreement>
syn delve (into), dig (into), go (into), inquire (into), investigate, look (into), probe, prospect, sift
rel burrow, mouse (out); quarry, search; examine, test, try; inquisite, question
idiom nose around

explosion *n* ***syn*** see OUTBURST 1

exponent *n* one who actively promotes or backs something <an *exponent* of arbitration in labor disputes>
syn advocate, champion, expounder, proponent, supporter
rel backer, booster, partisan, promoter, protagonist; defender, upholder
con antagonist, enemy; opposition
ant opponent

expose *vb* **1** to make accessible to something detrimental or dangerous <he needlessly *exposed* his troops to enemy fire>
syn lay (open), subject, uncover
rel endanger, hazard, imperil, jeopard, jeopardize, jeopardy, peril, risk
idiom put (*or* leave) in harm's way
con cover, shelter; guard, protect
ant shield
2 ***syn*** see OPEN 2
rel unfold, unshroud
3 ***syn*** see SHOW 4
rel advertise, air, broadcast, publish
4 to reveal the faults, frailties, unsoundness, or pretensions of <the monograph *exposed* the theory as being pure myth>
syn debunk, discover, show up, uncloak, undress, unmask, unshroud
rel disclose, reveal, uncover
idiom lay bare

exposé *n* ***syn*** see EXPLANATION 1

exposed *adj* **1** ***syn*** see OPEN 2
rel apparent, evident, manifest; unconcealed, unhidden; revealed; visible
idiom laid bare
con covered, enveloped, sheathed
2 ***syn*** see LIABLE 2
rel likely; menaced, threatened
con defended, guarded, protected, safeguarded, shielded

exposition *n* **1** ***syn*** see EXPLANATION 1
rel presentation; discourse, discussion, disquisition, expounding; statement; delineation, enunciation
2 ***syn*** see EXHIBITION 2
rel display, production

expositional *adj* ***syn*** see EXPLANATORY

expositive *adj* ***syn*** see EXPLANATORY
rel depictive, descriptive, graphic; illuminative; delineative

expository *adj* ***syn*** see EXPLANATORY
rel disquisitional; critical

expostulate *vb* ***syn*** see OBJECT 1
rel combat, fight, oppose, resist; argue, debate, discuss, dispute
idiom raise one's voice against

exposure *n* the condition of being exposed to something detrimental <*exposure* to attack>
syn liability, openness, vulnerability, vulnerableness
rel susceptibility, susceptiveness, susceptivity; defenselessness, helplessness, unprotection; danger, jeopardy, peril, risk
con bulwark, cover, protection, safeguard, shelter, shield, shielding

expound *vb* ***syn*** see EXPLAIN 1
rel express, present, state; comment, discourse; clarify, delineate, describe, exemplify, illustrate

expounder *n* ***syn*** see EXPONENT
rel explainer, expositor

express *adj* **1** ***syn*** see EXPLICIT
rel expressed, uttered, voiced; out-and-out, unmistakable; unconditional, unqualified
con unexpressed, unsaid, unstated; ambiguous, equivocal; conditional, qualified
2 of a particular or exact sort <came for the *express* purpose of buying a car>
syn especial, set, special, specific
rel individual; definite, particular; explicit; intended, intentional, premeditated
ant vague

express *vb* **1** ***syn*** see WORD
2 to give expression to (as a thought, an opinion, or an emotion) <*expressed* his views freely>
syn air, give, put, state, vent, ventilate; *compare* SAY 1, WORD
rel broach, circulate, put about; disclose, tell; frame; enunciate, phrase; announce, declare, proclaim, pronounce; discharge, drain
con hint, insinuate, intimate, suggest
ant imply
3 ***syn*** see MEAN 2
rel communicate, convey, impart
4 ***syn*** see PRESS 3

expression *n* **1** an act, process, or instance of expressing in words <his anger found *expression* in a string of oaths>

syn statement, utterance, vent, voice
rel issue; manifestation, representation; observation, reflection
con hint, insinuation, intimation, suggestion
2 ***syn*** see PHRASE 2
rel word; verbalism; idiom; clause
3 one thing that calls to mind another often symbolically <sent flowers as an *expression* of sympathy>
syn gesture, indication, reminder, sign, token
rel embodiment, manifestation, representation, symbol; demonstration, show
4 ***syn*** see ELOQUENCE
rel graphicness, vividness
5 ***syn*** see LOOK 2

expressionless *adj* lacking expression <cold *expressionless* eyes>
syn blank, deadpan, empty, inexpressive, unexpressive, vacant
rel dull, lackluster, lusterless, vacuous; impassive, inscrutable, stolid, wooden; dead
con lustrous; responsive; alive, vital
ant expressive

expressive *adj* clearly conveying or manifesting something <a forceful and *expressive* word>
syn eloquent, facund, meaningful, pregnant, rich, sententious, significant
rel revealing, revelatory, suggestive; graphic, pictorial, vivid; alive, demonstrative, lively, responsive, senseful, spirited
con banal, commonplace, drab, dull, flat, jejune, inane, insipid, vacuous, vapid; impassive, indifferent; austere, severe, stern, stiff, wooden; blank, deadpan, empty, expressionless, vacant; dead
ant inexpressive, unexpressive

expressiveness *n* ***syn*** see ELOQUENCE
ant inexpressiveness

expressivity *n* ***syn*** see ELOQUENCE

expressly *adv* **1** in direct and unmistakable terms <his beliefs *expressly* repudiate the church's teachings>
syn categorically, definitely, explicitly, specifically
rel directly; unmistakably
con ambiguously, equivocally; conditionally; likely, possibly, probably
2 for the express purpose <programs designed *expressly* to serve immediate political objectives>
syn especially, in specie, specially, specifically
3 ***syn*** see EVEN 1

expropriate *vb* ***syn*** see APPROPRIATE 1
rel dispossess; take (away)

expulse *vb* ***syn*** see BANISH
rel ||bounce; eject
con admit, receive

expulsion *n* ***syn*** see EXILE 1
rel driving out, forcing out; ejection, ousting; removal
idiom the boot, the old heave-ho

expunge *vb* ***syn*** see ERASE
rel discard, drop, exclude, omit; annihilate, eradicate

expurgate *vb* **1** ***syn*** see PURIFY 2
2 ***syn*** see CENSOR

expurgation *n* ***syn*** see PURIFICATION

expurgatorial *adj* ***syn*** see PURGATIVE

expurgatory *adj* ***syn*** see PURGATIVE

exquisite *adj* **1** ***syn*** see CHOICE
rel consummate, finished; faultless, flawless, impeccable
2 ***syn*** see IMPECCABLE 1
rel superb, superlative
con faulty, flawed, imperfect
3 ***syn*** see INTENSE 1
rel acute, extreme; consummate, transcending

exquisite *n* ***syn*** see FOP

exsect *vb* ***syn*** see EXCISE

exsiccate *vb* ***syn*** see DRY 1

extant *adj* **1** that is in existence <the most talented writer *extant*>
syn alive, around, existent, existing, living
con dead, defunct, destroyed, exterminated, extinct; departed, gone, lost
ant nonextant
2 ***syn*** see ACTUAL 1
rel current, immediate, present
con possible, potential
3 ***syn*** see PRESENT

extemporaneous *adj* composed, devised, or done at the moment rather than beforehand <made an *extemporaneous* speech after the dinner>
syn autoschediastic, extemporary, extempore, impromptu, improvised, offhand, spur-of-the-moment, unrehearsed, unstudied; *compare* UNINTENTIONAL
rel casual, informal; unprepared, unthought-out; impulsive, snap, spontaneous
idiom off the cuff, on the spur of the moment
con designed, planned, prepared, projected, schemed, thought-out; considered, deliberated, premeditated, studied

extemporary *adj* ***syn*** see EXTEMPORANEOUS

extempore *adj* ***syn*** see EXTEMPORANEOUS

extemporization *n* ***syn*** see IMPROVISATION

extemporize *vb* ***syn*** see IMPROVISE
rel dash off, knock off, toss off
idiom do offhand, play (it) by ear
con cook up, plan, prepare, think out

extend *vb* **1** ***syn*** see OPEN 4
con close, fold
2 ***syn*** see OFFER 1
rel allocate, allot; accord, advance, award, bestow, confer, grant; donate
idiom place at one's disposal
3 to make or become longer <*extended* her visit by a week>
syn draw, draw out, elongate, lengthen, prolong, prolongate, protract, spin (out), stretch
rel amplify, enlarge, expand, increase
con abridge; curtail
ant shorten

---

syn synonym(s) ***rel*** related word(s)
ant antonym(s) ***con*** contrasted word(s)
idiom idiomatic equivalent(s)
|| use limited; if in doubt, see a dictionary

4 ***syn*** see INCREASE 1
5 ***syn*** see RUN 8
rel advance, proceed; continue
6 ***syn*** see RANGE 3
7 to reach a certain point <his education doesn't *extend* beyond elementary school>
syn go
rel reach, run; advance; attain

extended *adj* **1** ***syn*** see LONG 1
rel prolonged, protracted, spread out, stretched out (*or* forth)
ant contracted
2 ***syn*** see EXTENSIVE 1
rel far-flung, widespread
con narrow; inextensive
ant unextended

extension *n* **1** the act or state of extending or being extended <a one-month *extension* of the price freeze seems likely>
syn elongation, lengthening, production, prolongation, prolongment, protraction
rel continuation, continuing; drawing out, stretch, stretch-out
con abridgment, shortening; contraction, curtailment, shrinking
2 ***syn*** see EXPANSION 2
rel augmentation, increase; spreading out
con abridgment, curtailment; reduction
ant contraction
3 ***syn*** see RANGE 2
rel magnitude, size, spread; comprehensiveness
4 ***syn*** see ANNEX

extensity *n* ***syn*** see RANGE 2

extensive *adj* **1** widely ranging in scope or application <*extensive* privileges>
syn broad, expansive, extended, scopic, scopious, wide
rel comprehensive, general, inclusive; far-reaching, far-spreading, spacious, wide-ranging; all-encompassing, all-inclusive, blanket, boundless, indiscriminate, unrestricted, wholesale
con circumscribed, constricted, limited, narrow, restricted; unextended
2 ***syn*** see BIG 1
con little, small

extent *n* **1** ***syn*** see RANGE 2
rel domain, field, province, sphere
2 ***syn*** see SIZE 1
rel compass, extension, orbit, radius, reach, scope, sweep
3 ***syn*** see ORDER 4

extenuate *vb* **1** ***syn*** see THIN 1
rel mitigate; moderate, qualify, temper
con aggravate, enhance, heighten
2 ***syn*** see PALLIATE
rel explain, justify, rationalize; apologize
idiom put a gloss on (*or* upon *or* over), put a good face upon

exterior *adj* ***syn*** see OUTER
rel outermost, outmost
con inner, ingrained, inherent, intrinsic
ant interior

exteriorize *vb* ***syn*** see EMBODY 1
ant interiorize

exterminate *vb* **1** ***syn*** see ANNIHILATE 2
rel finish off; execute; kill (off)
idiom do away with, put an end to, put out of the way
2 ***syn*** see SLAUGHTER 3
idiom wipe off the face of the earth, wipe off the map

external *adj* ***syn*** see OUTER
rel out, outermost, outmost, peripheral
con ingrained, inherent, intrinsic
ant internal

externalize *vb* ***syn*** see EMBODY 1
ant internalize

extinct *adj* **1** ***syn*** see DEAD 1
2 that has died out altogether <an *extinct* civilization>
syn bygone, dead, defunct, departed, gone, lost, vanished
rel nonexistent; collapsed, fallen, overthrown; disappeared
idiom gone from the face of the earth
con existent, existing, living; active; contemporary, current
ant extant
3 ***syn*** see OBSOLETE
rel antiquated, archaic, old-fashioned
con modern; contemporary
ant current

extinguish *vb* **1** to cause to cease burning <firemen *extinguishing* the blaze>
syn douse, ||dout, out, put out, quench, ||squench
rel blow out, snuff out; smother
con fire, kindle, start; torch
ant ignite
2 ***syn*** see ANNIHILATE 2
rel erase, expunge, obliterate
3 ***syn*** see CRUSH 5
rel check; smother, stifle; snuff (out); choke (out), trample (down)
idiom put the lid (*or* the kibosh) on
con encourage, fire (up)
ant inflame

extinguishment *n* ***syn*** see REPRESSION 1

extirpate *vb* **1** ***syn*** see ANNIHILATE 2
rel efface, erase, expunge, demolish, destroy, raze; kill off
con breed, engender, generate, propagate
2 ***syn*** see EXCISE

extol *vb* ***syn*** see PRAISE 2
idiom beat the drum for, make much of
ant decry

extort *vb* **1** to obtain something by pressure or intimidation <racketeers *extorting* protection money>
syn exact, gouge, pinch, screw, shake down, squeeze, wrench, wrest, wring; *compare* CHEAT, FLEECE 1
rel demand; coerce, force; extract, get, obtain, secure; bleed, fleece, skin
idiom bleed one white, make one pay through the nose, put the screws to
2 ***syn*** see EDUCE 1

extra *adj* ***syn*** see SUPERFLUOUS

rel added, additional, supplemental, supplementary

extra *adv* to a degree or extent beyond the usual <she was *extra* smart>
syn extremely, rarely, ‖uncommon, uncommonly, unusually
rel especially; particularly; considerably, markedly, noticeably
con barely, scarcely

extract *vb* **1** to draw out forcibly or with effort <*extract* a confession> <*extract* a tooth>
syn evulse, pull, tear, yank
rel pry; avulse
2 ***syn*** see EKE OUT 3
3 ***syn*** see GLEAN
4 ***syn*** see EDUCE 1
5 ***syn*** see EXCERPT
rel abridge, condense, shorten

extraction *n* ***syn*** see ANCESTRY

extraneous *adj* **1** ***syn*** see EXTRINSIC
rel accidental, adventitious, incidental
con constitutional, ingrained, inherent; germane, material, pertinent
2 ***syn*** see IRRELEVANT
rel incidental; unessential; unrelated; pointless; inappropriate
idiom beside the point
ant relevant

extraordinary *adj* ***syn*** see EXCEPTIONAL 1
rel amazing; stupendous, terrific, wonderful
idiom out of the ordinary
con customary, normal, regular, usual
ant ordinary

extravagance *n* **1** ***syn*** see LUXURY
2 the quality, state, fact, or an instance of being extravagant <by living simply and avoiding *extravagance* they saved enough for the trip>
syn extravagancy, lavishness, overdoing, prodigality, squander, unthrift, waste, wastefulness
rel improvidence, spendthriftness; excess, indulgence, overindulgence
con moderation, temperateness; care, forehandedness, frugality; austerity
ant economy

extravagancy *n* ***syn*** see EXTRAVAGANCE 2

extravagant *adj* **1** grossly exaggerated <*extravagant* accusations>
syn fantastic, preposterous, wild
rel unbalanced, unrestrained; absurd, foolish, ludicrous, nonsensical, ridiculous, silly; bizarre, crazy; exaggerated, implausible
con plausible, sensible; restrained
ant reasonable
2 ***syn*** see EXCESSIVE 1
rel exuberant, lavish, profuse; prodigal, profligate, wasteful
con economical, frugal, sparing
ant restrained

extreme *adj* **1** very great <the project demanded *extreme* secrecy>
syn utmost, uttermost
2 ***syn*** see ARDENT 2
rel deep, moving
3 departing sharply from the traditional or usual <*extreme* political views>
syn extremist, fanatic, rabid, radical, revolutional, revolutionary, revolutionist, ultra, ultraist; *compare* OUTLANDISH 3
rel excessive, immoderate; desperate, drastic; extravagant, unreasonable; violent, wild
con conservative, moderate, restrained; reasonable, sensible
4 ***syn*** see EXCESSIVE 1
rel intolerable, unwarranted
5 most distant from a center <the *extreme* edge of the city>
syn farthest, furthermost, furthest, outermost, outmost, remotest, utmost, uttermost

extreme *n* **1** an extreme state or condition <an *extreme* of poverty>
syn extremity
rel excess, inordinancy
2 something situated at or marking one end or the other of a range <*extremes* of heat and cold>
syn extremity, limit
rel climax, consummation, culmination; ceiling, crest, crown, height; peak, pinnacle, summit, top; maximum, utmost, uttermost

extremely *adv* **1** ***syn*** see EVER 6
2 ***syn*** see VERY 1
3 ***syn*** see EXTRA

extremist *n* ***syn*** see RADICAL

extremist *adj* ***syn*** see EXTREME 3

extremity *n* **1** ***syn*** see EXTREME 2
rel acme, apex, apogee, vertex, zenith
2 ***syn*** see EXTREME 1

extricate *vb* **1** ***syn*** see KNOW 4
2 to free from an undesirable situation or condition <*extricate* himself from financial difficulties>
syn clear, clear away, discumber, disembarrass, disembroil, disencumber, disentangle, disentwine, unentangle, unscramble, untangle, untie, untwine
rel unravel; abstract, detach, disengage; disburden, disemburden; deliver, disinvolve, free, liberate, release, rescue; resolve
con embroil, entangle, tangle; clog, fetter, hogtie, manacle, shackle, trammel; block, hamper, hinder, impede, obstruct

extrinsic *adj* not properly part of a thing <a point *extrinsic* to his basic thesis>
syn alien, extraneous, foreign
rel acquired, gained; exterior, external, outer, outside, outward
con native; inner, inside, interior, internal, inward; individual, personal
ant intrinsic

extrude *vb* ***syn*** see EJECT 1

exuberance *n* ***syn*** see EBULLIENCE
rel gayness; friskiness, life, liveliness, sprightliness, zest, zestfulness; abandon, ardor

exuberancy *n* ***syn*** see EBULLIENCE

---

syn synonym(s) ***rel*** related word(s)
ant antonym(s) ***con*** contrasted word(s)
idiom idiomatic equivalent(s)
‖ use limited; if in doubt, see a dictionary

exuberant *adj* **1** joyously unrestrained and enthusiastic <his warm *exuberant* personality>
syn brash, ebullient, effervescent, high-spirited, vivacious
rel gay, lively, spirited, sprightly, zestful; frolicsome; ardent, passionate
con constrained, inhibited, repressed, restrained, subdued; calm, impassive, quiet
ant austere
2 ***syn*** see PROFUSE
rel fecund, fertile, fruitful, prolific; rampant, rank; diffuse
con scant, scanty, spare

exude *vb* to flow slowly out <a sticky resin *exuded* from the bark>
syn bleed, ooze, percolate, ‖screeve, seep, ‖sew, ‖sicker, strain, sweat, transude, weep
rel emanate; discharge, emit; trickle

exult *vb* to rejoice especially with feelings or display of triumph or self-satisfaction <the players were *exulting* in their victory>
syn delight, glory, jubilate, triumph
rel rejoice; celebrate; boast, brag, crow, show off
con lament, mourn
ant bemoan

exultance *n* ***syn*** see EXULTATION

exultant *adj* manifesting proud elation <*exultant* over her successes>
syn cock-a-hoop, cock-a-whoop, exulting, jubilant, triumphal, triumphant
rel happy, joyous, overjoyed; delighting, rejoicing; elated, flushed
idiom in high feather
con depressed, mournful, unhappy

exultation *n* the act of exulting or the state of being exultant <the *exultation* of victory and the thrill of power>
syn exultance, jubilance, jubilation, triumph
rel delight, elation, satisfaction; celebration, rejoicing; gloating

exulting *adj* ***syn*** see EXULTANT

exuviate *vb* ***syn*** see SHED 2

eye *n* **1** an organ of sight <turned his *eyes* to the view>
syn lamp, ocular, oculus, ‖ogle, orb, peeper, winker
2 the faculty of seeing with or as if with the eyes <had a keen *eye* for details>
syn eyesight, seeing, sight, vision
3 very close watching or observation <kept an *eye* on him>
syn eagle eye, scrutiny, surveillance, tab, watch
4 *often* **eyes** *pl* a way of looking at something <in the *eyes* of the law, a man is innocent until proven guilty>
syn view, viewpoint; *compare* VIEWPOINT 2
rel attitude, position, thinking; conception, grasp; conclusion, judgment
5 ***syn*** see OPINION
6 ***syn*** see LOOP 1
7 ***syn*** see LOOP 2
‖**8** ***syn*** see DETECTIVE

eye *vb* **1** to fix the eyes on <the child *eyed* the presents with delight>
syn consider, contemplate, gaze (upon), look (at *or* upon), view; *compare* LOOK 7
rel regard; stare (at)
2 to keep a close watch on <the detective *eyed* the suspect>
syn eyeball, scrutinize, watch; *compare* TAIL
rel stare (at); size up
idiom keep a close (*or* an eagle) eye on
3 ***syn*** see LOOK 7

eyeball *vb* ***syn*** see EYE 2

eye–catching *adj* ***syn*** see NOTICEABLE

eyeful *n* ***syn*** see BEAUTY

eyeless *adj* ***syn*** see BLIND 1

eye–popping *adj* ***syn*** see EXCITING

eyesight *n* ***syn*** see EYE 2

eyesore *n* something offensive to the sight <the old abandoned house was a neighborhood *eyesore*>
syn desight, fright, mess, monstrosity, sight

eyewash *n* ***syn*** see NONSENSE 2

eyewitness *n* ***syn*** see SPECTATOR

F

fable *n* **1** ***syn*** see FICTION
2 ***syn*** see ALLEGORY 2

fabric *n* **1** ***syn*** see BUILDING
2 ***syn*** see TEXTURE 2

fabricate *vb* ***syn*** see MAKE 3
rel turn out; create, formulate, invent; concoct, contrive, devise

fabrication *n* ***syn*** see FICTION
rel creation; deceit, fib; artifact, opus, product, production, work

fabulous *adj* ***syn*** see MYTHICAL
rel amazing, astonishing, astounding, incredible, marvelous, unbelievable, wonderful; exorbitant, extravagant, inordinate, outrageous, preposterous; monstrous, prodigious, stupendous
con believable, colorable, credible

facade *n* ***syn*** see MASK 2

face *n* **1** the front part of the head including the eyes, nose, mouth, cheeks, chin, and forehead <hid his *face* from the camera>
syn countenance, ‖dial, features, ‖kisser, ‖map, mug, ‖mush, muzzle, ‖pan, phiz, ‖puss, visage
rel lineaments, physiognomy
2 ***syn*** see LOOK 2
3 ***syn*** see APPEARANCE 2
4 ***syn*** see MASK 2
5 ***syn*** see EFFRONTERY
6 a distortion of the face usually as an expression of contempt or distaste <the old man made a *face* at the flat beer>
syn grimace, moue, mouth, mouthing, mow, mug
rel frown, glower, lower, pout, scowl
idiom wry face, wry mouth
con grin, simper, smile, smirk
7 ***syn*** see MAKEUP 3
8 ***syn*** see TOP 2

face *vb* **1** to have the face or front in a specified direction <the house *faces* toward the river>
syn front, look
rel border, meet
ant back
2 ***syn*** see MEET 6
rel watch; gaze, glare, stare; await, expect, look (for)
3 to confront with courage or boldness <ready to *face* her accusers>
syn ‖banter, beard, brave, challenge, dare, defy, ‖double-dog dare, front, outdare, outface, venture
rel confront, encounter, meet; oppose, resist, withstand; contend, fight
idiom brazen it out, face the music, face up to, take the bull by the horns
con elude, escape, eschew, evade, shun
ant avoid
4 ***syn*** see CONFRONT 1
5 ***syn*** see ACCOST 2
rel beard, brave, challenge, dare, defy
idiom stand up to
6 ***syn*** see ENGAGE 5
7 ***syn*** see SHEATHE

facet *n* ***syn*** see PHASE
rel face, front

facetious *adj* ***syn*** see WITTY
rel jesting, joking, quipping, wisecracking; blithe, jocund, jolly, jovial, merry; comic, comical, droll, funny, laughable, ludicrous
con grave, serious, sober, solemn, somber
ant lugubrious

facile *adj* ***syn*** see EASY 1
rel adroit, deft, dexterous; fluent, glib, voluble; cursory, shallow, superficial, uncritical
con awkward, clumsy, constrained, cumbersome, labored, maladroit; tongue-tied; deep, profound, thorough
ant arduous

facilely *adv* ***syn*** see EASILY 1
ant arduously

facilitate *vb* ***syn*** see EASE 3

facility *n* **1** ***syn*** see READINESS 3
rel skill, wit; aptitude, bent, leaning, propensity, turn; abandon, spontaneity, unconstraint; address, poise, tact; effortlessness, lightness, smoothness
con awkwardness, clumsiness, ineptness, maladroitness; rigidity, stiffness, woodenness; effort, exertion, pains
2 ***syn*** see AMENITY 2
rel accommodation, advantage, aid, fitting
con difficulty, hardship, inconvenience

facing *prep* **1** ***syn*** see AGAINST 1
con side by side
2 ***syn*** see BEFORE 2

facsimile *n* ***syn*** see REPRODUCTION
con archetype, model, original, pattern, prototype, standard

fact *n* **1** the quality of being actual <the realm of *fact* is distinct from fancy>
syn actuality, reality
rel authenticity, genuineness, truth
con fancy, fantasy, fiction
2 something that has actual existence <stubborn *facts* that cannot be confuted>
syn event, phenomenon
rel circumstance, detail, episode, particular; happening, incident, occurrence; observable
con contingency, eventuality, hope, possibility, potentiality, probability
ant illusion

---

syn synonym(s) ***rel*** related word(s)
ant antonym(s) ***con*** contrasted word(s)
idiom idiomatic equivalent(s)
‖ use limited; if in doubt, see a dictionary

faction *n* ***syn*** see COMBINATION 2
rel camp, offshoot, wing
idiom splinter group

factious *adj* ***syn*** see INSUBORDINATE
rel contending, fighting, warring; belligerent, contentious, quarrelsome; alienated, disaffected, estranged
con companionable, gregarious, social; acquiescent, compliant; faithful, loyal, true
ant cooperative

factitious *adj* ***syn*** see SYNTHETIC
rel affected, assumed, counterfeited, false, feigned, forced, pretended, sham, shammed, simulated
con authentic, bona fide, genuine, veritable; artless, naive, simple, spontaneous
ant natural

factor *n* **1** ***syn*** see ELEMENT 2
rel antecedent, cause, determinant; agency, agent, instrument, instrumentality, means
2 ***syn*** see AGENT 2
rel bailiff, majordomo, seneschal, steward; adjutant, aid, assistant, coadjutor, helper

factory *n* an establishment for the manufacturing of goods <a shoe *factory*>
syn manufactory, mill, plant, works

factual *adj* ***syn*** see ACTUAL 2
rel certain, undoubted, veritable; authentic, legitimate, unquestionable, valid
con erroneous, false, questionable, wrong
ant illusory

facultative *adj* ***syn*** see OPTIONAL

faculty *n* **1** ***syn*** see GIFT 2
rel instinct; property, quality; leaning, penchant, proclivity, propensity; predilection
con inability, incapability, incapacity, ineptness
2 ***syn*** see POWER 3

facund *adj* ***syn*** see EXPRESSIVE

facundity *n* ***syn*** see ELOQUENCE

fad *n* ***syn*** see FASHION 3
rel caprice, conceit, fancy, vagary, whim, whimsy
con custom, habit, practice, usage

fade *vb* **1** ***syn*** see FAIL 1
2 ***syn*** see DULL 1
3 ***syn*** see VANISH
rel deliquesce, dissolve, melt; abate, diminish, dwindle, ebb, lessen, moderate, wane; attenuate, rarefy, thin
idiom fade like a shadow
con intensify; eternalize, immortalize, perpetuate

faded *adj* ***syn*** see SHABBY 1
rel haggard, washed-out, wasted, worn; dim, murky; achromatic, colorless; ashen, pale, pallid, wan
con energetic, lusty, vigorous; colorful; vivid

fag *n* ***syn*** see CIGARETTE

fag *vb* ***syn*** see EXHAUST 4
con refresh, relax, rest, restore

‖**fag** *n* ***syn*** see HOMOSEXUAL

‖**faggot** *n* ***syn*** see HOMOSEXUAL

fail *vb* **1** to lose strength, power, vitality, or intensity <his health *failed* and he retired early>
syn decline, deteriorate, ‖dwine, fade, flag, languish, weaken
rel jade, sink, slip, waste (away), worsen
idiom go downhill, hit the skids
con better, improve, strengthen
2 to become used up <food *failed* before they got back to civilization>
syn give out, run out
rel dwindle, shrink, wane
3 to be or become inadequate or deficient <the spring gradually *failed* as the drought persisted>
syn dwindle, shrink, wane, waste (away), weaken
rel decrease, diminish, lessen; give out, run out; short
idiom be found wanting
con appreciate, gain, grow, increase, wax
4 to be less than adequate or successful <the attack *failed*>
syn bomb, ‖flop, flummox, wash out
rel bankrupt, deplete, drain, exhaust, impoverish; bust out, flunk, ‖spin
idiom come to grief, fall flat (*or* short), go on the rocks, ‖lay an egg, ‖take the count
ant succeed
5 to be unable to meet financial engagements <the bank *failed*>
syn break, bust, crash, fold
rel gazette; close, end, finish, terminate
idiom be ruined, go bankrupt, go broke, go on the rocks, go to the wall, go under
con boom, prosper
6 ***syn*** see NEGLECT
idiom be found wanting, come (*or* fall) short of

failing *n* ***syn*** see FAULT 2
rel imperfection, shortcoming
idiom weak point

failing *adj* ***syn*** see SHORT 3

failure *n* **1** omission of performance of an action or task <the mechanic's *failure* to adjust the brakes>
syn default, delinquency, dereliction, neglect, oversight
rel laxity, negligence, remissness, slackness; indifference, unconcern
con accomplishment, achievement, discharge, effectuation, fulfillment
2 lack of satisfactory performance or effect <the *failure* of the candidate in the election>
syn defeat, insuccess, nonsuccess, unsuccess, unsuccessfulness
rel failing, fault, imperfection, shortcoming
idiom no go
ant success
3 the fact or state of being inadequate <the crop *failure* brought on a near famine>
syn defalcation, deficiency, deficit, inadequacy, insufficience, insufficiency, lack, scantiness, shortage, underage; *compare* ABSENCE, SCARCITY
rel inferiority, meagerness, poorness, skimpiness; dearth, paucity
con abundance, adequacy, sufficiency
4 a marked weakening <felt a gradual *failure* of physical strength>

syn declination, decline, deterioration, ebbing, waning
rel debilitation, enfeeblement, exhaustion, flagging, weakness
con improvement; invigoration, revitalization, strengthening
5 one that has failed <he is a *failure* in school because of inattention>
syn bomb, bummer, bust, dud, flop, lemon, loser
rel botch, fiasco, fizzle, hash, muddle, washout; has-been, might-have-been
ant success

fain *adj* *syn* see WILLING 1

faineant *n* *syn* see SLUGGARD

faineant *adj* *syn* see LAZY
rel apathetic, impassive, phlegmatic
con active, energetic, vigorous; busy, industrious

faint *adj* **1** *syn* see GENTLE 1
2 scarcely or imperfectly perceptible <he had only a *faint* idea of how he could help>
syn blear, bleary, dim, fuzzy, ill-defined, indistinct, obscure, shadowy, unclear, undefined, undetermined, undistinct, vague; *compare* OBSCURE 3
rel blurred, dusty, pale, wan, weak; hushed, inaudible, low, muffled, small, soft, stifled, thin
con bright, distinct, evident, obvious, patent, unmistakable; certain, sure
ant clear

faint *n* the act or condition of losing consciousness <was so frightened she fell into a *faint*>
syn blackout, coma, swoon, syncope
rel grayout, swim; dizziness, vertigo; knockout
idiom a dead faint

faint *vb* to lose consciousness <*fainted* at the sight of blood>
syn black out, ||crap out, pass out, ||swarf, ||swelt, swoon
rel gray out
idiom faint dead away, fall in a faint, go out like a light, pass out cold

faintly *adv* *syn* see SOTTO VOCE

fair *adj* **1** *syn* see BEAUTIFUL
rel dainty, delicate, exquisite; charming, enchanting; chaste, pure
con ill-favored, ugly
ant foul
2 not stormy <a *fair* day>
syn clarion, clear, cloudless, fine, pleasant, rainless, sunny, sunshine, sunshining, sunshiny, unclouded, undarkened
rel calm, placid, tranquil, unthreatening; balmy, clement, mild, pretty
con overcast, stormy, threatening
3 of light complexion <*fair* people often sunburn badly>
syn blond, light
rel ruddy, tawny
con brunet, dark, swarthy
4 characterized by honesty, justice, and freedom from improper influence <a *fair* decision by the judge>
syn candid, dispassionate, equal, equitable, impartial, impersonal, indifferent, just, nondiscriminatory, nonpartisan, objective, square, unbiased, uncolored, undistinctive, unprejudiced, unprepossessed
rel detached, disinterested; balanced, rational, reasonable, sane; open-minded, straight
con biased, inequitable, partial, partisan, prejudiced, prepossessed, unjust
ant unfair
5 observing the rules <a *fair* fight>
syn clean, sportsmanlike, sportsmanly
rel decent, honest, lawful
con dirty, dishonest, fixed
ant unfair
6 *syn* see EVEN 3
7 *syn* see MEDIUM
rel common, ordinary
con choice, good, prime, right; bad, poor, wrong

fair *n* *syn* see EXHIBITION 2
rel carnival, festival

fair–haired *adj* *syn* see FAVORITE 1

fairish *adj* *syn* see MEDIUM

fairly *adv* **1** *syn* see ENOUGH 2
2 *syn* see SOMEWHAT 2

fairy *n* a benevolent mythical being <children who believe in *fairies*>
syn brownie, elf, fay, nisse, pixie, sprite
rel gremlin, imp, leprechaun, puck; dwarf, gnome, goblin, kobold
con ogre, troll

fairyland *n* *syn* see UTOPIA

faith *n* **1** *syn* see BELIEF 1
con dubiety, dubiosity, skepticism, uncertainty
2 *syn* see TRUST 1
con disbelief, incredulity, unbelief; apprehension, misgiving
3 *syn* see RELIGION 1
4 *syn* see RELIGION 2
rel doctrines, dogmas, tenets

faithful *adj* **1** firm in adherence to whatever one is bound to by duty or promise <a *faithful* public official, conscientious and above reproach>
syn allegiant, ardent, constant, ||dinky-di, fast, liege, loyal, resolute, staunch, steadfast, steady, true
rel dependable, reliable, tried, trustworthy; affectionate, devoted, loving; dyed-in-the-wool
con disloyal, false, perfidious, traitorous, treacherous; fickle, inconstant, unstable
ant faithless
2 *syn* see TRUE 3
idiom at one with, on all fours with
3 *syn* see AUTHENTIC 1

faithfulness *n* **1** *syn* see ATTACHMENT 1
2 *syn* see FIDELITY 1

faithless *adj* not true to allegiance or duty <a *faithless* husband>

---

syn synonym(s) *rel* related word(s)
ant antonym(s) *con* contrasted word(s)
idiom idiomatic equivalent(s)
|| use limited; if in doubt, see a dictionary

syn disloyal, false, perfidious, recreant, traitorous, treacherous, unfaithful, unloyal, untrue
rel capricious, fickle, inconstant, unstable; fluctuating, wavering; changeable, changeful
con constant, loyal, resolute, staunch, steadfast, true
ant faithful

faithlessness *n* **1** ***syn*** see TREACHERY
2 ***syn*** see INFIDELITY

fake *vb* ***syn*** see ASSUME 4

fake *n* **1** ***syn*** see IMPOSTURE
2 ***syn*** see IMPOSTOR

fake *adj* **1** ***syn*** see COUNTERFEIT
rel fabricated, forged; concocted, framed, invented
con bona fide, genuine
2 ***syn*** see FICTITIOUS 2

faker *n* ***syn*** see IMPOSTOR
rel cheat, cheater, cozener, defrauder, swindler

fall *vb* **1** to pass downward <fruit *falling* off a tree> <the temperature *fell* sharply>
syn descend, drop, lower
rel decline, dip, plummet, sink; decrease, diminish, lessen; dangle, drag, droop, trail
ant rise
2 to come down suddenly and involuntarily <*fell* on the ice>
syn drop, go down, keel (over), pitch, plunge, slump, topple, tumble
rel slip, sprawl, stumble, trip
idiom come a cropper, take a header, take a spill
con ascend, climb
3 to suffer ruin, defeat, or failure <the city *fell* after a long siege>
syn go down, go under, submit, succumb, surrender
rel give up, yield
con endure, prevail, resist; conquer, triumph, vanquish, win
4 ***syn*** see ABATE 4
ant rise
5 ***syn*** see PLUMMET

fall (off *or* away) *vb* ***syn*** see SLIP 6

fall (on *or* upon) *vb* ***syn*** see ATTACK 1

fall *n* **1** ***syn*** see DESCENT 1
2 ***syn*** see DESCENT 4
3 *usu* **falls** *pl but sing or pl in constr* ***syn*** see WATERFALL

fallacious *adj* **1** ***syn*** see ILLOGICAL
ant sound, valid
2 ***syn*** see MISLEADING
ant veritable

fallaciousness *n* ***syn*** see FALLACY 1
rel ambiguity, equivocation; deception, deluding, misleading; faultiness, illogicality, unreasonableness
ant soundness, validity

fallacy *n* **1** a false or erroneous idea <his argument is based on a *fallacy*>
syn erroneousness, error, fallaciousness, falsehood, falseness, falsity, untruth
rel misconception, misconstrual, misinterpretation, misunderstanding
con comprehension, grasp, understanding; correctitude, correctness, truth
ant verity
2 unsound and misleading reasoning <the *fallacy* of her theory is clearly evident>
syn casuistry, deception, deceptiveness, delusion, equivocation, sophism, sophistry, speciousness, spuriousness
rel elusion, evasion, inconsistency, quibble, quibbling

fall back *vb* **1** ***syn*** see RETREAT 2
2 ***syn*** see RECEDE 1

fall flat *vb* ***syn*** see FAIL 4

fall guy *n* **1** ***syn*** see SCAPEGOAT
2 ***syn*** see FOOL 3

fallible *adj* liable or inclined to error <a *fallible* rule>
syn errable, errant
rel careless, faulty, heedless
con careful, heedful; inerrable, inerrant, unerring; exact, perfect, precise
ant infallible

falling–out *n* ***syn*** see QUARREL

falloff *n* ***syn*** see DECLINE 3

fall out *vb* **1** ***syn*** see HAPPEN 1
2 ***syn*** see QUARREL

fall to *vb* ***syn*** see PITCH IN 1

false *adj* **1** not in conformity with what is true <the information turned out to be *false*>
syn counterfactual, erroneous, inaccurate, incorrect, specious, unsound, untrue, wrong; *compare* ILLOGICAL
rel deceptive, delusive, delusory, distorted, fallacious, misleading; deceitful, dishonest, fraudulent, lying, mendacious, untruthful
idiom contrary to fact, off the mark
con accurate, correct, established, factual, truthful, veracious, veridical
ant true
2 ***syn*** see MISLEADING
3 ***syn*** see FAITHLESS
rel apostate, backsliding, renegade; crooked, devious; hollow
ant true
4 ***syn*** see COUNTERFEIT
rel apparent, ostensible, seeming
con bona fide, genuine
ant real
5 ***syn*** see ARTIFICIAL 2

false face *n* ***syn*** see MASK 1

false front *n* ***syn*** see MASK 2

falsehood *n* **1** ***syn*** see FALLACY 1
2 ***syn*** see LIE
rel fakery, feigning, pretense, sham; deceit, dissimulation, fraud
ant truth
3 ***syn*** see MENDACITY

falseness *n* **1** ***syn*** see FALLACY 1
2 ***syn*** see INFIDELITY
3 ***syn*** see DEFECTION

falsifier *n* ***syn*** see LIAR

falsify *vb* **1** ***syn*** see LIE
2 ***syn*** see MISREPRESENT
rel alter, change; cook, doctor; contort; contradict, contravene, deny, traverse

falsity *n* **1** ***syn*** see LIE

2 ***syn*** see FALLACY 1
rel bluff, fabrication, fake, sham; disingenuousness, hypocrisy, insincerity, uncandidness
ant verity
3 ***syn*** see INFIDELITY
falter *vb* **1** ***syn*** see TEETER
2 ***syn*** see HESITATE
rel blench, flinch, quail, recoil, shrink; quake, quaver, shake, shudder, tremble; tick over
con persevere, persist; decide, determine, resolve
faltering *adj* ***syn*** see VACILLATING 2
fame *n* **1** ***syn*** see REPUTATION 2
2 the state of being widely known for one's deeds <his *fame* was short-lived>
syn celebrity, éclat, notoriety, renown, ‖rep, reputation, repute
rel acclaim, acclamation, applause; acknowledgment, recognition; conspicuousness, prominence; distinction, eminence, glory, greatness, honor, illustriousness, note, preeminence
con disgrace, dishonor, disrepute, ignominy, obloquy, odium, opprobrium, shame
ant obscurity; infamy
famed *adj* ***syn*** see FAMOUS 2
ant obscure; ill-famed
familiar *n* ***syn*** see FRIEND
familiar *adj* **1** closely associated <time and interests have made them *familiar*>
syn chummy, close, confidential, intimate, thick
rel amicable, friendly, neighborly; affable, boon, cordial, genial, gracious, sociable; comfortable, cozy, easy, snug; forward, fresh, impertinent, intrusive, obtrusive, officious
con detached, disinterested, incurious, indifferent, remote, unconcerned; ceremonial, ceremonious, conventional, formal
ant aloof
2 ***syn*** see COMMON 4
rel accustomed, habitual, wonted; commonplace, prosaic
con new, newfangled, new-fashioned, novel; rare, strange, uncommon; chimerical, fantastic
ant unfamiliar
3 well-informed especially through study or experience <*familiar* with what is being taught in the schools>
syn abreast, acquainted, au courant, au fait, conversant, informed, up, versant, versed
rel aware, cognizant, conscious, mindful
con unacquainted, unconversant, uninformed, unversed; insensible, unaware, unconscious, unmindful; ignorant, unenlightened, unknowing
ant unfamiliar
familiarity *n* ***syn*** see ACQUAINTANCE 1
rel awareness, cognition, comprehension, knowledge, understanding
ant unfamiliarity
familiarize *vb* ***syn*** see ACCUSTOM
rel acquaint, adapt, adjust, condition, naturalize, season
family *n* **1** a group of persons of or regarded as of common ancestry <traditionally all people belong to the *family* of Noah>
syn clan, folk, house, kin, kindred, lineage, race, stock, tribe
rel brood, dynasty, line, stirp, strain; issue, offspring, progeny
idiom kith and kin, one's own flesh and blood
2 a group of usually related persons living in one house and under one head <was the only child in her *family*>
syn folks, house, household, ménage
family *adj* ***syn*** see DOMESTIC 1
family tree *n* ***syn*** see GENEALOGY
famished *adj* ***syn*** see HUNGRY
famous *adj* **1** ***syn*** see WELL-KNOWN
2 widely known and honored for achievement <a *famous* physician>
syn celebrated, celebrious, distinguished, eminent, famed, great, illustrious, notable, prestigious, prominent, redoubtable, renowned; *compare* WELL-KNOWN
rel estimable, honorable, reputable, respectable, well-thought-of
idiom held in esteem
con humble, inconspicuous, undistinguished, unimportant, unknown
ant obscure; infamous
3 ***syn*** see EXCELLENT
ant wretched
fan *n* **1** ***syn*** see ADDICT
2 ***syn*** see AMATEUR 1
fan *vb* **1** ***syn*** see BLOW 1
‖2 ***syn*** see SEARCH 2
fan (out) *vb* ***syn*** see OPEN 4
fanatic *adj* ***syn*** see EXTREME 3
fanatic *n* ***syn*** see ENTHUSIAST
fancied *adj* ***syn*** see IMAGINARY 1
fancier *n* ***syn*** see AMATEUR 1
fanciful *adj* **1** ***syn*** see IMAGINARY 1
rel apocryphal, fabulous, fictitious, legendary, mythical; bizarre, fantastic, grotesque; absurd, preposterous; false, wrong
con matter-of-fact, prosaic; truthful, veracious
ant realistic
2 ***syn*** see FICTITIOUS 1
ant veridical
fancy *n* **1** ***syn*** see WILL 1
2 ***syn*** see CAPRICE
rel idea; irrationality, unreasonableness; contrariness, perverseness
3 ***syn*** see IMAGINATION
rel envisagement, envisioning, objectification
idiom flight of fancy
con awareness, experience, perception
4 an idea or image present in the mind but having no concrete or objective reality <unable to tell fact from *fancy*>
syn daydream, dream, fantasy (*or* phantasy), nightmare, phantasm, vision
rel fable, fabrication, fiction, figment, invention; concept, conception, idea, notion; chimera, delu-

---

syn synonym(s) ***rel*** related word(s)
ant antonym(s) ***con*** contrasted word(s)
idiom idiomatic equivalent(s)
‖ use limited; if in doubt, see a dictionary

sion, illusion; fata morgana, hallucination, mirage
idiom figment of the imagination
con actuality, fact, reality
fancy *vb* **1** *syn* see LIKE
rel approve, endorse, sanction
idiom have a fancy (*or* hankering) for; have one's heart set on
con deprecate, disapprove; abhor, abominate, detest, dislike, hate, loathe
2 *syn* see THINK 1
con demonstrate, prove, test, try
fancy *adj* *syn* see ELABORATE 2
fancy–free *adj* *syn* see FREE 6
fancy house *n* *syn* see BROTHEL
fancy man *n* **1** *syn* see LOVER 1
2 *syn* see PIMP 1
fancy woman *n* *syn* see HARLOT 1
fanfare *n* *syn* see DISPLAY 2
fanny *n* *syn* see BUTTOCKS
fantastic *adj* **1** *syn* see FICTITIOUS 1
rel implausible, incredible, unbelievable; absurd, preposterous; irrational, unreasonable; deceptive, delusive, delusory, misleading
con common, commonplace, everyday, familiar, ordinary; customary, prevailing, universal, usual
2 conceived or made without reference to reality <their explanation was *fantastic*>
syn antic, bizarre, grotesque
rel adroit, clever, ingenious; eccentric, erratic, odd, queer, singular, strange; absurd, nonsensical, preposterous, ridiculous
con factual, solid, sound, valid, well-grounded; plausible, reasonable
3 *syn* see FOOLISH 2
4 *syn* see MONSTROUS 1
5 *syn* see EXTRAVAGANT 1
fantasy (*or* **phantasy**) *n* **1** *syn* see IMAGINATION
rel conceiving, envisioning, fancying, imagining; externalizing, objectifying
2 *syn* see FANCY 4
rel caprice, freak, vagary, whim, whimsy; bizarrerie, grotesquerie
con actuality, fact, reality
3 *syn* see PIPE DREAM
far *adv* *syn* see WELL 8
far *adj* *syn* see DISTANT 1
idiom a long day's journey
ant near
far and away *adv* by a considerable margin <he was *far and away* the best man for the job>
syn by all odds, by a long shot, by far, by long odds, by odds, out and away
rel decidedly, definitely; doubtless, unconditionally, undoubtedly, unequivocally, unquestionably; absolutely, positively; just, quite, very
con barely; slightly; possibly
far and near *adv* *syn* see EVERYWHERE 1
far and wide *adv* *syn* see EVERYWHERE 1
faraway *adj* **1** *syn* see DISTANT 1
ant near-at-hand
2 *syn* see ABSTRACTED
rel disregardful, heedless, oblivious, stargazing, unheeding, unmindful
idiom off one's guard
farce *n* *syn* see MOCKERY 2
farceur *n* *syn* see ZANY 2
farcical *adj* *syn* see LAUGHABLE
rel absurd, extravagant, nonsensical, outrageous, preposterous
fare *vb* **1** *syn* see GO 1
rel advance, progress
idiom make headway
con stay, stop
2 *syn* see SHIFT 5
farewell *interj* *syn* see GOOD-BYE
farewell *n* *syn* see PARTING
farewell *adj* *syn* see PARTING
farfetched *adj* *syn* see FORCED
rel bizarre, fantastic, grotesque; eccentric, erratic, queer, strange
con accustomed, usual, wonted
far–flung *adj* *syn* see DISTANT 1
far–gone *adj* *syn* see EFFETE 2
farming *n* *syn* see AGRICULTURE
rel cultivation, tillage; agronomy, geoponics, hydroponics
far–off *adj* *syn* see DISTANT 1
idiom behind the farthest range
ant nearby
far–out *adj* *syn* see OUTLANDISH 3
farther *adv* *syn* see BEYOND 1
farther *adj* *syn* see ADDITIONAL
farthest *adj* *syn* see EXTREME 5
ant nearest
fascinate *vb* **1** *syn* see ENTHRALL 2
2 *syn* see ATTRACT 1
rel affect, impress, influence, strike, sway, touch; delight, gladden, please, rejoice; absorb, engage, engross, occupy, preoccupy
con disgust, horrify, repel; affront, insult, offend, outrage, shame
3 *syn* see INTEREST
fascinated *adj* *syn* see ENAMORED 3
fascinating *adj* *syn* see ATTRACTIVE 1
rel delectable, delightful; seducing
fascination *n* *syn* see CHARM 3
fashion *n* **1** *syn* see METHOD 1
rel custom, habit, practice, usage, wont
2 *syn* see VEIN 1
3 the prevailing or accepted custom <follow the *fashion*>
syn bandwagon, chic, craze, cry, dernier cri, fad, furore, mode, rage, style, thing, ton, trend, ‖twig, vogue
rel drift, tendency; convention, form, usage
idiom the in thing, the last word, the latest thing
fashion *vb* *syn* see MAKE 3
rel contrive, devise; design, plan, plot; turn out
fashionable *adj* *syn* see STYLISH
rel current, popular, prevalent, up-to-the-minute
idiom all the rage
ant unfashionable
fast *adj* **1** *syn* see SURE 1
rel fixed, held, inextricable, stuck, wedged
con insecure, loose, shaky, unstable
2 *syn* see FAITHFUL 1

3 moving, proceeding, or acting with great celerity <a *fast* horse>
syn breakneck, expeditious, expeditive, fleet, harefooted, hasty, posthaste, quick, raking, rapid, snappy, speedy, swift
rel active, alert, brisk, keen, lively
idiom quick as lightning, quick as thought, swift as an arrow
con lethargic, logy, poky, sluggish, tardy, torpid; languid, languorous; deliberate, gradual
ant slow
4 persistent in adhering to something <a *fast* grip>
syn firm, fixed, secure, set, tenacious, tight; *compare* STABLE 4, SURE 1
idiom stuck fast
con insecure, loose, relaxed, unfirm, weak; free, unattached, unfixed
5 ***syn*** see WILD 7
6 ***syn*** see LICENTIOUS 2
7 sexually promiscuous—usually used of a woman <she's said to be *fast*>
syn easy, light, loose, ‖riggish, unchaste, wanton, whorish
rel careless, heedless, lax, slack; bawdy, indecent; lascivious, lecherous, lewd, libertine, licentious, lickerish, riotous
idiom no better than one should be, of easy virtue
con chaste, decent, decorous, modest, moral, pure, virtuous

fast *adv* **1** ***syn*** see HARD 7
2 in a rapid manner <run up the hill as *fast* as you know how>
syn apace, chop-chop, expeditiously, flat-out, fleetly, full tilt, hastily, lickety-split, posthaste, presto, promptly, pronto, quick, quickly, rapidly, soon, speedily, swift, swiftly
idiom by leaps and bounds, in a flash, in a twinkling, in nothing flat, in short order, like a bat out of hell, like a blue streak, like a flash, like a house afire, like a shot, like a streak, like greased lightning, like wildfire
con deliberately, leisurely; apathetically, lethargically, sluggishly
ant slow, slowly

fasten *vb* **1** to cause one thing to hold to another <*fasten* a feather to a hat>
syn affix, attach, fix, rivet
rel connect, join, link, unite; adhere, cleave, cling, cohere, stick
con divide, divorce, part, separate, sever, sunder; loose, loosen
ant unfasten
2 to fix in place or in a desired position <*fasten* the door>
syn anchor, catch, fix, moor, secure
rel bed, implant, infix, lodge, set, settle; embed, join, wedge; establish; bar, hitch, hook
idiom make fast (*or* secure *or* sure)
con loose, undo, unloose, unloosen
ant unfasten
3 to direct (as attention or hope) directly and steadily <*fastened* his whole mind on the problem>
syn concenter, concentrate, fix, fixate, focus, put, rivet
rel address, apply, devote, direct, train, turn
con falter, vacillate, waver

fastidious *adj* ***syn*** see NICE 1
rel demanding, exacting; captious, critical, hypercritical
con cursory, uncritical

fastigium *n* ***syn*** see TOP 1

fastness *n* ***syn*** see FORT
rel retreat, shelter; defense, guard, protection; adytum, sanctum

fat *adj* **1** ***syn*** see FATTY 1
2 having excess adipose tissue <a *fat* woman overflowing her chair>
syn corpulent, fleshy, gross, heavy, obese, overblown, overweight, porcine, portly, pursy, stout, upholstered, weighty; *compare* ROTUND 2
rel beefy, bulky, chunky, dumpy, full-bodied, heavyset, squat, stocky, stubby, thick, thickset; paunchy, potbellied; brawny, burly, husky
idiom broad in the beam, fat as a pig
con angular, gaunt, lank, lanky, rawboned, scrawny, skinny, spare; slender, slight, slim, thin
ant lean
3 ***syn*** see LARGE 1
rel broad, deep, wide
con narrow, skinny
4 ***syn*** see RESONANT
‖**5** ***syn*** see REMOTE 4

fat *n* **1** ***syn*** see BEST
2 ***syn*** see EXCESS 1

fatal *adj* **1** ***syn*** see DEADLY 1
2 bringing on an adverse fate <to accept his word was a *fatal* mistake>
syn calamitous, cataclysmic, catastrophic, disastrous, fateful, ruinous
rel baneful, pernicious; baleful, malefic, maleficent, malign, sinister; ill-fated, ill-starred, unlucky
con advantageous, beneficial, profitable; auspicious, benign, favorable, propitious

fatal *n* ***syn*** see FATALITY 2

fatality *n* **1** the condition of causing death <the tuberculosis *fatality* remains high>
syn deadliness, lethality, mortality
rel malignancy, noxiousness, perniciousness, poisonousness, virulence
2 an instance of dying especially as the result of accident or disaster <two *fatalities* over the weekend>
syn casualty, death, fatal

‖**fat cat** *n* ***syn*** see NOTABLE 1

fate *n* whatever is destined or inevitably decreed for one <the *fate* of the bill has not been decided>
syn circumstance, destiny, doom, kismet, lot, moira, portion, weird

---

syn synonym(s) ***rel*** related word(s)
ant antonym(s) ***con*** contrasted word(s)
idiom idiomatic equivalent(s)
‖ use limited; if in doubt, see a dictionary

rel consequence, effect, issue, outcome, result, upshot; end, ending, termination; ineluctability, inescapableness, inevitability, inevitableness, unavoidability
con accident, chance, fortune, hazard, luck

fate *vb* ***syn*** see PREDESTINE 1

fateful *adj* **1** ***syn*** see OMINOUS
rel important, momentous, significant; conclusive, decisive, determinative; acute, critical, crucial
con inconclusive, insignificant, trivial, unimportant
2 ***syn*** see FATAL 2

fathead *n* ***syn*** see DUNCE

fatheaded *adj* ***syn*** see STUPID 1

father *n* **1** a male human parent <scarcely knew his *father*>
syn dad, dada, daddy, ‖governor, ‖old man, pa, ‖pap, papa, ‖pappy, ‖pater, pop, poppa; *compare* MOTHER 1
2 one that originates or institutes <the *father* of radiotelegraphy>
syn architect, author, creator, founder, generator, inventor, maker, originator, patriarch, sire
rel builder, encourager, motor, mover, organizer, prime mover, producer, promoter, promulgator, supporter; inaugurator, initiator, introducer
con disciple, follower

father *vb* **1** to be the male parent in reproduction <didn't know who *fathered* the child>
syn beget, breed, get, procreate, progenerate, sire
rel engender, generate, ingenerate; spawn
2 ***syn*** see GENERATE 1

fatherland *n* ***syn*** see COUNTRY

fatherless *adj* ***syn*** see ILLEGITIMATE 1

fathom *vb* **1** ***syn*** see SOUND
2 ***syn*** see KNOW 1
rel penetrate, pierce, probe; perceive, recognize; ‖dig, savvy

fathomable *adj* ***syn*** see UNDERSTANDABLE

fathomless *adj* ***syn*** see BOTTOMLESS 2

fatidic *adj* ***syn*** see PROPHETIC

fatigue *n* complete depletion of strength <suffering from *fatigue*>
syn exhaustion, lassitude, tiredness, weariness
rel enervation, ennui, languor, listlessness; debilitation, faintness, feebleness, weakness
con briskness, energy, liveliness, vigor, vitality; endurance, strength

fatigue *vb* ***syn*** see TIRE 1
rel deplete; exhaust, fag, tucker, wear out; debilitate, disable, weaken; annoy, bother, irk, vex
con refresh, rejuvenate, renew, restore; assuage, relieve

fatigued *adj* ***syn*** see TIRED 1

fatness *n* ***syn*** see OBESITY

‖**fatso** *n* ***syn*** see FATTY

fatty *adj* **1** containing fat especially in unusual amounts <a rather *fatty* steak>
syn adipose, fat
rel blubbery, lardy, suety
ant lean
2 having the qualities of fat <the constant frying left a *fatty* deposit on the kitchen woodwork>
syn greasy, oily, oleaginous, unctuous

fatty *n* a fat person <*fatties* trying to diet>
syn blimp, butterball, dumpling, ‖fatso, ‖tub
rel overweight; pudge, roly-poly, strapper; potbelly
idiom tons of fun
ant skinny

fatuous *adj* ***syn*** see SIMPLE 3
rel idiotic, imbecile, moronic; besotted, fond, infatuated, insensate; absurd, dumb, silly, stupid
con judicious, prudent, sage, sane, sapient, wise
ant sensible

faucet *n* a fixture for controlling the passage of fluid <turn off the *faucet*>
syn cock, gate, hydrant, petcock, spigot, stopcock, tap, valve
rel bung, spile

fault *n* **1** ***syn*** see IMPERFECTION
rel infirmity, weakness
con faultlessness, impeccability; meticulousness, preciseness, precision
2 an imperfection in character or an ingrained moral weakness <he has few *faults*>
syn failing, foible, frailty, vice
rel infirmity, weakness; blemish, defect, flaw
con excellence, perfection, virtue; desirability, goodness, rightness
ant merit
3 ***syn*** see BLAME
rel accountability, answerability, liability, responsibility; crime, error, offense, sin, transgression

faultfinder *n* **1** ***syn*** see CRITIC
2 ***syn*** see GROUCH

faultfinding *adj* ***syn*** see CRITICAL 1
rel particular, pernickety; ultracritical
con appreciative, cherishing, prizing, valuing

faultily *adv* ***syn*** see AMISS 1
rel erroneously, fallaciously, inaccurately, mistakenly, unfairly
con correctly, right

faultless *adj* **1** ***syn*** see IMPECCABLE 1
rel entire, intact, perfect, whole; blameless
con defective, deficient, imprecise, inaccurate, inexact, uncorrect
ant faulty
2 ***syn*** see INNOCENT 2

faulty *adj* marked by a fault or defect <a *faulty* mechanism>
syn amiss, defective, flawed, imperfect, sick
rel imprecise, inaccurate, inexact, uncorrect; deficient, inadequate, incomplete; erroneous, fallacious, fallible, specious, wrong; blemished, damaged, defaced, disfigured, marred
con accurate, correct, exact, nice, precise, right; complete, entire, intact, perfect, whole; excellent, good; unflawed, unimpaired
ant faultless

faux pas *n* a breach of etiquette or of social convention <hustled him out of the room before he could commit another *faux pas*>
syn blooper, boner, ‖boo-boo, break, gaffe, impropriety, indecorum, solecism; *compare* ERROR 2

rel bungle, misstep, stumble; howler, screamer; indiscretion, misjudgment, oversight, pratfall

favor *n* **1** *syn* see REGARD 4
ant disfavor
2 *syn* see APPROBATION 1
con depreciation, derogation, disparagement
ant disfavor
3 *syn* see GIFT 1
rel aid, assistance, backing, encouragement, help, support
4 a special privilege <willing to grant a *favor* to a good friend>
syn courtesy, dispensation, indulgence, kindness, service
rel aid, assistance, cooperation, help

favor *vb* **1** *syn* see APPROVE 1
rel endorse, OK (*or* okay), sanction; appreciate, prize, value
idiom set great store by
con decry, depreciate, disparage
ant disfavor
2 *syn* see OBLIGE 2
rel humor, indulge, pamper
idiom do one a favor (*or* service), do right by
con baffle, circumvent, foil, frustrate, thwart
3 *syn* see ENCOURAGE 2
4 *syn* see RESEMBLE
con contradict, differ

favorable *adj* **1** expressing approval <a *favorable* recommendation>
syn approbative, approbatory, approving
rel benignant, kind, kindly; recommendatory, well-disposed; commendatory, complimentary, laudatory, praiseful
idiom in one's favor
con depreciative, disapprobatory, disapproving, disparaging, uncomplimentary; censorious, condemnatory, critical, faultfinding
ant unfavorable
2 *syn* see PLEASANT 1
3 *syn* see GOOD 1
rel healthful, salutary, wholesome
con disadvantageous, unpropitious; damaging, hampering
ant unfavorable
4 *syn* see TIMELY 1
5 indicative of a successful outcome <*favorable* conditions for opening a new business>
syn auspicious, benign, bright, dexter, fortunate, propitious, white
rel advantageous, beneficial, profitable; happy, lucky, promising, providential; cheering, encouraging, reassuring
idiom full of promise
con calamitous, cataclysmic, catastrophic, disastrous, fatal, fateful, ruinous; baleful, malefic, maleficent, malign, sinister; ill-fated, ill-starred, unlucky; inauspicious, unpromising, unpropitious
ant unfavorable

favorably *adv syn* see WELL 5

favored *adj syn* see FAVORITE 2

favoring *adj syn* see GOOD 1

favorite *adj* **1** accorded special treatment or attention <a *favorite* daughter>
syn beloved, blue-eyed, darling, dear, fair-haired, loved, pet, precious, white-haired, white-headed
rel admired, adored, esteemed, revered; cherished, prized, treasured
idiom dear as the apple of one's eye, dear to one's heart, held dear
con contemned, despised, disdained; abhorrent, detested, hated
2 constituting a favorite <*favorite* melodies>
syn favored, popular, preferred, well-liked
rel laudable, pleasant, praiseworthy; cherished, prized, treasured
con despised, detested, disliked, hated, unpopular; eschewed, rejected

fawn *vb* to act or behave with abjectness in the presence of a superior <*fawn* on the master>
syn apple-polish, bootlick, ||brownnose, cotton, cower, cringe, grovel, honey (up), kowtow, slaver, toady, truckle
rel blandish, cajole, coax, wheedle; butter (up), flatter, make up (to); cater (to), pander (to); crawl; abase, debase, demean; bow, cave, defer, submit, yield; court, invite, woo
idiom be at one's beck and call, curry favor, dance attendance, kiss one's feet, lick one's shoes (*or* boots), make a doormat of oneself
con contemn, despise, disdain, scorn, scout; reject, repudiate, spurn; flout, gibe, jeer, scoff; deride, mock, ridicule, taunt
ant domineer

fawning *adj* characteristic of one that fawns <sent *fawning* greetings>
syn bootlicking, cowering, cringing, groveling, kowtowing, parasitic, sycophant, sycophantic, sycophantical, sycophantish, toadying, toadyish, truckling
rel flunkyish, obsequious, servile, slavish, subservient; compliant, deferential, humble, submissive, yielding; ingratiating; adulatory, flattering, mealy-mouthed; crawling, spineless; abject, ignoble, mean
con arrogant, disdainful, haughty, insolent, lordly, overbearing, proud, supercilious; contemptuous, insulting, scathing, scornful; authoritative, imperious, magisterial, masterful
ant domineering

fay *n syn* see FAIRY

faze *vb syn* see EMBARRASS
rel confound, dumbfound, mystify, nonplus, perplex, puzzle; confuse, muddle; appall, daunt, dismay, horrify; annoy, bother, irritate, vex
con calm, compose, quiet, relax, soothe; ease, relieve

fealty *n syn* see FIDELITY 1
rel faith, trueness, truth; dependability, reliability, trustworthiness; devotedness, support
con disloyalty, traitorousness, treacherousness
ant perfidy

---

syn synonym(s) *rel* related word(s)
ant antonym(s) *con* contrasted word(s)
idiom idiomatic equivalent(s)
|| use limited; if in doubt, see a dictionary

fear *n* **1** agitation or dismay in the anticipation of or in the presence of danger <living in *fear* of what the future might hold>
syn alarm, cold feet, consternation, dismay, dread, fright, horror, panic, terror, trepidation, trepidity
rel apprehension, foreboding, misgiving, presentiment; angst, anxiety, concern, worry; agitation, discomposure, disquietude, perturbation; chickenheartedness, cowardice, cowardliness, faintheartedness, timidity, timorousness; funk, scare
idiom cold sweat
con boldness, bravery, courage, courageousness, dauntlessness, fortitude, gallantry, intrepidity, prowess, valiancy, valor
ant fearlessness
2 ***syn*** see REVERENCE 2
rel esteem, respect
con contempt, scorn

fearful *adj* **1** ***syn*** see AFRAID 1
rel agitated, alarmed, discomposed, disquieted, disturbed, perturbed
con audacious, bold, brave, courageous, dauntless, unafraid, valiant
ant fearless
2 inspired or moved by fear <*fearful* of loud noises>
syn afraid, apprehensive; *compare* AFRAID 1
rel alarmed, disquieted, disturbed; aflutter, agitated, jittery, nervous, perturbed, uneasy; anxious, concerned, solicitous, worried
con assured, confident, sanguine, sure; collected, composed, cool, imperturbable, nonchalant, unflappable, unperturbed
ant unafraid
3 causing fear <a *fearful* sight>
syn appalling, awful, dire, direful, dreadful, formidable, frightful, horrible, horrific, redoubtable, shocking, terrible, terrific, tremendous
rel alarming, frightening, terrifying; ghastly, grim, grisly, gruesome, lurid, macabre; baleful, malign, sinister; overwhelming, sublime
con attractive, charming, delightful, enchanting, pleasant, pleasing
ant reassuring

fearless *adj* ***syn*** see BRAVE 1
rel assured, confident, sanguine, sure
con afraid, frightened, scared, terrified
ant fearful

feasible *adj* ***syn*** see POSSIBLE 1
rel practical; advantageous, beneficial, profitable; appropriate, fit, fitting, suitable
con impossible, impracticable, unachievable, unattainable, unworkable; ambitious, pretentious, utopian
ant infeasible, unfeasible

feast *n* ***syn*** see DINNER
rel entertainment, festivity; refreshment, repast; meal

feat *n* **1** ***syn*** see ADVENTURE
idiom bold stroke, deed of derring-do
2 a remarkable act or performance <Washington's *feat* of tossing a dollar across the river>
syn achievement, deed, exploit, tour de force
rel act, action; accomplishment, consummation, execution, performance; conquest, triumph, victory
3 ***syn*** see TRICK 3

feather *n* ***syn*** see TYPE

featherbrain *n* ***syn*** see SCATTERBRAIN

featherbrained *adj* ***syn*** see GIDDY 1
rel capricious, fickle, impulsive, whimsical; shallow, superficial, unprofound

featherhead *n* ***syn*** see SCATTERBRAIN

featherlight *adj* ***syn*** see LIGHT 1

featherweight *n* ***syn*** see DUNCE

featherweight *adj* ***syn*** see LIGHT 1

feature *n* **1** ***syn*** see QUALITY 1
2 ***syn*** see CHARACTERISTIC 1
rel article, detail, item, particular; component, constituent, element, factor, ingredient; individuality, particularity, peculiarity, speciality, specialty; attribute, property, quality
3 **features** *pl* ***syn*** see FACE 1

feature *vb* ||**1** ***syn*** see RESEMBLE
2 ***syn*** see THINK 1
3 ***syn*** see EMPHASIZE

febrile *adj* ***syn*** see FEVERISH 1

feckless *adj* **1** having no real worth or purpose <after years of *feckless* negotiations>
syn fustian, good-for-nothing, meaningless, purposeless, unpurposed, useless, worthless
rel bootless, fruitless, futile, unavailing, vain; ineffective, ineffectual, inefficacious
con meaningful, purposeful, worthwhile; fruitful; effective, effectual, efficacious; consequential, important, momentous, significant, weighty
ant efficient, ||feckful
2 ***syn*** see CARELESS 1
rel carefree, easygoing, happy-go-lucky, lackadaisical, nonchalant; remiss; irresponsible, undependable, unreliable, untrustworthy
con attentive, considerate, thoughtful; meticulous, punctilious, punctual, scrupulous; dependable, reliable, responsible, trustworthy
3 ***syn*** see IRRESPONSIBLE
ant ||feckful

fecund *adj* ***syn*** see FERTILE
rel breeding, generating, propagating, reproducing
con infertile, sterile
ant barren

fecundity *n* **1** ***syn*** see FERTILITY
rel productiveness, productivity; exuberance, lavishness, lushness, luxuriance, prodigality, profuseness, profusion
con infertility, sterility, unproductiveness
ant barrenness, infecundity
2 ***syn*** see ELOQUENCE

federation *n* ***syn*** see ALLIANCE 2

fed up *adj* disgusted and completely out of patience <*fed up* with her bad behavior>
syn disgusted, sick, tired, weary
rel bored; glutted, sated, satiated, surfeited
idiom fed to the gills (*or* teeth), full up to here with, sick and tired of, sick (*or* tired) to death
con enchanted, enraptured, enthralled; delighted, excited, exhilarated, pleased, thrilled

fee *n* ***syn*** see WAGE
rel consideration; charge, cost, expense, price
||**feeb** *n* ***syn*** see FOOL 4
feeble *adj* **1** ***syn*** see WEAK 1
rel emasculated, enervated, unmanned, unnerved; helpless; aged, doddering, senile; ailing, sapless
con hale, healthy, sound; lusty, strenuous; strong
ant robust
2 ***syn*** see TENUOUS 3
feebleminded *adj* ***syn*** see RETARDED
ant strong-minded
feebleness *n* ***syn*** see INFIRMITY 1
feed *vb* ***syn*** see GIVE 3
feed (on) *vb* ***syn*** see EAT 1
idiom have (*or* take) a bite, ||put on the feed bag (*or* nose bag)
feed *n* **1** ***syn*** see MEAL
2 ***syn*** see FOOD 1
rel banquet, feast, meal, repast
feel *vb* **1** ***syn*** see TOUCH 1
rel manipulate, ply, wield; explore, sound; fumble, grope
2 to have as an emotional response <*felt* pleasure in her company>
syn experience, know, savor, taste
rel apprehend; notice, observe, perceive; encounter, meet; endure, suffer, undergo
idiom be aware (*or* conscious) of, be sensible of
con disregard, ignore
3 to view as right or true <we *feel* that he should retire soon>
syn believe, consider, credit, deem, hold, sense, think; *compare* CONSIDER 3
rel assume, presume, suppose, suspect; conclude, deduce, gather, infer, judge; conjecture, guess, surmise; esteem; repute
idiom take (it) into one's head
con challenge, distrust, doubt, misdoubt, mistrust, question
4 ***syn*** see GROPE
feel (for) *vb* ***syn*** see COMPASSIONATE
feel *n* **1** ***syn*** see TOUCH 3
2 ***syn*** see TOUCH 4
3 ***syn*** see AIR 3
con basis, essence, reality
feeler *n* an attempt to ascertain opinion <the letter was a *feeler* to see how they would react>
syn trial balloon
rel query, question; inquiry, probe, test; leader, leading question; sounding board; intimation, representation; prospectus; kiteflying
feeling *n* **1** ***syn*** see SENSATION 1
rel action, behavior, reaction; responsiveness; palpability, palpableness, perceptibility, perceptibleness, tangibility, tangibleness
con apathy, indifference, insensibility, numbness
2 ***syn*** see TOUCH 4
3 subjective response or reaction (as to a person or situation) <a *feeling* of sadness>
syn affection, affectivity, emotion, passion, sentiment
rel humor, mood, temper, vein; attitude, outlook; belief, opinion, view; concept, idea, impression, notion, thought
4 ***syn*** see OPINION
5 ***syn*** see AIR 3
rel impress, impression, imprint
feeling *adj* ***syn*** see EMOTIONAL 1
con numb, unmoved, unresponsive
ant unfeeling
feel out *vb* ***syn*** see PROBE 2
feign *vb* ***syn*** see ASSUME 4
feigned *adj* ***syn*** see ARTIFICIAL 3
rel counterfeit, false, sham
con heartfelt, hearty, sincere, wholehearted, whole-souled
feint *n* ***syn*** see TRICK 1
rel make-believe, pretense, pretension; befooling, hoax, hoodwinking; cheat, counterfeit, deceit, fake, humbug, imposture, sham; expedient, resort, shift
felicitate *vb* ***syn*** see CONGRATULATE
rel commend, compliment, recommend; salute
con comfort, console, solace; commiserate, condole (with), pity; gibe, jeer, scoff; deride, mock, ridicule, taunt; contemn
felicitous *adj* ***syn*** see FIT 1
rel convincing, telling; opportune, pat, seasonable, timely, well-timed; apposite, apropos, germane, pertinent, relevant
con awkward, clumsy, gauche, inept, maladroit; unfortunate, unhappy, unlucky
ant infelicitous
feline *adj* ***syn*** see STEALTHY 2
fell *vb* **1** to force an opponent off his feet <*felled* the heckler with a single blow>
syn bowl (down *or* over), bring down, down, drop, flatten, floor, ground, knock down, knock over, lay low, level, mow (down), prostrate, throw down, tumble
rel shoot, shoot down
idiom lay level with the ground
con pick up, raise
2 to bring down by cutting <*felled* the great oak by the driveway>
syn chop, cut, hew
rel flatten, level, raze; cleave, rive, split; sever, sunder; gash, hack, mangle, slash
fell *adj* **1** ***syn*** see FIERCE 1
rel baleful, malefic, maleficent, malign, sinister; implacable, relentless, unrelenting; fearful, horrible, horrific, terrific
con compassionate, sympathetic, tender; clement, forbearing, lenient, merciful; humane
2 ***syn*** see GRAVE 3
fell *n* ***syn*** see HIDE
fellow *n* **1** ***syn*** see PARTNER
2 ***syn*** see ACCOMPANIMENT 2
3 ***syn*** see MATE 5
4 ***syn*** see MAN 3

syn synonym(s) ***rel*** related word(s)
ant antonym(s) ***con*** contrasted word(s)
idiom idiomatic equivalent(s)
|| use limited; if in doubt, see a dictionary

fellow feeling *n* ***syn*** see SYMPATHY 2
fellowship *n* **1** ***syn*** see COMPANY 1
2 ***syn*** see ASSOCIATION 2
felo–de–se *n* ***syn*** see SUICIDE
felon *n* ***syn*** see CRIMINAL
female *n* ***syn*** see WOMAN 1
female *adj* ***syn*** see FEMININE
feminine *adj* of, relating to, or characterized by qualities considered typical of a woman <clothing for the career woman that manages to be both *feminine* and businesslike>
syn female, muliebral, womanish, womanlike, womanly
rel effeminate; ladylike
con male, manlike, manly, masculine, virile; manful, mannish
femme fatale *n* ***syn*** see SIREN
fen *n* ***syn*** see SWAMP
fence *n* ***syn*** see BAR 2
fence *vb* **1** ***syn*** see ENCLOSE 1
2 ***syn*** see DODGE 1
rel feint, maneuver; baffle, foil, outwit
fend *vb* **1** ***syn*** see DEFEND 1
2 ***syn*** see WARD 1
fend (off) *vb* to give a sharp check to <tried to *fend* off his attentions>
syn hold off, keep off, rebuff, rebut, repel, repulse, stave off, ward (off)
rel refuse, reject; snub, spurn; avert, avoid
idiom hold (*or* keep) at bay, keep at a distance, keep at arm's length
con allure, attract, captivate, charm, enchant, fascinate; embolden, hearten
feral *adj* **1** ***syn*** see BRUTISH
rel barbaric, barbarous, ferocious, fierce, inhuman, savage, vicious
con gentle, mild, tame
2 ***syn*** see SAVAGE 1
ferine *adj* ***syn*** see BRUTISH
ferment *vb* ***syn*** see SEETHE 4
ferment *n* **1** ***syn*** see UNREST
2 ***syn*** see COMMOTION 1
ferocious *adj* **1** ***syn*** see FIERCE 1
rel rapacious, ravening, ravenous, voracious; implacable, relentless
ant tender
2 ***syn*** see SAVAGE
ferret out *vb* ***syn*** see SEEK 1
rel elicit, extract; nose out, pry (out); penetrate, pierce, probe; chase, follow, pursue, trail; ascertain, determine, discover, learn
con conceal, hide, screen, secrete; camouflage, disguise; cover (up), hush (up), suppress
ant squirrel (away)
ferry *vb* ***syn*** see CARRY 1
fertile *adj* marked by abundant productivity <*fertile* soil><a *fertile* mind>
syn childing, fecund, fruitful, productive, proliferant, prolific, rich, spawning
rel bearing, producing, yielding; abundant, bountiful, copious, exuberant, generous, lush, luxuriant, plenteous, plentiful, teeming; creative, ingenious, inventive, pregnant, resourceful; exciting, galvanizing, provoking, quickening, stimulating
con barren, impotent, unfruitful; dull, imitative, stupid, unproductive
ant infertile, sterile
fertility *n* the quality or state of being fertile <insure the *fertility* of the soil>
syn fecundity, fruitfulness, prolificacy
rel abundance, copiousness, plentifulness; creativity, ingenuity, inventiveness, resourcefulness
con barrenness, impotence, unfruitfulness
ant infertility, sterility
fervent *adj* ***syn*** see IMPASSIONED
rel devout, pious, religious; responsive, tender, warm, warmhearted; heartfelt, hearty, sincere, unfeigned, wholehearted, whole-souled; earnest, serious; eager, enthusiastic
con apathetic, impassive, phlegmatic; aloof, detached, indifferent, unconcerned
fervid *adj* **1** ***syn*** see IMPASSIONED
con collected, composed, cool, imperturbable, nonchalant
ant gelid
2 ***syn*** see FEVERISH 2
fervor *n* ***syn*** see PASSION 6
rel devoutness, piety, piousness; earnestness, seriousness, solemnity; heartiness, sincerity, wholeheartedness; empressement, warmth
con apathy, impassiveness, impassivity; aloofness, detachment, indifference, unconcern; languor, lethargy, torpor
fescennine *adj* ***syn*** see OBSCENE 2
fess (up) *vb* ***syn*** see ACKNOWLEDGE 1
fester *vb* ***syn*** see RANKLE
festive *adj* ***syn*** see MERRY
festivity *n* ***syn*** see MERRYMAKING
fetch *vb* ***syn*** see SELL 4
fetching *adj* ***syn*** see ENTICING
fetch up *vb* ‖**1** ***syn*** see BRING UP 1
2 ***syn*** see STOP 4
fetid *adj* ***syn*** see MALODOROUS 1
rel loathsome, repugnant, repulsive, revolting
con aromatic, balmy, odorous, redolent
ant fragrant
fetish *n* **1** ***syn*** see CHARM 2
2 irrational reverence or attachment <had a *fetish* for red hair>
syn fixation, mania, obsession, thing
rel preoccupation, prepossession; bias, partiality, predilection, prejudice; leaning, penchant, proclivity, propensity
con antipathy, aversion, repugnance, repulsion; dislike, disrelish, distaste
fetter *n, usu* **fetters** *pl* ***syn*** see SHACKLE
fetter *vb* ***syn*** see HAMPER
con disembarrass, disencumber, disentangle, extricate, untangle; detach, disengage
fettle *n* ***syn*** see ORDER 10
feud *n* **1** ***syn*** see VENDETTA
2 ***syn*** see QUARREL
rel argument; combat, contest
fevered *adj* **1** ***syn*** see FEVERISH 1
ant afebrile
2 ***syn*** see FEVERISH 2
feverish *adj* **1** abnormally heated by fever <the child's forehead felt *feverish*>

syn febrile, fevered, fiery
rel burning, flushed, hectic, hot, inflamed, pyretic
ant afebrile
2 marked by intense emotion or activity <a *feverish* imagination>
syn burning, fervid, fevered, heated, hectic
rel excited, high-strung, nervous, overwrought; frenzied, furious, passionate
idiom keyed up
con calm, composed, cool, serene, tranquil; apathetic, languid, lethargic, listless, phlegmatic

few *adj syn* see INFREQUENT

few *n* a small quantity or number <sold a *few* of the books>
syn handful, scattering, smatch, smatter, smattering, spatter, spattering, sprinkling
con abundance, many, multitude, numbers

fiat *n syn* see SANCTION

fib *n syn* see LIE
rel equivocation, evasiveness; mendacity, untruthfulness
idiom tall tale

fib *vb syn* see LIE
rel concoct, fabricate, make up, trump up
idiom draw the long bow, stretch the truth

fibber *n syn* see LIAR

fibbery *n syn* see MENDACITY

fiber *n syn* see TEXTURE 2

fibrous *adj syn* see MUSCULAR 1

fibster *n syn* see LIAR

fickle *adj syn* see INCONSTANT 1
rel unfaithful; undependable, unreliable
con stable, unchanging
ant constant, true

fiction *n* a story, account, explanation, or conception which is an invention of the human mind <his belief was based on a *fiction*>
syn fable, fabrication, figment
rel concoction, fantasy, invention; falsehood, lie, misrepresentation, untruth; anecdote, narrative, story, tale, yarn; fish story
con actuality, reality
ant fact

fictional *adj syn* see FICTITIOUS 1

fictitious *adj* 1 suggestive of fiction especially in lacking a sound factual basis <*fictitious* values in logic>
syn chimerical, fanciful, fantastic, fictional, fictive, illusory, imaginary, suppositious, supposititious, unreal
rel concocted, created, invented, made; fabricated, fashioned; cooked-up, false, made-up, trumped-up, untrue; romantic
con actual, real, true; authentic, genuine; factual, veritable; truthful, veracious, verisimilar
2 not genuine <the gigolo wooed the heiress with *fictitious* ardor>
syn fake, mock, sham, simulated; *compare* ARTIFICIAL 2
rel deceptive, delusive, delusory, misleading; dishonest, unreal, untrue; artificial, ersatz, factitious, synthetic
con authentic, bona fide, veritable; actual, honest, real, true
ant genuine

fictive *adj syn* see FICTITIOUS 1

fiddle *vb* 1 to handle something nervously or absently <always *fiddling* with his tie>
syn fidget, play, trifle, twiddle
rel feel, handle, touch
2 to work aimlessly, fruitlessly, or pointlessly <*fiddled* around with the engine for hours>
syn doodle, mess, mess around, potter, puddle, putter, tinker
rel dabble, fool, monkey

fiddle *n syn* see IMPOSTURE

fiddle–faddle *n syn* see NONSENSE 2

fiddlesticks *n pl syn* see NONSENSE 2

fidelity *n* 1 constancy to something to which one is bound by a pledge or duty <we must practice *fidelity* to our word>
syn allegiance, ardor, devotion, faithfulness, fealty, loyalty, piety
rel constancy, staunchness, steadfastness; dependability, reliability, trustworthiness
con disloyalty, falseness, falsity, perfidiousness, traitorousness, treacherousness, treachery; undependableness, unreliability, untrustworthiness
ant perfidy; faithlessness
2 *syn* see ATTACHMENT 1
ant infidelity

fidget *vb syn* see FIDDLE 1

fidgety *adj syn* see NERVOUS

field *n* a limited area of knowledge or endeavor to which pursuits, activities, and interests are confined <a lawyer eminent in her *field*>
syn bailiwick, champaign, demesne, domain, dominion, precinct, province, region, sphere, terrain, territory, walk
rel bounds, confines, limits; area, department; compass, orbit, purview, range, reach, scope, sweep
con terra incognita

fiend *n syn* see DEVIL 1
2 *syn* see DEVIL 2
3 *syn* see ENTHUSIAST

fiendish *adj* having or manifesting qualities associated with devils, demons, and fiends <inflicted *fiendish* tortures on his captive>
syn demoniac, demonian, demonic, devilish, diabolic, diabolonian, satanic, serpentine, unhallowed
rel hellish, infernal; baleful, malefic, maleficent, malign, sinister; malevolent, malicious, malignant; atrocious, heinous, monstrous, outrageous; barbarous, cruel, ferocious, inhuman, savage, vicious
con benign, benignant, kind, kindly; gentle, mild; compassionate, sympathetic, tender

fierce *adj* 1 displaying fury or malignity in looks or actions <*fierce* native tribes>

---

syn synonym(s) *rel* related word(s)
ant antonym(s) *con* contrasted word(s)
idiom idiomatic equivalent(s)
|| use limited; if in doubt, see a dictionary

syn barbarous, cannibalic, cruel, fell, ferocious, grim, inhuman, inhumane, savage, truculent, wolfish
rel menacing, threatening; enraged, infuriated, maddened; aggressive, bellicose, belligerent, pugnacious; brutal, merciless, pitiless, ruthless, vicious, wild
con benign, benignant, gentle, kind, kindly; peaceful; subdued, submissive, tame
ant mild
2 *syn* see INTENSE 1
rel excessive, extreme, inordinate; penetrating, piercing; superlative, supreme, transcendent
con gentle, mild, subdued

fiercely *adv syn* see HARD 2

fiery *adj* **1** *syn* see BURNING 1
2 *syn* see HOT 1
ant frigid, icy
3 *syn* see FEVERISH 1
4 *syn* see SPIRITED 2
rel headlong, hotheaded, impetuous, madcap, precipitate; fervid, impassioned, perfervid; fierce, intense, vehement, violent; enthusiastic, excitable, impulsive, unrestrained; irascible, irritable
con deliberate, leisurely, slow; apathetic, dull, impassive, lethargic, phlegmatic, sluggish; enervated, listless, spiritless
5 *syn* see IMPASSIONED
ant icy

fifty–fifty *adv syn* see EVENLY 1

fifty–fifty *adj syn* see EVEN 4

fight *vb* **1** *syn* see CONTEND 1
rel strive, struggle; rowdy, scuffle, tussle; debate, dispute; altercate, bicker, quarrel, scrap, spat, squabble, tiff, wrangle
idiom ‖mix it, mix it up, put up a fight
con bow, capitulate, submit, succumb, yield
2 *syn* see RESIST
con abide, bear, endure, suffer; advocate, back, champion, support, uphold; defend, guard, protect, shield

fight *n* **1** *syn* see BRAWL 2
2 *syn* see QUARREL
3 *syn* see ATTACK 2

fighter *n syn* see SOLDIER

fighting man *n syn* see SOLDIER

figment *n syn* see FICTION
rel daydream, dream, fancy, nightmare; bubble, chimera, illusion; creation

figurant *n syn* see DANCER

figurante *n syn* see DANCER

figuration *n* **1** *syn* see OUTLINE
2 *syn* see ALLEGORY 1

figure *n* **1** *syn* see NUMBER
rel character, symbol
2 *syn* see FORM 1
rel delineation; appearance, build, frame, physique
3 a unit in a decorative composition (as in a fabric) <a rug with geometrical *figures* in blue and red>
syn design, device, motif, motive, pattern
rel decoration, embellishment, ornamentation

figure *vb* **1** *syn* see CALCULATE
2 *syn* see ADD 2
rel count, enumerate, number
3 *syn* see DECIDE

figure out *vb syn* see SOLVE 2
rel disentangle, unscramble, untangle; crack, decode
con obfuscate, obscure; conceal, hide, screen

figuring *n syn* see COMPUTATION

filch *vb syn* see STEAL 1

filcher *n syn* see THIEF

file *n syn* see LINE 5

filius nullius *n syn* see BASTARD 1

filius populi *n syn* see BASTARD 1

fill *vb* **1** to make full in a way or to a degree that prevents further entry or passage <*fill* a cavity in a tooth>
syn block, choke, clog, close, congest, obstruct, occlude, plug, stop, stopper
rel bar, dam, jam; ‖bung, pug
con clear, free
2 *syn* see LOAD 3
3 *syn* see SATISFY 5
4 *syn* see SATIATE
rel overfeed, overfill, overstuff

fille de joie *n syn* see PROSTITUTE

fillet *n syn* see STRIP 1

fill in *vb* **1** *syn* see INTRODUCE 6
2 *syn* see INFORM 2

fill–in *n syn* see SUBSTITUTE 1

film *n* **1** *syn* see HAZE 1
2 *syn* see MOVIE

filmy *adj* characterized by fineness and delicacy of texture <*filmy* curtains>
syn diaphanous, flimsy, gauzy, gossamer, sheer, tiffany, transparent
rel dainty, delicate, fine
con coarse, heavy, opaque, rough

filthy *adj* **1** *syn* see DIRTY 1
rel disheveled, slipshod, sloppy, slovenly, unkempt; loathsome, offensive, repulsive, revolting, verminous; coarse, gross, obscene, ribald, vulgar
con cleaned, cleansed; clean, cleanly; neat, shipshape, tidy, trig, trim
ant immaculate, spick-and-span
2 *syn* see OBSCENE 2

filthy lucre *n syn* see MONEY

finagle *vb syn* see ENGINEER

final *adj syn* see LAST
rel crowning, ending, finishing; conclusive, decisive, definitive, determinative; irrefutable, unanswerable, unappealable
con earliest, maiden, original, primary; beginning, incipient, introductory; inaugural
ant initial

finale *n* a final part or element (as of a sequence, series, or action) <the solution of the mystery forms the *finale* of the play>
syn close, conclusion, end, ending, finish, windup; *compare* END 2
rel climax, consummation, culmination; denouement, payoff; cessation, termination
con beginning, genesis, initiation, rise, start; inception, origin, root, source

ant prologue
finally *adv* ***syn*** see YET 2
idiom at last, at length, at long last, in the long run, when all is said and done
finance *vb* **1** ***syn*** see CAPITALIZE
idiom put up the money, raise the dough
2 ***syn*** see ENDOW 2
rel back, bank, bankroll, grubstake, stake, underwrite; patronize, promote, sponsor, support
financial *adj* of or relating to finance <the *financial* interests of the country>
syn fiscal, monetary, pecuniary, pocket
rel business, commercial, economic
find *vb* **1** to come upon <they soon *found* what they needed>
syn catch, descry, detect, encounter, espy, hit (on *or* upon), meet (with), spot, turn up
rel discern, discover, note, sight; distinguish, identify, recognize; dig up, scare up
idiom bring to light, come up with, fall in with, lay one's finger (on *or* upon), lay one's hand (on *or* upon)
con miss, overlook, pass (over)
ant lose
2 ***syn*** see GIVE 3
find *n* **1** one of unexpected worth or merit obtained or encountered more or less by chance <the young understudy proved to be a remarkable *find*>
syn treasure, treasure trove
rel boast, gem, jewel, pride
idiom one in a thousand (*or* million)
2 ***syn*** see DISCOVERY
find out *vb* ***syn*** see DISCOVER 3
fine *n* a pecuniary penalty exacted by an authority <paid a *fine* of ten dollars>
syn amercement, forfeit, mulct, penalty
rel damages, reparation; punishment; assessment
fine *vb* ***syn*** see PENALIZE
rel distrain, exact, levy, tax; confiscate, sequestrate
fine *adj* **1** marked by subtlety of perception or discrimination <I cannot follow these *fine* distinctions>
syn delicate, finespun, hairline, hairsplitting, nice, refined, subtle
rel abstruse, esoteric, recondite; cryptic, enigmatic, obscure; minute, petty, trifling
con definite, explicit, express, specific; clear, lucid, perspicuous; broad, extensive, general, generic, indefinite, wide
2 consisting of small particles <*fine* sand>
syn impalpable, powdery, pulverized
rel light, loose, porous
ant coarse
3 ***syn*** see EXCELLENT
rel beautiful, splendid; enjoyable, pleasant
idiom fine and dandy
con miserable, wretched; atrocious, awful, objectionable, unpleasant
4 ***syn*** see FAIR 2
finecomb *vb* ***syn*** see SCOUR 2
finery *n* dressy clothing <decked out in all her *finery*>
syn ‖best bib and tucker, bravery, frippery, full dress, ‖glad rags, regalia, Sunday best, war paint
rel apparel, clothes; foofaraw, frill, gewgaw, ornament, trimming
con rags, tatters
finespun *adj* ***syn*** see FINE 1
finesse *vb* ***syn*** see MANIPULATE 2
fine–tooth–comb *vb* ***syn*** see SCOUR 2
finger *vb* **1** ***syn*** see TOUCH 1
2 ***syn*** see DESIGNATE 2
3 ***syn*** see IDENTIFY
finical *adj* ***syn*** see NICE 1
con slipshod, sloppy, slovenly; blowsy, dowdy, frowzy, slatternly
finicking *adj* ***syn*** see NICE 1
finicky *adj* ***syn*** see NICE 1
finish *vb* **1** ***syn*** see CLOSE 3
rel accomplish, achieve, effect, fulfill
idiom have done with
2 ***syn*** see GO 4
3 ***syn*** see KILL 1
4 ***syn*** see MURDER 1
finish *n* **1** ***syn*** see END 2
2 ***syn*** see FINALE
3 ***syn*** see ACQUIREMENT
rel correctness, discrimination, propriety, refinement; elegance, grace, polish; cultivation, taste
finished *adj* **1** ***syn*** see COMPLETE 4
2 ***syn*** see THROUGH 3
3 ***syn*** see CONSUMMATE 1
rel cultivated, cultured, refined; smooth, suave, urbane; elegant, exquisite; all-around, many-sided, versatile
con imperfect, incomplete
ant crude; unfinished
finish off *vb* ***syn*** see CLIMAX
finite *adj* having definite or definable limits or boundaries <a *finite* thickness>
syn bound, bounded, limited
rel confined, restricted; definable, defined, definite, determinate, fixed, terminable; exact, precise, specific
con boundless, unbounded, unlimited; absolute, complete, total
ant infinite
‖**fink** *n* ***syn*** see INFORMER
fire *n* **1** a destructive burning <the house was destroyed by *fire*>
syn conflagration, holocaust, inferno
rel blaze, flame, flare, glare; burning, charring, scorching, searing
idiom sea of flames, sheet of fire
2 ***syn*** see PASSION 6
rel animation, exhilaration, liveliness; dash, drive, energy, ginger, gusto, heartiness, pep, punch, snap, spirit, starch, verve, vigor, vim, zest, zing, zip

---

syn synonym(s) *rel* related word(s)
ant antonym(s) *con* contrasted word(s)
idiom idiomatic equivalent(s)
‖ use limited; if in doubt, see a dictionary

con languor, lassitude, lethargy, listlessness, stupor, torpidity, torpor; apathy, impassivity, phlegm

fire *vb* **1** ***syn*** see LIGHT 1
idiom set fire to, set on fire
con extinguish, quench, smother
2 to stimulate (as mental powers) to higher or more intense activity <a painting that *fired* the viewer's imagination>
syn animate, exalt, inform, inspire; *compare* PROVOKE 4
rel arouse, enliven, rouse, stir; electrify, excite; heighten, intensify; enthuse, thrill
con appall, dismay; alarm, frighten, terrify
ant daunt
3 ***syn*** see DISMISS 3
rel eject, expel, oust
idiom give the pink slip, give the sack, strike off the rolls
con engage; appoint, designate, elect, name
ant hire
4 ***syn*** see SHOOT 1
5 ***syn*** see THROW 1
6 to dry or harden by subjecting to heat <*fire* bricks>
syn bake, burn, kiln

firebug *n* ***syn*** see INCENDIARY

fire–new *adj* ***syn*** see BRAND-NEW

firewater *n* ***syn*** see LIQUOR 2

firm *adj* **1** ***syn*** see FAST 4
2 ***syn*** see STABLE 4
3 having a texture or consistency that resists deformation by external force <*firm* flesh>
syn hard, solid
rel close, compact, dense, thick; inelastic, inflexible, rigid, stiff, unyielding; sturdy, substantial, tough
con flaccid, flimsy, floppy, limp, loose, slack, sleazy, soft, squishy
ant flabby
4 that has been established and is not usually subject to change <a *firm* price>
syn certain, fixed, set, settled, stated, stipulated
rel established, going, prevailing; consistent, stable, steady, unwavering; definite, exact, explicit, specific, undeviating; flat
con changeable, fluctuating, shaky, shifting, unsteady, variable
5 ***syn*** see SURE 1
6 ***syn*** see SURE 2

firm *adv* ***syn*** see HARD 7

firm *n* ***syn*** see ENTERPRISE 3

firmament *n* ***syn*** see SKY

firmly *adv* **1** ***syn*** see HARD 7
2 ***syn*** see HARD 9

firmness *n* **1** ***syn*** see STABILITY
2 ***syn*** see DECISION 2

first *adj* **1** being number one in a series <the *first* day of the week>
syn foremost, headmost, inaugural, initial, leading
con final, terminal, ultimate; interjacent, intermediary, intermediate, intervenient, intervening
ant last
2 preceding all others <succeeded at her *first* try>
syn earliest, initial, maiden, original, pioneer, primary, prime
rel early, pristine; primal, primogenial, primordial
con derivative, imitative, secondary
ant final
3 exceeding all others <he was the *first* statesman of his era>
syn arch, champion, chief, foremost, head, leading, premier, principal
rel eminent, highest, preeminent, primary, prime, supreme; dominant, paramount, predominant, sovereign; main, outstanding
con ancillary, auxiliary, secondary, subsidiary
ant subordinate
4 most rudimentary <had not the *first* chance of success>
syn least, slightest, smallest
rel measly, slight, slim, trifling, trivial
con considerable, goodly, significant, substantial, tolerable, worthwhile

first *adv* ***syn*** see FIRSTLY

first–class *adj* ***syn*** see EXCELLENT
idiom in a class by itself
con fair, indifferent, middling; unexceptional, unnoteworthy, unremarkable

firsthand *adj* ***syn*** see DIRECT 4

firstly *adv* as the first thing to be mentioned <*firstly,* we wish to consider the economic problem>
syn first, initially
rel incipiently, originally, primarily
idiom before all (*or* anything) else, first of all, first off, to begin with
con ultimately
ant finally, lastly

first off *adv* ***syn*** see AWAY 3

first–rate *adj* ***syn*** see EXCELLENT
con fair, indifferent, middling, poor; unexceptional, unnoteworthy, unremarkable

first–string *adj* ***syn*** see EXCELLENT

firth *n* ***syn*** see INLET

fiscal *adj* ***syn*** see FINANCIAL

fish *n* **1** ***syn*** see FOOL 3
‖**2** ***syn*** see DOLLAR

fish *vb* ***syn*** see HINT 4

fishwife *n* ***syn*** see VIRAGO

fishy *adj* ***syn*** see DOUBTFUL 1

fissure *n* **1** ***syn*** see CRACK 3
rel abyss, chasm, gorge, ravine; breach, rent, rupture; gash, hole, opening
2 ***syn*** see BREACH 3

fist *n* ***syn*** see HANDWRITING

fisticuffs *n pl* ***syn*** see BOXING

fit *n* ***syn*** see ATTACK 3

fit *adj* **1** adapted to an end or use by nature or art <food *fit* for a king>
syn applicable, appropriate, apt, befitting, felicitous, fitting, happy, just, meet, proper, right, rightful, suitable; *compare* JUST 3
rel adapted, adjusted; congruous, consonant; decent, decorous; acceptable, adequate, tolerable

con improper, inadequate, inappropriate, unsuitable; false, wrong
ant unfit
2 *syn* see ELIGIBLE
rel able, competent
3 *syn* see GOOD 2
4 *syn* see HEALTHY 1
idiom fit as a fiddle
ant unfit

fit *vb* **1 *syn*** see SUIT 4
2 *syn* see BELONG 1
3 *syn* see PREPARE 1
4 *syn* see ADAPT

fit (in) *vb* ***syn*** see AGREE 4

fitful *adj* lacking steadiness or regularity in course, movement, or succession <a *fitful* breeze>
syn catchy, desultory, on-again-off-again, spasmodic, sporadic, spotty
rel intermittent, interrupted, irregular, periodic, recurrent; haphazard, hit-or-miss, random; changeable, variable; capricious, inconstant, unstable
con equable, even, steady, uniform; methodical, orderly, regular, systematic
ant constant

fitly *adv* ***syn*** see WELL 1

fitness *n* **1 *syn*** see ORDER 10
2 *syn* see ORDER 11
rel decency, decorum, harmony
ant unfitness
3 *syn* see USE 3

fit out *vb* ***syn*** see FURNISH 1

fitted *adj* ***syn*** see ASSORTED 2

fitting *adj* **1 *syn*** see FIT 1
rel apposite, apropos, germane, pertinent, relevant, seemly; accordant, concordant, harmonious
2 *syn* see TRUE 7

fittingly *adv* **1 *syn*** see WELL 1
2 *syn* see WELL 4

fivefold *adj* ***syn*** see QUINTUPLE

five–star *adj* ***syn*** see EXCELLENT

fix *vb* **1 *syn*** see SET 1
rel stabilize, steady; decide, determine, rule; specify
con change, modify, vary
ant alter; abrogate
2 *syn* see ENTRENCH 1
rel inculcate, instill
con overthrow, overturn, subvert, upset
3 *syn* see FASTEN 1
4 *syn* see FASTEN 2
con dislodge, displace
5 *syn* see FASTEN 3
6 *syn* see PREPARE 1
7 *syn* see MEND 2
8 *syn* see ADJUST 2
rel mend, patch, rebuild, repair; amend, emend, revise
con disorganize, unsettle
9 *syn* see SOLVE 1
10 *syn* see STERILIZE
11 *syn* see BRIBE

fix *n* ***syn*** see PREDICAMENT

fixate *vb* ***syn*** see FASTEN 3

fixation *n* ***syn*** see FETISH 2
rel craze, fascination, infatuation
idiom bee in one's bonnet

fixed *adj* **1 *syn*** see FAST 4
2 *syn* see IMMOVABLE 1
3 *syn* see DEFINITE 1
4 *syn* see INFLEXIBLE 3
5 *syn* see FIRM 4
con changing, variable, varying
6 *syn* see SURE 2
7 *syn* see WHOLE 5
con distracted, erratic, wandering

fixedly *adv* ***syn*** see HARD 7
rel stubbornly, tenaciously

fixture *n* ***syn*** see INSTITUTION

fix up *vb* ***syn*** see DRESS UP 1

fizz *vb* ***syn*** see HISS

fizzle *vb* ***syn*** see HISS

flabbergast *vb* ***syn*** see SURPRISE 2
rel overwhelm, shock

flabby *adj* ***syn*** see LIMP 1
rel soft, yielding; impotent, powerless; enervated, languid, listless, spiritless
con taut, tense, tight; strong, sturdy, tenacious, tough; gritty, plucky
ant firm

flaccid *adj* ***syn*** see LIMP 1
rel emasculated, enervated, unnerved; debilitated, enfeebled, sapped, weakened
con elastic, flexible, springy, supple; limber, lithe; energetic, lusty, nervous, vigorous
ant resilient

flag *n* a piece of fabric that is used as a symbol (as of a nation) or as a signaling device <we respect the *flag* of our fathers>
syn banderole, banner, bannerol, burgee, color, ensign, gonfalon, gonfanon, jack, oriflamme, pendant, pennant, pennon, standard, streamer

flag *vb* ***syn*** see SIGNAL

flag *vb* **1 *syn*** see FAIL 1
2 *syn* see DROOP 3
rel abate, ebb, wane

flagellate *vb* ***syn*** see WHIP 1

flagitious *adj* ***syn*** see VICIOUS 2
rel criminal, scandalous, sinful, wicked; disgraceful, shameful; flagrant, glaring, gross
con good, upstanding, virtuous

flagrant *adj* ***syn*** see EGREGIOUS
rel bold, conspicuous, obvious, striking; heinous; flagitious, wicked; disgraceful, scandalous, shameful, shocking
con hidden, inconspicuous, obscure; excusable, unimportant

flagrante delicto *adv* ***syn*** see RED-HANDED

flag-waver *n* ***syn*** see PATRIOTEER

flair *n* ***syn*** see GIFT 2

flak *n* ***syn*** see CRITICISM 2

---

syn synonym(s) ***rel*** related word(s)
ant antonym(s) ***con*** contrasted word(s)
idiom idiomatic equivalent(s)
‖ use limited; if in doubt, see a dictionary

flake (off) *vb* ***syn*** see SCALE 2
‖**flake out** *vb* ***syn*** see COLLAPSE 2
flam *n* ***syn*** see IMPOSTURE
flamboyant *adj* **1** ***syn*** see ORNATE
2 ***syn*** see SHOWY
flame *n* **1** ***syn*** see SWEETHEART 1
2 ***syn*** see GIRL FRIEND 2
3 ***syn*** see BOYFRIEND 2
flame *vb* ***syn*** see BLAZE
rel coruscate, glint; fire, ignite, kindle, light
flaming *adj* **1** ***syn*** see BURNING 1
2 ***syn*** see IMPASSIONED
flammable *adj* ***syn*** see COMBUSTIBLE 1
ant incombustible, nonflammable
flap *n* ***syn*** see COMMOTION 2
flapdoodle *n* ***syn*** see NONSENSE 2
flare *vb* ***syn*** see BLAZE
rel dart, shoot; flicker, flutter
idiom burst into flame
ant gutter out
flare (up) *vb* ***syn*** see ANGER 2
idiom ‖blow one's stack (*or* top *or* lid), fly into a passion, fly off the handle
con calm (down), cool (off *or* down), simmer down
flare *n* ***syn*** see OUTBREAK 1
flare–up *n* ***syn*** see OUTBURST 1
flaring *adj* ***syn*** see BURNING 1
flash *vb* **1** to shoot forth light (as in rays or sparks) <lightning *flashed* in the sky>
syn coruscate, glance, gleam, glimmer, glint, glisten, glitter, scintillate, shimmer, spangle, sparkle, twinkle
rel dart, shoot; blare, blaze, burn, flame, flare, glare, glow, incandesce; blink, flicker, spark; dazzle; beam, radiate, shine
2 ***syn*** see BLINK 2
3 ***syn*** see SHOW 4
flash *n* **1** a sudden brief light <saw a *flash* sweep across the sky>
syn coruscation, glance, gleam, glimmer, glint, glisten, glitter, quiver, scintillation, shimmer, sparkle, twinkle
rel blare, blaze, flame, flare, glare, glow; flicker; beam, ray
2 ***syn*** see INSTANT 1
idiom half a second (*or* shake), twinkling of an eye
flashy *adj* ***syn*** see GAUDY
rel flamboyant, florid, ornate; flashing, glittering, sparkling
con dowdy, slatternly; natural, simple, unaffected; chic, modish, smart
flat *adj* **1** ***syn*** see LEVEL
idiom flat as a billiard table (*or* pancake)
con rugged, scabrous, uneven; hilly, mountainous
2 ***syn*** see PRONE 4
3 ***syn*** see DOWNRIGHT 2
4 ***syn*** see COLORLESS 2
5 ***syn*** see INSIPID 3
rel dull, lifeless; flavorless, stale, tasteless
6 ***syn*** see UNPALATABLE 1
7 ***syn*** see POOR 1
8 ***syn*** see DULL 7
flat *n* ***syn*** see APARTMENT 1
‖**flatfoot** *n* ***syn*** see POLICEMAN
flatly *adv* ***syn*** see EVENLY 3
flat–out *adj* ***syn*** see UTTER
flat–out *adv* ***syn*** see FAST 2
flatten *vb* **1** ***syn*** see EVEN 1
2 ***syn*** see FELL 1
flatter *vb* to be becoming to <a neckline designed to *flatter* the stylishly stout>
syn become, enhance, suit
rel adorn, beautify, decorate, embellish, ornament; finish, perfect
idiom put in the best light
con deface, disfigure; distort; mar, spoil
flattery *n* flattering speech or attentions <*flattery* will get you nowhere>
syn adulation, blandishment, blarney, incense, oil, soft soap
rel compliments; laud, laudation, praise; cajolery, coaxing, wheedling; fulsomeness, unctuousness; bootlicking, fawning, ingratiation, obsequiousness, sycophancy, toadying, truckling
idiom honeyed words
con censure, condemnation, criticism, reprehension, reprobation; castigation, excoriation; aspersion, insult; contempt, disdain, scorn; belittling, depreciation, derogation, detraction, disparagement
flatulent *adj* ***syn*** see INFLATED
rel empty, hollow, vain; shallow, superficial
con weighty; cogent, compelling, convincing, telling; forceful, forcible, potent
flaunt *vb* ***syn*** see SHOW 4
rel boast, brag, gasconade, vaunt; disclose, discover, divulge, reveal; advertise, broadcast, declare, proclaim, publish; flourish, wave
idiom dangle before the (*or* one's) eyes
con camouflage, cloak, disguise, dissemble, mask; bury, conceal, hide, screen, secrete
flavor *n* ***syn*** see TASTE 3
flavorless *adj* ***syn*** see UNPALATABLE 1
ant flavorsome
flavorsome *adj* ***syn*** see PALATABLE
con flat, insipid, vapid, wishy-washy; bland, mild; displeasing, tasteless, unflavored, unpalatable, unpleasant, unsavory
ant flavorless
flaw *n* ***syn*** see BLEMISH
rel cleavage, rent, rip, riving, split, tear
flawed *adj* **1** ***syn*** see DAMAGED
ant flawless
2 ***syn*** see FAULTY
ant flawless
flawless *adj* **1** ***syn*** see WHOLE 1
ant flawed
2 ***syn*** see PERFECT 2
3 ***syn*** see IMPECCABLE 1
con defective, faulty, flawed, imperfect, unsound
4 ***syn*** see IDEAL 3
flaxen *adj* ***syn*** see BLOND 1
flay *vb* ***syn*** see LAMBASTE 3
rel assail, attack, berate, tongue-lash

fleckless *adj* ***syn*** see PERFECT 2
flection *n* ***syn*** see TURN 4
fledgling *n* ***syn*** see NOVICE
flee *vb* **1** ***syn*** see ESCAPE 1
rel avoid, elude, evade, shun
idiom take a (runout) powder
2 ***syn*** see RUN 2
con stand, stay
fleece *vb* **1** to obtain something valuable from by improper means <a corrupt mayor who *fleeced* the town treasury>
syn bleed, milk, mulct, rook, stick, sweat; *compare* CHEAT, EXTORT 1
rel cheat, cozen, defraud, do, hustle, ||rope (in), swindle, take; pluck
idiom sell one a bill of goods, take for a sucker, take to the cleaner's
2 ***syn*** see OVERCHARGE 1
fleeceable *adj* ***syn*** see EASY 3
fleecy *adj* ***syn*** see HAIRY 1
fleer *vb* **1** ***syn*** see SNEER 1
2 ***syn*** see SCOFF
rel grin, smile, smirk
idiom cast in one's teeth, curl one's lip at, laugh one out of court
fleet *vb* **1** ***syn*** see WHILE
rel dally, fritter, idle, potter, squander, waste
2 ***syn*** see FLY 4
idiom go like the wind (*or* lightning), make (good) time
3 ***syn*** see HURRY 2
fleet *adj* ***syn*** see FAST 3
rel agile, brisk, nimble, spry; alert, animated, lively, spirited, sprightly, vivacious
fleeting *adj* ***syn*** see TRANSIENT
con abiding, enduring, persistent
ant lasting
fleetly *adv* ***syn*** see FAST 2
flesh *n* ***syn*** see MANKIND
fleshiness *n* ***syn*** see OBESITY
fleshliness *n* ***syn*** see ANIMALITY
fleshly *adj* **1** ***syn*** see BODILY
2 ***syn*** see CARNAL 2
rel epicurean, luxurious, sensuous, sybaritic, voluptuous; lay, profane, secular, temporal
con divine, religious, spiritual; intellectual, mental, psychic
fleshy *adj* ***syn*** see FAT 2
ant emaciated
flexible *adj* ***syn*** see ELASTIC 1
rel amenable, docile, manageable, tractable; acquiescent, compliant
con brittle, crisp, fragile, frangible; firm, hard, rigid, stiff, unyielding, wooden; intractable, recalcitrant, refractory, ungovernable; callous, hardened, indurated
ant inflexible
flexuous *adj* ***syn*** see WINDING
flexure *n* ***syn*** see TURN 4
flibbertigibbet *n* ***syn*** see SCATTERBRAIN
flick *n* ***syn*** see MOVIE
flicker *vb* **1** ***syn*** see FLIT 2
2 ***syn*** see BLINK 2
rel fluctuate, oscillate, swing, vibrate, waver; blaze, flame, flare, glare; coruscate, glance, gleam, glint, glitter, sparkle; quaver, quiver, tremble
flier *n* ***syn*** see PILOT 2
flight *n* ***syn*** see ESCAPE 1
flightiness *n* ***syn*** see LIGHTNESS
rel capriciousness, fickleness, inconstancy, instability, mercurialness
con constancy, equableness, steadfastness
ant steadiness
flighty *adj* ***syn*** see GIDDY 1
rel changeable, inconstant, mercurial, unstable; buoyant, effervescent, volatile; gay, lively, sprightly; irresponsible
con constant, dependable, reliable, responsible, trustworthy; stable; sedate
ant steady
flimflam *n* **1** ***syn*** see IMPOSTURE
2 ***syn*** see NONSENSE 2
flimflam *vb* **1** ***syn*** see DUPE
2 ***syn*** see CHEAT
flimflammer *n* ***syn*** see SWINDLER
flimsy *adj* **1** ***syn*** see FILMY
2 ***syn*** see IMPLAUSIBLE
ant substantial
3 ***syn*** see DELICATE 5
4 ***syn*** see WEAK 1
ant sturdy
5 ***syn*** see LIMP 1
flinch *vb* ***syn*** see RECOIL
rel avoid, elude, escape, eschew, evade, shun; retire, withdraw; recede, retreat
fling *vb* **1** ***syn*** see RUSH 1
2 ***syn*** see THROW 1
con catch, grab, receive
fling *n* **1** a casual attempt <I'm willing to take a *fling* at almost any job>
syn crack, go, pop, shot, slap, stab, ||stagger, try, whack, whirl
rel attempt, effort, essay, trial
con best, limit, maximum
ant utmost
2 ***syn*** see SPREE 1
flip (through) *vb* ***syn*** see BROWSE
flippancy *n* ***syn*** see LIGHTNESS
rel archness, pertness, sauciness; impishness, mischievousness, playfulness, roguishness, waggishness; cheekiness, cockiness, freshness
con earnestness, gravity, soberness, solemnity
ant seriousness
flirt *vb* ***syn*** see TRIFLE 1
rel disport, play, sport; caress, fondle, pet
flirt *n* a woman who trifles amorously <a charming girl but an outrageous *flirt*>
syn coquette, vamp
flit *vb* **1** ***syn*** see HURRY 2
2 to move briskly, irregularly, and usually intermittently <the hummingbird *flitted* from flower to flower>
syn dance, flicker, flitter, flutter, hover

---

syn synonym(s) ***rel*** related word(s)
ant antonym(s) ***con*** contrasted word(s)
idiom idiomatic equivalent(s)
|| use limited; if in doubt, see a dictionary

rel dart, float, fly, scud, skim
3 *syn* see FLY 4
flitter *vb* *syn* see FLIT 2
rel quaver, quiver, teeter
float *vb* 1 *syn* see DRIFT 1
2 *syn* see HANG 3
3 *syn* see FLY 1
rel drift, waft
floater *n* *syn* see VAGABOND
flock *n* 1 *syn* see MULTITUDE 1
2 *syn* see DROVE 2
flog *vb* *syn* see WHIP 1
flood *n* 1 *syn* see FLOW
2 a great or overwhelming flow of or as if of water <a *flood* of messages>
syn cataclysm, cataract, deluge, flooding, inundation, niagara, overflow, pour, spate, torrent
rel current, flow, stream, tide; excess, superfluity, surplus; outgushing, outpouring
con dribble, drip, dropping
ant trickle
flood *vb* 1 *syn* see DELUGE 1
2 *syn* see DELUGE 3
flooding *n* *syn* see FLOOD 2
floor *vb* *syn* see FELL 1
floozy *n* *syn* see DOXY 1
‖**flop** *vb* 1 *syn* see RETIRE 4
2 *syn* see FAIL 4
con come off, go over, succeed
flop *n* *syn* see FAILURE 5
floppy *adj* *syn* see LIMP 1
florid *adj* 1 *syn* see RHETORICAL
2 *syn* see ORNATE
rel ostentatious, pretentious, showy
con bald, bare, barren; austere, unadorned
3 *syn* see RUDDY
ant pallid
florilegium *n* *syn* see ANTHOLOGY
floss *n* *syn* see DOWN
flotsam *n* *syn* see DRIFTWOOD
flounce *vb* *syn* see SASHAY
flounder *vb* *syn* see WALLOW 2
rel strive, struggle; labor, toil, travail
flourish *vb* *syn* see SUCCEED 3
rel bloom, blossom, flower; augment, increase, multiply; amplify, expand; develop, grow, wax
con shrivel, wither; contract, shrink; abate, ebb, subside, wane
ant languish
flourishing *adj* enjoying a vigorous growth <a *flourishing* economy>
syn booming, prospering, prosperous, roaring, robust, thrifty, thriving; *compare* SUCCESSFUL
rel vigorous; rampant, rank; exuberant, lush, luxuriant, profuse
idiom going strong, in full swing
con decadent, declining, deteriorating; failing; decreasing, dwindling
ant languishing
flout *vb* *syn* see SCOFF
rel disregard, slight; repudiate, spurn; insult; defy
idiom thumb one's nose at
con admire, esteem, regard, respect
ant revere
flow *vb* 1 *syn* see POUR 2
rel cascade, jet, spout, spurt; well; course, ripple, run
2 *syn* see SPRING 1
3 *syn* see TEEM
4 *syn* see DISCHARGE 5
flow *n* something suggestive of running water <she expressed herself in a *flow* of words>
syn current, drift, flood, flux, rush, spate, stream, tide
rel progression, sequence, series, succession; continuance, continuation, continuity
flower *n* 1 the often showy part of a seed plant that bears reproductive organs <children picking *flowers* in the meadow>
syn bloom, blossom, posy
rel bud, floret; shoot, spray
2 *syn* see BEST
3 *syn* see ARISTOCRACY
flower *vb* *syn* see BLOSSOM
flowering *n* *syn* see DEVELOPMENT
ant fading
flowery *adj* *syn* see RHETORICAL
rel diffuse, prolix, redundant, verbose, wordy
con compendious, concise, laconic, pithy, succinct, summary, terse
flowing *adj* *syn* see EASY 9
flub *vb* *syn* see BOTCH
fluctuant *adj* 1 *syn* see WEAK 2
2 *syn* see UNCERTAIN 1
flue *n* *syn* see DOWN
fluent *adj* 1 *syn* see VOCAL 3
rel loquacious, talkative; easy, effortless, facile, smooth; apt, prompt, quick, ready
con stammering, stuttering; tongue-tied; dumb; fettered, hampered, trammeled
2 *syn* see EASY 9
fluff *n* 1 *syn* see DOWN
2 *syn* see ERROR 2
fluff *vb* *syn* see BOTCH
fluid *adj* *syn* see CHANGEABLE 1
fluky *adj* *syn* see ACCIDENTAL
flummadiddle *n* *syn* see NONSENSE 2
flummox *vb* *syn* see FAIL 4
flurry *n* *syn* see STIR 1
rel confusion, excitement, turbulence, turmoil; haste, hurry
flurry *vb* *syn* see DISCOMPOSE 1
rel bewilder, distract, perplex; excite, galvanize, provoke, quicken, stimulate
flush *n* 1 *syn* see BLOOM 3
2 *syn* see BLOOM 2
flush *vb* 1 *syn* see BLUSH
2 *syn* see EVEN 1
flush *adj* 1 *syn* see RICH 1
2 *syn* see RUDDY
3 *syn* see LEVEL
flushed *adj* *syn* see RUDDY
fluster *vb* 1 *syn* see DISCOMPOSE 1
rel bewilder, confound, distract, mystify, nonplus, perplex, puzzle; addle, confuse, fuddle, muddle
ant steady

2 syn see CONFUSE 2

flutter *vb* ***syn*** see FLIT 2
rel quaver, quiver, shake, tremble, wobble; beat, palpitate, pulsate, throb; fluctuate, oscillate, swing, vibrate; flap

flux *n* **1** ***syn*** see DIARRHEA
2 ***syn*** see FLOW

flux *vb* ***syn*** see LIQUEFY

fly *vb* **1** to pass lightly or quickly over or above a surface <clouds *flying* across the sky>
syn dart, float, sail, scud, shoot, skim, skirr
rel dance, flicker, flit, flitter, flutter, hover; arise, ascend, mount, rise, soar; glide, slide, slip
2 ***syn*** see RUN 2
rel hide; retreat, withdraw
3 ***syn*** see ESCAPE 1
4 to pass swiftly as if on wings <how time *flies* when we are happy>
syn fleet, flit, sail, sweep, wing
rel soar; hasten, hurry, speed; barrel, skim, whisk, whiz, zip; breeze, dart, dash, rush, tear
idiom go like the wind (*or* lightning), outstrip the wind
con dally, dawdle, dillydally, drift; lag, linger, loiter, trail; crawl, creep, poke
ant drag
5 ***syn*** see HURRY 2

fly–boy *n* ***syn*** see PILOT 2

fly–by–night *adj* ***syn*** see UNRELIABLE 1

flying colors *n pl* ***syn*** see SUCCESS

flyspeck *n* ***syn*** see POINT 11

foam *n* a mass of bubbles gathering in or on the surface of a liquid or something as insubstantial as such a mass <a *foam* of delicate lace at her throat>
syn froth, lather, spume, suds, yeast

fob off *vb* ***syn*** see FOIST 3

focal point *n* ***syn*** see CENTER 2

focus *n* ***syn*** see CENTER 2
idiom center of attraction (*or* interest), focus of attention

focus *vb* **1** ***syn*** see FASTEN 3
2 ***syn*** see CONVERGE
idiom come to a focus

foe *n* ***syn*** see ENEMY
con associate, companion, comrade
ant friend

fog *n* ***syn*** see HAZE 2

fog *vb* **1** ***syn*** see OBSCURE
rel bewilder, distract, mystify, perplex, puzzle
2 ***syn*** see CONFUSE 4
rel addle, muddle

foggy *adj* ***syn*** see HAZY
idiom in a fog

fogram *n* ***syn*** see FOGY

fogy *n* a person who is behind the times or overconservative <his father is an old *fogy*>
syn antediluvian, fogram, fossil, fuddy-duddy, mid-Victorian, moldy fig, mossback, square, stick-in-the-mud
rel conservative, diehard; back number
idiom regular old fogy
ant modern

fogyish *adj* ***syn*** see CONSERVATIVE 1

ant up-to-the-minute

foible *n* ***syn*** see FAULT 2
rel imperfection, shortcoming

foil *vb* ***syn*** see FRUSTRATE 1
rel discomfit, disconcert, embarrass, faze, rattle; curb, restrain

foist *vb* **1** ***syn*** see INSINUATE 3
2 ***syn*** see IMPOSE 4
3 to pass or offer (something spurious) as genuine or worthy <his theory was far more reasonable than many *foisted* on the public>
syn fob off, palm (on *or* upon), palm off, pass off, work off; *compare* IMPOSE 4
rel beguile, deceive, delude, mislead; bamboozle, dupe, gull, hoax, hoodwink, trick; cheat, defraud, overreach, swindle; impose, inflict, wish

fold *n* ***syn*** see WRINKLE

fold *vb* **1** ***syn*** see DOUBLE 2
2 ***syn*** see FAIL 5

fold up *vb* **1** ***syn*** see GIVE 12
2 ***syn*** see RUIN 3

foliage *n* the leaves of plants <a tree with handsome *foliage*>
syn leafage, umbrage, verdure
rel greenness, herbage; growth, vegetation

folk *n* **1** ***syn*** see FAMILY 1
2 folks *pl* ***syn*** see FAMILY 2

folklore *n* ***syn*** see LORE 2

follow *vb* **1** to come after in time <a juggling act *followed* the singer>
syn ensue, succeed, supervene
rel displace, replace, supersede, supplant; postdate
con herald, lead, preface, usher (in); antedate, predate
ant precede
2 to go after or on the track of <*followed* the boys to their hiding place>
syn chase, chivy, pursue, trail; *compare* TAIL
rel trace, track; hunt, search, seek; dog, hound, tag; accompany, attend, convoy; ape, copy, imitate; exercise, practice
con guide, lead, pilot, steer; elude, escape, evade; abandon, desert
ant precede; forsake
3 ***syn*** see OBEY
4 ***syn*** see APPREHEND 1

follower *n* one who attaches himself to another <he is a born *follower*>
syn adherent, cohort, disciple, henchman, partisan, satellite, sectary, sectator, supporter
rel addict, devotee, freak, habitué, votary; admirer, fan, fancier; advocate; bootlicker, hanger-on, lickspittle, parasite, sycophant, toady
ant leader

following *adj* ***syn*** see NEXT

following *n* **1** ***syn*** see ENTOURAGE
2 the body of persons who attach themselves to another especially as disciples, patrons, or ad-

---

syn synonym(s) *rel* related word(s)
ant antonym(s) *con* contrasted word(s)
idiom idiomatic equivalent(s)
|| use limited; if in doubt, see a dictionary

THESAURUS

mirers <he has a strong *following* in this country>
syn audience, clientage, clientele, public

following *prep* ***syn*** see AFTER 2

folly *n* ***syn*** see FOOLISHNESS
rel fatuity, stupidity
ant wisdom

foment *vb* ***syn*** see INCITE
rel goad, spur; cultivate, foster, nurse, nurture
con repress, suppress
ant quell

fomenter *n* ***syn*** see INSTIGATOR

fond *adj* **1** ***syn*** see OPTIMISTIC
2 ***syn*** see LOVING
rel responsive, romantic, sentimental, sympathetic, tender, warm; indulgent
idiom silly over

fondle *vb* ***syn*** see CARESS
rel clasp, embrace, hug; nestle, snuggle

fondness *n* **1** ***syn*** see LOVE 1
2 ***syn*** see APPETITE 3
rel partiality, predilection; relish
con disgust; hate

font name *n* ***syn*** see GIVEN NAME

food *n* **1** things that are edible <conserve a nation's supply of *food*>
syn bread, ‖chow, comestibles, ‖eats, edibles, feed, foodstuff, grub, meat, ‖muckamuck, nurture, provender, provisions, scoff, ‖tuck, viands, victuals, vivres
2 material which feeds and supports the mind or spirit <*food* for thought>
syn aliment, nourishment, nutriment, pabulum, pap, sustenance

foodstuff *n* ***syn*** see FOOD 1

foofaraw *n* ***syn*** see COMMOTION 3

fool *n* **1** a person lacking in judgment or prudence <stop acting like a *fool*>
syn ass, asshead, donkey, doodle, idiot, imbecile, jackass, jerk, madman, mooncalf, nincom, nincompoop, ninny, ninnyhammer, poop, ‖schmo, ‖schmuck, tomfool
rel blockhead, dimwit, dope, dumbbell, dummy, nitwit, numskull, pinhead; birdbrain, featherbrain, featherhead, rattlebrain, scatterbrain; goose, silly
2 a retainer formerly kept to provide casual entertainment <a king's *fool*>
syn idiot, jester, motley
rel buffoon, clown, comedian, comic, merry-andrew
3 one who is victimized or made to appear foolish <she's nobody's *fool*>
syn butt, chump, ‖come-on, ‖cull, dupe, easy mark, fall guy, fish, gudgeon, gull, mark, monkey, ‖mug, patsy, pigeon, sap, saphead, ‖schlemiel, simple, sucker, victim
rel pushover; laughingstock; loser; instrument, tool
4 one who is mentally deficient <a badly retarded child, little more than a *fool*>
syn ament, cretin, ‖feeb, half-wit, idiot, imbecile, moron, natural, simpleton, softhead, underwit, zany

fool *vb* **1** ***syn*** see TRIFLE 1
2 ***syn*** see MEDDLE
3 ***syn*** see BANTER
4 ***syn*** see DUPE

fool (around) *vb* ***syn*** see PHILANDER

fool (away) *vb* ***syn*** see WASTE 2

foolhardy *adj* ***syn*** see ADVENTUROUS
rel headlong, impetuous, precipitate
con calculating, cautious, circumspect; careful, prudent
ant wary

fooling *n* ***syn*** see HORSEPLAY

foolish *adj* **1** ***syn*** see SIMPLE 3
rel idiotic, imbecilic, moronic; daft, feebleminded, half-witted; half-cocked; irrational
con bright, clever, intelligent, quick-witted
ant smart
2 felt to be ridiculous because not exhibiting good or conventional sense <a *foolish* investment>
syn absurd, ‖balmy, cockamamie, crazy, daffy, ‖dilly, ‖dippy, donkeyish, dotty, fantastic, harebrained, idleheaded, insane, kooky, loony, loopy, lunatic, mad, nutty, ‖potty, preposterous, sappy, silly, tomfool, unearthly, wacky, zany
rel laughable, ludicrous, ridiculous; half-baked, headless, jerky, nonsensical; offbeat, unacceptable, unconventional, unorthodox
con judicious, sage, sapient; discreet, foresighted, prudent; canny, shrewd, slick
ant sensible; wise

foolishness *n* the quality or state of being foolish <the *foolishness* of so many of her schemes>
syn absurdity, craziness, dottiness, folly, inanity, insanity, lunacy, preposterousness, senselessness, silliness, witlessness
rel imprudence, indiscretion, injudiciousness, insensibility, unwiseness; irrationality, unreasonableness; impracticality; absurdness, ludicrousness, ridiculousness; bull, bunk, nonsense
con discretion, judiciousness, prudence, sensibility, wiseness; rationality, reasonableness; practicality; soundness; canniness, shrewdness
ant sense, wisdom

foot *n* ***syn*** see BOTTOM 3

foot *vb* ***syn*** see ADD 2

foot (it) *vb* **1** ***syn*** see DANCE 1
2 ***syn*** see WALK 1

footing *n* **1** ***syn*** see BASIS 1
2 ***syn*** see STATUS 1
3 ***syn*** see BASE 1
4 ***syn*** see TERM 5

footlicker *n* ***syn*** see SYCOPHANT

footlights *n pl* ***syn*** see DRAMA

footprint *n* the mark or impression made by a foot <*footprints* in the sand>
syn footstep, spoor, step, track, tract, vestige
rel sign, trace; pug, pugmark

footslog *vb* ***syn*** see PLOD 1

footstep *n* ***syn*** see FOOTPRINT

footstone *n* ***syn*** see TOMBSTONE

foozle *vb* ***syn*** see BOTCH

fop *n* a man who is conspicuously fashionable or elegant in dress or appearance <felt contempt for the mincing overdressed *fop*>

syn Beau Brummel, blood, buck, coxcomb, dandy, dude, exquisite, gallant, lounge lizard, macaroni, petit-maître, popinjay
rel fashion plate, silk stocking; blade, cavalier, man-about-town, spark, sport, swell; ladies' man, lady-killer, masher
idiom man of the world

for *prep* **1** *syn* see TO 5
2 on the side of <I'm *for* Smith all the way>
syn in favor of, pro, with
con anti, contra
ant against
3 *syn* see AFTER 1

for *conj* *syn* see BECAUSE

forage *vb* *syn* see SCOUR 2

forager *n* *syn* see MARAUDER

foray *vb* **1** *syn* see INVADE 1
2 *syn* see RAID 1

foray *n* *syn* see INVASION

forbear *vb* **1** *syn* see FORGO
rel bridle, curb, inhibit, restrain; avoid, escape, evade, shun; cease, desist
2 *syn* see REFRAIN 1
rel bear, endure, suffer, tolerate

forbearance *n* **1** *syn* see PATIENCE
rel restraint, temperance; endurance
2 the quality of being forbearing <she is known for her *forbearance* with children>
syn clemency, indulgence, lenience, leniency, mercifulness, tolerance, toleration; *compare* MERCY
rel longanimity, long-suffering, patience; charity, grace, lenity, mercy
con firmness, inflexibility, rigidity, sternness, strictness; austerity, harshness, inexorability
ant vindictiveness

forbearing *adj* disinclined to be severe or rigorous <*forbearing* toward her husband's weaknesses>
syn charitable, clement, easy, indulgent, lenient, merciful, tolerant
rel gentle, mild; longanimous, long-suffering, patient; considerate, thoughtful
con grim, implacable, merciless, relentless; impatient, nervous, restive; firm, inflexible, rigid, stern, strict; austere, harsh
ant unrelenting

forbid *vb* to debar one from using, doing, or entering or something from being used, done, or entered <smoking is *forbidden* here> <security regulations *forbid* the entry of unauthorized persons>
syn ban, enjoin, inhibit, interdict, outlaw, prohibit, taboo
rel debar, exclude, rule out, shut out; estop, obviate, preclude, prevent; forestall; proscribe, veto; check, curb, halt, restrain, stop; bar, block, hinder, impede, obstruct
con allow, let, suffer; authorize, license; approve, endorse, sanction; command, order; abide, bear, endure, tolerate
ant permit; bid

forbiddance *n* *syn* see TABOO

forbidden *adj* not permitted or allowed <accepting bribes is *forbidden*>
syn banned, prohibited, verboten
ant permitted

force *n* **1** *syn* see POWER 4
rel pressure, strain, stress, tension; headway, impetus, momentum, speed, velocity; vigor
2 *syn* see POINT 3
3 forces *pl* *syn* see TROOP 2
4 the exercise of power in order to impose one's will on a person or to have one's will with a thing <move a huge boulder by main *force*>
syn coercion, compulsion, constraint, duress, violence
rel fierceness, intensity, vehemence; effort, exertions, pains, trouble
con compliance, submission, yielding; impotence, powerlessness, weakness
ant forcelessness

force *vb* **1** *syn* see RAPE
2 to cause a person or thing to yield to pressure <hunger *forced* him to steal the food>
syn coerce, compel, concuss, constrain, make, oblige, shotgun
rel drive, impel, move; command, enjoin, order; demand, exact, require; press, pressure, sandbag; cause, occasion
con blandish, cajole, coax, wheedle; get, induce, persuade, prevail; entice, inveigle, lure, seduce, tempt

force (on *or* upon) *vb* *syn* see INFLICT 2

‖**force** *n* *syn* see WATERFALL

forced *adj* produced or kept up through effort <a *forced* laugh>
syn farfetched, labored, strained
rel coerced, compelled, constrained; artificial, factitious; unnatural; inflexible, rigid, stiff, wooden; exhausting, fatiguing
con easy, effortless, smooth; impulsive, instinctive, spontaneous; artless, natural, normal, unaffected, unsophisticated
ant unforced

forceful *adj* **1** *syn* see POWERFUL 2
rel compelling, constraining; manful, virile; cogent, telling
con decrepit, frail, infirm
ant feeble
2 *syn* see EMPHATIC

forcefully *adv* *syn* see HARD 1

forceless *adj* *syn* see WEAK 4

forcible *adj* *syn* see POWERFUL 2
rel intense, vehement, violent; aggressive, assertive, militant, self-assertive; coercive

forcibly *adv* *syn* see HARD 1

forcing bed *n* *syn* see BREEDING GROUND

forcing house *n* *syn* see BREEDING GROUND

fore *adv* *syn* see BEFORE 1

forebear *n* *syn* see ANCESTOR 1

forebode *vb* *syn* see AUGUR 2

foreboding *n* *syn* see APPREHENSION 3

---

syn synonym(s) *rel* related word(s)
ant antonym(s) *con* contrasted word(s)
idiom idiomatic equivalent(s)
‖ use limited; if in doubt, see a dictionary

rel augury, foretoken, omen, portent, prognostic; forewarning, warning

forecast *vb* ***syn*** see FORETELL
rel conjecture, guess, surmise; conclude, gather, infer

forecast *n* ***syn*** see PREDICTION

forecaster *n* ***syn*** see PROPHET

foredestine *vb* ***syn*** see PREDESTINE 2

forefather *n* ***syn*** see ANCESTOR 1

forefeel *vb* ***syn*** see FORESEE

foregoer *n* ***syn*** see FORERUNNER 2

foregoing *adj* ***syn*** see PRECEDING
ant following

forehandedness *n* ***syn*** see ECONOMY

forehead *n* the part of the face above the eyes <his broad noble *forehead*>
syn brow, frons, front

foreign *adj* **1** ***syn*** see EXOTIC 1
ant native
2 ***syn*** see EXTRINSIC
rel incompatible, incongruous, inconsistent, inconsonant; distasteful, obnoxious, repellent, repugnant; accidental, adventitious
con applicable, apposite, apropos, material, pertinent, relevant; akin, alike, uniform
ant germane
3 ***syn*** see IRRELEVANT

foreigner *n* ***syn*** see STRANGER

foreknow *vb* ***syn*** see FORESEE
rel conclude, gather, infer

foreland *n* ***syn*** see PROMONTORY

foremost *adj* **1** ***syn*** see FIRST 1
2 ***syn*** see FIRST 3

forename *n* ***syn*** see GIVEN NAME

forenoon *n* ***syn*** see MORNING 2

forensic *n* ***syn*** see ARGUMENTATION

foreordain *vb* **1** ***syn*** see PREDESTINE 1
2 ***syn*** see PREDESTINE 2

forerun *vb* **1** ***syn*** see PRECEDE 2
2 ***syn*** see ANNOUNCE 2

forerunner *n* **1** one that goes before and in some way announces the coming of another <a coma is often a *forerunner* of death>
syn harbinger, herald, outrider, precursor
rel anticipator; advertiser, announcer; advertisement, announcement, augury, foretoken, omen, portent, presage, prognostic; forewarning, warning; mark, sign, symptom, token; foreshadow
2 one belonging to an early developmental period of something contemporary or fully developed <the water-driven dynamo that was a *forerunner* of present-day giant atomic power plants>
syn ancestor, antecedent, antecessor, foregoer, precursor, predecessor, prototype
rel example, exemplar, model, pattern; pioneer; author, initiator, originator
con consequence, result; effect, event, issue, outgrowth; conclusion, consummation, culmination
ant end product

foresee *vb* to know or expect in advance that something will happen or come into existence or be made manifest <he had not *foreseen* his present problems>
syn anticipate, apprehend, divine, forefeel, foreknow, preknow, previse, prevision, see, visualize
rel forebode, forecast, foretell, predict, presage, prognosticate, prophesy; descry, discern, espy, perceive
idiom look for, look forward to

foreseer *n* ***syn*** see PROPHET

foreshadow *vb* **1** ***syn*** see ADUMBRATE 1
2 ***syn*** see AUGUR 2

foreshow *vb* **1** ***syn*** see AUGUR 2
2 ***syn*** see ANNOUNCE 2

foresight *n* ***syn*** see PRUDENCE
rel clairvoyance, discernment, perception
ant hindsight

forest *n* a heavily wooded area
syn timber, timberland, weald, wood(s), woodland
rel coppice, copse, grove, thicket; wildwood, woodlot
con field, meadow, plain, prairie

forestall *vb* **1** ***syn*** see PREVENT 2
con court, invite, woo; advance, forward, further, promote
2 ***syn*** see PREVENT 1

foretell *vb* to tell something before it happens through or as if through special knowledge or occult power <the prophet *foretold* the fall of the city>
syn adumbrate, augur, call, forecast, portend, predict, presage, prognosticate, prophesy, soothsay, vaticinate
rel anticipate, apprehend, divine, foreknow, foresee; announce, declare, proclaim; disclose, divulge, reveal; forewarn, warn; bode, forebode, foreshadow, foreshow, foretoken, promise; prefigure

foreteller *n* ***syn*** see PROPHET

foretelling *n* ***syn*** see PREDICTION

forethink *vb* ***syn*** see PREMEDITATE

forethought *n* ***syn*** see PRUDENCE 1
rel deliberation, premeditation; gumption, judgment, sense
ant rashness; impetuosity

foretime *n* ***syn*** see PAST

foretoken *n* something that serves as a sign of future happenings <they felt that her new job was a *foretoken* of good fortune>
syn augury, bodement, boding, omen, portent, presage, prognostic
rel badge, indication, mark, note, sign, symptom, token; forerunner, harbinger, herald, precursor; forewarning, shadow, warning; intimation, promise; ostent; hint, inkling, suggestion

foretoken *vb* ***syn*** see AUGUR 2

forever *adv* ***syn*** see EVER 2

forevermore *adv* ***syn*** see EVER 2

forewarn *vb* ***syn*** see WARN 1

forewarning *n* ***syn*** see WARNING

foreword *n* ***syn*** see INTRODUCTION

forfeit *n* ***syn*** see FINE

forfeit *vb* ***syn*** see LOSE 1

forfend *vb* ***syn*** see PREVENT 2

forgather *vb* ***syn*** see GATHER 6

forge *vb* ***syn*** see MAKE 3
rel beat, pound, turn out; copy, imitate

forget *vb* **1** to lose the remembrance of <I soon *forgot* his name>
syn disremember, ||misremember, unknow
rel misrecollect; blow up, fluff; unlearn
idiom clean forget, draw a blank
con recall, recollect
ant remember
2 ***syn*** see NEGLECT
con bethink, mind, recall, recollect
ant remember

forgetful *adj* tending to lose or let go from one's mind something once known or learned <she is growing *forgetful*>
syn oblivious, unmindful, unwitting
rel lax, neglectful, negligent, remiss, slack; careless, heedless, thoughtless; absent, absent-minded, abstracted, bemused
con alert, alive, awake, aware, cognizant, conscious, sensible; attentive, considerate, thoughtful

forgetfulness *n* ***syn*** see OBLIVION

forgivable *adj* ***syn*** see VENIAL

forgive *vb* ***syn*** see EXCUSE 1
idiom forgive and forget

forgo *vb* to deny oneself something for the sake of an end <he vowed to *forgo* all luxuries until the debt was paid>
syn eschew, forbear, sacrifice
rel abandon, relinquish, surrender, waive; abdicate, renounce, resign; forsake, give up

fork (out) *vb* ***syn*** see SPEND 1

forlorn *adj* **1** dejected and saddened especially by reason of being alone <a *forlorn* lost child>
syn lonely, lonesome, lorn
rel abandoned, deserted, desolate, forgotten, forsaken; miserable, wretched; friendless, homeless; defenseless, helpless; depressed, oppressed, weighed down; alone, solitary
2 ***syn*** see DESPONDENT
rel cynical, pessimistic; fruitless, futile, vain
con hopeful, optimistic, roseate, rose-colored

form *n* **1** outward appearance of something as distinguished from the substance of which it is made <the carefully graded *form* of the curves>
syn cast, configuration, conformation, figure, shape
rel contour, outline, profile, silhouette; anatomy, framework, skeleton, structure; economy, organism, scheme, system
2 conduct regulated by an external control (as custom or a formal protocol of procedure) <observing the *forms* of polite society>
syn ceremonial, ceremony, formality, liturgy, rite, ritual
rel procedure, proceeding, process; custom, habit, practice, usage; canon, law, precept, regulation, rule; method, mode; decorum, etiquette, propriety
3 a fixed or accepted way of doing or sometimes of expressing something <good *form* in swimming>
syn convenance, convention, usage
rel fashion, manner, mode, style, way

form *vb* **1** ***syn*** see MAKE 3
rel devise; create, invent; turn out; design, plan, plot, project, scheme; establish, found, organize
con demolish, destroy, ruin, wreck
2 ***syn*** see DEVELOP 4
3 ***syn*** see CONSTITUTE 1

formal *adj* **1** ***syn*** see CEREMONIAL
rel methodical, orderly, regular, systematic; decorous, proper, seemly; prim, unbending; distant, reserved
ant informal
2 ***syn*** see NOMINAL

formality *n* **1** ***syn*** see FORM 2
rel convenance, convention
ant informality
2 ***syn*** see RITE 2

formation *n* ***syn*** see MAKEUP 1

former *adj* **1** ***syn*** see PRECEDING
con following, succeeding, supervening
ant latter
2 having been such at some previous time <*former* friends>
syn bygone, erstwhile, late, old, once, onetime, past, quondam, sometime, whilom
con current, present; future, prospective

formerly *adv* ***syn*** see BEFORE 2

formidable *adj* **1** ***syn*** see FEARFUL 3
ant comforting
2 ***syn*** see HARD 6
ant simple

formless *adj* having no definite or recognizable form <a *formless* fear>
syn amorphous, inchoate, shapeless, unformed, unshaped
rel chaotic, orderless, unordered, unorganized; indistinct, obscure, unclear, vague; indefinite, indeterminate, undefined; crude, raw, rough, rude
con distinct, formed; definite, explicit, express, specific; ordered, organized

formulate *vb* **1** ***syn*** see WORD
2 ***syn*** see CONTRIVE 2
3 ***syn*** see DRAFT 3

||**fornent** *prep* ***syn*** see BESIDE 1

for real *adv* ***syn*** see SERIOUSLY 1

forsake *vb* ***syn*** see ABANDON 1
rel spurn; leave; abdicate, resign
ant return (to), revert (to)

forsaken *adj* ***syn*** see DERELICT 1

forswear *vb* **1** ***syn*** see ABJURE
2 ***syn*** see PERJURE

fort *n* a structure or place offering resistance to a hostile force <settlers fled to the *fort*>
syn citadel, fastness, fortress, redoubt, stronghold

forte *n* that in which one excels <writing is her strongest *forte*>

---

syn synonym(s) ***rel*** related word(s)
ant antonym(s) ***con*** contrasted word(s)
idiom idiomatic equivalent(s)
|| use limited; if in doubt, see a dictionary

syn eminency, long suit, medium, métier, oyster, strong suit
rel ableness, effectiveness, efficiency; ability, competence; bag, thing
idiom cup of tea, dish of tea, strong point
con inadequacy, incapability, incompetence, inefficiency; greenness, rawness

forth *adv* **1** ***syn*** see AHEAD 2
2 ***syn*** see ALONG 1

forthcome *vb* ***syn*** see LOOM 2

forthcoming *adj* being soon to appear or take place <the *forthcoming* holidays>
syn approaching, coming, nearing, oncoming, upcoming
rel future; imminent, impending, pending; anticipated, awaited, expected
con distant, far-off, remote; bygone, former, gone, gone-by, past

forthright *adj* **1** ***syn*** see STRAIGHTFORWARD 2
con covert, secret, stealthy, surreptitious, underhand; deceitful, mendacious, untruthful
ant furtive
2 ***syn*** see FRANK

forthwith *adv* **1** ***syn*** see AWAY 3
2 ***syn*** see SHORT 1

fortify *vb* **1** ***syn*** see STRENGTHEN 2
rel arouse, rally, rouse, stir; refresh, renew, restore
con dilute, thin
ant enfeeble
2 ***syn*** see GIRD 3

fortitude *n* a quality of character combining courage and staying power <she bore up under all her problems with admirable *fortitude*>
syn backbone, grit, guts, intestinal fortitude, ‖moxie, nerve, sand, spunk; *compare* COURAGE
rel courage, mettle, pith, resoluteness, resolution, spirit, stick-to-itiveness, tenacity; boldness, bravery, courageousness, dauntlessness, fearlessness, intrepidity, valiancy, valor, valorousness; endurance, stamina, strength; constancy, determination, perseverance; bottom
con cowardliness, fearfulness, timidity, timorousness; faintheartedness, milksoppiness, weakness; cowardice, yellowness
ant pusillanimity

fortress *n* ***syn*** see FORT

fortuitous *adj* ***syn*** see ACCIDENTAL
con activated, actuated, motivated; projected, schemed
ant deliberate

fortuitously *adv* ***syn*** see INCIDENTALLY 1
ant deliberately

fortuity *n* ***syn*** see ACCIDENT 1
ant deliberation

fortunate *adj* **1** ***syn*** see FAVORABLE 5
ant disastrous
2 ***syn*** see LUCKY
ant unfortunate

fortunately *adv* ***syn*** see WELL 5

fortunateness *n* ***syn*** see LUCK 3
ant unfortunateness

fortune *n* **1** ***syn*** see CHANCE 2
rel destiny, doom, portion
con design, intent, intention
2 ***syn*** see LUCK 3
ant misfortune
3 ***syn*** see WEALTH 2
4 a very large amount of money <those furs must have cost a *fortune*>
syn ‖bomb, boodle, bundle, mint, packet, pile, pot, ‖roll, wad
idiom king's ransom, pretty penny, tidy sum

fortuneless *adj* ***syn*** see POOR 1

forty winks *n pl but sing or pl in constr* ***syn*** see NAP

forward *adj* **1** ***syn*** see PRESUMPTUOUS
2 ***syn*** see WISE 5
ant bashful
3 ***syn*** see PRECOCIOUS
con regressive, retrograde, retrogressive
ant backward

forward *adv* **1** ***syn*** see BEFORE 1
2 ***syn*** see AHEAD 2
ant backward
3 ***syn*** see ALONG 1

forward *vb* **1** ***syn*** see ADVANCE 1
rel back, champion, support, uphold
con baffle, circumvent, foil, frustrate, outwit, thwart
ant balk
2 ***syn*** see SEND 1

fossil *n* ***syn*** see FOGY

foster *vb* **1** ***syn*** see NURSE 2
rel back, champion, support, uphold; entertain, harbor, house, lodge, shelter; accommodate, assist, favor, help, oblige
con combat, fight, oppose, resist, withstand; curb, inhibit, restrain; ban, forbid, interdict, prohibit; abuse, disregard, neglect
2 ***syn*** see ADVANCE 1

foul *adj* **1** ***syn*** see OFFENSIVE
2 ***syn*** see DIRTY 1
rel fetid, malodorous, noisome, putrid, stinking; loathsome, offensive, repulsive, revolting
ant fair; undefiled
3 ***syn*** see OBSCENE 2

foul *vb* **1** ***syn*** see SOIL 2
rel contaminate, defile, pollute; desecrate, profane
2 ***syn*** see CONTAMINATE 2

foul play *n* ***syn*** see MURDER

foul up *vb* ***syn*** see CONFUSE 5

found *vb* **1** ***syn*** see BASE
rel support, sustain; erect, raise, rear
2 to set going or to bring into existence <*founded* a new school for graduate studies>
syn constitute, create, establish, institute, organize, set up, start
rel begin, commence, inaugurate, initiate; fashion, form
con close, conclude, end, finish, terminate; arrest, check, halt, stay, stop

foundation *n* **1** ***syn*** see BASIS 1
2 ***syn*** see BASIS 3
3 ***syn*** see BASE 1

foundational *adj* ***syn*** see FUNDAMENTAL 1

foundationless *adj* ***syn*** see BASELESS

founder *n* ***syn*** see FATHER 2

founder *vb* ***syn*** see SINK 1
fount *n* ***syn*** see SOURCE
fountain *n* ***syn*** see SOURCE
fountainhead *n* ***syn*** see SOURCE
four *n* ***syn*** see QUARTET
fourberie *n* ***syn*** see DECEPTION 1
four–flush *vb* ***syn*** see DECEIVE
foursome *n* ***syn*** see QUARTET
foursquare *adj* ***syn*** see SQUARE 1
fourth *n* ***syn*** see QUARTER 1
foxiness *n* ***syn*** see CUNNING 2
foxy *adj* **1** ***syn*** see SLY 2
rel deceitful, dishonest
con aboveboard, forthright, straightforward
2 ***syn*** see BEAUTIFUL
foyer *n* ***syn*** see VESTIBULE
fracas *n* **1** ***syn*** see QUARREL
2 ***syn*** see BRAWL 2
fractional *adj* ***syn*** see INCOMPLETE 1
fractious *adj* **1** ***syn*** see UNRULY 1
ant orderly
2 ***syn*** see IRRITABLE
ant peaceable
fracturable *adj* ***syn*** see FRAGILE 1
fracture *n* ***syn*** see BREACH 3
fragile *adj* **1** easily broken <a *fragile* dish of the finest porcelain>
syn breakable, delicate, fracturable, frail, frangible, shatterable, shattery
rel brittle, crisp, crumbly, crunchy, friable, short
con infrangible, unbreakable; elastic, flexible, resilient; stout, strong, sturdy, tenacious
ant tough
2 ***syn*** see WEAK 1
ant durable
fragment *n* **1** ***syn*** see PARTICLE
2 ***syn*** see END 4
fragment *vb* ***syn*** see SHATTER 1
fragmentary *adj* ***syn*** see INCOMPLETE 1
fragrance *n* a sweet or pleasant odor <the *fragrance* of flowers>
syn aroma, balm, bouquet, incense, perfume, redolence, scent, spice
rel odor, smell
con fetidness, fetor, malodor, noisomeness, rancidness, rankness
ant stench, stink
fragrant *adj* ***syn*** see SWEET 2
rel delectable, delicious, delightful
ant fetid
frail *adj* **1** ***syn*** see WEAK 1
rel slender, slight, slim, tenuous, thin; petty, puny
con hale, healthy, sound
ant robust
2 ***syn*** see FRAGILE 1
con solid, substantial
frailty *n* ***syn*** see FAULT 2
frame *vb* **1** ***syn*** see CONTRIVE 2
2 ***syn*** see DRAFT 3
3 ***syn*** see MAKE 3
framework *n* ***syn*** see STRUCTURE 3
franchise *n* ***syn*** see SUFFRAGE
franchise *vb* ***syn*** see ENFRANCHISE
frangible *adj* ***syn*** see FRAGILE 1
frank *adj* marked by free, forthright, and sincere expression <a *frank* answer>
syn candid, direct, forthright, man-to-man, open, openhearted, plain, plainspoken, single, single-eyed, single-hearted, single-minded, straightforward, unconcealed, undisguised, undissembled, undissembling, unmannered, unreserved, unvarnished; *compare* COMMUNICATIVE, STRAIGHTFORWARD 2
rel ingenuous, naive, natural, simple, unsophisticated; bluff, blunt; heart-to-heart, sincere; honest, scrupulous, upright; dispassionate, fair, impartial, just, unbiased; barefaced, brazen, outspoken, uninhibited
con reserved, reticent, secretive, silent, taciturn, uncommunicative; covert, furtive, secret, sneaking, underhand; deceitful, deceptive, dishonest, evasive, false, lying, mendacious, tricky, untruthful; insincere
ant reticent
frank *n* ***syn*** see FRANKFURTER
frankfurter *n* a seasoned beef or beef and pork sausage <baked beans served with the obligatory *frankfurters*>
syn dog, frank, hot dog, wiener, wienerwurst, ‖wienie
frantic *adj* ***syn*** see FURIOUS 2
frantically *adv* ***syn*** see HARD 2
fraternity *n* ***syn*** see ASSOCIATION 2
fraud *n* **1** ***syn*** see DECEPTION 1
2 ***syn*** see IMPOSTURE
rel bamboozlement, bamboozling, dupery, duping, hoodwinking
3 ***syn*** see IMPOSTOR
fray *n* **1** ***syn*** see BRAWL 2
rel contention, discord, dissension, strife
2 ***syn*** see CLASH 2
frayed *adj* ***syn*** see RAGGED
frazzle *vb* ***syn*** see EXHAUST 4
frazzled *adj* ***syn*** see RAGGED
freak *n* **1** ***syn*** see CAPRICE
2 one that is physically abnormal <pitiful *freaks* displayed in sideshows>
syn abortion, lusus, miscreation, monster, monstrosity
rel aberration, chimera, malconformation, malformation, misshape, mosaic, mutation, sport; abnormality, anomaly, curiosity, oddity; rara avis, rarity; androgyne, hermaphrodite
idiom freak of nature
3 ***syn*** see ENTHUSIAST
freakish *adj* ***syn*** see ARBITRARY 1
freckle *vb* ***syn*** see SPECKLE 1
free *adj* **1** not subject to the rule or control of another <a *free* country>
syn autarchic, autarkic, autonomous, independent, separate, sovereign

---

syn synonym(s) ***rel*** related word(s)
ant antonym(s) ***con*** contrasted word(s)
idiom idiomatic equivalent(s)
‖ use limited; if in doubt, see a dictionary

rel free-born, unenslaved; delivered, emancipated, enfranchised, freed, liberated, released; democratic, self-directing, self-governing, self-ruling; sui juris; individualistic, unregimented
con coerced, compelled, constrained, forced, obliged; dependent, restricted, subject; inferior, subordinate, subservient; captive, enslaved, enthralled, subjugated
ant bond
2 not bound, confined, or detained by force <the prisoner was now *free*>
syn loose, unconfined, unrestrained
rel unbound, unchained, unfettered, unshackled, untied; clear, loose, scot-free; emancipated, freed, liberated; independent
idiom at liberty, free as a bird, free as air, free to come and go
con confined, restrained; impounded, imprisoned, incarcerated, interned, jailed; bound, chained, fettered, shackled, tied
3 *syn* see LIBERAL 1
ant close
4 *syn* see OUTSPOKEN
5 not costing or charging anything <a *free* public school>
syn chargeless, complimentary, costless, gratis, gratuitous
rel unpaid, unrecompensed, unremunerated
idiom for free, for love, for nothing, on the cuff, on the house
con charged, paid; costly, dear, expensive, high, high priced
6 not having the affections fixed on a particular object <she was happy to be *free* and in no hurry to fall in love again>
syn fancy-free, heart-whole

free *vb* to relieve from constraint or restraint <*free* an oppressed people>
syn discharge, disenthrall, disimprison, emancipate, liberate, loose, loosen, manumit, redeem, release, ‖spring, unbind, unchain, unshackle
rel clear, detach, disencumber, disengage, disentangle, extricate; deliver, ransom, redeem, rescue; affranchise, enfranchise
idiom cut loose
con fetter, hamper, hog-tie, manacle, shackle, trammel; immure, imprison, incarcerate, intern, jail; circumscribe, confine, limit, restrict; curb, inhibit, restrain; enslave, enthrall, subjugate

freebooter *n* **1** *syn* see MARAUDER
2 *syn* see PIRATE

freedom *n* the power or condition of acting without compulsion <*freedom* of the press>
syn liberty, license
rel exemption, immunity; prerogative, privilege, right; compass, latitude, scope, sweep
con coercion, compulsion, constraint; restraint
ant necessity

free–for–all *n syn* see BRAWL 2

free hand *n syn* see CARTE BLANCHE

freehanded *adj syn* see LIBERAL 1

freeloader *n syn* see PARASITE

freely *adv* EASILY 1, effortlessly, facilely, lightly, readily, smoothly, well

free–minded *adj syn* see HAPPY-GO-LUCKY

free–spoken *adj syn* see OUTSPOKEN

freezer *n syn* see JAIL

freezing *adj syn* see COLD 1
ant scorching

freight *n syn* see LOAD 1

frenetic *adj syn* see FURIOUS 2

frenzied *adj syn* see FURIOUS 2

frenziedly *adv syn* see HARD 2

frenzy *n syn* see DELIRIUM

frenzy *vb syn* see MADDEN 1

frequent *adj syn* see COMMON 4
ant infrequent, rare

frequent *vb* to go to or be in often <he *frequents* the bar down the street>
syn affect, hang around, hang out, haunt, resort
rel attend, go (to), visit; infest, overrun
con avoid, miss, sidestep
ant shun

frequenter *n syn* see HABITUÉ 1

frequently *adv* **1** *syn* see OFTEN
ant infrequently
2 *syn* see USUALLY 2

fresh *adj* **1** *syn* see NEW 1
rel gleaming, glistening, sparkling; striking, vital, vivid; virginal, youthful; crude, green, raw, uncouth; artless, naive, natural, unsophisticated
con hackneyed, shopworn, stereotyped, threadbare, trite
ant stale
2 *syn* see ADDITIONAL
3 *syn* see INEXPERIENCED
4 *syn* see WISE 5

freshman *n syn* see NOVICE

freshness *n syn* see INEXPERIENCE

fret *vb* **1** *syn* see WORRY 3
rel chafe, fume; brood, mope
idiom eat one's heart out
2 *syn* see ANNOY 1
3 *syn* see CHAFE 3
4 *syn* see RIPPLE

fretful *adj* **1** *syn* see IRRITABLE
rel captious, carping, caviling, critical, faultfinding; contrary, perverse
con forbearing, long-suffering, patient, resigned; subdued, submissive, tame
2 *syn* see IMPATIENT 1

friable *adj syn* see SHORT 6

fribble *adj syn* see GIDDY 1

fribbling *adj syn* see GIDDY 1

fried *adj syn* see INTOXICATED 1

friend *n* a person with whom one is on good and, usually, familiar terms <he is one of my closest *friends*>
syn acquaintance, amigo, cater-cousin, confidant, familiar, intimate, mate; *compare* ASSOCIATE 3
rel alter ego, best friend, bosom friend; ally, colleague, partner; nodding acquaintance
con enemy; adversary, antagonist, opponent; competitor, rival
ant foe

friendliness *n syn* see GOODWILL 1
rel affability, amiability, congeniality, cordiality, neighborliness, sociability

ant unfriendliness
friendly *adj* **1** *syn* see AMICABLE 1
rel close, familiar, intimate; affectionate, devoted, loving
ant unfriendly; belligerent
2 *syn* see HARMONIOUS 3
3 *syn* see SYMPATHETIC 2
ant unfriendly
friendship *n* *syn* see GOODWILL 1
rel affinity, attraction; empathy; accord, concord, consonance, harmony; alliance, coalition, federation, fusion, league
con antagonism, antipathy, hostility, rancor; hate
ant animosity
fright *n* **1** *syn* see FEAR 1
2 *syn* see EYESORE
fright *vb* *syn* see FRIGHTEN
frighten *vb* to strike or to fill with fear or dread <the puppy was *frightened* by the unfamiliar noises>
syn affright, alarm, awe, fright, scare, ‖spook, startle, terrify, terrorize
rel appall, astound, daunt, disconcert, dismay, faze, horrify, shock; demoralize, unman, unnerve; browbeat, bulldoze, cow, intimidate; agitate, discompose, disquiet, perturb, upset
idiom curdle the blood, curl the hair, freeze the blood, frighten one out of one's wits, give one a scare, give one a turn, make one's blood run cold, make one's flesh creep, make one's hair stand on end, make one's teeth chatter, make one tremble, put one's heart in one's mouth, scare hell out of, scare one spitless, scare one stiff, scare the life out of, scare the pants off of, scare to death, strike terror into, take one's breath away
con embolden, encourage, hearten, reassure
frightened *adj* *syn* see AFRAID 1
idiom in a fright
ant unfrightened
frightful *adj* *syn* see FEARFUL 3
frigid *adj* **1** *syn* see COLD 1
2 *syn* see COLD 2
3 free from or deficient in passion <claimed his wife was a *frigid* woman>
syn cold, inhibited, passionless, undersexed, unresponsive
idiom as cold as an iceberg
con affectionate, demanding, loving
ant ardent; amorous
frill *n* *syn* see LUXURY
fringe *n* *syn* see BORDER 1
fringe *vb* *syn* see BORDER 1
frippery *n* *syn* see FINERY
frisk *vb* **1** *syn* see GAMBOL
2 *syn* see SEARCH 2
frisky *adj* *syn* see PLAYFUL 1
fritter *vb* *syn* see WASTE 2
frivol away *vb* *syn* see WASTE 2
frivolity *n* *syn* see LIGHTNESS
rel coquetting, dallying, flirting, toying, trifling; fun, game, jest, play, sport
ant seriousness; staidness
frivolous *adj* *syn* see GIDDY 1
rel shallow, superficial, unprofound; gay, light, playful
ant serious
‖**frogskin** *n* *syn* see DOLLAR
frolic *vb* **1** *syn* see REVEL 1
2 *syn* see GAMBOL
frolic *n* *syn* see PRANK
frolicsome *adj* **1** *syn* see ANTIC 2
2 *syn* see PLAYFUL 1
from *prep* **1** *syn* see AFTER 1
2 in the face of <protect them *from* exploitation>
syn against
frondeur *n* *syn* see REBEL
frons *n* *syn* see FOREHEAD
front *n* **1** *syn* see FOREHEAD
2 *syn* see MASK 2
3 a person, group, or thing used to mask the identity or true character of a controlling agent <the export company was a *front* for illegal activities>
syn blind
rel disguise, facade, mask
front *vb* **1** *syn* see FACE 1
2 *syn* see FACE 3
3 *syn* see MEET 6
4 *syn* see ACCOST 2
frontier *n* **1** a region between two countries <lived on the *frontier* between Mexico and the U.S.>
syn border, borderland, march, marchland
2 a rural region that forms the margin of settled or developed territory <settlers found living on the *frontier* was a hard life>
syn backcountry, backland, ‖backveld, backwash, backwater, backwoods, ‖boondocks, ‖boonies, bush, hinterland, ‖outback, sticks, up-country
idiom the back of beyond
frontier *adj* *syn* see BACK 1
fronting *prep* *syn* see AGAINST 1
front-rank *adj* *syn* see EXCELLENT
frore *adj* *syn* see COLD 1
frosty *adj* *syn* see COLD 1
froth *n* *syn* see FOAM
rel flippancy, frivolity, levity, lightness
froward *adj* *syn* see CONTRARY 3
frown *vb* **1** to put on a dark or malignant countenance or aspect <he *frowned* at the naughty child>
syn gloom, glower, lower, scowl
rel glare; grimace; pout, sulk
idiom look black, look daggers
con grin, laugh
ant smile
2 *syn* see DISAPPROVE 1
frowsy *adj* **1** *syn* see SLATTERNLY
rel lax, neglectful, negligent, remiss, slack
ant trim; smart

---

syn synonym(s) *rel* related word(s)
ant antonym(s) *con* contrasted word(s)
idiom idiomatic equivalent(s)
‖ use limited; if in doubt, see a dictionary

2 ***syn*** see MALODOROUS 1
frugal *adj* ***syn*** see SPARING
rel careful, meticulous; discreet, prudent; conserving, preserving; cheeseparing, penny-pinching, scrimping, stinting
ant wasteful
frugality *n* ***syn*** see ECONOMY
‖**fruit** *n* ***syn*** see HOMOSEXUAL
fruitage *n* ***syn*** see HARVEST 2
fruitful *adj* ***syn*** see FERTILE
rel breeding, propagating, reproducing; abounding
con abortive, bootless, futile, vain
ant unfruitful; fruitless
fruitfulness *n* ***syn*** see FERTILITY
fruition *n* ***syn*** see PLEASURE 2
rel actualization, materialization, realization; accomplishment, fulfillment; achievement, attainment
fruitless *adj* ***syn*** see FUTILE
rel barren, infertile, sterile, unfruitful; foiled, frustrated, thwarted; infructuous, unprofitable
con fecund, fertile, prolific
ant fruitful
‖**fruity** *adj* ***syn*** see INSANE 1
frumpish *adj* ***syn*** see TACKY 2
frumpy *adj* ***syn*** see TACKY 2
frustrate *vb* **1** to come between a person and his aim or desire or to defeat another's plan <my efforts are *frustrated* at every turn>
syn baffle, balk, beat, bilk, buffalo, circumvent, dash, disappoint, foil, ruin, thwart; *compare* OUTWIT
rel annul, cancel, counteract, negative, neutralize, nullify; anticipate, forestall; conquer, defeat, lick, overcome; forbid, inhibit, prohibit; obviate, preclude, prevent; bar, block, hinder, impede, obstruct; arrest, check, halt, interrupt
idiom cut the ground from under one, dash one's hope, defeat expectation, throw a monkey wrench into the works, upset one's applecart
con accomplish, achieve, bring about, effect, perform; advance, forward, further, promote; abet, foment, incite, instigate
ant fulfill
2 ***syn*** see NEUTRALIZE
frying pan *n* a pan with a handle used for frying food <some still prefer the sturdy cast-iron *frying pan*>
syn skillet, spider
fuddle *vb* ***syn*** see CONFUSE 2
ant clarify, clear
fuddler *n* ***syn*** see DRUNKARD
fuddy-duddy *n* **1** ***syn*** see FOGY
2 ***syn*** see STUFFED SHIRT
3 ***syn*** see FUSSBUDGET
fudge *vb* ***syn*** see EMBROIDER
fudge *n* ***syn*** see NONSENSE 2
fugacious *adj* ***syn*** see TRANSIENT
fugitive *adj* ***syn*** see TRANSIENT
fugitive *n* ***syn*** see REFUGEE
fulfill *vb* **1** to do what is required by the terms of so as to make effective <found themselves unable to *fulfill* their contract>
syn complete, execute, implement, perform; *compare* EFFECT 2
rel effect, effectuate; discharge
2 ***syn*** see SATISFY 5
fulgent *adj* ***syn*** see BRIGHT 1
full *adj* **1** containing as much as is possible <the hamper is *full*>
syn awash, big, block and block, brimful, brimming, bung-full, chockablock, chock-full, cram-full, crammed, crowded, jam-full, jammed, jam-packed, loaded, packed, ‖packed out, replete, stuffed, ‖trig
rel abounding, teeming
idiom full to bursting (*or* overflowing), ready to burst
con blank, vacant, void; bare, barren
ant empty
2 ***syn*** see CIRCUMSTANTIAL
ant incomplete
3 ***syn*** see WHOLE 2
con denuded, dismantled, divested, stripped
4 ***syn*** see SATIATED
full-blooded *adj* **1** ***syn*** see PUREBRED
2 ***syn*** see RUDDY
full-blown *adj* **1** ***syn*** see MATURE 1
2 ***syn*** see TOTAL 5
full-bodied *adj* ***syn*** see STRONG 3
full-bosomed *adj* ***syn*** see BUXOM
full dress *n* ***syn*** see FINERY
full-dress *adj* ***syn*** see EXHAUSTIVE
full-fledged *adj* ***syn*** see MATURE 1
full-grown *adj* ***syn*** see MATURE 1
full-mouthed *adj* ***syn*** see LOUD 1
fullness *n* ***syn*** see BREADTH 2
full-out *adj* ***syn*** see TOTAL 5
full-scale *adj* ***syn*** see TOTAL 5
full tilt *adv* ***syn*** see FAST 2
fully *adv* **1** ***syn*** see DOWN 2
2 ***syn*** see WELL 3
fulsome *adj* too obviously extravagant or ingratiating to be accepted as genuine or sincere <offering sickeningly *fulsome* praise>
syn oily, oleaginous, slick, smarmy, soapy, unctious, unctuous
rel canting, holier-than-thou, hypocritical, pecksniffian, pharisaical, sanctimonious; bland, glib, honey-mouthed, honey-tongued, ingratiating, mealy-mouthed, oily-tongued, smooth, smooth-tongued, suave; buttery, flattering, wheedling; excessive, extravagant, exuberant, lavish, profuse; cloying, satiating, sating; bombastic, grandiloquent, magniloquent
con earnest, genuine, heartfelt, hearty, sincere, true, truthful, unfeigned, wholehearted, whole-souled
fumble *vb* **1** ***syn*** see GROPE
2 ***syn*** see BOTCH
rel flounder, stumble
3 ***syn*** see MUMBLE
fume *n* ***syn*** see SNIT
fume *vb* ***syn*** see ANGER 2
fun *vb* ***syn*** see BANTER
fun *n* **1** action or speech intended to amuse or arouse laughter <you know he only said it in *fun*>

syn game, jest, joke, play, sport
rel amusement, diversion, entertainment, recreation; blitheness; jocundity, joviality, merriment; glee, hilarity, jollity, mirth; mischief, teasing
con soberness, thoughtfulness
ant earnestness, seriousness
2 ***syn*** see PLAY 1

function *n* **1** the acts or operations expected of a person or thing <fulfill one's *function* as a mother>
syn business, duty, office, province, role
rel affair, concern; job, task, work
2 ***syn*** see USE 4
3 ***syn*** see POWER 3
rel action, behavior, operation

function *vb* **1** ***syn*** see ACT 4
2 ***syn*** see ACT 5
3 to operate in the proper or expected manner <finally succeeded in getting the motor to *function*>
syn act, go, run, work
rel do, operate, perform

functional *adj* ***syn*** see PRACTICAL 2
functioning *adj* ***syn*** see ACTIVE 1
fund *n* ***syn*** see SUPPLY
fund *vb* ***syn*** see ENDOW 2
fundament *n* ***syn*** see BUTTOCKS

fundamental *adj* **1** forming or affecting the groundwork, roots, or lowest part of something <the *fundamental* rules of poetry>
syn basal, basic, bottom, foundational, meat-and-potatoes, primary, radical, underlying
rel primal, prime, primordial; elemental, elementary
con incidental
2 ***syn*** see ELEMENTAL 1
3 ***syn*** see ESSENTIAL 2
rel indispensable, necessary, needful, requisite; dominant, paramount

fundamental *n* **1** ***syn*** see PRINCIPLE 1
rel component, constituent, element, factor
2 ***syn*** see ESSENTIAL 1
3 *usu* **fundamentals** *pl* ***syn*** see ALPHABET 2

fundamentalist *n* ***syn*** see DIEHARD 1
fundamentally *adv* ***syn*** see ESSENTIALLY 1
ant superficially
funeral director *n* ***syn*** see MORTICIAN
funereal *adj* ***syn*** see GLOOMY 3
rel grave, solemn
con animated, gay, lively, sprightly, vivacious; blithe, jocund, jolly, jovial, merry
ant festive
fungible *adj* ***syn*** see INTERCHANGEABLE
funk *vb* ***syn*** see SMELL 3
funk *n* ***syn*** see COWARD
funker *n* ***syn*** see COWARD
funky *adj* ***syn*** see MALODOROUS 1
funnel *vb* ***syn*** see CONDUCT 4
funniness *n* ***syn*** see HUMOR 4
funny *adj* ***syn*** see LAUGHABLE
rel antic, bizarre, fantastic, grotesque
idiom too funny for words
con doleful, dolorous, lugubrious, melancholy, plaintive
ant unfunny

||**funny farm** *n* ***syn*** see ASYLUM 3
funnyman *n* ***syn*** see HUMORIST 2
fur *n* **1** ***syn*** see HIDE
2 ***syn*** see DOWN
furbish *vb* ***syn*** see POLISH 1

furious *adj* **1** ***syn*** see WILD 6
2 marked by uncontrollable excitement often under the stress of a powerful emotion <in a state of *furious* activity>
syn corybantic, delirious, frantic, frenetic, frenzied, mad, rabid, wild
rel excited, provoked, stimulated; enthusiastic, fanatic; desperate, feverish, hasty, impetuous; fierce, intense, vehement, violent; excessive, extravagant, extreme, inordinate; enraged, incensed, infuriated, maddened; hysterical, irrational, unreasonable; bewildered, distracted, upset; crazed, demented, insane, mad, maniac
con calm, composed, peaceful, placid, quiet, serene, subdued, tranquil; apathetic, impassive, imperturbable, inexcitable
3 ***syn*** see INTENSE 1

furiously *adv* ***syn*** see HARD 2
furl *vb* ***syn*** see ROLL 3

furnish *vb* **1** to supply one with what is needed (as for daily living or a particular activity) <*furnished* him the papers for his application>
syn accouter, appoint, arm, equip, fit out, gear, outfit, rig, turn out
rel dower, endow, endue; apparel, array, clothe; mount; give, provide, supply
con denude, dismantle, divest, strip; despoil, spoliate; relieve (of), take away
2 ***syn*** see GIVE 3

furor *n* ***syn*** see DELIRIUM
furore *n* **1** ***syn*** see STIR 1
2 ***syn*** see FASHION 3
3 ***syn*** see COMMOTION 3
furrow *n* ***syn*** see WRINKLE
rel channel, groove, rut
further *adv* **1** ***syn*** see BEYOND 1
2 ***syn*** see AGAIN 4
further *adj* ***syn*** see ADDITIONAL
further *vb* ***syn*** see ADVANCE 1
rel engender, generate, propagate
con bar, block, impede, obstruct; forestall, prevent
ant hinder; retard
furthermore *adv* ***syn*** see ALSO 2
furthermost *adj* ***syn*** see EXTREME 5
furthest *adj* ***syn*** see EXTREME 5
furtive *adj* **1** ***syn*** see SECRET 1
rel artful, crafty, cunning, foxy, guileful, insidious, scheming, shifty, sly, sneaky, tricky, wily; calculating, cautious, circumspect, wary; cloaked, disguised, masked
con brash, impudent, presumptuous
ant forthright; barefaced, brazen

---

syn synonym(s) ***rel*** related word(s)
ant antonym(s) ***con*** contrasted word(s)
idiom idiomatic equivalent(s)
|| use limited; if in doubt, see a dictionary

2 *syn* see STEALTHY 2
ant open
furtively *adv syn* see SECRETLY
ant openly
furuncle *n syn* see ABSCESS
fury *n syn* see ANGER
rel passion; furor; acerbity, acrimony, asperity
fuse *vb* 1 *syn* see LIQUEFY
2 *syn* see MIX 1
rel compact, consolidate, unify
fusillade *n syn* see BARRAGE
fusion *n syn* see MIXTURE
fuss *n* 1 *syn* see STIR 1
rel fluster, perturbation; bother, flap, stew; racket, rumpus; haste, hurry, speed
2 *syn* see COMMOTION 3
3 *syn* see QUARREL
fuss *vb* 1 *syn* see WORRY 3
idiom fret and fume
2 *syn* see COMPLAIN
3 *syn* see GRIPE
4 *syn* see NAG
fussbudget *n* one who becomes upset over trifles <he is the biggest *fussbudget* I know, always going into a tizzy over nothing>
syn fuddy-duddy, fusser, fusspot, granny, old lady, old maid
rel perfectionist, precisionist, stickler
fusser *n syn* see FUSSBUDGET
fusspot *n syn* see FUSSBUDGET
fussy *adj* 1 *syn* see BUSTLING
2 *syn* see CAREFUL 2
3 *syn* see NICE 1
rel fretful, irritable, querulous
fustian *n syn* see BOMBAST
fustian *adj syn* see FECKLESS 1
fusty *adj* 1 *syn* see MALODOROUS 1
rel close, moldy; dirty, filthy, squalid; disheveled, slipshod, sloppy, slovenly, unkempt
2 *syn* see OLD-FASHIONED

futile *adj* barren of results <efforts to convince him were *futile*>
syn abortive, bootless, fruitless, ineffective, ineffectual, unavailable, unavailing, unprevailing, unproductive, useless, vain
rel empty, hollow, idle, nugatory, otiose; inadequate, inefficacious, inefficient, insufficient; unsatisfactory, unsuccessful
idiom in vain, no dice, of no avail, to no effect
con effectual, efficacious, fruitful; advantageous, beneficial, profitable
ant effective

future *n* time that is to come <you must try to do better in the *future*>
syn aftertime, afterward, by-and-by, hereafter, offing, to-be; *compare* PRESENT
idiom time to come
ant past
fuzz *n* 1 *syn* see DOWN
‖2 *syn* see POLICEMAN
fuzzy *adj syn* see FAINT 2

G

gab *vb* ***syn*** see CHAT 1
gab *n* ***syn*** see CHATTER
gabber *n* ***syn*** see CHATTERBOX
gabble *vb* **1** ***syn*** see GIBBER
2 ***syn*** see BABBLE 2
3 ***syn*** see CHAT 1
gabble *n* ***syn*** see CHATTER
gabby *adj* ***syn*** see TALKATIVE
gad *vb* ***syn*** see WANDER 1
gadget *n* **1** a usually small and often novel mechanical or electronic device or contrivance <a new kitchen *gadget* for separating egg whites>
syn concern, gimmick, gizmo, jigger, widget; *compare* DEVICE 2, DOODAD, WHAT-DO-YOU-CALL-IT
rel apparatus, appliance, contraption, tool, utensil
2 ***syn*** see DOODAD
gaffe *n* ***syn*** see FAUX PAS
gaffer *n* a man of advanced years <doddering *gaffers* on the park benches>
syn graybeard, patriarch; *compare* BELDAM 1, OLDSTER
rel duffer, geezer, grandfather, old boy, veteran
gag *vb* **1** ***syn*** see RETCH
2 ***syn*** see DEMUR
gag *n* ***syn*** see JOKE 1
rel ruse, trick, wile
gaiety *n* **1** ***syn*** see MERRYMAKING
2 ***syn*** see MIRTH
rel cheerfulness, gladness, happiness; geniality, pleasantness, winsomeness; animation, conviviality, entertainment, exhilaration, liveliness, merrymaking, radiance, spiritedness, vivacity
con blues, cheerlessness, dismalness, dreariness, gloom, grief, infelicity, joylessness, misery, moodiness, moroseness, pensiveness, solemnity, somberness, sorrow, sullenness, uncheerfulness, wistfulness, woe
gain *n* ***syn*** see PROFIT
rel cut, rake-off, share, take, winnings; ice
ant loss
gain *vb* **1** to arrive at a goal, point, or end <*gained* success in the theater>
syn accomplish, achieve, attain, rack up, reach, realize, score, win
rel complete, consummate, fulfill, perfect, produce; succeed
con falter, flop, flounder, flunk, lose
2 ***syn*** see IMPROVE 3
rel invigorate, renew, strengthen; cure, heal, remedy
3 ***syn*** see EARN 1
4 ***syn*** see GET 1
ant lose
5 ***syn*** see CLEAR 6
ant lose
gainful *adj* ***syn*** see ADVANTAGEOUS 1
rel fat, fruitful, generous, lush, productive, rich; satisfying, substantial
gainsay *vb* ***syn*** see DENY 4
rel combat, fight, oppose, resist, withstand
ant admit
gainsaying *n* ***syn*** see DENIAL 2
ant admission; admitting
gait *n* ***syn*** see SPEED 2
gal *n* **1** ***syn*** see GIRL 1
2 ***syn*** see GIRL FRIEND 1
3 ***syn*** see WOMAN 1
gall *n* ***syn*** see EFFRONTERY
rel arrogance, conceit, haughtiness, loftiness, lordliness, overbearance, pomposity, pride, priggishness, self-importance, smugness
con bashfulness, humbleness, humility, lowliness, modesty, shyness
ant meekness
gall *vb* **1** ***syn*** see ABRADE 1
rel bark, burn, file, fray, frazzle, grate, graze, scrape, scratch, scuff, skin
2 ***syn*** see CHAFE 3
rel distress, pain; cut, score, wound
3 ***syn*** see ANNOY 1
4 ***syn*** see IRRITATE
rel chide, disturb, harass, harry, torment, worry; bedevil, needle, trouble
gallant *n* **1** ***syn*** see FOP
2 an individual who is amorously attracted to the opposite sex <his fiancee accused him of being a trifling *gallant*>
syn amorist, Casanova, Don Juan, lothario, paramour, Romeo
rel dirty old man, lecher, libertine, rake, satyr; admirer, adorer, beau, date, escort, lover, sparker, suitor, swain, wooer
idiom gay blade
gallant *adj* **1** ***syn*** see COURTLY
rel suave, urbane; attentive, considerate, thoughtful
con heedless, inattentive, indifferent, thoughtless, unconcerned
ant ungallant
2 ***syn*** see BRAVE 1
ant dastardly
gallantry *n* **1** ***syn*** see COURTESY 1
rel deference, duty, homage, honor; reverence, suavity, urbanity; address, poise, savoir faire, tact
con boorishness, churlishness, clownishness, loutishness; discourteousness
ant discourtesy

2 ***syn*** see HEROISM
rel bravery, dauntlessness; mettle, resolution, spirit
ant dastardliness
gallery *n* ***syn*** see MUSEUM
galley slave *n* ***syn*** see SLAVE 2
gallimaufry *n* ***syn*** see MISCELLANY 1
galling *adj* ***syn*** see BITTER 2
gallivant *vb* ***syn*** see WANDER 1
||**gallows** *n pl* ***syn*** see SUSPENDERS
||**galluptious** *adj* ***syn*** see MARVELOUS 2
||**galluses** *n pl* ***syn*** see SUSPENDERS
galoot *n* ***syn*** see MAN 3
galumph *vb* ***syn*** see LUMBER
galvanize *vb* ***syn*** see PROVOKE 4
rel activate, energize, vitalize
gambit *n* ***syn*** see TRICK 1
rel design, plan, plot
gamble *vb* **1** to engage in a game of chance for something of value <swore he would never *gamble* for high stakes again>
syn bet, game, lay, play, put (on), set, stake, wager
rel chance, hazard, lot, risk, speculate, venture
idiom buck the odds, take a flyer (on), try one's luck
2 to take a chance on something <*gambled* on the train being late>
syn chance, hazard, risk, venture; *compare* VENTURE 1
rel brave, challenge, dare, defy, face; endanger, imperil, jeopardize
idiom go it blind, take a chance (*or* one's chances), tempt fortune, trust to luck
gambol *vb* to leap or tumble about playfully <young lambs *gamboling* in the meadow>
syn caper, cavort, frisk, frolic, rollick, romp
rel lark, revel, roister; bound, leap, spring
idiom kick up one's heels, let off steam
game *n* **1** ***syn*** see FUN 1
con business, duty, labor, study, toil
2 games *pl* ***syn*** see ATHLETICS
3 animals under pursuit <hunting big *game* is a risky and expensive sport>
syn chase, prey, quarry
rel kill, ravin, victim
game *vb* ***syn*** see GAMBLE 1
game *adj* ***syn*** see BRAVE 1
game plan *n* ***syn*** see PLAN 1
gamesome *adj* ***syn*** see PLAYFUL 1
gamin *n* ***syn*** see URCHIN
gamine *n* ***syn*** see TOMBOY
gammer *n* ***syn*** see BELDAM 1
gamut *n* ***syn*** see RANGE 5
gamy *adj* ***syn*** see MALODOROUS 1
||**gander** *n* ***syn*** see PEEP
gangling *adj* being tall, thin, and usually loose-jointed <a *gangling* high-school boy>
syn gangly, lanky, rangy, spindling, spindly
rel bony, gaunt, lank, lean, scrawny, skinny, spare, tall, thin
con low, low-set, low-statured, short, squat, stocky, sturdy, thickset
gangly *adj* ***syn*** see GANGLING
||**gangrel** *n* ***syn*** see VAGABOND
gap *n* **1** an open space in a barrier <the sheep got through a *gap* in the fence>
syn breach, break, discontinuity, hole, opening
rel fracture, rupture; chink, cleavage, cleft, crack, crevice, fissure, slit, slot; division, interspace, interval, separation; aperture, cranny, orifice
2 ***syn*** see RAVINE
3 a period of discontinuity <a *gap* of an hour between speakers>
syn breach, break, hiatus, interim, interruption, interval, lacuna; *compare* PAUSE
rel caesura, intermission, lull, pause, respite, rest
gape *vb* **1** ***syn*** see GAZE 1
2 ***syn*** see LOOK 7
3 ***syn*** see YAWN
gaping *adj* ***syn*** see CAVERNOUS 1
garb *vb* ***syn*** see CLOTHE
garbage *n* ***syn*** see REFUSE
rel dregs, rubble; filth, sewage, slop
garble *vb* ***syn*** see MISREPRESENT
rel becloud, conceal, hide, obfuscate, obscure
garden house *n* ***syn*** see SUMMERHOUSE
gargantuan *adj* ***syn*** see HUGE
ant lilliputian
garish *adj* ***syn*** see GAUDY
rel overdone, overwrought
con dark, dim, dreary, dull, dusky, murky; quiet, unpretentious
ant somber
garland *n* **1** ***syn*** see WREATH
2 ***syn*** see ANTHOLOGY
garment *vb* ***syn*** see CLOTHE
garner *vb* **1** ***syn*** see REAP
2 ***syn*** see GLEAN
3 ***syn*** see ACCUMULATE
rel gather, glean, harvest, reap; hoard, store
con disseminate, spread
garnish *vb* ***syn*** see ADORN
garrulous *adj* ***syn*** see TALKATIVE
rel blabbing, prattling, prolix, verbose, windy, wordy
con concise; terse; blunt, brusque, curt
ant taciturn
||**gas** *n* ***syn*** see NONSENSE 2
||**gas** *vb* ***syn*** see CHAT 1
||**gasbag** *n* ***syn*** see BRAGGART
gasconade *vb* ***syn*** see BOAST
gash *vb* ***syn*** see CUT 1
rel carve, split; injure, wound; furrow, mark, notch; lance, nip
gasp *vb* ***syn*** see PANT 1
||**gasper** *n* ***syn*** see CIGARETTE
gastronome *n* ***syn*** see EPICURE
rel aesthete, connoisseur, dilettante
gastronomer *n* ***syn*** see EPICURE
gastronomist *n* ***syn*** see EPICURE
gate *n* ***syn*** see FAUCET
gather *vb* **1** ***syn*** see GROUP 1
rel choose, cull, pick, select; accumulate, amass
idiom separate the wheat from the chaff (*or* the sheep from the goats)

con dispel, disperse, dissipate
ant scatter
2 syn see REAP
rel cull, pick, pluck; heap, mass, pile, stack
3 syn see GLEAN
4 syn see INFER
rel catch, fathom, follow, grasp, take in
idiom put two and two together
5 syn see UNDERSTAND 3
6 to bring or come together <a crowd *gathered* to watch the fight>
syn assemble, collect, congregate, congress, forgather, muster, raise, rendezvous; *compare* GROUP 1
rel aggregate, troop; affiliate, ally, associate, league; encounter, meet
con break up, disband, disperse, part, separate; disintegrate, disorganize, dissolve
ant scatter
7 syn see LOOM 2

gathering *n* **1 syn** see CONCOURSE
2 a number of individuals come or brought together <a *gathering* in the town park>
syn aggregation, assemblage, assembly, collection, company, congeries, congregation, crowd, group, muster, ruck; *compare* GROUP 1
rel bunch, crew, crush, flock, gang, horde, mass, press, rout, swarm, turnout
3 syn see HARVEST 1

gauche *adj* **syn** see AWKWARD 2
rel crude, green, unpolished
con bland, smooth, suave, urbane
ant adroit

gaudy *adj* cheaply or vulgarly showy <*gaudy* sideshow posters>
syn blatant, brazen, chintzy, flashy, garish, glaring, loud, meretricious, tawdry, tinsel
rel obtrusive, ostentatious, pretentious, showy, tasteless; coarse, crude, gross, vulgar; brummagem, fake, phony, sham
con restrained, tasteful, unobtrusive; factual, illuminating, informative
ant quiet

gauge *n* **syn** see STANDARD 3
rel check, mark, model, norm, pattern, rule, type

gauge *vb* **syn** see MEASURE 2

‖**gaum** *n* **syn** see OAF 2

gaunt *adj* **1 syn** see LEAN
2 syn see EMACIATED
ant bloated

‖**gaup** (*or* **gawp**) *vb* **1 syn** see LOOK 7
2 syn see GAZE 1

gauzy *adj* **syn** see FILMY

gawk *vb* **syn** see GAZE 1

gawk *n* **syn** see OAF 2

gawky *adj* **syn** see CLUMSY 1

gay *adj* **1 syn** see MERRY
2 syn see LIVELY 1
rel frolicsome, playful, sportive
con earnest, sedate, serious, solemn, somber, staid; quiet, silent, still
ant grave, sober
3 syn see COLORFUL
4 syn see WILD 7
5 syn see HOMOSEXUAL
6 syn see PRESUMPTUOUS

gaze *vb* **1** to look long and usually attentively <*gazed* out the window>
syn bore, gape, ‖gaup (*or* gawp), gawk, glare, gloat, goggle, peer, stare; *compare* LOOK 7
rel look, see, watch; peek, peep; contemplate, inspect, observe, scrutinize, survey; admire, ogle, regard
con glance, skim, skip
2 syn see LOOK 7

gaze (upon) *vb* **syn** see EYE 1

gazebo *n* **syn** see SUMMERHOUSE

gear *n* **syn** see EQUIPMENT
rel accessories, adjuncts, appendages, appurtenances; belongings, effects, means, possessions

gear *vb* **syn** see FURNISH 1

‖**gee** *n* **syn** see MAN 3

‖**gee** *vb* **syn** see AGREE 4

Gehenna *n* **syn** see HELL

gel *vb* **syn** see COAGULATE

gelastic *adj* **syn** see LAUGHABLE

gelate *vb* **syn** see COAGULATE

gelatinize *vb* **syn** see COAGULATE

geld *vb* **syn** see STERILIZE

gelid *adj* **syn** see COLD 1
con ardent, burning, fervent, scorching, sweltering, torrid
ant fervid

‖**gelt** *n* **syn** see MONEY

gem *vb* **syn** see BEJEWEL

‖**gendarme** *n* **syn** see POLICEMAN

genealogy *n* an account often in chart form recording a line of ancestors <decided to prepare a *genealogy* of his family>
syn ‖begats, family tree, pedigree, stemma

general *adj* **1** conforming to what is expected in the ordinary course of events <the *general* problems of everyday life>
syn common, commonplace, matter-of-course, natural, normal, prevalent, regular, run-of-the-mill, typic, typical, usual
rel everyday, popular; familiar, universal; habitual, humdrum, routine, uneventful
con abnormal, extraordinary, irregular, novel, strange, unexpected, unforeseeable, unusual
2 belonging or relating to the whole <a *general* change in the weather>
syn common, generic, universal
rel natural, normal, regular, typical; broad, inclusive, wide
con individual, particular, special; characteristic, distinctive, peculiar
3 syn see ALL-AROUND 2
4 syn see PUBLIC 4

generally *adv* **1** in a reasonably inclusive manner <the forest was *generally* coniferous>

syn chiefly, largely, mainly, mostly, overall, predominantly, primarily, principally
rel about, approximately, practically, roughly, roundly
con altogether, totally, wholly
2 *syn* see ALTOGETHER 3
3 *syn* see USUALLY 2

generate *vb* 1 to bring into existence <*generate* new business>
syn create, father, hatch, make, originate, parent, procreate, produce, sire, spawn
rel bring about, effect, impose, occasion; introduce; cause; found, inaugurate, institute, set up; develop, induce, whip (up)
idiom bring to pass, give birth to, give rise to
con demolish, destroy, extinguish, ruin; degenerate, deteriorate, impair, worsen
2 *syn* see PROCREATE 1
3 to be the cause or source of something immaterial <actions that *generated* a good deal of suspicion>
syn breed, cause, engender, get up, hatch, induce, muster (up), occasion, produce, provoke, work up
rel accomplish, achieve, perform
idiom give birth to, give rise to

generator *n syn* see FATHER 2

generic *adj syn* see GENERAL 2
ant specific

generous *adj* 1 marked by a noble or forbearing spirit <*generous* toward the weakness of others>
syn benevolent, big, chivalrous, considerate, greathearted, lofty, magnanimous
rel altruistic, charitable, kindhearted, kindly, thoughtful, ungrudging, unselfish; fair, honest; long-suffering, tolerant; helpful, willing
con base, ignoble, mean, self-centered, selfish; grim, hard, harsh, intolerant
ant ungenerous
2 *syn* see LIBERAL 1
ant stingy
3 *syn* see PLENTIFUL
rel lavish; luxuriant; affluent, wealthy
con scant, scanty, sparse

generously *adv syn* see WELL 2

genesis *n syn* see BEGINNING
rel provenance, provenience
con cessation, conclusion, culmination, end, finish, termination

genial *adj* 1 *syn* see GRACIOUS 1
rel amicable, friendly, neighborly; blithe, cheerful, jocund, jolly, jovial, merry
con discourteous, rude, uncivil, ungracious; crabbed, morose, sullen; ironic, sarcastic, sardonic, satiric
ant caustic (*remarks, comments*); saturnine (*manner, disposition, aspect*)
2 *syn* see GENTLE 2

geniality *n syn* see AMENITY 1

genitalia *n pl* the external components of the reproductive system <nude bathers were reminded of the local ordinance prohibiting public exposure of the *genitalia*>
syn genitals, parts, private parts, privates, privities, privy parts, pudendum (*usu* pudenda *pl*), secrets

genitals *n pl syn* see GENITALIA

genius *n syn* see GIFT 2
rel creativity, ingenuity, inventiveness, originality; astuteness, brains, grasp, intellect, intelligence, understanding

gent *n syn* see MAN 3

genteel *adj* 1 having characteristics or qualities befitting the upper classes <in those days croquet was a very *genteel* sport> <his manner was perfectly *genteel*>
syn cultivated, cultured, distingué, polished, refined, urbane, well-bred
rel elegant, fashionable, graceful, stylish; chivalrous, gentlemanly, knightly, ladylike, noble; mannerly, well-mannered
con coarse, common, crude, ill-bred, rough, rude, uncouth, uncultured, unpolished, vulgar
ant ungenteel
2 *syn* see CIVIL 2
rel well-behaved; aristocratic, cultured
con crude, discourteous, inconsiderate, rough, rude
3 involving or excessively preoccupied with the airs and forms of middle-class or upper-class proprieties <a shy *genteel* girl terrified of blundering socially>
syn affected, la-di-da, ||lardy-dardy, mincing, pretentious, stilted, too-too; *compare* PRECIOUS 4, PRIM 1
rel artificial, formal, highfalutin
con cultured, genuine, honest, refined; gracious, polished; gentlemanly, ladylike
4 *syn* see PRIM 1
rel narrow; intolerant, uncharitable; confined, insular, parochial, provincial
idiom nasty nice
con charitable, tolerant, understanding; broad-minded, easy, relaxed

gentile *adj syn* see HEATHEN

gentility *n syn* see ARISTOCRACY

gentle *adj* 1 free from all harshness, roughness, or intensity <a *gentle* summer breeze>
syn balmy, bland, faint, lenient, mild, smooth, soft
rel delicate, mellow, tender; hushed, low, soothing; calm, halcyon, peaceful, placid, quiet, serene, tranquil
con coarse, harsh, rough; exquisite, fierce, intense, savage, vehement, violent; forceful, forcible, powerful
2 having a pleasant easygoing nature <a *gentle* person in everything she does>
syn affable, amiable, genial
rel kind, pleasant, pleasing, tender; agreeable, benign, mild; compassionate, kindly, softhearted, sympathetic, warmhearted
con belligerent, cantankerous, contentious, ill-natured, petty, quarrelsome; aggressive, demanding, overbearing
ant harsh, stern

gentleman *n* **1** a person of good or noble birth <the contributions of the country *gentleman* to social stability>
syn ‖aristo, aristocrat, blue blood, patrician
rel Brahmin; chevalier; nob, swell
con churl, clown, lout
ant boor
2 ***syn*** see MAN 3

gentleman friend *n* ***syn*** see BOYFRIEND 1

gentlewoman *n* ***syn*** see WOMAN 1

gentry *n* ***syn*** see ARISTOCRACY

genuine *adj* **1** ***syn*** see AUTHENTIC 2
con artificial, ersatz, factitious; counterfeited, sham, simulated; sophisticated
ant fraudulent
2 ***syn*** see ACTUAL 2
con uncommon, unordinary, unusual; alleged, apocryphal, apparent, fabulous, fictitious, mythical
3 free from hypocrisy or pretense <a *genuine* love for his fellowman>
syn heart-whole, honest, real, sincere, true, undesigning, undissembled, unfeigned; *compare* NATURAL 5, SINCERE 1
rel reliable, trustworthy, unaffected, unimpeachable, veritable
con affected, hyprocritical
ant insincere

genuinely *adv* ***syn*** see VERY 2

germ *n* ***syn*** see SEED 2

germane *adj* ***syn*** see RELEVANT
con incompatible, incongruous, inconsonant
ant foreign

gest *n* ***syn*** see ADVENTURE

gestapo *adj* ***syn*** see TERRORISTIC

gestation *n* ***syn*** see PREGNANCY

gesture *n* ***syn*** see EXPRESSION 3

gesture *vb* ***syn*** see SIGNAL

get *vb* **1** to come into possession of <hoped to *get* a fortune from his invention>
syn acquire, annex, chalk up, compass, gain, have, land, obtain, pick up, procure, pull, secure, win
rel educe, elicit, evoke, extort, extract, ‖promote; accept, receive; clutch, grab, grasp, take; accomplish, achieve, effect; capture, carry; draw
idiom come by
con abnegate, eschew, forbear, forgo, give up, sacrifice; abandon, forsake, renounce
2 ***syn*** see EARN 1
3 ***syn*** see BECOME 1
rel achieve, attain, effect, realize
idiom get to be, turn out to be
4 ***syn*** see CONTRACT 1
5 ***syn*** see FATHER 1
6 ***syn*** see PREPARE 1
rel arrange, order, right; adjust, coordinate, organize
7 ***syn*** see CATCH 1
8 ***syn*** see AFFECT
rel bend, bias, dispose, predispose, prompt
con benumb, deaden, numb; blunt, dull, harden
9 ***syn*** see NONPLUS 1
rel bother, distress, disturb, perturb, upset; discomfit, disconcert, embarrass
10 ***syn*** see IRRITATE
idiom try one's temper
con calm, compose, cool, lull, soothe, subdue
11 ***syn*** see LEARN 1
idiom get into one's head
12 ***syn*** see MEMORIZE
13 ***syn*** see INDUCE 1
rel provoke; beg, coax, press, pressure, urge
14 ***syn*** see REACH 4
15 ***syn*** see COME 1

get along *vb* **1** ***syn*** see ADVANCE 5
rel depart, go
con recede, regress, retreat, retrogress, reverse, revert
2 ***syn*** see SHIFT 5
rel flourish, prosper, succeed, thrive

get away *vb* ***syn*** see GO 2

getaway *n* ***syn*** see ESCAPE 1

get back *vb* ***syn*** see RECOVER 1

get by *vb* ***syn*** see SHIFT 5

get in *vb* ***syn*** see COME 1

get off *vb* **1** ***syn*** see GO 2
rel advance, progress
2 ***syn*** see BEGIN 1

get on *vb* **1** ***syn*** see DON 1
2 ***syn*** see ADVANCE 5
3 ***syn*** see SHIFT 5

get out *vb* **1** to go away quickly, immediately, and often secretly <had to *get out* before the police arrived>
syn begone, bug off, buzz off, clear out, decamp, hightail, kite, scram, skedaddle, skiddoo, take off, ‖vamoose
rel depart, duck (out), egress, exit, go, leave, split
idiom beat it, be off, make tracks, take a powder, take a runout powder
con abide, remain, reside, stay
2 to become known <we can't let this story *get out*>
syn break, come out, leak, out, transpire
3 ***syn*** see PUBLISH 2

gettable *adj* ***syn*** see AVAILABLE 1

get up *vb* **1** ***syn*** see ROLL OUT
2 ***syn*** see RISE 1
3 ***syn*** see GENERATE 3

getup *n* **1** ***syn*** see COSTUME
2 ***syn*** see VIGOR 2

get–up–and–go *n* **1** ***syn*** see VIGOR 2
2 ***syn*** see ENTERPRISE 4

gewgaw *n* ***syn*** see KNICKKNACK

ghastly *adj* **1** disturbingly frightening or repellent in appearance or aspect <the *ghastly* sight of burned and rotting bodies>
syn grim, grisly, gruesome, hideous, horrible, horrid, horrifying, lurid, macabre, terrible, terrifying

---

rel appalling, awful, dreadful, frightening, frightful, shocking; disgustful, disgusting, nauseant, nauseating, sickening
con appealing, attractive, charming, pleasant, touching; acceptable, bearable; trivial, unimportant
2 resembling or suggestive of a ghost <a *ghastly* form slightly visible through the fog>
syn cadaverous, corpselike, deathlike, ghostlike, ghostly, shadowy, spectral
rel ashen, livid, lurid, pale; uncanny, weird; gruesome, haggard, macabre; dim, faint, weak; charnel, mortuary, sepulchral

ghost *n* ***syn*** see APPARITION
rel demon, devil

ghost *vb* ***syn*** see GHOSTWRITE

ghostlike *adj* ***syn*** see GHASTLY 2

ghostly *adj* ***syn*** see GHASTLY 2

ghostwrite *vb* to write for and in the name of another <a *ghostwritten* autobiography>
syn ghost, ‖spook

GI *n* ***syn*** see SOLDIER

giant *n* something of monstrous size, appearance, or power <a *giant* of a tractor>
syn behemoth, leviathan, mammoth, monster, whale
rel cyclops, polypheme

giant *adj* ***syn*** see HUGE
rel gross, hulking
con paltry, petty, puny, trifling, trivial
ant dwarf

gibber *vb* to utter or speak rapidly, inarticulately, and usually unintelligibly <a *gibbering* idiot>
syn babble, chatter, gabble, jabber
rel blather, drivel, prate, prattle, yammer; stammer, stutter; mumble, mutter; mow
idiom run off at the mouth
con articulate, enunciate, pronounce

gibberish *n* **1** unintelligible or meaningless talk <the *gibberish* of an imbecile>
syn babble, drivel, Greek, jabber, jabberwocky, nonsense, skimble-skamble; *compare* GIBBERISH 3
rel blather, bunkum, claptrap, twaddle; blabber, gabble, palaver, prattle
2 ***syn*** see GOBBLEDYGOOK
3 speech or actions that are esoteric in nature and suggest the magical, strange, or unknown <the shaman's strange *gibberish*>
syn abracadabra, hocus-pocus, mumbo jumbo, mummery
rel magic, sorcery, thaumaturgy

gibbet *vb* ***syn*** see HANG 2

gibble–gabble *n* ***syn*** see CHATTER

gibe *vb* ***syn*** see SCOFF
rel rail, rally, revile, scold, twit

giddy *adj* **1** having a lightheartedly silly nature <tried to teach a bunch of *giddy* Girl Scouts how to make a fire>
syn bird-witted, dizzy, empty-headed, featherbrained, flighty, fribble, fribbling, frivolous, harebrained, hoity-toity, light, light-headed, rattlebrained, scatterbrained, silly, skittish, volage, yeasty
rel capricious, fickle, impulsive, whimsical; brainless, exuberant, thoughtless, witless
idiom giddy as a goose
con earnest, pensive, sedate, serious, sober, solemn, staid, thoughtful
2 ***syn*** see DIZZY 2
rel bemused, flustered
idiom going around in circles, like a chicken with its head cut off, seeing double

gift *n* **1** something freely given by one person to another for his benefit or pleasure <the watch was a graduation *gift*>
syn benevolence, boon, ‖compliment, favor, largess, present
rel alms, benefaction, contribution, donation; award, bestowal, grant, presentation; legacy; offering, reward, tip; remembrance, souvenir, token
2 a natural or special facility or capableness <has a *gift* for electronics>
syn aptness, bent, bump, faculty, flair, genius, head, knack, nose, set, talent, turn; *compare* LEANING 2
rel ability, aptitude, capability; accomplishment, acquirement, attainment; instinct, numen, power; forte, leaning, propensity, specialty
con awkwardness, clumsiness, maladroitness

gigantean *adj* ***syn*** see HUGE

gigantesque *adj* ***syn*** see HUGE

gigantic *adj* ***syn*** see HUGE
rel hulking, stupendous
con paltry, petty, puny, trifling, trivial

giggle *vb* ***syn*** see LAUGH

gill *n* ***syn*** see CREEK 2

gimcrack *n* ***syn*** see KNICKKNACK

gimmick *n* **1** ***syn*** see GADGET 1
2 ***syn*** see TRICK 1
rel cheat, counterfeit, deceit, dodge, fake, humbug, imposture; fun, game, jest, method, sport

gimp *n* ***syn*** see SPIRIT 5

gingerly *adj* ***syn*** see CAUTIOUS

gingery *adj* ***syn*** see SPIRITED 2
con lethargic, listless, poky, slow; dead, dull, flat, insipid, stuffy; dreary; blasé, lackadaisical, nonchalant

‖**gin mill** *n* ***syn*** see BAR 5

gird *vb* **1** ***syn*** see BELT 1
ant ungird
2 ***syn*** see SURROUND 1
rel wrap, wreathe
3 to prepare oneself for action <*girded* himself for the coming trial>
syn brace, fortify, prepare, ready, steel, strengthen
rel bolster, buttress, support, sustain; harden, reinforce, shore (up); invigorate; dispose, forearm, prepare
idiom gird one's loins, whet the knife

gird *vb* ***syn*** see SCOFF

girdle *n* ***syn*** see BELT 1

girdle *vb* **1** ***syn*** see BELT
2 ***syn*** see SURROUND 1

girl *n* **1** a young unmarried female person <hired a *girl* to babysit>
syn ‖bird, damsel, gal, lass, lassie, maid, maiden, miss, missy, ‖quail, ‖quiff, wench

rel hoyden, tomboy; deb, debutante, subdeb, subdebutante; bobby-soxer; schoolgirl; gamine
‖**2** ***syn*** see WOMAN 1
3 ***syn*** see MAID 2
4 ***syn*** see GIRL FRIEND 1

girl Friday *n* ***syn*** see RIGHT-HAND MAN

girl friend *n* **1** a woman who is a man's usual or preferred companion <took his *girl friend* out every weekend>
syn best girl, ‖chick, ‖doney, gal, girl, lady friend, lass, mouse, popsy
2 a woman who shares with a man a strong and usually sexually oriented mutual attraction <his wife caught him with his *girl friend*>
syn ‖baby, beloved, flame, honey, inamorata, ladylove, steady, sweetheart, sweetie, truelove
3 ***syn*** see MISTRESS

gist *n* ***syn*** see SUBSTANCE 2
rel sap, soul, spirit; subject, theme, topic; bearing, drift, tenor

give *vb* **1** to provide gratuitously <*gave* their labor to rebuild the burned church>
syn bestow, devote, donate, give away, hand out, present; *compare* CONTRIBUTE 1
rel accord, award, confer, grant, hand; afford, contribute, furnish, provide; aid, assist, benefact, help
con keep, retain, withhold; lease, sell
2 to provide by or as if by formal action <he was *given* a diploma>
syn accord, award, confer, grant; *compare* GRANT 1
rel bestow, hand over, present; allocate, appropriate, assign
con decline, refuse; hold back, withhold
3 to put into the possession of another usually for use or consumption <*gave* the dog a drink of water>
syn deliver, dish out, dispense, feed, find, furnish, hand, hand over, provide, supply, transfer, turn over
rel administer, commit, offer; deal, disburse, disperse, distribute, divide, dole (out), lot (out); afford, lend
con have, hold, hold back, keep, keep back, reserve, retain, withhold
4 ***syn*** see OFFER 1
rel bestow, confer, render; administer, dispense, issue
5 ***syn*** see EXPRESS 2
6 ***syn*** see ALLOT
7 to furnish as a result or product <6 +6 *gives* 12>
syn produce, yield
rel be, equal, make; afford, furnish, offer, supply
8 ***syn*** see SPEND 1
9 ***syn*** see SELL 2
10 to bestow or dispense by some action <*gave* him a punch in the nose>
syn administer, deal, deliver, inflict, strike
rel bestow, dispense; fetch
11 ***syn*** see ADDRESS 3
12 to fail in response to physical stress <the bridge *gave* under the heavy load>
syn bend, break, cave, collapse, crumple, fold up, go, yield
rel fail, relax, relent, slacken, weaken
idiom cave in, give way
13 ***syn*** see HAPPEN 1

give away *vb* **1** ***syn*** see GIVE 1
2 ***syn*** see REVEAL 1

give back *vb* **1** ***syn*** see RETREAT 2
rel back out, backtrack, backwater; crumble, fail, falter, weaken
2 ***syn*** see RESTORE 5

given *adj* ***syn*** see APT 1

given name *n* the name that precedes one's surname <arguing over the baby's *given name*>
syn baptismal name, Christian name, font name, forename, personal name, prename
rel first name, middle name; appellation, appellative, compellation, denomination, style; praenomen; epithet, label, tag

give off *vb* **1** ***syn*** see EMIT 2
2 ***syn*** see DISCHARGE 5

give out *vb* **1** ***syn*** see EMIT 2
2 ***syn*** see COLLAPSE 2
3 ***syn*** see FAIL 2

give over *vb* ***syn*** see STOP 3

giver *n* ***syn*** see DONOR

give up *vb* **1** ***syn*** see RELINQUISH
2 ***syn*** see DESPAIR

gizmo *n* **1** ***syn*** see DOODAD
2 ***syn*** see GADGET

glabrous *adj* ***syn*** see HAIRLESS
rel beardless, shaven, smooth-shaven
con bristled, bristly, hairy, hirsute, stubbled, stubbly

glacial *adj* **1** ***syn*** see COLD 1
2 ***syn*** see COLD 2
rel aloof, distant, remote, reserved, standoffish, withdrawn; exclusive, inaccessible, seclusive, unapproachable
con affable, gregarious, sociable

glad *adj* **1** characterized by or expressing the mood of one who is pleased or delighted <she was *glad* to be on vacation>
syn happy, joyful, joyous, lighthearted
rel delighted, gratified, pleased, rejoiced, tickled; blithe, exhilarated, jocund, jolly, jovial, merry; gleeful, hilarious, mirthful
idiom filled with (*or* full of) delight
con blue, dejected, depressed, downcast, melancholy; despondent, dispirited, heavyhearted, sadhearted, unhappy; forlorn, joyless, sorrowful, woeful
ant sad
2 full of brightness and cheerfulness <a *glad* spring morning>
syn bright, cheerful, cheery, radiant
rel beaming, sparkling; beautiful; genial, pleasant
con dark, dim, dull, gloomy, somber

---

syn synonym(s) ***rel*** related word(s)
ant antonym(s) ***con*** contrasted word(s)
idiom idiomatic equivalent(s)
‖ use limited; if in doubt, see a dictionary

gladden *vb* ***syn*** see PLEASE 2
rel comfort, console, solace; animate, enliven, exhilarate, invigorate, liven, quicken, vivify
con depress, oppress, weigh; discourage, dishearten, dispirit; damp, dampen; bother, irk
ant sadden
gladiatorial *adj* ***syn*** see BELLIGERENT
||**glad rags** *n pl* ***syn*** see FINERY
glamorous *adj* ***syn*** see ATTRACTIVE 1
glamour *n* ***syn*** see CHARM 3
glance *vb* **1** to strike a surface obliquely so as to go off at an angle <the bullet *glanced* off the stone wall>
syn carom, dap, graze, ricochet, skim, skip
rel brush, kiss, scrape, shave, slant; contact, hit, strike, touch; bounce, careen, rebound
con center, focus
2 ***syn*** see BRUSH
3 ***syn*** see FLASH 1
glance (at *or* over) *vb* ***syn*** see BROWSE
glance *n* **1** ***syn*** see FLASH 1
2 ***syn*** see PEEP
glance *vb* ***syn*** see POLISH 1
glare *vb* **1** ***syn*** see BLAZE
rel dazzle, flash, gleam, glisten, glitter
2 ***syn*** see GAZE 1
rel frown, glower, lower, scowl
glaring *adj* **1** ***syn*** see EGREGIOUS
rel conspicuous, noticeable, outstanding; excessive, extreme, inordinate; obtrusive
ant unnoticeable
2 ***syn*** see GAUDY
rel cheap, coarse, crude, gross
con elegant, tasteful
glass *n* ***syn*** see MIRROR 1
glass *vb* ***syn*** see REFLECT 1
||**glasshouse** *n* ***syn*** see GREENHOUSE
glassy *adj* ***syn*** see SLEEK
glaze *vb* ***syn*** see POLISH 1
glaze *n* ***syn*** see LUSTER
gleam *n* ***syn*** see FLASH 1
gleam *vb* **1** ***syn*** see SHINE 1
2 ***syn*** see FLASH 1
rel burn
gleaming *adj* ***syn*** see LUSTROUS 1
glean *vb* to gather by effort and usually bit by bit <evidence *gleaned* from various testimonies>
syn cull, extract, garner, gather, pick up
rel sift, winnow; ascertain, conclude, deduce, learn
con amass, heap, pile
glee *n* ***syn*** see MIRTH
rel delectation, delight, enjoyment, joy, pleasure; blitheness; joyousness
ant gloom
gleeful *adj* ***syn*** see MERRY
glen *n* ***syn*** see VALLEY
glib *adj* characterized by very fluent often superficial address toward others <*glib* chatter>
syn silver-tongued, vocative, voluble, well-hung; *compare* TALKATIVE
rel articulate, eloquent, facile, fluent, vocal
con inarticulate, unfluent
glide *vb* **1** ***syn*** see SLIDE 1
rel float, fly, sail, scud, shoot, skim
2 ***syn*** see STEAL 3
3 ***syn*** see SNEAK
glimmer *vb* ***syn*** see FLASH 1
glimmer *n* ***syn*** see FLASH 1
glimpse *n* ***syn*** see PEEP
glint *vb* ***syn*** see FLASH 1
glint *n* **1** ***syn*** see FLASH 1
2 ***syn*** see LUSTER
glissade *vb* ***syn*** see SLIDE 1
rel float, fly, sail, scud, shoot, skim
glisten *vb* ***syn*** see FLASH 1
glisten *n* ***syn*** see FLASH 1
glistening *adj* ***syn*** see LUSTROUS 1
glitter *vb* **1** ***syn*** see FLASH 1
2 ***syn*** see SPANGLE 1
glitter *n* ***syn*** see FLASH 1
gloaming *n* ***syn*** see EVENING 1
gloat *vb* ***syn*** see GAZE 1
con begrudge, covet, envy, grudge
global *adj* **1** ***syn*** see UNIVERSAL 2
ant parochial
2 ***syn*** see ALL-ROUND 2
rel all-inclusive, blanket, catholic, grand, universal
globe *n* **1** ***syn*** see BALL
2 ***syn*** see EARTH 1
globule *n* ***syn*** see DROP 1
gloom *vb* **1** ***syn*** see FROWN 1
rel brood, mope
con smile; bubble, effervesce, enthuse, sparkle
2 ***syn*** see OBSCURE
gloom *n* ***syn*** see SADNESS
con hilarity, jollity, mirth; gaiety, gladness
ant glee
gloomy *adj* **1** ***syn*** see DARK 1
rel bleak, dismal, dreary
ant brilliant
2 ***syn*** see SULLEN
rel cheerless, dejected, depressed, downcast, joyless, melancholy, oppressed, solemn, unhappy, weary
con glad, happy, joyful, joyous, lighthearted; blithe, jocund, jovial, merry
ant cheerful
3 causing or marked by gloom <the *gloomy* atmosphere of the dungeon>
syn acheronian, acherontic, black, bleak, cheerless, cold, depressant, depressing, depressive, desolate, disconsolate, discouraging, disheartening, dismal, dispiriting, drear, dreary, dusky, funereal, joyless, lugubrious, morne, oppressive, somber, tenebrific, unhappy, woebegone
rel despondent, mirthless, pessimistic; melancholy, mournful, sad; drab, dull, muzzy
con bright, cheerful, happy; cheering, emboldening, encouraging, heartening, optimistic
ant gloomless
glorification *n* ***syn*** see APOTHEOSIS 2
glorify *vb* **1** ***syn*** see PRAISE 2
2 ***syn*** see EXALT 1
glorious *adj* **1** ***syn*** see SPLENDID 2
rel brilliant, effulgent, lustrous, radiant; imposing, impressive; majestic, noble; ravishing, stunning; beautiful

ant inglorious
2 *syn* see MARVELOUS 2
glory *vb syn* see EXULT
gloss *n syn* see LUSTER
rel glossiness, silkiness, sleekness, slickness; burnish
gloss *vb syn* see POLISH 1
gloss (over) *vb syn* see PALLIATE
rel account, explain, justify, rationalize; belie, falsify, miscolor, misrepresent
gloss *vb syn* see ANNOTATE
glossy *adj* 1 *syn* see LUSTROUS 1
2 *syn* see SLEEK
glow *vb* 1 *syn* see BLAZE
rel burn; ignite, kindle, light
2 *syn* see BLUSH
glow *n syn* see BLOOM 3
glower *vb syn* see FROWN 1
rel stare; look, watch
glowing *adj* 1 *syn* see RUDDY
2 *syn* see IMPASSIONED
rel enthusiastic; avid, desirous, eager, fierce, keen; burning, heated
gloze (over) *vb syn* see PALLIATE
rel account, explain, justify, rationalize; belie, falsify, miscolor, misrepresent
gluey *adj syn* see STICKY 1
glum *adj syn* see SULLEN
rel close-lipped, silent, taciturn, tight-lipped; depressed, oppressed, weighed down
con glad, happy, joyful, joyous, lighthearted
ant cheerful
glut *vb syn* see SATIATE
rel cram, feast, stuff
idiom make a pig of (oneself)
con scant, skimp
ant stint
glutted *adj syn* see SATIATED
gluttonous *adj syn* see VORACIOUS
rel hoggish, piggish; indulgent, intemperate
con sober, temperate; ascetic, austere; sparing
ant abstemious
gnaw *vb* 1 *syn* see WORRY 1
rel haunt, irritate, rankle
2 *syn* see EAT 3
rel abrade, fret; consume, crumble
gnome *n syn* see MAXIM
gnostic *adj syn* see WISE 1
go *vb* 1 to move on a course <they were glad to be *going* toward home>
syn ||cruise, fare, hie, journey, pass, proceed, ||process, push on, repair, travel, wend
rel advance; approach, near
idiom gain ground, get over the ground, make one's way
ant stay; stop
2 to move out of and away from where one is <it's time to *go* now>
syn ||blow, depart, exit, get away, get off, leave, ||mog, move, pop off, pull out, push off, quit, retire, run along, shove off, take off, withdraw
rel abscond, decamp, escape, flee, fly, hightail
idiom take a powder
con abide, remain, stay; arrive
ant come
3 *syn* see RUN 8
4 to be brought to or toward an end <his money will soon be *gone*>
syn consume, exhaust, expend, finish, run through, spend, use up, wash up
rel deplete, devour, dissipate, fritter (away), overspend, squander, waste
con conserve, preserve, save
5 *syn* see DIE 1
6 *syn* see PASS 3
7 *syn* see GIVE 12
8 *syn* see HAPPEN 1
9 *syn* see BECOME 1
10 *syn* see RANGE 3
11 *syn* see SUCCEED 3
12 *syn* see SUCCEED 2
13 *syn* see RESORT 2
14 *syn* see FUNCTION 3
15 *syn* see EXTEND 7
16 *syn* see AGREE 4
17 *syn* see BELONG 1
18 *syn* see BEAR 10
19 *syn* see ENJOY 1
go (for) *vb syn* see APPROVE 1
go (into) *vb syn* see EXPLORE
go (together *or* with) *vb syn* see SUIT 4
go *n* 1 *syn* see OCCURRENCE
2 *syn* see VIGOR 2
3 *syn* see ENERGY 2
4 *syn* see FLING 1
5 *syn* see SPELL 1
6 *syn* see SIEGE
7 *syn* see SUCCESS
goad *n syn* see STIMULUS
rel compulsion, drive, impulsion; desire, lust, passion, urge, zeal
ant curb
goad *vb syn* see URGE
rel impel, move; coerce, compel, force; instigate
go–ahead *adj syn* see ENTERPRISING 2
goal *n* 1 *syn* see AMBITION 2
2 *syn* see USE 4
goat *n syn* see SCAPEGOAT
goatish *adj syn* see LUSTFUL 2
gob *n* 1 *syn* see LUMP 1
2 *usu* **gobs** *pl syn* see SCAD
gob *n syn* see MOUTH 1
gobbet *n syn* see DROP 1
gobble *vb syn* see GULP
gobbledygook *n* wordy unintelligible language <the *gobbledygook* of bureaucrats>
syn double-talk, gibberish
rel double Dutch, Greek, jabberwocky; ||bull, bunkum, claptrap, drivel, garbage, malarkey, nonsense, poppycock, twaddle
go–between *n* 1 *syn* see MARRIAGE BROKER

---

syn synonym(s) *rel* related word(s)
ant antonym(s) *con* contrasted word(s)
idiom idiomatic equivalent(s)
|| use limited; if in doubt, see a dictionary

2 an intermediate agent between individuals or groups <served as a *go-between* in the labor dispute>
syn broker, entrepreneur, interagent, interceder, intercessor, intermediary, intermediate, intermediator, mediator, middleman
rel agent, attorney, deputy, factor, proxy; emissary, envoy, messenger; delegate, representative; arbitrator, negotiator

godless *adj* ***syn*** see IRRELIGIOUS
rel agnostic, atheistic, infidel
ant godly

godlike *adj* ***syn*** see DIVINE 2

godly *adj* **1** ***syn*** see DIVINE 1
2 ***syn*** see SAINTLY
3 ***syn*** see DEVOUT
ant godless

go down *vb* **1** ***syn*** see FALL 2
rel droop, sag, sink; cave (in), collapse, crumple, fold
2 ***syn*** see SET 12
3 ***syn*** see SINK 1
4 ***syn*** see FALL 3
5 ***syn*** see HAPPEN 1

God's acre *n* ***syn*** see CEMETERY

godsend *n* ***syn*** see GOOD 1

go–getter *n* ***syn*** see HUSTLER 1

goggle *vb* **1** ***syn*** see LOOK 7
2 ***syn*** see GAZE 1

go in *vb* ***syn*** see ENTER 1

Golconda *n* ***syn*** see BONANZA

goldarn *adj* **1** ***syn*** see DAMNED 2
2 ***syn*** see UTTER

goldbrick *n* ***syn*** see SLACKER

goldbrick *vb* ***syn*** see IDLE

golden *adj* **1** ***syn*** see BLOND 1
2 ***syn*** see MELLIFLUOUS

golden–ager *n* ***syn*** see OLDSTER

gold mine *n* ***syn*** see BONANZA

golem *n* ***syn*** see ROBOT 2

gone *adj* **1** ***syn*** see EXTINCT 2
2 ***syn*** see ABSENT 1
3 ***syn*** see LOST 2
4 ***syn*** see PREGNANT 1

gonfalon *n* ***syn*** see FLAG

gonfanon *n* ***syn*** see FLAG

goo *n* **1** a sticky substance <slipped on a patch of greasy *goo* on the walk>
syn gook, goop, gumbo, gunk, muck; *compare* CRUD
rel dope
2 ***syn*** see CRUD

good *adj* **1** having a helpful or auspicious character <a *good* wind>
syn advantageous, benefic, beneficial, brave, favorable, favoring, helpful, propitious, toward, useful
rel convenient, suitable; desirable, needed; appropriate, proper, right
con disadvantageous, unfavorable; damaging, hampering, harmful; unwanted
ant ill
2 adapted to the end in view <they doubted that the fruit was *good* to eat>
syn appropriate, convenient, fit, meet, proper, suitable, useful
rel all right, apt, becoming, conformable, congruous, fitting, seemly
con inadequate, inappropriate, undesirable, unfit, unsuitable, useless
3 ***syn*** see WHOLE 1
con blemished, damaged, defective, flawed, impaired, imperfect, unsound
ant bad
4 ***syn*** see ADVANTAGEOUS 1
5 ***syn*** see PLEASANT 1
6 ***syn*** see HEALTHFUL
7 ***syn*** see CLEVER 5
8 ***syn*** see CONSIDERABLE 2
9 ***syn*** see WELL-FOUNDED
10 ***syn*** see DECENT 4
11 conforming to a high standard of morality or virtue <if you can't be *good,* be careful>
syn blameless, exemplary, guiltless, inculpable, innocent, irreprehensible, irreproachable, lily-white, pure, righteous, unblamable, virtuous
rel incorrupt, sound, uncorrupted, untainted
con blameworthy, impure, unrighteous; evil, iniquitous, reprobate, sinful
ant bad
12 ***syn*** see CHARITABLE 1
13 behaving in an acceptable or desirable manner <a *good* child>
syn decorous, well-behaved
rel polite, proper; considerate, kindly, thoughtful
con ill-behaved, indecorous, naughty; careless, heedless, inconsiderate, mischievous, thoughtless
ant bad
14 ***syn*** see SKILLFUL 2
ant bad
15 ***syn*** see ABLE

good *n* **1** something that is desirable or beneficial <it's an ill wind that blows no *good*>
syn advantage, benediction, benefit, blessing, boon, godsend
con bane, harm, misfortune; detriment, jinx
ant evil, ill
2 ***syn*** see RIGHT 1
3 ***syn*** see WELFARE
4 **goods** *pl* ***syn*** see POSSESSION 2
5 **goods** *pl* ***syn*** see MERCHANDISE

good–bye *interj* — used as a conventional expression of good wishes at parting <the party was over; the time had come to say *good-bye*>
syn adieu, by, bye-bye, ‖cheerio, farewell, so long, ‖toodle-oo
rel good day, good evening, good morning, good night
idiom be good, be seeing you, fare you well, keep in touch, see you (later)
con hello, how do, howdy, hullo

good–bye *n* ***syn*** see PARTING

good–bye *adj* ***syn*** see PARTING

good faith *n* a state of mind characterizing one free from fraud, deceit, or misconduct <determined to act in *good faith*>

syn bona fides, sincereness, sincerity, uberrima fides
rel decency, decorum, propriety, seemliness; ethicality, morality, virtuousness
good-fellowship *n syn* see CAMARADERIE
good-for-nothing *n syn* see WASTREL 1
good-for-nothing *adj* **1** *syn* see FECKLESS 1
2 *syn* see WORTHLESS 1
ant precious
good-hearted *adj syn* see KIND
good-humored *adj syn* see AMIABLE 1
rel buoyant, cheerful, cheery, genial, smiling
ant ill-humored
good-looking *adj syn* see BEAUTIFUL
ant ill-looking
good-natured *adj syn* see AMIABLE 1
rel altruistic, benevolent, charitable; acquiescent, compliant
con choleric, cranky, cross, irascible, splenetic, touchy; crabbed, gloomy, glum, morose, splenetic
ant contrary; ill-natured
goodness *n* the quality or state of being morally excellent <that eternal *goodness* that burns away evil>
syn morality, probity, rectitude, righteousness, rightness, uprightness, virtue
rel honesty, honor, integrity; grace, merit, quality, superiority
ant badness, evil
good sense *n syn* see SENSE 6
good-tasting *adj syn* see PALATABLE
good-tempered *adj syn* see AMIABLE 1
con crabbed, surly; snappish, touchy; irascible
ant bad-tempered, ill-tempered
goodwill *n* **1** benevolent interest or concern <trying to promote interracial *goodwill*>
syn amity, benevolence, comity, friendliness, friendship, kindliness
rel altruism, charity, favor, generosity, helpfulness, kindness, rapport, sympathy, tolerance
con animus, disfavor, enmity, hatred, intolerance, malevolence
ant animosity, ill will
2 *syn* see ALACRITY
goody *n syn* see DELICACY
goody-goody *n syn* see PRUDE
gooey *adj* **1** *syn* see STICKY 1
2 *syn* see SENTIMENTAL
goof *n* **1** *syn* see DUNCE
2 *syn* see ERROR 2
‖**goof** (off) *vb syn* see IDLE
goof (up) *vb syn* see BOTCH
go off *vb syn* see EXPLODE 1
gook *n* **1** *syn* see GOO
2 *syn* see CRUD
3 *syn* see NONSENSE 2
go on *vb* **1** *syn* see PERSEVERE
2 *syn* see BEHAVE 1
‖**goon** *n syn* see DUNCE
goop *n syn* see GOO 1
goose egg *n syn* see ZERO 1
goosey *adj* **1** *syn* see STUPID 1
2 *syn* see NERVOUS

go over *vb syn* see SUCCEED 2
gordian *adj syn* see COMPLEX 2
gore *n syn* see BLOOD 1
gorge *n syn* see RAVINE
gorge *vb syn* see SATIATE
rel bolt, devour, gobble, guzzle, raven, wolf; overeat, overindulge, stuff
idiom eat like a horse, eat one out of house and home
gorged *adj syn* see SATIATED
gorgeous *adj* **1** *syn* see SPLENDID 2
rel elegant, luxurious, opulent, plush, sumptuous; flamboyant, garish, gaudy, ostentatious, pretentious, showy; beautiful, colorful
2 *syn* see GRAND 2
‖**gorilla** *n syn* see THUG 1
gory *adj syn* see BLOODY 1
gospel *n syn* see VERACITY 2
gossamer *adj syn* see FILMY
gossip *n* **1** a person who habitually retails private, scandalous, or sensational and often inaccurate information <her life ruined by a vicious old *gossip*>
syn carrytale, circulator, clack, gossiper, gossipmonger, ‖long tongue, mumblenews, newsmonger, quidnunc, rumorer, rumormonger, scandalizer, scandalmonger, sieve, tabby, talebearer, telltale; *compare* BUSYBODY, INFORMER
2 *syn* see REPORT 1
rel account, chronicle, conversation, story, tale; babble, banter, chatter, prate
gossip *vb* to disclose something, often of questionable veracity, that is better kept to oneself <*gossiped* about his neighbor's business>
syn blab, noise (about *or* abroad), rumor, talk, tattle
rel babble, chat, chatter, prate, prattle; hint, imply, insinuate, intimate, suggest
idiom dish the dirt, spill the beans, tell idle tales, tell tales out of school
gossiper *n syn* see GOSSIP 1
gossipmonger *n syn* see GOSSIP 1
Gothic *adj syn* see BARBARIAN 1
rel brutal, coarse, crude
gouge *vb syn* see EXTORT 1
rel cheat, con, swindle; overcharge
go under *vb* **1** *syn* see FALL 3
2 *syn* see SINK 1
gourmand *n syn* see EPICURE
gourmet *n syn* see EPICURE
govern *vb* **1** to exercise sovereign authority <a dictator may *govern* in a thoroughly enlightened manner>
syn overrule, reign, rule, sway
rel captain, command, head; administer, conduct, control, direct, manage, master; regulate, supervise
2 *syn* see ADMINISTER 1

---

syn synonym(s) *rel* related word(s)
ant antonym(s) *con* contrasted word(s)
idiom idiomatic equivalent(s)
‖ use limited; if in doubt, see a dictionary

3 to exercise a decisive role in influencing the actions and conduct of <parents who *govern* their children wisely>
syn control, direct, dominate, handle, manage
rel directionalize, guide, lead, shepherd, steer; boss, oversee, supervise
idiom be at the helm (*or* wheel), be in the driver's seat, hold the reins

‖**governor** *n syn* see FATHER 1

grab *vb syn* see SEIZE 2

grabble *vb syn* see GROPE

grabby *adj syn* see COVETOUS

grace *n* **1** a short prayer either asking a blessing before or giving thanks after a meal <taught each child a *grace* of his own>
syn benediction, blessing, thanks, thanksgiving
rel invocation, petition
2 *syn* see MERCY
rel compassionateness, responsiveness, tenderness; forbearance, indulgence, leniency; goodness
3 *syn* see ELEGANCE

graceless *adj* **1** *syn* see BARBARIC 1
2 *syn* see INFELICITOUS
ant graceful

gracious *adj* **1** marked by kindly courtesy <her *gracious* attitude toward those around her>
syn affable, congenial, cordial, genial, sociable, ‖sonsy
rel amiable, complaisant, easy, obliging; benign, benignant, kind, kindly; chivalrous, courteous, courtly; approachable, bonhomous, clubby, forthcoming, forthgoing, outgoing
con boorish, churlish; blunt, brusque, crabbed, crusty, curt, gruff, short, sullen, surly
ant ungracious
2 *syn* see COURTLY
rel mannered, starchy

gradation *n* the difference or variation between two things that are nearly alike <the *gradations* were too small to be seen with the unaided eye>
syn nuance, shade
rel difference, distinction, divergence; change, modification, variation

grade *n* **1** *syn* see DEGREE 1
2 *syn* see ESTATE 2
3 *syn* see CLASS 1
4 *syn* see QUALITY 3
5 *syn* see SLOPE

grade *vb syn* see CLASS 2
rel arrange, order; assort, sort

Grade A *adj syn* see EXCELLENT

gradient *n syn* see SLOPE

gradual *adj* proceeding slowly usually by minute or imperceptible steps or degrees <his health showed *gradual* improvement>
syn piecemeal, step-by-step
rel deliberate, dilatory, lagging, poky, sluggish
con acute, sharp, sudden
ant abrupt

gradually *adv* by small degrees or amounts <*gradually* he learned the new job>
syn bit by bit, little by little, piecemeal
idiom a little at a time, by degrees
con quickly, rapidly, speedily; at once, immediately, suddenly

grain *n syn* see PARTICLE

grainy *adj syn* see COARSE 1

grammar *n syn* see ALPHABET 2

grand *adj* **1** large and impressive in size, scope, extent, or conception <the platform provided a *grand* view of the canyon>
syn august, baronial, grandiose, imposing, lordly, magnific, magnificent, majestic, noble, princely, royal, stately; *compare* HUGE
rel monumental, prodigious, stupendous, tremendous; towering; gorgeous, splendid, sublime, superb
con measly, paltry, petty, puny, trifling, trivial
2 marked by great magnificence, display, and usually ceremony or formality <delighted to attend the *grand* presidential fete>
syn gorgeous, impressive, lavish, luxurious, splendid, sumptuous
rel magnificent, majestic; flashy, garish, gaudy, ornate, ostentatious, showy
con crude, meretricious, obtrusive, vulgar; flimsy, tawdry
3 noble in character or spirit <a *grand* outlook on life>
syn elevated, exalted, lofty, sublime, superb
rel magnificent, splendid
con average, common, commonplace, ordinary; base, lowly, mean, poor

grandam *n syn* see BELDAM 1

grande dame *n syn* see MATRIARCH

grandiloquent *adj syn* see RHETORICAL

grandiose *adj* **1** *syn* see GRAND 1
rel ostentatious, pretentious, showy; cosmic, overwhelming, unfathomable, vast
2 *syn* see AMBITIOUS 2

granny *n syn* see FUSSBUDGET

grant *vb* **1** to give as a favor or right <*granted* him an extension of payments>
syn accord, award, concede, vouchsafe
rel bestow, confer, donate, give, present; allow, permit; cede, relinquish, yield
con decline, refuse, turn down
2 *syn* see ACKNOWLEDGE 1
con differ, disagree, dissent; challenge, dispute, object, protest
3 *syn* see GIVE 2

grant *n syn* see APPROPRIATION
rel gift; assistance, benefaction, contribution, donation; alms, charity, dole, handout

granular *adj syn* see COARSE 1

grapevine *n syn* see REPORT 1

graph *n syn* see CHART 1
rel diagram, outline, sketch

graphic *adj* **1** giving a clear visual impression especially in words <gave a *graphic* description of the whole incident>
syn photographic, pictorial, picturesque, vivid
rel clear, lucid, perspicuous; clear-cut, incisive; cogent, compelling, convincing, telling; definite, explicit, precise, realistic, striking, visual
con confused, hazy, indistinct, obscure
2 *syn* see PICTORIAL 1

grapple *n* ***syn*** see HOLD
grapple *vb* **1** ***syn*** see SEIZE 2
2 ***syn*** see WRESTLE
grasp *vb* **1** ***syn*** see TAKE 4
2 ***syn*** see APPREHEND 1
rel envisage, fathom, perceive
3 ***syn*** see KNOW 1
grasp *n* ***syn*** see HOLD
graspable *adj* ***syn*** see UNDERSTANDABLE
ant ungraspable
grasping *adj* ***syn*** see COVETOUS
rel extorting, extortionate
grass *n* ***syn*** see MARIJUANA
grate *vb* **1** ***syn*** see SCRAPE 1
rel abrade, bark, chafe, fray, gall, scuff, skin
2 ***syn*** see IRRITATE
grateful *adj* **1** feeling or expressing gratitude <was *grateful* for the gift>
syn obliged, thankful
rel appreciative, beholden; gratified, pleased
idiom filled with gratitude
ant ungrateful
2 ***syn*** see PLEASANT 1
rel comforting, consoling, solacing; refreshing, rejuvenating, renewing, restorative, restoring; delectable, delicious, delightful
ant obnoxious
gratefulness *n* ***syn*** see AMENITY 1
gratify *vb* **1** ***syn*** see PLEASE 2
rel appease, baby, cater (to), coddle, favor, humor, indulge, oblige, pamper
con bother, irk; aggravate, exasperate, irritate, nettle, rile; agitate, disturb, perturb, upset
2 ***syn*** see SATISFY 3
3 ***syn*** see INDULGE 1
idiom do one proud
gratifying *adj* ***syn*** see PLEASANT 1
rel contenting, satisfying; delighting, gladdening, regaling, rejoicing
con invidious, obnoxious; offensive, revolting
grating *adj* ***syn*** see HARSH 3
gratis *adj* ***syn*** see FREE 5
gratuitous *adj* **1** ***syn*** see FREE 5
rel voluntary, willing
2 ***syn*** see SUPEREROGATORY
3 ***syn*** see BASELESS
rel indefensible, reasonless, unsupportable
gratuity *n* something given over and above what is due, generally in return for or expectation of good service <he found that an occasional *gratuity* smoothed his path>
syn cumshaw, lagniappe, largess, ‖palm grease, ‖palm oil, ‖perk(s), perquisite, pourboire, tip
rel alms, benefaction, contribution, donation; offering, reward
grave *vb* **1** ***syn*** see ENGRAVE 1
2 ***syn*** see IMPRESS 3
grave *n* a place of interment <his *grave* is in the church burial ground>
syn burial, ‖pit, sepulcher, sepulture, tomb
rel catacomb, crypt, vault; mausoleum; ossuary; cinerarium
idiom final resting place
grave *adj* **1** ***syn*** see SERIOUS 2
2 ***syn*** see SERIOUS 1
rel heavy, ponderous; grim, sad, saturnine; awful, dreadful, horrible, terrible
con flippant, light, light-minded
ant gay
3 involving marked risk of impairment or destruction <a *grave* illness>
syn dangerous, fell, grievous, major, serious, ugly; *compare* DANGEROUS 1
rel deadly, destructive, dire, fatal, killing, murderous; frightening, ghastly, terrible; afflictive, severe
con paltry, petty, trivial; harmless, innocuous; temporary, transitory
gravely *adv* ***syn*** see SERIOUSLY 2
grave marker *n* ***syn*** see TOMBSTONE
gravestone *n* ***syn*** see TOMBSTONE
graveyard *n* ***syn*** see CEMETERY
gravid *adj* ***syn*** see PREGNANT 1
gravidity *n* ***syn*** see PREGNANCY
graybeard *n* ***syn*** see GAFFER
gray matter *n* ***syn*** see MIND 1
graze *vb* **1** ***syn*** see BRUSH
2 ***syn*** see GLANCE 1
3 ***syn*** see ABRADE 1
rel harm, hurt, injure; bruise, contuse, wound
greasy *adj* **1** ***syn*** see FATTY 2
2 ***syn*** see SLICK 1
‖**greasy spoon** *n* ***syn*** see EATING HOUSE
great *adj* **1** ***syn*** see LARGE 1
con measly, paltry, petty, puny, trifling, trivial
ant little
2 ***syn*** see FAMOUS 2
rel superlative, supreme, surpassing, transcendent
great deal *n* ***syn*** see MUCH
greater *adj* **1** ***syn*** see BEST
2 ***syn*** see SUPERIOR 1
great gun *n* ***syn*** see NOTABLE 1
greathearted *adj* **1** ***syn*** see BRAVE 1
2 ***syn*** see GENEROUS 1
greatly *adv* ***syn*** see VERY 1
greatness *n* ***syn*** see SIZE 2
greed *n* ***syn*** see CUPIDITY
rel gluttonousness, gluttony, rapaciousness, ravenousness, voraciousness
greedy *adj* ***syn*** see COVETOUS
con bounteous, bountiful, generous, liberal, munificent, openhanded; exuberant, lavish, prodigal, profuse
Greek *n* ***syn*** see GIBBERISH 1
green *adj* **1** ***syn*** see YOUNG 1
2 ***syn*** see INEXPERIENCED
con grown-up, ripe, mature, matured; educated, instructed, trained; proficient, skilled, skillful
ant experienced
green *n* ***syn*** see COMMON 2
‖**greenbacks** *n pl* ***syn*** see MONEY
green–eyed *adj* ***syn*** see ENVIOUS

---

syn synonym(s) ***rel*** related word(s)
ant antonym(s) ***con*** contrasted word(s)
idiom idiomatic equivalent(s)
‖ use limited; if in doubt, see a dictionary

greenhorn *n* ***syn*** see RUSTIC

greenhouse *n* a glass-enclosed structure for the cultivation and protection of tender plants <a small window *greenhouse* full of bloom>
syn conservatory, ‖glasshouse
rel coolhouse, hotbed, hothouse

greenness *n* **1** ***syn*** see YOUTH 1
2 ***syn*** see INEXPERIENCE

greet *vb* ***syn*** see ADDRESS 7

greeting *n* the ceremonial words or acts of one who meets, welcomes, or formally addresses another <after the *greeting* the chairman called the roll>
syn salutation, salute
rel address, hail, hello, welcome
con farewell, good-bye
ant valediction

gregarious *adj* ***syn*** see SOCIAL 2

grief *n* ***syn*** see SORROW
rel bemoaning, bewailing, deploring, lamenting
con comfort, comforting, consolation, solace, solacing
ant joy

grievance *n* ***syn*** see INJUSTICE 2
rel hardship, rigor; affliction, cross, trial, tribulation

grieve *vb* **1** ***syn*** see DISTRESS 2
2 to feel or express deep distress <*grieved* at the loss of so many lives>
syn mourn, sorrow
rel bear, endure, suffer; bemoan, bewail, deplore, lament; cry, keen, wail, weep
ant rejoice
3 ***syn*** see DEPLORE 1

grievous *adj* **1** ***syn*** see ONEROUS
2 ***syn*** see BITTER 2
3 ***syn*** see GRAVE 3
4 ***syn*** see DEPLORABLE

‖**grifter** *n* ***syn*** see SWINDLER

grill *n* ***syn*** see CROSS-EXAMINATION

grilling *n* ***syn*** see CROSS-EXAMINATION

grim *adj* **1** ***syn*** see FIERCE 1
rel foreboding, ominous
2 forbidding in action or appearance <had a *grim* and determined expression on his face>
syn austere, bleak, dour, hard, harsh, severe, stringent
rel cold, forbidding, ‖off-putting; fixed, rigid, set; determined, firm, stern
con calm, mellow, mild, soft, warm; attractive, beautiful, pleasing
ant pleasant
3 being extremely obdurate or firm in action or purpose <fought with *grim* determination>
syn implacable, ironfisted, merciless, mortal, relentless, ruthless, unappeasable, unflinching, unrelenting, unyielding
rel adamant, inexorable, inflexible, obdurate, resolute, stubborn, unforgiving, vindictive; certain, inevitable; determined, dogged
con considerate, gentle, mild; clement, forbearing, indulgent
ant lenient
4 ***syn*** see GHASTLY 1
rel loathsome, offensive, repugnant, repulsive, revolting

grimace *n* ***syn*** see FACE 6

grimace *vb* to distort one's face by way of expressing a feeling <*grimaced* with pain>
syn mop, mouth, mow, mug, ‖mump
rel contort, deform, distort, misshape
idiom make a face (*or* mouth), make a wry face (*or* mouth), pull a face, screw up one's face

grime *vb* ***syn*** see SOIL 2

grim reaper *n* ***syn*** see DEATH 1

grimy *adj* ***syn*** see DIRTY 1

grin *vb* ***syn*** see SMILE
con frown, gloom
ant grimace

grind *vb* ***syn*** see DRUDGE

grind *n* **1** ***syn*** see WORK 2
2 ***syn*** see ROUTINE

grip *vb* **1** ***syn*** see TAKE 4
2 ***syn*** see ENTHRALL 2

grip *n* ***syn*** see HOLD
rel coercion, constraint, duress, restraint

gripe *vb* to complain emphatically and often petulantly <students *griping* about the cafeteria food>
syn ‖beef, ‖bellyache, bleat, ‖blow off, crab, ‖crib, fuss, kvetch, squawk, yammer, yawp (*or* yaup); *compare* COMPLAIN
rel brawl, kick, take on; croak, grouch, grouse, grumble, murmur, mutter
con applaud, approve, cheer; rejoice; accept, bear, endure, tolerate

gripe *n* **1** ***syn*** see HOLD
2 *usu* **gripes** *pl* ***syn*** see STOMACHACHE

griper *n* ***syn*** see GROUCH

grisette *n* ***syn*** see DOXY 1

grisly *adj* ***syn*** see GHASTLY 1
rel eerie, uncanny, weird

grit *n* ***syn*** see FORTITUDE
con faltering, hesitation, vacillation, wavering
ant faintheartedness

grobian *n* ***syn*** see BOOR 2

grog *n* ***syn*** see LIQUOR 2

‖**groggery** *n* ***syn*** see BAR 5

‖**grogshop** *n* ***syn*** see BAR 5

groove *n* ***syn*** see ROUTINE

groovy *adj* ***syn*** see MARVELOUS 2

grope *vb* to reach out or about blindly (as in testing or searching) <*groped* along the wall in search of a door>
syn feel, fumble, grabble
rel poke, pry, root; examine, explore, search

gross *adj* **1** ***syn*** see EGREGIOUS
rel excessive, exorbitant, extreme, immoderate, inordinate
con paltry, trifling, trivial
ant petty
2 ***syn*** see UTTER
3 ***syn*** see FAT 2
4 ***syn*** see WHOLE 4
ant net
5 ***syn*** see MATERIAL 1
6 ***syn*** see COARSE 3
7 ***syn*** see OBSCENE 2

rel animal, carnal, fleshy, sensual; loathsome, offensive, repulsive, revolting; improper, unrefined
con decent, decorous, proper, refined

gross *n* ***syn*** see WHOLE 1

grotesque *adj* ***syn*** see FANTASTIC 2
rel baroque, flamboyant, rococo; eerie, uncanny, weird; extravagant, extreme; comic, comical, droll, ludicrous

grotto *n* ***syn*** see CAVE

grouch *n* an habitually irritable or complaining person <it's hard to live with a *grouch*>
syn ‖bellyacher, complainer, crab, crabber, crank, crosspatch, faultfinder, griper, grouser, growler, grumbler, grump, kicker, malcontent, sorehead, sourpuss
con optimist, Pollyanna

grouch *vb* ***syn*** see GRUMBLE 1

ground *n* **1** ***syn*** see BASIS 1
2 ***syn*** see BASE 1
3 ***syn*** see REASON 3
rel evidence, testimony; antecedent, cause, determinant; demonstration, test, trial
4 grounds *pl* ***syn*** see SEDIMENT
5 ***syn*** see EARTH 2

ground *vb* **1** ***syn*** see FELL 1
2 ***syn*** see BASE
rel buttress, support, sustain

grounded *adj* ***syn*** see AGROUND

groundless *adj* ***syn*** see BASELESS
ant well-founded, well-grounded

groundwork *n* **1** ***syn*** see BASIS 1
2 ***syn*** see BASE 1

group *n* **1** a usually comparatively small assemblage of individuals <people gathered in *groups* about the hall>
syn assembly, band, bevy, bunch, cluster, covey, crew, party; *compare* COMPANY 4, GATHERING
rel circle, clique, coterie, set
con crowd, crush, horde, mob, press, rout, throng
2 ***syn*** see GATHERING 2
3 an assemblage of things constituting a unit <a *group* of houses behind the church>
syn array, batch, battery, body, bunch, bundle, clot, clump, cluster, clutch, lot, parcel, passel, platoon, set, sort, suite
rel assemblage, collection, mess, shooting match
4 ***syn*** see SET 5
5 ***syn*** see SYNDICATE
6 ***syn*** see CLASS 1

group *vb* **1** to make into or bring together in a group <*grouped* the children according to age>
syn assemble, cluster, collect, gather, round up; *compare* GATHER 6
rel adjust, arrange, harmonize, organize, systematize; allocate, dispose, distribute, place; bunch, crowd, huddle
idiom bring together, get together
con disband, disperse, scatter, separate
2 ***syn*** see ASSORT

‖**group grope** *n* ***syn*** see ORGY 2

grouping *n* ***syn*** see CLASS 1

grouse *vb* ***syn*** see GRUMBLE 1

grouser *n* ***syn*** see GROUCH

grovel *vb* ***syn*** see FAWN
idiom lick the dust (*or* one's boots)

groveler *n* ***syn*** see SYCOPHANT

groveling *adj* ***syn*** see FAWNING

grow *vb* **1** to cause (something living) to exist or flourish <*grew* a crop of wheat>
syn breed, cultivate, produce, propagate, raise
rel care (for), foster, nurse, nurture, rear, tend
2 ***syn*** see MATURE
3 ***syn*** see ESCALATE 2
4 ***syn*** see BECOME 1

growl *vb* ***syn*** see RUMBLE

growler *n* ***syn*** see GROUCH

grown *adj* **1** ***syn*** see MATURE 1
2 ***syn*** see OVERGROWN

grown–up *adj* ***syn*** see MATURE 1
ant childish; callow

growth *n* ***syn*** see DEVELOPMENT

grow up *vb* ***syn*** see MATURE

grub *vb* **1** ***syn*** see DIG 1
rel burrow, poke, root
2 ***syn*** see SCOUR 2
3 ***syn*** see DRUDGE

grub *n* **1** ***syn*** see HACK 2
2 ***syn*** see FOOD 1

grubber *n* ***syn*** see HACK 2

grubby *adj* ***syn*** see DIRTY 1
ant immaculate

grubstake *vb* ***syn*** see CAPITALIZE

grudge *vb* ***syn*** see ENVY
rel deny; refuse

grudge *n* ***syn*** see MALICE
rel grievance, injury, injustice

gruesome *adj* ***syn*** see GHASTLY 1
rel appalling, daunting; horrendous, horrific; baleful, sinister

gruff *adj* **1** ***syn*** see BLUFF
rel crabbed, dour, morose, saturnine, sullen, surly; boorish, churlish; fierce, truculent
con bland, smooth, suave, urbane; fulsome, oily, slick, soapy, unctuous
2 ***syn*** see HOARSE 1

grumble *vb* **1** to complain in a low harsh voice and often in a surly manner <workers *grumbling* about the low wages>
syn croak, grouch, grouse, ‖grunt, murmur, mutter, scold; *compare* COMPLAIN
rel ‖beef, ‖bellyache, brawl, crab, fuss, gripe, holler, squawk, whine; groan, moan; complain, kick
con applaud, cheer; rejoice
2 ***syn*** see RUMBLE

grumbler *n* ***syn*** see GROUCH

grump *n* **1 grumps** *pl* ***syn*** see SULK
2 ***syn*** see GROUCH

grump *vb* ***syn*** see SULK

---

syn synonym(s) ***rel*** related word(s)
ant antonym(s) ***con*** contrasted word(s)
idiom idiomatic equivalent(s)
‖ use limited; if in doubt, see a dictionary

Grundy *n* ***syn*** see PRUDE

grungy *adj* ***syn*** see DIRTY 1

‖**grunt** *vb* ***syn*** see GRUMBLE 1

guarantee *n* **1** an assurance for the fulfillment of a condition <gave him a *guarantee* that the work would be done according to specifications>
syn bail, bond, guaranty, security, surety, warranty; *compare* PLEDGE 1
rel earnest, pledge, promise, token, undertaking, word; oath, vow
2 ***syn*** see WORD 8

guarantee *vb* ***syn*** see WARRANT 2

guarantor *n* ***syn*** see SPONSOR

guaranty *n* ***syn*** see GUARANTEE 1
rel bargain, contract

guaranty *vb* ***syn*** see WARRANT 2

guard *n* **1** ***syn*** see DEFENSE 1
2 a person or group on sentinel duty <posted six *guards* around the diamond necklace><turned out the *guard*>
syn lookout, picket, sentinel, sentry, ward, watch, watchman
rel guardian, jailer, keeper, turnkey, warden, warder; patrolman; outguard, patrol

guard *vb* ***syn*** see DEFEND 1
rel attend, mind, tend, watch; accompany, chaperon, conduct, convoy, escort

guarded *adj* **1** ***syn*** see ULTERIOR
2 ***syn*** see CAUTIOUS
ant unguarded

guardian *n* ***syn*** see CUSTODIAN

guardianship *n* ***syn*** see CUSTODY

guardroom *n* ***syn*** see JAIL

gudgeon *n* ***syn*** see FOOL 3

guerdon *n* ***syn*** see REWARD

guerdon *vb* ***syn*** see PAY 1

guerrilla *n* ***syn*** see PARTISAN 2

guess *vb* **1** ***syn*** see CONJECTURE
rel reason, speculate; deduce; estimate, reckon
idiom venture a guess
2 ***syn*** see PREDICT 2

guest *n* **1** ***syn*** see VISITOR 1
2 guests *pl* ***syn*** see COMPANY 2

guff *n* **1** ***syn*** see NONSENSE 2
2 ***syn*** see BACK TALK

guffaw *vb* ***syn*** see LAUGH

guide *vb* to put or lead on a course or into the way to be followed <*guided* them safely through the minefields>
syn conduct, direct, escort, lead, pilot, route, see, shepherd, show, steer
rel accompany, chaperon, convoy; control, manage; contrive, engineer, maneuver
idiom set one on one's way
con bewilder, distract, mystify, perplex, puzzle; beguile, deceive, delude, mislead
ant misguide

guide *n* **1** ***syn*** see LEADER 1
2 ***syn*** see ESCORT 2
rel conductor, director, leader, pilot
3 ***syn*** see HANDBOOK

guidebook *n* ***syn*** see HANDBOOK

guild *n* ***syn*** see ASSOCIATION 2

guile *n* ***syn*** see DECEIT 1
ant ingenuousness; candor

guileful *adj* **1** ***syn*** see SLY 2
ant guileless
2 ***syn*** see UNDERHAND

guileless *adj* ***syn*** see NATURAL 5
ant guileful

guillotine *vb* ***syn*** see BEHEAD

guilt *n* ***syn*** see BLAME
rel crime, offense, sin; responsibility
ant innocence; guiltlessness

guiltless *adj* **1** ***syn*** see GOOD 11
2 ***syn*** see INNOCENT 2
ant guilty

guilty *adj* ***syn*** see BLAMEWORTHY
rel accountable, answerable, responsible; impeached, incriminated, indicted
ant innocent; guiltless

guise *n* **1** ***syn*** see COSTUME
2 ***syn*** see APPEARANCE 2
3 ***syn*** see MASK 2

gulch *n* ***syn*** see RAVINE

gulf *n* **1** ***syn*** see INLET
2 a hollow place of vast width and depth <a *gulf* extending deep into the earth>
syn abysm, abyss, chasm
rel cave, cavity, hollow; crevasse, gulch, ravine; pit, shaft, well

gull *vb* ***syn*** see DUPE

gull *n* ***syn*** see FOOL 3

gullible *adj* ***syn*** see EASY 3
ant astute

gulp *vb* to swallow hurriedly or greedily or in one swallow <*gulped* his lunch and ran off>
syn bolt, cram, englut, gobble, guzzle, ingurgitate, slop, slosh, wolf
rel devour, glut, stuff
con nibble, pick

gum (up) *vb* ***syn*** see BOTCH

gumbo *n* ***syn*** see GOO 1

gummy *adj* ***syn*** see STICKY 1

gumption *n* ***syn*** see SENSE 6
rel astuteness, perspicaciousness, perspicacity, sagaciousness, sagacity, shrewdness

gumptious *adj* ***syn*** see ENTERPRISING 2

gumshoe *n* **1** ***syn*** see DETECTIVE
2 ***syn*** see POLICEMAN

gumshoe *vb* ***syn*** see SNEAK

gun *n* ***syn*** see ASSASSIN

gung ho *adj* ***syn*** see ENTHUSIASTIC

gunk *n* **1** ***syn*** see GOO 1
2 ***syn*** see CRUD

gunman *n* ***syn*** see ASSASSIN

‖**gunsel** *n* ***syn*** see ASSASSIN

gunslinger *n* ***syn*** see ASSASSIN

gurge *vb* ***syn*** see SWIRL

gurgle *vb* ***syn*** see SLOSH 1

gush *vb* ***syn*** see POUR 2
rel flood, flush; emanate, issue, spring

gushing *adj* ***syn*** see EFFUSIVE

gushy *adj* ***syn*** see EFFUSIVE

gussy up *vb* ***syn*** see DRESS UP 1

gust *n* ***syn*** see OUTBURST 1

gusto *n* ***syn*** see TASTE 4
rel delectation, delight, enjoyment, pleasure; ardor, enthusiasm, fervor, passion, zeal

gusty *adj* ***syn*** see WINDY 1
‖**gusty** *adj* ***syn*** see PALATABLE
gut *n* **1** *usu* **guts** *pl* ***syn*** see ENTRAILS
‖**2** ***syn*** see ABDOMEN
3 guts *pl* ***syn*** see COURAGE
4 guts *pl* ***syn*** see FORTITUDE
gut *vb* **1** ***syn*** see EVISCERATE
2 ***syn*** see DRESS 3
gut *adj* ***syn*** see INNER 2
gutless *adj* ***syn*** see COWARDLY
ant ‖gutsy
‖**gutsy** *adj* ***syn*** see BRAVE 1
guy *n* ***syn*** see MAN 3
guzzle *vb* **1** ***syn*** see DRINK 3
2 ***syn*** see GULP
guzzler *n* ***syn*** see DRUNKARD
gyp *n* **1** ***syn*** see SWINDLER
2 ***syn*** see IMPOSTURE
gyp *vb* ***syn*** see CHEAT
gypper *n* ***syn*** see SWINDLER
gyrate *vb* **1** ***syn*** see TURN 1
2 ***syn*** see SPIN 1
gyration *n* ***syn*** see REVOLUTION 1
gyre *vb* **1** ***syn*** see TURN 1
2 ***syn*** see SPIN 1
gyre *n* ***syn*** see REVOLUTION 1
gyve *n, usu* **gyves** *pl* ***syn*** see SHACKLE

syn synonym(s) ***rel*** related word(s)
ant antonym(s) ***con*** contrasted word(s)
idiom idiomatic equivalent(s)
‖ use limited; if in doubt, see a dictionary

H

habiliment *n* **1 habiliments** *pl* ***syn*** see EQUIPMENT
2 *usu* **habiliments** *pl* ***syn*** see CLOTHES

habit *n* **1** a mode of behaving or doing fixed by constant repetition <it was his *habit* to rise early>
syn consuetude, custom, habitude, manner, practice, praxis, trick, usage, use, way, wont
rel bent, disposition, inclination, proclivity, tendency, turn; convention, fashion, form, mode, pattern, style; addiction; groove, rote, routine, rut, set
2 ***syn*** see PHYSIQUE
rel carcass; framework; contour, outline

habitable *adj* ***syn*** see LIVABLE 1
ant unhabitable, uninhabitable

habitant *n* ***syn*** see INHABITANT

habitat *n* the physical environment natural to a kind of being <the watery *habitat* of the eel>
syn haunt, home, locality, range, site, stamping ground
rel environment, locale, surroundings, territory

habitation *n* **1** the act of inhabiting or the state of being inhabited <places suitable for *habitation*>
syn inhabitancy, inhabitation, occupancy, occupation, residence, settlement
rel colonization, domiciliation, peopling; sojourning
2 the place where one lives <*habitations* unfit for human occupancy>
syn abode, commorancy, domicile, dwelling, home, house, residence, residency
rel apartment, flat, tenement; housing, lodging, lodgment, quarters; haunt, haven, homeplace, homestead, place, seat; ‖digs, nest, nook, ‖pad, ‖roost; astre, fireside, hearth, hearthside, hearthstone, roof, rooftree
idiom roof over one's head, where one hangs one's hat

habitual *adj* **1** ***syn*** see USUAL 1
rel constant, established, ingrained, inveterate, persistent, steady
con infrequent, irregular, sporadic, uncommon
ant occasional
2 acting by force of habit <*habitual* smokers who blue the air>
syn accustomed, chronic, confirmed, habituated
rel continual, inveterate, persistent, regular, steady; automatic, instinctive, involuntary; addicted; customary, wonted
con conscious, deliberate, premeditative, purposive, witting

habitually *adv* ***syn*** see USUALLY 1
ant occasionally

habituate *vb* **1** ***syn*** see ACCUSTOM
2 to make acceptable or desirable (as to oneself) through use <*habituate* oneself to poverty>
syn addict, adjust, confirm (in), devote (to), take (to)
rel bear, endure, inure, support, tolerate; condition, familiarize, season
con balk (at), object (to), resist

habituated *adj* ***syn*** see HABITUAL 2

habitude *n* ***syn*** see HABIT 1
rel attitude, position, stand; condition, situation, state
con humor, mood, temper; caprice, freak, vagary, whim

habitué *n* **1** one who frequents a place <an *habitué* of libraries>
syn denizen, frequenter, haunter
rel customer, devotee, patron, sojourner; employer, user
2 ***syn*** see ADDICT

habitus *n* ***syn*** see PHYSIQUE

hack *vb* to cut with repeated crude or ruthless blows <*hack* a path through the jungle>
syn hackle, haggle, slash
rel gash, mangle; chop, cut, fell, hew

hack *n* **1** ***syn*** see TAXICAB
2 one who surrenders intellectual or personal integrity for an assured reward (as a regular income) <party *hacks* and hangers-on>
syn drudge, grub, grubber, hireling, mercenary, slavey
rel grind, lackey, servant, slave; machine, plodder; potboiler

hack *adj* **1** ***syn*** see INFERIOR 2
rel commonplace, dull, ordinary, trite, usual; inconsequential, petty, trivial
con individual, original, uncommon, unusual
2 ***syn*** see TRITE
rel antiquated, old, outmoded, outworn
con lively; unfamiliar

hackle *vb* ***syn*** see HACK

hackneyed *adj* ***syn*** see TRITE
rel antediluvian, antiquated, archaic, obsolete, outmoded, out-of-date; conventional, everyday, quotidian, stock; moth-eaten
ant unhackneyed

Hadean *adj* ***syn*** see INFERNAL 1
rel gloomy, murky, stygian

hades *n* ***syn*** see HELL

hag *n* **1** ***syn*** see WITCH 1
2 an ugly or evil-looking old woman <a pitiful homeless *hag*>
syn ‖bag, ‖bat, beldam, biddy, crone, drab, trot, witch
rel gammer, grandam; ‖battle-ax, fishwife, gorgon, harpy, harridan, shrew, slattern, virago, vixen

haggard *adj* thin and contracted by or as if by fatigue or inner distress <*haggard* from their long vigil>
syn careworn, drawn, pinched, worn
rel angular, gaunt, lank, lean, scraggy, scrawny, skinny, spare; ashen, faded, pale, pallid, wan;

exhausted, fagged, fatigued, tired, wearied, worn-down
con energetic, lusty, strenuous, vigorous; easy, relaxed

haggle *vb* **1** ***syn*** see HACK
2 to argue as to terms <*haggle* over prices>
syn bargain, chaffer, dicker, higgle, huckster, palter
rel barter, deal, horse-trade, trade; bicker, cavil, dispute, quibble, squabble, stickle, wrangle

hagridden *adj* ***syn*** see OBSESSED

hagride *vb* ***syn*** see WORRY 1

hail *n* ***syn*** see BARRAGE

hail *vb* **1** ***syn*** see ADDRESS 7
rel hallo, hallow, holler, shout
2 ***syn*** see COMMEND 2
con belittle, depreciate, disparage, downgrade; berate, censure, condemn, libel, rap; dismiss, reject

hail (from) *vb* ***syn*** see ORIGINATE 5

hair *n* a minute distance, degree, or margin <won the election by a *hair*>
syn ace, hairbreadth, whisker; *compare* HINT 2
rel bit, fraction, jot, mite, particle, trace, trifle

hairbreadth *n* ***syn*** see HAIR

haircutter *n* ***syn*** see BARBER

hairless *adj* lacking hair <he had a shining *hairless* head>
syn bald, glabrous, smooth
rel baldish; shaved, shaven, shorn, tonsured
ant hairy

hairline *adj* ***syn*** see FINE 1

hairsplitting *adj* ***syn*** see FINE 1

hair-trigger *adj* ***syn*** see INSTANTANEOUS

hairy *adj* **1** covered with or as if with hair <wore a *hairy* overcoat>
syn fleecy, hirsute, pileous, pilose, whiskered, woolly
rel bristly, bushy, downy, fluffy, fuzzy, lanate, nappy, pubescent, rough, shaggy, tomentose, tufted, unshorn, villous
con bald, barefaced, beardless, glabrous, shaved, shaven, shorn, smooth
ant hairless
2 ***syn*** see DANGEROUS 1
3 ***syn*** see ROUGH 1

halcyon *adj* ***syn*** see CALM 1
con blustery, fevered, foul, raging, rough, stormy, tempestuous, troubled, tumultuous, wild

hale *adj* ***syn*** see HEALTHY 1
rel husky, stout, strapping
idiom hale and hearty
ant infirm

haleness *n* ***syn*** see HEALTH

half-blind *adj* ***syn*** see PURBLIND

half blood *n* ***syn*** see HYBRID
ant full blood

half-breed *n* ***syn*** see HYBRID
ant full blood

halfhearted *adj* ***syn*** see TEPID 2

‖**half-seas over** *adj* ***syn*** see INTOXICATED 1

halfway *adj* ***syn*** see MIDDLE 1

half-wit *n* ***syn*** see FOOL 4

half-witted *adj* ***syn*** see RETARDED

hall *n* ***syn*** see PASSAGE 4

hallo *vb* ***syn*** see CALL 1

hallow *vb* **1** ***syn*** see BLESS 1
2 ***syn*** see DEVOTE 1
con defile, desecrate, pollute, profane

hallowed *adj* ***syn*** see HOLY 1

hallucination *n* ***syn*** see DELUSION 1
rel apparition, fata morgana, phantom, wraith

hallway *n* ***syn*** see PASSAGE 4

halt *vb* ***syn*** see LIMP 1

halt *vb* **1** ***syn*** see STOP 4
ant proceed
2 ***syn*** see STOP 3
3 ***syn*** see ARREST 1
4 ***syn*** see HESITATE
5 ***syn*** see CLOSE 2

halting *adj* **1** ***syn*** see AWKWARD 2
2 ***syn*** see VACILLATING 2

ham-handed *adj* ***syn*** see AWKWARD 2

hammer *vb* **1** to strike or shape with or as if with a hammer <brass *hammered* into bowls and trays>
syn beat, malleate, pound
rel elaborate, fashion, form, shape
2 ***syn*** see BEAT 1
3 ***syn*** see IMPRESS 3
‖**4** ***syn*** see STAMMER 1

hammer (out) *vb* ***syn*** see ERECT 5

hammerhead *n* ***syn*** see DUNCE

hammerheaded *adj* ***syn*** see STUPID 1

hamper *vb* to impede in moving, progressing, or acting freely <the long dress *hampered* her escape>
syn clog, curb, entrammel, fetter, hobble, hogtie, leash, shackle, tie, tie up, trammel; *compare* HINDER, RESTRAIN 1
rel cumber, encumber, handicap, hinder, impede, lumber, obstruct; baffle, balk, bar, block, foil, frustrate, thwart; restrain, restrict, retard; discomfit, embarrass; check, inconvenience, inhibit
idiom tie one's hands
con free, liberate, loose, release, unfetter, unleash, unshackle
ant aid, facilitate

hamper *n* ***syn*** see OBSTACLE 1

hams *n pl* ***syn*** see BUTTOCKS

hand *n* **1** ***syn*** see SIDE 1
2 ***syn*** see PHASE
3 ***syn*** see HANDWRITING
4 ***syn*** see HELP 1
5 ***syn*** see WORKER
6 ***syn*** see TOUCH 6

hand *vb* **1** ***syn*** see GIVE 3
2 ***syn*** see PASS 9

handbill *n* ***syn*** see POSTER

handbook *n* a concise reference book <a *handbook* of wild flowers>

---

syn synonym(s) ***rel*** related word(s)
ant antonym(s) ***con*** contrasted word(s)
idiom idiomatic equivalent(s)
‖ use limited; if in doubt, see a dictionary

syn Baedeker, compendium, enchiridion, guide, guidebook, manual, vade mecum

con cyclopedia, encyclopedia

hand down *vb* to convey in succession <a skill *handed down* from father to son>

syn bequeath, hand on, pass (on), transmit

con get, obtain, receive

handful *n* ***syn*** see FEW

handicap *n* **1** ***syn*** see DISADVANTAGE

rel burden, encumbrance, load; embarrassment

ant asset

2 ***syn*** see ADVANTAGE 3

handicraft *n* ***syn*** see TRADE 1

hand in *vb* ***syn*** see SUBMIT 2

handkerchief *n* a small usually square piece of cloth used especially for blowing the nose <carry a pocket *handkerchief*>

syn hankie, kerchief, ‖wipe, ‖wiper

‖**handle** *n* **1** ***syn*** see NAME 1

2 ***syn*** see NICKNAME

handle *vb* **1** ***syn*** see TOUCH 1

rel test, try; manipulate

2 to deal with or manage usually with dexterity or efficiency <*handles* his tools with great skill>

syn dispense, maneuver, manipulate, ply, swing, wield

rel direct, guide, manage, operate, run, work; brandish, flourish, shake, wave; aim, lay, level, point

3 ***syn*** see OPERATE 3

4 ***syn*** see TREAT 2

rel conduct, control, direct, manage

5 ***syn*** see GOVERN 3

6 ***syn*** see USE 2

handling *n* ***syn*** see OVERSIGHT 1

handmaid *n* ***syn*** see MAID 2

hand on *vb* ***syn*** see HAND DOWN

hand out *vb* ***syn*** see GIVE 1

hand over *vb* **1** ***syn*** see RELINQUISH

2 ***syn*** see GIVE 3

3 ***syn*** see COMMIT 1

hand running *adv* ***syn*** see TOGETHER 2

handsome *adj* **1** ***syn*** see LIBERAL 1

con economical, frugal, sparing; scrimpy, skimpy

2 ***syn*** see BEAUTIFUL

rel august, majestic, noble, stately; chic, dashing, fashionable, modish, smart, stylish

con inelegant, unsightly

ant unhandsome

handwriting *n* writing in which the letters are formed by a hand-guided implement (as a pen) <legible *handwriting*>

syn calligraphy, chirography, ductus, fist, hand, penmanship, script

rel longhand

handy *adj* **1** ***syn*** see CONVENIENT 2

idiom at one's hand (*or* elbow), ready to hand

ant unhandy

2 ***syn*** see PRACTICAL 2

rel adaptable, advantageous, beneficial, wieldy

con clumsy, cumbersome, cumbrous, unwieldy

ant unhandy

3 ***syn*** see DEXTEROUS 1

hang *vb* **1** to place or be placed so as to be supported at one point or side usually at the top <*hang* the washing on the line>

syn dangle, depend, sling, suspend

rel attach, hook; fix, pin, tack (up); adhere, cling, stick

2 to put to death by suspending by the neck <was *hanged* for stealing a sheep>

syn gibbet, noose, scrag, string (up), turn off

rel execute, lynch

idiom bring to the gallows, hang by the neck, make dance on air (*or* nothing)

3 to remain poised or stationary as if suspended in midair <clouds *hanging* in the west>

syn float, hover, poise

4 to project outward or incline downward <children *hanging* out the windows to watch a parade>

syn beetle, bend (over), jut, lean (over), overhang

rel drape, droop, loll, lop, sag, trail

hang (on *or* upon) *vb* ***syn*** see DEPEND (on *or* upon) 1

hang *n* the special method of doing, using, or dealing with something <can't get the *hang* of this gadget>

syn knack, swing, trick

rel art, craft, skill

hang around *vb* ***syn*** see FREQUENT

hanger–on *n* ***syn*** see PARASITE

rel bystander, follower, spectator, sycophant

hanging *adj* ***syn*** see SUSPENDED

hand–loose *adj* ***syn*** see EASYGOING 3

hang on *vb* ***syn*** see PERSEVERE

hang out *vb* **1** ***syn*** see RESIDE 1

2 ***syn*** see FREQUENT

hangout *n* **1** ***syn*** see RESORT 2

2 ***syn*** see DIVE

hang up *vb* ***syn*** see DELAY 1

hanker *vb* ***syn*** see LONG

rel covet, desire, wish

hankie *n* ***syn*** see HANDKERCHIEF

hanky–panky *n* ***syn*** see DECEPTION 1

hap *n* ***syn*** see ACCIDENT 1

rel destiny, fate, lot, portion

hap *vb* ***syn*** see HAPPEN 1

‖**hap** *vb* ***syn*** see BUNDLE UP

haphazard *adj* ***syn*** see RANDOM

rel accidental; careless, helter-skelter, slipshod; unorganized, unsystematic

con deliberate, designed, intentional, voluntary, willful

ant planned

haphazard *adv* ***syn*** see ABOUT 4

rel accidentally, aimlessly, carelessly, casually, promiscuously

haphazardly *adv* ***syn*** see ABOUT 4

rel accidentally, aimlessly, carelessly, casually, promiscuously

hapless *adj* ***syn*** see UNLUCKY

rel infelicitous; miserable, woeful, wretched

happen *vb* **1** to take place or come about <the incident *happened* at midnight>

syn befall, betide, break, chance, come, come off, develop, do, fall out, give, go, go down, hap, occur, pass, rise, transpire
rel go off, turn out
idiom come to pass
2 to come by chance <he unexpectedly *happened* on a new method>
syn bump, chance, hit, light, luck, meet, stumble, tumble
rel befall

happening *n* ***syn*** see OCCURRENCE

happify *vb* ***syn*** see PLEASE 2

happily *adv* ***syn*** see WELL 5

happiness *n* a state of well-being or pleasurable satisfaction <felt *happiness* at her husband's success>
syn beatitude, blessedness, bliss, blissfulness
rel content, contentedness, satisfaction; cheer, cheerfulness, felicity, gladness; gaiety, jollity, joy; delectation, delight, enjoyment, pleasure
con discontent, dissatisfaction, vexation; cheerlessness, despair, desperation, despondency, hopelessness; distress, misery, wretchedness
ant unhappiness

happy *adj* **1** ***syn*** see LUCKY
rel accidental, casual, fortuitous, incidental; opportune, seasonable, timely
ant unhappy
2 ***syn*** see FIT 1
rel effective, effectual, efficacious, efficient; cogent, convincing, telling; pat, seasonable, well-timed; correct, nice, right
ant unhappy
3 ***syn*** see GLAD 1
rel content, contented, satisfied
ant unhappy; disconsolate

happy-go-lucky *adj* disposed to accept cheerfully whatever happens <enjoyed a *happy-go-lucky* existence without needlessly worrying>
syn carefree, free-minded, insouciant, lighthearted, lightsome; *compare* COOL 2
rel casual, easy, easygoing; blithe, careless, cheerful, feckless, heedless, lackadaisical; debonair, nonchalant, unconcerned; devil-may-care, reckless
con careful, cautious, circumspect, discreet, guarded, prudent

happy hunting ground *n* ***syn*** see HEAVEN 2

hara-kiri *n* ***syn*** see SUICIDE

harangue *n* ***syn*** see TIRADE

harangue *vb* ***syn*** see ORATE

harass *vb* **1** ***syn*** see RAID 1
2 ***syn*** see WORRY 1
rel badger, bait, bullyrag, chivy, devil, heckle, hector, hound, ride
idiom give a bad (*or* hard) time
3 ***syn*** see TRY 2

harassed *adj* ***syn*** see DISTRAUGHT

harasser *n* ***syn*** see BULLY 1

harassment *n* ***syn*** see ANNOYANCE 1
rel aggravation, disturbance, exasperation, irritation, perturbation

harbinger *n* ***syn*** see FORERUNNER 1

harbinger *vb* ***syn*** see ANNOUNCE 2

harbor *n* **1** ***syn*** see SHELTER 1
2 ***syn*** see INLET
3 a place where seacraft may ride secure <a small craft retreated to the safety of the *harbor*>
syn anchorage, ‖chuck, harborage, haven, port, riding, road(s), roadstead

harbor *vb* **1** to provide with shelter or a refuge <*harbored* the refugees in our homes>
syn chamber, haven, house, roof, shelter, shield
rel cherish, foster, nurse, nurture; conceal, hide, secrete; guard, protect, safeguard, screen
idiom give shelter (*or* asylum) to
con eject, evict, expel, oust; banish, deport, exile; eliminate, exclude, shut out
2 to provide with a usually temporary place to live <the miners were *harbored* in camps>
syn accommodate, bestow, billet, board, bunk, domicile, domiciliate, entertain, house, hut, lodge, put up, quarter, room, roost
rel cabin, camp, encamp

harborage *n* ***syn*** see SHELTER 1
2 ***syn*** see REFUGE 1
3 ***syn*** see HARBOR 3

hard *adj* **1** ***syn*** see FIRM 2
rel compacted, compressed, concentrated, consolidated, packed; callous, hardened, indurate, indurated, set; adamantine, flinty, granitic, iron, ironhard
con fluid, liquid; flabby, limp; ductile, malleable, plastic, pliable, pliant; elastic, flexible, limber, resilient, supple
ant soft
2 ***syn*** see SPIRITUOUS
ant soft
3 ***syn*** see REALISTIC
4 ***syn*** see INSENSIBLE 5
5 ***syn*** see INTENSIVE
6 demanding great toil and effort <a *hard* but rewarding task>
syn arduous, difficile, difficult, effortful, formidable, heavy, knotty, labored, laborious, operose, rough, rugged, serious, severe, slavish, sticky, strenuous, terrible, toilful, toilsome, tough, uphill
rel burdensome, exacting, onerous; complex, complicated, intricate, involved, scabrous; backbreaking, distressing, exhausting, fatiguing, grinding, tiring, wearing, wearisome, wearying; bothersome, demanding, irksome, rocky, straining, troublesome, trying; merciless, unsparing
con effortless, facile, light, simple, smooth
ant easy
7 ***syn*** see ACTUAL 2
8 ***syn*** see GRIM 2
9 ***syn*** see SEVERE 3

hard *adv* **1** with great or utmost force <hit the nail *hard*>

---

syn synonym(s) ***rel*** related word(s)
ant antonym(s) ***con*** contrasted word(s)
idiom idiomatic equivalent(s)
‖ use limited; if in doubt, see a dictionary

syn energetically, forcefully, forcibly, hardly, might and main, mightily, powerfully, strongly, vigorously
rel actively, animatedly, briskly, snappily, spiritedly, sprightly, vivaciously; earnestly, intensely, keenly, seriously, urgently, wholeheartedly
idiom with all one's might
con faintly, feebly, nervelessly, softly, strengthlessly, unenergetically, weakly
ant easily, easy
2 in a violent manner <the wind blew *hard* all the next day>
syn fiercely, frantically, frenziedly, furiously, hardly, madly, stormily, tumultuously, turbulently, violently, wildly
rel boisterously, exuberantly, rowdily, uproariously; angrily, brutally, ferociously, savagely, viciously
idiom like a house afire, like fury, like mad
con gently, mildly, softly
3 with intentness and determination <made up her mind to study *hard*>
syn assiduously, dingdong, earnestly, exhaustively, intensely, intensively, painstakingly, thoroughly, unremittingly
rel conscientiously, meticulously, punctiliously
con carelessly, casually, desultorily, fitfully, haphazardly
4 in a fixed and intensive manner <stared *hard* at the offender>
syn closely, intently, searchingly, sharply
con casually, cursorily, idly, offhand
5 in such manner as to cause hardship, difficulty, or defeat <things will go *hard* with him if he doesn't reform>
syn badly, hardly, harshly, painfully, rigorously, roughly, severely; *compare* AMISS 2
rel cruelly; relentlessly; meanly, shabbily, unfairly
con comfortably, pleasantly, smoothly; acceptably, satisfactorily, satisfyingly
ant easily, easy
6 with great or excessive resentment or grief <don't take your setback so *hard*>
syn bitterly, hardly, keenly, rancorously, resentfully, sorely
con casually, lightly, nonchalantly, offhandedly
7 in a firm manner <hold on *hard*>
syn fast, firm, firmly, fixedly, solidly, steadfastly, tight, tightly
con easily, easy, loose, loosely, slackly
8 with difficulty <breathing *hard* after the climb>
syn arduously, burdensomely, difficultly, hardly, laboriously, onerously, toilsomely
rel exhaustingly, gruelingly, painfully, tiredly; awkwardly, cumbersomely, cumbrously, inconveniently, ponderously, unhandily, unwieldily
con effortlessly, evenly, handily, readily, smoothly
ant easily, easy
9 to the point of hardness <the pond is frozen *hard*>
syn firmly, hardly, solid, solidly
10 ***syn*** see CLOSE

hard–boiled *adj* **1** ***syn*** see UNFEELING 2
rel coarse, crude, rough; seasoned, sophisticated, worldly-wise
idiom not born yesterday
con artless, guileless, naive, simple-hearted, unsophisticated; kindly, mild, soft
2 ***syn*** see REALISTIC

harden *vb* **1** to make or become physically hard or solid <this substance *hardens* immediately on exposure to air>
syn cake, concrete, congeal, dry, indurate, set, solidify
rel compact, consolidate, densify, firm, stiffen; anneal, caseharden, temper; calcify, fossilize, lithify, ossify, petrify
con deliquesce, dissolve, fuse, liquefy, melt
ant soften
2 to make proof against hardship, strain, or exposure <frontier life *hardened* most men quickly to rough conditions>
syn acclimate, acclimatize, climatize, season, toughen
rel accustom, habituate, indurate, inure; accommodate, adapt, adjust, conform
con emasculate, enervate; debilitate, devitalize, enfeeble, sap, undermine, weaken
ant soften

hardened *adj* ***syn*** see UNFEELING 2

hardfisted *adj* ***syn*** see STINGY
ant openhanded

hardhanded *adj* ***syn*** see STINGY
ant openhanded

hardheaded *adj* **1** ***syn*** see OBSTINATE
2 ***syn*** see REALISTIC

hardhearted *adj* ***syn*** see UNFEELING 2

hardihood *n* **1** ***syn*** see TEMERITY
rel boldness, intrepidity; brazenness, cockiness; fortitude, grit, guts, pluck, sand
ant cowardice; timidity
2 ***syn*** see INSOLENCE
3 ***syn*** see ENERGY 2

hardiness *n* ***syn*** see TEMERITY
ant cowardice; timidity

hard–line *adj* ***syn*** see TOUGH 3

hardly *adv* **1** ***syn*** see HARD 1
2 ***syn*** see HARD 2
3 ***syn*** see HARD 5
4 ***syn*** see HARD 6
5 ***syn*** see HARD 8
6 ***syn*** see JUST 2
7 ***syn*** see HARD 9

hardly ever *adv* ***syn*** see SELDOM

hardness *n* ***syn*** see DIFFICULTY 1
ant easiness

hardpan *n* ***syn*** see BASE 1

hardscrabble *adj* ***syn*** see BARREN 2

hard–shell *adj* ***syn*** see INVETERATE 1

hardship *n* ***syn*** see DIFFICULTY 1
rel adversity, mischance, misfortune; danger, hazard, peril; affliction, trial, tribulation; drudgery, toil, travail; discomfort, distress
con comfort, ease

hardy *adj* ***syn*** see TOUGH 4
ant tender
harebrain *n* **1** ***syn*** see SCATTERBRAIN
2 ***syn*** see CRACKPOT
harebrained *adj* **1** ***syn*** see GIDDY 1
2 ***syn*** see FOOLISH 2
harefooted *adj* ***syn*** see FAST 3
hark *vb* ***syn*** see LISTEN
rel mark, mind, note, notice, remark
idiom be all ears, not miss a trick
harlequin *n* ***syn*** see CLOWN 3
harlot *n* **1** a woman who engages in unlawful or socially unacceptable sexual intercourse often for material gain <ply the trade of a *harlot*>
syn blowen, courtesan, demimondaine, demimonde, demirep, fancy woman, hetaera, kept woman, paphian, whore
2 ***syn*** see PROSTITUTE
harlotry *n* ***syn*** see PROSTITUTION
harm *n* ***syn*** see INJURY 1
rel deleteriousness; banefulness, noxiousness, perniciousness; mischance, misfortune, misuse; impairment, marring
con aid, help; accommodation, benefaction; charity, favor, service
ant benefit
harm *vb* ***syn*** see INJURE 1
rel abuse, ill-use, maltreat, mistreat, misuse, molest; dilapidate, ruin; discommode, incommode, inconvenience; sabotage, sap, undermine
idiom do violence to
con ameliorate, better, improve; avail, profit
ant benefit
harmful *adj* inflicting or capable of inflicting injury <a *harmful* drug>
syn bad, damaging, deleterious, detrimental, evil, hurtful, ill, injurious, mischievous, nocent, nocuous, prejudicial, prejudicious
rel baleful, baneful, malefic, malign, malignant, noisome, noxious, pernicious, toxic; insalubrious, unhealthful, unhealthy, unwholesome; dangerous, hazardous, risky, unsafe
con innocuous, inoffensive, nontoxic; beneficent, beneficial, benign, benignant, favorable, helpful, salutary, useful; safe, unhazardous
ant harmless
harmless *adj* not having hurtful or injurious qualities <*harmless* pastimes>
syn innocent, innocuous, innoxious, inobnoxious, inoffensive, unoffending, unoffensive; *compare* SAFE 3
rel guiltless; nontoxic, painless, safe
con baneful, dangerous, malignant, noxious, pernicious, toxic, virulent; damaging, destructive, detrimental, hurtful, injurious; deadly, fell, ruinous; improper, unsuitable, wrong
ant harmful
harmonic *adj* ***syn*** see HARMONIOUS 1
harmonious *adj* **1** musically concordant <a *harmonious* morning chorus of birds>
syn blending, chiming, consonant, harmonic, musical, symphonic, symphonious
rel canorous, dulcet, euphonious, mellifluous, mellisonant, melodious, musical, silvery, sonorous, sweet, tuneful; chordal, contrapuntal, counterpointed, polyphonic
idiom in concert, in tune
con clashing, discordant, dissonant, grating, harsh, jangling, jarring, raucous, shrill, strident, tuneless, unmusical, untuneful; atonal
ant disharmonious, inharmonious, unharmonious
2 having the parts agreeably related <a building with *harmonious* proportions>
syn accordant, concordant, congruous; *compare* CONSONANT 1
rel agreeable, pleasing, satisfying; concinnate, symmetrical
con clashing, incongruous, unsymmetrical; askew, distorted, skewed
ant inharmonious, unharmonious
3 marked by accord in sentiment or action <a *harmonious* effort to reach a practicable agreement>
syn amicable, amical, congenial, friendly
rel coactive, collaborative, cooperative; empathetic, empathic, simpatico, sympathetic; calm, irenic, pacific, peaceful
idiom of one accord
con incompatible, uncongenial, uncooperative, unfriendly, unsympathetic; belligerent, contentious, pugnacious
ant inharmonious, unharmonious
harmonize *vb* **1** ***syn*** see AGREE 3
rel cooperate, match, unite
con differ, disagree
ant clash; conflict
2 ***syn*** see AGREE 4
ant differ (from)
3 to bring into consonance or accord <*harmonize* the factions of a political party>
syn accommodate, attune, conform, coordinate, integrate, proportion, reconcile, reconciliate, tune
rel adapt, adjust, correlate; coapt, relate
con alienate, disrupt, estrange
ant disharmonize
4 to combine or adapt so as to achieve a desired effect <*harmonize* the elements of a story>
syn arrange, blend, integrate, orchestrate, symphonize, synthesize, unify
rel coordinate, correlate
harmonizing *n* ***syn*** see RECONCILIATION
harmony *n* **1** musical agreement of sounds <singing in *harmony*>
syn accord, chorus, concert, concord, consonance, tune
rel mellifluousness, melodiousness, melody, musicality, sonority, tunefulness; diapason, polyphony
con cacophony, discord, discordance, discordancy, dissonance, harshness, inharmoniousness, jangle, stridency, tunelessness, unharmoni-

syn synonym(s) ***rel*** related word(s)
ant antonym(s) ***con*** contrasted word(s)
idiom idiomatic equivalent(s)
‖ use limited; if in doubt, see a dictionary

ousness, unmusicalness, untunefulness; atonality
ant disharmony, inharmony
2 the effect produced when different things come together without clashing or disagreement <goals that are in *harmony* with our capabilities>
syn accord, agreement, chime, concord, concordance, consonance, tune; *compare* CONSISTENCY
rel conformance, conformity, correspondence; articulation, coaptation, compatibility, congruity; concatenation, concurrence, integration, oneness, togetherness, unity
con disagreement, discord, disparity, dissidence, disunity, variance
ant conflict
3 the state of persons who are in full and perfect agreement <friends who live in *harmony*>
syn concord, rapport, unity
rel affinity, empathy, fellow-feeling, kinship; peace, tranquillity
idiom meeting of minds
con contention, dissension, strife
ant discord
4 ***syn*** see SYMMETRY
rel concinnity, consonance; dignity, elegance, grace; integrity, unity
con asymmetry, discordance, discordancy, imbalance
ant inharmony

harness *vb* ***syn*** see HITCH 2

||harness bull (*or* **cop**) *n* ***syn*** see POLICEMAN

harpy *n* ***syn*** see VIRAGO

harrier *n* ***syn*** see BULLY 1

harrow *vb* ***syn*** see AFFLICT
rel fret, irritate, pester; badger, bait, bedevil, devil, heckle, hector, needle, tantalize, tease

harrowing *adj* ***syn*** see EXCRUCIATING

harry *vb* **1** ***syn*** see RAVAGE
2 ***syn*** see RAID 1
3 ***syn*** see WORRY 1
rel disturb, irk, perturb, upset; badger, irritate

harsh *adj* **1** ***syn*** see ROUGH 1
rel coarse, granular, loose; bristly, scraggly, scratchy, shaggy, stubbly
con glossy, satiny, silken, silky, sleek, slick, velvety
2 ***syn*** see ACRID
rel acerb, acerbic, biting, burning, mordant; pungent, tangy; dry, sour, tart
con mild, smooth, sweet, velvety
3 disagreeable to the ear <many birds have *harsh* cries>
syn dry, grating, hoarse, jarring, rasping, raucous, rough, rugged, rusty, squawky, strident, stridulent, stridulous
rel discordant, dissonant, immelodious, ineuphonious, inharmonious, unmelodious, unmusical; grinding, jangling, scraping; blaring, brassy; ear-piercing, piercing, shrill, squeaky
con euphonious, harmonious, mellow, melodic, melodious, musical, sonorous, sweet; low, soft; agreeable, pleasing
4 ***syn*** see UNCOMFORTABLE
5 ***syn*** see GRIM 2
6 ***syn*** see SEVERE 3
ant mild

harshly *adv* ***syn*** see HARD 5
con considerately; gently, lightly, well; famously
ant smoothly

haruspex *n* ***syn*** see PROPHET

harvest *n* **1** the act, process, or occasion of gathering a crop <the time of *harvest*>
syn cropping, gathering, harvesting, ingathering, reaping
rel garnering, storing
con planting, seedtime, sowing
2 the gathered produce of land <a bountiful *harvest* saved the settlers>
syn crop, fruitage
rel yield; bearing, vintage

harvest *vb* ***syn*** see REAP
rel assemble, collect; accumulate, amass, bin, store (up), stow (away); cache, hide, hoard, squirrel, stash

harvesting *n* ***syn*** see HARVEST 1

hash *vb* ***syn*** see CHOP 2

hash *n* **1** ***syn*** see MISCELLANY 1
2 ***syn*** see CLUTTER 2
3 ***syn*** see MESS 3

||hashery *n* ***syn*** see EATING HOUSE

||hash house *n* ***syn*** see EATING HOUSE

hassle *n* **1** ***syn*** see QUARREL
2 ***syn*** see COMMOTION 4
3 ***syn*** see ATTEMPT

hassle *vb* **1** ***syn*** see ARGUE 2
rel cavil; brawl, fight, spar, struggle
2 ***syn*** see WORRY 1

haste *n* **1** rapidity of motion or action <we finished our job with great *haste*>
syn celerity, dispatch, expedition, expeditiousness, hurry, hustle, rustle, speed, speediness, swiftness
rel fastness, fleetness, quickness, rapidity; pace, velocity; dash, drive
con languidness, languor, leisureliness, reluctance, slowness; lethargy, sluggishness, torpor
ant deliberateness, deliberation
2 rash or headlong action <oversights due to *haste*>
syn hastiness, hurriedness, precipitance, precipitancy, precipitateness, precipitation, rush
rel impetuosity, impetuousness, impulsiveness
con care, carefulness, circumspection, hastelessness, unhurriedness
ant deliberateness, deliberation

haste *vb* ***syn*** see HURRY 2

hasten *vb* ***syn*** see SPEED 3
2 ***syn*** see HURRY 2

hastily *adv* ***syn*** see FAST 2
rel agilely, nimbly; impetuously, impulsively, unpremeditatedly; carelessly, recklessly, thoughtlessly; precipitately, prematurely, suddenly
con carefully, designedly, studiedly, thoughtfully; gradually, leisurely, slowly, sluggishly
ant deliberately

hastiness *n* ***syn*** see WASTE 2
hasty *adj* **1** ***syn*** see FAST 3
rel agile, brisk, nimble; hurried, quickened
con dilatory, laggard, leisured, leisurely
2 ***syn*** see PRECIPITATE 1
ant deliberate
3 ***syn*** see RASH 1
rel devil-may-care, slambang, slapdash
hatch *vb* **1** ***syn*** see GENERATE 3
2 ***syn*** see GENERATE 1
hatch (up) *vb* ***syn*** see CONTRIVE 2
hatchet man *n* ***syn*** see ASSASSIN
hate *n* **1** ***syn*** see ABOMINATION 2
rel animosity, animus, antipathy, hostility, ill will, rancor; disgust, scorn, spite
con affection; toleration; adoration, veneration
ant love
2 ***syn*** see ABOMINATION 1
rel bother, grievance, gripe, irritant, nuisance, ||pain, trouble
ant delight
hate *vb* to feel extreme enmity or dislike <Cain *hated* his brother> <*hate* to meet strangers>
syn abhor, abominate, detest, execrate, loathe
rel contemn, despise, disdain, dislike, scorn; deprecate, disapprove; resent
con cherish, enjoy, fancy, like, relish; favor, prefer, prize; esteem, respect, revere; dote; idolize, worship
ant love
hateable *adj* ***syn*** see HATEFUL 2
ant lovable
hateful *adj* **1** ***syn*** see MALICIOUS
rel acrimonious, ill-natured; bitter, resentful; mean
con benevolent, charitable, cordial, genial, good-humored, good-natured, kind, kindly, pleasant
2 deserving of or arousing hate <found herself in a *hateful* situation>
syn abhorrent, abominable, detestable, hateable, horrid, odious
rel distasteful, distressing, obnoxious, repellent, repulsive; contemptible, despicable, execrable, opprobrious, reprehensible, scurvy; foul, infamous, vile; accursed, blasphemous, damnable, unspeakable
con compatible, congenial, consonant; alluring, appealing, attractive, charming, enchanting; agreeable, delectable, delightful, likable, pleasant, pleasing
ant lovable; sympathetic
hatred *n* ***syn*** see ABOMINATION 2
rel antipathy, dislike; animosity, enmity, hostility, rancor
con affability, benevolence, benignity, charitableness, cordiality
ant love; admiration
haughtiness *n* ***syn*** see PRIDE 3
ant lowliness
haughty *adj* ***syn*** see PROUD 1
rel aloof, detached, distant, indifferent, reserved; egotistic; contemptuous, scornful
con humble; obsequious, servile, subservient
ant lowly
haul *vb* ***syn*** see PULL 2
rel move, remove, shift; boost, elevate, hoist, lift, raise
haul *n* ***syn*** see LOAD 1
haul up *vb* ***syn*** see STOP 4
haunches *n pl* ***syn*** see BUTTOCKS
haunt *vb* ***syn*** see FREQUENT
haunt *n* **1** ***syn*** see RESORT 2
2 ***syn*** see HABITAT
3 ***syn*** see APPARITION
haunter *n* ***syn*** see HABITUÉ 1
hauteur *n* ***syn*** see PRIDE 3
ant lowliness
haut monde *n* ***syn*** see ARISTOCRACY
have *vb* **1** to keep, control, or experience as one's own <can't *have* your cake and eat it too>
syn enjoy, hold, own, possess, retain
idiom to be possessed of, have in hand
con lack, need, want
2 ***syn*** see INCLUDE
rel admit, compose, comprise
3 ***syn*** see BEAR 3
4 ***syn*** see GET 1
5 ***syn*** see EXPERIENCE 1
6 ***syn*** see LET 2
7 ***syn*** see KNOW 1
8 ***syn*** see OUTWIT
9 ***syn*** see BRIBE
10 ***syn*** see MUST 2
haven *n* **1** ***syn*** see HARBOR 3
2 ***syn*** see SHELTER 1
haven *vb* ***syn*** see HARBOR 1
haversack *n* ***syn*** see BACKPACK
havoc *n* ***syn*** see RUIN 3
rel calamity, cataclysm, catastrophe; despoiling, pillaging, ravaging; vandalism
havoc *vb* ***syn*** see RAVAGE
hawk *vb* ***syn*** see PEDDLE 2
hawker *n* ***syn*** see PEDDLER
hawk–eyed *adj* ***syn*** see SHARP-EYED
hawkshaw *n* ***syn*** see DETECTIVE
haymaker *n* ***syn*** see CUFF
hayseed *n* ***syn*** see RUSTIC
ant city slicker, slicker
hazard *n* **1** ***syn*** see CHANCE 2
2 ***syn*** see DANGER
hazard *vb* **1** ***syn*** see VENTURE 1
2 ***syn*** see GAMBLE 2
3 ***syn*** see ENDANGER
hazardous *adj* ***syn*** see DANGEROUS 1
ant safe; unhazardous
haze *vb* ***syn*** see OBSCURE
haze *n* **1** an atmospheric condition that is characterized by the presence of fine particulate material in the air and that deprives the air of its transparency <*haze* obscured the distant hills>
syn brume, film, mist, smaze

---

syn synonym(s) ***rel*** related word(s)
ant antonym(s) ***con*** contrasted word(s)
idiom idiomatic equivalent(s)
|| use limited; if in doubt, see a dictionary

rel cloud, ‖drisk, fog, murk, ‖smeech, smog, smoke, vapor; cloudiness, mistiness, murkiness, smokiness
2 a state of mental vagueness or obtuseness <lived in a *haze* of pleasant memories>
syn befuddlement, daze, fog, ‖maze, muddledness, muddleheadedness, muddlement
rel dream, reverie, stupor, trance; absentmindedness, abstraction, bemusement, preoccupation, woolgathering
con alertness, attentiveness, awareness

hazy *adj* obscured or made dim by or as if by haze <had only a *hazy* idea of where they were>
syn cloudy, foggy, misty, mushy, vague, vaporous, vapory
rel blurred, clouded, dim, indefinite, indistinct, murky, nebulous, obscure; bemused, dreamy, tranced, stuporous; dazed, ‖mazed, muzzy

he *n* ***syn*** see MAN 3

head *n* **1** the upper division of the body that contains the brain, the chief sense organs, and the mouth <put your hat on your *head*>
syn ‖bean, ‖belfry, ‖chump, ‖coco, ‖coconut, ‖conk, ‖dome, headpiece, noddle, noggin, noodle, ‖nut, ‖pallet, pate, poll, sconce
rel brainpan, cranium, crown, scalp
2 ***syn*** see MIND 1
3 ***syn*** see GIFT 2
4 ***syn*** see LEADER 2
con subordinate; aide, assistant, helper
5 ***syn*** see PROMONTORY
6 ***syn*** see TOILET
7 ***syn*** see HEADLINE
8 ***syn*** see SUBJECT 2

head *adj* ***syn*** see FIRST 3

head *vb* **1** ***syn*** see BEHEAD
2 ***syn*** see DIRECT 2
3 to commence to go in an indicated direction <the cowboys *headed* for town>
syn bear, light out, make, set out, strike out, take off
rel go, proceed, start
idiom make a beeline for
4 ***syn*** see SPRING 1

heading *n* ***syn*** see HEADLINE

headland *n* ***syn*** see PROMONTORY

headline *n* a word or group of words usually in large type introducing and summarizing a newspaper story <*headlines* that screamed the news of the president's death>
syn head, heading
rel banner, banner head, bannerline, scarehead, screamer, spreadhead

headlong *adj* ***syn*** see PRECIPITATE 1
rel daredevil, daring, foolhardy, rash, reckless

headman *n* ***syn*** see LEADER 2

headmost *adj* ***syn*** see FIRST 1

headpiece *n* ***syn*** see HEAD 1

headshaker *n* ***syn*** see SKEPTIC

head start *n* ***syn*** see ADVANTAGE 3

headstone *n* ***syn*** see TOMBSTONE

headstrong *adj* ***syn*** see OBSTINATE
con subdued, tame; amenable, biddable, docile, meek, obedient, tractable

headway *n* **1** ***syn*** see ADVANCE 2

heady *adj* ***syn*** see SHREWD

heal *vb* ***syn*** see CURE

healing *adj* ***syn*** see CURATIVE

health *n* the state of being sound in body or mind <the patient was nursed back to *health*>
syn haleness, healthiness, soundness, wholeness
rel stamina, vitality, well-being; euphoria
con debility, decrepitude, feebleness; ill health, illness, sickliness
ant disease, infirmity

healthful *adj* conducive or beneficial to the health or soundness of body or mind <regular exercise is a *healthful* practice>
syn good, healthy, hygienic, salubrious, salutary, salutiferous, wholesome
rel advantageous, beneficial, profitable, useful; corrective, curative, remedial; aiding, alleviative, helpful, mitigative, restorative, sanative
con insalubrious, unhealthy, unhygienic, unwholesome; damaging, deleterious, detrimental, harmful, injurious, mischievous, pernicious
ant unhealthful

healthiness *n* ***syn*** see HEALTH
ant unhealthiness

healthy *adj* **1** enjoying or manifesting health <a *healthy* baby>
syn ‖bunkum, fit, hale, right, sane, sound, well, well-conditioned, well-liking, whole, wholesome
rel hearty, iron, lusty, robust, thriving, vigorous; rugged, stalwart, strong, sturdy, tough; agile, chipper, spry; blooming, rosy, thriving
idiom fit as a fiddle, in (top) condition, in fine fettle, in shape, in trim, sound as a dollar, up to snuff
con decrepit, delicate, feeble, fragile, frail, weak; infirm, ‖poorly, sickly
ant unhealthy
2 ***syn*** see HEALTHFUL
ant unhealthful
3 ***syn*** see SAFE 3

heap *n* **1** ***syn*** see PILE 1
rel congeries, gathering
2 ***syn*** see MUCH
3 ***syn*** see SCAD
4 ***syn*** see JALOPY

heap *vb* **1** to throw or collect in a pile <*heap* up leaves for a bonfire>
syn bank, cock, drift, hill, mound, pile, stack
rel cord, ‖dess, rick, shock; bunch, clump, lumber, lump, mass; deposit, dump; accumulate, amass, assemble, collect, gather, group
con broadcast, disperse, distribute, scatter, separate, spread, strew
2 ***syn*** see LOAD 3

hear *vb* **1** ***syn*** see LISTEN
idiom get wind of
2 ***syn*** see DISCOVER 3

hearing *n* **1** ***syn*** see EARSHOT
2 an opportunity to be heard <they finally obtained a *hearing* on their complaints>
syn audience, audition
rel conference, interview, meeting, parley; test, tryout; discussion, negotiation

hearken *vb* ***syn*** see LISTEN
hearsay *n* ***syn*** see REPORT 1
heart *n* **1** the seat or center of secret thoughts and emotions <in his *heart* he knew he was seriously in the wrong>
syn bosom, breast, soul
idiom bottom of the heart, cockles of the heart
2 ***syn*** see COURAGE
3 ***syn*** see TASTE 4
4 ***syn*** see CENTER 2
5 ***syn*** see CENTER 3
heartache *n* ***syn*** see SORROW
idiom aching heart, heavy heart
heartbreak *n* **1** ***syn*** see SORROW
rel agony, bale, torment
idiom bleeding heart
heartbreaking *adj* ***syn*** see DEPLORABLE
hearten *vb* ***syn*** see ENCOURAGE 1
rel energize, enliven; arouse, rally, rouse, stir
con damp, dampen; weigh
ant dishearten
heartfelt *adj* ***syn*** see SINCERE 1
rel bona fide, genuine, honest, true, unfeigned; deep, profound
con hypocritical, insincere; false, pretended
heartless *adj* ***syn*** see UNFEELING 2
heartrending *adj* ***syn*** see DEPLORABLE
heart–searching *n* ***syn*** see INTROSPECTION
heartsick *adj* ***syn*** see DOWNCAST
heartsore *adj* ***syn*** see DOWNCAST
heartthrob *n* ***syn*** see SWEETHEART 1
heart–whole *adj* **1** ***syn*** see FREE 6
2 ***syn*** see GENUINE 3
hearty *adj* ***syn*** see SINCERE 1
rel responsive, warm, warmhearted; deep, profound; exuberant, profuse
con cold, dispassionate, emotionless
ant hollow
‖**heat** *n* ***syn*** see POLICEMAN
heated *adj* **1** ***syn*** see HOT 1
ant chilled
2 ***syn*** see FEVERISH 2
3 ***syn*** see ANGRY
heathen *adj* of or relating to people who do not acknowledge the God of the Bible <ancient *heathen* sacrificial rites>
syn ethnic, gentile, infidel, infidelic, pagan, profane
rel heathenish, paganish
heave *vb* **1** ***syn*** see THROW 1
2 ***syn*** see TOSS 2
3 ***syn*** see PANT 1
4 ***syn*** see RETCH
‖**5** ***syn*** see VOMIT
heaven *n* **1** *usu* **heavens** *pl* ***syn*** see SKY
2 an abode of blissful spiritual life after death <the religious conceptions of *heaven* and hell>
syn Abraham's bosom, bliss, Canaan, Civitas Dei, elysium, empyrean, happy hunting ground, kingdom come, New Jerusalem, nirvana, paradise, Zion
rel afterworld, eternity, glory, hereafter, promised land; everlastingness, immortality
idiom Beulah Land (*or* Land of Beulah), City of God, Kingdom of God, Kingdom of Heaven
con earth, world; Gehenna, hades, inferno, netherworld, perdition, pit, Sheol, Tartarus, Tophet, underworld
ant hell
3 ***syn*** see UTOPIA
4 ***syn*** see ECSTASY
heavenly *adj* **1** ***syn*** see CELESTIAL
con hadean, Tartarean
ant hellish
2 ***syn*** see DELIGHTFUL
heavy *adj* **1** having great or relatively great weight <a *heavy* load>
syn hefty, massive, ponderous, weighty; *compare* UNWIELDY
rel awkward, bulky, clumsy, lumbering, lumbersome; unhandy, unmanageable, unwieldy; cumbersome, cumbrous
con airy, buoyant, weightless; handy, manageable, wieldy
ant light
2 ***syn*** see FAT 2
3 ***syn*** see SERIOUS 2
4 ***syn*** see RECONDITE
5 ***syn*** see PREGNANT 1
6 ***syn*** see LETHARGIC
7 ***syn*** see OVERCAST
8 ***syn*** see HARD 6
9 ***syn*** see RICH 3
heavy *n* ***syn*** see NOTABLE 1
heavy–footed *adj* ***syn*** see PONDEROUS 2
heavy–handed *adj* **1** ***syn*** see AWKWARD 2
2 ***syn*** see PONDEROUS 2
heavyhearted *adj* ***syn*** see SAD 1
ant lighthearted
heavyheartedness *n* ***syn*** see SADNESS
ant lightheartedness
heavyset *adj* ***syn*** see STOCKY
heavyweight *n* ***syn*** see NOTABLE 1
con lightweight
hebetate *vb* ***syn*** see DULL 5
hebetude *n* ***syn*** see LETHARGY 1
hebetudinous *adj* ***syn*** see LETHARGIC
heckle *vb* **1** ***syn*** see BAIT 2
rel plague, worry; discomfit, disconcert, embarrass, faze, rattle; tease, torment
2 ***syn*** see MOLEST
hectic *adj* ***syn*** see FEVERISH 2
hector *n* ***syn*** see BULLY 1
hector *vb* **1** ***syn*** see INTIMIDATE
2 ***syn*** see BAIT 2
hedge *vb* **1** ***syn*** see EQUIVOCATE 2
2 ***syn*** see ENCLOSE 1
hedonist *n* one given to the zealous pursuit of pleasure <lead the life of a *hedonist*>
syn carpet knight, pleasuremonger, sybarite
rel bon vivant, man-about-town; epicure, epicurean, gourmand, gourmet; debauchee, libertine, rake; sensualist, voluptuary; pleasure-seeker
ant ascetic

---

syn synonym(s) ***rel*** related word(s)
ant antonym(s) ***con*** contrasted word(s)
idiom idiomatic equivalent(s)
‖ use limited; if in doubt, see a dictionary

hedonistic *adj* ***syn*** see SYBARITIC
con austere, self-denying, self-disciplined, self-restricted
ant ascetic
heebie-jeebies *n pl* ***syn*** see JITTERS
heed *vb* ***syn*** see LISTEN
rel mark, mind, note; observe, see, watch
idiom give (*or* pay) heed to
heed *n* **1** ***syn*** see NOTICE 1
rel awareness, interest, mindfulness; audience, hearing
2 ***syn*** see ATTENTION 1
rel concern, interest
con inattention, unconcern
3 ***syn*** see CARE 4
heedful *adj* **1** ***syn*** see ATTENTIVE 1
ant heedless, unheeding
2 ***syn*** see MINDFUL 2
ant heedless, unheeding
3 ***syn*** see CAREFUL 2
heedfully *adv* ***syn*** see WELL 2
ant heedlessly, unheeding
heedfulness *n* ***syn*** see CARE 4
ant heedlessness
heedless *adj* ***syn*** see CARELESS 1
ant heedful, heeding
heedlessness *n* ***syn*** see APATHY 2
ant heedfulness
hee-haw *vb* ***syn*** see LAUGH
heel *n* **1** ***syn*** see REMAINDER
2 ***syn*** see VILLAIN 1
heel *vb* ***syn*** see SLANT 1
hefty *adj* **1** ***syn*** see HEAVY 1
2 ***syn*** see HUSKY 1
3 ***syn*** see BIG 1
height *n* the distance a thing rises above the level on which it stands <the *height* of a building>
syn altitude, elevation
rel highness, loftiness, rise, tallness, stature
con lowness, profundity
ant depth
heighten *vb* **1** ***syn*** see INCREASE 1
2 ***syn*** see INCREASE 2
rel elevate, lift, raise; better, improve; enlarge, increase
con diminish, lessen, shrink
3 ***syn*** see INTENSIFY
heinie (*or* **hiney**) *n* ***syn*** see BUTTOCKS
heinous *adj* ***syn*** see OUTRAGEOUS 2
con paltry, petty, trifling, trivial
ant venial
heinousness *n* ***syn*** see ENORMITY 1
heir *n* one who inherits <died without *heirs*>
syn heritor, inheritor
‖**heist** *vb* ***syn*** see STEAL 1
hell *n* a place or state of the dead or of the damned <went to *hell* for his sins>
syn abyss, barathrum, blazes, Gehenna, hades, inferno, netherworld, Pandemonium, perdition, pit, Sheol, Tophet
rel limbo, Styx, Tartarus
idiom the hot place, infernal regions, place of torment
ant heaven
hell *vb* ***syn*** see REVEL 1
hell-fired *adj* ***syn*** see UTTER
hellish *adj* ***syn*** see INFERNAL 2
helotry *n* ***syn*** see BONDAGE
help *n* **1** an act or instance of giving what will benefit or assist <the stranded travelers received *help* from passersby>
syn aid, assist, assistance, comfort, hand, lift, relief, secours, succor, support
rel benefit, cooperation, service
ant hindrance
2 something that is beneficial <the rain was a real *help* to late crops>
syn aid, support
rel benefit, use
3 ***syn*** see HELPER
help *vb* **1** to give assistance or support <*help* the children with their lessons>
syn abet, aid, assist, benefact, do for, help out, stead
rel back, bolster, boost, champion, second, support, uphold; avail, benefit, profit; advance, facilitate, forward, further, promote, serve; befriend, succor
idiom give a lift, lend a hand (*or* a helping hand), stand back of (*or* behind)
con bar, block, impede, obstruct, oppose; baffle, balk, foil, frustrate, thwart; discomfit, embarrass; damage, harm, hurt, injure
ant hinder
2 ***syn*** see IMPROVE 1
rel alleviate, mitigate, palliate, relieve
con harm, impair, worsen
helper *n* one that helps <was made boss and assigned a dozen *helpers*>
syn aid, ancilla, assistant, attendant, help, striker
rel helpmate, helpmeet; auxiliary, deputy, subordinate; associate, follower; employee, laborer, servant, worker
idiom helping hand, right-hand man
helpful *adj* **1** of service or assistance <*helpful* suggestions>
syn aidant, aiding, assistive, serviceable
rel beneficial, effective, profitable, salutary, usable; constructive, practical, useful
con timeserving, uncooperative, unreliable; impractical, ineffectual
ant unhelpful
2 ***syn*** see GOOD 1
helpless *adj* **1** lacking protection or support <*helpless* nestlings>
syn defenseless, unprotected
rel abandoned, desolate, forlorn, forsaken, friendless; feeble, weak
2 ***syn*** see POWERLESS
helplessly *adv* ***syn*** see WILLY-NILLY
help out *vb* ***syn*** see HELP 1
helter-skelter *adv* **1** ***syn*** see PELL-MELL
2 ***syn*** see ABOUT 4
hem *n* ***syn*** see BORDER 1
hem *vb* **1** ***syn*** see BORDER
2 ***syn*** see ENCLOSE 1
3 ***syn*** see SURROUND 1

hence *adv* **1** ***syn*** see AWAY 1
2 ***syn*** see THEREFORE
henceforth *adv* from this time forward <made up his mind to keep out of trouble *henceforth*>
syn henceforward, hereafter; *compare* THENCEFORTH
idiom from now on
henceforward *adv* ***syn*** see HENCEFORTH
henchman *n* ***syn*** see FOLLOWER
rel attendant; lackey, minion, stooge
henpeck *vb* ***syn*** see NAG
hep *adj* ***syn*** see WISE 4
herald *n* ***syn*** see FORERUNNER 1
rel courier, crier, messenger
herald *vb* **1** ***syn*** see ANNOUNCE 2
2 ***syn*** see TOUT
Herculean *adj* ***syn*** see HUGE
herd *n* ***syn*** see DROVE 2
herd *vb* ***syn*** see DRIVE 3
here *adv* ***syn*** see HITHERTO 2
hereafter *adv* ***syn*** see HENCEFORTH
hereafter *n* **1** ***syn*** see FUTURE
2 an existence or place of existence after this life <buried pots and tools with the dead for use in the *hereafter*>
syn afterlife, afterworld, beyond, otherworld
idiom great beyond (*or* hereafter), life after death, next world (*or* life), world beyond the grave, world to come
con here and now
here and there *adv* ***syn*** see SOMETIMES
heresy *n* defection from a dominant belief or ideology <the *heresy* of the flat-earth theory>
syn dissent, dissidence, heterodoxy, misbelief, nonconformism, nonconformity, schism, unorthodoxy
rel impiety, infidelity; apostasy, defection, revisionism; error, fallacy
heretic *n* one who is not orthodox in his beliefs <a *heretic* in religion>
syn dissenter, dissident, misbeliever, nonconformist, schismatic, schismatist, sectary, separatist
rel apostate, defector, iconoclast, recreant, recusant, renegade; infidel, unbeliever; deviationist, revisionist
ant orthodox
heretical *adj* of, relating to, or characterized by heresy <*heretical* beliefs>
syn dissident, heterodox, nonconformist, schismatic, sectarian, unorthodox
rel apostate, infidel, miscreant, revisionist; differing, disagreeing, dissentient, dissenting, dissentive, misbelieving, unbelieving
con conventional, established; agreeing, conforming, conformist
ant orthodox
heretofore *adv* ***syn*** see BEFORE 2
heritage *n* **1** something that one receives or is entitled to receive by succession (as from a parent) <the *heritage* of freedom>
syn birthright, heritance, inheritance, legacy, patrimony
2 ***syn*** see TRADITION 1
heritance *n* ***syn*** see HERITAGE 1
heritor *n* ***syn*** see HEIR
hermaphrodite *adj* ***syn*** see BISEXUAL
hermaphroditic *adj* ***syn*** see BISEXUAL
hermetic *adj* **1** ***syn*** see RECONDITE
2 ***syn*** see SECLUDED
hermit *n* ***syn*** see RECLUSE
heroic *adj* **1** ***syn*** see BRAVE 1
ant pusillanimous
2 ***syn*** see HUGE
heroism *n* conspicuous courage or bravery <received an award for *heroism*>
syn gallantry, prowess, valiance, valiancy, valor, valorousness
rel boldness, bravery, courage, doughtiness, fearlessness, intrepidity, spirit; chivalry, nobility
con cowardice, spiritlessness, timidity, timorousness, weakness
ant pusillanimity
hesitancy *n* ***syn*** see HESITATION
hesitant *adj* **1** ***syn*** see DISINCLINED
con resolute, staunch, steadfast
2 ***syn*** see VACILLATING 2
hesitate *vb* to show irresolution or uncertainty <*hesitate* to buy a new car just now>
syn dither, falter, halt, shilly-shally, stagger, vacillate, waver, whiffle, wiggle-waggle
rel balk, boggle, demur, scruple, stick, stickle; fluctuate, oscillate, swing; dawdle, delay, dilly-dally, hang back, procrastinate, stall, temporize; pause
hesitating *adj* ***syn*** see VACILLATING 2
hesitation *n* the act or action of hesitating <several persons volunteered without *hesitation*>
syn hesitancy, indecision, indecisiveness, irresolution, shilly-shally, to-and-fro, vacillation, wavering
rel doubt, dubiety, dubiosity, mistrust, uncertainty; dawdling, delay, procrastination; averseness, indisposition, reluctance
con alacrity, eagerness; courage, mettle, resolution, spirit, tenacity; aplomb, assurance, confidence
hetaera *n* ***syn*** see HARLOT 1
heteroclite *adj* ***syn*** see ABNORMAL 1
heterodox *adj* ***syn*** see HERETICAL
ant orthodox
heterodoxy *n* ***syn*** see HERESY
ant orthodoxy
heterogeneous *adj* ***syn*** see MISCELLANEOUS
ant homogeneous
hew *vb* ***syn*** see FELL 2
hex *vb* ***syn*** see BEWITCH 1
hex *n* **1** ***syn*** see JINX
2 ***syn*** see WITCH 1
hiatus *n* ***syn*** see GAP 3
hic jacet *n* ***syn*** see EPITAPH
hick *n* ***syn*** see RUSTIC
hick town *n* ***syn*** see BURG

syn synonym(s) ***rel*** related word(s)
ant antonym(s) ***con*** contrasted word(s)
idiom idiomatic equivalent(s)
‖ use limited; if in doubt, see a dictionary

hidden *adj* ***syn*** see ULTERIOR
ant open
hide *vb* to withdraw or withhold from sight or observation <they *hid* their loot in a cave>
syn bury, ||bush up, cache, conceal, cover, ||ditch, ensconce, occult, plant, screen, secrete, stash
rel mantle, mask, obscure, shade, shield; entomb, inter; cloak, curtain, shroud, veil; harbor, lodge, seclude, shelter
con bare, disclose, discover, display, exhibit, expose, reveal, show; uncover, unmask, unveil, unwrap; flaunt, parade, show off
hide *n* an animal skin <tanned *hides* for shoe leather>
syn fell, fur, jacket, pelt, skin
hide *vb* ***syn*** see WHIP 1
hideaway *n* ***syn*** see HIDEOUT
hidebound *adj* ***syn*** see ILLIBERAL
hideous *adj* **1** ***syn*** see UGLY 2
ant lovely
2 ***syn*** see OFFENSIVE
3 ***syn*** see GHASTLY 1
hideout *n* a place of retreat or concealment <a gangsters' *hideout*>
syn den, hideaway, lair
rel covert, haven, hermitage, refuge, retreat, sanctuary, shelter; robbers' roost
hie *vb* ***syn*** see GO 1
hierarch *n* ***syn*** see LEADER 2
hieratic *adj* ***syn*** see SACERDOTAL
higgle *vb* ***syn*** see HAGGLE 2
higgler *n* ***syn*** see PEDDLER
high *adj* **1** having a relatively great upward extension <a *high* building>
syn altitudinous, tall; *compare* LOFTY 6
rel aerial, eminent, lofty, soaring, towering; big, gigantic, grand, large, prominent
idiom tall (*or* high) as a steeple
con little, short, squat
ant low
2 ***syn*** see COSTLY 1
ant low
3 ***syn*** see MALODOROUS 1
4 ***syn*** see ELEVATED 4
5 ***syn*** see ACUTE 4
6 ***syn*** see DRUGGED
high and low *adv* ***syn*** see EVERYWHERE 1
high–and–mighty *adj* ***syn*** see PROUD 1
highball *vb* ***syn*** see HURRY 2
highbinding *n* ***syn*** see DECEPTION 1
highbrow *n* ***syn*** see INTELLECTUAL 2
highbrow *adj* ***syn*** see INTELLECTUAL 2
highbrowed *adj* ***syn*** see INTELLECTUAL 2
ant lowbrow, low-browed
higher *adj* ***syn*** see SUPERIOR 1
higher–up *n* ***syn*** see SUPERIOR
highest *adj* **1** ***syn*** see TOP 1
ant lowest
2 ***syn*** see EXALTED 1
highest–ranking *adj* ***syn*** see EXALTED 1
highfalutin *adj* ***syn*** see RHETORICAL
con down-to-earth, matter-of-fact
highfalutin *n* ***syn*** see BOMBAST
high–flown *adj* ***syn*** see RHETORICAL
high–handed *adj* ***syn*** see MASTERFUL 1
high hat *n* ***syn*** see SNOB
high–hat *adj* ***syn*** see SNOBBISH
high–hearted *adj* ***syn*** see SPIRITED 2
high jinks *n pl* **1** ***syn*** see HORSEPLAY
2 ***syn*** see REVELRY 2
highly *adv* ***syn*** see VERY 1
high–minded *adj* ***syn*** see ELEVATED 2
ant low-minded
high–muck–a–muck *n* ***syn*** see NOTABLE 1
high–principled *adj* ***syn*** see HONORABLE 1
high roller *n* ***syn*** see SPENDTHRIFT
high sign *n* **1** ***syn*** see SIGN 1
2 a private usually covert signal, warning, or cue <I gave him the *high sign* when I saw the police approaching>
syn ||office
rel tip, tip-off, wink; nod; alarm, SOS, warning
high–sounding *adj* ***syn*** see PRETENTIOUS 3
high–spirited *adj* **1** ***syn*** see SPIRITED 2
rel jolly, lighthearted, merry, mirthful
ant low-spirited
2 ***syn*** see EXUBERANT 1
high–strung *adj* **1** ***syn*** see TENSE 3
2 ***syn*** see NERVOUS
hightail *vb* ***syn*** see GET OUT 1
highway *n* ***syn*** see WAY 1
high yellow *n* ***syn*** see MULATTO
hike *vb* **1** ***syn*** see RAISE 9
2 to travel about or through on foot <*hiked* through the woods>
syn tramp, tromp
rel footslog; stroll, walk; ramble, rove, wander; explore
hike *n* **1** ***syn*** see TRAMP 3
2 ***syn*** see RISE 3
hilarity *n* ***syn*** see MIRTH
hill *n* ***syn*** see PILE 1
hill *vb* ***syn*** see HEAP 1
hillbilly *n* ***syn*** see RUSTIC
hillman *n* ***syn*** see RUSTIC
hind *adj* ***syn*** see POSTERIOR 2
hind end *n* ***syn*** see BUTTOCKS
hinder *vb* to put obstacles in the way of <their cause was *hindered* by the excesses of overzealous supporters>
syn bar, block, brake, dam, impede, obstruct, overslaugh; *compare* HAMPER
rel arrest, check, interrupt, retard; clog, entrammel, fetter, hamper, hog-tie, manacle, shackle, trammel; curb, deter, hamstring, inhibit, restrain, tie (down); embog, mire; burden, handicap, lumber; baffle, balk, frustrate, thwart
idiom bog down
con abet, advance, aid, assist, ease, encourage, facilitate, forward, promote; accelerate, hasten, quicken, speed
ant further, help
hinder *adj* ***syn*** see POSTERIOR 2
ant fore, front
||hinder *n* ***syn*** see BUTTOCKS
hindmost *adj* **1** ***syn*** see POSTERIOR 2
con foremost, headmost

2 ***syn*** see LAST

hindrance *n* ***syn*** see ENCUMBRANCE
ant help

hinge (on *or* upon) *vb* ***syn*** see DEPEND (on *or* upon) 1

hint *n* **1** a slight or indirect pointing out of something and especially of the way to an end <give me a *hint* on how you would deal with the matter>
syn clue, cue, indication, inkling, intimation, notion, suggestion, telltale, wind
rel innuendo, insinuation; inspiration, prompting; aiming, direction, pointing; key, pointer, tip; advice, assistance
con command, directive, instruction, order
2 a very small amount or admixture <add a *hint* of garlic to the salad>
syn breath, cast, dash, intimation, lick, shade, shadow, smack, smatch, smell, soupçon, spice, sprinkling, strain, streak, suggestion, suspicion, taste, tincture, tinge, touch, trace, trifle, twang, vein, whiff, whisper, wink; *compare* HAIR
rel adumbration, taint, vestige; particle, scintilla
con abundance, heap, lot
ant oodles
3 ***syn*** see ASSOCIATION 4

hint *vb* **1** ***syn*** see SUGGEST 1
2 ***syn*** see POINT 2
3 ***syn*** see ADUMBRATE 1
4 to seek to obtain by sly or indirect means <kept *hinting* for an invitation to the party>
syn angle, fish
rel beg, coax, plead; importune, press; seek, solicit
con ask (for), demand, insist (on *or* upon)

hinterland *n* ***syn*** see FRONTIER 2

hipped *adj* **1** ***syn*** see DOWNCAST
2 ***syn*** see OBSESSED

hire *n* ***syn*** see WAGE

hire *vb* **1** to take or engage something or grant the use of something for a stipulated price or rate <*hire* a conveyance>
syn charter, lease, let, rent
rel contract (for), engage; sublease, sublet, subrent
2 ***syn*** see EMPLOY 2
ant fire

hired girl *n* ***syn*** see MAID 2

hireling *n* ***syn*** see HACK 2

hiring *n* ***syn*** see EMPLOYMENT 4

hirsute *adj* ***syn*** see HAIRY 1
ant hairless

hiss *vb* to make a sibilant sound <he thought he heard a snake *hiss*>
syn buzz, fizz, fizzle, sibilate, sizz, sizzle, swish, wheeze, whish, whisper, whiz, whoosh

hiss *n* ***syn*** see RASPBERRY

history *n* **1** ***syn*** see ACCOUNT 7
2 a chronological record of events <a *history* of the American Revolution>
syn annals, chronicle
rel account, recital, relation, report; diary, journal, memoir; epic, saga, tale

histrionic *adj* ***syn*** see DRAMATIC 1

hit *vb* **1** ***syn*** see STRIKE 2
rel buffet, pound, stroke
idiom give one a clip
2 ***syn*** see OCCUR 2
3 ***syn*** see HAPPEN 2

hit (on *or* upon) *vb* ***syn*** see FIND 1

hit *n* **1** a stroke delivered with a part of the body or an instrument <gave the disobedient boy a *hit* on the head with her ruler>
syn ‖conk, knock, lick, rap, swat, swipe, wipe; *compare* BLOW 1, CUFF
2 ***syn*** see SMASH 6
3 ***syn*** see MURDER

hitch *vb* **1** ***syn*** see LIMP 1
2 to attach as a means of motive power <*hitched* the team to a wagon>
syn couple, harness, yoke
idiom make fast
con free, release, unfasten; uncouple, unharness, unyoke
ant unhitch
‖**3** ***syn*** see MARRY 2
4 ***syn*** see HITCHHIKE

hitchhike *vb* to travel by securing free rides <*hitchhiked* to California>
syn hitch, thumb
idiom bum (*or* hook) a ride

hitherto *adv* **1** up to this particular point or time <imposed order upon what was *hitherto* haphazard>
syn as yet, earlier, so far, thus far, yet
rel before, formerly, heretofore, once, previously
idiom up to now (*or* then)
2 to this place <the appointed delegate shall come *hitherto*>
syn here

hit man *n* ***syn*** see ASSASSIN

hit–or–miss *adj* ***syn*** see RANDOM

hive *vb* ***syn*** see ACCUMULATE

hoard *n* **1** ***syn*** see ACCUMULATION
2 ***syn*** see RESERVE

hoard *vb* to store up beyond one's present or reasonable need <*hoarding* sugar during war>
syn squirrel, stash; *compare* ACCUMULATE, SAVE 4
rel ‖sock away; garner, lay by, lay up
idiom take all one can lay one's hands on
con consume, use up; blow, dissipate, tool (away), fritter, frivol away, prodigalize, throw away, trifle (away), waste

hoarse *adj* **1** rough or dry in sound <developed a *hoarse* cough>
syn croaking, croaky, gruff, husky
rel coarse, dry, guttural, thick
2 ***syn*** see HARSH 3
con honeyed, mellifluent, mellifluous, smooth

hoary *adj* ***syn*** see ANCIENT 1

hoax *vb* ***syn*** see DUPE

---

syn synonym(s) ***rel*** related word(s)
ant antonym(s) ***con*** contrasted word(s)
idiom idiomatic equivalent(s)
‖ use limited; if in doubt, see a dictionary

hoax *n* ***syn*** see IMPOSTURE
hobble *vb* **1** ***syn*** see LIMP 1
2 ***syn*** see HAMPER
hobo *n* ***syn*** see VAGABOND
hoboism *n* ***syn*** see VAGRANCY
hock *vb* ***syn*** see PAWN
hocus–pocus *n* ***syn*** see GIBBERISH 3
‖**hodge** *n* ***syn*** see RUSTIC
hodgepodge *n* ***syn*** see MISCELLANY 1
hogback *n* ***syn*** see RIDGE 1
hogshead *n* ***syn*** see CASK
hog–tie *vb* ***syn*** see HAMPER
hogwash *n* ***syn*** see NONSENSE 2
hoi polloi *n* ***syn*** see RABBLE 2
hoist *vb* ***syn*** see LIFT 1
hoity–toity *adj* ***syn*** see GIDDY 1
hokum *n* ***syn*** see NONSENSE 2
hold *vb* **1** ***syn*** see KEEP 5
2 ***syn*** see ENTHRALL 2
3 ***syn*** see HAVE 1
4 ***syn*** see CONTAIN 2
5 ***syn*** see FEEL 3
hold (with) *vb* ***syn*** see APPROVE 1
hold *n* the act or manner of grasping or holding <lost his *hold* on the side of the boat>
syn clamp, clasp, clench, clinch, clutch, grapple, grasp, grip, gripe, tenure
rel handclasp, handhold; purchase
hold back *vb* **1** ***syn*** see RESTRAIN 1
2 ***syn*** see KEEP 5
3 ***syn*** see DENY 3
hold down *vb* ***syn*** see RESTRAIN 1
holder *n* ***syn*** see OWNER
hold in *vb* ***syn*** see RESTRAIN 1
hold off *vb* **1** ***syn*** see FEND (off)
2 ***syn*** see DEFER
hold out *vb* ***syn*** see OFFER 1
hold over *vb* ***syn*** see DEFER
hold up *vb* ***syn*** see DEFER
hole *n* **1** ***syn*** see APERTURE
2 ***syn*** see GAP 1
3 a space within the substance of a body or mass <buried their trash in a *hole* in the ground>
syn cavity, hollow, vacuity, void
rel gap, hiatus, lacuna; cranny, interstice, niche; fissure, rent, rift; vacancy, vacuum
4 ***syn*** see HOVEL
5 ***syn*** see PREDICAMENT
hole *vb* ***syn*** see OPEN 3
hole–and–corner *adj* ***syn*** see SECRET 1
holiday *n* ***syn*** see VACATION
holiness *n* a state of spiritual soundness and unimpaired virtue <the *holiness* of the saints>
syn saintliness, sanctity
rel blessedness, divineness, divinity, sacredness; consecration, devotion, devoutness, piety, piousness, spirituality
holler *vb* ***syn*** see CALL 1
hollo *vb* ***syn*** see CALL 1
hollow *adj* **1** having a muffled or reverberating quality <had a deep *hollow* gloomy voice>
syn cavernous, reverberant, sepulchral
rel echoing, resonant, resounding, reverberating, sounding
con dead, dull, flat, toneless
2 ***syn*** see VAIN 1
hollow *n* **1** ***syn*** see DEPRESSION 2
2 ***syn*** see HOLE 3
holocaust *n* ***syn*** see FIRE 1
holy *adj* **1** dedicated to the service of or set apart by religion <pilgrimages to *holy* places>
syn blessed, consecrated, hallowed, sacred, sanctified, unprofane; *compare* SACRED 2
rel adored, glorified, revered, reverenced, venerated, worshiped; divine, religious, spiritual
2 ***syn*** see SAINTLY
ant unholy
3 ***syn*** see DEVOUT
‖**Holy Joe** *n* ***syn*** see CLERGYMAN
holy place *n* ***syn*** see SHRINE
Holy Writ *n* ***syn*** see BIBLE
homage *n* ***syn*** see HONOR 1
home *n* **1** ***syn*** see HABITATION 2
2 ***syn*** see HABITAT
3 ***syn*** see COUNTRY
home *adj* **1** ***syn*** see DOMESTIC 1
2 ***syn*** see DOMESTIC 2
homeland *n* ***syn*** see COUNTRY
homely *adj* **1** ***syn*** see PLAIN 1
rel commonplace, familiar, intimate
2 ***syn*** see PLAIN 5
idiom homely as a mud (*or* hedge) fence, homely enough to sour milk
ant comely
homicidal *adj* ***syn*** see MURDEROUS
homicide *n* **1** ***syn*** see MURDERER
2 ***syn*** see MURDER
homilize *vb* ***syn*** see PREACH 1
hominine *adj* ***syn*** see HUMAN
hominoid *n* ***syn*** see ANTHROPOID
‖**homo** *n* ***syn*** see HOMOSEXUAL
homoerotic *adj* ***syn*** see HOMOSEXUAL
homophile *adj* ***syn*** see HOMOSEXUAL
Homo sapiens *n* ***syn*** see MANKIND
homosexual *adj* relating to or exhibiting sexual desire toward a member of one's own sex <*homosexual* acts between consenting adults>
syn gay, homoerotic, homophile, inverted, ‖queer, uranian
rel androgynous, bisexual, epicene; transvestite; lesbian, sapphic; camp, effeminate, ‖swishy
homosexual *n* one who is inclined to or practices homosexuality <a bar frequented by *homosexuals*>
syn ‖fag, ‖faggot, ‖fruit, ‖homo, invert, ‖queer, uranian, uranist
rel transvestite; ‖fairy, ‖nance, ‖nancy, ‖pansy, ‖queen, ‖swish; lesbian, sapphist
homunculus *n* ***syn*** see DWARF
honcho *n* ***syn*** see LEADER 2
hone *vb* ***syn*** see SHARPEN
honed *adj* ***syn*** see SHARP 1
honest *adj* **1** ***syn*** see GENUINE 3
rel reliable, unaffected, unimpeachable
2 ***syn*** see UPRIGHT 2
rel candid, forthright, frank, open, plain; dispassionate, objective; truthful, veracious
ant dishonest

honestness *n* ***syn*** see HONESTY
ant dishonesty

honesty *n* uprightness as evidenced in character and actions <he was generally known as a person of scrupulous *honesty*>
syn honestness, honor, honorableness, incorruption, integrity
rel conscientiousness, justness, probity, scrupulousness, uprightness; dependability, reliability, trustworthiness; goodness, morality, rectitude, virtue
con deceitfulness, mendaciousness, mendacity, untruthfulness; deceit, duplicity, guile
ant dishonesty

honey *n* **1** ***syn*** see SWEETHEART 1
2 ***syn*** see GIRL FRIEND 2

honey *vb* ***syn*** see SUGARCOAT 1

honey (up) *vb* ***syn*** see FAWN

honeybunch *n* ***syn*** see SWEETHEART 1

honeyed *adj* ***syn*** see MELLIFLUOUS

honky–tonk *n* ***syn*** see DIVE

honor *n* **1** respect or esteem shown one as his due or claimed by one as a right <received the *honor* due his rank>
syn deference, homage, obeisance, reverence
rel admiration, esteem; adoration, adulation, devotion, veneration, worship; acknowledgment, compliment, recognition, regard, respect
con contempt, despite, disdain, scorn; disregard, neglect, slighting
ant dishonor
2 an evidence or symbol of distinction <received many *honors* for her devoted public service>
syn accolade, award, badge, bays, decoration, distinction, kudos, laurels
rel deference, esteem, respect; admiration, approval
3 ***syn*** see HONESTY
con disgrace, ignominy, shame
ant dishonor, dishonorableness

honor *vb* ***syn*** see EXALT 1
ant dishonor

honorable *adj* **1** deserving of or entitled to honor (as because of rank, achievements, or service) <medicine is an *honorable* profession>
syn estimable, high-principled, noble, sterling, worthy; *compare* VENERABLE 1
rel august, illustrious, reverend, venerable, worshipful
ant dishonorable
2 ***syn*** see UPRIGHT 2
ant dishonorable

honorableness *n* ***syn*** see HONESTY
ant dishonor, dishonorableness

||**hooch** *n* **1** ***syn*** see LIQUOR 2
2 ***syn*** see MOONSHINE 2

||**hood** *n* ***syn*** see THUG 1

hoodlum *n* ***syn*** see THUG 1

hoodoo *n* ***syn*** see JINX

hoodwink *vb* ***syn*** see DUPE

hooey *n* ***syn*** see NONSENSE 2

hoof *vb* ***syn*** see WALK 1

hoof (it) *vb* ***syn*** see DANCE 1

hoofer *n* ***syn*** see DANCER

hook *vb* ***syn*** see STEAL 1

||**hooker** *n* ***syn*** see PROSTITUTE

||**hookshop** *n* ***syn*** see BROTHEL

hookup *n* ***syn*** see ASSOCIATION 1

hooligan *n* ***syn*** see THUG 1

||**hoosegow** *n* ***syn*** see JAIL

hoosier *n* ***syn*** see RUSTIC

hoot *n* **1** ***syn*** see RASPBERRY
2 ***syn*** see PARTICLE

||**hootenanny** *n* ***syn*** see DOODAD

hop *vb* **1** ***syn*** see SKIP 1
2 ***syn*** see JUMP 1

||**hop** *n* ***syn*** see DRUG 2

hope *vb* ***syn*** see EXPECT 1

hope *n* ***syn*** see TRUST 1

hopeful *adj* **1** full of hope or inclined to hope <the candidate was *hopeful* of winning>
syn hoping; *compare* CONFIDENT 1, EXPECTANT 1, OPTIMISTIC
rel anticipative, assured, satisfied, secure; cheerful, content, easy, undisturbed; fond, optimistic, Pollyannaish, rose-colored, sanguine, upbeat
con doubtful, insecure, pessimistic, uncertain; discouraged, disheartened, gloomy, glum
ant hopeless
2 exhibiting qualities that inspire hope <a *hopeful* prospect for improvement>
syn couleur de rose, encouraging, likely, promiseful, promising, roseate, rose-colored, rosy
rel advantageous, auspicious, propitious; bright, cheering, cheery, golden, halcyon, happy, sunny; budding, up-and-coming
con discouraging, disheartening, dismal, dreary, gloomy, pessimistic
ant hopeless

hopeful *n* ***syn*** see CANDIDATE

hopeless *adj* **1** ***syn*** see DESPONDENT
rel gloomy, glum, morose
con cheerful; assured, confident, optimistic, sanguine, sure
ant hopeful
2 offering no prospect of change for the better <his case was *hopeless* and beyond all human aid>
syn cureless, immedicable, impossible, incurable, insanable, irremediable, irreparable, uncorrectable, uncurable, unrecoverable
rel insoluble; incorrigible, irredeemable
idiom beyond hope (*or* remedy *or* repair), beyond human aid
con correctable, curable, medicable, remediable, reparable
ant hopeful

hoper *n* ***syn*** see OPTIMIST

hoping *adj* ***syn*** see HOPEFUL 1

hop–o'–my–thumb *n* ***syn*** see DWARF

hopped–up *adj* ***syn*** see DRUGGED

hopping *adj* ***syn*** see BUSTLING

---

syn synonym(s) ***rel*** related word(s)
ant antonym(s) ***con*** contrasted word(s)
idiom idiomatic equivalent(s)
|| use limited; if in doubt, see a dictionary

horde *n* ***syn*** see CROWD 1
horizon *n* ***syn*** see KEN
horn in *vb* **1** ***syn*** see MEDDLE
2 ***syn*** see INTRUDE 1
||**horning** *n* ***syn*** see SHIVAREE
hornswoggle *vb* ***syn*** see DUPE
horrible *adj* **1** ***syn*** see GHASTLY 1
rel abhorrent, abominable, detestable, hateful; loathsome, obnoxious, offensive, repulsive, revolting
con gratifying, pleasing, soothing
2 ***syn*** see FEARFUL 3
3 ***syn*** see OFFENSIVE
horrid *adj* **1** ***syn*** see GHASTLY 1
2 ***syn*** see HATEFUL 2
3 ***syn*** see OFFENSIVE
horrific *adj* ***syn*** see FEARFUL 3
horrify *vb* ***syn*** see DISMAY 1
horrifying *adj* ***syn*** see GHASTLY 1
horror *n* **1** ***syn*** see FEAR 1
rel distress, pain, shock, throe, wrench
2 ***syn*** see ABOMINATION 2
hors d'oeuvre *n* ***syn*** see APPETIZER
horse *n* ***syn*** see SAWHORSE
horse *vb* ***syn*** see CUT UP 2
||**horsefeathers** *n pl* ***syn*** see NONSENSE 2
horse opera *n* ***syn*** see WESTERN
horseplay *n* rough or boisterous play <their friendly *horseplay* almost ended in tragedy>
syn fooling, high jinks, roughhouse, roughhousing, rowdiness, skylarking
rel buffoonery, clowning
horseplay *vb* ***syn*** see CUT UP 2
horse sense *n* ***syn*** see SENSE 6
hospice *n* ***syn*** see HOTEL
hospitable *adj* ***syn*** see SOCIAL
ant inhospitable
host *n* ***syn*** see MULTITUDE 1
hostage *n* ***syn*** see PLEDGE
rel guaranty, security, surety
hostel *n* ***syn*** see HOTEL
hostelry *n* ***syn*** see HOTEL
hostile *adj* **1** marked by lack of friendliness or by opposition <takes a *hostile* view of a tax increase><*hostile* tribes>
syn ill, inimicable, inimical, unfriendly
rel argumentative, competitive, contrary, dim, disaffected, disapproving, opposed, opposite, unfavorable; dour, sour; bellicose, belligerent, contentious, pugnacious; militant, warlike
con amicable, benign, friendly
ant unhostile
2 ***syn*** see BITTER 3
hostility *n* ***syn*** see ENMITY
hot *adj* **1** marked by a notable amount of heat <a *hot* day>
syn ardent, baking, blistering, boiling, broiling, burning, fiery, heated, red-hot, scalding, scorching, sizzling, sultry, sweltering, sweltry, torrid, white-hot
rel febrile, fevered, feverish, feverous, hectic; summery, tropic, tropical; mild, warm
idiom hot as a firecracker (*or* furnace), hot as an oven, hot as hell
con chilly, cool, frigid, icy
ant cold
2 ***syn*** see LUSTFUL 2
3 ***syn*** see MARVELOUS 2
4 ***syn*** see CONTRABAND
hot air *n* ***syn*** see NONSENSE 2
hotbed *n* ***syn*** see BREEDING GROUND
hot-blooded *adj* ***syn*** see IMPASSIONED
con callous, hard, unfeeling
ant cold-blooded
hotchpotch *n* ***syn*** see MISCELLANY 1
hot dog *n* ***syn*** see FRANKFURTER
hotel *n* an establishment for the lodging and entertainment especially of transients <spent their vacation at a resort *hotel*>
syn auberge, caravansary, hospice, hostel, hostelry, inn, lodge, public house, roadhouse, tavern
rel boardinghouse, lodging house, pension, rooming house, spa; boatel, motel, motor inn; ||fleabag, ||flophouse
hotfoot *adv* ***syn*** see PELL-MELL
hotfoot *vb* ***syn*** see HURRY 2
hotheaded *adj* ***syn*** see RASH 1
ant cool
hothouse *n* ***syn*** see BREEDING GROUND
hot spot *n* ***syn*** see NIGHTCLUB
hot-tempered *adj* **1** ***syn*** see ILL-TEMPERED
2 ***syn*** see IRASCIBLE
hot water *n* **1** ***syn*** see PREDICAMENT
2 ***syn*** see TROUBLE 3
hound *n* **1** ***syn*** see DOG 1
2 ***syn*** see ADDICT
hound *vb* ***syn*** see BAIT 2
house *n* **1** ***syn*** see HABITATION 2
2 ***syn*** see FAMILY 2
3 ***syn*** see FAMILY 1
4 ***syn*** see ENTERPRISE 3
house *vb* **1** ***syn*** see HARBOR 1
2 ***syn*** see HARBOR 2
housebreak *vb* to commit an act of breaking open and entering with a felonious purpose the dwelling of another by day or night <was arrested again in September for *housebreaking*>
syn break in; *compare* BURGLARIZE, ROB 1
rel knock over, rob; ransack, rifle
idiom break and enter
household *n* ***syn*** see FAMILY 2
household *adj* ***syn*** see DOMESTIC 1
housemaid *n* ***syn*** see MAID 2
houseman *n* ***syn*** see BOUNCER 2
house of God ***syn*** see HOUSE OF WORSHIP
house of prayer ***syn*** see HOUSE OF WORSHIP
house of worship a building for religious exercises <there are many *houses of worship* in this city>
syn church, house of God, house of prayer, tabernacle, temple
rel abbey, basilica, bethel, cathedral, chantry, chapel, conventicle, ||fane, ||kirk, masjid, meetinghouse, minster, mosque, oratory, pagoda, sanctuary, shrine, stupa, synagogue
idiom the Lord's house
house trailer *n* ***syn*** see TRAILER
housing *n* ***syn*** see SHELTER 2
hovel *n* a small wretched dwelling place <migrants forced to live in *hovels*>

syn burrow, hole; *compare* HUT
rel hut, hutch, shack, shanty; pigpen, pigsty, sty

hover *vb* **1** ***syn*** see FLIT 2
2 ***syn*** see HANG 3

howbeit *adv* ***syn*** see HOWEVER

howbeit *conj* ***syn*** see THOUGH

however *conj* ***syn*** see ONLY

however *adv* in spite of that <I accept your decision; I cannot, *however,* approve of it>
syn after all, howbeit, nevertheless, nonetheless, notwithstanding, per contra, still, still and all, though, withal, yet
idiom all the same, be that as it may, for all that, on the other hand

howl *vb* **1** to utter or emit a loud sustained doleful sound or outcry <the dogs *howled* through the night>
syn bay, quest, ululate, wail
rel bark, growl, yelp; blubber, cry, keen, weep, whimper; bawl, squall, yowl
2 ***syn*** see YELL 2
3 ***syn*** see BAWL 2

howl *n* ***syn*** see RIOT 2

hoyden *n* ***syn*** see TOMBOY

hub *n* ***syn*** see CENTER 2

hubbub *n* **1** ***syn*** see DIN
2 ***syn*** see COMMOTION 4

‖**hubby** *n* ***syn*** see HUSBAND

hubristic *adj* ***syn*** see PROUD 1

huckster *n* ***syn*** see PEDDLER

huckster *vb* **1** ***syn*** see HAGGLE 2
2 ***syn*** see PEDDLE 2

huddle *vb* **1** ***syn*** see CROUCH
2 ***syn*** see CONFER 2

huddle (on) *vb* ***syn*** see DON 1

huddle *n* ***syn*** see CONFUSION 3

hue *n* ***syn*** see COLOR 1

huff *vb* **1** ***syn*** see PANT 1
2 ***syn*** see IRRITATE

huff *n* ***syn*** see OFFENSE 2

huffy *adj* **1** ***syn*** see PROUD 1
2 ***syn*** see IRRITABLE

hug *vb* ***syn*** see EMBRACE 1

huge *adj* exceedingly or excessively large <*huge* corporations> <ate a *huge* dinner>
syn Antaean, behemothic, Brobdingnagian, Bunyanesque, colossal, cyclopean, dinosauric, elephantine, enormous, gargantuan, giant, gigantean, gigantesque, gigantic, Herculean, heroic, immense, jumbo, leviathan, lusty, mammoth, massive, massy, mastodonic, mighty, monster, monstrous, monumental, mountainous, planetary, prodigious, pythonic, ‖swapping, Titan, titanic, tremendous, unfathomed, untold, vast, walloping, whacking, whaling, whopping; *compare* GRAND 1
rel bulky, extensive, great, immeasurable, magnificent, towering; outsize, oversize
con diminutive, little, miniature, minute, petite, small, teeny, tiny, wee, weeny

hugely *adv* ***syn*** see VERY 1

hugeness *n* ***syn*** see ENORMITY 2

hugger-mugger *n* **1** ***syn*** see SECRECY
2 ***syn*** see CLUTTER 2

hugger-mugger *adv* ***syn*** see SECRETLY

hugger-mugger *adj* ***syn*** see SECRET 1

hugger-muggery *n* ***syn*** see SECRECY

hull *n* an outer covering of a fruit or seed <peanut *hulls*>
syn case, husk, pod, shell, shuck, skin, ‖slough
rel chaff; bark, peel, rind

hull *vb* ***syn*** see SHUCK

hullabaloo *n* ***syn*** see DIN

hum *vb* to make a low prolonged sound <the wind *hummed* in the chimney>
syn bombinate, ‖bum, bumble, buzz, drone, ‖sowf, strum, thrum
rel moan, murmur, purr, vibrate, whisper
con howl, roar, shriek

human *adj* of, relating to, or characteristic of mankind <problems of *human* relationships>
syn hominine, mortal
rel anthropological, ethnologic, ethological; anthropoid, hominid, hominoid
con angelic, divine, superhuman; animal, brute, subhuman

human *n* a member of the human race <every *human* has a right to live>
syn being, body, ‖character, creature, individual, life, man, mortal, party, person, personage, soul, wight; *compare* MAN 3, MANKIND

humane *adj* ***syn*** see CHARITABLE 1
rel chickenhearted, compassionate, kindhearted, soft-hearted; benevolent, gentle, kind, kindly, mild
ant inhuman, inhumane

humanitarian *adj* ***syn*** see CHARITABLE 1

humanity *n* ***syn*** see MANKIND

humankind *n* ***syn*** see MANKIND

humanoid *adj* ***syn*** see ANTHROPOID

humble *adj* **1** lacking all signs of pride, aggressiveness, or self-assertiveness <accepted her success with *humble* appreciation>
syn lowly, meek, modest, unassuming
rel simple, unobtrusive, unostentatious, unpretentious; acquiescent, compliant, resigned; quiet, subdued, submissive
con ostentatious, pretentious, showy; vain, vainglorious; arrogant, disdainful, haughty, lordly, overbearing, proud, toplofty
ant conceited
2 ***syn*** see IGNOBLE 1

humble *vb* to make lower in status, prestige, or esteem <his devotion to duty *humbled* his critics>
syn abase, bemean, cast down, debase, degrade, demean, humiliate, lower, sink
rel chagrin, mortify; abash, discomfit, embarrass
idiom bring low, take down a peg or two
con aggrandize, exalt, magnify

humbug *n* **1** ***syn*** see IMPOSTURE
2 ***syn*** see IMPOSTOR
3 ***syn*** see NONSENSE 2

---

syn synonym(s) ***rel*** related word(s)
ant antonym(s) ***con*** contrasted word(s)
idiom idiomatic equivalent(s)
‖ use limited; if in doubt, see a dictionary

humbug *vb* ***syn*** see DECEIVE

humdinger *n* ***syn*** ‖DILLY, ‖corker, crackerjack, ‖daisy, dandy, jim-dandy, ‖lulu, nifty, peach, ‖pip

humdrum *adj* ***syn*** see DULL 9

humdrum *n* ***syn*** see MONOTONY

humid *adj* containing or characterized by an uncomfortable amount of atmospheric warmth and moisture <a *humid* climate>
syn mucky, muggy, soggy, sticky, sultry; *compare* STIFLING 1, STUFFY 1
rel clammy, dank, sodden; close, oppressive, stuffy; sweltering
con arid, dry; cool, crisp, fresh

humiliate *vb* ***syn*** see HUMBLE

humming *adj* ***syn*** see BUSTLING

humor *n* **1** ***syn*** see DISPOSITION 3
2 ***syn*** see MOOD 1
3 ***syn*** see CAPRICE
4 that quality or element which appeals to a sense of the ludicrous or incongruous <see the *humor* in a situation>
syn comedy, comicality, comicalness, drollery, drollness, funniness, humorousness, wittiness
rel jocosity, jocularity, jocundity, jocundness; flippancy, levity, lightness; banter, chaffing, jesting, joking, kidding
con earnestness, seriousness, solemnity; depth, profundity
5 something that is or is designed to be humorous <his heavy *humor* fell flat>
syn wit
rel banter, chitchat, pleasantry, repartee
6 ***syn*** see WIT 5
ant humorlessness

humor *vb* **1** ***syn*** see INDULGE 1
2 ***syn*** see BABY

humorist *n* **1** ***syn*** see WAG 1
2 a person noted for or specializing in humor <a writer best known as a *humorist*>
syn comedian, comic, droll, funnyman, jester, joker, jokester, quipster, wag, wit
rel buffoon, card, clown, cutup, gagman, gagster, jokesmith, merry-andrew, prankster, punster, zany; banterer, kidder

humorous *adj* ***syn*** see WITTY

humorousness *n* ***syn*** see HUMOR 4

humorsome *adj* ***syn*** see MOODY

‖**hump** *vb* ***syn*** see CARRY 1

hunch *vb* ***syn*** see CROUCH

hunch *n* ***syn*** see LUMP 1

hunger *vb* ***syn*** see LONG

hungry *adj* feeling distressed from lack of food <a group of *hungry* children>
syn famished, ‖peckish, ravenous, starved, starving
rel rapacious, voracious
con full, glutted, gorged, sated, satiated
ant surfeited

hunk *n* ***syn*** see LUMP 1

hunker (down) *vb* ***syn*** see SQUAT

hunkers *n pl* ***syn*** see BUTTOCKS

hunks *n pl but sing or pl in constr* ***syn*** see MISER

hunky–dory *adj* ***syn*** see MARVELOUS 2

Hunnic *adj* ***syn*** see BARBARIAN 1

Hunnish *adj* ***syn*** see BARBARIAN 1

hunt *vb* **1** to search for or pursue (game or prey) for the purpose of capturing or killing <*hunted* deer in bow-and-arrow season only>
syn chase, run
rel dog, ferret, hawk, hound; course, drive, stalk, start, still-hunt, track; capture, kill, snare; gun, shoot
idiom go hunting
2 ***syn*** see SEEK 1

hunt (down *or* out *or* up) *vb* ***syn*** see RUMMAGE 3

hunting *n* the act or practice of seeking and taking wild and especially game animals <lived by *hunting* and fishing>
syn chase, venery
rel angling, coursing, falconry, fishing, gunning, hawking, shooting

hurdle *n* ***syn*** see OBSTACLE

hurdle *vb* **1** ***syn*** see CLEAR 8
2 ***syn*** see JUMP 1
3 ***syn*** see OVERCOME 1

hurl *vb* ***syn*** see THROW 1

hurly–burly *n* ***syn*** see COMMOTION 4

hurrah *n* **1** ***syn*** see PASSION 6
2 ***syn*** see COMMOTION 3
3 ***syn*** see ARGUMENT 2

hurricane *n* a violent rotating storm or system of winds originating in the tropics and often moving into temperate latitudes <the *hurricane* struck the coast early today>
syn tropical cyclone, tropical storm, typhoon, ‖willy-willy; *compare* TORNADO, WHIRLWIND 1
rel williwaw

hurried *adj* ***syn*** see PRECIPITATE 1
ant unhurried

hurriedness *n* ***syn*** see HASTE 2

hurry *vb* **1** ***syn*** see SPEED 3
2 to proceed or move with dispatch <*hurry* home after school>
syn barrel, barrelhouse, beeline, bucket, bullet, bustle, ‖dust, fleet, flit, fly, haste, hasten, highball, hotfoot, hustle, ‖nip, pelt, rock, rocket, run, rush, scoot, scour, ‖skeet, skin, smoke, speed, stave, ‖tatter, whirl, whish, whisk, whiz, zip; *compare* RUSH 1
rel jog, peg, skelp, trot; bowl (along), breeze; dig in; post
idiom get a move on, go (*or* move) like lightning, make tracks, step on it, step on the gas
con creep, dally, dawdle, drag, lag, linger, loiter, poke, saunter, stroll

hurry *n* ***syn*** see HASTE 1

hurry–scurry *adv* ***syn*** see PELL-MELL

hurt *vb* **1** ***syn*** see INJURE 1
rel abuse, afflict, mistreat, misuse
ant benefit
2 ***syn*** see INJURE 3
3 ***syn*** see DISTRESS 2
4 to experience or be the seat of sharp physical distress <my arm still *hurts*>
syn ache, pain, ‖suffer; *compare* SMART

hurt *n* ***syn*** see INJURY 1

hurtful *adj* **1** ***syn*** see HARMFUL

con harmless, innocuous
2 *syn* see PAINFUL 1

hurting *adj syn* see PAINFUL 1

husband *n* the male partner in a marriage <neglected his responsibilities as a *husband*>
syn ‖hubby, lord, man, ‖master, mister, Mr., ‖old man
rel consort, helpmate, helpmeet, mate, other half, spouse; benedict, bridegroom

husbanding *n syn* see CONSERVATION 1
ant squandering

husbandry *n* 1 *syn* see ECONOMY
2 *syn* see AGRICULTURE

hush *vb syn* see SILENCE

hush (up) *vb syn* see SUPPRESS 3

hush *adj syn* see STILL 3

hush *n* 1 *syn* see QUIET 1
2 *syn* see SECRECY

hushed *adj* 1 *syn* see CALM 1
2 *syn* see PRIVATE 2

hushful *adj syn* see STILL 3

hush–hush *adj syn* see SECRET 1

hush–hush *n syn* see SECRECY

husk *n syn* see HULL

husk *vb syn* see SHUCK

husky *adj syn* see HOARSE 1

husky *adj* 1 big and muscular <a *husky* man carried in the trunks>
syn beefy, burly, hefty
rel brawny, muscular, well-built; stalwart, stout, strapping, strong, sturdy; Herculean, mighty, powerful; Bunyanesque, gigantic
con delicate, fragile, frail; puny, scrawny, slight; elfin; mousey
2 *syn* see LARGE 1

hussy *n* 1 *syn* see WANTON
2 *syn* see MINX

hustle *vb* 1 *syn* see PUSH 2
2 *syn* see HURRY 2

hustle *n syn* see HASTE 1

hustler *n* 1 an alert enterprising individual <he's a *hustler,* eager to get ahead in the world>
syn dynamo, go-getter, live wire, peeler, rustler, self-starter
rel humdinger, hummer; new broom; doer, powerhouse
idiom busy bee
con dawdler, idler; slow coach, slowpoke, stick-in-the-mud
2 *syn* see PROSTITUTE

hustling *adj syn* see BUSTLING

hut *n* a small, simply constructed dwelling often for temporary or intermittent occupancy <the shepherds lived in *huts* in the summer>
syn ‖box, cabin ‖caboose, camp, cot, cottage, lodge, shack, shanty; *compare* BUILDING, EDIFICE, HOVEL
rel bungalow, cabana, chalet, crib, dacha, hooch (*or* hootch), hovel, hutch, lean-to, shed, summer house

hut *vb syn* see HARBOR 2

Hyblaean *adj syn* see MELLIFLUOUS

hybrid *n* an offspring produced by parents of different strains, breeds, varieties, species, or genera <the mule is a *hybrid* of the ass and the horse>
syn bastard, cross, crossbred, crossbreed, half blood, half-breed, mongrel, mule
rel incross, incrossbred, outcross; combination, composite, mixture
con pureblood, purebred, thoroughbred

hybridize *vb syn* see CROSS 4

hydrant *n syn* see FAUCET

‖**hydro** *n syn* see SPA 1

hydroponics *n* the growing of plants in nutrient solution and without soil <tomatoes grown by *hydroponics*>
syn aquiculture, nutriculture
idiom soilless agriculture

hygienic *adj syn* see HEALTHFUL
ant unhygienic

hymeneal *adj syn* see MATRIMONIAL

hymn *n syn* see SONG 2

hymn *vb* 1 *syn* see PRAISE 2
2 *syn* see SING

hypaethral *adj syn* see OUTDOOR

hype *n syn* see PUBLICITY

hype *vb syn* see PUBLICIZE

hyperbole *n syn* see EXAGGERATION
con depreciation, minimization, understatement
ant litotes

hypercritical *adj syn* see CRITICAL 1

hypercriticize *vb syn* see QUIBBLE 1

hypnotic *adj syn* see SOPORIFIC 1

hypocorism *n syn* see NICKNAME

hypocrisy *n* the pretense or affectation of having virtues, principles, or beliefs that one does not actually have <political *hypocrisy*>
syn cant, hypocriticalness, pecksniffery, pharisaicalness, pharisaism, sanctimoniousness, sanctimony, sham, Tartuffery, Tartuffism
rel pietism, religiosity; casuistry, glibness, insincerity, self-righteousness, unctiousness; charlatanry, humbug, quackery
con candidness, fairness, openness; honesty, probity, truthfulness
ant sincerity

hypocrite *n* one who affects virtues, qualities, or attitudes he does not have <don't be a *hypocrite* — if you don't approve, say so>
syn dissembler, dissimulator, lip server, pharisee, Tartuffe, whited sepulcher
rel pietist; actor, attitudinizer, bluffer, charlatan, faker, four-flusher, fraud, humbug, impostor, masquerader, phony, poser, poseur, pretender, quack, sham

hypocritical *adj* 1 characterized by hypocrisy <*hypocritical* compliments>
syn canting, pecksniffian, pharisaic, pharisaical, sanctimonious, self-righteous
rel goody-goody, holier-than-thou, moralistic, pietistic, religiose; casuistic; affected, insincere;

---

syn synonym(s) *rel* related word(s)
ant antonym(s) *con* contrasted word(s)
idiom idiomatic equivalent(s)
‖ use limited; if in doubt, see a dictionary

bland, glib, mealymouthed, oily, smooth, smooth-spoken, smooth-tongued, unctuous
con honest, open, straightforward
ant sincere
2 *syn* see INSINCERE
hypocriticalness *n syn* see HYPOCRISY
ant sincerity
hypostatize *vb syn* see MATERIALIZE 2
hypothesis *n syn* see THEORY 1
hypothetical *adj* **1** *syn* see SUPPOSED 1
rel doubtful, problematic
2 *syn* see ABSTRACT 1

I

icky *adj* ***syn*** see OFFENSIVE
iconographic *adj* ***syn*** see PICTORIAL 1
icy *adj* **1** ***syn*** see COLD 1
ant fiery
2 ***syn*** see COLD 2
ant fiery
idea *n* what exists in the mind as a representation (as of something comprehended) or as a formulation (as of a plan) <that's not my *idea* of a good time>
syn apprehension, conceit, concept, conception, image, impression, intellection, notion, perception, thought
rel assumption, belief, conclusion, conviction, estimation, feeling, inclination, judgment, opinion, persuasion, presumption, reaction, reflection, sentiment, view; conjecture, guess, hypothesis, speculation, supposition, surmise, suspicion, theory; caprice, fancy, fantasy, vagary, whim, whimsy; brainstorm, inspiration
ideal *adj* **1** ***syn*** see ABSTRACT 1
ant actual
2 ***syn*** see CONCEPTUAL
3 constituting a standard (as of perfection or excellence) <the *ideal* man of letters>
syn flawless, indefectible, model
rel archetypal, archetypical, prototypal, prototypical
con average, normal, representative, typical
4 ***syn*** see PERFECT 3
5 ***syn*** see TYPICAL 1
ideal *n* **1** ***syn*** see MODEL 2
2 ***syn*** see PARAGON
idealist *n* ***syn*** see DREAMER
idealist *adj* ***syn*** see IDEALISTIC
idealistic *adj* characterized by idealism <made an *idealistic* speech on human rights>
syn idealist, utopian, visionary
rel impractical, poetical, quixotic, romantic, starry, starry-eyed, unrealistic
con empirical, matter-of-fact, practical, pragmatic, rational, realistic
ant unidealistic
ideational *adj* ***syn*** see CONCEPTUAL
identic *adj* ***syn*** see SAME 2
ant nonidentical
identical *adj* **1** ***syn*** see SAME 1
2 ***syn*** see SAME 2
ant nonidentical
identicalness *n* ***syn*** see IDENTITY 1
identification *n* ***syn*** see RECOGNITION 1
identify *vb* to establish the identity of <the culprit was *identified* by his fingerprints>
syn determinate, diagnose, diagnosticate, distinguish, finger, pinpoint, place, recognize, spot
rel find; determine, establish, make out, pick out, select, separate (out)
identity *n* **1** the quality of being the same in all that constitutes the objective reality of separate things <the *identity* of the two texts is exact>
syn identicalness, oneness, sameness, selfsameness
rel agreement, likeness, resemblance, semblance, similarity, similitude; correspondence, equality, equivalence; uniformity
con dissimilarity, dissimilitude, unlikeness, unsimilarity
ant nonidentity
2 ***syn*** see INDIVIDUALITY 4
ideologue *n* ***syn*** see DREAMER
ideology *n* an overall view of or attitude toward life <an *ideology* based on tolerance>
syn credo, creed, weltanschauung
rel outlook, philosophy, view
idiom *n* ***syn*** see LANGUAGE 1
idiosyncratic *adj* **1** ***syn*** see CHARACTERISTIC
2 ***syn*** see STRANGE 4
idiot *n* **1** ***syn*** see FOOL 1
2 ***syn*** see FOOL 2
3 ***syn*** see FOOL 4
4 ***syn*** see DUNCE
||idiot box *n* ***syn*** see TELEVISION
idle *adj* **1** ***syn*** see VAIN 1
2 ***syn*** see VACANT 4
3 ***syn*** see INACTIVE
ant busy
idle *vb* to spend time in idleness <people *idling* in the park>
syn ||brogue, bum, dawdle, diddle, diddle-daddle, drone, goldbrick, ||goof (off), ||lallygag, laze, lazy, loaf, loiter, loll, lounge
rel relax, repose, rest; amble, linger, mooch, mosey, saunter, stroll, tarry; hang around, sit around, sit back, sit by
idiom dog it, kill time, lie around, mark time
idleheaded *adj* ***syn*** see FOOLISH 2
idleness *n* ***syn*** see SLOTH 1
idler *n* ***syn*** see SLUGGARD
idolatry *n* ***syn*** see ADORATION
idolization *n* ***syn*** see ADORATION
idolize *vb* ***syn*** see ADORE 3
idiom worship the ground one walks on
iffy *adj* ***syn*** see UNCERTAIN 1
ignis fatuus *n* ***syn*** see DELUSION 1
ignitable *adj* ***syn*** see COMBUSTIBLE 1
ignite *vb* ***syn*** see LIGHT 1
ignited *adj* ***syn*** see BURNING 1
ignoble *adj* **1** belonging to or characteristic of socially or economically inferior classes <a person of *ignoble* antecedents>

syn synonym(s) ***rel*** related word(s)
ant antonym(s) ***con*** contrasted word(s)
idiom idiomatic equivalent(s)
|| use limited; if in doubt, see a dictionary

syn base, baseborn, humble, low, lowborn, lowly, mean, plebeian, unennobled, unwashed
rel coarse, common, homely, inferior, inglorious, modest, ordinary, peasant, plain, poor, popular, simple, vulgar
con highborn, highbred, wellborn, well-bred; eminent, high, lofty, proud, superior
ant noble
2 ***syn*** see BASE 3
ant noble

ignominious *adj* ***syn*** see DISREPUTABLE 1

ignominy *n* ***syn*** see DISGRACE
rel contempt, despite, disdain, scorn; chagrin, mortification
con glory, honor; esteem, respect

ignoramus *n* ***syn*** see DUNCE

ignorance *n* **1** the state of being unlearned <the blight of *ignorance*>
syn benightedness, illiteracy
rel callowness, greenness, inexperience, naiveté, rawness, simpleness, simplicity, uncouthness, uncultivation, unsophistication; empty-headedness, unintelligence, witlessness; know-nothingism, philistinism
con education, enlightenment, erudition, learning, literacy
2 the state of being unaware or uninformed <*ignorance* of the law>
syn innocence, inscience, nescience, unacquaintance, unacquaintedness, unawareness, unfamiliarity, unknowingness
con acquaintance, acquaintanceship, experience; awareness, familiarity, knowledgeableness

ignorant *adj* **1** lacking knowledge or education <an *ignorant* boy with no taste for school>
syn benighted, empty-headed, illiterate, know-nothing, rude, uneducated, uninstructed, unlettered, unschooled, untaught, untutored
rel lowbrow, uncultured, unintellectual; callow, green, inexperienced; crude, gross, raw, uncouth; ingenuous, naive, simple, unsophisticated
con educated, erudite, learned, literate
2 lacking information on or awareness of something <was *ignorant* of the circumstances surrounding the affair>
syn incognizant, inconversant, oblivious, unacquainted, unaware, unfamiliar, uninformed, uninstructed, unknowing, unwitting
idiom in the dark
con aware, conscious, conversant, informed, knowing, knowledgeable
3 ***syn*** see BACKWARD 5

ignore *vb* ***syn*** see NEGLECT
rel avoid, evade

ilk *n* ***syn*** see TYPE

ill *adj* **1** ***syn*** see EVIL 5
ant good
2 ***syn*** see HARMFUL
3 ***syn*** see SICK 1
4 ***syn*** see RUDE 6
5 ***syn*** see HOSTILE 1

ill *n* **1** ***syn*** see EVIL 1
ant benefit
2 ***syn*** see DISEASE 1

ill–adapted *adj* ***syn*** see UNFIT 1

ill–advised *adj* **1** ***syn*** see RASH 1
2 ***syn*** see INADVISABLE
ant well-advised
3 ***syn*** see UNWISE
ant well-advised

illation *n* **1** ***syn*** see INFERENCE 1
2 ***syn*** see INFERENCE 2

ill–behaved *adj* ***syn*** see NAUGHTY 1

ill–boding *adj* ***syn*** see OMINOUS

ill–bred *adj* **1** ***syn*** see BOORISH
ant well-bred
2 ***syn*** see RUDE 6
ant well-bred, well-mannered

ill–chosen *adj* ***syn*** see INFELICITOUS

ill–defined *adj* ***syn*** see FAINT 2
ant well-defined

illegal *adj* ***syn*** see UNLAWFUL
rel banned, forbidden, interdicted, prohibited, proscribed, outlawed, unauthorized, unlicensed, unwarranted; felonious; contraband, hot; actionable, irregular
con authorized, lawful, licensed, licit, permitted, regular, right
ant legal

illegality *n* the quality or state of being illegal <the *illegality* of an act>
syn illegitimacy, illicitness, unlawfulness
rel badness, impropriety, wrongness
con lawfulness, legitimacy, licitness; propriety
ant legality

illegible *adj* incapable of being read or deciphered <an *illegible* signature>
syn indecipherable, undecipherable, unreadable
rel faint, indistinct, obscure, unclear
ant legible, readable

illegitimacy *n* **1** the state or condition of being born out of wedlock <he accepted the fact of his *illegitimacy*>
syn bastardy, illegitimateness, supposititiousness
rel bar sinister
ant legitimacy, legitimateness
2 ***syn*** see ILLEGALITY
ant legitimacy, legitimateness

illegitimate *adj* **1** not recognized by law as lawful offspring <an *illegitimate* child>
syn baseborn, bastard, fatherless, misbegotten, natural, spurious, supposititious, unfathered
rel birthless; adulterine
ant legitimate
2 ***syn*** see UNLAWFUL
ant legitimate

illegitimate *n* ***syn*** see BASTARD 1
ant legitimate

illegitimateness *n* ***syn*** see ILLEGITIMACY 1
ant legitimacy, legitimateness

ill–famed *adj* ***syn*** see INFAMOUS 1

ill–fated *adj* ***syn*** see UNLUCKY

ill–favored *adj* **1** ***syn*** see UGLY 2
ant well-favored
2 ***syn*** see OBJECTIONABLE

ill–flavored *adj* ***syn*** see UNPALATABLE 1

ill–humored *adj* ***syn*** see ILL-TEMPERED

ant good-humored, good-natured

illiberal *adj* unwilling or unable to grasp the point of view of others <had the *illiberal* outlook of an old-time schoolmaster>
syn bigoted, brassbound, hidebound, intolerant, narrow, narrow-minded, small-minded, unenlarged
rel biased, jaundiced, one-sided, opinionated, partial, partisan, prejudiced; grudging, little, mean, paltry, petty, small, uncharitable, ungenerous; insular, parochial, provincial; rigid, rigorous, stringent
con broad-minded, open-minded, tolerant, unbigoted; advanced, progressive, radical
ant liberal

illicit *adj* ***syn*** see UNLAWFUL
ant licit

illicitness *n* ***syn*** see ILLEGALITY

illimitable *adj* ***syn*** see INFINITE 1
rel endless, interminable
ant limitable; limited

illiteracy *n* ***syn*** see IGNORANCE 1

illiterate *adj* ***syn*** see IGNORANT 1
ant literate; erudite

illiterate *n* one who cannot read or write <the training of adult *illiterates*>
syn analphabet
rel functional illiterate, semiliterate, subliterate
ant literate

ill-judged *adj* ***syn*** see UNWISE

ill-kempt *adj* ***syn*** see SLOVENLY 1

ill-looking *adj* ***syn*** see UGLY 2
ant good-looking, ||well-looked

ill-mannered *adj* ***syn*** see RUDE 6
ant well-bred, well-mannered

ill-natured *adj* ***syn*** see ILL-TEMPERED
ant good-humored, good-natured

illness *n* ***syn*** see SICKNESS 1
ant health

illogical *adj* contrary to or devoid of logic <came to an *illogical* conclusion from the facts presented>
syn fallacious, invalid, irrational, mad, nonrational, reasonless, sophistic, unreasonable, unreasoned; *compare* FALSE 1
rel inconsistent; specious; unscientific, unsound; absurd, meaningless, senseless
idiom without rhyme or reason
con rational, reasonable, sensible; plausible, sane, sound, valid
ant logical

ill-omened *adj* ***syn*** see OMINOUS
ant auspicious

ill-seasoned *adj* ***syn*** see UNSEASONABLE 1
ant seasonable

ill-starred *adj* ***syn*** see UNLUCKY
rel bodeful, fateful, foreboding, ominous, portentous; baleful, malefic, malign, sinister; unfavorable, unpromising, unpropitious

ill-suited *adj* ***syn*** see UNFIT 1

ill-tempered *adj* having a bad temper <an *ill-tempered* old man>
syn bad-tempered, dyspeptic, hot-tempered, ill-humored, ill-natured, ||rusty, tempersome
rel crabbed, surly; fractious, huffy, irritable, peevish, petulant, querulous, snappish, sour, waspish; shrewish, vixenish
con calm, easy, placid, serene, tranquil; amiable, complaisant, considerate, good-natured, kindly, obliging, tolerant
ant good-tempered, sweet-tempered, well-tempered

ill-timed *adj* **1** ***syn*** see UNSEASONABLE 1
ant seasonable
2 ***syn*** see IMPROPER 1

ill-treat *vb* ***syn*** see ABUSE 4
rel aggrieve, harass, harry, molest
con befriend, relieve, succor; countenance, encourage, favor, patronize

illude *vb* ***syn*** see DECEIVE

illume *vb* **1** ***syn*** see ILLUMINATE 1
2 ***syn*** see ILLUMINATE 2

illuminant *adj* ***syn*** see ENLIGHTENING

illuminate *vb* **1** to supply with physical light <a room dimly *illuminated* by firelight>
syn illume, illumine, light, lighten
rel brighten; irradiate; floodlight, highlight, spotlight; fire, ignite, kindle
con blur, cloud, darken, dim, dull, obscure, pale
2 to supply with spiritual or intellectual light <the worth of a truly *illuminating* book>
syn edify, enlighten, illume, illumine, improve, irradiate, uplift
rel better, improve; ennoble, exalt, refine; finish, mature, perfect, polish
con becloud, cloud, darken, obfuscate, obscure, overshadow, shadow
3 ***syn*** see CLARIFY 2
rel construe, define, dramatize, expound, express, gloss, interpret
idiom shed light on (*or* upon)
con baffle, confound, confuse, mystify, pose, puzzle, stump

illuminati *n pl* ***syn*** see INTELLIGENTSIA

illuminating *adj* ***syn*** see ENLIGHTENING

illuminative *adj* ***syn*** see ENLIGHTENING

illumine *vb* **1** ***syn*** see ILLUMINATE 1
2 ***syn*** see ILLUMINATE 2

illumining *adj* ***syn*** see ENLIGHTENING

ill-use *vb* ***syn*** see ABUSE 4
con befriend, relieve, succor; countenance, encourage, favor, patronize

illusion *n* **1** ***syn*** see DELUSION 1
rel invention; bubble, chimera, dream, will-o'-the-wisp; appearance, seeming, semblance
2 ***syn*** see PIPE DREAM

illusionist *n* ***syn*** see MAGICIAN 2

illusive *adj* ***syn*** see APPARENT 2

illusory *adj* **1** ***syn*** see FICTITIOUS 1
ant factual
2 ***syn*** see APPARENT 2

rel chimerical, fanciful, fantastic, imaginary, unreal, visionary; deceptive, delusive, delusory, misleading
con actual, real, veritable; authentic, true, valid
ant factual

illustrate *vb* **1** *syn* see CLARIFY 2
rel display, exhibit, expose, show; disclose, discover, reveal
con cloak, conceal, enshroud, mask, screen, shroud, veil
2 *syn* see EXEMPLIFY 1
rel elucidate, explain, expound, interpret; demonstrate, manifest, show; enliven, vivify
3 *syn* see REPRESENT 2
4 *syn* see SHOW 2

illustration *n* **1** *syn* see EXAMPLE 3
2 *syn* see INSTANCE

illustrational *adj* *syn* see PICTORIAL 1

illustrative *adj* *syn* see PICTORIAL 1

illustratory *adj* *syn* see PICTORIAL 1

illustrious *adj* *syn* see FAMOUS 2
rel glorious, resplendent, splendid, sublime; conspicuous, lofty, outstanding, signal, striking
con abject, inglorious, mean; disgraceful, dishonorable, ignoble, ignominious, shameful
ant infamous

illustriousness *n* *syn* see EMINENCE 1
ant infamy

ill will *n* *syn* see MALICE
rel hostility, rancor, venom
ant goodwill

image *n* **1** one strikingly like another especially in appearance or manner <she was the *image* of her mother>
syn double, picture, portrait, ringer, simulacrum, spit, spitting image
rel counterpart, equal, equivalent, match
idiom chip off the old block, dead ringer, speaking likeness, spit and image
2 *syn* see IDEA

image *vb* **1** *syn* see REPRESENT 1
2 *syn* see THINK 1
3 *syn* see REFLECT 1

imaginable *adj* *syn* see THINKABLE 2
ant unimaginable

imaginary *adj* **1** having no real existence but existing in imagination <elves are *imaginary* beings>
syn fancied, fanciful, imagined, notional, shadowy
rel imaginative; abstract, hypothetical, ideal, visionary; apparitional, chimerical, fantastic, figmental, hallucinatory, illusory, phantasmal, phantasmic, quixotic, spectral; unreal, unsubstantial
con genuine, true, valid
ant actual, real
2 *syn* see FICTITIOUS 1
ant actual, real

imagination *n* the power or function of the mind by which mental images are formed or the exercise of that power <children have great *imagination*>
syn fancy, fantasy (*or* phantasy), imaginativeness
rel creativity, inspiration, invention, inventiveness, visualization
con literalness, matter-of-factness, prosaism, unimaginativeness

imaginativeness *n* *syn* see IMAGINATION
ant unimaginativeness

imagine *vb* **1** *syn* see THINK 1
2 *syn* see UNDERSTAND 3

imagined *adj* *syn* see IMAGINARY 1
con known, recognized, seen

imbecile *adj* *syn* see RETARDED

imbecile *n* **1** *syn* see FOOL 4
2 *syn* see FOOL 1

imbibe *vb* **1** *syn* see ABSORB 1
2 *syn* see DRINK 1
3 *syn* see DRINK 3

imbricate *vb* *syn* see OVERLAP

imbroglio *n* *syn* see QUARREL

imbrued *adj* *syn* see BLOODY 1

imbue *vb* *syn* see INFUSE 1

imitate *vb* **1** *syn* see COPY
2 *syn* see MIMIC

imitation *adj* *syn* see ARTIFICIAL 2
ant real

imitation *n* something made or produced as an often inferior likeness of something else <usually wore *imitations* of her costly jewels>
syn copy, ersatz, simulacrum
rel counterfeit, fake, forgery, phony, sham, simulation; counterpart, duplicate, replica, reproduction; likeness, semblance
ant original

imitative *adj* **1** *syn* see ONOMATOPOEIC
2 *syn* see SLAVISH 3

immaculate *adj* **1** *syn* see CHASTE
ant maculate
2 *syn* see IMPECCABLE 1
3 *syn* see CLEAN 1

immalleable *adj* *syn* see STIFF 1
ant malleable

immaterial *adj* **1** not composed of matter <*immaterial* forces>
syn asomatous, bodiless, disbodied, discarnate, disembodied, incorporeal, insubstantial, metaphysical, nonmaterial, nonphysical, spiritual, unbodied, ||uncorporal, unembodied, unfleshly, unmaterial, unphysical, unsubstantial
rel impalpable, imponderable; psychic, subjective; aerial, airy, ethereal; insensible, unearthly, unworldly; supernatural; celestial, heavenly; apparitional, ghostly, shadowy
con bodily, corporeal, fleshly, incarnate; material, objective, palpable, physical, substantial; mundane, terrestrial, worldly
ant material
2 *syn* see IRRELEVANT
ant material

immature *adj* **1** *syn* see YOUNG 1
rel precocious, premature
ant mature
2 *syn* see CHILDISH
ant mature

immeasurable *adj* **1** *syn* see INCALCULABLE 1
2 *syn* see LIMITLESS

immediacy *n* ***syn*** see PROXIMITY
immediate *adj* **1** ***syn*** see DIRECT 4
ant distant (*of relatives*)
2 ***syn*** see INSTANTANEOUS
3 ***syn*** see CLOSE 6
immediately *adv* **1** in direct connection without intermediary <*immediately* in front of the viewers>
syn contiguously, directly
2 ***syn*** see AWAY 3
rel anon, shortly, soon
idiom right now
immedicable *adj* ***syn*** see HOPELESS 2
ant medicable
immense *adj* ***syn*** see HUGE
immensely *adv* ***syn*** see EVER 6
immensity *n* ***syn*** see ENORMITY 2
immerse *vb* **1** ***syn*** see DIP 1
rel saturate, soak
2 ***syn*** see BAPTIZE
3 ***syn*** see ENGAGE 4
immersed *adj* ***syn*** see INTENT
immigrant *n* ***syn*** see EMIGRANT
imminent *adj* **1** about to take place <their departure is *imminent*>
syn impending, proximate
rel approaching, coming, nearing, upcoming; brewing, gathering; pending; likely, possible, probable; ineluctable, inescapable, inevasible, inevitable, unavoidable, unescapable
idiom in prospect, in store, in the cards, in the offing, in the wind, in view
con distant, far-off, remote
2 menacingly near <a thunderstorm was *imminent*>
syn lowering (*or* louring), lowery (*or* loury), menacing, overhanging, threatening
rel alarming, ominous, sinister; brewing, gathering; minatory
immingle *vb* ***syn*** see MIX 1
immix *vb* ***syn*** see MIX 1
immixture *n* ***syn*** see MIXTURE
immobile *adj* **1** ***syn*** see IMMOVABLE 1
ant mobile, movable
2 ***syn*** see STATIC
immobilize *vb* ***syn*** see PARALYZE 1
immoderate *adj* **1** ***syn*** see EXCESSIVE 1
ant moderate
2 ***syn*** see EXCESSIVE 2
ant moderate
immoderation *n* ***syn*** see EXCESS 3
ant moderation
immolate *vb* ***syn*** see SACRIFICE 1
immoral *adj* **1** ***syn*** see IMPURE 1
ant moral
2 ***syn*** see WRONG 1
ant moral
immorality *n* ***syn*** see VICE 1
ant morality
immortal *adj* **1** not subject to death <the *immortal* gods>
syn deathless, undying; *compare* EVERLASTING 1
rel endless, enduring, imperishable, indestructible, perpetual, sempiternal, timeless
con ephemeral, evanescent, fleeting, fugitive, passing, short-lived, transient, transitory
ant mortal
2 ***syn*** see EVERLASTING 1
immortality *n* ***syn*** see ETERNITY 2
ant mortality
immortalize *vb* ***syn*** see PERPETUATE
immotile *adj* ***syn*** see IMMOVABLE 1
ant motile
immotive *adj* ***syn*** see IMMOVABLE 1
immovable *adj* **1** incapable of moving or being moved <an *immovable* rock>
syn fixed, immobile, immotile, immotive, irremovable, ‖sitfast, steadfast, unmovable
rel adamant, fast, rooted, stable, stationary, stuck, unmoving, unyielding
con portable, removable, transferable, transportable
ant movable
2 ***syn*** see INFLEXIBLE 3
immunity *n* ***syn*** see EXEMPTION
ant susceptibility
immure *vb* **1** ***syn*** see ENCLOSE 1
2 ***syn*** see IMPRISON
immusical *adj* ***syn*** see DISSONANT 1
ant musical
immutable *adj* ***syn*** see INFLEXIBLE 3
ant mutable
imp *n* **1** a small demon, devil, or wicked spirit <the *imps* of hell>
syn deviling, devilkin
rel elf, gnome, goblin, gremlin, ‖hob, hobgoblin, kobold, ouph, pixie, puck, sprite, troll
2 ***syn*** see URCHIN
impact *n* **1** a forcible or enforced contact between two or more things <a crater formed by the *impact* of a meteorite>
syn appulse, blow, bump, clash, collision, concussion, crash, impingement, jar, jolt, jounce, percussion, shock, smash, wallop
rel brunt; buffet, hit, pound, punch, rap, slap, smiting, strike, stroke; bounce, quake, quiver, rock, shake, tremble, tremor; encounter, meeting
2 ***syn*** see EFFECT 3
impair *vb* ***syn*** see INJURE 1
rel sap, undermine, weaken
con ameliorate, better
ant improve; repair
impaired *adj* ***syn*** see DAMAGED
impale *vb* to pierce or fix with or as if with something pointed <an insect *impaled* on a pin>
syn lance, skewer, skiver, spear, spike, spit, transfix, transpierce
rel perforate, pierce, prick, punch, puncture, stab
impalpable *adj* **1** ***syn*** see IMPERCEPTIBLE
ant palpable
2 ***syn*** see FINE 2
imparity *n* ***syn*** see DISPARITY

syn synonym(s) ***rel*** related word(s)
ant antonym(s) ***con*** contrasted word(s)
idiom idiomatic equivalent(s)
‖ use limited; if in doubt, see a dictionary

ant parity
impart *vb* ***syn*** see COMMUNICATE 1
impartial *adj* ***syn*** see FAIR 4
ant partial
impartially *adv* ***syn*** see EVENLY 2
impassable *adj* **1** not allowing passage <an *impassable* barrier>
syn impenetrable, impermeable, imperviable, impervious, unpierceable
con penetrable, permeable, pervious
ant passable
2 ***syn*** see INSUPERABLE
impasse *n* **1** ***syn*** see DEAD END
2 ***syn*** see PREDICAMENT
impassible *adj* ***syn*** see INSENSIBLE 5
rel cold, emotionless, passionless, unemotional, unfeeling; inert, unresponsive
ant passible
impassioned *adj* actuated by or showing intense feeling <*impassioned* oratory>
syn ardent, blazing, burning, dithyrambic, fervent, fervid, fiery, flaming, glowing, hot-blooded, overheated, passionate, perfervid, red-hot, torrid, white-hot
rel feverish, fierce, furious, intense, vehement, violent; deep, profound, warm, zealous; gushing, gushy, maudlin, melodramatic, mushy, overemotional, romantic, sentimental
con cold, cool, dispassionate, frigid, icy, unemotional; objective
ant unimpassioned
impassive *adj* **1** unresponsive to what might normally excite interest or emotion <*impassive* endurance of pain>
syn apathetic, dry, matter-of-fact, phlegmatic, stoic, stolid
rel calm, cold, cool; collected, composed, dispassionate, emotionless, imperturbable, inexcitable, unexcitable, unflappable; inexpressive, reserved, reticent, taciturn, unemotional, unexpressive; bovine, passionless, placid, spiritless, unconcerned, wooden; callous, hardened, indurated, insensible; cold-blooded, coldhearted, heartless
con compassionate, sympathetic, tender, warm, warmhearted
ant responsive
2 ***syn*** see INSUSCEPTIBLE
impassivity *n* ***syn*** see APATHY 1
impatient *adj* **1** lacking power to endure hardship, distress, or opposition <married to an *impatient* self-centered man>
syn chafing, fretful, unpatient
rel abrupt, hasty, headlong, impetuous; anxious, edgy, itchy, nervous; irascible, irritable
idiom all of a stew
con enduring, forbearing, tolerant; self-controlled, Spartan, stoic
ant patient
2 ***syn*** see INTOLERANT 1
rel demanding, harsh
3 ***syn*** see EAGER
ant patient
impeach *vb* ***syn*** see ACCUSE
impeccable *adj* **1** absolutely correct and beyond criticism <*impeccable* manners>
syn errorless, exquisite, faultless, flawless, immaculate, irreproachable
rel accurate, clean, correct, exact, nice, perfect, precise, right; infallible, unerring
con defective, deficient, faulty; blameworthy, censurable, criticizable, culpable; cursory, shallow, superficial, uncritical
ant peccant
2 ***syn*** see PERFECT 2
impecunious *adj* ***syn*** see POOR 1
ant affluent; flush
impecuniousness *n* ***syn*** see POVERTY 1
ant affluence; flushness
impedance *n* ***syn*** see ENCUMBRANCE
impede *vb* ***syn*** see HINDER
rel discomfit, disconcert, embarrass, faze, rattle
ant aid, assist
impediment *n* **1** ***syn*** see ENCUMBRANCE
ant aid, assistance
2 ***syn*** see OBSTACLE
impel *vb* ***syn*** see MOVE 5
rel compel, constrain, force; foment, incite, instigate; goad, spur; inspire, motivate
con check, curb, inhibit
ant restrain
impend *vb* ***syn*** see LOOM 2
impending *adj* ***syn*** see IMMINENT 1
impenetrable *adj* **1** ***syn*** see IMPASSABLE 1
rel firm, solid, substantial
ant penetrable
2 ***syn*** see INCOMPREHENSIBLE 1
ant penetrable
3 ***syn*** see MYSTERIOUS
impenetrate *vb* ***syn*** see PERMEATE
impenitent *adj* ***syn*** see REMORSELESS
ant penitent
imperative *adj* **1** ***syn*** see MASTERFUL 1
rel bidding, commanding, ordering; harsh, stern
con begging, entreating, imploring; lenient, mild, soft
2 ***syn*** see PRESSING
rel acute, critical, crucial
3 ***syn*** see ESSENTIAL 4
rel basic, fundamental; claimed, demanded, exacted
4 ***syn*** see MANDATORY
imperceptible *adj* incapable of being apprehended by the senses or intellect <*imperceptible* changes in temperature>
syn impalpable, imponderable, inappreciable, indiscernible, insensible, intangible, invisible, unapparent, unappreciable, undiscernible, unobservable, unperceivable
rel faint, inconspicuous, indistinct, indistinguishable, insignificant, obscure, undistinguishable, unnoticeable, vague; ephemeral, evanescent, fugitive, momentary; slight, trivial
con apparent, appreciable, discernible, observable, palpable, ponderable, sensible, visible
ant perceivable, perceptible

imperceptive *adj* lacking perception or insight <*imperceptive* criticism that misses the point of the play>
syn impercipient, unperceiving, unperceptive
rel unappreciative, undiscerning, unobservant; cursory, shallow, slapdash, superficial
con astute, discerning, discriminating, judicious, perspicacious; delicate, nice, refined, sensitive, subtle
ant perceiving, perceptive, percipient
impercipient *adj* ***syn*** see IMPERCEPTIVE
ant perceiving, perceptive, percipient
imperfect *adj* ***syn*** see FAULTY
ant perfect
imperfection *n* an instance of failure to reach a standard of excellence or perfection <watch for *imperfections* in the cloth>
syn deficiency, demerit, fault, shortcoming, sin
rel blemish, defect, flaw; failing, foible, frailty
ant perfection
imperial *adj* ***syn*** see MASTERFUL 1
imperil *vb* ***syn*** see ENDANGER
imperious *adj* **1** ***syn*** see MASTERFUL 1
rel heavy-handed, oppressive, strict, stringent; absolute, arbitrary
con considerate, easy, gentle, kindly
2 ***syn*** see MANDATORY
imperishable *adj* ***syn*** see INDESTRUCTIBLE
impermanent *adj* ***syn*** see TRANSIENT
ant permanent
impermeable *adj* ***syn*** see IMPASSABLE 1
ant permeable
impersonal *adj* **1** ***syn*** see NEUTRAL
2 ***syn*** see FAIR 4
3 ***syn*** see MATTER-OF-FACT 3
impersonate *vb* ***syn*** see ACT 1
impersonator *n* ***syn*** see ACTOR 1
impertinence *n* ***syn*** see INSOLENCE
impertinent *adj* **1** ***syn*** see IRRELEVANT
ant pertinent
2 going beyond what is proper or acceptable in thrusting oneself into the affairs of others <*impertinent* interference with her sister's family>
syn busy, intrusive, meddlesome, ‖nebby, obtrusive, officious, polypragmatic
rel arrogant, bold, brash, brazen, fresh, impudent, pert, presumptuous, saucy; inquisitive, interfering, meddling, nosy, prying; offensive, rude
con decent, decorous, proper, seemly; reserved, reticent, silent; apposite, germane, pertinent, relevant
3 ***syn*** see RUDE 6
4 ***syn*** see INSOLENT 2
imperturbability *n* ***syn*** see EQUANIMITY
imperturbable *adj* ***syn*** see COOL 2
rel complacent, self-satisfied, smug; unaffected, unmoved, untouched
con discomfited, disconcerted, fazed, rattled; irascible, splenetic, testy
ant choleric; touchy
imperviable *adj* ***syn*** see IMPASSABLE 1
impervious *adj* ***syn*** see IMPASSABLE 1
ant pervious
impetuous *adj* ***syn*** see PRECIPITATE 1
rel spontaneous; restive; ardent, fervid, impassioned, passionate
con equable, even, steady; advised, considered, deliberate, planned, premeditated
impetuously *adv* ***syn*** see PELL-MELL
impetus *n* ***syn*** see STIMULUS
impignorate *vb* ***syn*** see PAWN
impingement *n* ***syn*** see IMPACT 1
impious *adj* **1** lacking reverence for holy or sacred matters <made *impious* remarks about the church>
syn irreverent, irreverential, profane, ungodly, unhallowed, unholy
rel godless, iconoclastic, irreligious, sacrilegious, scandalous, undevout
con devout, godly, religious, spiritual
ant pious
2 lacking due respect (as toward one's parents) <an *impious* son>
syn unduteous, undutiful
rel disobedient, froward, unfaithful, wayward; contrary, perverse, wrongheaded
con duteous, dutiful
impish *adj* ***syn*** see PLAYFUL 1
rel arch, pert, saucy; flippant, fresh, giddy; casual, devil-may-care, free and easy, offhand
impishness *n* ***syn*** see MISCHIEVOUSNESS
implacable *adj* ***syn*** see GRIM 3
con peaceable, tractable; kindly, tolerant
ant placable
implant *vb* to introduce into the mind <*implanted* worthy ideals in their children>
syn inculcate, infix, inseminate, instill
rel imbue, infuse, ingrain, inoculate, leaven, root; impenetrate, impregnate, penetrate, permeate, pervade, saturate; inspire
implausible *adj* not plausible or readily believable <an *implausible* explanation>
syn flimsy, improbable, inconceivable, incredible, thick, thin, unbelievable, unconceivable, unconvincing, unsubstantial, weak; *compare* TENUOUS 3
rel doubtful, dubious, fishy; problematic, puzzling, suspect
idiom a bit thick
con meaty, pithy; solid, sound, substantial; believable, conceivable, credible; likely, probable
ant plausible
implement *n* a usually relatively simple device for performing a mechanical or manual operation <spades, hoes, and other gardener's *implements*>
syn instrument, tool, utensil
rel apparatus, appliance; contrivance, device; contraption, gadget
implement *vb* **1** ***syn*** see FULFILL 1
2 ***syn*** see ENFORCE
rel actualize, materialize, realize
implemental *adj* ***syn*** see INSTRUMENTAL

syn synonym(s) ***rel*** related word(s)
ant antonym(s) ***con*** contrasted word(s)
idiom idiomatic equivalent(s)
‖ use limited; if in doubt, see a dictionary

impliable *adj* ***syn*** see STIFF 1
ant pliable
implicate *vb* ***syn*** see INVOLVE 1
rel affect, concern; incriminate
con absolve, acquit, exculpate, exonerate
implicated *adj* ***syn*** see INTERESTED
implication *n* ***syn*** see ASSOCIATION 4
implicit *adj* **1** ***syn*** see TACIT 1
idiom taken for granted
ant explicit
2 being such in essential character <our *implicit* freedom is better than your nominal liberty>
syn constructive, practical, virtual
rel absolute, complete, unqualified, wholehearted; genuine, real
ant spelled out
implied *adj* ***syn*** see TACIT 1
imploration *n* ***syn*** see PRAYER
implore *vb* ***syn*** see BEG
imply *vb* **1** ***syn*** see POINT 2
2 ***syn*** see SUGGEST 1
con state; express; affirm, assert, declare
impolite *adj* ***syn*** see RUDE 6
ant polite
impolitic *adj* **1** ***syn*** see UNWISE
ant politic
2 ***syn*** see INADVISABLE
ant politic
3 ***syn*** see TACTLESS
imponderable *adj* ***syn*** see IMPERCEPTIBLE
ant appreciable, ponderable
imponderous *adj* ***syn*** see LIGHT 1
ant ponderous
import *vb* **1** ***syn*** see MEAN 2
2 ***syn*** see MATTER
import *n* **1** ***syn*** see MEANING 1
rel construction, interpretation
2 ***syn*** see IMPORTANCE
rel value, worth; design, intent, object, objective, purpose; emphasis, stress
importance *n* the quality or state of being of notable worth or influence <persons of national and worldwide *importance*>
syn consequence, import, magnitude, moment, momentousness, pith, significance, ‖signification, weight, weightiness
rel conspicuousness; distinction, eminence, mark, prominence, salience; notability, note, noteworthiness, reputation, standing; substance, value, worth, worthiness; gravity, seriousness
con inconsequence, insignificance, paltriness, pettiness, triviality
ant unimportance
important *adj* **1** marked by or indicative of notable worth or consequence <an *important* discovery> <his manner was grave and *important*>
syn big, consequential, considerable, material, meaningful, momentous, significant, substantial, weighty
rel conspicuous, distinctive, exceptional, impressive, marked, memorable, notable, noteworthy, noticeable, outstanding, prominent, remarkable, salient, unusual; essential; valuable, worthwhile; worthy; effective, potent, powerful, telling; big-time, first-class, first-rate, front-page, top-notch; distinguished, eminent, famous, noted
con inconsiderable, little, minor, paltry, petty, slight, trivial
ant unimportant
2 ***syn*** see POMPOUS 1
importunate *adj* ***syn*** see PRESSING
rel persevering, persistent; dogged, pertinacious
importune *vb* ***syn*** see BEG
impose *vb* **1** ***syn*** see DICTATE
rel charge, command, enjoin, order; demand, exact, require; compel, constrain, oblige
2 ***syn*** see LEVY
3 ***syn*** see INFLICT 2
4 to force another to accept <*imposed* all the dirty jobs on her sister>
syn foist, wish; *compare* FOIST 3, INFLICT 2
rel burden, lade, saddle; fob, fob off, palm off
idiom take advantage of
5 to take usually unwarranted advantage <did not wish to *impose* by turning up unannounced>
syn infringe, intrude, obtrude, presume
rel encroach, trespass
idiom make free, take liberties
impose (on *or* upon) *vb* ***syn*** see EXPLOIT 2
imposing *adj* **1** ***syn*** see GRAND 1
rel impressive, moving; imperial, regal
ant unimposing
2 ***syn*** see PRETENTIOUS 3
impossible *adj* **1** not capable of being realized or attained <*impossible* goals>
syn impracticable, impractical, infeasible, irrealizable, unattainable, unfeasible, unrealizable, unworkable
rel absurd, inexecutable, unobtainable, unreasonable, unthinkable
idiom out of the question
con attainable, feasible, realizable; practicable, practical, rational, reasonable
ant possible
2 ***syn*** see HOPELESS 2
impost *n* ***syn*** see TAX 1
impostor *n* one who passes himself off as something or someone he is not <the presumed heir was discovered to be an *impostor*>
syn fake, faker, fraud, humbug, phony, pretender; *compare* CHARLATAN
rel imitator, mimic; beguiler, deceiver, misleader; cheat, pettifogger, shyster, trickster; hypocrite; charlatan, mountebank, quack; bluffer, dissembler, four-flusher, shammer
idiom wolf in sheep's clothing
imposture *n* the act, practice, or an instance of imposing on another by use of an assumed character or name <his claims were based on *imposture*>
syn cheat, counterfeit, deceit, deception, fake, flam, flimflam, fraud, gyp, hoax, humbug, mare's nest, phony, put-on, ‖rig, sell, sham, spoof, swindle
rel copy, imitation; fabrication, forgery; artifice, feint, gambit, maneuver, ploy, ruse, sleight, stratagem, trick, wile; make- believe, pretense, pretension

impotent *adj* **1** ***syn*** see POWERLESS
rel crippled, disabled, enfeebled
con able, capable, competent
ant potent
2 ***syn*** see WEAK 4
con forceful, powerful, puissant, strenuous, vigorous
ant potent
3 ***syn*** see STERILE 1

impoverish *vb* **1** ***syn*** see DEPLETE
ant enrich
2 ***syn*** see RUIN 3

impoverished *adj* ***syn*** see POOR 1

impoverishment *n* ***syn*** see POVERTY 1

impracticable *adj* **1** ***syn*** see IMPOSSIBLE 1
ant feasible, practicable
2 incapable of being successfully used or turned to account <a route through the mountains that is *impracticable* in winter>
syn impractical, nonfunctional, unfunctional, unserviceable, unusable, unworkable, useless
rel disadvantageous, unacceptable, undesirable, unsatisfactory; awkward, inconvenient, troublesome
con functional, practical, serviceable, usable, useful, workable
ant practicable

impractical *adj* **1** incapable of dealing prudently with practical matters <a very *impractical* person whose checkbook never balanced>
syn ivory-tower, ivory-towered, ivory-towerish, nonrealistic, unpractical, unrealistic, viewy
rel idealistic, otherworldly, quixotic, romantic, starry-eyed, visionary
con commonsensible, commonsensical, realistic, sensible, worldly-wise
ant practical
2 ***syn*** see IMPRACTICABLE 2
ant practical
3 ***syn*** see IMPOSSIBLE 1

imprecate *vb* ***syn*** see SWEAR 3

imprecation *n* **1** ***syn*** see BLASPHEMY 1
2 ***syn*** see PRAYER
3 ***syn*** see CURSE 1
con blessing

impregnable *adj* ***syn*** see INVINCIBLE 1
rel safe, secure; defended, guarded, protected, safeguarded, shielded
con exposed, open, susceptible

impregnate *vb* **1** ***syn*** see PERMEATE
rel inoculate, leaven
2 ***syn*** see SOAK 1

impress *vb* **1** ***syn*** see ENGRAVE 2
2 ***syn*** see AFFECT
rel enthuse, electrify, thrill; excite, galvanize, pique, provoke, stimulate
idiom make (*or* leave) one's mark
3 to fix in the mind or memory by emphasis or repetition <the speaker *impressed* his principal thesis upon his audience>
syn drive, grave, hammer, pound, stamp
rel establish, fix, set
idiom drive home to one, fix in one's mind, get into one's head

impress *n* ***syn*** see IMPRESSION 1

impressible *adj* ***syn*** see SENTIENT 3

impression *n* **1** the perceptible trace or traces left by pressure <the *impression* made by a die>
syn impress, imprint, indentation, print, stamp
rel dent, dint, hollow; trace, track, vestige; mark, sign
2 ***syn*** see IDEA
3 ***syn*** see EDITION

impressionable *adj* ***syn*** see SENTIENT 3
rel affectable, influenceable

impressive *adj* **1** ***syn*** see MOVING 2
rel august, grand, imposing, majestic, noble; splendid, superb; arresting, notable, striking
ant unimpressive
2 ***syn*** see GRAND 2

imprint *vb* ***syn*** see ENGRAVE 2

imprint *n* **1** ***syn*** see IMPRESSION 1
2 ***syn*** see EFFECT 3

imprison *vb* to shut up closely so that escape is impossible or unlikely <the offender was quickly sentenced and *imprisoned*>
syn bastille, confine, constrain, immure, incarcerate, intern, jail, jug, ‖prison, ‖quod
rel circumscribe, limit, restrict; check, curb, restrain
idiom put under lock and key
con free, liberate, release

improbable *adj* **1** not likely to be true or to occur <the immediate success of their plan is *improbable*>
syn doubtful, dubious, questionable, unlikely
ant probable
2 ***syn*** see IMPLAUSIBLE

impromptu *n* ***syn*** see IMPROVISATION

impromptu *adj* ***syn*** see EXTEMPORANEOUS
rel prompt, quick

improper *adj* **1** unsuited to the circumstances or the occasion <wore quite *improper* dress for such a formal reception>
syn ill-timed, inadmissible, inappropriate, inapt, inept, intempestive, malapropos, unapt, unbecoming, unbefitting, uncomely, undue, unfitting, unseasonable, unseemly, unsuitable, untimely
rel infelicitous, unhappy; inapplicable, inapposite; fresh, impertinent, sassy; crude, gauche, tactless
idiom out of place, out of season
con apposite, appropriate, apropos, apt, becoming, befitting, felicitous, fitting, germane, happy, opportune, pat, pertinent, seasonable, suitable, timely, well-timed
ant proper
2 ***syn*** see INDECOROUS
rel informal, unceremonious, unconventional
con correct, right
ant proper

---

syn synonym(s) ***rel*** related word(s)
ant antonym(s) ***con*** contrasted word(s)
idiom idiomatic equivalent(s)
‖ use limited; if in doubt, see a dictionary

impropriety *n* **1** the quality or state of being improper (as in social behavior) <was shocked by the *impropriety* of their actions>
syn incorrectness, indecorousness, indecorum, inelegance, unbecomingness, unmeetness, unseemliness, untowardness
rel inadmissibility, objectionableness, unacceptableness
con becomingness, decency, decorousness, decorum, meetness
ant propriety, seemliness
2 *syn* see FAUX PAS; *compare* ERROR 2
3 *syn* see BARBARISM

improve *vb* **1** to make more acceptable or bring nearer to some standard <studied hard to *improve* her chances of success>
syn ameliorate, amend, better, help, meliorate
rel cultivate, develop, perfect; correct, emend, rectify, reform, remedy; edit, revise; enhance, enrich, refine, rub up, upgrade
con diminish, downgrade, lessen, lower
2 *syn* see ILLUMINATE 2
3 to grow or become better (as in health or well-being) <the invalid is steadily *improving*>
syn ameliorate, convalesce, gain, look up, mend, perk (up), recuperate
rel advance, better, progress; recover; rally, revive, strengthen
idiom gain ground, make progress
con decline, deteriorate, fail, flag, languish, run down, sink, weaken

improvident *adj* not foreseeing or providing for the future <an *improvident* way of life>
syn thriftless, unthrift, unthrifty
rel careless, heedless, imprudent; extravagant, prodigal, profligate, spendthrift; lavish, profuse, reckless; uneconomical, wasteful
con careful, economical, frugal, parsimonious, prudent, saving, sparing
ant provident, thrifty

improvisate *vb* *syn* see IMPROVISE

improvisation *n* something that is improvised <the pianist played several clever *improvisations*>
syn autoschediasm, extemporization, impromptu

improvise *vb* to perform or provide on the spur of the moment <*improvise* an excuse for being late>
syn ad-lib, extemporize, improvisate
rel concoct, contrive, devise, invent

improvised *adj* *syn* see EXTEMPORANEOUS

imprudent *adj* **1** *syn* see UNWISE
ant prudent
2 *syn* see INADVISABLE
ant prudent

impudence *n* *syn* see INSOLENCE

impudent *adj* **1** *syn* see WISE 5
2 *syn* see INSOLENT 2
3 *syn* see SHAMELESS

impugn *vb* *syn* see DENY 4
rel assail, attack
idiom call in (*or* into) question (*or* doubt), throw doubt on
con back, support, uphold
ant advocate; authenticate

impugnable *adj* *syn* see DOUBTFUL 1

impulse *n* *syn* see STIMULUS
rel excitant; lust, passion, urge; actuation, drive, impulsion

impulsive *adj* *syn* see SPONTANEOUS
rel abrupt, hasty, headlong, impetuous, precipitate, sudden
con considered, designed, premeditated; calculating, cautious, circumspect
ant deliberate

impulsiveness *n* *syn* see ABANDON 2

impunity *n* *syn* see EXEMPTION

impure *adj* **1** morally or mentally unclean <*impure* thoughts>
syn dirty, immoral, unchaste, unclean, uncleanly
rel belowstairs, carnal, immodest, indecent, indecorous, lascivious, lewd, lustful, prurient, scarlet, sensual; filthy, vile
con chaste, clean, cleanly, decent, decorous, immaculate, modest, virtuous; moral
ant pure
2 *syn* see DIRTY 1
3 made unfit for ceremonial purposes <altars overturned and sacred vessels made *impure* by the touch of profane hands>
syn common, defiled, desecrated, polluted, profaned, unclean
rel unhallowed, unholy
con clean, consecrated, undefiled
ant pure
4 *syn* see UNREFINED 3

impute *vb* *syn* see ASCRIBE
rel accuse, indict; adduce; hint, insinuate, intimate

in *adj* *syn* see STYLISH

in *n* *syn* see PULL 2

inability *n* lack of sufficient power, resources, or capacity to perform <suffered from an *inability* to make quick decisions>
syn inadequacy, incapability, incapacity, incompetence, ineffectiveness, ineffectualness, inefficacy
rel inadeptness, inaptitude, inaptness, inefficiency, ineptitude, ineptness
con adequacy, capability, capacity; competence, efficiency
ant ability

inaccessible *adj* not capable of being achieved <an *inaccessible* goal>
syn inapproachable, unapproachable, unattainable, un-come-at-able, ungetatable, unobtainable, unreachable
rel distant, far, faraway, far-off, out-of-the-way, remote
ant accessible

inaccurate *adj* *syn* see FALSE 1
con right, true
ant accurate

inaction *n* lack of action or activity <the delay was due to the committee's *inaction*>
syn inactiveness, inactivity

rel drift, idleness, indolence, inertness, lethargy, quiescence, slackness, slothfulness, torpidity
con activeness, activity

inactive *adj* not characterized by or engaged in usual or normal activity <forced by illness to lead an *inactive* life>
syn asleep, idle, inert, passive, quiet, sleepy
rel abeyant, dormant, inoperative, latent, quiescent; do-nothing, indolent, lethargic, lymphatic, slack, slothful, sluggish, torpid; motionless, sedentary, static; disengaged, jobless, unemployed, unoccupied, unworking; ossified
con busy, employed, engaged, occupied; energetic, strenuous, vigorous; animated, brisk, lively
ant active

inactiveness *n* ***syn*** see INACTION

inactivity *n* ***syn*** see INACTION
ant activity

in addition *adv* ***syn*** see AGAIN 4

inadept *adj* ***syn*** see UNSKILLFUL 1
ant adept

inadequacy *n* **1** ***syn*** see INABILITY
2 ***syn*** see FAILURE 3
ant adequacy

inadequate *adj* **1** ***syn*** see DEFICIENT 1
ant adequate
2 ***syn*** see SHORT 3
ant adequate
3 ***syn*** see MEAGER
ant adequate
4 ***syn*** see WEAK 4
ant adequate

inadmissible *adj* **1** ***syn*** see IMPROPER 1
2 ***syn*** see OBJECTIONABLE
ant admissible

in advance *adv* ***syn*** see BEFORE 1

in advance of *prep* **1** ***syn*** see BEFORE 1
2 ***syn*** see UNTIL

inadvertent *adj* **1** ***syn*** see CARELESS 1
ant advertent
2 ***syn*** see UNINTENTIONAL

inadvisable *adj* not likely to have a satisfactory outcome <it seemed *inadvisable* to go any farther because of threatening weather>
syn ill-advised, impolitic, imprudent, inexpedient, unadvisable, unexpedient
rel careless, inappropriate, incautious, rash, undesirable, unsensible; foolish, indiscreet, pointless, unwise; foolhardy, harebrained
con expedient, judicious, politic, prudent, sensible, wise
ant advisable

in all *adv* ***syn*** see ALTOGETHER 2

in all probability *adv* ***syn*** see PRESUMABLY

inalterable *adj* ***syn*** see INFLEXIBLE 3
ant alterable

inamorata *n* **1** ***syn*** see GIRL FRIEND 2
2 ***syn*** see MISTRESS

inamorato *n* ***syn*** see BOYFRIEND 2

in and out *adv* ***syn*** see THOROUGHLY 2

inane *adj* ***syn*** see INSIPID 3
rel asinine, fatuous, foolish, silly; idle, vain; blank, empty, hollow
con expressive, meaningful, pregnant, significant, weighty
ant deep, profound

inanimate *adj* **1** ***syn*** see INSENSATE 1
ant animate
2 ***syn*** see DEAD 1
ant animate; living

inanity *n* ***syn*** see FOOLISHNESS

inapplicable *adj* ***syn*** see IRRELEVANT
ant applicable

inapposite *adj* ***syn*** see IRRELEVANT
ant apposite

inappreciable *adj* **1** ***syn*** see IMPERCEPTIBLE
ant appreciable
2 ***syn*** see MEAGER

inapproachable *adj* ***syn*** see INACCESSIBLE
ant approachable

inappropriate *adj* **1** ***syn*** see UNFIT 1
rel indecorous, unseemly; inconsonant
con felicitous, fitting, happy, meet, proper; fit, suitable
ant appropriate
2 ***syn*** see IMPROPER 1

inapt *adj* **1** ***syn*** see UNFIT 1
rel awkward, clumsy, gauche, maladroit; banal, flat, insipid, jejune
con apposite, germane, pertinent, relevant
ant apt
2 ***syn*** see IMPROPER 1
ant apt
3 ***syn*** see UNSKILLFUL 1
ant adept

inarguable *adj* ***syn*** see POSITIVE 3
ant arguable

inarticulate *adj* **1** ***syn*** see DUMB 1
ant articulate
2 ***syn*** see TACIT 1
3 failing to give or incapable of giving clear or effective verbal expression to one's ideas or feelings <made some *inarticulate* explanation for being late> <was completely *inarticulate* when it came to expressing affection>
syn incoherent, maundering, tongue-tied, unvocal
rel faltering, halting, hesitating, mumbling, stammered, stammering; blurred, indistinct
con facile, glib, smooth
ant articulate

inartificial *adj* ***syn*** see NATURAL 5
ant artificial

inasmuch as *conj* ***syn*** see BECAUSE

inattentive *adj* not paying proper attention <an *inattentive* pupil dozing at his desk>
syn inobservant, unheeding, unnoticing, unobservant, unobserving, unperceiving, unwatchful
rel distracted, distrait, distraught; careless, heedless, thoughtless, undiscerning, unmindful, unthinking; bored, ennuyé
ant attentive; observant

---

inaugural *adj* ***syn*** see FIRST 1
inaugural *n* ***syn*** see INITIATION
inaugurate *vb* **1** ***syn*** see INITIATE 3
2 ***syn*** see BEGIN 1
3 ***syn*** see INTRODUCE 3
inauguration *n* ***syn*** see INITIATION
inauspicious *adj* **1** ***syn*** see OMINOUS
ant auspicious
2 ***syn*** see EVIL 6
in between *prep* ***syn*** see BETWEEN 2
inborn *adj* **1** ***syn*** see INNATE 1
ant acquired
2 ***syn*** see INHERENT
inbred *adj* ***syn*** see INHERENT
in brief *adv* ***syn*** see BRIEFLY
incalculable *adj* **1** being great beyond calculation <*incalculable* damage>
syn immeasurable, inestimable, measureless, uncountable, unmeasurable, unmeasured, unreckonable
rel countless, innumerable, unnumbered, untold; boundless, enormous, infinite, limitless, vast
con minimal, slight, trivial
ant infinitesimal
2 ***syn*** see UNCERTAIN 1
ant calculable
in camera *adv* ***syn*** see SECRETLY
incandescent *adj* ***syn*** see BRIGHT 1
incantation *n* **1** ***syn*** see SPELL
2 ***syn*** see MAGIC 1
incapability *n* ***syn*** see INABILITY
ant capability
incapable *adj* **1** ***syn*** see UNFIT 2
ant capable
2 ***syn*** see INEFFICIENT 2
ant capable
incapacitate *vb* **1** ***syn*** see PARALYZE 1
2 ***syn*** see DISQUALIFY
ant capacitate
incapacity *n* ***syn*** see INABILITY
ant capacity
incarcerate *vb* ***syn*** see IMPRISON
incarnadine *vb* ***syn*** see REDDEN 1
incarnate *vb* ***syn*** see EMBODY 1
incarnation *n* ***syn*** see EMBODIMENT
incautious *adj* **1** lacking in caution <made an *incautious* prediction>
syn unalert, unguarded, unvigilant, unwary, unwatchful; *compare* CARELESS 1
rel imprudent, indiscreet, injudicious; bold, brash, impetuous, rash, reckless; neglectful, negligent, regardless, thoughtless, unmindful; hasty
idiom caught napping, off one's guard
con careful, circumspect, judicious, wary, watchful; discreet, judicious, prudent; sensible, thoughtful, wise
ant cautious
2 ***syn*** see RASH 1
ant cautious
3 ***syn*** see IRRESPONSIBLE
incendiary *n* a person who deliberately and unlawfully sets fire to a building or other property <a fire set by an *incendiary*>
syn arsonist, firebug, torch
rel pyromaniac
incendiary *adj* ***syn*** see INFLAMMATORY
incense *n* **1** ***syn*** see FRAGRANCE
2 ***syn*** see FLATTERY
incense *vb* ***syn*** see ANGER 1
ant placate
incentive *n* ***syn*** see STIMULUS
inception *n* ***syn*** see SOURCE
con closing, completion, conclusion
ant termination
inceptive *adj* ***syn*** see INITIAL 1
ant terminal
incertitude *n* ***syn*** see UNCERTAINTY
ant certitude
incessant *adj* ***syn*** see CONTINUAL
ant intermittent
inchoate *adj* **1** ***syn*** see FORMLESS
2 ***syn*** see INCOHERENT 2
incident *n* ***syn*** see OCCURRENCE
incident *adj* **1** ***syn*** see CONCOMITANT
ant essential, fundamental
2 ***syn*** see RELATED
incidental *adj* ***syn*** see ACCIDENTAL
ant essential
incidentally *adv* **1** by chance <in this discussion grave questions were brought up *incidentally*>
syn accidentally, casually, fortuitously
ant deliberately
2 by way of interjection or digression <another leading industry, *incidentally*, has quadrupled its business in four years>
syn by the bye, by the way, in passing, obiter, parenthetically
idiom in the bygoing
incipient *adj* ***syn*** see INITIAL 1
incise *vb* **1** ***syn*** see CUT 1
2 ***syn*** see ENGRAVE 1
incisive *adj* having, manifesting, or suggesting a keen alertness of mind <a man well known for his *incisive* wit>
syn biting, clear-cut, crisp, cutting, ingoing, penetrating, trenchant
rel acute, drilling, keen, sharp; acerb, acerbic, caustic, mordant, scathing, slashing, tart; concise, laconic, succinct, terse
con diffuse, prolix, verbose, wordy; feeble, limp, pithless, sapless
ant unincisive
incisiveness *n* ***syn*** see EDGE 2
incitation *n* ***syn*** see STIMULUS
incite *vb* to aid or promote the activity or development of <*incite* a riot>
syn abet, foment, instigate, provoke, raise, set, set on, stir (up), whip (up)
rel forward, further, promote, stimulate; set off, trigger; agitate, solicit; encourage, motivate, motive; excite, inflame, rouse
con check, curb, discourage, inhibit, restrain; calm, quiet, subdue
incitement *n* ***syn*** see STIMULUS
ant restraint; inhibition
inciter *n* ***syn*** see INSTIGATOR
incivil *adj* ***syn*** see RUDE 6

ant civil
inclement *adj* ***syn*** see SEVERE 3
ant clement
inclination *n* **1** ***syn*** see LEANING 2
ant disinclination
2 ***syn*** see WILL 1
ant disinclination
3 ***syn*** see APPETITE 3
ant disinclination
4 ***syn*** see SLOPE
incline *vb* **1** ***syn*** see TEND 1
2 ***syn*** see SLANT 1
rel deflect, turn
3 to have an attitude toward or to influence one to take an attitude <*inclined* to believe the story> <his argument *inclined* me to share his view>
syn bend, bias, dispose, predispose; *compare* PREJUDICE 2, TEND 1
rel affect, influence, prompt, sway; drive, impel, induce, move, persuade
ant disincline, indispose
4 ***syn*** see DIRECT 2
incline *n* ***syn*** see SLOPE
inclined *adj* **1** ***syn*** see WILLING 1
ant disinclined
2 ***syn*** see APT 1
ant disinclined
3 sloping from the horizontal or perpendicular <cars running on an *inclined* track>
syn declivate, declivitous, inclining, leaning, oblique, pitched, pitching, sloped, sloping, tilted, tilting, tipped; *compare* DIAGONAL
rel dipping, graded, raked
inclining *n* ***syn*** see LEANING 2
inclining *adj* ***syn*** see INCLINED 3
include *vb* to possess as an integral part of a whole <the park *includes* a zoo and a botanical garden>
syn comprehend, contain, embody, embrace, encompass, have, involve, subsume, take in
rel comprise, cover, encircle, enclose, hold; number; admit, receive
con leave out, omit; preclude, reject; debar; eliminate, rule out
ant exclude
inclusive *adj* **1** ***syn*** see ALL-AROUND 2
2 ***syn*** see ENCYCLOPEDIC
incogitable *adj* ***syn*** see INCREDIBLE 1
ant cogitable
incogitant *adj* ***syn*** see RASH 1
incognizable *adj* ***syn*** see INCOMPREHENSIBLE 1
ant cognizable
incognizant *adj* ***syn*** see IGNORANT 2
ant cognizant
incoherent *adj* **1** ***syn*** see LOOSE 3
2 lacking cohesion or continuity <an *incoherent* presentation>
syn disconnected, discontinuous, disjointed, disordered, inchoate, incohesive, muddled, unconnected, uncontinuous, unorganized
rel discordant, incompatible, incongruous, inconsistent, inconsonant, inharmonious
con ordered, orderly; connected; organized, planned, plotted
ant coherent
3 ***syn*** see INARTICULATE 3
incohesive *adj* ***syn*** see INCOHERENT 2
ant cohesive
incombustible *adj* ***syn*** see NONCOMBUSTIBLE
ant combustible
income *n* ***syn*** see REVENUE
incommode *vb* ***syn*** see INCONVENIENCE
rel block, hinder, impede, obstruct; annoy, bother, irk, vex
con favor, oblige; humor, indulge; gratify, please
ant accommodate
incommodious *adj* **1** ***syn*** see INCONVENIENT
ant commodious
2 ***syn*** see CRAMPED
ant commodious
incommunicable *adj* **1** ***syn*** see UNUTTERABLE
ant communicable
2 ***syn*** see RESERVED 1
ant communicable, communicative
incomparable *adj* ***syn*** see SUPREME
rel matchless
con common, commonplace, ordinary; indifferent, mediocre, medium, middling
ant average
incompatible *adj* ***syn*** see INCONSONANT 1
rel adverse, antagonistic, counter; antipathetic; antipodal, antipodean, antithetical, contradictory, contrary, opposite; irreconcilable, unadaptable, unconformable
ant compatible
2 ***syn*** see IRRECONCILABLE
ant compatible
incompetence *n* ***syn*** see INABILITY
incompetent *adj* **1** ***syn*** see UNFIT 2
ant competent
2 ***syn*** see INEFFICIENT 2
ant competent
incomplete *adj* **1** lacking a part or parts <an *incomplete* text of a speech>
syn fractional, fragmentary, part, partial
rel broken, deficient, incoherent, lacking, short, wanting; bitty, composite, scrappy
con intact, undamaged, whole
ant complete
2 ***syn*** see DEFICIENT 1
ant complete
incompliant *adj* **1** ***syn*** see OBSTINATE
ant compliant
2 ***syn*** see STIFF 1
incomprehensible *adj* **1** lying above or beyond the reach of the human mind <the *incomprehensible* universe>
syn impenetrable, incognizable, uncomprehensible, unfathomable, ungraspable, unintelligible, unknowable

---

syn synonym(s) ***rel*** related word(s)
ant antonym(s) ***con*** contrasted word(s)
idiom idiomatic equivalent(s)
‖ use limited; if in doubt, see a dictionary

rel inscrutable, mysterious, mystifying, unsearchable; cryptic, enigmatic, obscure, unclear; imperceptible, indistinguishable
con cognizable, fathomable, graspable, intelligible, knowable; clear, lucid, plain, simple, straightforward; rational, reasonable
ant comprehensible, understandable
2 *syn* see INCONCEIVABLE 1
ant comprehensible, graspable

inconceivable *adj* **1** impossible to comprehend in the absence of actual experience or knowledge <color is *inconceivable* to those born blind>
syn incomprehensible, unimaginable, unknowable, ununderstandable
idiom beyond one's grasp
con comprehensible, imaginable, knowable, understandable
ant conceivable
2 *syn* see INCREDIBLE 1
ant conceivable
3 *syn* see IMPLAUSIBLE
con believable, convincing, credible, plausible
ant conceivable

inconclusive *adj* leading to no conclusion or definite result <the report was *inconclusive*>
syn indecisive
rel open, uncertain, undecided, unsettled; incomplete, unfinished
con clarifying, illuminating; decisive
ant conclusive

incondite *adj syn* see RUDE 6

inconformable *adj syn* see IRRECONCILABLE
ant conformable

incongruent *adj syn* see INCONSONANT 1
ant congruent, congruous

incongruous *adj syn* see INCONSONANT 1
rel alien, extraneous, foreign; bizarre, fantastic, grotesque
idiom out of place
con appropriate, fit, fitting, meet, seemly, suitable
ant congruent, congruous

inconnu *n syn* see STRANGER

inconquerable *adj* **1** *syn* see INVINCIBLE 1
2 *syn* see INSUPERABLE

inconscient *adj syn* see ABSTRACTED
ant conscient, conscious

inconscious *adj syn* see INSENSIBLE 2
ant conscious

inconsequent *adj syn* see PETTY 2

inconsequential *adj syn* see PETTY 2
ant consequential

inconsiderable *adj* **1** *syn* see LITTLE 3
ant considerable
2 *syn* see MEAGER
ant considerable
3 *syn* see PETTY 2
ant considerable

inconsiderate *adj* **1** *syn* see RASH 1
ant considerate
2 *syn* see SHORT 5
ant considerate

inconsistent *adj* **1** *syn* see INCONSTANT 1
ant consistent
2 *syn* see INCONSONANT 1
ant consistent
3 *syn* see IRRECONCILABLE
ant consistent

inconsolable *adj* incapable of being consoled <she was *inconsolable* over the loss of her child>
syn desolate, disconsolate, unconsolable
rel comfortless, dejected, forlorn, heartsick
ant consolable

inconsonant *adj* **1** not in agreement with one another or not agreeable one to the other <his actions are *inconsonant* with his words>
syn conflicting, disconsonant, discordant, discrepant, dissonant, incompatible, incongruent, incongruous, inconsistent, unmixable
rel ill-matched, ill-suited, mismated, uncongenial; inappropriate, unsuitable
con accordant, compatible, congenial, congruous, consistent
ant consonant
2 *syn* see INHARMONIOUS 2
ant consonant

inconspicuous *adj* not readily noticeable <occupied an *inconspicuous* position>
syn obscure, unconspicuous, unemphatic, unnoticeable
rel indistinct, insignificant, unnoticeable, unobtrusive, vague
con eye-catching, showy, striking; distinct, noticeable
ant conspicuous, prominent

inconstant *adj* **1** lacking firmness or steadiness (as in purpose or devotion) <depended too much on an *inconstant* friend>
syn capricious, changeable, fickle, inconsistent, lubricious, mercurial, temperamental, ticklish, uncertain, unstable, variable, volatile; *compare* CHANGEABLE 1, MUTABLE 2, UNCERTAIN 1
rel changeful, mutable, protean, unsettled, unsteady; elusive, erratic, vacillating, vagrant, wavering, wayward; irresolute, shifty, shilly-shally; undependable, unreliable; disloyal, faithless, false, perfidious, traitorous, treacherous, untrue; frivolous, light, light-minded
con dependable, reliable, trustworthy, trusty; faithful, loyal, resolute, staunch, steadfast, true
ant constant
2 *syn* see MUTABLE 2
ant constant

incontestable *adj syn* see POSITIVE 3
ant contestable

incontinent *adj syn* see LICENTIOUS 2
ant continent

incontinently *adv syn* see PELL-MELL

incontrovertible *adj syn* see POSITIVE 3
ant controvertible

inconvenience *n* the quality or state of being inconvenient <hated the *inconvenience* of not having a telephone>
syn bother, bothersomeness, ‖disconvenience, troublesomeness
rel aggravation, annoyance, exasperation, trial; fuss, pother, stew
ant convenience

inconvenience *vb* to subject to disturbance or discomfort <was not seriously *inconvenienced* by the bad weather>
syn discommode, ‖disconvenience, disoblige, incommode, put about, put out, trouble
rel discompose, disturb; interfere, intermeddle, meddle; aggravate, exasperate, try
idiom put to trouble
ant convenience

inconvenient *adj* not conducive to physical, mental, or social ease and comfort <he came at an *inconvenient* time>
syn awkward, discommoding, discommodious, embarrassing, incommodious
rel bothersome, pestiferous, troublesome; inexpedient; detrimental, disadvantageous, prejudicial
con appropriate, becoming, fitting, suitable; acceptable, bearable, tolerable; advantageous, desirable, helpful
ant convenient

inconversable *adj syn* see SILENT 3
ant conversable

inconversant *adj syn* see IGNORANT 2
ant conversant

incorporate *vb* **1** *syn* see ABSORB 1
2 *syn* see EMBODY 2

incorporeal *adj syn* see IMMATERIAL 1
ant corporeal

incorrect *adj syn* see FALSE 1
ant correct

incorrectly *adv syn* see AMISS 1
ant correctly

incorrectness *n syn* see IMPROPRIETY 1
ant correctitude, correctness

incorruptible *adj syn* see INDESTRUCTIBLE
ant corruptible

incorruption *n syn* see HONESTY
ant corruption

increase *vb* **1** to make greater or more numerous <*increase* crops by good cultural practices>
syn aggrandize, augment, beef (up), boost, build, compound, enlarge, expand, extend, heighten, magnify, manifold, multiply, plus, push
rel aggravate, enhance, intensify; amplify, dilate, distend, inflate, swell; elongate, lengthen, prolong, protract; reinforce, strengthen
con abate, abbreviate, condense, contract; depreciate, diminish, lessen, lower, reduce; curtail, shorten, shrink; minimize
ant decrease
2 to become greater or more numerous <his wealth *increased* over the years>
syn augment, build, burgeon, enlarge, expand, heighten, mount, multiply, rise, run up, snowball, upsurge, wax
rel dilate, distend, inflate, intensify, lengthen, strengthen, swell; pullulate, swarm, teem
con abate, condense, contract, diminish, lessen, lower, reduce, shorten, shrink; die off, die (out), end, terminate
ant decrease
3 *syn* see RAISE 9

increase *n* **1** *syn* see ADDITION
ant decrease
2 *syn* see RISE 3

increate *adj syn* see SELF-EXISTENT
ant created

incredible *adj* **1** too extraordinary or improbable to admit of belief <an *incredible* story of privations overcome>
syn incogitable, inconceivable, insupposable, unbelievable, unimaginable, unthinkable
rel absurd, outlandish, preposterous, ridiculous; impossible, untenable
idiom beyond belief, out of the question
con acceptable, believable, conceivable, likely, plausible, reasonable
ant credible
2 *syn* see IMPLAUSIBLE
ant credible

incredulity *n syn* see UNBELIEF
con gullibility, naiveté
ant credulity, credulousness

incredulous *adj* unwilling to admit or accept what is offered as true <his explanation met an *incredulous* response from his listeners>
syn aporetic, disbelieving, questioning, quizzical, show-me, skeptical, unbelieving
rel hesitant, suspicious, uncertain, wary; distrustful, distrusting, mistrustful; doubting, dubious, unconvinced, unsatisfied
con trustful, trusting; unsuspecting, unsuspicious, unwary; gullible, naive
ant credulous

increment *n syn* see ADDITION

incriminate *vb syn* see ACCUSE
rel implicate, involve
ant exonerate

incrustate *vb syn* see CAKE 1

inculcate *vb syn* see IMPLANT
rel educate, instruct, teach; communicate, impart

inculpable *adj* **1** *syn* see GOOD
ant culpable
2 *syn* see INNOCENT 2
ant culpable

inculpate *vb syn* see ACCUSE
ant exculpate

incult *adj syn* see COARSE 3

incur *vb* to bring (something usually unpleasant) upon oneself <he foolishly *incurred* debts beyond his ability to pay>
syn contract
rel acquire, get; bring on, induce
idiom bring down on (*or* upon)
con avoid, elude, escape, eschew, evade, shun; discharge, pay, settle

incurable *adj syn* see HOPELESS 2
ant curable

incurious *adj syn* see INDIFFERENT 2

---

syn synonym(s) *rel* related word(s)
ant antonym(s) *con* contrasted word(s)
idiom idiomatic equivalent(s)
‖ use limited; if in doubt, see a dictionary

THESAURUS

rel absent, absentminded, abstracted, distraught, preoccupied
con nosy, prying, snoopy; impertinent, intrusive, meddlesome; observant, observing
ant curious, inquisitive

incursion *n syn* see INVASION

indebted *adj* owing gratitude or recognition (as for a favor or service rendered) <was *indebted* to the book for most of her information>
syn beholden, obligated, obliged
rel duty-bound, honor-bound

indebtedness *n* **1** a state of owing something <unable to escape from *indebtedness*>
syn arrearage, debt, liability, obligation; *compare* DEBT 3
rel delinquency, nonpayment; bankruptcy, failure, insolvency
con discharge, liquidation, satisfaction; exoneration, freeing, release
2 *syn* see DEBT 3

indecent *adj* **1** *syn* see INDECOROUS
ant decent
2 *syn* see OBSCENE 2
ant decent

indecipherable *adj syn* see ILLEGIBLE
ant decipherable

indecision *n syn* see HESITATION
ant decision, decisiveness

indecisive *adj* **1** *syn* see INCONCLUSIVE
ant decisive
2 *syn* see DOUBTFUL 1
con certain, incontrovertible, undebatable, unequivocal
ant decisive
3 *syn* see VACILLATING 2
rel undecided, unsettled
idiom of two minds
con decided, determined, firm, positive, resolved, settled, unfaltering, unhesitant, unhesitating, unwavering
ant decisive

indecisiveness *n syn* see HESITATION
ant indecision, indecisiveness

indecorous *adj* not conforming with accepted standards of propriety or good taste <they regarded argument in public as *indecorous*>
syn improper, indecent, indelicate, malodorous, ridiculous, rough, unbecoming, undecorous, ungodly, unseemly, untoward
rel inappropriate, incorrect, unbefitting, unfit, unfitting; immodest, inelegant, undignified; coarse, gross, loose, offensive, shameful, tasteless, vulgar; discourteous, ill-mannered, impolite, rude, uncivil; irregular, unlawful
idiom in bad form
con becoming, courteous, decent, nice, proper, seemly; conventional, formal
ant decorous

indecorousness *n syn* see IMPROPRIETY 1
ant decorousness

indecorum *n* **1** *syn* see FAUX PAS
2 *syn* see IMPROPRIETY 1
ant decorum

indeed *adv* **1** *syn* see WELL 7
2 *syn* see EVEN 3

indefatigable *adj* capable of prolonged and arduous effort <a teacher who has *indefatigable* patience with slow learners>
syn inexhaustible, tireless, unflagging, untiring, unweariable, unwearying, weariless
rel assiduous, diligent, painstaking, sedulous; determined, dogged, patient, persevering, persistent, pertinacious, relentless, steadfast, stubborn, tenacious, unfaltering, unflinching, unrelenting, unwavering; energetic, strenuous, vigorous
con dawdling, dilatory, laggard, lagging, procrastinating; fainéant, indolent, lackadaisical, lazy, slothful, sluggish
ant fatigable

indefectible *adj* **1** *syn* see PERFECT 2
2 *syn* see IDEAL 3

indefensible *adj syn* see INEXCUSABLE
ant defensible

indefinable *adj syn* see UNUTTERABLE
ant definable

indefinite *adj* **1** having no exact limits <a region with *indefinite* boundaries>
syn indeterminate, indistinct, inexact, undeterminable
rel unclear, undefined, unfixed, unspecific; broad, loose, wide; general, obscure, vague
con exact, measured; known
ant definite
2 *syn* see LIMITLESS
ant definite

indelible *adj* that cannot be removed or erased <made an *indelible* impression on his hearers>
syn ineffaceable, ineradicable, inerasable, inexpungible, inextirpable, uneradicable, unerasable
rel indestructible, undestroyable; enduring, permanent
con effaceable, eradicable, erasable, removable; ephemeral, evanescent, passing, temporary, transitory
ant delible

indelicate *adj syn* see INDECOROUS
rel callow, crude, rude, uncouth; lewd, wanton
con chaste, modest, pure
ant delicate

indemnification *n syn* see REPARATION

indemnify *vb syn* see COMPENSATE 3

indemnity *n syn* see REPARATION

indentation *n* **1** *syn* see NOTCH 1
2 *syn* see IMPRESSION 1

indenture *n syn* see NOTCH 1

indentured *adj syn* see BOUND 2

independent *adj* **1** *syn* see FREE 1
2 *syn* see SELF-SUFFICIENT
ant dependent

independently *adv syn* see APART 1
idiom on one's own

indescribable *adj syn* see UNUTTERABLE
ant describable

indestructible *adj* incapable of being destroyed <*indestructible* idealism>
syn imperishable, incorruptible, inexterminable, inextinguishable, inextirpable, irrefragable, irre-

frangible, quenchless, undestroyable, unperishable
rel changeless, immutable, unalterable, unchangeable; deathless, immortal, perpetual, undying; durable, enduring, lasting, permanent; indelible, ineradicable; unextinguishable, unquenchable
con alterable, changeable, corruptible, impermanent, temporary, transient, unlasting; mortal, temporal; evanescent
ant destroyable, destructible, perishable

indeterminate *adj* ***syn*** see INDEFINITE 1
ant determinate

index *n* ***syn*** see INDICATION 3

Indian sign *n* ***syn*** see JINX

indicate *vb* **1** ***syn*** see POINT 2
2 to give evidence of or serve as ground for a valid or reasonable inference <several polls *indicate* a landslide for the incumbent>
syn announce, argue, attest, bespeak, betoken, testify, witness
rel denote, import, mean, signify; demonstrate, prove; evidence, evince, manifest, show; display, exhibit, express, illustrate; connote, hint, imply, suggest
3 ***syn*** see SHOW 5

indication *n* **1** ***syn*** see HINT 1
2 ***syn*** see EXPRESSION 3
3 something that is an outward manifestation of something else <such *indications* of prosperity as second cars and color TVs>
syn evidence, index, indicia, mark, sign, significant, symptom, token; *compare* SYMBOL 1, TESTIMONY
rel expression, manifestation; hint, suggestion; proof; prefiguration, type

indicative *adj* serving to indicate <the roar of the crowd was *indicative* of its approval>
syn denotative, denotive, designative, exhibitive, indicatory, indicial, significative
rel characteristic, demonstrative, evidential, evincive, expressive, suggestive, symbolic, symptomatic, testatory

indicatory *adj* ***syn*** see INDICATIVE

indicia *n pl* ***syn*** see INDICATION 3

indicial *adj* ***syn*** see INDICATIVE

indict *vb* ***syn*** see ACCUSE

indifference *n* ***syn*** see APATHY 2

indifferent *adj* **1** ***syn*** see FAIR 4
2 marked by a lack of interest or concern <was *indifferent* to suffering and poverty>
syn aloof, by-the-way, casual, detached, disinterested, incurious, numb, pococurante, remote, unconcerned, uncurious, uninterested, withdrawn; *compare* UNSOCIABLE
rel apathetic, impassive, insensible; dispassionate; careless, heedless, negligent, regardless, uncaring, unmindful; inattentive, unobserving
con attentive, considerate, heedful, interested, mindful, regardful, sympathetic
ant concerned
3 ***syn*** see COLD 2
4 ***syn*** see MEDIUM

indigence *n* ***syn*** see POVERTY 1
ant affluence, opulence

indigency *n* ***syn*** see POVERTY 1
ant affluence, opulence

indigenous *adj* **1** ***syn*** see NATIVE 2
con alien, extraneous, foreign
ant exotic; naturalized
2 ***syn*** see INNATE 1

indigent *adj* ***syn*** see POOR 1
ant affluent, opulent

indignant *adj* ***syn*** see ANGRY
ant gratified

indignation *n* ***syn*** see ANGER
ant gratification

indignity *n* ***syn*** see AFFRONT
rel grievance, injury, injustice, wrong

indirect *adj* **1** deviating from a direct line or straightforward course <made *indirect* inquiries about the new neighbor>
syn circuitous, circular, collateral, oblique, roundabout
rel circumlocutory, crooked, devious; meandering, serpentine, sinuous, tortuous, twisting, winding; errant, vagrant, wandering
ant direct; forthright, straightforward
2 ***syn*** see UNDERHAND
ant straight

indirection *n* ***syn*** see DECEPTION 1

indiscernible *adj* ***syn*** see IMPERCEPTIBLE
ant discernible, distinguishable

indiscreet *adj* ***syn*** see UNWISE
ant discreet

indiscriminate *adj* **1** including all or nearly all within the range of choice, operation, or effectiveness <her charity was *indiscriminate* but generous>
syn indiscriminating, indiscriminative, sweeping, undiscriminated, undiscriminating, undistinguishing, wholesale
rel assorted, heterogeneous, miscellaneous, promiscuous; shallow, superficial, uncritical; broad, extensive, wide
con discretionary, discriminative; choosy, picky; critical, perfectionist
ant selective; discriminate, discriminated
2 ***syn*** see RANDOM
3 ***syn*** see MISCELLANEOUS

indiscriminating *adj* ***syn*** see INDISCRIMINATE 1
ant discriminating

indiscriminative *adj* ***syn*** see INDISCRIMINATE 1
ant discriminative

indispensable *adj* ***syn*** see ESSENTIAL 4
rel cardinal, fundamental
ant dispensable

indisposed *adj* **1** ***syn*** see UNWELL
2 ***syn*** see DISINCLINED
rel antagonistic, antipathetic, hostile, inimical
con amicable, neighborly; responsive, sympathetic
ant disposed

---

indisposition *n* **1** ***syn*** see DISLIKE
2 ***syn*** see SICKNESS 1
indisputable *adj* **1** ***syn*** see POSITIVE 3
ant disputable
2 ***syn*** see REAL 3
indistinct *adj* **1** ***syn*** see INDEFINITE 1
ant distinct
2 ***syn*** see FAINT 2
ant distinct
indistinguishable *adj* ***syn*** see SAME 2
ant distinguishable
indite *vb* ***syn*** see WRITE
individual *adj* **1** ***syn*** see PERSONAL 1
ant common, popular
2 ***syn*** see SPECIAL 1
rel separate, single, sole
con generic, universal
ant general
3 ***syn*** see CHARACTERISTIC
ant common
4 ***syn*** see SEVERAL 1
individual *n* **1** ***syn*** see ENTITY 1
2 ***syn*** see THING 5
3 ***syn*** see HUMAN
individualism *n* **1** ***syn*** see DISPOSITION 3
2 ***syn*** see INDIVIDUALITY 3
individualist *adj* ***syn*** see EGOCENTRIC 1
individualistic *adj* ***syn*** see EGOCENTRIC 1
individuality *n* **1** ***syn*** see DISPOSITION 3
2 ***syn*** see UNITY 1
3 distinctive character <a person of marked *individuality*>
syn distinctiveness, individualism, particularity, singularity
rel character, personality
4 individual identity <a teacher who respects children's *individualities*>
syn identity, ipseity, personality, seity, selfdom, selfhood, selfness, singularity
rel independence, separateness, uniqueness; difference, dissimilarity, unlikeness
con likeness, resemblance, similarity
individualize *vb* ***syn*** see CHARACTERIZE 2
individually *adv* ***syn*** see APART 1
individuate *vb* ***syn*** see CHARACTERIZE 2
indocile *adj* ***syn*** see UNRULY 1
ant docile
indolence *n* ***syn*** see SLOTH 1
ant industry
indolent *adj* ***syn*** see LAZY
con active, diligent, energetic, vigorous
ant industrious
indomitable *adj* **1** ***syn*** see INVINCIBLE 1
ant domitable
2 ***syn*** see INSUPERABLE
rel dogged, pertinacious, stubborn; resolute, staunch, steadfast
ant domitable
3 ***syn*** see UNRULY 1
indoors *adv* in or into a building <stayed *indoors* during the storm>
syn inside, within, withindoors, withinside
con outdoors, outside, without, withoutdoors
ant outdoors
indubitable *adj* **1** ***syn*** see POSITIVE 3
ant dubitable, questionable
2 ***syn*** see AUTHENTIC 2
ant doubtful, dubious
3 ***syn*** see DOWNRIGHT 2
induce *vb* **1** to move another to do or agree to something <*induced* him to give up smoking for the sake of his health>
syn argue (into), bring around, convince, draw, draw in, draw on, get, oversway, persuade, prevail (on *or* upon), procure, prompt, talk (into), win (over)
rel influence, sway; abet, incite, lead; actuate, impel, move; activate, motivate
con check, curb, hold back, restrain
2 ***syn*** see GENERATE 3
inducible *adj* ***syn*** see INDUCTIVE
induct *vb* ***syn*** see INITIATE 3
induction *n* ***syn*** see INITIATION
inductive *adj* **1** derived or derivable by reasoning from a part to a whole, from particulars to generals, or from the individual to the universal <used an *inductive* approach to the problem>
syn a posteriori, inducible
rel Baconian, epagogic
2 ***syn*** see PRELIMINARY
indulge *vb* **1** to give free rein to (as curiosity or a desire) <*indulged* their taste for gourmet foods>
syn cater (to), gratify, humor
rel favor, oblige, satisfy; delight, please, regale
idiom give rein to
con bridle, check, constrain, curb, restrain
2 ***syn*** see BABY
3 ***syn*** see WALLOW 3
indulgence *n* **1** ***syn*** see FORBEARANCE 2
rel benignancy, benignity, benignness, kindliness, kindness; gentleness, mildness
con rigor, severity, sternness; rigidity, rigorousness; harshness
ant strictness
2 ***syn*** see FAVOR 4
indulgent *adj* ***syn*** see FORBEARING
rel cosseting, pampering, permissive; condoning, excusing, forgiving, pardoning; benign, benignant, kind, kindly
con severe, stern; harsh, rigorous, stringent
ant strict
indurate *vb* ***syn*** see HARDEN 1
industrious *adj* ***syn*** see ASSIDUOUS
rel active, busy, live, dynamic; persevering, persistent
con idle, inactive; lethargic, sluggish
ant indolent, slothful; unindustrious
industry *n* ***syn*** see BUSINESS 4
indwell *vb* ***syn*** see BELONG 3
indweller *n* ***syn*** see INHABITANT
indwelling *adj* ***syn*** see INHERENT
inebriant *n* ***syn*** see LIQUOR 2
inebriate *n* ***syn*** see DRUNKARD
inebriated *adj* ***syn*** see INTOXICATED 1
inebrious *adj* ***syn*** see INTOXICATED 1
inedible *adj* not fit for food <an *inedible* plant>
syn inesculent, uneatable
rel indigestible, unwholesome; insipid, unappetizing; baneful, noxious, poisonous

con eatable, esculent; digestible, wholesome; appetizing, savory, tasty; harmless, innocuous, innoxious, nonpoisonous
ant edible
ineffable *adj* ***syn*** see UNUTTERABLE
rel celestial, empyreal, empyrean, heavenly; ethereal; divine, holy, sacred, spiritual; abstract, ideal, transcendent, transcendental
con expressible; utterable
ineffaceable *adj* ***syn*** see INDELIBLE
ineffective *adj* **1** ***syn*** see FUTILE
ant effective
2 ***syn*** see WEAK 4
3 not producing or not capable of producing a required result <*ineffective* remedies>
syn ineffectual, inefficacious, inefficient
rel inadequate, incompetent, inferior; useless, worthless
con active, effectual, efficacious; esteemed, valuable
ant effective
ineffectiveness *n* ***syn*** see INABILITY
ant effectiveness
ineffectual *adj* **1** ***syn*** see FUTILE
ant effectual
2 ***syn*** see INEFFECTIVE 3
ant effectual
3 ***syn*** see WEAK 4
4 ***syn*** see LITTLE 2
ineffectualness *n* ***syn*** see INABILITY
ant effectualness
inefficacious *adj* ***syn*** see INEFFECTIVE 3
ant efficacious
inefficacy *n* ***syn*** see INABILITY
ant efficacy
inefficient *adj* **1** ***syn*** see INEFFECTIVE 3
ant efficient
2 incapable of the proper performance of duties <*inefficient* workmen>
syn incapable, incompetent, inept, inexpert, unexpert, unskilled, unskillful, unworkmanlike
rel careless, slipshod, slovenly; unfitted, unprepared, unqualified, untrained; unskilled, unskillful
con able, adept, capable, competent, expert, proficient, qualified, skilled, skillful, workmanlike
ant efficient
inelaborate *adj* ***syn*** see PLAIN 1
ant elaborate
inelastic *adj* ***syn*** see STIFF 1
ant elastic
inelegance *n* ***syn*** see IMPROPRIETY 1
ant elegance
inelegant *adj* ***syn*** see COARSE 3
ineligible *adj* ***syn*** see UNFIT 2
ant eligible
ineluctable *adj* ***syn*** see INEVITABLE
con doubtful, dubious, questionable; likely, possible, probable
ineludible *adj* ***syn*** see INEVITABLE
inenarrable *adj* ***syn*** see UNUTTERABLE
inept *adj* **1** ***syn*** see IMPROPER 1
ant apt
2 ***syn*** see INFELICITOUS
ant apropos, apt
3 ***syn*** see AWKWARD 2
ant apt; adept
4 ***syn*** see UNSKILLFUL 1
ant able
5 ***syn*** see INEFFICIENT 2
ant competent, efficient
inequable *adj* ***syn*** see INEQUITABLE
ant equable
inequality *n* **1** the quality of being uneven <hampered by the *inequality* of the ground>
syn asperity, irregularity, roughness, unevenness
rel cragginess, jaggedness, ruggedness, rugosity
con equality, evenness, levelness, smoothness
2 ***syn*** see DISPARITY
ant equality
inequitable *adj* not fair or just <an *inequitable* tax burden>
syn inequable, unequitable, unfair, unjust, unrighteous
rel undeserved, undue, unmerited; bad, wrong, wrongful; arbitrary, high-handed, oppressive
con fair, just
ant equitable
inequitableness *n* ***syn*** see INJUSTICE 1
ant equitableness
inequity *n* ***syn*** see INJUSTICE 1
ant equity
ineradicable *adj* ***syn*** see INDELIBLE
ant eradicable
inerasable *adj* ***syn*** see INDELIBLE
ant erasable
inerrable *adj* ***syn*** see INFALLIBLE 1
ant errable
inerrant *adj* ***syn*** see INFALLIBLE 1
rel accurate, correct, exact, precise; dependable, reliable, trustworthy
ant errant
inert *adj* ***syn*** see INACTIVE
rel impotent, powerless; apathetic, impassive, phlegmatic, stolid; dead, inanimate, lifeless
con animated, awake; alert, vigilant, watchful; live, operative
ant animated; dynamic
inerudite *adj* ***syn*** see UNSCHOLARLY
ant erudite, learned
inescapable *adj* ***syn*** see INEVITABLE
ant escapable
inescapably *adv* ***syn*** see WILLY-NILLY
inesculent *adj* ***syn*** see INEDIBLE
ant esculent
in essence *adv* **1** ***syn*** see ESSENTIALLY 1
2 ***syn*** see VIRTUALLY
inessential *adj* ***syn*** see UNNECESSARY
ant crucial, essential
inestimable *adj* **1** ***syn*** see INCALCULABLE 1
2 ***syn*** see PRECIOUS 1

---

syn synonym(s) ***rel*** related word(s)
ant antonym(s) ***con*** contrasted word(s)
idiom idiomatic equivalent(s)
‖ use limited; if in doubt, see a dictionary

inevasible *adj* ***syn*** see INEVITABLE
inevitable *adj* incapable of being avoided or escaped <the effect of the scandal on the election was *inevitable*>
syn certain, ineluctable, ineludible, inescapable, inevasible, necessary, returnless, unavoidable, unescapable, unevadable
rel ineliminable, sure, unpreventable; decided, settled; destined, foreordained; inexorable, inflexible
idiom as sure to follow as night follows day, in the cards
con eludible, escapable, evadable
ant avoidable, evitable
inevitably *adv* ***syn*** see WILLY-NILLY
inexact *adj* ***syn*** see INDEFINITE 1
ant exact
inexcusable *adj* being without excuse or justification <an *inexcusable* blunder>
syn indefensible, inexpiable, unforgivable, unjustifiable, unpardonable, untenable
rel blamable, blameworthy, censurable, criticizable; impermissible, unallowable, unpermissible; intolerable, reprehensible
con allowable, blameless, defensible, forgivable, justifiable, pardonable, venial
ant excusable
inexhaustible *adj* ***syn*** see INDEFATIGABLE
inexorable *adj* ***syn*** see INFLEXIBLE 2
rel resolute; immobile, immovable
con compassionate, responsive, sympathetic, tender; clement, forbearing, indulgent, lenient
inexpedient *adj* ***syn*** see INADVISABLE
ant expedient
inexpensive *adj* ***syn*** see CHEAP 1
ant expensive
inexperience *n* lack or serious deficiency of practical wisdom <his failure was due to his *inexperience*>
syn callowness, freshness, greenness, rawness
rel ignorance, naiveté; amateurishness; unfamiliarity; unsophistication, verdancy
con grasp, understanding; polish, sophistication; skill, training
ant experience
inexperienced *adj* lacking knowledge, skill, or practice based on direct observation and participation <hired *inexperienced* help>
syn callow, fresh, green, inexpert, raw, rude, unconversant, unexperienced, unfleshed, unpracticed, unseasoned, untried, unversed, young
rel ignorant, immature, inept, naive; prentice, unacquainted, unfamiliar, unskilled, untrained
con expert, old, practiced, seasoned, skilled, versed, veteran
ant experienced
inexpert *adj* **1** ***syn*** see INEXPERIENCED
ant expert
2 ***syn*** see UNSKILLFUL 1
ant expert
3 ***syn*** see INEFFICIENT 2
ant expert
4 ***syn*** see CRUDE 5
inexpiable *adj* ***syn*** see INEXCUSABLE
ant expiable
inexplainable *adj* ***syn*** see INEXPLICABLE
ant explainable, explicable
inexplicable *adj* not capable of being explained or accounted for <an *inexplicable* discrepancy in the accounts>
syn inexplainable, unaccountable, unexplainable; *compare* MYSTERIOUS
rel indecipherable, indescribable, inscrutable, undefinable, unfathomable, unsolvable; mysterious, odd, peculiar, strange
con clear, obvious, plain; comprehensible, graspable, intelligible
ant explainable, explicable
inexpressible *adj* ***syn*** see UNUTTERABLE
ant expressible
inexpressive *adj* ***syn*** see EXPRESSIONLESS
ant expressive
inexpugnable *adj* ***syn*** see INVINCIBLE 1
rel irresistible, unopposable
con assailable, attackable
ant expugnable
inexpungible *adj* ***syn*** see INDELIBLE
inexterminable *adj* ***syn*** see INDESTRUCTIBLE
inextinguishable *adj* ***syn*** see INDESTRUCTIBLE
ant extinguishable
inextirpable *adj* **1** ***syn*** see INDESTRUCTIBLE
2 ***syn*** see INDELIBLE
inextricable *adj* ***syn*** see INSOLUBLE
ant extricable
infallible *adj* **1** incapable of being in error <an *infallible* ear for pitch in music>
syn inerrable, inerrant, sure, unerring
rel faultless, flawless, impeccable, undeceivable; correct, exact, perfect
con deceivable, faulty, unsure; doubtful, dubious, questionable
ant fallible
2 not liable to mislead, deceive, or disappoint <an *infallible* remedy>
syn certain, sure, surefire, unfailing
rel effective, efficacious, efficient; handy, helpful, useful; acceptable, agreeable, satisfying; satisfactory
con doubtful, questionable, uncertain, unsure; useless, worthless; unacceptable, unsatisfying; unsatisfactory
ant fallible
infamous *adj* **1** having an extremely and deservedly bad reputation <one of the most *infamous* of the dictator's henchmen>
syn ill-famed, notorious, opprobrious
rel abominable, atrocious, evil, hateful, heinous, iniquitous, odious, scandalous, vile, villainous; contemptible, despicable, scurvy, sorry
con distinguished, eminent, esteemed, honored, illustrious, notable, prestigious, reputable
2 ***syn*** see VICIOUS 2
rel disgraceful, disreputable, ignominious, shameful
con glorious, splendid, sublime
ant illustrious
infamy *n* ***syn*** see DISGRACE
rel notoriety, notoriousness

infancy *n* **1** early childhood <the helplessness of *infancy*>
syn babyhood, infanthood
rel childhood, immaturity, juvenility, nonage
con adulthood, maturity, old age, senescence
2 the state or period of being under the age established by law for the attainment of full civil rights <his heirs were still in *infancy*>
syn minority, nonage
rel immaturity, juniority, juvenility
con adulthood, adultness, maturity, seniority
ant majority

infant *n* *syn* see BABY 1

infant *adj* *syn* see YOUNG 1

infanthood *n* *syn* see INFANCY 1

infantile *adj* *syn* see CHILDISH
ant adult

infantine *adj* *syn* see CHILDISH
ant adult

infatuate *adj* *syn* see INFATUATED

infatuated *adj* possessed with or marked by a strong attachment or foolish or unreasoning love or desire <*infatuated* with a woman he can't have>
syn besotted, dotty, enamored, infatuate
rel bewitched, captivated, enraptured, obsessed; foolish, silly
con detached, dispassionate, objective, undazzled, unprepossessed

infatuation *n* a strong and unreasoning but transitory attachment <went through a series of *infatuations* before she settled down>
syn béguin, crush, ‖pash, passion
rel ardor, craze, devotion, fascination, obsession, rage

in favor of *prep* *syn* see FOR 1

infeasible *adj* *syn* see IMPOSSIBLE 1
ant feasible

infectious *adj* **1** capable of causing infection <viruses and other *infectious* agents>
syn infective
rel mephitic, miasmic, noxious, pestilent, pestilential, poisonous, toxic, virulent
con healthful, hygienic, salutary, wholesome
2 transmissible by infection <*infectious* diseases>
syn catching, communicable, contagious
3 easily communicated or diffused <her enthusiasm was *infectious*>
syn catching, contagious, taking
rel irresistible, sympathetic

infective *adj* *syn* see INFECTIOUS 1

infecund *adj* *syn* see STERILE 1
ant fecund

infelicitous *adj* marked by a lack of appropriateness and grace of expression <made a very *infelicitous* remark>
syn awkward, graceless, ill-chosen, inept, unfortunate, unhappy
rel inappropriate, inapropos, inapt, malapropos, unapt; deplorable, gauche, regrettable
con fortunate, graceful, happy
ant felicitous

infer *vb* to arrive at by reasoning from evidence or from premises <we *inferred* from his questions that he was a stranger in the vicinity>
syn collect, conclude, deduce, deduct, derive, ‖dope out, draw, gather, judge, make, make out; *compare* CONJECTURE
rel induce; conjecture, glean, guess, reckon, speculate, surmise, think; ascertain, construe, interpret, reason, understand
idiom come to (*or* draw *or* reach) a conclusion; read between the lines

inference *n* **1** the deriving of a conclusion by reasoning <the answer was obtainable by *inference*>
syn deduction, illation, judgment, ratiocination
rel conjecture, guessing, reckoning, supposition, surmise
2 a determination arrived at by reasoning <a wrong *inference* based on incomplete evidence>
syn conclusion, deduction, illation, judgment, ratiocination, sequitur
rel assumption, conjecture, guess, presumption, reckoning, supposition, surmise

inferior *adj* **1** being or regarded as being below the level of another thing <the *inferior* latitudes of the northern hemisphere>
syn lesser, low, lower, nether, subjacent, under
rel junior, minor, secondary, subaltern, subordinate
con greater, higher, over, overlying
ant superior
2 of little or less importance, value, or merit <sold *inferior* goods at high prices>
syn common, déclassé, hack, low-grade, mean, poor, second-class, second-drawer, second-rate; *compare* CHEAP 2
rel average, fair, indifferent, mediocre, middling, ordinary; bad, base, paltry, punk, shoddy, sleazy, sorry, tawdry, tin-pot, wretched; good-for-nothing, lousy, ‖no-account, no-good, unworthy, valueless, worthless
con choice, excellent, first-class, first-rate, high-grade, prime
ant superior

inferior *n* one lower than another (as in station or worth) <a man inclined to be disdainful of his social *inferiors*>
syn poor relation, scrub, secondary, subaltern, subordinate, underling, understrapper
rel attendant, auxiliary, deputy; retainer, satrap, subject, vassal; hanger-on, heeler, henchman, hireling, minion, satellite, sycophant; adherent, disciple, follower
con chief, head, leader, master, principal
ant superior

infernal *adj* **1** of or relating to a nether world of the dead <the *infernal* regions>
syn chthonian, chthonic, Hadean, plutonian, plutonic, sulphurous, Tartarean

---

syn synonym(s) *rel* related word(s)
ant antonym(s) *con* contrasted word(s)
idiom idiomatic equivalent(s)
‖ use limited; if in doubt, see a dictionary

con celestial, elysian, Hesperidean, paradisaic, paradisal, paradisiacal
ant supernal
2 resembling or appropriate to hell or its inhabitants <an *infernal* glow in the sky>
syn avernal, cimmerian, hellish, pandemoniac, plutonian, plutonic, stygian
rel demoniac, devilish, diabolic, fiendish; sulphurous
ant celestial, heavenly
3 ***syn*** see DAMNED 2
4 ***syn*** see UTTER

inferno *n* **1** ***syn*** see HELL
2 ***syn*** see FIRE 1

inferred *adj* ***syn*** see TACIT 1

infertile *adj* **1** ***syn*** see STERILE 1
rel depleted, drained, exhausted, impoverished
con breeding, generating, propagating, reproducing
ant fertile
2 ***syn*** see BARREN 2
ant fertile

infest *vb* **1** to spread or swarm over in a troublesome manner <lawns *infested* with weeds>
syn beset, overrun, overspread, overswarm
rel abound, crawl, swarm, teem; annoy, harass, harry, pester, plague, worry
2 to live in or on as a parasite <a dog *infested* by fleas>
syn parasite, parasitize

infidel *adj* ***syn*** see HEATHEN

infidelic *adj* ***syn*** see HEATHEN

infidelity *n* betrayal of a moral obligation <a leader guilty of *infidelity* to the responsibilities he had accepted>
syn disloyalty, faithlessness, falseness, falsity, perfidiousness, perfidy, unfaithfulness; *compare* TREACHERY
rel fickleness, inconstancy; treacherousness, treachery, treason
idiom bad faith
con devotion, faithfulness, fealty; constancy, loyalty, steadfastness
ant fidelity

infiltrate *vb* ***syn*** see INSINUATE 3

infinite *adj* **1** being without known limits <the idea of an *infinite* universe>
syn eternal, illimitable, perdurable, sempiternal, supertemporal
rel everlasting, perpetual
con bounded, circumscribed, limited, restricted
ant finite
2 ***syn*** see LIMITLESS
ant finite

infinity *n* ***syn*** see ETERNITY 1

infirm *adj* ***syn*** see WEAK 1
ant hale

infirmity *n* **1** the quality or state of being enfeebled and weakened in health <suffering from old age and attendant physical *infirmity*>
syn debility, decrepitude, disease, feebleness, infirmness, malaise, sickliness, unhealthiness; *compare* DISEASE 1, SICKNESS 1
rel debilitation, decay, enfeeblement, failing, frailty, weakening, weakness; diseasedness, unwellness; illness, indisposition, sickness, unhealth
ant haleness
2 ***syn*** see DISEASE 1
3 ***syn*** see SICKNESS 1

infirmness *n* ***syn*** see INFIRMITY 1

infix *vb* **1** ***syn*** see ENTRENCH 1
2 ***syn*** see IMPLANT

inflame *vb* **1** ***syn*** see LIGHT 1
ant extinguish
2 ***syn*** see IRRITATE

inflammable *adj* ***syn*** see COMBUSTIBLE 1
ant nonflammable, noninflammable

inflammatory *adj* exciting or tending to excite anger, animosity, or disorder <*inflammatory* speeches designed to spark rebellion>
syn incendiary
rel exciting, incitive, instigative, provocative; revolutionary, seditionary, seditious
con calming, moderating, soothing, temperate

inflate *vb* ***syn*** see EXPAND 3
ant deflate

inflated *adj* swollen with or as if with something insubstantial <had an *inflated* idea of his own importance>
syn dropsical, dropsied, flatulent, overblown, tumescent, tumid, turgid, windy
rel aureate, bombastic, flowery, grandiloquent, magniloquent, rhetorical; ostentatious, pretentious, showy; fustian, ranting, rhapsodical; diffuse, prolix, verbose, wordy
con compendious, concise, laconic, pithy, succinct, summary, terse

inflatus *n* ***syn*** see INSPIRATION

inflection *n* a particular manner of employing the sounds of the voice in speech <questions end on a rising *inflection*>
syn accent, intonation, tone
rel articulation, enunciation, pronunciation; timbre, tonality
idiom tone of voice

inflexible *adj* **1** ***syn*** see STIFF 1
rel immobile, immovable
con elastic, resilient, springy, supple; ductile, malleable, plastic, pliable, pliant; fluid, liquid
ant flexible
2 rigidly firm in will or purpose <a person of *inflexible* resolution>
syn adamant, adamantine, brassbound, dogged, inexorable, iron, obdurate, relentless, rigid, rockbound, rock-ribbed, single-minded, steadfast, stubborn, unbendable, unbending, uncompliant, uncompromising, unswayable, unyielding; *compare* STIFF 1
rel intractable, obstinate; indomitable, invincible, unconquerable; grim, hard, implacable, unrelenting; dyed-in-the-wool, fixed, set, ‖sot
con agreeable, amenable, compliant, docile, pliant, responsive, swayable, yielding; mild, open
ant flexible
3 incapable of changing or being changed <*inflexible* rules>
syn constant, determinate, fixed, immovable, immutable, inalterable, invariable, ironclad, un-

alterable, unchangeable, unmodifiable, unmovable
rel strict; rigorous; established, set, settled; changeless, unchanging
con adaptable, adjustable, alterable, changeable, mutable, variable
ant flexible
4 *syn* see TOUGH 3

inflict *vb* **1** *syn* see GIVE 10
2 to cause one to endure (something damaging or painful) <*inflict* retribution>
syn force (on *or* upon), impose, visit, wreak, wreck; *compare* IMPOSE 4
rel expose, subject
idiom lay open to, put on the spot
con guard, protect, shelter, shield

inflow *n* *syn* see INFLUX
ant outflow, outflux

influence *n* **1** power exerted over the minds or behavior of others <a person of great *influence* in national politics>
syn authority, credit, prestige, weight; *compare* PULL 2
rel command, domination, dominion, mastery; ascendancy, dominance, eminence, predominance; consequence, importance, moment; ‖drag, in, pull
2 *syn* see PULL 2
3 *syn* see EFFECT 3

influence *vb* **1** *syn* see AFFECT
2 *syn* see PREJUDICE 2

influenceable *adj* *syn* see RECEPTIVE 1

influx *n* a flowing in <anticipated an *influx* of immigrants>
syn inflow, influxion, inpour, inpouring, inrush
rel accession, augmentation, increase; illapse
con outpour, outpouring, outrush; efflux, effluxion, exodus
ant outflow, outflux

influxion *n* *syn* see INFLUX
ant effluxion

inform *vb* **1** *syn* see FIRE 2
rel imbue, infuse, leaven, permeate; enlighten, illuminate; endow, endue
2 to make aware or cognizant of something <was kept *informed* of developments>
syn acquaint, advise, apprise, clue (*or* clew), fill in, notify, post, tell, warn, wise (up)
rel educate, enlighten, instruct, teach; familiarize; caution, forewarn
idiom keep posted
3 to give information about someone especially as an informer <his suspicions aroused, he *informed* on his neighbor to the police>
syn ‖nark, peach, ‖pimp, rat, ‖sing, snitch, squeak, squeal, ‖stool; *compare* TALK 6
rel blab, tattle, tell; betray, give away, turn in

informal *adj* **1** conducted or carried out without rigidly prescribed procedure <carried on an *informal* investigation>
syn irregular, unceremonious, unofficial
rel casual, spontaneous; unauthorized; unconventional; private, special
con authorized, ceremonious, conventional, official, regular
ant formal
2 *syn* see EASYGOING 3
rel familiar, natural, simple
con affected, mannered, prim, rigid, stiff, stilted
ant formal

information *n* **1** *syn* see KNOWLEDGE 2
2 *syn* see NEWS

informational *adj* *syn* see INFORMATIVE

informative *adj* imparting information <gave an *informative* talk>
syn educational, educative, informational, informatory, instructional, instructive
rel edifying, elucidative, enlightening, explanatory, illuminating
ant uninformative

informatory *adj* *syn* see INFORMATIVE

informed *adj* *syn* see FAMILIAR 3
ant uninformed

informer *n* one who informs against another <his arrest was brought about by an *informer*>
syn betrayer, ‖canary, ‖fink, ‖nark, ‖pimp, snitch, squawker, ‖squeaker, squealer, stool, stoolie, stool pigeon, talebearer, tattler, tattletale, tipster; *compare* BUSYBODY, DETECTIVE, GOSSIP 1, SPY

infra *adv* **1** *syn* see BELOW 2
ant above, supra
2 *syn* see AFTER

infract *vb* *syn* see VIOLATE 1

infraction *n* *syn* see BREACH 1
rel crime, offense, sin; error, faux pas, lapse, slip

infrastructure *n* **1** *syn* see BASE 1
ant superstructure
2 *syn* see BASIS 1

infrequent *adj* appearing, happening, or met with so seldom as to attract attention <held only *infrequent* press conferences>
syn few, occasional, rare, scarce, seldom, semioccasional, sporadic, uncommon, unfrequent
rel isolated, scattered; meager, scant, scanty, sparse; exceptional, limited, unusual; odd, spasmodic, stray
idiom few and far between
con abundant, common, numerous, regular; ordinary, routine
ant frequent

infrequently *adv* **1** *syn* see SELDOM
ant frequently
2 *syn* see OCCASIONALLY
ant frequently

infringe *vb* **1** *syn* see TRESPASS 2
2 *syn* see VIOLATE 1
3 *syn* see IMPOSE 5

infringement *n* *syn* see BREACH 1

infuriate *vb* *syn* see ANGER 1

infuse *vb* **1** to introduce one thing into another so as to change or affect it <a teacher who *infused* her pupils with the desire to learn>

---

syn synonym(s) *rel* related word(s)
ant antonym(s) *con* contrasted word(s)
idiom idiomatic equivalent(s)
‖ use limited; if in doubt, see a dictionary

syn imbue, ingrain, inoculate, invest, leaven, steep, suffuse
rel animate, fire, inform, inspire; implant, inculcate, instill; impregnate, permeate, pervade, saturate; indoctrinate
2 *syn* see INTERFUSE 2
ingather *vb* ***syn*** see REAP
ingathering *n* ***syn*** see HARVEST 1
ingeminate *vb* ***syn*** see REPEAT
ingenerate *adj* ***syn*** see INHERENT
ingenious *adj* **1 *syn*** see INVENTIVE
2 *syn* see CLEVER 4
ingenuous *adj* ***syn*** see NATURAL 5
con covert, furtive, stealthy, surreptitious, underhand; artful, crafty, foxy, guileful, insidious, sly, tricky, wily
ant disingenuous
ingest *vb* ***syn*** see EAT 1
inglorious *adj* ***syn*** see DISREPUTABLE 1
ant glorious
ingoing *adj* ***syn*** see INCISIVE
ingot *n* ***syn*** see BAR 1
ingrain *vb* **1 *syn*** see ENTRENCH 1
rel engrave, etch, grave, incise
2 *syn* see INFUSE 1
ingrained *adj* ***syn*** see INHERENT
rel chronic, confirmed, deep-rooted, inveterate
con exterior, external, outer, outside, outward
ingratiating *adj* intended or designed to gain favor <an *ingratiating* smile>
syn deferential, disarming, ingratiatory, insinuating, insinuative, saccharine, silken, silky
rel adulatory; fawning, sycophantic
ingratiatory *adj* ***syn*** see INGRATIATING
ingredient *n* ***syn*** see ELEMENT 2
ingress *n* **1 *syn*** see ENTRANCE 1
ant egress
2 *syn* see DOOR 2
ant egress
ingress *vb* ***syn*** see ENTER 1
ant egress
ingression *n* ***syn*** see ENTRANCE 1
ant egression
in–group *n* ***syn*** see CLIQUE
ant outgroup
ingurgitate *vb* ***syn*** see GULP
inhabit *vb* to dwell in as a place of settled residence <islands *inhabited* by Polynesians>
syn occupy, people, populate, tenant
rel settle; abide, dwell, live
inhabitable *adj* ***syn*** see LIVABLE 1
ant uninhabitable
inhabitancy *n* ***syn*** see HABITATION 1
inhabitant *n* one that occupies a particular place regularly <*inhabitants* of large cities>
syn denizen, dweller, habitant, indweller, liver, occupant, resident, ||residenter, resider
rel aborigine, autochthon, indigene, native
inhabitation *n* ***syn*** see HABITATION 1
inhale *vb* to draw (as air) into the lungs <*inhaling* smoke>
syn breathe (in), inspire
ant exhale, expire
inharmonic *adj* ***syn*** see DISSONANT 1
ant harmonic
inharmonious *adj* **1 *syn*** see DISSONANT 1
ant harmonious
2 lacking harmony especially in sentiment <the committee meeting was singularly *inharmonious*>
syn discordant, inconsonant, uncongenial, unharmonious
rel antagonistic, cat-and-dog, conflicting, conflictive, differing, disagreeing, incompatible, incongruous, quarrelsome
con concordant, congenial, consonant; amiable, compatible; collaborative
ant harmonious
inharmony *n* ***syn*** see DISCORD
ant harmony
inhaust *vb* ***syn*** see ABSORB 1
inhere *vb* **1 *syn*** see CONSIST 1
2 *syn* see BELONG 3
inherent *adj* being a part, element, or quality of a thing's inmost being <*inherent* rights of every citizen>
syn born, built-in, congenital, connate, constitutional, deep-seated, elemental, essential, inborn, inbred, indwelling, ingenerate, ingrained, innate, intimate, intrinsic
rel inner, internal, inward, resident; basic, elementary, fundamental, immanent, integral; characteristic, distinctive, individual, peculiar; natural, normal, regular, typical; bred-in-the-bone
con shallow, superficial; accidental, fortuitous, incidental; alien, extraneous, extrinsic, foreign
ant adventitious
inheritance *n* **1 *syn*** see HERITAGE 1
2 *syn* see LEGACY 1
inherited *adj* ***syn*** see INNATE 1
inheritor *n* ***syn*** see HEIR
inhibit *vb* **1 *syn*** see FORBID
rel avert, ward
ant allow
2 *syn* see RESTRAIN 1
ant activate; animate
inhibited *adj* ***syn*** see FRIGID 3
ant uninhibited
inhuman *adj* ***syn*** see FIERCE 1
rel malicious, malign, malignant; implacable, relentless, unrelenting; devilish, diabolical, fiendish
con altruistic, benevolent, charitable, eleemosynary, humanitarian, philanthropic; compassionate, tender
ant humane
inhumane *adj* ***syn*** see FIERCE 1
ant humane
inhumation *n* ***syn*** see BURIAL 2
ant exhumation
inhume *vb* ***syn*** see BURY 1
ant disinhume, exhume
inimicable *adj* ***syn*** see HOSTILE 1
inimical *adj* ***syn*** see HOSTILE 1
iniquitous *adj* ***syn*** see WRONG 1
iniquity *n* ***syn*** see EVIL 3
initial *adj* **1** marking a commencement or constituting a start <*initial* symptoms of the disease>

syn beginning, inceptive, incipient, initiative, initiatory, introductory, nascent
rel basic, elementary, first, fundamental; embryonic, germinal; early, infant; antecedent; earliest, introductory, primary
con closing; concluding, conclusive; terminal, terminative; last, ultimate
ant final
2 *syn* see FIRST 2
3 *syn* see FIRST 1
ant final

initially *adv* **1** in the beginning <*initially* we were confused but soon enough we fully understood>
syn originally, primarily, primitively
rel first, firstly, incipiently
idiom at first, at the first go-off, from the word go
con lastly, ultimately
ant finally
2 *syn* see FIRSTLY

initiate *vb* **1** *syn* see BEGIN 1
ant terminate
2 *syn* see INTRODUCE 3
3 to put through the formalities for becoming a member or official <the club *initiated* four new members>
syn inaugurate, induct, install, instate, invest
rel institute; admit, enter, introduce, take in

initiation *n* the process or an instance of being formally introduced into an office or made a member of an organization <a fraternity *initiation*>
syn inaugural, inauguration, induction, installation, investiture
rel baptism; institution, introduction

initiative *adj* *syn* see INITIAL 1

initiative *n* *syn* see ENTERPRISE 4

initiatory *adj* *syn* see INITIAL 1

injudicious *adj* *syn* see UNWISE
ant judicious

injunction *n* *syn* see COMMAND 1

injure *vb* **1** to deplete the soundness, strength, effectiveness, or perfection of something <*injured* her prestige by making rash statements>
syn blemish, damage, harm, hurt, impair, mar, prejudice, spoil, tarnish, vitiate
rel disserve; disadvantage; endamage, weaken; blight, queer; foul up, louse up; contort, deface, deform, disfigure, distort; bespatter, foul, smirch; disable, incapacitate
con assist, help, succor; better, enhance, improve; benefit; strengthen
ant aid
2 *syn* see DISTRESS 2
idiom do dirt to
3 to inflict bodily hurt on <was *injured* in an auto accident>
syn hurt, wound
rel damage, harm; afflict, torment, torture; batter, cripple, maim, mangle, mutilate
idiom draw blood

injurious *adj* *syn* see HARMFUL

injury *n* **1** an act or the result of inflicting something that causes loss or pain <we cannot forgive his *injury* of the painting> <his falsehood caused grave *injury* to his brother's reputation>
syn damage, harm, hurt, mischief, outrage, ruin
rel agony, discomfiture, distress, misery, suffering; pain, pang; detriment, disservice, loss; bad, evil, ill
2 *syn* see INJUSTICE 2

injustice *n* **1** absence of justice <preached against *injustice*>
syn inequitableness, inequity, unfairness, unjustness, wrong
rel crime, malfeasance, malpractice, villainy, wrongdoing; favoritism, inequality, partiality, partisanship
con equity, fairness, right
ant justice, justness
2 an act or instance of unjustness <pointed out various *injustices* in the law> <you do him an *injustice* when you call him lazy>
syn grievance, injury, wrong
rel damage, harm, hurt, mischief, outrage, ruin; breach, infraction, infringement, tort, transgression, trespass, violation

ink *vb* *syn* see SIGN 1

inkling *n* *syn* see HINT 1

inky *adj* *syn* see BLACK 1

||**inland** *adj* *syn* see DOMESTIC 2
ant foreign

inlet *n* a recess in the shores of a body of water <*inlets* of lakes and rivers>
syn arm, bay, bayou, bight, cove, ||creek, firth, gulf, harbor, ||loch, ||lough, slough

inn *n* *syn* see HOTEL

innards *n pl* *syn* see ENTRAILS

innate *adj* **1** existing in or belonging to an individual inherently <*innate* vigor>
syn congenital, connate, connatural, inborn, indigenous, inherited, native, natural, unacquired
rel constitutional, deep-seated, essential, ingrained, inherent, intrinsic; hereditary; normal, regular, standard, typical
con accidental, adventitious, fortuitous, incidental; affected, assumed, feigned, simulated; cultivated, fostered, nurtured
ant acquired
2 *syn* see INHERENT

inner *adj* **1** situated further in <the *inner* layers were less worn>
syn ||innermore, inside, interior, internal, intestine, inward
rel central, focal, middle, nuclear; close, familiar, intimate; constitutional, essential, inherent, intrinsic
con exterior, external, outside, outward
ant outer
2 arising from one's inmost self <*inner* thoughts and feelings>
syn gut, interior, internal, intimate, visceral, viscerous

---

syn synonym(s) *rel* related word(s)
ant antonym(s) *con* contrasted word(s)
idiom idiomatic equivalent(s)
|| use limited; if in doubt, see a dictionary

rel individual, personal, private; concealed, hidden, secret
con exterior, outer; open, public
||**innermore** *adj* ***syn*** see INNER 1
innervate *vb* ***syn*** see PROVOKE 4
innerve *vb* ***syn*** see PROVOKE 4
innholder *n* ***syn*** see SALOONKEEPER
innkeeper *n* ***syn*** see SALOONKEEPER
innocence *n* ***syn*** see IGNORANCE 2
innocent *adj* **1** ***syn*** see GOOD 11
rel unstained, unsullied, white, white-handed
2 free from legal guilt or fault <the defendant was found *innocent*>
syn blameless, clean, crimeless, faultless, guiltless, inculpable, unguilty
idiom in the clear
ant guilty
3 ***syn*** see LAWFUL
4 ***syn*** see DEVOID
5 ***syn*** see NATURAL 5
6 ***syn*** see HARMLESS
con harmful, injurious, mischievous
innocuous *adj* **1** ***syn*** see HARMLESS
con harmful, injurious; evil; troublesome
ant pernicious
2 ***syn*** see INSIPID 3
innominate *adj* ***syn*** see ANONYMOUS
innovation *n* ***syn*** see CHANGE 2
rel deviation, introduction, wrinkle
innovational *adj* ***syn*** see INVENTIVE
innovative *adj* ***syn*** see INVENTIVE
innovator *n* one who introduces something new <an *innovator* of bold ideas in the field of computers>
syn introducer, inventor, original, originator
rel author, creator, maker, producer; architect, builder, developer
innovatory *adj* ***syn*** see INVENTIVE
innoxious *adj* ***syn*** see HARMLESS
ant noxious
innuendo *n* ***syn*** see INSINUATION
innumerable *adj* too many to be counted <received *innumerable* requests for help>
syn countless, innumerous, numberless, uncountable, uncounted, unnumberable, unnumbered, untold
ant numberable, numerable
innumerous *adj* ***syn*** see INNUMERABLE
inobnoxious *adj* ***syn*** see HARMLESS
ant obnoxious
inobservant *adj* ***syn*** see INATTENTIVE
ant observant
inobtrusive *adj* ***syn*** see QUIET 4
ant obtrusive
inoculate *vb* ***syn*** see INFUSE 1
rel admit, enter, introduce
inodorous *adj* ***syn*** see ODORLESS
ant odorous; smelly
inoffensive *adj* ***syn*** see HARMLESS
con loathsome, repulsive, revolting; distasteful, obnoxious, repellent, repugnant
ant offensive
inopportune *adj* ***syn*** see UNSEASONABLE 1
ant opportune
inordinate *adj* **1** ***syn*** see EXCESSIVE 1
rel irrational, unreasonable; gratuitous, supererogatory, uncalled-for, wanton; extra, superfluous, surplus
con moderate, temperate; checked, curbed, inhibited, restrained
2 ***syn*** see EXCESSIVE 2
inordinately *adv* ***syn*** see EVER 6
inordinateness *n* ***syn*** see EXCESS 3
in passing *adv* ***syn*** see INCIDENTALLY 2
in perpetuum *adv* ***syn*** see EVER 2
inpour *n* ***syn*** see INFLUX
ant outpour, outpouring
inpouring *n* ***syn*** see INFLUX
ant outpour, outpouring
inquest *n* ***syn*** see INQUIRY 1
inquietude *n* ***syn*** see UNREST
rel anxiety, uneasiness
ant quiet, quietness, quietude
inquire *vb* ***syn*** see ASK 1
rel investigate, probe, search; scrutinize, study
inquire (into) *vb* ***syn*** see EXPLORE
inquiring *adj* ***syn*** see INQUISITIVE 1
inquiry *n* **1** the act or an instance of seeking truth, information, or knowledge about something <an exhaustive *inquiry* revealed no evidence of a conspiracy>
syn delving, inquest, inquisition, investigation, probe, probing, quest, research
rel catechizing, interrogation, questioning; audit, check, examination, inspection, scrutiny; hearing; inquirendo
2 a request for information <addressed his *inquiry* to the personnel director>
syn interrogation, interrogatory, query, question, questioning
inquisition *n* ***syn*** see INQUIRY 1
inquisitive *adj* **1** given to examination or investigation <an *inquisitive* child who was interested in everything around her>
syn curious, disquisitive, inquiring, investigative, questioning
rel nosy, prying, snoopy
con indifferent, unconcerned, uninquisitive, uninterested
ant incurious
2 ***syn*** see CURIOUS 2
ant incurious, uninquiring
inquisitorial *adj* ***syn*** see CURIOUS 2
inquisitory *adj* ***syn*** see CURIOUS 2
in re *prep* ***syn*** see APROPOS
in respect to *prep* ***syn*** see APROPOS
in reverse *adv* ***syn*** see ABOUT 6
inroad *n* ***syn*** see INVASION
inroad *vb* ***syn*** see INVADE 1
inrush *n* ***syn*** see INFLUX
ant outrush
insalubrious *adj* ***syn*** see UNWHOLESOME 1
ant salubrious, salutary
insalutary *adj* ***syn*** see UNWHOLESOME 1
ant salubrious, salutary
insanable *adj* ***syn*** see HOPELESS 2
ins and outs *n pl* characteristic peculiarities or technicalities <soon learned the *ins and outs* of his job>

syn minutiae, ropes
rel details, incidentals, particulars; ramifications; oddities, peculiarities, quirks

insane *adj* **1** being afflicted by or manifesting unsoundness of mind or an inability to control one's rational processes <adjudged *insane* after a period of observation>
syn bananas, ‖batty, bedlamite, ‖bonkers, brainsick, ‖buggy, ‖bughouse, ‖bugs, crackbrained, cracked, ‖crackers, ‖cracky, ‖cranky, crazed, crazy, cuckoo, daffy, daft, demented, deranged, disordered, distraught, ‖fruity, ‖loco, loony, lunatic, mad, maniac, ‖mental, mindless, non compos mentis, nuts, nutsy, nutty, reasonless, screwy, teched, unbalanced, unsane, unsound, wacky, witless, wrong
rel irrational, unreasonable; bewildered, distracted; dotty, eccentric, off, rocky, strange, touched; ‖dippy
idiom around the bend, crazy as a coot, not all there, not right in one's head, ‖off one's dot, off one's nut (*or* rocker), ‖off one's onion, out of (*or* off) one's head, out of one's mind, touched in the head
con judicious, sapient, sensible, wise; rational, reasonable; balanced; logical, subtle; healthy, sound; clear, lucid
ant sane
2 *syn* see FOOLISH 2
rel fanciful, fantastic, imaginary, visionary; impractical, unrealistic
con feasible, possible, practicable, usable; rational, reasonable, sane, sensible; practical, realistic

insaneness *n* *syn* see INSANITY 1
ant saneness, sanity

insanity *n* **1** grave disorder of mind that impairs one's capacity to function safely or normally in society <his *insanity* required confinement in a mental institution>
syn aberration, alienation, derangement, distraction, insaneness, lunacy, madness, psychopathy, unbalance
rel acromania; delirium, frenzy, hysteria; delusion, hallucination, illusion; irrationality, unreasonableness; dotage
con judiciousness, sageness, sensibility, wiseness; rationality, reasonableness; healthiness, soundness, wholesomeness
ant saneness, sanity
2 *syn* see FOOLISHNESS
rel asininity, fatuousness, stupidity; impracticality

insatiable *adj* incapable of being satisfied or appeased <an *insatiable* lust for glory>
syn insatiate, quenchless, unappeasable, unquenchable, unsatiate, unsatisfiable
rel unsatiated, unsatisfied; demanding, exigent, importunate, insistent, urgent; clamorous, crying, pressing, yearning
con appeasable, quenchable, satisfiable; satiate, satiated, satisfied; controlled, curbed, restrained
ant satiable

insatiably *adv* *syn* see VERY 1

insatiate *adj* *syn* see INSATIABLE
ant satiate, satiated

inscience *n* *syn* see IGNORANCE 2

inscribe *vb* **1** *syn* see WRITE
rel engrave, enscroll
2 *syn* see LIST 3
3 *syn* see ENGRAVE 2

inscrutable *adj* *syn* see MYSTERIOUS

insecure *adj* **1** not confident or sure <feels very *insecure* about his future>
syn unassured, unconfident, unsure
rel hesitant, questioning, uncertain
idiom in suspense, up in the air
con assured, confident, self-assured, self-confident, sure
ant secure
2 *syn* see WEAK 2
ant secure

inseminate *vb* *syn* see IMPLANT

insensate *adj* **1** lacking animate awareness or sensation <would often talk to stones and other *insensate* objects>
syn inanimate, insensible, insentient, senseless, unfeeling
rel exanimate, unanimated; anesthetic, insensitive
con aware, cognizant, conscious; feeling, sensible, sensient
ant sensate
2 *syn* see SIMPLE 3
3 *syn* see INSENSIBLE 5

insensibility *n* *syn* see APATHY 1
ant sensibility

insensible *adj* **1** *syn* see INSENSATE 1
ant sensible
2 deprived of consciousness <knocked *insensible* by a sudden punch>
syn cold, comatose, inconscious, senseless, unconscious
idiom out cold
3 *syn* see NUMB 1
4 *syn* see IMPERCEPTIBLE
ant sensible
5 devoid or insusceptible of emotion or passion <*insensible* to love or compassion>
syn anesthetic, bloodless, dull, hard, impassible, insensate, insensitive, rocky
rel blunt, obtuse; apathetic, impassive, phlegmatic, stoic, stolid; callous, hardened, indurated, pachydermatous, thick-skinned; absorbed, engrossed, intent, rapt
con alert, alive, awake, aware, cognizant, conscious; affected, impressed, influenced, touched
ant sensible

insensitive *adj* **1** *syn* see INSENSIBLE 5
rel aloof, incurious, indifferent, unconcerned
con compassionate, responsive, tender
ant sensitive
2 *syn* see NUMB 1
ant sensitive

---

syn synonym(s) *rel* related word(s)
ant antonym(s) *con* contrasted word(s)
idiom idiomatic equivalent(s)
‖ use limited; if in doubt, see a dictionary

3 *syn* see INSUSCEPTIBLE
ant sensitive

insentient *adj* **1** *syn* see INSENSATE 1
ant sentient
2 *syn* see INSUSCEPTIBLE

insert *vb* *syn* see INTRODUCE 6
rel interlope, intrude, obtrude; implant, inculcate, instill; admit, enter
con detach, disengage
ant abstract, extract

in short *adv* *syn* see BRIEFLY

inside *n* **1** *syn* see INTERIOR
ant outside
2 insides *pl* *syn* see ENTRAILS

inside *adj* **1** *syn* see INNER 1
ant outside
2 *syn* see PRIVATE 2

inside *adv* *syn* see INDOORS
ant outside

inside out *adv* *syn* see THOROUGHLY 2

insidious *adj* *syn* see SLY 2
rel perfidious, treacherous; dangerous, perilous; gradual, subtle

insight *n* **1** *syn* see SAGACITY
2 *syn* see INTUITION

insighted *adj* *syn* see WISE 1

insightful *adj* *syn* see WISE 1
rel discriminating, penetrating; inseeing

insignia *n* a distinguishing mark of authority, office, or honor <wore a coronet with the strawberry leaf *insignia* of his ducal rank > <displayed her military *insignia* with pride>
syn badge, emblem
rel decoration; regalia

insignificancy *n* *syn* see NONENTITY

insignificant *adj* **1** *syn* see SENSELESS 5
ant significant
2 *syn* see MINOR 2
3 *syn* see LITTLE 3
ant significant

insincere *adj* not being or expressing what one appears to be or express <an *insincere* person who could not be trusted>
syn ambidextrous, double, double-dealing, double-faced, doublehearted, double-minded, double-tongued, hypocritical, left-handed, mala fide
rel deceitful, dishonest, lying, mendacious, untruthful; shifty, slippery, tricky
con candid, frank, open, plain; direct, forthright, straight, straightforward
ant sincere

insinuate *vb* **1** *syn* see INTRODUCE 6
2 *syn* see SUGGEST 1
rel ascribe, impute
con affirm, assert, aver, avouch, avow, declare, profess; air, broach, express, state, voice
3 to introduce (as oneself) by stealthy, smooth, or artful means <*insinuated* himself into the confidence of others>
syn edge in, foist, infiltrate, work in, worm
rel insert, intercalate, interject, interpolate, interpose, introduce

insinuating *adj* *syn* see INGRATIATING

insinuation *n* a stealthy or indirect hinting or suggestion <*insinuations* about her opponent's probity>
syn innuendo, insinuendo
rel hint, hinting, implication, implying, intimation, suggestion; animadversion, aspersion, reflection; ascription, imputation

insinuative *adj* *syn* see INGRATIATING

insinuendo *n* *syn* see INSINUATION

insipid *adj* **1** *syn* see UNPALATABLE 1
rel bland, mild
con appetizing, flavorable, tasty
ant sapid, savory
2 *syn* see ARID 2
rel commonplace, ordinary, plain; mundane, prosaic, unimaginative
3 devoid of qualities that make for spirit and character <an *insipid* little story of teenage puppy love>
syn banal, bland, driveling, flat, inane, innocuous, jejune, milk-and-water, namby-pamby, sapless, swashy, vapid, waterish, watery, wishy-washy
rel slight, tenuous, thin; feeble, weak; subdued, tame; mild, soft; pointless
con piquant, poignant, pungent, racy, spicy; fiery, gingery, high-spirited, mettlesome, peppery, spirited, spunky; exciting, piquing, provocative, provoking
ant sapid

insistent *adj* **1** *syn* see PERSISTENT 1
2 *syn* see EMPHATIC
rel persevering, persistent, pressing; obtrusive
3 *syn* see PRESSING

insociable *adj* *syn* see UNSOCIABLE
ant sociable

insolate *vb* *syn* see SUN

insolence *n* the quality, state, or an instance of being insulting or grossly lacking in respect <court-martialed because of *insolence* to an officer>
syn boldness, disrespect, hardihood, impertinence, impudence, insolency, insolentness; *compare* EFFRONTERY
rel brazenness; presumption; arrogance; rudeness; contempt
con deference; correctness, decency, decorum, decorousness, properness, seemliness
ant respect, respectfulness

insolency *n* *syn* see INSOLENCE
ant respect, respectfulness

insolent *adj* **1** *syn* see PROUD 1
rel imperative, peremptory; dictatorial, magisterial
ant deferential
2 exhibiting boldness or effrontery <an *insolent* child with no respect or regard for anyone>
syn audacious, bold, ‖boldacious, brazen, contumelious, impertinent, impudent, procacious, saucy
rel arrogant, disdainful, overbearing; discourteous, impolite, rude, uncivil, ungracious
con humble, lowly, meek, modest, unassertive; civil, courteous, polite

ant deferential

insolentness *n* ***syn*** see INSOLENCE
ant respect, respectfulness

insoluble *adj* admitting of no solution <seemingly *insoluble* problems faced the city council>
syn inextricable, insolvable, irresoluble, irresolvable, unsoluble, unsolvable
rel inexplicable, unexplainable; inconceivable, unaccountable; mysterious
con answerable, explicable, understandable; resolvable; clear, plain, straightforward
ant soluble, solvable

insolvable *adj* ***syn*** see INSOLUBLE
ant soluble, solvable

insomnia *n* prolonged inability to obtain adequate sleep <sleeping pills failed to relieve his *insomnia*>
syn insomnolence, sleeplessness
rel restlessness, wakefulness; stress, tension

insomnolence *n* ***syn*** see INSOMNIA

insorb *vb* ***syn*** see ABSORB 1

insouciance *n* ***syn*** see APATHY 2

insouciant *adj* ***syn*** see HAPPY-GO-LUCKY

inspect *vb* ***syn*** see SCRUTINIZE 1
rel notice, observe; catechize, inquire, interrogate, question; review

inspection *n* ***syn*** see EXAMINATION
rel inquest, inquiry, inquisition, investigation, probe, research; oversight, supervision, surveillance

inspiration *n* a divine or seemingly divine imparting of knowledge or power <*inspiration* is the only plausible explanation for his exquisite work>
syn afflation, afflatus, inflatus
rel animus, genius, muse, vision; enlightenment, illumination; brainstorm, brain wave

inspire *vb* **1** ***syn*** see INHALE
ant expire
2 ***syn*** see FIRE 2
rel quicken, stimulate; infect, infuse; endow, endue
3 ***syn*** see ELATE
4 ***syn*** see AFFECT

inspiring *adj* ***syn*** see EXCITING
ant uninspiring

inspirit *vb* ***syn*** see ENCOURAGE 1
rel exalt, fire, inform, inspire
ant dispirit

in spite of *prep* ***syn*** see AGAINST 4

instability *n* the state or quality of not being firm or fixed <the *instability* of the economy>
syn precariousness, shakiness, unfixedness, unsettledness, unstability, unstableness, unsteadfastness, unsteadiness
rel undependability, unreliability; inconstancy, insecurity
con firmness, soundness, stoutness, sturdiness; fixity, solidity
ant stability, stableness

install *vb* **1** ***syn*** see INITIATE 3
2 ***syn*** see ENSCONCE 2

installation *n* ***syn*** see INITIATION

instance *n* an individual that clearly belongs to an indicated class <their rescue was an *instance* of great courage>
syn case, case history, example, illustration, representative, sample, sampling, specimen
rel ground, proof, reason; detail, item, particular; exponent

instance *vb* **1** ***syn*** see EXEMPLIFY 1
2 ***syn*** see MENTION
rel exemplify, illustrate

instant *n* **1** an infinitesimal space of time <came not an *instant* too soon>
syn breathing, crack, flash, ‖jiff, jiffy, minute, moment, second, shake, split second, ‖tick, trice, twinkle, twinkling, wink
2 ***syn*** see POINT 7
3 ***syn*** see OCCASION 5

instant *adj* **1** ***syn*** see PRESSING
2 ***syn*** see PRESENT
3 ***syn*** see INSTANTANEOUS

instantaneous *adj* done, occurring, or acting without any perceptible duration of time <*instantaneous* answers to tough questions>
syn hair-trigger, immediate, instant; *compare* QUICK 2
rel spontaneous; fast, quick, rapid; momentary, transitory
con late, tardy; slow, sluggish

instanter *adv* ***syn*** see AWAY 3

instantly *adv* ***syn*** see AWAY 3
idiom in a flash, on a dime, on the spot

instate *vb* ***syn*** see INITIATE 3

instead *adv* as an alternative to something expressed or implied <longed *instead* for a quiet country life>
syn alternately, alternatively, in lieu, rather

insteep *vb* ***syn*** see SOAK 1

instigate *vb* ***syn*** see INCITE
rel activate, actuate; hint, insinuate, suggest; plan, plot, scheme; goad, urge; fire, inflame

instigation *n* ***syn*** see STIMULUS

instigator *n* one that goads or urges forward <the *instigator* of the riot>
syn agitator, fomenter, inciter, mover
rel firebrand, incendiary, inflamer, rabble-rouser

instill *vb* ***syn*** see IMPLANT

instinctive *adj* **1** prompted by natural instinct or propensity <was quite unable to control her *instinctive* fear of snakes>
syn instinctual, intuitive, visceral
rel congenital, inborn, innate; ingrained, inherent, intrinsic; natural
ant reasoned
2 ***syn*** see SPONTANEOUS
rel natural, normal, regular, typical
ant intentional

instinctual *adj* ***syn*** see INSTINCTIVE 1

institute *vb* **1** ***syn*** see FOUND 2

---

syn synonym(s) ***rel*** related word(s)
ant antonym(s) ***con*** contrasted word(s)
idiom idiomatic equivalent(s)
‖ use limited; if in doubt, see a dictionary

ant abrogate
2 *syn* see INTRODUCE 3
institute *n* ***syn*** see LAW 1
institution *n* something or someone well established in a customary relationship <he's been in the office so long that he has become an *institution*>
syn fixture
rel custom, habit; establishment, rite
instruct *vb* **1 *syn*** see TEACH
rel acquaint, apprise, inform; engineer, guide, lead, pilot, steer
2 *syn* see COMMAND
rel assign, define, prescribe
instruction *n* ***syn*** see EDUCATION 1
instructional *adj* ***syn*** see INFORMATIVE
instructive *adj* ***syn*** see INFORMATIVE
rel didactic, moralistic, moralizing
instrument *n* **1 *syn*** see MEAN 2
2 *syn* see IMPLEMENT
rel equipment, gear, machinery, paraphernalia, tackle
instrumental *adj* serving as a means, agent, or tool <was *instrumental* in organizing the strike>
syn implemental, ministerial
rel conducive, helpful; serviceable, useful
instrumentality *n* ***syn*** see MEAN 2
rel energy, force, might, power
instrumentation *n* ***syn*** see MEAN 2
insubordinate *adj* unwilling to submit to authority <*insubordinate* soldiers are court-martialed>
syn contumacious, factious, insurgent, mutinous, rebellious, seditious
rel intractable, recalcitrant, refractory, ungovernable, unruly; indocile, uncompliant, uncomplying; disaffected, dissentious
con amenable, biddable, docile, obedient, tractable; subdued, submissive, tame
ant subordinate
insubstantial *adj* **1 *syn*** see IMMATERIAL 1
ant substantial
2 *syn* see WEAK 1
ant substantial
3 *syn* see TENUOUS 3
ant substantial
insuccess *n* ***syn*** see FAILURE 2
ant success, successfulness
insufferable *adj* incapable of being endured <that man is an *insufferable* bore>
syn insupportable, intolerable, unbearable, unbrookable, unendurable, unsufferable, unsupportable
rel distressing, painful; unacceptable
ant sufferable
insufficience *n* **1 *syn*** see FAILURE 3
ant sufficiency
2 *syn* see SCARCITY
ant sufficiency
insufficiency *n* **1 *syn*** see FAILURE 3
ant sufficiency
2 *syn* see SCARCITY
ant sufficiency
insufficient *adj* **1 *syn*** see DEFICIENT 1
ant sufficient
2 *syn* see SHORT 3
ant sufficient
insular *adj* having the narrow and limited outlook characteristic of geographic isolation <the *insular* thinking of peasant communities>
syn local, ‖parish-pump, parochial, provincial, sectarian, small-town
rel regional, sectional; insulated, isolated, secluded; circumscribed, confined, limited, restricted; illiberal, narrow, narrow-minded
con broad-minded, liberal; cosmopolitan, metropolitan, urban
insulate *vb* ***syn*** see ISOLATE
insult *vb* ***syn*** see OFFEND 3
rel abase, debase, degrade, humble, humiliate; fleer, flout, gibe, gird, jeer, scoff, sneer; deride, mock, ridicule, taunt; rump
con admire, esteem, respect
ant honor
insult *n* ***syn*** see AFFRONT
rel abuse, invective, obloquy, vituperation; disgrace, ignominy, opprobrium, shame; disdainfulness, insolence, superciliousness; contempt, disdain, scorn; unpleasantry
con deference, homage, honor, obeisance, reverence
insuperable *adj* incapable of being surmounted, overcome, or passed over <they met with *insuperable* difficulties>
syn impassable, inconquerable, indomitable, insurmountable, invincible, unconquerable, unsurmountable
rel unachievable, unattainable; unsurpassable; impenetrable, impregnable, invulnerable
con surmountable; achievable, negotiable
ant superable
insupportable *adj* ***syn*** see INSUFFERABLE
ant bearable, supportable
insupposable *adj* ***syn*** see INCREDIBLE 1
ant supposable
insuppressible *adj* ***syn*** see IRREPRESSIBLE
ant suppressible
insuppressive *adj* ***syn*** see IRREPRESSIBLE
insure *vb* ***syn*** see ENSURE
rel guard, protect, safeguard, shield
insurgent *n* ***syn*** see REBEL
insurgent *adj* ***syn*** see INSUBORDINATE
insurmountable *adj* ***syn*** see INSUPERABLE
ant surmountable
insurrect *vb* ***syn*** see REVOLT 1
insurrectionist *n* ***syn*** see REBEL
insusceptible *adj* incapable of being moved, affected, or impressed <*insusceptible* to flattery>
syn impassive, insensitive, insentient, unimpressible, unimpressionable, unresponsive, unsusceptible
con impressible, impressionable, responsive, sensitive, sentient
ant susceptible
intact *adj* **1 *syn*** see WHOLE 1
ant defective
2 *syn* see VIRGIN 1
ant deflowered
intangible *adj* **1 *syn*** see IMPERCEPTIBLE

rel rare, tenuous, thin; slender, slight; aerial, aeriform, airy, ethereal; eluding, elusive, evading, evasive; touchless
ant tangible
2 *syn* see ELUSIVE
integer *n* ***syn*** see NUMBER
integral *adj* ***syn*** see WHOLE 3
integral *n* ***syn*** see WHOLE 2
integrate *n* ***syn*** see WHOLE 2
integrate *vb* **1 *syn*** see HARMONIZE 4
2 *syn* see HARMONIZE 3
3 to join together systematically <an economic system that successfully *integrates* private gain with public responsibility>
syn articulate, concatenate
rel combine, conjoin, link, unite; compact, concentrate, consolidate, unify; blend, coalesce, fuse, merge; organize, systematize
con disperse, dissipate, scatter; analyze, break down, resolve
ant disintegrate
4 *syn* see UNIFY 1
5 *syn* see EMBODY 2
integrative *adj* tending to integrate <*integrative* forces in a fragmented society>
syn centralizing, centripetal, compacting, concentrating, consolidating, unifying
ant disintegrative
integrity *n* **1 *syn*** see HONESTY
rel forthrightness, straightforwardness
2 the quality or state of being complete or undivided <trying to maintain the *integrity* of the empire>
syn completeness, entireness, perfection, wholeness
rel soundness, stability; absoluteness, purity, simplicity
intellect *n* **1 *syn*** see REASON 5
rel comprehension; intuition
2 a person with great intellectual powers <one of the great *intellects* of his time>
syn brain, intellectual, intelligence
rel genius; egghead, pundit; thinker
intellection *n* ***syn*** see IDEA
intellective *adj* ***syn*** see MENTAL 1
intellectual *adj* **1 *syn*** see MENTAL 1
con animal, fleshly, sensual
ant carnal
2 devoted to or engaged in the creative use of the intellect <the play appealed to the *intellectual* members of the audience>
syn cerebral, highbrow, highbrowed, intellectualistic
intellectual *n* **1 *syn*** see INTELLECT 2
2 a person who possesses or has pretensions of strong intellectual interest or superiority <accused of being an *intellectual* and a snob>
syn Brahmin, double-dome, egghead, highbrow
3 intellectuals *pl* ***syn*** see INTELLIGENTSIA
intellectualistic *adj* ***syn*** see INTELLECTUAL 2
intelligence *n* **1** the ability to learn and to cope <what he lacked in education, he made up in *intelligence*>
syn brain(s), brainpower, mentality, mother wit, sense, wit
rel acumen, discernment, insight, judgment; perspicacity, sagacity, wisdom
2 *syn* see INTELLECT 2
3 *syn* see NEWS
intelligent *adj* **1 *syn*** see RATIONAL
con irrational, unreasonable
ant unintelligent
2 mentally keen or quick <quite *intelligent* for his age>
syn alert, brainy, bright, brilliant, clever, knowing, knowledgeable, quick-witted, ready-witted, sharp, smart; *compare* WISE 4
rel astute, perspicacious, sagacious, shrewd; acute, keen; adroit, cunning, ingenious
con foolish, idiotic, imbecilic, moronic; crass, dense, dull, dumb, slow, stupid
ant unintelligent
intelligentsia *n* a class of articulate persons devoted to intellectual, cultural, and social matters <the *intelligentsia* posed a threat to the new regime>
syn clerisy, illuminati, intellectuals, literati
rel avant-garde, vanguard
intelligible *adj* ***syn*** see UNDERSTANDABLE
ant unintelligible
intemperance *n* ***syn*** see EXCESS 3
rel drunkenness, insobriety; debauchery
ant temperance
intemperate *adj* **1 *syn*** see EXCESSIVE 2
rel bibacious, bibulous, crapulous, drunken; gluttonous
ant temperate, tempered
2 *syn* see SEVERE 3
ant temperate
intempestive *adj* ***syn*** see IMPROPER 1
intemporal *adj* ***syn*** see ETERNAL 4
ant temporal
intend *vb* **1 *syn*** see MEAN 2
2 to have in mind as a purpose <*intended* to read the book>
syn aim, contemplate, design, mean, ‖mind, plan, propose, purpose
rel attempt, endeavor, essay, strive, try; plot, scheme; assign, designate, destine
idiom figure on, have in mind to, look forward to
intendance *n* ***syn*** see OVERSIGHT 1
intended *adj* ***syn*** see ENGAGED 2
intended *n* ***syn*** see BETROTHED
intendment *n* **1 *syn*** see INTENTION
2 *syn* see MEANING 1
intensate *vb* ***syn*** see INTENSIFY
intense *adj* **1** extreme in degree, power, or effect <*intense* hatred>
syn concentrated, desperate, exquisite, fierce, furious, terrible, vehement, vicious, violent
rel aggravated, enhanced, heightened, intensified; accentuated, emphasized, stressed
ant subdued

---

syn synonym(s) ***rel*** related word(s)
ant antonym(s) ***con*** contrasted word(s)
idiom idiomatic equivalent(s)
‖ use limited; if in doubt, see a dictionary

2 ***syn*** see INTENSIVE
3 ***syn*** see ARDENT 2
ant slight

intensely *adv* **1** ***syn*** see HARD 3
rel fiercely, furiously, vehemently, viciously, violently
2 ***syn*** see SERIOUSLY 2

intensify *vb* to increase markedly in measure or degree <both companies *intensified* their efforts to win the contract> <the pain *intensified* sharply>
syn aggravate, deepen, enhance, heighten, intensate, magnify, mount, redouble, rise, rouse
rel accent, accentuate, emphasize, stress; aggrandize, exalt; sharpen
con moderate, qualify; alleviate, ease, lighten, relieve; decrease, diminish, lessen, reduce
ant abate; allay, mitigate; temper

intensive *adj* highly concentrated <an *intensive* study of the causes of the war>
syn blood-and-guts, deep, hard, intense, profound
con casual, shallow, superficial

intensively *adv* ***syn*** see HARD 3

intent *n* **1** ***syn*** see INTENTION
rel conation, volition, will
con chance, fortune, hap, hazard, luck
ant accident
2 ***syn*** see MEANING 1

intent *adj* **1** having one's mind or attention deeply fixed <the student was too *intent* on his work to hear the phone>
syn absorbed, deep, engaged, engrossed, immersed, preoccupied, rapt, wrapped, wrapped up
rel attending, attentive, minding, watching; concentrated, riveted
con absent, absent-minded, abstracted, bemused, faraway, preoccupied; daydreaming, napping, oblivious
ant distracted
2 ***syn*** see DECIDED 2

intention *n* what one purposes to accomplish or do <her *intention* was to finish by noon>
syn animus, design, intendment, intent, meaning, plan, purpose; *compare* AMBITION 2
rel project, scheme; desire, hope, wish

intentional *adj* ***syn*** see VOLUNTARY
rel intended, meant, proposed, purposed; advised, considered, designed, designful, premeditated, studied
con accidental, casual, fortuitous; careless, heedless, inadvertent, thoughtless
ant unintentional

intentionally *adv* with intention <hurt her *intentionally*>
syn ‖apurpose, deliberately, designedly, on purpose, prepensely, purposedly, purposely, purposively
ant unintentionally

intentive *adj* ***syn*** see ATTENTIVE 1

intently *adv* ***syn*** see HARD 4

intentness *n* ***syn*** see EARNESTNESS

inter *vb* ***syn*** see BURY 1
ant disinter

interact *vb* to act upon one another <humor and pathos *interacted* to make a moving drama>
syn coact, interplay, interreact
rel collaborate, cooperate; combine, join, merge, unite

interagent *n* ***syn*** see GO-BETWEEN 2

interblend *vb* ***syn*** see MIX 1

interbreed *vb* ***syn*** see CROSS 4

intercalate *vb* ***syn*** see INTRODUCE 6

intercede *vb* ***syn*** see INTERPOSE 2

interceder *n* ***syn*** see GO-BETWEEN 2

intercept *vb* to stop, seize, or interrupt in progress or course <*intercept* a forward pass>
syn block, catch, cut off
rel grab, seize, take; check, curb
con fumble, miss; loose, release

intercessor *n* ***syn*** see GO-BETWEEN 2

interchange *vb* ***syn*** see EXCHANGE 3
rel reverse, transpose

interchangeable *adj* permitting mutual substitution <*interchangeable* parts>
syn commutable, exchangeable, fungible, interconvertible, substitutable
rel changeable, convertible; reciprocal, reciprocative

interchurch *adj* ***syn*** see NONSECTARIAN

intercommunication *n* **1** ***syn*** see COMMUNICATION 3
2 ***syn*** see CONTACT 2

intercomparable *adj* ***syn*** see LIKE

interconnect *vb* ***syn*** see INTERJOIN

interconvertible *adj* ***syn*** see INTERCHANGEABLE

intercourse *n* **1** ***syn*** see COMMERCE 2
2 ***syn*** see COMMUNICATION 3
3 ***syn*** see CONTACT 2

intercreedal *adj* ***syn*** see NONSECTARIAN

intercross *vb* **1** ***syn*** see INTERSECT
2 ***syn*** see CROSS 4

interdenominational *adj* ***syn*** see NONSECTARIAN

interdict *vb* ***syn*** see FORBID
ant sanction

interdiction *n* ***syn*** see TABOO
ant sanction

interest *n* **1** participation in advantage, profit, and responsibility <he owned a half *interest* in a furniture store>
syn claim, share, stake
2 ***syn*** see WELFARE
3 readiness to be concerned with or moved by something <had an *interest* in art>
syn concern, curiosity, interestedness, regard
rel enthusiasm, excitement, passion; attention, care, concernment; absorption, engrossment
con apathy, indifference, unconcern
ant disinterest

interest *vb* to engage the attention and interest of <his appeal failed to *interest* his listeners>
syn appeal, attract, excite, fascinate, intrigue
rel arouse, tantalize, titillate; lure, pull, snare, tempt; pique
ant bore

interested *adj* having a share or concern in some affair <all *interested* parties met for the reading of the will>

syn affected, concerned, implicated, involved
rel biased, partial, partisan, prejudiced
con aloof, incurious, indifferent, unconcerned; apathetic, bored, ennuyé
ant detached, disinterested
interestedness *n syn* see INTEREST 3
interfere *vb* **1** *syn* see INTERPOSE 2
rel bar, block, hinder, impede, obstruct
2 *syn* see MEDDLE
rel discommode, incommode, inconvenience, trouble; baffle, balk, foil, frustrate, thwart
interflow *vb syn* see MIX 1
interfuse *vb* **1** *syn* see MIX 1
2 to cause to pass into or through <*interfused* illuminating anecdotes with the informative text>
syn diffuse, infuse, interlard, intersow, intersperse, intersprinkle
rel impenetrate, impregnate, interpenetrate, penetrate, pervade, saturate
3 *syn* see PERMEATE
interfusion *n syn* see MIXTURE
interim *n syn* see GAP 3
interim *adj syn* see TEMPORARY
interior *adj* **1** *syn* see INNER 1
con extraneous, extrinsic, foreign
ant exterior
2 *syn* see INNER 2
interior *n* the internal or inner part <the *interior* of the house>
syn inside, inward(s), within
rel center, heart; belly, bosom; innards, internals
ant exterior, outside
interject *vb syn* see INTRODUCE 6
interjoin *vb* to join mutually <*interjoined* several stations into a new system>
syn anastomose, interconnect, interlink, intertie
rel interdigitate, interlace, interlock, interrelate
con disunite, part, separate, sunder
ant disjoin
interknit *vb syn* see INTERWEAVE
interlace *vb syn* see INTERWEAVE
interlard *vb syn* see INTERFUSE 2
interlink *vb syn* see INTERJOIN
interlope *vb* **1** *syn* see INTRUDE
2 *syn* see MEDDLE
interlude *n* an intervening or interruptive period or space <an *interlude* of happiness in a tragic story> <woodland broken by *interludes* of meadow>
syn break, intermission, interregnum, interval, parenthesis
rel breather, lull, pause, respite, rest; episode, idyll; meantime, meanwhile, spell; entr'acte
intermeddle *vb syn* see MEDDLE
rel encroach, entrench, invade, trespass
intermeddler *n syn* see BUSYBODY
intermediary *adj syn* see MIDDLE 2
intermediary *n* **1** *syn* see GO-BETWEEN 2
2 *syn* see MEAN 2
intermediate *vb syn* see INTERPOSE 2
intermediate *adj* **1** *syn* see MIDDLE 2
2 *syn* see MEDIUM
intermediate *n syn* see GO-BETWEEN 2
intermediator *n syn* see GO-BETWEEN 2
interment *n syn* see BURIAL 2
ant disinterment
intermesh *vb syn* see ENGAGE 1
interminable *adj syn* see CONTINUAL
rel eternal, infinite; lasting, permanent
con intermittent, periodic; discontinued, stopped; closed, completed, ended, finished, terminated
intermingle *vb syn* see MIX 1
intermission *n* **1** *syn* see ABEYANCE
2 *syn* see INTERLUDE
intermit *vb syn* see DEFER
rel arrest, check, interrupt
con continue, persist; iterate, reiterate, repeat
intermittent *adj* occurring or appearing in interrupted sequence <they predict *intermittent* rain throughout the day>
syn alternate, isochronal, isochronous, periodic, periodical, recurrent, recurring
rel cyclic, cyclical, iterant, iterative, metrical, rhythmic, rhythmical, seasonal, serial; arrested, checked, interrupted; fitful, spasmodic; infrequent, occasional, sporadic; discontinuing, discontinuous
con constant, perpetual; everlasting, interminable
ant continual, continuous; incessant, unceasing
intermix *vb syn* see MIX 1
intermixture *n syn* see MIXTURE
intermutual *adj syn* see COMMON 1
intern *vb syn* see IMPRISON
internal *adj* **1** *syn* see INNER 1
ant external
2 *syn* see INNER 2
3 *syn* see DOMESTIC 2
ant external
internals *n pl syn* see ENTRAILS
internuncio *n syn* see MESSENGER
interpenetrate *vb syn* see PERMEATE
interplay *vb syn* see INTERACT
interpolate *vb syn* see INTRODUCE 6
rel admit, enter; interlope, intrude; add, annex, append, superadd
con cancel, delete, erase, expunge
interpose *vb* **1** *syn* see INTRODUCE 6
rel cast, throw, toss; push, shove, thrust
2 to come between disagreeing elements <forced to *interpose* when the argument grew heated>
syn intercede, interfere, intermediate, intervene, mediate, step in
rel butt in, interlope, intrude, obtrude; intermeddle, meddle; arbitrate, moderate, negotiate
interpret *vb* **1** *syn* see EXPLAIN 1
rel exemplify, illustrate; annotate, gloss; comment, commentate
con contort, deform, distort; garble, misrepresent; misconstrue, misunderstand

---

syn synonym(s) *rel* related word(s)
ant antonym(s) *con* contrasted word(s)
idiom idiomatic equivalent(s)
‖ use limited; if in doubt, see a dictionary

2 ***syn*** see REPRESENT 1

interpretation *n* **1** ***syn*** see EXPLANATION 1
2 manner of artistic presentation in performance or adaptation or an instance of this <*interpretation* involves a re-creative effort by the performer>
syn reading, rendering, rendition, version

interpretive *adj* ***syn*** see EXPLANATORY

interreact *vb* ***syn*** see INTERACT

interregnum *n* ***syn*** see INTERLUDE

interrogate *vb* ***syn*** see ASK 1

interrogation *n* **1** ***syn*** see CROSS-EXAMINATION
2 ***syn*** see INQUIRY 2

interrogatory *n* ***syn*** see INQUIRY 2

interrupt *vb* **1** ***syn*** see ARREST 1
rel defer, intermit, postpone, suspend
2 to ask questions or make remarks while another is speaking <a chatterbox who habitually *interrupts* everyone>
syn break in, chime in, chip in
rel cut in, put in
idiom break in on (*or* upon)

interruption *n* **1** ***syn*** see GAP 3
rel rent, rift, rupture, split
2 ***syn*** see ABEYANCE

intersect *vb* to divide by passing through or across <parallel lines can never *intersect*>
syn crisscross, cross, crosscut, decussate, intercross
rel traverse; bisect

intersow *vb* ***syn*** see INTERFUSE 2

intersperse *vb* ***syn*** see INTERFUSE 2

intersprinkle *vb* ***syn*** see INTERFUSE 2

intertangle *vb* ***syn*** see ENTANGLE 1

intertie *vb* ***syn*** see INTERJOIN

intertrude *vb* ***syn*** see INTRUDE 1

intertwine *vb* ***syn*** see INTERWEAVE

intertwist *vb* ***syn*** see INTERWEAVE

interval *n* **1** ***syn*** see PAUSE
2 ***syn*** see INTERLUDE
3 ***syn*** see GAP 3

intervene *vb* ***syn*** see INTERPOSE 2
rel divide, part, separate, sever

intervolve *vb* ***syn*** see INTERWEAVE

interweave *vb* to blend or unite intimately <joy and melancholy are often closely *interwoven*>
syn interknit, interlace, intertwine, intertwist, intervolve, interwind, interwork, interwreathe, inweave
rel associate, join, link; blend, fuse, mix

interwind *vb* ***syn*** see INTERWEAVE

interwork *vb* ***syn*** see INTERWEAVE

interwreathe *vb* ***syn*** see INTERWEAVE

intestinal fortitude *n* ***syn*** see FORTITUDE

intestine *adj* **1** ***syn*** see DOMESTIC 2
2 ***syn*** see INNER 1

intimacy *n* ***syn*** see ACQUAINTANCE 1

intimate *vb* ***syn*** see SUGGEST 1
rel attest, bespeak, betoken, indicate
con air, express, utter, vent, voice; affirm, assert, aver, avouch, declare, profess

intimate *adj* **1** ***syn*** see INHERENT
2 ***syn*** see INNER 2
3 ***syn*** see FAMILIAR 1
rel nearest, next; affectionate, devoted, fond, loving; privy, secret
con distant, remote
4 having or marked by a warm personal relation <*intimate* friends for many years><an *intimate* friendship>
syn ‖buddy-buddy, chummy, cozy, pally, ‖palsy-walsy
idiom thick as thieves

intimate *n* ***syn*** see FRIEND
rel associate, companion, comrade, crony
con outsider, stranger

intimation *n* **1** ***syn*** see HINT 1
2 ***syn*** see HINT 2

intimidate *vb* to frighten or coerce into submission or obedience <refused to be *intimidated* by the manager>
syn bludgeon, bluster, ‖bounce, browbeat, bulldoze, bully, bullyrag, cow, dragoon, hector, ‖ruffle, strong-arm, terrorize
rel alarm, disquiet, frighten, scare, terrify; badger, bait, chivy, hound, ride; coerce, compel, constrain, force, oblige; ‖ruffianize
con blandish, cajole, coax, wheedle; induce, persuade, prevail

intimidator *n* ***syn*** see BULLY 1

into *prep* ***syn*** see TO 1

intolerable *adj* ***syn*** see INSUFFERABLE
ant tolerable

intolerant *adj* **1** unwilling or unable to endure with composure <he was inclined to be very *intolerant* of interruption>
syn impatient, unforbearing, unindulgent
rel contemptuous, disdainful; fractious, irritable, snappish, waspish; indignant, irate, outraged, stuffy, upset, worked up
con forbearing, indulgent, long-suffering, patient; resigned, uncomplaining
ant tolerant
2 ***syn*** see ILLIBERAL
rel inflexible, obdurate; antipathetic, averse, unsympathetic
con forbearing, indulgent, lenient
ant tolerant

intonation *n* ***syn*** see INFLECTION

in toto *adv* ***syn*** see ALL 1

intoxicant *n* ***syn*** see LIQUOR 2

intoxicated *adj* **1** significantly under the influence of alcoholic liquor <some people become *intoxicated* more easily than others>
syn alcoholized, ‖bagged, blind, ‖blotto, ‖boiled, ‖bombed, ‖boozed, ‖boozy, ‖buffy, ‖buzzed, ‖canned, ‖capernoited, cockeyed, ‖crocked, cut, ‖deleerit, disguised, drunk, drunken, fried, ‖half-seas over, inebriated, inebrious, ‖jagged, ‖juiced, ‖lit, ‖lit up, ‖loaded, looped, ‖lushed, muddled, ‖oiled, ‖organized, ‖pickled, ‖pie-eyed, ‖piped, ‖pipped, pixilated, ‖plastered, polluted, ‖potted, rum-dum, ‖screwy, ‖shick, ‖shicker, ‖shot, slewed, slopped, sloppy, ‖smashed, soshed, sozzled, ‖spiflicated, squiffed, ‖stewed, stiff, ‖stinking, ‖stinko, stoned, ‖swacked, tanked, ‖tiddly, tight, unsober, wet, zonked

rel befuddled, bemused, besotted, dazed, dopey, fuddled, loopy, maudlin, sodden, soppy, sotted, tipsy
idiom disguised with drink, full as a tick, in drink (*or* liquor), in one's cups, in the bag, stewed to the gills, the worse for drink, three sheets in (*or* to) the wind, under the table, under the weather, with drink taken
con abstemious, abstinent, moderate, temperate
ant sober
2 profoundly and usually pleasantly moved <*intoxicated* with the beauty of the scene>
syn elated, excited, exhilarated, turned-on
rel affected, concerned, interested, moved; galvanized, piqued, quickened, stimulated
con disinterested, unconcerned; depressed, disheartened, distressed, saddened

intoxicating *adj* ***syn*** see EXCITING

intoxication *n* ***syn*** see EUPHORIA 2

intractable *adj* **1** ***syn*** see UNRULY 1
ant tractable
2 ***syn*** see OBSTINATE
ant tractable

intransigent *adj* ***syn*** see OBSTINATE

intrepid *adj* ***syn*** see BRAVE 1
ant craven

intricate *adj* **1** ***syn*** see COMPLEX 2
rel arduous, difficult, hard
2 ***syn*** see ELABORATE 2

intrigue *vb* **1** ***syn*** see INTEREST
2 ***syn*** see PLOT

intrigue *n* **1** ***syn*** see PLOT 2
2 ***syn*** see AMOUR 2

intrinsic *adj* ***syn*** see INHERENT
con added, annexed, appended, superadded
ant extrinsic

intrinsically *adv* ***syn*** see PER SE

introduce *vb* **1** ***syn*** see ENTER 2
rel inaugurate, induct, install; bring forward
2 ***syn*** see BROACH
3 to bring into practice or use <*introduce* reforms in the welfare system>
syn inaugurate, initiate, institute, launch, originate, set up, usher in
rel establish, found, organize; innovate, invent; unveil; pioneer
4 to cause to know each other personally <planned to *introduce* her to his mother>
syn acquaint, present, ‖quaint
5 ***syn*** see PRECEDE 3
6 to put among or between others <*introduced* several new lines of dialogue>
syn fill in, insert, insinuate, intercalate, interject, interpolate, interpose, throw in
rel inlay, inlet, inset; inject, instill; work in
con eject, evict, oust; eliminate, exclude
ant abstract; withdraw

introducer *n* ***syn*** see INNOVATOR

introduction *n* something that serves as a preliminary or antecedent <the crisis could be the *introduction* to a general war>
syn exordium, foreword, overture, preamble, preface, prelude, prelusion, proem, prolegomenon, prologue

introductory *adj* **1** ***syn*** see PRELIMINARY
ant closing, concluding
2 ***syn*** see INITIAL 1

introspection *n* the examination of one's own thought and feeling <a man much given to *introspection*>
syn heart-searching, self-contemplation, self-examination, self-observation, self-questioning, self-reflection, self-scrutiny, self-searching, soul-searching
rel contemplation, meditation, reflection; self-analysis
ant extrospection

intrude *vb* **1** to thrust or force in without permission, welcome, or fitness <constantly *intruded* himself into his sister's affairs>
syn butt in, chisel (in), cut in, horn in, intertrude, obtrude
rel encroach, entrench, infringe, invade, muscle, trespass; insinuate, intercalate, interject, interpolate, interpose, introduce; interfere, intervene; intermeddle, meddle; bother, disturb, pester
con retire, stand off, withdraw
2 ***syn*** see IMPOSE 5

intrusive *adj* ***syn*** see IMPERTINENT 2
rel butting in, intruding, obtruding
con bashful, coy, diffident, modest, retiring, shy
ant unintrusive

intuition *n* immediate apprehension or cognition <skeptical of the traditional woman's *intuition*>
syn anschauung, insight, intuitiveness
rel second sight, sixth sense
ant ratiocination

intuitive *adj* ***syn*** see INSTINCTIVE 1
rel direct, immediate, presentative
ant ratiocinative

intuitiveness *n* ***syn*** see INTUITION

inumbrate *vb* ***syn*** see SHADE

inundate *vb* ***syn*** see DELUGE 1

inundation *n* ***syn*** see FLOOD 2

inurbane *adj* ***syn*** see RUDE 6
ant urbane

inure *vb* ***syn*** see ACCUSTOM
rel discipline, train

inutile *adj* ***syn*** see WORTHLESS 1
ant utile

invade *vb* **1** to enter for conquest or plunder <the Danes *invaded* England>
syn foray, inroad, overrun, overswarm, raid
rel loot, pillage, plunder, ravage
2 ***syn*** see TRESPASS 2
rel impenetrate, interpenetrate, permeate, pervade

invalid *adj* **1** ***syn*** see ILLOGICAL
ant valid
2 ***syn*** see NULL

invalidate *vb* ***syn*** see ABOLISH 1
rel counteract, counterbalance, negative, neutralize, offset; discredit

---

syn synonym(s) ***rel*** related word(s)
ant antonym(s) ***con*** contrasted word(s)
idiom idiomatic equivalent(s)
‖ use limited; if in doubt, see a dictionary

ant validate
invaluable *adj* ***syn*** see PRECIOUS 1
ant worthless
invariable *adj* **1** ***syn*** see INFLEXIBLE 3
ant variable
2 ***syn*** see SAME 3
ant variable, varying
invariably *adv* **1** ***syn*** see ALWAYS 1
2 ***syn*** see EVER 3
invasion *n* a hostile entrance into the territory of another <Hitler's *invasion* of Poland>
syn foray, incursion, inroad, irruption, raid
rel aggression, attack, offense, offensive; breach, infraction, infringement, transgression, trespass, violation; encroachment, entrenchment
invective *adj* ***syn*** see ABUSIVE
rel censorious, condemnatory, damnatory, denunciatory, reproachful
invective *n* ***syn*** see ABUSE
rel diatribe, jeremiad, philippic, tirade
inveigh (against) *vb* ***syn*** see OBJECT 1
inveigle *vb* ***syn*** see LURE
inveiglement *n* ***syn*** see LURE 2
invent *vb* ***syn*** see CONTRIVE 2
rel conceive, envision, imagine; create, mint, produce, turn out; inaugurate, initiate
invention *n* a product of creative imagination <his most famous *invention* is the electric light bulb>
syn brainchild, coinage, contrivance
rel concoction, contraption, innovation, novelty; creation, opus, original
inventive *adj* adept or prolific at producing new things and ideas <had a very *inventive* turn of mind> <she was an *inventive* genius>
syn creative, demiurgic, deviceful, ingenious, innovational, innovative, innovatory, original, originative
rel fertile, fruitful, productive, teeming; causative, constructive, formative
con sterile, uncreative, unproductive
ant uninventive
inventor *n* **1** ***syn*** see INNOVATOR
2 ***syn*** see FATHER 2
inventory *n* **1** ***syn*** see SUPPLY
2 ***syn*** see RESERVE
inventory *vb* **1** to make an itemized report or record of <will *inventory* all office supplies>
syn catalog, itemize, tally
rel list, record, register; enumerate, tabulate
idiom take account (*or* stock) of
2 ***syn*** see ITEMIZE 1
3 ***syn*** see EPITOMIZE 1
inveracity *n* ***syn*** see LIE
ant veracity
inverse *vb* ***syn*** see REVERSE 1
inversion *n* ***syn*** see REVERSAL 1
invert *vb* ***syn*** see REVERSE 1
rel flip, turn down, turn over
invert *n* ***syn*** see HOMOSEXUAL
invertebrate *n* ***syn*** see WEAKLING
invertebrate *adj* ***syn*** see WEAK 4
rel disorganized, structureless
inverted *adj* **1** ***syn*** see UPSIDE-DOWN 1
2 ***syn*** see HOMOSEXUAL
invest *vb* **1** ***syn*** see INITIATE 3
rel endow, endue; consecrate, honor
ant divest, strip
2 to make a formal grant of power or authority <the Constitution *invests* the Congress with taxation powers>
syn authorize, empower, vest
rel bequeath, endow
con hold back, keep back, reserve, withhold
ant divest
3 ***syn*** see ENFOLD 1
4 ***syn*** see BESIEGE
5 ***syn*** see INFUSE 1
investigate *vb* ***syn*** see EXPLORE
rel muckrake, poke, pry
investigation *n* ***syn*** see INQUIRY 1
rel observation, observing; sounding, survey, surveying
investigative *adj* ***syn*** see INQUISITIVE 1
investigator *n* ***syn*** see DETECTIVE
investiture *n* ***syn*** see INITIATION
inveterate *adj* **1** firmly established or having something firmly established <the *inveterate* tendency to overlook the obvious>
syn bred-in-the-bone, confirmed, deep-dyed, deep-rooted, deep-seated, dyed-in-the-wool, entrenched, hard-shell, irradicable, settled, sworn
rel accustomed, addicted, chronic, habituated; customary, habitual, usual; hardened, indurated; established, fixed, set; inbred, innate; abiding, enduring, persistent, persisting
2 ***syn*** see OLD 2
invidious *adj* **1** ***syn*** see LIBELOUS
2 ***syn*** see ENVIOUS
rel bitter; hateful
3 ***syn*** see REPUGNANT 1
rel abominable, detestable, hateful, odious
con agreeable, grateful, gratifying, pleasant, pleasing
invidiousness *n* ***syn*** see ENVY
invigorate *vb* ***syn*** see STRENGTHEN 2
rel refresh, rejuvenate, renew, restore; rally, rouse, stir; activate, animate, stimulate, vitalize, vitaminize
ant debilitate
invigorating *adj* having an enlivening effect <an *invigorating* discussion>
syn animating, bracing, exhilarating, exhilarative, quickening, stimulating, stimulative, tonic, vitalizing
rel brisk, lively; fascinating, interesting
con anesthetic, numbing, somniferous.
ant deadening
invincible *adj* **1** incapable of being conquered <the team proved to be *invincible*>
syn impregnable, inconquerable, indomitable, inexpugnable, invulnerable, unassailable, unbeatable, unconquerable, undefeatable
rel inviolable, untouchable; unattackable
con conquerable, subduable, surmountable, vanquishable
ant vincible
2 ***syn*** see INSUPERABLE
ant vincible

inviolable *adj* ***syn*** see SACRED 3
rel consecrated, hallowed; blessed, divine, holy; chaste, pure
ant violable
inviolate *adj* ***syn*** see SACRED 3
rel intact, perfect; faultless, flawless
con desecrated, profaned; defiled, polluted
invisible *adj* ***syn*** see IMPERCEPTIBLE
rel hidden, unseeable
ant visible
invitation *n* ***syn*** see PROPOSAL
invite *vb* to request the presence or participation of <*invited* guests to dinner> <*invited* the major nations to confer>
syn ask, bid
rel call, call in, summon; court, solicit, woo; entice, inveigle, lure, tempt
invoice *n* ***syn*** see BILL 1
invoke *vb* **1** ***syn*** see BEG
2 ***syn*** see ENFORCE
involuntary *adj* ***syn*** see SPONTANEOUS
rel unintended, unintentional, unwitting
ant voluntary
involve *vb* **1** to bring a person or thing into circumstances or a situation from which extrication is difficult <nations *involved* in war>
syn embroil, implicate, mire, tangle; *compare* ENTANGLE 3
rel catch up; draw (into)
2 ***syn*** see INCLUDE
involved *adj* **1** ***syn*** see COMPLEX 2
rel confused, muddled
con easy, facile, simple
2 ***syn*** see INTERESTED
rel enmeshed, entangled
ant uninvolved
involvement *n* ***syn*** see ENTANGLEMENT 1
invulnerable *adj* ***syn*** see INVINCIBLE 1
ant vulnerable
inward *adj* ***syn*** see INNER 1
con alien, extraneous, extrinsic, foreign
ant outward
inward *n* **1** *often* **inwards** *pl* ***syn*** see INTERIOR
2 inwards *pl* ***syn*** see ENTRAILS
inwardness *n* ***syn*** see ACQUAINTANCE 1
inweave *vb* ***syn*** see INTERWEAVE
iota *n* ***syn*** see PARTICLE
ipseity *n* ***syn*** see INDIVIDUALITY 4
irascible *adj* easily aroused to anger <an *irascible* fellow and hard to get along with>
syn choleric, cranky, cross, hot-tempered, ireful, passionate, peppery, quick-tempered, ratty, ‖stomachy, temperish, testy, tetchy, touchy; *compare* CANTANKEROUS, IRRITABLE
rel fractious, huffy, irritable, peevish, petulant, querulous, snappish, waspish; impatient, jittery, jumpy, nervous, restive; bristly, crabbed, surly
con amiable, complaisant, good-natured, obliging; calm, quiet, relaxed; long-suffering, patient, tolerant
irate *adj* ***syn*** see ANGRY
ire *n* ***syn*** see ANGER
ire *vb* ***syn*** see ANGER 1
ireful *adj* **1** ***syn*** see ANGRY
2 ***syn*** see IRASCIBLE
irenic *adj* ***syn*** see PACIFIC
ant acrimonious
irk *vb* **1** ***syn*** see ANNOY 1
rel discommode, incommode, inconvenience, trouble
2 ***syn*** see TRY 2
irking *n* ***syn*** see ANNOYANCE 1
irksome *adj* tending to cause boredom or tedium <an *irksome* task>
syn boresome, boring, drudging, tedious, tiresome, tiring
rel dull, stupid; exhausting, fagging, fatiguing, wearisome
con exciting, inspiring, provocative, stimulative, stirring
ant absorbing, engrossing
iron *n, usu* **irons** *pl* ***syn*** see SHACKLE
iron *adj* ***syn*** see INFLEXIBLE 2
ironbound *adj* ***syn*** see ROUGH 1
ironclad *adj* ***syn*** see INFLEXIBLE 3
ironfisted *adj* **1** ***syn*** see STINGY
2 ***syn*** see GRIM 3
ironhanded *adj* ***syn*** see RIGID 3
ironhead *n* ***syn*** see DUNCE
ironhearted *adj* ***syn*** see UNFEELING 2
ant softhearted
ironic *adj* ***syn*** see SARDONIC
rel biting, cutting, incisive, trenchant; caustic, mordant, scathing
‖**iron man** *n* ***syn*** see DOLLAR
irradiate *vb* ***syn*** see ILLUMINATE 2
irradicable *adj* ***syn*** see INVETERATE 1
irrational *adj* ***syn*** see ILLOGICAL
rel crazy, demented, insane
con logical, reasonable, sensible
ant rational
irrealizable *adj* ***syn*** see IMPOSSIBLE 1
ant realizable
irrebuttable *adj* ***syn*** see POSITIVE 3
ant rebuttable
irreclaimable *adj* ***syn*** see IRRECOVERABLE
ant reclaimable
irreconcilable *adj* incapable of being made consistent <the two versions of the story are completely *irreconcilable*>
syn incompatible, inconformable, inconsistent
rel discordant, discrepant, dissonant, inaccordant, incongruent, incongruous, inharmonious
ant reconcilable
irrecoverable *adj* not capable of being recovered, regained, remedied, or rectified <suffered an *irrecoverable* loss in the fire>
syn irreclaimable, irredeemable, irremediable, irreparable, irretrievable
ant recoverable
irredeemable *adj* ***syn*** see IRRECOVERABLE
ant redeemable
irreflective *adj* ***syn*** see CARELESS 1

---

syn synonym(s) ***rel*** related word(s)
ant antonym(s) ***con*** contrasted word(s)
idiom idiomatic equivalent(s)
‖ use limited; if in doubt, see a dictionary

ant reflective

irrefragable *adj* ***syn*** see INDESTRUCTIBLE

irrefrangible *adj* ***syn*** see INDESTRUCTIBLE

irrefutable *adj* ***syn*** see POSITIVE 3
ant refutable

irregular *adj* **1** not according with or explainable by law, rule, or custom <unusual problems require *irregular* solutions>
syn abnormal, anomalous, deviant, divergent, off-key, unnatural, unregular
rel aberrant, atypical; exceptional, odd, peculiar, queer, singular, strange, unique
con natural, normal, typical; accustomed, customary, habitual, usual, wonted
ant regular
2 ***syn*** see INFORMAL 1
3 ***syn*** see LOPSIDED
ant regular
4 ***syn*** see RANDOM
rel occasional, sporadic; erratic, fitful, spasmodic; inconstant, uneven, unsteady
5 ***syn*** see SPOTTY 1

irregular *n* ***syn*** see PARTISAN 2

irregularity *n* ***syn*** see INEQUALITY 1
ant regularity

irregularly *adv* ***syn*** see OCCASIONALLY
ant regularly

irrelative *adj* ***syn*** see IRRELEVANT
ant relative

irrelevant *adj* not applicable or pertinent <age should be *irrelevant* to employability>
syn extraneous, foreign, immaterial, impertinent, inapplicable, inapposite, irrelative
rel inconsequential, insignificant, unimportant
idiom beside the point, neither here nor there, out of the question
con applicable, appurtenant, germane, material, pertinent, significant
ant relevant

irreligious *adj* lacking religious emotions, doctrines, or practices <an *irreligious* person but not openly hostile to organized religion>
syn godless, nonreligious, unreligious
rel indevout, undevout; ungodly, unholy, unsanctimonious; blasphemous, impious, profane, sacrilegious; amoral, unmoral
con devout, pious
ant religious

irremediable *adj* **1** ***syn*** see IRRECOVERABLE
ant remediable
2 ***syn*** see HOPELESS 2

irremovable *adj* ***syn*** see IMMOVABLE 1
ant removable

irreparable *adj* **1** ***syn*** see IRRECOVERABLE
ant reparable
2 ***syn*** see HOPELESS 2

irreprehensible *adj* ***syn*** see GOOD 11
ant reprehensible

irrepressible *adj* impossible to repress, restrain, or control <an *irrepressible* joy over his brother's good fortune>
syn insuppressible, insuppressive, irrestrainable, uncontainable, uncontrollable, unrestrainable
rel bubbling over, effervescent, enthusiastic, rhapsodical
ant repressible

irreproachable *adj* **1** ***syn*** see GOOD 11
2 ***syn*** see IMPECCABLE 1

irresoluble *adj* ***syn*** see INSOLUBLE
ant resoluble

irresolute *adj* ***syn*** see VACILLATING 2
ant resolute

irresolution *n* ***syn*** see HESITATION
ant resolution

irresolvable *adj* ***syn*** see INSOLUBLE
ant resolvable

irresponsible *adj* lacking in responsibility <*irresponsible* behavior>
syn carefree, careless, feckless, incautious, reckless, uncareful, wild
rel undependable, unreliable, untrustworthy; unaccountable, unanswerable
con careful, cautious, discreet, heedful; dependable, reliable, trustworthy
ant responsible

irrestrainable *adj* ***syn*** see IRREPRESSIBLE
ant restrainable

irretrievable *adj* ***syn*** see IRRECOVERABLE
ant retrievable

irreverent *adj* ***syn*** see IMPIOUS 1
ant reverent

irreverential *adj* ***syn*** see IMPIOUS 1
ant reverential

irreversible *adj* ***syn*** see IRREVOCABLE
ant reversible

irrevocable *adj* incapable of being recalled or revoked <an *irrevocable* decision of the Supreme Court>
syn irreversible, nonreversible, unrepealable
rel constant, established, fixed; immutable, unchangeable, unmodifiable
con repealable, reversible; alterable, changeable, modifiable
ant revocable

irritable *adj* easily exasperated <the miserable weather made us all *irritable*>
syn disagreeable, fractious, fretful, huffy, peevish, pettish, petulant, ||pindling, prickish, prickly, querulent, querulential, querulous, raspish, raspy, snappish, snappy, twitty, waspish, waspy, whiny; *compare* CANTANKEROUS, IRASCIBLE
rel cranky, cross, testy, touchy; choleric, irascible, splenetic
con amiable, complaisant, good-natured, obliging; affable, cordial, genial, gracious, sociable
ant easygoing

irritant *n* ***syn*** see ANNOYANCE 3

irritate *vb* to excite to angry annoyance <his rude interruptions really *irritated* her>
syn aggravate, burn (up), exasperate, gall, get, grate, huff, inflame, nettle, peeve, pique, provoke, put out, rile, roil; *compare* ANNOY 1
rel abrade, bother, ||bug, chafe, exercise, fret, irk, ruffle, try, vex; anger, enrage, incense, infuriate, madden; affront, offend
con appease, conciliate, mollify, pacify, placate, propitiate; delight, gladden, gratify, please

irrupt *vb* ***syn*** see ERUPT 1
irruption *n* ***syn*** see INVASION
Ishmael *n* ***syn*** see OUTCAST
Ishmaelite *n* ***syn*** see OUTCAST
island *vb* ***syn*** see ISOLATE
isochronal *adj* ***syn*** see INTERMITTENT
isochronous *adj* ***syn*** see INTERMITTENT
isolate *vb* to set apart from others <the jury was *isolated* for several days>
syn close off, cut off, enisle, insulate, island, segregate, separate, sequester
rel quarantine; block (off); abstract, detach, disengage, remove; divide, part, sever, sunder
con associate, connect, join, link, unite
isolate *adj* ***syn*** see ALONE 1
isolated *adj* ***syn*** see ALONE 1
rel retired, secluded, withdrawn; abandoned, deserted, forsaken, stranded
isolation *n* ***syn*** see SOLITUDE
issue *n* **1** ***syn*** see OFFSPRING
2 ***syn*** see EFFECT 1
3 ***syn*** see PROBLEM 2
rel matter; subject, topic
issue *vb* **1** ***syn*** see SPRING 1
2 ***syn*** see EMIT 2
3 ***syn*** see PUBLISH 2
italicize *vb* ***syn*** see EMPHASIZE
itch *n* **1** ***syn*** see DESIRE 1
2 ***syn*** see LUST 2
itch *vb* ***syn*** see LONG
itchy *adj* ***syn*** see COVETOUS
item *adv* ***syn*** see ALSO 2
item *n* ***syn*** see POINT 1
rel component, piece; incidental, minutia
itemize *vb* **1** to set down in detail or by particulars <*itemize* deductions on a tax form>
syn enumerate, inventory, list, particularize, specialize, specify; *compare* SPECIFY 3
rel circumstantiate, document; count, number; cite, instance, mention; spell out
ant summarize
2 ***syn*** see INVENTORY
itemized *adj* ***syn*** see CIRCUMSTANTIAL
ant summarized
iterate *vb* ***syn*** see REPEAT
itinerant *adj* traveling from place to place <*itinerant* preachers>
syn ambulant, ambulatory, deambulatory, itinerate, nomadic, perambulant, perambulatory, peripatetic, roving, vagabond, vagrant, wandering, wayfaring
rel rambling, ranging, roaming; moving, shifting
itinerate *adj* ***syn*** see ITINERANT
itsy–bitsy *adj* ***syn*** see TINY
itty–bitty *adj* ***syn*** see TINY
‖**ivory** *n often* **ivories** *pl* ***syn*** see DICE
ivory–tower *adj* ***syn*** see IMPRACTICAL 1
ant down-to-earth
ivory–towered *adj* ***syn*** see IMPRACTICAL 1
ivory–towerish *adj* ***syn*** see IMPRACTICAL 1

syn synonym(s) ***rel*** related word(s)
ant antonym(s) ***con*** contrasted word(s)
idiom idiomatic equivalent(s)
‖ use limited; if in doubt, see a dictionary

J

jab *vb* ***syn*** see POKE 1
jab *n* **1** ***syn*** see POKE 1
2 ***syn*** see PRICK
jabber *vb* ***syn*** see GIBBER
jabber *n* **1** ***syn*** see GIBBERISH 1
2 ***syn*** see CHATTER
jabberer *n* ***syn*** see CHATTERBOX
jabberwocky *n* ***syn*** see GIBBERISH 1
jack *n* **1** ***syn*** see MARINER
2 ***syn*** see FLAG
‖**3** ***syn*** see MONEY
jack (up) *vb* ***syn*** see RAISE 9
jackass *n* **1** ***syn*** see DONKEY 1
2 ***syn*** see FOOL 1
jacket *n* ***syn*** see HIDE
jackleg *adj* ***syn*** see AMATEURISH
jackleg lawyer *n* ***syn*** see PETTIFOGGER
jackpot *n* ***syn*** see POT 3
jack-tar *n* ***syn*** see MARINER
jade *n* **1** ***syn*** see WANTON
2 ***syn*** see MINX
jade *vb* **1** ***syn*** see TIRE 1
rel cloy, pall, sate, satiate, surfeit; emasculate, enervate, unman, unnerve; depress, oppress, weigh
con rejuvenate, renew, restore
ant refresh
2 ***syn*** see SATIATE
jaded *adj* **1** ***syn*** see TIRED 1
ant refreshed
2 ***syn*** see SATIATED
‖**jag** *n* ***syn*** see PRICK
jag *n* ***syn*** see BINGE 1
‖**jag** *vb* ***syn*** see CARRY 1
jagged *adj* ***syn*** see ROUGH 1
‖**jagged** *adj* ***syn*** see INTOXICATED 1
jail *n* a building or institution for the confinement of persons held in lawful custody <sent to *jail* for perjury>
syn bastille, ‖big house, bridewell, ‖brig, ‖bucket, ‖caboose, ‖calaboose, ‖can, ‖carcel, ‖chokey, ‖clink, ‖college, cooler, coop, freezer, guardroom, ‖hoosegow, jug, keep, lockup, pen, penitentiary, ‖pokey, prison, reformatory, rock pile, skookum-house, slammer, ‖stir, stockade
idiom house of correction
jail *vb* ***syn*** see IMPRISON
ant release
jailbird *n* ***syn*** see CONVICT
jake *n* ***syn*** see RUSTIC
jakes *n pl but sing or pl in constr* ***syn*** see PRIVY 1
jalopy *n* a dilapidated old automobile <bought a *jalopy* for $50>
syn clunker, crate, dog, heap, junker, wreck
jam *vb* **1** ***syn*** see PRESS 1
rel tamp, wad
2 ***syn*** see CRAM 1
3 ***syn*** see PRESS 7
jam *n* ***syn*** see PREDICAMENT
jam *n* a rich spread prepared by boiling fruit and sugar until the mixture thickens <enjoyed his mother's tasty berry *jams*>
syn confiture, conserve, preserve
rel jelly, marmalade
jam–full *adj* ***syn*** see FULL 1
jammed *adj* ***syn*** see FULL 1
jam–pack *vb* ***syn*** see CRAM 1
jam–packed *adj* ***syn*** see FULL 1
jangle *vb* ***syn*** see CLASH 2
jangle *n* ***syn*** see DIN
jape *n* ***syn*** see JOKE 1
jar *vb* **1** ***syn*** see CLASH 2
2 ***syn*** see SHAKE 2
jar *n* ***syn*** see IMPACT 1
rel fluctuation, sway, vibration; agitation, disturbance, upset
jargon *n* **1** ***syn*** see TERMINOLOGY
2 ***syn*** see DIALECT 2
rel idiom, speech; abracadabra, gibberish
jarring *adj* ***syn*** see HARSH 3
ant soothing
jaundiced *adj* ***syn*** see BIASED 2
jaunt *n* ***syn*** see EXCURSION 1
‖**jaw** *n* ***syn*** see BACK TALK
jaw *vb* **1** ***syn*** see SCOLD 1
2 ***syn*** see CHAT 1
jay *n* ***syn*** see RUSTIC
jazz *n* ***syn*** see NONSENSE 2
jealous *adj* **1** intolerant of rivalry or unfaithfulness <her husband was *jealous* of her flirting with other men>
syn possessive, possessory
rel covetous, demanding; grasping, grudging; envious, green-eyed, invidious; mistrustful, suspicious; doubting, questioning
con tolerant, trusting, understanding
2 ***syn*** see ENVIOUS
3 ***syn*** see SUSPICIOUS 2
jealousy *n* ***syn*** see ENVY
jeer *vb* ***syn*** see SCOFF
con fawn, toady, truckle; approve, endorse, OK, sanction
jejune *adj* ***syn*** see INSIPID 3
rel slight, slim, tenuous, thin; arid, dry
jell *vb* ***syn*** see COAGULATE
rel stiffen, thicken; cohere, stick
jellify *vb* ***syn*** see COAGULATE
jelly *vb* ***syn*** see COAGULATE
jellyfish *n* ***syn*** see WEAKLING
jeopard *vb* ***syn*** see ENDANGER
jeopardize *vb* ***syn*** see ENDANGER
jeopardous *adj* ***syn*** see DANGEROUS 1
jeopardy *n* ***syn*** see DANGER
rel exposure; liability, openness, sensitiveness, susceptibility; accident, chance, hap
ant safety

jeopardy *vb* ***syn*** see ENDANGER
jeremiad *n* ***syn*** see TIRADE
jerk *vb* to act on with or make a sudden sharp quick movement <*jerked* to one side> <*jerk* a root from the ground>
syn lug, lurch, snap, twitch, vellicate, yank
rel drag, pull; fling, sling, throw, toss; wrench, wrest, wring
jerk *n* ***syn*** see FOOL 1
jerkwater town *n* ***syn*** see BURG
jerry–build *vb* ***syn*** see THROW UP 1
jest *n* **1** ***syn*** see JOKE 1
rel banter, chaff, jolly; derision, ridicule, twit
2 ***syn*** see FUN 1
con gravity, seriousness, soberness
ant earnest
3 ***syn*** see LAUGHINGSTOCK
jest *vb* **1** ***syn*** see SCOFF
2 ***syn*** see BANTER
jestee *n* ***syn*** see LAUGHINGSTOCK
jester *n* **1** ***syn*** see FOOL 2
2 ***syn*** see HUMORIST 2
jet *adj* ***syn*** see BLACK 1
jet *vb* ***syn*** see SQUIRT
jetsam *n* ***syn*** see DRIFTWOOD
jet set *n* ***syn*** see SMART SET
jettison *n* ***syn*** see DISPOSAL 2
jettison *vb* ***syn*** see DISCARD
ant salvage
jetty *n* ***syn*** see WHARF
jetty *adj* ***syn*** see BLACK 1
jewel *n* ***syn*** see PARAGON
jewel *vb* ***syn*** see BEJEWEL
jezebel *n* ***syn*** see WANTON
jib *vb* ***syn*** see DEMUR
jibe *vb* ***syn*** see AGREE 4
‖**jiff** *n* ***syn*** see INSTANT 1
jiffy *n* ***syn*** see INSTANT 1
jig *n* ***syn*** see TRICK 1
jigger *n* **1** ***syn*** see DOODAD
2 ***syn*** see GADGET 1
‖**jiggery–pokery** *n* ***syn*** see NONSENSE 2
jiggle *vb* ***syn*** see SHAKE 3
jillion *n* ***syn*** see SCAD
jim–dandy *n* ***syn*** see ‖DILLY
‖**jimjams** *n* ***syn*** see JITTERS
‖**jimmies** *n* ***syn*** see JITTERS
jimmy *vb* ***syn*** see PRY
jingle *vb* to make a repeated sharp light ringing sound <the coins *jingled* in his pocket>
syn chink, chinkle, clink, tingle, tinkle
rel clack, clatter, rattle
jinx *n* something that is felt or meant to bring bad luck <her continual bad luck seemed due to a *jinx*>
syn hex, hoodoo, Indian sign, voodoo, whammy
rel charm, enchantment, spell; curse, evil eye
jitters *n pl* a sense of panic or extreme nervousness <got the *jitters* whenever he thought of the money he had lost>
syn ‖all-overs, dither, heebie-jeebies, ‖jimjams, ‖jimmies, jumps, shakes, shivers, whim-whams, willies
jittery *adj* ***syn*** see NERVOUS
‖**jive** *vb* ***syn*** see BANTER
job *n* **1** ***syn*** see TASK 1
rel affair, concern, matter, thing
2 a regular remunerative employment <held two *jobs* to make ends meet>
syn appointment, berth, billet, connection, office, place, position, post, situation, spot; *compare* WORK 1
rel assignment, engagement, posting; calling, employment, occupation, pursuit; profession, trade, vocation; niche, opening, slot
3 ***syn*** see WORK 1
4 ***syn*** see TASK 2
job *vb* ***syn*** see DUPE
jobless *adj* ***syn*** see UNEMPLOYED
jockey *vb* ***syn*** see MANIPULATE 2
jocose *adj* ***syn*** see WITTY
rel playful, roguish, sportive, waggish, whimsical; comic, comical, droll, laughable, ludicrous; blithe, jocund, jolly, jovial
con demure, earnest, grave, sedate, serious, sober, solemn, staid
ant lugubrious
jocular *adj* ***syn*** see WITTY
rel jolly, jovial, merry; playful, sportive; comic, comical, droll, laughable, ludicrous
con earnest, grave, serious, sober, solemn
jocularity *n* ***syn*** see MIRTH
jocund *adj* ***syn*** see MERRY
rel mischievous, playful, sportive
con dour, gloomy, glum, morose, saturnine, sullen; grave, sedate, serious, solemn, somber, staid
jocundity *n* ***syn*** see MIRTH
jog *vb* ***syn*** see POKE 1
rel agitate, shake
joggle *vb* ***syn*** see SHAKE 3
john *n* ***syn*** see TOILET
John Law *n* ***syn*** see POLICEMAN
johnny *n* ***syn*** see TOILET
join *vb* **1** to bring or come together into some manner of union <the couple were *joined* in marriage soon thereafter>
syn associate, bracket, coadunate, coagment, coalesce, combine, compound, concrete, conjoin, conjugate, connect, couple, link, marry, one, relate, unite, wed, yoke
rel agree, concur, cooperate; articulate, concatenate, integrate; affix, attach, fasten; knit, weave; bind, tie, tie up
con separate, sever, sunder; detach, disengage; disembarrass, disentangle, untangle
ant disjoin, part
2 ***syn*** see ADJOIN
join (up) *vb* ***syn*** see ENTER 3
joining *n* ***syn*** see JOINT 1
joint *n* **1** a place where two or more things are united <the leak was found at a *joint* in the pipeline>

---

syn synonym(s) ***rel*** related word(s)
ant antonym(s) ***con*** contrasted word(s)
idiom idiomatic equivalent(s)
‖ use limited; if in doubt, see a dictionary

syn connection, coupling, joining, junction, juncture, seam, union
rel crux, link, tie; interconnection; abutment, articulation, suture; concourse, confluence, meeting
2 *syn* see DIVE
joint *adj* *syn* see COMMON 1
jointly *adv* *syn* see TOGETHER 3
joke *n* **1** a remark, story, or action intended to evoke laughter <had a good memory for *jokes*>
syn crack, drôlerie, drollery, gag, jape, jest, quip, sally, waggery, wisecrack, witticism, ||yak
rel antic, caper, dido, monkeyshine, prank; bijouterie, bon mot; burlesque, caricature, parody, quiz, rib; badinage, persiflage, raillery; facetiousness, humorousness, jocoseness, jocularity, wittiness; humor, repartee, sarcasm, wit
2 *syn* see FUN 1
3 *syn* see LAUGHINGSTOCK
joke *vb* *syn* see BANTER
joker *n* **1** *syn* see WAG 1
2 *syn* see HUMORIST 2
3 *syn* see ZANY 2
jokester *n* **1** *syn* see HUMORIST 2
2 *syn* see ZANY 2
jollity *n* **1** *syn* see MIRTH
rel blitheness; disport, frolic, gambol, play, rollick, romp, sport
con earnestness, gravity, sedateness, seriousness, solemnity, staidness
ant somberness
2 *syn* see MERRYMAKING
jolly *adj* *syn* see MERRY
rel frolicsome, mischievous, playful, roguish, sportive, waggish
con earnest, grave, sedate, serious, solemn, staid; doleful, dolorous, lugubrious, rueful
ant somber
jolly *vb* *syn* see BANTER
rel blandish, cajole
jolt *vb* *syn* see SHOCK 2
jolt *n* **1** *syn* see IMPACT 1
2 *syn* see DRAM
jongleur *n* *syn* see BARD 1
josh *vb* *syn* see BANTER
joskin *n* *syn* see RUSTIC
jostle *vb* *syn* see PUSH 2
jot *n* *syn* see PARTICLE
jounce *n* *syn* see IMPACT 1
journal *n* a publication that appears at regular intervals <a monthly scientific *journal*>
syn magazine, newspaper, organ, periodical, review
journey *n* passing or a passage from one place to another <at that time it was a four day *journey* from Boston to New York> <she was tired though their *journey* was barely begun>
syn expedition, peregrination(s), travel(s), trek, trip; *compare* TRIP 1
rel excursion, jaunt, junket, sally, tour; cruise, voyage; pilgrimage, progress, safari
journey *vb* *syn* see GO 1
jovial *adj* *syn* see MERRY
rel facetious, humorous, jocose, jocular; affable, genial, sociable; amiable, good-natured; bantering, chaffing, jollying, joshing
con dour, gloomy, glum, morose, saturnine, sullen; grave, sedate, serious, solemn, staid
joviality *n* *syn* see MIRTH
joy *n* *syn* see PLEASURE 2
rel ecstasy, rapture, transport
ant sorrow; misery
joyance *n* *syn* see PLEASURE 2
joyful *adj* *syn* see GLAD 1
rel buoyant, effervescent, expansive
con despairing, desperate, despondent, forlorn, hopeless; depressed, oppressed, weighed down
ant joyless
||**joy girl** *n* *syn* see PROSTITUTE
||**joyhouse** *n* *syn* see BROTHEL
||**joy–juice** *n* *syn* see LIQUOR 2
joyless *adj* **1** *syn* see SAD 2
2 *syn* see GLOOMY 3
joyous *adj* *syn* see GLAD 1
rel ecstatic, rapturous, transported
con doleful, dolorous, melancholy; miserable, wretched
ant lugubrious
jubilance *n* *syn* see EXULTATION
jubilant *adj* *syn* see EXULTANT
jubilate *vb* *syn* see EXULT
jubilation *n* *syn* see EXULTATION
judge *n* **1** a person who impartially decides unsettled questions or controversial issues <the *judge* declared the ruling invalid>
syn arbiter, arbitrator, referee, umpire
rel intermediary, mediator, negotiator; conciliator, peacemaker, reconciler
2 an official entrusted with administration of laws <the *judge* gave the defendant a suspended sentence>
syn ||beak, court, justice, magistrate
judge *vb* **1** to decide something in dispute or controversy upon its merits and upon evidence <the committee will *judge* the truth of the testimony>
syn adjudge, adjudicate, arbitrate, referee, umpire
rel decide, determine, rule, settle
2 *syn* see INFER
rel demonstrate, prove, show; check, test, try
3 *syn* see ESTIMATE 3
judgmatic *adj* *syn* see WISE 2
judgment *n* **1** *syn* see INFERENCE 1
rel decision, determination, ruling; belief, conviction, opinion, persuasion, view
2 *syn* see INFERENCE 2
3 *syn* see ESTIMATION 1
4 *syn* see SENSE 6
rel astuteness, perspicacity, sagacity, shrewdness; acumen, discernment, insight, penetration
judicious *adj* *syn* see WISE 2
rel rational, reasonable; dispassionate, equitable, fair, objective
con irrational, thoughtless, unreasonable; ill-considered
ant injudicious; asinine
jug *n* *syn* see JAIL

jug *vb syn* see IMPRISON
juggle *vb syn* see DECEIVE
‖**juice** *n syn* see LIQUOR 2
‖**juiced** *adj syn* see INTOXICATED 1
juicy *adj syn* see SUCCULENT
juju *n syn* see CHARM 2
jumble *vb* **1** *syn* see CONFUSE 5
2 *syn* see DISORDER 1
jumble *n* **1** *syn* see CLUTTER 2
2 *syn* see MISCELLANY 1
jumbo *adj syn* see HUGE
jump *vb* **1** to move suddenly through space by or as if by muscular action <*jumped* across the open trench>
syn bounce, bound, hop, hurdle, leap, lop, saltate, spring, vault
2 *syn* see START 1
3 *syn* see RAISE 9
jump (in *or* into) *vb syn* see PITCH IN 1
jump (off) *vb syn* see BEGIN 1
jumps *n pl syn* see JITTERS
jumpy *adj syn* see NERVOUS
idiom on pins and needles
junction *n* **1** *syn* see CONCOURSE
2 *syn* see JOINT 1
juncture *n* **1** *syn* see JOINT 1
2 a critical or crucial time or state of affairs <was at a *juncture* where he had to make a decision>
syn contingency, crisis, crossroad(s), emergency, exigency, pass, pinch, strait, turning point, zero hour
rel condition, posture, situation, state, status; plight, predicament, quandary
3 *syn* see POINT 7
jungle *n* **1** *syn* see CLUTTER 2
2 *syn* see MAZE 1
junk *n syn* see REFUSE
junk *vb syn* see DISCARD
junker *n syn* see JALOPY
junket *n syn* see EXCURSION 1
junking *n syn* see DISPOSAL 2
Junoesque *adj syn* see CURVACEOUS
jurisdiction *n syn* see POWER 1
rel bounds, confines, limits; compass, range, reach, scope; bailiwick, domain, field, province, sphere, territory
just *adj* **1** *syn* see WELL-FOUNDED
2 *syn* see TRUE 3
3 being what is called for by circumstances or accepted standards <punishments once considered fair and *just* are now held to be cruel, excessive, and unreasonable>
syn appropriate, condign, deserved, due, merited, requisite, rhadamanthine, right, rightful, suitable; *compare* FIT 1
rel fit, fitting, meet, proper
con farfetched, irrelevant, remote, unconnected; improper, inapplicable, inapposite, inappropriate; abusive, cruel, harsh
ant unjust
4 *syn* see UPRIGHT 2
rel rigid, strict; dependable, reliable, tried, trustworthy
5 *syn* see FAIR 4
rel aloof; condign, due, rightful
ant unjust
6 *syn* see FIT 1
just *adv* **1** as stated or indicated without deviation <*just* six inches long>
syn accurately, bang, exactly, precisely, right, sharp, ‖smack-dab, spang, square, squarely
rel definitely, directly, expressly, unmistakably
con almost, nearly; approximately, imprecisely, inaccurately, inexactly, loosely
2 by a very small margin <*just* enough food for one meal>
syn barely, hardly, scarce, scarcely
rel almost, approximately, nearly
con copiously, fully, generously, lavishly, unstintedly, unstintingly
3 no more than <*just* a note to remind you>
syn but, merely, only, simply
idiom nothing but
4 *syn* see ALL 1
5 *syn* see EVEN 1
just about *adv syn* see NEARLY
justice *n* **1** the action, practice, or obligation of awarding each his just due <his *justice* was stern but absolutely fair>
syn equity
rel evenness, fairness, impartiality
con foul play, inequity, unjustness; bias, leaning, one-sidedness, partiality
ant injustice
2 *syn* see JUDGE 2
justifiable *adj* capable of being justified <thought her absence was not *justifiable*>
syn condonable, defensible, excusable, tenable, vindicable, warrantable
rel admissible, allowable, legitimate, reasonable; forgivable, pardonable, remissible
ant unjustifiable
justification *n* **1** *syn* see EXPLANATION 2
2 *syn* see APOLOGY 1
justified *adj syn* see WELL-FOUNDED
ant unjustified
justify *vb* **1** *syn* see MAINTAIN 2
rel demonstrate, prove; back, support, uphold
con confute, disprove, refute
2 *syn* see CONFIRM 2
3 *syn* see EXPLAIN 3
rel extenuate, gloss, gloze, palliate, whitewash
con accuse, arraign, incriminate, indict; blame, condemn, denounce
4 to constitute sufficient grounds <thought the storm warning *justified* his leaving early>
syn warrant
rel allow, permit; approve, authorize, sanction
justly *adv syn* see WELL 1
jut *vb* **1** *syn* see BULGE
rel elongate, extend, lengthen
2 *syn* see HANG 4
jut *n syn* see PROJECTION 1

---

syn synonym(s) *rel* related word(s)
ant antonym(s) *con* contrasted word(s)
idiom idiomatic equivalent(s)
‖ use limited; if in doubt, see a dictionary

juvenile *adj* ***syn*** see YOUNG 1
ant adult
juvenile *n* ***syn*** see CHILD 1
juvenility *n* ***syn*** see YOUTH 1
juxtaposed *adj* ***syn*** see ADJACENT 3

K

||**kale** *n* ***syn*** see MONEY
keck *vb* ***syn*** see RETCH
keel (over) *vb* ***syn*** see FALL 2
keen *adj* **1** ***syn*** see SHARP 1
2 ***syn*** see ENTHUSIASTIC
3 ***syn*** see EAGER
rel fervent, fervid, perfervid; fierce, intense, vehement; fired
con apathetic, impassive, phlegmatic, stolid; languid, listless
4 ***syn*** see SHARP 4
5 ***syn*** see ACUTE 3
con dull, obtuse
6 ***syn*** see LIVELY 1
||**7** ***syn*** see MARVELOUS 2
keenly *adv* ***syn*** see HARD 6
keenness *n* **1** ***syn*** see EDGE 2
2 ***syn*** see WIT 3
keep *vb* **1** ***syn*** see OBEY
ant neglect
2 to notice or honor a day, occasion, or deed <*keep* the Sabbath by refraining from work>
syn celebrate, commemorate, observe, solemnize
rel regard, respect; bless, consecrate, sanctify; honor, laud, praise
idiom keep the faith
con disregard, forget, ignore, neglect, omit, overlook, slight; contravene, infringe, transgress, violate
ant break
3 ***syn*** see STOCK
4 ***syn*** see RESTRAIN 1
ant release
5 to hold in one's possession or under one's control <*kept* all the money for himself>
syn detain, hold, hold back, keep back, keep out, reserve, retain, withhold
rel conserve, preserve, save; enjoy, have, own, possess; conduct, control, direct, manage
con cast, discard, junk; refuse, reject, repudiate, spurn; abandon, resign, surrender, yield
ant relinquish
6 ***syn*** see REFRAIN 1
7 ***syn*** see CONDUCT 3
keep *n* **1** ***syn*** see LIVING
2 ***syn*** see JAIL
keep back *vb* **1** ***syn*** see KEEP 5
2 ***syn*** see DENY 2
keeper *n* ***syn*** see CUSTODIAN
keeping *n* **1** ***syn*** see CUSTODY
2 ***syn*** see PRESERVATION 1
keep off *vb* ***syn*** see FEND (off)
keep out *vb* ***syn*** see KEEP 5
keepsake *n* ***syn*** see REMEMBRANCE 3
keep up *vb* ***syn*** see MAINTAIN 1
keg *n* ***syn*** see CASK
||**keister** *n* ***syn*** see BUTTOCKS
kelter *n* ***syn*** see REFUSE
ken *n* the extent of one's recognition, comprehension, perception, understanding, or knowledge <abstractions that are beyond the *ken* of small children>
syn horizon, purview, range, reach
rel comprehension, grasp, perception, understanding
kept woman *n* ***syn*** see HARLOT 1
kerchief *n* **1** a square of cloth used as a head covering or scarf <wore a *kerchief* around his neck>
syn babushka, bandanna
2 ***syn*** see HANDKERCHIEF
kernel *n* ***syn*** see SUBSTANCE 2
key *n* ***syn*** see PASSPORT
kibitzer *n* ***syn*** see BUSYBODY
kick *vb* **1** ***syn*** see OBJECT 1
rel combat, fight, oppose, resist, withstand; anathematize, condemn, curse, damn, execrate
idiom put up a fight (against)
2 ***syn*** see COMPLAIN
kick *n* ***syn*** see THRILL
||**kick around** *vb* ***syn*** see DISCUSS 1
kick back *vb* ***syn*** see BACKFIRE
kicker *n* ***syn*** see GROUCH
||**kick in** *vb* **1** ***syn*** see CONTRIBUTE 1
2 ***syn*** see DIE 1
kick off *vb* **1** ***syn*** see BEGIN 1
||**2** ***syn*** see DIE 1
kick out *vb* **1** ***syn*** see DISMISS 3
2 ***syn*** see EJECT 1
kickshaw *n* ***syn*** see DELICACY
kid *n* ***syn*** see CHILD 1
kid *vb* **1** ***syn*** see DUPE
2 ***syn*** see BANTER
kidnap *vb* to carry off a person surreptitiously for an illegal purpose <an ex-convict *kidnapped* the child for ransom>
syn abduct, ||snatch, spirit (away)
rel shanghai, waylay; coax, decoy, entice, inveigh, lure, seduce
idiom make off with
con deliver, ransom, redeem, rescue; bring (back), give back, restore, return
kidney *n* ***syn*** see TYPE
kid stuff *n* ***syn*** see SNAP 1
kill *vb* **1** to deprive of life <found it hard to *kill* animals>
syn carry off, cut off, destroy, dispatch, down, finish, lay low, put away, scrag, slay, take off; *compare* MURDER 1

---

syn synonym(s) ***rel*** related word(s)
ant antonym(s) ***con*** contrasted word(s)
idiom idiomatic equivalent(s)
|| use limited; if in doubt, see a dictionary

rel butcher, choke, drown, massacre, poison, shoot, slaughter, suffocate; knife, sacrifice, stifle; annihilate, exterminate, ruin
idiom do (*or* make) away with, do for, put out of the way, put (*or* do) to death, put to sleep, take one's life
2 *syn* see VETO
killer *n syn* see MURDERER
killing *n syn* see MURDER
kiln *vb syn* see FIRE 6
kilter *n syn* see ORDER 10
kin *n* **1** *syn* see FAMILY 1
2 the members of one's immediate or extended family <all our *kin* gathered to celebrate great grandma's birthday>
syn cousinage, cousinhood, kinfolk, kinsmen
3 *syn* see RELATIVE
kind *n syn* see TYPE
kind *adj* showing or having a gentle considerate nature <mother was a *kind* person, always willing to help others>
syn benign, benignant, good-hearted, kindly
rel altruistic, benevolent, charitable, eleemosynary, humane, humanitarian, openhearted, philanthropic, propitious; compassionate, kindhearted, responsive, sympathetic, tender, warm, warmhearted; clement, forbearing, indulgent, lenient, merciful, tolerant; affable, amiable, cordial, genial, good-humored, good-natured, good-tempered, sweet-tempered; complaisant, obliging; gentle, good
con cruel, fell, fierce, inhuman, savage; hard, harsh, rough; grim, implacable, merciless, unrelenting
ant unkind
kindhearted *adj syn* see TENDER
kindle *vb* **1** *syn* see LIGHT 1
rel blaze, flame, flare, glow; excite, provoke, stimulate; arouse, foment, incite, instigate, rouse, stir
ant smother
2 *syn* see STIR 1
ant stifle
kindless *adj syn* see ANTIPATHETIC 2
kindliness *n syn* see GOODWILL 1
ant unkindliness
kindly *adj syn* see KIND
rel gracious, sociable; friendly, neighborly; attentive, considerate, thoughtful
con malevolent, malicious, malign, spiteful
ant unkindly; acrid (*of temper, attitudes, comments*)
kindly *adv syn* see WELL 2
kindness *n syn* see FAVOR 4
kind of *adv syn* see SOMEWHAT 2
kindred *n syn* see FAMILY 1
kindred *adj syn* see RELATED
ant alien
kinfolk *n pl syn* see KIN 2
king *n syn* see MAGNATE
kingdom come *n syn* see HEAVEN 2
kinglike *adj syn* see KINGLY
kingly *adj* of, relating to, or befitting a king <a *kingly* entourage>
syn kinglike, majestic, monarchal, monarchial, monarchical, regal, royal, sovereign
rel imperious, lordly, masterful, powerful, puissant; imperial, princely, queenly
kinky *adj syn* see OUTLANDISH 3
kinsman *n* **1** *syn* see RELATIVE
2 kinsmen *pl syn* see KIN 2
kinswoman *n syn* see RELATIVE
kismet *n syn* see FATE
kiss *vb* **1** to touch with the lips especially as a sign of affection <*kissed* his mother good night>
syn buss, lip, osculate, peck, smack, smooch, ||smoodge, ||smouch
2 *syn* see BRUSH
||kisser *n syn* see FACE 1
kiss off *vb syn* see DISMISS 5
kite *vb syn* see GET OUT 1
kittenish *adj syn* see PLAYFUL 1
kitty *n syn* see POT 3
klutz *n syn* see OAF 2
knack *n* **1** *syn* see GIFT 2
rel quickness, readiness
ant ineptitude
2 *syn* see ABILITY 2
3 *syn* see HANG
knapsack *n syn* see BACKPACK
knave *n syn* see VILLIAN 1
knavish *adj syn* see DISHONEST
knell *vb syn* see RING
knickknack *n* a small or trivial ornamental article <a collection of pretty *knickknacks* was displayed on the mantel>
syn bauble, bibelot, curio, dido, gewgaw, gimcrack, novelty, objet d'art, pretty-pretty, rattletrap(s), toy, trifle, trinket, whatnot, whigmaleerie
rel souvenir; bric-a-brac, virtu; miniature; kickshaw, notion; trumpery
knifelike *adj syn* see SHARP 8
ant dull
knobkerrie *n syn* see CUDGEL
knock *vb* **1** *syn* see TAP 1
2 *syn* see CRITICIZE
ant boost
knock *n* **1** *syn* see HIT 1
2 *syn* see CRITICISM 2
knock about *vb syn* see MANHANDLE
knock down *vb* **1** *syn* see FELL 1
2 *syn* see EARN 1
knock–down–and–drag–out *n* **1** *syn* see BRAWL
2 *syn* see QUARREL
knocker *n syn* see CRITIC
knock off *vb* **1** *syn* see STOP 3
2 *syn* see DEDUCT 1
3 *syn* see MURDER 1
||4 *syn* see ROB 1
knock out *vb syn* see EXHAUST 4
knockout *n* **1** *syn* see ||DILLY
2 *syn* see BEAUTY
knock over *vb* **1** *syn* see FELL 1
2 *syn* see OVERTURN 1
3 *syn* see OVERWHELM 4
4 *syn* see ROB 1
knot *n* **1** *syn* see BOND 3

2 *syn* see BUMP 2
3 *syn* see MAZE 1
knothead *n* ***syn*** see DUNCE
knotty *adj* **1** ***syn*** see COMPLEX 2
2 *syn* see HARD 6

know *vb* **1** to possess an intellectual hold of <*knows* several languages>
syn appreciate, apprehend, cognize, comprehend, fathom, grasp, have, understand
rel apperceive; differentiate, discern, discriminate, distinguish, realize
idiom have at one's fingertips, see through
2 ***syn*** see EXPERIENCE 1
3 ***syn*** see FEEL 2
4 to recognize the differences between <*know* right from wrong>
syn difference, differentiate, discern, discrepate, discriminate, distinguish, extricate, separate, sever, severalize
con confound, mingle, mix
ant confuse, mix up
5 ***syn*** see RECOGNIZE 1

knowable *adj* ***syn*** see UNDERSTANDABLE
ant unknowable
know-how *n* **1** ***syn*** see ABILITY 2
2 ***syn*** see ART 1
knowing *adj* **1** ***syn*** see INTELLIGENT 2
rel vigilant, watchful; discerning, observant, perceptive
con blunt, obtuse
2 ***syn*** see WISE 1
3 ***syn*** see WISE 4
4 ***syn*** see AWARE
5 ***syn*** see SOPHISTICATED 2
know-it-all *n* ***syn*** see SMART ALECK
knowledge *n* **1** ***syn*** see EDUCATION 2
ant ignorance
2 the body of things known about or in science <made major contributions to scientific *knowledge*>
syn information, lore, science, wisdom
rel advice, intelligence, news; data, evidence, facts, input
knowledgeable *adj* **1** ***syn*** see INTELLIGENT 2
2 ***syn*** see WISE 1
know-nothing *adj* ***syn*** see IGNORANT 1
know-nothing *n* ***syn*** see DUNCE
knuckle *vb* ***syn*** see YIELD 2
knucklehead *n* ***syn*** see DUNCE
knuckle under *vb* ***syn*** see YIELD 2
kook *n* ***syn*** see CRACKPOT
kooky *adj* ***syn*** see FOOLISH 2
kowtow *vb* ***syn*** see FAWN
kowtowing *adj* ***syn*** see FAWNING
kudize *vb* ***syn*** see COMMEND 2
kudo *n* ***syn*** see COMPLIMENT 1
kudos *n* **1** ***syn*** see EMINENCE 1
2 ***syn*** see HONOR 2
kvetch *vb* ***syn*** see GRIPE

L

laager *vb* ***syn*** see CAMP
label *n* ***syn*** see TICKET 1
rel mark, marker
labor *n* **1** ***syn*** see WORK 2
rel endeavor, struggle
con ease, leisure, relaxation, repose, rest; amusement, diversion, entertainment, recreation; idleness, inactivity, inertia, inertness, passiveness
2 the physical activities involved in parturition <first *labors* are sometimes difficult>
syn birth pang(s), childbearing, childbirth, travail
labor *vb* **1** to exert one's powers of mind or body especially with painful or strenuous effort <*labored* all day to make a living>
syn drive, moil, strain, strive, toil, tug, work
idiom break one's neck
con idle, laze, loaf, lounge; goof (off), shirk; dawdle, poke, putter
‖**2** ***syn*** see TILL
labored *adj* **1** ***syn*** see HARD 6
2 ***syn*** see FORCED
rel heavy, ponderous, weighty; awkward, clumsy, inept, maladroit
laborer *n* ***syn*** see WORKER
laborious *adj* ***syn*** see HARD 6
ant easy, effortless
laboriously *adv* ***syn*** see HARD 8
ant easily, effortlessly
labyrinth *n* ***syn*** see MAZE 1
labyrinthine *adj* ***syn*** see COMPLEX 2
lacerated *adj* having jagged cuts or breaks <the *lacerated* area was badly swollen>
syn mangled, rent, torn
rel gashed, mutilated, ripped, slashed; jagged, ragged, saw-toothed, scalloped, scored; serrated
lachrymose *adj* ***syn*** see TEARFUL
lack *vb* to be without something and especially something essential or greatly needed <the building *lacks* a fire escape>
syn need, require, want
con enjoy, have, hold, own, possess
lack *n* **1** ***syn*** see ABSENCE
2 ***syn*** see FAILURE 3
lackadaisical *adj* ***syn*** see LANGUID
rel incurious, indifferent, unconcerned; faineant, indolent, lazy, slothful; idle, passive; emasculated; romantic, sentimental
con energetic, lusty, strenuous, vigorous; active, dynamic, live
lacking *adj* **1** ***syn*** see ABSENT 1
2 ***syn*** see DEFICIENT 1
lacking *prep* ***syn*** see WITHOUT 2
lackluster *adj* **1** ***syn*** see DULL 7
2 ***syn*** see COLORLESS 2
rel dead, leaden, rusty, tarnished
con lustrous
lackwit *n* ***syn*** see DUNCE
laconic *adj* ***syn*** see CONCISE
rel brusque
con garrulous, glib, loquacious, talkative
ant verbose, wordy
laconically *adv* ***syn*** see BRIEFLY
lacuna *n* ***syn*** see GAP 3
lad *n* ***syn*** see BOY 1
laddie *n* ***syn*** see BOY 1
lade *vb* **1** ***syn*** see BURDEN
2 ***syn*** see DIP 2
la–di–da *adj* **1** ***syn*** see PRECIOUS 4
2 ***syn*** see GENTEEL 3
ladies' man *n* ***syn*** see WOLF
lading *n* ***syn*** see LOAD 1
ladle *vb* ***syn*** see DIP 2
lady *n* **1** ***syn*** see WOMAN 1
2 ***syn*** see WIFE
lady friend *n* ***syn*** see GIRL FRIEND 1
lady–killer *n* ***syn*** see WOLF
ladylove *n* ***syn*** see GIRL FRIEND 2
lag *vb* ***syn*** see DELAY 2
rel retard, slacken, slow; stay
lag *adj* ***syn*** see LAST
‖**lag** *vb* ***syn*** see BANISH
‖**lag** *n* ***syn*** see CONVICT
laggard *adj* ***syn*** see SLOW 2
rel dawdling, delaying, loitering, procrastinating; comatose, lethargic, sluggish; apathetic, impassive, phlegmatic
con alert, vigilant, watchful, wide-awake; expeditious, fast, fleet, speedy
ant prompt, quick
laggard *n* one that delays unnecessarily or falls behind <no room for *laggards* on the expedition>
syn dawdler, lingerer, loiterer, slow coach, slowpoke, straggler
rel lazybones, loafer
con dynamo, go-ahead, go-getter, hustler, live wire, rustler; eager beaver
lagniappe *n* ***syn*** see GRATUITY
lair *n* **1** a resting or living place of a wild animal <photographed the wolf at the entrance to his *lair*>
syn burrow, couch, den, lodge
2 ***syn*** see HIDEOUT
‖**lalapalooza** *n* ***syn*** ‖DILLY, ‖corker, crackerjack, ‖daisy, dandy, humdinger, jim-dandy, ‖lulu, peach, ‖pip
‖**lallygag** *vb* ***syn*** see IDLE
lam *vb* ***syn*** see BEAT 1
lam *n* ***syn*** see ESCAPE 1
lambaste *vb* **1** ***syn*** see BEAT 1
2 ***syn*** see WHIP 2
3 to assail with withering oral or written denunciation <the senator has been publicly *lambasted* for taking bribes>

syn blister, castigate, ||crawl, drub, excoriate, flay, lash (into), roast, scarify, scathe, scorch, score, scourge, slam, slap, slash, ||slate; *compare* CRITICIZE, REPROVE, SCOLD 1
rel censure, criticize, denounce, pan; berate, scold, tongue-lash; assail, attack, squabash
idiom burn one's ears, ||crawl all over, give (one) a roasting, pin one's ears back, rake (one) over the coals, read the riot act, rip into
con applaud, extol, praise; approve, countenance, endorse

lambent *adj syn* see BRIGHT 1

lame–brain *n syn* see DUNCE

lament *vb syn* see DEPLORE 1
ant exult; rejoice

lamentable *adj* **1** *syn* see DEPLORABLE
2 *syn* see MELANCHOLY 2

lamia *n syn* see WITCH 1

lamp *n syn* see EYE 1

lampoonery *n syn* see SATIRE

lampooning *adj syn* see SATIRIC

lance *vb syn* see IMPALE

land *n* **1** *syn* see EARTH 2
2 *syn* see COUNTRY
3 *syn* see ESTATE 3

land *vb* **1** *syn* see DISEMBARK
2 *syn* see ALIGHT
3 *syn* see GET 1

||**lang syne** *n syn* see PAST

language *n* **1** a body or system of words and phrases used by a large community or by a people, a nation, or a group of nations <the English and French *languages*>
syn dialect, idiom, speech, tongue, vernacular
rel argot, cant, jargon, lingo, patois, slang
2 *syn* see TERMINOLOGY

languid *adj* lacking in vim or energy <doing the job in a slow and *languid* manner>
syn die-away, enervated, lackadaisical, languishing, languorous, limp, listless, spiritless
rel comatose, lethargic, sluggish, torpid; apathetic, impassive, phlegmatic; inactive, inert, supine
con alert, awake, ||fly, keen, lively, wide-awake
ant vivacious; chipper

languish *vb syn* see FAIL 1
ant flourish

languishing *adj syn* see LANGUID
rel debilitated, enfeebled, weakened; faineant, indolent; longing, pining, yearning
con hale, healthy, robust, sound; energetic, lusty, vigorous
ant flourishing, thriving; unaffected

languor *n syn* see LETHARGY 1
rel exhaustion, fatigue, weariness; blues, depression, dumps; doldrums, ennui, tedium
con celerity, legerity; gusto, zest
ant alacrity

languorous *adj syn* see LANGUID
rel dilatory, laggard, leisurely, slow; faineant, indolent, slothful; passive; lax, loose, relaxed, slack; indulged, pampered
ant vigorous; strenuous (*of times, seasons*)

lank *adj syn* see LEAN
rel attenuated, extenuated
con chubby
ant burly

lanky *adj* **1** *syn* see GANGLING
2 *syn* see LEAN

lap *vb syn* see OVERLAP

lap *vb* **1** *syn* see SLOSH 1
2 *syn* see BATHE 2

lapse *n* **1** *syn* see ERROR 2
rel crime, offense, sin, vice; failing, foible, frailty; breach, transgression, trespass, violation
2 a temporary deviation or fall especially from a higher to a lower state <a *lapse* into nonproductiveness> <ashamed of his *lapse* from grace>
syn backsliding, relapse
rel decadence, declension, decline, degeneration, deterioration, devolution; recession, retrogradation; regression, retrogression
con advance, progress; development, maturation; amendment; betterment, improvement

lapse *vb* to fall from a better or higher state into a lower or poorer one <*lapsed* into his old vulgar ways>
syn backslide, recidivate, relapse
rel return, revert; slide, slip; decline, degenerate, deteriorate; subside; descend; recede, retrograde; apostatize
con advance, progress; develop, mature; amend, mend; better, improve

larcener *n syn* see THIEF

larcenist *n syn* see THIEF

larcenous *adj* prone to committing larceny <*larcenous* employees were robbing the company blind>
syn sticky-fingered, thieving, thievish
rel burglarious; light-fingered

larceny *n syn* see THEFT

||**lardy–dardy** *adj syn* see GENTEEL 3

lares and penates *n pl syn* see POSSESSION 2

large *adj* **1** above the average of its kind in magnitude <a *large* increase in the tax rate>
syn big, bull, fat, great, husky, oversize
rel colossal, enormous, gigantic, huge, immense, mammoth, vast, voluminous; monstrous, monumental, prodigious, stupendous, tremendous; excessive, exorbitant, extravagant, extreme, immoderate, inordinate
con diminutive, little, minute, tiny, wee; slender, slight, slim, thin
ant small
2 *syn* see BIG 1

largely *adv syn* see GENERALLY 1

largeness *n syn* see SIZE 2

large–scale *adj syn* see BIG 1

largess *n* **1** *syn* see GIFT 1
2 *syn* see GRATUITY

largest *adj syn* see BEST

lark *n* **1** *syn* see ESCAPADE
2 *syn* see PRANK

---

syn synonym(s) *rel* related word(s)
ant antonym(s) *con* contrasted word(s)
idiom idiomatic equivalent(s)
|| use limited; if in doubt, see a dictionary

larkish *adj* ***syn*** see PLAYFUL 1
‖**larrup** *vb* **1** ***syn*** see WHIP 1
2 ***syn*** see WHIP 2
‖**larruping** *adv* ***syn*** see VERY 1
lascivious *adj* **1** ***syn*** see LICENTIOUS 2
rel coarse, gross, obscene
2 ***syn*** see LUSTFUL 2
lash *vb* **1** ***syn*** see RUSH 1
2 ***syn*** see POUR 3
3 ***syn*** see WHIP 1
4 ***syn*** see WAG
5 ***syn*** see SCOLD 1
lash (into) *vb* ***syn*** see LAMBASTE 3
lashings *n pl* ***syn*** see MUCH
lass *n* **1** ***syn*** see GIRL 1
2 ***syn*** see GIRL FRIEND 1
lassie *n* ***syn*** see GIRL 1
lassitude *n* **1** ***syn*** see FATIGUE
2 ***syn*** see APATHY 2
3 ***syn*** see LETHARGY 1
rel doldrums, ennui, tedium; blues, depression, dumps; impotence, powerlessness
con energy, force, might, power, strength
ant vigor
last *vb* ***syn*** see CONTINUE 1
last *adj* following all relevant others (as in time, order, or importance) <he was the *last* one in line>
syn closing, concluding, eventual, final, hindmost, lag, latest, latter, rearmost, terminal, terminating, ultimate
rel bottommost, end, extreme, furthest, outermost, remotest, utmost, uttermost
con beginning, inaugural, initial, introductory, original, primary, prime
ant first
lasting *adj* existing or continuing for so long a time as to seem fixed or established <his reading made a *lasting* impression on him>
syn diuturnal, durable, enduring, perdurable, perduring, permanent, stable; *compare* OLD 2
rel abiding, continuing, persisting; endless, everlasting, unceasing; continual, continuous, incessant, perennial, unremitting; eternal, sempiternal; indelible, indissoluble, inexhaustible, inexpugnable, inexpungible
con ephemeral, evanescent, fugitive, momentary, passing, short-lived, transient, transitory
ant fleeting
last word *n* ***syn*** see APOTHEOSIS 1
late *adj* **1** ***syn*** see TARDY
con opportune, seasonable, well-timed
ant early; prompt, punctual
2 ***syn*** see DEAD 1
3 ***syn*** see FORMER 2
4 ***syn*** see MODERN 1
lated *adj* ***syn*** see TARDY
lately *adv* ***syn*** see NEW
latency *n* ***syn*** see ABEYANCE
latent *adj* not now manifest or showing signs of existence or activity <a *latent* infection>
syn abeyant, dormant, lurking, potential, prepatent, quiescent
rel concealed, hidden; idle, inactive, inert; immature, unmatured, unripe
con active, dynamic, live, operative; activated, energized, vitalized
ant patent
later *adj* ***syn*** see SUBSEQUENT 1
later *adv* ***syn*** see AFTER
ant earlier
laterally *adv* ***syn*** see SIDEWAYS 1
latest *adj* ***syn*** see LAST
ant earliest
lather *n* **1** ***syn*** see FOAM
2 ***syn*** see COMMOTION 4
3 ***syn*** see COMMOTION 2
lather *vb* ***syn*** see WHIP 1
latitude *n* ***syn*** see ROOM 3
latrine *n* ***syn*** see TOILET
latter *adj* ***syn*** see LAST
ant former
latterly *adv* ***syn*** see AFTER
laud *vb* ***syn*** see PRAISE 2
rel adore, revere, reverence, venerate, worship; admire; flatter
con blame, condemn; anathematize, curse, damn, execrate, objurgate
ant revile
laudable *adj* ***syn*** see WORTHY 1
ant illaudable
laudative *adj* ***syn*** see EULOGISTIC
laudatory *adj* ***syn*** see EULOGISTIC
laugh *vb* to show mirth, joy, or scorn with a smile and a usually explosive sound <*laughed* at all the funny things that happened>
syn chortle, chuckle, giggle, guffaw, hee-haw, snicker, ‖sniggle, tehee, titter
rel cachinnate, cackle, crow, roar, whoop; beam, grin, simper, smile, smirk
laughable *adj* provoking laughter or mirth <the *laughable* antics of the clowns>
syn comic, comical, droll, farcical, funny, gelastic, ludicrous, ridiculous, risible
rel amusing, diverting, entertaining, rich; facetious, humorous, jocose, jocular, witty; derisive, derisory, mocking
con grave, serious, solemn; boring, irksome, tedious, tiresome, wearisome; affecting, impressive, moving, pathetic, poignant, touching
laughingstock *n* an object of ridicule <totally unaware that he was the *laughingstock* of the entire office>
syn butt, derision, jest, jestee, joke, mock, mockery, pilgarlic, sport
rel gazingstock; mark, target
launch *vb* **1** ***syn*** see THROW 1
2 ***syn*** see BEGIN 1
3 ***syn*** see INTRODUCE 3
laurels *n pl* ***syn*** see HONOR 2
lavatory *n* ***syn*** see TOILET
lave *vb* ***syn*** see BATHE 2
lavish *adj* **1** ***syn*** see PROFUSE
con scant, scanty; economical, frugal, thrifty; discreet, provident, prudent; miserly, niggardly, parsimonious, penurious, stingy
ant sparing
2 ***syn*** see GRAND 2
lavishness *n* ***syn*** see EXTRAVAGANCE 2

ant sparingness

law *n* **1** a principle governing conduct, action, or procedure <found it hard to live by outdated *laws*>
syn assize, canon, decree, decretum, edict, institute, ordinance, precept, prescript, prescription, regulation, rule, statute
rel command, dictate, mandate
2 *syn* see PRINCIPLE 1
rel exigency, necessity
ant chance

lawbreaker *n* *syn* see CRIMINAL

lawcourt *n* *syn* see COURT 2

lawful *adj* being in accordance with law <obtained *lawful* custody of the child>
syn innocent, legal, legitimate, licit
rel condign, due, rightful; allowable, permissible; justifiable, warrantable; bona fide
idiom of right
con flagitious, iniquitous, nefarious; improper, unjustifiable, wrong; criminal, guilty, peccant; illegitimate, illicit
ant lawless, unlawful

lawless *adj* *syn* see UNLAWFUL
ant lawful

lawlessness *n* *syn* see ANARCHY 1
rel conflict, contention, difference, discord, dissension, strife, variance

lawsuit *n* *syn* see SUIT 1

lawyer *n* a person authorized to practice law in the courts or to serve clients in the capacity of legal agent or adviser <took the problem to his family *lawyer*>
syn attorney, attorney-at-law; *compare* PETTIFOGGER
rel advocate, ‖barrister, counsel, counselor, ‖mouthpiece, pleader, ‖solicitor; jurisconsult, jurisprudent, jurist; legist

lax *vb* *syn* see LOOSE 5

lax *adj* **1** *syn* see LOOSE 1
con firm, hard, solid; elastic, resilient, springy
ant rigid
2 *syn* see NEGLIGENT
rel forgetful, oblivious, unmindful
con austere, severe, stern; rigid, rigorous; conscientious, honest, scrupulous, upright
ant strict, stringent

lay *vb* **1** *syn* see SET 1
2 *syn* see GAMBLE 1
3 *syn* see EVEN 1
4 *syn* see ASCRIBE
5 *syn* see DIRECT 2
6 *syn* see SET 5
7 *syn* see ADDUCE

lay (for) *vb* *syn* see SURPRISE 1

lay (open) *vb* *syn* see EXPOSE 1

lay *n* **1** *syn* see MELODY
2 *syn* see SONG 2

lay *adj* *syn* see PROFANE 1
con professional

lay aside *vb* **1** *syn* see DISCARD
2 *syn* see SAVE 4

lay away *vb* **1** *syn* see SAVE 4
2 *syn* see BURY 1

lay by *vb* *syn* see SAVE 4

lay down *vb* **1** *syn* see RELINQUISH
2 *syn* see PRESCRIBE 2
3 *syn* see DICTATE

layer *n* *syn* see BOOKMAKER

lay in *vb* *syn* see SAVE 4

lay low *vb* **1** *syn* see FELL 1
2 *syn* see KILL 1

lay off *vb* *syn* see REST 3

lay out *vb* **1** *syn* see DESIGN 3
2 *syn* see SPEND 1

lay over *vb* *syn* see DEFER

lay up *vb* **1** *syn* see ACCUMULATE
2 *syn* see SAVE 4

laze *vb* *syn* see IDLE
con drudge, grind, labor, toil, travail, work

laze *n* *syn* see SLOTH 1

laziness *n* *syn* see SLOTH 1
ant industriousness

lazy *adj* not easily aroused to action or activity <the hot humid weather made them *lazy*>
syn drony, easygoing, faineant, indolent, slothful, slowgoing, work-shy
rel idle, inactive, inert, passive, supine, trifling; comatose, lethargic, sluggish, torpid; lackadaisical, languid, languorous, listless, unenergetic, unindustrious; lax, neglectful, negligent, remiss, shiftless, slack
con diligent, hardworking; brisk, chipper, energetic, vigorous; active, animated, lively, spry, vivacious; prompt, quick, ready
ant industrious

lazy *vb* *syn* see IDLE

lazybones *n* *syn* see SLUGGARD

lead *vb* **1** *syn* see GUIDE
rel get, induce, persuade, prevail
con drive, impel; coerce, compel, constrain, force, oblige
ant follow
2 *syn* see PRECEDE 3
3 *syn* see CONVERT 1

lead *n* *syn* see LEADER 1

leader *n* **1** one that takes the lead or initiative <each group selected its own *leader* for the tour>
syn ‖bell cow, bellwether, dean, doyen, guide, lead, pilot
rel pacemaker, pacesetter; forerunner, harbinger, herald, precursor; conductor, director, rector
con adherent, dependent, hanger-on, henchman, satellite
ant follower
2 a person in whom resides authority or ruling power <the company had only one *leader*>
syn boss, chief, chieftain, cock, dominator, head, headman, hierarch, honcho, master

---

syn synonym(s) *rel* related word(s)
ant antonym(s) *con* contrasted word(s)
idiom idiomatic equivalent(s)
‖ use limited; if in doubt, see a dictionary

rel captain, commander, general; director, principal, superintendent, superior; foreman, manager, straw boss
con inferior, subaltern, subordinate, underling, understrapper
3 ***syn*** see NOTABLE 1
leading *adj* **1** ***syn*** see FIRST 1
2 ***syn*** see FIRST 3
ant subordinate
3 ***syn*** see WELL-KNOWN
lead off *vb* ***syn*** see BEGIN 1
lead on *vb* **1** ***syn*** see LURE
2 ***syn*** see TRIFLE 1
leaf (through) *vb* ***syn*** see BROWSE
leafage *n* ***syn*** see FOLIAGE
league *n* **1** ***syn*** see ALLIANCE 2
2 ***syn*** see ASSOCIATION 2
3 ***syn*** see CLASS 1
4 a group of sports clubs or teams that play one another competitively <the new baseball *league*>
syn association, circuit, conference, loop, wheel
rel division
league *vb* ***syn*** see UNITE 2
leak *vb* ***syn*** see GET OUT 2
lean *vb* **1** ***syn*** see SLANT 1
rel bend, curve; deflect, divert, sheer, turn
2 ***syn*** see TEND 1
lean (over) *vb* ***syn*** see HANG 4
lean *n* ***syn*** see SLOPE
lean *adj* thin because of absence of superfluous flesh <a *lean* strong horse>
syn angular, bony, gaunt, lank, lanky, meager, rawboned, scraggy, scrawny, skinny, spare; *compare* THIN 1
rel slender, slight, slim, spare-set, stringy, thin; cadaverous, haggard, pinched, wasted, worn; wizened
con brawny, burly, husky, muscular, sinewy; stalwart, stout, strong, sturdy; corpulent, fat, fatty, flabby, obese, plump, portly, rotund
ant fleshy
leaning *n* **1** ***syn*** see SLOPE
2 an attraction to a particular activity, thing, or end <a strong *leaning* toward liberal views>
syn bent, bias, disposition, drift, inclination, inclining, lurch, partiality, penchant, predilection, predisposition, proclivity, propensity, sentiment, tendency; *compare* GIFT 2, PREJUDICE
rel favor, favoritism, odds
con avoidance, evasion, shunning; disdaining, scorning, scouting, spurning; disinterest, dislike, distaste
leaning *adj* ***syn*** see INCLINED 3
leap *vb* **1** ***syn*** see JUMP 1
rel arise, ascend, mount, rise, soar
con drop, fall, sink, slump
2 ***syn*** see CLEAR 8
learn *vb* **1** to acquire knowledge of or skill in by study and experience <*learn* a trade>
syn get, master, pick up
rel con, peruse, study
idiom make oneself master of
2 ***syn*** see MEMORIZE
3 ***syn*** see DISCOVER 3
learned *adj* possessing or manifesting unusually wide and deep knowledge <a most *learned* scholar in his field>
syn erudite, scholarly, scholastic
rel cultivated, cultured; academic, bookish, pedantic, professorial; abstruse, esoteric, polymath, recondite
con ignorant, illiterate, uneducated, unlearned, unlettered, untutored
learnedness *n* ***syn*** see ERUDITION 2
learning *n* ***syn*** see EDUCATION 2
lease *vb* ***syn*** see HIRE 1
leash *vb* ***syn*** see HAMPER
least *adj* ***syn*** see FIRST 4
leave *vb* **1** ***syn*** see WILL
rel commit, confide, consign, entrust; allot, apportion, assign
2 ***syn*** see LET 2
3 ***syn*** see GO 2
4 ***syn*** see QUIT 6
5 ***syn*** see RELINQUISH
leave *n* **1** ***syn*** see PERMISSION
rel assent
con refusal, rejection; forbiddance, interdiction, prohibition
2 ***syn*** see VACATION
leaven *vb* ***syn*** see INFUSE 1
rel moderate, qualify, temper; enliven, quicken, vivify
leave off *vb* ***syn*** see STOP 3
leave–taking *n* ***syn*** see PARTING
leaving *n, usu* **leavings** *pl* ***syn*** see REMAINDER
rel fragments, pieces, portions; discards, junk, scrap
lecherous *adj* ***syn*** see LICENTIOUS 2
lecture *n* ***syn*** see SPEECH 2
lecture *vb* ***syn*** see TALK 7
ledger *n* ***syn*** see TOMBSTONE
leech *n* ***syn*** see PARASITE
leer *vb* ***syn*** see SNEER 1
lees *n pl* ***syn*** see SEDIMENT
leeway *n* ***syn*** see ROOM 3
left–handed *adj* ***syn*** see INSINCERE
legacy *n* **1** a gift by will especially of money or personal property <received a *legacy* of $5,000 from her late uncle>
syn bequest, devise, inheritance
2 ***syn*** see HERITAGE 1
legal *adj* ***syn*** see LAWFUL
ant illegal
legal tender *n* ***syn*** see MONEY
legate *vb* ***syn*** see WILL
legend *n* **1** ***syn*** see MYTH 1
2 ***syn*** see CAPTION
3 ***syn*** see LORE 2
legendary *adj* ***syn*** see MYTHICAL
legerdemain *n* ***syn*** see MAGIC 2
legion *n* ***syn*** see MULTITUDE 1
legion *adj* ***syn*** see MANY
legitimate *adj* **1** ***syn*** see LAWFUL
rel cogent, sound, valid; acknowledged, recognized; customary, usual; natural, normal, regular, typical

ant illegitimate
2 *syn* see TRUE 8
ant arbitrary
leisure *n* *syn* see REST 1
con drudgery, grind, labor
ant toil
leisurely *adj* *syn* see SLOW 2
rel lax, relaxed, slack; delayed, retarded, slackened; comfortable, easy, restful
con fast, hasty, quick, rapid, speedy; headlong, impetuous, precipitate
ant hurried; abrupt
leitmotiv *n* a dominant recurring thematic element or feature (as in a work of art) <the *leitmotiv* of man against nature often appears in his paintings>
syn motif
rel motive, theme
lemon *n* *syn* see FAILURE 5
lend *vb* to give into another's keeping for temporary use on condition that the borrower return the same or its equivalent <I do not have another copy of the book to give, but I can *lend* you mine>
syn advance, loan
rel lease-lend, lend-lease; allow, furnish, give; accommodate, oblige
length *n* 1 *syn* see DISTANCE 1
2 *syn* see RANGE 2
lengthen *vb* *syn* see EXTEND 3
ant shorten; abbreviate
lengthening *n* *syn* see EXTENSION 1
ant shortening
lengthways *adv* *syn* see LENGTHWISE
ant widthways, widthwise
lengthwise *adv* in the direction of the length <the students folded their papers *lengthwise*>
syn endways, endwise, lengthways, longitudinally, longways, longwise
con latitudinally, widthways; broadside, broadway, broadwise
ant widthways, widthwise
lengthy *adj* 1 *syn* see LONG 2
ant short
2 *syn* see LONG 1
lenience *n* *syn* see FORBEARANCE 2
leniency *n* *syn* see FORBEARANCE 2
lenient *adj* 1 *syn* see GENTLE 1
ant caustic
2 *syn* see FORBEARING
rel condoning, excusing, forgiving, pardoning; benign, benignant, kindly; compassionate, tender; humoring, indulging, pampering, mollycoddling, spoiling
con rigid, rigorous, stringent; austere, severe
ant stern; exacting
3 *syn* see AMIABLE 1
lenity *n* *syn* see MERCY
rel tenderness; benevolence, charitableness, humaneness
con rigidity, rigorousness, strictness, stringency; austerity, sternness
ant severity
leper *n* *syn* see OUTCAST
lessen *vb* 1 *syn* see ABRIDGE 1
rel amputate, clip, crop, truncate
2 *syn* see DECREASE
rel attenuate, dilute, thin, weaken
lesser *adj* 1 *syn* see INFERIOR 1
2 *syn* see MINOR 2
lesson *n* *syn* see EXERCISE 4
lesson *vb* *syn* see REPROVE
let *vb* 1 *syn* see HIRE 1
2 to neither forbid nor prevent <*let* the boy go to the movies>
syn allow, have, leave, permit, suffer
rel accredit, approve, certify, endorse, sanction; authorize, commission, license; concede, grant
con ban, enjoin, forbid, inhibit, interdict, prohibit; bar, block, hinder, impede, obstruct; circumvent, foil, frustrate, thwart
let down *vb* *syn* see LOWER 3
lethal *adj* *syn* see DEADLY 1
con renewing, restorative, restoring
lethality *n* *syn* see FATALITY 1
lethargic *adj* deficient in alertness or activity <became *lethargic* after taking the drug>
syn comatose, dopey, heavy, hebetudinous, sluggish, slumberous, stupid, torpid
rel dormant, idle, inactive, inert, passive, supine; apathetic, impassive, phlegmatic, spiritless, stolid; lackadaisical, languid, languorous, listless; dilatory, laggard, slow
con alert, aware, responsive; apt, prompt, quick, ready; brisk, gingery, peppery, spirited
ant energetic
lethargy *n* 1 physical and mental inertness <disgusted, he sank into a state of *lethargy*>
syn coma, dullness, hebetude, languor, lassitude, sleep, slumber, stupor, torpidity, torpidness, torpor
rel comatoseness, sluggishness; indolence, laziness, sloth, slothfulness; idleness, inactivity, inertia, inertness, passiveness, supineness; apathy, impassivity, inanition, phlegm
con aptness, promptness, quickness, readiness; alertness, quick-wittedness
ant vigor
2 *syn* see APATHY 2
lethe *n* *syn* see OBLIVION
let off *vb* *syn* see EXEMPT
let on *vb* 1 *syn* see ACKNOWLEDGE 1
2 *syn* see REVEAL 1
let out *vb* ||1 *syn* see REVEAL 1
2 *syn* see DISMISS 3
letter *n* 1 **letters** *pl* *syn* see ALPHABET 1
2 a direct or personal written or printed message addressed to a person or organization <wrote several *letters* to her friends>
syn epistle, missive, note
rel dispatch, memorandum, message, report
||**lettuce** *n* *syn* see MONEY
let up *vb* *syn* see ABATE 4

---

syn synonym(s) *rel* related word(s)
ant antonym(s) *con* contrasted word(s)
idiom idiomatic equivalent(s)
|| use limited; if in doubt, see a dictionary

levee *n* **1** ***syn*** see WHARF
2 ***syn*** see RED-LIGHT DISTRICT
level *vb* **1** ***syn*** see EVEN 1
2 ***syn*** see DIRECT 2
3 ***syn*** see FELL 1
level *adj* having a surface without bends, curves, or irregularities <looked for a *level* spot to land the plane>
syn even, flat, flush, planate, plane, smooth
rel akin, alike, identical, like, parallel, similar, uniform; aligned; regular; equal, equivalent, same
con bumpy, irregular, lumpy, uneven; unaligned, unparallel; changing, varying; fluctuating, rolling, swaying, undulating; coarse, rough
lever *vb* ***syn*** see PRY
leviathan *n* ***syn*** see GIANT
leviathan *adj* ***syn*** see HUGE
levity *n* ***syn*** see LIGHTNESS
rel absurdity, folly, foolishness, silliness
con collection, quietude, sobriety
ant gravity
levy *n* ***syn*** see TAX 1
levy *vb* to determine and require satisfaction of (as a tax or obligation) <several broad-based taxes were *levied*>
syn assess, exact, impose, put (on *or* upon)
rel extort, wrest, wring; charge, lay (on *or* upon), place, set
con remit; abate, diminish, lessen
lewd *adj* ***syn*** see LICENTIOUS 2
rel coarse, gross, obscene; improper, indecent, indelicate
con modest, proper, self-restrained; temperate
ant chaste
lexicon *n* **1** ***syn*** see VOCABULARY 1
2 ***syn*** see TERMINOLOGY
liability *n* **1** ***syn*** see DEBT 3
ant asset
2 ***syn*** see INDEBTEDNESS 1
3 ***syn*** see EXPOSURE
liable *adj* **1** ***syn*** see RESPONSIBLE
rel bound, tied
con exempt, immune; free, independent
2 being likely to be affected by some usually adverse contingency or action <without the heat shield he was *liable* to be burned>
syn exposed, obnoxious, open, prone, sensitive, subject, susceptible
rel assailable, penetrable, vulnerable; attackable, beatable, conquerable, vincible
ant unliable
3 ***syn*** see APT 1
ant unliable
liaison *n* ***syn*** see AMOUR 2
liar *n* one that tells lies <he is a compulsive *liar*>
syn Ananias, falsifier, fibber, fibster, perjurer, prevaricator, storyteller
libel *vb* ***syn*** see MALIGN
rel burlesque, caricature, travesty
libelous *adj* injurious to reputation <the campaign degenerated into an exchange of *libelous* statements>
syn backbiting, calumnious, defamatory, detracting, detractive, detractory, invidious, maligning, scandalous, slanderous, traducing, vilifying
rel depreciative, depreciatory, derogative, disparaging, pejorative; contumelious, debasing, malevolent, vituperative
con adulating, adulatory, applauding, commendatory, eulogistic, eulogizing, laudatory, praising
liberal *adj* **1** marked by generosity and openhandedness <a *liberal* allowance for his son>
syn bounteous, bountiful, free, freehanded, generous, handsome, munificent, openhanded, unsparing
rel exuberant, lavish, prodigal, profuse; benevolent, charitable, eleemosynary, philanthropic
con closefisted, miserly, niggardly, parsimonious, penurious, stingy, tight, tightfisted; meager, scanty
ant close
2 ***syn*** see PLENTIFUL
3 not bound by authoritarianism, orthodoxy, or traditional forms <modern young people usually have a *liberal* attitude toward sex>
syn advanced, broad, broad-minded, progressive, radical, tolerant, wide
rel forbearing, indulgent, lenient
con rigid, rigorous, strict, stringent; dictatorial, doctrinaire, dogmatic, oracular; conservative, reactionary
ant authoritarian
liberate *vb* ***syn*** see FREE
rel detach, unhook; untangle; disembarrass
con bind, tie; ensnare, entrap, snare, trap; constrain, restrain, restrict
libertine *adj* ***syn*** see LICENTIOUS 2
con ethical; continent, sober, temperate
ant straitlaced
liberty *n* ***syn*** see FREEDOM
rel autonomy, independence; delivery, emancipation, enfranchisement, liberation
con circumscription, confinement, limitation, restriction
ant restraint
libidinous *adj* **1** ***syn*** see LICENTIOUS 2
rel coarse, gross, obscene
2 ***syn*** see LUSTFUL 2
library *n* a place in which literary, musical, artistic, or reference materials (as books or films) are kept for use but not for sale <planned to study all evening in the *library*>
syn archive(s), athenaeum
rel reading room
license *n* ***syn*** see FREEDOM
rel laxity, looseness, relaxation, slackness
con duty, obligation; decency, propriety; continence, sobriety, temperance
ant decorum
license *vb* ***syn*** see AUTHORIZE 1
rel allow, let, permit, suffer; certify, sanction
con check, curb, restrain
ant ban
licentious *adj* **1** ***syn*** see ABANDONED 2
2 disregarding sexual restraints <a coarse *licentious* man>

syn fast, incontinent, lascivious, lecherous, lewd, libertine, libidinous, lustful, randy, salacious, satyric
rel animal, carnal, fleshly, oversexed, sensual; abandoned, dissolute, profligate, reprobate; corrupt, debauched, depraved, scabrous; amoral, immoral, unmoral; lax, loose, relaxed
con chaste, decent, pure; moral, virtuous; rigid, strict; ascetic, austere, severe
ant continent

licit *adj* ***syn*** see LAWFUL
rel approved, sanctioned; authorized, licensed
con banned, forbidden, inhibited, interdicted, prohibited
ant illicit

lick *vb* **1** ***syn*** see WHIP 2
2 ***syn*** see OVERCOME 1

lick *n* **1** ***syn*** see HINT 2
2 ***syn*** see HIT 1

lickerish *adj* ***syn*** see LUSTFUL 2

lickerishness *n* ***syn*** see LUST 2

lickety-split *adv* ***syn*** see FAST 2

licking *n* ***syn*** see DEFEAT 1

lickspit *n* ***syn*** see SYCOPHANT

lickspittle *n* ***syn*** see SYCOPHANT

lie *vb* **1** ***syn*** see REST 1
2 ***syn*** see CONSIST 1

lie *vb* to be untruthful directly or indirectly <*lying* under oath is a crime>
syn equivocate, falsify, fib, palter, prevaricate
rel beguile, deceive, delude, misguide, misinform, misinstruct, mislead; distort, exaggerate, misstate

lie *n* a statement or declaration that is not true <was sued for printing *lies* about the candidate>
syn ‖bouncer, canard, cock-and-bull story, falsehood, falsity, fib, inveracity, misrepresentation, misstatement, prevarication, ‖rapper, story, tale, taradiddle, untruism, untruth
rel deceitfulness, dishonesty, distortion, fraudulence, inaccuracy, mendacity; fable, flam, myth; falsification, forgery, libel, perjury; fish story, song and dance
con veracity, verisimilitude, verity
ant truth

lie by *vb* ***syn*** see REST 3

lied *n* ***syn*** see SONG 2

lie down *vb* ***syn*** see REST 1

liege *adj* ***syn*** see FAITHFUL 1

lieutenant *n* ***syn*** see ASSISTANT 2

life *n* **1** ***syn*** see BIOGRAPHY
2 ***syn*** see HUMAN
3 ***syn*** see SPIRIT 5

lifeless *adj* **1** ***syn*** see DEAD 1
ant living
2 ***syn*** see COLORLESS 2
ant lifeful

lifelong *adj* ***syn*** see OLD 2

lifework *n* ***syn*** see MISSION

lift *vb* **1** to remove from a lower to a higher place or position <*lifted* the sack to his shoulder>
syn elevate, hoist, pick up, raise, rear, take up, uphold, uplift, upraise, uprear
rel arise, ascend, levitate, mount, rise, rocket, soar, surge, tower; aggrandize, exalt, magnify
con decrease, diminish, lessen, reduce; abase, debase, degrade, demean, humble, humiliate; depress, oppress, weigh
ant lower
2 ***syn*** see REVOKE 2
ant invoke
3 ***syn*** see STEAL 1
4 ***syn*** see RISE 4

lift *n* **1** ***syn*** see THEFT
2 ***syn*** see HELP 1

lifted *adj* ***syn*** see ELEVATED 1

ligament *n* ***syn*** see BOND 3

ligature *n* ***syn*** see BOND 3

light *n* ***syn*** see DAWN 1

light *adj* ***syn*** see FAIR 3

light *vb* **1** to cause something to start burning <*lighted* the fuse on the dynamite>
syn enkindle, fire, ignite, inflame, kindle
con douse, ‖dout, put out, quench, snuff; damp (down), smother, stamp (out)
ant extinguish
2 ***syn*** see ILLUMINATE 1

light *adj* **1** having little weight <the package was *light*>
syn featherlight, featherweight, imponderous, lightweight, unheavy, weightless
rel inconsequential, trifling, trivial; little, petty, small; flimsy, meager, slender, slight
idiom light as a feather
con bulky, burdensome, cumbersome, huge, massive, overweight, ponderous, portly, unwieldy, weighty
ant heavy
2 ***syn*** see EASY 1
ant arduous
3 ***syn*** see FAST 7
4 ***syn*** see GIDDY 1
5 ***syn*** see LITTLE 3
6 ***syn*** see DIZZY 2

light *vb* **1** ***syn*** see ALIGHT
2 ***syn*** see HAPPEN 2

lighted *adj* ***syn*** see BURNING 1
ant unlighted, unlit

lighten *vb* ***syn*** see ILLUMINATE 1
ant darken

lighten *vb* ***syn*** see RELIEVE 1
rel attenuate, dilute, extenuate, thin
con depress, oppress, weigh

light-headed *adj* **1** ***syn*** see GIDDY 1
2 ***syn*** see DIZZY 2

lighthearted *adj* **1** ***syn*** see HAPPY-GO-LUCKY
ant heavyhearted
2 ***syn*** see GLAD 1
rel buoyant, effervescent, expansive, resilient, volatile; high-spirited, spirited; gay, lively, sprightly, vivacious
con gloomy, glum, morose, sullen
ant despondent
3 ***syn*** see MERRY

---

syn synonym(s) *rel* related word(s)
ant antonym(s) *con* contrasted word(s)
idiom idiomatic equivalent(s)
‖ use limited; if in doubt, see a dictionary

THESAURUS

ant heavyhearted

lighthouse *n* a building equipped to guide sea navigators by means of a powerful light <rowed out to the *lighthouse*>
syn beacon, pharos
rel direction, guidance

lightless *adj* ***syn*** see DARK 1
ant bright, ‖lightful

lightly *adv* ***syn*** see EASILY 1

light-mindedness *n* ***syn*** see LIGHTNESS

lightness *n* gaiety or indifference where seriousness and attention are called for <a crisis that allowed no room for *lightness*>
syn flightiness, flippancy, frivolity, levity, light-mindedness, volatility
rel buoyancy, effervescence, elasticity, expansiveness, resiliency; gaiety, liveliness, vivacity; cheerfulness, lightheartedness
con earnestness, gravity, sedateness, soberness, somberness, staidness
ant seriousness

light-o'-love *n* ***syn*** see DOXY 1

light out *vb* ***syn*** see HEAD 3

lightsome *adj* **1** ***syn*** see CHEERFUL 1
2 ***syn*** see HAPPY-GO-LUCKY

lightweight *adj* ***syn*** see LIGHT 1

like *vb* **1** ***syn*** see ENJOY 1
rel choose, elect, prefer, select; admire, esteem, regard, respect; approve, endorse; appreciate, comprehend, understand
ant dislike
2 ***syn*** see WILL

like *adj* being so similar as to appear to be the same or nearly the same (as in appearance, character, or quantity) <shirts of *like* design>
syn agnate, akin, alike, analogous, comparable, consonant, corresponding, equivalent, intercomparable, parallel, similar, such, suchlike, undifferenced, undifferentiated, uniform; *compare* SAME 2
rel equal, equivalent, identical, same, selfsame; allied, cognate, close, related, resembling; coextensive, commensurate
idiom of that ilk, on the order of
con different, disparate, divergent, diverse, various; dissimilar, distinct; discordant, discrepant, inconsistent, inconsonant
ant unlike

like *n* ***syn*** see EQUAL

likely *adj* **1** ***syn*** see PROBABLE
con problematic; certain, inevitable, necessary
ant unlikely
2 ***syn*** see APT 1
ant unlikely
3 ***syn*** see HOPEFUL 2

likely *adv* ***syn*** see PRESUMABLY

liken *vb* ***syn*** see EQUATE 2

likeness *n* agreement or correspondence in details (as of appearance, structure, or quality) <the remarkable *likeness* of the two cousins>
syn affinity, alikeness, analogy, comparison, resemblance, semblance, similarity, simile, similitude
rel equality, equivalence, identicalness, identity, sameness; agreement, conformity, correspondence; analogousness, comparableness, parallelism, uniformity
con difference, dissimilarity, distinction, divergence, divergency; disaffinity, opposition
ant unlikeness

likewise *adv* **1** ***syn*** see ALSO 1
2 ***syn*** see ALSO 2

liking *n* **1** ***syn*** see APPETITE 3
ant disliking
2 ***syn*** see WILL 1

lilliputian *adj* ***syn*** TINY, diminutive, minute, teensy, teensy-weensy, teenty, teeny, teeny-weeny, wee, weeny
ant Brobdingnagian

lilliputian *n* ***syn*** see DWARF

lily-livered *adj* ***syn*** see COWARDLY

lily-white *adj* ***syn*** see GOOD 11

limb *n* **1** a member of a woody plant that is an outgrowth from a main stem or from one of its divisions <hung the swing from a tree's *limb*>
syn bough, branch
rel shoot, spray, sprig, switch, twig; arm
2 ***syn*** see SCAMP

limber *adj* ***syn*** see SUPPLE 3
rel plastic, pliable, pliant; elastic, flexible, resilient, springy
con inflexible, rigid, stark, stiff, tense, wooden

limit *n* **1** a material or immaterial point beyond which something does not or cannot extend <there seemed no *limit* to the problems they faced>
syn bound, confine(s), end, limitation, term; *compare* ENVIRONS 1
rel circumscription, confinement, restriction, termination; border, brim, brink, edge, margin, rim, verge
2 limits *pl* ***syn*** see ENVIRONS 1
3 ***syn*** see EXTREME 2

limit *vb* **1** ***syn*** see DEMARCATE 1
2 to prescribe or serve as a restricting boundary <*limited* the naughty child to the house for three days> <ignorance that *limits* spiritual growth>
syn bar, circumscribe, confine, delimit, delimitate, prelimit, restrict
rel constrict, contract, lessen, narrow, pinch; check, curb, hinder, inhibit, restrain; appoint, assign, define, prescribe, set
con enlarge, expand, extend, increase, widen; develop, grow
ant broaden

limitation *n* **1** ***syn*** see LIMIT 1
2 ***syn*** see RESTRICTION 1

limited *adj* **1** ***syn*** see DEFINITE 1
rel inexhaustive, inextensive
con boundless, infinite
ant unlimited
2 ***syn*** see FINITE
3 ***syn*** see QUALIFIED 2
4 ***syn*** see LITTLE 2

limitless *adj* having no limits <the *limitless* black of deep space>
syn boundless, endless, immeasurable, indefinite, infinite, measureless, unbounded, unlimited, unmeasured

rel bottomless, countless, incalculable, incomprehensible, inexhaustible, innumerable, undrainable, unfathomable, vast, wasteless
con bound, bounded, finite, fixed, limited, measurable; comprehensible, fathomable; confined, restricted
ant limited

limn *vb* ***syn*** see REPRESENT 1

limp *vb* **1** to walk lamely <*limped* across the floor after his fall>
syn halt, hitch, hobble
rel toddle, totter, waddle; falter, stagger, stumble, wobble
2 ***syn*** see STUMBLE 6

limp *adj* **1** deficient in firmness of texture, substance, or structure <plants going *limp* from lack of water>
syn flabby, flaccid, flimsy, floppy, sleazy
rel lax, loose, relaxed, slack; limber, supple
con inflexible, rigid, stark, stiff, tense, wooden; firm, hard, solid; brittle, crisp
2 ***syn*** see LANGUID

limpid *adj* ***syn*** see TRANSPARENT 1

limpidity *n* ***syn*** see CLARITY

line *n* **1** ***syn*** see WAY 2
2 ***syn*** see COURSE 3
3 ***syn*** see WORK 1
||**4** ***syn*** see SPIEL
5 a series of things arranged in continuous or uniform order <a *line* of cars waiting at the light>
syn echelon, file, queue, rank, row, string, tier
rel column, progression, succession, train; sequence, series
6 ***syn*** see OUTLINE
7 ***syn*** see MERCHANDISE

line *vb* **1** to arrange in a line or lines <*lined* the bottles along the shelf>
syn align, allineate, line up, range
rel arrange, array, marshal, order, ordinate
con derange, disarrange, disorder, disturb; disperse, dissipate, scatter
2 ***syn*** see ADJOIN

lineage *n* **1** ***syn*** see ANCESTRY
2 ***syn*** see FAMILY 1

lineal *adj* ***syn*** see DIRECT 1

lineament *n* ***syn*** see OUTLINE

lineation *n* ***syn*** see OUTLINE

line up *vb* ***syn*** see LINE 1

linger *vb* **1** ***syn*** see STAY 2
2 ***syn*** see DELAY 2
3 ***syn*** see SAUNTER

lingerer *n* ***syn*** see LAGGARD

lingo *n* ***syn*** see DIALECT 2

link *n* ***syn*** see BOND 3

link *vb* ***syn*** see JOIN 1

lint *n* ***syn*** see DOWN

lion *n* ***syn*** see NOTABLE 1

lionhearted *adj* ***syn*** see BRAVE 1

||**lip** *n* ***syn*** see BACK TALK

lip *vb* **1** ***syn*** see KISS 1
2 ***syn*** see BATHE 2

lip server *n* ***syn*** see HYPOCRITE

liquefy *vb* to convert or to become converted to a liquid state <*liquefy* a block of ice by heating>
syn deliquesce, dissolve, flux, fuse, liquesce, melt, run, thaw
rel soften; thin
con clot, coagulate, congeal; harden, set; gel, jellify, jelly; condense, inspissate, thicken
ant solidify

liquesce *vb* ***syn*** see LIQUEFY

liquid *adj* ***syn*** see MELLIFLUOUS

liquidate *vb* **1** ***syn*** see CLEAR 5
2 ***syn*** see PURGE 3
3 ***syn*** see MURDER 1

liquor *n* **1** ***syn*** see DRINK 1
2 an intoxicating beverage usually distilled after being fermented <belted down a slug of *liquor*>
syn alcohol, aqua vitae, booze, ||budge, drink, firewater, grog, ||hooch, inebriant, intoxicant, ||joy-juice, ||juice, ||lush, ||sauce, spirit(s), ||strunt, tipple
idiom Demon Rum, the bottle

liquor (up) *vb* ***syn*** see DRINK 3

lissome *adj* ***syn*** see SUPPLE 3

list *n* a series of items (as names) written down or printed especially as a memorandum or record <all the people on the *list* were present>
syn catalog, register, roll, roll call, roster, schedule
rel checklist, handlist; index; inventory

list *vb* **1** ***syn*** see ENUMERATE 2
2 ***syn*** see ITEMIZE 1
3 to enter in a list <his name was not *listed* in the telephone book>
syn book, catalog, enroll, inscribe
rel file, index, note, post, schedule, tabulate; record, register, roster
4 ***syn*** see ENROLL 1

list *vb* ***syn*** see SLANT 1

listen *vb* to perceive by ear usually with careful or responsive attention <now hear me; *listen* to my words>
syn attend, hark, hear, hearken, heed
idiom give a hearing to, give ear to, hang upon the lips (*or* words) of, keep one's ears open, lend one's (*or* an) ear, prick up one's ears, strain one's ears

listless *adj* ***syn*** see LANGUID
rel careless, heedless, thoughtless
con agog, anxious, avid, keen; alert, vigilant, watchful; energetic, lusty, vigorous; prompt, quick, ready
ant eager

listlessness *n* ***syn*** see APATHY 2

||**lit** *adj* ***syn*** see INTOXICATED 1

literal *adj* ***syn*** see VERBATIM

literally *adv* ***syn*** see VERBATIM

literati *n pl* ***syn*** see INTELLIGENTSIA

literatim *adv* ***syn*** see VERBATIM

lithe *adj* ***syn*** see SUPPLE 3
rel slender, slight, slim, thin; lean, spare

syn synonym(s) *rel* related word(s)
ant antonym(s) *con* contrasted word(s)
idiom idiomatic equivalent(s)
|| use limited; if in doubt, see a dictionary

con awkward, clumsy, gauche, inept, maladroit; inflexible, stiff, tense, wooden

lithesome *adj* ***syn*** see SUPPLE 3

litigious *adj* ***syn*** see CONTENTIOUS 2

litter *n* **1** ***syn*** see REFUSE

2 ***syn*** see CLUTTER 2

little *adj* **1** ***syn*** see SMALL 1

ant big

2 contemptibly limited <men with *little* minds picking at flaws in a great leader>

syn borné, ineffectual, limited, mean, narrow, paltry, set, small

rel bigoted, hidebound, illiberal, narrow-minded, provincial; contemptible; niggard, niggardly, self-centered, selfish

ant great

3 lacking importance <the nagging *little* details of a job>

syn casual, inconsiderable, insignificant, light, minor, minute, petty, ‖potty, shoestring, small, small-beer, trivial, unimportant; *compare* PETTY 2

rel fortuitous; incidental; collateral, secondary, subordinate, subsidiary

con consequential, meaningful, significant, substantial, weighty; basal, basic, essential, foundational, fundamental

ant important

little *adv* ***syn*** see SELDOM

ant much

little by little *adv* ***syn*** see GRADUALLY

‖little woman *n* ***syn*** see WIFE

‖lit up *adj* ***syn*** see INTOXICATED 1

liturgy *n* **1** ***syn*** see FORM 2

2 ***syn*** see RITE 2

livable *adj* **1** suitable for living <a very *livable* apartment>

syn habitable, inhabitable, lodgeable, occupiable, tenantable

rel cozy, homelike, homey, snug; acceptable, bearable, tolerable

ant unlivable

2 ***syn*** see BEARABLE

live *vb* **1** ***syn*** see BE

2 ***syn*** see RESIDE 1

live *adj* ***syn*** see ACTIVE 1

rel effective, effectual, efficacious, efficient

ant inactive, inert; dormant (*as a volcano*); defunct (*as an institution, journal*)

livelihood *n* ***syn*** see LIVING

rel art, craft, handicraft, profession, trade; emolument, fee, pay, salary, stipend, wage

lively *adj* **1** keenly alive and brisk <always thought of as a *lively* teacher>

syn alert, animate, animated, bright, ‖cant, ‖canty, chipper, ‖chirk, dashing, gay, keen, ‖peart, peppy, pert, rousing, spirited, ‖spirity, sprightful, sprightly, unpedantic, vivacious; *compare* CHEERFUL 1

rel agile, brisk, nimble, spry; buoyant, effervescent, elastic, expansive, resilient, volatile; blithe, cock-a-hoop, jocund, jolly, merry; gleeful, hilarious, mirthful; chirping, chirpy, chirrupy

con lethargic, sluggish, torpid; lackadaisical, languid, languorous, listless; apathetic, impassive, phlegmatic, stolid; boring, irksome, tedious

ant dull, unlively

2 ***syn*** see AGILE

idiom full of pep

3 ***syn*** see ENERGETIC 2

4 ***syn*** see BUSTLING

ant unanimated

liven *vb* ***syn*** see QUICKEN 1

liver *n* ***syn*** see INHABITANT

live wire *n* ***syn*** see HUSTLER 1

livid *adj* **1** ***syn*** see PALE 1

rel grisly; dusky, gloomy, murky

con bright, brilliant, effulgent, lucent, luminous, lustrous, radiant

2 ***syn*** see SENSATIONAL 2

living *adj* **1** having or showing life <the *living* things of a locality>

syn alive, animate, animated, vital, zoetic

rel being, existing, subsisting; active, dynamic, live, operative

con dead, deceased, defunct, demised, departed, gone, inanimate

ant lifeless

2 ***syn*** see EXTANT 1

living *n* supplies or resources needed to live <kept trying to earn a *living* the honest way>

syn alimenation, alimony, bread, bread and butter, keep, livelihood, maintenance, salt, subsistence, support, sustenance

rel sustainment, sustentation

load *n* **1** something which is carried, conveyed, or transported from one place to another <a *load* of grain just arrived>

syn burden, cargo, freight, haul, lading, payload

rel bale, pack, parcel, shipment

2 something heavy <could not lift the *load*>

syn weight

3 a burdensome or laborious responsibility <considered taking care of the children a heavy *load*>

syn burden, charge, deadweight, duty, millstone, onus, task, tax, weight

rel care, liability, obligation, responsibility; drag, drain, pressure

idiom millstone around one's neck

con breeze, child's play, cinch, duck soup, picnic, ‖pipe, pushover, snap

ant sinecure

4 *usu* **loads** *pl* ***syn*** see SCAD

load *vb* **1** ***syn*** see BURDEN

rel bear, carry, convey, transport

ant unload

2 ***syn*** see ADULTERATE

3 to make full or overfull <a basket *loaded* with fresh fruit>

syn charge, choke, fill, heap, pack, pile; *compare* CRAM 1

rel glut, gorge, surfeit; flood, oversupply, swamp

loaded *adj* **1** ***syn*** see FULL 1

‖**2** ***syn*** see INTOXICATED 1

loaf *vb* ***syn*** see IDLE

con labor, toil, travail, work

loafer *n* ***syn*** see SLUGGARD

loan *vb* ***syn*** see LEND

loan shark *n* one who lends money to individuals at exorbitant rates of interest <got involved with *loan sharks*>
syn Shylock, usurer
rel lender, loaner, moneylender; shark
loath *adj* *syn* see DISINCLINED
ant anxious
loathe *vb* *syn* see HATE
rel decline, refuse, reject, repudiate, spurn
con covet, crave, desire, want, wish
ant tolerate
loathing *n* *syn* see ABOMINATION 2
ant tolerance
loathsome *adj* *syn* see OFFENSIVE
rel hateful, invidious, obnoxious
con bearable, endurable, sufferable, supportable; engaging, inviting; alluring, bewitching, charming, enchanting, fascinating
ant tolerable
lobby *n* *syn* see VESTIBULE
lobster *n* *syn* see OAF 2
local *adj* *syn* see INSULAR
ant cosmopolitan
locale *n* *syn* see SCENE 3
rel area, district, neighborhood, vicinage, vicinity
locality *n* **1** a more or less definitely circumscribed place or region <searched for the child in the *locality* of the waterfront>
syn area, district, neighborhood, vicinage, vicinity
rel belt, region, tract, zone; section, sector; bailiwick, domain, field, province, sphere, territory
idiom neck of the woods
2 *syn* see HABITAT
located *adj* *syn* see SITUATED
location *n* *syn* see PLACE 1
||**loch** *n* *syn* see INLET
lockup *n* *syn* see JAIL
||**loco** *adj* *syn* see INSANE 1
locum tenens *n* *syn* see SUBSTITUTE 1
locus *n* *syn* see PLACE 1
locution *n* *syn* see PHRASE 2
lodge *vb* **1** *syn* see HARBOR 2
rel accept, admit, receive, take; accommodate, contain, hold
2 *syn* see ENTRENCH 1
lodge *n* **1** *syn* see HUT
2 *syn* see HOTEL
3 *syn* see LAIR 1
lodgeable *adj* *syn* see LIVABLE 1
lodging *n* **1** *syn* see ACCOMMODATIONS
2 *usu* **lodgings** *pl* *syn* see APARTMENT 1
lodgment *n* *syn* see ACCOMMODATIONS
loftiest *adj* *syn* see TOP 1
loftiness *n* *syn* see PRIDE 3
lofty *adj* **1** *syn* see PROUD 1
2 *syn* see AMBITIOUS 2
3 *syn* see GRAND 3
4 *syn* see GENEROUS 1
5 *syn* see ELEVATED 4
6 extending or rising high in the air so as to have great or imposing height <a *lofty* monument to human aspiration>
syn aerial, airy, skyscraping, soaring, spiring, topless, towering, towery; *compare* HIGH 1
rel elevated, lifted, raised; aggrandized, exalted, magnified; august, imposing, majestic, stately
con humble, low, modest
logical *adj* **1** *syn* see RATIONAL
ant illogical
2 having or showing skill in thinking or reasoning <a *logical* argument>
syn analytic, analytical, ratiocinative, subtle
rel cogent, compelling, convincing, sound, telling, valid; clear, lucid, perspicuous; rational, reasonable; discriminating
con instinctive, intuitive; irrational, unreasonable; casuistical, sophistical
ant illogical
logo *n* *syn* see MARK 7
logotype *n* *syn* see MARK 7
loiter *vb* **1** *syn* see DELAY 2
2 *syn* see IDLE
loiterer *n* *syn* see LAGGARD
loll *vb* **1** *syn* see SLOUCH
2 *syn* see IDLE
||**lollop** *vb* *syn* see SLOUCH
lone *adj* **1** having no company <a *lone* figure walking through the snow>
syn alone, lonely, lonesome, solitary
rel single, sole, unique; abandoned, deserted, forsaken; isolated, secluded
con attended, chaperoned, companioned, convoyed, escorted
ant accompanied
2 *syn* see ONLY 2
3 *syn* see SINGLE 2
lonely *adj* **1** *syn* see LONE 1
2 *syn* see FORLORN 1
loneness *n* *syn* see SOLITUDE
lonesome *adj* **1** *syn* see LONE 1
2 *syn* see FORLORN 1
3 *syn* see OBSCURE 2
long *adj* **1** having considerable extension in space or time <a *long* road> <it has been a *long* time since we have seen you>
syn elongate, elongated, extended, lengthy
rel extensive, longish, outstretched
con brief, curtailed
ant short
2 unduly extended <went through many *long* days of misery>
syn dragging, drawn-out, ||dreich, lengthy, long-drawn-out, longsome, overlong, prolonged, protracted
rel diffuse, diffusive, long-winded, prolix; flatulent, verbose, wordy
con ephemeral, evanescent, fleeting, fugacious, fugitive, impermanent, passing, short-lived, transient, transitory; abbreviated, abridged, curtailed, shortened
ant brief

---

syn synonym(s) *rel* related word(s)
ant antonym(s) *con* contrasted word(s)
idiom idiomatic equivalent(s)
|| use limited; if in doubt, see a dictionary

long *n* ***syn*** see AGE 2

long *vb* to desire urgently <*long* for peace>
syn ache, crave, dream, hanker, hunger, itch, lust, pine, sigh, suspire, thirst, yearn, yen
rel aim, aspire, want; miss
idiom have an appetite (*or* a longing) for
con abhor, detest, dread, fear, loathe

longanimity *n* ***syn*** see PATIENCE

long-drawn-out *adj* ***syn*** see LONG 2
ant short; curtailed

‖long green *n* ***syn*** see MONEY

longitudinally *adv* ***syn*** see LENGTHWISE
ant horizontally

long-lasting *adj* ***syn*** see OLD 2
ant ephemeral

long-lived *adj* ***syn*** see OLD 2
ant short-lived

longsome *adj* ***syn*** see LONG 2

long–suffering *n* ***syn*** see PATIENCE
rel subduedness; humility, lowliness, meekness
con impatience, uneasiness; irksomeness, tediousness, wearisomeness; boredom, ennui, tedium

long suit *n* ***syn*** see FORTE
rel specialism, specialization, specialty

longtimer *n* ***syn*** see VETERAN
con apprentice, neophyte, novice; newcomer, rookie, tenderfoot

‖long tongue *n* ***syn*** see GOSSIP 1

longways *adv* ***syn*** see LENGTHWISE

long–winded *adj* ***syn*** see WORDY
rel extended, lasting, lengthy, long, long-drawn-out, prolonged, protracted
con brief, close, compact

longwise *adv* ***syn*** see LENGTHWISE

‖loo *n* ***syn*** see TOILET

looby *n* ***syn*** see OAF 2

look *vb* **1** to make sure or take care (that something is or is not done) <*look* that you accuse no one unjustly>
syn mind, see, watch
rel attend, heed, tend; note, notice, observe; beware
2 ***syn*** see SEE 2
rel note, notice, observe, spot
idiom get a load of, take a gander at
3 ***syn*** see EXPECT 1
rel divine, forecast, foretell
ant despair (of)
4 to make apparent by the expression of the eyes or countenance <*looked* her annoyance at this interruption>
syn exhibit, show; *compare* SHOW 2
rel display, express, indicate, manifest
5 ***syn*** see SEEM
idiom strike one as
6 ***syn*** see FACE 1
7 to gaze in wonder or surprise <you should have seen them *look*>
syn eye, gape, ‖gaup (*or* gawp), gaze, goggle, ogle, rubberneck, stare; *compare* GAZE 1
rel gawk; glare, gloat, glower; peer
8 ***syn*** see TEND 1

look (at *or* upon) *vb* ***syn*** see EYE 1

look (into) *vb* ***syn*** see EXPLORE

look *n* **1** the directing of one's eyes in order to see <he wanted one last *look* before departing>
syn sight, view
rel glance, glimpse, peek, peep, squint; cast, slant; eye, ‖gander, ‖look-see, regard; eyeful, gaze, stare, survey
2 facial aspect especially as indicative of mood or feeling <you should have seen the *look* on her face>
syn cast, countenance, expression, face, visage
rel mug, physiognomy, ‖puss
3 ***syn*** see APPEARANCE 1

look down *vb* **1** ***syn*** see OVERLOOK 2
2 ***syn*** see DESPISE
3 ***syn*** see STARE DOWN

looker *n* ***syn*** see BEAUTY

looker–on *n* ***syn*** see SPECTATOR

look in *vb* ***syn*** see VISIT 2

look–in *n* ***syn*** see OPPORTUNITY

looking glass *n* ***syn*** see MIRROR 1

look out *vb* ***syn*** see BEWARE

lookout *n* **1** ***syn*** see GUARD 2
2 an elevated place affording a wide view for observation <guards posted at a *lookout* to watch for enemy troops entering the valley>
syn observatory, outlook, overlook
rel watchtower; crow's nest; cupola, widow's walk; fire tower
3 a careful looking or watching <kept a constant *lookout* for new developments>
syn surveillance, tout, vigil, vigilance, watch, watch and ward
rel observance, observation
4 ***syn*** see VISTA
5 ***syn*** see BUSINESS 8

look up *vb* **1** ***syn*** see IMPROVE 3
2 ***syn*** see VISIT 2

loom *vb* **1** ***syn*** see APPEAR 1
2 to take shape as an impending occurrence <an international economic crisis *looms* ahead>
syn brew, forthcome, gather, impend
rel approach, come on, make up, near
con disappear, fade, pass, vanish; die (down *or* away), diminish, dwindle, wane; recede, retreat, withdraw
3 to appear in an impressively great or exaggerated form <the power of the enemy *loomed* in the soldiers' imagination>
syn bulk, stand out
rel lower, rear, threaten, tower
con die (down *or* away), diminish, dwindle, wane

loon *n* ***syn*** see LUNATIC 1

loony *adj* **1** ***syn*** see FOOLISH 2
2 ***syn*** see INSANE 1

loony *n* ***syn*** see LUNATIC 1

loony bin *n* ***syn*** see ASYLUM 3

loop *n* **1** a curving or doubling of a line so as to form a closed or partly open curve <the transit makes a *loop* around town>
syn eye, ring
rel circlet, circuit, circumference, hoop, wreath; curve

2 a circular or curved piece used often to form a fastening or a handle <one of his belt *loops* is broken>
syn eye, ring, staple
rel hook
3 ***syn*** see LEAGUE 4

loop *vb* ***syn*** see SURROUND 1
rel arc, arch, bend, coil, curve

looped *adj* ***syn*** see INTOXICATED 1

loopy *adj* ***syn*** see FOOLISH 2

loose *adj* **1** not tightly bound, held, restrained, or stretched <*loose* rope>
syn lax, relaxed, slack
rel detached, free; flabby, flaccid, limp; desultory, negligent, remiss
con rigid, rigorous, stringent, taut, tense; exact, precise; bound, checked, curbed, inhibited, restrained, tied
ant strict; tight
2 ***syn*** see FREE 2
rel clear; disconnected, unattached, unconnected, undone, unfastened
con fast
3 not dense, close, or compact in structure <*loose* soil>
syn incoherent, nonadhesive
rel disconnected, disjointed, separate, unconnected
con compressed, condensed, contracted; concentrated, crammed, crowded, localized; close, compact, dense, thick
4 ***syn*** see FAST 7
rel capricious, extravagant, free, inconstant, reckless, unrestrained

loose *vb* **1** ***syn*** see FREE
2 ***syn*** see TAKE OUT (on)
3 to set free from a fastened or fixed condition <*loose* a knot>
syn disengage, unbind, undo, unfasten, unfix, unloose, unloosen
rel unbandage, unbar, unbolt, unbuckle, unbutton, unchain, unclasp, unglue, unhitch, unhook, unlace, unlash, unlatch, unlock, unpin, unscrew, unsnap, unstick, unstrap, untie
con bind, engage, fasten, fix, secure
4 ***syn*** see SHOOT 1
5 to make less rigid or tight <exercise *loosed* his muscles>
syn ease, ease off, lax, loosen, relax, slack, slacken, untighten
rel abate, alleviate, bate, lessen, let up, mitigate
con anchor, cement, clamp, clinch, fasten, knit, secure, set, tauten
ant tighten

loose–lipped *adj* ***syn*** see TALKATIVE
ant closemouthed

loosen *vb* **1** ***syn*** see LOOSE 5
ant tighten
2 ***syn*** see FREE

loosen up *vb* ***syn*** see RELAX 2
ant tighten (up)

loose–tongued *adj* ***syn*** see TALKATIVE
ant closemouthed

loot *n* **1** ***syn*** see SPOIL
rel lift, pillage, seizure
2 ***syn*** see MONEY

loot *vb* ***syn*** see ROB 1

looter *n* ***syn*** see MARAUDER

lop *vb* **1** ***syn*** see SLOUCH
2 ***syn*** see JUMP 1

lope *vb* ***syn*** see SKIP 1
rel run, sprint; romp, trip

||**lopper** *vb* ***syn*** see CURDLE

lopsided *adj* lacking in balance, symmetry, or proportion <the arrangement of the furniture was *lopsided*>
syn asymmetric, difform, disproportional, disproportionate, irregular, nonsymmetrical, off=balance, overbalanced, proportionless, unbalanced, unequal, uneven, unproportionate, unsymmetrical
rel cockeyed, crooked, top-heavy, unsteady
con balanced, even, regular, symmetrical

loquacious *adj* ***syn*** see TALKATIVE
rel jabbering, overtalkative; prolix, verbose, wordy
con breviloquent, concise, succinct, taciturn, terse; abrupt, brusque, curt

lord *n* ***syn*** see HUSBAND

lord *vb* to affect an air of superiority and authority <nouveau riche love to *lord* it>
syn cock, peacock, pontificate, swagger, swank, swell
rel affect, pretend, put on; boss, order (about *or* around), overawe, overbear; tyrannize
idiom put on airs

Lord Harry *n* ***syn*** see DEVIL 1

lordly *adj* **1** ***syn*** see GRAND 1
2 ***syn*** see PROUD 1
rel egotistic, puffed; affected, snobbish, swollen; authoritarian, dictatorial, magisterial
con humble; abject, mean; subdued, submissive

lore *n* **1** ***syn*** see KNOWLEDGE 2
2 a body of traditions relating to a person, institution, or place <the Scottish Highlands are rich in local *lore*>
syn folklore, legend, myth, mythology, mythos, tradition
rel custom, folkway, traditionalism; fable, old wives' tale, saga, superstition, tale

Lorelei *n* ***syn*** see SIREN

lorn *adj* **1** ***syn*** see DERELICT 1
2 ***syn*** see FORLORN 1

lose *vb* **1** to suffer deprivation of <*lost* all his savings in a poor investment>
syn drop, forfeit, sacrifice
rel mislay, misplace, miss; give up, relinquish, surrender, yield
con cash in, profit; clear, make, realize, take in; obtain, win
ant gain
2 to fail to win, gain, or obtain <*lost* every contest she entered>

---

syn synonym(s) ***rel*** related word(s)
ant antonym(s) ***con*** contrasted word(s)
idiom idiomatic equivalent(s)
|| use limited; if in doubt, see a dictionary

syn drop, lose out
rel decline, fall, succumb, yield
ant win
3 *syn* see DEPRIVE 2
4 *syn* see SHAKE 5
5 *syn* see RID

lose out *vb syn* see LOSE 2

loser *n* **1** *syn* see FAILURE 5
rel also-ran, underdog
ant winner
2 *syn* see CONVICT

losing *n syn* see LOSS 1

loss *n* **1** the action of having something go out of one's control or possession <took precautions against *loss* or theft of his property>
syn losing, mislaying, misplacement, misplacing; *compare* PRIVATION 2
rel forfeit, forfeiture, sacrifice; bereavement, deprivation, deprivement, dispossession, divestiture, divestment, privation
2 *syn* see PRIVATION 2
3 *syn* see RUIN 3

lost *adj* **1** *syn* see DAMNED 1
rel incorrigible, irreclaimable, irredeemable, irreformable, unconverted, unregenerate; graceless
2 no longer possessed <earned his *lost* reputation by his outrageous behavior>
syn gone, missing
rel absent, lacking; past; irrecoverable, irretrievable, irrevocable
con cherished, protected, treasured
3 *syn* see EXTINCT 2
4 *syn* see ABSTRACTED
rel absorbed; daydreamy, musing, unconscious

lot *n* **1** *syn* see SHARE 1
2 *syn* see FATE
rel decree, fortune; foreordination, predestination, predetermination
3 a measured portion of land having fixed boundaries <building *lots*>
syn parcel, plat, plot, tract
rel clearing, field, patch; part, plottage; block, frontage, real estate
4 *syn* see GROUP 3
rel aggregate, aggregation, conglomerate, conglomeration
5 *syn* see SET 5
6 *syn* see TYPE
7 *syn* see MUCH

lot *vb syn* see ALLOT

||**lot** (on *or* upon) *vb syn* see RELY (on *or* upon)

lot (out) *vb syn* see DISTRIBUTE 1

lothario *n syn* see GALLANT 2

loud *adj* **1** marked by intensity or volume of sound <a *loud* blast on a trumpet>
syn blaring, earsplitting, full-mouthed, piercing, roaring, stentorian, stentorious, stentorophonic
rel booming, deafening, ear-piercing, fulminating, pealing, ringing, thunderous; resonant, resounding, sonorous; harsh, hoarse, raucous, stertorous, strident
con dulcet, gentle, mellifluous, mellow, quiet, smooth
ant low, soft
2 *syn* see GAUDY
rel brassy, vulgar; obnoxious, offensive; obtrusive

loudmouthed *adj syn* see VOCIFEROUS

||**lough** *n syn* see INLET

lounge *vb syn* see IDLE
rel drift, vegetate; dally, slack; lie, lie down, recline

lounge *n syn* see BAR 5

lounge car *n syn* see PARLOR CAR

lounge lizard *n* **1** *syn* see FOP
2 *syn* see PARASITE

louse *n syn* see SNOT 1

louse up *vb syn* see BOTCH

lout *n syn* see OAF 2
rel boor, bumpkin, churl, clodhopper, hayseed, hick, peasant, rube, rustic, yokel; dolt

lout *vb syn* see RIDICULE

loutish *adj syn* see BOORISH
rel awkward, bungling, clumsy, inept, maladroit, rusty; callow, crude, gauche, raw, rough, uncouth

lovable *adj* gifted with traits and qualities that attract affection <a *lovable* child>
syn adorable, lovesome
rel admirable, agreeable, attractive, desirable, genial, likable, pleasing, winning, winsome; alluring, appealing, bewitching, captivating, charming, enchanting, engaging, enthralling, entrancing, fetching, ravishing, seductive
con dislikable, displeasing, distasteful, unattractive, unlikable, unpleasing; odious, offensive; abhorrent, abominable, obnoxious, repellent; contemptible, despicable, detestable
ant hateful; unlovable

love *n* **1** the feeling which animates a person who is genuinely fond of someone or something <a mother's *love* for her child>
syn affection, attachment, devotion, fondness
rel like(s), liking, regard; adoration, idolatry, piety, worship; allegiance, fealty, fidelity, loyalty; emotion, sentiment; crush, infatuation, passion, yearning; ardency, ardor, enthusiasm, fervor, zeal
con antipathy, aversion; animosity, animus, enmity, hostility, rancor; abhorrence, detestation, hatred
ant hate
2 the affection and tenderness felt by lovers <the ability to distinguish between *love* and lust was the mark of her maturity>
syn amorousness, amour, passion
rel crush, infatuation; desire, lust, yearning; ardency, ardor, fervor
idiom (the) tender passion
3 *syn* see LOVE AFFAIR
4 *syn* see SWEETHEART 1

love *vb* **1** to like or desire actively <she *loves* her material possessions all too dearly>
syn adore, delight (in), ||eat up
rel appreciate, cherish, prize, treasure, value; dote (on *or* upon), fancy
idiom hold dear

con abjure, give up, reject, relinquish
2 to feel a lover's passion, devotion, or tenderness for <in spite of all their misfortunes, they continued to *love* each other devotedly>
syn adore, affection, worship
rel deify, exalt, idolize, revere, venerate; cherish, dote (on *or* upon); admire, fancy, like
con avoid, disregard, ignore, neglect, overlook, shun, slight
3 ***syn*** see CARESS

love affair *n* a romantic attachment or episode between lovers <saddened by the end of a summer *love affair*>
syn affair, amour, love, romance
rel flirtation, intrigue; triangle, ménage à trois

love child *n* ***syn*** see BASTARD 1

loved *adj* ***syn*** see FAVORITE 1

love letter *n* a letter expressing a lover's affection <she had never received a *love letter*>
syn billet-doux, mash note
rel valentine

loveling *n* ***syn*** see SWEETHEART 1

lovely *adj* ***syn*** see BEAUTIFUL
rel alluring, bewitching, captivating, charming, enchanting, engaging, entrancing, lovesome; delectable, delightful; dainty, delicate, exquisite, rare; graceful
ant hideous; unlovely

lovely *n* ***syn*** see BEAUTY

lover *n* **1** a man who is a woman's regular partner in nonmarital sexual activity
syn boyfriend, fancy man, man, master, paramour
rel cavalier servente, sugar daddy
2 ***syn*** see BOYFRIEND 2
3 ***syn*** see ADDICT
4 ***syn*** see MISTRESS

lovesome *adj* **1** ***syn*** see LOVABLE
2 ***syn*** see LOVING

lovey-dovey *adj* ***syn*** see SENTIMENTAL

loving *adj* feeling or expressing love <his *loving* son unfailingly waited upon him during his last years>
syn affectionate, dear, devoted, doting, fond, lovesome
rel adoring, attached, benevolent, cordial, kind, tender, warmhearted; attentive, caring, considerate, solicitous; amatory, amorous, erotic; enamored, infatuated; ardent, fervent, impassioned, passionate; faithful; bound up
con aloof, detached, indifferent, unconcerned; chilly, cold, frigid
ant unloving

low *adj* ‖**1** ***syn*** see SHORT 2
rel squatty; unelevated
2 ***syn*** see INFERIOR 1
3 ***syn*** see POOR 1
4 ***syn*** see IGNOBLE 1
rel lowbred, rude
5 ***syn*** see BASE 3
rel scrubby, scruffy; miserable, woebegone, woeful
con decent, decorous, proper, seemly; ethical, moral, noble; high, lofty
6 ***syn*** see COARSE 3
7 ***syn*** see UNWELL
rel declining, weak; dizzy, faint, feverish
8 ***syn*** see DOWNCAST
9 of lesser degree, size, or amount than average or ordinary <the energy crisis resulted in *lower* speed limits for all vehicles>
syn subaverage, subnormal
rel fallen, reduced; brief, short; mediocre, moderate; atypical
10 ***syn*** see CHEAP 1
rel economical; moderate, nominal; cut, cut-rate, marked down, slashed
con elevated, enhanced, increased, raised

lowborn *adj* ***syn*** see IGNOBLE 1
ant highborn

lowbred *adj* ***syn*** see BOORISH
ant highbred

low-cost *adj* ***syn*** see CHEAP 1

low-down *adj* ***syn*** see BASE 3

lower *vb* ***syn*** see FROWN 1
rel peer, stare; intimidate, menace, threaten

lower *adj* ***syn*** see INFERIOR 1
ant higher

lower *vb* **1** ***syn*** see FALL 1
ant rise
2 ***syn*** see DEPRECIATE 1
rel demote; de-escalate, deflate
con raise
3 to cause or allow to descend <*lowered* the landing gear of the aircraft>
syn couch, demit, depress, droop, let down, sink
rel detrude, submerge; debase, reduce
con elevate, hoist, lift, pull up, raise
4 ***syn*** see REDUCE 2
ant raise
5 ***syn*** see HUMBLE
ant elevate

lowering (*or* **louring**) *adj* **1** ***syn*** see IMMINENT 2
rel frowning, gloomy, sullen; black, dark; foreboding, impending, portentous
2 ***syn*** see OVERCAST

lowermost *adj* ***syn*** see BOTTOMMOST
ant uppermost

lowery (*or* **loury**) *adj* ***syn*** see IMMINENT 2

lowest *adj* ***syn*** see BOTTOMMOST
ant highest

low-grade *adj* ***syn*** see INFERIOR 2

low-key *adj* ***syn*** see SUBDUED 2

low-keyed *adj* ***syn*** see SUBDUED 2

lowlife *n* **1** ***syn*** see WRETCH 1
2 ***syn*** see VILLAIN 1

lowly *adj* **1** ***syn*** see HUMBLE 1
rel retiring, withdrawing; deferential, obeisant, reverential; obsequious, servile
ant haughty
2 ***syn*** see IGNOBLE 1
3 ***syn*** see PROSAIC 3

low-pressure *adj* ***syn*** see EASYGOING 3

---

syn synonym(s) ***rel*** related word(s)
ant antonym(s) ***con*** contrasted word(s)
idiom idiomatic equivalent(s)
‖ use limited; if in doubt, see a dictionary

ant high-pressure
low-priced *adj* ***syn*** see CHEAP 1
‖**low-rate** *vb* ***syn*** see DECRY 2
low-set *adj* ***syn*** see SHORT 2
low-spirited *adj* ***syn*** see DOWNCAST
ant high-spirited
low-statured *adj* ***syn*** see SHORT 2
loyal *adj* ***syn*** see FAITHFUL 1
con faithless; alienated, disaffected, estranged; contumacious, factious, insubordinate, mutinous, rebellious, seditious
ant disloyal
loyalist *n* ***syn*** see PATRIOT 1
loyalty *n* **1** ***syn*** see FIDELITY 1
rel trueness, truth
ant disloyalty
2 ***syn*** see ATTACHMENT 1
lubber *n* ***syn*** see OAF 2
lubberland *n* ***syn*** see UTOPIA
lubberly *adj* ***syn*** see BOORISH
‖**lubricate** *vb* ***syn*** see BRIBE
lubricious *adj* **1** ***syn*** see INCONSTANT 1
2 ***syn*** see SLICK 1
lucent *adj* **1** ***syn*** see BRIGHT 1
2 ***syn*** see CLEAR 4
lucid *adj* **1** ***syn*** see BRIGHT 1
2 ***syn*** see SANE 2
3 ***syn*** see UNDERSTANDABLE
4 ***syn*** see CLEAR 4
con dusky, gloomy, murky; muddy, turbid
lucidity *n* **1** ***syn*** see CLARITY
rel comprehensibility, intelligibility, understandability; distinctness, explicitness
ant ambiguity
2 ***syn*** see WIT 2
Lucifer *n* ***syn*** see DEVIL 1
luck *n* **1** ***syn*** see CHANCE 2
rel break, occasion, opportunity
2 ***syn*** see ACCIDENT 1
3 success dependent on chance <he had all the *luck* in the world and was greatly envied by every one of his associates>
syn fortunateness, fortune, luckiness
rel advantage, break, fluke, godsend, opportunity, windfall; weal; hap, kismet
ant ill-fortune
4 ***syn*** see CHARM 2
luck *vb* ***syn*** see HAPPEN 2
luckiness *n* ***syn*** see LUCK 3
luckless *adj* ***syn*** see UNLUCKY
rel miserable, wretched
ant lucky
lucky *adj* having a favorable outcome or an unforeseen or unpredictable success <he can only be described as *lucky*, as his success and fame are unearned>
syn fortunate, happy, providential, ‖sonsy, well
rel auspicious, benign, favorable, propitious; advantageous, beneficial, profitable; felicitous
idiom in luck
con baleful, malefic, maleficent, malign, sinister
ant luckless, unlucky
lucrative *adj* ***syn*** see ADVANTAGEOUS 1
lucre *n* **1** ***syn*** see PROFIT
2 ***syn*** see MONEY
luculent *adj* ***syn*** see CLEAR 4
ludicrous *adj* ***syn*** see LAUGHABLE
rel absurd, foolish, preposterous, silly; antic, bizarre, fantastic, grotesque
con doleful, dolorous, lugubrious, melancholy
lug *vb* **1** ***syn*** see PULL 2
2 ***syn*** see CARRY 1
3 ***syn*** see JERK
‖**lug** *n* ***syn*** see OAF 2
‖**lugs** *n pl* ***syn*** see POSE 2
lugubrious *adj* **1** ***syn*** see MELANCHOLY 2
rel depressing, oppressing, oppressive; dour, glum, morose, saturnine, sullen
con blithe, jocund, jolly, jovial, merry; cheerful, glad, joyful
ant facetious
2 ***syn*** see GLOOMY 3
lukewarm *adj* **1** ***syn*** see TEPID 1
2 ***syn*** see TEPID 2
rel irresolute, irresolved, uncommitted, unresolved; hesitant, indecisive, uncertain, undecided; cool; wishy-washy
ant icy; boiling
lull *vb* **1** ***syn*** see CALM
rel moderate, qualify, temper
ant agitate
2 ***syn*** see ABATE 4
lull *n* **1** ***syn*** see QUIET 1
2 ***syn*** see PAUSE
rel abeyance, quiescence
lullaby *n* a song to quiet children or lull them to sleep <sang a *lullaby* to the baby every night>
syn berceuse, cradlesong
‖**lulu** *n* ***syn*** see ‖DILLY
lumber *vb* to tread heavily or clumsily <the tired old man slowly *lumbered* home>
syn barge, clump, galumph, stumble, stump
rel plod, trudge; shamble, slog
lumber *vb* ***syn*** see BURDEN
lumbering *adj* **1** ***syn*** see CLUMSY 1
rel cumbersome, cumbrous, ponderous; hulking, hulky
2 ***syn*** see AWKWARD 2
luminary *n* **1** ***syn*** see CELEBRITY 2
rel leading light
2 ***syn*** see NOTABLE 1
luminous *adj* **1** ***syn*** see BRIGHT 1
2 ***syn*** see CLEAR 4
3 ***syn*** see UNDERSTANDABLE
lummox *n* ***syn*** see OAF 2
lump *n* **1** a compact mass of indefinite size and shape <dropped a large *lump* of butter into the steaming chowder>
syn chunk, clod, clump, gob, hunch, hunk, nugget, wad
rel particle, piece, portion; batch, bunch, ‖swad; bit, chip, crumb, morsel, scrap; wedge; block, bulk
2 ***syn*** see MUCH
3 ***syn*** see BUMP 2
rel bulge, protuberance, swelling
4 ***syn*** see OAF 2
5 **lumps** *pl* ***syn*** see DUE 1

lump *vb* ***syn*** see BEAR 10
lumpish *adj* **1** ***syn*** see BOORISH
2 ***syn*** see CLUMSY 1
lumpkin *n* ***syn*** see OAF 2
lumpy *adj* ***syn*** see RUDE 1
lunacy *n* **1** ***syn*** see INSANITY 1
rel absurdity, folly, foolery, foolishness; asininity, fatuity, inanity, ineptitude, stupidity
2 ***syn*** see FOOLISHNESS
lunatic *adj* **1** ***syn*** see INSANE 1
2 ***syn*** see FOOLISH 2
lunatic *n* **1** a person who is insane or of unsound mind <Bedlam was a famous old English asylum for *lunatics*>
syn bedlamite, dement, loon, loony, madling, madman, maniac, non compos, nut, Tom o' Bedlam
rel demoniac, energumen; raver; neuropath, neurotic, paranoid, psycho, psychoneurotic
2 ***syn*** see CRACKPOT
lunch counter (*or* **bar**) *n* ***syn*** see EATING HOUSE
luncheonette *n* ***syn*** see EATING HOUSE
lunchroom *n* ***syn*** see EATING HOUSE
lunch wagon (*or* **cart**) *n* ***syn*** see EATING HOUSE
lunge *vb* ***syn*** see PLUNGE 2
lunk *n* ***syn*** see DUNCE
lunkhead *n* ***syn*** see DUNCE
lupanar *n* ***syn*** see BROTHEL
lurch *n* ***syn*** see LEANING 2
lurch *vb* **1** ***syn*** see SEESAW
2 to move forward unsteadily while swaying from side to side <the sodden drunk *lurched* uncertainly toward the door>
syn careen, stagger, ‖stoit, ‖stoiter, ‖stot, sway, swing, weave, wobble; *compare* TEETER
rel reel, rock, roll, swag, toss, totter, whirl; bob; wave, waver
con march, stride
3 ***syn*** see TEETER
rel pitch, plunge
4 ***syn*** see JERK
5 ***syn*** see WALLOW 2
6 ***syn*** see STUMBLE 3
lure *n* **1** ***syn*** see ATTRACTION 1
2 something that leads an individual into a place or situation from which escape is difficult <used her charm as a *lure* to trap the unsuspecting youth>
syn allurement, bait, come-on, decoy, enticement, inveiglement, seducement, siren song, snare, ‖stale, temptation, trap
rel appeal, attraction, incentive, inducement; con game, gimmick, suck-in, trick; ambush, blind, camouflage, delusion, fake, illusion
con caution, caveat, warning
lure *vb* to draw from a usual, desirable, or proper course or situation into one felt as unusual, undesirable, or wrong <the promise of money *lured* him away from his steady job>
syn allure, bait, decoy, entice, entrap, inveigle, lead on, seduce, tempt, toll, train
rel bag, capture, catch, draw in, ensnare, rope, snare, suck in; attract, beguile, bewitch, captivate, charm, enchant, fascinate, invite; draw, draw on; blandish, cajole, wheedle
idiom bait the hook, give the come-on
con drive (away *or* off), rebuff, repulse
ant repel
lurid *adj* **1** ***syn*** see PALE 1
2 ***syn*** see GHASTLY 1
rel ashen, ashy, livid, pale, pallid, wan; baleful, malefic, maleficent, malign, sinister
3 ***syn*** see SENSATIONAL 2
luring *adj* ***syn*** see ENTICING
ant repellent, repelling
lurk *vb* ***syn*** see SNEAK
lurking *adj* ***syn*** see LATENT
luscious *adj* **1** ***syn*** see DELIGHTFUL
rel appetizing, flavorsome, nectarious, palatable, piquant; choice, distinctive, exquisite, rare, rich
ant austere
2 ***syn*** see LUXURIOUS 3
3 ***syn*** see SENSUOUS
4 ***syn*** see ORNATE
lush *adj* **1** ***syn*** see PROFUSE
rel luxurious, sumptuous
2 ***syn*** see DELIGHTFUL
3 ***syn*** see SENSUOUS
4 ***syn*** see LUXURIOUS 3
lush *n* ‖**1** ***syn*** see LIQUOR 2
2 ***syn*** see DRUNKARD
lush (**up**) *vb* ***syn*** see DRINK 3
‖**lushed** *adj* ***syn*** see INTOXICATED 1
‖**lusher** *n* ***syn*** see DRUNKARD
lust *n* **1** ***syn*** see DESIRE 1
rel coveting, yearning, yen
2 sexual appetency <they mistakenly thought that *lust* was lasting love>
syn aphrodisia, concupiscence, desire, eroticism, itch, lickerishness, lustfulness, passion, prurience, pruriency
rel nymphomania, priapism, satyriasis, satyrism; excitement, heat, hunger, libido, rut; fervor; carnality, lasciviousness, lecherousness, lechery, lubricity, salacity
lust *vb* ***syn*** see LONG
rel desire, wish
luster *n* the quality or condition of shining by reflected light <the satiny *luster* of fine pearls>
syn glaze, glint, gloss, polish, sheen, shine
rel iridescence, opalescence; brilliance, brilliancy, effulgence, luminosity, radiance, refulgence; afterglow, gleam, glow; candescence, incandescence
lusterless *adj* **1** ***syn*** see DULL 7
ant lustrous
2 ***syn*** see COLORLESS 2
lustful *adj* **1** ***syn*** see LICENTIOUS 2
2 sexually excited <*lustful* old man>
syn concupiscent, goatish, hot, lascivious, libidinous, lickerish, passionate, prurient, ruttish, rutty, satyric

---

syn synonym(s) ***rel*** related word(s)
ant antonym(s) ***con*** contrasted word(s)
idiom idiomatic equivalent(s)
‖ use limited; if in doubt, see a dictionary

rel burning, hot-blooded, itching; lecherous, salacious

lustfulness *n* ***syn*** see LUST 2

lustral *adj* ***syn*** see PURGATIVE

lustrate *vb* ***syn*** see PURIFY 2

lustration *n* ***syn*** see PURIFICATION

lustratory *adj* ***syn*** see PURGATIVE

lustrous *adj* **1** having a high gloss or shine <a *lustrous* star sapphire>
syn burnished, gleaming, glistening, glossy, polished, sheeny, shining, shiny
rel gleamy, glimmering, glinting, sparkling; radiant
con dull, flat, lackluster, mat
ant lusterless
2 ***syn*** see BRIGHT 1
rel glorious, resplendent, splendid

lusty *adj* **1** ***syn*** see VIGOROUS
rel hale, healthy
ant effete
2 ***syn*** see STRONG 3
3 ***syn*** see HUGE

lusus *n* ***syn*** see FREAK 2

luxuriant *adj* **1** ***syn*** see PROFUSE
rel fecund, fertile, fruitful, prolific; rampant, rank
con barren, infertile, sterile, unfruitful
2 ***syn*** see LUXURIOUS 3

luxuriate *vb* ***syn*** see WALLOW 3
rel overindulge, overdo; eat up, enjoy, feast, love, riot

luxurious *adj* **1** ***syn*** see SENSUOUS
rel self-indulging, self-pampering; languishing, languorous
con self-abnegating, self-denying; austere, severe, stern
ant ascetic
2 ***syn*** see GRAND 2
rel imposing, majestic, stately
3 ostentatiously rich or magnificent <the robber barons built *luxurious* homes which rivaled the palaces of Europe>
syn Capuan, deluxe, luscious, lush, luxuriant, opulent, palace, palatial, plush, plushy, sumptuous, upholstered
rel extravagant, grandiose, ostentatious, posh, pretentious, showy; awful, grand, imposing, magnificent, majestic, stately; Lucullan; elaborate, fancy; costly, expensive, precious
con economical, frugal, sparing, thrifty; exiguous, meager, scant, scanty, scrimpy, skimpy, spare

luxury *n* something adding to pleasure but not absolutely necessary <the poor cannot even afford the essentials, let alone occasional *luxuries*>
syn amenity, extravagance, frill, luxus, superfluity
rel comfort; embellishment, redundancy, self-indulgence; dainty, delicacy
con basics, essential(s), fundamental(s)

luxus *n* ***syn*** see LUXURY

lying *adj* ***syn*** see DISHONEST
rel false, wrong; deceptive, delusive, delusory, misleading

lying–in *n* ***syn*** see CONFINEMENT 2

lyncean *adj* ***syn*** see SHARP-EYED

lynx–eyed *adj* ***syn*** see SHARP-EYED

M

ma *n* ***syn*** see MOTHER 1
macabre *adj* ***syn*** see GHASTLY 1
rel deadly, deathlike, deathly; ghostlike, ghostly
macaroni *n* ***syn*** see FOP
mace *n* ***syn*** see CUDGEL
‖**mace** *n* ***syn*** see SWINDLER
‖**mace** *vb* ***syn*** see CHEAT
machinate *vb* **1** ***syn*** see ENGINEER
2 ***syn*** see PLOT
machination *n* ***syn*** see PLOT 2
machine *n* **1** ***syn*** see CAR
2 ***syn*** see ROBOT 2
machinery *n* ***syn*** see EQUIPMENT
rel agency, agent, channel, instrument, instrumentality, means, medium, organ, vehicle; contraption, contrivance, device, gadget; appliance, implement, instrument, tool, utensil
‖**mack** *n* ***syn*** see PIMP 1
macquereau *n* ***syn*** see PIMP 1
macrocosm *n* ***syn*** see UNIVERSE
ant microcosm
macrocosmos *n* ***syn*** see UNIVERSE
ant microcosm
mad *adj* **1** ***syn*** see INSANE 1
rel delirious, frantic, frenetic, furious, rabid, wild
2 ***syn*** see FOOLISH 2
3 ***syn*** see ILLOGICAL
4 ***syn*** see ANGRY
rel sore, worked up; affronted, offended, outraged
5 ***syn*** see FURIOUS 2
mad *vb* ***syn*** see ANGER 1
mad *n* ***syn*** see ANGER
mad–brained *adj* ***syn*** see RASH 1
madcap *adj* ***syn*** see RASH 1
madden *vb* **1** to make insane <prolonged solitary confinement had *maddened* the prisoners>
syn craze, derange, distract, frenzy, unbalance, unhinge
rel shatter; possess
idiom drive insane (*or* mad *or* crazy)
2 ***syn*** see ANGER 1
con allay, assuage, mitigate, relieve
made–to–order *adj* ***syn*** see CUSTOM-MADE
madhouse *n* ***syn*** see ASYLUM 3
madid *adj* ***syn*** see WET 1
madling *n* ***syn*** see LUNATIC 1
madly *adv* ***syn*** see HARD 2
rel foolishly, insanely, irrationally; hastily, rashly
madman *n* **1** ***syn*** see LUNATIC 1
2 ***syn*** see FOOL 1
madness *n* ***syn*** see INSANITY 1
maelstrom *n* ***syn*** see EDDY
rel commotion, confusion, fury, storm, turmoil
mafia *n* ***syn*** see CLIQUE
magazine *n* **1** ***syn*** see DEPOT 2
rel cache, lumber room
2 ***syn*** see ARMORY
3 ***syn*** see JOURNAL
rel publication; digest, gazette; annual, bimonthly, biweekly, daily, monthly, quarterly, semiweekly, weekly
mage *n* ***syn*** see MAGICIAN 1
maggot *n* ***syn*** see CAPRICE
magian *n* ***syn*** see MAGICIAN 1
magian *adj* ***syn*** see MAGIC
magic *n* **1** the use of means (as charms or spells) believed to have supernatural power over natural forces <the practice of *magic*>
syn bewitchment, conjuring, conjury, enchantment, ensorcellment, incantation, magicking, necromancy, sorcery, thaumaturgy, witchcraft, witchery, witching, wizardry
rel abracadabra, alchemy, augury, charm, divining, exorcism, fortune-telling, mumbo jumbo, occultism, soothsaying, sortilege, voodooism; devilry, deviltry, diablerie, diabolism, satanism; wicca
2 the art of producing mysterious effects by illusion and sleight of hand <the club presented a program of clever *magic* to raise funds>
syn conjuring, legerdemain
idiom sleight of hand
magic *adj* having seemingly supernatural qualities or powers <modern medicine has developed a host of *magic* drugs>
syn magian, magical, mystic, necromantic, sorcerous, thaumaturgic, witchy, wizardly
rel extraordinary, marvelous, prodigious, remarkable, stupendous, unbelievable, unprecedented
magical *adj* ***syn*** see MAGIC
magician *n* **1** one who practices magical arts <a *magician* cast a spell over the child>
syn archimage, charmer, conjurer, enchanter, mage, magian, magus, necromancer, sorcerer, voodoo, voodooist, warlock, wizard; *compare* WITCH 1
rel augurer, brujo, diviner, exorciser, exorcist, invocator, thaumaturge, thaumaturgist; medicine man, shaman; prophet, seer, soothsayer; fortune-teller, medium; diabolist, satanist
2 one who practices tricks of illusion and sleight of hand <a *magician* performed tricks for the children at the party>
syn conjurer, illusionist, trickster
magicking *n* ***syn*** see MAGIC 1
magisterial *adj* **1** ***syn*** see DICTATORIAL

---

syn synonym(s) ***rel*** related word(s)
ant antonym(s) ***con*** contrasted word(s)
idiom idiomatic equivalent(s)
‖ use limited; if in doubt, see a dictionary

rel disdainful, insolent, lordly, supercilious
2 *syn* see MASTERFUL 1
3 *syn* see POMPOUS 1

magistrate *n* *syn* see JUDGE 2

magnanimous *adj* *syn* see GENEROUS 1
rel altruistic, liberal, unselfish; great, high-minded, knightly, noble, nobleminded, princely
con measly, paltry, petty, picayune, picayunish

magnate *n* a businessman of exceptional wealth, influence, or power <the oil and steel *magnates* who controlled whole nations>
syn baron, czar, king, merchant prince, mogul, prince, tycoon
rel figure, name, personage; ‖biggie, big gun, big-timer, ‖big wheel, fat cat, lion, nabob; plutocrat
idiom captain of industry

magnetic *adj* *syn* see ATTRACTIVE 1
rel arresting, irresistible; charismatic
con repellent, repugnant, repulsive

magnetism *n* *syn* see CHARM 3

magnetize *vb* *syn* see ATTRACT 1

magnific *adj* *syn* see GRAND 1

magnificent *adj* **1** *syn* see GRAND 1
rel glorious, resplendent, splendid, sublime, superb; luxurious, opulent, sumptuous
con abject, ignoble, mean, sordid; humble, lowly, meek; paltry
ant modest
2 *syn* see SPLENDID 2
3 *syn* see SUPERB 3

magnify *vb* **1** *syn* see PRAISE 2
2 *syn* see EXALT 1
rel augment, enlarge, increase; amplify, dilate, distend, expand, inflate, swell
ant belittle, minimize
3 *syn* see INCREASE 1
ant minify
4 *syn* see INTENSIFY
5 *syn* see OVERPLAY 2
6 *syn* see EMBROIDER

magniloquent *adj* *syn* see RHETORICAL

magnitude *n* **1** *syn* see ENORMITY 2
2 *syn* see SIZE 1
3 *syn* see SIZE 2
4 *syn* see ORDER 4
5 *syn* see IMPORTANCE

magnum opus *n* *syn* see MASTERPIECE 1

magpie *n* *syn* see CHATTERBOX

magus *n* *syn* see MAGICIAN 1

mahogany *n* *syn* see TABLE 1

maid *n* **1** *syn* see GIRL 1
2 a woman hired to do housework <in addition to her other duties the *maid* was expected to care for the baby>
syn biddy, girl, handmaid, hired girl, housemaid, maidservant
rel au pair girl; chambermaid, nursemaid, parlormaid; handmaiden; domestic, factotum, ‖muchacha, servant
idiom maid of all work

maiden *n* *syn* see GIRL 1

maiden *adj* **1** *syn* see VIRGIN 1
rel husbandless; old-maidish, spinsterish, spinsterly
2 *syn* see FIRST 2

maidenhead *n* *syn* see VIRGINITY

maidenhood *n* *syn* see VIRGINITY

maiden lady *n* *syn* see SPINSTER

maidservant *n* *syn* see MAID 2

maim *vb* to wound so severely as to deprive of the use of or to cause loss of a limb or member <an arm hanging useless, *maimed* in an auto accident>
syn cripple, dislimb, dismember, mayhem, mutilate; *compare* PARALYZE 1
rel disable, disfigure, hamstring; batter, break, ‖bung up, mangle, massacre, maul
con rehabilitate, restore, salvage; cure, fix, heal, mend, remedy, repair

main *n* *syn* see OCEAN

main *adj* *syn* see CHIEF 2
rel foremost, head, leading, paramount; cardinal, controlling, essential, fundamental, vital; prevailing

‖**main** *adv* *syn* see VERY 1

‖**mainline** *vb* *syn* see SHOOT UP 2

mainly *adv* *syn* see GENERALLY 1

mainstay *n* a chief reliance <the *mainstay* of the organization held things together>
syn backbone, pillar, sinew(s)
rel brace, buttress, crutch, maintainer, prop, staff, standby, stay, support, supporter, sustainer, upholder

maintain *vb* **1** to keep in a state of repair, efficiency, or validity <he followed a careful regimen to *maintain* his good health>
syn keep up, preserve, save, sustain; *compare* SAVE 3
rel husband, manage; care (for), cultivate; guard, protect
con disregard, ignore, neglect, omit, overlook, slight
2 to uphold as true, right, proper, or acceptable often in the face of challenge or indifference <I *maintain* that his actions were justified by the circumstances>
syn argue, assert, claim, contend, defend, justify, vindicate, warrant
rel affirm, aver, avouch, avow, declare, profess, protest; emphasize, insist, persist, stress; correct, rectify, right
con contradict, deny, gainsay, traverse; challenge, query, question
3 *syn* see SUPPORT 3

maintenance *n* *syn* see LIVING

majestic *adj* **1** *syn* see GRAND 1
rel courtly, dignified; ceremonious; imperial
2 *syn* see KINGLY

major *adj* **1** *syn* see CHIEF 2
rel better, greater, higher, superior
2 *syn* see BIG 1
3 *syn* see GRAVE 3

make *vb* **1** *syn* see EFFECT 1
rel initiate, originate, start
2 *syn* see GENERATE 1
rel brew
3 to bring something into being by forming, shaping, combining, or altering materials <*made* a dress from odd bits of material>

syn assemble, build, construct, erect, fabricate, fashion, forge, form, frame, manufacture, mold, produce, put together, shape; *compare* BUILD 1
4 ***syn*** see DRAFT 3
5 ***syn*** see CONSTITUTE 1
6 ***syn*** see PREPARE 1
7 ***syn*** see DESIGNATE 2
8 ***syn*** see ENACT 1
9 ***syn*** see INFER
10 ***syn*** see EARN 1
rel harvest, reap
11 ***syn*** see CLEAR 6
12 ***syn*** see FORCE 2
13 ***syn*** see HEAD 3
rel break (for)
||**14** ***syn*** see MEDDLE
15 ***syn*** see RUN 8
make–believe *n* ***syn*** see PRETENSE 2
make off *vb* ***syn*** see RUN 2
rel depart, go, leave, quit, retire, withdraw; abscond, decamp, escape
make out *vb* **1** ***syn*** see APPREHEND 1
2 ***syn*** see ESTABLISH 6
3 ***syn*** see INFER
||**4** ***syn*** see SHIFT 5
5 ***syn*** see SUCCEED 3
make over *vb* ***syn*** see TRANSFER 4
make–peace *n* ***syn*** see PEACEMAKER
maker *n* ***syn*** see FATHER 2
rel executor, operator; manufacturer
makeshift *n* ***syn*** see RESOURCE 3
makeshift *adj* serving as a temporary expedient <forced to make *makeshift* plans>
syn provisional, rough-and-ready, rough-and-tumble, stopgap
make up *vb* **1** ***syn*** see CONTRIVE 2
2 ***syn*** see MIX 1
3 ***syn*** see PREPARE 1
4 ***syn*** see CONSTITUTE 1
5 ***syn*** see COMPENSATE 1
make up (to) *vb* ***syn*** see ADDRESS 8
makeup *n* **1** the way in which parts or constituents are related in an organized whole <the complex *makeup* of the eye>
syn architecture, composition, constitution, construction, design, formation
rel arrangement, ordering, organization, plan, setup; form, shape, style
2 ***syn*** see DISPOSITION 3
rel cast, fiber, grain, mold, stamp, stripe, vein; constitution, frame
3 cosmetics used to color and beautify the face or body <with *makeup* on, she didn't look bad>
syn face, maquillage, paint, war paint
rel powder; blackface, grease paint
maladroit *adj* **1** ***syn*** see AWKWARD 2
rel blundering, floundering, stumbling, ungraceful; left-handed, unskilled
con deft, dexterous, handy; clever, cunning, ingenious
ant adroit
2 ***syn*** see TACTLESS
malady *n* ***syn*** see DISEASE 1
mala fide *adj* ***syn*** see INSINCERE
ant bona fide
malaise *n* ***syn*** see INFIRMITY 1
malapert *adj* ***syn*** see SAUCY 1
malapert *n* ***syn*** see MINX
malapropos *adj* **1** ***syn*** see IMPROPER 1
ant apropos
2 ***syn*** see UNSEASONABLE 1
malarkey *n* ***syn*** see NONSENSE 2
malconformation *n* ***syn*** see DEFORMITY
malcontent *n* **1** ***syn*** see GROUCH
2 ***syn*** see REBEL
malcontent *adj* ***syn*** see DISCONTENTED
rel alienated, disaffected, estranged; disobedient, ungovernable, unruly; restless; contumacious, factious, insubordinate, mutinous, rebellious, seditious
malcontented *adj* ***syn*** see DISCONTENTED
male *adj* ***syn*** see VIRILE
rel macho
male *n* ***syn*** see MAN 3
malediction *n* ***syn*** see CURSE 1
ant benediction
malefactor *n* ***syn*** see CRIMINAL
rel blackguard, knave, miscreant, rascal, rogue, scoundrel; evildoer, sinner, wrongdoer
malefic *adj* ***syn*** see SINISTER
ant benefic
maleficent *adj* ***syn*** see SINISTER
ant beneficent
maleness *n* ***syn*** see VIRILITY
rel machismo, macho
malevolence *n* ***syn*** see MALICE
rel antagonism, hostility; abhorrence, abomination, detestation
ant benevolence
malevolent *adj* ***syn*** see MALICIOUS
rel baleful, malefic, maleficent, sinister
con benign, benignant, kind, kindly
ant benevolent
malformation *n* ***syn*** see DEFORMITY
malice *n* a desiring or wishing pain, injury, or distress to another <they sought to ruin his reputation out of pure *malice*>
syn despite, despitefulness, grudge, ill will, malevolence, maliciousness, malignancy, malignity, spite, spitefulness, spleen
rel bane, poison, venom; bile; animosity, animus, antipathy, down, enmity; hate, hatefulness, hatred, invidiousness, meanness; bitterness, resentment, umbrage
con benevolence, benignancy, benignity, charity, kindliness, kindness
malicious *adj* having, showing, or indicative of intense often vicious ill will <the helpless victim of *malicious* rumors>
syn catty, despiteful, evil, hateful, malevolent, malign, malignant, nasty, rancorous, spiteful, spitish, vicious, wicked

---

syn synonym(s) ***rel*** related word(s)
ant antonym(s) ***con*** contrasted word(s)
idiom idiomatic equivalent(s)
|| use limited; if in doubt, see a dictionary

rel poisonous, poison-pen, venomous, virulent; baneful, deleterious, detrimental, noxious, pernicious; envious, green, green-eyed, jealous; mean, petty
con benevolent, charitable, friendly, kind, kindly; considerate, thoughtful

maliciousness *n* ***syn*** see MALICE

malign *adj* **1** ***syn*** see SINISTER
rel baneful, deleterious, detrimental, injurious, noxious, pernicious
con auspicious, favorable, propitious; fortunate, happy, lucky, providential
ant benign
2 ***syn*** see MALICIOUS
rel antagonistic, antipathetic, hostile, inimical
con benignant, kind, kindly
ant benign

malign *vb* to speak evil of for the purpose of injuring and without regard for the truth <the candidates increasingly *maligned* each other as the campaign degenerated>
syn asperse, befoul, bespatter, blacken, calumniate, defame, denigrate, libel, ‖scandal, scandalize, slander, slur, smear, spatter, tear down, traduce, vilify, villainize
rel decry, depreciate, derogate, detract, disparage; opprobriate, revile, vituperate; backbite, besmirch, defile, pollute, smirch, soil, stain, sully, taint, tarnish
idiom blow upon, cast aspersion(s) on (*or* upon)
con acclaim, applaud, eulogize, extol, laud, praise; defend, justify, maintain, vindicate

malignancy *n* ***syn*** see MALICE

malignant *adj* ***syn*** see MALICIOUS
rel devilish, diabolical, fiendish
con altruistic, benevolent, charitable, humane
ant benignant

maligning *adj* ***syn*** see LIBELOUS

malignity *n* ***syn*** see MALICE
rel revengefulness, vengefulness, vindictiveness
ant benignity

malison *n* ***syn*** see CURSE 1
ant benison

‖**malkin** *n* ***syn*** see SLATTERN 1

malleable *adj* ***syn*** see PLASTIC
rel governable, manageable; transformable
con intractable, recalcitrant, ungovernable, unmanageable, unruly
ant refractory

malleate *vb* ***syn*** see HAMMER 1

malodorous *adj* **1** having an unpleasant smell <*malodorous* cheeses>
syn fetid, frowsy, funky, fusty, gamy, high, mephitic, musty, nidorous, noisome, olid, putrid, rancid, rank, reeking, reeky, ‖smellful, smelly, stale, stenchful, stenchy, stinking, stinky, strong, whiffy; *compare* ODOROUS
rel bad, foul, nauseating, offensive, vile; decayed, decomposed, fuggy, off, rotten, spoiled, tainted; nasty, noxious, pestilential, poisonous, polluted
con clean, deodorized, fresh
ant fragrant, sweet
2 ***syn*** see INDECOROUS

maltreat *vb* ***syn*** see ABUSE 4

‖**mam** *n* ***syn*** see MOTHER 1

mama (*or* **mamma**) *n* ***syn*** see MOTHER 1

‖**mammock** *vb* ***syn*** see DISORDER 1

mammoth *n* ***syn*** see GIANT

mammoth *adj* ***syn*** see HUGE

mammy *n* ***syn*** see MOTHER 1

mamzer (*or* **momzer** *or* **momser**) *n* ***syn*** see BASTARD 1

man *n* **1** ***syn*** see HUMAN
2 ***syn*** see MANKIND
3 a male human being <just an average *man* trying to get by>
syn ‖bloke, boy, buck, ‖cat, chap, cuss, fellow, galoot, ‖gee, gent, gentleman, guy, he, male, ‖mun, skate, snap, ‖stirra; *compare* HUMAN
4 ***syn*** see HUSBAND
5 ***syn*** see LOVER 1
6 ***syn*** see POLICEMAN

manage *vb* **1** ***syn*** see CONDUCT 3
rel superintend; guide
2 ***syn*** see GOVERN 3
3 ***syn*** see SHIFT 5
rel bring about, carry out, contrive, effect, execute; accomplish, achieve, succeed
idiom sink or swim on one's own
con collapse, fail, fall down; give up, poop (out)

management *n* ***syn*** see OVERSIGHT 1

manager *n* ***syn*** see EXECUTIVE
rel handler, impresario, producer

man-at-arms *n* ***syn*** see SOLDIER

mancipium *n* ***syn*** see SLAVE 1

mandarin *n* ***syn*** see BUREAUCRAT

mandate *n* ***syn*** see COMMAND 1
rel decree, fiat, imperative; authority, authorization

mandatory *adj* containing or constituting a command <*mandatory* entrance examinations>
syn compulsatory, compulsory, imperative, imperious, obligatory, required
rel essential, indispensable, irremissible, necessary, needful, requisite; binding, commanding, compelling, de rigueur; forced, involuntary
con discretionary, elective, voluntary
ant optional

maneuver *n* **1** ***syn*** see MEASURE 7
2 ***syn*** see TRICK 1
rel contrivance, device; intrigue, machination, manipulation, plot; demarche, movement, plan; finesse, subterfuge

maneuver *vb* **1** ***syn*** see ENGINEER
rel navigate; finesse; design
2 ***syn*** see HANDLE 2
rel navigate
3 ***syn*** see MANIPULATE 2

man Friday *n* ***syn*** see RIGHT-HAND MAN

manful *adj* ***syn*** see BRAVE 1

manfulness *n* ***syn*** see VIRILITY
rel machismo, macho

mangle *vb* ***syn*** see BATTER 1
rel damage, impair, injure, mar; deface, disfigure; contort, deform, distort; butcher, hack

mangled *adj* ***syn*** see LACERATED

mangy *adj* ***syn*** see SHABBY 1

manhandle *vb* to treat roughly <riot police *manhandled* innocent bystanders>
syn knock about, mishandle, rough (up), roughhouse, slap around
rel abuse, maltreat, mistreat; batter, ‖bung up, mangle, maul

mania *n* ***syn*** see FETISH 2
rel craze, enthusiasm, fancy, fascination, infatuation, passion; compulsion, fixed idea, hang-up, idée fixe

maniac *adj* ***syn*** see INSANE 1
rel berserk, delirious, frantic, frenetic, frenzied, furious, rabid, raging, ranting, violent, wild

maniac *n* **1** ***syn*** see LUNATIC 1
2 ***syn*** see ENTHUSIAST

manifest *adj* ***syn*** see CLEAR 5
rel disclosed, divulged, revealed, told; evidenced, evinced, shown; noticeable, prominent
con implicit; obscure

manifest *vb* **1** ***syn*** see EMBODY 1
2 ***syn*** see SHOW 2
rel display, expose; express, utter, vent, voice
con adumbrate, shadow
ant suggest

manifold *adj* comprehending or uniting various features <a *manifold* operation>
syn diverse, diversiform, multifarious, multifold, multiform, multiplex, multivarious
rel multiphase, polymorphic, polymorphous
con homogeneous, pure, uniform; plain, simple, straightforward, uncomplex, uncomplicated

manifold *vb* ***syn*** see INCREASE 1

manikin *n* ***syn*** see DWARF

manipulate *vb* **1** ***syn*** see HANDLE 2
2 to control or play upon by artful, unfair, or insidious means <the sycophant cleverly *manipulated* his master>
syn beguile, exploit, finesse, jockey, maneuver, play; *compare* ENGINEER
rel machinate, use; conduct, control, direct, engineer, manage

mankind *n* the human race <all *mankind* will benefit from this new discovery>
syn flesh, Homo sapiens, humanity, humankind, man, mortality; *compare* HUMAN

manlike *adj* **1** ***syn*** see ANTHROPOID
2 ***syn*** see VIRILE
rel macho

manliness *n* ***syn*** see VIRILITY
rel machismo, macho

manly *adj* **1** ***syn*** see VIRILE
rel macho
2 ***syn*** see BRAVE 1

man-made *adj* ***syn*** see SYNTHETIC

manner *n* **1** ***syn*** see HABIT 1
2 ***syn*** see METHOD 1
rel custom, habit, habitude, practice, usage, use, wont; form, style
3 ***syn*** see STYLE 4
4 ***syn*** see VEIN 1
rel form, turn; affectation, affectedness, mannerism; idiosyncrasy, peculiarity
5 manners *pl* habitual conduct or deportment in social intercourse evaluated according to some conventional standard of politeness or civility <a person with impeccable *manners*>
syn amenities, civilities, decorum(s), etiquette, mores, proprieties
rel formalities, protocol; elegancies; bearing, behavior, demeanor, deportment, mien, p's and q's; mannerliness
idiom conduct becoming a gentleman
con mannerlessness, unmannerliness

mannered *adj* ***syn*** see SELF-CONSCIOUS

mannerism *n* ***syn*** see POSE 2
rel eccentricity, idiosyncrasy; oddness, peculiarity, queerness, singularity

mannerless *adj* ***syn*** see RUDE 6
ant mannerly

mannerly *adj* ***syn*** see CIVIL 2
ant mannerless, unmannerly

manor *n* **1** ***syn*** see MANSION
2 ***syn*** see ESTATE 3

mansion *n* a large imposing residence <the governor's *mansion*>
syn castle, chateau, manor, villa
rel estate, hall, house

manslaughter *n* ***syn*** see MURDER

manslayer *n* ***syn*** see MURDERER

mantic *adj* ***syn*** see PROPHETIC

mantle *vb* ***syn*** see BLUSH

man-to-man *adj* ***syn*** see FRANK

manual *n* ***syn*** see HANDBOOK
rel abecedarium, hornbook, primer; text, textbook

manufactory *n* ***syn*** see FACTORY

manufacture *vb* ***syn*** see MAKE 3

manumit *vb* ***syn*** see FREE
ant enslave

many *adj* consisting of a goodly but indefinite number <*many* lives were lost in the flood>
syn legion, multifarious, multitudinal, multitudinous, numerous, populous, ‖several, sundry, various, voluminous
rel divers, manifold, multiple, multiplicate, multiplied, myriad; abounding, abundant, bounteous, bountiful, copious, plentiful
con meager, scant, scanty, sparse; only, sole
ant few

many *pron* ***syn*** see SUNDRY

many-sided *adj* **1** ***syn*** see MULTILATERAL
2 ***syn*** see VERSATILE

map *n* **1** ***syn*** see CHART 1
rel picture, portrayal; delineation, design, diagram, draft, outline, sketch, tracing
‖**2** ***syn*** see FACE 1

map (out) *vb* ***syn*** see DESIGN 3

maquillage *n* ***syn*** see MAKEUP 3

mar *vb* ***syn*** see INJURE 1
rel bruise, scar, scratch, warp; ruin, wreck
con adorn, beautify, decorate, embellish; mend, patch, repair; amend, correct, emend, rectify, reform, revise

---

syn synonym(s) ***rel*** related word(s)
ant antonym(s) ***con*** contrasted word(s)
idiom idiomatic equivalent(s)
‖ use limited; if in doubt, see a dictionary

maraud *vb* ***syn*** see RAID 1

marauder *n* one who raids in search of plunder <*marauders* sacked village after village>
syn bandit, brigand, bummer, cateran, depredator, despoiler, forager, freebooter, looter, pillager, plunderer, raider, ravager, ravisher, sacker, spoiler, spoliator
rel buccaneer, desperado, pirate; wrecker

marblehearted *adj* ***syn*** see UNFEELING 2
ant softhearted

marbles *n pl* ***syn*** see WIT 2

march *n* ***syn*** see FRONTIER 1
rel boundary, periphery; territory; outlands, provinces

march *vb* ***syn*** see ADJOIN
rel fringe, hem, rim, skirt; extend; parallel

march *vb* **1** ***syn*** see AGREE 4
2 ***syn*** see STRIDE 1
3 ***syn*** see ADVANCE 5

march *n* ***syn*** see ADVANCE 2

marchland *n* ***syn*** see FRONTIER 1

mare's nest *n* ***syn*** see IMPOSTURE
rel babel, clamor, din, hubbub, hullabaloo, racket, uproar

margin *n* **1** ***syn*** see BORDER 1
rel frame, trimming; shore; side
2 ***syn*** see ROOM 3
3 ***syn*** see MINIMUM

margin *vb* ***syn*** see BORDER 1
rel abut, connect, join, line, neighbor, touch

marijuana *n* the dried leaves and flowering tops of the pistillate hemp plant sometimes smoked for their intoxicating effect <*marijuana* was smoked by several students at the party>
syn boo, cannabis, grass, ‖Mary Jane, moocah, pot, ‖tea, weed
rel joint, reefer; hash, hashish

marine *adj* **1** of or relating to the sea <*marine* biology>
syn maritime, oceanic, thalassic
rel hydrographic, oceanographic; abyssal, bathyal, bathybic, bathysmal, benthic, dipsey, neritic, pelagic; aquatic, fluvial, fluviatile, lacustrine
2 of or relating to the navigation of the sea <*marine* charts and maps>
syn maritime, nautical, navigational
rel naval; seamanlike, seamanly; deep-sea, oceangoing, seafaring, seagoing

mariner *n* one engaged in sailing or handling a ship <the tanker crew was made up mostly of experienced *mariners*>
syn jack, jack-tar, sailor, sailorman, salt, seaman, tar, tarpaulin
rel bluejacket, gob, rating, ‖swab, ‖swabbie; ‖lascar, ‖limey; old salt, sea dog, shellback

marital *adj* ***syn*** see MATRIMONIAL

maritime *adj* **1** ***syn*** see MARINE 2
2 ***syn*** see MARINE 1

mark *n* **1** ***syn*** see AMBITION 2
2 ***syn*** see TARGET 1
3 ***syn*** see USE 4
4 ***syn*** see FOOL 3
5 ***syn*** see INDICATION 3
rel attribute, emblem, symbol, type; character, property, quality
6 ***syn*** see QUALITY 1
7 a device (as a word) pointing distinctly to the origin or ownership of merchandise to which it is applied and legally reserved to the exclusive use of the owner <the company was brought to court for illegally using the *mark* of its rival>
syn brand, brand name, logo, logotype, trademark
rel label, stamp
8 ***syn*** see CHARACTER 1
9 ***syn*** see NOTICE 1
10 ***syn*** see EFFECT 3

mark *vb* **1** ***syn*** see CHOOSE 1
2 ***syn*** see SHOW 5
3 ***syn*** see SHOW 2
4 ***syn*** see CHARACTERIZE 2
rel bespeak, betoken, denote, signify
idiom set apart
5 ***syn*** see SEE 1
rel record, register; attend, heed, regard

mark (out) *vb* ***syn*** see DEMARCATE 1
rel lay off, mark off; chart, lay out, map

mark down *vb* **1** ***syn*** see REDUCE 2
ant mark up
2 ***syn*** see DEPRECIATE 1

marked *adj* ***syn*** see NOTICEABLE
rel distinguished, noted; considerable

market *n* ***syn*** see STORE 4

market *vb* **1** ***syn*** see SELL 3
rel wholesale
2 ***syn*** see SELL 2

marketable *adj* capable of being sold <*marketable* commodities>
syn merchandisable, merchantable, salable, sellable, trafficable, vendible
rel commercial; profitable, selling; fit, good, sound, wholesome
con unmerchantable, unsalable
ant unmarketable

‖**maroon** *vb* ***syn*** see CAMP

marred *adj* ***syn*** see DAMAGED
rel banged-up, battered, bruised, mutilated; ruined, wrecked
ant unmarred

marriage *n* **1** the state of being united to a person of the opposite sex as husband or wife <*marriage* was not in the plans of this couple>
syn conjugality, connubiality, matrimony, wedlock
rel match, union
2 ***syn*** see WEDDING

marriage broker *n* one who arranges marriages <the old widow served as the town's *marriage broker*>
syn go-between, matchmaker
rel shadchan

marriage portion *n* ***syn*** see DOWRY

married *adj* ***syn*** see MATRIMONIAL

marrow *n* ***syn*** see ESSENCE 2
rel core, heart, kernel, meat

marrowy *adj* ***syn*** see PITHY

marry *vb* **1** to take as spouse <he *married* her for her money>

syn catch, espouse, wed

rel wive

idiom get hitched, get married, tie the knot

con annul, divorce, separate

2 to join in wedlock <the minister *married* all three daughters in one ceremony>

syn ‖hitch, mate, splice, tie, wed

idiom tie the knot, unite in marriage

3 ***syn*** see JOIN 1

marsh *n* ***syn*** see SWAMP

marshal *vb* **1** ***syn*** see ORDER 1

rel distribute, space; escort, guide, shepherd, usher

2 ***syn*** see MOBILIZE 3

marshland *n* ***syn*** see SWAMP

martial *adj* belonging to, engaged in, or appropriate to the affairs of war <the reviewing officer saw the company standing in *martial* array>

syn military, warlike

rel bellicose, belligerent, combative, pugnacious; aggressive, militant; high-spirited, mettlesome, spirited

con civil, civilian; irenic, pacific, peaceable, peaceful

ant unmartial

martyr *vb* ***syn*** see AFFLICT

martyrize *vb* ***syn*** see AFFLICT

marvel *n* ***syn*** see WONDER 1

marveling *n* ***syn*** see WONDER 2

rel surprise

marvelous *adj* **1** causing or exciting wonder <the way in which he could bring together opposing forces was truly *marvelous*>

syn amazing, astonishing, astounding, miraculous, prodigious, spectacular, staggering, strange, stupendous, surprising, wonderful, wondrous

rel awe-inspiring, awesome, awful, awing; incomprehensible, inconceivable, incredible, unimaginable; fabulous, phenomenal, supernatural; exceptional, extraordinary; bewildering, confounding, striking, stunning

con commonplace, ordinary, routine; blah, unexciting, uninteresting

2 superior or outstanding of its kind <had a *marvelous* weekend>

syn ‖cool, ‖dandy, divine, dreamy, ‖galluptious, glorious, groovy, hot, hunky-dory, ‖keen, ‖neat, nifty, peachy, ripping, sensational, super, swell, terrific, wonderful; *compare* EXCELLENT, SUPERIOR 4, SUPREME

rel agreeable, enjoyable, pleasant, pleasurable; rewarding, satisfying

con dreary, dull, humdrum, monotonous, tedious; inferior, low-grade, mean, poor, punk

‖**Mary Jane** *n* ***syn*** see MARIJUANA

mascot *n* ***syn*** see CHARM 2

masculine *adj* ***syn*** see VIRILE

ant effeminate, unmasculine

rel macho

masculinity *n* ***syn*** see VIRILITY

rel machismo, macho

mash *n* ***syn*** see CLUTTER 2

mash *vb* **1** ***syn*** see CRUSH 2

‖**2** ***syn*** see PRESS 1

mashed *adj* ***syn*** see ENAMORED 1

masher *n* ***syn*** see WOLF

mash note *n* ***syn*** see LOVE LETTER

mask *n* **1** a cover or partial cover for the face that has openings for the eyes and is used especially for disguise <on Halloween he wore a pirate's *mask*>

syn domino, doughface, false face, visor, vizard

rel disguise, masquerade; veil

2 an outward appearance that seeks to obscure an underlying true character <he was able to maintain a *mask* of dignity and tranquillity in his time of anxiety>

syn cloak, color, coloring, cover, disguise, disguisement, facade, face, false front, front, guise, masquerade, muffler, pretense, pretext, put-on, semblance, show, veil, veneer, window dressing; *compare* APPEARANCE 2

rel affectation, air, pose, posture; fakery, sham; dissembling, dissimulation, seeming, simulation; appearance, aspect

mask *vb* ***syn*** see DISGUISE

rel screen, secrete, veil; blur; defend, guard, protect, safeguard, shield

masquerade *n* ***syn*** see MASK 2

masquerade *vb* ***syn*** see POSE 4

mass *n* **1** ***syn*** see BODY 4

2 ***syn*** see PILE 1

3 ***syn*** see BULK 1

rel aggregate, aggregation, conglomerate, conglomeration; sum, whole

4 ***syn*** see BODY 3

5 ***syn*** see MUCH

6 *usu* **masses** *pl* ***syn*** see RABBLE 2

massacre *vb* ***syn*** see SLAUGHTER 3

massacre *n* the act or an instance of killing a considerable number of human beings under circumstances of atrocity or cruelty <the *massacre* of the Indians by the soldiers and settlers>

syn bloodbath, bloodshed, butchery, carnage, slaughter

rel blood purge, decimation, genocide, pogrom; internecion; assassination, killing, murder, slaying

massive *adj* **1** ***syn*** see HEAVY 1

rel hulking, hulky, massy

2 ***syn*** see HUGE

3 ***syn*** see MONSTROUS 1

massy *adj* ***syn*** see HUGE

master *n* **1** ***syn*** see EXPERT

rel maestro, savant; genius, mastermind; guru, swami

2 ***syn*** see LEADER 2

rel overlord, overman, overseer

3 ***syn*** see VICTOR 1

‖**4** ***syn*** see HUSBAND

5 ***syn*** see LOVER 1

master *vb* **1** ***syn*** see OVERCOME 1

syn synonym(s) ***rel*** related word(s)

ant antonym(s) ***con*** contrasted word(s)

idiom idiomatic equivalent(s)

‖ use limited; if in doubt, see a dictionary

THESAURUS

2 *syn* see DOMESTICATE
rel dominate, govern, predominate, rule
3 *syn* see CONQUER 2
4 *syn* see LEARN 1

master *adj* 1 *syn* see DOMINANT 1
2 *syn* see PROFICIENT

masterdom *n syn* see SUPREMACY

masterful *adj* 1 disposed to exercise or flaunt dictatorial authority in a way to override any protestation <the royal favorite was pompous and *masterful* when dealing with subordinates>
syn bossy, domineering, high-handed, imperative, imperial, imperious, magisterial, overbearing, peremptory
rel absolute, arbitrary, authoritarian, authoritative, dictative, dictatorial, doctrinaire, dogmatic; autocratic, despotic, tyrannical; high-and-mighty, self-willed
con humble, modest, unpretentious; indecisive, irresolute; submissive, yielding; feeble, weak
2 *syn* see PROFICIENT
rel adroit, deft, dexterous; preeminent, superlative, supreme, transcendent

master-hand *n syn* see EXPERT

masterly *adj syn* see PROFICIENT
rel preeminent, superlative, supreme, transcendent

masterpiece *n* 1 something done or made with extraordinary skill or brilliance <his latest work is unquestionably a *masterpiece*>
syn chef d'oeuvre, classic, magnum opus, masterwork, tour de force
rel objet d'art, masterstroke
con botch, disaster, fiasco
2 *syn* see SHOWPIECE

mastership *n syn* see ABILITY 2

masterwork *n syn* see MASTERPIECE 1

mastery *n* 1 *syn* see POWER 1
2 *syn* see ABILITY 2

masticate *vb syn* see CHEW 1
rel bruise, crush, macerate, mash, pulp, pulpify, smash, squash

mastodonic *adj syn* see HUGE

mat *adj syn* see DULL 7

matador *n syn* see BULLFIGHTER

match *n* 1 *syn* see OPPONENT
2 *syn* see EQUAL
rel analogue, parallel
3 *syn* see MATE 5
4 *syn* see PARALLEL
5 *syn* see EVENT 5
rel bout, engagement, game

match *vb* 1 *syn* see OPPOSE 1
2 *syn* see EQUATE 2
3 *syn* see AMOUNT 2
rel complement, supplement
4 *syn* see EQUAL 3
rel compare, stack up
idiom hold a candle to

matched *adj syn* see ASSORTED 2
rel balanced, equated, evened, similar; coordinated, harmonized; coupled, joined, mated, paired, yoked
ant unmatched

matchless *adj syn* see ALONE 3
ant matchable

matchmaker *n syn* see MARRIAGE BROKER

mate *n* 1 *syn* see PARTNER
2 *syn* see ACCOMPANIMENT 2
3 *syn* see FRIEND
rel bedmate, classmate, co-mate, helpmate, playmate, roommate, schoolmate, teammate
4 *syn* see SPOUSE
rel match, parti
5 one of a pair matched in one or more qualities <the *mate* of a shoe>
syn companion, coordinate, double, duplicate, fellow, match, reciprocal, twin
rel alter ego, complement, sosie; compeer, equal, equivalent, peer

mate *vb syn* see MARRY 2
rel breed, crossbreed, pair; generate, procreate

‖**mater** *n syn* see MOTHER 1

material *adj* 1 of or belonging to actuality <for him the *material* world is the only world>
syn corporeal, gross, objective, phenomenal, physical, sensible, substantial, tangible
rel actual, real, true; appreciable, palpable, perceptible; earthly, worldly; animal, carnal, fleshly, sensual
con impalpable, imperceptible, intangible, unsubstantial; spiritual
ant immaterial, nonmaterial
2 *syn* see IMPORTANT 1
ant immaterial
3 *syn* see RELEVANT
rel consequential, important, momentous, significant; cardinal, essential, fundamental, vital
ant immaterial

material *n* 1 *syn* see THING 5
rel component, constituent, element, ingredient; apparatus, equipment, machinery
2 *usu* **materials** *pl syn* see EQUIPMENT

materialistic *adj* of or relating to a preoccupation with or stress upon material rather than intellectual or spiritual things <*materialistic* values characterize the modern age>
syn banausic, earthy, mundane, sensual, temporal, worldly
rel carnal, profane; earthly, terrestrial; secular, unspiritual
con intellectual, mental; spiritual, unfleshly, unworldly; heavenly

materiality *n syn* see ACTUALITY 2

materialize *vb* 1 *syn* see EMBODY 1
rel appear, emerge, loom, show; issue, rise, spring
2 to convert mentally into something concrete <with the help of graphs and figures abstract ideas can be *materialized*>
syn entify, hypostatize, reify
rel actualize, pragmatize, realize; corporealize; symbolize, typify

matériel *n syn* see EQUIPMENT

matriarch *n* a dignified, usually elderly woman of some rank or authority <the local *matriarchs* controlled the town's social functions>
syn dame, dowager, grande dame, matron

rel materfamilias, mother

matrimonial *adj* of, relating to, or characteristic of marriage <the *matrimonial* bond between husband and wife>
syn conjugal, connubial, hymeneal, marital, married, nuptial, spousal, wedded
rel bridal, epithalamic

matrimony *n* ***syn*** see MARRIAGE 1

matron *n* ***syn*** see MATRIARCH

matter *n* **1** ***syn*** see SUBJECT 2
2 ***syn*** see AFFAIR 1
rel complication, grievance, to-do, worry; circumstance, predicament
3 ***syn*** see SUBSTANCE 2
4 ***syn*** see THING 5
5 ***syn*** see ORDER 4

matter *vb* to be of importance <being your own self is what really *matters*>
syn count, import, mean, signify, weigh
idiom carry weight

matter-of-course *adj* ***syn*** see GENERAL 1

matter-of-fact *adj* **1** ***syn*** see REALISTIC
rel objective, sound
2 ***syn*** see PROSAIC 1
3 involving no display of emotion <the *matter-of-fact* reading of the judge masked his inner anguish>
syn cold, cold-blooded, emotionless, impersonal, unimpassioned
rel unaffected, unsentimental; prosaic
con emotional, impassioned, personal
4 ***syn*** see IMPASSIVE 1

maturate *vb* ***syn*** see MATURE

mature *adj* **1** having attained the normal peak of natural growth and development <*mature* plants ready to bear fruit>
syn adult, full-blown, full-fledged, full-grown, grown, grown-up, matured, ripe, ripened
rel developed, ready
idiom of age
con childish, childlike; boyish, green, juvenile, maiden, puerile, youthful
ant immature
2 ***syn*** see DUE 2
3 ***syn*** see UNPAID 2

mature *vb* to become fully developed or ripe <she *matured* as an actress after several years of summer stock>
syn age, develop, grow, grow up, maturate, mellow, ‖ripe, ripen
rel blossom, flower; advance, progress, round; season; decline, deteriorate, olden, wane
idiom come of age

matured *adj* **1** ***syn*** see MATURE 1
rel completed, finished; advised, considered, deliberate, designed, premeditated, studied
con callow, crude, green, raw, rough, rude, uncouth
ant premature, unmatured
2 ***syn*** see RIPE 3

maudlin *adj* ***syn*** see SENTIMENTAL
rel addled, befuddled, confused, fuddled, muddled; silly

maul *n* ***syn*** see BRAWL 2

maul *vb* ***syn*** see BATTER 1
rel flagellate, flail, lash, whip; bang, bash, buffet, pound; abuse, maltreat, manhandle, molest, rough (up)

maunder *vb* ***syn*** see WANDER 1

maundering *adj* ***syn*** see INARTICULATE 3

maven *n* ***syn*** see EXPERT

maverick *n* ***syn*** see BOHEMIAN

mawkish *adj* ***syn*** see SENTIMENTAL
rel banal, flat; cloying, nauseating, sickening

maxim *n* a general truth or fundamental principle usually expressed sententiously <Francis Bacon is noted for his fondness for *maxims*>
syn aphorism, apothegm, axiom, brocard, dictum, gnome, moral, rule, truism
rel commonplace, motto, platitude; law, precept, prescript; theorem; proverb
idiom rule of thumb

maximal *adj* ***syn*** see MAXIMUM
ant minimal

maximize *vb* ***syn*** see OVERPLAY 2
ant minimize

maximum *adj* greatest in quantity or highest in degree attainable or attained <apply *maximum* pressure above the point of injury>
syn maximal, outside, top, topmost, utmost; *compare* SUPREME
rel greatest, highest, largest
con least, lowest, slightest, smallest
ant minimum

maybe *adv* ***syn*** see PERHAPS

mayhem *vb* ***syn*** see MAIM

maze *n* **1** something intricately or confusingly elaborate or complicated <the landscape soon became a *maze* of superhighways>
syn jungle, knot, labyrinth, mesh, mizmaze, morass, skein, snarl, tangle, web
rel fog, haze; gordian knot; conglomeration, hodgepodge, miscellany, mishmash
‖**2** ***syn*** see HAZE 2

‖**mazuma** *n* ***syn*** see MONEY

MD *n* ***syn*** see PHYSICIAN

meager *adj* **1** ***syn*** see LEAN
2 being smaller than what is normal, necessary, or desirable <the remains of dinner provided only a *meager* meal that evening>
syn exiguous, poor, scant, scanty, scrimp, scrimpy, skimp, skimpy, spare, sparse; *compare* SHORT 3
rel deficient, inadequate, insufficient; inappreciable, inconsiderable, slight; bare, mere, minimum; miserable, shabby
con adequate, enough, sufficient; appreciable, considerable; copious, plentiful
ant ample

meal *n* the portion of food taken at one time to satisfy appetite <the noonday dinner was the big *meal* of the day in those times>
syn ‖chow, feed, ‖nosh, refection, repast

rel feast, ‖nosh-up, spread; refreshment, regalement; collation, snack; fare, grub, meat, mess, victuals; board, table
meal *vb* ***syn*** see EAT 1
mean *adj* **1** ***syn*** see IGNOBLE 1
ant wellborn
2 ***syn*** see INFERIOR 2
3 ***syn*** see LITTLE 2
4 ***syn*** see CONTEMPTIBLE
5 ***syn*** see CHEAP 2
6 ***syn*** see STINGY
7 ***syn*** see TROUBLESOME
rel difficult, formidable, rough, rugged, tough
8 ***syn*** see UNWELL
mean *vb* **1** ***syn*** see INTEND 2
rel desire, want, wish
2 to convey (as an idea) to the mind <your answer *means* nothing to me>
syn add up (to), connote, denote, express, import, intend, signify, spell
rel designate, name; attest, betoken, indicate; hint, imply, intimate, suggest
3 ***syn*** see MATTER
mean *n* **1** ***syn*** see AVERAGE
2 *usu* **means** *sing or pl in constr* one by which work is accomplished or an end effected <careful planning is a major *means* of improving output> <use any *means* to secure peace>
syn agency, agent, channel, instrument, instrumentality, instrumentation, intermediary, medium, ministry, organ, vehicle
rel fashion, manner, method, mode, system, way; apparatus, equipment, machinery, paraphernalia
3 means *pl* one's total property including real property and intangibles <people of moderate *means* are feeling the effects of inflation worse>
syn assets, capital, resources, wealth
rel finances, fortune, funds, moneybags, pocket, purse; ‖bundle, nest egg, pile, reserves, savings; estate, holdings, possessions; intangibles
mean *adj* **1** ***syn*** see MIDDLE 2
2 ***syn*** see MEDIUM
meander *vb* ***syn*** see WANDER 1
rel snake, turn, twist, wind
meanderer *n* ***syn*** see ROVER
meandering *adj* ***syn*** see WINDING
meandrous *adj* ***syn*** see WINDING
meaning *n* **1** the idea that something conveys to the mind <critics have endlessly debated the *meaning* of the poem>
syn acceptation, import, intendment, intent, message, purport, sense, significance, significancy, signification, sum and substance, understanding; *compare* SUBSTANCE 2, TENOR 1
rel drift, effect, essence, tenor; force, point, value; hint, implication, intimation, suggestion; connotation, definition, denotation
2 ***syn*** see INTENTION
meaningful *adj* **1** ***syn*** see EXPRESSIVE
ant meaningless
2 ***syn*** see IMPORTANT 1
meaningless *adj* **1** ***syn*** see SENSELESS 5
rel blank, empty, vacant
ant meaningful
2 ***syn*** see FECKLESS 1
measly *adj* ***syn*** see PETTY 2
measure *n* **1** ***syn*** see RATION
2 ***syn*** see TEMPERANCE 1
3 ***syn*** see SIZE 1
4 ***syn*** see MELODY
5 ***syn*** see RHYTHM
6 ***syn*** see STANDARD 3
7 an action planned or taken toward the accomplishment of a purpose <developed a new set of safety *measures*>
syn maneuver, move, procedure, proceeding, step
rel effort, project, proposal, proposition; expedient, makeshift, resort, resource, shift, stopgap
measure *vb* **1** ***syn*** see DEMARCATE 1
2 to ascertain the quantity, mass, extent, or degree of in terms of a standard unit or fixed amount <*measure* the depth of the water>
syn gauge, scale
rel size, size up; calculate, compute, estimate, figure, reckon
measure (out) *vb* ***syn*** see DISTRIBUTE 1
measureless *adj* **1** ***syn*** see INCALCULABLE 1
ant measurable
2 ***syn*** see LIMITLESS
ant measurable
measure up *vb* ***syn*** see EQUAL 3
meat *n* **1** ***syn*** see FOOD 1
2 ***syn*** see SUBSTANCE 2
meat–and–potatoes *adj* ***syn*** see FUNDAMENTAL 1
meathead *n* ***syn*** see OAF 2
meaty *adj* ***syn*** see PITHY
mechanical *adj* ***syn*** see PERFUNCTORY
meddle *vb* to concern oneself with officiously, impertinently, or indiscreetly <continually *meddling* in other people's affairs>
syn busybody, butt in, fool, horn in, interfere, interlope, intermeddle, ‖make, mess around, monkey (with), tamper (with)
rel intervene, intrude, invade, obtrude; pry, snoop, trespass
idiom put (*or* shove *or* stick) one's oar in, stick one's nose into
con disregard, ignore, neglect, omit, overlook, slight; avoid, eschew, shun
meddler *n* ***syn*** see BUSYBODY
meddlesome *adj* ***syn*** see IMPERTINENT 2
Meddlesome Mattie *n* ***syn*** see BUSYBODY
medial *adj* **1** ***syn*** see MIDDLE 1
2 ***syn*** see MIDDLE 2
3 ***syn*** see MEDIUM
median *n* ***syn*** see AVERAGE
rel center, middle
median *adj* **1** ***syn*** see MIDDLE 1
2 ***syn*** see MIDDLE 2
mediate *vb* ***syn*** see INTERPOSE 2
mediator *n* **1** ***syn*** see GO-BETWEEN 2
rel arbitrator, judge; conciliator, peacemaker; negotiator, troubleshooter
2 ***syn*** see MODERATOR
medical *n* ***syn*** see PHYSICIAN
medicament *n* ***syn*** see REMEDY 1

medicant *n* ***syn*** see REMEDY 1
medication *n* ***syn*** see REMEDY 1
medicinal *n* ***syn*** see DRUG 1
medicine *n* ***syn*** see REMEDY 1
mediciner *n* ***syn*** see PHYSICIAN
medico *n* ***syn*** see PHYSICIAN
mediocre *adj* ***syn*** see MEDIUM
rel bad, inferior, poor; common, commonplace, ordinary, unexceptional
idiom no great shakes, nothing to write home about
meditate *vb* ***syn*** see PONDER 2
meditative *adj* **1** ***syn*** see THOUGHTFUL 1
rel musing, ruminant; wistful
2 ***syn*** see PENSIVE 2
medium *adj* midway between the extremes of a scale, measurement, or evaluation <bought a suit of *medium* quality>
syn average, fair, fairish, indifferent, intermediate, mean, medial, mediocre, middle-rate, middling, moderate, run-of-mine, run-of-the-mill, so-so
rel median, par; passable, tolerable; neutral; popular, vulgar; normal, standard
idiom fair to middling
con inferior, low-grade, poor; excellent, first-class, high-grade, prime, superior
medium *n* **1** ***syn*** see MEAN 2
rel intermediate, intermedium
2 ***syn*** see ENVIRONMENT
3 ***syn*** see FORTE
medley *n* ***syn*** see MISCELLANY 1
‖**meech** *vb* ***syn*** see SNEAK
meed *n* **1** ***syn*** see REWARD
rel recompensing, satisfaction
2 ***syn*** see RATION
rel desert, due, merit
meek *adj* ***syn*** see HUMBLE 1
rel gentle, mild; tame; forbearing, lenient, tolerant; long-suffering, patient
con high-spirited, mettlesome, spirited, spunky; contumacious, insubordinate, rebellious
ant arrogant
meet *vb* **1** ***syn*** see HAPPEN 2
2 ***syn*** see CONFRONT 1
3 ***syn*** see ENGAGE 5
rel brave, oppose
4 ***syn*** see EQUAL 3
5 ***syn*** see SATISFY 5
rel approach, equal, match, rival, tie, touch
6 to come together face-to-face or as if face-to-face <the two leaders agreed to *meet* in a series of summit talks>
syn close, encounter, face, front; *compare* CONFRONT 1
rel accost, greet, salute; bump, clash, collide, cross; grapple, tussle, wrestle; experience, suffer, sustain, undergo
con elude, escape, evade, shun
ant avoid
7 ***syn*** see CONVERGE
8 ***syn*** see CONVENE 1
meet (with) *vb* ***syn*** see FIND 1
meet *n* **1** ***syn*** see EVENT 5
2 ***syn*** see CONTEST 2
meet *adj* **1** ***syn*** see FIT 1
rel accommodated, conformed, reconciled; good, right; equitable, fair, just
ant unmeet
2 ***syn*** see GOOD 2
ant unmeet
meeting *n* **1** ***syn*** see CONTEST 2
2 ***syn*** see CONCOURSE
3 ***syn*** see TALK 4
rel congress, moot
meetness *n* ***syn*** see ORDER 11
ant unmeetness
megacosm *n* ***syn*** see UNIVERSE
ant microcosm
megrim *n* ***syn*** see CAPRICE
rel impulse, urge
melancholic *adj* ***syn*** see SAD 2
melancholy *n* ***syn*** see SADNESS
rel miserableness, misery, wretchedness; despair, desperation; boredom, ennui, tedium
con hopefulness, optimism
ant exhilaration
melancholy *adj* **1** ***syn*** see SAD 1
2 expressing or suggesting sorrow or mourning <the gloomy day led him to a *melancholy* train of thought>
syn doleful, dolesome, dolorous, lamentable, lugubrious, moanful, mournful, plaintive, rueful, sighful, sorrowful, wailful, woeful; *compare* SAD 1, SAD 2
rel pensive, reflective, thoughtful; discomposing, disquieting, disturbing, perturbing; dismal, dreary, funereal, gloomy, lachrymose, somber, sombrous
con cheerful, glad, happy, joyful, joyous, lighthearted; gay, lively, vivacious
3 ***syn*** see SAD 2
mélange *n* ***syn*** see MISCELLANY 1
meld *vb* ***syn*** see MIX 1
melding *n* ***syn*** see UNIFICATION
melee *n* **1** ***syn*** see CLASH 2
rel dogfight, scuffle
2 ***syn*** see BRAWL 2
3 ***syn*** see MISCELLANY 1
meliorate *vb* ***syn*** see IMPROVE 1
melisma *n* ***syn*** see MELODY
mellay *n* **1** ***syn*** see BRAWL 2
2 ***syn*** see CLASH 2
mellifluent *adj* ***syn*** see MELLIFLUOUS
mellifluous *adj* having a smooth rich flow <his *mellifluous* voice held his audience in a trance>
syn golden, honeyed, Hyblaean, liquid, mellifluent, mellow; *compare* MELODIOUS 1
rel accordant, canorous, euphonic, euphonious, harmonious, mellisonant, silvery; golden-tongued, silver-tongued; dulcet, sweet; resonant, sonorous

---

syn synonym(s) ***rel*** related word(s)
ant antonym(s) ***con*** contrasted word(s)
idiom idiomatic equivalent(s)
‖ use limited; if in doubt, see a dictionary

con blatant, boisterous, clamorous, obstreperous, strident, vociferous; discordant, grating, harsh

mellisonant *adj* ***syn*** see MELODIOUS 1

mellow *adj* **1** ***syn*** see RIPE 3
2 ***syn*** see MELLIFLUOUS

mellow *vb* ***syn*** see MATURE

melodia *n* ***syn*** see MELODY

melodic *adj* **1** ***syn*** see MELODIOUS 2
2 ***syn*** see MELODIOUS 1

melodious *adj* **1** pleasing to the ear <*melodious* sounds of the forest>
syn dulcet, euphonic, euphonious, mellisonant, melodic, sweet, tuneful; *compare* MELLIFLUOUS
rel canorous, harmonious
con discordant, grating, harsh
ant unmelodious
2 containing, constituting, or characterized by melody <her voice shows marked improvement and a new richly *melodious* quality>
syn melodic, musical, songful, tuned, tuneful
rel cantabile, lyric, melic

melody *n* a rhythmic succession of single tones organized as an aesthetic whole <took out his flute and played a simple *melody*>
syn air, descant, diapason, lay, measure, melisma, melodia, strain, tune, warble; *compare* SONG 2
rel song; bel canto, canto, vocalise; lyrics

melt *vb* **1** ***syn*** see LIQUEFY
rel heat, warm
con coagulate, harden, set
ant freeze; solidify
2 ***syn*** see BURN 3
rel perspire, sweat

member *n* ***syn*** see PART 1

memento *n* **1** ***syn*** see REMEMBRANCE 3
2 ***syn*** see VESTIGE 1

memo *n* **1** ***syn*** see NOTE 2
2 ***syn*** see MEMORANDUM 2

memoir *n* **1** ***syn*** see BIOGRAPHY
rel anecdote; memory, recollection, remembrance, reminiscence
2 ***syn*** see DISCOURSE 2

memoirist *n* ***syn*** see BIOGRAPHER

memorable *adj* ***syn*** see NOTEWORTHY
rel momentous, rememberable; deathless, unfadable, unforgettable
ant unmemorable

memorandum *n* **1** ***syn*** see NOTE 2
2 a communication that contains directive, advisory, or informative matter <the *memorandum* announced the holiday schedule>
syn directive, memo, notice
rel announcement, dispatch, minute; epistle, letter, missive, note; reminder, tickler; message; diary

memorial *adj* serving to preserve remembrance <a *memorial* plaque>
syn commemorative, commemoratory
rel celebrative, consecrative, dedicatory, enshrining

memorial *n* **1** ***syn*** see REMEMBRANCE 3
2 ***syn*** see MONUMENT 2

memorialize *vb* **1** ***syn*** see ADDRESS 4
2 to record or honor the memory of by or as if by a monument <the new library *memorializes* the late President>
syn commemorate, monument, monumentalize
rel etch, grave, impress, imprint; jog, nudge, remind
idiom bring to mind, fix in the (*or* one's) mind (*or* memory), impress on one's mind, treasure in one's heart
con forget, neglect, overlook

memorial park *n* ***syn*** see CEMETERY

memorize *vb* to commit to memory <the actors hadn't even *memorized* their lines>
syn con, get, learn
rel study
idiom get (*or* learn) by heart, get (*or* learn) word for word
con forget

memory *n* **1** the power or process of reproducing or recalling what has been learned <blessed with a good *memory*>
syn recollection, remembrance, reminiscence
rel reflection, retrospection; retention, retentiveness; mind, recall; mind's eye; awareness, cognizance, consciousness
con forgetfulness, obliviousness, unmindfulness; lethe, oblivion
2 a particular act of recalling <her *memory* of her wedding day remains vivid>
syn anamnesis, recall, recollection, remembrance, reminiscence
rel memento, souvenir

menace *vb* **1** ***syn*** see THREATEN
rel alarm, frighten, scare; endanger, torment; loom, lower
2 ***syn*** see ENDANGER

menacing *adj* ***syn*** see IMMINENT 2

ménage *n* ***syn*** see FAMILY 2
rel ménage à trois

mend *vb* **1** ***syn*** see CORRECT 1
2 to put into good shape or working order again <*mends* garments in her spare time>
syn doctor, do up, fix, overhaul, patch, rebuild, recondition, reconstruct, repair, revamp, ‖right, ‖rightle, vamp
rel condition, ready, service; refurbish, rejuvenate, renew, renovate, restore; correct, emend, rectify, redress, reform; heal
3 ***syn*** see IMPROVE 3

mendacious *adj* ***syn*** see DISHONEST
rel false, wrong; erroneous, fallacious, spurious; equivocating, fibbing, paltering, prevaricating
ant veracious

mendaciousness *n* ***syn*** see MENDACITY
ant veraciousness, veracity

mendacity *n* the practice or an instance of lying <he was ultimately caught by his own outrageous *mendacity*>
syn falsehood, fibbery, mendaciousness, truthlessness, untruthfulness, unveracity
rel boggling, caviling, dodging, equivocation, hedging, quibbling, shifting, sidestepping
ant veraciousness, veracity

mendicancy *n* the practice or act of begging <the city passed an ordinance against *mendicancy*>
syn beggary, bumming, cadging, mendicity, mooching, panhandling
rel sponging

mendicity *n* ***syn*** see MENDICANCY

menial *adj* ***syn*** see SUBSERVIENT 2

mental *adj* **1** of or relating to the mind <the *mental* aspects of the problem>
syn cerebral, intellective, intellectual, psychic, psychical, psychological
rel immaterial, inner, spiritual; telepathic; intelligent, rational, reasoning, thinking; ideological
con bodily, corporal, corporeal, physical, somatic; perceptive; sensual, sensuous
||**2** ***syn*** see INSANE 1

mentality *n* ***syn*** see INTELLIGENCE 1

mention *vb* to refer to someone or something in a clear unmistakable manner <several donors were *mentioned* in the article>
syn cite, instance, name, specify
rel denominate, designate; detail; advert, allude, refer; quote
idiom make mention of
con disregard, ignore, neglect, overlook, pass by, pass over, slight

menu *n* a list of the dishes that may be ordered (as at a restaurant) or that are to be served (as at a banquet) <hoped to find something tasty on the *menu*><he saved the elaborate *menu* as a souvenir of the awards banquet>
syn card, carte du jour
idiom bill of fare

Mephistophelian *adj* ***syn*** see SATANIC 1

mephitic *adj* **1** ***syn*** see MALODOROUS 1
2 ***syn*** see POISONOUS

mercenary *n* ***syn*** see HACK 2

mercenary *adj* ***syn*** see CORRUPT 2
ant unmercenary

merchandisable *adj* ***syn*** see MARKETABLE
ant unmerchantable, unsalable

merchandise *n* the products that are bought and sold in business <*merchandise* of inferior quality>
syn commodities, goods, line, vendible(s), wares
rel effects; job lot, stock; staples

merchandise *vb* ***syn*** see SELL 3
rel advertise, publicize

merchandiser *n* ***syn*** see MERCHANT

merchant *n* a buyer and seller of commodities for profit <a *merchant* of dry goods>
syn businessman, dealer, merchandiser, trader, tradesman, trafficker
rel jobber, retailer, wholesaler

merchantable *adj* ***syn*** see MARKETABLE
ant unmerchantable, unsalable

merchant prince *n* ***syn*** see MAGNATE

merciful *adj* ***syn*** see FORBEARING
rel compassionate, pitiful, softhearted; benign, kind, kindly; condoning, forgiving, pardoning
ant merciless, unmerciful

mercifulness *n* ***syn*** see FORBEARANCE 2
rel commiseration, pity, ruth
con severeness, severity, sternness
ant mercilessness, unmercifulness

merciless *adj* **1** ***syn*** see PITILESS
ant merciful
2 ***syn*** see GRIM 3
rel compassionless, cutthroat, pitiless; gratuitous, uncalled-for, wanton
con charitable, lenient, tolerant; easy, easygoing
ant merciful

mercurial *adj* ***syn*** see INCONSTANT 1
rel buoyant, effervescent, elastic, expansive, resilient; mobile, movable; adroit, clever, cunning, ingenious
ant saturnine

mercy *n* a show of or a disposition to show kindness or compassion <the *mercy* of the Lord knows all seasons>
syn caritas, charity, clemency, grace, lenity; *compare* FORBEARANCE 2
rel commiseration, compassion, pity, ruth; benevolence, benignancy, benignity, kindliness, kindness; generosity, goodwill
con reprisal, retaliation, retribution, revenge, vengeance; castigation, chastening, chastisement, punishment

mere *adj* ***syn*** see VERY 4

merely *adv* ***syn*** see JUST 3

meretricious *adj* ***syn*** see GAUDY
rel deceptive, delusive, delusory, misleading, spurious; insincere

meretrix *n* ***syn*** see PROSTITUTE

merge *vb* ***syn*** see MIX 1

mergence *n* ***syn*** see UNIFICATION

merger *n* **1** ***syn*** see CONSOLIDATION 2
2 ***syn*** see UNIFICATION

merging *n* ***syn*** see UNIFICATION

meridian *n* ***syn*** see APEX 2

merit *n* **1** ***syn*** see EXCELLENCE
ant fault
2 ***syn*** see QUALITY 2
3 ***syn*** see DUE 1
rel gaining(s), winning(s)

merit *vb* ***syn*** see EARN 2
rel award, reward; recompense, repay, requite; entitle, justify, warrant

meritable *adj* ***syn*** see WORTHY 1
ant meritless

merited *adj* ***syn*** see JUST 3
rel entitled, justified, warranted
ant unmerited

meritorious *adj* ***syn*** see WORTHY 1

merriment *n* **1** ***syn*** see MIRTH
2 ***syn*** see MERRYMAKING

merry *adj* indicative of or marked by high spirits or lightheartedness <the *merry* life of the town folk was a joy to see>
syn blithe, blithesome, boon, festive, gay, gleeful, jocund, jolly, jovial, lighthearted, mirthful, riant

---

syn synonym(s) ***rel*** related word(s)
ant antonym(s) ***con*** contrasted word(s)
idiom idiomatic equivalent(s)
|| use limited; if in doubt, see a dictionary

rel animated, lively, sprightly, vivacious; cheerful, glad, happy, joyful, joyous; hilarious, mad, unconstrained, wild
con gloomy, glum, melancholy; grave, sober, somber; earnest, sedate, serious, staid
merry–andrew *n* ***syn*** see CLOWN 3
merrymaking *n* gay or festive activity <a night of *merrymaking*>
syn festivity, gaiety, jollity, merriment, revel, reveling, revelment, revelry, whoopee
rel enjoyment, indulgence, pleasure, self-indulgence
mesh *n* **1** *usu* **meshes** *pl* ***syn*** see WEB 2
2 ***syn*** see MAZE 1
rel net, network
mesh *vb* ***syn*** see ENGAGE 1
meshuggaas *n* ***syn*** see NONSENSE 2
mesmeric *adj* ***syn*** see ATTRACTIVE 1
mesmerize *vb* ***syn*** see ENTHRALL 2
rel entrance, hypnotize
mess *n* ‖**1** ***syn*** see MUCH
2 ***syn*** see EYESORE
3 a confused or disordered state, condition, or situation <upon becoming president, he proceeded to make a *mess* of the government>
syn botch, botchery, hash, mess-up, mix-up, muddle, mull, muss, shambles; *compare* MISCELLANY 1
rel confusion, disorder; wreck, wreckage
idiom kettle of fish
mess *vb* **1** ***syn*** see BOTCH
rel confuse, disorder, jumble
idiom make a mess of
2 ***syn*** see FIDDLE 2
mess (up) *vb* ***syn*** see DISORDER 1
rel damage, mar, ruin, spoil; ‖muck, mucker, muff
message *n* **1** something (as information) conveyed by writing, speech, or signals <left a *message* before he went out>
syn communication, directive, word
rel communiqué, dispatch, report; memo, memorandum; epistle, letter, missive, note
2 ***syn*** see MEANING 1
mess around *vb* **1** ***syn*** see FIDDLE 2
2 ***syn*** see MEDDLE
3 ***syn*** see PHILANDER
messenger *n* one who bears a message or does an errand <blamed the *messenger* for the bad news he brought>
syn bearer, carrier, courier, emissary, envoy, internuncio
rel herald; go-between, intermediary, mediator; dispatcher, post
mess–up *n* ***syn*** see MESS 3
messy *adj* **1** ***syn*** see SLOVENLY 1
rel dirty, grimy, grubby
con clean
ant neat
2 ***syn*** see SLIPSHOD 3
metagrobolize *vb* ***syn*** see PUZZLE
metamorphize *vb* ***syn*** see TRANSFORM
metamorphose *vb* ***syn*** see TRANSFORM
rel age, develop, mature, ripen
metanoia *n* ***syn*** see CONVERSION 1
metaphor *n* ***syn*** see ANALOGY 2
rel comparison, trope; allegory, personification
idiom figure of speech
metaphysical *adj* **1** ***syn*** see IMMATERIAL 1
rel supernatural, transcendent, transcendental
2 ***syn*** see SUPERNATURAL 1
mete (out) *vb* **1** ***syn*** see ADMINISTER 2
rel measure
2 ***syn*** see ALLOT
meter *n* ***syn*** see RHYTHM
method *n* **1** the means or procedures used in attaining an end <he claimed that his ends justified his *methods*>
syn fashion, manner, mode, modus, system, technique, way, wise
rel design, plan, schema, scheme; form, style; course, line; modus operandi, practice, procedure, process, routine; wrinkle
2 ***syn*** see ORDER 8
methodic *adj* ***syn*** see ORDERLY 1
ant desultory, unmethodical
methodical *adj* ***syn*** see ORDERLY 1
rel methodized, organized, systematized; analytical, logical; careful, meticulous, scrupulous
con casual, hit-or-miss, random; confused, jumbled
ant desultory, unmethodical
methodize *vb* ***syn*** see ORDER 1
rel establish, fix, set, settle
meticulous *adj* ***syn*** see CAREFUL 2
rel fastidious, pernickety, picky; cautious, strict, thorough; microscopic
métier *n* **1** ***syn*** see TRADE 1
2 ***syn*** see FORTE
metropolitan *adj* ***syn*** see COSMOPOLITAN 1
mettle *n* ***syn*** see COURAGE
mettlesome *adj* ***syn*** see SPIRITED 2
rel edgy, excitable, high-strung, skittish, startlish
mew *vb* ***syn*** see ENCLOSE 1
Mickey Mouse *adj* ***syn*** see PETTY 2
mid *adj* **1** ***syn*** see MIDDLE 2
2 ***syn*** see MIDDLE 1
mid *prep* **1** ***syn*** see AMID 1
2 ***syn*** see AMONG 1
3 ***syn*** see DURING
middle *adj* **1** equally distant from the extremes <the *middle* finger>
syn center, centermost, equidistant, halfway, medial, median, mid, middlemost, midmost
2 being at neither extreme <paid a *middle* price for it>
syn center, central, intermediary, intermediate, mean, medial, median, mid
middle *n* ***syn*** see CENTER 1
middlebrow *n* ***syn*** see PHILISTINE
middleman *n* ***syn*** see GO-BETWEEN 2
middlemost *adj* ***syn*** see MIDDLE 1
middle–of–the–road *adj* ***syn*** see MODERATE 4
middle–rate *adj* ***syn*** see MEDIUM
middle–road *adj* ***syn*** see MODERATE 4
middling *adj* ***syn*** see MEDIUM
rel inferior, poor, second-rate

midge *n* ***syn*** see DWARF
midget *n* ***syn*** see DWARF
midget *adj* ***syn*** see TINY
midmost *adj* ***syn*** see MIDDLE 1
midpoint *n* ***syn*** see CENTER 1
midst *n* ***syn*** see CENTER 1
midst *prep* **1** ***syn*** see AMID 1
2 ***syn*** see AMONG 1
3 ***syn*** see DURING
mid-Victorian *n* ***syn*** see FOGY
rel bluenose, goody-goody, Mrs. Grundy, prig, prude, puritan; Victorian
mien *n* **1** ***syn*** see BEARING 1
rel expression, manner, mannerism
2 ***syn*** see APPEARANCE 1
miff *n* **1** ***syn*** see OFFENSE 2
rel conniption, fit
2 ***syn*** see QUARREL
might *n* **1** ***syn*** see POWER 1
2 ***syn*** see POWER 4
rel energeticness, lustiness, strenuousness, vigor, vigorousness; forcefulness, forcibleness, powerfulness
3 ***syn*** see ABILITY 1
4 ***syn*** see MUSCLE 1
might and main *adv* ***syn*** see HARD 1
mightily *adv* **1** ***syn*** see HARD 1
rel arduously, laboriously, strenuously, toilsomely
2 ***syn*** see VERY 1
mighty *adj* **1** ***syn*** see POWERFUL 2
2 ***syn*** see STRONG 1
3 ***syn*** see HUGE
rel eminent, illustrious, renowned; august, grand, imposing, impressive, moving
mighty *adv* ***syn*** see VERY 1
migrant *adj* ***syn*** see MIGRATORY
migrant *n* ***syn*** see EMIGRANT
rel in-migrant, out-migrant; drifter, mover, nomad, traveler, wanderer
migrate *vb* to move from one country, place, or locality to another <his father had *migrated* to the Far West years before>
syn emigrate, transmigrate
rel immigrate, in-migrate, out-migrate, remigrate; drift, trek; nomadize, range, roam, rove, wander
migrative *adj* ***syn*** see MIGRATORY
ant nonmigratory
migratorial *adj* ***syn*** see MIGRATORY
ant nonmigratory
migratory *adj* moving habitually or occasionally from one region or climate to another <the study of *migratory* birds>
syn migrant, migrative, migratorial, mobile, transmigratory
rel errant, nomad, nomadic, ranging, roving, wandering
ant nonmigratory
mild *adj* **1** ***syn*** see GENTLE 1
rel choice, dainty, delicate, exquisite; moderate, temperate; benign, benignant
con intense, severe, sharp, vehement
ant fierce, harsh
2 ***syn*** see AMIABLE 1
rel docile, meek; subdued, submissive; deferential, obeisant, subservient
milepost *n* ***syn*** see EVENT 2
milestone *n* ***syn*** see EVENT 2
milieu *n* ***syn*** see ENVIRONMENT
militant *adj* **1** ***syn*** see BELLIGERENT
rel martial, military
2 ***syn*** see AGGRESSIVE
military *adj* ***syn*** see MARTIAL
rel chauvinistic, jingoistic, militaristic, warmongering; soldierlike, soldierly
ant unmilitary
military *n* ***syn*** see TROOP 2
militate *vb* ***syn*** see WEIGH 3
milk *vb* **1** ***syn*** see FLEECE 1
rel exact, exploit, extort; drain, empty, exhaust, pump, suck, wring
2 ***syn*** see EDUCE 1
milk-and-water *adj* ***syn*** see INSIPID 3
milk-livered *adj* ***syn*** see COWARDLY
milksop *n* ***syn*** see WEAKLING
rel effeminate; coward
milk-warm *adj* ***syn*** see TEPID 1
mill *n* ***syn*** see FACTORY
million *n* ***syn*** see SCAD
millstone *n* ***syn*** see LOAD 3
Milquetoast *n* ***syn*** see WEAKLING
mime *n* ***syn*** see ACTOR 1
mimic *n* ***syn*** see ACTOR 1
mimic *vb* to copy or exaggerate (as manner or gestures) often by way of mockery <*mimicked* her halting speech>
syn ape, burlesque, imitate, mock, parody, take off, travesty
rel hit off, mime, mum; act, do, enact, impersonate, perform, personate, play; copycat; pantomime
mimicry *n* the art or practice of closely imitating another in speech, gestures, or manners <engaged in *mimicry* of café society>
syn apery
rel imitation, mimesis, mimetism; mock, mockery; caricature, parody
miminy-piminy *adj* ***syn*** see NICE 1
mince *vb* **1** ***syn*** see CHOP 2
2 ***syn*** see SASHAY
mincing *adj* ***syn*** see GENTEEL 3
rel dainty, delicate, fastidious, finical, finicking, finicky, fussy, nice, particular, pernickety, persnickety, squeamish
||**mincy** *adj* ***syn*** see NICE 1
mind *n* **1** the element or complex of elements in an individual that feels, perceives, thinks, wills, and especially reasons <sad to see such a *mind* dulled by drink and drugs>
syn brain, gray matter, head, ||upper story, ||upperworks, wit

rel brainpower, intellect, intelligence; consciousness, mentality; faculty, function, power
2 ***syn*** see WILL 1
rel disposition, temper, temperament
con aversion, disinclination, indisposition
3 ***syn*** see WIT 2
4 ***syn*** see OPINION
5 ***syn*** see MOOD 1
‖6 ***syn*** see NOTICE 1
mind *vb* ‖1 ***syn*** see REMEMBER
‖2 ***syn*** see ENJOY 1
3 ***syn*** see SEE 1
‖4 ***syn*** see INTEND 2
5 ***syn*** see OBEY
6 ***syn*** see LOOK 1
7 ***syn*** see BEWARE
8 ***syn*** see TEND 2
rel oversee, superintend, supervise; discipline, govern
con forget, slight
9 ***syn*** see CONSIDER 1
minded *adj* ***syn*** see WILLING 1
rel contemplating, intending, planning, purposing
mindful *adj* 1 ***syn*** see AWARE
ant unmindful
2 inclined to be aware <*mindful* of the ever-changing social scene>
syn heedful, observant, observative, observing, regardful, thoughtful
rel attentive, conscientious; aware, cognizant, conscious, conversant, sensible; alert, vigilant, watchful
con heedless, inattentive
ant mindless, unmindful
mindless *adj* 1 ***syn*** see SIMPLE 3
2 ***syn*** see INSANE 1
mine *n* ***syn*** see BONANZA
rel lode, quarry, vein; spring, well, wellspring
mine *vb* to dig into for the purpose of obtaining items of use or value <*mined* manuscripts looking for undiscovered masterpieces>
syn delve, quarry
rel burrow, drill, excavate, sap, scoop; work
mingle *vb* 1 ***syn*** see MIX 1
2 ***syn*** see SOCIALIZE
mingle-mangle *n* ***syn*** see MISCELLANY 1
mingy *adj* ***syn*** see STINGY
miniature *n* ***syn*** see MODEL 1
miniature *adj* ***syn*** see TINY
rel small-scale, subminiature
con large-scale
minify *vb* ***syn*** see ABRIDGE 1
rel dwarf, miniaturize, shrink
minikin *adj* ***syn*** see TINY
minim *n* ***syn*** see PARTICLE
minimal *adj* constituting the least possible <*minimal* differences of opinion>
syn minimum
rel littlest, lowest, slightest, smallest; basal, basic, essential, fundamental
con maximum, topmost, utmost; greatest, highest, largest, most
ant maximal
minimize *vb* ***syn*** see DECRY 2
rel dwarf, reduce
ant magnify, maximize
minimum *n* the least quantity assignable, admissible, or possible <testing the use of a *minimum* of security at the prison>
syn margin
rel dab, hair, iota, jot, modicum, particle, pittance, smidgen, speck, whit
con abundance, bushel(s), gob(s), ‖lashings, load(s), lot(s), mass(es), much, oodles, profusion, scads, slather(s), ton(s), world(s)
ant maximum
minimum *adj* ***syn*** see MINIMAL
ant maximum
minion *n* ***syn*** see SYCOPHANT
minister *n* ***syn*** see CLERGYMAN
minister (to) *vb* to attend to the wants and comforts of someone <*minister* to the sick and dying>
syn care (for), mother, nurse, serve, wait (on)
rel cure, heal, remedy; doctor, treat; pander
ministerial *adj* ***syn*** see INSTRUMENTAL
minister plenipotentiary *n* ***syn*** see ENVOY 1
ministry *n* ***syn*** see MEAN 2
minor *adj* 1 ***syn*** see LITTLE 3
rel dependent; inferior, piddling, trifling; junior, lower
con meaningful, significant
ant major
2 lower in standing or reputation than others of the same class <a *minor* poet of the late eighteenth century>
syn bush, bush-league, dinky, insignificant, lesser, minor-league, secondary, small, small-fry, small-time
rel average, fair, indifferent, mediocre, medium, middling, second-rate, undistinguished, unnoticeable; trivial, unimportant
con chief, foremost, leading, principal
ant major
minor *n* ***syn*** see INFANT 2
minority *n* ***syn*** see INFANCY 2
ant majority
minor-league *adj* ***syn*** see MINOR 2
minstrel *n* ***syn*** see BARD 1
rel balladist, singer, wait
mint *n* ***syn*** see FORTUNE 4
mint *adj* ***syn*** see BRAND-NEW
rel intact, original, perfect, unmarred
minus *prep* ***syn*** see WITHOUT 2
ant plus
minute *n* ***syn*** see INSTANT 1
minute *adj* 1 ***syn*** see TINY
2 ***syn*** see LITTLE 3
3 ***syn*** see CIRCUMSTANTIAL
rel careful, meticulous, punctilious, scrupulous
con abstract; general, universal; comprehending, comprehensive, embracing, embracive, including, inclusive
minutely *adj* ***syn*** see CONTINUAL
minutia *n, usu* **minutiae** *pl* 1 ***syn*** see INS AND OUTS
2 ***syn*** see TRIVIA
minx *n* a pert girl <her rivals called her a brazen *minx*>

syn hussy, jade, malapert, saucebox, slut, snip
rel broad, brat, upstart; baggage, chippy, drab, floozy, strumpet, tart, trollop, trull

miracle *n* ***syn*** see WONDER 1

miraculous *adj* **1** ***syn*** see SUPERNATURAL 1
2 ***syn*** see MARVELOUS 1
con natural, normal

mirage *n* ***syn*** see DELUSION 1

mire *n* ***syn*** see SWAMP
rel muck

mire *vb* **1** ***syn*** see DELAY 1
rel bemire, sink; adhere, cleave, cling, cohere, stick; enmesh, ensnare, entangle, entrap, involve, snare, trap
2 ***syn*** see INVOLVE 1

mirror *n* **1** a polished or smooth surface (as of glass) that forms images by reflection <spent hours looking at herself in the *mirror*>
syn glass, looking glass, ||seeing glass
rel cheval glass, pier glass, reflector, speculum
2 ***syn*** see MODEL 2

mirror *vb* **1** ***syn*** see REFLECT 1
2 ***syn*** see REPRESENT 2

mirth *n* a mood or temper characterized by joy and high spirits and usually manifested in laughter and merrymaking <a man of contentment, but seldom of *mirth*>
syn glee, hilarity, jocularity, jocundity, jollity, joviality, merriment
rel cheer, cheerfulness, joyfulness, lightheartedness; gladness, happiness; frivolity, levity
con blues, dejection, depression, dumps, gloom, sadness; boredom, ennui, tedium; anguish, misery, woe; infelicity, wretchedness
ant melancholy

mirthful *adj* ***syn*** see MERRY
ant mirthless

miry *adj* ***syn*** see MUDDY 1

misadventure *n* **1** ***syn*** see DISASTER
2 ***syn*** see ACCIDENT 2
rel blunder, boner, bull, error, faux pas, howler, lapse, slip

misanthropic *adj* ***syn*** see ANTISOCIAL
rel misogynic
con altruistic, benevolent, charitable, humane, humanitarian
ant philanthropic

misapply *vb* ***syn*** see ABUSE 2
rel misappropriate, misdirect, mismanage

misapprehend *vb* **1** ***syn*** see MISUNDERSTAND 1
ant apprehend
2 ***syn*** see MISUNDERSTAND 2
ant apprehend

misappropriate *vb* ***syn*** see EMBEZZLE

misbegotten *adj* ***syn*** see ILLEGITIMATE 1

misbehaving *adj* ***syn*** see NAUGHTY 1
ant well-behaved

misbehavior *n* ***syn*** see MISCONDUCT

misbelief *n* ***syn*** see HERESY

misbeliever *n* ***syn*** see HERETIC

miscalculate *vb* to calculate wrongly <*miscalculate* the distance> <he seriously *miscalculated* the effect of his remark>
syn misestimate, misjudge, misreckon
rel discount, disregard, overlook; misconstrue, misinterpret, misunderstand; overestimate, overprize, overrate, overvalue; underestimate, underprize, underrate, undervalue

miscarry *vb* to go wrong or amiss <her plans *miscarried* almost from the start>
syn misfire, miss
rel abort; fail, flop
idiom fall through, miss fire, miss the mark
con come off, prevail, succeed

miscellaneous *adj* consisting of diverse things or members <gathered together a *miscellaneous* lot of books for sale>
syn assorted, chowchow, conglomerate, heterogeneous, indiscriminate, mixed, motley, multifarious, promiscuous, unassorted, unsorted, varied
rel different, disparate, divergent, diverse, various; divers, many, sundry; odd; commingled, jumbled, mingled, scrambled
con akin, alike, identical, like, parallel, similar, uniform

miscellany *n* **1** an unorganized mixture of various dissimilar items or elements <sold a *miscellany* of old household effects>
syn assortment, brew, chowchow, colluvies, gallimaufry, hash, hodgepodge, hotchpotch, jumble, medley, mélange, melee, mingle-mangle, mishmash, mixed bag, motley, odds and ends, olio, olla podrida, omnium-gatherum, pasticcio, pastiche, patchwork, porridge, potpourri, rumble-bumble, salad, salmagundi, smorgasbord, stew
rel mess, muddle; accumulation, aggregation, congeries, conglomeration, cumulation; combination, mix, mixture
2 ***syn*** see ANTHOLOGY

mischance *n* **1** ***syn*** see MISFORTUNE
2 ***syn*** see ACCIDENT 2

mischief *n* **1** ***syn*** see INJURY 1
rel difficulty, hardship, trouble
2 ***syn*** see SCAMP
3 ***syn*** see MISCHIEVOUSNESS
4 ***syn*** see DISCORD

||**mischiefful** *adj* ***syn*** see PLAYFUL 1

mischief-maker *n* ***syn*** see TROUBLEMAKER

mischievous *adj* **1** ***syn*** see HARMFUL
rel dangerous, hazardous, perilous, precarious, risky
2 ***syn*** see NAUGHTY 1
rel annoying, bothering, bothersome, irking, irksome, vexatious, vexing
3 ***syn*** see PLAYFUL 1
rel artful, foxy, insidious, sly, tricky

mischievousness *n* action or conduct that annoys or irritates without causing or meaning serious harm <a wag who was forever engaging in *mischievousness*>

---

syn synonym(s) ***rel*** related word(s)
ant antonym(s) ***con*** contrasted word(s)
idiom idiomatic equivalent(s)
|| use limited; if in doubt, see a dictionary

syn devilment, devilry, deviltry, diablerie, impishness, mischief, roguery, roguishness, sportiveness, waggery, waggishness
rel doggery, odiousness, offensiveness; evil, harm, hurt, injury; annoying, pestering, teasing
miscolor *vb* ***syn*** see MISREPRESENT
miscomprehend *vb* ***syn*** see MISUNDERSTAND 1
misconceive *vb* ***syn*** see MISUNDERSTAND 2
misconduct *n* improper behavior <was charged with *misconduct*>
syn misbehavior, misdoing, wrongdoing
rel impropriety; malfeasance, malversation, misfeasance
misconstrue *vb* ***syn*** see MISUNDERSTAND 2
miscreant *adj* ***syn*** see VICIOUS 2
miscreant *n* ***syn*** see VILLAIN 1
miscreation *n* ***syn*** see FREAK 2
rel deformation, deformity
miscue *n* ***syn*** see ERROR 2
misdate *n* ***syn*** see ANACHRONISM 1
misdating *n* ***syn*** see ANACHRONISM 1
misdeed *n* ***syn*** see CRIME 1
misdeem *vb* **1** ***syn*** see MISJUDGE 2
2 ***syn*** see MISTAKE 1
misdoing *n* ***syn*** see MISCONDUCT
misdoubt *vb* ***syn*** see DISTRUST
rel apprehend, dread, fear
mise–en–scène *n* **1** ***syn*** see SCENE 1
2 ***syn*** see SCENE 3
3 ***syn*** see ENVIRONMENT
misemploy *vb* ***syn*** see ABUSE 2
miser *n* a mean grasping person <an old *miser* who loved only his bank account>
syn cheapskate, cheeseparer, chuff, hunks, moneygrubber, muckworm, nabal, niggard, ||nipcheese, penny pincher, piker, scrooge, skin, skinflint, stiff, tightwad
rel glutton, hog, pig
miserable *adj* ***syn*** see WOEFUL 1
rel despairing, despondent, forlorn, hopeless; piteous, pitiable, pitiful; melancholy
con cheerful, glad, happy, joyful, joyous, lighthearted
miserly *adj* ***syn*** see STINGY
rel avaricious, covetous, grasping, greedy; abject, ignoble, sordid
con bountious, generous; altruistic, benevolent, charitable
misery *n* **1** a state of suffering and want that is the result of poverty or conditions beyond one's control <the poor learn to live with *misery*> <*the utter misery* in which the flood victims survived>
syn unhappiness, woe, wretchedness
rel agony, anguish; despondency, grief, sorrow; desolation, squalor
con beatitude, blessedness, bliss, felicity, happiness; content, ease, satisfaction
2 ***syn*** see DISTRESS
rel adversity, misfortune; dejection, depression, melancholy, sadness
ant blessedness
||**3** ***syn*** see PAIN 1
misesteem *vb* ***syn*** see MISJUDGE 2
misestimate *vb* ***syn*** see MISCALCULATE
misfire *vb* ***syn*** see MISCARRY
misfortunate *adj* ***syn*** see UNLUCKY
ant fortunate
misfortune *n* adverse fortune or an instance of this <her hopes and dreams soon ended in *misfortune*> <unable to grasp why he had been struck by such a *misfortune*>
syn adversity, contretemps, ||dole, mischance, mishap, tragedy, ||unluck
rel calamity, cataclysm, catastrophe, disaster; accident, casualty; affliction, cross, trial, tribulation, visitation
con break, chance, luck, opportunity
ant fortune
misgiving *n* ***syn*** see APPREHENSION 3
rel doubt, fear, qualm, suspicion; distrust, mistrust
misguided *adj* ***syn*** see MISTAKEN
mishandle *vb* **1** ***syn*** see MANHANDLE
2 ***syn*** see ABUSE 2
mishap *n* **1** ***syn*** see MISFORTUNE
2 ***syn*** see ACCIDENT 2
mishmash *n* **1** ***syn*** see MISCELLANY 1
2 ***syn*** see CLUTTER 2
misidentify *vb* ***syn*** see MISTAKE 1
misimprove *vb* ***syn*** see ABUSE 2
misinterpret *vb* ***syn*** see MISUNDERSTAND 2
misjudge *vb* **1** ***syn*** see MISCALCULATE
2 to have a mistaken opinion of <her first impression led her to *misjudge* the girl>
syn misdeem, misesteem, mistake
rel misapprehend, miscomprehend, misconceive, misconstrue, misinterpret, misunderstand
con catch on (to), penetrate, tumble (to), wise (up)
misknow *vb* ***syn*** see MISUNDERSTAND 1
mislaying *n* ***syn*** see LOSS 1
mislead *vb* ***syn*** see DECEIVE
rel lie, misguide, misinform; entice, inveigle, lure, seduce, tempt
misleading *adj* having an appearance or character that leads one astray or into error <the president made several *misleading* statements to the people>
syn beguiling, deceiving, deceptive, deluding, delusive, delusory, fallacious, false
rel casuistical, sophistical, specious; wrong; bewildering, confounding, distracting, perplexing, puzzling; deceitful, inaccurate
con clarifying, elucidative, explanatory, illuminating
||**mismannered** *adj* ***syn*** see RUDE 6
mismatch *vb* ***syn*** see CLASH 2
misorder *n* ***syn*** see CONFUSION 3
misplacement *n* ***syn*** see LOSS 1
misplacing *n* ***syn*** see LOSS 1
misread *vb* ***syn*** see MISUNDERSTAND 2
misreckon *vb* ***syn*** see MISCALCULATE
||**misremember** *vb* ***syn*** see FORGET 1
misrepresent *vb* to give a false, imperfect, or misleading representation of <the summary totally *misrepresents* the facts of the case>

syn belie, color, confuse, distort, falsify, garble, miscolor, misstate, pervert, twist, warp, wrench, wrest
rel dress, embellish, embroider, gild, gloss, varnish; camouflage, cloak, disguise, dissemble, mask; counterfeit, feign, simulate; equivocate, lie, palter, prevaricate, weasel
idiom give a false coloring, put a false construction (*or* appearance) on

misrepresentation *n* ***syn*** see LIE

misrule *n* ***syn*** see DISORDER 2

miss *vb* **1** ***syn*** see NEGLECT
2 ***syn*** see MISUNDERSTAND 1
3 ***syn*** see MISCARRY

||**miss** *n* ***syn*** see ABSENCE

miss *n* ***syn*** see GIRL 1

misshape *vb* ***syn*** see DEFORM

misshape *n* ***syn*** see DEFORMITY

missing *adj* **1** ***syn*** see ABSENT 1
2 ***syn*** see LOST 2

mission *n* a continuing task or responsibility that one is destined or fitted to do or specially called upon to undertake <his *mission* in life was to serve humanity>
syn calling, lifework, vocation
rel goal, purpose; business, profession, trade

missionary *n* one who attempts to convert others to a specific way of life, set of ideas, or course of action <served as a *missionary* for the feminist cause>
syn apostle, colporteur, evangelist, missioner, propagandist
rel revivalist; promoter

missioner *n* ***syn*** see MISSIONARY

missish *adj* ***syn*** see PRIM 1

missive *n* ***syn*** see LETTER 2

Miss–Nancyish *adj* ***syn*** see EFFEMINATE

misstate *vb* ***syn*** see MISREPRESENT

misstatement *n* ***syn*** see LIE

misstep *n* ***syn*** see ERROR 2

||**missus** *n* ***syn*** see WIFE

missy *n* ***syn*** see GIRL 1

mist *n* ***syn*** see HAZE 1

mist *vb* ***syn*** see OBSCURE

mistake *vb* **1** to take one thing to be another <he *mistakes* sarcasm for wit>
syn confound, confuse, misdeem, misidentify, mix, mix up
rel misconceive, misknow; addle, jumble, muddle, tumble
con discern, distinguish, grasp, perceive; differentiate, separate
ant recognize
2 ***syn*** see MISUNDERSTAND 2
3 ***syn*** see MISJUDGE 2

mistake *n* **1** ***syn*** see ERROR 2
rel confounding, confusion, mistaking; inadvertence; disregarding, neglect, neglecting, omission, omitting, slight, slighting
2 ***syn*** see ERROR 1

mistaken *adj* acting, thinking, or judging in a manner at variance with truth or the facts <he is *mistaken* in his evaluation of the crisis>
syn erroneous, misguided, wrong
rel confounded, confused; deceived, deluded, misinformed
idiom all wet, off base, off the track
con accurate, correct, right, unerring; exact, precise

mister *n* ***syn*** see HUSBAND

mistimed *adj* ***syn*** see UNSEASONABLE 1
ant well-timed

mistiming *n* ***syn*** see ANACHRONISM 1

mistreat *vb* ***syn*** see ABUSE 4

mistress *n* a woman who is a man's regular partner in nonmarital sexual activity <gave up his *mistress* when he married>
syn ||doxy, girl friend, inamorata, lover, paramour, woman
rel bedmate; concubine; kept woman; dulcinea

mistrust *n* ***syn*** see UNCERTAINTY
rel apprehension, foreboding, misgiving, presentiment
con dependence, faith, reliance
ant assurance, trust

mistrust *vb* **1** ***syn*** see DISTRUST
rel anticipate, apprehend, foresee; alarm, frighten, scare; appall, dismay
ant trust
2 ***syn*** see QUESTION 2

mistrustful *adj* ***syn*** see SUSPICIOUS 2
ant trustful, trusting

mistrustfully *adv* ***syn*** see ASKANCE 2
ant trustfully, trustingly

misty *adj* ***syn*** see HAZY

misunderstand *vb* **1** to fail to understand <he *misunderstood* the full meaning of the novel>
syn misapprehend, miscomprehend, misknow, miss
rel misconceive, misconstrue, misinterpret, misread, mistake
con apprehend, conceive, know, realize; fathom, follow, grasp, seize, take in
ant comprehend, understand
2 to interpret incorrectly <*misunderstood* the instructions>
syn misapprehend, misconceive, misconstrue, misinterpret, misread, mistake
rel misexplain, mistranslate; miscomprehend, misknow
con fathom, follow, take in
ant understand

misuse *vb* **1** ***syn*** see ABUSE 2
2 ***syn*** see ABUSE 4

mite *n* ***syn*** see PARTICLE

mitigate *vb* ***syn*** see RELIEVE 1
rel extenuate, palliate
con aggravate, enhance, heighten; augment, increase
ant intensify

mitigation *n* ***syn*** see EASE 3

---

syn synonym(s) *rel* related word(s)
ant antonym(s) *con* contrasted word(s)
idiom idiomatic equivalent(s)
|| use limited; if in doubt, see a dictionary

mix *vb* **1** to combine or be combined into a more or less uniform whole <*mixed* the ingredients to make a thick sauce>
syn admix, amalgamate, blend, comingle, commingle, commix, compound, fuse, immingle, immix, interblend, interflow, interfuse, intermingle, intermix, make up, meld, merge, mingle
rel associate, combine, conjoin, inosculate, join, link, unite; braid, lump, work in; coalesce; blunge
con divide, part, separate, sever, sunder
2 *syn* see MISTAKE 1

mix *n* *syn* see MIXTURE

mixed *adj* *syn* see MISCELLANEOUS
rel amalgamated, blended, fused, merged, mingled

mixed bag *n* *syn* see MISCELLANY 1

mixologist *n* *syn* see BARTENDER

mixture *n* a product formed by the combination of two or more things <the tea is actually a *mixture* of several varieties>
syn admixture, alloy, amalgam, amalgamation, blend, commixture, composite, compost, compound, fusion, immixture, interfusion, intermixture, mix, mix-up
rel brew, concoction, confection, mélange

mix up *vb* **1** *syn* see CONFUSE 2
ant straighten (out)
2 *syn* see CONFUSE 5
3 *syn* see MISTAKE 1
4 *syn* see DISORDER 1
ant straighten (out *or* up)

mix–up *n* **1** *syn* see MESS 3
2 *syn* see MIXTURE

mizmaze *n* *syn* see MAZE 1

‖**mizzle** *vb* *syn* see SPRINKLE 5

‖**mizzle** *vb* *syn* see CONFUSE 2

moan *vb* *syn* see DEPLORE 1

moanful *adj* *syn* see MELANCHOLY 2

mob *n* **1** *syn* see RABBLE
2 a large disorderly crowd of people usually bent on riotous or destructive action <the *mob* screamed for a lynching>
syn rabble, rout
rel posse; crowd, crush, horde, press, push, throng; herd, swarm
3 *syn* see CLIQUE

‖**mob** *vb* *syn* see SCOLD 1

mobile *adj* **1** *syn* see MOVABLE
rel fluid, liquid; protean; capricious, fickle, inconstant, mercurial
con immutable, invariable, unchangeable
ant immobile
2 *syn* see CHANGEABLE 1
ant immobile, stable
3 *syn* see VERSATILE
4 *syn* see MIGRATORY

mobile home *n* *syn* see TRAILER

mobilize *vb* **1** to put into movement or circulation <an increase in prices *mobilizes* the whole cycle of inflation>
syn actuate, circulate, set off
rel activate; impel, propel
idiom set in motion
con inactivate, slow (down *or* up)
ant immobilize
2 *syn* see MOVE 5
3 to assemble (as resources) and make ready for use or action <the president tried to *mobilize* support for the new proposal>
syn marshal, muster, organize, rally

mobocracy *n* *syn* see ANARCHY 1

mock *vb* **1** *syn* see RIDICULE
rel buffoon, burlesque, caricature, parody, travesty
2 *syn* see DECEIVE
3 *syn* see MIMIC
rel affect, assume, counterfeit, feign, simulate

mock *n* **1** *syn* see LAUGHINGSTOCK
2 *syn* see MOCKERY 2

mock *adj* **1** *syn* see ARTIFICIAL 2
rel pseudo, quasi, so-called
2 *syn* see FICTITIOUS 2
rel bogus, phony

mockery *n* **1** *syn* see LAUGHINGSTOCK
2 an insincere, contemptible, or impertinent imitation of something worthwhile <arbitrary methods that make a *mockery* of justice>
syn burlesque, caricature, farce, mock, sham, travesty
rel derision, ridicule, sport; parody, satire, take-off; joke, laughingstock

mode *n* **1** *syn* see VEIN 1
2 *syn* see METHOD 1
3 *syn* see STATE 1

mode *n* *syn* see FASHION 3

model *n* **1** a miniature representation of something <a *model* of the dam that was accurate down to the last detail>
syn miniature, pocket edition
rel copy, mock-up, replica, reproduction; dummy, effigy
2 something set or held before one for guidance or imitation <Samuel Johnson's literary style is often used as a *model* for writers seeking precision and clarity>
syn archetype, beau ideal, ensample, example, exemplar, ideal, mirror, paradigm, pattern, standard; *compare* PARAGON
rel apotheosis, nonesuch, nonpareil, paragon; emblem, symbol, type; embodiment, epitome, quintessence; criterion, gauge, touchstone

model *adj* **1** *syn* see IDEAL 3
rel commendable, exemplary
2 *syn* see PERFECT 3
3 *syn* see TYPICAL 1

moderate *adj* **1** *syn* see SOBER 3
2 not excessive in degree, amount, or intensity <the new proposals were met with only *moderate* enthusiasm> <the snowfall is expected to be no more than *moderate*>
syn modest, reasonable, temperate
rel bland, gentle, mild, soft; inconsequential, inconsiderable, slight, small; paltry, piddling, trifling, trivial
con excessive, extreme, inordinate, intemperate, radical, unreasonable
ant immoderate

3 ***syn*** see MEDIUM
rel constant, equable, even, steady
4 avoiding extreme political or social measures <party policy became increasingly *moderate*>
syn middle-of-the-road, middle-road, soft-shell
con conservative, right, tory; left, radical, red; extremist, fanatical, ultra
5 ***syn*** see CONSERVATIVE 2

moderate *vb* **1** to modify as to avoid an extreme or keep within bounds <actors *moderate* their voices and gestures to fit the size of the theater>
syn modulate, restrain, temper
rel abate, decrease, diminish, lessen, reduce; alleviate, cushion, lighten, mitigate, mollify, relieve, slacken, slow; constrain, control, qualify; chasten, cool, subdue, tone (down)
con aggravate, enhance, heighten, intensify; augment, increase
2 ***syn*** see ABATE 4

moderately *adv* **1** ***syn*** see ENOUGH 2
2 ***syn*** see SOMEWHAT 2
ant extremely, immoderately

moderateness *n* ***syn*** see TEMPERANCE 1
ant immoderateness, immoderation

moderation *n* ***syn*** see TEMPERANCE 1
ant immoderateness, immoderation

moderator *n* one who arbitrates <the labor dispute was finally referred to a *moderator*>
syn arbitrator, mediator
rel arbiter, judge; conciliator, negotiator, peacemaker

modern *adj* **1** having taken place, existed, or developed in times close to the present <*modern* concepts of engineering made the bridge possible>
syn late, recent
rel contemporary, present-day; latter
con antiquated, old-fashioned, old hat, outdated, outmoded, outworn
ant old-time
2 ***syn*** see NEW 1
rel coincident, concomitant, concurrent, contemporaneous, contemporary; current, prevailing, prevalent
ant ancient, antique

modernistic *adj* ***syn*** see NEW 1
rel futuristic
ant antiquated

modernize *vb* ***syn*** see RENEW 1

modest *adj* **1** ***syn*** see HUMBLE 1
rel moderate, temperate; retiring, withdrawing; unboastful; unpresuming, unpresumptuous, unpretending
con barefaced, brazen, impudent, shameless
ant ambitious
2 ***syn*** see SHY 1
rel reticent, silent; nice, proper, seemly
3 ***syn*** see CHASTE
rel priggish, prim, prissy, prudish, puritanical, straitlaced, stuffy
con improper, indecent, indecorous, indelicate, unseemly
ant immodest
4 ***syn*** see MODERATE 2
5 ***syn*** see PLAIN 1

modicum *n* ***syn*** see PARTICLE

modification *n* ***syn*** see CHANGE 1
rel conversion, metamorphosis, transformation, transmogrification; qualification, tempering

modified *adj* ***syn*** see QUALIFIED 2

modify *vb* ***syn*** see CHANGE 1
rel modulate, restrain, temper; qualify

modish *adj* ***syn*** see STYLISH
rel voguish

modulate *vb* ***syn*** see MODERATE 1

modus *n* ***syn*** see METHOD 1

||**mog** *vb* ***syn*** see GO 2

mogul *n* ***syn*** see MAGNATE

moiety *n* ***syn*** see PART 1

moil *vb* **1** ***syn*** see LABOR 1
||2 ***syn*** see SEETHE 4

moil *n* **1** ***syn*** see WORK 2
2 ***syn*** see COMMOTION 4

moira *n* ***syn*** see FATE

moist *adj* **1** ***syn*** see DAMP
2 ***syn*** see SENTIMENTAL

moistureless *adj* ***syn*** see DRY 1
ant moist

moisty *adj* ***syn*** see DAMP

||**moke** *n* ***syn*** see DONKEY 1

mold *n* ***syn*** see TYPE

mold *vb* ***syn*** see MAKE 3

moldable *adj* ***syn*** see PLASTIC

molder *vb* ***syn*** see DECAY

moldy *adj* ***syn*** see OLD-FASHIONED

moldy fig *n* ***syn*** see FOGY

mole *n* ***syn*** see BIRTHMARK 1

molecule *n* ***syn*** see PARTICLE

molest *vb* to annoy or disturb with hostile intent or injurious effect <he was specifically warned by the court not to *molest* his former wife>
syn bait, heckle, persecute, torment
rel annoy, badger, bother, irk, pester; pother, tease; bedevil, beset, devil, trouble; harass, harry, vex

moll *n* ***syn*** see PROSTITUTE

mollify *vb* **1** ***syn*** see PACIFY
rel lighten; temper; abate, decrease, lessen, reduce
ant exasperate
2 ***syn*** see RELIEVE 1

||**molly** *n* ***syn*** see WEAKLING

mollycoddle *n* ***syn*** see WEAKLING
rel ||mollycot

mollycoddle *vb* ***syn*** see BABY
ant neglect; abuse

molt *vb* ***syn*** see SHED 2

mom *n* ***syn*** see MOTHER 1

||**momble** *vb* ***syn*** see CONFUSE 2

moment *n* **1** ***syn*** see INSTANT 1
ant eternity
2 ***syn*** see POINT 7
3 ***syn*** see OCCASION 5
4 ***syn*** see IMPORTANCE

---

rel advantage, avail, profit, use
momentaneous *adj syn* see TRANSIENT
momentary *adj syn* see TRANSIENT
rel brief, quick, short; impulsive
ant agelong
momentous *adj* **1** *syn* see IMPORTANT 1
ant trivial
2 *syn* see EPOCHAL
momentousness *n syn* see IMPORTANCE
ant triviality
mommy *n syn* see MOTHER 1
momus *n syn* see CRITIC
monarchal *adj syn* see KINGLY
monarchial *adj syn* see KINGLY
monarchical *adj syn* see KINGLY
mondaine *adj syn* see SOPHISTICATED 2
monetary *adj syn* see FINANCIAL
rel numismatic
money *n* something (as pieces of stamped metal or paper certificates) customarily and legally used as a medium of exchange <the only thing that he liked about his job was the *money*>
syn ‖blunt, ‖brass, ‖bread, ‖cabbage, cash, ‖chink, ‖chips, ‖coin, currency, ‖dibs, ‖dinero, ‖do-re-mi, dough, filthy lucre, ‖gelt, ‖greenbacks, ‖jack, ‖kale, legal tender, ‖lettuce, ‖long green, loot, lucre, ‖mazuma, ‖moolah, ‖mopus, needful, ‖ooftish, pelf, rhino, rocks, ‖scratch, ‖shekels, ‖smash, stuff, ‖stumpy, ‖sugar, swag, ‖wampum
rel bankroll, capital, coinage, finances, funds, mammon, resources, riches, treasure, wealth, wherewithal; boodle, hay; ‖stiff
moneyed *adj syn* see RICH 1
ant penniless, unmoneyed
moneygrubber *n syn* see MISER
moneymaking *adj syn* see ADVANTAGEOUS 1
monger *n syn* see PEDDLER
monger *vb syn* see PEDDLE 2
mongerer *n syn* see PEDDLER
mongrel *n syn* see HYBRID
‖**moniker** *n* **1** *syn* see NAME 1
2 *syn* see NICKNAME
monish *vb syn* see REPROVE
monition *n syn* see WARNING
monitorial *adj syn* see MONITORY
monitory *adj* giving a warning <the parents wrote their son a *monitory* letter>
syn admonishing, admonitory, cautionary, cautioning, monitorial, warning
rel advisory, counseling; critical, expostulatory, remonstratory; exhortatory, hortatory; moralistic, moralizing, preachy
monkey *n* **1** *syn* see FOOL 3
2 *syn* see URCHIN
monkey *adj syn* see SMALL 1
monkey (with) *vb syn* see MEDDLE
monkeyshine *n usu* **monkeyshines** *pl*
syn see PRANK
monocratic *adj syn* see ABSOLUTE 4
con democratic
monogram *n* a sign of identity usually formed of the combined initials of a name <everything he owned had his *monogram* on it>
syn cipher
rel device, initials; John Hancock, signature
monograph *n syn* see DISCOURSE 2
monography *n syn* see DISCOURSE 2
monopolize *vb* to take up completely <he would attempt to *monopolize* every conversation>
syn absorb, consume, engross, sew up
rel corner, hog; devour; have, hold, own, possess; employ, use, utilize; control, manage
con contribute, participate, share
monopolizing *adj syn* see ENGROSSING
monopoly *n* exclusive possession <neither party has a *monopoly* on morality>
syn corner
rel cartel, consortium, pool, syndicate, trust; copyright; ownership, possessorship, proprietorship
monotone *n syn* see MONOTONY
monotone *adj syn* see DULL 9
monotonous *adj syn* see DULL 9
rel samely, uniform, unvaried; repetitious; jog-trot, singsong
con changing, varying; fresh, new, novel; absorbing, engrossing, interesting
monotonousness *n syn* see MONOTONY
monotony *n* a tedious sameness or reiteration <the *monotony* of his job finally got to him>
syn humdrum, monotone, monotonousness
rel boredom, ennui, tedium; dryness, flatness, uniformity
con variability, variation; diversification, diversity, multifariousness, variety
monster *n* **1** *syn* see FREAK 2
rel demon, devil, fiend, hellhound; bandersnatch
2 *syn* see GIANT
monster *adj syn* see HUGE
monstrosity *n* **1** *syn* see FREAK 2
2 *syn* see EYESORE
monstrous *adj* **1** extremely impressive <the traditional burial ceremonies turned into a *monstrous* spectacle>
syn cracking, fantastic, massive, monumental, mortal, prodigious, stupendous, towering, tremendous
rel grandiose, impressive, magnificent, showy, splendid, superb; colossal, enormous, huge, immense, mammoth, vast
con mean, petty, picayune, poky, small-time
2 *syn* see HUGE
3 *syn* see OUTRAGEOUS 2
rel glaring, rank; fateful, ominous, portentous; flagitious, infamous
‖**monstrous** *adv syn* see VERY 1
monstrousness *n syn* see ENORMITY 1
Montezuma's revenge *n syn* see DIARRHEA
monument *n* **1** *syn* see DOCUMENT 1
2 a lasting evidence or reminder of someone or something notable <the whole body of students who learned from him form his *monument*>
syn memorial, testimonial
rel memento, tribute
3 *syn* see TOMBSTONE
monument *vb syn* see MEMORIALIZE 2

monumental *adj* **1** ***syn*** see HUGE
2 ***syn*** see MONSTROUS 1
3 ***syn*** see TOWERING 4
monumentalize *vb* ***syn*** see MEMORIALIZE 2
moocah *n* ***syn*** see MARIJUANA
mooch *vb* ***syn*** see WANDER 1
moocher *n* ***syn*** see BEGGAR 1
mooching *n* ***syn*** see MENDICANCY
mood *n* **1** a state of mind in which an emotion or set of emotions gains ascendancy <a melancholy *mood* induced by the sight of ancient ruins>
syn humor, mind, strain, temper, tone, vein
rel character, disposition, individuality, personality, temperament; soul, spirit; affection, emotion, feeling, response
2 ***syn*** see TEMPER 1
3 ***syn*** see AIR 3
moody *adj* subject to moods <a *moody* person whose behavior was erratic and whose actions were unpredictable>
syn humorsome, temperamental
rel capricious, fickle, inconstant, mercurial, unstable, whimsical; broody
con calm, dispassionate, stable, steady, unexcitable; bovine, impassive, stolid
‖**moolah** *n* ***syn*** see MONEY
mooncalf *n* ***syn*** see FOOL 1
‖**moonraker** *n* ***syn*** see DUNCE
moonshine *n* **1** ***syn*** see NONSENSE 2
2 illegally distilled liquor <his death was caused by bad *moonshine*>
syn bathtub gin, ‖blockade, bootleg, ‖busthead, ‖hooch, mountain dew, white lightning
rel homebrew; ‖bug juice, grappa, ‖jake, smoke, squareface
moor *vb* ***syn*** see FASTEN 2
moot *vb* **1** ***syn*** see BROACH
2 ***syn*** see DISCUSS 1
moot *adj* open to question <it is a *moot* point whether he would have been tried and convicted>
syn arguable, debatable, disputable, doubtful, dubious, mootable, problematic, questionable, uncertain; *compare* DOUBTFUL 1
rel controversial, suspect; unsettled
con confirmed, established, settled; inarguable, indisputable, undebatable, unproblematic, unquestionable; certain, sure
mooting *n* ***syn*** see ARGUMENTATION
mootable *adj* ***syn*** see MOOT
mop *vb* ***syn*** see GRIMACE
mop (up) *vb* ***syn*** see WHIP 2
mope *vb* **1** to become listless or dejected <*moped* for several days after the divorce>
syn brood, despond
rel ache, grieve, grump, pout, sulk
2 ***syn*** see SAUNTER
mopes *n pl* ***syn*** see SADNESS
mopey *adj* ***syn*** see DOWNCAST
moppet *n* ***syn*** see CHILD 1
‖**mopus** *n* ***syn*** see MONEY
moral *adj* **1** conforming to a standard of what is right and good <*moral* goodness may be distinguished from intellectual goodness>
syn ethical, moralistic, noble, principled, righteous, right-minded, virtuous
rel good, right; conscientious, honest, honorable, just, scrupulous, upright; chaste, decent, modest, pure
con amoral, nonmoral, unmoral
ant immoral
2 ***syn*** see DIDACTIC
3 ***syn*** see ELEVATED 2
moral *n* ***syn*** see MAXIM
morale *n* a sense of common purpose or a degree of dedication to a common task regarded as characteristic of or dominant in a group <*morale* was high among the troops>
syn esprit, esprit de corps
rel drive, spirit, vigor; assurance, confidence, self-confidence, self-possession
con enervation; aimlessness, purposelessness; egoism, egotism, self-centeredness
moralistic *adj* ***syn*** see MORAL 1
rel didactic
morality *n* **1** ***syn*** see GOODNESS
rel godliness, saintliness
2 ***syn*** see ETHIC 2
moralize *vb* to make moral reflections usually in an officious or tiresome manner <people avoided him as he was always *moralizing*>
syn preach, preachify, sermonize
rel lecture, pontificate
moralizing *adj* ***syn*** see DIDACTIC
morally *adv* ***syn*** see VIRTUALLY
morals *n pl* **1** ***syn*** see ETHIC 1
2 ***syn*** see ETHIC 2
rel conduct, habits, standards
morass *n* **1** ***syn*** see SWAMP
2 ***syn*** see MAZE 1
rel dunghill
moratorium *n* ***syn*** see SUSPENSION 2
morbid *adj* abnormally susceptible to or characterized by gloomy or unwholesome feelings <his *morbid* poetry is the product of his lifelong frustrations>
syn morose, sick, sickly
rel gloomy, melancholic; psychotic; dark, moody, saturnine, sullen
con healthy, sound, well, wholesome; solid, stable, stolid, sturdy
mordacious *adj* ***syn*** see CAUSTIC 1
mordancy *n* ***syn*** see ACRIMONY
rel incisiveness, pungency, trenchancy; acidity, acridity, causticity, mordacity
mordant *adj* ***syn*** see CAUSTIC 1
more *adj* ***syn*** see ADDITIONAL
more *adv* ***syn*** see ALSO 2
2 to a greater or higher degree <were *more* evenly matched>
syn better
more or less *adv* **1** ***syn*** see SOMEWHAT 2
2 ***syn*** see NEARLY

---

syn synonym(s) ***rel*** related word(s)
ant antonym(s) ***con*** contrasted word(s)
idiom idiomatic equivalent(s)
‖ use limited; if in doubt, see a dictionary

moreover *adv* ***syn*** see ALSO 2

mores *n pl* **1** ***syn*** see ETHIC 2
2 ***syn*** see MANNER 5

morgue *n* ***syn*** see PRIDE 3

moribund *adj* approaching death or a final end <found lying *moribund* in her bed> <with its mills shut down the city's economy was *moribund*>
syn dying
rel expiring, fading, going; decadent, deteriorating, regressing
idiom at death's door, on one's last legs, with one foot in the grave
con booming, flourishing, prospering, thriving; lively, viable

morn *n* **1** ***syn*** see DAWN 1
2 ***syn*** see MORNING 2

morne *adj* ***syn*** see GLOOMY 3

morning *n* **1** ***syn*** see DAWN 1
con sundown, sunset
2 the time before noon <it rained most of the *morning*>
syn forenoon, morn
con afternoon, evening; day, night

moron *n* **1** ***syn*** see FOOL 4
2 ***syn*** see DUNCE

moronic *adj* ***syn*** see RETARDED

morose *adj* **1** ***syn*** see SULLEN
rel choleric, cranky, irascible, splenetic, testy; irritable, waspish; brusque, gruff
con jocund, jolly, jovial, merry
ant blithe
2 ***syn*** see MORBID

morsel *n* **1** a small piece or quantity of food <tossed a *morsel* of meat to the dog>
syn bit, bite, mouthful
rel taste; tidbit; crumb, ort, scrap
2 ***syn*** see SNACK
3 ***syn*** see DELICACY

mort *n* ***syn*** see CORPSE

‖**mortacious** *adv* ***syn*** see VERY 1

mortal *adj* **1** ***syn*** see DEADLY 1
rel implacable, relentless, unrelenting
2 ***syn*** see GRIM 3
3 ***syn*** see MONSTROUS 1
4 ***syn*** see HUMAN
rel finite, temporal; frail, weak
5 ***syn*** see PROBABLE

mortal *n* ***syn*** see HUMAN

mortality *n* **1** ***syn*** see FATALITY 1
2 ***syn*** see MANKIND

mortally *adv* ***syn*** see VERY 1

mortgage *vb* ***syn*** see PAWN

mortician *n* one whose business is to prepare the dead for burial and to arrange and manage funerals <*morticians* must be certified>
syn funeral director, undertaker
rel embalmer

mortiferous *adj* ***syn*** see DEADLY 1

mortified *adj* **1** ***syn*** see SEVERE 1
2 ***syn*** see ASHAMED
rel annoyed, harassed, harried, worried

mortuary *adj* ***syn*** see SEPULCHRAL 1

mosey *vb* ***syn*** see SAUNTER

‖**moss** *n* ***syn*** see SWAMP

mossback *n* **1** ***syn*** see RUSTIC
2 ***syn*** see FOGY

most *adj* ***syn*** see BEST
rel greatest, highest, maximum, utmost, uttermost

most *adv* ***syn*** see VERY 1

most *adv* ***syn*** see NEARLY

mostly *adv* ***syn*** see GENERALLY 1
idiom for the most part

mote *n* ***syn*** see POINT 11

moth-eaten *adj* **1** ***syn*** see SHABBY 1
2 ***syn*** see OLD-FASHIONED

mother *n* **1** a female human parent <the *mother* of seven children>
syn ma, ‖mam, mama (*or* mamma), mammy, ‖mater, mom, mommy, ‖mum, mummy, ‖old lady, ‖old woman; *compare* FATHER 1
2 ***syn*** see SOURCE

mother *vb* ***syn*** see MINISTER (to)

mother country *n* ***syn*** see COUNTRY

motherland *n* ***syn*** see COUNTRY

mother-naked *adj* ***syn*** see NUDE 2

mother wit *n* ***syn*** see INTELLIGENCE 1

motif *n* **1** ***syn*** see LEITMOTIV
2 ***syn*** see SUBJECT 2
3 ***syn*** see FIGURE 3

motion *n* **1** the act or an instance of moving <the *motion* of the planets>
syn move, movement, stir, stirring
rel agitation, fluctuation, oscillation, sway, swing, wavering; locomotion
con inertia, inertness, passivity
2 an impulse or inclination of the mind or will <a *motion* of the will toward what appears good>
syn movement
rel goad, impulse, incentive, inducement, motive, spring, spur
con inertia, stagnation, vegetation

motion *vb* ***syn*** see SIGNAL

motionless *adj* being without motion <stood *motionless* so that he would remain undiscovered>
syn still, stock-still, stone-still
rel stagnant, static, stationary, unmoving; fixed, immobile, immotile, immotive, immovable, irremovable, ‖sitfast, steadfast, unmovable
con active, changing, mobile, moving

motion picture *n* ***syn*** see MOVIE

motivate *vb* ***syn*** see PROVOKE 4

motivation *n* ***syn*** see STIMULUS

motive *n* **1** the object influencing a choice or prompting an action <trying to discover what was his *motive* in killing the girl>
syn cause, consideration, reason, spring; *compare* STIMULUS
rel antecedent, determinant; emotion, feeling, passion; aim, end, intent, intention, purpose
2 ***syn*** see FIGURE 3
3 ***syn*** see SUBJECT 2

motley *adj* **1** ***syn*** see VARIEGATED
2 ***syn*** see MISCELLANEOUS
rel discrepant, incompatible, incongruous, uncongenial

motley *n* **1** ***syn*** see FOOL 2

2 ***syn*** see MISCELLANY 1
motor *n* ***syn*** see CAR
motor *vb* **1** ***syn*** see RIDE 1
2 ***syn*** see DRIVE 5
motorcar *n* ***syn*** see CAR
motor home *n* ***syn*** see TRAILER
motorist *n* a person who travels by automobile <the roads were crowded with *motorists* going to work>
syn autoist, automobilist, driver, operator
mottle *vb* ***syn*** see SPLOTCH
motto *n* ***syn*** see BATTLE CRY
rel byword, catchphrase, catchword, shibboleth, slogan, watchword, word
moue *n* ***syn*** see FACE 6
mound *vb* ***syn*** see HEAP 1
mound *n* ***syn*** see PILE 1
mount *n* ***syn*** see MOUNTAIN 1
mount *vb* **1** ***syn*** see INCREASE 2
2 ***syn*** see ASCEND 1
con descend, fall, lower
ant drop
3 ***syn*** see RISE 4
ant drop
4 ***syn*** see INTENSIFY
5 to get on (something) as a means of conveyance <*mount* a horse>
syn back, bestride
rel seat, settle
ant dismount
‖**6** ***syn*** see TESTIFY 2
7 ***syn*** see STAGE
mountain *n* **1** a relatively steep and high elevation of land <why are *mountains* in New England considered no more than hills in Colorado>
syn alp, mount, peak
rel butte, mesa; bald, dome; hill; bluff; volcano; sierra
con bottom, bottomland, dale, dell, vale, valley
2 ***syn*** see PILE 1
3 ***syn*** see MUCH
4 ***syn*** see OBSTACLE
mountain dew *n* ***syn*** see MOONSHINE 2
mountaineer *n* ***syn*** see RUSTIC
mountainous *adj* ***syn*** see HUGE
mountebank *n* **1** ***syn*** see CHARLATAN
2 ***syn*** see SWINDLER
mourn *vb* ***syn*** see GRIEVE 2
con delight, gladden, please, rejoice
mournful *adj* **1** ***syn*** see SAD 1
2 ***syn*** see SAD 2
3 ***syn*** see MELANCHOLY 2
4 ***syn*** see DEPLORABLE
mournfulness *n* ***syn*** see SADNESS
mouse *n* **1** ***syn*** see GIRL FRIEND 1
2 ***syn*** see BLACK EYE 1
mouse *vb* **1** ***syn*** see SNOOP
2 ***syn*** see STEAL 3
mousehole *n* ***syn*** see CUBBYHOLE
mousetrap *n* ***syn*** see PITFALL
mouth *n* **1** the opening through which food passes into the body of an animal <the *mouth* in vertebrates is one of the features of the face>
syn ‖bazoo, gob, ‖mush, ‖row, ‖trap, ‖yap
rel mug, muzzle
2 ***syn*** see FACE 6
3 ***syn*** see SPOKESMAN
4 ***syn*** see BACK TALK
5 the place where a tributary enters a larger stream or body of water <the *mouth* of the Mississippi river is in the Gulf of Mexico>
syn embouchement, embouchure
rel estuary; delta
mouth *vb* **1** ***syn*** see ORATE
2 ***syn*** see BOAST
3 ***syn*** see REVEAL 1
4 ***syn*** see GRIMACE
mouthful *n* ***syn*** see MORSEL 1
mouthing *n* ***syn*** see FACE 6
mouthpiece *n* ***syn*** see SPOKESMAN
mouth–watering *adj* ***syn*** see PALATABLE
‖**mouthy** *adj* **1** ***syn*** see TALKATIVE
2 ***syn*** see RHETORICAL
movable *adj* capable of moving or of being moved <a device with a *movable* attachment>
syn mobile, moving, unstable, unsteadfast, unsteady
rel remotive, removable; motile; changeable, changeful, mutable, variable; roving
con immobile, immotile, immotive, irremovable, steadfast; established, fixed, set, settled; stagnant, static, unmoving
movables *n pl* ***syn*** see POSSESSION 2
move *vb* **1** ***syn*** see GO 2
2 ***syn*** see ADVANCE 5
3 ***syn*** see BE
4 to change or cause to change from one place to another <he *moved* quickly down the staircase> <*move* the chair across the room>
syn dislocate, disturb, remove, shift, ship, transfer
rel displace, replace, supersede, supplant; bear, carry, convey, transmit, transport
5 to set or keep in motion or action <the mechanism that *moves* the locomotive>
syn actuate, drive, impel, mobilize, propel
rel activate, motivate
con bring up, draw up, fetch up, halt, haul up, pull up, stop
6 ***syn*** see PROVOKE 4
7 ***syn*** see AFFECT
rel induce, persuade, prevail
8 ***syn*** see CONVERT 1
9 ***syn*** see BEHAVE 1
move *n* **1** ***syn*** see MEASURE 7
2 ***syn*** see MOTION 1
rel alteration, change, modification, variation
movement *n* **1** ***syn*** see MOTION 1
rel act, action, deed; activity, dynamism, liveness, operation, operativeness
2 ***syn*** see MOTION 2
mover *n* ***syn*** see INSTIGATOR

---

syn synonym(s) ***rel*** related word(s)
ant antonym(s) ***con*** contrasted word(s)
idiom idiomatic equivalent(s)
‖ use limited; if in doubt, see a dictionary

THESAURUS

movie *n* a representation (as of a story) by means of motion pictures <tired old *movies* that appear on TV>
syn cine, ‖cinema, film, flick, motion picture, moving picture, photoplay, picture, picture show, show
rel cinematics, cinematography

moving *adj* **1** *syn* see MOVABLE
2 having the power to excite deep and usually somber emotion <made a *moving* appeal for help for the orphaned children>
syn affecting, impressive, poignant, touching; *compare* EMOTIONAL 2
rel eloquent, expressive, facund, meaningful, pregnant, sententious, significant; arousing, awakening, rallying, rousing, stirring; exciting, provoking, quickening, stimulating; breathless, gripping
con unaffecting, unimpressive, untouching; casual, cold, formal
ant unmoving
3 *syn* see EMOTIONAL 2

moving picture *n* *syn* see MOVIE

mow *n* *syn* see PILE 1

mow *vb* to cut down standing grass or grain with a tool or a machine <*mowed* the lawn every week>
syn clip, crop, cut
rel reap; pare, trim

mow (down) *vb* *syn* see FELL 1

mow *n* *syn* see FACE 6

mow *vb* *syn* see GRIMACE

moxie *n* **1** *syn* see ENERGY 2
2 *syn* see COURAGE
3 *syn* see FORTITUDE

‖**mozo** *n* *syn* see WORKER

Mr. *n* *syn* see HUSBAND

Mrs. *n* *syn* see WIFE

Mrs. Grundy *n* *syn* see PRUDE

much *adv* **1** *syn* see VERY 1
2 *syn* see OFTEN
3 *syn* see NEARLY

much *n* a great quantity, amount, extent, or degree <learned *much* worth remembering from his experiences in the army>
syn barrel, great deal, heap, lashings, lot, lump, mass, ‖mess, mountain, multiplicity, pack, peck, pile, plenty, ‖power, ‖sight; *compare* MULTITUDE 1, SCAD
rel excess, overage, oversupply, plethora, superfluity
idiom all kinds of
con bit, crumb, modicum, trifle; deficiency, inadequacy, insufficiency, undersupply
ant little

‖**much** *vb* *syn* see BABY

much as *conj* *syn* see THOUGH

muck *n* **1** *syn* see SLIME
2 *syn* see REFUSE
3 *syn* see GOO 1

muck *vb* **1** *syn* see SOIL 2
‖**2** *syn* see BOTCH
‖**3** *syn* see COMPLICATE
4 *syn* see DRUDGE
‖**5** *syn* see SAUNTER

‖**muckamuck** *n* *syn* see FOOD 1

muckamuck *n* *syn* see NOTABLE 1

mucker *vb* *syn* see BOTCH

mucker *n* **1** *syn* see BOOR
2 *syn* see WRETCH 1
3 *syn* see TOUGH

mucking *adj* *syn* see DAMNED 2

muckworm *n* *syn* see MISER

mucky *adj* **1** *syn* see DIRTY 1
2 *syn* see MURKY 3
3 *syn* see HUMID

‖**mucky** *vb* *syn* see SOIL 2

mucronate *adj* *syn* see POINTED 1

mud *vb* *syn* see ROIL 1

muddle *vb* **1** *syn* see ROIL 1
2 *syn* see MUMBLE
3 *syn* see CONFUSE 2
4 *syn* see DISORDER 1
5 *syn* see CONFUSE 5
6 *syn* see COMPLICATE
7 *syn* see STUMBLE 6

muddle (away) *vb* *syn* see WASTE 2

muddle *n* **1** *syn* see CONFUSION 3
2 *syn* see MESS 3
3 *syn* see CLUTTER 2

muddled *adj* **1** *syn* see INCOHERENT 2
2 *syn* see INTOXICATED 1

muddledness *n* *syn* see HAZE 2

muddlehead *n* *syn* see DUNCE

muddleheadedness *n* *syn* see HAZE 2

muddlement *n* *syn* see HAZE 2

muddle through *vb* *syn* see SHIFT 5

muddy *adj* **1** having a great deal of mud <playing in the wet field, he got his shoes all *muddy*>
syn bemired, ‖claggy, ‖clarty, miry, oozy
rel black, dirty, dungy, filthy, foul, grubby, impure, nasty, soily, sordid, squalid, unclean, uncleanly; bedraggled, draggled
con clean, cleanly, immaculate, spotless, taintless, unsoiled, unsullied
ant mudless
2 *syn* see TURBID
rel gloomy, murky; addled, confused, muddled
3 *syn* see DULL 8

muddy *vb* **1** *syn* see SOIL 2
2 *syn* see ROIL 1
3 *syn* see DULL 1
4 *syn* see CONFUSE 4
rel conceal, hide, screen
con illuminate, illumine, light, lighten

mudhole *n* **1** *syn* see POTHOLE
2 *syn* see BURG

muff *vb* *syn* see BOTCH

muffle *vb* **1** *syn* see BUNDLE UP
rel cover, envelop, overspread, shroud, veil
2 to dull the sound of <closed the door to *muffle* the outside noises>
syn dampen, deaden, mute, stifle
rel mellow, soften, soft-pedal, subdue, tone (down); smother
con amplify, enhance, heighten, magnify, reinforce, strengthen
3 *syn* see SUPPRESS 2

muffler *n* *syn* see MASK 2

mug *n* **1** ***syn*** see FACE 1
2 ***syn*** see FACE 6
3 ***syn*** see DUNCE
||**4** ***syn*** see FOOL 3
5 ***syn*** see TOUGH
mug *vb* ***syn*** see GRIMACE
||**mug** (up) *vb* ***syn*** see CRAM 4
muggins *n* ***syn*** see DUNCE
muggy *adj* ***syn*** see HUMID
rel damp, dampish, moist, moisty, wettish
con dry
mughouse *n* ***syn*** see ALEHOUSE
mug–up *n* ***syn*** see SNACK
mugwump *n* ***syn*** see NOTABLE 1
mulatto *n* a person of mixed Caucasian and Negro ancestry <the special conflicts faced by *mulattoes* with both whites and blacks>
syn high yellow
rel mulatta, mulattress; octoroon, quadroon; sambo, zambo; mustee; half-breed
mulct *n* ***syn*** see FINE
mulct *vb* **1** ***syn*** see PENALIZE
rel claim, demand, exact, require
2 ***syn*** see FLEECE 1
mule *n* ***syn*** see HYBRID
muleheaded *adj* ***syn*** see OBSTINATE
muley *adj* ***syn*** see OBSTINATE
muliebral *adj* ***syn*** see FEMININE
mulish *adj* ***syn*** see OBSTINATE
rel ungovernable, unruly; fixed, set
mull *n* ***syn*** see MESS 3
mull *vb* **1** ***syn*** see DEADEN 1
2 ***syn*** see CONFUSE 2
3 ***syn*** see DELAY 2
mull (over) *vb* ***syn*** see PONDER 2
mulligrubs *n pl* ***syn*** see SULK
rel blues, dejection, depression, (the) dismals, dumps, gloom, heavyheartedness, melancholy, mournfulness, sadness, unhappiness
||**mullock** *n* **1** ***syn*** see REFUSE
2 ***syn*** see CONFUSION 3
multeity *n* ***syn*** see VARIETY 1
multicolor *adj* ***syn*** see VARIEGATED
ant monotone
multicolored *adj* ***syn*** see VARIEGATED
ant monotone
multifarious *adj* **1** ***syn*** see MANY
2 ***syn*** see MANIFOLD
3 ***syn*** see MISCELLANEOUS
multifariousness *n* ***syn*** see VARIETY 1
multifold *adj* ***syn*** see MANIFOLD
multiform *adj* ***syn*** see MANIFOLD
ant uniform
multiformity *n* ***syn*** see VARIETY 1
ant uniformity
multihued *adj* ***syn*** see VARIEGATED
ant monotone
multilateral *adj* having many sides <*multilateral* figures>
syn many-sided
ant one-sided, unilateral
multiloquent *adj* ***syn*** see TALKATIVE
multiloquious *adj* ***syn*** see TALKATIVE
multiplex *adj* ***syn*** see MANIFOLD
multiplicity *n* **1** ***syn*** see VARIETY 1
ant unity
2 ***syn*** see MUCH
multiply *vb* **1** ***syn*** see INCREASE 1
2 ***syn*** see INCREASE 2
3 ***syn*** see PROCREATE 1
multitude *n* **1** a very large number of individuals or things <that child always asks a *multitude* of questions>
syn army, cloud, crowd, flock, host, legion, rout, scores; *compare* CROWD 1, MUCH, SCAD
rel numbers, oodles, quantities
con few, handful, scattering, smatter, smattering, sprinkling
ant none
2 ***syn*** see CROWD 1
multitudinal *adj* ***syn*** see MANY
rel countless, innumerable, innumerous, numberless, uncountable, uncounted, unnumberable, unnumbered, untold
multitudinous *adj* ***syn*** see MANY
rel countless, innumerable, innumerous, numberless, uncountable, uncounted, unnumberable, unnumbered, untold
multivarious *adj* ***syn*** see MANIFOLD
multivocal *adj* ***syn*** see VOCIFEROUS
mum *adj* ***syn*** see SILENT 2
||**mum** *n* ***syn*** see MOTHER 1
mumble *vb* to utter with a low inarticulate voice <embarrassed, he *mumbled* an apology>
syn ||chunter, fumble, muddle, ||mump, murmur, mutter, swallow
rel maunder; limp, shuffle, stumble; ||hammer, stammer, ||stut, stutter; speak, talk, utter, verbalize, vocalize, voice
idiom speak with mush in one's mouth
con speak out, speak up; clamor, cry out, shout, vociferate
mumble *n* ***syn*** see MURMUR 1
mumblenews *n pl but sing or pl in constr* ***syn*** see GOSSIP 1
mumbo jumbo *n* ***syn*** see GIBBERISH 3
||**mumchance** *adj* ***syn*** see SILENT 2
mummer *n* ***syn*** see ACTOR 1
mummery *n* ***syn*** see GIBBERISH 3
mummify *vb* ***syn*** see WITHER
mummy *n* ***syn*** see MOTHER 1
mummy *vb* ***syn*** see WITHER
||**mump** *vb* **1** ***syn*** see MUMBLE
2 ***syn*** see GRIMACE
3 ***syn*** see SULK
||**mump** *vb* ***syn*** see CHEAT
mumpish *adj* ***syn*** see SULLEN
mumps *n pl* ***syn*** see SULK
||**mun** *vb* ***syn*** see MUST 2
||**mun** *n* ***syn*** see MAN 3
munch *vb* ***syn*** see CHEW 1
mundane *adj* **1** ***syn*** see EARTHLY 1
rel profane, secular, temporal

syn synonym(s) ***rel*** related word(s)
ant antonym(s) ***con*** contrasted word(s)
idiom idiomatic equivalent(s)
|| use limited; if in doubt, see a dictionary

ant eternal
2 *syn* see MATERIALISTIC
rel animal, carnal, fleshly
3 *syn* see PROSAIC 3
municipal *adj* **1 *syn*** see DOMESTIC 2
2 *syn* see URBAN
munificent *adj* ***syn*** see LIBERAL 1
con close, mean, niggard, ungiving
murder *n* the crime of killing a person <a *murder* occurred during a gang shoot-out>
syn blood, ||bump-off, foul play, hit, homicide, killing, manslaughter
murder *vb* **1** to kill (a human being) unlawfully and with premeditated malice <planned a safe way to *murder* his rival>
syn assassinate, ||bump off, cool, do in, ||dust off, execute, finish, knock off, liquidate, put away, rub out, scrag, slay; *compare* KILL 1
rel asphyxiate, behead, decapitate, electrocute, garrote, guillotine, hang, lynch, smother, strangle
idiom take for a ride
2 *syn* see ANNIHILATE 2
murderer *n* one who kills a human being <a *murderer* who wouldn't hesitate to kill in cold blood>
syn homicide, killer, manslayer, slayer; *compare* ASSASSIN
rel butcher, slaughterer
murdering *adj* ***syn*** see MURDEROUS
murderous *adj* characterized by or of a kind to cause murder or bloodshed <made a *murderous* assault on his former friend>
syn bloodthirsty, bloody, homicidal, murdering, sanguinary, sanguine, sanguineous
rel deadly; destructive, devastating, ruinous
con harmless, innocuous, trivial
mure *vb* ***syn*** see ENCLOSE 1
murk *vb* **1 *syn*** see OBSCURE
2 *syn* see SOIL 2
murky *adj* **1 *syn*** see DARK 1
rel glooming, glowering, lowering
con bright, brilliant, effulgent, radiant
2 *syn* see OBSCURE 3
3 having visible material in suspension <a *murky* liquid>
syn cloudy, mucky
rel muddy, roily, turbid
con clear, limpid, lucent, translucent, transparent; clean, fresh, pure, unpolluted
4 *syn* see DULL 8
5 *syn* see DIRTY 1
murmur *n* **1** a low indistinct but often continuous sound (as of voices) <could hear the *murmur* of the audience throughout the entire performance>
syn mumble, mutter, rumor, susurration, undertone, whisper
rel murmuration; buzz, drone, hum, purr; brool
2 *syn* see REPORT 1
murmur *vb* **1 *syn*** see GRUMBLE 1
2 *syn* see COMPLAIN
3 *syn* see MUMBLE
muscle *n* **1** muscular strength <loading cargo calls for real *muscle*>
syn beef, brawn, might, sinew, thew
rel power, strength
con impotence
2 *syn* see POWER 4
muscle–bound *adj* ***syn*** see STIFF 4
muscular *adj* **1** marked by good well-developed musculature <his arms were lean but *muscular*>
syn fibrous, ropy, sinewy, stringy, wiry
rel flexible, elastic, resilient, springy, supple
con flabby, flaccid, flimsy, floppy, limp, sleazy; feeble, weak
2 strong and powerful in build or action <a *muscular* lad who could wield an ax like a man>
syn athletic, brawny, sinewy; *compare* STRONG 1
rel stalwart, stout, strong, sturdy; well-built, well-knit, well-set; beefy, burly, husky; Herculean, mighty, powerful
con faint, fragile, frail; delicate, feeble, weak; ||pindling, puny, slight
muse *vb* ***syn*** see PONDER 2
rel excogitate, study
muse *n* ***syn*** see REVERIE
muse *n* ***syn*** see POET
museum *n* a room, building, or locale where a collection of objects is put on exhibition <an art *museum* with a famous collection of jade>
syn gallery
rel salon; picture gallery, pinacotheka
||**mush** *n* **1 *syn*** see MOUTH 1
2 *syn* see FACE 1
||**mush** (up) *vb* ***syn*** see CRUSH 2
mushroom *vb* ***syn*** see EXPLODE 1
mushy *adj* **1 *syn*** see SOFT 6
2 *syn* see HAZY
3 *syn* see SENTIMENTAL
music *n* ***syn*** see DIN
musical *adj* **1 *syn*** see HARMONIOUS 1
ant unmusical; musicless
2 *syn* see MELODIOUS 2
ant unmusical; musicless
musician *n* one skilled in music <the one playing the sax is a real *musician*>
syn musicianer, ||musicker, musico, virtuoso
rel performer, player
musicianer *n* ***syn*** see MUSICIAN
||**musicker** *n* ***syn*** see MUSICIAN
musico *n* ***syn*** see MUSICIAN
muskeg *n* ***syn*** see SWAMP
muss *n* ||**1 *syn*** see BRAWL 2
2 *syn* see MESS 3
muss (up) *vb* ***syn*** see DISORDER 1
rel dishevel, rumple, wrinkle
mussy *adj* ***syn*** see SLOVENLY 1
must *verbal auxiliary* **1 *syn*** see WANT 3
2 — used to indicate requirement by immediate or future need or purpose <we *must* hurry if we want to catch the bus>
syn have, ||mun, need
rel ought, should want
idiom have got to, must needs
must *n* **1 *syn*** see OBLIGATION 2
2 *syn* see ESSENTIAL 2
muster *vb* **1 *syn*** see ENTER 3
2 *syn* see MOBILIZE 3

3 ***syn*** see GATHER 6

muster (up) *vb* ***syn*** see GENERATE 3

muster *n* **1** ***syn*** see GATHERING 2
2 ***syn*** see ROSTER 1

muster out *vb* ***syn*** see DISCHARGE 7
ant call up, draft

muster roll *n* ***syn*** see ROSTER 1

musty *adj* **1** ***syn*** see MALODOROUS 1
rel dirty, filthy, squalid
2 ***syn*** see TRITE

mutable *adj* **1** ***syn*** see CHANGEABLE 1
rel fluctuating, swaying, swinging, wavering; fickle, inconstant, unstable
con equable, even, steady, uniform; durable, lasting, permanent, stable
ant immutable
2 liable to change or to be changed <a flexible and perhaps too *mutable* policy>
syn changeable, inconstant, shifty, slippery, uncertain, unstable, unsteady, variable; *compare* CHANGEABLE 1, INCONSTANT 1
rel changeful, protean, unsettled; capricious, fickle, inconsistent, lubricious, mercurial, temperamental, ticklish, volatile; fluctuating, shilly-shally, vacillating, wavering
con constant, established, fixed, immovable, inalterable, invariable, set, unalterable, unchangeable, unmodifiable, unmovable
ant immutable

mutate *vb* **1** ***syn*** see TRANSFORM
2 ***syn*** see CHANGE 1

mutation *n* **1** ***syn*** see CHANGE 1
2 ***syn*** see CHANGE 2

mute *adj* **1** ***syn*** see DUMB 1
2 ***syn*** see SILENT 2
con articulate, eloquent, fluent, glib, vocal, voluble

mute *vb* ***syn*** see MUFFLE 2

muted *adj* ***syn*** see DULL 7

mutedly *adv* ***syn*** see SOTTO VOCE

mutilate *vb* **1** ***syn*** see MAIM
rel damage, hurt, injure, mar, spoil; deface
2 ***syn*** see STERILIZE

mutineer *n* ***syn*** see REBEL

mutinous *adj* ***syn*** see INSUBORDINATE
rel alienated, disaffected

mutiny *vb* ***syn*** see REVOLT 1

mutt *n* ***syn*** see DUNCE

mutter *vb* **1** ***syn*** see MUMBLE
2 ***syn*** see GRUMBLE 1
rel repine, wail

mutter *n* ***syn*** see MURMUR 1

muttonchops *n pl* ***syn*** see SIDE-WHISKERS

muttonhead *n* ***syn*** see DUNCE

mutual *adj* ***syn*** see COMMON 1
rel partaken, participated; associated, connected, related, united

mutually *adv* ***syn*** see TOGETHER 3

‖**mux** *vb* ***syn*** see DISORDER 1

muzzle *n* ***syn*** see FACE 1

myopic *adj* affected by a condition in which the visual images come to a focus in front of the retina of the eye resulting especially in defective vision of distant objects <so *myopic* that he used glasses even to read>
syn nearsighted, shortsighted
rel presbyopic; astigmatic
ant farsighted, hyperopic, longsighted

myriad-minded *adj* ***syn*** see VERSATILE

mysterial *adj* ***syn*** see MYSTERIOUS

mysterious *adj* being beyond one's powers to discover, understand, or explain <he had a *mysterious* sense of humor, laughing when other people did not>
syn arcane, cabalistic, impenetrable, inscrutable, mysterial, mystic, numinous, unaccountable, unexaminable, unguessed, unknowable; *compare* INEXPLICABLE, STRANGE 4
rel impenetrable, incognizable, incomprehensible, uncomprehensible, ungraspable, unintelligible, unknowable; abstruse, esoteric, occult, recondite; ambiguous, cryptic, enigmatic, equivocal, obscure
con explainable, explicable; apprehensible, comprehendible, comprehensible, fathomable, graspable, intelligible, knowable, lucid, scrutable; candid, frank, honest, straightforward
ant unmysterious

mystery *n* something which baffles or perplexes <the *mystery* of her disappearance has never been solved>
syn Chinese puzzle, closed book, conundrum, enigma, mystification, puzzle, puzzlement, riddle, why
rel poser, problem, stumper; perplexity; brainteaser, brain twister
con open book

mystic *adj* **1** ***syn*** see MYSTICAL 1
rel imaginary, visionary; quixotic
2 ***syn*** see MYSTERIOUS
3 ***syn*** see MAGIC

mystical *adj* **1** having a spiritual meaning or reality that is neither apparent to the senses nor obvious to the intelligence <the Church is the *mystical* body of Christ>
syn anagogic, mystic, telestic
rel abysmal, deep, profound; absolute, categorical, ultimate; divine, holy, sacred, spiritual; miraculous, supernatural, supranatural
2 ***syn*** see SECRET 1

mystification *n* ***syn*** see MYSTERY

mystifying *adj* ***syn*** see CRYPTIC

myth *n* **1** a traditional story of ostensibly historical content whose origin has been lost <the various Greek *myths* that have come down to us>
syn legend, mythos, mythus; *compare* ALLEGORY 2
rel saga; fable, fabrication, fiction, figment; creation, invention
2 ***syn*** see ALLEGORY 2
3 ***syn*** see LORE 2

mythical *adj* lacking factual basis or historical validity <a *mythical* account attributes the founding of the city to Noah>

---

syn synonym(s) ***rel*** related word(s)
ant antonym(s) ***con*** contrasted word(s)
idiom idiomatic equivalent(s)
‖ use limited; if in doubt, see a dictionary

syn fabulous, legendary, mythological
rel fictional, fictitious, fictive, imaginary, suppositious, unreal; fanciful, fantastic, visionary; created, invented
con actual, real, true; authentic, genuine, veritable; truthful, veracious, verisimilar
ant historical

mythological *adj* ***syn*** see MYTHICAL

mythology *n* ***syn*** see LORE 2

mythos *n* **1** ***syn*** see MYTH 1
2 ***syn*** see LORE 2

mythus *n* ***syn*** see MYTH 1

N

nab *vb* **1** ***syn*** see ARREST 2
2 ***syn*** see SEIZE 2
3 ***syn*** see STEAL 1
‖**nab** *n* **1** ***syn*** see POLICEMAN
2 ***syn*** see ARREST
nabal *n* ***syn*** see MISER
nabob *n* ***syn*** see NOTABLE 1
nada *n* ***syn*** see NOTHINGNESS
nadir *n* ***syn*** see BOTTOM 3
con acme, climax, culmination; peak, summit
ant apex, zenith
nag *vb* to find fault incessantly <stop *nagging* her over nothing>
syn carp (at), fuss, henpeck, peck (at)
rel annoy, harass, harry, pester, plague, tease, worry; bother, irk, vex; badger, bait, chivy, heckle, hector, hound, ride; egg, goad, needle, prod, urge
idiom give a bad (*or* hard) time, pick at (*or* on), take it out on
con commend, compliment, praise; acclaim, applaud, hail
nail *vb* **1** ***syn*** see CATCH 1
‖**2** ***syn*** see SEIZE 2
‖**3** ***syn*** see STEAL 1
‖**4** ***syn*** see STRIKE 2
naive *adj* **1** ***syn*** see NATURAL 5
rel fresh, original
ant sophisticated
2 ***syn*** see EASY 3
naked *adj* **1** ***syn*** see BARE 1
2 ***syn*** see NUDE 2
3 ***syn*** see OPEN 2
rel disclosed, discovered, revealed; evident, manifest, obvious, palpable; colorless, uncolored; pure, sheer, simple
namby-pamby *adj* **1** ***syn*** see INSIPID 3
2 ***syn*** see CHARACTERLESS
namby-pamby *n* ***syn*** see WEAKLING
name *n* **1** the word or combination of words by which something is called and by means of which it can be distinguished or identified <the *name* always given to the eldest son> <what is the *name* of that bird?>
syn appellation, appellative, cognomen, compellation, denomination, designation, ‖handle, ‖moniker, nomen, rubric, style, title
rel baptismal name, Christian name, font name, forename, personal name, prename; byname, byword, hypocorism, nickname, pet name, sobriquet; epithet, label, tag; alias, incognito, nom de guerre, nom de plume, pen name, pseudonym
2 ***syn*** see REPUTATION 2
3 ***syn*** see CELEBRITY 2
name *vb* **1** to give a name to <*named* the child for his grandfather>
syn baptize, call, christen, denominate, designate, dub, entitle, style, term, title
rel label, tag, ticket; nickname
idiom give a handle, pin a moniker on
2 ***syn*** see DESIGNATE 2
rel advertise, announce, declare, publish
3 ***syn*** see MENTION
rel identify, recognize
nameable *adj* ***syn*** see NOTEWORTHY
nameless *adj* **1** ***syn*** see OBSCURE 5
2 ***syn*** see ANONYMOUS
ant named
namely *adv* that is to say <understandably his wife disapproves of his bad habits, *namely* gambling and drinking>
syn scilicet, to wit, videlicet
rel especially, expressly, particularly, specially, specifically
nana *n* ***syn*** see NURSEMAID
‖**nanny** *n* ***syn*** see NURSEMAID
nap *n* a short sleep <generally took an hour's *nap* after lunch>
syn catnap, dog nap, ‖dover, forty winks, siesta, snooze; *compare* DOZE, SLEEP 1
rel dogsleep; break, interlude, intermission, let up, pause, respite, rest
nap *vb* to sleep briefly <*napped* for an hour after lunch>
syn catnap, ‖caulk (off), siesta, snooze; *compare* DOZE, SLEEP
rel drowse; relax, rest, unlax
idiom catch a wink of sleep, catch forty winks, take a nap (*or* siesta *or* snooze)
narcissism *n* ***syn*** see CONCEIT 2
narcissistic *adj* ***syn*** see VAIN 3
narcotic *n* **1** ***syn*** see DRUG 2
2 ***syn*** see ANODYNE 2
narcotic *adj* ***syn*** see SOPORIFIC 1
‖**nark** *n* ***syn*** see INFORMER
‖**nark** *vb* ***syn*** see INFORM 3
narrate *vb* ***syn*** see RELATE 1
rel descant, dilate, discourse, expatiate
narration *n* **1** ***syn*** see DESCRIPTION 2
2 ***syn*** see STORY 2
narrative *n* **1** ***syn*** see STORY 2
2 ***syn*** see ACCOUNT 7
narrow *adj* **1** ***syn*** see DEFINITE 1
2 ***syn*** see LITTLE 2
3 ***syn*** see ILLIBERAL
rel inexorable, inflexible, obdurate
con forbearing, indulgent, lenient, tolerant
ant broad
‖**4** ***syn*** see STINGY
narrow *vb* ***syn*** see CONSTRICT 2

syn synonym(s) ***rel*** related word(s)
ant antonym(s) ***con*** contrasted word(s)
idiom idiomatic equivalent(s)
‖ use limited; if in doubt, see a dictionary

narrow–fisted *adj syn* see STINGY
ant openhanded
narrowhearted *adj syn* see STINGY
ant openhearted
narrow–minded *adj syn* see ILLIBERAL
ant broad-minded
nascent *adj syn* see INITIAL 1
nasty *adj* **1** *syn* see DIRTY 1
rel coarse, gross, obscene, ribald, vulgar; improper, indecent, indecorous, indelicate, unseemly
2 *syn* see OFFENSIVE
3 *syn* see OBSCENE 2
4 *syn* see MALICIOUS
nates *n pl syn* see BUTTOCKS
national *adj* **1** *syn* see PUBLIC 1
2 *syn* see DOMESTIC 2
national *n syn* see CITIZEN 2
native *adj* **1** *syn* see INNATE 1
2 belonging to a locality by birth or origin <a *native* tradition> <delighted with the tasty *native* fruits>
syn aboriginal, autochthonous, endemic, indigenous
rel domestic, local
con adopted, introduced, naturalized
ant alien, foreign, nonnative
3 *syn* see DOMESTIC 2
4 *syn* see WILD 1
5 *syn* see UNREFINED 3
Nativity *n syn* see CHRISTMAS
||**natter** *vb syn* see CHAT 1
natty *adj syn* see DAPPER
natural *adj* **1** *syn* see ILLEGITIMATE 1
2 *syn* see INNATE 1
ant abnormal, unnatural
3 *syn* see GENERAL 1
4 *syn* see WILD 1
5 free from pretension or calculation <he spoke in a perfectly *natural* manner>
syn artless, guileless, inartificial, ingenuous, innocent, naive, simple, simplehearted, unaffected, unartful, unartificial, unschooled, unsophisticated, unstudied, untutored, unworldly; *compare* GENUINE 3
rel impulsive, instinctive, spontaneous; easy, unlabored; constitutional, ingrained, inherent; folksy, homespun, unpretentious; ignorant, primitive, undesigning; unconstrained, unembarrassed; candid, frank, open, plain; sincere, unfeigned; provincial, rustic
con ceremonial, ceremonious, conventional, formal; ostentatious, pretentious, showy; assumed, contrived, counterfeited, feigned, pretended; artful, sophisticated, studied
ant affected; artificial, unnatural
natural *n syn* see FOOL 4
natural child *n syn* see BASTARD 1
naturalness *n syn* see UNCONSTRAINT
ant unnaturalness
nature *n* **1** *syn* see TYPE
rel anatomy, framework, structure; conformation, figure, shape
2 *syn* see ESSENCE 1
3 *syn* see DISPOSITION 3
4 *syn* see UNIVERSE
naught (*or* **nought**) *n* **1** *syn* see NOTHING 1
2 *syn* see ZERO
naughty *adj* **1** guilty of misbehavior <a *naughty* boy who teased the cat and upset the milk>
syn bad, ill-behaved, misbehaving, mischievous, paw; *compare* DISOBEDIENT
rel contrary, froward, perverse, wayward; headstrong, intractable, recalcitrant, refractory, ungovernable, unruly, willful; disorderly, rowdy, ruffianly; evil, indecorous, wicked
con decorous, good, well-behaved; amenable, docile, obedient, tractable; amiable, complaisant, good-natured, obliging; polite, proper; considerate, kindly, thoughtful
2 *syn* see DISOBEDIENT
nausea *n* a stomach distress with an urge to vomit <overcome with *nausea* as the boat continued to pitch and wallow>
syn qualmishness, queasiness, squeamishness
nauseate *vb syn* see DISGUST
nauseated *adj* affected with nausea <was *nauseated* after taking the drug>
syn nauseous, squeamish; *compare* SQUEAMISH 1
rel choking, gagging; heaving; barfing, upchucking, vomiting
idiom ready (*or* about) to lose one's cookies
nauseating *adj syn* see OFFENSIVE
ant appetizing
nauseous *adj syn* see NAUSEATED
nautical *adj syn* see MARINE 2
navigable *adj syn* see PASSABLE
ant unnavigable
navigational *adj syn* see MARINE 2
nawob *n syn* see NOTABLE 1
nay *adv* **1** *syn* see NO
2 *syn* see EVEN 3
naze *n syn* see PROMONTORY
neanderthal *adj syn* see OLD-FASHIONED
near *adv* **1** *syn* see CLOSE
ant far
2 *syn* see ABOUT 5
near *prep* **1** *syn* see ABOUT 1
2 not far distant from <kept the boy *near* him>
syn ||aside, beside, by, nearby, nigh, round
idiom close to, hard by, within earshot, within reach, within sight
near *adj* **1** *syn* see CLOSE 6
ant far
2 *syn* see COMPARATIVE
near *vb syn* see APPROACH 1
rel equal, match, rival, touch
con alter, change, modify, vary; differ
||**nearabout** *adv syn* see NEARLY
near–at–hand *adj* **1** *syn* see NEIGHBORING
2 *syn* see CLOSE 6
3 *syn* see CONVENIENT 2
near–at–hand *adv syn* see ABOUT 5
nearby *adv* **1** *syn* see CLOSE
2 *syn* see ABOUT 5
nearby *prep* **1** *syn* see NEAR 2
2 *syn* see ABOUT 1
nearby *adj* **1** *syn* see CLOSE 6

2 ***syn*** see NEIGHBORING
3 ***syn*** see CONVENIENT 2
nearing *adj* ***syn*** see FORTHCOMING
nearly *adv* very close to <our work is *nearly* done for today>
syn about, all but, almost, approximately, as good as, just about, more or less, most, much, ||nearabout, nigh, practically, roughly, round, roundly, rudely, say, some, somewhere, well-nigh
rel virtually
idiom as near as never mind(s), in effect, in essence, in substance, in the main, nigh on (*or* onto *or* upon), to all (practical) intents and purposes
nearsighted *adj* ***syn*** see MYOPIC
neat *adj* **1** ***syn*** see STRAIGHT 3
2 manifesting care and orderliness <always kept a *neat* house>
syn chipper, orderly, prim, shipshape, snug, spick-and-span, tidy, trig, trim, uncluttered, well-groomed; *compare* DAPPER
rel clean, immaculate, spotless; dainty, fastidious, finicky, nice; methodical, regular, systematic; accurate, correct, exact, precise
idiom in good order, neat as a pin (*or* bandbox), neat as can be, neat as wax
con disheveled, disordered, slipshod, sloppy, slovenly, unkempt, untidy; dirty, filthy, foul, nasty; lax, negligent, remiss, slack
ant disorderly, messy
||3 ***syn*** see MARVELOUS 2
neat-handed *adj* ***syn*** see DEXTEROUS 1
neb *n* ***syn*** see BILL 1
nebbish *n* ***syn*** see WEAKLING
||**nebby** *adj* ***syn*** see IMPERTINENT 2
||**necessary** *n* ***syn*** see PRIVY 1
necessary *adj* **1** ***syn*** see ESSENTIAL 4
rel compelling, compulsory, constraining, mandatory, obligatory; important, momentous, significant; cardinal, fundamental
con insignificant, unessential, unimportant
ant unnecessary
2 ***syn*** see INEVITABLE
rel inerrable, inerrant, infallible, unerring
necessitate *vb* ***syn*** see DEMAND 2
necessitous *adj* **1** ***syn*** see POOR 1
rel depleted, drained, exhausted
2 ***syn*** see ESSENTIAL 4
necessity *n* **1** ***syn*** see NEED 4
rel coercion, compulsion, constraint, duress, obligation; indispensableness, needfulness, requisiteness
2 ***syn*** see OCCASION 3
3 ***syn*** see ESSENTIAL 2
neck *vb* ***syn*** see BEHEAD
necrology *n* ***syn*** see OBITUARY
necromancer *n* ***syn*** see MAGICIAN 1
necromancy *n* ***syn*** see MAGIC 1
necromantic *adj* ***syn*** see MAGIC
necropolis *n* ***syn*** see CEMETERY
necropsy *n* ***syn*** see AUTOPSY
||**neddy** *n* ***syn*** see DONKEY 1
need *n* **1** ***syn*** see OBLIGATION 2
2 ***syn*** see REQUIREMENT 1
3 opportunity or requirement to employ <found little *need* for his rifle>
syn demand, occasion, use
rel call, claim, exaction
4 a pressing lack of something essential <he is in *need* of food>
syn exigency, necessity
rel deficiency, deficit, lack, shortage, want
con adequacy, enough, sufficiency
5 ***syn*** see POVERTY 1
need *vb* **1** ***syn*** see LACK
rel claim, demand, exact; hanker, hunger, long, pine, thirst, yearn; covet, crave, desire, wish
2 ***syn*** see MUST 2
needed *adj* ***syn*** see NEEDFUL
ant unneeded
needful *adj* necessary for supply or relief <provided them with everything *needful*>
syn needed, required, requisite
rel essential, imperative, indispensable, necessary; lacked, wanted; cardinal, fundamental, vital
con excess, redundant, superfluous; nonessential, unessential; uncalled-for, unnecessary, unneeded
ant needless
needful *n* ***syn*** see MONEY
neediness *n* ***syn*** see POVERTY 1
needle *vb* ***syn*** see WORRY 1
needless *adj* ***syn*** see UNNECESSARY
ant needful
needy *adj* ***syn*** see POOR 1
ne'er *adv* ***syn*** see NEVER
ne'er-do-well *n* ***syn*** see WASTREL 1
nefarious *adj* ***syn*** see VICIOUS 2
rel atrocious, heinous, monstrous, outrageous; flagrant, glaring, gross, rank
ant exemplary
negate *vb* **1** ***syn*** see DENY 4
ant affirm
2 ***syn*** see ABOLISH 1
3 ***syn*** see NEUTRALIZE
negation *n* ***syn*** see DENIAL 2
ant affirmation
negative *adj* ***syn*** see ADVERSE 2
negative *vb* **1** ***syn*** see VETO
2 ***syn*** see DENY 4
ant affirm
3 ***syn*** see NEUTRALIZE
rel abrogate, invalidate, nullify
neglect *vb* to pass over without giving due attention <*neglected* his family for the sake of his mistress>
syn blink (at *or* away), discount, disregard, elide, fail, forget, ignore, miss, omit, overleap, overlook, overpass, pass, pass by, pass over, pretermit, slight, slough over, slur (over)
rel brush (off *or* aside), disdain, dismiss, reject, scant, scorn, shrug away, shrug off

syn synonym(s) ***rel*** related word(s)
ant antonym(s) ***con*** contrasted word(s)
idiom idiomatic equivalent(s)
|| use limited; if in doubt, see a dictionary

idiom pay no attention to, pay no heed (*or* mind), think little of

con appreciate, prize, treasure, value; cultivate, foster, nurse, nurture

ant cherish

neglect *n* ***syn*** see FAILURE 1

neglected *adj* not properly or sufficiently attended to or cared for <the whole property had a *neglected* appearance>

syn run-down, uncared-for, untended

rel disregarded, ignored, overlooked, slighted, unheeded

con prized, treasured; fostered, tended; guarded, supervised, watched

ant cherished

neglectful *adj* ***syn*** see NEGLIGENT

ant attentive

negligent *adj* failing to give proper attention or care <*negligent* in taking care of the children> <a *negligent* man, prone to forgetfulness>

syn behindhand, careless, delinquent, derelict, discinct, disregardful, lax, neglectful, regardless, remiss, slack

rel heedless, inadvertent, inattentive, inconsiderate, thoughtless, unheedful, unthinking; incurious, indifferent, unconcerned; slipshod, slovenly

con rigid, rigorous, strict; attentive, considerate, heedful, thoughtful; careful, exact, fussy, meticulous, punctilious, punctual, scrupulous

ant attentive

negligible *adj* ***syn*** see REMOTE 4

ant significant

negotiable *adj* ***syn*** see PASSABLE

ant nonnegotiable

negotiate *vb* **1** to bring about by mutual agreement <*negotiate* a treaty>

syn arrange, concert, settle

rel adjust, compose, transact; agree, bargain, contract, covenant

con break off, intermit, interrupt, suspend; differ, disagree, dissent

2 ***syn*** see CLEAR 8

neigh *vb* to make the cry typical of a horse <the frightened horse *neighed* and stamped>

syn nicker, whicker, ‖whinner, whinny

neighbor *vb* ***syn*** see ADJOIN

neighborhood *n* **1** ***syn*** see LOCALITY 1

2 ***syn*** see ORDER 4

neighboring *adj* not distant <the need for understanding between *neighboring* countries>

syn adjacent, close-at-hand, close-by, contiguous, near-at-hand, nearby; *compare* CLOSE 6

rel abutting, adjoining, bordering, conterminous, touching; close, near

con distant, far, faraway, far-off, remote, removed; parted, separated

neighborly *adj* ***syn*** see AMICABLE

rel cooperative, gregarious, hospitable, social; cordial, gracious, sociable

ant unneighborly; ill-disposed

neonate *n* ***syn*** see BABY 1

neophyte *n* ***syn*** see NOVICE

neoteric *adj* ***syn*** see NEW 1

nepenthe *n* ***syn*** see ANODYNE 2

ne plus ultra *n* ***syn*** see APEX 2

nerve *n* **1** ***syn*** see FORTITUDE

2 ***syn*** see TEMERITY

3 ***syn*** see EFFRONTERY

nerve *vb* ***syn*** see ENCOURAGE 1

nerve center *n* ***syn*** see CENTER 2

nervous *adj* easily upset or irritated <a *nervous* fretful woman>

syn fidgety, goosey, high-strung, jittery, jumpy, nervy, spooky, twittery, unrestful

rel agitated, edgy, excitable, skittish, volatile; fretful, irritable, querulous, snappish, waspish

con calm, placid, serene, steady, tranquil; collected, composed, cool, imperturbable, inexcitable, poised, unflappable, unruffled

ant nerveless

nervous breakdown *n* an emotional disorder often characterized by depression, tenseness, irritability, headache, and susceptibility to fatigue <worked and worried himself into a *nervous breakdown*>

syn breakdown, collapse, crack-up, nervous prostration

rel neurasthenia; prostration

nervous prostration *n* ***syn*** see NERVOUS BREAKDOWN

nervy *adj* **1** ***syn*** see WISE 5

2 ***syn*** see NERVOUS

rel excitable, fidgety, jerky, tense, twitchy

idiom tied up in knots

con composed, easy, relaxed

ant phlegmatic

3 ***syn*** see TENSE 2

nescience *n* ***syn*** see IGNORANCE 2

nest egg *n* ***syn*** see RESERVE

nestle *vb* ***syn*** see SNUGGLE

net *vb* ***syn*** see CLEAR 6

nether *adj* ***syn*** see INFERIOR 1

nethermost *adj* ***syn*** see BOTTOMMOST

ant uppermost

netherwards *adv* ***syn*** see DOWN 1

ant upwards

netherworld *n* ***syn*** see HELL

nettle *vb* ***syn*** see IRRITATE

rel agitate, discompose, disturb, perturb, upset

nettlesome *adj* ***syn*** see THORNY

neuter *vb* ***syn*** see STERILIZE

neutral *adj* not experiencing or generating a strong emotional commitment or response <made a *neutral* response to his challenge>

syn abstract, colorless, detached, disinterested, dispassionate, impersonal, poker-faced, unpassioned

rel clinical, collected, composed, cool, nonchalant; calm, easy, relaxed; aloof, indifferent

con intemperate, loaded; fervent, impassioned, passionate, vehement

neutralize *vb* to make inoperative or ineffective usually by means of an opposite force, influence, or effect <attacked by the kind of propaganda that is difficult to *neutralize*>

syn annul, cancel (out), counteract, countercheck, frustrate, negate, negative, redress

rel balance, compensate, counterbalance, counterpoise, countervail, offset; abrogate, invali-

date, nullify; conquer, defeat, overcome, subdue; override, overrule
con activate, animate, dynamize, vitalize

never *adv* not at any time <they had *never* seen him before>
syn ne'er
idiom never in all one's born days, never in one's life, never in the world, never on earth
con constantly, continuously, ever, invariably, perpetually
ant always

never–ending *adj* ***syn*** see EVERLASTING 1
ant ended; transitory

never–failing *adj* ***syn*** see SURE 2

nevertheless *adv* ***syn*** see HOWEVER

nevus *n* ***syn*** see BIRTHMARK 1

new *adj* **1** recently come into existence or use or a particular state or relation <*new* styles that flatter stout figures>
syn fresh, modern, modernistic, neoteric, newfangled, new-fashioned, new-sprung, novel, recent
rel first-hand, independent, primary
con dated, outdated, outmoded, out-of-date; shabby, worn; hackneyed, old hat, trite
ant old
2 ***syn*** see UNFAMILIAR 1
3 ***syn*** see ADDITIONAL
4 ***syn*** see REFRESHED

new *adv* within recent time <the scent of *new*-mown grass>
syn afresh, anew, lately, newly, of late, recently
con aforetime, before, earlier, formerly; heretofore, hitherto
ant once

newborn *n* ***syn*** see BABY 1

newcomer *n* ***syn*** see NOVICE

newfangled *adj* ***syn*** see NEW 1
ant oldfangled

new–fashioned *adj* ***syn*** see NEW 1
ant old-fashioned

New Jerusalem *n* ***syn*** see HEAVEN 2

newly *adv* ***syn*** see NEW

news *n pl but sing in constr* a report of events or conditions not previously known <her friend gave her the bad *news*>
syn advice, information, intelligence, speerings, tidings, word
rel announcement, report; dope, lowdown, ‖poop; gossip, rumor, tattle

newsmonger *n* ***syn*** see GOSSIP 1

newspaper *n* ***syn*** see JOURNAL

new–sprung *adj* ***syn*** see NEW 1

next *adj* being the one that comes immediately after another <the *next* day>
syn coming, ensuing, following; *compare* CONSECUTIVE
rel proximate

next *adv* ***syn*** see AFTER

next *prep* ***syn*** see AFTER 2

next to *prep* ***syn*** see BESIDE 1

nexus *n* ***syn*** see BOND 3

niagara *n* ***syn*** see FLOOD 2

nib *n* ***syn*** see BILL 1

‖**nibby** *adj* ***syn*** see CURIOUS 2

nice *adj* **1** having or displaying exacting standards <too *nice* about his food to like camp cooking>
syn ‖choicy, choosy, clerkish, dainty, delicate, fastidious, finical, finicking, finicky, fussy, miminy-piminy, ‖mincy, niminy-piminy, old-maidish, old-womanish, particular, pernickety, persnickety, picksome, picky, precious, squeamish, squeamy
rel discerning, discriminating, penetrating; overparticular; queasy; careful, meticulous, punctilious, scrupulous; judicious, sage, sapient, wise
con coarse, gross, vulgar; callow, crude, green, raw, uncouth; lax, neglectful, negligent, remiss, slack; careless, sloppy, slovenly
2 ***syn*** see FINE 1
3 ***syn*** see PLEASANT 1
4 ***syn*** see CORRECT 2
rel rigid, strict, stringent; exquisite, rare
con haphazard, happy-go-lucky, hit-or-miss, random; careless, heedless, inadvertent
5 ***syn*** see DECOROUS 1

nicely *adv* ***syn*** see WELL 1

nice Nelly *n* **1** ***syn*** see PRUDE
2 ***syn*** see EUPHEMISM

nice–nellyism *n* ***syn*** see EUPHEMISM

niche *n* ***syn*** see NOOK

nick *n* ***syn*** see NOTCH 1

‖**nick** *vb* ***syn*** see STEAL 1

nicker *vb* ***syn*** see NEIGH

nickname *n* a descriptive or familiar name that is used instead of or in addition to one's proper name <because he was a redhead his friends gave him the *nickname* "Red">
syn byname, byword, ‖handle, hypocorism, ‖moniker, sobriquet
rel first name, middle name; appellation, appellative, compellation, denomination, style; epithet, label, tag

nictate *vb* ***syn*** see WINK

nictitate *vb* ***syn*** see WINK

nidorous *adj* ***syn*** see MALODOROUS 1

nifty *adj* ***syn*** see MARVELOUS 2

nifty *n* ***syn*** see ‖DILLY

niggard *n* ***syn*** see MISER

niggard *adj* ***syn*** see STINGY

niggardly *adj* ***syn*** see STINGY
ant bounteous, bountiful

niggling *adj* ***syn*** see PETTY 2

nigh *adv* **1** ***syn*** see CLOSE
2 ***syn*** see NEARLY

nigh *adj* ***syn*** see CLOSE 6

nigh *prep* **1** ***syn*** see NEAR 2
2 ***syn*** see ABOUT 1

nigh *vb* ***syn*** see APPROACH 1

night *n* the time from dusk to dawn <stayed up all *night*>
syn nighttide, nighttime

---

con day, daytime

night *adj syn* see NIGHTLY

night and day *adv syn* see TOGETHER 2

nightclub *n* a restaurant serving liquor and providing entertainment <Las Vegas *nightclubs*>
syn bistro, cabaret, café, discotheque, hot spot, nightery, night spot, nitery, supper club, watering hole, watering place

nightery *n syn* see NIGHTCLUB

nightfall *n syn* see EVENING 1

nightly *adj* of, relating to, or associated with the night <*nightly* noises>
syn night, nocturnal
con daily, diurnal; matutinal, morning; evening, twilight, vespertine

nightmare *n syn* see FANCY 4

night spot *n syn* see NIGHTCLUB

nightstick *n syn* see CUDGEL

nighttide *n syn* see NIGHT

nighttime *n syn* see NIGHT

nightwalker *n syn* see PROSTITUTE

nihility *n syn* see NOTHINGNESS

nil *n syn* see NOTHING 1

nim *vb syn* see STEAL 1

nimble *adj* **1** *syn* see AGILE
rel light, lightsome; alert, vigilant, watchful, wide-awake
2 *syn* see DEXTEROUS 1

nimble-witted *adj syn* see WISE 4
ant slow-witted

niminy–piminy *adj syn* see NICE 1

nimmer *n syn* see THIEF

nincom *n syn* see FOOL 1

nincompoop *n syn* see FOOL 1

ninny *n syn* see FOOL 1

ninnyhammer *n syn* see FOOL 1

nip *vb* **1** *syn* see BLAST 1
rel arrest, check; press, squeeze; balk, frustrate, thwart
2 *syn* see STEAL 1
‖**3** *syn* see HURRY 2

nip *n syn* see DRAM

nip *vb syn* see DRINK 3

‖**nipcheese** *n syn* see MISER

‖**nipper** *n syn* see CHILD 1

nipping *adj syn* see COLD 1

nippy *adj syn* see COLD 1

nirvana *n syn* see HEAVEN 2

nisse *n syn* see FAIRY

‖**nit** *adv syn* see NO

nitery *n syn* see NIGHTCLUB

nitwit *n syn* see DUNCE

nitwitted *adj syn* see SIMPLE 3

‖**nix** *n syn* see NOTHING 1

‖**nix** *adv syn* see NO

‖**nix** *vb syn* see VETO

no *adv* — used as a function word to express negation, dissent, denial, or refusal <*no,* you can't come with me>
syn nay, ‖nit, ‖nix, ‖nope
idiom by no manner of means, by no means, in no case, no dice, not at any price, not for love or money, not for the life of me, not for the world, nothing doing, not on your life, no way, on no account, on no condition, under no circumstances
ant yes

‖**no-account** *adj syn* see WORTHLESS 1

Noachian *adj syn* see ANCIENT 1

noble *adj* **1** *syn* see GRAND 1
rel eminent, illustrious
con beggarly, contemptible, despicable, scurvy, sorry
ant cheap, ignoble, unnoble
2 *syn* see ELEVATED 2
ant base
3 *syn* see HONORABLE 1
ant ignoble
4 *syn* see MORAL 1

nobody *pron syn* see NO ONE
ant everybody; somebody

nobody *n syn* see NONENTITY
ant somebody

nocent *adj syn* see HARMFUL
ant innocent

nocturnal *adj syn* see NIGHTLY
con daily, diurnal

nocuous *adj syn* see HARMFUL
ant innocuous

nodding *adj syn* see SLEEPY 1

noddle *n syn* see HEAD 1

noddy *n syn* see DUNCE

noel *n syn* see CHRISTMAS

noggin *n syn* see HEAD 1

no–good *adj syn* see WORTHLESS 1

no–good *n* **1** *syn* see WASTREL 1
2 *syn* see WRETCH 1

noise *n syn* see SOUND 1
rel babel, clamor, din, hubbub, pandemonium, racket, uproar
con quiet, silence, stillness

noise (about *or* abroad) *vb syn* see GOSSIP

noiseful *adj syn* see NOISY
ant noiseless, silent

noiseless *adj syn* see STILL 3
con boisterous, clamorous, strident, vociferous
ant noiseful, noisy

noiselessness *n syn* see SILENCE 1
ant noisiness

noisome *adj* **1** *syn* see UNWHOLESOME 1
ant wholesome
2 *syn* see MALODOROUS 1
rel dirty, filthy, squalid; loathsome, revolting
ant balmy
3 *syn* see OFFENSIVE

noisy *adj* making noise <the *noisiest* car you ever heard>
syn clangorous, clattery, noiseful, rackety, sonorous, uproarious
rel blatant, boisterous, clamorous, obstreperous, strepitous, strident, vociferous; tumultuous, turbulent
con quiet, silent, still, stilly
ant noiseless

nomadic *adj syn* see ITINERANT

no man *pron syn* see NO ONE
ant everybody, everyman

nom de guerre *n syn* see PSEUDONYM

nomen *n* ***syn*** see NAME 1
nominal *adj* being something in name or form only <the *nominal* head of his party>
syn formal, so-called, titular
rel apparent, ostensible, seeming; alleged, pretended, professed
idiom in name only
con genuine, real, true
ant actual
nominate *vb* ***syn*** see DESIGNATE 2
rel intend, mean, propose, purpose; offer, present, proffer, tender
nonadhesive *adj* ***syn*** see LOOSE 3
nonage *n* ***syn*** see INFANCY 2
ant age
nonchalant *adj* ***syn*** see COOL 2
rel cheerful, glad, lighthearted; easy, effortless, light, smooth
con anxious, careful, concerned, solicitous, worried
noncombustible *adj* incapable of being burned <*noncombustible* material was used whenever possible>
syn apyrous, incombustible, nonflammable, noninflammable, uninflammable
rel fireproof, fire-resistant, fire-resistive, fire-retardant, flameproof
con flammable, inflammable
ant combustible
noncommittal *adj* ***syn*** see RESERVED 1
noncompos *n* ***syn*** see LUNATIC 1
non compos mentis *adj* ***syn*** see INSANE 1
nonconformism *n* ***syn*** see HERESY
ant conformism
nonconformist *n* **1** ***syn*** see HERETIC
ant conformist
2 ***syn*** see BOHEMIAN
ant conformist
nonconformist *adj* ***syn*** see HERETICAL
nonconformity *n* ***syn*** see HERESY
ant conformity
noncreative *adj* ***syn*** see UNORIGINAL
ant creative
nondiscriminatory *adj* ***syn*** see FAIR 4
ant discriminatory
none *pron* ***syn*** see NO ONE
nonentity *n* an utterly insignificant person <tired of dealing with subordinates and *nonentities*>
syn cipher, insignificancy, nobody, nothing, nullity, rushlight, whiffet, whippersnapper, whipster, zero, zilch
rel lightweight, obscurity, sad sack, small beer, small fry
idiom blank space in the rear rank, man in the street, no great shakes
nonesuch *n* ***syn*** see PARAGON
idiom one in a million
nonessential *adj* ***syn*** see DISPENSABLE
ant essential
nonetheless *adv* ***syn*** see HOWEVER
nonexistence *n* ***syn*** see NOTHINGNESS
ant existence; reality
nonflammable *adj* ***syn*** see NONCOMBUSTIBLE
ant flammable, inflammable
nonfunctional *adj* ***syn*** see IMPRACTICABLE 2
ant functional
noninflammable *adj* ***syn*** see NONCOMBUSTIBLE
ant flammable, inflammable
nonliterate *adj* ***syn*** see PRIMITIVE 6
nonmaterial *adj* ***syn*** see IMMATERIAL 1
ant material
nonobligatory *adj* ***syn*** see OPTIONAL
ant obligatory
no–nonsense *adj* ***syn*** see SERIOUS 1
nonpareil *n* ***syn*** see PARAGON
nonpartisan *adj* ***syn*** see FAIR 4
ant partisan
nonphysical *adj* ***syn*** see IMMATERIAL 1
ant physical
non–placet *vb* ***syn*** see VETO
nonplus *vb* **1** to cause to be at a total loss as to how to act or decide <was totally *nonplussed* by the economic problems>
syn beat, buffalo, get, stick, stump; *compare* PUZZLE
rel baffle, frustrate, stymie, thwart; confound, perplex; mystify; dumbfound; overcome, throw; paralyze; confuse, flurry, fluster, muddle, rattle
idiom put (*or* drive) to one's wit's end, put up a tree (*or* stump), throw on one's beam end
2 ***syn*** see STAGGER 5
rel faze, rattle; baffle, balk, frustrate
nonprofessional *n* ***syn*** see AMATEUR 2
ant professional
nonrational *adj* ***syn*** see ILLOGICAL
ant rational
nonrealistic *adj* ***syn*** see IMPRACTICAL 1
ant realistic
nonreligious *adj* ***syn*** see IRRELIGIOUS
rel lay, profane, secular, temporal
ant religious
nonresistant *adj* ***syn*** see PASSIVE 2
ant resistant, resisting
nonresisting *adj* ***syn*** see PASSIVE 2
ant resistant, resisting
nonreversible *adj* ***syn*** see IRREVOCABLE
ant reversible
nonsectarian *adj* not affiliated with or restricted to a particular religious group <the problems facing *nonsectarian* colleges>
syn interchurch, intercreedal, interdenominational, undenominational, unsectarian
con denominational
ant sectarian
nonsense *n* **1** ***syn*** see GIBBERISH 1
2 something uttered or proposed that seems senseless or absurd <his theories are mere *nonsense*>
syn ‖applesauce, balderdash, ‖baloney, bilge, blague, blah, blather, blatherskite, bosh, ‖bull, ‖bunk, bunkum, bushwa, claptrap, ‖cobblers, ‖cock, ‖codswallop, ‖crap, crock, double-talk, ‖drip, drivel, drool, eyewash, fiddle-faddle, fid-

---

syn synonym(s) ***rel*** related word(s)
ant antonym(s) ***con*** contrasted word(s)
idiom idiomatic equivalent(s)
‖ use limited; if in doubt, see a dictionary

dlesticks, flapdoodle, flimflam, flummadiddle, fudge, ‖gas, gook, guff, hogwash, hokum, hooey, ‖horsefeathers, hot air, humbug, jazz, ‖jiggery-pokery, malarkey, meshuggaas, moonshine, piffle, pishposh, poppycock, punk, rot, rubbish, slipslop, tomfoolery, tommyrot, tosh, trash, trumpery, twaddle, whangdoodle, windbaggery
idiom stuff and nonsense

nonsuccess *n* ***syn*** see FAILURE 2
ant success, successfulness

nonsymmetrical *adj* ***syn*** see LOPSIDED
ant symmetrical

nonviolent *adj* ***syn*** see PACIFIC
ant violent

noodle *n* **1** ***syn*** see DUNCE
2 ***syn*** see HEAD 1

nook *n* a secluded or sheltered place <resting in a shady *nook*>
syn byplace, cranny, niche
rel alcove, recess; cubbyhole, hole

noon *n* ***syn*** see APEX 2

no one *pron* no person <*no one* will be allowed to leave early>
syn nobody, no man, none
idiom never a one, nobody on earth, nobody under the sun, not a blessed soul, not a soul
con all, everyman; many, some
ant everybody, everyone

noontide *n* ***syn*** see APEX 2

noose *vb* ***syn*** see HANG 2

‖**nope** *adv* ***syn*** see NO
ant ‖yep, ‖yup

norm *n* ***syn*** see AVERAGE

normal *adj* **1** ***syn*** see SANE 2
2 ***syn*** see GENERAL 1

nose *n* **1** the prominent part of the human face that bears the nostrils and covers the nasal passage <had a large *nose*>
syn beak, ‖beezer, ‖boko, ‖conk, pecker, proboscis, ‖schnozzle, smeller, ‖sneezer, ‖snitch, snoot, snout
2 ***syn*** see BUSYBODY
3 ***syn*** see GIFT 2

nose *vb* **1** ***syn*** see SMELL 1
2 ***syn*** see SNOOP

nose-dive *vb* ***syn*** see PLUMMET

nosegay *n* ***syn*** see BOUQUET 1

nosey Parker *n* ***syn*** see BUSYBODY

nosh *n* ‖**1** ***syn*** see MEAL
2 ***syn*** see SNACK

Nostradamus *n* ***syn*** see PROPHET

nostrum *n* ***syn*** see PANACEA

nosy *adj* ***syn*** see CURIOUS 2

notability *n* **1** ***syn*** see NOTABLE 1
2 ***syn*** see CELEBRITY 2

notable *adj* **1** ***syn*** see NOTEWORTHY
2 ***syn*** see FAMOUS 2

notable *n* **1** a person of consequence or prominence <*notables* of Congress and the diplomatic corps>
syn big, big boy, ‖big bug, ‖big cheese, ‖big chief, ‖biggie, big gun, ‖big noise, big shot, big-timer, ‖big wheel, bigwig, character, chief, dignitary, eminence, ‖fat cat, great gun, heavy, heavyweight, high-muck-a-muck, leader, lion, luminary, muckamuck, mugwump, nabob, nawob, notability, personage, personality, pooh-bah, pot, somebody, VIP
rel figure; baron, czar, king, magnate, mogul, prince; light, star; power
idiom big-time operator, his nibs, Mr. Big
con cipher, nobody, nonentity; functionary, underling
2 ***syn*** see CELEBRITY 2

notably *adv* ***syn*** see VERY 1

notandum *n* ***syn*** see NOTE 2

notation *n* ***syn*** see NOTE 2

notch *n* **1** a usually V-shaped depression in an edge or surface <a *notch* in the table>
syn indentation, indenture, nick; *compare* DEPRESSION 2
rel cut, gash, incision, score, scratch; cleft, gap, nock
2 ***syn*** see DEGREE 1

note *vb* ***syn*** see SEE 1

note *n* **1** ***syn*** see CALL 1
2 a written reminder <made a *note* to return the call>
syn chit, memo, memorandum, notandum, notation
3 ***syn*** see REMARK 2
rel reminder
4 ***syn*** see LETTER 2
5 ***syn*** see NOTICE 1

noted *adj* ***syn*** see WELL-KNOWN
ant unnoted

note-perfect *adj* ***syn*** see PERFECT 2

noteworthy *adj* having a quality that attracts one's attention <a *noteworthy* event>
syn ‖bodacious, memorable, nameable, notable, observable, red-letter, rubric
rel conspicuous, noticeable, outstanding, prominent, remarkable; evident, manifest, patent; exceptional, extraordinary
con blah, common, commonplace, inconsequential, insignificant, ordinary, quotidian, unimportant, unremarkable
ant unnoteworthy

nothing *n* **1** something that does not exist <his hopes were based on *nothing*>
syn naught (*or* nought), nil, ‖nix, wind
idiom nothing at all, nothing whatever
con something
2 ***syn*** see ZERO 1
3 ***syn*** see NONENTITY
idiom (the) little end of nothing whittled down to a point

nothing *adj* ***syn*** see WORTHLESS 1

nothingness *n* the quality or state of being nothing <the house was blown into *nothingness* by the force of the explosion>
syn nada, nihility, nonexistence, nullity, vacuity
rel emptiness; vacuum, void
con concreteness, solidity, substantiality; materiality, reality
ant somethingness

notice *n* **1** a noting of or concerning oneself with something <take *notice* of the gathering clouds>

syn attention, cognizance, ear, heed, mark, ‖mind, note, observance, observation, regard, remark
rel care, concern, consideration, thought; apprehension, grasp, understanding
con disinterest, disregard, indifference, unconcern; carelessness, heedlessness, unmindfulness; insouciance, negligence, recklessness
2 ***syn*** see MEMORANDUM 2
3 ***syn*** see CRITICISM 1

notice *vb* ***syn*** see SEE 1
rel acknowledge, recognize; advert, allude, refer
con disregard, ignore, neglect, overlook, slight

noticeable *adj* attracting or compelling notice or attention <they both showed a *noticeable* aversion to his company>
syn arresting, arrestive, conspicuous, eye-catching, marked, outstanding, pointed, prominent, remarkable, salient, sensational, signal, striking
rel notable, noteworthy; evident, manifest, obvious, palpable, patent; spectacular
con obscure, vague; concealed, hidden, shrouded; insignificant, undistinguished
ant unnoticeable

notify *vb* ***syn*** see INFORM 2
rel announce, broadcast, declare, proclaim, promulgate, publish; disclose, discover, divulge, reveal

notion *n* **1** ***syn*** see IDEA
2 ***syn*** see CAPRICE
3 ***syn*** see HINT 1

notional *adj* **1** ***syn*** see CONCEPTUAL
2 ***syn*** see IMAGINARY 1
ant real

notoriety *n* ***syn*** see FAME 2
rel ballyhoo, promotion, propaganda, publicity

notorious *adj* **1** ***syn*** see WELL-KNOWN
2 ***syn*** see INFAMOUS 1

notwithstanding *prep* ***syn*** see AGAINST 4

notwithstanding *adv* ***syn*** see HOWEVER

nourish *vb* **1** ***syn*** see NURSE 1
2 ***syn*** see NURSE 2

nourishing *adj* ***syn*** see NUTRITIOUS
ant unnourishing

nourishment *n* ***syn*** see FOOD 2
rel keep, living, maintenance, support

nouveau riche *n* ***syn*** see UPSTART

novel *adj* ***syn*** see NEW 1
rel different, odd, peculiar, singular, special, strange, uncommon, unfamiliar, unique, unusual
con customary, habitual, usual; common, familiar, ordinary

novelty *n* **1** ***syn*** see CHANGE 2
con old story
2 ***syn*** see KNICKKNACK

novice *n* one who is just entering a field in which he has no previous experience <a *novice* in the theater —had never even had a walk-on role>
syn apprentice, beginner, boot, colt, fledgling, freshman, neophyte, newcomer, novitiate, prentice, punk, recruit, rookie, tenderfoot, tyro
rel amateur; cub; postulant, probationer; greenhorn, greeny; learner, student, trainee, undergraduate
con expert, pro, professional
ant doyen, old hand, old-timer, veteran

novitiate *n* ***syn*** see NOVICE

now *adv* **1** ***syn*** see TODAY
ant then
2 ***syn*** see AWAY 3

now *conj* ***syn*** see BECAUSE

now *n* ***syn*** see PRESENT

nowadays *adv* ***syn*** see TODAY

now and again *adv* ***syn*** see SOMETIMES

now and then *adv* ***syn*** see SOMETIMES

noxious *adj* **1** ***syn*** see UNWHOLESOME 1
ant wholesome; sanitary
2 ***syn*** see PERNICIOUS
rel fetid, noisome, putrid, stinking
ant innocuous, innoxious

nuance *n* ***syn*** see GRADATION
rel dash, soupçon, suggestion, suspicion, tinge, touch; nicety, refinement, subtlety

nub *n* ***syn*** see SUBSTANCE 2

nubbin *n* ***syn*** see SUBSTANCE 2

nubilous *adj* **1** ***syn*** see OVERCAST
2 ***syn*** see OBSCURE 3

nucleus *n* ***syn*** see SEED 2

nude *adj* **1** ***syn*** see BARE 1
con covered
2 not wearing any clothes <all the boys liked to swim *nude*>
syn au naturel, buff-bare, mother-naked, naked, raw, stark, ‖starkers, stark-naked, stripped, unclad, unclothed, undressed
rel peeled, uncovered; dishabille, garmentless, unattired, unrobed
idiom ‖buck naked, in a state of nature, in one's birthday suit, in one's skin, in the altogether, in the buff, in the raw, stripped to the buff, without a stitch on, without a stitch to one's name
con attired, robed; decent; covered
ant clad, clothed, dressed

nudge *vb* ***syn*** see POKE 1

nudnick *n* ***syn*** see PEST 2

nugatory *adj* ***syn*** see VAIN 1

nugget *n* ***syn*** see LUMP 1

nuisance *n* **1** ***syn*** see PEST 2
2 ***syn*** see ANNOYANCE 3

null *adj* having no legal or binding force or validity <a *null* ballot>
syn bad, invalid, null and void, void
rel ineffective, ineffectual, inefficacious, useless, worthless
con acceptable, good, valid

null and void *adj* ***syn*** see NULL

nullify *vb* ***syn*** see ABOLISH 1
rel counteract, neutralize; compensate, counterbalance, countervail, offset; confine, limit, restrict

nullity *n* **1** ***syn*** see NOTHINGNESS
2 ***syn*** see NONENTITY

---

syn synonym(s) ***rel*** related word(s)
ant antonym(s) ***con*** contrasted word(s)
idiom idiomatic equivalent(s)
‖ use limited; if in doubt, see a dictionary

numb *adj* **1** devoid of sensation or feeling <my arm is *numb*>
syn anesthetized, asleep, benumbed, dead, deadened, insensible, insensitive, numbed, senseless, unfeeling
rel insensate, insentient, stupefied; comatose, unconscious
con alert; aware, conscious; sensitive
2 *syn* see INDIFFERENT 2
numb *vb* *syn* see DEADEN 1
rel chill, freeze, frost
numbed *adj* *syn* see NUMB 1
number *n* a character by which an arithmetical value is designated <you must add the *numbers* of the first column>
syn chiffer, cipher, digit, figure, integer, numeral, whole number
number *vb* **1** *syn* see COUNT 1
2 *syn* see AMOUNT 1
numberless *adj* *syn* see INNUMERABLE
ant numberable
number one *adj* **1** *syn* see CHIEF 2
2 *syn* see EXCELLENT
numeral *n* *syn* see NUMBER
numerate *vb* **1** *syn* see ENUMERATE 2
2 *syn* see COUNT 1
numerous *adj* *syn* see MANY
rel big, great, large
numinous *adj* **1** *syn* see SUPERNATURAL 1
2 *syn* see SACRED 2
3 *syn* see SPIRITUAL 4
4 *syn* see MYSTERIOUS
numskull *n* *syn* see DUNCE
numskulled *adj* *syn* see STUPID 1
nuptial *adj* *syn* see MATRIMONIAL
nuptial *n, usu* **nuptials** *pl* *syn* see WEDDING
nurse *n* *syn* see NURSEMAID
nurse *vb* **1** to feed from the breast <decided to *nurse* her baby>
syn breast-feed, nourish, suckle
rel bottle-feed
2 to promote the growth, development, or progress of <*nursed* the flame into a blaze>
syn cherish, cultivate, foster, nourish, nursle, nurture
rel feed; advance, forward, further, promote; humor, indulge, pamper
con check, hold back, retard, slow
3 *syn* see MINISTER (to)
nursemaid *n* one who is regularly employed to look after children <the *nursemaid* had three children in her charge>
syn ||amah, ||ayah, nana, ||nanny, nurse, nurserymaid
rel babysitter, ||minder, sitter; chaperon; governess
nurserymaid *n* *syn* see NURSEMAID
nursle *vb* *syn* see NURSE 2
nurture *n* *syn* see FOOD 1
nurture *vb* *syn* see NURSE 2
rel bring up, raise, rear; discipline, educate, school, train; back, bolster, support, sustain, uphold
con disregard, ignore, neglect, overlook, pass over, slight

nut *n* **1** *syn* see PROBLEM 2
||**2** *syn* see HEAD 1
3 *syn* see CRACKPOT
4 *syn* see LUNATIC 1
5 *syn* see ENTHUSIAST
||**nuthouse** *n* *syn* see ASYLUM 3
nutriculture *n* *syn* see HYDROPONICS
nutrient *adj* *syn* see NUTRITIOUS

nutriment *n* *syn* see FOOD 2
rel bread, bread and butter, keep, livelihood, living, maintenance, subsistence, support

nutrimental *adj* *syn* see NUTRITIOUS
nutritional *adj* *syn* see NUTRITIVE 1

nutritious *adj* promoting growth and repairing natural waste <*nutritious* food>
syn nourishing, nutrient, nutrimental, nutritive
rel good, healthful, salubrious, salutary, wholesome; balanced
con indigestible; bad, insalubrious, unhealthful, unwholesome
ant innutritious

nutritive *adj* **1** relating to or concerned with nutrition <*nutritive* organs of the body>
syn alimentary, alimentative, nutritional
rel digestive, metabolic; constructive, creative, formative, productive
2 *syn* see NUTRITIOUS
nuts *adj* *syn* see INSANE 1
nutshell *vb* *syn* see EPITOMIZE 1
nutsy *adj* *syn* see INSANE 1
nutty *adj* **1** *syn* see ENTHUSIASTIC
2 *syn* see INSANE 1
3 *syn* see FOOLISH 2
nuzzle *vb* *syn* see SNUGGLE
nymph *n* *syn* see DOXY 1
nymphet *n* *syn* see DOXY 1

O

oaf *n* **1** ***syn*** see DUNCE
2 a big clumsy, usually slow-witted person <an *oaf* who bumped into everything he passed>
syn bohunk, ‖gaum, gawk, klutz, lobster, looby, lout, lubber, ‖lug, lummox, lump, lumpkin, meathead, palooka, schlepp (*or* schlepper), slouch
rel ‖baboon, beast, bruiser, brute, bull, gorilla, hulk, missing link, ox; clod, clown, dub, galoot, slob; blunderbuss, blunderer, blunderhead

oar *vb* ***syn*** see ROW

oater *n* ***syn*** see WESTERN

oath *n* ***syn*** see SWEARWORD

obdurate *adj* **1** ***syn*** see UNFEELING 2
con tender
2 ***syn*** see INFLEXIBLE 2
rel mulish, stiff-necked; immovable
con relenting, submitting

obedient *adj* submissive to the will, guidance, or control of another <children should always be *obedient* to their parents>
syn amenable, biddable, docile, ‖docious, tractable
rel acquiescent, compliant, sheeplike, submissive, yielding; duteous, dutiful, loyal; law-abiding; obeisant, subservient
con insubordinate, rebellious; contrary, froward, perverse, wayward, willful; headstrong, intractable, recalcitrant, refractory, uncontrollable, ungovernable, unruly
ant contumacious, disobedient

obeisance *n* ***syn*** see HONOR 1
rel allegiance, fealty, loyalty

obeisant *adj* ***syn*** see SUBSERVIENT 2

obese *adj* ***syn*** see FAT 2
ant skinny

obesity *n* a condition characterized by excessive bodily fat <could barely walk because of his *obesity*>
syn adiposity, corpulence, fatness, fleshiness
rel chubbiness, chunkiness, embonpoint, grossness, plumpness, portliness, pudginess, rotundity, stockiness, stoutness, tubbiness
con lankiness, leanness, scrawniness, slenderness, slimness
ant skinniness

obey *vb* to act or behave in conformity with (as an order) or in duty to (as a parent) <*obey* a superior's order>
syn comply, conform, follow, keep, mind, observe
rel bow, defer, submit, yield; accede, acquiesce, agree, assent; fulfill, satisfy; carry out; heed, regard
idiom abide by
con break, disregard, transgress, violate; command, order
ant disobey

obfuscate *vb* ***syn*** see OBSCURE
ant clarify

obit *n* ***syn*** see OBITUARY

obiter *adv* ***syn*** see INCIDENTALLY 2

obiter dictum *n* ***syn*** see REMARK 2

obituary *n* a notice of a person's death usually with a short biographical account <always read the *obituaries* in the paper>
syn necrology, obit

object *n* **1** ***syn*** see THING 3
rel doodad; gadget
2 ***syn*** see THING 5
3 ***syn*** see BODY 4
4 ***syn*** see VIEW 6
5 ***syn*** see USE 4

object *vb* **1** to oppose by arguing against <*objecting* because the evidence was unclear>
syn except, expostulate, inveigh (against), kick, protest, remonstrate
rel balk, boggle, demur, dissent, jib, stickle; complain; criticize; challenge; spurn; rail, rant, rave, storm
con accede, agree, assent, consent; accredit, approve, sanction
ant acquiesce
2 ***syn*** see DISAPPROVE 1

objectify *vb* ***syn*** see EMBODY 1

objection *n* ***syn*** see DEMUR 2

objectionable *adj* arousing or likely to arouse objection <the language in that movie is *objectionable*>
syn exceptionable, ill-favored, inadmissible, unacceptable, undesirable, unwanted, unwelcome
rel abhorrent, loathsome, offensive, repellent, repugnant, repulsive, revolting; disagreeable, distasteful, invidious, obnoxious, unpleasant; unfit, unsuitable; censurable, reprehensible
con acceptable, agreeable, gratifying, pleasant, pleasing, welcome
ant unobjectionable

objective *adj* **1** ***syn*** see MATERIAL 1
rel external, outer, outside, outward
ant subjective
2 ***syn*** see FAIR 4
ant subjective

objective *n* **1** ***syn*** see AMBITION 2
2 ***syn*** see USE 4

objectless *adj* ***syn*** see RANDOM

objet d'art *n* ***syn*** see KNICKKNACK

objurgate *vb* ***syn*** see EXECRATE 1
rel castigate, censure

obligated *adj* ***syn*** see INDEBTED

---

syn synonym(s) ***rel*** related word(s)
ant antonym(s) ***con*** contrasted word(s)
idiom idiomatic equivalent(s)
‖ use limited; if in doubt, see a dictionary

obligation *n* **1** ***syn*** see OCCASION 3
2 something one is bound to do or forbear <it is our *obligation* to obey the law>
syn charge, commitment, committal, devoir, duty, must, need, ought, ‖right
rel compulsion, constraint, restraint; burden, requirement, responsibility; business, part, place
con choice, discretion, free will, option; decision, determination, pleasure, will
3 ***syn*** see INDEBTEDNESS 1
obligatory *adj* ***syn*** see MANDATORY
ant nonobligatory
oblige *vb* **1** ***syn*** see FORCE 2
2 to do a service or courtesy <you will *oblige* me greatly if you will get there on time>
syn accommodate, convenience, favor
rel gratify, please; avail, benefit, profit; aid, assist, contribute, help
con bother, discommode, incommode, inconvenience, trouble
ant disoblige
obliged *adj* **1** ***syn*** see GRATEFUL 1
2 ***syn*** see INDEBTED
obliging *adj* ***syn*** see AMIABLE 1
ant disobliging
oblique *adj* **1** ***syn*** see INCLINED 3
2 ***syn*** see INDIRECT 1
ant straight
obliquely *adv* ***syn*** see ASIDE 1
ant straight
obliterate *vb* ***syn*** see ERASE
oblivion *n* a state of forgetting or the fact of having forgotten <the *oblivion* of sleep>
syn forgetfulness, lethe, obliviousness
rel nirvana; insensibleness
con alertness, awareness, consciousness; memory, recall, recalling, recollection, remembrance
oblivious *adj* **1** ***syn*** see FORGETFUL
rel absorbed, unaware, unconscious
idiom turned off
2 ***syn*** see IGNORANT 2
obliviousness *n* ***syn*** see OBLIVION
obloquy *n* **1** ***syn*** see ABUSE
2 ***syn*** see ANIMADVERSION
3 ***syn*** see DISGRACE
obnoxious *adj* **1** ***syn*** see LIABLE 2
ant unobnoxious
2 ***syn*** see REPUGNANT 1
con congenial, likable, simpatico
ant grateful; unobnoxious
obnubilate *vb* ***syn*** see OBSCURE
obscene *adj* **1** ***syn*** see OFFENSIVE
2 marked by the use of words regarded as taboo in polite usage <knew all the *obscene* expressions for the genitalia>
syn barnyard, coarse, crude, crusty, dirty, fescennine, filthy, foul, gross, indecent, nasty, paw, profane, rank, raunchy, ‖raw, rocky, scatological, scurrilous, smutty, vulgar; *compare* RISQUÉ
rel bawdy, ribald, smoking-room; impure, lascivious, lewd, warm; lurid, pornographic, salacious, scabrous, sultry; earthy, rich; unprintable; foulmouthed
con acceptable, proper, tolerable; appropriate, fit, suitable; clean, decent, decorous, seemly

obscure *adj* **1** ***syn*** see DARK 1
rel clouded, cloudy, fuliginous; shadowy, shady, umbrageous
con clear, lucid; bright, brilliant, luminous
2 withdrawn from the main centers of human activity <was exiled to an *obscure* Siberian village>
syn devious, lonesome, out-of-the-way, remote, removed, retired, secret
rel distant, far, far-off; close, hidden, odd, secluded, sequestered, solitary; blind; inaccessible
idiom back of beyond, off the beaten track (*or* path), in the boondocks (*or* sticks)
con central; urban; populous
3 not readily understood or grasped <an *obscure* textual reference>
syn ambiguous, amphibological, double-edged, double-faced, dusky, equivocal, murky, nubilous, opaque, sibylline, tenebrous, uncertain, unclear, unexplicit, unintelligible, vague; *compare* CRYPTIC, FAINT 2
rel difficult, incomprehensible, inexplicable, puzzling, unfathomable; illegible; abstruse, Delphian, enigmatic, esoteric, inscrutable, mysterious, mystic, mystical; inconclusive, indecisive, indefinite
con definite, explicit, obvious; clear, express, unambiguous, unequivocal
ant lucid
4 ***syn*** see INCONSPICUOUS
rel humble, lowly, minor, unimportant
5 lacking the prominence, showiness, or worth by which attention might be attracted <an *obscure* Roman poet>
syn nameless, uncelebrated, unfamed, unheard-of, unknown, unnoted, unrenowned
rel inconspicuous; minor, undistinguished, unimportant
con celebrated, distinguished, named, notable, noted, noteworthy, renowned, well-known
ant famed, famous
6 ***syn*** see FAINT 2
ant clear
obscure *vb* to make dark, dim, or indistinct <fog *obscured* our view>
syn adumbrate, becloud, bedim, befog, cloud, darken, dim, dislimn, eclipse, fog, gloom, haze, mist, murk, obfuscate, obnubilate, overcast, overcloud, overshadow, shadow
rel blear, blur, fuzz; blind, conceal, dim out, hide, screen, shade, shroud; bemask, camouflage, cloak, cover, disguise, mask, veil; belie, falsify, misrepresent
con brighten, light (up), lighten; clarify, enlighten; elucidate, exemplify, explain
ant illuminate, illumine
obscured *adj* ***syn*** see ULTERIOR
obsequious *adj* ***syn*** see SUBSERVIENT 2
rel deferential; parasitic, sycophantic, toadying
con self-assertive
observable *adj* **1** ***syn*** see PERCEPTIBLE
ant unobservable
2 ***syn*** see NOTEWORTHY
observance *n* **1** ***syn*** see RITE 2

2 ***syn*** see NOTICE 1
ant nonobservance, unobservance
observant *adj* **1** ***syn*** see ATTENTIVE 1
rel awake
ant unobservant
2 ***syn*** see MINDFUL 2
observation *n* **1** ***syn*** see NOTICE 1
2 ***syn*** see REMARK 2
observative *adj* ***syn*** see MINDFUL 2
observatory *n* ***syn*** see LOOKOUT 2
observe *vb* **1** ***syn*** see OBEY
2 ***syn*** see KEEP 2
rel revere, reverence, venerate
ant break, violate
3 ***syn*** see SEE 1
4 ***syn*** see REMARK 2
observer *n* ***syn*** see SPECTATOR
observing *adj* ***syn*** see MINDFUL 2
ant unobserving
obsessed *adj* preoccupied intensely or abnormally <*obsessed* with cleanliness>
syn hagridden, hipped, queer
rel bewitched, dominated, gripped, held, possessed, prepossessed; bedeviled, beset, dogged, harassed, haunted, plagued, troubled; overcome
idiom have on the brain
con detached, unconcerned, uninterested; indifferent, neutral; cool, easygoing
obsession *n* ***syn*** see FETISH 2
obsolesce *vb* ***syn*** see OUTDATE
obsolete *adj* no longer active or in use <*obsolete* social customs>
syn dead, disused, extinct, outmoded, outworn, passé, superseded; *compare* ANCIENT 1
rel old-fashioned, old hat, old-time, old-timey, out-of-date, unfashionable; dusty, fusty, moldy, moth-eaten, musty, stale, timeworn
idiom behind the times
con contemporary, modern, new-fashioned, up-to-date, up-to-the-minute; novel, original, unique
ant current
obsolete *vb* ***syn*** see OUTDATE
obstacle *n* something that seriously hampers action or progress <lack of education is an *obstacle* to advancement>
syn bar, Chinese wall, crimp, hamper, hurdle, impediment, mountain, obstruction, rub, snag, stumbling block, traverse
rel clog, encumbrance, handicap, hindrance; bump, difficulty, hardship, vicissitude; catch, hitch; disincentive
con aid, assist, assistance, help
ant advantage
obstinate *adj* unwilling to submit (as to reason or control) <he had an *obstinate* determination to live as he pleased>
syn bullheaded, closed-minded, deaf, hardheaded, headstrong, incompliant, intractable, intransigent, muleheaded, muley, mulish, pertinacious, perverse, pervicacious, pigheaded, refractory, self-willed, ‖sot, stiff, stiff-necked, stubborn, tough, unpliable, unpliant, unyielding, willful, wrongheaded; *compare* UNRULY 1
rel resistant, unsubmissive, withstanding; contrary, crabbed, recalcitrant, renitent; inexorable, inflexible, obdurate; opinionated; resolute, staunch, steadfast, unbudging
con acquiescent, complaisant, compliant; submissive, yielding; agreeable, cooperative, willing
ant pliable, pliant
obstipated *adj* ***syn*** see CONSTIPATED
obstreperous *adj* **1** ***syn*** see VOCIFEROUS
2 ***syn*** see DISOBEDIENT
obstruct *vb* **1** ***syn*** see FILL 1
2 ***syn*** see HINDER
3 ***syn*** see SCREEN 3
obstruction *n* ***syn*** see OBSTACLE
obtain *vb* ***syn*** see GET 1
obtainable *adj* **1** ***syn*** see AVAILABLE 1
rel derivable
2 ***syn*** see PURCHASABLE 1
obtrude *vb* **1** ***syn*** see IMPOSE 5
2 ***syn*** see INTRUDE 1
obtrusive *adj* ***syn*** see IMPERTINENT 2
ant unobtrusive
obtund *vb* ***syn*** see DULL 3
obtuse *adj* ***syn*** see DULL 6
obviate *vb* ***syn*** see PREVENT 2
rel anticipate; interfere, interpose, intervene
obvious *adj* ***syn*** see CLEAR 5
ant abstruse, obscure; unobvious
occasion *n* **1** ***syn*** see OPPORTUNITY
2 ***syn*** see CAUSE 1
3 something that provides a reason for something else <there is no *occasion* for alarm>
syn call, cause, necessity, obligation
rel basis, foundation, ground, warrant; justification, right; excuse
4 ***syn*** see OCCURRENCE
5 a particular point of time at which something takes place <we always spoke, but on that *occasion* we didn't>
syn instant, moment, time, while
idiom point in time
6 ***syn*** see NEED 3
7 **occasions** *pl* ***syn*** see BUSINESS 8
8 ***syn*** see EVENT 2
occasion *vb* ***syn*** see GENERATE 3
occasional *adj* ***syn*** see INFREQUENT
rel incidental; casual, random
con accustomed, habitual, usual; constant, continual, continuous
ant customary
occasionally *adv* on a few occasions <*occasionally* she'll walk instead of drive>
syn infrequently, irregularly, on occasion, sporadically, uncommonly; *compare* SOMETIMES
rel off and on, once or twice
idiom every now and then, from time to time, ‖once in a way, once in a while

---

syn synonym(s) ***rel*** related word(s)
ant antonym(s) ***con*** contrasted word(s)
idiom idiomatic equivalent(s)
‖ use limited; if in doubt, see a dictionary

con continually, continuously, frequently; commonly, customarily, habitually, often; hardly ever, rarely, scarcely, seldom; never
ant constantly

occlude *vb* ***syn*** see FILL 1

occult *vb* ***syn*** see HIDE

occult *adj* ***syn*** see RECONDITE
rel arcane, mysterious; cabalistic, mystical, supernatural; eerie, unearthly, weird

occupancy *n* ***syn*** see HABITATION 1

occupant *n* ***syn*** see INHABITANT

occupation *n* **1** ***syn*** see WORK 1
2 ***syn*** see HABITATION 1

occupiable *adj* ***syn*** see LIVABLE 1

occupied *adj* ***syn*** see BUSY 1
ant unoccupied

occupy *vb* **1** ***syn*** see ENGAGE 4
2 ***syn*** see INHABIT

occur *vb* **1** ***syn*** see HAPPEN 1
2 to enter one's mind <it just *occurred* to me: she can't drive>
syn hit, strike
idiom come into one's head, come to mind, cross one's mind, flash across one's mind, go through one's head

occurrence *n* something that happens or takes place <the chance encounter turned out to be a fortunate *occurrence*>
syn circumstance, episode, event, go, happening, incident, occasion, thing
rel contingency, emergency, exigency, juncture, pass; condition, situation, state; adventure, experience

ocean *n* the body of water that covers nearly three-fourths of the earth <pulled the downed pilot from the *ocean*>
syn blue, brine, ||briny, deep, drink, main, sea

oceanic *adj* ***syn*** see MARINE 1

ochlocracy *n* ***syn*** see ANARCHY 1

ocular *adj* **1** ***syn*** see VISUAL 2
2 ***syn*** see VISUAL 1

ocular *n* ***syn*** see EYE 1

oculus *n* ***syn*** see EYE 1

odd *adj* **1** being without a corresponding mate <had only an *odd* glove; the other was lost>
syn unmatched, unpaired
rel lone, only, single
con matched, paired
2 ***syn*** see ACCIDENTAL
3 ***syn*** see STRANGE 4

oddball *n* ***syn*** see ECCENTRIC

oddball *adj* ***syn*** see STRANGE 4

oddity *n* **1** ***syn*** see ECCENTRIC
2 ***syn*** see CURIOSITY 2

oddments *n pl* ***syn*** see SUNDRIES

odds *n pl* ***syn*** see ADVANTAGE 3

odds and ends *n pl* **1** ***syn*** see SUNDRIES
2 ***syn*** see MISCELLANY 1

odiferous *adj* ***syn*** see ODOROUS

odious *adj* ***syn*** see HATEFUL 2

odium *n* **1** ***syn*** see DISGRACE
rel hate, hatred
ant honor
2 ***syn*** see STIGMA

odor *n* ***syn*** see SMELL 1

odoriferous *adj* ***syn*** see ODOROUS

odorize *vb* ***syn*** see SCENT 2

odorless *adj* having no odor <*odorless* castor oil>
syn inodorous, scentless, smell-less
rel deodorant, deodorizing; unscented
con scented, smelly
ant odorous

odorous *adj* having or emitting an odor <*odorous* chemicals are often malodorous>
syn odiferous, odoriferous, scented; *compare* MALODOROUS 1, SWEET 2
rel redolent, reeking, smelling, smelly; heady, pungent, strong; olfactive, olfactory
ant inodorous, odorless, scentless

o'er *prep* ***syn*** see OVER 1

oeuvre *n* a substantial body of work constituting the lifework of a writer, composer, or artist <one of the more popular operas in the Mozart *oeuvre*>
syn corpus, opera omnia
rel output

off *adv* ***syn*** see AWAY 2

off *adj* **1** ***syn*** see REMOTE 4
2 ***syn*** see SLOW 3

offal *n* ***syn*** see REFUSE

off–balance *adj* ***syn*** see LOPSIDED

off–center *adj* ***syn*** see ECCENTRIC 1

off–color *adj* **1** ***syn*** see UNWELL
2 ***syn*** see RISQUÉ

offend *vb* **1** ***syn*** see TRESPASS 1
2 ***syn*** see VIOLATE 1
3 to cause hurt feelings or deep resentment <*offended* her by his cruel remark>
syn affront, insult, outrage
rel aggrieve, hurt, sting, wound; exasperate, gall, irritate, nettle; excite, provoke; appall, horrify, scandalize, shock; disoblige, displease, distress, disturb, miff, pique, upset
idiom hurt one's feelings, ruffle one's feathers, step (*or* tread) on one's toes
con delight, gratify, please, tickle; captivate, charm, enchant; flatter

offender *n* ***syn*** see CRIMINAL

offense *n* **1** ***syn*** see ATTACK 1
2 an emotional response to a slight or indignity <he is so sensitive that he takes *offense* at the slightest criticism>
syn dudgeon, huff, miff, pique, resentment, ||snuff, umbrage
rel affront, indignity, insult; anger, indignation; displeasure; catfit, conniption, fit, tantrum; pet, tizzy; explosion, flare-up, outburst, scene
con delight, pleasure
3 ***syn*** see CRIME 1

offensive *adj* utterly unpleasant or distasteful to the senses or sensibilities <the *offensive* odor of garbage> <her arrogant assurance was more than a little *offensive*>
syn atrocious, disgusting, evil, foul, hideous, horrible, horrid, icky, loathsome, nasty, nauseating, noisome, obscene, repellent, repugnant, repulsive, revolting, sickening, ungrateful, unwholesome, vile

rel abhorrent, bad, disagreeable, objectionable, uncongenial, unpleasant; abominable, detestable, fulsome, odious; rank; appalling, awful, beastly, dreadful, frightful, ghastly, grim, grisly, gruesome, lurid, shocking, terrible; unappetizing, unpalatable, unsavory
con agreeable, appealing, attractive, pleasant, pleasing; favorable, unobjectionable, welcome; appetizing, palatable, savory; divine
ant inoffensive, unoffensive

offensive *n syn* see ATTACK 1

offer *vb* **1** to put something before another for acceptance or consideration <he was soon *offered* another job>
syn extend, give, hold out, pose, present, proffer, tender
rel display, exhibit, show
con accept, receive, take; decline, refuse, reject
2 *syn* see ADDUCE
3 *syn* see TRY 5
4 *syn* see SHOW 1

offering *n* **1** *syn* see VICTIM 1
2 *syn* see DONATION

offgoing *n syn* see DEPARTURE 1

offhand *adj syn* see EXTEMPORANEOUS

office *n* **1** *syn* see JOB 2
2 *syn* see FUNCTION 1
‖**3** *syn* see PRIVY 1
‖**4** *syn* see HIGH SIGN 2

officer *n* **1** *syn* see POLICEMAN
2 *syn* see EXECUTIVE

official *n syn* see EXECUTIVE

official *adj* derived from the proper office, officer, or authority <the mayor's office issued an *official* statement>
syn authoritative, ex cathedra, ex officio
rel approved, authorized, certified, cleared, endorsed, OK'd, sanctioned; canonical, cathedral
ant officious (*in diplomatic use*), unofficial

officially *adv syn* see OSTENSIBLY

officiate *vb syn* see ACT 4

officious *adj syn* see IMPERTINENT 2

offing *n syn* see FUTURE

offish *adj* **1** *syn* see UNSOCIABLE
2 *syn* see UNWELL

off-key *adj syn* see IRREGULAR 1

off-load *vb syn* see UNLOAD

off-lying *adj syn* see DISTANT 1

offscouring *n syn* see OUTCAST

offset *vb syn* see COMPENSATE 1
rel check, stop

offshoot *n syn* see OUTGROWTH 2

offspring *n pl* those who follow in direct parental line <a mother of numerous *offspring*>
syn ‖begats, brood, children, descendants, issue, posterity, progeniture, progeny, scions, seed
rel hatch, swarm; produce, spawn, young
con antecedents, ascendants, forebears, forefathers, progenitors
ant ancestors

offstage *adj or adv syn* see BACKSTAGE
ant onstage

‖**off-the-peg** *adj syn* see READY-MADE

off-the-rack *adj syn* see READY-MADE

off-the-shelf *adj syn* see READY-MADE

of late *adv syn* see NEW

oft *adv syn* see OFTEN

often *adv* many times <we called *often* but still could not reach you>
syn again and again, frequently, much, oft, oftentimes, ofttimes, over and over, repeatedly, time and again
idiom a number of times, many a time, many times over, time and time again
con infrequently, rarely; now and then, occasionally
ant seldom

oftentimes *adv syn* see OFTEN

ofttimes *adv syn* see OFTEN

ogle *vb syn* see LOOK 7

‖**ogle** *n syn* see EYE 1

ogress *n syn* see VIRAGO

oil *n syn* see FLATTERY

‖**oiled** *adj syn* see INTOXICATED 1

oily *adj* **1** *syn* see FATTY 2
2 *syn* see FULSOME

ointment *n* a semisolid medicinal or cosmetic preparation for application to the skin <put *ointment* on the burned skin>
syn balm, cerate, chrism, cream, salve, unction, unguent
rel embrocation, liniment; demulcent, emollient; lotion; dressing

OK (*or* **okay**) *adv syn* see YES 1

OK (*or* **okay**) *vb syn* see APPROVE 2

OK (*or* **okay**) *n syn* see APPROBATION

‖**okeydoke** *adv syn* see YES 1

old *adj* **1** *syn* see ANCIENT 1
con contemporary, current, recent; advanced
ant new
2 of long standing <the ending of such an *old* friendship was tragic>
syn continuing, enduring, inveterate, lifelong, long-lasting, long-lived, perennial; *compare* LASTING
rel constant, perpetual, staying; established, firm, solid, steady
con newfound, recent; brief, short-lived; casual, temporary, transitory, weak
ant new
3 *syn* see OLD-FASHIONED
rel primitive; traditional
con newish
ant modern, new
4 *syn* see AGED 1
idiom along in years, getting on
con juvenile, young
ant youthful
5 *syn* see EXPERIENCED
con young
ant new
6 *syn* see FORMER 2

---

syn synonym(s) *rel* related word(s)
ant antonym(s) *con* contrasted word(s)
idiom idiomatic equivalent(s)
‖ use limited; if in doubt, see a dictionary

old age *n* the final stage of the normal life span <spent his *old age* in a nursing home>
syn age, caducity, elderliness, senectitude, senescence, years; *compare* DOTAGE
rel decrepitude, feebleness; infirmity
idiom advanced years, declining years, winter of life
ant youth

olden *adj* **1** ***syn*** see ANCIENT 1
2 ***syn*** see AGED 1

oldest profession *n* ***syn*** see PROSTITUTION

oldfangled *adj* ***syn*** see OLD-FASHIONED
ant newfangled

old–fashioned *adj* typical of an earlier time and often replaced by something more modern or fashionable <*old-fashioned* high-buttoned shoes>
syn antiquated, antique, archaic, belated, bygone, dated, démodé, demoded, dowdy, fusty, moldy, moth-eaten, neanderthal, old, oldfangled, old hat, old-time, old-timey, outdated, outmoded, out-of-date, passé, rococo, unmodern, vintage
rel aged, ancient; discarded, disused, obsolete; outworn, unfashionable; crusty, fogyish, fuddy-duddy, fusty, moss-backed, moss-grown, mossy, stodgy; Victorian; old-line
con modernistic, modish, newfangled, stylish, ‖trendy; current, recent, timely; new-fashioned, up-to-date, up-to-the-minute
ant contemporary; modern

Old Gooseberry *n* ***syn*** see DEVIL 1

Old Guard *n* ***syn*** see ESTABLISHMENT 2

old hand *n* ***syn*** see VETERAN

old hat *adj* **1** ***syn*** see OLD-FASHIONED
2 ***syn*** see TRITE

old lady *n* ‖**1** ***syn*** see WIFE
‖**2** ***syn*** see MOTHER 1
3 ***syn*** see FUSSBUDGET

old–line *adj* ***syn*** see CONSERVATIVE 1

old liner *n* ***syn*** see DIEHARD 1

old maid *n* **1** ***syn*** see SPINSTER
2 ***syn*** see FUSSBUDGET

old–maidish *adj* ***syn*** see NICE 1

‖**old man** *n* **1** ***syn*** see HUSBAND
2 ***syn*** see FATHER 1

Old Nick *n* ***syn*** see DEVIL 1

Old Scratch *n* ***syn*** see DEVIL 1

oldster *n* a person of advanced years <an *oldster* long retired from the business world>
syn ancient, elder, golden-ager, old-timer, senior, senior citizen; *compare* BELDAM 1, GAFFER
ant youngster, youth

old–time *adj* **1** ***syn*** see OLD-FASHIONED
2 ***syn*** see EXPERIENCED

old–timer *n* **1** ***syn*** see VETERAN
2 ***syn*** see OLDSTER

old–timey *adj* ***syn*** see OLD-FASHIONED

‖**old woman** *n* **1** ***syn*** see WIFE
2 ***syn*** see MOTHER 1

old–womanish *adj* ***syn*** see NICE 1

oleaginous *adj* **1** ***syn*** see FATTY 2
2 ***syn*** see FULSOME

olid *adj* ***syn*** see MALODOROUS 1

olio *n* ***syn*** see MISCELLANY 1

olla podrida *n* ***syn*** see MISCELLANY 1

omen *n* ***syn*** see FORETOKEN

omen *vb* ***syn*** see AUGUR 2

ominous *adj* indicative of future misfortune or calamity <dark *ominous* clouds preceded the storm>
syn apocalyptic, baleful, baneful, dire, direful, doomful, fateful, ill-boding, ill-omened, inauspicious, threatening, unlucky, unpropitious; *compare* EVIL 5, SINISTER
rel portentous; malefic, maleficent, malign, sinister; comminatory, forbidding, grim, lowering, menacing; hostile, inhospitable, unfriendly
con auspicious, benign, favorable, promising, propitious; beneficial

omission *n* something omitted or missing <several *omissions* in the list>
syn blank, chasm, overlook, oversight, preterition, pretermission, skip
rel inadvertence, inadvertency, lapse, slip; break, gap, hiatus, lacuna
con inclusion; accession, addition, augmentation, increase, reinforcement; superaddition

omit *vb* ***syn*** see NEGLECT

omitted *adj* ***syn*** see ABSENT 1
ant included

omnibus *n* ***syn*** see ANTHOLOGY

omnipotent *adj* having virtually unlimited authority or influence <an *omnipotent* leader>
syn all-powerful, almighty
rel divine, godlike; unlimited, unrestricted
con impotent, powerless; limited, restricted

omnipresent *adj* present at all places at all times <*omnipresent* God>
syn allover, ubiquitous, universal
rel boundless, endless, immeasurable, infinite, limitless, unending
con bounded, finite, limited, restricted; cramped, straitened; narrow, strait

omnium–gatherum *n* ***syn*** see MISCELLANY 1

on *prep* **1** ***syn*** see OVER 4
2 ***syn*** see OVER 3

on *adv* ***syn*** see ALONG 1

on–again–off–again *adj* ***syn*** see FITFUL

onanism *n* ***syn*** see SELF-GRATIFICATION

onanistic *adj* ***syn*** see SYBARITIC

once *adv* **1** ***syn*** see EVER 5
2 ***syn*** see BEFORE 2

once *adj* ***syn*** see FORMER 2

once and again *adv* ***syn*** see SOMETIMES

once more *adv* ***syn*** see OVER 7

oncoming *adj* ***syn*** see FORTHCOMING

on–dit *n* ***syn*** see REPORT 1

one *adj* ***syn*** see SINGLE 2

one *n* ***syn*** see DOLLAR

one *vb* ***syn*** see JOIN 1

one by one *adv* ***syn*** see APART 1

one–horse town *n* ***syn*** see BURG

oneness *n* **1** ***syn*** see UNITY 1
ant multiplicity
2 ***syn*** see UNIQUENESS
3 ***syn*** see ENTIRETY 1
4 ***syn*** see IDENTITY 1

onerous *adj* imposing great hardship or strain <found the care of his old mother an *onerous* task>
syn burdensome, demanding, exacting, exigent, grievous, oppressive, superincumbent, taxing, tough, trying, weighty
rel arduous, difficult, hard, laborious; heavy, hefty, ponderous; cumbersome, unruly, unwieldy; driving, heavy-handed
con easy, effortless; facile, light, simple, smooth, unexacting, untaxing

onerously *adv* ***syn*** see HARD 8

one-sided *adj* ***syn*** see BIASED 2
rel lopsided, weighted
con many-sided

one-sidedness *n* ***syn*** see PREJUDICE
con manysidedness

onetime *adj* ***syn*** see FORMER 2

onfall *n* ***syn*** see ATTACK 1

ongoing *n* ***syn*** see ADVANCE 2
rel development, growth

onlooker *n* ***syn*** see SPECTATOR

only *adj* **1** ***syn*** see ALONE 3
2 being one or more of which there exist no others <the *only* survivors of the wreck>
syn alone, lone, singular, sole, solitary, solo, unexampled, unique, unrepeatable
rel incomparable, inimitable, matchless, peerless, transcendent, unequaled, unparalleled, unrivaled; companionless, separate, unaccompanied, unattended, uncompanied, uncompanioned
con divers, many, multifarious, numerous, sundry, various
3 ***syn*** see SINGLE 2

only *adv* **1** to the exclusion of any alternative or competitor <he will confess *only* to you>
syn alone, but, entirely, exclusively, solely
2 ***syn*** see JUST 3

only *conj* in spite of which <it looks delicious, *only* I'm not hungry>
syn but, except, however, save, yet

on occasion *adv* ***syn*** see OCCASIONALLY

on offer *adj* ***syn*** see PURCHASABLE 1

onomatopoeic *adj* formed in imitation of a natural sound <*buzz* is an *onomatopoeic* word to describe the sound of bees>
syn echoic, imitative, onomatopoetic
rel emulative, simulative; mimetic, mimic, mimical

onomatopoetic *adj* ***syn*** see ONOMATOPOEIC

on purpose *adv* ***syn*** see INTENTIONALLY

onset *n* **1** ***syn*** see ATTACK 1
2 ***syn*** see BEGINNING

onslaught *n* ***syn*** see ATTACK 1

on the whole *adv* ***syn*** see ALTOGETHER 3

onus *n* **1** ***syn*** see LOAD 3
2 ***syn*** see BLAME
3 ***syn*** see STIGMA

onward *adv* **1** ***syn*** see AHEAD 2
2 ***syn*** see ALONG 1

onyx *adj* ***syn*** see BLACK 1

oodles *n pl but sometimes sing in constr* ***syn*** see SCAD

||**ooftish** *n* ***syn*** see MONEY

||**oofy** *adj* ***syn*** see RICH 1

ooid *adj* ***syn*** see OVAL

oomph *n* ***syn*** see SPIRIT 5

ooze *vb* ***syn*** see EXUDE

oozy *adj* ***syn*** see MUDDY 1

opaque *adj* ***syn*** see OBSCURE 3
ant transparent, transpicuous

ope *vb* ***syn*** see OPEN 1

open *adj* **1** not closed or obstructed <escaped through the *open* gate>
syn patent, unclosed, unobstructed
rel agape, dehiscent, gaping, patulous, ringent, wide, yawning; ajar; unbarred, unbolted, unfastened, unlocked, unsealed; clear, unimpeded
con blocked, obstructed; constricted, cramped, narrow, strait
ant closed, shut
2 lacking a cover or covering <an *open* wound that continued to ooze blood> <his chest *open* to the sun>
syn bare, denuded, exposed, naked, peeled, stripped, uncovered
3 ***syn*** see LIABLE 2
ant closed
4 not restricted to a particular group or situation <favored *open* enrollment in the schools>
syn accessible, open-door, public, unrestricted
rel attainable, available, obtainable, reachable, securable
idiom to be had, within reach
con limited, restricted; inaccessible, private
ant closed
5 available for use or consideration or decision <there are only two courses *open* to us>
syn accessible, employable, operative, practicable, usable
rel appropriate, fit, proper, suitable; acceptable, agreeable, pleasing
idiom within reach
con inaccessible, inoperative, unusable
ant closed
6 ***syn*** see DOUBTFUL 1
7 ***syn*** see FRANK
ant close; clandestine

open *vb* **1** to change from a closed to an open condition <*open* the window>
syn ope, unblock, unclose, undo, unshut, unstop
rel clear, free, release; bare, disclose, expose, reveal
idiom lay open, swing open, throw open
con block, occlude, stop
ant close, shut
2 to make physically or mentally visible <dawn *opened* a surprising scene to his startled eyes>
syn disclose, display, expose, reveal, unclothe, uncover, unveil
rel adumbrate, hint, shadow, suggest

---

syn synonym(s) ***rel*** related word(s)
ant antonym(s) ***con*** contrasted word(s)
idiom idiomatic equivalent(s)
|| use limited; if in doubt, see a dictionary

idiom bring to light, bring to (*or* into) view, lay bare, make plain, show forth
con cloak, conceal, hide, screen, secrete, shroud
3 to make an opening in <decided to *open* a can of beans>
syn breach, disrupt, hole, rupture
rel break, broach, tap, undo; cut, gash, slash; perforate, pierce
idiom lay open
con occlude, shut; fasten, secure
ant close
4 to spread out <the eagle slowly *opened* its mighty wings>
syn expand, extend, fan (out), outspread, outstretch, spread, unfold
rel billow, dilate, distend, swell; cover, mantle, overspread
con collect, concentrate, contract, gather (in)
ant close
5 *syn* see BEGIN 1
ant close
6 *syn* see CONVENE 1

open *n syn* see OUTDOORS

open air *n syn* see OUTDOORS

open–air *adj syn* see OUTDOOR
con indoor, inside; enclosed

open–and–shut *adj syn* see CLEAR 5

open–door *adj syn* see OPEN 4

open–eyed *adj syn* see WATCHFUL

openhanded *adj* **1** *syn* see LIBERAL 1
ant closefisted, tightfisted
2 *syn* see CLEAR 5

openhearted *adj syn* see FRANK

opening *n* **1** *syn* see BEGINNING
ant closing
2 *syn* see APERTURE
3 *syn* see GAP 1
4 *syn* see OPPORTUNITY

opening gun *n syn* see BEGINNING

openmouthed *adj syn* see VOCIFEROUS

openness *n syn* see EXPOSURE

open sesame *n syn* see PASSPORT

open up *vb syn* see OPERATE 2

opera omnia *n syn* see OEUVRE

operate *vb* **1** *syn* see ACT 5
2 to perform surgery <*operated* on him to remove a brain tumor>
syn cut, open up
3 to cause to function <knew how to *operate* earth-moving equipment>
syn handle, run, use, work
rel play; manage, maneuver; drive, pilot, steer; ply, wield
idiom make go
4 *syn* see CONDUCT 3

operation *n* **1** *syn* see EXERCISE 1
2 *syn* see USE 1

operative *adj* **1** *syn* see ACTIVE 1
ant inoperative
2 *syn* see OPEN 5

operative *n* **1** *syn* see WORKER
2 *syn* see PRIVATE DETECTIVE

operator *n syn* see MOTORIST

operose *adj* **1** *syn* see HARD 6
2 *syn* see ASSIDUOUS

opiate *adj syn* see SOPORIFIC 1

opiate *n* **1** *syn* see DRUG 2
2 *syn* see ANODYNE 2

opine *vb* to form or express an opinion <he *opined* that the story was true>
syn ‖opinion, opinionate
rel accept, believe, consider, hold, judge, regard, think, view; speculate
con deny, disclaim, disown, reject, repudiate; disbelieve, discredit, doubt

opinion *n* an idea or judgment held as true or valid <seek an expert *opinion* on the authenticity of the painting>
syn belief, conviction, eye, feeling, mind, persuasion, sentiment, view
rel attitude, impression, notion, think, thought; conclusion, estimate, estimation, judgment, reaction; assumption, conjecture, speculation, supposition, theory
idiom point of view
con disbelief, discredit, doubt, unbelief; distrust, mistrust, questioning, skepticism

‖opinion *vb syn* see OPINE

opinionate *vb syn* see OPINE

opponent *n* one who expresses or manifests opposition <her *opponent* in the debate>
syn adversary, antagonist, anti, con, match, opposer, oppugnant
rel enemy, foe; competitor, rival; assailant, combatant; counteragent
con ally, colleague, comrade, confederate, partner; advocate, champion
ant exponent, pro, proponent

opportune *adj syn* see TIMELY 1
rel appropriate, felicitous, happy
ant inopportune

opportunity *n* a state of affairs or combination of circumstances favorable to some end <all he asked was an *opportunity* to show what he could do>
syn break, chance, look-in, occasion, opening, shot, show, squeak, time
rel room, space; leisure, liberty; relief, spell, turn; juncture, pass; dog's chance, hope, prayer

oppose *vb* **1** to place over against something to provide resistance or counterbalance <*oppose* one military force with another>
syn counter, match, pit, play (off), vie
rel array, confront, face
idiom set over against
2 *syn* see RESIST

opposed *adj syn* see ADVERSE 1

opposer *n syn* see OPPONENT

opposing *adj syn* see ADVERSE 1

opposite *n* something that is exactly opposed or contrary <virtue and vice are *opposites*>
syn antipode, antipole, antithesis, contra, contradictory, contrary, converse, counter, counterpole, reverse
rel contrast, counterpoint, foil; contrapositive, inverse, obverse; antonym
idiom the other extreme, the other side of the coin

con analogon, analogue, counterpart, like, parallel, similar; equal, equivalent; correlate, correlative; carbon copy, duplicate, replica
ant same

opposite *adj* being so far apart as to be or to seem irreconcilable <held *opposite* views on the solution of the problem>
syn antipodal, antipodean, antithetical, contradictory, contrary, converse, counter, diametric, polar, reverse
rel contrasting; contrapositive, inverse, obverse; antonymous; different, dissimilar, divergent, opposed, unalike, unlike, unsimilar; independent, separate, unconnected, unrelated
con alike, analogous, equivalent, like, parallel, similar; equal; correlative
ant same

opposite *prep* ***syn*** see TO 6

oppositely *adv* ***syn*** see AGAIN 5

opposite number *n* one holding an equivalent or parallel position <the Secretary of State and his *opposite number,* the Foreign Minister>
syn coordinate, counterpart, vis-à-vis; *compare* EQUAL
rel complement, cousin, equal, equivalent, like, match, tally

opposition *n* ***syn*** see ANTAGONISM 2

opposure *n* ***syn*** see ANTAGONISM 2

oppress *vb* **1** ***syn*** see WRONG
rel harass, harry; afflict, torment, torture; conquer, overcome, overthrow, subjugate
2 ***syn*** see DEPRESS 2
rel burden, distress, trouble

oppressive *adj* **1** ***syn*** see ONEROUS
ant unoppressive
2 ***syn*** see GLOOMY 3

oppressor *n* ***syn*** see TYRANT

opprobriate *vb* ***syn*** see DECRY 2

opprobrious *adj* **1** ***syn*** see ABUSIVE
2 ***syn*** see INFAMOUS 1

opprobrium *n* ***syn*** see DISGRACE
rel abuse, scurrility, vituperation
con credit, prestige

oppugn *vb* ***syn*** see CONTEND 1

oppugnant *adj* ***syn*** see ADVERSE 1

oppugnant *n* ***syn*** see OPPONENT

opt (for) *vb* ***syn*** see CHOOSE 1

optate *vb* ***syn*** see CHOOSE 1

optic *adj* ***syn*** see VISUAL 1

optical *adj* ***syn*** see VISUAL 1

optimacy *n* ***syn*** see ARISTOCRACY

optimism *n* an inclination to put the most favorable construction on actions and events or to anticipate the best possible outcome <was a practitioner of *optimism* in his everyday life>
syn Pollyannaism, rose-colored spectacles, sanguineness, sanguinity
rel brightness, buoyancy, happiness; idealism, positivism
con hopelessness; despair, gloom, melancholy; malism; defeatism, fatalism; cynicism
ant pessimism

optimist *n* one given to optimism <was a jaunty *optimist*>
syn hoper, Pollyanna
rel dreamer, idealist, positivist
con defeatist, fatalist; cynic, doubter, skeptic
ant pessimist

optimistic *adj* anticipating only the best to happen and minimizing all other possibilities <was *optimistic* about book sales that year>
syn fond, Pollyannaish, sanguine, upbeat; *compare* HOPEFUL 1
rel bright, cheerful, merry, sunny; hopeful, hoping; assured, confident
idiom feeling on top of the world, looking on the bright side, riding (*or* sitting) on cloud nine
con cynical; doubtful, uncertain
ant pessimistic

option *n* ***syn*** see CHOICE 1
rel prerogative, privilege, right

optional *adj* not compulsory <attendance at the meeting is *optional*>
syn discretionary, elective, facultative, nonobligatory
rel free, voluntary; alternative
con demanded, imperative; enforced, involuntary; essential, necessary
ant compulsory, mandatory, obligatory, required

opulent *adj* **1** ***syn*** see RICH 1
rel lavish, prodigal, profuse; extravagant, ostentatious, pretentious, showy; plush, swank
con modest, simple, unpretentious
2 ***syn*** see LUXURIOUS 3
3 ***syn*** see PROFUSE

oracle *n* ***syn*** see REVELATION

oracular *adj* ***syn*** see PROPHETIC

oral *adj* **1** ***syn*** see VOCAL 1
2 expressed or transmitted vocally <stories of folk heroes kept alive in *oral* tradition>
syn spoken, traditional, unwritten, verbal, word-of-mouth
rel narrated, recounted, related, told
con chronicled, recorded, written, written down

orate *vb* to talk in a declamatory, grandiloquent, or impassioned manner <*orated* to the crowd about the flag and patriotism>
syn bloviate, declaim, harangue, mouth, perorate, rant, rave, soapbox
rel elocute; bombast, rodomontade, sermonize, speechify; blah-blah

oratorical *adj* ***syn*** see RHETORICAL

oratory *n* the art of speaking in public eloquently and effectively <a politician who was a master at *oratory*>
syn elocution, rhetoric, speechcraft

orb *n* **1** ***syn*** see BALL
2 ***syn*** see EYE 1

orbit *n* ***syn*** see RANGE 2

orchestra *n* a usually large group of musicians who perform together <a string *orchestra* played at the reception>

---

syn synonym(s) ***rel*** related word(s)
ant antonym(s) ***con*** contrasted word(s)
idiom idiomatic equivalent(s)
|| use limited; if in doubt, see a dictionary

syn band, philharmonic, symphony
rel combo, ensemble

orchestrate *vb* ***syn*** see HARMONIZE 4

orchidaceous *adj* ***syn*** see SHOWY

orchids *n pl* ***syn*** see COMPLIMENT 1

ordain *vb* **1** ***syn*** see CONDUCT 3
2 ***syn*** see DICTATE

ordeal *n* ***syn*** see TRIAL 1

order *n* **1** ***syn*** see ASSOCIATION 2
2 ***syn*** see TYPE
rel bracket, branch, pigeonhole, set; estate, grade, rank, status
3 sequential occurrence in space or time <changed the *order* of the books on the shelf>
syn arrangement, disposal, disposition, distribution, ordering, sequence
rel array, arrayal, collocation; allocation, allotment, apportionment, arrayment, proration
con disarrangement, disordering; chaos, confusion, disorder, mix-up, muddle
4 general or approximate size or amount <a loss on the *order* of seven million dollars>
syn extent, magnitude, matter, neighborhood, range, tune, vicinity
rel approach, approximation, closeness, nearness, proximity
5 manner of being arranged in space or of occurring in time <tell everything in the *order* in which it happened>
syn consecution, procession, sequence, succession
rel consecutiveness, following, successiveness; chain, progression, series, train
6 ***syn*** see SUCCESSION 2
7 orderly conduct <about to call the meeting to *order* when the interruption occurred>
syn correctitude, correctness, decorousness, decorum, orderliness, properness, propriety, seemliness
rel goodness, niceness, rightness; fitness, suitability; integrity, probity, rectitude, uprightness
con impropriety, indecorousness, indecorum, unseemliness
ant disorder
8 orderly arrangement or disposition <troubled by the lack of *order* in their daily lives>
syn method, orderliness, pattern, plan, system
con anarchy, chaos, confusion, muddle, ‖snafu
ant disorder
9 state with respect to quality, functioning, or status <the equipment was in very poor *order*>
syn case, condition, estate, repair, shape
rel fettle, fitness, kilter, trim
10 a state of soundness <had her car put in *order* for spring>
syn condition, fettle, fitness, kilter, repair, shape, trim
rel adjustment, amendment, correction, gear, rectification
idiom working order
con disrepair
11 the state of being appropriate to or required by the circumstances <that remark is definitely out of *order*>
syn appositeness, appropriateness, aptness, expediency, fitness, meetness, propriety, rightness, suitability, suitableness
rel opportuneness, seasonableness, timeliness; auspiciousness, favorableness; felicity, grace
con inappropriateness, unfitness, unsuitability, unsuitableness
12 ***syn*** see COMMAND 1
rel authorization, permission

order *vb* **1** to bring about an orderly disposition of individuals, units, or elements <*ordered* his affairs in preparation for marriage>
syn arrange, array, dispose, marshal, methodize, organize, systematize
rel adjust, fix, regulate, right; align, line, line up, range; classify, codify, hierarchize; regiment, routine, routinize; streamline
idiom put (*or* set) in order, put in shape, put (*or* set) to rights, reduce to order, whip into shape (*or* order)
ant disorder
2 ***syn*** see COMMAND

ordering *n* ***syn*** see ORDER 3

orderliness *n* **1** ***syn*** see ORDER 7
ant disorderliness
2 ***syn*** see ORDER 8
ant disorderliness

orderly *adj* **1** following a set arrangement, design, or pattern <work out an *orderly* procedure and stick to it> <an *orderly* row of houses surrounded the village green>
syn methodic, methodical, regular, systematic
rel accurate, correct, exact, precise; alike, uniform; businesslike; conventional, formal
idiom in apple-pie order
con haphazard, irregular, unmethodical, unsystematic; careless, casual, free and easy
ant chaotic, disorderly
2 ***syn*** see NEAT 2
rel picked up
ant disordered; disorderly

order up *vb* ***syn*** see CALL UP

ordinance *n* ***syn*** see LAW 1

ordinarily *adv* ***syn*** see USUALLY 2

ordinary *adj* **1** of the customary or common type encountered in the normal course of events <*ordinary* traffic had been stopped to let the marchers pass>
syn everyday, plain, plain Jane, quotidian, routine, unremarkable, usual, workaday
rel commonplace, natural, normal, regular; customary, familiar, frequent
con infrequent, rare, uncommon; accidental, casual, chance, fortuitous
ant extraordinary
2 ***syn*** see COMMON 6

organ *n* **1** ***syn*** see MEAN 2
2 ***syn*** see JOURNAL

organize *vb* **1** ***syn*** see FOUND 2
rel construct, put together
2 ***syn*** see ORDER 1
rel coordinate, integrate
3 ***syn*** see MOBILIZE 3

‖**organized** *adj* ***syn*** see INTOXICATED 1

orgulous *adj* ***syn*** see PROUD 1
orgy *n* **1** ***syn*** see BINGE 1
2 an act or occasion of excessive indulgence in sex <the infamous *orgies* of ancient Rome>
syn bacchanal, bacchanalia, debauch, ‖group grope, party, saturnalia
3 ***syn*** see SPREE 1
orifice *n* ***syn*** see APERTURE
oriflamme *n* ***syn*** see FLAG
origin *n* **1** ***syn*** see ANCESTRY
rel maternity, parentage, paternity
2 ***syn*** see SOURCE
original *n* **1** a first form from which copies or reproductions can be produced <students copying the da Vinci *original*>
syn archetype, protoplast, prototype
rel forerunner, mother, precursor; model, pattern; precedent
con dummy, imitation, simulacrum; counterfeit, fake, forgery
ant copy, reproduction
2 ***syn*** see INNOVATOR
3 ***syn*** see ECCENTRIC
original *adj* **1** ***syn*** see FIRST 2
rel archetypal, prototypal
2 ***syn*** see PRIMARY 5
3 ***syn*** see INVENTIVE
con banal, trite; derivative, initative
ant unoriginal
originally *adv* ***syn*** see INITIALLY 1
originate *vb* **1** ***syn*** see GENERATE 1
2 ***syn*** see INTRODUCE 3
3 ***syn*** see SPRING 1
4 ***syn*** see BEGIN 2
5 to have one's origin or home base in <he *originates* from Ohio>
syn come (from), hail (from)
rel derive (from), spring (from), stem (from)
originative *adj* ***syn*** see INVENTIVE
ant unoriginative
originator *n* **1** ***syn*** see FATHER 2
2 ***syn*** see INNOVATOR
orison *n* ***syn*** see PRAYER
ornament *vb* ***syn*** see ADORN
rel enrich; embroider
ornate *adj* elaborately and often pretentiously decorated or designed <a very *ornate* room—all marble, gilt, and brocade>
syn baroque, flamboyant, florid, luscious, rich, rococo
rel elaborate, high-wrought, resplendent; labored, overdone, overelaborated, overembellished, overworked, overwrought; luxuriant, luxurious, opulent, sumptuous; aureate, gilded
con natural, plain, quiet, simple; severe, unembellished, unornamented, unostentatious, unpretentious; restrained, subdued
ant austere; chaste
ornery *adj* ‖**1** ***syn*** see CHEAP 2
2 ***syn*** see CANTANKEROUS
3 ***syn*** see CONTRARY 3
orotund *adj* **1** ***syn*** see RESONANT
rel loud, stentorian
2 ***syn*** see RHETORICAL
orphan *adj* deprived by death of one and usually both parents <seeking homes for the countless *orphan* children from the disaster area>
syn orphaned, parentless, unparented
rel alone, solitary; abandoned, cast-off, forsaken, lost; disregarded, ignored, neglected, slighted
orphaned *adj* ***syn*** see ORPHAN
orphic *adj* ***syn*** see RECONDITE
orthodox *adj* **1** conforming to doctrines or practices that are held to be right or true by an authority, standard, or tradition <those who still hold an *orthodox* view about evolution>
syn accepted, authoritative, canonical, received, sanctioned, sound
rel acknowledged, admitted, approved; customary, official, recognized, standard, traditional; correct, proper, right
con heretical, heterodox, unauthoritative, uncanonical
ant unorthodox
2 ***syn*** see CONVENTIONAL 1
3 ***syn*** see CONSERVATIVE 1
ant unorthodox
oscillate *vb* ***syn*** see SWING 2
osculate *vb* ***syn*** see KISS 1
ostend *vb* ***syn*** see SHOW 2
ostensible *adj* **1** ***syn*** see APPARENT 2
2 ***syn*** see ALLEGED
ostensibly *adv* to all outward appearances <*ostensibly* it was a business trip but actually it was all pleasure>
syn apparently, evidently, officially, outwardly, professedly, seemingly
rel externally, superficially; sensibly
idiom on the face of it, on the surface, to the eye
con genuinely, really, truly; au fond, basically
ostentatious *adj* ***syn*** see SHOWY
ant unostentatious
ostracism *n* ***syn*** see EXILE 1
ostracize *vb* **1** ***syn*** see BANISH
con accept, entertain, receive, welcome; harbor, haven, refuge, shelter
2 ***syn*** see CUT 7
other *adj* **1** ***syn*** see DIFFERENT 1
2 ***syn*** see ADDITIONAL
‖**othergates** *adv* ***syn*** see OTHERWISE 1
other half *n* ***syn*** see RABBLE 2
otherness *n* ***syn*** see DISSIMILARITY
‖**otherways** *adv* ***syn*** see OTHERWISE 2
‖**otherwhile** *adv* ***syn*** see SOMETIMES
otherwise *adv* **1** in a different way or manner <he could not act *otherwise*>
syn differently, diversely, ‖othergates, variously
ant likewise
2 under different conditions <might *otherwise* have left>
syn else, ‖elseways, elsewise, ‖otherways
otherwise *adj* ***syn*** see DIFFERENT 1

otherworld *n* ***syn*** see HEREAFTER 2

otherworldly *adj* **1** of or relating to a world other than the actual world <believed in the existence of *otherworldly* phenomena>
syn transcendental, transmundane
rel exterrestrial, extramundane, extraterrestrial; unearthly, unworldly
2 ***syn*** see DREAMY 1

otiose *adj* ***syn*** see VAIN 1
rel purposeless, useless; inexcusable; superfluous, supernumerary, surplus

oubliette *n* ***syn*** see DUNGEON

ought *vb* ***syn*** see WANT 3

ought *n* ***syn*** see OBLIGATION 2

ounce *n* ***syn*** see PARTICLE

oust *vb* **1** ***syn*** see DEPRIVE 2
2 ***syn*** see BANISH

out *adv* ***syn*** see OUTDOORS

out *vb* **1** ***syn*** see EJECT 1
2 ***syn*** see EXTINGUISH 1
3 ***syn*** see GET OUT 2

out *n* ***syn*** see SHOWING 1

out and away *adv* ***syn*** see FAR AND AWAY

out–and–out *adj* ***syn*** see UTTER

||**outback** *n* ***syn*** see FRONTIER 2

outbalance *vb* ***syn*** see OUTWEIGH 1

outbloom *vb* ***syn*** see BLOSSOM

outbreak *n* **1** a sudden or violent beginning of activity <an *outbreak* of new housing starts>
syn burst, eruption, flare, outburst; *compare* EPIDEMIC
rel beginning, commencement, dawn, onset, outset
2 ***syn*** see EPIDEMIC

outbreathe *vb* ***syn*** see EXHALE

outburst *n* **1** a violent expression of emotion <an *outburst* of anger>
syn access, burst, eruption, explosion, flare-up, gust, sally
rel scene, storm, tantrum; frenzy, rapture transport(s)
2 ***syn*** see OUTBREAK 1

outcast *n* one who is cast out by society <a political *outcast*>
syn castaway, derelict, Ishmael, Ishmaelite, leper, offscouring, pariah, untouchable
rel hobo, tramp, vagabond, vagrant; displaced person; exile, expatriate; reprobate
con big name, bigwig, celebrity, lion, luminary, name, notable, personage, somebody

outcome *n* ***syn*** see EFFECT 1

outcomer *n* ***syn*** see STRANGER

out–country *adj* ***syn*** see RURAL

outcrier *n* ***syn*** see PEDDLER

outcry *n* ***syn*** see COMMOTION 1

outdare *vb* ***syn*** see FACE 3

outdate *vb* to make obsolete or out-of-date <the automobile *outdated* the horse and buggy>
syn antiquate, obsolesce, obsolete, outmode, superannuate
rel age, date, fossilize; replace, supersede

outdated *adj* ***syn*** see OLD-FASHIONED
ant up-to-the-minute

outdistance *vb* ***syn*** see OUTSTRIP 1

outdo *vb* **1** ***syn*** see SURPASS 1
idiom out-Herod Herod, steal (*or* get) a march on
2 ***syn*** see DEFEAT 2

outdoor *adj* taking place, done, or existing in the open air <an *outdoor* restaurant>
syn alfresco, hypaethral, open-air, out-of-door, outside
ant indoor, inside

outdoors *adv* in or into the open air <went *outdoors* for some fresh air>
syn out, out of doors, outside, without, withoutdoors
ant indoors, inside, withindoors

outdoors *n pl but sing in constr* the space where air is unconfined <every night he let the dog run in the *outdoors*>
syn open, open air, out-of-doors, outside, without
idiom God's good (*or* green) earth

outer *adj* being or located outside something <the sheep's thick *outer* coat of wool>
syn exterior, external, outside, outward, over
rel extraneous, extrinsic, superficial, surface; outlying, remote
con inside, interior, internal, inward
ant inner

outermost *adj* ***syn*** see EXTREME 5
ant inmost, innermost

outface *vb* ***syn*** see FACE 3

outfit *n* **1** ***syn*** see EQUIPMENT
2 ***syn*** see COSTUME
3 ***syn*** see COMPANY 4
4 ***syn*** see ENTERPRISE 3

outfit *vb* ***syn*** see FURNISH 1

outfox *vb* ***syn*** see OUTWIT

outgeneral *vb* ***syn*** see OUTWIT
rel outfight, outflank, outgame
idiom steal a march

outgo *vb* ***syn*** see SURPASS 1

outgoing *adj* ***syn*** see DEMONSTRATIVE
ant aloof

outgrowth *n* **1** a projecting part of an organism <a warty *outgrowth* on the skin>
syn excrescence, excrescency, process, processus
rel enlargement, prolongation, swelling; offshoot, shoot
2 something that develops or grows directly out of something else <the new TV series was an *outgrowth* of a popular movie>
syn by-product, derivative, descendant, offshoot, spin-off
rel branch, member; child, offspring, product; aftereffect, consequence, effect, issue, outcome, result
con origin, root, source; antecedent, cause, determinant

outhouse *n* ***syn*** see PRIVY 1

outing *n* ***syn*** see EXCURSION 1

outjockey *vb* ***syn*** see OUTWIT

outland *adj* ***syn*** see RURAL

outlander *n* ***syn*** see STRANGER

outlandish *adj* **1** ***syn*** see BARBARIC 1

rel foreign, strange
2 *syn* see STRANGE 4
rel monstrous; outré
con commonplace, everyday
3 marked by sharp departure from the traditional or usual <men who wear beads, earrings, and other *outlandish* ornaments>
syn far-out, kinky, outré, ultra; *compare* EXTREME 3
rel bizarre, extravagant, outrageous, wild; unconventional, unorthodox
con conservative, conventional; compliant, conformable; moderate
4 *syn* see BACK 1

outlast *vb syn* see OUTLIVE

outlaw *n* a criminal of the American Western frontier <*outlaws* held up stagecoaches>
syn badman, ‖bandido, bandit, desperado
rel gunman, gunslinger
idiom bad guy

outlaw *vb syn* see FORBID

outlay *vb syn* see SPEND 1

outlay *n syn* see EXPENSE 1

outlet *n* **1** *syn* see APERTURE
2 *syn* see EGRESS 2
rel escape; release
3 *syn* see STORE 4

outline *n* the line that gives form or shape to a body or a figure <saw only a dark *outline* of the house through the gloom>
syn contour, delineation, figuration, line, lineament, lineation, profile, silhouette
rel configuration, conformation, figure, form, shape; skyline
con bulk, hulk, mass

outline *vb* **1** *syn* see BORDER 1
2 *syn* see SKETCH

outlive *vb* to remain in existence longer than <the committee has *outlived* its usefulness>
syn outlast, outwear, survive
rel outstand, outstay

outlook *n* **1** *syn* see LOOKOUT 2
2 *syn* see VISTA
3 *syn* see VIEW 4
4 *syn* see VIEWPOINT 2

outlying *adj syn* see DISTANT 1

outmaneuver *vb syn* see OUTWIT
idiom steal a march (on)

outmatch *vb syn* see SURPASS 1

outmode *vb syn* see OUTDATE

outmoded *adj* **1** *syn* see OLD-FASHIONED
2 *syn* see OBSOLETE
3 *syn* see TACKY 2

outmost *adj syn* see EXTREME 5
ant inmost, innermost

out–of–date *adj* **1** *syn* see OLD-FASHIONED
ant up-to-date
2 *syn* see TACKY 2

out–of–door *adj syn* see OUTDOOR

out–of–doors *n pl but sing in constr syn* see OUTDOORS

out of doors *adv syn* see OUTDOORS

out–of–the–way *adj syn* see OBSCURE 2

outpace *vb syn* see OUTSTRIP 1

outplace *vb syn* see REPLACE 3

output *n* the amount of something produced <an annual *output* of 3,000,000 units>
syn outturn, product, production, turnout, yield
rel gain, get, profit, take; crop, harvest
con input; raw material

outrage *n syn* see INJURY 1

outrage *vb* **1** *syn* see RAPE
2 *syn* see ABUSE 4
3 *syn* see WRONG
4 *syn* see OFFEND 3

outrageous *adj* **1** exceeding the limits of what is normal or tolerable <*outrageous* prices that threaten our way of life>
syn barbarous, unchristian, uncivilized, unconscionable, ungodly, unholy, wicked
rel abominable, awful, beastly, dreadful, ghastly, horrible, horrid, impossible, intolerable, terrible, unreasonable; scandalous, shocking
con normal, reasonable, tolerable; acceptable, bearable, endurable, supportable
2 enormously or flagrantly bad or horrible <*outrageous* treatment of prisoners>
syn atrocious, crying, desperate, heinous, monstrous, scandalous, shocking
rel enormous, flagrant, gross; egregious, nefarious, notorious, villainous
con condonable, excusable, forgivable, pardonable; defensible, justifiable; legitimate, reasonable; comprehensible, plausible, understandable

outrank *vb syn* see PRECEDE 1

outré *adj syn* see OUTLANDISH 3

outreach *vb syn* see OUTWIT

outrecuidance *n syn* see CONCEIT 2

outrider *n syn* see FORERUNNER 1

outright *adj* **1** *syn* see UTTER
2 *syn* see WHOLE 4

outrun *vb syn* see OUTSTRIP 1

outset *n syn* see BEGINNING

outshine *vb syn* see SURPASS 1

outside *n syn* see OUTDOORS

outside *adj* **1** *syn* see OUTER
rel alien, foreign
ant inside
2 *syn* see OUTDOOR
3 *syn* see MAXIMUM
4 *syn* see REMOTE 4

outside *adv syn* see OUTDOORS

outside *prep* **1** *syn* see BEYOND 1
2 *syn* see EXCEPT

outside of *prep syn* see EXCEPT

outsider *n syn* see STRANGER
con insider

outskirt *n usu* **outskirts** *pl syn* see ENVIRONS 2

outslick *vb syn* see OUTWIT

outsmart *vb syn* see OUTWIT

outspeed *vb syn* see OUTSTRIP 1

---

syn synonym(s) *rel* related word(s)
ant antonym(s) *con* contrasted word(s)
idiom idiomatic equivalent(s)
‖ use limited; if in doubt, see a dictionary

THESAURUS

outspoken *adj* speaking without fear or reserve <quite *outspoken* in her views on mandatory retirement>
syn free, free-spoken, round, vocal
rel candid, direct, forthright, frank, open, plain, plainspoken, straightforward, unreticent; bluff, blunt; explicit, point-blank, unequivocal; strident
con reserved, restrained, reticent; private, retiring, shrinking; unassertive
outspread *vb* ***syn*** see OPEN 4
ant folded (*of wings or a fan*)
outstanding *adj* **1** ***syn*** see UNPAID 2
2 ***syn*** see NOTICEABLE
3 ***syn*** see CHIEF 2
4 ***syn*** see SUPERB 3
outstare *vb* ***syn*** see STARE DOWN
outstart *n* ***syn*** see BEGINNING
outstep *vb* ***syn*** see EXCEED 1
outstretch *vb* ***syn*** see OPEN 4
outstrip *vb* **1** to go faster than <could *outstrip* even the fastest horse>
syn distance, outdistance, outpace, outrun, outspeed
rel outfly, outsoar, outwing; outfoot, outrace, outride; outsail; outtravel; lose, shake off
con follow, trail; drag, hang back, lag
2 ***syn*** see SURPASS 1
outsweepings *n pl* ***syn*** see REFUSE
outthink *vb* ***syn*** see OUTWIT
outthrust *n* ***syn*** see PROJECTION 1
outtire *vb* ***syn*** see EXHAUST 4
outturn *n* ***syn*** see OUTPUT
outward *adj* ***syn*** see OUTER
ant inward
outwardly *adv* ***syn*** see OSTENSIBLY
ant inwardly
outwear *vb* **1** ***syn*** see EXHAUST 4
2 ***syn*** see OUTLIVE
rel endure, hold up
outweigh *vb* **1** to exceed in weight, value, or importance <her brother *outweighed* her by nearly fifty pounds> <the facts *outweigh* his argument>
syn outbalance, overbalance, overweigh, overweight
rel overbear
2 ***syn*** see COMPENSATE 1
outweighing *adj* ***syn*** see DOMINANT 1
outwit *vb* to defeat or get the better of by superior cleverness or ingenuity <*outwitted* the enemy by taking a different route>
syn have, outfox, outgeneral, outjockey, outmaneuver, outreach, outslick, outsmart, outthink, overreach, undo; *compare* FRUSTRATE 1
rel bamboozle, befool, dupe, gull, hoax, hoodwink, outtrick, outtrump, trick; outdo; outguess
outworn *adj* ***syn*** see OBSOLETE
oval *adj* having the shape of a longitudinal section of an egg <an *oval* pond>
syn ooid, ovate, oviform, ovoid
rel ovaloid; ellipsoidal, elliptic
ovate *adj* ***syn*** see OVAL
over *adv* **1** from one point to another across intervening space <sailed *over* to the island>
syn across, athwart, beyond, transversely
2 ***syn*** see AWAY 2
3 ***syn*** see EVER 6
4 at a higher point <the plane was directly *over*>
syn above, aloft, overhead
idiom on high
ant under
5 at or to an end <it's all *over* between them>
syn by, through
6 ***syn*** see THROUGH 1
7 yet another time <do the work *over*>
syn afresh, again, anew, de novo, once more
idiom over again
over *prep* **1** at a higher level <clouds hung *over* the town>
syn above, o'er
ant under
2 ***syn*** see ACROSS
3 with respect to <children squabbling *over* toys>
syn about, on, upon, with
4 so as to make contact with <hit him *over* the head>
syn on, upon
5 ***syn*** see DURING
6 as the result of <quarreled *over* money matters>
syn because of, due to, owing to, through
over *adj* **1** ***syn*** see SUPERIOR 1
ant under
2 ***syn*** see OUTER
over *vb* ***syn*** see CLEAR 8
overabounding *adj* ***syn*** see SUPERABUNDANT
overabundance *n* ***syn*** see EXCESS 1
overabundant *adj* ***syn*** see SUPERABUNDANT
overact *vb* to exaggerate in acting especially on the stage or screen <was criticized for *overacting* the part>
syn overplay
rel ham, mug; declaim, rant, spout
idiom chew the scenery
ant underact, underplay
over against *prep* **1** ***syn*** see AGAINST 1
2 ***syn*** see VERSUS 2
overage *n* ***syn*** see EXCESS 2
ant shortage, underage
overall *adv* **1** ***syn*** see EVERYWHERE 1
2 ***syn*** see GENERALLY 1
overall *adj* ***syn*** see ALL-AROUND 2
over and above *prep* ***syn*** see BESIDES 1
over and over *adv* ***syn*** see OFTEN
overbalance *vb* ***syn*** see OUTWEIGH 1
overbalanced *adj* ***syn*** see LOPSIDED
overbalancing *adj* ***syn*** see DOMINANT 1
overbearing *adj* **1** ***syn*** see MASTERFUL 1
2 ***syn*** see DOMINANT 1
3 ***syn*** see PROUD 1
rel absolute, autocratic, despotic, tyrannical
con passive, unassertive; acquiescent, compliant, unresisting
ant subservient
overblown *adj* **1** ***syn*** see FAT 2
2 ***syn*** see INFLATED
3 ***syn*** see RHETORICAL

4 ***syn*** see PRETENTIOUS 3
overbold *adj* ***syn*** see SHAMELESS
overbrim *vb* ***syn*** see OVERFLOW 2
overburden *vb* ***syn*** see OVERLOAD
overcast *vb* **1** ***syn*** see OBSCURE
2 ***syn*** see COVER 3
overcast *adj* clouded over <a gray *overcast* March day>
syn cloudy, ‖dowly, dull, heavy, lowering (*or* louring), nubilous, overclouded
rel brooding, dirty, oppressive, sullen
ant clear, cloudless
overcharge *vb* **1** to charge excessively for service or goods <a clip joint well known for *overcharging* customers>
syn clip, fleece, skin, soak, stick
ant undercharge
2 ***syn*** see OVERLOAD
3 ***syn*** see EMBROIDER
overcloud *vb* ***syn*** see OBSCURE
overclouded *adj* ***syn*** see OVERCAST
overcome *vb* **1** to get the better of <*overcome* a bad habit>
syn conquer, down, hurdle, lick, master, surmount, throw; *compare* CONQUER 2
rel beat, defeat; outlive, prevail
con adopt, embrace, take up; indulge
2 ***syn*** see CONQUER 2
3 ***syn*** see OVERWHELM 4
4 ***syn*** see WIN 1
overconfident *adj* ***syn*** see PRESUMPTUOUS
overcritical *adj* ***syn*** see CRITICAL 1
overdo *vb* to make excessive use or application of <he has *overdone* that joke to the point that it is no longer funny>
syn overplay, overuse, overwork
idiom go overboard, go to extremes, run into the ground
overdoing *n* ***syn*** see EXTRAVAGANCE 2
overdraw *vb* ***syn*** see EMBROIDER
overdue *adj* **1** ***syn*** see UNPAID 2
2 ***syn*** see TARDY
ant early
overearly *adj* ***syn*** see EARLY 2
overemphasize *vb* ***syn*** see OVERPLAY 2
ant underemphasize
overesteem *vb* ***syn*** see OVERVALUE
overestimate *vb* ***syn*** see OVERVALUE
ant underestimate
overfill *vb* ***syn*** see OVERFLOW 2
overflow *vb* **1** ***syn*** see DELUGE 1
2 to flow over the brim <the river *overflowed* its banks>
syn overbrim, overfill, overrun, run over, spill, well over
rel brim, cascade, slop, slosh
con drop, recede, withdraw
overflow *n* **1** ***syn*** see FLOOD 2
2 ***syn*** see EXCESS 1
overflowing *adj* **1** ***syn*** see ALIVE 5
2 ***syn*** see SUPERABUNDANT
overfull *adv* ***syn*** see EVER 6
overgrown *adj* covered with growth or herbage <a vacant lot *overgrown* with weeds>
syn grown, rank
rel braky, brambly, brushy, copsy, jungly, thicketed, thickety; dense, overrun, thick; lush
‖**overhand** *n* ***syn*** see ADVANTAGE 3
overhang *vb* **1** ***syn*** see BULGE
2 ***syn*** see HANG 4
overhanging *adj* ***syn*** see IMMINENT 2
overhaul *vb* **1** ***syn*** see MEND 2
2 ***syn*** see CATCH 7
overhead *adv* ***syn*** see OVER 4
ant underfoot
overheated *adj* ***syn*** see IMPASSIONED
overindulgence *n* ***syn*** see EXCESS 3
overindulgent *adj* ***syn*** see EXCESSIVE 2
overkill *n* ***syn*** see EXCESS 1
overlade *vb* ***syn*** see OVERLOAD
overlap *vb* to extend over and cover a part of <each course of shingles should *overlap* the preceding course by several inches>
syn imbricate, lap, overlie, override, ride, shingle
overlay *vb* ***syn*** see COVER 3
overleap *vb* **1** ***syn*** see CLEAR 8
2 ***syn*** see NEGLECT
overlie *vb* ***syn*** see OVERLAP
overload *vb* to load to excess <*overload* a ship>
syn overburden, overcharge, overlade, overtax, overweigh, overweight
con lighten
overlong *adj* ***syn*** see LONG 2
overlook *vb* **1** ***syn*** see SURVEY 3
2 to rise above and afford a view of <the tower *overlooks* the city>
syn dominate, look down, overtop, tower (above *or* over)
rel oversee
3 ***syn*** see NEGLECT
4 ***syn*** see SUPERVISE
overlook *n* **1** ***syn*** see OMISSION
2 ***syn*** see LOOKOUT 2
overly *adv* ***syn*** see EVER 6
overlying *adj* ***syn*** see SUPERIOR 1
ant underlying
overmuch *n* ***syn*** see EXCESS 1
overmuch *adv* ***syn*** see EVER 6
overnice *adj* ***syn*** see PRECIOUS 4
overpaint *vb* ***syn*** see EMBROIDER
overpass *vb* ***syn*** see NEGLECT
overpeopled *adj* ***syn*** see OVERPOPULATED
ant underpeopled
overplay *vb* **1** ***syn*** see OVERACT
ant underact, underplay
2 to give undue attention or emphasis to <*overplaying* the trivial at the expense of the significant>
syn magnify, maximize, overemphasize, overstress

---

syn synonym(s) ***rel*** related word(s)
ant antonym(s) ***con*** contrasted word(s)
idiom idiomatic equivalent(s)
‖ use limited; if in doubt, see a dictionary

rel accent, accentuate, point up; dramatize, exaggerate, hyperbolize, overdraw, overstate, stretch; overvalue
idiom lay it on thick
con downgrade, downplay; minimize
3 *syn* see OVERDO

overplus *n syn* see EXCESS 1

overpopulated *adj* populated too densely <*overpopulated* cities>
syn overpeopled
rel congested, dense, overcrowded
con empty, vacant, void; unpopulated
ant underpopulated

overpower *vb* 1 *syn* see CONQUER 1
2 *syn* see OVERWHELM 4

overpress *vb syn* see PRESSURE

overprize *vb syn* see OVERVALUE
ant underprize, undervalue

overrate *vb syn* see OVERVALUE
ant underrate

overreach *vb* 1 *syn* see CHEAT
2 *syn* see OUTWIT

overreckon *vb syn* see OVERVALUE

overrefined *adj syn* see PRECIOUS 4

override *vb syn* see OVERLAP

overriding *adj syn* see CENTRAL 1
rel primary, principal

overripe *adj syn* see EFFETE 3

overrule *vb syn* see GOVERN 1

overruling *adj syn* see CENTRAL 1

overrun *vb* 1 *syn* see WHIP 2
2 *syn* see INVADE 1
3 *syn* see INFEST 1
4 *syn* see EXCEED 1
5 *syn* see OVERFLOW 2

oversea *adj syn* see OVERSEAS

overseas *adv* beyond or across the sea <served *overseas* for two years>
syn abroad
con stateside

overseas *adj* situated, originating in, or relating to lands overseas <attempting to tap the potential of *overseas* markets>
syn oversea, transmarine, ultramarine
rel alien, exotic, foreign, strange
con domestic, home; stateside

oversee *vb* 1 *syn* see SURVEY 3
2 *syn* see SUPERVISE

overset *vb* 1 *syn* see OVERTURN 1
2 *syn* see OVERTHROW 2

overshadow *vb syn* see OBSCURE

oversight *n* 1 the function or duty of watching or guarding for the sake of proper direction or control <had *oversight* of the children as they played>
syn care, charge, conduct, handling, intendance, management, running, superintendence, superintendency, supervision
rel custody, guard, guardianship; keeping, maintenance; surveillance; aegis, tutelage; ciceronage; chaperonage; check, control
2 *syn* see FAILURE 1
3 *syn* see OMISSION

oversize *adj syn* see LARGE 1
ant undersized

overslaugh *vb syn* see HINDER

oversoon *adj syn* see EARLY 2

oversoon *adv syn* see EARLY 2

overspread *vb* 1 *syn* see COVER 3
2 *syn* see INFEST 1

overstate *vb syn* see EMBROIDER
ant understate

overstatement *n syn* see EXAGGERATION
ant understatement

overstep *vb syn* see EXCEED 1
rel infringe, transgress, trespass

overstock *n syn* see EXCESS 2
ant understock

overstress *vb syn* see OVERPLAY 2

oversupply *n syn* see EXCESS 2
ant undersupply

overswarm *vb* 1 *syn* see INFEST 1
2 *syn* see INVADE 1

oversway *vb syn* see INDUCE 1

overtake *vb syn* see CATCH 7

overtax *vb syn* see OVERLOAD

overthrow *vb* 1 *syn* see OVERTURN 1
2 to cause the downfall of <*overthrow* the government>
syn overset, overturn, topple, tumble, unhorse; *compare* CONQUER 1
rel depose, dethrone, oust, remove, unseat; liquidate, purge; conquer, defeat, destroy, ruin
con create, establish, found, set up

overthrow *n syn* see DEFEAT 1

overtone *n syn* see ASSOCIATION 4

overtop *vb syn* see OVERLOOK 2

overture *n* 1 action intended to attract favorable attention <made friendly *overtures* to the new member of the class>
syn advance, approach
rel bid, proposal, proposition, tender
2 *syn* see INTRODUCTION

overturn *vb* 1 to turn from an upright or level position <the embarrassed boy backed into the table and *overturned* a lamp>
syn knock over, overset, overthrow, tip (over), topple, turn over, upset
rel capsize, keel (over *or* up), upend, upturn; prostrate; down; roll (over)
con erect, right, set up, straighten (up)
2 *syn* see OVERTHROW 2

overturn *n syn* see SHAKE-UP

overuse *vb syn* see OVERDO
ant underuse

overvalue *vb* to set too high a value on <inclined to *overvalue* his own charm>
syn overesteem, overestimate, overprize, overrate, overreckon
rel cherish, prize, treasure; adore, idolize, worship
con belittle, depreciate
ant underprize, undervalue

overweening *adj syn* see PRESUMPTUOUS

overweigh *vb* 1 *syn* see OUTWEIGH 1
2 *syn* see OVERLOAD

overweighing *adj syn* see DOMINANT 1

overweight *vb* 1 *syn* see OUTWEIGH 1

2 ***syn*** see OVERLOAD

overweight *adj* ***syn*** see FAT 2
ant underweight

overwhelm *vb* **1** ***syn*** see DELUGE 1
2 ***syn*** see DELUGE 3
3 ***syn*** see WHIP 2
4 to subject to the grip of something overpowering and usually distressing or damaging <*overwhelmed* by the death of his only child> <human wants that tend to *overwhelm* environmental realities>
syn drown, knock over, overcome, overpower, prostrate, whelm
rel demoralize, devastate, dumbfound, shatter; floor, sink; disturb, upset; destroy, ruin, wreck; downgrade, lower, subordinate

overwhelmed *adj* ***syn*** see AGHAST 2

overwhelming *adj* ***syn*** see TOWERING 4

overwork *vb* ***syn*** see OVERDO

oviform *adj* ***syn*** see OVAL

ovoid *adj* ***syn*** see OVAL

owing *adj* ***syn*** see UNPAID 2

owing to *prep* ***syn*** see OVER 6

owl–light *n* ***syn*** see EVENING 1

own *vb* **1** ***syn*** see HAVE 1
2 ***syn*** see ACKNOWLEDGE 1
con deny, disclaim
ant disown, repudiate

owner *n* one that has the legal or rightful title <*owner* of the shop>
syn holder, possessor, proprietor
rel lord, master
con lessee, renter, tenant; squatter; interloper, intruder, trespasser

ownership *n* lawful claim or title <would soon have *ownership* of the house>
syn dominion, possession, possessorship, property, proprietary, proprietorship
rel hand

own up *vb* ***syn*** see ACKNOWLEDGE 1

oyster *n* ***syn*** see FORTE

P

pa *n* ***syn*** see FATHER 1
pablum *n* ***syn*** see PAP 2
pabulum *n* ***syn*** see FOOD 2
pace *n* **1** ***syn*** see TEMPO
2 ***syn*** see SPEED 2
3 ***syn*** see ROUTINE
pace *vb* **1** ***syn*** see WALK 1
2 ***syn*** see PRECEDE 2
pacific *adj* affording or promoting peace <a *pacific* policy>
syn irenic, nonviolent, pacificatory, pacifist, peaceable, peaceful
rel appeasing, conciliating, conciliatory, pacifying, propitiating, propitiatory; dovelike, gentle, inoffensive
con belligerent, combative, contentious, pugnacious, quarrelsome; unpeaceable, unpeaceful; hawkish, violent, warlike
ant bellicose, unpacific
pacificator *n* ***syn*** see PEACEMAKER
pacificatory *adj* ***syn*** see PACIFIC
pacificist *n* ***syn*** see PACIFIST
idiom man of peace
pacifist *n* one who opposes war or violence as a means of settling disputes <*pacifists* mounted a campaign against the war>
syn dove, pacificist
rel satyagrahi; ‖conchie, conscientious objector; peacemonger
con belligerent, combatant; chauvinist, hawk, jingo, jingoist, warmonger
ant bellicist
pacifist *adj* ***syn*** see PACIFIC
ant combative
pacify *vb* to allay anger or agitation <saw his mounting rage and tried to *pacify* him>
syn appease, assuage, conciliate, mollify, placate, propitiate, sweeten
rel dulcify, soften; allay, alleviate, mitigate, relieve; moderate, qualify, smooth (over), temper
idiom pour balm into, pour oil on (the) troubled waters
con arouse, stir (up)
ant anger
pack *n* **1** ***syn*** see BACKPACK
2 ***syn*** see MUCH
pack *vb* **1** ***syn*** see STOW
2 ***syn*** see LOAD 3
3 ***syn*** see CARRY 1
packed *adj* ***syn*** see FULL 1
idiom packed like sardines (*or* herrings)
‖packed out *adj* ***syn*** see FULL 1
packet *n* ***syn*** see FORTUNE 4
packman *n* ***syn*** see PEDDLER
packsack *n* ***syn*** see BACKPACK
pact *n* **1** ***syn*** see CONTRACT
rel settlement
2 ***syn*** see TREATY
‖pad *n* ***syn*** see PROTECTION 2
pad *vb* ***syn*** see EMBROIDER
paddle *vb* ***syn*** see ROW
‖paddy *n* ***syn*** see POLICEMAN
pagan *adj* ***syn*** see HEATHEN
pageant *n* ***syn*** see PRETENSE 2
pagoda *n* ***syn*** see SUMMERHOUSE
pain *n* **1** a bodily sensation that causes acute discomfort or suffering <suffering from chest *pains*>
syn ache, ‖misery, pang, stitch, throe, twinge
rel discomfort, distress, hurt, suffering; agony, torment, torture
2 pains *pl* ***syn*** see EFFORT 1
rel assiduousness, diligence, industry, sedulousness
pain *vb* **1** ***syn*** see HURT 4
rel agonize, convulse, crucify, excruciate, harrow, lacerate
2 ***syn*** see DISTRESS 2
rel afflict; distress, upset; wound; anguish
idiom ‖hit one where one lives
3 ***syn*** see TRY 2
painful *adj* **1** causing, marked by, or affected with pain <a *painful* wound>
syn aching, afflictive, algetic, hurtful, hurting, sore
rel raw; acute, piercing, sharp, shooting, stabbing, stinging; agonizing, excruciating, harrowing, racking, tormenting, torturous
ant painless, unpainful
2 ***syn*** see BITTER 2
rel unappetizing, unsavory
ant painless
painfully *adv* ***syn*** see HARD 5
ant painlessly
pain–killer *n* ***syn*** see ANODYNE 1
painstaking *adj* ***syn*** see CAREFUL 2
painstakingly *adv* ***syn*** see HARD 3
rel carefully, meticulously; lovingly
paint *n* ***syn*** see MAKEUP 3
pair *n* ***syn*** see COUPLE
paired *adj* ***syn*** see TWIN
pal *n* ***syn*** see ASSOCIATE 3
palace *adj* ***syn*** see LUXURIOUS 3
palace car *n* ***syn*** see PARLOR CAR
palatable *adj* agreeable or pleasant especially to the sense of taste <a *palatable* meal>
syn aperitive, appetizing, flavorsome, good-tasting, ‖gusty, mouth-watering, relishing, sapid, saporous, savorous, savorsome, savory, tasteful, tasty, toothsome, toothy
rel delectable, delicious, delightful, luscious, scrumptious, yummy; tempting; saporific
con bad-tasting, disagreeable, distasteful, ill-flavored, unappetizing
ant unpalatable
palate *n* ***syn*** see TASTE 4

palatial *adj* ***syn*** see LUXURIOUS 3
rel noble, regal; monumental; impressive; rich, splendid
palaver *n* **1** ***syn*** see CONFERENCE 2
rel dialogue, discussion; parley
2 ***syn*** see CHATTER
rel gas, guff, hot air
3 ***syn*** see TERMINOLOGY
4 ***syn*** see BUSINESS 8
palaverous *adj* ***syn*** see WORDY
pale *adj* **1** deficient in color or in intensity of color <a *pale* face>
syn ashen, ashy, blanched, colorless, complexionless, doughy, livid, lurid, pallid, paly, wan, waxen
rel sallow, sick, sickly; gray, pasty, pasty-faced, waxlike; white, whitened; deathlike, ghastly
con flushed, ruddy; bright, colorful, florid
2 being weak and thin in substance or in vital qualities <a *pale,* inadequate foreign policy>
syn anemic, bloodless, pallid, waterish, watery
rel inane, insipid, jejune, wishy-washy; insubstantial, unsubstantial; ineffective, ineffectual; faint, feeble, weak
con strong, substantial; effective, effectual; bright, colorful
ant brilliant
pale *vb* ***syn*** see DULL 1
Pale Horse *n, used with* the ***syn*** see DEATH 1
palinode *vb* ***syn*** see ABJURE
pall *vb* **1** ***syn*** see BORE
2 ***syn*** see SATIATE
rel disgust, weary
||**pallet** *n* ***syn*** see HEAD 1
palliate *vb* to give a speciously fine appearance to what is erroneous, base, or evil <did not try to conceal or *palliate* his errors>
syn blanch (over), extenuate, gloss (over), gloze (over), prettify, sugarcoat, varnish, veneer, white, whiten, whitewash
rel alleviate, lighten, mitigate; condone, excuse; moderate, qualify, soften, temper; camouflage, cloak, conceal, cover up, disguise, dissemble, mask; hush (up)
idiom paper over the cracks, put a good face on (*or* upon)
pallid *adj* **1** ***syn*** see PALE 1
2 ***syn*** see PALE 2
pally *adj* ***syn*** see INTIMATE 4
palm (on *or* upon) *vb* ***syn*** see FOIST 3
||**palm grease** *n* ***syn*** see GRATUITY
palm off *vb* ***syn*** see FOIST 3
||**palm oil** *n* ***syn*** see GRATUITY
palooka *n* ***syn*** see OAF 2
palpable *adj* **1** ***syn*** see TANGIBLE 1
2 ***syn*** see PERCEPTIBLE
rel apparent, ostensible, seeming; believable, colorable, credible, plausible
3 ***syn*** see CLEAR 5
rel certain, positive, sure; arresting, noticeable, remarkable, striking
con doubtful, dubious, problematic, questionable
ant impalpable

palpate *vb* ***syn*** see TOUCH 1
palpation *n* ***syn*** see TOUCH 2
palpitate *vb* ***syn*** see PULSATE
rel pitter-patter
||**palsy–walsy** *adj* ***syn*** see INTIMATE 4
palter *vb* **1** ***syn*** see LIE
rel evade, fence
idiom play false, play fast and loose
2 ***syn*** see HAGGLE 2
paltry *adj* **1** ***syn*** see CHEAP 2
rel beggarly, shabby; pitiful
2 ***syn*** see LITTLE 2
rel base, low, low-down, vile
3 ***syn*** see PETTY 2
rel insignificant, unimportant
paly *adj* ***syn*** see PALE 1
pamper *vb* ***syn*** see BABY
rel regale, tickle; caress, dandle, fondle, pet; overindulge
||**pan** *n* **1** ***syn*** see FACE 1
2 ***syn*** see CRITICISM 2
pan *vb* ***syn*** see CRITICIZE
panacea *n* a remedy for all ills or difficulties <bicycles are not a *panacea* for the traffic problem>
syn catholicon, cure-all, elixir, nostrum
rel relief; remedy
idiom universal (*or* sovereign) remedy
pandect *n* ***syn*** see COMPENDIUM 1
pandemoniac *adj* ***syn*** see INFERNAL 2
pandemonium *n* **1** *cap* **Pandemonium** ***syn*** see HELL
2 ***syn*** see SINK 1
3 ***syn*** see DIN
pander *n* ***syn*** see PIMP 1
panegyric *n* ***syn*** see ENCOMIUM
panegyrical *adj* ***syn*** see EULOGISTIC
panegyrize *vb* ***syn*** see PRAISE 2
pang *n* ***syn*** see PAIN 1
rel prick, stab, ||stang
||**pang** *vb* ***syn*** see CRAM 1
panhandler *n* ***syn*** see BEGGAR 1
panhandling *n* ***syn*** see MENDICANCY
panic *n* **1** ***syn*** see FEAR 1
rel frenzy, hysteria; stampede
con composure, equanimity, sangfroid, self-possession
||**2** ***syn*** see RIOT 2
||**pank** *vb* ***syn*** see PANT 1
panoply *n* ***syn*** see DISPLAY 2
panorama *n* ***syn*** see RANGE 2
pan out *vb* ***syn*** see SUCCEED 2
pansified *adj* ***syn*** see EFFEMINATE
pant *vb* **1** to breathe quickly, spasmodically, or in a labored manner <was *panting* after running up the stairs>
syn blow, gasp, heave, huff, ||pank, ||pegh, puff
rel gulp; wheeze; wind; chuff
idiom be out of breath
2 ***syn*** see AIM 2
rel hunger, long, pine, thirst; desire, want, wish

syn synonym(s) ***rel*** related word(s)
ant antonym(s) ***con*** contrasted word(s)
idiom idiomatic equivalent(s)
|| use limited; if in doubt, see a dictionary

idiom be consumed with desire (for)
pantywaist *n* ***syn*** see WEAKLING
pantywaist *adj* ***syn*** see CHARACTERLESS
pap *n* **1** ***syn*** see FOOD 2
2 something (as reading matter) lacking in solid value or substance <the sentimental *pap* that he offered his readers>
syn pablum, rubbish, slop
rel garbage, trash
||**pap** *n* ***syn*** see FATHER 1
papa *n* ***syn*** see FATHER 1
paper *n* **1** ***syn*** see ESSAY 2
2 *usu* **papers** *pl* ***syn*** see CREDENTIALS
paphian *n* ***syn*** see HARLOT 1
pappy *adj* ***syn*** see SOFT 6
||**pappy** *n* ***syn*** see FATHER 1
par *n* **1** ***syn*** see EQUIVALENCE
2 ***syn*** see AVERAGE
rel standard
parable *n* ***syn*** see ALLEGORY 2
rel comparison, similitude
parachronism *n* ***syn*** see ANACHRONISM 1
parade *n* ***syn*** see DISPLAY 2
rel exhibition
parade *vb* ***syn*** see SHOW 4
rel disclose, divulge, reveal; advertise, declare, proclaim, publish; boast, brag, gasconade
idiom parade one's wares
con camouflage, cloak, disguise, dissemble, mask
paradigm *n* ***syn*** see MODEL 2
paradigmatic *adj* ***syn*** see TYPICAL 1
paradise *n* **1** ***syn*** see HEAVEN 2
idiom the next world (*or* life)
2 ***syn*** see UTOPIA
paragon *n* an individual of unequaled excellence often serving as a model <she is a *paragon* of a caring physician>
syn ideal, jewel, nonesuch, nonpareil, phoenix; *compare* MODEL 2
rel apotheosis, epitome, last word, quintessence, ultimate; archetype, beau ideal, exemplar, pattern; ||beaut, beauty, crackerjack, gem, love, lovely, peach, trump; champ, champion; cream, pick, tops
paragon *vb* ***syn*** see EQUATE 2
parallel *adj* ***syn*** see LIKE
ant nonparallel, unparallel
parallel *n* one that corresponds to or closely resembles another <we seek in vain a *parallel* for this situation>
syn analogue, correlate, correspondent, counterpart, countertype, match; *compare* COUNTERPART 1, EQUAL
rel equivalent; double, duplicate, duplication
parallel *vb* **1** ***syn*** see EQUATE 2
2 to place (something) so as to be parallel with another <machines that combed and *paralleled* the fibers>
syn collimate, collocate, parallelize
rel align, line up
parallelize *vb* ***syn*** see PARALLEL 2
paralyze *vb* **1** to render completely powerless, ineffective, or inert <a general strike that *paralyzed* the nation>
syn cripple, disable, disarm, immobilize, incapacitate, prostrate; *compare* MAIM, WEAKEN 1
rel deaden, enfeeble, weaken; close, shut (down); freeze; demolish, destroy, knock out
idiom bring to a grinding halt, tie hand and foot
2 ***syn*** see DAZE 2
rel appall, daunt, dismay, horrify; cripple, disable, enfeeble, weaken; astound, flabbergast, nonplus
con animate, enliven, pep (up), stimulate
ant galvanize
paramount *adj* ***syn*** see DOMINANT 1
rel capital, headmost; commanding, controlling; cardinal, crowning
paramour *n* **1** ***syn*** see GALLANT 2
2 ***syn*** see LOVER 1
3 ***syn*** see MISTRESS
parapet *n* ***syn*** see BULWARK
paraphernalia *n pl but sometimes sing in constr*
syn see EQUIPMENT 1
paraphrase *n* ***syn*** see VERSION 1
paraphrase *vb* to express or interpret something (as a text or passage) in other words <*paraphrased* the complicated document>
syn rephrase, restate, reword, translate (into)
rel summarize; transcribe
con quote, reproduce
parasite *n* a person who is supported or seeks support from another without making an adequate return <lived as a *parasite* in his father's house>
syn barnacle, bloodsucker, freeloader, hanger-on, leech, lounge lizard, ||spiv, sponge, sponger, sucker; *compare* SYCOPHANT
rel dependent; smell-feast; deadbeat, idler, laze
parasite *vb* ***syn*** see INFEST 2
parasitic *adj* ***syn*** see FAWNING
rel freeloading, leechlike, sponging
parasitize *vb* ***syn*** see INFEST 2
parboil *vb* ***syn*** see BOIL 2
parcel *n* **1** ***syn*** see PART 1
2 ***syn*** see LOT 3
3 ***syn*** see GROUP 3
parcel *vb* ***syn*** see APPORTION 2
rel allocate, allot, assign; deal, disburse, disperse; dole (out), lot (out)
parch *vb* ***syn*** see DRY 1
||**pard** *n* ***syn*** see PARTNER
pardon *n* a remission of penalty or punishment <the governor granted the prisoner a *pardon*>
syn absolution, amnesty
rel acquittal, exculpation, exoneration, indemnification, indemnity; forgiveness, remission; justification, vindication
con conviction; condemnation
ant punishment
pardon *vb* ***syn*** see EXCUSE 1
rel justify; accept, tolerate; free, liberate, release
idiom let bygones be bygones, wipe the slate clean
con amerce, fine, mulct, penalize
ant punish
pardonable *adj* ***syn*** see VENIAL
ant unpardonable
pare *vb* **1** ***syn*** see CUT 6

rel flay, scalp, skin, strip
2 *syn* see REDUCE 2
parent *vb* *syn* see GENERATE 1
parenthesis *n* 1 *syn* see DIGRESSION
2 *syn* see INTERLUDE
parenthetically *adv* *syn* see INCIDENTALLY 2
parentless *adj* *syn* see ORPHAN
ant parented
par excellence *adj* *syn* see EXCELLENT
pariah *n* *syn* see OUTCAST
rel déclassé
‖**parish–pump** *adj* *syn* see INSULAR
parity *n* *syn* see EQUIVALENCE
rel analogy, parallelism, similitude; approximation, closeness, nearness
ant disparity, imparity
parlance *n* *syn* see WORDING
parley *vb* 1 *syn* see SPEAK 3
2 *syn* see CONFER 2
parley *n* 1 *syn* see TALK 4
rel rap session
2 *syn* see CONVERSATION 1
parlor car *n* a railroad passenger car equipped with individual revolving and reclining chairs and providing the services of an attendant
syn chair car, club car, lounge car, palace car, tavern car
parlor house *n* *syn* see BROTHEL
parlous *adj* *syn* see DANGEROUS 1
parlous *adv* *syn* see VERY 1
Parnassian *n* *syn* see POET
parochial *adj* *syn* see INSULAR
rel prejudiced; bigoted
con unprejudiced; uncircumscribed, unlimited; cosmic, universal
ant catholic
parody *n* *syn* see CARICATURE 2
rel spoof, spoofery, rib, ridicule
parody *vb* *syn* see MIMIC
paronomasia *n* *syn* see PUN
parous *adj* *syn* see PREGNANT 1
parry *vb* 1 *syn* see DODGE 1
rel preclude, prevent; anticipate, forestall
2 *syn* see WARD 1
parsimonious *adj* *syn* see STINGY
idiom penny-wise and pound-foolish
ant prodigal
parson *n* *syn* see CLERGYMAN
part *n* 1 something less than the whole to which it belongs <a *part* of the road was paved>
syn cut, division, member, moiety, parcel, piece, portion, section, segment
rel component, constituent, element, ingredient; detail, fraction, fragment; bit, chip, scrap
con aggregate, total; combination, complex; entirety, entity, totality, unity
ant whole
2 **parts** *pl* *syn* see GENITALIA
3 *syn* see RATION
4 *syn* see SHARE 1
rel chunk
5 *syn* see SIDE 4
part *vb* *syn* see SEPARATE 1
ant unite
part *adj* *syn* see INCOMPLETE 1
partage *n* *syn* see SHARE 1
partake *vb* *syn* see SHARE 2
rel accept, receive, take
idiom take part in
partake (of) *vb* 1 *syn* see EAT 1
2 *syn* see AMOUNT 2
idiom bear resemblance (to)
partaker *n* *syn* see PARTICIPANT
part and parcel *n* *syn* see ESSENTIAL 1
partial *adj* 1 *syn* see BIASED 2
ant impartial
2 *syn* see INCOMPLETE 1
rel halfway
ant whole
partiality *n* 1 *syn* see PREJUDICE
2 *syn* see LEANING 2
participant *n* one that takes part in something <were *participants* in the uprising>
syn actor, partaker, participator, party, sharer
rel aide, assistant, helper; colleague, confrere, fellow, partner
con bystander, looker-on, nonparticipant, observer, onlooker, spectator, watcher
participate *vb* *syn* see SHARE 2
rel enter (into), join (in)
idiom be a party to, be in on, be (*or* get) in the act, have to do with
con observe, watch; retire, withdraw
participator *n* *syn* see PARTICIPANT
particle *n* a tiny or insignificant amount, part, or piece <not a *particle* of sense>
syn ace, atom, bit, crumb, damn, ‖dite, doit, dram, drop, fragment, grain, hoot, iota, jot, minim, mite, modicum, molecule, ounce, ray, ‖rissom, scrap, scruple, shred, smidgen, smitch, snap, speck, spot, syllable, tittle, whit, whoop
rel morsel; snip; dribbet, dribble; dot
parti–color *adj* *syn* see VARIEGATED
parti–colored *adj* *syn* see VARIEGATED
ant unicolor, unicolorous
particular *adj* 1 *syn* see SINGLE 2
ant general
2 *syn* see CIRCUMSTANTIAL
rel careful, meticulous, punctilious, scrupulous
3 *syn* see SPECIAL 1
rel appropriate; distinct; singular
ant universal
4 *syn* see SEVERAL 1
5 *syn* see NICE 1
particular *n* *syn* see POINT 1
rel speciality, specific
con entirety
ant universal
particularity *n* *syn* see INDIVIDUALITY 3
particularize *vb* 1 *syn* see SPECIFY 3
idiom draw it fine
2 *syn* see ITEMIZE 1
particularized *adj* *syn* see CIRCUMSTANTIAL

---

syn synonym(s) *rel* related word(s)
ant antonym(s) *con* contrasted word(s)
idiom idiomatic equivalent(s)
‖ use limited; if in doubt, see a dictionary

ant generalized
particularly *adv* ***syn*** see ESPECIALLY 1
parting *n* a mutual separation of two or more persons <saddened by their approaching *parting*>
syn adieu, congé, farewell, good-bye, leave-taking
rel separation; departure
con joining, meeting; return
ant reunion
parting *adj* given, taken, or performed during leave-taking <remembered his father's *parting* advice>
syn departing, farewell, good-bye, valedictory
rel final, last
partisan *n* **1** ***syn*** see FOLLOWER
rel backer, champion, upholder; die-hard, stalwart
con adversary, antagonist, opponent
2 an irregular soldier who operates behind enemy lines <a train blown up by *partisans*>
syn guerrilla, irregular, patriot
partisan *adj* ***syn*** see BIASED 2
rel denominational, factional, sectarian; blind, devoted, die-hard, fanatic, unreasoning
con impartial, indifferent, unbiased, unprejudiced
ant nonpartisan
partition *n* ***syn*** see SEPARATION 1
partition *vb* ***syn*** see DISTRIBUTE 1
partner *n* one that is associated in any action with another <*partners* in crime>
syn associate, cohort, confrere, consociate, copartner, fellow, mate, ‖pard
rel assistant, helper, sidekick; bedfellow, buddy, chum, companion, comrade, crony, pal
partnership *n* ***syn*** see ASSOCIATION 1
rel consociation, fellowship
parturient *adj* ***syn*** see PREGNANT 1
parturition *n* ***syn*** see BIRTH 1
party *n* **1** ***syn*** see COMBINATION 2
rel alliance, union; side
2 ***syn*** see PARTICIPANT
3 ***syn*** see HUMAN
4 ***syn*** see GROUP 1
5 ***syn*** see COMPANY 4
6 ***syn*** see ORGY 2
party girl *n* **1** ***syn*** see DOXY 1
2 ***syn*** see PROSTITUTE
parvenu *n* ***syn*** see UPSTART
idiom codfish aristocrat, pig in clover
‖pash *vb* ***syn*** see SHATTER 1
‖pash *n* ***syn*** see INFATUATION
pass *vb* **1** ***syn*** see GO 1
rel jog, ‖mog
2 ***syn*** see DIE 1
idiom pass on to the Great Beyond
con linger
3 to move or come to a termination or end <as time *passes,* the pain too will *pass*>
syn elapse, expire, go, pass away
rel slip (by); roll (on); fade (away), peter (out); cease, close, discontinue, end, stop, terminate
con continue; linger
4 ***syn*** see HAPPEN 1
idiom come to pass
5 ***syn*** see SURPASS 1
idiom leave way behind, shoot ahead of
6 ***syn*** see SPEND 3
7 ***syn*** see NEGLECT
8 ***syn*** see PROMISE 1
9 to transfer by hand from one person to another <*pass* the salt>
syn buck, hand, reach, ‖shoot
rel give; fork (over)
pass (as *or* for) *vb* ***syn*** see POSE 4
pass (on) *vb* ***syn*** see HAND DOWN
pass (over) *vb* ***syn*** see TRAVEL 2
pass *n* ***syn*** see JUNCTURE 2
passable *adj* capable of being passed, crossed, or traveled <*passable* roads>
syn navigable, negotiable, travelable
rel open, unblocked; ‖motorable; accessible, attainable, reachable
con blocked, closed; unnavigable; inaccessible, unattainable, unreachable
ant impassable
passably *adv* ***syn*** see ENOUGH 2
passage *n* **1** movement or transference from one place or point to another <air *passage* from New York to London> <the *passage* of current through a wire>
syn transit, travel
rel traject, trajet, traverse, traversing; transfer, transference, transmission, transmittal, transmittance
2 ***syn*** see TRANSITION
3 ***syn*** see WAY 2
4 a typically long narrow way connecting parts of a building <the office building contained endless *passages*>
syn corridor, couloir, hall, hallway, passageway
rel areaway
passageway *n* ***syn*** see PASSAGE 3
pass away *vb* **1** ***syn*** see DIE 1
2 ***syn*** see PASS 3
pass by *vb* ***syn*** see NEGLECT
passé *adj* **1** ***syn*** see OBSOLETE
2 ***syn*** see OLD-FASHIONED
ant a la mode
passed master *n* ***syn*** see EXPERT
passel *n* ***syn*** see GROUP 3
passing *n* ***syn*** see DEATH 1
passing *adj* ***syn*** see TRANSIENT
con lingering
passion *n* **1** ***syn*** see DISTRESS
2 ***syn*** see DESIRE 1
rel coveting; aiming, aspiring, panting
3 ***syn*** see FEELING 3
ant dispassion
4 ***syn*** see TEMPER 4
rel outbreak, outburst
5 ***syn*** see LOVE 2
rel heartthrob
6 intense, high-wrought emotion that compels to action <the *passion* of an evangelist>
syn ardor, calenture, enthusiasm, fervor, fire, hurrah, zeal
rel dedication, devotion; eagerness, lust; lyricism; ecstasy, rapture, transport; fury, rage

7 ***syn*** see LUST 2
rel amorousness; sensuality, sensuousness
8 ***syn*** see INFATUATION

passionate *adj* **1** ***syn*** see IRASCIBLE
2 ***syn*** see IMPASSIONED
rel excited, quickened, stimulated; high-powered, high-pressure, steamed up; headlong, impetuous, precipitate
ant dispassionate
3 ***syn*** see LUSTFUL 2
rel steamy, sultry
ant passionless

passionless *adj* ***syn*** see FRIGID 3
rel detached, impassive, unsusceptible; unaffected, unmoved; apathetic, indifferent, uncaring, unconcerned, unfeeling; cold-blooded, cold-hearted, frozen, heartless
ant passionate, passionful

passive *adj* **1** ***syn*** see INACTIVE
rel apathetic, impassive, phlegmatic, stolid
ant active
2 receiving or enduring without resistance <a *passive* acceptance of her fate>
syn acquiescent, nonresistant, nonresisting, resigned, submissive, unresistant, unresisting, yielding
rel bearing, enduring, patient; compliant, docile, tractable; nonviolent
con resistant, resisting, unresigned, unsubmissive, unyielding

pass off *vb* **1** ***syn*** see FOIST 3
2 ***syn*** see POSE 4

pass on *vb* ***syn*** see COMMUNICATE 1

pass out *vb* **1** ***syn*** see FAINT
2 ***syn*** see DIE 1

pass over *vb* ***syn*** see NEGLECT

passport *n* a means of entry into a desirable group, society, or condition of life <her skill at sports was a *passport* to fame and fortune>
syn key, open sesame, password, ticket

password *n* **1** a word or phrase that must be spoken by a person before he may pass a guard <give the *password* before entering the fort>
syn countersign, watchword, word
rel tessera
2 ***syn*** see PASSPORT
3 something (as a short phrase) used as a sign of recognition among members of the same society, class, or group <a fraternity that has secret handshakes and *passwords*>
syn watchword, word

past *adj* **1** ***syn*** see PRECEDING
2 ***syn*** see FORMER 2
rel bypast, gone-by; late, previous
ant present

past *prep* **1** ***syn*** see BEYOND 1
rel by
ant before
2 ***syn*** see BEYOND 2

past *n* former time <reminisced about the *past*>
syn foretime, ‖lang syne, yesterday, yesteryear, yore; *compare* PRESENT
rel antiquity
idiom bygone days (*or* times), days gone by, the good old days
con here and now; tomorrow
ant present; future

paste *vb* ***syn*** see BEAT 1
idiom give one a pasting

‖**paste** *n* ***syn*** see CUFF

pasticcio *n* ***syn*** see MISCELLANY 1

pastiche *n* ***syn*** see MISCELLANY 1

past master *n* ***syn*** see EXPERT

pastoral *adj* ***syn*** see RURAL
rel agrarian

patch *vb* ***syn*** see MEND 2

patchwork *n* ***syn*** see MISCELLANY 1

patchy *adj* ***syn*** see SPOTTY 1

pate *n* ***syn*** see HEAD 1

patent *adj* **1** ***syn*** see OPEN 1
2 ***syn*** see CLEAR 5
rel prominent; flagrant, glaring, gross, rank
idiom patently obvious
con impalpable, imperceptible, insensible; concealed, hidden, secreted
ant latent

‖**pater** *n* ***syn*** see FATHER 1

path *n* **1** ***syn*** see TRAIL
2 ***syn*** see WAY 1
3 ***syn*** see WAY 2

pathetic *adj* ***syn*** see PITIFUL 1

pathos *n* a quality that moves one to pity and sorrow <the *pathos* of the play was rarely offset by moments of comedy>
syn poignance, poignancy
rel bathos

pathway *n* ***syn*** see TRAIL

patience *n* the power or capacity to endure without complaint something difficult or disagreeable <it took a lot of *patience* to put up with him>
syn forbearance, longanimity, long-suffering, patientness, resignation, uncomplainingness
rel composure, cool, equanimity, impeturbability, self-control; endurance, sufferance, suffering, tolerance, toleration; nonresistance, passiveness, passivity, submission, submissiveness
con fretfulness; restiveness, restlessness; hastiness; rebellion, resistance
ant impatience

patientness *n* ***syn*** see PATIENCE

patois *n* **1** ***syn*** see VERNACULAR 3
2 ***syn*** see DIALECT 2

patriarch *n* **1** ***syn*** see FATHER 2
2 ***syn*** see GAFFER

patriarchal *adj* ***syn*** see VENERABLE 1

patrician *n* ***syn*** see GENTLEMAN 1
ant plebeian

patriciate *n* ***syn*** see ARISTOCRACY
ant plebs

patrimony *n* ***syn*** see HERITAGE 1

patriot *n* **1** a person who loves his country and supports its interests <*patriots* who asked what they could do for their country>

---

syn synonym(s) ***rel*** related word(s)
ant antonym(s) ***con*** contrasted word(s)
idiom idiomatic equivalent(s)
‖ use limited; if in doubt, see a dictionary

syn loyalist
rel nationalist
ant traitor
2 *syn* see PATRIOTEER
3 *syn* see PARTISAN 2

patrioteer *n* one who is ostentatiously and chauvinistically patriotic <bloodthirsty *patrioteers* immersed in political witch-hunts>
syn flag-waver, patriot, superpatriot
rel jingo, jingoist

patrolman *n syn* see POLICEMAN

patron *n* 1 *syn* see PATRON SAINT
2 *syn* see SPONSOR
ant client; protégé
3 *syn* see CUSTOMER

patronage *n* 1 *syn* see BACKING
rel benefaction, guardianship, protection; subsidy
2 commercial transactions of customers and patrons <developed a large *patronage* by offering fair prices and courteous service>
syn business, custom, trade, traffic
rel clientage, clientele
3 the power to make appointments to government jobs on a basis other than merit alone <ousted his enemies from office and used *patronage* to support his policies>
syn pork-barreling
rel cronyism

patron saint *n* a saint to whose protection and intercession a person, society, church, or place is dedicated <Saint Christopher is the *patron saint* of travelers>
syn avowry, patron
rel titular; guardian angel

patsy *n* 1 *syn* see SCAPEGOAT
2 *syn* see FOOL 3

patter *vb syn* see CHAT 1

patter *n syn* see DIALECT 2

pattern *n* 1 *syn* see MODEL 2
rel original
2 *syn* see FIGURE 3
rel patterning
3 *syn* see ORDER 8
rel arrangement, constellation

paucity *n syn* see SCARCITY
rel fewness

Paul Pry *n syn* see BUSYBODY

paunch *n* 1 *syn* see ABDOMEN
2 *syn* see POTBELLY

paunch *vb syn* see EVISCERATE

pauper *n* a person having no financial resources except those derived from charity
syn beggar, down-and-out
rel have-not, indigent; ‖casual; almsman, lazarus
con have, millionaire, plutocrat

pauper *vb syn* see RUIN 3

pauperism *n syn* see POVERTY 1

pauperize *vb syn* see RUIN 3

pausation *n syn* see PAUSE

pause *n* a temporary cessation of activity or of an activity <a *pause* in the conversation>
syn comma, interval, lull, pausation; *compare* BREAK 4, GAP 3
rel caesura, hush, lapse, letup, suspension; interlude, intermission; recess, respite; wait; break, gap, interruption; cessation, ‖deval
con continuation, progression

paw *vb syn* see TOUCH 1

paw *adj* 1 *syn* see NAUGHTY 1
2 *syn* see OBSCENE 2

pawn *n syn* see PLEDGE 1

pawn *vb* to give or deposit as security for the payment of a loan or debt or for the fulfillment of an obligation <had to *pawn* all her jewels>
syn ‖dip, hock, impignorate, mortgage, pledge, ‖pop, ‖spout
ant redeem

pawn *n syn* see TOOL 2

pay *vb* 1 to discharge an obligation to usually with money <*paid* the doctor for his services>
syn compensate, guerdon, remunerate
rel indemnify, recompense, satisfy; cough (up), plunk down, pony (up), pungle (up), remit, render, tender; pay off
2 *syn* see CLEAR 5
3 *syn* see SPEND 1
4 *syn* see COMPENSATE 3
idiom make up for
5 *syn* see YIELD 5

pay *n syn* see WAGE

payable *adj* 1 *syn* see DUE 2
ant unpayable
2 *syn* see UNPAID 2

pay envelope *n syn* see WAGE

paying *adj syn* see ADVANTAGEOUS 1
rel productive; sound; solvent

payload *n syn* see LOAD 1

pay up *vb syn* see CLEAR 5

PDQ *adv syn* see AWAY 3

peaceable *adj syn* see PACIFIC
rel amicable, friendly, neighborly; amiable, complaisant
ant acrimonious; contentious; warlike

peaceful *adj syn* see PACIFIC
rel collected, composed, cool, unruffled; constant, equable, steady
con agitated, discomposed, disquieted, disturbed, perturbed, upset

peacemaker *n* one that makes or seeks to make peace <a president who was remembered as a great *peacemaker*>
syn make-peace, pacificator
rel arbitrator, mediator, negotiator; placater; appeaser, peacemonger; peacekeeper
con chauvinist, jingo, jingoist, militarist, war dog, warmonger; peacebreaker

peace officer *n syn* see POLICEMAN

peach *n syn* ‖DILLY, crackerjack, ‖daisy, dandy, humdinger, jim-dandy, ‖lalapalooza, ‖lulu, nifty, ‖pip
rel pearl

peach *vb syn* see INFORM 3

peachy *adj syn* see MARVELOUS 2

peacock *vb syn* see LORD

peacockish *adj syn* see SHOWY

peacocky *adj syn* see SHOWY

peak *n* 1 *syn* see VISOR 1

2 ***syn*** see TOP 1
3 ***syn*** see MOUNTAIN 1
4 ***syn*** see APEX 2
peak (out) *vb* ***syn*** see DECREASE
peaked *adj* ***syn*** see POINTED 1
peaked *adj* ***syn*** see SICKLY 2
‖**peaking** *adj* ***syn*** see SICKLY 2
peaky *adj* ***syn*** see POINTED 1
peaky *adj* ***syn*** see SICKLY 2
peal *vb* ***syn*** see RING
peanut *adj* ***syn*** see PETTY 2
‖**peart** *adj* ***syn*** see LIVELY 1
‖**pearten** (up) *vb* ***syn*** see ENCOURAGE 1
peasant *n* ***syn*** see RUSTIC
peck *n* ***syn*** see MUCH
peck *vb* **1** to strike at or pick up with the beak <a hen *pecking* the scattered grain from the ground>
syn beak, pick
2 ***syn*** see KISS 1
peck (at) *vb* ***syn*** see NAG
pecker *n* **1** ***syn*** see BILL 1
2 ***syn*** see NOSE 1
‖**peckish** *adj* ***syn*** see HUNGRY
pecksniffery *n* ***syn*** see HYPOCRISY
pecksniffian *adj* ***syn*** see HYPOCRITICAL
peculate *vb* ***syn*** see EMBEZZLE
peculiar *adj* **1** ***syn*** see CHARACTERISTIC
rel unique
2 ***syn*** see STRANGE 4
rel uncustomary
con normal
peculiarity *n* ***syn*** see QUALITY 1
pecuniary *adj* ***syn*** see FINANCIAL
pedantic *adj* too narrowly concerned with scholarly matters <intellectual life that was *pedantic* rather than broad and humane>
syn academic, bookish, book-learned, booky, quodlibetic, scholastic
rel erudite, learned; didactic, donnish, inkhorn, schoolish, schoolteacherish; arid, dry, dryasdust, dull
ant unpedantic
peddle *vb* **1** ***syn*** see PUSH 6
2 to sell or offer for sale from place to place <*peddled* fish from a pushcart>
syn hawk, huckster, monger, vend
rel sell; push
peddler *n* one who travels about with merchandise to sell <*peddlers* were once common in rural areas>
syn ‖arab, cheap-jack (*or* cheap-john), ‖duffer, hawker, higgler, huckster, monger, mongerer, outcrier, packman, piepoudre, roadman, vendor
rel colporteur, costermonger; pusher
peddling *adj* ***syn*** see PETTY 2
pedestal *vb* ***syn*** see EXALT 1
pedestrian *adj* ***syn*** see DULL 9
rel commonplace, platitudinous, truistic; banal, inane, jejune, wishy-washy; heavy
pedigree *n* **1** ***syn*** see GENEALOGY
2 ***syn*** see ANCESTRY
pedigree *adj* ***syn*** see PUREBRED
pedigreed *adj* ***syn*** see PUREBRED
peek (in *or* out) *vb* ***syn*** see PEEP
peek *n* ***syn*** see PEEP
peel *vb* **1** ***syn*** see SKIN 2
2 ***syn*** see SCALE 2
peeled *adj* ***syn*** see OPEN 2
peeler *n* **1** ***syn*** see STRIPTEASER
2 ***syn*** see HUSTLER
‖**peeler** *n* ***syn*** see POLICEMAN
peep *vb* ***syn*** see CHIRP
rel pip
peep *vb* to peer through or as if through a hole or crevice <*peeped* cautiously under the bed>
syn peek (in *or* out)
rel glance; look; peer, stare
idiom take a peep (*or* peek)
peep *n* a brief and sometimes furtive look <take a *peep* at the new neighbors>
syn ‖gander, glance, glimpse, peek
rel look-over, look-see; oeillade, ogle; stare
peeper *n* **1** ***syn*** see PEEPING TOM
2 ***syn*** see EYE 1
peeping tom *n* a pruriently prying person <a *peeping tom* spying on the couple>
syn peeper, voyeur
rel prowler, snoop, snooper
idiom porch climber, window (*or* transom) peeper
‖**peepy** *adj* ***syn*** see SLEEPY 1
peer *vb* ***syn*** see GAZE 1
rel eye, rubberneck; pry, snoop
peerless *adj* ***syn*** see ALONE 3
rel dominant, paramount, predominant, sovereign
peery *adj* ***syn*** see CURIOUS 2
peeve *vb* ***syn*** see IRRITATE
rel disturb; miff
idiom make one hot under the collar
peevish *adj* ***syn*** see IRRITABLE
rel captious, carping, caviling, critical, faultfinding
idiom being in a peeve
peewee *n* ***syn*** see DWARF
peewee *adj* ***syn*** see TINY
‖**peg** *n* ***syn*** see DRINK 3
‖**pegh** *vb* ***syn*** see PANT 1
peg out *vb* **1** ***syn*** see COLLAPSE 2
2 ***syn*** see DIE 1
pejorative *adj* ***syn*** see DEROGATORY
con acclaiming, extolling, lauding, praising; aggrandizing, exalting, magnifying
pelf *n* **1** ***syn*** see MONEY
‖**2** ***syn*** see REFUSE
pell–mell *adv* in or as if in confused haste <barged in *pell-mell* without thinking>
syn helter-skelter, hotfoot, hurry-scurry, impetuously, incontinently
rel hurriedly; indiscreetly; carelessly, heedlessly, rashly, thoughtlessly
idiom on the spur of the moment

syn synonym(s) ***rel*** related word(s)
ant antonym(s) ***con*** contrasted word(s)
idiom idiomatic equivalent(s)
‖ use limited; if in doubt, see a dictionary

pell–mell *n* ***syn*** see CONFUSION 3
pell–mell *vb* ***syn*** see STAMPEDE 2
pellucid *adj* **1** ***syn*** see TRANSPARENT 1
rel sheer
con muddy, roily, turbid
2 ***syn*** see CLEAR 4
pelt *n* ***syn*** see HIDE
pelt *vb* **1** ***syn*** see BEAT 1
2 ***syn*** see HURRY 2
pen *vb* ***syn*** see ENCLOSE 1
ant unpen
pen *n* ***syn*** see JAIL
penalize *vb* to inflict a penalty on <*penalize* a delinquent taxpayer with a stiff fine>
syn amerce, fine, mulct
rel castigate, chasten, chastise, correct, discipline, punish; condemn; judge
penalty *n* ***syn*** see FINE
penance *n* ***syn*** see PENITENCE
penchant *n* ***syn*** see LEANING 2
‖**pend** *vb* ***syn*** see DEPEND (on *or* upon) 1
pendant *n* **1** ***syn*** see FLAG
2 ***syn*** see COUNTERPART 1
pendent *adj* **1** ***syn*** see SUSPENDED
2 ***syn*** see PENDING
pending *adj* not yet settled or decided <a claim still *pending*>
syn pendent, undecided, undetermined, unsettled
idiom hanging in the balance, in suspense, up in the air
con decided, determined, settled
ant closed
pendulant *adj* ***syn*** see SUSPENDED
pendulate *vb* ***syn*** see SWING 2
pendulous *adj* **1** ***syn*** see SUSPENDED
2 ***syn*** see VACILLATING 2
penetrable *adj* ***syn*** see PERMEABLE
ant impenetrable
penetrate *vb* **1** ***syn*** see ENTER 1
rel encroach, invade, trespass
2 to enter or go through by or as if by overcoming resistance <the icy wind *penetrated* the heavy parka>
syn pierce
rel bore, perforate, prick, puncture; jab, knife, stab; drill, drive
3 ***syn*** see PERMEATE
rel insert, insinuate, interpolate, introduce
penetrating *adj* **1** ***syn*** see INCISIVE
rel penetrant, penetrative
2 ***syn*** see SHARP 4
penetration *n* ***syn*** see WIT 3
rel penetrativeness
penetrative *adj* ***syn*** see SHARP 4
penitence *n* regret for sin or wrongdoing <responded to true *penitence* with forgiveness>
syn attrition, compunction, contriteness, contrition, penance, penitency, remorse, remorsefulness, repentance, rue, ruth
rel qualm, scruple; self-accusation, self-castigation, self-punishment, self-reproach, self-reproof; anguish, distress, grief, regret, sadness, sorrow; debasement, degradation, humbling, humiliation
con adamancy, inexorableness, obduracy, obdurateness, stubbornness
penitency *n* ***syn*** see PENITENCE
penitent *adj* ***syn*** see REMORSEFUL
penitential *adj* ***syn*** see REMORSEFUL
penitentiary *n* ***syn*** see JAIL
idiom correctional institution
penmanship *n* ***syn*** see HANDWRITING
pennant *n* ***syn*** see FLAG
pennilessness *n* ***syn*** see POVERTY 1
pennon *n* ***syn*** see FLAG
penny dreadful *n* ***syn*** see DIME NOVEL
penny pincher *n* ***syn*** see MISER
penny–pinching *adj* ***syn*** see STINGY
penny–wise *adj* ***syn*** see STINGY
pennyworth *n* ***syn*** see BARGAIN
pensile *adj* ***syn*** see SUSPENDED
pension (off) *vb* ***syn*** see RETIRE 2
pensive *adj* **1** ***syn*** see THOUGHTFUL 1
rel musing, ruminating
2 being musingly sad and thoughtful <gazed out the window with a *pensive* expression on her face>
syn meditative, ‖pensy, wistful
rel absorbed, abstracted, contemplative, musing, preoccupied, thoughtful, withdrawn; blue, melancholy, sad, saddened
con alert, aware, interested, outgoing
‖**pensy** *adj* **1** ***syn*** see PENSIVE 2
2 ***syn*** see THOUGHTFUL 1
3 ***syn*** see SQUEAMISH 1
penumbra *n* ***syn*** see SHADE 1
penurious *adj* **1** ***syn*** see POOR 1
2 ***syn*** see STINGY
penury *n* ***syn*** see POVERTY 1
ant luxury
peon *n* ***syn*** see SLAVE 2
peonage *n* ***syn*** see BONDAGE
people *n* **1** ***syn*** see SOCIETY 3
2 ***syn*** see COMMONALTY
people *vb* ***syn*** see INHABIT
pep *n* **1** ***syn*** see ENERGY 2
2 ***syn*** see VIGOR 2
pepper *vb* ***syn*** see SPECKLE 1
peppery *adj* **1** ***syn*** see PUNGENT
2 ***syn*** see IRASCIBLE
3 ***syn*** see SPIRITED 2
rel pepperish; alert, keen, lively, peppy
peppy *adj* ***syn*** see LIVELY 1
per *prep* ***syn*** see VIA 2
‖**per** *adv* ***syn*** see APIECE
perambulant *adj* ***syn*** see ITINERANT
perambulate *vb* ***syn*** see TRAVERSE 5
‖**perambulator** *n* ***syn*** see BABY CARRIAGE
perambulatory *adj* ***syn*** see ITINERANT
per capita *adv* ***syn*** see APIECE
per caput *adv* ***syn*** see APIECE
perceive *vb* ***syn*** see SEE 1
rel divine, identify, realize, recognize; grasp, seize, take; apprehend
perceptible *adj* apprehensible as real or existent <a *perceptible* change in attitude>
syn appreciable, detectable, discernible, observable, palpable, sensible, tangible; *compare* TANGIBLE 1

rel distinguishable, recognizable; cognizable, understandable; clear, lucid, perspicuous; conspicuous, noticeable, signal
con impalpable, indiscernible, intangible, invisible, unappreciable, undetectable, undiscernible, unnoticeable, unobservable
ant imperceptible
perception *n* ***syn*** see IDEA
perceptive *adj* **1** ***syn*** see ACUTE 3
rel responsive
ant imperceptive, unperceptive
2 ***syn*** see WISE 1
rel prehensile, prehensive, prehensorial
ant imperceptive, unperceptive
perch *vb* ***syn*** see ALIGHT
perchance *adv* ***syn*** see PERHAPS
percipience *n* ***syn*** see WIT 3
percolate *vb* **1** ***syn*** see PERMEATE
2 ***syn*** see EXUDE
per contra *adv* ***syn*** see HOWEVER
percussion *n* ***syn*** see IMPACT 1
rel percussiveness
perdition *n* ***syn*** see HELL
perdurable *adj* **1** ***syn*** see LASTING
ant fleeting
2 ***syn*** see INFINITE 1
perdure *vb* ***syn*** see CONTINUE 1
perduring *adj* ***syn*** see LASTING
ant fleeting
peregrination *n, usu* **peregrinations** *pl* ***syn*** see JOURNEY
peremptory *adj* ***syn*** see MASTERFUL 1
rel certain, positive; decided, decisive; absolute, fixed, uncompromising; obstinate
perennial *adj* ***syn*** see OLD 2
rel durable, perdurable
perfect *adj* **1** ***syn*** see WHOLE 1
ant imperfect
2 being entirely without flaw and meeting supreme standards of excellence <a ballerina whose technique was *perfect*>
syn absolute, flawless, fleckless, impeccable, indefectible, note-perfect, unflawed; *compare* CONSUMMATE 1
rel excellent; consummate; expert, finished, masterful, masterly
con defective, faulty, flawed; deficient, inadequate, wanting; unfinished, unpolished; unsound
ant imperfect
3 precisely appropriate or right <found the *perfect* gift for him>
syn ideal, model, very
rel needed, required, requisite; appropriate, fit, proper, right, suitable; exact, express, precise
idiom being just the thing
con foolish, inappropriate, undesirable, unsuitable
4 ***syn*** see PURE 2
5 ***syn*** see WHOLE 3
rel consummate
6 ***syn*** see UTTER
perfect *vb* ***syn*** see POLISH 2
perfected *adj* ***syn*** see CONSUMMATE 1
ant unperfected
perfectibilian *n* ***syn*** see PERFECTIONIST
perfectibilist *n* ***syn*** see PERFECTIONIST
perfection *n* **1** ***syn*** see INTEGRITY 2
2 ***syn*** see EXCELLENCE
ant imperfection
perfectionist *n* one that demands or works to achieve perfection <a *perfectionist* who rehearsed one scene fifty times>
syn perfectibilian, perfectibilist, perfectist
rel precisian, precisionist, stickler
perfectist *n* ***syn*** see PERFECTIONIST
perfectly *adv* ***syn*** see WELL 3
perfervid *adj* ***syn*** see IMPASSIONED
rel enhanced, heightened, intensified
perfidious *adj* ***syn*** see FAITHLESS
rel mercenary, venal; alienated, disaffected, estranged; deceitful, dishonest
perfidiousness *n* **1** ***syn*** see INFIDELITY
2 ***syn*** see TREACHERY
perfidy *n* **1** ***syn*** see TREACHERY
rel foul play
idiom Judas' kiss
ant fealty
2 ***syn*** see INFIDELITY
rel betrayal, sellout
perforate *vb* to pierce through so as to leave a hole <*perforate* a sheet of postage stamps>
syn bore, drill, prick, ‖pritch, punch, puncture
rel pit; probe; drive, penetrate, pierce
perforce *adv* ***syn*** see WILLY-NILLY
perform *vb* **1** ***syn*** see FULFILL 1
2 to carry something (as a process) to a successful conclusion <*perform* a surgical procedure>
syn achieve, do, execute; *compare* EFFECT 2
rel accomplish, bring off; complete, end, finish, wind up
idiom carry to completion (*or* a successful conclusion), do to a turn, do up brown
3 ***syn*** see ACT 1
4 ***syn*** see ACT 5
performance *n* ***syn*** see EFFICIENCY 1
performer *n* ***syn*** see ACTOR 1
perfume *n* ***syn*** see FRAGRANCE
perfume *vb* ***syn*** see SCENT 2
perfumed *adj* ***syn*** see SWEET 2
perfumy *adj* ***syn*** see SWEET 2
perfunctory *adj* characterized by routine and often done merely as a duty <gave her his usual *perfunctory* nod>
syn automatic, mechanical
rel cursory, superficial; involuntary, unaware; routine, usual; standard, stock; cool, impersonal, indifferent; wooden; unconcerned, uninterested
con cordial, friendly, genial, hearty, warm
pergola *n* ***syn*** see ARBOR
perhaps *adv* conceivably but not certainly so <*perhaps* this is true, but I think it's debatable>

---

syn synonym(s) ***rel*** related word(s)
ant antonym(s) ***con*** contrasted word(s)
idiom idiomatic equivalent(s)
‖ use limited; if in doubt, see a dictionary

syn maybe, perchance, possibly
rel conceivably, feasibly, imaginably
idiom as it may be, as the case may be, for all one knows
con certainly, definitely, doubtlessly, surely, undoubtedly, unquestionably
perhaps *n* ***syn*** see THEORY 2
periapt *n* ***syn*** see CHARM 2
peril *n* ***syn*** see DANGER
rel exposure, liability, openness, subjection; endangerment
idiom cause for alarm, rocks (*or* breakers) ahead
peril *vb* ***syn*** see ENDANGER
perilous *adj* ***syn*** see DANGEROUS 1
rel shaky, tottery, unstable, unsteady; delicate, ticklish, touchy
perimeter *n* **1** ***syn*** see CIRCUMFERENCE
2 ***syn*** see BORDER 1
period *n* **1** ***syn*** see END 2
2 an extent of time set off or typified by someone or something <the Victorian *period*><a *period* of expansion>
syn age, day(s), epoch, era, time
periodic *adj* ***syn*** see INTERMITTENT
rel on-again-off-again
periodical *adj* ***syn*** see INTERMITTENT
periodical *n* ***syn*** see JOURNAL
peripatetic *adj* ***syn*** see ITINERANT
periphery *n* **1** ***syn*** see CIRCUMFERENCE
2 ***syn*** see BORDER 1
periphrase *n* ***syn*** see VERBIAGE 1
periphrasis *n* ***syn*** see VERBIAGE 1
perish *vb* **1** ***syn*** see DIE 1
ant survive
2 to suffer spiritual or moral death <nations *perishing* for lack of true leaders>
syn die
rel decline; collapse, go under; expire, succumb; disappear, vanish; cease, end
con flourish, prosper, thrive
ant endure
‖**3** ***syn*** see DECAY
perishing *adj* ***syn*** see DAMNED 2
perjure *vb* to make a false swearer of oneself by violating one's oath to tell the truth <a *perjured* witness>
syn forswear
rel equivocate; deceive, delude, mislead, trick; lie, prevaricate
idiom commit perjury, lie under oath, swear falsely
perjurer *n* ***syn*** see LIAR
perk (up) *vb* ***syn*** see IMPROVE 3
‖**perk** *n, usu* **perks** *pl* ***syn*** see GRATUITY
perlustrate *vb* ***syn*** see SCRUTINIZE 1
perlustration *n* ***syn*** see EXAMINATION
permanent *adj* ***syn*** see LASTING
rel imperishable, invariable
ant temporary
permeable *adj* capable of being permeated especially by fluids <a *permeable* membrane>
syn penetrable, pervious, porose, porous
rel passable
con impassable, impenetrable, impervious
ant impermeable
permeate *vb* to pass or cause to pass through every part of a thing <air *permeated* with cigar smoke>
syn charge, compenetrate, impenetrate, impregnate, interfuse, interpenetrate, penetrate, percolate, pervade, saturate, transfuse
rel invade; imbrue, imbue, infiltrate, infuse, ingrain; diffuse, suffuse; drench, soak, steep; fill
permissible *adj* that may be permitted <a *permissible* error>
syn admissible, allowable
rel unforbidden, unprohibited; allowed, permitted, tolerated; approved, authorized, endorsed, sanctioned; acceptable, bearable, tolerable
con banned, forbidden, disallowed, prohibited, unpermitted, verboten; unacceptable, unbearable
ant impermissible
permission *n* a sanctioning to act or do something that is granted by one in authority <received *permission* to leave work early>
syn allowance, authorization, consent, leave, permit, sanction, sufferance
rel acceptance, acquiescence; approbation, approval; endorsement
ant prohibition
permit *vb* ***syn*** see LET 2
rel tolerate
idiom give one his head
ant forbid, prohibit
permit *n* ***syn*** see PERMISSION
permutation *n* ***syn*** see CHANGE 2
rel alteration, modification
pernicious *adj* exceedingly harmful or destructive <*pernicious* gossip>
syn baneful, deadly, noxious, pestiferous, pestilent, pestilential; *compare* DEADLY 1
rel damaging, deleterious, detrimental, harmful, hurtful; baleful, malefic, maleficent, malign, sinister; miasmatic, miasmic, poisonous, toxic, venomous; malignant, swart, virulent; destructive, devastating, ruinous; fatal, killing, lethal, mortal
con harmless, uninjurious; nonmalignant, nonpoisonous, nontoxic
ant innocuous
pernickety *adj* ***syn*** see NICE 1
perorate *vb* ***syn*** see ORATE
perpend *vb* ***syn*** see CONSIDER 1
perpendicular *adj* ***syn*** see VERTICAL
rel stand-up, straight
ant horizontal
perpendicularity *n* ***syn*** see VERTICALITY
rel erectness, uprightness
ant horizontality
perpetrate *vb* ***syn*** see COMMIT 2
rel effect; inflict, wreak
idiom ‖up and do
perpetual *adj* ***syn*** see CONTINUAL
ant ephemeral, transient
perpetually *adv* ***syn*** see ALWAYS 1
perpetuate *vb* to make perpetual or cause to last indefinitely <*perpetuate* his memory for future generations>

syn eternalize, eternize, immortalize
rel bolster, conserve, keep, maintain, preserve, secure, support, sustain
con annihilate, blot out, erase, expunge
ant obliterate

perplex *vb* **1** *syn* see PUZZLE
rel discompose, perturb; balk, thwart; astonish, astound, surprise
idiom put (*or* drive) to one's wit's end
2 *syn* see COMPLICATE
3 *syn* see ENTANGLE 1

perquisite *n* **1** *syn* see GRATUITY
2 *syn* see RIGHT 2

per se *adv* by, of, or in itself or oneself or themselves <not opposed to the death penalty *per se*>
syn as such, intrinsically
rel alone, independently, solely

persecute *vb* **1** *syn* see WRONG
rel dragoon, rack, torment, torture
con back, champion, support, uphold
2 *syn* see MOLEST
rel worry; hound, ride
con humor, indulge, pamper; accommodate, favor, oblige

perseverant *adj syn* see PERSISTENT 1

perseverative *adj syn* see PERSISTENT 1

persevere *vb* to continue in a state, enterprise, or undertaking in spite of counter influences, opposition, or discouragement <*persevered* in her unpopular economic policy>
syn carry on, go on, hang on, persist
rel continue, get on, press (on), proceed
idiom hang in there, hang tough, keep at it, keep driving, never say die, stick (*or* tough) it out
con falter, hesitate, vacillate, waver; renounce, surrender, yield
ant give up

persevering *adj syn* see PERSISTENT 1

persiflage *n syn* see BANTER

persist *vb* **1** *syn* see PERSEVERE
con cease, discontinue, quit, stop
ant desist
2 *syn* see CONTINUE 1
rel go on; linger; obtain, prevail
ant desist

persistence *n* **1** *syn* see CONTINUATION 1
2 *syn* see RUN 2
rel course

persistent *adj* **1** continuing in a course of action without regard to discouragement, opposition, or previous failure <a *persistent* suitor>
syn dogged, insistent, perseverant, perseverative, persevering, persisting, persistive
rel determined, steadfast, tenacious, unshakable; relentless, unremitting
con malleable, pliant, tractable, yielding; infirm, invertebrate, spineless; vacillating, wavery, wobbling
2 *syn* see PRIMITIVE 3

persisting *adj syn* see PERSISTENT 1

persistive *adj syn* see PERSISTENT 1

persnickety *adj syn* see NICE 1

person *n syn* see HUMAN
rel chap, ||cookie, coot, fellow, galoot, guy, specimen, stick

personage *n* **1** *syn* see NOTABLE 1
2 *syn* see HUMAN

personal *adj* **1** of, relating to, or affecting a particular person <owed his *personal* allegiance to his wife>
syn individual
rel particular, peculiar, special
con general, universal; common, joint, mutual, shared; commonplace, everyday, ordinary
2 *syn* see PRIVATE 1

personal effects *n pl* privately owned items (as clothing and toilet articles) normally worn or carried on the person <packed his *personal effects* in a small bag>
syn ||plunder, stuff, things, traps, tricks
rel belongings, goods, possessions
idiom personal belongings

personality *n* **1** *syn* see INDIVIDUALITY 4
2 *syn* see DISPOSITION 3
3 *syn* see NOTABLE 1

personalize *vb* **1** *syn* see EMBODY 1
rel anthropomorphize
2 *syn* see REPRESENT 2

personal name *n syn* see GIVEN NAME

personate *vb* **1** *syn* see ACT 1
2 *syn* see REPRESENT 2

personification *n syn* see EMBODIMENT

personify *vb* **1** *syn* see EMBODY 1
rel reincarnate
2 *syn* see REPRESENT 2

personize *vb syn* see EMBODY 1

perspective *n syn* see VISTA

perspicacious *adj syn* see SHREWD
rel quick-sighted, sharp-sighted, sharp-witted

perspicacity *n syn* see WIT 3

perspicuity *n syn* see CLARITY
rel intelligibility; explicitness

perspicuous *adj syn* see CLEAR 4

perspiring *adj syn* see SWEATY

perspiry *adj syn* see SWEATY

persuadable *adj syn* see RECEPTIVE 1
ant unpersuadable

persuade *vb* **1** *syn* see INDUCE 1
rel affect, impress, touch; reason; convert
con discourage, hinder, prevent
ant dissuade
2 *syn* see CONVERT 1
3 *syn* see ASSURE 2
ant dissuade

persuasible *adj syn* see RECEPTIVE 1
ant unpersuasible

persuasion *n* **1** *syn* see OPINION
rel bias, partiality, predilection, prejudice, prepossession
2 *syn* see RELIGION 1
3 *syn* see RELIGION 2
rel affiliation; order
4 *syn* see TYPE

pert *adj* **1** *syn* see SAUCY 1

---

syn synonym(s) *rel* related word(s)
ant antonym(s) *con* contrasted word(s)
idiom idiomatic equivalent(s)
|| use limited; if in doubt, see a dictionary

rel bold, daring; audacious, brazen
con shy
ant coy
2 *syn* see WISE 5
rel disrespectful, rude
3 *syn* see LIVELY 1
pertain *vb* **1** *syn* see BELONG 2
2 *syn* see BEAR (on *or* upon)
rel associate, combine, connect, join
idiom be pertinent (*or* relevant) to
pertinacious *adj syn* see OBSTINATE
rel fixed, unshakable; dogged, tenacious
pertinent *adj syn* see RELEVANT
rel pertaining
ant impertinent
perturb *vb syn* see DISCOMPOSE 1
rel trouble; unsettle
ant compose
pervade *vb syn* see PERMEATE
idiom spread through and through
perverse *adj* **1** *syn* see VICIOUS 2
2 *syn* see OBSTINATE
rel cranky, irritable, unreasonable
3 *syn* see CONTRARY 3
pervert *vb* **1** *syn* see DEBASE 1
rel abuse, maltreat, mistreat, misuse, outrage; ruin
2 *syn* see ABUSE 2
rel ill-treat
3 *syn* see MISREPRESENT
perverted *adj syn* see DEBASED
rel defiled, polluted, tainted; contorted, distorted, warped; abused, misused, outraged
pervicacious *adj syn* see OBSTINATE
pervious *adj syn* see PERMEABLE
ant impervious
pesky *adj syn* see TROUBLESOME
pesky *adv syn* see VERY 1
pessimist *n* one who emphasizes adverse aspects or conditions and expects the worst <*pessimists* predicting another depression>
syn calamity howler, Cassandra, crepehanger, worrywart
rel fussbudget; Job's comforter; defeatist; killjoy; cynic, misanthrope
con positivist; idealist; Pollyanna
ant optimist
pest *n* **1** *syn* see ANNOYANCE 3
rel bane, trouble, vexation, worry
idiom pain in the neck, pea in the shoe, thorn in the flesh
2 one who pesters or annoys <a little *pest* who constantly asked questions>
syn nudnick, nuisance, pesterer
rel badgerer, heckler, tormentor
idiom pain in the neck
pester *vb syn* see WORRY 1
rel ride
idiom drive (one) crazy, drive (one) up the wall, pester to death
pester *n syn* see ANNOYANCE 3
pesterer *n syn* see PEST 2
‖**pesterment** *n syn* see ANNOYANCE 3
pesticide *n* a chemical agent used to destroy pests <the need to control indiscriminate use of *pesticides*>
syn biocide, economic poison
rel bactericide, fungicide, germicide, insecticide, microbicide, rodenticide, vermicide
pestiferous *adj syn* see PERNICIOUS
pestilence *n syn* see PLAGUE 1
pestilent *adj* **1** *syn* see DEADLY 1
2 *syn* see PERNICIOUS
pestilential *adj* **1** *syn* see DEADLY 1
2 *syn* see PERNICIOUS
pet *adj syn* see FAVORITE 1
pet *vb syn* see CARESS
rel embrace, hug
pet *vb syn* see SULK
petcock *n syn* see FAUCET
peter (out) *vb syn* see DECREASE
Peter Funk *n syn* see SWINDLER
petite *adj syn* see SMALL 1
rel diminutive, dwarf, lilliputian, miniature, wee
petition *n syn* see PRAYER
rel request
petition *vb* to make an earnest, formal, and often written request <*petitioned* for a hearing before the labor board>
syn appeal, sue (for *or* to)
rel ask, request; beg, beseech, entreat, implore, plead, pray, supplicate
con claim, demand, exact, press (for)
petitioner *n syn* see SUPPLIANT
petit–maître *n syn* see FOP
petrify *vb syn* see DAZE 2
rel alarm, frighten, startle, terrify; appall, dismay, horrify; numb
idiom turn to stone
pettifogger *n* an unscrupulous lawyer <done out of his rights by a slick *pettifogger*>
syn jackleg lawyer, shyster; *compare* LAWYER
rel ambulance chaser, Philadelphia lawyer; ‖bush lawyer
pettifogging *adj syn* see PETTY 2
pettish *adj syn* see IRRITABLE
petty *adj* **1** *syn* see LITTLE 3
2 being often contemptibly insignificant or unimportant <*petty* quarrels and intrigues>
syn inconsequent, inconsequential, inconsiderable, measly, Mickey Mouse, niggling, paltry, peanut, peddling, pettifogging, picayune, picayunish, piddling, piffling, pimping, puny, small, trifling, trivial, unconsequential, unconsidered, ungenerous, unvital; *compare* LITTLE 3
rel negligible, unimportant; hair-drawn, hairsplitting; impertinent, irrelevant
con consequential, considerable; big, gross; significant, vital
ant important, momentous
petulant *adj syn* see IRRITABLE
rel grouchy, sulky
phantasm *n* **1** *syn* see DELUSION 1
rel fabrication, fiction, invention
2 *syn* see APPARITION
3 *syn* see FANCY 4
phantom *n syn* see APPARITION

pharisaic *adj* ***syn*** see HYPOCRITICAL
pharisaical *adj* ***syn*** see HYPOCRITICAL
pharisaicalness *n* ***syn*** see HYPOCRISY
pharisaism *n* ***syn*** see HYPOCRISY
pharisee *n* ***syn*** see HYPOCRITE
pharmaceutic *n* ***syn*** see DRUG 1
pharmaceutical *n* ***syn*** see DRUG 1
pharmacist *n* ***syn*** see DRUGGIST
pharmacon *n* ***syn*** see REMEDY 1
pharos *n* ***syn*** see LIGHTHOUSE
phase *n* one of the possible ways of viewing or being presented to view <the moral *phase* of the problem>
syn angle, aspect, facet, hand, side
rel condition, situation, state; position, posture, view, viewpoint; appearance, look, semblance; color, complexion
phenomenal *adj* **1** ***syn*** see MATERIAL 1
con ontic
ant noumenal
2 ***syn*** see EXCEPTIONAL 1
phenomenon *n* **1** ***syn*** see FACT 2
rel experience; actuality, reality
2 ***syn*** see WONDER 1
rel abnormality; anomaly, paradox; peculiarity, singularity, uniqueness, unusualness
philander *n* ***syn*** see WOLF
idiom ‖skirt chaser
philander *vb* to have many love affairs <his reputation for *philandering* with married women>
syn fool (around), mess around, play (around), wolf, womanize
rel dally, flirt, trifle; chase, pursue; ‖tomcat (around)
idiom ‖chase skirts, play Don Juan, play the femmes
philanderer *n* ***syn*** see WOLF
philanthropic *adj* ***syn*** see CHARITABLE 1
rel bighearted, freehearted, greathearted, kindhearted, largehearted, openhearted; contributing, donating, freehanded, giving, magnanimous; civic-minded, public-spirited
ant misanthropic
philharmonic *n* ***syn*** see ORCHESTRA
philippic *n* ***syn*** see TIRADE
philistine *n* a crass, prosaic, often priggish individual guided by material rather than artistic or intellectual values <*philistines* who opposed everything new and creative in art>
syn Babbitt, boeotian, boob, middlebrow
rel bourgeois; capitalist; materialist; boor, clown, lout, vulgarian
ant aesthete
phiz *n* ***syn*** see FACE 1
phlegm *n* **1** ***syn*** see APATHY 1
2 ***syn*** see EQUANIMITY
rel nonchalance, unconcern
phlegmatic *adj* ***syn*** see IMPASSIVE 1
rel calm, undemonstrative; aloof, incurious, indifferent, unconcerned; lethargic, sluggish
phoebus *n* ***syn*** see SUN 1
phoenix *n* ***syn*** see PARAGON
phonate *vb* ***syn*** see ARTICULATE 2
phone *vb* ***syn*** see TELEPHONE
phony *adj* ***syn*** see COUNTERFEIT
phony *n* **1** ***syn*** see IMPOSTURE
2 ***syn*** see IMPOSTOR
photo *vb* ***syn*** see PHOTOGRAPH
idiom take a photo (of)
photog *n* ***syn*** see PHOTOGRAPHER
photograph *vb* to use a camera to make a picture, image, or likeness of <*photographed* the whole family>
syn photo, shoot
rel cinematize, ‖cinematograph, cinemize, film, filmize, picture; snap, snapshoot, snapshot; mug
idiom capture on film, take a picture (*or* photograph)
photographer *n* one who takes photographs <a newspaper *photographer*>
syn cameraman, camerist, photog, photographist, photoist
rel snapshooter, ‖snapshotter; shutterbug; paparazzo; photojournalist
photographic *adj* ***syn*** see GRAPHIC 1
rel accurate, detailed, exact
photographist *n* ***syn*** see PHOTOGRAPHER
photoist *n* ***syn*** see PHOTOGRAPHER
photoplay *n* ***syn*** see MOVIE
phrase *n* **1** ***syn*** see WORDING
rel styling
2 a group of words which, taken together, express a notion and may constitute part of a sentence <an adverbial *phrase*><a trite *phrase*>
syn expression, locution
rel phrasing; idiom; catchword, slogan
3 ***syn*** see CATCHWORD
phrase *vb* ***syn*** see WORD
phraseology *n* ***syn*** see WORDING
idiom choice of words
phrasing *n* ***syn*** see WORDING
phthisis *n* ***syn*** see TUBERCULOSIS
phylactery *n* ***syn*** see CHARM 2
physic *n* ***syn*** see REMEDY 1
physical *adj* **1** ***syn*** see MATERIAL 1
rel natural; elemental, elementary
ant spiritual
2 ***syn*** see BODILY
rel visceral; lusty; brute
ant mental
physician *n* a doctor of medicine <the shortage of *physicians* in rural areas>
syn ‖croaker, doc, doctor, MD, medical, mediciner, medico, ‖sawbones
rel medic; general practitioner, practitioner; surgeon; specialist
idiom medical doctor, medical man
physique *n* bodily makeup or type <a muscular *physique*>
syn build, constitution, habit, habitus
rel anatomy, structure; configuration, shape; body, figure, form, frame
picaroon *n* ***syn*** see PIRATE

syn synonym(s) ***rel*** related word(s)
ant antonym(s) ***con*** contrasted word(s)
idiom idiomatic equivalent(s)
‖ use limited; if in doubt, see a dictionary

picayune *adj* ***syn*** see PETTY 2
picayunish *adj* ***syn*** see PETTY 2
pick *vb* **1** ***syn*** see CHOOSE 1
idiom pick and choose
ant reject
2 ***syn*** see PECK 1
pick *n* ***syn*** see BEST
pick *adj* ***syn*** see SELECT 1
picked *adj* ***syn*** see SELECT 1
picket *n* ***syn*** see GUARD 2
pickle *n* ***syn*** see PREDICAMENT
idiom pretty pickle, ||sticky wicket, tight spot
||**pickled** *adj* ***syn*** see INTOXICATED 1
pick out *vb* ***syn*** see CHOOSE 1
pickpocket *n* one who steals from pockets <his wallet was lifted by a *pickpocket*>
syn ||cannon, cutpurse, ||dip, ||diver, purse cutter, ||wire
rel ||ganef, thief; ||mobsman, ||swell-mobsman
idiom ||pocket prowler
picksome *adj* ***syn*** see NICE 1
pick up *vb* **1** ***syn*** see LIFT 1
2 ***syn*** see GLEAN
3 ***syn*** see GET 1
4 ***syn*** see LEARN 1
5 ***syn*** see ARREST 2
rel book
idiom ||take (someone) downtown
6 ***syn*** see RESUME 2
idiom pick up the thread again
pickup *n* ***syn*** see ARREST
rel booking
picky *adj* ***syn*** see NICE 1
picnic *n* ***syn*** see SNAP 1
pictorial *adj* **1** consisting of or relating to pictures <a collection of *pictorial* materials>
syn graphic, iconographic, illustrational, illustrative, illustratory, pictoric
rel photographic, pictographic
2 ***syn*** see GRAPHIC 1
pictoric *adj* ***syn*** see PICTORIAL 1
picture *n* **1** ***syn*** see REPRESENTATION
2 ***syn*** see IMAGE 1
3 ***syn*** see MOVIE
picture *vb* ***syn*** see REPRESENT 1
rel draw
picture show *n* ***syn*** see MOVIE
picturesque *adj* ***syn*** see GRAPHIC 1
piddling *adj* ***syn*** see PETTY 2
pie *n* ***syn*** see SNAP 1
piece *n* **1** ***syn*** see PART 1
||**2** ***syn*** see SNACK
pièce de résistance *n* ***syn*** see SHOWPIECE
piecemeal *adv* ***syn*** see GRADUALLY
piecemeal *adj* ***syn*** see GRADUAL
||**pie–eyed** *adj* ***syn*** see INTOXICATED 1
piepoudre *n* ***syn*** see PEDDLER
pier *n* **1** ***syn*** see WHARF
rel pierage, wharfage
2 ***syn*** see PILLAR 1
pierce *vb* **1** ***syn*** see CUT 1
rel penetrate, perforate
2 ***syn*** see PENETRATE 2
rel run through
piercing *adj* **1** ***syn*** see SHARP 8
2 ***syn*** see LOUD 1
3 ***syn*** see ACUTE 4
pietistic *adj* ***syn*** see DEVOUT
rel reverencing, reverential
piety *n* ***syn*** see FIDELITY 1
rel docility, obedience; enthusiasm, fervor, passion, zeal; holiness, sanctity
piffle *n* ***syn*** see NONSENSE 2
piffling *adj* ***syn*** see PETTY 2
||**pig** *n* **1** ***syn*** see WANTON
2 ***syn*** see POLICEMAN
pigeon *n* ***syn*** see FOOL 3
pigeon *vb* ***syn*** see DUPE
pigeonhole *n* **1** ***syn*** see CUBBYHOLE
2 ***syn*** see CLASS 1
rel niche, slot
pigeonhole *vb* ***syn*** see ASSORT
rel identify, label, name; place, rank, rate; catalog; break down, subdivide
pigeon house *n* ***syn*** see DOVECOTE
pigeonry *n* ***syn*** see DOVECOTE
pigheaded *adj* ***syn*** see OBSTINATE
idiom not to be moved (*or* budged)
pigment *n* ***syn*** see COLOR 6
pigpen *n* ***syn*** see STY 1
pigsty *n* ***syn*** see STY 1
piked *adj* ***syn*** see POINTED 1
piker *n* ***syn*** see VAGABOND
piker *n* ***syn*** see MISER
pilaster *n* ***syn*** see PILLAR 1
pile *n* **1** a quantity of things heaped or stacked together <a *pile* of dirty clothes>
syn bank, ||bing, cock, drift, heap, hill, mass, mound, mountain, mow, pyramid, rick, ||rickle, ||ruck, shock, stack, stockpile, windrow
rel barrow, pyre, tumulus; ||dess, haycock, hayrick, haystack; accumulation, aggregate, aggregation, amassment, assemblage, collection, conglomeration, glomeration, hoard, jumble
2 ***syn*** see MUCH
3 ***syn*** see EDIFICE
4 ***syn*** see FORTUNE 4
idiom a pile of money
pile *vb* **1** ***syn*** see HEAP 1
2 ***syn*** see LOAD 3
pile (in) *vb* ***syn*** see RETIRE 4
pile (out) *vb* ***syn*** see ROLL OUT
idiom ||get the lead out, shake a leg, ||shake it out
pile *n* ***syn*** see DOWN
pileous *adj* ***syn*** see HAIRY 1
con bare; pileless
pile up *vb* ***syn*** see SHIPWRECK 1
pileup *n* ***syn*** see CRASH 3
pilfer *vb* ***syn*** see STEAL 1
pilferer *n* ***syn*** see THIEF
pilgarlic *n* ***syn*** see LAUGHINGSTOCK
||**pill** *n* **1** ***syn*** see CIGARETTE
2 ***syn*** see BORE
pillage *vb* **1** ***syn*** see RAVAGE
rel encroach, invade, trespass; appropriate, arrogate, confiscate, usurp
idiom lay waste
2 ***syn*** see STEAL 1

pillager *n syn* see MARAUDER
pillar *n* **1** a firm upright support for a superstructure <stone *pillars* supported the ceiling>
syn column, pier, pilaster
rel prop; pedestal; post
2 *syn* see MAINSTAY
pilose *adj syn* see HAIRY 1
pilot *n* **1** *syn* see LEADER 1
2 one who flies or is qualified to fly an airplane <jet *pilots*>
syn airman, aviator, birdman, flier, fly-boy
rel aerialist
pilot *vb* **1** *syn* see GUIDE
2 *syn* see DRIVE 5
pimp *n* **1** a man who solicits for a prostitute, lives off her earnings, and often lives with her <after dark, the *pimp* appeared on the street seeking clients for his girls>
syn bully, ‖cadet, ‖easy rider, fancy man, ‖mack, macquereau, pander
rel procurer; white slaver
‖**2** *syn* see INFORMER
‖**pimp** *vb syn* see INFORM 3
pimping *adj syn* see PETTY 2
pimple *n syn* see ABSCESS
rel ‖plouk
pimple *vb syn* see SPOT 2
pin *n syn* see BROOCH
pinch *vb* **1** *syn* see EXTORT 1
2 *syn* see STEAL 1
3 *syn* see ARREST 2
4 *syn* see SCRIMP
pinch *n* **1** *syn* see JUNCTURE 2
2 *syn* see THEFT
3 *syn* see ARREST
pinchbeck *adj syn* see COUNTERFEIT
pinched *adj syn* see HAGGARD
con stalwart, stout, strong, sturdy; healthy, robust
pinch hitter *n syn* see SUBSTITUTE 1
pinching *adj syn* see STINGY
pinchpenny *adj syn* see STINGY
‖**pindling** *adj syn* see IRRITABLE
pine *vb syn* see LONG
rel brood, fret, mope; grieve, mourn; agonize
pinhead *n syn* see DUNCE
pinhead *adj syn* see STUPID 1
pinheaded *adj syn* see STUPID 1
pink *vb syn* see BLUSH
pinken *vb syn* see BLUSH
Pinkerton *n syn* see PRIVATE DETECTIVE
pin money *n syn* see POCKET MONEY
pinnacle *n syn* see APEX 2
pinpoint *vb syn* see IDENTIFY
pint–size *adj syn* see TINY
pioneer *adj syn* see FIRST 2
rel pilot
pious *adj syn* see DEVOUT
rel priestlike, priestly
ant impious
pip *vb* ‖**1** *syn* see DEFEAT 2
2 *syn* see DIE 1
‖**pip** *n syn* ‖DILLY, ‖corker, crackerjack, ‖daisy, dandy, humdinger, jim-dandy, ‖lalapalooza, ‖lulu, nifty
pipe *n* **1** *syn* see CASK
‖**2** *syn* see PIPE DREAM
‖**3** *syn* see SNAP 1
pipe *vb* ‖**1** *syn* see CRY 2
2 *syn* see CONDUCT 4
‖**piped** *adj syn* see INTOXICATED 1
pipe down *vb syn* see SHUT UP 2
pipe dream *n* an illusory or fantastic plan or hope <*pipe dreams* of universal peace>
syn bubble, chimera, dream, fantasy (*or* phantasy), illusion, ‖pipe, rainbow
rel expectation, hope, prospect
pipeline *n* a person through whom information is transmitted <she was his news *pipeline* from the mayor's office>
syn channel, conduit
rel grapevine; origin, source, wellspring; supplier; connection, contact
piping *adj syn* see ACUTE 4
‖**pipped** *adj syn* see INTOXICATED 1
pippin *n syn* ‖DILLY, ‖corker, crackerjack, dandy, ‖dinger, ‖doozer, humdinger, jim-dandy, ‖lalapalooza, ‖pip
piquant *adj syn* see PUNGENT
rel high-flavored, well-flavored; appetizing, sparkling
con inane, jejune
ant banal
pique *n syn* see OFFENSE 2
rel annoyance, irk, irking, vexation; exasperation, irritation, provocation
pique *vb* **1** *syn* see IRRITATE
2 *syn* see PROVOKE 4
rel prick, punch; ignite
3 *syn* see PRIDE
pirate *n* a robber on the high seas <little boys dreaming of sailing as *pirates*>
syn buccaneer, corsair, freebooter, picaroon, rover, sea dog, sea robber, sea rover, sea wolf
rel viking; privateer; looter, marauder, pillager, plunderer, raider
‖**pirl** *vb syn* see SPIN 1
‖**piroot** *vb syn* see SNOOP
pirouette *vb syn* see SPIN 1
pishposh *n syn* see NONSENSE 2
pit *n* ‖**1** *syn* see GRAVE
2 *syn* see HELL
pit *vb syn* see OPPOSE 1
pitch *vb* **1** *syn* see THROW 1
rel hoist, raise; move
2 *syn* see THROW 2
‖**3** *syn* see PLANT 1
4 *syn* see FALL 2
idiom take a pitch
5 *syn* see PLUNGE 2
rel drop, fall, sink
6 *syn* see TOSS 2
7 *syn* see SEESAW
pitch *n syn* see SPIEL

---

syn synonym(s) *rel* related word(s)
ant antonym(s) *con* contrasted word(s)
idiom idiomatic equivalent(s)
‖ use limited; if in doubt, see a dictionary

rel persuasion

pitch–black *adj* ***syn*** see BLACK 1

pitch–dark *adj* ***syn*** see BLACK 1

pitched *adj* ***syn*** see INCLINED 3

pitch in *vb* **1** to set about doing something energetically <had a lot to do and decided to *pitch in*>
syn buckle (down), fall to, jump (in *or* into), set to, wade (in *or* into)
rel attack, tackle; launch, tee off; begin, commence, start (off *or* out *or* up)
idiom fall to it, fall to work, get busy (*or* cracking), get down to it, get going, get (*or* have) with it, go to it, hop (*or* jump) to it
con dally, dawdle, procrastinate, stall; vacillate
2 ***syn*** see CONTRIBUTE 1

pitching *adj* ***syn*** see INCLINED 3

pitchy *adj* ***syn*** see BLACK 1

piteous *adj* ***syn*** see PITIFUL 1
rel beseeching, entreating, imploring, supplicating; doleful, dolorous, melancholy, plaintive; ruined

pitfall *n* a hidden or obscure source of danger, error, or harm <*pitfalls* that trap the unwary investigator>
syn booby trap, deadfall, mousetrap, springe, trapfall
rel danger, hazard, peril, risk; cobweb, entanglement, mesh(es), toil(s), web; bait, lure, snare, trap

pith *n* **1** ***syn*** see ESSENCE 2
rel center, focus, nucleus; meaning, meaningfulness
2 ***syn*** see SUBSTANCE 2
idiom the long and (the) short
3 ***syn*** see CENTER 3
rel fulcrum; hub
4 ***syn*** see IMPORTANCE

pithy *adj* being rich in meaning and tersely cogent in expression <a *pithy* summary>
syn compact, epigrammatic, marrowy, meaty; *compare* CONCISE
rel brief, concise, lean, short, short and sweet, succinct; crisp, curt, terse; effective, forceful; meaningful, significant, substantial
idiom brief and to the point, down to brass tacks, right to the point
con flatulent, inflated, tumid, turgid; prolix, verbose, wordy
ant diffuse

pitiable *adj* **1** ***syn*** see PITIFUL 1
2 ***syn*** see CONTEMPTIBLE
rel miserable, wretched; deplorable, lamentable

pitiful *adj* **1** arousing or deserving pity <*pitiful* refugees driven from their homes>
syn commiserable, pathetic, piteous, pitiable, poor, rueful
rel affecting, moving, touching; miserable, woeful, wretched; heartrending
2 ***syn*** see CONTEMPTIBLE

pitiless *adj* devoid of or unmoved by pity <a *pitiless* concentration camp guard>
syn merciless, unmerciful, unpitying; *compare* UNFEELING 2
rel coldhearted, hardhearted, heartless, ironhearted, marblehearted, stony, stonyhearted, uncompassionate, unfeeling; barbarous, brutal, cruel, cutthroat, inhumane, savage
idiom lacking bowels of compassion, without an ounce of pity
con compassionate, humane, sympathetic; clement, merciful; tender, warmhearted
ant pitying

pittance *n* a small, often barely sufficient amount or allowance <a *pittance* of an education> <worked for a mere *pittance*>
syn dribble, driblet, ‖scrimption
rel bit, mite, scrap, smidgen, trace; inadequacy, insufficiency
idiom a drop in the bucket, cheeseparings and candle ends
con abundance, opulence, plenty, wealth

pity *n* sympathetic feeling for one suffering, distressed, or unhappy <felt the deepest *pity* for the prisoners>
syn commiseration, compassion, rue, ruth, sympathy
rel dejection, distress, melancholy, sadness, sorrow; charity, clemency, lenity, mercy
con contempt, disdain, disgust, scorn

pity *vb* ***syn*** see COMPASSIONATE

pivot *vb* ***syn*** see TURN 6

pivotal *adj* ***syn*** see CENTRAL 1
rel essential, vital; momentous; capital, principal

pixie *n* **1** ***syn*** see FAIRY
2 ***syn*** see SCAMP

pixie *adj* ***syn*** see PLAYFUL 1

pixieish *adj* ***syn*** see PLAYFUL 1

pixilated *adj* **1** ***syn*** see PLAYFUL 1
2 ***syn*** see INTOXICATED 1

placard *n* ***syn*** see POSTER

placard *vb* ***syn*** see POST

placate *vb* ***syn*** see PACIFY
rel comfort; tranquilize
idiom lay the dust
con anger, incense, infuriate, madden; excite, pique, provoke, stimulate
ant enrage

place *n* **1** the portion of space occupied by or chosen for something <the *place* where we'll meet>
syn location, locus, point, position, site, situation, spot, station, where
rel district, locality, vicinity; area, region, tract, zone; field, province, territory
2 ***syn*** see STATUS 1
3 ***syn*** see JOB 2

place *vb* **1** ***syn*** see SET 1
2 ***syn*** see ESTIMATE 3
3 ***syn*** see IDENTIFY
rel know, tell; nail, peg
idiom put one's finger on

placed *adj* ***syn*** see SITUATED
ant displaced

placid *adj* **1** ***syn*** see CALM 1
rel irenic, peaceful, serene, unagitated, unstirring
ant roiled
2 ***syn*** see CALM 2

rel detached, inexcitable, unmoved
con fidgety, jittery, jumpy, skittery; agitated
ant choleric

plague *n* **1** an epidemic disease causing a high mortality rate <smallpox finally ceased to be a *plague* in those nations>
syn curse, pestilence, scourge
rel infestation, invasion; affliction, disease; epidemic; ravage
2 ***syn*** see ANNOYANCE 3
rel bane, curse
3 ***syn*** see EPIDEMIC

plague *vb* ***syn*** see WORRY 1
rel chafe, gall; badger, bait, hassle, hector, hound, ride; afflict, torment

plain *adj* **1** free from all ostentation or superficial embellishment <just give the *plain* facts>
syn discreet, dry, homely, inelaborate, modest, simple, unadorned, unbeautified, undecorated, unelaborate, unembellished, unembroidered, ungarnished, unornamented, unostentatious, unpretentious
rel muted, restrained; austere, bald, bare, severe, spartan, stark, unluxurious; homespun
con adorned, beautified, elaborate, embellished, embroidered, exaggerated; high-flown, ostentatious, pretentious; flamboyant, rococo
ant rich
2 ***syn*** see STRAIGHT 3
3 ***syn*** see CLEAR 5
rel broad, unmistakable; legible
ant abstruse
4 ***syn*** see FRANK
rel unfeigned; abrupt
idiom plain and open
5 lacking allure without being positively ugly <a *plain* woman, drably dressed>
syn homely, unalluring, unattractive, unbeauteous, unbeautiful, uncomely, unhandsome, unpretty
rel plain-featured; inelegant; ordinary, plain Jane, unremarkable; ill-favored
idiom not much for looks, not much to look at, short on looks
con alluring, attractive, beautiful, comely, handsome; elegant; striking; knockout, sensational
6 ***syn*** see ORDINARY 1

plainclothesman *n* ***syn*** see DETECTIVE

plain dealing *adj* ***syn*** see STRAIGHTFORWARD 2

plain Jane *adj* ***syn*** see ORDINARY 1

plainness *n* ***syn*** see CLARITY
ant abstruseness

plainspoken *adj* ***syn*** see FRANK

plaintive *adj* ***syn*** see MELANCHOLY 2
rel deploring, lamenting, wailing; piteous, pitiful; sad, saddening

plan *n* **1** a method devised for making or doing something or attaining an end <each company had a *plan* for increasing profits>
syn blueprint, design, game plan, project, scheme, strategy
rel conception, idea, notion; ground plan, projection, projet; intent, intention, platform, purpose; means, method, way
idiom course (*or* plan) of action
2 ***syn*** see INTENTION
rel policy
3 ***syn*** see ORDER 8

plan *vb* **1** ***syn*** see DESIGN 3
2 to formulate a plan for arranging, realizing, or achieving something <*planned* next year's program>
syn arrange, blueprint, cast, chart, design, devise, ||dope out, project; *compare* DESIGN 3
rel contemplate, meditate; cut out, draft, outline, sketch; figure (out), think (out); formulate, work out; organize
3 ***syn*** see INTEND 2
idiom be planning (*or* counting) on, have all intentions of, have every intention of

planate *n* ***syn*** see LEVEL

plane *vb* ***syn*** see EVEN 1

plane *adj* ***syn*** see LEVEL

planet *n, used with the* ***syn*** see EARTH 1

planetary *adj* **1** ***syn*** see HUGE
2 ***syn*** see UNIVERSAL 2

plangent *adj* ***syn*** see RESONANT

plant *vb* **1** to put or set into the ground for growth <*plant* corn>
syn ||pitch, put in, seed, sow
rel drill; broadcast, dust, scatter; seed down
con crop, gather, harvest, reap
2 ***syn*** see HIDE
3 ***syn*** see BURY 1

plant *n* ***syn*** see FACTORY

plash *vb* ***syn*** see SPLASH

plaster *vb* ***syn*** see SMEAR 1

||**plastered** *adj* ***syn*** see INTOXICATED 1

plastic *adj* susceptible of being modified in form or nature <the *plastic* quality of modeling clay>
syn adaptable, ductile, malleable, moldable, pliable, pliant, supple
rel elastic, flexible, resilient, supple, workable; impressionable, influenceable, suggestible, susceptible; amenable, bending, giving, tractable, yielding
con inflexible, rigid, stiff; accepted, customary, prevailing, set, standard, wonted

plat *n* ***syn*** see LOT 3

plateau *n* a usually extensive level land area raised sharply above adjacent land on at least one side <the *plateaus* of central Bolivia>
syn table, tableland, upland
rel mesa
con dale, glen, vale, valley; bottom, bottomland, lowland

platitude *n* ***syn*** see COMMONPLACE
rel inanity, insipidity, vapidity; mawkishness, sentimentality

platoon *n* ***syn*** see GROUP 3

plaudit *n, usu* **plaudits** *pl* ***syn*** see APPLAUSE
rel kudos

plausibility *n* ***syn*** see VERISIMILITUDE

---

syn synonym(s) ***rel*** related word(s)
ant antonym(s) ***con*** contrasted word(s)
idiom idiomatic equivalent(s)
|| use limited; if in doubt, see a dictionary

plausible *adj* ***syn*** see BELIEVABLE
rel likely, possible, probable; presumable
con impossible, improbable, unlikely
ant implausible

play *n* **1** activity engaged in for amusement <children need periods of work and *play*>
syn disport, diversion, fun, recreation, sport
rel amusement, entertainment; frolic, gambol, romp; delectation, delight, enjoyment, pleasure
con business, duty, obligation; labor; drudgery
ant work
2 ***syn*** see FUN 1
rel sportiveness
ant earnest
3 ***syn*** see TRICK 1
4 ***syn*** see USE 1
5 ***syn*** see ROOM 3

play *vb* **1** to engage in an activity for amusement or recreation <*played* outside for hours>
syn disport, recreate, sport
rel amuse, divert, engage, entertain; frolic, gambol, rollick, romp
con labor, toil, travail; drudge, fag, slave
ant work
2 ***syn*** see FIDDLE 1
3 ***syn*** see TREAT 2
4 ***syn*** see MANIPULATE 2
5 ***syn*** see ACT 1
6 ***syn*** see GAMBLE 1

play (around) *vb* ***syn*** see PHILANDER

play (down) *vb* ***syn*** see SOFT-PEDAL
rel restrain; mute, soften
ant play (up)

play (off) *vb* ***syn*** see OPPOSE 1

play (up) *vb* ***syn*** see EMPHASIZE
idiom make a (big) production of
ant play (down)

playact *vb* ***syn*** see ACT 1

playactor *n* ***syn*** see ACTOR 1

player *n* ***syn*** see ACTOR 1

playful *adj* **1** given to or characterized by play, jests, or tricks <in a *playful* mood>
syn antic, coltish, elvish, frisky, frolicsome, gamesome, impish, kittenish, larkish, ||mischief-ful, mischievous, pixie, pixieish, pixilated, prankful, prankish, pranky, puckish, roguish, sportive, waggish, wicked
rel gay, lighthearted, whimsical; dashing, larking, lively, sprightly; blithe, jocund, jolly, jovial, merry; gleeful, hilarious, mirthful
idiom as playful as a kitten (*or* colt), feeling one's oats
con grim, stern, stolid; grave, serious
2 ***syn*** see ANTIC 2

||play–pretty *n* ***syn*** see TOY 2

plaything *n* ***syn*** see TOY 2

playwright *n* one who writes plays <a famous Broadway *playwright*>
syn dramatist, dramatizer, dramaturge
rel librettist; scenarist

plaza *n* ***syn*** see COMMON 2

plea *n* **1** ***syn*** see EXCUSE 1
rel extenuation, mitigation, palliation; apology; out; vindication
2 ***syn*** see PRAYER
rel overture; call, cry
idiom solemn entreaty (*or* plea)

plead *vb* ***syn*** see BEG

pleasance *n* ***syn*** see AMENITY 1

pleasant *adj* **1** highly acceptable to the mind or senses <a *pleasant* personality><a *pleasant* respite>
syn agreeable, congenial, favorable, good, grateful, gratifying, nice, pleasing, pleasurable, pleasureful, welcome
rel cheerful, cheering, cheery, glad, joyful, joyous; alluring, attractive, charming, pretty; convivial, engaging
con displeasing, distasteful; harsh; obnoxious, repellent, repelling, repugnant, repulsive
ant unpleasant
2 ***syn*** see FAIR 2

pleasantness *n* ***syn*** see AMENITY 1
rel goodness, niceness
ant unpleasantness

please *vb* **1** ***syn*** see WILL
2 to give or be a source of pleasure to <her work *pleased* him>
syn arride, delectate, delight, gladden, gratify, happify, pleasure
rel content, satisfy, suit; amuse, tickle, titillate; regale, rejoice; overjoy
con vex; annoy; anger
ant displease
3 ***syn*** see SUIT 6

pleasing *adj* ***syn*** see PLEASANT 1
rel satisfactory, suitable; enchanting, winning; adorable, darling, delightful
ant displeasing, repellent

pleasurable *adj* ***syn*** see PLEASANT 1
ant unpleasurable

pleasure *n* **1** ***syn*** see WILL 1
2 the agreeable emotion accompanying the expectation, acquisition, or possession of something good or desirable <the *pleasures* and pains of growing up>
syn delectation, delight, enjoyment, fruition, joy, joyance; *compare* ENJOYMENT 1
rel bliss, felicity, happiness; kick, thrill
con vexation; annoyance; anger; affliction, distress, sorrow, trouble
ant displeasure
3 ***syn*** see ENJOYMENT 1
ant displeasure

pleasure *vb* ***syn*** see PLEASE 2

pleasure dome *n* ***syn*** see RESORT 3

pleasureful *adj* ***syn*** see PLEASANT 1

pleasuremonger *n* ***syn*** see HEDONIST

pleb *n* **plebs** *pl* ***syn*** see COMMONALTY

plebeian *adj* ***syn*** see IGNOBLE 1
ant patrician

plebeians *n pl* ***syn*** see COMMONALTY
ant patricians

plebs *n* **plebes** *pl* ***syn*** see COMMONALTY
rel peasantry, peasants
ant patricians, patriciate

pledge *n* **1** something given or held as a sign of another's good faith or intentions <the new school

is the *pledge* given by the community to its children>
syn earnest, pawn, security, token, warrant; *compare* GUARANTEE 1, PROMISE
rel bail, bond, guarantee, guaranty, surety, warranty; promise, word; oath, vow
2 ***syn*** see WORD 8

pledge *vb* **1** ***syn*** see PAWN
2 ***syn*** see DRINK 2
3 ***syn*** see PROMISE 1
rel bind, tie; commit, confide, consign, entrust
idiom give (*or* make) a solemn pledge, pledge one's honor
4 ***syn*** see VOW

plenteous *adj* ***syn*** see PLENTIFUL
rel full, hearty; fruitful, galore, prolific; luxurious, opulent, sumptuous; lavish, prodigal, profuse, profusive, rampant, rife

plentiful *adj* being more than sufficient without being excessive <a *plentiful* harvest>
syn abundant, ample, bounteous, bountiful, copious, generous, liberal, plenteous, plenty
rel enough, sufficient; fulsome, rich, unstinted; excessive, extravagant, overabundant, overflowing, superabundant; abounding, bumper, bursting, swarming, swimming, teeming
con deficient, exiguous, meager, skimpy; inadequate, insufficient
ant scant, scanty

plenty *n* ***syn*** see MUCH
rel abundance, cornucopia

plenty *adj* ***syn*** see PLENTIFUL

pleonasm *n* ***syn*** see VERBIAGE 1

plethora *n* ***syn*** see EXCESS 1
rel much, plenty; many; deluge, flood

pliable *adj* ***syn*** see PLASTIC
rel manipulable, manipulatable
con unadaptable, unflexible, unmalleable, unpliant
ant unpliable

pliant *adj* ***syn*** see PLASTIC
rel spongy
ant unpliant

plica *n* ***syn*** see WRINKLE

plight *vb* ***syn*** see VOW
idiom plight one's honor

plight *n* ***syn*** see PROMISE

plight *n* ***syn*** see PREDICAMENT
rel quandary

plighted *adj* ***syn*** see ENGAGED 2

plink *vb* ***syn*** see TINKLE 1

plod *vb* **1** to walk laboriously and heavily <slowly *plodded* across the sodden field>
syn footslog, ‖plodge, plunther, slog, slop, stodge, toil, ‖trash, trudge; *compare* TRAMP 1
rel tramp, trample, tromp; stamp, stomp, stump; flounder, wallow
2 ***syn*** see DRUDGE
idiom plug away at it

plodding *adj* ***syn*** see DULL 9

‖**plodge** *vb* ***syn*** see PLOD 1

plot *n* **1** ***syn*** see LOT 3
2 a secret plan for accomplishing a usually evil or unlawful end <an assassination *plot*>
syn cabal, conspiracy, covin, intrigue, machination, practice, scheme
rel design, plan; connivance, conniving; collusion, complicity; contraption, contrivance, device; artifice, maneuver, ruse, stratagem, trick

plot *vb* to work out a plan especially for something unlawful or wrong <*plotted* the overthrow of the government>
syn cogitate, ‖collogue, collude, connive, conspire, contrive, devise, intrigue, machinate, scheme (out)
rel lay; brew, concoct, cook (up), hatch, set up; finagle, maneuver

plow *vb* to cut into and work the surface of (soil) <*plow* a field>
syn break, plow up, turn, turn over
rel cultivate, till; fallow; ‖backset; furrow, list, ridge, trench; harrow, rake

plow up *vb* ***syn*** see PLOW
rel plow out

ploy *n* ***syn*** see TRICK 1

pluck *n* ***syn*** see COURAGE

‖**plucked** *adj* ***syn*** see BRAVE 1

plucky *adj* ***syn*** see BRAVE 1
idiom full of pluck (*or* spunk)
con feeble, weak
ant pluckless

plug *n* ***syn*** see PUFF 3

plug *vb* **1** ***syn*** see FILL 1
rel pack; cork
2 ***syn*** see PROMOTE 3

plugging *n* ***syn*** see WORK 2

plug–ugly *n* ***syn*** see TOUGH

plum *n* ***syn*** see REWARD
rel catch, find

‖**plumb** *adv* ***syn*** see WELL 3

plumb *vb* ***syn*** see SOUND

plumb *adj* ***syn*** see VERTICAL

plumbless *adj* ***syn*** see BOTTOMLESS 2
con plumbable

plumb–line *vb* ***syn*** see SOUND

plumbness *n* ***syn*** see VERTICALITY

plume *vb* ***syn*** see PRIDE

plummet *vb* to decrease suddenly and sharply in financial value or price <the stock *plummeted* 60 points when the story broke>
syn dip, drop, fall, nose-dive, plunge, skid, tumble
rel decline, decrease, descend, sink; dump; precipitate; collapse, crash
idiom take a sudden downturn (*or* downtrend)
con increase; rise; shoot up
ant skyrocket, soar

plummetless *adj* ***syn*** see BOTTOMLESS 2

plump *adj* ***syn*** see ROTUND 2
rel fleshy, portly
idiom plump as a partridge
ant skinny

plumpish *adj* ***syn*** see ROTUND 2

---

syn synonym(s) ***rel*** related word(s)
ant antonym(s) ***con*** contrasted word(s)
idiom idiomatic equivalent(s)
‖ use limited; if in doubt, see a dictionary

idiom like a butterball

plumpy *adj* ***syn*** see ROTUND 2

plunder *vb* ***syn*** see ROB 1

plunder *n* **1** ***syn*** see SPOIL
‖**2** ***syn*** see PERSONAL EFFECTS

plunderage *n* ***syn*** see SPOIL

plunderer *n* ***syn*** see MARAUDER

plunge *vb* **1** ***syn*** see THRUST 2
2 to thrust or cast oneself or something into or as if into deep water <*plunged* into the crowd>
syn burst, dive, drive, lunge, pitch, ‖splunge; *compare* RUSH 1
rel dip, immerse, submerge; plump, plunk; propel, push, shove, thrust; boil, charge, fling, rush, tear
idiom plunge headlong
con ease, glide, slide, slip
3 ***syn*** see FALL 2
idiom take a plunge
4 ***syn*** see PLUMMET
idiom drop like a rock, take a downward plunge

plunther *vb* ***syn*** see PLOD 1

plus *n* ***syn*** see EXCESS 2

plus *vb* ***syn*** see INCREASE 1

plush *adj* ***syn*** see LUXURIOUS 3
idiom fit for the gods

plushy *adj* ***syn*** see LUXURIOUS 3

plutonian *adj* **1** ***syn*** see INFERNAL 1
2 ***syn*** see INFERNAL 2

plutonic *adj* **1** ***syn*** see INFERNAL 1
2 ***syn*** see INFERNAL 2

ply *vb* **1** ***syn*** see HANDLE 2
rel exercise; function
2 ***syn*** see EXERT

pneuma *n* ***syn*** see SOUL 1

pneumatic *adj* ***syn*** see AIRY 1

pocket *n* ***syn*** see DEAD END

pocket *vb* **1** ***syn*** see STEAL 1
2 ***syn*** see ACCEPT 2

pocket *adj* **1** ***syn*** see TINY
2 ***syn*** see CONDENSED
3 ***syn*** see FINANCIAL

pocket edition *n* ***syn*** see MODEL 1

pocket money *n* money for small personal expenses or incidentals <he had spent all his *pocket money* on candy and snacks>
syn pin money, spending money
rel petty cash; change, small change
con fortune, resources; income

pocket–size *adj* ***syn*** see TINY

pococurante *adj* ***syn*** see INDIFFERENT 2

pod *n* **1** ***syn*** see HULL
2 ***syn*** see POTBELLY

podex *n* ***syn*** see BUTTOCKS

podgy *adj* ***syn*** see ROTUND 2

Podunk *n* ***syn*** see BURG

poem *n* a particular example of metrical writing <recited a *poem* by Robert Frost>
syn poesy, poetry, rhyme, rune, verse

poesy *n* **1** ***syn*** see POEM
2 ***syn*** see POETRY 1

poet *n* a writer of verse <a *poet* to stir men's souls>
syn bard, muse, Parnassian
rel jongleur, rhapsodist, trouvère, trouveur; balladist, elegist, idyllist, lyricist, lyrist, odist, satirist, sonneteer, sonnetist

poetaster *n* a writer of mediocre or inferior verse <*poetasters* who churn out tasteless verse>
syn balladmonger, bardlet, bardling, poeticule, poetling, rhymer, rhymester, verseman, versemonger, verser, versesmith, versificator, versifier

poeticule *n* ***syn*** see POETASTER

poetling *n* ***syn*** see POETASTER

poetry *n* **1** metrical language or writing <studied the *poetry* of Milton>
syn poesy, rhyme, song, verse
2 ***syn*** see POEM

poignance *n* ***syn*** see PATHOS

poignancy *n* ***syn*** see PATHOS

poignant *adj* **1** ***syn*** see PUNGENT
ant dull
2 ***syn*** see MOVING 2
rel agitating, disturbing, perturbing

point *n* **1** one unitary part of a whole made up of two or more parts <listened to each *point* of his opponent's argument>
syn article, detail, element, item, particular, thing; *compare* ELEMENT 2
rel characteristic, feature, trait; constituent, material, part; circumstantial, circumstantiality
con aggregate, sum, total, whole
2 ***syn*** see CHARACTERISTIC 1
3 the quality of an utterance that arouses interest and produces an effect <a book that lacks *point*>
syn cogency, effectiveness, force, punch, validity, validness
rel appositeness, convincement, significance, suggestiveness; appeal, attraction, charm, fascination, interest
4 ***syn*** see SUBJECT 2
5 ***syn*** see TIP
6 ***syn*** see PLACE 1
7 a particular limited and often critical interval of time <at that *point* he was interrupted>
syn instant, juncture, moment
rel brink, threshold, verge
idiom point in time
8 ***syn*** see VERGE 2
9 a sharp or slender and tapering terminal part <the *point* of a sword>
syn apex, cusp, tip
rel awn, barb, jag, nib, prong, snag, spike, tag, tine
10 ***syn*** see PROMONTORY
11 a tiny mark or spot <saw a distant *point* of light>
syn dot, flyspeck, mote, speck
rel bit, fleck, iota, minim, mite, particle, scrap, tittle, trace

point *vb* **1** ***syn*** see PUNCTUATE
2 to tend to show something as probable <all signs *point* to an economic recovery>
syn hint, imply, indicate, suggest; *compare* SUGGEST 1
idiom lead one to expect, make (*or* give) promise of, offer a good prospect of
3 ***syn*** see DIRECT 2

point (out) *vb* ***syn*** see REFER 3
point (to) *vb* ***syn*** see TESTIFY 1
pointed *adj* **1** tapering to a thin tip <a *pointed* rock>
syn acicular, aciculate, acuminate, acuminous, acute, cuspidate, mucronate, peaked, peaky, piked, pointy, sharp
con dull, rounded
ant blunt
2 ***syn*** see NOTICEABLE
pointer *n* ***syn*** see TIP
pointful *adj* ***syn*** see RELEVANT
pointless *adj* ***syn*** see SENSELESS 5
||**pointsman** *n* ***syn*** see POLICEMAN
pointy *adj* ***syn*** see POINTED 1
poise *vb* **1** ***syn*** see STABILIZE
rel back, support, uphold
con agitate, disturb, upset; overthrow, overturn, subvert
2 ***syn*** see HANG 3
poise *n* **1** ***syn*** see BALANCE 1
2 ***syn*** see TACT
rel aplomb, assurance, confidence, self-possession; calmness, serenity, tranquillity; dignity, elegance, grace
poised *adj* ***syn*** see CALM 2
poison *n* something that harms, interferes with, or destroys the activity, progress, or welfare of something else <the negative publicity was *poison* for her political ambitions>
syn bane, contagion, venom, virus
rel adulteration, contamination, corruption, sophistication
con catholicon, elixir, panacea
ant antidote
poison *vb* ***syn*** see DEBASE 1
poison *adj* ***syn*** see POISONOUS
poisonous *adj* having the properties or effect of poison <*poisonous* propaganda>
syn mephitic, poison, toxic, toxicant, venomous, virulent
rel miasmal, miasmatic, miasmic, pestilent, pestilential; deadly, fatal, lethal, mortal; baneful, deleterious, detrimental, nocuous, noxious, pernicious
con corrective, countervailing, emendatory, healing, remedial
ant antidotal
||**poke** *n* ***syn*** see BAG 1
poke *vb* **1** to thrust something into so as to stir up, urge on, or attract attention <he *poked* the man in front of him to get his attention>
syn dig, jab, jog, nudge, prod, punch
rel push, shove, thrust; arouse, awaken, rouse, stir; excite, galvanize, provoke, quicken, stimulate
2 ***syn*** see SNOOP
3 ***syn*** see DELAY 2
4 ***syn*** see BULGE
poke *n* **1** a quick thrust with or as if with the hand <gave him a *poke* in the ribs with my finger>
syn dig, jab, punch, stab
rel bunt, butt; boost, push, shove
2 ***syn*** see CUFF
3 ***syn*** see DUNCE
poker-faced *adj* **1** ***syn*** see SERIOUS 1
2 ***syn*** see NEUTRAL
||**pokey** *n* ***syn*** see JAIL
poky *adj* ***syn*** see DULL 9
polar *adj* ***syn*** see OPPOSITE
polemical *adj* ***syn*** see CONTENTIOUS 2
polestar *n* ***syn*** see CENTER 2
police *n* ***syn*** see POLICEMAN
||**police constable** *n* ***syn*** see POLICEMAN
policeman *n* a member of a police force <ask the *policeman* for directions>
syn ||bluebottle, bluecoat, ||bobby, ||bull, ||constable, cop, ||copper, Dogberry, ||flatfoot, ||fuzz, ||gendarme, gumshoe, ||harness bull (*or* cop), ||heat, John Law, man, ||nab, officer, ||paddy, patrolman, peace officer, ||peeler, ||pig, ||pointsman, police, ||police constable, police officer, ||rozzer, ||trap
police officer *n* ***syn*** see POLICEMAN
policy *n* ***syn*** see COURSE 3
polish *vb* **1** to make smooth or glossy usually by friction <*polished* the silver>
syn buff, burnish, furbish, glance, glaze, gloss, rub, shine
rel brighten, scour, scrub
con roughen
2 to give an elegant finish to <attended classes to *polish* his manners>
syn perfect, refine, round, sleek, slick, smooth
rel better, improve, mend; brush up, furbish, touch up; mature, perfect
polish *n* **1** ***syn*** see LUSTER
2 ***syn*** see CULTURE
polished *adj* **1** ***syn*** see LUSTROUS 1
2 ***syn*** see SLEEK
3 ***syn*** see GENTEEL 1
polish off *vb* **1** ***syn*** see CONSUME 5
2 ***syn*** see EAT UP 1
polite *adj* ***syn*** see CIVIL 2
rel attentive, considerate, thoughtful
ant impolite
politic *adj* **1** ***syn*** see EXPEDIENT
rel astute, perspicacious, sagacious, shrewd
2 ***syn*** see TACTFUL
rel judicious, wise
polity *n* ***syn*** see COURSE 3
poll *n* ***syn*** see HEAD 1
pollard *vb* ***syn*** see TOP 1
polloi *n* ***syn*** see RABBLE 2
pollute *vb* **1** ***syn*** see CONTAMINATE 1
2 ***syn*** see CONTAMINATE 2
polluted *adj* **1** ***syn*** see IMPURE 3
2 ***syn*** see INTOXICATED 1
Pollyanna *n* ***syn*** see OPTIMIST
rel daydreamer, wishful thinker
Pollyannaish *adj* ***syn*** see OPTIMISTIC
Pollyannaism *n* ***syn*** see OPTIMISM
||**polly-fox** *vb* ***syn*** see SKIRT 3

---

syn synonym(s) ***rel*** related word(s)
ant antonym(s) ***con*** contrasted word(s)
idiom idiomatic equivalent(s)
|| use limited; if in doubt, see a dictionary

poltroon *n* ***syn*** see COWARD
poltroon *adj* ***syn*** see COWARDLY
poltroonish *adj* ***syn*** see COWARDLY
polyandrium *n* ***syn*** see CEMETERY
polychromatic *adj* ***syn*** see VARIEGATED
polychrome *adj* ***syn*** see VARIEGATED
polypragmatic *adj* ***syn*** see IMPERTINENT 2
polypragmatist *n* ***syn*** see BUSYBODY
pomp *n* ***syn*** see DISPLAY 2
rel ceremonial, ceremony, form, formality, liturgy, ritual
pom–pom girl *n* ***syn*** see PROSTITUTE
pompous *adj* **1** characterized by or exhibiting self-importance <a *pompous* old fool>
syn arrogant, bloated, important, magisterial, pontifical, puffy, self-important, stuffy, wiggy; *compare* EGOCENTRIC 2, PROUD 1
rel conceited, narcissistic, self-conceited, stuck-up, vain, vainglorious; affected, highfalutin, hoity-toity, pretentious; presumptuous, self-centered, selfish; flaunting, flossy, ostentatious
con natural, unaffected, unpretentious; humble, meek, plain, simple; modest, unassuming
2 ***syn*** see RHETORICAL
ponder *vb* **1** ***syn*** see CONSIDER 1
rel appraise, evaluate
2 to consider or examine attentively or deliberately <*ponder* the best way to do it>
syn ‖chaw, deliberate, meditate, mull (over), muse, revolve, roll, ruminate, turn over
rel cogitate, reason, reflect, speculate, think; brood, debate, dwell
pondering *adj* ***syn*** see THOUGHTFUL 1
ponderous *adj* **1** ***syn*** see HEAVY 1
rel substantial; burdensome, onerous, oppressive
2 lacking all lightness and grace <a *ponderous* prose style>
syn elephantine, heavy-footed, heavy-handed, uninspired
rel dreary, dry, dull, humdrum, lifeless, monotonous, pedestrian, plodding, stodgy, stuffy; arid, barren; flat, insipid, savorless, vapid; buckram, cardboard, muscle-bound, stiff, stilted, wooden
con sparkling, vivid; easy, natural, relaxed, supple, unlabored
3 ***syn*** see UNWIELDY
pontifical *adj* ***syn*** see POMPOUS 1
pontificate *vb* ***syn*** see LORD
pony *n* a literal translation of a foreign language text used especially surreptitiously by students in rendering a lesson <had his *pony* hidden in his lap>
syn crib, trot
‖**pooch** *n* ***syn*** see DOG 1
pooh *n* ***syn*** see RASPBERRY
pooh–bah *n* ***syn*** see NOTABLE 1
pooh–pooh *n* ***syn*** see RASPBERRY
pooh–pooh *vb* ***syn*** see DISMISS 5
pool *n* a small body of standing liquid <saw the *pool* of blood on the floor>
syn puddle
pool *n* **1** ***syn*** see POT 3
2 ***syn*** see SYNDICATE
poop *n* ***syn*** see FOOL 1
‖**poop** *vb* ***syn*** see EXHAUST 4
poor *adj* **1** lacking money or material possessions <they were so *poor* that the children had no winter coats>
syn beggared, broke, destitute, dirt poor, flat, fortuneless, impecunious, impoverished, indigent, low, necessitous, needy, penurious, poverty-stricken, stone-broke, stony, strapped, unprosperous
rel distressed, embarrassed, pinched, reduced, straitened; bankrupt, bankrupted, insolvent; hardscrabble; moneyless, penceless, penniless, unmoneyed; beggarly, down-and-out, pauperized; underprivileged
idiom down to one's bottom dollar, flat broke, hard up, in need, in penury, in rags, in want, on one's beam-ends, on one's uppers, out at elbows, out of pocket, poor as a church mouse, unable to keep the wolf from the door, unable to make ends meet
con affluent, comfortable, moneyed, ‖oofy, opulent, pecunious, prosperous, wealthy, well-fixed, well-heeled, well-off, well-to-do
ant rich
2 ***syn*** see MEAGER 2
3 ***syn*** see PITIFUL 1
4 ***syn*** see CHEAP 2
5 ***syn*** see INFERIOR 2
6 ***syn*** see BAD 1
poorly *adj* ***syn*** see UNWELL
poorness *n* ***syn*** see POVERTY 1
poor relation *n* ***syn*** see INFERIOR
poor–spirited *adj* ***syn*** see COWARDLY
pop *vb* **1** ***syn*** see STRIKE 2
‖**2** ***syn*** see PAWN
pop *n* ***syn*** see FLING 1
pop *n* ***syn*** see FATHER 1
pop (in) *vb* ***syn*** see VISIT 2
popinjay *n* ***syn*** see FOP
pop off *vb* **1** ***syn*** see GO 2
2 ***syn*** see DIE 1
poppa *n* ***syn*** see FATHER 1
popping *adj* ***syn*** see BUSTLING
poppycock *n* ***syn*** see NONSENSE 2
popsy *n* ***syn*** see GIRL FRIEND 1
populace *n* ***syn*** see COMMONALTY
popular *adj* **1** ***syn*** see PUBLIC 4
2 ***syn*** see DEMOCRATIC
3 ***syn*** see CHEAP 1
4 ***syn*** see PREVAILING
5 ***syn*** see FAVORITE 2
ant unpopular
6 ***syn*** see WELL-KNOWN
ant unpopular
populate *vb* ***syn*** see INHABIT
populous *adj* ***syn*** see MANY
porcine *adj* ***syn*** see FAT 2
pork–barreling *n* ***syn*** see PATRONAGE 3
porky *adj* ***syn*** see FATTY 2
porose *adj* ***syn*** see PERMEABLE
porous *adj* ***syn*** see PERMEABLE
porridge *n* ***syn*** see MISCELLANY 1
port *n* **1** ***syn*** see HARBOR 3

2 ***syn*** see SHELTER 1

port *n* ***syn*** see BEARING 1

portable *adj* capable of being carried or moved about <a *portable* TV>
syn carriageable, portative, transportable
rel convenient, handy, manageable, wieldy
con fixed, stationary

portal *n* ***syn*** see DOOR 1

portative *adj* ***syn*** see PORTABLE

portend *vb* 1 ***syn*** see AUGUR 2
2 ***syn*** see FORETELL

portent *n* 1 ***syn*** see FORETOKEN
2 ***syn*** see WONDER 1

porter *n* ***syn*** see BEARER 2

portion *n* 1 ***syn*** see SHARE 1
2 ***syn*** see FATE
3 ***syn*** see PART 1
4 ***syn*** see RATION

portion *vb* ***syn*** see APPORTION 2

portion (out) *vb* ***syn*** see ADMINISTER 2

portly *adj* ***syn*** see FAT 2

portrait *n* ***syn*** see IMAGE 1

portraiture *n* ***syn*** see REPRESENTATION

portray *vb* ***syn*** see REPRESENT 1
rel photograph; copy, duplicate, reproduce

portrayal *n* ***syn*** see REPRESENTATION

pose *vb* 1 ***syn*** see OFFER 1
2 ***syn*** see PROPOSE 1
rel ask, query, question; confound, puzzle; baffle
3 to assume a particular physical posture <they *posed* for a family portrait>
syn posture, sit
rel peacock, strut
4 to assume an artificial or pretended attitude or character usually to deceive or impress <*posed* as a salesman>
syn attitudinize, masquerade, pass (as *or* for), pass off, posture; *compare* ACT 1
rel fake, feign, pretend, sham; profess, purport; grandstand, show off

pose *n* 1 ***syn*** see POSTURE 1
2 an adopted way of speaking or acting <his reticence is just a *pose*>
syn affectation, air(s), lugs, mannerism, prettyism
rel dog, prettiness; fake, pretense, pretension

pose *vb* ***syn*** see OFFER 1

pose *vb* ***syn*** see PUZZLE

posh *adj* ***syn*** see STYLISH

posit *vb* ***syn*** see PRESUPPOSE

posit *n* ***syn*** see ASSUMPTION 2

position *n* 1 a firmly held point of view or way of regarding something <took a conservative *position* on educational issues>
syn attitude, color, stance, stand; *compare* SIDE 4
rel belief, judgment, opinion, view; angle, slant, standpoint, viewpoint
2 ***syn*** see PLACE 1
3 ***syn*** see STATUS 1
4 ***syn*** see STATUS 2
5 ***syn*** see JOB 2

positioned *adj* ***syn*** see SITUATED

positive *adj* 1 expressed clearly and usually peremptorily <her answer was a *positive* no>
syn categorical, decided, definite, unequivocal
rel clear, unmistakable; decisive, emphatic, energetic, firm, forceful, forcible; explicit, express, specific, unambiguous
con irresolute, uncertain, undecided, unsure
2 ***syn*** see SURE 5
ant doubtful
3 not subject to being disputed or called in question <gave *positive* proof that he had been there>
syn certain, inarguable, incontestable, incontrovertible, indisputable, indubitable, irrebuttable, irrefutable, sure, uncontestable, uncontrovertible, undeniable, undisputable, undoubtable, unequivocal, unquestionable; *compare* DOWNRIGHT 2
rel assured, clear, decisive
con contestable, controvertible, debatable, disputable, doubtful, dubious, inconclusive, questionable, unconvincing
4 ***syn*** see UTTER
5 ***syn*** see ACTUAL 2
6 capable of being constructively applied <*positive* proposals for improving the city>
syn affirmative
rel practical, reasonable, sound
con impractical, unsound, unusable
ant negative
7 ***syn*** see RIGHT-HANDED

positively *adv* ***syn*** see EASILY 2

positure *n* ***syn*** see POSTURE 1

possess *vb* 1 ***syn*** see HAVE 1
2 ***syn*** see BEAR 3

possessed *adj* ***syn*** see CALM 2

possession *n* 1 ***syn*** see OWNERSHIP
2 **possessions** *pl* things one owns usually excluding real property and intangibles <lost all their *possessions* in the fire>
syn belongings, chattels, effects, goods, lares and penates, movables, things
rel appointments, fixtures, furnishings, furniture; accessories, appurtenances, baggage, ||duds, duffle, equipment, impedimenta, paraphernalia, trappings, tricks; havings; tangibles

possessive *adj* ***syn*** see JEALOUS 1

possessor *n* ***syn*** see OWNER

possessorship *n* ***syn*** see OWNERSHIP

possessory *adj* ***syn*** see JEALOUS 1

possibilities *n pl* ***syn*** see POTENTIAL

possible *adj* 1 capable of being realized <a cure is still *possible*>
syn doable, feasible, practicable, viable, workable
rel advisable, expedient; achievable, attainable, available
con futile, hopeless, impracticable
ant impossible
2 ***syn*** see PROBABLE
rel dormant, latent, potential
3 ***syn*** see POTENTIAL 1

---

syn synonym(s) ***rel*** related word(s)
ant antonym(s) ***con*** contrasted word(s)
idiom idiomatic equivalent(s)
|| use limited; if in doubt, see a dictionary

possibly *adv* ***syn*** see PERHAPS
post *vb* to affix to a usual place (as a wall) for public notices <*posted* the notice on the bulletin board>
syn placard, poster
post *vb* ***syn*** see INFORM 2
post *n* ***syn*** see JOB 2
post *vb* ***syn*** see STATION
‖**post** *n* ***syn*** see AUTOPSY
poster *n* a notice or announcement for posting in a public place <nailed the *poster* to the side of the building>
syn affiche, bill, handbill, placard
rel advertisement, announcement, banner, broadside, notice, sign; billboard, signboard
poster *vb* ***syn*** see POST
posterior *adj* **1** ***syn*** see SUBSEQUENT 1
2 situated at or toward the back <the *posterior* part of the animal>
syn after, back, hind, hinder, hindmost, rear, retral
con fore, front
ant anterior
posterior *n* **1** ***syn*** see BACK 1
2 ***syn*** see BUTTOCKS
posterity *n* ***syn*** see OFFSPRING
ant ancestry
posthaste *adv* ***syn*** see FAST 2
posthaste *adj* ***syn*** see FAST 3
posthumous *adj* occurring after one's death <*posthumous* fame>
syn postmortal, postmortem, post-obit, post-obituary
rel delayed, late, retarded
con opportune, seasonable, timely
ant antemortem
postliminary *adj* ***syn*** see SUBSEQUENT 1
postmortal *adj* ***syn*** see POSTHUMOUS
postmortem *adj* ***syn*** see POSTHUMOUS
ant antemortem
postmortem *n* ***syn*** see AUTOPSY
postmortem examination *n* ***syn*** see AUTOPSY
post–obit *adj* ***syn*** see POSTHUMOUS
post–obituary *adj* ***syn*** see POSTHUMOUS
postpone *vb* ***syn*** see DEFER
postulate *vb* **1** ***syn*** see DEMAND 1
2 ***syn*** see PRESUPPOSE
rel affirm, assert, aver, predicate
postulate *n* ***syn*** see ASSUMPTION 2
postulation *n* ***syn*** see ASSUMPTION 2
posture *n* **1** the position or bearing of the body <erect *posture*>
syn attitude, carriage, pose, positure, stance
rel bearing, deportment, mien
2 ***syn*** see STATE 1
rel promptness, quickness, readiness
posture *vb* **1** ***syn*** see POSE 3
2 ***syn*** see POSE 4
posy *n* **1** ***syn*** see FLOWER 1
2 ***syn*** see BOUQUET 1
3 ***syn*** see ANTHOLOGY
pot *n* **1** ***syn*** see FORTUNE 4
2 ***syn*** see BET
3 the total of the bets at stake at one time <lost track of how much was in the *pot*>
syn jackpot, kitty, pool
4 ***syn*** see POTSHOT
‖**5** ***syn*** see POTBELLY
6 ***syn*** see NOTABLE 1
7 ***syn*** see MARIJUANA
‖**8** ***syn*** see TOILET
potable *adj* suitable for drinking <*potable* water>
syn drinkable
rel clean, fresh, pure, uncontaminated, unpolluted
con dirty, foul, impure, polluted, unclean
ant impotable
potable *n* ***syn*** see DRINK 1
potbelly *n* an enlarged, swollen, or protruding abdomen <he had the biggest *potbelly* we had ever seen>
syn bay window, corporation, paunch, pod, ‖pot
potency *n* **1** ***syn*** see POWER 4
ant impotence
2 ***syn*** see EFFICACY 1
3 ***syn*** see ENERGY 2
ant impotence
potent *adj* **1** ***syn*** see POWERFUL 2
ant impotent
2 ***syn*** see STRONG 3
potential *adj* **1** existing in possibility <a *potential* site for the new factory>
syn possible
rel conceivable, imaginable, likely, plausible, probable, thinkable
idiom within the realm (*or* range) of possibility
con existent, extant; doubtful, impossible, questionable; impracticable, unsuitable
ant actual
2 ***syn*** see LATENT
potential *n* something that can develop or become actual <industrial *potential*>
syn possibilities, potentiality
ant actuality, reality
potentiality *n* ***syn*** see POTENTIAL
ant actuality
pother *n* **1** ***syn*** see COMMOTION 4
2 ***syn*** see STIR 1
3 ***syn*** see ANNOYANCE 2
4 ***syn*** see COMMOTION 2
pother *vb* ***syn*** see WORRY 3
pothole *n* a hole, depression, or rut in a road surface <*potholes* all over that stretch of highway>
syn chuckhole, mudhole
pothouse *n* ***syn*** see BAR 5
potpourri *n* ***syn*** see MISCELLANY 1
potshot *n* a critical remark made in a random or sporadic manner <took a few *potshots* at his neighbor's argument>
syn pot, shy, sideswipe
rel cut, crack, dig; gibe, jeer; aspersion, criticism, insult
potted *adj* **1** ***syn*** see CONDENSED
‖**2** ***syn*** see INTOXICATED 1
potter *vb* ***syn*** see FIDDLE 2
potter (away) *vb* ***syn*** see WASTE 2
potter's field *n* ***syn*** see CEMETERY
potty *adj* ‖**1** ***syn*** see LITTLE 3

‖2 ***syn*** see FOOLISH 2
3 ***syn*** see SNOBBISH
‖**potty** *n* ***syn*** see TOILET
pouch *n* ***syn*** see BAG 1
pouch *vb* ***syn*** see BULGE
pouf *n* ***syn*** see QUILT
poule *n* ***syn*** see PROSTITUTE
poultice *n* a soft, usually heated, and sometimes medicated mass spread on cloth and applied to sores or other lesions <slapped a mustard *poultice* over the boil>
syn cataplasm
rel plaster; compress; dressing
pound *vb* **1** ***syn*** see HAMMER 1
2 ***syn*** see BEAT 1
3 ***syn*** see IMPRESS 3
pound *n* ***syn*** see BLOW 1
pour *vb* **1** ***syn*** see DISCHARGE 5
2 to send forth or come forth abundantly <medical supplies *poured* into the stricken area>
syn flow, gush, roll, sluice, stream, surge
rel issue, proceed, spring; course, rill, run, rush, swarm; cascade, cataract; deluge, flood, inundate
3 to rain heavily <it *poured* for two solid days>
syn drench, lash, teem
rel beat; deluge, flood, stream
idiom come down in buckets (*or* torrents), rain cats and dogs
pour *n* ***syn*** see FLOOD 2
pourboire *n* ***syn*** see GRATUITY
pout *vb* **1** ***syn*** see SULK
2 ***syn*** see BULGE
pouts *n pl* ***syn*** see SULK
poverty *n* **1** the state of one with insufficient resources <repeated crop failures had reduced the farmers to *poverty*>
syn beggary, borasca, destituteness, destitution, impecuniousness, impoverishment, indigence, indigency, need, neediness, pauperism, pennilessness, penury, poorness, privation, unprosperousness, want
rel exigency, necessity; juncture, pass, pinch, strait; difficulty, distress, embarrassment; hardship, suffering; mendicancy
idiom hand-to-mouth existence, straitened circumstances
con affluence, comfort, luxury, opulence, prosperity, richness, wealth
ant riches
2 ***syn*** see SCARCITY
poverty–stricken *adj* ***syn*** see POOR 1
powder *vb* **1** ***syn*** see SPRINKLE 1
2 ***syn*** see PULVERIZE 1
powdering *n* ***syn*** see DUSTING
powdery *adj* ***syn*** see FINE 2
power *n* **1** the right or prerogative of determining, ruling, or governing or the exercise of that right or prerogative <party in *power*>
syn authority, command, control, domination, jurisdiction, mastery, might, strings, sway
rel birthright, prerogative, privilege, right; direction, management; ascendancy, dominance, dominion, masterdom, sovereignty, supremacy; superiority; influence, prestige, weight; force, strength
con forcelessness, impotence, weakness
ant impuissance, powerlessness
‖2 ***syn*** see MUCH
3 the ability of a living being to perform in a given way or a capacity for a particular kind of performance <the *power* to think clearly>
syn faculty, function
rel ability, capability, capacity; aptitude, bent, turn; endowment, gift, talent
con inability, incapability, incapacity; inaptness, ineptitude
4 the ability to exert effort for a purpose <raised the productive *power* of the nation>
syn arm, beef, dint, energy, force, might, muscle, potency, puissance, sinew, steam, strength, strong arm, vigor, virtue
rel ability, capability, capacity; effectiveness; dynamism, powder, voltage; dynamis, potentiality; competence, qualification
con inability, incapability, incapacity; ineffectiveness; incompetence
powerful *adj* **1** ***syn*** see STRONG 1
2 having or manifesting power to effect great or striking results <a *powerful* leader>
syn forceful, forcible, mighty, potent, puissant
rel able, capable, competent; effective, effectual, efficacious, efficient; dynamic, energetic, strenuous, vigorous; convincing, great, invincible; authoritative, dominant, influential, weighty
con faulty, feeble, flawed; impotent, inadequate, incompetent, weak
ant powerless
powerfully *adv* ***syn*** see HARD 1
powerless *adj* unable to effect one's purpose, intention, or end <*powerless* to leave>
syn helpless, impotent
rel inactive, inert, passive, supine; decrepit, feeble, infirm, weak; incapable, incompetent, ineffective, unfit
con effective, effectual, efficient; able, capable, competent; potent, puissant
ant powerful
powwow ***syn*** see TALK 4
powwow *vb* ***syn*** see CONFER 2
‖**prabble** *n* ***syn*** see QUARREL
practic *adj* ***syn*** see REALISTIC
practicable *adj* **1** ***syn*** see POSSIBLE 1
ant impracticable
2 ***syn*** see PRACTICAL 2
3 ***syn*** see OPEN 5
ant impracticable
practical *adj* **1** ***syn*** see IMPLICIT 2
2 capable of being turned to use or account <a *practical* knowledge of auto mechanics>
syn functional, handy, practicable, serviceable, useful, utile
con abstract, academic, theoretical

syn synonym(s) ***rel*** related word(s)
ant antonym(s) ***con*** contrasted word(s)
idiom idiomatic equivalent(s)
‖ use limited; if in doubt, see a dictionary

THESAURUS

ant impractical, unpractical
3 *syn* see REALISTIC
ant impractical, unpractical
4 *syn* see EXPERIENCED
practically *adv* **1** *syn* see VIRTUALLY
2 *syn* see ALMOST 2
3 *syn* see NEARLY
practice *vb* *syn* see EXERCISE 3
rel execute, fulfill, perform; follow, pursue; iterate, repeat
practice *n* **1** *syn* see HABIT 1
rel procedure, proceeding, process; method, mode, system
2 *syn* see PLOT 2
3 *syn* see EXERCISE 3
rel use, usefulness, utility; convenance, convention, form, usage
ant theory; precept
practiced *adj* *syn* see EXPERIENCED
ant unpracticed
praetorian *adj* *syn* see CORRUPT 2
praetorian *n* *syn* see DIEHARD 1
pragmatic *n* *syn* see BUSYBODY
pragmatic *adj* *syn* see REALISTIC
pragmatical *adj* *syn* see REALISTIC
pragmatist *n* *syn* see BUSYBODY
praisable *adj* *syn* see WORTHY 1
praise *vb* **1** *syn* see COMMEND 2
ant censure, criticize
2 to glorify and exalt expecially in song or writing <*praised* God for all his blessings>
syn bless, celebrate, cry up, eulogize, extol, glorify, hymn, laud, magnify, panegyrize, psalm, psalmody, resound
rel aggrandize, dignify, distinguish, ennoble, erect, exalt, honor, sublime, uprear; enhance, heighten, intensify; apotheosize; proclaim
idiom sing the praises of
con asperse, calumniate, defame, libel, malign, traduce, vilify; belittle, decry, depreciate, derogate, detract (from), discount, disparage, minimize, opprobriate; censure, criticize, denounce, reprehend, reprobate; abuse, reproach, revile
ant dispraise; blame
praiseful *adj* *syn* see EULOGISTIC
praiseworthy *adj* *syn* see WORTHY 1
ant despicable
‖**pram** *n* *syn* see BABY CARRIAGE
prance *vb* **1** *syn* see SASHAY
2 *syn* see DANCE 1
‖**prang** *vb* *syn* see BUMP 1
‖**prang** *n* *syn* see CRASH 3
prank *n* a mischievous or roguish act <he was always playing *pranks* on his sister>
syn antic, caper, dido(es), frolic, lark, monkeyshine(s), ‖rig, shenanigan, shine(s), ‖skite, tomfoolery, trick, wheeze; *compare* ESCAPADE, TRICK 1
rel fooling, high jinks, horseplay, roughhouse, roughhousing, rowdiness, skylarking; gambol, play, rollick, sport; frivolity, levity, lightness; caprice, conceit, fancy, freak, vagary, whim, whimsy
prank *vb* **1** *syn* see ADORN
2 *syn* see DRESS UP 1
prankful *adj* *syn* see PLAYFUL 1
prankish *adj* *syn* see PLAYFUL 1
pranky *adj* *syn* see PLAYFUL 1
‖**prat** *n* *syn* see TRICK 1
prate *vb* **1** *syn* see CHAT 1
2 *syn* see BOAST
3 *syn* see BABBLE 2
prate *n* *syn* see CHATTER
prater *n* *syn* see CHATTERBOX
prattle *vb* **1** *syn* see CHAT 1
2 *syn* see BABBLE 2
prattle *n* *syn* see CHATTER
prattler *n* *syn* see CHATTERBOX
praxis *n* *syn* see HABIT 1
pray *vb* *syn* see BEG
prayer *n* an earnest and usually a formal request for something <the *prayer* in a bill in equity is the part that specifies the kind of relief sought>
syn appeal, application, entreaty, imploration, imprecation, orison, petition, plea, suit, supplication
rel begging, beseeching, imploring, pleading; adoration, worship
con claim, demand, exaction
prayer *n* *syn* see SUPPLIANT
prayerful *adj* *syn* see DEVOUT
preach *vb* **1** to discourse publicly on a religious subject <*preached* at Sunday services>
syn evangelize, homilize, sermonize
rel minister, mission, missionary; prophesy; address, lecture, speak, talk
2 *syn* see MORALIZE
preach *n* *syn* see SERMON
preacher *n* *syn* see CLERGYMAN
preachify *vb* *syn* see MORALIZE
preaching *n* *syn* see SERMON
preachment *n* *syn* see SERMON
preachy *adj* *syn* see DIDACTIC
preamble *n* *syn* see INTRODUCTION
precarious *adj* **1** *syn* see DOUBTFUL 1
2 *syn* see DELICATE 7
precariousness *n* *syn* see INSTABILITY
precaution *n* *syn* see PRUDENCE 1
precede *vb* **1** to go before in rank, dignity, or importance <the small countries at the conference were *preceded* by the large wealthy ones> <those who still feel that age should *precede* beauty>
syn outrank, rank
2 to go before in time <all-out war was *preceded* by many small raids>
syn antecede, antedate, forerun, pace, predate
rel announce, foreshadow, harbinger, herald, presage
con ensue, supervene
ant follow, succeed
3 to cause to be preceded <*preceded* her address with a welcome to the visitors>
syn introduce, lead, preface, usher
ant follow
precedence *n* *syn* see PRIORITY
precedency *n* *syn* see PRIORITY
precedent *adj* *syn* see PRECEDING
precedently *adv* *syn* see BEFORE 1

preceding *adj* being before especially in time or in arrangement <the *preceding* day>
syn antecedent, anterior, foregoing, former, past, precedent, previous, prior
rel other; preexistent; precursive, precursory; erstwhile, heretofore, hitherto
con coming, ensuing, next, sequent, sequential, subsequent, successive
ant following, succeeding

preceding *prep* ***syn*** see BEFORE 1

precept *n* ***syn*** see LAW 1
rel axiom, fundamental, principle; doctrine, dogma, tenet; behest, bidding, injunction
ant practice; counsel

précieux *adj* ***syn*** see PRECIOUS 4

precinct *n* **1** ***syn*** see QUARTER 2
2 ***syn*** see FIELD
3 precincts *pl* ***syn*** see ENVIRONS 1

precious *adj* **1** of such great value that a suitable price is hard to estimate <a *precious* twelfth century painting>
syn costly, inestimable, invaluable, priceless, valuable; *compare* COSTLY 1
rel choice, exquisite, rare, recherché; treasurable; rich; prizable
idiom of price
con base, common, mean, paltry, poor, rubbishy, shabby, trashy; contemptible, despicable, miserable; claptrap, gimcrack, trumpery
ant cheap; worthless
2 ***syn*** see FAVORITE 1
3 ***syn*** see NICE 1
4 excessively refined <too *precious* to mingle with the common people>
syn affected, alembicated, chichi, la-di-da, overnice, overrefined, précieux; *compare* GENTEEL 3
rel ostentatious, pretentious, showy; artful, sophisticated, studied
con artless, ingenuous, naive, natural, simple, unaffected, unartful, unschooled, unsophisticated, unstudied, untutored; down-to-earth, matter-of-fact, practical, pragmatic, rational

precipitance *n* ***syn*** see HASTE 2

precipitancy *n* ***syn*** see HASTE 2

precipitant *adj* ***syn*** see PRECIPITATE 1

precipitate *n* **1** ***syn*** see SEDIMENT
2 ***syn*** see EFFECT 1

precipitate *adj* **1** characterized by impetuous or unexpected haste <beat a *precipitate* retreat>
syn abrupt, hasty, headlong, hurried, impetuous, precipitant, precipitous, rushing, subitaneous, sudden
rel breakneck, headstrong, hotheaded, impatient, impulsive, madcap, refractory, uncontrolled, willful; unanticipated, unexpected, unforeseen, unlooked-for; overhasty
con leisurely, slow, unhurried
ant deliberate
2 ***syn*** see STEEP 1

precipitateness *n* ***syn*** see HASTE 2

precipitation *n* **1** ***syn*** see HASTE 2
2 ***syn*** see SEDIMENT

precipitous *adj* **1** ***syn*** see PRECIPITATE 1
2 ***syn*** see STEEP 1

précis *n* ***syn*** see COMPENDIUM 1

precise *adj* **1** ***syn*** see DEFINITE 1
2 ***syn*** see CORRECT 2
rel rigid, stringent
con careless, heedless; lax, slack
ant imprecise; loose
3 ***syn*** see PRIM 1
4 distinguished from every other <arrived just at the *precise* moment when he was needed>
syn exact, very
rel specific; individual; particular
con general, inexact, nonspecific
ant imprecise

precisely *adv* **1** ***syn*** see JUST 1
idiom on the button
ant imprecisely; approximately
2 ***syn*** see EVEN 1
3 ***syn*** see EXACTLY 3

preciseness *n* ***syn*** see PRECISION
ant impreciseness

precisian *n* ***syn*** see PURIST

precision *n* the quality or character of what is precise <the *precision* involved in close-tolerance machining>
syn accuracy, correctness, definiteness, definitiveness, definitude, exactitude, exactness, preciseness
rel care, carefulness; attention, heed
con inaccuracy, incorrectness, indefiniteness, inexactness; obscurity, unclearness, vagueness; unreliability, untrustworthiness
ant imprecision

precisionist *n* ***syn*** see PURIST

preclude *vb* ***syn*** see PREVENT 2
rel cease, discontinue, quit, stop

precocious *adj* exceptionally early in development <a *precocious* child, smart beyond her years>
syn advanced, forward; *compare* EARLY 2
rel ahead, early, overearly, oversoon, premature, previous, ‖soon; developed, mature
con backward, undeveloped; dull, slow, slow-witted, sluggish
ant retarded

precogitate *vb* ***syn*** see PREMEDITATE

preconception *n* an attitude, belief, or impression formed beforehand <had a lot of *preconceptions* about a man she'd never met>
syn prejudgment, prepossession; *compare* PREJUDICE
rel illusion; delusion
idiom preconceived notion (*or* idea *or* opinion)

precondition *n* ***syn*** see ESSENTIAL 2

precursor *n* **1** ***syn*** see FORERUNNER 1
2 ***syn*** see FORERUNNER 2

predacious *adj* ***syn*** see RAPACIOUS 1

predate *vb* ***syn*** see PRECEDE 2

predative *adj* ***syn*** see RAPACIOUS 1

predatorial *adj* ***syn*** see RAPACIOUS 1

predatory *adj* ***syn*** see RAPACIOUS 1

---

syn synonym(s) ***rel*** related word(s)
ant antonym(s) ***con*** contrasted word(s)
idiom idiomatic equivalent(s)
‖ use limited; if in doubt, see a dictionary

predecessor *n* ***syn*** see FORERUNNER 2
predestinate *vb* ***syn*** see PREDESTINE 2
predestine *vb* **1** to fix the future of in advance <his treasured scribblings were *predestined* to light a kitchen fire>
syn destine, determine, doom (to), fate, foreordain, predetermine, preform, preordain
rel predecide; prejudge; preestablish
2 to determine by or as if by divine decree or eternal purpose <some believe that God *predestines* individuals to eternal life or to eternal damnation>
syn foredestine, foreordain, predestinate, predetermine, preordain
predetermine *vb* **1** ***syn*** see PREDESTINE 2
2 ***syn*** see PREMEDITATE
3 ***syn*** see PREDESTINE 1
predicament *n* a difficult, perplexing, or trying situation <was in a *predicament,* trying to decide whether or not to take the job>
syn box, corner, deep water, dilemma, fix, hole, hot water, impasse, jam, pickle, plight, quagmire, scrape, soup, spot
rel emergency, exigency, juncture, pass, pinch, strait; asperity, difficulty, hardness, hardship, rigor, vicissitude; Dutch, trouble; condition, posture, situation, state
idiom ||in a bind
predicate *vb* **1** ***syn*** see ASSERT 1
2 ***syn*** see BASE
predict *vb* **1** ***syn*** see FORETELL
2 to conjecture correctly <*predicted* the turn of the market months in advance>
syn call, guess
rel conjecture, presume, suppose, surmise, think; conclude, gather, infer, judge
idiom hazard a conjecture (*or* guess)
prediction *n* something that is predicted <the *prediction* was for a good outcome>
syn cast, forecast, foretelling, prevision, prognosis, prognostication, prophecy, weird
rel conjecture, guess, surmising
predictor *n* ***syn*** see PROPHET
predilection *n* ***syn*** see LEANING 2
predispose *vb* ***syn*** see INCLINE 3
rel impress, strike, sway
con disaffect, disincline, disinterest, indispose
predisposed *adj* ***syn*** see WILLING 1
ant indisposed
predisposition *n* ***syn*** see LEANING 2
ant indisposition
predominant *adj* **1** ***syn*** see DOMINANT 1
ant subordinate
2 ***syn*** see CHIEF 2
predominantly *adv* ***syn*** see GENERALLY 1
predominate *adj* ***syn*** see DOMINANT 1
predominate *vb* ***syn*** see RULE 2
preeminence *n* **1** ***syn*** see SUPREMACY
2 ***syn*** see EMINENCE 1
preeminent *adj* **1** ***syn*** see SUPREME
2 ***syn*** see CHIEF 2
preempt *vb* **1** ***syn*** see APPROPRIATE 1
2 ***syn*** see ARROGATE 1
preen *vb* ***syn*** see PRIDE
preengage *vb* **1** ***syn*** see RESERVE 2
2 ***syn*** see PREPOSSESS 1
preface *n* ***syn*** see INTRODUCTION
preface *vb* ***syn*** see PRECEDE 3
prefatial *adj* ***syn*** see PRELIMINARY
prefatorial *adj* ***syn*** see PRELIMINARY
prefatory *adj* ***syn*** see PRELIMINARY
prefer *vb* **1** ***syn*** see ADVANCE 2
2 ***syn*** see CHOOSE 1
3 ***syn*** see PROPOSE 1
preferable *adj* ***syn*** see BETTER 2
preference *n* **1** ***syn*** see CHOICE 1
rel partiality, predilection, prepossession
2 ***syn*** see ADVANCEMENT 1
preferment *n* ***syn*** see ADVANCEMENT 1
preferred *adj* ***syn*** see FAVORITE 2
prefigurate *vb* ***syn*** see ADUMBRATE 1
prefigure *vb* ***syn*** see ADUMBRATE 1
preform *vb* ***syn*** see PREDESTINE 1
pregnance *n* ***syn*** see PREGNANCY
pregnancy *n* the condition of containing unborn young within the body <she was in the last trimester of her *pregnancy*>
syn gestation, gravidity, pregnance, situation
pregnant *adj* **1** containing unborn young within the body <she was *pregnant* with her second child>
syn big, childing, enceinte, expectant, expecting, gone, gravid, heavy, parous, parturient
idiom in an interesting condition, in the family way, with child (*or* young)
con barren, infertile; delivered; postpartum
2 ***syn*** see EXPRESSIVE
rel consequential, important, momentous, significant, weighty
prehend *vb* ***syn*** see CATCH 1
prehensile *adj* ***syn*** see COVETOUS
preindicate *vb* ***syn*** see ANNOUNCE 2
prejudgment *n* ***syn*** see PRECONCEPTION
prejudice *n* the inclination to take a stand (as in a conflict) usually without just grounds or sufficient information <could not review his competitor's work without *prejudice*>
syn bias, one-sidedness, partiality; *compare* LEANING 2, PRECONCEPTION
rel partisanship
idiom jaundiced eye
con detachment, dispassion, impartiality, indifference, neutrality
ant objectivity
prejudice *vb* **1** ***syn*** see INJURE 1
2 to cause to have opinions formed without due knowledge or examination <*prejudice* a man against his neighbor by innuendo>
syn bias, influence, prepossess; *compare* INCLINE 3, SLANT 3
rel bend, dispose, incline, predispose; angle, skew, slant; prejudge
prejudiced *adj* ***syn*** see BIASED 2
ant unprejudiced; disinterested
prejudicial *adj* **1** ***syn*** see HARMFUL
2 ***syn*** see DISCRIMINATORY
prejudicious *adj* ***syn*** see HARMFUL
prekindergarten *adj* ***syn*** see CHILDISH

preknow *vb* ***syn*** see FORESEE
prelation *n* ***syn*** see ADVANCEMENT 1
prelect *vb* ***syn*** see TALK 7
‖prelim *adj* ***syn*** see PRELIMINARY
preliminary *adj* serving to make ready the way for something that follows <held a *preliminary* discussion to set up the agenda of the conference>
syn inductive, introductory, prefatial, prefatorial, prefatory, ‖prelim, preludial, prelusive, preparative, preparatory, proemial
rel primal, primary; elemental, elementary; basic, fundamental; fitting, preparing, readying
ant postliminary
prelimit *vb* ***syn*** see LIMIT 2
preliterate *adj* ***syn*** see PRIMITIVE 6
prelude *n* ***syn*** see INTRODUCTION
preludial *adj* ***syn*** see PRELIMINARY
prelusion *n* ***syn*** see INTRODUCTION
prelusive *adj* ***syn*** see PRELIMINARY
premature *adj* ***syn*** see EARLY 2
prematurely *adv* ***syn*** see EARLY 2
premeditate *vb* to think on and revolve in the mind beforehand <carefully *premeditating* each step of his plan of campaign>
syn forethink, precogitate, predetermine
rel prearrange, preplan, set up; predecide; prepare
premeditated *adj* ***syn*** see DELIBERATE 1
ant unpremeditated; spontaneous
premier *adj* ***syn*** see FIRST 3
premise *n* ***syn*** see ASSUMPTION 2
premise *vb* ***syn*** see PRESUPPOSE
premium *n* ***syn*** see REWARD
premium *adj* ***syn*** see SUPERIOR 4
premonition *n* ***syn*** see APPREHENSION 3
prename *n* ***syn*** see GIVEN NAME
prenotion *n* ***syn*** see APPREHENSION 3
prentice *n* ***syn*** see NOVICE
prentice *adj* ***syn*** see CRUDE 5
preoccupied *adj* **1** ***syn*** see INTENT
2 ***syn*** see ABSTRACTED
rel absorbed; forgetful
ant unpreoccupied
preoccupy *vb* ***syn*** see PREPOSSESS 1
preordain *vb* **1** ***syn*** see PREDESTINE 1
2 ***syn*** see PREDESTINE 2
preparative *adj* ***syn*** see PRELIMINARY
preparatory *adj* ***syn*** see PRELIMINARY
prepare *vb* **1** to make ready in advance usually for a particular use or disposition <*prepared* rooms for the expected guests>
syn fit, fix, get, make, make up, ready
rel furnish, provide, supply; dower, endow, endue; equip, outfit; dispose, incline, predispose; prime
idiom set the stage (for)
ant unprepare
2 ***syn*** see DRAFT 3
3 ***syn*** see GIRD 3
prepared *adj* ***syn*** see READY 1
ant unprepared
prepatent *adj* ***syn*** see LATENT
prepense *adj* ***syn*** see DELIBERATE 1
prepensely *adv* ***syn*** see INTENTIONALLY
preponderance *n* ***syn*** see SUPREMACY
preponderancy *n* ***syn*** see SUPREMACY
preponderant *adj* ***syn*** see DOMINANT 1
preponderate *vb* ***syn*** see RULE 2
preponderation *n* ***syn*** see SUPREMACY
prepossess *vb* **1** to influence or affect strongly beforehand <was *prepossessed* with the notion of his own superiority>
syn preengage, preoccupy
rel busy, engage, engross, immerse, occupy, soak; absorb, imbue, involve
2 ***syn*** see PREJUDICE 2
prepossessed *adj* ***syn*** see BIASED 2
ant unprepossessed
prepossessing *adj* ***syn*** see ATTRACTIVE 1
prepossession *n* ***syn*** see PRECONCEPTION
preposterous *adj* **1** ***syn*** see FOOLISH 2
rel irrational, unreasonable
2 ***syn*** see EXTRAVAGANT 1
preposterousness *n* ***syn*** see FOOLISHNESS
prepotence *n* ***syn*** see SUPREMACY
prepotency *n* ***syn*** see SUPREMACY
prerequisite *n* ***syn*** see ESSENTIAL 2
prerequisite *adj* ***syn*** see ESSENTIAL 4
prerogative *n* ***syn*** see RIGHT 2
rel exemption, immunity
presage *n* **1** ***syn*** see FORETOKEN
2 ***syn*** see APPREHENSION 3
presage *vb* **1** ***syn*** see AUGUR 2
rel bespeak, indicate
2 ***syn*** see ANNOUNCE 2
3 ***syn*** see FORETELL
prescribe *vb* **1** ***syn*** see DICTATE
2 to fix arbitrarily or authoritatively for the sake of order or of a clear understanding <the Constitution *prescribes* the conditions under which it may be amended>
syn assign, define, lay down
rel establish, fix, set, settle; decide, determine; choose, pick out, select
prescript *n* ***syn*** see LAW 1
prescription *n* ***syn*** see LAW 1
presence *n* ***syn*** see BEARING 1
rel appearance, aspect, look, seeming
present *n* ***syn*** see GIFT 1
present *vb* **1** ***syn*** see INTRODUCE 4
2 ***syn*** see GIVE 1
3 ***syn*** see OFFER 1
4 ***syn*** see ADDUCE
5 ***syn*** see DIRECT 2
present *adj* now existing or in progress <the *present* state of the economy seems to be shaky from all reports>
syn contemporary, current, existent, extant, instant, present-day, todayish
rel contemporaneous, modern; newfashioned, up-to-date, up-to-the-minute
con bygone, erstwhile, late, old, once, onetime, quondam, sometime, whilom

---

syn synonym(s) ***rel*** related word(s)
ant antonym(s) ***con*** contrasted word(s)
idiom idiomatic equivalent(s)
‖ use limited; if in doubt, see a dictionary

ant past

present *n* the present time <the course covers U.S. history from 1900 to the *present*>
syn now, today; *compare* FUTURE, PAST
idiom here and now, this day and age
ant past; future

presentable *adj* ***syn*** see RESPECTABLE 5

present–day *adj* ***syn*** see PRESENT

presenter *n* ***syn*** see DONOR

presentiment *n* ***syn*** see APPREHENSION 3
rel discomposing, discomposure, disquietude, disturbance, perturbation

presently *adv* **1** without undue time lapse <the results will be evident *presently*>
syn anon, by and by, directly, shortly, soon
2 ***syn*** see TODAY

presentment *n* ***syn*** see REPRESENTATION

preserval *n* ***syn*** see CONSERVATION 1

preservation *n* **1** the act of preserving or the state of being preserved <the *preservation* of peace in the world>
syn conservation, keeping, safekeeping, salvation, saving, sustentation
rel defense, guard, protection, safeguard, shield; care, guardianship, ward
2 ***syn*** see CONSERVATION 1

preserve *vb* **1** ***syn*** see SAVE 3
2 ***syn*** see MAINTAIN 1

preserve *n* ***syn*** see JAM

preside *vb* to occupy the place of authority (as in an assembly) <the chief justice *presides* over the supreme court> <the *presiding* elders of the church>
syn chair
rel carry on, conduct, control, direct, keep, manage, operate, ordain, run; administer, handle, head, oversee, supervise

press *n* ***syn*** see CROWD 1

press *vb* **1** to act upon through steady pushing or thrusting force exerted in contact <*pressed* her nose against the window>
syn bear, compress, constrain, crowd, crush, jam, ‖mash, push, ‖squab, squash, squeeze, squish, squush
rel propel, shove, thrust; drive, impel, move
2 ***syn*** see DEPRESS 2
3 to squeeze out the juice or contents of <*press* grapes>
syn crush, express
rel compress, squeeze
4 ***syn*** see PUSH 2
5 ***syn*** see PRESSURE
6 ***syn*** see EMBRACE 1
7 to crowd closely against or around someone or something <hundreds *pressed* around the performer after the show>
syn cram, crowd, crush, jam, squash, squeeze; *compare* CRAM 1
rel pack, ram, stuff, tamp; mass, pile; assemble, collect, congregate, gather
8 to force or push one's way (as through a crowd or against obstruction) <had to *press* through the traffic to get to the other side of town>
syn bear, squeeze
rel force, push, shove

press–agent *vb* ***syn*** see PUBLICIZE

press–agentry *n* ***syn*** see PUBLICITY

pressing *adj* demanding or claiming especially immediate attention <he was barely able to pay his most *pressing* debts>
syn burning, clamant, clamorous, crying, dire, exigent, imperative, importunate, insistent, instant, urgent
rel direct, immediate; claiming, demanding, exacting, requiring; compelling, constraining, forcing, obliging; acute, critical, crucial

pressure *n* ***syn*** see STRESS 1

pressure *vb* to insist upon unduly <*pressured* him into making the wrong move>
syn overpress, press, push
rel drive, impel; rush

prestige *n* **1** ***syn*** see STATUS 2
2 ***syn*** see INFLUENCE 1
rel power, sway
3 ***syn*** see EMINENCE 1

prestigious *adj* ***syn*** see FAMOUS 2

presto *adv* ***syn*** see FAST 2

presumably *adv* by reasonable assumption <*presumably* the best qualified for the job should get it>
syn assumably, doubtless, likely, presumptively, probably
rel indubitably, surely, undoubtedly, unquestionably

presume *vb* **1** ***syn*** see CONJECTURE
2 ***syn*** see PRESUPPOSE
3 ***syn*** see IMPOSE 5

presuming *adj* ***syn*** see PRESUMPTUOUS
ant unassuming, unpresuming

presumption *n* **1** ***syn*** see EFFRONTERY
2 ***syn*** see PRESUPPOSITION 1
3 ***syn*** see ASSUMPTION 2

presumptively *adv* ***syn*** see PRESUMABLY

presumptuous *adj* marked by or based on bold and excessive self-confidence <in such company his demand for attention was utterly *presumptuous*>
syn brash, brassbound, confident, forward, gay, overconfident, overweening, presuming, pushful, pushing, ‖pushy, self-asserting, self-assertive, uppish, uppity
rel pretentious, self-assured, self-conceited; lofty, pompous, supercilious; complacent, self-satisfied, smug; inexcusable, outrageous
idiom too big for one's britches
con deferential, dutiful, respectful, submissive; appropriate, proper

presuppose *vb* to take something for granted or as true or existent especially as a basis for action or reasoning <a lecturer who talks above the heads of his listeners *presupposes* too extensive a knowledge on their part>
syn assume, posit, postulate, premise, presume
rel conjecture, guess, surmise; deduce, infer, judge; believe, expect, gather, imagine, reckon, suppose, suspect, take, think, understand; preconceive

presupposition *n* **1** an act of presupposing <going on her *presupposition* that they would succeed>

syn assumption, presumption
rel conjecture, guess, surmise; deduction, inference, judgment; belief, conviction, opinion, view
2 *syn* see ASSUMPTION 2

pretend *vb* **1** *syn* see ASSUME 4
rel beguile, deceive, delude, mislead; profess, purport
idiom make believe
2 *syn* see CONJECTURE

pretended *adj syn* see ALLEGED

pretender *n syn* see IMPOSTOR

pretense *n* **1** *syn* see CLAIM 1
2 the offering of something false as real or true <there is too much *pretense* in his piety>
syn charade, disguise, make-believe, pageant, pretension, pretentiousness
rel deceit, deception, fake, fraud, humbug, imposture, sham; affectation, air, mannerism, pose
con sincereness; reality, soundness, substantiality, validity; fairness, honesty
ant sincerity
3 *syn* see MASK 2

pretension *n* **1** *syn* see CLAIM 1
2 *syn* see AMBITION 1
3 *syn* see PRETENSE 2

pretentious *adj* **1** *syn* see SHOWY
ant unpretentious
2 *syn* see GENTEEL 3
ant unpretentious
3 flamboyant, turgid, or bombastic in manner or content <a *pretentious* literary style>
syn arty, arty-crafty, big, high-sounding, imposing, overblown
rel affected, feigned, put-on; pompier; aureate, bombastic, euphuistic, flowery, grandiloquent, magniloquent, rhetorical; inflated, tumid, turgid
con heartfelt, hearty, sincere, unfeigned, wholehearted, whole-souled; artless, genuine, natural, simple, unaffected
ant unpretentious
4 *syn* see AMBITIOUS 2

pretentiousness *n syn* see PRETENSE 2
ant unpretentiousness

preterition *n syn* see OMISSION

pretermission *n syn* see OMISSION

pretermit *vb syn* see NEGLECT

preternatural *adj* **1** *syn* see SUPERNATURAL 1
rel anomalous, unnatural; nonnatural
2 *syn* see ABNORMAL 1
ant natural

pretext *n* **1** *syn* see EXCUSE 1
2 *syn* see MASK 2

prettify *vb syn* see PALLIATE

pretty *adj* **1** *syn* see SKILLFUL 2
2 *syn* see BEAUTIFUL
rel darling, ducky; cunning, cute
ant unpretty

pretty *adv syn* see SOMEWHAT 2
idiom pretty much

||**pretty** *n syn* see TOY 2

prettyism *n syn* see POSE 2

pretty-pretty *n syn* see KNICKKNACK

preux *adj syn* see COURTLY

prevail *vb* **1** *syn* see CONQUER 2
2 *syn* see WIN 1
3 *syn* see RULE 2

prevail (on *or* upon) *vb syn* see INDUCE 1
rel affect, impress

prevailing *adj* general (as in circulation, acceptance, or use) in a given place or at a given time <the *prevailing* point of view among farmers>
syn current, popular, prevalent, rampant, regnant, rife, ruling, widespread
rel dominant, predominant, preponderant; common, familiar, ordinary; general, universal
con exceptional, uncommon, unusual

prevalent *adj* **1** *syn* see DOMINANT 1
2 *syn* see PREVAILING
3 *syn* see GENERAL 1
rel accustomed, customary, wonted

prevaricate *vb syn* see LIE
rel belie, garble, misrepresent

prevarication *n syn* see LIE

prevaricative *adj syn* see EVASIVE 1

prevaricator *n syn* see LIAR

prevaricatory *adj syn* see EVASIVE 1

prevent *vb* **1** to be or get ahead of or to deal with beforehand <many problems are *prevented* easily if one plans wisely>
syn anticipate, forestall
rel baffle, balk, foil, frustrate, thwart; arrest, check, interrupt
2 to stop from advancing or occurring <take steps to *prevent* war> <measures designed to *prevent* the spread of disease>
syn avert, deter, forestall, forfend, obviate, preclude, rule out, stave off, ward
rel bar, block, dam, hinder, impede, obstruct; debar, shut out; forbid, inhibit, interdict, prohibit
con allow, leave, let, suffer
ant permit

previous *adj* **1** *syn* see PRECEDING
ant subsequent; consequent
2 *syn* see EARLY 2

previous *adv syn* see BEFORE 1

previously *adv syn* see BEFORE 2
ant subsequently; consequently

previousness *n syn* see PRIORITY

previse *vb syn* see FORESEE

prevision *n syn* see PREDICTION

prevision *vb syn* see FORESEE

prey *n* **1** *syn* see GAME 3
2 *syn* see VICTIM 2

||**pribble** *n syn* see QUARREL

price *n* **1** the quantity of one thing that is exchanged or demanded in barter or sale for another <what is the *price* of this book>
syn charge, cost, price tag, rate, tab, tariff
2 *syn* see EXPENSE 2

priceless *adj syn* see PRECIOUS 1
rel cherished, prized, treasured, valued
idiom without price

---

syn synonym(s) *rel* related word(s)
ant antonym(s) *con* contrasted word(s)
idiom idiomatic equivalent(s)
|| use limited; if in doubt, see a dictionary

price tag *n* ***syn*** see PRICE 1

prick *n* a mark or shallow hole made by or as if by a pointed tool <a needle *prick* in his arm>
syn jab, ‖jag, puncture, stab
rel prickle; hole

prick *vb* **1** ***syn*** see PERFORATE
rel enter; cut, slash, slit
2 ***syn*** see URGE
rel excite, pique, stimulate

‖prick (up) *vb* ***syn*** see DRESS UP 1

prickish *adj* ***syn*** see IRRITABLE

prickly *adj* **1** ***syn*** see THORNY
rel annoying, bothersome
2 ***syn*** see IRRITABLE

pride *n* **1** ***syn*** see CONCEIT 2
rel bighead, cockiness, overconfidence, self-assurance
idiom overweening pride
ant humility
2 a reasonable or justifiable sense of one's worth or position <inhumane treatment in prison caused him to lose his *pride*>
syn amour propre, self-esteem, self-regard, self-respect
rel dignity, face, pridefulness, self-confidence, self-trust
con humiliation, mortification; shamefacedness
ant shame
3 proud or disdainful behavior or actions <her snobbishness and overbearing *pride* were offensive>
syn arrogance, disdain, disdainfulness, haughtiness, hauteur, loftiness, morgue, superbity, superciliousness
rel condescension, snobbishness; contempt, scorn; insolence; smugness; pretentiousness
idiom haughty airs
con humbleness, modesty, unpretentiousness
ant humility
4 ***syn*** see BEST
idiom pride of the herd

pride *vb* to congratulate (oneself) for something one is, has, or has done or achieved <he *prides* himself on his ancestry>
syn pique, plume, preen
rel boast, brag, crow, gasconade, vaunt; congratulate, felicitate
ant efface

‖pridy *adj* ***syn*** see PROUD 1

prier (*or* **pryer**) *n* ***syn*** see BUSYBODY

priestal *adj* ***syn*** see SACERDOTAL

priestish *adj* ***syn*** see SACERDOTAL

priestlike *adj* ***syn*** see SACERDOTAL

priestly *adj* ***syn*** see SACERDOTAL

‖prig *vb* ***syn*** see STEAL 1

prig *n* ***syn*** see THIEF

prig *n* ***syn*** see PRUDE

prig *adj* ***syn*** see PRIM 1

priggish *adj* **1** ***syn*** see COMPLACENT
rel self-righteous; self-esteeming, self-loving
2 ***syn*** see PRIM 1

prim *adj* **1** excessively concerned with what one regards as proper or right <a *prim* woman, easily shocked by vulgar language>
syn bluenosed, genteel, missish, precise, prig, priggish, prissy, proper, prudish, puritanical, straitlaced, stuffy, tight-laced, Victorian; *compare* GENTEEL 3
rel correct, nice, precise; decorous; rigid, stiff, wooden; ceremonial, ceremonious, conventional, formal, straight
idiom prim and proper
con lax, loose, slack; easy, easygoing, free
2 ***syn*** see NEAT 2

prima facie *adj* ***syn*** see SELF-EVIDENT

primarily *adv* **1** ***syn*** see GENERALLY 1
2 ***syn*** see INITIALLY 1

primary *adj* **1** ***syn*** see FIRST 2
2 ***syn*** see PRIMITIVE 4
3 ***syn*** see FUNDAMENTAL 1
4 ***syn*** see DIRECT 4
5 not based on or derived from something else <the *primary* studies in nuclear physics>
syn original, prime, primitive, underivative, underived
rel first, firsthand; basic, foundational, fundamental, principal, underlying
con derivate, derivational, derivative, derived; borrowed, secondhand
ant secondary

prime *n* **1** ***syn*** see MORNING 1
2 ***syn*** see YOUTH 1
3 ***syn*** see BEST

prime *adj* **1** ***syn*** see FIRST 2
2 ***syn*** see EXCELLENT
3 ***syn*** see PRIMARY 5

prime *vb* ***syn*** see PROVOKE 4

primeval *adj* ***syn*** see PRIMITIVE 4

primevous *adj* ***syn*** see PRIMITIVE 4

primitial *adj* ***syn*** see PRIMITIVE 4

primitive *adj* **1** ***syn*** see PRIMARY 5
2 ***syn*** see EARLY 1
3 closely approximating an early ancestral type <the opossums are *primitive* mammals>
syn archaic, persistent, undeveloped, unevolved
ant advanced
4 of or relating to earlier ages of the world or of human history <archaeology is concerned especially with the study of *primitive* man>
syn primary, primeval, primevous, primitial
ant unprimitive
5 ***syn*** see ELEMENTAL 1
6 characterized by a lack of written language, simple technology, and a relatively simple social organization
syn nonliterate, preliterate
rel barbarian, uncivilized, uncultivated
con advanced, civilized, cultivated

primitively *adv* ***syn*** see INITIALLY 1

primogenitor *n* ***syn*** see ANCESTOR 1

primordial *adj* **1** ***syn*** see EARLY 1
2 ***syn*** see FIRST

primp *vb* ***syn*** see DRESS UP 1

primrose *n* ***syn*** see BEST

prince *n* ***syn*** see MAGNATE

princely *adj* ***syn*** see GRAND 1

principal *adj* **1** ***syn*** see CHIEF 2
2 ***syn*** see FIRST 3

principally *adv* ***syn*** see GENERALLY 1

principium *n* ***syn*** see PRINCIPLE 1

principle *n* **1** a comprehensive and fundamental rule, doctrine, or assumption <the *principle* of free speech>
syn axiom, fundamental, law, principium, theorem
rel basis, foundation, ground; canon, precept, rule; convention, form, usage
2 principles *pl* ***syn*** see ETHIC 3
3 principles *pl* ***syn*** see ALPHABET 2

principled *adj* ***syn*** see MORAL 1
ant unprincipled

‖**prink** *vb* ***syn*** see SASHAY

prink (up) *vb* ***syn*** see DRESS UP 1

print *n* **1** ***syn*** see IMPRESSION 1
2 printed state or form <to see his name in *print*>
syn black and white, writing

printing *n* ***syn*** see EDITION

prior *adj* ***syn*** see PRECEDING
rel ahead, before, forward
con after, behind

priority *n* the act, the fact, or the right of preceding another <the right to inherit a title is dependent mainly on *priority* of birth>
syn antecedence, precedence, precedency, previousness
rel arrangement, order, ordering; ascendancy, supremacy; preeminence, transcendence

prior to *prep* **1** ***syn*** see BEFORE 1
2 ***syn*** see UNTIL

prison *n* ***syn*** see JAIL

‖**prison** *vb* ***syn*** see IMPRISON

prison bird *n* ***syn*** see CONVICT

prissy *adj* **1** ***syn*** see PRIM 1
rel fastidious, finicky, squeamish
2 ***syn*** see EFFEMINATE

‖**pritch** *vb* ***syn*** see PERFORATE

private *adj* **1** belonging to or concerning an individual person, company, or interest <*private* property>
syn personal, privy
rel intimate
con common, general, shared
ant public
2 known only to a select few <the group had *private* information about the strike>
syn closet, confidential, hushed, inside
rel secret; discreet; concealed, hidden
con common, general, open
ant public

private detective *n* a person concerned with the maintenance of lawful conduct or the investigation of crime either as a regular employee of a private interest (as a hotel) or as a contractor for fees <retained a *private detective* to report on his wife's associates>
syn operative, Pinkerton, ‖private eye, ‖shamus; *compare* DETECTIVE

‖**private eye** *n* ***syn*** see PRIVATE DETECTIVE

privately *adv* ***syn*** see SECRETLY

private parts *n pl* ***syn*** see GENITALIA

privates *n pl* ***syn*** see GENITALIA

privation *n* **1** ***syn*** see ABSENCE
2 the state of one deprived of something previously or normally possessed <suffered great *privation* during the famine>
syn deprivation, deprivement, dispossession, divestiture, loss; *compare* LOSS 1
rel distress, misery, suffering; losing, mislaying, misplacement, misplacing
3 ***syn*** see POVERTY 1

privilege *n* ***syn*** see RIGHT 2
rel allowance, concession; boon, favor

privilege (from) *vb* ***syn*** see EXEMPT

privities *n pl* ***syn*** see GENITALIA

privy *adj* **1** ***syn*** see PRIVATE 1
2 ***syn*** see ULTERIOR

privy *n* **1** an outdoor toilet <in less settled areas, *privies* often take the place of indoor plumbing>
syn backhouse, ‖biffy, ‖closet, jakes, ‖necessary, ‖office, outhouse
2 ***syn*** see TOILET

privy parts *n pl* ***syn*** see GENITALIA

prize *n* **1** ***syn*** see REWARD
2 ***syn*** see BEST

prize *vb* ***syn*** see APPRECIATE 1

prize *n* ***syn*** see SPOIL

prize *vb* ***syn*** see PRY

prizefighting *n* ***syn*** see BOXING

pro *prep* ***syn*** see FOR 2
ant anti, con

pro *n* ***syn*** see EXPERT

pro–and–con *vb* ***syn*** see DISCUSS 1

probable *adj* being such as may become true or actual <seems to be a *probable* candidate>
syn conceivable, earthly, likely, mortal, possible
rel believable, colorable, credible, plausible; rational, reasonable; apparent, illusory, ostensible, seeming
con doubtful, dubious, questionable, unlikely
ant improbable, unprobable

probably *adv* ***syn*** see PRESUMABLY
ant improbably

probe *n* ***syn*** see INQUIRY 1

probe *vb* **1** ***syn*** see EXPLORE
2 to try to find out (as by discreet questioning) the views or intentions of <*probed* the neighbors on the subject of political reform>
syn feel out, sound (out)
rel ask, catechize, examine, inquire, interrogate, query, quiz
idiom feel the pulse, launch a trial balloon, put out a feeler, see how the land lies, see which way the wind blows, test the water(s)
3 ***syn*** see SCOUT

probing *n* ***syn*** see INQUIRY 1

probity *n* ***syn*** see GOODNESS

problem *n* **1** ***syn*** see EXAMPLE 3
2 something requiring thought and skill to arrive at a proper conclusion or decision <what to do now is a *problem*>

---

syn synonym(s) ***rel*** related word(s)
ant antonym(s) ***con*** contrasted word(s)
idiom idiomatic equivalent(s)
‖ use limited; if in doubt, see a dictionary

syn issue, nut, question
rel enigma, mystery, puzzle; bugaboo, bugbear; count, point
idiom a hard nut to crack
problematic *adj* **1** *syn* see DOUBTFUL 1
ant unproblematic
2 *syn* see MOOT
ant unproblematic
proboscis *n* *syn* see NOSE 1
procacious *adj* **1** *syn* see INSOLENT 2
2 *syn* see WISE 5
procedure *n* **1** *syn* see COURSE 3
2 *syn* see MEASURE 7
3 *syn* see PROCESS 1
proceed *vb* **1** *syn* see SPRING 1
2 *syn* see GO 1
3 *syn* see ADVANCE 5
ant recede
proceeding *n* **1** *syn* see MEASURE 7
2 *syn* see PROCESS 1
proceeds *n pl* *syn* see PROFIT
process *n* **1** the series of actions, operations, or motions involved in the accomplishment of an end <the *process* of making sugar from sugarcane>
syn procedure, proceeding
rel fashion, manner, method, mode, modus, system, technique, way, wise; routine; operation
2 *syn* see OUTGROWTH 1
||**process** *vb* *syn* see GO 1
procession *n* *syn* see ORDER 5
processus *n* *syn* see OUTGROWTH 1
proclaim *vb* **1** *syn* see DECLARE 1
rel utter, vent, ventilate, voice
2 *syn* see SHOW 2
proclamation *n* *syn* see DECLARATION
proclivity *n* *syn* see LEANING 2
procrastinate *vb* *syn* see DELAY 2
rel defer, postpone, stay, suspend; prolong, protract
procreate *vb* **1** to produce offspring <*procreate* children>
syn bear, beget, breed, generate, multiply, produce, propagate, reproduce
rel mother; engender; hatch, spawn; proliferate
idiom give birth to, multiply the earth
2 *syn* see GENERATE 1
3 *syn* see FATHER 1
procumbent *adj* *syn* see PRONE 4
procurable *adj* *syn* see AVAILABLE 1
procure *vb* **1** *syn* see GET 1
2 *syn* see INDUCE 1
prod *vb* **1** *syn* see POKE 1
2 *syn* see URGE
rel instigate; excite, pique, provoke, stimulate
prodigal *adj* *syn* see PROFUSE
ant parsimonious; frugal
prodigal *n* *syn* see SPENDTHRIFT
prodigality *n* *syn* see EXTRAVAGANCE 2
ant parsimoniousness
prodigalize *vb* *syn* see WASTE 2
prodigious *adj* **1** *syn* see MARVELOUS 1
2 *syn* see MONSTROUS 1
3 *syn* see HUGE
prodigy *n* *syn* see WONDER 1
produce *vb* **1** *syn* see PROCREATE 1
2 *syn* see STAGE
3 *syn* see EFFECT 1
4 *syn* see GENERATE 1
5 *syn* see GENERATE 3
6 *syn* see MAKE 3
7 *syn* see BEAR 9
8 *syn* see GIVE 7
9 *syn* see GROW 1
produce *n* *syn* see PRODUCT 1
product *n* **1** something produced by physical labor or intellectual effort <the literary *products* of the Age of Reason>
syn produce, production
rel handiwork; consequence, effect, offshoot, outcome, outgrowth, result; fruit, harvest
2 *syn* see OUTPUT
production *n* **1** *syn* see PRODUCT 1
2 *syn* see EXTENSION 1
3 *syn* see OUTPUT
productive *adj* *syn* see FERTILE
ant unproductive
proem *n* *syn* see INTRODUCTION
proemial *adj* *syn* see PRELIMINARY
profanation *n* a violation or misuse of something normally held sacred <the *profanation* of a religious ritual>
syn blasphemy, desecration, sacrilege, violation
rel contamination, defilement, pollution; corruption, debasement, perversion, vitiation; transgression, trespass
con glorification, hallowing, sanctification
ant purification; consecration
profane *adj* **1** not concerned with religion or religious purposes <he was speaking of *profane* history, not the history found in the Bible>
syn lay, secular, temporal, unsacred
rel earthly, mundane, terrestrial, worldly
con consecrated, hallowed, holy, sanctified; divine, religious, spiritual
ant sacred
2 *syn* see HEATHEN
3 *syn* see IMPIOUS 1
4 *syn* see SACRILEGIOUS
5 *syn* see OBSCENE 2
profaned *adj* *syn* see IMPURE 3
ant unprofaned
profanity *n* *syn* see BLASPHEMY 1
profess *vb* *syn* see ASSERT 1
professed *adj* *syn* see ALLEGED
professedly *adv* *syn* see OSTENSIBLY
profession *n* *syn* see TRADE 1
professional *n* *syn* see EXPERT
ant amateur
proffer *vb* *syn* see OFFER 1
proffer *n* *syn* see PROPOSAL
proficiency *n* *syn* see ADVANCE 2
proficient *adj* having or manifesting the knowledge, skill, and experience needed for sucess in a particular field or endeavor <a *proficient* glider pilot>
syn adept, crack, crackerjack, expert, master, masterful, masterly, skilled, skillful; *compare* EXPERIENCED, SKILLFUL 2

rel checked-out, drilled, exercised, practiced; effective, effectual, efficient; able, capable, competent, qualified; accomplished, consummate, finished
con ignorant, untaught, untrained; inexperienced; unskilled
ant incompetent

proficient *n* ***syn*** see EXPERT

profile *n* ***syn*** see OUTLINE

profit *n* the excess of returns over expenditure in a transaction or a series of transactions <his *profits* from the business venture were rewarding>
syn earnings, gain, lucre, proceeds, return
rel cleaning, cleanup, killing; receipt(s); output, outturn, product, production, turnout, yield
con cost, expenditure, expense, outgo
ant loss

profit *vb* ***syn*** see BENEFIT
ant lose

profitable *adj* ***syn*** see ADVANTAGEOUS 1
ant profitless, unprofitable

profligate *adj* ***syn*** see ABANDONED 2

profligate *n* **1** ***syn*** see WASTREL 1
2 ***syn*** see SPENDTHRIFT

profound *adj* **1** ***syn*** see RECONDITE
2 ***syn*** see DEEP 1
3 ***syn*** see INTENSIVE

profoundness *n* ***syn*** see DEPTH 2

profundity *n* ***syn*** see DEPTH 2

profuse *adj* proffered in or characterized by great abundance <*profuse* apologies> <a *profuse* flow of blood>
syn exuberant, lavish, lush, luxuriant, opulent, prodigal, profusive, riotous
rel abundant, copious; abounding, swarming, teeming; excessive, extravagant, immoderate; bounteous, bountiful, generous, liberal, munificent, openhanded
con exiguous, meager, scrimpy, skimpy, slight, small, sparse
ant scant, scanty

profusive *adj* ***syn*** see PROFUSE

progenerate *vb* ***syn*** see FATHER 1

progenitor *n* ***syn*** see ANCESTOR 1

progeniture *n* ***syn*** see OFFSPRING

progeny *n* ***syn*** see OFFSPRING

prognosis *n* ***syn*** see PREDICTION

prognostic *n* ***syn*** see FORETOKEN

prognosticate *vb* ***syn*** see FORETELL

prognostication *n* ***syn*** see PREDICTION

prognosticator *n* ***syn*** see PROPHET

program *n* **1** a formulated plan listing things to be done or to take place especially in chronological order <the *program* of a concert>
syn agenda, calendar, card, docket, programma, schedule, sked, timetable
rel bill; slate; plan
idiom order of the day
2 ***syn*** see COURSE 3

programma *n* ***syn*** see PROGRAM 1

progress *n* **1** ***syn*** see ADVANCE 2
ant regression, retrogression
2 a movement onward (as in time or space) <the *progress* of a disease> <they made slow *progress* toward their destination>
syn advance, course, progression
rel passage
3 ***syn*** see DEVELOPMENT

progress *vb* ***syn*** see ADVANCE 5
ant retrogress

progression *n* **1** ***syn*** see PROGRESS 2
2 ***syn*** see SUCCESSION 2
3 ***syn*** see DEVELOPMENT
ant regression, retrogression

progressive *adj* ***syn*** see LIBERAL 3
ant reactionary

prohibit *vb* ***syn*** see FORBID
ant permit

prohibited *adj* ***syn*** see FORBIDDEN

prohibition *n* ***syn*** see TABOO
ant permission

project *n* **1** ***syn*** see PLAN 1
2 something (as a business operation) that one engages in or attempts <large-scale *projects* involving large sums of money>
syn enterprise, undertaking
rel affair, business, concern, matter, proposition, thing; adventure, emprise, exploit, feat, gest, venture

project *vb* **1** ***syn*** see PLAN 2
rel intend, propose, purpose; delineate, diagram
2 ***syn*** see THINK 1
||**3** ***syn*** see WANDER 1
4 ***syn*** see BULGE
rel extend, lengthen, prolong

projection *n* **1** something which extends beyond a level or a normal outer surface <buttresses are *projections* which serve to support a wall>
syn bulge, jut, outthrust, protrusion, protuberance
rel bump, bunch, swelling; extension, prolongation; hook, knob, point, spine, spur
ant depression
2 ***syn*** see EMINENCE 3

prolegomenon *n* ***syn*** see INTRODUCTION

proletariat *n* ***syn*** see RABBLE 2

proliferant *adj* ***syn*** see FERTILE

prolific *adj* ***syn*** see FERTILE
rel abounding, swarming; breeding, generating, propagating, reproducing, reproductive
ant barren, unfruitful

prolificacy *n* ***syn*** see FERTILITY
ant barrenness, unfruitfulness

prolix *adj* ***syn*** see WORDY
rel irksome, tedious, tiresome, wearisome; prolonged, protracted

prolixity *n* ***syn*** see VERBOSITY

prolixness *n* ***syn*** see VERBOSITY

prologue *n* ***syn*** see INTRODUCTION
ant epilogue

prolong *vb* ***syn*** see EXTEND 3
rel continue, endure, last, persist
con abbreviate, retrench, shorten
ant curtail

---

syn synonym(s) ***rel*** related word(s)
ant antonym(s) ***con*** contrasted word(s)
idiom idiomatic equivalent(s)
|| use limited; if in doubt, see a dictionary

prolongate *vb* ***syn*** see EXTEND 3
prolongation *n* ***syn*** see EXTENSION 1
prolonged *adj* ***syn*** see LONG 2
ant curtailed
prolongment *n* ***syn*** see EXTENSION 1
prominence *n* **1** ***syn*** see EMINENCE 1
2 ***syn*** see EMINENCE 3
prominency *n* ***syn*** see EMINENCE 1
prominent *adj* **1** ***syn*** see NOTICEABLE
ant inconspicuous
2 ***syn*** see FAMOUS 2
3 ***syn*** see WELL-KNOWN
promiscuous *adj* **1** ***syn*** see MISCELLANEOUS
2 ***syn*** see RANDOM
promise *vb* **1** to give one's word to do, bring about, or provide <*promised* to render all possible assistance to the flood victims>
syn engage, pass, pledge, undertake; *compare* VOW
rel accede, agree, assent, consent; bargain, compact, contract; covenant, plight, swear, vow; assure, ensure, insure; guarantee
idiom give (*or* make) a promise, pass one's word
2 ***syn*** see AUGUR 2
promise *n* a declaration that one will do or refrain from doing something specified <never gave a *promise* that he did not intend to keep>
syn engagement, plight, word; *compare* PLEDGE 1, WORD 8
rel earnest, guarantee, pawn, pledge, security, token; covenant, swear, vow; assurance, warrant
idiom word of honor
||**promised** *adj* ***syn*** see ENGAGED 2
promised land *n* ***syn*** see UTOPIA
promiseful *adj* ***syn*** see HOPEFUL 2
promising *adj* ***syn*** see HOPEFUL 2
ant unpromising
promontory *n* a high point of land or rock projecting into a body of water beyond the line of coast <stood on the *promontory* watching boats come in with the tide>
syn beak, bill, cape, foreland, head, headland, naze, point
promote *vb* **1** ***syn*** see ADVANCE 2
con break, bust, declass, degrade, demerit, disgrade, disrate, downgrade, reduce
ant bump, demote
2 ***syn*** see ADVANCE 1
3 to encourage public acceptance of (as a policy or merchandise) through publicity <official attempts to *promote* energy conservation> <television helped *promote* the new smaller cars>
syn advertise, boost, plug, push; *compare* PUBLICIZE
rel ballyhoo, propagandize; build up, cry, hype, press-agent, publicize, puff; communicate, impart
idiom make much of
con belittle, decry, depreciate, discredit, knock, run down
ant disparage
promotion *n* **1** ***syn*** see ADVANCEMENT 1
ant demotion
2 ***syn*** see PUBLICITY
rel advertisement
prompt *vb* **1** ***syn*** see INDUCE 1
2 ***syn*** see URGE
prompt *adj* **1** ***syn*** see QUICK 2
rel alert, vigilant, watchful, wide-awake; expeditious, speedy, swift
con lax, remiss, slack; dilatory
2 ***syn*** see PUNCTUAL 2
promptitude *n* ***syn*** see ALACRITY
promptly *adv* ***syn*** see FAST 2
promulgate *vb* ***syn*** see DECLARE 1
promulgation *n* ***syn*** see DECLARATION
prone *adj* **1** ***syn*** see WILLING 1
2 ***syn*** see LIABLE 2
3 ***syn*** see APT 1
4 lying down <lying *prone* on the floor>
syn decumbent, flat, procumbent, prostrate, reclining, recumbent
rel resupine, supine; level
con arrect, raised, stand-up, straight-up, upright, upstanding
ant erect
pronounce *vb* ***syn*** see ARTICULATE 2
pronounced *adj* ***syn*** see DECIDED 1
pronouncement *n* ***syn*** see DECLARATION
||**pronto** *adv* ***syn*** see FAST 2
pronunciamento *n* ***syn*** see DECLARATION
proof *n* **1** ***syn*** see REASON 3
2 ***syn*** see TESTIMONY
prop *n* ***syn*** see SUPPORT 3
prop *vb* **1** ***syn*** see SUPPORT 4
2 ***syn*** see SUPPORT 5
propagandist *n* ***syn*** see MISSIONARY
propagate *vb* **1** ***syn*** see PROCREATE 1
2 ***syn*** see GROW 1
3 ***syn*** see SPREAD 1
propel *vb* **1** ***syn*** see PUSH 1
2 ***syn*** see MOVE 5
3 ***syn*** see URGE
propellant *n* ***syn*** see STIMULUS
propensity *n* ***syn*** see LEANING 2
ant antipathy
proper *adj* **1** ***syn*** see FIT 1
ant improper
2 ***syn*** see TRUE 7
ant improper
3 ***syn*** see DECOROUS 1
ant improper
4 ***syn*** see ABLE
5 ***syn*** see GOOD 2
ant improper
6 ***syn*** see CHARACTERISTIC
||**7** ***syn*** see UTTER
8 ***syn*** see CORRECT 2
9 ***syn*** see PRIM 1
properly *adv* **1** ***syn*** see WELL 4
ant improperly
2 ***syn*** see WELL 1
idiom by rights
ant improperly
properness *n* ***syn*** see ORDER 7
ant improperness
property *n* **1** ***syn*** see QUALITY 1
2 ***syn*** see WEALTH 2

3 *syn* see OWNERSHIP
prophecy *n* **1** *syn* see REVELATION
2 *syn* see PREDICTION
prophesier *n syn* see PROPHET
prophesy *vb syn* see FORETELL
prophet *n* one who predicts events or developments <there have been many *prophets* foretelling the end of the world>
syn augur, auspex, forecaster, foreseer, foreteller, haruspex, Nostradamus, predictor, prognosticator, prophesier, seer, soothsayer
prophetic *adj* of, relating to, or characteristic of a prophet or prophecy <the old woman seemed to have *prophetic* powers>
syn apocalyptic, Delphian, fatidic, mantic, oracular, prophetical, sibylline, vatic, vaticinal
rel revelatory; interpretive; mysterious, mystic, strange, unexplainable
ant unprophetic
prophetical *adj syn* see PROPHETIC
propinquity *n syn* see PROXIMITY
propitiate *vb syn* see PACIFY
rel adapt, adjust, conform, reconcile; content, satisfy; intercede, mediate
propitiatory *adj syn* see PURGATIVE
propitious *adj* **1** *syn* see FAVORABLE 5
ant unpropitious; adverse
2 *syn* see TIMELY 1
ant unpropitious
3 *syn* see GOOD 1
ant unpropitious; adverse
‖**propone** *vb syn* see PROPOSE 1
proponent *n syn* see EXPONENT
ant opponent
proportion *n* **1** *syn* see DEGREE 2
2 *syn* see SYMMETRY
ant disproportion
3 *syn* see SIZE 1
proportion *vb syn* see HARMONIZE 3
proportional *adj* being in proportion <a starting salary *proportional* to her experience>
syn commensurable, commensurate, equal, symmetrical
rel correlative, corresponding, reciprocal; contingent, dependent, relative
con asymmetrical, disproportionate, irregular, lopsided, nonsymmetrical, off-balance, overbalanced, unbalanced, unequal, uneven, unsymmetrical
ant disproportional
proportionless *adj syn* see LOPSIDED
proposal *n* something which is proposed to another for consideration <his *proposal* for a new busing plan>
syn invitation, proffer, proposition, suggestion
rel motion; recommendation; idea, plan, project; outline, scheme
propose *vb* **1** to set before the mind for consideration <she *proposed* Mr. Smith for secretary of the club>
syn pose, prefer, ‖propone, proposition, propound, put, suggest
rel move (for); offer, present, submit, tender; ask, request, solicit
idiom put forth (*or* forward)
ant withdraw
2 *syn* see INTEND 2
proposition *n syn* see PROPOSAL
proposition *vb syn* see PROPOSE 1
propound *vb syn* see PROPOSE 1
proprietary *n syn* see OWNERSHIP
proprietor *n syn* see OWNER
proprietorship *n syn* see OWNERSHIP
propriety *n* **1** *syn* see ORDER 11
2 *syn* see DECORUM 1
ant impropriety
3 *syn* see ORDER 7
ant impropriety
4 proprieties *pl syn* see MANNER 5
prorate *vb syn* see APPORTION 2
prorogate *vb syn* see ADJOURN 2
prorogue *vb* **1** *syn* see DEFER
2 *syn* see ADJOURN 2
prosaic *adj* **1** belonging to or characteristic of prose as distinguished from poetry <his poetry is far more fanciful than his *prosaic* writings>
syn matter-of-fact, prose, prosing, prosy
rel actual, factual; literal
con figurative, metaphorical, symbolic; fanciful, florid, flowery, ornate
ant poetic
2 *syn* see COLORLESS 2
3 belonging to or suitable to the everyday world <the *prosaic* business of day-to-day housekeeping>
syn commonplace, everyday, lowly, mundane, workaday, workday
rel practicable, practical; boring, irksome, tedious
4 *syn* see COMMON 6
prosaicism *n syn* see COMMONPLACE
prosaism *n syn* see COMMONPLACE
proscribe *vb syn* see SENTENCE
proscription *n syn* see TABOO
prose *n syn* see CHAT 2
prose *adj syn* see PROSAIC 1
prosing *adj syn* see PROSAIC 1
prospect *n syn* see VISTA
prospect *vb syn* see EXPLORE
prosper *vb syn* see SUCCEED 3
rel augment, increase, multiply; bear, produce, turn out, yield
prospering *adj syn* see FLOURISHING
prosperity *n* **1** *syn* see SUCCESS
2 a state of good fortune and especially of financial success <his wise investments finally brought him a life of *prosperity*>
syn abundance, ease, easy street, prosperousness, thriving, well-being
rel affluence, riches, wealth
idiom bed of roses, comfortable (*or* easy) circumstances, life of ease, the good life

---

syn synonym(s) *rel* related word(s)
ant antonym(s) *con* contrasted word(s)
idiom idiomatic equivalent(s)
‖ use limited; if in doubt, see a dictionary

con misery, suffering; distress, embarrassment, indigence, poverty, straits
ant adversity
3 ***syn*** see WELFARE
4 a state of high general economic activity marked by relatively full employment <a war economy often generates *prosperity*>
syn boom, prosperousness
rel expansion; growth; inflation
con recession, slump, stagnation; bust
ant depression

prosperous *adj* **1** ***syn*** see TIMELY 1
rel appropriate, convenient, desirable; felicitous, fortunate, happy, lucky
con ill-seasoned, ill-timed, inauspicious, inopportune, unpropitious, unseasonable, untimely
ant unprosperous
2 ***syn*** see SUCCESSFUL
3 enjoying or marked by economic well-being <in *prosperous* circumstances>
syn comfortable, easy, ‖snug, substantial, well, well-fixed, well-heeled, well-off, well-to-do
rel affluent, opulent, rich, wealthy; halcyon
idiom comfortably off, comfortably situated, in (the) clover, in good case
con impecunious, necessitous, needy, poor; failing, unfortunate, unsuccessful
ant unprosperous
4 ***syn*** see FLOURISHING
rel lusty, strong
con decrepit, feeble, spindling, weak

prosperously *adv* ***syn*** see WELL 5
ant unprosperously

prosperousness *n* **1** ***syn*** see PROSPERITY 2
ant unprosperousness
2 ***syn*** see PROSPERITY 4

prostitute *vb* ***syn*** see ABUSE 2
rel corrupt, debase, debauch, deprave, vitiate

prostitute *n* a woman who engages in promiscuous sexual intercourse especially for money <streets haunted by *prostitutes*>
syn bawd, ‖callet, call girl, camp follower, cocotte, ‖cruiser, drab, fille de joie, harlot, ‖hooker, hustler, ‖joy girl, meretrix, moll, nightwalker, party girl, pom-pom girl, poule, quean, sporting girl, street girl, streetwalker, ‖tomato, whore
rel bar girl, B-girl, pickup; V-girl, victory girl; cocodette
idiom lady of pleasure, lady of the evening, woman of the street (*or* streets), woman of the town

prostitution *n* the act or practice of engaging in promiscuous sexual intercourse especially for money <the problem of *prostitution* around military installations>
syn harlotry, oldest profession, (the) social evil, streetwalking, whoredom

prostrate *adj* ***syn*** see PRONE 4

prostrate *vb* **1** ***syn*** see FELL 1
2 ***syn*** see PARALYZE 1
3 ***syn*** see OVERWHELM 4
4 ***syn*** see EXHAUST 4

prosy *adj* **1** ***syn*** see PROSAIC 1
2 ***syn*** see COLORLESS 2

protean *adj* ***syn*** see CHANGEABLE 1

protect *vb* ***syn*** see DEFEND 1
rel conserve, preserve, save; harbor, shelter

protection *n* **1** ***syn*** see DEFENSE 1
2 money paid under threat of depredation <offered *protection* to keep his store from being vandalized>
syn ‖pad
rel extortion, shakedown, squeeze; graft; bribe, payola

pro tem *adj* ***syn*** see TEMPORARY

pro tempore *adj* ***syn*** see TEMPORARY

protest *n* ***syn*** see DEMUR 2

protest *vb* **1** ***syn*** see ASSERT 1
2 ***syn*** see OBJECT 1
rel demonstrate; combat, fight, oppose, resist
ant agree

protoplast *n* ***syn*** see ORIGINAL 1

prototypal *adj* ***syn*** see TYPICAL 1

prototype *n* **1** ***syn*** see ORIGINAL 1
2 ***syn*** see FORERUNNER 2

prototypical *adj* ***syn*** see TYPICAL 1

protract *vb* ***syn*** see EXTEND 3
ant curtail

protracted *adj* ***syn*** see LONG 2
ant curtailed

protraction *n* ***syn*** see EXTENSION 1
rel dallying, dawdling, delay, lag; stay, suspension
ant curtailment

protrude *vb* ***syn*** see BULGE

protrusion *n* ***syn*** see PROJECTION 1

protuberance *n* ***syn*** see PROJECTION 1

protuberate *vb* ***syn*** see BULGE

proud *adj* **1** showing or feeling superiority toward others <a woman who was too *proud* to do her share of menial tasks>
syn arrogant, cavalier, disdainful, dismissive, haughty, high-and-mighty, hubristic, huffy, insolent, lofty, lordly, orgulous, overbearing, ‖pridy, proudhearted, supercilious, superior, toplofitical, toplofty; *compare* POMPOUS 1, VAIN 3
rel contemptuous, scornful; misproud; ostentatious, pretentious; bloated, important, pompous, self-important, stuffy, wiggy; conceited, narcissistic, self-conceited, stuck-up, vain, vainglorious; domineering, high-handed, imperious, masterful
con lowly, meek, modest, unassuming; chagrined, mortified
ant humble
2 ***syn*** see SPLENDID 2

proudhearted *adj* ***syn*** see PROUD 1

prove *vb* **1** to establish a point by appropriate objective means <gathered evidence that *proved* the need for better controls>
syn demonstrate, test, try
rel confirm, corroborate, substantiate, verify; argue, attest, bespeak, betoken, indicate
ant disprove; refute
2 ***syn*** see TRY 1
3 ***syn*** see ESTABLISH 6

provenance *n* ***syn*** see SOURCE

provender *n* ***syn*** see FOOD 1

provenience *n* ***syn*** see SOURCE
prove out *vb* ***syn*** see SUCCEED 2
proverb *n* ***syn*** see SAYING
provide *vb* ***syn*** see GIVE 3
provide (for) *vb* ***syn*** see SUPPORT 3
providence *n* **1** ***syn*** see ECONOMY
ant improvidence
2 ***syn*** see PRUDENCE 1
ant improvidence
provident *adj* ***syn*** see SPARING
ant improvident
providential *adj* ***syn*** see LUCKY
rel benignant, kind, kindly
province *n* **1** ***syn*** see FUNCTION 1
rel calling, pursuit, work
2 ***syn*** see FIELD
provincial *n* ***syn*** see RUSTIC
provincial *adj* **1** ***syn*** see RURAL
2 ***syn*** see INSULAR
rel bigoted, hidebound
con cosmic, universal; progressive
ant catholic
provision *n* ***syn*** see CONDITION 1
provisional *adj* **1** ***syn*** see CONDITIONAL 1
rel temporary; contingent, dependent
ant definitive
2 ***syn*** see MAKESHIFT
provisionary *adj* ***syn*** see CONDITIONAL 1
provisions *n pl* ***syn*** see FOOD 1
proviso *n* ***syn*** see CONDITION 1
provisory *adj* ***syn*** see CONDITIONAL 1
provocation *n* ***syn*** see ANNOYANCE 1
provocative *n* ***syn*** see STIMULUS
provoke *vb* **1** ***syn*** see IRRITATE
rel insult, outrage
ant gratify
2 ***syn*** see ANNOY 1
rel anger, incense, madden
3 ***syn*** see INCITE
rel perturb, upset
4 to lead one into doing or feeling or to produce by so leading a person <was *provoked* into finding a solution to the problem> <this foolish answer *provoked* an outburst of rage>
syn excite, galvanize, innervate, innerve, motivate, move, pique, prime, quicken, rouse, ‖roust, stimulate, suscitate; *compare* FIRE 2, STIR 1
rel arouse, awaken, bestir, build up, challenge, kindle, rally, stir, wake, waken, whet; animate, exalt, fire, inform, inspire; electrify, enthuse, thrill; titillate, titivate
idiom bring (one) to one's feet
con calm, relax, soothe
5 ***syn*** see GENERATE 3
provoking *n* ***syn*** see ANNOYANCE 1
prowess *n* **1** ***syn*** see HEROISM
2 ***syn*** see ADDRESS 1
proximate *adj* **1** ***syn*** see CLOSE 6
2 ***syn*** see IMMINENT 1
3 ***syn*** see RUDE 3
ant exact
proximity *n* the quality or state of being near <the two houses are in close *proximity*>
syn appropinquity, contiguity, contiguousness, immediacy, propinquity
rel togetherness; closeness, nearness; adjacency, juxtaposition
con farness, remoteness
ant distance
proxy *n* ***syn*** see AGENT 2
prude *n* a person who is excessively or priggishly attentive to propriety or decorum <in that narrow atmosphere she hardened into a rigid, inhibited, censorious person—a thorough *prude*>
syn bluenose, comstock, goody-goody, Grundy, Mrs. Grundy, nice Nelly, prig, puritan, ‖wowser
rel spoilsport, stick-in-the-mud, wet blanket; fuddy-duddy, old fogy, stuffed shirt; fussbudget, old maid
con freethinker, latitudinarian, libertarian
prudence *n* **1** a quality in a person that allows him to choose the sensible course <displayed *prudence* in setting up his business>
syn canniness, caution, discreetness, discretion, foresight, forethought, precaution, providence; *compare* WIT 3
rel acumen, astucity, astuteness, clear-sightedness, discrimination, keenness, penetration, percipience, perspicacity, shrewdness, wit; insight, sagaciousness, sagacity, sageness, sapience, wisdom; advisableness, expediency; calculation, circumspection
con indiscretion, unreasonableness, unwiseness
ant imprudence
2 ***syn*** see ECONOMY
prudent *adj* **1** ***syn*** see WISE 2
ant imprudent
2 ***syn*** see EXPEDIENT
prudish *adj* ***syn*** see PRIM 1
rel strict; austere, severe, stern
prune *n* ***syn*** see DUNCE
prune *vb* ***syn*** see CUT 6
rel brash, lop; thin; eliminate, exclude
prurience *n* ***syn*** see LUST 2
pruriency *n* ***syn*** see LUST 2
prurient *adj* ***syn*** see LUSTFUL 2
rel bawdy, erotic, lewd; sensual
pry *vb* ***syn*** see SNOOP
idiom nose into
pry *vb* to raise, move, or pull apart with or as if with a pry <*pry* up a floorboard>
syn jimmy, lever, prize
rel elevate, hoist, lift, pick up, raise, rear, take up, uphold, uplift, upraise, uprear; turn, twist; disengage, disjoin, divide, separate
prying *adj* ***syn*** see CURIOUS 2
rel obtrusive, officious
psalm *vb* ***syn*** see PRAISE 2
psalmody *vb* ***syn*** see PRAISE 2
pseudo *adj* ***syn*** see COUNTERFEIT
rel wrong
pseudonym *n* a fictitious or assumed name <used a *pseudonym* in many of his adventures>
syn alias, anonym, nom de guerre

---

syn synonym(s) ***rel*** related word(s)
ant antonym(s) ***con*** contrasted word(s)
idiom idiomatic equivalent(s)
‖ use limited; if in doubt, see a dictionary

rel ananym; nom de plume, pen name; stage name; incognito

psychal *adj* ***syn*** see PSYCHIC 1

psyche *n* ***syn*** see SOUL 1

psychic *adj* **1** sensitive to nonphysical forces and influences <because he foretold many things correctly, people regarded him as *psychic*>
syn psychal, psychical, supersensible, supersensory
rel telepathic; spiritual; impressible, impressionable, responsive, sensible, sensile, sensitive, sentient, susceptible, susceptive
2 ***syn*** see MENTAL 1

psychical *adj* **1** ***syn*** see PSYCHIC 1
2 ***syn*** see MENTAL 1

psychological *adj* ***syn*** see MENTAL 1

psychopathy *n* ***syn*** see INSANITY 1

pub *n* ***syn*** see BAR 5

puberty *n* ***syn*** see YOUTH 1

pubescence *n* ***syn*** see YOUTH 1

public *adj* **1** of, relating to, or affecting the people as an organized community <*public* affairs>
syn civic, civil, national
rel government, governmental; community; state; municipal, urban
2 ***syn*** see OPEN 4
rel common, general, universal
con private
3 ***syn*** see COMMON 1
con private
4 held by or applicable to the majority of the people <*public* opinion>
syn general, popular, vulgar
rel prevalent, usual, widespread
ant private

public *n* **1** ***syn*** see SOCIETY 3
2 ***syn*** see FOLLOWING 2
rel hangers-on, suite

‖**publican** *n* ***syn*** see SALOONKEEPER

publication *n* ***syn*** see DECLARATION
rel dissemination

public house *n* **1** ***syn*** see HOTEL
‖**2** ***syn*** see BAR 5

publicity *n* information with news value issued to gain public attention or support <$100,000 was allocated for new-product *publicity*>
syn advertising, buildup, hype, press-agentry, promotion, puffery
rel broadcasting, promulgation, skywriting; réclame; announcement, write-up; blurb, commercial, plug, promo, puff; ballyhoo, hoopla; propaganda; hard sell

publicize *vb* to give publicity to <*publicize* a new book>
syn advertise, build up, cry, hype, press-agent, puff; *compare* PROMOTE 3
rel announce, broadcast, headline, promulgate, skywrite; advance, boost, plug, push; extol; bruit, tout, trumpet; propagandize
idiom bring into the limelight, throw the spotlight on

publish *vb* **1** ***syn*** see DECLARE 1
rel broach, express, utter, vent, ventilate
idiom bring to public notice, lay before the public, publish (*or* noise *or* spread) abroad, put forth
2 to produce for publication and allow to be distributed and sold <*published* a newspaper>
syn get out, issue, put out
rel produce; bring out; market; distribute

puckfist *n* ***syn*** see BRAGGART

puckish *adj* ***syn*** see PLAYFUL 1

‖**pudding** *n, usu* **puddings** *pl* ***syn*** see ENTRAILS

puddle *n* ***syn*** see POOL

puddle *vb* ***syn*** see FIDDLE 2

puddy *adj* ***syn*** see ROTUND 2

pudendum *n, usu* **pudenda** *pl* ***syn*** see GENITALIA

pudgy *adj* ***syn*** see ROTUND 2
rel ‖chuffy, ‖chumpy, squab, squdgy, ‖stuggy, stumpy, thick-bodied

puerile *adj* ***syn*** see CHILDISH

puff *vb* **1** ***syn*** see PANT 1
idiom huff and puff, pant and blow
2 ***syn*** see BOAST
3 ***syn*** see PUBLICIZE

puff *n* **1** ***syn*** see DRAW 1
rel inhalation, inhaling
2 ***syn*** see QUILT
3 a commendatory and often extravagant publicity notice or review <this book fails to deliver what the *puff* promises>
syn blurb, plug, puffing, write-up
rel promo; boost, buildup, push; laudation, praise

puffery *n* ***syn*** see PUBLICITY

puffing *n* ***syn*** see PUFF 3

puffy *adj* ***syn*** see POMPOUS 1

‖**puggy** *adj* ***syn*** see SWEATY

pugilism *n* ***syn*** see BOXING

pugnacious *adj* ***syn*** see BELLIGERENT
rel pushing, pushy, self-assertive; defiant, rebellious; brawling
idiom itching for a fight, itching (*or* ready) to fight, ready to fight at the drop of a hat
con bland, easygoing, mild; calm, peaceful; quiet
ant pacific

pugnacity *n* ***syn*** see ATTACK 2

puissance *n* ***syn*** see POWER 4
rel clout, influence, sway
con powerlessness, weakness
ant impuissance

puissant *adj* ***syn*** see POWERFUL 2
rel influential; commanding, ruling
con ineffectual, inefficacious, powerless
ant impuissant

puke *n* ***syn*** see SNOT 1

pukka *adj* ***syn*** see AUTHENTIC 2

pulchritudinous *adj* ***syn*** see BEAUTIFUL

pule *vb* ***syn*** see WHIMPER

pull *vb* **1** ***syn*** see EXTRACT 1
2 to cause to move toward or after an applied force <*pull* a trunk across the floor>
syn drag, draw, haul, lug, tow, tug
rel strain; heave; jerk, wrench, yank; drive, impel, push, shove
3 ***syn*** see STRAIN 2
4 ***syn*** see ROW
idiom pull on the oar (*or* oars)
5 ***syn*** see COMMIT 2

idiom ||go and do
6 *syn* see DON 2
7 *syn* see GET 1
pull *n* **1** *syn* see DRAW 1
2 the power or ability to secure special favor or partiality <had lots of *pull* with the government>
syn clout, ||drag, in, influence; *compare* INFLUENCE 1
rel persuasion; wire-pulling
idiom backstairs influence
3 *syn* see ATTRACTION 1
pullback *n syn* see DIEHARD 1
pull down *vb syn* see DESTROY 1
pull in *vb* **1** *syn* see RESTRAIN 1
2 *syn* see ARREST 2
pull out *vb syn* see GO 2
ant pull in
pull through *vb syn* see SURVIVE 2
pullulate *vb syn* see TEEM
pull up *vb syn* see STOP 4
pulp *vb syn* see CRUSH 2
pulpitarian *n syn* see CLERGYMAN
pulpiteer *n syn* see CLERGYMAN
pulpiter *n syn* see CLERGYMAN
pulpous *adj syn* see SOFT 6
pulpy *adj syn* see SOFT 6
pulsate *vb* to course or move with or as if with rhythmic strokes <blood *pulsating* through his veins>
syn beat, palpitate, pulse, throb
rel fluctuate, oscillate, vibrate; pump; drum, pound, roar, thrum
pulse *vb syn* see PULSATE
pulverize *vb* **1** to reduce (as by crushing, beating, or grinding) to minute particles <*pulverized* the ore in a stamp mill>
syn bray, buck, comminute, contriturate, crush, powder, triturate; *compare* SHATTER 1
rel break up; abrade, grate, grind; crumble, crunch, mull; levigate; atomize, fragment, fragmentalize, fragmentize, micronize; beat, shatter, smash, smatter, splinter; flour, mill
2 *syn* see DESTROY 1
pulverized *adj syn* see FINE 2
rel pulverous, pulverulent; dusty, granular, splintery
ant unpulverized
pummel *vb syn* see BEAT 1
pump *vb syn* see DRAIN 1
pumpkin head *n syn* see DUNCE
||**pumpknot** *n syn* see BUMP 2
pun *n* the humorous use of a word so as to suggest different meanings, or of words having the same or similar sound but different meanings <"mourning shall come with approaching day" is a *pun*>
syn calembour, paronomasia
rel double entendre
idiom play on words
punch *vb* **1** *syn* see POKE 1
rel hit, slap, strike
2 *syn* see PERFORATE
punch *n* **1** *syn* see CUFF
2 *syn* see POKE 1
3 *syn* see POINT 3
4 *syn* see VIGOR 2
punctilious *adj syn* see CAREFUL 2
rel conventional, formal, observant; overconscientious, overscrupulous
punctual *adj* **1** *syn* see CAREFUL 2
ant unpunctual
2 marked by exact adherence to an appointed time <a *punctual* arrival>
syn prompt, timely
rel quick, ready
idiom on the dot, on time
con late, tardy
ant unpunctual
punctuate *vb* to mark or divide (written matter) with punctuation marks <*punctuated* the sentence>
syn point
rel divide, separate
puncture *n syn* see PRICK
rel perforation
puncture *vb* **1** *syn* see PERFORATE
rel riddle
2 *syn* see DISCREDIT 2
idiom shoot full of holes
pungent *adj* sharp and stimulating to the mind or senses <his *pungent* wit>
syn peppery, piquant, poignant, racy, snappy, spicy, zesty
rel acute, keen, salt, salty, sharp; biting, bitter, cutting, hot, incisive, trenchant; exciting, provocative, stimulating; rich
con banal, corny, dull, flat, hackneyed, insipid, old hat, platitudinous, prosaic, prosy, stale, stodgy, tasteless, unimaginative, uninteresting
ant bland
punish *vb* **1** to inflict a penalty on in requital for a wrongdoing <*punished* the child for misbehaving>
syn castigate, chasten, chastise, correct, discipline
rel criticize, reprove; amerce, fine, mulct, penalize; avenge, fix, revenge; lambaste, scourge
con overlook; absolve, acquit, exculpate, exonerate, vindicate; let off, release
ant excuse, pardon
2 *syn* see CONSUME 5
punishing *adj syn* see PUNITIVE
punishment *n* the act or an instance of punishing <a spanking was his *punishment*>
syn castigation, chastisement, correction, discipline, punition, rod
rel criticism, reproof; amercement, fine, mulct, penalty; avengement, revenge
idiom carrot-and-stick treatment, disciplinary action, dose of strap oil, what for
con overlooking; acquittal, exculpation, exoneration, vindication

---

syn synonym(s) *rel* related word(s)
ant antonym(s) *con* contrasted word(s)
idiom idiomatic equivalent(s)
|| use limited; if in doubt, see a dictionary

ant excuse, pardon

punition *n* ***syn*** see PUNISHMENT
idiom punitive measures

punitive *adj* inflicting, involving, or constituting punishment <took *punitive* action against him>
syn castigating, disciplinary, punishing, punitory
rel correctional, penal

punitory *adj* ***syn*** see PUNITIVE

punk *n* **1** ***syn*** see NONSENSE 2
2 ***syn*** see NOVICE
3 ***syn*** see TOUGH

||**punk** *adj* ***syn*** see BAD 1

puny *adj* **1** ***syn*** see PETTY 2
rel feeble, weak
2 ***syn*** see WEAK 1

pup *n* ***syn*** see TWERP

puppet *n* ***syn*** see TOOL 2
rel dupe; slave

puppy *n* ***syn*** see TWERP

purblind *adj* partly blind <*purblind* with cataracts>
syn dim-sighted, half-blind
rel myopic, nearsighted, shortsighted; dim; blind, dark, sightless

purchasable *adj* **1** capable of being bought <*purchasable* goods>
syn available, obtainable, on offer
rel marketable, salable
idiom on (*or* for) sale, on the market, to be had
con rare; unavailable, unobtainable
ant unpurchasable
2 ***syn*** see VENAL 1
rel undependable, unreliable; slippery, tricky; treacherous

purchase *vb* ***syn*** see BUY 1
idiom make a purchase
ant sell

purchaser *n* one to whom something is sold <instruction booklets for new-car *purchasers*>
syn buyer, emptor, vendee
rel marketer, shopper; client, customer, patron; consumer, user
con seller, vendor

pure *adj* **1** ***syn*** see STRAIGHT 3
ant impure
2 being such and no other <his solution of the problem was *pure* genius>
syn absolute, perfect, pure and simple, sheer, simple, unadulterated, unalloyed, undiluted, unmitigated, unmixed, unqualified; *compare* UTTER
rel complete, plenary, total; authentic, genuine; classic; out-and-out, plain, utter
con mixed, qualified; doubtful, dubious, questionable, uncertain
3 ***syn*** see UTTER
4 ***syn*** see GOOD 11
ant impure
5 ***syn*** see CHASTE
rel fresh, inviolate, unblighted, unprofaned
idiom as pure as the driven snow
con contaminated, dirty, sullied
ant immoral, impure

||**pure** *adv* ***syn*** see VERY 1

pure and simple *adj* ***syn*** see PURE 2

pureblood *adj* ***syn*** see PUREBRED

purebred *adj* being of unmixed ancestry <a *purebred* collie>
syn full-blooded, pedigree, pedigreed, pureblood, thoroughbred
rel registered
con bastard, hybrid, lowbred, mixed
ant mongrel

||**puredee** (*or* **pure–D**) *adj* ***syn*** see UTTER

purely *adv* ***syn*** see ALL 1

purgation *n* ***syn*** see PURIFICATION

purgative *adj* cleansing or purifying especially from sin <confession as a *purgative* ritual>
syn expiative, expiatory, expurgatorial, expurgatory, lustral, lustratory, propitiatory, purgatorial

purgatorial *adj* ***syn*** see PURGATIVE

||**purgatory** *n* ***syn*** see SWAMP

purge *vb* **1** ***syn*** see DISABUSE
rel absolve, cleanse; clear, rid
2 ***syn*** see PURIFY 2
3 to get rid of often by exile, imprisonment, or murder <Stalin *purged* all the Party dissidents>
syn eliminate, liquidate, remove
rel debar, exclude, shut out; dismiss, eject, expel, oust; erase, expunge, wipe (out); exterminate
con rehabilitate; reinstate; repatriate; accept, bear (with), tolerate
ant depurge

purification *n* a freeing from something morally harmful, offensive, or sinful <sought *purification* through repentance>
syn catharsis, cleansing, expurgation, lustration, purgation
rel atonement, expiation; absolution, forgiveness; grace, redemption, salvation; rebirth, regeneration; sanctification
con contamination, defilement

purify *vb* **1** to free from material impurities or noxious matter <*purify* the water for drinking>
syn clarify, clean, cleanse, depurate
rel elutriate; filter; refine
con dirty, foul, soil
ant contaminate, pollute
2 to free from guilt or moral blemish (often ceremonially) <*purify* one's heart through confession>
syn cleanse, expurgate, lustrate, purge
rel atone, expiate; absolve, remit
con defile, sully, tarnish

purist *n* one who adheres strictly and often excessively to a tradition <*purists* who believe in prescriptive grammar>
syn precisian, precisionist, traditionalist
rel Atticist, classicist; bitter-ender, conservative, diehard, Puritan
con liberal, radical, young Turk
ant revisionist

puritan *n* ***syn*** see PRUDE

puritanical *adj* ***syn*** see PRIM 1
rel rigorous, strict; bigoted, hidebound, illiberal, intolerant, narrow, narrow-minded
con liberal, tolerant; modern

purl *vb* ***syn*** see SWIRL
‖**purl** *vb* ***syn*** see SPIN 1
purlieu *n* **1** ***syn*** see RESORT 2
2 purlieus *pl* ***syn*** see ENVIRONS 1
3 purlieus *pl* ***syn*** see ENVIRONS 2
purloin *vb* ***syn*** see STEAL 1
purloiner *n* ***syn*** see THIEF
purloining *n* ***syn*** see THEFT
purple *adj* **1** ***syn*** see RISQUÉ
2 ***syn*** see RHETORICAL
purport *n* **1** ***syn*** see MEANING 1
2 ***syn*** see TENOR 1
rel connotation; implication
3 ***syn*** see SUBSTANCE 2
purported *adj* ***syn*** see ALLEGED
rel postulated, presupposed; suppositional, suppositive; academic, speculative, theoretical; reputed, rumored; suspected
purportless *adj* ***syn*** see SENSELESS 5
purpose *n* **1** ***syn*** see INTENTION
rel destination, direction; aim, goal, mission, objective, point; ambition, aspiration; proposal, proposition
2 ***syn*** see USE 4
rel mission
purpose *vb* ***syn*** see INTEND 2
rel meditate, ponder; consider; conclude, decide, determine, resolve
purposedly *adv* ***syn*** see INTENTIONALLY
purposefulness *n* ***syn*** see DECISION 2
rel certainty, confidence, sureness
con indecision, irresoluteness, irresolution, vacillation, waffling, wavering, weakness; aimlessness, indirection
ant purposelessness
purposeless *adj* **1** ***syn*** see FECKLESS 1
rel unhelpful, unprofitable; purportless, senseless; nonsensical
con helpful, profitable
ant purposeful
2 ***syn*** see RANDOM
ant purposeful
purposely *adv* ***syn*** see INTENTIONALLY
rel expressly; explicitly
con unintentionally
ant accidentally
purposively *adv* ***syn*** see INTENTIONALLY
purposiveness *n* ***syn*** see DECISION 2
purse cutter *n* ***syn*** see PICKPOCKET
pursual *n* ***syn*** see PURSUIT 2
pursuance *n* ***syn*** see PURSUIT 2
pursue *vb* **1** ***syn*** see FOLLOW 2
rel persevere, persist; oppress, persecute; badger, bait, hound, ride
idiom go in pursuit (of)
2 ***syn*** see ADDRESS 8
pursuing *n* ***syn*** see PURSUIT 2
pursuit *n* **1** ***syn*** see WORK 1
2 a following with a view to reach, accomplish, or obtain <the *pursuit* of happiness>
syn pursual, pursuance, pursuing, quest, search, seeking
rel following; reaching; obtaining; accomplishing, accomplishment
idiom a going all out (after)
pursy *adj* ***syn*** see FAT 2
purview *n* **1** ***syn*** see RANGE 2
2 ***syn*** see KEN
push *vb* **1** to use force so as to cause to move ahead or aside <*push* a wheelbarrow across the yard>
syn drive, propel, shove, thrust
rel launch; impel, move; force, ram
con brake, check, stay
ant pull
2 to do, effect, or accomplish by forcing aside obstacles or opposition <*pushed* her way through the crowd> <*pushed* the measure through congress>
syn bulldoze, elbow, hustle, jostle, press, ‖shog, shoulder, shove
rel dig, nudge; hunch; drive, force, thrust; bump, butt, ram
con ease, facilitate, slide (by), slip (through); expedite, help (along)
3 ***syn*** see INCREASE 1
4 ***syn*** see PRESSURE
5 ***syn*** see PROMOTE 3
rel oversell
6 to engage in the illicit sale of (narcotics) <*pushing* drugs to teenagers>
syn peddle, shove
7 ***syn*** see PRESS 1
push *n* **1** ***syn*** see ENTERPRISE 4
2 ***syn*** see VIGOR 2
3 ***syn*** see STIMULUS
4 ***syn*** see CROWD 1
5 ***syn*** see SET 5
push around *vb* ***syn*** see BAIT 2
pushful *adj* **1** ***syn*** see AGGRESSIVE
2 ***syn*** see PRESUMPTUOUS
rel imposing, intrusive, obtruding, obtrusive, officious; assured, confident, self-confident
pushing *adj* **1** ***syn*** see AGGRESSIVE
idiom ‖not backward in going forward
2 ***syn*** see PRESUMPTUOUS
push off *vb* ***syn*** see GO 2
push on *vb* ***syn*** see GO 1
pushover *n* ***syn*** see SNAP 1
pushy *adj* **1** ***syn*** see AGGRESSIVE
‖**2** ***syn*** see PRESUMPTUOUS
pusillanimous *adj* ***syn*** see COWARDLY
puss *n* ***syn*** see CHILD 1
‖**puss** *n* ***syn*** see FACE 1
pussyfoot *vb* **1** ***syn*** see SNEAK
2 ***syn*** see EQUIVOCATE 2
pustule *n* ***syn*** see ABSCESS
put *vb* **1** ***syn*** see SET 1
2 ***syn*** see FASTEN 3
3 ***syn*** see PROPOSE 1
4 ***syn*** see WORD
5 ***syn*** see TRANSLATE 1
6 ***syn*** see EXPRESS 2
7 ***syn*** see ESTIMATE 3

put (back) *vb syn* see RESTORE 5
put (on) *vb syn* see GAMBLE 1
put (on *or* upon) *vb syn* see LEVY
put *n syn* see DUNCE
put about *vb syn* see INCONVENIENCE
putative *adj syn* see SUPPOSED 1
put away *vb* **1** *syn* see DIVORCE 2
2 *syn* see CONSUME 5
3 *syn* see MURDER 1
4 *syn* see BURY 1
5 *syn* see KILL 1
put by *vb syn* see SAVE 4
put down *vb* **1** *syn* see CRUSH 5
2 *syn* see DEGRADE 1
3 *syn* see CONSUME 5
4 *syn* see DECRY 2
put in *vb syn* see PLANT 1
put off *vb* **1** *syn* see DELAY 2
idiom drag one's feet
2 *syn* see DEFER
idiom lay on the table, let the matter stand
3 *syn* see REMOVE 3
ant put on
put on *vb* **1** *syn* see DON 1
ant put off
2 *syn* see DON 2
rel affect, feign, sham, simulate; masquerade, pose
idiom make as if (*or* as though)
3 *syn* see ASSUME 4
idiom put on a (false) front, put on an act
4 *syn* see EMPLOY 2
5 *syn* see STAGE
put–on *adj syn* see ARTIFICIAL 3
rel mannered, posed; faked, sham
put–on *n* **1** *syn* see IMPOSTURE
2 *syn* see MASK 2
put out *vb* **1** *syn* see EXERT
2 *syn* see EXTINGUISH 1
3 *syn* see PUBLISH 2
4 *syn* see IRRITATE
5 *syn* see INCONVENIENCE
rel displease, dissatisfy; annoy, irritate
idiom put out of the way, put to it
put over *vb syn* see DEFER
putrefy *vb syn* see DECAY
putresce *vb syn* see DECAY
putrid *adj* **1** *syn* see BAD 5
2 *syn* see MALODOROUS 1
3 *syn* see VICIOUS 2
putter *vb syn* see FIDDLE 2
rel boondoggle; dawdle
||**put to** *vb syn* see CLOSE 1
put together *vb syn* see MAKE 3
put up *vb* **1** *syn* see HARBOR 2
2 *syn* see BUILD 1
rel forge, make, put together, shape
3 *syn* see ERECT 3
4 *syn* see RAISE 9
rel elevate, escalate
||**puxy** *n syn* see SWAMP
puzzle *vb* to baffle and disturb mentally <a persistent fever that *puzzled* her doctor>
syn befog, bewilder, ||cap, confound, confuse, metagrobolize, perplex, pose, stumble; *compare* NONPLUS 1
rel baffle, foil, frustrate; befuddle, ||bumfuzzle, fuddle; disconcert, distract, disturb, upset; addle, muddle; mystify; amaze, dumbfound, flabbergast
con enlighten, inform
puzzle *n syn* see MYSTERY
puzzlement *n syn* see MYSTERY
puzzle out *vb syn* see SOLVE 2
idiom find the key to, pick the lock
pygmy *n syn* see DWARF
ant giant
pygmy *adj syn* see TINY
pyramid *n syn* see PILE 1
Pyrrhonian *n syn* see SKEPTIC
Pyrrhonist *n syn* see SKEPTIC
pythonic *adj syn* see HUGE

Q

quack *n* ***syn*** see CHARLATAN
rel counterfeiter, pretender, shammer, simulator
‖**quackle** *vb* ***syn*** see SUFFOCATE
quacksalver *n* ***syn*** see CHARLATAN
quackster *n* ***syn*** see CHARLATAN
quad *n* ***syn*** see COURT 1
quadrangle *n* ***syn*** see COURT 1
quadrate *adj* ***syn*** see SQUARE 1
quadrate *vb* **1** ***syn*** see AGREE 4
2 ***syn*** see ADAPT
quadratic *adj* ***syn*** see SQUARE 1
quadratical *adj* ***syn*** see SQUARE 1
quaesitum *n* ***syn*** see AMBITION 2
quaff *vb* ***syn*** see DRINK 1
quag *n* ***syn*** see SWAMP
quaggy *adj* ***syn*** see SOFT 6
quagmire *n* **1** ***syn*** see SWAMP
2 ***syn*** see PREDICAMENT
quail *n* ***syn*** see GIRL 1
quail *vb* ***syn*** see RECOIL
rel cower, cringe
quaint *adj* ***syn*** see STRANGE 4
rel droll, funny, laughable; antiquated, antique, archaic
‖**quaint** *vb* ***syn*** see INTRODUCE 4
quake *vb* **1** ***syn*** see SHAKE 2
rel fluctuate, waver
2 ***syn*** see SHAKE 1
quake *n* ***syn*** see EARTHQUAKE
‖**quaker** *n* ***syn*** see EARTHQUAKE
quaking *adj* ***syn*** see TREMULOUS
quaky *adj* ***syn*** see TREMULOUS
qualification *n* ***syn*** see ABILITY 1
qualified *adj* **1** ***syn*** see ABLE
rel disciplined, instructed, trained; catechized, examined, quizzed; proved, tested, tried
con incapable, incompetent, unequipped, unfit
ant disqualified, unqualified
2 not unlimited and complete <gave only a *qualified* endorsement to the project>
syn limited, modified, reserved
rel circumscribed, definite, determined, fixed, restricted; partial
con complete, entire, full, total, utter, whole; unlimited, unrestricted
ant absolute, unqualified
qualifiedness *n* ***syn*** see ABILITY 1
qualify *vb* **1** ***syn*** see CHARACTERIZE 2
rel ascribe, assign, attribute, impute; predicate
2 ***syn*** see ENTITLE 2
quality *n* **1** something inherent and distinctive <learned the special *qualities* of the native herbs>
syn affection, attribute, character, characteristic, feature, mark, peculiarity, property, savor, trait, virtue; *compare* CHARACTERISTIC 1
rel individuality; affirmation, predication; element, factor, parameter
2 a usually high level of merit or superiority <merchandise of *quality*>
syn caliber, merit, stature, value, virtue, worth
rel arete, excellence, excellency, perfection, superbness, superiority
con inferiority, meanness, mediocrity, poorness; inadequacy; deficiency
3 degree of excellence <upgrading the *quality* of incoming students>
syn caliber, class, grade
rel capacity, character, footing, place, position, rank, situation, standing, state, station, status
4 ***syn*** see STATUS 1
5 ***syn*** see ARISTOCRACY
6 ***syn*** see EXCELLENCE
quality *adj* ***syn*** see EXCELLENT
qualm *n* a misgiving about what one is going to do <had *qualms* about the secret meeting>
syn compunction, conscience, demur, scruple, squeam
rel apprehension, foreboding, misgiving, presentiment; doubt, mistrust, suspicion, uncertainty; agitation, insecurity, perturbation; objection, remonstrance; reluctance, unwillingness; impatience, nervousness, unease, uneasiness
con aplomb, assurance, confidence, self-assurance, self-confidence, self-possession; certainty, certitude, conviction
qualmish *adj* ***syn*** see SQUEAMISH 1
qualmishness *n* ***syn*** see NAUSEA
qualmy *adj* ***syn*** see SQUEAMISH 1
quantity *n* **1** ***syn*** see BODY 5
2 quantities *pl* ***syn*** see SCAD
quantum *n* **1** ***syn*** see BODY 5
2 ***syn*** see RATION
quarrel *n* a usually verbal dispute marked by anger or discord <a *quarrel* over who would drive the car>
syn altercation, ‖barney, beef, bickering, brabble, brannigan, brawl, controversy, difficulty, dispute, dust, dustup, embroilment, falling-out, feud, fight, fracas, fuss, hassle, imbroglio, knock-down-and-drag-out, miff, ‖prabble, ‖pribble, rhubarb, row, ruckus, run-in, set-to, spat, squabble, squall, tiff, to-and-fro, word(s), wrangle; *compare* BRAWL 2
rel battle royal, catfight; affray, bobbery, broil, donnybrook, fray, free-for-all, melee, ruction, rumpus, scrap, scrimmage, scuffle; conflict, contention, difference, discord, dissension, strife, variance; disagreement, misunderstanding

syn synonym(s) ***rel*** related word(s)
ant antonym(s) ***con*** contrasted word(s)
idiom idiomatic equivalent(s)
‖ use limited; if in doubt, see a dictionary

idiom ||pribbles and prabbles
con accord, concord, harmony; agreement, like-mindedness, understanding, unity

quarrel *vb* to contend noisily or captiously <with his belligerent personality he was always *quarreling* with someone>
syn altercate, bicker, brabble, brawl, ||cast out, caterwaul, fall out, row, scrap, spat, squabble, tiff, wrangle; *compare* ARGUE 2
rel differ, disaccord, dissent, divide, vary; bump, clash, collide, conflict, thwart; battle, contend, fight, war
idiom have words with, pull caps
con agree, coincide, concur

quarrelsome *adj* **1** *syn* see BELLIGERENT
rel adverse, antagonistic, counter; antipathetic, hostile, inimical, rancorous
idiom having a chip on one's shoulder
2 apt or disposed to quarrel <when he's in a bad mood he becomes so *quarrelsome*>
syn battlesome, brawling, brawlsome, brawly, scrappy; *compare* BELLIGERENT
rel argumentative; disputatious; cankered, crabbed, irascible, irritable
con conciliatory, propitiatory

quarry *n* *syn* see GAME 3

quarry *vb* *syn* see MINE

quarter *n* **1** one of four equal parts <ate one *quarter* of the pie>
syn fourth, quartern
rel quadrant
2 a division or part of a town or city <the market *quarter* in Paris>
syn district, precinct, section, sector
rel division, part; area; locality; barrio

quarter *vb* **1** *syn* see HARBOR 2
2 *syn* see BILLET 1

quarterage *n* *syn* see SHELTER 2

quarterback *vb* *syn* see SUPERVISE

quartern *n* *syn* see QUARTER 1

quarter–witted *adj* *syn* see RETARDED

quartet *n* a group consisting of four individuals <a singing *quartet*>
syn four, foursome, quartetto, quaternion, quatuor, tetrad
rel quadruplet

quartetto *n* *syn* see QUARTET

quash *vb* **1** *syn* see ANNUL 4
2 *syn* see ABOLISH 1
3 *syn* see CRUSH 5

quashing *n* *syn* see REPRESSION 1

||**quat** *vb* *syn* see SQUAT

quaternion *n* *syn* see QUARTET

quatuor *n* *syn* see QUARTET

quaver *vb* *syn* see SHAKE 1
rel falter, hesitate, vacillate, waver

||**quawk** *vb* *syn* see SQUALL 1

quay *n* *syn* see WHARF

||**queak** *vb* *syn* see SQUEAK 1

quean *n* *syn* see PROSTITUTE

queasiness *n* *syn* see NAUSEA

queasy *adj* **1** *syn* see DOUBTFUL 1
2 *syn* see SQUEAMISH 1

queer *adj* **1** *syn* see STRANGE 4
rel doubtful, dubious, questionable; droll, funny, laughable
2 *syn* see OBSESSED
||**3** *syn* see HOMOSEXUAL
4 *syn* see SQUEAMISH 1

||**queer** *n* *syn* see HOMOSEXUAL

||**quelch** *vb* *syn* see SUPPRESS 2

quell *vb* *syn* see CRUSH 5
rel conquer, overcome, subjugate, vanquish
con abet, incite, instigate
ant foment

quench *vb* **1** *syn* see EXTINGUISH 1
2 *syn* see CRUSH 5
rel end, terminate
3 *syn* see DESTROY 1
4 to bring (as thirst) to an end with or as if with a refreshing drink <after being in the hot sun, he found it difficult to *quench* his thirst>
syn slake, ||squench
rel appease, content, gratify, satisfy; sate, satiate; allay, alleviate, assuage, lighten, mitigate, relieve; decrease, diminish, lessen, reduce

quenching *n* *syn* see REPRESSION 1

quenchless *adj* **1** *syn* see INSATIABLE
2 *syn* see INDESTRUCTIBLE

querulent *adj* *syn* see IRRITABLE

querulential *adj* *syn* see IRRITABLE

querulous *adj* *syn* see IRRITABLE
rel blubbering, crying, wailing, weeping, whimpering; bemoaning, deploring, lamenting

query *n* **1** *syn* see INQUIRY 2
2 *syn* see UNCERTAINTY

query *vb* *syn* see ASK 1

quest *n* **1** *syn* see INQUIRY 1
2 *syn* see PURSUIT 2

quest *vb* **1** *syn* see HOWL 1
2 *syn* see SEEK 1

question *n* **1** *syn* see INQUIRY 2
2 *syn* see PROBLEM 2
3 *syn* see DEMUR 2

question *vb* **1** *syn* see ASK 1
2 to express doubt about <*questioned* his decision to take a new job>
syn challenge, dispute, doubt, mistrust
rel suspect, ||suspicion; hesitate (over), puzzle (over), wonder (about)

questionable *adj* **1** *syn* see IMPROBABLE 1
ant unquestionable
2 *syn* see MOOT
rel refutable; equivocal, obscure, vague
con dependable, true, trustworthy, trusty; genuine, indubitable, real, undoubted, undubitable, veritable, very
ant authoritative; unquestionable, unquestioned
3 *syn* see UNRELIABLE 1

questioning *n* *syn* see INQUIRY 2

questioning *adj* **1** *syn* see INCREDULOUS
ant questionless, unquestioning
2 *syn* see INQUISITIVE 1

questionless *adj* *syn* see AUTHENTIC 2

queue *n* *syn* see LINE 5

quibble *vb* **1** to find fault with something usually on minor grounds <was a peevish critic, always ready to *quibble*>

syn cavil, chicane, hypercriticize
rel carp, criticize
idiom split hairs
con applaud, commend, compliment, recommend; approve, endorse, sanction
2 ***syn*** see ARGUE 2
quick *adj* **1** ***syn*** see FAST 3
rel agile, brisk, nimble; abrupt, impetuous
idiom quick on the trigger
con dilatory, laggard, leisurely, slow, unhasty, unhurried; comatose
ant sluggish
2 able to respond without delay or hesitation or indicative of such ability <very *quick* in perception> <his *quick* eye spotted the trouble>
syn apt, prompt, ready; *compare* INSTANTANEOUS
rel clever, intelligent, quick-witted, smart; adroit, deft, dexterous; acute, keen, sharp; able, capable, competent, effective, effectual
con comatose, lethargic, logy, poky, torpid; crass, dense, dull, dumb, stupid
ant slow; sluggish
3 ***syn*** see WISE 4
quick *adv* ***syn*** see FAST 2
quick *n* ***syn*** see CENTER 3
quicken *vb* **1** to make alive or lively <warm spring days that *quicken* the earth>
syn animate, enliven, liven, vivificate, vivify
rel activate, energize, vitalize; arouse, awaken, rouse, stir, wake
con blunt, dull; slow (down)
ant deaden
2 ***syn*** see PROVOKE 4
rel activate, actuate, motivate; goad, induce, spur
con check, halt, interrupt, stall, stay; curb, inhibit, restrain
ant arrest
3 ***syn*** see SPEED 3
con bog (down), detain, embog, hang up, mire
ant slacken
quickening *adj* ***syn*** see INVIGORATING
quick-lunch *n* ***syn*** see EATING HOUSE
quickly *adv* ***syn*** see FAST 2
quickness *n* ***syn*** see SPEED 2
ant slowness
quick-sighted *adj* ***syn*** see SHARP 4
quick-tempered *adj* ***syn*** see IRASCIBLE
quick-witted *adj* **1** ***syn*** see SHARP 4
2 ***syn*** see INTELLIGENT 2
rel apt, prompt, quick, ready
3 ***syn*** see WISE 4
rel acute, keen; facetious, humorous, witty
ant slow-witted
quidnunc *n* **1** ***syn*** see BUSYBODY
2 ***syn*** see GOSSIP 1
quiescence *n* ***syn*** see ABEYANCE
quiescency *n* ***syn*** see ABEYANCE
quiescent *adj* ***syn*** see LATENT
rel calm, halcyon, hushed, placid, quiet, still, stilly, untroubled
quiet *n* **1** a period of intensified silence <the *quiet* before the storm>
syn calm, hush, lull
rel cessation, stop, termination
con din, hubbub, racket, uproar
2 ***syn*** see SILENCE 1
quiet *adj* **1** ***syn*** see CALM 1
con harsh, rough; disquieted, disturbed, perturbed, upset
ant unquiet
2 ***syn*** see INACTIVE
3 ***syn*** see STILL 3
con blatant, boisterous, clamorous, strident, vociferous
4 not showy or obtrusive <always dressed in *quiet* good taste>
syn inobtrusive, restrained, subdued, tasteful, tasty, unobtrusive
rel homely, plain, simple, unpretentious
con blatant, brazen, flashy, garish, glaring, meretricious, tawdry, tinsel; elaborate
ant gaudy, loud
quiet *vb* **1** ***syn*** see SILENCE
rel abate, decrease, lessen
con excite, provoke, quicken, stimulate; awaken, rally, stir
2 ***syn*** see CALM
con agitate; unhinge, untune
ant disquiet; excite
‖**quieten** *vb* **1** ***syn*** see SILENCE
2 ***syn*** see CALM
ant arouse; excite
quietive *adj* ***syn*** see SEDATIVE
quietness *n* ***syn*** see SILENCE 1
quietude *n* ***syn*** see SILENCE 1
quietus *n* ***syn*** see DEATH 1
‖**quiff** *n* ***syn*** see GIRL 1
quilt *n* a bed coverlet made of two layers of cloth with a stuffing (as of cotton, wool, or feathers) between <a warm *quilt* is nice on a winter night>
syn ‖comfortable, comforter, pouf, puff
rel bedcover, bedspread, counterpane; eiderdown
quinary *adj* ***syn*** see QUINTUPLE
quinta *n* ***syn*** see ESTATE 3
quintessence *n* **1** ***syn*** see ESSENCE 2
2 ***syn*** see APOTHEOSIS 1
quintessential *adj* ***syn*** see TYPICAL 1
quintessential *n* ***syn*** see ESSENCE 2
quintuple *adj* consisting of five <the problem is viewed as having *quintuple* aspects>
syn fivefold, quinary
rel quintuplicate
quip *n* ***syn*** see JOKE 1
quip (at) *vb* ***syn*** see SCOFF
quipster *n* ***syn*** see HUMORIST 2
quit *vb* **1** ***syn*** see CLEAR 5
2 ***syn*** see BEHAVE 1
3 ***syn*** see GO 2
4 ***syn*** see ABANDON 1
rel relinquish, resign, surrender
5 ***syn*** see STOP 3

6 to give up (as a habit, activity, or employment) especially with finality <*quit* a job> <determined to *quit* smoking>
syn drop, leave, resign, terminate
rel retire, secede, withdraw
idiom draw one's time, give notice
con hire on, hire out

quite *adv* **1** ***syn*** see WELL 3
2 ***syn*** see ALTOGETHER 2
3 ***syn*** see ALL 1
4 ***syn*** see WELL 8

quittance *n* ***syn*** see REPARATION

quitter *n* ***syn*** see COWARD

quiver *n* ***syn*** see FLASH 1

quiver *vb* ***syn*** see SHAKE 1
rel beat, palpatate, pulsate, pulse, throb

quivering *adj* ***syn*** see TREMULOUS

quivery *adj* ***syn*** see TREMULOUS

quiz *n* ***syn*** see ECCENTRIC

quiz *vb* **1** ***syn*** see RIDICULE
2 ***syn*** see ASK 1

quizzical *adj* ***syn*** see INCREDULOUS
rel curious, inquisitive; probing, searching

‖**quod** *vb* ***syn*** see IMPRISON

quodlibetic *adj* ***syn*** see PEDANTIC

quondam *adj* ***syn*** see FORMER 2

quota *n* **1** ***syn*** see SHARE 1
2 ***syn*** see RATION

quota *vb* ***syn*** see APPORTION 2

quotidian *adj* **1** ***syn*** see DAILY
2 ***syn*** see ORDINARY 1

R

rabbity *adj* ***syn*** see SHY 1

rabble *n* **1** ***syn*** see MOB 2

2 the lowest class of people <the *rabble* of the city>

syn canaille, doggery, dreg(s), hoi polloi, mass(es), mob, other half, polloi, proletariat, raff, ‖ragabash, ragtag, ragtag and bobtail, riffraff, roughscuff, rout, scum, scurf, tag and rag, tagrag and bobtail, trash, unwashed

rel bourgeoisie, commonalty, many, people, populace, public, rank and file

idiom the great unwashed, the scum of the earth, the submerged tenth

con aristocracy, aristoi, elite, Four Hundred, gentility, nobility, upper class, upper crust, upper ten, upper ten thousand

rabble–rouser *n* ***syn*** see DEMAGOGUE

rabid *adj* **1** ***syn*** see FURIOUS 2

rel crazed, crazy, demented, deranged, insane

2 ***syn*** see EXTREME 3

rel enthusiastic, keen, obsessed, zealous

race *n* ***syn*** see CREEK 2

race *vb* **1** ***syn*** see RUSH 1

2 ***syn*** see COURSE

race *n* ***syn*** see FAMILY 1

rel culture, nation, nationality, people; breed, type, variety

rachis *n* ***syn*** see SPINE

rachitic *adj* ***syn*** see RICKETY

racial *adj* ***syn*** see ETHNIC 2

racialism *n* ***syn*** see RACISM

racism *n* racial prejudice or discrimination <an act of overt *racism*>

syn racialism

rel discrimination, prejudice; illiberality, unfairness; bias, one-sideness, partiality

con broad-mindedness, liberalness, open-mindedness, tolerance; indifference, neutrality

rack *vb* ***syn*** see AFFLICT

rel distress, pain; oppress, persecute

‖**rack back** *vb* ***syn*** see REPROVE

racket *n* **1** ***syn*** see DIN

‖**2** ***syn*** see WORK 1

racketry *n* ***syn*** see DIN

rackety *adj* **1** ***syn*** see NOISY

2 ***syn*** see RICKETY

racking *adj* ***syn*** see EXCRUCIATING

rel barbarous, cruel, ferocious, fierce, inhuman, savage

rack up *vb* ***syn*** see GAIN 1

racy *adj* **1** ***syn*** see PUNGENT

rel fiery, gingery, mettlesome, spirited

con banal, inane, jejune

2 ***syn*** see RISQUÉ

radiant *adj* **1** ***syn*** see BRIGHT 1

2 ***syn*** see GLAD 2

radiate *vb* **1** ***syn*** see SHINE 1

2 ***syn*** see SPREAD 1

rel diverge

radical *adj* **1** ***syn*** see FUNDAMENTAL 1

rel cardinal, essential, vital; constitutional, inherent, intrinsic

ant superficial

2 ***syn*** see EXTREME 3

3 ***syn*** see LIBERAL 3

radical *n* one who favors rapid and sweeping changes <the *radicals* advocated overthrow of the government>

syn extremist, revolutionary, revolutionist, ultraist; *compare* REACTIONARY

rel liberal, progressive, reformer; agitator, insurgent, insurrectionist, rebel; anarchist, nihilist, red, subversive; out-and-outer; secessionist, separatist

con bitter-ender, diehard, fogy, intransigent, mossback, reactionary, rightist, standpatter

ant conservative

radius *n* ***syn*** see RANGE 2

raff *n* ***syn*** see RABBLE 2

raffish *adj* ***syn*** see WILD 7

rag *vb* **1** ***syn*** see SCOLD 1

2 ***syn*** see BANTER

‖**ragabash** *n* ***syn*** see RABBLE 2

ragamuffin *n* a person dressed in ragged clothing <a poor *ragamuffin* found begging>

syn ragshag, scarecrow, tatterdemalion

rel hobo, tramp, vagabond, vagrant; bum, loafer, wastrel; orphan, waif

con buck, coxcomb, dandy, dude, fop

rage *n* **1** ***syn*** see ANGER

rel acerbity, acrimony, asperity; frenzy, hysteria, mania; agitation, perturbation, upset

2 ***syn*** see FASHION 3

rel caprice, conceit, crotchet, fancy, freak, vagary, whim

rage *vb* ***syn*** see ANGER 2

ragged *adj* torn or worn to tatters <never saw such *ragged* clothes>

syn frayed, frazzled, shreddy, tattered

rel rent, torn; battered, patched; dilapidated, dingy, faded, seedy, shabby, threadbare, worn-out

raging *adj* ***syn*** see WILD 6

rags *n pl* **1** poor or ragged clothing <a beggar in *rags*>

syn ‖duds, tatters

rel odds and ends, ribbons, shreds

2 ***syn*** see CLOTHES

ragshag *n* ***syn*** see RAGAMUFFIN

ragtag *n* ***syn*** see RABBLE 2

---

syn synonym(s) ***rel*** related word(s)
ant antonym(s) ***con*** contrasted word(s)
idiom idiomatic equivalent(s)
‖ use limited; if in doubt, see a dictionary

ragtag and bobtail *n* ***syn*** see RABBLE 2
raid *n* **1** ***syn*** see INVASION
rel assault, onset, onslaught
2 a sudden attack by officers of the law <a *raid* on a gambling joint>
syn ‖bust
raid *vb* **1** to make a raid on <Indians *raided* the settlers frequently>
syn foray, harass, harry, maraud
rel despoil, devastate, ravage, sack, spoliate, waste; loot, plunder, rifle, rob
2 ***syn*** see INVADE 1
raider *n* ***syn*** see MARAUDER
rail *n* ***syn*** see RAILING
rail *vb* ***syn*** see SCOLD 1
railing *n* a usually protective barrier consisting essentially of an elongated raised member <a staircase without a *railing*>
syn balustrade, banister, rail
raillery *n* ***syn*** see SATIRE
railroad station *n* a building containing accommodations for railroad passengers or freight <an old *railroad station* fallen into disrepair>
syn depot, station, station house
raiment *n* ***syn*** see CLOTHES
raiment *vb* ***syn*** see CLOTHE
rainbow *n* ***syn*** see PIPE DREAM
rainless *adj* ***syn*** see FAIR 2
ant rainy
raise *vb* **1** ***syn*** see LIFT 1
ant lower
2 ***syn*** see INCITE
3 ***syn*** see RESURRECT 1
4 ***syn*** see ERECT 3
5 ***syn*** see BUILD 1
6 ***syn*** see BRING UP 1
7 ***syn*** see GROW 1
8 ***syn*** see GATHER 6
9 to make larger in amount <*raised* the rent>
syn boost, hike, increase, jack (up), jump, put up, up
rel inflate
idiom send through the roof
con cut back, decrease, drop, lessen, reduce, roll back; minimize
ant lower
raise *n* ***syn*** see ADDITION
raised *adj* **1** ***syn*** see ELEVATED 1
2 ***syn*** see ERECT
rake *vb* ***syn*** see SCOUR 2
rakehell *adj* ***syn*** see WILD 7
raking *adj* ***syn*** see FAST 3
rakish *adj* ***syn*** see WILD 7
rally *vb* **1** ***syn*** see MOBILIZE 3
2 ***syn*** see STIR 1
rel fire; refresh, renew, restore
3 ***syn*** see RECOVER 2
rel brace (up), enliven, invigorate, perk (up), pick up
rally *vb* ***syn*** see RIDICULE
rel harass, harry, tantalize, tease, worry
rallying cry *n* ***syn*** see BATTLE CRY
ram *vb* **1** ***syn*** see THRUST 2
2 ***syn*** see CRAM 1
ramble *vb* **1** ***syn*** see WANDER 1
2 ***syn*** see DIGRESS 2
3 ***syn*** see SPRAWL 2
ramble *n* ***syn*** see WALK 1
rambler *n* ***syn*** see ROVER
rambunctious *adj* ***syn*** see TURBULENT 1
rampage *n* ***syn*** see SPREE 1
rel turmoil, uproar
rampant *adj* **1** ***syn*** see RANK 1
rel excessive, immoderate, inordinate
con moderate, temperate; checked, curbed, restrained
2 ***syn*** see PREVAILING
rampart *n* ***syn*** see BULWARK
rancid *adj* ***syn*** see MALODOROUS 1
rel ‖reasty; loathsome, repulsive
ant sweet
rancor *n* ***syn*** see ENMITY
rel bitterness, vindictiveness, virulence
rancorous *adj* **1** ***syn*** see MALICIOUS
2 ***syn*** see BITTER 3
rancorously *adv* ***syn*** see HARD 6
random *adj* lacking a definite plan, purpose, or pattern <a *random* choice>
syn aimless, designless, desultory, haphazard, hit-or-miss, indiscriminate, irregular, objectless, promiscuous, purposeless, slapdash, spot, unaimed, unconsidered, unplanned; *compare* ACCIDENTAL
rel contingent, fluky, fortuitous, incidental, odd
con arranged, organized, planned; methodical, systematic; deliberate, purposeful
ant purposive
random *adv* ***syn*** see ABOUT 4
ant orderly
randomly *adv* ***syn*** see ABOUT 4
ant orderly
randy *adj* ***syn*** see LICENTIOUS 2
range *vb* **1** ***syn*** see LINE 1
rel assort, classify, sort; bias, dispose, incline, predispose
2 ***syn*** see WANDER 1
3 to change or differ within limits <discounts *range* from 10% to 40%>
syn extend, go, run, vary
rel differ, fluctuate
range *n* **1** ***syn*** see HABITAT
2 sphere of action, expression, or influence <a political movement worldwide in its *range* and power>
syn ambit, circle, compass, confine(s), dimension(s), extension, extensity, extent, length, orbit, panorama, purview, radius, reach, realm, scope, stretch, sweep, width
rel area, space, span; domain, field, province, sphere, territory; amplitude, expanse, gamut, spread
3 ***syn*** see KEN
rel compass
idiom range of comprehension
4 ***syn*** see ORDER 4
5 the distance or extent between possible extremes <the *range* of exhibited photographs went from the extremely good to the extremely bad>

syn diapason, gamut, scale, spectrum
rel compass, radius, reach, scope, stretch, sweep

rangy *adj* ***syn*** see GANGLING
ant compact

rank *adj* **1** growing or increasing at an immoderate rate <*rank* weeds>
syn rampant
rel exuberant, lavish, lush, luxuriant, profuse
con scanty, sparse, thin
2 *syn* see OVERGROWN
3 *syn* see OBSCENE 2
4 *syn* see EGREGIOUS
rel conspicuous, noticeable, outstanding
5 *syn* see UTTER
6 *syn* see MALODOROUS 1
rel dank, humid; loathsome, repulsive

rank *n* **1** *syn* see LINE 5
2 *syn* see ESTATE 2
3 *syn* see STATUS 1
4 *syn* see STATUS 2

rank *vb* **1** *syn* see CLASS 2
rel arrange, order; assort, sort
2 *syn* see PRECEDE 1

rank and file *n* *syn* see COMMONALTY

rankle *vb* to produce continual or progressive anger, irritation, or bitterness <this decision has long *rankled* as an act of injustice>
syn fester
rel annoy, bother, irk, vex; aggravate, exasperate, irritate; harass, obsess, plague, torment

ransack *vb* **1** *syn* see SCOUR 2
2 *syn* see ROB 1

ransom *vb* to liberate by paying a price <*ransomed* the king>
syn buy, redeem
rel recover, regain, retrieve; emancipate, free, liberate; extricate, release

rant *vb* **1** *syn* see ORATE
rel bluster, huff; rage, storm
2 *syn* see SCOLD 1

rant *n* *syn* see BOMBAST

ran–tan *n* *syn* see BINGE 1

rantankerous *adj* *syn* see CANTANKEROUS

rap *n* **1** *syn* see HIT 1
2 *syn* see REBUKE

rap *vb* **1** *syn* see TAP 1
2 *syn* see CRITICIZE

rap *n* **1** *syn* see CHAT 2
2 *syn* see CONFERENCE 1
3 *syn* see CRITICISM 2

rapacious *adj* **1** subsisting on prey <the *rapacious* wolf seized the lamb>
syn predacious, predative, predatorial, predatory, raptorial, vulturine, vulturish, vulturous
2 *syn* see VORACIOUS
rel ferocious, fierce

rapacity *n* *syn* see CUPIDITY
rel claim, demand, exaction

rape *vb* to have sexual intercourse with a woman without her consent and chiefly by force or deception <*rape* a young girl>
syn defile, deflorate, deflower, force, outrage, ravish, spoil, violate
rel debauch, devirginate, dishonor, ruin; betray, deceive, mislead; entice, lure, seduce, tempt; compromise, shame, wrong

rapid *adj* *syn* see FAST 3
rel agile, brisk, nimble; hurried, quickened
ant deliberate; leisurely

rapidity *n* *syn* see SPEED 2

rapidly *adv* *syn* see FAST 2

rapidness *n* *syn* see SPEED 2

||**rapper** *n* *syn* see LIE

rapport *n* *syn* see HARMONY 3

rapprochement *n* *syn* see RECONCILIATION

rapscallion *n* *syn* see SCAMP

rap session *n* *syn* see CONFERENCE 2

rapt *adj* *syn* see INTENT

raptorial *adj* *syn* see RAPACIOUS 1

rapture *n* *syn* see ECSTASY

rare *adj* **1** *syn* see THIN 2
2 *syn* see CHOICE
rel excellent, fine, unique
3 *syn* see INFREQUENT
con accustomed, customary, habitual, usual, wonted; abounding, profuse
4 *syn* see EXCEPTIONAL 1

rarefied *adj* *syn* see THIN 2

rarefy *vb* *syn* see THIN 2

rarely *adv* **1** *syn* see SELDOM
2 *syn* see EXTRA

raring *adj* *syn* see EAGER

rascal *n* **1** *syn* see VILLAIN 1
2 *syn* see SCAMP

rash *adj* **1** acting, done, or expressed with undue haste or disregard for consequences <don't do anything *rash*> <that was a very *rash* statement>
syn brash, hasty, hotheaded, ill-advised, incautious, incogitant, inconsiderate, mad-brained, madcap, reckless, thoughtless, unadvised, unconsidered, unwary; *compare* CARELESS 1
rel abrupt, headlong, impetuous, precipitate, precipitous, sudden; foolhardy, foolish, impulsive, silly; careless, heedless, imprudent, indiscreet, injudicious, unthinking, unwise
con careful, cautious, chary, circumspect, wary; advised, considered, deliberate, designed, premeditated, studied; calm, cool, level-headed
ant calculating
2 *syn* see ADVENTUROUS

rash *n* *syn* see EPIDEMIC

rasp *vb* *syn* see SCRAPE 1

raspberry *n* a sound of disapproval, contempt, or derision <the crowd gave the umpire a *raspberry*>
syn bazoo, bird, boo, ||Bronx cheer, catcall, hiss, hoot, pooh, pooh-pooh, ||razz

rasping *adj* *syn* see HARSH 3

raspish *adj* *syn* see IRRITABLE

raspy *adj* *syn* see IRRITABLE

rat *n* **1** *syn* see RENEGADE

---

syn synonym(s) *rel* related word(s)
ant antonym(s) *con* contrasted word(s)
idiom idiomatic equivalent(s)
|| use limited; if in doubt, see a dictionary

2 *syn* see SNOT 1
rat *vb* **1** *syn* see DEFECT
2 *syn* see INFORM 3
rate *vb* *syn* see SCOLD 1
rate *n* **1** *syn* see PRICE 1
2 *syn* see DEGREE 2
rate *vb* **1** *syn* see ESTIMATE 1
2 *syn* see CLASS 2
3 *syn* see EARN 2
rather *adv* **1** *syn* see ENOUGH 2
2 *syn* see INSTEAD
3 *syn* see SOMEWHAT 2
4 *syn* see WELL 8
ratherish *adv* *syn* see SOMEWHAT 2
ratify *vb* to make something legally valid or operative usually by formal approval or sanctioning <agreed to *ratify* the treaty>
syn confirm
rel accredit, authorize, commission, license; approve, endorse, sanction; authenticate, validate
con disown, reject, repudiate
ratio *n* *syn* see DEGREE 2
ratiocination *n* **1** *syn* see INFERENCE 1
ant intuition
2 *syn* see INFERENCE 2
ratiocinative *adj* *syn* see LOGICAL 2
ration *n* an amount allotted or made available especially from a limited supply <saved up their gasoline *ration* for a vacation trip>
syn allotment, allowance, apportionment, measure, meed, part, portion, quantum, quota, share; *compare* SHARE 1
rel assignment, consignment, distribution, division
ration *vb* *syn* see APPORTION 2
rel allocate, allot, assign, mete (out)
rational *adj* agreeable to reason <offered a *rational* explanation>
syn consequent, intelligent, logical, reasonable, sensible, sound
rel calm, cool, level-headed, sober, stable; circumspect, judicious, prudent; lucid, normal, sane
con rash, reckless, wild; groundless, illogical, unreasonable, unreasoning, unsound; crazy, demented, deranged
ant animal, irrational; absurd
rationale *n* *syn* see EXPLANATION 2
rationalization *n* *syn* see EXPLANATION 2
rationalize *vb* *syn* see EXPLAIN 3
rattle *vb* **1** to make a rapid succession of short sharp noises <the window *rattled* in the wind>
syn bicker, clack, clatter, clitter, ‖ruttle, shatter
2 *syn* see CHAT 1
3 *syn* see EMBARRASS
rel addle, muddle; disturb, upset; bewilder, distract, perplex
rattlebrain *n* *syn* see SCATTERBRAIN
rattlebrained *adj* *syn* see GIDDY 1
rattlehead *n* *syn* see SCATTERBRAIN
rattletrap *n*, *usu* **rattletraps** *pl* *syn* see KNICKKNACK
rattletrap *adj* *syn* see RICKETY
rattling *adv* *syn* see VERY 1
ratty *adj* *syn* see IRASCIBLE
raucous *adj* **1** *syn* see HARSH 3
rel brusque, gruff
2 *syn* see TURBULENT 1
raunchy *adj* **1** *syn* see SLOVENLY 1
2 *syn* see OBSCENE 2
ravage *vb* to lay waste (as by plundering or destroying) <the countryside was *ravaged* by the invading soldiers>
syn deflower, depredate, desecrate, desolate, despoil, devast, devastate, devour, harry, havoc, pillage, sack, scourge, spoil, spoliate, strip, waste
rel demolish, destroy, raze; loot, plunder, ransack, rob; ruin, wreck; encroach, invade, trespass; crush, overpower, overrun, overthrow, overwhelm
idiom lay in ruins, lay waste
con build, improve, rehabilitate
ravager *n* *syn* see MARAUDER
rave *vb* **1** *syn* see ORATE
2 *syn* see ENTHUSE 2
ravel *vb* *syn* see COMPLICATE
raven *adj* *syn* see BLACK 1
ravening *adj* *syn* see VORACIOUS
ravenous *adj* **1** *syn* see VORACIOUS
2 *syn* see HUNGRY
ravine *n* a small narrow steep-sided valley <followed the *ravine* high up into the hills>
syn arroyo, chasm, cleft, clough, clove, gap, gorge, gulch
rel cut, notch; defile, pass; abyss, gulf; crevasse, crevice, fissure; ‖dry wash, gully, gutter, ‖wash; canyon
raving *adj* *syn* see DELIRIOUS 1
ravish *vb* **1** *syn* see TRANSPORT 2
2 *syn* see RAPE
ravisher *n* *syn* see MARAUDER
raw *adj* **1** not cooked <a *raw* egg>
syn uncooked
2 *syn* see UNREFINED 3
3 *syn* see RUDE 1
4 *syn* see NUDE 2
5 *syn* see INEXPERIENCED
rel untaught, untutored; unmatured, unripe
con drilled, exercised; hardened; adult, grown-up, mature, matured, ripe
6 *syn* see COARSE 3
‖7 *syn* see OBSCENE 2
rawboned *adj* *syn* see LEAN
rawhider *n* *syn* see SLAVE DRIVER
rawness *n* *syn* see INEXPERIENCE
ray *n* **1** one of the lines of light that appear to radiate from a bright or luminous object <the *rays* of the sun>
syn beam, shaft, shoot
rel raylet; pencil, streak, stream; moonbeam, sunbeam
con gleam, glow, incandescence, shine
2 *syn* see PARTICLE
raze *vb* *syn* see DESTROY 1
razor-sharp *adj* *syn* see SHARP 1
‖**razz** *n* *syn* see RASPBERRY
razz *vb* **1** *syn* see BANTER
2 *syn* see RIDICULE

re *prep* ***syn*** see APROPOS

reach *vb* **1** ***syn*** see COME 1
2 ***syn*** see GAIN 1
3 to get into contact with especially intellectually or emotionally <there was no common ground on which she could *reach* him>
syn approach
rel affect, influence, sway; get, move, touch
idiom establish contact with, find a common denominator, get through to, get to, have a meeting of minds, make advances to, make overtures to, make up to, reach (*or* share) common ground
4 to communicate with <you can *reach* me at this number>
syn contact, get
idiom get in touch (*or* contact) with, get through to, get to, keep in touch (*or* contact) with, maintain connections with
5 ***syn*** see PASS 9
6 ***syn*** see RUN 8

reach *n* **1** ***syn*** see RANGE 2
2 ***syn*** see KEN

react *vb* **1** ***syn*** see ACT 5
2 ***syn*** see RETURN 1

reactionarist *n* ***syn*** see REACTIONARY

reactionary *adj* ***syn*** see CONSERVATIVE 1

reactionary *n* one who strongly resists change and often favors a prior condition <he is a staunch political *reactionary*>
syn Blimp, Bourbon, Colonel Blimp, diehard, reactionarist, reactionist, royalist, ultraconservative, white; *compare* DIEHARD 1, RADICAL
rel bitter-ender, conservative, intransigent, rightist, right-winger, standpatter; fogy, mossback
con extremist, radical, revolutionary, revolutionist, ultraist; liberal, progressive, reformer

reactionist *n* ***syn*** see REACTIONARY

reactivate *vb* ***syn*** see REVIVE 3

read *vb* ***syn*** see SHOW 5

readily *adv* ***syn*** see EASILY 1

readiness *n* **1** ***syn*** see ALACRITY
2 ***syn*** see ADDRESS 1
3 the power of doing something without evidence of effort <his *readiness* in repartee>
syn ease, facility
rel eloquence, fluency, volubility
con effort, exertions, pains, trouble

reading *n* ***syn*** see INTERPRETATION 2

readjust *vb* ***syn*** see REORGANIZE

ready *adj* **1** in a state of mental or physical fitness for some experience or action <*ready* to leave at a moment's notice>
syn prepared, set
rel adjusted, fit, qualified; primed
idiom all ready, all set, champing at the bit
con unprepared, unqualified
ant unready
2 ***syn*** see WILLING 1
3 ***syn*** see QUICK 2
rel adept, expert, masterly, proficient, skilled, skillful; active, dynamic, live

ready *vb* **1** ***syn*** see PREPARE 1
2 ***syn*** see GIRD 3

ready–made *adj* made for general sale or use rather than prepared according to individual specifications <*ready-made* clothing>
syn bought, ||boughten, ||off-the-peg, off-the-rack, off-the-shelf, ready-to-wear, store, store-bought, ||store-boughten
con custom-built, made-to-order, tailor-made; handmade
ant custom-made

ready–to–wear *adj* ***syn*** see READY-MADE

ready–witted *adj* ***syn*** see INTELLIGENT 2

real *adj* **1** ***syn*** see AUTHENTIC 2
ant bogus
2 ***syn*** see GENUINE 3
3 corresponding to known facts <discovered the *real* reason for her hasty departure>
syn actual, indisputable, true, undeniable, unfabled, veridical
rel being, existing, subsisting; certain, inevitable, necessary; sound, valid, well-grounded
idiom deniable, disputable, doubtful, questionable; improbable, uncertain, unlikely
ant unreal; apparent; imaginary

realistic *adj* having no illusions and facing reality squarely <he made a *realistic* appraisal of his chances for advancement>
syn down-to-earth, earthy, hard, hard-boiled, hardheaded, matter-of-fact, practic, practical, pragmatic, pragmatical, sober, unfantastic, unidealistic, unromantic, unsentimental, utilitarian
rel rational, reasonable, sane, sensible, sound; astute, prudent, shrewd; nonacademic
con dreamy, fantastic, imaginative; idealistic, impractical, irrational, romantic, visionary; theoretical
ant unrealistic; fanciful

reality *n* **1** ***syn*** see FACT 1
2 ***syn*** see ACTUALITY 2

realize *vb* **1** ***syn*** see GAIN 1
2 ***syn*** see THINK 1

really *adv* **1** ***syn*** see VERY 2
2 ***syn*** see WELL 7

realm *n* ***syn*** see RANGE 2

ream *n, usu* **reams** *pl* ***syn*** see SCAD

ream *vb* ***syn*** see CHEAT

||ream out *vb* ***syn*** see SCOLD 1

reanimation *n* ***syn*** see REVIVAL

reap *vb* to do the work of collecting ripened crops <storms hampered his *reaping*>
syn garner, gather, harvest, ingather
rel glean

reaping *n* ***syn*** see HARVEST 1

reappearance *n* ***syn*** see RECURRENCE

rear *vb* **1** ***syn*** see BUILD 1
2 ***syn*** see ERECT 3
3 ***syn*** see LIFT 1
4 ***syn*** see BRING UP 1
rel foster, nurse, nurture; breed, propagate

---

syn synonym(s) ***rel*** related word(s)
ant antonym(s) ***con*** contrasted word(s)
idiom idiomatic equivalent(s)
|| use limited; if in doubt, see a dictionary

rear *n* **1** ***syn*** see BACK 1
ant front
2 ***syn*** see BUTTOCKS
rear *adj* ***syn*** see POSTERIOR 2
ant front
rear end *n* ***syn*** see BUTTOCKS
rearmost *adj* ***syn*** see LAST
rearrange *vb* ***syn*** see REORGANIZE
rearward *n* ***syn*** see BACK 1
reason *n* **1** ***syn*** see EXPLANATION 2
2 ***syn*** see MOTIVE 1
3 a point or points that support something open to question <he soon gave sensible *reasons* for the proposed change>
syn argument, ground, proof, wherefore, why, whyfor
rel explanation, justification, rationalization
4 ***syn*** see CAUSE 1
5 the power of the mind by which man attains truth or knowledge <we all must use *reason* to solve this problem>
syn intellect, understanding
rel inference, ratiocination
6 ***syn*** see WIT 2
reason *vb* ***syn*** see THINK 5
reasonable *adj* **1** ***syn*** see CONSERVATIVE 2
2 ***syn*** see MODERATE 2
3 ***syn*** see CHEAP 1
ant extravagant
4 ***syn*** see RATIONAL
ant unreasonable
reasoned *adj* ***syn*** see DEDUCTIVE
reasonless *adj* **1** ***syn*** see INSANE 1
2 ***syn*** see ILLOGICAL
reassume *vb* ***syn*** see RESUME 1
rebate *vb* ***syn*** see DECREASE
rebate *n* ***syn*** see DEDUCTION 1
rebel *n* one who breaks with or opposes constituted authority or the established order <he is a *rebel* among educators>
syn anarch, anarchist, frondeur, insurgent, insurrectionist, malcontent, mutineer, revolter
rel adversary, antagonist, opponent; assailant, attacker; extremist, radical, revolutionary, revolutionist, ultraist; debunker, iconoclast
con authoritarian, intransigent, traditionalist; conservative, reactionary, white
rebel *vb* ***syn*** see REVOLT 1
rebellious *adj* ***syn*** see INSUBORDINATE
rel alienated, disaffected, estranged
con acquiescent, resigned; submissive
rebirth *n* **1** ***syn*** see CONVERSION 1
2 ***syn*** see REVIVAL
rebound *vb* ***syn*** see RECOVER 3
rebuff *vb* ***syn*** see FEND (off)
idiom give the cold shoulder
rebuild *vb* ***syn*** see MEND 2
rebuke *vb* ***syn*** see REPROVE
rebuke *n* an expression of strong disapproval <his bad behavior earned him a sharp *rebuke*>
syn admonishment, admonition, chiding, rap, reprimand, reproach, reproof, wig, wigging
rel dressing down, earful, lecture, lesson, scolding, talking-to, tongue-lashing
idiom a flea in one's ear, slap on the wrist
con applause, compliment, praise
rebut *vb* **1** ***syn*** see FEND (off)
2 ***syn*** see DISPROVE 1
recalcitrance *n* ***syn*** see DEFIANCE 2
recalcitrant *adj* ***syn*** see UNRULY 1
rel obstinate, stubborn; opposing, resisting, withstanding
ant amenable
recall *vb* **1** ***syn*** see REMEMBER
rel educe, elicit, evoke, extract; arouse, awaken, rouse, stir, waken
2 ***syn*** see ABJURE
3 ***syn*** see REVOKE 2
4 ***syn*** see RESTORE 1
recall *n* ***syn*** see MEMORY 2
recant *vb* ***syn*** see ABJURE
recapitulation *n* ***syn*** see SUMMARY
recede *vb* **1** to move backward <they will return after the floodwaters *recede*>
syn back, fall back, retract, retreat, retrocede, retrograde
rel regress, retrogress; depart, retire, withdraw
ant proceed; advance
2 ***syn*** see DECREASE
receipts *n pl* ***syn*** see REVENUE
receive *vb* ***syn*** see TAKE 10
received *adj* ***syn*** see ORTHODOX 1
recension *n* ***syn*** see REVISION 1
recent *adj* **1** ***syn*** see NEW 1
2 ***syn*** see MODERN 1
recently *adv* ***syn*** see NEW
receptive *adj* **1** open to ideas, impressions, or suggestions <he has a most *receptive* mind>
syn acceptant, acceptive, influenceable, persuadable, persuasible, responsive, suasible, swayable
rel open, open-minded; accessible, amenable, suggestible
con closed, closed-minded, inhospitable
ant unreceptive
2 ***syn*** see SYMPATHETIC 2
recess *vb* ***syn*** see ADJOURN 2
recession *n* ***syn*** see DEPRESSION 3
recherché *adj* ***syn*** see CHOICE
rel fresh, new, novel, original; exotic, uncommon, unusual
ant commonplace
recidivate *vb* ***syn*** see LAPSE
reciprocal *n* ***syn*** see MATE 5
reciprocate *vb* to give back, usually in kind or quantity <they were glad of the chance to *reciprocate* her kindness>
syn recompense, requite, retaliate, return
rel exchange, interchange; compensate, repay; retort, serve out
con accept, acquire, pocket, take
recital *n* ***syn*** see DESCRIPTION 2
rel discourse, story; enumeration
recite *vb* ***syn*** see RELATE 1
rel count, enumerate, number, tell
reckless *adj* **1** ***syn*** see ADVENTUROUS
rel desperate, hopeless
2 ***syn*** see RASH 1

ant calculating
3 *syn* see IRRESPONSIBLE

reckon *vb* 1 *syn* see CALCULATE
rel count, enumerate, number; add, cast, foot, sum, total
2 *syn* see CONSIDER 3
rel conjecture, guess, surmise
3 *syn* see ESTIMATE 3
‖4 *syn* see UNDERSTAND 3

reckon (on) *vb syn* see RELY (on *or* upon)

reckoning *n* 1 *syn* see BILL 1
2 *syn* see COMPUTATION

reclaim *vb syn* see RESTORE 3

recline *vb* 1 *syn* see SLANT 1
2 *syn* see REST 1

reclining *adj syn* see PRONE 4

recluse *adj syn* see SECLUDED

recluse *n* a person who leads a secluded or solitary life <a man who led the life of a *recluse* although living in a busy city>
syn hermit, solitary
rel anchorite, cenobite, eremite

reclusion *n syn* see SECLUSION

reclusive *adj syn* see ANTISOCIAL

recognition *n* 1 a learning process that relates a perception of something new to knowledge already possessed <*recognition* of a genuine diamond>
syn apperception, assimilation, identification
rel cognizance, realization; awareness, consciousness, sensibility
ant irrecognition
2 *syn* see CREDIT 4
ant unrecognition

recognize *vb* 1 to make out as or perceive to be something previously known <said they would *recognize* that face anywhere>
syn know
rel recall, recollect, remember
2 *syn* see IDENTIFY
3 *syn* see ACKNOWLEDGE 2
rel note, notice, observe, remark

recoil *vb* to draw back usually through fear or disgust <*recoiled* from the snake>
syn blanch, blench, flinch, quail, shrink, squinch, start, wince
rel falter, hesitate, waver; balk, shy, stick, stickle; dodge, duck, swerve; quake, shake, shudder, tremble; reel (back)
con advance, approach, near
ant confront; defy

re–collect *vb syn* see COMPOSE 4

recollect *vb syn* see REMEMBER
rel arouse, awaken, rally, rouse, stir, waken

recollection *n* 1 *syn* see MEMORY 2
2 *syn* see MEMORY 1

recommence *vb syn* see RESUME 2

recommend *vb* 1 *syn* see COMMEND 2
ant discommend
2 *syn* see COUNSEL

recompense *vb* 1 *syn* see COMPENSATE 3
rel accord, award, grant, vouchsafe; balance, offset
2 *syn* see RECIPROCATE

recompense *n syn* see REPARATION

reconcile *vb* 1 *syn* see HARMONIZE 3
idiom bury the hatchet, make peace
ant estrange
2 *syn* see ADAPT

reconcilement *n syn* see RECONCILIATION

reconciliate *vb syn* see HARMONIZE 3

reconciliation *n* establishment of harmony <a *reconciliation* between the two countries was effected after ten years>
syn harmonizing, rapprochement, reconcilement
rel appeasement, conciliation, mollification, propitiation, satisfying
ant disagreement

recondite *adj* beyond the reach of the average intelligence <a *recondite* subject>
syn abstruse, acroamatic, deep, esoteric, heavy, hermetic, occult, orphic, profound, secret
rel erudite, learned, scholarly; academic, pedantic; difficult, hard; dark, enigmatic, obscure; anagogic, cabalistic, mystic, mystical; cryptic, runic, sibylline
con easy, facile, simple, straightforward

recondition *vb* 1 *syn* see RESTORE 3
2 *syn* see MEND 2

reconnoiter *vb syn* see SCOUT

reconsider *vb* to consider again with a view to changing or reversing <was asked to *reconsider* his decision>
syn reevaluate, reexamine, rethink, re-treat, review, reweigh, think (over)
rel draw off; sleep (on); amend, correct, revise
idiom revise one's thoughts, think better of, view in a new light

reconsideration *n syn* see REVIEW 5

reconstitute *vb syn* see REORGANIZE

reconstruct *vb* 1 *syn* see MEND 2
2 *syn* see REORGANIZE
3 *syn* see RESTORE 3

record *vb syn* see SHOW 5

record *n syn* see DOCUMENT 1

recount *vb syn* see RELATE 1

recountal *n syn* see DESCRIPTION 2

recounting *n syn* see DESCRIPTION 2

recoup *vb syn* see RECOVER 1

recourse *n syn* see RESOURCE 3

recover *vb* 1 to obtain again <*recover* a lost watch>
syn get back, recoup, recruit, regain, repossess, retrieve
rel reclaim, redeem; reacquire, recapture, retake, rewin; reoccupy, resume; rediscover; balance, compensate, offset
con lose, mislay, misplace; forfeit, sacrifice
2 to regain health <*recovering* from a bout of pneumonia>
syn come round, rally

rel convalesce, improve, mend, recuperate; perk (up), revive; heal; refresh, rejuvenate, renew, restore
idiom get back in shape, get better, sit up and take nourishment, take a turn for the better
con decline, fail, weaken, worsen; die, expire, perish
3 to regain a former or normal state <the textile industry was *recovering* quickly from the depression>
syn bounce (back), rebound, snap back
rel rally, revive
con decline, fail
ant worsen
4 *syn* see RESTORE 3

recreancy *n syn* see DEFECTION
recreant *adj syn* see FAITHLESS
recreant *n syn* see RENEGADE
recreate *vb* 1 *syn* see AMUSE
rel refresh, rejuvenate, renew, restore
2 *syn* see PLAY 1
recreation *n* 1 *syn* see ENTERTAINMENT
rel ease, relaxation, repose; frolic, rollick; hilarity, jollity, mirth
2 *syn* see PLAY 1
recreational vehicle *n syn* see TRAILER
recrementitious *adj syn* see SUPERFLUOUS
recrudesce *vb syn* see RETURN 1
rel refurbish, renew, renovate
con repress, suppress; cease, discontinue, stop
recruit *n syn* see NOVICE
recruit *vb syn* see RECOVER 1
rel refresh, renew, renovate, restore; mend, rebuild, repair
rectify *vb syn* see CORRECT 1
rel rebuild, repair
rectitude *n syn* see GOODNESS
rel conscientiousness, justness, scrupulousness
recumbent *adj syn* see PRONE 4
ant erect, upright
recuperate *vb syn* see IMPROVE 3
recur *vb* 1 *syn* see RETURN 1
rel iterate, reiterate, repeat
2 *syn* see RESORT 2
recurrence *n* a periodic or frequent returning <the *recurrence* of the nightmare upset him>
syn reappearance, reoccurrence, return
rel repetition, reproduction; crebrity, frequency
recurrent *adj syn* see INTERMITTENT
recurring *adj syn* see INTERMITTENT
Red *n syn* see COMMUNIST
red-blooded *adj syn* see VIGOROUS
redden *vb* 1 to make red <blood soon *reddened* the bandage>
syn incarnadine, rubify, rubric, ruby, rud, ruddle, ruddy
2 *syn* see BLUSH
redeem *vb* 1 *syn* see RANSOM
2 *syn* see FREE
3 *syn* see COMPENSATE 1
red-handed *adv* in the act of committing a misdeed <caught *red-handed*>
syn dead to rights, flagrante delicto
rel blatantly, openly
red-hot *adj* 1 *syn* see HOT 1
2 *syn* see IMPASSIONED
3 *syn* see UP-TO-DATE
red-letter *adj syn* see NOTEWORTHY
red-light district *n* a district characterized by brothels <sailors frequented the *red-light district*>
syn levee, stew(s), tenderloin
idiom street of fallen women
red-neck *n syn* see RUSTIC
redolence *n syn* see FRAGRANCE
redolent *adj* 1 *syn* see SWEET 2
2 *syn* see REMINISCENT
redouble *vb syn* see INTENSIFY
redoubt *n syn* see FORT
redoubtable *adj* 1 *syn* see FEARFUL 3
2 *syn* see FAMOUS 2
redound *vb syn* see CONTRIBUTE 2
redraft *n syn* see REVISION 1
redraft *vb syn* see REVISE
redraw *vb syn* see REVISE
redress *vb* 1 *syn* see AVENGE
2 *syn* see NEUTRALIZE
redress *n syn* see REPARATION
rel balancing, offsetting; retaliation, vengeance
reduce *vb* 1 *syn* see DECREASE
2 to decrease in amount <they decided to *reduce* prices to stimulate sales>
syn clip, cut, cut back, cut down, lower, mark down, pare, shave, slash
rel curtail, decrease, diminish, lessen; deflate, depreciate; scale (down), step down; roll back
con boost, hike, jack (up), jump, put up, raise, up
ant increase
3 *syn* see CONQUER 1
rel cripple, disable, enfeeble, undermine, weaken; debase, degrade, humble, humiliate
4 *syn* see DEGRADE 1
ant advance
5 to lose body weight especially by dieting <ate no cake while *reducing*>
syn slenderize, slim (down)
rel bant, diet
idiom lose flesh, take off weight
ant fatten
reduction *n* 1 *syn* see DEDUCTION 1
2 *syn* see DEMOTION
redundancy *n syn* see VERBIAGE 1
rel flatulence, inflatedness, inflation, tumidity, turgidity
redundant *adj syn* see WORDY
rel extra, spare, superfluous, supernumerary, surplus; iterating, reiterating, repetitious
ant concise
reduplicate *vb syn* see COPY
reduplication *n syn* see REPRODUCTION
reedy *adj syn* see THIN 1
reek *vb syn* see SMELL 3
reeking *adj syn* see MALODOROUS 1
reeky *adj syn* see MALODOROUS 1
reel *vb* 1 *syn* see SPIN 2
2 to move uncertainly or uncontrollably (as in intoxication) <*reeled* down the street>

syn stagger, titubate, totter, wheel
rel careen, lurch, ||swaver, sway, swing, weave, wobble; falter, ||stammer, stumble, teeter, topple; bob, waver
reestablish *vb* *syn* see RESTORE 1
reevaluate *vb* *syn* see RECONSIDER
reexamination *n* *syn* see REVIEW 5
reexamine *vb* *syn* see RECONSIDER
refashion *vb* *syn* see CHANGE 1
refection *n* *syn* see MEAL
refer *vb* **1** *syn* see ASCRIBE
2 *syn* see SUBMIT 2
3 to call or direct attention to something <no one *referred* to his recent divorce>
syn advert, allude, bring up, point (out)
rel insert, interpolate, introduce; cite, quote; instance, mention, name, specify; glance, touch
idiom make an allusion to
4 *syn* see RESORT 2
rel advise, commune, confer, consult
referee *n* *syn* see JUDGE 1
referee *vb* *syn* see JUDGE 1
refine *vb* *syn* see POLISH 2
refined *adj* **1** *syn* see GENTEEL 1
ant earthy
2 *syn* see FINE 1
refinement *n* *syn* see CULTURE
rel finish, suavity, urbanity; civility, courtesy, politeness; dignity, elegance, grace
ant vulgarity
reflect *vb* **1** to reproduce or show as a mirror does <the trees on the shore were *reflected* in the water>
syn glass, image, mirror
rel repeat, reproduce
2 *syn* see THINK 5
rel study, weigh
reflecting *adj* *syn* see THOUGHTFUL 1
reflection *n* **1** *syn* see ANIMADVERSION
rel assault, attack, onset, onslaught; depreciation, derogation, disparagement
2 *syn* see THOUGHT 1
reflective *adj* *syn* see THOUGHTFUL 1
reformatory *n* *syn* see JAIL
refractory *adj* *syn* see OBSTINATE
ant malleable
refrain *vb* **1** to hold oneself back from doing or indulging in something <*refrained* from speaking out of turn>
syn abstain, forbear, keep, withhold
rel arrest, check, halt, interrupt, stop; curb, inhibit, restrain
2 *syn* see DENY 3
refresh *vb* *syn* see RENEW 1
rel animate, enliven, quicken, vivify; recover, recruit, regain; amuse, divert, recreate
con exhaust, tire
ant addle; jade
refreshed *adj* made or become fresh <awoke a *refreshed* man>
syn new, regenerated, reinvigorated, renewed, revived
rel recreated, renovated; animated, exhilarated, invigorated, stimulated
con exhausted, fagged, fatigued, jaded, tired, tuckered, wearied, worn-down, worn-out
refuge *n* **1** the state of being covered or protected <exiles seeking *refuge* in neutral countries>
syn asylum, harborage, sanctuary, shelter; *compare* SHELTER 1
rel protection, shield; immunity
con exposure, liability, openness; vulnerability
2 *syn* see SHELTER 1
3 *syn* see RESOURCE 3
refugee *n* one who flees for safety <the villagers fed and housed the *refugees* from the bombed city>
syn displaced person, DP, émigré, evacuee, fugitive
rel exile; emigrant, expatriate
idiom stateless person
refulgent *adj* *syn* see BRIGHT 1
refurbish *vb* *syn* see RENEW 1
refusal *n* *syn* see DENIAL 1
refuse *vb* **1** *syn* see DECLINE 4
2 *syn* see DENY 2
refuse *n* matter that is regarded as worthless and fit only for throwing away <heaps of *refuse* left by the former tenant>
syn ||collateral, debris, dreck, ||dust, garbage, junk, kelter, litter, ||muck, ||mullock, offal, outsweepings, ||pelf, riffraff, rubbish, ||sculch, spilth, sweepings, swill, trash, waste
rel dump, dustheap; rejectamenta, scraps; lumber; offscouring(s)
refute *vb* *syn* see DISPROVE 1
regain *vb* *syn* see RECOVER 1
rel achieve, attain, compass, gain, reach; reclaim, redeem, save; renew, restore
regal *adj* *syn* see KINGLY
rel august, imposing, magnificent, stately; glorious, resplendent, splendid, sublime
regale *n* *syn* see DINNER
regalia *n pl* *syn* see FINERY
regard *n* **1** *syn* see NOTICE 1
2 *syn* see CONSIDERATION 3
ant disregard
3 *syn* see INTEREST 3
4 a feeling of deferential approval and liking <held in high *regard* by his neighbors>
syn account, admiration, consideration, esteem, estimation, favor, respect
rel deference, homage, honor, reverence; appreciation, cherishing, prizing, valuing; approbation, approval, satisfaction
con deprecation, disapproval; disfavor, disgust, dislike, distaste; contempt, disdain, scorn; detestation, hate, hatred
ant despite
5 *syn* see CARE 4
regard *vb* **1** *syn* see ADMIRE 2
con reject, repudiate, scorn
ant despise

---

syn synonym(s) *rel* related word(s)
ant antonym(s) *con* contrasted word(s)
idiom idiomatic equivalent(s)
|| use limited; if in doubt, see a dictionary

2 *syn* see CONSIDER 3
rel assay, assess, estimate, rate, value

regardful *adj* 1 *syn* see ATTENTIVE 1
2 *syn* see MINDFUL 2
3 *syn* see RESPECTFUL

regarding *prep syn* see APROPOS

regardless *adj syn* see NEGLIGENT

regardless of *prep syn* see AGAINST 4

regenerated *adj syn* see REFRESHED

region *n* 1 *syn* see AREA 1
rel neighborhood, vicinity; division, part, section, sector
2 *syn* see FIELD

register *n syn* see LIST

register *vb* 1 *syn* see ENROLL 1
2 *syn* see SHOW 5

regnant *adj* 1 *syn* see DOMINANT 1
2 *syn* see PREVAILING

regress *vb syn* see REVERT 2

regret *vb* to be very sorry for <*regrets* his mistakes> <*regret* the problems facing minorities>
syn deplore, repent, rue
rel bemoan, bewail, lament; grieve, mourn, sorrow; deprecate, disapprove

regret *n* 1 *syn* see SORROW
rel compunction, contrition, penitence, remorse, repentance; demur, qualm, scruple
2 **regrets** *pl syn* see APOLOGY 2

regretful *adj syn* see REMORSEFUL

regretless *adj syn* see REMORSELESS

regrettable *adj syn* see DEPLORABLE

regular *adj* 1 *syn* see GENERAL 1
rel customary, ordinary
ant irregular
2 *syn* see ORDERLY 1
rel fixed, set, settled; constant, equable, even, steady, uniform
ant irregular; sporadic
3 *syn* see UTTER

regulate *vb syn* see ADJUST 2
rel arrange, methodize, order, organize, systematize; moderate, temper

regulation *n syn* see LAW 1

rehabilitate *vb syn* see RESTORE 3

rehearse *vb* 1 *syn* see RELATE 1
rel iterate, reiterate, repeat
2 *syn* see EXERCISE 3
rel run through

reify *vb syn* see MATERIALIZE 2

reign *vb* 1 *syn* see GOVERN 1
idiom sit on the throne
2 *syn* see RULE 2

reimburse *vb syn* see COMPENSATE 3
rel recover; balance, compensate, offset
con default, dishonor, repudiate, welsh

rein *vb syn* see COMPOSE 4

reinforce *vb syn* see STRENGTHEN 2
rel augment, enlarge, increase, multiply; bolster, buttress, pillar, prop, sustain
ant undermine

reinstate *vb* 1 *syn* see RESTORE 5
2 *syn* see RESTORE 1

reintroduce *vb syn* see RESTORE 1

reinvigorated *adj syn* see REFRESHED

reissue *n syn* see EDITION

reiterate *vb syn* see REPEAT

reject *vb* 1 *syn* see DECLINE 4
rel debar, eliminate, exclude, shut out
ant accept; choose, select
2 *syn* see DISCARD

rejection *n syn* see DENIAL 1

rejoin *vb syn* see ANSWER 1

rejoinder *n syn* see ANSWER 1

rejuvenate *vb* 1 *syn* see RENEW 1
2 *syn* see RESTORE 3

rekindle *vb syn* see REVIVE 3

relapse *n syn* see LAPSE 2

relapse *vb syn* see LAPSE

relate *vb* 1 to tell orally or in writing the details or circumstances of a situation <*related* the story of his life>
syn describe, narrate, recite, recount, rehearse, report, state
rel disclose, divulge, reveal, tell; detail, itemize, particularize; depict, express, render; pronounce
idiom make public
2 *syn* see JOIN 1
rel ascribe, assign, credit, impute, refer
3 *syn* see BEAR (on *or* upon)

related *adj* connected by or as if by family ties <persons *related* in the first degree> <physics and mathematics are closely *related*>
syn affiliated, agnate, akin, allied, cognate, connate, connatural, consanguine, incident, kindred
rel associated, connected; complementary, convertible, correlative, corresponding, reciprocal; alike, analogous, identical; germane, pertinent, relevant
con different, dissimilar, divergent, unconnected, unlike
ant unrelated

relation *n syn* see RELATIVE

relative *n* a person connected with another by blood <all of his *relatives* live out of state>
syn kin, kinsman, kinswoman, relation
rel brother, half brother, half sister, sib, sibling, sister; father, mother, parent; child, daughter, son; grandfather, grandmother, grandparent; grandchild, granddaughter, grandson; aunt, half aunt, half uncle, uncle; half nephew, half niece, nephew, niece; cousin, cross-cousin, half cousin, ortho-cousin; agnate, cognate

relative *adj* 1 *syn* see DEPENDENT 1
2 *syn* see COMPARATIVE

relax *vb* 1 *syn* see LOOSE 5
2 to become less tense or reserved <couldn't *relax* in crowds>
syn ease off, loosen up, unbend, unlax, unwind
rel calm (down), collect (oneself), compose (oneself), cool (off), simmer down
idiom be at ease, breathe easily, feel at home, make oneself at home
con rack (oneself), tense (up)
3 *syn* see REST 2

relaxation *n syn* see REST 1
rel amusement, diversion, recreation; alleviation, assuagement, mitigation, relief
ant tension

relaxed *adj* **1** ***syn*** see LOOSE 1
rel flexuous, sinuous; gentle, lenient, mild, soft
ant stiff
2 ***syn*** see EASYGOING 3
con ascetic, austere, severe, stern
ant tense

release *vb* **1** ***syn*** see FREE
rel acquit, exculpate, exonerate; relinquish, resign, surrender, yield
idiom cast loose, set at large
ant detain
2 ***syn*** see EMIT 2
3 ***syn*** see TAKE OUT (on)
ant check

relegate *vb* **1** ***syn*** see BANISH
2 ***syn*** see COMMIT 1
rel accredit, charge, credit, refer

relegation *n* **1** ***syn*** see EXILE 1
2 ***syn*** see DISPOSAL 2

relent *vb* ***syn*** see ABATE 4

relentless *adj* **1** ***syn*** see GRIM 3
rel rigorous, strict, stringent; cruel, ferocious, fierce, inhuman
con submissive, yielding
2 ***syn*** see INFLEXIBLE 2

relevance *n* ***syn*** see USE 3

relevant *adj* relating to or bearing upon the matter in hand <*relevant* testimony>
syn ad rem, applicable, applicative, applicatory, apposite, apropos, germane, material, pertinent, pointful
rel allied, cognate, related; appropriate, apt, fit, fitting, proper, suitable; important, significant, weighty; admissible, allowable
idiom in point, in question, to the point
con impertinent, inadmissible, inapplicable, inapposite, inappropriate; unallied, unassociated, unconnected, unrelated; alien, extrinsic, foreign
ant irrelevant; extraneous

reliable *adj* **1** having qualities that merit confidence or trust <a *reliable* friend>
syn dependable, secure, tried, tried and true, trustworthy, trusty
rel safe; inerrable, inerrant, infallible, unerring; apposite, cogent, compelling, convincing, meaningful, significant, sound, telling, valid; attested, authenticated, circumstantiated, confirmed, proven, validated, verified; unimpeachable, unquestionable
con doubtful, dubious, problematic, questionable, suspect; independable, undependable, untried, untrustworthy; unattested, unauthenticated, unconfirmed, unvalidated
ant unreliable
2 ***syn*** see CERTAIN 3

reliance *n* ***syn*** see TRUST 1

reliant *adj* ***syn*** see DEPENDENT 1

relic *n* **1** ***syn*** see REMEMBRANCE 3
2 ***syn*** see VESTIGE 1

relief *n* **1** ***syn*** see EASE 3
rel lightening, softening; allayment, appeasement, assuagement, mollification
ant anguish
2 ***syn*** see HELP 1

relieve *vb* **1** to make less grievous or more tolerable <drugs that *relieve* pain>
syn allay, alleviate, assuage, ease, lighten, mitigate, mollify
rel comfort, console, solace; appease, palliate, soften; quiet, soothe, subdue; moderate, qualify, temper; decrease, diminish, lessen, reduce; aid, benefit, help
con aggravate, enhance, heighten, sharpen; reinforce
ant intensify
2 ***syn*** see ROB 1
3 to take the place of for a time <sent to *relieve* the sentry>
syn spell, take over
rel fill in, sub, substitute; replace, supply
4 ***syn*** see EXEMPT

religion *n* **1** a system of religious belief <tolerant of all *religions*>
syn creed, cult, faith, persuasion
rel belief, doctrine
2 the body of persons who accept a system of religious belief <Jerusalem is a city sacred to three great *religions*>
syn church, communion, connection, creed, cult, denomination, faith, persuasion, sect

religious *adj* ***syn*** see DEVOUT
rel faithful, staunch, steadfast, true; ethical, moral, noble, righteous, virtuous; honest, honorable, just, upright
con godless, ungodly
ant irreligious

relinquish *vb* to let out of one's possession or control completely <few leaders willingly *relinquish* power>
syn abandon, cede, give up, hand over, lay down, leave, resign, surrender, ‖turn up, waive, yield; *compare* ABDICATE 1
rel lay aside; quit, throw up; abdicate, renounce; desert, forsake; abnegate, forbear, forgo, sacrifice; cast, discard, shed
ant keep

relish *n* **1** ***syn*** see TASTE 3
2 ***syn*** see TASTE 4
rel enjoying, liking, loving; bias, prejudice; flair, leaning, penchant, propensity
3 ***syn*** see ENJOYMENT 1

relish *vb* **1** ***syn*** see ENJOY 1
2 to eat or drink with pleasure <so hungry that he will *relish* plain food>
syn savor
3 ***syn*** see ADMIRE 1

relishing *adj* ***syn*** see PALATABLE
rel delighting, gratifying, pleasing, regaling, rejoicing, tickling
con banal, flat, inane, insipid, jejune

reluct *vb* ***syn*** see DISGUST

reluctant *adj* ***syn*** see DISINCLINED

---

syn synonym(s) ***rel*** related word(s)
ant antonym(s) ***con*** contrasted word(s)
idiom idiomatic equivalent(s)
‖ use limited; if in doubt, see a dictionary

rel calculating, cautious, chary, circumspect, wary
rely (on *or* upon) *vb* to place full confidence <*relied* on the doctor for an accurate diagnosis>
syn bank (on *or* upon), build (on), calculate (on *or* upon), count (on), depend (on *or* upon), ‖lot (on *or* upon), reckon (on), trust (in *or* to)
rel commit, confide, entrust; await, expect, hope, look
idiom put faith in, swear by
con distrust, mistrust
remain *vb* ***syn*** see STAY 2
ant depart
remainder *n* a remaining group, part, or trace <he spent the *remainder* of his life in prison>
syn balance, heel, leavings, remains, remanet, remnant, residual, residue, residuum, rest
rel excess, surplus; hangover, leftover
remains *n pl* **1** ***syn*** see REMAINDER
2 ***syn*** see CORPSE
remanet *n* ***syn*** see REMAINDER
remark *vb* **1** ***syn*** see SEE 1
2 to make observations and pass on one's judgment <she *remarked* on the lack of modern paintings at the gallery>
syn animadvert, comment, commentate, observe
rel mention, note
remark *n* **1** ***syn*** see NOTICE 1
2 an expression of opinion or judgment <a *remark* that led to a vehement argument>
syn comment, commentary, note, obiter dictum, observation
rel assertion, reflection, saying, statement, utterance; clarification, elucidation, explanation, explication, exposition, interpretation; annotation, exegesis, gloss, postil, scholium
remarkable *adj* **1** ***syn*** see NOTICEABLE
rel exceptional; important, momentous, significant, weighty; peculiar, singular, strange, unique
2 ***syn*** see EXCEPTIONAL 1
remarkably *adv* ***syn*** see VERY 1
remedial *adj* ***syn*** see CURATIVE
remedy *n* **1** something used for the treatment of disease <a cold *remedy*>
syn cure, medicament, medicant, medication, medicine, pharmacon, physic
rel biologic, drug, medicinal, pharmaceutical
2 something that corrects or counteracts <no easy *remedy* for discontent>
syn antidote, corrective, counteractant, counteractive, counteragent, countermeasure, counterstep, cure
rel cure-all, elixir, panacea; nostrum
remedy *vb* ***syn*** see CURE
remedying *adj* ***syn*** see CURATIVE
remember *vb* to bring an image or idea from the past into the mind <*remembers* the old days>
syn bethink, cite, ‖mind, recall, recollect, remind, reminisce, retain, retrospect, revive, revoke
rel look back (on *or* upon), think (of), treasure; relive; educe, elicit, evoke, extract
con disregard, ignore, neglect, overlook; disremember, lose
ant forget
remembrance *n* **1** ***syn*** see MEMORY 1
2 ***syn*** see MEMORY 2
3 something that serves to keep a person or thing in mind <wanted to give her a small *remembrance*>
syn keepsake, memento, memorial, relic, remembrancer, reminder, souvenir, token, trophy
rel favor, gift, present
remembrancer *n* ***syn*** see REMEMBRANCE 3
remind *vb* ***syn*** see REMEMBER
rel hint, imply, intimate, suggest; admonish, advise, warn; jog, prompt
idiom put in mind
reminder *n* **1** ***syn*** see EXPRESSION 3
2 ***syn*** see REMEMBRANCE 3
rel memo, memorandum, note, notice; hint, intimation, suggestion; admonition, warning
remindful *adj* ***syn*** see REMINISCENT
reminisce *vb* ***syn*** see REMEMBER
reminiscence *n* **1** ***syn*** see MEMORY 1
2 ***syn*** see MEMORY 2
reminiscent *adj* tending to remind <shoes *reminiscent* of those worn fifty years ago>
syn redolent, remindful
rel evocative, suggestive
idiom bringing to mind
remise *vb* ***syn*** see TRANSFER 4
remiss *adj* ***syn*** see NEGLIGENT
rel faineant, indolent, lazy, slothful
ant scrupulous
remit *vb* **1** ***syn*** see EXCUSE 1
2 ***syn*** see DEFER
3 ***syn*** see SEND 1
remittable *adj* ***syn*** see VENIAL
remnant *n* ***syn*** see REMAINDER
remonstrance *n* ***syn*** see DEMUR 2
remonstrate *vb* ***syn*** see OBJECT 1
rel combat, fight, oppose, resist, withstand
remonstration *n* ***syn*** see DEMUR 2
remorse *n* ***syn*** see PENITENCE
remorseful *adj* motivated or marked by remorse <a *remorseful* confession>
syn apologetic, attritional, compunctious, contrite, penitent, penitential, regretful, repentant, sorry
rel mournful, rueful, sorrowful
con impenitent, regretless, unregretful; hard, obdurate
ant remorseless
remorsefulness *n* ***syn*** see PENITENCE
remorseless *adj* having no remorse <a *remorseless* villain>
syn impenitent, regretless, uncontrite, unregretful, unremorseful, unrepentant, unsorry
rel compassionless, merciless, pitiless, ruthless, uncompassionate, unmerciful
con penitent, regretful, sorry
ant remorseful
remote *adj* **1** ***syn*** see DISTANT 1
ant close; adjacent
2 ***syn*** see BACK 1
3 ***syn*** see OBSCURE 2
4 small in degree <a *remote* possibility>

syn ‖fat, negligible, off, outside, slender, slight, slim, small
con great, large; important, significant, weighty
5 *syn* see INDIFFERENT 2

remotest *adj* *syn* see EXTREME 5

remove *vb* **1** *syn* see MOVE 4
2 to take something from a place or position <*removed* the book from the shelf>
syn take away, take off, take out, withdraw
rel move, shift, transfer; extract
3 to take (as a hat) from one's person <*removed* her coat when she entered the house>
syn doff, douse, put off, take off
rel cast off, throw off
idiom off with
con don, put on, replace
4 to get rid of <*remove* the causes of poverty>
syn clear away, eliminate, take out
rel dispose (of), eradicate, exterminate, extirpate; blot out, efface, erase, expunge, obliterate
idiom do away with
5 *syn* see PURGE 3

removed *adj* **1** *syn* see DISTANT 1
ant adjoining
2 *syn* see OBSCURE 2
3 *syn* see ALONE 1

remunerate *vb* **1** *syn* see PAY 1
rel accord, award, grant, vouchsafe
2 *syn* see COMPENSATE 3

remunerative *adj* *syn* see ADVANTAGEOUS 1

renaissance *n* *syn* see REVIVAL

renascence *n* *syn* see REVIVAL

rencontre *n* *syn* see CONTEST 2

rend *vb* *syn* see TEAR 1
rel divide, separate

render *vb* **1** *syn* see RETURN 3
2 *syn* see REPRESENT 1
3 *syn* see TRANSLATE 1
4 *syn* see ADMINISTER 1

rendering *n* **1** *syn* see INTERPRETATION 2
2 *syn* see VERSION 1

rendezvous *n* **1** *syn* see ENGAGEMENT 3
2 *syn* see RESORT 2

rendezvous *vb* *syn* see GATHER 6

rendition *n* *syn* see INTERPRETATION 2

renegade *n* a person who forsakes his faith, party, cause, or allegiance and aligns himself with another <the *renegade* derided his former beliefs>
syn apostate, defector, rat, recreant, runagate, tergiversator, turnabout, turncoat
rel iconoclast, insurgent, rebel; abandoner, deserter, forsaker; heretic, schismatic
con liege man; disciple, follower
ant adherent

renege *vb* *syn* see BACK DOWN

renew *vb* **1** to make like new <rested to *renew* their strength>
syn modernize, refresh, refurbish, rejuvenate, renovate, restore, update
rel make over, remodel; mend, rebuild, repair; correct, rectify, reform, revise
con bankrupt, deplete, drain, exhaust, impoverish; consume
ant wear out
2 *syn* see RESTORE 1
3 *syn* see REVIVE 3
4 *syn* see REPEAT
5 *syn* see RESUME 2

renewed *adj* *syn* see REFRESHED

renounce *vb* **1** *syn* see ABDICATE 1
ant arrogate
2 *syn* see ABANDON 1
idiom wash one's hands of
3 *syn* see DEFECT

renouncement *n* *syn* see RENUNCIATION

renovate *vb* **1** *syn* see REVIVE 3
2 *syn* see RENEW 1
rel clean, cleanse

renown *n* **1** *syn* see FAME 2
2 *syn* see EMINENCE 1

renowned *adj* *syn* see FAMOUS 2
rel acclaimed, extolled, lauded, praised; outstanding, signal

rent *vb* *syn* see HIRE 1

rent *adj* *syn* see LACERATED

rent *n* *syn* see BREACH 3

rental *n* *syn* see APARTMENT 1

renunciation *n* voluntary surrender or putting aside of something desired or desirable <led a life of total *renunciation* as a monk>
syn abnegation, denial, renouncement, self-abnegation, self-denial, self-renunciation
rel abjurement, eschewing, forbearing, forgoing, forswearing, sacrifice, self-sacrifice; rejection, repudiation, surrender, yielding
con gripping, holding, keeping
ant retention

reoccupy *vb* *syn* see RESUME 1

reoccurrence *n* *syn* see RECURRENCE

reopen *vb* *syn* see RESUME 2

reorder *vb* *syn* see REORGANIZE

reorganization *n* *syn* see SHAKE-UP

reorganize *vb* to arrange in a different way <*reorganize* a bankrupt company>
syn readjust, rearrange, reconstitute, reconstruct, reorder, reorient, reorientate, reshuffle, retool
rel reestablish, refound, resettle; rebuild, regenerate, renovate
con disarrange, disorder, disorganize

reorient *vb* *syn* see REORGANIZE

reorientate *vb* *syn* see REORGANIZE

‖**rep** *n* **1** *syn* see FAME 2
2 *syn* see REPUTATION 2

repair *vb* **1** *syn* see GO 1
2 *syn* see RESORT 2

repair *vb* *syn* see MEND 2

repair *n* **1** *syn* see ORDER 9
2 *syn* see ORDER 10

reparation *n* a return for something lost or suffered, usually through the fault of another <war *reparations*>

---

syn synonym(s) *rel* related word(s)
ant antonym(s) *con* contrasted word(s)
idiom idiomatic equivalent(s)
‖ use limited; if in doubt, see a dictionary

syn amends, compensation, indemnification, indemnity, quittance, recompense, redress, reprisal, restitution
rel atonement, expiation; remuneration, requital, retribution, reward; adjustment, settlement

repartee *n* **1** *syn* see RETORT 2
2 *syn* see BANTER
rel humor, irony, sarcasm, satire, wit; rejoinder, response, retort

repast *n* *syn* see MEAL

repay *vb* *syn* see COMPENSATE 3
rel balance, offset; accord, award

repeal *vb* *syn* see REVOKE 2
ant establish; enact

repeat *vb* to say or do again <*repeat* a command>
syn ingeminate, iterate, reiterate, renew, reprise, resay
rel recite, recount, rehearse, relate; hash over, recapitulate, rehash, restate, retell; chime, din, echo, harp, ring; duplicate, reproduce; copy, ditto, imitate; recrudesce, recur, return, revert

repeatedly *adv* *syn* see OFTEN
idiom day after day, day by day, day in and day out

repel *vb* **1** *syn* see FEND (off)
2 *syn* see RESIST
3 *syn* see DISGUST
ant allure; attract

repellent *adj* **1** *syn* see REPUGNANT 1
con alluring, bewitching, captivating, charming; enticing, luring, seductive, tempting
ant attractive; pleasing
2 *syn* see OFFENSIVE
3 *syn* see ANTIPATHETIC 2

repent *vb* *syn* see REGRET

repentance *n* *syn* see PENITENCE
con complacency, self-complacency, self-satisfaction

repentant *adj* *syn* see REMORSEFUL

repercussion *n* *syn* see EFFECT 3

rephrase *vb* *syn* see PARAPHRASE

repine *vb* *syn* see COMPLAIN

replace *vb* **1** *syn* see RETURN 4
2 *syn* see RESTORE 5
3 to put out of a usual or proper place or into the place of another <the old bridge was *replaced* by a new one last year>
syn outplace, supersede, supplant
rel renew, restore; alter, change; recoup, recover, regain, retrieve
4 *syn* see CHANGE 5

replacement *n* *syn* see SUBSTITUTE 1

replete *adj* **1** *syn* see ALIVE 5
2 *syn* see FULL 1

replica *n* *syn* see REPRODUCTION

replicate *vb* *syn* see COPY

replication *n* *syn* see REPRODUCTION

reply *vb* *syn* see ANSWER 1
con accuse, charge, impeach, indict; address, greet, salute

reply *n* *syn* see ANSWER 1
con argument, dispute; greeting, salute

report *n* **1** common talk or an instance of it that spreads rapidly <spread a false *report*>
syn buzz, cry, gossip, grapevine, hearsay, murmur, on-dit, rumble, rumor, scuttlebutt, talk, tattle, tittle-tattle, whispering, word
rel conversation, speech; chat, chatter, chitchat, prating, small talk; canard, dirt, scandal; advice, intelligence, news, tidings
2 *syn* see REPUTATION 2
3 *syn* see ACCOUNT 7
rel declaration, statement; comment, notice, review; brief, bulletin

report *vb* *syn* see RELATE 1
rel communicate, impart

repose *vb* *syn* see REST 1

repose *n* *syn* see REST 1
rel refreshment, renewal, restoration
con strain, stress; agitation, discomposure, perturbation

repository *n* *syn* see DEPOT 2

repossess *vb* **1** *syn* see RECOVER 1
2 *syn* see RESUME 1
3 to resume possession of (an item purchased on installment) in default of payments due <*repossessed* the car>
syn take back
rel get back, reclaim, recover, retrieve

reprehend *vb* *syn* see CRITICIZE
rel admonish, chide, rebuke, reprimand, reproach, reprove; berate, rate, scold, upbraid

reprehensible *adj* *syn* see BLAMEWORTHY

represent *vb* **1** to present an image or lifelike imitation of (as in art) <the painting *represents* a spring scene>
syn delineate, depict, describe, image, interpret, limn, picture, portray, render
rel express, realize, show; display, exhibit; hint, suggest; draft, outline, sketch; narrate, relate
con color, distort, falsify, garble, misinterpret, pervert, twist, warp
2 to serve as the counterpart or image of <a movie hero who *represents* the ideals of the culture>
syn body (forth), emblematize, embody, epitomize, exemplify, illustrate, mirror, personalize, personate, personify, symbolize, typify; *compare* EMBODY 1
rel denote, mean, signify; impersonate, substitute; copy, imitate, reproduce
con belie, distort, garble, twist, warp
ant misrepresent

representant *n* *syn* see DELEGATE

representation *n* the act of delineating <an exponent of *representation* in art>
syn delineation, depiction, description, picture, portraiture, portrayal, presentment
rel demonstration, exemplification, illustration

representative *adj* *syn* see TYPICAL 1
ant atypical

representative *n* **1** *syn* see INSTANCE
2 *syn* see DELEGATE

repress *vb* **1** *syn* see SUPPRESS 2
2 *syn* see COMPOSE 4

repression *n* **1** the action or process of putting down by authority or force <the *repression* of unpopular opinions>

syn choking, extinguishment, quashing, quenching, smothering, squashing, squelching, stifling, strangling, suppression, throttling
rel check, control, curb, restraint; crushing, quelling, subdual
con emboldening, encouragement, support
2 an instance of putting down by authority or force <*repressions* of racial minorities>
syn clampdown, crackdown, suppression
rel crushing, extinction, smothering; limitation, restriction

reprieve *n* *syn* see RESPITE 1
reprimand *n* *syn* see REBUKE
reprimand *vb* *syn* see REPROVE
reprinting *n* *syn* see EDITION
reprisal *n* 1 *syn* see REPARATION
2 *syn* see RETALIATION
reprise *vb* *syn* see REPEAT
reproach *n* *syn* see REBUKE
rel blame, censure, discredit
reproach *vb* *syn* see REPROVE
reprobate *vb* 1 *syn* see CRITICIZE
2 *syn* see DECLINE 4
reprobate *adj* 1 *syn* see ABANDONED 2
2 *syn* see WRONG 1
reprobate *n* *syn* see VILLAIN 1
reproduce *vb* 1 *syn* see PROCREATE 1
2 *syn* see COPY
reproduction *n* one thing which closely or essentially resembles another that has already been made, produced, or written <printed *reproductions* of the great masters>
syn carbon, carbon copy, copy, ditto, duplicate, facsimile, reduplication, replica, replication
ant original
reproof *n* *syn* see REBUKE
reprove *vb* to criticize adversely, especially in order to warn of or to correct a fault <*reproved* him for talking in class>
syn admonish, call down, chide, lesson, monish, ‖rack back, rebuke, reprimand, reproach, ‖sneap, tick off; *compare* CRITICIZE, LAMBASTE 3, SCOLD 1
rel counsel, warn; blame, censure, criticize, reprehend, reprobate; chasten, correct, discipline, punish
idiom haul over the coals, slap one's wrist, take to task
reptile *n* *syn* see SYCOPHANT
repudiate *vb* 1 *syn* see DECLINE 4
con acknowledge, admit, avow, confess, own
ant adopt
2 *syn* see DEFECT
3 *syn* see DISCLAIM
rel abandon, desert, forsake; cast, discard
con allow, concede, grant
ant own
repugnance *n* *syn* see ABOMINATION 2
repugnancy *n* *syn* see ABOMINATION 2
repugnant *adj* 1 so alien or unlikable as to arouse antagonism and aversion <the idea of moving again became *repugnant* to her>
syn abhorrent, invidious, obnoxious, repellent, revulsive
rel alien, extraneous, extrinsic, foreign; incompatible, incongruous, inconsonant, uncongenial
con acceptable, bearable, tolerable; agreeable, gratifying, pleasant, pleasing, pleasurable
ant congenial
2 *syn* see OFFENSIVE
3 *syn* see ANTIPATHETIC 2
repulse *vb* 1 *syn* see FEND (off)
2 *syn* see DISGUST
ant captivate
repulsion *n* *syn* see ABOMINATION 2
repulsive *adj* *syn* see OFFENSIVE
ant alluring
reputable *adj* *syn* see RESPECTABLE 1
reputation *n* 1 *syn* see FAME 2
rel authority, credit, influence, prestige, weight
2 the estimation in which one is generally held <a good *reputation*>
syn character, fame, name, ‖rep, report, repute
repute *n* 1 *syn* see FAME 2
ant disrepute
2 *syn* see REPUTATION 2
reputed *adj* 1 *syn* see RESPECTABLE 1
2 *syn* see SUPPOSED 1
request *vb* *syn* see ASK 2
rel appeal, petition, pray, sue
requiescence *n* *syn* see REST 1
require *vb* 1 *syn* see DEMAND 1
2 *syn* see DEMAND 2
3 *syn* see LACK
required *adj* 1 *syn* see NEEDFUL
2 *syn* see MANDATORY
ant optional
requirement *n* 1 something wanted or needed <production was not sufficient to satisfy *requirements* for cars>
syn demand, need, want
2 *syn* see ESSENTIAL 2
requisite *adj* 1 *syn* see NEEDFUL
2 *syn* see JUST 3
requisite *n* *syn* see ESSENTIAL 2
requisition *vb* *syn* see DEMAND 1
requital *n* *syn* see RETALIATION
requite *vb* 1 *syn* see RECIPROCATE
rel content, satisfy; revenge
2 *syn* see COMPENSATE 3
resay *vb* *syn* see REPEAT
rescind *vb* *syn* see REVOKE 2
rescript *n* *syn* see REVISION 1
rescue *vb* to set free (as from confinement or risk) <*rescue* a drowning child>
syn deliver, save
rel emancipate, free, liberate, manumit, release; conserve, preserve; disembarrass, disentangle, extricate; recover, regain, retrieve; buy, ransom, redeem
research *n* *syn* see INQUIRY 1
resect *vb* *syn* see EXCISE
resemblance *n* *syn* see LIKENESS

syn synonym(s) *rel* related word(s)
ant antonym(s) *con* contrasted word(s)
idiom idiomatic equivalent(s)
‖ use limited; if in doubt, see a dictionary

rel parallel
ant dissemblance

resemble *vb* to be like or similar to <he *resembles* his father>
syn favor, ||feature, simulate
idiom be a dead ringer for, bear a resemblance to, be the spit and image of, be the very image of, bring to mind, have all the earmarks of, look like, put one in mind of, remind one of, take after
con differ, vary

resentfully *adv* ***syn*** see HARD 6

resentment *n* ***syn*** see OFFENSE 2
rel animosity, animus, antagonism, antipathy, rancor; ill will, malice, malignancy, malignity, spite

reservation *n* ***syn*** see CONDITION 1
rel circumscription

reserve *vb* **1** ***syn*** see KEEP 5
2 to set or have set aside or apart <*reserve* a hotel room>
syn bespeak, book, preengage
rel contract, engage, retain

reserve *n* something stored or kept available for future use or need <keep a *reserve* of canned foods on hand>
syn backlog, hoard, inventory, nest egg, reservoir, stock, stockpile, store
rel fund, supply
idiom something for a rainy day, something in the sock

reserved *adj* **1** inclined to cautious restraint in the expression of knowledge or opinions <too *reserved* to offer a spontaneous criticism>
syn constrained, incommunicable, noncommittal, restrained
rel bashful, diffident, modest, shy; ceremonious, conventional, formal
con demonstrative, expansive, unconstrained, unrestrained; boisterous, loud, ostentatious; extroverted, open, outgoing
ant unreserved
2 ***syn*** see SILENT 3
ant effusive
3 ***syn*** see UNSOCIABLE
ant affable
4 ***syn*** see ANTISOCIAL
5 ***syn*** see QUALIFIED 2

reservoir *n* ***syn*** see RESERVE

reshuffle *vb* ***syn*** see REORGANIZE

reside *vb* **1** to have as one's habitation or domicile <he *resides* in Boston>
syn abide, bide, ||dig, dwell, hang out, live
rel inhabit, occupy, people, tenant; continue, endure
2 ***syn*** see CONSIST 1

residence *n* **1** ***syn*** see HABITATION 1
2 ***syn*** see HABITATION 2

residency *n* ***syn*** see HABITATION 2

resident *n* ***syn*** see INHABITANT

||residenter *n* ***syn*** see INHABITANT

resider *n* ***syn*** see INHABITANT

residual *n* ***syn*** see REMAINDER

residue *n* ***syn*** see REMAINDER

residuum *n* ***syn*** see REMAINDER

resign *vb* **1** ***syn*** see RELINQUISH
2 ***syn*** see ABDICATE 1
3 ***syn*** see QUIT 6

resignation *n* **1** ***syn*** see ACQUIESCENCE
rel humbleness, lowliness, meekness, modesty
2 ***syn*** see PATIENCE

resigned *adj* ***syn*** see PASSIVE 2
ant rebellious

resile *vb* ***syn*** see BACK DOWN

resilient *adj* **1** ***syn*** see ELASTIC 1
2 ***syn*** see ELASTIC 2
ant flaccid

resist *vb* to stand firm against a person or influence <the criminal *resisted* the police> <we must learn to *resist* temptation>
syn buck, combat, contest, dispute, duel, fight, oppose, repel, traverse, withstand
rel assail, assault, attack; contradict, contravene, gainsay, impugn; baffle, balk, foil, frustrate, thwart; check, counter, hinder, obstruct, stem
con bow, capitulate, surrender
ant submit, yield

resolute *adj* **1** ***syn*** see DECIDED 2
rel obstinate, pertinacious, stubborn
2 ***syn*** see FAITHFUL 1

resoluteness *n* ***syn*** see DECISION 2

resolution *n* **1** ***syn*** see ANALYSIS 1
2 ***syn*** see DECISION 1
3 ***syn*** see DECISION 2
4 ***syn*** see COURAGE

resolve *vb* **1** ***syn*** see ANALYZE
ant blend
2 ***syn*** see SOLVE 1
3 ***syn*** see SOLVE 2
rel dispel, disperse, dissipate; clear, disabuse, purge, rid
4 ***syn*** see DECIDE

resolve *n* ***syn*** see DECISION 2

resolved *adj* ***syn*** see DECIDED 2

resonant *adj* marked by conspicuously full and rich sounds or tones (as of speech or music) <a deep *resonant* voice rang out>
syn consonant, fat, orotund, plangent, resounding, ringing, rotund, round, sonorant, sonorous, vibrant
rel full, mellow, rich; deep, profound; enhanced, heightened, intensified; earsplitting, loud, powerful, stentorian, strident; beating, pulsating, pulsing, throbbing; booming, clangorous, noisy, reverberant, reverberating, sounding, thundering, thunderous; electrifying, thrilling
con faint, low, murmurous, muted, smothered, soft, weak; flat, toneless, unmusical; cacophonous, discordant, inharmonious, off-key

resort *n* **1** ***syn*** see RESOURCE 3
2 a place that is habitually frequented <a favorite *resort* of teenagers>
syn hangout, haunt, purlieu, rendezvous, stamping ground, watering hole
rel harbor, haven, refuge, retreat; den, nest
3 a place providing recreation and entertainment especially to vacationers <returned to the same *resort* every year>

syn pleasure dome, spa, watering place
rel hotel, inn, lodge; bath(s), hot spring(s), mineral spring(s), spring(s), thermal spring(s)

resort *vb* **1** ***syn*** see FREQUENT
ant avoid
2 to betake oneself or to have recourse when in need of help or relief <they were unwilling to *resort* to her parents for aid>
syn apply, go, recur, refer, repair run, turn
rel address, devote, direct, employ, use, utilize
idiom avail oneself of, fall back on (*or* upon)

resound *vb* ***syn*** see PRAISE 2

resounding *adj* **1** ***syn*** see RESONANT
2 ***syn*** see EMPHATIC

resource *n* **1 resources** *pl* ***syn*** see MEAN 3
2 resources *pl* ***syn*** see WEALTH 2
3 something to which one turns for assistance in difficulty or need in the absence of a usual means or source of supply <has exhausted every *resource* he can think of>
syn dernier ressort, expediency, expedient, makeshift, recourse, refuge, resort, shift, stopgap, string, substitute, surrogate
rel contraption, contrivance, device, lash-up; creation, invention; fashion, manner, method, mode, system, way; means, measure, step; artifice, dodge, stratagem, subterfuge; hope, opportunity, possibility, relief

respect *n* ***syn*** see REGARD 4
rel awe, fear, reverence; adoration, veneration, worship
ant scorn

respect *vb* ***syn*** see ADMIRE 2
rel revere, reverence, venerate
ant abuse; misuse; scorn

respectable *adj* **1** worthy of esteem or deference <a *respectable* scientist>
syn creditable, estimable, reputable, reputed, well-thought-of
rel honorable, worthy
ant disreputable, unrespectable
2 ***syn*** see DECOROUS 1
3 ***syn*** see DECENT 4
4 ***syn*** see CONSIDERABLE 2
5 acceptable in appearance or standing <wore old but *respectable* clothes>
syn decent, presentable, tolerable; *compare* DECENT 4
rel adequate, satisfactory; acceptable, appropriate, proper, suitable
ant disreputable

respectful *adj* marked by or showing respect or deference <a *respectful* glance>
syn deferential, duteous, dutiful, regardful
rel reverent, reverential, venerating; attentive, civil, courteous, gracious, polite
con abusive, insolent, insulting, offensive; contemptuous, impudent, irreverent, rude
ant disrespectful

respecting *prep* ***syn*** see APROPOS

respective *adj* ***syn*** see SEVERAL 1

respire *vb* ***syn*** see BREATHE 3

respite *n* **1** a temporary suspension of the execution of a capital offender <the murderer won a *respite*>
syn reprieve
2 ***syn*** see BREAK 4
rel intermission, lull, pause, recess; ease, leisure, rest

resplendent *adj* ***syn*** see SPLENDID 2
rel blazing, flaming, glowing

respond *n* ***syn*** see ANSWER 1

respond *vb* ***syn*** see ANSWER 1
rel act, behave, react

response *n* ***syn*** see ANSWER 1

responsible *adj* subject to an authority which may exact redress in case of default <she is *responsible* for the safe delivery of the goods>
syn accountable, amenable, answerable, liable
rel exposed, open, subject
con clear, exempt, immune; irresponsible, unaccountable, unanswerable, unliable
ant irresponsible

responsive *adj* **1** ***syn*** see RECEPTIVE 1
ant unresponsive
2 ***syn*** see SENTIENT 3
rel answering, replying, responding
3 ***syn*** see TENDER
con cold, cool, indifferent

rest *n* **1** freedom from toil or strain <enjoyed his well-deserved *rest*>
syn ease, leisure, relaxation, repose, requiescence
rel deferring, intermission, suspension; quiet, silence, stillness; calm, peace, peacefulness, placidity, restfulness, serenity, tranquillity
con action, work; restlessness, strain
2 ***syn*** see BASE 1

rest *vb* **1** to dispose oneself at ease in order to relieve or avoid fatigue <she is *resting* in the bedroom after a hard day's work>
syn lie, lie down, recline, repose, stretch (out)
rel doze, nap, nod, sleep, slumber, snooze
2 to refrain from labor or exertion <planned to do nothing but *rest* during his vacation>
syn relax, rest up, unbend, unlax
rel loaf, loll, lounge; ease off, ease up, let down, let up, slacken, slack off
idiom take it easy, take life easy
con labor, toil, work; drudge, grind, slave
3 to allow an interval of rest from exertion <they *rested* for ten minutes before going back to work>
syn breathe, lay off, lie by, spell
idiom lie (*or* rest) on one's oars, stop for breath, take a break (*or* rest), take five (*or* ten), take time out
4 ***syn*** see BASE
rel depend, hang, hinge; count, rely

rest *n* ***syn*** see REMAINDER
rel excess, overplus, superfluity, surplus, surplusage

restart *vb* ***syn*** see RESUME 2

restate *vb* ***syn*** see PARAPHRASE

---

syn synonym(s) ***rel*** related word(s)
ant antonym(s) ***con*** contrasted word(s)
idiom idiomatic equivalent(s)
‖ use limited; if in doubt, see a dictionary

restatement *n* ***syn*** see VERSION 1
restitute *vb* **1** ***syn*** see RESTORE 3
2 ***syn*** see RETURN 4
restitution *n* ***syn*** see REPARATION
restive *adj* **1** ***syn*** see CONTRARY 3
2 ***syn*** see TENSE 2
restiveness *n* ***syn*** see UNREST
restless *adj* lacking rest or giving no rest <the patient was *restless* from pain> <*restless* sleep>
syn uneasy, unpeaceful, unquiet, unrestful, unsettled, untranquil
rel agitated, disturbed, perturbed, troubled; fidgety, jittery, jumpy, nervous, restive; fitful, intermittent, spasmodic
con easy, peaceful, quiet, tranquil
ant restful
restlessness *n* ***syn*** see UNREST
restorative *adj* **1** ***syn*** see CURATIVE
2 ***syn*** see TONIC 1
restore *vb* **1** to put or bring back (as into existence or use) <*restore* peace in the world>
syn recall, reestablish, reinstate, reintroduce, renew, revive
rel get back, recover, regain, retrieve, win (back)
2 ***syn*** see RENEW 1
3 to put into a previous good state <made plans to *restore* slum areas>
syn reclaim, recondition, reconstruct, recover, rehabilitate, rejuvenate, restitute
rel redeem, rescue, save; amend, reform, revise; recoup, recruit, regain, retrieve; better, improve; correct, rectify, remedy, right; return
ant deteriorate
4 to help or cause to regain signs of life and vigor <*restore* him to health>
syn resuscitate, revive, revivify
rel cure, heal, remedy; arouse, rally, rouse, stir
5 to put again in possession of something <*restore* the king to his throne>
syn give back, put (back), reinstate, replace, return
6 ***syn*** see RETURN 4
restrain *vb* **1** to prevent from or control in doing something <*restrained* the child from picking all the flowers>
syn bit, bridle, check, coarct, constrain, crimp, curb, hold back, hold down, hold in, inhibit, keep, pull in, withhold; *compare* HAMPER
rel arrest, interrupt, stop; prevent; forbear, refrain; block, hinder, impede, obstruct; gag, muzzle
idiom keep in line, put (*or* lay) under restraint
con countenance, encourage; incline, induce, move, prompt; persuade; allow, permit
ant impel; incite
2 ***syn*** see COMPOSE 4
ant abandon
3 ***syn*** see MODERATE 1
restrained *adj* **1** ***syn*** see QUIET 4
ant unrestrained
2 ***syn*** see UNDEMONSTRATIVE
3 ***syn*** see RESERVED 1
4 ***syn*** see CONSERVATIVE 2
ant extravagant

restraint *n* ***syn*** see RESTRICTION 2
restrict *vb* ***syn*** see LIMIT 2
rel bind, tie; shrink
restricted *adj* ***syn*** see DEFINITE 1
restriction *n* **1** something that restricts or restrains <they both wanted to be free of the *restriction* of the school>
syn ‖ball and chain, circumscription, cramp, limitation, stint, stricture
rel brake, check, control, curb
2 an act of restricting or the condition of being restricted <undue *restriction* of children>
syn circumscription, confinement, constrainment, constraint, cramp, restraint
rest up *vb* ***syn*** see REST 2
restyle *vb* ***syn*** see REVISE
result *n* **1** ***syn*** see EFFECT 1
rel close, conclusion, end, finish, termination; product, production
con origin, root, source
2 ***syn*** see ANSWER 2
resume *vb* **1** to assume or take again <*resumed* her place in society>
syn reassume, reoccupy, repossess, retake
rel reclaim, recoup, recover, regain, retrieve
2 to return to or begin again after interruption <*resumed* her work>
syn continue, pick up, recommence, renew, reopen, restart, take up
rel carry on, go on, keep up
con cease, discontinue, end, halt, postpone, quit, stop; check, intermit, interrupt
résumé *n* ***syn*** see SUMMARY
resurgence *n* ***syn*** see REVIVAL
resurrect *vb* **1** to restore to life <believed that his body would be literally *resurrected*>
syn raise
idiom raise from the dead
2 ***syn*** see REVIVE 3
resurrection *n* ***syn*** see REVIVAL
resuscitate *vb* **1** ***syn*** see RESTORE 4
2 ***syn*** see REVIVE 3
resuscitation *n* ***syn*** see REVIVAL
retail *vb* ***syn*** see SELL 3
retain *vb* **1** ***syn*** see HAVE 1
2 ***syn*** see KEEP 5
con abdicate, resign; abjure, forswear, recant, renounce, retract
3 ***syn*** see REMEMBER
retake *vb* ***syn*** see RESUME 1
retaliate *vb* ***syn*** see RECIPROCATE
rel avenge, revenge
idiom even the score, get back at, get even with, give in kind, give one a dose of his own medicine, give one tit for tat, pay one in his own coin, settle (*or* square) accounts, turn the tables on
retaliation *n* the act of inflicting or the intent to inflict injury in return for injury <they had no opportunity for *retaliation*>
syn avengement, avenging, counterblow, reprisal, requital, retribution, revanche, revenge, vengeance
rel correction, discipline, punishment; indemnification, recompense, repayment; amends, indemnity, redress, reparation, restitution

idiom an eye for an eye, blow for blow, measure for measure, tit for tat
con clemency, grace, lenity, mercy; forgiveness, pardon, remission

retard *vb* ***syn*** see DELAY 1
rel decrease, lessen, reduce; clog, fetter, hamper; baffle, balk
ant accelerate; advance

retarded *adj* limited in intellectual or emotional development <a *retarded* child>
syn backward, dim-witted, dull, feebleminded, half-witted, imbecile, moronic, quarter-witted, simple, simpleminded, slow, slow-witted; *compare* SIMPLE 3, STUPID 1
rel dim, ‖dough-baked, ‖dunny, opaque; exceptional, underachieving; touched
idiom not all there, soft in the head
con bright, capable, intelligent

retch *vb* to make an effort to vomit <started to *retch* after drinking it>
syn gag, heave, keck

rethink *vb* ***syn*** see RECONSIDER

reticent *adj* ***syn*** see SILENT 3
con candid, open, plain
ant frank, unreticent

retinue *n* ***syn*** see ENTOURAGE

retire *vb* **1** ***syn*** see RETREAT 2
2 ***syn*** see GO 2
rel recede, retreat; abandon, relinquish, surrender, yield
ant advance
3 to cause to withdraw from one's position or occupation <all employees are automatically *retired* at age sixty-five>
syn pension (off), superannuate
rel discharge, dismiss; drop, leave, quit, resign, terminate, vacate
4 to go to bed <youngsters should always *retire* before midnight>
syn bed, ‖flop, pile (in), roll in, turn in
idiom go beddie-bye, go night-night, hit the hay (*or* sack)
con arise, get out, get up, pile (out), roll out, turn out, uprise
ant rise

retired *adj* ***syn*** see OBSCURE 2

retirement *n* ***syn*** see SECLUSION

retiring *adj* **1** ***syn*** see SHY 1
ant assertive
2 ***syn*** see UNDEMONSTRATIVE
ant forward

retool *vb* ***syn*** see REORGANIZE

retort *vb* ***syn*** see ANSWER 1

retort *n* **1** ***syn*** see ANSWER 1
2 a quick, witty, or cutting reply <he made a very clever *retort*>
syn back answer, comeback, repartee, riposte
rel reprisal, retaliation, revenge; crack, gag, jape, jest, joke, quip, sally, wisecrack, witticism

retouch *vb* ***syn*** see TOUCH UP

retract *vb* **1** ***syn*** see RECEDE 1
ant protract
2 ***syn*** see ABJURE
rel eliminate, exclude, rule out, suspend

retral *adj* **1** ***syn*** see POSTERIOR 2
2 ***syn*** see BACKWARD 1

retreat *n* ***syn*** see SHELTER 1

retreat *vb* **1** ***syn*** see RECEDE 1
rel quail, recoil, shrink
ant advance
2 to draw back from action or danger <the army *retreated* in disarray>
syn fall back, give back, retire, withdraw
rel abandon, depart, evacuate, go, leave, pull out, quit, vacate; decamp, escape, flee, fly; back down, back out, bow out, climb down
idiom beat a retreat, drop back, give ground, give way, sound a retreat
con advance, move, proceed, progress
ant attack

re–treat *vb* ***syn*** see RECONSIDER

retrench *vb* ***syn*** see SHORTEN

retribution *n* ***syn*** see RETALIATION
rel affliction, trial, tribulation, visitation

retrieve *vb* **1** ***syn*** see RECOVER 1
2 ***syn*** see REVIVE 3

retrocede *vb* ***syn*** see RECEDE 1

retrograde *adj* ***syn*** see BACKWARD 1

retrograde *vb* **1** ***syn*** see RECEDE 1
rel return, revert; invert, reverse; backslide, lapse, relapse
2 ***syn*** see DETERIORATE 1

retrogress *vb* ***syn*** see REVERT 2

retrospect *n* ***syn*** see REVIEW 5

retrospect *vb* ***syn*** see REMEMBER

retrospection *n* ***syn*** see REVIEW 5

return *vb* **1** to go or come back (as to a person, place, or condition) <the converted sinner soon *returned* to his old ways>
syn react, recrudesce, recur, revert, turn back
rel advert; revolve, rotate, turn; renew, restore; recover, regain; rebound, reflect, repercuss, reverberate
con abandon, depart, leave, quit
ant forsake
2 ***syn*** see ANSWER 1
3 to bring back (as a writ or verdict) to an office or tribunal <*return* a verdict of not guilty>
syn render
4 to bring, send, or put back to a former or proper place <*return* the gun to its holster>
syn replace, restitute, restore, take back
ant remove
5 ***syn*** see RESTORE 5
6 ***syn*** see YIELD 5
7 ***syn*** see RECIPROCATE
rel bestow, give

return *n* **1** ***syn*** see RECURRENCE
2 ***syn*** see ANSWER 1
3 ***syn*** see PROFIT
ant outlay

returnless *adj* ***syn*** see INEVITABLE

revamp *vb* **1** ***syn*** see MEND 2

---

syn synonym(s) ***rel*** related word(s)
ant antonym(s) ***con*** contrasted word(s)
idiom idiomatic equivalent(s)
‖ use limited; if in doubt, see a dictionary

2 *syn* see REVISE

revanche *n syn* see RETALIATION

reveal *vb* **1** to make known what has been or should be concealed <he solemnly promised he would not *reveal* the truth>
syn betray, blab (out), disclose, discover, divulge, give away, let on, ‖let out, mouth, spill, tell, unbosom, unclose, uncover, uncurtain, unveil
rel break, communicate, impart; announce, blow (about *or* abroad), broadcast, declare, give out, publish, vent; breathe, whisper; leak; acknowledge, admit, avow, confess, let on; peach, rat, ‖split, squeak, squeal (on), ‖stool, talk
idiom let slip, let the cat out of the bag, spill the beans
con cover (up), hide, obscure, veil
ant conceal
2 *syn* see OPEN 2

revel *vb* **1** to be festive in a noisy or riotous manner <they *reveled* all night long>
syn carouse, frolic, hell, riot, roister, spree, wassail
idiom blow off steam, cut loose, kick up one's heels, let go, let loose, paint the town red, whoop it up
2 *syn* see WALLOW 3

revel *n* **1** *syn* see MERRYMAKING
2 *syn* see REVELRY 2

revelation *n* disclosure or something disclosed by or as if by divine or preternatural means <a *revelation* closely guarded by members of the sect>
syn apocalypse, oracle, prophecy, vision
ant adumbration

reveling *n syn* see MERRYMAKING

revelment *n* **1** *syn* see MERRYMAKING
2 *syn* see REVELRY 2

revelry *n* **1** *syn* see MERRYMAKING
2 boisterous partying <they were exhausted after the night of *revelry*>
syn high jinks, revel, revelment, skylarking, wassail, whoop-de-do, whoopee, whoopla, whoop-up

revenant *n syn* see APPARITION

revenge *vb syn* see AVENGE
rel defend, justify
idiom get one's own back, have one's revenge, take an eye for an eye

revenge *n syn* see RETALIATION

revengeful *adj syn* see VINDICTIVE
rel adamant, inexorable, inflexible, obdurate

revenue *n* amount received or gained usually measured in money <still holds property that yields a good *revenue*>
syn coming(s) in, income, receipts
rel earnings, gains, salary, wages; proceeds, profit, returns, yield
con expenditure, expense(s), outgoings, outlay

reverberant *adj syn* see HOLLOW 1

revere *vb* to honor and admire profoundly and respectfully <he is *revered* for his wisdom>
syn adore, reverence, venerate, worship
rel admire, esteem, regard, respect; appreciate, cherish, prize, treasure, value; exalt, magnify; enjoy, love
con contemn, despise, disdain, scorn, scout; insult, mock, scoff
ant flout

revered *adj syn* see VENERABLE 1

reverence *n* **1** *syn* see HONOR 1
rel devotion, fealty, loyalty, piety
2 the emotion inspired by what arouses one's deep respect or veneration <a deep *reverence* for honesty>
syn awe, fear
con contempt, despite, disdain, hatred, scorn; insult, mockery

reverence *vb syn* see REVERE
idiom hold in reverence

reverend *adj syn* see VENERABLE 1

reverend *n syn* see CLERGYMAN

reverential *adj syn* see VENERABLE 1

reverie *n* the condition of being lost in thought <spent the day in *reverie* before the fire>
syn brown study, muse, study, trance
rel absorption, abstraction, preoccupation; contemplation, meditation, thought; castle-building, daydreaming, dreaming

reversal *n* **1** a causing to move or face in an opposite direction or to appear in an inverted position <a *reversal* in policy> <the *reversal* of objects seen through a simple lens>
syn about-face, changeabout, inversion, reverse, reversement, reversion, right-about, right-about-face, turn, turnabout, turning, volte-face
rel bouleversement, overturning
2 *syn* see SETBACK

reverse *adj syn* see OPPOSITE

reverse *vb* **1** to change to the contrary or opposite side or position <the chairman *reversed* the order in which they would speak>
syn change, inverse, invert, revert, transplace, transpose, turn
rel capsize, overturn, upset; exchange, interchange; shift, transfer
2 *syn* see REVOKE 2

reverse *n* **1** *syn* see OPPOSITE
2 *syn* see REVERSAL 1
3 *syn* see SETBACK

reversement *n syn* see REVERSAL 1

reversion *n* **1** a return to an ancestral type or condition or an instance of such a return <the law was a shocking *reversion* to earlier times>
syn atavism, throwback
rel backsliding, lapse, relapse
con advance, amendment, bettering, betterment, improvement; reform
2 *syn* see REVERSAL 1

revert *vb* **1** *syn* see RETURN 1
2 to come or go back to a lower or worse condition <*reverted* to savagery>
syn regress, retrogress, throw back
rel backslide, lapse, relapse; decline, degenerate, deteriorate, retrograde
con advance, progress
3 *syn* see REVERSE 1

review *n* **1** *syn* see REVISION 1
2 *syn* see EXAMINATION
3 *syn* see CRITICISM 1

4 ***syn*** see JOURNAL
5 a retrospective view of or meditation on past events <an occurrence that in *review* did not surprise him>
syn afterlight, reconsideration, reexamination, retrospect, retrospection, revision
rel reflection, study; second thought
con anticipation, contemplation, foreseeing

review *vb* ***syn*** see RECONSIDER

reviewal *n* ***syn*** see CRITICISM 1

revile *vb* ***syn*** see SCOLD 1
rel asperse, calumniate, defame, libel, malign, slander, traduce, vilify
con acclaim, eulogize, extol, praise
ant laud

revisal *n* ***syn*** see REVISION 1

revise *vb* to make a new, amended, improved, or up-to-date version of <the many problems involved in *revising* a dictionary>
syn redraft, redraw, restyle, revamp, rework, rewrite, work over
rel overhaul, reorganize; perfect, polish, upgrade
con discard, disregard

revise *n* ***syn*** see REVISION 1

revision *n* **1** an act of revising <the *revision* of a manuscript>
syn recension, redraft, rescript, review, revisal, revise
rel amendment, correction, emendation, rectification
2 ***syn*** see REVIEW 5

revitalize *vb* ***syn*** see REVIVE 3

revival *n* a renewal of life, activity, or prominence <a *revival* of weaving>
syn reanimation, rebirth, renaissance, renascence, resurgence, resurrection, resuscitation, revivification, reviviscence, risorgimento
rel regeneration, rejuvenation, renewal, restoration

revive *vb* **1** ***syn*** see RESTORE 4
rel gain, improve, recuperate
2 ***syn*** see RESTORE 1
3 to restore from a depressed, inactive, or unused state <*revived* his hope of escape>
syn reactivate, rekindle, renew, renovate, resurrect, resuscitate, retrieve, revitalize, revivify
rel reanimate, regenerate, reinvigorate, rejuvenate; arouse, galvanize, quicken, stimulate; activate, energize, vitalize
con extinguish, put down, put out, quell, quench, suppress; inhibit
4 ***syn*** see REMEMBER

revived *adj* ***syn*** see REFRESHED

revivification *n* ***syn*** see REVIVAL

revivify *vb* **1** ***syn*** see REVIVE 3
2 ***syn*** see RESTORE 4

reviviscence *n* ***syn*** see REVIVAL

revoke *vb* **1** ***syn*** see REMEMBER
2 to annul by recalling or taking back <*revoke* a privilege>
syn dismantle, lift, recall, repeal, rescind, reverse
rel abrogate, annul, void; cancel, erase, expunge; invalidate, nullify; countermand, counterorder; abjure, forswear, recant, retract
ant confirm

revolt *vb* **1** to renounce allegiance or subjection <*revolted* against the king>
syn insurrect, mutiny, rebel, rise (against)
rel defy, oppose, resist; break, renounce, turn (against); boycott, strike; overthrow, overturn, riot
idiom kick over the traces, take up arms against
con obey, submit; aid, assist, help, succor, support; bolster, prop (up), sustain, uphold
2 ***syn*** see DISGUST

revolter *n* ***syn*** see REBEL

revolting *adj* ***syn*** see OFFENSIVE

revolute *vb* ***syn*** see REVOLUTIONIZE

revolution *n* **1** the action or an act of moving around an orbit or circular course <the *revolution* of the earth around the sun>
syn circuit, circulation, circumvolution, gyration, gyre, revolve, rotation, round, turn, wheel, whirl
rel cycle, pirouette, reel, roll, spin, twirl
2 ***syn*** see SHAKE-UP

revolution *vb* ***syn*** see REVOLUTIONIZE

revolutional *adj* ***syn*** see EXTREME 3

revolutionary *adj* ***syn*** see EXTREME 3

revolutionary *n* ***syn*** see RADICAL

revolutionist *n* ***syn*** see RADICAL

revolutionist *adj* ***syn*** see EXTREME 3

revolutionize *vb* to change fundamentally or completely <he *revolutionized* manufacturing processes>
syn revolute, revolution
rel alter, change, modify; recast, refashion, reform, remodel; redraw, restyle, revamp, revise; metamorphose, transfigure, transform, transmogrify; overthrow, overturn
idiom break with the past, make a clean sweep, make a radical change

revolve *vb* **1** ***syn*** see PONDER 2
2 ***syn*** see TURN 1

revolve *n* ***syn*** see REVOLUTION 1

revulsion *n* ***syn*** see ABOMINATION 2

revulsive *adj* ***syn*** see REPUGNANT 1

reward *n* something that is offered or given for some service or attainment <the miner received a *reward* for his hard work>
syn carrot, dividend, guerdon, meed, plum, premium, prize
rel compensation, recompense, remuneration, requital

reweigh *vb* ***syn*** see RECONSIDER

reword *vb* ***syn*** see PARAPHRASE

rework *vb* ***syn*** see REVISE

rewrite *vb* ***syn*** see REVISE

rhadamanthine *adj* ***syn*** see JUST 3

rhapsodize *vb* ***syn*** see ENTHUSE 2

---

syn synonym(s) ***rel*** related word(s)
ant antonym(s) ***con*** contrasted word(s)
idiom idiomatic equivalent(s)
|| use limited; if in doubt, see a dictionary

rel acclaim, extol, praise
con blame, condemn, denounce; decry, derogate, detract, minimize
rhapsody *n* **1** ***syn*** see BOMBAST
2 ***syn*** see ECSTASY
rhapsody *vb* ***syn*** see ENTHUSE 2
rhetoric *n* **1** ***syn*** see ORATORY
2 ***syn*** see BOMBAST
rhetorical *adj* emphasizing style often at the expense of thought <the candidate was given to windy *rhetorical* speeches>
syn aureate, bombastic, declamatory, euphuistic, florid, flowery, grandiloquent, highfalutin, high-flown, magniloquent, ‖mouthy, oratorical, orotund, overblown, pompous, purple, sonorous, stilted, swelling, swollen, tumescent, tumid, turgid
rel chichi, orchidaceous, ostentatious, pretentious, showy; gassy, inflated, windy; exaggerated, overdone, overwrought; grand, grandiose, high-sounding, imposing; flamboyant, ornate; embellished; articulate, eloquent, fluent, glib, vocal, voluble
con homely, literal, plain, simple, unpretentious; unadorned, undecorated, unembellished, ungarnished, unornamented
ant unrhetorical
rhino *n* ***syn*** see MONEY
rhubarb *n* ***syn*** see QUARREL
rhyme *n* **1** ***syn*** see POETRY 1
2 ***syn*** see POEM
3 ***syn*** see RHYTHM
rhyme *vb* ***syn*** see AGREE 4
rhymer *n* ***syn*** see POETASTER
rhymester *n* ***syn*** see POETASTER
rhythm *n* the regular rise and fall in intensity of sounds that is associated chiefly with poetry and music <the *rhythm* of the music made it easy to dance to>
syn beat, cadence, cadency, measure, meter, rhyme, rhythmus, swing
rel lilt; accent
rhythmus *n* ***syn*** see RHYTHM
riant *adj* ***syn*** see MERRY
‖**rib** *n* ***syn*** see WIFE
rib *vb* ***syn*** see BANTER 1
ribald *n* ***syn*** see SCAMP
ribbon *n* ***syn*** see STRIP 1
rich *adj* **1** having goods, property, and money in abundance <he was a *rich* man, having accumulated his wealth in business>
syn affluent, moneyed, ‖oofy, opulent, wealthy
rel comfortable, easy, independent, prosperous, well-fixed, well-heeled, well-off, well-to-do; fat, flush
idiom flush with money, having money to burn, in the money, rich as Croesus, rolling in money
con destitute, indigent, penurious, poverty-stricken
ant poor
2 ***syn*** see ORNATE
3 highly seasoned and fatty, oily, or sweet <ate *rich* desserts every day>
syn heavy
rel cloying, oversweet; filling, satiating, sating; fat
con natural, simple, unseasoned
ant plain
4 ***syn*** see FERTILE
5 ***syn*** see EXPRESSIVE
richen *vb* ***syn*** see ENRICH
riches *n pl* ***syn*** see WEALTH 2
rick *n* ***syn*** see PILE 1
‖**rick** *vb* ***syn*** see SPRAIN
rickety *adj* likely to give way or break down <a *rickety* old chair>
syn rachitic, rackety, rattletrap, shaky, wobbly; *compare* WEAK 2
rel unsound, unsteady
con firm, rugged, solid, sturdy, substantial, well-made
ant stable
‖**rickle** *n* ***syn*** see PILE 1
ricochet *vb* ***syn*** see GLANCE 1
rel bound, rebound, recoil
rid *vb* to set a person or thing free of something that encumbers <*rid* himself of his troubles>
syn clear, lose, shake (off), throw off, unburden
rel free, liberate, release; disembosom, unbosom; eradicate, exterminate, extirpate, remove, uproot; abolish, extinguish
con burden, charge, clog, cumber, encumber, lade, load, lumber, saddle, task, tax, weigh, weight
ant weigh down
riddance *n* ***syn*** see DISPOSAL 2
riddle *n* ***syn*** see MYSTERY
ride *vb* **1** to travel by automobile <often *rode* out to the countryside>
syn auto, motor
idiom go for a spin
2 ***syn*** see DRIFT 1
3 ***syn*** see BAIT 2
rel oppress, persecute; torment, torture
4 ***syn*** see OVERLAP
ride (out) *vb* ***syn*** see SURVIVE 2
ride *n* ***syn*** see DRIVE 1
rel excursion, expedition, journey, tour, trip
rider *n* ***syn*** see APPENDIX 1
ridge *n* **1** a top or upper part especially when long and narrow <topped the mountain *ridge*>
syn chine, crest, hogback
2 ***syn*** see WRINKLE
‖**ridge runner** *n* ***syn*** see RUSTIC
ridicule *vb* to make an object of laughter <*ridiculed* him for his inability to perform the feat>
syn deride, lout, mock, quiz, rally, razz, scout, taunt, twit
rel ‖barrack, flout, gibe, jape, jeer, scoff, sneer; burlesque, caricature, mimic, travesty; haze, ride, roast
idiom laugh out of court, make fun (*or* game *or* sport) of, poke fun at
ridiculous *adj* **1** ***syn*** see LAUGHABLE
rel absurd, foolish, preposterous, silly; antic, bizarre, fantastic, grotesque
2 ***syn*** see INDECOROUS
riding *n* **1** ***syn*** see SHIVAREE

2 ***syn*** see HARBOR 3
rife *adj* **1** ***syn*** see PREVAILING
2 ***syn*** see ALIVE 5
riff (through) *vb* ***syn*** see BROWSE
riffle *vb* ***syn*** see RIPPLE
riffle (through) *vb* ***syn*** see BROWSE
riffraff *n* **1** ***syn*** see RABBLE 2
2 ***syn*** see REFUSE
rifle *vb* ***syn*** see ROB 1
rift *n* **1** ***syn*** see CRACK 3
2 ***syn*** see BREACH 3
rel gap, hiatus, interruption, interval
rig *vb* ***syn*** see FURNISH 1
rig *n* ***syn*** see COSTUME
||**rig** *n* **1** ***syn*** see IMPOSTURE
2 ***syn*** see PRANK
||**rig** *vb* ***syn*** see DUPE
rigamajig *n* ***syn*** DOODAD, business, dingus, dofunny, doohickey, gadget, gizmo, thingum, thingumajig, thingumbob
rigging *n* ***syn*** see CLOTHES
||**riggish** *adj* ***syn*** see FAST 7
right *adj* **1** ***syn*** see UPRIGHT 2
2 ***syn*** see DECOROUS 1
3 ***syn*** see JUST 3
4 ***syn*** see TRUE 3
con specious, unsound; misguided, mistaken
ant unright, wrong
5 ***syn*** see CORRECT 2
6 ***syn*** see FIT 1
7 ***syn*** see AUTHENTIC 2
8 ***syn*** see SANE 2
9 ***syn*** see HEALTHY 1
10 ***syn*** see CONSERVATIVE 1
11 ***syn*** see DECENT 4
right *n* **1** qualities (as adherence to duty or obedience to lawful authority) that together constitute the ideal of moral propriety or merit moral approval <the *right* is not all on one side>
syn good, straight
rel correctitude, correctness, properness, propriety, rightness
con debt, sin, wickedness; improperness, impropriety, incorrectness, unrightness
ant unright, wrong
2 something to which one has a just claim <the *right* to life, liberty, and the pursuit of happiness>
syn appanage, birthright, perquisite, prerogative, privilege
rel claim, interest, title; freedom, liberty, license
3 *usu* **rights** *pl* ***syn*** see DUE 1
4 ***syn*** see DIEHARD 1
||5 ***syn*** see OBLIGATION 2
||6 ***syn*** see EXCUSE 1
right *adv* **1** ***syn*** see JUST 1
2 ***syn*** see WELL 4
ant wrong, wrongly
3 ***syn*** see DIRECTLY 1
4 ***syn*** see WELL 3
5 ***syn*** see AWAY 3
6 ***syn*** see VERY 1
right *vb* **1** ***syn*** see CORRECT 1
||2 ***syn*** see MEND 2
right–about *n* ***syn*** see REVERSAL 1
right–about–face *n* ***syn*** see REVERSAL 1
right away *adv* ***syn*** see AWAY 3
righteous *adj* **1** ***syn*** see MORAL 1
con corrupt, flagitious, nefarious; bad, evil, immoral, reprobate, sinful, vicious, wicked, wrong
ant iniquitous, unrighteous
2 ***syn*** see GOOD 11
ant unrighteous
righteousness *n* ***syn*** see GOODNESS
ant unrighteousness
rightful *adj* **1** ***syn*** see JUST 3
rel equitable, fair, impartial
ant unrightful
2 ***syn*** see TRUE 8
ant unrightful
3 ***syn*** see FIT 1
right hand *n* ***syn*** see RIGHT-HAND MAN
right–handed *adj* having the same direction or course as the movement of the hands of a watch viewed from in front <a *right-handed* propeller>
syn clockwise, dextrorotatory, positive
right–hand man *n* a reliable or indispensable person <the boss viewed his efficient assistant as his *right-hand man*>
syn girl Friday, man Friday, right hand
rightist *n* ***syn*** see DIEHARD 1
ant leftist
||**rightle** *vb* ***syn*** see MEND 2
rightly *adv* ***syn*** see WELL 1
right–minded *adj* ***syn*** see MORAL 1
rightness *n* **1** ***syn*** see GOODNESS
2 ***syn*** see ORDER 11
right off *adv* ***syn*** see AWAY 3
||**right smart** *adj* ***syn*** see CONSIDERABLE 2
||**right smart** *adv* ***syn*** see VERY 1
right wing *n* ***syn*** see DIEHARD 1
right–winger *n* ***syn*** see DIEHARD 1
ant left-winger
rigid *adj* **1** ***syn*** see STIFF 1
rel firm, hard, solid
ant elastic
2 ***syn*** see INFLEXIBLE 2
3 extremely severe or stern <was regarded as a *rigid* disciplinarian>
syn draconian, ironhanded, rigorist, rigorous, strict, stringent, unpermissive
rel austere, severe, stern; hard-line, inflexible, tough, uncompromising, unyielding; adamant, adamantine, inexorable, obdurate
con humoring, indulgent, pampering; loose, relaxed; easy, gentle, mild
ant lax
rigor *n* ***syn*** see DIFFICULTY 1
rel austerity, severity, sternness; harshness, roughness; affliction, trial, tribulation, visitation
ant amenity
rigorist *adj* ***syn*** see RIGID 3
rigorous *adj* **1** ***syn*** see RIGID 3

---

syn synonym(s) ***rel*** related word(s)
ant antonym(s) ***con*** contrasted word(s)
idiom idiomatic equivalent(s)
|| use limited; if in doubt, see a dictionary

rel inflexible, stiff; ascetic; burdensome, exacting, onerous, oppressive
con easy, effortless, facile, light, smooth
ant mild
2 *syn* see SEVERE 3
rel drastic
con bland, faint, lenient, smooth
3 *syn* see CORRECT 2
rigorously *adv syn* see HARD 5
rile *vb* 1 *syn* see ROIL 1
2 *syn* see IRRITATE
riley *adj syn* see TURBID
rim *n syn* see BORDER 1
rim *vb syn* see BORDER 1
rima *n syn* see CRACK 3
rimation *n syn* see CRACK 3
rime *n syn* see CRACK 3
rime *vb syn* see CAKE 1
rimple *n syn* see WRINKLE
rimple *vb syn* see CRUMPLE 1
‖**rimption** *n, usu* **rimptions** *pl syn* see SCAD
‖**rindle** *n syn* see CREEK 2
ring *n* 1 *syn* see LOOP 2
2 *syn* see LOOP 1
3 *syn* see BOXING
4 *syn* see CLIQUE
5 *syn* see COMBINATION 2
ring *vb syn* see SURROUND 1
ring *vb* to sound clearly and resonantly <the church bells were *ringing*>
syn bell, bong, chime, knell, peal, toll
rel resound, reverberate, sound
‖**ring** (up) *vb syn* see TELEPHONE
ringer *n syn* see IMAGE 1
ringing *adj syn* see RESONANT
‖**ring off** *vb syn* see SHUT UP 2
riot *n* 1 *syn* see DISORDER 2
2 something or someone wildly amusing <the new comedy is a *riot*>
syn howl, ‖panic, scream, sidesplitter
rel sensation, smash, wow
riot *vb syn* see REVEL 1
riot (away) *vb syn* see WASTE 2
riotous *adj syn* see PROFUSE
rip *vb syn* see TEAR 1
rip (out) *vb syn* see SPUTTER 1
ripe *adj* 1 *syn* see MATURE 1
rel seasonable, timely, well-timed; overdue
con callow, crude, raw, rude; immature, unmatured, unmellow
ant unripe; green
2 *syn* see CONSUMMATE 1
3 brought by aging to full flavor or the best state <*ripe* cheese>
syn aged, matured, mellow, ripened
rel ready
ant unripe
‖**ripe** *vb syn* see MATURE
ripen *vb syn* see MATURE
rel better, improve; enhance, heighten, intensify, season
ripened *adj* 1 *syn* see MATURE 1
ant unripened
2 *syn* see RIPE 3
rip–off *n syn* see THEFT
rip off *vb* 1 *syn* see ROB 1
rel abuse, exploit, impose (on *or* upon), use, bleed, fleece, gouge, skin, soak, stick
2 *syn* see STEAL 1
riposte *n syn* see RETORT 2
ripper *n syn* ‖DILLY, ‖corker, crackerjack, dandy, ‖dinger, humdinger, jim-dandy, ‖lulu, nifty, peach
ripping *adj syn* see MARVELOUS 2
ripple *vb* to become fretted or lightly ruffled on the surface (as water) <the pond was *rippled* by rain>
syn cockle, dimple, fret, riffle
ripsnorter *n syn* ‖DILLY, ‖corker, crackerjack, ‖daisy, dandy, ‖dinger, ‖doozer, humdinger, jim=dandy, ‖lulu
rise *vb* 1 to assume an upright or standing position <he *rose* from his chair>
syn get up, stand up, uprise, upspring
rel sit up; straighten up
idiom come to one's feet
con lie, lounge, recline, sit; loll, sprawl
2 *syn* see ROLL OUT
ant retire
3 *syn* see ADJOURN 2
ant sit
4 to move or come up from a lower to a higher level <smoke *rose* from the chimneys>
syn arise, ascend, aspire, lift, mount, soar, up, uprear
rel surge, tower; climb, scale; elevate, raise, rear
con descend, drop, lower; dip, plummet, sink
ant fall; decline
5 *syn* see INTENSIFY
6 *syn* see SURFACE
7 *syn* see INCREASE 2
ant abate; fall
8 *syn* see HAPPEN 1
9 *syn* see SPRING 1
rise (against) *vb syn* see REVOLT 1
rise (to) *vb syn* see APPLAUD 2
rise *n* 1 *syn* see ASCENT
ant fall
2 *syn* see ADDITION
3 an increment in amount, number, or volume <crime is on the *rise*>
syn boost, breakthrough, hike, increase, upgrade, wax
con declension, decline, lessening, letup, reduction, slump; decrement, loss
ant drop
rise and shine *vb syn* see ROLL OUT
risible *adj syn* see LAUGHABLE
ant lachrymose, larmoyant
rising *n syn* see ASCENT
ant falling
risk *n syn* see DANGER
rel accident, chance, fortune, luck; exposedness, exposure, liability, liableness, openness
risk *vb* 1 *syn* see ENDANGER
rel beard, brave, dare, defy, face; confront, encounter, meet
idiom go out of one's depth

2 ***syn*** see VENTURE 1
3 ***syn*** see GAMBLE 2
riskless *adj* ***syn*** see SAFE 2
risky *adj* **1** ***syn*** see DANGEROUS 1
rel delicate, precarious, sensitive, ticklish, touchy; speculative
idiom on thin ice
2 ***syn*** see RISQUÉ
risorgimento *n* ***syn*** see REVIVAL
risqué *adj* verging on impropriety or indecency <blushed at his *risqué* stories>
syn blue, broad, off-color, purple, racy, risky, salty, sexy, shady, spicy, suggestive, wicked; *compare* OBSCENE 2
rel naughty, warm; coarse, crude, earthy, gross, lewd, obscene, raunchy, raw, ribald, vulgar; dirty, foul; indecent, indecorous, indelicate, inelegant, unrefined
con clean, decent, proper; restrained; euphemistic
‖**rissom** *n* ***syn*** see PARTICLE
rite *n* **1** ***syn*** see FORM 2
2 forms (as religious rites) appropriate to a particular event <the marriage *rites*>
syn ceremonial, ceremony, formality, liturgy, observance, ritual, service
rel celebration, occasion, solemnity; sacrament, sacramental; form
‖**rithe** *n* ***syn*** see CREEK 2
ritual *n* **1** ***syn*** see RITE 2
2 ***syn*** see FORM 2
rival *n* one of two or more striving for what only one can possess <political *rivals* for the nomination>
syn competition, competitor, corrival
rel contender, contestant, entrant; adversary, antagonist, opponent
rival *vb* **1** ***syn*** see COMPETE 1
2 to strive to equal or surpass <*rivaling* each other for the most work done>
syn compete, emulate, rivalize
rel attempt, strive, struggle, try; contend, fight
3 ***syn*** see EQUAL 3
4 ***syn*** see AMOUNT 2
rivalize *vb* ***syn*** see RIVAL 2
rivalry *n* ***syn*** see CONTEST 1
rive *vb* **1** ***syn*** see TEAR 1
rel divide, separate; chop, hew
2 ***syn*** see SHATTER 1
rivel *n* ***syn*** see WRINKLE
rivet *vb* **1** ***syn*** see FASTEN 1
2 ***syn*** see FASTEN 3
rivulet *n* ***syn*** see CREEK 2
road *n* **1** *often* **roads** *pl* ***syn*** see HARBOR 3
2 ***syn*** see WAY 1
3 ***syn*** see WAY 2
roadblock *n* ***syn*** see BAR 2
roadhouse *n* ***syn*** see HOTEL
roadman *n* ***syn*** see PEDDLER
roadstead *n* ***syn*** see HARBOR 3
roadster *n* ***syn*** see VAGABOND
roam *vb* ***syn*** see WANDER 1
roamer *n* ***syn*** see ROVER

roar *vb* to make a very loud and often a continuous or protracted noise <the crowd *roared* their disapproval of the speech>
syn bawl, bellow, bluster, clamor, rout; *compare* BAWL 2
rel rebound, repercuss, reverberate; shout, vociferate, yell; din
con breathe, murmur, mutter, whisper
roaring *adj* **1** ***syn*** see LOUD 1
2 ***syn*** see FLOURISHING
roast *vb* **1** ***syn*** see BURN 3
2 ***syn*** see LAMBASTE 3
rob *vb* **1** to take possessions unlawfully <*rob* a bank><he was mugged and *robbed*>
syn ‖knock off, knock over, loot, plunder, ransack, relieve, rifle, rip off, stick up; *compare* BURGLARIZE, HOUSEBREAK
rel ‖heist, hold up; jackroll, roll; strong-arm; filch, hijack, lift, pilfer, purloin, steal, thieve; cheat, defraud, hustle, swindle; despoil, pillage, ravage, sack
2 ***syn*** see DEPRIVE 2
robber *n* one who commits the crime of robbery <only one *robber* was involved in the holdup>
syn yegg; *compare* THIEF
rel hijacker; sandbagger; crook, swindler; cat burglar, cat man, housebreaker, raffles, second-story man; rifler; holdup man, stickup man; ‖bushranger, highwayman, ‖sticker-up
roborant *adj* ***syn*** see TONIC 1
robot *n* **1** a machine that looks like a human being and performs various complex acts (as walking or talking) of a human being <a *robot* that performed household chores>
syn android, automaton
rel golem
idiom bionic man
2 an efficient, insensitive, often brutalized person <working on an assembly line can often turn people into *robots*>
syn automaton, golem, machine
robust *adj* **1** ***syn*** see FLOURISHING
2 ***syn*** see STRONG 3
robustious *adj* ***syn*** see BOORISH
rock *vb* **1** ***syn*** see SHAKE 4
rel oscillate, sway, swing, undulate; quake, totter, tremble
2 ***syn*** see TOSS 2
3 ***syn*** see HURRY 2
rock *n* **1** ***syn*** see ERROR 2
2 ***syn*** see DOLLAR
3 rocks *pl* ***syn*** see MONEY
rock bottom *n* ***syn*** see ESSENCE 2
rock–bottom *adj* ***syn*** see BOTTOMMOST
rockbound *adj* **1** ***syn*** see ROCKY 1
2 ***syn*** see INFLEXIBLE 2
rocket *vb* **1** ***syn*** see SKYROCKET
rel arise, ascend, levitate, mount, surge, tower
2 ***syn*** see HURRY 2

---

syn synonym(s) ***rel*** related word(s)
ant antonym(s) ***con*** contrasted word(s)
idiom idiomatic equivalent(s)
‖ use limited; if in doubt, see a dictionary

rock pile *n* ***syn*** see JAIL
rock-ribbed *adj* **1** ***syn*** see ROCKY 1
2 ***syn*** see INFLEXIBLE 2
rocky *adj* **1** abounding in or consisting of rocks <a *rocky* shore>
syn rockbound, rock-ribbed
rel bebouldered, bouldery; stony
2 ***syn*** see INSENSIBLE 5
rocky *adj* **1** ***syn*** see UNSTABLE 2
2 ***syn*** see OBSCENE 2
‖**Rocky Mountain canary** *n* ***syn*** see DONKEY 1
rococo *adj* **1** ***syn*** see OLD-FASHIONED
2 ***syn*** see ORNATE
rod *n* **1** ***syn*** see BAR 1
2 ***syn*** see PUNISHMENT
idiom rod in pickle
rodomont *n* ***syn*** see BRAGGART
rodomontade *n* **1** ***syn*** see BOMBAST
rel boasting, bragging, vaunting; pride, vainglory, vanity
2 ***syn*** see BRAGGART
rodomontade *vb* ***syn*** see BOAST
rodomontade *adj* ***syn*** see BOASTFUL
rogue *n* **1** ***syn*** see VILLAIN 1
rel culprit, delinquent
2 ***syn*** see SWINDLER
3 ***syn*** see SCAMP
roguery *n* ***syn*** see MISCHIEVOUSNESS
roguish *adj* **1** ***syn*** see DISHONEST
2 ***syn*** see PLAYFUL 1
3 ***syn*** see COY 2
roguishness *n* ***syn*** see MISCHIEVOUSNESS
roil *vb* **1** to make turbid <*roiled* the brook with his splashings>
syn mud, muddle, muddy, rile
rel befoul, contaminate, dirty, pollute
con clear, purify, settle
2 ***syn*** see IRRITATE
roily *adj* ***syn*** see TURBID
roister *vb* ***syn*** see REVEL 1
role *n* **1** characteristic exterior properties and aspects, style, and atmosphere in which something intangible is discerned <the moral *role* of the legislature>
syn character, clothing
rel appearance, face, guise, seeming, semblance, show; aspect, look
2 ***syn*** see FUNCTION 1
roll *n* **1** ***syn*** see LIST
2 ***syn*** see ROSTER 1
‖**3** ***syn*** see FORTUNE 4
roll *vb* **1** ***syn*** see PONDER 2
2 ***syn*** see SWATHE
3 to wrap around on itself or something else <this cloth *rolls* unevenly>
syn furl
4 ***syn*** see WALLOW 3
5 ***syn*** see TURN 1
6 ***syn*** see WANDER 1
7 ***syn*** see POUR 2
8 ***syn*** see RUMBLE
9 ***syn*** see TOSS 2
roll call *n* ***syn*** see LIST
rollick *vb* **1** ***syn*** see GAMBOL
2 ***syn*** see WALLOW 3
rollick *n* ***syn*** see ESCAPADE
rollicking *adj* ***syn*** see ANTIC 2
rel cheerful, glad, happy, joyful, joyous, lighthearted
roll in *vb* ***syn*** see RETIRE 4
ant roll out
rolling stone *n* ***syn*** see ROVER
roll out *vb* to leave one's bed <*rolled out* at dawn>
syn arise, get up, pile (out), rise, rise and shine, turn out, uprise
ant roll in
roll up *vb* ***syn*** see ACCUMULATE
roly-poly *adj* ***syn*** see ROTUND 2
romance *n* ***syn*** see LOVE AFFAIR
romanesque *adj* ***syn*** see EXOTIC 2
romantic *adj* ***syn*** see EXOTIC 2
2 ***syn*** see SENTIMENTAL
rel fanciful, fantastic, imaginary, quixotic, visionary; created, invented
ant unromantic; matter-of-fact
Romeo *n* ***syn*** see GALLANT 2
romp *n* ***syn*** see RUNAWAY
romp *vb* ***syn*** see GAMBOL
idiom cut capers, horse around
rondure *n* ***syn*** see BALL
roof *n* ***syn*** see TOP 1
roof *vb* ***syn*** see HARBOR 1
rook *vb* ***syn*** see FLEECE 1
rookie *n* ***syn*** see NOVICE
room *n* **1** space in a building enclosed or set apart by a partition <the house had seven *rooms*>
syn apartment, chamber
2 rooms *pl* ***syn*** see APARTMENT 1
3 enough space or range for free movement <no *room* for hope>
syn elbowroom, latitude, leeway, margin, play, scope
rel clearance; license, range, rein, sway; rope
room *vb* ***syn*** see HARBOR 2
room and board *n* ***syn*** see ACCOMMODATIONS
roomy *adj* ***syn*** see SPACIOUS
ant cramped
‖**roose** *vb* ***syn*** see COMMEND 2
roost *vb* **1** ***syn*** see ALIGHT
2 ***syn*** see HARBOR 2
root *n* **1** ***syn*** see SOURCE
rel basis, foundation, ground
2 ***syn*** see BASIS 1
3 ***syn*** see CENTER 3
4 ***syn*** see ESSENCE 2
root *vb* ***syn*** see ENTRENCH 1
ant uproot
root *vb* ***syn*** see APPLAUD 2
rootage *n* ***syn*** see SOURCE
rootless *adj* ***syn*** see WEAK 2
root out *vb* ***syn*** see ANNIHILATE 2
rel demolish, destroy, raze
ant enroot
rootstock *n* ***syn*** see SOURCE
roperipe *n* ***syn*** see VILLAIN 1
ropes *n pl* ***syn*** see INS AND OUTS
ropy *adj* ***syn*** see MUSCULAR 1
rose *vb* ***syn*** see BLUSH

roseate *adj* ***syn*** see HOPEFUL 2
rose–colored *adj* ***syn*** see HOPEFUL 2
rose–colored spectacles *n pl* ***syn*** see OPTIMISM
roster *n* **1** a list of officers or enlisted men <an army *roster*>
syn muster, muster roll, roll
2 ***syn*** see LIST
rosy *adj* ***syn*** see HOPEFUL 2
rot *vb* **1** ***syn*** see DECAY
rel corrupt, debase, vitiate
2 ***syn*** see DETERIORATE 1
3 ***syn*** see DEBASE 1
rot *n* ***syn*** see NONSENSE 2
rotate *vb* **1** ***syn*** see TURN 1
2 to succeed or cause to succeed each other in turn <the drivers in the car pool *rotated* each week>
syn alternate
rel bandy, exchange, interchange; ensue, follow, succeed; relieve, spell
rotation *n* ***syn*** see REVOLUTION 1
rote *n* ***syn*** see ROUTINE
rotten *adj* **1** ***syn*** see BAD 5
rel foul; tainted, touched; sour
2 ***syn*** see VICIOUS 2
3 ***syn*** see BAD 8
4 ***syn*** see BAD 1
rotter *n* ***syn*** see CAD
rotund *adj* **1** ***syn*** see RESONANT
2 rounded or swollen with fat <a wheezing *rotund* man lumbered by>
syn chubby, plump, plumpish, plumpy, podgy, puddy, pudgy, roly-poly, round, roundabout, spuddy, tubby; *compare* FAT 2
rel beefy, chunky, dumpy, heavyset, squat, stocky, stubby, thick, thickset; paunchy, potbellied; buxom, ‖crummy
idiom on the plump side
con angular, gaunt, lank, lanky, lean, rawboned, scrawny, skinny, spare; slender, slight, slim, thin
roturier *n* ***syn*** see UPSTART
rouge *vb* ***syn*** see BLUSH
rough *adj* **1** not smooth or even <a *rough* undressed block of stone>
syn asperous, cragged, craggy, hairy, harsh, ironbound, jagged, rugged, scabrous, scraggy, uneven, unlevel, unsmooth
rel bumpy, choppy; burred; firm, hard, solid; coarse, gross
con flat, flush, level, plain, plane
ant smooth
2 ***syn*** see WILD 6
con calm, halcyon, peaceful, placid, serene, tranquil
3 ***syn*** see TOUGH 8
4 ***syn*** see TIGHT 4
5 ***syn*** see INDECOROUS
6 ***syn*** see RUDE 1
idiom in the rough
7 ***syn*** see RUDE 3
8 ***syn*** see HARSH 3
9 ***syn*** see COARSE 3
rel discourteous, impolite, uncivil, ungracious
10 ***syn*** see BLUFF
11 ***syn*** see HARD 6
rough *n* ***syn*** see TOUGH
rough (out) *vb* ***syn*** see SKETCH
rough (up) *vb* ***syn*** see MANHANDLE
rough–and–ready *adj* ***syn*** see MAKESHIFT
rough–and–tumble *n* ***syn*** see BRAWL 2
rough–and–tumble *adj* ***syn*** see MAKESHIFT
roughhewn *adj* ***syn*** see RUDE 1
roughhouse *n* ***syn*** see HORSEPLAY
roughhouse *vb* ***syn*** see MANHANDLE
roughhousing *n* ***syn*** see HORSEPLAY
roughly *adv* **1** ***syn*** see HARD 5
ant smoothly
2 ***syn*** see NEARLY
roughneck *n* ***syn*** see TOUGH
roughness *n* ***syn*** see INEQUALITY 1
ant smoothness
roughscuff *n* ***syn*** see RABBLE 2
round *adj* **1** having every part of the circumference equally distant from a center within <flowers crowded in stiff *round* beds>
syn circular
rel annular, globular, orbed, orbicular, rounded, spherical, spiral
2 ***syn*** see CURVED
3 ***syn*** see ROTUND 2
4 ***syn*** see OUTSPOKEN
5 ***syn*** see RESONANT
round *adv* **1** ***syn*** see ABOUT 1
2 ***syn*** see NEARLY
3 ***syn*** see THROUGH 1
4 ***syn*** see ABOUT 6
round *prep* **1** ***syn*** see NEAR 2
2 ***syn*** see ABOUT 4
round *n* **1** ***syn*** see BALL
2 ***syn*** see REVOLUTION 1
3 ***syn*** see TOUR 2
4 ***syn*** see CYCLE 1
5 ***syn*** see CURVE
round *vb* **1** ***syn*** see BALL
2 ***syn*** see SURROUND 1
3 ***syn*** see POLISH 2
4 ***syn*** see CURVE
round about *adv* **1** ***syn*** see ABOUT 1
2 ***syn*** see ABOUT 6
3 ***syn*** see ABOUT 2
roundabout *n* **1** ***syn*** see DETOUR
2 ***syn*** see VERBIAGE 1
3 ***syn*** see TOUR 2
4 ***syn*** see EXCURSION 1
roundabout *adj* **1** ***syn*** see INDIRECT 1
2 ***syn*** see ROTUND 2
rounded *adj* **1** ***syn*** see CURVED
2 ***syn*** see CURVACEOUS
rounder *n* ***syn*** see WASTREL 1
roundly *adv* **1** ***syn*** see WELL 3
2 ***syn*** see NEARLY
round off *vb* ***syn*** see CLIMAX

---

syn synonym(s) ***rel*** related word(s)
ant antonym(s) ***con*** contrasted word(s)
idiom idiomatic equivalent(s)
‖ use limited; if in doubt, see a dictionary

round trip *n syn* see TOUR 2
round up *vb syn* see GROUP 1
rouse *vb* **1** *syn* see WAKE 1
rel animate, enliven, quicken, vivify; excite, provoke, stimulate; foment, incite, instigate
con calm, compose, lull, quiet, quieten, settle, soothe, still, tranquilize
2 *syn* see INTENSIFY
3 *syn* see PROVOKE 4
4 *syn* see STIR 1
rouser *n syn* see ‖DILLY
rousing *adj* **1** *syn* see EXCITING
2 *syn* see LIVELY 1
‖**roust** *vb syn* see PROVOKE 4
roustabout *n syn* see WORKER
rout *n* **1** *syn* see MOB 2
2 *syn* see RABBLE 2
3 *syn* see MULTITUDE 1
rout *vb syn* see ROAR
rout *vb syn* see RUMMAGE 3
rout *n* **1** *syn* see DEFEAT 1
2 *syn* see RUNAWAY
rout *vb* **1** to put to precipitate flight <the army regrouped and *routed* the enemy>
syn derout, stampede
rel chase, dispel, drive, expel
idiom put to flight
2 *syn* see WHIP 2
route *n syn* see WAY 2
route *vb* **1** *syn* see SEND 1
2 *syn* see GUIDE
routine *n* habitual or mechanical and sometimes monotonous performance of an established procedure <settled into the *routine* of factory work>
syn grind, groove, pace, rote, rut, treadmill
rel squirrel cage; ‖drill
idiom the beaten path, the drab monotony of habit
routine *adj* **1** *syn* see ORDINARY 1
2 *syn* see USUAL 1
rove *vb syn* see WANDER 1
rover *n syn* see PIRATE
rover *n* one who roams habitually <he spent most of his life as a *rover* always on the move>
syn drifter, meanderer, rambler, roamer, rolling stone, wanderer
rel gad, gadabout, gadder, runabout; itinerant, peripatetic; floater
idiom bird of passage
con homebody
ant stay-at-home
roving *adj syn* see ITINERANT
row *vb* to propel a boat by means of oars <*rowed* across the lake>
syn oar, paddle, pull
rel scull; punt; sail, scud
row *n* **1** *syn* see LINE 5
2 *syn* see SUCCESSION 2
row *n* **1** *syn* see BRAWL 2
2 *syn* see QUARREL
3 *syn* see MOUTH 1
row *vb* ‖**1** *syn* see SCOLD 1
2 *syn* see QUARREL

rowdiness *n syn* see HORSEPLAY
rowdy *adj syn* see TURBULENT 1
rowdy *n syn* see TOUGH
rowdydow *n* **1** *syn* see COMMOTION 4
2 *syn* see BRAWL 2
3 *syn* see BINGE 1
rowdydowdy *adj syn* see TURBULENT 1
rowdyish *adj syn* see TURBULENT 1
royal *adj* **1** *syn* see KINGLY
rel glorious, resplendent, splendid, superb; august, imposing, stately
2 *syn* see EASY 1
3 *syn* see GRAND 1
4 *syn* see EXCELLENT
royalist *n syn* see REACTIONARY
‖**rozzer** *n syn* see POLICEMAN
rub *vb* **1** *syn* see ABRADE 1
2 *syn* see CHAFE 3
rel aggravate, exasperate, nettle, peeve, provoke, rile; annoy, bother, irk, vex
3 *syn* see POLISH 1
rub *n syn* see OBSTACLE
rubber *n syn* see BUSYBODY
rubberneck *n* **1** *syn* see BUSYBODY
2 *syn* see TOURIST
rubberneck *vb syn* see LOOK 7
rubber stamp *n syn* see COMMONPLACE
rubbish *n* **1** *syn* see REFUSE
2 *syn* see NONSENSE 2
3 *syn* see PAP 2
rubbishing *adj syn* see CHEAP 2
rubbishly *adj syn* see CHEAP 2
rubbishy *adj syn* see CHEAP 2
rube *n syn* see RUSTIC
rubicund *adj syn* see RUDDY
rubify *vb syn* see REDDEN 1
rub out *vb* **1** *syn* see DESTROY 1
2 *syn* see MURDER 1
rubric *n syn* see NAME 1
rubric *adj syn* see NOTEWORTHY
rubric *vb syn* see REDDEN 1
ruby *vb syn* see REDDEN 1
ruck *n* ‖**1** *syn* see PILE 1
2 *syn* see GATHERING 2
ruck *n syn* see WRINKLE
ruck (up) *vb syn* see CRUMPLE 1
‖**ruckle** *vb syn* see CRUMPLE 1
rucksack *n syn* see BACKPACK
ruckus *n* **1** *syn* see COMMOTION 3
rel brawl, broil, melee, scrap
2 *syn* see QUARREL
ruction *n* **1** *syn* see BRAWL 2
2 *syn* see COMMOTION 4
‖**ructious** *adj syn* see BELLIGERENT
rud *vb syn* see REDDEN 1
ruddle *vb syn* see REDDEN 1
ruddy *adj* having a healthy reddish color <has a *ruddy* complexion after being out in the cold>
syn florid, flush, flushed, full-blooded, glowing, rubicund, sanguine
rel bronzed; blooming; blowsy
con ashen, ashy, livid, pale, pallid, wan, waxy; anemic, bloodless
ruddy *vb syn* see REDDEN 1

rude *adj* **1** lacking in craftsmanship or artistic finish <a *rude* sketch>
syn angular, crude, lumpy, raw, rough, rough-hewn, undressed, unfashioned, unfinished, unformed, unhewn, unpolished, unworked, unwrought
rel unlicked; unprocessed; primitive, rudimental, rudimentary
con dressed, fashioned, finished, formed, hewn, polished, worked, wrought
2 *syn* see DISSONANT 1
3 hastily executed and admittedly imperfect or imprecise <*rude* estimates for the cost of building the house>
syn approximate, proximate, rough
rel crude, imperfect, imprecise, inexact
idiom ||in the ball park
con accurate, correct; faultless, perfect; exact, precise; meticulous, scrupulous
4 *syn* see COARSE 3
5 *syn* see IGNORANT 1
6 lacking in social refinement <gave a *rude* reply to a polite question>
syn discourteous, disgracious, disrespectful, ill, ill-bred, ill-mannered, impertinent, impolite, incivil, incondite, inurbane, mannerless, ||mismannered, uncalled-for, uncivil, uncourteous, uncouth, ungracious, unhandsome, unmannered, unmannerly, unpolished
rel brusque, crusty, curt, gruff; harsh; intrusive, meddlesome; crabbed, surly; boorish, churlish, clownish, loutish
con courteous, genteel, mannerly, polite, well-mannered; bland, diplomatic, politic, smooth, suave; affable, considerate, gracious
ant civil; urbane
7 *syn* see BARBARIAN 1
8 *syn* see INEXPERIENCED

rudely *adv syn* see NEARLY

rudiment *n* **1** *syn* see ESSENTIAL 1
2 rudiments *pl syn* see ALPHABET 2

rudimental *adj syn* see ELEMENTARY 1

rudimentary *adj syn* see ELEMENTARY 1

rue *vb syn* see REGRET

rue *n* **1** *syn* see SORROW
2 *syn* see PENITENCE
3 *syn* see PITY

rueful *adj* **1** *syn* see PITIFUL 1
2 *syn* see WOEFUL 1
3 *syn* see MELANCHOLY 2
rel depressed, oppressed, weighed down; piteous, pitiful; despairing, despondent, hopeless

ruffian *n* **1** *syn* see TOUGH
2 *syn* see THUG 1

ruffle *vb* **1** *syn* see BLOW 1
2 *syn* see ABRADE 1
3 *syn* see ANNOY 1
||**4** *syn* see INTIMIDATE

rugged *adj* **1** *syn* see ROUGH 1
2 *syn* see SEVERE 3
rel arduous, difficult
3 *syn* see HARSH 3
4 *syn* see BOORISH
5 *syn* see TOUGH 4
rel brawny, burly, husky, muscular
ant fragile
6 *syn* see HARD 6

ruin *n* **1** *syn* see DETERIORATION 1
2 *syn* see DOWNFALL 2
3 the bringing about of or the results of disaster <met *ruin* at the hands of the enemy>
syn confusion, destruction, devastation, havoc, loss, ruination
rel crumbling, disintegration; break up, dissolution; disrepair; wreck
con rebuilding, reconstruction, re-creation
4 *syn* see INJURY 1

ruin *vb* **1** *syn* see DESTROY 1
rel deface, disfigure; maim, mangle, mutilate; depredate, desecrate, desolate, despoil, devastate, devour, pillage, sack, spoliate, waste
ant restore
2 to subject to forces that are destructive of soundness, worth, or usefulness <in danger of being *ruined* by prosperity>
syn bankrupt, dilapidate, do in, shipwreck, wreck
rel corrupt, debase, degenerate, vitiate
idiom play hob (*or* the devil) with
con rebuild, renew, restore; reclaim, redeem, retrieve, salvage
3 to overthrow the fortunes of <was *ruined* during the Great Depression>
syn bankrupt, break, bust, fold up, impoverish, pauper, pauperize
rel beggar, clean out, deplete, drain, draw, draw down, exhaust, use up; wipe (out); reduce
idiom go under, lose one's shirt (*or* pants), take to the cleaners
4 *syn* see FRUSTRATE 1

||**ruinate** *vb syn* see DESTROY 1

ruination *n* **1** *syn* see RUIN 3
2 *syn* see DOWNFALL 2

ruinator *n syn* see VANDAL

ruiner *n syn* see VANDAL

ruinous *adj* **1** *syn* see DESTRUCTIVE
2 *syn* see FATAL 2

rule *n* **1** *syn* see LAW 1
rel order; axiom, fundamental, principle; decorum, etiquette, propriety
2 *syn* see MAXIM
rel fundamental, principle

rule *vb* **1** *syn* see GOVERN 1
rel guide, lead
2 to hold preeminence in (as by ability, strength, or position) <an actor who rightfully *rules* the Shakespearian stage>
syn dominate, domineer, predominate, preponderate, prevail, reign
rel guide, lead; preside
idiom be number one, take first place (in *or* on)
3 *syn* see DECIDE
rel deduce, gather, infer, judge

---

syn synonym(s) *rel* related word(s)
ant antonym(s) *con* contrasted word(s)
idiom idiomatic equivalent(s)
|| use limited; if in doubt, see a dictionary

rule out *vb* **1** ***syn*** see EXCLUDE
2 ***syn*** see PREVENT 2
ruling *n* ***syn*** see EDICT 1
ruling *adj* **1** ***syn*** see CENTRAL 1
con peripheral
2 ***syn*** see PREVAILING
‖**rum** *adj* ***syn*** see STRANGE 4
rumble *vb* to make a low heavy rolling sound <thunder *rumbling* in the distance>
syn growl, grumble, roll
rel boom, roar, thunder; peal, resound; blast, burst, clap, crack, crash
rumble *n* ***syn*** see REPORT 1
rumble–bumble *n* ***syn*** see MISCELLANY 1
rumbustious *adj* ***syn*** see TURBULENT 1
rum–dum *adj* ***syn*** see INTOXICATED 1
rumdum *n* ***syn*** see DRUNKARD
‖**rum–hole** *n* ***syn*** see BAR 5
ruminate *vb* **1** ***syn*** see PONDER 2
rel consider, excogitate, weigh
2 ***syn*** see CHEW 1
ruminative *adj* ***syn*** see THOUGHTFUL 1
rummage *n* ***syn*** see CLUTTER 2
rel conglomeration, hash, hotchpotch, miscellany, patchwork, potpourri
rummage *vb* **1** ***syn*** see DISORDER 1
2 ***syn*** see SCOUR 2
3 to produce by searching <*rummaged* an old dress out of the attic>
syn dig out, hunt (down *or* out *or* up), rout
rel ferret (out), find; fish, search (out), spy (out); poke
rummery *n* ***syn*** see BAR 5
‖**rum–mill** *n* ***syn*** see BAR 5
rummy *adj* ***syn*** see STRANGE 4
rummy *n* ***syn*** see DRUNKARD
rumor *n* **1** ***syn*** see REPORT 1
2 ***syn*** see MURMUR 1
rumor *vb* ***syn*** see GOSSIP
rumorer *n* ***syn*** see GOSSIP 1
rumormonger *n* ***syn*** see GOSSIP 1
rump *n* ***syn*** see BUTTOCKS
rumple *vb* ***syn*** see CRUMPLE 1
‖**rumpot** *n* ***syn*** see DRUNKARD
rumpus *n* **1** ***syn*** see COMMOTION 3
2 ***syn*** see ARGUMENT 2
rumshop *n* ***syn*** see BAR 5
run *vb* **1** to move at a fast springing gait in which both feet are momentarily off the ground in the course of each pace <the boy *ran* down the walk>
syn dash, scamper, scoot, scurry, shin, sprint; *compare* SCUTTLE
rel career, course, race; bustle, hurry, hustle, rush, speed; scorch
con crawl, creep, drag, inch, mosey, poke, saunter, stroll, toddle
2 to hasten away from something that frightens or perturbs <afraid to fight but ashamed to *run*>
syn bolt, flee, fly, make off, scamper, scoot, ‖screw, skedaddle, skip, skirr
idiom ‖dog it, make a break, run for it, show a clean pair of heels, take flight, take French leave, take to one's heels
3 ***syn*** see HURRY 2
idiom go all out, go like (greased) lightning
4 ***syn*** see RESORT 2
5 ***syn*** see FUNCTION 3
6 ***syn*** see BECOME 1
7 ***syn*** see LIQUEFY
8 to lie in or take a certain course <the path *runs* along the crest of the hill>
syn extend, go, make, reach, stretch
9 ***syn*** see RANGE 3
10 ***syn*** see HUNT 1
11 ***syn*** see DRIVE 3
12 ***syn*** see THRUST 2
13 ***syn*** see SMUGGLE
14 ***syn*** see OPERATE 3
15 ***syn*** see CONDUCT 3
run (through *or* over) *vb* ***syn*** see BROWSE
run (to *or* into) *vb* ***syn*** see AMOUNT 1
run *n* **1** ‖***syn*** see CREEK 2
2 an uninterrupted course of occurrence or repetition especially of like things or events <the play had a long *run*>
syn continuance, continuation, duration, persistence
rel continuity, endurance, prolongation
3 ***syn*** see TENDENCY 1
rel course, set; bearing, direction, line, swing
4 ***syn*** see TRIP 1
‖**5 runs** *pl but sing or pl in constr* ***syn*** see DIARRHEA
runagate *n* **1** ***syn*** see RENEGADE
2 ***syn*** see VAGABOND
run along *vb* ***syn*** see GO 2
runaround *n* **1** ***syn*** see DETOUR
2 ***syn*** see ESCAPE 2
run away *vb* ***syn*** see ELOPE
runaway *n* a one-sided or overwhelming victory <the game was a *runaway,* the home team winning by 30 points>
syn cakewalk, romp, rout, walkaway, walkover
rel breather, cinch, duck soup, pushover; setup; shutout; conquest, triumph, victory, win
con photo finish, toss-up
run down *vb* ***syn*** see DECRY 2
run–down *adj* **1** ***syn*** see SHABBY 1
2 ***syn*** see NEGLECTED
rel abandoned, derelict, deserted, desolate, forsaken, lorn
rune *n* **1** ***syn*** see SPELL
2 ***syn*** see POEM
rung *n* ***syn*** see DEGREE 1
run in *vb* **1** ***syn*** see ARREST 2
2 ***syn*** see VISIT 2
run–in *n* **1** ***syn*** see ENCOUNTER
2 ***syn*** see QUARREL
runnel *n* ***syn*** see CREEK 2
running *n* ***syn*** see OVERSIGHT 1
running *adj* **1** ***syn*** see ACTIVE 1
2 ***syn*** see EASY 9
running *adv* ***syn*** see TOGETHER 2
running mate *n* ***syn*** see ASSOCIATE 3
run–of–mine *adj* **1** ***syn*** see UNREFINED 3
2 ***syn*** see MEDIUM
run–of–the–mill *adj* **1** ***syn*** see MEDIUM
rel uncommon, unexceptional

2 ***syn*** see GENERAL 1
run on *vb* ***syn*** see CHAT 1
run out *vb* **1** ***syn*** see FAIL 2
2 ***syn*** see BANISH
run over *vb* ***syn*** see OVERFLOW 2
runt *n* ***syn*** see DWARF
runted *adj* ***syn*** see STUNTED
run through *vb* ***syn*** see GO 4
runtish *adj* ***syn*** see STUNTED
runty *adj* ***syn*** see STUNTED
run up *vb* **1** ***syn*** see INCREASE 2
2 ***syn*** see THROW UP 1
rupture *n* **1** ***syn*** see BREACH 3
rel division, divorce, parting
2 ***syn*** see SEPARATION 1
rupture *vb* **1** ***syn*** see OPEN 3
rel divide, divorce, part, separate, sunder; cleave, rend, rive, split
2 ***syn*** see SEPARATE 1
rural *adj* relating to or characteristic of the country <a peaceful *rural* scene>
syn agrestic, bucolic, campestral, countrified, country, out-country, outland, pastoral, provincial, rustic
rel arcadian, idyllic; natural, simple, unsophisticated
con metropolitan, municipal, oppidan; crammed, crowded, packed, populous; bustling, busy, hustling; artificial, mundane, sophisticated, worldly
ant urban; citified
ruse *n* ***syn*** see TRICK 1
rush *vb* **1** to move or cause to move quickly, impetuously, and often heedlessly <*rushed* around madly trying to get things done>
syn boil, bolt, charge, chase, dash, fling, lash, race, shoot, ||swither, tear; *compare* COURSE, HURRY 2, PLUNGE 2, STAMPEDE 2
rel hasten, hurry, speed; dart, fly, scud; break
idiom go off half-cocked, not look before one leaps
2 ***syn*** see HURRY 2
3 ***syn*** see COURSE
rush *n* **1** ***syn*** see HASTE 2
2 ***syn*** see FLOW
rushing *adj* ***syn*** see PRECIPITATE 1
rushlight *n* ***syn*** see NONENTITY
rustic *adj* ***syn*** see RURAL
rustic *n* an inhabitant of a rural or remote area who is usually characterized by an utter lack of sophistication and cultivation <an unbelieving *rustic* gawking at the skyscrapers>
syn ||apple knocker, ||backwoodser, backwoodsman, bucolic, bumpkin, chawbacon, clodhopper, clown, country jake, countryman, greenhorn, hayseed, hick, hillbilly, hillman, ||hodge, hoosier, jake, jay, joskin, mossback, mountaineer, peasant, provincial, redneck, ||ridge runner, rube, ||wayback, woodsy, yap, ||yob, yokel
rel rural; exurbanite, suburbanite; agriculturalist, farmer, granger, husbandman
con burgher, oppidan, townsman; cityite, urbanite; cosmopolitan, cosmopolite
ant city slicker
rustle *n* ***syn*** see HASTE 1
rustler *n* ***syn*** see HUSTLER 1
rusty *adj* ***syn*** see HARSH 3
||**rusty** *adj* ***syn*** see ILL-TEMPERED
rut *n* ***syn*** see ROUTINE
ruth *n* **1** ***syn*** see PITY
2 ***syn*** see PENITENCE
ruthful *adj* ***syn*** see WOEFUL 1
ruthless *adj* ***syn*** see GRIM 3
ruttish *adj* ***syn*** see LUSTFUL 2
||**ruttle** *vb* ***syn*** see RATTLE 1
rutty *adj* ***syn*** see LUSTFUL 2
RV *n* ***syn*** see TRAILER

syn synonym(s) ***rel*** related word(s)
ant antonym(s) ***con*** contrasted word(s)
idiom idiomatic equivalent(s)
|| use limited; if in doubt, see a dictionary

S

sable *adj* ***syn*** see BLACK 1
rel dark, dusky, murky; gloomy, somber

sabotage *n* willful effort by indirect means to hinder, prevent, undo, or discredit (as a plan or activity) <*sabotage* of the project by disgruntled officials>
syn subversion, undermining, wreckage, wrecking
rel subversiveness, subversivism; damage, impairment, injury

sabotage *vb* to practice sabotage on <*sabotaged* his opponent's campaign with rumors and smears>
syn subvert, undermine, wreck
rel frustrate, hamper, hinder; block, obstruct; damage; break up, destroy
idiom throw a monkey wrench into
con assist, back, support

saccharine *adj* ***syn*** see INGRATIATING
rel candied, cloying, honeyed, oversweet, sugar-candy, sugar-coated, sugared, sugary, sweet, syrupy

sacerdotal *adj* of, relating to, or belonging to priests or priesthood <*sacerdotal* vestments>
syn hieratic, priestal, priestish, priestlike, priestly, sacerdotical
rel churchly, ecclesiastical, religious; clerical, ministerial; apostolic, papal

sacerdotical *adj* ***syn*** see SACERDOTAL

sack *n* ***syn*** see BAG 1
rel container; pocket

sack *vb* ***syn*** see DISMISS 3
rel expel, ship; ||bump, ||chuck
idiom give one the sack, send packing

sack *vb* ***syn*** see RAVAGE
rel forage, raid; strip

sacker *n* ***syn*** see MARAUDER

sacred *adj* **1** ***syn*** see HOLY 1
rel sacramental; angelic, godly, saintly; cherished
con lay, secular, temporal; earthly; unhallowed
ant profane
2 dedicated to or hallowed by association with a deity <*sacred* songs>
syn numinous, spiritual; *compare* HOLY 1
rel hallowed, sanctified
3 protected (as by law, custom, or human respect) against abuse <a fund *sacred* to charity>
syn inviolable, inviolate, sacrosanct
rel defended, guarded, protected, shielded; immune, untouchable

Sacred Writ *n* ***syn*** see BIBLE
idiom Good Book

sacrifice *n* ***syn*** see VICTIM 1
rel burnt offering, oblation; sacrification; hecatomb; sin offering

sacrifice *vb* **1** to offer as a victim in sacrifice <Abraham about to *sacrifice* Isaac>
syn immolate, victimize
rel offer (up); consecrate, dedicate, devote; donate, give, yield
2 ***syn*** see LOSE 1
idiom kiss good-bye
3 ***syn*** see FORGO
rel cede, yield
idiom part with

sacrilege *n* ***syn*** see PROFANATION
rel irreverence; heresy; crime, impiety, offense, sin

sacrilegious *adj* involving or marked by debasement or defilement of what is sacred <*sacrilegious* despoilers of ancient churches>
syn blasphemous, profane
rel impious, irreverent, ungodly; evil, sinful, wicked; irreligious
con godly, pious, reverent; religious

sacrosanct *adj* ***syn*** see SACRED 3
rel esteemed, regarded, respected

sad *adj* **1** affected with or expressing sadness <was *sad* to see him go>
syn heavyhearted, melancholy, mournful, saddened, sorry, unhappy; *compare* DOWNCAST, MELANCHOLY 2
rel blue, dejected, dispirited, down, downbeat, downcast, drear, dumpish, dumpy; grieving, unenjoying; depressed, morose; depressing, dismal, joyless, mirthless, saddening, triste; desolate
con happy, joyful, joyous; blithe, gay, lighthearted; exalted, fired, inspired, uplifted
ant glad
2 causing sadness <felt miserable after listening to that *sad* song>
syn depressing, joyless, melancholic, melancholy, mournful, saddening, triste; *compare* MELANCHOLY 2
rel dismal, gloomy; afflicting, doleful, dreary, lamentable, sorrowful; pathetic, tear-jerking
con bright, gay, lively; exhilarating, heartwarming, stimulating, stirring
ant happy

sadden *vb* ***syn*** see DEPRESS 2
idiom make blue, ||put into a funk
ant gladden

saddened *adj* ***syn*** see SAD 1

saddening *adj* ***syn*** see SAD 2

saddle *vb* ***syn*** see BURDEN
rel hamper, impede, restrict; impose, inflict
idiom hang like a millstone around one's neck

sadness *n* the quality, state, or an instance of being sad <her feelings of *sadness* and longing persisted long after he left>
syn blues, dejection, depression, dinge, (the) dismals, (the) dolefuls, dumps, dysphoria, gloom, heavyheartedness, melancholy, mopes, mournfulness, suds, unhappiness

rel dispiritedness, doldrums, downcastness, downheartedness, downs, ||funk, listlessness, moodiness; anguish, grief, sorrow, sorrowfulness, woe; desolation, disconsolateness, disconsolation, forlornness, misery, mourning; blue devils, despondency, hopelessness, megrims, melancholia
idiom slough of despond
con happiness, joy, joyfulness, joyousness; cheerfulness, cheeriness, gayness, lightheartedness, liveliness; exhilaration, ups
ant gladness

safe *adj* **1** having been freed from risk, danger, harm, or injury <refugees who found themselves *safe* at last in a neutral country>
syn scatheless, unharmed, unscathed
rel unhurt, uninjured; intact
idiom in (*or* with) a whole skin, out of harm's way, safe and sound
con damaged, harmed, hurt, injured
ant unsafe
2 affording security from threat of harm, injury, risk, or loss <found a *safe* place to hide>
syn riskless, secure
rel guarding, protecting, safeguarding, sheltering, shielding; defended, guarded, protected, sheltered, shielded; unthreatened; impregnable, inviolable, invulnerable, unassailable
idiom safe as a bank vault
con insecure, undefended, unguarded, unprotected, vulnerable; threatened; hazardous, risky
ant dangerous, unsafe
3 not threatening danger <it's *safe* to go there only in the daytime>
syn healthy, uninjurious, wholesome; *compare* HARMLESS
rel innocent, innocuous, inoffensive
con hazardous, perilous, precarious, risky; harmful, injurious, unhealthy
ant dangerous, unsafe
4 *syn* see CAUTIOUS

safeguard *n syn* see DEFENSE 1
rel palladium; buffer, screen

safeguard *vb syn* see DEFEND 1
rel conserve, preserve, save; assure, ensure, insure

safekeeping *n* **1** *syn* see CUSTODY
2 *syn* see PRESERVATION 1

safeness *n syn* see SAFETY

safety *n* the quality, state, or condition of being safe <there's *safety* in numbers>
syn assurance, safeness, security
rel cover, protection, shelter; defense; impregnability, inviolability, invulnerability
con hazard, jeopardy, peril, risk, threat; instability, vulnerability
ant danger

sag *vb* **1** *syn* see SLIP 6
2 *syn* see DROOP 3
rel bend, decline; dangle, flap, flop
idiom ||have a case of the sags
ant tauten

sag *n* **1** *syn* see DEPRESSION 2
rel settling, sinking
2 *syn* see DECLINE 3

sagacious *adj* **1** *syn* see WISE 1
rel clever, intelligent, smart; far-seeing; judicious, prudent, sapient
idiom wise as an owl
con dumb, stupid, unintelligent; ignorant, unlearned, untaught; unperceptive; unwise
2 *syn* see SHREWD
rel critical, discerning, discriminating
idiom wise in the ways of the world

sagaciousness *n syn* see SAGACITY
rel judgment, wiseness

sagacity *n* intelligent application of knowledge <*sagacity* acquired from years of learning and experience>
syn insight, sagaciousness, sageness, sapience, wisdom
rel discernment, penetration, perception, perceptiveness, sensitivity; understanding; judiciousness, prudence; comprehension, grasp

sage *adj* **1** *syn* see WISE 1
rel philosophic; learned; profound
2 *syn* see WISE 2
rel acute, penetrating, probing

sage *n* one distinguished for his breadth of knowledge, experience, wisdom, and sound judgment <was one of the renowned *sages* of constitutional law>
syn savant, scholar, wise man
rel expert, master

sageness *n syn* see SAGACITY

said *adj syn* see SUCH 1

sail *vb* **1** *syn* see FLY 1
2 *syn* see FLY 4

sailor *n syn* see MARINER

sailorman *n syn* see MARINER

saintliness *n syn* see HOLINESS
rel righteousness, worthiness

saintly *adj* being of deeply religious and wholly upright character <a *saintly* old couple>
syn angelic, godly, holy
rel righteous, upright, upstanding, virtuous, worthy; devout, God-fearing, pious; sainted; seraph, seraphic, seraphlike
idiom pure in mind and heart

salable *adj syn* see MARKETABLE
ant unsalable

salacious *adj syn* see LICENTIOUS 2

salad *n syn* see MISCELLANY 1

salad days *n pl syn* see YOUTH 1

salary *n syn* see WAGE

salient *adj syn* see NOTICEABLE
rel important, pertinent, significant, weighty; impressive, moving; obvious, pronounced; intrusive, obtrusive

saliferous *adj syn* see SALTY 1

saline *adj syn* see SALTY 1

---

syn synonym(s) *rel* related word(s)
ant antonym(s) *con* contrasted word(s)
idiom idiomatic equivalent(s)
|| use limited; if in doubt, see a dictionary

saliva *n* a liquid secreted into the mouth and helpful to digestion <*saliva* drooled down the baby's chin>
syn slaver, spit, spittle, water
rel sputum
salivate *vb* ***syn*** see DROOL 2
sally *n* **1** ***syn*** see OUTBURST 1
2 ***syn*** see JOKE 1
3 ***syn*** see EXCURSION 1
salmagundi *n* ***syn*** see MISCELLANY 1
salon *n* **1** a spacious elegant apartment or living room (as in a fashionable house) <her *salon* was decorated à la Louis XV>
syn drawing room, saloon
rel parlor; suite
2 a fashionable assemblage of notables held by custom at the home of a prominent person <was famous for her literary *salons*>
syn saloon
rel at home; reception; levee; evening, soiree
saloon *n* **1** ***syn*** see SALON 1
rel gallery; hall
2 ***syn*** see SALON 2
rel gathering, party
3 ***syn*** see BAR 5
saloonist *n* ***syn*** see SALOONKEEPER
saloonkeeper *n* one who owns or manages a bar <the traditional image of the fat cigar-smoking *saloonkeeper*>
syn barkeeper, boniface, innholder, innkeeper, ‖publican, saloonist, taverner; *compare* BARTENDER
rel victualler
salt *n* **1** ***syn*** see LIVING
2 ***syn*** see MARINER
salt *adj* ***syn*** see SALTY 1
saltate *vb* ***syn*** see JUMP 1
salt away *vb* ***syn*** see SAVE 4
saltimbanque *n* ***syn*** see CHARLATAN
rel impostor, pretender; cheat, fraud
salty *adj* **1** of, relating to, or containing salt <*salty* deposits>
syn saliferous, saline, salt
rel brackish, briny, saltish; salted
ant saltless
2 ***syn*** see RISQUÉ
3 ***syn*** see CAUSTIC 1
salubrious *adj* ***syn*** see HEALTHFUL
rel bracing, invigorating, stimulating
ant insalubrious
salutary *adj* ***syn*** see HEALTHFUL
rel restorative, sanative, sanatory, tonic
con debilitating, enfeebling, weakening; bad, evil
ant deleterious; unsalutary
salutation *n* **1** ***syn*** see GREETING
2 ***syn*** see ENCOMIUM
salute *vb* ***syn*** see ADDRESS 7
salute *n* ***syn*** see GREETING
salutiferous *adj* ***syn*** see HEALTHFUL
salvage *vb* to rescue and save from wreckage, destruction, or loss <*salvaged* the torpedoed vessel>
syn salve
rel deliver, redeem, rescue, save; reclaim, recover, regain, retrieve; ransom
con dump, jettison
salvation *n* **1** ***syn*** see PRESERVATION 1
2 ***syn*** see CONSERVATION 1
salve *n* ***syn*** see OINTMENT
rel emollient, lubricant; counterirritant; aid, remedy
salve *vb* ***syn*** see SALVAGE
salvo *n* **1** ***syn*** see BARRAGE
rel discharge; spray
2 ***syn*** see TESTIMONIAL 2
same *adj* **1** being one rather than another or more <went to the *same* hotel each summer>
syn exact, identical, selfsame, very
rel comparable, like, similar
ant different
2 agreeing fundamentally or absolutely <all the family have the *same* dark eyes>
syn duplicate, equal, equivalent, identic, identical, indistinguishable, tantamount; *compare* LIKE
rel comparable, like, similar; coequal
ant different
3 not changing or fluctuating <treated everyone with the *same* courtesy>
syn consistent, constant, invariable, unchanging, unfailing, unvarying
con changeable, fluctuant, inconsistent, inconstant, irregular, variable, varying
sameness *n* **1** ***syn*** see IDENTITY 1
rel alikeness; uniformity, uniformness, unity
2 ***syn*** see EQUIVALENCE
rel analogy; resemblance, similarity
sample *n* ***syn*** see INSTANCE
rel indication, sign; fragment, part, piece, portion, segment; constituent, element; individual, unit
sampling *n* ***syn*** see INSTANCE
sanative *adj* ***syn*** see CURATIVE
rel healthful, hygienic, salutary, sanitary
sanatory *adj* ***syn*** see CURATIVE
sanctified *adj* ***syn*** see HOLY 1
rel canonized, deified, sainted
ant unsanctified
sanctify *vb* ***syn*** see BLESS 1
sanctimonious *adj* ***syn*** see HYPOCRITICAL
rel deceiving, false; snuffling
ant unsanctimonious
sanctimoniousness *n* ***syn*** see HYPOCRISY
idiom odor of sanctity
ant unsanctimoniousness
sanctimony *n* ***syn*** see HYPOCRISY
sanction *n* **1** explicit authoritative permission or recognition that gives validity to acts of a subordinate <a colonial governor acting under the *sanction* of the king>
syn endorsement, fiat
rel approval, authorization, consent, permission; approbation, confirmation, encouragement, ratification, recommendation, support
con restraint; debarment; interdict, prohibition; disapprobation, disapproval, objection
ant interdiction
2 ***syn*** see PERMISSION

sanction *vb* ***syn*** see APPROVE 2
rel authorize, commission, license
con ban, disallow, forbid, prohibit
ant interdict
sanctioned *adj* ***syn*** see ORTHODOX 1
ant unsanctioned
sanctity *n* ***syn*** see HOLINESS
rel godliness; righteousness, uprightness
sanctorium *n* ***syn*** see SHRINE
sanctuary *n* **1** ***syn*** see SHRINE
2 ***syn*** see SHELTER 1
rel bamah; oasis
3 ***syn*** see REFUGE 1
sanctum *n* ***syn*** see SHRINE
sand *n* ***syn*** see FORTITUDE
rel chutzpah, gall
idiom true (*or* clear) grit
sandwich shop *n* ***syn*** see EATING HOUSE
sane *adj* **1** ***syn*** see HEALTHY 1
2 free from mental disorder <a thoroughly *sane* and well-balanced man>
syn all there, compos mentis, lucid, normal, right
rel balanced, oriented; levelheaded, rational, sensible, sober, sound
idiom of sound mind
con abnormal, unbalanced; neurotic, paranoid, psychopathic, psychotic, schizophrenic; balmy, crazy, ||cuckoo, non compos, non compos mentis, nuts, screwy; deranged, lunatic, mad, wild
ant insane
3 ***syn*** see WISE 2
rel logical, rational, reasonable; good, right; cogent, compelling, convincing, sound
con imprudent, injudicious, unwise
saneness *n* ***syn*** see WIT 2
rel clear-mindedness, perception; comprehension, ||smarts, understanding
sangfroid *n* ***syn*** see EQUANIMITY
rel self-containment, self-control; aloofness, coolheadedness, indifference, unconcern
sanguinary *adj* **1** ***syn*** see MURDEROUS
2 ***syn*** see BLOODY 1
ant unsanguinary
sanguine *adj* **1** ***syn*** see BLOODY 1
2 ***syn*** see MURDEROUS
3 ***syn*** see RUDDY
4 ***syn*** see CONFIDENT 1
rel expectant; hopeful, undespairing
idiom full of hope
ant hopeless
5 ***syn*** see OPTIMISTIC
ant unsanguine
sanguineness *n* ***syn*** see OPTIMISM
sanguineous *adj* **1** ***syn*** see BLOODY 1
2 ***syn*** see MURDEROUS
sanguinity *n* ***syn*** see OPTIMISM
sanity *n* ***syn*** see WIT 2
rel intelligence; comprehension
idiom sound mind
ant insanity
sans *prep* ***syn*** see WITHOUT 2
sap *n* ***syn*** see FOOL 3
sap *vb* ***syn*** see WEAKEN 1
rel deplete, drain, exhaust, knock out; ruin, wreck; destroy
saphead *n* ***syn*** see FOOL 3
rel ||boob, jerk
sapid *adj* ***syn*** see PALATABLE
idiom fit for a king
con bland, tasteless; repulsive, unpalatable
ant insipid
sapidity *n* ***syn*** see TASTE 3
ant insipidity
sapience *n* ***syn*** see SAGACITY
sapient *adj* ***syn*** see WISE 2
rel erudite, learned, scholarly; thinking; discriminating, sapiential
sapless *adj* ***syn*** see INSIPID 3
sapor *n* ***syn*** see TASTE 3
saporous *adj* ***syn*** see PALATABLE
sappy *adj* ***syn*** ||**1** ***syn*** SUCCULENT, juicy
2 ***syn*** see SENTIMENTAL
3 ***syn*** see FOOLISH 2
sarcasm *n* a savage bitter form of humor usually intended to hurt or wound <a speech full of personal jabs and *sarcasm*>
syn acerbity, causticity, corrosiveness, sarcasticness
rel humor, irony, raillery, satire, wit; jest, repartee; gibe, lampooning; mockery, ridicule, scorn, sneering; acrimony, invective; rancor, sharpness
con playfulness, waggishness, whimsicality
sarcastic *adj* marked by, expressive of, or given to sarcasm <a critic noted for his *sarcastic* comments on actors' performances>
syn acerb, acerbic, archilochian, caustic, corrosive, ||sarky; *compare* CAUSTIC 1
rel dry; cynical, ironic, sardonic, satiric; jeering, mocking, scornful; biting, cutting, incisive; mordant, scathing, sharp, stinging; pungent, tart, trenchant
con droll, playful, sportive, waggish, whimsical
sarcasticness *n* ***syn*** see SARCASM
rel bitingness, cuttingness, incisiveness, trenchancy; derision, mocking, taunting
sardonic *adj* characterized by or expressing disdainful, skeptical humor <had a *sardonic* smile that mirrored his fixed expectation of the worst from everyone>
syn cynical, ironic, wry
rel contemptuous, disdainful, scornful; derisive, jeering, mocking, saturnine, sneering; caustic, corrosive, sarcastic, satiric
||**sarky** *adj* ***syn*** see SARCASTIC
sash *n* ***syn*** see BELT 1
sashay *vb* to move about often self-consciously and usually in a conspicuous manner <*sashaying* around, trying to walk like a model>
syn flounce, mince, prance, ||prink, strut
rel swagger
sass *n* ***syn*** see BACK TALK
rel impertinence, insolence, sassiness

---

syn synonym(s) ***rel*** related word(s)
ant antonym(s) ***con*** contrasted word(s)
idiom idiomatic equivalent(s)
|| use limited; if in doubt, see a dictionary

sassy *adj* **1** ***syn*** see WISE 5
rel brazen, unabashed; audacious
2 ***syn*** see DAPPER

Satan *n* **1** ***syn*** see DEVIL 1
rel deuce; Mephistopheles; devil-god
idiom fallen angel, lord of the underworld, prince of darkness
2 ***syn*** see DEVIL 2
rel renegade, villain; beast, viper

satanic *adj* **1** of, relating to, or characteristic of Satan <*Satanic* rites>
syn devilish, diabolic, Mephistophelian
rel saturnine
2 ***syn*** see FIENDISH
rel evil, wicked

satanism *n* the worship of Satan usually marked by the travesty of Christian rites <interpreted *satanism* as an offshoot of the belief in two coequal and coeternal principles of good and evil>
syn diabolism
rel Black Mass

sate *vb* ***syn*** see SATIATE
rel overfill, overstuff, stuff
idiom have (*or* give) a bellyful of, have (*or* give) an overdose of

sated *adj* ***syn*** see SATIATED
ant unsated

satellite *n* ***syn*** see FOLLOWER
rel favorite, minion

satellite *adj* ***syn*** see CONCOMITANT

satiate *adj* ***syn*** see SATIATED
idiom stuffed to the gills
con insatiable, unsatiable
ant insatiate, unsatiate

satiate *vb* to satisfy fully or to repletion <tried to titillate rather than *satiate* his readers' interest>
syn cloy, fill, glut, gorge, jade, pall, sate, ‖stall, stodge, surfeit; *compare* SATISFY 3
rel content, fulfill, gratify, indulge, satisfy; overdose, stuff
con coax, court, invite, pique, tantalize, tempt, titillate

satiated *adj* filled to repletion <the mob, *satiated* with violence, finally dispersed>
syn full, glutted, gorged, jaded, sated, satiate, surfeited
rel fulfilled, gratified, indulged, satisfied
con avid, greedy, ravening; craving, hungering, hungry, lusting, thirsting, thirsty
ant unsatiated

satiny *adj* ***syn*** see SOFT 3

satire *n* humorous ridicule often used to convey rebuke or criticism or to expose folly or vice <a brilliant writer noted for her *satire*>
syn lampoonery, raillery, satiricalness
rel banter, chaffing; causticity, irony; mockery, ridicule; pasquinade, persiflage, squib; parody, spoof, spoofery, takeoff

satiric *adj* of, relating to, characterized by, or based on satire <witty, eloquent, and *satiric* plays>
syn lampooning, satirizing
rel bantering, chaffing; caustic, ironic; mocking, ridiculing; parodying, spoofing; farcical; Rabelaisian

satiricalness *n* ***syn*** see SATIRE

satirizing *adj* ***syn*** see SATIRIC

satisfactorily *adv* ***syn*** see WELL 4
rel competently, sufficiently
ant unsatisfactorily

satisfactory *adj* **1** ***syn*** see SUFFICIENT 1
ant unsatisfactory
2 ***syn*** see VALID
ant unsatisfactory
3 ***syn*** see DECENT 4
rel fair, goodish, passable
ant unsatisfactory

satisfy *vb* **1** ***syn*** see CLEAR 5
2 ***syn*** see SUIT 6
3 to satiate desires or longings <strove to *satisfy* his lust for money and power>
syn appease, content, gratify; *compare* SATIATE
rel gladden, humor, indulge, please; sate, satiate; pacify, placate
con tantalize, tease; excite, pique, provoke, stimulate; arouse
4 ***syn*** see ASSURE 2
rel induce, inveigle, win (over)
5 measure up to a set of criteria or requirements <courses taken to *satisfy* requirements for graduation>
syn answer, fill, fulfill, meet
rel comply (with), conform (to), serve; do, suffice
idiom fill the bill, make good

satisfying *adj* ***syn*** see VALID
ant unsatisfying

satisfyingly *adv* ***syn*** see WELL 5
rel gratifyingly, pleasingly
ant unsatisfyingly

saturate *vb* **1** ***syn*** see SOAK 1
rel bathe, douche, wash; imbue, infuse, suffuse
2 ***syn*** see PERMEATE
rel pierce, probe; inoculate, instill

saturate *adj* ***syn*** see WET 1

saturated *adj* ***syn*** see WET 1

saturnalia *n* ***syn*** see ORGY 2

saturnine *adj* ***syn*** see SULLEN
rel grave, serious, solemn, somber, staid; moping; dark, funereal; reserved, silent, taciturn, uncommunicative
con cheerful, cheery, happy; cordial, polite
ant genial

satyric *adj* **1** ***syn*** see LICENTIOUS 2
2 ***syn*** see LUSTFUL 2

sauce *n* **1** ***syn*** see BACK TALK
rel pertness, sauciness
‖**2** ***syn*** see LIQUOR 2

saucebox *n* ***syn*** see MINX

saucy *adj* **1** flippant and bold in manner or attitude <a *saucy* little flirt>
syn arch, bantam, ‖cocket, malapert, pert
rel flippant, frivolous, light-minded, volatile; bold, brash, combative; impertinent, impudent, insolent; intrusive, meddlesome, obtrusive; smart, smart-alecky, wise
con gentle, meek, mild, quiet, subdued
ant deferential
2 ***syn*** see INSOLENT 2

sault *n* ***syn*** see WATERFALL
saunter *vb* to walk slowly in an idle or leisurely manner <*sauntered* about the streets, stopping in at various shops>
syn amble, bummel, drift, linger, mope, mosey, ‖muck, stroll; *compare* WANDER 1
rel meander, ramble, roam, rove, spatiate, ‖stravage, wander; loiter, tarry
con bustle, chase, hustle, scurry, tear
saunter *n* ***syn*** see WALK 1
savage *adj* **1** being undomesticated and often destructive or ferocious through lack of restraints or human control <*savage* dogs>
syn feral, vicious, wild; *compare* WILD 1
rel uncivilized, undomesticated, unsocialized; unbroken, unsubdued, untamed; bestial, brutal, brute; ferocious, fierce
con civilized, domesticated, socialized; broken, subdued, tamed; domestic, tame
2 ***syn*** see FIERCE 1
rel coldhearted, heartless, implacable, relentless, unrelenting; rapacious, ravenous, voracious; bloodthirsty, bloody, butcherly, murderous, rabid
3 ***syn*** see BARBARIAN 1
rel primeval, primitive; uncontrolled, unharnessed; harsh, rough, rugged
savant *n* ***syn*** see SAGE
save *vb* **1** ***syn*** see RESCUE
rel unchain, unshackle
idiom snatch from the jaws of death
con desert, leave; condemn, damn
2 ***syn*** see MAINTAIN 1
3 to keep secure or maintain intact from injury, decay, or loss <regular painting helps *save* the wood>
syn conserve, preserve; *compare* MAINTAIN 1
rel defend, guard, protect, safeguard, shield
con draw (out), withdraw; consume, spend, use up
4 to accumulate and store up (a supply) for future use <*saved* his money for college>
syn lay aside, lay away, lay by, lay in, lay up, put by, salt away, ‖spare; *compare* HOARD
rel accumulate, cache, collect, stockpile, store (up); hoard, squirrel, stash (away); conserve, husband, manage; keep, reserve, set by; deposit, stow
idiom feather one's nest, keep as a nest egg, save for a rainy day, save to fall back on
con lose, squander, use up, waste
ant consume, spend
5 ***syn*** see ECONOMIZE
save *prep* ***syn*** see EXCEPT
save *conj* **1** ***syn*** see ONLY
2 ***syn*** see EXCEPT 1
save–all *adj* ***syn*** see STINGY
saving *n* **1** ***syn*** see PRESERVATION 1
2 ***syn*** see CONSERVATION 1
saving *prep* ***syn*** see EXCEPT
saving *conj* ***syn*** see EXCEPT 1
saving *adj* ***syn*** see SPARING
savoir faire *n* ***syn*** see TACT
rel manners; dignity, elegance, grace; refinement, savoir vivre, taste; aplomb, confidence, self-assurance, self-possession; blaséness, experience, sophistication
con awkwardness, clumsiness, gaucherie, ineptness, maladroitness
savor *n* **1** ***syn*** see TASTE 3
rel scent, tinge
2 ***syn*** see QUALITY 1
savor *vb* **1** ***syn*** see SMACK
2 ***syn*** see FEEL 2
3 ***syn*** see RELISH 2
savorless *adj* ***syn*** see UNPALATABLE 1
rel bland; thin, watery, weak; unpleasing
con appetizing, pleasing, tempting; piquant, spicy
ant savory
savorous *adj* ***syn*** see PALATABLE
savorsome *adj* ***syn*** see PALATABLE
savory *adj* **1** ***syn*** see PALATABLE
rel pleasing, tempting; gustful
con acrid, sharp, strong
ant unsavory
2 ***syn*** see SWEET 2
‖**savvy** *adj* ***syn*** see SHREWD
saw *n* ***syn*** see SAYING
‖**sawbones** *n* ***syn*** see PHYSICIAN
sawbuck *n* ***syn*** see SAWHORSE
saw–edged *adj* ***syn*** see SERRATE
sawhorse *n* a rack on which something (as a board) is laid for sawing <*sawhorses* in the carpentry shop>
syn buck, horse, sawbuck, trestle, workhorse
sawtooth *adj* ***syn*** see SERRATE
saw–toothed *adj* ***syn*** see SERRATE
say *vb* **1** to express in words <learn to *say* what you mean>
syn bring out, chime in, come out (with), declare, deliver, state, tell, throw out, utter; *compare* EXPRESS 2
rel breathe; articulate, enunciate, pronounce; announce, proclaim; animadvert, comment, give, remark; cite, quote, recite, repeat; affirm, assert, aver, avow, protest
idiom out with, put in (*or* into) words, put it
2 ***syn*** see ARTICULATE 2
rel speak, talk
3 ***syn*** see SHOW 5
say *n* ***syn*** see VOICE 2
rel authority; decision
say *adv* ***syn*** see NEARLY
saying *n* an oft-repeated statement usually involving common experience or observation <the old *saying* that ignorance is bliss>
syn adage, byword, proverb, saw, word
rel dictum, maxim; truism
say–so *n* ***syn*** see VOICE 2
scabrous *adj* ***syn*** see ROUGH 1
rel scabby, scaly, scurfy; downy; knobby, knotty; bristly, prickly, thorny
con bald, glabrescent

---

syn synonym(s) ***rel*** related word(s)
ant antonym(s) ***con*** contrasted word(s)
idiom idiomatic equivalent(s)
‖ use limited; if in doubt, see a dictionary

ant glabrous, smooth

scad *n, usu* **scads** *pl* a great number or abundance <*scads* of opportunities>
syn gob(s), heap, jillion, load(s), million, oodles, quantities, ream(s), ‖rimption(s), slather(s), slew, thousand, trillion, wad(s); *compare* MUCH, MULTITUDE 1
rel great deal, lot
con few, handful, scattering, sprinkle, sprinkling

scalawag *n syn* see SCAMP

scalding *adj syn* see HOT 1
ant freezing

scale *vb* **1** *syn* see SKIN 2
2 to shed scales or fragmentary surface matter <*scaling* skin>
syn desquamate, exfoliate, flake (off), peel
rel chip (off), spall (off)

scale *n* **1** *syn* see DEGREE 2
2 *syn* see RANGE 5

scale *vb* **1** *syn* see ASCEND 1
2 *syn* see MEASURE 2

‖**scamble** *vb syn* see SPRAWL 1

scamp *n* a pleasantly mischievous person <what have those little *scamps* done now>
syn devil, enfant terrible, limb, mischief, pixie, rapscallion, rascal, ribald, rogue, scalawag, skeezicks, slyboots, villain
rel bird, chap, dog, ‖duck; ‖bleeder; joker, prankster
con sobersides

scamper *vb* **1** *syn* see RUN 2
rel hasten (off), hurry (away *or* off), light out, speed (away); dash (off), rush (off), shoot, tear (off), whip (off), whiz (off)
2 *syn* see RUN 1
rel scud, scuddle, scuttle

scan *vb syn* see BROWSE
idiom pass one's eye over

scan *n syn* see EXAMINATION
rel perusal; observation, reconnaissance

scandal *n syn* see DETRACTION
rel aspersion; reproach; discredit, disrepute

‖**scandal** *vb syn* see MALIGN

scandalize *vb* **1** *syn* see MALIGN
2 *syn* see SHOCK 1

scandalizer *n syn* see GOSSIP 1
rel blabber, blabbermouth, talker

scandalmonger *n syn* see GOSSIP 1
rel meddler, snoop; backbiter; muckraker

scandalous *adj* **1** *syn* see LIBELOUS
2 *syn* see OUTRAGEOUS 2

‖**scant** *n syn* see SCARCITY

scant *adj* ‖**1** *syn* see STINGY
2 *syn* see SHORT 3
3 *syn* see MEAGER 2
ant ample

scant *vb syn* see SPARE 3

scantiness *n syn* see FAILURE 3
rel scarceness, scarcity; sparseness, sparsity
con excess, overage, surplus

scanty *adj* **1** *syn* see MEAGER 2
rel scarce, wanting
con ample, enough; profuse
ant plentiful
2 *syn* see SHORT 3

scape *vb syn* see ESCAPE 1

‖**scape** *n syn* see ESCAPE 1

scape *n syn* see VISTA

scapegoat *n* one that bears the blame for another or others <was made the *scapegoat* for his boss's errors>
syn fall guy, goat, patsy, whipping boy
rel mark, target; victim

scapegrace *n syn* see WASTREL 1

scar *n* a mark left by the healing of injured tissue <still had *scars* from the operation>
syn cicatrix, scarification
rel blemish, defect, flaw; blister, pockmark, scab; disfigurement

scar *vb* to mark with a scar <burns that had *scarred* her face>
syn cicatrize, scarify
rel cut, score, scratch; blemish, disfigure, flaw, mar; damage, deface

scarce *adj* **1** *syn* see SHORT 3
rel curtailed, shortened, truncated
con adequate, sufficient, unwanting
ant abundant
2 *syn* see INFREQUENT
idiom scarce as ice water in hell, scarcer than hen's teeth, seldom met with

scarce *adv syn* see JUST 2

scarcely *adv syn* see JUST 2
idiom just barely, only just

scarceness *n syn* see SCARCITY

scarcity *n* smallness of supply, quantity, or number in proportion to demand <a serious *scarcity* of grain>
syn insufficience, insufficiency, paucity, poverty, ‖scant, scarceness; *compare* FAILURE 3
rel deficiency, shortage, underage; meagerness; rareness, uncommonness; absence, dearth, lack
con sufficiency; great deal, much; overabundance, overage, oversupply, surplus
ant abundance

scare *vb syn* see FRIGHTEN
rel panic, shake up; freeze, paralyze, petrify
idiom give a scare to, strike terror into the heart of, throw a scare into

scarecrow *n syn* see RAGAMUFFIN

scared *adj syn* see AFRAID 1
rel startled; panicked, panicky, terror-stricken
con emboldened, heartened, reassured; aggressive, bold
ant unafraid, unscared

scarification *n syn* see SCAR

scarify *vb* **1** *syn* see SCAR
rel deform, disfigure, maim, mar
2 *syn* see LAMBASTE 3

scary *adj syn* see AFRAID 1

scathe *vb syn* see LAMBASTE 3
idiom ‖give holy hell, give the business, rip (someone) up one side and down the other

scatheless *n syn* see SAFE 1

scathing *adj syn* see CAUSTIC 1
rel brutal; burning, scorching, searing, sulphurous

scatological *adj* ***syn*** see OBSCENE 2
scatter *vb* **1** to cause to separate or break up <the rain *scattered* the crowd>
syn dispel, disperse, dissipate
rel break up, shatter; disband; diverge, divide, part, separate, sever
con assemble, congregate, convene; accumulate, amass, collect, concentrate, crowd
ant gather
2 ***syn*** see STREW 1
rel dispense, distribute; cast, discard, shed; besprinkle, sprinkle
con accumulate, amass, concentrate
ant collect
scatterbrain *n* a flighty thoughtless person <his wife is a *scatterbrain*>
syn birdbrain, featherbrain, featherhead, flibbertigibbet, harebrain, rattlebrain, rattlehead, shatterbrain
rel fool, goose, silly, simpleton
scatterbrained *adj* ***syn*** see GIDDY 1
scattergood *n* ***syn*** see SPENDTHRIFT
scattering *n* ***syn*** see FEW
scene *n* **1** the total arrangement of the objects that form the scenic environment in which a drama is enacted <spectacle plays that attempt a realistic, three-dimensional *scene*>
syn mise-en-scène, scenery, set, setting, stage set, stage setting
rel hangings, scene cloth; ||back cloth, backdrop, background; tableau
2 ***syn*** see VIEW 4
3 the place of an occurrence or action <the *scene* of the crime>
syn locale, mise-en-scène, site
rel locality, location, place, spot
4 a sphere of activity, interest, or controversy <the drug *scene*>
syn arena
rel compass, field, setting, sphere; culture, environment, milieu
scenery *n* ***syn*** see SCENE 1
rel decor; furnishings, furniture; properties, props
scent *vb* **1** ***syn*** see SMELL 1
2 to imbue or fill with an odor <air *scented* with herbs>
syn aromatize, odorize, perfume
scent *n* **1** ***syn*** see SMELL 1
rel essence, whiff
2 ***syn*** see FRAGRANCE
scented *adj* **1** ***syn*** see SWEET 2
2 ***syn*** see ODOROUS
ant scentless, unscented
scentless *adj* ***syn*** see ODORLESS
schedule *n* **1** ***syn*** see LIST
rel chart, table
2 ***syn*** see PROGRAM 1
schedule *vb* **1** to place in a schedule <*schedule* a new train>
syn card, sked
rel list, record, slate
2 ***syn*** see TIME 1
scheme *n* **1** ***syn*** see PLAN 1
rel presentation, proposal, proposition, suggestion; arrangement, order, ordering; contrivance, device, expedient
2 ***syn*** see PLOT 2
scheme (out) *vb* ***syn*** see PLOT
schism *n* **1** ***syn*** see BREACH 3
2 ***syn*** see HERESY
3 a division of a group into two discordant groups <a *schism* within a political party>
syn chasm, cleavage, cleft, split; *compare* BREACH 3
rel divergence, division, separation; breach, break, rupture; estrangement
con unification, unity; reconciliation
schismatic *n* ***syn*** see HERETIC
rel protester; skeptic; radical, Young Turk
schismatic *adj* ***syn*** see HERETICAL
rel rebellious; unconventional
schismatist *n* ***syn*** see HERETIC
||**schlemiel** *n* ***syn*** see FOOL 3
schlepp (*or* **schlepper**) *n* ***syn*** see OAF 2
||**schmo** *n* ***syn*** see FOOL 1
||**schmuck** *n* ***syn*** see FOOL 1
||**schnook** *n* ***syn*** see DUNCE
||**schnorrer** *n* ***syn*** see BEGGAR 1
||**schnozzle** *n* ***syn*** see NOSE 1
scholar *n* ***syn*** see SAGE
rel pupil, student; bookman; polymath
scholarliness *n* ***syn*** see ERUDITION 2
ant unscholarliness
scholarly *adj* ***syn*** see LEARNED
rel studious; intellectual, long-hair; educated, taught, trained
con untaught, untrained
ant unscholarly
scholarship *n* **1** ***syn*** see EDUCATION 2
2 ***syn*** see ERUDITION 2
scholastic *adj* **1** ***syn*** see PEDANTIC
rel lettered, literary; scholarly; formal
2 ***syn*** see LEARNED
rel conversant, versed
con unconversant, unscholarly
school *vb* ***syn*** see TEACH
rel inform; guide, lead, show; advance, cultivate; control, direct, manage
schooling *n* ***syn*** see EDUCATION 1
rel knowledge; book learning, booklore
schoolmasterish *adj* ***syn*** see DIDACTIC
science *n* **1** ***syn*** see KNOWLEDGE 2
2 ***syn*** see EDUCATION 2
scilicet *adv* ***syn*** see NAMELY
scintillate *vb* ***syn*** see FLASH 1
scintillating *adj* ***syn*** see CLEVER 5
scintillation *n* ***syn*** see FLASH 1
scions *n pl* ***syn*** see OFFSPRING
scoff *vb* to show contempt by derision or mockery <heard his tale and *scoffed* at it>
syn fleer, flout, gibe, gird, jeer, jest, quip (at), scout (at), sneer

---

rel pooh-pooh; deride, mock, rally, ridicule, taunt, twit; contemn, despise, disdain, scorn; boo
con accept, approve, commend; compliment; acclaim, laud, praise

scoff *n* ***syn*** see FOOD 1

scold *n* ***syn*** see VIRAGO

scold *vb* **1** to reproach angrily and abusively <loudly *scolded* him for staying out late>
syn baste, bawl out, berate, ‖bless out, ‖cample, ‖carpet, ‖chew, ‖chew out, dress down, jaw, lash, ‖mob, rag, rail, rant, rate, ‖ream out, revile, ‖row, tell off, tongue, tongue-lash, ‖tongue-walk, upbraid, vituperate, wig; *compare* CRITICIZE, LAMBASTE 3, REPROVE
rel blame, censure, criticize, denounce, reprehend, reprobate; admonish, chide, rebuke, reprimand, reproach, reprove; execrate, objurate; brace, grill, harass, hound; blister, excoriate
idiom jump down one's throat, rake over the coals, read one the riot act, walk into
2 ***syn*** see GRUMBLE 1

sconce *n* ***syn*** see HEAD 1

scoop *n* a news story first obtained and reported by only one source (as a newspaper) <the story was a *scoop* by just a few hours>
syn beat, exclusive

scoop *vb* **1** ***syn*** see DIP 2
rel gather; lift, pick up
2 ***syn*** see DIG 2
rel gouge, grub
3 to report a news item in advance of competitors <CBS *scooped* NBC on that story>
syn beat

scoot *vb* **1** ***syn*** see HURRY 2
2 ***syn*** see RUN 1
3 ***syn*** see RUN 2

scope *n* **1** ***syn*** see ROOM 3
2 ***syn*** see RANGE 2
3 ***syn*** see BREADTH 2

scopic *adj* ***syn*** see EXTENSIVE 1

scopious *adj* ***syn*** see EXTENSIVE 1

scorch *vb* **1** ***syn*** see LAMBASTE 3
2 ***syn*** see BURN 3
rel seethe, simmer, stew; ‖plot

scorching *adj* ***syn*** see HOT 1
idiom scorching hot, sizzling hot

score *n* **1** **scores** *pl* ***syn*** see MULTITUDE 1
2 a slight cut or line made with or as if with a sharp instrument <cut *scores* on the ham before baking it>
syn scotch, scratch
rel line, mark; nick, notch, serration; cut, slit; cleft, furrow, groove, indentation; gash
3 ***syn*** see BILL 1
4 an obligation or injury kept in mind for future reckoning <had a *score* to settle with him>
syn account
rel grudge
5 the number of points gained by contestants in a game or contest <a record *score* of 263 for 72 holes>
syn tally
rel account, record; summary, total
idiom the final count

score *vb* **1** ***syn*** see LAMBASTE 3
rel ream out
idiom tear to pieces
2 ***syn*** see GAIN 1
3 ***syn*** see SUCCEED 3

scorn *n* ***syn*** see DESPITE 1
rel flouting, gibing, jeering, scoffing; derision, mockery, ridicule, taunt, taunting
con consideration, respectfulness
ant respect

scorn *vb* ***syn*** see DESPISE
rel flout, gibe, jeer, scoff; mock, ridicule, taunt
idiom hold in utter contempt
con accept, acknowledge, welcome
ant respect

scotch *n* ***syn*** see SCORE 2

Scotch *adj* ***syn*** see SPARING

scoundrel *n* ***syn*** see VILLAIN 1

scour *vb* **1** ***syn*** see HURRY 2
2 to make a thorough search or examination of <*scoured* the neighborhood for the lost child>
syn beat, comb, finecomb, fine-tooth-comb, forage, grub, rake, ransack, rummage, search
rel rout; look (for), seek; fan, range; rifle; ferret (out), find
idiom beat the bushes, leave no stone unturned, look high and low, look up and down, turn inside out, turn upside down

scour *vb* **1** ***syn*** see SCRUB 1
2 ***syn*** see EAT 3

scour *n, usu* **scours** *pl* ***syn*** see DIARRHEA

scourge *n* ***syn*** see PLAGUE 1

scourge *vb* **1** ***syn*** see WHIP 1
rel hit; knout; flail, whop
idiom whip to ribbons
2 ***syn*** see RAVAGE
3 ***syn*** see LAMBASTE 3

scout *vb* to explore in order to obtain information <forward observers *scouted* the terrain before the attack>
syn probe, reconnoiter
rel look (over), survey; observe; check out, examine; ‖case, inspect
idiom run reconnaissance

scout *vb* **1** ***syn*** see RIDICULE
2 ***syn*** see DESPISE
rel mock, ridicule

scout (at) *vb* ***syn*** see SCOFF

scowl *vb* ***syn*** see FROWN 1
idiom look black as thunder, pull a face (*or* scowl)

scrabble *vb* **1** ***syn*** see SCRIBBLE
2 ***syn*** see SCRAMBLE 1

scrag *vb* **1** ***syn*** see HANG 2
2 ***syn*** see KILL 1
3 ***syn*** see MURDER 1

scraggy *adj* **1** ***syn*** see ROUGH 1
2 ***syn*** see LEAN
rel gangling, spindling, spindly; skeletal; dwarfed, scrubby, stunted, undersize

scram *vb* ***syn*** see GET OUT 1
idiom ‖beat it, ‖cheese it, ‖get the hell out

scramble *vb* **1** to move or climb hastily on all fours <*scrambled* across the rocks>

syn clamber, scrabble, ‖spartle, ‖sprauchle
rel scurry, scuttle
2 *syn* see SPRAWL 2
scramble *n* ***syn*** see CLUTTER 2
rel conglomeration
scrap *n* **1 *syn*** see END 4
rel chip, cutting; scrappage, waste
2 *syn* see PARTICLE
scrap *vb* ***syn*** see DISCARD
idiom consign to the scrap heap
scrap *n* ***syn*** see BRAWL 2
scrap *vb* ***syn*** see QUARREL
scrape *vb* **1** to rub or slide against something that is often harsh, rough, or sharp <chalk *scraping* on the blackboard>
syn grate, rasp, scratch
rel graze, rub, scuff; abrade, chafe, grind
2 *syn* see SCRIMP
3 to make one's way with great difficulty or succeed by a narrow margin <the student barely *scraped* through the exam>
syn shave
rel struggle; get along, get by
idiom cut it (*or* the corner) pretty close, have a close shave
scrape *n* ***syn*** see PREDICAMENT
rel trouble; discomfiture, embarrassment
scrapping *n* ***syn*** see DISPOSAL 2
scrappy *adj* **1 *syn*** see QUARRELSOME 2
2 *syn* see BELLIGERENT
scratch *vb* **1 *syn*** see SCRAPE 1
rel squeak, squeal
2 *syn* see SCRIBBLE
scratch *n* **1 *syn*** see SCORE 2
‖**2 *syn*** see MONEY
scrawl *vb* ***syn*** see SCRIBBLE
rel inscribe; doodle
scrawny *adj* ***syn*** see LEAN
idiom just (*or* nothing but) skin and bones
ant brawny
screak *vb* ***syn*** see SQUEAL 2
scream *vb* **1** to voice a sudden piercing loud cry often in shock, terror, or pain <*screamed* at the sight of the accident and then fainted>
syn screech, shriek, shrill, squeal; *compare* SHOUT 1
rel screak, squeak; cry, yell; bellow, roar; caterwaul, howl, wail, ‖yawl
idiom let out a scream (*or* shriek *or* screech)
2 *syn* see SQUEAL 2
3 *syn* see YELL 2
rel complain, grumble, protest; blare
idiom raise a howl
4 to produce a vivid, blatant, or startling effect <clothes and furnishings that *screamed* nouveau riche>
syn blare, shout, shriek
scream *n* ***syn*** see RIOT 2
screech *vb* **1 *syn*** see SCREAM 1
rel penetrate, pierce; vent, voice
2 *syn* see SQUEAL 2
screen *vb* **1 *syn*** see DEFEND 1
2 *syn* see SHADE
3 to cut off from view by interposing something resembling a screen <*screen* a view with a tall hedge>
syn block out, close, obstruct, shroud, shut off, shut out
rel conceal, hide; separate, wall off; protect, seclude; embosk
idiom throw up a screen
con bare, disclose, expose, open, reveal
4 *syn* see HIDE
rel defend, guard, protect, safeguard, shield; camouflage, cloak, cover up, disguise
5 to examine carefully and methodically in order to separate, select, or eliminate <the personnel department *screened* seventy candidates for ten jobs>
syn sieve, sift; *compare* SORT 2
rel choose, pick out, select; extract, filter (out), riddle, sort (out), winnow (out)
6 *syn* see CENSOR
‖**screeve** *vb* ***syn*** see EXUDE
screw *vb* **1 *syn*** see CRUMPLE 1
2 *syn* see EXTORT 1
‖**3 *syn*** see CHEAT
4 *syn* see SCRIMP
‖**5 *syn*** see RUN 2
‖**screw** (up) *vb* ***syn*** see BOTCH
rel confuse, muddle, snafu; spoil
screwball *n* ***syn*** see CRACKPOT
screwy *adj* ‖**1 *syn*** see INTOXICATED 1
2 *syn* see INSANE 1
idiom having a screw loose
scribble *vb* to write or draw hastily or roughly <*scribbled* a quick note to her on his way out>
syn scrabble, scratch, scrawl, squiggle
rel jot (down); scribe, write
scribe *vb* ***syn*** see WRITE
scrimmage *n* **1 *syn*** see CLASH 2
rel scuffle; fight; free-for-all
2 *syn* see BRAWL 2
scrimp *adj* ***syn*** see MEAGER 2
scrimp *vb* to be extremely frugal and parsimonious in an effort to economize <*scrimped* all year to buy that fur coat>
syn pinch, scrape, screw, skimp, ‖skinch, spare, stint; *compare* SPARE 3
rel scamp; scratch; save (up)
idiom pinch pennies
‖**scrimption** *n* ***syn*** see PITTANCE
scrimpy *adj* **1 *syn*** see MEAGER 2
2 *syn* see SHORT 3
3 *syn* see STINGY
scrimy *adj* ***syn*** see STINGY
script *n* ***syn*** see HANDWRITING
Scripture *n* ***syn*** see BIBLE
scrooch (down) *vb* ***syn*** see CROUCH
scrooge *n* ***syn*** see MISER
scrub *n* ***syn*** see INFERIOR

syn synonym(s) ***rel*** related word(s)
ant antonym(s) ***con*** contrasted word(s)
idiom idiomatic equivalent(s)
‖ use limited; if in doubt, see a dictionary

scrub *vb* **1** to clean by abrasive action <*scrubbed* the pots and pans>
syn scour
rel brush; rub; cleanse, wash; buff, polish
2 ***syn*** see CANCEL 2
scrubby *adj* ***syn*** see SHABBY 1
scruffy *adj* ***syn*** see SHABBY 1
scrumptious *adj* ***syn*** see DELIGHTFUL
scrunch *vb* **1** ***syn*** see CHEW 1
2 ***syn*** see CRUMPLE 1
‖**scrunty** *adj* ***syn*** see STUNTED
scruple *n* ***syn*** see PARTICLE
scruple *n* ***syn*** see QUALM
rel faltering, hesitancy, hesitation, pause; reconsideration, second thought
scruple *vb* ***syn*** see DEMUR
rel question; fret, worry
scrupulous *adj* **1** ***syn*** see UPRIGHT 2
rel fair-minded; strict; upstanding
con questionable; shifty, slippery; dishonorable, unprincipled; dishonest
ant unscrupulous
2 ***syn*** see CAREFUL 2
rel critical, fastidious
con careless; undiscriminating, unparticular
ant remiss
scrutinize *vb* **1** to look at or over critically and searchingly <the jeweler *scrutinized* the diamonds to see if they were fakes>
syn canvass, ‖case, check over, check up, con, examine, inspect, perlustrate, study, survey, vet, view
rel look over, overlook, peruse, pore (over), scan; consider, contemplate, weigh; penetrate, pierce, probe; analyze, dig (into), dissect; comb
idiom turn a careful (*or* heedful) eye to (*or* on)
2 ***syn*** see EYE 2
scrutiny *n* **1** ***syn*** see EXAMINATION
rel look-in, look-over, look-see
2 ***syn*** see EYE 3
scud *vb* ***syn*** see FLY 1
scuddle *vb* ***syn*** see SCUTTLE
scuff *vb* ***syn*** see SHUFFLE 3
scuffle *vb* **1** ***syn*** see WRESTLE
rel cuff, scuff
2 ***syn*** see SHUFFLE 3
scuffle *n* ***syn*** see BRAWL 2
‖**sculch** *n* ***syn*** see REFUSE
sculp *vb* ***syn*** see SCULPTURE
sculpt *vb* ***syn*** see SCULPTURE
sculpture *vb* to form an image or representation from solid material (as wood or stone) <*sculptured* a colossal statue of a horse>
syn carve, chisel, sculp, sculpt
rel cast, form; model, mold, shape
scum *n* **1** ***syn*** see RABBLE 2
idiom scum of the earth
2 ***syn*** see SNOT 1
‖**scumbag** *n* ***syn*** see SNOT 1
scummy *adj* ***syn*** see CONTEMPTIBLE
scurf *n* ***syn*** see RABBLE 2
scurrile *adj* ***syn*** see ABUSIVE
scurrility *n* ***syn*** see ABUSE
rel scurrilousness; maligning, traducing, vilification
scurrilous *adj* **1** ***syn*** see ABUSIVE
rel coarse, gross; filthy, foul; insulting, offending, offensive, outrageous, outraging
2 ***syn*** see OBSCENE 2
scurry *vb* **1** ***syn*** see SCUTTLE
2 ***syn*** see RUN 1
rel shoot, tear; dart, fly; scuffle, skelter
scurvy *adj* ***syn*** see CONTEMPTIBLE
rel base, low, vile
scutter *vb* ***syn*** see SCUTTLE
rel hasten, hurry, run, speed
scuttle *vb* to move with or as if with short rapidly alternating steps <armies of fiddler crabs *scuttled* across the road>
syn scuddle, scurry, scutter; *compare* RUN 1
rel scoot; scramble; scud
scuttlebutt *n* ***syn*** see REPORT 1
sea *n* ***syn*** see OCEAN
sea dog *n* ***syn*** see PIRATE
seal *n* an adhesive-backed device bearing a symbolic, pictorial, or official design <the *seal* on a diploma>
syn stamp, sticker
seam *n* ***syn*** see JOINT 1
rel bond
seaman *n* ***syn*** see MARINER
sear *vb* **1** ***syn*** see DRY 1
2 to burn or scorch with a sudden application of intense heat <*seared* the steaks in the broiler>
syn sizzle
rel parch, scorch, shrivel; burn (up)
search *vb* **1** ***syn*** see SCOUR 2
rel run down, scout (around), scrimmage, skirmish
idiom search high and low
2 to subject (a person) to a thorough check for concealed or contraband articles <police *searching* the suspects for weapons>
syn ‖fan, frisk, shake down
rel check, examine; inspect, look over, scan, scrutinize, study
search (for *or* out) *vb* ***syn*** see SEEK 1
rel pry (out), scout (out)
search *n* ***syn*** see PURSUIT 2
searchingly *adv* ***syn*** see HARD 4
sea robber *n* ***syn*** see PIRATE
sea rover *n* ***syn*** see PIRATE
season *n* a particular period of the year <the Christmas *season*>
syn time
rel period, term
season *vb* ***syn*** see HARDEN 2
rel discipline, school, train; fit, prepare; case harden, steel
seasonable *adj* ***syn*** see TIMELY 1
rel apropos, pertinent, relevant; appropriate, apt; convenient
con irrelevant; inappropriate, inapt; ill-timed, inconvenient, inopportune
ant unseasonable
seasonably *adv* ***syn*** see EARLY 1
ant unseasonably
seasoned *adj* ***syn*** see EXPERIENCED
rel acclimated, acclimatized, hardened, toughened; case-hardened, steeled

con inexperienced, unpracticed, unskilled, unversed; unacclimated, unacclimatized, unsteeled, untempered, untried
ant unseasoned

seat *n* **1** ***syn*** see BUTTOCKS
2 ***syn*** see CENTER 2
rel fulcrum
3 ***syn*** see BASE 1

seat *vb* to cause to be seated <an usher *seated* her in the third row>
syn sit
rel establish, place, put

seating *n* ***syn*** see BASE 1

sea wolf *n* ***syn*** see PIRATE

seclude *vb* to remove or separate (oneself or another) from external influences <in the convent she was *secluded* from secular life>
syn cloister, sequester
rel retire, separate, withdraw; closet, confine, enclose, immure, isolate; screen, shut off

secluded *adj* disposed to, living in, or characterized by seclusion <*secluded* monks> <they enjoyed *secluded* country living>
syn cloistered, hermetic, recluse, secluse, seclusive, sequestered
rel retired, withdrawn; close, hidden, private, screened, shy; alone, isolated, solitary
con communal, public

secluse *adj* ***syn*** see SECLUDED

seclusion *n* the act or condition of secluding or of being secluded <the queen went into *seclusion* when her husband died>
syn reclusion, retirement, sequestration; *compare* SOLITUDE
rel detachment, separation, withdrawal; reclusiveness, seclusiveness; privacy, privateness; aloneness, isolation, separateness, solitude

seclusive *adj* ***syn*** see SECLUDED

second *n* ***syn*** see INSTANT 1
idiom the flash of an eyelid

secondary *adj* **1** ***syn*** see SUBORDINATE
rel accessory, subservient
con major, prime; first, first-ranking, first-string
ant primary
2 formed from something original, primary, or basic <a *secondary* historical analysis based on original archives>
syn derivate, derivational, derivative, derived
rel borrowed, secondhand; consequent, resultant, subsequent
con basic, principle; first, firsthand, original, uncopied, underived
ant primary
3 ***syn*** see MINOR 2

secondary *n* ***syn*** see INFERIOR
rel second fiddle, second-in-command

second childhood *n* ***syn*** see DOTAGE

second–class *adj* ***syn*** see INFERIOR 2

second–drawer *adj* ***syn*** see INFERIOR 2

second–rate *adj* ***syn*** see INFERIOR 2
ant first-rate

secours *n* ***syn*** see HELP 1

secrecy *n* the practice or policy of keeping secrets or maintaining concealment <*secrecy* is an inherent feature of intelligence operations>
syn hugger-mugger, hugger-muggery, hush, hush-hush, secretiveness, secretness, silence
rel clandestineness, covertness, furtiveness; concealment, stealth, subterfuge; censorship, suppression
ant openness

secret *adj* **1** existing or done in such a way as to maintain concealment <was involved in *secret* negotiations with the enemy>
syn clandestine, covert, furtive, hole-and-corner, hugger-mugger, hush-hush, mystical, sneak, stealthy, sub-rosa, surreptitious, undercover, ‖underneath, under-the-table; *compare* STEALTHY 2, UNDERHAND
rel underhand, underhanded; unacknowledged, unavowed, undeclared; concealed, hidden, screened; classified, confidential, eyes only, restricted, top secret
con acknowledged, avowed, declared, revealed; aboveboard, straightforward, unconcealed; declassified, unclassified, unrestricted; clear, evident, manifest, obvious, patent, plain
ant open, public
2 ***syn*** see OBSCURE 2
3 ***syn*** see RECONDITE

secret *n* **secrets** *pl* ***syn*** see GENITALIA

secretaire *n* ***syn*** see DESK

secretary *n* ***syn*** see DESK

secrete *vb* ***syn*** see HIDE
rel deposit; withhold

secretiveness *n* ***syn*** see SECRECY

secretly *adv* in a secret manner <negotiated *secretly* with both sides>
syn by stealth, clandestinely, covertly, furtively, hugger-mugger, in camera, privately, stealthily, sub rosa, surreptitiously
rel confidentially; privatim, privily
idiom behind closed doors, on the qt, on the quiet, under the rose, under the table
con forthrightly, plainly, publicly; manifestly, overtly
ant openly

secretness *n* ***syn*** see SECRECY

sect *n* ***syn*** see RELIGION 2

sectarian *adj* **1** ***syn*** see HERETICAL
rel splinter
con unified, united
ant nonsectarian
2 ***syn*** see INSULAR

sectary *n* **1** ***syn*** see HERETIC
rel beatnik, Bohemian, hippie; maverick; liberal, radical, Young Turk; rebel, revolutionary
con advocate, conformist, follower
2 ***syn*** see FOLLOWER
rel bigot

sectator *n* ***syn*** see FOLLOWER

section *n* **1** ***syn*** see PART 1
rel district, locality, subdivision, vicinity; area, belt, zone; region, tract; field, sphere, territory

---

2 ***syn*** see QUARTER 2

section *vb* to divide into sections <*sectioned* the class on the basis of ability>
syn sectionalize, sectionize; *compare* SEGMENT
rel break up, divide, separate, slice, split; sector, segment

sectionalize *vb* ***syn*** see SECTION

sectionize *vb* ***syn*** see SECTION

sector *n* ***syn*** see QUARTER 2

secular *adj* ***syn*** see PROFANE 1
rel nonclerical, nonreligious
con clerical, ecclesiastical, ministerial, priestly, regular; eternal
ant religious

securable *adj* ***syn*** see AVAILABLE 1
rel convenient, handy, reachable, ready
idiom at one's disposal
con unavailable, unreachable

secure *adj* **1** ***syn*** see CONFIDENT 1
2 ***syn*** see SAFE 2
rel firm, stable, strong
con open, wide-open; assailable, weak; dangerous, precarious
ant insecure
3 ***syn*** see RELIABLE 1
4 ***syn*** see FAST 4
rel strong; iron
5 ***syn*** see STABLE 4
6 ***syn*** see SURE 1
rel established, settled; balanced
con precarious; unbalanced; unstable, wobbly
ant insecure

secure *vb* **1** ***syn*** see DEFEND 1
2 ***syn*** see ENSURE
rel underwrite
3 ***syn*** see CATCH 1
4 ***syn*** see FASTEN 2
rel batten (down), clamp, clinch, pinion, rivet, tie down; cement
con unfasten, untie
5 ***syn*** see GET 1
6 ***syn*** see EFFECT 1

security *n* **1** ***syn*** see SAFETY
ant insecurity
2 ***syn*** see STABILITY
3 ***syn*** see PLEDGE 1
4 ***syn*** see GUARANTEE 1
rel assurance; certification; pledge
5 ***syn*** see DEFENSE 1

sedate *adj* ***syn*** see SERIOUS 1
rel calm, placid, serene, tranquil; collected, composed, dispassionate, imperturbable, unruffled; decorous, dignified, proper, seemly
con indecorous, undignified, unseemly; airy, flippant, light
ant flighty

sedative *n* an agent or drug that relieves irritability, nervousness, or excitement <took a *sedative* to help her sleep>
syn calmant, calmative, quietive
rel balm; pacifier, tranquilizer; sleeping pill, sleeping tablet; depressant, ‖downer
con energizer; stimulant; ‖upper

sediment *n* matter which settles to the bottom of a liquid <rocks hidden by *sediment* spoiled the cove for diving>
syn deposit, dreg(s), grounds, lees, precipitate, precipitation, settlings
rel bottoms, dross, recrement, scoria, slag; draff, heeltap

sedition *n* an offense against official ruling authority (as a government or sovereign) to which one owes allegiance <considered the defense industry strike to be overt *sedition*>
syn seditiousness, treason
rel alienation, disaffection, estrangement; action, protest, strike; coup, coup d'etat, putsch; insurrection, mutiny, rebellion, revolt, revolution, uprising; quislingism
con allegiance, fealty, fidelity, loyalty; duty, respect, responsibility

seditious *adj* ***syn*** see INSUBORDINATE
rel alienated, disaffected, dissident; disloyal, faithless, perfidious, traitorous, treacherous; lawless, violent
con faithful, loyal, patriotic

seditiousness *n* ***syn*** see SEDITION

seduce *vb* **1** ***syn*** see LURE
rel coax, tease; betray, deceive, delude, mislead; enslave, entrance; overpower, overwhelm
2 to persuade or entice into sexual partnership <his pathetic attempts to *seduce* his female coworkers>
syn debauch, undo
rel deflower; rape, ravish, violate; corrupt, degrade, pervert, ruin

seducement *n* **1** ***syn*** see SEDUCTION 1
rel undoing
2 ***syn*** see LURE 2

seduction *n* **1** the act or an instance of seducing or being seduced into a sexual relationship <his locker-room accounts of innumerable *seductions* were never taken seriously>
syn seducement
rel deflowering; rape, ravishment, violation; corruption, degradation, perversion, ruin
2 ***syn*** see ATTRACTION 1
rel Lorelei, siren song, temptation

seductive *adj* ***syn*** see ATTRACTIVE 1
rel desirable, mouth-watering, provocative

seductress *n* ***syn*** see SIREN

sedulous *adj* ***syn*** see ASSIDUOUS
rel active; busy; hustling, persevering, persistent, unremitting

see *vb* **1** to take cognizance of by physical or mental vision <*saw* that the boat was being driven ashore> <the only one who *saw* the truth>
syn behold, descry, discern, distinguish, espy, mark, mind, note, notice, observe, perceive, remark, twig, view
rel sight; make out; examine, inspect, scan, scrutinize; penetrate, pierce, probe; consider, study; appraise, ponder, weigh
idiom fix one's eyes (*or* mind *or* thoughts) on, occupy oneself with, pay heed (*or* attention) to, take notice of
2 to perceive something by means of the eyes <she *sees* clearly with her new glasses>

syn ‖dekko, look, watch
rel gape, gaze, glare, peek, peep, peer, stare
idiom give the eye, hold in view, keep one's eye on, lay eyes on, turn one's eyes to
3 ***syn*** see EXPERIENCE 1
4 ***syn*** see DISCOVER 3
5 ***syn*** see THINK 1
6 ***syn*** see APPREHEND 1
rel discern, discriminate, recognize
7 ***syn*** see FORESEE
idiom see the day when
8 ***syn*** see LOOK 1
rel look out, watch out
idiom see to it that
9 ***syn*** see VISIT 2
10 ***syn*** see DATE
11 ***syn*** see GUIDE
rel accompany, go (with); attend

seeable *adj* ***syn*** see VISUAL 2
ant unseeable

seed *n* **1** ***syn*** see OFFSPRING
2 a beginning or source from which something (as a conception) may later develop <the growing *seeds* of suspicion in her mind>
syn bud, embryo, germ, nucleus, spark
rel rudiment; core, kernel; conceit, concept, conception, image, impression, notion

seed *vb* ***syn*** see PLANT 1

seedy *adj* ***syn*** see SHABBY 1
rel drooping, droopy, flagging, sagging, wilted, wilting; messy, slovenly, unkempt, untidy; neglected, overgrown
idiom gone to seed
con manicured, polished, shined

seeing *n* ***syn*** see EYE 2

seeing *conj* ***syn*** see BECAUSE
idiom ‖being as how, in that

‖**seeing glass** *n* ***syn*** see MIRROR 1

seek *vb* **1** to look for <has gone to *seek* a doctor>
syn cast about, ferret out, hunt, quest, search (for *or* out)
rel bird-dog, delve, dig, fish, mouse, nose, root, smell out, sniff
idiom go in quest (*or* search) of
2 ***syn*** see TRY 5

seeker *n* ***syn*** see CANDIDATE
rel bidder; petitioner; solicitant; claimant

seeking *n* ***syn*** see PURSUIT 2

seem *vb* to give the impression of being without necessarily being so in fact <things are not always the way they *seem*>
syn appear, look, sound
rel resemble, suggest; hint, imply, insinuate, intimate
idiom have (*or* show) every sign of, have the earmarks of

seeming *n* **1** ***syn*** see APPEARANCE 2
rel feigning, pretense, sham; facade; illusion
idiom false face (*or* front), outward show
2 ***syn*** see APPEARANCE 1
rel bearing, demeanor, posture; image, style; effect, impression

seeming *adj* ***syn*** see APPARENT 2

seemingly *adv* ***syn*** see OSTENSIBLY

seemliness *n* **1** ***syn*** see ORDER 7
2 ***syn*** see DECORUM 1
ant unseemliness

seemly *adj* ***syn*** see DECOROUS 1
rel compatible, congenial, congruous, consistent, consonant; pleasing
con inappropriate, unfit, unseasonable, unsuitable, untimely; incompatible, uncongenial; displeasing, unpleasing
ant unseemly

seep *vb* ***syn*** see EXUDE
rel drip; leak; flow

seer *n* ***syn*** see PROPHET

seesaw *vb* to move backward and forward or up and down from a central axis usually in a swaying often unsteady way <planes landing on the *seesawing* flight deck>
syn lurch, pitch, swag, tilt, tilter, yaw; *compare* TEETER, TOSS 2
rel cant, incline, lean, list; rock, roll, sway

seethe *vb* **1** ***syn*** see BOIL 2
2 ***syn*** see SOAK 1
3 ***syn*** see ANGER 2
idiom ‖do a slow burn
con calm (down), simmer (down)
ant cool (down)
4 to be in a state of internal and especially mental agitation, excitement, or turmoil <his brain *seethed* with unanswered questions>
syn boil, bubble, churn, ferment, ‖moil, simmer, smolder, stir
rel abound, swarm, teem; fret, fume, sizzle, steam; bubble over, erupt, overflow

see–through *adj* ***syn*** see TRANSPARENT 1

segment *n* ***syn*** see PART 1

segment *vb* to separate into segments <tried to *segment* the poem into understandable units>
syn segmentalize, segmentize; *compare* SECTION
rel categorize, compartmentalize; divide, separate; isolate, seclude, set off

segmentalize *vb* ***syn*** see SEGMENT

segmentize *vb* ***syn*** see SEGMENT

segregate *vb* ***syn*** see ISOLATE
rel disconnect; choose, select, single
con mix
ant desegregate

segregation *n* the quality, state, or condition of being socially or racially excluded or separated <fought against racial *segregation* in the schools>
syn apartheid, separateness, separation, separatism
rel discrimination, jim crowism; ghettoization; isolation, seclusion
ant desegregation

seity *n* ***syn*** see INDIVIDUALITY 4

seize *vb* **1** ***syn*** see APPROPRIATE 1
rel occupy; usurp

---

syn synonym(s) ***rel*** related word(s)
ant antonym(s) ***con*** contrasted word(s)
idiom idiomatic equivalent(s)
‖ use limited; if in doubt, see a dictionary

2 to take possession or control of usually suddenly and forcibly <the cat *seized* the fish and made off> <*seized* the rope and dragged the boat ashore>
syn catch, clutch, ‖cotch, grab, grapple, nab, ‖nail, snatch, take; *compare* CATCH 1
rel fasten (onto), grasp, latch (onto), snap (at); apprehend, arrest; capture, secure, take over; abduct, carry off, kidnap, spirit (away *or* off)
idiom get into one's clutches, get one's hands (*or* paws) on, lay hold (on *or* of)
con free, loose, release
3 to affect especially as if by laying hold of <was *seized* with a coughing fit>
syn catch, strike, take
rel overtake; afflict

seizure *n* ***syn*** see ATTACK 3
rel convulsion; breakdown

seldom *adv* in few instances <she *seldom* writes home anymore>
syn hardly ever, infrequently, little, rarely, unfrequently, unoften
rel occasionally; semioccasionally; irregularly, sporadically; hardly, scarcely
idiom once in a blue moon
con regularly; frequently; usually
ant often

seldom *adj* ***syn*** see INFREQUENT

select *adj* **1** singled out from a number or group by fitness or preference <this hotel caters to a *select* clientele>
syn chosen, elect, exclusive, pick, picked, selected
rel culled, screened, weeded (out), winnowed (out); favored, preferred; best, elite
con random; indiscriminate; average, commonplace, mediocre, run-of-the-mill
2 ***syn*** see CHOICE
rel blue-chip, fine; best; top
3 ***syn*** see ECLECTIC 1

select *vb* ***syn*** see CHOOSE 1
idiom make a choice (*or* selection)
con ignore, pass (over); drop
ant reject

selected *adj* ***syn*** see SELECT 1
rel singled (out); appointed, tagged, tapped

selection *n* ***syn*** see CHOICE 1
rel choosing, culling, draft, drafting, picking; acumen, discernment, discrimination, insight
ant rejection

selective *adj* ***syn*** see ECLECTIC 1
rel particular, scrupulous

self-abandoned *adj* ***syn*** see ABANDONED 2

self-abnegating *adj* ***syn*** see SELF-SACRIFICING

self-abnegation *n* ***syn*** see RENUNCIATION
rel abandonment, relinquishment, resignation

self-absorbed *adj* ***syn*** see EGOCENTRIC 2
rel arrogant, cocky, self-important

self-abuse *n* ***syn*** see SELF-REPROACH

self-accusation *n* ***syn*** see SELF-REPROACH

self-admiration *n* ***syn*** see CONCEIT 2

self-asserting *adj* ***syn*** see PRESUMPTUOUS
rel aggressive, militant
con meek, modest, unassuming; docile, passive
ant self-effacing

self-assertive *adj* **1** ***syn*** see AGGRESSIVE
rel impertinent, intrusive, meddlesome, obtrusive, officious; audacious, bold; cocksure, sure
2 ***syn*** see PRESUMPTUOUS

self-assurance *n* ***syn*** see CONFIDENCE 2
rel collectedness, coolness, imperturbability; composure, equanimity, sangfroid
con insecurity, uncertainness

self-assured *adj* ***syn*** see CONFIDENT 1
rel self-satisfied, smug

self-assuredness *n* ***syn*** see CONFIDENCE 2

self-centered *adj* **1** ***syn*** see SELF-SUFFICIENT
2 ***syn*** see EGOCENTRIC 2
idiom wrapped up in oneself

self-centeredness *n* ***syn*** see SELFISHNESS

self-command *n* ***syn*** see WILL 3
rel self-containment, uncommunicativeness

self-complacency *n* ***syn*** see CONCEIT 2

self-complacent *adj* ***syn*** see COMPLACENT

self-composed *adj* ***syn*** see CALM 2

self-conceit *n* ***syn*** see CONCEIT 2

self-conceited *adj* ***syn*** see VAIN 3

self-concern *n* ***syn*** see SELFISHNESS

self-concerned *adj* ***syn*** see EGOCENTRIC 2

self-confidence *n* ***syn*** see CONFIDENCE 2
rel sanguineness, sureness; cockiness, overconfidence
con diffidence, shyness; self-distrust; doubt, uneasiness
ant self-doubt

self-confident *adj* ***syn*** see CONFIDENT 1

self-conscious *adj* aware of the scrutiny of others to the point of not appearing natural or spontaneous <felt *self-conscious* about wearing platform shoes>
syn affected, conscious, mannered
rel self-aware; anxious, ill at ease, uncomfortable, uneasy; formal, stiff, stilted; artificial; ‖mim, prim; exhibitionist, flaunty, ostentatious
con unaware, unconcerned; blithe, easy; natural, spontaneous, unaffected

self-consequence *n* ***syn*** see CONCEIT 2

self-contained *adj* ***syn*** see SELF-SUFFICIENT

self-contemplation *n* ***syn*** see INTROSPECTION

self-contented *adj* ***syn*** see COMPLACENT

self-control *n* ***syn*** see WILL 3
rel constraint, reserve, self-containedness; balance, stability; dignity
idiom presence of mind
ant self-abandonment

self-criticism *n* ***syn*** see SELF-REPROACH

self-deceit *n* ***syn*** see SELF-DECEPTION

self-deception *n* the act or an instance of deceiving oneself or of being so deceived <to presume agreement where none exists is a dangerous form of *self-deception*>
syn self-deceit, self-delusion
rel misconception, misinterpretation, misunderstanding; deception, delusion, illusion
idiom kidding oneself

self-defense *n* an act, instance, or means of defending oneself, one's property, or a close relative <sought some measure of *self-defense* against society's lawless elements>

syn self-protection
rel self-preservation

self–delusion *n* ***syn*** see SELF-DECEPTION

self–denial *n* ***syn*** see RENUNCIATION
rel abstaining, abstemiousness, abstinence; asceticism, selflessness, self-sacrifice, self-sacrificing; self-forgetful, self-forgetting
ant self-indulgence

self–denying *adj* ***syn*** see SELF-SACRIFICING

self–dependence *n* ***syn*** see SELF-RELIANCE

self–destruction *n* ***syn*** see SUICIDE

self–discipline *n* ***syn*** see WILL 3

selfdom *n* ***syn*** see INDIVIDUALITY 4

self–educated *adj* ***syn*** see SELF-TAUGHT

self–effacing *adj* ***syn*** see SHY 1

self–esteem *n* **1** ***syn*** see PRIDE 2
rel self-content, self-contentment; self-satisfaction
con self-distrust, self-doubt; self-contempt
ant self-hate
2 ***syn*** see CONCEIT 2
rel self-flattery, self-glorification
con self-distrust, self-doubt; self-hate
ant self-contempt

self–evidencing *adj* ***syn*** see SELF-EVIDENT

self–evident *adj* evident in itself without need of argument or proof <*self-evident* truths>
syn prima facie, self-evidencing
rel clear, manifest, obvious, plain; unmistakable, unquestionable
con enigmatic, hidden, mysterious, obscure; doubtable, doubtful, questionable, uncertain

self–exaltation *n* ***syn*** see CONCEIT 2

self–examination *n* ***syn*** see INTROSPECTION

self–existent *adj* existing of or by itself and having no antecedent cause <argues backward to a first great cause, which is itself *self-existent*>
syn increate, self-existing, unbegotten, uncaused, uncreated, unoriginated
rel self-generated, self-originated, self-produced
con consequent, resultant, sequential
ant derivative

self–existing *adj* ***syn*** see SELF-EXISTENT

self–explaining *adj* ***syn*** see SELF-EXPLANATORY

self–explanatory *adj* capable of being understood without explanation <his actions are *self-explanatory:* he wants to resign>
syn self-explaining; *compare* CLEAR 5
rel clear, evident, obvious, manifest, plain, self-evident; comprehensible, understandable
con equivocal, obscure, uncertain, unclear, vague; complex; incomprehensible, mysterious; inexplicable, unexplainable

self–forgetful *adj* ***syn*** see SELFLESS

self–forgetting *adj* ***syn*** see SELFLESS

self–giving *adj* ***syn*** see SELF-SACRIFICING

self–glorifying *adj* ***syn*** see BOASTFUL

self–glory *n* ***syn*** see CONCEIT 2
rel self-aggrandizement, self-glorification

self–governing *adj* ***syn*** see DEMOCRATIC

self–government *n* ***syn*** see WILL 3

self–gratification *n* the act of pleasing oneself or of satisfying one's desires <human beings driven by unconscious forces toward *self-gratification*>
syn onanism, self-indulgence
rel self-abandonment; self-pleasing, self-satisfaction; autotheism, narcissism, self-worship

selfhood *n* **1** ***syn*** see INDIVIDUALITY 4
2 ***syn*** see SELFISHNESS

self–importance *n* **1** ***syn*** see CONCEIT 2
2 ***syn*** see EGOTISM 1
rel arrogance, pomposity

self–important *adj* ***syn*** see POMPOUS 1

self–imposed *adj* imposed by oneself or itself <insists on working under *self-imposed* handicaps>
syn self-inflicted
rel self-generated, self-produced

self–indulgence *n* ***syn*** see SELF-GRATIFICATION
rel indulgence; excess, intemperance, overindulgence
ant abstinence

self–indulgent *adj* ***syn*** see SYBARITIC

self–inflicted *adj* ***syn*** see SELF-IMPOSED
rel self-determined; accepted; voluntary

self–instructed *adj* ***syn*** see SELF-TAUGHT

self–interest *n* ***syn*** see SELFISHNESS

self–interested *adj* ***syn*** see EGOCENTRIC 2

self–involved *adj* ***syn*** see EGOCENTRIC 2

selfish *adj* ***syn*** see EGOCENTRIC 2
idiom ||looking out for number one
con self-denying, selfless, self-sacrificing; altruistic, benevolent, charitable, generous, magnanimous
ant unselfish

selfishness *n* a concern for one's own welfare at the expense of or in disregard of others <his *selfishness* was consummate: he cared for no one but himself>
syn self-centeredness, self-concern, self-hood, self-interest, self-regard, self-seeking
rel egoism, egotism, self-absorption; self, selfism, selfness; autotheism, self-worship
con self-denial, selflessness, self-sacrificing; benevolence, charity, generosity
ant unselfishness

self–knowledge *n* knowledge or understanding of one's own character, motivations, and capabilities <a poet whose verse reflected deep *self-knowledge* and honesty>
syn autognosis, self-understanding
rel self-awareness; introspection, self-examination, self-observation

selfless *adj* having no concern for oneself <*selfless* service to community, state, and nation>
syn self-forgetful, self-forgetting, unselfish
rel self-giving, self-sacrificing; self-renouncing; elevated, generous, high-minded, magnanimous
con self-devoted, self-loving, self-serving
ant self-centered, selfish

self–love *n* ***syn*** see CONCEIT 2
idiom the sixth insatiable sense
con self-abuse, self-accusation, self-reproach; self-forgetfulness, selflessness

---

syn synonym(s) ***rel*** related word(s)
ant antonym(s) ***con*** contrasted word(s)
idiom idiomatic equivalent(s)
|| use limited; if in doubt, see a dictionary

THESAURUS

ant self-hate
self–mastery *n syn* see WILL 3
self–murder *n syn* see SUICIDE
selfness *n syn* see INDIVIDUALITY 4
self–observation *n syn* see INTROSPECTION
self–opinion *n syn* see CONCEIT 2
self–pleased *adj syn* see COMPLACENT
self–possessed *adj syn* see CALM 2
rel aloof, reserved; self-contained, self-controlled; self-assured
self–possession *n syn* see EQUANIMITY
self–pride *n syn* see CONCEIT 2
self–proclaimed *adj syn* see SELF-STYLED
self–protection *n syn* see SELF-DEFENSE
self–questioning *n syn* see INTROSPECTION
self–recrimination *n syn* see SELF-REPROACH
self–reflection *n syn* see INTROSPECTION
self–regard *n* **1** *syn* see SELFISHNESS
2 *syn* see PRIDE 2
self–reliance *n* reliance on one's own resources, efforts, and ability <a strong people characterized by bravery and *self-reliance*>
syn self-dependence
rel confidence, self-assurance, self-confidence; self-sufficiency, self-support
self–renouncing *adj syn* see SELF-SACRIFICING
self–renunciation *n syn* see RENUNCIATION
self–reproach *n* an act or instance of reproaching oneself <experienced both guilt and *self-reproach* after the quarrel>
syn self-abuse, self-accusation, self-criticism, self-recrimination, self-reproof
rel contrition, regret, remorse; self-castigation, self-condemnation, self-flagellation, self-punishment; self-contempt
con self-contentment, self-satisfaction; self-applause
ant self-approbation
self–reproof *n syn* see SELF-REPROACH
self–respect *n syn* see PRIDE 2
self–restraining *adj syn* see ABSTEMIOUS
self–restraint *n syn* see WILL 3
ant abandon
self–righteous *adj syn* see HYPOCRITICAL
self–ruling *adj syn* see DEMOCRATIC
self–sacrificing *adj* sacrificing or denying oneself for others <a *self-sacrificing* love>
syn self-abnegating, self-denying, self-giving, self-renouncing
rel selfless, unselfish; charitable, generous, kindly, philanthropic
con self-centered, selfish, self-seeking
selfsame *adj syn* see SAME 1
rel alike, like
idiom (the) very same
con different, unalike
ant diverse
selfsameness *n syn* see IDENTITY
ant diverseness
self–satisfied *adj syn* see COMPLACENT
self–scrutiny *n syn* see INTROSPECTION
self–searching *n syn* see INTROSPECTION
self–seeking *n syn* see SELFISHNESS
self–seeking *adj syn* see EGOCENTRIC 2
self–serving *adj syn* see EGOCENTRIC 2
self–slaughter *n syn* see SUICIDE
self–starter *n syn* see HUSTLER 1
self–styled *adj* given a specified designation or title by oneself often without justification <a department cluttered with *self-styled* experts>
syn self-proclaimed, soi-disant
rel self-appointed, self-created, self-given; so-called; quasi; would-be
self–sufficient *adj* maintaining or able to maintain oneself without outside aid <organisms are not *self-sufficient*, closed systems>
syn closed, independent, self-centered, self-contained, self-sufficing, self-supported, self-supporting, self-sustained, self-sustaining
rel self-dependent, self-reliant; self-subsistent, self-subsisting; individual, one-man, unit
idiom one's own man, sufficient unto oneself (*or* itself)
con dependent
self–sufficing *adj syn* see SELF-SUFFICIENT
self–supported *adj syn* see SELF-SUFFICIENT
self–supporting *adj syn* see SELF-SUFFICIENT
self–sustained *adj syn* see SELF-SUFFICIENT
self–sustaining *adj syn* see SELF-SUFFICIENT
self–taught *adj* having knowledge or skills acquired by one's own efforts without formal instruction <a *self-taught* painter>
syn autodidactic, self-educated, self-instructed
self–trust *n syn* see CONFIDENCE 2
self–understanding *n syn* see SELF-KNOWLEDGE
self–violence *n syn* see SUICIDE
self–willed *adj syn* see OBSTINATE
con weak, weak-willed, wishy-washy; spineless
sell *vb* **1** *syn* see BETRAY 2
2 to give up (property) to another for money or other valuable consideration <can *sell* you the house now>
syn give, market, vend
ant buy, purchase
3 to deal in or offer (articles) for sale on a regular basis <he *sells* small appliances>
syn market, merchandise, retail
rel barter, deal (in), exchange, trade, traffic; hawk, peddle; vend
ant buy
4 to command a specified price <that coat *sells* for $300>
syn bring, bring in, fetch
rel command, draw; realize, return, yield; gross, net
sell *n syn* see IMPOSTURE
sellable *adj syn* see MARKETABLE
sell off *vb syn* see SELL OUT 1
sell out *vb* **1** to dispose of entirely by selling <*sold out* his share of the business>
syn close out, sell off, ||sell up
rel dump, move, unload; sacrifice
2 *syn* see DECEIVE
3 *syn* see BETRAY 2
||sell up *vb syn* see SELL OUT 1
selvage *n syn* see BORDER 1
semblance *n* **1** *syn* see AIR 3
rel aspect, look

2 ***syn*** see LIKENESS
3 ***syn*** see APPEARANCE 2
rel air, pose
4 ***syn*** see MASK 2
semblant *adj* ***syn*** see APPARENT 2
seminar *n* ***syn*** see CONFERENCE 2
semioccasional *adj* ***syn*** see INFREQUENT
sempiternal *adj* ***syn*** see INFINITE 1
sempiternity *n* ***syn*** see ETERNITY 1
send *vb* **1** to cause to go or be taken from one place, person, or condition to another <*send* a messenger to the bank> <his cold *sent* him to bed>
syn address, consign, dispatch, forward, remit, route, ship, transmit
rel allocate, assign, commit, delegate; advance, launch; expedite, rush
ant receive
2 ***syn*** see THRILL
senectitude *n* ***syn*** see OLD AGE
senescence *n* ***syn*** see OLD AGE
senile *adj* exhibiting the weakness and loss of mental faculties often associated with old age <a *senile* professor now unable to lecture coherently>
syn doddering, doddery, ‖doted, doting
rel aging, senescent; aged, ancient, old; enfeebled, feeble, weak; decrepit, doddered, shattered
idiom in one's second childhood
senility *n* ***syn*** see DOTAGE
rel decline; senescence
senior *n* **1** ***syn*** see OLDSTER
2 one older than another <he was her *senior* by eight years>
syn elder
ant junior
3 ***syn*** see SUPERIOR
con inferior, subordinate, underling
senior citizen *n* ***syn*** see OLDSTER
sensation *n* **1** the power to respond or an act of responding to stimuli <the stage of *sensation* precedes that of rational comprehension>
syn feeling, sense, sensibility, sensitivity
rel susceptibility; consciousness; sensitiveness, sensitivity; impression, perception, response
2 ***syn*** see WONDER 1
rel bomb, bombshell
sensational *adj* **1** ***syn*** see SENSORY
2 arousing or designed to arouse a quick, intense, and usually superficial emotional response <*sensational* crime reporting>
syn livid, lurid, sensationalistic, sensationist, sultry, tabloid
rel juicy, piquant, pungent; colored, extravagant; coarse, vulgar
con exact, factual; dignified, formal, proper, restrained
3 ***syn*** see NOTICEABLE
rel impressive, stunning
4 ***syn*** see MARVELOUS 2
rel boffo, crashing, rousing, slambang, smash, smashing, superfine
sensationalistic *adj* ***syn*** see SENSATIONAL 2
sensationist *adj* ***syn*** see SENSATIONAL 2
sensatory *adj* ***syn*** see SENSORY
sense *n* **1** ***syn*** see MEANING 1
rel gist, pith, substance; center, core, focus, nucleus
2 ***syn*** see SUBSTANCE 2
3 ***syn*** see SENSATION 1
rel awareness, cognizance; discernment, discrimination, penetration; appreciation; recognition
4 *usu* **senses** *pl* ***syn*** see WIT 2
rel consciousness
5 ***syn*** see INTELLIGENCE 1
6 ability to make intelligent choices and to reach intelligent conclusions or decisions <had enough *sense* to study something practical>
syn common sense, good sense, gumption, horse sense, judgment, wisdom
rel discretion, foresight, prudence; appreciation, comprehension, understanding; brains, intelligence, ‖smarts, wit
ant folly
sense *vb* ***syn*** see FEEL 3
rel anticipate; know, realize
senseless *adj* **1** ***syn*** see NUMB 1
rel oblivious, unaware; inanimate, wooden
2 ***syn*** see INSENSATE 1
3 ***syn*** see INSENSIBLE 2
4 ***syn*** see SIMPLE 3
rel irrational, surd
5 having no meaning <an ancient custom, now outdated and *senseless*>
syn insignificant, meaningless, pointless, purportless, unmeaning
rel purposeless; trivial, unimportant
idiom without rhyme or reason
con purposeful; important, meaning, meaningful, significant
senselessness *n* ***syn*** see FOOLISHNESS
rel illogicality, stupidity
sensibility *n* ***syn*** see SENSATION 1
rel discernment, discrimination, insight, keenness, penetration, responsiveness; affection, emotion, heart
con apathy, indifference, insensibleness, insentience, unfeelingness, unresponsiveness
ant insensibility
sensibilize *vb* ***syn*** see SENSITIZE
sensible *adj* **1** ***syn*** see MATERIAL 1
rel concrete, solid
con immaterial, insubstantial; unreal
2 ***syn*** see PERCEPTIBLE
rel imaginal, perceptual, sensational; weighable; evident, manifest, obvious, patent
con imperceptible; cloudy, unclear
ant insensible
3 ***syn*** see CONSIDERABLE 2
4 ***syn*** see SENTIENT 3
5 ***syn*** see AWARE

syn synonym(s) ***rel*** related word(s)
ant antonym(s) ***con*** contrasted word(s)
idiom idiomatic equivalent(s)
‖ use limited; if in doubt, see a dictionary

rel sensitive, susceptible; noting, observing, perceiving, remarking, seeing; appreciating, comprehending, understanding; intelligent, knowing
con anesthetic, insensate, insensitive
ant insensible
6 *syn* see RATIONAL
rel sensemaking
7 *syn* see WISE 2
rel rational, reasonable; down-to-earth, matter-of-fact
con unreasonable, unsound, unwise; asinine, fatuous
ant absurd, foolish

sensile *adj* *syn* see SENTIENT 3

sensitive *adj* 1 *syn* see SENTIENT 3
rel hypersensitive, supersensitive
con impervious, insensible, unfeeling, unimpressionable, unresponsive; wooden
ant insensitive, unsensitive
2 *syn* see EMOTIONAL 1
rel high-strung, irritable, nervous, tense; insultable, oversensitive, umbrageous; unstable
con impervious, insensate, insensible, unaffected, unemotional
ant insensitive, unsensitive
3 *syn* see ACUTE 3
rel perceiving, seeing; aware, cognizant, conscious; knowing, understanding
4 *syn* see LIABLE 2
rel affected, impressed, influenced; disposed, inclined, predisposed
ant insensitive
5 *syn* see DELICATE 7
6 *syn* see SENSORY

sensitivity *n* *syn* see SENSATION 1

sensitize *vb* to cause to become sensitive or more sensitive <*sensitizing* corporate officers to social and environmental problems>
syn sensibilize
rel animate, excite, quicken, sharpen, stimulate, whet
ant desensitize

sensorial *adj* *syn* see SENSORY

sensory *adj* of or relating to sensation or the senses <*sensory* perception>
syn sensational, sensatory, sensitive, sensorial, sensual
rel sensate; receptive

sensual *adj* 1 *syn* see SENSORY
2 *syn* see CARNAL 2
rel irreligious, unspiritual
3 *syn* see SENSUOUS
4 *syn* see MATERIALISTIC

sensualistic *adj* *syn* see SENSUOUS

sensuous *adj* producing or characterized by gratification of the senses <*sensuous* pleasures>
syn epicurean, luscious, lush, luxurious, sensual, sensualistic, voluptuous; *compare* CARNAL 2, SYBARITIC
rel bacchic, dionysiac, Dionysian, hedonistic, pleasure-loving, pleasure-seeking; self-indulgent, sybaritic; carnal, fleshly, fleshy
con ascetic, disciplined, restrained

sentence *vb* to decree the fate or punishment of one adjudged guilty, unworthy, or unfit <was *sentenced* to exile>
syn condemn, damn, doom, proscribe
rel adjudge, adjudicate, judge; ordain, rule; blame, denounce; penalize, punish; devote
idiom pass sentence on
con absolve, acquit, exculpate, exonerate, vindicate; discharge, free, liberate, release

sententious *adj* *syn* see EXPRESSIVE
rel aphoristic, concise, crisp, epigrammatic, piquant, pithy, terse

sentient *adj* 1 *syn* see AWARE
2 *syn* see EMOTIONAL 1
3 capable of receiving and of being readily affected by external stimuli <deeply disturbed in the most *sentient* reaches of her mind>
syn impressible, impressionable, responsive, sensible, sensile, sensitive, susceptible, susceptive
rel sensate; open, receptive, susceptive; reactive
con insensate; closed, unreceptive; unreactive

sentiment *n* 1 *syn* see LEANING 2
2 *syn* see OPINION
rel leaning, predilection, propensity; position, posture
idiom way of thinking
3 *syn* see FEELING 3
rel conception; sensation; emotionalism, sentimentality

sentimental *adj* unduly or affectedly emotional <*sentimental* love stories>
syn bathetic, drippy, gooey, lovey-dovey, maudlin, mawkish, moist, mushy, romantic, sappy, slushy, sobby, sobful, soft-boiled, ||soppy, soupy, sticky, syrupy, tear-jerking
rel dreamy, misty-eyed, moonstruck, nostalgic, oversentimental; inane, insipid, jejune, namby-pamby, schoolgirlish, vapid; rosewater, saccharine, soft, sugar-candy, sugary, sweet; loving, tender; affectionate, demonstrative, effusive; gushing, gushy; passionate
con unaffectionate, undemonstrative; dispassionate, emotionless, unemotional, unresponsive; unfeeling, unloving; dry
ant unsentimental

sentinel *n* *syn* see GUARD 2

sentry *n* *syn* see GUARD 2

separate *vb* 1 to become or cause to become disunited or disjoined <forces that *separate* families>
syn break up, dichotomize, disjoin, disjoint, dissect, dissever, disunite, divide, divorce, part, rupture, sever, split (up), sunder, uncombine
rel alienate, discontinue, disunify, estrange; dislink, uncouple, unjoin, unlink; disaggregate, disassemble, disgregate, dispel, disperse, dissolve, scatter; detach, disengage, disrelate, dissociate; halve, quarter
con assemble, associate, blend, mingle, mix; connect, couple, join, link; unify, unite; agglutinate, bind, cement, fuse, weld
ant combine
2 *syn* see KNOW 4

3 *syn* see SORT 2
rel compartment, compartmentalize
4 *syn* see DISCHARGE 7
5 *syn* see ISOLATE

separate *adj* **1** *syn* see SINGLE 2
rel distinctive, peculiar; detached, disconnected, disengaged
2 *syn* see FREE 1
3 *syn* see DISTINCT 1
rel free, independent

separately *adv syn* see APART 1
rel distinctly; solely
con conjointly, jointly
ant together

separateness *n syn* see SEGREGATION
ant togetherness

separation *n* **1** the act, process, or an instance of separating or of being separated <*separation* of church and state> <their *separation* was a sad occasion>
syn detachment, dissolution, disunion, division, divorce, divorcement, partition, rupture, split-up
rel disrelation, dissociation, disunity, parting, shedding; disconnection, disjointedness, disjointure; breakup, disjunction, dissection, sequestration; diffluence, dispersal; dichotomy, diremption, trichotomy
con combination; unification
ant union
2 *syn* see SEGREGATION

separatism *n syn* see SEGREGATION

separatist *n syn* see HERETIC

sepulcher *n syn* see GRAVE

sepulcher *vb* **1** *syn* see ENTOMB 1
2 *syn* see BURY 1

sepulchral *adj* **1** of, relating to, or serving as a sepulcher or a memorial to the dead <*sepulchral* inscriptions>
syn mortuary, tumulary
rel exequial, funebrial, funeral, funerary, funereal
2 *syn* see HOLLOW 1

sepulture *n* **1** *syn* see BURIAL 2
2 *syn* see GRAVE

sepulture *vb* **1** *syn* see ENTOMB 1
2 *syn* see BURY 1

sequel *n* **1** *syn* see SUCCESSION 2
2 *syn* see EFFECT 1
rel end, ending, termination; close, closing, finish, finishing
3 *syn* see EPILOGUE 2
rel continuation, development; aftermath, outcome, result

sequence *n* **1** *syn* see SUCCESSION 2
rel arrangement, disposition, ordering; procession
2 *syn* see ORDER 3
rel classification, grouping; placement
3 *syn* see EFFECT 1
4 *syn* see ORDER 5

sequent *adj syn* see CONSECUTIVE

sequential *adj syn* see CONSECUTIVE

sequester *vb* **1** *syn* see ISOLATE
2 *syn* see SECLUDE
rel hide, secrete
3 *syn* see APPROPRIATE 1
rel attach; impound; dispossess

sequestered *adj syn* see SECLUDED
rel sheltered; closeted

sequestration *n syn* see SECLUSION
rel retreat

sequitur *n syn* see INFERENCE 2

seraglio *n syn* see BROTHEL

sere *adj syn* see DRY 1

serene *adj syn* see CALM 2
rel noiseless, quiet, still; quiescent, resting; undisturbed
con agitated, disquieted, upset

serfage *n syn* see BONDAGE

serfdom *n syn* see BONDAGE

serial *adj syn* see CONSECUTIVE

series *n syn* see SUCCESSION 2
rel continuance, continuation, run; category, group, set; column, tier; gradation, scale

serious *adj* **1** not light or frivolous (as in disposition, appearance, or manner) <he was disturbed by her stern, *serious* look>
syn earnest, grave, no-nonsense, poker-faced, sedate, sober, sobersided, solemn, somber, staid, weighty
rel businesslike, ‖dern, determined, steady, steady-going; intent, serious-minded; contemplative, meditative, pensive, reflective, thoughtful; austere, severe, stern; humorless, unhumorous; grim
idiom serious as a judge
con flighty, ‖flip, flippant, frivolous, volatile; casual, easy, relaxed
ant light, unserious
2 expressing, involving, or characterized by seriousness or gravity (as of consequence) <a *serious* economic situation>
syn grave, heavy, severe, weighty
rel important, significant; sobering; unamusing, unfunny, unhumorous; grim
idiom no joke, no laughing matter
con inconsequential, insignificant, unimportant, unserious
ant trifling, trivial
3 *syn* see HARD 6
4 *syn* see GRAVE 3
rel menacing, threatening

seriously *adv* **1** in a serious manner <at last settled *seriously* to work>
syn actively, down, earnestly, for real
rel gravely, soberly, solemnly; intently; vigorously, zealously; determinedly, purposefully, resolutely; fervently, passionately
idiom all joking aside, in all seriousness, in earnest
con airily, casually, flippantly, lightly, unconcernedly; carelessly, haphazardly

---

syn synonym(s) *rel* related word(s)
ant antonym(s) *con* contrasted word(s)
idiom idiomatic equivalent(s)
‖ use limited; if in doubt, see a dictionary

2 to a serious extent <the cities are *seriously* overcrowded>
syn gravely, intensely, severely
rel decidedly, quite, very; dangerously; critically, deplorably, regrettably

serious–mindedness *n* ***syn*** see EARNESTNESS
rel thoughtfulness; sober-mindedness

seriousness *n* ***syn*** see EARNESTNESS
rel sedateness, sobriety, solemnity, staidness
con gaiety, jollity; lightness
ant flippancy, frivolity

sermon *n* a religious discourse delivered in public by a clergyman as part of a worship service <preached his first *sermon* on Sunday>
syn preach, preaching, preachment, sermonizing
rel preachification; sermonary, sermonology; sermonette; exhortation, harangue, lecture, tirade

sermonic *adj* ***syn*** see DIDACTIC

sermonize *vb* **1** ***syn*** see PREACH 1
2 ***syn*** see DISCOURSE 1
3 ***syn*** see MORALIZE

sermonizer *n* ***syn*** see CLERGYMAN

sermonizing *n* ***syn*** see SERMON

sermonizing *adj* ***syn*** see DIDACTIC

serpent *n* ***syn*** see DEVIL 1

serpentine *adj* **1** ***syn*** see FIENDISH
2 ***syn*** see WINDING
rel serpentiform, serpentile, serpentlike, snakelike; crooked, devious

serrate *adj* notched or toothed on the edge <jagged peaks and *serrate* ridges>
syn denticulate, saw-edged, sawtooth, saw-toothed, serrated, serried
rel indented, notched, scored, toothed; serrulate

serrated *adj* ***syn*** see SERRATE

serried *adj* ***syn*** see SERRATE

serve *vb* **1** ***syn*** see BENEFIT
2 ***syn*** see ACT 4
3 to prove adequate or sufficient <will not *serve* as a true translation >
syn do, suffice, suit
rel service; function, work; fit; satisfy; make
idiom fill the bill
4 ***syn*** see MINISTER (to)
5 to put in (a term of imprisonment) <*served* ten years for armed robbery>
syn do
rel put in, spend; undergo
idiom do a hitch (*or* stretch), serve (out) a sentence, serve time, ‖take a vacation
6 ***syn*** see ADVANCE 1
7 ***syn*** see TREAT 2

service *n* **1** the performance of military duty in wartime and especially in a combat zone <saw a year's *service* in Vietnam>
syn action, combat
rel active duty, duty; fighting
2 ***syn*** see FAVOR 4
3 ***syn*** see RITE 2
4 ***syn*** see USE 3

serviceability *n* ***syn*** see USE 3
rel serviceableness; durability

serviceable *adj* **1** ***syn*** see HELPFUL 1
ant unserviceable
2 ***syn*** see PRACTICAL 2
ant unserviceable

serviceman *n* **1** ***syn*** see SOLDIER
2 servicemen *pl* ***syn*** see TROOP 2

servile *adj* **1** ***syn*** see SUBSERVIENT 2
rel obedient, submissive; passive, unresisting; bootlicking, groveling, toadyish
con aggressive
ant authoritative
2 ***syn*** see BASE 3

servility *n* ***syn*** see BONDAGE

servitude *n* ***syn*** see BONDAGE
con freedom, independence

set *vb* **1** to position (something) in a specified place <*set* the lamp on the table>
syn establish, fix, lay, place, put, settle, stick
rel bestow, deposit, park; emplace, ensconce, install; affix, anchor, wedge
con displace, replace, supplant; remove, take (away); uproot
2 ***syn*** see DIRECT 2
idiom set one's sights on
3 ***syn*** see STATION
4 ***syn*** see DICTATE
rel designate, direct, instruct, specify, stipulate; establish; make, name
5 to put in order for a meal <she quickly *set* the table for dinner>
syn lay, spread
rel fix, prepare, ready; arrange
ant clear
6 ***syn*** see GAMBLE 1
7 ***syn*** see INCITE
‖**8** ***syn*** see SIT 1
9 ***syn*** see BELONG 1
10 ***syn*** see COAGULATE
11 *of a fowl* to incubate eggs by crouching upon them <a chicken house filled with hens *setting* on eggs>
syn brood, ‖clock, cover, sit
rel hatch, incubate; hover
12 *of a celestial body* to pass below the horizon <the sun *set* at seven o'clock>
syn decline, dip, go down, sink
rel descend, drop
con ascend, climb, come up
ant rise
13 ***syn*** see HARDEN 1
rel crystallize, granulate; fix

set (at) *vb* ***syn*** see ESTIMATE 1

set *adj* **1** ***syn*** see SITUATED
2 ***syn*** see DECIDED 2
3 ***syn*** see FIRM 4
rel confirmed, entrenched, established, inveterate, rooted, well-set, well-settled; prescribed, specified
4 ***syn*** see LITTLE 2
rel diehard, inflexible, obstinate, pigheaded, rigid, unbending, unyielding
5 ***syn*** see FAST 4
rel fastened; close; sound
6 ***syn*** see EXPRESS 2

7 ***syn*** see READY 1
set *n* **1** ***syn*** see GIFT 2
2 ***syn*** see BEARING 1
3 ***syn*** see SCENE 1
4 ***syn*** see GROUP 3
rel assortment, gaggle; kit, pack
5 a number of people having something (as habit, interest, occupation, or age) in common <the horsey *set* was gathered at the bar>
syn bunch, circle, crowd, group, lot, push; *compare* CLIQUE
rel clan, clique, crew, gang, mob; cénacle; camp, faction; company
set back *vb* ***syn*** see DELAY 1
setback *n* a checking of progress <loss of his fellowship was a serious *setback* to his education>
syn backset, check, reversal, reverse; *compare* COMEDOWN
rel delay, retardation, slowdown; hindrance, impediment, obstacle, stumbling block; disappointment; rebuff; defeat; regress, regression
idiom reverse of fortune
con advancement, forwarding, progressing
set down *vb* ***syn*** see ALIGHT
set off *vb* **1** ***syn*** see COMPENSATE 1
2 ***syn*** see MOBILIZE 1
set on *vb* ***syn*** see INCITE
set out *vb* **1** ***syn*** see DESIGN 3
2 ***syn*** see HEAD 3
idiom set one's course for
setout *n* **1** ***syn*** see COSTUME
2 ***syn*** see BEGINNING
setting *n* ***syn*** see SCENE 1
setting–out *n* ***syn*** see DEPARTURE 1
settle *vb* **1** ***syn*** see ENSCONCE 2
2 ***syn*** see CALM
rel assure, reassure
ant unsettle
3 ***syn*** see SET 1
rel found, ground, lodge, seat
con dislodge, unseat, uproot
ant unsettle
4 ***syn*** see DECIDE
rel fix, seal
idiom come to a decision (*or* conclusion), form a judgment, make a decision
5 ***syn*** see NEGOTIATE 1
rel mediate, reconcile, straighten (out)
idiom bring to terms (*or* agreement)
6 ***syn*** see CLEAR 5
idiom settle the score, settle up (*or* square) accounts
7 to put in order for final disposal <waiting to *settle* an estate>
syn clean up, wind up
8 ***syn*** see ALIGHT
rel flop (down), plop (down)
settled *adj* **1** ***syn*** see FIRM 4
rel decided, determined
con uncertain, undecided
ant unsettled
2 ***syn*** see INVETERATE 1
3 ***syn*** see DECIDED 2
rel certain, fixed
con irresolute, undecided, undetermined, unresolved, vacillating, wavering
ant unsettled
settlement *n* **1** ***syn*** see HABITATION 1
2 ***syn*** see DECISION 1
rel showdown; quietus
settlings *n pl* ***syn*** see SEDIMENT
set to *vb* **1** ***syn*** see BEGIN 1
2 ***syn*** see PITCH IN 1
set–to *n* **1** ***syn*** see BRAWL 2
2 ***syn*** see QUARREL
3 ***syn*** see ENCOUNTER
set up *vb* **1** ***syn*** see ERECT 5
ant tear down
2 ***syn*** see ELATE
3 ***syn*** see ERECT 3
con disassemble, take down
4 ***syn*** see FOUND 2
rel generate, originate; start up; open
5 ***syn*** see INTRODUCE 3
6 ***syn*** see TREAT 3
setup *n* ***syn*** see SNAP 1
seventh heaven *n* ***syn*** see ECSTASY
rel exhilaration; bliss, paradise
con sadness, unhappiness; blues, doldrums, dumps
sever *vb* **1** ***syn*** see SEPARATE 1
2 ***syn*** see KNOW 4
3 ***syn*** see CUT 5
several *adj* **1** possessed by or attributed to a specific individual <the debaters expressed their *several* opinions>
syn individual, particular, respective, singular
rel independent; personal, special, specific
2 ***syn*** see DISTINCT 1
3 consisting of an indefinite number more than two and less than many <*several* days passed>
syn divers, some, sundry, various
rel particular, separate, single; few; considerable; many, numerous
idiom not a few
‖**4** ***syn*** see MANY
‖**several** *pron* ***syn*** see SUNDRY
severalize *vb* ***syn*** see KNOW 4
severally *adv* ***syn*** see APART 1
rel discretely; exclusively
idiom one at a time
severe *adj* **1** given to or characterized by strict discipline and firm restraint <treated all the students with *severe* impartiality>
syn ascetic, astringent, austere, mortified, stern
rel exacting, heavy-handed, onerous, oppressive; disciplined, iron-willed, self-disciplined; inflexible, restrictive, rigid, rigorous, strict, stringent, uncompromising, unyielding
con easy, easygoing, gentle, mild, soft; clement, forbearing, indulgent, lax, lenient, merciful
ant tender, tolerant
2 ***syn*** see GRIM 2

---

syn synonym(s) ***rel*** related word(s)
ant antonym(s) ***con*** contrasted word(s)
idiom idiomatic equivalent(s)
‖ use limited; if in doubt, see a dictionary

rel serious, sober, stern
3 of a kind to cause discomfort or hardship <a *severe* winter storm>
syn bitter, brutal, hard, harsh, inclement, intemperate, rigorous, rugged
rel crimpy, unpleasant; forbidding, hostile, inhospitable; bleak, disagreeable, grim; painful, raw, sharp, smart; blistering, extreme, intense, savage; blustering, blustery, stormy, wintry
con balmy, calm, equable, gentle, moderate, soft, temperate
ant mild
4 *syn* see HARD 6
5 *syn* see SERIOUS 2
rel consequential; dear, sore

severely *adv* **1** *syn* see HARD 5
2 *syn* see SERIOUSLY 2
rel markedly

||**sew** *vb* *syn* see EXUDE

sew up *vb* ||**1** *syn* see EXHAUST 4
2 *syn* see MONOPOLIZE

sexy *adj* *syn* see RISQUÉ

shabby *adj* **1** being ill-kept and showing signs of wear and tear <a *shabby* neighborhood full of depressing tenements>
syn bedraggled, broken-down, decrepit, dilapidated, dingy, disreputable, down-at-heel, faded, mangy, moth-eaten, run-down, scrubby, scruffy, seedy, shoddy, sleazy, slipshod, squalid, tacky, tagrag, tattered, threadbare, tired
rel disfigured, dog-eared; decaying, deteriorated, deteriorating; ramshackle, ratty, rickety; bare, miserable, neglected, poor, poverty-stricken; sordid; worm-eaten; outworn, worn-out; abandoned, desolate, ruined, ruinous, wrecked
idiom gone to seed
con neat, spick-and-span, tidy, trig, trim, well-kept; brand-new, fresh, new; unused
ant spruce
2 *syn* see CONTEMPTIBLE
3 *syn* see DISREPUTABLE 1

||**shack** *n* *syn* see VAGABOND

shack *n* *syn* see HUT

shackle *n, usu* **shackles** *pl* something that confines the legs or arms so as to prevent free movement <slaves in *shackles*>
syn bond(s), chains, fetter(s), gyve(s), iron(s)
rel anklet, bilbo, leg-iron, trammel; bracelet, handcuff, manacle; straitjacket; collar, garrote

shackle *vb* *syn* see HAMPER
rel lash, rope, strap; chain, enchain, manacle; handcuff; pinion, secure
con unchain, unfetter, untie
ant unshackle

shade *n* **1** comparative darkness or obscurity due to interception of light rays <trees providing *shade* from the sunlight>
syn adumbration, penumbra, shadow, umbra, umbrage
rel blackness, darkness, dimness, obscuration, obscurity; cover, shelter
con brightness, brilliancy, effulgence, radiance; blaze, glare, glow
2 *syn* see APPARITION
3 *syn* see COLOR 1
rel intensity, saturation
4 *syn* see GRADATION
rel difference, distinction, variation
5 *syn* see HINT 2

shade *vb* to cast into shadow by intercepting light rays <avenues *shaded* by large trees>
syn inumbrate, screen, shadow, umbrage
rel shelter; cover
con roast, scorch, swelter; expose

shaded *adj* *syn* see SHADY 1
ant unshaded

shadow *n* **1** *syn* see SHADE 1
2 *syn* see APPARITION
3 *syn* see VESTIGE 1
4 *syn* see HINT 2

shadow *vb* **1** *syn* see SHADE
2 *syn* see OBSCURE
3 *syn* see TAIL

shadow (forth) *vb* **1** *syn* see SUGGEST 5
2 *syn* see ADUMBRATE 1
rel forecast, foretell, predict

shadow *adj* *syn* see SHADY 1

shadowed *adj* *syn* see SHADY 1
ant unshadowed

shadowy *adj* **1** *syn* see IMAGINARY 1
2 *syn* see GHASTLY 2
3 *syn* see FAINT 2
rel amorphous; foggy
4 *syn* see SHADY 1
ant bright

shady *adj* **1** producing, affording, or abounding in shade <a *shady* day> <cool, *shady* streets>
syn shaded, shadow, shadowed, shadowy, umbrageous, umbrous
rel bosky, screened, sheltered; dusky; dark
con exposed, unshaded, unshadowed; unsheltered; bright, light
ant sunny
2 *syn* see DOUBTFUL 1
3 *syn* see DISREPUTABLE 1
rel subreputable
4 *syn* see RISQUÉ
rel disreputable, shameful

shaft *n* **1** *syn* see RAY 1
2 a scornful, cutting, or pithily critical remark <the target of her latest *shaft* is the president himself>
syn barb, dart
rel cut, jab, thrust; potshot

shake *vb* **1** to move irregularly to and fro or up and down often in a wavering or oscillating manner <was so frightened that her hands *shook*>
syn ||didder, dither, quake, quaver, quiver, shiver, shudder, tremble, tremor, twitter
rel palpitate, quail, waver; flicker, flit, flitter, flutter; fluctuate, oscillate; chatter, shimmy, vibrate
idiom shake like an aspen leaf
2 to undergo strong vibration especially as the result of a physical blow or shock <the platform *shook* as the train passed>
syn jar, quake, tremble, tremor, vibrate

rel bounce, jounce; chatter, quiver, shimmy; rock, stagger
3 to cause to move in a quick, jerky manner <rattling and *shaking* the latch>
syn jiggle, joggle
rel bounce, ||chounse, jounce; jostle; rattle; jerk
4 to cause to move to and fro or up and down violently <an earthquake that *shook* the whole coast>
syn agitate, concuss, convulse, rock
rel jog, jostle, rattle, ||shog; commove, discompose, disorder, jar, jolt, unsettle; disquiet, disturb, perturb, upset; churn, roil, ruffle, stir up, whip
5 to get or keep away from (a pursuer) <tried unsuccessfully to *shake* the man tailing him>
syn lose, slip, throw off; *compare* ESCAPE 2
rel avoid, elude; outwit
idiom get rid of, give (someone) the shake (*or* slip), slip from under the eye of
6 ***syn*** see DISMAY 1
rel disturb, jar, rattle, unsettle, upset; bother, worry; unnerve, unstring

shake (off) *vb* ***syn*** see RID

shake *n* **1** ***syn*** see EARTHQUAKE
2 shakes *pl* ***syn*** see JITTERS
3 ***syn*** see INSTANT 1
4 ***syn*** see DEAL 2

shake down *vb* **1** ***syn*** see EXTORT 1
2 ***syn*** see SEARCH 2

shake up *vb* ***syn*** see SPEED 3

shake–up *n* an extensive and often drastic rearrangement <a personnel *shake-up* effected by new management>
syn overturn, reorganization, revolution, turnover
rel liquidation, purge; cleanout, cleanup, clearing out, clear-up; removal, riddance
idiom break with the past, clean sweep

shakiness *n* ***syn*** see INSTABILITY

shaking *adj* ***syn*** see TREMULOUS
rel unsettled, unstable, unsteady; tottering
con unshakable, unshaken

shaky *adj* **1** ***syn*** see WEAK 2
rel unsettled; infirm, unsound, unsteady; precarious, tottering, tottery
2 ***syn*** see DOUBTFUL 1
3 ***syn*** see TREMULOUS
4 ***syn*** see RICKETY

shallow *adj* **1** lacking physical depth <buried in a *shallow* grave>
syn shoal, superficial
rel shallowish; surface
idiom as deep as a mud puddle, no deeper than a heavy dew, not deep enough to float a match
con bottomless, unfathomable
ant deep
2 ***syn*** see SUPERFICIAL 2
rel paltry, petty, trifling, trivial; empty, hollow, idle, vain; bird-witted, featherbrained, flighty
con heavy, profound; discerning, penetrating
ant deep

shallow *n* ***syn*** see SHOAL
ant deep

sham *n* **1** ***syn*** see IMPOSTURE
rel facade, fakery, false front, Potemkin village
2 ***syn*** see HYPOCRISY
3 ***syn*** see MOCKERY 2

sham *vb* ***syn*** see ASSUME 4
rel ape, copy, imitate, mock; create, invent; lie, mislead

sham *adj* **1** ***syn*** see FICTITIOUS 2
rel affected, assumed, feigned; pseudo, so-called; make-believe, pretend
2 ***syn*** see COUNTERFEIT
3 ***syn*** see ARTIFICIAL 2
rel plaster, synthetic; adulterated; bogus

shamble *vb* ***syn*** see SHUFFLE 3

shambles *n pl but usu sing in constr* ***syn*** see MESS 3

shame *n* ***syn*** see DISGRACE
rel chagrin, embarrassment; guilt, mortification, self-reproach, self-reproof
con pride, self-admiration, self-love, self-respect
ant glory

shamed *adj* ***syn*** see ASHAMED
rel crestfallen; shamefaced, shamefast; crushed, disgraced
idiom loaded (*or* bowed down) with shame
ant proud

shameful *adj* ***syn*** see DISREPUTABLE 1

shameless *adj* characterized by or exhibiting boldness and a lack of shame <a *shameless* hussy>
syn arrant, barefaced, blatant, brassy, brazen, brazenfaced, impudent, overbold, unabashed, unblushing
rel audacious, bold, cheeky, presumptuous; baldfaced, high-handed; abandoned, dissolute, profligate; immodest, lewd; disgraceful, outrageous
idiom bold as brass, dead (*or* lost) to shame
con bashful, diffident, mousy, shy; chaste, decent, modest, pure

||shamus *n* ***syn*** see PRIVATE DETECTIVE

Shangri–la *n* ***syn*** see UTOPIA

shanty *n* ***syn*** see HUT

shape *vb* ***syn*** see MAKE 3
rel devise, plan, work up; tailor

shape *n* **1** ***syn*** see FORM 1
rel appearance, aspect, look, semblance
2 ***syn*** see ORDER 9
3 ***syn*** see ORDER 10
rel state, whack

shapeful *adj* ***syn*** see SHAPELY
ant shapeless

shapeless *adj* ***syn*** see FORMLESS
rel unshapely; deformed, misshapen
con proportional, proportionate, proportioned, shapeful, symmetrical
ant shapeful, shapely

shapely *adj* having a regular or pleasing shape <a *shapely* girl>

---

syn synonym(s) ***rel*** related word(s)
ant antonym(s) ***con*** contrasted word(s)
idiom idiomatic equivalent(s)
|| use limited; if in doubt, see a dictionary

syn clean-limbed, shapeful, statuesque, trim, well-proportioned, well-turned; *compare* CURVACEOUS
rel balanced, clean-cut, proportioned, regular, symmetrical; comely, pleasing; ‖built, full-figured, rounded, ‖stacked; buxom
con dumpy, squat, stumpy; angular, lank, lean; ill-favored, ill-looking
ant shapeless, unshapely

share *n* **1** something belonging to, assumed by, or falling to one (as in division or apportionment) <wanted his *share* of the prize money>
syn allotment, allowance, bite, cut, lot, part, partage, portion, quota, slice; *compare* RATION
rel proportion, quotient, quotum; commission, percentage; divide, ‖divvy; rake-off
idiom piece of the action, slice of the melon
2 ***syn*** see RATION
3 ***syn*** see INTEREST 1

share *vb* **1** ***syn*** see APPORTION 2
rel assign, deal (out), dispense, dole (out), give out, mete (out)
idiom ‖go snucks, share and share alike
con retain, withhold; combine, unite
2 to have, get, or use in common with another or others <she *shared* her husband's fate>
syn partake, participate
rel experience
idiom have a share (*or* part) in, have (*or* take) a hand in

shared *adj* ***syn*** see COMMON 1
ant unshared

share out *vb* ***syn*** see ADMINISTER 2

sharer *n* ***syn*** see PARTICIPANT

sharp *adj* **1** having a fine edge <a *sharp* knife makes a clean cut>
syn honed, keen, razor-sharp, unblunted, whetted
rel acute
idiom sharp as a razor blade
con blunted, dulled; unsharpened
ant blunt, dull
2 ***syn*** see POINTED 1
3 ***syn*** see INTELLIGENT 2
4 possessing or indicative of alert competence and clear understanding <people of *sharp* judgment and refined sensibilities>
syn acute, keen, penetrating, penetrative, quick-sighted, quick-witted, sharp-sighted, sharp-witted; *compare* SHREWD
rel alert, bright; clever, cute, ingenious, original, resourceful; fast, quick
idiom sharp as a knife (*or* tack)
con dull-witted; unintelligent; foolish, simple, slow, stupid
ant dull
5 ***syn*** see ACUTE 3
6 ***syn*** see WISE 4
rel adroit, nimble; clever, cute; sly, unethical
idiom nobody's fool
7 ***syn*** see SHORT 5
rel acrimonious, biting, double-edged, incisive, penetrating, piercing, stabbing, stinging; caustic, virulent, vitriolic
8 causing intense mental or physical distress <a *sharp* pain>
syn acute, knifelike, piercing, shooting, stabbing
rel intense, severe, smart; biting, drilling, stinging; penetrating; agonizing, excruciating; paralyzing
9 ***syn*** see ACRID
rel odorous; strong-scented, strong-smelling; suffocating
10 ***syn*** see ACUTE 4
11 ***syn*** see STYLISH

‖**sharp** *vb* ***syn*** see SHARPEN

sharp *adv* ***syn*** see JUST 1

sharpen *vb* to give a keen edge to <*sharpen* an ax>
syn edge, hone, ‖sharp, whet
rel dress, file, grind, stroke
idiom hone to a razor edge, hone to razor sharpness
ant blunt, dull

sharper *n* ***syn*** see SWINDLER

sharp–eyed *adj* having keen vision <the *sharp-eyed* child found all the Easter eggs>
syn eagle-eyed, hawk-eyed, lyncean, lynx-eyed, sharp-sighted
rel alert, attentive, aware, keen, lynxlike, observant, sharp, vigilant, watchful
con myopic, nearsighted, shortsighted; dim-sighted, purblind; blind

sharpie *n* ***syn*** see SWINDLER

sharply *adv* ***syn*** see HARD 4
rel intensely, penetratingly, piercingly

sharpness *n* ***syn*** see EDGE 2
ant bluntness, dullness

sharp practice *n* ***syn*** see DECEPTION 1

sharp–sighted *adj* **1** ***syn*** see SHARP-EYED
2 ***syn*** see SHARP 4

sharp–witted *adj* **1** ***syn*** see SHARP 4
2 ***syn*** see WISE 4

shatter *vb* **1** to break into small pieces by or as if by a blow <*shatter* a windowpane with a rock>
syn burst, fragment, ‖pash, rive, shiver, smash, ‖smatter, splinter, splinterize, splitter; *compare* PULVERIZE 1
rel break, crack, rend, snap, ‖spalt, split; crunch, crush; crash, dash; fragmentalize, fragmentize, pulverize; demolish, destroy, disintegrate, ruin, ‖total, wreck
idiom smash to smithereens (*or* bits)
2 ***syn*** see DESTROY 1
3 ***syn*** see RATTLE 1

shatterable *adj* ***syn*** see FRAGILE 1
ant shatterproof

shatterbrain *n* ***syn*** see SCATTERBRAIN

shattering *adj* ***syn*** see DESTRUCTIVE

shattery *adj* ***syn*** see FRAGILE 1
idiom as delicate as an eggshell

shave *vb* **1** ***syn*** see SLIVER
2 ***syn*** see CUT 6
rel shingle
3 ***syn*** see REDUCE 2
4 ***syn*** see BRUSH
idiom cut (*or* shave) it close
5 ***syn*** see SCRAPE 3

shaveling *n syn* see BOY 1
she *n syn* see WOMAN 1
shear *vb syn* see CUT 6
rel mow; barb, barber; manicure, snip
sheath *n syn* see SKIN 3
sheathe *vb* to cover (a surface) with something that protects <a house *sheathed* with aluminum siding>
syn clad, face, side, skin
rel envelop, surround, wrap; case, cover, encase, jacket; panel
con bare, expose, strip
sheathing *n syn* see SKIN 3
shed *vb* **1** *syn* see DISCARD
rel drop; divest
2 to cast off (a body covering) in a periodic process of growth or renewal <a snake *shedding* its skin>
syn exuviate, molt, slip, slough
rel cast off, discard; doff, take off
sheen *n syn* see LUSTER
rel finish; shininess
sheeny *adj syn* see LUSTROUS 1
sheepheaded *adj syn* see SIMPLE 3
sheer *adj* **1** *syn* see FILMY
rel airy, chiffon, thin; see-through
2 *syn* see UTTER
3 *syn* see PURE 2
rel arrant, bald-faced, complete, outright
4 *syn* see STEEP 1
sheer *vb* **1** *syn* see TURN 6
2 *syn* see SWERVE 1
||shekels *n pl syn* see MONEY
shell *n syn* see HULL
shell *vb* **1** *syn* see SHUCK
2 *syn* see BOMBARD
rel pepper; rake
idiom open fire on
shellac *vb syn* see WHIP 2
shellacking *n syn* see DEFEAT 1
rel ||clobbering, whipping
shell out *vb syn* see SPEND 1
shelter *n* **1** something (as a structure or place) that covers or affords protection <a bomb *shelter*>
syn asylum, cover, covert, harbor, harborage, haven, port, refuge, retreat, sanctuary; *compare* REFUGE 1
rel buen retiro, den, hermitage, hide, hideaway, hideout, hidey-hole, retirement, tower
2 dwellings provided for numbers of people or for a community <*shelter* for the aged>
syn housing, quarterage
rel dwellings, lodging; roof
3 *syn* see REFUGE 1
shelter *vb syn* see HARBOR 1
shelve *vb syn* see DEFER
rel dish, drop, give up
idiom put on the shelf
shenanigan *n* **1** *syn* see TRICK 1
rel fast one, game, legerdemain
2 *syn* see PRANK
rel frolic; goings-on, mischievousness; stunt
Sheol *n syn* see HELL
shepherd *vb syn* see GUIDE
Sherlock *n syn* see DETECTIVE
Sherlock Holmes *n syn* see DETECTIVE
shibboleth *n* **1** *syn* see CATCHWORD
rel platitude, truism
2 *syn* see COMMONPLACE
||shick *adj syn* see INTOXICATED 1
||shicker *adj syn* see INTOXICATED 1
||shicker *n syn* see DRUNKARD
shield *n syn* see DEFENSE 1
rel buffer, bumper, screen
shield *vb* **1** *syn* see HARBOR 1
idiom give cover (*or* shelter) to; take (*or* shield) under one's wing
ant expose
2 *syn* see DEFEND 1
shift *vb* ||**1** *syn* see APPORTION 2
2 *syn* see CHANGE 5
3 *syn* see MOVE 4
rel alter, change, vary; budge, stir; shuffle; relocate
idiom shift place
4 *syn* see CONSUME 5
5 to carry on one's affairs independently and self-sufficiently often under difficult circumstances <after the divorce, she was forced to *shift* for herself>
syn do, fare, get along, get by, get on, ||make out, manage, muddle through, stagger (on *or* along)
rel contrive, survive; freelance; progress, succeed
idiom fend for oneself, make do, make it alone, make shift, paddle one's own canoe, stand on one's own two feet
shift *n* **1** *syn* see CONVERSION 2
2 *syn* see RESOURCE 3
rel gambit, maneuver, ploy, strategy
3 *syn* see SPELL 1
4 *syn* see TRANSITION
5 *syn* see TURN 2
shifty *adj* **1** *syn* see EVASIVE 1
rel dodging, elusive; cagey, collusive, conniving, crafty, cunning; furtive, shifty-eyed, sneaky, tricky; insidious, shady; deceitful, dishonest, fraudulent; treacherous
idiom shifty as the sand
2 *syn* see DISHONEST
3 *syn* see UNDERHAND
4 *syn* see MUTABLE 2
shill *n syn* see DECOY 2
shillaber *n syn* see DECOY 2
||shillelagh *n syn* see CUDGEL
shilling shocker *n syn* see DIME NOVEL
shilly-shally *adj syn* see VACILLATING 2
shilly-shally *n syn* see HESITATION
shilly-shally *vb syn* see HESITATE
shilly-shallying *adj syn* see VACILLATING 2
rel halfhearted, lukewarm
shimmer *vb syn* see FLASH 1

---

syn synonym(s) *rel* related word(s)
ant antonym(s) *con* contrasted word(s)
idiom idiomatic equivalent(s)
|| use limited; if in doubt, see a dictionary

shimmer *n* ***syn*** see FLASH 1
rel blinking; spangle; spark, sparking

shin *vb* ***syn*** see RUN 1

shindig *n* **1** a large, festive, and often overly lavish party <threw the *shindig* of the year for the author>
syn bash, ‖blowout, shindy
rel fête, gala; ball, dance; blast, party; affair, shebang; ‖shivoo
2 ***syn*** see COMMOTION 3

shindy *n* **1** ***syn*** see SHINDIG 1
2 ***syn*** see COMMOTION 3

shine *vb* **1** to emit rays of light <the storm is over and the sun is *shining*>
syn beam, burn, gleam, radiate
rel glimmer, glow; incandesce, luminesce; flash, sparkle, twinkle; flare; glare
2 ***syn*** see POLISH 1

shine *n* **1** ***syn*** see DISPLAY 2
2 ***syn*** see LUSTER
rel finish
3 *usu* **shines** *pl* ***syn*** see PRANK

shiner *n* ***syn*** see BLACK EYE 1

shingle *vb* ***syn*** see OVERLAP

shining *adj* ***syn*** see LUSTROUS 1

shiny *adj* ***syn*** see LUSTROUS 1

ship *vb* **1** ***syn*** see SEND 1
rel direct; freight; export
ant receive
2 ***syn*** see MOVE 4

shipshape *adj* ***syn*** see NEAT 2

shipwreck *vb* **1** to destroy, disable, or seriously damage a ship (as by running aground or causing to founder) <the typhoon *shipwrecked* the entire fishing fleet>
syn beach, cast away, pile up, strand, wreck
rel break up; scuttle; founder; capsize; go down, sink
idiom go aground, go to the bottom (*or* Davy Jones's locker), run on the rocks
2 ***syn*** see RUIN 2

shirk *vb* **1** ***syn*** see SNEAK
2 ***syn*** see DODGE 1
rel bilk, burke; bypass, double, eschew, get around; shuffle off, shun

shirker *n* ***syn*** see SLACKER

shirty *adj* ***syn*** see ANGRY

shivaree *n* a noisy mock serenade to a newly married couple <*shivarees* and other such disappearing rural customs>
syn ‖belling, ‖bull band, ‖callithump, charivari, ‖horning, ‖riding, ‖skimmelton
rel entertainment, reception, welcome

shiver *vb* ***syn*** see SHATTER 1

shiver *vb* ***syn*** see SHAKE 1

‖**shivereens** *n pl* ***syn*** see SMITHEREENS

shivering *adj* ***syn*** see TREMULOUS

shivers *n pl* ***syn*** see JITTERS

shivery *adj* **1** ***syn*** see TREMULOUS
2 ***syn*** see COLD 1

shoal *adj* ***syn*** see SHALLOW 1

shoal *n* a place where a body of water (as a sea or river) is not deep <dangerous *shoals* in uncharted waters>
syn shallow
rel barrier, barrier reef, coral reef, fringing reef, reef, sand reef; bank, bar, sandbank, sandbar, tombolo; hook, spit; seamount
con abyss, deep, depth

shock *n* ***syn*** see PILE 1

shock *n* **1** ***syn*** see IMPACT 1
2 ***syn*** see EARTHQUAKE
3 ***syn*** see TRAUMA
rel prostration, stupefaction

shock *vb* **1** to offend the moral sense of <were *shocked* by pornography>
syn scandalize
rel astonish, astound, startle, surprise; jar, jolt, shake up; insult, offend, outrage; appall, horrify; floor, knock out; disgust, nauseate, sicken
idiom stink in one's nostrils, turn one's stomach
2 to cause to undergo a physical or psychological shock <his slap *shocked* her out of hysterics>
syn jolt, startle
rel shake; jar; electrify

shocked *adj* ***syn*** see AGHAST 2
rel jarred, jolted, shaken up, ‖shook up; offended, outraged; appalled, horrified

shocker *n* **1** ***syn*** see THRILLER
2 ***syn*** see DIME NOVEL

shocking *adj* **1** ***syn*** see FEARFUL 3
rel heinous, monstrous
2 ***syn*** see OUTRAGEOUS 2
rel burning, glaring; disgraceful, shameful; unspeakable

shoddy *adj* **1** ***syn*** see CHEAP 2
rel makeshift, scambling
2 ***syn*** see SHABBY 1
3 ***syn*** see DISREPUTABLE 1

shoeless *adj* ***syn*** see BAREFOOT 1
ant shod

shoestring *adj* ***syn*** see LITTLE 3

‖**shog** *vb* ***syn*** see PUSH 2

shoo–in *n* ***syn*** see SURE THING

‖**shool** *vb* ***syn*** see SHUFFLE

shoot *vb* **1** to cause (a weapon) to drive a projectile forward <*shoot* an arrow at a target>
syn discharge, fire, loose
rel trigger; launch, project; expel; blast; poop
idiom let fly
2 ***syn*** see DESTROY 1
3 ***syn*** see DISCREDIT 2
‖**4** ***syn*** see DISCARD
5 ***syn*** see VOMIT
‖**6** ***syn*** see PASS 9
7 ***syn*** see SHOOT UP 2
8 ***syn*** see FLY 1
9 ***syn*** see RUSH 1
rel gallop, highball, hotfoot; spurt
10 ***syn*** see PHOTOGRAPH

shoot *n* ***syn*** see RAY 1

shooting *adj* ***syn*** see SHARP 8
ant stationary

shooting match *n* ***syn*** see AFFAIR 1

shoot up *vb* **1** ***syn*** see SKYROCKET
2 to take (a drug) by hypodermic needle <had been *shooting up* heroin for weeks>
syn ‖mainline, shoot

shop *n* ***syn*** see STORE 4
rel boutique

shoplift *vb* to steal displayed goods from a store <the manager caught them *shoplifting* records>
syn ||boost
rel bag, cop, ||nick, palm, pilfer, pinch, rip off, snitch, swipe

shopworn *adj* ***syn*** see TRITE
rel overused, overworked, overworn

shore *n* the land bordering a usually large body of water <watched the ships while walking along the *shore*>
syn bank, beach, coast, strand
rel coastline, shoreline, waterfront, waterside; coastland, seacoast, seashore; foreshore, littoral, shoreface, shoreside; brink, embankment, riverbank, riverside

shore (up) *vb* ***syn*** see SUPPORT 4

shore *n* ***syn*** see SUPPORT 3

short *adj* **1** having little length in space or time <a *short* visit>
syn brief
rel abbreviate, abbreviated, abridged, curtailed, decreased, diminished, lessened, shortened; curtate, decurtate
con extensive, lengthy; drawn-out, overlong; extended, prolonged, protracted
ant long
2 having small physical stature <he was the *shortest* boy present>
syn ||low, low-set, low-statured
rel chunky, dumpy, squat, squatty, stubby, thick, thickset
con gangling, gangly, lanky, rangy; elevated, high, lofty, spiring, towering
ant tall
3 not coming up to a measure or need <fuel was very *short* that year>
syn deficient, failing, inadequate, insufficient, scant, scanty, scarce, scrimpy, shy, skimpy, slender, unsufficient, wanting; *compare* MEAGER 2
rel lacking, needing; exiguous, meager, sparse
con abounding, overflowing, teeming; abundant, ample, copious, plenteous, plentiful
ant long
4 ***syn*** see BLUFF
ant expansive
5 lacking in graciousness or consideration <her manner was *short* and abrupt>
syn inconsiderate, sharp, thoughtless, unceremonious, ungracious
rel bluff, blunt, brusque, crusty, curt; short-spoken; gruff, irascible
con considerate, gracious, kindly; bland, smooth; ceremonious
6 readily breaking or crumbling <a rich *short* pastry>
syn brittle, crisp, crumbly, ||crump, crunchy, friable
rel delicate, fragile
con soggy, tough
7 ***syn*** see CONCISE
rel compact; pointed
idiom to the point
con extended, protracted, spun-out
ant lengthy, long-drawn-out

short *adv* **1** without hesitation or delay <stopped *short*>
syn abruptly, asudden, forthwith, sudden, suddenly
con hesitantly; gradually, slowly
2 ***syn*** see UNAWARES

short *n* ***syn*** see SUBSTANCE 2

short *vb* ***syn*** see SPARE 3

shortage *n* ***syn*** see FAILURE 3
rel curtailment, pinch, tightness; shortfall
ant overage

short and sweet *adj* ***syn*** see CONCISE

shortcoming *n* ***syn*** see IMPERFECTION
idiom weak point
con forte, long suit

shortcut *n* a route shorter or more direct than the one ordinarily taken <they took a *shortcut* down the back roads>
syn cutoff
rel bypass
ant detour

shorten *vb* to reduce in extent (as of length or duration) <decided to *shorten* their visit> <*shorten* a skirt for summer wear>
syn abbreviate, abridge, curtail, cut, cut back, retrench, slash
rel decrease, diminish, elide, excerpt, lessen, reduce; compress, condense, contract, shrink; bobtail, clip, dock; minimize
idiom cut short
con draw out, protract
ant elongate; lengthen; extend, prolong

shorthanded *adj* short of the necessary number of people <the office was critically *shorthanded*>
syn underhanded, undermanned, understaffed
rel short, wanting
con overmanned, overstaffed

short–lived *adj* ***syn*** see TRANSIENT
rel short-haul, short-run, short-term
con long-run, long-term
ant agelong; long-lived

shortly *adv* **1** ***syn*** see BRIEFLY
2 ***syn*** see PRESENTLY 1
rel pronto, quickly

short–range *adj* ***syn*** see TACTICAL 1
ant long-range

shortsighted *adj* ***syn*** see MYOPIC
ant farsighted, longsighted

short–spoken *adj* ***syn*** see BLUFF
ant windy

shot *n* **1** ***syn*** see FLING 1
2 ***syn*** see OPPORTUNITY
3 ***syn*** see DRAM

||**shot** *adj* ***syn*** see INTOXICATED 1

shotgun *vb* ***syn*** see FORCE 2

should *vb* ***syn*** see WANT 3

shoulder *vb* ***syn*** see PUSH 2

---

syn synonym(s) ***rel*** related word(s)
ant antonym(s) ***con*** contrasted word(s)
idiom idiomatic equivalent(s)
|| use limited; if in doubt, see a dictionary

shout *vb* **1** to utter a sudden loud cry (as to express joy or triumph or to attract attention) <the mob *shouted* for a speech>
syn cry, whoop, yell; *compare* CALL 1, SCREAM 1
rel exclaim; howl, scream, shriek; bawl, bellow, clamor, roar, vociferate
con murmur, whisper
2 ***syn*** see SCREAM 4
3 ***syn*** see CALL 1
rel bark; bray
4 ***syn*** see TREAT 3

shove *vb* **1** ***syn*** see PUSH 1
rel cram, jam; dig, jab, poke, prod
idiom push and shove
2 ***syn*** see PUSH 2
3 ***syn*** see PUSH 6

shove (off) *vb* ***syn*** see GO 2
ant pull in

shovel *vb* **1** ***syn*** see DIG 1
2 ***syn*** see DIG 2

shovel *vb* ***syn*** see SHUFFLE

show *vb* **1** to set out or place on view for customers <we're *showing* lots of long dresses this fall>
syn display, offer
rel afford, supply; exhibit; present, proffer, submit; deal (in), sell
2 to reveal outwardly or make apparent <asked a question or two to *show* his intelligence>
syn demonstrate, evidence, evince, exhibit, illustrate, manifest, mark, ostend, proclaim; *compare* LOOK 4
rel disclose, discover, divulge, lay out, reveal, unveil; present, project
con camouflage, conceal, dissemble, hide, obscure
ant disguise
3 ***syn*** see STAGE
4 to present in such a way as to invite notice, attention, and admiration <she loved to *show* her jewels to everyone>
syn brandish, display, disport, exhibit, expose, flash, flaunt, parade, show off, trot out
rel air, lay out, set out, spread; blazon, flourish, sport, vaunt
con belittle, deprecate, depreciate, minimize
5 to give an exact and usually automatic reading or indication of <the speedometer *shows* 70 MPH>
syn indicate, mark, read, record, register, say
rel point (to); ring up
6 ***syn*** see LOOK 4
rel lay out, reveal, unveil
7 ***syn*** see GUIDE
8 ***syn*** see ESTABLISH 6
rel present; plead; allege
9 ***syn*** see APPEAR 1
rel come, show up; materialize
10 ***syn*** see COME 1
idiom ‖make the scene, put in an appearance, show one's face
11 ***syn*** see TURN UP 3

show *n* ***syn*** see APPEARANCE 2
rel likeness; effect, impression
idiom outward show
2 ***syn*** see MASK 2
3 ***syn*** see DISPLAY 2
4 ***syn*** see OPPORTUNITY
5 ***syn*** see EXHIBITION 1
6 ***syn*** see EXHIBITION 2
7 ***syn*** see MOVIE
8 ***syn*** see SHOWING 1

shower *n* ***syn*** see BARRAGE
rel shatter, spatter, spray

shower *vb* ***syn*** see BATHE 1

showing *n* **1** performance in a test of skill, power, or effectiveness <he made a good *showing* in the race>
syn out, show
rel record
2 ***syn*** see APPEARANCE 2

show–me *adj* ***syn*** see INCREDULOUS

show off *vb* ***syn*** see SHOW 4
rel boast, brag, swagger

showpiece *n* a prime or outstanding example used or suitable for exhibition <a Fabergé Easter egg was the *showpiece* of the collection>
syn chef d'oeuvre, masterpiece, pièce de résistance
rel gem, jewel; prize
con claptrap, rubbish, trash, trivia, truck

showroom *n* ***syn*** see STORE 4

show up *vb* ***syn*** see EXPOSE 4
rel discredit; invalidate
2 ***syn*** see TURN UP 3
3 ***syn*** see COME 1

showy *adj* given to or marked by excessive outward display <*showy* decorations>
syn chichi, flamboyant, orchidaceous, ostentatious, peacockish, peacocky, pretentious, splashy, swank
rel sporty; flashy, garish, gaudy, jazzy, meretricious, tawdry; gorgeous, resplendent; luxurious, opulent, ornate, sumptuous; overdone, overwrought; sensational
con muted, quiet, restrained, subdued; elegant, graceful, restrained; appropriate, seemly
ant unshowy

shred *n* ***syn*** see PARTICLE

shred *vb* ***syn*** see SLIVER

shreddy *adj* ***syn*** see RAGGED

shrew *n* ***syn*** see VIRAGO
rel she-devil, spitfire

shrewd *adj* marked by clever discerning awareness and hardheaded acumen <the captain was a *shrewd* judge of character>
syn argute, astucious, astute, cagey, heady, perspicacious, sagacious, ‖savvy; *compare* SHARP 4, WISE 2, 4
rel canny, crafty, foxy, ingenious, ‖pawky, slick, ‖sly, tidy; clever, intelligent, knowing, quick-witted, smart; polite, smooth; judicious, prudent, sensible, wise; penetrating, piercing, probing; acute, keen, sharp; farsighted, foresighted
con green, naive, simple, soft; foolable, gullible, slow

shrewdness *n* ***syn*** see WIT 3
rel canniness, foxiness

shriek *vb* **1** ***syn*** see SCREAM 1

rel squawk, ‖yarm
2 *syn* see SQUEAL 2
3 *syn* see SCREAM 4

shrill *vb syn* see SCREAM 1

shrill *adj syn* see ACUTE 4

shrine *n* a structure or place considered sacred by a religious group <pilgrims going to the *shrine* at Lourdes hoping to be healed>
syn holy place, sanctorium, sanctuary, sanctum
rel reliquary; enshrinement

shrink *vb* **1** *syn* see CONTRACT 3
rel shrivel (up), wither
con amplify, expand
ant swell
2 *syn* see FAIL 3
idiom shrink (*or* dwindle) down to nothing
3 *syn* see RECOIL
rel cower, cringe, crouch, huddle, slink; draw (back), recede, retire, retreat, withdraw; boggle, demur, scruple

shrinking *adj syn* see UNDEMONSTRATIVE

shrivel *vb syn* see WITHER
rel parch; fossilize

shroud *vb* **1** *syn* see ENFOLD 1
2 *syn* see SCREEN 3

shrouded *adj syn* see ULTERIOR

shuck *n syn* see HULL

shuck *vb* to strip, break off, or remove the enclosing case or cover of <*shuck* corn>
syn hull, husk, shell; *compare* SKIN 2
rel decorticate, peel, skin, strip

shuck (off) *vb syn* see DISCARD

shudder *vb syn* see SHAKE 1
rel gyrate, shimmy

shuffle *vb* **1** *syn* see DISORDER 1
2 *syn* see EQUIVOCATE 2
3 to walk awkwardly in a sliding, dragging way without lifting the feet <an old drunk *shuffling* along in filthy bedroom slippers>
syn scuff, scuffle, shamble, ‖shool, shovel
rel drag, pad, scrape, slipper, slip-slop, slur; draggle, straggle, trail (along)
4 *syn* see STUMBLE 6

shuffle *n syn* see CLUTTER 2

shuffling *adj syn* see EVASIVE 1

shun *vb syn* see ESCAPE 2
rel decline, refuse, reject; snub; despise, disdain, scorn
idiom have nothing to do with, keep away from, stand aloof from, steer clear of, turn away from, turn one's back upon
con accept, adopt, welcome

shunning *n syn* see ESCAPE 2

shunt *vb* **1** to push or turn off to one side <*shunt* a railroad car onto a siding>
syn sidetrack, switch; *compare* TURN 6
rel change, move, shift, transfer; avert, deflect, divert, head off
idiom push aside (*or* to the side)
2 *syn* see SHUTTLE

shush *vb* **1** *syn* see SILENCE
2 *syn* see SUPPRESS 2

shut *vb syn* see CLOSE 1
rel lock, seal; batten (down)
ant open

‖**shut–eye** *n syn* see SLEEP 1

shut in *vb syn* see ENCLOSE 1
ant shut out

shut–in *adj syn* see UNSOCIABLE

shut–mouthed *adj syn* see SILENT 3
ant openmouthed

shut off *vb syn* see SCREEN 3

shut out *vb syn* see SCREEN 3

shuttle *vb* to travel back and forth frequently <*shuttled* between New York and Washington every week>
syn shunt
rel shuttlecock; alternate

shut up *vb* **1** *syn* see SILENCE
2 to cease speaking <told the boy to sit down and *shut up*>
syn dry up, dumb (up), ‖dummy (up), pipe down, ‖ring off
rel hush, quiet (down), shush, soft-pedal
idiom button (*or* seal) one's lips, keep quiet

shy *adj* **1** disinclined to obtrude oneself <*shy* in the presence of strangers>
syn backward, bashful, coy, demure, diffident, modest, rabbity, retiring, self-effacing, timid, unassertive, unassured
rel backhanded, hesitant, reluctant; conscious, self-conscious, self-distrustful, shamefaced, sheepish; introversive, introvert, introverted, inturned; circumspect, reserved; cautious, chary, suspicious, wary; apprehensive, fearful, nervous, skittish, timorous
con brash, forward; aggressive, audacious, intrusive, obtruding, pushing, pushy; blunt, crass
ant bold, obtrusive
2 *syn* see DISINCLINED
3 *syn* see SHORT 3
con excess, over, surplus

shy *vb* **1** *syn* see DEMUR
rel blench, quail, recoil, shrink
2 *syn* see ESCAPE 2

shy *n syn* see POTSHOT

Shylock *n syn* see LOAN SHARK

shyster *n syn* see PETTIFOGGER

‖**sib** *adj syn* see SYMPATHETIC 2

sibilate *vb syn* see HISS

sibylline *adj* **1** *syn* see PROPHETIC
2 *syn* see OBSCURE 3

sic *vb syn* see URGE
rel agitate, catalyze, inspirit, instigate; abet, aid, countenance, favor

sick *adj* **1** affected with illness or disease <was *sick* with pneumonia>
syn down, ill; *compare* UNWELL
rel diseased, disordered, fevered; ailing, ‖cronk, ‖crook, funny, indisposed, unwell; debilitated, sickly, unhealthy; rocky, tottering, wobbly; confined, laid up; lousy, mean, rotten
idiom ‖on the sick list, sick as a dog

---

syn synonym(s) *rel* related word(s)
ant antonym(s) *con* contrasted word(s)
idiom idiomatic equivalent(s)
‖ use limited; if in doubt, see a dictionary

con healthy, strong
ant well
2 *syn* see MORBID
3 *syn* see FED UP
idiom ‖up to here with
4 *syn* see FAULTY
5 *syn* see SICKLY 2

sick (up) *vb syn* see VOMIT

sicken *vb* 1 *syn* see UPSET 5
2 *syn* see DISGUST

sicken (with *or* of) *vb syn* see CONTRACT 1

sickening *adj syn* see OFFENSIVE

‖**sicker** *vb syn* see EXUDE

sickliness *n syn* see INFIRMITY 1

sickly *adj* 1 *syn* see UNWELL
rel ‖cranky, down
con hale, hearty; healthy, well
ant robust
2 accompanying, indicating, or suggesting sickness <a *sickly* complexion>
syn peaked, ‖peaking, peaky, sick
rel ‖pimping, puny, sickish, weak; diseased; unhealthy
con healthy, hearty
3 *syn* see UNWHOLESOME 1
4 *syn* see MORBID

sickness *n* 1 the condition of being ill <finally recovered from her *sickness*>
syn affliction, diseasedness, disorder, illness, indisposition, infirmity, unhealth; *compare* DISEASE 1, INFIRMITY 1
rel indisposedness, unhealthfulness, unhealthiness, unwellness; affection, ailment, ill
idiom ill health
con haleness, healthiness, heartiness
ant health
2 *syn* see DISEASE 1

side *n* 1 a place, space, or direction with respect to a center or a line of division <lived on the north *side* of the street> <turned to one *side*>
syn hand
rel direction, flank, sector
2 *syn* see PHASE
3 *syn* see VIEWPOINT 2
4 the attitude, position, or action of one person or group as opposed to another <could understand her *side* as well as his in the quarrel>
syn part; *compare* POSITION 1
rel attitude, disposition; posture, stance, stand; position, standpoint, viewpoint

side *vb syn* see SHEATHE

side (with) *vb syn* see SUPPORT 2

side action *n syn* see SIDE EFFECT

sideboards *n pl syn* see SIDE-WHISKERS

sideburns *n pl syn* see SIDE-WHISKERS

side effect *n* a secondary and usually adverse effect (as of a drug) <drowsiness is a common *side effect* of antihistamines>
syn side action, side reaction
rel effect; reaction, response

side–glance *n* a look or glance directed to one side <she shot an impatient *side-glance* at him>
syn side-look
rel glance; stare

sideling *adv syn* see SIDEWAYS 1

sideling *adj syn* see STEEP 1

‖**sidelings** *adv syn* see SIDEWAYS 1

sidelong *adv syn* see SIDEWAYS 1

side–look *n syn* see SIDE-GLANCE

side reaction *n syn* see SIDE EFFECT

sidereal *adj syn* see STELLAR 1

sidesplitter *n syn* see RIOT 2

sidestep *vb* 1 *syn* see EQUIVOCATE 2
2 *syn* see SKIRT 3
3 *syn* see DODGE 1

sideswipe *n syn* see POTSHOT

sidetrack *vb syn* see SHUNT 1

sideward *adv syn* see SIDEWAYS 1

sideways *adv* 1 to, toward, or at one side <slipped *sideways* on the ice>
syn crabwise, laterally, sideling, ‖sidelings, sidelong, sideward, sidewise; *compare* ASIDE 1
rel obliquely; indirectly
con straight; directly
2 *syn* see ASIDE 1

side–whiskers *n pl* the usually shaped growth of whiskers on both sides of a man's face <grew *side-whiskers* and a moustache in order to look older>
syn burnsides, dundrearies, muttonchops, sideboards, sideburns

sidewise *adv* 1 *syn* see SIDEWAYS 1
2 *syn* see ASIDE 1

sidle *vb* to move sideways or obliquely especially in an unobtrusive or furtive manner <a suspicious-looking man *sidled* up to her>
syn edge, ‖slive
rel ease, slip

siege *n* a sometimes prolonged period of disorder or stress (as of body or mind) <endured a three-week *siege* of flu>
syn bout, go; *compare* ATTACK 3
rel attack, onslaught, seizure, spell

siesta *n syn* see NAP

siesta *vb syn* see NAP

sieve *n syn* see GOSSIP 1

sieve *vb syn* see SCREEN 5

sift *vb* 1 *syn* see SCREEN 5
2 *syn* see SORT 2
3 *syn* see EXPLORE

sigh *vb* 1 to take in and let out a deep audible breath (as in weariness, grief, or relief) <flopped down in the chair and *sighed* deeply>
syn ‖sock, sough, suspire
rel breathe, respire; exhale; gasp, pant, wheeze; groan, moan; sob
idiom heave a sigh
2 to make a sound like sighing <the wind *sighed* in the branches>
syn sough
rel blow; murmur, whisper; moan; whine; whistle; howl, roar
3 *syn* see LONG

sighful *adj syn* see MELANCHOLY 2

sight *n* 1 *syn* see EYESORE
‖2 *syn* see MUCH
3 *syn* see EYE 2
4 *syn* see LOOK 1

5 ***syn*** see VIEW 4
6 ***syn*** see VIEW 5
sightless *adj* ***syn*** see BLIND 1
ant sighted
sightseer *n* ***syn*** see TOURIST
sign *n* **1** a motion, action, gesture, or word by which a command, thought, or wish is expressed <put a finger to her lips as a *sign* to keep quiet>
syn high sign, signal
rel gesticulation, gesture, motion; hint, indication, suggestion, warning
2 ***syn*** see CHARACTER 1
3 ***syn*** see EXPRESSION 3
rel symbolization; attestation, evidence, proof
4 ***syn*** see INDICATION 3
rel earmark, exponent, indicator; exhibit, show
sign *vb* **1** to affix a signature to <he refused to *sign* a confession>
syn autograph, ink, signature, subscribe
idiom put one's John Hancock on, put one's John Henry down (*or* on)
2 ***syn*** see SIGNAL
sign (over) *vb* ***syn*** see TRANSFER 4
signal *n* ***syn*** see SIGN 1
rel alarm, alert, tocsin; movement
signal *vb* to notify by or as if by a signal <*signaled* his wife to keep quiet>
syn flag, gesture, motion, sign, signalize
idiom give the high sign (to)
signal *adj* ***syn*** see NOTICEABLE
rel characteristic, distinctive, individual, peculiar, significative; eminent, famous, illustrious, renowned
signalize *vb* **1** ***syn*** see CHARACTERIZE 2
2 ***syn*** see SIGNAL
signature *vb* ***syn*** see SIGN 1
significance *n* **1** ***syn*** see MEANING 1
2 ***syn*** see IMPORTANCE
rel authority, credit, influence, merit, prestige; excellence, perfection, virtue
con indifference; triviality, unimportance, worthlessness; irrelevance
ant insignificance
significancy *n* ***syn*** see MEANING 1
significant *adj* **1** ***syn*** see EXPRESSIVE
rel cogent, compelling, convincing, sound, telling, valid; forceful, powerful; important, momentous, weighty
con meaningless, unexpressive; unimportant
ant insignificant
2 ***syn*** see IMPORTANT 1
con inconsequential, meaningless, unimportant
ant insignificant
significant *n* ***syn*** see INDICATION 3
significantly *adv* ***syn*** see WELL 8
ant insignificantly
signification *n* **1** ***syn*** see MEANING 1
rel implying, signifying; construction, implication; essence, gist, substance
‖**2** ***syn*** see IMPORTANCE
significative *adj* ***syn*** see INDICATIVE
signify *vb* **1** ***syn*** see MEAN 2
rel bear, carry, convey; bespeak, purport
2 ***syn*** see MATTER
sign on *vb* ***syn*** see ENTER 3
sign up *vb* ***syn*** see ENTER 3
silence *n* **1** absence of sound or noise <the heavy *silence* of the night>
syn noiselessness, quiet, quietness, quietude, soundlessness, still, stillness
rel calm, hush, lull
con din, uproar
ant noise
2 ***syn*** see SECRECY
3 ***syn*** see DEATH 1
silence *vb* to compel or reduce to silence <*silenced* the courtroom chatter by pounding her gavel>
syn choke (off), hush, quiet, ‖quieten, shush, shut up, still
rel dampen, deaden, dumb, lull, muffle, mute; quash, quell, squash, squelch, suppress; gag, muzzle
silent *adj* **1** ***syn*** see DUMB 1
2 characterized by absence of speech <was *silent* as he faced the altar>
syn dumb, mum, ‖mumchance, mute, speechless, wordless; *compare* DUMB 1
rel inarticulate, muted, tongue-tied, voiceless
con speaking, talking
3 showing marked restraint in speaking <a stern, *silent* man>
syn close, close-lipped, closemouthed, close-tongued, dumb, inconversable, reserved, reticent, shut-mouthed, silentious, speechless, taciturn, tight-lipped, tight-mouthed, uncommunicative, wordless
rel checked, curbed, inhibited, restrained; unconversational, unsociable; inarticulate, incoherent; mute, voiceless; mum, secretive
con articulate, fluent, glib, vocal, voluble; babblative, garrulous, loquacious, windy; blabbering, blabbery, chattering
ant talkative
4 ***syn*** see STILL 3
idiom silent as a post (*or* stone), silent as the grave (*or* tomb)
ant noisy
5 ***syn*** see UNSPOKEN 1
silentious *adj* ***syn*** see SILENT 3
silhouette *n* ***syn*** see OUTLINE
rel ‖shade, shadow
silken *adj* **1** ***syn*** see SOFT 3
2 ***syn*** see INGRATIATING
silky *adj* **1** ***syn*** see SOFT 3
2 ***syn*** see INGRATIATING
silliness *n* ***syn*** see FOOLISHNESS
rel illogicality
con logic, logicality, logicalness, sanity, sensibleness; wisdom
silly *adj* **1** ***syn*** see SIMPLE 3
rel empty, empty-headed, vacuous; irrational, unreasonable; ignorant, unintelligent, unwise
ant sensible

---

syn synonym(s) ***rel*** related word(s)
ant antonym(s) ***con*** contrasted word(s)
idiom idiomatic equivalent(s)
‖ use limited; if in doubt, see a dictionary

2 ***syn*** see GIDDY 1
rel ‖balmy, crazy, ‖dippy, irrational, off, ‖wacked-out
idiom silly as a goose
con level-headed, practical, rational, serious
ant sensible
3 ***syn*** see FOOLISH 2
rel funny, senseless

silvern *adj* ***syn*** see SILVERY

silver–tongued *adj* ***syn*** see GLIB

silvery *adj* relating to, containing, or resembling silver <repeated polishings gave the wood a *silvery* sheen>
syn argent, argentate, argenteous, argentine, silvern
rel silver; brilliant, glittering, shimmering, shining

similar *adj* ***syn*** see LIKE
rel complementary, correlative; reciprocal
idiom much of a muchness, much the same
con antithetical, antonymous, contradictory, contrary, opposite
ant dissimilar

similarity *n* ***syn*** see LIKENESS
rel approximation; collation, correlation; association, interrelation; parallel; closeness; coincidence, synonymity
con unlikeness, variance
ant dissimilarity

similarly *adv* ***syn*** see ALSO 1
idiom by the same token

simile *n* **1** ***syn*** see ANALOGY 2
2 ***syn*** see LIKENESS

similitude *n* **1** ***syn*** see LIKENESS
rel copy, image, replica
ant dissimilitude
2 ***syn*** see ANALOGY 2

simmer *vb* **1** ***syn*** see BOIL 2
2 ***syn*** see SEETHE 4

simmer down *vb* ***syn*** see COMPOSE 4
rel quiet (down), subside
idiom ‖cool it, take it easy
con boil, seethe; explode, fulminate
ant boil over

Simon Legree *n* ***syn*** see SLAVE DRIVER

simon–pure *adj* ***syn*** see AUTHENTIC 2

simp *n* ***syn*** see DUNCE

simper *vb* ***syn*** see SMIRK

simple *adj* **1** ***syn*** see NATURAL 5
rel childish, childlike; amateur, green, unexperienced; trusting; ‖square
2 ***syn*** see PLAIN 1
ant elaborate
3 actually or apparently deficient in intelligence <a poor *simple* woman easily duped>
syn asinine, brainless, ‖buffle-headed, fatuous, foolish, insensate, mindless, nitwitted, senseless, sheepheaded, silly, soft, spoony, unintelligent, unwitty, weak-headed, weak-minded, witless; *compare* RETARDED, STUPID 1
rel amateur, green, inexperienced, inexpert; credulous, gullible; childish, childlike, naive; ignorant, illiterate, uneducated, unschooled, untaught; crass, dense, dopey, dull, dumb, slow, stupid; doting, feebleminded, idiotic, retarded, simpleminded
con able, competent; alert, clever, keen; bright, intelligent, understanding
ant wise
4 ***syn*** see RETARDED
5 ***syn*** see PURE 2
rel inelaborate, stark; bald, bare, mere; fundamental, uncompounded
6 ***syn*** see EASY 1
rel incomplex, incomplicate
idiom simple as ABC
ant complex, complicated

simple *n* ***syn*** see FOOL 3

simplehearted *adj* ***syn*** see NATURAL 5

simpleminded *adj* ***syn*** see RETARDED

simplest *adj* ***syn*** see ELEMENTARY 1

simpleton *n* **1** ***syn*** see FOOL 4
2 ***syn*** see DUNCE
rel bungler, ‖clot

simplify *vb* to make simple or simpler <*simplify* a manufacturing process>
syn boil down, streamline
rel clarify, clean up, disentangle, disinvolve, straighten (out), unscramble; abridge, cut down, reduce, shorten; oversimplify
ant complicate

simply *adv* ***syn*** see JUST 3

simulacrum *n* **1** ***syn*** see IMAGE 1
2 ***syn*** see IMITATION
3 ***syn*** see APPEARANCE 2

simulate *vb* **1** ***syn*** see ASSUME 4
rel ape, copy, imitate, mimic; play-act, pose
idiom ‖make out like (*or* as if)
2 ***syn*** see RESEMBLE

simulated *adj* **1** ***syn*** see FICTITIOUS 2
ant genuine
2 ***syn*** see ARTIFICIAL 2
ant genuine

simultaneous *adj* ***syn*** see CONTEMPORARY 1
rel agreeing, coinciding, concurring

simultaneously *adv* ***syn*** see TOGETHER 1
idiom in one breath

sin *n* **1** ***syn*** see EVIL 3
2 ***syn*** see EVIL 2
3 ***syn*** see IMPERFECTION

sin *vb* ***syn*** see TRESPASS 1

since *prep* ***syn*** see AFTER 2
ant before

since *conj* ***syn*** see BECAUSE

sincere *adj* **1** genuine in feeling or expression <had a *sincere* dislike for politics>
syn heartfelt, hearty, unfeigned, wholehearted, whole-souled; *compare* GENUINE 3
rel candid, frank, frankhearted, open, plain; faithful, honest, truthful; aboveboard, forthright, pretensionless, straightforward, unpretentious; dear, devout, heartful; meant, unaffected
con affected, artificial, feigned, put-on, unmeant
ant insincere
2 ***syn*** see GENUINE 3
rel authentic, bona fide; serious; actual
idiom honest to God
ant insincere

sincereness *n* ***syn*** see GOOD FAITH
sincerity *n* ***syn*** see GOOD FAITH
rel heart; goodwill; singleness, straightforwardness
con cunning, deceit, guile; ill will
ant insincerity
sine qua non *n* ***syn*** see ESSENTIAL 2
sinew *n* **1** ***syn*** see POWER 4
2 *usu* **sinews** *pl* ***syn*** see MAINSTAY
sinewy *adj* ***syn*** see MUSCULAR 1
rel strong, sturdy, tenacious, tough
ant flabby
2 ***syn*** see MUSCULAR 2
sinful *adj* **1** ***syn*** see WRONG 1
rel base, low, vile; disgraceful, shameful; culpable, damnable
2 ***syn*** see BLAMEWORTHY
ant sinless
sing *vb* **1** to utter words in musical tones and with musical inflections and modulations <children often can *sing* before they converse>
syn chant, tune, vocalize
rel descant; carol, serenade, troll; croon, hum, lull, lullaby; cantillate, hymn, intone; singsong; roar
2 ***syn*** see TALK 6
||**3** ***syn*** see INFORM 3
single *adj* **1** being without a spouse <enjoying life as a *single* girl>
syn sole, spouseless, unmarried, unwed
rel free, unattached, unfettered; celibate; maiden, virgin
idiom footloose and fancy-free
con attached; united; wed
ant married
2 one as distinguished from two or more or all others <a *single* instance of dishonesty has been cited>
syn lone, one, only, particular, separate, sole, solitary, unique
rel individual, singular; especial, special, specific; distinguished, singled-out; distinct
con several; manifold, many, numerous
ant multiple
3 ***syn*** see FRANK
4 ***syn*** see SOLE 4
single (out) *vb* ***syn*** see CHOOSE 1
rel screen, winnow (out); accept, admit, receive
single–eyed *adj* ***syn*** see FRANK
single–hearted *adj* ***syn*** see FRANK
single–minded *adj* **1** ***syn*** see FRANK
2 ***syn*** see INFLEXIBLE 2
rel diehard; bigoted
singleness *n* **1** ***syn*** see UNIQUENESS
2 ***syn*** see UNITY 1
ant multifariousness
singly *adv* ***syn*** see APART 1
ant together
singular *adj* **1** ***syn*** see SEVERAL 1
rel discrete; certain, definite; exclusive
2 ***syn*** see EXCEPTIONAL 1
ant usual
3 ***syn*** see ONLY 2
idiom first and last, one and only, one only
4 ***syn*** see STRANGE 4
idiom passing strange
singularity *n* **1** ***syn*** see INDIVIDUALITY 4
2 ***syn*** see INDIVIDUALITY 3
3 ***syn*** see UNITY 1
ant multiplicity
singularize *vb* ***syn*** see CHARACTERIZE 2
singularness *n* ***syn*** see UNITY 1
ant multifariousness
sinister *adj* seriously threatening disaster <a *sinister* plot>
syn baleful, malefic, maleficent, malign; *compare* OMINOUS
rel fateful, ill-omened, inauspicious, ominous, portentous, unpropitious; apocalyptic, dire, doomful, ill-boding, threatening; lowering, menacing; evil, malicious
con harmless, innocent, innocuous
sink *vb* **1** to become submerged <the overloaded raft *sank* below the surface>
syn founder, go down, go under, submerge, submerse
rel capsize, overturn, tip (over); dive, plunge; scuttle; shipwreck, wreck
idiom go to Davy Jones's locker, go to the bottom, sink like a rock
con come up, rise
ant float
2 ***syn*** see SET 12
3 ***syn*** see DETERIORATE 1
ant rise
4 ***syn*** see STOOP 2
5 ***syn*** see LOWER 3
6 ***syn*** see THRUST 2
7 ***syn*** see HUMBLE
ant uplift
sink *n* **1** a place marked by a staggering amount of corruption and filth <that area of the city was a *sink* of vice and crime>
syn Augean stable, cesspit, cesspool, den, pandemonium, Sodom, sty
rel hellhole; fleshpot
idiom Alsatian den, den of iniquity, sink of corruption
2 ***syn*** see DEPRESSION 2
sinkage *n* ***syn*** see DEPRESSION 2
sinkhole *n* ***syn*** see DEPRESSION 2
sinuous *adj* ***syn*** see WINDING
rel twisted; snake-shaped
idiom twisting and turning
sip *vb* ***syn*** see DRINK 1
siphon *vb* **1** ***syn*** see CONDUCT 4
2 ***syn*** see DRAIN 1
sire *n* ***syn*** see FATHER 2
sire *vb* **1** ***syn*** see FATHER 1
2 ***syn*** see GENERATE 1
siren *n* an enticingly attractive woman who lures men into dangerous or compromising situations <a slinky *siren* of the silent screen era>

syn synonym(s) ***rel*** related word(s)
ant antonym(s) ***con*** contrasted word(s)
idiom idiomatic equivalent(s)
|| use limited; if in doubt, see a dictionary

THESAURUS

syn femme fatale, Lorelei, seductress, temptress
rel charmer, vamp
siren *adj* ***syn*** see ATTRACTIVE 1
rel sirenic
siren song *n* ***syn*** see LURE 2
sissified *adj* ***syn*** see EFFEMINATE
sissy *n* ***syn*** see WEAKLING
sissy *adj* ***syn*** see EFFEMINATE
sissy–pants (*or* **sissy-britches**) *n pl but sing or pl in constr* ***syn*** see WEAKLING
sit *vb* **1** to rest on the buttocks or haunches <she was *sitting* in a chair>
syn ‖set
rel perch, rest; ‖plop (down), seat, sit down; squat
con arise, get up, rise, stand, stand up
2 ***syn*** see CONVENE 1
3 ***syn*** see POSE 3
4 ***syn*** see SET 11
5 ***syn*** see SEAT
rel ensconce, install, settle
sit down *vb* ***syn*** see ALIGHT
site *n* **1** ***syn*** see PLACE 1
2 ***syn*** see SCENE 3
3 a place where an archaeological excavation is made <a burial *site*>
syn dig
4 ***syn*** see HABITAT
sited *adj* ***syn*** see SITUATED
‖**sitfast** *adj* ***syn*** see IMMOVABLE 1
sitting duck *n* ***syn*** see TARGET 1
rel sitter
situate *adj* ***syn*** see SITUATED
situated *adj* having a site, situation, or location <a town *situated* on a hill>
syn located, placed, positioned, set, sited, situate
situation *n* **1** ***syn*** see PLACE 1
2 ***syn*** see PREGNANCY
3 ***syn*** see JOB 2
4 ***syn*** see STATUS 1
5 ***syn*** see STATE 1
rel bargain
sizable *adj* **1** ***syn*** see CONSIDERABLE 2
2 ***syn*** see BIG 1
rel man-sized; giant-sized
sizableness *n* ***syn*** see SIZE 2
size *n* **1** the amount of measurable space or area occupied by or comprising a thing <the *size* of the card is 3″x 5″>
syn admeasurement, dimension(s), dimensionality, extent, magnitude, measure, proportion
rel area; body, bulk, mass, volume; height; extension, length; amplitude, breadth, expanse, spread, stretch, width; measurement
2 considerable amount, proportion, volume, character, or importance <left an estate of some *size*>
syn amplitude, bigness, greatness, largeness, magnitude, sizableness
rel dimension, extent
con littleness, smallness; minuteness, tininess
sizz *vb* ***syn*** see HISS
sizzle *vb* **1** ***syn*** see SEAR 2
2 ***syn*** see HISS
sizzling *adj* ***syn*** see HOT 1
‖**skag** *n* ***syn*** see CIGARETTE
skate *n* ***syn*** see MAN 3
sked *n* ***syn*** see PROGRAM 1
sked *vb* ***syn*** see SCHEDULE 1
skedaddle *vb* **1** ***syn*** see RUN 2
rel ‖split; cut out
2 ***syn*** see GET OUT 1
idiom lift them up and set them down, ‖take off like a bat out of hell
‖**skeet** *vb* ***syn*** see HURRY 2
skeezicks *n* ***syn*** see SCAMP
skein *n* ***syn*** see MAZE 1
skeletal *adj* ***syn*** see EMACIATED
skeleton *vb* ***syn*** see SKETCH
skeletonize *vb* ***syn*** see SKETCH
‖**sken** *vb* ***syn*** see SQUINT
skeptic *n* a doubting or incredulous person <people of long experience are often *skeptics*>
syn doubter, doubting Thomas, headshaker, Pyrrhonian, Pyrrhonist, unbeliever, zetetic
rel questioner; agnostic; pessimist; scoffer; cynic, misanthrope; disbeliever
con accepter; apostle, disciple, follower; devotee, diehard
ant believer
skeptical *adj* ***syn*** see INCREDULOUS
rel freethinking; dissenting; suspicious; cynical
idiom ‖from Missouri
ant believing
skeptically *adv* ***syn*** see ASKANCE 2
idiom with a grain of salt, with a note of skepticism, with a skeptical eye
con trustingly
ant gullibly
skepticism *n* ***syn*** see UNCERTAINTY
rel qualm, qualmishness
idiom question in one's mind, shadow of doubt
con belief, trust
ant gullibility
sketch *n* ***syn*** see COMPENDIUM 1
sketch *vb* to present succinctly <let's *sketch* our plan of action>
syn adumbrate, block (out), chalk (out), characterize, draft, outline, rough (out), skeleton, skeletonize
rel depict; diagram, diagrammatize; blueprint, delineate, line; draw, plot, trace; design, develop; detail, lay out, map (out)
sketchy *adj* ***syn*** see SUPERFICIAL 2
skew *vb* **1** ***syn*** see SLANT 3
2 ***syn*** see SWERVE 1
rel skid, slide, slip
skewer *vb* ***syn*** see IMPALE
skid *vb* **1** ***syn*** see SLIDE 3
rel sheer, skew, slue, veer
idiom go into a skid
2 ***syn*** see PLUMMET
skiddoo *vb* ***syn*** see GET OUT 1
idiom go (*or* take) off like a shot
skid road *n* ***syn*** see SKID ROW
skid row *n* a city street or district notorious for cheap bars, flophouses, and homeless derelicts <boozy old men wandering the *skid row*>

syn bowery, skid road
skill *n* **1** *syn* see ABILITY 2
2 *syn* see ART 1
3 *syn* see ADDRESS 1
rel ease, skillfulness
skilled *adj* **1** *syn* see PROFICIENT
con skill-less, unproficient
ant unskilled, unskillful
2 *syn* see EXPERIENCED
rel prepared, primed, trained
con unfit, unqualified, untrained
ant unskilled
skillet *n* *syn* see FRYING PAN
skillful *adj* **1** *syn* see PROFICIENT
rel learned, versant, well-versed
ant unskillful
2 accomplished or done with proficiency or skill <his answer was a very *skillful* evasion>
syn adroit, clever, good, pretty, ‖skilly, wicked, workmanlike, workmanly; *compare* CLEVER 4, PROFICIENT
rel expert, masterful
con clumsy; unskilled
ant inept, unskillful
‖**skilly** *adj* *syn* see SKILLFUL 2
skim *vb* **1** *syn* see BRUSH
2 *syn* see GLANCE 1
3 *syn* see FLY 1
skim (through) *vb* *syn* see BROWSE
con examine, inspect, scrutinize
skimble–skamble *n* *syn* see GIBBERISH 1
‖**skimmelton** *n* *syn* see SHIVAREE
skimp *adj* *syn* see MEAGER 2
skimp *vb* **1** *syn* see SCRIMP
2 *syn* see SPARE 3
skimpy *adj* **1** *syn* see MEAGER 2
2 *syn* see SHORT 3
skin *n* **1** *syn* see HIDE
2 *syn* see HULL
3 a usually thin casing forming the outside surface of a structure or thing <aircraft *skins* made of aluminum alloys>
syn sheath, sheathing
rel facing, siding; case, casing, cover, jacket; shell
4 *syn* see MISER
5 *syn* see SWINDLER
‖**6** *syn* see DOLLAR
skin *vb* **1** *syn* see SHEATHE
2 to remove the surface, skin, or thin outer covering of <*skin* a Bermuda onion>
syn decorticate, excorticate, peel, scale, strip; *compare* SHUCK
rel cut off, pull off; pare, shave (off), trim; hull, husk, shuck; bark, rind; excoriate, flay, gall
3 *syn* see OVERCHARGE 1
4 *syn* see CRITICIZE
5 *syn* see HURRY 2
‖**skinch** *vb* **1** *syn* see SCRIMP
2 *syn* see SPARE 3
skinflint *n* *syn* see MISER
‖**skinhead** *n* *syn* see BALDHEAD
skinny *adj* *syn* see LEAN
rel twiggy, weedy; emaciated; skeletal
idiom mere skin and bones, skinny as a rail
ant fleshy
skip *vb* **1** to move or proceed with a light bounding step <children *skipping* home from school>
syn hop, lope, skitter, spring, trip
rel caper, cavort, curvet, frisk, gambol; bounce, hippety-hop; jump; leap; bound
con hobble, shamble, shuffle; hitch, limp, stagger, totter
2 *syn* see GLANCE 1
3 *syn* see RUN 2
idiom ‖split the scene
skip *n* *syn* see OMISSION
skirmish *n* **1** *syn* see CLASH 2
rel assault, attack; ambush
con pitched battle
2 *syn* see ENCOUNTER
skirr *vb* **1** *syn* see RUN 2
2 *syn* see FLY 1
skirt *n* **1** *syn* see BORDER 1
rel skirting
‖**2** *syn* see WOMAN 1
skirt *vb* **1** *syn* see BORDER 1
2 to make a detour or circuit (as around a congested area) <*skirted* the city to avoid traffic>
syn bypass, circumnavigate, circumvent, detour
idiom go around
3 to avoid (as a topic or question) because of difficulty, complexity, controversy, or danger <*skirted* all touchy issues>
syn burke, bypass, circumvent, ‖polly-fox, sidestep; *compare* EQUIVOCATE 2, ESCAPE 2
rel avoid, dodge, duck, evade, hedge; elude, escape; ignore, skip
idiom get around
con confront, face, meet, take on
‖**skite** *n* *syn* see PRANK
skitter *vb* *syn* see SKIP 1
skittery *adj* *syn* see EXCITABLE
skittish *adj* **1** *syn* see GIDDY 1
rel irresponsible, undependable, unreliable
2 *syn* see EXCITABLE
rel restive; nervous
skive *vb* *syn* see CUT 6
skiver *vb* *syn* see IMPALE
skookum *adj* *syn* see EXCELLENT
skookum–house *n* *syn* see JAIL
skulk *vb* *syn* see SNEAK
skunk *n* *syn* see SNOT 1
skunk *vb* *syn* see WHIP 2
sky *n* the expanse of space surrounding the earth <blue *sky* crisscrossed with jet trails>
syn empyrean, firmament, heaven(s), welkin
rel azure; celestial sphere
idiom the wild blue yonder
sky–high *adv* *syn* see APART 3
sky–high *adj* *syn* see EXCESSIVE 1
skylarking *n* **1** *syn* see HORSEPLAY
idiom ‖making whoopee

---

2 ***syn*** see REVELRY 2

sky pilot *n* ***syn*** see CLERGYMAN
rel chaplain; padre

skyrocket *vb* to rise abruptly and rapidly (as to an unprecedented level or amount) <when the election was over taxes and prices *skyrocketed*>
syn rocket, shoot up, soar
rel climb, rise; upsoar, upspring
con slide; fall; drop
ant crash, plummet

skyscraping *adj* ***syn*** see LOFTY 6

slab *n* ***syn*** see BAR 1
rel chunk, lump

‖**slab** *n* ***syn*** see SLIME

slabber *vb* ***syn*** see DROOL 2

slack *adj* **1** ***syn*** see NEGLIGENT
rel dilatory, lackadaisical, lethargic, sluggish; faineant, indolent, lazy, slothful; inert, stagnant
con assiduous, busy, diligent, industrious, sedulous
2 ***syn*** see LOOSE 1
rel feeble, infirm, soft, unsteady, weak; inactive, inert, passive, supine; laggard, leisurely, slow
con tensed, tightened; constant, equable, even, steady, uniform; firm, hard
ant taut, tight
3 ***syn*** see SLOW 3

slack *vb* ***syn*** see LOOSE 5
idiom ‖cut some slack, make slack
ant tighten

slack *n* ***syn*** see SLOWDOWN 1

slacken *vb* **1** ***syn*** see DELAY 1
idiom keep back
ant quicken
2 ***syn*** see ABATE 4
3 ***syn*** see LOOSE 5
ant tighten

slackening *n* ***syn*** see SLOWDOWN 1

slacker *n* one who shirks work, responsibility, or an obligation <didn't want any *slackers* in her office>
syn goldbrick, shirker, slinker, ‖spiv
rel idler, loafer; slugabed, sluggard

slack–spined *adj* ***syn*** see WEAK 4

slake *vb* ***syn*** see QUENCH 4

slam *n* **1** ***syn*** see BLOW 1
2 ***syn*** see BANG 2
3 ***syn*** see ANIMADVERSION
rel fling, swipe; crack, potshot; rap, slap; dig, jab

slam *vb* **1** to strike with extreme force or violence <*slammed* the ball out of the park><the car *slammed* into the fence>
syn belt, blast, clobber, slug, smash, wallop; *compare* STRIKE 2
rel bang, bat, hit, knock, slap, swat, thwack; cudgel, hammer, mace; batter, beat, pound
2 ***syn*** see LAMBASTE 3

‖**slam** *adv* ***syn*** see WELL 3

slammer *n* ***syn*** see JAIL

slander *n* ***syn*** see DETRACTION
rel black wash, muckraking, mud-slinging, roorback, scandal-mongering

slander *vb* ***syn*** see MALIGN
rel assail, attack; damage, hurt, injure; blackwash, muckrake; belie, strumpet
idiom dish the dirt, run a smear campaign, sling the mud
ant panegyrize

slanderous *adj* ***syn*** see LIBELOUS
rel blackwashing, muckraking, scandalmongering
ant panegyrical

slang *n* ***syn*** see DIALECT 2
rel slanginess, slanguage

slangism *n* ***syn*** see BARBARISM

slant *adv* ***syn*** see ASIDE 1

slant *vb* **1** to set or be set at an angle <*slanted* the ladder against the wall>
syn cant, heel, incline, lean, list, recline, slope, tilt, tip
rel bank, decline, descend; bend, deviate, diverge, splay, swerve, veer
2 to direct (written or spoken material) to the interests of a particular audience or group <a magazine *slanted* to farm families>
syn aim, angle
rel direct, orient, point, train; concentrate, focus; spoon-feed; bias, skew, warp
3 to orient (material) from objective presentation so as to favor a particular bias <accused the media of *slanting* the news against the president>
syn angle, bias, skew; *compare* PREJUDICE 2
rel influence, prejudice; color, distort, twist, warp
ant objectify, objectivize

slant *n* **1** ***syn*** see SLOPE
2 ***syn*** see VIEWPOINT 2
rel predilection, predisposition, prejudice

slanted *adj* ***syn*** see DIAGONAL

slanting *adj* ***syn*** see DIAGONAL

slantingly *adv* ***syn*** see ASIDE 1

slantingways *adv* **1** ***syn*** see ASIDE 1
2 ***syn*** see DIAGONALLY

slantly *adv* ***syn*** see ASIDE 1

slantways *adv* **1** ***syn*** see ASIDE 1
2 ***syn*** see DIAGONALLY

slantwise *adv* **1** ***syn*** see ASIDE 1
2 ***syn*** see DIAGONALLY

slap *n* **1** ***syn*** see CUFF
2 ***syn*** see AFFRONT
3 ***syn*** see FLING 1

slap *vb* **1** to strike quickly and sharply with the hand <*slapped* the hysterical girl>
syn blip, box, buffet, cuff, smack, spank, ‖wherret; *compare* STRIKE 2
rel ‖biff, ding, hit, sock, swat, whack; ‖wap, wham; bash
2 ***syn*** see LAMBASTE 3

‖**slap** *adv* ***syn*** see WELL 3

slap around *vb* ***syn*** see MANHANDLE

slapdash *adj* **1** ***syn*** see RANDOM
2 ***syn*** see SLIPSHOD 3

‖**slap–up** *adj* ***syn*** see EXCELLENT

slash *vb* **1** ***syn*** see CUT 1
2 ***syn*** see HACK
3 ***syn*** see LAMBASTE 3

idiom ‖light into
4 *syn* see REDUCE 2
5 *syn* see SHORTEN

slate *n syn* see TICKET 3

‖**slate** *vb syn* see LAMBASTE 3

slather *n, often* **slathers** *pl syn* see SCAD

slattern *n* **1** an untidy slovenly woman <two blowsy *slatterns* gossiping at the bar>
syn dowd, dowdy, drab, draggle-tail, ‖malkin, slut, ‖streel, traipse
rel frump; slob, ‖slommack, sloven; crone, gammer, hag, witch
2 *syn* see WANTON
rel prostitute, whore

slattern *adj syn* see SLATTERNLY

slatternly *adj* being habitually untidy and very dirty especially in dress or appearance <a filthy, *slatternly* old woman>
syn blowsy, dowdy, draggletailed, frowsy, slattern, sordid; *compare* SLOVENLY 1
rel careless, disordered, neglected, poky; bedraggled, disheveled, draggled, draggly, messy, mussy, slipshod, sloppy, slovenly, unkempt, untidy; dirty, filthy, foul, grimy, squalid
con clean, fresh, neat, tidy, trim; smart; immaculate, spotless
ant bandbox

slaughter *n syn* see MASSACRE
rel slaughtery; annihilation, destruction

slaughter *vb* **1** to kill (animals) for food <*slaughtered* a steer for the winter>
syn butcher, slay
rel stick
2 to kill (a person) in an especially bloody or barbarous manner <Jack the Ripper *slaughtered* his victims with a knife>
syn butcher, slay
rel kill, murder, ‖total, ‖waste; maim, mangle, mutilate, torture
3 to kill (people) in large numbers <millions *slaughtered* in death camps>
syn annihilate, decimate, exterminate, massacre, wipe (out)

‖**slaunchways** *adv* **1** *syn* see DIAGONALLY
2 *syn* see ASIDE 1

slave *n* **1** a person held in servitude or bondage <plantations worked by *slaves*>
syn bondman, bondslave, bondsman, chattel, mancipium
rel help, menial, retainer, servant; helot, serf, thrall, vassal
con freedman, freedwoman; ‖deditician
ant freeman
2 one who works at a hard, monotonous, usually menial task <*slaves* working all night for minimum wage>
syn ‖dogsbody, dray horse, drudge, galley slave, peon, slavey, toiler, workhorse
rel ‖coolie

slave *vb syn* see DRUDGE
idiom work like a slave

slave driver *n* a person in authority who exacts extreme effort from his subordinates <the chief proofreader was a real *slave driver*>
syn rawhider, Simon Legree, taskmaster
rel martinet
idiom a hard taskmaster

slaver *vb* **1** *syn* see DROOL 2
2 *syn* see FAWN

slaver *n syn* see SALIVA

slavery *n* **1** *syn* see WORK 2
2 *syn* see BONDAGE
idiom involuntary servitude, the yoke (*or* chains) of slavery

slavey *n* **1** *syn* see SLAVE 2
2 *syn* see HACK 2

slavish *adj* **1** *syn* see HARD 6
2 *syn* see SUBSERVIENT 2
rel spineless, subdued, tame; miserable, wretched
ant independent
3 copying obsequiously something superior <the painting was a *slavish* copy of an old master>
syn apish, emulative, imitative
rel uninspired; unoriginal
con fresh, new, novel, original; fanciful, imaginative, ingenious, inspired; extravagant, high-flown

slay *vb* **1** *syn* see KILL 1
2 *syn* see MURDER 1
3 *syn* see SLAUGHTER 2
4 *syn* see SLAUGHTER 1

slayer *n syn* see MURDERER

sleazy *adj* **1** *syn* see LIMP 1
rel slight, tenuous, thin; gossamery
2 *syn* see CHEAP 2
3 *syn* see SHABBY 1

sleek *vb syn* see POLISH 2

sleek *adj* having a very smooth or lustrous surface or texture <the car's *sleek* new paint job>
syn glassy, glossy, polished, ‖sleekit, sleeky, smarmy
rel smooth; glistening, lustrous

‖**sleekit** *adj syn* see SLEEK

sleeky *adj syn* see SLEEK

sleep *n* **1** the natural periodic suspension of consciousness during which the powers of the body are restored <needed eight hours of *sleep* to function efficiently>
syn ‖doss, ‖shut-eye, slumber; *compare* DOZE, NAP
rel repose, rest; slumberland
idiom land of Nod, the arms of Morpheus
con wakefulness
2 *syn* see LETHARGY 1
3 *syn* see DEATH 1

sleep *vb* to rest in a state of sleep <*slept* for over eight hours>
syn ‖doss, slumber; *compare* DOZE, NAP
rel relax, repose, rest; oversleep, sleep in
idiom be in the land of Nod, be sunk in sleep, pound one's ear, rest in the arms of Morpheus, sleep like a top (*or* log)

---

syn synonym(s) *rel* related word(s)
ant antonym(s) *con* contrasted word(s)
idiom idiomatic equivalent(s)
‖ use limited; if in doubt, see a dictionary

con arouse, awaken, wake (up)
sleeplessness *n* ***syn*** see INSOMNIA
sleepy *adj* **1** having an inclination for or affected by sleep <was *sleepy* after the long day>
syn dozy, drowsy, nodding, ||peepy, ||sloomy, slumberous, slumbery, snoozy, somnolent, soporific
rel heavy, heavy-eyed, lethargic, sluggish, torpid; dazed, dopey, listless, oscitant, yawning; asleep, sleeping, slumbering; nepenthean, poppied; comatose, ||out
con awake, conscious; restless, sleepless, unsleeping; alert, wide-awake
ant wakeful
2 ***syn*** see INACTIVE
3 ***syn*** see SOPORIFIC 1
||**sleer** *vb* ***syn*** see SNEER 1
sleight *n* **1** ***syn*** see ADDRESS 1
2 ***syn*** see TRICK 1
||**sleighty** *adj* ***syn*** see CLEVER 4
slender *adj* **1** ***syn*** see THIN 1
rel slenderish, slimmish; lithe, svelte, trim
idiom slender as a reed
2 ***syn*** see SHORT 3
3 ***syn*** see REMOTE 4
slenderize *vb* ***syn*** see REDUCE 5
sleuth *n* ***syn*** see DETECTIVE
slew *n* ***syn*** see SCAD
slewed *adj* ***syn*** see INTOXICATED 1
slice *n* ***syn*** see SHARE 1
rel segment
idiom a slice of the pie (*or* melon)
slice *vb* **1** ***syn*** see CUT 1
2 ***syn*** see CUT 5
slick *vb* **1** ***syn*** see POLISH 2
2 ***syn*** see DRESS UP 1
3 ***syn*** see SLIDE 1
slick *adj* **1** having a glassy surface that often offers insecure footing <a floor *slick* with wax>
syn greasy, lubricious, ||sliddery, ||slipper, slippery, slippy, slithery
rel oily; ||slape, smooth; soapy
idiom slick as a greased pig
con coarse, gritty, rough, uneven
2 ***syn*** see FULSOME
rel glossy; slippery
3 ***syn*** see WISE 4
slicker *n* ***syn*** see SWINDLER
||**slidder** *vb* **1** ***syn*** see SLIDE 3
2 ***syn*** see SLITHER 2
||**sliddery** *adj* ***syn*** see SLICK 1
slide *vb* **1** to go or progress with a smooth continuous motion <goldfish *slid* across the pool>
syn glide, glissade, slick, slip, slither
rel flow, stream
2 ***syn*** see SLIP 6
3 to fall or nearly fall because of loss of balance or footing <stumbled and *slid* on the ice>
syn skid, ||slidder, slip, ||slur
idiom take a slide (*or* a skid)
4 to shift or be shifted out of place or away from one's grasp <the packages *slid* from her arms>
syn slip
rel shift; move; fall, spill, tumble
5 ***syn*** see CREEP 1
6 to take a natural course <preferred to let the matter *slide* for a while>
syn coast, drift
rel glide
idiom run its course
7 ***syn*** see STEAL 3
8 ***syn*** see SNEAK
slide *n* ***syn*** see DECLINE 3
slight *adj* **1** ***syn*** see THIN 1
rel slightish, ||slighty; smallish; pint-sized
2 ***syn*** see DELICATE 5
rel gossamery, sleazy
3 ***syn*** see REMOTE 4
slight *vb* ***syn*** see NEGLECT
rel skip; contemn, despise; flout, scoff
slightest *adj* ***syn*** see FIRST 4
rel ||fat, negligible
slighting *adj* ***syn*** see DEROGATORY
slim *adj* **1** ***syn*** see THIN 1
rel lissome, lithe, lithesome, svelte
ant chubby
2 ***syn*** see CLEVER 4
3 ***syn*** see REMOTE 4
slim (down) *vb* ***syn*** see REDUCE 5
slime *n* a viscous and usually dirty or offensive substance <a layer of *slime* formed in the bottom of the pool>
syn muck, ||slab, slum
rel ooze, ||sleech, sludge; scum
sling *vb* **1** ***syn*** see THROW 1
rel catapult; sock
2 ***syn*** see STRIDE 1
sling *vb* ***syn*** see HANG 1
slink *vb* ***syn*** see SNEAK
slink *n* ***syn*** see SNEAK
slinker *n* ***syn*** see SLACKER
slip *vb* **1** ***syn*** see SLIDE 1
2 ***syn*** see SNEAK
3 ***syn*** see STEAL 3
4 ***syn*** see SLIDE 4
5 ***syn*** see SLIDE 3
6 to decline gradually from a standard or accustomed level <sales in some lines *slipped*>
syn drop (off), fall (off *or* away), sag, slide, slump
rel erode, soften; decline, go down, sink; dip, drop; nose-dive, plummet, topple; crash
con better, gain, improve, rally, rebound; ascend, climb, rise; skyrocket, soar
7 ***syn*** see SHAKE 5
8 ***syn*** see SHED 2
slip (on) *vb* ***syn*** see DON 1
ant slip (off)
slip *n* **1** ***syn*** see WHARF
2 ***syn*** see ESCAPE 1
3 ***syn*** see ERROR 2
4 ***syn*** see DECLINE 3
||**slipper** *adj* ***syn*** see SLICK 1
slippery *adj* **1** ***syn*** see SLICK 1
2 ***syn*** see MUTABLE 2
slippy *adj* ***syn*** see SLICK 1
slipshod *adj* **1** ***syn*** see SHABBY 1
2 ***syn*** see SLOVENLY 1

3 marked by indifference to exactness, precision, and accuracy <a *slipshod* piece of research>
syn botchy, careless, messy, slapdash, sloppy, slovenly, unthorough, untidy
rel neglected, negligent; haphazard, slaphappy, unmeticulous; botched-up, fouled-up, messed-up, ||screwed-up; faulty, imperfect, inaccurate, inexact
con fastidious, meticulous, neat; accurate, exact, precise; methodical, orderly, systematic; thorough

slipslop *n syn* see NONSENSE 2

slipup *n syn* see ERROR 2

slit *vb syn* see CUT 1

slither *vb* 1 *syn* see SLIDE 1
rel ||sluther
2 to walk or move in a sinuous way <the trout *slithered* among the smooth rocks>
syn ||slidder, snake, undulate
rel creep, glide, sidle, steal; lurk, prowl, slink, sneak

slithery *adj syn* see SLICK 1

||**slive** *vb syn* see SIDLE

sliver *vb* to cut into very thin slices <*slivered* cheese>
syn shave, shred
rel carve, haggle, slice
con chop, dice, mince; comminute, powder, pulverize; crush, mash

slobber *vb syn* see DROOL 2

slobbering *adj syn* see EFFUSIVE

slobbery *adj* 1 *syn* see EFFUSIVE
2 *syn* see SLOVENLY 1

slog *vb* 1 *syn* see STRIKE 2
2 *syn* see PLOD 1
3 *syn* see DRUDGE

slogan *n syn* see CATCHWORD
rel expression, idiom, locution

slogging *n syn* see WORK 2

||**slommacky** *adj syn* see SLOVENLY 1

||**sloom** *n syn* see DOZE

||**sloom** *vb syn* see DOZE

||**sloomy** *adj syn* see SLEEPY 1

slop *n syn* see PAP 2

slop *vb* 1 *syn* see SPILL 1
2 *syn* see SPLASH
3 *syn* see GULP
4 *syn* see PLOD 1

slope *vb syn* see SLANT 1

slope *n* a natural or artificial inclined surface <the steep *slope* of the hill>
syn grade, gradient, inclination, incline, lean, leaning, slant, tilt
rel acclivity, ascent, rise; declivity, descent; deflection, deviation, obliqueness, obliquity; pitch, swag, sway, tip; bend, skew
con champaign, flat, flatland, mesa, plain(s), plateau, tableland
ant level

sloped *adj syn* see INCLINED 3

slopeways *adv syn* see ASIDE 1

sloping *adj syn* see INCLINED 3

slopped *adj syn* see INTOXICATED 1

sloppy *adj* 1 *syn* see SLIPSHOD 3
rel amateurish; mediocre; awkward, clumsy; poor
ant exact, precise
2 *syn* see SLOVENLY 1
3 *syn* see EFFUSIVE
rel soft; oversentimental
4 *syn* see INTOXICATED 1

slosh *n syn* see BLOW 1

slosh *vb* 1 *of a liquid* to move with a gentle lapping motion or sound <heard water *sloshing* in the bottom of the boat>
syn bubble, burble, gurgle, lap, swash, wash
rel babble; ripple; dash, plash, splash, tumble; bespatter, spatter; churn, whirl; gush, rush; roar
2 *syn* see SPLASH
3 *syn* see GULP
||4 *syn* see STRIKE 2

sloth *n* 1 disinclination to action or labor <a hot summer day is likely to induce *sloth* in all of us>
syn idleness, indolence, laze, laziness, slothfulness, slouch, sluggishness
rel ergophobia, faineancy, idling, lazing, loafing; apathy, heaviness, languidness, languor, lassitude, lethargy, listlessness, torpidity; shiftlessness
con assiduity, assiduousness, busyness, diligence, sedulity, sedulousness
ant industriousness, industry
2 sluggishness and apathy in the practice of virtue <the deadly sin of *sloth*>
syn acedia
rel heedlessness, inattention, inattentiveness
con assiduity

slothful *adj syn* see LAZY
con assiduous, busy, diligent, sedulous
ant industrious

slothfulness *n syn* see SLOTH 1

slouch *n* 1 *syn* see OAF 2
2 *syn* see SLUGGARD
3 *syn* see SLOTH 1

slouch *vb* to assume, have, or move with an awkwardly drooping posture, carriage, or gait <three drunks *slouched* across the room>
syn droop, loll, ||lollop, lop, slump, trollop
rel loaf, lounge, saunter, shamble, shuffle; bend, lean, stoop; sag, wilt
con erect, straighten (up); sit up, stand up

slough *n* 1 *syn* see SWAMP
2 *syn* see INLET

||**slough** *n syn* see HULL

slough *vb* 1 *syn* see SHED 2
2 *syn* see DISCARD
idiom ||get shut (*or* shed) of

slough over *vb syn* see NEGLECT

sloven *adj syn* see SLOVENLY 1

slovenly *adj* 1 negligent of or marked by lack of neatness and order especially in appearance or dress <*slovenly* attire>

syn synonym(s) *rel* related word(s)
ant antonym(s) *con* contrasted word(s)
idiom idiomatic equivalent(s)
|| use limited; if in doubt, see a dictionary

syn careless, disheveled, ill-kempt, messy, mussy, raunchy, slipshod, slobbery, ‖slommacky, sloppy, sloven, uncombed, unfastidious, unkempt, unneat, untidy; *compare* SLATTERNLY
rel down-at-heel, shabby, sleazy, sluttish, slutty; blowsy, dowdy, frowsy, frumpish
con fastidious, neat, tidy, trim; combed, groomed, well-groomed; immaculate
ant neat
2 ***syn*** see SLIPSHOD 3

slow *adj* **1** ***syn*** see RETARDED
rel limited; ‖dunch
2 moving, flowing, or proceeding at less than the usual, desirable, or required speed <a *slow* advance toward mutual understanding>
syn deliberate, dilatory, laggard, leisurely, unhasty, unhurried
rel measured, slowish, steady; unhasting, unhurrying; slow-footed, slow-going, slow-paced; plodding, poky, rusty; dragging, flagging, halting, lagging, straggling; dawdling, delaying, postponing, procrastinating; leaden, sluggish; crawling, snaillike, snail-paced, ultra-slow
idiom as slow as a swamp turtle, as slow as molasses in January
con blitz, lightning, quick, rapid, swift; fast-going, fast-moving, fast-paced, rapid-paced
ant fast
3 marked by reduced economic activity (as in sales or patronage) <trading was *slow* on the commodity exchange today>
syn down, off, slack, sluggish
rel moderate; reduced; low; inactive, stagnant
con active; up; heavy

slow (up *or* down) *vb* ***syn*** see DELAY 1
rel moderate, qualify, temper; abate, decrease, lessen, reduce
ant speed

slow coach *n* ***syn*** see LAGGARD

slowdown *n* **1** a slowing or gradual decrease in activity <a *slowdown* in car sales this quarter>
syn slack, slackening, slow-up
rel decline, downtrend, downturn; drop, drop-off, falloff; inactivity, stagnation; freeze
con increase, rise, upswing, upturn; acceleration, quickening
ant speedup
2 a deliberate slowing down by workers in the rate and quantity of production <air traffic snarled by a controllers' *slowdown*>
syn ‖ca' canny
rel action; protest; slow-up; sit-down; strike, walkout; stoppage
ant speedup

slowgoing *adj* ***syn*** see LAZY

slowpoke *n* ***syn*** see LAGGARD

slow–up *n* ***syn*** see SLOWDOWN 1

slow–witted *adj* ***syn*** see RETARDED
ant quick-witted

‖**slubberdegullion** *n* ***syn*** see VILLAIN 1

slue *vb* ***syn*** see SWERVE 1

slug *n* ***syn*** see SLUGGARD
rel slacker, sloven

slug *n* ***syn*** see DRAM

slug *vb* ***syn*** see SLAM 1

slugabed *n* ***syn*** see SLUGGARD

sluggard *n* an habitually lazy, shiftless, and inactive person <a *sluggard* who wanted to sleep all day>
syn bum, dolittle, do-nothing, faineant, idler, lazybones, loafer, slouch, slug, slugabed
rel lie-abed, sleepyhead; dawdler, laggard, slow coach, slowpoke; goldbrick, shirker
idiom ‖his idleship, ‖Weary Willie
con go-getter, hustler, live wire
ant dynamo

sluggish *adj* **1** ***syn*** see LETHARGIC
rel dragging, draggy, leaden, lumpish; costive, stiff; apathetic, stupefied
con go-getting, hustling, vigorous; expeditious
ant brisk
2 ***syn*** see SLOW 3

sluggishness *n* ***syn*** see SLOTH 1

sluice *vb* ***syn*** see POUR 2
rel flush, wash; douse, drench, soak

slum *n* a densely populated usually urban area marked by run-down housing, poverty, and social disorganization <a *slum* full of vagrants, junkies, pimps, and pushers>
syn stew
rel slumdom, slumland; tobacco road; tenderloin; skid row; ghetto; hive, kennel, rookery, warren
idiom desolation row, the wrong side of the tracks

slum *n* ***syn*** see SLIME

slumber *vb* **1** ***syn*** see DOZE
2 ***syn*** see SLEEP

slumber *n* **1** ***syn*** see SLEEP 1
2 ***syn*** see DOZE
3 ***syn*** see LETHARGY 1

slumberous *adj* **1** ***syn*** see SLEEPY 1
2 ***syn*** see SOPORIFIC 1
3 ***syn*** see LETHARGIC

slumbery *adj* ***syn*** see SLEEPY 1

slump *vb* **1** ***syn*** see FALL 2
rel droop, flag, sag
idiom come down like a rock (*or* a ton of bricks)
2 ***syn*** see SLOUCH
rel cave in, collapse
3 ***syn*** see SLIP 6

slump *n* **1** ***syn*** see DECLINE 3
2 ***syn*** see DEPRESSION 3

slup *vb* ***syn*** see SLURP

‖**slur** *vb* ***syn*** see SLIDE 3

slur *vb* ***syn*** see MALIGN

slur (over) *vb* ***syn*** see NEGLECT

slur *n* **1** ***syn*** see ANIMADVERSION
2 ***syn*** see STIGMA

slurp *vb* to eat or drink noisily <*slurping* soup with a large spoon>
syn slup
rel guzzle, lap (up), slosh, swill; suck; wolf (down); smack
con nibble, pick (at); sip

slushy *adj* ***syn*** see SENTIMENTAL

slut *n* **1** ***syn*** see SLATTERN 1
2 ***syn*** see WANTON

3 ***syn*** see MINX

sly *adj* **1** ***syn*** see CLEVER 4
rel smart; cagey; masterful
2 attaining or seeking to attain one's ends by devious means <a *sly* way of upping sales>
syn artful, astute, crafty, cunning, deep, ‖downy, foxy, guileful, insidious, subdolous, subtle, tricky, vulpine, wily; *compare* UNDERHAND
rel disingenuous, unfrank; calculating, designing, Machiavellian, scheming; cagey, devious, shady, shifty, ‖slanter, slick, slippery, smooth; clandestine, covert, furtive, stealthy; underhand, underhanded, unscrupulous; predatory; crooked, dishonest
idiom crazy like a fox, cunning as a fox (*or* serpent), sly as a fox
con candid, forthright, frank, honest, open, sincere, straightforward

sly *vb* ***syn*** see SNEAK

slyboots *n pl but sing in constr* ***syn*** see SCAMP

slyness *n* ***syn*** see CUNNING 2

smack *n* **1** ***syn*** see TASTE 3
2 ***syn*** see HINT 2

smack *vb* to have a trace, vestige, or suggestion of something <that plan *smacks* of radicalism>
syn savor, smell
rel resemble, suggest; reek, stink

smack *vb* **1** ***syn*** see KISS 1
idiom ‖plant a juicy kiss on
2 ***syn*** see SLAP 1

smack *n* **1** ***syn*** see CUFF
2 ***syn*** see BLOW 1

‖**smack–dab** *adv* ***syn*** see JUST 1

‖**smacker** *n* ***syn*** see DOLLAR

‖**smackeroo** *n* ***syn*** see DOLLAR

small *adj* **1** being the opposite of large <a *small* white house>
syn bantam, little, monkey, petite, smallish; *compare* TINY
rel cramped, limited, narrow, two-by-four; puny, undersized; paltry, petty, piddling, trivial
con big, great; considerable, sizable; enormous, huge, immense, vast
ant large
2 ***syn*** see MINOR 2
3 ***syn*** see LITTLE 2
4 ***syn*** see LITTLE 3
5 ***syn*** see PETTY 2
6 ***syn*** see REMOTE 4

small beer *n* ***syn*** see TRIVIA

small–beer *adj* ***syn*** see LITTLE 3

small change *n* ***syn*** see TRIVIA

smallest *adj* ***syn*** see FIRST 4

small–fry *adj* ***syn*** see MINOR 2

smallish *adj* ***syn*** see SMALL 1
ant largish

small–minded *adj* ***syn*** see ILLIBERAL
ant large-minded

small potato *n, usu* **small potatoes** *pl but sing or pl in constr* ***syn*** see TRIVIA

small talk *n* light or casual conversation <had to make *small talk* at the cocktail party>
syn bavardage, by-talk, chitchat, chitter-chatter, trifling
rel badinage, banter, repartee; babble, babbling, bibble-babble, chatter, prattle, prattling, prittle-prattle

small–time *adj* ***syn*** see MINOR 2
ant big-time

small–town *adj* ***syn*** see INSULAR

‖**smarm** *vb* ***syn*** see SMEAR 1

smarmy *adj* **1** ***syn*** see SLEEK
2 ***syn*** see FULSOME

smart *vb* ***syn*** see HURT 4

smart *vb* to cause or produce a sharp stinging and usually localized pain <gave him a slap that was hard enough to *smart*>
syn bite, burn, ‖stang, sting; *compare* HURT 4
rel prick; tingle; hurt

smart *adj* **1** ***syn*** see INTELLIGENT 2
ant stupid
2 ***syn*** see WISE 4
idiom knowing the score, on the ball
ant dull, dumb
3 ***syn*** see CLEVER 5
rel pert, saucy
4 ***syn*** see WISE 5
5 ***syn*** see STYLISH
rel dapper, ‖dinky, spruce
ant dowdy
‖**6** ***syn*** see CONSIDERABLE 2

smart aleck *n* an obnoxiously conceited and self-assertive person with pretensions to smartness or cleverness <was heckled by a *smart aleck* in the back row>
syn know-it-all, smarty, smarty-pants, wiseacre, wisecracker, wise guy, wisehead, wisenheimer
rel blowhard, boaster, braggadocio, braggart, gasbag, windbag; exhibitionist, grandstander, show-off
idiom hot-air artist

smart–alecky *adj* ***syn*** see WISE 5

smarten (up) *vb* ***syn*** see DRESS UP 1

smart set *n* ultrafashionable often international society <the *smart set* that suns in Cannes and skis in St. Moritz>
syn beautiful people, jet set, ton
rel aristocracy, aristoi, blue bloods, bon ton, elite, Four Hundred, society, upper crust, who's who

smarty *n* ***syn*** see SMART ALECK

smarty–pants *n pl but sing in constr* ***syn*** see SMART ALECK

smash *vb* **1** ***syn*** see SHATTER 1
2 ***syn*** see SLAM 1
3 ***syn*** see DESTROY 1

smash *n* **1** ***syn*** see BLOW 1
2 ***syn*** see BANG 2
3 ***syn*** see IMPACT 1
4 ***syn*** see CRASH 3
5 ***syn*** see COLLAPSE 2
6 a striking success <the new musical was a box-office *smash*>

---

syn synonym(s) ***rel*** related word(s)
ant antonym(s) ***con*** contrasted word(s)
idiom idiomatic equivalent(s)
‖ use limited; if in doubt, see a dictionary

syn bang, bell ringer, hit, succès fou, ten-strike, wow
rel sensation; knockout
idiom howling (*or* roaring) success, smash hit
con disaster, dud, failure
ant flop

‖**smash** *n* ***syn*** see MONEY

‖**smashed** *adj* ***syn*** see INTOXICATED 1

smashup *n* **1** ***syn*** see COLLAPSE 2
2 ***syn*** see CRASH 3

smatch *n* **1** ***syn*** see HINT 2
2 ***syn*** see FEW

smatter *vb* ‖**1** ***syn*** see SHATTER 1
2 ***syn*** see CHAT 1

smatter *n* ***syn*** see FEW

smatterer *n* ***syn*** see AMATEUR 2

smattering *n* ***syn*** see FEW

smaze *n* ***syn*** see HAZE 1

smear *vb* **1** to overspread with something unctuous, viscous, or adhesive <*smeared* the crack with wet concrete>
syn bedaub, besmear, dab, daub, plaster, ‖smarm, smudge
rel rub; coat, cover, overlay, overspread, spread; smirch, soil
2 ***syn*** see TAINT 1
3 ***syn*** see MALIGN
idiom use smear tactics (on *or* against)
4 ***syn*** see WHIP 2
rel foil, frustrate; repulse
idiom mop up the floor (*or* earth) with

smell *vb* **1** to perceive by means of the olfactory organs <*smelled* a dead skunk>
syn nose, scent, sniff, ‖snift, snuff
rel detect, perceive, sense; whiff; ‖snaffle, snuffle
idiom get a whiff of
2 ***syn*** see SMACK
3 to have or emit an offensive odor <the canal *smells* today>
syn funk, reek, stench, stink
idiom offend the nostrils, smell (*or* stink) to high heaven

smell *n* **1** a quality that makes a thing perceptible to the olfactory sense <the *smell* of a ham cooking>
syn aroma, odor, scent
rel bouquet, fragrance, incense, perfume, redolence, spice; flavor, savor, stench, stink
2 ***syn*** see HINT 2

smeller *n* ***syn*** see NOSE 1

‖**smellful** *adj* ***syn*** see MALODOROUS 1
ant odorless, smell-less

smellfungus *n* ***syn*** see CRITIC

smell–less *adj* ***syn*** see ODORLESS
ant ‖smellful, smelly

smelly *adj* ***syn*** see MALODOROUS 1
con odorless, scentless, smell-less; fragrant, fresh, sweet

smidgen *n* ***syn*** see PARTICLE

smile *vb* to express amusement, satisfaction, or pleasure by brightening one's eyes and curving the corners of one's mouth upward <*smiled* as she greeted him>
syn beam, grin
rel simper, smirk
idiom break into a smile, crack a smile
con grimace; glare, glower, lower, scowl
ant frown

smirch *vb* ***syn*** see SOIL 2
rel discolor; smear

smirk *vb* to smile in an affected manner <*smirking* children imitating their teacher>
syn simper, ‖smirkle; *compare* SNEER 1
rel grin, smile; fleer, leer, sneer

‖**smirkle** *vb* ***syn*** see SMIRK

smitch *n* ***syn*** see PARTICLE

smite *vb* **1** ***syn*** see STRIKE 2
rel bat, belt, clobber; dash
idiom smite a blow
2 ***syn*** see AFFLICT

smithereens *n pl* very small particles or fragments <a house blown to *smithereens* by a bomb>
syn ‖shivereens, smithers
rel fragments, particles, pieces

smithers *n pl* ***syn*** see SMITHEREENS

smitten *adj* ***syn*** see ENAMORED 1
idiom bitten by the love bug

smoke *n* ***syn*** see CIGARETTE

smoke *vb* ***syn*** see HURRY 2

smolder *vb* ***syn*** see SEETHE 4
rel burst, erupt, explode; fulminate

smooch *vb* ***syn*** see SOIL 2

smooch *vb* ***syn*** see KISS 1
idiom ‖plant a smooch on

‖**smoodge** *vb* ***syn*** see KISS 1

smooth *adj* **1** ***syn*** see LEVEL
rel glossy, sleek, slick; rippleless, unbroken, unwrinkled
con harsh, rugged, scabrous, uneven
ant rough
2 ***syn*** see HAIRLESS
3 ***syn*** see EASY 9
4 ***syn*** see EASY 1
rel smooth-running
idiom smooth and easy
ant labored
5 ***syn*** see SUAVE
rel courteous, courtly, polite; smooth-faced, smooth-tongued
con bluff, blunt, brusque, crusty, curt, gruff, harsh
6 ***syn*** see GENTLE 1
rel agreeable, soothing

smooth *vb* **1** ***syn*** see EVEN 1
con corrugate; roughen; wrinkle
ant unsmooth
2 ***syn*** see POLISH 2

smooth *adv* ***syn*** see EVENLY 3

smoothen *vb* ***syn*** see EVEN 1

smoothly *adv* **1** ***syn*** see EVENLY 3
con unevenly, ununiformly
ant roughly
2 ***syn*** see EASILY 1
ant unsmoothly

smooth–spoken *adj* ***syn*** see VOCAL 3
ant rough-spoken

smorgasbord *n* ***syn*** see MISCELLANY 1

smother *vb* **1** ***syn*** see SUFFOCATE

2 ***syn*** see COMPOSE 4
rel hush up, muffle; cork; quash, quell, squelch; quench
3 ***syn*** see WHIP 2
smothering *adj* ***syn*** see STIFLING 1
smothering *n* ***syn*** see REPRESSION 1
smothery *adj* ***syn*** see STIFLING 1
‖**smouch** *vb* ***syn*** see KISS 1
smouch *vb* ***syn*** see STEAL 1
smudge *vb* **1** ***syn*** see SOIL 2
rel smear; blotch, splotch
2 ***syn*** see SMEAR 1
3 ***syn*** see TAINT 1
‖**smudgy** *adj* ***syn*** see STIFLING 1
smug *adj* ***syn*** see COMPLACENT
idiom pleased with oneself
smug *vb* ***syn*** see DRESS UP 1
smuggle *vb* to import or export secretly and in violation of the law <*smuggling* weapons into the country>
syn bootleg, contraband, run
idiom run contraband
smut *vb* **1** ***syn*** see STAIN 1
2 ***syn*** see TAINT 1
smutch *vb* **1** ***syn*** see SOIL 2
2 ***syn*** see TAINT 1
smutty *adj* ***syn*** see OBSCENE 2
snack *n* food served or taken informally and usually in small amounts and typically under other circumstances than a regular meal <a milk-and-cookie *snack* after school>
syn ‖bait, ‖bever, bite, ‖chack, morsel, mug-up, nosh, ‖piece, tapa
rel collation, refreshment, tea
idiom bite to eat
snack bar (*or* **counter**) *n* ***syn*** see EATING HOUSE
‖**snaffle** *vb* ***syn*** see STEAL 1
‖**snafu** *vb* ***syn*** see CONFUSE 5
snag *n* ***syn*** see OBSTACLE
rel brake, clog, curb, drag; hold-up
idiom ‖snags and sawyers
snake *n* ***syn*** see SNOT 1
snake *vb* ‖**1** ***syn*** see STEAL 1
2 ***syn*** see CREEP 1
3 ***syn*** see SLITHER 2
‖4 ***syn*** see SNEAK
snaky *adj* ***syn*** see WINDING
snap *vb* **1** to speak in a curt biting tone <*snapped* at his subordinates for inefficiency>
syn bark, snarl
rel growl, grumble, grunt, snort; roar, yell
idiom bite one's head off, snap off one's head (*or* nose)
2 ***syn*** see JERK
rel clutch, grab, grasp, seize, snaffle, snatch
snap *n* **1** something easily managed or accomplished <that exam was a *snap*>
syn breeze, child's play, cinch, duck soup, kid stuff, picnic, pie, ‖pipe, pushover, setup, ‖snip, soft touch
rel sinecure
idiom a simple twist of the wrist, simplicity itself, soft snap
con difficulty, headache, problem, trouble; bother, inconvenience, pain
ant chore
2 ***syn*** see PARTICLE
3 ***syn*** see MAN 3
4 ***syn*** see VIGOR 2
snap back *vb* ***syn*** see RECOVER 3
‖**snapper** *vb* ***syn*** see STUMBLE 3
snapping *adv* ***syn*** see VERY 1
snappish *adj* ***syn*** see IRRITABLE
rel curt, short, ungracious; crabbed, morose, surly
snappy *adj* **1** ***syn*** see IRRITABLE
2 ***syn*** see FAST 3
3 ***syn*** see PUNGENT
rel animated, lively, vivacious; prompt, quick, ready
4 ***syn*** see STYLISH
snare *n* ***syn*** see LURE 2
rel chicane, chicanery, deception; ensnarement, entrapment
snare *vb* ***syn*** see CATCH 3
rel seduce, tempt; involve; embrangle, enmesh, ensnarl, trammel
‖**snark** *vb* ***syn*** see SNORE
snarl *n* **1** ***syn*** see CONFUSION 3
rel entanglement, tangle; complexity, complication, intricacy, intricateness; labyrinth, maze; mishmash, swarm; jam
idiom tangled skein, wheels within wheels
2 ***syn*** see MAZE 1
snarl *vb* **1** ***syn*** see ENTANGLE 1
2 ***syn*** see COMPLICATE
snarl *vb* ***syn*** see SNAP 1
snarl up *vb* ***syn*** see CONFUSE 5
snatch *vb* **1** ***syn*** see SEIZE 2
rel jerk, wrench, yank; nip (up), whip (up)
‖2 ***syn*** see KIDNAP
sneak *vb* to move or go stealthily and furtively <*sneaked* into the garage and stole the car>
syn creep, glide, gumshoe, lurk, ‖meech, pussyfoot, shirk, skulk, slide, slink, slip, sly, ‖snake, ‖snook, steal; *compare* STEAL 3
rel crawl, slither, worm, prowl
idiom go on (little) cat's feet, move under cover
con barge, strut, swagger; clump, stamp, stump; stride; march, parade
sneak *n* a person who behaves in a stealthy, furtive, or shifty manner <found out that he was a liar, a cheat, and a *sneak*>
syn slink, sneaker, sneaksby, weasel
rel blackguard, knave, scoundrel; cur, heel, louse, reptile, skunk, snake; toad
idiom Jerry Sneak
sneak *adj* ***syn*** see SECRET 1
sneaker *n* ***syn*** see SNEAK
sneaking *adj* ***syn*** see UNDERHAND
ant forthright
sneaksby *n* ***syn*** see SNEAK
sneaky *adj* ***syn*** see UNDERHAND
‖**sneap** *vb* ***syn*** see REPROVE

---

syn synonym(s) ***rel*** related word(s)
ant antonym(s) ***con*** contrasted word(s)
idiom idiomatic equivalent(s)
‖ use limited; if in doubt, see a dictionary

sneer *vb* **1** to smile with attendant facial contortions expressing scorn or contempt <*sneered* haughtily at the beggar>
syn fleer, leer, ‖sleer; *compare* SMIRK
rel grin, smile
idiom curl one's lip, make a scornful (*or* mocking) face
2 *syn* see SCOFF
rel belittle, detract, disparage, underrate
idiom cock a snook at, give the Bronx cheer to, give the raspberry, sneeze at, thumb one's nose at

‖**sneezer** *n syn* see NOSE 1

snicker *vb syn* see LAUGH
idiom have a case of the snickers

snide *adj* **1** *syn* see COUNTERFEIT
2 *syn* see CROOKED 2

sniff *vb syn* see SMELL 1

‖**snift** *vb syn* see SMELL 1
rel ‖snifter

snifter *n syn* see DRAM

‖**sniggle** *vb syn* see LAUGH

snip *n* **1** *syn* see MINX
‖**2** *syn* see SNAP 1

snippety *adj syn* see BLUFF
rel impolite, insolent, rude

snippy *adj syn* see BLUFF

snip–snap *n syn* see BANTER

snit *n* a state of agitation or excited irritation especially over a trivial matter <was in a *snit* because the bus was one minute late>
syn fume, stew, sweat, swivet, tizzy
rel huff, pique; conniption, fit, frenzy, seizure, taking; dither, flap, panic, ‖swither

snitch *vb* **1** *syn* see INFORM 3
2 *syn* see STEAL 1

snitch *n* ‖**1** *syn* see NOSE 1
2 *syn* see INFORMER

snob *n* one inclined to rebuff or ignore people or things that he regards as inferior (as in culture or social status) <appeals to real lovers of music rather than musical *snobs*>
syn high-hat, snoot, snot
rel name-dropper, snobling; bootlicker, hanger-on, lickspittle, sycophant, toady

snob *vb syn* see CUT 7

snobbish *adj* of, relating to, or characteristic of a snob <a *snobbish* group of jet-set sophisticates>
syn ‖dicty, high-hat, potty, snobby, snooty
rel aloof, remote; high-flown, pretentious, snotty, supercilious; haughty, hoity-toity, pompous, ritzy; condescending, patronizing; insecure, uncertain, unconfident, unself-confident, unsure
con certain, confident, secure, self-confident

snobby *adj syn* see SNOBBISH
rel snubbing, snubby

‖**snook** *vb* **1** *syn* see SNOOP
2 *syn* see SNEAK

snoop *vb* to look, inquire, or search impertinently or intrusively <he knew he had no right to *snoop* into her private life>
syn busybody, mouse, nose, ‖piroot, poke, pry, ‖snook
rel peek, peep, peer, stare; interfere, intrude, meddle, mess
idiom stick (*or* poke) one's nose into

snoop *n syn* see BUSYBODY

snoopy *adj syn* see CURIOUS 2

snoot *n* **1** *syn* see NOSE 1
2 *syn* see SNOB

snooty *adj syn* see SNOBBISH

snooze *vb syn* see NAP

snooze *n syn* see NAP

‖**snoozle** *vb syn* see DOZE

snoozy *adj syn* see SLEEPY 1

snore *vb* to breathe during sleep with a rough hoarse noise due to vibration of the soft palate <driven to distraction by her sister's *snoring*>
syn ‖snark
rel wheeze; snuffle; snort, ‖snotter
idiom ‖drive pigs to market, ‖saw logs (*or* wood)

snort *n syn* see DRAM

snorter *n syn* see DRAM

snot *n* **1** an utterly contemptible person <a despicable *snot* whom everyone shunned>
syn ‖bugger, cur, dog, louse, puke, rat, scum, ‖scumbag, skunk, snake, sod, stinkard, stinkaroo, stinker, toad, wretch; *compare* VILLAIN 1
rel ‖creep, ‖crumb, lowlife; knave, rogue, scoundrel, ‖skite; pig, reptile
2 *syn* see SNOB

snout *n syn* see NOSE 1

snowball *vb syn* see INCREASE 2

snub *vb syn* see CUT 7
rel high-hat, ‖ritz, swank; put down
idiom look coldly upon, turn a cold shoulder (on *or* upon)

‖**snudge** *vb syn* see SNUGGLE

‖**snuff** *n syn* see OFFENSE 2

snuff *vb syn* see SMELL 1

‖**snuff** (out) *vb syn* see DIE 1

snug *adj* **1** *syn* see NEAT 2
2 *syn* see COMFORTABLE 2
idiom snug as a bug in a rug
‖**3** *syn* see PROSPEROUS 3

snug *vb syn* see SNUGGLE

snuggle *vb* to assume or be in a warm comfortable position usually near another person or thing <a baby *snuggling* close to his mother>
syn burrow, ‖croodle, cuddle, nestle, nuzzle, ‖snudge, snug, ‖snuzzle
rel curl up; huddle; spoon
idiom snuggle up like a bug in a rug
con flinch, recoil, shrink

‖**snuzzle** *vb syn* see SNUGGLE

‖**sny** *vb syn* see TEEM

so *adv* **1** *syn* see ALSO 1
2 *syn* see THUS 1
3 *syn* see VERY 1
4 *syn* see THEREFORE

so *conj* with the purpose that <repeated it aloud *so* there'd be no mistake>
syn so as, so that
idiom in order that, to the end that, with the intent that

soak *vb* **1** to permeate or be permeated with or as if with water <*soak* a sponge with water> <rain *soaked* her to the skin>

syn drench, ||drouk, impregnate, insteep, saturate, seethe, sodden, ||sog, sop, souse, steep, waterlog; *compare* WET
rel dip, immerse, submerge; draw, infuse; infiltrate, penetrate, permeate, pervade; water-soak; drown
2 *syn* see WET
3 *syn* see ENGAGE 4
4 *syn* see OVERCHARGE 1
5 *syn* see DRINK 3
idiom ||soak it up like a sponge
soak *n* **1** *syn* see DRUNKARD
2 *syn* see BINGE 1
soaked *adj syn* see WET 1
soaker *n syn* see DRUNKARD
soaking *adj syn* see WET 1
idiom soaking wet
so–and–so *adj syn* see DAMNED 2
soapbox *vb syn* see ORATE
soapy *adj syn* see FULSOME
soar *vb* **1** *syn* see RISE 4
rel climb; shoot
2 *syn* see SKYROCKET
ant plummet
soaring *adj syn* see LOFTY 6
idiom high as the sky
so as *conj syn* see SO
sob *vb syn* see CRY 2
sobby *adj syn* see SENTIMENTAL
sober *adj* **1** *syn* see ABSTEMIOUS
rel controlled, restrained; self-possessed
con indulgent, overindulgent; uncontrolled, unrestrained; immoderate, intemperate; excessive; profligate
2 *syn* see SERIOUS 1
rel decorous, proper; calm, placid, serene, tranquil
con flippant, light, light-minded; unstable, volatile
ant gay
3 having or exhibiting self-control and avoiding extremes of behavior <his bearing was *sober,* his comments judicious>
syn moderate, temperate, unimpassioned; *compare* ABSTEMIOUS
rel rational, reasonable; calm, collected, composed, cool, imperturbable; constrained, disciplined, inhibited, reserved, restrained, self-controlled, self-disciplined; abstaining, forbearing, refraining; abnegating, eschewing, forgoing
con irrational, unreasonable; emotional, hotheaded, impassioned, overemotional, passionate; intemperate, uncontained, uncontrolled; excited; drunk, intoxicated; abandoned
ant unsober
4 *syn* see SUBDUED 2
5 *syn* see REALISTIC
rel sober-eyed, sober-minded
sobersided *adj syn* see SERIOUS 1
sobful *adj syn* see SENTIMENTAL
sobriety *n syn* see TEMPERANCE 2
rel gravity, sedateness, seriousness, soberness
con excitement; drunkenness, intoxication; abandonment
ant insobriety
sobriquet *n syn* see NICKNAME
so–called *adj* **1** *syn* see NOMINAL
2 *syn* see ALLEGED
sociable *adj* **1** *syn* see SOCIAL 2
ant nonsocial
2 *syn* see GRACIOUS 1
rel companionable, convivial; gregarious; close, familiar, intimate; good-natured
ant unsociable
3 *syn* see SOCIAL 1
ant unsociable, unsocial
social *adj* **1** conducive to, marked by, or passed in pleasant companionship with one's friends or associates <a relaxed, *social* evening>
syn companionable, convivial, sociable
rel amusing, entertaining, pleasant, pleasurable; cordial, friendly, genial, gracious, hospitable
con unfriendly, unhospitable; eremitic, solitary
ant unsociable, unsocial
2 inclined by nature to association or community life with others of the same species <man is a *social* animal>
syn gregarious, sociable
rel social-minded; intersocial
con eremitic, solitary, unsociable; antisocial, asocial, unsocial; remote, withdrawn
ant nonsocial
social evil *n, used with* the *syn* see PROSTITUTION
socialize *vb* to participate actively in a social group <*socializes* with her colleagues>
syn mingle
rel associate, mix
society *n* **1** *syn* see COMPANY 1
2 *syn* see ASSOCIATION 2
3 an organized aggregate of persons who are responsible for a prevailing social order <rules made in the interests of *society* rather than for the chosen few>
syn community, people, public
rel masses, populace
idiom people in general, society at large, the general public
4 *syn* see ARISTOCRACY
idiom high society (*or* life)
sock *vb syn* see STRIKE 2
sock *n* **1** *syn* see BLOW 1
2 *syn* see CUFF
||sock *vb syn* see SIGH 1
sod *n syn* see SNOT 1
sodality *n syn* see ASSOCIATION 2
sodden *adj syn* see WET 1
sodden *vb syn* see SOAK 1
Sodom *n syn* see SINK 1
rel Babylon
so far *adv syn* see HITHERTO 1
idiom up till now
soft *adj* **1** *syn* see GENTLE 1
rel moderate, temperate

---

syn synonym(s) *rel* related word(s)
ant antonym(s) *con* contrasted word(s)
idiom idiomatic equivalent(s)
|| use limited; if in doubt, see a dictionary

2 ***syn*** see SUBDUED 2
ant loud
3 smooth or delicate in texture, grain, or fiber <the dog's fur was *soft*>
syn cottony, satiny, silken, silky, velvety
rel smooth; sleek
con coarse, rough
ant harsh
4 ***syn*** see COMFORTABLE 2
ant rough
5 ***syn*** see SIMPLE 3
idiom ‖soft in the head
6 giving way easily to physical touch or pressure <a *soft cheese*>
syn mushy, pappy, pulpous, pulpy, quaggy, spongy, squashy, squelchy, squishy, squushy, yielding
rel softish; compressible, malleable, pliable, pliant, workable; doughy, formless; flabby, fleshy
idiom soft as butter
con firm, solid; resistant, rigid, tough, unyielding; nail-hard, rock-hard
ant hard

soft (on) *adj* ***syn*** see ENAMORED 1

soft-boiled *adj* ***syn*** see SENTIMENTAL
ant hard-boiled

soften *vb* ***syn*** see DEPRECIATE 1

softened *adj* ***syn*** see SUBDUED 2

softhead *n* ***syn*** see FOOL 4

softhearted *adj* ***syn*** see TENDER
ant hardhearted

soft-pedal *vb* to reduce the emphasis, importance, or effect of something (as an issue) <tried to *soft-pedal* military spending>
syn de-emphasize, play (down)
rel tone (down), tune (down); cushion, dampen, muffle, subdue; hush (up), silence, suppress; conceal, disguise
con emphasize, play (up); focus (on), spotlight

soft-shell *adj* ***syn*** see MODERATE 4

soft soap *n* ***syn*** see FLATTERY
rel ‖snow job

soft-soap *vb* ***syn*** see COAX

soft spot *n* **1** ***syn*** see APPETITE 3
2 a vulnerable point <the major *soft spot* in the West's armor>
syn Achilles' heel
rel vulnerability, vulnerableness, weakness; chink, loophole
idiom heel of Achilles, weak link (*or* point), weak link in the chain
con impregnability, invulnerability; invincibility

soft touch *n* **1** someone who can be easily talked into giving help (as a loan) <recognized him as a *soft touch* when she was broke>
syn easy mark
rel softy; dupe, fool, pushover; sucker; mark, sitting duck, target
con cynic, doubting Thomas, hard case, skeptic
2 ***syn*** see SNAP 1

‖sog *vb* ***syn*** see SOAK 1

‖sog *vb* ***syn*** see DOZE

soggy *adj* ***syn*** see HUMID

soi-disant *adj* ***syn*** see SELF-STYLED

soil *vb* **1** ***syn*** see CONTAMINATE 1
ant purify
2 to make or become unclean <a shirt *soiled* with grease and grime>
syn begrime, besoil, dirty, foul, grime, muck, ‖mucky, muddy, murk, smirch, smooch, smudge, smutch, tarnish; *compare* STAIN 1
rel ‖becoom, ‖benasty, ‖nasty; bedaub, daub, smear; drabble, draggle; mess, spoil
con brighten, cleanse, freshen, renew; purify
ant clean
3 ***syn*** see TAINT 1

soil *n* **1** ***syn*** see EARTH 2
2 ***syn*** see COUNTRY

soily *adj* ***syn*** see DIRTY 1

soiree *n* ***syn*** see EVENING 3

sojourn *n* a temporary but sometimes extended stay <a summer *sojourn* in Nice>
syn stopover, tarriance, visit
rel stay, stop; layover

sojourn *vb* ***syn*** see VISIT 3
rel linger; abide

Sol *n* ***syn*** see SUN 1

solace *vb* ***syn*** see COMFORT
idiom offer (*or* give) solace to, wipe one's tears away

soldier *n* a person engaged in military service <*soldiers* fighting and dying in futile wars>
syn fighter, fighting man, GI, man-at-arms, serviceman, swad, ‖swaddy, ‖sweat, warrior
rel dogface, doughboy, ‖doughfoot, grunt, infantryman; trooper; guerrilla, partisan; condottiere, free companion, free lance, mercenary, soldier of fortune

soldierly *adj* ***syn*** see BRAVE 1
rel martial; aggressive, combative, militant, pugnacious, warlike
con unsoldierly

sole *n* ***syn*** see BOTTOM 1

sole *adj* **1** ***syn*** see SINGLE 1
2 ***syn*** see SINGLE 2
3 ***syn*** see ONLY 2
idiom one and only
4 belonging, granted, or attributed to the one person or group <*sole* rights of publication>
syn exclusive, single, unshared
con multiple; shared

solecism *n* **1** ***syn*** see ANACHRONISM 2
2 ***syn*** see BARBARISM
3 ***syn*** see FAUX PAS

solely *adv* ***syn*** see ONLY 1

solemn *adj* **1** ***syn*** see CEREMONIAL
rel full, plenary; august, grand, impressive, magnificent, majestic, overwhelming; ostentatious
2 ***syn*** see SERIOUS 1
idiom as solemn as an owl, grave as an undertaker

solemnize *vb* ***syn*** see KEEP 2
rel dignify, honor, solemnify, venerate

solicit *vb* **1** to seek (as advertising, orders, or votes) especially on a large scale <*solicited* contributions all over the district>

syn canvass, drum, drum up
rel ask, request; beg, beseech, implore; claim, demand, exact
2 *syn* see ASK 2
rel apply, go, refer, resort, turn
3 *syn* see DEMAND 1

solicitous *adj syn* see EAGER

solicitude *n* 1 *syn* see CARE 2
rel attention, heed, watchfulness; presentiment; compunction, qualm, scruple
con carelessness, heedlessness, indifference, neglect, negligence
ant unmindfulness
2 *syn* see CONSIDERATION 3

solid *adj* 1 *syn* see FIRM 2
rel compacted, concentrated, consolidated
con spongy; disintegrated; fluid, liquid
2 *syn* see STABLE 4
3 *syn* see VALID
rel firm, hard
ant insubstantial
4 *syn* see UNANIMOUS

solid *adv syn* see HARD 9

solidarism *n syn* see SOLIDARITY

solidarity *n* a feeling of unity (as in interests, standards, and responsibilities) that binds members of a group together <*solidarity* among union members is essential in negotiations>
syn cohesion, solidarism, togetherness
rel cohesiveness; oneness, singleness, undividedness; integrity, solidity, union, unity; esprit, esprit de corps; firmness, fixity
con separation; discord, dissension, schism; confusion, disorder, disorganization
ant division

solidify *vb syn* see HARDEN 1
rel compress, contract
idiom make (*or* become) hard as a rock
con soften; disintegrate, dissolve
ant liquefy

solidly *adv* 1 *syn* see HARD 9
2 *syn* see HARD 7

solitariness *n syn* see SOLITUDE

solitary *adj* 1 *syn* see ANTISOCIAL
ant gregarious
2 *syn* see UNSOCIABLE
3 *syn* see DERELICT 1
4 *syn* see LONE 1
rel companionless, unaccompanied, unattended
ant accompanied
5 *syn* see SINGLE 2
6 *syn* see ONLY 2

solitary *n syn* see RECLUSE

solitude *n* the state of one who is alone <a very social person who could not bear *solitude*>
syn aloneness, isolation, loneness, solitariness; *compare* SECLUSION
rel detachment, separateness; retirement, withdrawal; confinement, quarantine; loneliness, lonesomeness
con companionship, company

solo *adj syn* see ONLY 2

so long *interj syn* see GOOD-BYE

solution *n syn* see ANSWER 2

solve *vb* 1 to find an answer or solution for (a problem or difficulty) <mass transit partially *solved* the traffic problem>
syn fix, resolve, work, work out
rel decide, determine, settle
idiom hit upon a solution
2 to find an explanation or solution for something obscure, mysterious, or incomprehensible <the mystery of the missing cookies has been *solved*>
syn break, ||cipher, clear up, decipher, dissolve, ||dope out, figure out, puzzle out, resolve, unfold, unravel, unriddle
rel enlighten, illuminate; construe, elucidate, explain, interpret
idiom get to the bottom of, have it, put two and two together

somatic *adj syn* see BODILY

somber *adj* 1 *syn* see DARK 1
2 *syn* see GLOOMY 3
3 *syn* see SERIOUS 1
idiom as somber as an undertaker

some *adj* 1 *syn* see CERTAIN 2
2 *syn* see SEVERAL 3

some *adv* 1 *syn* see NEARLY
2 *syn* see SOMEWHAT 2

somebody *pron* one or some individual of no certain or known identity <*somebody* should be home>
syn someone
rel anybody, one
con none
ant nobody, no one

somebody *n* 1 *syn* see NOTABLE 1
ant nobody
2 *syn* see CELEBRITY 2

someday *adv syn* see YET 2

||somegate *adv syn* see SOMEHOW

somehow *adv* in some way not yet known or specified <this thing must be done *somehow*>
syn ||somegate, someway, somewise
rel anyhow, anyway, anywise
idiom by hook or by crook, in one way or another, in some such way, somehow or other (*or* another)
con nohow, noway, nowise

someone *pron syn* see SOMEBODY

someplace *adv syn* see SOMEWHERE 1
ant no place

something *adv syn* see SOMEWHAT 2

something *n syn* see ENTITY 1

sometime *adv syn* see YET 2
idiom one of these days

sometime *adj syn* see FORMER 2

sometimes *adv* at intervals <illustrated by beautiful and *sometimes* outstanding photographs>
syn at times, ||betimes, ever and again, ever and anon, here and there, now and again, now and

---

syn synonym(s) *rel* related word(s)
ant antonym(s) *con* contrasted word(s)
idiom idiomatic equivalent(s)
|| use limited; if in doubt, see a dictionary

then, once and again, ‖otherwhile; *compare* OCCASIONALLY
rel intermittently, periodically, recurrently; frequently; consistently, constantly
idiom every now and then (*or* again), every once in a while, every so often, from time to time
con continually, continuously, unceasingly, uninterruptedly; endlessly, ever, interminably

someway *adv* ***syn*** see SOMEHOW

somewhat *adv* **1** ***syn*** see WELL 8
2 to some extent or in some degree <felt *somewhat* better but not fine>
syn fairly, kind of, moderately, more or less, pretty, rather, ratherish, some, something, sort of
rel adequately, bearably, tolerably; insignificantly, slightly
idiom rather more than less

somewhen *adv* ***syn*** see YET 2

somewhere *adv* **1** to, at, or in some unknown or unspecified location <lived on a farm *somewhere* in the Midwest>
syn someplace, ‖somewheres
rel somewhither; elsewhere, otherwhere
idiom someplace or other
con anyplace, anywhere, ‖anywheres; no place, ‖nowheres
ant nowhere
2 ***syn*** see NEARLY

‖**somewheres** *adv* ***syn*** see SOMEWHERE 1
ant ‖nowheres

somewise *adv* ***syn*** see SOMEHOW

somnifacient *adj* ***syn*** see SOPORIFIC 1

somniferous *adj* ***syn*** see SOPORIFIC 1

somnific *adj* ***syn*** see SOPORIFIC 1

somnolent *adj* **1** ***syn*** see SOPORIFIC 1
2 ***syn*** see SLEEPY 1
rel inactive, passive, supine

somnorific *adj* ***syn*** see SOPORIFIC 1

so much as *adv* ***syn*** see EVEN 4

son *n* ***syn*** see BOY 1
rel sonny; junior

sonance *n* ***syn*** see SOUND 1

sonant *adj* ***syn*** see VOCAL 1

song *n* **1** ***syn*** see POETRY 1
2 music or a piece of music intended for vocal expression <played and sang a *song*>
syn aria, descant, ditty, hymn, lay, lied; *compare* MELODY
rel lyric; piece
3 ***syn*** see CALL 1

song and dance *n* ***syn*** see SPIEL

songful *adj* ***syn*** see MELODIOUS 2

sonorant *adj* ***syn*** see RESONANT

sonorous *adj* **1** ***syn*** see RESONANT
2 ***syn*** see RHETORICAL
3 ***syn*** see NOISY

‖**sonsy** *adj* **1** ***syn*** see LUCKY
2 ***syn*** see GRACIOUS 1
3 ***syn*** see EASYGOING 3

soon *adv* **1** ***syn*** see PRESENTLY 1
rel forthwith, instantly, pronto, quickly
idiom in the near future
2 ***syn*** see FAST 2
3 ***syn*** see EARLY 1

‖**soon** *adj* ***syn*** see EARLY 2

sooner *adv* ***syn*** see BEFORE 3

sooner or later *adv* ***syn*** see YET 2

soothe *vb* ***syn*** see CALM
rel comfort, console; hush, subdue
con annoy, irritate, vex
ant excite

‖**soother** *n* ***syn*** see CALM

soothsay *vb* ***syn*** see FORETELL

soothsayer *n* ***syn*** see PROPHET

sop *n* **1** ***syn*** see WEAKLING
2 a conciliatory or propitiatory gift or advance <provided the $400 raise as a *sop*> <the new office was a *sop* to his wounded feelings>
syn sugarplum
rel douceur, gratuity; ‖baksheesh, ‖boodle, bribe, ‖palm oil
idiom sop in the pan, sop to Cerberus

sop *vb* **1** ***syn*** see WET
2 ***syn*** see SOAK 1
3 ***syn*** see BRIBE

sophic *adj* ***syn*** see WISE 1

sophism *n* ***syn*** see FALLACY 2
rel illogicality, irrationality; invalidity, unsoundness; claptrap

sophistic *adj* ***syn*** see ILLOGICAL

sophisticate *adj* ***syn*** see SOPHISTICATED 2

sophisticate *vb* ***syn*** see ADULTERATE

sophisticated *adj* **1** ***syn*** see COMPLEX 2
ant unsophisticated
2 being experienced in the ways of the world <a *sophisticated*, well-traveled man>
syn blasé, disenchanted, disentranced, disillusioned, knowing, mondaine, sophisticate, worldly, worldly-wise, world-wise; *compare* COSMOPOLITAN 1
rel adult, mature; experienced, practiced, schooled, seasoned; salty, uncelestial; couth, well-bred; smooth, suave, svelte, urbane; bored, jaded, world-weary; brittle; cynical, skeptical
con artless, gee-whiz, ingenuous, natural; green, inexperienced, unseasoned, virginal; unworldly
ant naive, unsophisticated

sophistry *n* ***syn*** see FALLACY 2
rel ambiguity, tergiversation

soporiferous *adj* ***syn*** see SOPORIFIC 1

soporific *adj* **1** tending to induce sleep <a *soporific* drug><*soporific* prose>
syn hypnotic, narcotic, opiate, sleepy, slumberous, somnifacient, somniferous, somnific, somnolent, somnorific, soporiferous, soporifical
rel calming, quietening, sedative, tranquilizing; anesthetic, deadening, numbing
con arousing, waking; invigorating, stimulating
2 ***syn*** see SLEEPY 1

soporifical *adj* ***syn*** see SOPORIFIC 1

sopping *adj* ***syn*** see WET 1

soppy *adj* **1** ***syn*** see WET 1
‖**2** ***syn*** see SENTIMENTAL

sorcerer *n* ***syn*** see MAGICIAN 1

sorceress *n* ***syn*** see WITCH 1

sorcerous *adj* ***syn*** see MAGIC

sorcery *n* ***syn*** see MAGIC 1

sordid *adj* **1** ***syn*** see DIRTY 1
2 ***syn*** see SLATTERNLY
3 ***syn*** see BASE 3
rel foul, nasty, seamy, sodden
sore *adj* ***syn*** see PAINFUL 1
sorehead *n* ***syn*** see GROUCH
sorely *adv* ***syn*** see HARD 6
sorrow *n* distress of mind <felt great *sorrow* at the loss of her friend>
syn affliction, anguish, care, ‖dole, grief, heartache, heartbreak, regret, rue, woe
rel mournfulness, sadness, sorrowfulness, unhappiness; grieving, lamentation, mourning, sorrowing; dejection, depression, melancholy; agony, distress, dolor, misery, suffering, wretchedness
con cheerfulness, gaiety, gladness, happiness, joyfulness; ecstasy
ant joy
sorrow *vb* ***syn*** see GRIEVE 2
rel groan, moan, sob
idiom break one's heart over, eat one's heart out
ant rejoice
sorrowful *adj* **1** ***syn*** see WOEFUL 1
rel sorrow-laden, sorrow-stricken, sorrow-struck
idiom full of (*or* filled with) sorrow
con sorrowless
ant joyful
2 ***syn*** see MELANCHOLY 2
ant gay
sorry *adj* **1** ***syn*** see SAD 1
rel bad, regretful, remorseful; miserable, wretched
ant glad
2 ***syn*** see REMORSEFUL
3 ***syn*** see CONTEMPTIBLE
rel inadequate, paltry, poor, trifling; cheesy, scruffy, shoddy; disgraceful
sort *n* **1** ***syn*** see TYPE
2 ***syn*** see GROUP 3
sort *vb* **1** ***syn*** see ASSORT
2 to analyze and assort (as individuals or things) to obtain those desired or required <he knew he must *sort* out facts from fancy>
syn comb, separate, sift, winnow; *compare* SCREEN 5
rel riddle, screen; choose, cull, pick, select
con consolidate, join, lump, merge; aggregate, amalgamate, blend, fuse, mix; unify
sort of *adv* ***syn*** see SOMEWHAT 2
SOS *n* ***syn*** see ALARM 1
soshed *adj* ***syn*** see INTOXICATED 1
so–so *adv* ***syn*** see ENOUGH 2
so–so *adj* ***syn*** see MEDIUM
sot *n* ***syn*** see DRUNKARD
‖**sot** *adj* ***syn*** see OBSTINATE
so that *conj* ***syn*** see SO
sotto voce *adv* in an inaudible or barely audible voice <made a snide remark to her *sotto voce*>
syn faintly, mutedly, weakly
rel low, quietly, softly; muffledly; mutteringly; aside, privately
idiom below one's breath, between one's teeth, in an aside, in an undertone, in a whisper, out of earshot, under one's breath
con aloud, out, out loud
sough *vb* **1** ***syn*** see SIGH 2
2 ***syn*** see SIGH 1
soul *n* **1** an animating essence or principle held to be inseparably associated with life or living beings <philosophers who teach that life is a manifestation of *soul*>
syn anima, animus, élan vital, pneuma, psyche, spirit, vital force
rel life, vitality
idiom breath of life
2 the immortal part of man believed to have permanent individual existence <into God's hands I commit my *soul*>
syn spirit
rel life; noumenon
idiom one's immortal soul
con flesh
ant body
3 ***syn*** see HEART 1
rel character, personality, psyche; conscience; spirit
idiom heart of hearts, heart's core, one's inmost soul (*or* mind), one's secret (*or* inner) self, (the) secret recesses of the heart
4 ***syn*** see ESSENCE 2
5 ***syn*** see HUMAN
soul–searching *n* ***syn*** see INTROSPECTION
soul–sick *adj* ***syn*** see DOWNCAST
sound *adj* **1** ***syn*** see HEALTHY 1
rel intact, unimpaired; perfect
idiom sound as a bell (*or* whistle), sound of mind and body
con impaired; unfit
ant unsound
2 ***syn*** see WHOLE 1
3 ***syn*** see STABLE 4
ant unsound
4 ***syn*** see VALID
rel errorless, faultless, flawless, impeccable; accurate, correct, exact, precise; rational, reasonable; well-founded, well-grounded
con questionable, shaky; invalid
ant unsound
5 ***syn*** see ORTHODOX 1
6 ***syn*** see RATIONAL
rel right-minded, sober, sober-minded, sound-minded
ant unsound
sound *n* **1** a sensation or effect resulting from stimulation of the auditory receptors <the *sound* of thunder>
syn noise, sonance
rel vibration; resonance; sonancy; reverberation
con quiet, soundlessness
ant silence

syn synonym(s) ***rel*** related word(s)
ant antonym(s) ***con*** contrasted word(s)
idiom idiomatic equivalent(s)
‖ use limited; if in doubt, see a dictionary

2 ***syn*** see EARSHOT
sound *vb* **1** ***syn*** see SEEM
2 ***syn*** see DECLARE 1
sound *vb* to measure the depth of (as a body of water) typically with a weighted line <*sounding* the distance to the bottom>
syn fathom, plumb, plumb-line
idiom ‖cast (*or* sling) the lead, make a sounding, take soundings
sound (out) *vb* ***syn*** see PROBE 2
soundless *adj* ***syn*** see BOTTOMLESS 2
ant soundable
soundless *adj* ***syn*** see STILL 3
soundlessness *n* ***syn*** see SILENCE 1
soundness *n* **1** ***syn*** see HEALTH
ant unsoundness
2 ***syn*** see STABILITY
3 ***syn*** see WIT 2
rel level-headedness, sensibleness
idiom sound mind, soundness of mind
ant unsoundness
sound off *vb* ***syn*** see SPEAK UP
soup *n* ***syn*** see PREDICAMENT
soupçon *n* ***syn*** see HINT 2
soupy *adj* ***syn*** see SENTIMENTAL
sour *adj* **1** causing or characterized by the one of the basic taste sensations produced chiefly by acids <*sour* pickles>
syn acerb, acerbic, acetose, acid, acidulous, dry, tart
rel keen, sharp, tangy; ‖blinky, sourish; fermented, soured, turned; acrid, bitter, vinegary
ant sweet
2 ***syn*** see BAD 8
source *n* the point at which something begins its course or existence <the *source* of her wisdom was long practical experience>
syn derivation, fount, fountain, fountainhead, inception, mother, origin, provenance, provenience, root, rootage, rootstock, spring, well, wellhead, wellspring, whence
rel birthplace; beginning, commencement, dawn, dawning, onset, opening, start, starting; authorship, origination, rise, rising; antecedent, cause, determinant; parent, paternity
con end, ending, terminus
ant termination; outcome
sourpuss *n* ***syn*** see GROUCH
rel killjoy
souse *vb* **1** ***syn*** see DIP 1
2 ***syn*** see WET
3 ***syn*** see SOAK 1
souse *n* ***syn*** see BINGE 1
soused *adj* ***syn*** see WET 1
souvenir *n* ***syn*** see REMEMBRANCE 3
idiom token of remembrance
sovereign *adj* **1** ***syn*** see FREE 1
rel self-determined, self-governed
2 ***syn*** see DOMINANT 1
rel commanding, directing, guiding; highest, loftiest
3 ***syn*** see EXCELLENT
4 ***syn*** see KINGLY
sovereignty *n* ***syn*** see SUPREMACY
sow *vb* **1** ***syn*** see PLANT 1
2 ***syn*** see STREW 1
rel fling, toss; drill
‖**sowf** *vb* ***syn*** see HUM
sozzled *adj* ***syn*** see INTOXICATED 1
spa *n* **1** a locality featuring mineral springs or water cures <hoped a week at a *spa* would help his arthritis>
syn baths, ‖hydro, springs, watering place, wells
rel waters
idiom health spa
2 ***syn*** see RESORT 3
space *n* **1** ***syn*** see WHILE 1
rel lapse; interval, term; duration
2 ***syn*** see EXPANSE
rel room, roomage; spaciousness
spaced–out *adj* ***syn*** see DRUGGED
spacious *adj* larger in extent or capacity than the average <a mansion with *spacious* rooms and gardens>
syn ample, capacious, commodious, roomy, wide
rel big, generous, great, large, spacy; enormous, immense, vast; expansive, extended, extensive; boundless, spaceless
con circumscribed, confined, cramped, limited, narrow, restricted; small, tiny
ant strait
spade *vb* **1** ***syn*** see DIG 2
2 ***syn*** see DIG 1
span *n* ***syn*** see TERM 2
rel interval; space
spang *adv* ***syn*** see JUST 1
spangle *vb* **1** to adorn with small brilliant objects <a tutu *spangled* with sequins>
syn bespangle, glitter
rel adorn, decorate, ornament, trim
2 ***syn*** see FLASH 1
spang–new *adj* ***syn*** see BRAND-NEW
spaniel *n* ***syn*** see SYCOPHANT
spank *vb* ***syn*** see SLAP 1
spank *n* ***syn*** see CUFF
idiom a sound spank
spanking *adv* ***syn*** see VERY 1
spanking–new *adj* ***syn*** see BRAND-NEW
span–new *adj* ***syn*** see BRAND-NEW
spare *vb* **1** ***syn*** see EXEMPT
2 ***syn*** see SAVE 4
3 to refrain from the free use or consumption of <don't *spare* the syrup on my pancakes>
syn scant, short, skimp, ‖skinch, stint; *compare* SCRIMP
rel pinch
4 ***syn*** see SCRIMP
spare *adj* **1** ***syn*** see SUPERFLUOUS
idiom enough and to spare, more than enough
2 ***syn*** see LEAN
ant corpulent
3 ***syn*** see MEAGER 2
ant profuse
sparing *adj* careful in the use of money, goods, or resources <was *sparing* in his expenditures>
syn canny, chary, economical, frugal, provident, saving, Scotch, stewardly, thrifty, unwasteful, wary; *compare* STINGY

rel parsimonious, ‖scant, tight, tightfisted, ungiving
con exuberant, liberal, prodigal, profuse
ant lavish, unsparing
spark *n* ***syn*** see SEED 2
spark *n* ***syn*** see SUITOR 2
spark *vb* ***syn*** see ADDRESS 8
sparker *n* ***syn*** see SUITOR 2
sparkish *adj* ***syn*** see DAPPER
sparkle *vb* ***syn*** see FLASH 1
sparkle *n* ***syn*** see FLASH 1
sparse *adj* ***syn*** see MEAGER 2
rel dispersed, scattered; infrequent, occasional, sporadic; rare, scarce, uncommon
con close, compact, thick
‖**spartle** *vb* ***syn*** see SCRAMBLE 1
spasmodic *adj* ***syn*** see FITFUL
rel spurtive
con continual, continuous, uninterrupted
spat *n* **1** ***syn*** see QUARREL
‖**2** ***syn*** see CUFF
spat *vb* ***syn*** see QUARREL
spate *n* **1** ***syn*** see FLOOD 2
rel progression, series, succession; rain, river, spurt
2 ***syn*** see FLOW
spatter *vb* **1** ***syn*** see SPLASH
rel sparge
2 ***syn*** see SPOT 1
3 ***syn*** see MALIGN
4 ***syn*** see SPUTTER 2
spatter *n* ***syn*** see FEW
spattering *n* ***syn*** see FEW
spawn *vb* ***syn*** see GENERATE 1
spawning *adj* ***syn*** see FERTILE
speak *vb* **1** to articulate words in order to express thoughts <always *speak* clearly>
syn talk, utter, verbalize, vocalize, voice
rel drawl, gasp, mouth, mumble, murmur, mutter, shout, splutter, spout, whisper; descant, dilate (on *or* upon), expatiate, perorate; converse, discourse; allege, assert, aver, convey, declare, tell
idiom break silence, give voice (*or* tongue *or* utterance) to, let fall, make public (*or* known), open one's mouth (*or* lips), put in (*or* into) words, say one's say, speak one's piece
con gabble, gibber, jabber; maunder, mumble, mutter; mispronounce, misspeak
2 ***syn*** see TALK 7
3 to have oral command of (a language) <he *speaks* fluent German>
syn converse (in), parley, talk, use
idiom be at ease in
con falter, hesitate, stumble
speaker *n* ***syn*** see SPOKESMAN
speaking *n* ***syn*** see SPEECH 1
speak out *vb* ***syn*** see SPEAK UP
speak up *vb* to speak strongly, boldly, or vigorously <we'll never know how you feel if you don't *speak up*>
syn sound off, speak out
idiom come out with it, have one's say, let one's voice be heard, make oneself heard, speak one's mind, stand up and be counted

spear *vb* ***syn*** see IMPALE
rel stick; bore, drill, penetrate, pierce; gouge, ream
special *adj* **1** of or relating to one thing or class <*special* soap for infants>
syn especial, individual, particular, specific
rel characteristic, distinctive, peculiar; exceptional, occasional, rare, uncommon; unique
con common, familiar, ordinary; customary, habitual, usual
2 ***syn*** see EXPRESS 2
rel defined, determinate; designated, earmarked
special *adv* ***syn*** see ESPECIALLY 1
specialize *vb* ***syn*** see ITEMIZE 1
specially *adv* **1** ***syn*** see ESPECIALLY 1
2 ***syn*** see EXPRESSLY 2
species *n* ***syn*** see TYPE
specific *adj* **1** ***syn*** see SPECIAL 1
rel limited, reserved, restricted, specialized
con general, generic
ant nonspecific, unspecific
2 ***syn*** see EXPLICIT
con ambiguous, cloudy, indefinite, uncertain, unexplicit, unspecified, vague
ant nonspecific, unspecific
3 ***syn*** see EXPRESS 2
ant nonspecific, unspecific
specifically *adv* **1** ***syn*** see EXPRESSLY 2
2 ***syn*** see ESPECIALLY 1
3 ***syn*** see EXPRESSLY 1
specificate *vb* ***syn*** see SPECIFY 3
specificize *vb* ***syn*** see SPECIFY 3
specify *vb* **1** ***syn*** see MENTION
2 ***syn*** see ITEMIZE 1
3 to make something (as a condition or requirement) specific <his will *specified* how the money would be divided>
syn detail, particularize, specificate, specificize, stipulate; *compare* ITEMIZE 1
rel determine, establish, fix, settle; condition, limit, set; pin (down); enumerate, list; precise
specimen *n* ***syn*** see INSTANCE
rel sort, species, type, variety
specious *adj* ***syn*** see FALSE 1
rel apparent, seeming; colorable, plausible; beguiling; illogical, spurious; empty, hollow, idle, nugatory, vain
ant valid
speciousness *n* ***syn*** see FALLACY 2
rel speciosity
ant validity
speck *n* **1** ***syn*** see POINT 11
rel pinpoint; tick
2 ***syn*** see PARTICLE
speck *vb* ***syn*** see SPECKLE 1
speckle *vb* **1** to produce on or mark with small spots, speckles, or blemishes <a *speckled* egg>
syn bespeckle, dot, freckle, pepper, speck, sprinkle, stipple; *compare* SPOT 1

---

syn synonym(s) ***rel*** related word(s)
ant antonym(s) ***con*** contrasted word(s)
idiom idiomatic equivalent(s)
‖ use limited; if in doubt, see a dictionary

rel dapple, flake, fleck
2 ***syn*** see SPOT 2

spectacle *n* ***syn*** see EXHIBITION 1

spectacled *adj* ***syn*** see BESPECTACLED

spectacular *adj* ***syn*** see MARVELOUS 1
rel eye-popping, sensational, striking, thrilling; dramatic, histrionic, stagy, theatrical
ant unspectacular

spectator *n* one who sees or looks upon something <sports *spectators*>
syn beholder, by-sitter, bystander, eyewitness, looker-on, observer, onlooker, stander-by, viewer, watcher, witness
rel gazer; perceiver; seer

specter *n* ***syn*** see APPARITION

spectral *adj* ***syn*** see GHASTLY 2
rel phantom, phantomlike, shadowlike; disembodied, unearthly; spooky

spectrum *n* **1** ***syn*** see APPARITION
2 ***syn*** see RANGE 5

speculate *vb* ***syn*** see THINK 5
rel excogitate, review, study, weigh
idiom ‖beat one's brains, turn over in one's mind, ‖use the gray matter

speculation *n* **1** ***syn*** see THOUGHT 1
rel excogitation, review, studying, weighing
2 ***syn*** see THEORY 2

speculative *adj* **1** ***syn*** see THEORETICAL 1
2 ***syn*** see THOUGHTFUL 1
rel musing, ruminating; curious, inquiring, questioning
ant unspeculative

speech *n* **1** communication, expression, or interchange of thoughts in spoken words <considered *speech* as a means of reproducing for one's listeners the images in one's mind>
syn discourse, speaking, talk, utterance, verbalization; *compare* VOCALIZATION
rel articulation, uttering, vocalization, vocalizing, voice, voicing; expressing, expression; language
idiom oral communication, vocal expression
2 a usually formal discourse delivered to an audience <a televised *speech* to the nation>
syn address, allocution, lecture, talk
rel debate, parlance, parley; declamation, harangue, oration, speechification
3 ***syn*** see LANGUAGE 1

speechcraft *n* ***syn*** see ORATORY

speechless *adj* **1** ***syn*** see DUMB 1
rel aphonic
2 ***syn*** see SILENT 2
3 ***syn*** see SILENT 3

speed *n* **1** ***syn*** see HASTE 1
rel alacrity, legerity; headway
con dilatoriness, tardiness
2 rate of movement, performance, or occurrence <ran through the exercise at a high *speed*>
syn ‖bat, celerity, gait, pace, quickness, rapidity, rapidness, swiftness, velocity; *compare* TEMPO
rel fastness, fleetness; clip, hickory

speed *vb* **1** ***syn*** see HURRY 2
idiom make haste
ant slow (up *or* down)
2 ***syn*** see COURSE
3 to cause to move fast or faster <*sped* our craft forward>
syn accelerate, hasten, hurry, quicken, shake up, step up, swiften
rel advance, aid, ease, encourage, expedite, facilitate, forward, further, help (along), smooth; cheer (on), drive (on), goad (on), spur (on); burn (up)
idiom ‖get the lead out
con hamper, restrain, retard; check, stay; delay, postpone, put off
ant slow (up *or* down)

speedily *adv* ***syn*** see FAST 2
idiom against the clock, hell-bent for leather, like a bat out of hell, like all forty, ‖like all get-out, on the double, to beat the band
con deliberately, languidly, leisurely; lazily, lethargically, sluggishly; crawlingly, creepingly
ant slow, slowly

speediness *n* ***syn*** see HASTE 1
ant slowness

speedy *adj* ***syn*** see FAST 3
rel agile, brisk, nimble; prompt, ready
idiom fast as greased lightning, speedy as an arrow
ant dilatory; slow

speerings *n pl* ***syn*** see NEWS

‖spelder *vb* ***syn*** see SPRAWL 1

spell *n* a spoken word or set of words believed to have magic power <cause death by muttering *spells* over her>
syn charm, conjuration, ‖devil-devil, incantation, rune
rel bewitching, enchanting, hexing

spell *vb* ***syn*** see BEWITCH 1

spell *vb* ***syn*** see MEAN 2

spell *vb* **1** ***syn*** see RELIEVE 3
2 ***syn*** see REST 3

spell *n* **1** a limited period or amount of activity <each *spell* of work was followed by a brief rest>
syn bout, go, shift, stint, time, tour, trick, turn
rel streak; ‖patch, period; stretch; relay
2 ***syn*** see WHILE 1
3 ***syn*** see ATTACK 3

spellbind *vb* ***syn*** see ENTHRALL 2

spell out *vb* ***syn*** see EXPLAIN 1

spend *vb* **1** to distribute or consume in payment or expenditure <*spent* fifty dollars for that dress>
syn disburse, expend, fork (out), give, lay out, outlay, pay, shell out
rel blow, drop, hand out; contribute; consume, dissipate, lavish, squander, throw away, waste
ant save
2 ***syn*** see GO 4
3 to cause or permit to elapse <*spent* the summer at the beach>
syn pass, while (away)

spender *n* ***syn*** see SPENDTHRIFT
ant saver

spending money *n* ***syn*** see POCKET MONEY

spendthrift *n* one who dissipates his resources foolishly and wastefully <a *spendthrift* who lost his estate through gambling>

syn high roller, prodigal, profligate, scattergood, spender, squanderer, unthrift, waster, wastethrift, wastrel
con hoarder, miser, saver
spent *adj* *syn* see EFFETE 2
spew *vb* **1** *syn* see VOMIT
2 *syn* see ERUPT 1
rel flood, gush
sphere *n* **1** *syn* see BALL
2 *syn* see FIELD
rel circle, jurisdiction, realm
sphere *vb* *syn* see BALL
spice *n* **1** *syn* see HINT 2
2 *syn* see FRAGRANCE
spick–and–span *adj* **1** *syn* see BRAND-NEW
2 *syn* see NEAT 2
spicy *adj* **1** *syn* see SWEET 2
2 *syn* see PUNGENT
rel fiery, gingery, high-spirited, spirited, zestful
3 *syn* see RISQUÉ
rel sophisticated; piquant
spider *n* *syn* see FRYING PAN
spiel *n* voluble, glib, or extravagant talk often intended to impress, persuade, or deceive <gave her a long sales *spiel*>
syn ||line, pitch, song and dance
rel demagoguery; dramatics, pyrotechnics, sensationalism
||**spieler** *n* *syn* see SWINDLER
spiff *vb* *syn* see DRESS UP 1
spiffy *adj* *syn* see DAPPER
||**spiflicated** *adj* *syn* see INTOXICATED 1
spigot *n* *syn* see FAUCET
spike *vb* *syn* see IMPALE
spill *vb* **1** to cause or allow (something) to fall, flow, or run out and be lost or wasted <accidentally dropped the cup and *spilled* his tea>
syn slop, squab
rel dribble, drip, drop; spatter, splash, spray
2 *syn* see OVERFLOW 2
3 *syn* see REVEAL 1
spilth *n* *syn* see REFUSE
spin *vb* **1** to turn or cause to turn rapidly <pinwheels *spinning* in the wind>
syn gyrate, gyre, ||pirl, pirouette, ||purl, twirl, whirl, whirligig; *compare* TURN 1
rel revolve, rotate, wheel; swirl; oscillate, pendulate, vibrate
idiom spin like a top
2 to feel as if revolving <her head was *spinning* with figures>
syn reel, swim, turn, whirl
rel dizzy, giddy; fluster, mix up, muddle
idiom be in a whirl
spin (out) *vb* *syn* see EXTEND 3
spin *n* *syn* see DRIVE 1
spinal column *n* *syn* see SPINE
spindling *adj* *syn* see GANGLING
spindly *adj* *syn* see GANGLING
spine *n* the articulated column of bones that is the central and axial feature of a vertebrate skeleton <fractured his *spine*>
syn back, backbone, rachis, spinal column, vertebrae, vertebral column
rel spinal cord
spineless *adj* *syn* see WEAK 4
rel weak-kneed, weak-willed
idiom as spineless as an amoeba
con self-willed, strong-willed
spin–off *n* *syn* see OUTGROWTH 2
spinster *n* a woman who is past the common age for marrying or who seems unlikely ever to marry <a gentle *spinster*, happy in her solitary life>
syn maiden lady, old maid, spinstress, ||tabby
spinstress *n* *syn* see SPINSTER
spiny *adj* *syn* see THORNY
spiral *vb* *syn* see WIND 2
spiring *adj* *syn* see LOFTY 6
spirit *n* **1** *syn* see SOUL 1
2 *syn* see APPARITION
3 *syn* see SOUL 2
4 *syn* see TEMPER 1
5 a lively or brisk quality in a person or his actions <a man of great *spirit* and courage>
syn animation, brio, dash, élan, esprit, gimp, life, oomph, verve, vim, zing; *compare* VIGOR 2
rel ardor, briskness, enthusiasm, liveliness; drive, get-up-and-go, ginger, go, pep, snap, starch, vigor, vitality, zip; character, force, substance
6 *syn* see COURAGE
rel ardor, fervor, passion, zeal; energy, force, might, power, strength
7 *often* **spirits** *pl* *syn* see LIQUOR
spirit (away) *vb* *syn* see KIDNAP
spirit (up) *vb* *syn* see ELATE
spirited *adj* **1** *syn* see LIVELY 1
rel sharp; fiery, gingery, peppery
idiom full of life (*or* go)
ant spiritless
2 having or manifesting a high degree of vitality, spirit, and daring <the lawyer gave a *spirited* defense of his client>
syn beany, fiery, gingery, high-hearted, high-spirited, mettlesome, peppery, spunky
rel game, gritty, resolute; audacious, bold, brave, courageous, dauntless, fearless, intrepid, nervy, plucky, valiant; avid, eager, hot, keen; ardent, enthusiastic, fervent, hot, passionate, peppy, zealous
con unenthusiastic; flabby, languid, limp; boneless, spineless
ant spiritless
spiritless *adj* **1** *syn* see DEAD 1
2 *syn* see DOWNCAST
idiom down in the dumps
3 *syn* see LANGUID
rel tame; broken, subdued, submissive
ant spirited
spiritual *adj* **1** *syn* see IMMATERIAL 1
rel supernatural, supramundane
ant physical

---

syn synonym(s) *rel* related word(s)
ant antonym(s) *con* contrasted word(s)
idiom idiomatic equivalent(s)
|| use limited; if in doubt, see a dictionary

2 *syn* see SACRED 2
3 *syn* see ECCLESIASTICAL
4 appealing to, coming from, or related to the higher emotions or to the aesthetic senses <man's *spiritual* and intellectual life as opposed to his animal instincts>
syn numinous
rel cerebral, intellectual, mental; elevated, high, high-minded, lofty; saintly
con low, lower; base
ant animal

spirituous *adj* containing a considerable amount of alcohol <*spirituous* liquors>
syn alcoholic, ardent, hard, strong
rel spiked; inebriating, intoxicating, intoxicative; heady
con nonalcoholic, nonintoxicating, soft

‖**spirity** *adj syn* see LIVELY 1

spit *vb syn* see IMPALE

spit *n* **1** *syn* see SALIVA
2 *syn* see IMAGE 1
rel counterpart; look-alike; twin

spit *vb* **1** *syn* see SPUTTER 1
2 *syn* see SPUTTER 2

spite *n syn* see MALICE
rel rancor; revenge, revengefulness, vengeance, vengefulness, vindictiveness
con sympathy; affection, love, tenderness

spiteful *adj syn* see MALICIOUS
rel antagonistic, hostile; revengeful, vengeful, vindictive
con charitable; sympathetic; affectionate, loving
ant spiteless

spitefulness *n syn* see MALICE

spitish *adj syn* see MALICIOUS

spitting image *n syn* see IMAGE 1
rel mirror image

spittle *n syn* see SALIVA

spit up *vb syn* see VOMIT

‖**spiv** *n* **1** *syn* see PARASITE
2 *syn* see SLACKER

splash *vb* to dash a liquid or semiliquid substance upon or against <*splashed* water onto her face>
syn douse, plash, slop, slosh, spatter, splatter, splosh, splurge, spurtle, swash
rel dash, throw; spray; sprinkle; ‖sprent, squirt; drench, drown, soak, sop, wet

splashy *adj syn* see SHOWY

splathering *adj syn* see CLUMSY 1

splatter *vb syn* see SPLASH

splay *adj syn* see CLUMSY 1

spleen *n syn* see MALICE
rel revenge, revengefulness, vindictiveness; wrath

splendid *adj* **1** *syn* see GRAND 2
rel baroque, flamboyant
2 extraordinarily or transcendently impressive <a *splendid* new city>
syn glorious, gorgeous, magnificent, proud, resplendent, splendiferous, splendorous, sublime, superb
rel eminent, illustrious; grand, impressive, lavish, luxurious, royal, sumptuous; divine, exquisite, lovely; incomparable, matchless, peerless, superlative, supreme, unparalleled, unsurpassed; surpassing, transcendent
con common, ordinary, run-of-the-mill
ant unimpressive

splendiferous *adj syn* see SPLENDID 2
rel dazzling, marvelous; smashing, walloping; rattling, ripping, screaming, terrific

splendorous *adj syn* see SPLENDID 2

splice *vb syn* see MARRY 2

splinter *vb syn* see SHATTER 1

splinterize *vb syn* see SHATTER 1

split *vb* **1** *syn* see CUT 5
rel crack, rive
2 *syn* see TEAR 1
‖3 *syn* see BETRAY 2

split (up) *vb syn* see SEPARATE 1

split *n* **1** *syn* see CRACK 3
2 *syn* see SCHISM 3
3 *syn* see BREACH 3
rel alienating, estranging

split second *n syn* see INSTANT 1

splitter *vb syn* see SHATTER 1

split–up *n syn* see SEPARATION 1

‖**splodge** *vb syn* see SPLOTCH

splosh *vb syn* see SPLASH

splotch *vb* to mark or spot with irregular patches especially of contrasting color <a black horse *splotched* with white>
syn blotch, mottle, ‖splodge
rel blot, stain; dapple, fleck, marble, motley, variegate; bespot, spot; harlequin

‖**splunge** *vb syn* see PLUNGE 2

splurge *n syn* see SPREE 1
rel extravagance; splash

splurge *vb syn* see SPLASH

splurt *vb syn* see SQUIRT

splutter *vb* **1** *syn* see SPUTTER 2
2 *syn* see SPUTTER 1

spoil *n* something taken from another by force or craft <gold, jewels, and paintings are often *spoils* of war>
syn boodle, booty, loot, plunder, plunderage, prize, ‖spreaghery, ‖spulzie, swag
rel acquisition, grab, haul, take; pickings, stealings; pillage, spoliation

spoil *vb* **1** *syn* see RAVAGE
2 *syn* see INJURE 1
rel ‖snafu; ruin, wreck; demolish, destroy
3 *syn* see RAPE
4 *syn* see BABY
rel accommodate, favor, oblige
idiom spoil (one) rotten, spoil to death
5 *syn* see DECAY

spoiled *adj* **1** *syn* see DAMAGED
ant unspoiled
2 *syn* see BAD 5
rel off, tainted; putrefying, rotting
ant unspoiled

spoiler *n syn* see MARAUDER

spoken *adj* **1** *syn* see ORAL 2
ant written
2 *syn* see VOCAL 1
ant unspoken

spokesman *n* one who speaks as a representative of another <selected as *spokesman* for the party's views>
syn mouth, mouthpiece, speaker, spokesperson, spokeswoman
rel delegate, deputy, representative; champion, protagonist; prophet

spokesperson *n* ***syn*** see SPOKESMAN

spokeswoman *n* ***syn*** see SPOKESMAN

spoliate *vb* ***syn*** see RAVAGE
rel raid; maraud; gut, ravish, sweep

spoliator *n* ***syn*** see MARAUDER

sponge *n* **1** ***syn*** see DRUNKARD
2 ***syn*** see PARASITE

sponger *n* ***syn*** see PARASITE

spongy *adj* ***syn*** see SOFT 6
idiom as soft as a sponge

sponsor *n* one that accepts responsibility for another person or thing <the major *sponsor* of this project is the government>
syn angel, backer, backer-up, guarantor, patron, surety
rel advocate, champion, mainstay, supporter, upholder; preferrer, promoter; benefactor, Maecenas

sponsorship *n* ***syn*** see BACKING

spontaneity *n* ***syn*** see UNCONSTRAINT
rel extemporaneousness, offhandedness, unpremeditatedness

spontaneous *adj* acting or activated without apparent thought or deliberation <a *spontaneous* burst of applause>
syn automatic, impulsive, instinctive, involuntary, unmeditated, unpremeditated, unprompted, will-less
rel unconstrained, unforced; unreasoned, unstudied; extemporaneous, extempore, impromptu, improvised, offhand; natural, simple, unsophisticated
con deliberate, intended, intentional, planned, predetermined, preplanned, studied, thought-out, voluntary, willed, willful; forced, prompted; conventional, formal, stylized
ant premeditated

spontoon *n* ***syn*** see CUDGEL

spoof *vb* ***syn*** see DUPE

spoof *n* ***syn*** see IMPOSTURE

spook *n* ||**1** ***syn*** see APPARITION
||**2** ***syn*** see ECCENTRIC
3 ***syn*** see SPY

||**spook** *vb* **1** ***syn*** see FRIGHTEN
2 ***syn*** see GHOSTWRITE

spooky *adj* **1** ***syn*** see WEIRD 1
rel spookish; ominous
2 ***syn*** see NERVOUS

||**spoon** *n* ***syn*** see DUNCE

spoony *adj* ***syn*** see SIMPLE 3

spoony (over *or* on) *adj* ***syn*** see ENAMORED 1

spoor *n* ***syn*** see FOOTPRINT

sporadic *adj* **1** ***syn*** see FITFUL
ant regular
2 ***syn*** see INFREQUENT
rel separate, single
ant frequent

sporadically *adv* ***syn*** see OCCASIONALLY
ant regularly

sport *vb* ***syn*** see PLAY 1

sport *n* **1** ***syn*** see PLAY 1
2 sports *pl* ***syn*** see ATHLETICS
3 ***syn*** see FUN 1
rel jollification; antics, high jinks, horseplay
4 ***syn*** see LAUGHINGSTOCK
5 ***syn*** see CHANGE 2

sporting girl *n* ***syn*** see PROSTITUTE

sporting house *n* ***syn*** see BROTHEL

sportive *adj* ***syn*** see PLAYFUL 1

sportiveness *n* ***syn*** see MISCHIEVOUSNESS

sportsmanlike *adj* ***syn*** see FAIR 5
ant unsporting, unsportsmanlike

sportsmanly *adj* ***syn*** see FAIR 5
ant unsporting, unsportsmanlike

sporty *adj* ***syn*** see WILD 7

spot *n* **1** ***syn*** see STIGMA
2 ***syn*** see DRAM
3 ***syn*** see PARTICLE
4 ***syn*** see PLACE 1
rel scene; section, sector
5 ***syn*** see JOB 2
idiom job slot
6 ***syn*** see PREDICAMENT

spot *vb* **1** to mark or stain (something) with spots <a white dress *spotted* with red mud>
syn bespatter, bespot, spatter; *compare* SPECKLE 1
rel blot, blotch, mottle; fleck, marble, streak, stripe; dot, pepper, speck, speckle, sprinkle, stipple; splash; dirty, soil, stain
2 to form or appear as spots on <a bleak landscape *spotted* with cottages>
syn dot, pimple, speckle, sprinkle, stud
rel intersperse
3 ***syn*** see IDENTIFY
rel ascertain; see
4 ***syn*** see FIND 1

spot *adj* ***syn*** see RANDOM

spotless *adj* **1** ***syn*** see CLEAN 1
rel hygienic, sanitary
2 ***syn*** see CHASTE
ant spotted

spotty *adj* **1** lacking uniformity <*spotty* illumination>
syn irregular, patchy, uneven
rel unequal; flickering, fluctuating
con equal, even, regular, uniform
2 ***syn*** see FITFUL

spousal *n* ***syn*** see WEDDING

spousal *adj* ***syn*** see MATRIMONIAL

spouse *n* a marriage partner <consulted with her *spouse* before buying the car>
syn consort, mate

spouseless *adj* ***syn*** see SINGLE 1
con espoused

||**spout** *vb* ***syn*** see PAWN

---

syn synonym(s) ***rel*** related word(s)
ant antonym(s) ***con*** contrasted word(s)
idiom idiomatic equivalent(s)
|| use limited; if in doubt, see a dictionary

spout *n* ***syn*** see WATERFALL
spraddle *vb* ***syn*** see SPRAWL 1
sprain *vb* to injure (a joint) by a sudden twisting motion that stretches and lacerates the ligaments <*sprained* her ankle>
syn ‖rick, turn, twist, wrench
rel pull, strain, stretch; tear; dislocate, throw; break, fracture
sprangle *vb* ***syn*** see SPRAWL 2
sprat *n* ***syn*** see TWERP
‖**sprauchle** *vb* ***syn*** see SCRAMBLE 1
sprawl *vb* **1** to lie or sit with arms and legs stretched out carelessly and awkwardly <the dog lay *sprawled* out on the sofa>
syn drape, ‖scamble, ‖spelder, spraddle, spread-eagle
rel loll, lounge; slouch, slump
2 to grow, develop, or spread irregularly and without apparent design or plan <the city *sprawls* down the whole coast>
syn ramble, scramble, sprangle, spread-eagle, straddle, straggle
rel extend, stretch; spread
spread *vb* **1** to extend or cause to extend over a considerable area or space <they *spread* the news far and wide> <clouds *spread* over the sky>
syn circulate, diffuse, disperse, disseminate, distribute, propagate, radiate, strew; *compare* STREW 1
rel deal, dispense; broadcast, communicate, pass (on), transmit; dissipate, scatter, sow; peddle, push, retail
idiom spread abroad (*or* far and wide)
con hold (in); contain; compress
2 ***syn*** see OPEN 4
con fold; close
3 ***syn*** see SET 5
spread *n* **1** ***syn*** see EXPANSION 2
rel diffusion; profusion; stretch, sweep
2 ***syn*** see EXPANSE
3 ***syn*** see DINNER
4 ***syn*** see BEDSPREAD
spread–eagle *vb* **1** ***syn*** see SPRAWL 1
2 ***syn*** see SPRAWL 2
‖**spreaghery** *n* ***syn*** see SPOIL
spree *n* **1** an unrestrained indulgence in or outburst of an activity <a shopping *spree*>
syn binge, fling, orgy, rampage, splurge
2 ***syn*** see BINGE 1
spree *vb* ***syn*** see REVEL 1
sprightful *adj* ***syn*** see LIVELY 1
sprightly *adj* **1** ***syn*** see LIVELY 1
rel perky; breezy
2 ***syn*** see ANTIC 2
rel sportive; coltish, frisky
3 ***syn*** see AGILE
4 ***syn*** see CLEVER 5
rel pungent, sharp; keen-witted, quick-witted
spring *vb* **1** to have something as a source <the primitive cultures from which civilization *springs*>
syn arise, birth, come (from), derive (from), emanate, flow, head, issue, originate, proceed, rise, stem, upspring; *compare* BEGIN 2
rel appear, emerge, come out, loom; arrive, come; begin, commence, hatch, start
2 ***syn*** see SKIP 1
3 ***syn*** see JUMP 1
4 ***syn*** see START 1
‖**5** ***syn*** see FREE
spring *n* **1** *usu* **springs** *pl* ***syn*** see SPA 1
2 ***syn*** see SOURCE
3 ***syn*** see YOUTH 1
ant autumn
4 ***syn*** see MOTIVE 1
rel excitant, impetus, incitement, stimulant, stimulus
5 the season between winter and summer <planting flowers in the *spring*>
syn budtime, springtide, springtime
rel ‖blackberry winter
idiom prime of the year
con autumn, fall
spring *adj* ***syn*** see VERNAL
springe *n* ***syn*** see PITFALL
springlike *adj* ***syn*** see VERNAL
springtide *n* **1** ***syn*** see SPRING 5
2 ***syn*** see YOUTH 1
ant autumn
springtime *n* **1** ***syn*** see SPRING 5
2 ***syn*** see YOUTH 1
ant autumn
springy *adj* ***syn*** see ELASTIC 1
rel rebounding, recoiling
ant rigid; springless
sprinkle *vb* **1** to scatter (something) in small drops or particles <*sprinkle* chocolate shot on whipped cream>
syn besprinkle, dust, powder, ‖strinkle; *compare* STREW 1
rel shake; scatter; pepper; sparge
2 ***syn*** see SPECKLE 1
3 ***syn*** see SPOT 2
4 ***syn*** see BAPTIZE
5 to rain lightly <it's only *sprinkling*, so we can still take our walk>
syn drizzle, ‖mizzle
rel mist; shower; spit
con pour, stream
sprinkling *n* **1** ***syn*** see HINT 2
2 ***syn*** see DUSTING
3 ***syn*** see FEW
sprint *vb* ***syn*** see RUN 1
sprit *vb* ***syn*** see SQUIRT
sprite *n* ***syn*** see FAIRY
‖**spritz** *vb* ***syn*** see SQUIRT
spruce *adj* ***syn*** see DAPPER
ant slouchy
spruce (up) *vb* ***syn*** see DRESS UP 1
sprucy *adj* ***syn*** see DAPPER
spry *adj* ***syn*** see AGILE
rel prompt, quick, ready; energetic, vigorous; healthy, robust, sound
ant doddering
spuddy *adj* ***syn*** see ROTUND 2
‖**spulzie** *n* ***syn*** see SPOIL
spume *n* ***syn*** see FOAM
spunk *n* **1** ***syn*** see FORTITUDE

rel bulldoggedness, doggedness
idiom clear (*or* true) grit
ant funk
2 *syn* see COURAGE
spunkless *adj syn* see COWARDLY
ant spunky
spunky *adj* **1** *syn* see BRAVE 1
idiom full of spunk
ant spunkless; funky
2 *syn* see SPIRITED 2
ant funky
spur *n syn* see STIMULUS
rel excitant; activation, actuation
ant checkrein, curb
spur *vb syn* see URGE
rel rowel; arouse, awaken, rally, rouse, stir; instigate; countenance, favor
ant curb
spurious *adj* **1** *syn* see ILLEGITIMATE 1
2 *syn* see ARTIFICIAL 2
3 of doubtful authenticity <claimed they had bought a *spurious* painting>
syn apocryphal, bastard, unauthentic, ungenuine; *compare* ARTIFICIAL 2, COUNTERFEIT
rel bogus, counterfeit, fake, phony, pseudo, sham; false, unreal
idiom not what (*or* all) it's cracked up to be
con actual, real, true; bona fide, genuine, veritable
ant authentic
4 *syn* see ARTIFICIAL 3
rel make-believe, pretend, pretended, pseudo
5 *syn* see COUNTERFEIT
spuriousness *n syn* see FALLACY 2
spurn *vb syn* see DECLINE 4
rel conspue, contemn, despise, disdain, scorn, scout; flout, scoff, sneer
con crave, desire, want
ant embrace
spur-of-the-moment *adj syn* see EXTEMPORANEOUS
spurt *vb syn* see SQUIRT
spurtle *vb syn* see SPLASH
sputter *vb* **1** to utter (words or ejaculations) hastily, explosively, and sometimes indistinctly <pompously *sputtering* his objections>
syn rip (out), spit, splutter
rel ejaculate, eject, throw (out); gibber, jabber; bluster, heckle, hector, rage, rant, rave, storm
2 to make a series of sudden short crackling or popping sounds <bacon *sputtering* in the pan>
syn spatter, spit, splutter
rel crackle, pop; hiss
spy (on *or* upon) *vb* to make furtive, stealthy, or secret observations of <had private detectives *spying* on his wife>
syn ‖stag
rel stake out; watch
spy *n* one who keeps secret watch to obtain information <was convicted on evidence produced by a *spy*>
syn agent, spook, undercover man; *compare* INFORMER
rel detective, investigator, sleuth; ‖narc; scout; beagle
idiom inside man, secret agent
spying *n syn* see ESPIONAGE
squab *adj syn* see STOCKY
‖**squab** *vb syn* see PRESS 1
squab *vb syn* see SPILL 1
squabble *n syn* see QUARREL
squabble *vb* **1** *syn* see QUARREL
rel clash, encounter
idiom have a squabble over
2 *syn* see ARGUE 2
idiom get into (*or* have) a hassle, have a verbal wrestling match
squalid *adj* **1** *syn* see DIRTY 1
rel disheveled, slipshod, sloppy, slovenly, unkempt; frowzy, slatternly; dingy, shoddy, sleazy
2 *syn* see SHABBY 1
3 *syn* see BASE 3
squall *vb* **1** to make a raucous noise <angry street urchins fighting and *squalling* at each other>
syn caw, ‖quawk, squark, squawk, yawp (*or* yaup)
rel bellow, howl, roar, shout, yell; bark, yap, yip; croak
2 *syn* see BAWL 2
rel squeal; screech, shriek; yelp
squall *n syn* see QUARREL
squander *vb syn* see WASTE 2
idiom make ducks and drakes of, play ducks and drakes with
squander *n syn* see EXTRAVAGANCE 2
squanderer *n syn* see SPENDTHRIFT
square *n* **1** *syn* see COMMON 2
2 *syn* see FOGY
square *adj* **1** having four equal sides and four right angles <a large *square* box>
syn foursquare, quadrate, quadratic, quadratical
rel boxlike, boxy, squarish
2 *syn* see EVEN 5
3 *syn* see FAIR 4
4 *syn* see CONVENTIONAL 1
square *vb* **1** *syn* see ADAPT
2 *syn* see CLEAR 5
3 *syn* see BRIBE
4 *syn* see AGREE 4
rel balance; coincide
square *adv syn* see JUST 1
squarehead *n syn* see DUNCE
squarely *adv* **1** *syn* see EVENLY 1
2 *syn* see JUST 1
squark *vb syn* see SQUALL 1
squash *vb* **1** *syn* see PRESS 1
2 *syn* see CRUSH 2
3 *syn* see CRUSH 5
4 *syn* see PRESS 7
squash *n* **1** *syn* see SQUELCH
2 *syn* see CROWD 1
squashing *n syn* see REPRESSION 1
squashy *adj syn* see SOFT 6

---

syn synonym(s) *rel* related word(s)
ant antonym(s) *con* contrasted word(s)
idiom idiomatic equivalent(s)
‖ use limited; if in doubt, see a dictionary

ant firm

squat *vb* to sit on one's haunches <they were *squatting* around the fire>

syn hunker (down), ‖quat, ‖swat; *compare* CROUCH

rel crouch; hunch; stoop

squat *adj* ***syn*** see STOCKY

rel squattish, squatty

con long, tall; twiggy

ant lanky

‖squaw *n* **1** ***syn*** see WIFE

2 ***syn*** see WOMAN 1

squawk *vb* **1** ***syn*** see SQUALL 1

2 ***syn*** see GRIPE

rel yap, yip

squawker *n* ***syn*** see INFORMER

squawky *adj* ***syn*** see HARSH 3

con liquid, mellow, smooth

squdgy *adj* ***syn*** see STOCKY

squeak *vb* **1** to utter or make a short shrill cry or noise <mice *squeaking* in the barn>

syn ‖queak; *compare* SQUEAL 2

rel creak, grate, screak, screech, squeal; pipe; scream

2 ***syn*** see TALK 6

3 ***syn*** see INFORM 3

squeak *n* ***syn*** see OPPORTUNITY

‖squeaker *n* ***syn*** see INFORMER

squeal *vb* **1** ***syn*** see SCREAM 1

idiom squeal like a stuck pig

2 to make a harsh piercing sometimes rasping noise <tires *squealing* on wet pavement>

syn screak, scream, screech, shriek; *compare* SQUEAK 1

rel creak, grate, rasp

3 ***syn*** see INFORM 3

4 ***syn*** see TALK 6

5 ***syn*** see YELL 2

rel bitch, bleat, complain, gripe, squawk

idiom raise a howl, scream bloody murder

squealer *n* ***syn*** see INFORMER

squeam *n* ***syn*** see QUALM

squeamish *adj* **1** inclined to become nauseated <felt *squeamish* after the heavy meal on the ship>

syn ‖pensy, qualmish, qualmy, queasy, queer, ‖wambly; *compare* NAUSEATED

rel unsettled, upset; dizzy, shaky, vertiginous

2 ***syn*** see NAUSEATED

idiom sick at (*or* to) one's stomach

3 ***syn*** see NICE 1

squeamishness *n* ***syn*** see NAUSEA

squeamy *adj* ***syn*** see NICE 1

squeeze *vb* **1** ***syn*** see PRESS 1

rel contract, ‖scruze

2 ***syn*** see EMBRACE 1

3 ***syn*** see EXTORT 1

4 ***syn*** see EKE OUT 2

5 ***syn*** see PRESS 8

6 ***syn*** see PRESS 7

squeezy *adj* ***syn*** see CRAMPED

squelch *n* a sound of or as if of semiliquid matter under suction <the *squelch* of his feet in the mud>

syn squash, squidge, squish

squelch *vb* ***syn*** see SUPPRESS 2

squelching *n* ***syn*** see REPRESSION 1

squelchy *adj* ***syn*** see SOFT 6

‖squench *vb* **1** ***syn*** see EXTINGUISH 1

2 ***syn*** see QUENCH 4

squidge *n* ***syn*** see SQUELCH

squiffed *adj* ***syn*** see INTOXICATED 1

squiggle *vb* **1** ***syn*** see WRIGGLE

2 ***syn*** see SCRIBBLE

squinch *vb* **1** ***syn*** see RECOIL

2 ***syn*** see SQUINT

squinny *vb* ***syn*** see SQUINT

squinny *adj* ***syn*** see THIN 1

squint *vb* to look or peer with the eyes partly closed <*squinted* in the bright sunlight>

syn ‖sken, squinch, squinny

idiom look asquint, screw up one's eyes

ant goggle

squirm *vb* **1** ***syn*** see WRIGGLE

2 ***syn*** see WRITHE 1

squirrel *vb* ***syn*** see HOARD

squirt *vb* to come forth in a sudden rapid usually narrow stream <water *squirting* from the hose>

syn jet, splurt, sprit, ‖spritz, spurt, ‖squitter

rel pour, stream, surge; spatter; spray

con dribble, drip, trickle

squirt *n* **‖1 squirts** *pl* ***syn*** see DIARRHEA

2 ***syn*** see TWERP

squish *n* **1** ***syn*** see PRESS 1

2 ***syn*** see SQUELCH

squishy *adj* ***syn*** see SOFT 6

‖squit *n* ***syn*** see TWERP

‖squitter *vb* ***syn*** see SQUIRT

squush *vb* ***syn*** see PRESS 1

squushy *adj* ***syn*** see SOFT 6

stab *n* **1** ***syn*** see PRICK

2 ***syn*** see POKE 1

3 ***syn*** see FLING 1

stab *vb* ***syn*** see THRUST 2

rel dagger, dirk, poniard, prong

stabbing *adj* ***syn*** see SHARP 8

stabile *adj* ***syn*** see STEADY 2

stabilify *vb* ***syn*** see STABILIZE

stabilitate *vb* ***syn*** see STABILIZE

stability *n* the ability to withstand force or stress without alteration of position and without material change <the structural *stability* of the bridge>

syn firmness, security, soundness, stableness, steadiness, strength

rel dependability, durability, reliability; solidity, solidness, sturdiness; cohesion, toughness

con insecurity, undependability, unreliability, unsoundness, unsteadiness; weakness

ant instability, unstability

stabilize *vb* to make or keep stable, steadfast, or firm <a policy that *stabilized* the economy>

syn ballast, poise, stabilify, stabilitate, steady

rel balance, counterbalance, counterpoise, equalize, equipoise; prop, support, sustain; fix, secure, set, settle

ant unstabilize

stable *adj* **1** ***syn*** see SURE 1

rel balanced, poised; fixed, set, solid, sound, steadfast
con wobbling, wobbly
ant instable, unstable
2 *syn* see STEADY 2
3 *syn* see LASTING
rel constant, steady; safe, secure, sound; resolute, staunch, steadfast
4 marked by solidity, firmness, and stability especially in design or construction <a *stable* foundation for the building>
syn firm, secure, solid, sound; *compare* FAST 4, SURE 1
rel strong, sturdy; unassailable, unshakable
idiom as firm as (the rock of) Gibraltar, solid as a rock
con insecure, shaky, unsound, weak, wobbling, wobbly
ant instable, unstable

stableness *n* ***syn*** see STABILITY
ant unstableness

stack *n* ***syn*** see PILE 1

stack *vb* ***syn*** see HEAP 1

||**stacked** *adj* **1** ***syn*** see CURVACEOUS
2 *syn* see BUXOM

stade *n* ***syn*** see STADIUM

stadium *n* a large usually unroofed structure with tiered seats enclosing a field used especially for sports <a football *stadium*>
syn bowl, coliseum, stade
rel arena, garden, gymnasium

||**stag** *vb* ***syn*** see SPY (on *or* upon)

stage *n* **1** *used with the* ***syn*** see DRAMA
2 *syn* see DEGREE 1
rel level; phase; period

stage *vb* to present on the stage <*staged* a play>
syn mount, produce, put on, show
rel bring out, open; give, present; do, execute, perform, play

stage set *n* ***syn*** see SCENE 1

stage setting *n* ***syn*** see SCENE 1

stagger *vb* **1** ***syn*** see REEL 2
2 *syn* see LURCH 2
idiom pitch and plunge
3 *syn* see TEETER
rel ||stiver, ||stoit, ||stoiter, ||stot
4 *syn* see HESITATE
5 to affect with great wonder or bewilderment <a plot so bizarre as to *stagger* the imagination>
syn boggle, dumbfound, nonplus
rel perplex, puzzle, stump; amaze, astonish, astound, flabbergast; bowl (over), floor, knock over; devastate, overpower, overwhelm, shatter; paralyze
idiom take (one) aback

stagger (on *or* along) *vb* ***syn*** see SHIFT 5

||**stagger** *n* ***syn*** see FLING 1

staggering *adj* ***syn*** see MARVELOUS 1

stagnant *adj* ***syn*** see STATIC

stagnate *vb* **1** ***syn*** see VEGETATE
2 *syn* see STULTIFY

stagnation *n* ***syn*** see DEPRESSION 3

staid *adj* ***syn*** see SERIOUS 1
rel decorous, formal; collected, composed, cool; priggish, smug; starchy, stuffy
con breezy, devil-may-care, easy, frivolous; debonair, jaunty; playful, sportive; hoydenish, rakish; fresh, irreverent; uncontrolled, unrestrained
ant unstaid

stain *vb* **1** to soil often permanently with foreign matter <a shirt *stained* with grease>
syn bestain, blot, discolor, smut; *compare* SOIL 2
rel tinge; bedaub, daub, smear; besmirch, smirch, smudge, smutch
2 *syn* see TAINT 1
3 *syn* see DEBASE 1

stain *n* **1** ***syn*** see STIGMA
rel blemish, defect, flaw
idiom blot on the escutcheon
2 *syn* see COLOR 6

stainless *adj* ***syn*** see CHASTE
con tainted, tarnished
ant stained

stake *n* **1** ***syn*** see BET
2 *syn* see INTEREST 1

stake *vb* **1** ***syn*** see GAMBLE 1
rel stake down
2 *syn* see CAPITALIZE

stale *adj* **1** ***syn*** see MALODOROUS 1
2 *syn* see TRITE
rel dusty, fusty; dead
ant fresh

||**stale** *n* ***syn*** see LURE 2

stalemate *n* ***syn*** see DRAW 4

stalk *vb* **1** to pursue (game) stealthily or under cover <*stalk* deer>
syn still-hunt
rel follow, track; drive, chase, pursue; walk up; flush (out); ambush
2 *syn* see STRIDE 1

stalky *adj* ***syn*** see THIN 1

stall *vb* ||**1** ***syn*** see SATIATE
2 *syn* see ARREST 1
rel brake, slow (down); hold off, put off, stand off; suspend; shut down
idiom pull the checkstring
con spur

stalwart *adj* **1** ***syn*** see STRONG 2
rel athletic, brawny, husky, muscular, sinewy
2 *syn* see BRAVE 1

stamina *n* ***syn*** see TOLERANCE 1

stammer *vb* **1** to make involuntary stops and repetitions in uttering syllables and words <the frightened child *stammered* and fell silent>
syn ||hammer, ||stut, stutter
rel falter, hesitate; stumble; splutter, sputter; gibber, jabber
||2 *syn* see TEETER

stamp *vb* **1** ***syn*** see TRAMPLE 2
rel clomp, clump, stump
2 *syn* see IMPRESS 3
rel etch, imprint, infix, inscribe, print
idiom impress on the mind

stamp *n* **1** ***syn*** see IMPRESSION 1

---

syn synonym(s) *rel* related word(s)
ant antonym(s) *con* contrasted word(s)
idiom idiomatic equivalent(s)
|| use limited; if in doubt, see a dictionary

2 ***syn*** see TYPE
3 ***syn*** see SEAL
stampede *vb* **1** ***syn*** see ROUT 1
2 to take to sudden headlong flight in panic <cattle *stampeding* across the plain>
syn pell-mell; *compare* RUSH 1
rel bolt, charge, chase, crash, dash, fling, hurry, rush, shoot, tear
idiom run like a pack of scalded dogs
stamping ground *n* **1** ***syn*** see HABITAT
2 ***syn*** see RESORT 2
stance *n* **1** ***syn*** see POSTURE 1
2 ***syn*** see POSITION 1
stanch *vb* ***syn*** see STEM
stand *vb* **1** ***syn*** see BEAR 10
idiom ||hack it, take lying down
2 ***syn*** see TREAT 3
stand (on *or* upon) *vb* ***syn*** see DEPEND (on *or* upon) 1
idiom be contingent on
stand *n* ***syn*** see POSITION 1
standard *n* **1** ***syn*** see FLAG
2 ***syn*** see MODEL 2
3 a means of determining what a thing should be <each generation has its own *standards* of morality>
syn benchmark, criterion, gauge, measure, touchstone, yardstick
rel average, mean, median, norm, par; axiom, belief, fundamental, principle; law, rule; exemplar, model, pattern
idiom rule of thumb
4 a fixed, customary, or official measure (as of quantity, quality, or price) <governmental *standards* of weights and measures>
syn assize
rel ||dick
stander-by *n* ***syn*** see SPECTATOR
stand-in *n* ***syn*** see SUBSTITUTE 1
rel second; assistant
standing *n* **1** ***syn*** see TERM 5
2 ***syn*** see STATUS 1
3 ***syn*** see STATUS 2
standoff *adj* ***syn*** see UNSOCIABLE
standoff *n* ***syn*** see DRAW 4
standoffish *adj* **1** ***syn*** see UNSOCIABLE
2 ***syn*** see ANTISOCIAL
stand out *vb* **1** ***syn*** see BULGE
2 ***syn*** see LOOM 3
standout *adj* ***syn*** see SUPERB 3
stand over *vb* ***syn*** see DEFER
standpat *n* ***syn*** see DIEHARD 1
standpatter *n* ***syn*** see DIEHARD 1
standpoint *n* ***syn*** see VIEWPOINT 2
standstill *n* cessation of movement <the car came to a *standstill* in the mud>
syn stay, stillstand, stop
rel arrest, check; pause; cessation, halt
con start; movement
ant start-up
stand up *vb* ***syn*** see RISE 1
stand-up *adj* ***syn*** see ERECT
con lowered; flat, horizontal
||**stang** *vb* ***syn*** see SMART
staple *n* ***syn*** see LOOP 2
staple *n* ***syn*** see BODY 3
star *adj* ***syn*** see CHIEF 2
starch *n* ***syn*** see VIGOR 2
star-crossed *adj* ***syn*** see UNLUCKY
stare *vb* **1** ***syn*** see LOOK 7
idiom ||take a gander at
2 ***syn*** see GAZE 1
idiom fix (*or* rivet) one's eyes on
stare down *vb* to overcome (someone) by or as if by staring <the teacher could not *stare* the boy *down*>
syn look down, outstare
rel glare; master, quell, subdue, suppress; overcome, overwhelm
stark *adj* **1** ***syn*** see UTTER
2 ***syn*** see NUDE 2
3 ***syn*** see EMPTY 1
||**starkers** *adj* ***syn*** see NUDE 2
stark-naked *adj* ***syn*** see NUDE 2
idiom bare (*or* naked) as a newborn babe, ||naked as a jaybird, naked as the day one was born
||**starny** *adj* ***syn*** see STELLAR 1
starry *adj* ***syn*** see STELLAR 1
start *vb* **1** to move suddenly and violently from a state of stillness or rest <*started* from his bed at the sound of shots>
syn bolt, jump, spring, startle
rel dart; bounce; bound, leap; draw (back), flinch, recoil
idiom jump out of one's skin, start aside
ant stay
2 ***syn*** see RECOIL
3 ***syn*** see BEGIN 2
rel proceed, spring
ant end
4 ***syn*** see FOUND 2
5 ***syn*** see BEGIN 1
ant stop
start *n* **1** ***syn*** see BEGINNING
ant finish
2 ***syn*** see ADVANTAGE 3
startle *vb* **1** ***syn*** see START 1
2 ***syn*** see SHOCK 2
3 ***syn*** see FRIGHTEN
rel astonish, surprise
idiom make one jump out of one's skin, ||scare the pants off
startlish *adj* ***syn*** see EXCITABLE
starved *adj* ***syn*** see HUNGRY
rel underfed, undernourished; weakened; half-famished, half-starved
con fed, nourished; overfed
ant well-fed
starving *adj* ***syn*** see HUNGRY
rel craving, famishing, hungering; dying, perishing
idiom crazy for food
stash *vb* **1** ***syn*** see HOARD
2 ***syn*** see HIDE
rel hoard, squirrel
stasis *n* ***syn*** see BALANCE 1
state *n* **1** the way in which one manifests existence or the circumstances under which one exists or

by which one is given distinctive character <remained in a weakened *state* for weeks>
syn condition, mode, posture, situation, status
rel circumstances; attitude, position, stand
idiom state of being
2 ***syn*** see STATUS 1
3 ***syn*** see STATUS 2

state *vb* **1** ***syn*** see RELATE 1
rel elucidate, explain, expound, interpret; set forth
2 ***syn*** see ENUNCIATE 1
3 ***syn*** see SAY 1
4 ***syn*** see EXPRESS 2
ant imply

stated *adj* ***syn*** see FIRM 4

stately *adj* **1** ***syn*** see CEREMONIAL
rel dignified, grand, noble; imperial, kingly, princely, regal, royal
2 ***syn*** see COURTLY
3 ***syn*** see GRAND 1
con lowly, poor; shabby; cheap

statement *n* **1** ***syn*** see EXPRESSION 1
rel outgiving; articulation, presentation, presentment, verbalization, vocalization
2 ***syn*** see WORD 1
rel description, narrative, recital
3 ***syn*** see BILL 1

static *adj* characterized by relatively little or no movement, progression, or change (as in conditions) <a *static* economy>
syn immobile, stagnant, stationary, unmoving; *compare* STEADY 2
rel constant, stabile, stable, unchanging, unfluctuating; fixed, immovable, rigid, sticky; inactive, inert; stalled, stopped, stuck
idiom at a standstill, standing still
con active, changing, mobile, moving, progressing; erratic, fluctuating, inconstant, unstable
ant dynamic

station *n* **1** ***syn*** see PLACE 1
2 ***syn*** see RAILROAD STATION
3 ***syn*** see STATUS 1

station *vb* to appoint or assign to an office or duty <*stationed* guards around the camp>
syn post, set
rel appoint, assign; place, position

stationary *adj* ***syn*** see STATIC
rel motionless, stock-still
ant moving

station house *n* ***syn*** see RAILROAD STATION

statuesque *adj* ***syn*** see SHAPELY

stature *n* **1** ***syn*** see QUALITY 2
rel prestige, standing, status; ability, capacity; competence, qualification
2 ***syn*** see STATUS 2

status *n* **1** rating or positioning in relation to others (as in a social order, community, class, or profession) <his *status* as a slave>
syn capacity, character, footing, place, position, quality, rank, situation, standing, state, station
rel rating
2 social or professional importance or distinction <a lawyer of international *status*>
syn cachet, consequence, dignity, position, prestige, rank, standing, state, stature
rel caliber, merit, worth; distinction, renown; eminence, prominence
con inconsequence, insignificance, unimportance
3 ***syn*** see STATE 1
rel status quo
idiom state of affairs

statute *n* ***syn*** see LAW 1
rel act, enactment

staunch *adj* **1** ***syn*** see SURE 1
2 ***syn*** see FAITHFUL 1
rel firm, strong
idiom as staunch as an oak, tried and true
con mercurial; shaky, unsteady

stave *vb* ***syn*** see HURRY 2

stave off *vb* **1** ***syn*** see FEND (off)
rel beat off, drive (off), fight (off); block, parry
2 ***syn*** see PREVENT 2

staving *adv* ***syn*** see VERY 1
ant barely

stay *vb* **1** ***syn*** see ARREST 1
rel postpone, prorogue, put off
2 to continue to be in one place for a noticeable time <*stayed* late at the office>
syn abide, bide, linger, remain, stick around, tarry, wait
rel dally, delay, dillydally, lag, procrastinate; hang around, loiter; outstay, stay out
ant go
3 ***syn*** see VISIT 3
rel bide, dwell, live
4 ***syn*** see DEFER

stay *n* ***syn*** see STANDSTILL

stay *n* ***syn*** see SUPPORT 3

stay *vb* ***syn*** see BASE

stead *vb* ***syn*** see HELP 1

steadfast *adj* **1** ***syn*** see IMMOVABLE 1
2 ***syn*** see INFLEXIBLE 2
ant unsteadfast, vacillating
3 ***syn*** see SURE 2
ant capricious
4 ***syn*** see FAITHFUL 1
rel unfaltering, unflinching, unquestioning, unwavering

steadfastly *adv* ***syn*** see HARD 7
rel staunchly, strongly

steadiness *n* ***syn*** see STABILITY
ant unsteadiness

steady *adj* **1** ***syn*** see SURE 2
rel unswerving; eternal, never-ending
2 being neither markedly varying nor variable in course or extent <a *steady* rain> <*steady* prices>
syn constant, equable, even, stabile, stable, unchanging, unfluctuating, uniform, unvarying; *compare* STATIC
rel steady-going; certain, changeless, fixed, set, sure, unchangeable; unflickering, unwavering; durable, reliable

---

syn synonym(s) ***rel*** related word(s)
ant antonym(s) ***con*** contrasted word(s)
idiom idiomatic equivalent(s)
‖ use limited; if in doubt, see a dictionary

con inconstant, uneven, unstable; changeable; changing, fluctuating, uncertain, undependable, undulating, unsure, varying, wavering
ant unsteady
3 *syn* see FAITHFUL 1

steady *vb* *syn* see STABILIZE

steady *n* **1** *syn* see BOYFRIEND 2
2 *syn* see GIRL FRIEND 2

steal *vb* **1** to take another's possession illegally and without his knowledge <*stole* a car>
syn abstract, annex, appropriate, cabbage, ‖clout, ‖cly, collar, ‖coon, ‖cop, ‖crook, filch, ‖heist, hook, lift, nab, ‖nail, ‖nick, nim, nip, pilfer, pillage, pinch, pocket, ‖prig, purloin, rip off, smouch, ‖snaffle, ‖snake, snitch, swipe, thieve, vulture
rel mooch; fleece, frisk; grab, grasp, seize, snatch, take; plagiarize; hijack, shanghai; poach, rustle; burglarize, rob; loot, plunder, rifle
idiom make off (*or* away) with, run away (*or* off) with
2 *syn* see SNEAK
3 to move or go quietly so as not to disturb <*stole* out of the sickroom on tiptoe>
syn creep, glide, mouse, slide, slip; *compare* SNEAK
rel tiptoe
con clump, stamp, stomp, stump

steal *n* **1** *syn* see THEFT
2 *syn* see BARGAIN 1

stealage *n* *syn* see THEFT

stealer *n* *syn* see THIEF

stealing *n* *syn* see THEFT

stealthily *adv* *syn* see SECRETLY
ant openly

stealthy *adj* **1** *syn* see SECRET 1
rel crafty, cunning, sly, wily; skulking, slinking, sneaking; catlike
con direct, straight, straightforward
ant open
2 being so quiet, slow, and deliberate in movement as to escape observation <the *stealthy* movements of the cat burglar>
syn catlike, catty, feline, furtive; *compare* SECRET 1
rel noiseless, pantherine, pantherish, quiet, silent; shifty, skulking, sly, sneak, sneaking, sneaky

steam *n* *syn* see POWER 4

steamroller *vb* *syn* see WHIP 2

steam up *vb* *syn* see ANGER 1

steel *vb* **1** *syn* see GIRD 3
rel rally; nerve; buck up; reinforce
idiom grit one's teeth, set one's jaw, take the bit in one's teeth
ant unsteel
2 *syn* see ENCOURAGE 1

steep *adj* **1** having an incline approaching the perpendicular <a *steep* trail up the mountain>
syn abrupt, arduous, precipitate, precipitous, sheer, sideling, steepdown, steep-to, steep-up, ‖stickle
rel elevated, lifted, raised; steepish; high, lofty; prerupt; perpendicular, straight-up; breakneck
con easy, gentle, gradual, moderate; shelfy, shelving, shelvy
2 *syn* see EXCESSIVE 1

steep *vb* **1** *syn* see SOAK 1
2 *syn* see INFUSE 1

steepdown *adj* *syn* see STEEP 1

steep–to *adj* *syn* see STEEP 1

steep–up *adj* *syn* see STEEP 1

steer *vb* *syn* see GUIDE
idiom steer one's course

steer *n* *syn* see TIP

stellar *adj* **1** of, relating to, or suggestive of a star or group of stars <*stellar* light>
syn astral, sidereal, ‖starny, starry, stellular
rel gleaming, luminous, lustrous, shining, starlike, twinkling; star-spangled
con starless
2 *syn* see CHIEF 2

stellify *vb* *syn* see EXALT 1

stellular *adj* *syn* STELLAR 1, astral, sidereal, ‖starny, starry

stem *vb* *syn* see SPRING 1

stem *vb* to hinder or prevent by or as if by damming <*stem* the flow of blood>
syn stanch, stop
rel arrest, check, control

stemma *n* *syn* see GENEALOGY

stench *vb* *syn* see SMELL 3

stenchful *adj* *syn* see MALODOROUS 1

stenchy *adj* *syn* see MALODOROUS 1

stentorian *adj* *syn* see LOUD 1
rel orotund; clamorous, vociferous; gravelly, rough; clarion-voiced, loudmouthed, loud-voiced, trumpet-tongued

stentorious *adj* *syn* see LOUD 1

stentorophonic *adj* *syn* see LOUD 1

step *n* **1** *syn* see FOOTPRINT
2 *syn* see DEGREE 1
3 *syn* see MEASURE 7
rel act, action; motion

step *vb* **1** *syn* see WALK 1
2 *syn* see DANCE 1

step–by–step *adj* *syn* see GRADUAL

step in *vb* **1** *syn* see VISIT 2
2 *syn* see INTERPOSE 2

step up *vb* *syn* see SPEED 3
ant step down

stereotyped *adj* *syn* see TRITE
idiom worn thin

stereotypical *adj* *syn* see TRITE
ant original

sterile *adj* **1** lacking the power to bear offspring or produce fruit <a hybrid that is completely *sterile*>
syn barren, effete, impotent, infecund, infertile, unfruitful
rel sterilized; fallow, fruitless, unproductive; unprolific; arid, bare, dry; dead, desolate
con potent, productive, rich; bearing, fruiting, fruitive, producing, turning out, yielding; fecund, fruitful, prolific, teeming
ant fertile
2 *syn* see UNORIGINAL
rel flat, insipid, jejune, vapid; stale; effete, worn-out; impotent

con fertile, fruitful, potent, producing, productive, prolific
ant fecund
sterilize *vb* to make incapable of producing offspring <*sterilizing* animals in medical experiments>
syn alter, castrate, change, desexualize, fix, geld, mutilate, neuter, unsex
rel emasculate; caponize, poulardize; spay
sterling *adj* ***syn*** see HONORABLE 1
rel pure, true
stern *adj* ***syn*** see SEVERE 1
rel grim, implacable, unrelenting; inexorable, inflexible
ant lenient, soft
‖**stern** *n* ***syn*** see BUTTOCKS
stew *n* **1** ***syn*** see BROTHEL
2 *usu* **stews** *pl* ***syn*** see RED-LIGHT DISTRICT
3 ***syn*** see SLUM
4 ***syn*** see MISCELLANY 1
5 ***syn*** see SNIT
rel boil
6 ***syn*** see COMMOTION 2
stew *vb* **1** ***syn*** see BOIL 2
2 ***syn*** see WORRY 3
idiom be in a stew
stewardly *adj* ***syn*** see SPARING
‖**stewed** *adj* ***syn*** see INTOXICATED 1
stick *n* **1** ***syn*** see BAR 1
2 ***syn*** see DECOY 2
3 **sticks** *pl, used with* the ***syn*** see FRONTIER 2
idiom the middle of nowhere
stick *adv* ***syn*** see ALL 1
stick *vb* **1** ***syn*** see THRUST 2
2 to become or cause to become closely and firmly attached <papers all *stuck* together>
syn adhere, cleave, cling, cohere
rel affix, attach, fasten, fix; glue; cement; fuse, weld; braze, solder
idiom stick close, stick like a wet shirt, stick like the paper on the wall, stick like wax, stick to like a barnacle (*or* leech)
con loosen; detach, disengage
ant unstick
3 ***syn*** see SET 1
4 ***syn*** see NONPLUS 1
5 ***syn*** see FLEECE 1
6 ***syn*** see OVERCHARGE 1
‖**7** ***syn*** see BEAR 10
8 ***syn*** see DEMUR
stickage *n* ***syn*** see ADHERENCE 1
stick around *vb* ***syn*** see STAY 2
stick–at–nothing *adj* ***syn*** see UNSCRUPULOUS
sticker *n* ***syn*** see SEAL
sticking *n* ***syn*** see ADHERENCE 1
stick–in–the–mud *n* ***syn*** see FOGY
‖**stickle** *adj* ***syn*** see STEEP 1
stickle *vb* ***syn*** see DEMUR
rel hold out, stall; contend, kick, object, protest
stick out *vb* **1** ***syn*** see BULGE
rel outstretch, outthrust, protend, push
2 ***syn*** see STRIKE 1
3 ***syn*** see BEAR 10
stick up *vb* ***syn*** see ROB 1
sticky *adj* **1** having the quality of sticking by or as if by adhesion <*sticky* syrup>
syn adhesive, ‖claggy, ‖clarty, cloggy, gluey, gooey, gummy, stodgy
rel tacky; viscid, viscous
2 ***syn*** see HUMID
3 ***syn*** see HARD 6
4 ***syn*** see SENTIMENTAL
‖**stickybeak** *n* ***syn*** see BUSYBODY
sticky–fingered *adj* ***syn*** see LARCENOUS
stiff *adj* **1** incapable of or highly resistant to bending or flexing <a *stiff* cardboard packing box>
syn immalleable, impliable, incompliant, inelastic, inflexible, rigid, unbending, unflexible, unyielding; *compare* INFLEXIBLE 2
rel stiffish; hard, resistant; hardened, petrified; stark
idiom stiff as a board (*or* poker)
con soft, softened; yielding; bendable, pliable, pliant; limber, supple, willowy
ant flexible, flexile
2 ***syn*** see INTOXICATED 1
3 ***syn*** see OBSTINATE
4 characterized by a lack of ease, grace, or spontaneity especially in style <a play whose dialogue and characters were *stiff* and perfunctory>
syn buckram, cardboard, muscle-bound, stilted, wooden
rel rigid, set, studied; machine-made, mechanical, stereotyped, stock; arid, dry, dull
con expressive, graphic, vivid; easy, fluent, graceful, smooth
5 ***syn*** see EXCESSIVE 1
stiff *n* **1** ***syn*** see CORPSE
2 ***syn*** see DRUNKARD
3 ***syn*** see MISER
stiff–necked *adj* ***syn*** see OBSTINATE
stifle *vb* **1** ***syn*** see SUFFOCATE
2 ***syn*** see MUFFLE 2
3 ***syn*** see SUPPRESS 3
4 ***syn*** see STULTIFY
stifling *adj* **1** producing or seeming to produce suffocation <*stifling* heat>
syn smothering, smothery, ‖smudgy, suffocating, suffocative; *compare* HUMID, STUFFY 1
rel oppressive, overpowering; unbearable, unendurable
2 ***syn*** see STUFFY 1
stifling *n* ***syn*** see REPRESSION 1
stigma *n* a mark of shame or discredit <the *stigma* of personal cowardice>
syn bar sinister, black eye, blot, blur, brand, odium, onus, slur, spot, stain
rel besmirchment, disfigurement, smudge, smutch, taint, tainting; disgrace, dishonor, shame
con credit, distinction, glory, honor; bay(s), crown, laurel(s)
still *adj* **1** ***syn*** see MOTIONLESS

---

syn synonym(s) *rel* related word(s)
ant antonym(s) *con* contrasted word(s)
idiom idiomatic equivalent(s)
‖ use limited; if in doubt, see a dictionary

2 ***syn*** see CALM 1
rel peaceful, unperturbed
con roiled, roily, turbid
3 devoid of or making no stir, sound, or noise <the streets were *still* at 3:00 A.M.>
syn hush, hushful, noiseless, quiet, silent, soundless, stilly, whist
rel calm, hushed, peaceful, placid, serene, tranquil; deathlike, deathly
idiom deathly still, still as death
ant noisy

still *vb* **1** ***syn*** see CALM
ant agitate
2 ***syn*** see SILENCE

still *adv* **1** ***syn*** see HOWEVER
2 ***syn*** see YET 1
idiom still (*or* even) more
3 ***syn*** see ALSO 2

still *n* ***syn*** see SILENCE 1

still and all *adv* ***syn*** see HOWEVER

still–hunt *vb* ***syn*** see STALK 1

stillness *n* ***syn*** see SILENCE 1

stillstand *n* ***syn*** see STANDSTILL

stilly *adj* **1** ***syn*** see STILL 3
con agitated, disturbed, noisy
ant noiseful
2 ***syn*** see CALM 1

stilted *adj* **1** ***syn*** see RHETORICAL
2 ***syn*** see STIFF 4
3 ***syn*** see GENTEEL 3
rel conventional, formal; decorous; prim

stimulant *n* ***syn*** see STIMULUS

stimulate *vb* **1** ***syn*** see PROVOKE 4
rel enliven, vivify; activate, dynamize, energize, vitalize
idiom build a fire under, get one started (*or* moving)
con unnerve; deaden
2 ***syn*** see ELATE

stimulating *adj* **1** ***syn*** see EXCITING
rel enlivening, lively; provocative, seminal, suggestive; incitory, stimulative, stimulatory
2 ***syn*** see INVIGORATING

stimulative *adj* ***syn*** see INVIGORATING

stimulus *n* something that rouses the mind or spirits or incites to activity <the war proved a *stimulus* to the economy> <sought a *stimulus* to take her mind off her own troubles>
syn catalyst, goad, impetus, impulse, incentive, incitation, incitement, instigation, motivation, propellant, provocative, push, spur, stimulant; *compare* MOTIVE 1
rel boost, encouragement, inducement, invitation, urging; cause, motive; excitement, piquing, provocation, stimulation

sting *vb* ***syn*** see SMART

stingy *adj* being unwilling or showing unwillingness to share with others <too *stingy* to tip the waiter>
syn cheap, cheeseparing, ‖chinchy, chintzy, close, closefisted, costive, hardfisted, hard-handed, ironfisted, mean, mingy, miserly, ‖narrow, narrow-fisted, narrowhearted, niggard, niggardly, parsimonious, penny-pinching, penny-wise, penurious, pinching, pinchpenny, save-all, ‖scant, scrimpy, scrimy, tight, tightfisted, ungenerous, ungiving; *compare* SPARING
rel economical, frugal, Scotch, sparing, thrifty; scaly, screwy
idiom as close as a vise, as close (*or* tight) as paper on a wall, near (*or* close *or* tight) as the bark on a tree
con bountiful, giving, liberal, munificent, openhanded, philanthropic, unsparing, unstinting; prodigal
ant generous

stink *vb* ***syn*** see SMELL 3

stinkard *n* ***syn*** see SNOT 1

stinkaroo *n* ***syn*** see SNOT 1

stinker *n* ***syn*** see SNOT 1

stinking *adj* **1** ***syn*** see MALODOROUS 1
idiom stinking to high heaven
‖2 ***syn*** see INTOXICATED 1

‖**stinko** *adj* ***syn*** see INTOXICATED 1

stinky *adj* ***syn*** see MALODOROUS 1

stint *vb* **1** ***syn*** see SCRIMP
2 ***syn*** see SPARE 3

stint *n* **1** ***syn*** see RESTRICTION 1
2 ***syn*** see TASK 1
rel amount, quantity; allotment, apportionment; participation, share
3 ***syn*** see SPELL 1

stipend *n* ***syn*** see WAGE
rel award, consideration, payment

stipple *vb* ***syn*** see SPECKLE 1

stipulate *vb* ***syn*** see SPECIFY 3
rel designate; state; provide

stipulated *adj* ***syn*** see FIRM 3
rel designated, pinned down
con implied, unstated, unwritten

stipulation *n* ***syn*** see CONDITION 1
rel specification; circumscription, limit

stir *vb* **1** to cause to shift from quiescence or torpor into activity <a teacher who *stirred* the minds of his most sluggish students>
syn arouse, awaken, bestir, challenge, kindle, rally, rouse, wake, waken, whet; *compare* PROVOKE 4
rel excite, galvanize, inspire, provoke, quicken, stimulate; agitate, foment, incite, instigate; activate, energize, vitalize; actuate, drive, impel, move; ‖roust, rout
idiom make (*or* have) an impact on, set astir, set on fire
2 ***syn*** see WAKE 1
3 ***syn*** see SEETHE 4

stir (up) *vb* ***syn*** see INCITE
idiom add fuel to the flame, apply the torch, feed the fire, pour oil on the fire, stir the embers

stir *n* **1** signs of excited activity, hurry, or commotion <noticed a *stir* within the crowd>
syn ado, bustle, flurry, furore, fuss, pother, whirl, whirlpool, whirlwind; *compare* COMMOTION 4
rel agitation, disquiet, stir-up; commotion, disturbance; din, hubbub, pandemonium, stirabout, tumult
con calm, peace, placidity; inaction, inactivity
ant tranquillity

2 ***syn*** see MOTION 1

||**stir** *n* ***syn*** see JAIL

||**stirra** *n* ***syn*** see MAN 3

stirring *n* ***syn*** see MOTION 1

stirring *adj* ***syn*** see EXCITING
rel heart-stirring, soul-stirring

stitch *n* ***syn*** see PAIN 1

stivy *adj* ***syn*** see STUFFY 1

stock *n* **1** ***syn*** see FAMILY 1
2 ***syn*** see ESTIMATION 1
3 ***syn*** see TRUST 1
4 ***syn*** see SUPPLY
5 ***syn*** see RESERVE

stock *vb* to equip, furnish, supply, or have material requisites (as for sale) <a bar that *stocks* all the best brands of liquor>
syn carry, keep
rel have; furnish, supply
idiom have (*or* keep) in stock, keep on hand

stockade *n* ***syn*** see JAIL

stockpile *n* **1** ***syn*** see PILE 1
2 ***syn*** see RESERVE

stockpile *vb* ***syn*** see ACCUMULATE

stock–still *adj* ***syn*** see MOTIONLESS

stocky *adj* being compact and broad in build and often short in stature <a *stocky* but quick and hard-hitting catcher>
syn ||chuffy, ||chumpy, chunky, dumpy, heavyset, squab, squat, squdgy, stubby, ||stuggy, stumpy, thick, thick-bodied, thickset
rel plump, stout; bunty, low-set, short; lumpish, lumpy, pudgy; corpulent, fat
con lean, skinny, thin, wiry

stodge *vb* **1** ***syn*** see SATIATE
2 ***syn*** see PLOD 1

stodgy *adj* **1** ***syn*** see STICKY 1
2 ***syn*** see DULL 9
rel unexciting; pedantic; heavy, ponderous, weighty
3 ***syn*** see TACKY 2

stoic *adj* ***syn*** see IMPASSIVE 1
rel aloof, detached, indifferent, unconcerned; self-controlled, Spartan; indomitable, unassailable; long-suffering, patient, resigned

stoicism *n* ***syn*** see APATHY 1
rel backbone, fortitude, grit, guts, pluck, sand

||**stoit** *vb* ***syn*** see LURCH 2

||**stoiter** *vb* ***syn*** see LURCH 2

stolid *adj* ***syn*** see IMPASSIVE 1
rel blunt, dull, obtuse; dense, dull, dumb, slow, stupid; inactive, inert, passive, supine
ant sensitive

stolidity *n* ***syn*** see APATHY 1
rel dullness, dumbness, slowness, stupidity; inactiveness, inactivity, inertia, passivity
con aptness, quickness, readiness; animation, enlivening, quickening; ardor, enthusiasm, fervor, passion, zeal; fire
ant sensitivity

stomach *n* **1** ***syn*** see ABDOMEN
2 ***syn*** see APPETITE 1

stomach *vb* ***syn*** see BEAR 10

stomachache *n* abdominal pain <she has a terrible *stomachache*>
syn bellyache, colic, collywobbles, gripe(s)
rel distress, misery

||**stomachy** *adj* ***syn*** see IRASCIBLE

stomp *vb* ***syn*** see TRAMPLE 2

stone–blind *adj* ***syn*** see BLIND 1

stone–broke *adj* ***syn*** see POOR 1

stoned *adj* **1** ***syn*** see INTOXICATED 1
2 ***syn*** see DRUGGED

stone–still *adj* ***syn*** see MOTIONLESS

stony *adj* **1** ***syn*** see UNFEELING 2
ant soft
2 ***syn*** see POOR 1

stonyhearted *adj* ***syn*** see UNFEELING 2
rel flinty, hard, stonelike
idiom as cold as marble
ant softhearted

stooge *n* **1** one who plays a subordinate or compliant role to a principal <an executive who was only a *stooge* with no real power>
syn Charlie McCarthy, dummy, yes-man
2 ***syn*** see TOOL 2

stool *n* ***syn*** see INFORMER

||**stool** *vb* ***syn*** see INFORM 3

stoolie *n* ***syn*** see INFORMER

stool pigeon *n* ***syn*** see INFORMER

stoop *vb* **1** to descend from one's level (as of rank or dignity) usually to do something <a king who would not *stoop* to consider the common people>
syn condescend, deign
rel relax, thaw, unbend; accord, concede; accommodate, favor, oblige
idiom be so good as to, come (*or* get) down from one's high horse, lower oneself
2 to drop in status or dignity by indulgence in pettiness or unworthy behavior <a woman who would not *stoop* to tell a lie>
syn descend, sink
idiom act beneath oneself, debase (*or* demean) oneself, lower oneself
3 ***syn*** see DUCK 2

stop *vb* **1** ***syn*** see STEM
2 ***syn*** see FILL 1
rel disrupt, hinder, interrupt; cut off, shut off, turn off
ant unstop
3 to suspend or cause to suspend activity <the conversation *stopped*>
syn cease, desist, ||deval, discontinue, give over, halt, knock off, leave off, quit, surcease; *compare* ARREST 1
rel ||can, refrain (from); arrest, check, cut off, interrupt; stay, suspend; ||cheese, lay off; break off, break up, end, terminate
con continue, go on, keep (on), keep up, persist
ant start
4 to come to a standstill <the car *stopped* at the intersection>

syn bring up, draw up, fetch up, halt, haul up, pull up
con start; move; pull out
ant go

stop (in *or* by) *vb syn* see VISIT 2
stop (over) *vb syn* see VISIT 3
idiom make a stopover
stop *n* **1** *syn* see END 2
ant start
2 *syn* see BAR 2
3 *syn* see STANDSTILL
stopcock *n syn* see FAUCET
stopgap *adj syn* see MAKESHIFT
stopgap *n syn* see RESOURCE 3
stopover *n syn* see SOJOURN
stopper *vb syn* see FILL 1
ant unstopper
store *vb syn* see STOW
store (up) *vb syn* see ACCUMULATE
rel deposit; cache
store *n* **1** *syn* see RESERVE
2 *syn* see SUPPLY
3 *syn* see DEPOT 2
4 a business establishment where goods are shown for sale <a food *store*>
syn market, outlet, shop, showroom
rel discounter, discount house, discount store, emporium
store *adj syn* see READY-MADE
store–bought *adj syn* see READY-MADE
‖**store–boughten** *adj syn* see READY-MADE
storehouse *n syn* see DEPOT 2
storm *n* **1** *syn* see COMMOTION 4
2 *syn* see BARRAGE
storm *vb syn* see ATTACK 1
storm and stress *n syn* see UNREST
stormful *adj syn* see WILD 6
rel threatening; dusty, murky; foul; howling, riproaring, roaring
ant calm
stormily *adv syn* see HARD 2
stormy *adj syn* see WILD 6
rel threatening; dusty, murky; foul; howling, riproaring, roaring
ant calm
story *n* **1** *syn* see ACCOUNT 7
2 a recital of real or imaginary happenings that is less elaborate than a novel <told the *story* of his escape> <a simple *story* of heartwarming devotion>
syn anecdote, narration, narrative, tale, yarn; *compare* ACCOUNT 7
rel conte; description; fable; folktale, legend, märchen; Canterbury tale, cock-and-bull story, fabrication, fairy tale, fiction
3 *syn* see LIE
storyteller *n syn* see LIAR
‖**stot** *vb syn* see LURCH 2
stout *adj* **1** *syn* see BRAVE 1
idiom bold as a lion
con irresolute; fainthearted
2 *syn* see STRONG 2
rel resolute, steadfast; hard; indomitable, invincible
idiom as strong (*or* stalwart) as an English oak
3 *syn* see FAT 2
rel thick-bodied; ‖plenitudinous
ant spare
stouthearted *adj syn* see BRAVE 1
stow *vb* to put (articles) into a storage space <*stowed* his gear belowdecks>
syn bestow, pack, store, warehouse
ant unstow
straddle *vb* **1** *syn* see BESTRIDE 2
2 *syn* see SPRAWL 2
straggle *vb* **1** *syn* see WANDER 1
2 *syn* see SPRAWL 2
straggler *n syn* see LAGGARD
straight *adv* **1** *syn* see AWAY 3
2 *syn* see DIRECTLY 1
straight *adj* **1** *syn* see DIRECT 2
idiom as straight as an arrow
ant circuitous
2 *syn* see STRAIGHTFORWARD 2
3 free from admixture or extraneous matter <a shot of *straight* liquor>
syn neat, plain, pure, unadulterated, undiluted, unmixed
rel unmodified; concentrated; strong
con adulterated, blended, mixed; watered-down; weak
4 *syn* see CONVENTIONAL 1
straight *n syn* see RIGHT 1
straightaway *adv syn* see AWAY 3
straightforward *adj* **1** *syn* see DIRECT 2
2 free from all that is dishonest or secretive <a *straightforward* answer>
syn aboveboard, forthright, plain dealing, straight; *compare* FRANK
rel pretenseless; honest, honorable, just, upright, upstanding; candid, frank, open, plain, unequivocal; direct, outspoken
con equivocal, evasive, shuffling; indirect; prevaricative; dishonest, untruthful
ant devious
3 *syn* see FRANK
rel barefaced, straight-from-the-shoulder
4 *syn* see CLEAR 5
straightly *adv syn* see DIRECTLY 1
straight off *adv syn* see AWAY 3
straight–out *adj syn* see UTTER
straight–up *adj* **1** *syn* see ERECT
2 *syn* see VERTICAL
straightway *adv syn* see AWAY 3
strain *n* **1** *syn* see HINT 2
2 *syn* see MELODY
3 *syn* see MOOD 1
strain *vb* **1** *syn* see TRY 2
rel stretch
idiom put a strain on
2 to injure (as a body part) by overuse or misuse <*strained* a muscle while lifting weights>
syn pull
3 *syn* see LABOR 1
4 *syn* see EXUDE
5 *syn* see DEMUR
strain *n syn* see STRESS 1
strained *adj syn* see FORCED

rel taut, tense, tight
con unforced, unlabored; unconstrained
ant unstrained

strait *n* ***syn*** see JUNCTURE 2
rel bind, squeeze; difficulty, hardship, rigor, vicissitude; bewilderment, mystification, perplexity

straitlaced *adj* ***syn*** see PRIM 1
rel hidebound, intolerant, narrow, narrow-minded; rigorous, strict
idiom prim and proper
con easygoing, relaxed; broadminded, liberal, liberal-minded; libertine

strake *vb* ***syn*** see STREAK

||**stramash** *n* ***syn*** see CRASH 3

strand *n* ***syn*** see SHORE

strand *vb* ***syn*** see SHIPWRECK 1

stranded *adj* ***syn*** see AGROUND
idiom high and dry, run aground

strange *adj* **1** ***syn*** see EXOTIC 2
2 ***syn*** see UNFAMILIAR 1
rel unknown; alien
3 ***syn*** see MARVELOUS 1
4 deviating from what is ordinary, usual, or to be expected <a *strange*, unpredictable man>
syn bizarre, curious, eccentric, erratic, idiosyncratic, odd, oddball, outlandish, peculiar, quaint, queer, ||rum, rummy, singular, uncouth, unusual, weird; *compare* EXCEPTIONAL 1, MYSTERIOUS
rel aberrant, abnormal, atypical, off, off-the-wall; fishy, funny; far-out, freaky, ||kinky, kooky, offbeat, outré, ||scatty; crazy, nutty; fantastic, grotesque
idiom as strange as they come
con common, ordinary, unexceptional, usual; expected, predictable
ant familiar

stranger *n* a nonresident or an unknown person in a community <he felt he had become a *stranger* in a foreign land>
syn alien, auslander, foreigner, inconnu, outcomer, outlander, outsider
rel out-of-stater, outstater; transient; visitor; immigrant; wanderer
idiom stranger within the gates
con inhabitant, resident; aboriginal, aborigine, autochthon, indigene, native

strangle *vb* **1** ***syn*** see CHOKE 1
2 ***syn*** see SUPPRESS 2

strangling *n* ***syn*** see REPRESSION 1

strapped *adj* ***syn*** see POOR 1

stratagem *n* ***syn*** see TRICK 1
rel conspiracy, intrigue, machination, plot

strategy *n* ***syn*** see PLAN 1

stratospheric *adj* ***syn*** see EXCESSIVE 1

straw *adj* ***syn*** see BLOND 1
rel strawish, strawy

straw *vb* ***syn*** see STREW 1

stray *vb* **1** ***syn*** see WANDER 1
2 ***syn*** see ERR
idiom stray from the straight and narrow
3 ***syn*** see DIGRESS 2
idiom get off the track, get sidetracked

stray *adj* ***syn*** see ERRATIC 1
rel random, sporadic

streak *n* ***syn*** see HINT 2

streak *vb* to make irregular lines or stripes of contrasting colors on or in <hair *streaked* with gray>
syn strake, striate, stripe
rel dapple, fleck, spot; marble, variegate, vein

stream *n* **1** ***syn*** see CREEK 2
2 ***syn*** see FLOW

stream *vb* ***syn*** see POUR 2

streamer *n* ***syn*** see FLAG

streamline *vb* ***syn*** see SIMPLIFY

||**streel** *n* ***syn*** see SLATTERN 1

street *n* ***syn*** see WAY 1
rel ruelle, streetlet; drive

street arab *n* ***syn*** see VAGABOND

street girl *n* ***syn*** see PROSTITUTE

streetwalker *n* ***syn*** see PROSTITUTE

streetwalking *n* ***syn*** see PROSTITUTION

strength *n* **1** ***syn*** see POWER 4
rel brawn; sturdiness, toughness; healthiness, soundness
con feebleness
ant weakness
2 ***syn*** see STABILITY
3 ***syn*** see SUBSTANCE 2

strengthen *vb* **1** ***syn*** see ENCOURAGE 1
2 to make strong or stronger <exercise is needed to *strengthen* the body>
syn energize, fortify, invigorate, reinforce
rel brace, support, undergird; anneal, ruggedize, sinew, tone (up), toughen; cheer, embolden, encourage, enhearten, ensteel, hearten, inspirit, nerve, steel
con cripple, debilitate, disable, enfeeble, tear down, undermine; deject, discourage, dishearten, dispirit; emasculate, enervate, unman, unnerve
ant weaken
3 ***syn*** see GIRD 3
idiom gather one's resources, recruit one's strength

||**strengthy** *adj* ***syn*** see STRONG 1

strenuous *adj* **1** ***syn*** see VIGOROUS
2 ***syn*** see HARD 6
rel breathless, energy-consuming; mean, wicked; Herculean
idiom a long hard pull, an uphill climb, tough going
con comfortable, cushy, light, unburdensome
ant effortless

stress *n* the action or effect of force exerted within or upon a thing <the bridge trusses slowly yielded to *stress* and buckled under the weight of the deck>
syn pressure, strain, tension
rel pinch; burden, weight
2 ***syn*** see EMPHASIS

---

syn synonym(s) *rel* related word(s)
ant antonym(s) *con* contrasted word(s)
idiom idiomatic equivalent(s)
|| use limited; if in doubt, see a dictionary

THESAURUS

rel import, importance
stress *vb* **1** *syn* see TRY 2
2 *syn* see EMPHASIZE
stretch *vb* **1** *syn* see RUN 8
rel range, roll
2 *syn* see EXTEND 3
con abbreviate, shorten; condense, curtail, cut, trim
3 *syn* see EMBROIDER
stretch (out) *vb* *syn* see REST 1
stretch *n* **1** *syn* see RANGE 2
2 *syn* see DISTANCE 1
3 *syn* see EXPANSE
rel area, region, tract
4 *syn* see WHILE 1
stretch *adj* *syn* see ELASTIC 1
stretchy *adj* *syn* see ELASTIC 1
strew *vb* **1** to spread (something) loosely or at intervals usually over a substantial area <*strew* seed for birds>
syn bestrew, broadcast, disject, disseminate, scatter, sow, straw; *compare* SPREAD 1, SPRINKLE 1
rel dust, pepper; dissipate; cover
2 *syn* see SPREAD 1
striate *vb* *syn* see STREAK
strict *adj* **1** *syn* see RIGID 3
rel exacting, oppressive, unsparing; dour, forbidding, grim, hard-boiled, harsh, tough
idiom not to be trifled (*or* messed) with
con easy, easygoing; lax, loose; permissive
ant lenient
2 *syn* see TRUE 3
stricture *n* **1** *syn* see RESTRICTION 1
2 *syn* see ANIMADVERSION
‖**striddle** *vb* **1** *syn* see BESTRIDE 2
2 *syn* see STRIDE 1
stride *vb* **1** to move or walk with long often purposeful steps <*strode* to the door and slammed it>
syn march, sling, stalk, ‖striddle
rel clump, stamp, stomp, tramp, tromp
2 *syn* see BESTRIDE
strident *adj* **1** *syn* see HARSH 3
rel loud, stentorian, stertorous
2 *syn* see VOCIFEROUS
stridulent *adj* *syn* see HARSH 3
stridulous *adj* *syn* see HARSH 3
strife *n* **1** *syn* see DISCORD
rel argument, controversy, dispute; altercation, quarrel, squabble, wrangle; brawl, broil, fracas; affray, combat, fight, fray
ant accord
2 *syn* see CONTEST 1
strike *vb* **1** to engage in a temporary work stoppage to effect compliance with demands made on an employer <they *struck* for higher wages>
syn stick out, walk out
idiom go (*or* be) on strike
2 to deliver (a blow) in a strong, vigorous manner <angrily *struck* the boy>
syn ‖biff, catch, clout, ‖devel, ding, hit, ‖nail, pop, slog, ‖slosh, smite, sock, swat, whack; *compare* SLAM 1, SLAP 1
rel beat, pummel, ‖slat, ‖swap, ‖wap, whop; cudgel, hammer, mace; ‖plug, poke, ‖puck, punch; bang, bash, crash, ‖pandy, slam; ‖stoush, thrash
idiom hang one on, let one fly
3 *syn* see GIVE 10
4 *syn* see AFFLICT
5 *syn* see SEIZE 3
6 *syn* see ATTACK 1
7 *syn* see OCCUR 2
8 *syn* see AFFECT
9 *syn* see DON 2
strike *n* *syn* see DISCOVERY
strike out *vb* *syn* see HEAD 3
striker *n* *syn* see HELPER
striking *adj* *syn* see NOTICEABLE
rel showy; forceful, powerful; cogent, compelling, telling
strikingly *adv* *syn* see VERY 1
string *n* **1** *syn* see LINE 5
2 *syn* see RESOURCE 3
3 *syn* see SUCCESSION 2
4 strings *pl* *syn* see POWER 1
string (up) *vb* *syn* see HANG 2
string along *vb* *syn* see TRIFLE 1
idiom keep (someone) dangling
stringent *adj* **1** *syn* see RIGID 3
rel binding, confining, drawing
2 *syn* see GRIM 2
strings *n pl* *syn* see CONDITION 1
stringy *adj* *syn* see MUSCULAR 1
‖**strinkle** *vb* *syn* see SPRINKLE 1
strip *vb* **1** to remove the clothing of <guards *stripped* and searched the prisoners>
syn denude, disrobe, unclothe, undress
rel doff, peel, take off; bare, denudate, expose, uncover; disfrock, unfrock
idiom strip to the buff
con clothe, dress, robe; cover
2 to take something (as honors, privileges, functions, or trappings) away from <an exiled king now *stripped* of his power>
syn bankrupt, bare, denudate, denude, deprive, dismantle, disrobe, divest; *compare* DEPRIVE 2
rel bereave; deplenish, disfurnish, ‖displenish, dispossess; despoil, rob
con clothe, endow, furnish, grant, vest; install
ant invest
3 *syn* see RAVAGE
4 *syn* see SKIN 2
strip *n* *syn* see STRIPTEASE
strip *n* **1** a relatively long and narrow piece or section <tear old linen into *strips* for bandages>
syn band, bandeau, banding, fillet, ribbon, stripe
rel piece; section; segment; shred
2 *syn* see BAR 1
stripe *vb* *syn* see WHIP 1
stripe *n* **1** *syn* see STRIP 1
2 *syn* see TYPE
stripe *vb* *syn* see STREAK
stripling *n* *syn* see BOY 1
stripped *adj* **1** *syn* see NUDE 2
con attired; covered
ant clothed, dressed
2 *syn* see OPEN 2

con covered, unexposed; protected
stripper *n syn* see STRIPTEASER
stripping *n syn* see STRIPTEASE
striptease *n* entertainment in which a female performer removes her clothing piece by piece in view of an audience <a nightclub featuring *striptease*>
syn strip, stripping
idiom exotic dancing
stripteaser *n* one who performs a striptease <worked part-time as a model and *stripteaser*>
syn ecdysiast, peeler, stripper, stripteuse, teaser
idiom exotic dancer, ‖pantie peeler, ‖strip-and-shake artist, strip artist
stripteuse *n syn* see STRIPTEASER
strive *vb* **1** *syn* see LABOR 1
2 *syn* see TRY 5
rel labor, toil, travail, work; drive, strain
striving *n* **1** *syn* see CONTEST 1
rel contending; combat, fight
2 *syn* see ATTEMPT
rel labor, toil, travail, work
stroll *vb syn* see SAUNTER
stroll *n syn* see WALK 1
strong *adj* **1** having great physical strength <had the *strong* hands and arms of a wrestler>
syn mighty, powerful, ‖strengthy, wieldy; *compare* MUSCULAR 2
rel firm, robust, stark, strapping, sturdy, two-handed; able-bodied, tough; brawny, muscular, sinewy; lusty, vigorous
idiom strong as a bull (*or* ox)
con feeble, frail; puny, weak-bodied; forceless, impotent, powerless, strengthless
ant weak
2 having or manifesting great force or power (as in acting or resisting) <a *strong* constitution>
syn stalwart, stout, sturdy, tenacious, tough
rel hardy, robust, rugged, strapping; firm, solid, staunch; durable, enduring; forceful, potent, powerful; lusty, vigorous
con frail; forceless, impotent, powerless, strengthless; depleted, failing
ant weak
3 being rich in a characteristic ingredient <*strong* coffee>
syn concentrated, full-bodied, lusty, potent, robust
rel strong-flavored, strong-tasting; straight, undiluted, unmixed; rich; heroic, large, powerful
con diluted, mixed, watered-down
ant weak
4 *syn* see SPIRITUOUS
5 *syn* see SURE 1
rel solid, substantial, unmoving, unyielding
6 *syn* see MALODOROUS 1
strong arm *n* **1** *syn* see POWER 4
2 *syn* see THUG 1
strong-arm *vb syn* see INTIMIDATE
stronghold *n syn* see FORT
strongly *adv syn* see HARD 1
ant weakly
strong man *n syn* see TYRANT
strong suit *n syn* see FORTE
structure *n* **1** *syn* see BUILDING
rel construction, erection, pile
2 *syn* see EDIFICE
3 something made up of more or less interdependent elements and having a definite organizational pattern <the complex bureaucratic *structure* of modern government>
syn framework
rel anatomy, skeleton; build, construction, frame; arrangement, composition, form, format, makeup, morphology; complex, network, system
struggle *vb syn* see TRY 5
rel compete, vie
idiom make a valiant attempt (*or* try)
ant give up
struggle *n syn* see ATTEMPT
strum *vb syn* see HUM
strumpet *n syn* see WANTON
‖**strunt** *vb syn* see STRUT 2
‖**strunt** *n syn* see LIQUOR 2
strut *vb* **1** *syn* see SASHAY
2 to walk with an air of pomposity or affected dignity <a pompous general *strutting* off the parade ground>
syn ‖strunt, swagger
rel flaunt, parade
con cower, cringe; slink
stubborn *adj* **1** *syn* see OBSTINATE
rel contumacious, insubordinate, rebellious; cantankerous, ornery; ‖stunkard, ‖stunt
idiom set in one's ways, stubborn as a mule
con adaptable, pliable, pliant; amenable, tractable
ant docile
2 *syn* see INFLEXIBLE 2
stubbornness *n syn* see DEFIANCE 2
rel cantankerousness, orneriness
stubby *adj syn* see STOCKY
stube *n syn* see ALEHOUSE
stuck-up *adj syn* see VAIN 3
idiom too big for one's breeches, wise in one's own conceit
stud *vb syn* see SPOT 2
studied *adj syn* see DELIBERATE 1
rel thoughtful; intentional, voluntary, willful, willing
con natural, offhand
ant unstudied
studio *n* the working place of an artist (as a painter) <moved to a larger *studio*>
syn atelier, bottega
rel shop, workroom, workshop
studious *adj syn* see DELIBERATE 1
ant impromptu
study *n* **1** *syn* see REVERIE
2 *syn* see ATTENTION 1
rel contemplation, weighing; abstraction, meditation, musing, pondering, rumination

---

syn synonym(s) *rel* related word(s)
ant antonym(s) *con* contrasted word(s)
idiom idiomatic equivalent(s)
‖ use limited; if in doubt, see a dictionary

3 ***syn*** see EXERCISE 4

study *vb* **1** ***syn*** see CONSIDER 1
idiom give careful study to
2 ***syn*** see SCRUTINIZE 1

stuff *n* **1** ***syn*** see PERSONAL EFFECTS
2 ***syn*** see MONEY
3 ***syn*** see THING 5
4 ***syn*** see ESSENCE 2

stuff *vb* ***syn*** see CRAM 1
rel overfill, overstuff
idiom fill to overflowing, fill to the brim

stuffed *adj* ***syn*** see FULL 1

stuffed shirt *n* a smug usually pompous person with an inflexibly conservative or reactionary outlook <a *stuffed shirt* with a starched mind>
syn Blimp, Colonel Blimp, fuddy-duddy
rel diehard; prig, prude, smug
con freethinker, latitudinarian, liberal, libertarian, libertine; avant-garde

stuffing *n* ***syn*** see ENTRAILS
rel ‖tar

stuffy *adj* **1** marked by a heavy oppressive quality of air <a *stuffy* room that needed airing>
syn airless, breathless, close, stifling, stivy, suffocating, sultry; *compare* HUMID, STIFLING 1
rel heavy, oppressive, thick; stagnant; shut-up, unventilated
con airy, breezy; open, ventilated; bracing, invigorating, refreshing, stimulating
2 ***syn*** see PRIM 1
rel dull, humdrum, stodgy; hidebound, illiberal, narrow, narrow-minded
3 ***syn*** see POMPOUS 1

‖stuggy *adj* ***syn*** see STOCKY

stultify *vb* to deprive of vitality and render futile especially by enfeebling or repressive influences <artistic creativity *stultified* by the intrusion of propaganda>
syn constipate, stagnate, stifle, trammel
rel discourage, inhibit, restrain; check, stunt; enfeeble, impair, weaken; deaden, dull; repress, smother, suffocate, suppress; invalidate, nullify
con encourage, foster, nourish; pique, provoke, stimulate

stultiloquence *n* ***syn*** see CHATTER

stumble *vb* **1** ***syn*** see WALLOW 2
rel falter, waver; trip; fall
2 ***syn*** see DEMUR
3 to move so clumsily and awkwardly as to lose one's balance or trip and fall <*stumbled* across the darkened room and fell>
syn blunder, bumble, lurch, ‖snapper; *compare* WALLOW 2
rel reel, stagger, totter; trip; pitch, topple
4 ***syn*** see LUMBER
5 ***syn*** see TEETER
rel careen, swing
6 to act, proceed, or execute in a hesitant and clumsily faltering manner <*stumbled* through his Latin translation>
syn limp, muddle, shuffle
rel falter, hesitate, wobble; blunder, bumble; botch, bungle, ‖muck
ant breeze
7 ***syn*** see HAPPEN 2
idiom come (*or* run) up against, fall upon, stub one's toe upon (*or* on)
8 ***syn*** see PUZZLE

stumblebum *n* a clumsy inept or blundering person <a staff consisting of third-raters and *stumblebums*>
syn blunderbuss, blunderer, bungler
rel incompetent
con crackerjack, ‖dab, ‖darb, expert, topnotcher, whiz; natural; professional

stumbling block *n* ***syn*** see OBSTACLE

stump *vb* **1** ***syn*** see NONPLUS 1
2 ***syn*** see LUMBER

stump *n* ***syn*** see DEFIANCE 1

stumpy *adj* ***syn*** see STOCKY

‖stumpy *n* ***syn*** see MONEY

stun *vb* ***syn*** see DAZE 2
rel nonplus; amaze, astound, flabbergast; knock out
idiom strike dumb (*or* dead)

stunner *n* **1** ***syn*** see WONDER 1
2 ***syn*** see BEAUTY

stunning *adj* **1** ***syn*** see EXCELLENT
2 ***syn*** see BEAUTIFUL

‖stunpoll *n* ***syn*** see DUNCE

‖stunt *adj* ***syn*** see STUNTED

stunt *vb* to hinder the normal growth and development of <the inhospitable climate had *stunted* all vegetation>
syn dwarf, suppress
rel check, curb, hold back; impair

stunt *n* ***syn*** see TRICK 3

stunted *adj* having had one's growth and development hindered or arrested <the children were *stunted* from malnutrition>
syn runted, runtish, runty, ‖scrunty, ‖stunt
rel undersized; dwarf
con able-bodied, robust well-set, well-set-up; giant, oversize; healthy, strong, sturdy, vigorous

‖stupe *n* ***syn*** see DUNCE

stupefy *vb* **1** ***syn*** see DULL 5
2 ***syn*** see DAZE 2
rel addle, faze, rattle; nonplus

stupendous *adj* **1** ***syn*** see MARVELOUS 1
2 ***syn*** see MONSTROUS 1

stupid *adj* **1** lacking in or exhibiting a lack of power to absorb ideas or impressions <a willing boy but too *stupid* to succeed in school>
syn beefheaded, beef-witted, beetleheaded, blear-eyed, blear-witted, blockheaded, blockish, chuckleheaded, dense, doltish, dull, dumb, duncical, fatheaded, goosey, hammerheaded, numskulled, pinhead, pinheaded, thick, thickheaded, thick-witted; *compare* RETARDED, SIMPLE 3
rel asinine, fatuous, foolish, silly, simple; brute, brutish, dummel, lumbering, oafish, slow, slow-witted, sluggish; crass; backward, half-witted, retarded; idiotic, imbecilic
idiom ‖dead above (*or* between) the ears, ‖dead from the neck up, having a block for a head, having cotton between the ears, ‖muscle-bound between the ears

con acute, alert, bright, clever, keen, knowing, quick, quick-witted, sharp, smart; sage, wise; brilliant; able, competent
ant intelligent
2 *syn* see LETHARGIC
stupid *n syn* see DUNCE
stupor *n syn* see LETHARGY 1
rel sopor; anesthesia, insensibility
sturdy *adj syn* see STRONG 2
rel sound, substantial
ant decrepit
Sturm und Drang *n syn* see UNREST
‖stut *vb syn* see STAMMER 1
stutter *vb syn* see STAMMER 1
sty *n* **1** an extremely unkempt or filthy place <the basement was a rat-infested *sty*>
syn dump, pigpen, pigsty
2 *syn* see SINK 1
stygian *adj syn* see INFERNAL 2
style *n* **1** *syn* see VEIN 1
2 *syn* see NAME 1
3 *syn* see FASHION 3
4 an individual's characteristic attitudes and taste as expressed or indicated in his way of life <she liked the man's sophisticated *style*>
syn manner, way
rel behavior; bearing, carriage; characteristic, trait; idiosyncrasy, peculiarity
style *vb syn* see NAME 1
stylish *adj* being in accordance with or conforming to current fashion <she was a *stylish* dresser>
syn a la mode, chic, ‖classy, dashing, exclusive, fashionable, in, modish, posh, sharp, smart, snappy, swank, swish, tonish, tony, ‖trendy, trig, ultrafashionable, with-it; *compare* DAPPER
rel new, new-day, newfangled, new-fashioned; modern, modernistic, up-to-date; chichi, doggish, doggy, natty, rakish, sassy, swagger; ostentatious, pretentious, ritzy, showy, swell; sleek, slick
idiom in fashion, in the mode
con styleless; old-fashioned, outmoded, out-of-date; drab, tasteless
ant dowdy, unstylish
suasible *adj syn* see RECEPTIVE 1
suave *adj* being conspicuously and ingratiatingly tactful and well-mannered <a man of *suave*, well-bred equanimity>
syn bland, civilized, smooth, urbane; *compare* TACTFUL
rel affable, cordial, genial, gracious, sociable; courteous, courtly, polite; diplomatic, politic; cultivated, cultured, distingué, polished, refined, well-bred; sophisticated, worldly; ingratiating, soft, soft-spoken; fulsome, slick, unctuous
con clumsy, unpolished, unskilled; tactless, undiplomatic, untactful
ant bluff
sub *adj syn* see SUBORDINATE
sub *n syn* see SUBSTITUTE 1
subaltern *n syn* see INFERIOR
subaquatic *adj syn* see SUBMARINE
subaqueous *adj syn* see SUBMARINE
subaverage *adj syn* see LOW 9
subconscious *n* mental activities that occur just below the threshold of consciousness <a motive probably rooted in his *subconscious*>
syn underconsciousness, undersense
rel subconsciousness; subliminal self
idiom subconscious (*or* submerged) mind
con consciousness; awareness
subdolous *adj syn* see SLY 2
subdue *vb syn* see CONQUER 1
rel extinguish, put down, quash, quell, quench, squelch, suppress
subdued *adj* **1** *syn* see QUIET 4
2 reduced or lacking in force, intensity, or vividness <*subdued* colors> <the child answered his questions in a timid *subdued* voice>
syn low-key, low-keyed, sober, soft, softened, toned down
rel moderated, tempered; controlled, restrained; mellow; neutral; quiet
con enlivened, intensified; bright, intense, strong; brilliant, vivid; saturated; blaring, glaring, harsh, screaming
3 *syn* see TAME
ant unsubdued
subduer *n syn* see VICTOR 1
subfusc *adj syn* see DULL 8
subitaneous *adj syn* see PRECIPITATE 1
subjacent *adj syn* see INFERIOR 1
ant superjacent
subject *n* **1** *syn* see CITIZEN 2
2 the basic idea or the principal object of attention in a discourse or artistic composition <the Puritan ethic was the *subject* of her paper>
syn argument, head, matter, motif, motive, point, subject matter, text, theme, topic
rel material, substance; problem, question; leitmotiv; core, meat
con elaboration, enlargement, enlarging, expatiation; development, explication
subject *adj* **1** *syn* see SUBORDINATE
rel servile, slavish, subservient
ant dominant, sovereign
2 *syn* see LIABLE 2
rel apt, likely
subject *vb syn* see EXPOSE 1
subjective *adj* peculiar to a particular individual as modified by individual bias and limitations <*subjective* judgments>
syn unobjective
rel biased, prejudiced; abstract, nonobjective, nonrepresentational, nonrepresentative
ant objective
subject matter *n syn* see SUBJECT 2
subjoin *vb syn* see ADD 1
rel combine, conjoin, unite
con part, separate, sever
subjugate *vb* **1** *syn* see CONQUER 1
rel compel, coerce, force

---

syn synonym(s) *rel* related word(s)
ant antonym(s) *con* contrasted word(s)
idiom idiomatic equivalent(s)
‖ use limited; if in doubt, see a dictionary

2 ***syn*** see ENSLAVE
ant liberate
subjugator *n* ***syn*** see VICTOR 1
sublease *vb* ***syn*** see SUBLET
sublet *vb* to turn over to another one's right of occupancy of (rented or leased housing) <*sublet* her apartment to a friend>
syn sublease, underlease, underlet
sublime *vb* ***syn*** see EXALT 1
sublime *adj* **1** ***syn*** see GRAND 3
2 ***syn*** see SPLENDID 2
rel abstract, ideal, transcendent, transcendental; divine, holy, sacred, spiritual; august, majestic, noble, stately
sublimity *n* ***syn*** see APEX 2
sublunary *adj* ***syn*** see EARTHLY 1
submarine *adj* being, acting, growing, or used under water <a *submarine* camera>
syn subaquatic, subaqueous, underwater
submerge *vb* **1** ***syn*** see DIP 1
rel drench, impregnate, saturate, soak
2 ***syn*** see DELUGE 1
3 ***syn*** see SINK 1
submerse *vb* **1** ***syn*** see DIP 1
2 ***syn*** see SINK 1
submission *n* ***syn*** see SURRENDER
rel bowing, submitting; acquiescence, compliance, resignation; cringing, servility; prostration
ant resistance
submissive *adj* **1** ***syn*** see TAME
rel complying, conformable, obeying; bowing down, unerect; menial, servile, slavish, subservient
ant rebellious
2 ***syn*** see PASSIVE 2
submit *vb* **1** ***syn*** see YIELD 2
ant resist, withstand
2 to offer or commit (something) for consideration, study, or decision <*submitted* his report directly to the general>
syn hand in, refer
rel bring, deliver, present; offer, proffer, tender; send in; provide
3 ***syn*** see SUGGEST 4
4 ***syn*** see FALL 3
ant hold out, resist
subnormal *adj* ***syn*** see LOW 9
rel subpar
subordinate *adj* placed in or occupying a lower class, rank, or status <making the executive *subordinate* to the legislative branch>
syn collateral, dependent, secondary, sub, subject, tributary, under
rel adjuvant, auxiliary, contributory, subsidiary; satellite; inferior, subaltern, subalternate; accessory, parergal, supplementary
con chief, first, leading, main; dominant, master, superior
subordinate *n* ***syn*** see INFERIOR
sub rosa *adv* ***syn*** see SECRETLY
ant aboveboard
sub–rosa *adj* ***syn*** see SECRET 1
ant aboveboard
subscribe *vb* **1** ***syn*** see SIGN 1
2 ***syn*** see CONTRIBUTE 1
3 ***syn*** see ASSENT
rel approve, endorse, favor, sanction
subsequent *adj* **1** being, occurring, or carried out at a time after something else <*subsequent* events disproved his predictions>
syn after, ensuing, later, posterior, postliminary, subsequential
rel following, next, succeeding; consequential, resultant, resulting
con exordial, introductory, prefatory, preliminary, preludial; anterior, precedent, preceding, prior
ant antecedent
2 ***syn*** see CONSECUTIVE
ant antecedent
subsequential *adj* **1** ***syn*** see SUBSEQUENT 1
2 ***syn*** see CONSECUTIVE
ant antecedent
subsequently *adv* ***syn*** see AFTER
ant antecedently, priorly
subsequent to *prep* ***syn*** see AFTER 2
subservient *adj* **1** ***syn*** see AUXILIARY
2 showing extreme compliance or abject obedience <a *subservient* minor bureaucrat>
syn menial, obeisant, obsequious, servile, slavish
rel acquiescent, compliant, resigned, submissive; cowering, cringing, fawning, truckling; abject, ignoble, mean
idiom as obedient as a dog
con aggressive; arrogant, haughty; rebellious; independent, irrepressible, uncontainable
ant domineering, overbearing
subside *vb* ***syn*** see ABATE 4
idiom dwindle down
subsidiary *adj* ***syn*** see AUXILIARY
rel backup; minor, tributary
subsidize *vb* ***syn*** see ENDOW 2
rel back; promote; help
subsidy *n* ***syn*** see APPROPRIATION
rel subsidization; gift, reward
subsist *vb* ***syn*** see BE
subsistence *n* ***syn*** see LIVING
substance *n* **1** ***syn*** see TENOR 1
rel import, meaning
idiom the general drift
2 the inner significance or central meaning of something written or said <just give me the *substance* of his speech>
syn amount, body, burden, core, crux, gist, kernel, matter, meat, nub, nubbin, pith, purport, sense, short, strength, sum and substance, sum total, thrust, upshot; *compare* BODY 3, ESSENCE 2, MEANING 1, TENOR 1
rel center, focus, heart, nucleus; point; import, meaningfulness
3 ***syn*** see BODY 3
rel drift, tenor
4 ***syn*** see ESSENCE 2
5 ***syn*** see THING 5
6 ***syn*** see WEALTH 2
substantial *adj* **1** ***syn*** see MATERIAL 1
con airy, ethereal

ant unsubstantial
2 ***syn*** see IMPORTANT 1
rel key, principal; strong; serious
3 ***syn*** see PROSPEROUS 3
rel solid, solvent

substantiate *vb* **1** ***syn*** see EMBODY 1
rel substantialize, substantify
2 ***syn*** see CONFIRM 2
rel demonstrate, prove, test, try

substitutable *adj* ***syn*** see INTERCHANGEABLE

substitute *n* **1** a person who takes the place of or acts instead of another <found a *substitute* for the sick teacher>
syn alternate, backup, fill-in, locum tenens, pinch hitter, replacement, stand-in, sub, succedaneum, surrogate
rel relay, relief; deputy, procurator, proxy; supply; double, understudy
2 ***syn*** see RESOURCE 3

substitute *vb* ***syn*** see EXCHANGE 2

substitute *adj* **1** serving or fitted for use as a substitute <a *substitute* driver was needed for the long trip>
syn alternate, alternative, backup, surrogate
rel additional, another; other, second; reserve; supplemental, supplementary, suppletory
2 ***syn*** see ARTIFICIAL 2

substract *vb* ***syn*** see DEDUCT 1

substratal *adj* ***syn*** see ELEMENTAL 1

substratum *n* **1** ***syn*** see BASIS 1
rel core, meat, stuff, substance
2 ***syn*** see BASE 1

substruction *n* ***syn*** see BASE 1

substructure *n* ***syn*** see BASE 1
ant superstructure

subsume *vb* ***syn*** see INCLUDE

subterfuge *n* ***syn*** see DECEPTION 1

subterrane *n* ***syn*** see CAVE

subterranean *adj* being, lying, functioning, or operating under the surface of the earth <*subterranean* hot springs that emerge as geysers>
syn subterrestrial, underearth, underfoot, underground
con aboveground, surface, surficial

subterranean *n* ***syn*** see CAVE

subterrestrial *adj* ***syn*** see SUBTERRANEAN

subtile *adj* ***syn*** see THIN 2

subtle *adj* **1** ***syn*** see THIN 2
2 ***syn*** see FINE 1
ant unsubtle
3 ***syn*** see LOGICAL 2
rel dexterous, skillful
con blunt; dense
4 ***syn*** see SLY 2
ant unsubtle

subtract *vb* ***syn*** see DEDUCT 1
ant add

subtraction *n* ***syn*** see DEDUCTION 1
ant addition

suburbs *n pl* ***syn*** see ENVIRONS 2
rel fringes; suburbia

subvention *n* ***syn*** see APPROPRIATION

subversion *n* ***syn*** see SABOTAGE
rel demolishing, destroying, destruction

subvert *vb* ***syn*** see SABOTAGE
rel overthrow, overturn, upset; demolish, destroy, ruin; corrupt, debase, deprave, pervert
con sustain, uphold

succedaneum *n* ***syn*** see SUBSTITUTE 1

succedent *adj* ***syn*** see CONSECUTIVE

succeed *vb* **1** ***syn*** see FOLLOW 1
ant precede
2 to result favorably according to plans and desires <that advertising campaign really *succeeded*>
syn click, come off, go, go over, pan out, prove out
rel catch on; prevail
idiom go over big, go over with a bang, hit the mark, make a hit, turn out well
ant fail, flop
3 to attain or be attaining a desired end <how to *succeed* in big business>
syn arrive, flourish, go, make out, prosper, score, thrive
rel ‖dow; get ahead; boom; achieve, attain, gain, reach; accomplish, effect, fulfill; conquer, prevail, triumph, win (out)
idiom do all right by oneself, do well, gain one's end, get places, get somewhere, get to the top of the ladder, make a success, make it (big), make one's mark, ‖make the big time, make the grade
con dwindle, languish; fall down, flounder, founder; lose (out); bust
ant fail

succeeding *adj* ***syn*** see CONSECUTIVE

succès fou *n* ***syn*** see SMASH 6

success *n* a succeeding fully or in accordance with one's desires <attributed his business *success* to hard work and attention to detail>
syn arrival, ‖do, flying colors, go, prosperity, successfulness
rel accomplishment, achievement, attainment; triumph, victory
ant failure; nonsuccess, unsuccessfulness

successful *adj* resulting in or having gained success <a *successful* business venture>
syn prosperous, thriving; *compare* FLOURISHING
rel extraordinary, notable, noteworthy, outstanding, smash, smashing
idiom crowned (*or* blessed *or* flushed) with success, ‖out front
con failing, thriveless, unprosperous; defeated, disappointed, failed, frustrated; bankrupt, broken, destroyed, ruined
ant successless, unsuccessful

successfully *adv* ***syn*** see WELL 5
ant unsuccessfully

successfulness *n* ***syn*** see SUCCESS
ant nonsuccess, unsuccessfulness

succession *n* **1** ***syn*** see ORDER 5
2 a number of things that follow each other in some order <another *succession* of price hikes>

---

syn synonym(s) ***rel*** related word(s)
ant antonym(s) ***con*** contrasted word(s)
idiom idiomatic equivalent(s)
‖ use limited; if in doubt, see a dictionary

THESAURUS

syn alternation, chain, consecution, course, order, progression, row, sequel, sequence, series, string, suite, train; *compare* CYCLE 1
rel successiveness; round, round robin

successional *adj* *syn* see CONSECUTIVE

successive *adj* *syn* see CONSECUTIVE
rel alternating, rotating

successively *adv* *syn* see TOGETHER 2

succinct *adj* *syn* see CONCISE
rel blunt, brusque
idiom right to the point
ant discursive

succinctly *adv* *syn* see BRIEFLY
ant discursively

succor *n* *syn* see HELP 1
rel ministration, ministry; maintenance, nourishment, sustenance

succubus *n* *syn* see DEVIL 2

succulent *adj* full of juice <a *succulent* roast>
syn juicy, ‖sappy

succumb *vb* **1** *syn* see YIELD 2
rel abandon, relinquish, resign
2 *syn* see FALL 3
idiom hand over one's sword, meet one's Waterloo, show (*or* wave) the white flag, strike (*or* haul down) one's colors
3 *syn* see COLLAPSE 2
idiom bite the dust, ‖take the count
4 *syn* see DIE 1
idiom yield one's breath

such *adj* **1** being previously characterized or specified <authorized to seize illegally parked cars and impound *such* vehicles>
syn aforementioned, aforesaid, said
2 being of so extreme a degree or quality <*such* nonsense as I had never heard before>
syn that
3 *syn* see LIKE

such *pron* **1** *syn* see SUCH A ONE
2 *syn* see SUCHLIKE
idiom the like

such a one *pron* someone or something that has been, is being, or will be stated, implied, or exemplified <the area is full of caverns; *such a one* may be found here>
syn such

suchlike *adj* *syn* see LIKE

suchlike *pron* a person or thing of the same or similar kind <airplanes, missiles, rockets, and *suchlike*>
syn such

sucker *n* **1** *syn* see PARASITE
2 *syn* see FOOL 3
idiom easy pickings

sucker *vb* *syn* see CHEAT

suck in *vb* *syn* see DECEIVE

‖**suck–in** *n* *syn* see DECEPTION 1

suckle *vb* *syn* see NURSE 1

sudden *adj* *syn* see PRECIPITATE 1
rel accelerated, quickened, speeded; expeditious, fast, fleet, rapid, swift

sudden *adv* **1** *syn* see UNAWARES
2 *syn* see SHORT 1

suddenly *adv* **1** *syn* see SHORT 1
2 *syn* see UNAWARES
idiom of (*or* on) a sudden, on the sudden

suds *n pl but sing or pl in constr* **1** *syn* see SADNESS
2 *syn* see FOAM

sue *vb* *syn* see ADDRESS 8
idiom make (*or* pay) suit to, press one's suit

sue (for *or* to) *vb* *syn* see PETITION

suffer *vb* **1** *syn* see BEAR 10
rel accept, admit, receive
idiom grin and abide
2 *syn* see EXPERIENCE 1
3 *syn* see LET 2
rel countenance; accept, admit, receive; acquiesce, bow, submit, yield
‖**4** *syn* see HURT 4

sufferable *adj* *syn* see BEARABLE
ant insufferable

sufferance *n* *syn* see PERMISSION

suffering *n* *syn* see DISTRESS
rel adversity, misfortune

suffice *vb* *syn* see SERVE 3

sufficiency *n* *syn* see ENOUGH
ant insufficiency

sufficient *adj* **1** being what is requisite or needed especially without superfluity <there is *sufficient* bread left for breakfast>
syn adequate, comfortable, competent, decent, enough, satisfactory, sufficing; *compare* DECENT 4
rel ample, plenteous, plentiful, plenty; commensurable, commensurate, due, proportionate; acceptable, agreeable, pleasing
con inadequate, unsufficing; deficient; failing, lacking, missing, wanting
ant insufficient
2 *syn* see DECENT 4
idiom fair to middling

sufficient *n* *syn* see ENOUGH

sufficiently *adv* *syn* see ENOUGH 1
ant insufficiently

sufficing *adj* *syn* see SUFFICIENT 1

suffocate *vb* to stop the respiration of (as by asphyxiation) <the child was *suffocated* in an old refrigerator>
syn asphyxiate, choke, ‖quackle, smother, stifle; *compare* CHOKE 1
rel stive; strangle

suffocating *adj* **1** *syn* see STIFLING 1
2 *syn* see STUFFY 1

suffocative *adj* *syn* see STIFLING 1

suffrage *n* the right, privilege, or power of expressing one's choice or wish (as in an election or in the determination of policy) <universal *suffrage*>
syn ballot, franchise, vote
rel voice

suffuse *vb* *syn* see INFUSE 1
rel interject, interpose, introduce

‖**sugar** *n* *syn* see MONEY

sugar (over) *vb* *syn* see SUGARCOAT 1

sugarcoat *vb* **1** to make (something difficult or unpleasant) superficially easy or attractive <*sugarcoated* the reproach with a smile>
syn candy, honey, sugar (over), sweeten
rel edulcorate

2 *syn* see PALLIATE

sugarplum *n* *syn* see SOP 2

suggest *vb* **1** to convey an idea indirectly <designing attractive books with jackets that truly *suggest* their contents>
syn connote, hint, imply, insinuate, intimate; *compare* POINT 2
rel advert, allude, refer; denote
idiom bring to mind
con demonstrate, display, exhibit, manifest, set out, show
ant express
2 *syn* see POINT 2
rel promise
idiom be the sign of, point in the direction of
3 *syn* see PROPOSE 1
4 to offer (as an idea or theory) for consideration <this, I *suggest,* is what really happened>
syn submit, theorize
rel conjecture; imagine
5 to represent another thing indirectly, figuratively, and sometimes obscurely by evoking a thought, image, or conception of it <the meaning of a poem is often *suggested* in its title>
syn adumbrate, shadow (forth); *compare* ADUMBRATE 1
rel outline, sketch; betoken, symbolize; typify
con display, flaunt, parade
ant manifest

suggestion *n* **1** *syn* see PROPOSAL
2 *syn* see HINT 1
rel implication, innuendo
3 *syn* see ASSOCIATION 4
rel allusion; reminder
con demonstration, display, exhibition, manifestation, show
ant expression
4 *syn* see HINT 2

suggestive *adj* **1** *syn* see EVOCATIVE
rel significative
2 *syn* see RISQUÉ
rel erotic, sexy

suicide *n* the act or an instance of taking one's own life voluntarily and intentionally <committed *suicide* by shooting herself>
syn felo-de-se, hara-kiri, self-destruction, self-murder, self-slaughter, self-violence

suit *n* **1** a legal proceeding instituted for the sake of demanding justice or enforcing a right <filed a *suit* to recover her property>
syn action, case, cause, lawsuit
2 *syn* see PRAYER
rel asking, request, requesting, solicitation, soliciting

suit *vb* **1** *syn* see AGREE 4
idiom be in accord with, check out to the letter
2 *syn* see SERVE 3
3 *syn* see ADAPT
4 to be suitable for or to <the right word is the one that *suits* the occasion>
syn agree (with), become, befit, fit, go (together *or* with); *compare* SUIT 6
rel harmonize (with); benefit; please, satisfy
idiom answer a need (*or* the purpose), hit the spot
con clash, conflict, disaccord, disagree
5 *syn* see FLATTER
6 to meet the needs or desires of <this arrangement *suits* me fine>
syn please, satisfy; *compare* SUIT 4
con discontent, displease, dissatisfy; disappoint, fail, let down

suitability *n* *syn* see ORDER 11
ant unsuitability

suitable *adj* **1** *syn* see GOOD 2
ant unsuitable
2 *syn* see JUST 3
rel reasonable; advisable, expedient, politic
ant unsuitable
3 *syn* see FIT 1
rel nice, presentable, seemly
ant unbecoming, unsuitable
4 *syn* see ELIGIBLE
ant unsuitable

suitableness *n* *syn* see ORDER 11
ant unsuitableness

suitably *adv* *syn* see WELL 4
ant unsuitably

suite *n* **1** *syn* see ENTOURAGE
2 *syn* see GROUP 3
3 *syn* see APARTMENT 1
4 *syn* see SUCCESSION 2

suited *adj* *syn* see ASSORTED 2
ant unsuited

suitor *n* **1** *syn* see SUPPLIANT
2 one who courts a woman or seeks to marry her <a *suitor* for the king's daughter>
syn spark, sparker, swain, wooer
rel beau, boyfriend; cavalier, gallant; lover, man, paramour

sulk *vb* to be sullen or morose in mood usually because of a grievance <*sulked* all day when he didn't call>
syn ‖dort, grump, ‖mump, pet, pout, ‖sull
rel frown, glower, lower, scowl; brood, gloom, mope, take on
idiom be in a sulk, have the sulks, ‖take the dods

sulk *n, often* **sulks** *pl* the state, condition, or mood of one sulking <sat in a *sulk* all day after being reprimanded>
syn ‖dods, ‖dorts, grumps, mulligrubs, mumps, pouts, sullens
rel sourness, sulkiness, surliness; glumness, grouchiness
idiom a case of the sulks

sulky *adj* *syn* see SULLEN
rel cranky, testy, touchy; cantankerous, irritable, querulous
idiom having the sulks

‖sull *vb* *syn* see SULK

sullen *adj* showing a forbidding or disagreeable mood <stalked out in *sullen* silence>

---

syn synonym(s) *rel* related word(s)
ant antonym(s) *con* contrasted word(s)
idiom idiomatic equivalent(s)
‖ use limited; if in doubt, see a dictionary

syn ‖chuff, ‖chuffy, crabbed, crabby, ‖dorty, dour, gloomy, glum, morose, mumpish, saturnine, sulky, surly, ugly
rel moody; tenebrific, tenebrose, tenebrous; frowning, glowering, lowering, scowling; cross, fretful, grumpy, ill-humored, peevish, petulant, pouting, pouty, sour; black, hostile, malevolent, malicious, malign, mean, ‖runty; cynical, pessimistic
con easy, gay, high-spirited, insouciant, lighthearted, smiling
sullens *n pl* ***syn*** see SULK
sully *vb* ***syn*** see TAINT 1
rel disgrace, shame
sulphurous *adj* ***syn*** see INFERNAL 1
sultry *adj* **1** ***syn*** see HUMID
rel smothering, smothery, ‖smudgy, stifling, suffocating
2 ***syn*** see STUFFY 1
3 ***syn*** see HOT 1
idiom hot as Hades, ‖hot as old Billy Hell
4 ***syn*** see SENSATIONAL 2
sum *n* **1** ***syn*** see WHOLE 1
2 ***syn*** see WHOLE 2
rel body, bulk, mass; structure
3 ***syn*** see SUMMARY
sum *vb* **1** ***syn*** see ADD 2
2 ***syn*** see EPITOMIZE 1
sum (to *or* into) *vb* ***syn*** see AMOUNT 1
sum and substance *n* **1** ***syn*** see SUBSTANCE 2
2 ***syn*** see MEANING 1
summarize *vb* ***syn*** see EPITOMIZE 1
rel recapitulate, résumé, retrograde
summary *adj* **1** ***syn*** see CONCISE
rel compact, compacted
ant circumstantial
2 done or executed on the spot and without formality <a *summary* trial and speedy execution>
syn drumhead
summary *n* a short restatement of the main points <a *summary* of the news>
syn epitome, recapitulation, résumé, sum, summation, summing-up, sum-up
rel outline; run-through; roundup; inventory
con amplification, elaboration, enlargement, expansion
summate *vb* **1** ***syn*** see ADD 2
2 ***syn*** see EPITOMIZE 1
summation *n* ***syn*** see SUMMARY
summative *adj* ***syn*** see CUMULATIVE
summer *n* the season between spring and autumn <liked to swim during the *summer*>
syn summertide, summertime
rel midsummer
summer complaint *n* ***syn*** see DIARRHEA
summerhouse *n* a covered structure in a garden or park designed to provide a shady resting place <watched the sea from the *summerhouse*>
syn alcove, belvedere, garden house, gazebo, pagoda
summertide *n* ***syn*** see SUMMER
summertime *n* ***syn*** see SUMMER
summing–up *n* ***syn*** see SUMMARY
summit *n* **1** ***syn*** see TOP 1
2 ***syn*** see APEX 2
summon *vb* **1** ***syn*** see CONVOKE
2 to demand or request the presence or service of <were *summoned* to the principal's office>
syn call, call in, convene, summons; *compare* CONVOKE
rel bid, command, enjoin, order; cite, subpoena
idiom bid come
summons *vb* ***syn*** see SUMMON 2
‖**sump** *n* ***syn*** see SWAMP
sumptuous *adj* **1** ***syn*** see LUXURIOUS 3
rel gorgeous, resplendent, splendid, superb; lavish, rich
2 ***syn*** see GRAND 2
rel awe-inspiring, grandiose, imposing
sum total *n* **1** ***syn*** see WHOLE 1
2 ***syn*** see SUBSTANCE 2
sum up *vb* ***syn*** see EPITOMIZE 1
sum–up *n* ***syn*** see SUMMARY
sun *n* **1** the heavenly body about which the earth rotates <up in time to see the *sun* rise>
syn daystar, phoebus, Sol
rel celestial body, luminary, orb, star
idiom old Sol
2 the radiation of the sun <enjoying the warm spring *sun*>
syn sunlight, sunshine
rel daylight; radiance, radiation
sun *vb* to expose to sunshine <*sunned* himself too long and got badly burned>
syn bask, insolate
rel sunbathe; sunburn, sun-cure, sun-dry, tan
sunbeamy *adj* ***syn*** see CHEERFUL 1
Sunday best *n* ***syn*** see FINERY
idiom Sunday-go-to-meeting clothes
sunder *vb* **1** ***syn*** see SEPARATE 1
rel cleave, rend, rive
2 ***syn*** see CUT 5
‖**sundowner** *n* ***syn*** see VAGABOND
sundries *n pl* miscellaneous small articles, details, or items <supplied such *sundries* as needles, pins, and thread>
syn etceteras, oddments, odds and ends, this and that(s)
rel notions
sundry *adj* **1** ***syn*** MANY, legion, multifarious, multitudinal, multitudinous, numerous, populous, ‖several, various, voluminous
idiom all and sundry
2 ***syn*** see SEVERAL 3
idiom all sorts of
sundry *pron, pl in constr* an indeterminate number of more than one or two <*sundry* were interviewed; a few were selected>
syn divers, many, ‖several, various
idiom all and sundry, quite a few
sunk *adj* ***syn*** see DOWNCAST
sunlight *n* ***syn*** see SUN 2
sunny *adj* **1** ***syn*** see FAIR 2
rel bright, brilliant
idiom bright and sunny
2 ***syn*** see CHEERFUL 1
sunrise *n* ***syn*** see DAWN 1
sunset *n* ***syn*** see EVENING 2

sunshine *n* ***syn*** see SUN 2
sunshine *adj* ***syn*** see FAIR 2
sunshining *adj* ***syn*** see FAIR 2
sunshiny *adj* ***syn*** see FAIR 2
sunup *n* ***syn*** see DAWN 1
sup (off *or* up) *vb* ***syn*** see DRINK 1
super *adj* ***syn*** see MARVELOUS 2
idiom out of this world
super *adv* **1** ***syn*** see VERY 1
2 ***syn*** see EVER 6
superabundant *adj* abounding to a great, abnormal, or excessive degree <*superabundant* harvests had brought down prices>
syn overabounding, overabundant, overflowing
rel abounding, abundant, cornucopian, plenteous, plentiful; excess, excessive, overmuch, surplus; crawling, teeming; overspilling; epidemic, rampant
superadd *vb* ***syn*** see ADD 1
superannuate *vb* **1** ***syn*** see OUTDATE
2 ***syn*** see RETIRE 2
superb *adj* **1** ***syn*** see GRAND 3
rel noble; majestic
2 ***syn*** see SPLENDID 2
rel imposing, stately; opulent
3 consummately impressive and supremely excellent of its kind <the writer's style is brilliant and his command of words and imagery, *superb*>
syn magnificent, outstanding, standout, superexcellent, superlative; *compare* SUPREME
rel glorious, gorgeous, marvelous, resplendent; crashing, rousing, sensational, slambang, super, superfine, wonderful; best, optimal, optimum, prime; sublime
idiom very best
con inferior, mediocre, poor, substandard; atrocious, awful, dreadful, shocking; deplorable, dismal, lamentable, pitiful, woeful; abominable, execrable, outrageous, shameful
ant wretched
superbity *n* ***syn*** see PRIDE 3
supercilious *adj* ***syn*** see PROUD 1
rel sniffish, sniffy, snifty, snippy, snuffy; sneering
superciliousness *n* ***syn*** see PRIDE 3
supererogant *adj* ***syn*** see SUPEREROGATORY
supererogative *adj* ***syn*** see SUPEREROGATORY
supererogatory *adj* given or done without compulsion, need, or warrant <people who offer *supererogatory* advice>
syn gratuitous, supererogant, supererogative, unasked, uncalled-for, wanton
rel nonessential, superfluous, supernumerary, unnecessary, unneeded
con essential, indispensible, vital; compulsory, obligatory; called-for, needful, required, requisite, sought, wanted
superexcellent *adj* ***syn*** see SUPERB 3
rel incomparable, matchless, unparalleled, unsurpassed
superficial *adj* **1** ***syn*** see SHALLOW 1
2 lacking in depth, solidity, and comprehensiveness <wrote only a *superficial* report on the situation>
syn cursory, depthless, shallow, sketchy, uncritical
rel bird's-eye, general; one-dimensional, skin-deep; smattery
con comprehensive, full, inclusive; deep, detailed, in-depth, thorough; critical
ant exhaustive
superficies *n* ***syn*** see TOP 2
superfluent *adj* ***syn*** see SUPERFLUOUS
superfluity *n* **1** ***syn*** see EXCESS 1
rel overflowing, swarming, teeming
2 ***syn*** see LUXURY
superfluous *adj* exceeding what is needed or indispensable <omitted all *superfluous* information>
syn de trop, excess, extra, recrementitious, spare, superfluent, supernumerary, surplus
rel unnecessary, unneeded, unwanted; needless, useless; dispensable, nonessential; gratuitous, supererogatory, unasked, un- called-for
con critical, crucial, imperative; essential, fundamental, vital; consequential, important, momentous, notable, noteworthy; defective, inadequate
ant deficient
superhuman *adj* **1** ***syn*** see SUPERNATURAL 1
2 ***syn*** see SUPERNATURAL 2
superhuman *n* ***syn*** see SUPERMAN
superincumbent *adj* **1** ***syn*** see SUPERIOR 1
2 ***syn*** see ONEROUS
superintend *vb* ***syn*** see SUPERVISE
superintendence *n* ***syn*** see OVERSIGHT 1
rel direction, presidence
superintendency *n* ***syn*** see OVERSIGHT 1
rel direction, presidence
superior *adj* **1** being or regarded as being above the level of another <the new assistant received a *superior* rating for his work>
syn greater, higher, over, overlying, superincumbent, superjacent
rel major, primary, senior
con lesser, lower, nether, under
ant inferior
2 ***syn*** see SUPERNATURAL 1
3 ***syn*** see BETTER 2
ant inferior
4 being of higher quality, accomplishment, or merit <a class of *superior* students>
syn exceptional, premium; *compare* MARVELOUS 2
rel noteworthy, remarkable, unusual
con commonplace, ordinary, unexceptional, unremarkable
ant average
5 ***syn*** see CHOICE
6 ***syn*** see EXCELLENT
ant inferior
7 ***syn*** see PROUD 1
superior *n* one standing above another in a hierarchy of rank <was always respectful to his *superiors* in the department>

---

syn synonym(s) ***rel*** related word(s)
ant antonym(s) ***con*** contrasted word(s)
idiom idiomatic equivalent(s)
‖ use limited; if in doubt, see a dictionary

syn better, brass hat, elder, higher-up, senior
rel heavyweight
ant inferior

superiority *n* ***syn*** see BETTER 2
rel ascendancy, dominance, supremacy
ant inferiority

superjacent *adj* ***syn*** see SUPERIOR 1
ant subjacent

superlative *adj* ***syn*** see SUPERB 3
rel accomplished, consummate, finished

superman *n* a person of extraordinary power or achievement <a space program run by scientific *supermen*>
syn demigod, superhuman
idiom Triton among the minnows
con also-ran, loser, underdog
ant subhuman

supermundane *adj* ***syn*** see SUPERNATURAL 1

supernatural *adj* **1** of, relating to, or proceeding from an order of existence beyond the visible observable universe <many then believed in a *supernatural* force that directs history>
syn metaphysical, miraculous, numinous, preternatural, superhuman, superior, supermundane, suprahuman, supramundane, supranatural, unearthly
rel paranormal, rare, unusual; spiritual; celestial, heavenly; divine
2 being much more than is natural or normal <had a *supernatural* ability to win money>
syn superhuman, supernormal, superordinary, supranormal, uncanny, unnatural
rel extraordinary, outstanding, phenomenal, remarkable; paranormal
3 ***syn*** see EXCESSIVE 1

supernormal *adj* ***syn*** see SUPERNATURAL 2
ant subnormal

supernumerary *adj* ***syn*** see SUPERFLUOUS

superordinary *adj* ***syn*** see SUPERNATURAL 2
ant ordinary

superpatriot *n* ***syn*** see PATRIOTEER

superscribe *vb* ***syn*** see ADDRESS 6

supersede *vb* ***syn*** see REPLACE 3
rel reject, repudiate; abandon, desert, forsake; discard

superseded *adj* ***syn*** see OBSOLETE

supersensible *adj* ***syn*** see PSYCHIC 1

supersensory *adj* ***syn*** see PSYCHIC 1

supertemporal *adj* ***syn*** see INFINITE 1

supervene *vb* ***syn*** see FOLLOW 1

supervenient *adj* ***syn*** see ADVENTITIOUS

supervise *vb* to have or exercise the charge, direction, and oversight of <*supervised* the construction of the new stadium>
syn boss, chaperon, overlook, oversee, quarterback, superintend, survey
rel guide, steer; administer, conduct, direct; manage, run; control; monitor, proctor

supervision *n* ***syn*** see OVERSIGHT 1

supper club *n* ***syn*** see NIGHTCLUB

supplant *vb* **1** to supersede (another) by or as if by force, trickery, or treachery <a wife who found herself *supplanted* by another woman>
syn cut out, displace, usurp
rel crowd (out), force (out); bounce, cast (out), eject, expel, oust
idiom give the bum's rush, give the old heave-ho, step into the shoes of
2 ***syn*** see REPLACE 3

supple *adj* **1** ***syn*** see ELASTIC 1
ant stiff
2 ***syn*** see PLASTIC
3 showing freedom and ease of bodily movement (as in bending or twisting) <the light *supple* spring of a cat>
syn limber, lissome, lithe, lithesome
rel agile, graceful, willowy, wiry, withy
con awkward, clumsy, gawky, maladroit, unhandy; ungraceful; arthritic, creaky, decrepit
ant stiff

supplement *n* **1** ***syn*** see COMPLEMENT 1
2 ***syn*** see APPENDIX 1

suppliant *n* one who asks (as for a favor or gift) humbly <a room full of *suppliants* waiting to see the king>
syn asker, beggar, petitioner, prayer, suitor, supplicant, supplicator
rel solicitant, solicitor

supplicant *n* ***syn*** see SUPPLIANT

supplicate *vb* ***syn*** see BEG
idiom ask on bended knee, ||come down on one's marrowbones

supplication *n* ***syn*** see PRAYER

supplicator *n* ***syn*** see SUPPLIANT

supply *vb* ***syn*** see GIVE 3
rel fulfill, outfit, provision

supply *n* an accumulation of something that is a source from which things may be drawn <an unending *supply* of new talent>
syn armamentarium, fund, inventory, stock, store
rel accumulation; reserve, reservoir, stockpile, surplus; hoard

supply *adj* ***syn*** see TEMPORARY

support *vb* **1** ***syn*** see BEAR 10
2 to favor actively in the face of opposition <*support* an unpopular economic policy>
syn advocate, back, backstop, champion, side (with), uphold
rel applaud, approve, endorse, favor, plunk (for), pull (for), root; adopt, embrace, espouse; defend, maintain, sustain
idiom align oneself with, be on (someone's) side, take (someone's) side
con battle, combat, counter, fight, oppose; withstand
ant buck
3 to supply what is needed for sustenance <*support* his family>
syn maintain, provide (for)
idiom boil the pot, bring home the bacon, make a living for, take care of
4 to hold up in position by serving as a foundation or base for <pillars *supporting* an arch>
syn bear up, bolster, brace, buttress, carry, prop, shore (up), sustain, upbear, uphold
rel stand

5 to keep from yielding, sinking, or losing courage or stability <her friends *supported* her during the crisis>
syn bolster, buoy (up), prop, sustain, underprop, uphold; *compare* ENCOURAGE 1
rel encourage; fortify, stiffen, strengthen

support *n* **1** ***syn*** see HELP 1
2 ***syn*** see HELP 2
3 a supporting means, agency, medium, or device <girders as structural *supports*><strong economic *support* for the government>
syn brace, buttress, column, prop, shore, stay, underpinner, underpinning, underpropping
rel base, foundation; sustentation
4 ***syn*** see LIVING

supportable *adj* ***syn*** see BEARABLE
ant insupportable, unsupportable

supporter *n* **1** ***syn*** see FOLLOWER
2 ***syn*** see EXPONENT
ant antagonist

supposable *adj* ***syn*** see THINKABLE 2
ant insupposable

supposal *n* ***syn*** see THEORY 1

suppose *vb* **1** ***syn*** see UNDERSTAND 3
rel presuppose
2 ***syn*** see CONJECTURE

suppose *n* ***syn*** see THEORY 2

supposed *adj* **1** accepted or advanced as true or real on the basis of less than conclusive evidence <the *supposed* efficiency of the new machine>
syn conjectural, hypothetical, putative, reputed, suppositional, suppositious, supposititious, suppositive, suppository; *compare* ALLEGED
rel assumed, postulated, postulatory, presumed, presupposed; provisional, tentative; academic, speculative, theoretical; alleged
con sure; known, proved, proven; ascertained, demonstrated, observed, recognized
ant certain
2 ***syn*** see ALLEGED
ant proved, proven

supposition *n* **1** ***syn*** see ASSUMPTION 2
2 ***syn*** see THEORY 2

suppositional *adj* ***syn*** see SUPPOSED 1

suppositious *adj* **1** ***syn*** see FICTITIOUS 1
2 ***syn*** see SUPPOSED 1
rel doubtful, dubious, questionable; pretended, simulated

supposititious *adj* **1** ***syn*** see ILLEGITIMATE 1
2 ***syn*** see FICTITIOUS 1
3 ***syn*** see SUPPOSED 1

supposititiousness *n* ***syn*** see ILLEGITIMACY 1

suppositive *adj* ***syn*** see SUPPOSED 1

suppository *adj* ***syn*** see SUPPOSED 1

suppress *vb* **1** ***syn*** see CRUSH 5
idiom ride roughshod over
2 to hold back more or less forcefully someone or something that seeks an outlet <management tried to *suppress* the workers' discontent> <there was no way to *suppress* her short of murder>
syn muffle, ‖quelch, repress, shush, squelch, strangle; *compare* CRUSH 5
rel curb, restrain; arrest, check, interrupt; put down, slap down; quash, quell, squash; cut off, spike; abolish, annihilate, extinguish
idiom bring to naught, crack (*or* clamp) down on, put the kibosh on
3 to keep from public knowledge <*suppress* all news from the front>
syn burke, hush (up), stifle
rel repress; censor; silence
idiom put the lid on
con disclose, divulge, leak, ‖let out, reveal; broadcast, circulate, diffuse, publish, spread
4 ***syn*** see COMPOSE 4
rel drown; swallow
5 ***syn*** see STUNT

suppression *n* **1** ***syn*** see REPRESSION 1
2 ***syn*** see REPRESSION 2

supra *adv* ***syn*** see ABOVE 2
ant infra

suprahuman *adj* ***syn*** see SUPERNATURAL 1

supramundane *adj* ***syn*** see SUPERNATURAL 1

supranatural *adj* ***syn*** see SUPERNATURAL 1

supranormal *adj* ***syn*** see SUPERNATURAL 2

supremacy *n* the position of being first (as in rank, power, or influence) <Britain once enjoyed *supremacy* on the seas>
syn ascendancy, ascendant, dominance, domination, dominion, masterdom, preeminence, preponderance, preponderancy, preponderation, prepotence, prepotency, sovereignty
rel authority, control, driver's seat, power, sway; mastership, mastery, principality, superiority; transcendence

supreme *adj* developed to the utmost and not exceeded by any other in degree, quality, or intensity <dying for one's principles is an example of *supreme* sacrifice>
syn incomparable, preeminent, surpassing, towering, transcendent, ultimate, unequalable, unmatchable, unsurpassable; *compare* ALONE 3, EXCELLENT, MARVELOUS 2, MAXIMUM, SUPERB 3
rel crowning, master, sovereign; unequaled, unmatched, unparalleled, unrivaled, unsurpassed; final, last; absolute, perfect

surcease *vb* ***syn*** see STOP 3

sure *adj* **1** firmly settled or established <trying to find a *sure* footing on the rugged slope>
syn fast, firm, secure, stable, staunch, strong; *compare* FAST 4, STABLE 4
2 free from doubt, hesitation, or fear <upheld a *sure* faith>
syn abiding, enduring, firm, fixed, never-failing, steadfast, steady, unfaltering, unqualified, unquestioning, unshakable, unshaken, unwavering, wholehearted
rel assured, changeless, constant, unchangeable, unchanging, uncompromising, unfailing, unvarying; certain, fixed, set

---

syn synonym(s) ***rel*** related word(s)
ant antonym(s) ***con*** contrasted word(s)
idiom idiomatic equivalent(s)
‖ use limited; if in doubt, see a dictionary

con insecure, uncertain, unreliable; feeble, infirm, shaky, unsound; doubtful, dubious, hesitant
ant unsure
3 *syn* see INFALLIBLE 1
4 *syn* see INFALLIBLE 2
5 marked by unwavering assurance especially as to the rightness of one's views or actions <was *sure* he knew the answer>
syn certain, cocksure, confident, positive
rel assured, self-assured, self-possessed, self-satisfied; arrogant, cocky, pert; decided, decisive
con doubtful, hesitant, uncertain
ant unsure
6 *syn* see POSITIVE 3
rel convincing, telling; absolute, definite; genuine, real, valid

sure–enough *adj* 1 *syn* see ACTUAL 2
2 *syn* see AUTHENTIC 2

surefire *adj syn* see INFALLIBLE 2

sureness *n syn* see CERTAINTY
ant unsureness

sure thing *n* one that is bound to be successful <was deemed a *sure thing* in the race>
syn shoo-in
rel certainty; winner

surety *n* 1 *syn* see CERTAINTY
2 *syn* see GUARANTEE 1
3 *syn* see SPONSOR

surface *n syn* see TOP 2
rel exterior, outside; cover, covering
con body, mass; inside, interior; lining

surface *vb* to come to the surface (as of water) <a submarine *surfaced* outside the harbor>
syn rise
rel come up
con go down, go under; submerge; dive

surfeit *n syn* see EXCESS 1

surfeit *vb syn* see SATIATE
rel overfill, overindulge
idiom have all one can take (*or* stand)
ant whet

surfeited *adj syn* see SATIATED
ant unsatisfied

surge *vb syn* see POUR 2

surly *adj syn* see SULLEN
rel discourteous, ill-mannered, rude, ungracious; bearish, boorish, churlish; fractious, irritable, snappish, waspish
idiom as surly as a bear
con affable, cordial, genial, gracious
ant amiable

surmise *vb syn* see CONJECTURE
rel consider, regard; hypothesize, theorize
idiom risk assuming, venture a guess

surmount *vb* 1 *syn* see OVERCOME 1
rel best, better, outdo, outstrip, outtop, outtower, surpass
idiom rise superior to
2 *syn* see CLEAR 8
3 to stand or lie at the top of <a cross *surmounts* the cupola>
syn cap, crest, crown, top
rel finish; terminate
4 *syn* see TOP

surpass *vb* 1 to be or become greater than or superior to <*surpassed* all his fellows in scholarship>
syn ‖bang, beat, best, better, cap, cob, ding, exceed, excel, outdo, outgo, outmatch, outshine, outstrip, pass, top, transcend, trump
rel distance, outdistance, outpace, outperform, outpoint, outrange, outrival, outrun, outvie; eclipse, outrank, outtop, outtower, outweigh, overshadow, overtop, rank
idiom have it all over, put to shame
2 *syn* see EXCEED 1

surpassing *adj syn* see SUPREME

surpassingly *adv syn* see VERY 1

surplus *n* 1 *syn* see EXCESS 1
ant deficiency
2 *syn* see EXCESS 2
ant shortage

surplus *adj syn* see SUPERFLUOUS

surplusage *n* 1 *syn* see EXCESS 2
ant shortage, underage
2 *syn* see EXCESS 1
ant shortage

surprise *vb* 1 to attack unawares <hijackers *surprised* the truck driver and took his cargo>
syn ambush, lay (for), waylay
rel bushwhack, dry-gulch; capture, catch; grab, grasp, seize, take
2 to impress forcibly through unexpectedness, startlingness, or unusualness <was *surprised* by his violent jealousy>
syn amaze, astonish, astound, dumbfound, flabbergast
rel startle; bewilder, confound, discomfit, disconcert, dismay, nonplus, ‖swan; faze, rattle, rock; bowl (over), floor, stagger; stun, stupefy
idiom leave open-mouthed (*or* aghast), take aback (*or* by surprise)

surprising *adj syn* see MARVELOUS 1
rel unexpected, unforeseen, unlooked-for; eye-opening, eye-popping

surrender *vb* 1 *syn* see RELINQUISH
rel commit, consign, entrust
2 *syn* see FALL 3
rel give in, give up
idiom haul down one's colors, strike the (*or* one's) flag

surrender *n* the yielding of one's person, forces, or possessions to another <the victors demanded unconditional *surrender*>
syn capitulation, dedition, submission
rel appeasement, Munich; relenting, succumbing, yielding; white flag

surreptitious *adj syn* see SECRET 1
rel skulking, slinking, slinky, sneaking, sneaky
con obvious, open, overt
ant brazen

surreptitiously *adv syn* see SECRETLY
con openly, overtly, plainly
ant brazenly

surrogate *n* 1 *syn* see SUBSTITUTE
2 *syn* see RESOURCE 3

surrogate *adj syn* see SUBSTITUTE 1

surround *vb* **1** to close in or as if in a ring about something <a crowd *surrounded* the accident victim>
syn begird, beset, circle, compass, encircle, encompass, environ, gird, girdle, hem, loop, ring, round
rel embosom, enclave, enclose, envelop; circumscribe, circumvent, confine, limit
2 ***syn*** see BORDER 1

surroundings *n pl* ***syn*** see ENVIRONMENT

surveillance *n* **1** ***syn*** see EYE 3
idiom peeled eye
2 ***syn*** see LOOKOUT 3
rel surveyance
idiom watchful (*or* weather) eye

survey *vb* **1** ***syn*** see ESTIMATE 1
rel measure, size, size up
2 ***syn*** see SUPERVISE
3 to view from or as if from a high place or position <*surveyed* the view from her penthouse window>
syn overlook, oversee
4 ***syn*** see SCRUTINIZE 1

survey *n* **1** ***syn*** see EXAMINATION
2 ***syn*** see COMPENDIUM 1

‖**survigrous** *adj* ***syn*** see VIGOROUS

survive *vb* **1** ***syn*** see OUTLIVE
2 to continue to exist or function in spite of a usually adverse condition or development <a company that managed to *survive* the recession>
syn come through, pull through, ride (out)
rel carry on, carry through, continue, endure, last, persist; live down, outlast, outlive; recover, revive
idiom come out of it, live to fight again, make it through, ride out (*or* weather) the storm
con collapse, crash, fold, fold up, go down, go under; founder, sink; close (down), close up; bankrupt, bust
ant perish

susceptible *adj* **1** ***syn*** see LIABLE 2
rel disposed, inclined, predisposed
ant immune, unsusceptible
2 ***syn*** see EASY 3
rel nonresistant, soft; movable, persuadable
ant unsusceptible
3 ***syn*** see SENTIENT 3
rel affected, impressed, influenced, swayed, touched; aroused, roused, stirred
ant unsusceptible

susceptive *adj* ***syn*** see SENTIENT 3

suscitate *vb* ***syn*** see PROVOKE 4

suspect *adj* ***syn*** see DOUBTFUL 1
idiom ‖a bit thin (*or* thick), open to suspicion

suspect *vb* **1** ***syn*** see DISTRUST
idiom have doubts about
2 ***syn*** see UNDERSTAND 3
idiom be inclined to think

suspend *vb* **1** ***syn*** see EXCLUDE
2 ***syn*** see DEFER
rel arrest, check, interrupt; cease, discontinue, stop
idiom lay on the table, put on the shelf
3 ***syn*** see HANG 1

suspended *adj* hung or seeming as if hung from a support <bunches of grapes *suspended* from the vines>
syn hanging, pendent, pendulant, pendulous, pensile
rel dangling, swinging

suspenders *n pl* a pair of adjustable bands for holding up the front and rear of a pair of trousers or a skirt <every stockbroker seemed to be wearing *suspenders* and a yellow tie>
syn braces, ‖gallows, ‖galluses

suspense *n* ***syn*** see SUSPENSION 2

suspension *n* **1** ***syn*** see ABEYANCE
2 a temporary withholding of action or cessation of activity <asked for *suspension* of judgment until all the evidence was in>
syn moratorium, suspense
rel cessation, concluding, conclusion, end, ending, finish, period, termination
con resumption; continuance

suspicion *n* **1** ***syn*** see UNCERTAINTY
rel apprehension, foreboding, misgiving, presentiment; distrust
2 ***syn*** see HINT 2

‖**suspicion** *vb* ***syn*** see DISTRUST

suspicious *adj* **1** ***syn*** see DOUBTFUL 1
rel questionable; queer
2 given or prone to suspicion <was *suspicious* of everyone's motives>
syn distrustful, jealous, mistrustful
rel careful, cautious; leery, wary, watchful; skeptical, unbelieving
con trustful, trusting, unsuspecting; naive; dupable, easy, exploitable, gullible
ant unsuspicious

suspiciously *adv* ***syn*** see ASKANCE 2
rel distrustingly, mistrustingly
ant unsuspiciously

suspire *vb* **1** ***syn*** see SIGH 1
idiom draw a long breath
2 ***syn*** see LONG

sustain *vb* **1** ***syn*** see MAINTAIN 1
rel nourish, support; prolong
2 ***syn*** see SUPPORT 4
rel lug, pack, tote
3 ***syn*** see SUPPORT 5
rel befriend, favor
idiom stand by
con abandon, forsake; ignore
4 ***syn*** see BEAR 10
5 ***syn*** see EXPERIENCE 1
rel bear, endure

sustainable *adj* ***syn*** see BEARABLE
ant unsustainable

sustenance *n* **1** ***syn*** see FOOD 2
idiom bodily sustenance
2 ***syn*** see LIVING

sustentation *n* ***syn*** see PRESERVATION 1

susurration *n* ***syn*** see MURMUR 1

---

syn synonym(s)   ***rel*** related word(s)
ant antonym(s)   ***con*** contrasted word(s)
idiom idiomatic equivalent(s)
‖ use limited; if in doubt, see a dictionary

‖**swack** *n* ***syn*** see CUFF

‖**swacked** *adj* ***syn*** see INTOXICATED 1

swad *n* ***syn*** see SOLDIER

swaddle *vb* ***syn*** see SWATHE

rel ‖sweel

ant unswaddle

‖**swaddy** *n* ***syn*** see SOLDIER

swag *vb* **1** ***syn*** see SEESAW

2 ***syn*** see DROOP 3

swag *n* **1** ***syn*** see SPOIL

2 ***syn*** see MONEY

swagger *vb* **1** ***syn*** see LORD

rel swash, swashbuckle

2 ***syn*** see STRUT 2

rel bluster, brandish, flourish

con blench, quail; shrink, wince; truckle

‖**swagger** *n* ***syn*** see VAGABOND

‖**swagman** *n* ***syn*** see VAGABOND

swain *n* **1** ***syn*** see BOYFRIEND 1

2 ***syn*** see SUITOR 2

swainish *adj* ***syn*** see BOORISH

swallow *vb* **1** to receive through the esophagus into the stomach <*swallowed* the pills easily with a sip of water>

syn down, take

rel drop, gulp, ‖quilt, toss; ingest, ingurgitate

2 ***syn*** see DRINK 1

3 ***syn*** see BELIEVE 1

idiom swallow (something) hook, line, and sinker

4 ***syn*** see BEAR 10

5 ***syn*** see ACCEPT 2

6 ***syn*** see MUMBLE

swamp *n* wet spongy land saturated and sometimes partially covered with water <hunted alligators in the Florida *swamps*>

syn baygall, bog, fen, marsh, marshland, mire, morass, ‖moss, muskeg, ‖purgatory, ‖puxy, quag, quagmire, slough, ‖sump, swampland, ‖swang, ‖vlei

rel bottoms, ‖holm; ‖glade; ‖jheel; quake ooze; shaking prairie, trembling prairie

swamp *vb* **1** ***syn*** see DELUGE 1

2 ***syn*** see DELUGE 3

swampland *n* ***syn*** see SWAMP

‖**swang** *n* ***syn*** see SWAMP

swank *vb* ***syn*** see LORD

swank *adj* **1** ***syn*** see SHOWY

2 ***syn*** see STYLISH

swap *vb* **1** ***syn*** see EXCHANGE 2

2 ***syn*** see TRADE 1

idiom ‖swap horses, swap out of

‖**swap** *n* ***syn*** see BLOW 1

‖**swapping** *adj* ***syn*** see HUGE

‖**swarf** *vb* ***syn*** see FAINT

swarm *vb* ***syn*** see TEEM

idiom gather (*or* swarm) like bees

swarming *adj* ***syn*** see ALIVE 5

swart *adj* ***syn*** see DARK 3

swarth *adj* ***syn*** see DARK 3

swarthy *adj* ***syn*** see DARK 3

swash *vb* **1** ***syn*** see SLOSH 1

2 ***syn*** see SPLASH

swashy *adj* ***syn*** see INSIPID 3

swat *vb* ‖**1** ***syn*** see SQUAT

2 ***syn*** see STRIKE 2

rel blip, box, buffet, cuff, smack; belt, clobber, slug, smash, wallop

swat *n* ***syn*** see HIT 1

swathe *vb* to cover or bind completely with clothing or material <legs *swathed* in bandages> <the baby was *swathed* in a warm shawl>

syn drape, enswathe, envelop, enwrap, roll, swaddle, wrap (up); *compare* ENFOLD 1

rel enfold; encase; cover

con bare, denude, expose, strip, uncover, unswaddle, unwrap

ant unswathe

sway *vb* **1** ***syn*** see SWING 2

2 ***syn*** see LURCH 2

3 ***syn*** see GOVERN 1

4 ***syn*** see AFFECT

rel bias, dispose, incline, predispose; conduct, control, direct, manage; govern, rule

sway *n* ***syn*** see POWER 1

rel range, reach, scope, sweep; amplitude, expanse, spread, stretch

swayable *adj* ***syn*** see RECEPTIVE 1

swear *vb* **1** ***syn*** see VOW

idiom swear on a stack of Bibles, swear to God, swear up and down

2 ***syn*** see TESTIFY 2

3 to use profane, blasphemous, or obscene language <*swore* when the horse threw him>

syn bedamn, curse, cuss, damn, execrate, imprecate

rel blaspheme; rail, rant; abuse, revile, vilify, vituperate

idiom ‖chew the dirty rag, curse and swear, fall a-cursing, ‖let out religion, make the air blue, rip (*or* rap) out an oath, swear like a sailor (*or* trooper), use language

swear *n* ***syn*** see SWEARWORD

swearing *n* ***syn*** see BLASPHEMY 1

swearword *n* a profane, blasphemous, or obscene word <let loose with a string of *swearwords*>

syn curse, cuss, cussword, expletive, oath, swear

rel four-letter word, obscenity, scurrility

idiom blue word, one-horse oath, raw one, ripe (*or* juicy) word, sailor's blessing, six-cornered oath, strong word

sweat *vb* **1** ***syn*** see EXUDE

2 ***syn*** see FLEECE 1

sweat *n* **1** ***syn*** see WORK 2

2 ***syn*** see SNIT

‖**3** ***syn*** see SOLDIER

sweatful *adj* ***syn*** see SWEATY

sweating *adj* ***syn*** see SWEATY

sweat out *vb* ***syn*** see BEAR 10

sweaty *adj* producing, accompanied by, or characterized by sweat <he still held the racket tight in *sweaty* hands>

syn asweat, perspiring, perspiry, ‖puggy, sweatful, sweating

rel clammy; sticky; wet

idiom bathed in sweat, covered with sweat, drenched with (*or* in) sweat, in a muck of a sweat, wet with sweat (*or* perspiration)

sweep *vb* ***syn*** see FLY 4
sweep *n* ***syn*** see RANGE 2
sweeping *n* **sweepings** *pl* ***syn*** see REFUSE
sweeping *adj* **1** ***syn*** see ALL-AROUND 2
rel all-embracing, all-encompassing
2 ***syn*** see INDISCRIMINATE 1
rel all-out, out-and-out, whole-hog; across-the-board, blanket
sweet *adj* **1** distinctly pleasing or charming <a *sweet* smile>
syn dulcet, engaging, winning, winsome
rel agreeable, pleasant, pleasing; beautiful, fair, lovely; delectable, delicious, delightful, luscious; angelic, heavenly
con disagreeable, unpleasant; displeasing, obnoxious, repulsive
ant bitter
2 having a pleasant smell <the *sweet* odor of flowers and incense>
syn ambrosial, aromal, aromatic, balmy, fragrant, perfumed, perfumy, redolent, savory, scented, spicy; *compare* ODOROUS
rel clean, fresh; sweetish
con funky, fusty, musty, noisome, putrid, rancid, rotten, stale, stinking, strong, whiffy; fetid, foul, olid, rank, smelly
ant malodorous
3 ***syn*** see MELODIOUS 1
sweet *n* ***syn*** see SWEETHEART 1
sweeten *vb* **1** ***syn*** see PACIFY
2 ***syn*** see SUGARCOAT 1
sweetheart *n* **1** one who is dearly beloved — often used as a term of endearment <was her childhood *sweetheart*> <*sweetheart*, you know I'll wait>
syn beloved, darling, dear, flame, heartthrob, honey, honeybunch, love, loveling, sweet, sweetling, turtledove
rel ‖cutie pie, deary, pigsney; pet, puggy
2 ***syn*** see GIRL FRIEND 2
rel doll baby, lovey-dovey, ‖tootsie
3 ***syn*** see BOYFRIEND 2
rel paramour; ‖dreamboat
sweetheart *vb* ***syn*** see ADDRESS 8
sweetie *n* ***syn*** see GIRL FRIEND 2
rel sweetie pie
sweetling *n* ***syn*** see SWEETHEART 1
sweetness and light *n* ***syn*** see AMENITY 1
sweet–talk *vb* ***syn*** see COAX
swell *vb* **1** ***syn*** see EXPAND 3
rel balloon, belly, bloat, blow up, bosom; pouch, pout; overblow
con compress, condense, constrict, contract
ant shrink
2 ***syn*** see LORD
rel puff
idiom act the grand seigneur, swell it
swell *n* ***syn*** see EXPERT
swell *adj* ***syn*** see MARVELOUS 2
swelled head *n* ***syn*** see CONCEIT 2
swellheadedness *n* ***syn*** see CONCEIT 2
swelling *adj* ***syn*** see RHETORICAL
‖**swelt** *vb* **1** ***syn*** see DIE 1
2 ***syn*** see FAINT
swelter *vb* ***syn*** see BURN 3
sweltering *adj* ***syn*** see HOT 1
idiom ‖hot as the hinges of hell
ant frigid
sweltry *adj* ***syn*** see HOT 1
swerve *vb* **1** to turn or be turned away abruptly from a straight line or course <*swerved* the car to avoid collision>
syn dip, sheer, skew, slue, train off, veer
2 to be deflected from a fixed or right course of action or conduct <never *swerved* from the concept of duty, honor, country>
syn depart, deviate, digress, diverge
rel shift; waver; err, stray, wander
idiom deviate from the straight and narrow, get off the proper course (*or* path)
swift *adj* ***syn*** see FAST 3
rel headlong, precipitate, sudden; double-quick; supersonic
ant sluggish
swift *adv* ***syn*** see FAST 2
ant sluggishly
swiften *vb* ***syn*** see SPEED 3
swiftly *adv* ***syn*** see FAST 2
con slowly
ant sluggishly
swiftness *n* **1** ***syn*** see SPEED 2
ant sluggishness
2 ***syn*** see HASTE 1
ant slowness
swig *n* ***syn*** see DRINK 3
swig *vb* ***syn*** see DRINK 3
swill *vb* **1** ***syn*** see DRINK 3
2 ***syn*** see CONSUME 5
swill *n* **1** ***syn*** see REFUSE
2 ***syn*** see DRINK 3
swillbowl *n* ***syn*** see DRUNKARD
swiller *n* ***syn*** see DRUNKARD
swim *vb* ***syn*** see SPIN 2
idiom have one's head swim
swimming *adj* ***syn*** see DIZZY 2
rel fluctuating, swaying, wavering
swimmingly *adv* ***syn*** see WELL 5
swimmy *adj* ***syn*** see DIZZY 2
swindle *vb* ***syn*** see CHEAT
rel rogue; victimize
idiom sell one a bill of goods, take for a ride, take for a sucker
swindle *n* ***syn*** see IMPOSTURE
swindler *n* one who defrauds usually of money and especially by imposture or by gaining the victim's confidence <lost their savings to *swindlers* in a get-rich-quick scheme>
syn bunco steerer, cheat, cheater, chiaus, come-on, confidence man, con man, defrauder, diddler, double-dealer, flimflammer, ‖grifter, gyp, gypper, ‖mace, mountebank, Peter Funk, rogue, sharper, sharpie, skin, slicker, ‖spieler, trickster

---

syn synonym(s) ***rel*** related word(s)
ant antonym(s) ***con*** contrasted word(s)
idiom idiomatic equivalent(s)
‖ use limited; if in doubt, see a dictionary

rel bilk, bilker, blackleg, charlatan, chiseler, crook, deceiver, dodger, fraud, gouger, harpy, highbinder, hoaxer, operator, rook, shark, sharp, sharpster, tricker; scoundrel

swing *vb* **1** ***syn*** see HANDLE 2

2 to move rhythmically to and fro, up and down, or back and forth <the clock's pendulum *swung* slowly>

syn oscillate, pendulate, sway

rel undulate, wave; rock, roll; revolve, rotate, switch, wheel; jiggle, wag, waggle, wiggle, wigwag

3 ***syn*** see TURN 6

4 ***syn*** see LURCH 2

swing *n* **1** ***syn*** see RHYTHM

2 ***syn*** see HANG

‖swingeing *adj* ***syn*** see EXCELLENT

swinish *adj* ***syn*** see BRUTISH

swipe *n* **1** ***syn*** see HIT 1

2 ***syn*** see CRITICISM 2

swipe *vb* ***syn*** see STEAL 1

swirl *vb* to move swiftly in circles, eddies, or undulations <water *swirled* into the storm drains>

syn eddy, gurge, purl, swoosh, whirl, whirlpool, whorl

rel boil, roil; gush, surge

swish *vb* ***syn*** see HISS

swish *adj* ***syn*** see STYLISH

switch *vb* **1** ***syn*** see WAG

2 ***syn*** see EXCHANGE 2

3 ***syn*** see SHUNT 1

‖swither *vb* ***syn*** see RUSH 1

swivet *n* ***syn*** see SNIT

swizzle *vb* ***syn*** see DRINK 3

swollen *adj* ***syn*** see RHETORICAL

swoon *vb* ***syn*** see FAINT

rel die away, drown

swoon *n* ***syn*** see FAINT

swoosh *vb* ***syn*** see SWIRL

sworn *adj* ***syn*** see INVETERATE 1

sybarite *n* ***syn*** see HEDONIST

sybaritic *adj* marked by or given to luxury or voluptuous living <the *sybaritic* grandeur of a sultan's harem> <a man of *sybaritic* and self-indulgent habits>

syn hedonistic, onanistic, self-indulgent, sybaritical, sybaritish; *compare* SENSUOUS

rel apolaustic, pleasure-loving; epicurean, luxurious; carnal, sensual, voluptuous

sybaritical *adj* ***syn*** see SYBARITIC

sybaritish *adj* ***syn*** see SYBARITIC

sycophancy *n* ***syn*** see DETRACTION

sycophant *n* a base or servilely attentive flatterer and self-seeker <*sycophants* who slavishly curried favor with the king>

syn apple-polisher, bootlick, bootlicker, ‖brownnose, ‖brownnoser, ‖clawback, creature, ‖easy rider, footlicker, groveler, lickspit, lickspittle, minion, reptile, spaniel, toad, toadeater, toadier, toady, truckler, yes-man; *compare* PARASITE

rel flunky, gopher, lackey, slave, stooge; flatterer, self-seeker; snob, tuft-hunter

sycophant *adj* ***syn*** see FAWNING

sycophantic *adj* ***syn*** see FAWNING

sycophantical *adj* ***syn*** see FAWNING

sycophantish *adj* ***syn*** see FAWNING

syllable *n* ***syn*** see PARTICLE

syllabus *n* ***syn*** see COMPENDIUM 1

sylloge *n* ***syn*** see COMPENDIUM 1

symbol *n* **1** something that stands for something else by reason of relationship, association, convention, or accidental resemblance <the lion is often used as a *symbol* of courage>

syn attribute, emblem; *compare* INDICATION 3

rel indication, token, type; badge, mark, note, sign, stamp; character, design, device, figure, motif, pattern; representation

2 ***syn*** see CHARACTER 1

symbolism *n* ***syn*** see ALLEGORY 1

symbolization *n* ***syn*** see ALLEGORY 1

symbolize *vb* ***syn*** see REPRESENT 2

symmetrical *adj* ***syn*** see PROPORTIONAL

symmetry *n* beauty of form or arrangement arising from balanced proportions <the superb *symmetry* of the design>

syn balance, harmony, proportion

rel arrangement, order; agreement, conformity; equality, evenness, regularity; rhythm; finish

con asymmetry, dissymmetry; disproportion, imbalance, irregularity, unbalance

sympathetic *adj* **1** ***syn*** see CONSONANT 1

ant unsympathetic

2 favorably inclined <found his hearers *sympathetic* to his proposal>

syn friendly, receptive, ‖sib, well-disposed

rel agreeable, congenial, favorable; amenable, open, open-minded, receptive, responsive

con ill-disposed, unfriendly, unreceptive; cool, indifferent, lukewarm; neutral

ant unsympathetic

3 ***syn*** see TENDER

rel benign, benignant, kind, kindly; appreciating, comprehending, understanding

ant unsympathetic

sympathize (with) *vb* ***syn*** see COMPASSIONATE

rel appreciate, comprehend, understand

sympathy *n* **1** ***syn*** see ATTRACTION 2

ant antipathy

2 a feeling for or a capacity for sharing in the interests of another <he was in *sympathy* with her desire to succeed>

syn compassion, empathy, fellow feeling

rel responsiveness, sensitivity; feelings, heart; tenderness, warmheartedness, warmth; benignancy, benignness, kindliness, kindness

con disinterest, unconcern

3 ***syn*** see PITY

symphonic *adj* ***syn*** see HARMONIOUS 1

symphonious *adj* ***syn*** see HARMONIOUS 1

symphonize *vb* ***syn*** see HARMONIZE 4

symphony *n* ***syn*** see ORCHESTRA

rel concert band, symphony band; symphony orchestra

symptom *n* ***syn*** see INDICATION 3

synchronal *adj* ***syn*** see CONTEMPORARY 1

synchronic *adj* ***syn*** see CONTEMPORARY 1

synchronous *adj* ***syn*** see CONTEMPORARY 1

syncope *n* ***syn*** see FAINT
syndicate *n* a combination of interlocked companies or enterprises <a large newspaper *syndicate*>
syn cartel, chain, combine, conglomerate, group, pool, trust
rel association, organization; partnership, union
syndrome *n* ***syn*** see DISEASE 1
synergetic *adj* ***syn*** see COOPERATIVE
ant counteractive
synergic *adj* ***syn*** see COOPERATIVE
ant counteractive
synopsis *n* ***syn*** see ABRIDGMENT
synopsize *vb* ***syn*** see EPITOMIZE 1
idiom hit the high spots, put it in a nutshell
synthesize *vb* ***syn*** see HARMONIZE 4
synthetic *adj* formed or developed by human art, skill, or effort and not by natural processes <*synthetic* plastics>
syn artificial, factitious, man-made; *compare* ARTIFICIAL 2
rel manufactured; constructed, fabricated, made
con natural
syrupy *adj* ***syn*** see SENTIMENTAL
system *n* **1** an organized integrated whole made up of diverse but interrelated and interdependent parts <the capitalist *system*>
syn complex; *compare* WHOLE 2
rel aggregation, array; mesh, network; arrangement, disposition, scheme, setup; order, pattern
con disorganization; chaos
2 ***syn*** see WHOLE 2
3 ***syn*** see ORDER 8
rel procedure, proceeding, process
4 ***syn*** see METHOD 1
systematic *adj* ***syn*** see ORDERLY 1
rel arranged, ordered, organized, systematized; analytical, logical
con disorganized; chaotic
ant unsystematic
systematize *vb* ***syn*** see ORDER 1
rel contrive, frame
con confuse, disorder, jumble

syn synonym(s) ***rel*** related word(s)
ant antonym(s) ***con*** contrasted word(s)
idiom idiomatic equivalent(s)
‖ use limited; if in doubt, see a dictionary

THESAURUS

T

tab *n* **1** ***syn*** see EYE 3
2 ***syn*** see BILL 1
3 ***syn*** see CHECK 2
4 ***syn*** see PRICE 1
tabby *n* **1** ***syn*** see GOSSIP 1
‖**2** ***syn*** see SPINSTER
tabernacle *n* ***syn*** see HOUSE OF WORSHIP
table *n* **1** a piece of furniture on which food is customarily served <a feast on the *table*>
syn board, dining table, dinner table, mahogany, ‖table-board
rel bar, buffet, counter, sideboard
2 a condensed ordered enumeration of items usually arranged in columns <a *table* of weights and measures>
syn chart, tabulation
rel list; diagram
3 ***syn*** see PLATEAU
‖**table–board** *n* ***syn*** see TABLE 1
tableland *n* ***syn*** see PLATEAU
tabloid *adj* ***syn*** see SENSATIONAL 2
taboo *n* a restraint imposed by social usage or as a protective measure <a society rife with antiquated moral *taboos*>
syn ban, forbiddance, interdiction, prohibition, proscription
rel inhibition, limitation, reservation, restraint, restriction; regulation, sanction; don't
con acceptance, toleration; approval, authorization, permission, permit, permittance
taboo *vb* ***syn*** see FORBID
tabulation *n* ***syn*** see TABLE 2
tacit *adj* **1** expressed or conveyed without words, speech, or forthright reference <they made a *tacit* agreement to work together>
syn implicit, implied, inarticulate, inferred, undeclared, understood, unexpressed, unsaid, unspoken, unuttered, wordless
rel alluded (to), hinted (at), intimated, suggested; assumed
con expressed, spoken, verbal; categorical, explicit, express, unequivocal
2 ***syn*** see UNSPOKEN 1
taciturn *adj* ***syn*** see SILENT 3
rel laconic, unexpressive; brooding, dour
con chatty, communicative, loquacious, talkative; convivial, uninhibited, unreserved, unrestrained
ant garrulous
tack *n* ***syn*** see TURN 2
rel alteration; digression, tangent; swerve, zigzag
tackle *n* ***syn*** see EQUIPMENT
tackle *vb* ***syn*** see ATTACK 2
rel take on, undertake; plunge into, set about
idiom get on the job, put one's shoulder to the wheel, start the ball rolling
con avoid, delay, hesitate, put off

tackling *n* ***syn*** see EQUIPMENT
tacky *adj* **1** ***syn*** see SHABBY 1
rel dowdy, outmoded, unstylish; messy, sloppy, slovenly, unkempt, untidy; blowsy, frowsy, frumpish
idiom gone to seed
2 marked by a lack of style or good taste <an old *tacky* scarf spoiled her outfit>
syn dowdy, frumpish, frumpy, outmoded, out-of-date, stodgy, unstylish
rel unbecoming; crude, inelegant, tasteless; incorrect, unsuitable; cheap, gaudy
con ‖mod, modern, modish, smart, stylish, tasteful; elegant
tact *n* skill and grace in dealing with others <handled the embarrassing situation with great *tact*>
syn address, delicatesse, diplomacy, poise, savoir faire, tactfulness; *compare* ADDRESS 1
rel control, head, presence, repose; amenity, courtesy, gallantry; policy, politicness, smoothness, suavity, urbanity; adroitness, deftness, skill; acumen, finesse, perception, sensitivity
con abruptness, bluntness, coarseness, discourtesy, rudeness
ant tactlessness
tactful *adj* marked by or exhibiting tact <his *tactful* skill in handling negotiations>
syn delicate, diplomatic, politic, tactical; *compare* SUAVE
rel polished, suave, urbane; adroit, deft, skilled, skillful; perceptive, sensitive
con clumsy, unpolished, unskilled; discourteous, impolite, rude; undiplomatic
ant blunt, tactless, untactful
tactfulness *n* ***syn*** see TACT
rel civility, civilness, politeness; polish
ant tactlessness
tactic *adj* ***syn*** see TACTILE 2
tactical *adj* **1** made or carried out with only a limited or immediate end in view <had time only for *tactical* decisions and not strategic planning>
syn short-range
con long-range
ant strategic
2 ***syn*** see EXPEDIENT
3 ***syn*** see TACTFUL
tactile *adj* **1** ***syn*** see TANGIBLE 1
2 of or relating to the sense of touch <*tactile* responses>
syn tactic, tactual
tactility *n* ***syn*** see TOUCH 3
taction *n* ***syn*** see TOUCH 2
tactless *adj* marked by a lack of tact <his *tactless* remark hurt her>
syn brash, impolitic, maladroit, undiplomatic, unpolitic, untactful
rel impolite, inconsiderate, indelicate, rude; bungling, inept

con diplomatic, polite, tactical
ant tactful
tactual *adj* ***syn*** see TACTILE 2
tad *n* ***syn*** see BOY 1
tag *n* **1** ***syn*** see COMMONPLACE
2 ***syn*** see TICKET 1
tag *vb* ***syn*** see TAIL
tag and rag *n* ***syn*** see RABBLE 2
tag end *n* ***syn*** see TAIL END 2
tagrag *adj* ***syn*** see SHABBY 1
tagrag and bobtail *n* ***syn*** see RABBLE 2
tail *n* ***syn*** see BUTTOCKS
tail *vb* to follow (someone) for purposes of surveillance <detectives *tailing* the suspects>
syn bedog, dog, shadow, tag, trail; *compare* EYE 2, FOLLOW 2
rel hound, pursue
tail end *n* **1** ***syn*** see BUTTOCKS
2 the hindmost end of something <watched the *tail end* of the parade march off>
syn tag end
tailor *vb* ***syn*** see ADAPT
rel style; dovetail; shape up
tailor–made *adj* ***syn*** see CUSTOM-MADE
tailor–make *vb* ***syn*** see ADAPT
taint *vb* **1** to touch or affect with something bad or undesirable <his good reputation was *tainted* by the scandal>
syn besmear, besmirch, blur, cloud, defile, dirty, discolor, smear, smudge, smut, smutch, soil, stain, sully, tar, tarnish; *compare* CONTAMINATE 1
rel discredit; brand, stigmatize; blacken; damage, harm, hurt
idiom cast a slur upon; give a bad name to, give a black mark to
con brighten, cleanse, clear
2 ***syn*** see DECAY
rel befoul, contaminate, foul
3 ***syn*** see CONTAMINATE 1
taintless *adj* ***syn*** see CLEAN 1
ant tainted
take *vb* **1** ***syn*** see CATCH 1
2 ***syn*** see SEIZE 2
idiom make off with
con drop, dump, give up, relinquish, surrender
3 ***syn*** see APPROPRIATE 1
con relinquish, yield
4 to lay hold of (as with the hands or an instrument) <*took* the ax by the handle>
syn clasp, grasp, grip
rel hold; handle
idiom take hold of
con drop, release
5 ***syn*** see SEIZE 3
rel contract, get; harrow, reach, torment
6 ***syn*** see CATCH 7
7 ***syn*** see ATTRACT 1
8 ***syn*** see SWALLOW 1
9 ***syn*** see EAT 1
10 to bring into and accept in a particular capacity or relationship <*took* his son as a member of the firm>
syn admit, receive, take in
rel bring; accept; have, include
11 ***syn*** see BUY 1
12 ***syn*** see CHOOSE 1
13 ***syn*** see DEMAND 2
14 to obtain from another source by means of derivation <*takes* his name from his father's>
syn derive, draw
rel get, obtain; borrow
15 ***syn*** see BEAR 10
rel withstand; undergo; ‖hack
idiom take it lying down, take it on the chin
16 ***syn*** see CONTRACT 1
idiom take sick with
17 ***syn*** see APPREHEND 1
18 ***syn*** see UNDERSTAND 3
19 ***syn*** see DEDUCT 1
20 ***syn*** see TREAT 2
21 ***syn*** see CHEAT
rel bamboozle, hoodwink
idiom take for a ride
22 ***syn*** see ACT 5
take (from) *vb* ***syn*** see DECRY 2
take (to) *vb* ***syn*** see HABITUATE 2
rel enjoy, fancy, favor, like
idiom get used to
take away *vb* **1** ***syn*** see REMOVE 2
rel separate
2 ***syn*** see DEDUCT 1
3 ***syn*** see DECRY 2
take back *vb* **1** ***syn*** see RETURN 4
2 ***syn*** see REPOSSESS 3
3 ***syn*** see ABJURE
take down *vb* ***syn*** see DISMOUNT
take in *vb* **1** ***syn*** see TAKE 10
2 ***syn*** see INCLUDE
3 ***syn*** see APPREHEND 1
rel perceive; ‖savvy; absorb, assimilate, digest
4 ***syn*** see DECEIVE
rel flimflam, take; trick
take off *vb* **1** ***syn*** see REMOVE 2
2 ***syn*** see REMOVE 3
3 ***syn*** see DEDUCT 1
4 ***syn*** see KILL 1
5 ***syn*** see MIMIC
idiom do a takeoff on
6 ***syn*** see GET OUT 1
7 ***syn*** see HEAD 3
idiom hit the road (*or* trail)
8 ***syn*** see GO 2
takeoff *n* ***syn*** see CARICATURE 2
take on *vb* **1** ***syn*** see DON 2
2 ***syn*** see ADD 1
3 to proceed to deal with <*took on* a new job with more responsibilities>
syn take up, undertake
rel begin, commence, enter (upon); attempt, endeavor, try; launch, venture
idiom set about, take upon oneself
con abandon, drop, forsake
ant give up

syn synonym(s) ***rel*** related word(s)
ant antonym(s) ***con*** contrasted word(s)
idiom idiomatic equivalent(s)
‖ use limited; if in doubt, see a dictionary

4 ***syn*** see ENGAGE 5
5 ***syn*** see EMPLOY 2
6 ***syn*** see ADOPT
ant give up

take out *vb* **1** ***syn*** see REMOVE 2
2 ***syn*** see REMOVE 4
3 ***syn*** see DEDUCT 1
4 ***syn*** see DATE

take out (on) *vb* to find release for (as emotions) <*took out* her anger on the dog>
syn loose, release, unleash, vent
idiom give vent to, let loose (*or* fly)
con control, govern, restrain; bottle (up), check, keep down, quell, smother; repress, suppress

take over *vb* ***syn*** see RELIEVE 3

take up *vb* **1** ***syn*** see LIFT 1
2 ***syn*** see BEGIN 1
3 ***syn*** see TAKE ON 3
rel assume; tackle
idiom address oneself to
4 ***syn*** see ADOPT
rel support; affiliate
5 ***syn*** see RESUME 2

taking *adj* ***syn*** see INFECTIOUS 3

tale *n* **1** ***syn*** see STORY 2
rel myth, saga
2 ***syn*** see DETRACTION
3 ***syn*** see LIE
rel fiction; yarn
4 ***syn*** see WHOLE 1

tale *vb* ***syn*** see COUNT 1

talebearer *n* **1** ***syn*** see INFORMER
2 ***syn*** see GOSSIP 1

talent *n* ***syn*** see GIFT 2
rel art, craft, skill; endowment; expertise, forte

talisman *n* ***syn*** see CHARM 2
idiom good-luck piece, lucky piece (*or* charm)

talk *vb* **1** ***syn*** see SPEAK 3
2 ***syn*** see SPEAK 1
3 ***syn*** see CONVERSE
4 ***syn*** see CHAT 1
rel palaver, spout off
idiom talk one's arm (*or* ear *or* leg) off, flap (*or* wag) the (*or* one's) tongue
5 ***syn*** see GOSSIP
6 to reveal secret or confidential information usually concerning illegal acts <at last the suspect *talked* to the police>
syn sing, squeak, squeal; *compare* INFORM 3
rel inform (on); divulge, reveal; confess
idiom spill one's guts, spill the beans, tell all
7 to give a talk <he *talks* to community groups on ecology>
syn address, lecture, prelect, speak
rel declaim, harangue, hold forth, perorate, speechify, spout

talk (into) *vb* ***syn*** see INDUCE 1

talk *n* **1** ***syn*** see SPEECH 1
2 ***syn*** see CONVERSATION 2
3 ***syn*** see CHAT 2
4 a formal or prearranged discussion, exchange, or negotiation usually of a political nature <summit *talks* on nuclear arms>
syn conference, meeting, parley, powwow
rel dialogue, discussion, exchange; negotiation; deliberation
5 ***syn*** see REPORT 1
6 ***syn*** see SPEECH 2
rel spiel; conference, discussion

talkative *adj* given to talk or talking <a *talkative*, sociable man>
syn babblative, chatty, gabby, garrulous, loose-lipped, loose-tongued, loquacious, mouthy, multiloquent, multiloquious, talky, tonguey; *compare* GLIB
rel articulate, eloquent, fluent; vocal, voluble; buzzy, gossipy
con closemouthed, laconic, reserved, reticent, uncommunicative; speechless
ant silent

talkee–talkee *n* ***syn*** see CHATTER

talky *adj* ***syn*** see TALKATIVE

tall *adj* ***syn*** see HIGH 1
rel high-reaching, sky-high, skyscraping
idiom higher than a cat's back
con abbreviated, truncated; low
ant short

tally *n* ***syn*** see SCORE 5

tally *vb* **1** ***syn*** see INVENTORY
2 ***syn*** see COUNT 1
3 ***syn*** see AGREE 4
rel equal, match; balance, complement
con conflict (with), differ (from), disagree (with)

tame *adj* docilely tractable <a *tame* lion>
syn domestic, domesticated, domitae naturae, subdued, submissive
rel broken (in), ||busted, housebroken, trained; amenable, biddable, docile, obedient, tractable; pliable, pliant; meek, mild
idiom gentle as a lamb
con fierce, savage, tameless; undomesticated, untrained; unbridled, unbroken
ant untamed, wild

tame *vb* ***syn*** see DOMESTICATE

tamp *vb* ***syn*** see CRAM 1
rel fill up (*or* in), plug up; concentrate

tamper (with) *vb* **1** ***syn*** see BRIBE
2 ***syn*** see MEDDLE
rel interpose, intervene; doctor, manipulate

tang *n* ***syn*** see TASTE 3
rel bite, nip, piquancy, twang; aroma, pungency; spiciness, tanginess

tangible *adj* **1** capable of being perceived especially by the sense of touch <a stuffed animal that provides *tangible* as well as visual stimulation for infants>
syn palpable, tactile, touchable; *compare* PERCEPTIBLE
rel corporeal, physical; embodied, material, real, substantial
con ethereal, spiritual, unreal
ant intangible
2 ***syn*** see MATERIAL 1
3 ***syn*** see PERCEPTIBLE
rel distinct, evident, manifest, obvious, patent, plain
con clouded, cloudy, imperceptible, indistinct, unclear

ant intangible

tangle *vb* **1** ***syn*** see INVOLVE 1
idiom make a party to
ant untangle
2 ***syn*** see CATCH 3
ant untangle
3 ***syn*** see ENTANGLE 1
rel foul up, mix up
4 ***syn*** see COMPLICATE
ant untangle

tangle *n* ***syn*** see MAZE 1

tanked *adj* ***syn*** see INTOXICATED 1

tank town *n* ***syn*** see BURG

tank up *vb* ***syn*** see DRINK 3

tantalize *vb* ***syn*** see WORRY 1
rel badger, bait; frustrate

tantamount *adj* ***syn*** see SAME 2
rel alike, like, uniform; selfsame, very
idiom as much as to say

tap *n* **1** ***syn*** see FAUCET
2 ***syn*** see BAR 5

tap *vb* ***syn*** see DRAIN 1

tap *vb* **1** to strike or hit audibly and usually lightly <*tapped* her pencil on the desk>
syn bob, knock, rap, tunk
rel bang, beat, hammer, hit, pound, smite, strike, thud, thump
2 ***syn*** see DESIGNATE 2

tapa *n* ***syn*** see SNACK

taper *vb* ***syn*** see DECREASE

taper off *vb* ***syn*** see DECREASE

taproom *n* ***syn*** see BAR 5

tapster *n* ***syn*** see BARTENDER

tar *n* ***syn*** see MARINER

tar *vb* ***syn*** see TAINT 1

taradiddle *n* ***syn*** see LIE

tardy *adj* not arriving, occurring, or done at the set, due, or expected time <be *tardy* for school>
syn behindhand, belated, late, lated, overdue, unpunctual
rel delayed, detained; dilatory, laggard, slow; delinquent
con beforehand, early; convenient, opportune, seasonable, timely; precise, punctilious
ant prompt, punctual

target *n* **1** an object of ridicule, attack, or abuse <made him the chief *target* of political satire>
syn butt, mark, sitting duck
rel victim; fall guy, scapegoat, whipping boy
2 ***syn*** see AMBITION 2
3 ***syn*** see USE 4

tariff *n* **1** ***syn*** see TAX 1
2 ***syn*** see PRICE 1

‖**tarnation** *adj* ***syn*** see UTTER

tarnish *vb* ***syn*** see DULL 1
2 ***syn*** see SOIL 2
rel contaminate, defile, pollute, stain, taint
con clean, cleanse; shine (up)
ant polish
3 ***syn*** see INJURE 1
4 ***syn*** see TAINT 1
rel defame, disgrace, embarrass; slander

tarpaulin *n* ***syn*** see MARINER

tarriance *n* ***syn*** see SOJOURN

tarry *vb* **1** ***syn*** see DELAY 2
rel falter, flag
2 ***syn*** see STAY 2
rel dawdle; sojourn
3 ***syn*** see VISIT 3

tart *adj* ***syn*** see SOUR 1
rel piquant, pungent
ant flat

tart *n* ***syn*** see DOXY 1

Tartarean *adj* ***syn*** see INFERNAL 1

Tartuffe *n* ***syn*** see HYPOCRITE

Tartuffery *n* ***syn*** see HYPOCRISY

Tartuffism *n* ***syn*** see HYPOCRISY

task *n* **1** a piece of work assigned or to be done <laboratory *tasks* assigned to chemistry students>
syn assignment, chare, chore, devoir, duty, job, stint
rel enterprise, project, undertaking; errand, labor, toil, work; charge, function, mission, office, province; business, calling, employment, occupation, vocation
2 a necessary undertaking that is usually difficult, dull, disagreeable, or problematic <deciphering his handwriting is a real *task*>
syn chore, effort, job, taskwork
rel burden, onus, strain, tax; bother, headache, nuisance, pain, trouble
idiom a hard (*or* long) row to hoe
con child's play, cinch, duck soup, picnic, ‖pipe, sinecure, snap
3 ***syn*** see LOAD 3

task *vb* ***syn*** see BURDEN

taskmaster *n* ***syn*** see SLAVE DRIVER

taskwork *n* ***syn*** see TASK 2

taste *vb* ***syn*** see FEEL 2
idiom be exposed to, run up against

taste *n* **1** ***syn*** see HINT 2
rel bit, sample, sampling
2 ***syn*** see APPETITE 1
3 the property of a substance which makes it perceptible to the gustatory sense <children often dislike the *taste* of olives>
syn flavor, relish, sapidity, sapor, savor, smack, tang
4 a liking for or enjoyment of something because of the pleasure it gives <had a *taste* for fast cars>
syn gusto, heart, palate, relish, zest
rel appreciation, comprehension, understanding; partiality, predilection, prepossession; disposition, inclination, predisposition
con dislike, disrelish; allergy, aversion, repugnance, repulsion
ant antipathy; distaste
5 ***syn*** see APPETITE 3
ant distaste
6 the power or practice of discerning and enjoying whatever constitutes excellence (as in the fine

---

syn synonym(s) *rel* related word(s)
ant antonym(s) *con* contrasted word(s)
idiom idiomatic equivalent(s)
‖ use limited; if in doubt, see a dictionary

arts) <a room whose decoration reflected her exquisite *taste*>
syn tastefulness
rel correctness; finesse, polish, refinement; elegance, grace
con gracelessness, inelegance, unrefinement; incorrectness, vulgarity
ant tastelessness

tasteful *adj* **1** ***syn*** see PALATABLE
rel rich
ant savorless, tasteless
2 ***syn*** see QUIET 4
ant tasteless

tastefulness *n* ***syn*** see TASTE 6
ant tastelessness

tasteless *adj* **1** ***syn*** see UNPALATABLE 1
rel bland, dull, stale, vapid; unflavored; uninteresting
con flavorful, pleasing
ant tasteful, tasty
2 ***syn*** see BARBARIC 1
rel inelegant, unpolished, unrefined
idiom in bad taste
ant tasteful, tasty

tasty *adj* **1** ***syn*** see PALATABLE
idiom fit for a king
con unsavory; bland, flavorless, unpalatable
ant savorless, tasteless
2 ***syn*** see QUIET 4
ant tasteless

||**tats** *n pl* ***syn*** see DICE

||**tatter** *vb* ***syn*** see HURRY 2

tatterdemalion *n* ***syn*** see RAGAMUFFIN

tattered *adj* **1** ***syn*** see RAGGED
2 ***syn*** see SHABBY 1

tatters *n pl* ***syn*** see RAGS 1

tattle *vb* ***syn*** see GOSSIP
idiom tell tales out of school

tattle *n* ***syn*** see REPORT 1

tattler *n* ***syn*** see INFORMER

tattletale *n* ***syn*** see INFORMER

tatty *adj* ***syn*** see CHEAP 2

taunt *vb* ***syn*** see RIDICULE
rel banter, chaff; provoke; upbraid; disdain, scorn; affront, insult, offend, outrage

taut *adj* ***syn*** see TIGHT 3
rel firm, trim; stretched
con flabby; relaxed
ant slack

tautology *n* ***syn*** see VERBIAGE 1
rel reiteration, repetition, repetitiousness; padding

tavern *n* **1** ***syn*** see BAR 5
2 ***syn*** see HOTEL

tavern car *n* ***syn*** see PARLOR CAR

taverner *n* ***syn*** see SALOONKEEPER

tawdry *adj* ***syn*** see GAUDY
rel common, sleazy; flaring, screaming

tax *vb* **1** ***syn*** see BURDEN
rel overtax
idiom press hard upon, tax the strength of, weigh heavy on (*or* upon)
2 ***syn*** see ACCUSE

tax *n* **1** a charge usually of money imposed by authority upon persons or property for public purposes <federal, state, and local *taxes* bear heavily on the thrifty>
syn assessment, ||cess, duty, impost, levy, tariff
rel tithe, tribute; boodle, boondoggle, giveaway, pork barrel
2 ***syn*** see LOAD 3
rel difficulty, strain; demand, imposition

taxi *n* ***syn*** see TAXICAB

taxicab *n* an automobile that carries passengers for a fare <took a *taxicab* from the airport to his hotel>
syn cab, hack, taxi
rel ||crawler, nighthawk

taxing *adj* ***syn*** see ONEROUS
rel wearing; tedious, troublesome

TB *n* ***syn*** see TUBERCULOSIS

||**tea** *n* ***syn*** see MARIJUANA

teach *vb* to cause to acquire knowledge or skill <*teach* a child to read>
syn discipline, educate, instruct, school, train
rel communicate, impart; implant, inculcate, instill; edify, enlighten, indoctrinate; fit, ground, prepare, rear; drill, exercise, practice; coach, tutor; lesson
idiom give instruction

teaching *n* ***syn*** see EDUCATION 1

teachy *adj* ***syn*** see DIDACTIC

tear *vb* **1** to separate (one part of a substance or object from another) forcibly <*tore* a chunk from the loaf on the table>
syn cleave, rend, rip, rive, split
rel cut, gash, incise, slash, slit; devil, pull (apart), rift, sever, sunder; ribbon, shred; break, crack, rupture; damage, impair, injure
2 ***syn*** see EXTRACT 1
3 ***syn*** see RUSH 1
4 ***syn*** see COURSE

tear *n* ***syn*** see BINGE 1

tear down *vb* **1** ***syn*** see DESTROY 1
ant build up
2 ***syn*** see MALIGN
ant build up

teardrops *n pl* ***syn*** see TEARS

tearful *adj* flowing with or accompanied by tears <*tearful* entreaties>
syn lachrymose, teary, weeping, weepy
rel lamenting, mournful; sniveling; bawling, blubbering, crying, sobbing
con dry-eyed
ant tearless

tearing *adj* ***syn*** see EXCRUCIATING

tear–jerking *adj* ***syn*** see SENTIMENTAL

tears *n pl* a profuse secretion of saline fluid that overflows the eyelids and dampens the face <a blow that brought *tears* to his eyes>
syn teardrops, water

teary *adj* ***syn*** see TEARFUL
ant tearless

tease *vb* ***syn*** see WORRY 1
rel disturb, importune
idiom give a bad time

teaser *n* ***syn*** see STRIPTEASER

tease up *vb* ***syn*** see TOUCH UP

||**tec** *n* ***syn*** see DETECTIVE

teched *adj* ***syn*** see INSANE 1
technique *n* ***syn*** see METHOD 1
tedious *adj* **1** ***syn*** see IRKSOME
2 ***syn*** see ARID 2
rel dragging, mortal, slow, tiresome
tedium *n* a state of dissatisfaction and weariness <incessant routine without variety breeds *tedium*>
syn boredom, doldrums, ‖dullsville, ennui, yawn
rel irksomeness, tediousness, tiresomeness, wearisomeness; dullness, monotony
con enlivenment, interest, invigoration, refreshment
teem *vb* to be abundantly stocked or provided <rivers *teeming* with fish>
syn abound, crawl, flow, pullulate, ‖sny, swarm
rel bristle, bustle; cram, crowd, jam, pack; overbrim, overflow, overrun
con lack, want
teem *vb* ***syn*** see POUR 3
teeming *adj* ***syn*** see ALIVE 5
rel multitudinous, populous, pregnant; bristling
con rare, sparse, uncommon; empty, lacking, void, wanting
teensy *adj* ***syn*** see TINY
teensy–weensy *adj* ***syn*** see TINY
teenty *adj* ***syn*** see TINY
teeny *adj* ***syn*** see TINY
teeny–weeny *adj* ***syn*** see TINY
tee off *vb* ***syn*** see BEGIN 1
teeter *vb* to progress (as by walking) unsteadily <*teetered* along on 4-inch heels>
syn falter, lurch, stagger, ‖stammer, stumble, topple, totter, wobble; *compare* LURCH 2, SEESAW
rel sway, weave
teethy *adj* ***syn*** see TOOTHY 1
teetotal *adj* ***syn*** see DRY 3
tehee *vb* ***syn*** see LAUGH
telephone *vb* to communicate with (a person) by telephone <*telephoned* him yesterday>
syn ‖buzz, call, phone, ‖ring (up)
idiom ‖get (one) on the horn, give (one) a buzz (*or* ring)
telestic *adj* ***syn*** see MYSTICAL 1
television *n* a medium of communication involving the transmission and reproduction of images by radio waves <it's fashionable to put down *television*>
syn boob tube, box, ‖idiot box, ‖telly, tube, TV, video
tell *vb* **1** ***syn*** see COUNT 1
2 ***syn*** see SAY 1
rel communicate, convey, impart
3 ***syn*** see REVEAL 1
rel recite, recount, rehearse, relate; acquaint, apprise, inform
4 ***syn*** see INFORM 2
5 ***syn*** see COMMAND
6 ***syn*** see WEIGH 3
telling *adj* ***syn*** see VALID
rel power-packed; influential, weighty; significant, striking
tell off *vb* ***syn*** see SCOLD 1
rel call down; denounce
idiom give (one) a piece of one's mind, tell (one) a thing or two, tell (one) where to get off
telltale *n* **1** ***syn*** see GOSSIP 1
2 ***syn*** see HINT 1
tellurian *adj* ***syn*** see EARTHLY 1
telluric *adj* ***syn*** see EARTHLY 1
‖**telly** *n* ***syn*** see TELEVISION
temblor (*or* **tremblor**) *n* ***syn*** see EARTHQUAKE
temerarious *adj* ***syn*** see ADVENTUROUS
rel heedless, imprudent, incautious, injudicious
temerity *n* conspicuous or flagrant boldness (as in speech, behavior, or action) <had the *temerity* to order an attack when hopelessly outnumbered>
syn assurance, audacity, brashness, hardihood, hardiness, nerve
rel daring, foolhardiness, heedlessness, rashness, recklessness, venturesomeness; impetuosity, precipitateness; impertinence, intrusiveness
con deliberation, judgment, judiciousness, prudence; heed, heedfulness
ant caution
temper *vb* ***syn*** see MODERATE 1
rel dilute, season; ease, pacify, soften; adjust, modify; curb, tone (down)
idiom take the edge off
temper *n* **1** a general or prevailing quality or characteristic (as of moral or social attitudes and behavior) <the wild fashions reflected the *temper* of the times>
syn mood, spirit, timbre, tone
rel atmosphere, aura, climate; orientation, outlook; disposition, drift, leaning, tendency, trend; character, nature, peculiarity
2 ***syn*** see DISPOSITION 3
rel condition, posture, state; attribute, property, quality; style, type, way
idiom turn of mind
3 ***syn*** see MOOD 1
idiom frame (*or* state) of mind
4 an outbreak or display of anger <a childish fit of *temper*>
syn passion
rel anger, fury, ire, rage; conniption, fit, outburst, tantrum
temperament *n* ***syn*** see DISPOSITION 3
rel mentality, mind; kind, type, way
idiom inner nature
temperamental *adj* **1** ***syn*** see MOODY
2 ***syn*** see INCONSTANT 1
ant steady
temperance *n* **1** an avoidance of extremes (as in action, thought, or feeling) <a man who knew no *temperance* in his opinions>
syn measure, moderateness, moderation
rel reasonableness; constraint, restraint
idiom happy medium

---

syn synonym(s) ***rel*** related word(s)
ant antonym(s) ***con*** contrasted word(s)
idiom idiomatic equivalent(s)
‖ use limited; if in doubt, see a dictionary

con extremeness, radicalness; excess, excessiveness; immoderateness, immoderation, unconstraint, unreasonableness, unrestraint
ant intemperance, intemperateness
2 strict habitual and usually complete self-denial in the gratification of appetites or passions <an ascetic who practiced complete *temperance*>
syn abstinence, continence, sobriety
rel abnegation, eschewal, forbearance, forgoing, refrainment, sacrifice, self-denial, self-deprivation; control, restraint, self-control, self-discipline; asceticism, austerity, mortification
con intemperance, intemperancy, intemperateness, prodigality
ant excess

temperate *adj* **1** ***syn*** see MODERATE 2
rel constant, equable, even, steady; checked, curbed, regulated, restrained
ant intemperate
2 ***syn*** see ABSTEMIOUS
rel indulgent; self-indulgent
con intemperate; dissipated, prodigal, profligate
ant excessive
3 ***syn*** see CONSERVATIVE 2
4 ***syn*** see SOBER 3

temperish *adj* ***syn*** see IRASCIBLE

tempersome *adj* ***syn*** see ILL-TEMPERED

tempestuous *adj* ***syn*** see WILD 6
rel tumultuous, unbridled, unrestrained, violent
ant calm, quiet

temple *n* ***syn*** see HOUSE OF WORSHIP

tempo *n* rate of performance or delivery <increased sales and production *tempo*>
syn pace, time; *compare* SPEED 2
rel speed; momentum

temporal *adj* **1** ***syn*** see MATERIALISTIC
ant nontemporal
2 ***syn*** see PROFANE 1
rel material, physical; nonsacred, nonspiritual, unhallowed, unsanctified, unspiritual
con celestial, heavenly
ant spiritual

temporary *adj* lasting, continuing, or serving for a limited time <was *temporary* president of the company for nine months>
syn acting, ad interim, interim, pro tem, pro tempore, supply; *compare* TRANSIENT
rel alternate, substitute; interimistic, provisional, provisory; jackleg, make-do, makeshift, stopgap
ant permanent

tempt *vb* ***syn*** see LURE
rel provoke, rouse; court, invite, solicit, vamp, woo
idiom whet the appetite
con discourage; dissuade; repel, repulse, revolt

temptation *n* ***syn*** see LURE 2

tempting *adj* ***syn*** see ENTICING
rel appetizing, mouth-watering; provoking, rousing, tantalizing
con repellent, repulsive
ant untempting

temptress *n* ***syn*** see SIREN

ten *n* ***syn*** see BREAK 4

tenable *adj* **1** capable of being defended against attack <the platoon's position was no longer *tenable*>
syn defendable, defensible
rel impregnable, secure
con insecure, vulnerable; defenseless, helpless, unprotected; dangerous, precarious, risky
ant untenable
2 ***syn*** see JUSTIFIABLE
rel believable, credible, maintainable, plausible
con indefensible, inexcusable, unbelievable, unjustifiable
ant untenable

tenacious *adj* **1** ***syn*** see STRONG 2
rel bulldogged, bulldoggish, bulldoggy, dogged, obstinate, pertinacious, stubborn; resolute, steadfast, true; persevering, persisting
2 ***syn*** see VISCOUS
rel cohesive; tacky; sticky
3 ***syn*** see FAST 4
con lax, slack

tenant *vb* ***syn*** see INHABIT

tenantable *adj* ***syn*** see LIVABLE 1
idiom fit to live in
con uninhabitable

tend *vb* **1** ***syn*** see TILL
2 to supervise or take charge of <employed a girl to *tend* the children each day>
syn attend, care (for), mind, watch
rel cherish, cultivate, foster, minister, nurse, nurture, serve; defend, guard, protect, safeguard, shield; supervise
idiom look after, see after, see to, take care of, take under one's wing
con disregard, ignore, neglect

tend *vb* **1** to have or exhibit an inclination or tendency <he *tends* to praise people too highly>
syn incline, lean, look; *compare* INCLINE 3
idiom be disposed
2 ***syn*** see CONTRIBUTE 2

tendency *n* **1** a movement or course having a particular direction and character <a growing *tendency* to underestimate the potential strength of that nation>
syn current, drift, run, tenor, trend
rel curve, inclination, leaning, propensity; turn; shift; custom, habit, usage, way
2 ***syn*** see LEANING 2

tendentious *adj* ***syn*** see BIASED 2

tender *adj* showing or expressing affectionate interest in another <his mother was very *tender* with her wayward son>
syn compassionate, kindhearted, responsive, softhearted, sympathetic, warm, warmhearted
rel gentle, lenient, mild, soft, yielding; considerate, solicitous, thoughtful; affectionate, fond, loving; benevolent, charitable, humane, mild; commiserative; forgiving, merciful, tolerant
con callous, hard, harsh; inhumane, uncharitable, unfeeling
ant rough, severe

tender *vb* ***syn*** see OFFER 1
rel propose, purpose, submit, suggest

tenderfoot *n* ***syn*** see NOVICE

tenderloin *n* ***syn*** see RED-LIGHT DISTRICT
tenebrific *adj* ***syn*** see GLOOMY 3
tenebrous *adj* **1** ***syn*** see DARK 1
2 ***syn*** see OBSCURE 3
tenement *n* ***syn*** see APARTMENT 1
tenet *n* ***syn*** see DOCTRINE
rel belief, conviction, persuasion, view
tenor *n* **1** the course of thought that is retained through something spoken or written <the *tenor* of the book is first expressed in the introduction>
syn drift, purport, substance; *compare* BODY 3, MEANING 1, SUBSTANCE 2
rel intent; inclination, trend; mood, tone; core, gist, meat, stuff
2 ***syn*** see TENDENCY 1
tense *adj* **1** ***syn*** see TIGHT 3
rel strained, stretched
ant relaxed
2 feeling or showing nervous tension <the soldiers were *tense* as they waited for the order to advance>
syn edgy, nervy, restive, uneasy, uptight
rel queasy; jittery, rusty, unquiet; anxious, concerned, overanxious
con easy; calm, cool, ‖loose, placid, unconcerned; firm, nerveless, unshaken
ant relaxed
tension *n* **1** ***syn*** see STRESS 1
rel tautness, tenseness, tightness
idiom stress and strain
ant relaxation
2 emotional strain <was suffering from nervous *tension*>
syn unease, uptightness
rel strain, stress; anxiety, nerves, nervousness, uneasiness; agitation, discomfort, disquiet, misease
ten–strike *n* ***syn*** see SMASH 6
tent *vb* ***syn*** see CAMP
tentative *adj* **1** ***syn*** see CONDITIONAL 1
rel acting, ad interim, makeshift, temporary; probationary; experimental, test, trial
con conclusive, decisive, definitive
ant final
2 ***syn*** see VACILLATING 2
rel disinclined, reluctant
tenue *n* ***syn*** see BEHAVIOR
tenuous *adj* **1** ***syn*** see THIN 2
2 ***syn*** see THIN 1
rel aerial, airy, ethereal, fine
con abundant
ant dense
3 having little substance or strength and usually not firmly based <only a *tenuous* link in the chain of evidence>
syn feeble, insubstantial, unsubstantial; *compare* IMPLAUSIBLE
rel flimsy, weak; insignificant
con significant, sound, strong
ant substantial
tenure *n* ***syn*** see HOLD
tepid *adj* **1** moderately warm <a *tepid* bath>
syn lukewarm, milk-warm, warmish
rel mild, temperate, warm
con cold, cool, freezing, frozen; heated, hot, steaming
2 lacking in animation, force, passion, conviction, or commitment <gave only a *tepid* endorsement to the candidate>
syn halfhearted, lukewarm, unenthusiastic; *compare* ARID 2
rel indifferent; colorless, dull, lifeless, unlively; feeble, marrowless, pithless, sapless, spiritless; dim, faint, forceless, weak
con animated, forceful; fiery, impassioned, passionate, spirited
tergiversate *vb* **1** ***syn*** see DEFECT
idiom fall away from
2 ***syn*** see EQUIVOCATE 2
idiom beg the question
tergiversation *n* **1** ***syn*** see DEFECTION
rel about-face, reversal, reverse; denial, disavowal, forswearing, renunciation, repudiation
2 ***syn*** see AMBIGUITY
tergiversator *n* ***syn*** see RENEGADE
tergiverse *vb* **1** ***syn*** see DEFECT
2 ***syn*** see EQUIVOCATE 2
term *n* **1** ***syn*** see LIMIT 1
rel terminus
2 a limited, definite, or measurable extent of time during which something exists, lasts, or is in progress <the office has a *term* of four years>
syn duration, span, time
rel phase; go, period, spell, stretch; hitch, tour, turn; standing
3 ***syn*** see WORD 2
4 terms *pl* ***syn*** see CONDITION 1
rel detail, item, particular, point; limit
5 terms *pl* mutual social relationship or relative position <fight on equal *terms*> <the two were on *terms* of great intimacy>
syn footing, standing
rel coequality, equipollence, status; equality, equivalence, par, parity; balance
term *vb* ***syn*** see NAME 1
termagant *n* ***syn*** see VIRAGO
termagant *adj* ***syn*** see TURBULENT 1
terminable *adj* liable to be terminated or subject to termination <marriage is a *terminable* institution>
syn determinable, endable
rel finite, limited; limitable
terminal *adj* ***syn*** see LAST
con beginning, starting
ant initial
terminate *vb* **1** ***syn*** see CLOSE 3
rel abolish, extinguish; discontinue, wind down
idiom put the lid on
ant initiate
2 ***syn*** see ADJOURN 2
3 ***syn*** see DISMISS 3
4 ***syn*** see QUIT 6

---

syn synonym(s) ***rel*** related word(s)
ant antonym(s) ***con*** contrasted word(s)
idiom idiomatic equivalent(s)
‖ use limited; if in doubt, see a dictionary

terminated *adj* ***syn*** see COMPLETE 4

terminating *adj* ***syn*** see LAST

ant initial

termination *n* ***syn*** see END 2

rel issue, outcome, ‖pay-off, result

con source; beginning, start

ant initiation

terminology *n* the specialized or technical terms and expressions peculiar to a field, subject, or trade <the *terminology* of the plastics industry>

syn cant, dictionary, jargon, language, lexicon, palaver, vocabulary; *compare* DIALECT 2

rel shoptalk; gibberish, gobbledygook

terminus *n* ***syn*** see END 2

terra firma *n* ***syn*** see EARTH 2

terrain *n* **1** the physical configuration and features of a tract of land <made an analysis of the *terrain* via aerial photos>

syn topography

rel contour, form, profile, shape

2 an area devoted to a specified activity <the whole county had become breeding and racing *terrain*>

syn territory, turf

3 ***syn*** see FIELD

terrene *adj* **1** ***syn*** see EARTHLY 1

2 ***syn*** see EARTHY 1

terrestrial *adj* **1** ***syn*** see EARTHLY 1

rel earthbound, prosaic; profane, secular, unspiritual

ant empyreal

2 ***syn*** see EARTHY 1

terrible *adj* **1** ***syn*** see FEARFUL 3

2 ***syn*** see HARD 6

3 ***syn*** see INTENSE 1

4 ***syn*** see GHASTLY 1

terribly *adv* ***syn*** see VERY 1

terrific *adj* **1** ***syn*** see FEARFUL 3

rel terrorizing; agitating, disquieting, upsetting

2 ***syn*** see MARVELOUS 2

rel magnificent, superb; rattling, screaming

terrified *adj* ***syn*** see AFRAID 1

rel horrified, shocked; terrorized; frozen, paralyzed

con unfearful, unfearing, unfrightened

ant unafraid

terrify *vb* ***syn*** see FRIGHTEN

rel freeze, paralyze, petrify, stun, stupefy

idiom put the fear of God into, strike fear into the heart of

terrifying *adj* ***syn*** see GHASTLY 1

ant unterrifying

territory *n* **1** ***syn*** see AREA 1

2 ***syn*** see FIELD

3 ***syn*** see TERRAIN 2

terror *n* ***syn*** see FEAR 1

rel awe, fearfulness

terroristic *adj* characterized by or practicing terror as a means of coercion <used torture and other *terroristic* tactics to extract confessions>

syn gestapo

rel coercive, strong-arm; brutal, cruel, merciless; immoral, improper, unsanctioned

terrorize *vb* **1** ***syn*** see FRIGHTEN

idiom scare to death

2 ***syn*** see INTIMIDATE

idiom use gestapo tactics on

terse *adj* ***syn*** see CONCISE

rel close, compact; lean, precise; clear-cut, crisp, incisive; taut

con circuitous; pleonastic, redundant, repetitious

tersely *adv* ***syn*** see BRIEFLY

rel closely, compactly; crisply, incisively, precisely; abruptly, curtly

idiom in as few words as possible

ant prolixly

test *n* ***syn*** see EXPERIMENT

rel inspection, scrutiny; confirmation, corroboration, substantiation, verification

test *vb* **1** ***syn*** see TRY 1

rel assay, essay; confirm, substantiate, verify

idiom bring to test

2 ***syn*** see PROVE 1

test (out) *vb* ***syn*** see EXPERIMENT

test *adj* ***syn*** see EXPERIMENTAL 2

rel proving, testing, trying; probationary, speculative

testament *n* ***syn*** see TESTIMONY

testify *vb* **1** to serve as evidence of <present conditions *testify* to the accuracy of his predictions>

syn attest, point (to)

rel affirm; demonstrate, show; prove

con discredit, disprove, invalidate; confute, refute

2 to make a solemn declaration under oath for the purpose of establishing a fact (as in court) <*testified* against the defendant>

syn depone, depose, ‖mount, swear

idiom give testimony

3 ***syn*** see INDICATE 2

testimonial *n* **1** ***syn*** see TESTIMONY

rel indication, manifestation, show, sign, symbol, token

2 an expression of great approval and high esteem <a dinner was planned as a *testimonial* in her honor>

syn appreciation, salvo, tribute

rel salute; triumph; jubilee; commemoration, memorialization, remembrance

3 ***syn*** see MONUMENT 2

testimony *n* something that serves as tangible verification <the results are remarkable *testimony* to the accuracy of his predictions>

syn attestation, confirmation, evidence, proof, testament, testimonial, witness; *compare* INDICATION 3

rel demonstration, illustration; affirmation, corroboration, documentation, substantiation, verification

testy *adj* ***syn*** see IRASCIBLE

rel annoyed, exasperated, grouchy, irritable

tetchy *adj* ***syn*** see IRASCIBLE

rel ill-humored; cantankerous

tête–à–tête *n* a private conversation between two people <had a *tête-à-tête* with her in a quiet corner>

syn vis-à-vis

rel causerie, chat, coze; conversation, talk; argument, discussion
tetrad *n* ***syn*** see QUARTET
‖**tew** *vb* ***syn*** see WORRY 3
text *n* ***syn*** see SUBJECT 2
rel consideration, issue; fundamentals; idea
texture *n* **1** ***syn*** see ESSENCE 1
2 a basic often highly complex underlying scheme, structure, or pattern <war destroys the very *texture* of a society>
syn fabric, fiber, web
rel framework, structure; composition, constitution, makeup; pattern, scheme
thalassic *adj* ***syn*** see MARINE 1
thankful *adj* ***syn*** see GRATEFUL 1
con unappreciative, ungrateful
ant thankless, unthankful
thankless *adj* **1** not inclined to give thanks <a *thankless* guest>
syn unappreciative, ungrateful, unthankful
rel self-centered; careless, heedless, thoughtless; unappreciative, ungrateful, unmindful
con appreciative, grateful, mindful; careful, heedful, thoughtful
ant thankful
2 not likely to obtain thanks <a *thankless* job>
syn unappreciated, ungrateful, unthankful
rel disagreeable, distasteful, unpleasant; miserable, wretched
con thankworthy
thanks *n pl* ***syn*** see GRACE 1
thanksgiving *n* ***syn*** see GRACE 1
thankworthy *adj* ***syn*** see WORTHY 1
thank–you–ma'am *n* ***syn*** see BUMP 3
that *adj* **1** being the other <we argued it this way and we argued it *that* way>
syn another
ant this
2 ***syn*** see SUCH 2
thaumaturgic *adj* ***syn*** see MAGIC
thaumaturgy *n* ***syn*** see MAGIC 1
thaw *vb* ***syn*** see LIQUEFY
theater *n* ***syn*** see DRAMA
theatral *adj* ***syn*** see DRAMATIC 1
theatric *adj* ***syn*** see DRAMATIC 1
theatrical *adj* **1** ***syn*** see DRAMATIC 1
2 having qualities resembling a stage play or an actor's performance <he slowly made an exaggerated *theatrical* bow>
syn dramatic
rel histrionic, melodramatic, staged; affected, artificial, exaggerated, mannered, unnatural
theft *n* the unlawful taking and carrying away of property without the consent of its owner <was found guilty of auto *theft*>
syn larceny, lift, pinch, purloining, rip-off, steal, stealage, stealing, thievery, thieving, ‖touch
rel filching, pilferage, pilfering, swiping; robbery, robbing, ‖stouth, ‖stouthrief; ‖score
theme *n* **1** ***syn*** see SUBJECT 2
2 ***syn*** see ESSAY 2
then *adv* **1** at another time <science as it was taught *then*>
syn again, anon, when; *compare* BEFORE 2
rel before, formerly
2 ***syn*** see AGAIN 4
3 ***syn*** see THEREFORE
thence *adv* **1** ***syn*** see AWAY 1
2 ***syn*** see THEREFROM
thenceforth *adv* from that time forward <the island which was *thenceforth* to be their home>
syn thenceforward, thereafter; *compare* HENCEFORTH
idiom from then on
thenceforward *adv* ***syn*** see THENCEFORTH
theorem *n* ***syn*** see PRINCIPLE 1
theoretical *adj* **1** concerned principally with abstractions and theories <*theoretical* versus applied physics>
syn academic, closet, speculative
rel conjectural, hypothetical, notional, suppositional, unproved; analytical, problematical
con practical; factual; proved
ant applied
2 ***syn*** see ABSTRACT 1
rel idealized, ivory-tower
ant concrete
theorize *vb* ***syn*** see SUGGEST 4
theory *n* **1** a belief, policy, or procedure proposed or followed as the basis of action <an educational system that was based on the *theory* that men learn best by experience>
syn hypothesis, supposal; *compare* ASSUMPTION 2
rel base, basis, grounds, position, premise, understanding
ant practice
2 something taken for granted especially on trivial or inadequate grounds <her *theory* that the house was haunted>
syn conjecture, perhaps, speculation, suppose, supposition
rel guess, guesswork, surmise; feeling, hunch, impression, presentiment, suspicion
con assurance, certainty, knowledge
there *adv* to or into that place <they seldom go *there* anymore>
syn thither, thitherward, yon
rel yonder
ant here
thereafter *adv* ***syn*** see THENCEFORTH
thereby *adv* in consequence of that <lied to the jury, *thereby* negating his testimony>
syn therethrough; *compare* THEREFROM
therefore *adv* for this or that reason <I think, *therefore* I am>
syn accordingly, consequently, ergo, hence, so, then, thereupon, thus
rel thence, therefrom
therefrom *adv* from that thing, fact, or circumstance <public opinion and a policy deriving *therefrom*>
syn thence, thereof; *compare* THEREBY
thereof *adv* ***syn*** see THEREFROM

---

syn synonym(s) ***rel*** related word(s)
ant antonym(s) ***con*** contrasted word(s)
idiom idiomatic equivalent(s)
‖ use limited; if in doubt, see a dictionary

thereon *adv* on or upon that <knew both the text and commentary *thereon*>
syn thereupon
rel therein, thereof, thereto

therethrough *adv syn* see THEREBY

theretofore *adv* up to that time <*theretofore* obscure communities>
syn thereuntil
rel ||afore, before, previously
idiom before then

thereuntil *adv syn* see THERETOFORE
idiom until then

thereupon *adv* **1** *syn* see THEREON
2 *syn* see THEREFORE

thesis *n* **1** a position assumed or a point made especially in controversy <her *thesis* about the assassination was arguable>
syn contention, contestation
rel point, position; argument; belief, opinion, sentiment(s), view(s)
2 *syn* see ASSUMPTION 2
3 *syn* see DISCOURSE 2
rel exposition; argument, argumentation

thespian *adj syn* see DRAMATIC 1

thespian *n syn* see ACTOR 1

thew *n syn* see MUSCLE 1

thick *adj* **1** *syn* see STOCKY
rel broad, wide; bulky, burly, husky; blubber, blubbery, massive, obese
con slender, slight, slim; lanky, spare; skeletal
2 *syn* see CLOSE 4
rel concentrated, crammed; localized
con dispersed, scattered
ant diffuse
3 *syn* see STUPID 1
4 *syn* see FAMILIAR 1
idiom hand in glove, thick as thieves
5 *syn* see IMPLAUSIBLE
idiom a little too thick

thick-bodied *adj syn* see STOCKY

thickhead *n syn* see DUNCE
rel ||clot

thickheaded *adj syn* see STUPID 1

thickset *adj syn* see STOCKY
rel fleshy, portly

thickskull *n syn* see DUNCE
rel lout

thick-witted *adj syn* see STUPID 1

thief *n* one who steals <a *thief* took her money>
syn filcher, larcener, larcenist, nimmer, pilferer, prig, purloiner, stealer; *compare* ROBBER
rel burglar, cat burglar, cat man, housebreaker; hijacker, robber; ||booster, ||dip, lifter, shoplifter; nip, pickpocket

thieve *vb syn* see STEAL 1

thievery *n syn* see THEFT

thieving *adj syn* see LARCENOUS

thieving *n syn* see THEFT

thievish *adj syn* see LARCENOUS

thin *adj* **1** not thick, heavy, or broad (as in configuration or physique) <a *thin* body>
syn attenuate, reedy, slender, slight, slim, squinny, stalky, tenuous, twiggy; *compare* LEAN
rel lank, lanky, lathy, lean, macilent, spare; cadaverous, gaunt, pinched, skeletal, wasted; meager, puny, small, twiglike
con broad, wide; compact, dense, solid; heavy, massive; corpulent, fat, obese
ant thick
2 characterized by wide separation of component particles <*thin* air at high altitudes>
syn attenuate, attenuated, rare, rarefied, subtile, subtle, tenuous
rel diffuse, diluted, dispersed; fine, refined
con heavy, thick
ant dense
3 *syn* see DILUTE
4 *syn* see ACUTE 4
rel high-pitched
con low, low-pitched; guttural; deep
5 *syn* see IMPLAUSIBLE
rel vapid; transparent; questionable; untenable
idiom a bit thin
con believable, convincing, sound, substantial

thin *vb* **1** to make thin or thinner <a once powerful frame *thinned* by privation>
syn attenuate, extenuate, wiredraw
rel diminish, reduce; weaken
con broaden, enlarge; strengthen
ant thicken
2 to make or become less dense <the air *thinned* at high altitudes>
syn attenuate, rarefy
ant densify
3 *syn* see DILUTE

thing *n* **1** *syn* see AFFAIR 1
2 *syn* see OCCURRENCE
3 *syn* see ACTION 1
rel exploit, feat, stunt
4 whatever is apprehended as having actual, distinct, and demonstrable existence <there is a place for each *thing* in the lab>
syn article, object
rel entity, item
5 that which can be known as having existence in space or time <virtue is not a *thing*, but an attribute of a *thing*>
syn being, entity, individual, material, matter, object, stuff, substance
rel item, particular
con attribute, characteristic, property, quality
6 *syn* see ENTITY 1
ant nonentity, nonexistence
7 things *pl syn* see POSSESSION 2
8 things *pl syn* see PERSONAL EFFECTS
9 things *pl syn* see CLOTHES
10 *syn* see POINT 1
11 *syn* see FASHION 3
12 *syn* see FETISH 2

thingum *n syn* see DOODAD

thingumajig *n syn* see DOODAD

thingumbob *n syn* see DOODAD

thingummy *n syn* see DOODAD

think *vb* **1** to form an idea of something in the mind <try to *think* exactly how the accident happened>

syn conceive, envisage, envision, fancy, feature, image, imagine, project, realize, see, vision, visualize
rel consider, contemplate, study, weigh; appreciate, comprehend, understand; cerebrate, ideate; conjecture, guess, surmise
2 ***syn*** see UNDERSTAND 3
3 ***syn*** see CONJECTURE
4 ***syn*** see FEEL 3
rel estimate; regard
5 to use one's powers of conception, judgment, or inference <the power to *think* sets humans apart from other animals>
syn cerebrate, cogitate, deliberate, reason, reflect, speculate
rel consider, contemplate; brood, meditate, mull, muse, ponder, ruminate; intellectualize, logicalize, logicize, rationalize; conclude, deduce, infer, judge
idiom put on one's thinking cap, set one's brain to work, use one's head, use the old bean

think (out *or* over) *vb* ***syn*** see CONSIDER 1

think (over) *vb* ***syn*** see RECONSIDER

thinkable *adj* **1** capable of being thought about <concepts that are easy enough to be *thinkable*>
syn cogitable
rel imaginable, presumable, supposable; comprehendible, comprehensible
con unimaginable; incomprehensible, uncomprehensible
ant unthinkable
2 capable of being made actual <nationalism at this time would be scarcely *thinkable*>
syn conceivable, imaginable, supposable
rel likely, possible; convincing, plausible; feasible, practicable, practical
con inconceivable, unimaginable; impossible, unlikely; implausible; impractical, unfeasible
ant unthinkable

thinking *adj* ***syn*** see THOUGHTFUL 1
ant unthinking

third degree *n* ***syn*** see CROSS-EXAMINATION

third estate *n* ***syn*** see COMMONALTY

thirst *vb* ***syn*** see LONG
rel covet; desire, wish

thirsting *adj* ***syn*** see THIRSTY 1

thirsty *adj* **1** experiencing a desire for drink <the long hot walk had made him *thirsty*>
syn athirst, dry, thirsting
rel juiceless, parched, sapless
2 ***syn*** see DRY 1
3 ***syn*** see EAGER
idiom hungry for, itching for, wild for
ant sated, satiated

this and that *n, often* **this and thats** *pl* ***syn*** see SUNDRIES

thither *adv* ***syn*** see THERE
ant hither

thitherward *adv* ***syn*** see THERE
ant hitherward

thorny *adj* bristling with perplexities, points of controversy, or other conflicting elements <the *thorny* question of states' rights>
syn nettlesome, prickly, spiny
rel troublesome, vexatious; difficult; tricky

thorough *adj* **1** ***syn*** see EXHAUSTIVE
rel absolute
2 ***syn*** see CIRCUMSTANTIAL

thoroughbred *adj* ***syn*** see PUREBRED
con mixed, mongrel

thoroughfare *n* ***syn*** see WAY 1

thoroughgoing *adj* **1** ***syn*** see EXHAUSTIVE
2 ***syn*** see UTTER

thoroughly *adv* **1** ***syn*** see WELL 3
2 in a detailed and complete manner <*thoroughly* investigated the accusations>
syn completely, detailedly, exhaustively, in and out, inside out, up and down
idiom item by item, to the last detail
con casually, offhandedly, sketchily, superficially
ant cursorily
3 ***syn*** see VERY 1
4 ***syn*** see HARD 3

though *adv* ***syn*** see HOWEVER

though *conj* in spite of the fact that <*though* they know the war is lost, they continue to fight>
syn albeit, although, howbeit, much as, when, whereas, while

thought *n* **1** the act or process of thinking <sat immersed in deep *thought*>
syn brainwork, cerebration, cogitation, deliberation, reflection, speculation
rel contemplation; meditation, musing, pondering, rumination
2 ***syn*** see IDEA

thoughtful *adj* **1** characterized by or exhibiting the power to think <the doctor had a shrewd rather than a *thoughtful* face>
syn cogitative, contemplative, meditative, pensive, ‖pensy, pondering, reflecting, reflective, ruminative, speculative, thinking
rel analytical, calculating, logical, rational; earnest, grave, melancholy, serious, sober, studious; brainy, intellectual; deep, inseeing, introspective
con irrational; dull, slow, stupid, unthinking; empty-headed, shallow, vacuous
ant thoughtless
2 ***syn*** see MINDFUL 2
3 mindful of others <the thank-you note was a *thoughtful* gesture>
syn attentive, considerate
rel anxious, careful, concerned, heedful, mindful, solicitous; chivalrous, civil, courteous, gallant, gracious, polite, well-bred
con careless, heedless, inattentive, negligent, remiss, unconcerned, unmindful, unthinking; inconsiderate; discourteous, impolite
ant thoughtless, unthoughtful

thoughtfully *adv* ***syn*** see WELL 2
rel courteously, politely, solicitously
con discourteously, impolitely; inconsiderately, heedlessly, unkindly

---

syn synonym(s) ***rel*** related word(s)
ant antonym(s) ***con*** contrasted word(s)
idiom idiomatic equivalent(s)
‖ use limited; if in doubt, see a dictionary

ant thoughtlessly, unthoughtfully
thoughtless *adj* **1** ***syn*** see RASH 1
2 ***syn*** see CARELESS 1
con mindful
ant thoughtful
3 ***syn*** see SHORT 5
rel discourteous, impolite, rude; selfish
ant thoughtful
thought–out *adj* ***syn*** see DELIBERATE 1
rel investigated; analyzed
idiom thought over (*or* through)
thousand *n* ***syn*** see SCAD
thrall *n* ***syn*** see BONDAGE
thralldom *n* ***syn*** see BONDAGE
thrash *vb* **1** ***syn*** see BEAT 1
2 ***syn*** see WHIP 2
3 ***syn*** see WHIP 1
rel strike; paddywhack, ‖pail
thrashing *n* ***syn*** see DEFEAT 1
thrash out *vb* ***syn*** see DISCUSS 1
threadbare *adj* **1** ***syn*** see SHABBY 1
rel damaged, impaired, injured; frayed, ragged; shopworn, timeworn, worn
idiom the worse for wear, worn to rags (*or* threads)
2 ***syn*** see TRITE
rel common, familiar; imitative, uncreative; set, stock; banal, corny
con fresh, new; different, novel, original, unconventional, unusual; memorable
threaten *vb* to announce or forecast impending danger or evil <bullies *threatening* the child with a beating>
syn menace
rel browbeat, bulldoze, cow, intimidate; augur, forebode, portend, presage; caution, forewarn, warn
idiom make (*or* utter) threats against
threatening *adj* **1** ***syn*** see IMMINENT 2
rel impending; forthcoming, upcoming; close, near
2 ***syn*** see OMINOUS
threesome *n* ***syn*** see TRIAD
threshold *n* ***syn*** see VERGE 2
thrift *n* ***syn*** see ECONOMY
rel austerity, economizing; saving; parsimony
ant waste
thriftiness *n* ***syn*** see ECONOMY
ant thriftlessness
thriftless *adj* ***syn*** see IMPROVIDENT
ant thrifty
thrifty *adj* **1** ***syn*** see FLOURISHING
rel blooming, burgeoning; growing
2 ***syn*** see SPARING
rel foresighted, prudent; conserving, preserving
con extravagant, improvident
ant wasteful
thrill *vb* to fill with emotions that stir or excite or to be so excited <an audience *thrilled* by the brilliant spectacle>
syn electrify, enthuse, send
rel animate, excite, galvanize, move, quicken, stimulate; arouse, inspire, rally, rouse, stir
idiom thrill to pieces (*or* to bits)
con bore, ennui, weary
thrill *n* sudden emotional stimulation, excitement, or enjoyment <they both got a *thrill* out of small-boat racing>
syn bang, boot, kick, wallop
rel excitement, lift, stimulation, titillation
thriller *n* a work of fiction or drama designed to hold the interest by use of a high degree of intrigue, adventure, or suspense <wrote cheap detective *thrillers*>
syn chiller, shocker, thriller-diller
rel gothic, mystery; dime novel, penny dreadful, shilling shocker
thriller–diller *n* ***syn*** see THRILLER
thrive *vb* **1** ***syn*** see BOOM
rel come on, develop, grow; increase; prosper
con stagnate; fail; bust
2 ***syn*** see SUCCEED 3
rel advance, progress
idiom make a go, turn out well
thriving *adj* **1** ***syn*** see FLOURISHING
rel blooming, growing; advancing, progressing
idiom going strong
con shriveling; dying
2 ***syn*** see SUCCESSFUL
thriving *n* ***syn*** see PROSPERITY 2
throb *vb* ***syn*** see PULSATE
rel thump; resonate
throe *n* **1** ***syn*** see ATTACK 3
rel convulsion
2 ***syn*** see PAIN 1
rel stab
throne *n* ***syn*** see TOILET
throng *n* ***syn*** see CROWD 1
rel assemblage, assembly, collection, congregation, gathering; bunch, flock, group, pack
thronged *adj* ***syn*** see ALIVE 5
rel crawling
throttle *vb* ***syn*** see CHOKE 1
rel garrote
throttling *n* ***syn*** see REPRESSION 1
through *prep* **1** ***syn*** see VIA 1
2 ***syn*** see VIA 2
3 ***syn*** see OVER 6
4 ***syn*** see ABOUT 4
idiom clear through
through *adv* **1** from beginning to end <the region has a mild climate the whole year *through*>
syn around, over, round, throughout
2 ***syn*** see OVER 5
through *adj* **1** ***syn*** see DIRECT 2
con obstructed; interrupted
2 ***syn*** see COMPLETE 4
3 having no further value, strength, or resources <when he lost his voice, his singing career was *through*>
syn done for, finished, washed-up
rel ended; over
4 being at the very end of a course, concern, or relationship <was *through* with his wife>
syn done, washed-up
rel finished
through–and–through *adv* ***syn*** see DOWN 2
throughout *adv* **1** ***syn*** see EVERYWHERE 1

2 ***syn*** see THROUGH 1

throughout *prep* **1** ***syn*** see ABOUT 4

2 ***syn*** see DURING

throw *vb* **1** to cause to move swiftly through space by a propulsive movement or a propelling force <*throw* a ball to first base>
syn ‖bung, cast, chuck, fire, fling, heave, hurl, launch, pitch, sling, toss
rel ding, drive, impel, precipitate, shoot; project, propel, push, shove, thrust; flick, flip; shy, tumble; lift, lob

2 to dislodge from one's seat especially in horseback riding <was *thrown* while taking a fence>
syn buck (off), pitch, unhorse, unseat
rel ding (off), fling (off)

3 ***syn*** see OVERCOME 1

4 ***syn*** see DON 1

5 ***syn*** see EXERT

6 ***syn*** see ADDRESS 3

throw away *vb* **1** ***syn*** see DISCARD
ant salvage

2 ***syn*** see WASTE 2
con lay away, lay by, lay up

throw back *vb* ***syn*** see REVERT 2

throwback *n* ***syn*** see REVERSION 1

throw down *vb* ***syn*** see FELL 1
rel cast down

throw in *vb* ***syn*** see INTRODUCE 6
rel contribute

throwing away *n* ***syn*** see DISPOSAL 2
ant salvaging

throw off *vb* **1** ***syn*** see RID

2 ***syn*** see SHAKE 5

3 ***syn*** see EMIT 2
rel disgorge, eject, exhaust, expel

4 ***syn*** see CONFUSE 2

throw out *vb* **1** ***syn*** see EJECT 1

2 ***syn*** see DISCARD

3 ***syn*** see SAY 1

4 ***syn*** see CONFUSE 2

throw over *vb* ***syn*** see ABANDON 1

throw up *vb* **1** to construct or erect hastily and often carelessly <makeshift buildings *thrown up* almost overnight>
syn jerry-build, run up
rel roughcast, roughhew
idiom slap together, throw together

2 ***syn*** see VOMIT

thrum *vb* ***syn*** see HUM
rel ‖birr, purr

thrust *vb* **1** ***syn*** see PUSH 1
rel crowd, jam; bump, elbow, jostle, nudge, prod, shoulder

2 to cause (as a pointed instrument) to penetrate forcibly <*thrust* the dagger through her heart>
syn dig, drive, plunge, ram, run, sink, stab, stick
rel jab, shove; impale; pierce; embed; put

thrust *n* ***syn*** see SUBSTANCE 2

thud *vb* to make a dull sound by or as if by striking a surface with something thick and heavy <heard footsteps *thudding* down the hall>
syn clonk, clunk, thump
rel tunk; hit, smite, strike; beat, pound

thug *n* **1** a person inclined or hired to treat another roughly, brutally, or murderously <was beaten and robbed by *thugs*>
syn ‖gorilla, ‖hood, hoodlum, hooligan, ruffian, strong arm; *compare* TOUGH
rel bully, ‖larrikan, plug-ugly, roughneck, rowdy, tough; punk; cutthroat, gangster, gunman, mobster; goon, hatchet man

2 ***syn*** see TOUGH

thumb *vb* ***syn*** see HITCHHIKE
idiom thumb a ride

thumb (through) *vb* ***syn*** see BROWSE

thump *vb* ***syn*** see THUD
rel hammer, knock

thunder *n* the sound that follows a flash of lightning and is caused by sudden expansion of the air in the path of the electrical discharge <he was more afraid of *thunder* than of lightning>
syn thunderclap, thundercrack, thundering
rel fulmination

thunderbolt *n* a single discharge of lightning with the accompanying thunder <she was startled by the *thunderbolt*>
syn bolt, thunderstroke

thunderclap *n* ***syn*** see THUNDER

thundercrack *n* ***syn*** see THUNDER

thundering *n* ***syn*** see THUNDER

thunderstroke *n* ***syn*** see THUNDERBOLT

thunderstruck *adj* ***syn*** see AGHAST 2
rel bewildered, staggered; breathless, stunned
idiom struck dumb

thus *adv* **1** in this or that manner <summoned his counselors and spoke *thus* to them>
syn so, thus and so, thus and thus, thusly

2 ***syn*** see THEREFORE

thus and so *adv* ***syn*** see THUS 1

thus and thus *adv* ***syn*** see THUS 1

thus far *adv* ***syn*** see HITHERTO 1

thusly *adv* ***syn*** see THUS 1

thwack *n* ***syn*** see BLOW 1

thwart *adj* ***syn*** see TRANSVERSE

thwart *vb* ***syn*** see FRUSTRATE 1
rel curb, restrain, scotch; cross; foul up, gum up, queer; stymie; counter, match, oppose, pit, play(off), vie
con aid, assist, help, support; abet, encourage

‖**tick** *n* ***syn*** see INSTANT 1

ticket *n* **1** a slip giving information (as of ownership, identity, or price) <the price of the iron is on the *ticket*>
syn label, tag
rel card; slip; sticker

2 a card of admission <theater *tickets*>
syn carte d'entrée
rel pass

3 a list of candidates for appointment, nomination, or election <vote the party *ticket*>
syn slate
rel choice; lineup; list

---

syn synonym(s) ***rel*** related word(s)
ant antonym(s) ***con*** contrasted word(s)
idiom idiomatic equivalent(s)
‖ use limited; if in doubt, see a dictionary

4 ***syn*** see BALLOT 1
5 ***syn*** see PASSPORT
ticklish *adj* **1** ***syn*** see UNSTABLE 2
2 ***syn*** see DELICATE 7
rel critical
3 ***syn*** see INCONSTANT 1
tick off *vb* **1** ***syn*** see ENUMERATE 2
2 ***syn*** see REPROVE
tidbit (*or* **titbit**) *n* ***syn*** see DELICACY
‖**tiddly** *adj* ***syn*** see INTOXICATED 1
tide *n* ***syn*** see FLOW
tidings *n pl* ***syn*** see NEWS
tidy *adj* ***syn*** see NEAT 2
rel sleek, spruce
ant untidy
tie *n* **1** ***syn*** see BOND 3
rel fastener, fastening; attachment
2 ***syn*** see DRAW 4
tie *vb* **1** to make fast and secure <*tie* a bundle with strong cord>
syn bind, tie up
rel attach, fasten; connect, join, link; anchor, moor, rivet, secure; lash, truss (up); band, cinch, gird, rope
con loose, loosen; disconnect
ant untie
2 ***syn*** see MARRY 2
3 ***syn*** see HAMPER
idiom tie hand and foot, tie one's hands
ant untie
4 ***syn*** see EQUAL 3
tier *n* **1** ***syn*** see LINE 5
rel layer
2 ***syn*** see CLASS 1
tie up *vb* **1** ***syn*** see TIE 1
2 ***syn*** see HAMPER
tie–up *n* ***syn*** see ASSOCIATION 1
rel linkup
tiff *n* ***syn*** see QUARREL
tiff *vb* ***syn*** see QUARREL
tiffany *adj* ***syn*** see FILMY
tight *adj* **1** ***syn*** see FAST 4
rel clasped; solid, steadfast
con lax, limp; shaky
ant loose
2 ***syn*** see CLOSE 4
ant loose
3 fitting, drawn, or stretched so that there is no slackness or looseness <a *tight* drumhead>
syn close, taut, tense
rel skintight; constricted, contracted, drawn, tightened; inflexible, rigid, stiff
con loosened, slack, unconstricted
ant loose
4 difficult to cope with, get through, or circumvent <a very *tight* diplomatic situation>
syn arduous, rough, tricksy, trying
rel difficult; exacting; tense; critical; punishing; distressing, disturbing, upsetting
5 ***syn*** see STINGY
6 ***syn*** see INTOXICATED 1
idiom tight as a tick
tight *adv* ***syn*** see HARD 7
tightfisted *adj* ***syn*** see STINGY
rel grudging, mean, shabby
tight–laced *adj* ***syn*** see PRIM 1
tight–lipped *adj* ***syn*** see SILENT 3
idiom with one's lips sealed
tightly *adv* ***syn*** see HARD 7
tight–mouthed *adj* ***syn*** see SILENT 3
tightwad *n* ***syn*** see MISER
till *prep* ***syn*** see UNTIL
till *conj* up to the time when <be sure to wait *till* I come>
syn until
till *vb* to prepare (soil) for the raising of crops <*till* the soil>
syn cultivate, dress, ‖labor, tend, work
rel harrow, hoe, mulch, plow, turn; plant, sow
tillable *adj* ***syn*** see ARABLE
ant untillable
tilt *vb* **1** ***syn*** see SLANT 1
2 ***syn*** see SEESAW
tilt *n* ***syn*** see SLOPE
tilted *adj* ***syn*** see INCLINED 3
tilter *vb* ***syn*** see SEESAW
tilting *adj* ***syn*** see INCLINED 3
timber *n* **1** ***syn*** see FOREST
2 a large squared or dressed piece of wood <roof *timbers*>
syn balk, beam
rel girder, rafter
timberland *n* ***syn*** see FOREST
timbre *n* ***syn*** see TEMPER 1
time *n* **1** ***syn*** see WHILE 1
rel season
2 ***syn*** see OCCASION 5
3 ***syn*** see OPPORTUNITY
idiom the proper moment
4 ***syn*** see PERIOD 2
5 ***syn*** see TERM 2
6 ***syn*** see SEASON
7 ***syn*** see TEMPO
8 ***syn*** see SPELL 1
‖**9** ***syn*** see BINGE 1
time *vb* **1** to arrange or set the time of <*timed* his visits to coincide with her vacations>
syn book, schedule
rel plan, program, set up
2 to ascertain or record the time, duration, or rate of <*timed* the car at 100 mph>
syn clock
idiom hold the clock on
time and again *adv* ***syn*** see OFTEN
timeless *adj* **1** ***syn*** see CONTINUAL
2 ***syn*** see ETERNAL 4
timely *adv* ***syn*** see EARLY 1
timely *adj* **1** done or occurring at a suitable time <await a more *timely* moment>
syn auspicious, favorable, opportune, propitious, prosperous, seasonable, timeous, well-timed
rel appropriate, fit, fitting, meet, proper, suitable; likely, promising
con improper, inappropriate, unfitting; inauspicious, inopportune, unfavorable, unpropitious, unsuitable; ill-timed
ant untimely

2 *syn* see PUNCTUAL 2
timeous *adj* *syn* see TIMELY 1
timetable *n* *syn* see PROGRAM 1
rel table; plan
timeworn *adj* 1 *syn* see ANCIENT 1
2 *syn* see TRITE
timid *adj* 1 *syn* see SHY 1
rel humble; shrinking
ant bold
2 marked by or exhibiting a lack of boldness, courage, or determination <was too *timid* to ski>
syn timorous, ‖timorsome, undaring
rel gentle, mild, milk-toast, milky; cautious, chary, wary; jumpy, nervous, skittish; afraid, apprehensive, fainthearted, fearful; chicken, chickenhearted, henhearted, mouselike, mousy, pigeonhearted; cowardly, yellow; funky, panicky
con audacious, brave, courageous, daring, doughty, fearless, intrepid, lionhearted, unafraid, valiant, valorous
ant bold
3 *syn* see VACILLATING 2
timorous *adj* *syn* see TIMID 2
rel quailing, recoiling, shrinking; quivering, shivering, shuddering, trembling
ant assured
‖**timorsome** *adj* *syn* see TIMID 2
tincture *n* 1 *syn* see COLOR 6
2 *syn* see HINT 2
rel smattering
tincture *vb* *syn* see TINT
rel pigment; stain
ting *vb* *syn* see TINKLE 1
tinge *vb* *syn* see TINT
rel streak
tinge *n* 1 *syn* see COLOR 1
rel coloration, coloring, tincture; stain
2 *syn* see HINT 2
tingle *vb* 1 *syn* see TINKLE 1
rel chime
2 *syn* see JINGLE
tinker *vb* *syn* see FIDDLE 2
idiom play around
tinkle *vb* 1 to make a repeated light high-pitched ringing sound <wind-bells *tinkling* in the breeze>
syn plink, ting, tingle
rel clink, jangle, jingle
2 *syn* see JINGLE
3 *syn* see CHAT 1
tinsel *adj* *syn* see GAUDY
tint *n* *syn* see COLOR 1
rel tincture, touch; coloration, pigmentation; dye, stain, wash
tint *vb* to color with a slight shade or stain <white blossoms *tinted* with pale pink>
syn complexion, tincture, tinge
rel color, dye; shade, touch (up); stain, wash
tintamarre *n* *syn* see DIN
tiny *adj* exceptionally or remarkably small <the first *tiny* buds of spring flowers>
syn ‖bitsy, diminutive, dwarf, dwarfish, itsy-bitsy, itty-bitty, lilliputian, midget, miniature, minikin, minute, peewee, pint-size, pocket, pocket-size, pygmy, teensy, teensy-weensy, teenty, teeny, teeny-weeny, wee, weensy, weeny; *compare* SMALL 1
rel minuscular, minuscule; infinitesimal, microscopic, minim
con colossal, enormous, gigantic, immense, mammoth, vast
ant huge
tip *n* *syn* see POINT 9
tip *vb* *syn* see SLANT 1
tip *vb* *syn* see TIPTOE
rel creep, mince, pussyfoot, steal
tip (over) *vb* *syn* see OVERTURN 1
idiom turn upside down
tip *n* *syn* see GRATUITY
tip *n* a piece of advice or confidential information given by one thought to have access to special or inside sources <gave him a *tip* on which horse would win>
syn point, pointer, steer, tip-off
rel advice; information; clue, cue, hint; forecast, prediction
idiom a bit of inside advice, a bug in the ear, a word to the wise
tip–off *n* *syn* see TIP
tipped *adj* *syn* see INCLINED 3
tipple *vb* *syn* see DRINK 3
idiom drown one's cares (*or* sorrows)
tipple *n* *syn* see LIQUOR 2
tippler *n* *syn* see DRUNKARD
tipster *n* *syn* see INFORMER
tipsy *adj* *syn* see INTOXICATED 1
rel dazed, unsteady
tiptoe *vb* to walk or proceed quietly on or as if on the ends of the toes <*tiptoed* through the dark house>
syn tip, toe
rel creep, gumshoe, pussyfoot, steal
con clomp, clump, stamp, stomp, stump
tirade *n* a violent, often protracted, and usually denunciatory speech or writing <lashed out with a vicious *tirade* of angry protest>
syn diatribe, harangue, jeremiad, philippic
rel rant, rodomontade, screed; abuse, invective, revilement, vituperation; censure, condemnation, denunciation; berating, tongue-lashing; lecture, sermon
tire *vb* 1 to deplete the strength and energy of <the plane trip *tired* him>
syn drain, fatigue, jade, wear, wear down, weary; *compare* EXHAUST 4
rel debilitate, enervate, enfeeble, sap, weaken; exhaust, wear out
con brace (up), invigorate, strengthen; animate, energize, enliven, pep (up), quicken, stimulate, vitalize
2 *syn* see BORE
rel jade, wear; irk; disgust, nauseate, sicken

---

idiom make one tired, put one to sleep
tired *adj* **1** being depleted of strength and energy <was too *tired* to go on>
syn ‖clapped-out, fatigued, jaded, wearied, weary, worn, worn-down, worn-out
rel overtaxed, overworked; drained, run-down; ‖beat, ‖bushed, dog-tired, exhausted, fagged, frazzled, overworn, ‖pooped, ‖tucked up, tuckered; collapsing, consumed, knocked out, prostrate, spent
idiom worn to a frazzle
con active, energetic, lively, strong, tireless
ant rested; fresh, untired
2 ***syn*** see SHABBY 1
3 ***syn*** see FED UP
rel annoyed, bothered, displeased, irked
idiom having a bellyful of, having about enough of
4 ***syn*** see TRITE
tiredness *n* ***syn*** see FATIGUE
rel collapse, prostration
tireless *adj* ***syn*** see INDEFATIGABLE
rel active, enthusiastic
con inactive, listless, tired, unenergetic, unenthusiastic, weak
tiresome *adj* ***syn*** see IRKSOME
rel dull; jading; burdensome, onerous, oppressive; difficult, hard
tiring *adj* ***syn*** see IRKSOME
Titan *adj* ***syn*** see HUGE
titanic *adj* ***syn*** see HUGE
title *n* **1** ***syn*** see CLAIM 1
rel argument, ground, justification, proof, reason; desert, due, merit
2 ***syn*** see NAME 1
title *vb* ***syn*** see NAME 1
titter *vb* ***syn*** see LAUGH
rel twitter
idiom laugh behind (*or* in) one's hand, laugh in one's beard
tittle *n* ***syn*** see PARTICLE
rel fleck, flyspeck, speck; crumb, grain, scrap, snippet
tittle–tattle *n* **1** ***syn*** see CHATTER
2 ***syn*** see REPORT 1
titubate *vb* ***syn*** see REEL 2
titular *adj* ***syn*** see NOMINAL
tizzy *n* ***syn*** see SNIT
to *prep* **1** in the direction of and as far as <was driving *to* the city>
syn into
rel toward
ant from
2 ***syn*** see AGAINST 2
rel on, over, upon
3 ***syn*** see BEFORE 1
4 ***syn*** see UNTIL
5 for the particular purpose of <a market study tailored *to* your needs>
syn for
idiom in contemplation (*or* consideration) of, with an eye to, with a view to
6 in complement to <played Romeo *to* her Juliet>
syn opposite
toad *n* ***syn*** see SNOT 1
toad *n* ***syn*** see SYCOPHANT
toadeater *n* ***syn*** see SYCOPHANT
toadier *n* ***syn*** see SYCOPHANT
toady *n* ***syn*** see SYCOPHANT
toady *vb* ***syn*** see FAWN
rel follow, tag, tail, trail
toadying *adj* ***syn*** see FAWNING
toadyish *adj* ***syn*** see FAWNING
to–and–fro *n* **1** ***syn*** see HESITATION
2 ***syn*** see QUARREL
toast *n* ***syn*** see DRINK 2
to–be *n* ***syn*** see FUTURE
tocsin *n* ***syn*** see ALARM 1
rel sign, signal
today *adv* at the present time <youth *today* do not know what poverty is>
syn now, nowadays, presently
idiom in this day and age, these days
con then, yesteryear
today *n* ***syn*** see PRESENT
todayish *adj* ***syn*** see PRESENT
to–do *n* **1** ***syn*** see COMMOTION 4
2 ***syn*** see COMMOTION 3
toe *vb* ***syn*** see TIPTOE
tog (out *or* up) *vb* ***syn*** see DRESS UP 1
together *adv* **1** at one and the same time <events that occurred *together*>
syn at once, coincidentally, coincidently, coinstantaneously, concurrently, simultaneously
idiom all at once, all together
ant separately
2 in succession usually without intermission <was moody for days *together*>
syn consecutively, continually, continuously, hand running, night and day, running, successively, unintermittedly, uninterruptedly
idiom on end
3 in or by combined action or effort <students and faculty protested *together*>
syn conjointly, jointly, mutually
rel collectively, concertedly, unanimously
idiom in one breath, in the same breath, with one accord, with one voice
ant separately
togetherness *n* **1** ***syn*** see ASSOCIATION 1
2 ***syn*** see SOLIDARITY
‖toggle *vb* ***syn*** see DRESS UP 1
togs *n pl* ***syn*** see CLOTHES
toil *n* ***syn*** see WORK 2
idiom sweat of one's brow, toil and trouble
toil *vb* **1** ***syn*** see LABOR 1
2 ***syn*** see DRUDGE
3 ***syn*** see PLOD 1
toil *n, usu* **toils** *pl* ***syn*** see WEB 2
toiler *n* ***syn*** see SLAVE 2
toilet *n* a fixture for defecation and urination
syn ‖can, convenience, ‖donicker, head, john, johnny, latrine, lavatory, ‖loo, ‖pot, ‖potty, privy, ‖throne, water closet
rel hopper
toilful *adj* ***syn*** see HARD 6
toilsome *adj* ***syn*** see HARD 6

toilsomely *adv* ***syn*** see HARD 8
token *n* **1** ***syn*** see INDICATION 3
rel harbinger, omen, portent; characteristic, earmark; indicator, smack
2 ***syn*** see REMEMBRANCE 3
3 ***syn*** see EXPRESSION 3
4 ***syn*** see PLEDGE 1
‖**tokus** *n* ***syn*** see BUTTOCKS
tolerable *adj* **1** ***syn*** see BEARABLE
ant intolerable
2 ***syn*** see RESPECTABLE 5
3 ***syn*** see DECENT 4
rel fair, goodish, OK, tidy
idiom better than nothing, good enough
ant intolerable
tolerably *adv* ***syn*** see ENOUGH 2
tolerance *n* **1** the capacity to bear something unpleasant, painful, or difficult <had always had a high *tolerance* to pain>
syn endurance, stamina, toleration
rel fortitude, grit, guts; strength, vigor; long-suffering, patience, sufferance; steadfastness, steadiness; opposition, resistance
ant intolerance
2 ***syn*** see FORBEARANCE 2
rel liberality, liberalness, open-mindedness, permissiveness
con narrow-mindedness; prejudice; dogmatism; bigotry
ant intolerance
tolerant *adj* **1** ***syn*** see LIBERAL 3
rel open-minded; permissive
con narrow, narrow-minded; prejudiced; dogmatic; bigoted
ant intolerant
2 ***syn*** see FORBEARING
rel benevolent, humane; condoning, excusing, forgiving, sympathetic, understanding
con severe, stern; uncompromising, unforgiving, unsympathetic
ant intolerant
tolerate *vb* **1** ***syn*** see ACCEPT 2
rel condone, countenance; allow, consent (to), permit; have, hear (to)
2 ***syn*** see BEAR 10
rel sustain
toleration *n* **1** ***syn*** see FORBEARANCE 2
2 ***syn*** see TOLERANCE 1
toll *n* ***syn*** see EXPENSE 2
toll *vb* ***syn*** see LURE
toll *vb* ***syn*** see RING
‖**tomato** *n* ***syn*** see PROSTITUTE
tomb *n* ***syn*** see GRAVE
rel box, coffin, ‖trough
tomb *vb* **1** ***syn*** see BURY 1
ant untomb
2 ***syn*** see ENTOMB 1
ant disentomb, untomb
tomboy *n* a girl exhibiting boyish behavior <a *tomboy* who still rode, fished, and fought with her brothers>
syn gamine, hoyden
rel romp
tombstone *n* an inscribed memorial stone set at a place of interment <read the epitaph on the *tombstone* of her ancestor>
syn footstone, grave marker, gravestone, headstone, ledger, monument
rel memorial; cenotaph
tome *n* ***syn*** see BOOK 1
tomfool *n* ***syn*** see FOOL 1
tomfool *adj* ***syn*** see FOOLISH 2
tomfoolery *n* **1** ***syn*** see NONSENSE 2
2 ***syn*** see PRANK
tommyrot *n* ***syn*** see NONSENSE 2
Tom o' Bedlam *n* ***syn*** see LUNATIC 1
Tom Thumb *n* ***syn*** see DWARF
ton *n* **1** ***syn*** see FASHION 3
2 ***syn*** see SMART SET
tone *n* **1** ***syn*** see INFLECTION
2 ***syn*** see VEIN 1
3 ***syn*** see COLOR 1
rel blend
4 the state of a living body or any of its organs or parts in which the functions are healthy and performed with due vigor <diet and exercise contributed to her good muscle *tone*>
syn tonicity, tonus
rel health, healthiness; elasticity, resiliency; strength, vigor
5 ***syn*** see TEMPER 1
rel current, movement
idiom (the) state of things
6 ***syn*** see MOOD 1
toned down *adj* ***syn*** see SUBDUED 2
tongue *n* ***syn*** see LANGUAGE 1
tongue *vb* ***syn*** see SCOLD 1
tongue–lash *vb* ***syn*** see SCOLD 1
idiom give one the rough side of one's tongue
tongue–tied *adj* ***syn*** see INARTICULATE 3
con loose-lipped, loose-tongued
‖**tongue–walk** *vb* ***syn*** see SCOLD 1
idiom give one the rough side of one's tongue
tonguey *adj* ***syn*** see TALKATIVE
tonic *adj* **1** increasing or restoring physical or mental tone <the *tonic* effect of a vacation>
syn astringent, restorative, roborant
rel invigorating, refreshing, renewing, strengthening; bracing, sharp
con debilitating, enfeebling, weakening; enervating; exhausting, grueling, sapping
2 ***syn*** see INVIGORATING
tonicity *n* ***syn*** see TONE 4
tonish *adj* ***syn*** see STYLISH
tonus *n* ***syn*** see TONE 4
tony *adj* ***syn*** see STYLISH
too *adv* **1** ***syn*** see ALSO 2
2 ***syn*** see EVER 6
rel exorbitantly, immoderately, unconscionably, unmeasurably
3 ***syn*** see VERY 1
‖**toodle–oo** *interj* ***syn*** see GOOD-BYE

syn synonym(s) ***rel*** related word(s)
ant antonym(s) ***con*** contrasted word(s)
idiom idiomatic equivalent(s)
‖ use limited; if in doubt, see a dictionary

tool *n* **1** ***syn*** see IMPLEMENT
rel machine, mechanism
2 one used or manipulated by another to accomplish his purposes <had no intention of being used as a *tool* by either faction>
syn cat's-paw, pawn, puppet, stooge
rel agent, hireling, vehicle; chump, sucker

tool *vb* ***syn*** see DRIVE 5

toot *vb* ***syn*** see DECLARE 1

toot *n* ***syn*** see BINGE 1

toothful *n* ***syn*** see DRAM

toothsome *adj* ***syn*** see PALATABLE
rel agreeable, pleasant, pleasing

toothy *adj* **1** having or showing prominent teeth <a wide *toothy* grin>
syn teethy
2 ***syn*** see PALATABLE

too–too *adj* ***syn*** see GENTEEL 3
rel chichi

‖**tootsie** *n* ***syn*** see DOXY 1

top *n* **1** the highest point <hiked to the *top* of the mountain>
syn apex, crest, crown, fastigium, peak, roof, summit, vertex
rel acme, climax, culmination, height, pinnacle; cusp, head, point, tip
con base, foot, sole; nadir
ant bottom
2 the outer or upper part <the *top* of the table>
syn face, superficies, surface
3 ***syn*** see BEST
ant bottom

top *vb* **1** to remove or cut back the top of <*top* a tree>
syn crop, detruncate, pollard, truncate
rel clip, dock, prune, trim; curtail, shorten
2 ***syn*** see SURPASS 1
3 ***syn*** see SURMOUNT 3

top *adj* **1** of, relating to, or being at the top <the *top* floor of the house>
syn apical, highest, loftiest, topmost, uppermost
con bottommost, lowest
ant bottom
2 ***syn*** see EXCELLENT
3 ***syn*** see MAXIMUM

top–drawer *adj* ***syn*** see EXALTED 1

tope *vb* ***syn*** see DRINK 3

toper *n* ***syn*** see DRUNKARD

Tophet *n* ***syn*** see HELL

topic *n* ***syn*** see SUBJECT 2
rel proposition; issue

topless *adj* ***syn*** see LOFTY 6

toploftical *adj* ***syn*** see PROUD 1

toplofty *adj* ***syn*** see PROUD 1
rel inflated, puffed; egotistic
con crestfallen

topmost *adj* **1** ***syn*** see TOP 1
ant bottommost
2 ***syn*** see MAXIMUM

top–notch *adj* ***syn*** see EXCELLENT

top off *vb* ***syn*** see CLIMAX

topography *n* ***syn*** see TERRAIN 1

topple *vb* **1** ***syn*** see FALL 2
2 ***syn*** see TEETER
3 ***syn*** see OVERTURN 1
4 ***syn*** see OVERTHROW 2

top–ranking *adj* ***syn*** see EXALTED 1

topsy–turviness *n* ***syn*** see CONFUSION 3

topsy–turvy *adj* **1** ***syn*** see UPSIDE-DOWN 1
2 ***syn*** see UPSIDE-DOWN 2
rel cockeyed, disarranged, disjointed, disordered, unhinged

torch *n* ***syn*** see INCENDIARY

toreador *n* ***syn*** see BULLFIGHTER

torero *n* ***syn*** see BULLFIGHTER

torment *vb* **1** ***syn*** see AFFLICT
rel distress, trouble; hurt, pain, punish
2 ***syn*** see MOLEST

tormented *adj* ***syn*** see DISTRAUGHT

tormenting *adj* ***syn*** see EXCRUCIATING

torn *adj* ***syn*** see LACERATED

tornado *n* a violent destructive whirling wind accompanied by a funnel-shaped cloud extending downward from a cumulonimbus cloud <the *tornado* caused extensive destruction>
syn cyclone, twister; *compare* HURRICANE, WHIRLWIND 1

torpedo *n* ***syn*** see ASSASSIN

torpid *adj* ***syn*** see LETHARGIC
rel dull, leaden, sodden; motionless, static; numb
con lively; frisky, sprightly, vigorous; fast
ant active

torpidity *n* ***syn*** see LETHARGY 1
rel listlessness, passivity, stagnation

torpidness *n* ***syn*** see LETHARGY 1
ant activeness

torpor *n* ***syn*** see LETHARGY 1
rel stolidity; passivity
ant activity; animation

torrent *n* ***syn*** see FLOOD 2
rel flux, rush

torrid *adj* **1** ***syn*** see HOT 1
idiom burning hot, hot enough to roast an ox
ant arctic
2 ***syn*** see IMPASSIONED
rel sultry
ant frigid

tort *n* ***syn*** see EVIL 3

tortuous *adj* ***syn*** see WINDING
rel involute, vermiculate; cranky; involved

torture *vb* **1** ***syn*** see AFFLICT
rel oppress, persecute, wrong; hurt, wound; maim, mangle, mutilate
idiom put on the rack, put to torture
2 ***syn*** see DEFORM

torturing *adj* ***syn*** see EXCRUCIATING

torturous *adj* ***syn*** see EXCRUCIATING

tory *n* ***syn*** see DIEHARD 1
rel loyalist, traditionalist

tory *adj* ***syn*** see CONSERVATIVE 1

tosh *n* ***syn*** see NONSENSE 2

toss *vb* **1** ***syn*** see THROW 1
2 to rise and fall often rhythmically or with alternate motions <a small boat *tossing* in heavy seas>
syn heave, pitch, rock, roll; *compare* SEESAW
rel bob; sway

3 ***syn*** see DRINK 1
4 ***syn*** see WRITHE 1
idiom toss and turn

toss (around) *vb* ***syn*** see DISCUSS 1
rel bandy (about)

tosspot *n* ***syn*** see DRUNKARD

tot *n* ***syn*** see DRAM

tot *vb* ***syn*** see ADD 2

total *adj* **1** ***syn*** see WHOLE 4
rel overall; comprehensive, full, inclusive, plenary; teetotal
ant partial
2 ***syn*** see UTTER
3 ***syn*** see TOTALITARIAN 1
rel authoritative; absolute, arbitrary, despotic; omnipotent
4 ***syn*** see TOTALITARIAN 2
rel monopolistic
5 concentrating and employing all resources on a single objective <a *total* offensive>
syn all-out, full-blown, full-out, full-scale, totalitarian, unlimited
rel out-and-out, unreserved, unrestricted
con hampered, impeded, trammeled; restrained, restricted; stinted
ant limited

total *n* **1** ***syn*** see WHOLE 1
2 ***syn*** see BODY 5

total *vb* **1** ***syn*** see ADD 2
2 ***syn*** see AMOUNT 1
rel comprise, consist (of); stack up; equal, result (in), yield
idiom mount up to, pile up to
3 to make a total wreck of <*totaled* his car when he hit the wall>
syn demolish, wreck; *compare* DESTROY 1
rel crack up, smash

totalistic *adj* ***syn*** see TOTALITARIAN 1
con democratic; individualistic

totalitarian *adj* **1** of or relating to centralized control by one autocratic leader or party considered to be infallible <Nazi Germany was a *totalitarian* state>
syn authoritarian, total, totalistic; *compare* ABSOLUTE 4, DICTATORIAL
con democratic, popular; constitutional
2 having or exercising dictatorial powers often tending toward monopoly <antitrust legislation reversing the trend toward the *totalitarian* collectivism of big business>
syn total
3 ***syn*** see TOTAL 5

totalitarianism *n* ***syn*** see TYRANNY

totality *n* **1** ***syn*** see WHOLE 1
2 ***syn*** see ENTIRETY 1
3 ***syn*** see WHOLE 2
rel configuration, form

totalize *vb* ***syn*** see ADD 2

totally *adv* ***syn*** see ALL 1

tote *vb* ***syn*** see CARRY 1
rel cart, haul; shoulder

||**tote** *n* ***syn*** see WHOLE 1

tote *vb* ***syn*** see ADD 2

totter *vb* **1** ***syn*** see TEETER
rel shimmy
2 ***syn*** see REEL 2
rel blunder, stumble, trip; dodder, ||dotter; flounder

touch *vb* **1** to probe with a sensitive part of the body (as a finger) so as to get or produce a sensation often in the course of examining or exploring <*touch* an iron to test its temperature>
syn feel, finger, handle, palpate, paw
rel brush, graze; caress, fondle, rub, stroke, toy (with); palm, thumb; examine, inspect, probe, scrutinize; investigate
2 ***syn*** see ADJOIN
3 ***syn*** see EQUAL 3
4 ***syn*** see AFFECT
rel arouse, stir; excite, quicken, stimulate
idiom touch a chord
5 ***syn*** see AMOUNT 2
rel come (to), verge (on)

touch *n* **1** ***syn*** see CONTACT 1
rel junction; communication
2 an act of touching or feeling <woke her with a light *touch* on her hand>
syn palpation, taction
rel brush, pat, stroke; contact
3 tactile sensitivity <a blanket soft to the *touch*>
syn feel, tactility
rel feeling
4 a specified sensation conveyed through the tactile receptors <the velvety *touch* of a fabric>
syn feel, feeling
5 ***syn*** see HINT 2
6 distinctive manner or method <this house needs a woman's *touch*>
syn hand
rel manner, style, way
||**7** ***syn*** see THEFT

touchable *adj* ***syn*** see TANGIBLE 1
ant untouchable

touch down *vb* ***syn*** see ALIGHT

touching *prep* **1** ***syn*** see AGAINST 2
idiom up against
2 ***syn*** see APROPOS

touching *adj* **1** ***syn*** see ADJACENT 3
rel meeting; impinging; overlapping
2 ***syn*** see MOVING 2
rel compassionate, responsive, sympathetic, tender; piteous, pitiable, pitiful, tear-jerking

touch-me-not-ish *adj* ***syn*** see UNSOCIABLE

touchstone *n* ***syn*** see STANDARD 3
rel check, test, trial; barometer, scale; demonstration, proof

touch up *vb* to improve or perfect by small additional strokes or alterations <*touch up* a picture>
syn brush up, retouch, tease up
rel improve, perfect, polish; do (up), fix (up)
idiom put finishing touches on

touchy *adj* **1** ***syn*** see IRASCIBLE

---

syn synonym(s) ***rel*** related word(s)
ant antonym(s) ***con*** contrasted word(s)
idiom idiomatic equivalent(s)
|| use limited; if in doubt, see a dictionary

rel hypersensitive, oversensitive, sensitive, thin-skinned; temperamental, volatile; miffy
ant imperturbable
2 *syn* see DELICATE 7
rel dicey, risky, unpredictable; harmful, hazardous, unsafe

tough *adj* **1** *syn* see STRONG 2
rel flinty, hard, unyielding; resistant, unbreakable, withstanding
idiom tough as leather (*or* nails)
con breakable; brittle; yielding
ant fragile
2 *syn* see VISCOUS
3 advocating a persistently firm course of action <a *tough* foreign policy>
syn hard-line, inflexible, uncompromising, unyielding
rel stiff, taut; fixed, confirmed, hard-shell, narrow, rigid; arbitrary, immutable, unalterable; hard-boiled, hardened, obdurate; harsh, procrustean, rigorous, severe, strict; drastic
con liberal, relaxed; compromising, flexible, laissez-faire, yielding
ant soft
4 having or exhibiting great physical endurance (as to strain, hardship, or labor) <the rigorous climate created a *tough* people>
syn hardy, rugged
rel conditioned, hard-bitten, hardened, seasoned, steeled; fit, healthy, lusty, robust, vigorous; stalwart, strong, sturdy
con delicate, fragile, frail, tender; half-hardy, puny; weakened
ant weak
5 *syn* see OBSTINATE
rel hardfisted, hardhanded, hardheaded, tough-minded
6 *syn* see HARD 6
ant soft
7 *syn* see ONEROUS
ant soft
8 frequented by rowdy or criminal elements <lived in a *tough* neighborhood>
syn bad, rough
rel disorderly, rowdy; dangerous, unsafe; ghetto, inner-city, underprivileged
con orderly, quiet, safe

tough (out) *vb* *syn* see ACCEPT 2

tough *n* a rough or unruly person often taking part in bullying or violent behavior <attacked by a gang of *toughs*>
syn ||b'hoy, bullyboy, mucker, mug, plug-ugly, punk, rough, roughneck, rowdy, ruffian, thug, toughie, yahoo; *compare* BULLY 1, THUG 1
rel goon, hood, hoodlum, hooligan

toughen *vb* *syn* see HARDEN 2
rel develop, strengthen
ant weaken

toughie *n* *syn* see TOUGH
rel ||heavy

tour *n* **1** *syn* see SPELL
2 a journey in which one eventually returns to the starting point <made a quick *tour* of all the bars>
syn circuit, round, roundabout, round trip; *compare* TRIP 1
rel turn; circle tour

tour de force *n* **1** *syn* see FEAT 2
2 *syn* see MASTERPIECE 1

tourist *n* one who makes a tour for pleasure or culture <*tourists* going through the castle>
syn rubberneck, sightseer, ||tripper
rel day-tripper, excursionist; traveler; visitor

tout *n* *syn* see LOOKOUT 3

tout *vb* to overly publicize <was *touted* as the world's most modern shopping center>
syn ballyhoo, herald, trumpet
rel proclaim, publicize; plug, promote; acclaim, laud, praise
idiom praise to the skies

tow *vb* *syn* see PULL 2
rel propel; push
idiom take in tow

toward *adj* *syn* see GOOD 1
ant untoward

toward *prep* **1** *syn* see APROPOS
2 *syn* see AGAINST 1

tower (above *or* over) *vb* *syn* see OVERLOOK 2

towering *adj* **1** *syn* see LOFTY 6
rel altitudinous, high, tall; stratospheric
2 *syn* see SUPREME
3 *syn* see MONSTROUS 1
4 reaching a high point of greatness, intensity, or violence <a *towering* rage>
syn monumental, overwhelming
rel ||crashing; overpowering; mind-blowing
con minor, petty, piddling, puny, trivial
5 *syn* see EXCESSIVE 1

towery *adj* *syn* see LOFTY 6

to wit *adv* *syn* see NAMELY

towner *n* *syn* see TOWNSMAN

townish *adj* of, relating to, or characteristic of a town or of urban life <enjoyed a fast-paced, competitive, *townish* life-style>
syn towny
rel city, metropolitan, urban
con bucolic, rural; isolated, lonely, solitary

townman *n* *syn* see TOWNSMAN

townsman *n* a town dweller <population composed mostly of *townsmen* and a few countrymen>
syn burgher, cit, citizen, towner, townman, towny

towny *n* *syn* see TOWNSMAN

towny *adj* *syn* see TOWNISH

tow–row *n* *syn* see COMMOTION 4

toxic *adj* *syn* see POISONOUS
ant nontoxic

toxicant *adj* *syn* see POISONOUS

toy *n* **1** *syn* see KNICKKNACK
2 something for a child to play with <games, dolls, and other *toys*>
syn ||die, ||play-pretty, plaything, ||pretty

toy *vb* *syn* see TRIFLE 1
rel disport, frolic, play, sport; fiddle (with), tease; caress, cosset, cuddle, dandle, pet
idiom fool (*or* mess) around with

trace *n* **1** *syn* see TRACK 1

rel evidence, proof
2 *syn* see VESTIGE 1
rel mark, token
3 *syn* see HINT 2
trace *vb* *syn* see TRACK 1
track *n* **1** detectable evidence that something has passed <the *track* of a sleigh in the snow>
syn trace, tread
rel impress, imprint, mark, print; sign, vestige
2 *syn* see TRAIL
rel footpath, footway, walk
idiom beaten path
3 *syn* see WAY 1
rel roadway, trackway
4 *syn* see FOOTPRINT
rel scent, slot
track *vb* **1** to follow the tracks or traces of <*track* a wounded deer>
syn trace, trail
rel follow; dog, shadow, tail; chase, pursue; find, hunt (down), smell (out)
idiom be hot on the trail of
2 *syn* see TRAVEL 2
tract *n* **1** *syn* see AREA 1
rel amplitude, spread, stretch; part, portion, section, sector
2 *syn* see LOT 3
3 *syn* see FOOTPRINT
tractable *adj* *syn* see OBEDIENT
rel flexible, pliable, pliant; manageable; subdued
con headstrong, unmanageable, willful; obstinate, refractory, stubborn
ant intractable, unruly
tractate *n* *syn* see DISCOURSE 2
trade *n* **1** a pursuit followed as an occupation or means of livelihood and requiring technical knowledge and skill <the *trade* of a carpenter>
syn art, calling, craft, handicraft, métier, profession, vocation
rel employment, occupation, pursuit, work
con avocation, hobby
2 *syn* see BUSINESS 4
rel market
3 *syn* see PATRONAGE 2
trade *vb* **1** to give one thing in return for another with an expectation of gain <*traded* furs for beads and cloth>
syn bargain, barter, exchange, swap, traffic, truck; *compare* EXCHANGE 2
rel market, merchandise, sell; deal; argue, chaffer, dicker, haggle, wrangle
idiom make (*or* strike) a bargain, make a deal
2 *syn* see EXCHANGE 2
trademark *n* *syn* see MARK 7
trader *n* *syn* see MERCHANT
tradesman *n* *syn* see MERCHANT
tradition *n* **1** an inherited or established way of thinking, feeling, or doing <America's puritanical *tradition* is still very much alive>
syn heritage
rel culture; convention, custom, ethic, form; birthright, inheritance, legacy
2 *syn* see LORE 2
traditional *adj* **1** of or relating to tradition <a *traditional* interpretation of the Bible>
syn conventional, tralatitious; *compare* CONVENTIONAL 1
rel ancestral, immemorial, old; customary, habitual, usual; acknowledged, established, establishmentarian, fixed; common, popular
con new; unconventional, unusual; individualistic, original, personal
2 *syn* see ORAL 2
traditionalist *n* *syn* see PURIST
traditionalistic *adj* *syn* see CONSERVATIVE 1
traduce *vb* *syn* see MALIGN
rel mock; disgrace; betray; violate
traducing *adj* *syn* see LIBELOUS
traffic *n* **1** *syn* see BUSINESS 4
2 *syn* see COMMERCE 2
rel relations, relationship; closeness, connection, familiarity, intimacy
3 *syn* see PATRONAGE 2
4 the number or volume of vehicles or pedestrians moving along a route <freeway *traffic* is heavy during the rush hour>
syn travel
traffic *vb* **1** *syn* see TRADE 1
2 to engage in illegal or disreputable business or activity <*trafficked* in drugs>
syn truck
rel deal (in), push, shove; black-market; bootleg, moonshine; fence
idiom handle (*or* deal in) under the counter
trafficable *adj* *syn* see MARKETABLE
trafficker *n* *syn* see MERCHANT
tragedy *n* **1** *syn* see DISASTER
rel blow, shock
2 *syn* see MISFORTUNE
rel unluckiness; curse, lot; woe(s)
con prosperity, success
ant triumph
trail *vb* **1** *syn* see DRAG 3
2 *syn* see DELAY 2
rel plod, trudge; falter, flag; halt
3 *syn* see TRACK 1
rel nose (out), sniff (out)
idiom follow a scent
4 *syn* see TAIL
5 *syn* see FOLLOW 2
trail *n* a rough course or way formed by or as if by repeated chance footsteps <an old Indian *trail*>
syn path, pathway, track, ||trod
rel footpath, footwalk, footway
trailer *n* a motor-equipped or motor-drawn highway vehicle designed to serve as a place for dwelling or business <toured the country in a *trailer*>
syn camper, ||caravan, house trailer, mobile home, motor home, recreational vehicle, RV
rel van
train *vb* *syn* see LURE

---

syn synonym(s) *rel* related word(s)
ant antonym(s) *con* contrasted word(s)
idiom idiomatic equivalent(s)
|| use limited; if in doubt, see a dictionary

train *n* **1** ***syn*** see ENTOURAGE
2 ***syn*** see SUCCESSION 2
rel course, run; line, thread; gradation, scale, tier
train *vb* **1** ***syn*** see TEACH
rel cultivate, develop, shape; accustom, habituate; harden, season
2 ***syn*** see DIRECT 2
training *n* ***syn*** see EDUCATION 1
train off *vb* ***syn*** see SWERVE 1
traipse *vb* **1** ***syn*** see WANDER 1
2 ***syn*** see WALK 1
3 ***syn*** see DRAG 3
traipse *n* ***syn*** see SLATTERN 1
trait *n* **1** ***syn*** see QUALITY 1
2 ***syn*** see CHARACTERISTIC 1
rel denominator; attribute, quality
traitorous *adj* ***syn*** see FAITHLESS
rel apostate, renegade; mutinous, rebellious, seditious; alienated, disaffected, estranged; unpatriotic
con faithful; patriotic
traject *vb* ***syn*** see CONDUCT 4
tralatitious *adj* ***syn*** see TRADITIONAL 1
idiom handed down from time immemorial
tralucent *adj* ***syn*** see TRANSLUCENT 3
trammel *vb* **1** ***syn*** see ENTANGLE 3
2 ***syn*** see HAMPER
rel circumscribe, confine, limit; bind, enchain, handcuff, manacle
3 ***syn*** see STULTIFY
tramp *vb* **1** to walk, tread, or step especially heavily <heard hobnailed boots *tramping* across the square>
syn trample, tromp; *compare* PLOD 1
rel march; thud; footslog, stodge, trudge; stamp, stomp
2 ***syn*** see HIKE 2
3 ***syn*** see TRAMPLE 2
tramp *n* **1** ***syn*** see VAGABOND
2 ***syn*** see WANTON
3 a journey on foot or a walking trip <took a long *tramp* through the woods>
syn hike, walkabout
rel ramble, saunter, stroll, walk; traipse
tramper *n* ***syn*** see VAGABOND
trample *vb* **1** ***syn*** see TRAMP 1
2 to tread on forcibly and repeatedly so as to crush or injure <was *trampled* to death by his horse>
syn stamp, stomp, tramp, tromp
rel ‖stoach, ‖stramp, ‖stunt; pound; tread (on); override
trance *vb* ***syn*** see TRANSPORT 2
trance *n* ***syn*** see REVERIE
tranquil *adj* ***syn*** see CALM 2
rel irenic, pacific, peaceful; quiet, still; stable, steady
con stirred up, troubled
ant agitated
tranquilize *vb* ***syn*** see CALM
rel hush; sedate; subdue
idiom pour oil on troubled waters
ant agitate
transaction *n* ***syn*** see CONTRACT
transcend *vb* ***syn*** see SURPASS 1
idiom go beyond, rise above
transcendent *adj* **1** ***syn*** see SUPREME
rel accomplished, consummate, finished; entire, intact, perfect, whole
2 ***syn*** see ABSTRACT 1
rel absolute, ultimate; boundless, eternal, infinite
transcendental *adj* **1** ***syn*** see OTHERWORLDLY 1
2 ***syn*** see ABSTRACT 1
rel supernatural, supranatural, ultimate
transfer *vb* **1** ***syn*** see MOVE 4
rel carry, convey; relocate
2 ***syn*** see GIVE 3
rel convey, transmit
3 ***syn*** see TRANSFORM
4 to shift the title of (property) from one owner to another <to preserve the farm intact he *transfers* it to a single heir>
syn abalienate, alien, alienate, assign, cede, convey, deed, make over, remise, sign (over)
transfigure *vb* ***syn*** see TRANSFORM
transfix *vb* ***syn*** see IMPALE
transform *vb* to make over to a radically different form, composition, state, or disposition <the interaction of social forces *transforms* custom and produces a new tradition>
syn change, commute, convert, metamorphize, metamorphose, mutate, transfer, transfigure, translate, transmogrify, transmute, transpose, transubstantiate; *compare* CHANGE 1
rel alter; denature
transformation *n* ***syn*** see CONVERSION 2
transfuse *vb* ***syn*** see PERMEATE
transgress *vb* **1** ***syn*** see VIOLATE 1
2 ***syn*** see TRESPASS 1
transgression *n* ***syn*** see BREACH 1
rel erring, error, lapse, slip; overstepping; misbehavior, misstepping
transient *adj* lasting or staying only a short time <features of a *transient* culture now extinct>
syn ephemeral, evanescent, fleeting, fugacious, fugitive, impermanent, momentaneous, momentary, passing, short-lived, transitory, volatile; *compare* TEMPORARY
rel deciduous, flitting, unstable; temporal, temporary; insubstantial
idiom as transient as the clouds, here today and gone tomorrow
con lasting, perdurable, permanent, substantial; durable, stable
ant perpetual
transit *n* **1** ***syn*** see PASSAGE 1
2 ***syn*** see TRANSITION
3 ***syn*** see TRANSPORTATION 1
4 public conveyance of passengers or goods as a commercial enterprise <mass *transit*>
syn transport, transportation
transition *n* passage from one state or condition to another <the *transition* from boyhood to manhood>
syn alteration, passage, shift, transit

rel change, conversion, metamorphosis, transformation; development, evolution; growth, progress

transitional *adj* involving or characterized by passage from one stage, condition, or state to another <a *transitional* phase of social development>
syn transitive, transitory
rel developing, evolving; altering, changing, shifting
idiom being in a state of flux

transitive *adj* ***syn*** see TRANSITIONAL

transitory *adj* **1** ***syn*** see TRANSIENT
rel changeable; nonpermanent, unenduring; brief, short-term
2 ***syn*** see TRANSITIONAL

translate *vb* **1** to make a version of in another language <*translated* many secret documents from French to English>
syn put, render, transpose, turn
rel transliterate; transcribe; interpret; metaphrase, paraphrase
2 ***syn*** see TRANSFORM

translate (into) *vb* ***syn*** see PARAPHRASE

translation *n* ***syn*** see VERSION 1

translucent *adj* **1** ***syn*** see TRANSPARENT 1
2 ***syn*** see CLEAR 4
rel apparent, obvious, unmistakable
3 admitting and diffusing light so that objects beyond cannot be clearly distinguished <*translucent* amber>
syn clear, tralucent, translucid, transparent; *compare* TRANSPARENT 1
rel lucent, lucid

translucid *adj* ***syn*** see TRANSLUCENT 3

transmarine *adj* ***syn*** see OVERSEAS

transmigrate *vb* ***syn*** see MIGRATE

transmigratory *adj* ***syn*** see MIGRATORY

transmit *vb* **1** ***syn*** see SEND 1
rel convey, transport
2 ***syn*** see COMMUNICATE 1
3 ***syn*** see HAND DOWN
rel instill; transfuse, translate
4 ***syn*** see CONDUCT 4

transmogrify *vb* ***syn*** see TRANSFORM

transmundane *adj* ***syn*** see OTHERWORLDLY 1

transmute *vb* ***syn*** see TRANSFORM

transparent *adj* **1** admitting light without appreciable diffusion or distortion so that objects beyond are entirely visible <a sheet of *transparent* plastic>
syn clear, limpid, pellucid, see-through, translucent; *compare* TRANSLUCENT 3
rel crystal, crystalline, glassy; diaphanous
idiom clear as glass (*or* crystal)
con dark, smoky; cloudy, foggy hazy, misty, nubilous
ant opaque
2 ***syn*** see FILMY
3 ***syn*** see TRANSLUCENT 3
4 ***syn*** see CLEAR 4
rel distinguishable, recognizable; articulate, distinct, plain; unambiguous, unequivocal
con muddy, turbid

transpicuous *adj* ***syn*** see CLEAR 4

transpierce *vb* ***syn*** see IMPALE

transpire *vb* **1** ***syn*** see GET OUT 2
2 ***syn*** see HAPPEN 1
rel eventuate, result

transplace *vb* ***syn*** see REVERSE 1
rel remove; rearrange

transport *vb* **1** ***syn*** see CARRY 1
2 to carry away by strong and usually pleasant emotion <*transported* with ecstasy>
syn enrapture, enravish, entrance, ravish, trance
rel excite, move, provoke, quicken, stimulate; agitate, inflame, stir (up); elevate, uplift; carry away, delight, imparadise, ||send, slay, thrill, ||wow
3 ***syn*** see BANISH

transport *n* **1** ***syn*** see TRANSPORTATION 1
2 ***syn*** see ECSTASY
rel ardor, enthusiasm, fervor, passion; happiness
3 ***syn*** see VEHICLE 3
4 ***syn*** see TRANSIT 4

transportable *adj* ***syn*** see PORTABLE

transportation *n* **1** an act, process, or instance of transporting or being transported <arranged for the *transportation* of his luggage>
syn carriage, carrying, conveyance, transit, transport, transporting
rel hauling, moving
2 ***syn*** see VEHICLE 3
3 ***syn*** see TRANSIT 4

transporting *n* ***syn*** see TRANSPORTATION 1

transpose *vb* **1** ***syn*** see TRANSFORM
2 ***syn*** see TRANSLATE 1
3 ***syn*** see REVERSE 1

transubstantiate *vb* ***syn*** see TRANSFORM

transude *vb* ***syn*** see EXUDE

transversal *adj* ***syn*** see TRANSVERSE
rel bent; intersecting

transverse *vb* ***syn*** see TRAVERSE 4

transverse *adj* extended or lying in a direction across something else <the *transverse* arches of the cathedral ceiling>
syn crossing, crosswise, thwart, transversal, traverse
rel diagonal, oblique; across, crossed
con perpendicular
ant longitudinal

transversely *adv* ***syn*** see OVER 1

transversely *adv* ***syn*** see OVER 1

trap *n* **1** ***syn*** see LURE 2
rel artifice, feint, gambit, maneuver, ploy, ruse, stratagem, wile; birdlime, net; ambuscade, ambush; conspiracy, intrigue, machination, plot
||**2** ***syn*** see POLICEMAN
||**3** ***syn*** see MOUTH 1

trap *vb* ***syn*** see CATCH 3
rel mousetrap, snag

trapfall *n* ***syn*** see PITFALL

---

syn synonym(s) ***rel*** related word(s)
ant antonym(s) ***con*** contrasted word(s)
idiom idiomatic equivalent(s)
|| use limited; if in doubt, see a dictionary

traps *n pl* ***syn*** see PERSONAL EFFECTS
trash *n* **1** ***syn*** see REFUSE
rel leavings
2 ***syn*** see NONSENSE 2
3 ***syn*** see RABBLE 2
‖**trash** *vb* ***syn*** see VANDALIZE
trash *vb* ***syn*** see PLOD 1
trashy *adj* ***syn*** see CHEAP 2
rel third-rate
trauma *n* intense mental, emotional, or physical disturbance resulting from stress <a broken home may produce persistent *trauma* in children>
syn shock, traumatism
rel blow, stress; traumatization; derangement, disturbance, upset; collapse
traumatism *n* ***syn*** see TRAUMA
travail *n* **1** ***syn*** see WORK 2
rel task; struggle
idiom toil and trouble
con relaxation, rest
2 ***syn*** see LABOR 2
rel contractions, pains
idiom birth throe
travel *vb* **1** ***syn*** see GO 1
rel move (on); voyage; roam, trek; explore
2 to journey over (as by conveyance) <certain roads can be *traveled* only on horseback>
syn cover, do, pass (over), track, traverse
rel cross
travel *n* **1** ***syn*** see PASSAGE 1
2 *often* **travels** *pl* ***syn*** see JOURNEY
3 ***syn*** see TRAFFIC 4
travelable *adj* ***syn*** see PASSABLE
‖**traveler** *n* ***syn*** see VAGABOND
traverse *n* ***syn*** see OBSTACLE
traverse *vb* **1** ***syn*** see RESIST
2 ***syn*** see DENY 4
rel oppose; dismiss; squash, squelch
3 ***syn*** see TRAVEL 2
4 to extend or lie across (something) <a highway *traversing* the entire state>
syn cross, transverse
rel crisscross, intersect, quarter
idiom cut across
5 to pass over, along, or to and fro especially on foot <deep in thought he *traversed* the terrace again and again>
syn perambulate, walk
rel peregrinate; track, tread; pace
traverse *adj* ***syn*** see TRANSVERSE
travesty *n* **1** ***syn*** see CARICATURE 2
rel mimicry; distortion, exaggeration; ridicule
2 ***syn*** see MOCKERY 2
travesty *vb* ***syn*** see MIMIC
treacherous *adj* **1** ***syn*** see FAITHLESS
rel undependable, unreliable, untrustworthy; betraying, deceptive, double-crossing, falsehearted, misleading, Punic
ant dependable; trustworthy
2 ***syn*** see DANGEROUS 1
rel deceptive, ticklish, tricky; precarious
treacherousness *n* ***syn*** see TREACHERY
ant dependability; trustworthiness

treachery *n* betrayal of a trust or confidence <corruption in public office is little short of *treachery*>
syn disloyalty, faithlessness, perfidiousness, perfidy, treacherousness, treason; *compare* INFIDELITY
rel falseheartedness, falseness; double cross, double-dealing; sellout
idiom dirty pool, dirty work at the crossroads
con incorruptibility, reliability; probity, rectitude, uprightness; constancy, fidelity, loyalty, staunchness
ant dependability; trustworthiness
tread *vb* **1** ***syn*** see DANCE 1
2 ***syn*** see WALK 1
rel march, stride; tromp
tread *n* ***syn*** see TRACK 1
treadmill *n* ***syn*** see ROUTINE
treason *n* **1** ***syn*** see TREACHERY
rel deceit, deceitfulness; duplicity; Machiavellianism
idiom breach of trust (*or* faith)
con allegiance, loyalty
ant staunchness
2 ***syn*** see SEDITION
rel disloyalty, treacherousness, treachery; high treason; misprision
ant allegiance
treasure *n* ***syn*** see FIND 1
rel catch, plum, prize; pearl
treasure *vb* ***syn*** see APPRECIATE 1
rel conserve, guard, preserve, save; idolize, revere, reverence, venerate, worship
idiom hold dear
treasure–house *n* **1** ***syn*** see TREASURY 1
2 ***syn*** see BONANZA
treasure trove *n* **1** ***syn*** see FIND 1
2 ***syn*** see BONANZA
treasury *n* **1** a place (as a room or building) where valuables are kept <priceless gold candlesticks kept in the *treasury* of the cathedral>
syn treasure-house
rel archive(s), gallery, museum; depository, repository, storehouse
idiom treasure room
2 the place of deposit, retention, and disbursement of collected funds <the union *treasury* held emergency strike funds>
syn chest, coffer, exchequer, war chest
rel depositary, depository
3 ***syn*** see BONANZA
treat *vb* **1** ***syn*** see CONFER 2
rel consider, study, weigh; deliberate, reason, think
2 to have to do with or behave toward (a person or thing) in a specified manner <*treat* all employees fairly and impartially>
syn deal (with), handle, play, serve, take, use
rel conduct, do with, manage, ‖wield; regard, respect; account, consider, hold; appraise, estimate, evaluate, rate, value
idiom act with regard to, conduct oneself toward, do by
3 to pay for another's entertainment <*treated* her to a few drinks>

syn blow, set up, ‖shout, stand
rel stake
idiom go treat, pick up the tab for, stand treat
4 to give medical treatment to <was *treated* by an eye specialist>
syn doctor
rel attend, care (for), minister (to), nurse

treat *n* ***syn*** see DELICACY

treatise *n* ***syn*** see DISCOURSE 2
rel writing; book; argument, discussion, exposition

treaty *n* a formal, usually written, arrangement made by negotiation between two or more political authorities <the two nations finally signed an arms-limitation *treaty*>
syn agreement, concord, convention, pact; *compare* CONTRACT
rel arrangement, entente, understanding; bargain, contract; charter, compact, concordat, covenant; alliance, cartel, league; accord, reconciliation, settlement

treble *adj* ***syn*** see ACUTE 4
ant bass

tree *vb* ***syn*** see CORNER

trek *n* ***syn*** see JOURNEY

tremble *vb* **1** ***syn*** see SHAKE 1
rel shrink, wince
idiom tremble like a leaf
2 ***syn*** see SHAKE 2

trembling *adj* ***syn*** see TREMULOUS
ant steady

tremendous *adj* **1** ***syn*** see FEARFUL 3
2 ***syn*** see MONSTROUS 1
3 ***syn*** see HUGE
rel amazing, astounding, flabbergasting; terrific
idiom great big
ant minute

tremendousness *n* ***syn*** see ENORMITY 2
rel bigness, largeness

tremor *n* ***syn*** see EARTHQUAKE

tremor *vb* **1** ***syn*** see SHAKE 1
2 ***syn*** see SHAKE 2

tremorous *adj* ***syn*** see TREMULOUS

tremulant *adj* ***syn*** see TREMULOUS

tremulous *adj* characterized by or affected with trembling or tremors <her *tremulous* hands could scarcely hold the book>
syn aquake, aquiver, ashake, ashiver, quaking, quaky, quivering, quivery, shaking, shaky, shivering, shivery, trembling, tremorous, tremulant
rel aguish; aspen; palpitating; vibrating
idiom having the shakes
con firm, settled, stable, steady, unmoving

trench *n* a long narrow furrow in the ground <dig a *trench* for a sewer pipe>
syn cut, ditch
rel gully; drill, furrow; fosse; trough; drain, sink

trench *vb* ***syn*** see BORDER 3

trenchant *adj* **1** ***syn*** see INCISIVE
rel piercing, probing, razor-sharp; sarcastic, sardonic, satiric; acrid; piquant, poignant, pungent
2 ***syn*** see CAUSTIC 1
rel scalding, scorching

trend *n* **1** ***syn*** see TENDENCY 1
rel movement; flow; direction, orientation; swing, wind; progression
2 ***syn*** see FASHION 3

‖**trendy** *adj* ***syn*** see STYLISH
rel ultramodern
con dated, outmoded

trepidation *n* ***syn*** see FEAR 1
ant unapprehensiveness

trepidity *n* ***syn*** see FEAR 1
ant intrepidity, intrepidness

trespass *n* ***syn*** see BREACH 1
rel encroachment, entrenchment, invasion; intrusion, obtrusion

trespass *vb* **1** to commit an offense <exhibited scrupulous fairness even to those who *trespassed* against him>
syn offend, sin, transgress
rel deviate, err, lapse
idiom do wrong by
2 to make inroads on the property, territory, or rights of another <warned the hunters not to *trespass* on his land>
syn encroach, entrench, infringe, invade
rel enter, penetrate, pierce, probe; interlope, intermeddle, intrude; transgress
idiom crash the gate

trestle *n* ***syn*** see SAWHORSE

triad *n* a union or group of three often closely related individuals or things <a *triad* of deities>
syn threesome, trine, trinity, trio, triple, triumvirate, triune, troika; *compare* TRIUMVIRATE 1

trial *n* **1** the state or fact of being tested (as by suffering) <the Vietnam war period was a time of great national *trial*>
syn affliction, calvary, cross, crucible, ordeal, tribulation, visitation
rel agony, distress, misery, suffering; anguish, grief, heartbreak, sorrow, woe; adversity, misfortune; difficulty, hardship, rigor, vicissitude
idiom crown of thorns, fiery ordeal, trial and tribulation
2 a source of vexation or annoyance <living in a crowded hotel is a real *trial*>
syn care, trouble, worry
rel complication, difficulty; annoyance, distress, misfortune; ordeal
3 ***syn*** see EXPERIMENT
4 ***syn*** see ATTEMPT

trial *adj* ***syn*** see EXPERIMENTAL 2

trial and error *n* ***syn*** see EXPERIMENT

trial balloon *n* ***syn*** see FEELER
rel trial

trial run *n* ***syn*** see EXPERIMENT

tribe *n* ***syn*** see FAMILY 1

tribulation *n* ***syn*** see TRIAL 1
rel oppression, persecution, wronging

tribunal *n* ***syn*** see COURT 2

tributary *adj* ***syn*** see SUBORDINATE

---

syn synonym(s) *rel* related word(s)
ant antonym(s) *con* contrasted word(s)
idiom idiomatic equivalent(s)
‖ use limited; if in doubt, see a dictionary

rel conquered, subdued, subjugated, vanquished; accessory, minor; satellite

tribute *n* **1** ***syn*** see TESTIMONIAL 2
rel recognition; monument
2 ***syn*** see ENCOMIUM

trice *n* ***syn*** see INSTANT 1

trick *n* **1** an indirect, ingenious, and often cunning means to gain an end <used every *trick* in the bag to cover up the scandal>
syn artifice, chouse, device, feint, gambit, gimmick, jig, maneuver, play, ploy, ‖prat, ruse, shenanigan, sleight, stratagem, whizzer, wile; *compare* PRANK
rel contrivance, craft, expediency; blind, bluff, diversion, dodge, dodgery, red herring; curve, deception, sham, stall; fraud, ‖rort, scheme, shift, skin game
2 ***syn*** see PRANK
rel boutade; escapade; practical joke
3 an ingenious or dexterous act or procedure designed to puzzle or amuse <a juggler's *trick*>
syn feat, stunt
rel accomplishment
4 tricks *pl* ***syn*** see PERSONAL EFFECTS
5 ***syn*** see HANG
6 ***syn*** see HABIT 1
7 ***syn*** see SPELL

trick *adj* somewhat defective and inclined to function abnormally on occasion <a *trick* lock that doesn't always catch>
syn tricky, undependable
rel catchy, touchy; unreliable, untrustworthy; insecure, shaky, unstable; defective, dysfunctioning, malfunctioning

trick *vb* ***syn*** see DUPE
rel outtrick, outtrump, outwit; have
idiom take (someone) for a ride

trick (off, out, *or* up) *vb* ***syn*** see DRESS UP 1

trickery *n* ***syn*** see DECEPTION 1
rel double-cross; underhandedness
idiom underhand dealing

trickle *vb* ***syn*** see DRIP
ant gush

trickster *n* **1** ***syn*** see SWINDLER
idiom gyp artist
2 ***syn*** see MAGICIAN 2

tricksy *adj* ***syn*** see TIGHT 4

tricky *adj* **1** ***syn*** see SLY 2
rel deceptive, delusive; delusory, misleading; deceitful, dishonest
2 ***syn*** see UNSTABLE 2
rel catchy, difficult, trappy; quirky
3 ***syn*** see DELICATE 7
4 ***syn*** see TRICK

tried *adj* ***syn*** see RELIABLE 1
rel constant, faithful, staunch, steadfast; demonstrated, proved, tested; approved, certified
ant untried

tried and true *adj* ***syn*** see RELIABLE 1

trifle *n* **1** ***syn*** see KNICKKNACK
rel rope yarn
2 ***syn*** see HINT 2

trifle *vb* **1** to behave amorously without serious intent <was interested only in *trifling* with her, not marrying her>
syn coquet, dally, flirt, fool, lead on, string along, toy, wanton
rel play (with); mess around, ‖muck, mucker; philander; mash
2 ***syn*** see FIDDLE 1

trifle (away) *vb* ***syn*** see WASTE 2
rel misuse; burn (up), use up
con retain, save

trifling *n* ***syn*** see SMALL TALK

trifling *adj* ***syn*** see PETTY 2
rel banal, inane, insipid, jejune, vapid; empty, frivolous, hollow, idle, nugatory, otiose, vain; insignificant, unimportant

trig *adj* **1** ***syn*** see NEAT 2
2 ***syn*** see STYLISH
‖**3** ***syn*** see FULL 1

triggerman *n* ***syn*** see ASSASSIN

trill *vb* ***syn*** see DRIP

trillion *n* ***syn*** see SCAD

trim *vb* **1** ***syn*** see ADORN
2 ***syn*** see WHIP 2
rel ‖skin
3 ***syn*** see CUT 6

trim *adj* **1** ***syn*** see NEAT 2
rel clean, clean-cut, fit, spruce; shapely, streamlined, symmetrical
con disordered, shapeless, straggly
ant frowsy
2 ***syn*** see SHAPELY

trim *n* ***syn*** see ORDER 10
rel commission; whack

trine *n* ***syn*** see TRIAD

trinity *n* ***syn*** see TRIAD

trinket *n* ***syn*** see KNICKKNACK
rel plaything; frippery, showpiece, tinsel; trinketry, trinkums

trio *n* ***syn*** see TRIAD

trip *vb* ***syn*** see SKIP 1

trip *n* **1** a single passage of a vehicle between two points or to a point and return <a regular bus *trip* to and from the city>
syn run; *compare* DRIVE 1, JOURNEY, TOUR 2
rel drive; progress
2 ***syn*** see JOURNEY
rel run
3 ***syn*** see ERROR 2

tripes *n pl* ***syn*** see ENTRAILS

triple *n* ***syn*** see TRIAD

tripped out *adj* ***syn*** see DRUGGED

‖**tripper** *n* ***syn*** see TOURIST

triste *adj* ***syn*** see SAD 2

trite *adj* used or occurring so often as to have lost interest, freshness, or force <unrequited love has become a *trite* theme>
syn bathetic, chain, cliché, clichéd, commonplace, corny, hack, hackneyed, musty, old hat, shopworn, stale, stereotyped, stereotypical, threadbare, timeworn, tired, twice-told, warmed-over, well-worn, worn-out
rel common, ordinary; banal, dull, flat, jejune, mildewed, vapid; bedridden, drained, exhausted, used-up; bromidic, platitudinous, prosaic, ready-made, set, stock
con first, new, seminal; novel, unique; creative, imaginative; uncopied; memorable; distinctive

ant fresh, original

triturate *vb* ***syn*** see PULVERIZE 1

triumph *n* **1** ***syn*** see VICTORY 1
rel ascendancy, gain; surmounting, vanquishing, vanquishment
ant defeat
2 ***syn*** see EXULTATION
rel joy; festivity, merriment, reveling

triumph *vb* **1** ***syn*** see EXULT
rel gloat
2 ***syn*** see WIN 1
rel prosper, succeed; conquer, surmount
idiom get the best (*or* better) of
con lose
ant fail
3 ***syn*** see CONQUER 2

triumphal *adj* ***syn*** see EXULTANT

triumphant *adj* ***syn*** see EXULTANT
rel rejoicing, triumphing

triumvirate *n* **1** an administrative or ruling body of three <a monarchy replaced by a *triumvirate* of generals>
syn troika; *compare* TRIAD
rel junta
2 ***syn*** see TRIAD

triune *n* ***syn*** see TRIAD

trivia *n pl but sometimes sing in constr* unimportant matters <they became bored with the *trivia* of everyday life>
syn minutia(e), small beer, small change, small potato(es), triviality

trivial *adj* **1** ***syn*** see LITTLE 3
rel slight; negligible
idiom no great shakes
con considerable
ant momentous, weighty
2 ***syn*** see PETTY 2
rel captious, fribbling, frivolous; shallow, superficial

triviality *n* ***syn*** see TRIVIA
rel shallowness, superficiality, unimportance
con basic(s), essential(s), fundamental(s)

‖**trod** *n* ***syn*** see TRAIL

troika *n* **1** ***syn*** see TRIUMVIRATE 1
2 ***syn*** see TRIAD

trollop *n* ***syn*** see WANTON
idiom (a) fast number

trollop *vb* ***syn*** see SLOUCH

tromp *vb* **1** ***syn*** see TRAMP 1
2 ***syn*** see HIKE 2
rel slog, trudge
3 ***syn*** see TRAMPLE 2
4 ***syn*** see BEAT 1

troop *n* **1** ***syn*** see COMPANY 4
rel assemblage, assembly, collection, gathering; army, host, legion, multitude
2 troops *pl* members of a nation's military units <Marines, GI's, and Seabees were among the *troops* sent to war>
syn armed forces, forces, military, servicemen
rel combatants; soldiers, troopers
idiom fighting men

troop *vb* ***syn*** see WALK 1

trophy *n* ***syn*** see REMEMBRANCE 3

tropic *adj* ***syn*** see TROPICAL
rel baking, broiling, scorching, sweltering
con arctic

tropical *adj* of, relating to, or occurring in the tropics <*tropical* fruits>
syn tropic
rel equatorial, semitropical, subtropical; warm; hot, sultry, torrid
con temperate

tropical cyclone *n* ***syn*** see HURRICANE

tropical storm *n* ***syn*** see HURRICANE

trot *n* **1** ***syn*** see HAG 2
2 ***syn*** see PONY
‖**3 trots** *pl* ***syn*** see DIARRHEA

troth *n* ***syn*** see ENGAGEMENT 2

trot out *vb* ***syn*** see SHOW 4

troubadour *n* ***syn*** see BARD 1
rel balladist; rhymer, rhymester

trouble *vb* **1** to cause to be uneasy or upset <sorrows that *trouble* the strongest of men>
syn ail, cark, distress, upset, worry
rel agitate, concern, discompose, disquiet, disturb, perturb, rowel, ‖worrit; annoy, bother, fret, irk, vex; ‖destroy, haunt
2 ***syn*** see TRY 2
rel upset, worry; discompose, disconcert, disturb; harry, irritate; afflict, torment
3 ***syn*** see INCONVENIENCE
rel annoy, pester, plague, worry; impose (on *or* upon), intrude

trouble *n* **1** ***syn*** see TRIAL 2
2 ***syn*** see EFFORT 1
rel ado, bustle, flurry, fuss, pother; bother, inconvenience; difficulty, hardship, rigor; strain, stress
3 a condition of annoyance, disturbance, or distress <got him into *trouble* by repeating gossip>
syn Dutch, hot water
rel bind, difficulty, predicament

troubled *adj* ***syn*** see DISTRAUGHT

troublemaker *n* a person who consciously or unconsciously causes trouble <a *troublemaker* who set father against daughter>
syn bad actor, mischief-maker
rel agitator, inciter, inflamer, instigator

troublesome *adj* giving trouble or anxiety <a *troublesome* infection>
syn mean, pesky, troublous, ugly, vexatious, wicked
rel annoying, bothersome, vexing; alarming, disquieting, disturbing, upsetting; infestive; painful
con untroublesome
ant innocuous

troublesomeness *n* ***syn*** see INCONVENIENCE
rel difficulty; irritation, vexation

troublous *adj* ***syn*** see TROUBLESOME
rel troubling

trounce *vb* ***syn*** see WHIP 2

---

syn synonym(s) ***rel*** related word(s)
ant antonym(s) ***con*** contrasted word(s)
idiom idiomatic equivalent(s)
‖ use limited; if in doubt, see a dictionary

THESAURUS

idiom walk all over
trouncing *n* ***syn*** see DEFEAT 1
troupe *n* ***syn*** see COMPANY 4
trouper *n* ***syn*** see ACTOR 1
rel entertainer; artiste
trove *n* ***syn*** see ACCUMULATION
truce *n* a suspension of or an agreement for suspending hostilities <the high command ordered a *truce* for the holidays>
syn armistice, cease-fire
rel break, ||breather, letup, lull, pause, respite; de-escalation, ||wind-down; accord, reconciliation; peace
truck *vb* **1** ***syn*** see TRADE 1
rel handle; peddle, retail
2 ***syn*** see TRAFFIC 2
idiom have truck with
truck *n* ***syn*** see COMMERCE 2
truckle *vb* ***syn*** see FAWN
rel knuckle down, knuckle under, succumb; follow, tag, tail, trail
idiom kiss (*or* lick) one's boots, lick the feet of, make a doormat of oneself
truckler *n* ***syn*** see SYCOPHANT
truckling *adj* ***syn*** see FAWNING
truculent *adj* **1** ***syn*** see FIERCE 1
rel browbeating, bullying, cowing, intimidating; frightening, terrifying, terrorizing
2 ***syn*** see ABUSIVE
rel caustic, mordacious, mordant, scathing, sharp, trenchant; harsh, rough, severe; vitriolic
3 ***syn*** see BELLIGERENT
trudge *vb* ***syn*** see PLOD 1
true *adj* **1** ***syn*** see FAITHFUL 1
rel sincere, unfeigned, whole-hearted, whole-souled
ant false, fickle
2 ***syn*** see UPRIGHT 2
rel creditable, estimable, worthy; high-principled, right-minded, truehearted
3 conformable to fact or to a standard, rule, or model <gave a *true* account of the accident>
syn faithful, just, right, strict, undistorted, veracious, veridical
rel careful, conscientious, meticulous, punctilious, scrupulous; finicky, fussy, overnice; accurate, precise; absolute, mathematical
idiom true to the letter
con imprecise, inaccurate, incorrect, inexact; erroneous, false
ant untrue
4 ***syn*** see GENUINE 3
con deceitful
5 ***syn*** see AUTHENTIC 2
rel genuine, kosher; sincere, unfaked, unfeigned
con artificial, fake, faked, feigned; insincere
ant false
6 ***syn*** see REAL 3
rel natural, normal, regular, typical
ant false
7 being such as it should be <meanings presented in their *true* relationship>
syn appropriate, desired, fitting, proper
rel acceptable; applicable, befitting, likely, suitable
con inappropriate, unfitting
8 being such by right <the *true* heir>
syn legitimate, rightful
rel lawful, legal, proper
con illegitimate, spurious, supposititious
ant false
9 that can be relied on <polls can provide a *true* projection of public sentiment>
syn authoritative, dependable, trustable, trustworthy
rel meaningful, significant; expressive, indicative, suggestive
con independable, undependable, untrustworthy; doubtful, questionable
truelove *n* **1** ***syn*** see GIRL FRIEND 2
2 ***syn*** see BOYFRIEND 2
idiom one and only
true–tongued *adj* ***syn*** see TRUTHFUL
truism *n* **1** ***syn*** see VERACITY 2
2 ***syn*** see MAXIM
3 ***syn*** see COMMONPLACE
trull *n* ***syn*** see WANTON
truly *adv* **1** ***syn*** see VERY 2
rel absolutely, positively
2 ***syn*** see EVEN 3
rel confidently, really
3 ***syn*** see WELL 7
rel probably; surely
trump *n* ***syn*** see TRUMP CARD
trump *vb* ***syn*** see SURPASS 1
trump card *n* something decisive or telling often held in reserve <kept a political *trump card* up her sleeve till election eve>
syn clincher, trump
rel ace; coup, coup de grace, coup de main
idiom ace in the hole
trumpery *n* ***syn*** see NONSENSE 2
trumpery *adj* ***syn*** see CHEAP 2
trumpet *vb* ***syn*** see TOUT
truncate *vb* ***syn*** see TOP 1
rel abbreviate, abridge; cut off, lop; shear
truncheon *n* ***syn*** see CUDGEL
trust *n* **1** complete assurance and certitude regarding the character, ability, strength, or truth of someone or something <they continue to have *trust* in his judgment>
syn confidence, dependence, faith, hope, reliance, stock
rel assurance, certainty, certitude, conviction; belief, credence, credit; positiveness, sureness; entrustment; overconfidence, oversureness
con doubt, dubiety, dubiosity, skepticism, suspicion, uncertainty
ant mistrust
2 ***syn*** see SYNDICATE
3 ***syn*** see CUSTODY
trust *vb* ***syn*** see ENTRUST 1
rel commit, consign, hand over
trust (in *or* to) *vb* ***syn*** see RELY (on *or* upon)
rel assume, imagine, presume
idiom have no reservations
trustable *adj* ***syn*** see TRUE 9
ant trustless
trustless *adj* ***syn*** see UNRELIABLE 1

rel unworthy; unfaithful; suspect, suspicious; dishonest; deceitful; treacherous
ant trustable, trustworthy

trustworthy *adj* **1** ***syn*** see RELIABLE 1
rel truthful, veracious; honest, scrupulous, upright
con deceitful; dishonest
ant untrustworthy
2 ***syn*** see TRUE 9
rel accurate, exact; valid; realistic
con inaccurate, inexact; invalid; unrealistic; suspect
ant untrustworthy
3 ***syn*** see AUTHENTIC 1

trusty *adj* **1** ***syn*** see RELIABLE 1
rel predictable, stable; firm, sound; responsible, ||straight
con capricious
ant untrusty
2 ***syn*** see AUTHENTIC 1
ant untrusty

truth *n* **1** ***syn*** see VERACITY 1
rel precision, rightness, trueness; authenticity, genuineness, veritableness; candor
idiom unvarnished truth (*or* truthfulness)
con equivocation, evasion, hedging; deception, deceptiveness, falseness
ant falsity, untruth
2 ***syn*** see VERACITY 2
rel reality
idiom (the) gospel truth, (the) truth of the matter
ant lie, untruth

truthful *adj* observant of or telling the truth <a *truthful* witness>
syn true-tongued, truth-speaking, truth-telling, veracious, veridical
rel candid, frank, honest, sincere; accurate, factual; real, realistic
con false, insincere, truthless, uncandid; inaccurate; unrealistic
ant untruthful

truthfulness *n* ***syn*** see VERACITY 1
ant untruthfulness

truthlessness *n* ***syn*** see MENDACITY

truth–speaking *adj* ***syn*** see TRUTHFUL

truth–telling *adj* ***syn*** see TRUTHFUL

try *vb* **1** to subject to testing <*try* the door to be sure it's locked>
syn check, examine, prove, test
rel inspect, scrutinize; appraise, judge, weigh
idiom make trial of, put to proof, put to the test
2 to subject to stress <the fine print *tried* her eyes>
syn distress, harass, irk, pain, strain, stress, trouble
rel annoy, bother, vex
3 ***syn*** see AFFLICT
4 ***syn*** see PROVE 1
5 to make an effort to do or accomplish something <the baby is *trying* to walk>
syn assay, attempt, endeavor, essay, offer, seek, strive, struggle, undertake
rel aim, aspire, hope, strike
idiom do one's best (*or* utmost) to, have a go at

try (out) *vb* ***syn*** see EXPERIMENT
rel examine, inspect, scrutinize; demonstrate, prove
idiom cut and try, put to trial, try for size

try *n* **1** ***syn*** see ATTEMPT
2 ***syn*** see FLING 1
rel dab, jab

trying *adj* **1** ***syn*** see TIGHT 4
rel annoying, bothersome, irksome, irritating, troublesome, vexing; strenuous; sticky, tricky
2 ***syn*** see ONEROUS

try on *vb* ***syn*** see EXPERIMENT

tryst *n* ***syn*** see ENGAGEMENT 3

||**tub** *n* ***syn*** see FATTY

tub *vb* ***syn*** see BATHE 1

tubby *adj* ***syn*** see ROTUND 2
idiom plump as a dumpling (*or* partridge)

tube *n* ***syn*** see TELEVISION

tuberculosis *n* a communicable bacterial disease typically marked by wasting, fever, and formation of cheesy tubercles often in the lungs <Victorian heroines fading away with *tuberculosis*>
syn consumption, phthisis, TB, white plague

tuck (in) *vb* ***syn*** see BED
rel snug (down *or* up), snuggle

||**tuck** *n* ***syn*** see FOOD 1

tuck *n* ***syn*** see ENERGY 2

||**tucked up** *adj* ***syn*** see CRAMPED

tucker *vb* ***syn*** see EXHAUST 4
rel gruel; wilt; drop
idiom take the tuck out of

tug *vb* **1** ***syn*** see CONTEND 1
2 ***syn*** see LABOR 1
3 ***syn*** see PULL 2

tug–of–war *n* ***syn*** see CONTEST 1

tuition *n* ***syn*** see EDUCATION 1

tumble *vb* **1** ***syn*** see FALL 2
rel trip; come (down), descend
2 ***syn*** see PLUMMET
rel depreciate; sag, slump
idiom take a downward spiral, take a nosedive
3 ***syn*** see HAPPEN 2
4 ***syn*** see DISCOVER 3
5 ***syn*** see OVERTHROW 2
6 ***syn*** see FELL 1
7 ***syn*** see CONFUSE 5
8 ***syn*** see DISORDER 1

tumble (to) *vb* ***syn*** see APPREHEND 1

tumble *n* ***syn*** see CLUTTER 2

tumescent *adj* **1** ***syn*** see INFLATED
rel bloated; bulging
2 ***syn*** see RHETORICAL

tumid *adj* **1** ***syn*** see INFLATED
rel dilated, distended, expanded, swollen
2 ***syn*** see RHETORICAL

tummy *n* ***syn*** see ABDOMEN

tumulary *adj* ***syn*** see SEPULCHRAL 1

tumult *n* **1** ***syn*** see COMMOTION 1

---

syn synonym(s)   ***rel*** related word(s)
ant antonym(s)   ***con*** contrasted word(s)
idiom idiomatic equivalent(s)
|| use limited; if in doubt, see a dictionary

rel disturbance, turmoil, uproar
2 *syn* see COMMOTION 4
rel babel, din, hullabaloo, pandemonium, racket
con calm, hush, lull, quietude
3 *syn* see COMMOTION 2
rel seething; disorder, unsettlement; ferment, maelstrom, paroxysm
4 *syn* see DIN
rel noise; ‖corroboree
idiom ‖all hell broken loose

tumultuous *adj syn* see TURBULENT 1

tumultuously *adv syn* see HARD 2

tun *n syn* see CASK
rel vat

tune *n* **1** *syn* see MELODY
rel carol; composition, number, piece
2 *syn* see HARMONY 1
3 *syn* see HARMONY 2
4 *syn* see ORDER 4

tune *vb* **1** *syn* see SING 1
2 *syn* see HARMONIZE 3
rel fix, regulate
3 to adjust with respect to resonance <*tune* a TV set to a local station>
syn dial

tune (up) *vb syn* see ADJUST 2

tuned *adj syn* see MELODIOUS 2

tuneful *adj* **1** *syn* see MELODIOUS 2
2 *syn* see MELODIOUS 1
ant tuneless

tunk *vb syn* see TAP 1

turbid *adj* clouded with or as if with roiled sediment <a *turbid* stream>
syn muddy, riley, roily
rel dark, dense, obscure; mucky, thick; clouded, cloudy, murky, opaque, smoky; dull
con translucent; lucid, pellucid, transparent; crystal, crystalline; clean, pure, undefiled
ant clear, limpid

turbulence *n syn* see COMMOTION 2
rel babel, din, pandemonium, uproar; unruliness; fight, fracas
con calmness, composure, placidity, quiet

turbulent *adj* **1** given to insubordination and disorder <a *turbulent* and irresponsible group>
syn boisterous, disorderly, rambunctious, raucous, rowdy, rowdydowdy, rowdyish, rumbustious, termagant, tumultuous, unruly; *compare* UNRULY 1
rel mutinous; fast, roisterous, uncontrollable, uninhibited, wild; clamorous, loudmouthed; brawling, quarrelsome, rough, roughhouse; hell-for-leather, rip-roaring, tempestuous
con calm, placid, quiet, tranquil; controlled, orderly, peaceful, restrained
2 *syn* see WILD 6
rel agitated, convulsed, moiling, stirred up; boiling, roily, ruffled, swirling; howling, riotous, roaring; tempest-tossed

turbulently *adv syn* see HARD 2
rel blusteringly

turf *n syn* see TERRAIN 2
rel area, region, sphere

turgid *adj* **1** *syn* see INFLATED
rel swelling, turgescent
2 *syn* see RHETORICAL

turmoil *n* **1** *syn* see COMMOTION 2
rel jitteriness, nervousness, restlessness, unease, uneasiness; disorder, disruption; moil; riot, strife, uproar
2 *syn* see UNREST
rel distress; anxiety, anxiousness
ant tranquillity
3 *syn* see COMMOTION 4

turn *vb* **1** to move or cause to move in a curved or circular path on or as if on an axis <*turned* the wheel sharply to avoid a collision>
syn circle, circumduct, gyrate, gyre, revolve, roll, rotate; *compare* SPIN 1
rel orbit; pirouette, spin, twirl, whirl; twist, weave, wind; circulate, eddy, swirl; oscillate, sway, swing, vibrate
2 *syn* see SPRAIN
3 *syn* see REVERSE 1
4 *syn* see PLOW
5 *syn* see UPSET 5
rel discompose, undo; unbalance
6 to change or cause to change course or direction <*turned* his car down a side road>
syn avert, deflect, divert, pivot, sheer, swing, veer, volte-face, wheel, whip, whirl; *compare* SHUNT 1
rel depart, detract, deviate, digress, diverge; move, shift; switch, swivel, twist, zigzag; call off, double (back), reverse; shunt, sidetrack; bend, curve, sway; detour, rechannel, turn away
7 *syn* see DIRECT 2
con call off, detract (from), distract, divert (from), draw (away)
8 *syn* see ADDRESS 3
rel employ, use; plunge (into), undertake
idiom turn one's hand (*or* energies) to
con avoid, dodge, shy (away)
9 *syn* see CURDLE
10 *syn* see DECAY
11 *syn* see CHANGE 1
12 *syn* see TRANSLATE 1
13 *syn* see DULL 3
14 *syn* see SPIN 2
15 *syn* see DEFECT
16 *syn* see RESORT 2
17 *syn* see BECOME 1
rel change (into), pass (into)

turn (on *or* upon) *vb syn* see DEPEND (on *or* upon) 1

turn *n* **1** *syn* see REVOLUTION 1
2 an often sudden change in course or trend <his health took a *turn* for the better>
syn bend, deflection, deviation, double, shift, tack, yaw
rel course, drift, trend
3 *syn* see REVERSAL 1
4 a point at which a change of course takes place <hidden by a *turn* in the road>
syn angle, bend, bow, flection, flexure, turning
rel curve, twist; corner
5 *syn* see WALK 1
6 *syn* see DRIVE 1

7 ***syn*** see SPELL 1
8 ***syn*** see CHANGE 1
9 ***syn*** see GIFT 2
rel bias, disposition, predisposition
10 an unusual, unexpected, or special interpretation or construction <gave a new *turn* to the old joke>
syn twist
rel construction, interpretation; device, gimmick, trick
11 ***syn*** see ATTACK 3
turnabout *n* **1** ***syn*** see REVERSAL 1
2 ***syn*** see RENEGADE
rel backslider, coward, quitter, turnback
turn back *vb* ***syn*** see RETURN 1
turncoat *n* ***syn*** see RENEGADE
rel deserter, straggler; betrayer, quisler, quisling, traitor; spy
turn down *vb* ***syn*** see DECLINE 4
turned on *adj* ***syn*** see DRUGGED
turn in *vb* ***syn*** see RETIRE 4
ant turn out
turning *n* **1** ***syn*** see TURN 4
2 ***syn*** see DEVIATION 1
rel detour
3 ***syn*** see REVERSAL 1
turning point *n* ***syn*** see JUNCTURE 2
rel climax, culmination, peak
idiom moment of truth
turnip *n* ***syn*** see DUNCE
turn off *vb* **1** ***syn*** see DISMISS 3
2 ***syn*** see HANG 2
turn out *vb* **1** ***syn*** see FURNISH 1
rel deck, dress (out)
2 ***syn*** see BEAR 9
3 ***syn*** see ROLL OUT
turnout *n* **1** ***syn*** see COSTUME
2 ***syn*** see OUTPUT
turn over *vb* **1** ***syn*** see OVERTURN 1
2 ***syn*** see PLOW
3 ***syn*** see PONDER 2
idiom turn over in one's mind
4 ***syn*** see GIVE 3
rel assign, confer, consign, convey, delegate, relegate; give up, relinquish, ||turn up
idiom come across with, put into the hands of
con get back, reclaim, recover, regain, retrieve, take back
5 ***syn*** see COMMIT 1
turnover *n* ***syn*** see SHAKE-UP
turn up *vb* **1** ***syn*** see FIND 1
rel see; uncover, unearth; track (down)
idiom come across
||**2** ***syn*** see RELINQUISH
3 to arrive when or where expected <*turned up* for dinner promptly at seven o'clock>
syn show, show up
rel appear, arrive, come, materialize; blow in, pop (in), punch in, roll (in), weigh in
idiom make one's appearance, put in an appearance
4 ***syn*** see COME 1
turtledove *n* ***syn*** see SWEETHEART 1
tussle *vb* ***syn*** see WRESTLE
rel scrap, skirmish, spar; hassle
idiom get into a tussle
tutelage *n* ***syn*** see EDUCATION 1
TV *n* ***syn*** see TELEVISION
twaddle *n* ***syn*** see NONSENSE 2
rel gabble; wish-wash
twaddle *vb* **1** ***syn*** see BABBLE 2
2 ***syn*** see CHAT 1
twang *n* ***syn*** see HINT 2
tweedle *vb* ***syn*** see CHIRP
tween *prep* ***syn*** see BETWEEN 2
tweet *vb* ***syn*** see CHIRP
twerp *n* a usually young or insignificant upstart who meddles beyond his competence or concern <ignored the protests of that insolent *twerp*>
syn pup, puppy, sprat, squirt, ||squit
rel upstart; ||squib; fool, jerk, ||twit; brat
idiom small-time big shot
twice–told *adj* ***syn*** see TRITE
twiddle *vb* ***syn*** see FIDDLE 1
rel finger, manipulate, palpate; monkey (with), toy (with)
idiom twiddle around with
twiddle *vb* ***syn*** see CHAT 1
twig *vb* **1** ***syn*** see SEE 1
2 ***syn*** see APPREHEND 1
||**twig** *n* ***syn*** see FASHION 3
twiggy *adj* ***syn*** see THIN 1
twilight *n* **1** ***syn*** see EVENING 1
rel afterglow, afterlight
2 ***syn*** see EVENING 2
rel decline; end
twin *adj* made up of two very closely matched or identical aspects, elements, individuals, or parts <the *twin* threats of inflation and recession>
syn double, dual, paired
rel bifold, binary, twofold; identical, matched, matching; like, similar
con independent, separate; dissimilar, unlike
twin *n* ***syn*** see MATE 5
twine *vb* ***syn*** see WIND 2
rel interweave; undulate; enmesh, entangle, tangle
twinge *n* ***syn*** see PAIN 1
twinkle *vb* **1** ***syn*** see BLINK 2
rel illuminate, light, light up; shine
2 ***syn*** see FLASH 1
3 ***syn*** see WINK
twinkle *n* **1** ***syn*** see INSTANT 1
2 ***syn*** see FLASH 1
twinkling *n* ***syn*** see INSTANT 1
idiom the twinkling of an eye
twirl *vb* ***syn*** see SPIN 1
twist *vb* **1** ***syn*** see SPRAIN
2 ***syn*** see MISREPRESENT
3 ***syn*** see WIND 2
ant untwist
twist *n* ***syn*** see TURN 10
twister *n* ***syn*** see TORNADO

---

syn synonym(s) ***rel*** related word(s)
ant antonym(s) ***con*** contrasted word(s)
idiom idiomatic equivalent(s)
|| use limited; if in doubt, see a dictionary

twisting *adj* ***syn*** see CROOKED 1
twit *vb* ***syn*** see RIDICULE
rel jive, josh, tease; chide, reproach, reprove; blame, censure, reprehend
twitch *vb* ***syn*** see JERK
rel clutch, grasp, pluck, snatch; nip, pinch
twitter *vb* **1** ***syn*** see CHIRP
2 ***syn*** see CHAT 1
3 ***syn*** see SHAKE 1
twittery *adj* ***syn*** see NERVOUS
rel flustered; twittering
idiom all atwitter, all fluttery, all of a twitter
twitty *adj* ***syn*** see IRRITABLE
twixt *prep* ***syn*** see BETWEEN 2
twofold *adj* **1** having two parts, elements, or aspects <the problem is *twofold:* to find gasoline and to be able to pay for it>
syn bifold, binary, double, double-barreled, dual, dualistic, duple, duplex
rel dyadic; paired, twin
con distinct, separate
2 being twice as large, as great, or as many <a *twofold* increase in enrollment>
syn double, double-barreled
idiom twice over
two-handed *adj* **1** designed for or requiring the use of both hands <a *two-handed* sword>
syn bimanual
2 having or being efficient with two hands <*two-handed* tennis players are rare>
syn ambidextrous, bimanual
twosome *n* ***syn*** see COUPLE
two-time *vb* ***syn*** see DECEIVE
two-wheeler *n* ***syn*** see BICYCLE
tycoon *n* ***syn*** see MAGNATE
tyke *n* ***syn*** see DOG 1
type *n* a number of individuals thought of as a group because of a common quality or qualities <political radicals of whatever *type*>
syn breed, cast, character, class, cut, description, feather, ilk, kidney, kind, lot, mold, nature, order, persuasion, sort, species, stamp, stripe, variety, way
rel blazon, brand, form; sample, specimen; category, group, rubric
typhoon *n* ***syn*** see HURRICANE
typic *adj* ***syn*** see GENERAL 1
rel average, ordinary
typical *adj* **1** constituting or having the nature of a type <a *typical* instance of guilt by association>
syn archetypal, classic, classical, exemplary, ideal, model, paradigmatic, prototypal, prototypical, quintessential, representative
rel characteristic; emblematic, symbolic; absolute, consummate, perfect
con uncharacteristic; unusual
ant atypical, untypical
2 ***syn*** see GENERAL 1
rel old hat, unexceptional; collective, quintessential, representative; characteristic, specific
idiom being the rule and not the exception
con distinctive; exceptional, extraordinary, unusual; abnormal
ant atypical, untypical
typification *n* ***syn*** see ALLEGORY 1
typify *vb* **1** ***syn*** see REPRESENT 2
2 ***syn*** see EPITOMIZE 2
rel model
tyrannical *adj* ***syn*** see ABSOLUTE 4
rel brutal, harsh, oppressive; roughshod
tyrannize *vb* to exercise arbitrary power over often with unjust and oppressive severity <a country *tyrannized* by a dictator and his secret police>
syn despotize
rel dictate, dominate, domineer, overlord; crush, oppress, trample; shackle; terrorize
tyrannous *adj* ***syn*** see ABSOLUTE 4
rel lordly; fascistic, totalitarian
tyranny *n* absolute government in which unlimited power is vested in a single usually severe and oppressive ruler <the *tyranny* of Hitler>
syn autocracy, despotism, dictatorship, totalitarianism
rel monocracy; absolutism, authoritarianism, fascism; domination, oppression, totality; terrorism
idiom iron heel (*or* boot)
con democracy; freedom; anarchy
tyrant *n* a ruler who exercises absolute power oppressively and brutally <Hitler and Stalin as twentieth-century *tyrants*>
syn despot, dictator, duce, oppressor, strong man
rel autocrat, totalitarian
idiom man on horseback
tyro *n* **1** ***syn*** see AMATEUR 2
2 ***syn*** see NOVICE

U

uberrima fides *n* ***syn*** see GOOD FAITH
ubiquitous *adj* ***syn*** see OMNIPRESENT
ugly *adj* **1** ***syn*** see GRAVE 3
2 unpleasing to the sight <an *ugly* decaying neighborhood>
syn hideous, ill-favored, ill-looking, unbeautiful, uncomely, unsightly
rel homely, plain; bizarre, grotesque; repelling, repugnant, repulsive; unattractive, uninviting, unpleasing, unprepossessing
idiom homely as a mud (*or* hedge) fence, not much to look at, short on looks
con comely, fair, good-looking, handsome, lovely, pretty; attractive, prepossessing
ant beautiful
3 ***syn*** see BASE 3
4 ***syn*** see TROUBLESOME
5 ***syn*** see SULLEN
ukase *n* ***syn*** see EDICT 1
ulterior *adj* lying behind what is manifest or avowed <an *ulterior* motive>
syn buried, concealed, covert, guarded, hidden, obscured, privy, shrouded
rel ambiguous, cryptic, dark, enigmatic, equivocal, obscure
idiom hidden under the rug, kept behind a screen, under cover, under wraps
con clear, open, overt, plain, straightforward; explicit, expressed
ultimate *adj* **1** ***syn*** see LAST
2 ***syn*** see SUPREME
3 being so fundamental as to stand at the extreme limit of the actually or conceivably knowable <*ultimate* realities>
syn absolute, categorical
rel empyreal, empyrean, sublime, transcendental; exalted, grand, lofty
ultimate *n* ***syn*** see APOTHEOSIS 1
ultimate *vb* ***syn*** see CLOSE 3
ultimately *adv* ***syn*** see YET 2
ultra *adj* **1** ***syn*** see EXTREME 3
2 ***syn*** see OUTLANDISH 3
ultraconservative *n* ***syn*** see REACTIONARY
ultrafashionable *adj* ***syn*** see STYLISH
ultraist *n* ***syn*** see RADICAL
ultraist *adj* ***syn*** see EXTREME 3
ultramarine *adj* ***syn*** see OVERSEAS
ululate *vb* ***syn*** see HOWL 1
rel bewail, lament
umbra *n* **1** ***syn*** see APPARITION
2 ***syn*** see SHADE 1
umbrage *n* **1** ***syn*** see SHADE 1
2 ***syn*** see FOLIAGE
3 ***syn*** see OFFENSE 2
rel annoyance, irking, vexation; exasperation, irritation, nettling, provoking; fury, ire, rage, wrath
umbrage *vb* **1** ***syn*** see SHADE
2 ***syn*** see ANGER 1
umbrageous *adj* ***syn*** see SHADY 1
umbrous *adj* ***syn*** see SHADY 1
umpire *n* ***syn*** see JUDGE 1
umpire *vb* ***syn*** see JUDGE 1
unabashed *adj* ***syn*** see SHAMELESS
ant abashed
unabbreviated *adj* ***syn*** see UNABRIDGED
ant abbreviated
unabridged *adj* not shortened by omission of parts (as words) <published an *unabridged* edition of Shakespeare's plays>
syn complete, unabbreviated, uncondensed, uncut, undocked, whole-length
rel entire, intact, whole
con condensed, cropped, curtailed, cut, incompleted, shortened, trimmed
ant abridged
unacceptable *adj* ***syn*** see OBJECTIONABLE
ant acceptable
unaccompanied *adj* ***syn*** see ALONE 1
ant accompanied, companioned
unaccomplished *adj* ***syn*** see AMATEURISH
ant accomplished, skilled
unaccountable *adj* **1** ***syn*** see INEXPLICABLE
ant accountable
2 ***syn*** see MYSTERIOUS
unaccustomed *adj* ***syn*** see UNFAMILIAR 1
ant accustomed, familiar
unacquaintance *n* ***syn*** see IGNORANCE 2
ant acquaintance
unacquainted *adj* ***syn*** see IGNORANT 2
ant acquainted
unacquaintedness *n* ***syn*** see IGNORANCE 2
ant acquaintance
unacquired *adj* ***syn*** see INNATE 1
ant acquired
unadorned *adj* ***syn*** see PLAIN 1
ant adorned
unadulterated *adj* **1** ***syn*** see PURE 2
2 ***syn*** see STRAIGHT 3
ant adulterated
unadvisable *adj* ***syn*** see INADVISABLE
ant advisable
unadvised *adj* ***syn*** see RASH 1
ant advised, thought-out
unaffable *adj* ***syn*** see UNDEMONSTRATIVE
ant affable
unaffected *adj* ***syn*** see NATURAL 5
ant affected, artificial
unafraid *adj* ***syn*** see BRAVE 1
rel composed, cool, imperturbable; assured, confident, sure

---

syn synonym(s) ***rel*** related word(s)
ant antonym(s) ***con*** contrasted word(s)
idiom idiomatic equivalent(s)
|| use limited; if in doubt, see a dictionary

con apprehensive, fearful
ant afraid
unaimed *adj* ***syn*** see RANDOM
unalert *adj* ***syn*** see INCAUTIOUS 1
ant alert
unalike *adj* ***syn*** see DIFFERENT 1
ant alike
unalloyed *adj* ***syn*** see PURE 2
unalluring *adj* ***syn*** see PLAIN 5
ant alluring, attractive
unalterable *adj* ***syn*** see INFLEXIBLE 3
ant alterable
unambiguous *adj* **1** ***syn*** see CLEAR 4
ant ambiguous, obscure
2 ***syn*** see EXPLICIT
ant ambiguous
3 ***syn*** see CLEAR 5
unanimated *adj* ***syn*** see DEAD 1
unanimous *adj* being of one mind <they were *unanimous* in their determination to win>
syn consentaneous, consentient, solid
rel agreed, agreeing, concordant, concurrent, harmonious
idiom of one accord, of one (*or* the same) mind, with one voice
con differing, disagreed, disagreeing, discordant, inharmonious
unanticipatedly *adv* ***syn*** see UNAWARES
unapparent *adj* ***syn*** see IMPERCEPTIBLE
ant apparent, detectable
unappeasable *adj* **1** ***syn*** see INSATIABLE
ant appeasable
2 ***syn*** see GRIM 3
ant appeasable, placable
unappetizing *adj* ***syn*** see UNPALATABLE 1
ant appetizing
unappreciable *adj* ***syn*** see IMPERCEPTIBLE
ant appreciable
unappreciated *adj* ***syn*** see THANKLESS 2
ant appreciated
unappreciative *adj* ***syn*** see THANKLESS 1
ant appreciative
unapproachable *adj* **1** ***syn*** see INACCESSIBLE
ant approachable, attainable
2 ***syn*** see UNSOCIABLE
ant accessible, approachable
unapt *adj* **1** ***syn*** see IMPROPER 1
2 ***syn*** see UNSKILLFUL 1
ant apt
unarm *vb* ***syn*** see DISARM 2
unartful *adj* ***syn*** see NATURAL 5
ant artful
unarticulate *adj* ***syn*** see DUMB 1
ant articulate
unartificial *adj* ***syn*** see NATURAL 5
ant affected, artificial
unasked *adj* **1** not asked or invited <annoyed by his *unasked* advice>
syn unbidden, uninvited, unrequested, unsought
rel arrogant, impudent, overbearing, presumptuous; spontaneous, voluntary; unacceptable, unwanted, unwelcome
con desired, invited, sought, wanted; acceptable, welcome
ant asked
2 ***syn*** see SUPEREROGATORY
unassailable *adj* ***syn*** see INVINCIBLE 1
rel stalwart, stout, strong, sturdy, tenacious, tough
ant assailable
unassertive *adj* ***syn*** see SHY 1
ant aggressive, assertive
unassorted *adj* ***syn*** see MISCELLANEOUS
unassuming *adj* ***syn*** see HUMBLE 1
ant assuming, presumptuous
unassured *adj* **1** ***syn*** see UNSAFE
2 ***syn*** see SHY 1
ant assured
3 ***syn*** see INSECURE 1
unattainable *adj* **1** ***syn*** see INACCESSIBLE
ant attainable
2 ***syn*** see IMPOSSIBLE 1
unattractive *adj* ***syn*** see PLAIN 5
ant alluring, attractive
unauthentic *adj* ***syn*** see SPURIOUS 3
ant authentic, genuine
unavailable *adj* ***syn*** see FUTILE
unavailing *adj* ***syn*** see FUTILE
unavoidable *adj* ***syn*** see INEVITABLE
ant avoidable
unavoidably *adv* ***syn*** see WILLY-NILLY
unaware *adv* ***syn*** see UNAWARES
unaware *adj* ***syn*** see IGNORANT 2
ant aware, conscious
unawaredly *adv* ***syn*** see UNAWARES
unawareness *n* ***syn*** see IGNORANCE 2
ant awareness, consciousness
unawares *adv* without warning <caught *unawares* by company>
syn aback, short, sudden, suddenly, unanticipatedly, unaware, unawaredly, unexpectedly
rel unprepared, unready
idiom like a bolt from the blue, off base, out of a clear sky, out of the blue
unbalance *vb* ***syn*** see MADDEN 1
unbalance *n* ***syn*** see INSANITY 1
rel disorientation, instability
unbalanced *adj* **1** ***syn*** see LOPSIDED
ant balanced
2 ***syn*** see INSANE 1
unbearable *adj* ***syn*** see INSUFFERABLE
ant bearable, supportable
unbearing *adj* ***syn*** see BARREN 2
unbeatable *adj* ***syn*** see INVINCIBLE 1
ant beatable, defeatable
unbeauteous *adj* ***syn*** see PLAIN 5
ant beauteous
unbeautified *adj* ***syn*** see PLAIN 1
ant beautified, embellished
unbeautiful *adj* **1** ***syn*** see PLAIN 5
ant beautiful
2 ***syn*** see UGLY 2
ant beautiful
unbecoming *adj* **1** ***syn*** see INDECOROUS
rel awkward, clumsy, gauche, inept, maladroit
ant becoming, seemly
2 ***syn*** see IMPROPER 1
unbecomingness *n* ***syn*** see IMPROPRIETY 1

ant becomingness, seemliness
unbefitting *adj* ***syn*** see IMPROPER 1
ant apropos, befitting
unbegotten *adj* ***syn*** see SELF-EXISTENT
unbelief *n* the attitude or state of mind of one who does not believe <after so much deception, so many lies, she could offer nothing but *unbelief* to his words>
syn disbelief, incredulity, unbelievingness, unfaith
rel doubt, dubiety, dubiosity, skepticism, uncertainty; distrust, mistrust, suspicion; apprehension, misgiving, qualm
con assurance, certitude, security, trust; dependence, reliance, stock, store
ant belief
unbelievable *adj* **1** ***syn*** see INCREDIBLE 1
ant believable, credible
2 ***syn*** see IMPLAUSIBLE
ant believable, credible
unbelieve *vb* ***syn*** see DISBELIEVE
ant believe, credit
unbeliever *n* ***syn*** see SKEPTIC
ant believer
unbelieving *adj* ***syn*** see INCREDULOUS
ant believing
unbelievingness *n* ***syn*** see UNBELIEF
unbend *vb* **1** ***syn*** see RELAX 2
2 ***syn*** see REST 2
unbendable *adj* ***syn*** see INFLEXIBLE 2
ant bendable
unbending *adj* **1** ***syn*** see STIFF 1
ant bendable
2 ***syn*** see INFLEXIBLE 2
3 ***syn*** see UNSOCIABLE
unbiased *adj* ***syn*** see FAIR 4
rel aloof, uninterested
ant biased
unbidden *adj* ***syn*** see UNASKED
unbind *vb* **1** ***syn*** see LOOSE 3
ant bind
2 ***syn*** see FREE
ant bind
unblamable *adj* ***syn*** see GOOD 11
ant blamable, blameworthy
unblemished *adj* **1** ***syn*** see WHOLE 1
ant blemished, flawed
2 ***syn*** see CHASTE
unblenched *adj* ***syn*** see BRAVE 1
unblenching *adj* ***syn*** see BRAVE 1
unblock *vb* ***syn*** see OPEN 1
ant block
unblunted *adj* ***syn*** see SHARP 1
ant blunt, blunted
unblurred *adj* ***syn*** see CLEAR 4
ant blurred
unblushing *adj* ***syn*** see SHAMELESS
unbodied *adj* ***syn*** see IMMATERIAL 1
ant bodied, incarnate
unbookish *adj* ***syn*** see UNSCHOLARLY
ant bookish
unbosom *vb* ***syn*** see REVEAL 1
unbounded *adj* ***syn*** see LIMITLESS
ant bounded, limited

unbrace *vb* ***syn*** see WEAKEN 1
ant brace, reinforce
unbroken *adj* ***syn*** see WHOLE 1
ant broken
unbrookable *adj* ***syn*** see INSUFFERABLE
unbuild *vb* ***syn*** see DESTROY 1
ant build
unburden *vb* ***syn*** see RID
rel discharge, disencumber, unload
con encumber, lade, load, saddle, tax, weight
ant burden
unbury *vb* ***syn*** see EXHUME
ant bury
uncalled–for *adj* **1** ***syn*** see UNNECESSARY
ant required
2 ***syn*** see SUPEREROGATORY
3 ***syn*** see BASELESS
rel absurd, foolish, preposterous, silly; impertinent, intrusive, officious
ant well-founded
4 ***syn*** see RUDE 6
uncandid *adj* ***syn*** see DISINGENUOUS
ant candid
uncanny *adj* **1** ***syn*** see WEIRD 1
2 ***syn*** see SUPERNATURAL 2
uncared–for *adj* ***syn*** see NEGLECTED
ant cared-for
uncareful *adj* ***syn*** see IRRESPONSIBLE
ant careful
uncaring *adj* ***syn*** see CARELESS 1
ant careful
uncaused *adj* ***syn*** see SELF-EXISTENT
unceasing *adj* ***syn*** see CONTINUAL
uncelebrated *adj* ***syn*** see OBSCURE 5
ant celebrated, noted
uncelestial *adj* ***syn*** see EARTHLY 1
ant celestial
unceremonious *adj* **1** ***syn*** see INFORMAL 1
ant ceremonious
2 ***syn*** see SHORT 5
uncertain *adj* **1** not stable, consistent, or predictable <was in very *uncertain* health>
syn capricious, chancy, dicey, erratic, fluctuant, iffy, incalculable, unpredictable, whimsical; *compare* INCONSTANT 1
rel questionable, undependable, unsettled; fickle, inconstant, insecure, unstable, unsure; changeable, mutable, protean, variable; unexpectable, unforeseeable
idiom in a state of uncertainty, in suspense
2 ***syn*** see INCONSTANT 1
3 ***syn*** see MUTABLE 2
4 ***syn*** see DOUBTFUL 1
ant certain
5 ***syn*** see MOOT
ant certain
6 ***syn*** see OBSCURE 3
7 ***syn*** see VACILLATING 2
idiom at a loss

---

syn synonym(s) *rel* related word(s)
ant antonym(s) *con* contrasted word(s)
idiom idiomatic equivalent(s)
‖ use limited; if in doubt, see a dictionary

ant certain, set

uncertainty *n* a feeling of unsureness about someone or something <troubled by a growing *uncertainty* about the future>
syn concern, doubt, doubtfulness, dubiety, dubiosity, dubitancy, incertitude, mistrust, query, skepticism, suspicion, uncertitude, wonder
rel anxiety, bother, disquiet, trouble, worry; agitation, distress, perturbation, uneasiness; disfaith, distrust; hesitation, reserve, salt
con assurance, certitude, confidence, conviction; complacency, content, satisfaction
ant certainty

uncertitude *n* ***syn*** see UNCERTAINTY
ant certitude

unchain *vb* ***syn*** see FREE
ant chain

unchangeable *adj* ***syn*** see INFLEXIBLE 3
ant changeable

unchanging *adj* **1** ***syn*** see STEADY 2
2 ***syn*** see SAME 3
ant changeable, changing

uncharnel *vb* ***syn*** see EXHUME

unchaste *adj* **1** ***syn*** see IMPURE 1
ant chaste
2 ***syn*** see FAST 7
ant chaste

unchristian *adj* ***syn*** see OUTRAGEOUS 1
ant ‖Christian

uncivil *adj* **1** ***syn*** see BARBARIAN 1
2 ***syn*** see RUDE 6
rel coarse, crass, crude
con polished, smooth, urbane
ant civil

uncivilized *adj* **1** ***syn*** see BARBARIAN 1
ant civilized
2 ***syn*** see BOORISH
ant civilized
3 ***syn*** see OUTRAGEOUS 1

unclad *adj* ***syn*** see NUDE 2

unclean *adj* **1** ***syn*** see IMPURE 1
ant clean, pure
2 ***syn*** see DIRTY 1
ant clean, cleanly
3 ***syn*** see IMPURE 3
ant clean; purified

uncleanly *adj* **1** ***syn*** see IMPURE 1
ant cleanly
2 ***syn*** see DIRTY 1
ant clean, cleanly

unclear *adj* **1** ***syn*** see OBSCURE 3
ant clear
2 ***syn*** see FAINT 2
ant clear, distinct
3 ***syn*** see DOUBTFUL 1
ant clear

uncloak *vb* ***syn*** see EXPOSE 4
ant cloak

unclose *vb* **1** ***syn*** see OPEN 1
ant close
2 ***syn*** see REVEAL 1

unclosed *adj* ***syn*** see OPEN 1
ant closed

unclothe *vb* **1** ***syn*** see STRIP 1
ant clothe, dress
2 ***syn*** see OPEN 2

unclothed *adj* ***syn*** see NUDE 2
ant clothed, dressed

unclouded *adj* ***syn*** see FAIR 2
ant clouded, cloudy

uncluttered *adj* ***syn*** see NEAT 2
ant cluttered

uncolored *adj* ***syn*** see FAIR 4
ant colored, partial

uncombed *adj* ***syn*** see SLOVENLY 1

uncombine *vb* ***syn*** see SEPARATE 1
ant combine

un–come–at–able *adj* ***syn*** see INACCESSIBLE
ant come-at-able

uncomely *adj* **1** ***syn*** see IMPROPER 1
2 ***syn*** see PLAIN 5
ant comely
3 ***syn*** see UGLY 2
ant comely

uncomfortable *adj* causing or likely to cause discomfort <kept an *uncomfortable* chair for uninvited callers>
syn comfortless, discomforting, harsh, uncomforting, uncomfy
rel distressing, easeless, uneasy
con comforting, easy, soothing
ant comfortable

uncomforting *adj* ***syn*** see UNCOMFORTABLE
ant comforting

uncomfy *adj* ***syn*** see UNCOMFORTABLE
ant comfy

uncommon *adj* **1** ***syn*** see INFREQUENT
con commonplace, everyday, ordinary
ant common
2 ***syn*** see EXCEPTIONAL 1
ant common, commonplace

‖uncommon *adv* ***syn*** see EXTRA

uncommonly *adv* **1** ***syn*** see OCCASIONALLY
ant commonly
2 ***syn*** see EXTRA

uncommunicative *adj* **1** ***syn*** see SILENT 3
ant communicative
2 ***syn*** see UNSOCIABLE

uncompanionable *adj* ***syn*** see UNSOCIABLE
ant companionable

uncompassionate *adj* ***syn*** see UNFEELING 2
ant compassionate

uncompensated *adj* ***syn*** see UNPAID 1
ant compensated

uncomplainingness *n* ***syn*** see PATIENCE
ant complainingness, discontent

uncomplete *adj* ***syn*** see DEFICIENT 1
ant complete

uncompliant *adj* ***syn*** see INFLEXIBLE 2
ant compliant

uncomplimentary *adj* ***syn*** see DEROGATORY
ant complimentary

uncomprehensible *adj* ***syn*** see INCOMPREHENSIBLE 1
ant comprehensible, graspable

uncompromising *adj* **1** ***syn*** see INFLEXIBLE 2
2 ***syn*** see TOUGH 3

unconcealed *adj* ***syn*** see FRANK

unconceivable *adj* ***syn*** see IMPLAUSIBLE

ant conceivable
unconcern *n* ***syn*** see APATHY 2
ant concern
unconcerned *adj* ***syn*** see INDIFFERENT 2
rel collected, composed, cool, nonchalant
con anxious, careful, solicitous, worried
ant concerned
uncondensed *adj* ***syn*** see UNABRIDGED
ant condensed
unconfident *adj* ***syn*** see INSECURE 1
ant confident
unconfined *adj* ***syn*** see FREE 2
ant confined
uncongenial *adj* **1** ***syn*** see ANTIPATHETIC 2
rel displeasing, unattractive, unlikable, unpleasing
ant congenial
2 ***syn*** see INHARMONIOUS 2
unconnected *adj* ***syn*** see INCOHERENT 2
ant connected, ordered
unconquerable *adj* **1** ***syn*** see INVINCIBLE 1
rel insuperable, unsurmountable; proof, resistant, secure, tight
idiom more than a match for
con beatable, vincible; expugnable, pregnable, vulnerable; insecure, open, unprotected
ant conquerable
2 ***syn*** see INSUPERABLE
ant conquerable
unconscionable *adj* **1** ***syn*** see UNSCRUPULOUS
ant conscientious, conscionable
2 ***syn*** see EXCESSIVE 1
3 ***syn*** see UNREASONABLE 2
4 ***syn*** see OUTRAGEOUS 1
unconscious *adj* ***syn*** see INSENSIBLE 2
ant conscious
unconsequential *adj* ***syn*** see PETTY 2
ant consequential
unconsidered *adj* **1** ***syn*** see PETTY 2
2 ***syn*** see RANDOM
ant considered, planned
3 ***syn*** see RASH 1
ant considered
unconsolable *adj* ***syn*** see INCONSOLABLE
ant consolable
unconspicuous *adj* ***syn*** see INCONSPICUOUS
ant conspicuous
unconstrained *adj* **1** ***syn*** see EASYGOING 3
2 ***syn*** see DEMONSTRATIVE
ant constrained
unconstraint *n* freedom from constraint or pressure <had always been used to the *unconstraint* of a happy affectionate family>
syn abandon, ease, naturalness, spontaneity, unrestraint; *compare* ABANDON 2
rel impulsiveness, instinctiveness; ingenuousness, naiveté, simplicity, unsophistication
con pressure, strain, stress, tension; formality, rigidity; sophistication
ant constraint
uncontainable *adj* ***syn*** see IRREPRESSIBLE
uncontent *adj* ***syn*** see DISCONTENTED
ant content, contented
uncontented *adj* ***syn*** see DISCONTENTED
ant content, contented
uncontestable *adj* ***syn*** see POSITIVE 3
ant contestable
uncontinuous *adj* ***syn*** see INCOHERENT 2
uncontrite *adj* ***syn*** see REMORSELESS
ant contrite
uncontrollable *adj* **1** ***syn*** see UNRULY 1
ant controllable
2 ***syn*** see IRREPRESSIBLE
ant controllable
uncontrovertible *adj* ***syn*** see POSITIVE 3
ant controvertible, disputable
unconversant *adj* ***syn*** see INEXPERIENCED
ant conversant, versed
unconvincing *adj* ***syn*** see IMPLAUSIBLE
ant convincing
uncooked *adj* ***syn*** see RAW 1
ant cooked
‖**uncorporal** *adj* ***syn*** see IMMATERIAL 1
uncorrectable *adj* ***syn*** see HOPELESS 2
ant correctable
uncostly *adj* ***syn*** see CHEAP 1
ant costly
uncountable *adj* **1** ***syn*** see INNUMERABLE
ant countable
2 ***syn*** see INCALCULABLE 1
uncounted *adj* ***syn*** see INNUMERABLE
uncouple *vb* ***syn*** see DETACH
ant couple
uncourteous *adj* ***syn*** see RUDE 6
ant courteous
uncouth *adj* **1** ***syn*** see STRANGE 4
2 ***syn*** see DERELICT 1
3 ***syn*** see COARSE 3
ant couth
4 ***syn*** see RUDE 6
uncover *vb* **1** ***syn*** see REVEAL 1
2 ***syn*** see EXPOSE 1
3 ***syn*** see OPEN 2
ant cover
uncovered *adj* ***syn*** see OPEN 2
uncreate *vb* ***syn*** see ANNIHILATE 2
uncreated *adj* ***syn*** see SELF-EXISTENT
ant created
uncreative *adj* ***syn*** see UNORIGINAL
ant creative
uncritical *adj* ***syn*** see SUPERFICIAL 2
rel imprecise, inaccurate, inexact; careless, casual, offhand, perfunctory, slipshod
con accurate, exact, precise; careful; discerning, discriminating, penetrating
ant critical
uncrown *vb* ***syn*** see DEPOSE 1
ant coronate, crown
unction *n* ***syn*** see OINTMENT
unctious *adj* ***syn*** see FULSOME
unctuous *adj* **1** ***syn*** see FATTY 2
2 ***syn*** see FULSOME
uncultivated *adj* **1** ***syn*** see COARSE 3

---

syn synonym(s) ***rel*** related word(s)
ant antonym(s) ***con*** contrasted word(s)
idiom idiomatic equivalent(s)
‖ use limited; if in doubt, see a dictionary

ant cultivated
2 ***syn*** see BARBARIAN 1
ant cultivated
3 ***syn*** see WILD 1
ant cultivated
uncultured *adj* **1** ***syn*** see BOORISH
ant cultured
2 ***syn*** see COARSE 3
uncurable *adj* ***syn*** see HOPELESS 2
ant curable
uncurbed *adj* ***syn*** see AUDACIOUS 4
ant curbed
uncurious *adj* ***syn*** see INDIFFERENT 2
ant curious
uncurtain *vb* ***syn*** see REVEAL 1
uncustomary *adj* ***syn*** see EXCEPTIONAL 1
ant customary
uncut *adj* ***syn*** see UNABRIDGED
ant cut
undamaged *adj* ***syn*** see WHOLE 1
ant damaged
undaring *adj* ***syn*** see TIMID 2
ant daring
undarkened *adj* ***syn*** see FAIR 2
undauntable *adj* ***syn*** see BRAVE 1
undaunted *adj* ***syn*** see BRAVE 1
ant daunted
undear *adj* ***syn*** see CHEAP 1
ant dear
undeceive *vb* ***syn*** see DISABUSE
ant deceive
undecided *adj* **1** ***syn*** see PENDING
ant decided
2 ***syn*** see DOUBTFUL 1
undecipherable *adj* ***syn*** see ILLEGIBLE
ant decipherable
undecisive *adj* ***syn*** see VACILLATING 2
ant decisive
undeclared *adj* ***syn*** see TACIT 1
undecorated *adj* ***syn*** see PLAIN 1
ant decorated
undecorous *adj* ***syn*** see INDECOROUS
ant decorous
undefeatable *adj* ***syn*** see INVINCIBLE 1
ant defeatable
undefiled *adj* ***syn*** see CHASTE
undefined *adj* ***syn*** see FAINT 2
ant defined
undeflowered *adj* ***syn*** see VIRGIN 1
ant deflowered
undelude *vb* ***syn*** see DISABUSE
ant delude
undemonstrated *adj* ***syn*** see UNTRIED 1
ant demonstrated
undemonstrative *adj* not socially outgoing <a shy *undemonstrative* person yet capable of deep feeling>
syn aseptic, restrained, retiring, shrinking, unaffable, unexpansive, withdrawn; *compare* UNSOCIABLE
rel chill, cold, frigid, glacial, icy; emotionless, indifferent, unemotional, uninterested; aloof, distant, reserved, standoffish
con free and easy, hail-fellow-well-met, outgiving, outgoing, palsy-walsy; sociable
ant demonstrative
undeniable *adj* **1** ***syn*** see POSITIVE 3
ant deniable
2 ***syn*** see REAL 3
undenominational *adj* ***syn*** see NONSECTARIAN
ant denominational
undependable *adj* **1** ***syn*** see UNRELIABLE 1
ant dependable
2 ***syn*** see UNSAFE
ant dependable
3 ***syn*** see TRICK
ant dependable
under *adv* ***syn*** see BELOW 1
ant above, over
under *prep* ***syn*** see BELOW 1
ant over
under *adj* **1** ***syn*** see INFERIOR 1
2 ***syn*** see SUBORDINATE
underage *n* ***syn*** see FAILURE 3
ant overage
underconsciousness *n* ***syn*** see SUBCONSCIOUS
undercover *adj* ***syn*** see SECRET 1
undercover man *n* ***syn*** see SPY
undercroft *n* ***syn*** see CRYPT
underdeveloped *adj* ***syn*** see BACKWARD 6
underdog *n* ***syn*** see VICTIM 2
ant overdog, top dog
underearth *adj* ***syn*** see SUBTERRANEAN
underfoot *adj* **1** ***syn*** see SUBTERRANEAN
2 ***syn*** see DOWNTRODDEN
undergo *vb* ***syn*** see EXPERIENCE 1
rel abide, bear, endure, tolerate; bow, defer, submit, yield
underground *adj* ***syn*** see SUBTERRANEAN
underhand *adj* characterized by sly unobtrusive craft or deceit <ready to use the most *underhand* methods to gain his ends>
syn devious, duplicitous, guileful, indirect, shifty, sneaking, sneaky, underhanded; *compare* SECRET 1, SLY 2
rel deceitful, dishonest; crooked, oblique; crafty, cunning, insidious, sly, tricky, wily; furtive, hangdog
con candid, frank, open, plain; forthright, straightforward
ant aboveboard
underhanded *adj* **1** ***syn*** see UNDERHAND
ant aboveboard
2 ***syn*** see SHORTHANDED
underivative *adj* ***syn*** see PRIMARY 5
ant derivative
underived *adj* ***syn*** see PRIMARY 5
ant derived
underlease *vb* ***syn*** see SUBLET
underlet *vb* ***syn*** see SUBLET
underline *vb* ***syn*** see EMPHASIZE
underline *n* ***syn*** see CAPTION
underling *n* ***syn*** see INFERIOR
underlying *adj* **1** ***syn*** see FUNDAMENTAL 1
rel cardinal, essential, vital; critical, crucial; indispensable, necessary, needful
2 ***syn*** see ELEMENTAL 1
undermanned *adj* ***syn*** see SHORTHANDED
ant overmanned

undermine *vb* **1** ***syn*** see WEAKEN 1
rel ruin, wreck; foil, frustrate, thwart
idiom bore from within
ant reinforce
2 ***syn*** see SABOTAGE
undermining *n* ***syn*** see SABOTAGE
undermost *adj* ***syn*** see BOTTOMMOST
ant uppermost
underneath *prep* ***syn*** see BELOW 1
underneath *adv* ***syn*** see BELOW 1
‖**underneath** *adj* ***syn*** see SECRET 1
underneath *n* ***syn*** see BOTTOM 1
underpinner *n* ***syn*** see SUPPORT 3
underpinning *n* **1** ***syn*** see BASIS 1
2 ***syn*** see BASE 1
3 ***syn*** see SUPPORT 3
underprivileged *adj* deficient in basic economic and social resources <the role of the school in bettering the lot of *underprivileged* children>
syn depressed, deprived, disadvantaged
rel handicapped; hapless, ill-fated, ill-starred, unfortunate, unlucky; impoverished, needy, poor
idiom badly off, in adverse circumstances, out of luck
con advantaged, fortunate, privileged; coddled, indulged, spoiled
underprize *vb* ***syn*** see DEPRECIATE 1
ant overprize
underprop *vb* ***syn*** see SUPPORT 5
underpropping *n* ***syn*** see SUPPORT 3
underrate *vb* ***syn*** see DEPRECIATE 1
ant overrate
underscore *vb* ***syn*** see EMPHASIZE
undersense *n* ***syn*** see SUBCONSCIOUS
undersexed *adj* ***syn*** see FRIGID 3
ant oversexed
underside *n* ***syn*** see BOTTOM 1
understaffed *adj* ***syn*** see SHORTHANDED
ant overstaffed
understand *vb* **1** ***syn*** see APPREHEND 1
idiom get the drift
ant misunderstand
2 ***syn*** see KNOW 1
idiom get the hang of
3 to view as plausible or likely <I *understand* he is expected home soon>
syn assume, believe, ‖conceit, conceive, expect, gather, imagine, ‖reckon, suppose, suspect, take, think, ‖wit; *compare* CONJECTURE
rel conclude, deduce, infer; conjecture, guess, presume, surmise; fancy; consider
con know; challenge, doubt, question
understandable *adj* of a kind to be readily understood <her style was smooth and easy, her language *understandable*>
syn apprehensible, comprehendible, comprehensible, fathomable, graspable, intelligible, knowable, lucid, luminous; *compare* CLEAR 4, 5
rel clear-cut, unambiguous, unblurred; plain, simple, straightforward; exoteric, lay, popular
con mysterious, obscure, strange, vague; cryptic, esoteric, hidden
understanding *n* **1** ***syn*** see REASON 5
rel discernment, discrimination, insight, penetration; awareness, intuition; apprehension, comprehension, grasp
2 ***syn*** see AGREEMENT 2
3 ***syn*** see MEANING 1
understood *adj* ***syn*** see TACIT 1
understrapper *n* ***syn*** see INFERIOR
understructure *n* ***syn*** see BASE 1
ant superstructure
undersurface *n* ***syn*** see BOTTOM 1
undertake *vb* **1** ***syn*** see TRY 5
rel begin, commence, start
idiom put (*or* set) one's hand to
2 ***syn*** see TAKE ON 3
3 ***syn*** see PROMISE 1
rel certify, warrant
idiom stand back of (*or* behind)
undertaker *n* **1** ***syn*** see ENTREPRENEUR 1
2 ***syn*** see MORTICIAN
undertaking *n* **1** ***syn*** see ATTEMPT
2 ***syn*** see PROJECT 2
under–the–table *adj* ***syn*** see SECRET 1
ant aboveboard
undertone *n* **1** ***syn*** see MURMUR 1
2 ***syn*** see ASSOCIATION 4
undervalue *vb* ***syn*** see DEPRECIATE 1
ant overvalue
underwater *adj* ***syn*** see SUBMARINE
underwit *n* ***syn*** see FOOL 4
underworld *n* ***syn*** see HELL
undescribable *adj* ***syn*** see UNUTTERABLE
ant describable
undesignated *adj* ***syn*** see ANONYMOUS
undesigned *adj* ***syn*** see UNINTENTIONAL
ant designed
undesigning *adj* ***syn*** see GENUINE 3
ant designing
undesirable *adj* ***syn*** see OBJECTIONABLE
ant desirable
undesired *adj* ***syn*** see UNWELCOME 1
ant desired
undestroyable *adj* ***syn*** see INDESTRUCTIBLE
ant destroyable, destructible
undeterminable *adj* ***syn*** see INDEFINITE 1
ant determinable
undetermined *adj* **1** ***syn*** see PENDING
ant determined
2 ***syn*** see FAINT 2
undeveloped *adj* **1** ***syn*** see BACKWARD 6
ant developed
2 ***syn*** see PRIMITIVE 3
ant advanced
undeviatingly *adv* ***syn*** see DIRECTLY 1
undevised *adj* ***syn*** see UNINTENTIONAL
ant devised
undexterous *adj* ***syn*** see UNSKILLFUL 1
ant dexterous
undifferenced *adj* ***syn*** see LIKE
undifferentiated *adj* ***syn*** see LIKE

---

syn synonym(s) ***rel*** related word(s)
ant antonym(s) ***con*** contrasted word(s)
idiom idiomatic equivalent(s)
‖ use limited; if in doubt, see a dictionary

ant differentiated
undiluted *adj* **1** ***syn*** see STRAIGHT 3
ant diluted
2 ***syn*** see PURE 2
undiplomatic *adj* ***syn*** see TACTLESS
ant diplomatic
undiscernible *adj* ***syn*** see IMPERCEPTIBLE
ant discernible
undisciplinable *adj* ***syn*** see UNRULY 1
undisciplined *adj* ***syn*** see UNRULY 1
ant disciplined
undiscriminated *adj* ***syn*** see INDISCRIMINATE 1
ant discriminate, discriminated
undiscriminating *adj* ***syn*** see INDISCRIMINATE 1
undisguised *adj* ***syn*** see FRANK
undisputable *adj* ***syn*** see POSITIVE 3
ant controvertible, disputable
undissembled *adj* **1** ***syn*** see GENUINE 3
ant dissembled, feigned
2 ***syn*** see FRANK
undissembling *adj* ***syn*** see FRANK
ant dissembling
undistinct *adj* ***syn*** see FAINT 2
ant clear, distinct
undistinctive *adj* ***syn*** see FAIR 4
undistinguishing *adj* ***syn*** see INDISCRIMINATE 1
undistorted *adj* ***syn*** see TRUE 3
ant distorted
undistracted *adj* ***syn*** see WHOLE 5
undivided *adj* ***syn*** see WHOLE 5
ant divided
undo *vb* **1** ***syn*** see LOOSE 3
2 ***syn*** see OPEN 1
rel loose, untie
3 ***syn*** see ABOLISH 1
4 ***syn*** see DESTROY 1
5 ***syn*** see OUTWIT
idiom bring down (*or* low), bring to naught
6 ***syn*** see SEDUCE 2
undocked *adj* ***syn*** see UNABRIDGED
ant docked
undoing *n* ***syn*** see DOWNFALL 2
undomesticated *adj* ***syn*** see WILD 1
ant domesticated
undoubtable *adj* ***syn*** see POSITIVE 3
ant doubtable, questionable
undoubted *adj* ***syn*** see AUTHENTIC 2
ant doubtful, questionable
undoubtedly *adv* ***syn*** see WELL 7
undoubtful *adj* ***syn*** see CONFIDENT 1
ant doubtful
undress *vb* **1** ***syn*** see STRIP 1
ant dress
2 ***syn*** see EXPOSE 4
ant dress up
undressed *adj* **1** ***syn*** see NUDE 2
ant dressed
2 ***syn*** see RUDE 1
ant dressed, finished
undubitable *adj* ***syn*** see AUTHENTIC 2
ant dubitable
undue *adj* **1** ***syn*** see IMPROPER 1
2 ***syn*** see EXCESSIVE 1
3 ***syn*** see UNREASONABLE 2

undulate *vb* ***syn*** see SLITHER 2
unduly *adv* ***syn*** see EVER 6
ant duly
unduteous *adj* ***syn*** see IMPIOUS 2
ant duteous
undutiful *adj* ***syn*** see IMPIOUS 2
ant dutiful
undying *adj* ***syn*** see IMMORTAL 1
rel continuing, persistent; interminable, unceasing; inextinguishable, unquenchable
ant mortal
uneager *adj* ***syn*** see DISINCLINED
ant eager
unearth *vb* ***syn*** see DISCOVER 3
rel exhibit, expose, show; disclose, reveal; delve, dig
unearthing *n* ***syn*** see DISCOVERY
unearthly *adj* **1** ***syn*** see SUPERNATURAL 1
2 ***syn*** see WEIRD 1
3 ***syn*** see FOOLISH 2
unease *n* **1** ***syn*** see CARE 2
2 ***syn*** see TENSION 2
3 ***syn*** see EMBARRASSMENT
ant ease, easiness
uneasiness *n* **1** ***syn*** see CARE 2
2 ***syn*** see EMBARRASSMENT
ant ease, easiness
uneasy *adj* **1** ***syn*** see TENSE 2
rel anxious, careful, concerned, solicitous, worried; agitated, disquieted, disturbed, perturbed
idiom on pins and needles
ant easy
2 ***syn*** see RESTLESS
3 ***syn*** see DOUBTFUL 1
uneatable *adj* ***syn*** see INEDIBLE
ant eatable
uneducated *adj* ***syn*** see IGNORANT 1
ant educated, lettered
unelaborate *adj* ***syn*** see PLAIN 1
ant elaborate
unembellished *adj* ***syn*** see PLAIN 1
ant embellished
unembodied *adj* ***syn*** see IMMATERIAL 1
unembroidered *adj* ***syn*** see PLAIN 1
unemotional *adj* **1** ***syn*** see COLD 2
rel dispassionate; unfeeling; impassive
con affective, feeling; affectionate, demonstrative
ant emotional
2 ***syn*** see UNFEELING 2
unemphatic *adj* ***syn*** see INCONSPICUOUS
unemployed *adj* lacking a gainful occupation <the problems of *unemployed* workers>
syn jobless, workless
rel free, unengaged, unoccupied; underemployed; fired, laid off
idiom at liberty, let go, on layoff, out of work
ant employed
unending *adj* **1** ***syn*** see EVERLASTING 1
2 ***syn*** see CONTINUAL
unendurable *adj* ***syn*** see INSUFFERABLE
ant endurable
unenlarged *adj* ***syn*** see ILLIBERAL
unenlightened *adj* ***syn*** see BACKWARD 5

ant enlightened
unennobled *adj syn* see IGNOBLE 1
ant ennobled, noble
unentangle *vb syn* see EXTRICATE 2
ant entangle
unenthusiastic *adj syn* see TEPID 2
ant enthusiastic
unequal *adj* **1** *syn* see DIFFERENT 1
2 *syn* see LOPSIDED
unequalable *adj syn* see SUPREME
unequaled *adj syn* see ALONE 3
ant equaled
unequipped *adj syn* see UNFIT 2
unequitable *adj syn* see INEQUITABLE
ant equitable
unequivocal *adj* **1** *syn* see CLEAR 5
ant equivocal
2 *syn* see POSITIVE 1
ant equivocal
3 *syn* see POSITIVE 3
unequivocally *adv syn* see EASILY 2
uneradicable *adj syn* see INDELIBLE
ant eradicable
unerasable *adj syn* see INDELIBLE
ant erasable
unerring *adj syn* see INFALLIBLE 1
unescapable *adj syn* see INEVITABLE
ant escapable
unessential *adj* **1** *syn* see UNNECESSARY
ant essential
2 *syn* see DISPENSABLE
ant essential
unethical *adj syn* see CORRUPT 2
ant ethical
unevadable *adj syn* see INEVITABLE
ant evadable
uneven *adj* **1** *syn* see ROUGH 1
ant even
2 *syn* see LOPSIDED
ant even
3 *syn* see SPOTTY 1
rel differing, disparate, unequal; discrepant, inconsistent
con consistent, equal, regular
unevenness *n* **1** *syn* see DISPARITY
2 *syn* see INEQUALITY 1
uneventful *adj syn* see COMMON 6
ant eventful
unevolved *adj syn* see PRIMITIVE 3
ant advanced, evolved
unexaminable *adj syn* see MYSTERIOUS
unexampled *adj syn* see ONLY 2
unexceptionable *adj syn* see DECENT 4
ant exceptionable
unexceptional *adj* **1** *syn* see DECENT 4
2 *syn* see COMMON 6
ant exceptional
unexcessive *adj syn* see CONSERVATIVE 2
ant excessive
unexpansive *adj syn* see UNDEMONSTRATIVE
ant expansive
unexpectedly *adv syn* see UNAWARES
unexpedient *adj syn* see INADVISABLE
ant expedient
unexperienced *adj syn* see INEXPERIENCED
ant experienced
unexpert *adj syn* see INEFFICIENT 2
ant expert
unexplainable *adj syn* see INEXPLICABLE
ant explainable, explicable
unexplicit *adj syn* see OBSCURE 3
ant explicit
unexpressed *adj* **1** *syn* see UNSPOKEN 1
ant expressed
2 *syn* see TACIT 1
ant expressed
unexpressible *adj syn* see UNUTTERABLE
ant expressible
unexpressive *adj syn* see EXPRESSIONLESS
ant expressive
unextreme *adj syn* see CONSERVATIVE 2
unfabled *adj syn* see REAL 3
ant fabled
unfacile *adj syn* see UNSKILLFUL 1
unfailing *adj* **1** *syn* see SAME 3
2 *syn* see INFALLIBLE 2
ant fallible
unfair *adj syn* see INEQUITABLE
ant fair
unfairness *n syn* see INJUSTICE 1
ant fairness
unfaith *n syn* see UNBELIEF
ant faith
unfaithful *adj syn* see FAITHLESS
ant faithful
unfaithfulness *n syn* see INFIDELITY
ant faithfulness
unfaltering *adj syn* see SURE 2
unfamed *adj syn* see OBSCURE 5
ant famed
unfamiliar *adj* **1** not well known <trying to find her way about the *unfamiliar* room in the dark>
syn new, strange, unaccustomed
rel exotic, foreign; curious, peculiar, remarkable; unknown
con accustomed, commonplace, customary, ordinary, usual, wonted
ant familiar
2 *syn* see IGNORANT 2
ant familiar
unfamiliarity *n syn* see IGNORANCE 2
unfantastic *adj syn* see REALISTIC
ant fantastic
unfashioned *adj syn* see RUDE 1
unfasten *vb syn* see LOOSE 3
ant fasten
unfastidious *adj syn* see SLOVENLY 1
ant fastidious
unfathered *adj syn* see ILLEGITIMATE 1
unfathomable *adj* **1** *syn* see BOTTOMLESS 2
ant fathomable
2 *syn* see INCOMPREHENSIBLE 1
ant fathomable

---

syn synonym(s) *rel* related word(s)
ant antonym(s) *con* contrasted word(s)
idiom idiomatic equivalent(s)
‖ use limited; if in doubt, see a dictionary

THESAURUS

unfathomed *adj* ***syn*** see HUGE
unfavorable *adj* **1** ***syn*** see ADVERSE 2
ant favorable
2 ***syn*** see EVIL 5
unfavorably *adv* ***syn*** see AMISS 2
unfearful *adj* ***syn*** see BRAVE 1
ant fearful
unfearing *adj* ***syn*** see BRAVE 1
ant fearing
unfeasible *adj* ***syn*** see IMPOSSIBLE 1
ant feasible, practicable
unfeeling *adj* **1** ***syn*** see INSENSATE 1
ant feeling
2 lacking in normal human sympathy <an *unfeeling* response to a plea for help>
syn callous, cold-blooded, coldhearted, compassionless, hard-boiled, hardened, hardhearted, heartless, ironhearted, marblehearted, obdurate, stony, stonyhearted, uncompassionate, unemotional, unsympathetic; *compare* PITILESS
rel brutal, cruel, indurated, merciless, roughhearted, ruthless, tough; exacting, severe; unamiable, uncordial, unkind; cantankerous, churlish, crotchety, curmudgeonly, surly
idiom hard of heart
con considerate, gentle, thoughtful; kind, merciful; compassionate, sympathetic, warmhearted
ant feeling
3 ***syn*** see NUMB 1
unfeigned *adj* **1** ***syn*** see SINCERE 1
ant feigned
2 ***syn*** see GENUINE 3
ant dissembled, feigned
unfertile *adj* ***syn*** see BARREN 2
ant fertile
unfinished *adj* **1** ***syn*** see RUDE 1
ant dressed, finished
2 ***syn*** see AMATEURISH
ant finished
unfit *adj* **1** not adapted or appropriate to a particular end <land *unfit* for farming>
syn ill-adapted, ill-suited, inappropriate, inapt, unfitted, unmeet, unsuitable, unsuited
rel discordant, inharmonious; improper, infelicitous, unbecoming; incompatible, incongruous, uncongenial
idiom out of drawing, out of one's element, out of place
con adapted, appropriate, apt, suitable, suited; congruous, harmonious
ant fit
2 lacking essential qualifications <politicians *unfit* to govern>
syn disqualified, incapable, incompetent, ineligible, unequipped, unfitted, unqualified
rel awkward, blundering, bungling; butterfingered, heavy-handed, maladjusted, maladroit, unhandy; inefficient, inexpert, unproficient, unskillful
con capable, competent, qualified; adroit, dexterous, handy; expert, skilled
unfitted *adj* **1** ***syn*** see UNFIT 1
2 ***syn*** see UNFIT 2
ant fitted
unfitting *adj* ***syn*** see IMPROPER 1
ant fitting
unfix *vb* **1** ***syn*** see LOOSE 3
ant fix
2 ***syn*** see DETACH
unfixedness *n* ***syn*** see INSTABILITY
unflagging *adj* ***syn*** see INDEFATIGABLE
rel constant, steady
ant flagging
unflappable *adj* ***syn*** see COOL 2
rel easy, relaxed
unflawed *adj* ***syn*** see PERFECT 2
ant flawed
unfledged *adj* ***syn*** see YOUNG 1
ant fledged
unfleshed *adj* ***syn*** see INEXPERIENCED
unfleshly *adj* ***syn*** see IMMATERIAL 1
ant fleshly
unflexible *adj* ***syn*** see STIFF 1
ant flexible
unflinching *adj* ***syn*** see GRIM 3
unfluctuating *adj* ***syn*** see STEADY 2
ant fluctuant, fluctuating
unfold *vb* **1** ***syn*** see OPEN 4
ant fold
2 ***syn*** see SOLVE 2
3 to disclose by degrees to the sight or understanding <shyly she *unfolded* her hopes for the future>
syn develop, elaborate, evolve
rel demonstrate, evidence, evince, manifest, show; disclose, display, exhibit, expose, reveal
unfolding *n* ***syn*** see DEVELOPMENT
unforbearing *adj* ***syn*** see INTOLERANT 1
ant forbearing
unforced *adj* ***syn*** see VOLUNTARY
ant forced
unforgivable *adj* ***syn*** see INEXCUSABLE
ant forgivable
unformed *adj* **1** ***syn*** see FORMLESS
rel unfinished
ant formed
2 ***syn*** see RUDE 1
unfortunate *adj* **1** ***syn*** see UNLUCKY
rel infelicitous; deplorable, miserable, sad, wretched; malefic
con auspicious, favorable, propitious
ant fortunate
2 ***syn*** see INFELICITOUS
3 ***syn*** see DEPLORABLE
unfounded *adj* ***syn*** see BASELESS
rel deceptive, misleading; dishonest, mendacious, untruthful
ant well-founded
unframe *vb* ***syn*** see DESTROY 1
unfrank *adj* ***syn*** see DISINGENUOUS
ant frank
unfrequent *adj* ***syn*** see INFREQUENT
ant frequent
unfrequently *adv* ***syn*** see SELDOM
ant frequently
unfriendly *adj* ***syn*** see HOSTILE 1
ant friendly
unfruitful *adj* ***syn*** see STERILE 1

con fecund, fertile
ant fruitful, prolific
unfunctional *adj* ***syn*** see IMPRACTICABLE 2
ant functional
unfussy *adj* ***syn*** see EASYGOING 3
ant fussy
ungainly *adj* ***syn*** see CLUMSY 1
rel blundering, lubberly, maladroit
con graceful, supple, willowy; gainly
ungarnished *adj* ***syn*** see PLAIN 1
ant garnished
ungenerous *adj* **1** ***syn*** see PETTY 2
ant generous
2 ***syn*** see STINGY
ant generous
ungenial *adj* ***syn*** see ANTIPATHETIC 2
ant genial
ungenuine *adj* ***syn*** see SPURIOUS 3
ant genuine
ungetatable *adj* ***syn*** see INACCESSIBLE
ant getatable
ungifted *adj* ***syn*** see AMATEURISH
ant gifted
ungiving *adj* ***syn*** see STINGY
ungodly *adj* **1** ***syn*** see IMPIOUS 1
ant godly
2 ***syn*** see INDECOROUS
3 ***syn*** see OUTRAGEOUS 1
ungovernable *adj* ***syn*** see UNRULY 1
ant governable
ungoverned *adj* ***syn*** see AUDACIOUS 4
ungracious *adj* **1** ***syn*** see RUDE 6
ant gracious
2 ***syn*** see SHORT 5
ant gracious
ungraded *adj* ***syn*** see UNREFINED 3
ungraspable *adj* ***syn*** see INCOMPREHENSIBLE 1
ant comprehensible, graspable
ungrateful *adj* **1** ***syn*** see THANKLESS 1
ant grateful
2 ***syn*** see THANKLESS 2
3 ***syn*** see OFFENSIVE
ungratified *adj* ***syn*** see DISCONTENTED
ant gratified
ungrounded *adj* ***syn*** see BASELESS
unguarded *adj* ***syn*** see INCAUTIOUS 1
ant guarded
unguent *n* ***syn*** see OINTMENT
unguessed *adj* ***syn*** see MYSTERIOUS
unguilty *adj* ***syn*** see INNOCENT 2
ant guilty
unhallowed *adj* **1** ***syn*** see IMPIOUS 1
2 ***syn*** see FIENDISH
unhampered *adj* ***syn*** see AUDACIOUS 4
ant hampered
unhandsome *adj* **1** ***syn*** see PLAIN 5
ant handsome
2 ***syn*** see RUDE 6
unhandy *adj* **1** ***syn*** see UNWIELDY
2 ***syn*** see UNSKILLFUL 1
ant handy
3 ***syn*** see AWKWARD 2
ant handy
unhappiness *n* **1** ***syn*** see MISERY 1
ant happiness
2 ***syn*** see SADNESS
ant happiness
unhappy *adj* **1** ***syn*** see UNLUCKY
ant happy
2 ***syn*** see INFELICITOUS
ant happy
3 ***syn*** see AWKWARD 2
4 ***syn*** see SAD 1
ant happy
5 ***syn*** see BAD 8
6 ***syn*** see GLOOMY 3
unharmed *adj* ***syn*** see SAFE 1
unharmonious *adj* **1** ***syn*** see DISSONANT 1
ant harmonious
2 ***syn*** see INHARMONIOUS 2
ant harmonious
unhasty *adj* ***syn*** see SLOW 2
ant hasty
unhealth *n* ***syn*** see SICKNESS 1
ant health
unhealthful *adj* ***syn*** see UNWHOLESOME 1
ant healthful
unhealthiness *n* ***syn*** see INFIRMITY 1
ant healthiness
unhealthy *adj* **1** ***syn*** see UNWHOLESOME 1
ant healthy
2 ***syn*** see DANGEROUS 1
3 ***syn*** see VICIOUS 2
unheard–of *adj* ***syn*** see OBSCURE 5
unheavy *adj* ***syn*** see LIGHT 1
ant heavy
unheeding *adj* **1** ***syn*** see INATTENTIVE
ant heedful, heeding
2 ***syn*** see CARELESS 1
ant heedful, heeding
unhewn *adj* ***syn*** see RUDE 1
unhinge *vb* **1** ***syn*** see UPSET 5
2 ***syn*** see MADDEN 1
3 ***syn*** see DISCOMPOSE 1
unholy *adj* **1** ***syn*** see IMPIOUS 1
ant holy
2 ***syn*** see BLAMEWORTHY
3 ***syn*** see OUTRAGEOUS 1
unhonest *adj* ***syn*** see DISHONEST
ant honest
unhorse *vb* **1** ***syn*** see THROW 2
2 ***syn*** see OVERTHROW 2
unhurried *adj* ***syn*** see SLOW 2
ant hurried
unhurt *adj* ***syn*** see WHOLE 1
unicity *n* ***syn*** see UNIQUENESS
unidealistic *adj* ***syn*** see REALISTIC
ant idealistic
unification *n* a bringing together or being brought together into an integrated whole <*unification* of mass transit facilities is increasingly needed>

---

syn synonym(s) ***rel*** related word(s)
ant antonym(s) ***con*** contrasted word(s)
idiom idiomatic equivalent(s)
‖ use limited; if in doubt, see a dictionary

THESAURUS

syn coadunation, coalition, combination, consolidation, melding, mergence, merger, merging, union; *compare* ALLIANCE 2
rel affiliation, connection, interlocking, joining, linkage; coupling, hookup
con dissociation, disunion, division, parting, partition, separation
ant disunification

uniform *adj* **1** ***syn*** see LIKE
ant various
2 ***syn*** see STEADY 2
rel compatible, consistent, consonant; ordered, orderly, regular
ant multiform

uniformly *adv* ***syn*** see EVENLY 3
ant variably

unify *vb* **1** to gather or combine parts or elements into a close mass or a coherent whole <minorities that are *unified* by persecution>
syn compact, concentrate, consolidate, integrate; *compare* UNITE 2
rel articulate, concatenate; order, organize, systematize; bind, tie
idiom make one
con divide, part, scatter; disorder, disorganize; disunite, divide, separate
ant break up, disunify
2 ***syn*** see HARMONIZE 4
ant disunify

unifying *adj* ***syn*** see INTEGRATIVE
ant disunifying

unilluminated *adj* ***syn*** see DARK 1
ant illuminated

unimaginable *adj* **1** ***syn*** see INCONCEIVABLE 1
ant imaginable
2 ***syn*** see EXCEPTIONAL 1
3 ***syn*** see INCREDIBLE 1

unimpaired *adj* ***syn*** see WHOLE 1
ant impaired

unimpassioned *adj* **1** ***syn*** see MATTER-OF-FACT 3
ant impassioned
2 ***syn*** see SOBER 3
rel impassive, phlegmatic, stoic, stolid; calm, placid, tranquil
con ardent, fervent, fervid, heated, keen
ant impassioned, passionate

unimpeachable *adj* ***syn*** see DECENT 4

unimportant *adj* ***syn*** see LITTLE 3
ant important

unimpressible *adj* ***syn*** see INSUSCEPTIBLE
ant impressible

unimpressionable *adj* ***syn*** see INSUSCEPTIBLE
ant impressionable

unindifferent *adj* ***syn*** see BIASED 2
ant indifferent

unindulgent *adj* ***syn*** see INTOLERANT 1
ant indulgent

uninflammable *adj* ***syn*** see NONCOMBUSTIBLE
ant flammable, inflammable

uninformed *adj* ***syn*** see IGNORANT 2
ant informed

uninhibited *adj* ***syn*** see AUDACIOUS 4
ant inhibited

uninhibitedness *n* ***syn*** see ABANDON 2

uninitiate *n* ***syn*** see AMATEUR 2

uninjured *adj* ***syn*** see WHOLE 1
ant injured

uninjurious *adj* ***syn*** see SAFE 3

uninspired *adj* **1** ***syn*** see UNORIGINAL
ant inspired
2 ***syn*** see PONDEROUS 2
ant inspired

uninstructed *adj* **1** ***syn*** see IGNORANT 2
2 ***syn*** see IGNORANT 1

unintelligent *adj* ***syn*** see SIMPLE 3
ant intelligent

unintelligible *adj* **1** ***syn*** see INCOMPREHENSIBLE 1
ant intelligible
2 ***syn*** see OBSCURE 3
ant intelligible

unintended *adj* ***syn*** see UNINTENTIONAL
ant intended

unintentional *adj* not the result of intent or design <her slight of the newcomer was quite *unintentional*>
syn inadvertent, undesigned, undevised, unintended, unplanned, unpremeditated, unpurposed, unthought; *compare* ACCIDENTAL, EXTEMPORANEOUS
rel causeless, chance, haphazard, purposeless, random; unanticipated, unexpected, unforeseen, unlooked-for; unthinking, unwitting
con deliberate, designed, devised, intended, planned, premeditated, purposed
ant intentional

uninterested *adj* ***syn*** see INDIFFERENT 2
ant interested

uninteresting *adj* ***syn*** see ARID 2
ant interesting

unintermitted *adj* ***syn*** see CONTINUAL
ant intermitted, intermittent

unintermittedly *adv* ***syn*** see TOGETHER 2

unintermittent *adj* ***syn*** see CONTINUAL
ant intermitted, intermittent

uninterrupted *adj* **1** ***syn*** see CONTINUAL
ant interrupted
2 ***syn*** see DIRECT 2

uninterruptedly *adv* ***syn*** see TOGETHER 2
ant interruptedly

uninventive *adj* ***syn*** see UNORIGINAL
ant inventive

uninvited *adj* ***syn*** see UNASKED
ant invited

union *n* **1** ***syn*** see UNIFICATION
ant disunion
2 ***syn*** see ASSOCIATION 2
3 ***syn*** see JOINT 1
4 ***syn*** see ALLIANCE 2

unique *adj* **1** ***syn*** see ONLY 2
2 ***syn*** see SINGLE 2
3 ***syn*** see ALONE 3
4 ***syn*** see EXCEPTIONAL 1

uniqueness *n* the quality or state of standing alone and without a peer <the time she rode in an old-time sleigh — never would she forget the *uniqueness* of that experience>
syn oneness, singleness, unicity, uniquity
rel curiousness, oddity, peculiarity, quaintness, singularity, strangeness; import, mark, moment,

note, significance; memorability, notability, remarkableness, unusualness
con commonness, commonplaceness, ordinariness, routineness; monotony, sameness, tediousness

uniquity *n* ***syn*** see UNIQUENESS

unite *vb* **1** ***syn*** see JOIN 1
rel amalgamate, blend, merge, mix
ant alienate; disunite, divide
2 to join forces especially in order to act more effectively <citizen groups *uniting* to further the fight against crime>
syn band, coadjute, combine, concur, conjoin, cooperate, league; *compare* UNIFY 1
rel affiliate, ally, associate, confederate; coalesce, commingle, fuse, mingle, weld
idiom draw together, hook up with, join forces (with), make common cause (with), throw in with
con break up, disband, separate, split (up)
ant disunite, part

unity *n* **1** the condition of being or consisting of one <*unity* — the idea conveyed by whatever we visualize as one thing>
syn individuality, oneness, singleness, singularity, singularness
rel identity, selfsameness, soleness, uniqueness, uniquity
ant multiplicity
2 ***syn*** see HARMONY 3
rel agreement, identity, oneness, union; solidarity; conformance, congruity
ant disunity

universal *adj* **1** ***syn*** see OMNIPRESENT
2 present or significant throughout the world <*universal* aspirations for a better world>
syn catholic, cosmic, cosmopolitan, ecumenical, global, planetary, worldwide
rel all-embracing, all-inclusive; broad, extensive, sweeping; all, entire, total, whole
con narrow, petty, provincial
ant parochial
3 ***syn*** see GENERAL 2
ant particular

universe *n* the totality of physical entities <theories of the expanding *universe*>
syn cosmos (*or* kosmos), creation, macrocosm, macrocosmos, megacosm, nature, world

univocal *adj* ***syn*** see CLEAR 5
ant ambiguous

unjust *adj* ***syn*** see INEQUITABLE
ant just

unjustifiable *adj* **1** ***syn*** see UNREASONABLE 2
ant justifiable
2 ***syn*** see INEXCUSABLE
ant justifiable

unjustness *n* ***syn*** see INJUSTICE 1
ant justice, justness

unkempt *adj* ***syn*** see SLOVENLY 1
ant kempt

unknow *vb* ***syn*** see FORGET 1

unknowable *adj* **1** ***syn*** see INCOMPREHENSIBLE 1
ant knowable
2 ***syn*** see INCONCEIVABLE 1
ant knowable
3 ***syn*** see MYSTERIOUS

unknowing *adj* ***syn*** see IGNORANT 2
ant knowing

unknowingness *n* ***syn*** see IGNORANCE 2
ant knowingness

unknown *adj* ***syn*** see OBSCURE 5
ant well-known

unlade *vb* ***syn*** see UNLOAD
ant lade, load

unlawful *adj* contrary to or prohibited by law <the spread of *unlawful* wiretapping>
syn criminal, illegal, illegitimate, illicit, lawless, wrongful
rel flagitious, iniquitous, nefarious; black-market, bootleg, under-the-counter; exceptionable, improper, intolerable, objectionable
idiom against the law
con condign, due, rightful; allowable, justifiable, permissible
ant lawful

unlawfulness *n* ***syn*** see ILLEGALITY
ant lawfulness

unlax *vb* **1** ***syn*** see RELAX 2
2 ***syn*** see REST 2

unlearned *adj* ***syn*** see UNSCHOLARLY
ant erudite, learned

unleash *vb* ***syn*** see TAKE OUT (on)

unless *conj* ***syn*** see EXCEPT 1

unlettered *adj* ***syn*** see IGNORANT 1
ant educated, lettered

unlevel *adj* ***syn*** see ROUGH 1
ant level

unlike *adj* ***syn*** see DIFFERENT 1
ant like

unlikely *adj* ***syn*** see IMPROBABLE 1
ant likely

unlikeness *n* ***syn*** see DISSIMILARITY
rel incompatibility, incongruousness, inconsistence
ant likeness

unlimited *adj* **1** ***syn*** see LIMITLESS
ant limited, measured
2 ***syn*** see TOTAL 5
ant limited

unload *vb* to remove cargo or the cargo of <*unload* cattle from a truck>
syn disburden, discharge, off-load, unlade, unship, unstow
rel disencumber, dump, jettison, lighten; stevedore; debark, disembark, land
idiom break bulk
ant lade, load

unloose *vb* ***syn*** see LOOSE 3

unloosen *vb* ***syn*** see LOOSE 3

unloyal *adj* ***syn*** see FAITHLESS
ant loyal

||**unluck** *n* ***syn*** see MISFORTUNE
ant luck

---

syn synonym(s) *rel* related word(s)
ant antonym(s) *con* contrasted word(s)
idiom idiomatic equivalent(s)
|| use limited; if in doubt, see a dictionary

unlucky *adj* **1** ***syn*** see OMINOUS
2 involving or suffering misfortune that results from chance <in spite of careful planning the expedition was *unlucky* from the start>
syn hapless, ill-fated, ill-starred, luckless, misfortunate, star-crossed, unfortunate, unhappy, untoward
rel calamitous, cataclysmic, catastrophic, dire, disastrous, tragical
idiom down on one's luck, out of luck
con fortunate, happy, providential; prosperous, successful; coming, made
ant lucky

unmake *vb* **1** ***syn*** see DESTROY 1
2 ***syn*** see DEPOSE 1
ant make

unman *vb* ***syn*** see UNNERVE
rel deplete, drain, exhaust, impoverish; abase, degrade; disqualify, paralyze, prostrate, unfit
idiom knock the bottom (*or* stuffing) out of
con brace, fortify
ant man

unmanageable *adj* ***syn*** see UNRULY 1
ant manageable

unmanly *adj* **1** ***syn*** see COWARDLY
ant manly
2 ***syn*** see EFFEMINATE
ant manly

unmannered *adj* **1** ***syn*** see RUDE 6
2 ***syn*** see FRANK

unmannerly *adj* ***syn*** see RUDE 6
ant mannerly

unmarred *adj* ***syn*** see WHOLE 1
ant marred

unmarried *adj* ***syn*** see SINGLE 1
ant married, wed

unmarry *vb* ***syn*** see DIVORCE 2

unmask *vb* ***syn*** see EXPOSE 4

unmatchable *adj* ***syn*** see SUPREME

unmatched *adj* **1** ***syn*** see ALONE 3
2 ***syn*** see ODD 1
ant matched

unmaterial *adj* ***syn*** see IMMATERIAL 1
ant material

unmeaning *adj* ***syn*** see SENSELESS 5
ant meaningful

unmeasurable *adj* **1** ***syn*** see INCALCULABLE 1
ant measurable
2 ***syn*** see EXCESSIVE 1

unmeasured *adj* **1** ***syn*** see INCALCULABLE 1
ant measurable
2 ***syn*** see LIMITLESS
ant limited, measured

unmeditated *adj* ***syn*** see SPONTANEOUS
ant meditated

unmeet *adj* ***syn*** see UNFIT 1
ant meet

unmeetness *n* ***syn*** see IMPROPRIETY 1

unmellowed *adj* ***syn*** see YOUNG 1
con developed, matured, ripened
ant mellow, mellowed

unmerciful *adj* ***syn*** see PITILESS
ant merciful

unmindful *adj* ***syn*** see FORGETFUL
con anxious, careful, concerned
ant mindful; solicitous

unmindfulness *n* ***syn*** see APATHY 2
ant mindfulness

unmistakable *adj* ***syn*** see CLEAR 5
ant mistakable

unmitigated *adj* **1** ***syn*** see PURE 2
2 ***syn*** see UTTER

unmixable *adj* ***syn*** see INCONSONANT 1

unmixed *adj* **1** ***syn*** see STRAIGHT 3
ant blended, mixed
2 ***syn*** see PURE 2

unmodern *adj* ***syn*** see OLD-FASHIONED
ant modern

unmodifiable *adj* ***syn*** see INFLEXIBLE 3
ant modifiable

unmovable *adj* **1** ***syn*** see IMMOVABLE 1
ant mobile, movable
2 ***syn*** see INFLEXIBLE 3

unmoving *adj* ***syn*** see STATIC
ant mobile

unmusical *adj* ***syn*** see DISSONANT 1
ant musical

unnamed *adj* ***syn*** see ANONYMOUS

unnatural *adj* **1** ***syn*** see IRREGULAR 1
2 ***syn*** see SUPERNATURAL 2
ant natural

unneat *adj* ***syn*** see SLOVENLY 1
ant neat

unnecessary *adj* not needed <*unnecessary* loss of life>
syn inessential, needless, uncalled-for, unessential, unneeded, unneedful, unrequired
rel excess, redundant, superfluous, surplus; lavish, prodigal, profuse; gratuitous, supererogatory
con essential, needed, required, vital; inevitable, unescapable
ant necessary; unavoidable

unneeded *adj* ***syn*** see UNNECESSARY
ant needed; unavoidable

unneedful *adj* ***syn*** see UNNECESSARY
ant needful; unavoidable

unnerve *vb* to deprive of strength, spirit, and vigor <a man so *unnerved* as to be bereft of sense and judgment>
syn castrate, emasculate, enervate, unman, unstring
rel enfeeble, sap, undermine, weaken; bewilder, confound, distract; agitate, perturb, upset
con brace (up), inspirit, invigorate, reinforce, strengthen; encourage, hearten, steel
ant nerve

unneutral *adj* ***syn*** see BIASED 2
ant neutral

unnoted *adj* ***syn*** see OBSCURE 5
rel unconsidered, unobserved, unremarked
ant noted

unnoteworthy *adj* ***syn*** see COMMON 6
ant noteworthy

unnoticeable *adj* ***syn*** see INCONSPICUOUS
ant noticeable

unnoticing *adj* ***syn*** see INATTENTIVE
ant noticing

unnumberable *adj* ***syn*** see INNUMERABLE
unnumbered *adj* ***syn*** see INNUMERABLE
ant numbered
unobjectionable *adj* ***syn*** see DECENT 4
ant objectionable
unobjective *adj* ***syn*** see SUBJECTIVE
ant objective
unobservable *adj* ***syn*** see IMPERCEPTIBLE
unobservant *adj* ***syn*** see INATTENTIVE
ant observant, observing
unobserving *adj* ***syn*** see INATTENTIVE
ant observant, observing
unobstructed *adj* ***syn*** see OPEN 1
con clogged, plugged
ant obstructed
unobtainable *adj* ***syn*** see INACCESSIBLE
unobtrusive *adj* ***syn*** see QUIET 4
ant obtrusive
unoffending *adj* ***syn*** see HARMLESS
ant offending
unoffensive *adj* ***syn*** see HARMLESS
ant offensive
unofficial *adj* ***syn*** see INFORMAL 1
unoften *adv* ***syn*** see SELDOM
ant often
unordinary *adj* ***syn*** see EXCEPTIONAL 1
ant ordinary
unorganized *adj* ***syn*** see INCOHERENT 2
ant organized
unoriginal *adj* lacking or manifesting a lack of capacity for originality <a good man but with a mind stolid and *unoriginal*>
syn noncreative, sterile, uncreative, uninspired, uninventive, unoriginative; *compare* ARID 2
rel arid, barren, dry; dull, prosaic, staid, stodgy, stuffy, unfired
con creative, inspired, inventive, originative; alert, aware, keen; constructive, productive
ant original
unoriginated *adj* ***syn*** see SELF-EXISTENT
unoriginative *adj* ***syn*** see UNORIGINAL
ant originative
unornamented *adj* ***syn*** see PLAIN 1
unorthodox *adj* ***syn*** see HERETICAL
ant orthodox
unorthodoxy *n* ***syn*** see HERESY
ant orthodoxy
unostentatious *adj* ***syn*** see PLAIN 1
ant ostentatious
unpaid *adj* **1** serving without pay <a charity manned by *unpaid* assistants>
syn uncompensated, unrecompensed, unremunerated
rel freewill, gratuitous, voluntary, volunteer
con compensated, recompensed, remunerated
ant paid
2 not cleared by payment <an *unpaid* bill>
syn due, mature, outstanding, overdue, owing, payable, unsettled
idiom in arrears
con cleared, discharged, liquidated, settled
ant paid
unpaired *adj* ***syn*** see ODD 1
ant paired
unpalatable *adj* **1** lacking appeal to the sense of taste <threw together a greasy *unpalatable* meal>
syn distasteful, flat, flavorless, ill-flavored, insipid, savorless, tasteless, unappetizing, unsavory
rel loathsome, nauseous, sickening; thin, washy, watery, weak
con appetizing, delectable, delicious, flavorsome, sapid, savory, tasty
ant palatable
2 ***syn*** see BITTER 2
unparagoned *adj* ***syn*** see ALONE 3
ant paragoned
unparalleled *adj* ***syn*** see ALONE 3
ant paralleled
unpardonable *adj* ***syn*** see INEXCUSABLE
ant pardonable
unparented *adj* ***syn*** see ORPHAN
unpassioned *adj* ***syn*** see NEUTRAL
ant impassioned, passionate
unpatient *adj* ***syn*** see IMPATIENT 1
ant patient
unpeace *n* ***syn*** see DISCORD
ant peace
unpeaceful *adj* ***syn*** see RESTLESS
ant peaceful
unpedantic *adj* ***syn*** see LIVELY 1
ant pedantic
unperceivable *adj* ***syn*** see IMPERCEPTIBLE
unperceiving *adj* **1** ***syn*** see IMPERCEPTIVE
ant perceiving, perceptive, percipient
2 ***syn*** see INATTENTIVE
unperceptive *adj* ***syn*** see IMPERCEPTIVE
ant perceiving, perceptive, percipient
unperishable *adj* ***syn*** see INDESTRUCTIBLE
ant perishable
unpermissive *adj* ***syn*** see RIGID 3
ant permissive
unphysical *adj* ***syn*** see IMMATERIAL 1
ant physical
unpierceable *adj* ***syn*** see IMPASSABLE 1
ant pierceable
unpitying *adj* ***syn*** see PITILESS
ant pitying
unplanned *adj* **1** ***syn*** see RANDOM
ant planned
2 ***syn*** see UNINTENTIONAL
ant planned
unpleasant *adj* ***syn*** see BAD 8
unpliable *adj* ***syn*** see OBSTINATE
ant pliable, pliant
unpliant *adj* ***syn*** see OBSTINATE
ant pliable, pliant
unpolished *adj* **1** ***syn*** see RUDE 1
idiom in the rough
ant polished
2 ***syn*** see RUDE 6
3 ***syn*** see BOORISH

---

syn synonym(s) ***rel*** related word(s)
ant antonym(s) ***con*** contrasted word(s)
idiom idiomatic equivalent(s)
‖ use limited; if in doubt, see a dictionary

ant polished
unpolitic *adj syn* see TACTLESS
ant politic
unpractical *adj syn* see IMPRACTICAL 1
ant practical
unpracticed *adj* **1** *syn* see UNTRIED 1
2 *syn* see INEXPERIENCED
ant practiced
unpredictable *adj syn* see UNCERTAIN 1
ant predictable
unprejudiced *adj syn* see FAIR 4
ant prejudiced
unpremeditated *adj* **1** *syn* see SPONTANEOUS
2 *syn* see UNINTENTIONAL
ant premeditated
unprepossessed *adj syn* see FAIR 4
ant prepossessed
unprescribed *adj syn* see VOLUNTARY
ant prescribed
unpretentious *adj syn* see PLAIN 1
ant pretentious
unpretty *adj syn* see PLAIN 5
ant pretty
unprevailing *adj syn* see FUTILE
unprincipled *adj* **1** *syn* see UNSCRUPULOUS
ant principled
2 *syn* see ABANDONED 2
rel corrupt, crooked, unscrupulous; dishonest, unconscientious, unethical
3 *syn* see CORRUPT 2
ant principled
unproductive *adj* **1** *syn* see BARREN 2
rel impotent, infecund, unprolific
ant productive
2 *syn* see FUTILE
ant productive
unprofane *adj syn* see HOLY 1
ant profane
unproficient *adj syn* see UNSKILLFUL 1
ant proficient, skilled
unprogressive *adj* **1** *syn* see BACKWARD 6
ant progressive
2 *syn* see BACKWARD 5
ant progressive
unprompted *adj syn* see SPONTANEOUS
unpropitious *adj syn* see OMINOUS
rel adverse, antagonistic, counter
con cheering, encouraging, reassuring
ant propitious
unproportionate *adj syn* see LOPSIDED
ant proportionate
unprosperous *adj syn* see POOR 1
ant prosperous
unprosperousness *n syn* see POVERTY 1
ant prosperousness
unprotected *adj syn* see HELPLESS 1
rel undefended, unguarded, unsheltered, unshielded; insecure, unsafe
ant protected
unproved *adj syn* see UNTRIED 1
ant proved
unpunctual *adj syn* see TARDY
ant punctual
unpurposed *adj* **1** *syn* see UNINTENTIONAL
2 *syn* see FECKLESS 1
unqualified *adj* **1** *syn* see UNFIT 2
rel unskilled; unsuitable
ant qualified
2 *syn* see SURE 2
rel unconditional, unlimited, unreserved; clear, explicit, express; entire, perfect, utter
ant qualified
3 *syn* see UTTER
4 *syn* see PURE 2
unquenchable *adj syn* see INSATIABLE
ant quenchable
unquestionable *adj* **1** *syn* see AUTHENTIC 2
ant doubtable, questionable
2 *syn* see POSITIVE 3
rel dependable, reliable; established, well-founded, well-grounded
ant doubtable, questionable
3 *syn* see DOWNRIGHT 2
unquestionably *adv syn* see EASILY 2
ant questionably
unquestioning *adj syn* see SURE 2
ant questioning
unquiet *adj syn* see RESTLESS
ant quiet
unravel *vb syn* see SOLVE 2
rel disentangle, extricate, untangle
unreachable *adj syn* see INACCESSIBLE
ant reachable
unreadable *adj syn* see ILLEGIBLE
ant legible, readable
unreal *adj syn* see FICTITIOUS 1
ant real
unrealistic *adj syn* see IMPRACTICAL 1
ant realistic
unrealizable *adj syn* see IMPOSSIBLE 1
ant realizable
unreasonable *adj* **1** *syn* see ILLOGICAL
rel incongruous, loose, self-contradictory
ant reasonable
2 exceeding the bounds of reason or right <the constitutional guarantees against *unreasonable* searches and seizures>
syn unconscionable, undue, unjustifiable, unwarrantable, unwarranted
rel arbitrary, peremptory; excessive, immoderate, inordinate, overmuch; improper, unlawful, unrightful, wrongful
con lawful, licit; proper, right, tolerable
ant reasonable
unreasoned *adj syn* see ILLOGICAL
ant reasoned
unrecking *adj syn* see CARELESS 1
unreckonable *adj syn* see INCALCULABLE 1
unrecompensed *adj syn* see UNPAID 1
ant recompensed
unrecoverable *adj syn* see HOPELESS 2
unrefined *adj* **1** *syn* see BOORISH
ant refined
2 *syn* see COARSE 3
ant refined
3 not freed from unwanted material <shipped the *unrefined* ore>
syn crude, impure, native, raw, run-of-mine, ungraded, unsorted

rel rough, roughcast, roughhewn; coarse, natural, undressed, unprocessed
idiom in the rough
con dressed, processed
ant refined

unreflective *adj* ***syn*** see CARELESS 1

unregretful *adj* ***syn*** see REMORSELESS
ant regretful

unregular *adj* ***syn*** see IRREGULAR 1
ant regular

unrehearsed *adj* ***syn*** see EXTEMPORANEOUS
ant rehearsed

unrelenting *adj* ***syn*** see GRIM 3
ant relenting

unreliable *adj* **1** not to be counted on <it is certain that much of the testimony was *unreliable*>
syn dubious, fly-by-night, questionable, trustless, undependable, unsure, untrustworthy, untrusty
rel fickle, inconstant, unstable, vacillating; faithless, false, untrue; falsehearted, perfidious; shifty, slick, slippery, tricky; inaccurate, inexact, unfaithful
idiom not to be depended (*or* relied) on
con dependable, trustworthy, trusty; constant; faithful, true
ant reliable
2 *syn* see UNSAFE
ant reliable

unreligious *adj* ***syn*** see IRRELIGIOUS
ant religious

unremarkable *adj* ***syn*** see ORDINARY 1

unremitting *adj* ***syn*** see CONTINUAL

unremittingly *adv* ***syn*** see HARD 3

unremorseful *adj* ***syn*** see REMORSELESS
ant remorseful

unremunerated *adj* ***syn*** see UNPAID 1
ant remunerated

unrenowned *adj* ***syn*** see OBSCURE 5
ant renowned

unrepealable *adj* ***syn*** see IRREVOCABLE
ant repealable

unrepeatable *adj* ***syn*** see ONLY 2

unrepentant *adj* ***syn*** see REMORSELESS
ant repentant

unrepresentative *adj* ***syn*** see ABNORMAL 1

unrequested *adj* ***syn*** see UNASKED

unrequired *adj* **1** *syn* see UNNECESSARY
ant required
2 *syn* see DISPENSABLE
ant required

unreserved *adj* **1** *syn* see FRANK 1
ant reserved
2 *syn* see DEMONSTRATIVE
ant reserved
3 *syn* see EASYGOING 3

unresistant *adj* ***syn*** see PASSIVE 2
ant resistant, resisting

unresisting *adj* ***syn*** see PASSIVE 2
ant resistant, resisting

unresolved *adj* ***syn*** see VACILLATING 2
ant resolved

unrespectable *adj* ***syn*** see DISREPUTABLE 1
ant respectable

unresponsive *adj* **1** *syn* see INSUSCEPTIBLE
ant responsive
2 *syn* see FRIGID 3

unresponsiveness *n* ***syn*** see APATHY 1
ant responsiveness

unrest *n* a disturbed uneasy state <that popular *unrest* that, unchecked, can lead to insurrection and anarchy>
syn ailment, disquiet, disquietude, ferment, inquietude, restiveness, restlessness, storm and stress, Sturm und Drang, turmoil
rel agitation, commotion, confusion, convulsion, tumult, turbulence, upheaval; anarchy, chaos, disorder
con calm, easiness, peace, quiet

unrestful *adj* **1** *syn* see RESTLESS
ant restful
2 *syn* see NERVOUS

unrestrainable *adj* ***syn*** see IRREPRESSIBLE
ant restrainable

unrestrained *adj* **1** *syn* see EXCESSIVE 2
2 *syn* see FREE 2
ant restrained
3 *syn* see AUDACIOUS 4
rel candid, frank, open; forthright, plainspoken, straightforward; bluff, blunt, brusque
ant restrained
4 *syn* see DEMONSTRATIVE
ant restrained

unrestraint *n* **1** *syn* see UNCONSTRAINT
ant restraint
2 *syn* see ABANDON 2

unrestricted *adj* ***syn*** see OPEN 4

unriddle *vb* ***syn*** see SOLVE 2

unrighteous *adj* ***syn*** see INEQUITABLE
ant righteous

unripe *adj* ***syn*** see YOUNG 1

unrivaled *adj* ***syn*** see ALONE 3

unromantic *adj* ***syn*** see REALISTIC
ant romantic

unruffled *adj* ***syn*** see COOL 2
ant discomposed, ruffled

unruly *adj* **1** resistant to discipline or control <a stubborn *unruly* boy>
syn fractious, indocile, indomitable, intractable, recalcitrant, uncontrollable, undisciplinable, undisciplined, ungovernable, unmanageable, untoward, wild; *compare* OBSTINATE, TURBULENT 1
rel contumacious, incorrigible, insubordinate, rebellious; contrary, froward, perverse, wayward; boisterous, obstreperous, rampageous; disorderly, raffish, rambunctious, rowdy, turbulent
idiom out of hand
con controlled, easy, mild, restrained; disciplined, governable, manageable; amenable, biddable, obedient; correct, proper
ant docile, tractable
2 *syn* see TURBULENT 1

---

syn synonym(s) *rel* related word(s)
ant antonym(s) *con* contrasted word(s)
idiom idiomatic equivalent(s)
‖ use limited; if in doubt, see a dictionary

rel hard, ruffianly, tough
3 *syn* see DISOBEDIENT
unsacred *adj* *syn* see PROFANE 1
ant sacred
unsafe *adj* not to be depended on or trusted <an *unsafe* investment>
syn unassured, undependable, unreliable, untrustworthy
rel insecure, shaky, tottery, unsound, unstable; chancy, hazardous, risky; dangerous, jeopardous, perilous; erratic, uncertain
con dependable, trustworthy; secure, sound, stable, substantial
ant safe
unsaid *adj* *syn* see TACIT 1
unsalutary *adj* *syn* see UNWHOLESOME 1
ant salutary
unsandaled *adj* *syn* see BAREFOOT 1
ant sandaled
unsane *adj* *syn* see INSANE 1
ant sane
unsatiate *adj* *syn* see INSATIABLE
ant satiate, satiated
unsatisfactory *adj* *syn* see BAD 1
ant satisfactory
unsatisfiable *adj* *syn* see INSATIABLE
ant satisfiable
unsavory *adj* *syn* see UNPALATABLE 1
ant savory
unsay *vb* *syn* see ABJURE
unscathed *adj* *syn* see SAFE 1
unscholarly *adj* not devoted to scholarly pursuits <*unscholarly* concerns>
syn inerudite, unbookish, unlearned, unstudious
rel unenlightened, uninformed, uninitiated; callow, green, unripe; inexperienced, naive
con bookish, erudite, learned; enlightened, informed; experienced
ant scholarly
unschooled *adj* **1** *syn* see IGNORANT 1
2 *syn* see NATURAL 5
unscramble *vb* *syn* see EXTRICATE 2
unscrupulous *adj* **1** lacking in moral scruples <*unscrupulous* conduct of political leaders>
syn conscienceless, stick-at-nothing, unconscionable, unprincipled
rel crafty, deceitful, scheming; improper, unseemly, wrongful; corrupt, crooked, dishonest; questionable, shady, sinister, underhand
con conscientious, dutiful, proper, upright; dependable, reliable, responsible
ant scrupulous
2 *syn* see CORRUPT 2
con meticulous, particular, punctilious, strict
ant scrupulous
unseasonable *adj* **1** involving or occurring at an inappropriate or unexpected time <his wife's sudden return proved most *unseasonable*>
syn ill-seasoned, ill-timed, inopportune, malapropos, mistimed, untimely
rel deplorable, inappropriate, inconvenient, unsuitable; inauspicious, infelicitous, undesirable, unfavorable, unfortunate
con apropos, opportune, timely, well-timed
ant seasonable
2 *syn* see IMPROPER 1
unseasoned *adj* *syn* see INEXPERIENCED
ant seasoned
unseat *vb* *syn* see THROW 2
unsectarian *adj* *syn* see NONSECTARIAN
ant sectarian
unseemliness *n* *syn* see IMPROPRIETY 1
ant propriety, seemliness
unseemly *adj* **1** *syn* see INDECOROUS
rel coarse, crude, inelegant, unrefined; raffish, rowdy, ruffianly
con prim, restrained, starchy, stiff, stilted; elegant, gracious, polished, refined
ant seemly
2 *syn* see IMPROPER 1
ant seemly
unselfish *adj* *syn* see SELFLESS
ant selfish
unsentimental *adj* *syn* see REALISTIC
ant sentimental
unserviceable *adj* *syn* see IMPRACTICABLE 2
ant serviceable
unsettle *vb* **1** *syn* see DISORDER 1
rel agitate, disquiet, perturb; discommode, incommode, trouble
con calm, ease, quiet, stabilize, steady
ant settle
2 *syn* see UPSET 5
ant settle
3 *syn* see DISCOMPOSE 1
unsettled *adj* **1** *syn* see RESTLESS
2 *syn* see CHANGEABLE 1
ant settled
3 *syn* see DOUBTFUL 1
4 *syn* see PENDING
ant settled
5 *syn* see BACK 1
6 *syn* see UNPAID 2
ant settled
unsettledness *n* *syn* see INSTABILITY
unsex *vb* *syn* see STERILIZE
unshackle *vb* *syn* see FREE
ant shackle
unshakable *adj* *syn* see SURE 2
ant shakable
unshaken *adj* *syn* see SURE 2
ant shaken
unshaped *adj* *syn* see FORMLESS
ant shaped
unshared *adj* *syn* see SOLE 4
ant shared
unship *vb* *syn* see UNLOAD
unshod *adj* *syn* see BAREFOOT 1
ant shod
unshroud *vb* *syn* see EXPOSE 4
ant shroud
unshut *vb* *syn* see OPEN 1
ant shut
unsightly *adj* *syn* see UGLY 2
rel ill-shaped, unshapely; unesthetic; drab, dull, lackluster
ant sightly

unsimilar *adj* ***syn*** see DIFFERENT 1
ant similar
unskilled *adj* **1** ***syn*** see AMATEURISH
ant skilled
2 ***syn*** see INEFFICIENT 2
ant skilled
unskillful *adj* **1** lacking in skill or proficiency <an ardent but *unskillful* home mechanic>
syn inadept, inapt, inept, inexpert, unapt, undexterous, unfacile, unhandy, unproficient
rel incapable, incompetent; unfitted, unqualified, unready
con adept, apt, dexterous, expert, handy, proficient
ant skillful
2 ***syn*** see INEFFICIENT 2
unsleeping *adj* ***syn*** see WATCHFUL
ant sleeping
unsmooth *adj* ***syn*** see ROUGH 1
ant smooth
unsober *adj* ***syn*** see INTOXICATED 1
ant sober
unsociable *adj* disinclined to active social intercourse <tried to hide his basically shy *unsociable* nature under a professional heartiness of manner>
syn aloof, cool, distant, insociable, offish, reserved, shut-in, solitary, standoff, standoffish, touch-me-not-ish, unapproachable, unbending, uncommunicative, uncompanionable, withdrawn; *compare* INDIFFERENT 2, UNDEMONSTRATIVE
rel self-contained, self-sufficient; exclusive, inaccessible, remote; prickly, sensitive; brooding, secretive; diffident, shy, timid
con cordial, genial, hearty, outgoing; companionable, friendly, gregarious
ant sociable, social
unsoiled *adj* ***syn*** see CLEAN 1
ant soiled, sullied
unsoluble *adj* ***syn*** see INSOLUBLE
ant soluble, solvable
unsolvable *adj* ***syn*** see INSOLUBLE
ant soluble, solvable
unsophisticated *adj* ***syn*** see NATURAL 5
rel authentic, bona fide, genuine; callow, crude, green, uncouth
con finished, polished, smooth, suave
ant sophisticated
unsorry *adj* ***syn*** see REMORSELESS
ant sorry
unsorted *adj* **1** ***syn*** see MISCELLANEOUS
2 ***syn*** see UNREFINED 3
ant sorted
unsought *adj* **1** ***syn*** see UNASKED
2 ***syn*** see UNWELCOME 1
unsound *adj* **1** ***syn*** see INSANE 1
ant sound
2 ***syn*** see WEAK 1
rel damaged, faulty, flawed, imperfect
con solid, strong, substantial
ant sound
3 ***syn*** see FALSE 1
ant sound
4 ***syn*** see DANGEROUS 1
unsparing *adj* ***syn*** see LIBERAL 1
ant close, sparing
unspeakable *adj* ***syn*** see UNUTTERABLE
rel loathsome, offensive, repulsive, revolting; abominable, detestable, hateful, odious; distasteful, obnoxious, repellent, repugnant; atrocious, disgusting, outrageous
unspoiled *adj* ***syn*** see VIRGIN 2
unspoken *adj* **1** not put into words <met regularly by a sort of *unspoken* agreement>
syn silent, tacit, unexpressed, unuttered, unvoiced, wordless
rel implicit, implied, understood; hinted, intimated, suggested; mute, unsaid, unstated
con mentioned, said, stated, told, voiced
ant spoken
2 ***syn*** see TACIT 1
ant spoken
unstability *n* ***syn*** see INSTABILITY
ant stability
unstable *adj* **1** ***syn*** see MOVABLE
ant stable
2 difficult to manage because of lack of physical steadiness <the canoe is an inherently *unstable* craft>
syn rocky, ticklish, tricky
rel insecure, uncertain, unsteady
con secure, steady
ant stable
3 ***syn*** see WEAK 2
ant stable
4 ***syn*** see INCONSTANT 1
rel buoyant, effervescent, elastic, resilient; freakish
ant stable
5 ***syn*** see CHANGEABLE 1
ant stable
6 ***syn*** see MUTABLE 2
ant stable
7 ***syn*** see DOUBTFUL 1
unstableness *n* ***syn*** see INSTABILITY
ant stability, stableness
unsteadfast *adj* ***syn*** see MOVABLE
ant steadfast
unsteadfastness *n* ***syn*** see INSTABILITY
ant steadfastness
unsteadiness *n* ***syn*** see INSTABILITY
ant steadiness
unsteady *adj* **1** ***syn*** see MOVABLE
2 ***syn*** see CHANGEABLE 1
ant steady
3 ***syn*** see MUTABLE 2
ant steady
unsteel *vb* ***syn*** see DISARM 2
unstop *vb* ***syn*** see OPEN 1
ant stop
unstow *vb* ***syn*** see UNLOAD
unstrengthen *vb* ***syn*** see WEAKEN 1
ant strengthen

---

syn synonym(s) ***rel*** related word(s)
ant antonym(s) ***con*** contrasted word(s)
idiom idiomatic equivalent(s)
|| use limited; if in doubt, see a dictionary

unstring *vb* ***syn*** see UNNERVE
unstudied *adj* **1** ***syn*** see NATURAL 5
ant studied
2 ***syn*** see EXTEMPORANEOUS
unstudious *adj* ***syn*** see UNSCHOLARLY
ant studious
unstylish *adj* ***syn*** see TACKY 2
ant stylish
unsubstantial *adj* **1** ***syn*** see TENUOUS 3
ant substantial
2 ***syn*** see IMPLAUSIBLE
3 ***syn*** see IMMATERIAL 1
ant substantial
4 ***syn*** see WEAK 1
rel insecure, shaky, undependable
ant substantial
unsuccess *n* ***syn*** see FAILURE 2
ant success, successfulness
unsuccessfulness *n* ***syn*** see FAILURE 2
ant success, successfulness
unsufferable *adj* ***syn*** see INSUFFERABLE
ant sufferable
unsufficient *adj* ***syn*** see SHORT 3
ant sufficient
unsuitable *adj* **1** ***syn*** see UNFIT 1
rel undesirable, unhappy
ant suitable
2 ***syn*** see IMPROPER 1
ant suitable
unsuited *adj* ***syn*** see UNFIT 1
rel inadmissible, objectionable, unacceptable; disappointing, inadequate
ant suited
unsullied *adj* **1** ***syn*** see CHASTE
ant sullied
2 ***syn*** see CLEAN 1
ant soiled, sullied
unsupportable *adj* ***syn*** see INSUFFERABLE
ant bearable, supportable
unsure *adj* **1** ***syn*** see INSECURE 1
ant sure
2 ***syn*** see WEAK 2
3 ***syn*** see DOUBTFUL 1
ant sure
4 ***syn*** see UNRELIABLE 1
unsurmountable *adj* ***syn*** see INSUPERABLE
ant surmountable
unsurpassable *adj* ***syn*** see SUPREME
ant surpassable
unsusceptible *adj* ***syn*** see INSUSCEPTIBLE
ant susceptible
unsuspecting *adj* ***syn*** see CREDULOUS
ant suspecting, suspicious
unsuspicious *adj* ***syn*** see CREDULOUS
ant suspecting, suspicious
unswayable *adj* ***syn*** see INFLEXIBLE 2
ant suasible
unswerving *adj* ***syn*** see WHOLE 5
rel constant, steadfast, steady, unremitting; firm, unfaltering, unwavering
unsymmetrical *adj* ***syn*** see LOPSIDED
ant symmetrical
unsympathetic *adj* **1** ***syn*** see ANTIPATHETIC 2
rel dislikable, unlikable; displeasing, unpleasant, unpleasing
con appealing, congenial, likable; pleasant, pleasing
ant sympathetic
2 ***syn*** see UNFEELING 2
rel cold, cool, frigid; disinterested, halfhearted, indifferent, lukewarm
ant sympathetic
untactful *adj* ***syn*** see TACTLESS
ant tactful
untangle *vb* ***syn*** see EXTRICATE 2
ant entangle, tangle
untapped *adj* ***syn*** see VIRGIN 2
untaught *adj* ***syn*** see IGNORANT 1
untellable *adj* ***syn*** see UNUTTERABLE
ant expressible
untempered *adj* ***syn*** see EXCESSIVE 2
ant temperate, tempered
untenable *adj* ***syn*** see INEXCUSABLE
untended *adj* ***syn*** see NEGLECTED
untested *adj* ***syn*** see UNTRIED 1
ant tested, tried
unthankful *adj* **1** ***syn*** see THANKLESS 2
2 ***syn*** see THANKLESS 1
ant thankful
unthinkable *adj* **1** ***syn*** see EXCEPTIONAL 1
2 ***syn*** see INCREDIBLE 1
ant thinkable
unthinking *adj* ***syn*** see CARELESS 1
unthorough *adj* ***syn*** see SLIPSHOD 3
ant thorough
unthought *adj* ***syn*** see UNINTENTIONAL
ant aforethought
unthrift *n* **1** ***syn*** see EXTRAVAGANCE 2
ant thrift
2 ***syn*** see SPENDTHRIFT
unthrift *adj* ***syn*** see IMPROVIDENT
unthrifty *adj* ***syn*** see IMPROVIDENT
ant thrifty
untidy *adj* **1** ***syn*** see SLOVENLY 1
ant tidy
2 ***syn*** see SLIPSHOD 3
untie *vb* ***syn*** see EXTRICATE 2
untighten *vb* ***syn*** see LOOSE 5
ant tighten
until *prep* up to a stipulated time <we never met him *until* last night>
syn before, in advance of, prior to, till, to, up till, up to; *compare* BEFORE 1
until *conj* ***syn*** see TILL
untimely *adj* **1** ***syn*** see EARLY 2
ant timely
2 ***syn*** see UNSEASONABLE 1
con opportune, pat, seasonable, well-timed
ant timely
3 ***syn*** see IMPROPER 1
ant timely
untiring *adj* ***syn*** see INDEFATIGABLE
con casual, disinterested, intermittent
untold *adj* **1** ***syn*** see HUGE
2 ***syn*** see INNUMERABLE
untouchable *n* ***syn*** see OUTCAST
rel déclassé, outcaste, outsider
untouched *adj* **1** ***syn*** see WHOLE 1
2 ***syn*** see VIRGIN 2

untoward *adj* **1** ***syn*** see UNRULY 1
2 ***syn*** see UNLUCKY
3 ***syn*** see INDECOROUS
untowardness *n* ***syn*** see IMPROPRIETY 1
untrammeled *adj* ***syn*** see AUDACIOUS 4
untranquil *adj* ***syn*** see RESTLESS
untried *adj* **1** not subjected to test or proof (as by experience or use) <the fledgling's *untried* wings>
syn undemonstrated, unpracticed, unproved, untested
rel inexperienced, unseasoned; callow, green, immature; fresh, half-baked, unripe
con practiced, proven, tested; accomplished, finished, skilled; initiated
ant tested, tried
2 ***syn*** see INEXPERIENCED
untroubled *adj* ***syn*** see CALM 1
ant troubled
untroublesome *adj* ***syn*** see EASY 1
untrue *adj* **1** ***syn*** see FAITHLESS
ant true
2 ***syn*** see FALSE 1
rel imprecise, inexact, unprecise; forsworn, perjured
con exact, precise
ant true
untruism *n* ***syn*** see LIE
ant truism
untrustworthy *adj* **1** ***syn*** see UNRELIABLE 1
ant trustworthy
2 ***syn*** see UNSAFE
ant trustworthy
untrusty *adj* ***syn*** see UNRELIABLE 1
ant trusty
untruth *n* **1** ***syn*** see FALLACY 1
ant truth
2 ***syn*** see LIE
ant truth
untruthful *adj* ***syn*** see DISHONEST
rel deceptive, delusive, delusory, misleading; false, wrong; inaccurate, incorrect
ant truthful
untruthfulness *n* ***syn*** see MENDACITY
ant truthfulness
untune *vb* ***syn*** see DISCOMPOSE 1
untutored *adj* **1** ***syn*** see IGNORANT 1
2 ***syn*** see NATURAL 5
untwine *vb* ***syn*** see EXTRICATE 2
untypical *adj* ***syn*** see ABNORMAL 1
ant typical
ununderstandable *adj* ***syn*** see INCONCEIVABLE 1
ant understandable
unusable *adj* ***syn*** see IMPRACTICABLE 2
ant usable
unused *adj* ***syn*** see VACANT 4
unusual *adj* **1** ***syn*** see EXCEPTIONAL 1
idiom the exception rather than the rule
ant usual
2 ***syn*** see STRANGE 4
ant usual
unusually *adv* ***syn*** see EXTRA
unutterable *adj* being beyond human power to tell or describe <*unutterable* spiritual bliss>
syn incommunicable, indefinable, indescribable, ineffable, inenarrable, inexpressible, undescribable, unexpressible, unspeakable, untellable
rel inconceivable, incredible, unbelievable, unimaginable; awesome, awful, marvelous, prodigious, wonderful, wondrous
idiom beyond expression
con commonplace, humdrum, ordinary; monotonous, samely, unvarying
unuttered *adj* **1** ***syn*** see UNSPOKEN 1
ant uttered
2 ***syn*** see TACIT 1
ant uttered
unvarnished *adj* ***syn*** see FRANK
unvarying *adj* **1** ***syn*** see STEADY 2
ant varying
2 ***syn*** see SAME 3
ant variable, varying
unveil *vb* **1** ***syn*** see OPEN 2
ant veil
2 ***syn*** see REVEAL 1
ant veil
unveracity *n* ***syn*** see MENDACITY
ant veracity
unversed *adj* ***syn*** see INEXPERIENCED
ant versed
unvigilant *adj* ***syn*** see INCAUTIOUS 1
ant vigilant
unvital *adj* ***syn*** see PETTY 2
ant vital
unvocal *adj* ***syn*** see INARTICULATE 3
ant vocal
unvoiced *adj* ***syn*** see UNSPOKEN 1
ant voiced
unwanted *adj* **1** ***syn*** see UNWELCOME 1
ant wanted
2 ***syn*** see OBJECTIONABLE
unwarrantable *adj* ***syn*** see UNREASONABLE 2
ant warrantable
unwarranted *adj* **1** ***syn*** see BASELESS
2 ***syn*** see UNREASONABLE 2
unwary *adj* **1** ***syn*** see INCAUTIOUS 1
ant wary
2 ***syn*** see CREDULOUS
3 ***syn*** see RASH 1
ant wary
unwashed *adj* ***syn*** see IGNOBLE 1
unwashed *n* ***syn*** see RABBLE 2
unwasteful *adj* ***syn*** see SPARING
ant wasteful
unwatchful *adj* **1** ***syn*** see INATTENTIVE
ant watchful
2 ***syn*** see INCAUTIOUS 1
ant watchful
unwatered *adj* ***syn*** see DRY 1
ant watered
unwavering *adj* ***syn*** see SURE 2
ant wavering
unweariable *adj* ***syn*** see INDEFATIGABLE

syn synonym(s) ***rel*** related word(s)
ant antonym(s) ***con*** contrasted word(s)
idiom idiomatic equivalent(s)
‖ use limited; if in doubt, see a dictionary

ant wearisome

unwearying *adj* ***syn*** see INDEFATIGABLE
rel constant, steady; interminable, unceasing

unwed *adj* ***syn*** see SINGLE 1
ant married, wed

unwelcome *adj* **1** not of a kind to be welcome <an *unwelcome* interruption that scattered his train of thought>
syn undesired, unsought, unwanted, unwished
rel distasteful, obnoxious, repellent; unasked; undesirable, unpleasant, unpleasing
con desired, sought, wanted; agreeable, desirable, pleasant, pleasing
ant welcome
2 ***syn*** see OBJECTIONABLE
ant welcome

unwell *adj* somewhat disordered in health <had felt *unwell* from the moment she got up>
syn ailing, ‖donsie, indisposed, low, mean, off-color, offish, poorly, sickly; *compare* SICK 1
rel rocky, shaky, wobbly; feeble, frail, infirm, weakly; ill, sick; qualmish, queasy, squeamish
idiom out of sorts, under the weather
ant well

unwholesome *adj* **1** likely to be detrimental to physical, mental, or moral health <an *unwholesome* crime-ridden neighborhood>
syn insalubrious, insalutary, noisome, noxious, sickly, unhealthful, unhealthy, unsalutary
rel baneful, deleterious, detrimental, pernicious; harmful, hurtful, injurious, mischievous
con healthful, hygienic, salubrious, salutary
ant wholesome
2 ***syn*** see OFFENSIVE
ant wholesome

unwieldy *adj* clumsy and difficult to handle usually because of excessive weight and awkward form <a massive *unwieldy* sledgehammer>
syn cumbersome, cumbrous, ponderous, unhandy; *compare* HEAVY 1
rel awkward, inconvenient; uncontrollable, unmanageable; bulky, clumsy, lumbering, massive; burdensome, encumbering, onerous
con compact, neat, trig, trim; adaptable, convenient, handy; easy, facile, light
ant wieldy

unwilling *adj* ***syn*** see DISINCLINED
ant willing

unwind *vb* ***syn*** see RELAX 2

unwise *adj* not marked by or according with good sense or sound judgment <his decision to quit school was most *unwise*>
syn ill-advised, ill-judged, impolitic, imprudent, indiscreet, injudicious
rel senseless, thoughtless, witless; impractical, unsound; fatuous, inane, inept; inappropriate, undesirable, unfortunate; foolish, misguided, unintelligent; childish, immature, naive
idiom penny-wise and pound-foolish
con discreet, judicious, prudent; sane, sensible, sound; appropriate, apt, desirable
ant wise

unwished *adj* ***syn*** see UNWELCOME 1

unwishful *adj* ***syn*** see DISINCLINED
ant wishful

unwitting *adj* **1** ***syn*** see FORGETFUL
ant witting
2 ***syn*** see IGNORANT 2
ant witting

unwitty *adj* ***syn*** see SIMPLE 3
ant ‖witty

unwonted *adj* ***syn*** see EXCEPTIONAL 1
ant wonted

unworkable *adj* **1** ***syn*** see IMPOSSIBLE 1
2 ***syn*** see IMPRACTICABLE 2
ant workable

unworked *adj* ***syn*** see RUDE 1
ant worked, wrought

unworkmanlike *adj* ***syn*** see INEFFICIENT 2
ant workmanlike, workmanly

unworldly *adj* **1** ***syn*** see DREAMY 1
2 ***syn*** see NATURAL 5
ant worldly

unworthy *adj* ***syn*** see WORTHLESS 1
ant worthy

unwritten *adj* ***syn*** see ORAL 2
ant written

unwrought *adj* ***syn*** see RUDE 1
ant worked, wrought

unyielding *adj* **1** ***syn*** see STIFF 1
ant yielding
2 ***syn*** see OBSTINATE
rel firm, fixed, rigid
ant yielding
3 ***syn*** see GRIM 3
4 ***syn*** see TOUGH 3
ant yielding
5 ***syn*** see INFLEXIBLE 2

up *adj* **1** ***syn*** see BAD 1
2 ***syn*** see FAMILIAR 3
3 ***syn*** see UP-TO-DATE

up *vb* **1** ***syn*** see RISE 4
2 ***syn*** see RAISE 9

up–and–coming *adj* ***syn*** see ENTERPRISING 2
rel alert, eager, keen, ready

up and down *adv* ***syn*** see THOROUGHLY 2

up–and–down *adj* ***syn*** see DOWNRIGHT 2

upbear *vb* ***syn*** see SUPPORT 4

upbeat *adj* ***syn*** see OPTIMISTIC

upbraid *vb* ***syn*** see SCOLD 1

upchuck *vb* ***syn*** see VOMIT

upclimb *vb* ***syn*** see ASCEND 1

upcoming *adj* ***syn*** see FORTHCOMING
rel foreseen, prospective
idiom in prospect, on the horizon

up–country *n* ***syn*** see FRONTIER 2

update *vb* ***syn*** see RENEW 1

upend *vb* ***syn*** see WHIP 2

upgo *vb* ***syn*** see ASCEND 1

upgrade *vb* ***syn*** see ADVANCE 2
ant downgrade

upgrade *n* ***syn*** see RISE 3

upgrading *n* ***syn*** see ADVANCEMENT 1
ant downgrading

upgrowth *n* ***syn*** see DEVELOPMENT

upheaval *n* ***syn*** see COMMOTION 1
rel cataclysm, catastrophe, disaster; alteration, change; churning, heaving, stirring

upheaved *adj* ***syn*** see ELEVATED 1
ant downthrown
uphill *adj* ***syn*** see HARD 6
uphold *vb* **1** ***syn*** see SUPPORT 5
rel defend, justify, maintain, vindicate; aid, assist, help
ant contravene; subvert
2 ***syn*** see SUPPORT 2
3 ***syn*** see SUPPORT 4
4 ***syn*** see LIFT 1
upholstered *adj* **1** ***syn*** see LUXURIOUS 3
2 ***syn*** see FAT 2
upland *n* ***syn*** see PLATEAU
uplay *vb* ***syn*** see ACCUMULATE
uplift *vb* **1** ***syn*** see LIFT 1
2 ***syn*** see ILLUMINATE 2
ant degrade
uplifted *adj* ***syn*** see ELEVATED 1
upon *prep* **1** ***syn*** see OVER 3
2 ***syn*** see OVER 4
upper class *n* ***syn*** see ARISTOCRACY
upper crust *n* ***syn*** see ARISTOCRACY
rel (the) Four Hundred
upper hand *n* ***syn*** see BETTER 2
uppermost *adj* ***syn*** see TOP 1
ant lowermost
‖**upper story** *n* ***syn*** see MIND 1
‖**upperworks** *n pl* ***syn*** see MIND 1
uppish *adj* ***syn*** see PRESUMPTUOUS
uppity *adj* ***syn*** see PRESUMPTUOUS
upraise *vb* **1** ***syn*** see LIFT 1
2 ***syn*** see COMFORT
ant depress
upraised *adj* ***syn*** see ELEVATED 1
uprear *vb* **1** ***syn*** see LIFT 1
2 ***syn*** see BUILD 1
3 ***syn*** see EXALT 1
con bust, demote, downgrade
ant degrade
4 ***syn*** see RISE 4
upright *adj* **1** ***syn*** see ERECT
2 having or manifesting a strict regard for what is morally right <an *upright* man ready to give even the devil his due>
syn conscientious, honest, honorable, just, right, scrupulous, true
rel ethical, moral, principled, righteous, virtuous; equitable, fair, impartial; elevated, high-minded, noble; blameless, exemplary, good, pure
con crooked, devious, oblique; depraved; base, low, vile; ignoble, mean
ant corrupt
uprightness *n* ***syn*** see GOODNESS
rel nobility, reputability, worthiness; honesty, integrity
ant corruption
uprise *vb* **1** ***syn*** see RISE 1
2 ***syn*** see ROLL OUT
uprisen *adj* ***syn*** see ELEVATED 1
uproar *n* **1** ***syn*** see DIN
rel chaos, confusion, disorder; brawl, broil, fracas, melee; commotion, confusion, turbulence, turmoil
con calm, peace, quiet
2 ***syn*** see COMMOTION 4
3 ***syn*** see COMMOTION 3
uproarious *adj* ***syn*** see NOISY
uproot *vb* ***syn*** see ANNIHILATE 2
rel demolish, destroy; overthrow, overturn, subvert; displace, replace, supersede, supplant; move, shift, transplant
ant establish; inseminate
upset *vb* **1** ***syn*** see OVERTURN 1
rel invert, reverse; bend, curve, turn
2 ***syn*** see DISCOMPOSE 1
rel bewilder, confound, distract; unman, unnerve
idiom rock the boat
3 ***syn*** see TROUBLE 1
4 ***syn*** see DISORDER 1
5 to disturb the normal functioning especially of body or mind <her stomach was badly *upset* by too many sweets>
syn derange, disorder, sicken, turn, unhinge, unsettle
rel afflict, indispose, lay up; ail, suffer; debilitate, incapacitate, invalid
upshot *n* **1** ***syn*** see EFFECT 1
rel ending, termination; climax, culmination; completion, conclusion, finish
2 ***syn*** see SUBSTANCE 2
upside-down *adj* **1** having the upper and lower parts reversed in position <*upside-down* letters>
syn inverted, topsy-turvy
rel reversed
2 confused utterly even to the point of inversion of the normal or reasonable <*upside-down* logic that confused cause with effect>
syn arsy-varsy, downside-up, topsy-turvy
rel inverted, reversed; chaotic, confused, helter-skelter, jumbled, mixed-up; fouled-up, haywire, ‖snafu
con orderly, well-ordered; logical, reasonable, sensible, sound; legitimate, plausible
upspring *vb* **1** ***syn*** see SPRING 1
2 ***syn*** see RISE 1
upstanding *adj* ***syn*** see ERECT
upstart *n* a usually crude and pushing person who has recently reached a position of prominence, power, or wealth <declared the new executive an *upstart* lacking all breeding and culture>
syn arriviste, nouveau riche, parvenu, roturier
rel bounder, cad, outsider; guttersnipe, mucker, slob, vulgarian; boor, lout, roughneck, rowdy; comer; social climber
upsurge *vb* ***syn*** see INCREASE 2
uptight *adj* ***syn*** see TENSE 2
uptightness *n* ***syn*** see TENSION 2
up till *prep* ***syn*** see UNTIL
up to *prep* ***syn*** see UNTIL
up-to-date *adj* completely modern (as in style or outlook) <using *up-to-date* methods of study>

syn abreast, au courant, contemporary, down-to-date, red-hot, up, up-to-the-minute
rel convenient, opportune, timely; expedient, fitting, suitable; advanced, modern, stylish; a la mode, dashing, modish
idiom abreast of the times
con dusty, rusty, stale, timeworn; antiquated, outmoded, superannuated
ant out-of-date; archaic

up–to–the–minute *adj syn* see UP-TO-DATE

upturn *n syn* see COMMOTION 1

uranian *adj syn* see HOMOSEXUAL

uranian *n syn* see HOMOSEXUAL

uranist *n syn* see HOMOSEXUAL

urban *adj* of, relating to, or characteristic of a city <*urban* disorders>
syn burghal, city, municipal
rel inner city; metropolitan; civic, popular, public; oppidan, town, village
ant rural

urbane *adj* **1** *syn* see COSMOPOLITAN 1
2 *syn* see SUAVE
rel balanced, poised
ant bucolic, clownish
3 *syn* see GENTEEL 1
rel affable, civil, courteous, gracious, obliging
ant rude

urchin *n* a pert or roguish youngster <*urchins* pilfering apples on their way from school>
syn gamin, imp, monkey
rel brat, bratling, cub, dickens, pup, whelp, whippersnapper; guttersnipe, mudlark, ragamuffin, street arab; hobbledehoy

urge *vb* to press or impel to action, effort, or speed <his conscience *urged* him to tell the truth>
syn egg (on), exhort, goad, prick, prod, prompt, propel, sic, spur
rel hurry, hustle, push, rush, shove; blandish, cajole, coax, encourage, incite, needle, solicit, wheedle; constrain, drive, high-pressure, press, pressure; provoke, set (on), tar (on)
idiom bring pressure to bear on, twist one's arm
con brake, check, constrain, curb, hold back, inhibit, restrain

urge *n syn* see DESIRE 1
rel goad, incentive, motive, spring, spur

urgent *adj syn* see PRESSING
rel driving, impelling; demanding

usable *adj syn* see OPEN 5
ant unusable

usage *n* **1** *syn* see HABIT 1
rel choice, preference; procedure, proceeding, process; guidance, guiding, lead
2 *syn* see FORM 3
rel ceremony, formality

usance *n syn* see USE 1

use *n* **1** the act or practice of using something or the state of being used <all tools must be kept ready for instant *use*>
syn appliance, application, employment, operation, play, usance; *compare* EXERCISE 1
con desuetude, disuse
ant nonuse
2 *syn* see EXERCISE 1
3 the quality of being appropriate or valuable to some end <even the scraps had some *use*>
syn account, advantage, applicability, appropriateness, avail, fitness, relevance, service, serviceability, usefulness, utility
rel adaptability, availability, benefit, efficacy; profit, value, worth
con inadequacy, inapplicability, inappropriateness, insufficiency, unfitness, unserviceability, uselessness, worthlessness
4 a particular service or end <industrial *uses* of atomic energy>
syn duty, function, goal, mark, object, objective, purpose, target
5 *syn* see HABIT 1
rel ceremony, formality
6 *syn* see NEED 3

use *vb* **1** *syn* see ACCUSTOM
2 to put into action or service <it is necessary to *use* resources wisely>
syn apply, bestow, employ, exercise, exploit, handle, utilize
rel manipulate, operate, ply, wield; control, govern, manage, regulate
idiom avail oneself of, bring into play, fall back (on *or* upon), make use of, press into service, put into action, put to use
con dissipate, exhaust, use up; waste
3 *syn* see OPERATE 3
4 *syn* see SPEAK 3
5 *syn* see EXPLOIT 2
idiom make the most of, make use of
6 *syn* see TREAT 2

used up *adj syn* see EFFETE 2

useful *adj* **1** *syn* see PRACTICAL 2
2 *syn* see GOOD 1
ant useless
3 *syn* see GOOD 2
ant useless

usefulness *n syn* see USE 3
ant uselessness

useless *adj* **1** *syn* see FUTILE
ant useful
2 *syn* see IMPRACTICABLE 2
ant useful
3 *syn* see FECKLESS 1

use up *vb* **1** *syn* see CONSUME 1
2 *syn* see GO 4
3 *syn* see DEPLETE

usher *vb syn* see PRECEDE 3

usher in *vb syn* see INTRODUCE 3

usual *adj* **1** familiar through frequent or regular repetition <the sort that would perform her *usual* chores while waiting for the end of the world>
syn accepted, accustomed, chronic, customary, habitual, routine, wonted
rel natural, normal, regular, typical; common, familiar, ordinary; current, prevailing, prevalent, rife
idiom that make up one's daily round
con exceptional, rare, unaccustomed; remarkable, strange, unexpected
ant unusual

2 ***syn*** see GENERAL 1
3 ***syn*** see ORDINARY 1
usually *adv* **1** by or in accord with habit or custom <establishments of a kind *usually* restricted to back streets>
syn as usual, consistently, customarily, habitually, wontedly
2 more often than not <he is *usually* late for work>
syn as a rule, by ordinary, commonly, frequently, generally, ordinarily
rel now and again (*or* now and then), occasionally, once and again, sometimes
idiom for the most part, in the main
con infrequently, seldom, uncommonly
ant rarely
usurer *n* ***syn*** see LOAN SHARK
usurp *vb* **1** ***syn*** see ARROGATE 1
ant abdicate
2 ***syn*** see SUPPLANT 1
utensil *n* ***syn*** see IMPLEMENT
utile *adj* ***syn*** see PRACTICAL 2
ant inutile
utilitarian *adj* ***syn*** see REALISTIC
utility *n* ***syn*** see USE 3
ant inutility
utilize *vb* ***syn*** see USE 2
rel advance, forward, further, promote
utmost *adj* **1** ***syn*** see EXTREME 5
2 ***syn*** see MAXIMUM
3 ***syn*** see EXTREME 1
utopia *n* an often imaginary place or situation of perfection and delight <as far back as Plato, writers have attempted to portray their notion of *utopia*>
syn arcadia, Cockaigne, fairyland, heaven, lubberland, paradise, promised land, Shangri-la, wonderland, Zion
rel dreamland, dreamworld, never-never land
utopian *adj* **1** ***syn*** see IDEALISTIC
rel abstract, ideal, transcendental
2 ***syn*** see AMBITIOUS 2
rel impossible, impracticable, unfeasible; arcadian, edenic, millennial, otherworldly
utopian *n* ***syn*** see DREAMER
utter *adj* being such without qualification — used especially to intensify the noun modified <acted like an *utter* idiot>
syn absolute, all-fired, arrant, black, blamed, blank, blankety-blank, blasted, bleeding, blessed, blighted, blinding, ‖blinking, blithering, ‖blooming, blue, complete, confounded, ‖consarned, consummate, crashing, dad-blamed, dad-blasted, dad-burned, damned, dang, darn (*or* durn), dashed, deuced, doggone, double-distilled, double-dyed, downright, flat-out, goldarn, gross, hell-fired, infernal, out-and-out, outright, perfect, positive, ‖proper, pure, ‖puredee (*or* pure-D), rank, regular, sheer, stark, straight-out, ‖tarnation, thoroughgoing, total, unmitigated, unqualified; *compare* PURE 2
utter *vb* **1** ***syn*** see SPEAK 1
idiom give utterance to
2 ***syn*** see SAY 1
utterance *n* **1** ***syn*** see WORD 1
2 ***syn*** see VOCALIZATION
3 ***syn*** see EXPRESSION 1
4 ***syn*** see SPEECH 1
uttering *n* ***syn*** see VOCALIZATION
utterly *adv* **1** ***syn*** see WELL 3
2 ***syn*** see ALL 1
uttermost *adj* **1** ***syn*** see EXTREME 5
2 ***syn*** see EXTREME 1

syn synonym(s) ***rel*** related word(s)
ant antonym(s) ***con*** contrasted word(s)
idiom idiomatic equivalent(s)
‖ use limited; if in doubt, see a dictionary

V

vacancy *n* ***syn*** see VACUITY 2
rel desertedness
ant occupancy

vacant *adj* **1** ***syn*** see EMPTY 1
rel tenantless, unfilled, unoccupied, untaken
con inhabited, tenanted
ant occupied
2 ***syn*** see VACUOUS 2
3 ***syn*** see EXPRESSIONLESS
rel empty-headed, inane, thoughtless, witless
4 not being put to normal or appropriate use <*vacant* land>
syn idle, unused
rel bare, empty; unfilled, unoccupied
con filled; used
ant occupied

vacate *vb* **1** ***syn*** see ANNUL 4
rel repeal, rescind, retract, reverse, revoke
idiom declare null and void
2 to make something (as an office, post, or dwelling) vacant or empty <*vacate* a house>
syn clear, empty, void
rel abandon, give up, part (with *or* from), relinquish; leave, quit

vacation *n* a period spent away from one's usual activity or work often in travel or recreation <took a two-week *vacation* to Florida>
syn holiday, leave
rel break, breathing space (*or* breathing spell), intermission, recess; time off; respite, rest; furlough

vacillant *adj* ***syn*** see VACILLATING 2

vacillate *vb* ***syn*** see HESITATE
rel swag, sway, ‖swither; alternate, seesaw, teeter, teeter-totter, wag, waggle, wigwag, wobble; dally, dawdle, fiddle-faddle
idiom blow hot and cold, hem and haw, swing from one thing to another
con decide, resolve, settle

vacillating *adj* **1** ***syn*** see WEAK 2
rel unfixed; unsettled, unsteady; changeable, fickle, inconstant; eccentric, erratic, mercurial, volatile
con constant, steady, unchanging; strong
2 given to or manifesting hesitation or vacillation <a *vacillating* witness>
syn double-minded, faltering, halting, hesitant, hesitating, indecisive, irresolute, pendulous, shilly-shally, shilly-shallying, tentative, timid, uncertain, undecisive, unresolved, vacillant, vacillatory, wavering, weak-kneed, whiffling, wiggle-waggle, wobbly
rel doubtful, doubting, unsure; fluctuating, oscillating, shifting; dallying, dawdling, demurring, dillydallying, stalling
con certain, decisive, resolute, resolved, sure; definite, positive

vacillation *n* ***syn*** see HESITATION
rel dallying, demurral, dillydallying, stalling

vacillatory *adj* ***syn*** see VACILLATING 2
rel alternating, seesawing, varying; indecisive, irresolute, uncertain

vacuity *n* **1** ***syn*** see HOLE 3
2 the condition, fact, or quality of being vacuous <the utter *vacuity* of his expression>
syn blankness, emptiness, vacancy, vacuousness, voidness
rel bareness, barrenness, bleakness, desolateness, hollowness; dullness, inaneness, inanity, stupidity
3 ***syn*** see NOTHINGNESS

vacuous *adj* **1** ***syn*** see EMPTY 1
2 characterized by a lack of substance, thought, or intellectual content <a *vacuous* mind>
syn empty-headed, vacant; *compare* STUPID 1
rel shallow, superficial; blank, empty; dull, foolish, inane, silly

vacuousness *n* ***syn*** see VACUITY 2

vade mecum *n* ***syn*** see HANDBOOK

vag *n* ***syn*** see VAGABOND

vagabond *adj* ***syn*** see ITINERANT
rel vagabondish

vagabond *n* a person who wanders at will or as a habit <a park full of *vagabonds* sleeping on benches>
syn arab, ‖bindle stiff, bum, canter, clochard, derelict, drifter, floater, ‖gangrel, hobo, piker, roadster, runagate, ‖shack, street arab, ‖sundowner, ‖swagger, ‖swagman, tramp, tramper, ‖traveler, vag, vagrant, Weary Willie
rel roamer, rover, wanderer; boomer, migrant, runabout, straggler, stray, transient; bohemian, gypsy, picaro, picaroon; ‖casual; stiff; beggar, rogue
idiom knight of the road

vagabond *vb* ***syn*** see WANDER 1

vagabondage *n* ***syn*** see VAGRANCY

vagabondia *n* ***syn*** see VAGRANCY

vagabondism *n* ***syn*** see VAGRANCY

vagabondize *vb* ***syn*** see WANDER 1

vagarious *adj* ***syn*** see ARBITRARY 1
rel unreasonable; kinky

vagary *n* ***syn*** see CAPRICE
rel daydream, dream, fantasy; kink, quirk
idiom passing fancy

vagrancy *n* the act or state of wandering from place to place usually with no means of support <dropped out of society and lived a life of *vagrancy*>
syn hoboism, vagabondage, vagabondia, vagabondism
rel itineracy, itinerancy, nomadism; rambling, roaming, roving, wandering

vagrant *n* ***syn*** see VAGABOND

vagrant *adj* ***syn*** see ITINERANT

rel aimless, errant, erratic; straying; sauntering, strolling

vague *adj* **1** *syn* see OBSCURE 3
rel indeterminate, indistinct, unplain; cloudy, dim, hazy, nebulous; muddy
con clear, distinct
ant express
2 *syn* see FAINT 2
rel nebulous, unsubstantial; indefinite, unplain; uncertain, unrecognizable; dreamlike, dreamy
3 *syn* see HAZY
rel bleared, bleary, blurry

vain *adj* **1** devoid of worth or significance <the *vain* pursuits of a luxurious life>
syn empty, hollow, idle, nugatory, otiose
rel profitless, unprofitable, useless, valueless, void, worthless; ineffective, ineffectual, inefficacious; bootless, fruitless; abortive, futile
con useful, valuable, worthy; effective, effectual, efficacious
2 *syn* see FUTILE
rel paltry, petty, puny, trifling, trivial; delusive, delusory, misleading
3 having or exhibiting undue or excessive pride especially in one's appearance or achievements <was *vain* about his clothes>
syn conceited, ‖conceity, narcissistic, self-conceited, stuck-up, vainglorious; *compare* PROUD 1
rel arrogant, egocentric, egoistic, haughty, ‖pensy, proud, self-important, swollen-headed; boastful, self-exalting; coxcombical, dandyish, foppish
idiom stuck on oneself
con humble, meek, modest; bashful, diffident, retiring, shy

vainglorious *adj syn* see VAIN 3
rel boastful, bragging, vaunting; disdainful, insolent, supercilious

vainglory *n syn* see CONCEIT 2
rel arrogance, haughtiness; boastfulness, bombast; exhibition, flaunting, parading
con lowliness, meekness; bashfulness, diffidence, self-effacement, shyness; modesty
ant humility

vainness *n syn* see CONCEIT 2

vale *n syn* see VALLEY

valedictory *adj syn* see PARTING

valiance *n syn* see HEROISM
con feebleness, ineffectiveness; fear

valiancy *n syn* see HEROISM
con feebleness, ineffectiveness; fear

valiant *adj syn* see BRAVE 1
ant pusillanimous

valid *adj* having the power to impress others as right and well-founded <a *valid* conclusion>
syn cogent, convincing, satisfactory, satisfying, solid, sound, telling
rel persuasive, potent, strong; attested, confirmed, corroborated, demonstrated, determined, established, substantiated, validated, verified; lawful, legal, licit; effective, effectual; conclusive, decisive, definitive, determinative; acceptable
con groundless, shaky, unconvincing, unfounded, unsound; fallacious, false, misleading, sophistical; counterfeit, fictitious
ant invalid

validate *vb syn* see CONFIRM 2
rel approve, endorse, legalize, ratify, rubber-stamp, sanction
con abolish, abrogate, annul, cancel, repeal; void
ant invalidate

validity *n syn* see POINT 3
rel efficacy, gravity, soundness; persuasiveness, potency
con inconsistency; unsoundness; fallacy, falsity
ant invalidity, invalidness

validness *n syn* see POINT 3
ant invalidity, invalidness

valley *n* an elongate depression of the earth's surface commonly situated between ranges of hills or mountains <small farms dotted the floor of the *valley*>
syn ‖combe, dale, glen, vale
rel dell, dingle, hollow; ‖rincon; canyon

valor *n syn* see HEROISM
rel mettle, resolution, spirit, tenacity; indomitableness, invincibility, unconquerableness; backbone, fortitude, guts, sand
con cowardliness, fear
ant pusillanimity, pusillanimousness

valorous *adj syn* see BRAVE 1
ant pusillanimous

valorousness *n syn* see HEROISM
rel chivalrousness, chivalry; manliness
con cowardliness
ant pusillanimity, pusillanimousness

valuable *adj syn* see PRECIOUS 1
rel dear, expensive; appreciated, prized, treasured, valued; admired, esteemed, respected
idiom of great value
con cheap, inexpensive, trashy; unmarketable, unsalable; unworthy
ant valueless, worthless

valuate *vb syn* see ESTIMATE 1

valuation *n* **1** *syn* see ESTIMATE 1
rel judgment, opinion, rating
2 *syn* see WORTH 1
rel charge, cost, price

value *n* **1** *syn* see WORTH 1
rel appraisal, assessment; charge, cost, expense, price
2 *syn* see QUALITY 2

value *vb* **1** *syn* see ESTIMATE 1
rel compute, figure, gauge, reckon
idiom place a value (*or* price) on
2 *syn* see APPRECIATE 1
rel care (for); revere, reverence, venerate
idiom set much by

valueless *adj syn* see WORTHLESS 1
ant valuable

---

syn synonym(s) *rel* related word(s)
ant antonym(s) *con* contrasted word(s)
idiom idiomatic equivalent(s)
‖ use limited; if in doubt, see a dictionary

valve *n* ***syn*** see FAUCET
rel shutoff
‖**vamoose** *vb* ***syn*** see GET OUT 1
vamp *vb* ***syn*** see MEND 2
rel brush up, fix up, touch up; furbish, refurbish
vamp (up) *vb* ***syn*** see CONTRIVE 2
vamp *n* ***syn*** see FLIRT
rel charmer, enchantress, enticer, femme fatale, gold digger, inveigler, seductress, siren, temptress
vandal *n* one who willfully destroys or mars something valuable <*vandals* had knocked off the head of the statue>
syn defacer, despoiler, destroyer, ruinator, ruiner, wrecker
rel hoodlum, hooligan, lout, ruffian; devastator, ravager, spoiler, spoliator; looter, pillager, plunderer; iconoclast
vandalize *vb* to destroy or deface (as public or private property) willfully or maliciously <youths *vandalized* the shop>
syn ‖trash, wreck
rel ‖rip off; destroy, tear up
vanish *vb* to pass from view or out of existence <the moon *vanished* behind a cloud>
syn clear, disappear, evanesce, evanish, evaporate, fade
rel dematerialize, dissolve, melt (away); die
idiom do the vanishing act, vanish from sight, vanish into thin air, vanish like a dream
con arise, break out (*or* through), come (forth *or* out), emerge, issue, loom (up), materialize, show (up)
ant appear
vanished *adj* ***syn*** see EXTINCT 2
rel expired, passed away; annihilated, no more, perished
vanity *n* ***syn*** see CONCEIT 2
rel autotheism, self-worship
vanquish *vb* ***syn*** see CONQUER 1
rel surmount; overturn, subvert; humble, trample
vanquisher *n* ***syn*** see VICTOR 1
rel champ, champion
con loser
vanquishment *n* ***syn*** see DEFEAT 1
rel mastery, subdual, subjugation
vantage *n* ***syn*** see ADVANTAGE 3
ant disadvantage
vapid *adj* ***syn*** see INSIPID 3
rel flavorless, milk-toast, tasteless, weak; dull, unimaginative, uninteresting
idiom neither hot nor cold, neither one thing nor the other
con brisk, lively, tangy, zesty; crisp, forceful, incisive, trenchant; expressive, meaningful, pregnant, significant, telling
vaporous *adj* **1** ***syn*** see HAZY
2 ***syn*** see AIRY 3
rel unsubstantial, wispy; illusory, unreal
vapory *adj* **1** ***syn*** see HAZY
2 ***syn*** see AIRY 3
rel gaseous
variable *adj* **1** ***syn*** see CHANGEABLE 1
rel fitful, spasmodic; irregular, unequable, unequal, ununiform
con unchanging, unvarying; immobile, stable, unmoving; equable, equal, uniform
ant constant, invariable
2 ***syn*** see MUTABLE 2
3 ***syn*** see INCONSTANT 1
variance *n* **1** the quality, state, or fact of being variable <a daily *variance* of 1°F.>
syn difference, variation
rel change, deviation, fluctuation
ant invariance
2 ***syn*** see DISCORD
rel division, separation, severing, sundering
variation *n* **1** ***syn*** see CHANGE 1
rel difference, dissimilarity; deflection, discrepancy
con stability, unchangeableness
2 ***syn*** see VARIANCE 1
rel shift; divergence; discrepancy, disparity
con uniformity
varicolored *adj* ***syn*** see VARIEGATED
ant solid
varied *adj* ***syn*** see MISCELLANEOUS
variegated *adj* having a pattern involving different colors or shades of color <*variegated* leaves>
syn dappled, discolor, motley, multicolor, multicolored, multihued, parti-color, parti-colored, polychromatic, polychrome, varicolored, versicolor, versicolored
rel checked, checkered; piebald, pied, skewbald; freaked, streaked; flecked; stippled; marbled; mottle, mottled, spattered, speckled, spotted; calico; pinto
ant solid
variety *n* **1** the quality or state of being composed of different parts, elements, or individuals <the *variety* of the city's cultural life>
syn diverseness, diversity, multeity, multifariousness, multiformity, multiplicity, variousness
rel diversification, heterogeneity, variation
2 a collection of different things, forms, or qualities especially of a particular class <had a great *variety* of jobs in his lifetime>
syn assortment
rel conglomeration, medley, miscellany
3 ***syn*** see TYPE
rel classification; grade, rank
various *adj* **1** ***syn*** see MANY
rel assorted, heterogeneous, miscellaneous, omnifarious, omnigenous
2 ***syn*** see DIFFERENT 1
rel changing, variant, varied, varying; distinct, separate; distinctive, individual, peculiar
ant uniform
3 ***syn*** see SEVERAL 3
ant many, numerous
4 ***syn*** see DISTINCT 1
5 ***syn*** see CERTAIN 2
various *pron, pl in constr* ***syn*** see SUNDRY
variously *adv* ***syn*** see OTHERWISE 1
variousness *n* ***syn*** see VARIETY 1
varnish *vb* ***syn*** see PALLIATE
vary *vb* **1** ***syn*** see CHANGE 1

rel modulate, qualify
2 ***syn*** see DIFFER 1
3 ***syn*** see DIFFER 2
rel depart, deviate, digress, diverge; divide, part, separate
ant agree
4 ***syn*** see RANGE 3

vast *adj* ***syn*** see HUGE
rel big, large; ample, capacious, spacious; broad, expansive, far-flung, wide, widespread; astronomical, cosmic
con confined, limited, narrow, restricted

vastness *n* ***syn*** see ENORMITY 2

vatic *adj* ***syn*** see PROPHETIC

vaticinal *adj* ***syn*** see PROPHETIC

vaticinate *vb* ***syn*** see FORETELL

vault *n* ***syn*** see CRYPT

vault *vb* **1** ***syn*** see JUMP 1
rel upleap, upspring; overjump, overleap; clear; rise, soar; ascend, mount; surmount
2 ***syn*** see CLEAR 8

vaulting *adj* ***syn*** see AMBITIOUS 1
rel enthusiastic; opportunistic

vaunt *vb* ***syn*** see BOAST
rel brandish, display, exhibit, expose, flaunt, parade, show off
idiom puff oneself

vaunter *n* ***syn*** see BRAGGART

vaunting *adj* ***syn*** see BOASTFUL

vector *n* an agent capable of transmitting a pathogen from one organism to another <fleas are *vectors* of bubonic plague>
syn carrier, vehicle

veer *vb* **1** ***syn*** see TURN 6
2 ***syn*** see SWERVE 1
rel depart, deviate, digress, diverge; angle off, bear off; twist; pivot, turn, wheel

vegetate *vb* to lead a passive existence without exertion of body or mind <he never really lived his life—he merely *vegetated*>
syn stagnate
rel idle; languish; hibernate
idiom idle life away, live the life of a clam, pass the time

vehement *adj* ***syn*** see INTENSE 1
rel emphatic, pronounced; energetic, hearty, lively, zealous; forceful, potent, powerful; ardent, fervent, fervid, heated, impassioned, passionate, perfervid; delirious, frantic, furious, rabid, wild

vehicle *n* **1** ***syn*** see VECTOR
rel agent
2 ***syn*** see MEAN 2
rel implement, tool
3 a means of transporting goods or passengers <his *vehicle* was an old battered coupe>
syn conveyance, transport, transportation

veil *n* ***syn*** see MASK 2

veil *vb* ***syn*** see ENFOLD 1
rel mantle, overspread, spread (over); blanket, curtain; camouflage, cloak, cover (up), disguise, mask; conceal, hide, screen, secrete
con exhibit, lay (open), open up, reveal, uncover, unmask; bare, expose, show
ant unveil

vein *n* **1** a distinctive method of expression <wrote her speech in the proper *vein* for a very sophisticated audience>
syn fashion, manner, mode, style, tone
rel way; line; mood, tenor
2 ***syn*** see HINT 2
3 ***syn*** see MOOD 1
rel complexion, disposition, fettle, temperament; character, nature, spirit

velitation *n* ***syn*** see ENCOUNTER

velleity *n* ***syn*** see WILL 1
rel volition; wish

vellicate *vb* ***syn*** see JERK
rel nip, pinch; fidget, jig, jiggle

velocipede *n* ***syn*** see BICYCLE

velocity *n* ***syn*** see SPEED 2
rel headway, impetus, momentum; dispatch, expedition, haste, hurry

velutinous *adj* ***syn*** see VELVETY

velvetlike *adj* ***syn*** see VELVETY
idiom soft as velvet

velvety *adj* **1** having the extreme softness associated with the surface or appearance of velvet <wore a *velvety* red flower in her hair>
syn velutinous, velvetlike
rel plush, plushy, smooth, soft; glossy, sleek, slick; satiny, silken, silky
2 ***syn*** see SOFT 3

venal *adj* **1** open to corrupt influence and especially bribery <a *venal* legislator>
syn bribable, buyable, corruptible, purchasable; *compare* CORRUPT 2, CROOKED 2
rel corrupt, flagitious, infamous, iniquitous, nefarious, vicious; hack, hireling, mercenary, paid; ignoble, sordid; unethical, unprincipled, unscrupulous
2 ***syn*** see CORRUPT 2

vend *vb* **1** ***syn*** see SELL 2
2 ***syn*** see PEDDLE 2
3 ***syn*** see DECLARE 1

vendee *n* ***syn*** see PURCHASER

vendetta *n* a prolonged mutual enmity marked by bitter hostility and conflict <a long-standing *vendetta* between two rival gangs>
syn feud
rel dispute, quarrel; rhubarb, row, wrangle; conflict, fight, set-to; blood feud, blood vengeance

vendible *adj* ***syn*** see MARKETABLE
ant unvendible

vendible *n, usu* **vendibles** *pl* ***syn*** see MERCHANDISE

vendor *n* ***syn*** see PEDDLER

veneer *n* ***syn*** see MASK 2

veneer *vb* ***syn*** see PALLIATE

venerable *adj* **1** deserving to be venerated usually by reason of prolonged testing (as of character) <a *venerable* judge with an impressive knowledge of the law>

---

syn synonym(s) *rel* related word(s)
ant antonym(s) *con* contrasted word(s)
idiom idiomatic equivalent(s)
|| use limited; if in doubt, see a dictionary

syn patriarchal, revered, reverend, reverential; *compare* HONORABLE 1
rel dignified, imposing, stately; admirable, estimable; honored, reverenced; worshipful; sacred
ant unvenerable
2 *syn* see ANCIENT 1
rel elderly; patriarchal, reverenced, reverend, venerated
con contemporary, current; fresh, inexperienced, new, untried, unused

venerate *vb* ***syn*** see REVERE
rel honor; idolize
idiom put on a pedestal

venery *n* ***syn*** see HUNTING

venge *vb* ***syn*** see AVENGE
idiom even (up) the score, repay in kind, settle accounts (*or* an account)

vengeance *n* ***syn*** see RETALIATION
rel return; repayment; revengefulness, vengefulness

vengeful *adj* ***syn*** see VINDICTIVE
rel antagonistic, hostile, inimical, rancorous
con charitable, forgiving, kind; benevolent, benign, inoffensive

venial *adj* of a kind that can be remitted and that does not warrant punishment or penalty <the *venial* indiscretions of youth>
syn excusable, forgivable, pardonable, remittable
rel allowable, unobjectionable; insignificant, minor, trifling, trivial; harmless, tolerable
con criminal, damning, deadly, mortal; grievous, outrageous, serious; inexcusable, unforgivable, unpardonable, unremittable
ant heinous

venom *n* ***syn*** see POISON
rel ill will, malignity, rancor, venomousness, virulence, vitriol
con antidote, remedy

venomous *adj* ***syn*** see POISONOUS
rel malevolent, malign, malignant; baleful, malefic, maleficent; viperish, viperlike, viperous

vent *vb* **1 *syn*** see EMIT 2
rel cast out, discharge, exhaust
2 *syn* see EXPRESS 2
rel utter, voice; assert, declare
idiom come out with, give vent to
con check, curb, inhibit, restrain; repress, suppress
3 *syn* see TAKE OUT (on)

vent *n* **1 *syn*** see APERTURE
2 *syn* see EXPRESSION 1
rel articulation, verbalization, vocalization

venter *n* ***syn*** see ABDOMEN

ventilate *vb* **1 *syn*** see BROACH
2 *syn* see EXPRESS 2
rel go into, take up; debate, deliberate, discourse (about), discuss, ‖rap (about), talk over (*or* of *or* about), thresh out; advertise, broadcast, publish
idiom chew the fat (*or* the rag)

ventilation *n* ***syn*** see CONFERENCE 1

venture *vb* **1** to expose to risk or loss <*ventured* their capital in foreign trade>
syn adventure, chance, hazard, risk, wager; *compare* GAMBLE 2
rel endanger, imperil, jeopard, jeopardize, jeopardy, peril; expose, lay (open)
idiom take chances (*or* risks) on (*or* with)
2 *syn* see GAMBLE 2
rel bet, operate, play (for), speculate, stake; jeopard, jeopardize, jeopardy
idiom luck it
3 *syn* see FACE 3

venture *n* ***syn*** see ADVENTURE
rel attempt, undertaking; crack, fling; dare, gamble, risk, speculation
idiom leap in the dark

venturesome *adj* ***syn*** see ADVENTUROUS
rel stalwart, stout, sturdy; brave; overbold
con timid, timorous; afraid, apprehensive, fearful

venturous *adj* ***syn*** see ADVENTUROUS
rel aggressive, enterprising, hustling

veracious *adj* **1 *syn*** see TRUTHFUL
rel direct; undeceitful, undeceptive
con equivocal; deceitful, dishonest, insincere; false, untruthful
ant unveracious
2 *syn* see TRUE 3
rel unquestionable, valid
con illusory, invalid, wrong
ant unveracious

veraciousness *n* ***syn*** see VERACITY 1
rel artlessness, openness; trustworthiness
con falseness, insincerity

veracity *n* **1** the quality or state of keeping close to fact and avoiding distortion or misrepresentation <questions the *veracity* of that witness>
syn truth, truthfulness, veraciousness, veridicality, verity
rel accuracy, correctness, exactness, factualness; frankness, honesty
con inaccuracy, incorrectness; deception, dishonesty, untruth, untruthfulness
ant unveracity
2 something that is true <can make lies sound like *veracities*>
syn gospel, truism, truth, verity
rel verisimilitude; actuality; fact
con lie, untruth
ant unveracity

verbal *adj* **1 *syn*** see ORAL 2
2 *syn* see VERBATIM

verbalism *n* **1 *syn*** see WORDING
rel styling
2 *syn* see VERBOSITY

verbality *n* ***syn*** see VERBIAGE 1
rel verbalism, verboseness, verbosity, wordiness

verbalization *n* ***syn*** see SPEECH 1

verbalize *vb* ***syn*** see SPEAK 1
rel air, express, give, say, state, vent, ventilate, word
idiom couch in terms, find words to express

verbatim *adv* in the same words <repeated their earlier conversation *verbatim*>
syn direct, directly, literally, literatim, word for word

rel accurately, exactly, precisely
idiom to the letter
con basically, essentially, in essence; carelessly, imprecisely, inaccurately, inexactly

verbatim *adj* using the same words <court stenographers took down the *verbatim* testimony>
syn literal, verbal, word-for-word
rel close, faithful, strict; exact, precise
idiom following the letter, true to the letter
con careless, imprecise, inaccurate, inexact

verbiage *n* **1** a stylistic fault involving excessive wordiness that obscures or unduly complicates expression <the florid *verbiage* of the dissertation>
syn circumambages, circumbendibus, circumlocution, periphrase, periphrasis, pleonasm, redundancy, roundabout, tautology, verbality; *compare* VERBOSITY
rel nimiety; repetition; expansiveness, floridity, floridness; longiloquence, long-windedness
idiom purple prose
con breviloquence, brevity, briefness, terseness
ant concision
2 *syn* see WORDING

verbose *adj syn* see WORDY
rel flowery, grandiloquent, magniloquent; circumlocutory, periphrastic, pleonastic, tautologous
con precise; close, compact, lean, tight
ant concise; laconic

verboseness *n syn* see VERBOSITY
ant conciseness

verbosity *n* the quality or state or an instance of being wordy <his two-hour lecture was the epitome of *verbosity*> <flowery *verbosities* weakened his speech>
syn prolixity, prolixness, verbalism, verboseness, windiness, wordiness; *compare* VERBIAGE 1
rel bombast, grandiloquence; long-windedness; redundancy
con conciseness, preciseness, succinctness, terseness; leanness, tightness

verboten *adj syn* see FORBIDDEN
rel disallowed, disapproved; unauthorized, unlicensed, unsanctioned; outlawed, taboo
con allowed, permitted; authorized, licensed; approved, endorsed, sanctioned

verdure *n syn* see FOLIAGE

verge *n* **1** *syn* see BORDER 1
2 a time interval or set of circumstances marking the imminent beginning of a new state, condition, or action <on the *verge* of war>
syn brink, edge, point, threshold
rel border line

verge *vb* **1** *syn* see BORDER 1
rel approach; incline, lean, tend (to *or* toward); touch (on *or* upon)
2 *syn* see ADJOIN
3 *syn* see BORDER 3

veridical *adj* **1** *syn* see TRUTHFUL
2 *syn* see REAL 3
3 *syn* see TRUE 3
rel uncolored, undistorted, unvarnished; actual, real
con invalid; illusory, unreal

veridicality *n syn* see VERACITY 1
rel genuineness

verificatory *adj syn* see CORROBORATIVE

verify *vb syn* see CONFIRM 2
rel demonstrate, prove, test, try; document, establish, settle

verily *adv syn* see EVEN 3

verisimilitude *n* the quality of a representation that causes it to appear true <her characters are too stilted for *verisimilitude*>
syn color, plausibility, verisimility
rel authenticity, genuineness, veritableness; likeness, resemblance, similarity

verisimility *n syn* see VERISIMILITUDE

veritable *adj syn* see AUTHENTIC 2
rel undenied, unrefuted; actual, factual
con doubtful, questionable; imaginary, unreal, untrue; artificial, factitious; counterfeit, false, spurious

veritably *adv syn* see VERY 2

verity *n* **1** *syn* see VERACITY 2
ant falsity
2 *syn* see VERACITY 1

vernacular *adj* of or relating to everyday speech <*vernacular* Welsh differs greatly from literary Welsh>
syn colloquial, vulgar, vulgate

vernacular *n* **1** *syn* see LANGUAGE 1
rel mother tongue
idiom native tongue
2 *syn* see DIALECT 2
3 a commonly spoken as opposed to a prestige variety of a language <literary Chinese and the various *vernaculars*>
syn colloquial, patois, vulgate; *compare* DIALECT 2
rel dialect, lingo, slang

vernacularism *n syn* see BARBARISM

vernacularity *n syn* see BARBARISM

vernal *adj* of, relating to, or resembling the spring of the year <*vernal* sunshine>
syn spring, springlike

versant *adj syn* see FAMILIAR 3
ant unversed

versatile *adj* having a wide range of skills, aptitudes, or interests <a *versatile* artist, who is at home in any medium>
syn adaptable, all-around, ambidextrous, many-sided, mobile, myriad-minded
rel elastic, flexible, plastic, pliable; adroit, dexterous, facile; able, skilled, skillful; accomplished, conversant; gifted, talented; well-rounded
con inadequate, limited

verse *n* **1** *syn* see POETRY 1
2 *syn* see POEM
rel jingle; ballad, lay; sonnet; lyric; ode; epic

versed *adj* **1** *syn* see EXPERIENCED

---

syn synonym(s) *rel* related word(s)
ant antonym(s) *con* contrasted word(s)
idiom idiomatic equivalent(s)
‖ use limited; if in doubt, see a dictionary

rel competent
con incompetent
ant unversed
2 ***syn*** see FAMILIAR 3
ant unversed

verseman *n* ***syn*** see POETASTER

versemonger *n* ***syn*** see POETASTER

verser *n* ***syn*** see POETASTER

versesmith *n* ***syn*** see POETASTER

versicolor *adj* ***syn*** see VARIEGATED

versicolored *adj* ***syn*** see VARIEGATED

versificator *n* ***syn*** see POETASTER

versifier *n* ***syn*** see POETASTER

version *n* **1** a restating often in simpler language of something previously stated or written <a simple *version* of "Tom Sawyer" for the use of children>
syn paraphrase, rendering, restatement, translation
rel rendition; clarification, interpretation; condensation, simplification; rewording; restipulation
2 ***syn*** see ACCOUNT 7
rel tale
3 ***syn*** see INTERPRETATION 2

versus *prep* **1** in conflict with <the case of John Doe *versus* Richard Roe>
syn against
rel con, contra
idiom at cross-purposes with (*or* to), at odds with, at outs with, at variance with, on the outs with
2 in contrast with <the age-old argument about free trade *versus* protection>
syn over against, vis-à-vis
idiom as opposed to

vertebrae *n* ***syn*** see SPINE

vertebral column *n* ***syn*** see SPINE

vertex *n* ***syn*** see TOP 1
rel cap; tip-top; apogee, zenith
idiom upper extremity

vertical *adj* situated at right angles to the plane of the horizon or extending from that plane at such an angle <*vertical* walls>
syn perpendicular, plumb, straight-up
rel erect, upright; steep, up-and-down
con flat, plane
ant horizontal

verticalism *n* ***syn*** see VERTICALITY

verticality *n* the quality or state of being vertical <the soaring *verticality* of the spires>
syn perpendicularity, plumbness, verticalism, verticalness
rel erectness, uprightness
con flatness, lowness
ant horizontality

verticalness *n* ***syn*** see VERTICALITY

vertiginous *adj* ***syn*** see DIZZY 2

verve *n* ***syn*** see SPIRIT 5
rel liveliness, vivacity; bounce, buoyancy, elasticity, resiliency, spring; fire, gusto, zest

very *adj* **1** ***syn*** see AUTHENTIC 2
rel hundred-percent, perfect; correct, exact, right
con fake, fraudulent, mock, sham
2 ***syn*** see PRECISE 4
rel especial, express, special
3 ***syn*** see PERFECT 3
4 being as stated without addition or superfluity <the *very* thought of it makes me ill>
syn bare, mere
5 ***syn*** see SAME 1
idiom (the) very same

very *adv* **1** to a high or exceptional degree <a *very* successful meeting>
syn ‖awful, awfully, ‖big, ‖crazy, damned, ‖dreadful, dreadfully, eminently, exceedingly, exceptionally, extremely, greatly, highly, hugely, insatiably, ‖larruping, ‖main, mightily, mighty, ‖monstrous, ‖mortacious, mortally, most, much, notably, parlous, pesky, ‖pure, rattling, remarkably, right, ‖right smart, snapping, so, spanking, staving, strikingly, super, surpassingly, terribly, thoroughly, too, vitally, whacking, whopping
rel passing, quite, somewhat; perfectly, seriously, significantly, tellingly
idiom nothing if not
con inconsiderably, little, scarcely, slightly
2 in actual fact <told the *very* same story>
syn actually, de facto, genuinely, really, truly, veritably
rel exactly, precisely; almost, nearly, practically, well-nigh
idiom in point of fact, in truth
con apparently, ostensibly, outwardly, seemingly

vest *vb* **1** ***syn*** see INVEST 2
2 ***syn*** see BELONG 2

vestibule *n* an entrance chamber between the outer door and the interior of a building <the *vestibule* of a theater>
syn foyer, lobby
rel entrance hall, entry, entryway; portal, portico; antechamber, anteroom; narthex

vestige *n* **1** something (as a mark or visible sign) left by a material thing formerly present but now lost or unknown <digging for the *vestiges* of past civilizations>
syn memento, relic, shadow, trace
rel remainder, remains; rag, remnant, scrap, tag
2 ***syn*** see FOOTPRINT
rel path; trail

vet *vb* ***syn*** see SCRUTINIZE 1
idiom go over with a fine-tooth comb

vet *adj* ***syn*** see EXPERIENCED

vet *n* ***syn*** see VETERAN

veteran *n* one having knowledge or ability gained through long experience <was a political campaign *veteran* of long standing>
syn longtimer, old hand, old-timer, vet
rel expert, master, past master
con amateur, freshman, youngster
ant novice

veteran *adj* ***syn*** see EXPERIENCED
rel wise; sophisticated, worldly
idiom dry behind the ears, not born yesterday, wise in the ways of the world
con inexperienced, unpracticed, unversed; unqualified, unskilled, untrained

veto *vb* to refuse to admit or approve <the President *vetoed* the bill>
syn kill, negative, ‖nix, non-placet
rel decline, deny, disallow, forbid, prohibit, refuse, reject; defeat
idiom put one's veto on
con admit, approve, assent (to); pass

vex *vb* ***syn*** see ANNOY 1
rel ‖chaw, embarrass; plague; anger, infuriate
con appease, mollify, pacify, propitiate, smooth (over); please, regale
ant soothe

vexation *n* ***syn*** see ANNOYANCE 1
rel aggravation, irritation

vexatious *adj* ***syn*** see TROUBLESOME

vexing *n* ***syn*** see ANNOYANCE 1

via *prep* **1** over a route that passes through <shipped to New York *via* the Panama Canal>
syn by, by way of, through
rel along; over
2 using as a means of approach or action <reached the voters *via* mass-media advertising>
syn by, by dint of, by means of, by virtue of, by way of, per, through, with
idiom through the medium of

viable *adj* ***syn*** see POSSIBLE 1

viands *n pl* ***syn*** see FOOD 1
rel fare

vibrant *adj* ***syn*** see RESONANT

vibrate *vb* ***syn*** see SHAKE 2

vice *n* **1** degrading or immoral habits and practices <an exposé of *vice* and crime in the city>
syn corruption, depravity, immorality, wickedness
rel decay, rot, squalor; evil, ill, sin, wrong; indecency, unchastity; debasement, debauchery, licentiousness, perversion
con morality; respectability; uprightness
ant virtue
2 ***syn*** see FAULT 2
rel shortcoming
idiom weak point
3 ***syn*** see BLEMISH

vice versa *adv* ***syn*** see AGAIN 5

vicinage *n* ***syn*** see LOCALITY 1

vicinity *n* **1** ***syn*** see LOCALITY 1
2 ***syn*** see ORDER 4

vicious *adj* **1** ***syn*** see WRONG 1
2 highly offensive or reprehensible in character, nature, or conduct <*vicious* parents who were a bad influence on their children>
syn corrupt, degenerate, depraved, flagitious, infamous, miscreant, nefarious, perverse, putrid, rotten, unhealthy, villainous
rel bad, faulty, poor, unsound; opprobrious, reprehensible; contaminated, obnoxious, septic
con good, moral, righteous, right-minded
ant virtuous
3 ***syn*** see SAVAGE 1
rel brutish; bloodthirsty
4 ***syn*** see MALICIOUS
5 ***syn*** see INTENSE 1
rel severe

vicissitude *n* **1** ***syn*** see CHANGE 2
rel alternation; reversal; transposition; progression; diversity, variety
2 ***syn*** see DIFFICULTY 1
rel chop and change, ups and downs; adversity, mischance, misfortune; affliction, trial, tribulation

victim *n* **1** a living being sacrificed (as in a religious rite) <offered up human *victims* to appease their bloodthirsty gods>
syn offering, sacrifice
2 one subjected to oppression, loss, or suffering <*victims* of social injustice>
syn bottom dog, casualty, prey, underdog
rel quarry
3 ***syn*** see FOOL 3
idiom easy mark, easy pickings

victimize *vb* **1** ***syn*** see SACRIFICE 1
2 ***syn*** see DUPE

victor *n* **1** one that defeats an enemy <the Allies were the *victors* of World War II>
syn conqueror, defeater, master, subduer, subjugator, vanquisher
rel winner
con conquered, defeated, subjugated; loser
ant vanquished
2 a successful contender <emerged as *victor* in the swimming meet>
syn winner
rel champ, champion; first, top
idiom conquering hero
ant loser

Victorian *adj* ***syn*** see PRIM 1
rel old-fashioned, old-maidish; hidebound; starchy
con easy going; trendy, with-it

victory *n* **1** the overcoming of an opponent <won a knockout *victory* in the first round>
syn conquest, triumph, win
rel command, control, dominion, mastery, subjugation; superiority, supremacy; walkaway, walkover
idiom a feather in one's cap
con loss; bust, failure, fizzle, flop, ‖floperoo, washout; comedown, cropper
ant defeat
2 ***syn*** see BETTER 2

victuals *n pl* ***syn*** see FOOD 1

videlicet *adv* ***syn*** see NAMELY

video *n* ***syn*** see TELEVISION

vie *vb* **1** ***syn*** see COMPETE 1
rel challenge; match; outvie
2 ***syn*** see OPPOSE 1

view *n* **1** ***syn*** see LOOK 1
rel examination, inspection, scan, scrutiny
2 ***syn*** see EXAMINATION
3 ***syn*** see EYE 4
4 what is revealed to the vision or can be seen <the *view* from the window>

---

syn synonym(s) ***rel*** related word(s)
ant antonym(s) ***con*** contrasted word(s)
idiom idiomatic equivalent(s)
‖ use limited; if in doubt, see a dictionary

syn outlook, scene, sight
rel panorama, picture, prospect, vista
5 extent or range of vision <there were still no ships in *view*>
syn sight
rel look; apprehension, scan
6 something (as an aim, end, or motive) to or by which the mind is directed <kept this *view* in mind while negotiating>
syn object
rel intent, intention, purpose; aim, ambition, goal, objective; design, plan, project; consideration, notion; expectation
7 *syn* see OPINION
rel concept, conception; deduction, inference

view *vb* 1 *syn* see SCRUTINIZE 1
2 *syn* see EYE 1
rel observe
3 *syn* see SEE 1
4 *syn* see CONSIDER 3

viewable *adj syn* see VISUAL 2

viewer *n syn* see SPECTATOR

viewpoint *n* 1 *syn* see EYE 4
2 the position or attitude that determines how something is seen, presented, or evaluated <from this *viewpoint* the picture looks askew> <consider totalitarianism from the German *viewpoint*>
syn angle, direction, outlook, side, slant, standpoint; *compare* EYE 4
rel estimation; attitude, position, posture, stand; long view, perspective
idiom frame of reference, point of view, vantage point

viewy *adj syn* see IMPRACTICAL 1

vigil *n syn* see LOOKOUT 3

vigilance *n syn* see LOOKOUT 3

vigilant *adj syn* see WATCHFUL
rel agog, anxious, avid, eager, keen; acute, sharp, sharp-eyed; attentive
idiom on one's guard, with a weather eye open
con lax, neglectful, negligent, remiss, slack; forgetful, oblivious, unmindful

vigor *n* 1 *syn* see POWER 4
2 a quality of physical or mental force or forcefulness <the *vigor* of youth>
syn bang, drive, getup, get-up-and-go, go, pep, punch, push, snap, starch, vitality; *compare* ENERGY 2, ENTERPRISE 4, SPIRIT 5
rel bounce, energy, force, might, muscularity, power, strength; healthiness, soundness; lustiness, manliness, virility
con slowness, sluggishness
ant weakness
3 *syn* see ENERGY 2
rel dash, drive, dynamism, fire, punch, starch, steam, vim, zing, zip; ability, capability, capacity
con ineffectiveness; impotence; incompetence, uselessness, worthlessness

vigorous *adj* having or manifesting great vitality and force <seemed as *vigorous* as a youth half his age>
syn dynamic, energetic, lusty, red-blooded, strenuous, ‖survigrous, vital
rel brisk, dashing, lively, slashing; exuberant, mettlesome, proud, spirited; driving, hard-driving, hard-hitting, robust, rough-and-ready, zealous; bouncing, hardy, healthy, hearty, masterful, potent, powerful, strong, tough; rude, stout, sturdy; athletic, husky, muscular, sinewy
con languorous, unenergetic; decrepit, feeble, infirm, weak; impotent
ant lethargic

vigorously *adv syn* see HARD 1
rel alertly, eagerly; boldly, firmly, purposefully, resolutely, unfalteringly, zealously; lustily, robustly
con aimlessly, languorously; falteringly, indecisively; impotently

vile *adj* 1 *syn* see BASE 3
rel corrupted, debased, debauched, depraved, perverted; coarse, gross, obscene, vulgar; disgusting, foul, nasty; abhorrent, contemptible, loathsome, offensive, repulsive, revolting
2 *syn* see OFFENSIVE

vilify *vb syn* see MALIGN
rel abuse, mistreat, misuse, outrage; assail, attack, berate; denounce
con commend, compliment; acclaim, exalt; celebrate, glorify, honor; adore, worship
ant eulogize

vilifying *adj syn* see LIBELOUS

villa *n syn* see MANSION

villain *n* 1 a low, mean, reprehensible person utterly lacking in principle <was an insufferable bully, a tyrant, and a *villain* in general>
syn blackguard, heel, knave, lowlife, miscreant, rascal, reprobate, rogue, roperipe, scoundrel, ‖slubberdegullion; *compare* SNOT 1, DEVIL 2
rel meanie; evildoer, offender, sinner; criminal, malefactor
2 *syn* see SCAMP

villainize *vb syn* see MALIGN
ant eulogize

villainous *adj syn* see VICIOUS 2
rel contrary, detestable, objectionable, offensive; debased, perverted; atrocious, heinous, outrageous; abandoned, dissolute, profligate

villenage *n syn* see BONDAGE

vim *n syn* see SPIRIT 5
rel pepper; kick, push

vinculum *n syn* see BOND 3

vindicable *adj syn* see JUSTIFIABLE
rel inoffensive, unobjectionable, venial
con indefensible, unjustifiable; inexcusable, unforgivable; heinous, mortal

vindicate *vb* 1 *syn* see AVENGE
2 *syn* see MAINTAIN 2
rel advocate, plead (for), second, support, uphold; rationalize; bear out, prove
3 *syn* see EXCULPATE
rel confute, disprove, refute; defend, guard, protect, shield
con accuse, attack, calumniate
ant convict

vindictive *adj* showing or motivated by a desire for vengeance <*vindictive* hatred for his brother>

syn revengeful, vengeful, wreakful
rel grim, implacable, merciless, relentless, unrelenting; malicious, malign, malignant, spiteful
con charitable, forgiving, merciful, relenting
ant unvindictive

vinegarish *adj* ***syn*** see CANTANKEROUS

vinegary *adj* ***syn*** see CANTANKEROUS

vintage *adj* **1** being of old, recognized, and enduring interest, importance, or quality <a *vintage* comedy from the silent movie era>
syn classic, classical
2 ***syn*** see OLD-FASHIONED

violate *vb* **1** to fail to keep <people who thoughtlessly *violate* the law>
syn breach, break, contravene, infract, infringe, offend, transgress
rel disregard, trample (on *or* upon); err, sin; overpass, trespass
con abide by, carry out, fulfill, submit (to); heed, keep, mind
ant observe; obey
2 ***syn*** see RAPE

violation *n* **1** ***syn*** see BREACH 1
rel break; encroachment; illegality, misdemeanor, offense, wrong
ant observance
2 ***syn*** see PROFANATION
rel defacement, defacing

violence *n* ***syn*** see FORCE 4
rel frenzy, fury, savagery; assault, attack, clash, foul play, onslaught, rampage, struggle, tumult, uproar
con passiveness, passivity; peace, peacefulness
ant nonviolence

violent *adj* ***syn*** see INTENSE 1
rel forceful, forcible, mighty, potent, powerful, strong; extreme, immoderate, inordinate; acute, cutting, piercing, splitting
con calm, moderate, peaceful
ant nonviolent

violently *adv* ***syn*** see HARD 2
rel combatively; destructively, ruinously
idiom like fury, with a vengeance

VIP *n* ***syn*** see NOTABLE 1

virago *n* a woman of extremely pugnacious temperament <an overbearing *virago* who screamed at her children and squabbled with her neighbors>
syn amazon, fishwife, harpy, ogress, scold, shrew, termagant, vixen, Xanthippe
rel cat; dragon; fury

virgin *adj* **1** never having had sexual relations <*virgin* girls were sacrificed>
syn intact, maiden, undeflowered, virginal
rel innocent, untouched; single, spouseless, unmarried, unwed; abstinent, celibate
2 not marred or altered from a natural or original state <a *virgin* forest>
syn unspoiled, untapped, untouched, virginal
rel primeval, pristine; fresh, new; unmarred, unsullied

virginal *adj* **1** ***syn*** see VIRGIN 1
2 ***syn*** see VIRGIN 2

virginity *n* the quality or state of being a virgin <lost her *virginity*>
syn maidenhead, maidenhood
rel chasteness, chastity, purity

virile *adj* characterized by the energy and drive considered typical of a man or of men <developed a strong *virile* prose style>
syn male, manlike, manly, masculine
rel macho, manful, mannish; decisive, driving, forceful; energetic, potent, robust; ultramasculine, ultravirile
con effeminate, womanish; emasculated, weak, weakened; impotent

virility *n* the vigor or agressiveness held to be typical of males <pundits decided that the candidate's conspicuous *virility* appealed to voters>
syn maleness, manfulness, manliness, masculinity
rel courage, dauntlessness, guts, machismo, macho, mettle, ||moxie, pluck, resolution, spirit, spunk
con effeminacy, unmanliness; impotence, weakness; prissiness, sissiness

virtual *adj* ***syn*** see IMPLICIT 2
rel basic, essential, fundamental
ant actual

virtuality *n* ***syn*** see ESSENCE 2

virtually *adv* not absolutely or actually, yet so nearly so that the difference is negligible <that request is *virtually* an order>
syn in essence, morally, practically; *compare* ALMOST 2
rel basically, essentially, fundamentally; absolutely, actually
idiom for all practical purposes, in effect, in substance, to all intents and purposes

virtue *n* **1** ***syn*** see GOODNESS
rel fealty, fidelity, loyalty, piety; virtuousness
con dishonesty; disloyalty, infidelity; evil; immorality; depravity
ant vice
2 ***syn*** see EXCELLENCE
rel attribute, characteristic, feature, property; effectiveness, effectualness, efficacy; force, might, power, strength
3 ***syn*** see QUALITY 1
4 ***syn*** see QUALITY 2
5 ***syn*** see POWER 4

virtuosic *adj* ***syn*** see CONSUMMATE 1

virtuoso *n* **1** ***syn*** see EXPERT
2 ***syn*** see MUSICIAN

virtuous *adj* **1** ***syn*** see EFFECTIVE
ant virtueless
2 ***syn*** see MORAL 1
rel spotless, unsullied, untainted, untarnished; worthy
con dishonest; unjust; unworthy; impure, tainted; immodest, immoral, indecent; vicious, wicked
ant unvirtuous, virtueless
3 ***syn*** see GOOD 11

---

syn synonym(s) — *rel* related word(s)
ant antonym(s) — *con* contrasted word(s)
idiom idiomatic equivalent(s)
|| use limited; if in doubt, see a dictionary

rel faultless, sinless
idiom innocent as a lamb, in the clear, without reproach
con bad, impure, unrighteous
ant unvirtuous, virtueless; vicious

virulent *adj* **1** *syn* see POISONOUS
rel malign, malignant
2 *syn* see BITTER 3
rel biting, cutting, scathing, sharp, stabbing; hateful, spiteful, unfriendly

virus *n syn* see POISON
rel corruption, taint

visage *n* **1** *syn* see FACE 1
2 *syn* see LOOK 2

vis–à–vis *n* **1** *syn* see OPPOSITE NUMBER
2 *syn* see TÊTE-À-TÊTE

vis–à–vis *prep* **1** *syn* see AGAINST 1
rel opposite
2 *syn* see VERSUS 2

viscera *n pl syn* see ENTRAILS

visceral *adj* **1** *syn* see INNER 2
2 *syn* see INSTINCTIVE 1

viscerous *adj syn* see INNER 2

viscid *adj syn* see VISCOUS
rel jellylike, slabby

viscose *adj syn* see VISCOUS
rel smeary

viscous *adj* having a glutinous adhesive consistency or quality <a *viscous* scum covered the surface of the platter>
syn tenacious, tough, viscid, viscose
rel ‖slab, slimy, thick; glutinous, gummy, ropy, sticky; semifluid; stiff

visibility *n* the quality or state of being visible <very poor *visibility* due to fog>
syn visuality

visible *adj syn* see VISUAL 2
rel seen

vision *n* **1** *syn* see REVELATION
rel apparition, phenomenon, presence
2 *syn* see FANCY 4
rel muse
idiom phantom of the mind
3 *syn* see EYE 2

vision *vb syn* see THINK 1

visional *adj syn* see VISUAL 1

visionary *adj* **1** *syn* see DREAMY 1
rel abstracted, introspective, musing; impractical
idiom out of this world, up in the clouds
2 *syn* see IDEALISTIC
rel exalted, grandiose, lofty, noble, pretentious
ant pragmatic, pragmatical
3 *syn* see AMBITIOUS 2
rel radical

visionary *n syn* see DREAMER
ant pragmatist

visionless *adj syn* see BLIND 1

visit *vb* **1** *syn* see INFLICT 2
rel afflict, bother, pain, trouble; avenge, punish
idiom bring down upon
2 to make a social call upon <*visited* friends briefly in the evening>
syn call, come by, come over, drop (in *or* by), look in, look up, pop (in), run in, see, step in, stop (in *or* by)
3 to reside with temporarily as a guest <*visited* with friends in the country for a few weeks>
syn sojourn, stay, stop (over), tarry
rel frequent; reside
4 *syn* see CONVERSE

visit *n* **1** a coming to stay with another temporarily and usually briefly <pay a *visit* to friends>
syn call, visitation
2 *syn* see SOJOURN

visitant *n syn* see VISITOR 1

visitation *n* **1** *syn* see VISIT 1
2 *syn* see TRIAL 1
rel mischance; calamity, catastrophe, disaster

visitor *n* **1** one who visits another <there are *visitors* in the living room>
syn caller, guest, visitant; *compare* COMPANY 2
rel invitee
2 visitors *pl syn* see COMPANY 2

visor *n* **1** a projecting front brim on a cap or hat for shading the eyes <the *visor* kept out the sun>
syn bill, peak
rel eyeshade
2 *syn* see MASK 1

vista *n* an extensive or distant view <a long flat tree-lined *vista*>
syn lookout, outlook, perspective, prospect, scape
rel panorama, scene, sight, view; range, scope, survey
idiom long view

visual *adj* **1** of or relating to or used in vision <the *visual* sense>
syn ocular, optic, optical, visional
2 capable of being seen <*visual* objects>
syn ocular, seeable, viewable, visible
rel discernible, perceivable, perceptible

visuality *n syn* see VISIBILITY

visualize *vb* **1** *syn* see THINK 1
rel picture, view; objectify; call up, conjure (up)
idiom bring (*or* call) to mind, conjure up a mental image (*or* picture) of, see in the mind's eye
2 *syn* see FORESEE

vital *adj* **1** *syn* see LIVING 1
rel breathing
2 *syn* see VIGOROUS
3 *syn* see ESSENTIAL 2
rel indispensable, needed, needful, required, requisite; integral, prerequisite

vital force *n syn* see SOUL 1

vitality *n syn* see VIGOR 2
rel animation, life, liveliness, pulse; endurance, energy, spirit, vim

vitalize *vb* to arouse to activity, animation, or life <atomic energy is a force that can *vitalize* or destroy human civilization>
syn actify, activate, activize, energize
rel animate, enliven, invigorate, quicken, vivify; dynamize, excite, galvanize, provoke, stimulate; pep up, strengthen
idiom put life into
con eviscerate, weaken

ant atrophy; devitalize
vitalizing *adj **syn*** see INVIGORATING
ant devitalizing
vitally *adv **syn*** see VERY 1
vitiate *adj **syn*** see DEBASED
ant purified
vitiate *vb* **1** ***syn*** see INJURE 1
rel twist, warp
2 ***syn*** see DEBASE 1
rel defile, soil, sully, taint; prostitute; contaminate
idiom drive to the dogs
ant purify
3 ***syn*** see ABOLISH 1
vitiated *adj **syn*** see DEBASED
rel contaminated, defiled, polluted, tainted; impaired, injured, spoiled
ant purified
vitriolic *adj **syn*** see BITTER 3
vituperate *vb **syn*** see SCOLD 1
rel condemn, lambaste; asperse, calumniate, malign, traduce; bark (at), growl (at), yell (at); abuse, curse
idiom rip into
con applaud, commend, compliment; eulogize, extol, praise
ant acclaim
vituperation *n **syn*** see ABUSE
rel blame, censure, revilement, scolding, tongue-lashing
con eulogy, extolment
ant acclaim, praise
vituperative *adj **syn*** see ABUSIVE
rel censorious, critical; severe; railing, scolding
vituperatory *adj **syn*** see ABUSIVE
rel censorious, critical; severe; railing, scolding
vituperous *adj **syn*** see ABUSIVE
rel censorious, critical; severe; railing, scolding
vivacious *adj* **1** ***syn*** see LIVELY 1
rel breezy, vibrant, zesty; frolicsome, playful, sportive
idiom gay as a lark
ant languid
2 ***syn*** see EXUBERANT 1
viva voce *adj **syn*** see VOCAL 1
vivid *adj* **1** ***syn*** see COLORFUL
2 ***syn*** see GRAPHIC 1
rel acute, intense, keen, sharp; dramatic, dramaturgic, theatrical; eloquent, expressive, meaningful, rich; animated, lively, spirited, vigorous
vivificate *vb **syn*** see QUICKEN 1
rel revive
vivify *vb **syn*** see QUICKEN 1
rel refresh, renew, restore; excite, galvanize
idiom give life to, imbue with life, put new life into
vivres *n pl **syn*** see FOOD 1
vixen *n **syn*** see VIRAGO
vizard *n **syn*** see MASK 1
‖**vlei** *n **syn*** see SWAMP
vocable *n **syn*** see WORD 2
rel verbalism
vocabulary *n* **1** the sum or set of words employed by a language, group, individual, or work or in relation to a subject <Latin contributes heavily to the *vocabulary* of English>
syn lexicon, word-hoard, word-stock
idiom stock of words
2 ***syn*** see TERMINOLOGY
rel phraseology
vocal *adj* **1** uttered by the voice or having to do with such utterance <the infant's primitive *vocal* sounds from which language develops>
syn articulate, oral, sonant, spoken, viva voce, voiced
rel intonated; expressed, uttered
con unexpressed, unuttered, unvoiced
ant nonvocal
2 ***syn*** see VOCALIC
ant consonantal
3 being able to express oneself clearly or easily <he was hardly *vocal:* he could scarcely express the simplest concepts>
syn articulate, eloquent, fluent, smooth-spoken
rel expressing, voicing; expressive; outspoken, stentorian, venting
con faltering, halting, hesitant, stumbling
4 ***syn*** see OUTSPOKEN
vocalic *adj* marked by, consisting of, or functioning as a vowel or vowels <*vocalic* and consonantal sounds>
syn vocal, vowel, vowely
rel vowellike
vocalism *n **syn*** see VOCALIZATION
vocalization *n* the exercise of the vocal organs in song or speech <her *vocalization* of a previously unstated thought>
syn articulation, utterance, uttering, vocalism; *compare* SPEECH 1
rel mouth, mouthing; sounding, voice, voicing; diction, enunciation, verbalization; speaking, speech
vocalize *vb* **1** ***syn*** see SPEAK 1
rel emit, let out; express; enunciate, pronounce; communicate, convey, impart
idiom execute vocally
2 ***syn*** see SING 1
vocation *n* **1** ***syn*** see TRADE 1
2 ***syn*** see MISSION
vocative *adj **syn*** see GLIB
rel chatty, garrulous, loquacious, talkative, windy; slick, smooth
vociferant *adj **syn*** see VOCIFEROUS
vociferate *vb **syn*** see CALL 1
vociferous *adj* so loud, noisy, and insistent as to compel attention <the crowd made *vociferous* protests against the speaker's statement>
syn blatant, boisterous, clamorous, ‖dinsome, loudmouthed, multivocal, obstreperous, openmouthed, strident, vociferant
rel distracting; loud, noisy, shrill
con close-lipped, reserved, silent, uncommunicative; noiseless, quiet, still

---

vogue *n* ***syn*** see FASHION 2
rel bon ton, fashionableness, stylishness
voice *n* **1** ***syn*** see EXPRESSION 1
rel speech
2 the right to express a wish, choice, or opinion or to influence a situation <even the youngest had a *voice* in planning the party>
syn say, say-so
voice *vb* ***syn*** see SPEAK 1
rel sound; articulate, enunciate, pronounce; formulate, phrase, present, put; recount, tell
voiced *adj* ***syn*** see VOCAL 1
voiceless *adj* ***syn*** see DUMB 1
void *adj* **1** ***syn*** see EMPTY 1
ant full
2 ***syn*** see DEVOID
rel scant, short, shy; bare, bereft, denuded, deprived
3 ***syn*** see NULL
rel negated
void *n* ***syn*** see HOLE 3
void *vb* **1** ***syn*** see VACATE 2
rel evacuate; deplete, drain, eliminate; eject, remove, throw out
2 ***syn*** see DISCHARGE 5
void *vb* ***syn*** see ANNUL 4
idiom declare (*or* make) null and void
voidness *n* ***syn*** see VACUITY 2
ant fullness
volage *adj* ***syn*** see GIDDY 1
volant *adj* ***syn*** see AGILE
volatile *adj* **1** ***syn*** see ELASTIC 2
rel capricious, fickle, inconstant, mercurial, unstable; flighty, flippant, frivolous, light-minded; changeable, protean, variable
2 ***syn*** see EXCITABLE
rel explosive
3 ***syn*** see INCONSTANT 1
4 ***syn*** see TRANSIENT
volatility *n* ***syn*** see LIGHTNESS
rel animation, sprightliness; inconstancy, instability, mercurialness; changeability, variability
volition *n* ***syn*** see WILL 2
rel choice, election, option, selection; desire, preference
con coercion, compulsion, duress, force
volley *n* ***syn*** see BARRAGE
volte–face *n* ***syn*** see REVERSAL 1
volte–face *vb* ***syn*** see TURN 6
rel about-face, face (about), right-about-face
voluble *adj* ***syn*** see GLIB
volume *n* **1** ***syn*** see BOOK 1
2 ***syn*** see BULK 1
rel amount, content, quantity
3 ***syn*** see BODY 4
voluminous *adj* ***syn*** see MANY
voluntary *adj* consisting of or proceeding from an exercise of free will <the law requires that a confession be *voluntary*>
syn deliberate, intentional, unforced, unprescribed, willful, willing, witting
rel chosen, elected, opted, volitional; autonomous, free, independent
con coerced, compelled, forced; unintentional, unplanned, unwilling, unwitting
ant involuntary
voluptuous *adj* ***syn*** see SENSUOUS
rel indulgent, self-gratifying; abandoned, dissipated, dissolute, excessive, wanton
con self-contained, self-denying
ant ascetic
vomit *vb* to discharge the contents of the stomach through the mouth <the churning seas made several passengers *vomit*>
syn barf, bring up, ‖cack, ‖cascade, ‖cast, ‖cat, disgorge, ‖heave, shoot, sick (up), spew, spit up, throw up, upchuck
rel gag, regurgitate, retch; keck; eject, expel
idiom ‖blow one's lunch, holler New York, lose one's cookies
voodoo *n* **1** ***syn*** see MAGICIAN 1
2 ***syn*** see JINX
voodoo *vb* ***syn*** see BEWITCH 1
voodooist *n* ***syn*** see MAGICIAN 1
voracious *adj* excessively greedy (as in appetite, reactions, or behavior) <the wolverine is an extremely *voracious* eater>
syn edacious, gluttonous, rapacious, ravening, ravenous
rel acquisitive, covetous, grasping, greedy; devouring, gorging, satiating, sating, surfeiting; avid, insatiable
vortex *n* ***syn*** see EDDY
rel spiral, spout
votary *n* **1** ***syn*** see ADDICT
rel disciple; freak
2 ***syn*** see AMATEUR 1
rel hound
vote *n* **1** ***syn*** see BALLOT 1
2 ***syn*** see SUFFRAGE
vote (in) *vb* ***syn*** see ELECT 2
rel choose, decide
idiom cast one's vote for
vouch *vb* ***syn*** see CERTIFY 1
rel support, uphold; confirm, corroborate, prove, substantiate, verify; assure, guarantee
vouchsafe *vb* ***syn*** see GRANT 1
rel condescend, deign, stoop; accommodate, favor, oblige
vow *vb* to promise solemnly <*vowed* never to leave each other>
syn covenant, pledge, plight, swear; *compare* PROMISE 1
rel assert, declare, ‖swan; promise
idiom give (*or* make) a solemn promise, give one's word of honor
vowel *adj* ***syn*** see VOCALIC
vowely *adj* ***syn*** see VOCALIC
voyage *n* a journey by water <took the new ship on a long *voyage*>
syn cruise
rel journey, tour, trip
voyeur *n* ***syn*** see PEEPING TOM
vulgar *adj* **1** ***syn*** see VERNACULAR
rel conversational, spoken; idiomatic
2 ***syn*** see PUBLIC 4
3 ***syn*** see COARSE 3
4 ***syn*** see OBSCENE 2
rel base, low, vile; loathsome, offensive, repulsive, revolting; indecorous, indelicate, uncouth

con decent, delicate, refined; high-minded, lofty, noble
5 *syn* see BARBARIC 1
rel inelegant, ungraceful; improper, incorrect, unseemly; uncouth, unpolished, unrefined
idiom in very poor taste
con elegant, graceful; correct, proper, seemly
vulgarism *n* *syn* see BARBARISM
vulgate *adj* *syn* see VERNACULAR
vulgate *n* *syn* see VERNACULAR 3
vulnerability *n* *syn* see EXPOSURE
rel vincibility
vulnerableness *n* *syn* see EXPOSURE
rel weakness
vulnerary *adj* *syn* see CURATIVE
vulpine *adj* *syn* see SLY 2
vulture *vb* *syn* see STEAL 1
vulturine *adj* *syn* see RAPACIOUS 1
vulturish *adj* *syn* see RAPACIOUS 1
vulturous *adj* *syn* see RAPACIOUS 1

syn synonym(s) *rel* related word(s)
ant antonym(s) *con* contrasted word(s)
idiom idiomatic equivalent(s)
‖ use limited; if in doubt, see a dictionary

THESAURUS

W

‖**wack** *n* ***syn*** see ECCENTRIC
wacky *adj* **1** ***syn*** see FOOLISH 2
2 ***syn*** see INSANE 1
wad *n* **1** ***syn*** see LUMP 1
2 *often* **wads** *pl* ***syn*** see SCAD
3 ***syn*** see FORTUNE 4
wade (in *or* into) *vb* ***syn*** see PITCH IN 1
‖**waffle** *vb* ***syn*** see BABBLE 2
wag *vb* to move to and fro <the dog *wagged* his tail briskly>
syn beat, lash, switch, waggle, wave, woggle
rel shake, twitch, wiggle; oscillate; wigwag
wag *n* **1** a person full of sportive humor <a gay young *wag*, always full of fun>
syn card, comedian, humorist, joker, zany
rel clown, cutup, madcap, prankster, show-off; jester, kidder, quipster, wisecracker, wit
idiom life of the party
2 ***syn*** see ZANY 2
3 ***syn*** see HUMORIST 2
wage *n, often* **wages** *pl* the price paid a person for his labor or services <high *wages* are often seen as a factor in inflation>
syn emolument, fee, hire, pay, pay envelope, salary, stipend
rel compensation, recompense, remuneration, reward; earnings, income, receipts, return(s), take
wager *n* ***syn*** see BET
wager *vb* **1** ***syn*** see VENTURE 1
2 ***syn*** see GAMBLE 1
idiom lay a wager
waggery *n* **1** ***syn*** see MISCHIEVOUSNESS
2 ***syn*** see JOKE 1
waggish *adj* ***syn*** see PLAYFUL 1
rel facetious, humorous, jocose, jocular, witty; comic, comical, droll, funny, laughable, ludicrous; arch, pert, saucy
con earnest, grave, sedate, serious, sober, staid
waggishness *n* ***syn*** see MISCHIEVOUSNESS
waggle *vb* ***syn*** see WAG
rel sway, waddle, wobble
wail *vb* **1** ***syn*** see CRY 2
idiom make an outcry
2 ***syn*** see HOWL 1
3 ***syn*** see BAWL 2
4 ***syn*** see COMPLAIN
wailful *adj* ***syn*** see MELANCHOLY 2
waistband *n* ***syn*** see BELT 1
wait *vb* ***syn*** see STAY 2
rel anticipate, foresee; await, expect
idiom bide one's time, cool one's heels, look forward to, mark time
con depart, go, leave
wait (on) *vb* ***syn*** see MINISTER (to)
waive *vb* **1** ***syn*** see RELINQUISH
rel allow, concede, grant
con claim, demand, exact, require; assert, defend, maintain
2 ***syn*** see DEFER
wake *vb* **1** to stop sleeping <she usually *woke* before dawn>
syn awake, awaken, rouse, stir, waken
rel arise, get up, roll out
con catnap, doze, drowse, nap, nod, snooze; sleep, slumber
2 ***syn*** see STIR 1
rel freshen, renew
con calm, ease, mollify, relax
waken *vb* **1** ***syn*** see STIR 1
rel freshen, renew
con calm, ease, mollify, relax
2 ***syn*** see WAKE 1
wale *n* ***syn*** see WHEAL
walk *vb* **1** to advance on foot step by step <often *walked* to work on pleasant mornings>
syn ambulate, foot (it), hoof, pace, step, traipse, tread, troop
rel circumambulate, perambulate, promenade, ramble, stroll; hike, tramp; lumber, plod, slog, stride, stump, trudge; leg, race, run
idiom beat one's feet, heel and toe it, ride shanks' mare
con drive, ride
2 ***syn*** see TRAVERSE 5
walk *n* **1** a usually brief journey on foot for pleasure or exercise <always took a *walk* before breakfast>
syn constitutional, ramble, saunter, stroll, turn
rel hike, march, tramp; deambulation, parade, promenade; airing, stretch
2 ***syn*** see FIELD
walkabout *n* ***syn*** see TRAMP 3
walkaway *n* ***syn*** see RUNAWAY
walk out *vb* ***syn*** see STRIKE 1
walkover *n* ***syn*** see RUNAWAY
wall *n* ***syn*** see BAR 2
wall *vb* ***syn*** see ENCLOSE 1
wallop *n* **1** ***syn*** see BLOW 1
2 ***syn*** see IMPACT 1
3 ***syn*** see THRILL
wallop *vb* **1** ***syn*** see BEAT 1
2 ***syn*** see WHIP 2
3 ***syn*** see SLAM 1
walloping *adj* ***syn*** see HUGE
wallow *vb* **1** to roll or move in an indolent and ungainly yet comfortable fashion <hogs *wallowing* in a cool mudhole>
syn welter
rel flounder, roll, tumble; cuddle, nestle, snuggle
2 to move or progress unsteadily and clumsily as if beset by obstacles <*wallowed* through the mire for miles trying to get help>

syn blunder, flounder, lurch, stumble; *compare* STUMBLE 3
rel reel, stagger, sway, totter, wamble, welter
idiom make heavy weather (of)
3 to become deeply or excessively involved in or with something subjectively felt as pleasant <*wallowing* in luxury>
syn bask, indulge, luxuriate, revel, roll, rollick, welter
rel baby, humor, pamper, spoil; appreciate, delight (in), enjoy, relish
con abstain, refrain; avoid, eschew, shun

waltz *vb* ***syn*** see BREEZE
||wambly *adj* ***syn*** see SQUEAMISH 1
||wampum *n* ***syn*** see MONEY
wan *adj* **1** ***syn*** see PALE 1
rel cadaverous, haggard, worn; blanched, bleached, washed-out; anemic, bloodless
2 ***syn*** see WEAK 4
wander *vb* **1** to move about from place to place more or less aimlessly and without obvious plan <*wandering* through the forest>
syn bat, circumambulate, drift, gad, gallivant, maunder, meander, mooch, ||project, ramble, range, roam, roll, rove, straggle, stray, traipse, vagabond, vagabondize; *compare* SAUNTER
rel amble, saunter, stroll; divagate, diverge; trail; boom, bum, tramp
2 ***syn*** see DIGRESS 2
3 ***syn*** see ERR
wanderer *n* ***syn*** see ROVER
wandering *adj* **1** ***syn*** see ITINERANT
2 ***syn*** see ERRATIC 1
3 ***syn*** see DELIRIOUS 1
wane *vb* **1** ***syn*** see ABATE 4
ant wax
2 ***syn*** see FAIL 3
ant wax
wangle *vb* ***syn*** see ENGINEER
rel outflank, outgeneral, outmaneuver, overreach
waning *n* ***syn*** see FAILURE 4
ant waxing
||wanky *adj* ***syn*** see WEAK 1
want *vb* **1** ***syn*** see LACK
idiom be found wanting, fall short, feel the want of
2 ***syn*** see DESIRE 1
rel choose, prefer
idiom could do with, have a mind (*or* an eye) to
3 to have as a duty or responsibility <you *want* to behave yourself>
syn must, ought, should
rel become, befit, behoove; need (to)
idiom be wise to, had better (*or* best)
want *n* **1** ***syn*** see ABSENCE
rel exigency, necessity, need
con sufficiency
2 ***syn*** see POVERTY 1
rel exiguousness, meagerness, scantiness, skimpiness; inadequacy, insufficiency
con riches
3 ***syn*** see REQUIREMENT 1
wanting *adj* ***syn*** see ABSENT 1
2 ***syn*** see SHORT 3
3 ***syn*** see DEFICIENT 1
wanting *prep* ***syn*** see WITHOUT 2
wanton *adj* **1** ***syn*** see FAST 7
rel lax, slack, wayward
idiom of easy virtue, of loose morals
con austere, puritanical, restrained, self-restrained
ant chaste
2 ***syn*** see SUPEREROGATORY
rel malevolent, malicious, spiteful; contrary, perverse, wayward
wanton *n* a woman who engages in lewd unseemly conduct <giddy *wantons* flaunting themselves in bars>
syn baggage, ||bim, ||bimbo, cyprian, hussy, jade, jezebel, ||pig, slattern, slut, strumpet, tramp, trollop, trull, wench
idiom loose woman
wanton *vb* ***syn*** see TRIFLE 1
wantwit *n* ***syn*** see DUNCE
war *vb* ***syn*** see CONTEND 1
rel attempt, endeavor, essay, strive, struggle; challenge, engage, take on
idiom draw the sword against, lift one's hand against, take up the cudgels
warble *n* ***syn*** see MELODY
war chest *n* ***syn*** see TREASURY 2
war club *n* ***syn*** see CUDGEL
war cry *n* ***syn*** see BATTLE CRY
ward *n* **1** ***syn*** see GUARD 2
2 ***syn*** see DEFENSE 1
3 ***syn*** see CUSTODY
ward *vb* **1** to cause to miss an objective by or as if by turning aside <*warded* the stroke of his enemy's sword with his shield>
syn deflect, fend, parry
rel block, check, halt, stay, stymie; avert, divert, turn
idiom keep at arm's length, turn aside
2 ***syn*** see PREVENT 2
rel balk, foil, frustrate, thwart; check, interrupt
ant conduce (to)
ward (off) *vb* ***syn*** see FEND (off)
ant bring on
warden *n* ***syn*** see CUSTODIAN
ware *adj* ***syn*** see AWARE
warehouse *vb* ***syn*** see STOW
rel accommodate; guard, protect, shelter
wares *n pl* ***syn*** see MERCHANDISE
warfare *n* ***syn*** see CONTEST 1
warhorse *n* ***syn*** see COURSER
warlike *adj* **1** ***syn*** see BELLIGERENT
ant peaceable
2 ***syn*** see MARTIAL
rel battling, contending, fighting, warring
ant unwarlike
warlock *n* ***syn*** see MAGICIAN 1
warm *adj* **1** ***syn*** see ENTHUSIASTIC

---

syn synonym(s) ***rel*** related word(s)
ant antonym(s) ***con*** contrasted word(s)
idiom idiomatic equivalent(s)
|| use limited; if in doubt, see a dictionary

2 syn see TENDER
rel ardent, fervent, passionate; affable, cordial, gracious; heartfelt, hearty, sincere, wholehearted
ant cool; austere

warmed–over *adj syn* see TRITE

warmhearted *adj syn* see TENDER
rel benign, benignant, kind, kindly, outgoing
con austere, cold, cool, frigid, frosty, severe, stern
ant coldhearted

warming *n syn* see DEFEAT 1

warmish *adj syn* see TEPID 1

warn *vb* **1** to let one know of approaching danger or risk <police and the weather service join to *warn* travelers of hazardous road conditions>
syn caution, forewarn
rel advise, alert, apprise, inform, notify, tip; counsel, direct, guide
idiom address a warning to, give warning, put a flea in one's ear, put one on guard
2 syn see INFORM 2
3 syn see COMMAND

warning *n* something and especially a statement that warns or is intended to warn <gave them *warning* that disobedience would lead to punishment>
syn admonition, caution, caveat, commonition, forewarning, monition
rel advice, counsel, guidance, recommendation; hint, suggestion, tip
idiom flea (*or* word) in the ear, word to the wise

warning *adj syn* see MONITORY

warp *vb* **1** *syn* see DEBASE 1
rel contort, crook, distort, twist
con disentangle, rectify, straighten, unkink
2 syn see DEFORM
rel bend, crook, kink, twist
3 syn see MISREPRESENT

war paint *n* **1** *syn* see FINERY
2 syn see MAKEUP 3

warped *adj syn* see BIASED 2
ant unwarped

warrant *n* **1** *syn* see PLEDGE 1
2 syn see BASIS 3
3 syn see WORD 8

warrant *vb* **1** *syn* see MAINTAIN 2
rel state; assure, ensure, insure
2 to give assurance of the worth of something especially in respect to quality, quantity, or condition <*warranted* the merchandise to be exactly as described in the catalog>
syn certify, guarantee, guaranty
rel assure, insure, secure; back, sponsor, stipulate; affirm, claim, state
idiom stand behind
3 syn see JUSTIFY 4
rel endorse; call (for), need, require

warrantable *adj syn* see JUSTIFIABLE
ant unwarrantable

warranty *n syn* see GUARANTEE 1

warrior *n syn* see SOLDIER

wary *adj* **1** *syn* see CAUTIOUS
rel distrustful, doubting, leery, suspicious; vigilant, watchful
idiom on one's guard
con careless, heedless, thoughtless; devil-may-care, reckless, venturesome
ant foolhardy; unwary
2 syn see SPARING

wash *vb* **1** *syn* see BATHE 1
2 syn see BATHE 2
3 syn see DRIFT 1
4 syn see SLOSH 1

washed–out *adj syn* see EFFETE 2

washed–up *adj* **1** *syn* see THROUGH 3
2 syn see THROUGH 4

wash out *vb* **1** *syn* see FAIL 4
2 syn see DISCARD

wash up *vb syn* see GO 4

washy *adj syn* see DILUTE

waspish *adj* **1** *syn* see IRRITABLE
rel contrary, impatient, perverse; malicious, sharp, spiteful; crabbed, cross-grained
2 syn see CANTANKEROUS

waspy *adj* **1** *syn* see IRRITABLE
rel contrary, impatient, perverse; malicious, sharp, spiteful; crabbed, cross-grained
2 syn see CANTANKEROUS

wassail *n* **1** *syn* see BINGE 1
2 syn see REVELRY 2

wassail *vb syn* see REVEL 1

waste *n* **1** an area of the earth unsuitable for cultivation or general habitation <the scattered dwellers of southern Africa's dry *wastes*>
syn badland, barren, desert, wasteland, wild, wilderness, wild land, wildness
rel brush, brushland, bush; jungle
2 syn see EXTRAVAGANCE 2
3 syn see REFUSE
rel rubble, rummage

waste *vb* **1** *syn* see RAVAGE
idiom reduce to a shambles
ant conserve
2 to spend or expend freely and usually foolishly or futilely <*wasted* his inheritance on women and gambling> <*waste* one's time on trifles>
syn blow, blunder (away), cast away, consume, dissipate, dribble (away), drivel, fool (away), fritter, frivol away, muddle (away), potter (away), prodigalize, riot (away), squander, throw away, trifle (away)
rel disburse, expend, spend; dispense, distribute; deplete, drain, exhaust, impoverish; dispel, disperse, scatter; misspend
idiom let slip through one's fingers, pour down the drain, throw good money after bad
ant save; conserve

waste (away) *vb syn* see FAIL 3

wasted *adj syn* see EMACIATED
rel meager; shriveled, withered, wizened
con healthy, robust; stalwart, stout, strong, sturdy

wastefulness *n syn* see EXTRAVAGANCE 2
ant frugality

wasteland *n syn* see WASTE 1

waster *n* **1** *syn* see SPENDTHRIFT
rel dissipater, fritterer; idler, loafer, lounger
2 syn see WASTREL 1

wastethrift *n* ***syn*** see SPENDTHRIFT
wastrel *n* **1** a worthless, self-indulgent, and reprehensible person <loafers and other *wastrels* lounging on the corner>
syn ‖bad lot, good-for-nothing, ne'er-do-well, no-good, profligate, rounder, scapegrace, waster
rel lecher, libertine, rake, rip, roué; blackguard, black sheep, knave, rascal, rogue, scoundrel; rapscallion, scalawag, scamp
idiom sad case
2 ***syn*** see SPENDTHRIFT
rel dissipater, fritterer; idler, loafer, lounger
watch *vb* **1** ***syn*** see SEE 2
rel examine, follow, inspect, scan, scrutinize
idiom keep an eye on, keep tabs on
2 ***syn*** see EYE 2
3 ***syn*** see TEND 2
idiom keep watch over
4 ***syn*** see LOOK 1
watch *n* **1** ***syn*** see LOOKOUT 3
2 ***syn*** see GUARD 2
3 ***syn*** see EYE 3
watch and ward *n* ***syn*** see LOOKOUT 3
watchdog *n* ***syn*** see CUSTODIAN
watcher *n* ***syn*** see SPECTATOR
watchfire *n* ***syn*** see BEACON 1
watchful *adj* paying close attention usually with a view to anticipating approaching danger or opportunity <adopted a policy of *watchful* waiting>
syn alert, open-eyed, unsleeping, vigilant, wakeful, wide-awake
rel cautious, chary, circumspect, wary; prompt, quick, ready
idiom keeping one's eyes peeled (*or* open), on the watch (*or* lookout)
con careless, heedless, thoughtless; inadvertent; absentminded, abstracted, faraway
ant unwatchful
watchman *n* ***syn*** see GUARD 2
watch out *vb* ***syn*** see BEWARE
watchword *n* **1** ***syn*** see PASSWORD 1
2 ***syn*** see PASSWORD 3
3 ***syn*** see CATCHWORD
water *n* **1** ***syn*** see TEARS
2 ***syn*** see SALIVA
water *vb* ***syn*** see DROOL 1
water closet *n* ***syn*** see TOILET
watercourse *n* ***syn*** see CHANNEL 1
watered–down *adj* ***syn*** see DILUTE
waterfall *n* a precipitous descent of water or the site of this <heard the roar of the *waterfall*>
syn cascade, cataract, chute, fall(s), ‖force, sault, spout
rel rapid(s), riffle, shoot; eddy, surge, vortex, whirlpool
watering hole *n* **1** ***syn*** see RESORT 2
2 ***syn*** see BAR 5
3 ***syn*** see NIGHTCLUB
watering place *n* **1** ***syn*** see SPA 1
2 ***syn*** see RESORT 3
3 ***syn*** see BAR 5
4 ***syn*** see NIGHTCLUB
waterish *adj* **1** ***syn*** see DILUTE
2 ***syn*** see PALE 2
3 ***syn*** see INSIPID 3
waterless *adj* ***syn*** see DRY 1
ant watered
waterlog *vb* ***syn*** see SOAK 1
watery *adj* **1** ***syn*** see DILUTE
2 ***syn*** see PALE 2
3 ***syn*** see INSIPID 3
wave *vb* ***syn*** see WAG
waver *vb* ***syn*** see HESITATE
rel palter, shift, trim; seesaw, teeter
idiom back and fill, hem and haw
wavering *n* ***syn*** see HESITATION
wavering *adj* **1** ***syn*** see VACILLATING 2
ant unwavering
2 ***syn*** see WEAK 2
wax *vb* **1** ***syn*** see INCREASE 2
ant wane
2 ***syn*** see BECOME 1
wax *n* ***syn*** see RISE 3
ant wane
waxen *adj* ***syn*** see PALE 1
waxy *adj* ***syn*** see ANGRY
way *n* **1** a public and unobstructed passage leading from one place to another <tracing the remains of an old lumberman's *way*>
syn artery, avenue, boulevard, ‖drag, highway, path, road, street, thoroughfare, track
rel course, line, passage, route; alley, byway, lane, ride, row
2 that along which one passes in going from one place to another <his *way* led through wooded hills>
syn course, line, passage, path, road, route
3 ***syn*** see DOOR 2
4 ***syn*** see METHOD 1
rel custom, habit, habitude, practice, usage, use, wont
5 ***syn*** see STYLE 4
6 ***syn*** see HABIT 1
7 ***syn*** see DISTANCE 2
8 ***syn*** see TYPE
‖**wayback** *n* ***syn*** see RUSTIC
wayfaring *adj* ***syn*** see ITINERANT
waylay *vb* ***syn*** see SURPRISE 1
rel lurk, prowl, skulk, slink
idiom lay wait for, lie in wait for
ways *n pl but sing in constr* ***syn*** see DISTANCE 2
wayward *adj* **1** ***syn*** see CONTRARY 3
rel capricious, fickle, inconstant, unstable, variable
con complaisant, good-natured
2 ***syn*** see ARBITRARY 1
weak *adj* **1** lacking physical, mental, or moral strength <a *weak* spirit in a *weak* body>
syn decrepit, feeble, flimsy, fragile, frail, infirm, insubstantial, puny, unsound, unsubstantial, ‖wanky, weakly

---

syn synonym(s) ***rel*** related word(s)
ant antonym(s) ***con*** contrasted word(s)
idiom idiomatic equivalent(s)
‖ use limited; if in doubt, see a dictionary

rel debilitated, enfeebled, sickly, spindly, weakened; forceless, impotent, impuissant, powerless
con stalwart, stout, sturdy, tenacious, tough; dynamic, energetic, forceful, vigorous
ant strong
2 deficient in stability <a love too *weak* to bear the trials of daily life>
syn dickey, fluctuant, insecure, rootless, shaky, unstable, unsure, vacillating, wavering, wobbly; *compare* RICKETY
rel hesitant, irresolute, trimming, uncertain; insubstantial, undependable, unreliable
con certain, secure, solid, stable, sure; dependable, reliable, substantial
ant strong
3 ***syn*** see IMPLAUSIBLE
4 not equal to the requirements and demands of a situation <a *weak* executive>
syn boneless, emasculate, forceless, impotent, inadequate, ineffective, ineffectual, invertebrate, slack-spined, spineless, wan
rel unfit, unqualified, unsuitable; bungling, incompetent, inept
con able, competent, effective, efficient; adequate, fit, qualified, satisfactory, sufficient, suitable; manly, masculine, virile
ant strong
5 ***syn*** see DILUTE
ant strong

weaken *vb* **1** to lose or cause to lose strength, vigor, or energy <his hesitation *weakened* the force of his argument>
syn attenuate, blunt, cripple, debilitate, disable, enfeeble, sap, unbrace, undermine, unstrengthen; *compare* PARALYZE 1
rel emasculate, enervate, incapacitate, unman, unnerve; damage, impair, injure; lessen, minimize, reduce; dilute, thin
con better, improve; activate, energize, invigorate, vitalize
ant strengthen
2 ***syn*** see FAIL 1
3 ***syn*** see FAIL 3
4 ***syn*** see DILUTE

weak–headed *adj* ***syn*** see SIMPLE 3

weak–kneed *adj* ***syn*** see VACILLATING 2

weakling *n* a person lacking in stamina and character <her speech deplored the characterless *weaklings* in critical positions>
syn baby, doormat, invertebrate, jellyfish, milksop, Milquetoast, ‖molly, mollycoddle, namby-pamby, nebbish, pantywaist, sissy, sissy-pants (*or* sissy-britches), sop, wimp
rel butt, mark, pushover, sucker; drip, mama's boy, misfit, mother's boy, nerd, sad sack, weak sister
idiom shrinking violet

weakly *adv* ***syn*** see SOTTO VOCE
ant strongly

weakly *adj* ***syn*** see WEAK 1

weak–minded *adj* ***syn*** see SIMPLE 3

weakness *n* ***syn*** see APPETITE 3

weal *n* ***syn*** see WHEAL

weald *n* ***syn*** see FOREST

wealth *n* **1** ***syn*** see MEAN 3
2 one's worldly possessions <at that point his *wealth* consisted of the clothes he stood in and a solitary quarter>
syn fortune, property, resources, riches, substance, worth
rel assets, estate, goods, holdings, possessions

wealthy *adj* ***syn*** see RICH 1
con impoverished, penniless, poor
ant indigent

wean *vb* ***syn*** see ESTRANGE
ant addict

wear *vb* **1** ***syn*** see ABRADE 1
2 ***syn*** see TIRE 1

wear (away) *vb* ***syn*** see EAT 3

wear down *vb* ***syn*** see TIRE 1

wearied *adj* ***syn*** see TIRED 1
ant refreshed; unwearied, unweary

weariful *adj* ***syn*** see ARID 2

weariless *adj* ***syn*** see INDEFATIGABLE

weariness *n* ***syn*** see FATIGUE

wearisome *adj* ***syn*** see ARID 2

wear out *vb* **1** ***syn*** see EXHAUST 4
‖**2** ***syn*** see WHIP 1

weary *vb* **1** ***syn*** see TIRE 1
rel debilitate, enfeeble, weaken; depress, oppress, weigh
con animate, energize, vitalize; enliven, quicken, vivify
ant refresh
2 ***syn*** see BORE

weary *adj* **1** ***syn*** see TIRED 1
ant refreshed, unwearied, unweary
2 ***syn*** see FED UP

Weary Willie *n* ***syn*** see VAGABOND

weasel *n* ***syn*** see SNEAK

weasel *vb* ***syn*** see EQUIVOCATE 2

weathery *adj* ***syn*** see CHANGEABLE 1

weave *vb* ***syn*** see LURCH 2

web *n* **1** ***syn*** see TEXTURE 2
2 something by which one is ensnared, held fast, or inextricably involved <diplomacy caught in its own *web* of double-dealing>
syn cobweb, entanglement, mesh(es), toil(s); *compare* ENTANGLEMENT 1
rel complexity, complication; labyrinth, maze, morass, skein, snarl, tangle; embroilment, enmeshment, ensnarement, entrapment, involvement
idiom a tangled web
3 ***syn*** see MAZE 1

wed *vb* **1** ***syn*** see MARRY 1
2 ***syn*** see MARRY 2
3 ***syn*** see JOIN 1

wedded *adj* ***syn*** see MATRIMONIAL
con unwed, unwedded

wedding *n* the marriage ceremony usually with its accompanying festivities <one of the most elaborate *weddings* of the social season>
syn bridal, espousal(s), marriage, nuptial(s), spousal

wedlock *n* ***syn*** see MARRIAGE 1

wee *adj* ***syn*** see TINY

weed *n* ***syn*** see MARIJUANA

weensy *adj* ***syn*** see TINY
weeny *adj* ***syn*** see TINY
weep *vb* **1** ***syn*** see DEPLORE 1
2 ***syn*** see EXUDE
3 ***syn*** see CRY 2
4 ***syn*** see DRIP
weeping *adj* ***syn*** see TEARFUL
weepy *adj* ***syn*** see TEARFUL
weigh *vb* **1** ***syn*** see CONSIDER 1
rel appraise, evaluate, rate
2 ***syn*** see BURDEN
3 to carry intellectual weight <this evidence *weighed* heavily against him>
syn count, militate, tell
rel import, matter, register, signify
idiom amount to some shucks, be something, carry weight, cut (some) ice
4 ***syn*** see MATTER
weigh down *vb* ***syn*** see DEPRESS 2
ant raise (*one's spirits*)
weight *n* **1** ***syn*** see LOAD 2
2 ***syn*** see IMPORTANCE
3 ***syn*** see INFLUENCE 1
rel effectiveness, efficacy; forcefulness, forcibleness, potency, powerfulness
4 ***syn*** see LOAD 3
weight *vb* **1** ***syn*** see ADULTERATE
rel burden, cumber, encumber; contaminate, corrupt, foul up, spoil
2 ***syn*** see BURDEN
weightiness *n* ***syn*** see IMPORTANCE
weightless *adj* ***syn*** see LIGHT 1
ant weighty
weighty *adj* **1** ***syn*** see IMPORTANT 1
2 ***syn*** see SERIOUS 1
3 ***syn*** see SERIOUS 2
4 ***syn*** see HEAVY 1
ant weightless
5 ***syn*** see FAT 2
6 ***syn*** see ONEROUS
weird *n* **1** ***syn*** see FATE
2 ***syn*** see PREDICTION
weird *adj* **1** fearfully and mysteriously strange or fantastic <shuddered at the *weird* unearthly glow that swept across the sky>
syn eerie, spooky, uncanny, unearthly
rel creepy, haunting, unnatural; preternatural, supernatural; supernal; curious, odd, peculiar, queer, strange; inscrutable, mysterious; awe-inspiring, awful, dreadful, fearful, horrific
con common, commonplace, everyday, quotidian; natural, normal, ordinary
2 ***syn*** see STRANGE 4
welcome *adj* ***syn*** see PLEASANT 1
rel congenial, cordial, genial, sympathetic; contenting, satisfying
ant unwelcome
welfare *n* a state of thriving and progress <parents who seek their children's *welfare*>
syn advantage, benefit, good, interest, prosperity, well-being
rel fortune, luck, success; contentment, felicity, happiness, satisfaction
ant illfare
welkin *n* ***syn*** see SKY
well *n* **1 wells** *pl* ***syn*** see SPA 1
2 ***syn*** see SOURCE
well *adv* **1** in a good, proper, or acceptable manner <the children behaved very *well* at the party>
syn aright, befittingly, correctly, decently, decorously, fitly, fittingly, justly, nicely, properly, rightly
rel bearably, passably, tolerably, unobjectionably; considerately, pleasantly, thoughtfully, white; appropriately
con badly, improperly, objectionably, obnoxiously, outrageously
ant ill
2 in a pleasant, cooperative, or thoughtful manner <he speaks *well* of your new proposal>
syn considerately, generously, heedfully, kindly, thoughtfully
rel concernedly, interestedly; approvingly
con contemptuously, disdainfully, scornfully
3 to a full extent or degree <you are *well* aware of the problems we face>
syn à fond, altogether, clear, ‖cleverly, completely, entirely, fully, perfectly, ‖plumb, quite, right, roundly, ‖slam, ‖slap, thoroughly, utterly, wholly
rel certainly, obviously, surely, undoubtedly, unquestionably; sublimely
idiom all the way
con barely, hardly, scarcely
4 in an adequate or appropriate manner <any large box will answer our need very *well*>
syn acceptably, adequately, amply, appropriately, becomingly, fittingly, properly, right, satisfactorily, suitably
5 in a desirable or pleasing manner <everything went *well* on the trip>
syn favorably, fortunately, happily, prosperously, satisfyingly, successfully, swimmingly
rel comfortably, easily, smoothly
con amiss, wrong
ant badly
6 ***syn*** see EASILY 1
7 in all likelihood <the fighting may *well* continue for years>
syn doubtlessly, easily, indeed, really, truly, undoubtedly
rel conceivably, perhaps, possibly; likely, probably
8 to a considerable extent or degree <they landed *well* beyond the wharf>
syn considerably, far, quite, rather, significantly, somewhat
idiom by a long way, by a wide margin
well *adj* **1** ***syn*** see PROSPEROUS 3
2 ***syn*** see HEALTHY 1
ant ill, unwell
3 ***syn*** see LUCKY
well–behaved *adj* ***syn*** see GOOD 13

---

syn synonym(s) ***rel*** related word(s)
ant antonym(s) ***con*** contrasted word(s)
idiom idiomatic equivalent(s)
‖ use limited; if in doubt, see a dictionary

well–being *n* **1** ***syn*** see PROSPERITY 2
ant ill-being
2 ***syn*** see WELFARE
ant ill-being
well–bred *adj* ***syn*** see GENTEEL 1
ant ill-bred
well–conditioned *adj* ***syn*** see HEALTHY 1
well–developed *adj* ***syn*** see CURVACEOUS
well–disposed *adj* ***syn*** see SYMPATHETIC 2
ant ill-disposed
well–favored *adj* ***syn*** see BEAUTIFUL
ant ill-favored
well–fixed *adj* ***syn*** see PROSPEROUS 3
ant badly off
well–founded *adj* having a firm foundation in fact or logic <offered *well-founded* arguments to support his position>
syn cogent, good, just, justified, well-grounded
rel sound, substantial, telling, valid; rational, reasonable, reasoned; fundamental, meaty, pithy
con unjustified; insubstantial, invalid, unsound; irrational, unreasonable
well–groomed *adj* **1** ***syn*** see NEAT 2
2 ***syn*** see DAPPER
well–grounded *adj* ***syn*** see WELL-FOUNDED
wellhead *n* ***syn*** see SOURCE
well–heeled *adj* ***syn*** see PROSPEROUS 3
ant badly off
well–hung *adj* ***syn*** see GLIB
well–known *adj* much talked about <a *well-known* hospital>
syn famous, leading, noted, notorious, popular, prominent; *compare* FAMOUS 2
rel conspicuous, important, outstanding
idiom on everyone's tongue
con inconspicuous, obscure, unheard-of, unimportant, unnoted, unpopular
ant unknown
well–liked *adj* ***syn*** see FAVORITE 2
well–liking *adj* ***syn*** see HEALTHY 1
well–mannered *adj* ***syn*** see CIVIL 2
ant ill-mannered
well–nigh *adv* **1** ***syn*** see NEARLY
2 ***syn*** see ALMOST 2
well–off *adj* ***syn*** see PROSPEROUS 3
ant badly off
well over *vb* ***syn*** see OVERFLOW 2
well–paying *adj* ***syn*** see ADVANTAGEOUS 1
well–proportioned *adj* ***syn*** see SHAPELY
wellspring *n* ***syn*** see SOURCE
well–thought–of *adj* ***syn*** see RESPECTABLE 1
well–timed *adj* ***syn*** see TIMELY 1
con premature, untimely; behindhand, late, tardy
ant ill-timed
well–to–do *adj* ***syn*** see PROSPEROUS 3
ant badly off
well–turned *adj* ***syn*** see SHAPELY
well–worn *adj* ***syn*** see TRITE
welsh *vb* ***syn*** see BACK DOWN
welt *n* **1** ***syn*** see WHEAL
‖**2** ***syn*** see BLOW 1
weltanschauung *n* ***syn*** see IDEOLOGY
welter *vb* **1** ***syn*** see WALLOW 1
rel strive, struggle; toss, tumble, writhe; grovel
2 ***syn*** see WALLOW 3
welter *vb* ***syn*** see WITHER
wench *n* **1** ***syn*** see GIRL 1
2 ***syn*** see WANTON
wend *vb* ***syn*** see GO 1
western *n* a motion picture or radio or television play with its scene laid in the western U.S. and having cowboys as its main characters <young boys delighting in Saturday morning *westerns*>
syn horse opera, oater
rel shoot-'em-up
wet *vb* to make wet by or as if by saturating with water <they were *wet* thoroughly by the pouring rain>
syn deluge, douse, drench, drown, soak, sop, souse; *compare* SOAK 1
rel damp, dampen, moisten; humidify, humify; fill, impregnate, saturate; irrigate; lave, rinse, wash
ant desiccate, dry
wet *adj* **1** containing or impregnated with liquid <change *wet* clothing for dry>
syn drenched, dripping, madid, saturate, saturated, soaked, soaking, sodden, sopping, soppy, soused, wringing-wet
rel soggy, water-logged; damp, dank, moist, wettish
idiom dripping (*or* soaking *or* sopping) wet
con bone-dry, dehydrated, desiccated, parched, sere, waterless
ant dry
2 ***syn*** see INTOXICATED 1
‖**wet** *n* ***syn*** see DRAM
wettish *adj* ***syn*** see DAMP
whack *vb* ***syn*** see STRIKE 2
whack *n* **1** ***syn*** see BLOW 1
2 ***syn*** see FLING 1
whacking *adj* ***syn*** see HUGE
whacking *adv* ***syn*** see VERY 1
whale *n* ***syn*** see GIANT
whale *vb* ***syn*** see WHIP 1
whaling *adj* ***syn*** see HUGE
wham *n* ***syn*** see BANG 2
whammy *n* ***syn*** see JINX
whangdoodle *n* ***syn*** see NONSENSE 2
wharf *n* a structure used by boats and ships for taking on or landing cargo and passengers <brought the boat alongside the *wharf* and moored her>
syn berth, dock, jetty, levee, pier, quay, slip
what–do–you–call–it *n* a thing or person that the speaker cannot (as from not knowing or from forgetting) name <hand me one of those little *what-do-you-call-its*> <went to *what-do-you-call-her's* house last week>
syn what-is-it, whatsis, what's its name, what-you-call-it, what-you-may-call-it, whatyoumay-jigger; *compare* DOODAD, GADGET 1
what–is–it *n* ***syn*** see WHAT-DO-YOU-CALL-IT
whatnot *n* ***syn*** see KNICKKNACK
whatsis *n* ***syn*** see WHAT-DO-YOU-CALL-IT
what's its name *n* ***syn*** see WHAT-DO-YOU-CALL-IT
what–you–call–it *n* ***syn*** see WHAT-DO-YOU-CALL-IT

what-you-may-call-it *n* ***syn*** see WHAT-DO-YOU-CALL-IT
whatyoumayjigger *n* ***syn*** see WHAT-DO-YOU-CALL-IT
wheal *n* a ridge raised on the skin by or as if by a stroke of a lash <the convict's back was covered with *wheals* and old scars>
syn wale, weal, welt, whelk, ||whelp
rel strake, streak, stripe
wheedle *vb* ***syn*** see COAX
wheel *n* **1** ***syn*** see CYCLE 1
2 ***syn*** see REVOLUTION 1
3 ***syn*** see LEAGUE 4
wheel *vb* **1** ***syn*** see REEL 2
2 ***syn*** see DRIVE 5
3 ***syn*** see TURN 6
wheeze *vb* ***syn*** see HISS
wheeze *n* ***syn*** see PRANK
whelk *n* ***syn*** see WHEAL
whelm *vb* **1** ***syn*** see DELUGE 1
2 ***syn*** see DELUGE 3
3 ***syn*** see OVERWHELM 4
||**whelp** *n* ***syn*** see WHEAL
when *adv* ***syn*** see THEN 1
when *conj* ***syn*** see THOUGH
whence *n* ***syn*** see SOURCE
where *adv* **1** ***syn*** see WHEREVER
2 ***syn*** see WHITHER 1
where *n* ***syn*** see PLACE 1
whereabouts *adv* ***syn*** see WHITHER 1
con hereabouts, thereabouts
whereas *conj* **1** ***syn*** see BECAUSE
2 ***syn*** see THOUGH
||**whereaway** *adv* ***syn*** see WHITHER 1
wherefore *n* ***syn*** see REASON 3
whereto *adv* ***syn*** see WHITHER 2
whereunto *adv* ***syn*** see WHITHER 2
wherever *adv* at, in, or to any or every place in or to which <he goes *wherever* he is needed>
syn everywhere, where
con here, there
||**wherret** *vb* ***syn*** see SLAP 1
||**wherret** *vb* ***syn*** see WORRY 1
whet *vb* **1** ***syn*** see SHARPEN
2 ***syn*** see STIR 1
whet *n* ||**1** ***syn*** see WHILE 1
2 ***syn*** see APPETIZER
whether or no *adv* ***syn*** see WILLY-NILLY
whetted *adj* ***syn*** see SHARP 1
whicker *vb* ***syn*** see NEIGH
whiff *n* ***syn*** see HINT 2
whiffet *n* ***syn*** see NONENTITY
whiffle *vb* ***syn*** see HESITATE
whiffling *adj* ***syn*** see VACILLATING 2
whiffy *adj* ***syn*** see MALODOROUS 1
whigmaleerie *n* **1** ***syn*** see CAPRICE
2 ***syn*** see KNICKKNACK
while *n* **1** a somewhat indefinite period of time <sat down to rest for a *while*>
syn bit, space, spell, stretch, time, ||whet
2 ***syn*** see OCCASION 5
3 ***syn*** see EFFORT 1
while *conj* ***syn*** see THOUGH
while *vb* to pass time and especially leisure time without boredom or in pleasant ways <*whiled* odd hours away in dreaming>
syn beguile, fleet, wile
rel amuse, divert, entertain; brighten, enliven, lighten
while (away) *vb* ***syn*** see SPEND 3
whilom *adj* ***syn*** see FORMER 2
whim *n* ***syn*** see CAPRICE
rel idea; disposition, inclination, thought; dream, fantasy, vision
whimper *vb* to cry feebly and often plaintively or peevishly <a baby *whimpering* in his sleep>
syn pule, whine; *compare* CRY 2
whimsical *adj* **1** ***syn*** see ARBITRARY 1
2 ***syn*** see UNCERTAIN 1
whimsied *adj* ***syn*** see ARBITRARY 1
whimsy *n* ***syn*** see CAPRICE
rel idea; disposition, inclination, thought; dream, fantasy, vision
whim-whams *n pl* ***syn*** see JITTERS
whine *vb* **1** ***syn*** see WHIMPER
2 ***syn*** see COMPLAIN
||**whinner** *vb* ***syn*** see NEIGH
whinny *vb* ***syn*** see NEIGH
whiny *adj* ***syn*** see IRRITABLE
whip *vb* **1** to strike repeatedly with or as if with a lash or rod <*whip* a dog for stealing from the table>
syn flagellate, flog, hide, ||larrup, lash, lather, scourge, stripe, thrash, ||wear out, whale, ||yerk
rel beat, belabor, drub, wallop; bastinado, birch, bludgeon, cane, cudgel, quirt, switch
2 to defeat utterly <*whipped* their traditional rival by a score of 40 to 7>
syn beat, blast, ||bowl (down *or* out), ||clean up (on), ||clobber, ||cream, curry, drub, dust, lambaste, ||larrup, lick, mop (up), overrun, overwhelm, rout, shellac, skunk, smear, smother, steamroller, thrash, trim, trounce, upend, wallop, whomp; *compare* CONQUER 1, DEFEAT 2
rel conquer, defeat, overcome, subdue, vanquish
idiom cook one's goose, deal a crushing defeat, settle one's hash, snow one under
3 to agitate with an instrument so as to stiffen and increase the bulk of by incorporation of air <*whip* cream for a shortcake>
syn beat, whisk
4 ***syn*** see TURN 6
whip (up) *vb* ***syn*** see INCITE
ant calm (down)
whip hand *n* ***syn*** see BETTER 2
whippersnapper *n* ***syn*** see NONENTITY
whipping boy *n* ***syn*** see SCAPEGOAT
whippy *adj* ***syn*** see ELASTIC 1
whipster *n* ***syn*** see NONENTITY
whirl *vb* **1** ***syn*** see SPIN 1
2 ***syn*** see SWIRL
3 ***syn*** see TURN 6
4 ***syn*** see HURRY 2
5 ***syn*** see SPIN 2

whirl *n* **1** ***syn*** see REVOLUTION 1
2 ***syn*** see EDDY
3 ***syn*** see COMMOTION 4
4 ***syn*** see STIR 1
5 ***syn*** see FLING 1
whirlblast *n* ***syn*** see WHIRLWIND 1
whirligig *vb* ***syn*** see SPIN 1
whirlpool *n* **1** ***syn*** see EDDY
2 ***syn*** see STIR 1
whirlpool *vb* ***syn*** see SWIRL
‖whirlpuff *n* ***syn*** see WHIRLWIND 1
whirlwind *n* **1** a rotating windstorm of limited extent that is often accompanied by a column of dust or vapor <*whirlwinds* moved across the plowed land>
syn whirlblast, ‖whirlpuff, whirly; *compare* HURRICANE, TORNADO
rel dust devil, rainspout, sand column, sand spout, waterspout
2 ***syn*** see STIR 1
whirly *n* ***syn*** see WHIRLWIND 1
whish *vb* **1** ***syn*** see HISS
2 ***syn*** see HURRY 2
whisk *vb* **1** ***syn*** see HURRY 2
2 ***syn*** see WHIP 3
whisker *n* ***syn*** see HAIR
whiskered *adj* **1** ***syn*** see BEARDED
2 ***syn*** see HAIRY 1
whiskers *n pl* ***syn*** see BEARD
whisper *vb* **1** ***syn*** see HISS
2 ***syn*** see CONFIDE 1
whisper *n* **1** ***syn*** see MURMUR 1
2 ***syn*** see HINT 2
whispering *n* ***syn*** see REPORT 1
whist *adj* ***syn*** see STILL 3
whistle–stop *n* ***syn*** see BURG
whit *n* ***syn*** see PARTICLE
white *adj* ***syn*** see FAVORABLE 5
ant black
white *n* ***syn*** see REACTIONARY
ant red
white *vb* **1** ***syn*** see WHITEN 1
2 ***syn*** see PALLIATE
whited sepulcher *n* ***syn*** see HYPOCRITE
white–haired *adj* ***syn*** see FAVORITE 1
white–headed *adj* ***syn*** see FAVORITE 1
white–hot *adj* **1** ***syn*** see HOT 1
2 ***syn*** see IMPASSIONED
white lightning *n* ***syn*** see MOONSHINE 2
hite–livered *adj* ***syn*** see COWARDLY
ten *vb* **1** to free from color and make white or
er <*whiten* linen in the sun>
lanch, bleach, blench, decolor, decolorize,

ull, fade, lighten, pale; etiolate; frost,

ken

e TUBERCULOSIS
see PALLIATE
what place <*whither* did they

e, whereabouts, ‖whereaway

2 to what point, conclusion, or end <*whither* is our nation drifting?>
syn whereto, whereunto
whiz *vb* **1** ***syn*** see HISS
2 ***syn*** see HURRY 2
whiz *n* ***syn*** see EXPERT
ant dub, dud, duffer
whiz–bang *adj* ***syn*** see EXCELLENT
whizzer *n* ***syn*** see TRICK 1
whole *adj* **1** free from damage, defect, or flaw <feared the eggs were broken but found them *whole*>
syn entire, flawless, good, intact, perfect, sound, unblemished, unbroken, undamaged, unhurt, unimpaired, uninjured, unmarred, untouched
rel complete, plenary; healthy, well
con broken, damaged, defective, impaired, injured, marred
2 ***syn*** see HEALTHY 1
3 lacking nothing that properly belongs to it <the effect of the *whole* mural>
syn choate, complete, entire, full, integral, perfect
rel orbicular, rounded, well-rounded
ant partial
4 including every constituent element or individual <the *whole* community rose to his defense>
syn all, complete, entire, gross, outright, total
ant partial
5 not scattered or dispersed <gave the matter her *whole* attention>
syn concentrated, exclusive, fixed, undistracted, undivided, unswerving
whole *n* **1** the total supply or amount <the *whole* of our creative literature>
syn aggregate, all, be-all and end-all, entirety, gross, sum, sum total, tale, total, totality, ‖tote
rel amount, supply; result, resultant, summation; bulk, mass, quantity, quantum
con detail, division, fraction, fragment, portion, section, segment, share
ant part
2 an organized array of parts or elements forming or functioning as a unit <stars, planets, galaxies — all but parts of one stupendous *whole*, the universe>
syn entity, integral, integrate, sum, system, totality; *compare* SYSTEM 1
rel being, organism, organization; coherence, cohesion, linkage; unity
con accumulation, aggregation, heap, pile, mass; section, segment; selection
ant part; agglomeration
wholehearted *adj* **1** ***syn*** see SURE 2
2 ***syn*** see SINCERE 1
rel ardent, fervent, impassioned, passionate; earnest, serious; authentic, bona fide, genuine
whole–hog *adj* ***syn*** see EXHAUSTIVE
whole–length *adj* ***syn*** see UNABRIDGED
wholeness *n* **1** ***syn*** see HEALTH
rel integrity; heartiness, robustness, vigor
2 ***syn*** see ENTIRETY 1
3 ***syn*** see INTEGRITY 2
whole number *n* ***syn*** see NUMBER

wholesale *adj* ***syn*** see INDISCRIMINATE 1
wholesome *adj* **1** ***syn*** see HEALTHFUL
ant noxious; unwholesome
2 ***syn*** see CURATIVE
3 ***syn*** see HEALTHY 1
4 ***syn*** see SAFE 3
ant noxious
whole-souled *adj* ***syn*** see SINCERE 1
rel ardent, fervent, impassioned; earnest, intense, serious
wholly *adv* **1** ***syn*** see WELL 3
2 ***syn*** see ALL 1
whomp *vb* ***syn*** see WHIP 2
whoop *vb* ***syn*** see SHOUT 1
whoop *n* ***syn*** see PARTICLE
whoop-de-do *n* ***syn*** see REVELRY 2
whoopee *n* **1** ***syn*** see REVELRY 2
2 ***syn*** see MERRYMAKING
whoopla *n* **1** ***syn*** see COMMOTION 4
2 ***syn*** see REVELRY 2
whoop-up *n* ***syn*** see REVELRY 2
whoosh *vb* ***syn*** see HISS
whop *vb* ***syn*** see BEAT 1
whop *n* ***syn*** see BLOW 1
whopping *adj* ***syn*** see HUGE
whopping *adv* ***syn*** see VERY 1
whore *n* **1** ***syn*** see HARLOT 1
2 ***syn*** see PROSTITUTE
whoredom *n* ***syn*** see PROSTITUTION
whorehouse *n* ***syn*** see BROTHEL
whoreson *n* ***syn*** see BASTARD 1
whorish *adj* ***syn*** see FAST 7
whorl *vb* ***syn*** see SWIRL
who's who *n* ***syn*** see ARISTOCRACY
why *n* **1** ***syn*** see REASON 3
2 ***syn*** see MYSTERY
whyfor *n* ***syn*** see REASON 3
wicked *adj* **1** ***syn*** see WRONG 1
ant upright
2 ***syn*** see PLAYFUL 1
3 ***syn*** see RISQUÉ
4 ***syn*** see MALICIOUS
5 ***syn*** see DANGEROUS 1
6 ***syn*** see TROUBLESOME
7 ***syn*** see OUTRAGEOUS 1
8 ***syn*** see SKILLFUL 2
9 ***syn*** see ABLE
wickedness *n* **1** ***syn*** see EVIL 2
2 ***syn*** see VICE 1
wide *adj* **1** ***syn*** see SPACIOUS
2 ***syn*** see EXTENSIVE 1
3 ***syn*** see LIBERAL 3
wide-awake *adj* ***syn*** see WATCHFUL
rel alive, awake, aware, conscious, sensible
widen *vb* ***syn*** see BROADEN
wideness *n* ***syn*** see BREADTH 2
widespread *adj* ***syn*** see PREVAILING
widget *n* ***syn*** see GADGET 1
width *n* ***syn*** see RANGE 2
wield *vb* **1** ***syn*** see HANDLE 2
rel conduct, control
2 ***syn*** see EXERT
wieldy *adj* ***syn*** see STRONG 1
wiener *n* ***syn*** see FRANKFURTER
wienerwurst *n* ***syn*** see FRANKFURTER
‖**wienie** *n* ***syn*** see FRANKFURTER
wife *n* the female partner in a marriage <a sense of humor is a requirement for his potential *wife*>
syn ‖ball and chain, lady, ‖little woman, ‖missus, Mrs., ‖old lady, ‖old woman, ‖rib, ‖squaw, ‖woman
rel consort, helpmate, helpmeet, mate, other half, spouse; bride, dowager, matron; concubine
idiom better half
con maid, maiden; widow
wig *n* ***syn*** see REBUKE
wig *vb* ***syn*** see SCOLD 1
wigging *n* ***syn*** see REBUKE
wiggle *vb* ***syn*** see WRIGGLE
wiggle-waggle *adj* ***syn*** see VACILLATING 2
wiggle-waggle *vb* ***syn*** see HESITATE
wiggy *adj* ***syn*** see POMPOUS 1
wight *n* ***syn*** see HUMAN
wild *adj* **1** living and growing in a state of nature and without human intervention <lived on *wild* plants and game animals>
syn agrarian, agrestal, native, natural, uncultivated, undomesticated; *compare* SAVAGE 1
rel escaped, feral; unsubdued, untamed
ant cultivated, domesticated
2 ***syn*** see SAVAGE 1
ant tame, tamed
3 ***syn*** see IRRESPONSIBLE
rel adventurous, audacious, daring, dashing; brash, cocksure, rash
4 ***syn*** see FURIOUS 2
rel bewildered, distracted, perplexed; agitated, perturbed, upset; addled, confused, muddled; crazy, demented, deranged, mad
con easy, relaxed
5 ***syn*** see UNRULY 1
6 marked by turmoil and fury especially of natural elements <a *wild* night of howling winds and driving snow>
syn blustering, blustery, ‖coarse, dirty, furious, raging, rough, stormful, stormy, tempestuous, turbulent
rel blatant, boisterous, clamorous, ungovernable, unruly; brutal, harsh, severe
con calm, peaceful, placid, quiet, stormless; halcyon, irenic, serene
7 given to unrestrained self-indulgence and pursuit of pleasure <her son got in with a *wild* bunch and took to drink>
syn devil-may-care, fast, gay, raffish, rakehell, rakish, sporty
rel boisterous, roisterous, rollicking, swaggering; careless, heedless, irresponsible, thoughtless; lewd, loose, unchaste, wanton
con moderate, restrained, sober, sparing, temperate; bridled, controlled, curbed; self-controlled
8 ***syn*** see EXTRAVAGANT 1

syn synonym(s) ***rel*** related word(s)
ant antonym(s) ***con*** contrasted word(s)
idiom idiomatic equivalent(s)
‖ use limited; if in doubt, see a dictionary

9 ***syn*** see BARBARIAN 1
ant cultivated, cultured
10 ***syn*** see BARBARIC 1

wild *n* ***syn*** see WASTE 1

wilderness *n* ***syn*** see WASTE 1
rel backcountry, backland(s), hinterland
idiom back of beyond

wild land *n* ***syn*** see WASTE 1

wildly *adv* ***syn*** see HARD 2

wildness *n* ***syn*** see WASTE 1

wile *n* ***syn*** see TRICK 1
rel chicane, chicanery, trickery; cunning, deceit, dissimulation, guile
con candor, frankness, openness, plain dealing, straightforwardness, unconstraint; artlessness, naturalness, sincerity

wile *vb* **1** ***syn*** see ATTRACT 1
2 ***syn*** see WHILE

wiliness *n* ***syn*** see CUNNING 2

will *vb* to be inclined <you may decide whichever way you *will*>
syn choose, elect, like, please, wish
rel crave, desire, want
idiom have a mind to, see (*or* think) fit

will *n* **1** a desire to act in a particular way or have a particular thing <I've no *will* to be sociable tonight>
syn fancy, inclination, liking, mind, pleasure, velleity
rel appetite, desire, passion, urge; hankering, longing, pining, yearning
idiom heart's desire
con aversion, dislike, distaste, repugnance, repulsion, revulsion
2 the aspect of mind involved in choosing or deciding <problems arise when one's *will* and judgment come in conflict>
syn volition
rel design, intent, purpose, wishes; character, disposition, temper
3 power of controlling one's actions, impulses, or emotions <a self-indulgent man of feeble character and little *will*>
syn discipline, self-command, self-control, self-discipline, self-government, self-mastery, self-restraint, willpower
l aplomb, assurance, confidence, poise, self-
ession; control, discretion, restraint
ratification, indulgence, self-indulgence
give to another by will <*will* family
a relative>
h, devise, leave, legate
see OBSTINATE
, factious
it in one's teeth, not yielding
bedient, tractable
ve; decided, determined,
stinate, pertinacious, stub-
, chance, involuntary, uninten-
nned

willies *n pl* ***syn*** see JITTERS

willing *adj* **1** prepared in mind or by disposition <*willing* to help>
syn disposed, fain, inclined, minded, predisposed, prone, ready
rel agreeable, compliant, favorable; forward, game, prompt
idiom in the mood
con averse, disinclined, indisposed, loath, reluctant, unminded
ant unwilling
2 ***syn*** see VOLUNTARY
rel disposed, inclined, predisposed; open, prone

will–less *adj* ***syn*** see SPONTANEOUS

willpower *n* ***syn*** see WILL 3

willy–nilly *adv* surely and without regard to plans or inclination <it seems that we must drift *willy-nilly* toward disaster>
syn helplessly, inescapably, inevitably, perforce, unavoidably, whether or no
idiom as a matter of course, come what may, of necessity, without let or choice

‖**willy–willy** *n* ***syn*** see HURRICANE

wilt *vb* **1** ***syn*** see WITHER
2 ***syn*** see COLLAPSE 2
3 ***syn*** see DROOP 3

wily *adj* ***syn*** see SLY 2
rel sagacious, shrewd; clever, knowing
con aboveboard, forthright, straightforward; guileless, open, trusting

wimp *n* ***syn*** see WEAKLING

win *vb* **1** to gain the victory <the home team *won* by a wide margin>
syn beat, overcome, prevail, triumph; *compare* CONQUER 1
idiom bear off the palm (*or* prize), bring home the bacon, carry the day, come out first (*or* ahead), finish in front
ant lose
2 ***syn*** see GAIN 1
3 ***syn*** see EARN 1
rel produce, yield
4 ***syn*** see GET 1
ant lose

win (over) *vb* **1** ***syn*** see DISARM 2
2 ***syn*** see INDUCE 1

win *n* ***syn*** see VICTORY 1

wince *vb* ***syn*** see RECOIL
rel dodge, duck, jib, sheer, swerve, turn; cower, cringe

wind *n* **1** ***syn*** see NOTHING 1
2 ***syn*** see HINT 1

wind *vb* ***syn*** see BLOW 1

wind *vb* **1** ***syn*** see DEFORM
2 to follow a circular, spiral, or writhing course <the vine *wound* its way up the pillar>
syn coil, corkscrew, curl, entwine, spiral, twine, twist, wreathe; *compare* CURVE
rel bend, curve, meander, weave; circle, encircle, enlace, gird, girdle, surround; enclose, envelop

windbaggery *n* ***syn*** see NONSENSE 2

windiness *n* ***syn*** see VERBOSITY

winding *adj* curving repeatedly first one way then another <a *winding* country road>

syn anfractuous, convoluted, flexuous, meandering, meandrous, serpentine, sinuous, snaky, tortuous; *compare* CROOKED 1
rel bending, curving, twisting; crooked, devious; circuitous, indirect, roundabout
con direct, straight
window dressing *n syn* see MASK 2
windrow *n syn* see PILE 1
wind up *vb* **1** *syn* see CLOSE 3
2 *syn* see SETTLE 7
windup *n syn* see FINALE
windy *adj* **1** marked by more wind than usual <a *windy* March day>
syn airy, blowy, breezy, gusty
rel brisk, fresh; drafty
con breathless, motionless, still
ant windless
2 *syn* see INFLATED
3 *syn* see WORDY
wing *n syn* see ANNEX
rel expansion, prolongation; bulge, projection, protrusion, protuberance
wing *vb syn* see FLY 4
wink *vb* to close and open the eyelids quickly <*winking* involuntarily as the light struck his eyes>
syn bat, blink, nictate, nictitate, twinkle
rel squinch, squinny, squint; flutter
wink (at) *vb syn* see CONNIVE 1
wink *n* **1** *syn* see INSTANT 1
2 *syn* see HINT 2
winker *n syn* see EYE 1
winner *n syn* see VICTOR 2
ant loser
winning *adj syn* see SWEET 1
winnow *vb* **1** *syn* see BLOW 1
2 *syn* see SORT 2
winsome *adj syn* see SWEET 1
rel adorable, lovable, lovesome
wipe (out) *vb* **1** *syn* see ERASE
2 *syn* see ANNIHILATE 2
3 *syn* see SLAUGHTER 3
wipe *n* **1** *syn* see HIT 1
‖**2** *syn* see HANDKERCHIEF
‖**wiped out** *adj syn* see DRUGGED
‖**wiper** *n syn* see HANDKERCHIEF
‖**wire** *n syn* see PICKPOCKET
wiredraw *vb syn* see THIN 1
wiry *adj syn* see MUSCULAR 1
wisdom *n* **1** *syn* see KNOWLEDGE 2
2 *syn* see SAGACITY
3 *syn* see SENSE 6
rel judiciousness, sageness, saneness, sapience; perspicacity, sagacity, shrewdness
ant folly
wise *n syn* see METHOD 1
wise *adj* **1** having or exhibiting a capacity for discernment and the intelligent application of knowledge <to be *wise* is to use knowledge well>
syn discerning, gnostic, insighted, insightful, knowing, knowledgeable, perceptive, sagacious, sage, sophic, wisehearted
rel aware, grasping, intuitive, sensing; acute, keen, perspicacious; cogitative, contemplative, reflective, thoughtful; astute, sharp, shrewd
con dull, obtuse, slow, slow-witted; insensitive, unaware, unknowing
ant unwise
2 exercising or involving sound judgment <*wise* management of scarce resources>
syn judgmatic, judicious, prudent, sage, sane, sapient, sensible; *compare* SHREWD
rel canny, discreet, foresighted, provident; astute, perspicacious, sagacious, shrewd; alert, bright, intelligent, keen, smart
con careless, heedless, injudicious; improvident, imprudent, indiscreet, short-sighted
ant foolish, unwise
3 *syn* see EXPEDIENT
4 shrewdly aware and subtly resourceful <a *wise* operator with his eye always on the main chance>
syn canny, hep, knowing, nimble-witted, quick, quick-witted, sharp, sharp-witted, slick, smart; *compare* INTELLIGENT 2, SHREWD
rel cagey, foresighted, shrewd; artful, crafty, cunning, slippery, smooth, tricky, wily; steel-trap
idiom in the groove, not born yesterday, on the beam
con narrow, prim, puritanical, straitlaced; conservative, plodding, ‖square
5 presumptuously confident and self-assured <a bunch of *wise* kids tearing up the neighborhood>
syn ‖biggety, bold, bold-faced, cheeky, forward, fresh, impudent, nervy, pert, procacious, sassy, smart, smart-alecky
rel arrogant, brash, cocky, insolent; flip, flippant, impertinent, lippy, saucy
con demure, mannerly, modest, proper; dull, priggish, stuffy
wise (up) *vb syn* see INFORM 2
wiseacre *n syn* see SMART ALECK
wisecrack *n syn* see JOKE 1
wisecracker *n syn* see SMART ALECK
wise guy *n syn* see SMART ALECK
wisehead *n syn* see SMART ALECK
wisehearted *adj syn* see WISE 1
wise man *n syn* see SAGE
wisenheimer *n syn* see SMART ALECK
wish *vb* **1** *syn* see DESIRE 1
rel expect, hope; fancy
2 *syn* see WILL
3 *syn* see IMPOSE 4
wishy-washy *adj* **1** *syn* see INSIPID 3
rel enervated, languid, listless, spiritless; flavorless, savorless
idiom neither flesh, fowl, nor good red herring, neither one thing nor the other
2 *syn* see CHARACTERLESS
wistful *adj syn* see PENSIVE 2
‖**wit** *vb syn* see UNDERSTAND 3
wit *n* **1** *syn* see MIND 1

syn synonym(s) *rel* related word(s)
ant antonym(s) *con* contrasted word(s)
idiom idiomatic equivalent(s)
‖ use limited; if in doubt, see a dictionary

rel perspicacity, sagacity; apprehension, awareness, comprehension
2 *often* **wits** *pl* mental soundness and health <frightened nearly out of her *wits*>
syn lucidity, ||marbles, mind, reason, saneness, sanity, sense(s), soundnesss
rel balance, rationality
con aberration; craziness, derangement, insanity, lunacy, madness, mania
ant witlessness
3 acuteness of perception or judgment <had the *wit* to know that he was out of his depth in such a discussion>
syn acumen, astucity, astuteness, clear-sightedness, discernment, discrimination, keenness, penetration, percipience, perspicacity, shrewdness; *compare* PRUDENCE 1
rel awareness, comprehension, grasp, insight, perception, understanding; prudence, sagaciousness, sagacity, sageness, sapience, wisdom; clairvoyance, divination, ESP, sensing
con aridity, dullness, prosaicness, unimaginativeness; fatuity, foolishness, inanity, silliness, stupidity
4 ***syn*** see INTELLIGENCE 1
5 a talent for banter or persiflage <a jolly man, noted for his kindly *wit*>
syn esprit, humor
rel alertness, keenness, quick-wittedness; brilliance, cleverness, intelligence, smartness
6 ***syn*** see HUMOR 5
7 ***syn*** see HUMORIST 2

witch *n* **1** a woman who practices the black arts <ancient laws against *witches*>
syn bruja, enchantress, hag, hex, lamia, sorceress, witchwoman; *compare* MAGICIAN 1
2 ***syn*** see HAG 2

witch *vb* ***syn*** see BEWITCH 1

witchcraft *n* **1** ***syn*** see MAGIC 1
2 ***syn*** see CHARM 3

witchery *n* **1** ***syn*** see MAGIC 1
2 ***syn*** see CHARM 3

witching *n* ***syn*** see MAGIC 1

witchwoman *n* ***syn*** see WITCH 1

witchy *adj* ***syn*** see MAGIC

with *prep* **1** ***syn*** see OVER 3
2 ***syn*** see FOR 2
3 ***syn*** see VIA 2

withal *adv* **1** ***syn*** see ALSO 2
2 ***syn*** see HOWEVER

withdraw *vb* **1** ***syn*** see REMOVE 2
ant deposit
2 ***syn*** see ABJURE
3 ***syn*** see GO 2
rel quail, recoil, retreat, shrink; recede
idiom give ground, give way
con advance, progress; arrive, come
4 ***syn*** see RETREAT 2
ant advance

withdrawal *n* ***syn*** see DEPARTURE 1
ant approach

withdrawn *adj* **1** ***syn*** see UNDEMONSTRATIVE
ant outgiving
2 ***syn*** see INDIFFERENT 2
3 ***syn*** see UNSOCIABLE
ant outgoing

wither *vb* to lose substance and freshness by or as if by loss of natural moisture <projects that *wither* and die from lack of popular interest>
syn dry up, mummify, mummy, shrivel, welter, wilt, wizen
rel cave in, collapse, deflate, fold; constrict, contract, shrink; decline, wane
con freshen, revive, revivify; develop, grow, increase, wax
ant flourish

withhold *vb* **1** ***syn*** see RESTRAIN 1
2 ***syn*** see KEEP 5
con award, concede, grant, vouchsafe
ant accord
3 ***syn*** see DENY 2
4 ***syn*** see REFRAIN 1

within *adv* ***syn*** see INDOORS
ant without

within *n* ***syn*** see INTERIOR
ant without

withindoors *adv* ***syn*** see INDOORS
ant withoutdoors

withinside *adv* ***syn*** see INDOORS
ant withoutside

with–it *adj* ***syn*** see STYLISH

without *prep* **1** ***syn*** see BEYOND 1
2 not having <living *without* decent housing or adequate food>
syn awanting, lacking, minus, sans, wanting

without *adv* ***syn*** see OUTDOORS
ant within

without *n* ***syn*** see OUTDOORS

||**without** *conj* ***syn*** see EXCEPT 1

withoutdoors *adv* ***syn*** see OUTDOORS
ant indoors, withindoors

with respect to *prep* ***syn*** see APROPOS

withstand *vb* ***syn*** see RESIST
rel bear, endure, stand, suffer, tolerate
con capitulate, submit, yield

witless *adj* **1** ***syn*** see SIMPLE 3
2 ***syn*** see INSANE 1

witlessness *n* ***syn*** see FOOLISHNESS

witness *n* **1** ***syn*** see TESTIMONY
2 ***syn*** see SPECTATOR

witness *vb* **1** ***syn*** see CERTIFY 1
rel affirm; endorse, subscribe
2 ***syn*** see INDICATE 2

witticism *n* ***syn*** see JOKE 1

wittiness *n* ***syn*** see HUMOR 4

witting *adj* **1** ***syn*** see AWARE
ant unwitting
2 ***syn*** see VOLUNTARY
ant unwitting

witty *adj* provoking or intended to provoke mirth <a whimsical *witty* discussion on the foreignness of honesty to politics>
syn facetious, humorous, jocose, jocular
rel amusing, diverting, entertaining; scintillating, sparkling; penetrating, piercing, probing; funny, ridiculous, risible
con foolish, senseless, silly; brash, cheeky, fresh; earnest, serious, sober, solemn

ant unwitty
wiz *n* ***syn*** see EXPERT
ant dub, dud, duffer
wizard *n* **1** ***syn*** see MAGICIAN 1
2 ***syn*** see EXPERT
ant dub, dud, duffer
wizardly *adj* ***syn*** see MAGIC
wizardry *n* ***syn*** see MAGIC 1
wizen *vb* ***syn*** see WITHER
rel decrease, diminish, dwindle, reduce
wobble *vb* **1** ***syn*** see LURCH 2
2 ***syn*** see TEETER
3 ***syn*** see SHAKE
wobbly *adj* **1** ***syn*** see RICKETY
2 ***syn*** see WEAK 2
3 ***syn*** see VACILLATING 2
woe *n* **1** ***syn*** see SORROW
rel bemoaning, bewailing, deploring, lamentation
con bliss, felicity, happiness
2 ***syn*** see MISERY 1
3 *usu* **woes** *pl* ***syn*** see DISASTER
woebegone *adj* **1** ***syn*** see DOWNCAST
rel lugubrious, melancholy
con alert, concerned, interested, spirited; lively, vigorous; avid, eager, keen
2 ***syn*** see GLOOMY 3
rel dilapidated, outworn, shabby, worn
con bright, crisp, fresh, gay
woeful *adj* **1** full of or expressive of woe <a *woeful* countenance>
syn afflicted, doleful, dolent, dolorous, miserable, rueful, ruthful, sorrowful, wretched
rel harrowed, racked, tortured, wrung; crushed, overcome, stricken; disconsolate, heartsick, inconsolable; dejected, depressed, dispirited, downcast, downhearted, low-spirited
idiom cut to the heart, cut up, in the dumps (*or* depths *or* doldrums), on the rack
con content, satisfied; easy, peaceful, quiet; cheerful, gay, lighthearted
ant joyful
2 ***syn*** see MELANCHOLY 2
3 ***syn*** see DEPLORABLE
rel dismal, grave, sad; unprecedented
woggle *vb* ***syn*** see WAG
wolf *n* a man forward, direct, and zealous in amorous pursuit of women <known far and wide as a lecherous old *wolf*>
syn Casanova, chaser, Don Juan, ladies' man, lady-killer, masher, philander, philanderer, womanizer
rel amorist; lecher, libertine, Lothario, profligate, rip, roué, rounder
idiom man on the make, skirt chaser
wolf *vb* **1** ***syn*** see GULP
2 ***syn*** see PHILANDER
wolfish *adj* ***syn*** see FIERCE 1
woman *n* **1** a female human being <a health club that caters to *women*>
syn ‖dame, ‖doll, female, gal, gentlewoman, ‖girl, lady, she, ‖skirt, ‖squaw
rel ‖bird, ‖chick; milady
‖**2** ***syn*** see WIFE
3 ***syn*** see MISTRESS
womanish *adj* ***syn*** see FEMININE
womanize *vb* ***syn*** see PHILANDER
womanizer *n* ***syn*** see WOLF
womanlike *adj* ***syn*** see FEMININE
womanly *adj* ***syn*** see FEMININE
wonder *n* **1** something that causes fascinated astonishment or admiration <the seven *wonders* of the ancient world>
syn marvel, miracle, phenomenon, portent, prodigy, sensation, stunner
rel curiosity, cynosure, gazingstock, spectacle
idiom one for the book(s), something to shout (*or* write home) about
2 the complex emotion aroused by the strange and incomprehensible and especially the awe-inspiring <stood gazing in wide-eyed *wonder* at the scene unveiled before her>
syn admiration, amaze, amazement, marveling, wonderment
rel awe, fear, reverence; bewilderment, perplexity, puzzlement; astonishment, marvel, shock
con disinterest, incuriosity, indifference, unconcern; dispassion, impassivity; casualness, offhandedness; boredom, ennui
3 ***syn*** see UNCERTAINTY
rel assailability, vulnerability
con unconcern
wonderful *adj* **1** ***syn*** see MARVELOUS 1
2 ***syn*** see MARVELOUS 2
ant lousy
wonderland *n* ***syn*** see UTOPIA
wonderment *n* ***syn*** see WONDER 2
wondrous *adj* ***syn*** see MARVELOUS 1
wont *n* ***syn*** see HABIT 1
wont *vb* ***syn*** see ACCUSTOM
wonted *adj* ***syn*** see USUAL 1
ant unwonted
wontedly *adv* ***syn*** see USUALLY 1
ant unwontedly
woo *vb* ***syn*** see ADDRESS 8
idiom bill and coo, pitch woo
wood *n, often* **woods** *pl but sing or pl in constr* ***syn*** see FOREST
wooden *adj* **1** ***syn*** see STIFF 4
rel awkward, clumsy; heavy, ponderous, weighty
con limber, supple; plastic, pliable, pliant
2 ***syn*** see AWKWARD 2
woodenhead *n* ***syn*** see DUNCE
woodland *n* ***syn*** see FOREST
woods colt *n* ***syn*** see BASTARD 1
woodsy *n* ***syn*** see RUSTIC
wooer *n* ***syn*** see SUITOR 2
woolly *adj* ***syn*** see HAIRY 1
word *vb* to convey (as an impression, a thought, or a need) in words <seemed scarcely to know how to *word* her appeal>

---

syn synonym(s) ***rel*** related word(s)
ant antonym(s) ***con*** contrasted word(s)
idiom idiomatic equivalent(s)
‖ use limited; if in doubt, see a dictionary

syn couch, express, formulate, phrase, put; *compare* EXPRESS 2
rel convey, offer, submit; say, state, tell

word *n* **1** something that is said <didn't tell a *word* about his plans>
syn statement, utterance
rel announcement, declaration, pronouncement
2 a pronounceable sound or combination of sounds that expresses and symbolizes an idea <be sure you learn the meaning of each *word*>
syn term, vocable
rel expression, idiom, locution, phrase
3 *syn* see COMMAND 1
4 *syn* see NEWS
5 *syn* see REPORT 1
6 *syn* see MESSAGE 1
7 *syn* see SAYING
8 a statement whose weight or worth depends on the truthfulness or authority of its maker <had the doctor's *word* that no operation would be needed>
syn assurance, guarantee, pledge, warrant; *compare* PROMISE
rel commitment, engagement, undertaking; oath, vow; promise
9 *syn* see PROMISE
10 *usu* **words** *pl syn* see QUARREL
11 *syn* see PASSWORD 3
12 *syn* see PASSWORD 1

wordage *n syn* see WORDING

word for word *adv syn* see VERBATIM

word–for–word *adj syn* see VERBATIM

word–hoard *n syn* see VOCABULARY 1

wordiness *n syn* see VERBOSITY
con crispness, pithiness, trenchancy
ant laconicism, laconism

wording *n* manner or style of verbal expression <take care with the *wording* of a formal invitation>
syn diction, parlance, phrase, phraseology, phrasing, verbalism, verbiage, wordage
rel language, mode, style

wordless *adj* **1** *syn* see TACIT 1
2 *syn* see SILENT 2
3 *syn* see SILENT 3
4 *syn* see UNSPOKEN 1
ant wordy

word–of–mouth *adj syn* see ORAL 2

word–stock *n syn* see VOCABULARY 1

wordy *adj* using or marked by the use of more words than are needed to express an idea <tired of dull *wordy* editorials>
syn diffuse, long-winded, palaverous, prolix, redundant, verbose, windy
rel flatulent, inflated, tumid, turgid; garrulous, glib, loquacious, talkative, voluble; bombastic, highfalutin, rhetorical
con compendious, concise, pithy, succinct, summary, terse; lean, taut
ant laconic

work *n* **1** the activity that affords one his livelihood <laborers hurrying to *work* at dawn>
syn business, calling, employment, job, line, occupation, pursuit, ‖racket; *compare* JOB 2
rel art, craft, handicraft, métier, profession, trade, vocation, walk
2 strenuous activity that involves difficulty and effort and usually affords no pleasure <had done much hard *work* during her life>
syn bullwork, donkeywork, drudge, drudgery, grind, labor, moil, plugging, slavery, slogging, sweat, toil, travail
rel effort, exertion, pains, trouble; chore, duty, job; elucubration; striving; spadework
ant play
3 **works** *pl syn* see FACTORY

work *vb* **1** *syn* see OPERATE 3
2 *syn* see TILL
3 *syn* see SOLVE 1
4 *syn* see LABOR 1
5 *syn* see FUNCTION 3
6 *syn* see ACT 5

work (for) *vb syn* see BENEFIT

workable *adj syn* see POSSIBLE 1
rel applicable, exploitable, usable
ant unworkable

workaday *adj* **1** *syn* see PROSAIC 3
2 *syn* see ORDINARY 1

workday *adj syn* see PROSAIC 3

worker *n* one who earns a living by labor and especially by manual labor <weary *workers* straggling home each night>
syn hand, laborer, ‖mozo, operative, roustabout, workhand, workingman, workman
rel artisan, craftsman, handicraftsman, mechanic; employee
ant idler

workhand *n syn* see WORKER

workhorse *n* **1** *syn* see SLAVE 2
2 *syn* see SAWHORSE

work in *vb syn* see INSINUATE 3

working *adj* **1** *syn* see ACTIVE 1
2 *syn* see BUSY 1

workingman *n syn* see WORKER

workless *adj syn* see UNEMPLOYED

workman *n syn* see WORKER

workmanlike *adj syn* see SKILLFUL 2
ant unworkmanlike

workmanly *adj syn* see SKILLFUL 2

work off *vb syn* see FOIST 3

work out *vb syn* see SOLVE 1

work over *vb syn* see REVISE

work–shy *adj syn* see LAZY

work up *vb syn* see GENERATE 3

world *n* **1** *syn* see EARTH 1
2 *syn* see UNIVERSE

worldly *adj* **1** *syn* see EARTHLY 1
ant otherworldly
2 *syn* see MATERIALISTIC
ant otherworldly, unworldly
3 *syn* see SOPHISTICATED 2
ant unworldly

worldly–wise *adj syn* see SOPHISTICATED 2
rel callous, hard-boiled, hardened
con naive, unsophisticated, unworldly

worldwide *adj syn* see UNIVERSAL 2
con parochial

world–wise *adj syn* see SOPHISTICATED 2

world–without–end *adj syn* see EVERLASTING 1
world–without–end *n syn* see ETERNITY 2
worm *n syn* see WRETCH 1
worm *vb* **1** *syn* see INSINUATE 3
2 *syn* see WRIGGLE
wormling *n syn* see WRETCH 1
worn *adj* **1** *syn* see TIRED 1
2 *syn* see HAGGARD
worn–down *adj syn* see TIRED 1
worn–out *adj* **1** *syn* see EFFETE 2
2 *syn* see TIRED 1
3 *syn* see TRITE
worried *adj syn* see DISTRAUGHT
ant unworried
worry *vb* **1** to disturb one or destroy one's peace of mind by repeated or persistent tormenting attacks <vain regrets that *worry* his spirit>
syn annoy, bedevil, beleaguer, dun, gnaw, hagride, harass, harry, hassle, needle, pester, plague, tantalize, tease, ‖wherret
rel beset, bother, fret, pelt, trouble, vex; goad, test, try; afflict, torment, torture; aggrieve, oppress, persecute, wrong
idiom give one gyp
con comfort, console, solace; alleviate, assuage, ease, relieve
2 *syn* see TROUBLE 1
3 to experience concern, disquietude, or anxiety <*worrying* over her children's health>
syn cark, fret, fuss, pother, stew, ‖tew
rel carry on, take on; despair, give up; bother, concern (oneself); agitate, disquiet, disturb, trouble
idiom be upset, bite one's nails
con accept, submit; abide, bear, endure, stand, support; disregard, ignore, overlook, pass over
worry *n* **1** *syn* see CARE 2
rel presentiment; doubt, mistrust, uncertainty; anguish, heartache, woe
con composure, equanimity, sangfroid; assurance, certainty, certitude, confidence, security
2 *syn* see TRIAL 2
worrywart *n syn* see PESSIMIST
worsen *vb syn* see DETERIORATE 1
rel blast, blight, debase, degrade, humble, lower; corrupt, foul, taint
idiom get worse, grow worse
ant better
worship *n syn* see ADORATION
worship *vb* **1** *syn* see REVERE
con contemn, despise, disdain, flout, scorn; curse, execrate, vilify
2 *syn* see ADORE 3
ant abominate; scorn
3 *syn* see LOVE 2
worst *vb syn* see DEFEAT 2
worth *n* **1** equivalence in good qualities (as utility, importance, or desirability) express or implied <impossible to estimate the *worth* of such a man to the community>
syn account, valuation, value
rel class, excellence, merit, perfection, quality, virtue; rate; use, usefulness, utility; consequence, importance, mark, moment, note, significance, weight
con baseness, meanness, paltriness, poorness
ant worthlessness
2 *syn* see QUALITY 2
3 *syn* see WEALTH 2
worthless *adj* **1** lacking all excellence or value <gave me a *worthless* check>
syn draffy, drossy, good-for-nothing, inutile, ‖no-account, no-good, nothing, unworthy, valueless
rel inferior, mediocre, poor, second-rate; defective, flawed, imperfect; bootless, ineffectual, unavailing, useless; contemptible, dusty, mean, sad, sorry
idiom dear at any price, of no earthly value (*or* worth)
con esteemed, precious; useful, valuable, worthwhile; invaluable, priceless
ant worthful
2 *syn* see FECKLESS 1
rel incapable, incompetent, unqualified
worthwhile *adj syn* see ADVANTAGEOUS 1
worthy *adj* **1** having worth or merit <a *worthy* custom handed down from our ancestors>
syn admirable, commendable, deserving, estimable, laudable, meritable, meritorious, praisable, praiseworthy, thankworthy
rel invaluable, precious, priceless; desirable, pleasing, satisfying; divine
con good-for-nothing, ‖no-account, no-good, valueless; contemptible, sad, sorry
ant worthless
2 *syn* see HONORABLE 1
ant unworthy
wound *vb syn* see INJURE 3
wow *n syn* see SMASH 6
‖**wowser** *n syn* see PRUDE
wrack *vb syn* see DESTROY 1
wrackful *adj syn* see DESTRUCTIVE
wraith *n syn* see APPARITION
wrangle *vb* **1** *syn* see QUARREL
2 *syn* see ARGUE 2
wrangle *n syn* see QUARREL
wrap *vb syn* see ENFOLD 1
rel camouflage, cloak, mask
ant unwrap
wrap (up) *vb* **1** *syn* see BUNDLE UP
2 *syn* see SWATHE
wrapped *adj syn* see INTENT
wrapped up *adj syn* see INTENT
wrap up *vb syn* see CLOSE 3
wrath *n syn* see ANGER
rel acerbity, acrimony, asperity; offense, resentment
wrathful *adj syn* see ANGRY
wrathy *adj syn* see ANGRY
‖**wraxle** *vb syn* see WRESTLE
wreak *vb syn* see INFLICT 2
wreakful *adj syn* see VINDICTIVE

---

syn synonym(s) *rel* related word(s)
ant antonym(s) *con* contrasted word(s)
idiom idiomatic equivalent(s)
‖ use limited; if in doubt, see a dictionary

wreath *n* a circlet of intertwined leaves or flowers worn upon the head as an ornament or as a mark of honor or esteem <received the laurel *wreath* of victory from the emperor's own hand>
syn chaplet, coronal, coronet, crown, garland
rel bay(s), laurel
wreathe *vb syn* see WIND 2
wreck *n* **1** *syn* see CRASH 3
2 *syn* see COLLAPSE 2
3 *syn* see JALOPY
wreck *vb* **1** *syn* see VANDALIZE
2 *syn* see DESTROY 1
rel despoil, loot, plunder, ravage; cripple, disable
3 *syn* see TOTAL 3
4 *syn* see SABOTAGE
5 *syn* see SHIPWRECK 1
6 *syn* see RUIN 2
7 *syn* see INFLICT 2
wreckage *n* **1** *syn* see SABOTAGE
2 *syn* see DRIFTWOOD
wrecker *n syn* see VANDAL
wreckful *adj syn* see DESTRUCTIVE
wrecking *n syn* see SABOTAGE
wrench *vb* **1** to shift the position of or move by or as if by vigorous twisting <suddenly *wrenched* her around to face him>
syn wrest, wring, wry
rel bend, twist; coerce, compel, constrain, force; drag, rend, tear; contort, distort
2 *syn* see SPRAIN
3 *syn* see MISREPRESENT
4 *syn* see EXTORT 1
wrest *vb* **1** *syn* see WRENCH 1
rel arrogate, confiscate, usurp; elicit, extort, extract
2 *syn* see EXTORT 1
3 *syn* see MISREPRESENT
wrestle *vb* to struggle with an opponent at close quarters <determined to solve the problem if he had to *wrestle* with it all night>
syn grapple, scuffle, tussle, ‖wraxle
rel contend, fight, struggle; endeavor, essay; labor, moil, toil, travail, work; exert, strain, stretch, strive
wretch *n* **1** a worthless and often vicious or contemptible person <a treacherous drink-sodden *wretch*>
syn ‖blighter, lowlife, mucker, no-good, worm, wormling
rel good-for-naught, good-for-nothing, ne'er-do-well; blackguard, caitiff, devil, knave, rapscallion, rascal, rogue, rotter, scalawag, scoundrel, villain
idiom sad case
2 *syn* see SNOT 1
wretched *adj* **1** *syn* see WOEFUL 1
rel melancholy; abject, mean, sordid; piteous, pitiable, pitiful; despairing, despondent, forlorn, hopeless
con animated, gay, lively; content, contented, satisfied; gratified, pleased
2 *syn* see BASE
wretchedness *n syn* see MISERY 1
wriggle *vb* to move or advance with wormlike motions <the attackers *wriggled* stealthily through the underbrush>
syn squiggle, squirm, wiggle, worm, writhe
rel flow, glide, ooze, slide, slip
wring *vb* **1** *syn* see EXTORT 1
2 *syn* see WRENCH 1
rel press, squeeze
3 *syn* see AFFLICT
wringing–wet *adj syn* see WET 1
wrinkle *n* a small linear prominence or depression on a surface <a benign old face netted with *wrinkles*>
syn corrugation, crease, crinkle, fold, furrow, plica, ridge, rimple, rivel, ruck
rel crow's foot; pleat, pucker
wrinkle *vb syn* see CRUMPLE 1
write *vb* to form characters or words on a surface (as of paper) usually with pen or pencil <learned to *write* at an early age>
syn engross, indite, inscribe, scribe
rel dot (down), jot, note; chalk, pen, pencil; scratch, scrawl, scribble; draft, draw, make out; write down, write up
idiom push one's pen, put in writing, take down
write down *vb syn* see DEPRECIATE 1
ant write up
write off *vb* **1** *syn* see DEPRECIATE 1
2 *syn* see DECRY 2
write–up *n syn* see PUFF 3
writhe *vb* **1** to twist and turn in physical or mental distress <*writhing* in anguish with a throbbing toothache>
syn agonize, squirm, toss
rel blench, flinch, recoil, shrink, wince; contort, distort; bend, twist; thrash, tumble
2 *syn* see WRIGGLE
writing *n syn* see PRINT 2
writing desk *n syn* see DESK
wrong *n* **1** *syn* see INJUSTICE 2
2 *syn* see EVIL 2
3 *syn* see EVIL 3
4 *syn* see INJUSTICE 1
wrong *adj* **1** rejecting or deviating from the dictates of moral or divine law <had a *wrong* outlook on life> <*wrong* principles of conduct>
syn bad, evil, immoral, iniquitous, reprobate, sinful, vicious, wicked
rel blamable, blameworthy, censurable, reprehensible; corrupt, debauched, depraved; abandoned, dissolute, infamous, villainous; blasphemous, unholy, unrighteous; accursed, unblessed
con ethical, high-principled, moral, righteous, upright; chaste, innocent, pure, virtuous
ant right
2 *syn* see FALSE 1
idiom at fault, barking up the wrong tree, in error, on the wrong track
con exact, precise
ant right
3 *syn* see BAD 1
rel improper, inappropriate, inapt, infelicitous, unfit, unfitting, unhappy, unsuitable
con appropriate, fit, fitting, proper, suitable

4 ***syn*** see MISTAKEN
ant right
5 ***syn*** see INSANE 1
wrong ***adv*** ***syn*** see AMISS 2
ant right
wrong *vb* to inflict injury on another without justification <these men who have *wronged* the public trust deserve no consideration>
syn aggrieve, oppress, outrage, persecute
rel abuse, ill-treat, maltreat, mistreat; harm, hurt, injure; offend
idiom do wrong to (*or* by)
con guard, protect, safeguard; care (for), cherish; honor, love, respect
wrongdoing *n* **1** ***syn*** see EVIL 3
2 ***syn*** see MISCONDUCT
wrongful *adj* ***syn*** see UNLAWFUL
ant rightful
wrongheaded *adj* **1** ***syn*** see OBSTINATE
2 ***syn*** see CONTRARY 3
wrongly *adv* ***syn*** see AMISS 1
ant rightly
wroth *adj* ***syn*** see ANGRY
wrothful *adj* ***syn*** see ANGRY
wrothy *adj* ***syn*** see ANGRY
wry *vb* ***syn*** see WRENCH 1
wry *adj* ***syn*** see SARDONIC

XYZ

x *n* ***syn*** see ERROR 1
x (out) *vb* ***syn*** see ERASE
Xanthippe *n* ***syn*** see VIRAGO
Xmas *n* ***syn*** see CHRISTMAS
yahoo *n* ***syn*** see TOUGH
yak *n* ***syn*** see CHATTER
yak *vb* ***syn*** see CHAT 1
‖**yak** *n* ***syn*** see JOKE 1
yakety–yak *n* ***syn*** see CHATTER
yakety–yak *vb* ***syn*** see CHAT 1
yak–yak *n* ***syn*** see CHATTER
yak–yak *vb* ***syn*** see CHAT
yammer *vb* **1** ***syn*** see GRIPE
2 ***syn*** see CHAT 1
yank *vb* **1** ***syn*** see JERK
rel tug; clutch, grab, snatch
2 ***syn*** see EXTRACT 1
yap *n* **1** ***syn*** see RUSTIC
‖**2** ***syn*** see MOUTH 1
yard *n* ***syn*** see COURT 1
yardstick *n* ***syn*** see STANDARD 3
yare *adj* ***syn*** see AGILE
yarn *n* **1** ***syn*** see STORY 2
2 ***syn*** see CHAT 2
yarn *vb* ***syn*** see CONVERSE
yatter *n* ***syn*** see CHATTER
yatter *vb* ***syn*** see CHAT 1
yaw *n* ***syn*** see TURN 2
yaw *vb* ***syn*** see SEESAW
yaw *vb* ***syn*** see YAWN
yawn *vb* to breathe deeply with jaws widespread usually in reaction to fatigue or boredom <*yawned* again and again in the stuffy room>
syn gape, yaw
rel doze, drowse, nap, snooze
yawn *n* ***syn*** see TEDIUM
yawning *adj* ***syn*** see CAVERNOUS 1
yawp (*or* **yaup**) *vb* **1** ***syn*** see SQUALL 1
2 ***syn*** see GRIPE
yea *adv* **1** ***syn*** see ALSO 2
2 ***syn*** see YES 1
3 ***syn*** see EVEN 3
yearbook *n* a book issued yearly to chronicle a particular part of the preceding year's activities <sports editor of his school *yearbook*>
syn annual, annuary
yearn *vb* ***syn*** see LONG
rel covet, desire, wish; pant
ant dread
years *n pl* ***syn*** see OLD AGE
yeast *n* ***syn*** see FOAM
yeasty *adj* ***syn*** see GIDDY 1
yegg *n* ***syn*** see ROBBER
yell *vb* **1** ***syn*** see SHOUT 1
2 to complain vigorously or vociferously <let the opposition *yell;* we got the vote>
syn howl, scream, squeal, yip, yowl
rel cry, lament, squall, wail, weep; bemoan, bewail, deplore
idiom beat one's breast, make an outcry, tear one's hair, yell to high heaven
con acclaim, applaud, cheer, hail
3 ***syn*** see CALL 1
yellow *adj* ***syn*** see COWARDLY
yellowback *n* ***syn*** see DIME NOVEL
yellowbelly *n* ***syn*** see COWARD
rel fink, rat, stinker
yellow dog *n* ***syn*** see CAD
yen *vb* ***syn*** see LONG
‖**yep** *adv* ***syn*** see YES 1
ant ‖nope
‖**yerk** *vb* ***syn*** see WHIP 1
yes *adv* **1** —used as a function word to express assent, agreement, understanding, or acceptance <*yes,* I can do that>
syn agreed, all right, aye, OK (*or* okay), ‖okeydoke, yea, ‖yep
rel assuredly, certainly, gladly, willingly; undoubtedly, unquestionably
idiom beyond a doubt, beyond any shade (*or* shadow) of doubt, with all my heart, without the least doubt
2 ***syn*** see EXACTLY 3
yes *vb* ***syn*** see ASSENT
yes–man *n* **1** ***syn*** see STOOGE 1
2 ***syn*** see SYCOPHANT
yesterday *n* ***syn*** see PAST
ant tomorrow
yesteryear *n* ***syn*** see PAST
yet *adv* **1** beyond this — used as an intensive to stress the comparative degree <in spite of her protest he went *yet* faster>
syn even, still
2 at some future time <just wait, we'll get there *yet*>
syn eventually, finally, someday, sometime, somewhen, sooner or later, ultimately
idiom after a while, in due course, in the course of time
3 ***syn*** see ALSO 2
4 ***syn*** see HITHERTO 1
5 ***syn*** see HOWEVER
yet *conj* ***syn*** see ONLY
yield *vb* **1** ***syn*** see RELINQUISH
con appropriate, arrogate, confiscate
2 to give way before a force that one can no longer resist <*yielded* to temptation>
syn bow, buckle (under), capitulate, cave, defer, knuckle, knuckle under, submit, succumb
rel accord, award, concede, grant; cede, surrender, waive; break, fail
idiom give ground, give place, give way
con bear up, hold out, resist
ant withstand
3 ***syn*** see BEAR 9

4 ***syn*** see GIVE 7
rel discharge, eject, emit, vent
5 to produce as return or revenue <an investment that *yields* 10 percent>
syn bring in, pay, return
rel afford, furnish, provide, supply; hold out, offer, proffer, tender
idiom afford (*or* give *or* provide) a return of, put at one's disposal
6 ***syn*** see GIVE 12

yield *n* ***syn*** see OUTPUT

yielding *adj* **1** ***syn*** see SOFT 6
ant unyielding
2 ***syn*** see PASSIVE 2

yip *vb* ***syn*** see YELL 2

‖**yob** *n* ***syn*** see RUSTIC

yoke *n* **1** ***syn*** see BONDAGE
2 ***syn*** see BOND 3

yoke *vb* **1** ***syn*** see HITCH 2
2 ***syn*** see JOIN 1

yokel *n* ***syn*** see RUSTIC

yon *adv* **1** ***syn*** see BEYOND 1
2 ***syn*** see THERE

yonder *adv* ***syn*** see BEYOND 1

yore *n* ***syn*** see PAST

young *adj* **1** being in an early stage of life, growth, or development <interested in molding *young* minds>
syn callow, green, immature, infant, juvenile, unfledged, unripe, youthful
rel fresh, new; crude, raw, unfinished, unformed
con full-grown, grown-up, mature, ripe; aged, elderly, superannuated
ant old; adult
2 ***syn*** see INEXPERIENCED

youngling *n* ***syn*** see CHILD 1

young man *n* ***syn*** see BOYFRIEND 1

young one *n* ***syn*** see CHILD 1

youngster *n* ***syn*** see CHILD 1

youth *n* **1** the period of life in which one passes from childhood to maturity <the thought of regaining one's *youth*>
syn adolescence, greenness, juvenility, prime, puberty, pubescence, salad days, spring, springtide, springtime, youthfulness, youthhood
rel callowness, immaturity, inexperience, unripeness; dewiness
idiom awkward age, flower (*or* springtime *or* May) of life
ant age
2 ***syn*** see CHILD 1

youthful *adj* ***syn*** see YOUNG 1
rel beardless, boyish, puerile; maiden, virgin, virginal
con adult, matured
ant aged, elderly

youthfulness *n* ***syn*** see YOUTH 1

youthhood *n* ***syn*** see YOUTH

yowl *vb* **1** ***syn*** see YELL 2
2 ***syn*** see BAWL 2

yule *n* ***syn*** see CHRISTMAS

yuletide *n* ***syn*** see CHRISTMAS

yummy *adj* ***syn*** see DELIGHTFUL

zakuska *n* ***syn*** see APPETIZER

zany *n* **1** ***syn*** see CLOWN 3
rel comic, farceur, funnyman
2 one who makes an exhibition of himself for the amusement of others <tired of having her parties spoiled by drunken *zanies*>
syn clown, cutup, farceur, joker, jokester, wag
rel practical joker, pranker, prankster, trickster; exhibitionist, show-off
3 ***syn*** see WAG 1
4 ***syn*** see FOOL 4

zany *adj* ***syn*** see FOOLISH 2

zeal *n* ***syn*** see PASSION 6
rel energy, gusto, spirit, zest; fierceness, intensity, vehemence; avidity, keenness, readiness, urgency; earnestness, seriousness, sincerity
con coolness, halfheartedness, indifference, lukewarmness; carelessness, heedlessness, insouciance, negligence, unmindfulness; disinterest, lackadaisy, unconcern
ant apathy

zealot *n* ***syn*** see ENTHUSIAST
rel adherent, disciple, follower, partisan, sectary

zealous *adj* ***syn*** see ENTHUSIASTIC
rel afire, ardent, fervent, fervid, fired; avid, eager; dedicated, fanatic, frenetic, rabid, wild-eyed; infatuated, obsessed, possessed
con cool, halfhearted, indifferent, lukewarm; careless, heedless, insouciant, negligent, unmindful; disinterested, lackadaisical, uninterested
ant apathetic

zemi *n* ***syn*** see CHARM 2

zenith *n* ***syn*** see APEX 2
ant nadir

zero *n* **1** a numerical symbol 0 denoting the absence of all magnitude or quantity <wrote a row of *zeros* after the decimal point>
syn aught (*or* ought), cipher, goose egg, naught (*or* nought), nothing, zilch
rel blank, nil, void
2 ***syn*** see NONENTITY

zero (in) *vb* ***syn*** see DIRECT 2

zero hour *n* ***syn*** see JUNCTURE 2

zest *n* ***syn*** see TASTE 4
rel ardor, eagerness, enthusiasm, fervor, passion, zeal; delectation, delight, enjoyment, pleasure, satisfaction; bliss, ecstasy, elation

zesty *adj* ***syn*** see PUNGENT

zetetic *n* ***syn*** see SKEPTIC

zilch *n* **1** ***syn*** see ZERO 1
2 ***syn*** see NONENTITY

zing *n* **1** ***syn*** see EAGERNESS
2 ***syn*** see SPIRIT 5

Zion *n* **1** ***syn*** see HEAVEN 2
2 ***syn*** see UTOPIA

zip *vb* **1** ***syn*** see BREEZE
2 ***syn*** see HURRY 2

zippy *adj* ***syn*** see AGILE
rel alert, keen, ready; dynamic, forceful, intense

---

syn synonym(s) ***rel*** related word(s)
ant antonym(s) ***con*** contrasted word(s)
idiom idiomatic equivalent(s)
‖ use limited; if in doubt, see a dictionary

zoetic *adj* ***syn*** see LIVING 1
Zoilus *n* ***syn*** see CRITIC
zombie *n* **1** ***syn*** see DUNCE
2 ***syn*** see ECCENTRIC
zone *n* ***syn*** see AREA 1
rel section, sector, segment
zonked *adj* **1** ***syn*** see INTOXICATED 1
2 ***syn*** see DRUGGED